Who's Who in the West

Biographical Titles Currently Published by Marquis Who's Who

Who's Who in America
  Who's Who in America supplements:
    Geographic/Professional Area Index
    Supplement to Who's Who in America
    Who's Who in America Classroom Project Book
Who Was Who in America
  Historical Volume (1607–1896)
  Volume I (1897–1942)
  Volume II (1943–1950)
  Volume III (1951–1960)
  Volume IV (1961–1968)
  Volume V (1969–1973)
  Volume VI (1974–1976)
  Volume VII (1977–1981)
  Volume VIII (1982–1985)
  Index Volume (1607–1985)
Who's Who in the World
Who's Who in the East
Who's Who in the Midwest
Who's Who in the South and Southwest
Who's Who in the West
Who's Who in American Law
Who's Who of American Women
Who's Who of Emerging Leaders in America
Who's Who in Finance and Industry
Index to Who's Who Books
Directory of Medical Specialists

Who's Who
in the West ®

Including Alaska, Arizona, California, Colorado, Hawaii, Idaho,
Montana, Nevada, New Mexico, Oregon, Utah, Washington, and
Wyoming; and in Canada, the provinces of Alberta, British
Columbia, and Saskatchewan.

21st edition
1987-1988

MARQUIS
Who'sWho

Macmillan Directory Division
3002 Glenview Road
Wilmette, Illinois 60091 U.S.A.

Library of Congress Catalog Card Number 49-48186
International Standard Book Number 0-8379-0921-X
Product Code Number 030457

Distributed in Asia by
United Publishers Services Ltd.
Kenkyu-Sha Bldg.
9, Kanda Surugadai 2-Chome
Chiyoda-Ku, Tokyo, Japan

Manufactured in the United States of America

Table of Contents

Preface

The twenty-first edition of *Who's Who in the West* is a current compilation of biographical information on men and women of distinction in the western sector of North America. Such individuals are of decided reference interest locally and, in many instances, nationally.

The volume contains approximately 21,000 names from the western region of the United States including Alaska, Arizona, California, Colorado, Hawaii, Idaho, Montana, Nevada, New Mexico, Oregon, Utah, Washington, and Wyoming, and from the Canadian provinces of Alberta, British Columbia, and Saskatchewan. Reviewed, revised, and amended, the twenty-first edition offers up to date coverage of a broad range of Westerners based on position or individual achievement.

The persons sketched in this volume represent virtually every important field of endeavor. Included are executives and officials in government, business, education, religion, the press, civic affairs, the arts, cultural affairs, law, and other fields. This edition also includes significant contributors in such areas as contemporary art, music, and science.

Each candidate for inclusion in *Who's Who in the West* is invited to submit biographical data about his or her life and career. This information is reviewed by the Marquis editorial staff before being written into sketch form. A prepublication proof of the sketch is sent to the biographee for verification. The verified sketch, when returned and accepted by Marquis Who's Who, is rechecked and put into final Who's Who format.

In the event that a reference-worthy individual fails to submit biographical data, the Marquis staff compiles the information through independent research. Such sketches are donated by an asterisk. Brief key information is provided in the sketches of selected individuals who did not submit data.

The question often is asked, "How do people get into a Who's Who volume?" Name selection is based on one fundamental principle: reference value.

Biographees of *Who's Who in the West* can be classified into two basic categories: (1) Persons who are of reference importance to researchers, scholars, the press, historians, biographers, participants in business and civic affairs, colleagues, librarians, and others with specific or general inquiry needs; (2) Individuals of national reference interest who are also of such regional or local importance that their inclusion in the book is essential.

In the editorial evaluation that resulted in the ultimate selection of the names in this directory, an individual's desire to be listed was not sufficient reason for inclusion. Only occupational stature or achievement in a field within the western region of North America influenced selection.

Marquis Who's Who editors exercise the utmost care in preparing each biographical sketch for publication. Occasionally, however, errors do occur despite all precautions taken to minimize such occurrences. Users of this directory are requested to draw to the attention of the publisher any errors found so that corrections can be made in a subsequent edition.

Board of Advisors

Marquis Who's Who gratefully acknowledges the following distinguished individuals who have made themselves available for review, evaluation, and general comment with regard to the publication of the twenty-first edition of *Who's Who in the West*. The advisors have enhanced the reference value of this edition by the nomination of outstanding individuals for inclusion. However, the Board of Advisors, either collectively or individually, is in no way responsible for the final selection of names appearing in this volume, nor does the Board of Advisors bear responsibility for the accuracy or comprehensiveness of the biographical information or other material contained herein.

Toney Anaya
Former Governor
New Mexico

Duncan Ferguson Cameron
Director
Glenbow-Alberta Institute

Edward W. Carter
Chairman of the Board Emeritus
Carter Hawley Hale Stores, Inc.

Marion Irvine Lederer
Cultural Administrator
Los Angeles, California

James A. Mason
Dean
College of Fine Arts and Communications
Brigham Young University

Joseph A. McElwain
Consultant and Director
Montana Power Company

Most Reverend Robert F. Sanchez
Archbishop
Albuquerque, New Mexico

Carl H. Stoltenberg
Dean
College of Forestry
Oregon State University

Board of Nominators

Marquis Who's Who gratefully acknowledges the following distinguished nominators for their assistance with regard to the publication of the twenty-first edition of *Who's Who in the West*. They have enhanced the reference value of this edition by the recommendation of outstanding individuals from their respective states or local areas. However, the Board of Nominators, either collectively or individually, is in no way responsible for the final selection of names appearing in this volume, nor does the Board of Nominators bear responsibility for the accuracy or comprehensiveness of the biographical information or other material contained herein.

Dickwin D. Armstrong
President
Bellevue Chamber of Commerce
Bellevue, Washington

John C. Bowers
President and General Manager
Lakewood/South Jeffco Chamber of Commerce
Lakewood, Colorado

David W. Graybill
President and Chief Executive Officer
Tacoma-Pierce County Chamber of Commerce
Tacoma, Washington

Lee Grissom
President
Greater San Diego Chamber of Commerce
San Diego, California

Jim Haynes
President and General Manager
Phoenix Metropolitan Chamber of Commerce
Phoenix, Arizona

Allan B. Hughes
Executive Director
Anaheim Chamber of Commerce
Anaheim, California

Dave Kilby
Executive Vice President
Modesto Chamber of Commerce
Modesto, California

Terri L. Maisel
Executive Vice President
Greater Albuquerque Chamber of Commerce
Albuquerque, New Mexico

Michael Metzler
President
Greater Santa Ana Chamber of Commerce
Santa Ana, California

Dorothy Perkins
Executive Vice President
Casper Area Chamber of Commerce
Casper, Wyoming

Art Pick
Executive Vice President
Greater Riverside Chambers of Commerce
Riverside, California

George Reitemeier
General Manager
Spokane Area Chamber of Commerce
Spokane, Washington

Ray Remy
President
Los Angeles Area Chamber of Commerce
Los Angeles, California

Robert B. Robinson
President
The Chamber of Commerce of Hawaii
Honolulu, Hawaii

D. David Smith
Executive Vice President
Greater Stockton Chamber of Commerce
Stockton, California

Harry L. York
Executive Vice President
Concord Chamber of Commerce
Concord, California

Standards of Admission

The foremost consideration in selecting biographees for *Who's Who in the West* is the extent of an individual's reference interest. Such reference interest is judged on either of two factors: (1) the position of responsibility held, or (2) the level of significant achievement attained.

Admissions based on the factor of position include:

Members of the U.S. Congress

Federal judges

Governors of states covered by this volume

Premiers of Canadian provinces covered by this volume

State attorneys general

Judges of state and territorial courts of highest appellate jurisdiction

Mayors of major cities

Heads of major universities and colleges

Heads of leading philanthropic, educational, cultural, and scientific institutions and associations

Chief ecclesiastics of the principal religious denominations

Principal officers of national and international businesses

Others chosen because of incumbency or membership

Admission based on individual achievement is based on objective qualitative criteria. To be selected, a person must have attained conspicuous achievement.

Key to Information

❶ ASHTON, HARDY AMES, ❷ lawyer; **❸** b. Topeka, Aug. 3, 1934; **❹** s. Samuel Taylor and Barbara (Hanson) A.; **❺** m. Nancy Richardson, June 20, 1955; **❻** children: Marilyn Ashton Heim, Barbara Anne, William Marc. **❼** BA, Pa. State U., 1955; JD, Syracuse U., 1960. **❽** Bar: Calif. 1960, U.S. Supreme Ct. 1968. **❾** Assoc. Prine, Belden and Coates, Sacramento, 1960-67; mem. Johnson, Randolph, Sikes and Bord, Sacramento, 1967—, ptnr., 1969-74, sr. ptnr., 1974—; legal cons. Sacramento Urban League. **❿** Author: Urban Renewal and the Law, 1975, Changes in California Zoning Laws: A Perspective, 1987. **⓫** Commr. Sutter County Park Dist., 1971-78; mem. planning com. Arroyo Seco Redevel. Project, Sacramento, 1980—; bd. dirs. Hargrave Inst. **⓬** Served with U.S. Army, 1956-57. **⓭** Named Man of Yr., Sacramento C. of C., 1986. **⓮** Mem. ABA, Calif. Bar Assn., Sacramento Bar Assn., Am. Judicature Soc., Order of Coif. **⓯** Democrat. **⓰** Episcopalian. **⓱** Clubs: Twelve Trees Country, Tuesday Luncheon. **⓲** Lodge: Lions (Sacramento). **⓳** Avocations: sailing, woodworking. **⓴** Home: 3080 Grant St Sacramento CA 95814 **㉑** Office: Johnson Randolph Sikes & Bord 10 Saint Paul St Sacramento CA 95822

KEY

❶ Name
❷ Occupation
❸ Vital statistics
❹ Parents
❺ Marriage
❻ Children
❼ Education
❽ Professional certifications
❾ Career
❿ Writings and creative works
⓫ Civic and political activities
⓬ Military
⓭ Awards and fellowships
⓮ Professional and
 association memberships
⓯ Political affiliation
⓰ Religion
⓱ Clubs
⓲ Lodges
⓳ Avocations
⓴ Home address
㉑ Office address

Table of Abbreviations

The following abbreviations and symbols are frequently used in this book.

*An asterisk following a sketch indicates that it was researched by the Marquis Who's Who editorial staff and has not been verified by the biographee.

AA, A.A. Associate in Arts
AAAL American Academy of Arts and Letters
AAAS American Association for the Advancement of Science
AAHPER Alliance for Health, Physical Education and Recreation
AAU Amateur Athletic Union
AAUP American Association of University Professors
AAUW American Association of University Women
AB, A.B. Arts, Bachelor of
AB Alberta
ABA American Bar Association
ABC American Broadcasting Company
AC Air Corps
acad. academy, academic
acct. accountant
acctg. accounting
ACDA Arms Control and Disarmament Agency
ACLU American Civil Liberties Union
ACP American College of Physicians
ACS American College of Surgeons
ADA American Dental Association
a.d.c. aide–de–camp
adj. adjunct, adjutant
adj. gen. adjutant general
adm. admiral
adminstr. administrator
adminstrn. administration
adminstrv. administrative
ADP Automatic Data Processing
adv. advocate, advisory
advt. advertising
AE, A.E. Agricultural Engineer
A.E. and P. Ambassador Extraordinary and Plenipotentiary
AEC Atomic Energy Commission
aero. aeronautical, aeronautic
aerodyn. aerodynamic
AFB Air Force Base
AFL–CIO American Federation of Labor and Congress of Industrial Organizations
AFTRA American Federation of TV and Radio Artists
agr. agriculture
agrl. agricultural
agt. agent
AGVA American Guild of Variety Artists
agy. agency
A&I Agricultural and Industrial
AIA American Institute of Architects

AIAA American Institute of Aeronautics and Astronautics
AID Agency for International Development
AIEE American Institute of Electrical Engineers
AIM American Institute of Management
AIME American Institute of Mining, Metallurgy, and Petroleum Engineers
AK Alaska
AL Alabama
ALA American Library Association
Ala. Alabama
alt. alternate
Alta. Alberta
A&M Agricultural and Mechanical
AM, A.M. Arts, Master of
Am. American, America
AMA American Medical Association
A.M.E. African Methodist Episcopal
Amtrak National Railroad Passenger Corporation
AMVETS American Veterans of World War II, Korea, Vietnam
anat. anatomical
ann. annual
ANTA American National Theatre and Academy
anthrop. anthropological
AP Associated Press
APO Army Post Office
apptd. appointed
Apr. April
apt. apartment
AR Arkansas
ARC American Red Cross
archeol. archeological
archtl. architectural
Ariz. Arizona
Ark. Arkansas
ArtsD, ArtsD. Arts, Doctor of
arty. artillery
AS American Samoa
AS Associate in Science
ASCAP American Society of Composers, Authors and Publishers
ASCE American Society of Civil Engineers
ASHRAE American Society of Heating, Refrigeration, and Air Conditioning Engineers
ASME American Society of Mechanical Engineers
assn. association
assoc. associate
asst. assistant
ASTM American Society for Testing and Materials
astron. astronomical
astrophys. astrophysical
ATSC Air Technical Service Command

AT&T American Telephone & Telegraph Company
atty. attorney
Aug. August
AUS Army of the United States
aux. auxiliary
Ave. Avenue
AVMA American Veterinary Medical Association
AZ Arizona

B. Bachelor
b. born
BA, B.A. Bachelor of Arts
BAgr, B.Agr. Bachelor of Agriculture
Balt. Baltimore
Bapt. Baptist
BArch, B.Arch. Bachelor of Architecture
BAS, B.A.S. Bachelor of Agricultural Science
BBA, B.B.A. Bachelor of Business Administration
BBC British Broadcasting Corporation
BC, B.C. British Columbia
BCE, B.C.E. Bachelor of Civil Engineering
BChir, B.Chir. Bachelor of Surgery
BCL, B.C.L. Bachelor of Civil Law
BCS, B.C.S. Bachelor of Commercial Science
BD, B.D. Bachelor of Divinity
bd. board
BE, B.E. Bachelor of Education
BEE, B.E.E. Bachelor of Electrical Engineering
BFA, B.F.A. Bachelor of Fine Arts
bibl. biblical
bibliog. bibliographical
biog. biographical
biol. biological
BJ, B.J. Bachelor of Journalism
Bklyn. Brooklyn
BL, B.L. Bachelor of Letters
bldg. building
BLS, B.L.S. Bachelor of Library Science
Blvd. Boulevard
bn. battalion
B.&O.R.R. Baltimore & Ohio Railroad
bot. botanical
BPE, B.P.E. Bachelor of Physical Education
BPhil, B.Phil. Bachelor of Philosophy
br. branch
BRE, B.R.E. Bachelor of Religious Education
brig. gen. brigadier general
Brit. British, Brittanica
Bros. Brothers
BS, B.S. Bachelor of Science
BSA, B.S.A. Bachelor of Agricultural Science
BSD, B.S.D. Bachelor of Didactic Science

BST, B.S.T. Bachelor of Sacred Theology
BTh, B.Th. Bachelor of Theology
bull. bulletin
bur. bureau
bus. business
B.W.I. British West Indies

CA California
CAA Civil Aeronautics Administration
CAB Civil Aeronautics Board
Calif. California
C.Am. Central America
Can. Canada, Canadian
CAP Civil Air Patrol
capt. captain
CARE Cooperative American Relief Everywhere
Cath. Catholic
cav. cavalry
CBC Canadian Broadcasting Company
CBI China, Burma, India Theatre of Operations
CBS Columbia Broadcasting System
CCC Commodity Credit Corporation
CCNY City College of New York
CCU Cardiac Care Unit
CD Civil Defense
CE, C.E. Corps of Engineers, Civil Engineer
cen. central
CENTO Central Treaty Organization
CERN European Organization of Nuclear Research
cert. certificate, certification, certified
CETA Comprehensive Employment Training Act
CFL Canadian Football League
ch. church
ChD, Ch.D. Doctor of Chemistry
chem. chemical
ChemE, Chem.E. Chemical Engineer
Chgo. Chicago
chirurg. chirurgical
chmn. chairman
chpt. chapter
CIA Central Intelligence Agency
CIC Counter Intelligence Corps
Cin. Cincinnati
cir. circuit
Cleve. Cleveland
climatol. climatological
clin. clinical
clk. clerk
C.L.U. Chartered Life Underwriter
CM, C.M. Master in Surgery
CM Northern Mariana Islands
C.&N.W.Ry. Chicago & North Western Railway
CO Colorado
Co. Company
COF Catholic Order of Foresters
C. of C. Chamber of Commerce
col. colonel

coll. college
Colo. Colorado
com. committee
comd. commanded
comdg. commanding
comdr. commander
comdt. commandant
commd. commissioned
comml. commercial
commn. commission
commr. commissioner
condr. conductor
Conf. Conference
Congl. Congregational, Congressional
Conglist. Congregationalist
Conn. Connecticut
cons. consultant, consulting
consol. consolidated
constl. constitutional
constn. constitution
constrn. construction
contbd. contributed
contbg. contributing
contbn. contribution
contbr. contributor
Conv. Convention
coop. cooperative
CORDS Civil Operations and Revolutionary Development Support
CORE Congress of Racial Equality
corp. corporation, corporate
corr. correspondent, corresponding, correspondence
C.&O.Ry. Chesapeake & Ohio Railway
CPA, C.P.A. Certified Public Accountant
C.P.C.U. Chartered Property and Casualty Underwriter
CPH, C.P.H. Certificate of Public Health
cpl. corporal
C.P.R. Cardio-Pulmonary Resuscitation
C.P.Ry. Canadian Pacific Railway
C.S. Christian Science
CSB, C.S.B. Bachelor of Christian Science
C.S.C. Civil Service Commission
CSD, C.S.D. Doctor of Christian Science
CT Connecticut
ct. court
ctr. center
CWS Chemical Warfare Service
C.Z. Canal Zone

D. Doctor
d. daughter
DAgr, D.Agr. Doctor of Agriculture
DAR Daughters of the American Revolution
dau. daughter
DAV Disabled American Veterans
DC, D.C. District of Columbia
DCL, D.C.L. Doctor of Civil Law
DCS, D.C.S. Doctor of Commercial Science
DD, D.D. Doctor of Divinity

DDS, D.D.S. Doctor of Dental Surgery
DE Delaware
Dec. December
dec. deceased
def. defense
Del. Delaware
del. delegate, delegation
Dem. Democrat, Democratic
DEng, D.Eng. Doctor of Engineering
denom. denomination, denominational
dep. deputy
dept. department
dermatol. dermatological
desc. descendant
devel. development, developmental
DFA, D.F.A. Doctor of Fine Arts
D.F.C. Distinguished Flying Cross
DHL, D.H.L. Doctor of Hebrew Literature
dir. director
dist. district
distbg. distributing
distbn. distribution
distbr. distributor
disting. distinguished
div. division, divinity, divorce
DLitt, D.Litt. Doctor of Literature
DMD, D.M.D. Doctor of Medical Dentistry
DMS, D.M.S. Doctor of Medical Science
DO, D.O. Doctor of Osteopathy
DPH, D.P.H. Diploma in Public Health
DPhil, D.Phil. Doctor of Philosophy
D.R. Daughters of the Revolution
Dr. Drive, Doctor
DRE, D.R.E. Doctor of Religious Education
DrPH, Dr.P.H. Doctor of Public Health, Doctor of Public Hygiene
D.S.C. Distinguished Service Cross
DSc, D.Sc. Doctor of Science
D.S.M. Distinguished Service Medal
DST, D.S.T. Doctor of Sacred Theology
DTM, D.T.M. Doctor of Tropical Medicine
DVM, D.V.M. Doctor of Veterinary Medicine
DVS, D.V.S. Doctor of Veterinary Surgery

E. East
ea. eastern
E. and P. Extraordinary and Plenipotentiary
Eccles. Ecclesiastical
ecol. ecological
econ. economic
ECOSOC Economic and Social Council (of the UN)
ED, E.D. Doctor of Engineering
ed. educated
EdB, Ed.B. Bachelor of Education
EdD, Ed.D. Doctor of Education
edit. edition
EdM, Ed.M. Master of Education
edn. education
ednl. educational

EDP Electronic Data Processing
EdS, Ed.S. Specialist in Education
EE, E.E. Electrical Engineer
E.E. and M.P. Envoy Extraordinary and Minister Plenipotentiary
EEC European Economic Community
EEG Electroencephalogram
EEO Equal Employment Opportunity
EEOC Equal Employment Opportunity Commission
E.Ger. German Democratic Republic
EKG Electrocardiogram
elec. electrical
electrochem. electrochemical
electrophys. electrophysical
elem. elementary
EM, E.M. Engineer of Mines
ency. encyclopedia
Eng. England
engr. engineer
engring. engineering
entomol. entomological
environ. environmental
EPA Environmental Protection Agency
epidemiol. epidemiological
Episc. Episcopalian
ERA Equal Rights Amendment
ERDA Energy Research and Development Administration
ESEA Elementary and Secondary Education Act
ESL English as Second Language
ESSA Environmental Science Services Administration
ethnol. ethnological
ETO European Theatre of Operations
Evang. Evangelical
exam. examination, examining
exec. executive
exhbn. exhibition
expdn. expedition
expn. exposition
expt. experiment
exptl. experimental

F.A. Field Artillery
FAA Federal Aviation Administration
FAO Food and Agriculture Organization (of the UN)
FBI Federal Bureau of Investigation
FCA Farm Credit Administration
FCC Federal Communications Commission
FCDA Federal Civil Defense Administration
FDA Food and Drug Administration
FDIA Federal Deposit Insurance Administration
FDIC Federal Deposit Insurance Corporation
FE, F.E. Forest Engineer
FEA Federal Energy Administration

Feb. February
fed. federal
fedn. federation
FERC Federal Energy Regulatory Commission
fgn. foreign
FHA Federal Housing Administration
fin. financial, finance
FL Florida
Fla. Florida
FMC Federal Maritime Commission
FOA Foreign Operations Administration
found. foundation
FPC Federal Power Commission
FPO Fleet Post Office
frat. fraternity
FRS Federal Reserve System
FSA Federal Security Agency
Ft. Fort
FTC Federal Trade Commission

G-1 (or other number) Division of General Staff
GA, Ga. Georgia
GAO General Accounting Office
gastroent. gastroenterological
GATT General Agreement of Tariff and Trades
gen. general
geneal. genealogical
geod. geodetic
geog. geographic, geographical
geol. geological
geophys. geophysical
gerontol. gerontological
G.H.Q. General Headquarters
G.N. Ry. Great Northern Railway
gov. governor
govt. government
govtl. governmental
GPO Government Printing Office
grad. graduate, graduated
GSA General Services Administration
Gt. Great
GU Guam
gynecol. gynecological

hdqrs. headquarters
HEW Department of Health, Education and Welfare
HHD, H.H.D. Doctor of Humanities
HHFA Housing and Home Finance Agency
HHS Department of Health and Human Services
HI Hawaii
hist. historical, historic
HM, H.M. Master of Humanics
homeo. homeopathic
hon. honorary, honorable
Ho. of Dels. House of Delegates
Ho. of Reps. House of Representatives

hort. horticultural
hosp. hospital
HUD Department of Housing and Urban Development
Hwy. Highway
hydrog. hydrographic

IA Iowa
IAEA International Atomic Energy Agency
IBM International Business Machines Corporation
IBRD International Bank for Reconstruction and Development
ICA International Cooperation Administration
ICC Interstate Commerce Commission
ICU Intensive Care Unit
ID Idaho
IEEE Institute of Electrical and Electronics Engineers
IFC International Finance Corporation
IGY International Geophysical Year
IL Illinois
Ill. Illinois
illus. illustrated
ILO International Labor Organization
IMF International Monetary Fund
IN Indiana
Inc. Incorporated
Ind. Indiana
ind. independent
Indpls. Indianapolis
indsl. industrial
inf. infantry
info. information
ins. insurance
insp. inspector
insp. gen. inspector general
inst. institute
instl. institutional
instn. institution
instr. instructor
instrn. instruction
intern. international
intro. introduction
IRE Institute of Radio Engineers
IRS Internal Revenue Service
ITT International Telephone & Telegraph Corporation

JAG Judge Advocate General
JAGC Judge Advocate General Corps
Jan. January
Jaycees Junior Chamber of Commerce
JB, J.B. Jurum Baccalaureus
JCB, J.C.B. Juris Canoni Baccalaureus
JCD, J.C.D. Juris Canonici Doctor, Juris Civilis Doctor
JCL, J.C.L. Juris Canonici Licentiatus
JD, J.D. Juris Doctor
jg. junior grade

jour. journal
jr. junior
JSD, J.S.D. Juris Scientiae Doctor
JUD, J.U.D. Juris Utriusque Doctor
jud. judicial

Kans. Kansas
K.C. Knights of Columbus
K.P. Knights of Pythias
KS Kansas
K.T. Knight Templar
KY, Ky. Kentucky

LA, La. Louisiana
lab. laboratory
lang. language
laryngol. laryngological
LB Labrador
lectr. lecturer
legis. legislation, legislative
LHD, L.H.D. Doctor of Humane Letters
L.I. Long Island
lic. licensed, license
L.I.R.R. Long Island Railroad
lit. literary, literature
LittB, Litt.B. Bachelor of Letters
LittD, Litt.D. Doctor of Letters
LLB, LL.B. Bachelor of Laws
LLD, LL.D. Doctor of Laws
LLM, LL.M. Master of Laws
Ln. Lane
L.&N.R.R. Louisville & Nashville Railroad
LS, L.S. Library Science (in degree)
lt. lieutenant
Ltd. Limited
Luth. Lutheran
LWV League of Women Voters

M. Master
m. married
MA, M.A. Master of Arts
MA Massachusetts
mag. magazine
MAgr, M.Agr. Master of Agriculture
maj. major
Man. Manitoba
Mar. March
MArch, M.Arch. Master in Architecture
Mass. Massachusetts
math. mathematics, mathematical
MATS Military Air Transport Service
MB, M.B. Bachelor of Medicine
MB Manitoba
MBA, M.B.A. Master of Business Administration
MBS Mutual Broadcasting System
M.C. Medical Corps
MCE, M.C.E. Master of Civil Engineering
mcht. merchant
mcpl. municipal
MCS, M.C.S. Master of Commercial Science
MD, M.D. Doctor of Medicine

MD, Md. Maryland
MDip, M.Dip. Master in Diplomacy
mdse. merchandise
MDV, M.D.V. Doctor of Veterinary Medicine
ME, M.E. Mechanical Engineer
ME Maine
M.E.Ch. Methodist Episcopal Church
mech. mechanical
MEd, M.Ed. Master of Education
med. medical
MEE, M.E.E. Master of Electrical Engineering
mem. member
meml. memorial
merc. mercantile
met. metropolitan
metall. metallurgical
MetE, Met.E. Metallurgical Engineer
meteorol. meteorological
Meth. Methodist
Mex. Mexico
MF, M.F. Master of Forestry
MFA, M.F.A. Master of Fine Arts
mfg. manufacturing
mfr. manufacturer
mgmt. management
mgr. manager
MHA, M.H.A. Master of Hospital Administration
M.I. Military Intelligence
MI Michigan
Mich. Michigan
micros. microscopic, microscopical
mid. middle
mil. military
Milw. Milwaukee
mineral. mineralogical
Minn. Minnesota
Miss. Mississippi
MIT Massachusetts Institute of Technology
mktg. marketing
ML, M.L. Master of Laws
MLA Modern Language Association
M.L.D. Magister Legnum Diplomatic
MLitt, M.Litt. Master of Literature
MLS, M.L.S. Master of Library Science
MME, M.M.E. Master of Mechanical Engineering
MN Minnesota
mng. managing
MO, Mo. Missouri
moblzn. mobilization
Mont. Montana
M.P. Member of Parliament
MPE, M.P.E. Master of Physical Education
MPH, M.P.H. Master of Public Health
MPhil, M.Phil. Master of Philosophy
MPL, M.P.L. Master of Patent Law
Mpls. Minneapolis
MRE, M.R.E. Master of Religious Education

MS, M.S. Master of Science
MS, Ms. Mississippi
MSc, M.Sc. Master of Science
MSF, M.S.F. Master of Science of Forestry
MST, M.S.T. Master of Sacred Theology
MSW, M.S.W. Master of Social Work
MT Montana
Mt. Mount
MTO Mediterranean Theatre of Operations
mus. museum, musical
MusB, Mus.B. Bachelor of Music
MusD, Mus.D. Doctor of Music
MusM, Mus.M. Master of Music
mut. mutual
mycol. mycological

N. North
NAACP National Association for the Advancement of Colored People
NACA National Advisory Committee for Aeronautics
NAD National Academy of Design
N.Am. North America
NAM National Association of Manufacturers
NAPA National Association of Performing Artists
NAREB National Association of Real Estate Boards
NARS National Archives and Record Service
NASA National Aeronautics and Space Administration
nat. national
NATO North Atlantic Treaty Organization
NATOUSA North African Theatre of Operations
nav. navigation
NB, N.B. New Brunswick
NBC National Broadcasting Company
NC, N.C. North Carolina
NCCJ National Conference of Christians and Jews
ND, N.D. North Dakota
NDEA National Defense Education Act
NE Nebraska
NE Northeast
NEA National Education Association
Nebr. Nebraska
NEH National Endowment for Humanities
neurol. neurological
Nev. Nevada
NF Newfoundland
NFL National Football League
Nfld. Newfoundland
NG National Guard
NH, N.H. New Hampshire
NHL National Hockey League
NIH National Institutes of Health
NIMH National Institute of Mental Health
NJ, N.J. New Jersey
NLRB National Labor Relations Board

NM New Mexico
N. Mex. New Mexico
No. Northern
NOAA National Oceanographic and Atmospheric Administration
NORAD North America Air Defense
Nov. November
NOW National Organization for Women
N.P.Ry. Northern Pacific Railway
nr. near
NRC National Research Council
NS, N.S. Nova Scotia
NSC National Security Council
NSF National Science Foundation
N.T. New Testament
NT Northwest Territories
numis. numismatic
NV Nevada
NW Northwest
N.W.T. Northwest Territories
NY, N.Y. New York
N.Y.C. New York City
NYU New York University
N.Z. New Zealand

OAS Organization of American States
ob–gyn obstetrics–gynecology
obs. observatory
obstet. obstetrical
Oct. October
OD, O.D. Doctor of Optometry
OECD Organization of European Cooperation and Development
OEEC Organization of European Economic Cooperation
OEO Office of Economic Opportunity
ofcl. official
OH Ohio
OK Oklahoma
Okla. Oklahoma
ON Ontario
Ont. Ontario
ophthal. ophthalmological
ops. operations
OR Oregon
orch. orchestra
Oreg. Oregon
orgn. organization
ornithol. ornithological
OSHA Occupational Safety and Health Administration
OSRD Office of Scientific Research and Development
OSS Office of Strategic Services
osteo. osteopathic
otol. otological
otolaryn. otolaryngological

PA, Pa. Pennsylvania
P.A. Professional Association
paleontol. paleontological
path. pathological

P.C. Professional Corporation
PE Prince Edward Island
P.E.I. Prince Edward Island (text only)
PEN Poets, Playwrights, Editors, Essayists and Novelists (international association)
penol. penological
P.E.O. women's organization (full name not disclosed)
pfc. private first class
PHA Public Housing Administration
pharm. pharmaceutical
PharmD, Pharm.D. Doctor of Pharmacy
PharmM, Pharm.M. Master of Pharmacy
PhB, Ph.B. Bachelor of Philosophy
PhD, Ph.D. Doctor of Philosophy
PhM, Ph.M. Master of Philosophy
Phila. Philadelphia
philharm. philharmonic
philol. philological
philos. philosophical
photog. photographic
phys. physical
physiol. physiological
Pitts. Pittsburgh
Pkwy. Parkway
Pl. Place
P.&L.E.R.R. Pittsburgh & Lake Erie Railroad
P.O. Post Office
PO Box Post Office Box
polit. political
poly. polytechnic, polytechnical
PQ Province of Quebec
PR, P.R. Puerto Rico
prep. preparatory
pres. president
Presbyn. Presbyterian
presdl. presidential
prin. principal
proc. proceedings
prod. produced (play production)
prodn. production
prof. professor
profl. professional
prog. progressive
propr. proprietor
pros. atty. prosecuting attorney
pro tem pro tempore
PSRO Professional Services Review Organization
psychiat. psychiatric
psychol. psychological
PTA Parent–Teachers Association
ptnr. partner
PTO Pacific Theatre of Operations, Parent Teacher Organization
pub. publisher, publishing, published
pub. public
publ. publication
pvt. private

quar. quarterly

qm. quartermaster
Q.M.C. Quartermaster Corps
Que. Quebec

radiol. radiological
RAF Royal Air Force
RCA Radio Corporation of America
RCAF Royal Canadian Air Force
RD Rural Delivery
Rd. Road
REA Rural Electrification Administration
rec. recording
ref. reformed
regt. regiment
regtl. regimental
rehab. rehabilitation
Rep. Republican
rep. representative
Res. Reserve
ret. retired
rev. review, revised
RFC Reconstruction Finance Corporation
RFD Rural Free Delivery
rhinol. rhinological
RI, R.I. Rhode Island
RN, R.N. Registered Nurse
roentgenol. roentgenological
ROTC Reserve Officers Training Corps
R.R. Railroad
Ry. Railway

S. South
s. son
SAC Strategic Air Command
SALT Strategic Arms Limitation Talks
S.Am. South America
san. sanitary
SAR Sons of the American Revolution
Sask. Saskatchewan
savs. savings
SB, S.B. Bachelor of Science
SBA Small Business Administration
SC, S.C. South Carolina
SCAP Supreme Command Allies Pacific
ScB, Sc.B. Bachelor of Science
SCD, S.C.D. Doctor of Commercial Science
ScD, Sc.D. Doctor of Science
sch. school
sci. science, scientific
SCLC Southern Christian Leadership Conference
SCV Sons of Confederate Veterans
SD, S.D. South Dakota
SE Southeast
SEATO Southeast Asia Treaty Organization
SEC Securities and Exchange Commission
sec. secretary
sect. section
seismol. seismological

sem. seminary
Sept. September
s.g. senior grade
sgt. sergeant
SHAEF Supreme Headquarters Allied Expeditionary Forces
SHAPE Supreme Headquarters Allied Powers in Europe
S.I. Staten Island
S.J. Society of Jesus (Jesuit)
SJD Scientiae Juridicae Doctor
SK Saskatchewan
SM, S.M. Master of Science
So. Southern
soc. society
sociol. sociological
S.P. Co. Southern Pacific Company
spl. special
splty. specialty
Sq. Square
S.R. Sons of the Revolution
sr. senior
SS Steamship
SSS Selective Service System
St. Saint, Street
sta. station
stats. statistics
statis. statistical
STB, S.T.B. Bachelor of Sacred Theology
stblzn. stabilization
STD, STD Doctor of Sacred Theology
subs. subsidiary
SUNY State University of New York
supr. supervisor
supt. superintendent
surg. surgical
SW Southwest

TAPPI Technical Association of the Pulp and Paper Industry
Tb Tuberculosis
tchr. teacher
tech. technical, technology
technol. technological
Tel.&Tel. Telephone & Telegraph
temp. temporary
Tenn. Tennessee
Ter. Territory
Terr. Terrace
Tex. Texas
ThD, Th.D. Doctor of Theology
theol. theological
ThM, Th.M. Master of Theology
TN Tennessee
tng. training
topog. topographical
trans. transaction, transferred
transl. translation, translated
transp. transportation
treas. treasurer
TT Trust Territory
TV television

TVA Tennessee Valley Authority
twp. township
TX Texas
typog. typographical

U. University
UAW United Auto Workers
UCLA University of California at Los Angeles
UDC United Daughters of the Confederacy
U.K. United Kingdom
UN United Nations
UNESCO United Nations Educational, Scientific and Cultural Organization
UNICEF United Nations International Children's Emergency Fund
univ. university
UNRRA United Nations Relief and Rehabilitation Administration
UPI United Press International
U.P.R.R. United Pacific Railroad
urol. urological
U.S. United States
U.S.A. United States of America
USAAF United States Army Air Force
USAF United States Air Force
USAFR United States Air Force Reserve
USAR United States Army Reserve
USCG United States Coast Guard
USCGR United States Coast Guard Reserve
USES United States Employment Service
USIA United States Information Agency
USMC United States Marine Corps
USMCR United States Marine Corps Reserve
USN United States Navy
USNG United States National Guard
USNR United States Naval Reserve
USO United Service Organizations
USPHS United States Public Health Service
USS United States Ship
USSR Union of the Soviet Socialist Republics
USV United States Volunteers
UT Utah

VA Veterans' Administration
VA, Va. Virginia
vet. veteran, veterinary
VFW Veterans of Foreign Wars
VI, V.I. Virgin Islands
vice pres. vice president
vis. visiting
VISTA Volunteers in Service to America
VITA Volunteers in Technical Service
vocat. vocational
vol. volunteer, volume
v.p. vice president
vs. versus

VT, Vt. Vermont

W. West
WA Washington (state)
WAC Women's Army Corps
Wash. Washington (state)
WAVES Women's Reserve, US Naval Reserve
WCTU Women's Christian Temperance Union
we. western
W.Ger. Germany, Federal Republic of
WHO World Health Organization
WI Wisconsin
W.I. West Indies
Wis. Wisconsin
WSB Wage Stabilization Board
WV West Virginia
W.Va. West Virginia
WY Wyoming
Wyo. Wyoming

YK Yukon Territory
YMCA Young Men's Christian Association
YMHA Young Men's Hebrew Association
YM & YWHA Young Men's and Young Women's Hebrew Association
yr. year
YT, Y.T. Yukon Territory
YWCA Young Women's Christian Association

zool. zoological

Alphabetical Practices

Names are arranged alphabetically according to the surnames, and under identical surnames according to the first given name. If both surname and first given name are identical, names are arranged alphabetically according to the second given name. Where full names are identical, they are arranged in order of age—with the elder listed first.

Surnames beginning with De, Des, Du, however capitalized or spaced, are recorded with the prefix preceding the surname and arranged alphabetically under the letter D.

Surnames beginning with Mac and Mc are arranged alphabetically under M.

Surnames beginning with Saint or St. appear after names that begin Sains, are arranged according to the second part of the name, e.g. St. Clair before Saint Dennis.

Surnames beginning with Van, Von or von are arranged alphabetically under letter V.

Compound hyphenated surnames are arranged according to the first member of the compound. Compound unhyphenated surnames are treated as hyphenated names.

Parentheses used in connection with a name indicate which part of the full name is usually deleted in common usage. Hence Abbott, W(illiam) Lewis indicates that the usual form of the given name is W. Lewis. In such a case, the parentheses are ignored in alphabetizing. However, if the name is recorded Abbott, (William) Lewis, signifying that the entire name William is not commonly used, the alphabetizing would be arranged as though the name were Abbott, Lewis.

Who'sWho in the West

AADAHL, JORG, business executive; b. Trondheim, Norway, June 16, 1937; came to U.S., 1966; s. Ottar P. and Gurli (Lockra) A.; M.Sc.M.E., Tech. U. Norway, 1961; M.B.A., U. San Francisco, 1973; m. Inger R. Holst, July 13, 1973; children—Erik, Nina. Research fellow Tech. U. Norway, Trondheim, 1961-62; mgr. arc welding devel. NAG, Oslo, 1964-66; mfg. engr. Varian Assocs., Palo Alto, Calif., 1966-67; bus. mgr. United Airlines, San Francisco, 1974-75, sr. systems analyst, 1977-81; strategic planning specialist Magnex Corp., San Jose, 1981-82; cons. in mgmt., 1982-84; founder, pres. Safeware, Inc., Santa Clara, Calif., 1984—. Developer Safechem II. Recipient Certificate of Honor, San Francisco Bd. Suprs., 1973. Mem. Am. Inst. Indsl. Engrs. (sr.), Leif Erikson League (pres. 1973), Assn. M.B.A. Execs., Norwegian Soc. Profl. Engrs. Club: Young Scandinavians (v.p. 1971). Author: Strength Analysis, Welded Structures, 1967, 81; contbr. articles in various fields to profl. jours.; editor Nordic Highlights, 1972. Office: Safeware Inc 4677 Old Ironsides Dr Santa Clara CA 95054

AADLAND, DONALD INGVALD, engineer; b. Britton, S.D., Apr. 20, 1936; s. Ingvald Martin and Mabel Laverne (Hickok) A.; B.S. in Engring. Physics, S.D. State U., 1959; m. Georgia Doris Miller, Jan. 1957; children—Elizabeth, Donald, Kirsten, Danon, Darren. Electronic engr., govt. electronics div. Motorola, Inc., Scottsdale, Ariz., 1962-66, project mgr., 1966-69, sect. mgr. semicondr. div., 1970; prin. Donald I. Aadland Engrs., Scottsdale, 1971—; expert witness forensic investigations; instr. math. Allen Hancock Jr. Coll., 1960-62; researcher interior ballistics of small arms. Served as lt. USAF, 1959-62. Mem. Nat. Soc. Profl. Engrs., ASHRAE, ASME. Designer solar air conditioning systems and equipment, exptl. energy generation devices, ultrasonic systems and transducers, biomass powered elec. generation systems. Office: PO Box 340 Scottsdale AZ 85252

AAGAARD, CARL MUNK JENSEN, forensic pathologist; b. San Francisco, Mar. 18, 1922; s. Viktor M.J. and N. Fay (Shepard) A.; m. Earla Gardner; children: Carla, Earl, Victor, Lola. BA, Pacific Union Co., 1942; MD, Loma Linda U., 1945. Diplomate Am. Bd. Pathology. Intern Los Angeles County Gen. Hosp., 1945-46; general practice medicine San Mateo and Ukiah, Calif., 1948-51; with pathology tng. dept. Stanford U., San Francisco, 1951-53, Mt. Zion Hosp., San Francisco, 1953-55; practice medicine specializing in pathology Ukiah, 1955—; coroner's surgeon San Francisco Coroner's Office, 1953-55. Corp. bd. dirs. Am. Cancer Soc., San Francisco, 1960-80. Served to capt. Med. Service Corp, AUS, 1946-48. Fellow Coll. Am. Pathology, Am. Soc. Clin. Pathology; mem. AMA, Mendo Lakes Med. Soc. (pres. 1958), Calif. Soc. Pathology, Calif. Med. Assn. Libertarian. Lodge: Rotary. Avocation: pilot. Office: PO Box 450 Ukiah CA 95482-0450

AAGAARD, EARL MUNK JENSEN, biology educator; b. San Francisco, Oct. 17, 1947; s. Carl Munk Jensen and Earla (Gardner) A.; m. Gail LuAnn Selby, June 22, 1969; children: Thorvald, Laura. BA, Pacific Union Coll., 1969, MA, 1971; PhD, Colo. State U., 1982. Cert. community coll. tchr., Calif.; cert. secondary tchr., Adventist Ch. Tchr. sci. Modesto (Calif.) Adventist Acad., 1978-82; assoc. prof. biology Pacific Union Coll., Angwin, Calif., 1982—. Mem. Am. Soc. Mammalogists, Calif. Acad. Sci., N.Am. Fruit Explorers, San Francisco Zoological Soc., Angwin C. of C. Office: Pacific Union Coll Biology Dept Angwin CA 94508

AARON, ROY HENRY, lawyer, entertainment company executive; b. Los Angeles, Apr. 8, 1929; s. Samuel Arthur and Natalie (Krakauer) A.;' m. Theresa Gesas, Dec. 20, 1953; 1 child, Jill. B.A., U. Calif.-Berkeley, 1951; LL.B., U. So. Calif., 1956. Bar: Calif. 1957. Mem. Pacht, Ross, Warne, Bernhard & Sears, Inc., Los Angeles, 1957-79, of counsel, 1979-83; sr. v.p., gen. counsel Plitt Theatres, Inc. and Plitt Theatre Holdings, Inc., Los Angeles, 1978-80, pres., chief operating officer, 1980-85; pres. Plitt Entertainment Group, Inc., Los Angeles, 1985—; pres., chief exec. officer Showscan Film Corp., Los Angeles, 1985—; lectr. Calif. Continuing Edn. of Bar; lectr. continuing legal edn. Loyola U. Law Sch., Los Angeles. Mem. editorial bd. U. So. Calif. Law Rev., 1954-56. Trustee, mem. exec. com. Vista Del Mar Child-Care Service, 1968-80, Reiss-Davis Child Study Center, 1977-80; bd. dirs. Jewish Fedn. Council Greater Los Angeles, 1970-75, UCLA Found.; vice chmn. lawyers div. United Crusade Campaigns, 1971, 72; mem. adv. bd. dirs. Rape Treatment Center of Santa Monica Hosp.; mem. exec. com. Royce Two Seventy, pres. 1986; mem. exec. com. UCLA Performing Arts. Served with USAF, 1951-53. Fellow Am. Bar Found., Los Angeles County Bar Found. (life); mem. ABA, State Bar Calif., Los Angeles County Bar Assn. (trustee 1977-83, v.p. 1979-80, pres. 1982-83), Beverly Hills Bar Assn., Women Lawyers Los Angeles, U. So. Calif. Law Alumni Assn., Legion Lex, Found. Motion Picture Pioneers, Order of Coif, Am. Judicature Soc., Chancery Club Los Angeles. Office: Plitt Entertainment Group Inc 1801 Century Park E Suite 1225 Los Angeles CA 90067

AARON, SHIRLEY MAE, tax consultant; b. Covington, La., Feb. 28, 1935; d. Morgan and Pearl (Jenkins) King; m. Michael A. Aaron, Nov. 27, 1976; m. Richard L. King, Feb. 16, 1952 (div. Feb. 1965); children—Deborah, Richard, Roberta, Keely. Adminstrv. asst. South Central Bell, Covington, La., 1954-62; acct. Brown & Root, Inc., Houston, 1962-75; timekeeper Alyeska Pipeline Co., Fairbanks, Alaska, 1975-77; adminstrv. asst. Boeing Co., Seattle, 1979—; pres. Aaron Enterprises, Seattle, 1977—. Bd. dirs. Burien 146 Homeowners Assn., Seattle, 1979—, pres., 1980-83. Mem. Nat. Assn. Female Execs. Avocation: singing.

AARONSON, MARC A., astronomer, educator; b. Los Angeles, Aug. 24, 1950; s. Simon and Rena (Silverstein) A.; m. Marianne Gabrielle Kun, Aug. 20, 1972; children: Laura, Jamie. BS, Calif. Inst. Tech., 1972; MA, Harvard U., 1974, PhD, 1977. Research asst. Harvard Coll. Obs., Cambridge, 1974-76; research assoc. U. Ariz. Steward Obs., Tucson, 1977-80, asst. astronomer, 1980-82, assoc. astronomer, 1982-83, assoc. prof. astronomy, 1983—. Contbr. articles to profl. jours. Recipient Bart J. Bok prize Harvard U., 1983, George Van Bresbroeck prize U. Ariz., 1981, Newton Lacy Pierce prize Am. Astron. Soc., 1984; grantee Smithsonian Astrophys. Obs., 1976. Avocation: skiing. Office: U Ariz Steward Obs Tucson AZ 85721

ABARBANEL, GAIL, social service administrator, educator; b. Los Angeles, Apr. 17, 1944; d. Sam and Sylvia (Cramer) A.; m. Stephen P. Klein, Jan. 31, 1975. BA magna cum laude, UCLA, 1966; MSW, U. So. Calif., 1968. Lic. clin. social worker. Clin. social worker Mental Health Agy., Los Angeles, 1968-74; founder, dir. Rape Treatment Ctr. and Dept. Social Services Santa Monica (Calif.) Hosp. Med. Ctr., Los Angeles, 1974—; cons., educator in field. Contbr. articles to profl. jours.; author successful legislation to change rape laws. Bd. dirs. Clare Found., 1975-77; active Am. Cancer Soc., 1975-79; Child Trauma Council, 1978-81; Sr. Health Ctr., 1981-82. Recipient Gov.'s Victim Services award, 1985, Coro Found. Pub. Affairs award, 1985, Woman of Year Leadership award YWCA, 1980, 82, Status of Women award AAUW, 1978, Nat. Outstanding Achievement award Am. Cancer Soc., 1977; named Outstanding Alumni, U. So. Calif., 1979. Fellow Soc. for Clin. Social Work; mem. Nat. Assn. Social Workers (Agy. of Yr. award 1977), Nat. Orgn. for Victim Assistance (Exemplary Program award 1985), Women in Health, Phi Beta Kappa, Pi Gamma Mu. Office: Santa Monica Hospital 1225 15th St Santa Monica CA 90404

ABARBANELL, GAYOLA HAVENS, financial advisor, consultant; b. Chgo., Oct. 21, 1939; d. Leonard M. and Lillian L. (Leviten) Havens; m. Burton Abarbanell, June 1, 1967 (div. 1972); children—Jeffrey and Dena Reddick. Student, UCLA, 1975, San Joaquin Coll. Law, 1976-77. Lic. real estate broker, Calif.; lic. life ins. broker, Calif., Wash., Nev., N.Y., Ill.; lic. securities broker, all states. Postal clk., Van Nuys, Calif., 1966-69; regional mgr. Niagara Cyclo Massage, Fresno, Calif., 1969-72; owner, mgr. AD Enterprises, Fresno, 1972-73; agt., Field supr. Equitable of Iowa, Fresno, 1973-74; rep. Ciba Pharms., Fresno, 1976-76; owner, operator Creativity Unltd., Fresno, 1975-76; fin. Advisor Univ. Securities Corp., Los Angeles, 1976—; Fin. Network Investment Corp., 1983—; lectr. seminars for civic orgns. Past nat. CR coordinator NOW. Recipient award Women in Ins., 1972; Top Producer award Univ. Club-Univ. Securities, 1980, 81, 82, No. 1 Producer, 1982, 83; Top Producer, Fin. Network Investment Corp., 1983, 84, 85, 86. Mem. Bus. and Profl. Assn. Los Angeles, Central Calif., Bus. and Profl. Assn., ACLU, So. Calif. Women for Understanding, Gay Acad. Union, Nat. Gay Task Force. Democrat. Jewish. Co-author: Guidelines to Feminist Consciousness Raising, 1975. Home and Office: 1181 Hi Point St Los Angeles CA 90035 Home and Office: Northfork CA

ABBATE, PAUL J., judge; b. N.Y.C., Mar. 28, 1919; s. Salvatore and Mary (Clemente) A.; married, Sept. 8, 1946; children: Michael, Paul, Greg (dec.), Maria. B.S., U.S. Mcht. Marine Acad., 1943; LL.B., St. Johns U., 1949; LL.M., Bklyn. Law Sch., 1952. Bar: U.S. Supreme Ct. bar 1956. Practiced law N.Y.C., 1952-66; atty. gen. Guam, Agana, 1966-68; judge Island Ct., 1968-74; presiding judge Superior Ct. of Guam, 1974—; prof. law Coll. Guam; chmn. Jud. Council, 1979—, Bd. Law Examiners, 1979—. Ordained deacon Roman Catholic Ch. Served with USN. Decorated Bronze Star, Purple Heart. Office: Presiding Judge Superior Ct of Guam Judiciary Bldg Agana GU 96910

ABBEY, JAY MANNING, judge; b. Columbus, Kans., Mar. 21, 1932; s. William and Virginia (Janes) A.; 1 child, Jay Christopher; m. Anne M. McCormick, Mar. 21, 1981; children—William, Laura. B.A., Ariz. State U., 1957; LL.B., U. Ariz., 1960. Bar: Ariz. 1960. City prosecutor, Tucson, 1962; asst. city atty., Tucson, 1963-64; asst. utility dir. for Ariz. Corp. Com., Phoenix, 1965-66; spl. asst. atty. gen. for Corp. Com. and Ins. Dept., Phoenix, 1965-67, acting dir.; sole practice, Phoenix and Pinetop, Ariz., 1969-80; judge Navajo County Superior Ct., Holbrook, Ariz., 1980—; judge Hopi Tribal Ct., Hopi Ct. Appeals, Apache Tribal Ct., Apache Ct. Appeals; mem. Gov.'s Juvenile Justice and Delinquency Prevention Adv. Council, Phoenix, 1981—, Gov.'s Council on Children, Youth and Families, 1984—, Gov.'s Task Force on Child Abuse, 1984—; mem. adv. council to Dept. of Children, faculty for jud. edn. State of Ariz., 1985—. Served with U.S. Army, 1951-54, Korea. Mem. VFW. Democrat. Episcopalian. Lodges: Elks, Kiwanis. Home: PO Box 369 Pinetop AZ 85935 Office: Navajo County Superior Cts South Hwy 77 Holbrook AZ 86025

ABBOTT, ANTON DWIGHT, aerospace engineer; b. Indpls., Aug. 28, 1936; s. Horace Emerson and Evelyn (Goff) A.; m. Janet Mavis Kyseth, June 27, 1964; children: Steven, Douglas. BS in Aero. Engring., Purdue U., 1958, MS in Indsl. Adminstrn., 1965. Mgr. systems definition Aerospace Corp., San Bernadino, Calif., 1965-68; dir. advanced projects Aerospace Corp., Los Angeles, 1968-75; prin. dir. Eastern tech. div. Aerospace Corp., Washington, 1975-82; prin. dir. Space Transp. Plans and Architecture Aerospace Corp., Los Angeles, 1982—. Patentee in field. Mem. AIAA, AAAS, Purdue U. Gimlet Club. Avocations: private airplane pilot, running. Home: 1825 Via Estudillo Palos Verdes Estates CA 90274 Office: Aerospace Corp PO Box 92957 Los Angeles CA 90009

ABBOTT, H(ORACE) PORTER, English literature educator; b. Balt., Nov. 21, 1940; s. Horace Porter and Barbara (Trueblood) A.; m. Anita Vaivods, June 25, 1966; children: Jason, Byram. BA, Reed Coll., 1962; MA, U. Toronto, Ont., Can., 1964, PhD, 1968. Asst. prof. English U. Calif., Santa Barbara, 1966-73, assoc. prof., 1973-81, prof., 1981—, chmn. dept., 1983—. Author: The Fiction of Samuel Beckett, 1973, Diary Fiction, 1984; (dramatic anthology) Beckett This Evening, 1985. Office: U Calif Dept English Santa Barbara CA 93106

ABBOTT, ISABELLA AIONA, biology educator; b. Hana, Maui, Hawaii, June 20, 1919; d. Loo Yuen and Annie Patsue (Chung) Aiona; m. Donald P. Abbott, Mar. 3, 1943 (dec.); 1 dau., Ann Kaiue Abbott. A.B., U. Hawaii, 1941; M.S., U. Mich., 1942; Ph.D., U. Calif., Berkeley, 1950. Prof. biology Stanford U., 1972-82; G.P. Wilder prof. botany U. Hawaii, 1978—; vis. research biologist and tchr., Japan and Chile. Author: (with G.J. Hollenberg) Marine Algae of California, 1976; contbr. articles to profl. jours. Co-recipient N.Y. Bot. Garden award for best book in botany, 1978. Mem. Internat. Phycological Soc. (treas. 1964-68), Western Soc. Naturalists (sec. 1962-64, pres. 1977), Phycological Soc. Am., Brit. Phycological Soc., Hawaiian Bot. Soc. Office: 3190 Maile Way Botany Dept Univ of Hawaii Honolulu HI 96822

ABBOTT, JOHN RODGER, elec. engr.; b. Los Angeles, Aug. 2, 1933; s. Carl Raymond and Helen Catherine (Roche) A.; B.S. with honors, UCLA, 1955; M.S., U. So. Calif., 1957; m. Theresa Andrea McQuaide, Apr. 20, 1968. Advanced study engr. Lockheed Missile Systems, Los Angeles, 1955-56; radar systems engr. Hughes Aircraft Co., Los Angeles, 1956-59; devel. engr. Garrett Airesearch Co., Los Angeles, 1959-63, instr. plant tng. program, 1962-63; asst. project engr. Litton Industries, Los Angeles, 1963; space power systems engr. TRW Systems, Los Angeles, 1963-65; engr. specialist Los Angeles Dept. Water and Power, 1965—; frequency coordination chmn. Region X, Utilities Telecommunications Council, 1977-79, sec.-treas. Utilities Telecommunication Council, 1979-80; instr. electronics course Los Angeles City Schs., 1965-66, Birmingham High Sch., Van Nuys, Calif. Registered profl. engr., Calif. Mem. IEEE, Am. Radio Relay League (Pub. Service award 1971), Tau Beta Pi. Contbr. articles to profl. jours. Office: PO Box 71 Cambria CA 93428

ABBOTT, MITCHEL THEODORE, chemistry educator; b. Los Angeles, June 6, 1930; s. Chester and Judith T. (Wasserman) A.; m. Florine Ruth Lutze, Oct. 27, 1962; children: Valerie Michele, Mark Nelson, Chester Bruce. BS in Chemistry, UCLA, 1957, PhD in Biol. Chemistry, 1962. Postdoctoral fellow NYU Sch. Medicine, 1962-64; prof. chemistry San Diego State U., 1964—; vis. scientist Roche Inst. Molecular Biology, Nutley, N.J., 1972-73; mem. staff Molecular Biology Inst. San Diego State U., 1980—. Contbr. articles to profl. jours. Served with M.C., U.S. Army, 1953-55. Grantee NIH, 1965-83, Calif. Metabolic Research Found., 1985—. Mem. AAAS, Am. Soc. Biol. Chemists. Office: San Diego State U Dept Chemistry San Diego CA 92182

ABBOTT, ROBERT DEAN, educational psychology educator; b. Twin Falls, Idaho, Dec. 19, 1946; s. Charles Dean and Billie June (Moore) A.; m. Sylvia Patricia Keim, Dec. 16, 1967; children: Danielle, Matthew. B.A., Calif. Western U., San Diego, 1967; M.S., U. Wash., 1968, Ph.D., 1970. Asst. prof., assoc. prof. Calif. State U.-Fullerton, 1970-75; asst. prof., prof. ednl. psychology U. Wash., Seattle, 1975—. Author: Elementary Multivariate Statistics, 1983; contbr. articles to profl. jours. Calif. State scholar, 1964-67. Mem. Am. Psychol. Assn., Am. Ednl. Research Assn., Am. Stats. Assn., Psychometric Soc. Methodist. Office: U Wash Ednl Psychology DQ-12 Seattle WA 98195

ABBRUZZESE, CARLO ENRICO, physician, writer, educator; b. Rome, Italy, May 28, 1923; s. Aurelio and Maria (Sbriccoli) A.; Liceo-Ginnasio Dante Alighieri, Roma, 1935-43; Facoltà di Medicina e Chirurgia, Università di Roma, 1943-49; m. Jovanka N. Vasin, Feb. 14, 1976; children by previous marriage—Marco A., Carlo M., Eric L., Christopher E. Came to U.S., 1951, naturalized, 1959. Resident in tropical subtropical diseases U. Rome, 1950-51; intern Woman's and Highland Park Gen. hosps., Detroit, 1951-53; resident in family practice Saratoga Gen. Hosp., Detroit, Columbus Hosp., Newark, 1953-57; gen. practice occupational, sport medicine, Rome, 1949-51, Oakland, Calif., 1958-75, Santa Ana, Calif., 1975-84; dir. emergency and outpatients depts. Drs. Hosp. of Santa Ana (Calif.), 1975-77. Founder, leader polit. youth movements, Rome, 1943-47. Co-founder, nat. chmn. divorce reforms orgns., 1975; UN rep. on domestic human rights, 1977. Decorated Commendatore di Merito, 1950. Fulbright fellow, 1951-53. Fellow Am. Acad. Family Physicians; mem. Am. Acad. Gen. Practice, Ordine dei Medici di Roma Società Italiana di Chirurgia, Am. Coll. Emergency Physicians, Union Am. Physicians. Author: Storia della Psicologia, 1949; L'ascoltazione stetoscopica, 1955, 56, 83, 86; Esercitazioni di diagnostica ascoltatoria, 1983, 86; founder, pub., editor-in-chief ESDNA, Rome, 1983, ESDI, Rome, 1986; pub. Med. Newsletter, 1987. Contbr. articles to profl. jours. Office: 328 N Newport Blvd Suite 104 Newport Beach CA 92663

ABDUL-JABBAR, KAREEM (LEWIS FERDINAND ALCINDOR), professional basketball player; b. N.Y.C., Apr. 16, 1947; s. Ferdinand Lewis and Cora Alcindor; m. Habiba (Janice Brown), 1971 (div. 1973); children: Habiba, Kareem, Sultana, Amir. B.A., UCLA, 1969. Basketball player with Milw. Bucks, 1969-75, Los Angeles Lakers, 1975—. Appeared on TV in episodes of Mannix, The Man from Atlantis, Diff'rent Strokes, Tales from the Darkside, Pryor's Place, The ABC Aftersch. Spl.; appeared in movies: The Fish that Saved Pittsburgh, 1979, Airplane, 1980, Fletch, 1985; author: (with Peter Knobler) Giant Steps: An Autobiography of Kareem Abdul-Jabbar, 1983. Named Rookie of Year NBA, 1970; recipient Maurice Podoloff Cup, named Most Valuable Player NBA, 1971, 72, 74, 76, 77, 80; player NBA All-Star game, 1970-87; named to NBA 35th Anniversary All-Time Team, 1980; NBA Playoff Most Valuable Player, 1971, 85; mem. NBA Championship Team, 1971, 80, 82, 85, 87; NCAA Tournament Most Outstanding Player, 1967, 68, 69. Muslim. Became NBA all-time leading scorer, 1984. Avocation: jazz. Address: care Los Angeles Lakers The Forum PO Box 10 Inglewood CA 90306 *

ABE, NOEL KEN, chemist; b. Lahaina, Hawaii, Dec. 25, 1957; s. Hideo and Nobuko (Tabata) A. BS in Chemistry, Adams State Coll., 1980. Chemist Core Labs., Aurora, Colo., 1980-82; lab. technician City of Longmont, Colo., 1982—. Mem. Am. Chem. Soc., Colo. Water Wastewater Analyst Assn. Democrat. Mormon. Avocations: golf, backpacking, cycling, hunting, fishing. Office: City of Longmont 1100 S Sherman St Longmont CO 80501

ABEGGLEN, RICKI LEE, electrical engineer; b. LaCrosse, Wis., Aug. 6, 1960; s. James Frederick and Corrine Thelma (Peterson) A. BSEE, U. Wis., 1982, MSEE, 1984. Engr. Intel Corp., Santa Clara, Calif., 1984—. Mem. Beta Theta Pi (song chmn.). Avocations: guitar, frisbee.

ABEJO, SISTER MARIA ROSALINA, nun; b. Tagoloan, Philippines, July 13, 1922; came to U.S., 1977, naturalized, 1985; d. Don Pedro Abejo y Villegas and Dona Beatriz Zamarro de Abejo. AA in Music, St. Scholastica's Coll., Manila, 1949; MusB, Philippine Womens U., 1956, MusM, 1958; postrad. Cath. U. Am., 1962-64; postrad. studies in theory and composition, Eastman Sch. Music, 1962; studies with Fritz Mahler, N.Y.C., summers 1964, 65, 68, Maestro Franco Ferrara, Rome, 1972-75. Dean Lourdes Coll., Manila, 1958-61, Immaculate Coll., Manila, 1961-62, St. Mary's Coll., Manila, 1964-76; music dir. Holy Spirit Ch., Fremont, Calif., 1978-82, St. Leonard's Ch., Fremont, 1982—; sec. Nat. Liturgical Commn. Sacred Music, Manila, 1964-76; rep. Cath. ch. Ecumenical Council Chs., Manila, 1966-76; founder, dir., conductor Nuns Concerts For Charities, 1967-76; lectr. music Kans. U., Lawrence, 1977-79, Consular Wives and All Nations Group, San Francisco, 1980-82; head music dept. St. Pius X Sem., Covington, Ky., 1978-79; founder, dir., conductor Ars Nova Symphony Orchestra and Ars Nova Concert Chorus, Fremont, 1979—; cultural officer U.N. Assn., Manila, 1967-77, Dr. J.P. Rizal Found., MacArthur Found. Composer: Why Should We Weep So, 1968, First Oratorio in Pilipino, 1969, Ode to the Statesmen, 1971, Guerilla Symphony, 1971, Onward Ye Women, 1975, Death and Victory, 1976, Loops Circles & Squares, 1979, Five Wedding Songs, 1983, Surge of the Fair Sex, 1984, Explosion of the Pyramids, 1985, Brotherhood Symphony and Muslim Diver, 1986, The Mutiny and The Woman: Bloodless Revolution, 1987, over 500 others; commd. works include: The Conversion of King Humabon, 1967, Panahon, 1969, Fanfare For 8 Instruments, 1970, Overture 1081, 1972, (ballet) The Ritual, 1976, Eternal Memory, 1978, Strings on the Dignity of Man, 1980, Jubilee Cantata, 1984, The Absent Baritone, 1985; various compositions recorded on discs and tapes; author: (textbooks) Learning To Read and Write Music, Music for Philippine High Schools, Kantahin Pilipino, Our Own Choruses. Recipient numerous awards including: Republic Heritate award, Govt. of Manila, 1967, U.N. award, 1972, Pontifical Plaque of Recognition, 1972, Plaque of Recognition Zonta, 1973, Dr. J.P. Rizal-MacArthur award, 1974, Internat. Womens award In Womens Yr., 1975, Bay Area Recognition plaque, 1984, Contbrg.-Activities-Participating-Achievement Internat. award Philippine Women's Univ. Centennial Celebration, 1986. Mem. Conductors Assn. (v.p.), League of Filipino Composers (sec.-treas. 1966-77), Internat. Music Council (bd. dirs.), Internat. Soc. Music Edn., League of Asian Composers. Avocations: reading, composing. Home and Office: 37950 #62 Fremont Blvd Fremont CA 94536

ABEL, ALLAN BERNARD, mgmt. cons.; b. Williams, Calif., Dec. 22, 1924; s. Allen and Consuelo (Benham) A.; student U. Calif., Berkeley, 1943-50, Golden Gate Coll., 1947, Instituto Cultural Mexicano-Americano, Guadalajara, Mexico, 1961; m. Maria Socorro; children—Allan Bernard, Allen Raymond, Sonya. Practice in Reno, 1954-69, Las Vegas, 1969—; investment adviser, tax cons., rare coinbroker, 1963-67; asso., bus. cons. Bus. Consultants, Inc., bus. and mgmt. cons. in 11 Western states and Mexico, 1967—; pres. SUMCO, Inc.; officer, dir. Centro de Vivienda para Retirados, S.A., Abel de Mexico, S.A.; sec.-treas. Magic Valley Enterprises, Inc.; sec.-treas. Central Devel. Co., Las Vegas, also dir.; sec. Gastrox Constrn. Co., Las Vegas. Agt., Nev. Gaming Control Bd., Nev. Gaming Commn., 1956; dir. So. Nev. conf. Pop Warner Jr. Football, 1st v.p., 1981—; mem. nat. com. Young Democrats Clubs Am., 1955-57, bd. dirs., 1957-59; mem. exec. bd. Clark County Dem. Central Com., 1970—; mem. Nev. State Dem. State Central Com., 1970—, vice chmn., 1957-58; gen. mgr. retirement housing project, Mexico, 1965-67; pres. chpt. 15 Mother Earth News; state chmn. com. select del. Humphrey; chmn. Lucy Branch Kidney Fund; counselor Family Abuse Center; pres. Flame Soccer Club; dir. Las. Las Vegas Under 23 Select Soccer Team; Lic. pub. accountant, Nev. Mem. Nat. Soc. Pub. Accountants, U. Calif. Alumni Assn. (life), Inst. Indsl. Relations Alumni Assn., Internat. Platform Assn., Am. Numis. Assn. Democrat. Spaceite. Clubs: Calif. 23 (Berkeley); Tower and Flame, Daily Californian, Am. Soc. Jalisco. Pub.: Nev. Report. Research on problems of aged living in fgn. country, 1963-64. Home: 811 Upland Blvd Las Vegas NV 89107 Office: 3540 W Sahara Suite 298 Las Vegas NV 89104

ABEL, ELIZABETH A., dermatologist; b. Hartford, Conn., Mar. 16, 1940; d. Frederick A. and Rose (Borovicka) A.; m. Barton Lane; children: Barton, Geoffrey, Suzanne. Student, Colby-Sawyer Coll., 1957-60; BS, Wash. Hosp. Ctr. Sch. Med. Tech., 1961, U. Md., 1965; MD cum laude, U. Md., 1967. Diplomate Am. Bd. Dermatology. Intern San Francisco Gen. Hosp., 1967-68; resident, fellow in oncology U. Calif. Med. Ctr., San Francisco, 1968-69; resident in dermatology NYU Med. Ctr., 1969-72, USPHS research trainee in dermatology, 1972-73; dep. chief dept. dermatology USPHS Hosp., S.I.,

N.Y., 1973-74; instr. clin. dermatology Columbia U. Coll. Physicians and Surgeons, N.Y.C., 1974-75; instr. clin. dermatology Stanford (Calif.) U. Sch. Medicine, 1975-77, clin. asst. prof. dermatology, 1977-82, asst. prof. dermatology, 1982—; cons. Palo Alto (Calif.) VA Hosp., 1977—; dir. Psoriosis Day Care Ctr. and Phototherapy Unit, Stanford U. Med. Ctr., 1978—; adj. faculty Pacific Grad. Sch. Psychology, Palo Alto, 1984—. Contbr. articles to sci. jours. Mellon Found. fellow, 1983. Fellow Am. Acad. Dermatology; mem. Soc. Investigative Dermatology, San Francisco Dermatologic Soc., Internat. Soc. Dermatology Surgery, Dermatology Found., Pacific Dermatologic Assn., Women's Dermatologic Soc., Alpha Omega Alpha. Episcopalian. Avocations: piano, skiing. Office: Stanford U Med Ctr Dept Dermatology Stanford CA 94305

ABEL, RICHARD WAYNE, marketing communications consultant; b. San Luis Obispo, Calif., July 4, 1941; s. John William and Olive Mae (Bickmore) A. B.F.A., Cornell U., 1963; M.F.A., U. Hawaii, 1966. Advt. trainee Persons Advt., N.Y.C., 1963-64; campaign dir. Am. Cancer Soc., San Francisco, 1966-67; instr. theatre Occidental Coll., Los Angeles, 1967-69; pres., owner COMM/COORD, Los Angeles, 1969-72; dir. communications TRAN Corp., El Segundo, Calif., 1972-74; communications cons., Laguna Beach, Calif., 1974-84; founder Accomplishmence Systems & Cons., Inc., San Juan Capistrano, Calif., 1984—, also pres., Opera Pacific, also bd. dirs. and strategic planning com. Co-founder Nautical Heritage Mus.; founder Heritage Players; capt. California, Ofcl. Tallship Ambassador State of Calif. Address: 3531 Calle La Quinta San Clemente CA 92672 Office: Accomplishmence Systems & Cons Inc 27292 Calle Arroyo San Juan Capistrano CA 92675

ABELL, JAMES IRVINE, personnel management consultant; b. Louisville, May 14, 1923; s. Philip and Elsie (Schneider) A.; m. Aileen Towe, Dec. 30, 1945; children—Kevin P., Karen E. B.A., U. Louisville, 1947; Pre-Metereology Cert., Vanderbilt U., 1944; postgrad. UCLA, Calif. State U. Personnel mgr. H.J. Scheirich Co., Louisville, 1947-54; office mgr. Star Times Pub. Co., Santa Barbara, Calif., 1954-55; mgr. employee benefits adminstrn. Beckman Instruments, Fullerton, Calif., 1955-84; cons. in personnel mgmt., Fullerton, 1984—. Active numerous community activities. Served to sgt. USAF, 1943-46. Recipient Edn. award Fullerton C. of C., 1977. Mem. Electronic Salary and Wage Assn. (past pres.), Kappa Alpha. Republican. Home: 3001 Milagro Way Fullerton CA 92635

ABELS, ROBERT FREDERICK, tax consultant; b. West Palm Beach, Fla., Nov. 18, 1926; s. John Frederick and Nelly (Bulfin) A.; m. Shirley Mae Larsen, May 31, 1953; children: Robert Frederick, Steven John, Richard Alan. BS, U.S. NavaL Postgrad. Sch., 1965; MBA in Finance, U. West Fla., 1971. Enlisted USN, 1944, commd. ensign, 1949, advanced through grades to comdr., 1963, aviator in Korea and Vietnam; dir. Naval Officer Candidate Sch. USN, Pensacola, Fla., 1966-68; ret. USN, 1969; tchr. math. and bus. Skyline High Sch., Lemon Grove, Calif., 1971-83; tax counselor, real estate salesman. Decorated Bronze Star, Air medal, Commendation medal; Vietnamese Cross Gallantry. Mem. Nat. Assn. Enrolled Agts., Inland Soc. Tax. Cons., Nat. Assn. Tax Consultors. Republican. Lutheran. Address: 10633 Canyon Lake Dr San Diego CA 92131

ABERNATHIE, DONALD HARRY, software engineering specialist; b. Anna, Ill., May 6, 1934; s. Howard Wallace and Edith L. (Sanders) A.; m. Verdean Molly Neill, Dec. 27, 1952; children: Debra, Jan, Donna. B.A. in Math., U. Ill., 1956, M.A. in Stats., 1957. Research engr. Gen. Dynamics/Convair, San Diego, 1957-63, sr. research engr., 1963-68, design specialist Gen. Dynamics/Data Systems Services, 1968-80, software engring. specialist, 1980—. Mem. IEEE (mem. ATLAS lang. standardization com. 1979—), Phi Beta Kappa, Phi Eta Sigma. Democrat. Methodist. Home: 5040 Colina Dr La Mesa CA 92041 Office: Gen Dynamics MZ 7134-N PO Box 85808 San Diego CA 92138

ABERNATHY, ROBERT NOEL, chemist; b. San Rafael, Calif., Dec. 25, 1952; s. Jack Percy and Theresa Leona (Distel) A.; m. Susan Marie Beatty, Aug. 16, 1975 (div. Dec. 1982); m. Maureen Ann O'Neill, Feb. 10, 1983. BA in Chemistry, Biology, Calif. State Coll., 1976; PhD in Chemistry, Pa. State U., 1980. Mem. tech. staff The Aerospace Corp., El Segundo, Calif., 1980—. Contbr. articles to profl. jours. Mem. AAAS, Am. Chem. Soc. Home: 1706-B Marshallfield Ln Redondo Beach CA 90278 Office: The Aerospace Corp PO Box 92957 M5/754 Los Angeles CA 90009

ABERNETHY, JOHN LEO, chemistry educator; b. San Jose, Calif., Mar. 6, 1915; s. Elmer Robert and Margaret May (Scott) A. B.A., UCLA, 1936; M.S., Northwestern U., 1938, Ph.D., 1940. Instr. U.Tex., 1940-42, asst. prof., 1942-44, assoc. prof., 1944-45; fellow Northwestern U., Evanston, Ill., 1946; mem. faculty Washington and Lee U., 1948-49, Calif. State U., 1947-59; research assoc. UCLA, 1959-69; prof. chemistry Calif. State Poly. U., Pomona, 1969—. Author: Principles of Organic Chemistry, 1949. Mem. editorial bd. Jour. Chem. Edn., 1956—. Contbr. articles to chem. jours. Adv., Intervarsity Christian Fellowship, 1956-59. Fulbright fellow San Marcos U., Lima, Peru, 1962-63. Mem. Am. Chem. Soc., Am. Sci. Affiliation, Calif. Assn. Chemistry Tchrs. (editor proc. 1966—) Sigma Xi (local pres.), Alpha Chi Sigma, Phi Lambda Upsilon.

ABILDSKOV, J.A., cardiologist, educator; b. Salem, Utah, Sept. 22, 1923; s. John and Annie Marie (Peterson) A.; m. Mary Helen McKell, Dec. 4, 1944; children—Becky, Alan, Mary, Marilyn. B.A., U. Utah, 1944, M.D., 1946. Diplomate Am. Bd. Internal Medicine. Intern Latter-day Saints Hosp., Salt Lake City, 1947-48; resident Charity Hosp. La., New Orleans, 1948-51; instr. Tulane U., New Orleans, 1948-54; asst. prof. to prof. SUNY-Syracuse, 1955-68; prof. medicine U. Utah, Salt Lake City, 1968—; dir. Nora Eccles Harrison Cardiovascular Research and Tng. Inst., Salt Lake City, 1970—. Contbr. articles to profl. jours. Served to capt. USAR, 1954-56. Recipient Disting. Research award U. Utah, 1976. Fellow Am. Coll. Cardiology; mem. Assn. Am. Physicians, Am. Soc. Clin. Investigation (emeritus), Assn. Univ. Cardiologists (founding), Western Assn. Physicians, Venezuelan Cardiology Soc. (hon.), Cardiology Soc. Peru (corresponding). Republican. Mormon. Home: 1506 Canterbury Dr Salt Lake City UT 84112 Office: U Utah Cardiology Div Bldg 100 Salt Lake City UT 84112

ABKEN, PAMELA JO, advertising agency executive; b. Eldora, Iowa, Dec. 9, 1951; d. Glenn A. Gilbert and Audrey Laura (Brightwell) Comfort; m. Harvey James Abken, May 7, 1983 (div. June 1986). Student in psychology, N.Mex. State U., 1970-72. Dir. Weight Loss Clinic, Portland, Oreg., 1976-78; classified mgr. Community Press Inc., Tigard, Oreg., 1978-79; sales mgr. Columbia Broadcasting, Kennewick, Wash., 1979-84; dir. mktg. Wash. Baseball Inc., Richland, 1984-85; v.p., co-owner CNA Direct Inc., Seattle, 1985—; cons. Conley, Nealy & Assocs., Kennewick, 1985—. Unit chmn. Am. Cancer Soc., Kennewick, 1984; foster parent Cath. Family Services, Kennewick, 1981-82; vol. Spl. Olympics, Pasco, Wash., 1981; with advt./mktg. Tri-Cities Wine Festival, Kennewick, 1982—, Tri-Cities Vis. and Conv. Bur. Assn., Kennewick, 1982—. Named an Outstanding Young Woman of Am., OYM, Montgomery, Ala., 1986. Mem. Am. Advt. Fedn. (founding mem. 1981-82, bd. dirs. 1981—), Nat. Assn. Female Execs., Chi Omega. Mem. Four Sq. Church. Club: Toastmasters. Avocations: swimming, softball, snowmobiling. Home: 20435 14th Ave So Seattle WA 98148 Office: CNA Direct Inc 2815 2 Ave #523 Seattle WA 98121

ABLES, ERNEST DAVID, wildlife educator; b. Hugo, Okla., Jan. 13, 1934; s. Ernest Elmer and Annie Mae (Cooper) A.; m. Juanita Covington, Aug. 21, 1960; children: Christopher David, Brian Allen. BS in Zoology, Okla. State U., 1961; MS in Wildlife Mgmt., U. Wis., 1964, PhD in Zoology and Wildlife, 1968. Asst. prof. Tex. A&M U., College Station, 1968-71, assoc. prof., 1971-73; prof. wildlife U. Idaho, Moscow, 1973—, assoc. dean coll. forestry, 1974-82, head dept. wildlife, 1982—, acting dean coll. forestry, 1984-85. Author/editor Axis Deer in Texas, 1977 (pub. award 1977). Served with U.S. Army, 1954-57. Recipient Outstanding Tchr. award Coll. Forestry U. Idaho, 1973, Disting. Faculty award U. Idaho, 1983, Alumni award for Excellence, U. Idaho, 1982. Mem. The Wildlife Soc. (cert.), The Wilderness Soc. Democrat. Baptist. Avocations: photography, hunting, fishing. Home: 847 Nylarol Moscow ID 83843 Office: U Idaho Coll Forestry Moscow ID 83843

ABLOW, CLARENCE MAURICE, mathematician; b. N.Y.C., Nov. 6, 1919; s. Abraham and Bertha (Wolters) A.; m. Stella Jane Kahn, Aug. 6, 1945. BA, UCLA, 1940, MA, 1942; PhD, Brown U., 1951. Mathematician Boeing Airplane Co., Seattle, 1951-55, SRI Internat., Menlo Park, Calif., 1955-84. Served to lt. USNR, 1942-46. Mem. Indsl. and Applied Math. (pres. No. Calif. Sect. 1970-79), Am. Math. Soc. Democrat. Home: 193 Portola Rd Portola Valley CA 94025

ABO, RONALD KENT, architect; b. Rupert, Idaho, July 10, 1946; s. Isamu and Ameria (Hachiya) A.; m. Bekka Wright, June 29, 1968 (div. June 1975). BArch, U. Colo., 1969. Lic. architect, Colo. Designer SLP & Ptnrs., Denver, 1968-71; dir. Community Design Ctr., Denver, 1971-72; assoc. Barker, Rinker, Seacat, Denver, 1972-76; pvt. practice architecture Denver, 1976-80; pres. Abo Gude Architects, Denver, 1980-84, Ron Abo Architects, Denver, 1984—. Prin. works include Morrison Horiculture Ctr., 1983 (AIA citation 1983), Highland Square, 1982 (AIA citation 1983). Bd. dirs. Washington Park Community Ctr., Denver, 1978-80; advisor 38th Ave. Mcht.'s Assn., Denver, 1985; active Denver Community Leadership Forum, Denver, 1985. Mem. AIA. Democrat. Avocation: aikido (2d degree black belt). Home: 1448 Pennsylvania Denver CO 80203 Office: Ron Abo Architects 2536 S 15th St Denver CO 80211

ABRAHAM, EDWARD, research physician; b. Chgo., Apr. 17, 1952; s. Willard and Shirley Dale (Wiener) A.; m. Dawn Wood, Oct. 17, 1982. BA, Stanford U., 1974, MD, 1978. Diplomate Am. Bd. Internal Medicine, Am. Bd. Emergency Medicine. Intern in internal medicine UCLA Hosp., 1978-79, resident in internal medicine, 1979-81, fellow emergency medicine, 1981-82; fellow critical care Harbor/UCLA Hosp., Torrence, 1982-83; asst. prof. critical care medicine UCLA Med. Sch., 1983—. Contbr. articles to profl. jours.; chpts. to books. Fellow Am. Coll. Chest Physicians; mem. Soc. Critical Care Medicine (Young Investigator award 1985), ACP, Western Soc. Clin. Investigators, Shock Soc., Am. Fedn. Clin. Research. Avocation: jogging. Office: UCLA Med Ctr Emergency Medicine Ctr Los Angeles CA 90024

ABRAHAM, WILLARD, educator; b. Chgo., May 18, 1916; s. Edward and Sadie (Weiss) A.; m. Shirley Dale Wiener, June 13, 1948; children—Edward, Andrew, Amy Rebecca. B.S., Ill. Inst. Tech., 1940; M.Ed., Chgo. Tchrs. Coll., 1942; Ph.D., Northwestern U., 1950. With Postal Telegraph Co., Chgo., 1935-39, Roosevelt U., Chgo., 1946-53; mem. faculty Coll. Edn., Ariz. State U., Tempe, 1953—, now prof. spl. edn.; Cons. numerous orgns.; ednl. collaborator Coronet Films, Grolier Ednl. Services; assoc. editor Teaching Exceptional Children. Author: Your Post-War Career, 1945, Get the Job, 1946, A Guide for the Study of Exceptional Children, 1956, A Look at Reading, 1957, Barbara-A Prologue, 1958, Common Sense about Gifted Children, 1958, The Slow Learner, 1964, A Time for Teaching, 1964, A Study of the Devereux Found, 1970, Living With Preschoolers, 1976, A Dictionary of Special Education Terms, 1980, You Always Lag One Child Behind, 1980; Editor: The Preparation of B(ur.) (of) I(ndian) A(ffairs) Teacher and Dormitory Aides, 1968; Author: weekly column Our Children; monthly article Parent Talk; Contbr. profl. jours. Served with AUS, 1942-46. Recipient Faculty Achievement award Ariz. State U., 1965, Centennial Medallion Of Merit award Ariz. State U., 1985, Disting. Teaching award Coll. Edn. Ariz. State U., 1986, Cert. of Merit award Assn. for Gifted Council for Exceptional Children, 1985. Mem. Council Exceptional Children, Am. Assn. U. Profs., Phi Delta Kappa. Home: 6402 E Chaparral Rd Scottsdale AZ 85253 Office: Coll Edn Ariz State Univ Tempe AZ 85287

ABRAM, JOHN CHARLES, energy consultant; b. Des Moines, Sept. 1, 1920; s. John C. and Mary (Jones) A.; m. Dorothy Jean Buettner, Dec. 28, 1946; children: James Morgan, Susan Diane. AA, Glendale Coll., 1940; BS in Engring, UCLA, 1949; postgrad., U. Calif., Berkeley, 1949. With Pacific Lighting Service Co., 1959-69, v.p., 1969-71; with So. Calif. Gas Co., Los Angeles, 1951-57, 71-85, v.p., 1972-74, sr. v.p., 1974-81, vice chmn., 1980-81, chmn. bd., chief exec. officer, 1981-85; chief exec. officer AEA Internat. Ltd., Los Angeles, 1985—. Pres. Calif. Mus. Sci. and Industry Found., Los Angeles, 1985-86; vice chmn. Econ. Devel. Corp. Los Angeles County, 1984-86, Cen. City Assn., 1983-85. Mem. Internat. Gas Union, Internat. Energy Economists, The Atlantic Council, U.S.-Japan Energy Conf., Pacific Coast Gas Assn. (dir. 1973-82, chmn. 1980-81), Am. Gas Assn. (dir. 1981-85, Disting. Service award 1984), Gas Research Inst. (bd. dirs. 1980-87, chmn. 1981-83), UCLA Alumni Assn., U. Calif. at Berkeley Alumni Assn., Australian Gas Assn., Japan Am. Soc., Asia Soc., Japanese Am. Cultural and Community Ctr., The Los Angeles Club. Republican. Congregationalist. Clubs: California (Los Angeles); Oakmont Country (Glendale, Calif.). Avocations: photography, golf, art. Office: AEA Internat Ltd 810 S Flower St Los Angeles CA 90017

ABRAMS, ANDREW, II, chemist; b. Cin., Nov. 11, 1946; s. Stanley Jack and Betty (Schiff) A.; m. Monica Krasnick, Oct. 1, 1978. AA with honors, N.Mex. Mil. Inst., 1966; BS, U. Mo., 1973; MS, U. Cin., 1975. Chief chemist Biomed. Products, Ft. Lauderdale, Fla., 1976-77; mfg. chemist Calbiochem-Behering, La Jolla, Calif., 1977-78; environ. mgr. San Bernardino (Calif.) County, 1978-81; mgr. chem. control Discovision Assocs., Costa Mesa, Calif., 1981-82; mfg. engr. IBM, San Jose, Calif., 1982-83; mgr. safety health Fairchild Research Ctr., Palo Alto, Calif., 1984-87; mgr. safety, health and security Semiconductor div. Gould Electronics Semiconductor div. (AMI), Pocatello, Idaho, 1987—; cons. chem. compliance, San Jose, 1983-87. Author: Chemical Waste Disposal Section, 1983. Vol. trainer Santa Clara (Calif.) County Fire Depts., 1983—. Recipient First Place award IBM Photography Contest, 1982, Corp. Suggestion award IBM, 1983, First Place award Fairchild Corp. Photography Contest, 1985; named to Ski Team, U.S. Ski Assn., 1966-68. Fellow Am. Inst. Chemists; mem. Am. Inst. Chem. Engrs., Am. Chem. Soc., Am. Indsl. Hygiene Assn., Laser Inst. Am., N.Y. Acad. Scis., Palo Alto C. of C. (com. mem. 1986). Avocations: photography, raising and training field-trial retrievers, skiing. Home: PO Box 4765 Pocatello ID 83205 Office: Gould Electronics Semiconductor Div 2300 Buckskin Rd Pocatello ID 83205

ABRAMS, JORY MILLER, civil engineer; b. Corvallis, Oreg., Apr. 13, 1950; d. Herbert William and Kathleen Rose (Ramsby) Miller; m. Gerald Frank Abrams, Sept. 3, 1977. BSCE, Portland State U., 1979. Registered profl. engr., Oreg., Wash. Design technician CH2M Hill, Portland, Oreg., 1976-78, design engr., 1979-83, project mgr., 1983—; lectr. in field, Oreg., 1979—. Contbr. tech. papers to profl. jours. Mem. ASCE (bd. dirs. 1982—, sec. bd. dirs. 1984—, assoc., Outstanding Young Engr. 1984, v.p. Oreg. sect. 1986—). Avocations: golfing, snow skiing, traveling. Office: CH2M Hill 2020 SW Fourth Portland OR 97201

ABRAMS, LOIS M., psychotherpist, professional society officer; b. Chgo., May 20, 1936; s. Charles and Florence (Goldstein) Gould; m. Herbert I. Abrams, Aug. 21, 1955; children: Floree Lucas, Mark Alan. BA, Pepperdine U., 1956; MA, Calif. State U., Long Beach, 1969; PhD, U.S. Internat. U., 1974. Pres. Calif. Assn. Marriage and Family Therapists, San Diego, 1980-81, pres. edn. found., 1981-82, fellow, 1982—, chairperson honors com., 1984-86; chairperson elections com. Am. Assn. Marriage and Family Therapists, Washington, 1983-85; bd. dirs. So. Calif. chpt. Am. Assn. Marriage and Family Therapists, Los Angeles, 1986—; sec. Abrams Devel. Inc., Los Alamitos, Calif., 1985—; cons. Interval House, Seal Beach, Calif., 1981—, Casa de Bienvenidos, Los Alamitos, 1982—, Hospice, Los Alamitos, 1983—; sec., bd. dirs. Abrams Devel. Inc., 1983—. Author: Humanizing Student-Teacher Relationship, 1974, The ABC's of Marriage, 1985. Chairperson Long Beach Heart Assn., 1984-85, Am. Cancer Soc., 1984-85; bd. dirs. United Way, Garden Grove, Calif., 1985—. Club: Old Ranch Tennis (Seal Beach). Avocations: music, travel, reading, tennis, marine aquariums. Home: Box 306 Surfside CA 90743 Office: Los Alamitos Counseling Ctr 10861 Cherry St 202 Los Alamitos CA 90720

ABRAMS, PAUL GORDON, biotechnology company executive; b. N.Y.C., Jan. 10, 1948; s. Raymond Michael and Leonora (Grossman) A.; m. Marguerite Lindström Johnstone. BA suma cum laude, Yale U., 1969, MD, 1976, JD, 1976. Diplomate Am. Bd. Internal Medicine; subspecialty bds. in med. oncology. Sr. investigator Nat. Cancer Inst., Bethesda, Md., 1981-85; v.p., med. dir. NeoRx Corp., Seattle, 1985—; bd. dirs. NeoRx Corp., Seattle, 1985—. Co-editor: Immunology of Lung Cancer, 1986; contbr. articles to profl. jours. Mem. ACP, AAAS, Internat. Assn. Study Lung Cancer, Seattle C. of C. Office: NeoRx Corp 410 W Harrison St Seattle WA 98119

ABRAMS, STEPHEN L., state agency administrator, lawyer; b. Colorado Springs, Colo., May 18, 1946; s. John M. and Harriet (Yaffe) A.; m. Sherry J. Luchinske; children: Aaron Joseph, Jonathon Logan. BS in Edn., U. Kans., 1971, JD, 1974. Bar: Colo. 1974, Kans. 1976. Pub. affairs mgr. U.S. C. of C., Mpls., 1979-83; exec v.p. Greeley (Colo.) C. of C., 1983-85; dir. bus. devel. State of Colo., Denver, 1985—. Served to sgt. U.S. Army, 1967-69. Mem. Econ. Developers Council of Colo., Colo. C. of C., Indsl. Devel. Research Council, Am. Economic Devel. Council, Kans. Bar Assn. Avocations: skiing, horses, antique cars. Home: 1120 75th Ave Greeley CO 80634 Office: Bus Devel div Commerce & Devel Suite 1700 1625 Broadway Denver CO 80202

ABRAMSON, NORMAN JAY, marine biologist, science administrator; b. Los Angeles, May 4, 1927; s. Maurice Jacob and Anne Gertrude Abramson; m. Joan Delman, Mar. 30, 1951; 1 child, Jill. BS, U. Wash., 1955. Biologist Calif. Dept. Fish and Game, San Pedro, 1955-60, statistician, 1960-70; biologist Nat. Marine Fisheries Service, Tiburon, Calif., 1971-73, dir. lab., 1973—; cons. Fisheries Research Inst., U. Wash., 1969, UN Food and Agriculture Orgn., Rome, 1970, 86. Named Fishery Scholar, Seattle Times newspaper, 1954. Fellow Am. Inst. Fishery Research Biologists; mem. Am. Statis. Assn., Biometric Soc., Am. Fisheries Soc., Inst. Biol. Exploration (bd. dirs.). Avocations: tennis, fishing. Office: Nat Marine Fisheries Service 3150 Paradise Dr Tiburon CA 94920

ABRASSART, JOANNE YOCUM, speech pathologist, educator; b. Oakland, Calif., May 29, 1950; d. Richard Stone and Martha Lois (Dickerhoof) Yocum; m. Richard Allen Abrassart, Aug. 11, 1973; children: Joseph Richard, Jenna Marie. BA, U. Redlands, 1972, M.A., 1973. cert. clin. competent, Calif. Speech pathologist Los Angeles County schs., Downey, Calif., 1973-78; asst. prof. Chapman Coll., Orange, Calif., 1978-84; lectr. Whittier (Calif.) Coll., 1977-82, Calif. State U., Fullerton, 1984—; cons. Brea, Calif., 1986—, Rossier Ednl. and Assessment Ctr., Garden Grove, Calif., 1984—. Inspector registrar of voters, Brea, 1986. Recipient Profl. Contbn. award Speech and Lang. Devel. Ctr., Buena Park, Calif., 1983. Mem. Am. Speech Lang. Hearing Assn., Calif. Speech Lang. Hearing Assn. (bd. dirs. elect protem Orange County dist., 1983, chmn. nominating com., 1983-84, adv. bd. dirs. 1982-84), Delta Kappa Psi. Republican. Avocations: reading, sewing, gardening, cake decorating, sports.

ABRAVANEL, ELLIOT DON, physician, medical clinic administrator; b. N.Y.C., Oct. 13, 1942; s. Jack Don and Paula (Misshoula) A.; m. Elizabeth King Marsh, Nov. 16, 1975. BA, U. Calif., Berkeley, 1964; MD, U. Cin., 1969. Dir. med. services Maharishi Internat. U., Seelisberg, Switzerland, 1970-75; gen. practice medicine Beverly Hills, Calif., 1975-83; dir., pres. Skinny Sch. Med. Clinics, Los Angeles, 1983—. Author: Body Type Diet, 1983, Body Type Program, 1985; contbr. articles to profl. jours. Mem. AAAS. Republican. Jewish. Avocations: computers, backpacking. Office: Skinny Sch Med Clinic 6511 Van Nuys Blvd Suite 2 Van Nuys CA 91401

ABSHER, HENRY JERRELL, educator; b. Comanche, Okla., May 5, 1914; s. Lewis Olvie and Lucindy Elizabeth (Turner) A.; m. Hazel Maurine Proctor; children—Harold, Richard, Phyllis, Terry, Henry Jerrell, David. B.S., Okla. State U., 1957, M.S., 1959; Teaching cert., Okla., Tex., Ariz. Elem. tchr., Okla., 1936-42; aircraft mechanic, Ft. Worth, Tex., 1942-43, Goodyear Aircraft, Phoenix, 1944-45; tchr. high sch., Clifton, Ariz., 1945-47; instr. engring. drawing, Okla. State U., 1948-49, 56-58; tchr. Shidler (Okla.) High Sch., 1949-50, Miami (Okla.) High Sch., 1958-76; dir. bldg. trades program Labette Community Jr. Coll., Parsons, Kans., 1976-79; instr. drafting Eastern Ariz. Coll., Thatcher, 1980-81; tchr. drafting, organizer computer-aided drafting program Lamson Bus. Coll., Tucson, 1981—; tchr. bldg. trades Pima County Community Coll., Tucson, 1984-85. Mem. NEA, Am. Vocat. Assn., Okla. Vocat. Assn., Okla. Edn. Assn., Iota Lambda Sigma (life). Democrat. Baptist. Patentee drafting instrument. Home: 960 N Independence Ave Tucson AZ 85748 Office: Lamson Bus Coll 5320 E Pima St Tucson AZ 85712

ABT, BRUCE ALAN, psychologist; b. Buffalo, Aug. 17, 1940; s. Gerald N. and Emma (Shaupp) A.; m. Evet Loewen, June 12, 1973. Student, U. Madrid, 1960; BA, Hamilton Coll., 1962; MBA, Columbia U., 1964; PhD in Clin. Psychology, U. Tenn., 1975. Instr. psychology U. Tenn., Knoxville, 1971, San Jose (Calif.) State U., 1976, West Valley Coll., Los Gatos, Calif., 1976; clin. intern Palo Alto (Calif.) Veterans Hosp., 1975; group therapist San Jose Hosp., 1975-78; pvt. practice psychology specializing in work-related problems Sunnyvale, Calif., 1977—. Served with USAR. Mem. Assn. Labor-Mgmt. Adminstrs. and Cons.'s on Alcoholism, Am. Psychol. Assn. Home: 66 Pasa Robles Los Altos CA 94022 Office: 877 W Fremont Ave #K-5 Sunnyvale CA 94087

ABTS, JOANN SUE, parent educator; b. Monticello, Minn., Nov. 17, 1937; d. Roy E. and Hazel M. (Taft) Tyler; m. Donald H. Abts, Dec. 28, 1957; children: Dale, Douglas, David, Daniel. AS, Clark Coll., 1976; B in Liberal Arts, Evergreen State Coll., 1980. Cert. early childhood edn. Educator of early childhood edn. Clark Coll., Vancouver, Wash., 1971—; sec. Health Systems Agy., Vanc, Wash., 1981-84; presenter seminars to profl. assns; coordinator parent edn. scholarship com., also fundraising events, 1984-86. Mem. Nat. Assn. for the Edn. Young Children (v.p. 1976, presentor, 1980, 1982). Avocations: traveling, hiking, gourmet cooking, weight-lifting. Home: 6910 Tennessee Ln Vancouver WA 98664 Office: Clark Coll 1800 E McLoughlin Blvd Vancouver WA 98663

ABUL-HAJ, SULEIMAN KAHIL, pathologist; b. Jordan, Apr. 20, 1925; s. Sheik Khalil and S. Buteina (Oda) Abul-H.; B.S., U. Calif. at Berkeley, 1949; M.S., U. Calif. at San Francisco, 1951, M.D., 1955; m. Elizabeth Abood, Feb. 11, 1948; children—Charles, Alan, Cary; came to U.S., 1946, naturalized, 1955. Intern, Cook County Hosp., Chgo., 1955-56; resident U. Calif. Hosp., San Francisco, 1949, Brooke Gen. Hosp., 1957-59; chief clin. and anatomic pathology Walter Reed Army Hosp., Washington, 1959-62; assoc. prof. U. So. Calif. Sch. Medicine, Los Angeles, 1963—; sr. surg. pathologist Los Angeles County Gen. Hosp., 1963; dir. dept. pathology Community Meml. Hosp., Ventura, Calif., 1964-80, Gen. Hosp. Ventura County, 1966-74; dir. Pathology Service Med. Group, 1970—; cons. Calif. Tumor Tissue Registry, 1962—, Camarillo State Hosp., 1964-70, Tripler Gen. Hosp., Hawaii, 1963-67, Armed Forces Inst. Pathology, 1960—. Bd. dirs. Tri-Counties Blood Bank, Am. Cancer Soc. Served to maj., M.C., U.S. Army, 1956-62. Recipient Borden award Calif. Honor Soc., 1949; Achievement cert. Surgeon Gen. Army, 1962. Fellow Am. Soc. Clin. Pathologists, Coll. Am. Pathologists; mem. AMA, N.Y. Acad. Scis., Internat. Coll. Surgeons, AAAS, Calif. Med. Assn., Internat. Platform Assn., World Affairs Council. Clubs: Commonwealth of Calif. (San Francisco); Jonathan. Contbr. articles to profl. jours. Research in cardiovascular disease, endocrine, renal, skin diseases, also cancer. Home: 105 Encinal Way Ventura CA 93001 Office: 105 Encinal Way Ventura CA 93001

ACEVEDO-RUIZ, MANUEL, mechanical engineer; b. Madrid, Spain, June 5, 1963; came to U.S., 1977; s. Manuel Acevedo-Rodriguez and Victoria (Ruiz) Acevedo. BS, Calif. Inst. Tech., 1985. Mfg. engr. IBM Corp., Tucson, 1985; systems engr. IBM Corp., San Francisco, 1986—. Mem. Am. Soc. Mech. Engrs. Club: España of Tucson (sec. 1985—). Avocations: soccer, tennis, poetry, music, backgammon. Home: 520 Parker #302 San Francisco CA 94118 Office: IBM Corp 425 Market St B/O 396 21st Floor San Francisco CA 94105

ACHESON, LOUIS KRUZAN, JR., aerospace engineer; b. Brazil, Ind., Apr. 2, 1926; s. Louis Kruzan and Irene Ruth (Morrison) A.; m. Hyla Armstrong Cook, July 12, 1958; children: Mari Ruth, William Louis. B.S. in E.E., Case Inst. Tech., 1946; Ph.D. in Theoretical Physics, MIT, 1950. Mem. tech. staff Hughes Aircraft Co., Los Angeles, 1950—, chief scientist systems analysis and design labs Space and Communications Group;, 1985; with Inst. Def. Analyses, Washington, 1958-59. Contbr.: articles to profl. pubs. Mem. Soc. Gen. Systems Research, Am. Phys. Soc., Am. Geophys. Union, AIAA, Brit. Interplanetary Soc., AAAS, Mensa, Sigma Xi, Tau Beta Pi, Eta Kappa Nu, Theta Tau, Sigma Chi, Worldview Exploration Seminar,

Unity-in-Diversity Council, Bertrand Russell Soc. Home: 17721 Marcello Pl Encino CA 91316 Office: Hughes Aircraft Co PO Box 92919 Los Angeles CA 90009

ACHTEL, ROBERT ANDREW, pediatric cardiologist; b. Bklyn., May 5, 1941; s. Murray and Amelia (Ellian) A.; m. Erica Noel Woods, Mar. 10, 1063; children: Bergen Alison, Roland Hugh. BA, Adelphi U., 1963; MD, U. Cin., 1967. Diplomate Am. Bd. Pediatric Cardiology. Intern, Cin. Children's Hosp., 1967-68; resident in pediatrics Yale U., 1968-69, fellow in pediatric cardiology, 1969-71; clin. instr. pediatrics U. Calif.-Davis, 1972-73, clin. asst. prof., 1977-83; asst. prof. pediatrics, U. Ky., 1973-76; dir. pediatric ICU, Sutter Meml. Hosp., Sacramento, 1977-85, dir. pediatric Cardiology, 1982—, chmn. instl. rev. com., 1981-85; chmn. dept. pediatrics Mercy Hosp., Sacramento, 1981-83, vice chmn. pediatrics, 1983-85; dir. pediatric ICU, 1982-83; dir. Laurel Hills Devel. Ctr., 1985—. Contbr. articles in cardiovascular research. Bd. dirs. Sutter Meml. Hosp. Found., 1986—. Served as major M.C., USAF, 1971-73. Recipient grants from Heart Assn., U. Ky. Tobacco and Health Research Found. Mem. Am. Heart Assn. (dir. Sacramento chpt., mem. councils congenital heart disease and atherosclerosis and cardiovascular surgery), Am. Coll. Chest Physicians, Am. Acad Pediatrics, SW Pediatric Cardiology Soc., So. Soc. Pediatric Research. Office: 5609 J St Suite A Sacramento CA 95819

ACKERLEY, BARRY, professional basketball team executive. Chmn. bd. dirs. Seattle Supersonics; pres Sta. KJR. Office: Seattle Supersonics 190 Queen Anne Ave N Box C-900911 Seattle WA 98109 *

ACKERMAN, RICHARD C., Mayor, city of Fullerton, Calif. Office: Office of Mayor 303 W Commonwealth Ave Fullerton CA 92632 *

ACKLEY, DIANE DENISE, elementary educator; b. Boston, Feb. 21, 1951; d. Donald Lee and Beverly Dawn (Ruder) A. BA, Loma Linda U., Riverside, Calif., 1968; MA, U. Denver, 1973. Tchr. Riverside Unified Sch. Dist., 1973—; asst. prof. Loma Linda U., Riverside, 1980; mentor tchr. U. Redlands, Calif., 1986. Mem. Am. Speech and Hearing Assn. (cert.), Inland Empire Reading Assn. Democrat. Adventist. Avocations: reading, traveling. Home: 1723 Kingston Circle Redlands CA 92374 Office: Riverside Unified Sch Dist Fremont Sch 1925 Orange Riverside CA 92501

ACKLEY, DUNCAN RAY, JR., computer consultant; b. Chippewa Falls, Wis., Dec. 5, 1921; s. Duncan Ray and Anna Sarah (Magnan) A.; m. Rosemary Magdalen Mantych, Jan. 8, 1945; 1 child, Duncan Joseph. B.Chem. Engring., U. Minn., 1948. Registered profl. engr., Colo. Sales engr. Stapp Engring. Co., Denver, 1948-50; chief chem. br. Rocky Mountain Arsenal, U.S. Army, Denver, 1950-56; chief ops. br. Rocky Flats Area Office, AEC, Denver, 1956-69; chief weapons program br. Albuquerque Ops. Office, U.S. Dept. Energy, 1969-77; owner, mgr. Ackley & Assocs., Denver, 1978—; cons. in field. Contbr. articles to profl. jours. Scoutmaster Boy Scouts Am., Denver, 1959; dist. coordinator Gary Hart for Pres. campaign, 1984; del. Colo. Democratic Party Conv., 1984. Served to capt. USAAF, 1941-45. Mem. Am. Soc. Quality Control (sect. chmn. 1957-62), Am. Soc. Pub. Adminstrn., Am. Ordnance Assn., Am. Inst. Chem. Engrs., C.B.I. Hump Pilots Assn. Democrat. Roman Catholic. Address: 5 Dunbarton Ct Highlands Ranch CO 80126

ADA, JOSEPH F., territorial governor. Elected gov. of Guam, 1986. Republican. Office: Office of the Governor Territory of Guam Agana GU 96910 *

ADACHI, ATHAN KEN, civil engineer, county official; b. Honolulu, July 18, 1951; s. Kenneth Korji and Dorothy Takako (Fujioka) A.; m. Maude Miyo Migita, May 10, 1980. BS, U. Hawaii, 1974. Registered profl. engr., Hawaii. Project engr. Avanti Constrn. Co., Honolulu, 1974-77; engr. cons. Unemori Engring. Co., Wailuku, Hawaii, 1977-79; civil engr. IV, County of Maui, Wailuku, 1979-85; design engr. State of Hawaii, Kahului, 1985-86, asst. dist. engr., 1986—. Vol. Kahului Young Democratic Party; bd. dirs. Maui Assn. for Retarded Citizens, 1984. Mem. Water Pollution Control Fedn., NSPE. Buddhist. Club: Toastmasters. Home: 102 Kawelea Pl Kula HI 96790 Office: State Hawaii Dept Tranps Hwys Div 650 Palapala Dr Kahului HI 96732

ADAIR, JAMES ALLEN, Canadian provincial government official; b. Edmonton, Alta., Can., Mar. 13, 1929; s. James Wilfred and Beatrice (Shewfelt) A.; m. Joyce Helen Adair, Oct. 31, 1960; children—Richard, Catherine, Robert. Student pub. schs., Edmonton. Feed mill operator Searle Grain Co., St. Paul, 1948-49, grain buyer, 1949; seed buyer Peace Milling Co. Ltd., Peace River, Alta., 1953-59; catering supr. Fortier & Assocs., Peace River, 1960-64; salesman, sports dir. Sta. CKYL, Peace River, 1964-71, ptnr., 1971—; mem. Legis. Assembly for Peace River, 1971—; cabinet minister Alta Provincial Govt., Edmonton, 1971—. Progressive Conservative. Anglican. Home: 9634 83d Ave, Peace River, AB Canada T0H 2X0 Office: Minister Transp & Utilities, Legislature Bldg Room 208, 96th Ave and 108th St, Edmonton, AB Canada

ADAIR, JAMES SCOTT, small business owner; b. Valley City, N.D., Dec. 30, 1955; s. James W. Adair and Verna R. Landy; m. Kim Adair, Dec. 27, 1980; children: Melissa, Sadie, James. Student, U. Colo., 1974-76, Calif. State U., Fresno, 1976-78. Mgr. Schubach Jewelers, Missoula, Mont., 1979-82; co-owner, operator Adair Jewelers, Missoula, 1982-84; prin. James Adair Jewelers Ltd., Helena, Mont., 1984—. Pres. Southgate Mall Mchts. Assn., Missoula, 1984, bd. dirs. 1982-85; mem. 1st class Leadership Missoula, 1984. Mem. Nat. Rifle Assn. Republican. Mem. Christian Ch. Avocations: hunting, fishing, snowmobiling, rafting.

ADAIR, JAY CARLTON, broadcasting executive; b. Evanston, Ill., Jan. 6, 1946; s. Claude and Ruby (Lemke) A. Student, U. Wis.-Madison, 1964-67; student U. So. Calif., 1970, UCLA, 1974; B.A., Calif. Western U., 1979, M.B.A., 1982. Mgr., Meeker T.V., San Francisco, 1974-78; v.p. sta. relations Meeker T. V., 1978-79, v.p. West Coast ops., Los Angeles, 1979-81; mgr. West Coast Network Sales, CBS Radio Network, Hollywood, Calif., 1981-82; mgr. West Coast sales Broadcast Week, Beverly Hills, Calif., 1982-83; gen. sales mgr. Sta. KFYI All News Radio, Oakland, Calif., 1983-85; gen. sales mgr. Sta. KSTS-TV, San Jose, Calif., 1985—; co-owner Sta. KLRB-FM, Carmel, Calif., 1977-80; co-chmn. TVB/LA, 1980. lectr. in field. Served with USMCR and USNR, 1967-74. Mem. Hollywood Radio and TV Soc. Republican. Lutheran. Clubs: Olympic, Commonwealth. Office: Sta KSTS-TV 2349 Bering Dr San Jose CA 95131

ADAM, LAVERN LESTER, magnetic design executive; b. Leola, S.D., July 2, 1943; s. Fred John and Viola (Mehlhaff) A.; m. Barbara Jane Hammrich; children—Jim Dean, Kay Lee. Student in Indsl. Mgmt., North Orange Jr. Coll., 1970-71. Trainee Honeywell-Deburring, Gardena, Calif., 1963-66; prodn. control expeditor Indsl. Tectonics, Compton, Calif., 1966-68; materials mgr. Permag Pacific, Los Angeles, 1968-71; quality control mgr. MPC, Irvine, Calif., 1971-72; pres., chmn. bd. AZ Industries, Inc., Temecula, Calif., 1972—; lectr. in field. Founding pub. Magnets In Your Future mag. Mem. career activities bd. Lake Elsinore High Sch.; chmn. econ. devel. com., Rancho, Calif., local feasibility study com. Mem. Internat. Platform Assn., Temecula C. of C. (v.p., dir.), 500 Automobile Execs. Club, Meeting of the Minds (chmn. convs. 1986, 87). Republican. Lutheran. Magnetic designer for major corps. throughout world. Office: 28065 Diaz Rd Temecula CA 92390

ADAMEC, LUDWIG WARRAN, academic director; b. Vienna, Austria, Mar. 10, 1924; came to U.S., 1954; s. Ludwig and Emma (Kubicek) A.; m. Ena A. Vargas, June 16, 1962; 1 child, Eric. BA in Polit. Sci., UCLA, 1960, MA in Journalism, 1961, PhD in Near Eastern Studies, 1966. Asst. prof. history and politics of Middle East U. Ariz., Tucson, 1967-70, assoc. prof., 1970-74, prof., 1974—, dir. Near East Ctr., 1975-85; v.p. Am. Inst. Iranian Studies, 1979-81; bd. govs. Am. Research Ctr. Egypt, 1978-80, Am. Research Inst. Turkey, 1980-82; Fulbright cons. U. Baluchistan, Quetta, Pakistan, 1981. Author: Afghanistan 1900-23: A Diplomatic History, 1967, Afghanistan's Foreign Affairs to the Mid-20th Century: Relations with the USSR, Germany, and Britain, 1974, Historical and Political Who's Who of Afghanistan, 1975, Historical and Political Gazetteer of Afghanistan, 6 Vols., 1985, Historical Gazetteer of Iran, 3 Vols., 1979, Biographical Dictionary of Contemporary Afghanistan, 1986; assoc. editor Afganistan Jour., 1973-75. NDEA fellow, UCLA, 1961-63; grantee Social Sci. Research Council, 1968, 75, 79, 85, Denver Grad. Sch. Internat. Studies, 1969, Am. Philos. Soc., 1969, Fulbright Hayes, 1973. Democrat. Office: U Ariz Near East Ctr Franklin #80 Tucson AZ 85721

ADAMIAK, PATRICK ANTHONY, computer software professional; b. Pitts., Oct. 4, 1955; s. John Stanislaus and Eileen Mary (Cannon) A.; m. Janet Kathryn Whelan, July 25, 1981; children: Patrick John, Kathryn Sarah. BSEE, Pa. State U., 1978; MS in Indsl. Adminstrn., Carnegie-Mellon U., 1984. Mem. mfg. mgmt. program Gen. Electric, San Jose, Calif. and Waynesboro, Va., 1978-80; project leader interactive graphics Gen. Electric, Schenectady, N.Y., 1980-81, supr. computer aided design, computer aided mfg., 1981-82; product mgr. Computer Systems div. Hewlett-Packard, Cupertino, Calif., 1984-87, product line mgr., 1987—. Avocations: golf, tennis, guitar, reading. Home: 1682 Stardust Ct Santa Clara CA 95050 Office: Hewlett-Packard 19447 Pruneridge Ave M/C 44MF Cupertino CA 95014

ADAMS, ANDREW MARTIN, vineyard executive; b. Canastota, N.Y., May 20, 1943; s. Andrew Martin and Helen (Thurlow) A.; m. Maureen Burke, July 26, 1966; children: Katherine Grace, Andrew Burke. BA, Marquette U., 1965. With distbn. sales dept. Procter and Gamble, Ewing, N.J.; with prodn. and mktg. dept. Johnson and Johnson, New Brunswick, N.J.; with sales and mktg. support Baxter-Travenol, Deerfield, Ill.; sales mgr. Foremost KcKesson, Kansas City & Chgo., Federated Distbrs.; pres. Cray Wholesale, Kansas City, Mo., 1978-81, McCormick Distilling Co., Weston, Mo., 1981-86, Sebastiani Vineyards, Sonoma, Calif., 1986—. Mem. Young Pres. Orgn., Am. Mktg. Assn. Pres. Club, Distilled Spirits Council, Wine and Spirits Wholesalers Assn., Am. Beverage Alcohol Assn. Home: 20415 5th St E Sonoma CA 95476 Office: Sebastiani Vineyards PO Box AA 389 4th St E Sonoma CA 95476

ADAMS, BERNARD SCHRODER, college president; b. Lancaster, Pa., July 20, 1928; s. Martin Ray and Charlotte (Schroder) A.; m. Natalie Virginia Stout, June 2, 1951; children: Deborah Rowland, David Schroder. B.A., Princeton, 1950; M.A., Yale, 1951; Ph.D., U. Pitts., 1964; LL.D. (hon.), Lawrence U., 1967. Asst. dir. admissions, instr. English Princeton, 1953-57; dir. admissions and student aid U. Pitts., 1957-60, spl. asst. to chancellor, 1960-64; dean students, lectr. English Oberlin (Ohio) Coll., 1964-66; pres. Ripon (Wis.) Coll., 1966-85, Ft. Lewis Coll., Colo., 1985—; dir. Wis. Power & Light Co., Newton Funds, 1970-85; cons., examiner Commn. on Instns. Higher Edn., North Central Assn. Colls. and Secondary Schs., 1972—, exec. commr., 1981-86. Bd. dirs. Four Corners Opera Assn., 1985—, pres., 1986—. Author articles. Served to 1st lt. USAF, 1951-53. Woodrow Wilson fellow, 1951. Mem. Assoc. Colls. Midwest (bd. dirs. 1966-85, pres. 1973-75), Wis. Assn. Ind. Colls. and Univs. (dir. 1966-85, pres. 1969-71, 83-85). Home: 205 Hillcrest Dr Durango CO 81301

ADAMS, BROCK, U.S. Senator; b. Atlanta, Jan. 13, 1927; s. Charles Leslie and Vera Eleanor (Beemer) A.; m. Mary Elizabeth Scott, Aug. 16, 1952; children: Scott, Leslie, Lewis Dean, Katherine Elizabeth, Aleen Mundy. BA in Econs. summa cum laude, U. Wash., 1944; LLB, Harvard U., 1952. Bar: Wash. 1952, D.C. Ptnr. LeSourd, Patten and Adams (formerly Little, LeSourd, Patten and Adams), Seattle, 1952-61; U.S. atty. U.S. Dist. Ct. (we. dist.) Wash., Seattle, 1961-64; mem. 89th-94th Congresses from 7th Wash. dist., 1965-77, mem. sci. and astronautics com., interstate and fgn. commerce com., chmn. budget com.; U.S. Sec. Transp. Washington, 1977-79; ptnr. Garvey, Schubert, Adams and Barer, 1979-86; U.S. Senator from Wash. 1987—; instr. Am. Inst. Banking, 1954-60. Chmn. Western Wash. dist. Kennedy for Pres. campaign, 1960; former pres. Neighborhood House, Seattle; exec. dir. Wash. dist. Carter for Pres. campaign ; past trustee Civic Unity Commn., Seattle. Served with USN, 1944-46. Recipient Disting. Service award Seattle Jr. C. of C., 1960. Mem. ABA, Fed. Bar Assn., Wash. Bar Assn., Seattle-King County Bar Assn., Puget Sound Assn. (pres. 1962-63), U. Wash. Alumni Assn. (past trustee), Phi Beta Kappa. Democrat. Episcopalian. Office: US Senate 513 Hart Senate Office Bldg Washington DC 20510

ADAMS, CHARLES ARTHUR, municipal financial analyst; b. Caldwell, Idaho, July 25, 1933; s. John Woodrow and Eileen (Vail) A.; B.A., Coll. Idaho, 1962; m. Susan Rae Donovan, Jan. 30, 1960; children—Michael C., Teresa M. Sales mgr. Hoppins Ins. Agy., Nampa, Idaho, 1961-63; auditor Indsl. Indemnity Ins. Co., Boise, Idaho, 1964-65, Argonaut Ins. Co., Portland, 1966-67; br. mgr. Am. Mut. Ins. Co., Portland, 1968-70; underwriting mgr. Alaska Pacific Assurance Co., Juneau, 1970-73; pres. A.I.M. Ins. Inc., Anchorage, 1973-78, pres. parent co. A.I.M. Corp., 1977-78, also sr. v.p. A.I.M. Internat., Tokyo, 1975-78; fin. officer City of Petersburg (Alaska), 1978, City of Homer (Alaska), 1979; fin. analyst Municipality of Anchorage, 1980—. Vol. in corrections, State of Alaska, 1981; mem. central com. Libertarian Party of Alaska, 1981-84, vice chmn., 1985—, chmn., Anchorage, 1982-83. Served with AUS, 1955-58, ETO. Mem. Resource Devel. Council Alaska, Homebuilders Alaska (dir. 1974-78), Homeowners Warranty Council Alaska (v.p. 1977), Porsche Club Am., Alaska Council Sports Car Clubs (dir. 1976-78), Alaska World Affairs Council (chmn. fin. and devel. com. 1983-84, dir. 1984—, univ. and coll. liaison com. 1985—). Clubs: Toastmasters (named Summit Club Speaker of Yr. 1969), Wednesday Club, Captain Cook Athletic. Lodge: KC. Author: fin. procedures and master policy to insure constrn. of Alaska pipeline. Home: 3258 Montpelier Ct Anchorage AK 99503 Office: Pouch 6-650 Anchorage AK 99502

ADAMS, CHARLES FRANCIS, advertising and real estate executive; b. Detroit, Sept. 26, 1927; s. James R. and Bertha C. (DeChant) A.; m. Helen R. Harrell, Nov. 12, 1949; children: Charles Francis, Amy Ann, James Randolph, Patricia Duncan. BA, U. Mich., 1948; postgrad., U. Calif., Berkeley, 1949. With D'Arcy-MacManus & Masius, Inc., San Francisco, 1947-80, exec. v.p., dir., 1970-76, pres., chief operating officer, 1976-80; pres. Adams Enterprises, 1971—; exec. v.p., dir. Washington Office, Am. Assn. Advt. Agys., 1980-84; chmn., chief exec. officer Wajim Corp., Detroit; past mem. steering com. Nat. Advt. Rev. Bd.; mem. mktg. com. U.S. Info. Agy. Author: Common Sense in Advertising, 1965, Heroes of the Golden Gate, 1987. Past chmn. exec. com. Oakland U. Mem. Am. Assn. Advt. Agys. (dir., mem. govt. relations com.), Advt. Fedn. Am. (past dir.), Nat. Outdoor Advt. Bur. (past chmn.), Theta Chi, Alpha Delta Sigma (hon.). Republican. Roman Catholic. Clubs: Bloomfield Hills Country; Carmel Valley Ranch (Calif.); Nat. Golf Links Am. (Southampton, L.I.); Olympic, The Family (San Francisco). Home: 2240 Hyde St San Francisco CA 94109 also: 25450 Loma Robles Carmel CA 93923 Office: 10 W Long Lake Rd Bloomfield Hills MI 48013 also: 14 E 64th St New York NY

ADAMS, C(LAWDE) HARRIS, electronics company executive; b. Palo Alto, Calif., Oct. 27, 1926; s. Claude Harris and Audene Clarissa (Merrill) A.; m. Dorothy Renaud, Jan. 27, 1951; children: Donald, David, Allen. BS, Calif. Inst. Tech., 1949. Pres. Coast Magnetics, Inglewood, Calif., 1961—. Patentee in field. Republican. Mormon. Avocations: hiking, backpacking, pvt. pilot. Office: Coast Magnetics 1207 N La Brea Ave Inglewood CA 90302

ADAMS, DAVID BENNION, psychologist; b. Salt Lake City, May 21, 1945; s. Ferrell Harrison and Maurine (Bennion) A. B.A., U. Utah, 1968, M.S. (Kappa Sigma fellow), 1972, Ph.D. in Psychology cum laude, 1976. Staff psychologist Granite Mental Health Center, 1972-74; dir. Juvenile Alcohol Program, 1974-75; clin. supr. Adolescent Residential Treatment Ctr., 1974-79; pvt. practice clin. psychology, Salt Lake City, 1976—, also clin. dir. Am. Community Youth Services, 1979-82, Intermountain Youth Care, 1982—; instr. U. Utah, Brigham Young U.; program coordinator Children's div. Charter Summit Hosp. Local dist. Dem. del., 1972. Served with USAR, 1963-71. Lic. and cert. psychologist, Utah; cert. marriage and family counselor, Utah. Mem. Am. Psychol. Assn., Utah Psychol. Assn., Utah Psychologists in Pvt. Practice, Zero Population Growth, Nat. Register for Health Service Providers in Psychology, Friends of the Earth, Sierra Club, Utah Assn. Juvenile and Adult Corrections, Kappa Sigma. Contbr. articles to profl. jours. Home: 1036 E Countrylane Rd Holladay UT 84117 Office: 195 W 7200 S Midvale UT 84047

ADAMS, DAVID STANFORD, venture capitalist; b. St. Thomas, V.I., July 4, 1943; s. Eustice Noah and Elizabeth Jane (Princeton) A. BA in Math., U. Heidelberg, Fed. Republic Germany, 1964; MA in Math., MIT, 1970; MA in Anthropology, U. Calif., Irvine, 1972; PhD in Math. (hon.), U. Nev., 1975. Asst. prof. math. U. London, 1964-65; cryptgrapher U.S. Dept. Def., Republic Vietnam, 1965-68; asst. prof. math. U. Calif., Irvine, 1970-72; mathematician Rand Corp., McLean, Va., 1972-78; analyst Bessemer Investment Co., Menlo Park, Calif., 1978-83; chief exec. officer EPI, Mt. View, Calif., 1983—; cons. Arthur D. Little, Cambridge, Mass., 1968-70, U. Irvine, 1970-72; advisor Spl. Prosecutor's Office, Washington, 1974. Author: Mathematical Theorems of Cryptography, 1975; inventor in field, 1969. MIT scholar, 1969-70. Republican. Mem. Soc. Friends. Clubs: Olympic (San Francisco); Los Altos (Calif.) Country. Lodge: Masons. Office: EPI PO Box 391806 Mountain View CA 94039

ADAMS, DAVID VINCENT, robotics engineer; b. Lake Forest, Ill., Feb. 4, 1957; s. James Anthony and Wilma Louise (Pellizzari) A. BS in Engring., U. Ill., 1980; MSME, U. Calif., Berkeley, 1983. Percussion clinician Corps Style, Inc., Sylva, N.C., 1979; assoc. engr. Lockheed Space Systems Div., Sunnyvale, Calif., 1980-82; sr. engr. Applied Materials, Inc., Santa Clara, Calif., 1984-87; mem. tech. staff KLA Instruments Corp., San Jose, Calif., 1987—. Percussion instr. U. Ill. Marching Band, 1977-79; mem. Phantom Regt. Drum and Bugle Corps, Rockford, Ill., 1978. Democrat. Roman Catholic. Club: Santa Clara Decathlon. Avocations: rock climbing, bicycling, golf, volleyball, skiing. Home: 1024 Valencia St #6 Sunnyvale CA 94086 Office: KLASIC div KLA Instruments Corp PO Box 58016 MS 2-831 Santa Clara CA 95052

ADAMS, DAYTON WARREN, JR., developer company executive; b. Denison, Tex., June 10, 1941; s. Dayton Warren and Amelia Francis (Roots) A; m. Shelley Annette West, Oct. 10, 1968. B.A., Tex. Tech U., 1965; M. Fgn. Trade, Am. Grad. Sch. Internat. Mgmt., 1967. Auditor Ernst and Ernst, Phoenix, 1965-66, Touche, Ross, Baily and Smart, Phoenix, 1966-67; with internat. mgmt. dept. Am. Internat. Groups, N.Y.C., Milan, Italy and London, 1967-71; assoc. v.p. Coldwell Banker & Co., Phoenix, 1972-84; gen. ptnr. The WESTCOR Co., Phoenix, 1984—; bd. dirs. Compas, Phoenix. Mem. corp. bd. dirs. YMCA, Phoenix, 1980-86; trustee Claremont Sch. Theology, Calif. Named one of Country's Top 20 in Sales, Coldwell Banker & Co., 1968, 69. Mem. Sigma Chi. Republican. Club: Phoenix Country. Office: The Westcor Co 11411 N Tatum Blvd Phoenix AZ 85028

ADAMS, EDWIN CARROLL, electronics engineer; b. Chgo., Aug. 9, 1927; s. Edward and Esther (Mecsery) A.; m. Lillian Uebel, Sept. 4, 1948; children—Donald Edward, Nancy Adams Richards. B.S. in Electrical Engring., Ill. Inst. Tech., 1955. Engring. asst. Ill. Testing Labs., Chgo., 1949-51; devel. engr. Motorola Inc., Chgo., 1951-57; sr. engr. Cook Research Labs., Morton Grove, Ill., 1957-60; project engr. Zenith Radio Corp., Chgo., 1960-65; engr. mgr. Sierra Research Corp., Buffalo, 1965-79; engr. mgr. Thermal Tech. Lab., Buffalo, 1979-80; staff engr. Unisys (formerly Sperry Corp.), Salt Lake City, 1980—. Served with USN, 1945-46. Mem. IEEE, AIAA, Assn. Unmanned Vehicle Systems. Presbyterian. Patentee Doppler target simulator, 1967. Home: 8744 Acorn Ln Sandy UT 84092 Office: Unisys 640 N Sperry Way Salt Lake City UT 84116

ADAMS, GAIL HAYES, interior designer, exec.; b. Bronxville, N.Y., Nov. 18, 1944; d. Samuel Eugene and Kathryn Minnette (Hayes) A.; m. Gilbert Johnson, Oct. 25, 1968; m. 2d, Jay Martin Goodfarb, Nov. 5, 1978. B.S. in Fine Arts, Ariz. State U., 1967. Interior designer Mehagians Furniture Galleries Co., Phoenix, 1967-1979; pres., interior designer Gail Adams Interiors, Ltd., Phoenix, 1979—; v.p. Rocky Mt. region, Am. Soc. Interior Designers, 1981-82, nat. v.p. 1984, nat. pres. 1985. Active Phoenix Art Mus.; mem. steering com. Ariz. Theatre Co. Mem. Am. Soc. Interior Designers (cert., nat. pres. 1985, nat. 1st v.p. 1984, v.p. Rocky Mountain region 1981-82), Nat. Council Interior Design Qualification (nat. treas. 1987). Home: 110 E San Miguel Phoenix AZ 85012 Office: 1906 N 16th St Phoenix AZ 85006

ADAMS, GENE WYLIE, physicist; b. Los Angeles, Aug. 13, 1938; s. Garland Bernard and Martha Lois (Vernon) A.; m. Judith Marguerite Page, Aug. 15, 1959 (div. 1972); children: Carolyn Elizabeth Adams Welch, Martha Gail, Janis Marie Adams Vasquez; m. Lucretia Clara Elledge, Jan. 1, 1983. BS in Physics, Tex. A&M U., 1960; MS in Physics, U. N.H., 1962; PhD in Astrogeophysics, U. Colo., 1973. Research physicist Douglas Aircraft Co., Santa Monica, Calif., 1962-66, NOAA, Boulder, Colo., 1966-75, 1977-81; program dir. aeronomy NSF, Washington, 1975-77; sr. research assoc. Utah State U., Logan, 1981—, research prof. physics, 1986—. Contbr. articles to profl. jours.; patentee in field. Grantee NSF, 1982, 85, Air Force Geophys. Lab., 1985-86, Air Force Office of Sci. Research, 1983. Mem. AAAS, Am. Geophys. Union. Libertarian. Avocation: music. Home: 610 S 250 E Richmond UT 84333 Office: Utah State U Ctr for Atmospheric & Space Scis UMC 34 Logan UT 84322

ADAMS, GEORGE BAKER, physical chemist; b. Kentfield, Calif., Feb. 23, 1919; s. George Baker and Edith Belle (Johnson) A. BS, U. Calif., Berkeley, 1941, MS, 1947; PhD, Ohio State U., 1951. Research assoc. U. Oreg., 1953-55, instr., then asst. prof. chemistry, 1955-58; with Lockheed Missiles & Space Co., Palo Alto, Calif., 1958—, sr. mem. reasearch labs., 1962—; cons. scientist, 1971—. Patentee in field. Served to capt. AUS, 1941-46. Mem. Internat. Soc. Electrochemistry, Electrochem. Soc. (chmn. Pacific NW sect. 1957-58), Sigma Xi, Phi Lambda Upsilon. Republican. Home: 22069 McClellan Rd Cupertino CA 95014 Office: Lockheed Missiles & Space Co 3251 Hanover St Palo Alto CA 94304

ADAMS, GERALD ROBERT, professor; b. Fremont, Nebr., June 2, 1946; s. Arthur Edward and Florence (Schuett) A.; m. Jane E. Adams, July 15, 1973 (div. Feb. 1986); children: Shawnelle, Sheryl, Shelli, Elizabeth; m. Carol Ann Markstrom, Mar. 20, 1987. BE, Midland Coll., 1968; MA in Psychology, U. Nebr., 1971; PhD in Human Devel., Pa. State U., 1975. Prof. Utah State U., Logan, 1975—; bd. dirs. Lab. Research on Adolescent Research, Utah State U., chmn. 1979-81, acting chmn. 1986—. Author: (with others) Adolescent Life Experiences, 1983, Understanding Research Method, 1985, Today's Marriages and Families, 1986; author over 100 research pub. publs., 1971-86; contbr. articles to profl. jours. Project leader USDA Grant Adolescent Research, 1985—. Recipient James D. Moran Research award Am. Home Econs. Assn., 1985. Fellow Am. Psychology Assn.; Soc. Research Adoloescent (archivist 1986—), Soc. Research on Human Devel. (Southwestern) (sec./treas. 1986—), Utah Council Family Relations (pres. 1986—), Am. Sociology Assn., Nat. Council Family Relations, Soc. Research Child Devel. Democrat. Presbyterian. Avocations: writing, fishing, cross-country skiing, travel. Home: 1235 N 225 E Logan UT 84321 Office: Dept Family and Human Devel Utah State U Logan UT 84321

ADAMS, J. MACK, computer science educator; b. Marfa, Tex., Aug. 14, 1933; s. Glen Wayne and Albene Angie (Hughes) A.; m. Joe Ann Davis, Mar. 31, 1952; children: Mack Lane, Mark Wayne. BS, U. Tex., El Paso, 1954; MS, N.Mex. State U., 1960, PhD, 1963. Assoc. scientist Westinghouse Electric Corp., Pitts., 1954-56; supervising mathematician Flight Stimulation Lab., White Sands Missile Range, N.Mex., 1956-60; dir. computer directorate Electronics R&D Activity, White Sands Missile Range, N.Mex., 1963-64; assoc. prof. U. Tex., El Paso, 1964-65; dir. computer ctr. N.Mex. State U., Las Cruces, 1965-70, prof., 1970—; sr. Fulbright lectr., Cath. U., Santiago, Chile, 1972; vis. fellow Wolfson Coll., Oxford, England, 1978. Author: (with others) Introduction to Computer Science, 1970, Computers: Appreciation, Application, Implications, 1973, Social Effects of Computer Use and Misuse, 1976; also articles. Univ. fellow N.Mex. State U., Las Cruces, 1960. Mem. IEEE (computer sect.), Assn. Computing Machinery, Math. Assn. Am., Internat. Student Pugwash, Sigma Xi. Democrat. Methodist. Avocation: running. Home: 905 Conway #7 Las Cruces NM 88005 Office: N M State U Computer Sci Dept Las Cruces NM 88003

ADAMS, JAY CONKLIN, designer; b. East Lansing, Mich., July 7, 1953; s. William Conklin and Patricia Burr (Bergen) A.; m. Piper Hisano Murakami, July 8, 1983. Exchange student, Poly. Cen. London, 1975; BArch, U. Va., 1976. Designer, builder T. van Groll, Architect, Charlottesville, Va., 1977-78; designer various firms Santa Cruz, Calif., 1978-79; designervarious firms Landor Assocs., San Francisco, 1980-81; designer, various firms The Burdick

Group, San Francisco, 1982-83; designer, prin. Jay Adams Interior Architecture, San Francisco, 1983—; lectr. U. Va., Charlottesville, 1986, Calif. Coll. Arts and Crafts, San Francisco, 1986. Recipient Best in Design 1985 award Interiors mag., 1986. Club: Bay (San Francisco). Office: 42 1/2 Langton St San Francisco CA 94103

ADAMS, JO-ANN MARIE, data processing systems engineer; b. Los Angeles, May 27, 1949; d. Joseph John and Georgia S. (Wein) A.; A.A., Pasadena City Coll., 1968; B.A., Pomona Coll., 1970; M.A., Calif. State U., Los Angeles, 1971; M.B.A., Pacific Luth. U., 1973. Secondary tchr. South Pasadena (Calif.) Unified Schs., 1970-71; appraiser Riverside County (Calif.) Assessor's Office, 1972-74; systems and procedures analyst Riverside County Data Processing Dept., 1974-76, supervising systems analyst, 1976-79; systems analyst computer Boeing Computer Services Co., Seattle, 1979-81; sr. systems analyst Thurston County Central Services, Olympia, Wash., 1981-83, data processing systems mgr., 1983-84; data processing systems engr. IBM Corp., 1984—; instr. Riverside City Coll., 1977-79. Chairperson legis. task force Riverside/San Bernardino chpt. NOW, 1975-76, chpt. co-chairperson, 1978; mem. ethics com. Calif. NOW Inc., 1978; alt. del. Calif Democratic Caucus, 1978. Mem. Nat. Abortion Rights Action League, Nat. Assn. Female Execs., Assn. Systems Mgrs., Am. Mgmt. Assn., Nat. Assn. Computing Machinery, Pomona Coll. Alumni Assn. Home: 10807 41st Ave SW Seattle WA 98146 Office: IBM Corp 10807 41st Ave SW Seattle WA 98146

ADAMS, JOHN PHILLIPS, JR., economics educator, forensic economics consultant; b. Dothan, Ala., June 29, 1920; s. John Phillips Sr. and Lucile (Brown) A.; m. Flavienne Marcelle David, Dec. 5, 1946; children—Gilles David, Sidney Michel. Student Ga. Sch. Tech., 1939-43, U. S.C., 1964-65; M.A., Claremont Grad. Sch., 1968, Ph.D., 1972. Commd. 2d lt. U.S. Army, 1943, advanced through grades to lt. col., 1963, ret., 1963; lectr. econs. Calif. State Poly. U., Pomona, 1968-70; prof. econs., Calif. Poly. State U., San Luis Obispo, 1970—; trustee Calif. Council on Econ. Edn., 1972-78; forensic econs. cons., San Luis Obispo, 1976—. Pres. Calif. Cen. Coast chpt. Mended Hearts, Inc., Arroyo Grande, 1983-84. Mem. Am. Econ. Assn., Western Econ. Assn. Internat., Atlantic Econ. Soc., Indsl. Relations Research Assn., Western Soc. Scis. Assn., Nat. Assn. Forensic Economists (charter mem., West regional dir. 1986—), Ret. Officers Assn. (life), White Sands Pioneer Group (life), Aircraft Owners and Pilots Assn., Omicron Delta Epsilon, Delta Sigma Pi, Alpha Tau Omega. Home: 2000 Wilding Ln San Luis Obispo CA 93401 Office: Econs Dept Calif Poly State Univ San Luis Obispo CA 93407

ADAMS, JONATHAN EDWARDS, III, corporate policy executive; b. Bangor, Maine, Sept. 9, 1947; s. Jonathan Edwards Jr. and Ruth Mia (Abenheimer) A.; m. Marcia Ruth Howe, June 20, 1970; children: Natalie Marie, Emily Ruth. AB, Dartmouth Coll., 1969; MBA, U. Pa., 1974. CPA, Calif. Staff acct. Haskins & Sells, San Francisco, 1974-76; corp. controller Logic Bus. Machines, Sunnyvale, Calif., 1976-77; supr. cost acctg. Hewlett-Packard Corp., Palo Alto, Calif., 1977-80; mgr. corp. policy Hewlett-PackardCorp., Palo Alto, Calif., 1980—. Served to 1st lt. USAF, 1969-72. Mem. Calif. Soc. CPA's, Jane Austin Soc. N.Am. Republican. Presbyterian. Club: Toastmasters (Palo Alto). Avocation: magazine collecting.

ADAMS, KAREN GUNHILD, provincial librarian; b. Eriksdale, Man., Can., May 3, 1946; d. Everet Harold and Margaret Anna (Goranson) Sidwall; children—Karina Richard. B.A. with honors, U. Man., 1967; M.L.S., U. Western Ont., 1975. Dir. spl. projects Evergreen Sch. Div., Gimli, Man., Can., 1975-76; librarian Teshmont Cons., Winnipeg, Man., 1977; cataloguer Man. Public Library Service, Winnipeg, 1977-78, cons., 1978-79, dir., 1979-84; provincial librarian Sask. Library, Regina, Can., 1984—; cons. Teshmont Cons., 1977-78; instr. Red River Community Coll., Winnipeg, 1978. Mem. Can. Library Assn. (councillor 1984-87), Group on Nat. Library Services for Handicapped Persons (chair 1985-86), Inst. Public Adminstrn. Can., Sask. Library Assn. Office: Saskatchewan Library, 1352 Winnipeg St, Regina, SK Canada S4R 1J6

ADAMS, KENNETH DALE, psychologist, educator; b. Cloud Chief, Okla., Feb. 9, 1929; s. Alvin Rowe and Leona Sarah (Carpenter) A.; m. E. El Wanda Janes; 1 son, K. Dale. B.S. in Math., Southwestern State U., 1950; M.Ed. in Adminstrn and Guidance, U. Okla., 1957, Ph.D. in Counseling Psychology, 1982. Cert. psychologist, counselor, adminstr., tchr. Math tchr., Cowden, Okla., 1948-49, Mountain View, Okla., 1949-57; math tchr., counselor S. Kitsap Schs., Port Orchard, Wash., 1957-64, psychologist, 1965-70, adminstr., 1970-82; profl. counselor and psychologist Sound Counseling Services, Port Orchard, 1980—; adj. prof. counseling Central Wash. State U., Ellenburg, Seattle Pacific U., 1967-82. Active Democratic legis. campaign, 1982; bd. dirs. South Kitsap Sch. Dist., 1984—, pres. 1986-87. Recipient NDEA Counseling Insts. awards 1961, 62, 63, 64. Mem. Am. Personnel and Guidance Assn., Wash. State Counseling and Guidance Assn., Am. Mental Health Counselors Assn., Wash. Mental Health Counselors Assn., Phi Delta Kappa. Democrat. Methodist. Clubs: Bremerton Yacht. Lodges: Elks, Kiwanis (pres. South Kitsap chpt. 1985-86). Home: 2422 Parkwood Dr SE Port Orchard WA 98366 Office: Sound Counseling Services 502 High Ave S-203 Port Orchard WA 98366

ADAMS, LEON DAVID, author; b. Boston, Feb. 1, 1905; s. Nathan and Gussie (Lager) A.; m. Corinne Leona Adams (div. 1953); children: Gerald David, Brian Arthur; m. Eleanor Rittman (div. 1975); children: Timothy Rittman, Susan Campbell. Student, U. Calif., Berkeley, 1923-25. From reporter to marine editor San Francisco News and San Francisco Bulletin, 1923-28; bur. chief McClatchy Newspapers, San Francisco, 1928-35; with Organized Grape Growers League of Calif., San Francisco, 1931-33, Organized Wine Inst., San Francisco, 1934-54, Organized Wine Adv. Bd., San Francisco, 1938-54; organizer, exec. sec., editor Soc. Med. Friends of Wine, San Francisco, 1939—, editor, 1956—. Author: Striped Bass Fishing in California and Oregon, 1952, 2d rev. edit. 1954, Commonsense Book of Wine, 1958, 4th rev. edit., 1986, Commonsense Book of Drinking, 1960, The Wines of America, 1973, 3d rev. edit., 1985. Mem. Am. Wine Soc. (Merit award 1974), Am. Soc. of Viticulture and Enology (Merit award 1974), Wine and Food Soc. Republican. Avocations: fishing, judging wines. Home and Office: 230 Woodward Ave Box 218 Sausalito CA 94965

ADAMS, LYNNE ADELE, secondary education counselor; b. Seattle, May 8, 1952; d. Ralph Wilbur and Lorraine Evelyn (Lee) A. BA in Communication Disorders, Cen. Wash. U., 1974; MS in Communication Disorders, Eastern Wash. U., 1980; postgrad., Wash. State U., 1984—. Cert. ednl. staff assoc.; counseling initial level ednl. staff assoc. Communication disorders specialist Walla Walla (Wash.) Ednl. Service Dist. 123, 1974-77, Pasco (Wash.) Sch. Dist., 1977-86; counselor Prosser (Wash.) Sch. Dist., 1986—. Mem. NEA, Wash. Edn. Assn., Am. Speech Lang. Hearing Assn., Wash. Assn. Sch. Counselors, Delta Kappa Gamma. Avocations: running, collecting antiques, reading, piano. Home: 100 N Irving Pl #62 Kennewick WA 99336

ADAMS, MARILYN (MARTY) LEE, counselor, social work educator; b. Mpls., June 29, 1955; d. Vincent and Myrtle Ida Helena (Saline) K.; m. Keith Micheal Adams, Aug. 29, 1981; 1 child, Lindsey Marie. BA, Concordia Coll., 1976; MSW, U. Minn., 1979. Cert. social worker. Dir. programs Platte County Recreation Dept., Wheatland, Wyo., 1978; social worker Elk River (Minn.) Sch. Dist., 1979-80; dir. programs Geneva Glen Camp, Indian Hills, Colo., 1979-80; parent coordinator Wyo. Infant Stimulation Project, Laramie, 1980-81; assoc. prof. social work U. Wyo., Laramie, 1985—; sch. social worker Laramie Jr. High Sch., 1981—; cons. research Arrowhead Regional Devel. Ctr., Duluth, Minn., 1978-79, Minn. Pub. Info. Research Group, Duluth, 1978-79, The Legal Group, Duluth, 1979. Co-Author: A Baby Care Book for Young Parents, 1981 (named best seller by Internat. Childbirth Edn. Assn. 1985). Bd. dirs. Big Brothers and Big Sisters, Laramie, 1985—; active Cowboy Joe Club, Laramie, 1984—; active spl. projects com. and coach Spl. Olympics, Laramie, 1982-84. Mem. Nat. Assn. Social Workers (cert., Wyo. chpt.), Albany County Edn. Assn., Wyo. Edn. Assn., Nat. Assn. Secondary School Prins., Alpha Delta Kappa, Pi Gamma Mu, Lambda Delta Sigma. Methodist. Lodge: Jobs Daughters (hon. queen 1973). Avocations: Ukranian egg decorating, traveling, Hardanger embroidery. Home: 1801 Symons Laramie WY 82070 Office: Laramie Jr High Sch 1355 N 22nd St Laramie WY 82070

ADAMS, MARK F., industrial engineer; b. Hoquiam, Wash., Aug. 4, 1914; s. Harry John and Nellie Florence (Lamb) A.; m. Ruth L. Zier, June 7, 1942; children: Russel Mark, Charles Francis, Paul David, Sylvia Ruth. AS, Grays Harbor Coll., 1938; BS, Wash. State Coll. (later Wash. State U.), 1940, MS, 1942, PhD, 1951. With state dept. conservation and devel. Olympia, Wash., 1941-45; research chemist Wash. State U., Pullman, 1945-51, head dept. materials engring., div. indsl. research, 1945-74; indsl. cons. Consulting Assocs., Inc., Tacoma, 1974—. Contbr. chpts. to books, articles to profl. jours.; patentee in field. Active Sch. Bd. N. Beach Dist. 64, Copalis, Wash., 1978-82. Invited delegate Citizen Ambassador Program to China, 1986. Mem. Nat. Assn. Corrosion Engrs. (cert., chmn. nat. edn. com. 1961-63), Western Region of Nat. Assn. Corrosion Engrs., N.W. Sci. Assn. (pres. 1969, OUtstanding Scientist 1968), N.W. Electrolysis Council (underground elec. distbrn. test steering com. 1973), Am. Chem. Soc., Sigma Xi. Lutheran. Lodge: Kiwanis (lt. gov. Ocean Shores, Wash. club 1977-78). Avocations: singing, woodworking. Home and Office: 7406 S Cushman Tacoma WA 98408

ADAMS, NORMAN JOSEPH, economist, corporate mergers broker; b. Los Angeles, Feb. 21, 1930; s. Joseph O'Neil and Florence Mary (Michalek) A.; B.S., U. So. Calif., 1951; diploma Oxford U., 1953; postgrad. Harvard U., 1956; Ph.D., U. Karachi (Pakistan), 1958; m. Julia Jewell, Oct. 16, 1960; children—Darlene, Janet. Pres., Adams & Co., mergers and aquisitions, Los Angeles.

ADAMS, PATRICIA ANN, educator; b. Pasadena, Calif., Jan. 29, 1926; d. Alfred Corrin and Thelma (Genivieve (Sprigel) Jack; m. Norman Robert Stanger, Nov. 3, 1945; children—Randall, Robyn Stanger Clever; m. Robert Doyal Adams, Aug. 22, 1964. A.A., Pasadena City Coll., 1945; B.A., Calif. State U.-Fullerton, 1964; M.Ed., U. Ariz., 1972. Cert. techr., Calif., Ariz. Tchr. dist. 1, Yuma, Ariz., 1964-69, Wilson dist., Phoenix, 1969-72, Mesa Sch. Dist., Ariz., 1972-77, Herperia dist., Calif., 1977-80; program resource coordinator Hesperia dist., 1980-82, tchr., 1982—; trainer, profl. devel. tng. and clin. supr.; facilitator pilot reading programs; coordinator compensatory programs. Named Outstanding Tchr. of Yr., Mesa Sch. Dist., 1977. Mem. Internat. Reading Assn., Assn. Supervision and Curriculum Devel., NEA, Calif. Edn. Assn., Foothill Reading Council, Mountain-Desert Reading Council, U. Ariz. Alumni Assn., Hesperia Tchrs. Assn., Beta Sigma Phi (service award 1977, Girl of Yr. award 19787), Delta Kappa Gamma (pres., area dir.). Republican. Presbyterian. Club: Spring Valley Lake Country. Home: PO Box 1606 Apple Valley CA 92307 Office: 9144 3d St Hesperia CA 92345

ADAMS, PETER FREDERICK, civil engineer, educator; b. Halifax, N.S., Can.; m. Barbara Adams, Oct. 11, 1957; 3 sons. B.Eng., N.S. Tech. Coll., 1958, M.Engr., 1961; Ph.D., Lehigh U., 1966. With Internat. Nickel Co. Can., 1958-59, Dominion Bridge Co., 1974-75; mem. faculty U. Alta., Edmonton, 1960—; prof. civil engring. U. Alta., 1971—; dean Faculty of Engring., 1976-84; pres. Ctr. for Frontier Engring. Research, 1984—; lectr. in field. Author: (Krentz & Kulak) Canadian Structural Steel Design, 1973, (Krentz & Kulak) Limit States Design in Structural Steel, 1977. Past pres. Aspen Gardens Community League. Mem. Can. Soc. Civil Engring., ASCE, Internat. Assn. Bridge and Structural Engring., Can. Standards Assn. Club: Toastmasters (past pres.). Office: Centre For Frontier Engring C-FER-Building, Univ of Alberta, Edmonton, AB Canada T6G 2G2

ADAMS, PETER JULIAN, physicist; b. Hawkhurst, Eng., Sept. 4, 1941; came to Can., 1949; s. Mervyn Francis and Gladys Lillian (Redman) A.; m. Shari Madden, Dec. 28, 1975; children: Bryce Jacob, Myles Edward (twins). BS, U. Oreg., 1963, MS, 1968, PhD, 1973. Research assoc. Goddard Inst. for Space Studies, N.Y.C., 1973-76, U. B.C., Vancouver, Can., 1976-79; asst. prof. physics U. Puget Sound, Tacoma, 1979-80, 83-84, Wash. State U., Pullman, 1980-81; research assoc. Jet Propulsion Lab., Pasadena, Calif., 1981-83; staff scientist Los Alamos (N.Mex.) Nat. Lab., 1984—. Contbr. articles to profl. jours. Served with U.S. Army, 1965-67. Republican. Office: Los Alamos Nat Lab MS B220 Los Alamos NM 87544

ADAMS, PHILIP, lawyer; b. Los Angeles, July 18, 1905; s. Thaddeus Lafayette and Lena (Kelly) A.; m. Alice Rahman, 1933; children—Stephen, Judith, Deborah, Kate; m. Elaine Margaret Anderson, 1968. Student, Pomona Coll., 1924-27; J.D., Hastings Coll. Law, U. Calif., 1938; LL.D. (hon.), Ch. Div. Sch. of Pacific, Berkeley, Calif., 1965. Bar: Calif. bar 1938. Purser Panama Mail S.S. Line, 1928-29; profl. investigator 1930-38; individual practice law San Francisco, 1938—; atty. U.S. Govt., 1942-46; instr. domestic relations Golden Gate Law Sch., 1971-72. Author: Adoption Practice in California, 1956. Dir. Children's Protective Soc., 1939-44, United Cerebral Palsy Assn., San Francisco, 1952-72, Assn. for Mental Health, 1952—, United Bay Area Crusade, 1955-61, United Community Fund, San Francisco, 1957-62, San Francisco State Coll., 1964-69, Am. Democratic Action; trustee Ch. Div. Sch. of Pacific, 1951-76; nat. v.p. Episcopal Evang. Fellowship, 1952-61; chancellor Episcopal Diocese of Calif., 1960-67; dep. Episcopal Gen. Conv., 1946-70; pres. bd. trustees Grad. Theol. Union, Berkeley, 1963-66. Fellow Am. Acad. Matrimonial Lawyers (dir. No. Calif. chpt. 1968—); mem. ABA (chmn. com. on adoption, family law sect. 1959-60), Calif., San Francisco bar assns., Lawyers Club San Francisco (gov. 1956), Am. Acad. Polit. and Social Sci., San Francisco Symphony Assn., Soc. Genealogists (London). Clubs: Villa Taverna, Commonwealth. Home: 2170 Jackson St San Francisco CA 94115 Office: 220 Montgomery St San Francisco CA 94104

ADAMS, PHILLIP ANTHONY, entomology educator, researcher; b. Los Angeles, Jan. 13, 1929; s. Edwin Brown and Jeanette M. (Mc Pherson) A. BS, U. Calif., Berkeley, 1951; AM, PhD, Harvard U., 1958. From instr. to asst. prof. entomology U. Calif., Santa Barbara, 1958-63; from asst. prof. to assoc. prof. Calif. State U., Fullerton, 1963-67, from assoc. prof. to prof., 1969—; vis. assoc. prof. Yale U., 1968-69; cons. U.S. Nat. Mus. Natural History, Washington, 1978—. Contbr. articles to profl. jours. Shipmaster Orange County council Boy Scouts Am., Newport, Calif., 1972—. Mem. Assn. Mondiale des Névroptèristes (Am. editor 1982—), Entomol. Soc. Am., Sociedade Brasileira de Entomologia, Am. Sail Tng. Assn. Republican. Avocation: renaissance music (lute). Home: 17091 Saga Dr Yorba Linda CA 92686 Office: Calif State U Dept Biology Fullerton CA 92634

ADAMS, RICHARD CRITTENDEN, secondary school educator; b. Brevard County, Fla., May 4, 1945; s. Claude Willard Jr. and Jeanne (Cassels) A.; m. Nancy Payne, Nov. 28, 1975; children: Colin Cameron, Gabrielle Jeanne. BA in Chemistry, History, Calif. State U., Los Angeles, 1970; MA in Biology, Computers, Physics, U. Oreg., 1975. High sch. tchr. Pleasant Hill (Oreg.) High Sch., 1970—; pres. Adams' Soft Enterprises, Springfield Oreg.; lectr. U. Oreg., Eugene, Marylhurst (Oreg.) Coll. Author: (with Hendrik Keyzer) Misiones de California en Caligrafia, 1971, Science with Computers, 1987; contbr. articles to profl. jours. Named Outstanding Educator, 1972. Mem. Oreg. Sci. Tchrs. Assn. (lectr. 1983—), Oreg. Assn. Talented and Gifted (lectr. 1976—), Northwest Council for Computers in Edn. (lectr. 1981—). Club: Appleugene (Eugene) (v.p. 1983—). Avocations: photography, calligraphy, trivia, reading, cross-country skiing. Home: 894 W 11th Ave Eugene OR 97402 Office: PO Box 386 Springfield OR 97477 also: Pleasant Hill High Sch 36386 Hwy 58 Pleasant Hill OR 97455

ADAMS, RICHARD LEONARD, cotton gin executive; b. Porterville, Calif., Sept. 4, 1932; s. Richard Leonard and Leta (Crumal) A.; student Bakersfield Coll., 1953-54; m. Mary Ann Gordon, Sept. 9, 1954; children—Thomas Lee, Richard Leonard. Office mgr. Laton Coop. Gin. (Calif.), 1954-58; gen. mgr. Raisin City Coop. Gin. (Calif.), 1958—; alt. del. Nat. Cotton Council of Am., 1978—. Active Boy Scouts Am., Pop Warner Football League, 1970s. Served with U.S. Army, 1949-53; Korea. Decorated Bronze Star, Purple Heart (2); recipient Community Service award Caruthers C. of C., 1982. Mem. Caruthers C. of C. (pres. 1974-75), Laton C. of C. (pres. 1957-58), Calif. Coop. Gin Assn. (pres. 1978-79), Calif. Gin Assn., Nat. Soc. Accounts for Coop., Calif. State U.-Fresno Alumni Assn., 25th Inf. Div. Assn. Methodist. Club: Lions. Home: 13170 S Marsh St Caruthers CA 93609 Office: Raisin City Coop Gin 10833 S Cornelia Ave Raisin City CA 93652

ADAMS, ROLAND ANTHONY, periodontology educator, consultant; b. Adelaide, Australia, Nov. 22, 1945; came to U.S., 1975; s. Roland Harry and Valerie (Arnold) A.; children: Roland Stephen, Benjamin Sidney. DDS, U. Adelaide, 1969; specialty degree oral surgery, U. Melbourne, Victoria, Australia, 1973; specialty degree periodontology, Eastman Dental Ctr., 1975; MS, U. Rochester, 1975; MA, Miss. State U., 1983. Registrar oral surgery Royal Melbourne (Australia) Hosp., 1970-71; research fellow Eastman Dental Ctr., Rochester, N.Y., 1975-78; assoc. prof. periodontology U. Miss., Jackson, 1978-85; assoc. prof. periodontology Oreg. Health Sci. U., Portland, 1985—, dir. research, grad. periodontology, 1985—; research trainee NIH, Rochester, 1975-78; research cons. Kaiser Permanente Med. Ctr., Portland, 1985—; research investigator Proctor-Gamble Drug Corp., Portland, 1986—; cons. Warner-Lambert Drug Corp., Melbourne, 1971-73. Author: Preventive Dentistry, 1981, Health Care for Aging People, 1986; contbr. articles to profl. jours. Adv. bd. Lake Oswego (Oreg.) Sch. Dist. Uplands Sch., 1986—; coach youth soccer Oreg. Soccer Assn., Lake Oswego, 1985-86. Mem. ADA, Am. Acad. Periodontology, Internat. Assn. Dental Research, Am. Assn. Dental Schs. Episcopalian. Avocations: flying, scuba diving, climbing. Home: 22 Othello Lake Oswego OR 97035 Office: Oreg Health Sci U 611 SW Campus Dr Portland OR 97201

ADAMS, TERRI RUTH, speech-language pathologist, consultant; b. Germany, Sept. 11, 1957; d. Enzor Edward and Nancy Lee (Fenimore) A. AA, Chipola Jr. Coll., 1977; MS, U. S. Fla., 1981. Speech therapist Bonifay (Fla.) Pub. Schs., 1981-82, Navajo Community Coll., Tsaile, Ariz., 1982-84, Chinle (Ariz.) Pub. Schs., 1984—; cons. USPHS, 1983—; adj. instr. No. Ariz. U., Flagstaff, Ariz., 1983-85; parent advisor Ariz. Sch. for Deaf and Blind, Tucson, 1984—. Vol. Spl. Olympics, Chinle, 1982—; ch. tchr., Chinle, 1984—; ch. treas., Chinle, 1985—; active in community choir. Mem. Am. Speech-Lang.-Hearing Assn. (cert.), Ariz. Edn. Assn. Democrat. Club: OMC (Bonifay) (sec., treas. 1975—). Avocations: hiking, reading. Home: PO Box 7 Chinle AZ 86503 Office: Chinle Sch Dist PO Box 587 Chinle AZ 86503

ADAMS, VICKI PORTER, computer publications specialist; b. Wheeling, W. Va., Apr. 10, 1939; d. Clyde Scott and Helen (McClure) Porter; m. Theodore Cecil Adams, Nov. 20, 1971. B.E., Waynesburg Coll., 1961; postgrad. W.Va. U., 1962. Elem. tchr. Los Angeles Bd. Edn., 1961-63; tchr. jr. high sch. Thousand Oaks (Calif.) Unified Sch. Dist., 1963-66; computer programmer System Devel. Corp., Santa Monica, Calif., 1966-70; sr. programmer NCR Corp., San Diego, 1971-75; mem. staff testing Litton Mellonics, San Diego, 1975-76; mgr. tech. publs. TRW Communications, San Diego, 1976-78; sr. cons. publs. specialist NCR Corp., 1978-83; cons., writer, speaker in field. Pub. relations mem. Crime Victims Fund, DAR. Recipient Cert. of Achievement scholarship Nat. U., San Diego, 1982. Mem. Calif. Press Women (pres., editor, bd. dirs., 4 writing awards 1980, 5 awards 1981, 2 awards 1984, 4 awards 1985, 8 awards 1986), Nat. Fedn. Press Women, San Diego Republican Businesswomen, San Diego Writers/Editors Guild. Republican. Methodist. Contbr. articles to mags. Home and office: 4461 Moraga Ave San Diego CA 92117

ADAMS, WILLIAM MANSFIELD, educator; b. Kissimmee, Fla., Feb. 19, 1932; s. Shirah Devoy and Olive (Goding) A.; m. Roberta Kay Blackwell, July 23, 1955; children: William Mansfield, Johnathan Blackwell, Christopher Daniel; m. Naoko Nakashizuka, 1976; children: Henele Iitaka, Alden Fernald. A.B. (Univ. scholar), U. Chgo., 1951; B.A., U. Calif., 1953; M.S. (Gulf scholar), St. Louis U., 1955, Ph.D., 1957; M.B.A., Santa Clara U., 1964; postgrad., M.I.T., 1967-70. Instrument man Shell Oil Co., Merced, Calif., 1953; geophys. trainee Stanolind Oil Co., New Orleans, 1953, Western Geophys. Co., Rankin, Tex., 1954; tech. officer Govt. Can., Ottawa, 1956; chief seismologist Geotech Corp., Laramie, Wyo., 1957-59; program tech. dir. U. Calif., Livermore, 1959-62; pres. Planetary Scis., Inc., Santa Clara, Calif., 1962-64; prof. geophysics U. Hawaii, Honolulu, 1964—; exchange prof. Ind. U., Bloomington, 1975-76; UNESCO expert seismology Internat. Inst. Seismology and Earthquake Engring., Bldg. Research Inst., Tokyo, 1971-72; vis. fellow Co-op. Inst. Research in Environ. Scis., U. Colo., Boulder, 1970-71; research oceanographer Atlantic Marine and Environ. Lab., NOAA, Miami, Fla., 1979-80; cons. Del E. Webb, Kahuku Point, Oahu, Hawaii, 1969, Oceanic Properties, Lanai City, Lanai, Hawaii, 1969, C. Brewer Co., Punaluu, Hawaii, 1970, 74, Desert Research Inst. U. Nev., 1983. Contbr. numerous articles to profl. jours. Fulbright grantee, 1956-57; NATO grantee Internat. Inst. Geothermal Research, Pisa, Italy, 1973. Mem. Am. Geophys. Union, Geol. Soc. Am., Seismol. Soc. Am. (editor Bull 1962-65), Acoustical Soc. Am., Soc. Exploration Geophysicists, AAUP, European Assn. Exploration Geophysicists, Tsunami Soc. (founder), Fulbright Alumni Assn., Assn. Geoscientists for Internat. Devel., Sigma Xi. Patentee in field. Office: U Hawaii Dept Geophysics 2525 Correa Rd Honolulu HI 96822

ADAMSON, ALBERT SCOTT, JR., consumer products company executive; b. Cin., Sept. 30, 1947; s. Albert Scott Sr. and Betty Ann (Gaither) A.; m. Robin Ann Tarter, July 1, 1969. Perfumer Procter & Gamble, Cin., 1967-75; perfumer The Dial Corp., Scottsdale, Ariz., 1975-77, mgr. perfume dept., 1977-86, dir. perfumery, 1986—; lectr. Am. Chem. Soc., Phoenix, 1986, Am. Inst. Chem. Engrs., Phoenix, 1986, dept. chem. and bio engring. Ariz. State U., Tempe, 1986; guest speaker Sta. WELI, Conn., 1985. Mem. Am. Soc. Perfumers. Home: 1614 E Candlestick Dr Tempe AZ 85283 Office: The Dial Corp 15101 N Scottsdale Rd Scottsdale AZ 85254

ADAMSON, ARTHUR WILSON, chemistry educator; b. Shanghai, Republic of China, Aug. 15, 1919; s. Arthur Quintin and Ethel (Rhoda) A.; m. Virginia Louise Dillman, Mar. 24, 1942; children—Carol Ann, Janet Louise, Jean Elizabeth. B.S. with honors, U. Calif.-Berkeley, 1940; Ph.D. in Phys. Chemistry, U. Chgo., 1944. Research assoc. Manhattan Project, Oak Ridge, 1944-46; asst. prof. U. So. Calif., 1946-49, assoc. prof., 1949-53, prof., 1953—, chmn. dept. chemistry, 1972-75. editor Langmuir Washington, 1984—; author: Textbook of Physical Chemistry, 1986; Physical Chemistry of Surfaces, 1982; Understanding Physical Chemistry, 1980; Concepts of Inorganic Photochemistry, 1975; contbr. articles to profl. jours. Fellow Am. Inst. Chemists; mem. Am. Chem. Soc. (councillor So. Calif. sect. 1964-80, chmn. 1964, Tolman award 1966, Kendall award 1979, Disting. Service in Inorganic Chemistry award 1982, Chem. Edn. award 1984), AAAS. Republican. Club: Palos Verdes Tennis. Avocations: tennis; photography. Office: U So Calif Dept Chemistry Los Angeles CA 90089

ADAMSON, GEOFFREY DAVID, reproductive endocrinologist, surgeon; b. Ottawa, Ont., Can., Sept. 16, 1946; came to U.S., 1978, naturalized, 1986; s. Geoffrey Peter Adamson and Anne Marian Allan; m. Rosemary C. Adamson, Apr. 28, 1973; children: Stephanie, Rebecca, Eric. BSc with honors, Trinity Coll., Toronto, Can., 1969; MD, U. Toronto, 1973. Diplomate Am. Bd. Ob-Gyn; cert. Bd. Reproductive Endocrinology. Resident in ob-gyn Toronto Gen. Hosp., 1973-77, fellow in ob-gyn, 1977-78; fellow reproductive endocrinology Stanford (Calif.) U. Med. Ctr., 1978-80; practice medicine specializing in infertility Los Gatos, Calif., 1980-84, Palo Alto, Calif., 1984—; clin. asst. prof. Stanford (Calif.) U. Sch. Medicine, 1980—. Mem. editorial adv. bd. Can. Doctor mag., 1977-83; contbg. editor Fertility Rev.; contbr. articles to sci. jours. Ontario Ministry of Health fellow, 1977-78. Fellow ACS, Royal Coll. Surgeons Can., Am. Coll. Ob-Gyns.; mem. AAAS, AMA, Soc. Reproductive Endocrinologists (charter), Soc. Reproductive Surgeons (charter), Fallopius Soc. (charter), Pacific Coast Fertility Soc., Am. Assn. Gynecol. Laparoscopists, Gynecologic Laser Soc., N.Y. Acad. Scis., Shufelt Gynecologic Soc. San Mateo Med. Assn., Peninsula Gynecol. Soc., Calif. Med. Assn., Santa Clara County Med. Assn., Santa Clara County Med. Assn., No. Calif. Resolve (bd. dirs.), Am. Fedn. Clin. Research, Can. Assn. Internes and Residents (hon. life, pres. 1977-79, bd. dirs. 1974-79, rep. AMA resident physician sect. 1978-79, rep. Can. Med. Protective Assn. 1975-78, rep. Can. Med. Assn. 1975-78, Disting. Service award 1980), Profl. Assn. Internes and Residents Ont. (bd. dirs. 1973-74, v.p. 1974-75, pres. 1975-76), Royal Coll. Physician and Surgeons Can. (com. examinations 1977-80), Ont. Med. Assn. (sec. internes and residents sect. 1973-74). Avocations: personal computers, snow skiing. Home: 16520 S Kennedy Rd Los Gatos CA 95030 Office: 540 University Ave #200 Palo Alto CA 94301

ADAMS-SELICO, SHIRLEY LUCILE, nurse; b. Marshall, Tex., Feb. 22, 1941; d. Gerald Hugo and Ella Mary (Hodges) Adams; B.S., Howard U., 1962; grad. Los Angeles County Sch. Nursing, 1975; postgrad. Calif. State U.; children—Sherilyn Marie Lum-Bird, E. Gerald Steven Lum, Michael J. Premmer. Staff nurse spl. care nurseries, newborn intensive care unit Los

Angeles-U. So. Calif. Med. Center Women's Hosp., 1975-81, critical care nurse neonatalogy, 1976-81, clin. instr. nursing; staff nurse Queen of Valley Hosp. Nursery. Social vice chmn. Young Democrats Am., Washington, 1962. Mem. Nat. Assn. Negro Women, Nat. Assn. Female Execs., Philathias Soc., ACLU, Psi Chi. Roman Catholic. Home: 851 S Sunset Ave Apt 70 West Covina CA 91790

ADCOCK, RONALD PORTER, state official; b. Bklyn., Jan. 22, 1941; s. Porter Trout and Virginia Marie (Wilhelm) A.; B.A., Union Coll., Barbourville, Ky., 1963; M.Div., Boston U., 1969; m. Jo Ann Gulley, May 24, 1964; 1 child, Jerald Michael. Ordained to ministry United Methodist Ch., 1969; pastor chs., R.I., Idaho, 1965-70; trainer Idaho Dept. Spl. Services, 1970-72; nursing home ombudsman Idaho Office Aging, Boise, 1972-74; salesman Standard Ins. Co., Boise, 1974-75; dep. dir. Idaho Econ. Opportunity Office, Boise, 1975—; cons. on fed. grand mgmt. to non-profit orgns. Mem. Idaho Commn. Women's Programs, 1972-78; mem. Idaho Gov.'s Task Force on Emergency Med. Services, 1974; chairperson Area Tng. and Employment Adv. Council, Weiser, Idaho, 1974-77; mem. Idaho Gov.'s Vol. Citizen Participation Adv. Council, Nat. Task Force on Low Income Energy Utilization and Conservation. bd. dirs. Canyon County (Idaho) Hotline, 1970-75, Planned Parenthood Idaho, 1972-74, Canyon County Ret. Sr. Vol. Program, 1978-79; assoc. pastor Southside Blvd. United Meth. Ch. Recipient cert. recognition Gov. Idaho, 1974. Mem. Am. Soc. Tng. and Devel. (past pres. Treasure Valley chpt.), Nat. Assn. State Community Services Programs (chmn. grants mgmt. com.), Idaho Community Action Assn., Oreg.-Idaho Ann. Conf. United Meth. Ch. (hon. located), Nat. Model R.R. Assn. (life). Democrat. Home: 602 Fletcher Dr Nampa ID 83651 Office: Statehouse Boise ID 83720

ADDAMS, ROBERT JEAN, business and financial consultant; b. Salt Lake City, Sept. 24, 1942; s. Harvey J. and Virginia (Dutson) A.; m. Mary A. Watkins, Feb. 10, 1973; children—Ryan, Kelley, Amy, Michael. B.S., U. Utah, 1968, M.B.A., 1969. Fin. analyst Western Airlines, Inc., Los Angeles, 1969-72, mgr. budgets and cost control, 1972-74, controller mktg. div., 1974-76, dir. budgets and cost control, 1976-80; v.p., gen. mgr. Ball Bros., Inc., Everette, Wash., and Anchorage, 1980-82; pres., cons. Addams & Assocs., Redmond, Wash., 1982—. Author: Care and Handling of Wetsalted Cod Fish, 1984. Scoutmaster, Explorer advisor Gt. Salt Lake and Los Angeles councils Boy Scouts Am., 1973-75; served 2-yr. mission for Ch. Jesus Christ Latter-day Saints, 1962-64. Served with U.S. Army, 1961-62. Named Outstanding Grad., Coll. Bus., 1968, Beehive Honor Soc., 1969. Mem. U. Utah Alumni Assn. (pres. So. Calif. chpt. 1976-80), U. Utah Coll. of Bus. Alumni (pres. So. Calif. group 1978-79), Alpha Kappa Psi. Republican. Home and Office: Addams & Assocs 17003 NE 136th Pl Redmond WA 98052

ADDICOTT, WARREN OLIVER, geologist, educator; b. Fresno, Calif., Feb. 17, 1930; s. Irwin Oliver and Astrid (Jensen) A.; m. Suzanne Aubin, Oct. 2, 1976; m. Susanne Smith, Aug. 20, 1956 (div. 1974); children—Eric Oliver, Carol. BA cum laude, Pomona Coll., Calif., 1951; MA, Stanford U., Calif., 1952; PhD, U. Calif.-Berkeley, 1956. Teaching asst. U. Calif.-Berkeley, 1952-54; paleontologist Standard Oil Co. Calif., 1953; geologist Mobil Oil Co., Los Angeles, 1954-62; research geologist U.S. Geol. Survey, Menlo Park, Calif., 1962—; cons. prof. Stanford U., Calif., 1971-82; dep. chmn. Circum-Pacific Map Project, Menlo Park, Calif., 1979-82, gen. chmn., 1982-86, project advisor, 1986—. Contbr. artilces to profl. jours. Bd. dirs. Pacific Council Energy and Mineral Resources, 1983-86. Fellow AAAS, Geol. Soc. Am., Calif. Acad. Scis.; mem. Paleontol. Soc. (pres. 1979-80), Am. Assn. Petroleum Geologists, Paleontol. Res. Instn. (bd. dirs. 1980-81). Congregationalist. Home: 351 Everett St Palo Alto CA 94301 Office: US Geol Survey 345 Middlefield Rd Menlo Park CA 94025

ADDIS, RICHARD BARTON, lawyer; b. Columbus, Ohio, Apr. 9, 1929; s. Wilbur Jennings and Leila Olive (Grant) A.; m. Marguerite C. Christjohn, Feb. 9, 1957; children—Jacqueline Carol, Barton David. B.A., Ohio State U., 1954, J.D., 1955. Bar: Ohio 1956, U.S. Dist. Ct. (no. dist.) Ohio 1957, N.Mex. 1963, U.S. Dist. Ct. (N.Mex. 1963. Sole practice, Canton, Ohio, 1956-63, Albuquerque, 1963—. Served with USMC, 1946-48, 50-52. Mem. Ohio Bar Assn., N.Mex. Bar Assn., Am. Arbitration Assn. (arbitrator 1968—), Soc. Mining Engrs. Address: 1336 Wyoming Blvd NE Albuquerque NM 87112

ADDIS, THOMAS HOMER, III, professional golfer; b. San Diego, Nov. 30, 1945; s. Thomas H. and Martha J. (Edwards) A.; student Foothill Jr. Coll., 1963, Grossmont Jr. Coll., 1965; m. Susan Tera Buckley, June 13, 1966; children—Thomas Homer, IV, Bryan Michael. Head golf profl., mgr. Sun Valley Golf Course, La Mesa, Calif., 1966-67; asst. golf profl. Singing Hills Golf Course, El Cajon, Calif., 1967-69, head golf profl., dir. golf ops., 1969—; area cons. Nat. Golf Found.; gen. chmn. Nat. Jr. Golf championship U.S. Golf Assn., 1973—; mem. policy bd. Jr. World Golf Championships, rules chmn.; lectr. Bd. dirs. San Diego County Open, West Coast Golf Conf. and Mdse. Show, El Cajon Pony Baseball, 1981-82; trustee Calif. State Open, pres., 1980-84; chmn. Nat. Com. Liaison for Physically Limited. Recipient Retailer award Golf Industry mag., 1985; named to Lady Aztec San Diego State U. Hall of Fame. Mem. Profl. Golfers Assn. (pres. San Diego chpt. 1978-79, v.p. chpt. 1980-81; sec. So. Calif. sect. 1978-79, pres. sect. 1980-82, bd. dirs. sect. 1974—, speaker, long-range planning com. 1983—, chmn. mem. service com. 1986—, bd. dirs. San Diego sect. 1974—, assn. coordinator bus. schs. and seminars; named Profl. of Yr., So. Calif. sect. 1979, Nat. Golf Day Contbn. Leader, So. Calif. sect. 1973-76, 79; Horton Smith award So. Calif. sect. 1980-81, Nat. Horton Smith award 1981, Resort Merchandiser of Yr., So. Calif. sect. 1978, 83; ofcl. del. nat. meeting, annually 1978-85, mem. nat. bd. control 1978-85, membership com. 1978, 79; nat. edn. com. 1980-85, mem. jr. world championship com., long-range planning com. 1983-85, nat. bd. dirs., rules com. 1986—, championship com. 1986—), Nat. Amputee Golf Assn. (hon. mem.), San Diego Jr. Golf Assn. (dir.), Golf Collector's Soc. Club: Singing Hills Tennis. Lodge: Rotary. Author articles. Office: Singing Hills Golf Course 3007 Dehesa Rd El Cajon CA 92021

ADDISON, MARK P., dye manufacturer; b. Chgo., Sept. 22, 1934; m. Mary Kamps, Dec. 28, 1957; children: Douglas, Susan, Ann, Timothy, Sarah. BA, U. Colo., 1960. Cert. ski instr. Pres. Colo. Dye & Chem. Inc., Boulder, 1961—; owner Art Matters, Boulder, 1978—; bd. dirs. Hydrosol Inc.; fin. cons., Boulder, 1970—. Contbr. articles to profl. jours. Active City of Boulder Arts Commns., 1984—; bd. dirs. Colo. Bus. Com. Arts., Denver, 1985—; trustee Colo. Music Festival, Boulder, 1985—, Boulder Ctr. Visual Arts, 1981—. Served with U.S. Army, 1954-57. Mem. Am. Inst. Floral Designers (hon.), Bur. Conf. Services, Am. Acad. Floriculture (chmn. 1981-84), Wholesale Florists and Florist Suppliers Assn. (chmn. edn. com. 1969-71), Soc. Am. Florists (mem. council 1971-73). Republican. Avocation: mountaineering. Office: Colo Dye & Chem Co PO Box 601 Boulder CO 80306

ADEGBOLA, SIKIRU KOLAWOLE, nuclear engineer, educator; b. Ibadan, Nigeria, Jan. 21, 1949; came to U.S., 1971; s. Lasisi and Moriamo Abeke (Akinyemi) A. BSME, Calif. State U., Fullerton, 1974; MBA, Calif. State U., Dominguez Hills, 1984—; MSME, U. Ariz., 1975; MS in Applied Mechanics, U. So. Calif., 1977; PhD in Engring., Calif. Coast U., 1983. Registered profl. mech. engr., Calif., Ariz. Research engr. Jet Propulsion Lab., Pasadena, Calif., 1976-78; stress analyst Bechtel Power Corp., Norwalk, Calif., 1978—; prof. engring. Calif. State U., Fullerton, 1984—. Leopold Schepp Found. fellowship, 1972-74. Mem. ASME (assoc.), NSPE, Calif. Soc. Profl. Engrs. Home: 8710 E Rosecrans Apt 215 Paramount CA 90723 Office: Bechtel Power Corp 12440 E Imperial Hwy Norwalk CA 90650

ADEL, MARK ALAN, retail executive; b. Niagara Falls, N.Y., Sept. 11, 1956; s. Jerome and Hazel Maxine (Smith) A.; m. Mary Margaret Henige, Aug. 23, 1976; children: Michael, Jessica. Student, Oakland U., 1974-79. Area mgr. Associated Amusements, Rochester, Mich., 1976-79; store mgr. Van Horn's Menswear, Novi, Mich., 1979-83; owner Bomar Casuals, Durango, Colo., 1983—; chief exec. officer A.A. Bus. Services, Durango, 1985—. Adv. Bnai Brith Youth Orgn., Southfield, Mich., 1981-83; com. mem. Durango X-mas Com., Southfield, Mich., 1982; active Durango Mall Promotions, 1983—. Recipeint Gold Shield of David Bnai Brith Youth Orgn., 1974; named Adv. of Yr. Bnai Brith Youth Orgn., 1982, Most Creative Mcht., Durango Mall, 1985. Mem. Durango C. of C., Four Corners Better Bus. Bur. Democrat. Jewish. Avocations: fitness, skiing, softball, hiking, golf. Home: 2719 Colorado Ave Durango CO 81301 Office: Bomar Casuals 800 S Camino Del Rio Durango CO 81301

ADELMAN, IRMA GLICMAN, economics educator; b. Cernowitz, Rumania, Mar. 14, 1930; came to U.S., 1949, naturalized, 1955; d. Jacob Max and Raissa (Ettinger) Glicman; m. Frank L. Adelman, Aug. 16, 1950 (div. 1979); 1 son, Alexander. B.S., U. Calif., Berkeley, 1950, M.A., 1951, Ph.D., 1955. Teaching asso. U. Calif., Berkeley, 1955-56; instr. U. Calif., 1956-57, lectr. with rank asst. prof., 1957-58; vis. asst. prof. Mills Coll., 1958-59; acting asst. prof. Stanford, 1959-61, asst. prof., 1961-62; asso. prof. Johns Hopkins, Balt., 1962-65; prof. econs. Northwestern U., Evanston, Ill., 1966-72, U. Md., 1972-78; prof. econs. and agrl. econs. U. Calif. at Berkeley, 1979—; cons. div. indsl. devel. UN, 1962-63, AID, U.S. Dept. State, Washington, 1963—, Internat. Bank Reconstrn. and Devel., 1968—, ILO, Geneva, 1973—. Author: Theories of Economic Growth and Development, 1961, (with A. Pepelasis and L. Mears) Economic Development: Analysis and Case Studies, 1961, (with Eric Thorbecke) The Theory and Design of Economic Development, 1966, (with C.T. Morris) Society, Politics and Economic Development—A Quantitative Approach, 1967, Practical Approaches to Development Planning-Korea's Second Five Year Plan, 1969, Economic Development and Social Equity in Developing Countries, 1973, (with Sherman Robinson) Planning for Income Distribution, 1977. Fellow Center Advanced Study Behavioral Scis., 1970-71. Fellow Am. Acad. Arts and Scis., Econometric Soc.; mem. Am. Econ. Assn. (mem. exec. com., v.p. 1969—), Social Sci. Research Council (dir.-at-large), Comparative Econ. Assn. (exec. com.), Am. Statis. Assn. Office: Dept Agr and Natural Resources Univ Calif Berkeley CA 94720

ADELMAN, JONATHAN REUBEN, political science educator, consultant; b. Washington, Oct. 30, 1948; s. Benjamin and Kitty (Sandler) A.; m. Nancy Sloane, Jan. 9, 1983; 1 child, Joshua Sloane. BA, Columbia U., 1969, MA, 1972, M in Philosophy, 1974, PhD, 1976. Vis. asst. prof. Columbia U., N.Y.C., 1977; vis. asst. prof. U. Ala., Tuscaloosa, 1977-78; asst. prof. Grad. Sch. Internat. Studies, U. Denver, 1978-85, assoc. prof., 1985—; sr. research analyst Sci. Applications, Inc., Denver, 1981—; Lady Davis vis. assoc. prof. Hebrew U. Jerusalem, 1986. Author: The Revolutionary Armies, 1980, Revolution, Armies and War, 1986; co-author: The Dynamics of Soviet Foreign Policy, 1987; editor: Communist Armies in Politics, 1982, Terror and Communist Politics, 1984, Superpowers and Revolution, 1986; contbr. numerous articles in field to profl. jours. Charles Phelps Taft fellow U. Cin., 1976-77; Am. Philos. Soc. grantee, 1980. Mem. Am. Polit. Sci. Assn., Am. Assn. Advancement Slavic Studies, Inter-Univ. Sem. Armed Forces and Soc. Democrat. Jewish. Home: 6336 S Florence Way Englewood CO 80111 Office: U Denver Grad Sch Internat Studies Denver CO 80210

ADELSON, DANIEL, psychology educator; b. N.Y.C., Sept. 19, 1918; s. Louis Hirsch and Esther Fay (Edelson) A.; m. Suzanne B. Maricq, July 23, 1948; children: Isabelle Rachel, Ann Deborah, Mark David. BA, CCNY, 1940, postgrad., 1941-42; postgrad., U. Chgo., 1948, U. Calif., Berkeley, 1949-50; MA, New Sch. Social Research, 1953; PhD, Columbia U., 1957. Mem. dept. social and behavioral Sci. U. Calif. Med. Ctr. Sch. Nursing, San Francisco, lectr. psychology, 1960-67; assoc. prof. psychology in residence U. Calif. Med. Ctr. Sch. Nrusing, 1967-82, prof. emeritus in residence, 1983—; mem. psychology group 1967-74; research assoc. Inst. Human Devel., U. Calif., Berkeley, 1960-70; asst. dir. Ctr. Tng. Community Psychiatry, Berkeley, 1961-65; social sci. assoc. Jewish Bd. Guardians, N.Y, 1954-55; research assoc., social psychologist Altro Health and Rehab. Services, Inc., N.Y., 1953-54, 55-56; research cons. Child Welfare League Am., N.Y., 1956; prin. investigator, project dir., Calif. Dept. Mental Hygiene, 1957-64. Founding editor: Community Psychology Series; editor, Volume Man as the Measure: The Crossroads; and (with B.L. Kalis) Community Psychology and Mental Health: Perspectives and Challenges; mem. editorial bd. Jour. Rural Community Psychology. UNRRA team officer Children's Ctr., U.S. Zone, Fed. Republic Germany, 1946; vol. agy. liaison officer, dep. chief U.S. Zone Vol. Agy. Div., Fed. Republic Germany, UN Relief and Rehab. Administrn., and Internat. Ref. Org., 1946-48. Served with U.S. Army, 1943-45. Decorated Bronze Star with oak leaf cluster. Fellow Am. Psychol. Assn., AAAS, Soc. for Psychol. Study Social Issues. Home: 299 The Uplands Berkeley CA 94705 Office: U Calif Dept Social and Behavioral Scis N-631-Y San Francisco CA 94143

ADELSON, MARVIN, architecture educator; b. Bklyn., May 29, 1926; s. Isidore and Mollie (Gassner) A.; m. Ellen Arendale Denham, Apr., 1, 1961 (div. Apr. 18, 1975); 1 child, David William; m. Yolande Hargrave Chambers, Aug. 11, 1979. Student, Bklyn. Coll., 1942-43, Harvard U., 1943-44; BS, Va. Poly. Inst. and State U., 1947; AM, U. Ill., 1950, PhD, 1952. Asst. prof. psychology, research assoc. aviation psychology lab. U. Ill., Urbana, 1952-55; mgr. command control and info. systems dept. Hughes Aircraft Co., Los Angeles and Fullerton, Calif., 1955-61; prin. scientist System Devel. Corp., Santa Monica, Calif., 1961-69; co-founder, v.p., dir. Info. Transfer Corp., Santa Monica, 1969-70; lectr. architecture and urban design Sch. Architecture and Urban Planning UCLA, 1969-70, prof., 1970—, dir. creative problem solving program, 1971-76; exec. dir. com. utilization sci. and engring. manpower Nat. Acad. Scis., 1963-64; dir. Urban Innovations Group, Los Angeles, 1971-72, 77-86; cons. planning, manpower, systems devel., edn., futures studies, to firms, govt. agys., univs., found., non-profit orgns.; founder, mem. adv. bd. Inst. for the Future, Menlo Park, Calif., 1969—; mem. study group on alternatives Los Angeles Goals Project, 1969; program mgr. Calif. Gov.'s Commn. on Los Angeles Riots, 1965; mem. Los Angeles regional task force on corrections Calif. Council Criminal Justice, 1968-71; mem. study group on an Inst. for Applied Sci. and Social Change in a Rural Area, Nat. Acad. Scis., 1969-71. Mem. editorial bd. (jours.) Jour. Systems Engring., 1970—, Tech. Forecasting and Social Change, 1969—, Edn. and Urban Soc., 1970—, Instructional Sci., 1971—, Jour. Edn. Tech., 1971—, The Info. Soc., 1980—.; contbr. articles to profl. jours. Pres. bd. dirs. Westside Fair Housing Council, Los Angeles; bd. dirs., pres. Family Service, Los Angeles, 1967-74, Westside Fair Housing Council 1986—, Urban Innovations Group 1980-86. Served with AUS, 1944-46. Mem. AAAS, AAUP, N.Y. Acad. Sci., Sigma Xi. Home: 228 Monte Grigio Dr Pacific Palisades CA 90272 Office: UCLA Grad Sch Architecture & Urban Planning Los Angeles CA 90024

ADELSON, MERVYN LEE, entertainment and communication industry executive; b. Los Angeles, Oct. 23, 1929; s. Nathan and Pearl (Schwarzman) A.; m. Gail Kenaston, 1974 (div.); m. Barbara Walters, May 10, 1986; children from previous marriage: Ellen, Gary, Andrew. Student, Menlo Park Jr. Coll. Pres. Markettown Supermarket and Builders Emporium, Las Vegas, 1953-63; mng. ptnr. Paradise Devel., Las Vegas, 1958—; pres. Realty Holdings, 1962—, La Costa, Inc., 1983—; chmn. bd. dirs. Lorimar Inc., Culver City, Calif., 1969-86; chmn. bd. dirs., chief exec. officer Lorimar Telepictures Corp., Culver City, 1986—. Co-founder Nathan Adelson Hospice Found. Mem. Am. Film Inst. (trustee), Am. Mus. of Moving Images (trustee), Entertainment Industries Council (trustee), Acad. Motion Pictures, Acad. TV Arts and Sciences, Nat. Acad. Cable Programming, Alliance for Capital Access (bd. dirs.), Com. Publicly Owned Cos. (bd. dirs.).

ADELSTONE, JEFFREY ALAN, accountant, tax law specialist, educator; b. Los Angeles, Feb. 15, 1947; s. James and Joyce S. (Waldman) A.; m. E. Ruth Wilcox, Apr. 6, 1968; children—Kimberley, Stacey, Toni. B.S., U. Ariz., 1969; M.Edn., 1971. Cert. Jr. Coll. Instr., Ariz; cert. instr. Ariz. Dept. Real Estate, accredited Accreditation Council for Accountancy, enrolled to practice, IRS; cert. fin. planner. Tchr., Tucson High Sch., 1969-72; instr. Pima Community Coll., Tucson, 1970-78; pres., owner Adelstone Assocs., Inc. Tucson, 1970—. Active Republican Task Force. Named Nat. Acct. of Yr., 1985. Mem. Nat. Soc. Pub. Accts. (mem. fed. taxation com., assoc. state dir. for Ariz. 1983-84), Nat. Assn. Enrolled Agts., Ariz. Soc. Practicing Accountants (dir. credit union, pres. Tucson chpt., state v.p. 1983-84, pres. 1984-86), Cen. Ariz. Soc. Enrolled Agents (dir.), U.S. C. of C., Ariz. C. of C., Tucson Better Bus. Bur., Nat. Fedn. Ind. Bus., Inst. Cert. Fin. Planners, Internat. Assn. Fin. Planners. Contbr. articles to profl. jours. Office: Adelstone Assocs Inc 165 Sarnoff St Tucson AZ 85710

ADEN, JAMES STEPHEN, chemical engineer; b. Oregon City, Oreg., Sept. 28, 1958; s. Alton Keith and Ina Mae (Monroe) A. BSChemE with honors, Oreg. State U., 1981. Devel. engr. Hewlett-Packard, Inc., Crovallis, Oreg., 1981—. Contbr. articles to profl. jours. Discussion leader Beyond War Found., Corvallis, 1985—. Mem. Am. Vacuum Soc., Am. Inst. Chem. Engrs., U.S. Hang Gliding Assn., Aircraft Owners and Pilots Assn. Democrat. Avocations: hang gliding, gen. aviation, windsurfing, mountain climbing. Home: 2440 NW Rolling Green #25 Corvallis OR 97330 Office: Hewlett Packard Inc 1000 NE Circle Blvd Corvallis OR 97333

ADENIRAN, DIXIE DARLENE, library administrator; b. Los Angeles, May 26, 1943; d. Alfred and Madge (Clare) Harvey. BA, U. Calif., Santa Barbara, 1965; MA, Mich. State U., 1968; MLS, U. Mich., 1970. Librarian Free Library of Phila., 1970-72, Coll. Sci. and Tech., Port Harcourt, Nigeria, 1972-73; librarian Ventura (Calif.) County Library Services Agy., 1974-79, library dir., 1979—. Pres. Ventura County Master Chorale and Opera Assn., 1985. Mem. ALA, Calif. Library Assn., Calif. County Librarians' Assn. Lodge: Soroptimists (pres. Ventura club 1984). Home: 3700 Dean Dr #3003 Ventura CA 93003 Office: Ventura County Library Services 651 E Main St Ventura CA 93003

ADERTON, JANE REYNOLDS, lawyer; b. Riverside, Calif., Dec. 22, 1913; d. Charles Low and Verna Mae (Marshall) Reynolds; m. Robert Granville Johnson (div. 1959); children: Marshall Fallon, Jeannette Townsend; m. Thomas Radcliffe Aderton, Oct. 18, 1964. BS in Merchandising, U. So. Calif., 1935; JD, Southwestern U., Los Angeles, 1965. Bar: Calif. 1968. Sole practice Beverly Hills, Calif., 1968-79; jud. sec. U.S. Dist. Ct. Calif., Los Angeles, 1960-65; sole practice Riverside, 1979—; assoc. Wyman, Bautzer, Rothman & Kuchel, 1970-79; del. Calif. Bar Conf., 1976, 77, 78. Mem. Founders' Club, Riverside Community Hosp., 1980—; mem. women's aux. Salvation Army, 1981-83, pres., adv. bd., 1983—; v.p., pres.-elect Art Alliance of the Riverside Art Mus., 1984-85, pres. 1985-86; mem.. Riverside Hospice, 1983—, Riverside Opera Guild; bd. dirs. Friends of Mission Inn, 1986—, San Gorgonio Girl Scout Council, 1987-88. Mem. ABA, Calif. Bar Assn., Riverside Bar Assn., Beverly Hills Bar Assn. (bd. govs. 1976-79, chmn. probate and trust com. 1975-77, chmn. del. to Calif. bar conf. 1978), World Affairs Council Inland So. Calif., Riverside Art Alliance, Calif. Mus. Photography, Affiliates of U. Calif. at Riverside, Phi Alpha Delta, Pi Beta Phi (pres. Riverside alumni club 1981-83). Clubs: Victoria Country (Riverside); Newport Harbor Yacht (Newport Beach, Calif.). Lodge: Soroptimist Internat. Home: 5190 Stonewood Dr Riverside CA 92506 Office: Riverside CA

ADICOFF, ARNOLD, aerospace scientist; b. N.Y.C., Oct. 13, 1923; s. Louis and Rebecca (Brower) A.; m. Margaret Carroll Farrer, Jan. 27, 1950; children: Keith David, Laurie Carroll. BS in Chemistry, UCLA, 1949; PhD in Phys. Chemistry, Poly. Inst. Bklyn., 1955. Project leader Air Reduction Co., Murray Hill, N.J., 1954-56; research engr. Ford Motor Co., Dearborn, Mich., 1956-57, chemist, 1957-68; with Naval Weapons Ctr., China Lake, Calif., 1957-83; head polymer sci. br. Ford Motor Co., Dearborn, Mich., 1968-79, assoc. head chemistry div., 1973-79, sr. scientist, 1982-83; assoc. dir. research Office Dep. Under Sec. Def., Washington, 1979-81; tech. advisor propulsion Naval Sea Systems Command, Washington, 1981-82; scientist TRW Inc., Redondo Beach, Calif., 1983—; cons. Space Ordnance Systems, Canyon Country, Calif., 1982-83; chmn. subcom. JANNAF Structure and Mech. Behavior, 1968, 73, 75-78. Contbr. articles to profl. jours.; patentee in field. Served as cpl. USAAF, 1942-46. Mem. AAAS, Am. Chem. Soc., Research Soc. Am., Rheology Soc. Avocations: camping, fishing. Office: TRW Inc 1 Space Park Redondo Beach CA 90278

ADKINS, MARILYN BIGGS, lawyer, consultant; b. East Greenwich, R.I., July 3, 1945; d. John Elmer and Merle Bonita (Irish) Biggs; m. John C. Adkins, Oct. 12. 1965 (div. Feb. 1978). BA, U. Denver, 1967, JD, 1982. Bar: Colo. 1982, U.S. Dist. Ct. Colo. 1982, U.S. Ct. Appeals (10th cir.) 1982. Owner Texaco Service Stas., Denver, 1971-78; legal asst., paralegal Law Offices of Hubert M. Safran, Denver, 1974-82; pvt. practice bookkeeping Denver, 1978-81; ptnr. Safran & Adkins, Denver, 1982—; leg. dir. Colo. Trial Lawyers Assn., Denver, 1982—; mem. Dist. Atty.'s Arbitration Panel, Denver, 1976; active Colo. Supreme Ct. Pub. Edn. Com., 1984—. Instr. Denver Inner City Parish, 1970-75; mem. Anti-Defamation League Civil Rights Commn., Denver, 1983—; del. Democratic County Convs., Denver, 1975-78, 86; advisor U.S. Senate Com., Washington, 1978; trustee Temple Sinai, Denver, 1986—. Mem. ABA, Colo. Bar Assn., Denver Bar Assn., Assn. Trial Lawyers Am., Colo. Trial Lawyers Assn. (bd. dirs. 1983—), Trial Lawyers for Pub. Justice, U. Denver Alumni Assn. Democrat. Jewish. Avocations: musician, gardening. Office: Safran & Adkins 1832 Clarkson St Denver CO 80218

ADLER, ARTHUR BUDDY, actor, purchasing agent; b. Queens, N.Y., May 5, 1932; s. Arthur Leoplod and Ethel Ann (Dietz) A. Cert. purchasing mgr. Lab. technician Am. Cyanamid, Bound Brook, N.J., 1951-53; test engr. Bowen Engring. Co., North Branch, N.J., 1955-59; plant forman Nichols Engring. and Research Corp., Netcong, N.J., 1959-61; purchasing agt. Am. Weldery/Steel, Dover, N.J., 1961-67, Kraft Foods (Metro Glass), Jersey City, 1967-74; sr. contract adminstr. Walt Disney Orgn., Fla. and Calif., 1974-84; Founder, 1st chmn. The Friends of Walt Disney, 1982—; founder, organizer The Heather Templeton Childrens Wish Fund Inc., 1985. Author: The Old Garage that Nobody Wanted, 1985, Tribute to the Flag; appearnace Shields and Yarnell Xmas at Walt Disney, 1978, Jerry Eden Show, 1979; film reviewer Orlando, Fla., 1979-81. Lay minister Crystal Cathedral Congregation, Garden Grove, Calif.; founder, past chmn. Fla. Childrens Home com. 23d Dist., 1978, sec., treas., 1978; local zone chmn. youth activities, 1980-81; past pres. Dover Jaycees, past state v.p., past nat. dir. Served as cpl. U.S. Army, 1953-55. Mem. AFTRA, VFW, Purchasing Mgmt. Assn., Contract Mgmt. Assn., Screen Actors Guild, Actors Equity Assn., Screen Actors Guild, Orange County, Am. Legion, So. Calif. Motion Picture Council. Republican. Lodges: Masons, Shriners.

ADLER, CHARLES SPENCER, psychiatrist; b. N.Y.C., Nov. 27, 1941; s. Benjamin H. and Anne (Greenfield) A.; m. Sheila Noel Morrissey, Oct. 8, 1966. B.A., Cornell U., 1962; M.D., Duke U., 1966. Diplomate Nat. Bd. Med. Examiners, Am. Bd. Psychiatry and Neurology. Intern Tucson Hosps. Med. Edn. Program, 1966-67; psychiat. resident U. Colo. Sch. Medicine, Denver, 1967-70; practice medicine specializing in psychiatry and psychosomatic medicine, Denver, 1970—; chief div. psychiatry Rose Med. Center, 1982-87; co-founder Applied Biofeedback Inst., Denver, 1972-75; prof. pro tempore Cleve. Clinic, 1977. Recipient Award of Recognition, Nat. Migraine Found., 1981; N.Y. State regents scholar, 1958-62. Fellow Am. Psychiat. Assn.; mem. AAAS (rep. med. sect. com.), AMA, Am. Assn. Study Headache, Internat. Headache Soc. (chmn. subcom. on classifying psychiatric headaches), Am. Acad. Psychoanalysis (sci. assoc.), Colo. Psychiatry Soc., Biofeedback Soc. Colo. (pres. 1977-78), Biofeedback Soc. Am. (chmn. ethics com. 1983-87). Jewish. Author: (with Gene Stanford and Sheila M. Adler) We Are But a Moment's Sunlight, 1976; editor: (with Sheila M. Adler and Russell Packard) Psychiatric Aspects of Headache, 1987; contbr. chpts. to books, articles to profl. jours.; mem. editorial bd. Cephalalgia: an Internat. Jour. of Headache. Office: 955 Eudora St Suite 1605 Denver CO 80220

ADLER, ERWIN ELLERY, lawyer; b. Flint, Mich., July 22, 1941; s. Ben and Helen M. (Schwartz) A.; m. Stephanie Ruskin, June 8, 1967; children—Lauren, Michael, Jonathan. B.A., U. Mich., 1963, LL.M., 1967; J.D., Harvard U., 1966. Bar: Mich. 1966, Calif. 1967. Assoc. Pillsbury, Madison & Sutro, San Francisco, 1967-73; assoc. Lawler, Felix & Hall, Los Angeles, 1973-76, ptnr., 1977-82; ptnr. Rogers & Wells, Los Angeles, 1982-84, Richards, Watson & Gershon, Los Angeles, 1984—. Bd. dirs. Hollywood Civic Opera Assn., 1975-76, Children's Scholarships Inc., 1979-80. Mem. ABA (vice chmn. appellate advocacy com. 1982-86), Calif. Bar Assn., Phi Beta Kappa, Phi Kappa Phi. Jewish. Office: Richards Watson & Gershon 333 S Hope St 38th Floor Los Angeles CA 90071

ADLER, HOWARD IAN, company executive; b. N.Y.C., June 22, 1943; s. Simon Benjamin and Gladys (Stein) A.; m. Louise Cromwell, Apr. 1, 1967; children—Leah J., Rachel L. B.A., Calif. State U.-Long Beach, 1966. Legis. asst. U.S. Ho. of Reps., Washington, 1967-74; pres. Gt. Am. Land and Housing, Santa Ana, Calif., 1974—; chmn. Englander, Adler Droz, Newport Beach, Calif., 1976—; lectr. U. Calif.-Irvine, 1982-83; bd. dirs. Ins. Co. Inspection Bur., Orange, Calif., 1980—; mem. energy commn. County of Orange, Santa Ana, 1978-80. Contbr. articles to profl. jours. Chmn. Orange

County Dems., 1982-84, treas., 1975-78; co-chmn. rule com. Calif. Dems., 1983; active Dem. Nat. Fin. Council, 1984, Dem. Found. Recipient Outstanding Young Men of Am. award, 1970, 77; Disting. Service award Orange County Indsl. Suppliers, 1974. Mem. Pi Sigma Alpha. Club: Orange County (bd. dirs. 1982-84). Home: 22676 Waterway Ln El Toro CA 92630 Office: Gt Am Land and Housing Business Center Dr Suite 290 Irvine CA 92630

ADLER, LAUREL ANN, educational administrator, consultant; b. Cleve., Sept. 6, 1948; d. Clarence Linsley and Margaret Ann (Roberts) Wheeler; m. Thomas Jay Johnson, June 6, 1981; children—David, Anthony, Jennifer. B.A., U. Calif.-Irvine, 1968; M.A., Calif. State U.-Los Angeles, 1972; Ed.D., U. La Verne, 1980. Audlt Edn. adminstr. Hacienda La Puente Unified Sch. Dist., 1972-79; dir. career and vocat. edn. El Monte Union High Sch. Dist., 1979-83; dir. East San Gabriel Valley Regional Occupational Ctr., West Covina, Calif., 1984—; instr. Calif. State U.-Los Angeles, 1979-81; cons. Trust Ty. Pacific Islands, 1979—. Active El Monte Coordinating Council. Recipient Nat. Vol. Action award 1974; Calif. Consortium Ind. Study Recognition award of Outstanding Ednl. Program, 1983, Calif. Sch. Adminstrs. award, 1981; named Citizen of Yr., La Puente C. of C., 1977, Outstanding Vocat. Educator, Hoffman Ednl. Systems, 1983. Mem. Assn. Calif. Sch. Adminstrs., Internat. Reading Assn., Assn. Supervision and Curriculum Devel., Calif. Consortium Ind. Study, Phi Delta Kappa. Club: Soroptomist. Author: A Self Evaluation Model for Micronesian Education Programs, 1980; pub. Essential English for Micronesians, Beginning, 1980; Essential English for Micronesians, 1980; Reading Exercises for Micronesians, 1980; contbr. articles to profl. jours. Home: 3366 Garden Terr Hacienda Heights CA 91745 Office: East San Gabriel Valley Regional Occupational Ctr 1024 W Workman West Covina CA 91790

ADLER, ROBERT GARBER, research chemist; b. Upland, Calif., July 11, 1929; s. Robert and Amelia Anna (Garber) A.; m. Marilyn Jean Canfield, Nov. 29, 1963; children: Charles Robert, Paul Damon, Amelia Marie. AA, Chaffey Jr. Coll., 1949; BS, Calif. Inst. Tech., 1951; MS, U. So. Calif., 1955; PhD, U. Calif., Riverside, 1968. Cert. indsl. hygienist. Sr. chemist Am. Potash and Chem. Corp., Whittier, Calif., 1957-63; chemist Jet Propusion Lab., Pasadena, Calif., summer 1963, N.Am. Aviation Sci. Ctr., Thousand Oaks, Calif., 1963-64; asst. prof. Bethel Coll., North Newton, Kans., 1968-71; quality control dir., analytical and inorganic methods research chemist U.S. Dept. Labor-Occupational Safety & Health Adminstrn., Salt Lake City, 1972—. Served with U.S. Army, 1955-57. Mem. Am. Chem. Soc., Am. Indsl. Hygiene Assn., Am. Conf. Govt. Indsl. Hygienists, Phi Lambda Upsilon. Republican. Methodist. Club: Toastmasters. Avocations: piano, organ, railroads. Home: 3947 S 3075 E Salt Lake City UT 84124 Office: US Dept Labor Occupational Safety Health Adminstrn 1781 S 300 W Salt Lake City UT 84115

ADLER, ROY DOUGLAS, consumer psychologist; b. Detroit, Sept. 9, 1943; s. Roy Alvin and Ruth Louise (Potz) A.; m. Cecilia Canales, Mar. 9, 1968; children: Douglas, Davidson. BA, Bucknell U., 1965; MA, Western Mich. U., 1971; MBA, Xavier U., 1973; PhD, U. Ala., 1982. Mktg. mgr. Procter & Gamble, Cin., 1969-71; cons. Levi Strauss & Co., Cin., 1972-75; assoc. prof. Xavier U., Cin., 1973-84; prof. Pepperdine U., Malibu, Calif., 1984—; dir. Malibu Ctr. Consumer Trends, 1984—. Co-author: Marketing and Society, 1981; contbr. Marketing Megaworks, 1987. Chief pollster Springer for Gov., Ohio, 1982. Served to lt. U.S. Army, 1967-69. Recipient Emmy award for Best Instructional Series, 1985; named Outstanding Faculty Mem., Pepperdine U., 1985. Mem. Acad. Mktg. Sci. (v.p. 1984—), Am. Mktg. Assn., Am. Psychol. Assn. Republican. Avocations: sailing, motor sports. Home: 3031 Blondell Pl Newbury Park CA 91320 Office: Pepperdine U Pacific Coast Hwy Malibu CA 90265

ADLER, SYLVIA MARIE, psychotherapist, educator; b. Rochester, N.Y., June 6, 1932; d. Harold and Dorothy (Popick) Adler; m. Jay Schmidt, Dec. 1955 (div. July 1964). BA, U. Rochester, 1950-54; MSS, Smith Coll. Sch. for Social Work, 1954-56. Psychiat. social worker Inst. Juvenile Research, Chgo., 1957-59, 61-65; social work cons. Kramer Found., Palatine, Ill., 1965-71; dir. Profl. Edn. Family Inst. Chgo., Oak Park, Ill., 1969-71; lectr. continuing edn. nursing U. Calif., San Francisco, 1972-77; pvt. practice specializing in family, individual and somatic psychotherapy Berkeley, Calif., 1972—; assoc. Ctr. Energetic Studies, Berkeley, 1974—; cons. family therapy Loyola U. Guidance Ctr., Chgo., 1966-71; assoc. prof. Calif. Inst. Integral Studies, San Francisco, 1981-83; tchr., presenter of workshops on family therapy, U.S. and Europe, 1965—. Contbr. articles to profl. jours. Fellow Am. Orthopsychiat. Assn.; mem. Smith Coll. Sch. Social Work Alumnae Assn. (nat. v.p. 1963-65), Nat. Assn. Social Workers (cert., chmn. No. Calif. pvt. practice counsel 1975-77), No. Calif. Council Psychiatry Psychology and Social Work (cert., rep. 1975-78), Assn. Family Therapists of No. Calif. Office: 2045 Francisco St Berkeley CA 94709

ADRIAN, CHARLES RAYMOND, political science educator; b. Portland, Oreg., Mar. 12, 1922; s. Harry Raymond and Helen K. (Petersen) A.; m. Audrey Jean Nelson, Apr. 2, 1946; children: Kristin, Nelson. B.A., Cornell (Iowa) Coll., 1947, LL.D., 1973; M.A., U. Minn., 1948, Ph.D., 1950; postdoctoral fellow, U. Copenhagen, Denmark, 1954-55. Instr., then asst. prof. govt. Wayne State U., 1949-55; from asst. prof. to prof. polit. sci. Mich. State U., 1955-66, chmn. dept., 1963-66; dir. Inst. Community Devel., 1958-63; prof. polit. sci. U. Calif.-Riverside, 1966—, chmn. dept., 1966-70, acad. asst. to v.p. acad. affairs, 1973-74; cons. fed., state and local govt. ABC; research cons. Mich. Constl. Conv., 1961-62; Adminstrv. asst. to gov. Mich., 1956-57; mem. Meridian Twp. (Mich.) Planning Commn., 1957-60. Author: (with O. P. Williams) Four Cities: A Comparative Study in Community Politics, 1963, State and Local Governments, 2d edit., 1967, 3d edit., 1971, 4th edit., 1976, (with Charles Press) American Political Process, 1965, 2d. edit., 1969, Governing Urban America, 4th edit., 1972, 5th edit., 1977, American Politics Reappraised, 1974, (with E.S. Griffith) History of American City Government 1775-1870, 1976; also articles. Mem. Riverside Environ. Protection Commn., 1976-78, Riverside Mayor's Charter Revision Commn., 1985. Served with USAAF, 1943-46, PTO. Faculty fellow Fund Advancement Edn., 1954-55.; Mem. Am. Polit. Sci. Assn., Am. Soc. Pub. Adminstrn., Phi Beta Kappa. Office: Dept Polit Sci U Calif Riverside CA 92521

ADROUNY, ADOUR RICHARD, physician; b. Aleppo, Syrian Arab Republic, May 7, 1952; came to U.S., 1955; s. George Adour and Alice (Karamanookian) A.; m. Karen Alyce Tamzarian, May 1, 1982; 1 child, Melissa Knar. BS magna cum laude, Duke U., 1973; MPH, MD, Tulane U., 1978. Cert. Am. Bd. Internal Medicine. Intern Los Angeles County Gen. Hosp., 1978-79, resident, 1979-81; fellow in med. oncology Harbor Gen. Hosp., Torrance, Calif., 1981-84; fellow in hemtology Kaiser Found. Hosp., Los Angeles, 1984-85; pvt. practice medicine San Jose, Calif., 1985—; mem. staff Good Samaritan Hosp., San Jose, 1985—, Santa Teresa Community Hosp. (assoc.), San Jose, 1985—, Wheeler Hosp. (cons.), Gilroy, Calif., 1986—. Contbr. articles to profl. jours. Mem. profl. edn. com. Am. Cancer Soc., Santa Clara County, Calif., 1985—. Mem. AAAS, AMA, ACP, Am. Soc. Clin. Oncology, Calif. Med. Assn. (blood banks com. 1985—), Santa Clara County Med. Soc. (AIDS task force com. 1986—). Avocations: photography, music. Office: 275 Hospital Pkwy San Jose CA 95119

ADUJA, PETER AQUINO, lawyer, business executive; b. Vigan, Philippines, Oct. 19, 1920; came to U.S., 1927, naturalized, 1944; s. Dionicio and Francisca (Aquino) A.; m. Melodie Cabalona, July 31, 1949; children—Jay, Rebecca. B.A., U. Hawaii, 1944; J.D., Boston U., 1951. Bar: Hawaii 1953, U.S. Supreme Ct. 1983. Individual practice law Hilo, Hawaii, 1953-60, Honolulu, from 1960; dep. atty. gen. State of Hawaii, 1957-60; judge Hawaii Dist. Ct., 1960-62; prin. broker AAP Realty, Inc., Honolulu, 1970—; pres. Aduja Corp., Las Vegas, Nev., 1972—, Travel-Air Internat., Honolulu, 1975—; mem. Hawaii Ho. of Reps., 1954-56, 67-74; del. Hawaii Constl. Conv., 1968; sec.-treas. Melodie Aduja, Inc., 1979—. Troop committeeman Aloha council Boy Scouts Am., 1959—; active ARC; chmn. Salvation Army Adult Rehab. Center, Honolulu, 1965—, Goodwill Industries, 1972. Served with U.S. Army, 1944-46. Mem. Bar Assn. Hawaii, Hawaii Bd. Realtors. Democrat. Methodist. Home: 49 Niniko Pl Honolulu HI 96817 Office: AAP Realty Inc 1414 Dillingham Blvd Suite 102 Honolulu HI 96817

ADVANI, GULU NANIK, diversified electronics company executive; b. Calcutta, Bengal, India, July 27, 1953; came to U.S., 1976; s. Nanik Bulchand and Pushpa Nanik (Jhuremalani) A.; m. Claire Ann Piroli, June 21, 1980. BS, Barla Inst. Tech., Ranchi, Bihar, India, 1975; MS, Carnegie-Mellon U., 1977, PhD, 1979. Mgr. product devel. Sierra Monitor Corp., Sunnyvale, Calif., 1980-82; v.p. research Calif. Micro Devices, Milpitas, 1982-84; sect. mgr. research Hewlett Packard Co., San Jose, Calif., 1984—; v.p. Advanced Thin Films, San Jose, 1985-87. Contbr. articles to profl. jours.; patentee in field. Mentor East Side Schs. Hewlett Packard, 1986—. Mem. IEEE, Electro Chem. Soc., Sigma Xi. Avocations: classical music, guitar, gardening. Home: 3825 Ramirez Ct San Jose CA 95121

AERTS, ELIANE MARIE, research sociologist; b. Brussels, Aug. 15, 1943; came to U.S., 1971; d. Jean-Henri and Catherine (Hoffmann) A.; m. Guy Edwin Swanson, Aug. 19, 1977. Lic. polit. and social scis., Cath. U., Louvain, Belgium, 1967; MA in Sociology, U. Calif., Berkeley, 1973, PhD in Sociology, 1979. Research sociologist U. Calif., Berkeley, 1980—. Author: On Moral Grounds, 1985. Mem. AAAS, Am. Sociol. Assn., Pacific Sociol. Assn., Soc. Psychol. Study of Social Issues. Office: U Calif Inst Human Devel Tolman Hall Berkeley CA 94720

AFFELDT, ARNO MARCUS, JR., steel mill sales and heavy manufacturing executive; b. San Bernardino, Calif., Nov. 16, 1927; s. Arno Marcus and Evelyn Rose (Roberts) A.; m. Cora Nell Watkins, June 25, 1949; children—Arno Marcus, III, Laura Allison, Bruce Lawrence, Sherry Ann. B.A., U. Calif.-Berkeley, 1950; LL.B., LaSalle U., Chgo., 1971. Export trader Otis, McAllister Co., San Francisco, 1951-52; with Kaiser Steel Corp., various locations, 1953-70, Internat. Mill Service, Fontana, Calif., 1971-73; with Marathon Steel Co., Los Angeles, 1974-78, mgr. mill sales, Phoenix, 1978-85; mgr. sales, founder Sav-Trac of Ariz., Inc., 1986—; industry rep. to trade assns.; speaker in field. Served with U.S. Navy, 1946-47. Mem. Concrete Steel Reinforcing Inst., Phoenix C. of C., Pi Kappa Alpha. Republican. Congregationalist. Home: 8576 Via De Dorado E Scottsdale AZ 85258

AFFLECK, JULIE KARLEEN, accountant; b. Upland, Calif., Dec. 23, 1944; d. Karl W. and Juliette O. (Oppegaard) Hall; m. William J. Affleck, Aug. 29, 1964; children: Stephen, Tamara. BS in Bus., U. Colo., 1967; MBA, U. Denver, 1972. CPA, Colo. Cost acct. IBM, Boulder, Colo., 1967-71; audit supr. Ernst & Whinney, Denver, 1972-79, Rosemary E. Weiss & Co., Denver, 1979-80; ptnr. Affleck, Businga & Assocs., Denver, 1980—; pres. Affleck & Assoc., P.C., Denver, Colo., 1982—; tchr. Colo. Soc. CPA's., U. Denver; dir., corp. sec. Better-Way Electric, Inc. Bd. dirs. Bal Swan Children's Ctr. for Handicapped, Broomfield, Colo. Mem. Am. Inst. CPA's., Colo. Soc. CPA's., Am. Soc. Women Accts. (pres. chpt. 1980-81), Women Bus. Owners Assn. (treas., dir., pres. -elect). Republican. Lutheran. Home: 3193 W 12 Ave Ct Broomfield CO 80020

AFZAL, SAYED MOHAMMAD JAVED, laboratory staff scientist; b. Saharanpur, India, Oct. 4, 1952; came to U.S., 1979; s. S.M. Afzal and Ahmer (Jehan) H.; m. Veena Afzal, Oct. 28, 1977. BS in Biology, Meerut U., India, 1969; MS in Botany, Aligarh Muslim U., India, 1971; MPhil in Radiobiology, Jawaharlal Nehru U., New Delhi, 1975, PhD in Radiobiology, 1978. Pool officer Scientist Pool, Council for Sci. and Indsl. Research, New Delhi, 1979; research scientist Cancer Research and Treatment Ctr., U. N.Mex., Albuquerque, 1979-80; staff scientist Lawrence Berkeley Lab., U. Calif., 1980—. contbr. articles to profl. jours. Mem. Am. Soc. Therapeutic Radiology and Oncology, N.Y. Acad. Scis., Soc. for Free Radical Research, Radiation Research Soc., Environ. Mutagen Soc., AAAS. Home: 3380 Chamberlain Ct Walnut Creek CA 94598 Office: U Calif Lawrence Berkeley Lab 1 Cyclotron Rd Bldg 74 Berkeley CA 94720

AFZALI, ABDI, alumni association administrator, infosystems specialist; b. Tehran, Iran, Apr. 29, 1955; came to U.S., 1977; s. Ahmad and Nayer (Etemad) A.; m. Faranak M. Ghobadifard, July 16, 1983. BS in Pub. Health, Inst. Paramed. Scis., Tehran, 1977; MBA in Health Care, Nat. U., San Diego, 1980, MBA in Computer Info. Systems, 1982, MS in Advanced Mgmt., 1986. Asst. dir. graphic communications Nat. U. Alumni Assn., San Diego, 1980-81, dir. graphics communications, 1981-83, dir. word processing, 1983-85, dir. adminstrn. and info. systems, 1985—; cons. ARYA Micro-Applications, San Diego, 1985—. Mem. Nat. U. Alumni Assn. (assoc. mem. bd. dirs. 1985—). Avocations: ping-pong, tennis, soccer. Home: 3677 Caminito Cielo del Mar San Diego CA 92130 Office: Nat U Alumni Assn 4005 Camino del Rio S San Diego CA 92108

AGAJANIAN, STEPHEN ARAM, electrical engineer, educator; b. Istanbul, Turkey, Nov. 18, 1951; came to U.S., 1972, naturalized, 1985; s. Haygaz and Julyet Agajanian. BSEE, U. Rochester, 1974; MSEE, Syracuse U., 1982. Power engr. Foster Wheeler Corp, Livingston, N.J., 1974-78, Gen. Foods Corp., Terrytown, N.Y., 1978-79; quality engr. IBM Corp., Endicott, N.Y., 1979-81; instr. Syracuse (N.Y.) U., 1981-83; assoc. prof. Calif. State Poly. U., Pomona, 1983—. Active Inter-Varsity Christian Fellowship, Pomona, 1983—. Mem. IEEE, Am. Soc. Engring. Edn., Eta Kappa Nu. Avocations: hiking, swimming, bicycling, camping, cross-country skiing. Home: 190 Valley Oak Ln Pomona CA 91767

AGAWA, THOMAS TETSUO, architect; b. Shimane, Japan, Oct. 26, 1941; came to U.S., 1955, naturalized, 1960; s. Yoshie (Nakasako) Agawa; m. Linda Moriyama, June 20, 1970; children—Leanne Rika, Grant Satoshi. B.Arch., U. Hawaii, 1979. Registered architect, Hawaii. Project architect Boone & Assocs., Honolulu, 1973-78, Media Five Ltd., Honolulu, 1979, Louis Fulton AIA, Honolulu, 1980; architect, pres. Thomas T. Agawa & Assocs. AIA, Honolulu, 1980—. Rep., United Japanese Soc. Honolulu; treas. Hiroshima Kenjin Kai, Honolulu, 1983; bd. dirs. Kotohira Jinsha Temple, Honolulu, 1983. Mem. AIA. Home: 1472 Ala Iolani St Honolulu HI 96819 Office: Thomas T Agawa AIA and Assocs 1200 College Walk Suite 115 Honolulu HI 96817

AGERBEK, SVEN, mechanical engineer; b. Soerabaya, Dutch Indies, Aug. 2, 1926; came to U.S., 1958, naturalized, 1964; s. Niels Magnus and Else Heidam (Nielsen) Agerbek-Poulsen; m. Helen Hadsbjerg Gerup, May 30, 1963; 1 child, Jesper. MSME, Tech. U., Denmark, 1952; LLB, LaSalle Estension U., 1967; postgrad., UCLA, 1969. Registered profl. engr., Calif., Ohio, Fla. With Danish Refrigeration Research Inst., Copenhagen, 1952; engr. B.P. Oil Co., Copenhagen, 1952-54; refrigeration insp. J. Lauritzen, Copenhagen, 1954-56; engr. Danish-Am. Gulf Oil Co., Copenhagen, 1956-58; instr. Ohio U., Athens, 1958-60; asst. prof. Calif. State Poly. U., San Luis Obispo, 1960-62; prin. engr., environment dept. Ralph M. Parsons Co., Los Angeles, 1962-73; engring. supr. Bechtel Power Co., Norwalk, Calif., 1973-85; pres., owner Woodcraft Cabinets, Inc., Rancho Cordova, Calif., 1985—. Past mem. Luth. Ch. council, pres. Luth. Sch. bd. Served with Danish underground movement, World War II. Mem. ASHRAE, Danish Engring. Soc. Home: 5201 Vista del Oro Way Fair Oaks CA 95628 Office: Woodcraft Cabinets Inc 11386 Amalgam Way Rancho Cordova CA 95670

AGGARWAL, UMA NANDAN, distribution company executive; b. Amritsar, Punjab, India, July 15, 1944; came to U.S., 1968; s. Trilok Chand and Raj Rani (Bansal) A.; m. Pawan Rekha Gupta, Nov. 22, 1971; children: Amit, Anjali. BME with honors, Indian Inst. Tech., Bombay, 1966; MME in Indsl. Engring., U. Calif., Berkeley, 1969; MBA, U. Chgo., 1976. Apprentice engr. Larsen and Toubro, Bombay, 1966-68; ops. research analyst Armour and Co., Chgo., 1969-71; assoc. Theo Barry and Assocs., Los Angeles, 1971-72; mgmt. specialist Axia Inc., Oak Brook, Ill., 1973-77; pres., gen. mgr. Jensen Tools div. Axia Inc., Phoenix, 1977-87, corp. v.p., 1983—. Office: Axia Inc 7815 S 46th St Phoenix AZ 85044

AGNEW, HAROLD MELVIN, physicist; b. Denver, Mar. 28, 1921; s. Sam E. and Augusta (Jacobs) A.; m. Beverly Jackson, May 2, 1942; children: Nancy E. Agnew Owens, John S. A.B., U. Denver, 1942; M.S., U. Chgo., 1948, Ph.D., 1949. With Los Alamos Sci. Lab., 1943-46, alt. div. leader, 1949-61, leader weapons div., 1964-70, dir., 1970-79; pres. GA Techs. Inc., San Diego, 1979-85, dir., 1985—; dir. Blaws Corp., 1967-72; dir. DBA Systems, Inc.; sci. adviser Supreme Allied Comdr. in Europe, Paris, France, 1961-64; Chmn. Army Sci. Adv. Panel, 1965-70, mem., 1970-74; mem. aircraft panel Pres.'s Sci. Adv. Com., 1965-73; mem. USAF Sci. Adv. Bd., 1957-69, Def. Sci. Bd., 1965-70, Gov. N.Mex. Radiation Adv. Council, 1959-61; sec. N.Mex. Health and Social Services, 1971-73; chmn. gen. adv. com. ACDA, 1974-77, mem., 1977-81; mem. aerospace safety adv. panel NASA, 1964-70, 86—; mem. U.S. Army Sci. Bd., 1978-80, White House Sci. Council, 1982—. Mem. council engring. NRC, 1978-82, trustee council engring., 1982—, Los Alamos Bd. Ednl. Trustees, 1950-55, pres., 1955; trustee San Diego Mus. Art, 1983-87; mem. Woodrow Wilson Nat. Fellowship Found., 1973—; N.Mex. State senator, 1955-61; sec. N.Mex. Legis. Council, 1957-61; chmn. N.Mex. Senate Corp. Commn., 1957-61; mem. Fed. Emergency Agy., 1982—; bd. dirs. Fedn. Rocky Mountain States, Inc., 1975-77. Recipient Ernest Orlando Lawrence award AEC, 1966; Enrico Fermi award Dept. Energy, 1978. Fellow Am. Phys. Soc., AAAS; mem. Nat. Acad. Scis., Nat. Acad. Engring. (Assembly of Engring.), Council on Fgn. Relations, Phi Beta Kappa, Sigma Xi, Omicron Delta Kappa. Home: 322 Punta Baja Solana Beach CA 92075

AGNEW, STEPHEN FRANCIS, chemist; b. Lewiston, Idaho, Oct. 7, 1952; s. Edward John and Mary Ann (Schroeder) A.; m. Patricia Jo Rose, Sept. 20, 1975; children: Christopher Stephen, Corrie Frances, Peter Edwin. Student, U. Wash., 1971-72; BA, Evergreen State Coll., 1976; PhD in Chem. Physics, Wash. State U., 1981. Postdoctoral fellowship Wash. State U., Pullman, 1981, Max-Planck Institüt für Strahlenchemie, Mülheim, Ruhr, Fed. Republic Germany, 1981-82; postdoctoral fellow Los Alamos (N. Mex.) Nat. Lab., 1982-84, staff member, 1984—. Contbr. articles to profl. jours. Mem. Am. Chem. Soc. Home: 531 Paul Pl Los Alamos NM 87544 Office: Los Alamos Nat Lab Group INC-4 M/S C346 Los Alamos NM 87545

AGNOST, FRANK PETER, publishing executive, editor; b. Chgo., June 15, 1918; s. Peter and Effie (Kellar) A.; m. Mildred Corby, Aug. 31, 1940; children—Frank Peter, Adrienne Verreos; m. 2d, Melissa Caravellas, Sept. 24, 1970. Student U. Calif.-Berkeley, 1940. Commr. dept. pub. welfare City and County of San Francisco, 1951-58; copy boy, reporter, asst. fgn. editor, then asst. to pub. San Francisco Chronicle, 1940-61; pres. Falcon Assocs. Inc., San Francisco, 1961—; editor, pub. Hellenic Jour., San Francisco, 1975—. Served to capt. USAAF, 1942-46. Decorated Gold Cross, Order of Phoenix (Greece), Meml. Medal 1971, Archon, Order of St. Andrew, Ecumenical Patriarchate (Constantinople), recipient Award of Honor, United Greek Orthodox Charities N.Y., 1971; Disting. Service Award, Greek Orthodox Archdiocese N.Y., 1976; Axion award Hellenic Am. Profl. Soc. of San Francisco, 1978; Extraordinary Community Service award Calif. Assembly, 1982; medal of St. Paul, Greek Orthodox Archdiocese, 1982. Mem. ASCAP, Am. Legion, Clubs: San Francisco Press, Bohemian, Masons, Ahepa. Home: 1170 Sacramento St San Francisco CA 94108 Office: Falcon Assocs 527 Commercial St San Francisco CA 94111

AGOGINO, GEORGE ALLEN, anthropologist, educator; b. West Palm Beach, Fla., Nov. 18, 1920; s. Andrew and Beulah Mae A.; m. Mercedes Merner, Dec. 1, 1952; children: Alice, Karen. BA, U. N.Mex., 1948, MA, 1951; PhD, Syracuse U., 1958; postgrad., Harvard U., 1962-63. Asst. prof. anthropology Syracuse U., N.Y., 1956-58; asst. prof. anthropology U. S.D., Vermillion, 1958-59, U. Wyo., Laramie, 1959-61; Wenner-Gren postdoctoral fellow Harvard U., Cambridge, Mass., 1961-62; assoc. prof. Baylor U., Waco, Tex., 1962-63; assoc. prof. anthropology Eastern N.Mex. U., Portales, 1963-68, prof., 1968-85, disting. research prof. in anthropology, 1985—, dir. Indian Inst., 1963—, dir. Anthropology Mus., Blackwater Draw Mus., Miles Mus., 1967-86, chmn. dept. anthropology, 1963-80, dir. spl. programs, 1972-73, dir. humanities div., 1973-74; appointed disting. research prof. in anthropology Eastern N.Mex. U., 1985. Author monographs in field; contbr. numerous articles on Mexican anthropology, primitive religion and folklore to profl. jours. Served with Signal Corps, U.S. Army, 1942-46. Recipient Pres.'s award Eastern N.Mex. U., 1971; numerous research grants. Fellow Explorers Club Am., Am. Anthrop. Assn., AAAS, Instituto Interamericana. Republican. Avocations: fishing, tennis. Home: 1600 S Main Portales NM 88130 Office: Dept Anthropology Eastern NMex Univ Portales NM 88130

AGONIA, BARBARA ANN, English educator; b. St. Louis, June 11, 1934; d. Robert Lewis and Suzanne (Carter) Klinefelter; m. Robert James Agonia, Mar. 25, 1972. Student, U. Exeter, Devon, Eng., 1954-55; BA, Hanover Coll., 1957; MA, U. Nev., Las Vegas, 1971; postgrad., U. Nev., Reno, 1983—. Tchr. Carrollton (Ill.) Community Unit High Sch., 1955-56, 59-61, White Hall (Ill.) Community Unit High Sch., 1957-59; tchr., chmn. dept. English ROVA Community Unit High Sch., Oneida, Ill., 1961-69; prof. English Clark County Community Coll., North Las Vegas, Nev., 1971—, chmn. dept., 1972-75, dir. re-entry ctr., 1980-83; speaker in field, Ind., Ill., Nev., Eng., 1952—. Author poems. Vol. Opportunity Village, Las Vegas, Nev., 1985—; bd. dirs. Friends of Nev. Wilderness, Las Vegas, 1985—. Mem. Western Lit. Assn. (Golden award 1984), Shakespeare Assr Am., Coll. Conf. Composition and Communication (exec. com.), Nev. State Edn. Assn. (exec. bd. 1975-79), League of United Latin Am. Citizens (nat. parliamentarian 1978-82). Methodist (various offices held). Lodge: Soroptimists (parliamentarian Las Vegas club 1984—, pres.-elect 1986-87, Women Helping Women award 1983, named Woman of Distinction 1986), Order of Eastern Star (Worthy Matron 1960-61). Avocations: fishing, swimming, theatre. Home: 3411 Frontier St Las Vegas NV 89102 Office: Clark County Community Coll 3200 Cheyenne Ave North Las Vegas NV 89030

AGOSTINO, ELENA JEAN, marketing professional; b. San Francisco, Apr. 21, 1944; s. Ted A. and Mary M. (Canavero) Cinelli; m. Norman R. Agostino, Aug. 27, 1966; 1 child, Michael. BA, Gonzaga U., 1966; MBA with distinction, Santa Clara U., 1981. Br. mgr. Sun Electric Corp., Cin., 1972-74; product mktg. mgr. Tempress/Gen. Signal, Los Gatos, Calif., 1975-82; mktg. adminstrv. mgr. CMX/ORROX, Santa Clara, Calif., 1983; product mgr. Micro Automation, Sunnyvale, Calif., 1983-84; dir. ops. Micro Automation, Fremont, Calif., 1984-85; dir. mktg. Micro Automation/Gen. Signal, Santa Clara, 1985—. Mem. Internat. Soc. Hybrid Microelectronics, Am. Electroplaters Soc., Semiconductor Equipment and Materials Inst., Beta Gamma Sigma. Democrat. Roman Catholic. Avocation: gardening. Home: 3111 Coronado Dr Santa Clara CA 95054 Office: Micro Automation/Gen Signal 48603 Warm Springs Blvd Fremont CA 94539

AGRAS, WILLIAM STEWART, psychiatry educator; b. London, May 17, 1929; came to U.S., 1959; s. Harry and Isabel (Stewart) A.; m. Mary J. Jenkins, Jan. 7, 1955; children: Alison, Peter, Andrew, Catrin. MS, U. London, 1955; diploma in psychiatry, McGill U., Montreal, Que., Can., 1962. From instr. to prof. psychiatry U. Vt. & State Agrl. Coll., Burlington, 1962-69; prof., chmn. dept. U. Miss., University, 1969-73; prof. Stanford (Calif.) U., 1973—. Author: Behavior Therapy: Toward an Applied Clinical Science, 1979, Panic, 1985; editor Jour. Applied Behavioral Analysis; contbr. numerous articles to profl. jours. Fellow Royal Coll. Physicians, Ctr. Advanced Study Behavioral Sci.; mem. Soc. Behavioral Medicine (pres. 1979), Assn. for Advancement Behavioral Therapy (pres. 1986). Home: 515 Gerona Rd Stanford CA 94305 Office: Stanford U Dept Psychology Stanford CA 94305

AGRAWALLA, BIJAY SHANKAR, research physical chemist; b. Rairangpur, Orissa, India, Oct. 5, 1952; came to U.S., 1979; s. Madan Lal and Parmeshwari Devi (Shah) A.; m. Meena Hiranand Bachwani, Dec. 4, 1978; children: Amit Kumar, Anil Kumar. BS, Ravenshaw Coll., Cuttack, India, 1971; MS in Chemistry, Utkal U., Orissa, India, 1973; diploma, Bhabha Atomic Research Ctr. Tch. Sch., Bombay, 1975; PhD in Chemistry, Kans. State U., 1984. Sci. officer Bhabha Atomic Research Ctr., Bombay, 1975-78; research, teaching asst. Kans. State U., Manhattan, 1979-84, postdoctoral fellow, summer 1984; research scientist U. So. Calif., Los Angeles, 1984—. Contbr. articles to profl. jours. Mem. Am. Chem. Soc., Sigma Xi. Hindu. Avocations: tennis, badminton. Home: 1717 N Verdugo Rd Apt 233 Glendale CA 91208 Office: U So Calif Ctr Laser Studies DRB-17 Los Angeles CA 90089-1112

AGUILAR, ISABEL CHAVELA, counselor, academic administrator; b. Calexico, Calif., Nov. 5, 1936; d. Silbestre Macias and Petra (Soria) Badajós; m. Ruben Aguilar, Apr. 7, 1956; children: Ruben Anthony, John Xavier. AA, Imperial Valley Coll.; BA, San Diego State U., MS. Cert. community coll. counselor, adminstr., instr., personnel worker, Calif. Receptionist, interpreter Imperial County Hosp., El Centro, Calif., 1955-58; clerk typist Immigration and Naturalization Service, Calexico, 1958-60; med. clinic mgr. M.P. Ajalat Clinic, Calexico, 1961-72; admissions and records clk. San Diego State U.-Imperial Valley Campus, Calexico, 1972-77, admissions officer, 1977-80, admissions counselor and vet., 1980-83, outreach coordinator, counselor, alumni dir., scholarship coordinator, test coordinator, 1983—; Campus test coordinator, 1977—; campus liaison Imperial Valley Coll., Imperial, Calif., 1980—. Chmn. City Beautification Com., Calexico, 1980—; chmn. Affirmative Action Adv. Cons. to Bd. of Suprs., El Centro, 1983—. Recipient San Diego State U. Annual Alumna award, 1980; Delta Kappa Gamma scholar, 1978. Mem. Advocated for Women in Academia, Imperial Valley Guidance Assn. (sec. 1985-86), Raza Advocates for Calif. Higher Edn., Western Assn. of Ednl. Opportunty Personnel. Democrat. Roman Catholic. Lodge: Soroptimists (pres. Calexico club 1983-84, v.p. 1982-83, sec. 1984-85, publicity mgr. 1981-82, alternate del. 1985-86). Home: 814 Rockwood Ave Calexico CA 92231 Office: San Diego State U Imperial Valley 720 Heber Ave Calexico CA 92231

AGUILAR, MARTIN VELEZ, JR., manufacturing company executive, engineer; b. Mexico City, Mar. 12, 1944; came to U.S., 1969, naturalized, 1973; s. Martin V. and Esther Velez (Villalba) A.; m. Patricia E. Moran, Oct. 1969; children: Lauren, Cheryl, Robert, Pamela. BS in Archit. Engring., Universidad Nacional Autonoma de Mexico, Mexico City, 1968; MS in Bus. Mgmt., UCLA, 1980. Registered profl. engr. Research and devel. mgr. Ford Motor Co., Mexico City, 1968-69, Union Oil Co., Huntington Park, Calif., 1969; mgr. automation devel. and tooling Price Pfister Inc., Pacoima, Calif., 1970—; from tooling engr. to tooling supt., then tooling mgr. Norris Industries, Pacoima, 1970-83; div. mgr. Signa Molds and Engring., Sylmar, Calif., 1980—. Patent hydraulic stabilizer. Mem. rep. presdl. task force, Washington, 1981—. Recipient Toastmaster Speech Craft award, 1972. Mem. AAAS, N.Y. Acad. Sci., Soc. Plastic Engrs., Soc. Mfg. Engrs., Soc. Carbide Engrs., Am. Machinest Adv. Panel. Republican. Roman Catholic. Avocations: polo, swimming, collecting electric trains. Home: 1620 W Farlington St West Covina CA 91790 Office: Price Pfister Inc 13500 Paxton St Pacoima CA 91790

AGUIRRE, MARGUERITE, speech-language pathologist; b. Las Cruces, N.Mex., Oct. 31, 1959; s. Theodore Marquez Aguirre and Rosie T. Volz. BA, N.Mex. State U., 1981, MA, 1983. Dept. head spl. edn. Armijo Elem. Sch., Albuquerque, 1983-85; speech-lang. pathologist Albuquerque Pub. Schs., 1983-85, InSpeech, Inc., San Antonio, 1985, Las Cruces (N.Mex.) Pub. Schs., 1986—; conflict mediation coordinator Conflict Mgrs. Program, Albuquerque, 1984-85. Mem. Albuquerque Speech and Audiology Profls., N.Mex. Speech-Lang.-Hearing Assn., Am. Speech-Lang.-Hearing Assn. (cert.), Nat. Student Speech-Hearing Assn. (pres. 1982-83), Internat. Reading Assn., Delta Zeta (v.p. 1979). Democrat. Roman Catholic. Avocations: needlework, guitar, gardening, weaving. Home: 1767 Royal Dr Las Cruces NM 88001 Office: Las Cruces Pub Schs 301 Amador Las Cruces NM 88001

AGUIRRE, VUKOSLAV ENEAS, soils engineer; b. Santiago, Chile, Nov. 2, 1941; came to U.S., 1960; s. Eneas and Tonka (Domic) A.; m. Emma Jeannette Bendana, Nov. 15, 1970; children: Sergio Eneas, Tonka Lily. BS, U. S. Mil. Acad., 1964; MS, U. Ill., 1965, postgrad., 1968-67. Registered profl. engr. Pa., Va., Md., Mich., D.C., Colo., Ill., Ill., Utah, Wyo. Project engr. Ackenheil Assocs., Pitts., 1965-69; soils specialist Harza Internat., Chgo., 1969-70; project mgr. Law Engring. Testing, Washington, 1971-74; pres. Colo. Testing Lab., Denver, 1974-75, Geotek Inc., Denver, 1975-77; pres., owner Aguirre Engrs. Inc., Englewood, Colo., 1977—. Mem. Internat. Soc. Soil Mechanics and Found. Engring., Internat. Soc. Soil Mechanics, ASCE, Assn. Soil and Found. Engrs., Colo. Cons. Engrs. Council. Roman Catholic. Avocation: skiing. Office: Aguirre Engrs Inc 13276 E Fremont Pl Englewood CO 80112-3927

AGUZZI-BARBAGLI, DANILO LORENZO, educator; b. Arezzo, Italy, Aug. 1, 1924; came to U.S., 1950; s. Guglielmo and Marianna (Barbagli) Aguzzi-B. Dottore in Lettere, U. Florence (Italy), 1949; Ph.D., Columbia U., 1959. Instr., asst. U. Chgo., 1959-64; asso. prof. Tulane U., New Orleans, 1964-71; prof. U. B.C., Vancouver, 1971—; Mem. Fulbright-Hayes final scholarship com., 1970—; adviser on scholarship application Can. Council, 1972-75. Author: Critical Edition of Della Poetica of Francesco Patrizi, 3 vols, 1969, 70, 71, 72, Critical Edition of Francesco Patrizi's Lettere ed opuscoli inediti, 1975; contbr. articles in field to profl. jours. Newberry Library fellow Chgo., 1974; Folger Shakespeare Library fellow Washington, 1975. Fellow Am. Philos. Soc.; mem. Newberry Library Assn., Dante Soc. Am., Italian Honor Soc. (regional rep.), Accademia Petrarca, Medieval Soc. Am., Renaissance Soc. Am., Modern Lang. Assn., AAUP, Am. Assn. Tchrs. Italian. Office: Univ of British Columbia, Vancouver, BC Canada V6T 1W5

AHERN, ARLEEN FLEMING, librarian; b. Mt. Harris, Colo., Oct. 15, 1922; d. John R. and Josephine (Vidmar) Fleming; B.A., U. Utah, 1943; M.A., U. Denver, 1962; postgrad. U. Colo., 1967; m. George Irving Ahern, June 14, 1944; 1 son, George Irving. Library asst. Army Air Force Library, Salt Lake City, 1943-44; library asst. Colo. Women's Coll. Library (now U. Denver/CWC Campus), 1952-60, acquisitions librarian, 1960—, rep. Adult Edn. Council Denver, 1960—, reference librarian Penrose Library, WEC librarian, assoc. prof. librarianship. Committeewoman, Republican Com., Denver, 1958-59. Mem. ALA, Mountain Plains Library Assn., Colo. (1st v.p., pres. 1969-70, dir. 1971—), Library Assn., Altrusa Club of Denver (2d v.p. 1968-69, dir. 1971-74, 76, 78), Soc. Am. Archivists, Mountain Plains Adult Edn. Assn., AAUP. Home: 746 Monaco Pkwy Denver CO 80220 Office: U Denver Penrose Library University Park Denver CO 80208

AHERN, KENNETH EUGENE, podiatrist; b. Calif., June 25, 1943. BA, Chico State Coll., 1966; BS, Calif. Coll. Podiatric Medicine, 1969, D in Podiatric Medicine, 1971. Diplomate Am. Bd. Podiatric Surgery. Staff mem. Coast Plaza Med. Ctr., Norwalk, Calif., 1984—; chief podiatric dept. Norwalk Community Hosp. Mem. Am. Podiatric Med. Assn., Calif. Podiatric Med. Assn., Orange County Podiatric Med. Assn. Home: 1815 Clear Creek Dr Fullerton CA 92633 Office: Coast Plaza Med Ctr 13330 Bloomfield Ave Suite 216 Norwalk CA 90650-3296 Office: 18327 Gridley Rd Suite E Cerritos CA 90701

AHLGREN, GIBSON-TAYLOR, real estate broker; b. Memphis, Sept. 7, 1940; s. Frank Richard and Nona Elizabeth (Alley) A. B.S., U. Md., 1967; J.D., Western State U., San Diego, 1978. Legis. clk. U.S. Senate, Washington, 1963-67, spl. asst., 1970-71; legis. rep. Associated Gen. Contractors, Washington, 1971-73, San Diego, 1973-74; campaign dir. Brown for Gov. Calif., 1974; mgmt. cons. Ahlgren, Peters & Assocs., La Jolla, Calif., 1975-77; v.p., dir. pub. affairs Gt. Am. First Savs. Bank, San Diego, 1977-84; polit. cons., 1984-85; real estate broker, 1986—; cons. 1984-86; Served to lt. USN, 1967-70; Vietnam. Mem. Pi Kappa Alpha.

AHLSTROM, JOHN KEITH, computer infosystem engineer, educator; b. Jamestown, N.Y., July 1, 1942; s. Paul A. and Ruth M. (Conner) A.; m. Anne D. Pemberton, Dec. 15, 1964 (div. June 1976); m. Janice Tribe, June 17, 1982; 1 child, Michele. BA in Internat. Relations, Am. U., Washington, 1964, MA in Internat. Relations, 1968. Founder, systems mgr. Data Resources Inc., Lexington, Mass., 1969-74; operating systems programmer Burroughs Corp., Goleta, Calif., 1974-76; computer micro architect Data Gen. Corp., Mass. and Calif., 1976-78; mgr. software devel. Olivetti Corp., Cupertino, Calif., 1978-79; founder CompuShop Inc., Dallas, 1976-85; mgr. systems architecture Bell-No. Research, Mountain View, Calif., 1979-82; founder, dir. systems engring. DAVID Systems, Sunnyvale, Calif., 1982—; adj. prof. computer sci. San Francisco State U., 1976-86, assoc. prof. computer sci., 1986—. Inventor in field. Mem. Assn. Computing Machinery, Computer Soc. of IEEE (affiliate). Office: DAVID Systems 701 E Evelyn Sunnyvale CA 94086

AHMAD, MOGHISUDDIN, research chemist; b. Dhanbad, India, July 1, 1950; came to U.S., 1979; s. Moinuddin Ahmad and Zaibun Nesa; m. Athar Bano Hussain, Mar. 23, 1985. BS with honors, Aligarh (India) Muslim U., 1971, MS, 1973, MPhil., 1975, PhD, 1978. Postdoctoral fellow Aligarh Muslim U., 1978-79; research assoc. dept. biochemistry and biophysics Tex. A&M U., College Station, 1979-81; research assoc. dept. food sci. Oregon State U., Corvallis, 1981—. Contbr. articles to profl. jours. Mem. Am. Oil Chemists Soc., Am. Chem. Soc., Indian Sci. Congress Assn., Internat. Union Pure and Applied Chemistry, Sigma Xi. Avocations: reading, writing, music, TV. Office: Oreg State U Dept Food Sci and Tech Corvallis OR 97331

AHMADIEH, AZIZ, metallurgy materials science educator; b. Bam, Kerman, Iran, Sept. 25, 1930. BS, U. Tehran, Iran, 1955, U. Idaho, 1958; MS, U. Kans., 1960; PhD, U. Calif., Berkeley, 1964. Prof., head dept. U. Pahlavi, Shiraz, Iran, 1966-80, 1966-80, dean engring., 1978-79; prof. U. So. Colo., Pueblo, 1981—, head. dept., 1982-86. Author: Science of Materials Engineering; contbr. articles to profl. jours. Mem. Am. Soc. Metals (sec., treas. vice chmn. 1984—), Metall. Soc. AIME, Am. Soc. Engring. Edn. Avocations: reading, jogging, traveling. Home: 1042 Quail Vista Ct #E Salt Lake City UT 84117 Office: U So Colo 2200 N Bonforte Pueblo CO 81001

AHMED, SAAD ATTIA, research engineer; b. Giza, Egypt, July 28, 1950; d. Attia Ahmed and Hamida Muhammad El-Behwashy; m. Asmahan Munir Ahmed, Feb. 21, 1982; children: Rashad, Fatima, Muhammad. BS, Cairo U., Giza, Egypt, 1973; M in Engring., Carleton U., Ottawa, Ont., Can., 1978; PhD, Ga. Inst. Tech., 1981. Post-doctoral fellow Ga. Inst. Tech., Atlanta, 1981-83; research assoc. Ariz. State U., Tempe, 1983-84, research analyst, 1984-86; sr. research engr. Garrett Turbine Engine Co., Phoenix, 1986—. Contbr. articles to profl. jours. Mem. AIAA, Am. Soc. Engring. Edn., Am. Phys. Soc., ASME, Sigma Xi. Avocations: reading, playing soccer. Home: 4530 E McDowell Apt 239 Phoenix AZ 85008

AHMED, SAIYED IQBAL, marine biology educator; b. Desna, Pakistan, Jan. 5, 1941; s. Abdul Khalique and Asghari Khatoon; m. Zahida Begum; children: Ansa, Mahira. BS, D.J. Sci. Coll., Karachi, Pakistan; PhD, J.W. Goethe U., Frankfurt, Fed. Republic Germany. Sr. research officer Council of Sci. and Industry Research, Lahore, Pakistan, 1964; NRC postdoctoral fellow U. Man., Can., 1964-66; NIH postdoctoral fellow Yale U., New Haven, Conn., 1966-68, spl. NIH postdoctoral fellow, 1968-70, NIH postdoctoral fellow, 1966-68; vis. scientist U. B.C., Vancouver, Can., 1970-73; vis. scientist U. Wash., Seattle, 1970-73, from research assoc. to prof. oceanography, 1973—; assoc. prog. dir. marine biotech. NOAA/Nat. Sea Grant, Rockville, Md., 1985—. Contbr. articles to profl. jours. Grantee NSF, 1975—. Mem. AAAS, Am. Soc. Microbiology, Am. Soc. Limnology and Oceanography. Office: U Wash Dept Oceangraphy Seattle WA 98195 Office: NOAA/Nat Sea Grant Program 6010 Executive Blvd Rockville MD 20852

AHN, YOUNG SOO, research chemist; b. Seoul, Republic of Korea, July 21, 1943; came to U.S., 1974, naturalized, 1980; s. Dae Won and Won Rang (Kim) A.; m. Kun Hee Cho, Nov. 18, 1972; children: Silas, Sinclair, Sylvester. BS, Seoul Nat. U., 1970, MS, 1973. Instr. Yonsei U. Coll Medicine, Seoul, 1973-74; teaching asst. U. N.Mex., Albuquerque, 1975-76; chief chemist So. Union Co., Hobbs, N.Mex., 1976-79; research chemist Unichem Internat., Hobbs, 1979—. Contbr. articles to sci. jours. Served to sgt. Republic of Korea Marine Corps, 1964-67. Mem. Am. Chem. Soc. (Permian Basin sect. sec. 1986—), Soc. Applied Spectroscopy, Korean Scientists and Engrs. Assn. Am. Lutheran. Home: 218 E Llano Dr Hobbs NM 88240 Office: Unichem Internat Inc 707 N Leech St Hobbs NM 88240

AHRENS, RUSSEL FREDERICK, JR., advertising executive; b. Highland Park, Ill., Sept. 13, 1941; s. Russel Frederick and Frances Olive (Yeager) A. BFA, Claremont McKenna Coll., 1963. Account exec. BBDO Inc., San Francisco, 1964-67; supr. United Airlines, N.Y.C., 1968-71; regional sales mgr. St. Joseph (Mo.) Packaging, 1971-74; account exec. Dixon Paper Co., Denver, 1974-80; v.p. Brock & Assocs., Denver, 1981-83; pres. Ahrens & Whitlock Advt. Ltd., Denver, 1983—; cons. AT&T Mktg. Com., Denver, 1984—. Bd. dirs. ARTREACH Inc., Denver, 1984—; creative judge Portland (Oreg.) Advt. Club, 1984. Mem. Denver Advt. Fedn. (com. chmn. 1984-85), Denver C. of C., Aurora (Colo.) C. of C., Better Bus. Bur., Advt. Golf Assn. (chmn. 1985-86). Republican. Episcopalian. Avocations: art appreciation, golf, traveling. Office: Ahrens & Whitlock Advt Ltd 1860 Blake St Suite 640 Denver CO 80202

AHUJA, JAGDISH CHAND, mathematics educator; b. Rawalpindi, West Pakistan, Dec. 24, 1927; came to U.S., 1966, naturalized 1972; s. Nihal Chand and Ishwardai (Chhabra) A.; m. Sudarshan Sachdeva, May 18, 1955; children—Naina, Anita. B.A., Banaras U., 1953, M.A., 1955; Ph.D., U. B.C., 1963. Sr. math. tchr. D.A.V. High Sch., Nairobi, Kenya, 1955-56; tchr. math. Tanzania, 1956-58; teaching asst. U. B.C., 1958-61, teaching fellow, 1961-63, stats. lab. instr., 1959-61, lectr. stats., 1961-63; asst. prof. math. U. Calgary, Can., 1963-66; assoc. prof. math. Portland State U., Oreg., 1966-69, prof. math., 1969—. Contbr. articles to profl. jours.; referee profl. jours., reviewer profl. jours. Mem. Am. Statis. Assn., Inst. Math. Stats. Home: 9914 SW 30th Ave Portland OR 97219 Office: Portland State U Dept Math PO Box 751 Portland OR 97207

AIGNER, DENNIS JOHN, economics educator, consultant; b. Los Angeles, Sept. 27, 1937; s. Herbert Lewis and Della Geraldine (Balasek) A.; m. Vernita Lynne White, Dec. 22, 1957 (div. May 1977); children: Mitchell A., Annette N., Anita L., Angela D. B.S., U. Calif.-Berkeley, 1959, M.A., 1962, Ph.D., 1963. Asst. prof. econs. U. Ill., Urbana, 1962-67; from assoc. prof. to prof. U. Wis., Madison, 1967-76; prof., chmn. dept. econs. U. So. Calif., Los Angeles, 1976—; pres. Dennis Aigner Inc., Los Angeles, 1978—. Author: Introduction to Statistical Decision Making, 1968, Basic Econometrics, 1971; editor: Latent Variables in Socio-Economic Models, 1977; Co-editor Jour. Econometrics, 1972—. Fulbright fellow Belgium, 1970; Fulbright fellow Israel, 1983; NSF grantee, 1968-70, 70-72, 73-76, 79-81, 84-86. Fellow Econometric Soc.; mem. Am. Statis. Assn., Am. Econ. Assn. Office: Dept Econs U So Calif University Park CA 90089

AIKAWA, JERRY KAZUO, physician, educator; b. Stockton, Calif., Aug. 24, 1921; s. Genmatsu and Shizuko (Yamamoto) A.; m. Chitose Aihara, Sept. 20, 1944; 1 son, Ronald K. A.B., U. Calif., 1942; M.D., Wake Forest Coll., 1945. Intern, asst. resident N.C. Baptist Hosp., 1945-47; NRC fellow in med. scis. U. Calif. Med. Sch., 1947-48; NRC, AEC postdoctoral fellow in med. scis. Bowman Gray Sch. Medicine, 1948-50, instr. internal medicine, 1950-53, asst. prof., 1953; established investigator Am. Heart Assn., 1952-58; exec. officer lab. service Univ. Hosps., 1958-61, dir. lab. services, 1961-83, dir. allied health program, 1969—, assoc. dean allied health program, 1983—, pres. med. bd.; assoc. dean clin. affairs asst. prof. U. Colo. Sch. Medicine, 1953- 60, asso. prof. medicine, 1960-67, prof., 1967—, prof. biometrics, 1974—, assoc. dean clin. affairs, 1974—; Pres. Med. bd. Univ. Hosps. Fellow ACP, Am. Coll. Nutrition; mem. Western Soc. Clin. Research, So. Soc. Clin. Research, Soc. Exptl. Biology and Medicine, Am. Fedn. Clin. Research, AAAS, Central Soc. Clin. Research, AMA, Assn. Am. Med. Colls., Phi Beta Kappa, Sigma Xi, Alpha Omega Alpha. Home: 619 S Poplar Way Denver CO 80224 Office: U Colo Sch Medicine 4200 E 9th Ave Denver CO 80262

AIKEN, SUSAN HARDY, English educator; b. Bklyn., Nov. 4, 1943; d. Sutton Labon and Mae (Eppinger) Hardy; m. Christopher Franklin Carroll, Jan. 1, 1978; children: James Buchanan Aiken, Alden Hardy Carroll. BA, Furman U., 1964; MA, Duke U., 1966, PhD, 1971. Instr. English U. Ga., Athens, 1966-69; asst. prof. SUNY, Stony Brook, 1971-72, Suffolk Coll., Selden, N.Y., 1972-73; asst. prof. U. Ariz., Tucson, 1973-77, assoc. prof., 1977—; cons. U. Ariz. Press, 1984-85, U. Ariz. Women's Studies Program, 1981—; referee John Simon Guggenheim Meml. Found., 1985, 86, Signs: Jour. Women in Culture and Soc. Editor: (with others) Changing Our Minds: Feminist Transformations of Knowledge, 1987; contbr. articles to profl. jours. Fellow Ford Found., 1964-65, Woodrow Wilson II, 1965-66, Duke U., 1969-70; grantee U. Ariz., 1984; recipient U. Ariz. Creative Teaching award, 1985, Women's Studies Adv. Council award, 1987. Mem. MLA (adv. com. publs. 1985—), Nat. Women's Studies Assn., Browning Inst. Avocations: hiking, camping. Office: U Ariz Dept English Tucson AZ 85721

AIKEN, WILLIAM DAVID, lawyer; b. Sunnyside, Wash., Aug. 28, 1923; s. William Jerome and Louisa Gertrude (Nichols) A.; student Wash. State U., 1941-43, 46-47; J.D., George Washington U., 1949; m. Dorothy Louise Snyder, May 28, 1948; children—Katherine Aiken Schwartz, Mary L. Aiken Fishback, Sally S. Aiken Fetterer, Jerome Ross. Admitted to Wash. bar, 1951; asso. firm Chaffee & Aiken, Sunnyside, Wash., 1951-60; sole practice law, Sunnyside, 1960—; mcpl. judge City of Sunnyside, 1951-58; justice of peace Yakima County, Wash., 1951-58. Mem. Yakima County Civil Service Com., 1969—, chmn., 1975-77; mem. Yakima County Boundary Rev. Bd., 1985—, Selective Service Bd. 31 Yakima and Klickitat Counties, 1982—. Served to with U.S. Army, 1943-46, lt. col. JAG Wash. State N.G. Decorated Bronze Star. Mem. ABA, Wash. State Bar Assn. (exec. com. family law sect. 1974-76), Yakima County Bar Assn. (pres. 1985-86), Am. Judicature Soc., Am. Acad. Polit. and Social Sci. Episcopalian. Clubs: Masons (32 deg.), Shriners, Coll., Seattle. Home: 1241 Sunset Pl Sunnyside WA 98944 Office: 1001 E Edison Ave Sunnyside WA 98949

AINSLIE, RICHARD GEORGE, life insurance agent; b. Los Angeles, Apr. 4, 1916; s. Edgar and Elizabeth (Chesney) A.; B.S., Purdue U., 1939, M.S., 1940; postgrad. U. So. Calif., 1943-44; children—Paul R., Susan C. Instr., coach Purdue U., W. Lafayette, Ind., 1939-40; instr., head football and basketball coach Whitman Coll., Walla Walla, Wash., 1940-42; safety engr. Consol. Steel., Wilmington, Calif., 1942-44; recreation dir. AirService Command, Fairfield, Ohio, 1944-46; head football coach Wittenberg Coll., Springfield, Ohio, 1946; prof., basketball-baseball coach Creighton U., Omaha, 1947-48; agt. Minn. Mut. Life Ins. Co., Los Angeles, 1948-58, gen. agt., 1958—, field council, 1961, 63, 75, 76. Chmn. war and bond drive Patterson Field, Ohio, 1944-46, Community Chest and Red Cross drive, 1945-46. Named outstanding profl. salesman Am., 1967-68; registered profl. disability and health ins. underwriter. Mem. Million Dollar Round Table (life and qualifying, honor roll, 1952-87), Internat. Assn. Health Underwriters (leading producers Round Table, Health, Life and Qualifying 1969-83, nat. quality award 1955-81), Los Angeles Life Underwriters Assn., Life Ins. and Trust Council Los Angeles, Nat. Football Found. and Hall of Fame, Purdue Alumni Assn. (life), Internat. Srs. Amateur Golf Soc. (N.Y.C. chpt.), Assn. Ret. Profl. Basketball Personnel (charter mem. 1985-86). Clubs: Los Angeles Athletic, Oakmont Country (Glendale), Quarter Century. Lodge: Elks. Contbr. articles in field to publs. Home: 3000 Country Club Dr Glendale CA 91208 Office: 3000 Country Club Dr Glendale CA 90039

AINSWORTH, CAMERON, health care consultant; b. Three Hills, Alta., Can., Nov. 13, 1920; came to U.S., 1946; s. Francis and Sadie (Moore) A.; m. Jeanette Freeborn, Aug. 7, 1948; 1 child, John Victor. BS, U. Alta., Edmonton, 1945; PhD, U. Rochester, 1949; MD, U. Ciudad Juarez, Mex., 1980; MPH, U. Hawaii, 1983. Instr. U. Colo., Boulder, 1949-51; research chemist Eli Lilly & Co., Indpls., 1951-65; prof. Colo. State U., Ft. Collins, 1965-72, San Francisco State U., 1972-78; health care cons. Redwood City, Calif., 1983—. Contbr. numerous articles to sci. jours. Grantee NIH, NSF, 1965-78. Mem. AAAS, AMA, Am. Pub. Health Assn., Physicians for Social Responsibility, Sigma Xi. Lutheran. Avocations: gardening, reading, golf. Home and Office: 3879 Vineyard Dr Redwood City CA 94061

AINSWORTH, THOMAS HARGRAVES, JR., physician, medical administrator, author; b. Schenectady, June 16, 1920; s. Thomas Hargraves and Flora Cameron (MacCracken) A.; m. Shirley Ann Sanford, Dec. 23, 1950; children—Ann Louise McFarland, Thomas Hargraves III. B.S., Pa. State U., State Coll., 1941; M.D., Temple U., 1944; postgrad. exec. program in health services mgmt. Harvard Bus. Sch., 1977. Diplomate Am. Bd. Surgery. Intern Bryn Mawr Hosp., Pa., 1944-45, mem. staff, 1951-70, chief gen. surgery, 1964-70; resident in surgery Bellevue Med. Ctr., N.Y.C., 1948-51; practice medicine specializing in surgery, Bryn Mawr, 1951-70; assoc. dir. Am. Hosp. Assn., Chgo., 1970-74; med. dir. Ill. Masonic Hosp., Chgo., 1974-79; chmn. bd. Hale, Inc., Carmel Valley, Calif., 1979—; asst. prof. surgery and anatomy Temple U., Phila., 1964-70; prof. clin. surgery U. Ill., Chgo., 1974-79, prof. health care services Sch. Pub. Health, 1975-79; cons. Ainsworth Assocs., Chgo., Phila., Carmel Valley, 1974—. Author: Quality Assurance: Medical Care in Hospitals, 1972; Quality Assurance in Long Term Care, 1976; Live or Die, 1983; Health Promotion in the Workplace, 1984. Editor Hosp. Med. Staff, 1972-74. Patentee Ainsworth (hip) Nail, 1967. Elder Presbyn. Ch. in U.S.A., Bryn Mawr, 1960—. Served to capt. USMC, 1946-48. Recipient Award of Honor, Am. Hosp. Assn., 1969. Fellow ACS (com. on cancer 1970-79); mem. Coll. Physicians Phila., Am. Coll. Preventive Medicine, Acad. Surgery Phila., Inst. Medicine of Chgo., Am. Acad. Med. Dirs., Carmel Valley Garden Assn. (pres. 1982-83). Republican. Club: Phila. Country. Home: PO Box 1201 Carmel Valley CA 93924 Office: Hale Inc PO Box 223580 Carmel CA 93922

AIRD, STEVEN DOUGLAS, zoologist, biochemist; b. Ann Arbor, Mich., June 12, 1952; s. John Shields and Laurel (Jandy) A.; m. Mary Ellen Whiting, May 6, 1978; children: Benjamin Steven, Jonathan Isaac, Joshua Ethan. BS in Zoology, Mont. State U., 1974; MS in Biology, No. Ariz. U., 1977; PhD in Zoology, Colo. State U., 1984. Postdoctoral research assoc. U. Wyo., Laramie, 1983—; asst. curator Deaver Herbarium, No. Ariz. U., Flagstaff, 1974-75; pub. relations seminarian Johnson Wax Inc., western U.S., 1979; judge Colo.-Wyo. Jr. Acad. Sci., Ft. Collins, 1982; mem. herpetologists panel Colo. Div. Wildlife, Denver, 1985. contbr. articles to profl. jours. Pres. Stake Mission Mormon Ch., Laramie, 1984—. Colo. State U. fellow, 1979-81; cited for excellence in teaching Associated Students Colo. State U., 1979-81; biomed. research support grantee Colo. State U., 1983, U. Wyo., 1986. Mem. Herpetologist's League, Soc. Study Amphibians and Reptiles, Internat. Soc. Toxinology (full mem.), Sigma Xi (full mem.). Mormon. Avocations: backpacking, camping, hiking, photography. Office: U Wyo Dept Molecular Biology University Station Box 3944 Laramie WY 82071

AKAKA, DANIEL KAHIKINA, congressman; b. Honolulu, Sept. 11, 1924; s. Kahikina and Annie (Kahoa) A.; m. Mary Mildred Chong, May 22, 1948; children: Millannie, Daniel, Gerard, Alan, Nicholas. Grad., U. Hawaii, postgrad., 1966. Tchr. schs. in Hawaii, 1953-60; vice prin., then prin. Ewa Beach Elementary Sch., Honolulu, 1960-64; prin. Pohakea Elementary Sch., 1964-65, Kaneohe Elementary Sch., 1965-68; program specialist Hawaii Compensatory Edn., 1978-79, 85—; dir. Hawaii OEO, 1971-74; spl. asst. human resources Office Gov. Hawaii, 1975-76; mem. 95th-99th Congresses from 2d Dist., Hawaii, 1977—; chmn. Hawaii Prins. Conf. Bd. dirs. Hanahauoli Sch.; mem. Act 4 Ednl. Adv. Council, Library Adv. Council.; Trustee Kawaiahao Congl. Ch. Served with U.S. Army, 1945-47. Life mem. NEA; mem. Musicians Assn. Hawaii. Democrat. Address: Rayburn Office Bldg Washington DC 20515

AKATSUKA, CLAYTON KAZUMI, mathematics educator; b. Honolulu, Jan. 20, 1953; s. Roland Minoru and Haruko (Yonezaki) A.; m. Lynn Kayoko Murakami, July 6, 1980. BEd, U. Hawaii, 1975, profl. diploma, 1977, MEd, 1984. Cert. pvt. sch. tchr., Hawaii. Tchr. math. Kailua (Hawaii) High Sch., 1975-76; tchr. math., chmn. dept. Mid Pacific Inst., Honolulu, 1976—; coach math. team Mid Pacific Inst., 1976-84, co-coach, 1985—; coach math. team Kailua High Sch., 1975-76. Mem. Nat. Council Tchrs. Math., Hawaii Council Tchrs. Math., Am. Spaniel Club, Hawaii Cocker Spaniel Club (sec. 1975—, v.p. bd. dirs., editor). Democrat. Buddhist. Avocation: raising, tng. and exhibiting Am. Cocker Spaniels. Home: 45-606 Keole St Kaneohe HI 96744 Office: Mid-Pacific Inst 2445 Kaala St Honolulu HI 96822

AKBARI, HASHEM, scientist; b. Qazvin, Iran, Aug. 13, 1949; came to U.S., 1975; s. Ali Asghar and Fatemeh (Shakeri) A.; m. Mehrokh Moradi; children: Saman, Shahla Melody. BSc in Gas Engring., Abadan (Iran) Inst. Tech., 1971; MSc in Nuclear Engring., MIT, 1977; MSc in Indsl. Engring., Op. Research, U. Calif., Berkeley, 1978, PhD in Nuclear Engring., 1979. Sr. engr. Iranian Oil Service, Ahwaz, Iran, 1971-75; staff scientist Lawrence Berkeley (Calif.) Lab., 1977-79, 83—; assoc. prof. Abadan Inst. Tech., 1979-81; head refining engr. Enerchimi Cons. Engrs., Tehran, Iran, 1981-83; gen. mgr. Jahan Energy Cons. Engrs., Tehran, 1981-83; cons. energy conservation U. Tex., Austin, 1984-85. Contbr. articles to profl. jours. Mem. ASME. Office: Lawrence Berkeley Lab 1 Cyclotron Rd Berkeley CA 94720

AKERS, SCOTT ROGER, librarian, media specialist; b. Oakland, Calif., Sept. 11, 1946; s. Harry Albert and Edith Genevieve (Cleveland) A.; m. Suzanne Selberg, Aug. 25, 1973; 1 child, Steven. BA, Calif. State U., Chico, 1968; MA, San Diego State U., 1972. Cert. tchr. secondary level and jr. coll., Calif. Librarian/media specialist Dos Palos (Calif.) Joint Union High Sch., 1973-74; librarian/media specialist Calixico (Calif.) Unified Sch. Dist., 1974—, librarian, resource specialist Adult Basic Edn., 1974—; lectr. San Diego State U., Calexico, 1979-85, cons., 1985-86; travel counselor/tour guide Am. Inst. Fgn. Study, Greenwich, Conn., 1984—. Contbr. articles to mags. Bd. dirs. San Diego Model Cities, 1971-72, Literacy Vols. of Am., El Centro, Calif., 1984-85, Imperial County Sch. Resource Ctr., El Centro, 1978-79; coordinator southeastern Calif. World Food Day, 1982-83.

Recipient Amicus Poloniae award Poland mag., 1970. Mem. Assn. Edn. Communications and Tech., Calif. Media Library Educators Assn., Internat. Com. Library Info. (pres. 1979-80), Desert Valleys Library Assn. (pres. 1974-75, 86—), Nat. Edn. Assn., Calif. Tchrs. Assn. (Calexico site rep. 1987—). Democrat. Methodist. Club: United Meths., Inc. (El Centro). Lodge: Native Sons of Golden West (pres. 1984-85, sec. 1986—). Avocations: traveling, postcard and stamp collecting, swimming, photography. Home: 1850 Lincoln Ave #149 El Centro CA 92243 Office: Calexico High Sch 1030 Encinas Calexico CA 92231

AKERS, SUZANNE SELBERG, social worker; b. San Francisco, Jan. 5, 1947; d. Henry Edward and Barcy Pearl (Allsup) Selberg; m. Scott Roger Akers, Aug. 25, 1973; 1 child, Steven. BA, Calif. State U., Chico, 1983; MSW, Calif. State U., San Diego, 1984. Social worker Trinity County Welfare, Weaverville, Calif., 1969-73; hotline dir. Econ. Opportunity Commn., El Centro, Calif., 1975-76; health educator Am. Lung Assn., El Centro, Calif., 1976—; counselor Am. Inst. Fgn. Study, Greenwich, Conn., 1984—. Mem. AAUW, Nat. Assn. Social Workers, Congress of Lung Assn. Staff. Democrat. Methodist. Lodges: Order Eastern Star (organist 1981), Native Daughters of Golden West (organist 1984—). Avocations: writing, photography, travel.

AKIN, GWYNN COLLINS, pharmaceutical company executive; b. Century, Fla., Mar. 24, 1939; d. Edward John and Carrie Gwynn (Jones) Collins; m. John R. Akin, June 1, 1963 (div. Dec. 1985); children: Carrie Catherine, Margaret Marie; m. Albert Bowers, Dec. 23, 1985. BS in Biol. Scis., Fla. State U., 1961; PhD in Human Anatomy, Tulane U., 1965. Instr. gross anatomy Loyola U. Sch. Dentistry, New Orleans, 1965-66, instr. physiology, 1966; asst. to dean La. State U. Sch. Medicine, Shreveport, 1966-71, asst. prof. anatomy, 1968-71; head. spl. studies Office of Chancellor U. Calif., San Francisco, 1970-72, dir. spl. projects Office of Chancellor, 1972; acad. asst. U. Calif., Berkeley, 1971-75; sec., treas. A.F. Akin, Inc., Shreveport, 1973-86; spl. asst. to dir. Neuropsychiat. Inst. UCLA, 1975-76; policy and planning cons. to pres. U. Wash., Seattle, 1976-79; sr. profl. assoc. Assn. Acad. Health Ctrs., Washington, 1979-81; exec. asst. to pres., chief exec. officer Syntex Corp., Palo Alto, Calif., 1981, exec. asst. to chmn., pres. and chief exec. officer, 1982, asst. to chmn. and chief exec. officer, 1982-85, dir. health policy, 1986—; adj. prof. human anatomy and physiology U. W. Fla., Pensacola, 1968-69, asst. prof. dept. biol. and marine scis., 1969-70; cons. Fla. Bd. Regents, 1974-75, Ctr. for Collaborative Studies in Mental Health Delivery and Financing, 1975-76, Nat. Sci. Bd., Washington, 1978—; mem. sch. nursing vis. com., U. Wash., Seattle, 1976-79; adv. Bay Med. Research and Edn. Found., San Francisco, 1983-85. Contbr. articles to sci. jours. Mem. Cancer Research Inst. External Adv. Com., U. Calif., San Francisco, 1985—. Tulane U. Grad. Sch. scholar, 1961-62, 62-63; NIH Predoctoral fellow, 1961-65. Mem. AAUP, AAAS, Assn. Am. Med. Colls., Am. Assn. Anatomists, So. Soc. Anatomists, New Orleans Embryology Club, Shreveport Med. Soc. (assoc.), Calif. Assn. Instn. Research, Nat. Rehab. Assn., NIH Alumni Assn., Tulane U. Med. Alumni Assn., Fla. State U. Alumni Assn., Found. for Advanced Edn. in Scis. Inc., Calif. Bus. Roundtable, Pharm. Mfrs. Assn., Phi Beta Kappa, Sigma Xi, Phi Kappa Phi, Alpha Lambda Delta, Phi Sigma. Office: Syntex Corp 3401 Hillview Ave Palo Alto CA 94304

AKINS, GEORGE CHARLES, accountant; b. Willits, Calif., Feb. 22, 1917; s. Guy Brookins and Eugenie (Swan) A.; A.A., Sacramento City Coll., 1941; m. Jane Babcock, Mar. 27, 1945. Accountant, auditor Calif. Bd. Equalization, Dept. Finance, Sacramento, 1940-44; controller-treas. DeVons Jewelers, Sacramento, 1944-73, v.p., controller, 1973-80, v.p., chief fin. officer, dir., 1980-84; individual accounting and tax practice, Sacramento, 1944—. Accountant, cons. Mercy Children's Hosp. Guild, Sacramento, 1957-77. Served with USAAF, 1942. Mem. Soc. Calif. Pioneers, Nat. Soc. Pub. Accountants, U.S. Navy League, Calif. Hist. Soc., English Speaking Union, Drake Navigators Guild, Internat. Platform Assn., Mendocino County Hist. Soc., Sacramento County Hist. Soc. Republican. Roman Catholic. Clubs: Commonwealth of Calif., Comstock. Contbg. author: Portfolio of Accounting Systems for Small and Medium-Sized Business, 1968, rev., 1977. Home and Office: 96 S Humboldt St Willits CA 95490

AKITA, RICHARD MITSUO, electronics engr.; b. Honolulu, Nov. 13, 1939; s. Mitsuyoshi and Tomoyo (Sueoka) A.; B.S. in Math., Oreg. State U., 1961; M.S.E.E., Naval Postgrad. Sch., 1968; m. Gwen Harumi Tateno, June 14, 1964; children—Michael T., Andrea N. Electronics engr. command and control div. Naval Ocean Systems Center, 1970-77, supervisory engr., br. head navigation systems br., 1977—; instr. engring. Calif. Community Colls., 1977—. Mem. sch. site council Wangeheim Jr. High Sch., 1978-80. Served with USN, 1961-70. Mem. IEEE, Sigma Xi. Republican. Club: Lions. Home: 1738 Sorrel Ct Carlsbad CA 92008 Office: Naval Ocean Systems Center Code 434 San Diego CA 92152

AKIYAMA, CAROL LYNN, motion picture industry executive; b. Chgo., Dec. 5, 1946; s. Makio M. Akiyama and Mary (Uyeda) Maruyama; m. Peter Richard Bierstedt, Aug. 23, 1980. BA magna cum laude, U. So. Calif., 1968, JD, 1971. Bar: Calif. Atty. NLRB, Los Angeles, 1971-75, ABC TV, Hollywood, Calif., 1975-79, So. Calif. Edison, Rosemead, 1980-81; asst. gen. atty. CBS Inc., Los Angeles, 1981-82; sr. v.p. Alliance of Motion Picture and TV Producers, Sherman Oaks, Calif., 1982—. Mem. Los Angeles County Bar Assn. (chmn. labor law sect. 1981-82, exec. com. 1975-85), Phi Kappa Phi, Phi Beta Kappa. Office: AMPTP 14144 Ventura Blvd Sherman Oaks CA 91423

AKLONIS, JOHN JOSEPH, chemistry educator; b. Elizabeth, N.J., Sept. 28, 1940; s. Joseph John and Anna M. (Krusis) A.; m. Jo Ann Swaaley, Dec. 27, 1985. B.S., Rutgers U., 1962; M.A., Princeton U., 1964, Ph.D., 1965. Faculty U. So. Calif., Los Angeles, 1966—, prof. chemistry, 1976—; dir. Loker Hydrocarbon Research Inst. Los Angeles, 1983—. Author: Introduction to Polymer Viscoelasticity, 1984. Fellow Am. Phys. Soc.; mem. Am. Chem. Soc. Home: PO Box 187 San Pedro CA 90733 Office: U So Calif Loker Hydrocarbon Research Inst Los Angeles CA 90089

AKUBUILO, FRANCIS EKENECHUKWU, architect; b. Ebe-Udi, Anambra, Nigeria, Mar. 25, 1952; came to U.S., 1984; s. Robert O. and Regina N. (Agada) A. AS, Fachhochschule, Stuttgart, Fed. Republic of Germany; MArch, Fachhochschule, Frankfurt, Fed. Republic of Germany; D in Bus., Pacific State U. Asst. archtl. engr. Albrecht Assocs., Stuttgart, 1978-83; asst. lectr. Fachhochschule, Frankfort, 1981-83; legal researcher Control Data, Los Angeles, 1984; legal edn. researcher Am. Legal, Los Angeles, 1984—; cons. Udi Divisional Schs., Udi-Anambra, Nigera, 1981—, Akubuilo Designers, Enugu, Nigera, 1983—. Mem. German Architects Engrs. Assn. Roman Catholic. Avocations: table tennis, soccer. Home: 3664 W 59th St Los Angeles CA 90043

ALABACK, PAUL BERNARD, forest ecologist; b. La Grange Park, Ill., June 15, 1953; s. Glenn James and Lavinia Jean (Elliott) A.; m. Judy Kathryn Hall, Aug. 24, 1980; 1 child, Sean Muir. BS in Forest Sci., BS in Botany, U. Wash., 1976; PhD in Forest Sci., Oreg. State U., 1980. Research asst. Oreg. State U., Corvallis, 1976-80, research assoc., 1980-85; research ecologist USDA Forest Service, Juneau, Alaska, 1986—, cons. wildlife habitat, 1981-85; working group leader Long Term Ecol. Research Data Mgmt., 1983. Mem. editorial bd. NSF Long Term Ecol. Research Data Mgmt., 1984-85; contbr. articles to profl. jours; contributor edn. film Geography and Natural History of Alaska, 1985. Recipient Nat. Conservation award Izaak Walton League, Washington, 1971, Merit Pay and Acknowledgement award Oreg. State U., 1985. Mem. Brit. Ecol. Soc., AAAS, Audubon Soc. (scholar 1971). Democrat. Avocations: photography, backpacking, kayaking, fgn. langs. Home: 11220 N Douglas Juneau AK 99801 Office: USDA Forest Service Forestry Sci Lab PO Box 20909 Juneau AK 99802

ALAMEDA, GEORGE KEVIN, research chemical physicist; b. N.Y.C., Apr. 30, 1955; s. George and Mary (Schmitt) A.; m. Susan Jo O'Donnell, July 12, 1980. BS in Physics, BA in Math., Humboldt State U., 1978; MS in Chemistry, U. Calif., Riverside, 1980, PhD in Physical Chemistry, 1981. Research chemist Chevron Oil Field Research, La Habra, Calif., 1981-85, sr. research chemist, 1985-87; sr. reservoir engr Chevron U.S.A., Midland, Tex., 1987—. Mem. Soc. Petroleum Engrs., Sigma Xi (assoc.).

ALAMEDA, RUSSELL RAYMOND, JR., radiologic technologist, X-ray service company executive; b. San Jose, Calif., Oct. 13, 1945; s. Russell Raymond and Rose Margaret (Manzone) A.; m. Gayle Evileen Allison, Feb. 16, 1969 (div. 1975); children—Lynda Rae, Anthony David. Student San Jose City Coll., 1963-65. Served with U.S. Navy, 1966-75; x-ray technician VA Hosp., Palo Alto, Calif., 1975-78; office mgr., radiologic tech. orthopedic surgery Mountain View (Calif.), 1978—; owner, operator Ren-Tech, San Jose, 1982—. Recipient Mallinckrodt Outstanding Achievement award Mallinckrodt Corp., 1971. Mem. Am. Registry of Radiologic Technologists, Calif. Radiologic Technologists, DAV. Republican. Lutheran. Home: 165 Blossom Hill Rd SP76 San Jose CA 95123 Office: Orthopedic Surgery 2500 Dr Suite 7 Mount View CA 94040

ALANEN, JACK DAVID, computer scientist, educator; b. Painesville, Ohio, Aug. 27, 1938; s. Tauno Mattius and Lina Elenor (Bell) A.; m. Grace Marie Whipple, Nov. 14, 1969; 1 child, Julia. BS, Case Inst. Tech., 1960, MS, 1962; MS, Yale U., 1966, PhD, 1972. Head computing ctr. U. Nairobi, Kenya, 1973-74; assoc. prof. U. Buffalo, 1974-75; sci. collaborator U. Utrecht, The Netherlands, 1975-78; dir. acad. computing Case Western Res. U., Cleve., 1978-80; prof. computer sci. Calif. State U., Northridge, 1980-85; mem. tech. staff Litton Guidance and Control Systems, Woodland Hills, Calif., 1983-86; dir. software engring. Litton Aero Products, Moorpark, Calif., 1986—; part-time instr. UCLA, 1982—, Calif. State U. Northridge, 1986—. Contbr. articles to profl. jours. Mem. IEEE, Assn. for Computing Machinery, Math. Assn. Am., Am. Statis. Assn., Sigma Xi. Home: 9555 White Oak Ave Northridge CA 91325 Office: Litton Aero Products 6101 Condor Dr Moorpark CA 93021

ALARCON, ARTHUR LAWRENCE, federal judge; b. Los Angeles, Aug. 14, 1925; s. Lorenzo Marques and Margaret (Sais) A.; m. Sandra D. Paterson, Sept. 1, 1979; children—Jan Marie, Gregory, Lance. B.A. in Polit. Sci, U. So. Calif., 1949, J.D., 1951. Bar: Calif. 1952. Dep. dist. atty. Los Angeles County, Los Angeles, 1952-61; exec. asst. to Gov. Pat Brown State of Calif., Sacramento, 1962-64, legal adv. to gov., 1961-62; judge Los Angeles Superior Ct., 1964-78; assoc. justice Calif. Ct. Appeals, Los Angeles, 1978-79; judge U.S. Ct. Appeals for 9th Circuit, Los Angeles, 1979—. Served with U.S. Army, 1943-46, ETO. Office: US Ct Appeals 312 N Spring St Los Angeles CA 90012 *

ALBAUGH, PAMELA ANN, medicinal chemist; b. Columbus, Ga., Dec. 19, 1956; d. David Hinson and Martha Evalina (Anderson) A.; m. Michael Wayne Robertson, June 7, 1980 (div. May 1986). Student, Purdue U., 1974-76; BA in Chemistry, BS in Biology, U. Calif., Irvine, 1978; PhD in Organic Chemistry, U. Ill., 1982. Postdoctoral fellowship Ind. U., Bloomington, 1982-84; scientist Allergan Pharms., Irvine, Calif., 1984—; research assoc. U. Calif., Irvine, 1978. Contbr. articles to profl. jours. Alternate to bd. dirs. Capistrano Garden Homes Assn., San Juan Capistrano, Calif., 1986. NIH fellow, 1983. Mem. Am. Chem. Soc., Phi Lambda Upsilon, Alpha Epsilon Delta (v.p. 1981-82), Alpha Lambda Delta. Avocations: sewing, reading, sports, cooking. Office: Allergan Pharms 2525 Dupont Dr Irvine CA 92713

ALBERT, EDWARD GEOFFREY, consulting aerospace systems engineer; b. Staten Island, N.Y., Nov. 12, 1931; s. William Henry and Alice Sargent (Merrick) A.; A.B., Wagner Coll., 1953; postgrad. U. N.Mex., 1954; M.S., NYU, 1960; m. Stella L. Girten, Jan. 3, 1977; children by a previous marriage—James E., Bruce H. With, U.S. Weather Bur., Satellite Center, Suitland, Md., 1959-66, OIC, TIROS I and III joint data teams, 1960-61, NIMBUS Data Utilization mgr., 1962-65; chief GSFC Project Office ESSA, Rockville, Md., 1966-69; chief spacecraft systems Nat. Oceanic and Atmospheric Adminstrn., Greenbelt, Md., 1969-74; with NASA, 1974-81, SMS/GOES Spacecraft mgr., Palo Alto, Calif., 1974-76, TDRSS systems engr., Redondo Beach, Calif., 1977-80, LANDSAT western region mgr., Santa Barbara, Calif., 1980-81; sr. staff engr. Martin Marietta, Vandenberg AFB, Calif., 1982—, space shuttle ops. planning, 1982-83, shuttle cargo integrator, 1984-86; cons., 1981—. Guest lectr. on meteorol. satellites U. Md., 1965-68. Served with USAF, 1953-57. Mem. AAAS, Am. Meteorol. Soc., Smithsonian Assn., Met. Opera Guild, San Francisco Opera Guild, Friends Am. Ballet. Contbr. articles in field to profl. jours. Home: 714 St Andrews Way Lompoc CA 93436

ALBERT, JERRY DAVID, research biochemist; b. Milw., June 6, 1937; s. Leo Paul and Mildred Lydia (Voissem) A.; m. Judith Josephine Brown, Dec. 30, 1961; children: Jill Janeen, Jennifer Dawn. BA, Occidental Coll., 1959; PhD, Iowa State U., 1964. Sr. scientist Philco-Ford, Newport Beach, Calif., 1964-67; postdoctoral fellow Salk Inst., La Jolla, Calif., 1967-68; asst. dir. clin. chemistry U. Hosp., San Diego, 1968-73; research biochemist Mercy Hosp., San Diego, 1973—; instr. chemistry Mesa Coll., San Diego, 1976-83. Contbr. articles to profl. jours. Grantee Phi Lambda Upsilon, 1964. Fellow Am. Sci. Affiliation; mem. The Endocrine Soc., Am. Chem. Soc., Nat. Registry in Clin. Chemistry, Am. Inst. Chemists (sr.). Democrat. Lutheran. Avocation: running. Home: 11223 Cascada Way San Diego CA 92124-2878 Office: Mercy Hosp and Med Ctr Med Research Facility 4077 5th Ave San Diego CA 92103-2180

ALBERTONI, KATHLEEN HELEN, speech pathologist; b. Inglewood, Calif., Oct. 27, 1955; d. Richard William and Lidia Margaret (Miretti) A. BA, Calif. State U., Long Beach, 1978; MA, Calif. State U., Los Angeles, 1982. Cert. clin. competence speech pathology. Speech and lang. specialist Los Angeles Unified Sch. Dist., 1982—; pvt. practice speech pathologist Los Angeles, 1984—. Mem. Am. Speech and Hearing Assn., Calif. Speech and Hearing Assn. Home and Office: 339 S Pomelo Apt H Monterey Park CA 91754

ALBERTSON, DAVID L., retail store management executive, consultant; b. Denver, July 1, 1942; s. Vernon Albertson and Dorothy (McCabe) Gibson; m. Barbara Howe, July 10, 1961 (div. 1975); children—Derik, Jeffrey, Douglas; m. Theresa G. Jarmuth, Dec. 14, 1976. Grad. Clover Park High Sch. Store mgr. The Bon Colombia Ctr., Kennewick, Wash., 1977-78, dir. central group stores, Seattle, 1978-79, v.p., store mgr. South Ctr., Seattle, 1979-80, v.p. stores, 1980-81; store mgr. Lamonts, Bellevue, Wash., 1981-82; v.p., dist. mgr. Lamonts and Sportswest, Trump Group, Seattle, 1982—. Mem. Transit Adv. Bd., Everett, Wash., 1975-76; chmn. United Way, Tri-Cities, Wash., 1976-77. Recipient Outstanding Service award Everett C. of C., 1975. Home: 30809 38th Ave S Auburn WA 98001

ALBERTY, RON L., federal agency administrator, meteorologist; b. Mt. Vernon, Mo., Feb. 4, 1937; s. Loy Gerald and Cleva Irene (Palmer) A.; married; children: Bryon Keith, Dea Ann. AS, Kans. City Jr. Coll., 1961; BS in Physics, U. Mo., 1963, MS in Meteorology, 1965, PhD in Atmospheric Physics, 1967. Prof. meteorology Naval Postgrad. Sch., Monterey, Calif., 1967-72; chief meteorol. research, sr. scientist Nat. Severe Storms Lab., Norman, Okla., 1972-80; dep. dir. Program for Regional Observing and Forecasting Services, Boulder, Colo., 1980-82, chief advanced systems, 1982-83, chief exploratory devel., 1983-85; area mgr. Ariz. Nat. Weather Service, Phoenix, 1985—; cons. Naval Weapons Ctr., 1969-72; adj. assoc. prof. U. Okla., Norman, 1975-83; adj. prof. Met. State, Denver, 1982-86; adj. prof. Ariz. State U., Phoenix, 1986—. Contbr. articles to profl. jours. Served with USAF, 1956-60. Recipient Excellence in Teaching award U.S. Naval Postgrad. Sch., 1972, Silver medal U.S. Dept. Commerce, 1983; NDEA Title IV fellow Dept. Edn., 1967. Fellow Coop. Inst. for Research in Atmosphere Colo. State U.; mem. Am. Meteorol. Soc. Democrat. Avocations: nutrition, health, fitness, travel, music. Home: 7866 E Cactus Wren Rd Scottsdale AZ 85253 Office: Nat Weather Service 2633 E Buckeye Rd Phoenix AZ 85034

ALBRECHT, GEOFFREY JOHN, safety engineer; b. Patrick AFB, Fla., Aug. 17, 1955; s. Stanley F. and Joan M. (Winter) A.; m. Shirlee A. Keyes, Aug. 4, 1979. BS in Environ. Health, Colo. State U., 1977. Cert. indsl. hygienist-in-tng. Am. Bd. Indsl. Hygiene. Sr. safety environ. health specialist Storage Tech., Louisville, Colo., 1978-84; corp. safety mgr. Pacific Resources, Inc., Honolulu, 1984-86, mgr. environ. and govtl. services, 1986—. Active Rep. Party, Honolulu, 1985—; fund raiser Jr. Achievement, Honolulu, 1985—. Mem. Am. Indsl. Hygiene Assn. (cert., treas. 1986—), Am. Soc. Safety Engrs. (sec. Hawaii chpt. 1986—). Avocations: snow skiing, golf, tennis, racquetball, reading. Home: 1487 Hiikala Pl 42 Honolulu HI 96816 Office: Pacific Resources Inc 733 Bishop St Honolulu HI 96813

ALBRIGHT, TED LYNN, banker; b. Grand Junction, Colo., July 15, 1946; s. Howard W. and Hazel E. (Lambert) A.; m. Sharon E. Stoker, June 29, 1966; children: Heidi E., Heather L. AC in Data Processing and Bus. Adminstrn., Mesa Coll., 1968. Programmer Valley Fed. Savs. and Loan, Grand Junction, 1968-74, asst. sec.-treas., 1974-76, asst. v.p., 1976-80, v.p., 1980-86, sr. v.p., 1986—; pres. Home Water Supply Co., Whitewater, Colo., 1970-74. Judge data processing Mesa Coll. Sci. Fair, Grand Junction, 1981-83; coach Little League Softball, Grand Junction, 1978-82. Mem. Fin. Mgrs. Soc. Inc., Data Processing Mgmt. Assn., Micro Computer Users Group, Classic Chevy Club (pres. 1984—). Avocations: old cars, hunting, skiing, softball.

ALCINDOR, LEWIS FERDINAND See ABDUL-JABBAR, KAREEM

ALCORN, STANLEY MARCUS, plant pathology educator; b. Modesto, Calif., June 18, 1926; s. Timothy Marshall and Marian (Boehne) A.; m. Esther Irene Eastvold, June 19, 1949; children: Steven R., Joseph M., Eric E., Mark B. AA, Modesto Jr. Coll., 1946; BS, U. Calif., Berkeley, 1948, PhD, 1954. Research asst. U. Calif., Berkeley, 1949-53, postdoctoral researcher, 1953-55; plant pathologist USDA, Tucson, 1955-63; assoc. prof. plant pathology U. Ariz., Tucson, 1963-65, prof., 1965—; cons. USDA, Australia, 1982; participant site rev. teams; reviewer grant proposals. Contbr. articles to profl. jours. Served with USAAC, 1944-45. Fellow AAAS; mem. Am. Phytopathol. Soc. (chmn. fin. com. 1976-82), Am. Soc. Hort. Sci., Agronomy Soc. Am., Guayule Rubber Soc. (pres. 1986—), Am. Soc. Microbiology, Sigma Xi (local pres. 1964-65). Republican. Methodist. Avocations: traveling, reading, ptnr. in peach ranch. Office: U Ariz Dept Plant Pathology Tucson AZ 85721

ALCORN, TROY GENE, clergyman; b. Sulphur Springs, Tex., Aug. 4, 1930; s. Mahlon Winifield and Quincy Blanche (Shrode) A.; m. Bobbie Yvonne McCrady, Sept. 1, 1950; children—Karen L. Havens, Chris Alan Alcorn, Gayle M. Haggard, Cynthia J. Morris. B.A., East Tex. State U., 1952; postgrad. Indsl. Coll. Armed Forces, 1972-73. Commd. U.S. Air Force, 1952, advanced through grades to col., 1971, ret., 1976; ordained to ministry, Christian Assembly, 1974; asst. pastor Christian Assembly, Vienna, Va., 1976-77, pastor, Colorado Springs, Colo., 1977—; mem. adv. bd. Mission to Am., Humble, Tex., Colorado Springs, Christian Homes, El Paso, Tex. Decorated Legion of Merit with oak leaf cluster, Meritorious Service medal, Air Force Commendation medal with oak leaf cluster. Home: 3812 Templeton Gap Rd Colorado Springs CO 80907 Office: 3812 Templeton Gap Rd Colorado Springs CO 80907

ALDEN, ELEANOR SPACKMAN, health science facility director, educator, psychotherapist; b. Coatesville, Pa., Feb. 7, 1947; d. John Worth and Ethel Shoemaker (Farley) Spackman; m. Thomas Cowan Manning, Oct. 19, 1985. BA, Earlham Coll., 1967; MBA, U. Puget Sound, 1976; MSW, U. Wash., 1976. Lic. social worker II. Social worker Planned Parenthood, Bucks County, Pa., 1972-73, Harborview Hosp., Seattle, 1976, 1978-80, St. Luke's Hosp., Denver, 1980-82; dir. behavioral sci. Mercy Family Medicine, Denver, 1982—; pvt. practice psychotherapy Denver, 1983—. Mem. Soc. Tchrs. of Family Medicine, Colo. Pub. Health Assn., Physicians for Social Responsibility, Nat. Assn. Social Workers, Acad. Cert. Social Workers (cert.). Democrat. Mem. Soc. of Friends. Avocations: camping, sailing, cycling, travel, crafts. Home: 1794 S Ivy St Denver CO 80224 Office: Mercy Family Medicine Residency Program 16th at Milwaukee St Denver CO 80206

ALDER, HENRY LUDWIG, mathematics educator; b. Duisburg, Fed. Republic Germany, Mar. 26, 1922; came to U.S., 1941; s. Ludwig and Otti (Gottschalk) A.; m. Benne B. Daniel, Apr. 8, 1963; 1 child, Lawrence J. AB in Chemistry and Math., U. Calif., Berkeley, 1942, PhD in Math., 1947. Instr. U. Calif., Berkeley, 1947-48; instr. U. Calif., Davis, 1948-49, asst. prof., 1949-55, assoc. prof., 1955-65, prof. math., 1965—; mem. Calif. State Bd. Edn., Sacramento, 1982-85. Author: (with Edward B. Roessler) Introduction to Probability and Statistics, 1960; contbr. articles to profl. jours. Served with USAF, 1944-45. Recipient Cert. of Merit, Nat. Council Tchrs. Maths., 1975. Mem. Math. Assn. Am. (sec. 1960-75, pres. 1977-78, Lester R. Ford award 1970, Disting. Service to Math. award 1980), Am. Math. Soc., Mu Alpha Theta (pres. 1956-59). Avocation: stamp collecting. Home: 724 Elmwood Dr Davis CA 95616 Office: U Calif Dept Math Davis CA 95616

ALDERETE, EDWARD CHARLES, neonatologist; b. El Paso, Tex., Nov. 26, 1946; s. Francisco and Esperanza (Rodriguez) A.; m. Sue Ann Myers, Aug. 12, 1978; children—Natalie Sue, Michelle Christine, Julie Ann. B.A., U. Tex.-El Paso, 1969; M.D., Stanford U., 1974. Diplomate Am. Bd. Pediatrics, Am. Bd. Neonatal/Perinatal Medicine. Intern Stanford U. Med. Ctr., Calif., 1974-75, resident in pediatrics, 1975-77, chief resident in pediatrics, 1977-78; practice medicine specializing in pediatrics, Santa Barbara, Calif., 1978-81, in neonatol/perinatal medicine, Anchorage, 1983—; fellow in neonatology U. Calif.-San Diego, 1981-83; dir. neonatal ICU, Providence Hosp., Anchorage, 1984-86; cons. neonatologist Anchorage Native Med. Ctr., 1983—; staff neonatologist Humana Hosp., Anchorage, 1983—. Fellow Am. Acad. Pediatrics; mem. AMA, Calif. Med. Assn., Alaska State Med. Assn., Santa Barbara Med. Soc. Democrat. Roman Catholic. Clubs: Stanford, Alaska Athletic (Anchorage). Home: 6710 Lawlor Circle Anchorage AK 99502 Office: Alaska Neonatal/Perinatal Assocs 3340 Providence Suite 366 Anchorage AK 99508

ALDERMAN, ROBERT FRANK, civil engineer; b. Los Angeles, Aug. 1, 1932; s. Frank Edward and Frances Louise (Adams) A.; m. Eunice Estrid Anderson, Sept. 11, 1953; children: Jeffrey, Karen. BCE, Stanford U., 1954. Registered profl. engr. Calif.; cert. fall out shelter analyst, water treatment operator, Calif. Engring. aide Calif. Div. Hwys., Los Angeles, 1952-53; design engr. Alderman and Swift, South Pasadena, Calif., 1955-58; asst. water supt. City of Alhambra, Calif., 1958-64; project engr. Toups Engring., Santa Ana, Calif., 1964-65; v.p. Willdan Assocs., Anaheim, Calif., 1966-79; dir. engring. San Luis Engring., Arroyo Grande, Calif., 1979—; instr. math and hydraulics Santa Ana Coll., 1970-79, water treatment Allen Hancock Coll., Santa Maria, Calif., 1980-83. Mem. ASCE (br. pres. 1983-85), Am. Pub. Works Assn. (chpt. v.p. 1983), Am. Water Works Assn., Inst. Transp. Engrs. (chmn. pub. relations com. 1978, award of Merit 1978), Coastal Counties Water Assn., Alpha Sigma Phi. Republican. Mem. Ch. of Nazarene. Lodge: Toastmasters. Avocations: golf, photography, travel, skiing, gardening. Home: 6080 Joan Pl San Luis Obispo CA 93401 Office: San Luis Engring Inc PO Box 1127 Arroyo Grande CA 93420

ALDERSON, GARY DEAN, biology educator; b. Pasadena, Calif., Sept. 20, 1950; s. Murry Dean Alderson and Dorothy Lorraine (Thomas) Carroll; children: Kristina Marie, Julie Marie; m. Pamela Ann Langguth, Jan. 22, 1983; stepchildren: Karen Lynn Wanzung, Lisa Ann Wanzung. BS, U. Redlands, 1972; MA in Biology, U. Calif., Santa Barbara, 1975, PhD in Biology, 1976. Instr. biology Palomar Coll., San Marcos, Calif., 1976—; faculty advisor Life Sci. Soc., Palomar Coll., 1976-83. Author: (book) Microbiology: Experiments and Lab Techniques, 1986, (computer programs) Quikxam, 1985, Micro ID, 1985. Named one of Outstanding Young Men of Am., 1978. Democrat. Home: 860 Hill Lane San Marcos CA 92069 Office: Palomar Coll 1140 W Mission Rd San Marcos CA 92069

ALDISSI, MAHMOUD ALI YOUSEF, research chemist; b. Jalameh, Jordan, Sept. 15, 1952; came to U.S., 1981.; s. Ali and Amneh (Hussein) A.; m. Barbara E. Townsend, Sept. 16, 1983; one child, Andrew A.T. BS in Chemistry, Université des Sciences et Techniques du Languedoc, Montpellier, France, 1976, MS in Polymer Chemistry, 1978, PhD in Polymer Sci., 1981. Postdoctoral fellow U. Pa., Phila., 1981-83; postdoctoral fellow Los Alamos (N.Mex.) Nat. Lab., 1983-84, research chemist, 1984—; instr. Ctr. Profl. Advancement, E. Brunswick, N.J., 1982—. Contbr. articles on polymer sci. to profl. jours.; patentee in field. Mem. Am. Chem. Soc. (mem. polymer and polymeric materials sci. and engring. divs.). Home: 2982 Corte de Espuelas Santa Fe NM 87505 Office: Los Alamos Nat Lab PO Box 1663 Los Alamos NM 87545

ALDOUS, MARY ELIZABETH KIDWELL, medical librarian; b. L.I., N.Y., July 8, 1942; d. Howard Grove and Muriel C. (O'Neill) K.; m.

Edmund Preston Aldous Jr., May 21, 1966; children: Sarah Mary, Brian Edmund, Rachel Elizabeth. BA in English, St. Joseph Coll., Emmitsburg, Md., 1964; MLS, Peabody Coll., 1965. Music cataloger Nashville Pub. Library, 1962-65; readers services librarian Marquette U., Milw., 1965-66; asst. reference librarian Calif. Western U., San Diego, 1966-67, Marine Corps Devel. and Edn. Command, Quantico, Va., 1967-68; reference librarian Naval Electronics Lab. Ctr., San Diego, 1969-78; librarian Naval Health Research Ctr., San Diego, 1978—; cons. in field, San Diego, 1970—. Leader Girl Scouts USA San Diego Imperial council, 1983—. Mem. Med. Library Assn. (vice-chmn., mil. sect. 1982-83), Med. Library Group, Spl. Libraries Assn. (bulletin editor San Diego chpt. 1973-76), Assn. Mental Health Librarians, Lambda Iota Tau, Beta Phi Mu. Democrat. Roman Catholic. Office: Wilkins Biomed Library Naval Health Research Ctr PO Box 85122 San Diego CA 92138-9174

ALDRICH, DANIEL GASKILL, JR., university chancellor; b. Northwood, N.H., July 12, 1918; s. Daniel Gaskill and Marian (Farnum) A.; m. Jean Hamilton, Aug. 23, 1941; children: Daniel Gaskill III, Elizabeth, Stuart Hamilton. B.S., U.R.I., 1939, D. Sc. (hon.), 1960; M.S., U. Ariz., 1941, D.H.L. (hon.), 1985; Ph.D., U. Wis., 1943, D.Sc. (hon.), 1982; D.H.L., U. Redlands, 1978, Chapman Coll., 1980, Nat. U., 1981. Research chemist U. Calif. Citrus Expt. Sta., Riverside, 1943-55; chmn. dept. soils and plant nutrition U. Calif., Davis and Berkeley, 1955-59; univ. dean agr. U. Calif.-Berkeley, 1959-62; chancellor U. Calif.-Irvine, 1962-84, chancellor emeritus, 1984—; acting chancellor U. Calif., Riverside, 1984-85, Santa Barabara, 1986—; dir. Pacific Mut. Co. Mem. exec. bd. Orange County council Boy Scouts Am.; bd. dirs. Big Brothers Orange County, SRI Internat., Internat. Vol. Services; trustee Pacific Sch. Religion. Served as maj., inf. AUS; lt. col. Res. Mem. AAAS (past pres. Pacific div.), Western Soc. Soil Sci. (pres.), Am. Soc. Agronomy (dir.), Nat. Acad. Scis. (agrl. edn. policy com., commn. on edn. in agr. and nat. resources), Nat. Assn. State Univs. and Land-Grant Colls., Soil Conservation Soc., Soil Sci. Soc. Am., Am. Soc. Hort. Sci. Mem. United Ch. Christ.

ALDRICH, DAVID LAWRENCE, public relations executive; b. Lakehurst Naval Air Sta., N.J., Feb. 21, 1948; s. Clarence Edward and Sarah Stiles (Andrews) A.; m. Benita Susan Massler, Mar. 17, 1974. B.A. in Communications, Calif. State U.-Dominguez Hills, 1976. Pub. info. technician City of Carson (Calif.), 1973-77; pub. relations dir./adminstrv. asst. Calif. Fed. Savs., Los Angeles, 1977-78; v.p., group supr. Hill & Knowlton, Los Angeles, 1978-81; v.p., mgr. Ayer Pub. Relations western div. N.W. Ayer, Los Angeles, 1981-84; pres. Aldrich and Assocs., Los Angeles, 1984—. Served with USAF, 1968-72. Democrat. Club: Los Angeles Athletic. Office: 550 Orange Ave #125 Long Beach CA 90802

ALDRICH, FRANKLIN DALTON, research physician; b. Detroit, Jan. 25, 1929; s. George Franklin and Ruth Markham (Dalton) A.; m. Margaret Joan Pearson, Mar. 22, 1952; children: Allison Aldrich Cobb, Janet D., George P.; m. Gertrude Melsom, Mar. 24, 1984. BS, Mich. State U., 1950; MA, Oreg. State U., 1953, PhD, 1954; MD, Case Western Res. U., 1962. Diplomate Am. Bd. Med. Toxicology. Intern U. Iowa Hosps., Iowa City, 1962-63; fellow in medicine U. Colo., Boulder, 1964-65; resident and chief resident Lemuel Shattuck Hosp., Boston, 1969-71; physician Colo. Dept. Pub. Health, Denver, 1966-69; asst. med. dir. MIT, Cambridge, 1971-76; med. dir. Climax (Colo.) Molybdenum Co., 1976-77; health effects research mgr. IBM, Boulder, Colo., 1977—; mem. com. mil. environ. research Nat. Acad. Scis., 1976-80; mem. toxicology adv. com. U.S. Consumer Product Safety Com., 1982-85; clin. asst. prof. medicine U. Colo. Health Scis. Ctr., Denver, 1978—. Contbr. articles to profl. jours. Served with AUS, 1954-56. Case Meml. scholar, Mich. State Coll., 1948. Fellow ACP (Mead Johnson resident scholar 1970), Am. Acad. Clin. Toxicology (pres. 1980-82). Episcopalian. Avocations: fishing, amateur radio. Office: IBM 415/021 PO Box 1900 Boulder CO 80302

ALDRICH, MICHAEL RAY, organization executive; b. Vermillion, S.D., Feb. 7, 1942; s. Ray J. and Lucile W. (Hamm) A.; A.B., Princeton, 1964; M.A., U. S.D., 1965; Ph.D., SUNY, 1970; m. Michelle Cauble, Dec. 26, 1977. Fulbright tutor Govt. Arts and Commerce Coll., Indore, Madhya Pradesh, India, 1965-66; founder Lemar Internat., 1966-71; mem. faculty Sch. Critical Studies, Calif. Inst. Arts, Valencia, 1970-72; workshop leader Esalen Inst., San Francisco, 1972; co-founder, co-dir. AMORPHIA, Inc., The Cannabis Coop., non-profit nat. marijuana research and reform group, Mill Valley, Calif., 1969-74; exec. curator Fitz Hugh Ludlow Meml. Library, San Francisco, 1974—. Freelance writer, photographer, lectr., cons. on drug research, and sociolegal reform specializing in drug laws and history to various colls., drug confs., publishers, service groups; cons. Commn. of Inquiry into Non-Med. Use of Drugs, Ottawa, Ont., 1973; research aide, select com. on control marijuana Calif. Senate, 1974. Bd. dirs. Ethno-Pharmacology Soc., 1976—. Calif. Marijuana Initiative, 1971-74; mem. nat. adv. bd. Nat. Orgn. for Reform of Marijuana Laws, 1976—. Author: The Dope Chronicles 1850-1950, 1979, Coricancha, The Golden Enclosure, 1983; co-author: High Times Ency. of Recreational Drugs, 1978, Fiscal Costs of California Marijuana Law Enforcement, 1986; editor: Marijuana Review, 1968-74, Ludlow Library Newsletter, 1974—; contbg. author Cocaine Handbook, 1981; mem. editorial rev. bd. Jour. Psychoactive Drugs, 1981—; research photographer Life mag., 1984; contbg. editor High Times, 1979-86; contbr. articles to profl. publs. Office: PO Box 640346 San Francisco CA 94164

ALDRIDGE, NOEL HENRY, radiologist; b. Durban, S.Africa, Dec. 19, 1924; s. Percy Verey and Isaleine (Wilson) A.; came to U.S., 1955, naturalized, 1967; M.B., Ch.B., U. Cape Town (S.Africa), 1951; D.M.R.D., Roy Coll., London, 1955; L.M.C.C., Royal Coll. Can., 1958, m. Theresa Horton, Dec. 19, 1981; children by previous marriage—Anthony Mark, Andrea Marie. Intern, Groot Schuur Hosp., Cape Town, 1951-52; asst. govt. pathologist, Cape Town, 1952-53; sr. house officer Leeds (Eng.) Gen. Hosp., 1953-55; postgrad. tng. Karolinska Sjukhusset, Stockholm, 1955; fellow Johns Hopkins Hosp., 1955, instr. radiology, 1956; asso. radiologist, instr. Victoria Hosp.-U. Western Ont., 1956-59; clin. fellow in radiology Mass. Gen. Hosp. and Harvard Med. Sch., 1960-61, asso. radiologist, 1961-62; radiologist with pvt. group, Seattle, 1962-63; dir. dept. radiology Stevens Meml. Hosp., Edmonds, Wash., 1963—; pres. Stevens Radiologists, Inc. Diplomate Am. Bd. Radiology. Fellow Royal Coll. Physicians Can., Am. Coll. Radiology; mem. AMA, Canadian, Brit., Wash. State med. assns., King County Med. Soc., Am. Coll. Radiology, Royal Coll. Radiologists (London), Brit. Inst. Radiology, Canadian Assn. Radiologists, Johns Hopkins Radiologic Alumni Assn., Wash. State Radiologic Assn., Coll. Physicians and Surgeons of B.C., Coll. Physicians and Surgeons of Ont., Aircraft Owners and Pilots Assn., Wash. Pilots Assn., Am. Forestry Assn., Wildlife Fedn., Les Amis du Vin. Episcopalian. Club: Elks. Contbr. articles to profl. jours. Office: Dept Radiology Stevens Meml Hosp Edmonds WA 98020

ALDRIDGE, SUSAN COCKINGS, public administrator; b. Dodgeville, Wis., Nov. 24, 1951; d. Kenneth Gordon and Mary Patricia (Davis) Cockings; m. M. Gene Aldridge, June 16, 1981. BA, Colo. Women's Coll., 1977; M of Pub. Adminstrn., U. Colo., 1987 . Research assoc. Swedish Med. Ctr., Englewood, Colo., 1973; v.p. internat. health planning and policy research Aldridge & Assocs., Denver, 1974-78; planner, aging services div. Denver Regional Council Govts., 1978-80, dir. aging services, 1980—. Mem. policy bd. United Way, 1980-84; bd. dirs. Nat. Assn. Area Agys. on Aging, 1982-86; chmn. fiscal com. Colo. Assn. Area Agys. on Aging, 1981-83; mem. Mile-High Cable Coordinating Council, Denver, 1987. Recipient Recognition award Gov. Lamm, 1981. Office: 2480 W 26th Ave Suite 200 B Denver CO 80211

ALERU, JAMES ADEBAYO, accountant; b. Igbaja, Kwara, Nigeria, June 6, 1947; came to U.S., 1969; s. Joshua and Ruth Aleru. BA, Tabor Coll., 1973; postgrad., Calif. State U., Fresno, 1974-1976. Auditor, appraiser Fresno County Assessors Office, 1977—; acct. Davis and Lotia, Fresno, 1984, Shakir Lotia CPA, Fresno, 1985—. Avocations: tennis, soccer, carpentry, philosophical dialogue. Home: 5739 N Cedar #104 Fresno CA 93710 Office: Fresno County Assessors Office PO Box 1146 Fresno CA 93710

ALEXANDER, CHARLES MICHAEL, endocrinologist; b. N.Y.C., May 5, 1952; s. Saunders P. and Anna (Stein) A.; m. Lynn Suzanne Pollyea, Sept. 12, 1982; children: Danielle Cory, Michael J.. BA, Johns Hopkins U., 1973; MD, U. So. Calif., 1977. Diplomate Am. Bd. Internal Medicine, Am. Bd. Endocrinology and Metabolism. Intern U. So. Calif. Med. Ctr., Los Angeles, 1977-78, resident, 1978-80, fellow, 1980-82; asst. clin. prof. U. So. Calif. Sch. Medicine, 1982—; gen. practice medicine Inglewood, Calif., 1982—; med. dir. diabetes unit Daniel Freeman Marina Hosp., Marina Del Rey, Calif.; med. dir. diabetes dept. Daniel Freeman Meml. Hosp., Inglewood. Contbr. articles on internal medicine to profl. jours. Mem. ACP (fellow 1983), AAAS, Am. Diabetes Assn. (Los Angeles chpt. pres.-elect 1985-86, pres. 1986-87, chmn. patient edn. com.), The Endocrine Soc., Am. Fedn. Clin. Research, N.Am. Assn. Advancement Sci., Am. Soc. Internal Medicine, Calif. Med. Soc., Los Angeles Acad. Medicine, Los Angeles Soc. Internal Medicine, Los Angeles County Med. Assn., Crosstown Endocrine Club. Avocations: tennis, racquetball, hiking, bicycling. Office: 323 N Prairie Ave Suite 334 Inglewood CA 90301

ALEXANDER, DAVID DEAN, interior architect, designer; b. Phoenix, July 15, 1954; s. William Plato Alexander and Sophia (Felakos) Simos. BS, U. Utah, 1978; assoc. interior design, Parson's Sch. Design, N.Y.C., 1980. Assoc. designer Shean Nesbitt, Inc., N.Y.C., 1979-81; dir. Waldorf Astoria, N.Y.C., 1981-83; pres. David Alexander Design, N.Y.C. and Salt Lake City, 1983—; assoc. Wertheim & Assoc., N.Y.C., 1982—. Bd. dirs. Salt Lake City C. of C., 1985. Mem. Am. Soc. Interior Designers, U. Utah Alumni Assn. (bd. dirs. 1986—), Pres. Club, Kappa Sigma. Greek Orthodox. Avocations: snow and water skiing, sailing. Home: 2322 Walker Ln Salt Lake City UT 84117 Office: David Alexander Design PO Box 17729 Salt Lake City UT 84117

ALEXANDER, FRED SHARPE, III, architect, general contractor; b. Houston, July 21, 1941; s. Fred Sharpe and Bessie Grace (Tauber) A.; m. Carolyn Ann Compton, Apr. 16, 1966; 1 child, Katherine Rene; m. 2d, Susan Elinor Hjertman, June 11, 1977; children—Zachary Lee, Andrew Tauber. Student Tex. A&M U., 1960; B.Arch., Tex. Tech. Coll., 1967. Registered architect, Colo., N.Mex., Nebr., Ariz., Wyo., Kans. Draftsman archtl. firms, Denver, 1967-72; project architect W. C. Muchow Assocs., Denver, 1970-72; prin. Alexander Assocs. Architects, Denver, 1972-85; v.p. architecture and enging. Internat. design and Construction Corp., Denver, 1985—; chmn. bd. Constrn. 4 Inc., Denver, 1976-86; pres. Comml. Design Assocs., Denver, 1981—; pres. Alexander Industries; instr. U. Colo.-Denver Grad. Sch., 1975-77. Active Boy Scouts Am., 1968-73. Mem. AIA (sec. Denver chpt. 1976, dir. 1974, membership chmn. 1974-76), Nat. Council Archtl. Registration Bds. (grader nat. exams. 1984-86), Eastern Rockies Rugby Football Union (sec. 1975-77). Republican. Home: 1193 S Biscay St Aurora CO 80017 Office: Comml Design Assocs PO Box 440128 Aurora CO 80044

ALEXANDER, GEORGE JONATHON, legal educator, former dean; b. Berlin, Germany, Mar. 8, 1931; s. Walter and Sylvia (Grill) A.; m. Katharine Violet Sziklai, Sept. 6, 1958; children: Susan Katina, George Jonathon II. A.B. with maj. honors, U. Pa., 1953, J.D. cum laude, 1969; LL.M., Yale U., 1965, J.S.D., 1969. Bar: Ill. 1960, N.Y. 1961, Calif. 1974. Instr. law, Bigelow fellow U. Chgo., 1959-60; instr. internat. relations Naval Res. Officers Sch., Forrest Park, Ill., 1959-60; prof. law Syracuse U. Coll. Law, 1960-70, assoc. dean, 1968-69; vis. prof. law U. So. Calif., 1963; prof. law U. Santa Clara (Calif.) Law Sch., 1970—, dean, 1970-85; vis. scholar Stanford Law Sch., 1985-86; dir. Inst. Internat. and Comparative Law, 1986—; cons. in field. Author: Civil Rights, U.S.A., Public Schools, 1963, Honesty and Competition, 1967, Jury Instructing on Medical Issues, 1966, Cases and Materials on Space Law, 1971, The Aged and the Need for Surrogate Management, 1972, Commercial Torts, 1973, U.S. Antitrust Laws, 1980, also articles, chpts. in books, one film. Dir. Domestic and Internat. Bus. Problems Honors Clinic, Syracuse U., 1966-69, Regulations in Space Project, 1968-70; ednl. cons. Comptroller Gen., U.S., 1977—; Nat. Sr. Citizens Law Center, 1983—, pres., 1986—; co-founder Am. Assn. Abolition Involuntary Mental Hospitalization, 1970, dir., 1970-83. Served with USN, 1953-56. U.S. Navy scholar U. Pa., 1949-52; Law Boards scholar, 1956-59; Sterling fellow Yale, 1964-65; recipient Ralph E. Kharas Civil Liberties award, 1970, Owens award as Alumnus of Yr., 1984. Mem. Calif. Bar Assn. (first chmn. com. legal problems of aging), Assn. Am. Law Schs., Soc. Am. Law Tchrs. (dir., pres. 1979), AAUP (chpt. pres. 1962), N.Y. Civil Liberties Union (chpt. pres. 1965, dir., v.p. 1966-70), Am. Acad. Polit. and Social Sci., Order of Coif, Justinian Honor Soc., Phi Alpha Delta (chpt. faculty adviser 1967-70). Home: 11600 Summit Wood Rd Los Altos Hills CA 94022 Office: Univ Santa Clara Santa Clara CA 95053

ALEXANDER, JAMES HERBERT, III, cognitive engineer, researcher; b. Endicott, N.Y., Oct. 4, 1954; s. James Herbert and Laverne M. (Zorn) A.; m. Laurie Jane Wadman, July 29, 1978; 1 child, Jamie Zoe. BS in Psychology, Syracuse U., 1976; MA in Psychology, U. Colo., 1978, PhD in Psychology, 1982. Mem. tech. staff Bell Labs, Piscataway, N.J., 1978-80; sr. scientist Tektronix, Beaverton, Oreg., 1983-87; mem. tech. staff U.S. West Advanced Techs., Englewood, Co., 1987—. Contbr. articles to profl. jours. Mem. IEEE, Assn. Computing Machinery, Am. Assn. Artificial Intelligence. Democrat. Methodist. Avocations: skiing, running, writing. Home: 9429 Yale Ln Highlands Ranch CO 80126 Office: US West Advanced Techs 6200 S Quebec St Englewood CO 80111

ALEXANDER, JOHN DAVID, JR., college president; b. Springfield, Tenn., Oct. 18, 1932; s. John David and Mary Agnes (McKinnon) A.; m. Catharine Coleman, Aug. 26, 1956; children: Catharine McKinnon, John David III, Julia Mary. BA, Southwestern at Memphis, 1953; student, Louisville Presbyn. Theol. Sem., 1953-54; D.Phil. (Rhodes Scholar), Oxford (Eng.) U., 1957; LL.D., U. So. Calif., Occidental Coll., 1970, Centre Coll. of Ky., 1971; L.H.D., Loyola Marymount U., 1983; LittD, Rhodes Coll., 1986. Assoc. prof. San Francisco Theol. Sem., 1957-65; pres. Southwestern at Memphis, 1965-69, Pomona Coll., Claremont, Calif., 1969—; Am. sec. Rhodes Scholarship Trust, 1981—; mem. commn. liberal learning Assn. Am. Colls., 1966-69, Assn. Am. Colls. (commn. instl. affairs), 1971-74; mem. commn. colls. So. Assn. Colls. and Schs., 1966-69; mem. Nat. Commn. on Acad. Tenure, 1971-72; dir. Gt. Western Fin. Corp.; Bd. dirs. Community TV of So. Calif., Louisville Presbyn. Theol. Sem., 1966-69; trustee Tchrs. Ins. and Annuity Assn., 1970—, Woodrow Wilson Nat. Fellowship Found., 1978—; bd. dirs. Am. Council on Edn., 1981-84, Nat. Assn. Ind. Colls. and Univs., 1984—. Mem. Am. Oriental Soc., Soc. Bib. Lit., Soc. Religion in Higher Edn., Phi Beta Kappa Alumni in So. Calif. (pres. 1974-76), Phi Beta Kappa, Omicron Delta Kappa, Sigma Nu. Clubs: Century (N.Y.C.); University (Los Angeles), Calif. (Los Angeles); Bohemian (San Francisco).

ALEXANDER, NANCY TOLAND, personnel and administration director; b. San Francisco, June 18, 1934; d. John Charles and Florence Jane (Williamson) T.; m. Alex Ashur Alexander, June 11, 1952; children: Denise Longacre, Steven, William, Celeste Godfrey, Suzanne. Personnel mgr. Books, Inc., San Francisco, 1965-79; asst. dir. adminstrn. and personnel Toshiba Semiconductor, Sunnyvale, Calif., 1979—. Mem. Am. Soc. Personnel Adminstrs. Avocations: book collecting. Home: 3990 Blue Gum Dr San Jose CA 95127 Office: Toshiba Semiconductor USA Inc 1220 Midas Way Sunnyvale CA 94086

ALEXANDER, NICHOLAS MICHAEL, research biochemist, educator; b. Boise, Idaho, June 30, 1925; s. Michael A. and Bella (Mastoris) A.; m. Penny Angelides, Feb. 1, 1953; children: Leon, Michael, George. AA, Boise Jr. Coll., 1947; AB, U. Calif., Berkeley, 1950, PhD, 1955. Cert. Am. Bd. Clin. Chemistry. Prin. scientist VA Hosp., West Haven, Conn., 1955-63; lectr. biochemistry Yale U. Sch. Medicine, New Haven, 1955-63, assoc. prof. biochemistry, 1963-70; prof. pathology U. Calif., San Diego, 1970—, dir. clin. chemistry, 1979—. Served as sgt. U.S. Army, 1943-45. Mem. AAAS, Am. Assn. Clin. Chemists (editorial bd. 1985—), Am. Soc. Biol. Chemists, Am. Thyroid Assn. (Van Meter award 1960), Am. Chem. Soc., Endocrine Soc.. Office: U Calif Med Ctr 225 Dickinson St San Diego CA 92103

ALEXANDER, THOMAS GLEN, history educator, cultural center administrator; b. Logan, Utah, Aug. 8, 1935; s. Glen M. and Violet Bird Alexander; m. Marilyn Johns; children: Brooke Ann, Brenda Lynn, Tracy Lee, Mark Thomas, Paul Johns. AS, Weber State Coll., 1955; BS, Utah State U., 1960, MS, 1961; PhD, U. Calif., Berkeley, 1965. Asst. prof. history Brigham Young U., Provo, Utah, 1964-68, assoc. prof., 1968-73, prof. 1973—, assoc. dir. Charles Redd Ctr., 1973-80, dir. Charles Redd Ctr., 1980—; adj. assoc. prof. history, So. Ill. U., Carbondale, 1970-71; vis. prof. Utah State U., Logan, 1965; vis. instr. NDEA, Kearney (Nebr.) State Coll., 1966; instr. Salzburg, Austria, 1968. Author: Clash of Interests, 1977, Mormonism in Transition, 1986; co-author: Mormons and Gentiles, 1985. Grantee Utah Endowment for Humanities, 1975, 76, 70-80. Fellow Utah State Hist. Soc.; mem. Orgn. Am. Historians (membership com. 1972—), Mormon History Assn. (pres. 1974-75, Best Article award 1968, 76, 80), Assn. Utah Historians (pres. 1983-85), Western History Assn. (parlimentarian 1978—), Utah Bd. State History (chmn. 1985—, bd. editors 1968-79). Democrat. Mormon. Home: 3325 Mohican Ln Provo UT 84604 Office: Brigham Young U Charles Redd Ctr 4069 HBLL Provo UT 84602

ALEXANDERSON, GERALD LEE, mathematician, educator, writer; b. Caldwell, Idaho, Nov. 13, 1933; s. Albert William and Alvina (Gertlar) A. B.A., U. Oreg., 1955; M.S., Stanford U., 1958. Instr. math. Santa Clara U., Calif., 1958-62, asst. prof., 1962-68, coordinator honors program, 1965-67, assoc. prof., 1968-72, prof., 1972—, Michael and Elizabeth Valeriote prof., 1979—, chmn. dept., 1967—, dir. Div. Math. and Natural Scis., 1981—; lectr. Stanford U., summers 1958, 59, Geneva, 1964-65; assoc. dir. William Lowell Putnam Math. Competition, 1975—. Author: (with Hillman) Functional Trigonometry, 1961, rev. edit., 1971, Algebra and Trigonometry, 1963, Algebra Through Problem Solving, 1966, First Undergraduate Course in Abstract Algebra, 1973, rev. edit., 1983, (with Hillman, Klosinski and Logothetti) The Santa Clara Silver Anniversary Contest Book, 1985, (with Albers) Mathematical People, 1985, (with Klosinski and Larson) The William Lowell Putnam Mathematical Competition, Problems and Solutions, 1965-1984, 1985, (with Albers and Reid) International Mathematical Congresses/ An Illustrated History 1893-86, 1986, (with Hillman and Grassl) Discrete and Combinatorial Mathematics, 1987; assoc. editor: Two-Year College Math. Jour., 1979-84, Am. Math. Monthly, 1983-86; editor: Math. Mag., 1986—; contbr. articles to math. jours. Trustee Santa Clara U., 1979-86. Recipient Pres.'s Spl. Recognition award Santa Clara U., 1978. Mem. Am. Math. Soc., Math. Assn. Am. (sec.-treas. No. Calif. sect. 1967-70, chmn. 1971-72, nat. bd. govs. 1975-78, 84—, com. on undergrad. program in math. 1977-86, com. on Dolciani Math. Exposition series 1977-84, 1st v.p. 1984-86 com. on publs.), Math. Assn. Am. (bd. cons. 1982—), Fibonacci Assn. (pres. 1980-84), Phi Beta Kappa, Sigma Xi, Pi Mu Epsilon, Pi Delta Phi, Phi Eta Sigma. Home: 1133 Highland Ave Santa Clara CA 95050

ALEXIS, JODY RAE, real estate broker; b. Langdon, N.D., Mar. 2, 1940; d. Raymond and Ada (Widwick) Armstrong; student Stephens Coll., 1959-61; B.A., U. Nebr., 1963; M.A., U. Colo., 1968; J.D., U. Denver, 1971; div.; 1 son, Clark Kendall. Asst. dir. USO, Colorado Springs, Colo., 1964-65; asst. to dir. adminstrn. Aircraft Mechanics, Inc., Colorado Springs, 1965-67; pub. relations dir. Red Ram of Am. Corp., Colorado Springs, 1967-70, The Woodmar Corp., 1971; admitted to Colo. bar, 1971; exec. dir. Rocky Mountain Land Devel. Assn., Denver, 1970-74; pres. Alexis & Assocs., Denver, 1974—; individual practice law, Denver, 1974—; broker assoc. cons. Indian Mountain Corp., 1977—; broker assoc. Rimax of Cherry Creek; dir. Colo. Mgmt. Rocky Mountain Log Homes Inc., Designs Internationale. Bd. dirs. Colo. Conventions and Reservations, 1974—; chmn. Denver Art Mus. Mem. Denver Center for Performing Arts, Jr. Symphony Guild. Republican. Roman Catholic. Home: 1313 Williams St Denver CO 80218

ALF, EDWARD ALFRED, telecommunications management consultant; b. Great Falls, Mont., Oct. 17, 1930; s. Alfred I. Alf and Ruth (Walker) Alvarez; m. Marianne Ruth Billaud, May 6, 1961; 1 child, Lee Joanne. Student Mont. Sch. Mines, 1948-49, Mont. State Coll., 1953-55. Cert. engr. Chief communications Holmes & Narver, Las Vegas, Nev., 1969-72; chief engr. City of Portland, Oreg., 1972-76; cons., Portland, 1976-77; prin. engr. Fluor Engrs., Irvine, Calif., 1977-83, project mgr., 1983—. Pres. Mahana Homeowners Assn., Orange, Calif., 1978-83, 85-86. Served with USAF, 1951-52. Mem. Radio Club Am., Telecommunications Assn., Internat. Platform Assn. Republican. Episcopalian. Home: 400 S Flower St Apt 84 Orange CA 92668 Office: Fluor Engrs 3333 Michelson Dr Irvine CA 92730

ALFARO, FELIX BENJAMIN, physician; b. Managua, Nicaragua, Oct. 22, 1939; came to U.S., 1945, naturalized, 1962; s. Agustin Jose and Amanda Julieta (Barillas) A.; student (State scholar) U. San Francisco, 1958-59, 61-62; M.D., Creighton U., 1967; m. Carmen Heide Meyer, Aug. 14, 1965; children—Felix Benjamin, Mark. Clk., Pacific Gas & Electric Co., San Francisco, 1960-61; intern St. Mary's Hosp., San Francisco, 1967; resident Scenic Gen. Hosp., Modesto, Calif., 1970; practice family medicine, Watsonville, Calif., 1971—; active staff Watsonville Community Hosp., 1971—. Served to capt., M.C., U.S. Army, 1968-69. Lic. physician, Nebr., La., Calif. Diplomate Am. Bd. Family Practice. Fellow Am. Acad. Family Practice; mem. AMA, Calif. Med. Assn., Santa Cruz County Med. Soc., 38th Parrallel Med. Soc. of Korea Nat Rifle Assn., VFW. Republican. Roman Catholic. Office: 30 Brennan St Watsonville CA 95016

ALFING, NORMAN LEE, mechanical engineer; b. South Haven, Mich., May 31, 1933; s. William Edward and Geraldine S. (Brooks) A.; m. Nancy Mae Zook, Aug. 22, 1953 (div. May 1976); children Gwen Lee Yeaman, Brian David. Student, Western Mich. U., BS in Indsl Supervision and Bus., 1959. Tool and die maker Bohn Alum and Brass Corp., South Haven, Mich., 1952-59; fuel and electronics machinist Ordnance Stas., Aberdeen, Md., Ft. Carson, Colo., Orleans, France, 1955-57; engr. process and devel. St. Regis Panalyte div., Kalamazoo, Mich., 1953-61; indsl. engr. Borg Warner-Ingersoll div., Kalamazoo, 1961-62; engr. applications and sales Armstrong Machine Works, Three Rivers, Mich., 1974-77; asst. to chief engr. Armstrong Mach. Works, Three Rivers, Mich., 1962-69, mgr. European facility, 1969-71; with Sturgis (Mich.) Foundry, 1972-74; mgr. plant Packless Industries, Mt. Wolf, Pa. and Waco, Tex., 1977; pvt. practice constrn. Three Rivers, 1978; project mgr. Gen. Motors plan Miller Davis Constrn. Mgrs., Three Rivers, 1978; engr. and mgr. tech. service Dock Foundry, Three Rivers, 1979; manuf. engr. Hughes Aircraft Co., Tucson, 1979-83, mem. tech. staff, 1983-84, staff engr., 1984—. Patentee in field. Pres. PTA, Portage, Mich., 1967. Served with U.S. Army, 1955-57. Mem. Soc. Manuf. Engrs., Soc. Advancement Mgmt. Congregationalist. Lodges: Masons (Steward 1958-59), Elks. Home: 2750 Camino Iturbide Green Valley AZ 85614 Office: Hughes Aircraft Co PO Box 11337 Bldg 808 K6 Tucson AZ 85734

ALFIN-SLATER, ROSLYN BERNIECE, biochemist, nutritionist, educator; b. Bklyn., July 28, 1916; d. Sam and Lillian (Rubinsky) A.; m. Grant G. Slater, July 30, 1948. B.A., Bklyn. Coll., 1936; A.M., Columbia U., 1942, Ph.D., 1946. Asst. in charge lecture div., chemistry dept. Bklyn. Coll., 1938-43, tutor gen. inorganic chemistry, 1943, instr. inorganic chemistry, qualitative analysis, evenings 1946-48; asst. instr. inorganic chemistry, exptl. phys. chemistry, food analysis Columbia U., 1943-45; research fellow Corn Industries Research Found., 1945-46; instr. biochemistry NYU Coll. Dentistry, 1945-46; research chemist indsl. enzymes Takamine Labs., Clifton, N.J., 1946-47; research fellow Sloan Kettering Inst. Cancer Research, 1947-48; research assoc. dept. biochemistry and nutrition U. So. Calif. Sch. Medicine, 1948-52, vis. asst. prof., 1952-56, vis. asso. prof., 1956-59; asso. prof. nutrition UCLA, 1959-65, prof., 1965—, prof. biol. chemistry, 1971—, div. head, environ. and nutritional sci. Sch. Pub. Health, 1969-77, asst. dean acad. affairs Sch. Pub. Health, 1983—; Mem. nutrition study sect. NIH, 1968-72; mem. com. for dietary allowances, food and nutrition bd. NRC, 1970-74, mem. nat. com., internat. union nutritional scis., 1974—, mem. food and nutrition bd., 1975-81, vice chmn., 1978-79. Editor: Human Nutrition—A Comprehensive Treatise, 5 vols., 1980; Contbr. to sci. books, jours.; mem. editorial bd. Jour. Nutrition, 1966-70, Advances in Lipid Research, 1970-74, Am. Jour. Clin. Nutrition, 1975-78; Assoc. editor: jour. Lipids, 1972-78, AGE, Jour. Am. Aging Assn, 1977—, Nutrition & the M.D, 1974—, Drug-Nutrient Interactions, 1980—. Recipient nat. merit award for outstanding achievement in pub. health Delta Omega, 1985. Fellow AAAS, Am. Heart Assn. (council on arteriosclerosis), Am. Pub. Health Assn., Am. Inst. Nutrition (Osborne and Mendel award 1970, Borden award 1981); mem. N.Y. Acad. Scis., Am. Soc. Biol. Chemists, Soc. Exptl. Biology and Medicine, Am. Oil Chemists Soc., Am. Inst. Nutrition (treas. 1977-80), Soc. Nutrition Edn. (pres. 1978-79), Internat. Soc. Cardiology, Am. Dietetic

Assn. (hon.), Sigma Xi, Phi Sigma, Iota Sigma Pi, Omicron Nu (hon.). Home: 986 Somera Rd Los Angeles CA 90077

ALFORD, ROBERT ROSS, sociologist; b. Stockton, Calif., Apr. 18, 1928; s. Ellsworth and Grace (Ross) A.; m. Gloria Kramer, June 18, 1949; children—Heidi, Jonathan, Elissa. A.B., U. Calif., Berkeley, 1950, M.A., 1952, Ph.D., 1961. Lectr. sociology U. Calif., Berkeley, 1959-61; mem. faculty U. Wis., 1961-74, prof. sociology, 1966-74; asso. dir. Survey Research Lab., 1961-63; vis. prof. govt. U. Essex, Eng., 1966-67; vis. fellow Netherlands Inst. Advanced Study, 1981-82; vis. prof. sociology Columbia U., 1970-71, 80-81; prof. sociology U. Calif.-Santa Cruz, 1974—, chmn. bd. studies in sociology, 1974-76, dir. Interdisciplinary Grad. Program in Sociology, 1976-79, acad. adminstr. research unit in instl. analysis and social policy, 1982—. Author: Party and Society, 1963, Bureaucracy and Participation: Political Cultures in Four Wisconsin Cities, 1969, Health Care Politics, 1975, Powers of Theory, 1985; editor: Stress and Contradiction in Advanced Capitalist Societies, 1975. Mem. Am. Sociol. Assn., Am. Polit. Sci. Assn. (Woodrow Wilson Found. award 1976). Office: Univ Calif Merrill Coll Dept Sociology Santa Cruz CA 95064

ALFVÉN, HANNES OLOF GOSTA, physicist; b. May 30, 1908; Ph.D., U. Uppsala, 1934. Prof. theory of electricity Royal Inst. Tech., Stockholm, 1940-45, prof. electronics, 1945-63, prof. plasma physics, 1963-73; prof. dept. applied physics and info. sci. U. Calif.-San Diego, 1967—; mem. Swedish Sci. Adv. Council, 1963-67; past mem. Swedish AEC; past gov. Swedish Def. Research Inst., Swedish Atomic Energy Co.; past sci. adv. Swedish Govt.; pres. Pugwash Confs. on Sci. and World Affairs, 1970-75; mem. panel on comets and asteroids NASA. Recipient Nobel prize for physics, 1970; Lomonsov gold medal USSR Acad. Scis., 1971; Franklin medal, 1971, Bowie Gold medal Am. Geophysical Union, 1987. Fellow Royal Soc. (Eng.); mem. Swedish Acad. Scis., Akademia NAUK (USSR), Nat. Acad. Scis. (fgn. asso.), others. Author: Cosmical Electrodynamics, 1950; On the Origin of the Solar System, 1954; Cosmical Electrodynamics: Fundamental Principles, 1963; Worlds-Antiworlds, 1966; The Tale of the Big Computer, 1968; Atom, Man and the Universe, 1969; Living on the Third Planet, 1972; Evolution of the Solar System, 1976; Cosmic Plasma, 1981. Office: Univ Calif Dept Elec Engring & Computer Scis La Jolla CA 92093 Other: Dept Plasma Physics,, Royal Inst of Tech,, S-100-44 Stockholm 70 Sweden

ALI, MIR KURSHEED, mathematician; b. Hyderabad, India, Apr. 16, 1926; came to U.S., 1961, naturalized, 1974; s. Mir Warris and Haleema (Begum) A.; m. Mohammadi Begum, Jan. 13, 1952; 2 children. B.Sc., Osmania U., Hyderabad, 1947, M.A., 1949; M.S., Mont. State U., 1964; Ph.D., Wash. State U., 1968. Lectr. math. City Coll. Hyderabad, 1949-52; lectr. math. Sci. Coll., Saifabad, India, 1952-58; head dept. Sci. Coll., 1958-61; part time faculty Mont. State U., 1961-64; instr. Wash. State U., 1964-66, part time faculty, 1966-68; mem. faculty Calif. State U., Fresno, 1968—; prof. math. Calif. State U., 1975—; vis. prof. Abadan (Iran) Inst. Tech., 1976-77. Author articles. NSF fellow, 1965; Edwin W. Rice fellow, 1966. Mem. Am. Math. Soc., Math. Assn. Am., AAUP, Soc. Muslim Scientists U.S. and Can., World Affairs Council. Office: Dept Math Calif State U Fresno CA 93740

ALIAGA, IGNACIO, architect; b. Santiago, Chile, July 28, 1953; came to U.S., 1978; s. Ignacio and Julia (Vazquez) A.; m. Mercedes Uribe, Jan. 12, 1979; 1 child, Sean. Student, Universidad de Chile, Santiago, 1971; BA, Escuela de Artes Decorativas, Madrid, 1977; M, Calif. State Poly. U., Pomona, 1986. Interior designer Expomueble, Madrid, 1974-77; pvt. practice gen. contractor Los Angeles, 1978-80; constrn. specialist Barrio Planners Inc, Los Angeles, 1980-85; housing rehabilitation specialist City of Lawndale, Calif., 1985—; archtl. designer Spacios, Los Angeles, 1985—. Dir., producer and writer video programs Constrn. in Lawndale, 1985-86, illustrator book Didactronia, Madrid, 1973-75; prin. works include design and sculpture Madrid Amusement Park, 1976-78. Recipient Comml. Rehabilitation award NAHRO, 1984. Mem. Los Angeles Mus. Modern Art, Smithsonian Inst., AIA (affiliate). Avocations: drawing, painting, photography. Home: 4730 W 167th St Lawndale CA 90260 Office: City of Lawndale 14717 Burin Ave Lawndale CA 90260

ALIBRANDI, JOSEPH FRANCIS, diversified industrial company executive; b. Boston, Nov. 9, 1928; s. Paul and Anna (Amendolia) A.; m. Lambertha A. Araskiewicz, May 12, 1957; children: Paul, Ann-Marie, Carolyn. B.S.M.E., MIT, 1952. With Fairchild Engring. & Airplane Corp., 1951; mgr. indsl. engring. dept. Raytheon Co., Lexington, Mass., 1952-56; asst. plant mgr. Raytheon Co., Lowell, Mass., 1956-58, plant mgr., 1958-62, ops. mgr., 1962-65, v.p., gen. mgr., 1965-68, sr. v.p., gen. mgr., 1968-70; exec. v.p., dir. Whittaker Corp., Los Angeles, 1970, pres., 1970-86, chief exec. officer, 1974—, chmn., 1986—; dir. Fed. Res. Bank of San Francisco, 1973-76, chmn., 1977-79; dir. Daniel, Mann, Johnson & Mendenhall, Los Angeles, from 1979; mem. Western region adv. bd. Arkwright-Boston Ins., San Francisco, from 1978. Mem. corp. vis. com. Sloan Sch. Mgmt., MIT, from 1972, corp. vis. com. dept. biology, from 1979, mem. corp. devel. com., from 1973, mem. nat. bus. com., from 1977; chmn. bus. adv. council UCLA, from 1976, exec. com. bd. visitors Grad. Sch. Mgmt., from 1979; bd. councilors Sch. Bus. Adminstrn., U. So. Calif., from 1977; bd. dirs. Los Angeles World Affairs Council, from 1980. Served with U.S. Army, 1946-48. Mem. U.S. C. of C. (internat. policy com. from 1978). Office: Whittaker Corp 10880 Wilshire Blvd Los Angeles CA 90024 *

ALIRE, RICHARD MARVIN, scientist; b. Mogote, Colo., July 5, 1932; s. Richard Alire and Adelina (Martinez) Griego; m. Kathleen Helen Moffatt, Aug. 31, 1957; chidlren: Roderick, Bradley. BS, York Coll., 1954; MS, U. Nebr., 1956; PhD, U. N.Mex., 1962. Staff mem. Los Alamos (N. Mex.) Nat. Lab., 1961-65, sect. leader, 1965-76; tech. leader Livermore (Calif.) Nat. Lab., 1976-82, dep. dept. head, 1982-85, dept. head, 1985-87, mgr. process devel., 1987—. Chmn. McCurdy Sch. Bd., Espanola, N.Mex., 1968-76. Fellow Am. Inst. Chems.; mem. AAAS, Am. Chem. Soc. Republican. Methodist. Avocations: square dancing, skiing, tennis. Home: 1462 Groth Circle Pleasanton CA 94566 Office: Lawrence Livermore Lab PO Box 808-L128 Livermore CA 94550

ALISKY, MARVIN M., political science educator; b. Kansas City, Mo., Mar. 12, 1923; s. Joseph and Bess June (Capp) A.; m. Beverly Kay, June 10, 1955; children: Sander Michael, Joseph. BA, U. Tex., 1946, MA, 1947, PhD, 1953; cert., Instituto Tecnologico, Monterey, Mex., 1951. News corr. S.W. and Latin Am. NBC, 1947-49, news corr. Midwest, 1954-56; news corr. NBC and Christian Sci. Monitor, Latin Am., 1957-72; asst. prof. Ind. U., 1953-57; assoc. prof. journalism and polit. sci. Ariz. State U., Tempe, 1957-60; prof. polit. sci. Ariz. State U., 1960—, founding chmn. dept. mass communication, 1957-65, founding dir. Ctr. Latin Am. Studies, 1965-72; vis. fellow Princeton U., 1963-64, Hoover Inst., Stanford, 1978; Fulbright prof. Cath. U., Lima, Peru, 1958, U. Nicaragua, 1960; researcher U.S.-Mex. Interparliamentary Conf., Baja, Calif., 1965, Latin Am. Inst., Chinese Acad. Social Scis., Beijing, 1986, European Inst. Def. and Strategic Studies, London, 1985, Politics Inst., Copenhagan, Denmark, 1987, U. So. Calif., 1982—. Author: Governors of Mexico, 1965, Uruguay: Contemporary Survey, 1969, The Foreign Press, 1964, 70, Who's Who in Mexican Government, 1969, Political Forces in Latin America, 1970, Government in Nuevo Leon, 1971, Government in Sonora, 1971, Peruvian Political Perspective, 1975, Historical Dictionary of Peru, 1979, Historical Dictionary of Mexico, 1981, Latin American Media: Guidance and Censorship, 1981, Global Journalism, 1983; co-author: Political Systems of Latin America, 1970, Political Parties of the Americas, 1982, Yucatan: A World Apart, 1980; (with J.E. Katz) Arms Production in Developing Nations, 1984; (with Phil Rosen) International Handbook of Broadcasting Systems, 1987; contbr. numerous articles to profl. jours. and mags. Bd. dirs. Gov.'s Ariz.-Mex. Commn., 1975—, Ariz. Acad. Town Hall, 1981, Tempe Pub. Library, 1974-80; U.S. del. UNESCO Conf., Quito, Ecuador, 1960; U.S. State Dept. lectr., Costa Rica, Peru, Argentina and Chile, 1983; mem. U.S. Bd. Fgn. Scholarships, 1984—. Served as ensign USNR, 1944-45. NSF grantee, 1984; Ariz. State U. research grantee, 1962, 65, 70; Southwestern Studies Ctr. research grantee, 1983; Latin Am. Research in China grantee, 1986. Fellow Hispanic Soc. Am.; mem. Am. Polit. Sci. Assn., Western Polit. Sci. Assn., Latin Am. Studies Assn., Pacific Coast Council Latin Am. Studies (dir.), Inter-Am. Press Assn., Inter-Am. Broadcasters Assn., Assos. Liga de Municipios de Sonora, Friends of Mex. Art, Southwestern Polit. Sci. Assn. (chmn. 1976-77), Inter-Am. Broadcasters Assn. (research assoc.), Sigma Delta Chi. Club: Tempe Rep. Men's. Lodge: Knights of Sq. Roundtable. Home: 44 W Palmdale St Tempe AZ 85282 Office: Ariz State U Dept Polit Sci Tempe AZ 85287

ALKANA, RONALD LEE, neuropsychopharmacologist, psychobiologist; b. Los Angeles, Oct. 17, 1945; s. Sam Alkana and Madelyn Jane Davis; student UCLA, 1963-66; Pharm.D., U. So. Calif., 1970; Ph.D., U. Calif., Irvine, 1975; m. Linda Anne Kelly, Sept. 12, 1970; 1 son, Alexander Philippe Kelly. Postdoctoral fellow Nat. Inst. Alcohol Abuse and Alcoholism, U. Calif., Irvine, 1974-76; resident asst. dir. div. neurochemistry, dept. psychiatry and human behavior U. Calif., Irvine, 1976; asst. prof. pharmacy (pharmacology) U. So. Calif., Los Angeles, 1976-82, assoc. prof. pharmacy (pharmacology and toxicology), 1982—. Recipient various scholarships and grants. Mem. Soc. Neurosci., Am. Coll. Clin. Pharmacology, Am. Soc. Pharmacology and Exptl. Therapeutics, Internat. Soc. Biomed. Research on Alcoholism, Research Soc. Alcoholism, AAAS, Sigma Xi, Phi Delta Chi. Contbr. chpts. to books, articles to profl. jours. Office: 1985 Zonal Ave Los Angeles CA 90033

ALKIRE, LELAND GEORGE, JR., librarian, consultant; b. San Diego, May 11, 1937; s. Leland George Sr. and Emma Alice (Greene) A.; m. Maria Belen Bradbury, Sept. 10, 1958 (div. 1971); 1 child, Kathleen; m. Cheryl Irene Westerman, Apr. 25, 1987. AA, No. Idaho Coll., 1960; BA, U. Idaho, 1962; postgrad., Gonzaga U., 1963; MLS, U. Wash., 1966. Cert. acad. librarian, Wash. Tchr. social studies Kellogg (Idaho) Pub. Schs., 1963-64; librarian Eastern Wash. U., Cheney, 1966—; cons. Gale Research Co., Detroit, 1985—. Author: Writer's Advisor, 1985 (selected Outstanding Reference Book ALA); editor: New Periodical Abbreviations, 1983, 4th rev. edit., 1985, Periodical Title Abbreviations (2 vols.), 1986. Mem. AAUP, Assn. Coll. and Research Libraries, Am. Library Assn., Phi Delta Kappa. Unitarian. Avocations: skiing, sailing, gardening, lexicographical study. Home: 3105 S Howard Spokane WA 99203 Office: Eastern Wash U Kennedy Library Cheney WA 99004

ALKON, ELLEN SKILLEN, physician; b. Los Angeles, Apr. 10, 1936; d. Emil Bogen and Jane (Skillen) Rost; m. Paul Kent Alkon, Aug. 30, 1957; children: Katherine Ellen, Cynthia Jane, Margaret Elaine. BA, Stanford U., 1955; MD, U. Chgo., 1961; MPH, U. Calif., Berkeley, 1968. Diplomate Nat. Bd. Med. Examiners, Am. Bd. Pediatrics, Am. Bd. Preventive Medicine in Pub. Health. Chief sch. health Anne Arundel County Health Dept., Annapolis, Md., 1970-71; practice medicine specializing in pediatrics Mpls. Health Dept., 1971-73, dir. MCH, 1973-75, commr. health, 1975-80; chief preventive and pub. health Coast Region of Los Angeles County Dept. Health Services, 1980-81; chief pub. health West Area Los Angeles County Dept. Health Services, 1981-85; acting med. dir. pub. health Los Angeles County Dept. Health, 1986-87, med. dir. pub. health, 1987—; adj. prof. UCLA Sch. Pub. Health, 1981—; adminstr. vis. nurses service, Mpls., 1975-80. Fellow Am. Coll. Preventive Medicine, Am. Acad. Pediatrics; mem. So. Calif. Pub. Health Assn. (pres. 1985-86), Minn. Pub. Health Assn. (pres. 1978-79), Am. Pub. Health Assn., ACIP, Delta Omega. Office: Los Angeles County Dept Health Services 313 N Figueroa Los Angeles CA 90012

ALL, STEPHEN ANTHONY, broadcaster, educator, consultant, realtor; b. Flint, Mich., June 13, 1930; s. Stephen and Mary Rosalie (Suhajda) A.; m. Jean Mary Opiola, Sept. 4, 1954; children: Wendy, Elizabeth, Suzanne, Stephen Albert, Michal John. Student, Universidad Mexico, Mexico, 1955; BA in Radio and TV, U. Mich.-Ann Arbor, 1957, MA in Radio and TV, 1963. Cert. secondary tchr., Mich. High sch. tchr. Flint Cen., Mich., 1957-62; station mgr. Flint Community Sch. WFBE-FM, 1962-66; dir. ednl. TV for sch. dists, in San Diego County San Diego TV Authority, 1966-71; dir. communications HEW Right to Read, Washington, 1971-72; exec. producer, v.p. TeleMedia, Inc., San Diego, 1972-74; pres. Steve All Productions, San Diego, 1974— ; vis. prof. computer uses U.S. Internat. U., Nairobi, Kenya, 1986—. Author: SDITV Authority, 1969; (novel) We Always Led the Way, 1987. Contbr. articles to prof. jours. Producer, dir. children's TV programs. Served with U.S. Army, 1951-53. Recipient Armstrong award, Armstrong Found., 1964, Cert. of Excellence, Associated Press, 1968. Lodge: Kiwanis (Flint) (v.p. 1965-66). Home: 7025 Regner Rd San Diego CA 92119

ALLAN, JACKSON STEPHENS, accountant; b. Calgary, Alta., Can., July 2, 1944; s. Edward Burritt and Frances (Young) A.; m. Marjorie Jean MacNab, June 29, 1973; children—Thoburn Burritt, Warde Stephens, Morgan Catherine. B.Comm., U. Calgary, 1967. Chartered acct., Alta. Acct., cons. Price Waterhouse Co., 1967-74; pvt. practice acctg., 1975; mng. ptnr. Collins Barrow Co., Calgary, 1976—; chmn. Collins Barrow Ltd., 1984—. Bd. dirs. Calgary Elbow P.C. Constituency Assn., 1977-79, Centre P.C. Constituency Assn., 1977-81; assoc. bd. dirs. Exhibition and Stampede, 1978—; vol. fin. cons. Save Our Stampedes Com., 1986; dir., treas. Scouts Can. Project Challenge, 1986; dir. Scouts Can., Calgary region, 1987—. Mem. Inst. Chartered Accts. Can. Insolvency Assn., Inst. Mgmt. Cons. (dir. 1978-79), Alta. Insolvency Assn. (dir. 1982-86), Calgary Zool. Soc. (trustee 1987—). Anglican. Clubs: Calgary Golf and Country (bd. dirs. 1978—, pres. 1987—), Glencoe. Lodges: Masons, Rotary. Office: Collins Barrow Co, 800 401 9th Ave SW, Calgary, AB Canada T2P 3C5

ALLAN, JAMES COLLIN, banker, rancher; b. Mapleton, Utah, May 13, 1933; s. James G. and Gwen (Williams) A.; m. Peggie L. Bingham, June 17, 1957; children—Scott, Marian, Clark, Leisel, Melinda. B.S., Brigham Young U., 1958, postgrad., 1966. Auditor, Utah Savs., Provo, 1958-61; v.p., controller Utah Savs. & Loan, Provo, 1961-66; conf. dir. Brigham Young U., 1966-70; v.p. First Security Bank, Springville and Spanish Fork, Utah, 1970—, br. mgr., Springville, 1970-80, Spanish Fork, 1980-84, area mgr., 1984—; dir. Ft. Knox Security Products, Orem, Utah. Councilman, City of Mapleton, 1968-80; bd. dirs. Nebo Sch. Dist., Utah County, 1980-84, 85—, pres., 1983; bishop 1st ward ch. service Ch. Jesus Christ of Latter-day Saints, Mapleton, 1964-68, bishop 4th Ward, 1968-72, bishop youth, 1982—. Recipient Disting. Service award Jaycees Utah, 1966; Spl. Service award Utah State Div. Wildlife, 1984. Mem. Springville Wildlife Fedn. (pres. 1966-68, bd. dirs. 1970-82), Utah County Bankers. Republican. Lodge: Rotary (pres. Spanish Fork chpt. 1985-86). Home: 460 W 1600 S Mapleton UT 84663 Office: First Security Bank Utah 99 N Main St Spanish Fork UT 84660

ALLAN, ROBERT MOFFAT, JR., educator; b. Detroit, Dec. 8, 1920; s. Robert M. and Jane (Christman) A.; m. Harriet Spicer, Nov. 28, 1942; children—Robert M. III, Scott, David, Marilee. B.S., Stanford U., 1941; postgrad. Stanford Grad. Sch., 1941-42; M.S., UCLA, 1943; postgrad. Loyola Law Sch., 1947-50. Economist research dept. Security First Nat. Bank, 1942; exec. Marine Ins., 1946-53; asst. to pres., work mgr. Zinsco Elec. Products, 1953-55, v.p., dir., 1956-59; asst. to pres. The Times-Mirror Corp., 1959-60, corp. v.p., 1961-64; pres., dir. Cyprus Mines Corp., 1964-67; pres. Litton Internat., 1967-69; pres. U.S. Naval Postgrad. Sch. Found., prof. internat. mgmt. 1969-85. Bd. dirs., advisor U.S. Naval Acad.; trustee Boys Republic, Pomona Grad. Sch., Claremont Grad. Sch., Del Monte Forest Homeowners. Served with USAF, 1942-45. Recipient award Helms Athletic Found., 1947, 49; named Outstanding Businessman of Yr., Los Angeles, Nat. Assn. Accts., 1966; elected to Sailing Hall of Fame, 1969; recipient Meritorious Service award U.S. Navy, 1976; named Monterey Inst. Fgn. Studies trustee and sr. fellow, 1976. Mem. Mchts. and Mfrs. Assn. (dir.), Intercollegiate Yachting Assn. (regional dir. 1940-55), Phi Gamma Delta, Phi Delta Phi. Clubs: Newport Harbor Yacht (commodore 1962), Trans-Pacific Yacht, Monterey Country, Carmel Valley Country. Home: 169 Del Mesa Carmel CA 93921

ALLARD, JOHN BRERETON, school superintentent; b. Willows, Calif., July 8, 1925; s. Howard Rose and Louise Elizabeth (Brereton) A.; m. Betty LaRue Brown, June 25, 1950; children—Walter Howard, Gayle Jean, John Brereton II. A.A., Sacramento Jr. Coll., 1948; B.A., Sacramento State Coll., 1950, M.A., 1951. Cert. tchr., adminstr. Tchr. Turlock High Sch., Calif., 1951-54, Turlock Elem. Sch., 1954-55; prin. Turlock Sch. Dist., 1955-66; supt. Denair Unified Sch. Dist., Calif., 1966-70, Delta Island Sch. Dist., Stockton, Calif., 1970-76, Waterford Sch. Dist., Calif., 1976-78; county supt. Stanislaus County Dept. Edn., Modesto, Calif., 1979—. Chmn. bd. dirs. Salvation Army, Modesto, 1982; chmn. Scenic Gen. Hosp. Found., Modesto, 1983, Stanislaus County Human Services Council, Modesto, 1979—; mem. job tng. program Pvt. Industry Council, Modesto, 1983—; mem. steering com. Stanislaus County Jr. Achievement, 1984—. Served with U.S. Army, 1943-45, ETO. Decorated Purple Heart, Bronze Star; recipient Hon. Chpt. Farmer award Future Farmers Am., Denair, 1968; hon. Life Membership award Calif. Congress of Parents and Tchrs., 1966; Hats Off award Order of DeMolay, Turlock, 1974. Mem. Calif. State Assn. Local Elected Ofcls. (pres. 1981, outstanding service award 1982), Assn. Calif. Sch. Adminstrs. (Stanislaus chpt. Adminstr. of Yr. 1982, 83), Calif. County Supts. Schs. (chmn. area IV chmn.), Turlock C. of C., Modesto C. of C., Vets. of Battle of Bulge, Phi Delta Kappa (pres. Stanislaus State U. chpt. 1988). Republican. Presbyterian. Club: Commonwealth (Calif.). Lodge: Rotary (pres. 1988-89), Royal Arch (High Priest), Knights Templar (comdr.), Masons (Master). Office: Stanislaus County Dept Edn 801 County Ctr 3 Ct Modesto CA 95355

ALLARD, ROBERT WAYNE, geneticist, educator; b. Los Angeles, Sept. 3, 1919; s. Glenn A. and Alma A. (Roose) A.; m. Ann Catherine Wilson, June 16, 1944; children: Susan, Thomas, Jane, Gillian, Stacie. B.S., U. Calif. at Davis, 1941; Ph.D., U. Wis., 1946. From asst. to assoc. prof. U. Calif. at Davis, 1946—, prof. genetics, 1955—. Author books; contbr. articles to profl. jours. Served to lt. USNR. Recipient Crop Sci. award Am. Soc. Agronomy, 1964, DeKalb Disting. Career award Crop Sci. Soc. Am., 1983; Guggenheim fellow, 1954, 60; Fulbright fellow, 1955. Mem. Nat. Acad. Scis., Am. Acad. Arts and Scis., Am. Soc. Naturalists (pres. 1974-75), Genetics Soc. Am. (pres. 1983-84), Phi Beta Kappa, Sigma Xi, Alpha Gamma Rho, Alpha Zeta. Democrat. Unitarian. Home: 2515 Bombadil Ln Davis CA 95616 Office: U Calif Dept Genetics 204 Briggs Hall Davis CA 95616

ALLARD, WAYNE A., state senator, veterinarian; b. Ft. Collins, Colo., Dec. 12, 1943; m. Joan Malcolm, Mar. 23, 1967; children—Cheryl, Christie. D.V.M., Colo. State U., 1968. Veterinarian, Allard Animal Hosp.; mem. Colo. State Senate, 1982—, chmn. health, environment and instn. com., chmn. senate majority caucus; health officer Loveland, Colo.; mem. regional adv. council on vet. medicine Western Interstate Commn. Higher Edn.; mem. Colo. Low-level Radioactive Waste Adv. Com. Chmn. United Way; active 4-H Found. Mem. Loveland C. of C., AVMA, Colo. Vet. Medicine Assn., Latimer County Vet. Medicine Assn. (past pres.), Bd. Vet. Practitioners (charter mem.), Am. Animal Hosp. Assn., Nat. Conf. State Legislatures (vice chmn. human resources com. 1987—, healthcare cost containment com.). Methodist. Office: 1203 Jennifer Dr Loveland CO 80537

ALLBEE, NANCY JO, editor; b. Grand Prairie, Tex., Apr. 25, 1941; d. Wilson Ben and Audrey Naomi (Hoskins) Aughenbaugh; m. Charles Eugene Allbee, Dec. 23, 1961; children—Brian Dean, Janet Lynn. B.A., Adams State Coll., 1963; postgrad. U. No. Colo., 1973-74. Staff assoc. Nat. Ctr. for State Cts., Williamsburg, Va., 1974-78; with Harcourt Brace Jovanovich Plastics Publs. (formerly Industry Media), Denver, 1978—, mng. editor Plastics Compounding, 1980—, Advanced Composites, 1986—. Contbr. articles to profl. jours. Mem. Am. Bus. Press, Soc. Plastics Engrs. (assoc.; bd. dirs. 1984—, nat. council rep. 1985—). Office: HBJ Plastics Publs 1129 E 17th Ave Denver CO 80218

ALLDREDGE, LEROY ROMNEY, geophysicist; b. Mesa, Ariz., Feb. 6, 1917; s. Leo and Ida (Romney) A.; m. Larita Williams, Dec. 27, 1940; children—Carol, David Leroy, Joseph Leo, Gary Dean, Mark Evans, Janice, Luann. B.S., U. Ariz., 1939, M.S., 1940; M.Sc. in Engring, Harvard, 1953; Ph.D., U. Md., 1955. Instr. physics U. Ariz., 1940-41; fed. radio insp. FCC, Los Angeles, also Washington, 1941-44; radio engr. dept. terrestrial magnetism Carnegie Inst. of Washington, 1944-45; chief electricity and magnetism div. Naval Ordnance Lab., White Oak, Md., 1945-55; analyst operations research office Johns Hopkins, 1955-59; research geophysicist Coast and Geodetic Survey, Dept. Commerce, Washington, 1959-66; acting dir. Inst. Earth Scis., Environmental Sci. Services Adminstrn., Boulder, Colo., 1966; dir. Earth Scis. Labs., 1967-69, Earth Sci. Lab. Nat. Oceanographic and Atmospheric Adminstrn., 1969-73; research geophysicist U.S. Geol. Survey, 1973—; gen. sec., dir. central bur. Internat. Assn. Geomagnetism and Aeronomy, 1963-75. Asso. editor: Jour. Geophys. Research, 1966-69. Mem. Am. Geophys. Union (sect. on geomagnetism and aeronomy 1950-56, v.p. sect. 1956-59, pres. sect. 1959-61, chmn. Eastern meeting com. 1962-66), Sigma Xi, Phi Kappa Phi. Mem. Ch. of Jesus Christ of Latter-day Saints. Home: 4475 Chippewa Dr Boulder CO 80303 Office: USGS Br Global Seismology and Geomagnetism Denver Fed Ctr Mail Stop 968 Denver CO 80225

ALLDREDGE, ROBERT LOUIS, manufacturing company executive; b. Johnston City, Ill., Feb. 11, 1922; s. Samuel and Mary Elizabeth (Kreie) A.; B.S. in Chem. Engring., U. Denver, 1942; m. Shirley Alice Harrod, Dec. 15, 1944; children—Alice Louise, Mark Harrod. Research assoc. E.I. DuPont de Nemours & Co., Eastern Lab., Gibbstown, N.J., 1942-44; engring. research assoc. Manhattan Project, Los Alamos (N.Mex.) Sci. Lab., 1944-46; chem. engr. Denver Research Inst., U. Denver, 1946-50; pres. Alldredge & McCabe, Denver, 1950-81, exec., 1981—; pres. Serpentix Conveyor Corp., Denver, 1969—, Serpentix, Inc., Denver, 1969—; dir. Beryl Ores Co., Broomfield, Colo. Served with C.E., U.S. Army, 1944-46. Mem. Nat. Soc. profl. Engrs. (founding mem. Colo. div.), U. Denver Alumni Assn. (dir. 1965-72), Am. Chem. Soc., Profl. Engrs. Colo., AAAS, Sigma Alpha Epsilon. Methodist. Contbr. articles to profl. jours. Home: 130 Pearl St 1108 Denver CO 80203 Office: Alldredge & McCabe 9085 Marshall Ct Westminster CO 80030

ALLDRITT, VIRGIL EVERETT, data processing executive; b. Twin Falls, Idaho, Nov. 6, 1954; s. Everett Eugene and Elena Marie (Norris) A.; m. Kathleen Rose Haner, July 27, 1973 (div. Jan. 1983); 1 child, Ryan. AA in Bus., Coll. S. Idaho, 1975; BA in Computer Infosystems with high honors, Idaho State U., 1986. Systems analyst Computerized Farm, Twin Falls, 1975-79; ptnr. Idaho Computer Services, Twin Falls, 1979-82; mgr. data processing Bannock County, Pocatello, Idaho, 1982—. Mem. Data Processing Mgmt. Assn., Assn. Computing Machinery, Phi Kappa Phi, Beta Gamma Sigma. Republican. Mem. United Pentecostal Ch. Avocations: micros, fishing, softball, basketball, music. Home: 344 S 12th #1-B Pocatello ID 83201 Office: Bannock County 624 E Center Pocatello ID 83205-4777

ALLEMAND, DIANE MOORE, social worker; b. San Francisco, Nov. 22, 1951; d. Albert Paul and Gloria G. (Gerth) Moore; m. Justin L. Allemand, June 15, 1974. BA in Social Work with high honors, Eastern Wash. U., 1973, MSW, 1978. Office coordinator Pregnancy Care Ctr., Spokane, Wash., 1974-76; practicum asst. Eastern Wash. U., Cheney, 1978-79; social worker Spokane Div. Devel. Disabilities, 1979-84, Interlake Sch., Medical Lake, Wash., 1984—; field student supr. Eastern Wash. U., 1984-86. Vol. Am. Cancer Crusade, Spokane, 1977-86, Spokane County Health Dist., 1978, Pregnancy Care Ctr., Spokane, 1977-86; bd. dirs. Foster Grandparent Adv. Council, Spokane, 1984-86. Scholar AAUW, 1977, N. Marin PTA Council, 1969; named Outstanding Employee of Yr. Interlake Sch., 1985. Mem. Nat. Assn. Social Workers, Assn. Retarded Citizens, Sch. Social Work Alumni Assn. Democrat. Lutheran. Avocations: organic gardening, aerobics, reading. Home: N 123 Moffitt Spokane WA 99206 Office: Interlake Sch PO Box B Medical Lake WA 99022

ALLEN, ARTHUR DAVID, math educator; b. Provo, Utah, Oct. 18, 1940; s. Austin Douglas and Ruth Emma (Hanks) A.; m. Janet Larson, Aug. 7, 1964; children: Ruth, Jennifer, Ann Marie, Andrew, Abigail. BS, Utah State U., 1964; MS, Oreg. State U., 1965. Cert. tchr., Idaho, Utah, Oreg. Tchr. Reynolds Sch. Dist., Portland, Oreg., 1967-68; prof. Ricks Coll., Rexburg, Idaho, 1968—. Author: Physical Science Problem Guide, 1973. Mem. Selective Service Draft Bd., Rexburg, 1982—. Served to 1st lt. U.S. Army, 1965-67, Vietnam. Mem. Am. Assn. Physics Tchrs. (exec. bd. dirs. 1985—). Mormon. Avocation: antique automobiles. Home: 370 S 5th E Rexburg ID 83440 Office: Ricks Coll Dept Math Rexburg ID 83440

ALLEN, BONNIE LYNN, pension actuary; b. Los Angeles, Oct. 2, 1957; d. David and Lucille M. (Scott) A. B.A. summa cum laude, UCLA, 1979. Math. tutor, Los Angeles, 1971—; reader math. dept. UCLA, 1977-79; pension actuary Martin E. Segal Co., Los Angeles, 1980—. Author short stories and poetry. Active mentor program UCLA Alumni Assn., 1978-79. Mem. Math. Assn. Am., Am. Math. Soc., Acad. Sci. Fiction, Fantasy and Horror

Films, UCLA Alumni Assn. (life), Los Angeles Actuarial Club, Phi Beta Kappa. Office: Martin E Segal Co 500 S Virgil Ave Los Angeles CA 90020

ALLEN, BYRON SEDRIC, JR., physician; b. Center, Tex., Mar. 23, 1923; s. Byron Sedric and Thelma (Daugherty) A.; student S.W. Mo. State Tchrs. Coll., 1942-43, U. Houston, 1944-47; M.D., Tulane U., 1951; m. Alice Harrison, Aug. 21, 1947; children—Kathryn, Byron John, Diane. Intern, Fresno County (Calif.) Gen. Hosp., 1951-52, resident in obstetrics, 1952-53; gen. practice medicine and surgery, Fresno, Calif., 1953-63, Apple Valley Calif., 1963—; pres. med. staff St. Mary Desert Valley Hosp., Apple Valley, 1982-83; med. staff Victor Valley Hosp., Victorville, Calif., 1966—; vis. attending staff dept. family practice San Bernardino (Calif.) County Med. Center, 1973-76; guest lectr. in hypnosis Fresno State Coll., 1960-63; asst. prof. family medicine La. State U., 1976-77, clin. asst. prof., 1978-85. Trustee St. Mary Hosp., 1987-88. Served with USAAF, 1941-43. Named Outstanding Family Physicians in San Bernardino County, 1981-82; recipient Gierman-McKee Meml. award San Bernardino County Med. Ctr., 1982. Diplomate Am. Bd. Family Practice. Fellow Am. Acad. Family Physicians; mem. AMA, Calif. Acad. Family Physicians (chpt. pres. 1961, 80-81, del. Congress of Dels. 1982—, bd. dirs. 1985—), Calif. Med. Assn., San Bernardino County Med. Soc. (sec. 1976—, dir. 1972-83), Calif. Med. Assn. (del. 1974-80). Club: Rotary (pres. 1972—, Man of Year 1973). Home: 19004 Munsee Rd Apple Valley CA 92307 Office: 18327 Hwy 18 Apple Valley CA 92307

ALLEN, CHARLES RAY, chemical engineer, nuclear waste engineering administrator; b. Delta, Utah, Mar. 2, 1940; s. Charles Rial and Agness Emorett (Skidmore) A.; m. Diane Jensen, Dec. 18, 1965; children: Kevin, Debra, Rebecca, Elizabeth. BSChemE, Brigham Young U., 1966; MSChemE, U. Calif., Davis, 1968. Synthetics chem. engr. Procter and Gamble Mfg. Co., Dallas, 1969-71, mgr. soap processing dept., 1971-73; prin. engr. Westinghouse Hanford Co., Richland, Wash., 1974-75, mgr. engring. demonstration, 1975-82, mgr. process devel. and demonstration, 1982-83, mgr. BRET equipment engring., 1983-84, mgr. waste programs, 1984-86; mgr. hanford waste vitrification program Battelle Pacific N.W. Lab., Richland, 1986—; mem. incineration tech. assessment U.S. Dept. Energy, 1978; tech. liaison in acid digestion field, W.Ger., U.K. Inventor nuclear waste treatment, 1977, 78; shockwave atenuation, 1979. Contbr. articles to profl. jours. V.p. Cystic Fibrosis Found., Dallas, 1971-72, bd. dirs., 1973; com. chmn. Boy Scouts Am., Dallas and Richland, 1970, 77; treas. Garden Park Recreation Club, Richland, 1982-83. Mem. Am. Inst. Chem. Engrs., Am. Nuclear Soc. Home: 1950 Forest Ave Richland WA 99352 Office: Battelle Pacific NW Lab Battelle Blvd Richland WA 99352

ALLEN, DAVID CHARLES, educator; b. Syracuse, N.Y., Jan. 15, 1944; s. Charles Robert and Jane Loretta (Doolittle) A.; m. Mary Ann Stanke, June 15, 1968; children—Meredith Rae, Amelia Kathrine, Carl James. B.Tech. Edn., Nat. U., San Diego, 1983, M.A. in Human Behavior, 1984. Dir. retail sales Nat. U. Alumni Assn., 1981-83; audiovisual technician Grossmont Union High Sch. Dist., La Mesa, Calif., 1983-84; spl. project instr. San Diego Community Coll., 1985—. Mem. Presdl. Task Force; mem. Congl. Adv. Com. on Vets. Benefits for congressmen 44th and 45th dists. Served with USN, 1961-81. Mem. Am. Soc. Tng. and Devel., Am. Vocat. Assn., Nat. Assn. Performance and Instrn., Calif. Assn. Vocat. Edn., DAV, Vietnam Vets. Am., San Diego Zool. Soc., Am. Tech. Edn. Assn., Beta Sigma Phi (hon.). Republican. Roman Catholic. Club: K.C. Home: 8318 Blossom Hill Dr Lemon Grove CA 92045 Office: San Diego Community Coll Dist Mil Tng Program 3375 Camino del Rio S San Diego CA 92108

ALLEN, DEAN KENNETH, mechanical engineer; b. Glendale, Calif., Oct. 12, 1935; s. Reginal Virgil and Evelyn Geniveve A.; m. Margo Louise Oliphant, Mar. 29, 1958; children: Catherine L., Craig D., Ryan J. BSME, U. So. Calif., 1957; MBA, U. Pa., 1962. V.p., mgr. Fluor Engrs. Inc., Irvine, Calif., 1962-81, group v.p., 1981-82, pres., 1982-84; chmn. Fluor E&C Group, Irvine, Calif., 1984-86; exec. v.p. Fluor Corp., Irvine, Calif., 1986—, also bd. dirs. and exec. com. V.p. Boy Scouts Am., Orange County, Calif., 1984. Served to lt. USN, 1957-62. Fellow Inst. Advancement Engring.; mem. Am. Soc. Macro Engring. (bd. dirs.), Am. Assn. Cost Engrs. (pres.), Project Mgmt. Inst. ASME, El Niguel C. of C. Clubs: Huntington Harbour Yacht (Huntington Beach, Calif.).

ALLEN, DONALD BRUCE, public relations consulting firm executive; b. Rochester, N.Y., Aug. 23, 1941; s. Robert Thomas and Helen (Rife) A.; m. Irene Macinski, July 12, 1964 (div. 1984); children—Leigh Anne, Leslie Jennifer; m. Debra L. DeVore, Nov. 17, 1984. B.A., SUNY-Albany, 1963; postgrad. in bus. adminstrn. U. So. Calif. Bur. mgr. UPI, Rochester, 1962-65; pub. relations mgr. Xerox Corp., Rochester and N.Y.C., 1965-69; account mgr. Hutchins Young & Rubicam, Rochester, 1969-71; pub. relations dir. Digital Equipment Corp., Maynard, Mass., 1971-72, Gen. Automation, Anaheim, Calif., 1972-75; ptnr. DeSpain & Allen, North Hollywood, Calif., 1975-79; pres. The Allen Group, Santa Ana, Calif., 1979—. Author: Buying Your First Computer, 1976. Contbr. articles to profl. jours. Mem. Pub. Relations Soc. Am. (Counselor's Acad.), Nat. Investor Relations Inst., Fedn. Fly Fishermen, Calif. Trout Assn., Trout Unltd., Hell's Anglers (pres., bd. dirs.). Republican. Office: The Allen Group 31877 Del Obispo St #205 San Juan Capistrano CA 92675

ALLEN, EDMUND WALTER, structural engineer, surveyor, civil engineer, consultant; b. Vernal, Utah, Nov. 18, 1927; s. A. Edgar and Edith (McCoy) A.; m. Barbara Seegmiller, Mar. 17, 1950; children: Gregory L., Patti K., Ted W. BSCE, U. Utah, 1952. Cert. land surveyor, Utah; registered profl. engr. Utah, Nev., Idaho, Wyo., Colo., N.Mex. Surveyor Roger W. Sheridan Co., Salt Lake City, 1951-52, Harsh Devel. Corp., Portland, Oreg., 1952-53, Bechtel Corp., Salt Lake City, 1953-54; struct. engr. H.C. Hughes Co., Salt Lake City, 1954-57; engr. Alfred Brown Co., Salt Lake City, 1957-60; pres. E.W. Allen & Assocs., Salt Lake City, 1960—; chmn. Salt Lake City Bd. Appeals for Housing and Constrn., 1979, 84; mem. Mayor's Task Force on Preservation and Devel., Salt Lake City, 1983; mem. Landmarks Com. Salt Lake City, 1984—. Prin. works include: Met. Hall of Justice building, Salt Lake City; Chase Fine Arts ctr., the Spectrum, Utah State U., Logan; Skaggs Coll. of Pharmacy building, behavioral sci. building, art and architecture building, addition to hosp. med. ctr U. Utah, Salt Lake City; clock tower Weber State Coll, Ogden, Utah; Valley Fair Mall, West Valley City, Utah; Snowbird tram sta., comml. plaza, hotel and Mid Gad restaurant; Rampton sci. building, Utah Tech. Coll., Salt Lake City; bridge across Green River near Vernal, Utah; 15 high schs., 80 elem. schs., 50 ch. buildings, various locations; J.C. Penney office building, Salt Lake City; Eaton-Kenway office tower, Salt Lake City; Gov.'s Plaza offices and condominiums, Salt Lake City; conv. and exhibit hall for the Salt Palace, Salt Lake City; also, restoration of the Devereaux House, Salt Lake City, Salt Lake City and County building. Served with U.S. Army, 1946-48. Recipient Disting. Alumnus award U. Utah, 1975, Engring. Excellence Honor award Consulting Engrs. Council Utah, 1983, Merit award Am. Inst. Steel Constrn., 1985, Award for Excellence in Masonry Engring. Utah Masonry Promotion, 1983, Engring. Excellence award; named Outstanding Utah Engr. of Yr. Utah Engrs. Council, 1985. Mem. ASCE, Am. Concrete Inst., Am. Inst. Steel Constrn., Consulting Engrs. Council Utah (v.p. 1977-78, pres.-elect 1978-79, pres. 1979-80, nat. dir. 1984-85), Masonry Soc., Earthquake Engring. Research Inst. Struct. Engers. Assn. So. Calif. (allied), Struct. Engrs. Assn. Utah (founding, pres. 1980-81), Internat. Cof. Building Officials. Mormon. Avocations: swimming, hunting, boating, antique cars. Home: 2567 S 150 E Bountiful UT 84010 Office: EW Allen & Assocs 16 Exchange Pl Salt Lake City UT 84111

ALLEN, EDWARD RAYMOND, educator, accountant; b. Indpls., Sept. 30, 1913; s. Edward L. and Emmeline (Rice) A.; B.S. in Commerce, Drake U., 1950, M.A. in Accounting, 1951; m. Norma D. M. Brennan, May 10, 1941. Asst. prof. bus. adminstrn. Parsons Coll., Fairfield, Iowa, 1952-56; faculty Coll. of Idaho, Caldwell, 1956—, prof. bus. adminstrn., 1956-73, head dept., 1962-70, chmn. dept., 1970-73, emeritus, 1973—, vis. lectr., 1976—; practicing C.P.A., Caldwell, 1958—. Served to capt. AUS, 1942-46; lt. col. Res. ret. Decorated Bronze Star with 1 palm; C.P.A., Iowa, Idaho. Mem. Am. Inst. C.P.A.s, Idaho Soc. C.P.A.s (dir., regional v.p. 1958-61, mem. standards of practice com. 1974-83, chmn. com. 1980-83, chmn. relations with ednl. instns. com. 1984-86), AAUP (past pres. Coll. of Idaho chpt.), C. of C., Pi Kappa Phi. Clubs: Elks. Contbr. articles to profl. jours. Home: PO Box 336 Caldwell ID 83606

ALLEN, GARY KING, aerospace advance development consultant; b. Buffalo, June 27, 1944; s. Howard W. and Ethel M. (King) A.; m. Catherine Reardon, July 12, 1969; children—Matthew W., Sarah A. BSCE, Clarkson U., 1966; MBA with distinction, Nat. U., San Diego, 1977. Sr. structural analysis engr. Boeing Co., Seattle, 1966-73; lead preliminary design engr. Rohr Industries, Chula Vista, Calif., 1974-78; advanced devel. specialist RHO Co., Bellevue, Wash., 1978-82; sr. specialist on assignment to Lockheed Corp., Burbank, Calif., 1982-83, on assignment to Boeing, Seattle, 1978-82, 83—. Mem. nat. adv. bd. Am. Security Council, 1970-76. Recipient Pride in Excellence award Boeing Co., 1980, 86. Mem. AIAA, Lutheran. Home: 13400 SE 42d Pl Bellevue WA 98006 Office: RHO Co Inc 4034 148th Ave NE Redmond WA 98052

ALLEN, GARY MICHAEL, manufacturing executive; b. Columbus, Ohio, May 21, 1943; s. Harry Ethan and Mildred Lola (Perfect) A.; m. Gayle Delene Bogovich, Aug. 8, 1981. B.M.E., Ohio State U., 1966, M.B.A., 1969; postgrad. U. Wash., 1969-73. Staff supr. AT&T, Cin., 1966-67; teaching asst. U. Wash., 1969-73; asst. prof. U. Oreg., 1973-74; pres. D. O. Mills Inc., Sacramento, 1974-80, also dir.; pres. G.T.M. Enterprises, San Diego, 1980—; chief fin. officer Tech. Assocs., Inc., also bd. dirs.; cons. Jeffrey Mfg. Co., 1969. Named Small Businessman of Yr., Calif. SBA, 1978; recipient award Journey for Prospective, 1970. Mem. Sacramento C. of C., Nat. Restaurant Assn., Am. Philatelic Soc., Am. Numis. Assn., Am. Econ. Soc., ASME, Sigma Pi. Republican. Methodist. Editor: Financial Management (Robert Higgins), 1972.

ALLEN, GEORGE WINFIELD, JR., transportation professional; b. Norfolk, Va., Mar. 10, 1926; s. George Winfield Sr. and Alma Virginia (Fischer) A.; m. Bobbie Porter, May 18, 1945; children George Winfield III, Robert G., Delma R., Janice L. AA, Am. U., Washington. Supr. Capitol Airlines, Washington, 1954-61; supr. United Airlines, Washington, 1961-67; supr. United Airlines, San Francisco, 1967-69, prodn. controller, 1979—. Pres. PTA, Md., 1957. Served to sgt. USAF, 1943-46, PTO. Recipient Spl. Recognition award United Airlines, 1986. Mem. Calif. Sheriffs Assn., Brotherhood Ry. Clks. Union (nat. pres. 1953, vice gen. chmn. 1954). Republican. Baptist. Club: Singing Cedars (Washington) (pres. 1969-70). Lodges: Masons, Shriners. Avocations: private pilot, masonic research. Home: 2832 Camino Del Rey San Jose CA 95132 Office: United Airlines San Francisco Internat Airport San Francisco CA 94128

ALLEN, GERALD L., broadcast educator, business consultant; b. Hyrum, Utah, Aug. 29, 1933; s. Earle Wesley and Delores (Larsen) A.; m. Janet Louise Jorgensen, Dec. 19, 1958; children—Athena, Matthew, Toni, Eric, Byron, Alys, Ruth. B.S., Utah State U., 1961, M.S., 1965. Staff announcer Sta. KLGN, Logan, Utah, 1956-57, Sta. KWHO, Salt Lake City, 1958; office mgr. news and sports Sta. KVNU, Logan, Utah, 1959-62; station mgr. Sta. KUSU, Logan, 1962—; prof. Utah State U., Logan, 1962—; bd. dirs. Rocky Mountain Corp. Pub. Broadcasting, treas., 1986—; bd. govs. Rocky Mountain Pub. Radio, 1984—; pres. Utah Assn. Edn. Broadcasters, 1967-68; v.p. Rocky Mountain Pub. Radio, 1976-78, pres., 1978-80, bd. govs., 1978-80. Mormon. Home: 469 North 400 East Logan UT 84321 Office: Utah State U UMC 85 Logan UT 84322

ALLEN, HOWARD PFEIFFER, electric utility executive; b. Upland, Calif., Oct. 7, 1925; s. Howard Clinton and Emma Maud (Pfeiffer) A.; m. Dixie Mae Illa, May 14, 1948; 1 child, Alisa Cary. B.A. cum laude, Pomona Coll., 1948; J.D., Stanford U., 1951; LLD (hon.), Pepperdine U. Bar: Calif. 1952, U.S. Supreme Ct. Asst. dean, asst. prof. law Stanford Law Sch., 1951-54; with So. Calif. Edison Co., 1954—, v.p., 1962-71, sr. v.p., 1971-73, exec. v.p., 1973-80, pres., 1980-84, chmn., 1984—, also dir.; dir. Calif. Fed. Savs. & Loan Assn., Pacific S.W. Airlines, PS Group, MCA, Inc., ICN Pharms., Inc., Northrop Corp., Computer Scis., Inc., MCA, Inc.; mem. Bus. Council. Bd. dirs. Los Angeles County Fair Assn., Com. for Econ. Devel.; trustee, mem. exec. com. Pomona Coll., 1978—, Los Angeles County Mus. Art, NCCJ; vice chmn. bd. dirs.; mem. Los Angeles County Amateur Athletic Found. of Los Angeles. Mem. Los Angeles C. of C. (dir., pres. 1978, chmn. 1979), ABA, Los Angeles County Bar Assn., State Bar Calif., Bar Assn. San Francisco, Pacific Coast Elec. Assn. (pres. 1984-85), Los Angeles World Affairs Council (bd. dirs.), Edison Electric Inst. (bd. dirs.), Inst. for Resource Mgmt. (bd. dirs.), Phi Beta Kappa, Phi Delta Phi. Clubs: California (Los Angeles); Pacific-Union, Bohemian (San Francisco). Office: So Calif Edison Co 2244 Walnut Grove Ave Rosemead CA 91770

ALLEN, JEFFREY BLYNNE, real estate developer, consultant; b. Abington, Pa., Mar. 26, 1948; s. Francis Blynne and Julia (Obuhanych) A.; m. Carol Ann Imrie, June 28, 1975; 1 child, Julia Jane. BS, Cornell U., 1970; MBA, Harvard U., 1974. Project engr. Dravo Corp., Pitts., 1970-71, Metcalf & Eddy, Boston, 1971-72; project mgr. Cabot Cabot & Forbes, Los Angeles and Boston, 1974-77; v.p. Cabot Cabot & Forbes, Los Angeles, 1979-81; devel. mgr. The Koll Co., Newport Beach, Calif., 1977-79; mng. ptnr. Paragon Group, Los Angeles, 1981—, also bd. dirs.; cons. Fed. Home Loan Bank San Francisco, 1985—. Active Los Angeles Hdqrs. City Assn. (past bd. dirs.). Fellow Chrysler Corp., Harvard U. Sch. Bus., 1973; recipient scholarship Owens- Ill. Corp., Cornell U., 1966. Mem. Harvard Bus. Sch. Assn. (v.p. 1977-79), Los Angeles C. of C. Republican. Club: Jonathan (Los Angeles). Avocations: skiing, scuba diving, tennis, golf, reading. Home: 852 Sussex Rd San Marino CA 91108 Office: Paragon Group 523 W 6th St Los Angeles CA 90014

ALLEN, JOE HASKELL, physicist, geomagnetician; b. Okla. City, June 6, 1939; s. William Haskell and Gertrude L. (Arrington) A.; m. Charlotte Anne Moody, Sept. 1, 1961; children: Melissa Anne, Susan Michelle, Melinda Kay. BS in Physics, U. Okla., 1961; MS in Engring. Geoscis., U. Calif., Berkeley, 1966. Tchr. math. Casady Sch, Oklahoma City, 1961-63; geophysicist U.S. Coast and Geod. Survey, Washington, 1963-66; physicist NOAA, Boulder, Colo., 1966—; head Internat. Magnetospheric Study Cen. Info. Exchange Office, Boulder, 1976-79; dir. World Data Ctr.-A for Solar Terrestrial Physics, Boulder, 1981—; asst. sec. Internat. Council Sci. Unions panel on World Data Ctrs., 1986—. Editor Internat. Magnetospheric Study newsletter, 1976-79. Exec. bd. dirs. Colo. State Sci. Fair, Denver, 1968—, Soviet Sister City Project, Boulder, 1985—; deacon E. Boulder Baptist Ch. Recipient Silver medal U.S. Dept. Commerce, 1978, Cert. Service, Colo. State Sci. Fair, 1977. Mem. Am. Geophys. Union, Sci. Com. Solar Terrestrial Phys. (service award 1984), Internat. Assn. Geomagnetism and Aeronomy. Democrat. Avocations: history, fly fishing, tennis, skiing, choir. Home: 2880 Colby Dr Boulder CO 80303 Office: NOAA/NGDC E/GC2 325 Broadway Boulder CO 80303

ALLEN, LEW, JR., laboratory executive, former air force officer; b. Miami, Fla., Sept. 30, 1925; s. Lew and Zella (Holman) A.; m. Barbara Frink Hatch, Aug. 19, 1949; children: Barbara Allen Miller, Lew III, Marjorie Allen Dauster, Christie Allen Jameson, James Allen. BS, U.S. Mil. Acad., 1946; MS, U. Ill., 1952, PhD in Physics, 1954. Commd. 2d lt. USAAF, 1946; advanced through grades to gen. USAF, 1977, ret., 1982; physicist test div. AEC, Los Alamos, N.Mex., 1954-57; sci. advisor Air Force Spl. Weapons Lab., Kirkland, N.Mex., 1957-61; with office of spl. tech. Sec. of Def., Washington, 1961-65; from dir. spl. projects to dep. dir. adv. plans Air Force Space Program, 1965-72; dir. Nat. Security Agy., Ft. Meade, Md., 1973-77; comdr. Air Force Systems Command, 1977-78; vice chief of staff USAF, Washington, 1978, chief of staff, 1978-82; dir. Jet Propulsion Lab., Calif. Inst. Tech., Pasadena, Calif., 1982—; chmn. COSEPUP (Nat. Acad. Scis.) panel on impact of nat. security controls on internat. tech. transfer, 1985-87. Decorated D.S.M. with 3 oak leaf clusters, Legion of Merit with 2 oak leaf clusters, Joint Service Commendation medal. Mem. Am. Phys. Soc., Am. Geophys. Union, Nat. Acad. Engring., Council on Fgn. Relations, Sigma Xi. Republican. Episcopalian. Clubs: Sunset (Los Angeles); Alfalfa (Washington). Avocations: ballooning, rafting. Office: Jet Propulsion Lab Calif Inst Tech 4800 Oak Grove Dr Pasadena CA 91109

ALLEN, LEXIS MAC FADDEN, curriculum consultant; b. London, Mar. 31, 1937; d. Harry Alexander and Ruth Gloria (Lawlor) Mac Fadden; came to U.S., 1939; m. John Armstrong Hendricks, July 16, 1961; 1 son, Jonathan Armstrong; m. 2d, David Allen, Mar. 31, 1979. B.A. in History, Pomona Coll., 1958; postgrad. U. Calif.-Berkeley, 1958-59; M.A. in Elem. Edn., U. Nev.-Las Vegas, 1970; postgrad. U. Pacific, 1986—. Cert. tchr., Calif., adminstr., Nev. Tchr., Nev. and Calif., also team leader Tchr. Corps, 1970-72; curriculum writer, cons. lang. arts Clark County Sch. Dist., Las Vegas, 1974—; cons. educator Harcourt, Brace, Jovanovich; cons. in field. Active Assistance League Las Vegas. Mem. Assn. Supervision and Curriculum Devel., Nat. Council Tchrs. English, Women's Caucus, Women Lawyers of Sacramento, Mus. Soc. San Francisco, Phi Delta Kappa, Kappa Delta Pi. Republican. Club: Mesquite (past pres. jr. club). Author: (with Frances Van Wert) The Write Way, 1981; Wits, Whys and Wonders, 1983. Home: 7217 Mission Hills Dr Las Vegas NV 89113 Mailing: 1450 42d St Sacramento CA 95819

ALLEN, MARCUS, professional football player; b. San Diego, Mar. 26, 1960. Student, U. So. Calif. Running back with Los Angeles Raiders, NFL, El Segundo, Calif., 1982—; established NFL season record for most combined yards, 1985; played in NFL championship game, 1984; Pro Bowl, 1983, 85, 86. Recipient Heisman Trophy Downtown Athletic Club of N.Y.C., 1981; named The Sporting News NFL Rookie of Yr., 1982, Player of Yr., 1985. Office: care Los Angeles Raiders 332 Center St El Segundo CA 90245 *

ALLEN, MICHAEL E., staff engineer, project manager; b. Laplata, Md., Sept. 3, 1958; s. Carter E. and Maria (Ridi) A.; m. Joanne Winter, Aug. 18, 1979. BS in Computer Sci., U. Ga., 1980. Programmer Shaw Industries, Dalton, Ga., 1980-81, programmer, analyst, 1981; systems rep. Honeywell Info. Systems, Ft. Wayne, Ind., 1981-83, sr. systems rep., 1983-85; system design specialist, Mfg. Systems div. Honeywell Info. Systems, Phoenix, 1985-86, staff engr., Mfg. Systems div., 1986—. Recipient Tech. Merit award East Cen. Region, 1984, Mfg. Systems Div. Honeywell Info. Systems Dirs. award, 1986; named Systems Rep. of Yr. East Cen. Region, 1983. Republican. Roman Catholic. Home: 6922 W Kerry Ln Glendale AZ 85308 Office: Honeywell Info Systems 5115 N 27th Ave Phoenix AZ 85017

ALLEN, MICHAEL JOHN BRIDGMAN, English educator; b. Lewes, Eng., Apr. 1, 1941; came to U.S., 1966; m. Elena Hirshberg; children: William, Benjamin. BA, Oxford (Eng.) U., 1964, MA, 1966; PhD, U. Mich., 1970; DLitt, Oxford U., Eng., 1987. Asst. prof. UCLA, 1970-74, assoc. prof., 1974-79, prof. English, 1979—; assoc. dir. Ctr. for Medieval and Renaissance Studies UCLA, 1974—. Author: Marsilio Ficino: The Philebus Commentary, 1975, Marsilio Ficino and the Phaedran Charioteer, 1981, The Platonism of Marsilio Ficino, 1984; co-editor Shakespeare's Plays in Quarto. Guggenheim fellow, 1977; recipient, Eby award for Disting. Teaching, UCLA, 1977. Office: UCLA Dept English Los Angeles CA 90024

ALLEN, PATRICK D(AVID), research professional; b. Redwood City, Calif., May 15, 1955; s. Robert J. and Anne C. A. BS, Harvey Mudd Coll., 1977; MS, U. Calif., Berkeley, 1978; PhD, Colo. Sch. Mines, 1980; disting. mil. grad., ROTC, 1977; disting. grad., Officer Basic Course, 1981. Spectrophotometer operator Royco Instruments, Menlo Park, Calif., 1974; ops. research analyst Jet Propulsion Lab., Pasadena, Calif., 1977-78; commd. 2d lt. U.S. Army, 1977, advanced through grades to capt., 1982; ops. research analyst U.S. Army Concepts Analysis Agy., Bethesda, Md., 1981-84; research analyst The Rand Corp., Santa Monica, Calif., 1984—; cons. in field to cos. Recipient Meritorious Service medal U.S. Army. Mem. AIME, Ops. Research Soc. Am., Inst. Mgmt. Scis., Res. Officer's Assn. (liaison 1981-82).ub 19. Club: Toastmasters (charter, pres. 1982). Home: 3744 Delmas Terr #2 Los Angeles CA 90034 Office: The Rand Corp 1700 Main St Santa Monica CA 90406

ALLEN, PHYLLIS ADELLE GRISHAM, public relations and fund raising executive; b. Stockton, Calif., Aug. 11, 1927; d. Clarence William and Norma Grace (Collins) Grisham; children—Carole Hilles, Susan Allen Yonas, Stephen, Thomas, Patrica Allen Ruff. Student Long Beach City Coll., 1945-46, U. Oreg., 1957, Portland State U., 1967. Women's dir., broadcaster KMED Radio and TV, Medford, Oreg., 1957-65; copywriter, account exec. Williams Parma Advt., Portland, Oreg., 1965-66; sec.-treas., account exec. Williams Advt. and Pub. Relations, Portland, 1966-68; pub. relations dir. United Fund, Akron, Ohio, 1969-70; asso. pub. relations dir. Akron Gen. Med. Center, 1972-73; exec. dir. Akron Gen. Devel. Found., 1973-80; dir. community relations and devel. Children's Hosp. of San Francisco, 1980-83; dir. resource devel. Scripps Meml. Hosps., La Jolla, Calif., 1983—. Recipient 1st place Pillsbury invitational recipe contest for food editors, 1964. Fellow Nat. Assn. Hosp. Devel.; mem. Pub. Relations Soc. Am. (accredited). Home: 3567 Voyager Circle San Diego CA 92130 Office: Scripps Meml Hosps 9888 Genesee Ave La Jolla CA 92038

ALLEN, SHEILA ROSALYND, television and motion picture writer, novelist; b. Elmira, N.Y., Mar. 8, 1942; d. Charles Judson and Doris Elizabeth (Beers) A. Ptnr. Allen & Ukra, Los Angeles, 1974-75; owner Allen Enterprises, Venice Beach, Calif., 1975-84; pres., chief exec. officer S.R.A., Inc., Venice Beach, 1984—, also bd. dirs.; writer Columbia Studios TV, 1983-84, Aaron Spelling Prodns., 1984; mem. adv. bd. Whole Ocean Catalog, Dana Point, Calif., 1986, Insight for Learning, Ventura, Calif., 1978; bd. dirs. We the People, Santa Monica; speaker pub. TV, 1982. Author: (books) Fire and Innocence, 1984, Victoria's Secret Masquerade of Hearts, 1986, The Mars Kill, 1987; author: (screenplay) Honeymoon, 1986; author: (TV series) Cops and Riders, 1987, also movies of the week, documentaries and films. Speechwriter Calif. Dem. Kick-Off Campaign, 1976. Recipient Teacher's award Insight for Learning, Ventura, 1978, Silver award Houston Film Festival, 1984; named Best New Novelist, R.T. Book Conf., N.Y.C., 1986. Mem. Writers Guild Am. (west arbitrator credits 1984-86), Authors Guild, Authors League, Romance Writers Am. (awards judge 1986-87), Mystery Writers Am., Nat. Writers Club (critiquing cons). Anglican Catholic. Club: Rose Ave. Beach (Venice, Calif.). Avocations: painting, cycling, volunteer programs for disadvantaged would-be writers, classical music, culinary arts. Office: SRA Inc PO Box 5749 Santa Monica CA 90405

ALLEN, SPENCER FIRTH, civil engineer, consultant; b. Seattle, Feb. 9, 1926; s. Arthur Spencer and Gladys (Firth) A.; m. Doris Ann Stowell, Aug. 29, 1948; children: Susan, Janet, Steven, Timothy, Craig, Jonathon. BA, U. San Francisco, 1980, MS, 1985. Registered profl. civil engr., Calif., Oreg., Wash., Colo., Fla., Ariz., quality engr., Calif.; lic. gen. contractor, Calif. Resident engr. Calif. Div. Hwys., San Francisco, 1947-65; constrn. mgr. Green, Hensel, Phelps, Bechtel, various locations, 1965-80; civil engring. cons. Morrison-Knudsen Engrs., San Francisco, 1980—. Contbr. articles to profl. jours. Pres. Homeowners Assn., Moraga, Calif., 1982-84. Served to air cadet U.S. Army, 1944-45. Fellow ASCE. Avocations: sailing, mountaineering. Office: Morrison-Knudson Engrs 3131 35th Ave Suite P Phoenix AZ 85017

ALLEN, THOMAS JOSEPH, physician, medical clinic administrator; b. Oklahoma City, Apr. 4, 1946; s. Clarence M. and A. Rosemary (Wernsing) A.; m. Leslie D. Morgan, June 8, 1968; children: Joshua, Christopher, Lisa, Ryan. AB in Econs. and Math., Wabash Coll., 1968; MD, Ind. U., 1972. Diplomate Am. Bd. Family Practice. Physician emergency dept. Hancock County Meml. Hosp., Ind., 1973-74; physician emergency dept., dir. emergency services Henry County Meml. Hosp., 1974-75; physician emergency dept. Providence Hosp., Medford, Oreg., 1978-79, Cheyenne (Wyo.) Meml. Hosp., 1979-82; gen. practice medicine Conifer, Colo., 1975-78; prin., physician First-Care Med. Clinic, Loveland, Colo., 1982—; staff mem. McKee Med. Ctr., Loveland, 1979—. Fellow Am. Acad. Family Physicians; mem. Colo. Med. Soc. Avocations: running, camping, bicycling. Office: First Care Med Clinic 249H E 29th St Loveland CO 80538

ALLEN, WILLIAM RICHARD, economist; b. Eldorado, Ill., Apr. 3, 1924; s. Oliver Boyd and Justa Lee (Wingo) A.; m. Frances Lorraine Swoboda, Aug. 15, 1948; children: Janet Elizabeth, Sandra Lee. A.B., Cornell Coll., Iowa, 1948; Ph.D., Duke U., 1953. Faculty, Washington U., St. Louis, 1951-52; faculty UCLA, 1952—, prof., 1963—; vis. prof. Northwestern U., 1952, U. Wis., 1964, U. Mich., 1965, So. Ill. U., 1969, Tex. A&M, 1971-73; cons. Dept. Commerce, 1962; v.p. Found. Research in Econs. and Edn., 1971-73; pres. Internat. Inst. Econ. Research, 1974-86; v.p. Inst. for Contemporary Studies, 1986—; nationally syndicated radio commentator and newspaper columnist. Author: (with others) Foreign Trade and Finance, 1959, Essays in Economic Thought, 1960, University Economics, 3d edit., 1972, Exchange and Production, 3d edit., 1983, International Trade Theory, 1965, Midnight Economist, 1981; Adv. bd.: (with others) History of Polit. Economy, 1969-84, Social Sci. Quar, 1975—; contbr. articles to profl. jours. Served with USAAF, 1943-46. Social Sci. Research Council grantee, 1950-51, 62; Ford Found. grantee, 1958-59, 72-74; NSF grantee, 1965-66; Earhart Found. grantee, 1972, 74-75. Mem. Western Econ. Soc. (pres. 1970-71), So. Econ. Assn. (v.p. 1978-79), History of Econs. Soc. (v.p. 1974-75), Phi Beta Kappa. Home: 11809 Allaseba Dr Los Angeles CA 90066

ALLER, SONIA KONIALIAN, speech and language pathologist, psychologist; b. Aleppo, Syria, Sept. 10, 1944; came to U.S., 1968, naturalized, 1976; d. Assadour and Yeghisapet (Bizdikian) Konialian; m. Wayne Kendall Aller, Apr. 8, 1969. B.A. in Psychology, Beirut Coll. for Women, 1966; Ph.D. in Psychology, Ind. U., 1978. Cert. in speech and lang. pathology. Research assoc. Ctr. Behavior Research, Am. U. of Beirut, 1974-75; asst. prof. psychology, chmn. dept. St. Mary-of-the-Woods Coll., Ind., 1978-82; univ. affiliated fellow in clin. linguistics UCLA Neuro-psychiat. Inst., 1982-83; speech/lang. pathologist II, Los Angeles County-U. So. Calif. Med. Ctr., Los Angeles, 1983—; v.p. CompuLearn, Learning Unltd., Reseda, Calif., 1982—. Contbr. chpt. in book. Grantee Ford Found., 1974-75, NSF, 1979-81, NEH, 1982. Mem. Linguistics Soc. Am., Calif. Speech-Lang.-Hearing Assn., Calif. Neuropsychology Soc., Am. Speech, Lang. and Hearing Assn. (cert.). Armenian Orthodox.

ALLER, WAYNE KENDALL, psychology educator, researcher, computer education company executive; b. Slyvia, Kans., Feb. 20, 1933; s. Alvin Ray and Florence Dorothy (Snowbarger) A.; m. Sharon Cecelia Forray, Aug. 21, 1962 (div.); children—Jay Ramzi, Joyce Amal; m. Sonia Y. Konialian, Apr. 8, 1969. B.A. in Physics, N.W. Nazarene Coll., Nampa, Idaho, 1955; M.S. in Psychology, U. Wash., 1960, Ph.D. in Psychology, 1964. Asst. prof. psychology Pacific Lutheran U., 1962-64; asst. prof., chmn. div. behavioral scis. Beirut Coll. for Women, 1964-67; assoc. prof. Mankato State Coll., Minn., 1967-68; assoc. prof. Ind. State U., Terre Haute, from 1968, prof., to 1985; pres. CompuLearn, Learning Unlimited, 1985—; tech. writer, BMDP Statistical Software, 1986-87; sr. research adv. Ctr. Ednl. Research and Devel., Ministry Planning, Republic Lebanon, Beirut, 1974-75; sr. research assoc. Ctr. Behavioral Research, Am. U. of Beirut, 1974-75; vis. scholar dept. psychology UCLA, 1982-83; cons., tchr. English as fgn. lang. Vietnamese Affairs Ctr., Terre Haute, 1976-78. Author: Readings and Experiments in General Psychology, 1970, rev. edit., 1971. Ford Found. grantee, 1974-75. Mem. Am. Psychol. Assn., Western Psychol. Assn., N.Y. Acad. Scis., Soc. for Computers in Psychology, Sigma Xi, Psi Chi, Sigma Phi Iota. Presbyterian. Club: Wabash Valley Apple Byters (pres. 1981-82) (Terre Haute). Home: 17745 Stagg St Reseda CA 91335 Office: 12403 Ventura Ct Studio City CA 91604

ALLEY, CURTIS JOHN, viticulturist, researcher, consultant; b. Stockton, Calif., Aug.13, 1918; s. William Curtis and Emily Henrietta (Bareilles) A.; m. Elsie Sophie Frank, May 30, 1943; children—Michael C., Patricia A., John W., Kathy M. B.S., U. Calif.-Davis, 1940, Ph.D., 1951; cert. Boeing Sch. Aeronautics, Oakland, Calif., 1943. Research asst. dept. viticulture U. Calif.-Davis, 1938-41, 46-51; peach breeder Grant Merrill Orchards, Red Bluff, Calif., 1951-53; mgr. Calif. Grape Cert. Assn., Davis, 1953-57; mgr. Found. Plant Materials Service, Davis, 1957-71; specialist dept. viticulture and enology U. Calif.-Davis, 1971-82. Contbr. articles to profl. jours. Served as cpl. USAF, 1943-45, PTO. Mem. Internat. Plant Propagators Soc. (sec.-treas. 1962-83, disting. service award 1974, award of merit 1980), Am. Soc. Hort. Sci., Am. Soc. Enologists (hon.), Sigma Xi. Roman Catholic. Office: U Calif Dept Viticulture Davis CA 95616

ALLEY, WILLIAM EDWARD, III, physicist, researcher; b. Palo Alto, Calif., June 28, 1943; s. William Edward Jr. and Annabel Marie (Getzin) A.; m. Caryn Chiatovich, Oct. 18, 1969 (div. 1980); children: Lisa Marie, Jeffrey Edward, Jordan Clark Alley; m. Melanie Dawn Clark, Mar. 21, 1982; stepchildren: Lance Clark Adams, Guy Clark Adams. BA in Math. and Physics, San Jose State Coll., 1966; MS in Applied Sci., U. Calif., Davis, 1972, PhD, 1979. Programmer Lawrence Livermore (Calif.) Nat. Lab., 1966-74, physicist, 1974—. Contbr. articles to profl. jours. Mem. Am. Phys. Soc., AAAS, Phi Kappa Phi. Avocations: golf, sports, amateur astronomy. Office: U Calif Lawrence Livermore Nat Lab Livermore CA 94550

ALLIES, VICTORIA ROSSINI, electronics plant/process design consultant, chemical engineer; b. Southington, Conn., May 27, 1950; d. Leon and Lillian (Wanagus) Rossini; m. James M. McCarron, June 18, 1980; stepchildren—James Roy, Dolores, Lynn. Student Middlebury Coll., 1968-70; B.A. with honors, U. Conn., 1972, M.S., 1979; postgrad. U. Phoenix, 1980-81. Adhesive chemist Loctite Corp., Newington, Conn., 1972-76, adhesives engr., 1976-78; market devel. mgr. laminated materials dept. Gen. Electric, Coshocton, Ohio, 1978-79; process/p.c.b. start-up engr. ITT-Courier Terminal Systems, Inc., Tempe, Ariz., 1979-80; sr. chem. process engr., environ. engring. supr. Digital Equipment Corp., Tempe, 1980-82; pres., cons. Tng. 'n' Tech., Inc., Tempe, 1982—; facility design, review and implementation cons. Digitran Co. div. Becton Dickinson, Kodak, Hewlett-Packard, Xebec, Bechtel, L.M. Ericson, Sweden, 1982-84, Sino-CAD, Republic of China; sec.-treas. MCW Assocs., Inc., 1983-85; instr. chemistry Maricopa Community Coll., Phoenix 1981—; tech. expert cons. to joint venture of SWC and People's Republic of China, 1986—. Mem. Am. Chem. Soc., Ariz. Printed Circuit Bd. Assn., Soc. Women Engrs. Patentee temp. bonding adhesives. Home: 11455 S Half Moon Dr Phoenix AZ 85044 Office: 2121 W University Dr #108 Tempe AZ 85281

ALLIK, TIINA KATRIN, religious studies educator; b. Mpls., June 13, 1951; d. Erich Johannes and Anadie (Saluste) A. BS, MIT, 1972; MAR, Westminster Theol. Sem., 1974; PhD, Yale U., 1982. Asst. prof. theology Loyola Marymount U., Los Angeles, 1982—. Douglas Clyde Macintosh fellow for Theology and Philosophy of Religion, 1979-80;Kanzer fellow Kanzer Fund for Psychoanalysis and the Humanities, 1980-81; Deutsche Akademische Austauschdienst grantee, 1982; Loyola Marymount U. Summer Research grantee, 1985. Mem. Am. Acad. Religion (Narrative Theology Group, Person, Culture and Religion Group). Lutheran. Office: Loyola Marymount U Theology Dept Loyola Blvd at W 80th St Los Angeles CA 90045

ALLIONE, JODY ANN, management consultant; b. Tupper Lake, N.Y., May 3, 1952; d. Donald Paul and Nancy Margaret (Everest) La Barge; m. Milton S. Allione, June 4, 1977; 1 child, Eric Christopher. BS in Engring., Clarkson U., 1974; MBA, Pepperdine U., 1981. Sales trainee ABE Pump and Compressor, Allentown, Pa., 1974-75; sales engr. Worthington Pump Corp., Anaheim, Calif., 1975-78; dir. mktg. Brinderson Corp., Irvine, Calif., 1978-82; cons. K/A Assocs., Inc., Newport Beach, Calif., 1982-86; pres. Computer Temps., Inc., Newport Beach, 1984—; v.p. planning & mktg. Owl Energy Resources, Newport Beach, 1987—; cons. Ebasco Services, Inc., 1985-86, Owl Cos., 1983-86, Wolder Engring., 1983-85, POD, Inc., 1986, Metcalf and Eddy, 1984, Grunau Cos., 1983-85, Ficker and Ruffing, 1985. Named Outstanding Young Woman of Yr., 1978. Mem. Soc. Mktg. Profl. Services, Bus. Devel. of Orange County, Pacific Energy Assn. (chmn. arrangements com. 1984-85, Cert. Merit 1983), Newport Harbor C. of C., Orange County C. of C. Club: Newport Beach Tennis. Avocations: skiing, tennis, sailing, scuba, windsurfing. Home: 126 Via Xanthe Newport Beach CA 92663 Office: 4901 Birch St Newport Beach CA 92660

ALLISON, MARVIN LAWRENCE (LARRY), journalist; b. Phoenix, Aug. 8, 1934; s. George Lewis and Dorothy (Kinsella) A.; m. Patricia Ann Kiley, Apr. 2, 1954; 1 child, Marvin Lawrence. Student, Sorbonne, Paris, 1952-53, Long Beach State Coll., 1953-54. Reporter Downey (Calif.) Live Wire, 1955-57; copy editor Stars & Stripes newspaper, Darmstadt, Fed. Republic Germany, 1962, Press Telegram (formerly Ind. Press-Telegram), Long Beach, Calif., 1957-62; reporter Press Telegram (formerly Ind. Press-Telegram), 1963-66; copy editor Press Telegram (formerly Ind. Press-Telegram), Long Beach, 1966-68, mng. editor, 1969-76, editor, 1978—; asst. to pub. Lexington (Ky.) Herald-Leader, 1976-77; assoc. editor Detroit Free Press, 1977-78. Nieman fellow Harvard U., 1968-69. Mem. AP Mng. Editors Assn. (pres. 1981), Sigma Delta Chi. Club: Harvard (Los Angeles). Office: Ind Press Telegram 604 Pine Ave Long Beach CA 90844

ALLISON, RICHARD CASE, geology educator; b. Seattle, Oct. 19, 1935; s. Charles William and Bertha Helen (Lance) A.; m. Carol Kathleen Daily Wagner, Oct. 20, 1967; stepchildren: Ruth Elizabeth Wagner, Paul Barnaby Wagner. BS in Geology, U. Wash., 1957, MS in Geology, 1959; PhD in Paleontology, U. Calif., Berkeley, 1967. Assoc. prof. geology U. Alaska, Fairbanks, 1968-75, prof., 1975—, head geology/geophysics program, 1981-84, chmn. dept. geology and geophysics, 1984; affiliate in malacology and invertebrate paleontology U. Alaska Mus., Fairbanks, 1973—; cons. to State of Alaska and various energy corps., 1969—; com. co-chmn. 1st Internat. Congress on Pacific Neogene Stratigraphy, 1976-79; appointee U.S. Geol. Survey, 1979-82. Contbr. articles to profl. jours. Mem. Paleontol. Soc., Palaeontol. Assn. (Eng.), Internat. Paleontol. Union, Paleontol. Research Instn., Alaska Geol. Soc., Pacific Coast Sect. Soc. Econ. Paleontologists and Mineralogists, Sigma Xi, Phi Kappa Phi. Republican. Home: 1055 Kodiak Fairbanks AK 99709 Office: U Alaska Dept Geology and Geophysics Fairbanks AK 99775

ALLMAN, JOHN MORGAN, neurobiology educator; b. Columbus, Ohio, May 17, 1943; m. Evelyn McGuiness, June 26, 1977. BA, U. Va., 1965; PhD, U. Chgo., 1970. Asst. prof. biology Calif. Inst. Tech., Pasadena, 1974-77, assoc. prof., 1977-84, prof., 1984—. Grantee NIH, 1974—. Mem. Soc. for Neurosci. Avocation: conservation of nature. Office: Calif Inst Tech 216-76 Pasadena CA 91125

ALLMON, MICHAEL BRYAN, accountant; b. Oceanside, Calif., July 14, 1951; s. William Bryan and Cecelia Audrey (Wright) A.; m. Monika Ann Arth, Sept. 15, 1979. BBA, U. Tex., 1975; MBT U. So. Calif. CPA, Calif. Staff acct. Alexander Grant & Co., Los Angeles, 1976-77; acct. Laventhol & Horwath, CPA's, Los Angeles, 1977-85; ptnr. Zusman, Cameron and Allmon, CPA's, 1985—;chief exec. officer, dir. Essential Profl. Services, Inc., 1985—. Mem. Am. Inst. CPA's (fed. tax div.), Calif. Soc. CPA's (taxation com.), Internat. Assn. for Fin. Planning, Acctg. Circle U. So. Calif. Clubs: Walnut Track (pres. team) (Los Angeles), Manhattan Country (Manhattan Beach, Calif.).

ALLOWAY, ANNE MAUREEN SCHUBERT, industrial waste administrator; b. Martinez, Calif., Oct. 19, 1954; d. James Benjamin and Mariel Ann (Phillips) Schubert; m. William Glenn Alloway, Jr., Apr. 27, 1974 (div.); children: Joseph Benjamin, Odinn Glenn, Aaron Dean. AS in Life Sci., Allan Hancock Coll., 1982, AA in Liberal Arts, 1982. Cert. indsl. waste insp., 1984. Indsl. waste insp. City of Santa Maria, Calif., 1982-86; mgr. indsl. pretreatment program, collection systems Simi Valley (Calif.) County Sanitation Dist., 1986—; sect. chmn. Tri-Counties Pub. Edn. Mem. Calif. Water Pollution Control Assn. (state com.), Water Pollution Control Fedn. Republican. Roman Catholic. Club: Santa Maria Racquetball, Coast and Valley Health. Lodge: Keepers of the Flame. Avocations: painting, writing, sports, reading. Home: 1763 Cochran #G Simi Valley CA 93065 Office: Simi Valley County Sanitation Dist 500 W Los Angeles Ave Simi Valley CA 93065

ALLOWAY, BRUCE DONALD, broadcasting executive; b. Edmonton, Alta., Can., June 15, 1923; s. Frank Elmer and Edna May (Arndt) A.; m. Joan Christina Paterson, June 8, 1946; children—Susan Barry, Gordon, Christine Bradbury. Grad., U. Alta., 1944; postgrad. Banff Sch. Art, Alta., 1968. Account exec. Stas. CJCA/CFAC, Edmonton and Calgary, 1944-46, All-Can. Radio, Toronto, 1947-49; gen. sales mgr. Sta. CKXL, Calgary, 1950-54; gen. sales mgr. Sta. CFRN-TV, Edmonton, 1955-60, mgr., 1961-81; v.p., gen. mgr. Sunwapta Broadcasting Ltd., Edmonton, 1982—; dir. CTV TV Network, Toronto, Guaranty Trust, Edmonton, 1983—. Recipient Can. Centennial medal Govt. Can., 1967. Mem. Edmonton/Harbin China Friendship Soc. Progressive Conservative. Mem. United Ch. Can. Club: Royal Glenora (Edmonton). Lodge: Rotary. Home: 14007 89A Ave, Edmonton, AB Canada T5R 4S4 Office: Sta CFRN TV, Box 5030 Sta E, Edmonton, AB Canada T5P 4C2

ALLRED, JAMES L., architect. BArch, Idaho State U., 1965. Lic. architect, Colo., Ariz. Dir. design, sec.-treas., founding ptnr. Allred/Fisher Architects, Engrs., Littleton, Colo. Named Small Businessman of Yr., Colo. Mem. AIA. Home: 3481 S Fenton St H308 Denver CO 80227 Office: Allred Fisher Architects Engrs 26 W Dry Creek Circle Suite 250 Littleton CO 80210

ALLSWANG, JOHN MYERS, computer science educator, historian; b. Chgo., Jan. 16, 1937; s. Eugene Allen and Katherine (Myers) A.; m. Suzanne Menzel, Dec. 19, 1964; children: Eden, Yael. BA, U. Ill., 1959; MA, U. Iowa, 1960; PhD, U. Pitts., 1967. Instr. No. Ill. U., Dekalb, 1965-66; asst. prof. No. Mich. U., Marquette, 1966-68; prof. Calif. State U., Los Angeles, 1968—; vis. prof. Hebrew U., Jerusalem, 1971-72, U. Leiden, The Netherlands, 1977-78; prin. Computer Explanations, Los Angeles, 1982—. Author: Bosses, Machines and Urban Voters, 1986, Physician's Guide to Computers, 1985, New Deal and American Politics, 1978, House for All Peoples, 1972; columnist Rx Home Care mag., Los Angeles, 1985—; contbg. editor Interface Age mag., Cerritos, Calif., 1982-84, IBM PC Update mag., Indpls., 1984—. Adult vol. SafeRides program, Los Angeles, 1986. IBM fellow, 1968; recipient Merit award Calif. State U., Los Angeles, 1985, 86. Mem. Orgn. Am. Historians, Computer Press Assn. Democrat. Jewish. Avocations: travel, food. Home: 2438 La Condesa Dr Los Angeles CA 90049 Office: Calif State U 5151 State University Dr Los Angeles CA 90049

ALMGREN, HOWARD HANS, sanitary engineer; b. Chgo., May 1, 1938; s. Hans and Edna (Risberg) A.; m. Jeanette Elizabeth Treat, Sept. 30, 1972. BSCE with distinction, Northwestern U., 1961; MS in Sanitary Engring., U. Calif., Berkeley, 1962, PhD in Sanitary Engring., 1966. Registered profl. engr., Calif., Ariz., Hawaii, Nev. Project engr. U. Calif., Berkeley, 1963-66; postgrad. research fellow Norwegian Govt.; project engr. Norwegian Inst. Water Research, Oslo, 1966-69, Santee County (Calif.) Water Dist., 1969-72; cons. Govt. of Singapore, 1972-73; sr. san. engr. Boyle Engring. Corp., Newport Beach, Calif., 1973-74; pvt. practice san. engring. cons. La Jolla, Calif., 1974-80; prin. engr. Neste, Brudin & Stone, Inc., San Diego, 1980-85; v.p. Almgren & Koptionak, Inc., San Diego, 1985—; lectr. San Diego State U., 1974-75. Mem. ASCE, Am. Water Works Assn., Am. Pub. Works Assn., Water Pollution Control Fedn., Am. Acad. of Environ. Engrs., Soc. Am. Mil. Engrs., Sigma Xi, Tau Beta Pi, Chi Epsilon. Home: 2075 Caminito Circulo Sur La Jolla CA 92037 Office: Almgren & Koptionak Inc 9968 Hibert St Suite 102 San Diego CA 92131

ALMGREN, LOUIS EDGAR, engineer, fire protection consultant; b. San Diego, Apr. 2, 1926; s. Louis Robert Almgren and Virginia Lucile (Austin) Dougherty; m. Ruth Helena Fisher, Aug. 24, 1950; Christine A., Louis N., Theresa R., Jon M. BA, San Diego State Coll., 1947; MS, Stanford U., 1949. Registered fire protection engr. and civil engr., Calif. Fire protection engr. Pacific Fire Rating Bur., Los Angeles, 1949-61; fire protection engr., v.p. Gage Babcock & Assoc., San Francisco, 1961-72; mgr., engr. The Ansul Co., Marriette, Wis., 1972-74, The FPE Group, San Francisco, 1974-80, Sierra Cons. Internat., San Francisco, 1980—. Mem. Soc. Fire Protection Engrs. (bd. dirs. 1973-79), Am. Soc. Civil Engrs. Republican. Office: Sierra Cons Internat 145 Natoma St San Francisco CA 94109

ALMQUIST, ROBERT DEAN, lawyer; b. Weyburn, Sask., Can., Jan. 17, 1957; came to U.S., 1985; s. Henry Robert and Mynra Louise (Hoium) A. B in Adminstrn., U. Regina, Sask., 1980; LLB, U. Sask., Saskatoon, 1981; JD, U. Detroit, 1983. Bar: Sask. 1982, Ariz., 1984, U.S. Dist. Ct. Ariz. 1985, U.S. Ct. Appeals (9th cir.) 1985. Assoc. barrister, solicitor Hill, McLellan, Ball, Cundall & Bridges, Estevan, Sask., Can., 1982; sole practice Weyburn, 1983-84; assoc. Murphy & Posner, Phoenix, 1985—. Mem. ABA, State Bar Ariz., Law Soc. Sask., Maricopa County Bar Assn., Assn. Trial Lawyers Am., Ariz. Trial Lawyers Assn. Home: 16801 N 49th St Apt 216 Scottsdale AZ 85254 Office: Murphy & Posner 320 Biltmore Commerce Ctr 3200 E Camelback Phoenix AZ 85018

ALOIA, ROLAND CRAIG, research scientist; b. Newark, Dec. 21, 1943; s. Roland S. and Edna M. (Mahan) A.; m. Kathyrn A. Platt, June 15, 1974. BS, St. Mary's Coll., 1965; PhD, U. Calif., Riverside, 1970. Postdoctoral fellow City of Hope, Duarte, Calif., 1971-75; research biologist U. Calif., Riverside, 1975-76; asst. prof. biology Loma Linda (Calif.) U., 1976-79, assoc. prof., 1979—; chemist Vets. Hosp., Loma Linda, 1979—. Editor: Membrane Fluidity in Biology vols. 1-4, 1983, 85. Pres. Riverside chpt. Calif. Heart Assn., 1979-80, 1984-86, bd. dirs., exec. com. mem., 1973-86. Calif. Heart Assn. fellow, 1971-73. Mem. Am. Chem. Soc., N.Y. Acad. Scis., Soc. Cell Biology, Sigma Xi. Avocations: jogging, piano, reading, marksmanship. Office: Loma Linda U Med Ctr Dept Anesthesiology Loma Linda CA 92354 address: Jerry Pettis Vets Hosp Anesthesiology Service Loma Linda CA 92357

ALONSO, CARLOS RAUL, architectural project manager, designer; b. Tijuana, Mexico, July 20, 1957; came to U.S., 1975; s. Jose and Rebeca (Martinez) A.; m. Virginia Luna, Sept. 13, 1978; 1 child, Sarit Sigrid. AA in Architecture, Southwestern Coll., Chula Vista, Calif., 1977; BS in Architecture, U. So. Calif., 1980. Draftsman Alfredo Larin, AIA, San Diego, 1977; jr. designer John V. Mutlow, AIA, Los Angeles, 1978-79; designer Sheldon B. Caris, AIA, Los Angeles, 1979-81; project designer Marvin Berman, AIA, Encino, Calif., 1980-81; project mgr. Archiplan, Los Angeles, 1981-85, TNP Constrn. Co, Camarillo, Calif., 1985—. Editor So. Calif. Assocs. Newsletter; mem. editorial bd. L.A. Architect mag., 1984. Served with Mex. armed forces, 1981-82. Recipient hon. mention San Diego Lumber and Wood Products Assn., 1977. Mem. Los Angeles Conservancy, U. So. Calif. Archtl. Guild, Nat. Trust Hist. Preservation, Voyage 4 Design Forum (chmn. 1985-86), AIA (assoc., Los Angeles chpt. assoc. dir. 1985, assoc. dir. So. Calif. Council 1986). Jewish. Avocations: piano, cartooning, photography, camping, basketball. Office: TNP Constrn Co 155 Granada St Suite B Camarillo CA 93010

ALPER, MARSHALL EDWARD, aerospace program manager; b. N.Y.C., Feb. 9, 1930; s. Isidore H. and Estelle Sarah (Drazien) A.; m. Marcia Edith Ufland, June 7, 1956; children: Ian Howard, Robin Emily, Julia Lynn, Sharon Amy. SB, MIT, 1951, ScD, 1962. Teaching asst. MIT, Boston, 1951-55; research engr. Jet Propulsion Lab., Pasadena, Calif., 1955-64, section mgr. applied mech., 1964-71, mgr. civil and solar energy programs, 1971-85, mgr. energy, environ. and health programs, 1985—. Contbr. articles to profl. jours.; inventor Automated Parking Structure. Pres. Pasadena Jewish Temple, 1965-67, various positions held since 1965; chmn. energy com. Community Relations Com., Los Angeles, 1982-84. Recipient Exceptional Service medal NASA, 1982, D. Michel Achievement award, NASA/Cosmic, 1986. Mem. AIAA, AAAS. Avocations: camping, sailing, photography, reading. Home: 2286 Lambert Dr Pasadena CA 91107 Office: Jet Propulsion Lab 4800 Oak Grove Dr Pasadena CA 91109

ALPERS, EDWARD ALTER, history educator; b. Phila., Apr. 23, 1941; s. Bernard Jacob and Lillian (Sher) A.; m. Ann Adele Dixon, June 14, 1963; children—Joel Dixon, Leila Sher. A.B. magna cum laude, Harvard U., 1963; Ph.D., U. London, 1966. Lectr. history Univ. Coll., Dar es Salaam, Tanzania, 1966-68; from asst. prof. to prof. history UCLA, 1968—, dean div. honors Coll. Letters and Sci., UCLA, 1985—. Author: Ivory and Slaves in East Central Africa, 1975. Editor: Walter Rodney: Revolutionary and Scholar, 1982; editor newsletter Assn. Concerned Africa Scholars, 1983-85; contbr. articles to scholarly jours. Ford Found. fellow, 1972-73; NEH fellow, 1978-79; Fulbright fellow, 1980; Fundacao Calouste Gulbenkian grantee, Lisbon, Portugal, 1975. Mem. Africa Studies Assn. (bd. dirs. 1985—), Assn. Concerned Africa Scholars (exec. bd. 1983—), Brit. Inst. in Eastern Africa, Can. Assn. African Studies, Somali Studies Internat. Assn. Office: UCLA Dept History Div Honors 405 Hilgard Ave Los Angeles CA 90024

ALPERS, W. FRANK, concert baritone; b. Los Angeles, Apr. 10, 1924; s. Benjamin Francis and Lora Audrey (Gipson) A.; m. Roberta Vern Johns, Dec. 17, 1948; children—Sharon Vern, Debra Lynne. Student Los Angeles City Coll., 1941-42, 46-47, Art Center Sch., 1947-48, Ohio U., 1943, Calif. State U.-Los Angeles, 1950-52, Mt. San Antonio Coll., 1955-56. Soloist, Ralph Carmichael Singers, 1950-60; soloist, Laymen Singers, 1947—, Roger Wagner Chorale and Old Fashioned Revival Hour 1955-58, Old Fashioned Revival Hour, 1950-60, Frank Alpers Trio, 1960-66, Haven of Rest Radio, 1969-76, The King is Coming telecast, What's Your Question telecast, Teaching the Bible radio broadcast World Prophetic Ministry, Colton, Calif., 1976—; various solo recs. for Capitol, Coral, World, Tempo, Dial, Word labels; choral dir. Baptist chs., Greater Los Angeles area, 1947-77. Served with U.S. Army, 1943-46; ETO. Named Best Male Vocalist, Nat. Evang. Film Found., 1972. Mem. Am. Fedn. TV and Radio Artists, Am. Guild Mus. Artists. Republican. Baptist. Club: Kiwanis. Home: 244 S Wilbur Ave Covina CA 91724 Office: PO Drawer 907 Colton CA 92324

ALPERT, BETH ROSENBERG, speech pathologist, consultant; b. N.Y.C., Sept. 20, 1954; d. Fredrick and Rose (Ochstein) Rosenberg; m. Phillip Steven Alpert, Oct. 9, 1983; 1 child, David Alpert. BS, Northwestern U., 1976; M Med. Sci., Emory U., 1978. Cert. of clin. competence in speech pathology, Calif. Speech pathologist San Diego City Schs., 1978—; pvt. practice specializing in speech pathology San Diego, 1979—; guest lectr. San Diego State U., 1981, 84; supr. for cert. condidates San Diego City Schs., 1983-84; cons. in field., San Diego, 1979—. Chmn. pub. relations. Stride-Women's Orgn., San Diego, 1984-85, social com. San Diego City Schs., 1980—. Mem. Am. Speech and Hearing Assn., Calif. Speech and Hearing Assn. Democrat. Office: San Diego City Schs 4100 Normal St San Diego CA 92130

ALPERT, MICHAEL EDWARD, lawyer; b. Annapolis, Md., Nov. 13, 1942; s. Myron M. and Mary A. (Byrnes) A.; m. Deirdre Lehn Whittleton, Jan. 1, 1964; children—Lehn Patricia, Kristin Anne, Alison Daley. A.B., Pomona Coll., 1965; J.D., UCLA, 1969. Bar: Calif. 1970. Assoc., Gibson, Dunn & Crutcher, Los Angeles, 1969-72; chief dep. commr. corps. State of Calif., 1972-74; assoc. Gibson, Dunn & Crutcher, Los Angeles and San Diego, 1974-77, ptnr., 1977—. Bd. dirs. San Diego Repertory Theatre, 1978—; mem. San Diegans, Inc., 1976—, San Diego Econ. Devel. Corp., 1981—. Mem. ABA, State Bar Calif., San Diego County Bar Assn., San Diego Corp. Fin. Council (chmn. 1982-83), San Diego Central City Assn., Order of Coif, Phi Sigma Alpha. Mem. UCLA Law Rev., 1967-69. Democrat. Clubs: University Lomas Santa Fe Country (San Diego). Office: Gibson Dunn & Crutcher 600 B St San Diego CA 92101

ALPINIERI, LOUIS JOSEPH, aerospace company executive; b. Bklyn., Aug. 12, 1936; s. Salvatore and Virginia (Figurito) A.; m. Brenda Lee Porter, Sept. 15, 1962; children: Andrea, Steven. BA in Engring., Poly. Inst. N.Y., 1957, PhD, 1963; MS, Calif. Inst. Tech., 1960. Mem. tech. staff Aerospace Corp., El Segundo, Calif., 1963-65; prin. engr. Ford Aerospace, Newport Beach, Calif., 1965-67; sr. v.p. group, gen. mgr. Acurex Corp., Mountain View, Calif., 1968-79; pres. Vantage Assocs., Los Altos Hills, Calif., 1979-84, Vantage Assocs. Inc., San Diego, 1984—; bd. dirs. Flow Systems Inc., Seattle, Flowind Corp, Pleasanton, Calif., Sigma Research Inc., Seattle, Alten Corp., Mountain View, Life Support Systems Inc., Mountain View. Mem. Am. Elec. Assn., Soc. Aerospace Materials and Process Engring. Club: Commonwealth. Avocation: running. Home: 2678 Prestwick Ct La Jolla CA 92037 Office: Vantage Assocs Inc 6355 Nancy Ridge Dr San Diego CA 92121

ALSAKER, DANIEL LEE, small business owner; b. Moscow, Idaho, Aug. 12, 1950; s. Donald Ray and Bernice Ellen (Johnson) A.; m. Anne Virginia Murphy, Apr. 28, 1973; children: Dyche, Kama, Britt, Kjell. BA in Bus. Mgmt., U. Idaho, 1972. Pres. Alsaker Corp., Spokane, Wash., 1973—, Broadway Truck Stops, Spokane, 1980—. Active Cen. Valley Sch. Dist., Spokane, 1982—. Mem. Western Assn. Truck Stop Operators (bd. dirs. 1983—), Pvt. Industry Council Bd., Spokane Valley C. of C. (chmn. transp. sect. 1985-86), Sigma Alpha Epsilon (chmn. alumni com. 1983—). Lutheran. Lodge: Elks. Office: PO Box 14646 Spokane WA 99214

ALSTON, LELA, Ariz. state senator; b. Phoenix, June 26, 1942; d. Virgil Lee and Frances Mae Koonse Mulkey; B.S., U. Ariz., 1967; M.S., Ariz. State U., 1971; children—Brenda Susan, Charles William. Tchr. high sch., 1968—; mem. Ariz. State Senate, 1977—. Named Disting. Citizen, U. Ariz. Alumni Assn., 1978. Mem. NEA, Ariz. Edn. Assn., Am. Home Econs. Assn., Ariz. Home Econs. Assn., Am. Vocat. Assn. Methodist. Office: Capitol Bldg Senate Wing Phoenix AZ 85007

ALTAMURA, MICHAEL VICTOR, physician; b. Bklyn., Sept. 28, 1923; s. Frank and Theresa (Inganamorte) A.; BS, L.I. U., 1949; MA, Columbia U.,

1951; DO, Kirksville Coll., 1961; MD, Calif. Coll. Medicine, 1962; m. Emily Catherine Wandell, Sept. 21, 1948; children: Michael Victor, Robert Frank. Intern, Los Angeles County Gen. Hosp., 1961-62; practice medicine specializing in family practice, Sunnyvale, Calif., 1962—; staff El Camino Hosp., chief family practice dept., 1972-73; preceptor family practice Stanford Sch. Medicine, 1972-73, clin. asst. prof., 1974-81, clin. assoc. prof., 1982—; assoc. prof. family medicine Calif. Coll. Osteopathic Medicine, 1985—; preceptor family practice Davis (Calif.) Sch. Medicine, 1974-75. Served to 1st lt. AUS, 1942-45, 51-53; ETO. Recipient Order of Golden Sword, Am. Cancer Soc., 1973. Diplomate Am. Bd. Family Practice. Fellow Am. Acad. Family Physicians (pres. Santa Clara County chpt. 1972-73), Royal Soc. Health, Am. Geriatric Soc.; mem. AMA, Calif., Santa Clara County socs., Internat. Platform Assn. Republican. Lutheran. Author: (with Mary Falconer and Helen Behnke) Aging Patients: A Guide for Their Care. Office: 500 E Remington St Sunnyvale CA 94087

ALTER, EDWARD T., state treasurer; b. Glen Ridge, N.J., July 26, 1941; s. E. Irving and Norma (Fisher) A.; m. Patricia R. Olsen, 1975; children: Christina Lyn, Ashly Ann, Darci Lee. B.A., U. Utah., 1966; M.B.A., U. Utah, 1967. C.P.A., Calif., Utah. Sr. acct. Touche Ross & Co., Los Angeles, 1967-72; asst. treas. U. Utah, Salt Lake City, 1972-80; treas. State of Utah, Salt Lake City, 1981-87; pres. Nat. Assn. State Treas., 1987—. Bd. dirs. Utah Housing Fin. Agy.; bd. dirs. Utah State Retirement Bd.; mem. Utah State Republican Central Com., from 1981. Served to sgt. USAR, 1958-66. Mem. Am. Inst. CPAs, Nat. Assn. State Treas. (past sr. v.p., pres. 1987), Delta Sigma Pi, Delta Phi Kappa. Club: Utah Bond (pres. 1981-82). Office: 215 State Capitol Salt Lake City UT 84114

ALTER, GERALD L., business executive; b. Rensselaer, Ind., Aug. 24, 1910; s. Leslie and Lettie (Willis) A.; m. Margaret A. Davis, Sept. 15, 1929; children: Judith Ann (dec.), John Edward. Student Bus. Coll., 1927-28. Clk. and office mgr., 1929-35; bldg. contractor, 1936-45; real estate broker and ins. agt., 1946—; pres. Alter Realty & Ins., Leads, Inc., investments, Alter Ins. Agy., Inc., REMCO Real Estate Mgmt. Co., Alter Devel. Co.; pres. Developers & Builders. Planning commr. City of Torrance, 1966-83, chmn. Torrance Planning Commn. 1982-83; water commr. City of Torrance, 1984—; former bd. dirs. Harbor Area United Way. Mem. Torrance-Lomita-Carson Bd. Realtors (pres. 1978, v.p. 1980-81), Calif. Assn. Realtors (dir. 1978-81), Nat. Assn. Realtors, Torrance C. of C. (past dir.), Am. Legion. Republican. Clubs: OX-5 (pioneer airman), Rotary. Home: 1337 Engracia Ave Torrance CA 90501 Office: 2305 Torrance Blvd Torrance CA 90501

ALTFELD, MERWIN RICHARD, artist, educator; b. Elyria, Ohio, Sept. 19, 1913; s. Otis Charles and Kate Gertrude (Klein) A.; m. Mildred Frances Kirschbaum, June 23, 1936; children—Linda Voorsanger, Pamela Malone. B.A., Case Western Res. U., 1934; postgrad. UCLA, 1966-68. Cert. tchr., Calif. One-man shows: Calif. State U., Sacramento, 1978, SUNY, Alfred, 1979, Nylander Mus., Caribou, Maine, 1979; Loyola U., New Orleans, 1980, Santa Monica Library (Calif.), 1983; Senior Eye, Long Beach, Calif. 1984; group shows include: San Diego Mus., 1963, Swedish Mus., Stockholm, 1972, Nat. Acad. Design, N.Y.C., 1972, Watercolor U.S.A., Springfield, Mass., 1973, Palm Desert Mus., Palm Springs, Calif., 1974, San Diego Internat., 1984; represented in permanent collections: Queen Mary ship, Long Beach, Calif., Brugger Collection, Los Angeles; gen. mgr. Ford's Drug Stores, Buffalo, 1940-47; owner Merwin R. Altfeld & Assocs., Los Angeles, 1948-86. Active Jewish Big Bros., Los Angeles, 1965-74; hon. mem. Long Beach (Calif.) Mus., 1986—; bd. dirs. Artists for Ednl. Action, Los Angeles, 1978-82. Recipient Am. Traditional awards, 1955; Santa Monica ann. award, 1964; Delmar ann. graphics award 1964; Westwood ann. award, 1963, Nat. Watercolor Soc. award, 1974. Mem. Los Angeles Contemporary Art Gallery, (bd. dirs.), Westwood Centre of Arts (pres. 1965), Hollywood Press Club, Hollywood Media Assn. Nat. Watercolor Soc. (pres. 1972). Home: 18426 Wakecrest Dr Malibu CA 90265

ALTGELT, KLAUS HERMANN, physical chemist consultant; b. Wiesbaden, Fed. Republic Germany, Jan. 30, 1927; came to U.S., 1959; m. Sigrid M. Adolph, Aug. 11, 1952; children: K. Thomas, Claudia Christine. BS, U. Mainz, Fed. Republic Germany, 1952, MS in Phys. Chemistry, 1955, PhD in Phys. Chemistry, 1958. Instr. phys. chemistry U. Mainz, 1954-59; research assoc. dept. biology MIT, Cambridge, 1959-61; research chemist Chevron Research Co. subs. Standard Oil Calif., 1961-65, sr. research chemist, 1965-86, sr. research assoc., 1986; lectr. on phys. chemistry; cons. in field. Editor: Gel Permeation Chromatography, 1971, Chromatography in Petroleum Analysis, 1977; contbr. articles to profl. jours.; patentee in field. Recipient Bundesverdienstkreuz. Mem. Am. Chem. Soc. (chmn. GPC symposium 1972, petroleum chemistry div.), German Sch. San Francisco (v.p. 1967, pres. 1968-71, trustee 1971-74). Democrat. Unitarian. Avocations: hiking, kayaking, sailing, Classical music, traveling. Home and Office: 555 Appleberry Dr San Rafael CA 94903

ALTHERR, LAWANDA, educational consultant, Realtor; b. Ajo, Ariz., Jan. 27, 1926; d. Jesse Hoyt and Mayme Ellen (Amerson) Smith; m. Robert Kenneth Altherr, Aug. 5, 1946 (div.); children—Gary, Larry, Gregory, Brenda, Bryan, Robert. Assoc. in Nursing, Phoenix Coll., 1970; B.S. in Nursing, Ariz. State U., 1975; M.A. in Vocat. Edn., U. No. Ariz., 1978. Staff nurse surg. intensive care unit Maricopa County Gen. Hosp./Maricopa Med. Center 1970-72, inservice instr. 1973-75, dir. tng. and devel. 1975-83, dir. bio-med. communication dept. 1980-83, ret., 1983; ednl. cons., asst. project dir. U. Ariz., 1983-86; part time Realtor, Exec. Assocs., 1983—. Mem. Ariz. Vocat. Assn., Ariz. Assn. Realtors, Phoenix Bd. Realtors. Home: 1307 W Thomas St Phoenix AZ 85013 Office: 5533 N 19th Ave Suite 123 Phoenix AZ 85015

ALTMAN, ADELE ROSENHAIN, physician; b. Tel Aviv, Israel, June 4, 1924; came to U.S., 1933, naturalized, 1939; d. Bruno and Salla (Silberzweig) Rosenhain; m. Emmett Altman, Sept. 3, 1944; children: Brian R., Alan L., Karen D. Diplomate Am. Bd. Radiology. Intern Queens Gen. Hosp., N.Y.C., 1949-51; resident Hosp. for Joint Diseases, N.Y.C., 1951-52, Roosevelt Hosp., N.Y.C., 1955-57; clin. instr. radiology Downstate Med. Ctr., SUNY, Bklyn., 1957-61; asst. prof. radiology N.Y. Med. Coll., N.Y.C., 1961-65, assoc. prof., 1965-68; assoc. prof. radiology U. Okla. Health Sci. Ctr., Oklahoma City, 1968-78; assoc. prof. dept. radiology U. N.Mex. Sch. Medicine, Albuquerque, 1978-85. Author: Radiology of the Respiratory System: A Basic Review, 1978; contbr. articles to profl. jours. Fellow Am. Coll. Angiology, N.Y. Acad. Medicine; mem. Am. Coll. Radiology, Am. Roentgen Ray Soc., Assn. Univ. Radiologists, Radiol. Soc. N.Am. Clubs: Hadassah, B'nai B'rith Women.

ALTMAN, BRUCE ALLAN, city official; b. Milw., Dec. 13, 1937; s. Harry and Janet (Nemacheck) A.; m. Barbara Lou Altman, June 14, 1960; children—Tom, Tim. B.S., Ariz. State U., 1961; postgrad. U. So. Calif., 1961-64. Asst. city mgr. City of Claremont, Calif., 1961-64; city mgr. City of Newark, Calif., 1968-69, City of Brisbane, Calif., 1969-73, Pub. of Simi Valley, Calif., 1974-80, City of Palm Desert, Calif., 1983—; pub. adminstr. Los Angeles County, 1974-80; dir. pub. sector cons. Coopers & Lybrand, Los Angeles, 1980-83; mgr. City of Palm Desert, Calif., 1983—. Contbr. articles to profl. jours. Vice chmn. Project Star, Sacramento, 1971-73; bd. dirs. Ariz. Clean and Beautiful, 1985—; bd. dirs. bus. and industry council Glendale Community Coll., 1986—. Named Outstanding Mgmt. Innovator, Internat. City Mgrs. Assn., 1971; Recipient Stephen Maither Regional award 1986. Mem. Nat. Park and Conservation Assn., Adminstrv. Achievement award Am. Soc. Pub. Adminstrn., 1971. Mem. Am. Soc. Pub. Adminstrn. (v.p. 1982-83). Home: 48240 Beverly Dr Palm Desert CA 92260 Office: City of Palm Desert 73 510 Fred Waring Dr Palm Desert CA 92260

ALTROCK, RICHARD CHARLES, astrophysicist; b. Omaha, Dec. 20, 1940; s. Raymond John and Ada Ann (Baumann) A.; m. Janice Carol Reed, Mar. 23, 1963 (div. 1977); children—Craig Edward and Christopher Raymond (twins); m. Sally K. Neidig, Mar. 10, 1979; 1 child, Kristin Ann. B.S. In Physics and Math., U. Nebr., 1962; Ph.D. in Astro-Geophysics, U. Colo., 1968. Research asst. U. Nebr., Lincoln, 1959-61; teaching asst. U. Nebr., 1962; mathematician U.S. Army Engrs., Omaha, 1962; grad. asst. High Altitude Obs., Boulder, Colo., 1963-67; astrophysicist Air Force Geophysics Lab., Nat. Solar Obs., Sunspot, N.Mex., 1967—; work unit mgr. Air Force Geophysics Lab., 1976—, contract mgr., 1976—; co-investigator NASA High Resolution Solar Observatory, 1981—; guest investigator NASA Solar Maximum Mission, 1984-86; vis. research fellow U. Sydney, Australia, 1971-72; proposal reviewer NASA, 1978, NSF, 1980—. Contbr. articles to profl. jours. Bd. govs. N.Mex. Civil Liberties Union, 1974-76. Woodrow Wilson fellow, 1962-63; High Altitude Obs. fellow, 1962-63; Australian Commonwealth Sci. and Indsl. Research Orgn. travel grantee, 1971-72. Fellow AAAS; mem. Internat. Astron. Union, Am. Astron. Soc., Am. Geophys. Union, ACLU, Sigma Xi, Pi Mu Epsilon, Phi Beta Kappa, Delta Phi Alpha, Phi Gamma Delta. Home: PO Box 645 Cloudcroft NM 88317 Office: Nat Solar Obs Sunspot NM 88349

ALTUS, GRACE MERRIMAN THOMPSON, psychologist; b. Santa Barbara, Calif., Jan. 6, 1924; d. James Roderick and Mary Augusta (Merriman) Thompson; B.A., Santa Barbara Coll., 1944; M.A. (Allan D. Wilson Jr. Meml. scholar 1947-48), U. Calif.-Berkeley, 1947, Ph.D., 1949; m. William David Altus, Dec. 24, 1951 (dec. 1986); children—Martha Helen, Elizabeth Diane, Deborah Elaine. Tchr. Redlands (Calif.) Jr. High Sch., 1944-46; psychologist Santa Barbara (Calif.) County schs., 1949-53, dir. guidance, 1953-56; psychologist Goleta (Calif.) Union Sch. dist., 1966—. Fellow AAAS, Am. Psychol. Assn.; mem. Calif. Tchrs. Assn., NEA, Goleta Edn. Assn., U. Calif. at Santa Barbara Faculty Women (pres. 1958), Sierra Club. Club: Channel City Women's Forum (Santa Barbara). Contbr. articles to profl. jours. Home: 767 Las Palmas Dr Santa Barbara CA 93110 Office: Goleta Union Sch Dist 401 N Fairview Ave Goleta CA 93117

ALVARADO, MARILYN DEL MAR, paralegal; b. Los Angeles, Dec. 5, 1960; d. Eliud Eric Del Mar; m. Vicente Rolando Alvarado, Jr., Nov. 1, 1984. ABA paralegal cert. in litigation U. West Los Angeles Sch. Paralegal Studies, 1983; student Calif. State U., Los Angeles, 1978-80; BA in Psychology, Calif. State U., Northridge, 1982. Litigation paralegal Overton, Lyman & Prince, Los Angeles, 1982; litigation and bankruptcy paralegal Loeb & Loeb, Los Angeles, 1983-85; litigation and collections paralegal Graham & James, Los Angeles, 1985—; cosmetic rep. Avon Products, Inc., Los Angeles, 1985-86. Intern Los Angeles Mayor's Office, 1980-81. Recipient cert. appreciation Los Angeles Mayor's Office, 1981; Calif. Scholarship Bd. grantee Calif. State U.-Los Angeles, then Calif. State U.-Northridge, 1978-82. Mem. Los Angeles Paralegal Assn., Nat. Paralegal Assn., Nat. Assn. Female Execs., Am. Film Inst. Republican. Baptist. Avocations: photography; music; horses; painting. Home: 4416 Maplewood Ave Los Angeles CA 90004 Office: Graham & James Citicorp Plaza 725 S Figueroa St 34th Floor Los Angeles CA 90017

ALVAREZ, ANNE MAINO, plant pathologist; b. Rochester, Minn., Apr. 14, 1941; d. Charles Runston and Jeannette (Gould) Maino; m. Robustiano Alvarez. BA, Stanford U., 1962; MS, U. Calif., Berkeley, 1966, PhD, 1972. Instr. U. Neuquen, Argentina, 1969-71, Windward Community Coll., Kaneohe, Hawaii, 1973; extension specialist U. Hawaii, Honolulu, 1973-75, from asst. to assoc. plant pathologist, 1975-86, plant pathologist, 1986—. Assoc. editor Jour. Plant Disease, 1985—; contbr. articles to profl. jours. Research fellow Internat. Inst. Ciencias Agrarias, Costa Rica, 1966; grantee USDA, 1981-87. Mem. Am. Soc. Microbiology, Am. Phytopath. Soc., Sigma Xi, Gamma Sigma Delta. Office: U Hawaii Dept Plant Pathology 3190 Maile Way Honolulu HI 96822

ALVAREZ, LUIS W., physicist; b. San Francisco, June 13, 1911; s. Walter C. and Harriet S. (Smyth) A.; m. Geraldine Smithwick, 1936; children: Walter, Jean; m. Janet L. Landis, 1958; children: Donald and Helen. B.S., U. Chgo., 1932, M.S., 1934, Ph.D., 1936, Sc.D., 1967; Sc.D., Carnegie-Mellon U., 1968, Kenyon Coll., 1969, Notre Dame U., 1976, Ain Shams U., Cairo, 1979, Pa. Coll. Optometry, 1982. Research asso., instr., asst. prof., asso. prof. U. Calif., 1936-45, prof. physics, 1945-78, prof. emeritus, 1978—; asso. dir. Lawrence Radiation Lab., 1954-59, 75-78; radar research and devel. Mass. Inst. Tech., 1940-43, Los Alamos, 1944-45; dir. Hewlett Packard Co. Recipient Collier Trophy, 1946; Medal for Merit, 1948; John Scott medal, 1953; Einstein medal, 1961; Nat. Medal of Sci., 1964; Michelson award, 1965; Nobel prize in physics, 1968; Wright prize, 1981; Rockwell medal, 1986; named Calif. Scientist of Year, 1960; named to Nat. Inventors Hall of Fame, 1978. Fellow Am. Phys. Soc. (pres. 1969); mem. Nat. Acad. Scis., Nat. Acad. Engring., Am. Philos. Soc., Am. Acad. Arts and Scis., Phi Beta Kappa, Sigma Xi; asso. mem. Institut D'Egypte. Office: Univ of Calif Dept of Physics Berkeley CA 94720

ALVAREZ, RODOLFO, sociology educator, consultant; b. San Antonio, Oct. 23, 1936; s. Ramon and Laura (Lobo) A.; m. Edna Rosemary Simons, June 25, 1960 (div. 1984); children—Anica, Amira. B.A., San Francisco State U., 1961; cert. European Studies, Inst. Am. Univs., Aix-en-Provence, France, 1960; M.A., U. Wash., 1964, Ph.D., 1966. Teaching fellow U. Wash., Seattle, 1963-64; asst. prof. Yale U., New Haven, 1966-72; assoc. prof. UCLA, 1972-80, prof. sociology, 1980—, dir. Chicano Studies Research Ctr., 1972-74; vis. lectr. Wesleyan U., Middletown, Conn., 1970; founding dir. Spanish Speaking Mental Health Research Ctr., 1973-75. Author: Discrimination in Organizations: Using Social Indicators to Manage Social Change, 1979; Racism, Elitism, Professionalism: Barriers to Community Mental Health, 1976; mem. editorial bd. Social Sci. Quar., 1971-86. Pres. ACLU So. Calif., 1980, 81; trustee Inst. for Am. Univs., Aix-en-Provence, France, 1968—; bd. dirs. Mex. Am. Legal Def. and Ednl. Fund, 1975-79; mem. adv. commn. on housing 1984 Olympic Organizing Com., 1982-84; chmn. bd. dirs. Narcotics Prevention Assn., Los Angeles, 1974-77; mem. bilingual adv. com. Children's Television Workshop, N.Y.C., 1979-82; pres. Westwood Dem. Club, Calif., 1977-78; candidate rep. Nat. Dem. Platform Com., Washington, 1976; alt. del. Nat. Dem. Conv., N.Y.C., 1976. Served to sgt. USMC, 1954-57. Recipient citation meritorious service for devel. Nat. Fed. Offenders Rehab. and Research Program, State of Wash., 1967. Mem. Internat. Sociol. Honor Soc. (pres. 1976-79), Am. Sociol. Assn. (mem. council 1982—), Soc. Study Social Problems (bd. dirs. 1982-87, pres. 1985-86), Pacific Sociol. Assn. (council 1979-83, 87-89), Marines Meml. Club. Lodge: Westwood Village Rotary. Office: UCLA Dept Sociology Los Angeles CA 90024

ALVAREZ-SANDOVAL, EMANUEL, language educator, realtor; b. Santander, Colombia, Dec. 25, 1935; came to U.S., 1963; s. Anastacio and Martina (Sandoval) Alvarez; m. Olga Linda Flores, June 18, 1972; children—Barbara, Marta Emerald. B.A., Calif. State U.-Los Angeles, 1971, B.A., 1972; M.A., Am. Baptist Sem., West Covina, Calif., 1973; B.S. in Law, J.D., Valley U., Los Angeles, 1978; Ph.D., Walden U., Mpls., 1984. Ordained to ministry Victory New Testament Fellowship/Internat., 1984; pastor Bapt. Ch., San Cristobal, Venezuela, 1958-63, Los Angeles, 1963-66; ins. rep. Cert. Life Ins. Co. of Calif., Los Angeles, 1966-67; ind. income tax preparer, Los Angeles, 1967-78; tchr. Spanish, Los Angeles Sch. Dist., 1975—; instr. Los Angeles Community Coll., 1974—; instr. Citrus Community Coll., 1986—; owner, operator EMANUEL'S REALTY CO., Covina, Calif., 1980—. Inventor board games Trick, Star. Pres. West Covina Christian Ctr., 1982—. Recipient Pres.'s award Cert. Life Ins. Co. Calif., 1967, Pres. Reagan Spl. award Republican Nat. Com., 1983. Mem. Société Internationale d'Echanges Educatifs, Culturels at Scientifiques, Am. Fedn. Tchrs. Coll. Guild, Walden U. Alumni Assn., Nu Beta Epsilon. Mem. Assemblies of God Ch. Office: PO Box 1352 West Covina CA 91793

ALVARIÑO, ANGELES, biologist; b. El Ferrol, Spain, Oct. 3, 1916; came to U.S., 1958; d. Antonio and Alvariño-Grimaldos and Da Carmen Gonzalez Diaz-Saavedra de Alvariño; m. Eugenio Leira Manso, Mar. 16, 1940; 1 child, Angeles Leira-Alvariño. BS, BL summa cum laude, U. Santiago de Compostela, Spain, 1933; M in Natural Scis. with honors, U. Madrid, 1941, Certificado Doctoral, 1951, DSc summa cum laude, 1967; cert. biologist, oceanographer, Spanish Inst. Oceanography, Madrid, 1952. Prof. U. Coll., El Ferrol, 1941-48; fishery research biologist Dept. Sea Fisheries, Madrid, 1948-52; histologist Superior Council Sci. Research, Madrid, 1948-52; biologist, oceanographer Spanish Inst. Oceanography, Madrid, 1950-57; biologist Scripps Inst. Oceanography, La Jolla, Calif., 1958-69; fishery research biologist NOAA and Nat. Marine Fisheries Service, Southwest Fisheries Ctr., La Jolla, Calif., 1970—; vis. prof. U. Nat. Auton. UNAM, Mex., 1976—, Nat. Poly. Inst. Mex., 1980—; assoc. prof. San Diego State U., 1979-81; assoc. researcher U. San Diego, 1982-85; coordinator Oceanic Research Hispano-Am. countries, 1977-79; lectr. dir. PhD theses, dir. oceanic research for various instns. Discovered 22 new species of oceanic animals; contbr. articles to profl. jours. Fellow Fulbright, 1956-57, Brit. Council, 1953-54; grantee Marine Life Research, 1958-69, Office Naval Research, 1958-69, NSF, 1961-69, Smithsonian Instn., 1979-85. Fellow San Diego Mus. Natural History, Am. Inst. Fishery Research Biologists; mem. Calif. Acad. Scis., Biol. Soc. Washington, Sigma Xi. Avocations: hist. research on early Spanish navigators, lit., world art, music, painting. Home: 7535 Cabrillo Ave La Jolla CA 92037 Office: US Dept Commerce NOAA SW Fisheries Ctr PO Box 271 La Jolla CA 92038

ALVINO, ERIC, interior designer; b. N.Y.C., May 22, 1950; s. Eligio Alvino Perez and Marcha (Arquer) Alvino; m. Marni Jo Zats, Apr. 11, 1975; 1 child, Vanessa Joi. BA, Pratt Inst., Hans Kriek & Assocs., N.Y.C. Interior designer Gil Robert's Interior Designs, N.Y.C., 1973-75; interior designer Rapport Co., Los Angeles, 1975-80, art dir., residential and comml. designer, 1983—; art cons. Gallery Hawaii, Honolulu, 1980-81; furniture designer Skipper, Milan, Italy, 1981—. Mem. Am Soc. Furniture Designers. Republican. Avocations: basketball, tennis, swimming. Home: 13331 Moorpack #307 Sherman Oaks CA 91423 Office: Rapport Co 435 N LaBrea Los Angeles CA 90038

ALYANAK, KURKEN, real estate developer; b. Istanbul, Turkey, May 11, 1951; came to U.S., 1975; s. Levon and Sona (Mardirosyan) A.; m. Talin Bohcali, June 9, 1985. MArch, Istanbul Tech. U., 1979, UCLA, 1982. Owner, pres. Alyanak Constrn. Co., Marina del Rey, Calif., 1982—. Trustee Ararat Home of Los Angeles, Inc., 1985, Armenian Assembly of Am., Washington, 1986. Mem. Nat. Assn. Contractors, Nat. Assn. Housing Officials, Nat. Assn. Homebuilders. Home: 14007 Palawan Way 116 Marina del Rey CA 90292

AMADOR, RAYMOND ANDREW, aerospace engineer; b. Bogota, Colombia, Aug. 3, 1952; came to U.S., 1955; s. Raymond Howell and Ursula Julie (Wolf) A.; B.S. in Mech. Engring., Tulane U., 1974; M.S. in Aero/Astro (Hughes Aircraft Co. fellow), Stanford U., 1975; m. Margaret Marie Yvonne Ruiterman, June 24, 1978; children—Raymond Michael, Steven Andrew. Registered profl. mech. engr., Calif. Mem. tech. staff space and communications group Hughes Aircraft Co., El Segundo, Calif., 1975-76, electro-optical and data systems group, Culver City, Calif., 1976-77; staff engr. Santa Barbara Research Center, Goleta, Calif., 1977-80, sr. staff engr., lectr. advanced tech. edn. program, 1980-82, tech. sect. head, 1983, sr. scientist, 1986; pres. AMHOF Engring. Assocs., Inc., Goleta, 1982—; cons. in field. Mem. AIAA, The Planetary Soc. Republican. Roman Catholic. Club: Cathedral Oaks Tennis. Author papers in field; co-inventor quiet dental drill. Office: PO Box 1426 Goleta CA 93016

AMASH, CHARLES ELIAS, business executive; b. Lydda, Pacestine, Nov. 5, 1932, came to U.S., 1956, naturalized, 1962; s. Elias Yousef and Victoria (Rantisi) A.; m. Nadia Abu Dayyeh, Mar. 30, 1985; 1 child, Rosalinda Victoria. Student in acctg., Los Angeles City Coll., 1957-59; A.A. in Bus. Law, Orange Coast Coll., 1982, A.A. in Real Estate, 1983. Chief teller Bank Am., Los Angeles, 1957-61; owner, mgr. Vic's Market, Los Angeles, 1961-67, various liquor stores, 1967—, several restaurants, 1969—. Republican. Greek Orthodox. Mem. USCG Aux. (skipper Santa Ana 1981—). Office: Sir Charles Liquor 2981 Bristol St Costa Mesa CA 92626

AMATO, CAROL JOY, technical publications consulting company executive, writer; b. Portland, Oreg., Apr. 9, 1944; d. Sam Lawrence and Lena Dorothy (Dindia) A.; m. Neville Stanley Motts, Aug. 26, 1967 (div. 1978); children—Tracy, Damon. B.A., U. Portland, 1966; M.A., Calif. State U., 1986. Freelance writer, Westminster, Calif., 1969—; human factor cons. Design Sci. Corp., Los Angeles, 1979—; dir. software documentation Trans-Ed Communications, Westminster, 1980-84, pres. Advanced Profl. Software, Inc., Westminster, 1984-86, Systems Research Analysis, Inc., Westminster, 1986—; dir. Oasis, Redondo Beach, Calif. Editor, Cultural Futuristics, 1975-80; author numerous articles and short stories, 1978—; participant in numerous radio and TV interviews. Sec. bd. dirs. Am. Space Meml. Found., Los Angeles, 1986—. Mem. Am. Anthrop. Assn., L-5 Soc., Human Factor Soc., Writers' Club of Whittier, Inc., Soc. for Applied Anthropology, Southwestern Anthrop. Assn., Oasis. Avocation: environmental anthropology. Home: 10151 Heather Ct Westminster CA 92683

AMERI, JAMSHID, investment banker; b. Tehran, Iran, Jan. 23, 1955; came to U.S., 1974; s. Assadollah and Homa (Akhavan) A.; m. Golrokh Yazdi, Aug. 10, 1979; 1 child, Darius. BS, Calif. State Poly. U., 1977; MS, Stanford U., 1978. Registered profl. engr., Calif., securities prin., Calif. Engr. Cygna Energy Services, San Francisco, 1979-82; pres. Cento Energy, San Francisco, 1982-83; prin. Capital Concepts Investment Corp., San Francisco, 1983—. Avocations: tennis, skiing, reading. Office: Capital Concepts 50 California St Suite 3300 San Francisco CA 94111

AMERINE, ANNE FOLLETTE, aerospace engineer; b. San Francisco, Sept. 27, 1950; d. William T. and Wilma (Carlson) F.; m. Jorge Armando Verdi D'Eguia, July 4, 1970 (div.); m. Donald Amerine, Dec. 18, 1983. AA, Coll. Marin, 1977; BA in Math. with honors, Mills Coll., 1979. Sr. computer operator Bank of Am. Internat. Services, San Francisco, 1972-74; mathematician Pacific Missile Test Ctr., Pt. Mugu, Calif., 1979-80; engr. Grumman Aerospace Corp., Pt. Mugu, 1979-83; engr. Litton Guidance and Control Systems, 1984-86, product support and assurance dept. project mgr., 1986—. Chmn. Marina West Neighborhood Council, 1982-84; mem. NOW; chmn. subcom. Ventura County Community Coll. Dist. Citizen's Adv. Com. on Status of Women, 1983-84. Aurelia Henry Reinhart scholar, 1978-79; recipient Project Sterling award Grumman Aerospace Corp., 1982. Mem. Nat. Assn. Female Execs., Soc. Women Engrs. (chmn. career guidance com. and speaker Ventura County sect.), Litton Women's Enhancement Orgn. (founder, v.p. and chmn. info. and edn. com. 1985-86, editor newsletter 1986-87), Assn. Old Crows, Mills Coll. Alumni, Alpha Gamma Sigma (life). Office: Litton Guidance & Control Systems 5500 Canoga Ave MS 80 Woodland Hills CA 91367-6698

AMERINE, MAYNARD ANDREW, educator, enologist; b. San Jose, Calif., Oct. 30, 1911; s. Roy Reagan and Tennie (Davis) A. B.S., U. Calif.-Berkeley, 1932, Ph.D. in Plant Physiology, 1936. Mem. faculty U. Calif., Davis, 1935—, prof. enology, enologist Exptl. Sta., 1952-74, emeritus Exptl. Sta., 1974—, chmn. dept. viticulture and enology, 1957-62; cons. Wine Inst., 1974-85. Author: (with M. A. Joslyn) Table Wines: The Technology of Their Production in California, 1951, 2d edit., 1970, (with Louise Wheeler) A Check-List of Books and Pamphlets on Grapes and Wines and Related Subjects, 1951, A Short Check-List of Books and Pamphlets in English on Grapes, Wine and Related Subjects, 1949-1959, 1959, (with others) The Technology of Wine Making, 4th edit., 1980, (with G. L. Marsh) Wine Making at Home, 1962, (with M.A. Joslyn) Dessert, Appetizer and Related Flavored Wines: The Technology of Their Production, 1964, (with V.L. Singleton) Wine: An Introduction for Americans, 1965, 2d edit., 1977, (with Rose M. Pangborn and E. B. Roessler) Principles of Sensory Evaluation of Food, 1965, A Check List of Books on Grapes and Wines, 1960-68, (with supplement for), 1949-59, 1969, (with G.F. Stewart) Introduction to Food Science and Technology, 1973, 2d edit., 1982, (with C.S. Ough) Wine and Must Analyses, 1974, 80, (with E.B. Roessler) Wines: Their Sensory Evaluation, 1976, 2d edit., 1983; (with H. Phaff) Bibliography of Publications, 1876-1980, on Grapes, Wines, and Related Subjects, 1986; editor and contbr.: Wine Production Technology in the U.S, 1981; co-editor (with D. Muscatine and B. Thompson) The University of California/Sotheby Book of California Wine, 1984. Served to maj. AUS, 1942-46. Decorated chevalier de Merite Agricole France, 1947, officier Ordre National du Merite, (France), 1976; recipient diplôme d'honneur Office Internat. du Vin, 1952, 65, 84; 2d prize Oberly award A.L.A., 1953; Guggenheim fellow, 1954-55; Merit award Am. Soc. Enologists, 1967; Am. Wine Soc., 1976; Man of Year award Les Amis du Vin, 1976, The Wine Spectator, 1985. Mem. Am. Soc. Enologists (pres. 1958-59), AAAS, Am. Chem. Soc., Inst. Food Technologists. Republican. Baptist. Club: Bohemian (San Francisco). Home: PO Box 208 Saint Helena CA 94574

AMES, EVELYN E., health education educator; b. Elko, Nev., Oct. 9, 1937; d. Orval Connor and Esther Lillian (Sauer) A. BS, U. Nev., 1959; MS, Wash. State U., 1963; PhD, U. Md., 1972. Tchr. phys. edn. Tahoe-Truckee (Calif.) High Sch., 1959-61; counseling asst. Wash. State U., Pullman, 1961-62; instr. health and phys. edn. U. Portland, Oreg., 1962-64; from instr. to assoc. prof. phys. health edn. Western Wash. State Coll., later Western Wash. State U., Bellingham, 1966-86, prof. health edn., 1986—; grad. asst. in health edn. U. Md., College Park, 1969-70; pres. Wash. Cos. Against Health Fraud, Bellingham, 1984—; prof. adv. com. Home Health St. Joseph Hosp., Bellingham, 1985—. Co-author: (book) Becoming Male and Female, 1987, (tchrs. manual) Intstructional Resource Kit, 1982; assoc. editor health edn. jour. AAHPERD, 1978-81; contbr. articles to profl. jours. Recipient Recognition award Comprehensive Health Edn. Found., 1982, Cert. Appreciation AAHPERD, 1985. Mem. Am. Pub. Health Assn. (chmn. sch. health edn. and service com. 1985—), Assn. Advancement Health Edn. (recognition of service award 1983), Am. Council on Sci. and Health, Am. Sch. Health Assn., Eta Gamma Sigma. Avocations: opera, hiking, biking, skiing, golf, gardening. Home: 134 Sudden Valley Bellingham WA 92226 Office: Western Wash U Dept Health Edn Bellingham WA 98225

AMES, LYNFORD LENHART, chemistry educator; b. Fresno, Ohio, May 20, 1938; s. Robert J. and Magdalene (Miller) A.; m. Judith Kilbourne, Mar. 23, 1963; children: Graham Geoffrey, Constance Elaine. BS, Muskingum Coll., 1960; PhD, Ohio State U., 1965. Asst. prof. chemistry N.Mex. State U., Las Cruces, 1966-70, assoc. prof., 1970-77, dept. head, 1976—, prof. chemistry, 1977—. Officer First Presbyn. Ch., Las Cruces, 1966—. Fellow NSF, 1965-66. Fellow AAAS (chmn. local chpt.); mem. Am. Chem. Soc., N.Mex. Acad. of Scis., Sigma Xi. Republican. Lodge: Rotary. Avocations: ham radio, square dancing, computers. Home: 685 Farney Rd Las Cruces NM 88005 Office: NMex State U Chemistry Dept Box 3C Las Cruces NM 88003

AMES, MICHAEL MCCLEAN, university museum administrator, anthropology educator; b. Vancouver, B.C., Canada, June 19, 1933; s. Ernest Oliver Francis and Elsie (McClean) A.; m. Elinor Stetson, May 1964; children: Daniel J., Kristin Julia. BA with honors, U. B.C., 1956; PhD, Harvard U., 1961. Asst. prof. sociology McMaster U., Hamilton, Canada, 1962-64; from asst. prof. to full prof. of anthropology U. B.C., Vancouver, 1964—; dir. Mus. Anthropology U. B.C., Vancouver, B.C., Canada, 1974—. Author: Museums, The Public and Anthropology, 1986; co-editor: Man-like Monsters on Trial, 1980; contbr. articles to profl. jours. Guggenheim fellow, 1970-71; Nat. Mus. Can. grantee, 1976—. Fellow Royal Soc. Can., Am. Anthrop. Soc., Can. Ethnology Soc., Can. Asia Studies Assn.; mem. Indian Sociol. Assn., Assn. Asian Studies, Internat. Council Mus. Office: Mus Anthropology, Univ BC, 6393 NW Marine Dr, Vancouver, BC Canada V6T 1W5

AMES, NORMA HARRIET, wildlife consultant, researcher; b. Buffalo, Aug. 17, 1920; d. Robert Martin and Flora Mary (Wiener) Knipple; m. Donald Fairbanks Ames, July 8, 1944 (div. 1956); 1 child, Karyn Roberta. BA, Smith Coll., 1942; postgrad., Wellesley Coll., 1942, U. Colo., 1964. Asst. chief game mgmt. N.Mex. Dept Game and Fish, Santa Fe, 1956-76, asst. chief pub. affairs, 1976-82; leader Mex. wolf recovery team U.S. Fish and Wildlife Service, Santa Fe, 1979—; wildlife cons. Santa Fe, 1982—; wolf breeder and researcher Rancho Ma'ii-tsoh, Santa Fe, 1971—. Author: My Path Belated, 1970, Whisper in the Forest, 1971, (book revs.) Science Books and Films, 1970—; author/illustrator booklets, 1960-82; author/editor: New Mexico Wildlife Management, 1967 (conservation edn. award 1968); Named Conservationist of Yr., Sta. KOB TV and Radio, Albuquerque, 1980; recipient Leopold Conservation award The Nature Conservancy, 1983. Mem. AAAS, The Wildlife Soc. (cert.), Am. Soc. Mammalogists, Sierra Club (lectr.), Nat. Audubon Soc. (lectr.), Phi Beta Kappa, Sigma Xi. Avocation: raising cattle and other livestock. Home and Office: Rancho Ma'ii-tsoh Rt 7 Box 124NA Santa Fe NM 87505

AMES, WILLIAM CLARK, college financial administrator; b. Macomb, Ill., July 11, 1950; s. Clark Earl and Betty Amelia (Hegstrom) A.; B.A., Knox Coll., 1972; M.S., Western Ill. U., 1974; Ph.D., Ariz. State U. Asst. to dean students, instr. human interaction Knox Coll., Galesburg, Ill., 1974-75; instr. human interaction, counselor edn. Western Ill. U., Macomb, 1974-75; resident area coordinator Western Carolina U., Cullowhee, N.C., 1975-77; dir. Sahuaro Complex, Ariz. State U., Tempe, 1977-78, dir. housing office vending programs, 1978-79, asst. dir. housing-adminstrn., 1979-80, grad. assoc. for student leadership programs, 1980-81, research assoc., office of pres., 1981-82; asst. to chancellor Maricopa Community Coll., Phoenix, 1982-84, dir. mgmt. and budget, 1984—. Mem. Western Carolina Council on Alcohol and Use and Abuse, 1975-77. NSF grantee, 1970-72; recipient Leadership award Elks Ill., 1968; Robert Cunningham Taylor Jr. scholar, 1968-72. Mem. Nat. Assn. student Personnel Adminstrs., Am. Personnel and Guidance Assn., Am. Coll. Personnel Assn., Am. Council Univ. Housing Officers, Southeastern Assn. Housing Officers, Smithsonian Inst. (asso.), Knox Coll., Western Ill. U. alumni assns. Contbr. articles to student personnel and mgmt. jours. Home: 538 W Vaughn St Tempe AZ 85283 Office: Maricopa Community Coll 3910 E Washington St Phoenix AZ 85034

AMEZCUA, CHARLIE ANTHONY, counselor, educator; b. Los Angeles, Sept. 1, 1928; s. Carlos and Inez (Nunez) A.; B.A., UCLA, 1958; M.S., Calif. State U., Los Angeles, 1961; m. Kathleen Joyce Greene, Mar. 7, 1964; children—Colleen Alvita, Charles Anthony. Student psychologist Rancho Los Amigos Hosp., Downey, Calif., 1959-60; instr. in psychology East Los Angeles Coll., 1962-72, asst. prof. counseling, 1972-74, assoc. prof. counseling, 1974—, prof. psychology, 1980—, spl. edn. counselor, 1981—, coordinator vet. affairs, 1972—; personnel asst. Los Angeles City Sch. Dist., 1963-64; counselor Youth Tng. and Employment Project, Los Angeles, 1965-66, counseling supr., 1966, project dir., 1966-67; counseling psychologist VA, Los Angeles, 1967-70; dir. Head Start, Los Angeles County Econ. and Youth Opportunities Agy., 1970-71; bd. dirs. Tng. and Research Found., Child and Family Resources Centers; lectr. counselor edn. Calif. State U., Los Angeles. Mem. Calif. Gov.'s Adv. Com. on Children and Youth, 1966-67; judge blue ribbon panel Nat. Acad. TV Arts and Scis., 1966-76. Served with USN, 1948-52; Korea; cert. community coll. counselor, supr.-adminstrn., jr. coll. teaching in psychology. Mem. Am. Psychol. Assn., Calif. State Psychol. Assn., Assn. Chicano Educators, Calif. Assn. Post-Secondary Educators of the Disabled, Nat. Assn. Vets. Program Adminstrs., Western Psychol. Assn. Democrat. Home: 8348 Fable Ave Canoga Park CA 91304 Office: East Los Angeles Coll 1301 Brooklyn Ave Monterey Park CA 91754

AMIDON, CHESTER DALE, JR., childcare service administrator; b. Austin, Tex., July 16, 1953; s. Chester Dale and Juanita (Forehand) A.; m. Debbie Kay Mund, May 17, 1974; children: Cory Dale, Keisha Ann. B in Psychology, Tex. A&M U., 1975; MSW, U. Tex., Arlington, 1977. Lic. childcare adminstr., Tex.; lic. profl. counselor, Tex.; lic. advanced clin. practitioner, Tex. Youth minister Cen. Ch. Christ, Bryan, Tex., 1974-75; dir. family services Sherwood & Myrtie Foster Home, Stephenville, Tex., 1976-83; dir. group care Children's Home of Lubbock, Tex., 1983-85; exec. dir. Mountain States Children's Home, Longmont, Colo., 1985—; bd. pubs. Christian Childcare Conf., 1986-89. Instr. CPR and First Aid ARC, 1981—. Recipient Gayle Oler Childcare award Sherwood & Myrtie Foster Home, 1983; Inez Baucum-Chester Amidon scholar Sherwood & Myrtie Foster Home, 1983. Mem. Nat. Assn. Social Workers (cert.). Mem. Ch. of Christ. Lodge: Longmont Breakfast Optimists (Stephenville) (sec., chmn. toy drive 1977-83). Home and Office: Mountain States Childrens Home PO Box 1097 Longmont CO 80502

AMINI, FARIBORZ, med. educator; b. Tehran, Iran, July 23, 1930; s. Mirza and Farkhondeh (Rezai) A.; came to U.S., 1949, naturalized, 1963; B.S. in Math. with highest honors, U. Calif. at Berkeley, 1953; M.D., U. Calif. at San Francisco, 1957; m. Elizabeth Ann Cunningham, Feb. 5, 1972; children—Kim Shareen, Lisa Roshan, Dawn Parvaneh, Ariana Shereen, Christina Maheen, Elita Farine. Intern, Detroit Receiving Hosp., 1957-58; research fellow Cancer Research Inst., U. Calif. at San Francisco, 1958-59; resident in psychiatry Neuropsychiat. Inst., U. Mich., Children's Psychiat. Hosp., 1959-62; fellow in child psychiatry U. Calif. at Los Angeles Neuropsychiat. Inst., 1962-63; psychoanalytic tng. San Francisco Psychoanalytic Inst., 1964-71, mem. faculty, 1973—; mem. faculty Langley Porter Neuropsychiat. Inst., U. Calif. at San Francisco, 1963—, prof., dir. youth service dept. psychiatry, 1970-77, dir. residency tng. dept. psychiatry, 1976-81, dir. out-patient dept., 1977—, dir. clin. services, 1981—, pres. exec. med. bd.; vis. lectr. Boalt Hall, U. Calif. at Berkeley, 1965, also Sch. Criminology; cons. Aid to Retarded Children San Francisco, Family Life Edn. and Parent Edn. programs, San Francisco, Foster Parent Program, San Francisco, 1975, others. Diplomate Am. Bd. Psychiatry and Neurology. Fellow Am. Psychiat. Assn.; mem. Calif. Med. Assn., San Francisco Med. Soc., No. Calif. Psychiat. Soc., San Francisco Psychoanalytic Inst. and Soc. (pres.), Phi Beta Kappa, Sigma Xi, Nu Sigma Nu. Contbr. numerous articles to profl. jours. Home: 202 Lagunitas Rd Ross CA 94957 Office: 401 Parnassus Ave San Francisco CA 94143

AMIOKA, WALLACE SHUZO, ret. petroleum co. exec.; b. Honolulu, June 28, 1914; s. Tsurumatsu and Reye (Yoshimura) A.; B.A., U. Hawaii, 1966, M.B.A., 1968; m. Ellen Misao Honda, Aug. 9, 1942; children—Carol L. Amioka Price, Joanne M. Amioka Chikuma. With Shell Oil Co., 1931—, fin. services mgr., Honolulu, 1973-77; lectr. econs. U. Hawaii, 1969-79. Mem. Honolulu Police Commn., 1965-73, vice chmn., 1966, 68, chmn., 1971; U.S. civil adm. Ryuku Islands, 1950-52. Mem. City and County of Honolulu Charter Commn., 1981-82; bd. dirs. Honolulu Symphony Soc., 1968. Served with M.I., AUS, 1944-48. Mem. M.I. Service Vets. (pres. 1981-82), Hawaii C. of C. (chmn. edn. com. 1963-64, chmn. pub. health com. 1966-67), Phi Beta Kappa, Phi Kappa Phi. Clubs: Hui 31; Hui Aikane, Honolulu Police Old Timers. Home: 4844 Matsonia Dr Honolulu HI 96816 Office: Shell Oil Co 711 Keeaumoku St Honolulu HI 96814

AMMAN, JOHN CHARLES, accountant; b. Colorado Springs, Colo., Mar. 15, 1935; s. George Clarence and Mary Charlotte (Wilson) A.; m. SaraAnn Cameron, Sept. 6, 1958; children—Bradford Kevin, Brice Cameron, Barry Douglas. B.S. in Acctg., Colo. U., 1957; M.B.A., Denver U., 1962. C.P.A., Colo. With Arthur Andersen & Co., 1961-85; audit mgr. Arthur Andersen & Co., Denver, 1966-71; ptnr. Arthur Andersen & Co., 1971-85, Concord Assocs., 1986—; bd. dirs., pres. Bow-Mar Owners, Inc.; bd. dirs. Denver Partnership, 1st Nat. Bank Lowell, Wyo.; pres. N.Mex. Escrow Services Co. 1986—; v.p. N.Mex. Trading Corp., 1986—. Past chmn. alumni adv. council U. Colo. Bus. Sch.; mem. adv. council Acctg. Sch., mem. adv. council Bus. Sch., U. Denver; bd. dirs., past treas. Artreach; mem. council Western Regional Council; mem. adv. council Colo. Uplift; bd. dirs. Am. Lung Assn. Colo. Served with Security Agy., U.S. Army, 1957-60. Mem. Am. Inst. C.P.A.s, Colo. Soc. C.P.A.s, Wyo. Soc. C.P.A.s, Denver C. of C. (chmn. retirement plan trustees), Beta Alpha Psi (mem. nat. adv. forum). Republican. Clubs: Univ., Denver; Colo. Elephant; Cherry Hills Country (Englewood, Colo.); Garden of Gods (Colorado Springs, Colo.). Lodges: Masons, Rotary. Office: Concord Associates 3 Park Central 1515 Arapahoe Suite 900 Denver CO 80202

AMMON, CAROL KAY, social worker; b. Albion, Nebr., Dec. 11, 1949; d. Arthur and Mary Susan (King) Fleming; m. Eugene T. Ammon, Sept. 3, 1971; children: Jennifer, Analisa. BA magna cum laude, Macalester U., 1970; MA, Stanford U., 1972; MSW, San Francisco State U., 1977. Lic. clin. social worker. Employment counselor Snelling & Snelling, Mpls., 1971; social worker Santa Clara (Calif.) Dept. Social Services, 1973-80; med. social worker Santa Clara Valley Med. Ctr., San Jose, Calif., 1981—. Vol. therapist Santa Clara County Cen. Mental Health Ctr., San Jose, 1979-80; vol. classroom aid Eisenhower Sch., Santa Clara, 1984-87; brownie asst. to leader, Girl Scouts U.S., Santa Clara, 1986-87; pres. Holy Redeemer Luth. Ch. Council, San Jose, 1986-88; mem. Macalester Coll. Alumni Admissions Com., 1976—. Nat. Fgn. Def. Lang. fellow, 1971-72. Mem. Nat. Assn. Social Workers (registered clin. social worker), Nat. Assn. Perinatal Social Workers, Bay Area Social Workers in Health Care, Phi Beta Kappa. Club: Forest Park Cabana (treas. 1985-87). Avocations: swimming, skiing. Office: Santa Clara Valley Med Ctr 751 S Bascom Ave San Jose CA 95128

AMMONS, CAROL HAMRICK, psychologist, editor; b. Tampa, Fla., Feb. 22, 1927; d. Joe Fred and B. Carolyn (Patton) Hamrick; m. Robert Bruce Ammons, Aug. 26, 1949; children: Carl, Bruce, Douglas, Beth, Richard, Stephanie, Glenyss. BA, Hariette Sophie Newcomb Coll. for Women, 1947; MA, Tulane U., 1949; PhD, U. Ky., 1955. Lectr. U. Louisville, 1949-55; pvt. practice cons. psychologist Louisville, 1949-55, pvt. practice editor mag./tech. jour., 1949-55; pvt. practice editor mag./tech. jour. Grand Forks, N.D., 1955-56; pvt. practice editor mag. Missoula, Mont., 1956—. Contbr. numerous articles to profl. jours. Grantee U. Ky., Lexington, 1952-54, Tulane U., Nola, 1947-49. Mem. AAAS, Am. Psychol. Assn., Internat. Council Psychologists (sec. 1965-68). Home: 411 Keith Ave Missoula MT 59801 Office: PO Box 9229 Missoula MT 59807

AMOR, ROBERT HENRY, architect; b. Chgo., July 23, 1933; s. William Henry and Pearl (Scholten) A.; m. Alyce Mae Kolence, Aug. 20, 1955; children—Robert Alan, William Andrew, Andrew Gregory, Constance Lynn. B.Arch., U. Mich., 1963. Archtl. draftsman Paul Hazelton, Architect, Traverse City, Mich., 1961-62; project architect, designer Gordon Cornwell, Architect, Traverse City, 1962-65; designer, project architect Daverman Assocs., Grand Rapids, Mich., 1965-68; prin., owner Robert H. Amor, Architect, Grand Rapids, 1968-75, Grand Haven, Mich., 1975-82; prin., owner Robert H. Amor, Ch. Architect, Aptos, Calif., 1982—; officer Mission Land Constrn. Mgrs., Inc., Aptos. Lectr. ch. architecture; chmn. Conf. on Religious Art, Music and Architecture, Grand Haven, 1978-80. Prin. works include: United Meth. Ch., Evart, Mich., Manistee, Mich.-Bear Lake, Mich., Cath. Info. Ctr., Grand Rapids, 1st Bapt. Ch., Manistee, Foothills United Meth. Ch., Cameron Park, Calif., Hope United Meth. Ch., Sacramento, Bethany Lutheran Ch., Kaleva, Mich., Peace Lutheran Ch., Sparta, Mich., Mt. Pleasant Community Ch., Mich., Seventh-Day Adventist Ch., Fremont, Calif., St. Paul's United Meth. Ch., Fremont. Mem. art as worship task force Muskegon Cooperating Ch. Served with AUS, 1953-54. Recipient AIA design award for Bethany Lutheran Ch., Kaleva, 1970. Mem. Interfaith Forum Religion, Art and Architecture, Guild for Religious Architecture, Tau Sigma Delta. Home: 2395 Delaware Ave #169 Santa Cruz CA 95060 Office: 3040 Valencia Ave Aptos CA 95003

AMOR, WILLIAM ANDREW, architect; b. Ann Arbor, Mich., Aug. 22, 1959; s. Robert Henry and Alyce Mae (Kolence) A.; m. Carol Ann Kovats, Aug. 22, 1981; 1 child, Mary Ann. BS, U. Mich., 1981, MArch, 1983. Draftsman Robert H. Amor, Architects, Grand Rapids, Mich., 1978-79; ptnr. Robert H. Amor, Grand Rapids, 1979-82; draftsman Herrman and Holman Inc., Ann Arbor, 1982; lead draftsman Hobbs & Black Assoc., Ann Arbor, 1983-85; assoc. Robert H. Amor, Aptos, Calif., 1985; designer/draftsman Cobb & Morton Architects, Los Gatos, Calif., 1986—. Avocations: running, golf, hiking, model building.

AMPARAN, MARIA ELENA, personnel executive; b. Los Angeles, Aug. 19, 1945; d. John S. and Concepcion (Mendez) A. AA, East Los Angeles Coll., 1967; BA in Journalism, Calif. State U., Los Angeles, 1969. Sec., coordinator press and publicity Sta. KNBC, 1969-70; prin. public relations rep. model cities program East N.E. neighborhood City of Los Angeles, 1970-72; pub. info. aide Housing Authority, Los Angeles, 1972; editor So. Calif. Rapid Transit Dist., 1972-73; coordinator dept. community services County of Los Angeles, 1973-76; employment specialist Kaiser Permanente Med. Care Program, Los Angeles, 1976-79; personnel supr. McDonald's Corp., Denver, 1979-85; personnel spvr. Foster Farms, 1986—; mem. adv. council West San Gabriel Valley Consortium, 1986—. Vol., coordinator Youth Motivation Task Force, 1976-79; mem. employer adv. com. Career Planning Ctr., Inc., 1978-79; bd. dirs. Denver Pvt. Industry Council; mem. Denver Mayor's Task Force on Youth; mem. West San Gabriel Valley Consortium Adv. Council. Recipient commendation award Los Angeles County Bd. Supervisors. Mem. Personnel Mgmt. Assn. San Diego, Personnel Mgmt. Assn. of Aztlan (chairperson ad hoc placement com., pres. San Diego chpt. 1982-84, nat. publicity chmn. 1982-84), Profl. Women's Journalism Soc., Beta Phi Gamma. Democrat. Roman Catholic. Home: 2110 India St Los Angeles CA 90039 Office: 1913 Frank Stiles Rd PO Box 3247 South El Monte CA 91733

AMSBURY, CLIFTON, anthropology educator; b. Longton, Kans., July 16, 1910; s. Glenn Holman and Annie Keith (Allen) A.; m. Shirley Wooldridge, June 12, 1943; children: Raymona, Raymond, Merry Lynn, Sally. BA, U. Calif., Berkeley, 1932; MA, Calif. State U., Hayward, 1973. Cert. community coll. instr., Calif. Case aide Calif. Relief Adminstrn., Bakersfield, Fresno and Oakland, 1936, 39, 40; interviewer Calif. Employment Service, Ft. Bragg and Richmond, 1945-71; instr. Contra Costa Coll., Richmond, Calif., 1971—. Co-author: War: Its Causes and Correlates, 1975, Discussions On War, 1976. Del. EOC, Contra Costa County, 1981-86; del. cen. labor council Am. Fedn. Tchrs. Served with U.S. Army, 1941-45, PTO. Mem. Am. Anthrop. Assn., Southwestern Anthrop. Assn., Vets. Abraham Lincoln Brigade, First Fandom, Am. Ethnologocal Assn. Democrat. Home: 768 Amador St Richmond CA 94805 Office: Contra Costa Coll 2600 Mission Bell Dr San Pablo CA 94806

AMUNDSEN, JOANNE ELAINE, speech pathologist; b. Chgo., Mar. 30, 1954; d. Alvin Norman and Elaine June (Thompson) A. BA, U. Mich., 1975; MA, Cen. Mich. U., 1976, San Diego State U., 1981. Speech pathologist Northern Trails Edn. Agy., Clear Lake, Iowa, 1976-78, San Diego City Schs., 1978—; pvt. practice speech pathology San Diego, 1980—. group exhibits include Midsummer Award Show San Diego Art Inst., 1986, Point Loma Art and Design Ctr. Dem. vol., San Diego. Mem. Am. Speech and Hearing Assn. (cert. clin. competence), Assn. Calif. Sch. Adminstrs., Calif. Speech and Hearing Assn., Nat. Tchrs. Assn., Calif. Tchrs. Assn., Humane Soc., Pastel Soc. San Diego, Walkabout Internat., Amnesty Internat., Sierra Club, U. Mich. Alumni Club. Lutheran. Office: Lang Speech Hearing Whittier Ctr 3401 Clairemont Dr Room 25 San Diego CA 92117

AMUNDSON, ELLIE ELAINE, aerospace business executive; b. Austin, Minn., Aug. 28, 1948; d. Fred A. and Ella M. (Lukes) Radloff; m. Robert L. Amundson, Apr. 23, 1977. AA, Austin State Jr. Coll., 1966; BS, U. Minn., 1968, MA, 1970; postgrad., Calif. State U., Northridge, 1983—. Tchr. Franklin Jr. High Sch., Mankato, Minn., 1970-71; film distbr. Universal Studios, Universal City, Calif., 1972-75; ednl. evaluator Orcutt & Assocs., North Hollywood, Calif., 1975-77; with Volt Temporaries Co., Van Nuys, Calif., 1977-78; adminstrv. asst. The Marquardt Co., Van Nuys, 1979-84, fin. analyst, bus. mgr., 1985-87, project coordinator, 1987—; cons. Marquardt Recreation Council, Van Nuys, 1982; bd. dirs. Marquardt Fed. Credit Union. Avocations: aerobics, skiing, tennis. Office: The Marquardt Co 16555 Saticoy St Van Nuys CA 91409

AMUNDSON, EVA DONALDA, civic worker; b. Langdon, N.D., Apr. 23, 1911; d. Elmer Fritjof and Alma Julia (Nelson) Hultin; m. Leif Amundson, Mar. 1, 1929 (dec. 1974); children—Constance, Eleanor, Ardis, Priscilla. Bd. dirs. Opportunity Workshop, Missoula, Mont., 1950—, Rockmont Group Homes, Missoula, 1976—, Bethany L'Arche (group home for girls), 1976—; mem. Missoula Sr. Citizen's Ctr., 1980-82, pres., 1982-85; tchr. Norwegian cooking and baking, 1954-56, Norweigan Rosemaling, 1975-79; treas. Sacakawea Homemakers Club, 1979-81; mem. Am. Luth. Ch. Women St. Pauls' Lutheran Ch., 1951—; active Easter Seal Program, Heart Fund, March of Dimes, United Way, Campfire Girls; mem. adv. council Area Agy. on Aging, Missoula, 1984—. Recipient Outstanding Sr. award Missoula Jr. C. of C., 1984. Mem. Sons. of Norway. Club: Orchard Homes Country (mem. art judging com.). Lodges: Order of Eastern Star, Elks. Avocations: rosemaling; oil painting; poetry. Home: 324 Kensington Ave Missoula MT 59801

ANAND, RAJEN SINGH, physiologist; b. Kohat, India, June 8, 1937; came to U.S., 1963; s. Dial Singh and Daya Kaur (Kohli) A.; m. Asha Angela Bawa, Oct. 29, 1969; children: Shawn, Shabeen. BS, Meerut U., 1956; DVM, M.P. Vet. Coll., 1960; PhD, U. Calif., 1969. Demonstrator M.P. Vet. Coll., Mhow, India, 1960-63; research asst. U. Calif., Davis, 1963-68, P.G. research physiologist, 1968-69; prof. physiology Calif. State U., Long Beach, 1970-85, chmn. dept. anatomy and physiology, 1985—; postdoctoral fellow UCLA Harbor Med. Ctr., Torrance, 1977-78. Contbr. articles to profl. jours. Mem. state Dem. cen. com., 1986-88. Named Outstanding Prof., Calif. State U., Long Beach, 1983, Outstanding Student, U. Calif., Davis, 1967, 68; recipient Hertzendorf prize in physiology, 1969. Mem. Am. Physiol. Soc., AAAS, Sigma Xi, Fedn. of Indian Assns. (pres. 1984-86, chmn. 1986-88), Indo-Am. Polit. Assn. (pres. 1986—). Avocations: writing, hiking. Home: 8391 Satinwood Circle Westminster CA 92683 Office: Calif State U Dept Anatomy & Physiology Long Beach CA 90840

ANAND, SURESH CHANDRA, physician; b. Mathura, India, Sept. 13, 1931; s. Satchit and Sumaran (Bai) A.; came to U.S., 1957, naturalized, 1971; M.B., B.S., King George's Coll., U. Lucknow (India), 1954; M.S., U. Colo., 1962; m. Wiltrud, Jan. 29, 1966; children—Miriam, Michael. Fellow pulmonary diseases Nat. Jewish Hosp., Denver, 1957-58, resident in chest medicine, 1958-59, chief resident allergy-asthma, 1960-62; intern Mt. Sinai Hosp., Toronto, Ont., Can., 1962-63, resident in medicine, 1963-64, chief resident, 1964-65, demonstrator clin. technique, 1963-64, U. Toronto fellow in medicine, 1964-65; research assoc. asthma-allergy Nat. Jewish Hosp., Denver, 1967-69; clin. instr. medicine U. Colo., 1967-69; pres. Allergy Assocs. & Lab., Ltd., Phoenix, 1974—; mem. staff Phoenix Bapt. Hosp., chmn. med .records com., 1987; mem. staff St. Joseph's Hosp., St. Luke's Hosp., Humana Hosp., Phoenix Bapt., John C. Lincoln, Maryvale Meml., Good Samaritan, Phoenix Children's Hosp., Tempe St. Luke, Desert Samaritan, Mesa Luth., Scottsdale Meml. Mem. Camelback Hosp. Mental Health Center Citizens Adv. Bd., Scottsdale, Ariz., 1974-80; mem. council Phoenix Symphony; mem. Ariz. Opera Co. Diplomate Am. Bd. Allergy and Immunology. Fellow ACP, Am. Coll. Chest Physicians, Am. Acad. Allergy, Am. Coll. Cert. Allergists, Am. Assn. Clin. Immunology and Allergy; mem. AAAS, AMA, Ariz. Med. Assn., Maricopa County Med. Soc., West Coast Soc. Allergy and Immunology, Ariz. Soc. Allergists, Greater Phoenix Allergy Soc. (v.p. 1984-86, pres. 1986—), AAAS, Phoenix Zoo, N.Y. Acad. Scis., World Med. Assn., Internat. Assn. Asthmology, Assn. Care of Asthma, Ariz. Thoracic Soc., Nat. Geog. Soc., Ariz. Hist. Soc., Smithsonian Instn., Phoenix Art Mus., Nat. Audobon Soc. Clubs: Sertoma Internat. Contbr. articles in field to profl. jours. Office: 2200 W Bethany Home Rd Phoenix AZ 85015 Other: 1006 E Guadalupe Rd Tempe AZ 85283

ANANEH-FIREMPONG, OWUSU, physician; b. Ashanti, Ghana, Feb. 18, 1951; came to U.S., 1972, naturalized, 1986; s. Benjamin and Margaret (Appeah) Ananeh-Firempong; divorced; children: Owusu II, Adoma, Nana Frema. BA in Biology, Brandeis U., 1975; MD, U. So. Calif., 1979. Diplomate Nat. Bd. Med. Examiners, Am. Bd. Internal Medicine; cert. med. disability evaluator. Residency, internship White Meml. Med. Ctr., Los Angeles, 1979-82; admitting physician Lancaster (Calif.) Community Hosp., 1978—; attending physician Antelope Valley Hosp. Med. Ctr., Lancaster, 1982—, Palmdale (Calif.) Gen. Hosp., 1982—; pvt. practice Urgent Care Med. Ctr., Lancaster, 1982—; pres., chief exec. officer O. Ananeh-Firempong M.D., Inc., Lancaster, 1982—. Wein Internat. scholar, 1972-75. Fellow InterAm. Coll. of Physicians and Surgeons; mem. ACP, Am. Pub. Health Assn., Nat. Assn. Disability Evaluation Physicians, Am. Coll. Preventive Medicine, Nat. Acad. Scis. Avocations: soccer, ping-pong, weight lifting, karate, lawn tennis. Office: 907 W Lancaster Blvd Suite 101 Lancaster CA 93534

ANANE-SEFAH, JOHN CAMARA, physician; b. Bepong, Ghana, June 27, 1941; came to U.S., 1963, naturalized, 1979; s. Sam Kwabena Mireku and Akua (Gyafo) Mawu; B.S., Yale U., 1967; M.D., Harvard U., 1970; m. Patricia Anne Lawrence, June 2, 1973; children—Jason, John. Intern in surgery U. Colo., Denver, 1970-71, resident in surgery, fellow in trauma surgery, 1971-75; practice medicine specializing in gen. and vascular surgery; pres. Mid-County Surg./Med. Group, Inc., 1983—; mem. staffs Dominican Hosp., Community Hosp. Diplomate Am. Bd. Surgery. Fellow ACS, Royal Soc. Medicine (London), Internat. Coll. Surgeons, Internat. Acad. Proctology; mem. Santa Cruz C. of C. Contbr. articles to profl. jours. Office: 603 Capitola Ave Capitola CA 95010

ANANTH, JAMBUR, psychiatrist, educator; b. Hassan, Mysorg, India, Apr. 27, 1932; s. Venkata Subbaiah and Gundamma (Nanjundaiah) A.; m. Kamala Maroor, Apr. 23, 1971; 1 child, Kartik. MD, Kasturba Med. Sch., Manipal, India, 1960; Diploma in Psychol. Medicine, Nat. Inst. Mental Health, Bangalore, India, 1963. Diplomate Am. Bd. Psychiatry and Neurology. Asst. prof. McGill U., Montreal, Que., Can., 1969-74, assoc. prof., 1974-81; prof. UCLA, 1981—; chief clin. investigations dept. psychiatry McGill U., 1969-71, dir. edn. and research dept. psychiatry, 1971-72; dir. edn. and research St. Mary's Hosp., Montreal, 1972-76; dir. biol. psychiatry Allan Meml. Inst., Montreal, 1976-81. Contbr. articles to profl. jours.; adv. editor: Psychosomatics, 1978. Grantee Med. Research Council, Can., 1981, Dept. Mental Health, State of Calif., 1983. Fellow Collegeum Internat. Neuropharmocologicum, Royal Coll. Psychiatrists , Am. Psychiat. Assn. (pres. Que. dist. br. 1978-79). Avocations: photography, stamps. Home: 2709 Via Pacheco Palos Verdes Estates CA 90274 Office: Harbor-UCLA Med Ctr Dept Psychiat 1000 W Carson St Torrance CA 90509

ANARGYROS, NEDRA FLORENCE HARRISON, cytotechnologist; b. N.Y.C., Dec. 3, 1915; d. Leverette Roland and Florence Martha (Pickard) Harrison; student Emerson Coll., 1936; cert. in cytology U. Calif., San Francisco, 1957; m. Spero Drosos Anargyros, Oct. 21, 1940 (div. 1969). Supr. cytology San Francisco Gen. Hosp., 1957—. Mem. Am. Soc. Clin. Pathologists (affiliate mem.), Am. Soc. for Cytotech. (affiliate mem., cert. cytologist), Women Flyers of Am., DAR (1st vice regent La Puerta de Ora chpt., San Francisco), Nat. Soc. Colonial Dames of Am. in Calif., Huguenot Soc. of Calif. Republican. Christian Scientist. Club: Presidents of Mercer U. (Macon, Ga.). Home: 2503 Clay St San Francisco CA 94115 Office: San Francisco Gen Hosp 22d and Potrero Sts San Francisco CA 94110

ANAST, DAVID GEORGE, editor, publishing executive; b. Joliet, Ill., Oct. 9, 1955; s. George F. and Athey (Kusunis) A. Student, Ariz. State U., 1973-74; B. in Pub. Adminstrn., Calif. State Coll., Bakersfield, 1975-79, M. in Pub. Adminstrn., 1979. Corr. The Bakersfield Californian Daily Newspaper, 1975-79; mktg. and publs. mgr. U. So. Calif., Los Angeles, 1979; assoc. editor Calif. Good Life mag., Los Angeles, 1979-80, Worldwide Meetings and Incentives mag., Los Angeles, 1980-81; from assoc. editor to mng. editor Contemporary Dialysis and Nephrology mag., Los Angeles, 1980-85, editor, assoc. pub., 1985-86; exec. editor, pub. Nephrology News and Issues mag., Huntington Beach, Calif., 1986—. Author: (chpt.) Clinical Vascular Surgery, 1986; contbr. articles to profl. jours. Bd. dirs. NOW, San Fernando Valley, Calif., 1984, publs. advisor, 1984. Recipient Pub. Service award Nat. Kidney Found., 1984. Mem. Western Publs. Assn. (Maggie awards judge 1983-85). Greek Orthodox. Club: Hellenic U. of So. Calif. (sec. 1985). Avocations: photography, painting, reading, travel, films. Home: 6600 Warner Blvd #69 Huntington Beach CA 92647 Office: Nephrology News and Issues Mag 18582 Beach Blvd Suite 201 Huntington Beach CA 92648

ANASTOLE, DOROTHY JEAN, electronics company executive; b. Akron, Ohio, Mar. 26, 1932; d. Leonard L. and Helen (Sagedy) Dice; student De Anza Jr. Coll., Cupertino, Calif., spring 1969; children—Kally, Dennis, Christopher. Various secretarial positions in mfg., 1969-75; office mgr. Sci. Devices Co., Mountain View, Calif., 1975-76; exec. adminstrv. sec. corp. office Cezar Industries, Palo Alto, Calif., 1976-77; office and personnel mgr. AM Bruning Co., Mountain View, 1977-81; dir. employee relations Consol. Micrographics, Mountain View, 1981-83; personnel mgmt. cons., 1983-84; mgr. adminstrn./employee relations Mitsubishi Electronics Am., Inc., Sunnyvale, Calif., 1984—. Bd. dirs. Agnew State Hosp., San Jose, Calif., 1966-72, div. chmn. program mentally retarded, 1966-72, staff tutor, 1966-72. Recipient Service award Agnew State Hosp., 1972. Mem. Am. Soc. Profl. and Exec. Women, Am. Soc. Personnel Adminstrn. Office: Mitsubishi Electronics Am 1050 E Argues Ave Sunnyvale CA 94086

ANAYA, TONEY, governor of State of New Mexico; b. Moriarty, N. Mex., Apr. 29, 1941; s. Lauriano and Eufracia (Martinez) A.; m. Elaine Bolin, 1963; children—Kimberly, Toney, Kristina. B.A., Georgetown U., 1963; J.D., Washington Coll. Law, 1967. Bar: N.Mex. 1968, D.C. 1968, U.S. Supreme Ct. 1968. Atty. gen. State of N.Mex., Santa Fe, 1975-78; sr. ptnr. Anaya, Strumor, Gonzales & Fruman, Santa Fe, N.Mex., 1979-82; gov. State of N.Mex., Santa Fe, 1983-87; chmn. State Investment Council, State Bd. Fin., Community Devel. Council, Econ. Devel. and Tourism Bd.; co-chmn. Western Gov. Assn. Internat. Competitiveness Task Force; mem. Interstate Mining Commn., Reciprocity Commn., Edn. Commn. of States. Guest columnist Albuquerque Jour., Vista Mag., Fresno Bee, Capper's Weekly, Miami News, Denver Post, San Francisco Chronicle, Boston Jewish Times, Cath. Post; TV appearances include: ABC's Nightline, NBC Meet The Press, David Brinkley Show, NBC Today Show, C-SPAN Network, SIN Network. Mem. adv. bd. Central Am. Peace Campaign; chmn. Hispanic Force '84; co-chmn. Mondale for Pres., 1984; hon. chmn. N.Mex. Mothers Against Drunk Driving, 1984; mem. ex officio bd. regents all N.Mex. State Univs. Recipient Friend of Journalism award Sigma Delta Chi, 1976, Disting. Service award N.Mex. Broadcasters, 1977, Internat. award WW II Mexican Fighter Squadron, 1984, Outstanding Achievement award Ams. for Indian Opportunity, 1984, Outstanding Am. award Am. GI Forum, 1985, Hispanic Achievement award Colo. State U., 1986, Nat. Council of La Raza award, 1986; named one of Outstanding Young Men in Am. N.Mex. Jaycees, 1975, one of Top 10 Govs. Nat. Womens Polit. Caucus, 1986. Mem. Nat. Govs. Assn. (co-leader hazardous materials task force, co-leader telecommunications subcom., chmn. subcom. on environment). Democrat. Roman Catholic. Avocations: outdoors activities. Address: PO Box 8230 Santa Fe NM 87504

ANCELL, MARY KATHERINE ZIEG, property renovation company executive; b. Lincoln, Nebr., Apr. 10, 1943; d. Henry J. and Lydia B. Zieg; m. Ivan D. Ancell, Oct. 15, 1966. B.A., U. Iowa, 1966; M.A., Stanford U., 1974, Ph.D., 1978. Instr., U. Pa. Sch. Dental Medicine, 1969-70, project dir. NIH, 1970-72; instr. biol. scis. div. Foothill Coll., 1972-73; cons., subject matter expert NIH, San Francisco, 1970-74; research asst. Stanford (Calif.) Ctr. for Research and Devel. in Teaching, 1973-74; prin. operator Ancell Properties, Woodside, Calif., 1973—; owner Paradox Interiors, Woodside, Calif., 1978—; owner Paradox Assocs., div. Paradox Interiors, 1981—. Dir. pub. relations Woodside-Atherton Aux. to Children's Hosp. at Stanford; chmn. radio and TV publicity Stanford U. Mus. Art, 1986; publicity dir. Children's Miracle Network Telethon, Children's Hosp. Stanford, 1986; promotions rep. March of Dimes, 1987. Recipient Recognition award Alpha Kappa Gamma, 1966; Certificates of Appreciation, Am. Assn. Dental Schs., 1972-76; grantee Div. Health Manpower, NIH, 1970; Recognition award Periodontics Dept. of U. Pa. Sch. Dental Medicine, 1972. Mem. AAUP, Am. Assn. Dental Schs., Am. Thoroughbred Racing Assn., Friends of Filoli, Peninsula Humane Soc. Office: PO Box 620150 Woodside CA 94062

ANCOLI-ISRAEL, SONIA, psychologist, researcher; b. Tel Aviv, Israel, Dec. 25, 1951; came to U.S., 1955.; m. Andrew G. Israel; 2 children. BA, SUNY, Stony Brook, 1972; MA, Calif. State U., Long Beach, 1974; PhD, U. Calif., San Francisco, 1979. Lic. psychologist, Calif. Staff psychologist U. Calif.-San Diego, La Jolla, 1979-84, asst adj. prof., 1984—; asst. dir. Sleep Disorders Clinic VA Med. Ctr., San Diego, 1981—. Contbr. numerous articles to profl. jours. Bd. mgrs. Jewish Community Ctr., La Jolla, 1985—. Recipient Robert E. Harris Meml. award, U. Calif. San Franicsco, 1978. Mem. Sleep Research Soc., Clin. Sleep Soc., Gerontol. Soc. Am., Biofeedback Soc. Am. (mem. program com. 1978, chairperson Profl. Edn. Bulletin com., 1978, mem. cert. sub-com. of the profl. affairs com. 1979-80, mem. nominating com. 1985—), Biofeedback Soc. Calif. (bd. dirs. 1977-80, chairperson cert. com. 1978-80, chairperson fin. com. 1977, cert. examiner 1977-80), Internat. Assn. Psychophysiology, Soc. for Psychophysiol. Research , N.Y. Acad. Sci., AAAS.

ANDARY, THOMAS JOSEPH, biochemist; b. Sault Sainte Marie, Mich., Oct. 8, 1942; s. Joseph Boula and Marion (Schwifetti) A. B.S., No. Mich. U., 1966, M.A., 1968; Ph.D., Wayne State U., 1974. Instr. biology No. Mich. U., Marquette, 1967-69; research asso. physiology Wayne State U., Detroit, 1973-76; sr. research scientist, mgr. coagulation research Hyland Labs., Costa Mesa, Calif., 1976-83; dir. quality control Hyland Therapeutics, Glendale, Calif., 1983—; lectr. in field. Recipient Research award Sigma Xi, 1973; NDEA fellow, 1969-72. Mem. Am. Chem. Soc., N.Y. Acad. Sci., Sigma Xi. Roman Catholic. Contbr. over 25 articles to profl. publs. Home: 531 N Canyon Monrovia CA 91016 Office: 4501 Colorado Blvd Los Angeles CA 90039

ANDERBERG, ROY ANTHONY, journalist; b. Camden, N.J., Mar. 30, 1921; s. Arthur R. and Mary V. (McHugh) A.; A.A., Diablo Valley Coll., 1975; m. Louise M. Brooks, Feb. 5, 1953; children—Roy, Mary. Enlisted USN, 1942, commd. officer, 1960, ret., 1970; waterfront columnist Pacific Daily News, Agana, Guam, 1966-67; pub. relations officer Naval Forces, Mariana Islands, 1967; travel editor Contra Costa (Calif.) Times, 1968-69; entertainment and restaurant editor Concord (Calif.) Transcript, 1971-75; entertainment editor Contra Costa Advertiser, 1975-76; free-lance non-fiction journalist, 1976—. Mem. U.S. Power Squadron, DAV, Ret. Officers Assn., Am. Legion, VFW, U.S. Submarine Vets. World War II Assn. Democrat. Clubs: Martinez Yacht; Contra Costa Press; Toastmasters. Home: 2720 Lyon Circle Concord CA 94518 Office: Box 52 Concord CA 94522

ANDERS, BEATRICE BRYANT, art studio executive; b. Wichita, Kans., Sept. 30, 1950; d. Joseph Harmon and Beatrice (Sautter) Bryant; m. Barry Edward Johnston, Dec. 21, 1971 (div. July 1981); m. Robert Allen Anders, June 5, 1982 (div. Dec. 1986). BA in Art, Austin Coll., 1972; BS in Geology, Geophysics, No. Ariz. U., 1976; MS in Geology, Tex. A&M U., 1979. Research asst. Ctr. for Tectonophysics Tex. A&M U., College Station, 1976-77, research asst., 1977, research asst. NSF, 1978-79; research asst. Wash. State U., Pullman, 1979, Rockwell-Hanford, Richland, Wash., 1979-80; geologic aide Idaho Bur. Mines, Moscow, 1981; asst. geologist Richard Nielson Geocons., Evergreen, Colo., 1981-82; geologist, geochemist Marathon Resources, Denver, 1982; freelance sales rep. for artists Golden, Colo., 1982—; prin. Axis Studio, Golden, 1983—; lectr. on Mt. Saint Helens, 1980—; cons. Marathon Oil Co., Littleton, Colo., 1983. Contbr. articles to profl. jours. Sigma Pi Sigma. Democrat. Avocations: travelling, hiking, painting, rock collecting, photography. Home: 18200 W 3rd Ave #1 Golden CO 80401 Office: Axis Studio 4444 Gladiola St Golden CO 80403

ANDERS, DONALD EDWARD, research geochemist; b. Jacksonville, Ill., May 27, 1935; s. Alva and Nina Gertrude (Baird) A.; m. Rose Marie Morris, July 1, 1956; children: Mark Edward, Carrie Lynette. BS, Ill. Coll., 1958; MS, U. Wyo., 1971. Chemist No. Region Research Lab., Peoria, Ill., 1958-64, Laramie Energy Research Sta., 1964-74; chemist U.S. Geol. Survey, Denver, 1974-76, lab. mgr., 1976-85, project chief, 1976-85, prin. chemist, 1976—; cons. petroleum geochemistry, 1960—. Contbr. articles to profl. jours; patentee in field, 1963. Mem. Am. Chem. Soc., Colo. Sect. Am. Chem. Soc., Geochem. Soc. Am. (chmn. nomination com. 1975-76), Honor Soc. Agriculture, Gideons Internat. Soc. (pres. Laramie chpt. 1970-72), Sigma Xi. Republican. Baptist. Avocations: golf, skiing. Home: 11473 W Briarwood Dr Lakewood CO 80226 Office: US Geol Survey PO Box 25046 MS 977 Denver CO 80225

ANDERSEN, BARBARA DORIS, advertising executive; b. Mineola, N.Y., Aug. 25, 1946; d. Frederick W. and Ruth W. (Trebing) A.; m. John Patterson III, Nov. 30, 1968 (div.); 1 child, Andrew Oliver. BS, U. Vt., 1968. Sales promotion mgr. Advalloy, Inc., Palo Alto, Calif., 1968-70; media dir. Anderson-Madison Advt. Firm, Mnpls., 1970-71; mktg. mgr. Getz Bros., Inc., San Francisco, 1971-76; pub. relations dir. Logical Machine Corp., Sunnyvale, Calif., 1976-77; exhibits mgr. Smith-Kline Instruments Co., Sunnyvale, 1977-78; mktg. communications mgr. Durango Systems, Inc., San Jose, Calif., 1978-80; mktg. services mgr. Tandem Computers Co., Cupertino, Calif., 1980-83; account supr. Battenberg, Fillhardt & Wright, 1983-86; mktg. mgr. Convergent Techs., San Jose, 1986—; cons. Andersen Assocs., Cupertino; guest instr., lectr. local colls. Mem. Bus. and Profl. Advt. Assn., Peninsula Mktg. Assn. (dir.), Peninsula Women in Advt. (dir.), U. Vt. Alumnae Assn., Delta Delta Delta. Office: Convergent Techs 2700 N First St San Jose CA 95150-6685

ANDERSEN, BRENT MERRILL, mechanical engineer; b. Bell, Calif., Sept. 18, 1940; s. Kenneth Merrill Andersen and Margaret Jeanne (Rowley) Cook; m. Judith DiAnne Meadows, May 30, 1976; children: Tammy, Lee, Todd, Kevin. BSME, Heald Engring. Coll., 1969. Plant engr. Clorox Co., Tampa, Fla., 1974-76; plant engr. Kingsford div. Clorox Co., Springfield, Oreg., 1976-78, region engr., 1978-82, div. engr., 1983-85, plant engr., 1985—. Served with U.S. Army, 1962-65. Mem. Am. Inst. Plant Engrs. Republican. Avocations: hunting, fishing, golf. Office: Kingsford Products Co 3315 Marcola Rd Springfield OR 97478

ANDERSEN, CHARL PAUL, college administrator, theatre director; b. Lehi, Utah, Oct. 25, 1936; s. Charl Jens and Lizzie Leona (Clark) A.; m. Kathleen Ramsay, Aug. 29, 1959; children—Lisa, Jill, Wendy, Paul Ramsay. B.A., Brigham Young U., 1958, M.A., 1959, Ph.D., 1974. Instr. theatre arts Brigham Young U., 1958-59; tchr. West High Sch., Salt Lake City, 1959-61; asst. prof. Church Coll. Hawaii, Laie, 1961-62; tchr. Am. Fork High Sch., American Fork, Utah, 1962-65; prof. fine and performing arts Dixie Coll., St. George, Utah, 1965—, dir. theatre, 1968—; founder dir. Pioneer Courthouse Players, St. George, 1975—; dir. Old Barn Theatre, Kanab, Utah, 1978. Author: (plays) How Made Me Thus, 1959, Lilly, Prisoner of the Past, 1962, Dracula and Company, 1980, Revenge of the Southern Belle, 1984. Mem. Washington County Bi-Centennial Com., St. George, 1976; bd. dirs. O.C. Tanner Amphitheatre, St. George, 1980-82; mem. Dixie Ctr. Control Bd., St. George, 1984—. Mem. Utah Speech Arts Assn. (sec. 1963-64, pres. 1964-65), Wasatch Front Edn. council (sec. 1964-65), Am. Theatre Assn., Utah Theatre Assn. (dir. 1982-83), Screen Actors Guild, Dramatist's Guild, Bertolt Brecht Soc., Rocky Mountain Theatre Assn. Democrat. Mormon. Lodge: Kiwanis. Home: 830 E Fort Pierce Dr Saint George UT 84770 Office: Dixie Coll 225 S 700 E Saint George UT 84770

ANDERSEN, DORIS EVELYN, real estate broker; b. Christian County, Ky., Oct. 30, 1923; d. William Earl and Blanche Elma (Withers) Johnston; m. Roger Lewis Shirk, July 9, 1944 (div. 1946); 1 child, Vicki Lee Shirk Sanderson; m. DeLaire Andersen, July 6, 1946; children: Craig Bryant, Karen Rae, Kent DeLaire, Chris Jay, Mardi Lynn. Diploma, South Bend Coll. Commerce, 1942; diploma in banking Notre Dame U., 1946; student Ind. U., 1942-44. Tng. dir. First Nat. Bank, Portland, Oreg., 1963-69; assoc. broker Stan Wiley, Inc., Portland, 1969-79; prin. Doris Andersen & Assocs., Portland, 1979—; speaker at seminars; mem. Gov.'s Task Force Council on Housing, Salem, Oreg., 1985-86. Contbr. articles to profl. jours. Mem. task force Oreg. Dept. Energy, Salem, 1984-85. Mem. Nat. Assn. Realtors (dir. 1983—), Oreg. Assn. Realtors (dir. 1979—, pres. 1986—), Portland Bd. Realtors (pres. 1982), Women's Council Realtors (local pres. 1977, state pres. 1978, gov. nat. orgn. 1979). Avocations: reading, traveling. Home: 459 Chestnut St Ashland OR 97520 Office: PO Box 6770 Portland OR 97228

ANDERSEN, ELLEN MARIE, social worker; b. Kingman, Ariz., Jan. 25, 1948; d. William Franklin Cummings and Beatrice Ellen (Vanderberg) Kohlhase; m. Larry Harold Andersen, Feb. 16, 1973; children: Hans Harold, Anna Marie. Student, U. Puget Sound, 1966-68; BA, U. Oreg., 1970; MSW, U. Mich., 1972. Family services specialist Municipality of Anchorage, 1972-75; clinic coordinator River Bluffs Child Guidance Ctr., Council Bluffs, Iowa, 1975-78; social worker Bur. Indian Affairs, Anchorage, 1978, Indian Health Service, Anchorage, 1978—; active in child devel. and child health subjects, 1978—. Mem. Anchorage Child Abuse Bd., 1974-75. Health Careers grant March of Dimes, 1971-72. Mem. Nat. Assn. Social Workers (sec. Anchorage 1979-80, co-editor newsletter 1979-80), Acad. Cert. Social Workers (diplomate), Registry Clin. Social Workers (diplomate), Soc. Hosp. Social Work Dirs., Phi Beta Kappa. Avocations: figure skating, cross country skiing, movies, books. Office: Alaska Native Med Ctr 250 Gambell St Anchorage AK 99508

ANDERSEN, ERNEST CHRISTOPHER, lawyer; b. Minden, Nebr., Sept. 10, 1909; s. Dines Peter and Marie (Jensen) A.; m. Audrey Etta Robertson, Sept. 10, 1954; 1 dau., Elaine Carolyn Andersen Smith; 1 stepson, Albert Henry Whitaker. J.D., U. Denver, 1952, B.S. in Bus. Adminstrn., 1956. Bar: Colo. 1954, U.S. Supreme Ct. 1960. With U.S. Treasury Dept., Denver, 1935-39; accountant, Denver, 1939-41; with Civilian Prodn. Adminstrn., Denver, 1946-49; dep. state auditor Colo., 1949-51; with U.S. Commerce Dept., Denver, 1951-52; mgmt. cons., Denver, 1953-54; sole practice law, Denver, 1955-56, 69-75; asst. dir. GAO, Los Angeles, 1957-58, Denver, 1959, Washington, 1960-69, cons., 1969-75; sole practice law, Cedaredge, Colo., 1975—; owner Cedar Crest Farm, 1983—, Stand Sure Press (later Christopher Pub. Co.), 1977—; mem. faculty U. Denver, 1948-56; mcpl. judge Cedaredge, 1977-86; exec. in residence Tulane U., spring 1973. Bd. dirs. Delta Montrose Electric Assn., 1976-84, Colo.-Ute Electric Assn., 1980-84. Served to lt. col. U.S. Army, 1941-46. Recipient Meritorious Service award GAO, 1968. Republican. Presbyterian. Clubs: Masons, Shriners. Home: 1856 Road 2375 Cedaredge CO 81413 Office: PO Box 747 Cedaredge CO 30747

ANDERSEN, GARY KENT, television producer; b. Omaha, Aug. 6, 1939; s. Jacob Christian and Christine Marie (Albertsen) A.; m. Emily Hall, Nov. 23, 1962 (div. Dec. 1963); 1 child, John Christian. BA, U. Hawaii. Mammal behaviorist Sea Life Park, Honolulu, 1963-65; human behaviorist Sta. KPOI-FM, Honolulu, 1965-66; dir. photography Young Hawaii Mag., Honolulu, 1967-69; mem. crew Beach CAT, Honolulu, summers 1967-71; producer TV Oceanic Info. Services, Honolulu, 1971—. Executed mural for Trade Pub. Co., 1971; author TV spl. Abstract on Tape, 1981 (1st Place Internat. Videographers award); creative cons. Childrens' TV Workshop, 1980. Media cons. Honolulu Dems., 1975—. Served to capt. USAF, 1959-62. Recipient Presdl. Merit award, Pres. Gerald Ford, Washington, 1976. Fellow Am. Soc. Animal Behaviorists; mem. Nat. Soc. Arts and Letters, Assn. Honolulu Artists, Soc. Naval Architects and Marine Engrs., Sierra Club (chmn. conservation com. 1985—), Hawaii Wilderness Runners (pres. 1981—). Clubs: Hui Hani Hawaii Civic, Kaumaualii Hawaii Civic, Sierra Club (chmn. Honolulu exec. com.). Avocations: running marathons, Scottish drums, bird watching, 3-D chess. Office: Oceanic Info Services PO Box 61691 Honolulu HI 96822

ANDERSEN, JAMES A., justice; b. Auburn, Wash., Sept. 21, 1924; s. James A. and Margaret Cecilia (Norgaard) A.; m. Dolphina R. Novelli; children: James Blair, Tia Louise. BA, U. Wash., 1949, JD, 1951. Bar: Wash. 1952, U.S. Dist. Ct. (we. dist.) Wash. 1957, U.S. Ct. Appeals 1957. Dep. pros. atty. King County, Seattle, 1953-57; assoc. Lycette, Diamond & Sylvester, Seattle, 1957-61; ptnr. Clinton, Andersen, Fleck & Glein, Seattle, 1961-75; judge Wash. State Ct. of Appeals, Seattle, 1975-84; justice Wash. State Supreme Ct., Olympia, 1984—. Mem. Wash. State Ho. of Reps., 1958-67, Wash. State Senate, 1967-72. Served with U.S. Army, 1943-45, ETO. Decorated Purple Heart. Mem. ABA, Wash. State Bar Assn. Episcopalian. Office: Wash State Supreme Ct Temple of Justice Olympia WA 98504-0511

ANDERSEN, MARK GERALD, business educator; b. Riverside, Calif., July 29, 1959; s. Elton E. and Ruby Lee (Bagley) A. BA, Point Loma Coll., 1981; MBA, Calif. State U., San Bernardino, 1984. Account adminstr. IBM Corp., Riverside, 1981-84; owner Mark Andersen Resume Service, Riverside, 1984—; staff musician U. Calif., Riverside, 1984-86; instr. Riverside Community Coll., 1984—. Republican. Office: Mark Andersen Enterprises PO Box 5025 Riverside CA 92517

ANDERSEN, ROBERT DAVID, biochemist; b. Bellingham, Wash., Dec. 3, 1945; s. Jack Eli Andersen and Judith Rose (Greenberg) Spindler; m. Christhild Melchinger, Feb. 26, 1980; 1 child, Kimball Eberhard. BS, Harvey Mudd Coll., 1967; PhD in Biochemistry, U. Mich., 1972. Research technician Parke Davis and Co., Ann Arbor, Mich., summer 1967; assoc. research biochemist UCLA, 1978-83, new NIH investigator, 1983—. Contbr. articles to profl. jours. NIH fellow U. Mich., Ann Arbor, 1973-75, Alexander V. Humboldt fellow U. Tübingen, Fed. Republic Germany, 1976-78. Mem. AAAS. Democrat. Jewish. Avocations: mountaineering, bicycling. Office: Lab Biomed & Environ Scis 900 Veteran Ave Los Angeles CA 90024

ANDERSEN, SHIRLEY ANN, educator; b. Centertown, Mo., Nov. 2, 1929; d. Edward Elmer and Olive W. (Wagner) Keso; m. Kenwood Martin Andersen, Oct. 10, 1958; children—Maureen Kaye, Teresa Louise. B.S., Okla. A & M U., 1950, M.S., 1955; postgrad. Colo. State U., U. No. Colo., Adams State U., Cert. vocat. tchr., Okla., Nebr., Colo. Tchr. home econs. Perkins (Okla.) High Sch., 1950-52, Marlow (Okla.) High Sch., 1952-55; instr. food and nutrition U. Nebr., Lincoln, 1955-59, tchr. home econs. Potter (Nebr.) High Sch., 1960-61, Dalton (Nebr.) High Sch., 1962-68, Sterling (Colo.) High Sch., 1968—. Judge local, state contests; mem. Extension Service Adv. Bd., North Central Evaluation Teams; mem. local library bd. Mem. Am. Vocat. Assn., Colo. Vocat. Assn., Colo. Edn. Assn. NEA, South Platte Edn. Assn., Delta Kappa Gamma, Omicron Nu. Republican. Lutheran. Club: Order of Eastern Star (Sterling, Colo.). Office: Sterling High Sch Bengal Blvd Sterling CO 80751

ANDERSEN, SYLVIA, nurse, educator; b. Mesa, Ariz., Aug. 31, 1953; d. Darl Edwin and Erma (Farnsworth) A. BS in Nursing, Brigham Young U., 1977, MS, 1982. Registered nurse, Utah. RN various locations, Utah, Calif., Ariz., 1975-80, Utah, Ariz., 1980—; nursing instr. Ariz. State U., Tempe, 1981—; vol. family nurse practitioner Ariz. State U. Nursing Clinic, 1983; developer new staff orientation program Utah Valley Hosp., 1977. Author: Assignment Wheels, 1983. Vol. various Rep. candidates, Mesa, 1983-84; missionary Mormon Ch., Hong Kong, 1979-80. Mem. Cen. Ariz. Nurse Practitioners, Relief Soc., Sigma Theta Tau. Avocations: music, cooking, group sports, crafts. Home: 850 S River Dr #2067 Tempe AZ 85281 Office: Ariz State U Coll Nursing Tempe AZ 85287

ANDERSOHN, NATHAN L., lawyer; b. Sturgis, Mich., Aug. 11, 1955; s. Emerson L. and Betty Lou (Lederman) A. BS in Acctg., U. Denver, 1977; JD, Drake U., 1980. Bar: Colo. Gen. counsel Wedgcor Inc., Denver, 1983-84, Cersonsky Realty, Denver, 1985; house counsel ABC Supply Co., Inc., Aurora, Colo., 1986—. Mem. ABA, Colo. Bar Assn., Denver Bar Assn. Republican. Avocations: bow hunting, skiing, fishing. Home: 4380 E Mexico Ave Denver CO 80222 Office: 14805 E Moncrieff Pl Aurora CA 80011

ANDERSON, ALDON J., judge; b. Salt Lake City, Jan. 3, 1917; s. Aldon J. and Minnie (Egan) A.; m. Virginia Barbara Weilenmann, Nov. 5, 1943; children—Jeffrey Lance, Aldon Scott, Craig W., Paul Christian, Kevin E., Rebecca C., Douglas K. B.A., U. Utah, 1939, J.D., 1943. Bar: Utah 1943. Ptnr. King, Anderson & Durham, King, Anderson & Brown, 1943-57; state dist. atty. State of Utah, 1953-57, judge state dist. ct., 1957-71; judge U.S. Dist. Ct. Utah, 1971—, chief judge, 1978—; vice chmn. State Bar Com. on Uniform Cts., Utah, 1970, chmn.; subcom. on Jud. Improvement, Jud. Adminstrv. Conf., 1979—; vice chmn. State Bar Com. on Compiling State Rules of Edn.; chmn. ad hoc com. of judicial conf. Am. Inns of Ct.; past chmn. Amm. Inns of Ct. Found. Active Mormon Ch. Named Judge of Yr., Utah State Bar Assn., 1980. Mem. ABA, Dist. Attys. Assn. Utah, U.S. Dist. Judges Assn. (past pres. 10th cir.), Am. Bar Found., Pi Kappa Alpha, Delta Phi, Phi Delta Phi. Address: US Dist Ct Dist of Utah Salt Lake City UT 84101

ANDERSON, ALLAN JEFFREY, computer software engineer; b. Anchorage, Feb. 10, 1950; s. Arthur Oscar and Thelma Marie (Montgomery) A. BS, U. Ariz., 1974, MS, 1983. Chemist Jones Blair Co., Dallas, 1976-80; mem. tech. staff Hughes Aircraft Co., Tucson, 1983—. Vol. Murphy for Mayor campaign, Tucson, 1971; Rep. precinct capt., Tucson, 1972-74. Mem. Am. Chem. Soc., Assn. Computing Machinery. Club: SUNHUG (Tucson)(treas. 1983-85). Avocations: home computers, electronics, cryptology.

ANDERSON, ARTHUR ROLAND, civil engr.; b. Tacoma, Wash., Mar. 11, 1910; s. Eivind and Aslaug (Axness) A.; B.S., U. Wash., 1934; M.S., Mass. Inst. Tech., 1935, D.Sc., 1938; J.D. (hon.), Gonzaga U., 1983; m. Barbara Hinman Beck, June 5, 1938; children—Martha Anderson Nelson, Karl, Richard, Elisabeth Anderson Zerzan, Deborah Anderson Ray. Mem. staff MIT, Cambridge, 1936-38, 39-41, mem. ednl. council, 1954—; design engr. Klonne Steel Co., Dortmund, Germany, 1938-39; head tech. dept. Cramp Shipyard, U.S. Navy Bur. Ships, Phila., 1941-46; cons. civil engr., Stamford, Conn., 1946-51; co-founder Concrete Tech. Corp., Tacoma, 1951, sr. v.p., 1956—; pres. Anderson Enterprises Corp., Tacoma, 1957—; vis. lectr. U. Wash., 1954-55; chmn. bd. Anderson, Birkeland, Anderson & Mast, Engrs., Inc. (now ABAM Engrs. Inc.), Tacoma, 1951-77. Pres. Puget Sound (Wash.) Sci. Fair, 1954-58; mem. Tacoma Public Utility Bd., 1954-69, chmn., 1968-69; mem. Pacific Lutheran U. Collegium, 1976—; mem. vis. com. U. Wash.; mem. Wash. State Council for Post-Secondary Edn., 1977-84. Registered profl. engr., Wash., Conn., B.C., Can.; named Alumnus Summa Laude Dignatus, U. Wash., 1980. Mem. Am. Concrete Inst. (hon. mem.; dir. 1962-69, pres. 1966-67, Constrn. Practice award 1962, Alfred E. Lindau medal 1970, Roger Corbetta award 1974, Charles S. Whitney award 1975, Turner medal 1977, Arthur J. Boase award 1979), ASCE (hon., life mem., mem. tech. com. 1963-66, T.Y. Lin award 1971), Soc. Exptl. Stress Analysis (charter), ASTM, Nat. Soc. Profl. Engrs., Soc. Naval Architects and Marine Engrs., Internat. Assn. Bridge and Structural Engrs. (hon.), Prestressed Concrete Inst. (pres. 1970-71), N.E. Coast Shipbuilders and Engrs., Japan Concrete Inst. (hon.), Fedn. Internat. de la Precontrainte (F.I.P. medal 1974), Comité European de Beton, Nat. Acad. Engring., Sigma Xi, Chi Epsilon, Beta Gamma Sigma, Tau Beta Pi. Contbr. numerous articles in tech. of concrete and research on welded steel ships to profl. jours.; patentee in field. Home: 502 Tacoma Ave North Tacoma WA 98403 Office: 1123 Port of Tacoma Rd Tacoma WA 98421

ANDERSON, BARBARA KAYE, purchasing executive; b. Long Beach, Calif., Apr. 13, 1943; d. Jesse M. Anderson and Nell M. (Schramer) Huston-Curtiss; m. Eugene E. Buttery, July 1, 1967 (div. Apr. 1968); m. Erik

Ferguson, July 11, 1987. Student, St. Cloud State Coll., 1961-62. Sr. purchasing specialist MGM Grand Hotel, Las Vegas, Nev., 1973-77; dir. purchasing MGM Grand Hotel, Reno, 1977-79, Penthouse Boardwalk, Atlantic City, 1979-80, Del Webb's Claridge, Atlantic City, 1980-83; sr. purchasing agt. Ramada Corp. Hdqrs., Phoenix, 1983-86; dir. purchasing Tropicana Hotel, Las Vegas, 1986—; cons. Guest Supply Inc., North Brunswick, N.J., 1986. Mem. Purchasing Mgmt. Assn. Ariz., Food Service Execs. Assn. Republican. Club: Las Vegas Ski (sec. 1968-69). Avocations: skiing, dancing, reading, cards, Trivial Pursuit. Office: Tropicana Hotel and Casino 3801 Las Vegas Blvd S Las Vegas NV 89109

ANDERSON, BARBARA LOUISE, library director; b. San Diego, Jan. 5, 1933; d. Lorenzo and Louise (Morgan) A.; 1 child, Sean Allen. B.S., San Diego State U., 1954; M.L.S., Kans. State Teachers Coll., 1955. Br. librarian Los Angeles Pub. Library, 1956-59; br. librarian, reference, young adult librarian San Diego Pub. Library, 1959-64; librarian U.S. Army, Europe, 1964-69; coordinator Serra Reference Project, Serra Regional Library System, San Diego, 1969-71; head readers services Riverside (Calif.) City and County Pub. Library, 1972-74; county librarian San Bernardino County (Calif.) Library, 1974—; del. White House Conf. on Libraries and Info. Services, 1979. Bd. dirs. Inland Empire Symphony, 1982-84, Riverside Mental Health Assn., 1975-79. Mem. ALA, Calif. Library Assn., Black Caucus of Calif. Library Assn., Congress of Pub. Library Systems (pres. 1984), Calif. County Librarians Assn., Calif. Soc. Librarians (pres. 1974-75, mem. OCLC Users Council 1984-85), AAUW (pres. Riverside Br. 1976-77), NAACP, Bus. and Profl. Women San Bernardino. Democrat. Baptist. Contbr. articles to publs. in field. Office: San Bernardino County Library 104 W 4th St San Bernardino CA 92415

ANDERSON, BRADFORD WILLIAM, food company sales executive; b. Redlands, Calif., Feb. 17, 1956; s. B.W. and Helen Louise (Wisel) A.; m. Diane Elizabeth Hutt, Aug. 22, 1981. BS in Mgmt., U. Redlands, 1978; MBA in Mktg. Mgmt., Calif. State U., 1982. Cert. instr. in bus. edn., Calif. Store mgr. Fringer's Market, Redlands, Calif., 1978-80; ter. mgr. Carnation Co., Fullerton, Calif., 1980-82, sr. ter. mgr., trainer, 1982-84, dist. sales coordinator, 1984-85; nat. mgr. sales planning Carnation Co., Los Angeles, 1985—, implementation coordinator, 1984; instr. Chaffey Coll., Alta Loma, Calif., 1984-85. Named one of Outstanding Young Men in Am., Jaycees, 1984; recipient P. Pat Patterson Meml. Award, Santa Fe Fed. Savs., 1978; Harris Meml. scholar Harris Dept. Stores, 1978. Mem. Food Industry Sales Club, Alumni Assn. San Bernardino, Calif., Young Alumni Com. U. Redlands, Alpha Gamma Nu. Democrat. Methodist. Home: 24442 Rosegate Pl Diamond Bar CA 91765 Office: Carnation Co 5045 Wilshire Blvd Los Angeles CA 90036

ANDERSON, CARL DAVID, scientist; b. N.Y.C., Sept. 3, 1905; s. Carl David and Emma Adolfina (Ajaxson) A.; m. Lorraine Elvira Bergman; children—Marshall David, David Andrew. B.S., Calif. Inst. of Tech., 1927, Ph.D. magna cum laude, 1930; hon. Sc.D., Colgate U., 1937, Gustavus Adolphus Coll., 1963; LL.D. (hon.), Temple U., 1948. Coffin research fellow Calif. Inst. Tech., 1927-28, teaching fellow in physics, 1928-30, research fellow in physica, 1930-33, asst. prof. physics, 1933-37, asso. prof., 1937-39, prof., 1939-76, prof. emeritus, 1976—, chmn. div. physics, math. and astronomy, 1962-70. Awarded gold medal Am. Inst. of City of N.Y., 1935; Nobel prize in physics, 1936; Elliott Cresson medal of the Franklin Inst., 1937; John Ericsson medal Am. Soc. Swedish Engrs., 1960. Mem. Am. Phys. Soc., Am. Philos. Soc., Nat. Acad. Scis., Sigma Xi, Tau Beta Pi. Research on X-Ray photoelectrons, 1927-30; research on gamma rays and cosmic-rays since 1930. Address: Dept Physics Calif Inst of Tech Pasadena CA 91109

ANDERSON, CARL EDGAR, orthopaedic surgeon; b. Templeton, Calif., Apr. 11, 1914; s. Carl Frederick and Mabel Theodora (Berry) A.; m. Beatrice Anderson, Aug. 12, 1946; children: Carol, C. Lawrence, Susan. AB, U. Calif., Berkeley, 1930-34; MD, U. Calif., San Francisco, 1939. Intern San Francsico City and County Hosp., 1938-39, fellow in orghopaedic surgery, 1941-42; resident in orthopaedic surgery U. Calif. Hosp., 1939-41; clin. instr. orthopaedic surgery U. Calif. Sch. Medicine, San Francisco, 1942-52, asst. clin. prof., 1952-60, assoc. clin. prof., 1960-67, clin. prof., 1967-81, emeritus clin. prof., 1981—; practice medicine specializing in orthopaedic surgery San Francisco, 1942-49, Santa Rosa, 1949—; lectr. surg. anatomy Coll. Physicians and Surgeons, San Francisco, 1942; instr. in scis. basic to nursing and medicine Santa Rosa (Calif.) Coll. Sch. Nursing, 1949-58; med. advisor rehab. services Santa Rosa Meml. Hosp., 1978; med. dir. rehab. Brookwood Hosp., Santa Rosa, 1981; chmn. S.R. Health Systems Sisters of St. Joseph, Orange, Calif.; med. dir. phys. therapy and occupational therapy S.R. Meml. Hosp., S.R. Gen. Hosp.; con. medicare regulations HEW, 1965-69, mem. health ins. benefits adv. council, 1969-74. Contbr. articles to sci. jours. Cons. Calif. Legis. on Workers Compensation, Rehab., etc. 1962-75, Assembly Com. on Emergency Med. Care, 1968-69, Dept. Health Care Services on Med-Cal Regulations, 1967-68; mem. Gov.'s Task Force on Efficiency and Cost Control, 1967; chmn. div. indsl. accidents Med. Adv. Com., 1976-78. Fellow Am. Acad. Orthopaedic Surgeons (exec. com. 1967-72, Kappa Delta award 1972), Am. Coll. Surgeons; mem. Am. Congress of Rehab. Medicine, Am. Orthopaedic Assn. (v.p. 1974), AAAS, Nat. PTA (hon. life), AMA, Calif. Med. Assn. (council chmn. 1962-67), San Francisco County Med. Assn., Western Orthopaedic Assn. (pres. No. Calif. chpt.), Sonoma County Med. Assn., Orthopaedic Research Soc., Calif. Physicians Service, N.Y. Acad. Scis., Latin-Am. Soc. Orthopaedic and Traumatology, Pam Pacific Surg. Assn., Santa Rosa C. of C. Club: Santa Rosa Golf and Country. Lodge: Elks. Avocations: gardening, cooking. Home: 444 Laguna Vista Rd Santa Rosa CA 95401 Office: 983 Sonoma Ave Santa Rosa CA 95404

ANDERSON, CHARLES EDWARD, lawyer; b. Milw., Aug. 14, 1941; s. Edward Walter and Edna Alice A.; m. Sally J. Moriarty, Aug. 29, 1964; children: Erika, Seth. BBA, U. Wis., Madison, 1963, JD, 1966. Bar: Wis. 1966, U.S. Ct. Appeals (10th cir.) 1970, U.S. Ct. Appeals (9th cir.) 1972, N.Mex. 1974, U.S. Dist. Ct. N.Mex. 1974, U.S. Tax Ct. 1974, U.S. Supreme Ct. 1974. Tax atty., Arthur Anderson & Co., Milw., 1966-67; trial atty. appellate sect. tax div. U.S. Dept. Justice, Washington, 1970-74; ptnr. Schlenker, Parker, Wellborn & Anderson, Albuquerque, 1974-77; prin. Charles E. Anderson, P.A., 1977-83; shareholder, Eaves, Darling, Anderson & Porter, P.A., 1983—; adj. prof. law U. N.Mex., 1981-82. Served to 1st lt. USAF, 1967-70. Mem. ABA. Republican. Office: 6501 Americas Pkwy NE Suite 800 Albuquerque NM 87110

ANDERSON, CHARLES RAY, health science facility administrator; b. Big Spring, Tex., Mar. 4, 1943; s. William Madison and Lucille Irene (Plew) A.; m. Tommye Lela Whitehead, Dec. 22, 1967; children: Janice, Leah, Christopher, Clay, Timon. BA, Tex. Tech U., 1966; MEd, Eastern N.Mex. U., 1979. Asst. supt. N.Mex. Christian Children's Home, Portales, 1972—; exec. dir. Christian Child Placement Services div. N.Mex. Christian Children's Home, Portales, 1979—. Served to capt. USAF, 1966-70. Mem. N.Mex. Christian Child Care Assn. (pres. 1984—), N.Mex. Alliance Adoption Service Providers (sec., treas. 1978—), Am. Assn. Counseling and Devel. Avocations: building, gardening, landscaping. Office: NMex Christian Children's Home W Star Rt Box 48 Portales NM 88130

ANDERSON, CHARLES ROSS, civil engineer, surveying and cartography executive; b. N.Y.C., Oct. 4, 1937; s. Biard Eclare and Melva (Smith) A.; m. Susan Breinholt, Aug. 29, 1961; children: Loralee, Brian, Craig, Thomas, David. BSCE, U. Utah, 1961; MBA, Harvard U., 1963. Registered profl. engr.; cert. land surveyor. Owner, operator AAA Engring. and Drafting, Inc., Salt Lake City, 1960—. Mayoral appointee Housing Devel. com., Salt Lake City, 1981-86; bd. dirs., cons. Met. Water Dist., Salt Lake City, 1985—; bd. dirs. Utah Mus. Natural History, Salt Lake City, 1980—; asst. dist. commr. Sunrise Dist. Boy Scouts Am., Salt Lake City, 1985-86; fund raising coordinator architects and engrs. United Fund. Fellow Am. Gen. Contractors, Salt Lake City, 1960; recipient Hamilton Watch award, 1961. Mem. ASCE, Am. Congress on Surveying and Mapping, Harvard U. Bus. Sch. Club (pres. 1970-72), Pres. Club U. Utah, Pi Kappa Alpha (internat. pres. 1972-74, trustee endowment fund 1974-80, Oustanding Alumnus 1967, 72), Phi Eta Sigma, Chi Epsilon, Tau Beta Pi. Clubs: The Country, Bonneville Knife and Fork (Salt Lake City). Lodge: Rotary (chmn. election com. 1980— Salt Lake City chpt.). Avocations: fly fishing, golfing, hunting. Home: 2689 Comanche Dr Salt Lake City UT 84108 Office: AAA Engring & Drafting Inc 1865 S Main St Salt Lake City UT 84115

ANDERSON, CHRISTINA SUSANNE, speech and language therapist; b. Long Beach, Calif., Mar. 15, 1950; d. John Edwin and Mary Belle (Olson) Hockett; m. Robert George Anderson, June 9, 1973; children: Michelle, Marc, Brian. BS, Ariz. State U., 1972, MS, 1976. Speech therapist Rio Linda Sch. Dist., Sacramento, 1973-76, Washington Elem. Sch. Dist., Phoenix, 1976—; pvt. practice speech therapy Phoenix, 1978—. Active St. Helen's Ch., Glendale, Ariz., 1980-86, St. Paul's Ch., 1986—. Elks Found. scholar, 1968-71. Mem. NEA, Am. Speech and Hearing Assn. (Clin. Competency Cert.), Washington Dist. Edn. Assn., Maricopa County Bar Assn. (Womans Aux. Club), Sigma Alpha Eta, Alpha Lambda Delta, Phi Kappa Phi. Democrat. Roman Catholic. Avocations: skiing, aerobics, needlecrafts. Home: 215 W Kathleen Phoenix AZ 85023

ANDERSON, COURTNEY LEON CORBIN, information service executive; b. Lakeland, Fla., Dec. 15, 1944; d. Zeno Leon Anderson and Kathleen (Camp) Stokes; divorced. BS, U. Fla., 1968; MS, Princeton U., 1972, PhD, 1974. Dir. mktg. and sales Dionex Corp., Sunnyvale, Calif., 1975-82, mgr. spl. programs, 1982-84; pres. Coalesce Corp., Saratoga, Calif., 1984—; bd. dirs. XA Systems, Los Gatos, Calif. Contbr. articles to tech. jours. Mem. AAAS, Am. Chem. Soc., Am. Mgmt. Assn. Republican. Methodist. Club: Decathalon. Avocations: outdoor sports. Home: 18335 Lexington Ave Monte Sereno CA 95030 Office: Coalesce Corp PO Box 3527 Saratoga CA 95070

ANDERSON, CRAIG STEPHEN, engineering firm executive; b. Long Beach, Calif., July 20, 1946; s. Andy Q. and Clara E. (Ross) A.; m. Susan L. Gardner, Aug. 7, 1971; children—Jeffery, April, Kari. Student Long Beach City Coll., 1964-65, 66-67; B.S. in Indsl. Tech., Calif. Poly. State U., San Luis Obispo, 1969; M.S. in Mgmt. Sci., West Coast U., 1976. Mfg. engr. Robertshaw Controls, Anaheim, Calif., 1970-73; indsl. engr. U.S. Divers Co., Santa Ana, Calif., 1973-74; mfg./facilities engring. mgr. Anaconda Co., Anaheim, 1974-78; v.p. Reel Grobman & Assocs., Santa Ana, Calif., 1978—, co. v.p., 1982—. Mem. Soc. Mfg. Engrs., Am. Inst. Indsl. Engrs. Republican. Office: Reel Grobman & Assocs 3720 S Susan St Santa Ana CA 92704

ANDERSON, DAN ROGERS, economist; b. Geneva, Ill., Dec. 12, 1951; s. John Rogers and Clara Idele (Brelsford) A.; m. Jane Frances Stricklin, June 15, 1974. B.A. in Math. and Econs., Blackburn U., 1974; M.S. in Econs., Ariz. State U., Tempe, 1976. Economist dept. econ. security, State of Ariz., Phoenix, 1975—, research supr., 1977-80, sr. economist, 1980-84, research adminstr., 1984—; mem. fin. adv. com. state of Ariz.; interagy. policy com. Ariz. Econ. Roundtable; cons. in field. Recipient U.S. Dept. Labor internship award, 1979. Mem. Am. Econ. Assn., Western Regional Sci. Assn., Omicron Delta Epsilon. Contbr. articles to profl. jours. Office: PO Box 6123-733A Phoenix AZ 85005

ANDERSON, DANIEL RICHARD, chemist, oceanographer; b. St. Anthony, Idaho, Nov. 26, 1935; s. Daniel Milton and Anna Grace (Bryant) A.; m. Shirly Hendricks; children: Kirk, Tonya, Trena; m. Marcia Ann Fernandez, May 24, 1984; children: Antonio, Miguel, Louis. BS, Idaho State Coll., 1957; PhD, Oreg. State U., 1961. Mem. staff Sandia Nat. Labs., Albuquerque, 1961-75, div. supr., 1975—. Editor Radioactive Waste Mgmt. and the Nuclear Fuel Cycle; contbr. articles to profl. jours. Mem. Am. Chem. Soc., Am. Nuclear Soc., Linanology and Oceanography, Cousteau Soc., Sigma Xi. Republican. Lodge: Masons. Avocations: skiing, hunting, travel. Office: Sandia Nat Labs Seabed Programs Div # 6334 Albuquerque NM 87185

ANDERSON, DARRELL EDWARD, psychologist, educator; b. Coleridge, Nebr., May 2, 1932; s. Roy Blenton and Ruby Grace (Cisney) A.; m. Violeta Salazar, Sept. 3, 1951; children: Robert, James, Timothy. AB, York Coll., 1953; PhD, U. Nebr., 1958. Cert. psychologist, N.Mex. Counselor, asst. prof. U. Nebr., Lincoln, 1957-59; asst. prof. psychology Wittenberg U., Springfield, Ohio, 1959-61; chief psychologist Weld County Mental Health Ctr., Greeley, Colo., 1961-62; asst. prof. U. No. Colo., Greeley, 1962-66, assoc. prof., 1966-70, prof., 1970-77, chmn. dept. psychology, 1972-77; prof. counselor edn. U. N.Mex., Albuquerque, 1977—, chmn. dept., 1977-85; cons. psychologist Dulce (N.Mex.) Pub. Schs., 1984-85. Contbr. articles to profl. jours. Mem. Am. Psychol. Assn., Am. Assn. for Counseling and Devel., Assn. Counselor Edn. and Supervision, Rocky Mountain Psychol. Assn., Rocky Mountain Assn. Counselor Edn. and Supervision, N.Mex. Psychol. Assn., N.Mex. Assn. for Counseling and Devel. Democrat. Methodist. Avocation: golf. Home: 9712 Admiral Emerson NE Albuquerque NM 87111 Office: U NMex Dept Counselor Edn Albuquerque NM 87131

ANDERSON, DAVID EDMOND, telecommunications company executive; b. Sioux City, Iowa, Nov. 17, 1926; s. David E. and Ella S. (Geneva) A.; m. Marilyn G. Hoefer, May 28, 1949; children—Susan Sonye, Nancy J. Anderson. B.S.E.E., Iowa State U., 1948. Plant engr. Gen. Telephone Wis., Sun Prairie, 1948, div. mgr., Black River Falls, 1961, chief engr., Sun Prairie, 1965-67, Gen. Telephone Ohio, Marion, 1967-68; v.p. operations Gen. Telephone Ill., Bloomington, 1968-77, pres., 1978-79; v.p. network engring. & constrn. Gen. Telephone Calif., Santa Monica, 1977-78, pres., chief exec. officer, 1979—. Trustee Santa Monica Hosp., Calif., 1979—; bd. dirs. Barclays Bank Calif., San Francisco, 1983—, Calif. State U. Found., Long Beach, 1982—, Independent Colls. So. Calif., 1982—, Los Angeles United Way, Los Angeles Opera Theatre; chmn. 1982 Hispanic Women's Council awards dinner, Coro Found. awards dinner, 1983, Nat. Hispanic Scholarship Fund annual awards dinner, 1983. Served with USN, 1944-46. Mem. Calif. Roundtable, Nat. Soc. Profl. Engrs., Calif. C. of C. (bd. dirs.), Los Angeles Area C. of C. (bd. dirs., chmn. 1985). Methodist. Office: Gen Telephone Co Calif One GTE Pl Thousand Oaks CA 91362 *

ANDERSON, DAVID RICHARD, research chemistry educator; b. St. Paul, June 2, 1952; s. Richard Willis and Donna Mae Muriel (Feist) A.; m. Linda Maria Kish, May 27, 1978. BS in Chemistry, U. Minn., 1974; PhD, U. Colo., 1978. Postdoctoral research Columbia U., N.Y.C., 1978-79; staff engr. IBM Corp., Poughkeepsie, N.Y., 1979-81; vis. asst. prof. chemistry U. Colo., Boulder, 1981-83, Colo. Sch. Mines, Golden, 1983-84; asst. prof. U. Colo., Colorado Springs, 1984—. Contbr. articles to profl. jours. U. Colo. grad. fellow, Boulder, 1976. Mem. Am. Chem. Soc., Springs Organic Chemists, Sigma Xi, Phi Lambda Upsilon (pres. 1976-77), Tau Beta Pi. Avocations: woodworking, backpacking, cross-country skiing, handball. Office: U Colo Dept Chemistry Austin Bluffs Pkwy Colorado Springs CO 80907

ANDERSON, DONALD NORTON, JR., retired electrical engineer; b. Chgo., Aug. 15, 1928; s. Donald Norton and Helen Dorothy (Lehmann) A.; B.S., Purdue U., 1950, M.S., 1952. With Hughes Aircraft Co., Culver City and El Segundo, Calif., 1952-84, sect. head, sr. project engr., 1960-65, tech. mgr. Apollo program, 1965-66, mgr. visible systems dept., 1966-69, 70-73, project mgr., 1969-70, mgr. space sensors lab., 1973-79, mgr. space electro-optical systems labs., 1979-80, mgr. space electro-optical systems labs., 1980-84, ret., 1984. Recipient Apollo Achievement award, 1970; Robert J. Collier Landsat award, 1974. Mem. Research Soc. Am., Nat. Speleological Soc., Am. Theatre Organ Soc., Sigma XI (sec. Hughes Labs. br. 1974-75), Eta Kappa Nu, Sierra Club. Home: 2625 Topanga Skyline Dr Topanga CA 90290

ANDERSON, DOROTHY FISHER, social worker, psychotherapist; b. Funchal, Madeira, May 31, 1924; d. Lewis Mann Anker and Edna (Gilbert) Fisher (adoptive father David Henry Fisher); m. Theodore W. Anderson, July 8, 1950; children: Robert Lewis, Janet Anderson Yang, Jeanne Elizabeth. BA, Queens Coll., Flushing, N.Y., 1945; AM, U. Chgo., 1947. Lic. clin. social worker, Calif.; registered cert. social worker, N.Y.; cert. Nat. Bd. Examiners Social Workers. Intern Cook County (Ill.) Bur. Pub. Welfare, Chgo., 1945-46, Ill. Neuropsychiat. Inst., Chgo., 1946; clin. caseworker, Neurol. Inst. Presbyn. Hosp., N.Y.C., 1947; therapist, Mental Hygiene Clinic VA, N.Y.C., 1947-50; therapist, Child Guidance Clinic Pub. Elem. Sch. 42, N.Y.C., 1950-53; social worker, counselor Cedarhurst (N.Y.) Family Service Agy., 1954-55; psychotherapist, counselor Family Service of the Midpeninsula, Palo Alto, Calif., 1971-73, 79-86, George Hexter, M.D., Inc., 1972-83; clin. social worker Tavistock Clinic, London, 1974-75, El Camino Hosp., Mountain View, Calif., 1979; pvt. practice clin. social work 1978—; cons. Human Resource Services, Sunnyvale, Calif., 1981-86. Hannah G. Solomon scholar U. Chgo., 1945-46; Commonwealth fellow U. Chgo., 1946-47. Fellow Soc. Clin. Social Work (Continuing Edn. Recognition award 1980-83); mem. Nat. Assn. Social Workers (register of clin. social workers), Nat. Registry Health Care Providers in Clin. Social Work (bd. cert.). Avocations: sculpture, tennis, travel. Home and Office: 746 Santa Ynez St Stanford CA 94305

ANDERSON, EDWARD FREDERICK, biology educator; b. Covina, Calif., June 17, 1932; s. Edward White and Dorothy (Kaiser) A.; m. Adele Bowman, Mar. 31, 1956; children: Clark E., Adrienne K., Duc D., Erica R., Monica T., Stephen P., Bruce K. BA, Pomona Coll., 1954; MA, Claremont Grad. Sch., 1959, PhD, 1961. Instr. biology Pomona Coll., Claremont, Calif., 1961-62; asst. prof. Whitman Coll., Walla Walla, Wash., 1962-67, assoc. prof., 1967-76, prof., 1976—. Author: Peyote: The Divine Cactus, 1980. Elder Presbyn. Ch., Walla Walla, 1970—. Served to capt. U.S. Army, 1955-57. Recipient Town and Gown award Walla Walla C. of C., 1974, Fulbright lectureship Ecuador, 1965-66, Malaysia, 1969-70; Garrett fellow Whitman Coll., 1972-76. Fellow Linnean Soc. London; mem. Internat Orgn. Succulent Plant Study (v.p. 1984—), Bot. Soc. Am., Soc. Econ. Botany, Sigma Xi. Republican. Presbyterian. Lodge: Rotary (pres. Walla Walla club 1978-79). Avocation: photography. Home: 221 Newell St Walla Walla WA 99362 Office: Whitman Coll Dept Biology Walla Walla WA 99362

ANDERSON, ELISABETH MADGE KEHRER, physician, state administrator; b. Aberdeen, S.D.; d. Robert Ewald and Oriole (Johnston) Kehrer; m. Page Morris Anderson, Jan. 6, 1951; children: Bruce Statham, Catherine Mercer, Mary Elisabeth. BA, U. Louisville, 1946, MD, 1949; MPH, U. Hawaii, 1971. Intern Queen's Hosp., Honolulu, 1949-50, resident, 1950-51; physician, dir. research Pacific Inst. Rehab. Medicine, Honolulu, 1960-69; asst. to pres. Hawaii Med. Assn., Honolulu, 1972-75; chief med. health services div. Hawaii Dept. Health, Honolulu, 1980—; mem. Hawaii Cancer Commn., 1984—; mem. adv. bd. Hawaii Cancer Research Ctr., 1986—; mem. staff Queen's Hosp. Contbr. articles to profl. jours. Sec. bd. trustees Hawaii Loa Coll., Kaneohe, 1962-76; mem. exec. com. Women's Assn., ABA Conv., 1966-67; mem. exec. bd. Community Scholarship Program, Honolulu, 1966-71; mem. Stanford Biol. Preserve Docent Council (Calif.), 1978—; chmn. bd. Hawaii Nature Ctr., Honolulu, 1983—; past vice chmn., trustee Multiple Sclerosis Found. Hawaii; mem. exec. bd. Health and Community Service Council Hawaii, Jr. League of Honolulu. Mem. Yosemite Nat. History Assn., Am. Coll. Preventive Medicine, Am. Pub. Health Assn., Hawaii Med. Assn., Honolulu County Med. Soc., Sierra Club, Honolulu Acad. Arts, Outdoor Circle, Hawaii Bot. Soc. Clubs: Punahou Tennis, Trail and Mountain, Outrigger Caroe. Office: Hawaii Dept Health 1250 Punchbowl St Honolulu HI 96813

ANDERSON, E(MILE) PHILIP, physics educator; b. Denver, Mar. 6, 1953; s. Emile Philip and Betty June (Reynolds) A.; m. Patricia Lynn Hedrick, Aug. 18, 1979. BA in Chemistry and Math., Met. State Coll., 1980; postgrad., U. Colo., 1984-86. Instr. physics and laser tech. Met. State Coll., Denver, 1983-84, Denver Inst. Tech., 1984-86; physics engr. Hughes Aircraft Co., Manhattan Beach, Calif., 1986—. Co. chmn. United Way, Denver, 1985. Mem. Alpha Beta Kappa. Avocations: computers, skiing, tennis, reading. Home: 15224 S Wilton Pl Gardena CA 90249 Office: Hughes Aircraft Co 1240 Rosecrans Ave Manhattan Beach CA 90266

ANDERSON, ERIC GEORGE, physician, writer, photographer; b. Crieff, Scotland, Apr. 22, 1932; came to U.S., 1960; s. George Frederick and Jessie (Thom) A.; m. Margaret Innes Hunter, Sept. 14, 1955; children: Gillian, Carolyn, Michael. MD, Faculty of Medicine, Edinburgh, Scotland, 1958. Diplomate Am. Bd. Family Practice. Intern surgery Royal Infirmary, Edinburgh, Scotland, 1958-59; residency in medicine and ob/gyn Western Gen. Hosp., Edinburgh, 1959-60; gen. practice medicine Groveton, Tex., 1960-64; founder, staff mem. Derry (N.H.) Med. Ctr., 1964-85; chief of staff Alexander Eastman Hosp., Derry, 1968; staff mem. Sharp Rees-Stealy Med. Group, San Diego, 1985—. Author: Lightplane Vacationing, 1976, Plane Safety and Survival, 1978, The Pilot's Health, 1984; contbr. articles to profl. jours. Served to lt. Royal Scots Fusiliers, 1950-52. Fellow. Am. Acad. Family Physicians; mem. Am. Soc. Journalists and Authors, N.H. Acad. Family Physicians (pres. 1974). Republican. Presbyterian. Avocations: flying, history, travel. Home: 10205 Rue Touraine San Diego CA 92131 Office: Sharp Rees Stealy Med Group 16870 W Bernardo Dr San Diego CA 92127

ANDERSON, FLOYD M., psychologist, educator; b. Springville, Utah, Apr. 21, 1923; s. Thomas L. and Ellen E. (Whitmore) A.; m. Alice Ann Wilkinson Mangum, Mar. 23, 1974; children from previous marriage: Jennifer, Alicia, Devin Lincoln. BA, Brigham Young U., 1950; EdD, Columbia U., 1956. Marriage counselor Lucas County Ct. Domestic Relations, Toledo, 1953-56; lectr. U. Toledo, 1954-56; assoc. prof. human devel. and family Brigham Young U., Provo, Utah, 1956-61; exec. dir. Am. Inst. Family Relations, Hollywood, Calif., 1961-63; pres. Calif. Family Guidance Ctr., Los Angeles, 1963-74; sr. lectr. U. So. Calif., Los Angeles, 1963-68, vis. prof., 1967-74; lectr. U. Utah Sch. Medicine, 1974-75; psychologist, marriage counselor Salt Lake City, 1974—; pres. High Country Sales and Devel. Corp., 1975—; mng. ptnr. Anderson bus. Enterprises, 1985—; cons. Utah County Juvenile Ct., 1958-61; adminstrv. advisor Utah State Dept. Pub. Welfare, 1957. Mem. med. adv. bd. Los Angeles Planned Parenthood Assn., 1969-71; bd. dirs. Sawyer bus. Sch., Westwood, Calif., 1967-68; chmn. bd. dirs. Friends of Children, 1977-78; mem. Utah Legis. Task Force on Family Ct., 1978—. Served with USAAF, 1943-45. Grand Found. fellow, 1953. Fellow Am. Assn. Marriage and Family Counselors (chmn. admissions com. So. Calif. area 1968-70); mem. Mental Health Assn. Utah (chmn. com. children and youth), So. Calif. Assn. Marriage and Family Counselors (v.p. 1964-65), Utah Assn. Marriage and Family Counselors (exec. bd. 1976-78), Am. Psychol. Assn., Calif. Psychol. Assn. (com. family life 1967-70), Utah Psychol. Assn. (legis. chmn. 1976-79), Utah Psychologists in Pvt. Practice (pres. 1982-83), Assn. Humanistic Psychology. Republican. Mormon. Home: 1354 E 33d South Salt Lake City UT 84109 Office: 1354 E 33d S Salt Lake City UT 84016

ANDERSON, FRED EVERETT, accounting and business educator; b. San Francisco, May 3, 1927; s. Fred Everett and Hazel (Langendorfer) A.; m. Deborah D. Daughaday, Dec. 29, 1956; children: Keith Freer, Leslie Jean, Mark Stuart. BBA, Golden Gate Coll., 1950; MBA, Golden Gate U., 1978. CPA, Calif. Controller CTC Computer Corp. and Lockheed Missiles, 1956-70; asst. gen. mgr. U.S. Filter Corp.-Califilco, Burlinghame, Calif., 1970-73; instr. community colls., Hayward and Fremont, Calif., 1975-79, Armstrong Coll., Berkeley, Calif., 1975-76; controller Cal-Nev Meth. Homes, Oakland, Calif., 1976-78; assoc. prof. St. Mary's Coll., Moraga, Calif., 1978—; pvt. practice acctg, Calif., 1973-74, 75-78; bus. ins. cons. N.Y. Life Ins. Co., Fremont, 1974. Treas. "Save the Hills" campaign, 1982, Zlanik for Councilman campaign, 1979, Pimentel for Mayor campaign, 1984. Mem. Fin. Execs. Inst., Calif. Soc. CPA's. Republican. Congregationalist. Lodge: Lions (treas. 1984-86). Home: 646 Posada Way Fremont CA 94536 Office: Saint Mary's Coll of Calif Saint Mary's Rd Moraga CA 94575

ANDERSON, GEORGE CORLISS, aerospace engring. mgr.; b. Los Angeles, Dec. 3, 1921; s. Gustave Emil and Nellie Elizabeth (Bengtson) A.; B.S. in Applied Physics, U. Calif., Los Angeles, 1949; m. Edna Dorothy Westergard, Aug. 2, 1952; 1 dau., Judith Annette Anderson Hindes. Research engr. sound and acoustics Don Lee Broadcasting System, Hollywood, Calif., 1948-51; engring. mgr. field dir., asst. to exec. v.p. N.Am. Aviation, Inc., Downey, Calif., 1951-64; engring. dir. Saturn II/Apollo program Space div. N.Am. Rockwell, Inc., Downey, 1964-72; engring. mgr. strategic missile systems Autonetics div. Rockwell Internat. Corp., Anaheim, Calif., 1972—; cons. acoustics and electronics; instr. math. and electronics Compton (Calif.) Coll., 1952-55; comml. airplane pilot. Served with USNR, 1944-46. Recipient Apollo program achievement award NASA, 1969. Mem. Am. Inst. Physics, Acoustical Soc. Am., Aircraft Owners and Pilots Assn., Am. Radio Relay League. Republican. Presbyterian. Clubs: East Whittier Radio, Autonetics Radio, Airventurers So. Calif. Patentee precision frequency regulator. Home: 14462 Linda Vista Dr Whittier CA 90602 Office:

Autonetics div Rockwell Internat Corp 3370 Miraloma Ave Anaheim CA 92803

ANDERSON, GERALD MARSHALL, electrical engineer; b. Shanghai, China, Oct. 14, 1935; s. Gerald Carl Anderson and Lillian Ruth (Marshall) Gillen; m. Edith Calista Feiss. BS, U.S. Naval Acad., 1957; MS, MIT, 1961; PhD, U. Mich., 1966. Registered profl. engr. Commd. 2d lt. USAF, 1957; advanced through grades to maj. USAF, Wright-Patterson AFB, Ohio, 1969; retired USAF, 1977; prof. USAF Inst. Tech., Wright-Patterson AFB, Ohio, 1966-77; program mgr. Orincon Corp., La Jolla, Calif., 1977-86, dir. div., 1986—. Contbr. articles to profl. jours. Fellow Brit. Interplanetary Soc.; mem. IEEE, AIAA, Am. Astronaut. Soc. Home: 14185 Boquita Dr Del Mar CA 92014 Office: Orincon Corp 3366 N Torrey Pines Ct La Jolla CA 92037

ANDERSON, GLENDA GALE, technical manager; b. Turlock, Calif., June 28, 1957; d. Glenn Walter Anderson and Jacqueline Ann (Elliott) Aitken. B.S. in Indsl. Engring., Stanford U., 1979; M.B.A., Harvard U., 1983. Applications engr. Packard Electric, Warren, Ohio, 1979-80, methods engr., 1980-81; asst. to controller CFS Continental, Chgo., 1982; asst. to v.p., engr. Travenol Labs., Round Lake, Ill., 1983-84, molded product control mgr., 1984-85, internat. bus. mgr., 1985-86; sr. program mgr. research and devel. Am. Pharmaseal, 1986—; research assoc. Harvard Bus. Sch., Boston, 1983. Pres. Hawaii State Achiever's Assn., Honolulu, 1974; adviser Jr. Achievement, Warren, Ohio, 1980; v.p. Women Student Assn., Harvard Bus. Sch., 1983. Jr. Achievement scholar, 1981-83. Mem. Stanford Alumni Assn., Harvard Alumni Assn. Democrat. Avocation: travel. Home: 524 E Sierra Madre Blvd Sierra Madre CA 91024 Office: Am Pharmaseal 27200 Tourney Rd Valencia CA 60073

ANDERSON, GLENN MALCOLM, congressman; b. Los Angeles; m. Lee Dutton; children: Melinda (Mrs. Michael Keenan), Evan, Glenn Michael. B.A., UCLA. Mayor Hawthorne, Calif., 1940-43; mem. Calif. Assembly from South Bay Area, Los Angeles, 1943-51; lt. gov. Calif., 1958-67; mem. 91st-100th Congresses from 32d Dist. Calif., 1969—; mem. pub. works and transp. com., Mcht. Marine and fisheries com.; chmn. State Lands Commn., 1959-67; past mem. Commn. Califs., Calif. Council Urban Growth; past chmn. Calif. Interstate Cooperation Commn. Hon. life mem. PTA.; Regent U. Calif., 1959-67. Served with AUS, World War II. Mem. Secondary Sch. Adminstrs. Assn., Am. Legion, DAV, Amvets, Native Sons Golden West, Redmen, Hawthorne C. of C. Democrat. Clubs: Elks, Kiwanis. Office: 2329 Rayburn House Office Bldg Washington DC 20515

ANDERSON, GORDON DUANE, physicist; b. Turlock, Calif., June 26, 1931; s. Reuben William and Evangeline (Carlson) A.; m. Gertrude Ann Vieker, Aug. 15, 1954; children: Bruce, Bonnie, Paul, Peter. AA, Modesto Jr. Coll., 1951; BS, Iowa State U., 1954; MS, Wash. State U., 1956, PhD, 1963. Physicist SRI Internat., Menlo Park, Calif., 1956-60, 63-68, S-Cubed, La Jolla, Calif., 1968-72, SAI, La Jolla, Calif., 1972-73, Lawrence Livermore (Calif.) Nat. Lab., 1974—. Mem. AAAS, Am. Phys. Soc., Am. Geophys. Union, Soc. Petroleum Engrs., Calif. Acad. Sci. Home: 5446 Betty Circle Livermore CA 94550 Office: Lawrence Livermore Nat Lab PO Box 808 Livermore CA 94550

ANDERSON, GORDON MACKENZIE, petroleum service contractors executive; b. Los Angeles, Mar. 25, 1932; s. Kenneth C.M. and Edith (King) A.; m. Elizabeth Ann Pugh, Mar. 21, 1959; children: Michael James, Greg Mark, Jeffrey Stevens. AA, Glendale Coll., 1951; BSME, U. So. Calif., 1954; grad., Officers Candidate Sch., Newport, R.I., 1955; student, various Navy Schs. including CIC Sch. Mgr. Santa Fe Drilling Co., Chile, 1960-63, Libya, 1963-67; mgr. contracts adminstrn. Santa Fe Drilling Co., Calif., 1967-70; pres. Santa Fe Drilling Co., Orange, Calif., from 1970; sr. v.p. Santa Fe Internat. Corp., Alhambra, Calif., 1974-80, pres., chief operating officer, 1980—, also dir.; bd. dirs. Baker Internat., Orange. Mem. adv. bd. U. So. Calif. Sch. Engring.; bd. dirs. St. Jude Hosp., Fullerton, Calif. Served to lt. (j.g.) USN, 1955-58. Mem. Young Pres.'s Orgn. (chmn. 1978-79), Internat. Assn. Oilwell Drilling Contractors. Office: Santa Fe Internat Corp 100 S Fremont Ave Box 4000 Alhambra CA 91802 *

ANDERSON, GRANT LAMONT, engineer, mining researcher; b. Thornton, Idaho, Aug. 30, 1933; s. Oscar Eliason and Laura Selma (Carlson) A.; m. Betty Jean Woodruff, June 29, 1956 (div. Aug. 1984); children: Karla, John, David. BSME, U. Idaho, 1960. Registered profl. engr., Wash. Structural engr. C.E., Walla Walla, Wash., 1960-71; research structural engr. U.S. Bur. Mines, Spokane, Wash., 1971—; co-chmn. tech. transfer project between U.S. Bur. of Mines, Can. and Ont. Ministry of Labour, 1983—. Served as pvt. U.S. Army, 1954-56. Mem. ASME, Am. Soc. Safety Engrs. Presbyterian. Lodge: Eagles. Avocations: rockhound, leaded glass, silver jewelry fabrication. Office: US Bur Mines E 315 Montgomery Spokane WA 99207

ANDERSON, HAROLD PAUL, historian, archivist, bank executive; b. Darby, Pa., Oct. 4, 1946; s. Harold P. and Mary Ann A.; B.A., Villanova U., 1968; M.A., Ohio State U., 1969, Ph.D., 1978. Teaching and research fellow Stanford U., 1973-75; archives and library specialist Hoover Instn., Stanford, Calif., 1975-77; asst. archivist dept. history Wells Fargo Bank, N.A., San Francisco, 1977-79, pub. relations officer and corp. archivist dept. history, 1979, asst. v.p. and corp. archivist dept. history, 1979—, v.p. dept. history, 1984—; lectr. Stanford U., 1981; bd. dirs. Nat. Council on Pub. History, 1981-83. Mem. Am. Hist. Assn., Orgn. Am. Historians, Soc. Am. Archivists. Office: Wells Fargo Bank 420 Montgomery St San Francisco CA 94163

ANDERSON, HERSCHEL VINCENT, librarian; b. Charlotte, N.C., Mar. 14, 1932; s. Paul Kemper and Lillian (Johnson) A. B.A., Duke U., 1954; M.S., Columbia U., 1959. Library asst. Bklyn. Public Library, 1954-59; asst. bookmobile librarian King County Public Library, Seattle, 1959-62; asst. librarian Longview (Wash.) Public Library, 1962-63; librarian N.C. Mus. Art, Raleigh, 1963-64; audio-visual cons. N.C. State Library, Raleigh, 1964-68; dir. Sandhill Regional Library, Rockingham, N.C., 1968-70; asso. state librarian Tenn. State Library and Archives, Nashville, 1970-72; unit dir. Colo. State Library, Denver, 1972-73; state librarian S.D. State Library, Pierre, 1973-80; dir. Mesa (Ariz.) Public Library, 1980—; dir. Bibliographical Center for Research, Denver, 1974-80, v.p., 1977; mem. Western Council State Libraries, 1975-80, v.p., 1978, pres., 1979; mem. Ariz. State Library Adv. Council, 1981-84, pres., 1982-83; mem. library technician tng. adv. com. Mesa Community Coll., 1982-85; chmn. Serials On-Line in Ariz. Consortia, 1985-86; mem. Maricopa County Library Council, 1981—, treas. 1981—, pres. 1983. Jr. warden St. Mark's Episcopal Ch., Mesa, 1985-87, vestryman 1987-90. Served with AUS, 1955-57. Mem. ALA, S.D. Library Assn. (Librarian of Yr. 1977, hon. life 1980), Mountain Plains Library Assn. (pres. 1974, dir. 1974-77, 86—), Ariz. Library Assn. (exec. com. 1986-87), Chief Officers of State Library Agys. (dir. 1974-76, exec. com. 1986-87), Phi Kappa Psi. Lodge: Kiwanis (dir. Mesa club 1981-86, v.p. 1983, pres. 1985-86). Home: Durango CO also: Mesa AZ Office: Mesa Public Library Mesa AZ 85201

ANDERSON, J. BLAINE, judge; b. Trenton, Utah, Jan. 19, 1922; s. Leslie Howard and Theo Ellen (Stocking) A.; m. Grace Little, Nov. 14, 1944; children—J. Eric, J. Blaine, Leslie Ann, Dirk Brian. Student, U. Idaho, 1940-41, U. Wash., 1945-46; LL.B., U. Idaho, 1949; J.D. (hon.), Lewis and Clark Coll., 1978. Bar: Idaho bar 1949. Practiced in Blackfoot, 1949-71; partner firm Furchner and Anderson (and predecessor law firms), 1955-71; U.S. dist. judge Dist. Idaho, Boise, 1971-76; U.S. circuit judge U.S. Ct. Appeals, 9th Circuit, 1976—. Chmn. Idaho Air Pollution Commn., 1959-60. Served with USCG, 1942-45. First Recipient Faculty award of Legal Merit, U. Idaho Coll. Law, 1974. Fellow Am. Coll. Trial Lawyers; mem. Am. Bar Assn. (mem. ho. of dels. 1959-60, 64-71, gov. 1971-74, mem. council gen. practice sect. 1962-66, 70-71, mem. adv. bd. editors Jour. 1969-71), Idaho State Bar (bd. commrs. 1958-61, pres. 1960-61, chmn. unauthorized practice of law com. 1955-58), S.E. Idaho Dist. Bar (pres. 1957-58), Am. Judicature Soc. (dir. 1961-66), Am. Coll. Probate Counsel. Office: US Court Bldg 550 Fort St Boise ID 83724

ANDERSON, JACK JOE, communications executive; b. Lipan, Tex., Oct. 22, 1928; s. William Amon and Tommie Lucille (Roberts) A.; B.A., San Jose State U., 1965, M.A., 1967; postgrad. in bus. adminstrn. Pepperdine U., Los Angeles; m. Maria I. Kamantauskas, Mar. 13, 1976; children—Mark, Douglas, Craig. Asst. mgr. edn. systems Lockheed Missiles & Space Co., Sunnyvale, Calif., 1966-69; v.p. Learning Achievement Corp., San Jose, Calif., 1969-74; mgr. instrnl. systems Ford Aerospace & Communications Corp., Pasadena, Calif., 1974-83; pres. Anderson & Assocs., Alta Loma, Calif., 1983—; cons. tng. programs and systems, 1969-74. Served with USAF, 1946-66. Decorated 2 Air Force commendation medals; recipient nat. award for tng. program design Indsl. TV Assn., 1974. Mem. Am. Mgmt. Assn., Am. Soc. Tng. and Devel. Contbr. tech. and gen. instrnl. materials in field. Office: Anderson & Assocs 9155 Carrari Ct Alta Loma CA 91701

ANDERSON, JACK WAYNE, marine science researcher, administrator; b. San Diego, Mar. 15, 1938; s. Neil S. Anderson and Ethel (Wills) Archer; m. Marilyn Sue Wallace, Sept. 1964 (div. 1974); m. Mary Linda McLain, Feb. 19, 1978; children: Amanda Lynn, Jacquelyn Lindsey. AA, El Camino Coll., 1960; BA, Calif. State U., Long Beach, 1964, MA, 1966; PhD, U. Calif., Irvine, 1969. Asst. prof. Tex. A&M U., College Station, 1969-74, assoc. prof., 1974-76; sr. research scientist Battelle Northwest Lab., Sequim, Wash., 1976-83, assoc. mgr. Marine Research Lab., 1983-85; dir. So. Calif. Coastal Water Research Project, Long Beach, 1985—; cons. EXXON Prodn. Research Co., Houston, 1973-76; chmn. com. biol. effects program NSF/IDOE, 1974-75; mem. 5 man NOAA adv. com. on Amoco Cadiz oil spill, 1978-81; mem. sci. adv.c om. U.S. Sec. of Interior, 1979-81. Author 5 books on marine science; founding co-editor Marine Environ. Research, 1978-80; contbr. over 80 articles to profl. jours. Grantee Am. Petroleum Inst., U.S. Dept. Energy, Sea Grant, NSF, 1974-76. Mem. Am. Soc. Zoologists, AAAS, Western Soc. Naturalists, So. Calif. Acad. Scis., Sigma Xi. Avocations: skiing, windsurfing, volleyball. Office: So Calif Coastal Water Research Project Authority 646 W Pacific Coast Hwy Long Beach CA 90806

ANDERSON, JAMES CHARLES, podiatrist; b. Valentine, Nebr., Nov. 29, 1952; s. Oliver James and Ione Irene (Toelle) A.; m. Adriann Philips Douthett, Dec. 20, 1980; 1 child, Kathryn Lauren. BA in Biology, U. Colo., 1976; D in Podiatric Medicine, Calif. Coll. Podiatric Medicine, 1980. Diplomate Am. Bd. Podiatric Surgery. Med. and surg. resident VA Hosp., Albuquerque, 1980-81; mem. staff Highland Ctr. Hosp., Denver, 1981—, Poudre Valley Hosp., Ft. Collins, Colo., 1983—; med. dir. Rawhide Marathon, Ft. Collins, 1982—. Med. coordinator Ft. Collins Diabetes Assn. Triathlon, 1985—, bd. dirs. 1983—, chmn. pub. edn. com., 1984—; com. mem. Ft. Collins Multiple Sclerosis Soc., 1982-84; elder St. John's Luth. Ch., Ft. Collins, 1985—. Fellow Am. Coll. Foot Surgeons; mem. Am. Podiatry Assn., Colo. Podiatry Assn. (sports medicine com. 1984—), Am. Acad. Podiatric Sports Medicine. Republican. Avocations: skiing, running, tennis, windsurfing. Office: Poudre Valley Hosp 1355 Riverside Suite C Fort Collins CO 80524

ANDERSON, JAMES K., savings bank executive; b. 1936. BA, Whitman Coll., 1958. With Time Sharing Corp. and CTC Edn. Systems, Inc., 1968-73; asst. to pres. Computer Scis. Corp., 1973; group sr. v.p. Calif. Fed. Savs. and Loan, 1974-81; pres. Pacific 1st Fed. Savs. Bank, Tacoma, 1981-86, chmn. bd. dirs., chief exec. officer, 1984—, also bd. dirs. Served with U.S. Army, 1958-62. Office: Pacific 1st Fed Savs Bank Office of Chmn Tacoma Fin Ctr Tacoma WA 98402 *

ANDERSON, JAMES LELAND, art director, trade association executive; b. Orion, Ill., Nov. 29, 1925; s. James Reed and Hattie Lillian (Berg) A.; m. Delores Beulah O'Connell, June 25, 1947 (dec. Sept. 1961); children: Colleen Delores, Noreen Shelly; m. Myrna Kay Hooe, June 6, 1963; children: Kent Leon, Karen Darcey. BFA, Bradley U. Graphics designer Bawden Advt., Davenport, Iowa, 1950-63; prin., art dir. J. Anderson Advt., Denver, 1964-74; art dir. Am. Water Works Assn., Denver, 1974—; creative art supplier Gates Rubber Co., Denver, 1964-74, Am. Sch. Food Service, Denver, 1964-74, Data Core, Denver, 1971-74, Denver Humane Soc. (Disting. Merit award). Served with inf. and Q.M.C. U.S. Army, 1944-46, PTO. Recipient Honor award Kansas City Art Dir. Club, 1970, Distinctive Merit award Art Dir. Club of Denver, 1970, Honor award Art Dir. Club of Denver, 1968-69, Maggie awards Am. Water Works Assn. 1978-81. Republican. Mem. Christian Ch. Home: 8595 E Radcliff Ave Denver CO 80237 Office: Am Water Works Assn 6666 W Quincy Ave Denver CO 80235

ANDERSON, JAMES LEROY, insurance company executive; b. Wichita, Kans., Dec. 18, 1943; s. Harold and Freda (Windhorst) A.; m. Carolyn Thompson, Oct. 25, 1980; children—Raif, Ingrid. B.S., Fort Hays Kans. State Coll., 1965. Regional supr. Travelers Ins. Co., 1965-75; pres. Nat. Am. Ins. Co. Calif., Lakewood, 1975-82; exec. v.p., chief operating officer Stuyvesant Life Ins. Co. & Nat. Am. Ins. Co. N.Y., Allentown, Pa., 1980-82; pres., chief exec. officer Hosp. Hosp. Ins. Services, Inc., Los Angeles, 1982-86; chmn., chief exec. officer Physician and Surgeons Underwriting Corp., Pasadena; sr. v.p. Fremont Indemnity Co., 1984-86; pres. Comml. Bankers Life Ins. Co., Newport Beach, Calif., 1986—; chief operating officer Fremont Ins. Services, 1984—; mem. Orange County Chief Exec. Officers Roundtable. Recipient Gen. Ins. cert. Ins. Inst. Am., 1970. Mem. Young Pres.'s Orgn., Alpha Kappa Psi. Republican. Lutheran. Home: 21837 Tenderfoot Way Diamond Bar CA 91765 Office: Comml Bankers Life Ins Co Newport Beach CA 92658

ANDERSON, JANET NYE, trade school administrator, insurance underwriter; b. Logan, Utah, Sept. 28, 1949; d. William P. and Helen F. (Paulsen) Nye; m. Rodney R. Anderson; May 19, 1978; children: Christopher R., Jonathan R., Benjamin C. Ins. agt. various cos., Logan, 1973—; dir. Inst. Med.-Dental Technology, Logan, 1983—. Mem. Cache Valley Underwriters Assn. (sec. 1975-77, v.p. 1977-78). Mormon. Avocations: creative writing, computers, oilpainting, collecting miniatures. Office: Inst Med Dental Tech 2600 N Main Logan UT 84321

ANDERSON, JOHN LEONARD, chemical company executive; b. Chgo., July 27, 1927; s. Elmer G. and Florence (Peterson) A.; m. Patricia Ann Burtwell, Oct. 30, 1954 (div. Jan. 1986); children—Bryan John, Kimberly Sconce; m. Leslie Wallace, Apr. 26, 1986. B.S. in Chem. Engring., Northwestern U., 1951, M.B.A., 1960. Tech. developer Diversey Corp., Chgo., 1951-53; salesman George C. Peterson Co., Chgo., 1955-57, Am. Potash & Chem., Chgo., N.Y.C., 1957-66; sales mgr. Cominco Am., Spokane, Wash., 1966-73, v.p. mktg., 1973-82, pres., chief exec. officer, 1982-85, also bd. dirs.; pres. Chemicals and Fertilizers div., Cominco Ltd., Calgary, Alta., Can., 1986—, also bd. dirs. Served to cpl. U.S. Army, 1953-55. Mem. Potash Phosphate Inst. (dir.), The Fertilizer Inst. (dir.). Republican. Episcopalian. Clubs: Union League (Chgo.); Calgary Golf and Country. Avocations: tennis, golf, skiing, fishing, gardening. Office: Cominco Ltd, 10333 Southport Rd, Calgary, AB Canada 2TW 3X6 *

ANDERSON, JOHN RICHARD, educator; b. Fargo, N.D., May 5, 1931; s. John Raymond and Mary Ann (Beaulieu) A.; m. Shereen V. Erickson, Mar. 26, 1955; children: Scott F., Lisa K., Steven F. B.S., Utah State U., 1957; M.S., U. Wis., 1958, Ph.D., 1960. Asst. prof. entomology U. Calif.-Berkeley, 1961-66, assoc. prof., 1967-70, prof., 1970—, chmn. div. parasitology Coll. Natural Resources, 1970-71, assoc. dean research, 1979-85; Trustee, past chmn. Alameda County (Calif.) Mosquito Abatement Dist., 1961-73, 79—. Editoral bd.: Jour. Med. Entomology, 1968-72, Jour. Econ. Entomology, 1977-81, Thomas Say Found, 1968-72. Served with USN, 1950-54. Research grantee. Mem. AAAS, Entomol. Soc., Am., Can., Pacific Coast entomol. socs., Am., Calif. mosquito control assns., Calif. Acad. Sci., N.Y. Acad. Sci., No. Calif. Parasitologists, Oakland Mus. Assn., Soc. Vector Ecologists, Soc. Nature Conservancy, Wilderness Soc. Home: 2881 Shasta Rd Berkeley CA 94708 Office: U Calif Berkeley CA 94720

ANDERSON, JUDITH JAN, account executive; b. Cascade, Idaho, June 15, 1955; d. Dale Vernon and Audrey Isabella (Harvey) A. AA in Gen. Sci., Cottey Coll.; BS in Home Econs. (Mary Hall Niccolls scholar, PEO scholar), U. Idaho, 1977; MA in Counseling, Coll. Idaho, 1985. Cert. secondary edn., voc. home econs. tchr., Idaho. Substitute tchr. pub. schs., Boise and Meridian, Idaho, 1978; co-mgr. Vans Catering Co., Boise, 1978; tchr. home econs. Meridian Jr. High Sch., 1977-84; receptionist weekend Sta. KTVB-TV; hall dir. Coll. of Idaho, 1983-85; sr. op. specialist employee relations Morrison-Knudsen Co., 1984-86; account exec. Mgmt. Recruiters Internat., 1986—; mem. adv. com. spl. edn. curriculum, Meridian. Strike officer Jr. League Boise. Mem. PEO, AAUW, Beaux Arts Societe, Phi Beta Kappa, Phi Upsilon Omicron, Kappa Alpha Theta (alumni chpt. officer). Republican. Methodist. Lodge: Job's Daus. Home: 300 S Straughan #801 Boise ID 83712

ANDERSON, KAREN ANN, public affairs executive; b. Presque Isle, Maine, July 27, 1944; d. Henning Walter and Jean Reynolds (Taylor) Swanseen; m. Thomas Ellsworth Anderson, Apr. 27, 1968; children; Peter, Joshua, Mark. Student, Northwestern U., 1962; BA cum laude, Montclair State, N.J., 1966; MA with honors, NYU, 1975. Pub. relations freelancer N.Y.C., 1965-70; ednl. therapist N.Y. Inst. for Child Devel., N.Y.C., 1970-75, clin. therapist, 1975-77; v.p. pub. affair, co. spokesperson Gymboree Corp., Burlingame, Calif., 1981—; media cons. non-profit agys., N.Y.C., San Francisco, 1970-86. Editor Gymboree Gazette, 1982—; nationally syndicated columnist of Gymboree, It's Child's Play, 1984—. Active Interfaith Commmunications Commn., San Francisco, 1978—, host of Lightworks Sta. Kron-TV, 1978—; mem. media ministry com. Luth. Ch., Calif., 1978—, mgmt. com. Luth. Ch. Am., 1980—. Mem. Am. Women in Radio and TV, Kappa Delta Pi. Democrat. Club: Lutheran Ch. Women's (v.p. 1986—). Avocations: playing piano, oil painting. Home: 236 Moncada Way San Francisco CA 94127 Office: Gymboree Corp 872 Hinckley Rd Burlingame CA 94010

ANDERSON, KARL RICHARD, human factors engr.; b. Vinita, Okla., Sept. 27, 1917; s. Axel Richard and Hildred Audrey (Marshall) A.; B.S., Calif. Western U., 1964, M.A., 1966; Ph.D., U.S. Internat. U., 1970; m. Jane Shigeko Hiratsuka, June 20, 1953; 1 son, Karl Richard. Engr. personnel subsystems Atlas Missile Program, Gen. Dynamics, San Diego, 1960-63; design engr. Solar div. Internat. Harvester, San Diego, 1964-66, sr. design engr., 1967-69, project engr., 1970-74, product safety specialist, 1975-78; aerospace engring. cons., 1979-86; lectr. Am. Indian Sci. and Engring. Soc. Served to maj. USAF, 1936-60. Recipient Spl. Commendation San Diego County Bd. Supervisors, 1985, Spl. Commendation San Diego City Council, 1985. Registered profl. engr., Calif. Republican. Episcopalian. Home: 5886 Scripps St San Diego CA 92122

ANDERSON, KELLEY PIERCE, cardiologist; b. Chgo., Nov. 21, 1951; s. Herbert Lawrence and Jean Betty (Clough) A.; m. Susan E. Mann, Aug. 20, 1983. Intern, Michael Reese Hosp., Chgo., 1977-78, resident, 1978-80; BA in Psychology, U. Rochester, 1973, MD, 1977; intern, Michael Reese Hosp., Chgo., 1977-78, resident, 1978-80. Diplomate Am. Bd. Internal Medicine. Fellow in cardiology Stanford (Calif.) U., 1980-83; asst. prof. medicine U. Utah, Salt Lake City, 1983—; dir. Electrophysiology Lab. U. Utah Med. Ctr., 1983—. Contbr. articles to profl. jours. Advanced Research fellow Am. Heart Assn., 1982; recipient New Investigator Research award NIH, 1986. Fellow Am. Coll. Cardiology; mem. Am. Heart Assn. Home: 4439 S Parkhill Dr Salt Lake City UT 84124 Office: U Utah Sch Medicine Cardiology Div 4A100 50 Medical Dr Salt Lake City UT 84132

ANDERSON, LEE ROGER, solar, environmental, recreation and site planner; b. Boone, Iowa, July 24, 1945; s. Carl Donald and Hazel Irene (Erickson) A.; m. Linda Jean Parker, May 28, 1966; children—Eric Lee, Tai Denise. B.S. in Landscape Architecture, Iowa State U., 1967, M. Landscape Architecture, 1968. Registered landscape architect Calif. Dept. Consumer Affairs. Designer, draftsman H&F Builders, Ames, Iowa, 1966-68; landscape architect Simonds & Simonds, Pitts., 1968-70, Shasta-Trinity Nat. Forest, Redding, Calif., 1970-73, Klamath Nat. Forest, Yreka, Calif., 1973-81; prin. Designs for Living, Yreka, 1981—, Solid Rock Prodns, 1983-86, Lee Roger Anderson, Environ. Cons., Planning and Design, 1986—; promoter contemporary Christian concerts, 1983-85; environ. and visual resource planner Celeron/All-Am. Pipeline Project, 1986-87; planner Eddy Meadow Resort, 1985, Mt. Shasta Ski Area, 1985—, other nat. recreation area resorts; designer solar houses. Mem. Yreka City Planning Commn., 1976-80. Recipient award for design of children's playground Yreka Lions Club, 1976. Mem. Am. Soc. Landscape Architects, Tau Sigma Delta. Democrat. Club: Rotary. Author: (with others) Visual Absorption Capability, 1979, Visual Management Support Systems, 1979, Environmental Impact Report, Environmental Impact Statement Proposed Celeron All American and Getty Pipeline Projects, 1985. Office: Designs for Living 2270 Belle Ave Yreka CA 96097

ANDERSON, LEO JOSEPH, internat. mechanization planner; b. Kanwaka, Kans., Aug. 15, 1921; s. Michael Alexander and Helen Marie (O'Brien) A.; student engring. U. Kans., 1939-41, Wichita State U., 1958-59; m. Henrietta Slavens, Oct. 20, 1943; children—Leo Joseph, II, Kathleen Lynn. Planning engr. Kans. Hwy. Commn., 1946-49; elec. supervisory engr. U.S. Army C.E., 1950-52; chief engr. constrn. Hdqrs. SAC, USAF, Omaha, 1952-59; dir. engring. and facilities U.S. Dept. Post Office, 1959-67; dir. process engring. Hdqrs. U.S. Postal Service, 1967-71; pres., chmn. bd. Mechanized Systems Designs Inc., San Diego and Washington, 1971—; chmn. Engrs. in Govt., Kans., 1965-67. Served to capt. AUS, 1942-46. Registered profl. engr., Kans., Calif. Mem. Nat. Soc. Profl. Engrs., Calif. Soc. Profl. Engrs. Democrat. Roman Catholic. Home: 17021 Palacio Pl San Diego CA 92127 Office: Mechanized Systems Designs Inc 8361 Vickers St Suite 208 San Diego CA 92111

ANDERSON, LLOYD HAROLD, architect; b. Wichita, Kans., Aug. 21, 1945; s. Willard Harold and Ruby Treva Edith (Rymph) A.; m. Linda Jane Proctor, Dec. 27, 1965; children: Scott Dirk, Tadari Ciel. Student, Okla. State U., 1964-67; BArch., U. Colo., 1970. Lic. architect, Colo. Designer Charles Deaton, Assocs., Denver, 1967-71; chief design architect Bur. Reclamation, Denver, 1971-76; ptnr. Deaton, Anderson Design, Denver, 1975—; dir. design Zuhair Fayez & Assocs., Jeddah, Saudi Arabia, 1976-78; cons. internat. design, Lakewood, Colo., 1978—. Executed numerous bldgs. in U.S., Saudi Arabia and Jordan; prin. works include Dallah Group Office Bldg., Jeddah, Saudi Arabia, 1977, Royal Mountain Retreat, Taif, Saudi Arabia, 1979, Durr Mosque, Jeddah, 1980, NADEC Hdqrs., Riyadh, Saudi Arabia, 1984; patentee in furniture design and bldg. products. Recipient Emerson Meml. Prize Nat. Inst. Archtl. Edn., 1965. Avocations: scuba diving, painting. Home and Office: 12791 W Jewell Circle Lakewood CO 80228

ANDERSON, LOUISE STOUT, crime analyst; b. Wellsville, N.Y., Aug. 11, 1952; d. Carlton C. and Mary (Gasdik) Stout; m. Leonard M. Anderson, June 2, 1973. BA in German Lit., Polit. Sci., Mt. Holyoke Coll., 1974; MA in Polit. Sci., San Diego State U., 1977. Cert. community coll. tchr., Calif. Statistician Grossmont Coll., El Cajon, Calif., 1976-78; crime analyst San Diego Police Dept., 1978-80; crime analyst Career Criminal Apprehension Program, Marin County Sheriff's Office, San Rafael, Calif., 1980-83; crime analyst CCAP Unit, Sonoma County Sheriff's Office, Santa Rosa, Calif., 1983-85; mktg. services mgr. Command Data Systems, Dublin, Calif., 1985—; cons. Search Group Inc. for Automated Crime Analysis. Contbr. articles in field. Alumna recruiter Mt. Holyoke Club No. Calif., 1981—. Mem. Am. Polit. Sci. Assn., Assn. Police Planners Research Officers, Calif. Women in Govt., Nat. Assn. Criminal Justice Stats. Assn. Office: Command Data Systems 6250 Village Pkwy Dublin CA 94568

ANDERSON, MARILYN NELLE, educator; b. Las Animas, Colo., May 5, 1942; d. Mason Hadley Moore and Alice Carrie (Dwyer) Coates; m. George Robert Anderson, Sept. 3, 1974; children: Lisa Lynn, Edward Alan, Justin Patrick. BEd magna cum laude, Adams State Coll., 1962, postgrad., 1965; MEd, Ariz. State U., 1967; postgrad., Idaho State U., 1971, 86. Cert. elem. tchr., K-12 sch. counselor. Tchr. Wendell (Idaho) Sch. Dist. 232, 1962-66, Union-Endicott (N.Y.) Sch. Dist., 1967-68; counselor, librarian West Yuma (Colo.) Sch. Dist., 1968-69; elem. sch. counselor Am. Falls (Idaho) Sch. Dist. 381, 1969-73; project dir. Gooding County (Idaho) Sr. Citizens Orgn., 1974-75; tchr. Castleford (Idaho) Sch. Dist. 417, 1982—; mem. Castleford Schs. Merit Pay Devel. program, 1983-84, Accreditation Evaluation com., 1984-85, Math. Curriculum Devel. com., 1985-86. Leader Brownie Scouts, Endicott, 1967-68; chmn. fundraising com. Am. Falls Kindergarten, 1971-73; leader Gooding County 4-H Council, Wendell, 1983-86. Recipient Leader's award Nat. 4-H Conservation Natural Resources Program, 1984. Mem. NEA, Idaho Edn. Assn., Castleford Parent-Tchr. Youth Orgn., Castleford Tchr.'s Orgn. (sec.-treas. 1984-86). Republican. Baptist. Avocations: reading, painting, writing short stories, photography. Home: Rt 1 PO Box 293 Wendell ID 83355 Office: Castleford Schs Castleford ID 83355

ANDERSON, MARY ELIZABETH, nurse, educator; b. Silver City, N.Mex., Sept. 26, 1948; d. Harry Ernest and Dorothea Mabel (Silverthorne) Dines; m. William Bayne Anderson, Dec. 20, 1975; children—Sarah Marie, Phillip Wesley. Grad. Hotel Dieu Sch. Nursing, 1971; B.A. in Home Econs. and Health, Western N.Mex. U., 1973, M.A. in Sch. Adminstrn., 1982. R.N., N.Mex.; cert. tchr. N.Mex. Sch. nurse Deming (N.Mex.) pub. schs., 1973-74, tchr., 1974—, emergency med. tech.; high sch. sponsor, state bd. dirs. Vocat. Indsl. Clubs Am.; instr./coordinator U. N.Mex. Sch. Medicine, Albuquerque; mem. textbook adoption com., past. pres. Vocat. Health Occupation div. N.Mex. Dept. Edn., treas., 1986—. Leader Girl Scouts U.S., Brownies, 1986—. Mem. Am. Vocat. Assn., N.Mex. Vocat. Assn. (Tchr. of Yr. 1981, 83, pres. elect health occupations div.), NEA, N.Mex. Edn. Assn., N.Mex. Nurses Assn., N.Mex. Pilot Club, Beta Sigma Phi. Democrat. Methodist. Lodges: Order Eastern Star, Dau. of the Nile, White Shriner, Order of the Rainbow for Girls. Office: Deming High Sch Deming NM 88030

ANDERSON, MAUREEN ANNE, librarian; b. Fresno, Calif., Aug. 9, 1935; d. Harry Burney and Edna Grace (Jacobsen) Thorpe; m. Edward Dan Anderson, Sept. 15, 1964; 1 child, David Burke. BA, U. Calif., Santa Barbara, 1957, MA in History, 1960; MSLS, U. So. Calif., 1963. Asst. librarian Coll. of Sequoias, Visalia, Calif., 1959-62; librarian U.S. Army Spl. Services, Babenhausen and Aschaffenburg, Republic of Germany, 1963-64, Mt. Whitney High Sch., Visalia, Calif., 1966—. Active Tulare County Republican Council, Visalia, Calif., 1961-62. Mem. Calif. Tchrs. Assn., Visalia Unified Tchrs. Assn. (chmn. bd. dirs. 1975-76, sec. 1984-85), NEA. Democrat. Avocations: history, writing, needlework. Home: 1201 W Westcott Visalia CA 93277

ANDERSON, MAURICE CHARLS, lawyer; b. Kincaid, Sask., Can., June 30, 1940; s. Herman T. and Elizabeth (Jennings) A.; m. Carolle E.A. Anderson, Aug. 25, 1962; children—Keira, Dean, Ryan. B.Comm., U. Sask., 1964; LL.B., U. Alta., 1967. Bar: Alta. 1968. Ptnr. Gill Cook, and predecessors, Calgary, Alta., Can., 1971-81, Mccleod Lyle Smith McManns, Calgary, 1982—. Bd. dirs., past pres. Springbank Park for All Seasons, Calgary, pres. 1985-86. Mem. Can. Bar Assn., Calgary Bar Assn., Can. Condominium Assn., Can. Homebuilders Assn., Urban Devel. Inst. Liberal. Anglican, Calgary C. of C. (bldg. com.). Clubs: Glencoe, Men's Canadian (Calgary). Home: Box 17, Site 6, Rural Route 1, Calgary, AB Canada T2P 2G4 Office: 2200 Bow Valley Sq IV, 250 6th Ave SW, Calgary, AB Canada T2P 3H7

ANDERSON, MICHAEL GEORGE, quality assurance executive; b. Boulder, Colo., Aug. 3, 1951; s. George Martin and Annette Elizabeth (Girmann) A.; m. Susan Elliott, Mar. 19, 1977; children: Gregory Michael, Richard Charles. BS in Aero. Engring., U. Colo., 1973, MBA in Fin., 1978. Design engr. Beech Aircraft, Boulder, 1976-78, liaison engr., 1978-79; mech. engr. Dieterich Standard, Boulder, 1979-80, mgr. engring. design, 1980-84, quality assurance mgr., 1984—. Author (computer software) Tektronix Header Program, 1982. Recipient NPT Stamp and Cert., ASME, Boulder, 1986. Mem. ASTM, Am. mgmt. Assn., Am. Soc. Metals, Am. Soc. Quality Control, Boulder Flycasters Club, U. Colo. Alumni Assn. (bd. dirs. 1985—, v.p. bd. dirs. Boulder chpt. 1985—). Republican. Lutheran. Club: Buff (Boulder) (v.p. 1985—). Lodge: Elks. Avocations: fly tying, fly fishing. Home: 7400 Mount Meeker Rd Longmont CO 80501 Office: Dieterich Standard PO Box 9000 Boulder CO 80301

ANDERSON, MICHAEL ROBERT, marketing representative; b. Mpls., Nov. 3, 1953; s. Arthur Robert Anderson and Patricia Roberta Carlson; m. Rebecca Ellan Pierce, June 6, 1981; 1 child, Jenna Courtney. BSEE, U. Minn., 1976; MS in Systems Mgmt., U. So. Calif., 1981. Microelectronics engr. Hughes Aircraft Co., Fullerton, Calif., 1977; mktg. rep. Hewlett Packard, Orange County, Calif., 1977-81; regional mgr. Group III Elec., Orange County, 1981-85; mktg. rep. Lisp Machines Inc., Los Angeles, 1985-87, SUN Microsystems, Inc., Orange, Calif., 1987—. Big Brother, Big Bros. Inc., Orange, Calif., 1979-81. Fellow mem. AAAS, Am. Assn. Artificial Intelligence. Avocations: reading, piano, family activities, bicycling, travel. Home: 28152 Bedford Dr Laguna Niguel CA 92677 Office: SUN Microsystems 625 Century Suite 330 Orange CA 92668

ANDERSON, MOIRA KATHARINE, editor, writer; b. Santa Rosa, Calif., Jan. 1, 1959; d. Victor Roland and Muriel Ann (Drake) A.; m. Patrick D. Allen, Mar. 17, 1984. BA, U. Calif., Berkeley, 1981. Sec. NSF, Washington, 1982-84; tech. writer NIH, Bethesda, Md., 1984; freelance writer Los Angeles, 1979—; editor Fancy Pubs., San Juan Capistrano, Calif., 1985—. Editor: Dog Fancy, 1985-87, Best All-Breed Canine mag., 1986; assoc. editor: Cat Fancy, 1985-87, Horse Illustrated, 1985-87, Bird Talk, 1985-87; cons. editor Rand Corp., 1987—; contbg. editor: Pet Health News, 1985—; contbr. articles to profl. publs. Campaign editor Rich Taylor for City Council, Cerritos, 1986. Honorable Mention, Writer's Digest, 1982. Mem. Dog Writer's Assn. Am. Republican. Episcopalian. Avocations: photography, travel, anthropology, folklore studies, archaeology. Home and Office: 3744 Delmas Terr #2 Los Angeles CA 90034

ANDERSON, N. CHRISTIAN, III, newspaper editor; b. Montpelier, Idaho, Aug. 4, 1950; s. Nelson C. and Esther Barbara (Yackley) A.; m. Sara Ann Coffenberry, Dec. 11, 1971 (div.); children—Ryan, Erica; m. Aletha Ann Yurewicz, May 3, 1986. B.A. in Liberal Studies with honors, Oreg. State U., 1972. Asst. city editor, city editor Albany Democrat-Herald, Oreg., 1972-75; mng. editor Walla Walla Union-Bull., Wash., 1975-77; assoc. mng. editor Seattle Times, 1977-80; editor The Orange County (Calif.) Register, 1980—; instr. Calif. State U.-Fullerton, 1983. Bd. dirs. Santa Ana Rotary Found., 1984. Mem. AP Mng. Editors, Soc. Profl. Journalists (Barney Kilgore Finalist award 1971), Am. Soc. Newspaper Editors, Calif. Soc. Newspaper Editors (bd. dirs. 1984—, v.p. 1985, pres. 1986-87), Soc. Newspaper Design (steering com. 1978). Roman Catholic. Office: The Register 625 N Grand Ave Santa Ana CA 92711

ANDERSON, NED, SR., Apache tribal chairman; b. Bylas, Ariz., Jan. 18, 1943; s. Paul and Maggie (Rope) A.; m. Delphina Hinton; children—Therese Kay, Linette Mae, Magdalene Gail, Ned, Sean. A.A., Eastern Ariz. Coll., 1964; B.S., U. Ariz., 1967, J.D., 1973. Field dir. Nat. Study Indian Edn., dept. anthropology U. Ariz., Tucson, 1968-70; tech. asst. Project Head Start, Ariz. State U., Tempe, 1970; ethnographer Smithsonian Instn., Washington, 1970-73; dir. Jojoba Project, Office of Arid Land Studies, U. Ariz. Tucson, 1973-76; with Jojoba devel. project San Carlos Apache Tribe, Ariz., 1976-78, tribal chmn., 1978-86; dir. Southwestern Indian Devel., Inc., 1971; mem. affirmative action com. City of Tucson, 1975-76; bd. dirs. Indian Enterprise Devel. Corp., 1976-78; mem. study panel Nat. Acad. Scis., 1975-77; pres. Inter-Tribal Council Ariz., 1979—; mem. supervisory bd. Ariz. Justice Planning Commn., 1978—, Indian adv. bd. Intergovtl. Personnel Program, 1978—; pres. bd. Ft. Thomas High Sch. Unified Dist., 1987—; trustee Bacone Coll., 1986—; mem. adv. bd. Am. Indian Registry for Performing Arts, 1985—. Mem. San Carlos Fish and Game Commn., 1975—, chmn., 1976—; mem. exec. com. San Carlos Apache Tribal Council, 1976-78, budget, fin. com., 1976—, constn. and ordinance com. 1976-78, chmn. law and order com., 1976-78; adv. bd. Gila Pueblo Community Coll. ext. Eastern Ariz. Coll., 1979—; mem. sch. bd. Ft. Thomas High Sch. Unified Dist., 1977—; adv. bd. Indian Edn., Ariz. State U., Tempe, 1978—, U. Ariz., Tucson, 1978—. Contbr. articles and papers to publs. Mem. Nat. Tribal Chmn.'s Assn. (bd. edn. 1978—, adv. bd. 1978—), Ariz. Acad., Globe C. of C.

ANDERSON, NORMAN HENRY, psychology educator, researcher; b. Mpls., July 23, 1925. BS in Physics, U. Chgo., 1946, MS in Math., 1949; MS in Psychology, U. Wis., 1955, PhD in Psychology, 1956. Mathematician ERA/Sperry Rand, Arlington, Va., 1951-53; asst. prof. psychology UCLA, 1958-62, assoc. prof., 1962-65; prof. U. Calif.-San Diego, La Jolla, 1965—; vis. asst. prof. Yale U., New Haven, Conn., 1957-58, Ind. U., Bloomington, 1962-63; mem psychobiology panel NSF, 1963-65, mem. social psychology panel, 1973-75. Author: Foundations of Information Integration Theory, 1981, Methods of Information Integration Theory, 1982; mem. editorial bd. Jour. Math. Psychology, 1964-73, Behavior Research Methods and Instrumentation, 1968-80; contbr. numerous articles to profl. jours. Served with U.S. Army, 1946-47. Recipient Socio-Psychol. prize AAAS, 1972; fellow Ctr. Advanced Study in Behavioral Scis., Stanford U., 1968-69. Mem. Soc. Exptl. Psychologists. Avocations: Shakespeare, hiking. Office: U Calif Psychology C-009 La Jolla CA 92093

ANDERSON, PAUL MAURICE, electrical engineering educator, researcher, consultant; b. Des Moines, Jan. 22, 1926; s. Neil W. and Buena Vista (Thompson) A.; m. Virginia Ann Worswick, July 8, 1950; children: William, Mark, James, Thomas. B.S.E.E., Iowa State U., 1949, M.S.E.E., 1958, Ph.D. in Elec. Engring., 1961. Registered profl. engr., Ariz., Calif., Iowa registered control systems engr., Calif. Elec. engr. Iowa Pub. Service Co., Sioux City, 1949-55; prof. elec. engring. Iowa State U., Ames, 1955-75; program mgr. Electric Power Research Inst., Palo Alto, Calif., 1975-78; cons. Power Math Assocs. Inc., Palo Alto, Tempe and Del Mar, 1978—; prof. elec. engring. Ariz. State U., Tempe, 1980-84. Author: Analysis of Faulted Power Systems, 1973, (with others) Power Control and Stability, 1977; editor: Ency. Sci. and Tech., 1979; contbr. articles to profl. jours. NSF faculty fellow, 1960-61; recipient Faculty citation Iowa State U. Alumni Assn., 1973, Profl. Achievement citation Iowa State U., 1981. Fellow IEEE (pres. Iowa sect. 1959-60), Conf. Internat. des Grands Reseaux Electriques, Sigma Xi, Phi Kappa Phi, Eta Kappa Nu, Pi Mu Epsilon. Republican. Lodge: Masons. Home: 13335 Roxton Circle San Diego CA 92130 Office: Power Math Assocs Inc 2002 Jimmy Durante Blvd Suite 314 Del Mar CA 92014

ANDERSON, PAUL NATHANIEL, physician; b. Omaha, May 30, 1937; s. Nels Paul E. and Doris Marie (Chesnut) A.; BA, U. Colo., 1959, MD, 1963; m. Dee Ann Hipps, June 27, 1965; children:Mary Kathleen, Anne Christen. Intern Johns Hopkins Hosp., 1963-64, resident in internal medicine, 1964-65; research asso., staff assoc. NIH, Bethesda, Md., 1965-70; fellow in oncology Johns Hopkins Hosp., 1970-72, asst. prof. medicine, oncology Johns Hopkins U. Sch. Medicine, 1972-76; attending physician Balt. City Hosps., Johns Hopkins Hosp., 1972-76; dir. dept. med. oncology Penrose Cancer Hosp., Colorado Springs, Colo., 1976-86; clin. asst. prof. dept. medicine U. Colo. Sch. Medicine, 1976—; dir. Penrose Cancer Hosp., 1979-86; founding dir. Cancer Ctr. of Colorado Springs; med. dir. So. Colo. Cancer Program, 1979-86; mem., chmn. treatment com. Colo. Cancer Control and Research Panel, 1980-83; prin. investigator Cancer Info. Service of Colo., 1981-86. Mem. Colo. Gov.'s Rocky Flats Employee Health Assessment Group, 1983-84; mem. Gov.'s Breast Cancer Control Commn. Colo., 1984—; pres., founder Oncology Mgmt. Network, Inc., 1985—; founder, bd. dirs. Timberline Med. Assocs., 1986—; founder So. Colo. AIDS project 1986—; mem. adv. bd. Colo. State Bd. Health Tumor Registry, 1984—; chmn., bd. dirs. Preferred Physicians, Inc.; bd. dirs. Share Devel. Co. of Colo., Share Health Plan of Colo., Preferred Health Plan, Inc. Served with USPHS, 1965-70. Diplomate Am. Bd. Internal Medicine. Mem. Am. Soc. Clin. Oncology, Am. Assn. Cancer Research, Am. Assn. Cancer Insts. (liaison mem. bd. trustees 1980—), Am. Acad. Med. Dirs., Nat. Cancer Inst. (com. for community hosp. oncology program evaluation 1982—), Assn. Community Cancer Centers (chmn. membership com. 1980—, chmn. clin. research com. 1983-85, sec. 1983-84, pres.-elect 1984-85, pres. 1986-87, trustee 1981—), AAAS, N.Y. Acad. Scis., Johns Hopkins Med. Soc., AMA, Colo. Med. Soc., Am. Mgmt. Assn., Am. Assn. Profl. Cons., El Paso County Med. Soc., Coalition for Cancer, Alpha Omega Alpha. Contbr. articles to med. jours. Home: 32 Sanford Rd Colorado Springs CO 80907 Office: Cancer Ctr Colorado Springs 320 E Fontanero St Suite 100 Colorado Springs CO 80907 Address: 32 Sanford Rd Colorado Springs CO 80906

ANDERSON, RAYMOND HARTWELL, JR., metallurgical engineer; b. Staunton, Va., Feb. 25, 1932; s. Raymond Hartwell and Virginia Boatwright (Moseley) A.; m. Dana Bratton Wilson, Sept. 5, 1959; children: Kathryn, Margaret, Susan. BS in Ceramic and Metall. Engring., Va. Poly. Inst. and State U., 1957, MSMetE, 1959. Registered profl. engr. Asst. prof. metall. engring. Va. Poly. Inst. and State U., Blacksburg, 1957-59; metall. engr. Gen. Dynamics Corp., Ft. Worth, 1959-61; sr. engr. Babcock & Wilcox Co., Lynchburg, Va., 1961-65; tech. specialist McDonnell Douglas Astronautics Co., Huntington Beach, Calif., 1965—; cons. in field Los Angeles Area, 1967-71. Author, patentee Roll Diffusion Bonding of Beryllium, 1970-71, Increased Ductility of Beryllium, 1971-72. Served to 1st lt. U.S. Army, 1954-56. Mem. Am. Soc. Metals (lectr. 1968-70), Nat. Soc. Corrosion Engrs., Bolting Tech. Council., Am. Ceramic Soc., Alpha Sigma Mu, Tau Beta Pi, Sigma Gamma Epsilon. Republican. Avocations: gardening, antique cars, music, bicycling. Home: 1672 Kenneth Dr Santa Ana CA 92705 Office: McDonnell Douglas Astronautics Co 5301 Bolsa Ave Huntington Beach CA 92647

ANDERSON, RICHARD BRADFORD, economist; b. Mpls., July 31, 1931; s. Francis Xavier and Evelyn (Hanson) A.; B.BA magna cum laude, Nat. U., 1977, MBA, 1978; D.B.A., U.S. Internat. U., 1981; m. Mary Kathryn Schwenn; children: Jacquelyn Sue, Marta Jean, Richard Bradford, Ariana M. Asst. cashier First Nat. Bank San Diego, 1949-62; v.p., cashier Bank La Jolla (Calif.), 1962-64; broker Hayden-Stone & Co., Inc., San Diego, 1965-71; v.p., ptnr. Roberts-Scott & Co., Inc., San Diego, 1971-73; asst. to pres., sec.-treas. Commodore Resources, Inc., San Diego, 1974-75; sr. ptnr. Bradford Anderson Assocs., Salt Lake City, 1976-77; ptnr. Schwenn Anderson, Inc., Carson City, Nev., 1978—; mem. faculty U.S. Internat. U., Salt Lake City, 1980-81; domestic and internat. cons., 1976—. Pres., San Diego County Young Reps., 1958; bd. dirs. Mother Goose Parade Assn., 1955-62; chmn. Reps. of La Jolla, 1973-74; maj. U.S. Mormon Bn., 1978—, nat. donations officer, nat. liaison officer, gen. staff, 1981—; mem. nat. adv. bd. Am. Security Council, 1979-83. Mem. Am. Enterprise Inst. (assoc.), Nat. Geog. Soc., Smithsonian Instn. Mormon. Office: 26341 Houston Trail Laguna Hills CA 92653

ANDERSON, RICHARD ERNEST, energy and chemical research and development company executive, rancher; b. North Little Rock, Ark., Mar. 8, 1926; s. Victor Ernest and Lillian Josephine (Griffin) A.; m. Mary Ann Fitch, July 18, 1953; children: Vicki Lynn, Lucia Anita. B.S.C.E., U. Ark., 1949; M.S.E., U. Mich., 1959; Registered profl. engr., Mich., Va., Tex., Mont. Commd. ensign U.S. Navy, 1952, advanced through grades to capt., 1968; ret., 1974; v.p. Ocean Resources, Inc., Houston, 1974-77; mgr. maintenance and ops. Holmes & Narver, Inc., Orange, Calif., 1977-78; pres. No. Resources, Inc., Billings, Mont., 1978-81; v.p. Holmes & Narver, Inc., Orange, Calif., 1981-82; owner, operator Anderson Ranches, registered Arabian horses and comml. Murray Grey cows, Pony, Mont., 1982—; pres., dir. Carbon Resources Inc., Manhattan, Mont., 1983—. Trustee Lake Barcroft-Virginia Watershed Improvement Dist., 1973-74; pres. Lake Barcroft-Virginia Recreation Center, Inc., 1972-73. Served with USAAF, 1944-45. Decorated Silver Star, Legion of Merit with Combat V (2), Navy Marine Corps medal, Bronze Star with Combat V, Meritorious Service medal, Purple Heart; Anderson Peninsula in Antarctica named in his honor. Mem. ASCE, Soc. Am. Mil. Engrs. (Morrell medal 1965). Republican. Methodist. Clubs: Billings Petroleum, Elks. Home: PO Box 247 Pony MT 59747 Office: Carbon Resources Inc 105 S 5th Ave Manhattan MT 59741

ANDERSON, RICHARD PAUL, music educator; b. Bakersfield, Calif., Feb. 6, 1946; s. Arthur Gene and Eileen (Hubbs) A.; m. Susan Rae Hogan, Aug. 7, 1973; children: Michael, Geralyn, Stephanie, Julie, Stacey. BA, Ariz. State U., 1968; MusM, Northwestern U., 1970; student, Mus. Acad. of West, 1967; D in Mus. Arts, U. Colo., Boulder, 1986. Asst. prof. music Brigham Young U., Provo, Utah, 1972—; coordinator group piano Brigham Young U. Dept. Mus., 1975—; lectr., adjudicator. Composer numerous children's piano pieces; co-author: First Experience at the Piano (6 vols.), 1986; author: Keyboard Patterns. Coach Little League Baseball, Soccer, Orem, Utah. Republican. Mormon. Avocations: sports, writing, reading. Home: 111 W 1040 S Orem UT 84058 Office: Brigham Young U Dept Mus E-378 HFAC Provo UT 84602

ANDERSON, ROBERT, manufacturing company executive; b. Columbus, Nebr., Nov. 2, 1920; s. Robert and Lillian (Devlin) A.; m. Constance Dahlun Severy, Oct. 2, 1942 (div.); children: Robert, Kathleen D.; m. Diane Clark Lowe, Nov. 2, 1973. B.S. in Mech. Engring, Colo. State U., 1943, LL.D., 1966; M. Automotive Engring., Chrysler Inst. Engring., 1948. With Chrysler Corp., 1946-68, v.p. corp., gen. mgr. Chrysler-Plymouth div., 1965-67; with Rockwell International Corp., 1968—, pres. comml. products group, 1968-69, v.p. corp., 1968-69, exec. v.p., 1969-70, pres., chief operating officer, 1970-74, pres., 1974-79, chief exec. officer, 1974—, chmn., 1979—, dir., 1968—; dir. Security Pacific Corp. and subs. Security Pacific Nat. Bank, Los Angeles, Celanese Corp., Owens-Ill., Inc., Hosp. Corp. Am. Trustee Calif. Inst. Tech., bd. of overseers Exec. Council Fgn. Diplomats; chmn. bus.-higher edn. forum Am. Council on Edn., 1982-84; chmn. Western Hwy. Inst., 1983-84. Served to capt. F.A. AUS, 1943-46. Named Exec. of Yr. Nat. Mgmt. Assn., 1980. Mem. Soc. Automotive Engrs., Phi Kappa Phi, Tau Beta Pi, Sigma Nu. Clubs: Rolling Rock (Ligonier, Pa.), Laurel Valley Golf (Ligonier, Pa.); Fox Chapel (Pa.) Golf, Eldorado (Calif.) Country, Desert Horizons (Calif.), Country; Duquesne (Pitts.); Los Angeles Country.*

ANDERSON, ROBERT CHARLES, engineering consultant, retired diversified electronics and aerospace company executive; b. Greeley, Colo., Dec. 5, 1921; s. William Earl and Elizabeth (Doland) A.; m. Mary Connally Laird; children: Rebecca, Richard, Tamara, Gabriel, Susan. BME, U. Colo., 1943; postgrad., UCLA, 1954-60, U. So. Calif., 1969-70. Engr. rockets div. Naval Weapons Ctr., China Lake, Calif., 1946-56; mgr. minuteman propulsion div. TRW Corp., Redondo Beach, Calif., 1956-64, project mgr., Lunar Excursion Module Descent Engine, 1964-67, mgr. project ops. Applied Tech. div., 1967-72, v.p., asst. gen. mgr. Energy Devel. group, 1980-85; v.p., gen. mgr. Ballistic Missile div. TRW Corp., San Bernardino, Calif., 1973-79; chmn. indsl. liason com. U. Calif., Riverside, 1974-76, univ. relations com. Inland Action, San Bernardino, 1973-77. Contbr. articles to profl. jours. Ruling elder, com. chmn. Presbyn. Ch., Rancho Palos Verdes, Calif., 1950-84; bd. dirs. Little Co. Mary Hosp., Torrance, Calif., 1984. Served to lt. USN, 1943-46. Fellow AIAA (assoc., chmn. local sect. 1954-84, program devel. 1973-77); mem. World Affairs Council. Republican. Home: 840 55th Ave NW Salem OR 97304 Office: TRW Corp Electronics and Def 1 Space Park Redondo Beach CA 90278

ANDERSON, ROBERT CURTIS, biology educator; b. Columbus, Ohio, May 10, 1941; s. Ralph Curtis and Thelma Marie (Leach) A.; m. Marianne Elizabeth Bieniek, Apr. 1, 1967; children: Aran Edward, April Rebecca. BS, Calif. State U., Long Beach, 1963; MS, Purdue U., 1966, PhD, 1968. Instr. entomology Purdue U., West Lafayette, Ind., 1968-69; asst. prof. biology Idaho State U., Pocatello, 1969-74, assoc. prof., 1974-82, chmn. biology dept., 1975-82, prof., 1982—. Contbr. articles to profl. jours. Mem. adv. council Bur. Land Mgmt. Shoshone (Idaho) Dist., 1983—, NIH Environ. Health Scis. Council, Bethesda, Md., 1986—. Sr. Fulbright scholar, Egypt, 1983-84. Mem. AAAS, Am. Soc. Zoologists, Entomol. Soc. Am., Idaho Acad. Sci. (trustee 1973-76), Western Soc. Naturalists. Avocations: beekeeping, camping, gardening, photography. Home: 1611 Shane Pocatello ID 83204 Office: Idaho State U Dept Biol Scis Pocatello ID 83209

ANDERSON, ROBERT EMRA, chemical executive; b. Mentone, Ind., Jan. 6, 1924; s. Emra D. and Lenna (Coplen) A.; m. Wilma Rae Hanna, Jan. 13, 1945; children: Kenneth R., Keith R. BS in Chemistry, Ind. U., 1949, MA in Inorganic Chemistry, 1951. Phys. chemist Dow Chem. Co., Midland, Mich., 1951-56, group leader, 1956-68; group leader Diamond Shamrock Corp., Redwood City, Calif., 1968-78, sr. research scientist, 1978-82; cons. Sunnyvale, Calif., 1982—; chmn. Gordon Research Conf. on ion exchange, 1971. Served with U.S. Army, 1943-46. Mem. Am. Chem. Soc., Profl. Tech. Cons. Assn., Sunnyvale Stamp Soc. (pres. 1974-75, 86). Presbyterian. Lodge: Kiwanis. Avocations: stamp collecting. Home and Office: 1617 Wright Ave Sunnyvale CA 94087

ANDERSON, ROBERT ERNEST, sales executive; b. Heavener, Okla., July 30, 1926; s. Ernest L. and Dewey M. (Vaught) A., m. Eleanor Jeanne Mauzy, Sept. 15, 1948; children: Robert, Sarah, David, Hans. BS, Okla. State U., 1949, MS, 1950. Registered profl. engr., Calif.; cert. safety profl. Instr. Okla. State U. Agr. and Applied Sci., Stillwater, 1950-51, asst. prof., 1951-52; with Mine Safety Appliances Co., Beaumont, Tex., Gary, Ind., and Little Rock, 1952-63; mgr. safety products MSA Internat., Pitts., 1963-67; mgr. intermountain dist. MSA Internat., Salt Lake City, 1967—. Served with USNR, 1944-46. Mem. AIME, Am. Indsl. Hygiene Assn., Am. Soc. Safety Engrs. (v.p. region II 1986-87). Democrat. Methodist. Lodge: Masons. Home: 3372 Pioneer St Salt Lake City UT 84109

ANDERSON, ROBERT HELMS, computer and management consultant; b. Richmond, Calif., June 7, 1939; s. Oscar Nels and Elsie (Helms) A.; m. Lynn Shallenberger, Oct. 1965; children—Blythe, Kevin. B.A., U. Calif.-Berkeley, 1962; M.A., Harvard U., 1965, Ph.D., 1968. Head info. sci. dept. The Rand Corp., Santa Monica, Calif., 1976-79, dir. inst. for research on interactive systems, 1985—; exec. v.p. Interactive Systems Corp., Santa Monica, 1979-81; pres. Robert H. Anderson and Assocs., Inc., Pacific Palisades, Calif., 1981—; adj. assoc. prof. U. So. Calif., 1968-75. Contbr. articles to computer sci. jours. Served to 1st lt. U.S. Army, 1962-64. Mem. Assn. Computing Machinery, (nat. lectr. 1972-73), Am. Assn. for Artificial Intelligence, Soc. Office Automation Profls. Office: Robert H Anderson and Assocs Inc 16566 Chalet Terr Pacific Palisades CA 90272

ANDERSON, ROBERT ORVILLE, industrialist; b. Chgo., Apr. 13, 1917; s. Hugo A. and Hilda (Nelson) A.; m. Barbara Phelps, Aug. 25, 1939; children: Katherine, Julia, Maria, Robert Bruce, Barbara Burton, William Phelps, Beverley. B.A., U. Chgo., 1939. With Am. Mineral Spirits Co., Chgo., 1939-41; pres. Malco Refineries, Inc. (now Hondo Oil and Gas Co.), Roswell, N.Mex., 1941-63; chmn. exec. com. Atlantic Richfield Co., Los Angeles, retired chmn. bd., chief exec. officer; owner Diamond A Cattle Co., Roswell; mem. Com. Econ. Devel., Washington. Chmn. Aspen Inst. for Humanistic Studies; chmn. Lovelace Found.; trustee Calif. Inst. Tech., U. Chgo. Mem. Am. Petroleum Inst. Clubs: Century (N.Y.C.); California (Los Angeles); Metropolitan (Washington); Chicago; Pacific-Union (San Francisco).

ANDERSON, ROBERT UDDEN, university administrator; b. Balt., Dec. 6, 1943; s. Robert Bernard and Jane Elizabeth (Udden) A.; m. Sandra Marie Schauer, Mar. 31, 1984. Cert. Russian lang., Ind. U., 1967. Researcher U. N.Mex., Albuquerque, 1970-75, dir. div. govt. research, 1975—. Served with USAF, 1966-69. Democrat. Avocations: tennis, skiing. Home: 1809 Bryn Mawr NE Albuquerque NM 87106 Office: U NMex Div Govt Research Albuquerque NM 87131

ANDERSON, RONALD ALBERT, electronics technician; b. Detroit, June 13, 1941; s. Albert Walter and Jeannette Faubert A.; m. Vicki Ann Johnson, June 7, 1982; children: Christopher Walter, Delanie Ann. BS, So. Oreg. Coll., 1971; MS, U. Vt., 1974; AA, Portland Community Coll., 1984. Research assoc. U. Oreg. Med. Sch., Portland, 1975-83; mem. staff hardware electronics Intel Corp., Hillsboro, Oreg., 1983—; research asst. Frederic Burk Found. Research Ctr., San Francisco, 1965-66; lab. asst. Case-Western Res. U. Devel. Biol. Ctr., 1963-65. Contbr. articles to profl. jours. Served with USAF, 1967-70. NSF grantee, 1961, 62, 63. Mem. Sigma Xi. Avocations: fishing, hiking. Home: 2020 NW 29th Apt 10 Portland OR 97210 Office: Intel Corp 5200 NE Elam Young Pkwy Hillsboro OR 97124

ANDERSON, ROSEMARY BURDETTE, magazine editor; b. Phoenix, June 1, 1953; d. Houston Scarborough and Jess R. (Bradley) Burdette; m. Steven R. Anderson, Nov. 18, 1973; 1 child, Burdette Gavin. BA in History and Journalism, San Diego State U., 1976. Assoc. editor People's Pub. Co., Inc., Compton, Calif., 1976-82; mng. editor People's Pub. Co., Inc., Arcata, Calif., 1982—; vol. newsletter producer YWCA, Eureka, Calif. 1985-86; graphics vol. Eureka chpt. Am. Cancer Soc., 1979-83. Avocations: tennis, snow skiing. Office: People's Pub Co Inc PO Box 1095 Arcata CA 95521

ANDERSON, ROY ARNOLD, aerospace company executive; b. Ripon, Calif., Dec. 15, 1920; s. Carl Gustav and Esther (Johnson) A.; m. Betty Leona Boehme, June 10, 1948; children: Ross David, Karyn Dale, Debra Elayne, James Patrick. A.B., Stanford U., 1947, M.B.A., 1949. C.P.A., Calif. With Westinghouse Electric Corp., 1952-56; mgr. accounting and finance, then dir. mgmt. controls Lockheed Missiles & Space Co., 1956-65; dir. finance Lockheed-Ga. Co., 1965-68; asst. treas. Lockheed Corp., 1968-69, v.p., controller, 1969-71, sr. v.p. finance, 1971-75, Vice chmn. bd., chief financial and adminstrv. officer, 1975-77, chmn. bd., chief exec. officer, 1977-85, chmn. exec. com. bd., 1986—; dir. ARCOsystems, Inc., 1st Interstate Bank Calif., 1st Interstate Bancorp., Los Angeles, So. Calif. Edison Co.

Trustee Occidental Coll.; chmn. bd. Greater Los Angeles United Way; bd. dirs. Los Angeles Music Ctr., Los Angeles County Mus. Art. Served with USNR, 1942-46, 50-52. Recipient James Forrestal Meml. award Nat. Security Indsl. Assn., 1984; Mfr. of Yr., Calif. Mfrs. Assn., 1984; Good Scout award Los Angeles Council Boy Scouts Am., 1985. Mem. Phi Beta Kappa. Office: 4500 Park Granada Blvd Calabasas CA 91399

ANDERSON, ROYAL J., advertising agency executive; b. Portland, Oreg., Sept. 12, 1914; s. John Alfred and Martha Marie (Jacobsen) A.; B.A., Albany Coll., 1939; postgrad. U. Oreg., summers 1939-41, Oreg. Inst. Tech., 1940-41; m. Leticia Anderson; children: Michael, Johnny, Dora Kay, Mark Roy, Stan Ray, Ruth Gay, Janelle A., Jennifer T., Joseph, Daisy, Dina; 1 adopted dau., Muoi-Muoi. Corp. cons. Dupont Corp., Beverly Hills, Calif., 1967-68; editor-pub. Nev. State Democrat, Carson City, Nev. State Pub. Observer, Nev. State Congl. Assn., Carson City, 1962-78; pres. Allied-Western Produce Co., Yuma, Ariz., Nev. Dem. Corp., 1966-78; pres. Western Restaurant Corp., 1978-81, Nev. State Sage Co., 1979—, Midway Advt. Co., Environ. Research Corp., 1983—, Mid-City Advt. Agy., 1983—, Nat. Newspaper Found., 1969, 71-76, The Gt. North Banks Seafood Co., 1984—, Food Services Corp., 1985—, Sterlind Cruise Lines, 1986—, No-Tow Mfg. Inc.; chmn. bd. Press/Register Daily Newspapers, Foster Mortgage Co., 1983—. Bishop, Ch. of Palms, Mexico. Dep. registrar voters, Washoe County, Nev., 1966. Recipient Heroism award for rescue, 1933. Research fellow, Alaska, 1936. Mem. Am. Hort. Soc., Sparks (pres. 1970-81), Nev. chambers commerce, C. of C. of U.S., Chatso Farm Assn. (pres. 1962-81), Smithsonian Assos., N.Am. C. of C. Execs., Nat. Geog. Soc., Am. Newspaper Alliance (v.p. 1976), Club: Millionare. Lodges: Kiwanis, Elks, Lions. Designer prefabricated milk carton container, 1933, well water locating under-stream device, 1938. Home: PO Box 4349 North Las Vegas NV 89030 Home: 5600 E Sundance Ave Las Vegas NV 89116

ANDERSON, SCOTT CHARLES, computer programmer; b. Frankfurt, Fed. Republic Germany, Jan. 8, 1951; came to U.S., 1952; s. William Charles and Dortha Marie (Power) A.; m. Candyce Marie Pearson, Aug. 27, 1979. BS in Physics, Sonoma State U., 1977. Freelance artist San Diego, Calif., 1970-73; computer cons. Sonoma State U., Rohnert Park, Calif., 1974-77; pvt. practice computer programming Santa Rosa, Calif., 1977—. Developer various computer programs. NSF grantee Washington State U., 1975, Sonoma State U., 1976. Avocations: photography, painting.

ANDERSON, SHEILA BOTTORFF, natural resource consultant; b. Reno, Sept. 4, 1952; d. Glen Allen and Catherine Faye (Houck) Bottorff; m. Michael Bridges Dean, Dec. 18, 1971 (div. Mar. 1983); m. Peter Hanbury Anderson, Sept. 15, 1984; 1 child, Daniel Hanbury. BS in Wildlife Mgmt., U. Nev., 1978; MS in Range Mgmt., U. Wyo., 1983. Research assoc. U. Nev., Reno, 1978-80; grad. research assoc. U. Wyo., Laramie, 1981-83; resource specialist and planner Resource Concepts Inc., Carson City, Nev., 1980—; pres. Sweetwater Plant Co., Carson City, 1985—. Contbr. articles to profl. jours. Mem. Soc. Range Mgmt. (chmn. youth activities 1984-85, zone councilman 1987—), Soil Conservations Soc. Am. (chmn. pub. affairs com. 1984—), No. Nev. Native Plant Soc., Sigma Xi, Gamma Sigma Delta. Avocations: outdoor recreation, Western history. Office: Resource Concepts Inc 340 N Minnesota St Carson City NV 89701

ANDERSON, STANLEY HELMER, zoology researcher; b. San Francisco, Aug. 6, 1939; s. Helmer and Tyra (Sahlin) A.; m. Donna L. Lawrence, Feb. 27, 1965; children: Rebecca, Gregory. BS, U. Redlands, 1961; MS, Oreg. State U., 1968; PhD, Oreg. State. U., 1970. Asst. prof. Kenyon Coll., Gambier, Ohio, 1970-75; scientist Oak Ridge (Tenn.) Assn. U., 1975-76; chief nongame section Patuxent Res. Ctr., Laurel, Md., 1976-80; leader Wyo. Coop. Unit, U. Wyo., Laramie, 1980—; prof. U. Wyo., Laramie, 1980—. Author: Environmental Science, 1980, 86, Managing our Wildlife Resources, 1985; contbr. numerous articles to profl. jours. Served to lt. USN, 1963-66. Mem. Am. Ornithologists Union, Ecol. Soc. Am., Wildlife Soc., Cooper Ornithol. Soc., Wilson Ornithol. Soc., Sigma Xi. Avocations: backpacking, photography. Home: 1062 Arapaho Dr Laramie WY 82070 Office: U Wyo University Station Box 3166 Laramie WY 82071

ANDERSON, STEVEN CLEMENT, biology educator; b. Grand Canyon, Ariz., Sept. 7, 1936; s. Howard Theordore and Lois Belle (Patterson) A.; m. Kay Allison Bratsch, June 29, 1960; 1 child, Malcolm Ross. BA, U. Calif., 1957; MA, San Francisco State U., 1962; PhD, Stanford U., 1966. From asst. to assoc. curator of herpetology Calif. Acad. Scis., San Francisco, 1963-70, research assoc., 1975—; prof. biology U. Pacific, Stockton, Calif., 1970—. Cons. editor Ency. Iranica, 1978—; contbr. articles to sci. jours. Fellow Calif. Acad. Scis., Herpetologists' League; mem. Am. Soc. Ichthyologists and Herpetologists, Soc. Study of Amphibians and Reptiles, Sigma Xi. Avocations: scuba insts., martial arts. Office: U Pacific Dept Biology Stockton CA 95211

ANDERSON, SUSAN HOLLIDAY, coastal planner, consultant; b. Laconia, N.H., Aug. 23, 1944; d. Edmund Gilmore, Jr. and Marguerite (Pardee) A. B.A. (scholar), Mt. Holyoke Coll., 1966; M.S. in Marine Affairs (Noyes fellow), U. R.I., 1973. Regional rep. Expt. Internat. Living, Washington, 1968-70; adminstrv. asst. Ocean Affairs Bd., Nat. Acad. Scis., Washington, 1971-72; project coordinator French-Am. Mid-Ocean Study, Woods Hole (Mass.) Oceanographic Inst., 1973-74; marine recreation specialist Marine Adv. Program, U. So. Calif. Sea Grant Program, 1974-78; planner, legal asst. Nossaman, Krueger and Marsh, Los Angeles, 1978-80; coastal planner, project mgr. Moffatt & Nichol, Engrs., Long Beach, Calif., 1980-84; pvt. cons. Susan H. Anderson, Cons., 1984-86; owner Nautistitch, 1986—; cons. spl. projects Can., U.S. Mem. County Los Angeles Beach Adv. Com., 1975-82. Mem. Marine Tech. Soc., Am. Shore and Beach Preservation Assn., Orange County Coast Assn., Calif. Marine Parks and Harbors Assn. (pres. 1980-81). Republican. Episcopalian. Club: Mt. Holyoke of San Diego. Contbr. articles to profl. jours. Office: Nautistitch Cardiff by the Sea CA 92007

ANDERSON, SUSAN LORETTA MOUNT, manufacturing company executive; b. Lake Charles, La., Nov. 9, 1947; d. Joseph Buchanan and Loretta Odalie (Lowrey) Mount; m. Ronald Martin Anderson, June 30, 1978; children: Joseph Buchanan Lowrey, Ronald Martin Mount. BA, McNeese U., 1969; MA, U. Denver, 1971. Conv. sales Holiday Denver Downtown, 1973-74; tchr. East Grand Schs., Granby, Colo., 1974-78; salesperson Associated Real Estate Winter Park, Colo., 1978-80; pres., broker, gen. mgr. Mountain Brokerage, Inc., Granby, 1980-82; pres., gen. mgr., broker Silvercreek Central, Granby, 1982-83; ptnr., sec.-treas., v.p. St. Louis Creek Trading Co., Winter Park, Colo., 1983—, also dir. Author: Conversations With Bestfriends, 1983, Conversations with Hal's Pals, 1986. Founding bd. dirs., chmn. bd. dirs. Fraser Planning Commn., Colo., 1979-81; bd. dirs. East Grand Sch. Bd., 1978-82, Challenged Kids, Mattel, Inc., 1986—. Mem. Nat. Assn. Realtors, Grand County Realtors, Nat. Assn. Ind. Appraisers, Winter Park C. of C., Grand County Theatre Assn., Grand County Hist. Assn. Home: 800 County Rd 519 PO Box 648 Fraser CO 80442 Office: Hal's Pals PO Box 315 420 Railroad Ave Winter Park CO 80482

ANDERSON, THEODORE WILBUR, statistics educator; b. Mpls., June 5, 1918; s. Theodore Wilbur and Evelynn (Johnson) A.; m. Dorothy Fisher, July 8, 1950; children: Robert Lewis, Janet Lynn, Jeanne Elizabeth. B.S. with highest distinction, Northwestern U., 1939; M.A., Princeton U., 1942, Ph.D., 1945. Asst. dept. math. Northwestern U., 1939-40; instr. math. Princeton U., 1941-43, research assoc., 1943-45; research assoc. Cowles Commn., U. Chgo., 1945-46; staff Columbia U., 1946-67, successively instr. math. stats., asst. prof., assoc. prof., 1946-56, prof., 1956-67, chmn. math. stats. dept., 1956-60, 64-65, acting chmn., 1950-51, 63; prof. stats. and econs. Stanford U., 1967—; dir. project Office Naval Research, 1968-82; prin. investigator NSF project, 1969—, Army Research Office project, 1982—; vis. prof. math. U. Moscow, 1968; vis. prof. stats. U. Paris, 1968; vis. prof. econs. NYU, 1983-84; acad. visitor math. Imperial Coll. Sci. and Tech., U. London, 1967-68, London Sch. Econs. and Polit. Sci., 1974-75; research visitor Tokyo Inst. Tech., 1977; sabbaticant IBM Systems Research Inst., 1984; cons. RAND Corp., 1949-66; mem. com. on basic research adv. Office Ordnance Research, Nat. Acad. Scis.-NRC, 1955-58; mem. panel on applied math. adv. Nat. Bur. Standards, 1964-65; chmn. com. on stats. NRC, 1961-63; mem. exec. com. Conf. Bd. Math. Scis., 1963-64; mem. com. on support research in math. scis. Nat Acad. Scis., 1965-68; mem. com. Pres.'s Statis. Socs., 1962-64; sci. dir. NATO Advanced Study Inst. on Discriminant Analysis and Its Applications, 1972. Author: An Introduction to Multivariate Statistical Analysis, 1958, 2d edit., 1984, The Statistical Analysis of Time Series, 1971, (with Somesh Das Gupta and George P.H. Styan) A Bibliography of Multivariate Statistical Analysis, 1972, (with Stanley Sclove) Introductory Statistical Analysis, 1974, An Introduction to the Statistical Analysis of Data, 1978, 2d edit., 1986 (with Barry P. Eynon) MINITAB Guide to the Statistical Analysis of Data, 1986; mem. adv. bd. Econometric Theory, 1985—; editor: Annals of Math. Statistics, 1950-52; editorial bd.: Psychometika, 1954-72; assoc. editor: Jour. Time Series Analysis, 1980—. Named Wesley C. Mitchell Vis. Prof. Columbia U., 1983-84; Guggenheim fellow, 1947-48; fellow Center for Advanced Study in Behavioral Scis., 1957-58; vis. scholar, 1972-73, 80; Sherman Fairchild disting. scholar Calif. Inst. Tech., 1980; Abraham Wald Meml. lectr., 1982, R.A. Fisher award Pres.'s Statis. Socs., 1985; R.A. Fischer lectr. Am. Statis. Assn., 1985; P.C. Mahalanobis Meml. lectr., 1985; S.N. Roy Meml. lectr. Calcutta U., 1985. Fellow Am. Statis. Assn. (v.p. 1971-73), Econometric Soc., Royal. Statis. Soc., AAAS, Inst. Math. Stats. (pres. 1963), Am. Acad. Arts and Scis.; mem. Am. Math. Soc., Indian, Internat. statis. insts., Statistical Soc. Can., Psychometric Soc. (council dirs.), Nat. Acad. Scis., Bernouilli Soc. for Math. Stats. and Probability, Phi Beta Kappa. Home: 746 Santa Ynez St Stanford CA 94305 Office: Dept Statistics Sequoia Hall Stanford U Stanford CA 94305

ANDERSON, WARREN EARL, computer company executive; b. Pitts., May 22, 1951; s. Warren E. and Mary Kay (Fletcher) A. BSME, U. Cinn., 1974; MBA, Santa Clara U., 1982. Cert. community coll. tchr., Calif. Computer programmer Mitre Corp., Boston, 1974-75; mgr. sales and mktg. systems, sr. systems analyst Intel Corp., Santa Clara, Calif., 1975-80; database adminstr. Capital Preservation Fund, Palo Alto, Calif., 1980-82; pres., chmn Anderson Soft-Teach, San Jose, Calif., 1982—. Herman Schnieder scholar, 1973, Cooper-Bessemer scholar, 1969. Mem. Delta Tau Delta. Home: 2161 Blossom Valley Dr San Jose CA 95124 Office: Anderson Soft-Teach 2680 N 1st St San Jose CA 95134

ANDERSON, WARREN ROLAND, hotel executive; b. Kalispell, Mont., Nov. 2, 1929; s. Adolphe Emanuel and Marion (Frier) A.; m. Susan Morrow, Feb. 2, 1952; children—John Frederick, Jaynee Sue Anderson Fordham. B.S. in Hotel Adminstrn., Wash. State U., 1951. Cert. hotel adminstr. Asst. mgr. Davenport Hotel, Spokane, Wash., 1953-56, gen. mgr., 1964-66, co-owner, operating ptnr., 1979-84; asst. mgr. Finlen Hotel, Butte, Mont., 1956-57; exec. asst. mgr. Benjamin Franklin Hotel, Seattle, 1957-60; mgr. Rainbow Hotel, Great Falls, Mont., 1962-64; gen. mgr. No. Hotel, Billings, Mont., 1964-66; gen. mgr. Bonaventure Hotel, Western Internat. Hotels (now Westin Inc.), Montreal, Que., Can., 1966-68, v.p., gen. mgr. Dusit Thani Hotel, Bangkok, 1968-70, gen. mgr. Bayshore Inn, Vancouver, B.C., Can., 1970-72, Olympic Hotel, Seattle, 1972-77; co-owner, operator Colonial Inn, Helena, Mont., 1972-79; trustee Spokane Area Hotel and Resort Trust, 1980—; cons. Westerberg Inn., Wenatchee, Wash., 1983—, Grouse Mountain Lodge, Whitefish, Mont., 1983—. Mem. Wash. Gov.'s Council on Tourism, 1980—. Served to capt. U.S. Army, 1951-53, Korea. Decorated Bronze Star, also others. Fellow Am. Hotel and Motel Assn. (pres. 1982-83), Restaurant Assn. State Wash. (1st v.p. 1972-83), Soc. de Bon Table, Soc. Internat. Innkeepers, Western Acad. Internat. Innkeepers, Scabbard and Blade, Sigma Iota, Alpha Tau Omega. Clubs: Spokane; Overlake (Bellevue, Wash.); Capilano (Vancouver); LaValle Sur Le Lav (Montreal); Highlands (Billings); Meadowlark (Great Falls); Green Meadow (Helena). Lodges: Rotary, Kiwanis, Lions, Exchange, Optimists, Masons, Jesters, Elks. Home: W 807 Sprague Ave Spokane WA 99204 Office: W-3704 Grandview Rd D Spokane WA 99204

ANDERSON, WARREN RONALD, electrical engineering educator; b. Houston, July 31, 1914; s. Wallace Roy and Helen Adelia (Abrahamson) A.; m. Dantza Peinovich, May 28, 1945; children—Richard Godfrey, John Warren, Deborah Annete. A.A., Bethel Coll., 1935; B.S., U. Minn., 1939; B.S.E.E., La. State U., 1944. Registered profl. engr., Calif. Design engr. Plant Engring. Agy., Phila., 1945-46; circuits engr. Automatic Electric, Chgo., 1946; prof. elec. engring. Calif. Polytech. State U., San Luis Obispo, Calif., 1946-76, head elec. engring. dept., 1976-79, prof. emeritus, 1979—; design engr. Gen. Electric, Ft. Wayne, Ind., 1951; research analyst Northup Aircraft, Hawthorne, Calif., 1952; systems engr. Western Gear Corp., Lynwood, Calif., 1955; edn. cons. Gen. Electric, Schenectady, 1956. Leader Boy Scouts Am., San Luis Obispo, 1958-64. Served with U.S. Army, 1942-45. Recipient Cert. of Appreciation, AIEE, 1963. Mem. IEEE, Am. Soc. Engring. Edn., Nat. Soc. Profl. Engrs., Calif. Soc. Profl. Engrs. (dir. 1949-55), Calif. State Employees Assn. (dir. 1955-59), Eta Kappa Nu. Democrat. Baptist. Home: 573 Jeffrey Dr San Luis Obispo CA 93401 Office: Calif Poly State Univ Electronic and Elec Engring Dept San Luis Obispo CA 93407

ANDERSON, WILLIAM, retail company executive, business education educator; b. Los Angeles, May 21, 1923; s. William Bert and Marie (Novotney) A.; m. Margaret Lillian Phillips, Aug. 16, 1951; children: Margaret Gwen, Deborah Kay, William Keven, Denise Marie. BA in Econs., UCLA, 1948, MEd, 1957. Cert. secondary tchr. (life), Calif. Tchr. bus. edn. Big Bear Lake (Calif.) High Sch., 1949-52, Ventura (Calif.) Unified Sch. Dist. Buena High Sch., 1952—; mgr. Day's Aircraft Co., Santa Paula, Calif., 1967—; cons. micro computers Calif. State Dept. Edn., 1983-85. Crew chief Olympic Games basketball stats., 1984, basketball stats. World Games for the Deaf, 1985. Served as cpl. USAAF, 1943-45, PTO. Mem. NEA (life), Calif. Bus. Edn. Assn. (pres. So. sect. 1959-60, state sec. 1960-61), Calif. Assn. Work Experience Educators, Internat. Soc. Bus. Edn. (voting del. to Soc. Internat. Pour l'Enseignemer Comml.), Am. Aviation Hist. Soc., Calif. Assn. Work Experience Educators (life), Air Force Assn., So. Calif. Badminton Assn. (bd. dirs.), Inplant Printing Mgmt. Assn., Phi Delta Kappa, Delta Phi Epsilon. Democrat. Lutheran. Avocations: photography, aviation history, badminton, UCLA basketball stats. Home: 334 Manzanita Ave Ventura CA 93001 Office: Buena High Sch 5670 Telegraph Rd Ventura CA 93003

ANDERSON, WILLIAM LEVERE, data processing executive; b. Tacoma, Jan. 27, 1947; s. James William and Marion Estelle (Jones) A.; m. Paula Jeanne Smith, May 20, 1966; children: William, Shawn, Tyler, Aimee, Zachary, Jessica, Jill. Cert., Clover Park Tech. Sch., 1969; AA, Tacoma Community Coll., 1970; MBA, U. Wash., 1986. Tech. mgr. Pacific Nat. Bank, Seattle, 1968-74; supr. telecommunications Firemans Fund. Ins., San Francisco, 1974-75; v.p., mgr. Rainier Bank, Seattle, 1975-85, SeaFirst Bank, Seattle, 1985—. Republican. Roman Catholic. Avocations: running, woodworking. Home: 28626 11th Ave S Federal Way WA 98003 Office: SeaFirst Bank 800 Fifth Ave Seattle WA 98124

ANDERSON, WILLIAM WALTER, aerosapce scientist, consultant; b. Tacoma, Feb. 26, 1933; s. Walter Morton and Cora Louisa (Darnell) A.; m. Anne Jeanette LaPointe, Oct. 30, 1954; children: David, Carolyn, Kevin. BS, MS, MIT, 1956; PhD, Stanford U., 1959. Mem. tech. staff Bell Labs., Murray Hill, N.J., 1959-60; asst. prof. elec. engring. Stanford (Calif.) U., 1960-65; prof. Ohio State U., Columbus, 1965-75; scientist, cons. Lockheed Research and Devel. Div., Palo Alto, Calif., 1975—. Contbr. articles to profl. jours. Mem. IEEE, Sci. Research Soc., Am. Sci. Affiliation. Home: 1046 Pendleton Ave Sunnyvale CA 94087 Office: Lockheed R & DD 3251 Hanover St B202 Palo Alto CA 94304

ANDERSSON, GUNNAR EINAR, lawyer; b. El Paso, Tex., Mar. 10, 1926; s. Kingsley Sherman and Laurella Florence (Hollis) A.; m. Anne N. H. Williams, June 26, 1948; children—Laura Anne Andersson Kirkland, Norman Hill. B.S., U.S. Mil. Acad., 1946; J.D., U. Denver, 1978. Bar: Colo. 1978, U.S. Dist. Ct. Colo. 1978, U.S. Ct. Appeals (10th cir.) 1978, U.S. Supreme Ct. 1986. Commd. 2d lt. U.S. Army, 1946, advanced through grades to lt. col., 1965, ret., 1973; ptnr. firm Andersson & Conter, Colorado Springs, 1978-80, Barber, Gross & Andersson, Colorado Springs, 1980-81, Gross & Andersson, 1981-85, Andersson, Gerig, Gross & Lederer, P.C., 1985-86; sole practice Gunnar E. Andersson, P.C., 1986—. Dist. chmn. Colorado Springs Rep. Com., 1978—. Decorated Legion of Merit, Meritorious Service medal, Bronze Star medal. Fellow Explorer's Club; mem. Am. Trial Lawyers Assn., Phi Alpha Delta. Episcopalian. Clubs: Torch Internat. (past pres.). Lodge: Elks (advocate 1982—). Home: 716 Scorpio Circle Colorado Springs CO 80906 Office: 318 E Cimarron Colorado Springs CO 80903

ANDERSSON, LAURA ANNE, biochemist; b. Sendai, Japan, May 17, 1949; d. Gunnar Einar and Anne (Williams) A.; m. Robert Gaillard Kirkland, Apr. 16, 1981. BS, Auburn U., 1978; PhD, U. S.C., 1982. Postdoctoral research assoc. Oreg. Grad. Ctr., Beaverton, 1982-83, sr. research assoc., 1984, mem. faculty, research scientist, 1985—. Contbr. articles to profl. jours. NIH fellow 1982. Mem. AAAS, N.Y. Acad. Scis., Am. Chem. Soc. (research grantee 1985—), Sigma Xi (Cert. Recognition 1981, 1st Pl. Research award 1982). Episcopalian. Avocations: flower gardening, knitting, reading. Home: 405 SW Cedar St Hillsboro OR 97123 Office: Oreg Grad Ctr 19600 NW Von Neumann Dr Beaverton OR 97006

ANDONOV, VIKTOR, engineer; b. Radovish, Macedonia, Yugoslavia, Apr. 12, 1932; came to U.S., 1965; s. Boris and Zorka (Kaleova) A.; m. Elsbeth Hansigk, May 25, 1968; children: Walter Boris, Brian. Diploma in Engring., Engring. Coll., Zagreb, Yugoslavia, 1950; student U. Belgrade, Yugoslavia, 1954-57; spl. courses in radiol. instrumentation and equipment U. Erlangen, 1959-65. Electromed. engr. Siemens A.G., Fed. Republic Germany, 1959-65, Siemens Corp., Union, N.J., 1965-69, Pitts., 1969-72, Glendale, Calif., 1972-73; sr. tech. rep. Siemens Med. Systems, Las Vegas, Nev., 1973—. Republican. Methodist. Home and office: 3929 Cedaredge Ct Las Vegas NV 89120

ANDRE, HARVIE, Canadian government official; b. Edmonton, Alta., Can., July 27, 1940; s. John and Doris (Ewasiuk) A.; m. Joan Roberta Smith, May 15, 1965; children—Coryn, Lauren, Peter Harvie. B.Sc., U. Alta., 1962; M.S., Calif. Inst. Tech., 1963; Ph.D., U. Alta., 1966. Assoc. prof. chem. engring. U. Calgary, 1966-72; mem. Ho. of Commons, Ottawa, Ont., Can., 1972—, minister of supply and services, 1984, assoc. minister nat. defense, 1985, minister consumer and corporate affairs, 1986—; sworn to Queen's Privy Council, 1984. Past bd. dirs. Clifford E. Lee Found.; past v.p. Social Planning Council Calgary. Mem. Chem. Inst. Can. (chmn. Calgary sect. 1970). Mem. United Church. Clubs: Calgary Petroleum, Calgary Commerce. Avocations: gardening, politics, golf. Office: House of Commons, Confederation Bldg Rm 558, Ottawa, ON Canada K1A OA6

ANDREEN, BRIAN H., research foundation administrator; b. Superior, Wis., Aug. 15, 1934; s. Earl Herbert and Esther Elizabeth (Hawkins) A.; m. Jacqueline Ramona Johnson, June 15, 1956; children: Karin Lynn, Laurie Beth, Carole Ann, Eric Brian. BS, U. Wis., Superior, 1956; MS, Fla. State U., 1959. Assoc. chemist IGT Co., Chgo., 1959-60, research chemist, 1961-62, supr. chem. research, 1962-64; rep. midwest Research Corp., Chgo., 1964-69; midwest regional dir. Research Corp., Tucson/Mpls., 1969—, grant dir., 1986—; exec. sec. Council Undergrad. Research, Tucson, 1978—; chmn. Seaver Sci. com., Pomona Coll., Claremont, Calif., 1985—; bd. visitors U. N.C., Ashville, 1986—. Editor: Research in Chemistry at Private Undergraduate Colleges., 1979, 3d rev. edit., 1985, Research in Physics and Astronomy at Undergraduate Institutions, 1986. Fellow AAAS; mem. Am. Chem. Soc. Office: Research Corp 6840 E Broadway Blvd Tucson AZ 85710

ANDREN, SHEILA JOY, cultural association administrator; b. Cody, Wyo., Apr. 26, 1942; d. Earl James and Jacque LaVerne (Ridley) Corder; m. Robert Laurence Andren, Apr. 9, 1961 (div. Aug. 1975); children: Mark Laurence, Scott Jason, Aimee Christine; m. Frederick Robert vonPingel, Aug. 1986. Student, Mont. State U., 1960, Eastern Mont. Coll., 1972-75. Prodn. copy writer Sta. KGHL, Billings, Mont., 1975-76; media buyer, copywriter, acct. exec. West Advt. Sta. KOA-TV, Billings, 1976-77; acct. exec. Sage Advt., Billings, 1980-81; with mktg. dept. CTA Architects-Engrs., Billings, 1981-82; with pub. relations, advt. and mktg. dept. Buffalo Bill Hist. Ctr., Cody, 1983-86; interim dir. pub. relations Colo. Springs (Colo.) Fine Arts Ctr., 1986-87. Mem. task force on Tourism Wyo. Futures Council. Mem. Pub. Relations Soc. Am. (cert.), C. of C. Conv. and Visitors Com., Nat. Tour Assn., Travel Industry Assn. Am. (edn. com. Nat. Council Travel Attractions 1985), Yellowstone Teton Travel Assn. (bd. dirs. 1985-86). Episcopalian. Avocations: sports, art, horseback riding, hiking, crafts. Office: Buffalo Bill Hist Ctr 720 Sheridan Ave Cody WY 82414

ANDREOPOULOS, SPYROS GEORGE, writer; b. Athens, Greece, Feb. 12, 1929; s. George S. and Anne Levas) A.; came to U.S., 1953, naturalized, 1962; A.B., Wichita State U., 1957; m. Christiane Loesch Loriaux, June 6, 1958; 1 dau., Sophie. Pub. info. specialist USIA, Salonica, Greece, 1951-53; asst. editorial page editor Wichita (Kans.) Beacon, 1955-59; asst. dir. info. services, editor The Menninger Quar., The Menninger Found., Topeka, 1959-63; info. officer Stanford U. Med. Ctr., 1963-83, dir. communications and editor Stanford Medicine, 1983—; editor Sun Valley Forum on Nat. Health, Inc. (Idaho), 1972-83, 85—. Served with Royal Hellenic Air Force, 1949-50. Mem. AAAS, Assn. Am. Med. Colls., Nat. Assn. Sci. Writers, Am. Med. Writers Assn., Am. Hosp. Assn., Am. Soc. Hosp. Pub. Relations, Council for Advancement Edn. Co-author, editor: Medical Cure and Medical Care, 1972; Primary Care: Where Medicine Fails, 1974; National Health Insurance: Can We Learn from Canada? 1975; Heart Beat, 1978. Contbr. articles to profl. jours. Home: 1012 Vernier Pl Stanford CA 94305

ANDRESHAK, JOHN LEO, research chemist; b. Joliet, Ill., Mar. 3, 1961; s. Leon and Angela (DeSandre) A. BS in Chemistry, USAF Acad., 1983. Commd. capt. USAF, Edwards AFB, Calif., 1983—; research chemist Air Force Rocket Propulsion Lab., Edwards AFB, Calif., 1983-85, sr. research chemist, 1985—. Mem. Am. Chem. Soc. (div. organic chemistry). Avocation: sports. Office: Air Force Rocket Propulsion Lab LKLR Stop 24 Edwards AFB CA 93523

ANDRESS, VERN RANDOLPH, psychologist, marriage and family therapist; b. Boulder, Colo., Mar. 29, 1935; s. Victor William and Frances Willette (Boyer) A.; children: Vivian Monica, Kimberley Dawn; m. Linda Kathleen Delgardo, Nov. 29, 1986. A.A., Southwestern Coll., Chula Vista, Calif., 1967; B.A., San Diego State Coll., 1969; M.S., San Diego State U., 1971; Ph.D., U.S. Internat. U., 1976. Pres. Beauty Boutique, Inc., San Diego, 1961-67; counselor San Diego Acad., 1969-70; dir. adminstrn. of justice Loma Linda U., Riverside, Calif., 1970-80, asst. prof. psychology, 1972-76, assoc. prof., 1976-79, prof., 1979—, chmn. dept. psychology, 1977-80, dean Coll. Arts and Sci., 1980-84; psychologist Riverside County Coroner's Office, 1976—; cons. psychology to law enforcement and industry, 1970—. Contbr. numerous articles to profl. jours., popular publs.; editor: Jour. Adventist Behavioral Scientists, 1974-79. Mem. Grand Terrace Planning Commn., Calif., 1978-86. Served with U.S. Army, 1954-56, France. Named Disting. Researcher Inland Counties Psychol. Assn., 1980; recipient Disting. Service award Calif. Sex Crimes Investigators, 1983. Mem. Am. Assn. Suicidology, Am. Psychol. Assn., Calif. State Psychol. Assn., Calif. Assn. Marriage and Family Therapists, Am. Orchid Soc., John Steinbeck Soc., Sigma Xi. Adventist. Office: Loma Linda U 4700 Pierce St Riverside CA 92515

ANDREW, JANE HAYES, ballet company executive; b. Phila., Jan. 1, 1947; d. David Powell and Vivian Muriel (Saeger) Hayes; m. Brian David Andrew, June 14, 1977; 1 child, Kevin Hayes. AB, Barnard Coll., 1968. Theatre mgr. Minor Latham Playhouse, Barnard Coll., N.Y.C., 1970-74; co. mgr. Houston Ballet, 1974-77, Ballet West, Salt Lake City, 1978-83; gen. mgr. Pacific N.W. Ballet, Seattle, 1983—; panelist NEA Dance Program.Presentors, 1987—; cons. Ariz. Arts Commn., Phoenix, 1985-86; com. mem. 25th Anniversary of World's Fair, Seattle, 1986-87. Editor (directory) Philadelphia Cultural Organizations, 1977. Bd. dirs. Good Shepherd Adv. Bd., Seattle, 1985—. Recipient Dorothy D. Spivack award Barnard Coll., N.Y.C., 1972. Mem. Dance/USA (chmn. Mgrs. Council 1986—). Democrat. Office: Pacific Northwest Ballet 4649 Sunnyside Ave N Seattle WA 98103

ANDREW, JOHN HENRY, lawyer, retail corporation executive; b. Duluth, Minn., May 23, 1936; s. Frederick William and Florence Elizabeth (Phillips) A.; m. Floretta Claudette Townsend; children—Sean Townsend, Brett Townsend. B.A. cum laude with distinction, U. Minn., Duluth, 1958; J.D., Northwestern U., 1961. Bar: Ill. 1961, Calif. 1975, N.Y. 1980. Assoc., Pattishall, McAuliffe & Hofstetter, Chgo., 1961-71; sr. atty. J.C. Penney Co., Inc., N.Y.C., 1971-74, gen. atty., Western regional counsel, Los Angeles, 1974—. Chmn. pub. affairs com. Planned Parenthood Assn. of Chgo., 1970-71; mem. Calif. State Democratic Central Com., 1976-82. Mem. ABA, Ill. State Bar Assn. (chmn. internat. law sect. 1969-70), Calif. State Bar (com. on consumer fin. services 1982-84), Royal Instn. Cornwall, Am. Philatelic Soc., Calif. C. of C. (regulatory, consumer and legal affairs com. 1974—). Home:

5930 S LaCienega Blvd Los Angeles CA 90056 Office: JC Penney Co Inc 350 S Figueroa St Suite 257 Los Angeles CA 90071

ANDREW, LUCIUS ARCHIBALD DAVID, III, business executive; b. Highland Park, Ill., Mar. 5, 1938; s. Lucius Archibald David Jr. and Victoria (Rollins) A.; m. Susan Ott, June 1, 1963 (div. 1973); children—Ashley W., L.A. David IV; m. Phoebe Haffner Kellogg, Dec. 21, 1974; children—Gaylord M., Charles H., Matthew K., Louise M. Kellogg. B.S., U. Pa., 1962; M.B.A., NYU, 1965. Asst. treas. The Bank of N.Y., N.Y.C., 1962-68; instl. salesman Drexel, Harriman, Ripley, N.Y.C., 1968-70; v.p., br. mgr. Drexel, Firestone, Inc., Chgo., 1970-72; ptnr., br. mgr. Fahnestock & Co., Chgo., 1972-74; vice chmn. Viner's, Ltd., Sheffield, Eng., 1981-82; pres. N.E.A., Inc., 1975-85; chmn. exec. com. Cert. Mfg. Co., Shelton, Wash., 1975-85; bddirs. First Am. Bank, Skokie, Ill., 1965—, chmn., 1982—; dir. First Am. Bank Corp., 1985—, First Am. Data Corp., 1982—; chmn. FGI, Inc., Forest Grove, Oreg., 1985—, Union St. Capital Corp., Seattle, Wash., 1986—. Trustee Brooks Sch. Past trustee Seattle Repertory Theatre. Clubs: The Brook, Racquet and Tennis (N.Y.C.); Racquet (Chgo.); Rainier, University, Golf, Tennis. Home: The Highlands Seattle WA 98177 Office: 1001 Fourth Ave Plaza Suite 3020 Seattle WA 98154

ANDREW, ROBERT LYNAL, Canadian provincial official; b. Eston, Sask., Can., Apr. 13, 1944; s. Robert Elvin and Elizabeth Ann (Ellis) A.; m. N. Lynne Tunall, Dec. 22, 1964; children—Quinn, Kalen, Sharmen, Dreeson. B.A., U. Sask., 1966, LL.B., 1970. Bar: Sask. With supply and transp. dept. Pacific Petroleums, Calgary, Alta., Can., 1967-68; programmer IBM, Saskatoon, 1968; with personnel dept. Allan Potash Mine, 1969-70; mem. Andrew, Ritter, Chinn, Kindersley, Sask., 1970-80, sr. ptnr., 1973-80; minister of fin., chmn. Treasury Bd., Govt. of Sask., Regina, 1982-85; vice chmn. Crown Mgmt. Bd., 1983-86, mem., 1986—; atty. gen. Minister of Justice, 1986—; minister Econ. Devel. and Trade, 1985—. Mem. Eston Town Council, 1972-74. Progressive Conservative. Contbr. articles to parliamentary jours. Office: Govt Sask, 355 Legislative Bldg, Regina, SK Canada S4S 0B3

ANDREWS, CLINTON TOMS, JR., small business owner, retired publishing company executive; b. Hickory, N.C., Apr. 29, 1933; s. Clinton Toms and Eugenia Faye (Rigsbee) A.; m. Susan Katharine Stoffel, Nov. 25, 1960; children—Christina, Faye, Clinton Toms, III, Paul Christian, Christopher Sherwood. B.A. in Journalism, U. N.C., 1955; M.B.A., U. Vt., 1972. News editor Pullman Herald, Wash., 1962-65; reporter Chronicle-Advertiser, Mansfield, Nottinghamshire, Eng., 1965-66; mng. editor Burlington Free Press, Vt., 1966-73, Anchorage Times, Alaska, 1973-80, Alaska Mag., 1980-82; editorial page editor Anchorage Times, 1982-85; owner Stems Inc., Anchorage, 1985—. Chmn. Mcpl. Arts Adv. Commn., Anchorage, 1981-82; sr. warden Christ Episcopal Ch., 1981-83, mem. U.S. Citizen Stamp Adv. Com. U.S. Postal Service, Washington, 1983—. Mem. Anchorage Philatelic Soc. (hon.). Republican. Lodge: Rotary (bd. dirs. 1982—). Home: PO Box 212 Anchorage AK 99510 Office: 530 E Benson Blvd Anchorage AK 99503

ANDREWS, DAVID FRANK, physician, researcher; b. Abbeville, S.C., May 15, 1951; s. David Frank and Mary Jane (Vail) A.; m. Rasa Elena Bobelis, Sept. 13, 1975. BA with honors, Emory U., 1973, MD, 1977. Diplomate Am. Bd. Internal Medicine. Intern Emory U. Hosps., Atlanta, 1977-78; resident La. State U. Med. Ctr., Shreveport, 1978-80; sr. fellow Fred Hutchinson Cancer Ctr., Seattle, 1984—; attending physician Seattle VA Med. Ctr., 1986—; instr. medicine U. Wash., Seattle, 1986—. Contbr. articles to sci. jours. Served to maj. USAF, 1980-84. Mem. AAAS, ACP, AMA (recipient Physician's Recognition award 1981, 83), N.Y. Acad. Scis., So. Med. Assn., Delta Phi Alpha, Phi Gamma Delta. Methodist. Avocations: photography, traveling, history. Home: 2502 Canterbury Ln E Apt 411 Seattle WA 98112

ANDREWS, ERIC EDWIN, construction inspector; b. Windsor, Colo., June 27, 1936; s. Nathan Edwin and Ellen Margaret (Samson) A.; m. Lura May Robertson, July 19, 1969. Distbn. engr. assoc. Los Angeles County Engrs., 1961-78; sr. constrn. inspector Theodore Barry and Assocs., Los Angeles, 1979-84, Dennis Lykins and Assocs., Los Angeles, 1984-85; quality control engr. Crown Contracting Inc., Lemon Grove, Calif., 1985—; tchr. uniform bldg. codes IUSD, Ingelwood, Calif., 1975-77. Served with USAF, 1953-57. Mem. Internat. Conf. Bldg. Officials (cert.), Nat. Rifle Assn., Am. Legion, VFW. Republican. Avocations: shooting, fishing, leatherwork. Home: 3260 W Ave L-2 Lancaster CA 93536

ANDREWS, J. DAVID, lawyer; b. Decatur, Ill., July 5, 1933; s. Jesse D. and Louise Glenna (Mason) A.; m. Helen Virginia Migely, July 12, 1958; children: Virginia, Robert, Michael, Betsy. B.A. magna cum laude, U. Ill., 1955, J.D., 1960. Bar: Wash. 1961. Partner firm Perkins Coie, Seattle, 1960—; Bd. dirs. Cornish Inst., Seattle, 1977-83, pres., 1981-83; bd. dirs. Am. Bar Endowment, 1981—, pres., 1985—; bd. visitors Law Sch., U. Puget Sound., 1976—; trustee AEF Pension Fund, 1975-79; bd. govs. Am. Bar, 1975-79; bd. dirs. Leukemia Soc. Washington, 1985—. Bd. dirs. Am. Bar Jour, 1975-79, Am. Bar Found., 1985—; contbr. articles to profl. jours. Served to capt. USAF, 1955-57. Fellow Am. Bar Found. (former treas.), Am. Coll. Trial Lawyers; mem. Am. Bar Assn. (ho. of dels. 1967-69, 75—, asst. treas. 1972-74, treas. 1975-79, bd. govs. 1975-79, fed. judiciary standing com.), Wash. Bar Assn. (chmn. pub. relations com. 1971-73), Seattle-King County Bar Assn., Am. Judicature Soc. (bd. dirs. 1985—), Phi Beta Kappa, Phi Kappa Phi, Phi Eta Sigma. Home: 1519 3d Ave Seattle WA 98101 Office: Perkins Cole 1900 Washington Bldg Seattle WA 98101

ANDREWS, JAMES WHITMORE, JR., theatre producer, director; b. New Haven, Sept. 30, 1950; s. James Whitmore Andrews and Nancy Lee (Peery) Levin; m. Sharon Gray Mills, Nov. 6, 1971; 1 child, Jesse Leigh. Student, U. N.C., 1968-71. Mng. dir. Homestead Arts Inc., Colorado Springs, Colo., 1970-73; mgr. Record Ctr. Inc., Colorado Springs, 1973-76; producing dir. Theatreworks, Colorado Springs, 1977—; bd. dirs. Shakespeare In The Park, Colorado Springs; founder, dir. Playwrights Forum awards, Colorado Springs, 1981—. Mem. Pike's Peak Arts Council, Colorado Springs, 1983—; mem. grant rev. panels Colo. Council on Arts and Humanities, 1987. Mem. Colo. Found. for the Arts, Colo. Citizens for the Arts, Am. Theatre Assn., Colo. Theatre Producer's Guild, Rocky Mountain Theatre Guild. Democrat. Avocations: travel, music. Home: 436 Franklin Colorado Springs CO 80903 Office: U Colo Austin Bluffs Pkwy Colorado Springs CO 80907

ANDREWS, LAUREL MARIE, economist; b. Seattle, Dec. 31, 1953; d. Arthur Francis and Grace Elizabeth (Moats) A. BA in Econs. summa cum laude, U. Wash., 1976; MA in Econs., UCLA, 1977. Economist Math. Scis. Northwest, Bellevue, Wash., 1979-80, city of Seattle, 1980-81, Seattle City Light, 1981-84; sr. economist Synergic Resources Corp., Seattle, 1984—. Author: Reference Manual of Data Sources for Load Forecasting, 1981. Mem. Internat. Assn. of Energy Economists, Seattle Economists Club., Salnonberry Contra Dance Soc. (sec. 1984—), Phi Beta Kappa. Democrat. Office: Synergic Resources Corp 1511 3rd Ave Suite 1018 Seattle WA 98101

ANDREWS, LAWRENCE JAMES, chemistry educator, academic administrator; b. San Diego, Sept. 27, 1920; s. Elmer James and Florence (Brown) A.; m. Elizabeth Merriam Heggelund, Apr. 24, 1944; children: Robin Elizabeth, Carol Jeanne. BS, U. Calif., Berkeley, 1940; MA, UCLA, 1941, PhD, 1943. Lectr. chemistry UCLA, 1943-44; chemist Tenn. Eastman Corp., Oak Ridge, 1944-45; instr. chemistry U. Calif., Davis, 1945-46, from asst. prof. to prof. chemistry, 1946—, dean, Coll. Letters and Sci., 1964-85. Co-author Organic Molecular Complexes, 1964; contbr. articles to profl. jours. Ford fellow, Harvard U., MIT, 1953-54, Fulbright, U. Hull, Eng., 1967-68. Mem. Am. Chem. Soc. (chmn. Sacramento sect. 1959), Phi Kappa Phi, Sigma Xi, Pi Mu Epsilon. Home: 350 W 8th St Davis CA 95616 Office: U Calif Dept Chemistry Davis CA 95616

ANDREWS, THOMAS EARL, accountant; b. Payson, Utah, Oct. 19, 1944; s. James Erva and Rita (Schofield) A.; m. Barbara J. Dover, May 24, 1968; children: Rita Carolin, Thomas E. BS, U. Utah, 1963; M in Acctg., Utah State U., 1975. CPA, Utah. Mgr. acctg. and systems design Orscheln Farm and Home Supply, Moberly, Mo., 1971-74; instr. Humphrey's Coll., Stockton, Calif., 1975-77, U. Pacific, Stockton, 1977; supervising sr. audit staff Fox and Co., Stockton, 1975-77; mng. ptnr. Roberts, Parker and Andrews, CPA's, Salt Lake City, 1977-81; ptnr. Andrews, Hymas and Co., CPA's, Salt Lake City, 1981-85; mng. ptnr. Andrews and Co., CPA's, Salt Lake City, Midvale and Nephi, Utah, 1985—; pres. SRI Co., Salt Lake City, 1980—, Cen. Utah Gas Co., 1983—; v.p. Style Realty, 1978—, Techna Industries, 1977—. Br. pres. Ch. Jesus Christ Latter-Day Sts., Key West, Fla., 1969-70. Served with USN, 1968-71, comdr. Res. Mem. Res. Officers Assn (Navy v.p. Utah 1980-81, 87—), Utah Assn. Pub. Accts. (mgmt. adv. services com.), Am. Inst. CPA's, Navy Res. Assn. Republican. Home: 7128 Pine Cone St Salt Lake City UT 84121 Office: 1200 Beneficial Life Tower 36 S State St Salt Lake City UT 84111 Office: 1275 E Ft Union Blvd #205 Midvale UT 84047 Office: 245 N Main St Nephi UT 84648

ANDROS, STEPHEN JOHN, architect; b. Joliet, Ill., July 21, 1955; s. Stephen Benedict and Jacquelyn M. (Schoob) A.; m. Vicki Lee McCaffery, June 24, 1978; children: Jeffrey Kenneth, Christopher John. BArch cum laude, Ariz. State U., 1978. Registered architect, Ariz. Project architect, specifier, contract adminstr. Cornoyer-Hedrick Architect and Planners Inc., Phoenix, 1978-83; ptnr. Perrell-Andros Cons. Architects, Scottsdale, Ariz., 1983-85; dir. specifications Haver, Nunn and Collamer Inc., Phoenix, 1985-86; dir. specifications and quality control Gilleland, Hunt, Rehse, Ltd. Architects, Phoenix, 1986—; instr. Phoenix Inst. Tech., 1983-84; guest lectr. materials Ariz. State U., Tempe, 1984; mem. ad hoc contracting com. City of Phoenix, 1982. Prin. works include Banking and Revenue Bldg. State of Ariz., Phoenix, F-16 Squadron Ops., Luke AFB, Ariz., Scottsdale (Ariz.) Horseman's Park, McDonnell-Douglas Helicopter Co. Mesa (Ariz.) Facility, Spl. Mgmt. Unit for Ariz. Dept. Corrections, By Design at Ghiradelli Sq., San Francisco, Desert Valley Med. Ctr., Phoenix, Anasazi Bus. Park, Phoenix, Papago High Sch. BIA, San Simeon, Ariz., Student Activities Ctr. No. Ariz. U., Flagstaff, Remodel of Terminal 2 Sky Harbor Internat. Airport, Phoenix, Tempe Minicomputer Maintenance Ops. Ctr., Cen. One Thomas High Rise, Phoenix, Valley Nat. Bank, Phoenix. Recipient Cert. Recognition Copper Devel. Assn., 1977. Mem. AIA (profl. Cen. Ariz. chpt.), Constrn. Specifications Inst. (profl. Phoenix chpt., moderator Pres.'s forum, 1985, leader cert. workshop S.W. region, 1986, rep. to Constrn. Industry Council Ariz., 1981-84, chmn. Phoenix chpt. program, 1979-80, sec. Phoenix chpt., 1980-81, 1st v.p. Phoenix chpt., 1981-82, pres. Phoenix chpt., 1982-83, 83-84, program chmn. S.W. region conf., 1985, mem. inst. cert. com., 1984—, chmn., 1986—, others), Specifications Cons. in Ind. Practice (corr., nat. v.p., 1984-85, editor newsletter, 1983-85). Republican. Methodist. Avocations: computers, hiking, camping, handbell ringing. Home: 7321 N 19th Dr Phoenix AZ 85021

ANDRUS, CECIL D., governor of Idaho; b. Hood River, Oreg., Aug. 25, 1931; s. Hal Stephen and Dorothy (Johnson) A.; m. Carol Mae May, Aug. 27, 1949; children: Tana Lee, Tracy Sue, Kelly Kay. Student, Oreg. State U., 1948-49; LLD (hon.), Gonzaga U., U. Idaho, U. N.Mex. State gen. mgr. Paul Revere Life Ins. Co., 1969-70; gov. State of Idaho, 1971-77, 87—; sec. of interior 1977-81; dir. Albertson's, Inc., 1985—; Mem. Idaho Senate, 1961-66, 69-70; Mem. exec. com. Nat. Gov.'s Conf., 1971-72, chmn., 1976; chmn. Fedn. Rocky Mountain States, 1971-72. Chmn. bd. trustees Coll. of Idaho, 1985—; bd. dirs. Sch. Forestry, Duke U. Served with USN, 1951-55. Recipient Disting. Citizen award Oreg. State U., 1980, Collier County Conservancy medal, 1979; named Conservationist of Yr., Nat. Wildlife Fedn., 1980, Idaho Wildlife Fedn., 1972, Man of Yr., VFW, 1959. Mem. V.F.W., Idaho Taxpayers Assn. (dir. 1964-66). Democrat. Home: 1805 N 21st Boise ID 83702 Office: Office of Gov State Capitol 2d Floor Boise ID 83720

ANDRUS, DAVID CLIFFORD, electrical engineer; b. Los Angeles, Feb. 27, 1953; s. Dale Clifford and Patricia Mae (Johnson) A.; m. Deborah Diane Carlson, Dec. 17, 1977; 1 child, David Clifford Jr. Student, Brigham Young U., 1974, Calif. State Poly. U., Pomona, 1975-77. Missionary Ch. Jesus Christ Latter-day Saints, São Paulo, Brazil, 1972-74; supr. electronic maintainence So. Calif. Rapid Transit, Los Angeles, 1975-82; project engr. Linear Corp., Carlsbad, Calif., 1982—; cons. Hofco Electronics, Culver City, Calif., 1984—, Knight Protective Industries, Encino, Calif., 1984—. Inventor low power transmitter stabilization, low radiation receiver. Scoutmaster Boy Scouts Am., Walnut, Calif., 1984. Republican. Avocations: hiking, computer construction and programming. Home: 1186 Drifting Circle Dr Vista CA 92083 Office: Linear Corp 2055 Corte Del Nogal Carlsbad CA 92008

ANEMA, DURLYNN CAROL, communications educator, author, journalist; b. San Diego, Dec. 23, 1935; d. Durlin L. and Carolyn L. Flagg; m. Charles J. Anema, Jan. 18, 1955; children: Charlynn Ann, Jay, Richard F. Student Stanford U., 1953-55, U. Calif.-Berkeley, 1955; B.A., Calif. State U.-Hayward, 1968, M.S., 1977; Ed.D., U. Pacific, 1984. Cert. adminstr., supv., Calif. Tchr. journalism, history San Leandro Sch. Dist., 1970-72; tchr. journalism Hayward (Calif.) Unified Sch. Dist., 1972-75, adminstr., 1975-77; adminstr. Lodi Unified Sch. Dist., 1977-80; research asst. U. Pacific, Stockton, Calif., 1980-81, dir. lifelong learning, 1981-84, asst. prof. communications, 1984—; cons. social studies, adult learning, 1982-85. Pres., PTA, San Leandro, 1961, 63, hon. life mem., 1966; pres. San Leandro Library Bd., 1974, commendation, 1974; bd. dirs. Valley Community Counseling Ctr., 1981—, pres. 1987—; youth leader Grace Presbyterian Ch., Lodi, 1982-84, elder, 1986—; bd. dirs. econ. edn. com. San Joaquin County, 1982-84; mem. exec. com. San Joaquin County Hosp. 125th Anniversary; bd. dirs. San Joaquin County Authors Symposium. Recipient commendations San Leandro City Council, 1974, 77. Mem. Nat. Council Social Studies, Calif. Council Social Studies, Calif. Council for Adult Edn. (exec. dir. 1984-85), Phi Kappa Phi, Coll. Media Advisers, Phi Delta Kappa, Delta Kappa Gamma. Author: Don't Get Fired, 1977; Get Hired, 1979; Sharing an Apartment, 1982; California Yesterday and Today, 1983; Designing Effective Brochures and Newsletters, 1986. Home: 1782 W Vine St Lodi CA 95240 Office: U Pacific Communications Dept Stockton CA 95211

ANFUSO, VICTOR L'EPISCOPO, lawyer, business consultant; b. Bklyn., Sept. 17, 1932; s. Victor L'Episcopo and Frances (Stallone) A.; m. Kathy Ann Shea, Apr. 8, 1967; children—Dina, Michelle, Victor T., William P., Adrienne. A.B. magna cum laude, St. John's U., 1954, J.D., 1959. Bar: N.Y. 1959, Oreg. 1986. Ptnr., Warner Birdsall & Anfuso, N.Y.C., 1959-62, Anfuso & Kroll, N.Y.C., 1965-69, Anfuso & Posmantur, N.Y.C., 1971-73; sole practice, N.Y.C., 1974-80; ptnr. Wildes Weinberg & Anfuso, N.Y.C., 1980-84; ch. adminstr. Bible Temple, Portland, Oreg., 1984-86; prin. Anfuso & Assocs., Portland, 1987—; sr. cons. Anfuso Cons., Yuba City, Calif., 1981-82. Contbr. articles to law jours. Pres., N.Y. State Young Citizens for Johnson, 1964; bd. dirs. World Rehab. Fund, 1972-78. Served to lt. USNR, 1955-57. Mem. N.Y. State Bar Assn., Assn. Immigration and Nationality Lawyers, Full Gospel Businessmen's Assn. Mem. Christian Ch. Home: 352 NE 78th Portland OR 97213 Office: Bible Temple 7600 NE Glisan Portland OR 97213

ANGEL, ARMANDO CARLOS, internist; b. Las Vegas, N.Mex., Mar. 25, 1940; s. Edmundo Clemente and Pauline Teresa (Flores) Sanchez A.; m. Judith Lee Weedin, Aug. 5, 1961; children—Stephanie, Renee. B.A., San Jose State U., 1963; M.S., U. Ariz., 1970, Ph.D., 1971, M.D., 1977. Chemist Tracerlab, Inc., Richmond, Calif., 1963-67; prof. chemistry Pima Coll., Tucson, Ariz., 1971-74; intern U. N.Mex., Albuquerque, 1977-78, resident, 1978-80; resident VA Hosp., Lovelace Med. Ctr., Albuquerque, 1978-80; practice medicine specializing in internal medicine, Las Cruces, N.Mex., 1980—; cons. minority biomed. sci. project NIH, Washington, 1970-74, Ednl. Assocs., Tucson, 1971-74. Author: Llevve Tlaloc No. 2, 1973. Treas. Nat. Chicano Health Orgn., Los Angeles, 1974-75; v.p. Mexican-Am. Educators, Tucson, 1973-74; pres. N.Mex. affiliate Am. Diabetes Assn., Albuquerque, 1983-85. Mem. AMA, Am. Diabetes Assn., ACP, Dona Ana County Med. Soc. (pres. 1983), Alpha Chi Sigma. Office: Dona Ana Med Group 2437 Telshor Ave Las Cruces NM 88005

ANGEL, JAMES ROGER PRIOR, astronomer; b. St. Helens, Eng., Feb. 7, 1941; came to U.S., 1967; s. James Lee and Joan (Prior) A.; m. Ellinor M. Goonan, Aug. 21, 1965; children—Jennifer, James. B.A., Oxford (Eng.) U., 1963, D.Phil., 1967; M.S., Calif. Inst. Tech., 1966. From research asso. to asso. prof. physics Columbia U., 1967-74; vis. asso. prof. astronomy U. Tex., Austin, 1974; mem. faculty U. Ariz., Tucson, 1974—; prof. astronomy U. Ariz., 1975—, prof. optical sci., 1984—. Sloan fellow, 1970-74. Mem. Am. Astron. Soc. (Pierce prize 1976, v.p. 1987—), Optical Soc. Am. Research on white dwarf stars, quasars, astron. instruments and telescopes. Office: Steward Obs Univ Ariz Tucson AZ 85721

ANGEL, PHYLLIS JEAN, financial executive; b. North Platte, Nebr., Aug. 10, 1947; d. Ralph Henry and Lucille (Bussell) Shinn; m. Lewis Worth Angel, Jan. 11, 1969 (div. 1975). A.A., North Eastern Jr. Coll., 1967; student cosmetology Mile Hi Beauty Sch., 1969. Office rep. Standard Quarter Horse Assn., Lakewood, Colo., 1967-69; info. operator Mountain Bell, Denver, 1967; sec. King Soopers Bakery, Denver, 1973, Prudential Ins. Co., Denver, 1973-76; owner/operator Phyl's Styling Salon, Sedalia, Colo., 1976-77; fin. adminstr. Martin Marietta, Denver, 1978—; cons. Self Images, Denver, 1973-79, Frisbie & Frisbie, Denver, 1973-80; owner A & B Enterprises, Denver, 1974-76; owner Shaklee Product Distbn., Denver, 1982—. Author: A Wolf Pup Was Born, 1983; Grandma, 1984; Wax Doll, 1984. Coach, Wagon Wheel Softball Team, Champion, Nebr., 1963-65; active Muscular Dystrophy Telethon, Littleton, Colo., 1974, Multiple Sclerosis Ride-A-Thon, Cheyenne, Wyo., 1975; sponsor Little League Baseball Team, Sedalia, 1976. Recipient Grand Cross of Colors, Rainbow Girls, 1965; Golden Poet award, 1985, Silver Poet award, 1986. Mem. Career Womens Assn., Internat. Platform Assn., Nat. Mus. Women in Arts Club: Square Dance. Methodist. Clubs: 4-H, Rodeo. Lodges: Order Eastern Star. Home: PO Box 620215 Littleton CO 80162

ANGELETTI, MARIA CLAIRE, lawyer; b. Shankill, Ireland, Dec. 10, 1937; came to U.S., 1969; d. William Francis and Mary Ethel (O'Rourke) Power; m. Varo Antonio Angeletti, Mar. 25, 1965; 1 child, Kevin. BA with honors, U. Coll., Dublin, Ireland, 1958; JD, Loyola U., Los Angeles, 1983. Bar: Calif. 1984. Paralegal MGM Studios, Culver City, Calif., 1970-84, assoc. counsel, 1984-86, sr. counsel, 1986-87; sr. counsel MGM/UA Communications Co., Beverly Hills, Calif., 1987—. Recipient Merito, Inst. Cen. di Statistica, Rome, 1959. Mem. Women Lawyers of Los Angeles, Calif. Bar Assn. (corp. sect.). Roman Catholic. Avocations: horseback riding, body surfing. Office: MGM/UA Communications Co 450 N Roxbury Dr Beverly Hills CA 90210

ANGELOFF, DANN V., investment banker; b. Hollywood, Calif., Nov. 15, 1935; married; 3 children. BS in Fin., U. So. Calif., 1958, MBA, 1963. Trainee Dean Witter & Co., Inc., Los Angeles, 1957-60; v.p. Dempsey-Tegeler & Co., Inc., Los Angeles, 1960-70; v.p., bd. dirs. West Coast corp. fin. dept. Reynolds Securities, Inc., 1970-76; pres., bd. dirs. The Angeloff Co., Los Angeles, 1976—; bd. dirs., corp. fin. adv. Bobby McGee's U.S.A., Inc., Phoenix; bd. dirs. Core Mgmt. Co., Los Angeles, Storage Equities, Pasadena, Calif., Marine Nat. Bank, Irvine, Calif., Evalucom, Beverly Hills, Calif., KDI Corp., Cin. Bd. dirs. Trojan Club, 1969-73, pres. jr. bd.; bd. dirs. Nicholas-Applegate Growth Fund, San Diego, Royce Med. Co., Culver City, Calif.; membership chmn. U. So. Calif. Assocs., 1973—; bd. govs., trustee U. So. Calif., 1979-86; mem. Los Angeles Olympic Citizens Adv. Commn. Mem. Bond Club Los Angeles, Gen. Alumni Assn. U. So. Calif. (pres.), Commerce Assocs. U. So. Calif., Skull and Dagger, Cardinal and Gold, Kappa Beta Phi. Clubs: California, Jonathan, Pacific. Office: Angeloff Co 727 W 7th St Los Angeles CA 90017

ANGIER, KEITH A(LAN), former state official; b. Morris, Minn., Mar. 29, 1934; s. Roland S. and Edythe B. (Landes) A.; m. Joan Kay Foehlinger, Apr. 18, 1954; children—Kent, Tom, Megan. B.A., Drake U., 1957; M.P.A., Ind. U., 1967. Intelligence officer CIA, Washington, 1957-69; dir. data processing State of Alaska, Juneau, 1969-71; adminstr. U. Wash., Seattle, 1971-73; v.p. adminstrn. Crowley Maritime Corp., Seattle, 1977-78; pres., owner Pacific Commerce Co., Mercer Island, Wash., 1978-81; dir. Applied Audio Video, Tacoma, 1978-81; dir. Dept. Gen. Adminstrn., State of Wash., Olympia, 1973-77, 81-85; assoc. Pacific Inst., Seattle, 1985—; mem. exec. com. Wash. Corrections Standards Bd., Olympia, 1981-84, Wash. Data Processing Authority, Olympia, 1981-84; chmn. State Supply Mgmt. Adv. Bd., Olympia, 1981-84. Co-chmn. Wash. State/City of Olympia Commn., 1984; mem. exec. com. Olympia Regional/Urban Design Assistance Team, 1981-83; bd. dirs. Olympia Downtown Devel. Corp., 1984; state govt. coordinator United Way, Olympia, 1983-84; bd. dirs. United Way Thurston County, 1984—. Fellow Nat. Inst. for Pub. Affairs, Washington, 1967. Republican. Presbyterian. Office: Pacific Inst 1201 Western Ave Seattle WA 98101

ANGLEA, RALPH MAYHEW, savings and loan exec.; b. Pueblo, Colo., May 14, 1921; s. William P. and Ethel S. (Mayhew) A.; student So. Colo. State U., 1938-40, Denver U., 1940; Asso. Engring., U. Calif., Berkeley, 1950; postgrad. UCLA, 1970-71; m. Harriette Hopkins, June 30, 1943; children—Robert R., Carolyn Anglea Henderson. Air traffic controller FAA, 1941-55, supr., chief controller, 1956-58, staff air traffic control procedures, ops. and evaluation Los Angeles, 1959-61, spl. projects coordinator nat. and western region, 1962-77; sr. v.p., mng. assoc. State Savs. & Loan, Encino, Calif., 1978-84. Mem. Los Angeles World Affairs Council, 1979-87. Recipient Superior and Outstanding awards FAA, 1958-76; named Most Outstanding Account Exec., State Savs. & Loan, 1979. Mem. AIAA, Air Traffic Control Assn., Am. Ordinance Assn. Methodist. Clubs: Lions, Nat. Rocket, Cal Tech Assocs.

ANGLIN, NOAH LEE, electronics company executive; b. Frankfort, Ky., July 4, 1938; s. Noah L. and Olivia L. (Sheets) A.; m. Mary F. Markley, Oct. 2, 1962; children: Julie Ann, Steven Mark. BSME, U. Ky., 1965. Dir. engring. Memorex, Corp., Santa Clara, Calif., 1974-76; v.p. engring. and mfg. Atari, Inc., Sunnyvale, Calif., 1976-81; pres. Exidy, Inc., Sunnyvale, 1981-82; pres., chief exec. officer Simutrek, Inc., San Jose, Calif., 1982-85; v.p. engring. Greyhawk Systems, Milpitas, Calif., 1986—. Patentee in field. Republican. Avocations: antique and sports cars, golfing. Home: 11100 Enchanto Vista San Jose CA 95127 Office: Greyhawk Systems 1601 Centre Pointe Milpitas CA 95127

ANGLIN, RICHARD LEE, JR., lawyer; b. Herrin, Ill., July 31, 1945; s. Richard Lee and Helen (Yanulavich) A. BSCE, Case Inst. Tech., 1967; M in Regional Planning, Cornell U., 1969; JD, Loyola U., Los Angeles, 1981. Bar: Calif. 1981, D.C. 1982, U.S. Supreme Ct. 1985. Sole practice Calif. Office: 8601 Falmouth Ave #309 PO Box 5415 Playa Del Rey CA 90296

ANGUS, ROSALIE JOANN, social worker, educator; b. Garretson, S.D., Apr. 18, 1939; d. Joseph Einer and Evelene Margaret (Sittig) Erickson; m. Robert Leigh Angus, Aug. 29, 1965; children: Leigh James, Phillip John. BA, Augustana Coll., Sioux Falls, S.D., 1963, Colo. State U., 1982; MSW, Denver U., 1984. Cert. tchr. Tchr. pub. schs. Madison, Wis., 1963-69; homebound tchr. pub. schs. Longmont, Colo., 1969—; parent aide coordinator Boulder County Social Services, Longmont, 1975-76, state unemployment ins. rep., 1976-78, eligibility technician, 1978-80, social worker, 1980—; social worker Luth. Social Services, Longmont, 1985-86; with resource personnel dept. Augsburg Pub. Co., 1986—; parent aide coordinator Boulder County Social Services, Longmont, 1975-76. Mem. St. Vrain community council, Longmont, 1974—; vol. coordinator 1st Luth. Ch., Longmont, 1976; vice chmn. Longmont Interfaith Team, 1985—; vol. hospice tng., 1985—; lay worker Evang. Luth. Ch. Am., 1987—. Mem. Nat. Assn. Social Workers, AAUW (edn. chmn. 1986—). Democrat. Club: Longmont Newcomers (publicity com. 1969-71). Avocations: reading, hiking, cooking, piano. Home: 2142 Wright Ct Longmont CO 80501 Office: Boulder County Social Services 529 Coffman Longmont CO 80501

ANGWIN, JEFFREY ROBERT, engineering manager; b. Palo Alto, Calif., Apr. 3, 1955; s. Robert Raymond and Pamela Louise (Nickerson) A. BSEE, Stanford U., 1977. Project engr. Telesensory Systems Co., Palo Alto, 1974-80; design engr. Fairchild Test Systems, Billerica, Mass., 1980-82; product engr. Nat. Semiconductor Corp., Santa Clara, Calif., 1982-83; sr. applications engr. Test div. Marconi Instruments, Sunnyvale, Calif., 1983; engring. mgr. Automatic Test div. Marconi Instruments, Sunnyvale, Calif., 1983—. Contbr. articles to profl. jours. Mem. IEEE, Am. Soc. Test Engrs. Home: 2138 Avenida Flores Santa Clara CA 95050 Office: Marconi ATE 292 Gibraltar Dr A-2 Sunnyvale CA 94089

ANKLAM, JAMES RICHARD, pipe manufacturing and sales company sales executive, geophysical engineer, mining engineer, exploitation engineer; b. Tucson, July 26, 1933; s. Joseph Ralph and Jessie (Paddock) A.; m.

Markie Katrine Barker, June 18, 1933; children—Deborah Anklam Benedict, James Lawrence, Mark Richard. B.S. in Mining Engring. and Geology with high distinction, U. Ariz., 1955. Exploration engr. Shell Oil Co., Calif., Tex., Utah, N.Mex. and Wyo., 1955-58; sales rep. Johns-Manville, Scottsdale, Ariz., 1958-65, area mgr., western states, San Francisco, 1965-68, dist. mgr., western U.S., San Mateo, Calif., 1969-85; v.p., gen. mgr., co-owner Pipeline Materials Inc. of Tuscon, 1985—; mem. statewide water resources com. and legis. subcom. Calif. C. of C. Deacon, Community Presbyn. Ch., Danville, Calif., 1970-73, bd. moderator, 1973, elder, 1974-77, 81-84; co-founder troop Mt. Diablo council Boy Scouts Am., 1971, active council, 1971-83; coach Little League, Danville, Catholic Youth Basketball, Danville; invitational cross country and track ofcl., 50 schs., 1972-83. Named Outstanding Young Men Am., U.S. Jr. C. of C., 1965; recipient Dir.'s award U. Ariz., 1970, Service award Boy Scouts Am., 1980; Baird scholar, 1951-55. Mem. Nat. Utility Contractors Am. (bd. dirs. Tucson chpt. 1987—), Am. Soc. Testing Materials (taskforce chmn. 1983-85), Am. Waterworks Assn., Nat. Assn. Corrosion Engrs., Ariz. Alumni Assn. (dir.), Tucson C. of C. (local govt. com. 1985—), Tau Beta Pi, Theta Tau, Phi Kappa Phi, Phi Gamma Delta. Republican. Clubs: Toastmasters (pres. club 1963-64, area gov. 1965); Elks (Phoenix). Home: 4906 E Oakmont Dr Tucson AZ 85718

ANNESTRAND, STIG ALVAR, electrical engineer; b. Husby, Sweden, Sept. 18, 1933; came to U.S., 1967, naturalized, 1972; s. August Erik and Frida Linnea (Carlsson) Johansson; m. Britta Viviann Olsson, June 28, 1958; children: Peter N., Thomas A. MS, Royal Inst. Tech., Stockholm, 1958. Registered profl. engr., Oreg. Lab. engr. Almanna Svenska Elektriska Aktiebolaget, elec. equipment mfg. co., Ludvika, Sweden, 1958-61, mgr. research, 1962-67; tchr. Tech. High Sch., Borlange, Sweden, 1961-62; elec. engr. Bonneville Power Adminstrn., Dept. Interior, Portland, Oreg., 1967, head high voltage unit, 1967-74; head elec. investigations sect. Bonneville Power Adminstrn., Dept. Interior, Vancouver, Wash., 1974-77; chief br. labs. Bonneville Power Adminstrn., Dept. Energy, Portland, 1977-81, mgr. research and devel., 1981-85; Congl. fellow U.S. Congress, 1986; mgr. research and devel. Dept. Energy Bonneville Power Adminstrn., Portland, 1987—. Author: Standard Handbook for Electrical Engineers, 11th edit., 1978, The Encyclopedia of Physical Science and Technology, 1st edit., 1987; contbr. articles to profl. jours. Scoutmaster Boy Scouts Am., Lake Oswego, Oreg. 1971-77. Served to capt. Swedish Army, 1953-54. Fellow IEEE (sr. active various coms.; 1st prize Portland sect. 1970); mem. Am. Nat. Standards Inst. (chmn. subcom. on contamination 1969-75), Internat. Conf. Large High Tension Electric Systems. Democrat. Lutheran. Club: Toastmasters (pres. 1973). Avocation: photography. Home: 5392 SW Tree St Lake Oswego OR 97034 Office: PO Box 3621 Portland OR 97208

ANSBACHER, CHARLES ALEXANDER, conductor, musician; b. Providence, Oct. 5, 1942; s. Heinz L. and Rowena (Ripin) A.; m. Swanee Hunt, 1986; 1 son, Henry Lloyd. B.A., Brown U., 1965; M.Music, U. Cin., 1968, D.M.A., 1979. nat. adv. bd. Avery Fisher awards music, 1974—; mem. Colo. State Festival Council for Centennial-Bicentennial Commn., 1974-76; chmn. White House Fellows Regional Selection Com. Asst. condr., Kingsport (Tenn.) Symphony Orch., 1965-66, condr., mus. dir., Middletown (Ohio) Symphony Orch., 1967-70, Colorado Springs Symphony Orch., 1970-89 , condr. laureate, Colorado Springs Symphony Orch., 1989—, music dir., Rockefeller Found., Apprentice Musicians Program, Cin. Playhouse in Park, 1967, guest condr., Cin. Symphony Orch., Denver Symphony Orch., Frysk Orkest in Leeuwarden, Holland, Indpls. Symphony, Omaha Symphony, Ft. Worth Symphony, San Jose Symphony, Seoul Philharm., Young Musicians Symphony Orch. of London, 1985; condr., music dir., Young Artists Orch. Denver, 1980-84. White House fellow, 1976-77. Mem. Urban League Pike's Peak Region (treas.), Pike's Peak Musicians Assn. (v.p. 1974-76), Condrs. Guild of Am. Symphony Orch. League (chmn. 1979-81, pres. 1986—), Am. Symphony Orch. League (dir. 1979-81), Colo. Council Arts and Humanities (1978-84, chmn. 1987—), Colo. Pub. Edn. Partnership (1984—), Pub. Edn. Coalition of the Pikes Peak Region (co-pres. 1984—), Music Educators Nat. Conf., World Affairs Council Colorado Springs (pres. 1980-84, chmn. design constrn. subcom.), Pikes Peak Ctr. (founding bd. mem. charter fund), Conr.'s Guild, Inc. (pres. 1986—), Pub. Edn. Coalition Pikes Peak Region (bd. dirs. Colo. pub. edn. partnership, co-pres. 1985-86, chmn. design and constrn. subcom. Pikes Peak Ctr., founding bd. mem. charter fund). Clubs: Rotary, El Paso. Office: Colorado Springs Symphony Box 1692 Colorado Springs CO 80901

ANSCHUTZ, PHILLIP F., diversified company executive; b. 1939. B.S., Univ. Kansas, 1961. Chmn., pres. Anschutz Corp., Denver, 1965—, also dir. Office: Anschutz Corp 555 17th St Suite 2400 Denver CO 80202 *

ANSELL, GEORGE STEPHEN, metallurgy educator; b. Akron, Ohio, Apr. 1, 1934; s. Frederick Jesse and Fanny (Soletsky) A.; m. Marjorie Boris, Dec. 18, 1960; children: Frederick, Laura, Benjamin. B in Metall. Engring., Rensselaer Poly. Inst., 1954, M in Metall. Engring., 1955, PhD, 1960. Physcial metallurgist USN Research Lab., Washington, 1957-58; mem. faculty Rensselaer Poly. Inst., Troy, N.Y., 1960-84, Robert W. Hunt prof., 1965-84, chmn. materials div., 1969-74, dean engring., 1974-84; pres. Colo. Sch. Mines, Golden, 1984—. Editor books; patentee in field; contbr. articles to profl. jours. Served with USN, 1955-58. Recipient Hardy Gold Medal AIME, 1961, Curtis W. McGraw award Am. Soc. Engring. Edn., 1971. Fellow Metall. Soc. (pres. 1986-87), Am. Soc. Metals (Bradley Stoughton award 1968); mem. NSPE, Sigma Xi, Tau Beta Pi, Phi Lambda Upsilon. Office: Colo Sch of Mines Office of the President Golden CO 80401 *

ANSELMI, RUDOLPH RUDY, construction company executive; b. Rock Springs, Wyo., May 1, 1904; s. Joseph A. and Mary (Menghini) A.; B.S., U. Wyo., 1925, LL.D. (hon.), 1977; m. Shuster, July 10, 1929; children—Mary Lou Anselmi Unguren, Lynn Anselmi Lockhart, Jerl Anselmi Kirk. Pres., mgr. Miners Merc. Co., Rock Springs, 1931-65; exec. v.p. Cheyenne Service Corp., 1973-75; sec.-treas. HMA Realty, KOA Kampgrounds, Rock Springs; dir. North Side State Bank, Wyo., Cheyenne Fed. Savs. & Loan Assn.; sec. Huntley Constrn. Co., Rock Springs. Chmn. exec. com. Wyo. Cancer Soc., 1970-72. Mem. Sch. Bd., Rock Springs, 1936-65, pres., 1942-65; mem. Wyo. Senate, 1937-65; mem. Gov.'s Com. on Edn., 1963-64, Gov.'s Re-orgn. Com., 1967-68, 69-71; state committeeman Democratic party, 1944-66; mem. Legislative Interim Com., 1945-65; chmn. Wyo. Tax Commn. and State Bd. Equalization, 1975-87; mem. Wyo. state treas. investment adv. com., 1973-75. Named Distinguished Alumnus, U. Wyo. Coll. Commerce and Industry, 1961-62, Disting. Alumnus, U. Wyo., 1984; recipient Disting. Service award Nat. Govs. Assn., 1980. Mem. Sigma Chi, Phi Kappa Phi. Roman Catholic. Clubs: Elks, Eagles; K.C. (past grand knight); Vocations (pres.), Lions (past pres.) (Rock Springs). Home: 2608 House Cheyenne WY 82001 Office: Herschler Bldg 125 W 25th St Cheyenne WY 82001

ANSLEY, BETTY JOANNE, public health program manager, nurse; b. Kaufman, Tex., May 19, 1938; d. Thurman Monroe and Daisy Evelyn (Anderson) Dixson. BS, Loma Linda U., 1961. RN, Calif. Head nurse Loma Linda (Calif.) U. Hosp., 1961-64; pub. health nurse San Bernardino (Calif.) Pub. Health Dept., 1965-69, sr. pub. health nurse, 1969-80, pub. health nurse dist. mgr., 1980-83, program mgr., 1984—. Mem. Inland Counties Hypertension Control Coordinating Council of Health Systems Agy. Mem. Am. Pub. Health Assn., So. Calif. Pub. Health Assn. (sec. Inland Counties chpt. 1977-78), Am. Diabetes Assn. Republican. Club: Altrusa (Upland, Calif.) (sec. 1972-73). Office: San Bernardino County Pub Health 320 E D St Ontario CA 91764

ANSON, FRED COLVIG, chemistry educator; b. Los Angeles, Feb. 17, 1933; m. Roxana Anson; children: Alison, Eric. BS, Calif. Inst. Tech., 1954; MS, Harvard U., 1955, PhD, 1957. Instr. chemistry Calif. Inst. Tech., Pasadena, 1957-58, asst. prof., 1958-62, assoc. prof., 1962-68, prof. chemistry, 1968—, chmn. div. chemistry and chem. engr., 1984—. Contbr. numerous articles to profl. jours. Fellow J.S. Guggenheim Found. U. Brussels, 1964, Alfred P. Sloan Found., 1965-69; scholar Fulbright-Hays Found. U. Florence, Italy, 1972, A. von Humboldt Found. Fritz Haber Inst., Berlin, 1984-86. Mem. AAAS, Am. Chem. Soc., Am. Electrochem. Soc., Internat. Soc. Electrochemistry, Soc. Electroanalytical Chemistry, Tau Beta Pi. Home: Altadena CA 91001 Office: Calif Inst Tech Div Chemistry MS 127-72 Pasadena CA 91125

ANSPAUGH, LYNN RICHARD, research biophysicist; b. Rawlins, Wyo., May 25, 1937; s. Solon Earl and Alice Henrietta (Day) A.; m. Barbara Anne Corrigan, Nov. 2, 1965; children: Gregory, Heidi. BA, Nebr. Wesleyan U., 1959; M in Bioradiology, U. Calif., Berkeley, 1961, PhD, 1963. Biophysicist Lawrence Livermore (Calif.) Nat. Lab., 1963-74, group leader, 1974-75, sect. leader, 1976-82, div. leader, 1982—; tchr. extension U. Calif., Berkeley, 1966-69; lectr. San Jose (Calif.) State U., 1975; faculty affiliate Colo. State U., Ft. Collins, 1979-83; cons. EPA, Washington, 1984-85, U. Utah, Salt Lake City, 1983—; mem. U.S. del. UN Sci. Com. on Effects of Atomic Radiation, Vienna, 1987—. Contbr. articles to profl. jours. Mem. task group Nat. Council on Radiation Protection and Measurements, Bethesda, Md., 1985—. AEC fellow, 1959-61; fellow NSF, 1961-63. Mem. AAAS, Health Physics Soc. (pres. environ. radiation sect. 1984-85, pres. No. Calif. chpt. 1986-87), Soc. for Risk Analysis, Sigma Xi. Republican. Mem. Evangelical Free Ch. Club: Mt. Diablo Dog Tng. (Walnut Creek) (pres. 1960). Home: 2342 Brantford Ct Walnut Creek CA 94596 Office: Lawrence Livermore Nat Lab 7000 East Ave Livermore CA 94550

ANSUINI, PAT, SR., building contractor; b. La Prada, Italy, Jan. 17, 1946; s. Dominico and Guilia (Armillei) A.; m. Joann Hall, 1964 (div. 1967); 1 child, Pat. Jr.; m. Jane A. Johnston, Nov. 9, 1969 (div. Oct. 1973); 1 child, Thomas James (dec.); m. Pat. A. Jones, May 2, 1975; children: Marc. A. Juliano. Student pub. schs., San Jose, Calif. Auto mechanic J&M Automotive, San Jose, 1960-63; truck driver Can. Dry Beverages, San Jose, 1964-69; carpenter A&R Constrn., San Jose, 1969-75; contractor A. P. Constrn., San Jose, 1975—. Active San Jose Civic Club, Better Bus. Bur. of San Jose. Mem. Associated Builders and Contractors (labor pool), Am. Quarter Horse Assn., Pacific Coast Cutting Horse Assn., U.S. C. of C. Home: 19055 Malaguerra Ave Morgan Hill CA 95037 Office: AP Constn Co Inc 54 San Jose Ave San Jose CA 95125

ANTAL, MICHAEL JERRY, JR., educator; b. Monroe, Mich., May 18, 1947; s. Michael Jerry and Carolyn Sarah (McAdam) A.; m. Ann Gorsuch Slaughter, June 8, 1972; children: Dickinson James, Rachel Caroline. AB, Dartmouth Coll., 1969; MS, Harvard U., 1970, PhD, 1973. Mem. tech. staff Los Alamos (N.Mex.) Nat. Lab., 1973-75; asst. prof. thermosci. Princeton (N.J.) U., 1975-81; disting. prof. U. Hawaii, Honolulu, 1982—; cons. Council Environ. Quality, Washington, 1978, Office Tech. Assessment, Washington, 1979, Aerospace Corp., Washington, Exxon Corp., Newark, 1979-80. Contbr. articles to profl. jours. Chmn. Gov.'s Task Force Alternative Transp. Fuels, Honolulu, 1984—. Served to capt. U.S. Army, 1969-74. Grantee in field. Mem. AAAS, Am. Inst. Chem. Engrs., Am. Chem. Soc., Am. Phys. Soc., Soc. Indsl. Applied Math. Christian Scientist. Office: Hawaii Natural Energy Inst 2540 Dole St Honolulu HI 96822

ANTHES, RICHARD ALLEN, meteorologist; b. Saint Louis, Mar. 9, 1944; s. Harrison Inman and Virginia Louise (Kennedy) A.; m. Susan Quigley Hill, June 3, 1966; children: David Inman and Catherine Quigley. BS, U. Wis., 1966, MS, 1967, PhD, 1970. Research meteorologist Nat. Hurricane Lab., NOAA, Miami, Fla., 1968-71; prof. meteorology Pa. State U., University Park, Pa., 1971-81; dir. Atmospheric Analysis and Prediction div. Nat. Ctr. Atmospheric Research, Boulder, Colo., 1981—, dir. ctr., 1986—. Recipient Jule G. Charney award, 1987. Mem. Am. Meteorol. Soc. (councilor 1986—, Clarence L. Meisinger award 1980). Avocations: skiing, photography, cycling, tennis, running. Home: 1631 Gillespie Dr Boulder CO 80306 Office: Nat Ctr Atmospheric Research PO Box 3000 Boulder CO 80307

ANTHONY, WILMA TYLINDA, customer representative; b. Friars Point, Miss., July 11, 1954; d. John Thomas and Ellen (Ward) A. B.S. in Edn., Langston U., 1979; postgrad. in Interdisciplinary Studies, U. Oreg. Salesperson, Meier & Frank, Eugene, Oreg., 1976-78; vault teller 1st Interstate Bank, Portland, Oreg., 1979-80; mapping analyst Portland Gen. Electric Co., from 1980, now customer rep. Telethon div. chief Mt. Hood Council Campfire, Inc., Gladstone, Oreg., 1982; loaned exec. Columbia-Willamette United Way, 1982, in-house campaigner, Portland Gen. Electric Co., 1981. Active Nat. Fedn. Rep. Women, Portland; sec. Multnomah Young Reps., 1986; elected committee person Precinct 7, Washington County, 1986; line mem. Marshall for All Join Hands, 1986. Recipient Leadership in Community Services award Portland Gen. Electric, 1986; Honorable Mention Vol. of Yr. award Portland Gen. Electric, 1986. Mem. Kappa Delta Pi. Baptist. Club: Toastmasters (v.p. 1984, Competence cert. 1984). Office: Portland Gen Electric Co 121 SW Salmon St Portland OR 97204

ANTIA, SHIRIN DARA, special education teacher; b. Bombay, Jan. 26, 1952; came to U.S., 1972; d. Dara Pirojshaw and Jeroo Dara (Wania) A.; m. George Edmund Price, Jan. 2, 1983. BA, Calcutta U., 1971; MEd, U. Pitts., 1973, PhD, 1979. Tchr. Western Pa. Sch. for Deaf, Pitts., 1973-77; sr. teaching asst. U. Pitts., 1977-79; asst. prof. No. Ill. U., DeKalb, 1979-80; asst. prof. U. Ariz., Tucson, 1980-86, assoc. prof., 1986—; mem. Council Exceptional Children div. for children with communicative disorders., 1986, 87; cons. Ariz. Sch. for Deaf and Blind, Tucson, 1982-85. Contbr. articles to profl. jours. Research grantee U. Pitts., 1979; U.S. Office Edn. grantee, 1983, 84, 85. Mem. Assn. Coll. Educators of Hearing Impaired (pres. 1986-87). Zoroastrian. Avocations: hiking, music. Office: U Ariz Coll Edn Tucson AZ 85701

ANTIERI, PAUL JOSEPH, mechanical engineer, consultant; b. Bklyn., May 18, 1955; s. Salvatore Louis and Marie (Filippone) A.; m. Patricia Lynn Brozyna, May 6, 1978. BE, Stevens Inst. Tech., Hoboken, N.J., 1977. Registered profl. engr., Calif., N.Y., Ill. Assoc. Jaros, Baum & Bolles Cons. Engrs., N.Y.C., 1977-82; ptnr. I&N Cons. Engrs., Los Angeles, 1982—. Mem. Mech. Engrs. Calif. (pres. 1986—), ASME, ASHRAE, Am. Soc. Plumbing Engrs., Sigma Nu (treas. 1975-76). Republican. Catholic. Club: Wilshire Country (Los Angeles). Avocations: golf, skiing. Home: 516 Beirut Ave Pacific Palisades CA 90272 Office: I&N Cons Engrs 417 S Hill St Suite 1085 Los Angeles CA 90013

ANTIPORDA, HIPOLITO, surgeon; b. Vigan, Ilocos Sur, Philippines, Jan. 30, 1937; came to U.S., 1962; s. Proceso P. and Felicidad B. A.; M.D., U. Santo Tomas, Manila, 1961; m. Teresa McInerney, May 9, 1964; children—Maria, Catherine, Michael. Intern, Mary Immaculate Hosp., Jamaica, N.Y., 1962-63; resident in surgery Mary Immaculate Hosp., also Bridgeport (Conn.) Hosp., 1963-67; practice medicine specializing in surgery, N.Y.C., 1969-78, Carlsbad, N.Mex., 1979—; mem. staff, past chief of surgery Guadalupe Med. Center, Carlsbad. Diplomate Am. Bd. Surgery. Fellow ACS, Southwestern Surg. Congress, Am. Soc. Abdominal Surgeons, Soc. Philippine Surgeons in Am.; mem. AMA, N.Mex. Med. Soc., Eddy County Med. Soc. Clubs: Riverside Country, Elks. Office: 2402 W Pierce Suite 3A Carlsbad NM 88220

ANTOCH, ZDENEK VINCENT, electronic engineering educator; b. Prague, Czechoslovakia, Oct. 16, 1943; came to U.S., 1950; s. Zdenek Antoch and Marta (Smidova) Frank; m. Maureen O. Shaw, June 24, 1968; 1 child, Anna Marie. BS, Portland State U., 1971, postgrad. in Engring., 1971-73, postgrad. in Physics, 1973-75. Research asst. Portland (Oreg.) State U., 1972-75; electronics instr. Portland (Oreg.) Community Coll., 1975-80, 81—; design engr. Coast TV Terminals, Inc., Florence, Oreg., 1980-81; cons., Transat Microwave Systems, Los Angeles, 1984—, dir. research and devel., 1984-85. Inventor in field. NSF grantee. Mem. IEEE, Am. Soc. Engring. Edn. Democrat. Avocation: sailing. Office: Portland Community Coll 12000 SW 49th Ave Portland OR 97219

ANTONELLI, ARTHUR LOUIS, research entomologist; b. Vancouver, B.C., Can., Feb. 4, 1944; came to U.S., naturalized 1984; s. Ottorino and Audrey (Odlum) A.; m. Lois Marie Kuenkel, Jan. 4, 1980; children: David, Antony, Vincent. Research asst., bio-illustrator dept. biology Seattle U., 1967; teaching asst. Cen. Wash. State Coll., Ellensburg, 1968-69; instrnl. asst. entomology U. Idaho, Moscow, 1969-70, grad. asst., 1971-73, research assoc., 1973-74; research technologist Wash. State U., Pullman, 1974-76; extension entomologist Wash. State U. Research and Extension Ctr., Puyallup, 1976—; mem. tech. adv. com. wash. State Poison Prevention, 1976-82; mem. Wash., State Agrl. Pesticide Adv. Bd., 1983—; guest lectr. pest control and entomology to various profl. confs. and workshops, 1976—. Contbr. articles to profl. jours. Mem. Entomol. Soc. Am., Wash. State Entomol. Soc., Sigma Xi. Roman Catholic. Home: 18008 79th Ave E Puyallup WA 98373 Office: Western Wash Research and Extension Ctr Puyallup WA 98371

ANTONOFF, STEVEN ROSS, educational consultant, university dean, communication consultant, civic leader; b. Waukon, Iowa, Dec. 14, 1948; s. Ben H. and Florence R. A.; B.S., Colo. State U., 1967; M.A., U. Denver, 1970, Ph.D., 1979. Spl. asst. to dean U. Denver, 1970-71, dean student life, 1971-74, dean Center for Prospective Students, 1974-75, exec. dir. admissions and student affairs, 1975-78, dean admissions and fin. aid, 1978-81, adj. prof. speech communication, 1979—; dir., now pres. Antonoff Assocs., Inc.; owner Denver Nuggets Basketball, Inc., 1970-82. Chmn., Mayor's Commn. on Arts, Denver, 1979-81; trustee Congregation Emanuel, 1977-82; chmn. bd. dirs. Hospice of Met. Denver, 1970-84; mem. Denver Commn. on Cultural Affairs, 1984-86 ; mem. scholarship com. Mile High Cablevision, 1982—. Mem. Ind. Edn. Counselors Assn., Rocky Mountain Assn. Coll. Admissions Counselors, Ind. Ednl. Counselors Assn., Internat. Communication Assn., Speech Communication Assn., Assn. Student Personnel Adminstrs., Soc. Profl. Mgmt. Consultants, Nat. Assn. Coll. Admissions Counselors, Acad. Mgmt. Author various articles. Office: 425 S Cherry St Suite 215 Denver CO 80222

ANTONOPLOS, PATRICIA ANN, instrumentation manufacturing company executive, chemist; b. Erie, Pa., June 24, 1949; d. Frank Joseph and Marian Elsa (Puskas) Borkowski; B.S. cum laude, U. Pitts., 1970; M.S. in Organic Chemistry, Northwestern U., 1972, Ph.D. in Organic Chemistry, 1976; m. Timothy L. Antonoplos, June 27, 1973. Research chemist Gulf Oil Chems. Co., Houston, 1976-79; sr. engr. Beckman Instruments, Inc., Fullerton, Calif., 1979-80, research and devel. mgr. 1980—. Northwestern U. fellow, 1975-76. Mem. AAAS, Am. Chem. Soc., Am. Assn. Clin. Chemistry, Sigma Xi. Patentee in field. Office: Beckman Instruments Inc 200 S Kraemer Blvd Brea CA 92621

ANTONSON, THOMAS FREUND, chemical service company executive; b. McHenry, Ill., Feb. 29, 1944; s. Carl Leonard and Carmen Patricia (Freund) A.; m. Judith Ann Sorensen, June 10, 1972; children: Jenelle, Brett, Todd. BA in Biology, U. N.Colo., 1973; Indsl. Hygiene, Johns Manville Corp., 1973-76. Indsl. hygienist Abex Corp., Chgo., 1976-77; mgr. indsl. hygiene CF&I Corp., Pueblo, Colo., 1977-83; dir. indsl. hygiene Poly. Corp., Lincolnwood, Ill., 1984-85; pres. Asbestos Removal Corp., Colorado Springs, Colo., 1985—; owner Occupational Health Tech., Pueblo, 1985—, also bd. dirs. Mem. subcom. air pollution-asbestos State of Colo. Dept. Health, Denver. Served U.S. Army, 1966-68, Vietnam. Mem. Am. Indsl. Hygiene Assn. (sec. Rocky Mountain sect. 1980-81), Brit. Occupational Hygiene Soc., Am. Soc. Safety Engrs., Am. Pollution Control Assn. Roman Catholic. Lodge: KC. Avocations: fishing, gardening, carpentry, skiing, golf.

ANVARI, MORTEZA, computer science and mathmatics educator; b. Tehran, Iran, Jan. 29, 1931; came to U.S., 1956; s. Kazem and Fatemeh (Salimi) A.; m. Nancy Ann Hutchison, Jan. 26, 1958; children: Alexander, Lawrence. BS, U. Tehran, 1953; MS, U. Ill., 1959, PhD, 1962. Prof. math. U. B.C., Can., 1963-68; chmn. math. computer sci. U. Tech., Tehran, 1968-71; pres., founder Computer Coll., Tehran, 1972-79; prof. computer sci. Calif. State U., Northridge, 1980-83; prof., chmn. dept. computer sci. Calif. State U., Fullerton, 1983—; cons. BDM Internat. Inc., Va., 1985—, Ashton-Tate, 1987. Contbr. numerous articles to profl. jours. Smith-Mundt fellow U.S. State Dept., 1956-58. Mem. IEEE, Assn. Computing Machinery. Avocations: tennis, skiing, bridge.

ANZ, REG DEAN, architect; b. Clifton, Tex., Jan. 21, 1942; s. Edward Walter and Elizabeth Helen (Holman) A.; student U. Tex., Arlington, 1960-62, BS in Archtl. Studies, Austin, 1965; m. Patrice Ann Niehaus, Jan. 9, 1977; children: Adrian Van, Marisa Santana. Project architect Envirodynamics Inc., Dallas, 1971-72, Dahl/Braden/Jones/Chapman, Dallas, 1973-74, Dan Dworsky, Beverly Hills, Calif., 1974; assoc. Martin Stern, Jr., Beverly Hills, 1975-79, Maxwell Starkman, Beverly Hills, 1979-83; pvt. practice cons., 1983-84; cons. Lee & Sakahara, Costa Mesa, Calif., 1985; with Jones Cons. Mgmt., Beverly Hills, Calif., 1986—. Lic. architect, Tex., Calif. Mem. AIA (corp.), Constrn. Specifications Inst., Am. Arbitration Assn., Nat. Council Archtl. Registration Bds. (cert.). Supervising architect M.G.M. Grand Hotel, Reno, 1977-78; project architect Sahara Hotel & Casino, Las Vegas and Atlantic City, 1978-79; project dir. Sheraton Grande Hotel, Los Angeles, 1979-83; project mgr. UCLA Med. Ctr., 1986—. Office: 1008 5th St Santa Monica CA 90403

ANZEL, SANFORD H., orthopaedic surgeon; b. Bayonne, N.J., Feb. 17, 1929; s. Jules and Faye (Morganstein) A.; m. Darlene J. Wilson, July 14, 1937; children: Linda, Jon. BA, Yale U., 1950; MD, N.Y. Med. Coll., 1954; MS in Mrthopaedic surgery, U. Minn., 1959; cer. Cert. Am. Bd. Orthopaedic Surgery; lic. Nat. Bd. Med. Examiners, Bd. Med. Examiners, Calif., Minn. State Bd. Med. Examiners. Intern U. Calif. Med. Ctr., San Francisco, 1954-55; fellow in orthopaedic surgery Mayo Clinic, Rochester, Minn., 1955-59; chief orthopaedic surgery Orange (Calif.) County Med. Ctr., 1965-71; assoc. clin. prof. orthopaedic surgery U. Calif., Irvine, 1971-79, clin. prof., 1979—; chief orthopaedic sect. Children's Hosp. Orange County, 1977-78; state co-chmn. Orthopaedic Research and Edn. Found., 1982-84; chief orthopaedics Long Beach (Calif.) Vet's. Hosp., 1986—; cons. Baden Powell Orthopaedic Unite, Anaheim, Calif., Foothill High Sch., Katella High Sch., Univ. High Sch., Mater Dei High Sch., Los Angeles Rams; 7th ann. former alumnus vis. prof. Mayo Clinic and Found., 1975. Contbr. numerous articles to profl. jours. Served to maj. USAF, 1959-64. S.H. Anzel Soc. named in his honor, 1985. Fellow ACS (select membership com. 1969-76), Am. Acad. Orthopaedic Surgeons (regional admission com. 11 1969-76, com. ann. meeting press relations 1975-77, 82, co-vice chmn. sci. com. 1981, chmn. sci. com. 1983, bd. councilors); mem. AMA, Western Orthopaedic Assn. (membership com. 1975-78, v.p. Orange County chpt. 1976, pres.-elect Orange County chpt. 1977, pres. Orange County chpt. 1978, bd. dirs. Orange County chpt. 1985—), Calif. Med. Assn. Orange County Med. Assn., Am. Orthopaedic Soc. Sports Medicine, Arthritis Found. (Disting. Service award So. Calif. chpt. 1974, Humanitarian award Orange County chpt. 1968-79, Nat. Vol. Service Citation, 1981) Wilson-Bost Interurban Club. Home: 1066 Regis Way Tustin CA 92680 Office: Orthopaedic Surgery Med Group Inc 1201 W La Veta Ave Suite 501 Orange CA 92668

APOSHIAN, ARNO, real estate executive; b. Salt Lake City, Oct. 29, 1935; s. James J. and Louise (Boehme) A. BS, U. Utah, 1960. Pres., founder Aztec Investment Corp., Salt Lake City, 1962-66; chmn., pres. Century Properties Inc., Salt Lake City, 1967—, Century Internat. Corp., Salt Lake City, 1970—; chmn. Viva Corp., Salt Lake City, 1972—; pres. Equity Land Co. Inc., Salt Lake City, 1968—. Republican. Mormon. Home and Office: 3905 Parkview Dr Salt Lake City UT 84124

APP, JOHN O'NEAL, real estate developer; b. Hammond, Ind., Nov. 24, 1938; s. John Maximilian and Lurline (Burch) A.; m. Janet Elizabeth Manderson, June 22, 1979; children: Arielle Elizabeth, John Maximilian III, Konrad Alexandre, Friedrich Wilhelm. BA, Brown U., 1961. Agt. Underwriters Nat. Assurance Co., Orange, Calif., 1969-74; prin. John O. App & Assocs., Newport Beach, Calif., 1974-78; pres., chief exec. officer Corp. Pension Funding, Inc., Laguna Hills, Calif., 1978—; bd. dirs. Orange Rental Enterprises, Inc., El Toro, Calif., pres., 1984-86, chmn. 1986—, Default Service Co. Inc., Laguna Hills, Calif. Mem. Orange County Bd. Edn., 1974-78, Orange County Marine Inst., Dana Point, Calif., 1978, Pacific Ocean Found., Dana Point, 1978—, pres. 1980-84. Served to maj. USMC, 1962-67, Vietnam. Mem. Vietnam Combat Pilots Assn., Inc. Republican. Club: Toastmasters (named Outstanding Area Gov., 1974). Avocations: gardening, woodworking, skiing, reading. Office: Corp Pension Funding Inc PO Box 1655 San Juan Capistrano CA 92693

APPELL, ALLEN L., marketing educator; b. Worcester, N.Y., Aug. 2, 1943; s. William A. and Martha (Moraht) A.; m. Katherine Appell, Jan. 30, 1963 (div. Mar. 1982); children: Elizabeth, Jacquelyn. BA, U. Calif., Santa Barbara, 1965, U. Calif.-Hastings Coll. Law, San Francisco, 1966; MBA, San Francisco State U., 1969; PhD, Golden Gate U., 1981. Cert. tchr., Calif.; lice real estate broker, Calif. Mktg. specialist Wells Fargo Bank, San Francisco, 1967-69; dir. mktg. Hyatt Corp., Burlingame, Calif., 1969-72, Tia Maria Restaurants, San Francisco, 1972-74; instr. Skyline Coll., San Bruno,

Calif., 1974-83; prof. mktg. San Francisco State U., 1983—; cons. Paschal & Co., Burlingame, 1983, Patin Vineyard Mgmt., Santa Rosa, Calif., 1986. Author: A Practical Approach to Human Behavior in Business, 1984; contbr. articles to mktg. jours. Mem. Am. Mktg. Assn. Republican. Clubs: Corinthian Yacht (Tiburon, Calif.); Sausalito (Calif.) Sailing; Commonwealth (San Francisco). Avocations: running, diving, traveling, sailing, rowing. Home: 20 Arana Circle Sausalito CA 94965 Office: San Francisco State U 1600 Holloway Ave San Francisco CA 94132

APPLE, DAINA DRAVNIEKS, management, administrative systems designer; b. Kuldiga, Latvia, USSR, July 6, 1944; came to U.S., 1951; d. Albins Dravnieks and Alina A. (Bergs) Zelmenis; divorced; 1 child, Almira Moronne; m. Martin A. Apple, Sept. 2, 1986. BS, U. Calif., Berkeley, 1977, MA, 1980. Economist U.S. Forest Service, Berkeley, 1974-84; mgmt. analyst U.S. Forest Service, San Francisco, 1984—. Author: Public Involvement In the Forest Service-Methodologies, 1977, Public Involvement-Selected Abstracts for Natural Resources, 1979, The Management of Policy and Direction in the Forest Service, 1982, An Analysis of the Forest Service Civil Rights Program, 1984, Organization Design-Abstracts for Natural Resources Users, 1985. Mem. AAUW, Am. Forestry Assn., Assn. Women Geographers (local chmn. 1977-79), Commonwealth Club of Calif., Sigma Xi, Phi Beta Kappa (nat. sec. 1985—, pres. No. Calif. chpt. 1982-84, 1st v.p. 1981). Avocations: dancing, tennis, films, music, art. Home: 2040 Clemens Rd Oakland CA 94602 Office: US Forest Service Planning and Budgeting Office 630 Sansome St San Francisco CA 94111

APPLE, MARTIN ALLEN, high technology company executive; b. Duluth, Minn., Sept. 17, 1938; children—Deborah Dawn, Pamela Ruth, Nathan, Rebeccah Lynn. A.B., A.L.A., U. Minn., 1959, M.Sci., 1962; Ph.D., U. Calif., 1968. Pres., Internat. Plant Research Inst., San Carlos, Calif., 1978-81; with EAN-Tech., Inc., Daly City, Calif., 1982-84, chmn. bd., 1983-84; with Adytum Internat., Mountain View, Calif., 1982—, chief exec. officer, 1983—; cons. MIT, Stanford U., U. Calif., 1981-83; adj. prof. computers in medicine U. Calif. San Francisco, 1982—. Author: (with F. Myers) Review Medical Pharmacology, 1976; (with M. Fink) Immune RNA in Neoplasia, 1976; (with F. Becker et al) Cancer: A Comprehensive Treatise, 1977; (with M. Keenberg et al) Investing in Biotechnology, 1981; (with F. Ahmad et al) From Genes to Proteins: Horizons in Biotechnology, 1983. Mem. Calif. Council Indsl. Innovation, 1982. Mem. Assn. Venture Founders Internat. (bd. govs. 1982-83), East-West Center Alumni Assn. (bd. trustees, vice chmn. 1983-85), Profl. Software Programmers Assn., Phi Beta Kappa (Disting. Service award 1984, 85). Home: PO Box 391043 Mountain View CA 94039 Office: PO Box 2629 San Francisco CA 94126

APPLEBY, ARNOLD PIERCE, crop science educator; b. Formoso, Kans., Oct. 24, 1935; s. Howard L. and Argie V. (Pierce) A.; m. Geraldine Alice Smith, Apr. 1, 1956; children: Brian Dennis, Brent David. BS, Kans. State U., 1957, MS, 1958; PhD, Oreg. State U., 1962. Tchr. math. and sci. Bazine (Kans.) High Sch., 1958-59; instr. Oreg. State U., Corvallis, 1959-62, asst. prof., 1962-67, assoc. prof., 1967-72, prof., 1972—. Contbr. articles to profl. jours. Recipient Agr. Disting. Prof. award Coll. Agr. Oreg. State U., 1983, Oreg. Disting. Prof. award Alumni Assn., 1985. Fellow Weed Sci. Soc. Am. (Outstanding Tchr. 1971, Outstanding Researcher 1983), Western Soc. Weed Sci. (pres. 1971-72), Am. Soc. Agronomy, Crop Sci. Soc. Am. Home: 1665 SW Martin St Corvallis OR 97333 Office: Oreg State U Crop Sci Dept Corvallis OR 97331

APPLEGATE, EDNA (KAY), civic worker; b. Las Vegas, N.Mex., May 15, 1919; d. George Washington and Dora Maude (Bearce) Howell; m. George Edward Applegate, Nov. 30, 1945 (dec. 1980); 1 child, Nancy Kay. R.N., Hotel Dieu Sch. Nursing, 1942; B.S., Columbia U., 1956, M.S., 1963. Sch. nurse tchr. Garden City Pub. Sch., N.Y., 1960-73; pub. health nurse Nassau County Dept. Health, Garden City, 1953-60. Author: Breakfast Book, 1976; Little Book of Baby Foods, 1979. Bd. dirs. Maternal and Child Health Ctr., Santa Fe, 1978-80, Myasthenia Gravis Found. N.Mex. chpt., 1986—, LWV, Santa Fe, 1974-80, Vol. Involvement Service, Santa Fe, 1977-83, Santa Fe Opera Guild, 1982-82, Santa Fe Cancer Soc., 1983-84; mem. steering com. March of Dimes Birth Defects Found., Santa Fe, 1979-85, vol. coordinator N.Mex. chpt., 1985-86; mem. adv. bd. women's unit Charter Sunrise Hosp., Albuquerque, 1985—; mem. fin. com. St. John's Coll., Santa Fe, 1978-83, mem. fine arts com., 1979-83; co-founder The Gilbert & Sullivan Soc., Santa Fe, 1984; charter mem. Compadres de las Casas Reales, 1986; chmn. N.Mex. com. to restore the Montezuma (N.Mex.) Hotel, 1986—. Served as 2d lt. Army Nurse Corp, 1942-44. Fellow Am. Sch. Health Assn., Royal Soc. Health; mem. N.Y. Mental Health Assn. Democrat. Mailing Address: PO Box 2688 Santa Fe NM 87504

APPLEGATE, GARY BERT, psychologist; b. Los Angeles, Dec. 5, 1941; s. Bert and Yvonne (Stephan) A.; m. Suzy Frances VonSchanbl, May 24, 1981. BA, Loyola U., Los Angeles, 1963; MA, Calif. State U., Los Angeles, 1966; PhD, Wash. State U., 1970. lic. clin. psychologist, Calif. Ass. prof. psychology Mt. St. Mary's Coll., Los Angeles, 1968-71; resident faculty Inst. for Reality Therapy, Los Angeles, 1971-82; pres. Ctr. for Skill Devel., Sherman Oaks, Calif., 1982—; nat. speaker, 1971—; clin. dir. Life Skills, Los Angeles, 1985—; cons. to various mental health ctrs., 1975—. Author: What Are You Doing, 1980, Happiness, It's Your Choice, 1985. Recipient Service award Mensia, Los Angeles, 1978, Service award Kiwanis, Los Angeles, 1973. Mem. Am. Psychol. Assn., Calif. Assn. Psychologists. Club: PGA West (Palm Desert, Calif.). Office: Ctr for Skill Devel 15335 Morrison St #100 Sherman Oaks CA 91403

APTEKAR, ROBERT GARY, surgeon; b. Detroit, Aug. 14, 1944. Student, Johns Hopkins U., 1962-65; MD, U. Mich., 1969. Asst. prof. orthopedic surgery Stanford (Calif.) U.; cons. Arthritis and Orthopedic Med. Clinic, Advanced Rehab. Ctr. Contbr. articles to profl. jours. Pres. Arthritis Found. Santa Clara County. Served as surgeon USPHS, 1971-73. Mem. AMA, Calif. Med. Assn., Am. Acad. Orthopedic Surgeons, Am. Coll. Sports Medicine, Am. Rheumatism Assn., Am. Acad. Cerebral Palsy and Devel. Medicine.

APTER, ROBERT LYNN, emergency physician; b. Hartford, Conn., Aug. 17, 1949; s. Stanley Merriam and Penny (Zeidman) A.; m. Diane K. Sawyer, Apr. 4, 1981; 1 child, Ethan. Student, Wesleyan U., Middletown, Conn., 1966-68; AB, U. Calif., Berkeley, 1970; MD, U. Colo., Denver, 1974. Cert. Am. Bd. Emergency Medicine. Intern Virginia Mason Hosp., Seattle, 1974-75; emergency physician United Gen. Hosp., Sedro Woolley, Wash., 1976-78; resident Va. Mason Hosp., Seattle, 1975-76; dir. emergency dept. United Gen. Hosp., Sedro Woolley, Wash., 1978—. Bd. dirs. Skagit Valley YMCA, Mount Vernon, Wash., 1982—. Fellow Am. Coll. Emergency Physicians (pres. Wash. chpt. 1984-85, bd. dirs. 1978—); mem. Skagit-Island Counties Med. Soc., Wash. State Med. Assn. Club: Skagit Alpine (pres. 1982-83). Lodge: Rotary. Avocations: skiing, backpacking, mountain climbing, running. Office: United Gen Hosp Hwy 20 PO Box 410 Sedro-Woolley WA 98284

APURON, ANTHONY SABLAN, archbishop; b. Agana, Guam, Nov. 1, 1945; s. Manuel Taijito and Ana Santos (Sablan) P. BA, St. Anthony Coll., 1969; MDiv, Maryknoll Sem., 1972, M Theology, 1973; MA in Lituary, Notre Dame U., 1974. Ordained priest Roman Catholic ch, 1972, ordained bishop, 1984, installed archbishop, 1986. Chmn. Diocesan Liturgical Commn., Agana, 1974-86; vice chmn. Chamorro Lang. Commn., Agana, 1984-86; aux. bishop Archdiocese of Agana, 1984-85, archbishop, 1986-; chmn. Interfaith Vols. Caregivers, Agana, 1984-; mem. Civilian Adv. com., Agana, 1986-. Author: A Structural Analysis of the Content of Myth in the Thought of Mircea Eliade, 1973. Named Most Outstanding Young Man, Jaycees of Guam, 1984. Avocations: jogging, walking, swimming . Office: Archbishop's Office Cuesta San Ramon Agana GU 96910

ARAI, MASATSUGU, advertising company executive; b. Tokyo, Dec. 1, 1935; s. Goichi and Chiyoko (Takigawa) A.; m. Hiroko Arai Mizukami, May 7, 1967. BA in Journalism, Doshisha U., Kyoto, Japan, 1959. Mgr. TV dept. Kyodo Advt. Co., Tokyo, 1965-68; producer Japan Color Movie Co., Tokyo, 1968-75; pres., exec. producer, prin. M. Arai Corp., Los Angeles, 1975-84; v.p. Kyodo Advt. Am. Corp., Los Angeles, 1984—. Producer comml. films (grand prix Cannes Film Festival, 1974, grand prix All Japan Comml. Com., Internat. Broadcasting award Japan Air Lines-Jalpak, 1977, Clio award, 1973, Mother and Child award, 1975). Avocations: cruise travel, soccer. Home: 5923 Costello Ave Van Nuys CA Office: Kyodo Advt Am Corp 9454 Wilshire Blvd Penthouse Beverly Hills CA 90212

ARANGNO, DEBORAH CATHERINE, mathematics educator, writer; b. Rockville Center, N.Y., Nov. 27, 1956; s. Louis J. and Maria T. Arangno. BS, Mercer U., 1977; MS, Emory U., 1980. Teaching asst. Emory U., Atlanta, 1979-80; adj. prof. math. Dekalb Coll., Clarkston, Ga., 1980-81; mathematician Norad/Spacecom, Colorado Springs, Colo., 1981-83; hon. prof. math. U. Colo., Colorado Springs, 1982—; tutor Mercer U., Macon, Ga., 1975-77. Author: Arangno/Calculus Handbook, 1985, Water Comets, 1978. Organizer, model Benefit Fashion Shows, Macon, 1975-79. Grad. fellow Emory U., 1977. Avocations: fashion design, composing music, sculpture, running. Home: 230 Rockrimmon Colorado Springs CO 80919 Office: U Colo Dept Math Austin Bluffs Pkwy Box 7150 Colorado Springs CO 80933

ARANT, DAVID EUGENE, real estate broker, educator; b. Southgate, Calif., Apr. 17, 1935; s. Francis Marian and May Laveigh (Morris) A.; B.S., Pepperdine U., 1957; M.S., U. So. Calif., 1960; children—Brenda, Bradford. Treas., Vet. Escrow Co., Inc., Los Angeles, 1958-61; prof. accounting Los Angeles Met. Coll. of Bus., 1961-66; prof. real estate Los Angeles Harbor Coll., 1966—, prof. real estate, 1984—; owner, realtor, operator Dave Arant Realty, Rancho Palos Verdes, Calif., 1979—; also painter and musician. VA grantee, 1972, 74. Mem. Calif. Real Estate Assn., Delta Pi Epsilon, Pi Gamma Mu, Alpha Gamma Sigma. Democrat. Home: 1890 Peninsula Verde Dr Rancho Palos Verdes CA 90717

ARASHIRO, MICHAEL ANTHONY, real estate executive; b. Waimea, Hawaii, Jan. 6, 1951; s. Masaichi Arashiro and Jane (Oyadomari) Sadamitsu; B.S., Hawaii Pacific Coll., 1973; M.B.A., Pepperdine U., 1977. Lic. real estate broker, Hawaii. Mgr. devel. and fin. Blackfield Hawaii Corp., Honolulu, 1973-76; div. gen. mgr. Service Properties, Honolulu, 1976-78; dir. ops. McDonald's Devel. Co., Honolulu, 1978-80; v.p., dir. Home Properties, Inc., Honolulu, 1980-86, dir., 1981—, sr. v.p. 1986—. Trustee, Hawaii Pacific Coll., 1978—. Mem. Nat. Assn. Realtors, Internat. Council Shopping Ctrs., Hawaii Assn. Realtors, Hawaii Pacific Coll. Alumni Assn. (pres. 1977-79). Office: PO Box 539 Honolulu HI 96809

ARATA, MICHAEL JOSEPH, JR., fire prevention specialist; b. Bklyn., Jan. 3, 1951; s. Michael Joseph and Josephine (Cinquemani) A.; m. Karla Renee Newkirk, June 19, 1977; children: James Michael, Kristen Nicole. AS, St. Pete Jr. Coll., 1977; BA in Pub. Adminstrn., U. South Fla., 1979, MPA, 1982. Cert. Fire Protection Specialist, Calif. Firefighter Town of Wilton, Conn., 1971-73; patrolman N.Y. Bd. Fire Underwriters, N.Y.C., 1973; firefighter Clearwater (Fla.) Fire Dept., 1973-78, lt., 1978-83; fire chief, marshal Fla. Power Corp., Crystal River, 1983-85; safety and fire protection specialist Sacramento Mcpl. Utilities Dist. Rancho Seco Nuclear Generating Sta., Herald, Calif., 1985—; developer, mgr. corp. fire protection program Sacramento Mcpl. Utilities Dist., 1986—; cons. Impact Forecast Assocs., 1979-83; instr. Pinellas Fire Acad., 1978-83, St. Pete Jr. Coll., 1979, 81; chmn. cen. region Hazardous Materials Emergency Response Team Task Force, 1985. Chmn. Clearwater Affirmative Action Com., 1978-81; mem. study com. for incorporation of Elk Grove, 1986—. Named Firefighter or Yr., Clearwater Jaycees, 1979; Internat. Assn. Fire Chiefs scholar, 1978. Mem. Internat. Soc. Fire Service Instrs., Soc. Fire Protection Engrs., Am. Soc. Safety Engrs., Nat. Fire Protection Assn., Pi Sigma Alpha. Democrat. Roman Catholic. Avocations: fishing, hiking, guitar. Office: Sacramento Mcpl Utilities Dist 1708 59th St Sacramento CA 95819-4628

ARAVE, CLIVE WENDELL, animal scientist; b. Idaho Falls, Idaho, May 12, 1931; s. Joseph Clarence and Rhoda Elvera (Peterson) A.; m. Carley McMurtrey, Oct. 10, 1950; children: Wendy, Stephanie, Joe, Christine, Lorraine, James. BS, Utah State U., 1956, MS, 1957; PhD, U. Calif., Davis, 1963. Asst. mgr. Lavacre Farms, Modesto, Calif., 1957-59; asst. prof. Calif. State U., Chico, 1963-65; asst. prof. Utah State U., Logan, 1965-81, assoc. prof., 1981—; vis. prof. Purdue U., West Lafayette, Ind., 1972-73; vis. scientist Ruakura Agrl. Research Ctr., Hamilton, New Zealand, 1980-81; cons. in field. Contbr. articles to profl. jours. NSF grantee, 1980. Mem. Am. Dairy Sci. Assn., Animal Behavior Soc., Sigma Xi, Phi Kappa Phi. Republican. Mormon. Home: 1460 E 2100 N Logan UT 84321 Office: Utah State U Dept Animal Sci Logan UT 84322

ARBOGAST, JON DAVID, federal agency administrator; b. Bay City, Mich., May 22, 1942; s. Kenneth G. and Bessie P. (Peck) A.; m. Connie L. Brown, Sept. 16, 1978; children: Dawn, Michelle, Karen; 1 adopted child, Shana. BS in Math., Ill. State U., 1968. Tchr. math. Bloomington (Ill.) High Sch., 1968-70; spl. agt. FBI, New Orleans, 1970-71, Little Rock, 1971-74; supervisory spl. agt. FBI Hdqrs., Washington, 1974-83, cryptanalyst, 1974-76, ops. research mgr., 1976-78, automation long range plans mgr., 1978-81, internal mgmt. auditor, 1981-83; supervisory spl. agt. FBI, San Antonio, 1983-85, white collar crime program mgr., 1983-85; spl. agt. administr. FBI, Pocatello, Idaho, 1985—, regional ctr. adminstr., 1985—. Served with USAF, 1962-66. Mem. EDP Auditors Assn., Greater Pocatello C. of C. (adv. econ. devel., chmn. fed. campaign S.E. Idaho chpt. 1986). Avocations: scuba diving, flying, hunting. Office: FBI We Regional Computer Support PO Box 2860 Pocatello ID 83206

ARCADI, JOHN ALBERT, physician, surgeon, researcher; b. Whittier, Calif., Oct. 23, 1924; s. Antonio and Josephine (Ramirez) A; m. Doris M. Bohanan, Apr. 11, 1951; children: Patrick, Michael, Judith, Timothy, Margaret, William, Catherine. BS cum laude, U. Notre Dame, 1947; MD, Johns Hopkins U., 1950. Diplomate Am. Bd. Urology. Intern The Johns Hopkins Hosp., Balt., 1950-51, resident, 1951-52, 53-55; instr. urology Johns Hopkins U., Balt., Md., 1953-55, U. So. Calif., Los Angeles, 1955-60; research assoc. Whittier (Calif.) Coll., 1957-70, research prof., 1970—; staff mem. urology sect. Presbyn. Hosp., Whittier, 1960—. Fellow AAAS, Am. Coll. Surgeons; mem. Endocrine Soc., Am. Urology Assn., Am. Assn. Anatomy, Am. Soc. Cell Biology, Am. Micro Soc., Internat. Urol. Soc., Am. Assn. Clin. Anatomy. Republican. Roman Catholic. Avocations: photography, stamp and coin collecting, fishing. Home: 6202 S Washington Ave Whittier CA 90608 Office: PO Box 9220 Whittier CA 90608

ARCHAMBAULT, OLLIE MARIA, educator; b. Ardmore, Okla., Apr. 25, 1945; d. John and Luella Pearl (French) Hansen; m. John Henry Archambault, Dec. 20, 1969; children: Margaret Maria, Eric John. BA in Edn., Wayne State Coll., 1966; postgrad., U. Ariz., 1966-68; MA in Edn., No. Ariz. U., 1972, postgrad., 1982—; postgrad., Ariz. State U., 1973-81. Lic. elem. tchr., Ariz. Tchr. Casa Grande (Ariz.) Elem. Sch. Dist., 1966-85, coordinator K-3d grade programs, 1985—, holder numerous com. and adminstrv. positions, 1966—. Chmn. crusade com. Casa Grande chpt. Am. Cancer Soc., 1981-84; com. chmn. Casa Grande council Cub Scouts, Boy Scouts Am., 1982-85, mem. com. 1985—. Named Vol. of Yr. Am. Cancer Soc., 1983. Mem. NEA (life), Ariz. Edn. Assn., Casa Grande Elem. Edn. Assn., VFW (pres. local post 1970-80, Delta Kappa Gamma. Democrat. Baptist. Avocations: reading, sewing, traveling, sight-seeing, family and friends. Office: Cottonwood Sch Casa Grande Elem Sch Dist 4 1667 N Kadota Casa Grande AZ 85222

ARCHAMBEAU, JOHN ORIN, radiation oncologist, research administrator; b. Portland, Maine, Aug. 5, 1925. AB, Stanford U., 1950, MD, 1955. Cert. radiation therapist. Intern U. Chgo., 1954-55, resident in pathology, 1955-58; NIH fellow in therapeutic radiology Swedish Hosp. Tumor Inst., Seattle, 1958-60; research collaborator Brookhaven Nat. Lab., Upton, N.Y., 1966—; dir. radiation oncology Nassau County Med. Ctr., East Meadow, N.Y., 1966-77; radiation oncologist VA Hosp., Northport, N.Y., 1974-77; chmn. radiation and oncology City of Hope Med. Ctr., Duarte, Calif., 1977-81, dir. radiation research, 1981-84; dir. radiation research Loma Linda (Calif.) U. Med. Ctr., 1985—; mem. steering com. The Proton Working Group, 1985—, chmn. clin. applications com., 1985—. Contbr. articles to profl. jours. Fellow Am. Cancer Soc., 1960-61, Harvard, 1960-61, Nat. Cancer Inst., 1958-60; scholar Newhouse Found., 1950-53, San Francisco Found., 1953-54, Fulbright, 1960-61. Fellow Am. Coll. Radiology; mem. Am. Soc. Therapeutic Radiologsts and Oncologists, Radiation Research Soc., Cell Kinetics Soc., Am. Radium Soc., Calif. Soc. Therapeutic Radiologists, N.Y. Roentgen Soc., Sigma Xi.

ARCHDEACON, JOHN ROBERT, orthopedic surgeon; b. N.Y.C., Aug. 1, 1919; s. Thomas Francis and Mary (O'Connor) A.; m. Molly Taylor Sinclair, Sept. 18, 1948; children—Patricia Archdeacon Holland, Douglas, John, Richard, Moira, Kenneth. student Fordham U., 1939-41; M.D., N.Y.U., 1950. Diplomate Am. Bd. Orthopedic Surgery Am. Bd. Preventive Medicine. Served with USAAF, 1942-45; commd. 1st lt. USAF, 1952, advanced through grades to col., 1965; intern St. Lukes Hosp., N.Y.C., 1950-51; resident orthopedic surgery N.Y. U.-Bellevue Med. Center, 1955-59; chief orthopedic surgery Carswell AFB Hosp., Ft. Worth, 1959-61; dir. orthopedic pathology course Armed Forces Inst. Pathology, 1963-64; chief of surgery, cons. to surgeon gen. Maxwell Air Force Hosp., Ala., 1964-66; chief profl. services, sr. med. adviser Air Evacuation Squadron, USAF Hosp., Clark Hosp., Philippines, 1966-68, hosp. comdr., 1967-68; hosp. comdr. 78th USAF Hosp., Hamilton AFB, Calif., 1968-69; ret., 1969; practice medicine, specializing in orthopedic surgery, Los Gatos-Saratoga, Calif., 1969—. Decorated D.F.C., Air medal with 3 oak leaf clusters, Air Force Commendation medal, Legion of Merit. Fellow ACS, Am. Acad. Orthopedic Surgeons, Am. Coll. Preventive Medicine; mem. Am., Calif. med. assns., Santa Clara County Med. Soc., Brit. Assn. Aviation Med. Examiners. Office: 800 Pollard Rd Los Gatos CA 95030

ARCHER, GUY PHILIP DODSON, lawyer; b. N.Y.C., Jan. 18, 1943; s. Robert Palin and Dorothy Louise (Dodson) A.; m. Jeanne B. Graham; children: Kristen, Gina, Richard, Brandon. BA with honors, Wesleyan U., 1965; JD, Columbia U., 1968. Bar: N.Y. 1968, Hawaii 1974. Assoc. Marshall, Bratter, Greene, Allison & Tucker, N.Y.C., 1969-72; ptnr. Langa & Archer, Wailuku, Hawaii, 1975-76; sole practice Kula, Hawaii, 1977-80, Wailuku, Maui, Hawaii, 1981; dep. corp. counsel County of Maui, 1981-84, 86—; assoc. Bernard, Overton & Russell, Albany, N.Y., 1984-85; hearing officer N.Y. State Bd. Equalization and Assessment, Albany, 1985; br. mgr. Hawaii Escrow & Title Inc., Maui, 1974; legis. counsel NORML, N.Y.C., 1972-73. George F. Baker scholar, 1961-65; Davenport fellow, 1964. Mem. ABA, Hawaii Bar Assn. Congregationalist. Lodge: Rotary. Office: County of Maui Dept Corp Counsel 200 S High St Wailuku HI 96793 Mailing: PO Box 805 Wailuku HI 96793

ARCHER, RICHARD JOSEPH, lawyer; b. Virginia, Minn., Mar. 24, 1922; s. William John and Margaret Leanore (Duff) A.; m. Kristina Hanson, Jan. 29, 1977; children: Alison P., Cynthia J. A.B., U. Mich., 1947, J.D., 1948. Bar: Calif. 1949, U.S. Supreme Ct. 1962, Hawaii 1982. Partner firm Morrison and Foerster, San Francisco, 1954-71, Sullivan, Jones and Archer, San Francisco, 1971-81, Archer Rosenak & Hanson, San Francisco, 1981-85, Archer & Hanson, San Francisco, 1985—. Served with USN, 1942-45. Decorated Bronze Star. Mem. ABA, Am. Law Inst. (life), Am. Coll. Trial Lawyers, Assn. Trial Lawyers Am., ACLU, Am. Soc. Internat. Law. Republican. Clubs: Stock Exchange (San Francisco), Bankers (San Francisco). Home: 3110 Bohemian Hwy Occidental CA 95465 Office: 255 Kearny St San Francisco CA 94108

ARCHIBALD, JAMES DAVID, biology educator, paleontologist; b. Lawrence, Kansas, Mar. 23, 1950; s. James R. and Donna L. (Accord) A. B.Sc. in Geology, Kent State U., 1972; Ph.D. in Paleontology, U. Calif.-Berkeley, 1977. Gibb's instr. dept. geology Yale U., New Haven, 1977-79, asst., assoc. prof. dept. biology, 1979-83; curator of mammals Peabody Mus. Natural Hist., New Haven, 1979-83; assoc. prof. then prof. dept. biology San Diego State U., 1983—; extensive field expeditions in Mont., Colo., N.Mex., Pakistan, 1973—. Author: A Study of Mammalia and Geology Across the Cretaceous-Tertiary Boundary, 1982. Contbr. articles to profl. jours. Scholar Yale U., San Diego State U.; fellow Alcoa Found., U. Calif.-Berkeley; grantee Sigma Xi, Nat. Geog. Soc., NSF, Petroleum Research Found., San Diego State U. Mem. Soc. Vertebrate Paleontology, Geol. Soc. Am., Paleontol. Soc., Soc. Systematic Zoologists, Am. Soc. Mammalogists, Willi Hennig Soc., Sigma Xi. Office: San Diego State Univ Dept Biology San Diego CA 92182

ARCIERI, DEBORAH ANN, social worker; b. Berkeley, Calif., Dec. 20, 1951; d. Robert Van Eaton and Ethel (Drummond) Finley; m. Robert Joseph Arcieri, June 21, 1980; children: Anthony, Nicole. BA, Wheaton Coll., 1973; MSW, U. Denver, 1980. Cert. social worker, Colo. Family therapist Alpine Counseling Ctr., Grand Junction, Colo., 1976-82, team leader, 1981-82; home health/hospice social worker St. Mary's Home Health and Hospice, Grand Junction, Colo., 1985—; coordinator bereavement program St. Mary's Home Health and Hospice, Grand Junction, 1985—. Author: Bereavement Training Manual, 1985; co-editor The First Steps of Living with Loss, 1985. Mem. Nat. Assn. Social Workers.

ARD, SARADELL, art educator; b. Macon, Ga., Mar. 22, 1920; d. John and Lillian (Garrett) A.; m. Robert Allen Frederick, Sept. 10, 1969 (div. Apr. 29, 1983). BA, Asbury Coll., 1942; MA, U. Mich., 1943; DEd, Columbia U., 1970. Instr. art. Asbury Coll., Wilmore, Ky., 1942-47; asst. prof. Wheaton (Ill.) Coll., 1947-52; edn. supr. U.S. Army, Whittier, Alaska, 1952-54; arts and crafts supr. U.S. Army, Governors Island, N.Y., 1954-56; arts and crafts dir. U.S. Army, Europe, 1956-62; from assoc. prof. to prof. Alaska Meth. U., Anchorage, 1962-73; prof. U. Alaska, Anchorage, 1973-85, dean Coll. of Arts and Scis., 1976-77, prof. emeritus, 1985—; cons. Nat. Endowment for Arts, Washington, 1978, Nat. Mus. Natural History Smithsonian Inst., Washington, 1981-82, Art Gallery of Ontario, Toronto, 1981, Alaska State Council on Arts, Anchorage, 1978-83; adv. bd. Alaska State Mus., Juneau, 1970. Author: An Introduction to the Native Art of Alaska, 1972, Inuitkunst, Kunst der Eskimo, 1983, (mus. catalog) Inua: Spirit World of the Bering Sea Eskimo, 1982; contbr. articles to profl. jours. Bd. dirs. Anchorage Fine Arts Mus. Assn., 1974—, pres. 1981-82; commn. mem. Anchorage Hist. and Fine Arts Commn., 1972-82; bd. dirs. Visual Arts Ctr. Alaska, Anchorage, 1973-75, 85—; co-dir. All Alaska Juried Art Exhibition, 1969-73. Recipient Gov's award in Art Gov. Alaska, 1980; named Artist of Yr. Anchorage Fine Arts Mus. Assn., 1984. Mem. Coll. Art Assn., Alaska Artists Guild, Inst. Alaska Native Arts. Methodist. Avocations: painting, gardening. Home: 12400 Toilsome Hill Rd Anchorage AK 99516

ARDITTI, JOSEPH, biology educator; b. Sofia, Bulgaria, May 1, 1932; came to U.S., 1954; s. Solomon Joseph and Rebecca (Haimowitch) A.; m. Mastura Abdullah, June 2, 1983; 1 child, Jonathan Omar. BS, UCLA, 1959; PhD, U. So. Calif., 1966. Prof. devel. and cell biology U. Calif., Irvine, 1966—. Author: Experimental Plant Physiology, 1969; editor: Orchid Biology, vol. I, 1977, vol. II, 1982, vol. III, 1984, vol. IV, 1987. Mem. AAAS, Bot. Soc. Am., Am. Soc. Plant Physiologists, Am. Inst. Biol. Sci., Linnean Soc. London, Am. Orchid Soc. Office: U Calif Dept Devel and Cell Biology Irvine CA 92717

ARDLEY, HARRY MOUNTCASTLE (MIKE), mathematical statistician, operations research consultant; b. Oakland, Calif., Jan. 22, 1926; s. Harry Mountcastle and Anne Alvina (Meyer) A.; m. Jane Partridge, June 24, 1948; children: David Michael, Douglas Mountcastle, Mary Elizabeth. AB, U. Calif., Berkeley, 1950, postgrad., 1950-51, 58-59, 62-63. Econ. statistician U.S. Dept. Commerce, Washington, 1951-53; math. statistician Pacific Telephone Co., San Francisco, 1953-59; gen. statistician San Diego, 1959-63; supr. math. and statis. research San Francisco, 1963-83; pvt. practice cons. 1984—. Active citizens com. to establish Foothill Coll., 1957-58, San Francisco Symphony Assn.; exec. com. Santa Clara County Dem. Council, 1957-59; pres. Palo Alto-Stanford Dem. Club, 1965; pres. Greenmeadow Community Assn., 1969. Served with USAAF, 1943-46. Mem. Am. Statis. Assn. (pres. San Francisco Bay area chpt. 1981-82), Ops. Research Soc. Am., Inst. Mgmt. Sci., Sierra Club, Western Wheelers Club. As amateur bicyclist, rode from San Francisco to N.Y.C., 1986. Home and Office: 352 Parkside Dr Palo Alto CA 94306

ARDREY, ROSS JAMES, management consultant; b. N.Y.C., Jan. 4, 1943; s. Robert and Helen (Johnson) A.; m. Janet Kathleen Leslie, June 20, 1970; children—Robert Thornton, Janet Elizabeth. A.B., U. Chgo., 1963; M.A., U. Wash., 1966, J.D., 1970; Mgmt. cons. Harry J. Prior & Assocs., Bellevue, Wash., 1972—. Bd. trustees Villa Acad., 1986—, Friends of Seattle Pub. Library, 1985—; bd. dirs. Pacific N.W. chpt. Inst. Mgmt. Cons., 1985—; mem. Mcpl. League of Seattle and King County, Wash., 1976—; mem. exec.

com. nat. fund bd. U. Chgo., Ill., 1979-81. Mem. Inst. Mgmt. Cons., Pacific Northwest Personnel Mgmt. Assn. Office: Harry J Prior & Assocs Inc 700 112th Ave NE Bellevue WA 98104

ARENA, ALAN JOSEPH, manufacturing executive; b. Chgo., June 23, 1950; s. Joseph James and Madelyn Adele (Castrovillari) A.; m. Mary Ann Guglielmo, Nov. 26, 1972 (dec. Dec. 1977); m. Donna Kaye Albertson, Sept. 4, 1982; 1 child, Monica Kristen. BS in Mech. and Aerospace Engring., Ill. Inst. Tech., 1972; MME, Calif. State U., Los Angeles, 1984. Research and devel. engr. Fiat-Allis CMI, Deerfield, Ill., 1973-80; sr. project engr. Signet Sci. Co., El Monte, Calif., 1980-83; project mgr. def. electronics ops. Autonetics Strategic Systems div. Rockwell Internat., Anaheim, Calif., 1983—; Instr. Calif. Poly. Inst., Pomona, 1983—. Patentee in field. Roman Catholic. Avocations: model railroading, roller coaster driver. Home: 12515 Sterling Pl Chino CA 91710 Office: Rockwell Internat Autonetics Strategic Systems Div Def Electronics Ops 3370 Miraloma Ave Anaheim CA 92803

ARENA, JOHN I., publisher, reading specialist; b. Alameda, Calif., Sept. 12, 1929; s. Anthony and Nina Helen (Culotta) A.; m. Anna Maria Arena, Oct. 31, 1964; 1 son, James Anthony. A.B., San Francisco State Coll., 1951, M.A., 1959; postgrad., U. San Francisco, 1951-52, U. Calif., Berkeley, 1959-62. Tchr. Ashland Sch., San Lorenzo, Calif., 1954-56, Sunset Sch. for Physically Handicapped Children, San Lorenzo, 1956-59; prin. Marindale Sch., San Rafael, Calif., 1959-61; home tchr. Oakland Pub. Schs., 1961-62; instr., program dir. Dewitt Reading Clinic, San Rafael, Calif., 1961-68; editor, publisher Academic Therapy Publs., Inc. and High Noon Books, Novato, Calif., 1965—; exec. dir. Arena Sch. and Learning Center, remedial center and school, San Rafael, 1970-77; lectr. in Edn., Reading Dominican Coll. of San Rafael, 1972—; cons. in field to various sch. dists. Editor: Jour. Spl. Edn, 1968—, Bull. of Orton Soc, 1968-74, many others. Recipient award Calif. Assn. Neurologically Handicapped Children, 1971, pres.'s award, 1977; award Assn. Children with Learning Disabilities, 1970; also Pioneer-Profl. award, 1979. Mem. Optometric Extension Program Found., Inc. (hon.). Home: 50 Corte Morada Greenbrae CA 94904 Office: Academic Therapy Publs Inc & High Noon Books 20 Commercial Blvd Novato CA 94947

AREND, WILLIAM PHELPS, medical researcher; b. Utica, N.Y., Aug. 24, 1937; s. Ralph Wilcox and Frances Elizabeth (Clapp) A.; m. Ann Elizabeth Manes, June 5, 1964; children: Thomas Clapp, Christopher Austin, Jeffrey Phelps. BA, William Coll., 1959; MD, Columbia U., 1964. Intern U. Wash., Seattle, 1964-66, residency, 1968-69, fellow, 1969-71, asst. prof. medicine, 1971-75, assoc. prof. medicine, 1975-81; prof. medicine U. Tex. Health Scis. Ctr., Houston, 1981-82, dir. div. rheumatology, 1981-82; prof. medicine U. Colo. Health Scis. Ctr., Denver, 1983—, head. div. of rheumatology, 1983—; chief. arthritis sect. VA Hosp., Seattle, 1971-80; vis. scholar Corpus Christi Coll., 1980-81. Contbr. numerous articles to profl. jours. Served to lt. commdr. USPHS, 1966-68. Guggenheim Found. fellow, 1980-81. Fellow ACP; mem. Am. Soc. Clin. Investigation, Am. Assn. Immunologists, Am. Rheumatism Assn., Western Assn. Physicians, Western Soc. Clin. Investigation (councilor 1976-79), Phi Beta Kappa. Episcopalian. Avocations: hiking, skiing, gardening, reading. Office: U Colo health Scis Ctr 4200 E 9th Ave Denver CO 80262

ARENDELL, FRANCES HUSSEY, chemist, researcher; b. N.Y.C., Mar. 19, 1918; d. Erwin Howard and Nellie Frances (Phillips) Hussey; m. William H. Arendell. BA, BS, Barnard U., 1943. Research engr. Johns-Manville, N.J., 1944-53; info. scientist E.R. Squibb & Sons, Princeton, N.J., 1955-58; supr., cons. Warner-Lambert, Mead Johnson, Morris Plains, N.J. and Evansville, Ind., 1958-70; process engr. Rogers Corp., Mesa, Ariz., 1978-85; cons. Water and Waste Regulatory Affairs, Phoenix, 1986—; chmn. water and waste com. Ariz. Printed Circuits Assn. Mem. Am. Chem. Soc., Am. Electroplaters and Surface Finishers Soc. (cons.). Republican. Avocations: desert hiking, rock hunting, cooking, knitting. Home: Rt 1 Box 727 Maricopa AZ 85239

ARENOWITZ, ALBERT HAROLD, psychiatrist; b. N.Y.C., Jan. 12, 1925; s. Louis Isaac and Lena Helen (Skovron) A.; m. Betty Jane Wiener, Oct. 11, 1953; children: Frederick Stuart, Diane Helen. BA with honors, U. Wis., 1948; MD, U. Va., 1951. Diplomate Am. Bd. Psychiatry, Am. Bd. Child Psychiatry. Intern Kings County Gen. Hosp., Bklyn., 1951-52; resident in psychiatry Bronx (N.Y.) VA Hosp., 1952-55; postdoctoral fellow Youth Guidance Ctr., Worcester, Mass., 1955-57; dir. Ctr. for Child Guidance, Phila., 1962-65, Hahnemann Med. Service Eastern State Sch. and Hosp., Trevose, Pa., 1965-68; dir., tng. dir. Child and Adolescent Psychiat. Clinic, Phila. Gen. Hosp., 1965-67; asst. clin. prof. psychiatry Jefferson Med. Coll., Phila., 1974-76; exec. dir. Child Guidance and Mental Health Clinics, Media, Pa., 1967-74, Intercommunity Child Guidance Ctr., Whittier, Calif., 1976—; clin. asst. prof. child psychiatry Hahnemann Med. Coll., Phila., 1966-74; asst. clin. prof. psychiatry U. Wis., Madison, 1960-62, clin. asst. prof. psychiatry, behavioral scis., and family medicine U. So. Calif., Los Angeles, 1976—; mem. med. staff Presbyn. Intercommunity Hosp., Whittier, 1976—. Pres. Whittier Area Coordinating Council, 1978-80. Served with USAF, 1943-45. Fellow Am. Psychiat. Assn., Am. Acad. Child Psychiatry; mem. AMA, AAAS, Los Angeles County Med. Assn., So. Calif. Psychiat. Soc., So. Calif. Soc. Child Psychiatry, Phila. Soc. Adolescent Psychiatry (pres. 1967-68). Avocations: study of violence and aggression, ethnic travels, ethnic folk music. Office: Intercommunity Child Guidance Ctr 8106 S Broadway Whittier CA 90606

ARGENBRIGHT, ED FRANK, school administrator; b. Cut Bank, Mont., Dec. 3, 1934; s. Frank Paul Argenbright and Cleo (Newman) Glass; m. Betty Jane Fuller, June 30, 1956; children—Mark E., Bret F. B.A., U. Mont., 1956; M.A., San Jose State Coll., 1964. Cert. tchr., adminstr., Mont. Tchr., coach Granite County High Sch., Philipsburg, Mont., 1956-57; tchr. Campbell Union Schs., Calif., 1960-66; tchr., prin., supt. Sch. Dist. #1, Big Timber, Mont., 1966-80; co-owner McLeod Resort Corp., Mont., 1966-70; supt. pub. instrn. State of Mont., Helena, 1980—; dir. Carnegie Library Bd., Big Timber, 1972-80, Northwest Edn. Lab., Portland, Oreg., 1980—; mem. Mont. Land Bd., Tchr. Retirement Bd., Bd. Govs., Helena, 1980—, Council Chief State Sch. Officers, Washington, 1980—; mem., sec. Mont. Bd. Edn., Helena, 1980—; nat. adv. council Statue of Liberty Ellis Island Found., N.Y.C., 1983—. Active in Community Mental Health Bd., Big Timber, 1974-80; exec. com. Mont. Rep. Party, Helena, 1980—; v.p. Mont. Council Econ. Edn., Helena, 1984. Served to capt. USAF, 1957-60. Recipient Degree Hon. State Farmer Future Farmers Am., 1984, Sec. Regional award Dept. Edn., 1983; named to Basketball Hall Fame U. Mont., 1968. Mem. Sch. Adminstrs. Mont. (pres. so. central adminstrs. group 1977-78), Am. Assn. Sch. Adminstrs., U. Mont. Alumni Assn., Phi Delta Kappa, Sigma Nu. Presbyterian. Clubs: Big Timber Flying (pres. 1969-71), Toastmasters (pres. 1978). Lodges: Masons, (master 1976), Lions. Office: Supt Pub Instrn Room 106 State Capitol Helena MT 59620

ARGUE, JOHN CLIFFORD, lawyer; b. Glendale, Calif., Jan. 25, 1932; s. J. Clifford and Catherine Emily (Clements) A.; m. Leah Elizabeth Moore, June 29, 1963; children: Elizabeth Anne, John Michael. A.B. in Commerce and Finance, Occidental Coll., 1953; LL.B., U. So. Calif., 1956. Bar: Calif. 1957. Since practiced in Los Angeles; mem. firm Argue & Argue, 1958-59, Flint & MacKay, 1960-72, Argue, Freston, Pearson, Harbison & Myers, 1972—; bd. dirs. Cal Fed Inc., Calif. Fed. Savs. and Loan Assn. LAACO, Ltd., Trust Services Am., Inc. Pres. So. Calif. Com. Olympic Games, 1972—; founding-chmn. Los Angeles Olympic Organizing Com., 1978-79; bd. dirs. Amateur Athletic Found. Los Angeles; trustee, vice chmn. Pomona Coll., U. So. Calif., Mus. Sci. and Industry; chmn. bd. Greater Los Angeles affiliate Am. Heart Assn., 1982, chmn. adv. bd. 1985—; chmn. Verdugo Hills Hosp., chmn., 1979, chmn. adv. bd., 1983—; bd. govs. Alumni Occidental Coll., 1962-64; pres. Town Hall Calif., 1985; chmn. PGA Championship, 1983; vice chmn., sec. Los Angeles 2000 Com.; bd. dirs. Boy Scouts Am. Served with U.S. Army, 1956-58. Mem. ABA, Los Angeles Bar Assn., State Bar Calif., Nat. Club Assn. (dir.) So. Calif. Golf Assn. (pres. 1979), Calif. Golf Assn. (v.p. 1979), Los Angeles Area C. of C. (dir., vice chmn.), Cen. City Assn. (bd. dirs.), Phi Delta Phi, Alpha Tau Omega. Clubs: Chancery (pres. 1985-6), California (pres. 1983-84), Los Angeles Athletic, Riviera Country, Oakmont Country (pres. 1972), Los Angeles Country (Los Angeles), Automobile of Los Angeles (adv. bd.); Flint Canyon Tennis (La Canada, Calif.). Lodge: Rotary (Los Angeles). Home: 1314 Descanso Dr La Canada LA 91011 Office: 801 S Flower St Suite 5000 Los Angeles CA 90017

ARGYROS, GEORGE L., development company executive, professional sports team owner; b. Detroit; m. Judie Argyros. Student, Mich. State U.; B.S. in Bus. and Econs., Chapman Coll., 1959. Pres. Arnel Devel. Co.; chmn. bd. Arnel Mgmt.; chmn., dir. Air Cal, 1981—; dir. comml. financing services Newport bancorp and Coast Thrift and Loan Co.; prin. owner Seattle Mariners Baseball Team, 1981—; mem. Baseball's Revenue sharing Com., Restructuring Com., Commr. Selection Com.; bd. dirs. Am. League. Chmn. Western Wash.'s United Cerebral Palsy Telethon; chmn. fundraising Nat. Multiple Sclerosis Soc., Puget Sound chpt.; active NCCJ, Boy Scouts Am., World Affairs Council, Young Pres.'s Orgn.; chmn. bd. trustees Chapman Coll. Office: Seattle Mariners Baseball Club PO Box 4100 Seattle WA 98104 *

ARITA, GEORGE SHIRO, biology educator; b. Honolulu, Oct. 9, 1940; s. Ichimatsu and Natsu (Kimoto) A.; m. Harriet Yooko Ide, Dec. 26, 1964; children: Laurie Reiko, Daren Shizuo. BA, U. Hawaii, 1962, MS, 1964; MS, U. B.C., Vancouver, 1967; postgrad., U. Calif., Santa Barbara, 1967-71. Cert. community coll. tchr., Calif. Prof. biology Ventura (Calif.) Coll., 1971—, curator fish collection, 1976—. Author: (with others, lab. manual) Basic Concepts in Biology, 1981; contbr. articles on ichthyology to profl. jours. Fushiminomiya Meml. scholar U. Hawaii, 1961-62, Fisheries Assn. B.C. scholar U. B.C., 1964-65; NSF grad. trainee U. Calif. Santa Barbara, 1969-71. Mem. AAAS, Am. Soc. Ichthyologists and Herpetologists, Sigma Xi. Avocations: fishing, hiking, camping, gardening, photography. Home: 94 Howard Ave Oak View CA 93022 Office: Ventura Coll Dept Biology Ventura CA 93003

ARIYOSHI, GEORGE RYOICHI, lawyer, business consultant, former governor Hawaii; b. Honolulu, Mar. 12, 1926; s. Ryozo and Mitsue (Yoshikawa) A.; m. Jean Miya Hayashi, Feb. 5, 1955; children: Lynn Miye, Todd Ryozo, Donn Ryoji. Student, U. Hawaii, 1944-45, 47; B.A., Mich. State U., 1949, LL.D. (hon.), 1979; J.D., U. Mich., 1952; LL.D. (hon.), U. Philippines, 1975, U. Guam, 1975; H.H.D. (hon.), U. Visayas, Philippines, 1977, U. Hawaii, 1986. Bar: Hawaii 1953. Sole practice Honolulu, 1953-70; mem. T.H. Ho. of Reps., 1954-58, T.H. Senate, 1958, Hawaii State Senate, 1959-70; chmn. Senate Ways and Means Com., 1963-64, Senate majority leader, 1965-66, majority floor leader of State Senate, 1969-70; lt. gov. Hawaii, 1970-73; acting gov. 1973-74, gov., 1974-86; sole practice Honolulu, 1986—; chmn. Western Govs. Conf., 1977-78; chmn. Western Govs. Assn., 1984-85; dir. Hawaiian Ins. & Guaranty, Ltd., 1966-70, First Hawaiian Bank, 1962-70, Honolulu Gas Co., Ltd. (Pacific Resources, Inc.), 1964-70; bus. cons. Chmn. small bus. div. Community Chest, 1963; fund raiser pub. employees div. Aloha United Fund, 1971-72; exec. bd. Aloha council Boy Scouts Am., 1970-72; chmn. Citizenship Day Com., 1971; pres. Pacific Basin Devel. Council, 1980-81; bd. mgrs. YMCA, 1955-57. Served with M.I. Service AUS, 1945-46. Recipient Distinguished Alumni awards U. Hawaii, 1975, Distinguished Alumni awards Mich. State U., 1975. Mem. Am. Bar Assn. (ho. dels. 1969—), Hawaii Bar Assn. (pres. 1969), Hawaii Bar Found. (charter mem., pres. 1969—). Democrat. Club: Military Intelligence Service Vets (pres. 1968-69).

ARKIN, MICHAEL BARRY, lawyer, rancher; b. Washington, Jan. 11, 1941; s. William Howard and Zenda Lillian (Liebermann) A.; m. Gay Callan, July 3, 1982; children: Tracy Renee, Jeffrey Harris, Marcy Susan, Chatom Callan, Michael Edwin, Samuel Hopkins. A.A., George Washington U., 1961; B.A. in Psychology, U. Okla., 1962, J.D., 1965. Bar: Okla. 1965, U.S. Ct. Claims 1968, U.S. Supreme Ct. 1968, Calif. 1970, U.S. Tax Ct. 1970, U.S. Ct. Appeals (3d, 5th, 6th, 9th, 10th cirs.) 1970, U.S. Dist. Ct. (cen. dist.) Calif. 1970, U.S. Dist. Ct. (so. dist.) Calif. 1970, U.S. Dist. Ct. (ea. dist.) Calif. 1987. Trial atty. tax div. U.S. Dept. Justice, 1965-68, appellate atty., 1968-69; ptnr. Surr & Hellyer, San Bernardino, Calif., 1969-79; mng. ptnr. Wied, Granby Alford & Arkin, San Diego, 1979-82, Lorenz Alhadeff Fellmeth Arkin & Multer, San Diego, 1982, Finley, Kumble, Heine, Underberg, Manley & Casey, San Diego, 1983; sole practice Sacramento and San Andreas (Calif.), 1984-86; ptnr. McDonough Holland & Allen, Sacramento, 1986-87; sole practice San Andreas, Calif., 1987—. Bd. dirs. San Bernardino County Legal Aid Soc., 1971-73, sec., 1971-72, pres., 1973; mem. Calaveras County Adv. Com. on Alcohol and Drug Abuse, 1985—; treas. Calaveras County Legal Assistance Program, 1987—. Named to Hon. Order of Ky. Cols., 1967. Mem. ABA, Calif. Bar Assn. (com. on taxation), Sacramento County Bar Assn., San Diego County Bar Assn., San Bernardino County Bar Assn. (bd. dirs., sec.-treas. 1973-75, pilot drug abuse program 1970), Calaveras County Bar Assn., Am. Arbitration Assn. Republican. Jewish. Office: PO Box 1210 7 N Main St Suite 206 San Andreas CA 95249 Office: 7 N Main St Suite 206 San Andreas CA 95249

ARLIDGE, JOHN WALTER, utility company executive; b. Rochester, N.Y., Feb. 4, 1933; s. Harold Wesley and Grace Elizabeth (Kempshall) A.; m. Sandra Marie Koswar, Feb. 4, 1955; children—James William, Edward John. B.S., Los Angeles State Coll., 1962. Registered profl. engr., Calif., Nev., Utah. With City of Los Angeles, 1961-74, communications systems engring. design and purchase, 1961-62, power system resource planning research and devel., 1962-74; asst. to v.p. Nev. Power Co., Las Vegas, 1974—, v.p. resource planning and power dispatch, 1982—; v.p., dir. Nev. Electric Investment Co.; mem. State Engr.'s Adv. Com. on Geothermal Devel., 1974-76. State of Nev. Solar Energy Devel. Adv. Group, 1976—; mem. energy task force WEST, 1972-84, mem. energy engring. planning com., 1978; mem. advanced energy systems divisional com. Electric Power Research Inst., 1973—; mem. Western Utility Group on Fed. Land, 1977; endangered species subcom., rail issues group Edison Elec. Inst., 1977; cons. on air, land and water Western Regional Council, 1977; Nev. adv. bd. U.S. Bur. Land Mgmt., 1975-77, adv. council Las Vegas dist., 1980—. Contbr. articles on energy resources to publs. Served with USMC, 1950-54. Mem. IEEE, Geothermal Resources Council (dir.), utility Coal Gasification Assn. (chmn.), Internat. Solar Energy Assn., Pacific Coast Elec. Assn., So. Nevada Off-Road Vehicle Assn., Slurry Transp. Assn. (dir. 1979). Clubs: Masons. Office: PO Box 230 Las Vegas NV 89151

ARLOW, SETH MARTIN, anesthesiologist, physician; b. N.Y.C., Nov. 11, 1946; s. Jacob A. and Alice (Diamond) A.; m. Victoria Lynn Preciado, Aug. 19, 1985; children: Ferdinand B., Oelete L. Bert, Shiva P. AB cum laude, Syracuse U., 1968; MD, SUNY, Bklyn., 1972. Diplomate Am. Bd. Anesthesiology. Intern Providence Hosp., Seattle, 1972-73; resident in anesthesiology Mason Clinic, Seattle, 1973-75, research anesthesiologist, 1975-76; mem. med. staff Evergreen Gen. Hosp., Kirkland, Wash., 1978—, chief dept. anesthesiology, 1983-85. Contbr. articles to profl. jours. Served to maj. USAF, 1976-78. Fellow Am. Coll. Anesthesia; mem. Am. Soc. Anesthesia, Wash. State Soc. Anesthesia, Seattle Anesthesia Soc., Am. Soc. Regional Anesthesiology. Jewish. Avocations: kayaking, cross country skiing, running, profl. photographer. Home: 12040 NE 128th St Kirkland WA 98034

ARMANTROUT, NEIL BRANT, fisheries biologist; b. Salt Lake City, Apr. 22, 1941; s. Clo Elton and Bonnie Laura (Robinson) A. BS in Zoology, Oreg. State U., 1963, MS in Gen. Sci., 1964, PhD in Fisheries, 1981. Research biologist Game and Fish Dept., Tehran, Iran, 1967-68; lectr. postgrad. dept. U. Tabriz, Iran, 1973-74; biologist dist. fisheries Moab Dist. BLM, Utah, 1975-82; biologist state fisheries Oreg. State Office BLM, Portland, 1978-82; biologist dist. fisheries Eugene (Oreg.) Dist. BLM, 1982—; research cons. U.S Fish and Wildlife Service with Bombay Nat. History Soc. 1980—. Editor: Proceeding of Symposium on Aquatic Habitat Inventory, 1982; contbr. articles to profl. jours. Mem. McKenzie Adv. Com., Lane County, Oreg., 1985—. Recipient Spl. Achievement award Dept. Interior, 1978, 85, 87; named First Fed. Employee of Yr., Lane County Fed. Council, 1985. Mem. Am. Fisheries Soc. (pres. Western div., com. chmn. 1975—), Bombay Nat. History Soc., Asian Fisheries Soc., AAAS, Northwest Sci. Assn., Audubon Soc., Nat. Wildlife Fedn. Mormon. Avocations: photography, reading, music, gardening, cooking. Home: PO Box 10582 Eugene OR 97440 Office: Eugene Dist BLM PO Box 10226 Eugene OR 97440

ARMENTROUT, PETER BRUCE, chemistry educator; b. Dayton, Ohio, Mar. 13, 1953; s. Harry Martin and Lorraine (Johnson) A.; m. Mary Ann White, Aug, 6, 1983; children: Matthew Martin, Patricia Christine. BS, Case Western Res. U., 1975; PhD, Calif. Inst. Tech., 1980. Postdoctoral fellow Bell Telephone Labs., Murray Hill, N.J., 1980-81; asst. prof. chemistry U. Calif., Berkeley, 1981-87; assoc. prof. chemistry U. Utah, Salt Lake City, 1987—. Contbr. articles to profl. jours. Named Presdl. Young Investigator, NSF, 1984; Dreyfus Found. grantee, 1981; A.P. Sloan fellow, 1986. Mem. Am. Chem. Soc., Am. Phys. Soc., AAAS, Am. Assn. Mass Spectrometry. Office: U Utah Dept Chemistry Salt Lake City UT 84112

ARMENTROUT, STEVEN ALEXANDER, physician; b. Morgantown, W.Va., Aug. 22, 1933; s. Walter W. and Dorothy (Gasch) A.; m. Barbara Jean Lamson, July 18, 1977; children—Marc, Susan, Sandra, Nancy, Julie, Chris, Victor. A.B., U. Chgo., 1953, M.D., 1959. Intern U. Hosp., Cleve., 1959-60; resident in medicine, fellow Am. Cancer Soc. Western Res. U. Hosp., 1960-63; project dir. USPHS, 1963-65; asst. prof. Case Western Res. U. Med. Sch., 1965-71; mem. faculty U. Calif. Med. Sch., Irvine, 1971—; prof. medicine, chief div. hematology-oncology U. Calif. Med. Sch., 1978—, also dir. program in oncology.; pres. med. staff U. Calif.-Irvine Med. Ctr., 1983-85. Mem. Am. Assn. Cancer Research, AAUP, A.C.P., Am. Cancer Soc. (chmn. bd. 1973, pres. Orange County chpt. 1985-86), AMA, Am. Soc. Clin. Oncology, Am. Soc. Hematology, Orange County Med. Assn., Am. Soc. Internal Medicine, Calif. Med. Assn., Cen. Soc. Clin. Research, Leukemia Soc. Am., Orange County Chief of Staff Council. Research in multiple sclerosis. Office: 101 City Dr S Orange CA 92668 *

ARMENTROUT, VIVIENNE NIX, plant pathology educator; b. Comanche, Okla., Oct. 7, 1943; d. Theo Marion and Ethel Imogene (Inman) Nix; m. Charles Jesse Armentrout, Dec. 28, 1963. BA, Park Coll., 1965; MS, U. Ark., 1967; PhD, U. Wis., 1976. Instr. Donnelly Coll., Kansas City, Kans., 1969-70; research asst. U. Wis., Madison, 1970-76, research assoc., 1976-77; asst. prof. Calif. State Poly. U., Pomona, 1977-80, assoc. prof., 1981-86, prof. plant pathology, 1986—. Contbr. articles to sci. jours. Pres. North Shores Dem. Club, San Diego, 1983. Research grantee Kellogg Found., 1977-85, Ednl. grantee NSF, 1985. Mem. AAAS, Am. Phytopathol. Soc., Mycol. Soc. Am., Am. Soc. Plant Physiologists. Presbyterian. Avocations: gardening, hiking, camping. Home: PO Box 2778 Ann Arbor MI 48106 Office: Calif State Poly U Pomona CA 91768

ARMIJO, JACQULYN DORIS, interior designer; b. Gilmer, Tex., July 2, 1938; d. Jack King and Iris Adele (Cook) Smith; children—John, Christy, Mike. Student North Tex. State Coll., U. N.Mex. Profl. model, 1961-75; sec. State Farm Ins., Albuquerque, 1965-71; life ins. agt. Mountain States, Albuquerque, 1980; owner Interiors by Jacqulyn, Albuquerque, 1961—; cons., lectr. in field. Mem. Alby Little Theatre, Friends of Little Theatre, Symphony Women; fund raiser for Old Town Hist. Com., Arthritis Fund. Mem. Am. Soc. Interior Design (chmn. historic restoration Albuquerque), Internat. Soc. Interior Design, Internat. Platform Assn. Republican. Roman Catholic. Clubs: Albuquerque Jr. Women's, Los Amapolas Garden. Home: 509 Chamiso Ln NW Albuquerque NM 87107 Office: Interiors by Jacqulyn 509 Chamiso NW Albuquerque NM 87107

ARMON, NORMA, educational company producer, writer, editor; b. Mexico, July 22, 1937; came to U.S. 1977; d. Abraham and Gertrude (Cohen) Kreimerman; m. Moises Itzkowich, Dec. 17, 1955 (div. 1971); children—Ricardo, Rebeca, Carla. B.A. in English, U. of Americas, 1955; B.A. in Spanish Lit., Nat. U. Mex., 1968, M.A., 1970, Ph.D. in Linguistics, 1976; student London (Eng.) U., 1974, Cambridge (Eng.) U., 1980. Prof. linguistics and lit. Nat. U. Mex., 1968-76; writer, producer Mundo Latino, Spanish Internat. Network, Los Angeles, 1977-79; pres., Sispi Prodns., Inc., Los Angeles, 1979—; dir. curriculum devel. Summit, Inc., Los Angeles, 1980-82; creative dir. Eye Contact; editor-in-chief, Metamorphoses quar.; books include: Charles Dickens, 1970, Computers For Those Over Forty, 1983. Office: 474 Merritt #4 Oakland CA 94610

ARMSTRONG, AUGUSTUS KEATHLY, research geologist; b. Charleston, W.Va., June 6, 1930; s. John Westley and Eloise (Keathly) A.; m. Shirley Hutchinson, Mar. 9, 1953; children: Sharon, Augustus Jr., Christina. BS in Geology, U. N.Mex., 1953; PhD, U. Cin., 1960. Asst. prof. geology Portland (Oreg.) State U., 1960-62; petroleum geologist Shell Oil Co., Seattle and Farmington, N.Mex., 1961-66; research geologist U.S. Geol. Survey, Menlo Park, Calif., 1966—. Contbr. articles on geology to profl. publs. Served to 1st lt. USAF, 1953-55. Mem. AAAS, Am. Assn. Petroleum Geologists (cert.), Soc. Econ. Paleontologists and Mineralogists, Sedimentol. Assn. (Eng.). Presbyterian. Avocations: gardening, waterfowl. Home: 753 Silvertip Way Sunnyvale CA 94086 Office: US Geol Survy 345 Middlefield Rd Menlo Park CA 94025

ARMSTRONG, BRUCE DOUGLAS, veterinarian; b. Los Angeles, Aug. 26, 1953; s. William Bruce and Betty Ann (Martin) A.; m. Debbie Lynn Buck, Apr. 6, 1974; 1 child, Carissa Lynn. BS in Biology, U. Nebr., 1978; DVM, U. Minn., 1982. Staff veterinarian Northridge Vet. Clinic, Yucca Valley, Calif., 1982; owner, veterinarian Vet. House Call Services, Redding, Calif., 1983-85; staff veterinarian Cow Creek Vet. Hosp., Palo Cedro, Calif., 1983-85, Shasta Emergency Vet. Services, Redding, 1983-85, Trinity County Vet. Clinic, Hayfork, Calif., 1983-85, Tulare-Kings Vet. Emergency Service, Visalia, Calif., 1985-87, Your Pet Hosp., San Diego, 1987—; cons., relief veterinarian Redwood Vet. Hosp., Visalia, 1985-87, Lone Oak Vet. Hosp., Visalia, 1985-87. Named Small Animal Clinician of Yr., Upjohn Co., 1982. Mem. AVMA, Calif. Vet. Med. Assn., Tulare-Kings Vet. Med. Assn., Am. Arbitration Assn. Republican. Methodist. Lodge: Elks. Avocations: fishing, reading. Office: Your Pet Hosp 9870 Hibert D-9 San Diego CA 92131

ARMSTRONG, CHARLES G., baseball executive, lawyer; b. Louisville, Aug. 31, 1942; m. Susan; children—Dorrie, Katherine, Chuck. B.S., Purdue U., 1964; J.D., Stanford U., 1967. Bar: Calif. Practice law Hill Farrer & Burrill, Calif., 1971—; pres., chief operating officer Seattle Mariners Baseball Team, 1983—. Served with USN, 1967-70. Office: Seattle Mariners 100 S King St Suite 300 Seattle WA 98104 *

ARMSTRONG, DAVID MICHAEL, biology educator; b. Louisville, July 31, 1944; s. John D. and Elizabeth Ann (Horine) A.; divorced; children: John D., Laura C. BS, Colo. State U., 1966; MA in Teaching, Harvard U., 1967; PhD, U. Kans., 1971. From asst. prof. natural sci. to full prof. U. Colo., Boulder, 1971—; sr. scientist Rocky Mountain Biol. Lab., Gothic, Colo., 1977, 79; resident naturalist Sylvan Dale Ranch, Loveland, Colo., 1984—; cons. ecologist. Author: Distribution of Mammals in Colorado, 1972, Rocky Mountain Mammals, 1975, Mammals of the Canyon Country, 1982; coauthor: Mammals of the Northern Great Plains, Mammals of the Plains States. Mem. non-game adv. council Colo. Div. Wildlife, 1972-76, Colo. Natural Areas Council, 1975-80. Mem. AAAS, Am. Soc. Mammalogists (editor 1981—), Southwestern Assn. Naturalists (editor 1976-80), Rocky Mountain Biol. Lab. (trustee 1979-83), Sigma Xi. Avocations: ski-touring, music, conservation activities. Office: U Colo Natural Sci Program Box 331 Boulder CO 80309

ARMSTRONG, DICKWIN DILL, chamber of commerce executive; b. Muncie, Ind., Aug. 18, 1934; s. Colby Cooler and Elizabeth A. (Houck) A.; m. Janice A. Flora, June 2, 1957; children—Brent D., Stacey J. B.S. in Gen. Bus, Ind. U., 1956. Chief exec. officer Madison C. of C., Ind., 1959-61; chief exec. officer Frankfort C. of C., Ind., 1961-63, Marion C. of C., Ind., 1963-66, Lakeland C. of C., Fla., 1966-80; chief exec. officer Portland C. of C., Oreg., 1980-86, treas. polit. action com.; pres. Bellevue C. of C., Wash., 1987—. Served to capt. AUS, 1957-59. Mem. Am. C. of C. Execs. (cert. chamber exec., past officer), U.S. C. of C., Oreg. Chamber Execs. (dir., com. chmn.), Sigma Alpha Epsilon. Republican. Methodist. Club: Waverly Country. Lodge: Rotary, Masons, Shriners. Home: 15804 NE 65th Redmond WA 98052 Office: Bellevue C of C 110-110th Ave NE Suite 300 Bellevue WA 98004

ARMSTRONG, GENE LEE, retired aerospace company executive; b. Clinton, Ill., Mar. 9, 1922; s. George Dewey and Ruby Imald (Dickerson) A.; B.S. with high honors, U. Ill., Urbana, 1948, M.S., 1951; m. Lael Jeanne Baker, Apr. 3, 1946; children—Susan Lael, Roberta Lynn, Gene Lee. With Boeing Aircraft, 1948-50, 51-52; chief engr. astronautics div., corp. dir. Gen. Dynamics, 1954-65; chief engr. Def. Systems GroupTRW, Redondo Beach,

Calif., 1956-86, pvt. cons. systems engring., 1986—. Served to 1st lt. USAAF, 1942-45. Decorated Air medal; recipient alumni awards U. Ill., 1965, 77; registered profl. engr., Calif. Mem. Am. Math. Soc., AIAA, Nat. Mgmt. Assn., Am. Def. Preparedness Assn. Club: Masons. Contbr. chpts. to books, articles to profl. publs. Home: 5242 Bryant Circle Westminster CA 92683 Office: Armstrong Systems Engring Co PO Box 86 Westminster CA 92684-0086

ARMSTRONG, JENNIFER TAYLOR, publisher; b. Perth Amboy, N.J., Jan. 19, 1954; d. Joan D. (Vorhauer) McCarthy. BA in Journalism and Psychology, Marquette U., 1975. Pvt. practice pub. relations Los Angeles and Phoenix, 1978—; publisher, editor FootPrints Publs., Phoenix, 1985—ž. Contbr. articles to popular mags. and publs. Avocations: reading, writing, TV, movies. Home and Office: PO Box 41467 Phoenix AZ 85080

ARMSTRONG, ORVILLE A., lawyer; b. Austin, Tex., Jan. 21, 1929; s. Orville Alexander and Velma Lucille (Reed) A.; m. Mary Dean Macfarlane; children. B.B.A., U. Tex., Austin, 1953; LL.B., U. So. Calif., 1956. Bar: Calif., 1957, U.S. Ct. Appeals (9th cir.) 1958, U.S. Supreme Ct. 1980. Ptnr., Gray, Binkley & Pfaelzer, 1956-61, Pfaelzer, Robertson, Armstrong & Woodard, Los Angeles, 1961-66, Armstrong & Lloyd, Los Angeles, 1966-74, Macdonald, Halsted & Laybourne, Los Angeles, 1975—; lectr. Calif. Continuing Edn. of Bar. Served with USAF, 1946-49. Fellow Am. Coll. Trial Lawyers; mem. State Bar Calif. (gov. 1983-87, pres. 1986-87), ABA, Los Angeles County Bar Assn. (trustee 1971-72), Am. Judicature Soc., Chancery Club, Assn. Bus. Trial Lawyers, Am. Arbitration Assn. Democrat. Baptist. Clubs: Calif. Home: 2385 Coniston Pl San Marino CA 91108 Office: 725 S Figueroa St 36th Fl Los Angeles CA 90017

ARMSTRONG, RICHARD LEROY, business owner, executive; b. Normal, Ill., Feb. 24, 1940; s. Roy Kenner and Alice Ruth (Thompson) A.; m. Susan E. Buchwalter, Apr. 22, 1962 (div. Sept. 1968); m. Charlotte Ann Wolf, Nov. 10, 1968; children: Kimberly Ann, Michael Wolf. BS in Bus., U. Ariz., 1963. Asst. mgr., loan officer Bank of Calif., Los Angeles, 1963-70; asst. v.p. loans Valley Nat. Bank, Phoenix, 1970-73; sales mgr. Sahuaro Petroleum & Asphalt Co., Phoenix, 1973-82; pres. Daycor Inc., Yorba Linda, Calif., 1982—. Bd. dirs. Maricopa County chpt. ARC, Phoenix, 1971-73, local chpts. of U. Ariz., Los Angeles, Phoenix and Orange County, 1963—, U. Ariz. Nat. Alumni Bd., Tucson, 1983—. Mem. Am. Pub. Works Assn., Am. Assn. Airport Execs. (assoc.), Associated Gen. Contractors. Avocations: skiing, sailing, golf, racquetball. Home: 4358 Mahogany Circle Yorba Linda CA 92686 Office: Daycor Inc PO Box 1156 Paramount CA 90723

ARMSTRONG, ROBERT WALTER, electrical engineer, consultant; b. Newport News, Va., Sept. 29, 1946; s. Robert Walter and Mary Ray (Kuykendall) A.; m. Alice Louise Talley, Sept. 2, 1972; children: Robert Sloan, Diana Kathryn. BSEE, U. Va., 1974, MSEE, 1976, PhDEE, 1978. Registered profl. engr., Calif., Ariz. Sr. engr. Jet Propulsion Lab., Pasadena, Calif., 1978-80, mem. tech. staff, 1980-83; owner Armstrong Engring., San Gabriel, Calif., 1983—; sr. instr. Integrated Computer Systems, Santa Monica, Calif., 1982-85. Contbr. articles to profl. jours. Bd. dirs. Upper Hastings Ranch Housing Assn., Pasadena, 1980, block capt., 1979. Served to lt. (j.g.) USNR, 1968—. Recipient Cert. Recognition (4), NASA, 1981-86. Mem. IEEE, NSPE, Nat. Acad. Forensic Engrs., Calif. Soc. Profl. Engrs., Profl. Engrs. Pvt. Practice, Aircraft Owners and Pilots Assn., Eta Kappa Nu. Avocations: flying, photography. Home: 1175 Rexford Ave Pasadena CA 91107 Office: Armstrong Engring 9020 Greenwood Ave San Gabriel CA 91775

ARMSTRONG, ROGER JOSEPH, cartoonist, educator; b. Los Angeles, Oct. 12, 1917; s. Roger Dale and Elizabeth Theresa (Eliason) A.; 1 child, Julie Ann Vance. Student Pasadena City Coll., 1932-38, Chouinard Art Inst., 1938-40, 48-50. Illustrator, writer children's books and comic books Western Pub. Co., 1940-49; cartoonist Ella Cinders comic strip United Feature Syndicate, 1950-60; cartoonist, writer Napoleon and Uncle Elby comic strip Times Mirror Syndicate, 1950-61; cartoonist Little Lulu comic strip Western Pub. Co., 1964-66; dir. Laguna Beach (Calif.) Mus. Art, 1963-66; instr. Laguna Beach Sch. of Art, 1967-85; pvt. instr., 1985—; cartoonist Scamp comic strip Walt Disney Prodns., 1978—; mem. faculty Orange Coast Coll., Costa Mesa, Calif., 1980—; one-man shows include: Ettinger Gallery, Laguna Beach, 1980-82, Challis Galleries, Laguna Beach, 1982, Anaheim (Calif.) Cultural Ctr., 1983; group shows include: Dalzell Hatfield Galleries, Los Angeles, 1975, Desert Mus., Palm Springs, Calif., 1981; represented in permanent collections including: Laguna Beach Art Mus. Served with U.S. Army, 1944. Recipient 1st prize for oil painting Pico Rivera Festival of Arts, 1967; 1st Bicentennial award for meritorious achievement Cypress (Calif.) Coll., 1976. Mem. Nat. Watercolor Soc. (pres. 1984-85), Artists Equity, Nat. Cartoonists Soc., Comic Artists Profl. Soc. Home: 34202 Del Obispo Apt 24 Dana Point CA 92629 Office: Laguna Beach Coll Art 2222 Laguna Canyon Rd Laguna Beach CA 92651

ARMSTRONG, SCOTT ELLIOTT, TV director; b. Choteau, Mont., July 11, 1955; s. Robert Samuel and Dorothy Ann (Jackson) A. BS, Mont. State U., 1978, postgrad., 1981-84. TV dir. Sta. KXMC-TV, Minot, N.D., 1978-79, Sta. KXMB-TV, Bismarck, N.D., 1979-80; spl. effects technician Warner Photo Lab., Kansas City, Mo., 1980-81, Sta. KVEW-TV, Kennewick, Wash., 1984—; engring. asst. Mont. State U., Bozeman, 1983-84. Camera dir., editor Don't Drink and Drive, 1985 (Tri-Cities Advt. award 1986); prodn. technician Dr. Frankenstein, 1986 (3d Place award TV Bur. Advt.). Gt. Falls Advt. Fedn. scholar, 1983. Roman Catholic. Avocations: photography, skiing, bicycling, hiking. Home: 100 N Irving Pl #61 Kennewick WA 99336 Office: Sta KVEW-TV 601 N Edison Kennewick WA 99336

ARMSTRONG, WALLACE DOWAN, JR., data processor; b. Los Angeles, Feb. 9, 1926; s. Wallace Dowan and Vina Edith (Kreinbring) A.; B.S. cum laude, U. So. Calif., 1951; postgrad. U. Oslo (Norway), 1955; 1 son, Erik Bentung. Supr. accounting Ramo Wooldridge Corp., 1955-60; mgr. programmers, systems analyst Aerospace Corp., El Segundo, Calif., 1960-80, mgr. bus. systems, 1980—. Served with USMCR, 1944-46, 51. Mem. Data Processing Mgmt. Assn. Home: 25713 Crest Rd Torrance CA 90505 Office: Aerospace Corp 2350 E El Segundo Blvd El Segundo CA 90245

ARMSTRONG, WILLIAM L., senator; b. Fremont, Nebr., Mar. 16, 1937; s. William L. and Dorothy (Steen) A.; m. Ellen M. Eaton, July 15, 1962; children: Anne Elizabeth, William. Student, Tulane U., 1954-55, U. Minn., 1956. Pres. Sta. KPV1-TV, Pocatello, Idaho; mem. 93d-95th Congresses from 5th Dist. Colo.; mem. U.S. Senate from Colo., 1979—, chmn. Republican Policy Com., 1984—. dir. mem. Colo. Senate, 1965-72, majority leader, 1969-72; mem. Colo. Ho. of Reps., 1963-64. Served with U.S. Army N.G., 1957-63. Mem. AP Broadcasters Assn. (dir. 1971-72, v.p. 1972). Office: 528 Hart Senate Office Bldg Washington DC 20510 *

ARMSTRONG-SEWARD, CATHERINE, pediatrician; b. Denver, Feb. 12, 1915; d. Robert Francis and Frances Evelyn (Coe) Armstrong; m. John Lee Seward, Aug. 30, 1942 (div. Oct. 1946); children—Robert Coe Seward. A.A., Stephens Coll., 1935; B.A., U. Okla., 1938; M.D., U. Chgo., 1942. Diplomate Am. Bd. Pediatrics. Pediatrician Travis Clinic and Hosp., Jacksonville, Tex., 1947-50; practice medicine specializing in pediatrics, Carlsbad, N.Mex., 1950—. Recipient A.J. Crawford award Carlsbad Found., 1979. Fellow Am. Acad. Pediatrics; mem. AMA, N.Mex. State Med. Soc., Eddy County Med. Soc., AAUW Club: Altrusa. Republican. Episcopalian. Home: 919 N Alameda St Carlsbad NM 88220 Office: 515 W Fox St Carlsbad NM 88220

ARNAUD, CLAUDE DONALD, JR., physician, educator; b. Hackensack, N.J., Dec. 4, 1929; s. Claude Donald and Alice Marie (Minnet) A.; children: Claude Michael, Ellen Marie. B.A., Columbia Coll., 1951; M.D., N.Y. Med. Coll., 1955. Intern St. Luke's Hosp., N.Y.C.; also resident; resident, endocrine fellow Milwaukee County Hosp.; fellow U. Wis.; instr. biochemistry U. Pa., 1959-66; cons. dept. endocrine research Mayo Clinic, Rochester, Minn., 1967-77; head mineral research unit Mayo Clinic, 1972-74, head endocrine research unit, mineral research lab., 1974-77, asso. prof. medicine Grad. Sch. Medicine, 1970-74, prof., 1974-77; prof. medicine and physiology U. Calif., San Francisco, 1977—; chief endocrine unit San Francisco VA Med. Center, 1977—. Contbr. numerous articles to profl. jours. Served with M.C. U.S. Navy, 1957-59. NIH grantee, 1968—. Mem. Am. Fedn. Clin. Research, Am. Soc. Biol. Chemists, Am. Soc. Clin. Investigation, Am. Physiol. Soc., Assn. Am. Physicians, Endocrine Soc., Western Assn. Physicians, AAAS., Am. Soc. Bone Mineral Research (past pres.), Nat. Research Council, Nat. Acad. Sci., NIH (study sect. musculoskeletal 1985—, com. diet, health and chronic disease).

ARNELL, WALTER JAMES WILLIAM, engineering educator, consultant; b. Farnborough, Eng., Jan. 9, 1924; came to U.S., 1953, naturalized, 1960; s. James Albert and Daisy (Payne) A.; m. Patricia Catherine Cannon, Nov. 12, 1955; children—Sean Paul, Victoria Clare, Sarah Michele Arnell. Aero. Engr., Royal Aircraft Establishment, 1946; BSc, U. London, 1953, PhD, 1967; MA, Occidental Coll., Los Angeles, 1956; MS, U. So. Calif., 1958. Lectr. Poly. and Northampton Coll. Advance Tech., London, 1948-53; instr. U. So. Calif., Los Angeles, 1954-59; asst. prof. mech. engring. Calif. State U., Long Beach, 1959-62, assoc. prof., 1962-66, prof., 1966-71, chmn. dept. mech. engring., 1964-65, acting chmn. div. engring., 1964-66, dean engring., 1967-69, researcher Ctr. Engring. Research; affiliate faculty dept. ocean engring. U. Hawaii, 1970-74; adj. prof. systems and insdl. engring. U. Ariz., 1981—; pres. Lenra Assocs. Ltd., 1973—; chmn., project mgr. Hawaii Environ. Simulation Lab., 1971-72. Contbr. articles to profl. jours. Trustee, Rehab. Hosp. of the Pacific, 1975-79. Mem. Royal Aero. Soc., AIAA, IEEE Systems Man and Cybernetics Soc., AAUP, Am. Psychol. Assn., Soc. Engring., Psychology, Human Factors Soc., Ergonomics Soc., Psi Chi, Alpha Pi Mu, Tau Beta Pi, Phi Kappa Phi, Pi Tau Sigma. Home: 4491 E Fort Lowell Tucson AZ 85712

ARNETT, ROBERT WILLIAM, research engineer, retired; b. Steamboat Springs, Colo., Oct. 23, 1920; s. Robert Ashburnham and Charlotte May (Ives) A.; m. Louise S. Scott, Apr. 22, 1944; children: Selesta Jane, Clinton Douglas. AA, Trinidad State Jr. Coll., 1942; BSME, U. Colo., 1947, BS in Aero. Engring., 1948, MSME, 1958. Registered profl. engr., Wyo., Colo. From design engr. to head engr. Standard Oil Co., Casper, Wyo., 1948-53; research engr. Gates Rubber Co., Denver, 1954; design engr. Stanley Aviation, Aurora, Colo., 1954-55; research engr., sect. chief Nat. Bur. Standards, Boulder, Colo., 1955-73; cons. in field. Contbr. articles to profl. jours. Served to capt. USAF, 1943-58, PTO. Named Alumnus of Yr., Trinidad State Jr. Coll., 1966. Mem. ASME, Sigma Xi, Tau Beta Pi. Avocations: farming, skiing, hiking.

ARNETT, THOMAS L., management consulting executive; b. Mapleton, Utah, June 14, 1933; s. Leonard L. and Clara J. Arnett; m. Marilyn Salie, May 26, 1955; children: Tim, Troy, Todd. BS, Utah State U., 1955; MBA, Stanford U., 1957; postgrad., U. Calif., Berkeley, 1958. Sr. v.p. Creative Strategies Internat.; mktg. and human resource exec. Raychem Corp., Ford Aerospace Corp.; pres. Arnett Assocs., Los Altos, Calif., 1982—. Contbr. numerous books and research studies. Recipient Wall Street Jour. award. Avocations: skiing, tennis. Office: Arnett Assocs 101 First St Suite 403 Los Altos CA 94022

ARNEY, JEFFREY ALAN, social worker; b. Grand Junction, Colo., May 13, 1957; s. James Morrison and Dixie Margaret (Hall) A. BA, Oral Roberts U., 1979; MSW, U. Utah, 1984. Lic. social worker, Utah. Counselor Human Services, Inc., Westminster, Colo., 1980-81, Courthouse, Inc., Aurora, Colo., 1982; parent and child therapist The Children's Ctr., Salt Lake City, 1982-83, group home therapist, 1983; med. social work intern Primary Children's Med. Ctr., Salt Lake City, 1983-84; social worker pub. schs. Sch. Dist. 2, Green River, Wyo., 1984—; parent and child therapist The Children's Ctr., Salt Lake City, 1982-83, also group home therapist, 1983; vol. Denver Children's Hosp., 1981-82. Mem. Nat. Assn. Social Workers. Avocations: sports, travel, dining, books. Home: 145 D Monroe Ave Green River WY 82935 Office: Sch Dist #2 400 N First E Green River WY 82935

ARNEY, PAT WILSON, lawyer; b. Coeur d'Alene, Idaho, Mar. 3, 1927; s. J. Ward and Lillian Mae (Coon) A.; m. Jo Marie Cramer, July 23, 1956; children: Susan Gage, Sally, John; Elizabeth Chamberlain, Catherine Jones, Robert. BA, U. Wash., 1950, JD, 1954. Bar: Idaho 1954, U.S. Dist. Ct. Idaho 1954. Ptnr. Arney & Arney, Coeur d'Alene, 1954-68; sole practice, Coeur d'Alene, 1968—; pres. atty. Kootenai County, Idaho, Coeur d'Alene, 1965-69; grader Idaho State Bar Graders, various cities, 1956-80; mem. bar xamination com. Idaho State Bar, 1972-78; mem. med. malpractice screening panel Idaho State Bd. of Medicine, Coeur d'Alene, and Boise, 1979-84. Pres., Kootenai County United Crusade, 1948, IHM High Sch. Boosters, Coeur d'Alene, 1970-71; bd. dirs. Coeur d'Alene Homes, Inc., 1976-78; pub. relations officer, past membership v.p., charter mem. Soc. for Preservation and Encouragement of Barbershop Quartet Singing in Am., Inc. " Lake City Harmonizers" , Coeur d'Alene, 1981—. Served with USN, 1945-46; Guam. Mem. Idaho State Bar (unauthorized practice of law com. 1962-64, criminal laws com. 1968-70, legal aid services, ins. liaison coms. 1970-71). Democrat. Roman Catholic. Lodges: Lions, Elks (exalted ruler 1965-66) (Coeur d'Alene). Home: 607 S 11th St Coeur d'Alene ID 83814 Office: 111 N Second St Suite 10-M PO Box 758 Coeur d'Alene ID 83814

ARNEY, REX ODELL, lawyer, state senator; b. Ashland, Ky., Jan. 11, 1940; s. Harold Leat and Frances (Odell) A.; student U. Mich., 1958-59; B.A., U. Wyo., 1962, M.A., 1963; J.D., U. Ill., 1968; m. Marion Carroll Roberts, July 23, 1979; children—Dana, Jill, Michele, Ryan, Michael, Kelly, Emily. Instr., Black Hawk Coll., Moline, Ill., 1963-65; admitted to Wyo. bar, 1968; partner firm Redle, Yonkee & Arney, Sheridan, Wyo., 1968—; mem. Wyo. Ho. of Reps., 1973-77, senator Wyo. Senate, 1977—. Bd. dirs. Sheridan County YMCA, Sheridan County Hospice. Mem. Am. Bar Assn., Am. Judicature Soc., Am. Trial Lawyers Assn., Wyo. Bar Assn. Republican. Episcopalian. Lodges: Elks, Lions. Office: PO Box 6288 Sheridan WY 82801

ARNOLD, DALE EUGENE, wastewater management administrator; b. Spokane, Wash., July 4, 1953; s. Clarence Eugene and Ruth Selma (Broberg) A.; m. Julie Ann Cullen, Sept. 1, 1974; 1 child: Genevieve Jane. BA in Biology, Gonzaga U., 1975. Chemist Wastewater Lab., Spokane, 1976-79; supr. Wastewater Treatment Plant, Spokane, 1979-85, Wastewater Mgmt., Spokane, 1986—; internship advisor U. Wis., Stevens Point, 1986, Spokane Community Coll., 1986—. Rep. City of Spokane Inland Northwest Govt. Task Force, 1983-86; mem. budget com. Spokane Credit Union, 1986—. Mem. Inland Empire Pollution Control Assn. (pres. 1985—, dir. wastewater cert. tng. 1985—, bd. dirs. 1985—), Inland Empire Pacific Northwest Pollution Control Assn. (v.p. 1984-85), Nat. Mgmt. Assn. (pub. relations dir. 1983—), Spokane Bicycle Club, Missoula Bicycle Club. Avocations: ultra distance bicycle touring, bicycle collecting, collecting antiques. Home: W 457 15th Spokane WA 99203 Office: Wastewater Mgmt N 4401 Al White Pkwy Spokane WA 99205

ARNOLD, ESTHER FRANCES, social welfare administrator, dietitian; b. Berkeley, Calif., Feb. 20, 1934; d. Fred Clifford and Ruth (Ambs) Klingbeil; m. Earl Byron Arnold, June 7, 1959; children: Kathleen Reneé, Shauna Louise. BS in Foods and Nutrition, Pacific Union Coll., 1955. Registered dietitian. Food adminstr. Dept. Health, Sonoma, Calif., 1959-63; clin. dietitian Dept. Vets. Affairs, Yountville, Calif., 1963-65; dir. dietetics Dept. Mental Hygiene, Napa, Calif., 1965-71; dir. dietetics Dept. Devel. Services, Sonoma, 1971-75, asst. adminstr., 1974—; instr. Napa Community Coll, 1970-71. Active Norman Skeels Chorale, Angwin, Calif., 1976-85; supervisory com. Calif. State Cen. Credit Union., Eldridge, 1983—. Mem. Am. Dietetic Assn., Mem. Bay Area Dietetic Assn. Office: Sonoma State Hosp Box 121 Eldridge CA 95431

ARNOLD, HARRY LOREN, JR., dermatologist, editor, author; b. Owosso, Mich., Aug. 7, 1912; s. Harry L. and Meda (Sheldon) A.; m. Blanche G. Wetherald, 1934 (div. 1941); children—Sara Joan, Charles R.; m. Jeanne M. Prevost, July 11, 1942 (dec. Jan. 1983); children: Harry Loren III, John P., Susan M.; m. Jeanne S. Herman, Dec. 16, 1983. A.B. cum laude, U. Mich., 1932, M.D. cum laude, 1935; M.S., 1939. Diplomate: Am. Bd. Dermatology (mem. bd. 1966-76, pres. 1972-73). Intern U. Mich. Hosp., 1935-36, resident, 1936-37, instr. dermatology, 1937-39; chief dermatology Straub Clinic, Honolulu, 1939-69; clin. prof. medicine U. Hawaii.; clin. prof. dermatology U. Calif., San Francisco; pres. Straub Med. Research Inst., 1961-63; Frederick G. Novy, Jr. vis. scholar in dermatology U. Calif. Med. Sch., Davis, 1975; cons. emeritus U.S. Army Health Services Command, 1980. Author: Modern Concepts of Leprosy, 1953, Raibyo Gentaiteki Gainen, 1956, (with P. Fasal) Leprosy, 1973, (with A. Domonkos and R.B. Odom) Andrews' Diseases of the Skin, 7th edit, 1981; also numerous articles, editorials, columns, and chpts. in textbooks.; Editor: Hawaii Med. Jour, 1941-83, Founding editor, 1983—, Straub Clinic Procs, 1941-77, editor emeritus, 1978—; The Schoch Letter, 1975—, Soc. Sci. Assn. Trans., Internat. Jour. Dermatology, 1978—; corr. editor: Internat. Jour. of Leprosy, 1950—; editorial bd.: Cutis, 1965—, Group Practice, 1966-74, Jour. Internat. Med. Research, 1972—, Archives Dermatology, 1973-83, Jour. AMA, 1973-74. Named Practitioner of Yr. Dermatol. Found., 1983. Fellow ACP, AAAS, Royal Soc. Medicine; mem. Hawaii Med. Assn. (past pres.), Honolulu County Med. Assn. (past pres.), Hawaiian Acad. Sci. (past pres.), Am. Acad. Dermatology (hon.; pres. 1975-76), Internat. Soc. Tropical Dermatology (past v.p.), Internat. Leprosy Assn., Hawaii Dermatol. Soc. (hon. 1986), Pacific Dermatol. Soc. (hon. mem., pres. 1968), AMA (past del., sect. chmn., del. sect. dermatology), Am. Dermatol. Assn. (bd. dirs. 1969-70, pres. 1971), Sociedad Argentina de Leprologia (corr.), Sociedad Cubana de Dermatologia y Sifilografía (corr.), Asociacion Argentina de Dermatología (corr.), Sociedad Venezolana de Dermatología, Venereología y Leprologia (corr.), Sociedad Mexicana de Dermatología (hon.), Sociedad Brasileira de Dermatologia (hon.), S. African Dermatol. Assn. (hon.), N.Y. Dermatol. Assn. (hon.), Swedish Dermatol. Soc. (corr.), Honolulu chpt. Internat. Wine and Food Soc. (pres. 1977), Social Sci. Assn. Honolulu (pres. 1984, hon. mem.), Sigma Xi, Kappa Beta Phi, Alpha Omega Alpha, Nu Sigma Nu, Phi Kappa Psi, Zeta Psi. Home: 250 Laurel St Apt 301 San Francisco CA 94118 Office: 450 Sutter Suite 1432 San Francisco CA 94108

ARNOLD, JAMES RICHARD, chemist, educator; b. New Brunswick, N.J., May 5, 1923; s. Abraham Samuel and Julia (Jacobs) A.; m. Louise Clark, Oct. 11, 1952; children: Robert C., Theodore J., Kenneth C. A.B., Princeton U., 1943, M.A., 1945, Ph.D., 1946. Postdoctoral fellow Inst. Nuclear Studies, U. Chgo., 1946-47, mem. faculty, 1948-55; NRC fellow Harvard U., 1947-48; mem. faculty chemistry Princeton U., 1955-58; assoc. prof. chemistry U. Calif., San Diego, 1958-60; prof. U. Calif., 1960—, Harold C. Urey prof., 1983—, chmn. dept. chemistry, 1960-63; asso. Manhattan Project, 1943-46; dir. Calif. Space Inst., 1980—; mem. various bds. NASA, 1959—; mem. space sci. bd. Nat. Acad. Sci., 1970-74, mem. com. on sci. and public policy, 1973-77. Mem. editorial bd.: Ann. Rev. Nuclear Chemistry, 1972; asso. editor: Revs. Geophysics and Space Physics, 1972-75, Moon, 1972—; contbr. articles to profl. jours. Pres. Torrey Pines Elem. Sch. PTA, 1964-65; pres. La Jolla Democratic Club, 1965-66; mem. nat. council World Federalists-U.S.A., 1970-72. Recipient E.O. Lawrence medal AEC, 1968; Leonard medal Meteoritical Soc., 1976; asteroid 2143 named Jimarnold in his honor, 1980; Guggenheim fellow India, 1972-73. Mem. Nat. Acad. Sci., Am. Acad. Arts and Scis., Internat. Acad. Astronautics, Am. Chem. Soc., AAAS, Fedn. Am. Scientists, World Federalist Assn. Office: U Calif San Diego Dept Chemistry Code B-017 La Jolla CA 92037

ARNOLD, JOHN MILLER, biomedicine researcher, educator; b. St. Paul, Oct. 6, 1936; s. Arthur Henry and Lucile (Miller) A.; divorced; 1 dau., Kathrine Elizabeth. B.A., U. Minn., 1958, Ph.D., 1963. Mem. staff Am. Mus. Natural History, 1963-64; asst. prof. Iowa State U., 1965-67; faculty U. Hawaii, 1967—, now prof. biomed. research U. Hawaii; instr., trustee Marine Biol. Lab., Woods Hole, Mass., 1977-81; 1973 vis. prof. Silliman U., Philippines, 1982. NSF fellow, 1962, Am. Mus. Natural History fellow, 1963-64, Sigerfoos fellow, 1961; Nautilus research corp. grantee; NIH grantee, NSF grantee, Grass Found. grantee; recipient E.G. Conklin award, 1960. Fellow AAAS; mem. Marine Biol. Lab., Am. Inst. Biol. Scis., Am. Soc. Devel. Biologists, Am. Soc. Cell Biology, Western Soc. Naturalists, Internat. Soc. Devel. Biology, Internat. Soc. Cell Biology. Contbr. numerous articles to profl. jours. Office: U Hawaii 209 Snyder Hall Honolulu HI 96813 Office: Marine Biology Lab Woods Hole MA 02540

ARNOLD, KATHLEEN SPELTS, state senator; b. Miami, Fla., Oct. 25, 1941; d. John Keith and Mary Fay (Webber) Shay; m. Harold G. Arnold, Jan. 31, 1982; children by previous marriage—Melinda Kathleen, Meghan Shay, Richard John. B.A., U. Colo., 1963. Tchr., Bear Creek High Sch., Jefferson County, Colo., 1963-64, 65-67; asst. prodn. control mgr. Fordwerke, Cologne, Fed. Republic Germany, 1964-65; state rep. Colo. Gen. Assembly, Denver, 1978-83, state senator, 1983—, chmn. judiciary com., 1980-83, state affairs com., 1985-86; del. Nat. Conf. State Legislatures, 1980-83; candidate for Lt. Gov., 1986. Bd. dirs. Lane House, Littleton, Colo., 1982—, U. Colo. Alumni Bd., Denver, 1976; mem. curriculum council Jefferson County Schs.; sec. Littleton Fire Bd. Mem. South Jeffeo-Kalewood C. of C. Republican. Presbyterian. Office: Lane House 6436 W Frost Dr Littleton CO 80123

ARNOLD, R. STEVEN, sports promoter; b. N.Y.C., Mar. 15, 1938; s. Arnold H. and Matilda (Ostrow) A. AB, Brown U., 1959; JD, Columbia U., 1962. Dir. Am. Basketball Assn., N.Y.C., 1970-72, World Team Tennis, San Francisco, 1972-73, Internat. Basketball Assn., Geneva, 1973-74; dir., owner World Football League, Newport Beach, Calif., 1973-74; dir. World Hockey Assn., Newport Beach, 1971-72, Nat. Women's Volleyball League, Tiburon, Calif., 1985—; pres. Steve Arnold Enterprises, 1971—, World Telemedia Co., Corte Madera, Calif., 1981—; chmn. bd. dirs. ProSports, Inc., New Orleans; pres., commr. major league volleyball, 1986—; instr. Practicing Law Inst., N.Y.C., 1973—; arbitrator Am. Arbitration Assn., N.Y.C., 1970-73. Mem. N.Y. State Bar Assn., Calif. Real Estate Brokers. Home: 4386 Paradise Dr Tiburon CA 94920

ARNOLD, ROCKY RICHARD, structures engineer; b. Iola, Kans., Dec. 27, 1948; s. Dick William Virgil and Betty Jean (Rhodes) A.; m. Nazmiye Ertan, Jan. 6, 1972; 1 child, Sevgi Zübeyde. BSME, U. Mo., Rolla, 1970; MSME, MIT, 1972; MSCE, Stanford U., 1980, PhD in Civil Engring., 1983. Registered profl. engr., Calif. Asst. structures engr. United Tech. Corp., Sunnyvale, Calif., 1972-73, sr. engr., 1978-81; staff engr. Acurex Corp., Mountain View, Calif., 1973-75; sr. engring specialist Ford Aero. & Communications Corp., Palo Alto, Calif., 1981-83; cons. engr. Anamet Labs., Inc., San Carlos, Calif., 1975-78, prin. engr., 1983—. Contbr. articles to profl. jours. Served to capt. USAR, 1970-78. Mem. AIAA, Am. Helicopter Soc., ASME, Soc. for Advancement of Materials and Processes in Engring., Kappa Mu Epsilon, Phi Kappa Phi, Pi Tau Sigma, Sigma Xi. Republican. Avocations: bowling, basketball, tennis. Home: 799 Bounty Dr #2037 Foster City CA 94404 Office: Anamet Labs Inc 3400 Investment Blvd Hayward CA 94545

ARNOLD, SHEILA, state legislator; b. N.Y.C., Jan. 15, 1929; d. Michael and Eileen (Lynch) Keddy; coll. courses; m. George Longan Arnold, Nov. 12, 1960; 1 son, Peter; 1 son by previous marriage, Michael C. Young; stepchildren—Drew, George Longan, Joe. Mem. Wyo. Ho. of Reps., 1978—, mem. com. on appropriations, com. on rules and procedures; dir. First Interstate Bank of Laramie. Former mem., sec. Wyo. Land Use Adv. Coms.; past pres. Dem. Women's Club, Laramie; past vice-chmn. Albany County Dem. Cen. Com.; past mem. Dem. State Com.; mem. Nat. Conf. State Legislatures Spl. Task Force on Fiscal Affairs and Oversight. Recipient Spl. Recognition award for developmentally disabled citizens of Wyo., 1985. Mem. Laramie Area C. of C. (pres. 1982; Top Hand award 1977), LWV, Internat. Platform Assn. Clubs: Faculty Women's (past pres.), Zonta, Laramie Women's, Cowboy Joe. Office: Capitol Bldg Cheyenne WY 82002

ARNOLD, TERRENCE EUGENE, project engineer; b. Hiawatha, Kans., Dec. 27, 1955; s. Harold Eugene and Mary Elizabeth (Farrell) A.; m. Ruth Ann Ferguson, May 29, 1976; children: Ashleigh Marie, Andra Nicole, Chelsey Ann. BS, Kans. State U., 1977, MS, 1978. Staff engr. Woodward-Clyde Cons., Denver, 1978-84, project engr., 1984—. Mem. ASCE (assoc., asst. to sec. 1982-83, asst. to pres. 1984-85, Outstanding Young Profl. for Achievement 1986). Roman Catholic. Avocations: hunting, skiing, model airplanes. Office: Woodward-Clyde Cons 4582 S Ulster St Pkwy Suite 1000 Stanford Pl 3 Denver CO 80237

ARNOLD, THOMAS EADS, JR., real estate management executive; b. Oakland, Calif., June 29, 1944; s. Thomas Eads and Jean (Carson) A.; m. Kimball Clark, Apr. 8, 1972; children: Anne Elizabeth, Thomas Eads III, Charles Clark. BA, U. Ariz., 1970. Leasing agt. Del E. Webb Realty and Mgmt. Co., Phoenix, 1973-75, pres., 1981-84; pres. Del E. Webb Comml. Properties Corp., Phoenix, 1984; chmn., pres. Del E. Webb Realty and

Mgmt. Co., Phoenix, 1984-85; chmn. Del E. Webb Comml. Properties Corp., Phoenix, 1984-85; exec. v.p. real estate ops. Del E. Webb Corp., Phoenix, 1985-86, pres., 1986-87; leasing agt. Murdock Mgmt. Co., Phoenix, 1975, v.p. leasing, 1976, exec. v.p., 1977, pres., 1977-81; pres. Allen Tenant Services, Inc., Phoenix, 1987—. Chmn. corp. giving com. St. Luke's Med. Ctr. Toxicology Program, 1985, streets com. Phoenix Bond Com., 1984—, Cen. Phoenix Redevel. Com.; mem. Mayor's Com. High-Rise Zoning, 1983-84; exec. com. Phoenix Bond Election, 1984—, Luke's Men, 1978-84, Ariz. Acad. of Ariz. Town Halls, 1979—, bd. dirs. 1986-86; bd. dirs. Prescott (Ariz.) Coll., 1984—. Served with U.S. Army, 1967-69, Korea. Mem. Ariz. Real Estate Inst. (exec. com), Iron Springs Assn. (bd. dirs. 1984—), Desert Bot. Gardens (nominating com. 1985-86), Phoenix Met. C. of C. (vice chmn. econ. devel. exec. com., bd. dirs. 1984—), Conv. Bur./C. of C. (facilities com.), Phoenix Art Mus., Heard Mus. (trustee 1986—), Phoenix Town Hall, U. Ariz Coll. of Bus. (nat. bd. advisors), Real Estate Soc., Lambda Alpha. Republican. Avocations: tennis, gardening, outdoor activities. Office: Del E Webb Corp 3800 N Central Ave Phoenix AZ 85012

ARNOLD, WILLIAM OSCAR, data processing executive; b. Buckeye, Ariz., Mar. 24, 1938; s. Lee Odis and Lillie Mae (Keith) A.; m. Lynda Carol DeBerry, Aug. 8, 1962; children: Shaun, Shane, Shannon. BBA, U. Phoenix, 1986. Real estate salesman Red Carpet Realtors, Phoenix, 1975-77; EDP ops. mgr. Utah State U., Logan, 1968-75, Smitty's Super Value, Phoenix, 1977—. Served with USAF, 1961-62. Mem. Ch. of Christ. Office: Smitty's Super Value 2626 S 7th St Phoenix AZ 85034

ARNOLD, WILLIAM WRIGHT, III, hospital administrator; b. Long Beach, Calif., Dec. 10, 1948; s. William Busey and Virginia Eloise (Moore) A.; m. Joan Doell, Dec. 18, 1971; children—Brandon Wright, Justin Menefee. B.A. in English and Bus., U. Wash., 1972; M.H.A., UCLA, 1974. Asst. adminstr. Santa Barbara (Calif.) Cottage Hosp., 1975-79; asst. dir. Stanford U. Hosp., Palo Alto, Calif., 1979-82, assoc. dir., 1982-83, sr. assoc. dir., 1983-84, dep. dir., 1984-85; exec. v.p. Stanford U. Hosp., Palo Alto, 1985—. Bd. dirs. St. Joseph's Hosp., San Francisco. Mem. Am. Coll. Hosp. Adminstrs. Office: 300 Pasteur Dr C-204 Palo Alto CA 94305

ARNSAN, DANIEL CARLTON, college librarian, educator; b. Detroit, Aug. 28, 1946; s. David Leroy and Jane Virginia (Parsley) A.; m. Barbara Lynn Gribbin, Aug. 30, 1974; children: Priscilla, Thomas. AA, Mira Costa Coll., 1969; BA with high honors, San Diego State U., 1971; MA with high honors, San Jose State U., 1973. Bookmobile librarian Oceanside (Calif.) Pub. Library, 1970-72; head children's services Carlsbad (Calif.) City Library, 1973-80; librarian, head pub. services and instr. library tech. program Palomar Coll., San Marcos, Calif., 1980—; instr. children's lit. Palomar Coll., 1975-85. Active San Diego Speakers Bur., 1982—. Served as sgt. USMC, 1963-67, Vietnam. Mem. Calif. Tchrs. Assn. (chpt. v.p. 1984-86, pres. 1986—), Stained Glass Guild, Phi Kappa Phi. Democrat. Avocations: stained glass, art, reading, model railroading. Home: 1060 Vale View Dr Vista CA 92083 Office: Palomar Coll 1140 W Mission Rd San Marcos CA 92069

ARNST, ALBERT, editor, forester; b. Portland, Oreg., July 9, 1909; s. David and Alwina (Lorenz) A.; B.S. in Forestry, Oreg. State U., 1931; m. Della Coleen Irwin, May 1, 1939; children—Audrey Karen, Robert Craig, Rosemary. Forester, Forest Service, U.S. Dept. Agr., Portland, Oreg., 1931-35, Medford, Oreg., 1935-36, Lakeview, Oreg., 1937, public info. officer, Washington, 1962-75, with Soil Conservation Service, Dayton, Spokane and Sedro-Woolley, (all in Wash.), 1937-45, Corvallis and Portland, Oreg., 1941-43; sales rep Skagit Steel & Iron Works, Sedro-Woolley, 1945-46; public info. rep. Weyerhaeuer Co., Tacoma, 1946-52; editor Timberman mag., Portland, 1952-53; editor Miller Freeman Publs., Portland, 1954-62; mng. editor Western Conservation Jour., Portland, 1975-82. Fellow Soc. Am. Foresters (53-yr. mem.); mem. Soil Conservation Soc. Am., Oreg. Logging Conf. (hon. life), Internat. Assn. Bus. Communicators (Rodney Adair Meml. award 1978, pres. 1962, 71, 79, named Communicator of Yr. 1966 nat. Pres.'s award 1983), Nat. Assn. Govt. Communicators. Democrat. Clubs: Foggy Bottom (pres. 1971) (Washington), Willamette Writers. Lodge: Lions. Contbr. articles on forestry to profl. jours. Address: 2430 NE Stanton Portland OR 97212

AROFF, LEATRICE (JOY), fabric artist, dress designer; b. Portland, Oreg., Feb. 4, 1925; d. Elmer Walter and Margeurite Hedvig (Koch) Vinton; m. Maurice Nathaniel Aroff, Aug. 21, 1952 (div. Mar. 1970); children: Michael, Libbie, Kipp, Steve, Duke, Patrick. Student, Names Boling, Portland; studied under, Lenard Kester. Proofreader, copywriter The Oregonian Newspaper, Portland, 1943-44; radio announcer, copywriter Sta. KVAN-Radio, Vancouver, Wash., 1944-47; sec. to program dir. NBC Radio and TV, Hollywood, Calif., 1947-49; prodn. sec. NBC Network TV, Hollywood, Calif., 1950-52; sec. to prodn. mgr. Young & Rubicam Advt. Agy., Hollywood, Calif., 1949-50; owner, dir. Joya Design Studio, Los Angeles, 1982—. Democrat. Presbyterian. Avocations: running, cooking, embroidery, beading. Studio: Joya Design Studio 1131 Montana Ave Suite C Santa Monica CA 90403

ARONSON, HARVEY BEAR, social worker, educator; b. Bklyn., Mar. 26, 1945; s. George and Bessie Aronson; m. Anne C. Klein, Jan. 11, 1976. BS, Bklyn. Coll., 1966; PhD, U. Wis., 1975; MSW, Boston U., 1984. Asst. prof. U. Va., Charlottesville, 1975-82, Stanford U., Calif., 1984-86; clin. social worker Emergency Treatment Ctr., Palo Alto, Calif., 1984-86, Children's Hosp., Stanford, 1986—. Author: Love and Sympathy in Theravada Buddhism, 1980. Mem. Am. Acad. Religion, Nat. Assn. Social Workers. Home: 1294 Meadowlark Ave San Jose CA 95128 Office: Social Services Childrens Hosp Stanford Stanford CA 94304

ARONSON, JEROME MELVILLE, plant physiology educator; b. Oakland, Calif., May 20, 1930; s. Arthur and Tillie (Quint) A.; m. Danielle Esther Bourla, Oct. 27, 1955; children: Arthur Maurice, Vickie Charmaine. AB, U. Calif., Berkeley, 1952, PhD, 1958. Asst. prof. biology Wayne State U., Detroit, 1959-63; lectr. botany U. Calif., Berkeley, 1964-66; assoc. prof. botany Ariz. State U., Tempe, 1966-71, prof., 1971—, acting chmn. dept. botany and microbiology, 1976. Assoc. editor Exptl. Mycology, 1979—; contbr. articles to profl. jours. Fellow NIH, 1956-57, 58-59; grantee USDA, 1982-84, NIH, NSF, 1960-82. Mem. Am. Soc. Plant Physiologists, Mycol. Soc. Am. (chmn. awards com. 1981-82), Bot. Soc. Am. (chmn. microbiol. sect. 1972-73, 83-85), Sigma Xi. Avocation: jogging. Office: Ariz State U Dept Botany and Microbiology Tempe AZ 85287

ARONSON, JOHN GERALD, environmental scientist, water resource consultant; b. Omaha, May 20, 1949; s. Gerald Everett and Elizabeth Ann (Wood) A.; m. Jeanie Ann Greeno, Jan. 2, 1974; children: Christopher John Greeno, Alexandra Jean Greeno. B.S. with highest distinction in Biology, Nebr. Wesleyan U., 1971; M.S. in Zoology, U. Nebr., 1973; Ph.D. candidate in Botany, Colo. State U., 1974—. Aquatic ecologist, project mgr., lab. mgr. Environ. Research & Tech. Inc., Ft. Collins, Colo., 1973-78, mgr. tech. devel., 1978-80, regional mktg. mgr., 1980-82, sr. cons., 1982-85, div. mgr. biostratigraphy, 1982—; pres., dir. Riverside Tech., Inc., Ft. Collins, 1985—. Author: Earth Chords, 1983; contbr. articles to profl. jours. Fund raiser United Way Campaign, Ft. Collins, 1983, 84. Recipient Ten Yr. Service award ERT, Inc., 1984. Mem. Am. Fisheries Soc. (cert. fisheries scientist), Am. Soc. Limnology and Oceanography, Ecology Soc. Am., Phycol. Soc. Am., N.Am. Diatom Symposium, Am. Assn. Petroleum Geologists, Am. Inst. Biol. Scis., AAAS, Nebr. Acad. Sci., N.Am. Benthological Soc. Democrat. Lutheran. Club: Ft. Collins. Avocations: running, skiing, tennis, bicycling. Office: Riverside Tech Inc 375 E Horsetooth Rd Fort Collins CO 80525

ARRIGONI, LOUIS, cooperative food distributor; b. S. Cle Elum, Wash., Aug. 4, 1916; s. Joseph and Esther (Paganelli) A.; m. Evelyn I. Pierson, Apr. 26, 1944; children: Nancy, Evelyn, James. B.S., U. Wash., 1938, M.S., 1940, Ph.D., 1945. Asst. prof. chemistry U. Wash., Seattle, 1943-49; with Consol. Dairy Products Co., Seattle, 1949-67, v.p., 1962-67, dir., 1962—, pres., 1971—; pres. Assoc. Grocers Inc., Seattle, 1967-71, also dir., chmn. exec. com.; dir. Rainier Internat. Bank, Dairy Export Co., Inc., Rainier Nat. Bank. Mem. Am. Pharm. Assn., Sigma Xi. Clubs: Wash. Athletic (Seattle), Rainier (Seattle). Lodge: Elks. Home: 4845 NE 85th St Seattle WA 98115 Office: Consolidated Dairy Products Co 635 Elliott Ave Seattle WA 98119 •

ARRINGTON, LEONARD JAMES, history educator; b. Twin Falls, Idaho, July 2, 1917; s. Noah Wesley and Edna Grace (Corn) A.; m. Grace Fort, Apr. 24, 1943 (dec. Mar. 10, 1982); children: James Wesley, Carl Wayne, Susan Grace; m. Harriet Ann Horne, Nov. 19, 1983. B.A. in Econs, U. Idaho, 1939, L.H.D. (hon.), 1977; Ph.D. in Econ. History, U. N.C., 1952; H.H.D. (hon.), Utah State U., 1982. Prof. econs. Utah State U., 1946-72; summer prof. Brigham Young U., Provo, Utah, 1956, 58, 66; Lemuel H. Redd prof. Western history, dir. Charles Redd Center for Western Studies, 1972-80; dir. Joseph Fielding Smith Inst. for Ch. History, 1980-86; ch. historian Ch. of Jesus Christ of Latter-day Saints, 1972-80, dir. history div., 1978-80; Fulbright prof. Am. econs. U. Genoa, Italy, 1958-59; vis. prof. history UCLA, 1966-67. Author: Great Basin Kingdom: An Economic History of the Latter-day Saints, 1830-1900, 1958, The Changing Economic Structure of the Mountain West, 1850-1950, 1963, Beet Sugar in the West: A History of the Utah-Idaho Sugar Company, 1891-1966, 1966, Charles C. Rich, Mormon General, Western Frontiersman, 1974, David Eccles, Pioneer Western Industrialist, 1975, Building the City of God: Community and Cooperation Among the Mormons, 1976, From Quaker to Latter-day Saint: Bishop Edwin D. Woolley, 1976, The Mormon Experience: A History of the Latter-day Saints, 1979, Sunbonnet Sisters: A History of Mormon Women, 1984, Brigham Young, American Moses, 1985, History of the Hotel Utah, 1986, Mothers of the Prophets, 1987; editor: Western Hist. Quar., 1969-72, Jour. Mormon History, 1986—; bd. editors: Pacific Hist. Rev, 1959-62; adv. editor: Dialogue: A Jour. of Mormon Thought, 1966-69. Served with AUS, 1943-46. Recipient Charles Redd Humanities award Utah Acad. Scis., Arts and Letters, 1966, David O. McKay Humanities award Brigham Young U., 1969; Huntington Library fellow, 1956-57. Mem. Mormon History Assn. (pres. 1965-66), Western History Assn. (pres. 1968-69), Am. Hist. Assn. (pres. Pacific Coast br. 1981-82), Agrl. History Soc. (pres. 1969-70), Soc. Am. Historians, Sons Utah Pioneers, SAR, Am. Legion. Club: Rotary. Home: 2236 South 2200 E Salt Lake City UT 84109 Office: 301 Knight Mangum Bldg Brigham Young U Provo UT 84602

ARRIOLA, DAVID BRUCE, resort, hotel marketing executive; b. Winnemucca, Nev., June 18, 1950; s. Mario M. and Barbara M. (Metcalf) A.; m. Elizabeth S. Peterson, Apr. 28, 1979; 1 child, Brittany. B.A. U. Nev., Reno, 1973; postgrad., Ariz. State U., 1979, 83. Dir. pub. relations Mt. Rose Resort, Reno, Nev., 1971-73; dir. mktg. Heavenly Valley Ski Resort, Lake Tahoe, Calif., 1973-75; dir. mktg. Crested Butte (Colo.) Devel. Corp., 1975-77; gen. sales mgr. Best Western Internat., Inc., Phoenix, Ariz., 1977-84; v.p. mktg. Recreational Properties div. Del Webb Corp., 1984—. Mem. Fiesta Bowl Com., 1983—; bd. dirs. Scottsdale Arts Ctr. Assn., 1985—. Mem. Phoenix Valley of the Sun Visitors and Conv. Bur. (chmn. mktg. com. 1981-85, planning com. 1983-84), Am. Bus. Assn. (travel adv. com. 1982-83), Nat. Tour Assn. (mktg. and communications com. 1985-86), Scottsdale Arts Ctr. Assn. (bd. dirs.). Republican. Office: Del Webb Corp Recreational Properties PO Box 29040 Phoenix AZ 85038

ARROW, KENNETH JOSEPH, economist, educator; b. N.Y.C., Aug. 23, 1921; s. Harry I. and Lillian (Greenberg) A.; m. Selma Schweitzer, Aug. 31, 1947; children: David Michael, Andrew. B.S. in Social Sci., CCNY, 1940; M.A., Columbia U., 1941, Ph.D., 1951, D.Sc., 1973; LL.D. (hon.), U. Chgo., 1967, City U. N.Y., 1972, Hebrew U. Jerusalem, 1975, U. Pa., 1976; D.Social and Econ. Scis. (hon.), U. Vienna, Austria, 1971; D.Social Scis. (hon.), Yale, 1974; Doctor (hon.), Université René Descartes, Paris, 1974, U. Aix-Marseille III, 1985; Dr.Pol., U. Helsinki, 1976; M.A. (hon.), Harvard U., 1968; D.Litt., Cambridge U., 1985. Research assoc. Cowles Commn. for Research in Econs., 1947-49; asst. prof. econs. U. Chgo., 1948-49; acting asst. prof. econs. and stats. Stanford, 1949-50, assoc. prof., 1950-53, prof. econs., statistics and ops. research, 1953-68; prof. econs. Harvard, 1968-74, James Bryant Conant univ. prof., 1974-79; exec. head dept. econs. Stanford U., 1954-56, acting exec. head dept., 1962-63, Joan Kenney prof. econs. and prof. ops. research, 1979—; economist Council Econ. Advisers, U.S. Govt., 1962; cons. RAND Corp. Author: Social Choice and Individual Values, 1951, Essays in the Theory of Risk Bearing, 1971, The Limits of Organization, 1974, Collected Papers, Vols. I-VI, 1983-85; co-author: Mathematical Studies in Inventory and Production, 1958, Studies in Linear and Nonlinear Programming, 1958, Time Series Analysis of Inter-industry Demands, 1959, Public Investment, The Rate of Return and Optimal Fiscal Policy, 1971, General Competitive Analysis, 1971, Studies in Resource Allocation Processes, 1977, Social Choice and Multicriterion Decision Making, 1985. Served as capt. AUS, 1942-46. Social Sci. Research fellow, 1952; fellow Center for Advanced Study in the Behavioral Scis., 1956-57; fellow Churchill Coll., Cambridge, Eng., 1963-64, 70, 73, 86; Guggenheim fellow, 1972-73; Recipient John Bates Clark medal Am. Econ. Assn., 1957; Alfred Nobel Meml. prize in econ. scis., 1972, von Neumann prize, 1986. Fellow Am. Acad. Arts and Scis. (v.p. 1979-81), Econometric Soc. (v.p 1955, pres. 1956), Am. Statis. Assn., Inst. Math. Stats., Am. Econ. Assn. (mem. exec. com. 1967-69, pres. 1973), AAAS (chmn. sect K 1983), Internat. Soc. for Inventory Research (pres. 1983—); mem. Internat. Econs. Assn. (pres. 1983-86), Nat. Acad. Scis., Am. Philos. Soc., Inst. Mgmt. Scis. (pres. 1963, chmn. council 1964), Finnish Acad. Scis. (fgn. hon.), Brit. Acad. (corr.), Western Econ. Assn. (pres. 1980-81).

ARTERS, LINDA BROMLEY, public relations consultant, writer; b. Phila., Dec. 18, 1951; d. Edward Pollard and Rosalyn Irene (Bromley) A. BA, Thiel Coll., 1973. Dir. customer relations Artmann Devel. Corp. Inc., Media, Pa., 1973-74; with S.E. Nat. Bank, Malvern, Pa., 1974-78, coordinator pub. relations, 1976-78; pvt. practice pub. relations consultant Media, 1978-84, Tempe, Ariz., 1984—; lectr. in field; past mem. pvt. industry council County De. (Pa.) CETA Program. free lance writer for local, regional and nat. mags. and newspapers. Chmn. Emergency Dept. Vols. Chandler Regional Hosp; past bd. dirs. South Chester County Advanced Life Support Inc., United Cerebral Palsy of Del County; mem. Phila. Indoor Tennis Corp., 1977-82. Mem. Internat. Assn. Bus. Communicators, Nat. Fedn. Ind. Bus., Nat. Assn. Female Execs., Pub. Relations Soc. Am. (eligibility com. Phoenix chpt., mem. counselors group), U.S. Tennis Writers Assn., Phoenix C. of C. (communications council), Tempe C. of C. (chmn. communications council), Cen. Ariz. Mountain Rescue Assn. (chmn. pub. relations). Republican. Presbyterian. Office: Arters & Assocs PO Box 27848 Tempe AZ 85282

ARTHUR, ALLEN A., public relations counsel, writer; b. Ft. Scott, Kans., Jan. 24, 1920; s. Louis R. and Mary J. (Allen) Divilbiss. B.S. cum laude, U. So. Calif., 1952. Promotion dir. U. So. Calif., 1955-57; exec. mgr. San Diego Conv. and Tourist Bur., 1957-58; ind. counsel in pub. relations, Los Angeles and San Francisco, 1958-83; dir. advt. Crowell-Collier Broadcasting Corp., 1961; dir. univ. relations/spl. projects U. So. Calif., Los Angeles, 1974-76; pub. relations counsel, 1976—. Assoc. mem. Calif. Republican Central Com., 1965-76. Mem. Am. Philatelic Soc., Am. Theatre Organ Soc., Internat. Wine and Food Soc., Soc. Wine Educators, Les Amis Du Vin, Les Grand Crus, Am. Wine Soc., Wine and Food Soc. Tulsa (founder 1983), Blue Key, Alpha Kappa Psi, Beta Gamma Sigma, Alpha Delta Sigma, Alpha Phi Omega, Alpha Tau Omega. Presbyterian. Home: 30072 Andromeda Ln Malibu CA 90265

ARTHUR, GREER MARTIN, maritime container leasing firm executive; b. Champaign, Ill., Feb. 15, 1935; s. Greer Martin and Olive Loretta (Simard) A.; m. Veronica Lattman, Nov. 30, 1968; children—Alexandra, Vincent, Tanya, Greer III. B.A., Lafayette Coll., 1956; J.D., Columbia U., 1961. Account exec. tng. program Young & Rubicam, 1957-58; assoc. Havens, Wandless, Stitt & Tighe, N.Y.C., 1961-62; mgmt. cons. McKinsey & Co., 1962-67; asst. to v.p. internat. Scovil Mfg. Co., Waterbury, Conn.; internat. market mgr. Scovil France, Paris, market mgr. Hamilton Beach div. Scovil, Waterbury, 1967-69; pres., chief exec. officer SSI Container Corp., subs. Itel Corp., San Francisco, 1969-73; pres., chief exec. officer, dir. Trans Ocean Ltd., San Bruno, Calif., 1973—. Treas., trustee Phillips Brooks Sch., Menlo Park, Calif., 1980-83; mem. Lafayette Coll. Nat. Council, 1981-83. Mem. Bus. Edn. Council, Inst. Internat. Container Lessors Assn. Corp. Growth, Bus. Edn. Council, Inst. Internat. Container Lessors (pres. 1982-84), N.Y. State Bar, Young Pres. Orgn., Chief Exec. Orgn., World Bus. Forum. Clubs: Bankers, World Trade (San Francisco); Club at World Trade Center (N.Y.C.); Family, Commonwealth. Office: Trans Ocean Ltd 851 Traeger Ave San Bruno CA 94066

ARTHUR, JENNIFER LEE, hospital planner, marketer; b. San Juan, Puerto Rico, Sept. 11, 1951; d. Henry Harrison and Margaret Ann (Penning) A. BA in Econs., Smith Coll., 1974; MBA, Stanford U., 1978. Account exec. Ketchum Advt., San Francisco, 1978-81; mgmt. cons. Bain and Co., San Francisco, 1981-83; asst. v.p., planning and mktg. Mills-Peninsula Hosps., Burlingame and San Mateo, Calif., 1983-85; dir. planning and mktg. Acute Care Affiliates div. Alta Bates Corp., Berkeley, Calif., 1986—; adj. faculty mem. U. San Francisco Masters in Health Services Program, 1986—. Mem. No. Calif. Health Care Mktg. Assn. (bd. dirs.), Bay Area Planners Group, AMA Acad. Health Services Mktg., Am Hosp. Assn. Soc. Hosp. Planners and Marketers. Democrat. Avocations: racquetball, chinese and thai cooking. Office: Acute Care Affiliates 2855 Telegraph Ave Suite 210 Berkeley CA 94705

ARTHUR, JOHN READ, JR., electrical engineering educator; b. Omaha, Dec. 17, 1931; s. John Read and Edith Lisle A.; m. Beverly B. Bentzinger, Aug. 14, 1954; children—John Read, III, Stephen M., Michael W., Mary A. B.S. in Chem. Tech., Iowa State U., 1954, Ph.D. in Phys. chemistry, 1961. Mem. tech. staff Bell Labs., Murray Hill, N.J., 1961-77; with phys. electronics div. Perkin-Elmer Corp., Eden Prairie, Minn., 1977-83, sr. project scientist, 1978-83; Tektronix prof. elec. engring. Oreg. State U., Corvallis, 1983—. Contbr. articles to profl. jours. Patentee in field. Served to lt. USNR, 1954-56. Recipient Morris Leibmann award IEEE, 1982. Mem. Am. Phys. Soc. (IBM prize 1982), Am. Vacuum Soc. (pres. 1983). Clubs: Sierra, Appalachian Mountain. Office: Oregon State Univ Dept Elec and Computer Engring Corvallis OR 97331

ARTHUR, JOHN SCRIPTURE, thoracic and vascular surgeon; b. Rome, N.Y., Nov. 30, 1942; s. William Maurice and Ruth Priscilla (Scripture) A.; m. Ellen Doris Creeley, Apr. 29, 1967; children: Kelly Allison, Rachael Kimberly, Jason Andrew, Rebecca Susan, Benjamin Douglas, Sara Gamble, Luke William, Jesse Richard. AB, Dartmouth Coll., 1964; MD, Albany Med. Coll., 1968. Diplomate Am. Bd. Surgery. Intern in surgery U. Wash. Affiliated Hosps., 1968-69, resident in gen., thoracic and vascular surgery, 1969-75; practice medicine specializing in thoracic and vascular surgery Bremerton, Wash., 1977—; mem. staff Harrison Meml. Hosp., Bremerton, 1977-84, chief of surgery, 1984-86; founder Narrows Vascular Lab., 1982. Served with M.C. USN, 1975-77. Fellow ACS; mem. AMA, Wash. State Med. Assn., Pacific N.W. Vascular Soc. (founding), Puget Sound Vascular Soc. (founding), Personal Care Physicians (sec.), U. Wash. Surg. Soc., Kitsap County Med. Soc. Club: Bremerton Tennis and Swim. Office: 1225 Campbell Way Suite 101 Bremerton WA 98310

ARTHUR, PAUL KEITH, electronic engineer; b. Kansas City, Mo., Jan. 14, 1931; s. Walter B. and Frieda J. (Burckhardt) A.; m. Joy N. Lim, Apr. 26, 1958; children—Gregory V., Lia F. Student Ohio No. U., 1947, Taylor U., Upland, Ind., 1948-49; B.S.E.E., Purdue U., 1956; postgrad. N.Mex. State U., 1957-78. Registered profl. engr., N.Mex. With White Sands Missile Range, N.Mex., 1956—, electronic engr. field engring. group missile flight surveillance office, 1956-60, chief field engring. group, 1960-62, project engr. Pershing weapon system Army Missile Test and Evaluation Directorate, 1962-74, chief high altitude air def. projects br., 1974-82, chief air def. material test div., 1982—, mem. exec. devel. group, career program mgr. for engrs. and scientists. Served with USN, 1949-53, rear admiral Res., 1954—. Decorated Meritorious Service medal U.S. Navy, Navy Achievement medal. Mem. Am. Def. Preparedness Assn. (past pres.), AIAA (past vice chmn.), Assn. Old Crows (dir.), Naval Res. Assn., Res. Officers Assn. (pres. 1983-85), United Vets. Council (chmn. 1984-85), Am. Soc. Naval Engrs., Naval Inst., Navy League, Purdue Alumni Assn. (past pres.), N.Mex. State U. Alumni Assn., Sierra Club, Mesilla Valley Track Club, Bujutsukan Acad. Martial Arts. Author numerous plans and reports on weapon systems tests and evaluation. Home: 2050 San Acacio Las Cruces NM 88001 Office: STEWS-TE-M White Sands Missile Range NM 88002

ARTHURS, GARY ALAN, quality assurance engineer; b. Akron, Ohio, Feb. 21, 1947; s. David Franklin and Shirley Ann (Ohlson) A.; m. Margaret Anne Flanigan, Feb. 14, 1981; children: Brian Conal Flanigan-Arthurs, Lisa Marie Flanigan-Arthurs. Student, Phoenix Coll., 1965-67; AA, Glendale Community Coll., 1968; BS in Mfg. Engring. Tech., Ariz. State U., 1977. Quality control inspector Beckman Instruments, Scottsdale, Ariz., 1972-73, quality control auditor, 1973-77, quality control analyst, 1977-79, quality assurance coordinator, 1979, process quality engr., 1979-81; quality engr. Garrett Turbine Engine Co., Phoenix, 1981—. Mem. Consol. Coop. Scottsdale East, bd. dirs. 1974-80, pres., 1975-78. Recipient Reliabiligy Maintainability and Quality Assurance award Naval Material Command, 1985. Mem. Am. Soc. Quality Control (cert.), Soc. Mfg. Engrs., Cen. Ariz. Speculative Fiction Soc. (sec. 1980-81). Avocations: programming, reading, woodworking. Office: Garrett Turbine Engine Co 84-51 404-2K 111 S 34th St Box 5217 Phoenix AZ 85010

ARTINGSTALL, THOMAS, electrical and mechanical engineer; b. Chgo., Oct. 28, 1920; s. William Thomas and Louise Mary (Hanson) A.; m. Laura Ann Swanson, June 23, 1946 (div. June 1955)); m. Arloah Darlene Norelius, June 25, 1965. BME, Ill. Inst. Tech., 1944; postgrad., U. So. Calif., 1956. Registered profl. engr., Calif., Ill. Designer Solar Capacitator Co., Los Angeles, 1945-48; chief designer, developer Kollsman Instrument, Los Angeles, 1948-55; mem. radar/antenna/transmitter devel. staff Autonetics, Anaheim, Calif., 1956-70; tech. research staff Los Angeles Aircraft, 1970-71; chief engr. Space Div. So. Calif., Yorba Linda, 1980-86; engring. specialist Rockwell Internat., Downey, Calif., 1977-86; cons. engr. Pace-Arrow, Pomona, Calif., 1970-78; engring. developer and researcher Swanson Electronics, Arcadia, Calif., 1965-70. Patentee in field. Mem. Archtl. com. City of Yorba Linda, 1968; mem. com. Ad Hoc City Incorp., 1966; mem. bd. parks and recreation City of Yorba Linda, 1975. Mem. ASME, Nat. Mgmt. Assn., Profl. Engrs., Langlauflers Ski Club. Democrat. Roman Catholic. Avocations: photography, snow skiing, camping, fishing. Home: 19622 Larkridge Dr Yorba Linda CA 92686

ARUNDEL, IAN BRESSON, art dealer; b. Mitchell, S.D., Feb. 22, 1914; s. Charles Henry and Mary Porter (Bresson) A.; student U. Mich., 1934-37; m. Millie Lewis Waugh, Nov. 8, 1952; children—Ann Waugh, Colin Waugh. Restorer paintings and art objects, Detroit, 1937-43; dealer antique art, conservator, Los Angeles, 1945-52; art dealer, appraiser, Los Angeles, 1952—; expert primitive tribal art, appraiser U.S. govt.; exhibited tribal art in group shows at Santa Barbara (Calif.) Mus. Art, Los Angeles County Mus. Art, Miami U., Pomona Coll., U. Calif. at Fullerton, Otis Art Inst. Served with AUS, 1943-45. Fellow Am. Inst. for Conservation Historic and Artistic Works; mem. Smithsonian Instn., Brit. Mus. Soc., Archives Am. Art, Mus. Alliance Los Angeles County Mus., Victorian Soc. Office: 7152 SE 13th Ave Portland OR 97202

ARVAY, NANCY JOAN, insurance companey executive; b. Pitts., Aug. 27, 1952; d. William John and Cornelia (Prince) A. BA in History, Duke U., 1974; postgrad., Columbia U., 1974-75. Polit. and internat. communications specialist U.S. Senate Fgn. Relations Com., Washington, 1975-77; broadcast media relations rep. Am. Petroleum Inst., Washington, 1977-79; broadcast media relations rep. Chevron U.S.A., San Francisco, 1979-82, coordinator electronic news media relations, 1982-85; sr. media relations rep. Chevron Corp., San Francisco, 1985-87; dir. pub. relations Fireman's Fund Corp., Novato, Calif., 1987—; lectr. Dept. Interior-Park Service, Beckley, W.Va., 1983; chmn. pub. relations Internat. Oil Spill Conf., Washington, 1984-85. Author, coordinator: Research Studies in Business and the Media, 1980-83; contbg. author This Is Public Relations, 1985. Founding mem. San Francisco chpt. Overseas Edn. Group; mem. pub. relations com. World Affairs Council San Francisco. Mem. Am. Women in Radio and TV, Nat. Assn. Broadcasters (assoc.), Radio/TV News Dirs. Assn. (assoc.), San Francisco Women in Bus. Office: Fireman's Fund Corp 777 Marin Dr Novato CA 94998

ARY, BONNITA ELLEN, bookkeeper, government official; b. Walden, Colo., July 26, 1932; d. Burney Grover and Maude Velisa (Bulis) Dowdell; m. Leo D. Ary, Aug. 16, 1950 (div.); children—Kristy L. Ary Ackerson, R. Craig. Student pub. schs., Jackson County, Colo.; cert. med. asst. Am. Assn. Med. Assts. Sec., Mountain Park REA, Walden, 1950-51; dep. treas. Jackson County, Walden, 1955-61, registrar of vital stats., 1965—; med. asst., Walden, 1961-66; bus. mgmt. assn. U.S. Forest Service, Walden, 1967-84, support services specialist, 1985—; bookkeeper for small businesses, 1950-83. Mem. Walden Sch. Bd., 1971-79; chmn. fin. bd. North Park Community United Meth. Ch., 1980-84. Recipient cert. of merit U.S. Forest Service, 1978, 81, 85. Home: 496 McKinley St Walden CO 80480 Office: 612 5th St Walden CO 80480

ARZOUMANIAN, ARAM S., electromech. engr.; b. Cairo, Mar. 16, 1917; came to U.S., 1966, naturalized, 1974; s. Sarkis and Makrouhi (Melkonian) A.; French baccalaureat in Math., Coll. St. Joseph, Cairo, 1936; Electromech. Engr. (Master's degree) with mention excellent, Poly. Inst., Yerevan, Armenia, 1952; m. Darakjian Rosa, Oct. 1, 1950; children—Sarkis, Margaret. Sr. engr. designer Electrotech. Plant, Yerevan, 1952-57; chief engr. Research and Devel. Inst. of Computers, Yerevan, 1957-66; sr. project engr. Bryant Computer Products, Walled Lake, Mich., 1966-67; mem. tech. staff Dataproduct Corp., Woodland Hills, Calif., 1968—, now advance developer spl. projects. Mem. Evereg Fenesse Ednl. Soc. (pres. central com.). Developer disc printer for banking ops.; developed 1st memory magnetic drum with flying heads, USSR, 1962; contbr. tech. papers to profl. publs.; patentee in field. Home: 24326 Caris St Woodland Hills CA 91367 Office: Dataproducts Corp 6250 Canoga Ave Woodland Hills CA 91365

ARZUBE, JUAN ALFREDO, bishop; b. Guayaquil, Ecuador, June 1, 1918; came to U.S., 1944, naturalized, 1961; s. Juan Bautista and Maria (Jaramillo) A. B.S. in Civil Engring, Rensselaer Poly. Inst., 1942; B.A., St. John's Sem., 1954. Ordained priest Roman Catholic Ch., 1954; asso. pastor St. Agnes Ch., Los Angeles, Resurrection Ch., Los Angeles, Ascension Ch., Los Angeles, Our Lady of Guadalupe Ch., El Monte, Calif.; aux. bishop of Los Angeles, 1971—, Episcopal vicar for Spanish speaking, 1973—; mem. nat. bishops coms. Ad Hoc Com. for Spanish Speaking; chmn. Com. for Latin Am. Recipient Humanitarian award Mexican Am. Opportunity Found., 1978, John Anson Ford award Los Angeles County Commn. Human Relations, 1979. Address: 3149 Sunset Hill Dr West Covina CA 91791 *

ASCH, SUNNY CHARLA, arts administrator, consultant; b. N.Y.C.; d. Charles and Sunny (Goetz) A. BS in Edn., U. So. Calif., 1959; MA in Arts Adminstrn., Occidental Coll., 1975; JD, Whittier Coll., 1980. Bar: Calif., 1982. Adminstrv. intern Ford Found., N.Y.C. Ballet, N.Y.C., 1969-70; asst. mgr. Balt. Symphony, 1970-71; assoc. concert mgr. UCLA Fine Arts Prodns., 1971-75; concert mgr. Ambassador Internat. Cultural Found., Pasadena, 1975-76; dir. Arlington Celebrity Series, Santa Barbara, Calif., 1975—, Celebrity Presentations, La Canada, Calif., 1975—. Mem. ABA, State Bar Calif., Western Alliance of Arts Adminstrs., Assoc. Coll., Univ. and Community Arts Adminstrs., Internat. Soc. Arts Adminstrs., Am. Symphony Orchestra League. Office: Celebrity Presentations Inc PO Box 457 La Canada CA 91101

ASCHAUER, MARY ANN, university administrator, English educator; b. Oklahoma City, Jan. 14, 1947; d. Paul James and Helen (Atherton) B.; m. Mark L. Aschauer; children: Christopher, Noah, Casey. BA in English, Santa Clara U., 1969, MA in English and Folklore, 1974. Teaching asst. UCLA, 1969-71; adj. lectr. Santa Clara U., 1971-74, lectr., 1974-85, sr. lectr., 1986—, dir. freshman writing program, 1982—, dir. NEH summer faculty writing seminar, 1984—, cons. to MBA Leavey Sch. Bus., 1986—, cons. to Grad. Sch. Edn., 1986—. Contbr. articles to profl. jours. Grantee Santa Clara U., 1983, NEH, 1984, IBM, 1985. Mem. MLA, Assn. for Supervision and Curriculum Devel., Calif. Assn. Tchrs. of English, Nat. Council Tchrs. English. Democrat. Roman Catholic. Avocations: cross-country and downhill skiing, ice skating, hiking. Office: Santa Clarea U Dept English Santa Clara CA 95053

ASCHER, EVERETT S., music company executive; b. N.Y.C., Apr. 3, 1936; s. Morton and Ruth (Klein) A.; m. Ann Fine, June 25, 1958; 1 dau., Allison. B.A., U. Rochester, 1957. Pres., Regent Recorded Music, Emil Ascher, Inc., Los Angeles, 1959—; vice-chmn. Westwood Bancorp., Los Angeles, 1982-84. Trustee U. Rochester; v.p., bd. dirs. Los Angeles Chamber Orch.; founder Los Angeles Music Ctr.; mem. Citizens Adv. Commn. for 1984 Olympics, Blue Ribbon CItizens Adv. Com., Increase Police Protection in City Los Angeles; bd. dirs. Holmby-Westwood Property Owners Assn., pres. 1976-77. Served to lt. (j.g.) USN, 1957-59. Mem. ASCAP, Los Angeles West Regional C. of C. (v.p., chmn. bd. dirs. 1986-87), Music Ctr. Frat. of Friends (charter). Republican. Club: Regency (Los Angeles). Office: 6255 Sunset Blvd Suite 911 Los Angeles CA 90028

ASCHMANN, H(AROLD) HOMER, geography educator; b. San Francisco, May 5, 1920; s. George Henry and Julia (Keay) A.; m. Louise Goodale, Sept. 1, 1943; children: Stefanie Gail, Erika Louise, Jean Elise, Sara Margaret, Harold Konrad, Carl Edward. AA, Los Angeles Jr. Coll., 1938; AB, UCLA, 1940, MA, 1942; PhD, U. Calif., Berkeley, 1954. From instr. to asst. prof. San Diego State Coll., 1946-48; instr. U. Nebr., Lincoln, 1950-51; asst. prof. Los Angeles State Coll., 1951-54; from asst. prof. to assoc. prof. geography U. Calif., Riverside, 1954-64, prof., 1964—. Author: Central Desert of Baja California—Demography and Ecology, 1958; editor, translator: Natural and Human History of Baja California, 1966. Served to 1st lt. USAAF, 1942-46, ETO. Mem. Southwestern Anthropol. Assn. (v.p., then pres. 1952-54), Assn. Am. Geographers (Meritorious Achievement award 1972), Assn. Pacific Coast Geographers (pres. 1965-66). Home: 4757 Kansas Ave Riverside CA 92507

ASH, LAWRENCE ROBERT, public health educator, administrator; b. Holyoke, Mass., Mar. 5, 1933; s. Lawrence Clifton and Alice (Sartini) A.; m. Luana Lee Smith, Aug. 4 1960; 1 child, Leigh I. BS in Zoology, U. Mass., 1954, MA in Zoology, 1956; PhD in Parasitology, Tulane U., 1960. Asst. parasitologist U. Hawaii, Honolulu, 1960-61; instr. Tulane U., New Orleans, 1961-65; med. parasitologist South Pacific Commn., Noumea, New Caledonia, 1965-67; asst. prof. pub. health UCLA Sch. Pub. Health, 1967-71, assoc. prof., 1971-75, prof., 1975—, chmn. dept., assoc. dean, 1979-84; mem. panel U.S. Panel on Parasitic Diseases, U.S.-Japan Program, Washington, 1972-78, chmn. 1978-84; cons. Naval Med. Research Unit #2, Taipei, Republic of China, Manila, 1970—. Sr. author: Atlas of Human Parasitology, 2d rev. edit., 1984; jr. author: Diagnostic Parasitology Clinical Laboratory Manual, 1979. NIH grantee, 1970-84. Fellow Royal Soc. Tropical Medicine and Hygiene; mem. Am. soc. Tropical Medicine and Hygiene (councilor 1974-77), Am. Soc. Parasitologists (councilor 1972-75, v.p. 1982-83). Home: 10400 Northvale Rd Los Angeles CA 90064 Office: UCLA Sch Pub Health Los Angeles CA 90024

ASH, ROY LAWRENCE, business executive; b. Los Angeles, Oct. 20, 1918; s. Charles K. and Fay E. (Dickinson) A.; m. Lila M. Hornbek., Nov. 13, 1943; children—Loretta Ash Danko, James, Marilyn Ash Hodge, Robert, Charles. M.B.A., Harvard, 1947. With Bank of Am., 1936-42, 47-49; chief fin. officer Hughes Aircraft Co., 1949-53; co-founder Litton Industries, Inc., Beverly Hills, Calif., 1953-72; dir. Litton Industries, Inc., 1953-72, pres., 1961-72; asst. to Pres. U.S.; dir. Office Mgmt. and Budget, Washington, 1973-75; chmn. bd., chief exec. officer AM Internat., 1976-81; dir. Global Marine, Inc., 1965-72, 75-81, BankAmerica Corp., Bank of Am. NT & SA, Sara Lee Corp., Trus-Joist Corp.; chmn. Pres.'s Adv. Council on Exec. Orgn., 1969-71; co-chmn. Japan-Calif. Assn., 1965-72, 80-81; mem. Bretton Woods Com.; dir. Inst. for Contemporary Studies. vice chmn. Los Angeles Olympic Organizing Com., 1980-85. Trustee Calif. Inst. Tech., 1967-72; trustee Com. for Econ. Devel., 1970-72, 75—; dir. Los Angeles World Affairs Council, 1968-72, 78—, pres., 1970-72; chmn. adv. council on gen. govt. Rep. Nat. Com., 1977-80. Mem. C. of C. U.S. (bd. dirs. 1979-85), Conf. Bd. Clubs: Bel Air Country, Harvard, California (Los Angeles). Office: 1900 Ave of Stars #1600 Los Angeles CA 90067

ASH, SIDNEY ROY, geology educator; b. Albuquerque, Nov. 25, 1928; s. Oliver Knox and Ellen Rosene (Tavernier) A.; m. Shirley Martha Arviso, Jan. 25, 1963; children: Kathy Ellen, Randolph Henry. BA, Midland Luth. Coll., 1951, U. N.Mex., 1957; MS, U. N.Mex., 1961; PhD, U. Reading, Eng., 1966. Phys. sci. aid U.S. Geol. Survey, Albuquerque, 1956-58, geologist, 1958-64; asst. prof. earth sci. Midland Luth. Coll., Fremont, Nebr., 1966-69; assoc. prof. geology Ft. Hays State U., Hays, Kans., 1969-70; prof. geology Weber State Coll., Ogden, Utah, 1970—; cons. Petrified Forest Nat. Park, Ariz., 1980—, N.Mex. Mus. Natural History, Albuquerque, 1982—. Contbr. articles to profl. jours. Served to lt. USNR, 1952-55. Research grantee NSF, 1971, 73, 79, 83, U.S.-Australia Coop. Sci. Program, 1976. Mem. Palentol. Soc., Palentol. Assn., Bot. Soc. Am., Internat. Orgn. Paleontology, Paleobot. sect. of Bot. Soc. Am. Lutheran. Home: 1341 Henderson Dr Ogden UT 84404 Office: Weber State Coll Dept Geology Ogden UT 84404

ASHBY, CAROL IRIS HILL, chemist; b. Idaho Falls, Idaho, Aug. 3, 1953; d. George Arlington and Iris (Jones) H.; m. Jim Frank Ashby, June 3, 1975. BS in Chem., U. Idaho, 1975; PhD in Inorganic Chem., U. Ill., 1979. Mem. tech. staff Sandia Nat. Labs., Albuquerque, 1979—. Contbr. numerous articles to profl. jours.; patentee in field. NSF graduate fellow, 1975-78. Mem. Am. Chem. Soc., Am. Vacuum Soc., Materials Research Soc. Episcopalian. Avocations: aviculture, horticulture, herpetology, fishing, music. Office: Sandia Nat Labs PO Box 5800 Albuquerque NM 87185

ASHCRAFT, DANIEL WAYNE, industrial designer; b. Los Angeles, Apr. 3, 1948; s. Lloyd Eldon and Velma (Durrant) A.; m. Heidi Ann Koch, Sept. 19, 1970; children—Heather Ann, Dru Colin, Seth Cory, Britt Cullen. B.S. with great distinction, Art Ctr. Coll. Design, Pasadena, Calif., 1973. Designer Albert C. Martin & Assocs., Los Angeles, 1968; indsl. designer Klepa Design Assocs., Los Angeles, 1973-74; instr. design Pasadena City Coll., Calif., 1974-75; indsl. designer S.G. Hauser & Assocs., Woodland Hills, Calif., 1975-77; assoc. designer Selje, Bond, Stewart & Romberger, Pasadena, 1976-78; v.p., prin. Kaneko Metzgar Ashcraft Design, Venice, Calif., 1978-86; pres. Ashcraft Design, Los Angeles, 1986—. Patentee in field. Pres., founder. R.E.D.I. Preparedness Inc., Los Angeles, 1981; v.p. sch. site com. Torrance Unified, Calif., 1982; sr. pres. Ch. of Jesus Christ of Latter-day Saints, Torrance, 1984. Served with USNG, 1971-77. Recipient cert. of excellence Am. Inst. Graphic Arts, 1982, cert. of merit Art Ctr. 6th Ann. Internat., 1975, Exhibit 7th Ann., 1976, Excellence award Communication Arts, 1985, Gold Sound award, 1986, cert. of merit, Art Dir.'s Club of Los Angeles, 1985; Ford Motor Co. scholar, 1971. Mem. Indsl. Design Soc. Am. (cert.). Democrat. Office: Ashcraft Design 11832 W Pico Blvd Los Angeles CA 90064

ASHE, HILARY, biochemistry and clinical chemistry educator; b. Chgo., Apr. 16, 1934; d. Norman and Golia (Kritchevsky) A.; m. Mary Frances Knowles, July 4, 1959; children: Elizabeth Anne, Rebecca Marie, Norah Emily, Benjamin Norman. BSc, UCLA, 1955; PhD, U. So. Calif., 1962; postgrad., Purdue U., 1962-63, Brandeis U., 1963-65. Asst. prof. pharmacology U. Calif., Irvine, 1965-70; Phd clin. chem. trainee Reference Lab., North Hollywood, Calif., 1970-71; dir. pharmacology Ecological Systems Corp., Santa Monica, Calif., 1971-78; lectr. chemistry UCLA summer session, 1975—, Calif. State U., Los Angeles, 1978—; lectr. Pepperdine U., Los Angeles, 1973, U. So. Calif. Sch. Pharmacy, Los Angeles, 1974, UCLA Extension, 1974—, U. Bridgeport, Conn., 1985-86. Contbr. articles to sci. jours.; patentee in field. Pres. Friends of Library, Palms-Rancho, Los Angeles, 1985-86. Grantee Dept. Health, Edn., Welfare, 1966-69, fellow, 1975-76. Mem. AAAS, N.Y. Acad. Scis., Am. Chem. Soc. Univ. Profls. Avocation: book collecting. Office: Calif State U Dept Chemistry 5151 State University Dr Los Angeles CA 90032

ASHER, EUGENE LEON, historian, educator; b. Cleve., Nov. 23, 1929; s. Samuel H. and Dorothy Denise (LePon) A.; A.B., UCLA, 1952, M.A., 1955, Ph.D., 1958; postgrad. (Fulbright fellow) U. Paris, 1956-57, U. Toulouse, 1957; m. Bonnie Jane Anderson, June 9, 1956; children—Allyson Elizabeth, Christine Marie. Asst. prof. history U. Wichita (Kans.), 1957-59; mem. faculty history Calif. State U.-Long Beach, 1959-67, 71—, prof., chmn. dept. history, 1971-76, exec. asst. to pres., 1976-80, exec. officer, 1980—, dir. univ. relations, 1984—; exec. dir. KLON-FM public radio, 1981—; dir. Am. Hist. Assn. History Edn. Project, 1968-75; prof. history Ind. U., Bloomington, 1969-71. Pres., Casa Dorado Mng. Agt. Inc., Palm Springs, Calif., 1975. Vice chmn. Long Beach Am. Revolution Bicentennial Commn., 1973-76; co-chmn. history adv. panel, mem. Calif. State Social Scis. Commn., 1965-68; chmn. Joint Anglo-U.S. Commn. Confs. History, Dept. State, 1972-75; trustee Los Angeles Theater Ctr., 1983—, v.p. bd. trustees, 1985-86, pres. 1986-87, chmn. bd. 1987—. Trustee Sloan Found. Notre Dame U. Program; Am. Council Learned Socs. fellow, 1962-63, 66-67; Social Sci. Research Council grantee, 1962, 66-67; HEW grantee, 1969-75. Mem. Soc. History Edn. (chmn bd. 1972-78), Am. Hist. Assn., Nat. Council Social Studies, Orgn. Am. Historians, Societe d'Histoire Moderne et Contemporaine, Phi Beta Kappa Alumni Assn. (council Calif. 1979—, v.p. 1982-84, pres. 1984-86). Author: The Resistance to the Maritime Classes: the Survival of Feudalism in the France of Colbert, 1960: (with others) A Framework for the Social Sciences: Report of the Statewide Social Science Study Commission, 1968. Contbr. articles to profl. publs.; producer film: Oil: The Pioneering Years, 1978. Home: 38 58th Pl Long Beach CA 90803 Office: Office of Pres Calif State U 1250 Bellflower Blvd Long Beach CA 90840

ASHER, HOWARD RALPH, medical products executive; b. Long Beach, Calif., Sept. 29, 1947; s. Ralph Eugene Asher and Joyce Colleen (Johnson) Fry; m. Carol P. Yokota, Mar. 28, 1965; children: Stacey L., Randy M. BA in Bus. Adminstrn., UCLA, 1969. Sales rep. Howmedica, Inc., Rutherford, N.J., 1970-72; eastern area sales mgr. Am. Hosp. Supply, V. Mueller Innomed Orthopedics, Chgo., 1972-75; mktg. mgr. Cutter Biomed., San Diego, 1975-78; dir. sales and mktg. Hexcel Med., Dublin, Calif., 1978-79; pres. Advanced Biosearch Assocs., Danville, Calif., 1979—. Contbr. articles to profl. jours. Mem. Regulatory Affairs Profls. Soc. (internat. sect.), Med. Mktg. Assn., Food and Drug Law Inst., Assn. for Advancement Med. Instrumentation, Assn. for Advancement of Sci., Soc. for Biomaterials. Republican. Avocations: swimming, woodworking, golfing, gardening. Home: 30 Hidden Oak Ct Danville CA 94526 Office: Advanced Biosearch Assocs 3880 Blackhawk Rd Danville CA 94526-4617

ASHER, JAMES EDWARD, consulting forester, engineer, arborist; b. Los Angeles, July 22, 1931; s. John Edward and Dorothy (Ingraham) A.; student Pasadena City Coll., 1949-50; B.S., Oreg. State U., 1954; m. Marilyn Lee Struebing, Dec. 28, 1953; children—Lynne Marie, Laure Ann. With U.S. Forest Service, San Bernardino (Calif.) Nat. Forest, summers 1950-53, forester, 1956-57; prin. James E. Asher, ACF, Cons. Forester, 1957—; capt., bn. chief, asst. chief, fire prevention officer Crest Forest Fire Protection Dist., Crestline, Calif., 1960-69, chief, 1969-71; forester Big Bear div. Golden State Bldg. Products, Redlands, 1972, timber mgr., 1972-74; mem. profl. foresters exam. com. Calif. Bd. Forestry, 1978—, vice chmn., 1982—; mem. Calif. Integrated Hardwood, Calif. Forest Pest Control Action Council; chmn. Profl. Foresters Ad Hoc Task Force, 1983—. Vol. firewarden State of Calif., 1967—; mem. adv. com. Range Mgmt. Program, 1986—; chmn. Tree Conservation Subcom., Fire Dist. Suprs. Ad Hoc Com. on Soil Erosion and Sediment Control, County of San Bernardino, 1984—. Served with AUS, 1954-56. Recipient certificate of merit Nat. Fire Protection Assn., San Bernadino Mountains Assn.; Resolution of Commendation, County Bd. Suprs.; Forester of Year award So. Calif. sect. Soc. Am. Foresters, 1977; others. Registered profl. forester, registered profl. engr., Calif.; lic. pest control advisor, pest control operator, Calif. Mem. So. Calif. Assn. Foresters and Fire Wardens, Soc. Am. Foresters (chmn. licensing and ethics com. So. Calif. sect., chmn. So. Calif. 1983), Assn. Cons. Foresters, Internat. Soc. Arboriculture, Sierra-Cascade Logging Conf., Am. Forestry Assn., Tau Kappa Epsilon. Presbyterian. Club: Masons. Contbr. articles to profl. Office: PO Box 2326 Lake Arrowhead CA 92352

ASHER, ROBERT BERNARD, aerospace engineer; b. Chgo., June 15, 1941; s. Ben and Edwina R. (Deutschle) A.; m. Linda L. Parker, May 15, 1965; children—Christina Dawn, Kimberly Diane, Heidi Darlene. B.S., Okla. State U., 1969, M.S., 1971, Ph.D. in Engring., 1974. Commd. 2d lt. U.S. Air Force, 1969, advanced through grades to capt., 1972; computer analyst AF Satellite Control Facility, Sunnyvale, Calif., 1964-66; tech. mgr. AF Avionics Lab., Wright Patterson AFB, Ohio, 1971-74; vis. scientist Info. Scis. Lab., Stanford U., Calif., 1975; research assoc. F.J. Seiler Research Lab., USAF Acad., Colo., 1974-77; resigned, 1977; cons. Optical Scis. Co., Placentia, Calif., 1977-78; asst. prof. dept. elec. engring. Tex. Tech U., Lubbock, 1978; program mgr. Orincon Corp., San Diego, 1978-79; sr. staff scientist, tech. supr. optics group Lockheed Palo Alto Research Labs., Calif., 1979-81; program dir. Sandia Nat. Labs., Albuquerque, 1981-85; assoc. dir. Space Flight Systems Lab., U. Colo.-Colorado Springs, 1985—. Contbr. articles to profl. jours. Elder, Pulpit Rock Ch., Colorado Srings, Colo., 1976-77; adult edn. dir. Grace Bible Ch., Albuquerque, 1981-83. Decorated Meritorious Service medal, others. Mem. IEEE, Optical Soc. Am. Republican. So. Baptist. Home: 5410 Candlewood Ct NE Albuquerque NM 87111 Office: Sandia Nat Labs Albuquerque NM 87111

ASHLEY, ANNE, data processing executive, consultant; b. Glen Ridge, N.Y., May 5, 1942; d. Walter Quay and Virginia Anne Ashley; m. James Lee Hieronymus, May 30, 1964 (div.). B.S. in Engring., U. Mich., 1964. Research engr. Gen. Dynamics, San Diego, 1964-66; systems engr. Control Data, 1966-67; sr. systems programmer Cornell U., 1968-71; mgr. operating systems Stanford (Calif.) Linear Accelerator Ctr., 1971-75; systems programming mgr. Western States Bank, San Francisco, 1975-77; mgr. systems devel. and support Boole & Babbage, Sunnyvale, Calif., 1977-79, 79-80; pvt. cons., San Mateo, Calif., 1979-81; systems cons. mgr., mgr. benchmark and performance analysis Amdahl Corp., Sunnyvale, 1980-84, also mgr. Amdahl Performance Evaluation Ctr., dir. user group mgmt. liaison; mgr. advanced info. systems planning Coopers & Lybrand, San Jose, Calif., 1984-85; pres. Bet Your Bus. Techs., Woodside, Calif., 1980—; mktg. dir. Zerodne Systems, Santa Clara, 1986—. Mem. Am. Mgmt. Assn., Assn. Systems Mgrs., IBM User Groups. Democrat. Club: Decathlon. Composer and lyricist MVS Is Breaking My Heart (song), 1975. Home: 20 Medway Rd Woodside CA 94062 Office: 2995 Woodside Rd Suite 400 Woodside CA 94061

ASHLEY, HOLT, aero. scientist, educator; b. San Francisco, Jan. 10, 1923; s. Harold Harrison and Anne (Oates) A.; m. Frances M. Day, Feb. 1, 1947. Student, Calif. Inst. Tech., 1940-43; B.S., U. Chgo., 1944; S.M., Mass. Inst. Tech., 1948, Sc.D., 1951. Faculty Mass. Inst. Tech., 1946-67, prof. aero., 1960-67; prof. aeros. and astronautics Stanford U., 1967-; spl. research aeroelasticity, aerodynamics; cons. govt. agys., research orgns., indsl. corps.; dir. office of exploratory research and problem assessment and div. advanced tech. applications NSF, 1972-74; mem. sci. adv. bd. USAF, 1958-80; research adv. com. structural dynamics NASA, 1952-60, research adv. com. on aircraft structures, 1962-70, chmn. research adv. com. on materials and structures, 1974-77; mem. Kanpur Indo-American program Indian Inst. Tech., 1964-65; AIAA Wright Bros. lectr., 1981. Co-author: Aeroelasticity, 1955, Principles of Aeroelasticity, 1962, Aerodynamics of Wings and Bodies, 1969, Engineering Analysis of Flight Vehicles, 1974. Mem. Greater Boston coordinating council Boy Scouts Am., also mem.-at-large and adviser air explorer squadron. Recipient Goodwin medal M.I.T., 1952; Exceptional Civilian Service award U.S. Air Force, 1972, 80; Public Service award NASA, 1981; named one of 10 outstanding young men of year Boston Jr. C. of C., 1956. Fellow Am. Acad. Arts and Scis.; hon. fellow AIAA (assoc. editor jour., v.p. tech. 1971, pres. 1973, Structures, Structural Dynamics and Materials award 1969); mem. Am. Meterol. Soc. (profl., recipient 50th Anniversary medal 1971), AAAS, Nat. Acad. Engring. (aeros. and space engring. bd. 1977—), Nat. Acad. Engring. (mem. council 1985), Phi Beta Kappa, Sigma Xi, Tau Beta Pi. Address: 475 Woodside Dr Woodside CA 94062

ASHLEY, JOSEPH LAVON, III, mechanical engineer; b. Tallulah, La., Nov. 26, 1942; s. Joseph Lavon Jr. and Marion Delois (Lindsey) A.; m. Sophia Kokkinos, May 15, 1965; children: Natalie Christiana. BS in Physics, U. Northeast La., 1965; MS in Engring., Old Dominion U., 1978; postgrad., U. La Vern, 1985—. Registered profl. engr., Wis. Head noise reduction engrs. Ingalls Nuclear Shipbuilding, Pascagoula, Miss., 1969-71; head maintenance dept. Union Tank Car Co., Baton Rouge, 1971-72; research engr. Newport News (Va.) Shipbuilding Co., 1972-74; mech. engr. Naval Facilities Engring. Command, Norfolk, Va., 1974-79; sr. research engr. Naval Civil Engring. Labs., Port Hueneme, Calif., 1979—. Contbr. articles to profl. jours.; patentee in field. Pres. St. Demetrios Greek Orthodox Ch., Camarillo, Calif., 1982. Served with USN, 1965-68, ATO, Vietnam. Recipient Sustained Superior Performance award Naval Civil Engring. Lab., Port Hueneme, 1982, 83, 84, 86, Outstanding Performance award Naval Civil Engring. Lab., 1984, 86. Mem. Am. Soc. Am. Mil. Engrs., Am. Hellenic Edn. Progressive Assn. (pres. Ventura chpt. 1983-85, chmn. bd. govs. 1985-86, sec. 1980-83), Sigma Xi. Avocations: golf, astronomy, oil painting. Home: 1461 Brookhaven Ave Camarillo CA 93010 Office: Naval Civil Engring Lab Code L64 Port Hueneme CA 93043

ASHLEY, MARK JAMES, speech pathologist, health facility administrator; b. Ogdenburg, N.Y., Aug. 9, 1956; s. Cecil Erwin and Mary (Bernier) A.; m. Susan Marie Hess, Sept. 12, 1975; children: Matthew James, Nicholas Anthony. BS in Speech Pathology, SUNY Coll., Genesco, 1977; MS in Speech Pathology, So. Ill. U., 1978. Lic. speech pathologist, Calif., Fla., Tex. Rehab. asst. Ctr. for Comprehensive Services, Carbondale, Ill., 1977-78; clin. supr. Speech Pathology, Inc., Bakersfield, Calif., 1979-80; co-dir. Ctr. for Neuro Skills, Bakersfield, 1980—; lectr. numerous assns., agys., 1978—; instr. U. Calif., Santa Barbara, 1980; adj. prof. So. Ill. U., Dept. Communication Disorders and Scis., Carbondale, 1985. Bd. dirs. Kern County (Calif.) chpt. Am. Cancer Soc., 1980-82, service com. mem. 1979-82; cons. Bakersfield Assn. Retarded Citizens, 1981. Regents scholar State N.Y., 1974-77. Mem. Am. Speech Lang. Hearing Assn. (cert.), Calif. Speech and Hearing Assn., Nat. Rehab. Assn., Nat. Rehab. Counselors, Nat. Rehab. Adminstrn. Assn., Nat. Assn. Ind. Living, Am. Congress Phys. Medicine and Rehab. (chmn. subcom. post-acute care and rehab. standards with head injury task force), Nat. Head Injury Found., Traumatic Head Injury Profl. Assn. Calif., Internat. Assn. Laryngectomies (founder Kern County chpt. 1980-81). Avocations: music, racquetball, salt water aquaria. Home: 1901 Haggin Oaks Bakersfield CA 93311 Office: Ctr for Neuro Skills 2658 Mt Vernon Bakersfield CA 93306

ASHMEAD, ALLEZ MORRILL, speech pathologist, consultant; b. Provo, Utah, Dec. 18, 1916; d. Laban Rupert and Zella May (Miller) M.; m. Harvey Harold Ashmead, Sept. 24, 1940; children: Harve DeWayne, Sheryl Mae Harames, Zeltha Janeel Henderson, Emma Allez Moss. BS, Utah State U., 1938; MS summa cum laude, U. Utah, 1952, PhD summa cum laude, 1970; postgrad., Idaho State U., Oreg. State Coll., U. Denver, U. Utah, Brigham Young U., Utah State U. Cert. secondary edn., remedial reading, spl. edn., learning disabilities; cert. clin. competence speech pathology and audiology; profl. cert. in orofacial myology. Tchr. pub. schs. Utah, Idaho, 1938-43; speech and hearing pathologist Bushnell Hosp., Brigham City, Utah, 1943-45; sr. speech correctionist Utah State Dept. Health, Salt Lake City, 1945-52; dir. speech and hearing dept. Davis County Sch. Dist., Farmington, Utah, 1952-65; clin., field supr. U. Utah, Salt Lake City, 1965-70, 75-78; speech pathologist Box Elder Sch. Dist., Brigham City, 1970-75, 78-84; teaching specialist Brigham Young U., 1970-73; speech pathologist Primary Children's Med. Ctr., 1975-77; pvt. practice speech pathology and orofacial myology, 1970-86. Author: Physical Facilities for Handicapped Children, 1957, A Guide for Training Public School Speech and Hearing Clinicians, 1965, A Guide for Public School Speech Hearing Programs, 1959, Impact of Orofacial Myofunctional Treatment on Orthodontic Correction, 1982, Meeting Needs of Handicapped Children, 1975, Relationship of Trace Minerals to Disease, 172, Macro and Trace Minerals in Human Metabolism, 1971, Electromotive Potential Differences Between Stutterers and Non-stutterers, 1970, Learning Disability, An Educational Adventure, 1969, New Horizons in Special Education, 1969, Developing Speech and Language in the Exceptional Child, 1961, Parent Teacher Guidance in Primary Stuttering, 1951, numerous others; contbr. research articles to profl. jours. Student Placement chair Am. Field Service, Kaysville, Utah, 1962-66; ednl. del. Women's State Legis. Council, Salt Lake City, 1958-70; chairwoman fund raising Utah Symphony Orch., Salt Lake City, 1970-71; sec., treas. Utah chpt. U.S. Council for Exceptional Children, 1958-62, membership com. chair, 1962-66, program com. chair, 1966-68. Recipient Scholarship award for Higher Edn. U. Utah, Salt Lake City, 1969; Delta Kappa Gamma scholar, 1968; grantee Utah Dept. Edn., 1962. Mem. NEA, Utah Ednl. Assn., Am. Speech, Lang. Hearing Assn. (life, continuing edn. com. 1985), Western Speech Assn., Internat. Assn. Orofacial Myology (bd. examiners, Sci. Contribution award 1982), Utah Speech Hearing Assn. (sec., treas. 1956-60), AAUW (Utah state bd. chair status of wom n 1959-62, Kaysville br. 1957-60), Delta Kappa Gamma (state scholarship award 1968, del. Woman's State Legis. Council 1958-70, profl. affairs chair 1963-67, tchr. of yr. award 1978), Sigma Alpha Eta, Theta Alpha Phi, Psi Chi, Zeta Phi Eta, Phi Kappa Phi. Republican. Mormon. Lodges: Daus. Utah Pioneers (parlimentarian Kaysville chpt. 1980-86, historian 1975-80), Soroptimist Internat. (charter mem. 1954, bd. dirs. 1954-56, pres. Davis County chpt. 1965-69, treas. 1956-54, Rocky Mountain regional bd. dirs. 1965-70, community service award 1968, pub. service award 1970). Avocations: internat. travel, reading, boating, sports, performing arts. Home: 719 E Center St Kaysville UT 84037 Office: Harrison Profl Ctr 3293 Harrison Blvd Ogden UT 84403

ASHMEAD, HARVE DEWAYNE, nutritionist, executive, educator; b. Brigham City, Utah, June 6, 1944; s. Harvey Harold and Allez (Morrill) A.; m. Eugele Baird, June 24, 1966; children—Stephen, Jilane, Brett, Angelique, Heidi. B.S., Weber State Coll., 1969; Ph.D., Pacific Inst., 1970; Ph.D. magna cum laude, Donsbach U., 1981. Cert. nutritional, dietary cons. With Ch. Jesus Christ of Latter Day Saints, Paris, 1963-66; v.p. Albion Labs., Ogden, Utah, 1966-71, exec. v.p., Clearfield, Utah, 1971-82, pres., 1982—, also bd. dirs.; pres. Albion Internat.; adj. prof. Weber State Coll., also adv. council; advisor Weber County Sch. Dist.; bd. dirs. various corps.; guest lectr. Adv. Fruit Heights City (Utah); pres. PTA; adv. bd. Donsbach U. Fellow Am. Coll. Nutrition; mem. Am. Soc. Animal Sci., Am. Assn. Nutrition and Dietary Cons., Internat. Acad. Nutritional Cons., Am. Assn. Nutritional Cons., Am. Acad. Applied Health Scis., AAAS, Am. Biographical Inst. (bd. govs.), Clearfield C. of C. (bd. dirs.), Delta Sigma Pi. Mormon. Author: Chelated Mineral Nutrition, 1981; Mineral Absorption Mechanisms, 1981; Chelated Mineral Nutrition in Plants, Animal and Man, 1982; A New Era in Plant Nutrition, 1982; Intestinal Absorption of Metal Ions and Chelates, 1985; Foliar Feeding of Plants with Amino Acid Chelates; contbr. numerous articles to profl. jours. Office: Albion Labs 101 N Main St Clearfield UT 84015

ASHMORE, RHEA ANN, university program administrator, education educator; b. Cleve., July 4, 1949; d. LeRoy Crantz and Albina Anne (Turcznowicz) Jones; m. Gary Wayne Ashmore, Apr. 23, 1982. BA in Edn., U. R.I., 1971, MA in Reading Edn., 1974; cert. advanced grad. study in secondary reading, Boston U., 1977; EdD in Curriculum and Instrn., U. Mont., 1981. Cert. tchr. supervision, reading K-12, elem. edn., secondary English and Spl. Edn., Mont. Tchr. English and reading Chariho Regional High Sch., Wood River Junction, R.I., 1971-73; tchr. reading, cons. South Kingstown Jr. High Sch., Peacedale, R.I., 1973-81; tchr. classroom resource Missoula (Mont.) Sch. Dist. 1, 1981-82; instr. Upward Bound Reading U. Mont., Missoula, 1982-83, adj. asst. prof. Sch. Edn., 1982—, dir. reading and study skills ctr., 1982—; in-service presenter study skills, various sch. dists., 1982—; cons. study skills, Crook County (Oreg.) Sch. Dist., Prineville, 1985—. Contbr. articles to profl. jours. Grantee Faculty Devel. Com. U. Mont., 1985. Mem. Internat. Reading Assn., Western Coll. Reading and Learning Assn. (state dir. 1985-86), Mont. State Reading Assn. (corresponding sec. 1984-86), Five Valleys Reading Assn. (state rep. 1984-86), Phi Delta Kappa. Avocations: outdoor activities, running, reading, horseback riding. Office: U Mont Reading & Study Skills Program Corbin Hall Missoula MT 59812

ASHOR, LESLIE KAY, space planner, designer, consultant; b. Missoula, Mont., Jan. 3, 1959; d. Lester Tony and Kay Louise (Wallinder) Vierra; m. Michael Fremont Ashor, June 18, 1983; 1 child, Ariel Michelle. BS, BArch, Wash. State U., 1983. Owner, design cons. Ashor Design Group, Soldotna, Alaska, 1983-86, San Diego, 1986—. Active Kenai (Alaska) Old Town Com., 1985. Grantee Wash. Water Power Co., 1982. Republican. Mem. Pentecostal ch. Home and Office: 13256 Birch Tree Ln Poway CA 92064

ASHTON, CLIFFORD LINDSAY, lawyer; b. Salt Lake City, Dec. 29, 1908; s. Edward Treharne and Cora (Lindsay) A.; m. Myriel Cluff, June 29, 1940 (dec. June 1979); children: Edward C., Julie, Coralee, Deborah, Anne. BA, U. Mich., 1935, JD, 1937. Bar: Utah 1938, U.S. Supreme Ct. 1950. Ptnr. McCullough & Ashton, Salt Lake City, 1938-41; judge Salt Lake City, 1946-47; ptnr. Van Cott, Bagley et al, Salt Lake City, 1948—; spl. prosecutor Salt Lake County Grand Jury, 1948; spl. counsel in Gt. Salt Lake case, 1948-80. Author: Seeds of Promise, 1983. Mem. Cen. Utah Conservancy Dist., 1968-80; adv. mem. Salt Lake County Water & Sewer Dist., 1980-84. Served to 1st lt. (j.g.) U.S. Army, 1945-46. Fellow Am. Coll. Trial Lawyers; mem. ABA, Utah State Bar Assn. (commr.), Utah County Bar Assn., Bamberger Found. (chmn. 1960—). Republican. Clubs: Alta, Cottonwood Country (Salt Lake City). Office: Van Cott Bagley Cornwall & McCarthy PO Box 45340 50 S Main St Salt Lake City UT 84144

ASHTON, RICK JAMES, librarian; b. Middletown, Ohio, Sept. 18, 1945; s. Ralph James and Lydia Marie (Thornbery) A.; m. Marcia K. Zuroweste, Dec. 23, 1966; children: Jonathan Paul, David Andrew. A.B., Harvard U., 1967; M.A., Northwestern U., 1969, Ph.D., 1973; M.A., U. Chgo., 1976. Instr., asst. prof. history Northwestern U., Evanston, Ill., 1972-74; curator local and family history Newberry Library, Chgo., 1974-77; asst. dir. Allen County Pub. Library, Ft. Wayne, Ind., 1977-80, dir., 1980-85; city librarian Denver Pub. Library, 1985—; mem. Ind. Coop Library Services Authority, 1980-85, pres., 1984-85; mem. Ft. Wayne Cable TV Adv. Council, 1982-85; cons. Nat. Endowment Humanities, Nat. Ctr. Edn. Stats., Northwestern U. Office Estate Planning. Author: The Life of Henry Ruiter, 1742-1819, 1974, The Genealogy Beginner's Manual: A New Edition, 1977. Bd. dirs. Community Coordinated Child Care, Evanston, 1972-74; bd. dirs. Three Rivers Montessori Sch., Ft. Wayne, 1977-80; bd. dirs., sec. Allen County-Ft. Wayne Hist. Soc., 1977-83. Conscientious objector. Recipient Nat. Merit scholar, 1963-67; NDEA fellow, 1967-69; Woodrow Wilson fellow, 1971-72. Mem. ALA, Colo. Library Assn. Home: 2974 S Verbena Way Denver CO 80231 Office: Denver Pub Library 1357 Broadway Denver CO 80203

ASIRE, JOSEPH JUNIOR, chemistry educator; b. Elyria, Ohio, Feb. 20, 1936; s. Joseph Stanley and Pearl (Shank) A.; m. Donna Helen Givan, June 12, 1960; children: Mark Joseph, Scott John. BS, Ohio State U., 1958; MS, Kent State U., 1964; M in Natural Sci., Ariz. State U., 1964. Cert. tchr., Ohio, Calif. Tchr. biology Elyria Pub. Schs., 1958-63; tchr. chemistry Santa Maria (Calif.) Unified Sch. Dist., 1963-67; tchr. chemistry Cuesta Coll., San Luis Obispo, 1967—, staff devel. coordinator, 1967—. Named Father of Yr. United Meth. Women, Los Osos, Calif., 1983. Mem. Am. Chem. Soc., Nat. Sci. Tchrs. Assn., Calif. Chemistry Tchrs. Assn., Calif. Tchrs. Assn., NEA. Methodist. Avocations: woodworking, gardening. Home: 989 Highland Dr Los Osos CA 93402 Office: Cuesta Coll PO Box 8106 San Luis Obispo CA 93406-8106

ASKANAS-ENGEL, VALERIE, neurologist, educator, researcher; b. Poland, May 28, 1937; came to U.S., 1969, naturalized, 1975; d. Marian and Leontyne A.; m. W. King Engel; 1 dau., Eve Monique. M.D., Warsaw Med. Sch., Poland, 1960; Ph.D., Warsaw Med. Sch., 1967. Rotating intern Univ. Hosp. Warsaw Med. Sch., 1960-61, resident in neurology, 1961-64, fellow in neuromuscular diseases, 1964-65; asst. prof. neurology Warsaw Med. Sch., 1965-69; assoc. mem. Inst. Muscle Diseases, N.Y.C., 1969-73; asst. prof. NYU Med. Sch., 1973-77; sr. investigator NIH, Bethesda, Md., 1977-81; prof. neurology and pathology U. So. Calif., Los Angeles, 1981—; co-dir. Neuromuscular Ctr. at Hosp. Good Samaritan, 1981—, Muscular Dystrophy Assn. Clinic, 1981—; v.p. 6th Internat. Congress on Neuromuscular Diseases, 1986; vis. prof. internat. congresses, Europe, S.Am., Can., Far East. Contbr. numerous articles, chpts., abstracts to med. publs. Recipient Dean's prize for outstanding research, 1967; Premio Associazione Stampa Medica Italiana Di Giurnal ItalianaIsmo Medico, 1980; grantee NIH, 1974-77, 83—, Muscular Dystrophy Assn., 1969-77, 81—. Mem. Am. Acad. Neurology, Soc. for Neurosci., Am. Soc. Cell Biology, Am. Assn. Neuropathology, Histochem. Soc., Los Angeles County Med. Assn., Société Française de Neorologie (hon.). Home: 527 S Arden Blvd Los Angeles CA 90020 Office: Hosp Good Samaritan U So Calif Neuromuscular Ctr 637 S Lucas Ave Los Angeles CA 90017

ASKIN, LEON, director, actor, producer, writer; b. Vienna, Austria, Sept. 18, 1907; came to U.S., 1940, naturalized, 1943; s. Samuel and Malvine (Susman) Aschkenasy; m. Annelies Ehrlich, Apr. 12, 1955; 1 stepdau., Irene Hartzell. Grad., New Sch. for Dramatic Arts (later called Reinhardt-Seminar), Vienna, 1927; postgrad., Columbia U., summer 1951. Artistic dir. Washington Civic Theatre, 1940-42; tchr. modern play analysis Am. Theater Wing, 1946-47; directing Dramatic Workshop, N.Y.C., 1947-48; lectr. The Denver Ctr. for Performing Arts Conservatory, 1985; founder Actors Equity Community Theater, 1948; chmn. various coms. Actors Equity Library Theatre, 1947-52; hon. life dir. Equity Library Theatre. Actor, Dumont Playhouse, Dusseldorf, Germany, 1927, cabaret dir., writer, actor, Paris, 1933-35, dir. First Legion, Linz, Austria, 1935, artistic dir. lit. and polit. cabaret, ABC, Vienna, 1935-38; writer: motion pictures including Rappel Immediat, Paris, 1938-40; artistic dir. Washington Civic Theatre; dir. Troilus and Cressida (Most Outstanding Prodn. 1941), The Applecart (Shaw), American Way; Broadway actor and dir., 1946-52; staged: Faust for, Goethe Festival, 1948-49; dir., played Shylock in: Merchant of Venice, 1952; motion picture appearances as co-star in The Robe, 1953, One, Two, Three, 1962, Guns for San Sebastian, 1967, Do Not Disturb, 1966, Hammersmith is Out, Going Ape, 1980, Horror Star, 1981, Airplane II, 1982; starred in First Strike, Savage Island, and Summer Jobs, 1984, Stiffs, 1985, Deshima, 1986; starred as Gen. Burkhalter in: TV series Hogan's Heroes, 1966-71; starred as Martin Luther and Karl Marx: Meeting of Minds TV series; dir.: West Coast plays St. Joan (Bernard Shaw), 1954, Julius Caesar (Shakespeare), 1960, The Egg (Felicien Marceau), 1975, Fever in the Brain (Marvin Aron), 1980; played Othello (in German), Hamburg and Berlin, 1957 (acclaimed as greatest German Othello of 20th Century); Contbr. articles to Los Angeles Times, Der Morgen and Die Furche, Vienna, Austria.; essays to U. Hamburg Arbeitastelle fur Exilliteratur. Served with U.S. Army, 1942-46; editor-in-chief The Orientation Digest Air Tech. Service Command (15 citations). Recipient Medal of honor City of Vienna, 1983. Mem. Actors Equity (dir. West Coast adv. com. 1952-55), Screen Actors Guild (dir. 1973), AFTRA; mem. Am. Film Inst.; Mem. Acad. Motion Picture Arts and Scis., Acad. TV Arts and Scis., ANTA (nat. bd.), Am. Nat. Theatre and Acad. West (chmn. bd. 1976-78, pres. 1979-82, pres. emeritus 1983—, organized, presented Nat. Artist award to Fred Astaire, Henry Fonda, Bob Hope, Jimmy Stewart, and Roger Stevens.

ASKIN, RICHARD HENRY, JR., television syndication company executive; b. Flushing, N.Y., Feb. 11, 1947; s. Richard H. and Anne Margaret A.; B.A. in Econs., Rutgers U., 1969; M.A. in Communications, U. Tex., 1971; M.B.A. in Fin., Fordham U., 1976; m. Carol Ann Reilly, Aug. 16, 1969; children—Jennifer Leigh, Michael Richard. Sales rep. Proctor & Gamble Distbg. Co., Jericho, N.Y., 1969; account exec. CableRep, Inc., N.Y.C., 1973-74, WNBC-TV Nat. Broadcasting Co., N.Y.C., 1974-75, NBC-TV, NBC, N.Y.C., 1975-76, sales mgr. KNBC-TV, Los Angeles, 1976-79, dir. sales, 1979-85; v.p. domestic sales Fries Distbn. Co., Los Angeles, 1985-86, sr. v.p. distbn., 1986-87; pres. TV distbn. The Samuel Goldwyn Co., Los Angeles; pres. The Breckford Group, Inc. Served to 1st lt. Adj. Gen. Corps, U.S. Army, 1971-73. Decorated Army Commendation medal; Alcoa fellow, 1969-70. Mem. Hollywood Radio and TV Soc., Advt. Industry Emergency Fund (pres., bd. dirs.), Alpha Rho Alumni Assn., Chi Psi. Republican. Roman Catholic. Home: 32177 Sailview Ln Westlake Village CA 91361 Office: Fries Distbn Co 10203 Santa Monica Blvd Los Angeles CA 90067

ASPEY, FREDERICK MORRIS (FRITZ), lawyer; b. Phoenix, Jan. 12, 1947; s. Frederick Morris and Madge (Gieszl) A.; m. Antonette Elaine Puch, July 26, 1969; children: Tyler Jordan, Matthew Logan. B.S., No. Ariz. U., 1969; J.D., Ariz. State U., 1972. Bar: Ariz. 1972., U.S. Dist. Ct. Ariz. 1973, U.S. Ct. Appeals (9th cir.) 1974, U.S. Supreme Ct. 1978. Assoc. Law Office J.R. Babbitt, Flagstaff, Ariz., 1972-75; ptnr. firm Aspey, Watkins, & Diesel, Flagstaff, 1975—. Mem. Big Bros., Flagstaff, 1974—; mem. bd. visitors Ariz. State U. Coll. Law, Tempe, 1980—; cert. holder Flagstaff Med. Ctr., 1984—. Mem. ABA, Ariz. Bar Assn. (adminstrn. com. 1978-82, bd. govs. 1982—), Coconino County Bar Assn. (pres. 1980), Ariz. Trial Lawyers Assn., Assn. Trial Lawyers Am. Democrat. Methodist. Office: Aspey Watkins & Diesel 123 N Leroux St Flagstaff AZ 86001

ASPINWALL, DAVID CHARLES, lawyer; b. Denver, Apr. 15, 1955; s. Darrell David and Gwendolyn Beth (Skeels) A.; m. Inez Bussey Merritt, Dec. 5, 1981; children: Courtney Merritt, Johnathan Westbrook. B.Arts and Sci., Denver U., 1977, J.D., 1980. Bar: Colo. 1980. Mem. Dunn, Crane & Burg, Denver, 1980-81, Michael S. Burg, P.C., Denver, 1981-83, Burg & Aspinwall, P.C., Denver, 1983—. Mem. ABA, Arapahoe County Bar Assn., Def. Research Inst., Colo. Bar Assn., Phi Beta Kappa. Democrat. Episcopalian. Office: Burg & Aspinwall PC Regency Tower One 4643 S Ulster #900 Denver CO 80237

ASSINK, ROGER ALYN, polymer chemist; b. Zeeland, Mich., Sept. 28, 1945; s. William and Hattie (Jacobsen) A.; m. Anne Hoekstra, Sept. 22, 1967; children: Ryan J., Corry R. BS, Mich. State U., 1967; MS, U. Ill., 1969, PhD, 1972. Mem. tech. staff Sandia Nat. Lab., Albuquerque, 1972—. Office: Sandia Labs Div 1812 Albuquerque NM 87185

ASTIN, ALEXANDER WILLIAM, educator; b. Washington, May 30, 1932; s. Allen Varley and Margaret L. (Mackenzie) A.; m. Helen Stavridou, Feb. 11, 1956; children: John Alexander, Paul Allen. A.B., Gettysburg (Pa.) Coll., 1953, Litt.D. (hon.), 1981; M.A., U. Md., 1956, Ph.D., 1958; LL.D. (hon.), Alderson-Broaddus Coll., 1982, Whitman Coll., 1986; LHD, Chapman Coll., 1987; D of Pedagogy, R.I. Coll., 1987. Dep. chief psychology service USPHS Hosp., Lexington, Ky., 1957-59; dep. chief psychology research unit VA Hosp., Balt., 1959-60; research asso., dir. research Nat. Merit Scholar Corp., Evanston, Ill., 1960-64; dir. research Am. Council Edn., Washington, 1965-73; prof. higher edn. UCLA, 1973—; pres. Higher Edn. Research Inst., Los Angeles, 1973-83. Author: The College Environment, 1968, The Educational and Vocational Development of College Students, 1969, The Invisible Colleges, 1971, The Power of Protest, 1975, Preventing Students from Dropping Out, 1975, Four Critical Years, 1977, Maximizing Leadership Effectiveness, 1980, Minorities in American Higher Education, 1982; Achieving Educational Excellence, 1985; others. Trustee St. Xavier Coll., Chgo., Marjorie Webster Jr. Coll., Washington, Gettysburg Coll., 1983-86, Eckerd Coll., Fla., 1986—. Recipient Disting. Research award Am. Personnel and Guidance Assn., 1965, Disting. Research award Nat. Assn. Student Personnel Adminstrs., 1976, Outstanding Service award Am. Coll. Personnel Assn., 1978, Lindquist award for outstanding research on college students Am. Ednl. Research Assn., 1983, Excellence in Edn. award Nat. Assn. Coll. Admissions Counselors, 1985, Outstanding Research award Am. Coll. Personnel Assn., 1985, Outstanding Service award Council of Ind. Colls., 1986, Outstanding Research award Assn. for Study of Higher Edn., 1987; fellow Center Advanced Study Behavioral Sci. Fellow Am. Psychol. Assn., AAAS; mem. Am. Assn. Higher Edn. (dir.). Home: 2681 Cordelia Rd Los Angeles CA 90049 Office: Grad Sch Edn UCLA Los Angeles CA 90024

ASTIN, CURTIS SUMMERS, banker; b. Salt Lake City, Nov. 16, 1944; s. Rufus B. and Phyllis (Summers) A.; m. Carolyn Bowers, Jan. 21, 1965; 1 child, Kimberly D. Student U. Utah, 1963-65. With First Security Bank, Salt Lake City, 1965-74, asst. v.p., 1974-79, v.p. mortgage service mgr., 1979-84, v.p. spl. loans dept., 1984-85, v.p. mgr. income property fin. dept., 1985-86; v.p., mgr. loan servicing Western Savs. & Loan Co., Salt Lake City, 1986—. Bd. dirs. March of Dimes, Salt Lake City, 1974—; dir., officer Salt Lake County Sheriff's Search & Rescue, 1979—; vol. Utah Heart Assn., 1975. Served with U.S. Army, 1963. Mem. Utah Mortgage Bankers Assn., Am. Inst. Banking, Mortgage Bankers Assn., Sigma Nu. Republican. Mormon. Home: 3617 Canyon Way Salt Lake City UT 84106 Office: Western Savs and Loan Co 41 E 1st South Salt Lake City UT 84111

ASTON, EDWARD ERNEST, IV, dermatologist; b. Jersey City, Jan. 14, 1944; m. Kirsten Anita. B.A., U. Md.-College Park, 1968; M.D., U. Md.-Balt., 1969. Diplomate Am. Bd. Dermatology. Intern, Orange County Med. Ctr., Orange, Calif., 1969-70; resident U. Calif.-Irvine-Orange County Med. Ctr., 1971-74; practice medicine specializing in dermatology Fullerton Med. Clinic of Dermatology, Calif., 1974—. Office: 301 W Bastanchury Rd Fullerton CA 92631

ASTORGA, TONY M(ANUEL), accountant; b. Superior, Ariz., Dec. 14, 1945; s. Antonio Astorga and Esther L. (Luevano) Castro; divorced; children from previous marriage: Renee, Denise, Michelle; m. Milena Dora Cuellar, Apr. 29, 1984; children: Tabatha, Farah. BS in Acctg., Ariz. State U., 1970. CPA. Tax auditor II Ariz. Dept. Revenue, Phoenix, 1965-70; supervising sr. Peat, Marwick & Mitchell, Phoenix, 1970-75; ptnr. Astorga, Maurseth & Co., Phoenix, 1975—; bd. dirs. Blue Cross Blue Shield, Phoenix, Ariz. Acad., Phoenix, Ariz. Bd. dirs. Community Council, Phoenix, Friendly House, Phoenix, Info. and Referral Services, Phoenix, Valle del Sol, Phoenix, Ariz.-Mex. Commn., Phoenix; chmn., bd. dirs Ariz. Coliseum and Exposition Ctr., Phoenix, 1983—. Named one of Outstanding Young Men Am., U.S. Jaycees, Phoenix, 1980. Mem. Am. Inst. CPA's, Ariz. Soc. CPA's, Ariz. Hispanic C. of C. (Profl. of Yr. 1981-82), Ariz. State U. Acctg. Circle, Pi Kappa Alpha. Roman Catholic. Office: Astorga Maurseth and Co PC 4004 N 7th St Phoenix AZ 85014

ASWANI, PRAKASH, engineering executive; b. Nawabshah, Pakistan, Mar. 5, 1943; s. Gangaram N. and Kalawanti G. (Raichandani) A.; m. Shakuntala P. Jethmalani, July 30, 1971; children—Prashant, Aparna. B.S. with honors in Physics, U. Delhi, 1963; B.S. in Elect. Engring., Madras Inst. Tech., 1966; M.B.A., Ind. No. Grad. Sch., 1980. Test engr. Meril Ltd., Bombay, India, 1966-71; sr. product engr. Adcor Electronics Inc., Atlanta, 1972-78; mgr. Test Ctr., Burroughs Corp., Plymouth, Mich., 1978-80; pres., chief exec. officer Microtest Systems Inc., Sunnyvale, Calif., 1981-85; founder, pres. Mega Pro Inc., San Jose, Calif., 1986—; mgmt. cons. Mem. Am. Mgmt. Assn. (exec. con.). Home: 1596 Lewiston Dr Sunnyvale CA 94087

ATAIE, ATA JENNATI, oil products mktg. exec.; b. Mashad, Iran, Mar. 15, 1934; s. Hamid Jennati and Mohtaram (Momeni) A.; came to U.S., 1957, naturalized, 1969; B.S. in Agr., Fresno (Calif.) State U., 1964; B.A. in Econs., San Francisco State U., 1966; m. Judith Garrett Bush, Oct. 7, 1961; children—Ata Jennati, Andrew J. Mktg. exec. Shell Oil Co., Oakland, Calif., 1966-75; pres. A.J. Ataie & Cos., Concord, Calif., 1975—; Am. Value Inc., 1976—. Served as 2d lt. Iranian Army, 1953. Mem. Nat. Petroleum Retailers Assn. Democrat.

ATCHESON, SUE HART, business educator; b. Dubuque, Iowa, Apr. 12; d. Oscar Raymond and Anna (Cook) Hart; m. Walter Clark Atcheson, Dec. 18; children: Christine A. Hischer, Moffet Zoe, Claye Williams. BBA, Mich. State U.; MBA, Calif. State Poly. U., Pomona, 1973. Cert. tchr. and adminstr. Instr. Mt. San Antonio Coll., Walnut, Calif., 1968—; bd. dirs. faculty assn. Mt. San Antonio Coll.; mem. acad. senate Mt. San Antonio Coll.; originator vol. income tax assistance Mt. San Antonio Coll. Author: Fractions and Equations on Your Own, 1975. Speaker Howard Ruff Nat. Conv., San Diego, 1983, Mike DeFalco Numismatics Seminar, Claremont, Calif., 1986. Office: Mount San Antonio Coll 1100 N Grand Ave Walnut CA 91789

ATCHISON, CARLA JOAN, political scientist; b. Denver, May 24, 1948; d. Lowell Chrysler and Jerry Louise (Stephens) A.; m. Michel N. Schuh. BA, Willamette U., 1970; MA, U. Colo., 1972. Teaching asst. U. Colo., Boulder, 1971-72, lectr., 1976-80; adj. instr. U. Colo., Colorado Springs, 1985—; vis. instr. U. Denver, 1980. Recipient George M. Putnam award in Journalism, 1969; NSF predoctoral trainee, 1970-71; U. Colo. doctoral fellow 1980-81. Mem. Am. Polit. Sci. Assn., Acad. Polit. Sci., Phi Beta Kappa, Alpha Lambda Delta, Pi Gamma Mu, Alpha Kappa Nu, Dobro Slovo. Presbyterian. Club: Order Eastern Star. Home: 1200 Cody St Lakewood CO 80215

ATCHLEY, ANTHONY C., hotel executive; b. Live Oak, Fla., Feb. 6, 1942; s. James Fred and Billie Sue (Dupree) A.; m. Linda Lou Atchley, Apr. 29, 1962; children: Kelli Lynn Labate, Michael James, Staci Marie. Grad. high sch., Las Vegas, Nev. Dir. publicity and advt. Thunderbird Hotel and Casino, Las Vegas, 1965-67, asst. gen. mgr., 1968-71; dir. publicity and advt. Sahara Tahoe Hotel and Casino, Stateline, Nev., 1967-68, exec. dir. mktg., 1973, asst. gen. mgr., 1973-75, pres., 1983-85; dir. spl. projects Mint Hotel and Casino, Las Vegas, 1972-73; gen. mgr. Fresno (Calif.) Townehouse, 1973; v.p. ops. Sahara Nev. Corp., Las Vegas, 1975-76; v.p., gen. mgr. Del Webb's Hotel Sahara, Las Vegas, 1976; dir. pub. relations Del Webb Hotels, Las Vegas, 1978-79; v.p. Del E. Webb New Jersey Inc., Atlantic City, 1979; v.p., gen. mgr. Del Webb's Sahara Reno (Nev.) Hotel and Casino, 1979-81, Del Webb's Sahara Hotel and Casino, Las Vegas, 1982; exec. v.p. Del Webb Hotels, Las Vegas, 1982-83, pres., 1985—; v.p., gen. mgr. Showboat Hotel and Casino, Las Vegas, 1976-78; pres., gen. mgr. Claridge Hotel and Casino, Atlantic City, 1982. Mem. Nev. Resort Assn. (exec. com. 1985—). Office: Del Webb Hotels 2300 Paseo Del Prado #A206 Las Vegas NV 89102

ATHA, GEORGE CRAWFORD, petroleum geologist; b. Fairmont, W.Va., Nov. 25, 1902; s. William Hunter and Jessie Julia (Dougan) A.; student in geology Ohio State U., 1922, Muskingum Coll., 1927; m. Gladys R. Wray, Apr. 7, 1948. Civil engr., Sebring, Fla., 1927; salesman, mgr. real estate, Lorain, Ohio, 1927-28; staff Midwest Re '29 Co., Roswell, l.Mex., 1928-29; staff City of Palos Verdes Estates (Calif.), 1930-37; pres. Hiawatha Exploration Co., San Marino, Calif., 1943—; pvt. practice petroleum geologist San Marino, 1947—. Recipient hon. award Muskingum Coll., 1983. Mem. Internat. Oil Scouts (bd. dirs. oil securities). Club: Long Beach Petroleum, Elks (life), Los Angeles Athletic. Address: 2221 California Blvd San Marino CA 91108

ATHERTON, ALEXANDER SIMPSON, newspaper executive; b. Honolulu, Mar. 29, 1913; s. Frank Cooke and Eleanore Alice (Simpson) A.; m. LeBurta Marie Gates, Oct. 8, 1941; children—Burta Lee, Frank Cooke II, Marjory Gates. Grad., Tabor Acad., Marion, Mass., 1931; B.A., Dartmouth, 1936. With Hawaiian Trust Co., Honolulu, 1954-66; asst. v.p. Hawaiian Trust Co., 1958-66; pres. Honolulu Star-Bull., 1963—. past campaign chmn. Honolulu Community Chest.; trustee Atherton Family Found.; bd. dirs. Africare, Inc., Bishop Mus. Pres. Mid-Pacific Inst., 1955—. Mem. Royal Philatelic Soc. London, Theta Delta Chi. Republican. Mem. United Ch. Christ. Clubs: Pacific (Honolulu), Adventurers (Honolulu), Waialae Country (Honolulu); Oahu Country; Collectors (N.Y.C.). Home: 2150 Puualii Pl Honolulu HI 96822

ATHEY, ROBERT DOUGLAS, JR., consulting chemist; b. Washington, Aug. 27, 1936; s. Robert Douglas and Elizabeth Jennings (Pitkin) A.; m. Barbara Josephine Cress, Jan. 10, 1958 (div. May 1980); children: Ashley Elizabeth Jorgensen, Carol Scott DeRiggi, Jane Kelsey Satryan; m. Patricia Abigail Blankenship Shaw, Jan. 1, 1981. BS, U. Md., 1964; PhD, U. Del., 1974. Sr. research chemist Gen. Tire & Rubber Co., Akron, Ohio, 1973-77; assoc. dir., mgr. research Mellon Inst., Pitts., 1977-80; sr. research assoc. Swedlow, Inc., Garden Grove, Calif., 1980-82; pres. Athey Techs., El Cerrito, Calif., 1982—; extension instr. U. Calif., Berkeley, 1984—. Contbr. articles on chemistry and computers to profl. mags. and jours.; patentee in field. Served with U.S. Army, 1958-61. Recipient VOSS award Fedn. Socs. for Coating Tech., 1982, 84. Mem. ASTM, Am. Chem. Soc., Tech. Assn. Pulp and Paper Industry (Man of Month Nonwovens Industry mag., 1978, Best Speaker award 1976), Golden Gate Soc. for Coating Tech., Bay Area Kay Pro Users and Programmers (pres. 1986—). Republican. Episcopalian. Avocations: duplicate bridge, computer games, reading, hiking, snorkeling. Office: Athey Techs PO Box 1459 El Cerrito CA 94530

ATIYEH, VICTOR GEORGE, former governor of Oregon; b. Portland, Oreg., Feb. 20, 1923; s. George and Linda (Asley) A.; m. Dolores Hewitt, July 5, 1944; 2 children. Student, U. Oreg., 1941-43. With Atiyeh Bros., Inc., Portland, until 1979, resigned as pres.; gov. State of Oreg., Salem, 1979-86; mem. Oreg. Ho. of Reps., 1959-65, Oreg. Senate, 1965-78, minority leader, 1971-78; past chmn. Western Govs. Conf. Past regional council pres. Columbia-Pacific council Boy Scouts Am.; past mem. Nat. Explorer Bd.; mem. United Fund, St. Vincent Med. Found., Tuality Community Hosp. Found.; dir.-at-large U. Oreg. Devel. Fund; del. Republican Nat. Conv., 1968, 72, 76, mem. nat. platform com., 1968, 72. Served with USCGR, 1944-45. Recipient Silver Beaver and Silver Antelope awards Boy Scouts Am., Oreg. Disting. Pub. Service award B'nai Brith, Pub. Service Honor award U.S. Dept. Justice. Mem. Rep. Govs. Assn. (chmn.). Episcopalian.

ATKIN, J. MYRON, educator; b. Bklyn., Apr. 6, 1927; s. Charles Z. and Esther (Jaffe) A.; m. Ann Spiegel, Dec. 25, 1947; children—David, Ruth, Jonathan. B.S., CCNY, 1947; M.A., NYU, 1948, Ph.D., 1956. Tchr. sci. Ramaz High Sch., N.Y.C., 1948-50; tchr. elem. sch. sci. Great Neck (N.Y.) pub. schs., 1950-55; prof. sci. edn. Coll. Edn., U. Ill., Urbana, 1955-79, assoc. dean, 1966-70, dean, 1970-79; prof. Sch. Edn., Stanford (Calif.) U., 1979-86, dean, 1979-86; cons. OECD, Paris, Nat. Inst. Edn.; mem. edn. adv. bd. NSF, 1973-76, 84-86, vice chmn., 1984-85, sr. advisor, 1986-87; mem. Ill. Tchr. Certification Bd., 1973-76; Sir John Adams lectr. U. London Inst. Edn., 1980. Author children's sci. textbooks. Served with USNR, 1945-46. Fellow AAAS (v.p. sect. Q 1973-74); mem. Council Elementary Sci. Internat. (pres. 1969-70), Am. Ednl. Research Assn. (exec. bd. 1972-75, chmn. govt. and profl. liaison com.). Office: Sch Edn Stanford U Stanford CA 94305

ATKINS, GARY LESLIE, journalism educator; b. Terrell, Tex., Aug. 22, 1949; s. Leslie Roy and Adele Jane (Koska) A. BA, Loyola U., New Orleans, 1971; MA, Stanford U., 1972. Journalist Press-Enterprise, Riverside, Calif., 1972-78; journalism educator Seattle U., 1978—; participant investigative journalism seminar Am. Press Assn., 1974. Co-author: Reporting with Understanding, 1986; contbr. articles to profl. jours. Mem.

exec. com. Am. Friends Pacific NW, Seattle, 1985—; bd. dirs. Seattle Media Project, Seattle, 1984—. Fellow Seattle U., 1983, Precision Journalism, NSF, 1974. Mem. Investigative Reporters and Editors, Am. Educators in Journalism and Mass Communications, Sigma Delta Chi. Mem. Soc. of Friends. Home: PO Box 12261 Seattle WA 98102 Office: Seattle U Dept Journalism Seattle WA 98122

ATKINS, WILLIAM RONALD, hotel executive; b. Mound City, Mo., May 14, 1933; s. William Stanley and Alta May (Hagloch) A.; m. Beverly Joan Lynn, Aug. 6, 1950 (div.); children—Jacqua Lyn, Brian Allan, Koby Vaughn, Dawn Michelle. Cert. in bus. adminstrn. La Salle Extension U., Chgo., 1968. Asst. mgr. hardware dept. Sears Roebuck & Co., Battle Creek, Mich., 1954-57; sr. illustrator art dept., manuals and statistics div. Clark Equipment Co., Battle Creek, 1957-62; ptnr., mgr. Duncan's Oak Hills restaurant and motel, Mayer, Ariz., 1962-80; pres. D&A Enterprises Inc., Mayer, 1980—. Mem. Mayer Unified sch. dist. bd., 1968-78, pres., 1972-74, bd. dirs. Yavapai County (Ariz.) br. Ariz. Sch. Bds. Assn., 1974-78; fire chief Mayer vol. fire dist. Served with Mich. N.G., 1951-55. Recipient VFW Aux. Commendable Service award, 1979. Mem. Nat. Restaurant Assn., Ariz. Fire Fighters Assn., Ariz. Fire Chiefs, Nat. Fire Chiefs Assn. Democrat. Baptist. Clubs: Mayer Centennial Lions (Charter), Soc. Preservation and Encouragement Barber Shop Quartette Singing in Am. (past pres. Prescott chpt.). Office: PO Box 97 Mayer AZ 86333

ATKINSON, DANIEL EDWARD, educator, biochemist; b. Pawnee City, Nebr., Apr. 8, 1921; s. Max and Amy (Neiswanger) A.; m. Elsie Ann Hemmingson, 1948; children: Kristine Ruth, Owen Rolf, Joyce Elaine, Ellen Lee, David Eric. B.Sc., U. Nebr., 1942, D.Sc., 1975; Ph.D., Iowa State U., 1949. Research fellow Calif. Inst. Tech., 1949-50; asso. scientist Argonne Nat. Lab., 1950-52; mem. faculty UCLA, 1952—, prof. chemistry, 1962-81, prof. biochemistry, 1981—; vis. prof. MIT, 1966-67, U. B.C., 1975. Author: Cellular Energy Metabolism and Its Regulation, 1977; assoc. editor: Jour. Biol. Chemistry, 1972-77; Contbr. articles to profl. jours. Served with USNR, 1943-46. Guggenheim fellow, 1966-67. Mem. Am. Soc. Biol. Chemists, Am. Chem. Soc. (chmn. div. biol. chemistry 1978), Am. Soc. Microbiology, Am. Soc. Plant Physiologists. Home: 3123 Malcolm Ave Los Angeles CA 90034

ATKINSON, DAVID LEE, chiropractic physician, biotechnology consultant; b. Sturgis, Mich., Sept. 20, 1957; s. Stanley T. and Patricia (Daly) A. BS in Biology, Stanford U., 1979; D in Chiropractic Medicine, Palmer Coll. Chiropractic, 1987. Bichemist SRI Internat., Menlo Park, Calif., 1979-83; biotech. research assoc. Dugan Assocs., Inc., Palo Alto, Calif., 1984—. Contbr. articles to profl. jours. Mem. Am. Chiropractic Assn., Calif. Chiropractic Assn., Internat. Kenpo Karate Assn. Avocations: martial arts, bicycling, music. Home: 26070 Newbridge Los Altos Hills CA 94022

ATKINSON, FREDA MAE, social worker; b. Colorado Springs, Colo., June 23, 1948; d. Fred Louis Atkinson and Dorothy Leona (Justice) Granger. Student, Otero Jr. Coll., 1968-69; AA, Pikes Peak Community Coll., 1970; BS, U. So. Colo., 1977; MSW, U. Denver, 1985. Vocat. edn. coordinator City of Colorado Springs, 1977-84; employee relations specialist Inmos Corp., Colorado Springs, 1984-85; vocat. coordinator Cheyenne Village, Manitou Springs, Colo., 1971-77, Pikes Peak Mental Health Ctr., Colorado Springs, 1985—. Mem. Am. Soc. Tng. and Devel., Nat. Assn. Social Workers. Democrat. Baptist. Avocations: music, classic cars, collecting rocks and minerals. Home: 14 Waltham Ave Manitou Springs CO 80829 Office: Pikes Peak Mental Health Ctr 875 W Moreno Ave Colorado Springs CO 80905

ATKINSON, KATHY JO, physician; b. Missoula, Mont., June 2, 1951; d. Dale Eugene and Audrey Jane (Underhill) A. AB cum laude, Cornell U., 1973; MD, U. Wash., 1977. Resident in family practice U. Utah, Salt Lake City, 1977-80; emergency room physician Holy Cross Hosp., Salt Lake City, 1980—. Vol. physician, India, 1983, 84, 85. Fellow Am. Acad. Family Physicians (cert.); mem. Physicians for Social Responsibility, Am. Coll. Emergency Physicians (cert.), Sierra Club, Alpha Omega Alpha. Avocations: skiing, windsurfing, travel. Home: 600 Standel Dr Salt Lake City UT 84108

ATKINSON, RICHARD CHATHAM, educator, experimental psychologist, university chancellor; b. Oak Park, Ill., Mar. 19, 1929; s. Herbert and Margaret (Feuerbach) A.; m. Rita Loyd, Aug. 20, 1952; 1 dau., Lynn Loyd. Ph.B., U. Chgo., 1948; Ph.D., Ind. U., 1955. Lectr. applied math. and stats. Stanford (Calif.) U., 1956-57, assoc. prof. psychology, 1961-64, prof. psychology, 1964-80; asst. prof. psychology UCLA, 1957-61; dep. dir. NSF, 1975-76, acting dir., 1976-77; dir., 1977-80; chancellor U. Calif., San Diego, 1980—; Mem. Pres.'s Com. Nat. Medal Sci. Author: (with Atkinson, Smith and Hilgard) Introduction to Psychology, 9th edit, 1987, Computer Assisted Instruction, 1969, An Introduction to Mathematical Learning Theory, 1965, Studies in Mathematical Psychology, 1964, Contemporary Developments in Mathematical Psychology, 1974, Mind and Behavior, 1980. Served with AUS, 1954-56. Guggenheim fellow, 1967; fellow Center for Advanced Study in Behavioral Scis., 1963; recipient Distinguished Research award Social Sci. Research Council, 1962. Fellow Am. Acad. Arts and Scis., Am. Psychol. Assn. (pres. exptl. div. 1974-75, Disting. Sci. Contbn. award 1977, Thorndike award 1980), AAAS (chmn. psychology sect. 1975-76); mem. Soc. Exptl. Psychologists, Nat. Acad. Scis. (council 1982-85), Am. Philos. Soc., Nat. Acad. Edn., Inst. of Medicine, Psychonomic Soc. (chmn. 1973-74), Western Psychol. Assn. (pres. 1975-76), Psychometric Soc., Sigma Xi. Clubs: Cosmos (Washington); Explorers (N.Y.C.). Home: 9630 La Jolla Farms Rd La Jolla CA 92037 Office: Chancellor's Office U Calif at San Diego La Jolla CA 92093

ATKINSON, SHERIDAN EARLE, lawyer, financial and management consultant; b. Oakland, Calif., Feb. 14, 1945; s. Arthur Sheridan and Esther Louise (Johnson) A.; m. Margie Ann Lehtin, Aug. 13, 1966. 1 son, Ian Sheridan. B.S., U. Calif.-Berkeley, 1966, M.B.A., 1971; J.D., U. San Francisco, 1969. Bar: Calif. 1970. Prin. Atkinson & Assocs., fin. and mgmt. cons., corp. and bus. valuations, San Francisco, 1968—; assoc. Charles O. Morgan, Jr., San Francisco, 1972-76; sole practice, San Francisco Bar Area, 1976—. Served with USAR, 1970-76. Mem. Calif. Bar Assn., ABA. Republican. Office: The Watergate 4 Commodore Dr #227 Emeryville CA 94608

ATKINSON, STAN, newscaster, international reporter; b. Santa Barbara, Calif.; married. Student, Pasadena City Coll. Documentary producer, writer, dir. for David Wolper, Hollywood, Calif., 1963-76; anchorman, reporter NBC, Los Angeles, San Francisco, Oakland, Calif.; reporter Sta. KCRA, Sacramento, 1980—; corr., reporter Sta. KCRA, Honduras, Guatemala, Angola, Afghanistan, Switzerland, Thailand, Somalia, Peoples Republic of Kampuchea, El Salvador, 1980—. Master of Ceremonies, Labor Day Muscular Dystrophy telethon; chmn. San Sierra Celebrity Tennis Tournament; bd. dirs. Mercy Hosps. Found., Leukemia Soc., Muscular Dystrophy Assn., People Reaching Out, Rescue Now, Life Extension Inst.; mem., advisor Emergency Relief Fund Internat., Jr. Achievement, Calif. Com. Free Afghanistan, Internat. Med. Corps, Jr. League, Com. Free Angola. Served with U.S. Army. Named Humanitarian of Yr., United Way, 1981; recipient World Affairs Council Internat. Reporting award, Albert and Mary Lasker Med. Journalism award; Ford Found. fellow. Mem. Radio-TV News Dirs. Assn., Nat. Acad. TV Arts Scis., Sigma Delta Chi. Club: Sacramento Press. Office: Sta KCRA TV 310 Tenth St Sacramento CA 95814

ATKINSON, WALTER LEE, JR., business educator; b. Rocky Mount, N.C., Feb. 20, 1950; s. Walter Lee Sr. and Francis Olivia (Lawrence) A.; m. Deborah Faye Mitchell, Aug. 28, 1971; children: Jonnae Olivia, Eric Darnell. BEd, Seattle U., 1974, M in Pub. Adminstrn., 1977. Cert. tchr., Wash. Tchr. Seattle Pub. Schs., 1983—, Seattle Upward Bound, 1983—; tng. cons. Seattle Pub. Schs. Inter-Cultural Tng., 1983-84; mem. adv. bd. St. Therese Sch., Seattle, 1983—. Adminstr. Boys Clubs Am., Seattle, 1978-83; counselor II Summer Youth Employment Program, Seattle, 1977; mem. adv. bd. Western Region Casey Family Program, Seattle, 1983—, Minority Exec. Dirs. Coalition, SEattle, 1982-83, King County Dept. Youth Services, Seattle, 1980-83, chmn. city wide planning com., 1972. Fellow Robert W. Woodruff, Boys Clubs Am., N.Y.C., 1975, Urban Fellow, Boys Clubs Am., N.Y.C., 1975; recipient Outstanding Service in Edn. award Seattle U. Minority Affairs, 1986. Mem. Kappa Alpha Psi (named Outstanding Undergrad., 1974). Avocations: reading, jogging, sports, jazz. Home: 942 27th Ave Seattle WA 98122

ATKINSON, WILLIAM WILDER, lawyer; b. Little Rock, May 18, 1910; s. William Wilder and Mary Byrne (Parrish) A.; m. Josephine Elizabeth Foster, Oct. 20, 1934; children—William Wilder, Richard Foster. B.A., U. N.Mex., 1936; J.D., U. Colo., 1948. Bar: N.Mex. 1948, U.S. Supreme Ct. 1975. Sole practice, Albuquerque, 1948-62; ptnr. Hernandez & Atkinson, Albuquerque, 1962-73; sr. ptnr. Atkinson & Kelsey, P.A., Albuquerque, 1973—. Mem. Albuquerque City Commn., 1955-63, vice chmn., 1962-63; chmn. City of Albuquerque Personnel Bd., 1964-65; mem. Albuquerque Human Rights Commn., 1974-80; del. N.Mex. Constl. Conv., 1969; mem. Gov.'s Task Force on Mcpl. Fin., 1976; mem. U. N.Mex. Governance Adv. Commn., 1970; mem. Albuquerque Community Council, 1963-78, pres., 1964-65; mem. Albuquerque-Bernalillo County Econ. Opportunity Bd., 1965-68, pres., 1967-68; trustee Bernalillo County Mental Health/Mental Retardation Ctr., 1968-73; bd. dirs. Goodwill Industries N.Mex., 1968-84, pres., 1973-76; mem. exec. com. Presbyn. Hosp. Found., 1977-80; bd. dirs. N.Mex. chpt. NCCJ, 1974-79, Sr. Citizens Legal Services, 1984—, Arthritis Found., 1987—. Recipient Brotherhood award NCCJ, 1972. Mem. ABA, N.Mex. Bar Assn., Albuquerque Bar Assn. (pres. 1970-71), Albuquerque Lawyers Club (pres. 1954), U. N.Mex. Alumni Assn. (dir. 1960-66), Order of Coif, Phi Kappa Phi, Phi Delta Phi. Democrat. Congregationalist. Clubs: Optimists, Knife and Fork (Albuquerque). Home: 1637 Kit Carson Ave SW Albuquerque NM 87104 Office: 1300 First Interstate Bank Bldg PO Box 1126 Albuquerque NM 87103

ATKINSON, WILLIAM WILDER, JR., geology educator; b. Albuquerque, Dec. 16, 1935; s. William Wilder and Josephine Elizabeth (Foster) A.; m. Carol Ann Bambrook, June 9, 1957; children: William W. IV, Ellen Annalies. BS, U. N.Mex., 1957, MS, 1960; postgrad., Hamburg U., Fed. Republic Germany, 1960-61; PhD, Harvard U., 1973. Geologist Anaconda Co., Salt Lake City, 1967-78, cons., 1978—; prof. geology U. Colo., Boulder, 1978—. Contbr. articles to sci. jours. NSF scholar, 1961; Deutsche Acad. Austausch Dienst fellow, 1960. Mem. Soc. Econ. Geologists (com. mem.), Geol. Soc. Am., Geol. Soc. Chile, Sigma Xi. Avocations: lang. study, reading, photography. Home: 255 Cimmaron Way Boulder CO 80303 Office: U Colo Dept Geol Sci Campus Box 250 Boulder CO 80309

ATTEBERY, BRIAN LEONARD, English language educator; b. Ontario, Oreg., Dec. 8, 1951; s. Louie W. and Barbara (Olson) A.; m. Jennifer Eastman, Dec. 31, 1975. BA, Coll. Idaho, 1974; MA, Brown U., 1976, PhD, 1979. Vis. asst. prof. Coll. Idaho, Caldwell, 1979-81; instr. Boise (Idaho) State U., 1981-82; grant dir. Idaho State U., Pocatello, 1982-85, asst. prof., 1982—; cons. Idaho Hist. Soc., Boise, 1979-81, Boise Gallery of Art, 1980-81. Author: The Fantasy Tradition in American Literature, 1980; mem. editorial bd. Idaho Folklife Assocs., 1981-84; contbr. articles to profl. publs. Grantee Assn. for Humanities in Idaho, 1980. Mem. Am. Folklore Soc., Am. Studies Assn., Pacific Northwest Am. Studies Assn., Sci. Fiction Research Assn., Internat. Assn. for the Fantastic in Arts (mem. awards com.). Office: Idaho State U Am Studies Box 8056 Pocatello ID 83209

ATTLES, ALVIN A. (AL ATTLES), professional basketball team executive; b. Newark, Nov. 7, 1936; m. Wilhemina Rice; children: Alvin III, Erica. Grad., N.C. A & T State U., 1960. Player Phila. Warriors, Nat. Basketball Assn., 1960-62, San Francisco Warriors, Nat. Basketball Assn., 1962-71; coach Golden State Warriors, Nat. Basketball Assn., 1970-83; gen. mgr. Golden State Warriors, Nat. Basketball Assn., Oakland, Calif., 1983-86, now v.p., cons. Coach Nat. Basketball Assn. championship team, 1975. Office: Golden State Warriors Oakland Coliseum Arena Oakland CA 94621 *

ATWELL, MARGARET ANN, education educator; b. Milw., Jan. 26, 1949; d. Vincent C. and Margaret M. (McCormack) Abaravich. BA, Marquette U., 1971; MS, Ind. U., 1977, EdD, 1980. Cert. tchr., Wis., Mich. Tchr. Milw. Pub. Schs., 1971-75; vis. lectr. U. Wis., Milw., 1978-79; vis. prof. Ind. U., Bloomington, 1979-80; prof., assoc. dean, chmn. dept. grad. edn. Calif. State U., San Bernardino, 1981—; asst. dir. Ind. U. Learning Ctr., 1979-80. Author: Learning in College: Integrating Information, 1981; contbr. articles to profl. jours. Bd. dirs. YWCA, San Bernardino, 1981—, Am. Cancer Soc., San Bernardino, 1986—. Recipient F. Mote Disting. Researcher award Calif. State U., San Bernardino, 1981, Meritorious Performance award Calif. State U., San Bernardino, 1985. Mem. Internat. Reading Assn., Nat. Council Tchrs. English (Promising Researcher 1981), Nat. Council Research English, Ctr. for Excellence in Language and Teaching, Arrowhead Reading Council (bd. dirs. 1985-86). Office: Calif State U 5500 University Pkwy San Bernardino CA 92407

ATWOOD, MARY SANFORD, author; b. Mt. Pleasant, Mich., Jan. 27, 1935; d. Burton Jay and Lillian Belle (Sampson) Sanford; B.S., U. Miami, 1957; m. John C. Atwood, III, Mar. 23, 1957. Author: A Taste of India, 1969. Mem. San Francisco/N. Peninsula Opera Action, Hillsborough-Burlingame Newcomers, Suicide Prevention and Crisis Center, DeYoung Art Mus., Internat. Hospitality Center, Peninsula Symphony, San Francisco Art Mus., World Affairs Council, Mills Hosp. Assos. Mem. AAUW, Suicide Prevention Aux. Republican. Club: St. Francis Yacht. Address: 40 Knightwood Ln Hillsborough CA 94010

ATWOOD, ROBERT BRUCE, publisher; b. Chgo., Mar. 31, 1907; s. Burton H. and Mary Beach (Stevenson) A.; m. Evangeline Rasmuson, Apr. 2, 1932; children: Marilyn A. Odom, Sara Elaine. A.B., Clark U., 1929; Litt.D. (hon.), Alaska Meth. U., 1967; D.Journalism (hon.), U. Alaska, 1979. Reporter Worcester (Mass.) Telegram, 1926-29, 34-35, Ill. State Jour., Springfield, 1929-34; pres. and pub. Anchorage Times, 1935—. Author pamphlets, articles, editorials pub. in various jours. Chmn. Alaska Statehood Com., 1949-59; hon. Norwegian consul at Anchorage, 1960-86; mem. civilian affairs bd. Alaskan Air Command, 1962—, now chmn.; chmn. Chancellor's Circle U. Alaska. Decorated knight of first rank Order of St. Olaf, 1976. Mem. AP, Am. Newspaper Pubs. Assn., Pacific N.W. Newspaper Assn., Nat. Mcpl. League (v.p.), Allied Daily Newspapers, Am. Soc. Newspaper Editors, Am. Polar Soc. (bd. govs.), C. of C. (pres. 1944, 48), Sigma Delta Chi. Republican. Presbyterian. Clubs: Explorers, Nat. Press. Lodges: Sons of Norway, Rotary. Home: 2000 Atwood Dr Anchorage AK 99503 Office: Anchorage Times 820 4th Ave Anchorage AK 99501

ATWOOD, RONALD WAYNE, lawyer; b. Eugene, Oreg., Nov. 25, 1950; s. Wayne Riley and Phoebe Hall (Smith) A.; m. Rebecca Ada Youngstrom, Sept. 9, 1978; 1 child, Kira Juda Phoebe. BA, Lewis & Clark Coll., 1973; JD, U. Oreg., 1978. Bar: Oreg. 1978, U.S. Dist. Ct. Oreg. 1978, U.S. Ct. Appeals (9th cir.) 1980. Assoc. Gearin, Landis & Aebi, Portland, Oreg., 1978-79; ptnr. Rankin, Vav Rosky, Doherty, MacColl and Mersereau, Portland, Oreg., 1979—. Contbr. (book) Workers Compensation, 1980. Mem. ABA, Oreg. State Bar, Am. Soc. Law and Medicine, Assn. Workers Compensation Def. Attys. (mem. exec. com.), Mult County Bar Assn., Internat. Brotherhood of Knights of Vine, Oreg. Wine Tasters Guild (cellarmaster, v.p.). Democrat. Presbyterian. Club: City (chair bus. and labor standing com.) (Portland). Avocations: wine tasting, sculling, reading, video.

ATWOOD, SONIA EILEEN, analytical chemist; b. Warren, Pa., June 16, 1951; d. Claude Stockdill and Edna Katherine (Gregerson) A. BS, U. Pitts., 1973; MS, U. Colo., 1981. Assoc. scientist Marathon Oil Co., Littleton, Colo., 1974-75, scientist, 1977—; assoc. scientist Atlantic Richfield Co., Harvey, Ill., 1976-77; computer sci. instr. Arapahoe Community Coll., Littleton, 1984—. Mem. ASTM (chairwoman 1984—), Am. Chem. Soc. (chairwoman 1983), Ion Chromatography Users Group (sec. 1985-86), Soc. for Applied Spectroscopy, Rocky Mt. Chromatography Discussion Group, Sigma Xi. Avocations: U.S. Soccer Fedn. referee, scubadiving, water skiing, skiing, running. Office: Marathon Oil Co PO Box 269 Littleton CO 80160-0269

AU, ALICE MAN-JING, chemist; b. Canton, People's Republic of China; d. Ying-Tak and Yeuk-Suet Au. BS, U. Calif., Riverside, 1972, PhD, 1976. Postdoctoral scholar U. Calif., San Diego, 1976-78; postgrad. researcher U. Calif., San Francisco, 1978-80, research biochemist, 1980-81; chemist Calif. State Dept. Health Service, Berkeley, 1981-84, supervising chemist, 1984—; cons. Sci. Innovations, San Francisco, 1983—. Contbr. articles to profl. jours. dir. adv. com. Calif. State Dept. Health Services EEO Com., Sacramento, 1986. Fellow NSF, 1972; DAR scholar 1970; Disting. Acad. scholar U. Calif., Riverside, 1972-76. Mem. AAAS, Am. Chem. Soc., N.Y. Acad. Scis., Phi Beta Kappa.

AU, ANTHONY D., computer scientist, petroleum engineer; b. Hong Kong, July 18, 1947; came to Can., 1977; s. Jacob and S.Y. (Leung) A. BSc, U. Utah, 1970, MSc, 1972, PhD, 1977. Registered profl. engr., Alta, Can. Research assoc. U. Utah, Salt Lake City, 1974-77; research engr. Computer Modelling Group, Calgary, Alta., 1977-78, simulation engr., 1978-79, sr. simulation engr., 1979-81, asst. mgr., 1981-82, mgr., 1982—. Mem. Assn. Profl. Engrs. Geologists Geophysicists Alta., Soc. Petroleum Engrs., Petroleum Soc. Can. Inst. Mining (bd. dirs. 1985—). Home: 4802 Dalhousie Dr NW, Calgary Can T3A 1B2 Office: Computer Modelling Group, 3512-33 St NW, Calgary Can T2L 2A6

AUCOIN, LES, congressman; b. Portland, Oreg., Oct. 21, 1942; s. Francis Edgar and Alice (Atkinson) AuC.; m. Susan Swearingen, June 11, 1963; children: Stacy, Kelly. B.A., Pacific U., 1969. Reporter, editor Redmond (Oreg.) Spokesman, 1964; with Portland Oregonian, 1965-66; dir. pub. info. and publs. Pacific U., 1966-73; adminstr. Skidmore, Owings & Merrill, Portland, 1973-74; mem. 94th-100th Congresses from 1st Oreg. Dist., Com. on Appropriations, Subcom. on Interior, Def. and D.C.; chmn. House Task Force on Indsl. Innovation and Productivity., House Dem. Trade Caucus, 1983—; Mem. Oreg. Ho. of Reps., 1971-74, majority leader, 1973-74; chmn. Oreg. Ho. of Reps. (Com. on State and Fed. Affairs), 1973, Oreg. Ho. of Reps. (Com. on Rules), 1974; mem. State Emergency Bd., 1973-74; leader Whip Task Force on Arms Control. Served with inf. U.S. Army, 1961-64. Recipient One of 10 Outstanding Young Men of Am. award U.S. Jaycees, 1977; Brotherhood award B'nai, B'rith, 1978. Office: 2159 Rayburn House Office Bldg Washington DC 20515 *

AUDET, HAROLD HUDSON, physician; b. Newburyport, Mass., Oct. 10, 1918; s. Oliver J. and Edith Mary (Hudson) A.; m. Dorothea Schubert, May 6, 1956. AB, Colgate U., 1942; MD, CM, McGill U., 1945; MPH, Tulane U., 1956. Diplomate Am. Bd. Preventive Medicine. Intern Royal Victoria Hosp., Montreal, Que., Can., 1945-46; resident Camp Hill Hosp., Halifax, N.S., Can., 1948-51; commd. U.S. Army, 1942, advanced through grades to col., 1967, ret., 1972; area med. dir. Springs Mills Inc., Chester, S.C., 1974-77; occupational medicine physician Philip Morris U.S.A., Richmond, Va., 1977-85; practice medicine specializing in occupational medicine Pacific Grove, Calif., 1985—. Decorated Bronze Star, Dept. Def. Commendation medal, Army Commendation medal with oak leaf cluster. Mem. Assn. Mil. Surgeons, Am. Pub. Health Assn., Va. Med. Soc., Richmond Acad. Medicine, Royal Asiatic Soc. (Seoul, Republic of Korea). Club: Royal Okinawa Yacht. Lodge: Order of the Boar. Home: 511 Crocker Ave Pacific Grove CA 93956

AUERBACH, ARTHUR MICHAEL, orthopedic surgeon; b. N.Y.C., Feb. 19, 1937; s. Samuel and Gertrude (Steinberg) A.; m. Judith Ann Bernstein, June 1963 (div. 1977); m. Odette Tara Rauch, June 23, 1985; children: Adam Mark, Amy Lynn, Stefan David. BA, Cornell U., 1957; MD, U. Chgo., 1961. Intern N.Y. Hosp., N.Y.C., 1961-62, resident surgery, 1962-63; orthopedic resident Mayo Clinic, Rochester, Minn., 1965-68; orthopedic surgeon Oakland (Calif.) Orthopaedic Med. Group, Inc., 1968—; bd. dirs. Trans Pacific Nat. Bank, San Francisco, Fairmont Hosp. Amputation Prosthetics Clinic, Fairmont Hosp. Orthopedic Consultative Dept. Rehab., Fairmont Hosp. Orthopedic Clinic, Oakland; mem. exec. bd. Trans Pacific Nat. Bank, San Francisco, 1986; gen. ptnr. Redwood Athletic Club, Oakland; founder Summit Bank, Oakland; staff mem. Fairmont Hosp., San Leandro, Oakland Hosp., Providence Hosp., Oakland, Merritt Hosp., Oakland, Peralta Hosp., Oakland, Children's Hosp. of East Bay. Served to lt. commdr. USNR, 1963-65. Fellow Am. Acad. Orthopedic Surgery, Am. Coll. Surgeons, Internat. Coll. Surgeons; mem. Western Orthopedic Assn., Am. Coll. Sports Medicine, Am. Occupational Med. Assn., Royal Soc. Medicine, Bay Area Knee Soc., Mem. Am. Running and Fitness Assn., Alpha Epsilon Delta, Phi Beta Kappa, Alpha Omega Alpha. Republican. Avocations: reading, running, skiing, music. Office: Oakland Orthopaedic Med Group 3300 Webster St Suite 803 Oakland CA 94609

AUERBACH, DANIEL J., physicist; b. N.Y.C., Nov. 29, 1942; s. Samuel and Edith (Grossman) A.; m. Valerie M. Waldhorn, June 28, 1969; children: Jesse, Emma, Lisa. BS, U. Chgo., 1964, MS, 1966, PhD, 1970. Vis. scientist FOM Inst. for Atomic and Molecular Physics, Amsterdam, The Netherlands, 1971-72; teaching postdoctoral fellow U. Western Ont., Can., 1972-73; sr. research assoc. U. Chgo., 1973-76; asst. prof. Johns Hopkins U., Balt., 1977-78; mem. research staff IBM, San Jose, Calif., 1978-86; mgr. phys. sci. IBM Almaden Research Ctr., San Jose, Calif., 1986—. Mem. adv. editorial bd. Chem. Physics Letters, 1982—; contbr. articles to profl. jours. Fellow Am. Phys. Soc.; mem. Am. Chem. Soc., Am. Vacuum Soc. Office: IBM Research K31/802 650 Harry Rd San Jose CA 95120-6099

AUERBACH, IRVING, chemist; b. Cleve., May 24, 1919; s. Jacob and Fannie (Rothmen) A.; m. Hertha Bienes, July 4, 1969. BS in Chemistry, Ohio State U., 1942, PhD in Chemistry, 1948. Research assoc. Case Western Res. U., Cleve., 1948-49, Cleve. Indsl. Research, 1949-51; mem. research staff Goodyr. Research, Akron, Ohio, 1951-57; mem. tech. staff Sandia Nat. Labs., Albuquerque, 1957—. Contbr. articles to profl. jours. Fellow AAAS (chmn. phys. scis. div. 1982-84), N.Mex. Acad. Scis. (pres. 1960-62), Am. Inst. Chemists; mem. Sigma Xi. Avocations: hiking, climbing, skiing, gardening. Home: 3425 Tahoe NE Albuquerque NM 87111 Office: Sandia Nat Labs PO Box 5800 Albuquerque NM 87185

AUERBACH, ROGER MICHAEL, labor union executive; b. Bklyn., March 21, 1946; s. George and Helene Janice (Siegel) Auerbach Sparber. B.A., Alfred U., 1968; J.D., Boston U. Law Sch., 1971. Bar: Mass. 1971. Atty., HUD, Boston, 1971-72; buyer, organizer, New Eng. Food Co-op Orgn., Boston, 1973-74; researcher, Oreg. Student Public Interest Research Group, Portland, 1975-76; pres. Oreg. Fedn. Tchrs. AFL-CIO, Portland, 1977-84; pres. Oreg. Fedn. Public Employees, AFL-CIO, 1980-83; v.p. Oreg. State Indsl. Union Council, AFL-CIO, 1979-84; v.p. Pacific NW Labor Coll. Assn., 1977-84; bd. advisors Working Assets Money Fund, 1985—; exec. bd. Multnomah County Labor Council, AFL-CIO, 1980-84; council rep. Am. Fedn. State, County and Mcpl. Employees, AFL-CIO, Portland. Precinct committeeperson Democratic party, dist. 10 leader; exec. bd. Multnomah County Dems., 1984—; chmn. community relations com. Jewish Fedn. of Portland, also bd. dirs., 1985—; past pres. NW Oreg. Health Systems; bd. dirs. Food Front Coop. Grocery, 1982-86.

AUERBACK, SANDRA JEAN, social worker; b. San Francisco, Feb. 21, 1946; d. Alfred and Molly Loy (Friedman) A.; m. Joseph Gauthier, June 10, 1968 (div. Aug. 1978). BA, U. Calif., Berkeley, 1967; MSW, Hunter Sch. Social Work, 1972. Lic. clin. social worker, Calif. Case aide Spaulding Youth Ctr., Tilton, N.H., 1968-69; case worker Lakeside Sch., Spring Valley, N.Y., 1969-70; clin. social worker Jewish Family Services, Bklyn., 1972-73, Hackensack, N.J., 1973-78; pvt. practice psychotherapy San Francisco, 1978—; dir. intake adult day care Jewish Home for the Aged, San Francisco, 1979—. Bd. dirs. Demarest (N.J.) Little Theater, 1977-78. Mem. Nat. Assn. Social Workers (cert., bd. dirs. Bay Area Referral Service 1983—, chmn. referral service 1984—), Spouses of Gays (founder), Am. Group Psychotherapy Assn., Am. Soc. Aging. Home: 1100 Gough St Apt 8C San Francisco CA 94109 Office: 450 Sutter San Francisco CA 94108

AUERSWALD, DAVID CHRISTIAN, chemical engineer; b. Rocky Mount, N.C., July 11, 1946; s. Charles Gustave and Julia Moore (Scarborough) A.; m. Margery Jeanne Wilson, Nov. 28, 1971; 1 child, Steven Brett. BS in Chemistry, Purdue U., 1968. Jr. chemist So. Calif. Edison, Redondo Beach, 1968-69, asst. chemist, 1969-71, startup engr., 1971-72; supr. stm. gen. chemist So. Calif. Edison, Paramount, 1972-78, chem. engr., 1978-84, sr. chem. engr., 1984—; cons. to various utilities, Kans. Ariz., Calif., 1983—; researcher Electric Power Research Inst., Palo Alto, 1979-84; cons., process engr. San Onofre Nuclear Generating Sta., San Clemente, 1981-86. Author: International Water Conference, 1982; contbr. articles to profl. jours.; patentee water regeneration method, 1985. Mem. ASME (research and tech. sect., mem. com. on water in thermal power systems), Am. Chem. Soc. Jehovah's Witness. Avocations: stamp collecting, coin collecting, motorcycling, skiing. Home: 908 Firmona Ave Redondo Beach CA 90278 Office: So Calif Edison 7103 Marcelle St Paramount CA 90723

AUGSBURGER, WILSON LEE, army officer; b. Salem, Oreg., Feb. 19, 1939; s. William Ray and Billie (Polstra) A.; m. Frieda Bleich, June 17, 1967; children: Gretchen, Nikola. MusB, Wheaton Coll., 1960; MS, Juilliard Sch. Music, 1963; MA in Health Adminstrn., Baylor U., 1979. Commd. 1st lt. U.S. Army, 1963, advanced through graded to lt. col., 1984; platoon leader comdr. 46th Med. Bn., Fed. Republic of Germany, 1963-66; asst. registrar U.S. Army Hosp., Ft. Gordon, Ga., 1966-67; chief patient adminstrn. div. Frankfurt, Fed. Republic of Germany, 1969-72; patient adminstr. Office of Surgeon Gen., Washington, 1973-77; chief patient adminstrn. div. Blanchfield Army Hosp., Ft. Campbell, Ky., 1979-83, Acad. Health Scis., Ft. Sam Houston, Tex., 1983-84; dir. patient adminstrn. Fitzsimons Army Med. Ctr., Aurora, Colo., 1984—. Decorated Meritorious Service medal with oak leaf cluster. Mem. Am. Coll. Healthcare Execs., Assn. Mil. Surgeons U.S., Julliard Alumni Assn. Baptist. Home: 16 Halloran Circle Aurora CO 80045 Office: Fitzsimons Army Med Ctr Aurora CO 80045

AUGUST, RICHARD BRUCE, elec. engr., cons.; b. Miami, Fla., June 19, 1952; s. John Joseph and Patricia Adele (Beaton) A.; B.S.E.E., U. So. Calif. 1973; M.S.E.E., M.I.T., 1974; m. Kathleen Leslie Perez, May 15, 1977; children: Richard Bruce II, Lesley Brooke. Pres., chmn. bd. dirs. Paradigm Techs. Corp., 1984—. Developer imaging systems for Viking and Voyager Space probes; mem. Viking and Voyager imaging team NASA Jet Propulsion Lab.; developer instrumentation telemetry system USAF Global Positioning System; developer TACFIRE/CCS arty. fire direction system for U.S. Army, developer communications systems for all source analysis system/enemy situation correlation element for U.S. Army, USAF Intelligence System. Inventor paradigm sphere. Mem. exec. com. Internat. Boxing Hall of Fame, Las Vegas; trustee Rep. Presdl. Task Force. Served with USNR. Mem. Am. Soc. Engrs. and Architects (former pres.). Contbr. papers to profl. insts. Home: 2680 Monterey Rd San Marino CA 91108

AUGUSTIN, JORG ALOIS L., food scientist; b. Heerbrugg-Au, Switzerland, Jan. 5, 1930; came to U.S., 1960; s. Georg and Anna (Bossard) A. Grad., Swiss Fed. Inst. Tech., 1950-55; MS in Food Tech., U. Ill., 1957; PhD in Food Sci., Mich. State U., 1965. Research assoc. Hero Konserven, Lenzburg, Switzerland, 1957-60; sect. head. Armour Food Research, Oak Brook, Ill., 1964-68; assoc. prof. Agrl. Exptl. Sta., U. Idaho, Moscow, 1968-75, prof. food sci. and biochemistry, 1975—. Editor: Methods of Vitamin Assay; contbr. articles on food sci. and nutrition to profl. jours. Mem. Inst. Food Technologists, Am. Assn. Cereal Chemists, Assn. Ofcls. Analytical Chemists, Am. Chem. Soc., Sigma Xi. Roman Catholic. Avocations: skiing, fishing. Home: 914 West A St Moscow ID 83843 Office: U Idaho Food Research Ctr Moscow ID 83843

AULD, SAMUEL HAYWARD, JR., aircraft and electronics company executive; b. Pasadena, Calif., Sept. 16, 1925; s. Samuel Hayward and Wilda (Jackson) A.; m. Evelyn Lorraine Maydeck, June 15, 1952; children—John, James, Kathleen. BSEE Calif. Poly. State U., San Luis Obispo, 1955. Elec. engr. Lear, Inc., 1956-62; gen. mgr. Avionics div. Lear Jet Corp., Wichita, Kans., 1962-65, v.p., 1965-67; v.p. Static Power div., Newport Beach, Calif., 1967-72, pres., chief operating officer Static Power Inc., 1972-76; pres., chief exec. officer Lear Avia Corp., Reno, 1976-86, also dir.; vice chmn., dir. Lear Fan Ltd., London. Patentee in field. Served to capt. USAF, 1943-48. Republican. Home: 1324 Dartmouth Dr Reno NV 89509

AUMILLER, JAMES CARLTON, chemist, educator; b. Denver, Feb. 18, 1942; s. Dallas Dale Aumiller and Anita Marcile (Shaw) Hagerty; m. Linda Kathleen McCauley, Aug. 24, 1968; children: Stacy Michelle, Jared James. BS, Ft. Lewis Coll., 1967; MS, W. Wash. U., 1969; PhD, U. Wyo., 1973. Research assoc. Lamar U., Beaumont, Tex., 1973-75; instr. chemistry Western Wyo. Coll., Rock Springs, 1975-77, assoc. prof., 1977-81, prof., 1981—; Bd. dirs. Water Quality Lab., Western Wyo. Coll.; environ. cons. Rock Springs, 1975—; adv. West Wyo. Coll. and Meml. Hosp. programs, Rock Springs, 1976—. Contbr. articles to profl. jours. and outdoor mags. Served with USN, 1959-63. Mem. Am. Chem. Soc., Bowhunters of Wyo., Sigma Xi. Republican. Methodist. Avocations: backpacking, hunting, fishing, skiing, boating. Home: 1032 Elm Way Rock Springs WY 82901 Office: Western Wyo Coll 2500 College Dr Rock Springs WY 82901

AUSTAD, LORRAINE BLANCHE, interior designer, consultant; b. Las Vegas, Nev., June 21, 1947; d. Willard E. and Phyllis L. (Scott) Baldwin; 1 son, Paul K. B.A. in Design, U. Calif.-Irvine, 1970. Chief designer Dunes Hotel, Las Vegas, 1980-81; project designer Sheraton Hotel, Industry Hills, Calif., 1981; designer Golden Nugget Hotel, Las Vegas and Atlantic City, N.J., 1981-82; cons., South Laguna, Calif., 1968—; cons./designer Bel Age Hotel, Los Angeles, 1983—. Mem. Am. Soc. Interior Designers, Color Mktg. Group (host regional meeting 1981, chmn. Capt. of Living home workshop). Address: PO Box 645 South Laguna CA 92677-0645 Office: 1112 Noria St Laguna Beach CA 92651

AUSTIN, EDWARD MARVIN, mechanical engineer; b. Rome, Ga., Nov. 15, 1933; s. Marvin Hart and Sarah Katherine (Youngblood) A.; m. Elizabeth Maria Geisz, Dec. 17, 1955; children: Jean, Diane, Judy. BME, Ga. Inst. Tech., 1955, MSME, 1957. Registered profl. engr., N.C. Assoc. aircraft engr. Lockheed Aircraft Corp., Marietta, Ga., 1955; sr. engr. Western Electric Co., Greensboro, N.C., 1968-71; disting. mem. tech. staff Sandia Nat. Labs., Albuquerque, 1957—. Pres. Heights Br. YMCA, Albuquerque, 1974-75. Mem. ASME, Sigma Xi, Tau Beta Pi. Home: 3017 Matador Dr NE Albuquerque NM 87111 Office: Sandia Nat Labs PO Box 5800 Albuquerque NM 87185

AUSTIN, ERIC STUART, accountant; b. Bethesda, Md., Aug. 24, 1957; s. James Monteith and Mitzi Carolyn (Lux) A.; m. Lucille Sanae Shinno, Sept. 5, 1982. B.S., Ariz. State U., 1979. C.P.A., Hawaii. Auditor, Peat, Marwick & Mitchell, Honolulu, 1980-83; instr. Becker C.P.A. Review, 1981-82; internat. acctg. mgr. Dillingham Constrn., 1983-85, controller Rock Products Pacific div., 1985—; dir. Inta-Cell Nutrition, Inc. Mem. Nat. Assn. Accts., Beta Alpha Psi. Club: Toastmasters (pres. 1983). Home: 98-943 Moanalua Rd #1101 Aiea HI 96701

AUSTIN, EUGENE HOWARD, writer; b. Poughkeepsie, N.Y., Sept. 1, 1926; s. Eugene Hiram and Florence A.; ed. Coll. of Sequoias; m. Lucy Mary Ruggiero, Nov. 18, 1950; children—Lucyanne, Eugene John. Free lance writer, poet, 1972—. Mem. Kings County Grand Jury, 1979-80, Kings County Parole Commn., 1980—. Served with USN, 1943-46; served as master sgt. U.S. Army, 1951-57. Recipient Disting. Service citation Conn. dept. Am. Legion. Mem. Am. Security Council (nat. adv. bd.), Am. Def. Preparedness Assn., U.S. Naval Inst., DAV (life, charter mem. comdrs. club), VFW (past comdr. Nisei Liberty Post, 24th dist., sr. vice comdr. Dept. Calif.). Club: K.C. (4th deg.). Home: 8606 La Vaca Way Hanford CA 93230

AUSTIN, JOHN NORMAN, classics educator; b. Anshun, Kweichow, China, May 20, 1937; s. John Alfred and Lillian Maud (Reeks) A. B.A., U. Toronto, Ont. Can., 1958; M.A., U. Calif.-Berkeley, 1959, Ph.D., 1965. Vis. lectr. Yale U., New Haven, 1971; asst. prof., then assoc. prof. UCLA, 1966-76; Aurelio prof. Greek Boston U., 1976-78; prof., chmn. dept. classics U. Mass., Amherst, 1978-80; prof. classics U. Ariz., Tucson, 1980-84. Author: Archery at the Dark of the Moon, 1974; editor (with others) Works of John Dryden, vol. III; sr. editor Calif. Studies Classical Antiquity, vol. VI & VII. Jr. fellow Ctr. for Hellenic Studies, 1968-69, J.S. Guggenheim Found. fellow, 1974-75. Mem. Am. Philol. Assn. (bd. dirs. 1983—), Ariz. Homer Inst. Episcopalian. Home: 5846 E 2d St Tucson AZ 85711 Office: U Ariz Dept of Classics Tucson AZ 85721

AUSTIN, LORA EVELYN, med. technologist; b. Grand Rapids, Mich., Sept. 6, 1926; d. Carlton and Florence Evelyn (Tyson) Austin; BA, Olivet Coll., 1948; MS, Calif. State U., Dominguez Hills, 1981. Intern in med. tech. Butterworth Hosp., Grand Rapids, Mich., 1948-49, staff med. technologist, 1949-52; staff So. Calif. Permanente Med. Group Lab., Los Angeles, 1952—, regional chief immuno-serologist, 1970—; mem. adj. faculty Calif. State U., Dominquez Hills, 1974—. Leader, Campfire Girls, Grand Rapids, Mich., 1949-52; asst. leader Girl Scouts U.S.A., Los Angeles, 1970-81. Recipient Disting. Alumni award Olivet Coll., 1978; lic. med. technologist, Calif., Nat. Cert. Agy. Mem. Am. Soc. Clin. Pathologists (assoc.), Calif. Assn. Med. Lab. Technologists, Am. Soc. Med. Technologists, Olivet Coll. Alumni Assn., Smithsonian Assos., Nat. Wildlife Fedn., Nat. Rifle Assn. Republican. Presbyterian. Home: 10707 Moorpark St Toluca Lake CA 91602

AUSTIN, ROBERT B., consultant, records manager; b. Kansas City, Mo., Oct. 4, 1919; s. Harry W. Austin and Margurite G. McClune; m. Edna Frances Darwin, Feb. 17, 1946; children: Robert B., Mary M. BS in Geology, U. Okla., 1941, MS in Geology, 1946. Geologist Chevron, U.S.A., Denver, 1946-70, records mgr., 1970-76; pres. Austin Assocs., Englewood, Colo., 1976—. Contbr. articles to profl. jours. Served to major C.E., U.S. Army, 1941-46, ETO. Mem. Inst. Cert. Records Mgrs., Assn. Cert. Systems Profls.,Assn. Records Mgrs. and Adminstrs.(pres. 1979-80, chmn. standards com. 1981—, award of merit 1974, 81, Disting. Achievement award 1982), Am. Nat. Standard Inst., Info. Systems Standards Bd. Republican. Methodist. Avocation: golf. Home: 7112 S Harrison Way Littleton CO 80122 Office: Austin Assocs Cons Inc 5299 DTC Blvd Prentice Point Suite 500 Englewood CO 80111

AUSTIN, THEODORE ORIS, mechanical engineer; b. Hillsboro, Oreg., May 21, 1943; s. Mitchel Earl and Devona Lee (Carey) A.; m. Charline Nalley, June 11, 1966. B.S.M.E., U. Wash., 1976. Registered mech. engr. Marine pipefitter Puget Sound Naval Shipyard, Bremerton, Wash., 1961-72; design engr. Naval Undersea Warfare Engring. Sta., Keyport, Wash., 1972-78, sr. project engr., 1978—; cons. underwater recovery and marine salvage, 1978—. Big bro. Kitsap County Companion Program, Bremerton, 1978. Served with USAR, 1965-72. Fellow Dept. Def., U. Wash., 1975-76. Club: Rolls Royce Owners. Office: Code 7041 Keyport WA 98345

AUSTIN, WAYNE GARY, aerospace company executive; b. Mpls., Dec. 21, 1936; s. Theodore Morris and Eloise Ida (Morgan) A.; m. Michiko Hashimoto, May 10, 1965; children—Cassie, Brett. B.A. in Social Sci., Park Coll., 1974; M.A. in Mgmt./Human Relations, Webster Coll., 1975; M.A. in Multicultural Edn., Pepperdine U., 1978. Mgr., Davies Linen Co., San Diego, 1958-60; entered U.S. Air Force, 1961, advanced through grades to sr. master sgt.; air traffic controller, 1969-80, ret., 1980; human resources adminstr. TRW, Redondo Beach, Calif., 1980-81, dir. tng. and devel., space and tech. group, 1982—; cons. organizational devel.; tchr. mgmt. courses. Served with USMC, 1954-58. Decorated Meritorious Service medal with 2 oak leaf clusters; Air Force Commendation medal with 4 oak leaf clusters. Mem. Am. Soc. Tng. and Devel., Air Force Sgts. Assn., Pepperdine U. Alumni Assn. Republican. Home: 13442 Grinnel Circle Westminster CA 92683 Office: TRW E1/4006 Redondo Beach CA 90278

AUTH, DAVID CHRISTOPHER, manufacturing executive, biophysicist; b. Akron, Ohio, Dec. 5, 1940; s. Leo Christopher and Elsie Marie (Lauter) A.; children: Deborah, Christopher, Sharon. AB in Physics, Catholic U. of Am., 1962; MS in Physics, Georgetown U., 1966, PhD in Physics, 1969. Lic. profl. elec. engr., Wash.; diplomate Am. Bd. of Laser Surgery. Aerospace technologist NASA, Cape Canaveral, Fla., 1963; physicist U.S. Army, Washington, 1963-69; asst. prof. elec. engring. U. Wash., Seattle, 1969-73, assoc. prof., 1973-77, prof., 1977-85; dir. Biophysics Internat. div. Squibb Corp., Bellevue, Wash., 1985—; cons. Nat. Cancer Inst., Bethesda, Md., 1977—, Am. Hosp. Supply, Evanston, Ill., 1980-82; mem. scientific adv. bd. Pacific. Sci. Ctr., Seattle, 1982-84, Laserscope Biomed., Santa Clara, Calif., 1982—, Resound Corp., Palo Alto, Calif., 1985—. Contbr. articles to profl. jours.; patentee in field. Grantee NIH, 1978-81. Fellow Am. Soc. Laser Medicine and Surgery (chmn. instrumentation com. 1983-85); mem. IEEE, AAUP. Avocations: radio controlled model airplanes, skiing, photography, automobile restoration. Home: 12000 NE 8th St #505 Bellevue WA 98005 Office: Biophysics Internat 1555 132d NE Bellevue WA 98005

AUTRY, ORVON GENE, singer, actor, radio entertainer, broadcasting executive, baseball team executive; b. Tioga, Tex., Sept. 29, 1907; s. Delbert and Elnora (Ozment) A.; m. Ina Mae Spivey, Apr. 1, 1932; m. Jacqueline Ellam, 1981. Grad., Tioga (Tex.) High Sch., 1925. Began as r.r. telegraph operator Sapulpa, Okla., 1925; owner, chmn. bd. Calif. Angels; pres. Flying A Prodns.; owner Stas. KMPC & KUTE Radio, Hollywood, Calif., Stas. KVI & KPLZ Radio, Seattle, Golden West Broadcasters; pres. several music and publ. cos. Made first phonograph record of cowboy songs, 1929; radio artist Sta. WLS, Chgo., 1930-34; motion picture actor, 1934-53, including In Old Santa Fe; starred in 88 musical Western feature pictures, 91 half-hour TV pictures 1950-55; has written or co-written over 200 songs including That Silver-Haired Daddy of Mine, 1931, You're the Only Star in My Blue Heaven, 1938, Dust, 1938, Tears On My Pillow, 1941, Be Honest With Me, 1941, Tweedle O'Twill, 1942, Here Comes Santa Claus, 1948. Served with USAAF, 1942-45. Mem. Internat. Footprinters. Clubs: Masons (33 deg.), Shriners, Elks. Address: PO Box 710 Los Angeles CA 90078 Office: c/o Calif Angels PO Box 2000 Anaheim CA 92803

AVEDIAN, LEONARD V., physician; b. Fresno, Calif., July 21, 1934; s. George M. and Lily (Tarpinian) A.; m. Bonny Lou Krause; children: Kristen Elizabeth, Gabrielle Suzanne. AB, Calif. State U., Fresno, 1956; MD, U. Wis., 1970. Diplomate Am. Bd. Plastic Surgery. Practice medicine specializing in plastic surgery Newport Beach, Calif., 1970—. Served with USAF, 1957-59. Fellow ACS; mem. Am. Soc. Plastic and Reconstructive Surgery. Republican. Mem. Ch. Assemblies of God. Avocations: music, swimming, tennis, camping. Office: 1441 Avocado Ave Suite 602 Newport Beach CA 92660-7707

AVERSA, ANDRE ANTHONY, accountant; b. Messina, Italy, Mar. 1, 1934; came to U.S., 1956; s. Paolo Giunta and Giovanna Aversa; m. Marilyn A. Schroeder, Sept. 6, 1958 (div. 1969); children—Joanne Tonette, Harriet Elise; m. Susan E. Spoth, June 24, 1982; 1 child, Andre Anthony II. B.Div., Seminaire Adventiste-Haute Savoie, France, 1956; M.Th., Andrews U., 1958; LL.B., Am. U., 1961; postgrad. U. Houston, 1969-70. Bar: Va. 1961, Calif. 1963; C.P.A., Calif., Tex. Law clk. to dean Acheson-Covington & Burling, Washington, 1959-61; atty. Procter & Gamble, Cin., 1961-62; atty. internat. tax IRS, Washington, 1963-65; internat. tax ptnr. Peat, Marwick, Mitchell, Houston, 1965-71; dir. internat. tax Touche Ross & Co., N.Y.C., 1974-82, internat. tax ptnr., San Francisco, 1972—, internat. tax dir., 1972-86; owner East West Resources, Inc., real estate devel. co., San Francisco. Contbr. articles to profl. jours. Mem. legis. com. mem. World Trade Assn., Houston, 1965-71; chmn. Italy in Am. Assn., Houston, 1969-71; vice chmn. Houston Opera Assn., 1969-71; mem. internat. com. C. of C., Houston, 1970-71. Mem. Calif. Soc. C.P.A.s, Calif. Bar Assn., Va. Bar Assn., Tex. C.P.A. Soc. Club: St. Francis. Home: 320 Seacliff San Francisco CA 94121

AVERY, VALEEN TIPPETTS, history educator, researcher, writer; b. Great Falls, Mont., Dec. 22, 1936; d. Blake May and Maurine (Christensen) Tippetts; m. Charles C. Avery, Sept. 13, 1961 (div. Jan. 1986); children: Christopher, Maureen, Nathan, Thad. BA, Rocky Mountain Coll., 1959; MA, No. Ariz. U., 1981, PhD, 1983. Rep. World Univ. Services, N.Y.C. and Geneva, 1959-61; biographer, writer Flagstaff, Ariz., 1974-84; asst. prof. history No. Ariz. U., Flagstaff, 1983—; dir. Ctr. for Colo. Plateau Studies at No. Ariz. U., 1984—. Author: Mormon Enigma: Emma Hale Smith- 1804-1877, 1984 (Best Book of Yr. Mormon History Assn., 1985). Bd. dirs. Raymond Ednl. Found., Flagstaff, 1983-86; certificate holder Flagstaff Hosp., 1984—. Recipient Evans award Brigham Young Univ., Provo, Utah, 1985. Mem. Western History Assn., Mormon History Assn. (Reese History award 1983). Republican. Mormon. Avocations: writing, hiking. Home: Rt 4 Box 888 Flagstaff AZ 86001 Office: No Ariz Univ Ctr for Colo Plateau Studies Box 5613 Flagstaff AZ 86011

AVITAN, ISAAC, electromechanical engineer; b. Hadera, Israel, Jan. 9, 1950; came to U.S., 1982; s. David and Rachel (Harash) A.; m. Sherrie Michelle Glassman, June 16, 1974; children: Joshua Adam, Aaron Daniel. BS, U. Toronto, Ont., Can., 1979; postgrad., Ga. Inst. Tech., 1983—. Registered profl. engr., Ont., B.C. Tool and die maker Magna Internat., Downsview, Ont., Can., 1974-77; engring. devel. trainee Ont. Hydro Port Credit, Downsview, Ont., Can., 1978; mech. design engr. group leader Sentrol Systems Ltd., Downsview, Ont., Can., 1979-81; asst. tech. supr. Ont. Hydro-Nuclear, Toronto, 1981-82; engring. mgr. Pak-It Mfg. Co. Inc., Norcross, Ga., 1982-83; project engr. Raymond Carousel, Atlanta, 1983-85; sr. project engr. Raymond Prodn. Systems, Hollister, CA, 1985-86; mgr. control systems devel. Raymond Corp., Greene, N.Y., 1986—. Inventor, patentee electronically scanned, non-contacting reel hardness sensor. Served with Israeli Army, 1971-74. Grantee Can. Fed. Govt., 1976-78, Province of Ont., 1978. Mem. ASME, ASHRAE, Am. Soc. Metals. Jewish.

AVNER, BARRY PAUL, pharmacology educator, medical company executive; b. Chgo., June 19, 1944; s. Alex and Beatrice (Gerber) A.; m. Belina Rothman, Dec. 28, 1973; children: Jeremy, Michael. BA, SUNY, Buffalo 1966, PhD, 1970. Postdoctoral fellow dept. pharmacology SUNY, Buffalo Sch. Medicine, 1971, U. Calif., San Francisco Med. Ctr., 1972-73; asst. prof. pharmacology U. N.Mex. Sch. Medicine, Albuquerque, 1973-81, adj. asst. prof. physiology, 1981—; assoc. scientist dept. cell biology research div. Lovelace Med. Found., Albuquerque, 1981-83; dir. research, asst. v.p. sci. affairs Summa Med. Corp., Albuquerque, 1983-84; dir. head Biotherapeutics, Inc., Franklin, Tenn., 1985—, dir. monoclonal antibody projects tech. acquisition; speaker. Contbr. articles to sci. jours. N.Y. State Regents scholar, 1962-66; NIH fellow, 1970-71; San Francisco Bay Area Heart Research Com. fellow, 1972-73. Mem. Am. Soc. Pharmacology and Exptl. Therapeutics, Am. Chem. Soc., N.Y. Acad. Scis., Western Pharmacology Soc., AAAS, Soc. Analytical Cytology, Rho Chi.

AVOLIO, WENDY FREEDMAN, speech-language pathologist; b. Phila., Feb. 24, 1953; s. Harold Stanley and Phyllis Maxine (Broodno) Freedman; m. Michael Howard Strauss, Aug. 31, 1975 (Nov. 1981); 1 child, Nicole Erin; m. Mark Richard Avolio, Mar. 24, 1985. BS, Bradley U., 1973; MA, No. Ill. U., 1975. Speech-lang. pathologist Bartlett (Ill.) Sch. Dist., 1975-76, Proviso Area for Exceptional Children, Maywood, Ill., 1976-77, Cen. Reading and Speech Clinic, Mt. Prospect, Ill., 1977-78, Tucson Unified Sch. Dist., 1978-79, Handmaker Jewish Geriatric Ctr., Tucson, 1981; mgr. speech-lang. therapy program Dept. Econ. Security/Div. Devel. Disabilities, Tucson, 1981-86, So. Ariz. Spl. Edn. Coop., Vail, 1986—; cons. speech-lang. Parent Support Group, Tucson, 1981—, Ariz. Adv. Com. For Deaf-Blind, Tucson, 1983—; lang. cons. Community Outreach Program for Deaf, Tucson, 1983. Com. mem. Jewish Community Ctr. Youth and Children Com., Tucson, 1986—. Mem. Am. Speech Lang. and Hearing Assn. (cert.), Ariz. Speech and Lang. Assn. Avocations: dancing, skiing, swimming. Home: 3532 N Fiesta Del Sol E Tucson AZ 85715 Office: So Ariz Spl Edn Coop PO Drawer #8 Vail AZ 85641

AVSHALOMOV, DAVID, conductor, composer; b. N.Y.C., May 6, 1946; s. Jacob David and Doris (Felde) A.; m. Cheryl Lee Stray, June 9, 1968 (div. Aug. 1975); m. Carrie James Kourkoumelis, June 25, 1976 (div. Aug. 1980); m. Randi Lynn Grafman, June 18, 1982; chuildren: Jesse Alexander, Zachary Aaron. BA magna cum laude, Harvard U., 1967; Dr. Musical Arts, U. Wash., 1976; conducting studies with Leo Mueller, Peabody Conservatory of Music, 1969-72; studies with Leonard Bernstein, Seiji Ozawa and Gunther Schuller, Tanglewood Sch. Music, 1979; studies with Jean Morel, Werner Torkanowsky and Herbert Blomstedt, Aspen Sch. Music, 1972. Condr. opera workshop Highline Community Coll., Midway, Wash., 1975-76; staff condr. Tacoma Opera, 1975-76; condr., music dir. Bremerton (Wash.) Symphony Orch., 1973-75, Missoula (Mont.) Symphony Orch. and Chorale, 1976-78, Los Angeles Drs. Symphony Orch., 1981-85; founding condr., music dir. Santa Monica (Calif.) Chamber Orch., 1981—; guest condr. Japan Nat. Music Camp Orch., Tokyo, 1979, Spokane (Wash.) Symphony Orch., 1978, Helena (Mont.) Symphony Orch., 1977-78, S.E. Alaska Orch. Festival, 1976; timpanist and percussionist various orgns.; asst. prof. music U. Mont., Missoula, 1976-78. Composer works for orch., string quartet, band, chorus, chamber ensembles. Served with USAF, 1968-72. NDEA fellow, 1967, 72-74; recipient 1st prize Aspen Student Composition Contest, 1972. Mem. Phi Beta Kappa. Democrat. Jewish. Home: 2402 4th St Apt 5 Santa Monica CA 90405 Office: PO Box 5474 Santa Monica CA 90405

AWTRY, NELL CATHERINE, real estate executive; b. Dallas, Sept. 29, 1900; d. Henry Hibbler and Laura Jane (Harris) Jacoby; B.A., So. Meth U., 1935; postgrad. Columbia, 1941-42; m. John Hix Awtry, Apr. 24, 1922; 1 dau., Nell C. (Mrs. William W. Gilchrist) (dec.). Real estate saleswoman Prince & Ripley, Scarsdale, N.Y., 1948, Midgeley Parks, Scarsdale, 1949, Cleveland E. Van Wert, Inc., Scarsdale, 1954-60, Julia B. Fee, Inc., Scarsdale, 1960-73. Former mem. Scarsdale Realty Bd., Westchester Realty Bd. Mem. Am. Legion Aux. (vice comdr.), Leisure World Am. Aux., Zeta Tau Alpha. Republican. Baptist. Mem. Order Eastern Star (worthy matron 1961, 67). Clubs: Scarsdale Golf, Dallas Athletic, Leisure World Republican. Author poems and lyrics. Home: 3337-2A Punta Alta Rossmoor Leisure World PO Box 2833 Laguna Hills CA 92653

AXELROD, TODD MICHAEL, historical document expert, investment banker; b. Bklyn., Oct. 25, 1949; s. Herbert Richard Axelrod and Ruth (Levy) Canvasser; m. Pamela Joy Ring, Apr. 1, 1984. B.S., NYU, 1973. Lic. gen. securities prin. Sr. v.p. Bache Halsey Stuart Shields, La Jolla, Calif., 1980-81; pres. Am. Mus. Hist. Documents, Las Vegas, 1981—; cons. curator to corp. and institutional hist. document collections; adj. prof. fin. U. Nev.-Las Vegas, 1980—. Author: Collecting Historical Documents: A Guide to Owning History, 1984, 2d rev. edit., 1986. Mem. Manuscript Soc., Nat. Assn. Securities Dealers (membership com. 1986—). Office: Am Mus Hist Documents 3601 W Sahara Ave Promenade Suite Las Vegas NV 89102

AXELSON, JOSEPH ALLEN, professional athletics executive; b. Peoria, Dec. 25, 1927; s. Joseph Victor A. and Florence (Ealen) Massey; m. Malcolm Rae Smith, Oct. 7, 1950; children: David Allen, Mark Stephen, Linda Rae. B.S., Northwestern U., 1949. Sports info. dir. Ga. So. Coll., Statesboro, 1957-60, Nat. Assn. Intercollegiate Athletics, Kansas City, Mo., 1961-62; tournament dir. Bowling Proprs. Assn. Am., Park Ridge, Ill., 1963-64; asst. exec. sec. Nat. Assn. Intercollegiate Athletics, Kansas City, Mo., 1964-68; exec. v.p., gen. mgr. Cin. Royals Profl. Basketball Team, Cin., 1969-72; mgr. Cin. Gardens, 1970-72; pres., gen. mgr. Kansas City Kings Profl. Basketball Team, Kansas City, Mo., 1972-79, 82-85, Sacramento Kings Profl. Basketball Team, 1985—; pres. Arco Arena, Sacramento, 1985—; v.p. ops. NBA, N.Y.C., 1979-82, chmn. competition and rules com., 1975-79; trustee Naismith Basketball Hall of Fame. Served to capt. Signal Corps. AUS, 1949-54. Named Nat. Basketball Exec. of Yr. The Sporting News, St. Louis, 1973; recipient Annual Dirs. award Downtown, Inc., Kansas City, Mo., 1979. Mem. Am. Philatelic Soc., Phi Kappa Psi. Republican. Presbyterian. Lodge: Rotary. Home: 2950 Pasatiempo Pl Sacramento CA 95833 Home: 230 B Ave Coronado CA 92118 Office: Sacramento Kings 1515 Sports Dr Sacramento CA 95834

AYA, RODERICK HONEYMAN, tax consultant; b. Portland, Oreg., Sept. 17, 1916; s. Alfred Anthony and Grace Myrtle (Honeyman) A.; student U. Oreg., 1935-36, Internat. Accts. Soc., 1937-39, LaSalle Extension U., 1940-42, Walton Sch. Commerce, 1942, U. Calif. Extension, 1945; m. Helen Marjorie Riddle, June 16, 1945; children—Roderick Riddle, Deborah Germaine Aya Reynolds, Ronald Honeyman. Chief statistician Hotel Employers Assn., San Francisco, 1939-42; acct. Pacific Tel. & Tel. Co., San Francisco, 1942-52, spl. acct., 1952-63; tax acct., 1963-65; spl. acct. AT&T, N.Y.C., 1965-68, mgr. tax studies, 1968-73, div. mgr. tax research and planning, 1973-80; public acct., San Francisco, 1940—; music tchr., 1959—; v.p., treas., dir. Snell Research Assos., Inc., 1974-79; guest lectr. on taxes Westchester County Adult Edn. Program. Committeeman, Marin County council Boy Scouts Am., 1959-60, com. chmn., 1959-61; mem. Marin County Sheriffs' Reserve, 1963-65; law enforcement liaison com. on Juvenile Control; sec. Am. Nat. Standards Inst. Com. on Protective Headgear, 1967-80. Vice pres., treas., bd. dirs. Snell Meml. Found., 1957-80; trustee Snell Meml. Found. (U.K.), Ltd.; mem. chmn.'s com. U.S. Senatorial Bus. Adv. Bd.; mem. Republican Presdl. Task Force; dir., past pres. Stuart Highlanders Pipe Band of San Francisco. Recipient Wisdom award of honor Wisdom Soc., 1970; Pres.'s Medal of Merit, 1981. Mem. ASTM, Nat. Soc. Pub. Accts., St. Andrews Soc., Telephone Pioneers Am., Soc. for Ethnomusicology (contbr. to jour.), U.S. Naval Inst., Phi Chi, Sigma Nu. Clubs: Corinthian Yacht (Tiburon, Calif.); Sports Car of Am. (San Francisco region treas. 1957-58, dir. 1957-59); U.S. Yacht Racing Union. Author: The Legacy of Pete Snell, 1965; Determination of Corporate Earnings and Profits for Federal Income Tax Purposes, 2 vols., 1966. Home: PO Box 668 Seaside OR 97138

AYAD, BOULOS AYAD, archaeology educator; b. Egypt, May 3, 1928; came to U.S., 1967; s. Ayad A.; m. Suzanne E., Feb. 14, 1970; children:

Mary, Thereza, Boulos. B.A., U. Cairo, 1952, M.A., 1957, Ph.D. with honors, 1963; M.A., U. Ain Shams, 1953, Higher Inst. Coptic Studies, 1960. Asst. prof. U. Utah, 1967-68; asst. prof. U. Colo., Boulder, 1968-72, assoc. prof., 1972-77, prof. archaeology and ancient langs. of Middle East, 1977—, univ. fellow, 1974-75. Author: Coptic Grammar and Texts, 1971, The Jewish-Aramaean Communities in Ancient Egypt, 1975, The Aramaeans in Egypt, 1975, The Aramaeans in the Ancient Middle East, 1983, The Jewish-Aramaean Civilization and Its Relationship to the Ancient Egyptian Civilization, 1982, The Four Gospels, 1983; translator: Book of Job (from Syriac into Arabic), 1975; contbr. articles to profl jours. Mem. African Studies Assn., Societe d'Archeologie Copte, AAUP, Am. Assn. Tchrs. Arabic, Smithsonian Instn., Soc. Bible Friends. Coptic Orthodox. Home: 1332 Scrub Oak Circle Boulder CO 80303 Office: U Colo Dept Anthropology Boulder CO 80309

AYAKAWA, CLAUDE SHIGEAKI, professional photographer; b. Waipahu, Hawaii, Aug. 4, 1939; s. Toshio and Fumiko (Yokono) A. Cert., Brooks Inst. Photography, 1962; degree in photog. craftsman, Profl. Photographers Am., 1979, M in Photography, 1985. Prin. Claude's Photography, Waipahu, 1965—; lectr. Profl. Photography of Japan, Osaka and Tokyo, 1983, Profl. Photography N.Y., Syracuse, 1977, Profl. Photography Calif., Anaheim, 1984; tchr. U. Hawaii, Honolulu, 1984-86; print judge Profl. Photography N.Y., Montecello, 1986. Prin. works (photography) Beyond the Camera, 1976, Wedding Photography World, 1984. Served with U.S. Army, 1960-66. Mem. Hawaii Profl. Photographers (treas. 1972-75, pres. 1975-76), Profl. Photographers Am. (councilman 1970-76, 85-86). Home: 94-981 Awalai St Waipahu HI 96797 Office: 94-889 Waipahu St Waipahu HI 96797

AYALA, RUBEN SAMUEL, state senator; b. Chino, Calif., Mar. 6, 1922; s. Mauricio R. and Erminia (Martinez) A.; student Pomona Jr. Coll., 1941-42; grad. Nat. Electronic Inst. Los Angeles, 1948; m. Irene Morales, July 22, 1945; children—Bud, Maurice Edward, Gary. Mem. sch. bd. Chino (Calif.), 1955-62; councilman City of Chino, 1962-64, mayor, 1964-66; bd. suprs., 1966-73; chmn. San Bernardino County Bd. Suprs., 1968-72; mem. Calif. Senate, 1974—, chmn. agrl. and water resources com., 1976—, mem. govt., revenue and taxation com., pub. utilities com., mem. transp. com., 1981, mem. joint legis. audit com., com. fairs allocations. Mem. Chino Sch. Bd., 1955-62; chmn. San Bernardino County Health Com., 1968-72, Chino Police Commn., 1964-66, Chino Parks and Recreation Commn., 1962-64; mem. Nat. Alliance of Businessmen Com., Washington, 1970; chmn. West Valley Planning Agy., 1968-72; mem. steering com. County Hwy. Safety Orgn., 1968-72; bd. dirs. Pomona Freeway Assn., 1968; life mem. PTA, Chino. Served with USMC, World War II; PTO. Recipient Outstanding Civil Leaders of Am. award, 1967; Citizen of Year award Chino Valley C. of C., 1970, VFW of San Bernardino County, Mex. Am. Polit. Assn., Kiwanis Club, Disting. Citizens awardClaf. Inland Empire council Boy Scouts Am., 1985; named Calif. Legislator of Yr. Democrats United, 1982; named Citizen of Yr. Assn. Calif. Water Agys. and Am. Public Works Assn., San-Bernardino-Riverside branch, hon. City of Pomona, 1971, 80; parks named in his honor, Chino and Bloomington, Calif. Mem. Assn. Calif. Water Agys., Assn. Calif. Engrs., Am. Legion, Native Sons of Golden West. Club: Kiwanis. Office: State Capitol Sacramento CA 95814

AYCOCK, JOEL, astronomical telescope technician; b. Seattle, June 30, 1950; s. Marcus Hillman and Shirley Elaine (Williams) A. BA in Physics, Reed Coll., 1972; postgrad., U. Hawaii, 1976-77. Fire fighter USDA Forest Service, Portland, Oreg., 1969-72; data processor Sta. KGW TV, Portland, 1972-73; chief of consumer services Data Internat., Honolulu, 1975-76; laser ranger LURE Obs., Kula, Hawaii, 1977-85, chief opto-mech. technician, 1983-85; telescope technician UK Infrared Telescope, Hilo, Hawaii, 1985—. Co-discoverer Supernova 1986G, 1986. Prodn. support Videololo II, Honolulu, 1976—; contact video technician Ohlmeyer Prodn., ABC Sports, NBC Sports, ESPN, Los Angeles, 1976—; co-producer (video) Lanikai Tennis Tournament, 1983. Home: PO Box 1659 Keaau HI 96749 Office: UKIRT 655 Komohana Hilo HI 96720

AYCOCK, LINDA LOU, school administrator; b. Brunswick, Mo., Aug. 27, 1933; d. Frederick Cowell and Dorothy A. (Trosper) Heimer; m. Hartwell Boncile Aycock, Aug. 19, 1956; children: Angela, Anthony Ben, Alicia Lynn. BA, BS, N.E. Mo. State U., 1951; MA, Eastern N.Mex. U., 1972, edn. specialist, 1981. Tchr. English Carlsbad (N.Mex.) Schs., 1955-73, coordinator lang. arts, 1973-76, coordinator Title IV, 1975-85, coordinator elem. and secondary edn., 1976-83, dir. instrn., 1983-86, asst. supt. instrn., 1986—; cons. Women in Adminstrn., N.Mex., 1981-86, sex roles and sex desegregation, Austin, Tex., 1978-81; program coordinator artists in schs., Santa Fe, 1973-84, quality edn. conf. I-IV N.Mex. State U., Las Cruces, 1980-86. Bd. dirs. City Spirit Arts Community Arts, Carlsbad, 1979-85, Carlsbad Art Mus., 1978-81, Carlsbad Found., 1986—, Campfire, 1986—; trustee Carlsbad Mcpl. Library, 1965-81. Mem. AAUW (state pres. 1975-77, nat. program developer 1973-75, fellowship named in her honor 1978), N.Mex. Sch. Adminstrs., Eastern N.Mex. Sch. Research and Study Council (pres. 1982), Assn. Supervision and Curriculum Devel., Phi Delta Kappa. Democrat. Methodist. Home: 1213 Riverside Dr Carlsbad NM 88220 Office: Carlsbad Mcpl Schs 408 N Canyon Carlsbad NM 88220

AYER, JOHN DEMERITT, law educator; b. Manchester, N.H., Feb. 18, 1936; s. Demeritt Colby and Esther Annette (Nordstrom) A.; m. Sue Flesher, June 21, 1958 (div. 1978); children: Katherine Elizabeth, David Colby. BA, U. Louisville, 1963, JD, 1968; LLM, Yale U., 1969. Bar: Ky. 1968, Calif. 1973. Reporter, Washington corr. Louisville newspapers, 1960-68; mem. law faculty U. Calif., Davis, 1969—; judge U.S. Bankruptcy Ct., Los Angeles, 1983-84; of counsel Stutman, Treister & Glatt, Los Angeles, 1975, 80-81; vis. prof. U. Tex., Austin, 1979-80; acad. visitor London Sch. Econ., 1976. Author: Secured Transactions in California; contbr. articles to profl. jours. Served with USAR, 1958. Recipient Silver Gavel award ABA, 1965. Mem. Calif. Bar Assn. Office: U Calif Sch of Law Davis CA 95616

AYERS, CHARLES WILLIAM, military officer, educator; b. Nampa, Idaho, June 6, 1949; s. Zack William and Caroline B. (Ridnour) A.; m. Joyce Elaine Puncochar, Oct. 22, 1982; children: Sarah J.M., Zachary Edward, Marcus William. AS in Indsl. Mechanics, Lane Community Coll., Eugene, Oreg., 1970; BS in Occupational Safety and Health, Cen. Wash. U., Ellensburg, 1980; MS in Systems Mgmt., U. So. Calif., Los Angeles, 1985. Commd. 2d. lt. U.S. Army, 1977, advanced through grades to capt., 1982, various assignments in areas of safety, supply, tng., logistics and ops., 1977-83; asst. prof. mil. sci. U.S. Army, U. Guam, 1983-87; tng. instr. N.G. Profl. Edn. Ctr., North Little Rock, Ark., 1987—; safety cons. Wausau Ins. Co., Beaverton, Oreg., 1980-83. Mem. Am. Soc. Safety Engrs., Safety and Health Counsel No. Marianas, N.G. Assn. Avocation: hiking. Home: 212 3d St NAS FPO San Francisco CA 96637 Office: PO Box 73 NAS FPO San Francisco CA 96637

AYERS, EVERETTE LEE, highway patrol director; b. Bowling Green, Va., Dec. 20, 1940; s. Everette L. and Hauzie (Rouse) A.; m. Donna Rae Rose, Aug. 24, 1961; children: Jeff, Shelley. Student, Laramie County Community Coll., 1976-77. Patrolman Why. Hwy. Patrol, Wheatland, 1964-72; sgt. Why. Hwy. Patrol, Rawlins, 1972-76; sgt. Why. Hwy. Patrol, Laramie, 1976-78, lt., 1978-81; maj. Why. Hwy. Patrol, Cheyenne, 1982-85, col., 1985—. Served with USAF, 1959-63. Mem. Peace Officer's Standards Tng. Commn., Internat. Assn. Chiefs of Police, Am. Assn. Motor Vehicle Adminstrs., Wyo. Hwy. Patrol Assn. Methodist. Lodge: Odd Fellows. Avocations: electronics, fishing, restoring cars. Office: Wyo Hwy Patrol PO Box 1708 5300 Bishop Blvd Cheyenne WY 82002-9019

AYERS, JAMES LEE, consulting company executive; b. Fort Worth, May 28, 1919; s. I. Edwin and Anna May (Houck) A.; m. Rennie Kay, Dec. 20, 1943; 1 child, Avril Rennie. Higher B.Tech. Sic. with 1st class honors in Elec. Engring., Manchester U., Eng., 1950, also assoc. Manchester Coll. Tech., 1950; postgrad. Imperial Coll., London, 1951-52, UCLA, Westwood, 1960-61. With Lockheed Overseas Corp., Langford Lodge Base, No. Ireland, 1942-44, research labs. GEC Ltd., Stanmore, Middlesex, Eng., 1950-56; head advanced devel. electronic systems Convair, San Diego, 1956-59; chief engr. electronics Lear, Inc., Santa Monica, Calif., 1959-63; space systems design, planning and mgmt. positions Hughes Aircraft Co., Los Angeles, 1963-76, mgr. advanced program ops. Space and Communications Group, 1967-76, mgr. advanced proposals Electro Optical and Data Systems Group, 1976-82; dir. Laser Tech., Inc., North Hollywood, Calif., v.p., 1964; v.p. Total Bus. Cons., Oceanside, Calif., 1983—; mgmt. and cost analysis cons. Patentee in field; predesign and proposal mgr. Early Bird (Intelsat I), 1964-65. Pres. Malibu Freeway Com., Calif., 1962-66; mem. Malibu Community Coordinating Com., 1970-79; dir. Eastern Malibu precinct Malibu Twp. Council, 1970-77, treas. council, 1973-75. Served with Signal Corps, USAAF, 1944-46. Registered chartered eng., U.K. Fellow Instn. Elec. Engrs., Eng.; mem. IEEE (life), AIAA, Manchester Tech. Assn. (life), UCLA Alumni Assn. (life), Big Rock Assn. Malibu (pres. 1962-63, 70-72). Club: Ocean Hills Country (bd. dirs., v.p. 1984-86). Home and Office: 4662 Barcelona Way Oceanside CA 92056

AYERS, RENDALL PAUL, public relations consultant; b. Wichita Falls, Tex., Aug. 25, 1937; s. Richard Kelly and Gertrude Christine (Paul) A.; m. Sara Lee Hoffman, Aug. 27, 1960; children—Sydney Lynn, Reed A. B.A. in Journalism, U. Colo., 1961. Asst. bur. chief AP, Helena, Mont., 1960-61; asst. city editor Denver Post, 1962-67; dist. mgr. Ins. Info. Inst., Denver, 1968-69; pub. relations mgr. Denver div. Safeway Stores, Inc., 1970-74; pres. William Kostka & Assocs., Denver, 1975-80; prin. Rendall Ayers Pub. Relations, Denver, 1980—; ptnr. Ayers, Grimm, Starzel & Assocs., Denver, 1985—; lectr. in field. Bd. dirs. Men's Assistance Ctr., 1970-82, pres., 1974-76; bd. dirs. Colo. Heart Assn., 1970—, pres., 1977-78, chmn. Colo. Heart Fund campaign, 1971-73; bd. dirs. Goodwill Industries Denver, 1970-84, v.p. 1981-84; bd. dirs. Colo. Retail Council, 1972-74, Kempe Nat. Ctr. for Prevention and Treatment Child Abuse, 1984—. Recipient award Outstanding Reporting, Denver Newspaper Guild, 1966; Outstanding Vol. award Colo. Heart Assn., 1973. Mem. Pub. Relations Soc. Am. (accredited, pres. Colo. chpt. 1978), Pub. Relations Soc. Am. Counselors Acad., Sigma Delta Chi, Alpha Delta Sigma. Republican. Unitarian. Clubs: Press, Lakewood Country, Meadow Creek Racquet (Denver). Office: 2480 W 26th Ave Suite 110B Denver CO 80211

AYRES, JAMES EDWARD, archaeologist, educator; b. Eau Claire, Wis., Sept. 30, 1936; s. Wayne Perry and Alice Pearl (Gutow) A. B.A., Fresno State Coll., 1964; M.A., U. Ariz., 1970. Cert. Soc. Profl. Archaeologists. Asst. archaeologist, U. Ariz., Tucson, 1965-70, assoc. archaeologist, 1970-79; Ariz. state hist. preservation officer Ariz. State Parks, Phoenix, 1979-81; archaeol. cons. Archaeol. Research Services, Inc., Tempe, 1981-85; archaeol. cons., Tucson, 1985—; adj. instr. Ariz. State U., 1982—; mem. Gov.'s Commn. Ariz. Environment, 1979-80, Ariz. Hist. Adv. Commn., 1974—. Editorial advisor Historical Archaeology, 1978—; regional advisor newsletter Soc. Hist. Archaeology, 1971—; regional adv. editor North American Archaeologist, 1979—; author profl. articles and publs. Served with USAF, 1955-59. NEH research grantee, 1975-78. Fellow Explorers Club; mem. Soc. Am. Archaeology (sec. 1980-81), Soc. Hist. Archaeology (dir. 1972-75, pres. 1977), Am. Soc. Ethnohistory (sec. treas. 1971-79), Nat. Trust for Hist. Preservation (Ariz. advisor 1973-82), Sigma Xi. Democrat. Home: 1702 E Waverly Tucson AZ 85719 Office: Archaeol Cons 1702 E Waverly Tucson AZ 85719

AZARI, PARVIZ, research biochemist; b. Baku, USSR, Feb. 3, 1930; came to U.S., 1948; s. Reza and Zina Azari; m. Harriet Ann Coates; children: Aaron, Nina, Katerine, Doran, Victoria. BA in Biochemistry, U. Calif., Berkeley, 1955; MS in Chemistry, U. Nebr., 1958, PhD in Chemistry, 1961. Teaching asst. U. Nebr., Lincoln, 1957-58, research asst., 1958-61; asst. prof. biochemistry Colo. State U., Ft. Collins, 1962067, assoc. prof., 1967-75, prof., 1975—. Contbr. articles to profl. jours. Predoctoral fellow USPHS, 1960-61, postdoctoral fellow USPHS, 1961-63, sr. postdoctoral fellow USPHS, 1969-70. Mem. Am. Chem. Soc., Am. Soc. Biol. Chemists, Assn. Research in Vision and Ophthalmology, Sigma Xi. Democrat. Research interests include biochemistry of lens and role of iron in cellular differentiation; avocations: painting, gardening. Home: 1825 Essex Dr Fort Collins CO 80526 Office: Colo State U Dept Biochemistry Fort Collins CO 80523

AZAROW, CHARLES, sugar corporation; b. Jersey City, Dec. 12, 1918; s. Isaac and Ruth (Laurie) A.; m. Dolores Marie Willcockson. Student, Hudson Coll. With B.W. Dyer & Co., N.Y.C., 1937-52; v.p. sugar div. Pepsico, Purchase, N.Y., 1952-68; pres. sweetener div. Sucrest Corp., N.Y.C., 1968-77; pres. Revere Sugar Corp., N.Y.C., 1977-81; pres., chief exec. officer Nat. Sugar Refining, N.Y.C., 1981-82; vice chmn. Holly Sugar Corp., Colorado Springs, Colo., 1982-86; pres., chief exec. officer Holly Sugar Corp., Colorado Springs, 1986—. Counsilman Demarest, N.J., 1975-77. Served with U.S. Army, 1941-45. Mem. U.S. Beet Sugar Assn., Sugar Assn., Inc., Internat. Sugar Club (past pres.), Sugar Industry Technologists, N.Y. Coffee/Sugar Exchange (on spot com.). Office: Holly Sugar Corp 100 Chase Stone Center Colorado Springs CO 80903

BAADH, VALERIE, producer, designer, choreographer, dancer; b. Burbank, Calif., Sept. 16, 1952; d. Uffe and Shirley (Goldberg) B.; m. Michael Earl Garrett, May 20, 1979; children—John David Garrett, Rose Kaiulani Garrett. B.F.A., Calif. Inst. Arts, 1973. Choreographer Dancers' Group, San Francisco, 1981-83; ind. choreographer, San Francisco, 1984—; dir. Kadeka Dances for Kids, San Francisco, 1982-84, Dancers Group/Footwork, San Francisco, 1983. Choreographer: Half Past Eight, 1981, White Dance, 1982, Spy in the House of Love, 1983, Mother Goose Suite, 1984; producer: Bay Area Theatre Week, 1986, Event of the Year, San Francisco, 1986; prodn. designer: An Evening of Comedy and Dance with Robin Williams and Friends, San Francisco, 1985; producer Nina Watt Solos, 1986, Rosa Montoya Bailes Flamencos, 1987.a. Home: 120 Solano St Brisbane CA 94005

BABAYANS, EMIL, financial planner; b. Tehran, Iran, Nov. 9, 1951; came to U.S., 1969; s. Hacob and Jenik (Khatchatourian) B.; m. Annie Ashjian. B.S., U. So. Calif., 1974, M.S., 1976; m. Annie Ashjian. Cert. fin. planner. Pres. Babtech Internat., Inc., Sherman Oaks, Calif., 1975-85; sr. ptnr. Emil Babayans & Assocs., Woodland Hills, Calif., 1985—. Mem. Am. Mgmt. Assn., Nat. Assn. Life Underwriters, Inst. Cert. Fin. Planners, Internat. Assn. Fin. Planners. Armenian Orthodox. Office: 21041 Burbank Blvd Suite 200 Woodland Hills CA 91367

BABBITT, BRUCE EDWARD, former governor of Ariz.; b. June 27, 1938; m. Hattie Babbitt; children-Christopher, T.J. BS magna cum laude, U. Notre Dame; MS, U. Newcastle, Eng., 1962; LL.B., Harvard U., 1965. Bar: Ariz bar. Assoc. Brown and Bain, Phoenix, 1965-74; atty. gen. State of Ariz., Phoenix, 1975-78; gov. State of Ariz., 1978-87; mem. President's Commn. on Accident at Three Mile Island, 1979-80, chmn. Nuclear Saftey Oversight Com., 1980-81, Western Gov's Policy Office, 1982; mem. Adv. Commn. on Intergovtl. Relations, 1980-84; chmn. task force on fed. budget deficit Roosevelt Ctr. for Am. Policy Studies, 1984; chmn. Nat. Groundwater Policy Forum, 1984-. Author: Color and Light: The Southwest Canvases of Louis Akin, 1973, Grand Canyon: An Anthology, 1978. Trustee Dougherty Found. Recipent Thomas Jefferson award Nat. Wildlife Fedn., 1981, spl. conservation award Nat. Wildlife Fedn. 1983. Mem. Nat. Govs. Assn. (chmn. subcom. on water resources), Democratic Govs. Assn. (chmn. 1985). Democrat. Office: Office of Gov West Wing State Capital Phoenix AZ 85007 *

BABCOCK, NELLIE JO, clinical social worker; b. Bozeman, Mont., Mar. 26, 1951; d. Harold C. and Patricia A. (Alexander) B.; m. Christopher J. Krenk, July 3, 1977; 1 child, Hanna Jo. Student, St. Andrews Presbyn. Coll., 1968-70; BA summa cum laude, U. Minn., 1972, MSW, 1974. Registered clin. social worker, Oreg. Psychiat. social worker Lane County Mental Health, Eugene, Oreg., 1974-75, Benton County Mental Health, Corvallis, Oreg., 1975-77, Clackamas County Mental Health, Marylhurst, Oreg., 1978; pvt. psychotherapist and cons. Lake Oswego, Oreg., 1979—; dir. Family Growth Alternatives, Marylhurst, 1980-84; co-founder, dir. Portland Family Inst., 1983—; NIMH trainee, 1972-74. Mem. Nat. Assn. Social Workers, Acad. Cert. Social Workers, Am. Assn. Marriage and Family Therapy. Democrat. Office: 425 SW 2d St Lake Oswego OR 97034

BABCOCK, WILLIS, engr.; b. Waukesha, Wis., May 31, 1922; s. Barney and Helen (Reuter) B.; student Northland Coll., 1941-42, M.I.T., 1945-48, Cornell U., 1948; M.S.M.E., Century U., 1982; m. Elizabeth Anne Zimmerman, Sept. 26, 1947; children—Rudolph, Kathryn, Willis W., Gregory, Janet, Deborah. Chief engr. Domestic Engine and Pump Co., Shippensburg, Pa., 1948-53; chief engr. research and devel. Aurora Pump Co. (Ill.), 1953-59; v.p. engring., exec. v.p., gen. mgr. Carver Pump Co., Muscatine, Iowa, 1959-63, cons., 1963-64; chief engr. Mission Valve & Pump Co., Houston, 1964-66; dir. research and devel. Mech. Equipment Co., New Orleans, 1966-68; program mgr. Battelle N.W. Labs., Richland, Wash., 1968-71; sr. project engr. Emco Wheaton Inc., Conneant, Ohio, 1971-72; chief engr. Sta-Rite Industries, Inc., Delavan, Wis., 1972-77; mgr. engring. Wayne Home Equipment Co., Ft. Wayne, Ind., 1977-80; with Rockwell Internat., Richland, Wash., 1980—. Served with AUS, 1942-45. Mem. ASME, Nat. Soc. Profl. Engrs. Baptist. Home: 3937 Austin St West Richland WA 99352 Office: Rockwell Internat 3937 Austin St West Richland WA 99352

BABER, HARRIET ERICA, philosophy educator; b. Paterson, N.J., Jan. 6, 1950; d. Peter Philip and Gertrude (Schneider) F.; m. Roger S.M. Baber, June 10, 1972; children: John Locke Meyers Baber, Paul Christopher Meyers Baber. BA in Philosophy, Lake Forest Coll., 1971; MA in Philosophy, Johns Hopkins U., 1976, PhD in Philosophy, 1980. Instr. philosophy No. Ill. U., DeKalb, 1980-81; vis. asst. prof. Western Wash. U., Bellingham, 1981-82; asst. prof. U. San Diego, 1982—. Contbr. articles to scholarly jours. Recipient McPherson award in Philosophy Lake Forest (Ill.) Coll., 1971, Scott prize in Philosophy Lake Forest Coll., 1971; Gilman Fellow Johns Hopkins U. Mem. Am. Philosophical Assn., Soc. Christian Philosophers, Soc. Women in Philosophy, San Diego Computer Soc., Apple Corps, Phi Beta Kappa. Democrat. Episcopalian. Avocations: bikeriding, computers. Home: 1147 Edgemont St San Diego CA 92102-2331 Office: U San Diego Dept Philosophy Alcala Park San Diego CA 92110

BABICH, ALAN FRANCIS, computer scientist; b. Sewickley, Pa., Nov. 21, 1943; s. John and Hedwig Joanna (Bitautos) B. BS in Physics, Carnegie Inst. Tech., 1965, MSEE, 1966; PhDEE, Carnegie-Mellon U., 1972. With Burroughs Corp., 1971-79; mgmt. systems analyst Burroughs Corp., Mission Viejo, Calif., 1975, project leader, 1975-79; architect large systems Basic Four Corp., Tustin, Calif., 1979-83; system architect File Net Corp., Costa Mesa, Calif., 1983—. Mem. Capt. Hook and the Sky Pirates sport Parachuting team, Elsinore, Calif., 1974-76. Recipient awards in parachuting accuracy competitions, 1967-72, including 1st Pl. award, Tucumseh, Mich., 1970. Mem. IEEE, Assn. Computing Machinery, Mensa, Sigma Xi. Office: FileNet Corp 3530 Hyland Ave Costa Mesa CA 92626

BABLONKA, JOSEPH PAUL, management consultant; b. Derby, Conn., Mar. 30, 1950; s. Joseph Paul and Helen Alice (Murray) B. BA, So. Conn. State Coll., 1973; postgrad., Conn. Sch. Broadcasting, 1975; MA, U. New Haven, 1981; postgrad., Columbia U., 1982. Quality circle facilitator/tng. coordinator Sperry Gyroscope div. Sperry Corp., Waterbury, Conn., 1980-82; mgr. tng. and devel. instrument div. Dresser Industries, Stratford, Conn., 1982-85; sr. mgmt. cons. ARCO of Alaska, Anchorage, 1985—; adj. prof. Waterbury State Tech. Coll., 1982. Former treas., v.p. indsl. mgmt. club YMCA. Mem. Am. Psychol. Assn. (assoc.), Am. Soc. Tng. and Devel., Internat. Assn. Quality Circles (founder Conn. chpt.), Greater Bridgeport Personnel Assn. Home: 9827 Little Diomede Circle Eagle River AK 99577 Office: ARCO of Alaska PO Box 100360 Anchorage AK 99510-0360

BABU, MUTHIYALIAH, nephrology physician; b. India, Aug. 22, 1947; came to U.S., 1971; MD, Madras U., India. Diplomate Am. Bd. Internal Medicine, Am. Bd. Nephrology. Intern Madras U. Affiliated Hosps., 1970-71; intern N.Y. Med. Coll. at Westchester Med. Ctr., Valhalla, N.Y., 1972-73, resident in internal medicine, 1973-76, fellow in nephrology, 1976-78, research fellow in nephrology and physiology, 1978-79; assoc. clin. prof. medicine Mich. State U., East Lansing, 1983-85; med. dir. Marian Kidney Disease Ctr., Santa Maria, Calif., 1985—. Mem. Am. Soc. Hypertension, Internat. Soc. Artificial Internal Organs, Am. soc. Nephrology, Internat. Soc. Nephrology. Office: Marian Kidney Disease Ctr 220 S Palisades Dr Suite 204 Santa Maria CA 93455

BACA, LINDA TODD, psychotherapist, social worker; b. Ft. Madison, Iowa, Dec. 4, 1946; d. Marcus Clayton and Eugenia Armina (Foresman) Todd; m. Bernard Joseph Baca, Aug. 22, 1981. BS in Home Econs., So. Ill. U., 1969; MS in Social Work, U. Wis., 1975. Child welfare supr. Ill. Dept. Children and Family Services, Champaign, 1969-72; adminstr. day care services 1st Congl. Ch., Madison, Wis., 1973-74; cons. social work N.Mex. Human Services Dept., Santa Fe, 1975-80, 83-84; research and devel. coordinator Gratiot County Child Advocacy Assn., Alma, Mich., 1982-83; planner dir. N.Mex. Human Services Dept., Santa Fe, 1984-86; pvt. practice psychotherapy Sante Fe, 1987—; co-founder, bd. dirs. N.Mex. Com. for Prevention of Child Abuse, Albuquerque, 1984-87, v.p. coalitions 1985-86; mgr. guest house for Santa Fe visitors. Mem. Nat. Assn. Social Workers, Acad. Cert. Social Workers (cert.), NOW, Kappa Omicron Phi. Democrat. Mem. Ch. of Religious Sci. Avocations: color consulting, walking, gardening. Home and Office: 1320 Escalante Santa Fe NM 87501

BACA, MARCOS JOSE, bacteriologist; b. Portales, N.Mex., Dec. 27, 1961; s. Isaias and Leonela Ramona (Salguero) B.; m. Terri Ann Nials, June 4, 1983; children: Marcos Leandro, Mikel Abel. BS, Eastern N.Mex. U., 1984. Cert. water operator II and wastewater II, N.Mex. Becteriologist City of Hobbs, N.Mex., 1984-86; lab. technician Twining Water and Sanitation Dist., Taos Ski Valley, N.Mex., 1986—. Mem. Am. Chem. Soc., Am. Water Works Assn., Alpha Phi Omega. Democrat. Roman Catholic. Avocations: racquetball, photography, entomology. Home: PO Box 52 San Cristobal NM 87564 Office: Twining Water and Sanitation Dist Boxx 66 Taos Ski Valley NM 87571

BACA, OSWALD GILBERT, microbiologist, educator; b. Belen, N.Mex., July 6, 1942; s. Herman Jose and Susana (Sanchez) B.; children: John Michael, Paul Gregory. BS, U. N.Mex., 1966, MS, 1969; PhD, U. Kans., 1973. Postdoctoral fellow Friedrich Miescher Institute, Basel, Switzerland, 1973-75; research assoc. dept. biochemistry U. Minn. Med. Sch., Mpls., 1975; asst. prof. microbiology U. N.Mex., Albuquerque, 1976-81, assoc. prof., 1981-86, prof., 1986—, assoc. dean grad. studies, 1986—; co-chmn. 3d Internat. Symposium on Rickettsiae and Rickettsial diseases in Smolenice, Czechoslovakia, 1984. Contbr. articles to profl. jours. Research grantee NSF, NIH. Mem. Am. Soc. Microbiology (pres. N.Mex. br. 1981-83), Am. Soc. Biol. Chemists, Am. Soc. Microbiology, Am. Soc. Rickettsiology and Rickettsial Diseases (sec., treas. 1986—), Internat. Coll. of Rickettsiologists, AAAS, Sigma Xi, Phi Beta Kappa, Phi Kappa Phi. Democrat. Avocations: running, fishing, cross-country skiing. Office: U N Mex Dept Biology Albuquerque NM 87131

BACARD, ANDRÉ, author, professional society administrator; b. Montreal, Can., Nov. 21, 1947; s. Christine Memry. Student, U. Tex., 1965-69, Harvard U., 1969-74, U. Calif., Berkeley, 1982. Dir. Modern Studies Group, Stanford, Calif., 1977-82, Affirmist Soc., Stanford, 1983—; mem. editorial bd. Humanist Mag., Amherst, N.Y., 1984—, press rep., 1986—. Author: Affirmist Manifesto, 1981, Hunger for Power, 1986; contbr. articles to profl. jours. Bd. dirs. ACLU. Mem. World Affairs Council, World Future Soc., Bertrand Russell Soc. Office: Affirmist Soc PO Box 3009 Stanford CA 94305

BACASTOW, JACK LEROY, safety engr.; b. Arkansas City, Kan., Aug. 25, 1925; s. Alvin Hemperly and Mary Esther (Gribble) B.; m. Diane Edith Janicek, Sept. 22, 1951; children: Laurie Jean, Daniel Jack. Student U. Ill., 1946-47, Spartan Sch. Aeros., Tulsa, 1947-48; Los Alamos Grad. Ctr., U. N.Mex., 1960-70; BS in Indsl. Engring., N.Mex. State U., 1973. Research technician, pilot plant operator Universal Oil Products, McCook, Ill., 1949-50; research/instrument technician Argonne (Ill.) Nat. Lab., 1950-59; electronics/instrument technician Los Alamos Nat. Lab., 1959-70, staff mem., 1972-79, dep. safety group leader, 1979—. Served with USN, 1943-46; PTO. Registered profl. engr., Calif. Mem. Am. Soc. Safety Engrs. (cert. safety profl.), Am. Ins. Insl. Engrs., IEEE, System Safety Soc., Laser Inst. Am. Democrat. Editor Nat. Safety Council Research and Devel. Sect. Newsletter, 1987—; contbr. articles to profl. jours. Office: Los Alamos Nat Lab Safety Group HSE-3 Mail Stop K-489 Los Alamos NM 87545

BACH, DAVID RUDOLPH, physicist, consultant; b. Shimonoseki, Japan, Apr. 24, 1924; Came to U.S., 1941; s. Ditlev G.M. and Ellen Sigrid (Knudsen) B.; m. Barbara Ann Batteurs, June 26, 1948 (dec. Mar. 1975); children:

Catherine, Constance, Timothy, Thomas; m. Jacqueline Anne Larsen, Apr. 19, 1975; stepchildren: Susan, Louis. BA, U. Mich., 1948, MS in Physics, 1950, PhD in Physics, 1955. Physicist, mgr. Knolls Atomic Power Lab., Schenectady, N.Y., 1955-64; cons. Knolls Atomic Power Lab., 1964-66; prof. nuclear engring. U. Mich., Ann Arbor, 1964-79; staff physicist Los Alamos (N.M.) Nat. Lab., 1979-84, cons., 1984—; physics cons. Ventura, Calif., 1984—; cons. Lawrence Livermore (Calif.) Nat. Lab., 1985—, Kaman Tempo, Santa Barbara, Calif., 1986—. Contbr. numerous articles to profl. jours. Served to 1st lt. U.S. Army, 1943-46, CBI. Mem. IEEE, AAAS, Am. Phys. Soc. Avocations: tennis, sailing, Japanese language. Home and Office: 915 Tennyson Ln Ventura CA 93003

BACH, MARTIN WAYNE, stockbroker, owner antique clock stores; b. Milw., Mar. 30, 1940; s. Jack Baer and Rose (Weiss) B.; m. Roberta Sklar, Aug. 19, 1962; children: David Louis, Emily Elizabeth. BA, U. Wis., 1963. Stockbroker J. Barth & Co., Oakland, Calif., 1966-72, v.p., 1970-72; sr. v.p., stockbroker Dean Witter & Co., Oakland, 1972—; founder The TimePeace, Carmel, Calif., 1972-83, San Francisco, 1975—, La Jolla, 1977—; instr. fin. San Leandro and Hayward (Calif.) Adult Sch., 1970—. Chmn. bd. dirs. Diabco Light Opera Co., 1985—; bd. dirs. East Bay Hosp., 1985—. Served to 1st lt., U.S. Army, 1963-65. Mem. Calif. Thoroughbred Breeders Assn., Calif. Thoroughbred Assn., Nat. Assn. Clock & Watch Collectors, Am. Horse Council. Clubs: East Bay Brokers, Moraga Country, Dean Witter Chairmen's. Lodge: B'nai B'rith. Avocations: breeder, owner thoroughbred race horses. Home: 180 Sandringham S Moraga CA 94556 Office: 1 Kaiser Plaza Suite 1950 Oakland CA 94556

BACHA, JOHN DONALD, research chemist; b. Mpls., Aug. 21, 1941; s. George Thomas and Veronica Mary (Fabian) B.; m. Jane Beatrice Downey, June 25, 1966; children: Jeffrey, Jay, Joel, Jennifer. BA, St. Mary's Coll., 1963; PhD, Case Inst. Tech., 1967. Research chemist Gulf Research and Devel. Co., Harmarville, Pa., 1967-72; sr. research chemist Gulf Research and Devel. Co., Harmarville, 1972-78, research assoc., 1978-85; sr. research chemist Chevron Research Co., Richmond, Calif., 1985—. Contbr. articles to profl. jours.; patentee in field. Mem. AAAS, AIME, Am. Chem. Soc., Am. Carbon Soc., Metall. Soc., Am. Soc. Testing and Materials. Republican. Roman Catholic. Avocations: woodworking, landscape gardening. Home: 810 Arthur St Novato CA 94947 Office: Chevron Research Co 576 Standard Ave Richmond CA 94802

BACHER, ROSALIE WRIDE, sch. adminstr.; b. Los Angeles, May 25, 1925; d. Homer M. and Reine (Rogers) Wride; A.B., Occidental Coll., 1947, M.A., 1949; m. Archie O. Bacher, Jr., Mar. 30, 1963. Tchr., English, Latin, history David Starr Jordan High Sch., Long Beach, Calif., 1949-55, counselor, 1955-65, Lakewood (Calif.) Sr. High Sch., 1965-66; research asst., counselor Poly. High Sch., Long Beach, 1966-67; counselor, office occupational preparation, vocational guidance sect. Long Beach Unified School Dist., Long Beach, 1967-68; vice prin. Washington Jr. High Sch., Long Beach, 1968-70; asst. prin. Lakewood Sr. High Sch., Long Beach, spring 1970; vice prin. Jefferson Jr. High Sch., Long Beach, 1970-81, Marshall Jr. High Sch., Long Beach, 1981—; chmn. vocat. guidance steering com. Long Beach Unified Sch. Dist., 1963—. Mem. Internat. Platform Assn., AAUW, Long Beach Personnel and Guidance Assn. (dir. 1958-60), Long Beach Sch. Counselors Assn. (sec. high sch. segment 1963-64), Phi Beta Kappa, Delta Kappa Gamma (pres. Delta Psi chpt., area dir.; Calif. profl. affairs com. chmn. 1972-74), Phi Delta Gamma (pres. chpt. 1977-78, nat. chmn. bylaws com. 1980-81), Pi Lambda Theta (pres. chpt. 1974-76, v.p. So. Calif. council 1974-76), Phi Delta Kappa (sec. Long Beach chpt. 1977-80). Home: 265 Rocky Point Rd Palos Verdes Estates CA 90274 Home: 17721 Misty Lane Huntington Beach CA 92649 Office: John Marshall Jr High Sch 5870 E Wardlow Rd Long Beach CA 90808

BACHRACH, CHARLES LEWIS, advertising agency executive; b. N.Y.C., Feb. 22, 1946; s. Herbert and Lilla Clare (Blumberg) B.; m. Lois Susan Davis, Sept. 12, 1968; 1 dau., Jennifer Leigh. B.S., Ithaca (N.Y.) Coll., 1968. Assoc. producer MPO Sports Co., N.Y.C., 1968-69; unit mgr. NBC, N.Y.C., 1969; with Ogilvy & Mather, Inc., N.Y.C., 1969—; sr. v.p. broadcast Ogilvy & Mather, Inc., 1978-83, dir. Network and Programming Dept; sr. v.p. network and programming Western Internat. Media, 1983—; pres. Western Internat. Syndication, 1983—; vis. prof. Ithaca Coll. Sch. Communications; vis. lectr. New Sch. Contbr. articles to profl. publs. Judge Internat. Emmy Awards.; Lobbyist N.Y. State pvt. colls. Recipient Disting. Alumni award Ithaca Coll., 1980; named One of Top 100 Young People in Advt., 1985. Home: 3121 Dona Marta Dr Studio City CA 91604 Office: Western Internat Syndication 8544 Sunset Blvd Los Angeles CA 90069

BACHSTEIN, HARRY SAMUEL, lawyer, educator; b. Oakland, Calif., Aug. 6, 1943; s. Elizabeth (Rodenhouse) B.; m. Kathy Ann Hill; children—Harry S. III, David Jason, Shane Thomas, Jacob William, Gretchen Leah. BS in Bus. Adminstrn., No. Ariz. U., 1966; JD with honors, U. Ariz., 1969. Bar: Ariz. 1969, U.S. Supreme Ct. 1973, U.S. Ct. Customs and Patent Appeals, U.S. Dist. Ct. Ariz., U.S. Ct. Appeals (9th cir.), U.S. Bankruptcy Ct. Spl. investigator ethics com. Pinal County Bar Assn., 1971; juvenile ct. referee Ariz. Superior Ct., 1972-76; mem. Superior Ct. Med. Liability Rev. Panel, 1981; lawyer arbitrator Better Bus. Tucson. Mem. Devel. Authority for Tucson's Expansion, 1970-76; mem. U.S. Presdl. Task Force, 1981—; faculty Pima Coll., 1982-83. Mem. State Bar of Ariz. (sec., exec. council young lawyers' sect. 1972-73), ABA (Ariz. rep. com. on div. law and procedures 1976), Pima County Bar Assn. (grievance com. 1978—, spl. investigator for ethics com. 1971), Profl. Assn. of Diving Instrs. (cert. divemaster), Delta Chi (sec., pledgemaster 1961-65). Clubs: Optimist Internat. (state gov. Ariz. 1976, lt. gov. 1972-73, pres. 1971-72, Outstanding Gov. and Disting. Gov. 1976), Mason. Editor: Ariz. Law Rev., 1967-69. Avocations: hunting, deep sea diving (cert. openwater scuba diver). Office: PO Box 43188 Tucson AZ 85733-3188

BACHTEL NASH, ANN ELIZABETH, educational consultant, researcher, educator; b. Winnipeg, Man., Can., Dec. 12, 1928; d. John Wills and Margaret Agnes (Gray) Macleod; m. Richard Earl Bachtel, Dec. 19, 1947; children—Margaret Ann, John Macleod, Bradley Wills; m. 2d, Louis Philip Nash, June 30, 1978. A.B., Occidental Coll., 1947; M.A., Calif. State U.-Los Angeles, 1976. Cert. tchr., adminstr., Calif. Elem. tchr. pub. and pvt. schs. in Calif., 1947-50, 64-77; dir. Emergency Sch. Aid Act program, spl. projects, spl. arts State of Calif., 1977-80; leader, mem. program rev. team Calif. State Dept. Edn., 1981—; cons. Pasadena Unified Sch. Dist., 1981—; teaching asst., adj. prof. U. So. Calif.; cons. sch. dists., state depts. edn.; presenter workshops/seminars; mem. legis. task forces. Chmn. resource allocation com. City of Pasadena, Pasadena-Mishima (Japan) Sister Cities Internat. Com.; mem. Los Angeles World Affairs Council, docent council Pasadena Hist. Soc., Pasadena Philharm. Com., women's com. Pasadena Symphony Assn.; Emergency Sch. Aid Act grantee, 1977-81. Mem. World Council Gifted and Talented Children, Internat. Soc. Edn. Through Art, Council Exceptional Children, Am. Edn!. Research Assn., Assn. Supervision and Curriculum Devel., Nat. Art Educators Assn., Calif. Art Educators Assn., Calif. Humanities Edn. Assn., AAUW, Phi Delta Kappa, Kappa Delta Pi, Assistance League of Pasadena. Contbr. articles to publs.; writer/editor: Arts for the Gifted and Talented, 1981; author Nat. Directory of Programs for Artistically Gifted and Talented Students, K-12. Office: Pasadena Unified Sch Dist 732 Pinehurst Dr Pasadena CA 91106

BACKSTROM, DORIS IONE, school adminstrator; b. American Falls, Idaho, Oct. 18, 1939; d. Walter Rudolph and Emma June (Hofmeister) H.; m. Nicholas Charles Backstrom, May 23, 1960; children—Leslie Ann, Eric Glen. B.A., Idaho State U., 1966, Ed.M. Administr., 1978. Cert. tchr., Idaho. Tchr. Central Jr. High Sch., Idaho Falls, Idaho, 1964-66, Skyline High Sch., 1966-70; media dir. Skyline High Sch., 1970-78; asst. prin. Idaho Falls High Sch., 1978-84; prin. Clair E. Gale Jr. High Sch., 1984—; accreditation com. State Dept. Edn., Boise, Idaho, 1984—; adv. council, 1976-82. Contbr. articles to profl. jours. Pres. Bonneville County Hist. Soc., Idaho Falls, Idaho, 1976; mem. Idaho Falls City Study Com. Recipient Cert. of Recognition Idaho Com. on Women's Programs, Boise, Idaho, 1976; Service award State Supt. Pub. Instr., Boise 1982. Mem. Idaho Library Assn. (chmn. 1976), Idaho Edn. Assn. (local pres. 1975), Northwest Women in Edn. Administrn. (bd. dirs. 1982-84), Idaho Assn. Sch. Administrs. (com. chmn. 1982-84), Delta Kappa Gamma. Democrat. Lutheran. Office: Clair E Gale Jr High Sch 955 Garfield St Idaho Falls ID 83401

BACKUS, GEORGE EDWARD, theoretical geophysicist; b. Chgo., May 24, 1930; s. Milo Morlan and Dora Etta (Dare) B.; m. Elizabeth Evelyn Allen, Nov. 15, 1961 (div. 1971); children—Benjamin, Brian, Emily; m. Varda Esther Peller, Jan. 8, 1977. Ph.B., U. Chgo., 1947, B.S. in Math., 1948, M.S. in Math. and Physics, 1950, 53, Ph.D. in Physics, 1956. Jr. mathematician Inst. for Air Weapons, Chgo., 1951-53; physicist Project Matterhorn, Princeton, N.J., 1957-58; asst. prof. math. MIT, Cambridge, 1958-60; assoc. prof. geophysics U. Calif.-San Diego, La Jolla, 1960-62, prof. geophysics, 1962—; mem. vis. com. Institut de Physique du Globe de Paris, 1987—; co-chmn. Internat. Working Group on Magnetic Field Satellites, 1983—. Contbr. articles to profl. jours. Guggenheim Found. fellow, 1963, 71; Royal Soc. Arts fellow, London, 1970—. Fellow Royal Astron. Soc. (Gold medal 1986), Am. Geophys. Union (John Adam Fleming medal 1986); mem. Nat. Acad. Scis. (com. on grants and fellowships Day Fund 1974-79, Com. on Sci. and Pub. Policy 1971-74), Am. Acad. Arts and Scis., N.Y. Acad. Scis., Am. Phys. Soc., Am. Math. Soc., Soc. for Indsl. and Applied Math., Seismol. Soc. Am. Avocations: skiing; swimming; bicycling; hiking; history. Office: Inst of Geophysics and Planetary Physics A-025 U Calif La Jolla CA 92093

BACON, EARL RICHARD, mathematics educator; b. Hamilton, Mont., June 21, 1950; s. Alvin Alonzo and Margaret Jeanne (Partridge) B.; m. Gwendolyn Z. Kadar, Oct. 23, 1982; 1 child, Eric Richard. AA, Highline Community Coll.; BEd, Cen. Wash. State Coll.; postgrad., U. Wash. Instr. math. Federal Way (Wash.) Sch. Dist., 1974—, also swim coach, 1976—. Author: Primary Cursive Instruction, 1975. Mem. Dem. Caucus, Auburn, Wash., 1976, Citizens for Incorporation, Federal Way, 1975. Mem. NEA (negotiator 1975-76), Nat. Coaches Assn. Home: 32821 42d Ave SW Federal Way WA 98023

BACON, JAN GARVER, social worker; b. Flint, Mich., Jan. 20, 1950; s. Paul Jr. and Alyce Lucille (Barker) B.; m. Paula Frances Smith, Sept. 4, 1971 (div. Oct. 1976); m. Shirley Marie Nutt, Dec. 5, 1981; children: Autumn Star, Dusti Rose; 1 stepchild, Steven Dale. BA, U. Mich., 1972, MSW, 1976. Ordained priest Reorganized Ch. Jesus Christ of Latter-day Sts., 1985; lic. clin. social worker. Psychiat. social worker VA Hosp., Ann Arbor, Mich., 1976-78; mental health specialist Indian Health Service, Rocky Boy, Mont., 1978-79; chief social worker Indian Health Service, Parker, Ariz., 1979-82; pvt. practice clin. social work Logan, Utah, 1983—; coordinator alcohol program Utah State U., Logan, 1984—; bd. dirs. Citizens Against Phys. and Sexual Abuse, Logan. Mem. Internat. Transactional Analysis Assn., Nat. Assn. Social Workers. Democrat. Clubs: Cache Valley Soccer Club, Sun and Snow Runners (Logan). Avocations: soccer, marathon running, singing. Home: 55 W 400 S Logan UT 84321 Office: Utah State U Alcohol & Substance Abuse Program Logan UT 84321

BACON, LEONARD ANTHONY, accounting educator; b. Santa Fe, June 10, 1931; s. Manuel R. and Maria (Chavez) Baca; m. Patricia Balzaretti; children—Bernadine M., Jerry A., Tiffany A. B.E., U. Nebr.-Omaha, 1965; M.B.A., U. of the Americas, Mexico City, 1969; Ph.D., U. Miss., 1971. CPA; cert. mgmt. acct., internal auditor. Commd. 2d lt. U.S. Army, 1951, advanced through grades to maj., 1964, served fin. and acctg. officer mainly Korea, Vietnam; resigned, 1966; asst. prof. Delta State U., Cleveland, Miss., 1971-76; assoc. prof. West Tex. State U., Canyon, 1976-79; prof. acctg. Calif. State Coll., Bakersfield, 1979—; cons. Kershen Co. (now Atlantic Richfield Oil Co.), Canyon, 1979-80. Contbr. articles to profl. jours. U.S., Mex., Can., papers to profl. confs. Leader Delta area Boy Scouts Am., Cleveland, 1971-76; dir. United Campus Ministry, Canyon, 1976-79; minister Kern Youth Facility, Bakersfield, 1983-84. Paratrooper Brazilian Army, 1955. Mem. Am. Acctg. Assn., Am. Inst. CPA's, Am. Assn. Spanish Speaking CPA's, Nat. Assn. Accts. (pres. Bakersfield chpt. 1981-82, Most Valuable Mem. award 1981), Am. Mgmt. Assn., Inst. Mgmt. Acctg., Calif. Faculty Assn., Inst. Internal Auditors, Inst. Cost Analysts, Alpha Kappa Psi (Dedicated Service award 1979). Clubs: Jockey (Rio de Janeiro). Lodges: Lions (v.p. Cleveland 1971-73), Kiwanis (v.p. 1974-79, A Whale of a Guy award, Cleveland 1975). Office: Calif State College Bakersfield 9001 Stockdale Hwy Bakersfield CA 93309

BACON, VICKY LEE, lighting services executive; b. Oregon City, Oreg., Mar. 25, 1950; d. Herbert Kenneth and Lorean Betty (Boltz) Rushford; student Portland Community Coll., 1974-75, Mt. Hood Community Coll., 1976, Portland State Coll., 1979; m. Dennis M. Bacon, Aug. 7, 1971; 1 dau., Randene Tess. With All Electric Constrn., Milwaukie, Oreg., 1968-70; with Lighting Maintenance Co., Portland, Oreg., 1970-78; service mgr. GTE Sylvania Lighting Services, Portland, 1978-80, br. mgr., 1980-83; div. mgr. Christenson Electric Co. Inc., Portland, 1983—. Mem. Nat. Secs. Assn., Illuminating Engring. Soc., Nat. Assn. Lighting Maintenance Contractors. Office: Christenson Electric Co Inc 111 SW Columbia Suite 480 Portland OR 97201

BACON, WALTER LAURENCE, III, elec. engr.; b. Phila., Nov. 2, 1912; s. Walter Laurence and Elisabeth V. (Ford) B.; M.S., Calif. Inst. Tech., 1936; m. Ada Gwendolyn Perkin, Aug. 31, 1944; children—Cheryl Elizabeth, Walter Laurence IV. With Tex. Co., 1936-41; sr. staff engr. Gen. Telephone & Electronics Corp. Calif., Pomona, 1947-77; owner Ocean Electronics Research Studies, cons. firm, 1968—. Supr. edn., tng. Retarded Children's Assn. San Gabriel Valley, 1959-65, pres., 1957-58. Served as comdr. USNR, 1942—. Recipient Dr. Elenora Preston award for research, devel. methods in teaching retarded children, 1964. Mem. Am. Inst. E.E. (chmn. communications Los Angeles chpt.), IEEE (chmn. communications soc. profl. group Los Angeles Council, vice chmn. oceanic engring. council 1979—). Contbr. articles to profl. jours. Home: 323 N Elizabeth Ave Monterey Park CA 91754

BADANI, MAHESH PRANLAL, engineering management executive; b. Jetpur, India, Nov. 9, 1944; came to U.S., 1967; s. Pranlal D. and Dhiraj Badani; m. Preeti M. Badani, July 16, 1974; children: Mona, Ami, Romish. B in Tech. Engring., Indian Inst. Tech., Bombay, 1967; PhD in Engring., U. Calif., Berkeley, 1980; postgrad., Purdue U., U. Calif., Irvine, 1969-73. Sr. engr., project engr. C.F. Braun & Co., Alhambra, Calif., 1970-80; mgr. mktg. SMA, Inc., Newport Beach, Calif., 1980-81; pres. Concept Tech., Inc., Newport Beach, 1981—. Mem. Sigma Xi, Phi Kappa Phi. Republican. Home: 13 Sunlight Irvine CA 92715 Office: Concept Tech Inc 4000 Mac Arthur Blvd Newport Beach CA 92660

BADASH, LAWRENCE, science history educator; b. Bklyn., May 8, 1934; s. Joseph and Dorothy (Langa) B.; children: Lisa, Bruce. BS in Physics, Rensselaer Poly. Inst., 1956; PhD in History of Sci., Yale U., 1964. Instr. Yale. U., New Haven, Conn., 1964-65, research assoc., 1965-66; from asst. to assoc. prof. U. Calif., Santa Barbara, 1966-79, prof. history of sci., 1979—; bd. dirs. Summer Seminar on Global Security and Arms Control, U. Calif., 1983, 86; cons. Nuclear Age Peace Found., Santa Barbara, 1984—. Author: Radioactivity in America, 1979, Kapitza, Rutherford, and the Kremlin, 1985; editor: Rutherford and Boltwood, Letters on Radioactivity, 1969, Reminiscences of Los Alamos, 1943-45, 1980. Bd. dirs. Santa Barbara chpt. ACLU, 1971-86, pres., 1982-84; nat. bd. dirs. Com. for a Sane Nuclear Policy, Washington, 1972-81; mem. Los Padres Search and Rescue Team, Santa Barbara, 1981—. Served to lt. (j.g.) USN, 1956-59. Grantee, NSF, Cambridge, Eng., 1965-66, 69-72, Am. Philos. Soc., New Zealand, 1979-80, Inst. on Global Conflict and Cooperation, U. Calif., 1983-87; J.S. Guggenheim fellow, 1984-85. Fellow AAAS; mem. History of Sci. Soc. (founder West Coast chpt., chpt. bd. dirs. 1971-73, nat. council 1975-78), Am. Phys. Soc. Democrat. Jewish. Avocation: backpacking. Office: Univ of Calif Dept of History Santa Barbara CA 93106

BADCOCK, CHARLES CORYDON, aerospace company executive; b. Long Beach, Calif., Nov. 16, 1942; s. Ralph Wyant and Fern Margaret (Fulton) B.; m. Linda Kay Youde, Sept. 6, 1961; children: Eric Wyant, Melissa Ann. BS, Oreg. State U., 1965; PhD, U. Calif., Santa Barbara, 1969. Chemist Nat. Council for Stream Improvement, Corvallis, Oreg., 1963-65; postdoctoral fellow Ohio State U., Columbus, 1969-72; mem. tech. staff The Aerospace Corp., Los Angeles, 1972-77, mgr. labs., 1977-83, head energy scis. dept., 1983—. Contbr. articles to jours. Postdoctoral fellow EPA, 1969-71. Mem. Am. Chem. Soc., Electrochem. Soc., AAAS, AIAA (mem. aerospace power systems com. 1981-84, chmn. 1984-86), Sigma Xi. Avocations: fishing, swimming, travel, reading. Home: 20935 Conradi Ave Torrance CA 90502 Office: The Aerospace Corp PO Box 92957 Chemistry Physics Bldg A6 M2/275 Los Angeles CA 90009

BADER, JENNIE SUEKO TAKAHASHI, telecommunications administrator; b. Long Beach, Calif., Dec. 14, 1959; d. George M. and Valerie Hanako (Kishimoto) T.; m. Jeff Louis Bader, Sept. 1, 1984. BS in Bus. Mgmt., San Jose State U., 1981; postgrad., Golden Gate U., 1984—. Data processing adminstr. Equatorial Communications Co., Mountain View, Calif., 1982-84; supr. telecommunications Robert A. McNeil Corp., San Mateo, Calif., 1984-85; systems engr. Rolm Corp. div. IBM, Irvine, Calif., 1985—. Mem. Telecommunications Assn. (sect. edn. com. 1984-85), Soc. Advancement Mgmt. (sect. program dir. 1982-84). Methodist.

BADGER, LAURENE LAURITZEN, nurse; b. Salt Lake City, Jan. 24, 1955; d. Vaughn Kent and Lona Mae Stratford (Hyde) Lauritzen; m. Karl Franklin Badger, Dec. 14, 1978 (div.) A.D. in Med. Scis., Brigham Young U., 1975; A.D. in Nursing, Weber State Coll., 1978. Registered nurse, Utah. Registered nurse cons. Procter & Gamble, Salt Lake City, 1980-82, Knoll Pharmaceutical, Salt Lake City, 1983-84; profl. services analyst Control Data Corp., 1984—; nurse St. Mark's Hosp., Salt Lake City, 1976—; Mem. Utah Soc. for Post Anesthesia Nurses. Republican. Mormon. Office: 5965 S 900 E Salt Lake City UT 84121

BADGLEY, THEODORE MCBRIDE, psychiatrist, neurologist; b. Salem, Ala., June 27, 1925; s. Roy Joseph and Fannie (Limbaugh) B.; m. Mary Bennett Wells, Dec. 30, 1945; children: Justice Badgley O'Neil, Jan Badgley Wolkov, Mona Jean Badgley Covey, Jason Wells, James John, Mary Rose. Student, Occidental Coll., 1942-44; M.D., U. So. Calif., 1949. Diplomate: Am. Bd. Psychiatry and Neurology. Intern Letterman Gen. Hosp., San Francisco, 1949-50; resident in psychiatry Letterman Gen. Hosp., 1950-53; commd. capt. M.C. U.S. Army, 1950, advanced through grades to lt. col., 1967; chief mental hygiene cons. service Ft. Gordon, Ga.; and asso. clin. prof. psychiatry and neurology Med. Coll. Ga., 1954-55; resident in neurology Walter Reed Gen. Hosp., Washington, 1955-57; asst. chief psychiatry service Walter Reed Gen. Hosp., 1957-59, chief psychiatry service, 1959-62, asst. chief dept. psychiatry and neurology, 1962-63, dir. edn. and tng. psychiatry, 1957-63; chief dept. psychiatry and neurology U.S. Army Gen. Hosp., Landstuhl, Germany, 1963-66; chief psychiatry outpatient dept. Letterman Gen. Hosp., 1966-67; ret. 1967; dir. Kern View Mental Health Center, Bakersfield, Calif., 1967-69; pvt. practice medicine specializing in psychiatry Bakersfield, 1967—; pres. Sans Doloroso Inst., Bakersfield, 1969—; lectr. community health service orgns., profl. confs., seminars. Contbr. articles to profl. jours. Fellow Am. Psychiat. Assn. (life). Home: 1733 Crestmont Dr Bakersfield CA 93306 Office: 1901 Truxtun Ave Bakersfield CA 93301

BADHAM, ROBERT E., congressman; b. Los Angeles, June 9, 1929; s. Byron J. and Bess (Kissinger) B.; m. Anne Carroll; children: Sharon, Robert, William, Phyllis, Jennifer. A.B., Stanford U., 1951. Vice pres., dir. Hoffman Hardware Co., Los Angeles, 1955-69; mem. Calif. Assembly from 71st Dist., 1962-76, 95th-100th Congresses from 40th Calif. Dist., 1977—. Author articles. Mem. Orange Empire Area council Boy Scouts Am.; del. So. Pacific Dist. conv. Am. Lutheran Ch., 1967, Nat. conv., 1968; alt. del. Republican Nat. Conv., 1964-68; mem. Calif. Rep. Central Com., 1962—, Orange County Rep. Central Com., 1962—. Served to lt. (j.g.) USNR, 1952-54. Mem. Am. Soc. Archtl. Hardware Cons., Orange Coast Assn., Orange County Assn. Chambers Commerce, Am. Legion, Nat. Rifle Assn., Phi Gamma Delta. Office: 2438 Rayburn House Office Bldg Washington DC 20515 *

BADUA, RAYMOND MARTIN, air force officer; b. Washington, May 31, 1960; s. Romulo Obra and Isidora Ventura (Martin) B.; m. May Baclig Salamanca, Jan. 26, 1985; 1 child, Lauren Marie. BSEE, Marquette U., 1982; postgrad., U. So. Calif., 1985—. Commd. 2d lt. USAF, Lackland AFB, Tex., 1982; advanced through grades to capt. USAF, 1986; space system effectiveness div., 1986—; cons. Naval Research Lab., Washington, 1983—; instr. aerobics Los Angeles Air Force Sta., 1983—. Mem. IEEE, Air Force Assn. Republican. Roman Catholic. Avocations: photography, computers, basketball, racquetball, running. Office: USAF Space Div PO Box 92960 Los Angeles AFS CA 90009-2960

BAEHL DE LESCURE, PATRICK JEAN, hospital administrator; b. Paris, Dec. 8, 1949; came to Can., 1966; s. Jean H. Baehl and Genevieve Suzanne (de Lescure) Baehl de Lescure; m. Wendy L. Roberts, Oct. 6, 1973 (div. 1978); 1 child, Chantal; m. Jerri Lynne Olson, Mar. 2, 1983; children: Matthew, Mark. Cert. in journalism Caribou Coll., 1971; cert. in health care adminstrn. U. Sask., 1985. Br. coordinator Burns Foods, Vancouver, B.C., 1975-76, asst. provision mgr., Calgary, Alta., 1976-77, provision mgr., Edmonton, Alta., 1977-79; head buyer Edmonton and Rural Hosp. Dist. #24, 1979-81; equipment coordinator Alta. Hosp. Assn., 1981-84; adminstr. Daysland Gen. Hosp., Alta., 1984—; pres. Master Planning Centre, Inc., Edmonton, 1982—, Baehl Enterprises, Edmonton, 1979-83; cons. Health and Welfare Can., Ottawa, Ont., 1983. Contbr. articles to profl. jours. Mem. Recreation Bd., Daysland, 1984—, chmn. bd., 1984—; mem. chmn. Beverly Progressive Conservative Assn., Edmonton, 1983-84, area chmn., 1982-83; bd. dirs. Camrose Progressive Conservative Assn., 1984—, 1st v.p., 1986—; active Opimian Soc., Edmonton, 1983—. Mem. Can. Coll. Health Service Execs., Alta. Hosp. Purchasing Assn. (treas. 1980-83). Vancouver Aquarium Soc. (dir. 1973-76), Calgary Chess Club (pres. 1976-77). Lutheran. Lodge: Masons. (Grieshbach sr. steward 1982-83, chaplain 1983-84) Exelsior sr. deacon 1984-85. Home: PO Box 54, Daysland, AB Canada T0B 1A0 Office: Daysland Gen Hospital, Box 27, Daysland, AB Canada T0B 1A0

BAENDER, MARGARET WOODRUFF, free lance writer; b. Salt Lake City, Apr. 1, 1921; d. Russell Kimball and Margaret Angline (McIntyre) Woodruff; m. Phillip Albers Baender, Aug. 17, 1946 (dec.); children—Kristine Lynn, Charlene Anne, Michael Phillip, Russell Richard. B.A., U. Utah, 1944. In clerical, personnel work various firms, San Francisco Bay area, 1970-75; reporter, columnist Valley Pioneer, Danville, Calif., 1975-77; editor Diablo (Calif.) Inferno, 1971-76; author Shifting Sands, 1981, Tail Waggings of Maggie, 1982. Mem. Nat. Writers Club, AAUW, Soc. Children's Book Writers, Internat. Women's Writers Guild, Alpha Delta Pi. Republican. Episcopalian.

BAER, DONALD RAY, research physicist; b. Warren, Ohio, Nov. 12, 1947; s. Ray Burdell and Ethel (Seifert) B.; m. Janet Lovelock, Oct. 5, 1971; children: Nathaniel, Stephen. BS in Physics, Carnegie-Mellon U., 1969; PhD in Physics, Cornell U., 1974. Research assoc. U. Ill., Urbana, 1974-76; research scientist Batelle Northwest Labs., Richland, Wash., 1976-79, sr. research scientist, 1980—; vis. research fellow U. Surrey, Guildford, Eng., 1984-85. Contbr. articles to profl. jours. Ruling elder Kennewick (Wash.) Presbyn. Ch., 1980—. Mem. Am. Sci. Affiliation, Am. Phys. Soc., AAAS, The Metals Soc., Am. Vacuum Soc. (dir. applied surface sci. div.), ASTM (chmn. subcom. 1983—), Am. Assn. Physics Tchrs. Avocations: running, hiking. Office: Battelle Northwest Labs Box 999 Richland WA 99352

BAERLOCHER, WILLIAM GEORGE, data processing executive; b. Greencreek, Idaho, Apr. 13, 1932; s. Bernard A. and Katherine B. (Nuxoll) B.; m. Iva J. Housner, Dec. 21, 1962; children: Eva J., Anthony J. BA in Bus. Adminstrn., U. Wash., 1970. Quality assurance mgr. The Boeing Co., Renton, Wash., 1955-70; data processing ops. mgr. State of Nev., Carson City, 1970—. Vol. Youth Activities, Carson City, 1972—. Served to cpl. U.S. Army, 1953-55. Clubs: Carson Aquatic (Carson City) (pres. 1978-80), NV-CAL Swim League (N. Nev., N. Calif.) (v.p. 1978). Avocations: swimming, little league baseball. Home: 601 W Adaline St Carson City NV 89701 Office: Computer Facility 575 E Third St Carson City NV 89710

BAGDASARIAN, ANDRANIK, biochemist; b. Tehran, Iran, Dec. 5, 1935; s. Mamegon and Satenik (Gregorian) B.; m. Vilma T. Rincon, Mar. 15, 1979; children—Patrick, Armen, Levon. Ph.D. in Biochemistry, U. Louisville, 1967; Doctorate in Pharmacy, U. Tehran, Iran, 1962. Research asst. prof. U. Pa., Phila., 1975-78; sr. research scientist Hyland Therapeutics, Costa Mesa, Calif., 1978-80, research mgr., Costa Mesa, 1980-83, assoc. dir. research, Duarte, Calif., 1983—. NIH grantee, 1975-78; Nat. Cancer Inst. grantee,

1975-78; Am. Cancer Soc. grantee, 1975-77. Mem. Am. Soc. Biol. Chemists, Sigma Xi. Republican. Armenian Apostolic Ch. Office: Hyland Therapeutic Research 1710 Flower Ave Duarte CA 91010 Home: 1227 Calle Estrella San Dimas CA 91773

BAGLEY, JAMES EDWARD, hospital administrator; b. Waterloo, Iowa, Sept. 21, 1930; s. William Franklin and Margaret Cecilia (Craig) B.; m. Kathie Rebecca Smith, Nov. 30, 1968; children: Cheryl, Debra, Kathleen, Vicki, Sharri, Lauri. Diploma, Albia Community Coll., 1948; B.A. in Pub. Adminstrn., Upper Iowa U., 1975; M. Hosp. Adminstrn., U. Minn., 1977. Sr. patrolman State of Iowa, Iowa Falls, 1956-63; adminstr. Ellsworth Hosp., Iowa Falls, 1963-68; pres. Greene County Med. Ctr., Jefferson, Iowa, 1968-83; sr. exec. v.p., bd. dirs. Phoenix Bapt. Hosp., 1983—. Pres. Greene County Arts Council, Jefferson, 1980; bd. dirs. Greenwood Homes, Inc., Jefferson, 1981; del. Republican County Conv., Greene County, Iowa, 1982. Served with USN, 1948-52. Named Boss of Yr., Jefferson Jaycees, 1978. Fellow Am. Acad. Med. Adminstrs. (chmn. 1983—, Med. Adminstr. Yr. 1977, Regional Dir. of Yr. 1980), Am. Coll. Health Care Adminstrs. (cert.), Royal Soc. Health; mem. Am. Soc. Hosp. Personnel Adminstrs., Iowa Hosp. Assn. (chmn. 1982-83, Seaman Meml. award 1980). Republican. Methodist. Lodges: Lions, Elks. Home: 15012 N 46th St Phoenix AZ 85032 Office: Phoenix Bapt Hosp and Med Ctr 6025 N 20th Ave Phoenix AZ 85015

BAGLEY, RONALD LAIRD, air force officer, educator; b. Indiana, Pa., May 31, 1947; s. Ronald Dale and Sarah (Macpherson) B.; m. Ellen Louise Isaksen, June 26, 1971; children—Ross Andrew, Melissa Anne. B.S., MIT, 1969, M.S., 1971; Ph.D., Air Force Inst. Tech., 1979; postgrad. Air Command and Staff Coll., Maxwell, AFB, Ala., 1983—. Commd. 2d lt. U.S. Air Force, 1971, advanced through grades to lt. col., 1982; instr. U.S. Air Force Acad., 1979-80, asst. prof., 1980-82, assoc. prof., 1982-83, lab. dir. civil engrng. and engrng. mechanics lab., 1981-83; cons. in field. Decorated Air Force Commendation medal with oak leaf cluster, Air Force Meritorious Service medal. Mem. ASME. Presbyterian. Contbr. articles to profl. jours.

BAHN, IRENE ELIZA SCHUYLER, author; b. Borodino, N.Y., June 19, 1895; d. William Scott and Carrie Eugene (Kennedy) Schuyler; A.B., Syracuse U., 1918; m. Chester Bert Bahn, June 25, 1921 (dec. 1962); children—Gilbert Schuyler, Chester Bert, Jerrold Philip. News reporter Syracuse (N.Y.) Jour., 1918-21; free lance poet and news corr. various newspapers, N.Y., Pa., 1921-32; publicity agt. Loew's Theatre, Syracuse, 1932-34, RKO Theatres, Syracuse, 1934-36; vol. publicity agt. various charitable orgns., Malverne, N.Y., 1936-60, Thousand Oaks, Calif., 1960—. Vol., S. Nassau Communities Hosp. Malverne Aux., 1944-62, pres., 1956-57; organizer Save the Name referendum upon incorporation Thousand Oaks, 1964; founding pres. Conejo Valley Hosp. Aux., 1963-68; vol. Los Robles Hosp. Aux., 1968—; founding mem. Conejo Valley Debutantes Ball Com., 1968-81; bd. dirs. Conejo Valley Hist. Soc., 1968-80, named Dona Conejo, 1970. Recipient Community Service medal Thousand Oaks C. of C., 1963; life mem. Conejo Players, 1976. Mem. AAUW, Alpha Chi Omega. Republican. Presbyterian. Clubs: Conejo Valley Garden (hon. mem. 1975); Las Patronas. Home: 238 Encino Vista Dr Thousand Oaks CA 91362 Mailing Address: 615 Brandywine Dr Newport News VA 23602

BAHNEMANN, DETLEF WERNER, chemistry educator; b. Berlin, Apr. 20, 1953; came to U.S., 1985; s. Dietrich Emil Karl and Stephanie Martha (Jaensch) B.; m. Marion Gisela Zimmer, May 6, 1984; children: Bastian Arne, Janina Stephanie. Diplom Chemiker, Tech. U., Berlin, 1977, PhD, 1981. Sr. research fellow Hahn-Meitner Inst., Berlin, 1981-85; research assoc. Calif. Inst. Tech., Pasadena, 1985—; Contbr. articles to profl. jours. Mem. Am. Chem. Soc., Gesellschaft Deutscher Chemiker, Assn. Radiation Research, Soc. Free Radical Research. Lutheran. Home: 1273 Dominion Ave Pasadena CA 91104 Office: Calif Inst Tech 1201 California Blvd #138/78 Pasadena CA 91125

BAI, MONTY WOOSOON, mechanical engineer; b. Chung Ju, Republic of Korea, Feb. 2, 1940; came to U.S., 1966; s. Suck Chang and Gee Soo (Han) B.; m. Sue Elizabeth Stoll, Dec. 28, 1971; children: Monica, Dena. BSME, In-Ha Inst. Tech., Inchon, Republic of Korea, 1964; MSEM, U. Mo., Rolla, 1970, PhDME, 1974. Research engr. Vibro/Dynamics, La Grange, Ill., 1974-76; prin. staff engr. mech. engring. lab. Motorola Inc., Scottsdale, Ariz., 1976-84, mem. tech. staff tactical electronics div., 1984—. Patentee in field. Avocations: sculpture, painting. Home: 8107 E Cholla Rd Scottsdale AZ 85260 Office: Motorola Tactical Electronics Div 8220 E Roosevelt Scottsdale AZ 85252

BAILEY, BERNARD ALLEN, food supplement manufacturing executive; b. Grinnell, Iowa, Feb. 1, 1918; s. Harvey Manzel and Harriett Myrtle (Black) B.; m. Grace Ellerton, Mar. 21, 1947; children—Brent Ellerton, Elaine Ellerton Denault. B.A., Grinnell Coll., 1939. Adjuster State Farm Ins., Pasadena, Calif., 1946-48; gen. sales mgr. Mytinger Corp., Long Beach, Calif., 1948-63; gen. sales mgr. Nutrilite Products, Inc., Buena Park, Calif., 1963-68, v.p. sales, 1968-76, v.p. mktg. and sales services, 1976—. Pres. Travelers Aid, Long Beach, 1956-58; bd. dirs. Campfire Girls, Long Beach, 1964-78, mem. personnel com., 1978—; bd. dirs. Community Chest, Long Beach, 1953-57; trustee Lutheran Ch., Long Beach, 1964-73. Served with USCG, 1942-46. Decorated Air Medal. Club: Old Ranch Country (Los Alamitos, Calif.). Office: Nutrilite Products Inc 5600 Beach Blvd Buena Park CA 90622

BAILEY, BRIAN DENNIS, management consultant, author, publisher; b. Tacoma, June 10, 1952; s. Hugh Charles and Elsie Denise (Hinds) B.; B.B.A., Pacific Luth. U., Tacoma, 1975; M.B.A., City U. Seattle, 1982; Th.D. (hon.), Shekinah Sch. of Ministries, Tacoma, 1983; Ph.D. in Bus. Adminstrn., Century U., Beverly Hills, Calif., 1985. Prin. Brian D. Bailey, Mgmt. Cons., Tacoma, 1975—; pres. and chief exec. officer Bailey & Ellis, Inc., Tacoma, 1985—; adj. instr. City U., Seattle, 1986—. Mem. corp. bd., pres. Shekinah Ministries, Tacoma; pres. Young Democrats So. Pierce County, 1975-76. Served with USAF, 1971-73, with res. Mem. Full Gospel Businessmen's Fellowship Internat., World Bible Way Fellowship, Inc., Christian Writers Guild, Grange of Washington State. Home: PO Box 44757 Tacoma WA 98444 Office: Bailey & Ellis Inc PO Box 44757 Tacoma WA 98444-0757

BAILEY, BROWNELL MONROE, real estate development consultant; b. Concord, Mass., Aug. 3, 1953; s. Bruce Monroe and Joan Merril (Gesner) B.; m. Frances Louise Lockwood, Sept. 16, 1978; children: Brandon Little, Spencer Carleton, Trent Davis. BA in Modern Lang., Union Coll., 1976; cert., Université de Rennes, France, 1977; BS in Urban Planning and Engrng. with highest honors, Worcester Poly. Inst., 1980. Teaching. asst. Républic de France, Rennes, 1976-77; research asst. Transam. Computer Corp., San Francisco, 1977-78; land evaluator Commonwealth of Mass., Boston, 1978-80; project engr. Robillard and Assocs., Dillon, Colo., 1980-83; project mgr. Sawmill Sta. Assocs., Breckenridge, Colo., 1983—; sec.-treas. Breck-Air Inc., Breckenridge, 1982—. Mem. council Town of Breckenridge, 1983—; vice-chmn. Upper Blue Planning Commn., Breckenridge, 1983-86; bd. dirs. Summit Stage Transit Bd., Dillon, 1984-86; rep. Colo. Mcpl. League, Denver, 1984-86. NSF grantee, 1979. Mem. Urban Land Inst., Am. Planning Assn., Alliance Francaise. Episcopalian. Avocations: racquet sports, skiing, sailing, rafting. Home: 5380 Ridge Trail Littleton CO 80123 Office: Sawmill Sta Assocs Ltd 130 Ski Hill Rd Box 2177 Breckenridge CO 80424

BAILEY, CARL BOWMAN, industrial hygienist; b. Balt., May 31, 1949; s. Carl Elliott and Sara Kathryn (Bowman) B.; m. Rosemarie Therese Smith, Sept. 17, 1979. BS, U. Md., 1971; M in Health Sci., Johns Hopkins U., 1976. Staff scientist Enviro Control, Inc., Rockville, Md., 1976-80; indsl. hygienist Molycorp, Inc., Questa, N.Mex., 1980-85; sr. indsl. hygienist Unocal, Inc., Questa, 1985-86, Brea, Calif., 1986—. Mem. Am. Indsl. Hygiene Assn. (bd. dirs. Rio Grande Sect. 1985—), AAAS. Democrat. Avocations: travel, photography, gardening, hiking. Home: 6906 Eureka Dr Riverside CA 92503 Office: Unocal 376 S Valencia Ave PO Box 76 Brea CA 92621

BAILEY, DANA KAVANAGH, radiophysicist, botanist; b. Clarendon Hills, Ill., Nov. 22, 1916; s. Dana Clark and Dorothy (Kavanagh) B. B.S. with highest distinction, U. Ariz., 1937; postgrad., Harvard U., 1940; B.A. (Rhodes scholar) Queen's Coll., Oxford U., 1940, M.A., 1943, D.Sc., 1967. Astronomer expdn. to Peru for Hayden Planetarium, N.Y.C., 1937; physicist Antarctic expdn. U.S. Antarctic Service, 1940-41; project engr. Project RAND Douglas Aircraft Co., Santa Monica, Calif., 1946-48; physicist Nat. Bur. Standards, Washington, 1948-55; physicist, cons. Nat. Bur. Standards, Boulder, Colo., 1959-66; radiophysicist, research botanist Space Environment Lab., Environ. Research Labs., Nat. Oceanic and Atmospheric Adminstrn., Boulder, 1966-76; sci. dir. Page Communications Engrs., Inc., Washington, 1955-59; U.S. Exchange rep. Brit. Antarctic Survey Falkland Islands and Antarctica, 1967-68; research assoc. in physics Rhodes U., Grahamstown, Republic South Africa, 1970-71; assoc. in gymnosperms U. Colo. Mus., 1972—; internat. chmn. study group internat. radio consultative com. Internat. Telecommunication Union, Geneva, 1956-78. Contbr. articles to profl. jours. Served to maj., Signal Corps AUS, 1941-46. Decorated Legion of Merit; recipient Arthur S. Flemming govt. award Washington Jr. C. of C., 1951; Silver medal Dept. Commerce, 1952; Gold medal, 1956. Fellow AAAS, Am. Phys. Soc., Am. Geog. Soc., Royal Astron. Soc., Royal Geog. Soc.; mem. Sci. Research Soc. Am. (pres. Boulder br. 1967-68), Am. Geophys. Union, Am. Astron. Soc., Geog. Soc. Lima (hon.), Phi Beta Kappa., Sigma Xi. Clubs: Cosmos (Washington); Explorers (N.Y.C.). Home: 1441 Bluebell Ave Boulder CO 80302 Office: Univ Colo Museum Boulder CO 80309

BAILEY, DOUGLAS KENT, data processing manager; b. Pensacola, Fla., Mar. 16, 1949; s. Homer Dwight and Marjorie Louise (Shaw) B.; m. Wynette Lynn Kau, Apr. 26, 1986. BS cum laude, Wake Forest U., 1971; JD, Case Western Res. U., 1974. Bar: Ohio. Bus. analyst Union Carbide Corp., N.Y.C., 1974-76; legal analyst Fed. Jud. Ctr., Washington, 1976-81; court mgmt. analyst Jud. Council Calif., San Francisco, 1981-82, mgr. court mgmt. services unit, 1982, mgr. data processing unit, 1982—. Home: 1434 Saint Charles St Alameda CA 94501 Office: Jud Council Calif 350 McAllister St #3154 San Francisco CA 94102

BAILEY, ELAINE KVES, personnel consultant; b. Sacramento, July 21, 1943; d. George James and Gladys Goldie (Wood) Kves; divorced; children: Stacy, Erik. BA in Speech and Communications, Calif. State U.-Sacramento, 1966; MA in Mgmt. and Personnel Adminstrn., Cen. Mich. U., 1978; postgrad. U. So. Calif. Trainer, recruiter ARC, Washington, 1966-68; edn. counselor, ctr. dir. U.S. Army, W. Ger., 1969-71; program dir., instr. Hawaii Pacific Coll., Honolulu, 1977-79, mgmt. trainer, cons. Hawaii State Personnel Dept., Honolulu, 1979-83; instr. U. Hawaii-Manoa Coll. Bus. Adminstrn.; mgr., Personnel and Indsl. Relations Dept.; pres. Pacific-Rim Mgmt. Assocs. Inc. Author numerous tng. and personnel manuals. Mem. local bd. SSC; mem. Neighborhood Bd. 25 Edn., Planning and Zoning com. Mem. Bus. Women's Assn., Women Pacific Assn., AAUW, Honolulu Bd. Realtors, Am. Soc. Tng. and Devel., Nat. Assn. Female Execs., SBA Hawaii, Acad. Mgmt., Am. Soc. Personnel Adminstrs., Cen. Mich. U. Alumni Assn., Am. Overseas Assn., Sigma Iota Epsilon. Clubs: Mililani Tennis. Home: 1415 Victoria St #506 Honolulu HI 96822 Office: 2404 Maile Way Mail Box C Honolulu HI 96822

BAILEY, HENRY JOHN, III, lawyer, educator; b. Pitts., Apr. 4, 1916; s. Henry J. and Lenore Powell Bailey Cahoon; m. Marjorie Jane Ebner, May 30, 1949; children: George W., Christopher G., Barbara W., Timothy P. Student, U.S. Naval Acad., 1934-36; B.A., Pa. State U., 1939; J.D., Yale U., 1947. Bar: N.Y. 1948, Mass. 1963, Oreg. 1974. Ins. investigator Liberty Mut. Ins. Co., N.Y.C., 1941-42; atty. Fed. Res. Bank of N.Y., N.Y.C., 1947-55; asst. v.p. Empire Trust Co., N.Y.C., 1955-56; atty., legal dept. Am. Bankers Assn., N.Y.C., 1956-62; editor Banking Law Jour., Boston, 1962-65; asso. prof. law Willamette U., Salem, Oreg., 1965-69; prof. Willamette U., 1969-81, prof. emeritus, 1981—, adj. prof., 1981—; counsel firm Churchill, Leonard, Brown & Donaldson, Salem, 1981-85; vis. prof. U. Akron Sch. Law, 1983-84, Fla. State U. Coll. Law, 1984-85, Rutgers Sch. Law, Camden, N.J., 1985—; cons., lectr. to bar and banking groups; lectr. Banking Sch. of South, Baton Rouge, 1972, 73, 75. Author: The Law of Bank Checks, 1960, 5th edit., 1979; periodic supplements Modern Uniform Commercial Code Forms, 1963; (with Clarke and Young) Bank Deposits and Collections, 1972, UCC Deskbook: A Short Course in Commercial Paper, 1973, (with Robert D. Hursh) The American Law of Products Liability, 3d edit, 1984, (with William D. Hawkland) The Sum and Substance of Commercial Paper, 1976, 80, Secured Transactions in a Nutshell, 1976, 2d edit., 1981, Oregon Uniform Commercial Code, 3 vols., 1983, 84, 86; Contbr. articles on sales, products liability, comml. paper and secured transactions to legal jours. Served to 1st lt. USAAF, 1942-45; lt. col. Res.; ret. Mem. Am. Bar Assn. (chmn. subcom. on comml. paper 1965-66, 79-81), Am. Law Inst. (mem. editorial bd. The Practical Lawyers 1981—), Oreg. State Bar, Lambda Chi Alpha. Republican. Roman Catholic. Office: 530 Center St NE PO Box 804 Salem OR 97308 Office: Fla State U Coll Law Tallahassee FL 32306

BAILEY, JAMES EDWARD, industrial engineer, educator; b. Detroit, Jan. 16, 1942; s. Edward Durbin and Frieda (Kriewall) B.; m. Petra Kapahnke, Feb. 6, 1966; children: Michael, Heidi. BS Indsl. Engring., Wayne State U., 1964, MS Indsl. Engring., 1966, PhD, 1975. Cert. profl. engr., Ariz. Mfg. engr. Gen. Motors, Detroit, 1965-67; systems analyst Nat. Bank Detroit, 1967-68; instr. engring. Wayne State U., Detroit, 1968-74; prof. Ariz. State U., Tempe, 1974—; chief exec. officer Kurta Corp., Tempe, 1981. Author: Integrated Production Control Systems, 1982, Scheduling Computers, 1984; editor: Energy Systems, 1978; contbr. articles to profl. jours. Grantee Energy Mgmt. U.S. Dept. Energy, Health Care Info. systems U.S. Dept. Health, 1985, Energy Mgmt. Ariz. Dept. Energy, Phoenix, 1978-83. Mem. Inst. Mgmt. Sci., Soc. Mgmt. Info. Systems (editor jour. 1982-86), Am. Prodn. Inventory Control, Inst. Indsl. Engring. (v.p., dir. Southwest U.S. states 1980-82), Soc. Ariz. Artificial Intelligence (founder, dir. 1985-86), Tau Beta Pi, Alpha Pi Mu. Home: 2032 N Gentry Mesa AZ 85203 Office: Ariz State U Dept Indsl Engring Tempe AZ 85287

BAILEY, KAREN ANN, marketing executive; b. Hobart, Ind.; d. Cecil Alonzo and Florence Elizabeth (Cihonski) Bailey. B.S. in Bus. Adminstrn. and Econs., Regis Coll., 1982. Various acctg. and fin. positions, Chgo. and Denver, 1975-78; fin. analyst II, Adolph Coors Co., Golden, Colo., 1979-82, distbr. econs./expansion analyst, 1982-83, supr. young adult mktg., 1983-84, sr. distbr. econs./expansion analyst, 1984-86, area sales mgr., San Diego, 1986—. Office: Adolph Coors Co SW Div 24022 Calle De La Plata #580 San Diego CA 92653

BAILEY, KENNETH P., education educator, administrator; b. Benton Harbor, Mich., Feb. 17, 1912; s. Elton James and Lula Mae and Irene Marie Passarini, Aug. 11, 1936 children: Kenneth James, Darlene Marie. BA, UCLA, 1934, MA, 1936, PhD, 1938. Instr. history UCLA, 1938-39; chmn. social science department Oceanside (Calif.)-Carlsbad Coll., 1939-44, dir., 1948-50; supr. Oceanside-Carlsbad High Sch. and Jr. Coll., 1945-48; dean of students, prof. history, chmn. social scis. dept. Humboldt State Coll., Arcata, Calif., 1945-48; coordinator community services Long Beach (Calif.) City Coll., 1950-53; prin. Pacific High Sch., San Bernardino, Calif., 1953-67; dir. office tchr. edn. U. Calif., Irvine, 1967-83, sr. lectr. dept. history, 1983—; instr. dept. edn. U. Redlands, Calif., 1954—, U. Calif., Riverside, 1955—; with personnel Lockheed Aircraft, Burbank, 1942-43. Author books; editor profl. jours.; contbr. articles to profl. jours. Chmn. YMCA, San Bernardino, 1958-62, United Way, San Bernardino, 1965, Police Adv. Com., U. Calif., Irvine, 1978-82; active Liaison Com. on Liberal Studies, U. Calif. and Calif. State U., Berkeley, 1981-84, Cen. Dem. Com., Humboldt County, Calif., 1948. Recipient Am. Hist. Assn. award, 1939, Calif. State Legis. award, 1967,. Mem. Internat. Reading Assn., Calif. Guidance Assn., Calif. Council for Social Studies, Assn. Calif. Adminstrs., Am. Assn. Higher Edn., Am. Hist. Assn., Assn. for Supr. and Curriculum Devel., NEA, Calif. Council on Ednl. Tchrs., Western Assn. Schs. and Colls. (assoc. evaluator, 1968), Calif. Statewide Social Sci. Framework Com. (chmn. 1959-62), Phi Delta Kappa. Lodge: Kiwanis (Long Beach club pres. 1952-53, San Bernardino club pres. 1973-74). Avocations: research, coaching football, fishing. Home: 18751 Via Siena Irvine CA 92715 Office: U Calif Dir Office Tchr Edn Social Sci Tower 479 Irvine CA 92717

BAILEY, LEONARD LEE, surgeon; b. Takoma Park, Md., Aug. 28, 1942; s. Nelson Hulburt and Catherine Effie (Long) B.; B.S., Columbia Union Coll., 1960-64; postgrad NIH, 1965; M.D., Loma Linda U., 1969; m. Nancy Ann Schroeder, Aug. 21, 1966; children—Jonathan Brooks, Charles Connor. Intern, Loma Linda U. Med. Center, 1969-70, resident in surgery, 1970-73, resident in thoracic and cardiovascular surgery, 1973-74; resident in pediatric cardiovascular surgery Hosp. for Sick Children, Toronto, Ont., Can., 1974-75; resident in thoracic and cardiovascular surgery Loma Linda U. Med. Sch., 1975-76, asst. prof. surgery, 1976—, asst. prof. pediatrics, 1978—, dir. pediatric cardiac surgery, 1976—. Diplomate Am. Bd. Surgery, Am. Bd. Thoracic Surgery. Mem. Am. Coll. Cardiology, Soc. Thoracic Surgery, Am. Assn. Thoracic Surgery, Western Thoracic Surg. Assn., Western Soc. Pediatric Research, Walter E. McPherson Soc. (clin. investigator of year 1976, 85). Democrat. Seventh-day Adventist. Office: Loma Linda U Med Center Loma Linda CA 92350

BAILEY, NORMA JEAN, museum director; b. Cin., Dec. 29, 1930; d. Carl Edward and Juanita Grace Moore; m. Louis Ray Sandefur, Jan., 1953 (div.); 1 child, Jeffrey Mark; m. William Holcomb Hughes, Apr. 18, 1964 (div.); 1 child, Melinda Ann; m. William J. Bailey, Mar. 29, 1986. B.S., Western Ky. U., 1952. Cytotechnologist, Cancer Control Unit, field investigation Nat. Cancer Inst., NIH, Memphis, 1954-57; supr. cytotechnology lab., pathology dept. Bapt. Meml. Hosp., Memphis, 1957-60, Barger and Likos Med. Lab., Phoenix, 1960-63; tchr. Flagstaff, Ariz., Memphis, Twin Falls, Idaho, 1965-71; cytotechnologist Automated Pathology Services, Phoenix, 1973-75, supr., 1975-76; dir. Mohave Mus. of History and Arts, Kingman, Ariz., 1979—. Mem. exec. bd. Kingman Centennial Commn., 1979-83; mem. Kingman Hist. Preservation Commn., 1979-84, 86—, Kingman Econ. and Tourism Devel. Commn., 1987—, Kingman Republican Women. Named Citizen of Yr. Elks, 1986. Mem. AAUW, Ariz. Hist. Soc., Ariz. Paper and Photograph Conservation Group, LWV, Mohave Artists and Craftsmen's Guild (bd. dirs.), Mohave County Geneal. Soc., Mohave Archeol. Soc. (bd. dirs.). Methodist. Clubs: Soroptimists Internat. of Kingman (sec. 1981, pres. 1985-86), 1982), Toastmasters (edn. v.p. 1984-85). Home: 300 Astor Kingman AZ 86401 Office: Mohave Mus of History and Arts 400 W Beale Kingman AZ 86401

BAILEY, PALMER KENT, geologist; b. Bismarck, N.D., Oct. 27, 1947; s. Raymond Romeo and Helen Lorraine (Palmer) B.; m. Bonnie Linae Norell, June 14, 1970; 1 child, Laura. BS in Geology, U. N.D., 1970, BS in Geol. Engring., 1980, MS in Geology, 1980; grad. with honors, Army Command and Gen. Staff Coll., Fort Leavenworth, Kans., 1984. Registered profl. engr., Va. Commd. 2nd lt. U.S. Army, 1970, advanced through grades to lt. col., 1987; commdr. engr. and support cos. U.S. Army, Alaska and Fed. Republic of Germany, 1971-77; chief mil. engr. U.S. Army, Fort Richardson, Alaska, 1977-78; assoc. prof. U.S. Mil. Acad., West Point, N.Y., 1980-83; exec. officer 4th Engr. Battalion U.S. Army, Fort Carson, Colo., 1984-86; geol. sci. advisor Astronaut Office NASA, Houston, 1986—; leader on five geol. field expeditions in Alaska, 1979-83. Contbr. West Point Atlas of Landforms, 1984; contbr. articles to profl. jours. Recipient Henry Hines scholarship U. N.D., 1969, award for scholastic excellence U.N.D. alumni Assn., 1979. Mem. Geol. Soc. Am., Am. Scientific Affiliation, Sigma Gamma Epsilon (v.p. 1968-69), Sigma Xi (award of merit 1980), Phi Beta Kappa. Avocations: hiking, camping, skiing, woodworking, reading.

BAILEY, PATRICIA SUSAN, physician; b. N.Y.C., Dec. 18, 1943; d. Joel and Ethel (Miller) Salzburg; B.S. magna cum laude, Central Mich. U., 1970, M.A., 1972; M.D., Mich. State U., 1977 . Clin. instr. Mich. State U. Coll. Human Medicine, 1976-77; resident Los Angeles County-Harbor Gen. Hosp., UCLA Med. Center, Torrance, 1977-78; partner, physician in emergency medicine Kaiser-Permanente Hosp., Harbor City, Calif., 1978—; instr. Am. Heart Assn.; clin. instr. U. So. Calif. Coll. Medicine. Trustee, Delta Coll., 1972-74. Mem. Am. Coll. Emergency Medicine, Am. Physicians for Human Rights, Am. Physicians for Social Responsibility, Gay Acad. Union, So. Calif. Women for Understanding, NOW. Jewish. Author: (novel) The Summer of the Flea, 1980; contbr. to Echoes from the Heart (poetry anthology), 1982; contbr. articles to various publs. Office: Kaiser Permanente Hosp 1050 W Pacific Coast Hwy Harbor City CA 90710

BAILEY, PHILIP MARTIN, domestic service executive; b. Peterborough, N.H., Oct. 25, 1935; s. Herbert Martin and Edna Marie (Nelson) B.; m. Charlotte Rita Cooney, Sept. 1, 1972; children: Michael, Lisa, Timothy Bailey, Charles E. Cooney. BA, Northeastern Ill. U., 1972; MPH, U. Ill. Med. Ctr., Chgo., 1977. Enlisted USN, 1953, advanced through grades to chief petty officer, ret., 1976; mgr. housekeeping Red Top, Inc., Denver, 1976-77; dir. housekeeping Rehab. Inst. Chgo., 1977-79; mem. faculty City Wide Coll., Chgo., 1979-82; v.p. Housekeeping Tng. Assocs., Scottsdale, Ariz., 1980—. Author: Cleaning Public Buildings, 1980; co-author Manual for Clin. Chemistry, 1965; contbr. articles to profl. jours. Recipient Certificate of Appreciation City Wide Coll., Chgo., 1979, 81. Mem. Nat. Exec. Housekeepers Assn., Inc. (gov. Pacific S.W. dist. 1985—, 2d vice gov. Pacific S.W. dist. 1983-85, pres. Chgo. chpt. 1979-82, cert., Certificate of award 1984, Outstanding Member award 1985), Fleet Res. Assn., VFW. Lutheran. Avocations: swimming, traveling, reading, sports.

BAILEY, RAY THEODORE, marketing consultant; b. Clifton, N.J., Aug. 26, 1913; s. James Garfield and Anna (Pedersen) B.; grad. Clifton High Sch.; m. Laura Jean Schanze, Dec. 1, 1948; children—Cynthia, Raymond, James, Gretchen, Guy, Laurie. Editor, pub. 3 Weekly Newspapers, Flemington, N.J., 1943-46; publs. and sales promotion dir. Thermoid Co., Trenton, N.J., 1946; advt. mgr. Borden Foods Co., N.Y.C., 1947-54; mktg. dir. This Week mag., N.Y.C., 1954-60; group mktg. dir. J. Walter Thompson, N.Y.C., 1960-65; v.p. Gift Stars, Inc., Mpls., 1965-67; pres. Luncheon Is Served, Inc., Tucson, 1967-77, chmn. bd., dir., 1967-83; chmn. bd. Party Line, Inc., 1968-77; chmn. bd. Internat. Mktg. Assos., Ariz.; chmn. Ariz. Territory Land Investment Co., Good Life Inc.; dir. in charge U.S. and Can., United Survival Products Internat. (U.K.) Ltd.; lectr. univs. including Mich. State U., So. Calif., Cornell U.; del. White House Conf. on Small Bus., 1979; U.S. del., speaker Internat Small Bus. Symposium, Berlin, 1979, 1st World Assembly on Small Bus., New Delhi, 1980; trustee, Nat. Citizens Com. Working with Congress on Paperwork Reduction, 1977-78. Recipient top award in America for weekly, 1943; gen. excellence award NEA. Mem. Nat. Small Bus. Assn. (trustee emeritus, v.p., exec. com.). Home and Office: 7022 Blue Lake Dr Tucson AZ 85715

BAILEY, ROBERT C., opera company executive; b. Metropolis, Ill., Dec. 28, 1936; m. Sally McDermott, July 13, 1958. B.A. in Speech, U. Ill., 1958, M.A. in English, 1960; B.M. in Applied Voice, Eastman Sch. Music, 1965; M.M. in Applied Voice, New Eng. Conservatory Music, 1969. Music producer Nat. Pub. Radio, Washington, 1971-73, dir. cultural programming, 1973-75; mgr. Western Opera Theater, San Francisco, 1975-79; instr. arts mgmt. Golden Gate U., San Francisco, 1977-82; cons. arts mgmt., San Francisco, 1980-82; gen. dir. Portland Opera Assn., Oreg., 1982—; dir. Oreg. Advocates Arts, Portland, 1982—; cons. On-Site Program Nat. Endowment Arts, Washington, 1982—; judge Met. Opera Auditions, 1977—. Clubs: Bohemian (San Francisco); City (Portland). Lodge: Rotary. Office: Portland Opera Assn 1530 SW 2d St Portland OR 97201

BAILEY, ROBERT TERRY, landscape contracting company executive; b. Detroit, Oct. 9, 1938; s. Winfield Walter and Florance Marie (Griffen) B.; m. Marilyn Marie Evans, Nov. 8, 1958; children—Deborah Marie, Terry Robert. Co-owner Bailey-Sperber, Inc. (doing bus. as Century Landscape Contractors, Hydro West Landscape Contractors, Robert T. Bailey Landscape Constrn.), Agoura, Calif., 1968—. Recipient state landscape awards Calif. Landscape Contractors Assn., 1970, 71, Los Angeles bus. and industry award, 1973-74, 85, 86; Nat. Instl. Landscaping award Mrs. Patricia Nixon, 1973. Mem. Am. Landscape Contractors Assn. (nat. environ. grand award 1976, 80, 82, 84, 86, 87), Am. Assn. Nurserymen. Major projects include UCLA, U. Calif-Irvine, Los Angeles Internat. Airport, freeway systems State of Calif., Hughes Aircraft Nat. Hdqrs., U.S. Olympic Com. Field and Track, others.

BAILEY, ROLENE MARIE, lawyer; b. San Francisco, Feb. 13, 1938; d. Roland Herman Eichman and Alice Roberta (Wreath) Sloman; m. James E. Bailey, June 15, 1956 (div. 1981); children: Christopher E., Norene L.; m. William J. Kiesling. BA in History, San Jose State U., MA in Librarianship, MA in History; JD, Lincoln U. Bar: Calif. 1984. Tech. services librarian Santa Clara County Law Library, San Jose, Calif., 1973-86; reference librarian Sunnyvale (Calif.) Pub. Library, 1974-75, Heafy Law Library Santa

Clara U., 1985—; atty. Los Gatos, Calif., 1984—. Vol. Time Out Respite Care Program, San Jose, 1985—. Fellow Ralph Lutz Meml., San Jose State U., 1972; Alice Schroeder scholar, 1955. Mem. ABA, State Bar Calif., Am. Assn. Law Libraries, No. Calif. Assn. Law Libraries. Democrat. Roman Catholic. Avocations: needlework, photography, golfing, fishing. Home: 336 Penn Way Los Gatos CA 95030

BAILEY, STEVEN CLIFFORD, state official; b. Yuba City, Calif., Sept. 30, 1951; s. Richard Darwin and Irma Bailey; m. Kathleen Briggs, Dec. 11, 1976; children—John, Kristine. BA in Govt., Calif. State U.-Sacramento, 1976, JD, Lincoln Sch. Law., 1987; Legis. asst. to Senator John V. Briggs, Fullerton, Calif., 1975-77; pres. Starburst Consulting, Fullerton, 1977-80, Steven Bailey & Assocs., Sacramento, 1980-83; dep. dir. Calif. State Dept. Social Services, Sacramento, 1983—; treas. Found. Constitutional Edn., Sacramento, 1978—. Chmn. Western Fedn. Coll. Republicans, 1975; active Calif. State Republican Central Com., 1978—; pres. Golden West Paradise Property Owners Assn., Diamond Springs, Calif., 1983-85, Golden West Community Services Dist., Diamond Springs, 1984—; commr. Diamond Springs/El Dorado Fire Protection Dist., 1985—. Mem. Calif. Wool Growers Assn. Republican. Baptist. Club: Calif. Rep. Assembly. Office: Calif State Dept Social Services 744 P St MS 17-32 Sacramento CA 95814

BAILIN, TOBY, business executive; b. Cleve., June 7, 1941; d. Hayman Edward and Annette (Shor) Bailin; m. John W. Gilje, Aug. 22, 1965 (div. 1970). B.A., U. Mich., 1963, M.A., 1964; now postgrad. U. Hawaii. Copywriter Sta. KGMB, CBS, Honolulu, 1969-72; mem. pub. relations dept. Milici Advt. affiliate Doyle, Dane Bernbach, Honolulu, 1972-73, First Hawaiian Bank, Honolulu, 1973-78; asst. to pub. relations dir. Amfac, Inc., Honolulu, 1978; asst. v.p., asst. to chmn. and pres., 1978-82; v.p., asst. to chmn., 1983—. Editor co. mag. Panako (Best Overall Publ. award 1977). Bd. dirs. Hawaii Pub. Radio, Honolulu, 1985, Relationship Tng. Inst., Honolulu, 1985, Jewish Fedn. Hawaii, Honolulu, 1985; chmn. Dem. for Reagan, Honolulu, 1984, publicity com. The Outdoor Circle, Honolulu, 1983—; mem. adv. bd. Hawaii State Dept. Social Services and Housing, Correction Industries. Mem. Pub. Relations Soc. Am., Honolulu C. of C. (bd. dirs. 1985—, pub. affairs com.), Navy League, Orgn. Women Leaders (dir.), Japan Am. Soc. Honolulu. Clubs: Honolulu, Plaza. Office: Amfac Inc 700 Bishop St 21st Floor PO Box 3230 Honolulu HI 96801

BAILY, NORMAN A., radiology educator; b. N.Y.C., July 2, 1915; s. Louis D. and Ida (Bolet) B.; m. Rose Levine, Nov. 21, 1940; children: Philip, Barbara Baily Black. BS in Sci., St. Johns Univ., 1941; MA in Edn., NYU, 1943; PhD in Physics, Columbia U., 1952. Diplomate Am. Bd. Radiology, Am. Bd. Health Physics. Chief physicist, prin. cancer research scientist Roswell Park Meml. Inst., Buffalo, 1954-59; mgr. space sci. dept. Hughes Research Labs., Malibu, Calif., 1959-67; prof. radiology UCLA, 1959-68, Emory U., Atlanta, 1967-68; prof. U. Calif., San Diego, 1968—; cons. USN Regional Med. Ctr., San Diego, 1968—, VA Med. Ctr., San Diego, 1971—; vis. scientist CERN European Orgn. Nuclear Research, Switzerland, 1970; vis. prof. Hebrew U. Hadassah Med. Ctr., Israel, 1972; vis. prof. Korea Advanced Inst. of Sci. and Tech., 1982. Contbr. numerous articles to profl. jours. Named Henry Goldberg Prof., The Technion, 1980. Fellow: Am. Coll. Radiology; mem. AAAS, Am. Assn. Physicists in Medicine (mem. So. Calif. chpt.), Am. Phys. Soc., Am. Endocurietherapy Soc., Radiation Research Soc., Radiol. Soc. N.Am., Soc. Photo-Optical Instrumentation Engrs. Home: 8656 Cliffridge Ave La Jolla CA 92037 Office: U Calif San Diego Dept Radiology M-010 La Jolla CA 92093

BAIM, DEAN VERNON, economist, educator; b. Rockville Centre, N.Y., Dec. 3, 1949; s. Vernon Blyman and Lillian Bernice (Cornwell) B. BA in Econs. and Polit. Sci. with high honors, U. Calif., Santa Barbara, 1972; MA in Econs., UCLA, 1976, PhD, 1983. Cert. community coll. instr., Calif.; cert. elem. and secondary tchr., Calif. Adj. prof. econs. Pepperdine U., Malibu, Calif., 1977-83, instr., 1983-84, asst. prof., 1984—; dir. spl. projects Pacific Acad. for Advanced Studies, Los Angeles, 1979-86; cons. Internat. Assn. Auditorium Mgrs., Chgo., 1986—; instr. Acad. Econ. Edn., Richmond, Va., 1985—; mem. adv. bd. Ctr. Econ. Research and Edn., Northridge, Calif., 1984-85. Editor: Contemporary Econ. Issues, 1982—, econs. edn. newsletter, 1982—. Named Outstanding Prof. of Yr., Soc. Advancement Mgmt., Pepperdine U. chpt., 1984, Outstanding Young Man of Am., 1986. Mem. Western Econ. Assn., Assn. Pvt. Enterprise Educators, Omicron Delta Epsilon (co-founder, treas. Pi chpt. 1970-71; pres. 1971-72). Home: 21315 Bellini Dr Topanga CA 90290 Office: Pepperdine U Dept Bus Adminstrn Malibu CA 90265

BAIN, CONRAD STAFFORD, actor; b. Lethbridge, Alta., Can., Feb. 4, 1923; came to U.S., 1946, naturalized, 1946; s. Stafford Harrison and Jean Agnes (Young) B.; m. Monica Marjorie Sloan, Sept. 4, 1945; children: Kent Stafford, Mark Alexander, Jennifer Jean. Grad., Am. Acad. Dramatic Art, 1948. founder Actors Fed. Credit Union, 1962. Broadway appearances include Candide, 1957, Lost in the Stars, 1958, Hot Spot, 1963, Advise and Consent, 1961, Twigs, 1971, Uncle Vanya, 1973; off-Broadway appearances include The Iceman Cometh, 1957, Hogan's Goat, 1966, Scuba Duba, 1967, The Kitchen, 1968, Steambath, 1969; film appearances A Lovely Way to Die, 1967, Who Killed Mary Whats er Name, 1968, Up the Sand Box, 1970, C.H.O.M.P.S, 1979, Child Bride of Short Creek, 1982; co-star: TV series Maude, 1971-78; star: TV series Diff'rent Strokes, 1978-86, Mr. President, 1987—. Served with Canadian Army, World War II. Mem. Actors Equity Assn. (councilor 1962-76), ANTA West (dir. since 1977). Club: Players (N.Y.C.). Office: 1901 Ave of Stars Los Angeles CA 90067

BAIN, WILLIAM JAMES, JR., architect; b. Seattle, June 26, 1930; s. William James and Mildred Worline (Clark) B.; m. Nancy Sanford Hill, Sept. 21, 1957; children: David Hunter, Stephen Fraser (dec.), Mark Sanford, John Worthington. B.Arch., Cornell U., 1953. Partner NBBJ Group (formerly Naramore, Bain, Brady & Johanson), Seattle; juror, lectr. U. Wash., Seattle, Wash. State U. Prin. works include various research insts., mcpl. bldgs., office complexes, and community plans. Bd. dirs. Downtown Seattle Assn., 1980—, Arboretum Found., 1971-74; bd. dirs. Seattle Symphony Orch., 1974—, pres., 1977-79; mem. affiliate program steering com. Coll. Architecture and Urban Planning, U. Wash., 1969-71. Served to 1st lt., C.E. U.S. Army, 1953-55. Recipient cert. of achievement Port of Whittier, Alaska, 1955, Disting. Alumnus award Lakeside Sch., 1985. Fellow AIA (pres. Seattle chpt. 1969, chmn. N.W. Regional Student-Profl. Fund 1971, pres. Wash. State council 1974), N.W. Regional Archtl. Found. (pres. 1975); mem. Seattle C. of C. (dir. 1980-83), Nat. Assn. Indsl. and Office Parks, Urban Land Inst., Nat. Assn. Corp. Real Estate Execs., Downtown Seattle Assn. (dir. 1980—, exec. com. 1983—), Northwest Forum, Am. Arbitration Assn. (comml. panel 1975—), L'Ogive Soc., Lambda Alpha, Phi Delta Theta. Episcopalian. Clubs: Rainier, Wash. Athletic, University, Tennis (Seattle); University, Columbia Tower. Lodge: Rotary. Home: 1631 Rambling Ln Bellevue WA 98004 Office: NBBJ Group 111 S Jackson St Seattle WA 98104

BAIR, WILLIAM J., radiation biologist; b. Jackson, Mich., July 14, 1924; s. William J. and Mona J. (Gamble) B.; m. Barbara Joan Sites, Feb. 16, 1952; children: William J., Michael Braden, Andrew Emil. B.A. in chemistry, Ohio Wesleyan U., 1949; Ph.D. in Radiation Biology, U. Rochester, 1954. NRC-AEC fellow U. Rochester, 1949-50, research asso. radiation biology, 1950-54; biol. scientist Hanford Labs. of Gen. Electric Co., Richland, Wash., 1954-56, mgr. inhalation toxicology sect., biology dept., 1956-65; mgr. inhalation toxicology sect., biology dept. Battelle Meml. Inst., 1965-68; mgr. biology dept. Pacific Northwest Labs., Richland, Wash., 1968-74, dir. life scis. program, 1973-75, mgr. biomed. and environ. research program, 1975-76, mgr. environ. health and safety research program, 1976-86, mgr. life scis. ctr., 1986—; lectr. radiation biology Joint Center Grad. Study, Richland, 1955—; cons. to advisory com. on reactor safeguards Nuclear Regulatory Commn., 1971—; also mem. several coms. on plutonium toxicology; mem. subcom. inhalation hazards, com. pathologic effects atomic radiation Nat. Acad. Sci., 1957-64; mem. ad hoc com. on hot particles of subcom. biol. effects of ionizing radiation Nat. Acad. Scis.-NRC, 1974-76, vice chmn. Com. on Biol. Effects of Ionizing Radiation IV Alpha Radiation, 1985—; chmn. task force on biol. effects of inhaled particles Internat. Commn. on Radiol. Protection, 1970-79, mem. com. 2 on permissible dose for internal radiation, 1973—; chmn. Task Group on Respiratory Tract Models, 1984—; chmn. Hanford Symposium Inhaled Radioactive Particles and Gases, 1964; co-chmn. Hanford Symposium Biol. Implications of Transuranium Elements, 1971; chmn. Life Scis. Symposium on Radiation Protection—A Look to the Future, 1986; chmn. Am. Inst. Biol. Scis.-AEC-Energy Research and Devel. Adminstrn. Transuranium Tech. Group, 1972-75; mem. Nat. Council on Radiation Protection and Measurements, 1974—, bd. dirs., 1976-82, mem. com. of radionuclides on maximum permissible concentrations for occupational and non-occupational exposure, 1970-77, mem. com. basic radiation protection criteria, 1975—, chmn. ad hoc com. on hot particles, 1974, chmn. ad hoc com. internal emitter activities, 1976-77, mem. com. 57 on internal emitter standards, 1977—; U.S. participant and rep. numerous internat. confs., invited lectr. Japan AEC, Nat. Radiol. Health Inst., Chiba, 1969, South African Assn. Physicists in Medicine and Biology, Pretoria, 1980, North China Inst. Radiation Protection, 1984; mem. rev. com. Argonne Univs. Assn., 1977-80; chmn. Marshall Islands radiol. adv. group Dept. Energy, 1978-81; mem. staff Pres.'s Commn. on Accident at Three Mile Island, 1979-80; mem. regional steering com. on health effects from eruption of Mt. St. Helens, 1980-84; chmn. Dept. Energy task group on health and envrion. consequences of Soviet nuclear accident, 1986—. Author 100 books, articles, reports, chpts. in books.; lectr. Japan AEC. Recipient E.O. Lawrence Meml. award, 1970; cert. of appreciation AEC, 1975; Alumni Disting. Achievement citation Ohio Wesleyan U., 1986. Fellow AAAS, Health Physics Soc. (dir. 1970-73, pres.-elect 1983-84, pres. 1984-85); mem. Radiation Research Soc., N.Y. Acad. Sci., Soc. Exptl. Biology and Medicine (vice chmn. N.W. sect. 1967-70, 74—), Reticuloendothelial Soc., Soc. Occupational and Environ. Health, Sci. Soc. Pres. (council 1984-85), Sigma Xi. Club: Kiwanis (dir.). Demonstrated toxicology of plutonium and carcinogenisis of radioactive particles in lung. Home: 102 Somerset St Richland WA 99352 Office: Battelle Pacific NW Labs PO Box 999 Richland WA 99352

BAIRD, ALAN C., TV producer, writer; b. Waterville, Maine, Jan. 5, 1951; s. Chester A. and Beverly E. (Gilbert) B.; m. Lori J. Finn, July 29, 1983. BA, Mich. State U., 1973. Pres. Souterrain Teeshirts, Nice, France, 1977-78; page NBC, N.Y.C., 1979-80; producer, dir. Random Prodns., Hollywood, Calif., 1981; writer, producer Preview STV, N.Y.C., 1982-83, Sta. KCOP-TV, Hollywood, 1983-84; writer Vidiom Prodns., Hollywood, 1985—. Author: ATS Operations, 1976; producer (TV script) Live at the Palomino, 1981; writer (TV scripts) Night Court, 1986, 20/60, 1986, Golden Girls, 1986, Family Ties, 1986, Max Headroom, 1987. Crisis counselor San Francisco Suicide Prevention, 1975; prodn. asst. March of Dimes Telethon, Hollywood, 1985. Recipient Harvard Book prize Harvard U., Cambridge, Mass., 1969. Avocations: flying, running, sky diving, competitive driving.

BAIRD, BRUCE MARSHALL, banker; b. Salt Lake City, Oct. 19, 1946; s. Robert M. and Be-ty J. (Brown) B.; m. Jacqueline A. Shumway, July 27, 1968; children—Jeffrey, Marcie. B.S., U. Utah, 1970; postgrad. Pacific Coast Sch. Banking, 1976-78. Mgmt. trainee First Security Bank Utah, N.A., Salt Lake City, 1970-71, asst. br. mgr., 1971-73, br. mgr., 1973-78, asst. v.p., comml. loan officer, 1978-80, v.p., comml. loan officer, 1980-81, v.p., div. credit mgr., 1981-83, sr. v.p., mgr. Salt Lake div., 1983—, dir., 1983—. Mem. exec. com. Salt Lake Clearinghouse Assn., 1983; trustee Fin. Found., Salt Lake City, 1983; bd. dirs. Salt Lake chpt. ARC, 1984—. Mem. Robert Morris Assocs. Office: First Security Bank 79 S Main St Salt Lake City UT 84111

BAIRD, DALE SETH, retired state department administrator; b. Salt Lake City, Nov. 2, 1931; s. Seth and Leila Lavon (Bird) B.; m. Norma Jean Nelson, Mar. 27, 1951 (dec. Dec. 1981); children—Bradley Dale, Teri Lyn; m. 2d, Gloria Diane Barnes, May 22, 1982. Grad. high sch. Conservation officer Dept. Fish and Game, State of Idaho, 1956-65, regional conservation officer, 1965-74, chief enforcement, Boise, 1974-84; pres. Western States Law Enforcement Tech. Com., 1977; chmn. Peace Officer Standard Council, Boise, 1982-83. Contbr. articles to profl. jours. Dist. chmn. Teton Peaks council Boy Scouts Am., 1972. Served as cpl. U.S. Army, 1952-54. Recipient Cert. of Appreciation, Wash. State Sportsman's Assn., 1981. Mem. Idaho Peace Officers Assn., Nat. Wildlife Soc. Mormon. Lodges: Toastmasters (sec. treas. 1967-70), Rotary. Home: 6257 Morris Hill Boise ID 83704

BAIRD, JOHN JEFFERS, biology educator; b. North English, Iowa, Jan. 1, 1921; s. William Simon and Ruth Caroline (Jeffers) B.; m. Grace Geraldine Garner, Oct. 13, 1946; 1 child, Stephanie Lynn. BA in Sci., Iowa State Tchrs. Coll., 1948; MS in Zoology, U. Iowa, 1953, PhD, 1957. Cert. tchr., Iowa. Chief pilot M&T Aerial Spray Co., Cedar Falls, Iowa, 1948; tchr. Muscatine (Iowa) High Sch., 1948-54; from asst. prof. to prof. Calif. State U., Long Beach, 1956-67, dept. chmn., 1960-67; dep. dean, instr. State U., Long Beach, 1967-78; prof. biology Calif. Chancellors Office, Calif. State U., Long Beach, 1967-78; prof. biology Calif. State U., Long Beach, 1978—, prof. emeritus, 1984—. Mem., trustee Savanna Sch. Dist., Anaheim, Calif., 1965-81; mem. of session 1st Presbyn. Ch., Anaheim, 1975-78, pres. 1985—. Served to capt. USAFR, 1942-46, ETO, lt. col. Res. Named one of Outstanding Profs., Calif. State U. Associated Students, 1984. Fellow So. Calif. Acad. Sci.; mem. AAAS, Am. Soc. Zoologists, So. Calif. Acad. Sci. (pres. 1974-76, bd. dirs. 1968-81), Sigma Xi. Avocations: model airplanes, reading, travel. Office: Calif State U 1250 Bellflower Blvd Long Beach CA 90840

BAIRD, ROBERT ROY, real estate executive; b. Colorado Springs, Colo., Sept. 3, 1937; s. Eldred D. and Alice Eudora (Havens) B.; B.S. magna cum laude, Woodbury U., 1969; postgrad. Calif. State U., Northridge, 1970-71; m. Sally Ann Baird, Oct. 3, 1959; children—J. Brian, Sean Christopher, Robert Roy. Life agt. Manhattan Life Ins. Co., Encino, Calif., 1961-62; v.p. Red Top div. Am. Hosp. Supply Co., Los Angeles, 1962-73; pres. Baird Industries, Inc., Montrose, Calif., 1973-79; pres. Central Security Trust, Glendale, Calif., 1981—, Pension Vest Inc., 1982—, Cluck-in-a-Bucket, Inc, 1984—; dir. Baird Industries, Inc.; TV talk show host Channel 22, Los Angeles, 1981-83. Lector, St. Bede's Catholic Ch., LaCanada, Calif., 1977-81; mem. Long Beach Redevel. Agy., 1976; chmn. bd. Local 117 Selective Service; dist. chmn. Am. Cancer Soc., 1962; v.p. Lakeview Terrace (Calif.) Little League, 1974. Served with U.S. Army, 1955-57; ETO. Decorated Letter of Commendation; recipient Outstanding State Vice Pres. award Jr. C. of C., 1962, Phi Gamma Kappa award Woodbury U., 1969, Dora E. Kirby award Woodbury Coll., 1969; named Outstanding Mktg. Dir., Red Top, Inc., 1971-73. Mem. Assn. Interior Environmentalists (charter), Calif. Assn. Realtors, U.S. Olympic Volleyball Assn. (charter), Crescenta Valley C. of C. (pres. 1985), Nat. Assn. Pvt. Placement Syndicators (pres. 1985). Club: Crown City Kiwanis (dir.) (Pasadena, Calif.). Author: The Checkerboard Theory of Life, 1985; contbg. author: Young Men Can Change the World, 1966. Pioneer Tele Tissue, roller ski poles. Home: 1040 S Orange Grove Pasadena CA 91105 Office: 2335 Honolulu Ave Montrose CA 91020

BAKEMAN, CAROL ANN, administrative services manager, singer; b. San Francisco, Oct. 27, 1934; d. Lars Hartvig and Gwendolyne Beatrice (Zimmer) Bergh; student UCLA, 1954-62; m. Delbert Clifton Bakeman, May 16, 1959; children—Laurie Ann, Deborah Ann. Singer, Roger Wagner Chorale, 1954—, Los Angeles Master Chorale, 1964-86; librarian Hughes Aircraft Co., Culver City, Calif., 1954-61; head econs. library Planning Research Corp., Los Angeles, 1961-63; corporate librarian Econ. Cons., Inc., Los Angeles, 1963-68; head econs. library Daniel, Mann, Johnson & Mendenhall, architects and engrs., Los Angeles, 1969-71, corporate librarian, 1971-77, mgr. info. services, 1978-81, mgr. info. and office services, 1981-83, mgr. adminstrv. services, 1983—. Pres., Creative Library Systems, Los Angeles, 1974—; library cons. ArchiSystems, div. SUMMA Corp., Los Angeles, 1972—, Property Rehab. Corp., Bell Gardens, Calif., 1974-75, VTN Corp., Irvine, Calif., 1974, William Pereira & Assos., 1975. Mem. Assistance League, So. Calif., 1956—, mem. nat. auxilaries com. 1968-72, 75-78, mem. nat. by laws com. 1970-75, mem. asso. bd. dirs., 1966-76. Mem. Am. Guild Musical Artists, AFTRA, Screen Actors Guild, Adminstrv. Mgmt. Soc. (v.p. Los Angeles chpt. 1984-86, pres. 1986—), Los Angeles Master Chorale Assn. (bd. dirs. 1978-83). Office: DMJM 3250 Wilshire Blvd Los Angeles CA 90010

BAKER, ALTON FLETCHER, JR., newspaper editor; b. Cleve., Nov. 15, 1919; s. Alton Fletcher and Mildred (Moody) B.; m. Genevieve Mertzke, 1947 (div. 1975); m. Jeannette Workman Vollstedt, Feb. 14, 1976; children: Sue Baker Diamond, Alton Fletcher, III, Sarah Moody, Robin Louise. A.B., Pomona Coll., 1942. Reporter Eugene (Oreg.) Register-Guard, 1946-50, mng. editor, 1950-54, editor, 1954—, pub., 1961-82, chmn. bd., 1982—; chmn. Oreg. Press Conf., 1973. Chmn. fund drive United Way, Eugene, 1965, pres., 1966-67; bd. dirs., pres. YMCA, Eugene. Served to capt. USAAF, World War II. Mem. Oreg. Newspaper Pubs. Assn. (dir. 1965-70), Am. Soc. Newspaper Editors, Am. Newspaper Pubs. Assn. Republican. Clubs: Eugene Country, De Anza Country. Home: 2410 W 23d Ave Eugene OR 97405 Office: 975 High St PO Box 10188 Eugene OR 97440

BAKER, BEVERLY JEAN, hypnotherapist; b. Nampa, Idaho, Apr. 11, 1938; d. Clarence Steven Pilcher and Palma Mae (Bowman) Wilson; m. Paul A. Baker, May 3, 1958 (div. Mar. 1978); children: Jeff, Barbara, Carole; m. Robert Herman Van Zee, Mar. 31, 1984. Student, George Fox Coll., 1957, Linfield Coll., 1958, Hypnotism Tng. Inst. Washington, 1982-83. Producer, hostess, writer various radio stations, Oreg. and Wash., 1954-73; merchandising and pub. relations mgr. Herfy's Corp., Seattle, 1973-74; hostess daily program for women Sta. KGDN Radio, Edmonds, Wash., 1974-76; mgr. Am. Clinic Inc., Seattle, 1976-79; hostess daily telephone-in talk show Sta. KXA Radio, Seattle, 1977-79; account exec. Continental Inc., Edmonds, 1979-82; br. mgr. TransAm. Title Ins., 1982-84; pvt. practice hypnotherapy Seattle, 1984—. Trustee Seattle Crisis Clinic, 1969-74, v.p. 1973. Mem. Hypnosis Examining Council (cert. Washington chpt.), Better Bus. Bur., Queen Anne C. of C. Home and Office: 1907 Queen Anne Ave N Seattle WA 98109

BAKER, BRUCE LEE, psychology educator, consultant; b. Cambridge, Mass., July 23, 1940; s. Karl Watson and Elizabeth Cole (Bland) B.; m. Patricia McNeal, Feb. 24, 1966 (div. Oct. 1978); children—Kristen, Jason; m. Jan Blacher, Jan. 27, 1985; 1 child, Alexander. A.B. in Psychology, Brown U., 1962, Ph.D. in clin. Psychology, Yale U., 1966. Lic. psychologist, Calif. Asst. prof. psychology and social relations Harvard U., Cambridge, 1966-69, assoc. prof. edn., lectr. social relations, 1969-75; assoc. prof. psychology UCLA, 1975-77, prof., 1977—, chmn. Clinical Psychology, dir. training program in clinical psychology, 1985—, vis. prof. Harvard U. Med. Sch., Boston, 1982-83; pvt. practice psychology, Los Angeles, 1979—; founder, dir. Camp Freedom, Ossipee, N.H., 1969-75. Co-author: Abnormal Psychology, 1980, 2d rev. edit., 1986; Readings in Abnormal Psychology, 1981; As Close As Possible, 1977; Steps to Independence, 1975-83; mem. editorial bd. Jour. Behavior Therapy and Exptl. Psychology, 1975—, Am. Jour. Mental Deficiency, 1981-83, 85—, Family Process, 1979-85. Recipient Young Psychologist award Am. Psychol. Assn., 1969; grantee Dept. Edn., 1984—, Nat. Inst. Child Health and Human Devel., 1971-75, 77-83, Social and Rehab. Services Adminstrn., 1970-75. Mem. Western Psychol. Assn., Am. Assn. on Mental Deficiency. Democrat. Home: 8294 Gould Ave Los Angeles CA 90046 Office: Dept Psychology UCLA Los Angeles CA 90024

BAKER, CHARLES DEWITT, medical manufacturing company executive; b. Dayton, Ohio, Jan. 5, 1932; s. Donald James and Lillian Mae (Pund) B.; m. June Thordis Tandberg, June 25, 1954; children: Charles, Robert, Thomas, Michael. AA in Electrical Engring., Long Beach City Coll., 1953; Boston U., 1954, Pacific Coast U., 1963, U. Utah, 1980. Registered profl. mfg. engr., Calif. Chemist Shell Oil, Torrance, Calif., 1957-60; materials and process engr. Northrop Corp., Hawthorne, Calif., 1960-63; packaging engr. Jet Propulsion Lab., Pasadena, Calif., 1963-71; med. design engr. Utah Biomed. Test Lab., Salt Lake City, 1971-78, sect. mgr., 1978-83; v.p. Tech. Research Assocs., Salt Lake City, 1983—; pres. Thordis Corp., 1980—. Patentee in field. Pres. Utah Autistic Soc., 1984. Recipient Cost Reduction award NASA, 1969, New Tech. award, 1969, 71, 75. Republican. Mormon. Avocations: teaching, reading, car rebuilding. Office: Technical Research Assocs 410 Chipeta Way Suite 222 Salt Lake City UT 84108

BAKER, CHRISTOPHER JOSEPH, speech pathologist; b. Wheeling, W.Va., Sept. 21, 1956; s. Melvin Charles and Suzanne (Frank) B. BS, Wheeling Coll., 1978; MS, W.Va. U., 1981. Lic. speech pathologist, State Bd. Registration for Healing Arts, Mo., 1985, Bd. Examiners for Speech Pathology and Audiology, Oreg., 1984, State Com. Examiners Speech and Lang. Pathology, Tex., 1985; cert. Bd. Med. Quality Assurance, Calif., 1982. Supr. Cen. Calif. In Speech Inc./Lehrhoff div., Beverly Hills, Calif., 1981—. Mem. Am. Speech Lang. and Hearing Assn. (cert.), Calif. Speech-Lang.-Hearing Assn. Democrat. Office: InSpeech Inc/Lehrhoff Div 6701 Center Dr W #755 Los Angeles CA 90045

BAKER, DANIEL NEIL, space plasma physicist; b. Postville, Iowa, Nov. 10, 1948; s. Joseph N. and Alvira H. (Amundson) B.; m. A. Victoria Vaughan, Aug. 14, 1971. BA, U. Iowa, 1969, MS, 1973, PhD, 1974. Research aide dept. physics U. Iowa, Iowa City, 1967-69, grad. research asst., 1970-74, postdoctoral research assoc., 1974-75; research fellow Calif. Inst. Tech., Pasadena, 1975-78; mem. staff Los Alamos (N.Mex.) Nat. Lab., 1978-81, group leader, 1981—; chmn. data systems users group NASA, Washington, 1982—, tech. cons., 1985—; mem. com. solar and space physics Nat. Acad. Sci., Washington, 1983—, com. data mgmt. and computing 1986—; mem. panel on long-term observations, Nat. Research Council, Washington, 1985—. Assoc. editor Geophys. Research Letters, Washington, 1986—; mem. space tech. rev. bd. Los Alamos Nat. Lab.; contbr. numerous articles to profl. jours. NSF research fellow U. Iowa, 1970-74; grantee Inst. Geophys. and Planetary Physics U. Calif., 1980—. Mem. AAAS, Am. Geophys. Union, Sigma Xi. Avocations: jogging, creative writing, basketball, cinema. Office: Los Alamos Nat Lab MS D438 Los Alamos NM 87545

BAKER, DAVID KENNETH, coll. pres.; b. Glasgow, Scotland, Oct. 2, 1923; came to U.S., 1946, naturalized, 1956; s. David Thomas and Edith (Horner) B.; m. Vivian Christian Perry, Sept. 13, 1947; children—Paul D. (dec.), Richard R. B.Sc., McMaster U., 1946; Ph.D., U. Pa., 1953. Prof. physics Union Coll., Schenectady, 1953-65; mgr. profl. personnel, research and devel. lab. Gen. Electric Co., 1965-67; v.p., dean St. Lawrence U., Canton, N.Y., 1967-76; pres. Harvey Mudd Coll., Claremont, Calif., 1976—; mem. NSF. Author: (with A.T. Goble) Elements of Modern Physics. Mem. Am. Inst. Physics, AAUP, Newcomen Soc. Clubs: Rotary; Calif. (Los Angeles); Univ. (Claremont). Home: 495 E 12th St Claremont CA 91711 Office: Pres's Office Harvey Mudd Coll Claremont CA 91711

BAKER, DON ROBERT, chemist; b. Salt Lake City, Apr. 6, 1933; s. Ralph H. and Ruth Eve (Thalmann) B.; m. Shirley May Nelson, Nov. 20, 1954; children: Robert, David, George, Barbara. AA, Sacramento City Coll., 1953; AB, Calif. State U., Sacramento, 1955; PhD, U. Calif., Berkeley, 1959. Sr. research chemist Stauffer Chem. Co., Richmond, Calif., 1958-72, research assoc., 1970-74, supr., 1974-85, sr. research assoc., 1985—. Editor: California Chemists Alert, 1986, Advances in the Synthesis and Chemistry of Agrochemicals, 1986; contbr. articles to profl. jours.; patentee in field. Mem. Am. Chem. Soc. (chmn. Calif. sect. 1973, councilor Calif. sect. 1971—, chmn. nat. div. profl. relations 1980, coordinating com. Calif. sects. 1970—), Plant Growth Regulator Soc., Orchid Soc. Calif. (pres. 1979-80), Oakland Genealogy Library (librarian 1967—). Republican. Mormon. Avocations: orchid growing, mineralogy, genealogy. Home: 15 Muth Dr Orinda CA 94563 Office: Stauffer Chem Co 1200 S 47th St Richmond CA 94804

BAKER, EDWIN MOODY, newspaper publisher; b. Cleve., Dec. 20, 1923; s. Alton Fletcher and Mildred Elizabeth (Moody) B.; children—Bridget, Amanda Baker Barber, Jonathan. B.S. in Bus. Adminstrn., U. Oreg., 1948. With Eugene (Oreg.) Register-Guard, 1948—, successively advt. mgr., bus. mgr., gen. mgr., pub., pres. Guard Pub. Co.; pres. Times Newspapers, Inc., Beaverton, Oreg. Mem. exec. bd. Oreg. Trail Council, Boy Scouts Am., 1953—, pres. 1960-61, chmn. Region XI Area I (Northwest) 1971, pres., 1972, mem. nat. exec. bd., 1971-72, nat. adv. council, 1972—; trustee U. Oreg. Found., 1975—; chmn., trustee Eugene Arts Found., 1980—; pres. Oreg. Pacific Econ. Devel. Corp., 1984-85; 2d v.p. Eugene Springfield Met. Ptnrship.; mem., chmn. Mayan Sister City com., 1986—. Served with AUS, World War II. Decorated Bronze Star, Purple Heart; recipient Silver Beaver award, Boy Scouts Am., 1962, Silver Antelope, 1965, Disting. Eagle Scout award, 1982; Pioneer award U. Oreg., 1982; named Eugene First Citizen, 1983. Mem. Am. Newspaper Pubs. Assn. (research inst. lab. com. 1978-79), Oreg. Newspaper Pubs. Assn. (dir. 1982-83), U. Oreg. Pres. Assocs. Clubs: Rotary, Country (Eugene); Willow Creek Racquet. Home: 2121 Kimberly Circle Eugene OR 97405 Office: PO Box 10188 Eugene OR 97440

BAKER, FLOYD WAYNE, highway engineer; b. Beaver, Okla., June 4, 1934; s. Clarence Hubert and Myra Amy (Bayliff) B.; m. Myrtle Lou Aldridge, Mar. 27, 1955; children—Lori Ann Filter, Lisa Gaye. Student Yuba (Calif.) Jr. Coll., 1951-53; Chico State Coll., 1953. Lic. real estate agt., Calif. Asst. hwy. engr. Calif. Dept. Transp., Marysville, 1953-63; mgr. hwy. div. Baldwin Contracting Co., Inc., Marysville, 1962—, v.p., 1986. Served in U.S. Army, 1957-59. Mem. Associated Gen. Contractors of Calif., Marysville C. of C., Real Estate Assn. Democrat. Club: Rotary. Clubs: Peach Tree Country (bd. dirs.), Elks (Marysville). Office: 8th and Yuba Sts Marysville CA 95901

BAKER, FREDERICK CHARLES, JR., research biochemist; b. North Shields, Eng., July 30, 1948; came to U.S., 1969; s. Frederick Charles and May Rumney Broderick (Waldon) B.; m. Barbara Lorraine Lumsden, Apr. 14, 1978; children: Steven David, Stuart Alexander. BSc with honors, U. Newcastle, Eng., 1969; PhD, N.C. State U., 1974. Postdoctoral researcher dept. chemistry U. Glasgow, Scotland, 1974-76; postdoctoral researcher dept. biochemistry Zoecon Corp. (later Zoecon Research Inst.), Palo Alto, Calif., 1977, sr. biochemist, 1978—. Contbr. numerous articles to profl. jours. Mem. AAAS, Am. Soc. Biol. Chemists, Phyto Chem. Soc. Avocations: horticulture, plant ecology and taxonomy, collecting cacti and other succulents, soccer, squash. Home: 1084 S Blaney Ave San Jose CA 95129 Office: Zoecon Research Inst 975 California Ave Palo Alto CA 94304

BAKER, GEORGE ALLEN, JR., physicist; b. Alton, Ill., Nov. 25, 1932; s. George Allen and Grace Elizabeth (Cummins) B.; m. Elizabeth Ann Coles, Sept. 9, 1956; children: Constance Jean, Linda Ann, Deborah Jane. BS, Calif. Inst. Tech., 1954; PhD, U. Calif., Berkeley, 1956. Mem. staff Los Alamos Sci. Lab., N.Mex., 1957-66, 75-83, assoc., group leader, 1976-81, Los Alamos fellow, 1983—; physicist Brookhaven Nat. Lab., Upton, N.Y., 1966-71, sr. physicist, 1971-75; cons. Gen. Dynamics Corp., San Diego, 1962, Bell Telephone Labs., Murray Hill, N.J., 1964, Los Alamos Sci. Lab., 1968-75; assoc. research physicist U. Calif.-San Diego, 1961-62; vis. prof. King's Coll. U. London, 1964-65; materials research ctr. fellow Cornell U., Ithaca, N.Y., 1971-72; vis. scientist SUNY-Stony Brook, 1973-74; vis. physicist Centre d'Etudes Nucleaires de Saclay, Gif-sur-Yvette, France, 1976-77, 82-83; vis. lectr. Princeton U., N.J., 1983. Author: (with P.R. Graves-Morris) Pade Approximants, Part I: Basic Theory, Part II: Extensions and Applications, 1982; The Essentials of Padé Approximants, 1975. Editor: (with J.L. Gammel) The Padé Approximant in Theoretical Physics, 1970. Mem. editorial bd. Jour. Math. Physics, 1975-77, 82-84, Jour. Statis. Physics, 1979-81. Trustee South Country Central Sch. Dist., Bellport, N.Y., 1973-75. NSF fellow, 1956-57. Fellow Am. Phys. Soc.; mem. Tau Beta Pi. Office: Theoretical Div Los Alamos Nat Lab T-11 MS-B262 Los Alamos NM 87545

BAKER, GEORGE ALLEN, mathematics educator; b. Robinson, Ill., Oct. 31, 1903; s. Edward Sheridan and Ida (Everingham) B.; m. Grace Elizabeth Cummins, June 12, 1930; children: George Allen Jr., John Cummins. BS, U. Ill., 1926, PhD, 1929. Research fellow Columbia U., N.Y.C., 1929-30; assoc. statistician USPHS, Washington, 1929; prof. math. Shurtleff Coll., Alton, Ill., 1931-34, Miss. Women's Coll., Hattiesburg, 1934-36; statistician Dept. Agr. Bur. Home Econs., Birmingham and Washington, 1936-37; prof. math., stats. U. Calif., Davis, 1937—, faculty research lectr., 1955-56. Author: Statistical Techniques Based on Probabilistic Models, 1962; contbr. articles to profl. jours. Fellow Inst. Math. Stats.; mem. Biometric Soc. (v.p. 1950), Am. Math. Soc., Math. Assn. Am., Am. Statis. Assn., Econometric Soc., AAAS, Sigma Xi, Pi Mu Epsilon, Gamma Sigma Delta. Home: 507 Eisenhower St Davis CA 95616 Office: U Calif Dept Math Davis CA 95616

BAKER, GLADYS ELIZABETH, retired microbiologist, educator; b. Iowa City, Iowa, July 22, 1908; d. Richard Philip and Katherine (Riedelbauch) B. BA, U. Iowa, 1930, MS, 1932; PhD, Washington U., St. Louis, 1935. Biology instr. Hunter Coll., N.Y.C., 1936-40; instr., then asst. prof. Vassar Coll., Poughkeepsie, N.Y., 1940-45; assoc. prof., then prof., chmn. dept. plant scis. Vassar Coll., Poughkeepsie, 1945-61; prof. botany U. Hawaii, Honolulu, 1961-73; acting chmn. botany dept., U. Hawaii, 1965-66. Illustrator: The Myxomycetes, 1934; contbr. articles on mycology to profl., sci. jours. Recipient 3 research grants NSF, 1952-60, others. Fellow AAAS; mem. Mycol. Soc. Am., British Mycol. Soc., Med. Mycol. Soc. of the Ams. (charter). Episcopalian. Home: 10134 W Mohawk Ln Apt 2023 Peoria AZ 85345

BAKER, GORDON F., health care administrator; b. Corry, Pa., Mar. 4, 1941; s. Edward M. and Annabelle F. (Pratt) B.; m. Sandra J. Stevens, Mar. 25, 1967; children—J. Todd, Steven E. B.A., U. Md., 1970; M.H.A., George Washington U., 1972. Adminstrv. resident Med. Ctr. at Princeton U., 1971-72; asst. adminstr. Pascack Valley Hosp., Westwood, N.J., 1972-74; assoc. dir. Bellevue Hosp. Ctr., N.Y.C., 1974; v.p. Frederick Meml. Hosp., Md., 1976-80; v.p., adminstr. Schick Shadel Hosp., Santa Barbara, Calif., 1980-86, regional coordinator, 1986—. Served with USAF, 1963-67. Fellow Am. Coll. Alcoholism Treatment Adminstrs.; mem. Am. Coll. Hosp. Adminstrs., Am. Hosp. Assn. Lodge: Rotary.

BAKER, HARRY LUTHER, insurance broker; b. Butte, Mont., Apr. 28, 1939; s. Harry Willard and Isabelle Lois (Storey) B.; BS, Mont. State U., 1961; m. June Judy Langworthy, May 23, 1964 (div.); children: Gregory, Matthew, Jennifer. Underwriter, Safeco Ins. Co., Seattle, 1965-74; gen. mgr. spl. programs div. Providence-Wash. Ins. Co., 1974-78; pres. Profl. Ins. Consultants, Seattle, 1978—; cons. in field. Contbr. articles to profl. jours. Mem. Comml. Market Masters Club (life), Ins. Inst. Am., Profl. Ins. Agts., WAIB, Internat. Halfway House Assn., Ind. Ins. Agts. Am., Soc. for Ambulatory Surgery. Republican. Episcopalian. Office: 2601 4th Ave Seattle WA 98121

BAKER, JAMES LEONARD, electronics engineer, consultant; b. San Francisco, June 11, 1940; s. James Elbert Baker and Dorothy Edith (Hartlett) Bowman; m. Leah Mildred Crary, Oct. 27, 1962; children: Renee Fay Salazar, Daniel Leonard. AA in Electromech. Engring. Tech., Chabot Coll., 1974; BSEE, San Jose State U., 1982. Aircraft electrician Naval Air Rework Facility, Alameda, Calif., 1966-75; writer tech. manuals NAVAIR Engring. Support Office, Alameda, 1975-77, editor tech. manuals, 1977-80, electronics technician, 1980-82, electronics engr., 1982—. Author: Transmission Line Testing, 1978. Sustaining mem. Rep. Nat. com., Washington., 1982—, Calif. Reps., 1984—. Served with USAF, 1958-62. Mem. IEEE, Tape-head Interface Com., USN Anti-Submarine, Warfare Tape Recorder Steering Group. Methodist. Avocations: backpacking, fishing, hunting, camping, hiking. Office: NAVAIR Engring Support Office Alameda CA 94501-5021

BAKER, JOAN MARIAN, city official; b. Balt., Mar. 23, 1936; d. Charles Rowland and Iola (Sellers) Mitchell; m. James H. Baker, June 2, 1956; children—James Charles, Jay Herbert, Jack Marion, Jon William. Student Butler U., Indpls., 1954-55, Macalester Coll., 1955-56, Colo. U., 1980. Cert. mcpl. clk., advanced mcpl. clk. With Sunlife Assurance Co. of Can., Indpls., 1954-55; with Conrad Sheveland, atty., St. Paul, 1955-56; tax cons. Lawrence Bookkeeping, Indpls., 1966-70; legal sec. City of Northglenn (Colo.), 1975-80, city clk., 1980—. Mem. Colo. Clks. Assn. (pres. 1986), Internat. Inst. Mcpl. Clks., Women in Mcpl. Govt., Colo. Mcpl. League. Meth. Office: 11701 Community Ctr Dr #204 Northglenn CO 80233

BAKER, JOANNE, publishing executive; b. Toronto, Ont., Can., Sept. 16, 1957; d. Raymond H. and Mildred (Sussman) B.; m. Richard Lee Wynne, May 27, 1978. BS, Ind. U., 1979; MBA, U. So. Calif., 1988. Sales mgr. Bill Communications, N.Y.C., 1979-80; telemarketer The New York Times, 1980-81, presentation writer, 1981-85, prodn. mgr., 1985; assoc. pub. Bus. Today Publs., Burbank, Calif., 1986—; mktg. cons. Ron Bennett Enterprises, Los Angeles, 1986. Producer, writer multi-media presentation Welcome to the Times (award Internat. Assn. Bus. Communicators 1984, Silver award Internat. Film and TV Festival 1985, N.Y. Times Pub.'s award 1985). Club: Toastmasters (N.Y.C.). Avocations: cooking, walking, traveling. Home: 2871 Angelo Dr Los Angeles CA 90077

BAKER, JOHN ALBERT, JR., accountant; b. Port Angeles, Wash., July 2, 1919; s. John Albert and Rose (Anderson) B.; B.A., Wash. State U., 1943; m. P. Pasha Prossen, Nov. 25, 1978; children—Raymon Edward, Carlton Crawford, Cameron John, Peggy Melinda, Fred Albert. Sr. acct., audit supr., sr. tax cons. Cameron & Johnstone, Honolulu, 1946-50; partner Cameron, Tennent & Greaney, Honolulu, 1950-51, Baker & Gillette, Honolulu, 1951-65, Coopers & Lybrand, 1965-81; chmn. Pasha Pacific Properties, Inc., 1981—. Served with USMCR, 1943-46. Mem. Nat. Assn. Accountants, Hawaii Soc. C.P.A.s, Hawaii Estate Planning Council, Nat. Tax Assn., Hawaii Bd. of Accountancy (pres., disting. pub. service award 1984), Am. Inst. C.P.A.s (bd. examiners 1964-68), Nat. Assn. State Bds. Accountancy, Am. Acctg. Assn. Home: PO Box 3919 Honolulu HI 96812

BAKER, LAURA ANN, psychology educator; b. Kansas City, Mo., Oct. 25, 1955; d. John Patrick Baker and Frances Elnora (Knight) Evans. BA, Kans. U., 1978; MA, Colo. U., 1982, PhD, 1983. Research asst. U. Kans., Lawrence, 1977-79, U. Colo., Boulder, 1979-83; asst. prof. U. So. Calif., Los Angeles, 1984—; computing cons. U. Colo., 1980-83. Contbr. articles to profl. jours. NIMH predoctoral fellow, 1982-83; U. So. Calif. Faculty Research and Innovation Fund grantee, 1985—, Biomed. Research Support grantee, 1984-86, NIMH grantee, 1984-86. Mem. Am. Psychol. Assn., AAAS, Behavior Genetics Assn. (exec. com. mem. 1982-84), Psychometric Soc., Sigma Xi. Office: Dept Psychology U So Calif SGM 501 Los Angeles CA 90089-1061

BAKER, LEE WENDELL, public relations consultant; b. Bowen, Ill., Dec. 27, 1919; d. Samuel Albert and Ethel May (Nash) B.; m. George Ann McGreevy, June 9, 1945 (dec. Aug. 1972); Jean Hammond Otto, Nov. 23, 1973. BS, Bradley U., 1942. Pub. relations rep. Allis-Chalmers Corp., Milw., 1945-55, mgr., 1955-65; v.p. Owen King & Assocs., Milw., 1965-67; pres. Lee Baker Assocs., Milw., 1967-83, Denver, 1983—. Contbr. articles to profl. jours. Bd. dirs. Milw. Ballet Co., 1970-79, Artists Series at the Pabst, Mllw., 1979-83, Wis. Consumer League, Madison, 1979-83, Colo. Ballet, 1984—, Denver chpt. Am. Cancer Soc., 1986—; bd. dirs., sec. Found. Med. Care Evaluation, Milw., 1978-83. Mem. Pub. Relations Soc. Am. (cert., pres. Wis. chpt. 1965—), Milw. Mental Health Assn. (pres. 1974), Colo. Assn. Fund Raisers. Club: Milw. Press (v.p., sec. 1950-53).

BAKER, LILLIAN, author, historian, artist, polit. activist, lecturer; b. Yonkers, N.Y., Dec. 12, 1921; student El Camino (Calif.) Coll., 1952, UCLA, 1968, 77, m. Roscoe A. Baker; children: Wanda Georgia, George Riley. Continuity writer Sta. WINS, N.Y.C., 1945-46; columnist, freelance writer, reviewer Gardena (Calif.) Valley News, 1964-76; freelance writer, editor, 1971—; lectr. in field. founder/editor Internat. Club for Collectors of Hatpins and Hatpin Holders, monthly and semi-ann. Pictorial Jour., 1977—, conv. and seminar coordinator 1979-86; founder Ams. for Hist. Accuracy, 1972, Com. for Equality for All Draftees, 1973; chair S. Bay primary campaign S.I. Hayakawa, for U.S. Senator from Calif., 1976; witness U.S. Commn. Wartime Relocation, 1981, U.S. Senate Judiciary Com., 1983, U.S. Ho. Reps. Judiciary Com., 1986. Recipient award Freedoms Found., 1971; Ann. award Conf. Calif. Hist. Socs., 1983; monetary award Hoover Instn. Stanford (Calif.) U., 1985. Fellow Internat. Biographical Assn.; mem. Nat. League Am. Pen Women, Nat. Writers Club, Art Students League N.Y. (life), Nat. Historic Soc. (founding), Nat. Trust Historic Preservation (founding), other orgns. Author: Collector's Encyclopedia of Hatpins and Hatpin Holders, 1976, 100 Years of Collectible Jewelry 1850-1950, 1978, rev. edit., 1986, Jewelry: Art Nouveau and Art Deco, 1980, rev. edit. 1985, The Concentration Camp Conspiracy: A Second Pearl Harbor, 1981 (Scholarship Category award of Merit, Conf. of Calif. Hist. Socs. 1983), Hatpins and Hatpin Holders: An Illustrated Value Guide, 1983, Creative and Collectible Miniatures, 1984, Fifty Years of Collectible Fashion Jewelry: 1925-1975, 1986; also articles poetry; editor: Insider; contbg. author Vol. VII Time-Life Encyclopedia of Collectibles, 1979; numerous radio and TV appearances. Home and office: 15237 Chanera Ave Gardena CA 90249

BAKER, MARC ANTHONY, marketing professional; b. Hollywood, Calif., May 30, 1962; s. John Frederick and Mary Ann (Ross) B. BSEE, Stanford U., 1984. Mktg. engr. Monolithic Memories, Inc., Santa Clara, Calif., 1984—. Mem. IEEE. Democrat. Home: 245 Bush St #18 Mountain View CA 94041 Office: Monolithic Memories Inc 2175 Mission College Blvd Santa Clara CA 95054

BAKER, MARY, mechanical engineer; b. Madison, Wis., July 30, 1944; d. John Gordon Baker and Elizabeth Theadora (Nelson) B.; m. Wayne Wallace Pfeiffer, July 4, 1974; children: Elizabeth Ann, Gordon Jay. B.S., U. Wis., 1966; M.S. in Applied Mechanics, Calif. Inst. Tech., Pasadena, 1967, Ph.D. 1972. Registered profl. mech. engr., Calif., 1977. Mem. tech. staff IBM Research Ctr., Yorktown Heights, N.Y., 1972; sr. engr. Rohr Industries, Chula Vista, Calif., 1973-75; mem. sci. staff Systems Science and Software, 1975-77; project mgr., mgr. analytical services, tech. dir. western ops., Structural Dynamics Research Corp., San Diego, 1977—. Mem. ASME, AIAA, Sigma Xi, Phi Kappa Phi, Tau Beta Pi. Contbr. articles to profl. jours. Home: 13864 Boquita Dr Del Mar CA 92014 Office: Structural Dynamics Research Corp 11055 Roselle St San Diego CA 92121

BAKER, MICHAEL PHILLIP, social worker; b. Springfield, Ill., July 21, 1949; s. Herbert Charles and Dorothy Marie (Gaines) B.; m. Dianna Grace Goff, June 21, 1972 (div. Oct. 1974); children: Michael Phillip II, Mark Anthony; m. Pamela Jane Swearengen, Oct. 13, 1979 (div. 1982). BA, U. Minn., 1982. Clk. Ill. Sec. of State, Springfield, 1973-79; youth counselor Springfield Community Action, 1980; mental health technician People Inc., Mpls., 1984-85; child care worker St. George Homes, Berkeley, Calif., 1986—; child counselor Children's Home Soc., San Francisco, 1986—. Fellow Nat. Assn. Social Workers. Democrat. Roman Catholic.

BAKER, RICHARD EARL, architect, state official; b. Portland, Oreg., Oct. 8, 1931; s. Ralph Lowell and Isla Grace (Dayton) B.; m. Marlene Elaine Turner, Feb. 16, 1957; children—Russell A., Claudia G., Alison A. B.Archtl. Engring., Wash. State U., 1954. Registered architect, Nev., Calif. Design engr., Atomics Internat. div. N.Am. Aviation Co., Downey and Canoga Park, Calif., 1954-57; archtl. draftsman J. Arthur Drielsma, AIA, Los Angeles, 1957-58, Leo P. Raffaelli, AIA, Studio City, Calif., 1958, Nelson P. Rice, AIA, Studio City, 1959-60, State Pub. Works Bd., Carson City, Nev., 1960, chief asst., 1961, project architect, 1967-75, dep. mgr., 1975-83, sec., mgr., 1984—. Mem. AIA. Republican. Methodist. Lodge: Masons. Home: 2704 Marvin Dr Carson City NV 89701 Office: Nev Pub Works Bd 505 E King St Room 403 Kinkead Bldg Carson City NV 89710

BAKER, RICHARD LOUIS, electrical engineering educator; b. Los Angeles, Apr. 3, 1953; s. Ariel Rufus and Mabel Catherine (Pamp) B.; m. Robin Zenger, May 2, 1981. BS with Honors, Calif. Inst. Tech., 1974; MS, U. So. Calif., 1978; PhDEE, Stanford U., 1984. Mem. tech. staff Hughes Aircraft Co., Fullerton, Calif., 1976-81; research asst. Stanford (Calif.) U., 1982-83; asst. prof. elec. engring. Brigham Young U., Provo, Utah, 1983-84; asst. prof. UCLA, 1984—; cons. R.L. Baker Cons. Co., Los Angeles, 1984—. Recipient Donald S. Clark award Calif. Tech. U. Alumni Assn., 1973. Mem. IEEE. Office: UCLA Dept Elec Engring Los Angeles CA 90024

BAKER, RICHARD WILLIAM, chemist; b. Boreham Wood, Eng., Aug. 18, 1941; came to U.S., 1966; s. Leslie and Lillian Margaret (Hall) B. BSc in Chemistry, Chelsea Coll. London U., 1963; PhD in Phys. Chemistry, Imperial Coll. London U., 1966; postdoctoral, Poly. Inst. Bklyn., 1968-71. Sr. scientist Amicon Corp., Lexington, Mass., 1966-68; research scientist Alza Corp., Palo Alto, Calif., 1971-74; co-founder, dir. research Bend (Oreg.) Research, Inc., 1974-81; pres. Membrane Tech. and Research, Inc., Menlo Park, Calif., 1982—. Author: Controlled Release of Biologically Active Agents, 1986; editor: Controlled Release of Bioactive Materials, 1980; mem. editorial bd. Jour. Membrane Sci., Jour. Controlled Release, Biomed. Polymers, Topics in Controlled Release Sci.; contbr. numerous articles to profl. jours.; patentee in field. Recipient IR-100 award Indsl. Research, 1984; Innovative Small Bus. award SBA, San Francisco, 1985. Mem. AAAS, Am. Chem. Soc., European Soc. Membrane Sci. and Tech., N.Am. Membrane Soc. (bd. dirs.), Controlled Release Soc. (pres. 1981-82, Founders' award 1985). Office: Membrane Tech and Research Ind 1030 Hamilton Ct Menlo Park CA 94025

BAKER, RINA JOAN, social work agency administrator; b. Lith, The Netherlands, Apr. 19, 1948; came to U.S., 1962, naturalized, 1967; d. Anthony and Rina (Arnoldussen) Vander Wielen; m. John Tom Baker, June 21, 1969; children: Jude, Dane. BA in Psychology with honors, San Diego State U., 1976; MSW, U. Calif., Berkeley, 1978, D in Social Welfare, 1983. Lic. clin. social worker, Calif.; pupil personnel services credential, 1978. Intern psychotherapy Family Services, Berkeley, 1976-77; intern cons. Children's Council, San Francisco, 1977-78; intern psychiatric social work Kaiser, Walnut Creek, Calif., 1978-79; research asst. Inst. Human Devel., Berkeley, 1979-80; dir. social services Easter Seal Soc., Oakland, Calif., 1981-86; exec. dir. Aid to Adoption of Spl. Kids, Oakland, 1986—; student supr. dept. social welfare U. Calif., Berkeley, 1981-86; pub. speaker in field, Oakland, 1980—; researcher Single Parent Resource Ctr., San Francisco, 1977-78; coordinator Community Friends Mental Health Assn., Contra Costa County, Calif., 1973-74. Neighborhood coordinator Crime Prevention Com., Contra Costa County, 1978; mem. friends of El Sobrante, Calif., 1979, local chpt. Boys' Club of Am. Fellow Nat. Assn. Social Workers (cert., exec. com. 1985—); mem. Rehab. Social Workers Network (steering com. 1983-85), Social Welfare Alumni Assn. and Conf. Workshop, Calif. Assn. Sch. Social Workers, Pvt. Adoption Agy. Coalition, NOW, ERA, Phi Beta Kappa. Democrat. Roman Catholic. Avocations: singing, hiking, photography.

BAKER, ROBERT FRANK, molecular biologist, educator; b. Weiser, Idaho, Apr. 9, 1936; s. Robert Clarence and Beulah (Hulet) B.; m. Mary Margaret Murphy, May 29, 1965; children—Allison Leslie, Steven Mark. B.S., Stanford U., 1959; Ph.D., Brown U., 1966. Postdoctoral research assoc. Stanford U., Calif., 1966-68; asst. prof. dept. biol. scis. U. So. Calif., Los Angeles, 1968-72, assoc. prof., 1972-83, prof., 1983—, dir. molecular biology div., 1978-80; mem. Comprehensive Cancer Ctr. U. So. Calif., 1984—; vis. assoc. prof. Harvard U. Med. Sch. Boston 1975-76; mem. genetic study sect. NIH, Bethesda, Md., 1977-79, 82. Contbr. articles to profl. jours. Grantee NIH, NSF, 1968—. Mem. Am. Soc. Zoologists, Am. Soc. for Microbiology, Sigma Xi. Avocations: amateur radio; electronics. Home: 607 Almar Ave Pacific Palisades CA 90272 Office: U So Calif Dept Molecular Biology MC1481 Los Angeles CA 90089

BAKER, ROBERT KERRY, library director, author, editor; b. Glendale, Calif., Nov. 24, 1948; s. Robert Klein and Louise Eleanor (Winters) B.; m. Linda Jean Voorhees, Jan. 14, 1972 (div. 1978). B.A. in French, Calif. State U.-Northridge, 1971; M.A. in French, UCLA, 1973, M.L.S., 1976; postgrad. U. Paris, 1971-72. Cert. life librarian, Wash., Community Coll. instr., Calif. Asst. catalog librarian, Gonzaga U., Spokane, Wash., 1976-77; pub. services librarian Spokane Community Coll., 1977-80, tech. services librarian, 1980-83; library dir. Lower Columbia Coll., Longview, Wash., 1983—. Author: Introduction to Library Research in French Literature, 1978; Doing Library Research, 1981; editor Westview Guides to Library Research, Boulder, Colo., 1979—; contbr. articles to publs. in field. Marjorie Sether Mardellis fellow, UCLA, 1975. Mem. ALA, Wash. Library Assn., Assn. Coll. and Research Libraries, Pacific N.W. Library Assn. Democrat. Roman Catholic. Home: 120 Selix Ln Longview WA 98632 Office: Lower Columbia Coll 1600 Maple St Longview WA 98632

BAKER, ROBERT M. L., JR., university president; b. Los Angeles, Sept. 1, 1930; s. Robert M.L. and Martha (Harlan) B.; m. Bonnie Sue Vold, Nov. 14, 1964; children—Robert Randall, Robert M.L., Robin Michele Leslie. B.A., UCLA, 1954, M.A., 1956, Ph.D., 1958. Cons., Douglas Aircraft Co., Santa Monica, Calif., 1954-57; sr. scientist Aeronutronic, Newport Beach, Calif., 1957-60; head Lockheed Aircraft Research Center, West Los Angeles, 1961-64; assoc. mgr. Math. analysis Computer Scis. Corp., El Segundo, Calif., 1964-80; pres. West Coast U., Los Angeles, 1980—; faculty UCLA, 1958-72; dir. Internat. Info. Systems Corp., Pasadena, Calif., Transp. Scis. Corp., Los Angeles. Served to maj. USAF, 1960-61. Named Outstanding Young Man of Year, 1965; recipient Dirk Brouwer award, 1976. Fellow Am. Astro. Soc., Meteoritical Soc., Brit. Astro. Soc., AIAA; mem. Am. Phys. Soc., Phi Beta Kappa, Sigma Xi, Sigma Pi Sigma. Author: An Introduction to Astrodynamics, 1960; 2d edit., 1967; Astrodynamics-Advanced and Applied Topics, 1967, 87; editor: Jour. Astron. Scis., 1961-76.

BAKER, STEVEN LEE, data processing executive; b. Salem, Oreg., Feb. 11, 1943; s. Milbert Franklin and Florence Elaine (Drake) B.; m. Earletta Marie Blank, Apr. 8, 1967; children: Leslie Marie, Travis Lee. BS in Broadcasting, U. Oreg., 1966; AS in Computer Sci., Lane Community Coll., 1975. Commd. 2d lt. USAF, 1966, advanced through grades to maj.; programmer Multnomah County Info. Services, Portland, Oreg., 1973-76, programmer, analyst, 1976-80, sr. systems analyst, 1980-84, data adminstr., 1984—; prin. Data Design Services, Portland, 1978—. Mem. Data Processing Mgmt. Assn. (chmn. 1985-86). Republican. Methodist. Home: 28 SE 44th Ave Portland OR 97215 Office: Multnomah County Info Services 4747 E Burnside Portland OR 97215

BAKER, VICTOR RICHARD, geology researcher, educator, planetary sciences researcher; b. Waterbury, Conn., Feb. 19, 1945; s. Victor A. Baker and Doris Elizabeth (Day) MacGregor; m. Pauline Marie Heaton, June 10, 1967; children: Trent Heaton, Theodore William. BS, Rensselaer Poly. Inst., 1967; PhD, U. Colo., 1971. Geophysicist U.S. Geol. Survey, Denver, 1967-71; asst. prof. geology U. Tex., Austin, 1971-76, assoc. prof., 1976-81; prof. U. Ariz., Tucson, 1981—; cons. Lunar and Planetary Inst., Houston, 1983—, Salt River Project, Phoenix, 1984—, Argonne (Ill.) Nat. Lab., 1983—; com. Nat. Research Council, Washington, 1978—. Author: The Channels of Mars, 1982, co-author: Surficial Geology, 1981; editor: Catastrophic Flooding, 1981, co-editor: The Channeled Scabland, 1978. Served to capt. U.S. Army, 1971-72. Fulbright sr. research fellow, 1979-80, vis. fellow Australian Nat. U., Canberra, 1979-80; research grantee NASA, 1975—, NSF, 1977—. Fellow Geol. Soc. Am. (chmn. planetary geology div. 1986); mem. Am. Geophys. Union, AAAS. Am. Quarternary Assn. Office: U Ariz Dept Geoscis Tucson AZ 85721

BAKER, WARREN J(OSEPH), university president; b. Fitchburg, Mass., Sept. 5, 1938; s. Preston A. and Grace F. (Jarvis) B.; m. Carol Ann Fitzsimons, Apr. 28, 1962; children: Carrie Ann, Kristin Robin, Christopher, Brian. B.S., U. Notre Dame, 1960, M.S., 1962; Ph.D., U. N.Mex., 1966. Research assoc., lectr. E. H. Wang Civil Engring. Research Facility, U. N.Mex., 1962-66; assoc. prof. civil engring. U. Detroit, 1966-71, prof., 1972-79, Chrysler prof., dean engring., 1973-78, acad. v.p., 1976-79; NSF faculty fellow M.I.T., 1971-72; pres. Calif. Poly. State U., San Luis Obispo, 1979—; judge Internat. Sci. and Engring. Fair, 1974, 75, 77, 80; mem. adv. bd. Jr. Humanities and Sci. Symposium, 1976-78, Nat. Sci. Bd.; mem. Bd. Internat. Food and Agr. Devel., 1983-86; mem. Nat. Sci. Bd., 1985—. Contbr. articles to profl. jours. Mem. Detroit Mayor's Mgmt. Adv. Com., 1975-76; mem. engring. adv. bd. U. Calif., Berkeley, 1984—; bd. dirs. Calif. Council for Environ. and Econ. Balance, 1980-85. Fellow Engring. Soc. Detroit; mem. ASCE (chmn. geotech. div. com. on reliability 1976-78, civil engring. edn. and research policy com. 1985—), NSPE (pres. Detroit chpt. 1976-77), Am. Soc. Engring. Edn., Am. Assn. State Colls. and Univs. (bd. dirs. 1982-84). Office: Pres's Office Calif Poly State U San Luis Obispo CA 93407

BAKER, WILLIAM ALLISON, architect; b. Wheatland, Wyo., May 24, 1944; s. Wallace Allison and Ruth (Hill) B.; m. Constance Henriette Francisca de Vos, Dec. 27, 1970; children: Garrett, Eileen, Jesse, Hillary. B.C.E. with hons., U. Wyo., 1967; M.Arch., Princeton U., 1973. Registered profl. engr., Wyo.; registered architect, Wyo., S.D., Colo. Architect Banner Assocs., Inc., Laramie, Wyo., 1973-77, head archtl. dept., 1985—; asst. prof. dept. civil & archtl. engring. U. Wyo., 1977-79; ptnr. Malone, Baker & Assocs., Sheridan, Wyo., 1980-84; v.p. Wyo. Bd. Architects, 1984-85, pres. 1986—. Mem. Laramie Code appeals Bd., 1978-79. Served as 1st lt. U.S. Army, 1967-70, Vietnam. Recipient award of merit Soc. Mil. Engrs., 1968, teaching award, Amoco Corp., 1979. Mem. AIA, Nat. Trust Historic Preservation, Wyo. Hist. Soc., U. Wyo. Alumni Assn. Princeton Grad. Alumni, Sigma Tau, Phi Epsilon Phi, Phi Kappa Phi, Omicron Delta Kappa. Office: Banner Assocs Inc 620 Plaza Ct Laramie WY 82070

BAKER-LIEVANOS, NINA GILLSON, jewelry store executive; b. Boston, Dec. 19, 1950; d. Rev. John Robert and Patricia (Gillson) Baker; m. Jorge Alberto Lievanos, June 6, 1981; children—Jeremy John Baker, Wendy Mara Baker, Raoul Salvador Baker-Lievanos. Student Mills Coll., 1969-70; grad. course in diamond grading Gemology Inst. Am., 1983; student in diamondtology designation Diamond Council Am., 1986—. Artist, tchr., Claremont, Calif., 1973-78; escrow officer Bank of Am., Claremont, 1978-81; retail salesman William Pitt Jewelers, Puente Hills, Montclair, Calif., 1981-83, asst. mgr., Montclair, 1983, mgr., 1983—. Artist tapestry hanging

Laguna Beach Mus. Art, 1974. Recipient Cert. Merit Art Bank Am., 1968, High Sales award William Pitt Jewelers, 1983, 84. Mem. Nat. Assn. Female Execs., C. of C., Compassion Internat. Democrat. Unitarian. Avocations: tapestry weaving, creative writing. Office: William Pitt Jewelers 158 Towne Ctr Santa Maria CA 93454

BAKEWELL, PETER JOHN, history educator; b. Oldham, Eng., Dec. 3, 1943; came to U.S., 1975; s. Weeder and Irene Mary (Shaw) B.; m. Susan Benforado, Feb. 14, 1985; 1 child, Max Louis. BA, Cambridge (Eng.) U., 1965, MA, 1968, PhD, 1969. Vis. asst. prof. history U. N.Mex., Albuquerque, 1975-76, assoc. prof. history, 1976-85, prof. history, 1985—; presdl. lectr. history U. N.Mex., Albuquerque, 1984-86. Author: Silver Mining and Society in Colonial Mexico: Zacatecas, 1546-1700, 1971 (Herbert Eugene Bolton award), Miners of the Red Mountain: Indian Labor in Potosi 1550-1650, 1984; editor (with John J. Johnson and Meredith D. Dodge), Readings in Latin American History Volume I, The Formative Centuries, 1985, assoc. editor Hispanic American Historical Review, 1980-85. Prize Research Fellow Trinity Coll. Cambridge U., 1968-72. Mem. Conf. Latin Am. History, Latin Am. Studies Assn., Sch. Hist. Studies Inst. for Advanced Study. Avocations: woodworking, house maintenance, cooking, piano, gliding. Home: 514 12th St NW Albuquerque NM 87102 Office: U NMex Dept History Albuquerque NM 87131

BAKEY, THOMAS, computer graphics consultant. B.S. in Elec. Engring., Northeastern U., 1958, postgrad. in elec. engring., 1960-62. Dir. graphics mktg. Varian Assocs., Palo Alto, Calif., 1971-76; dir. market research and devel. Calma, Sunnyvale, Calif., 1976-81; founder, v.p. Tricad, Campbell, Calif., 1981-83; pres. Tom Bakey and Assocs., CAD Cons., 1983—; lectr. in field. Author several books, numerous articles on computer graphics systems and their application. Home: 1142 Quince Sunnyvale CA 94087

BAKIN, IRWIN IRA, police officer; b. N.Y.C, Apr. 29, 1948; s. Julius and Shirley (Friedman) B.; m. Joan Karen Debbins, Sept. 3, 1972; children: Jared, Jeremy. BA in Mgmt., U. Phoenix, 1979, MBA, 1985. Dir. computer services Phoenix Police Dept., 1980-85; commandr. patrol precinct Phoenix police dept., 1985—; dir. Phoenix Regional Police Acad., 1985; chmn. innovation team City of Phoenix, 1985-86, chmn. awards com., 1985, chmn. regulatory team, 1985. Bd. dirs. Anti Defamation League, Phoenix, 1984—, Ariz. Found. for the Handicapped, Phoenix, 1986, Phoenix Boys Club, 1986. Mem. Internat. Chiefs of Police Assn., Assn. Pub. Safety Communications Officers, Internat. City Mgrs. Assn. Lodge: Rotary. Avocations: running, classical music. Office: Maryvale Precinct 4020 W Glenrosa Phoenix AZ 85019

BALAICH, MICHAEL KERRY, microbiologist; b. Ogden, Utah, June 16, 1951; s. James Robert and Betty Bernice (Kilgrow) B.; m. Joyce Ann Volk, July 17, 1981; children: Samantha, Micki. BS in Microbiology cum laude, Weber State Coll., 1981. Prodn./research technician Microbiol. Research Corp., Bountiful, Utah, 1981—. Served as cpl. USMC, 1970-72. Mem. Am. Blade Assn., Sigma Xi. Avocations: classical guitar, collecting knives. Office: Microbiol Research Corp 40 W 500 S Bountiful UT 84010

BALBINDER, ELIAS, biologist; b. Warsaw, Poland, Jan. 22, 1926; s. Aaron Lajba and Chaja Pessa (Kratka) B.; m. Evelyn Weissman, May 10, 1955 (dec. 1974); children: Rachel Naomi, Sara Elizabeth; m. Glory Hirshfeld, May 17, 1980. BS, U. Mich., 1949; PhD, U. Ind., 1957. Research assoc. Carnegie Inst. Wash., Cold Spring Harbor, N.Y., 1957-60; Am. Cancer Soc. postdoctoral research fellow U. Calif. San Diego, La Jolla, 1960-62; asst. prof. genetics Syracuse (N.Y.) U., 1962-67, assoc. prof., 1967-71, prof., 1971-76; dir. genetics and carcinogenesis Am. Med. Ctr.-Cancer Research Ctr. and Hosp., Lakewood, Colo., 1976-82; adj. prof. biochemistry, biophysics and genetics U. Colo. Health Scis. Ctr., Denver, 1982—; mem. genetic biology panel NSF, 1977-79. Contbr. articles to profl. jours. NSF, NIH grantee, 1963-78; Fulbright Hays awardee Argentina, 1963, Colombia, 1982; NIH spl. fellow Osaka (Japan) U., 1970. Fellow AAAS; mem. Am. Soc. Microbiology, Genetics Soc. Am., Environ. Mutagen Soc., Sigma Xi. Home: 2160 E Columbia Pl Denver CO 80210 Office: 4200 E 9th Ave Denver CO 80262

BALCH, GLENN MCCLAIN, JR., minister, former university president; b. Shattuck, Okla., Nov. 1, 1937; s. Glenn McClain and Marjorie (Daily) B.; student Panhandle State U., 1958-60, So. Meth. U., summers 1962-64; B.A., S.W. State U. Okla., 1962; B.D., Phillips U., 1965; M.A., Chapman Coll., 1973, M.A. in Edn., 1975, M.A. in Psychology, 1975; Ph.D., U.S. Internat. U., 1978; postgrad. Claremont Grad. Sch., 1968-70, U. Okla., 1965-66; m. Diana Gale Seeley, Oct. 15, 1970; children—Bryan, Gayle, Wesley, Johnny. Ordained to ministry Methodist Ch., 1962; sr. minister First Meth. Ch., Eakly, Okla., 1960-63, First Meth. Ch., Calumet, Okla., 1963-65, Goodrich Meml. Ch., Norman, Okla., 1965-66, First Meth. Ch., Barstow, Calif., 1966-70; asst. dean Chapman Coll., Orange, Calif., 1970-76; v.p. Pacific Christian Coll., Fullerton, Calif., 1976-79; pres. Newport U., Newport Beach, Calif., 1979-82; sr. pastor Brea United Meth. Ch., 1978—; edn. cons. USAF, 1974-75; mental health cons. U.S. Army, 1969. Mem. Community Adv. Bd. Minority Problems, 1975; Mayor's rep. to County Dependency Prevention Commn., 1968-69; bd. dirs. For Kid's Sake. Served with USMC, 1956-57. Recipient Eastern Star Religious Tng. award, 1963, 64; named Man of Year, Jr. C. of C., Barstow, 1969; Broadhurst fellow, 1963-65. Mem. CalifAssn. Marriage and Family Therapists, Doctoral Soc. U.S. Internat. U. Lodges: Rotary (pres. 1969-70, 83-84, dist. gov. 1987—), Masons, Shriners, Elks. Home: 1016 Steele Dr Brea CA 92621 Office: 480 N State College Brea CA 92621

BALCOM, GLORIA DARLEEN, computer administrative and marketing consultant; b. Porterville, Calif., July 23, 1939; d. Orel A. and Eunice E. Stadtmiller; A.A., El Camino Coll., 1959; student computer sci. Harbor Coll., 1976-77; m. Orville R. Balcom, July 23, 1971; stepchildren—Cynthia Lou, Steven Raymond. Personnel trainee AiResearch div. Garrett Corp., Los Angeles, 1959-60, sales promotion adminstr., 1960-64; sales rep. Volt Temporary Services, El Segundo, Calif., 1965-69, mgr., Tarzana, Calif., 1969-71; co-owner, co-operator Brown Dog Engring., Lomita, Calif., 1972-77; pres., owner, cons. MicroSly Mktg., Lomita, 1977—. Mem. Ind. Computer Cons. Assn., Am. Soc. Profl. and Exec. Women, Nat. Assn. Female Execs., LWV. Club: Torrance Athletic. Home and Office: 24521 Walnut St Lomita CA 90717

BALCOM, ORVILLE, engineer; b. Inglewood, Calif., Apr. 20, 1937; s. Orville R. and Rose Mae (Argo) B.; B.S. in Math., Calif. State U., Long Beach, 1958, postgrad., 1958-59; postgrad. UCLA, 1959-62; m. Gloria Stadtmiller, July 23, 1971; children—Cynthia, Steven. Engr., AiResearch Mfg. Co., 1959-62, 64-65; chief engr. Meditron, El Monte, Calif., 1962-64; chief engr. Astro Metrics, Burbank, Calif., 1965-67; chief engr., gen. mgr. Varadyne Power Systems, Van Nuys, Calif., 1968-71; owner, chief engr. Brown Dog Engring., Lomita, Calif., 1971—. Mem. IEEE Computer Group, Independent Computer Cons. Assn. Patentee in field. Club: Torrance Athletic. Home: 24521 Walnut St Lomita CA 90717 Office: PO Box 427 Lomita CA 90717

BALDERI, NICOLA, designer; b. Pietrasanta, Lucca, Italy, May 19, 1951; came to U.S., 1954; s. Michelangelo and Alba (Venturelli) B; m. Karen Ann Schilling, Sept 22, 1973; children: Michael, Sara. BFA with honors, Wayne State U., 1973. Cert. Nat. Council for Interior Design Qualification. Designer Rossetti Assoc., Detroit, 1973-77; assoc. SH&G Inc., Detroit, 1977-81, HOK, Inc., Denver, 1981-83; pres. NB Assocs., Englewood, Colo., 1983—; instr. Wayne State U., Detroit, 1979-81; juror U. Colo., Denver, 1983—. Furniture designer; patentee in field. V.P. Our Father Luth. Ch., Littleton, Colo., 1985, pres. 1986. Avocations: photography, skiing. Office: NB Assocs Inc 7353 S Alton Way A103 Englewood CO 80112

BALDESCHWIELER, JOHN DICKSON, chemist, educator; b. Elizabeth, N.J., Nov. 14, 1933; s. Emile L. and Isobel (Dickson) B.; m. Marcia Ewing, June 20, 1959; children—John Eric, Karen Anne, David Russell. B. Chem. Engring., Cornell U., 1956; Ph.D., U. Calif. at Berkeley, 1959. From instr. to asso. prof. chemistry Harvard U., 1960-65; faculty Stanford (Calif.) U., 1965-71, prof. chemistry, 1967-71; chmn. adv. bd. Synchrotron Radiation Project, 1972-75; vis. scientist Synchrotron Radiation Lab., 1977; dep. dir. Office Sci. and Tech., Exec. Office Pres., Washington, 1971-73; prof. chemistry Calif. Inst. Tech., Pasadena, 1973—; chmn. div. chemistry and chem. engring. Calif. Inst. Tech., 1973-78; OAS vis. lectr. U. Chile, 1969; spl. lectr. in chemistry U. London, Queen Mary Coll., 1970; vis. scientist Bell Labs., 1978; Mem. Pres.'s Sci. Adv. Com., 1969—, vice chmn., 1970-71; mem. Def. Sci. Bd., 1973-80, vice chmn., 1974-76; mem. carcinogenesis adv. panel Nat. Cancer Inst., 1973—; mem. com. planning and intl. affairs NSF, 1973-77; adv. com. Arms Control and Disarmament Agy., 1974-76; mem. Nat. Acad. Sci. Bd. Sci. and Tech. for Internat. Devel., 1974-76, ad hoc com. on fed. sci. policy, 1979, task force on synfuels, 1979; mem. Pres.'s Com. on Nat. Medal of Sci., 1974-76, ,pres., 1987—, Pres.'s Adv. Group on Sci. and Tech., 1975-76; mem. governing bd. Reza Shah Kabir U., 1975-79; mem. Sloan Commn. on Govt. and Higher Edn., 1977-79, U.S.-USSR Joint Commn. on Sci. and Tech. Coop., 1977-79; vice chmn. del. on pure and applied chemistry to People's Republic of China, 1978; mem. com. on scholarly communication with People's Republic of China, 1978-84; mem. research adv. council Ford Motor Co., 1979—, mem. chem. and engring. adv. bd., 1981-83. Mem. editorial adv. bd. Chem. Physics Letters, 1979-83. Served to 1st lt. AUS, 1959-60. Sloan Found. fellow, 1962-64, 64-65; recipient Fresenius award Phi Lambda Upsilon, 1968. Mem. Nat. Acad. Scis., Am. Chem. Soc. (award in pure chemistry 1967), Council on Sci. and Tech. for Devel., Am. Acad. Arts and Scis., Am. Philos. Soc. Home: 619 S Hill Ave Pasadena CA 91106 Office: Div Chemistry and Chem Engring Calif Inst Tech Pasadena CA 91125

BALDINELLI, MICHAEL ARTHUR, safety engineer; b. Casablanca, Morrocco, July 6, 1952; came to U.S., 1954; s. Edward Lewis and Kathleen (May) B.; m. Joanne Marie Baldinelli, Aug..10, 1985; children: Frank, Shelly, Gina. AA, Merritt Coll., 1975; BA, San Francisco State U., 1978. CPA. Safety supr. Kaiser Engrs., Ispheming, Mich., 1973-74; safety cons. Barnes & Assocs., Oakland, Calif., 1974-77; safety mgr. Peterbilt Motor Co., Newark, Calif., 1977-81; regional safety mgr. Browning-Ferris Industries Inc., San Jose, Calif., 1981—; creative cons. Tom McCann Assocs., Boston, 1983-85. Inventor comml. winemaker, 1982. 1st aid instr. ARC, Berkeley, 1970, CPR instr., 1975. Mem. Am. Soc. Safety Engrs. (profl.), Safety Profls. Ams. (cert.), Wings of Rogollo. Roman Catholic. Avocations: winemaking, hang gliding, camping, cooking. Office: Browning Ferris Industries 55 Almaden Blvd San Jose CA 95113

BALDON, CLEO, interior designer; b. Leavenworth, Wash., June 1, 1927; d. Ernest Elsworth and Esther Jane (Hannan) Chute; m. Lewis Smith Baldon, Nov. 20, 1948 (div. July 1961); 1 child, Dirk; m. Ib J—rgen Melchior, Jan. 18, 1964; 1 stepson, Leif Melchior. BS, Woodbury Coll., 1948. Ptnr. Interior Designs Ltd., Los Angeles, 1948-50; freelance illustrator Los Angeles, 1952-54; prin. Cleo Baldon & Assocs., Los Angeles and Venice, Calif., 1954—; ptnr. Galper/Baldon Assocs., Venice, 1970—. Contbr. articles to profl. jours.; patentee in field. Recipient City Beautification awards Los Angeles 1974-77, 80, 83, 85-87, Beverly Hills 1982, Calif. Landscape Contractors, 1975, 79, Pacifica award Resources Council, Calif., 1979. Avocations: photography, collecting Colonial Am. documents. Home: 8228 Marmont Ln Los Angeles CA 90069 Office: Galder/Baldon Assocs 723 Ocean Front Walk Venice CA 90291

BALDRIDGE, WILLIAM KING, crisis intervention specialist, psychotherapist; b. San Luis Obispo, Calif., Mar. 14, 1946; s. Robert Harvey and Clara Kathryn (King) B.; divorced; children: Heather, Kimberly, Brett. BSW, San Diego State U., 1976; MSW, Calif. State U., Fresno, 1978. Lic. clin. social worker, psychiatric technician. Psychiat. technician Atascadero (Calif.) State, 1969-72, 77-78, social worker, 1978-80; psychiat. technician San Diego Mental Health Dept., 1972-76; crisis officer Fresno Police Dept., 1976-77, cons., 1978-80; crisis specialist San Luis Obispo/Santa Barbara County, 1980—; cons. N.Y.C. Police, 1981, Dallas Police, 1982. Bd. dirs. Sexual Response Team Victim Advocate, San Luis Obispo, 1980-83, Domestic Violence, San Luis Obispo, 1980-83, Sexual Assault Response Team, Santa Barbara, 1980—. Served with USNR, 1964-68, Vietnam. Recipient 1st World Congress on Victomology award, 1982. Mem. Nat. Assn. Social Workers. Republican. Avocations: sailing, running, bike riding, family. Home and Office: 2102 Red Rose Way Santa Barbara CA 93109

BALDWIN, GLADYS JANE, community services administrator; b. Conde, S.D., Jan. 6, 1924; d. Ransom H. and Edna Inez (Cunningham) W.; m. Theron Scott Knapp, Apr. 21, 1945 (div. Sept. 1969); children: Terry S. Knapp, Betty J. Baker, Lois A. Thurber, Donna J. Akins (dec.), Cheryl Knapp; m. Gilbert Ralph Baldwin, Feb. 14, 1974. AA, Highline Community Coll., 1978; B cum laude, Eastern Wash. U., 1981, MSW cum laude, 1985. Adminstrv. sec. Social and Health Services, Ephrata, Wash., 1960-62, clerical supr. 2, 1962-70; fin. supr. Social and Health Services, Seattle, 1970-72, fin. mgr., 1972-77; adminstr. Social and Health Services, Colfax, Wash., 1977-82, Spokane, Wash., 1982—. Mem. Nat. Assn. Social Welfare, Wash. Assn. Social Work, Nat. Notaries Assn. Republican. Avocations: painting, sewing. Home: 13413 E 9th Spokane WA 99216 Office: Dept Social and Health Services 1313 N Maple Spokane WA 99201

BALDWIN, JANICE ELAINE, buyer; b. Omaha, Oct. 11, 1934; d. James H. and Frances Cecelia (Hon) Wagner; m. Valder Dee Baldwin, Oct. 9, 1954 (div.); children—Robin (Mrs. R. Beckes), Kenneth, Jill. B.A. in Mktg., Western Wash. U.-Bellingham, 1978. Lic. real estate, Wash. Export mgr. Wham-O Mfg., San Gabriel, Calif., 1964-65; sales rep. HPH, Inc., Rosemead, Calif., 1968-74; dir. Personal Advocacy Services, Seattle, 1975-78; buyer Boeing Comml. Airplane Co., Renton, Wash., 1977-82, Seattle, 1984—; real estate agt. Realty World-Beeman & Assocs., Bellevue, Wash., 1983-84. Mem. model project Nat. Assn. for Retarded/King County ARC, 1974-75. Precinct committeeman Dem. Party, Bellevue. Mem. Nat. Assn. Female Execs., Nat. Assn. Realtors. Office: Boeing Comml Airplane Co PO Box 3707 Seattle WA 98124-2207

BALDWIN, JIM D., supermarket chain executive. Pres. King Soopers Inc., Denver. Office: King Soopers Inc 65 Tejon St Denver CO 80223 *

BALDWIN, JOHN DAVID, sociologist, educator; b. Cin., June 24, 1941; s. Herman Jackson and Helen Thomas (Scrivner) B.; m. Janice Irene Whiteside, Aug. 26, 1967. BA, Johns Hopkins U., 1963, PhD, 1967. From asst. to assoc. to prof. sociology U. Calif., Santa Barbara, 1967—. Author: Behavior Principles in Everyday Life, 1981, 2d rev. edit., 1986, Beyond Sociology, 1981, George Herbert Mead, 1986; contbr. numerous articles to profl. jours. Alfred Ludwig U. fellow, 1963-64. Mem. Am. Sociol. Assn., AAAS. Avocations: music, gardening. Office: U Calif Sociology Dept Santa Barbara CA 93106

BALDWIN, LARELL HARDISON, insurance company executive; b. Hanford, Calif., May 12, 1940; s. Leo H. and Bernice (Gash) B.; m. Kathleen L. Hardison, June 23, 1979; children: Jennifer Lin, Leslie Kari, Richard Allen, Michael Maxwell. Student Pasadena Coll., 1958-61; grad. Alexander Hamilton Inst. Bus., 1967. V.p. mortgage lending div. Standard Life & Accident Ins. Co. of Okla., Phoenix, 1961-64; sales mgr. Peterson Baby Products Inc., Burbank, Calif., 1964-67; v.p. sales Rotorway Aircraft Corp., Tempe, Ariz., 1967-69; pres. Trans World Arts Inc., San Jose, Calif., 1969-75, Baldwin Assocs. Devel. Corp., Santa Cruz, Calif., 1975-80; ptnr., v.p. Assurance Distbg. Co. Ltd., Santa Ana, Calif., 1979-82; pres. Baldwin Assurance Mktg. Corp., 1982—; nat. cons. ins. cos., author, lectr.; bd. dirs. Am. Acrylic Industries. Author in field. Office: PO Box 66972 Scotts Valley CA 95066

BALDWIN, MARK LEWIS, aerospace engineer; b. Detroit, Jan. 29, 1952; s. William Lewis and Bette Louis (McNear) B. BS, MS in Engring., Purdue U., 1974. Task mgr. McDonnell Douglas, Houston, 1979-86; group engr. Martin Marietta Corp., Denver, 1986—; owner, pres. Beacon Tech. Services, Littleton, Colo., 1980—. Contbr. articles to profl. jours. Served with USAF, 1975-79. Recipient Cert. Recognition NASA, 1982, Group Achievement award, 1984, 85. Mem. AIAA, Denver Mgmt. Assn. Club: Rocky Mountain Orienteering (Colorado Springs, Colo.). Office: 7711 S Curtice Way Apt E Littleton CO 80120

BALES, PAMELA JANE, public relations assistant; b. Hartford City, N.J., Aug. 6, 1962; d. Robert L. and Nancy Jane (Ewbank) Bales. BS in Journalism, Ball State U., 1980. Pub. relations asst. Netech Communications Corp., Denver, 1984-85, U.S. West CCI (merger Netech Communications Corp.), Denver, 1985-86; corp. communications specialist Cen. Bancorp. Inc., Denver, 1986—; vol. pub. relations Nat. Repertory Orch., Evergreen, Colo., 1985—. Mem. Pub. Relations Soc. Am. (newsletter editor 1986—), Kappa Tau Kappa, Kappa Alpha Theta. Republican. Avocations: pottery, skiing, hiking, reading.

BALESTRERY, FRANK GEORGE, optometrist; b. Oakland, Calif., Nov. 10, 1950; s. George D. and Esther D. (Close) B.; m. Sharon Lee Calkins, Aug. 23, 1975; children: Scott, James, Ryan. BS in Physiology, U. Calif., Davis, 1972, MS in Physiology, 1977; BS in Optometry, U. Calif., Berkeley, 1981, OD, 1983. Lic. optometrist, Calif. Ptnr., optometrist Eaton Ave. Optometric Group, Tracy, Calif., 1984—; guest lectr. U. Calif. Sch. Optometry, Berkeley, 1982—, asst. clin. instr., 1984—, asst. clin. prof., 1985. Contbr. articles to profl. jours. Recipient Jastro Research award U. Calif., Davis, 1975, Golden Retinoscope award U. Calif. Optometry Alumni Assn., 1983; scholar Peter Schields U. Calif., Davis, 1975, Mary Phleger U. Calif., Berkeley, 1981, Rupert Flower U. Calif., Berkeley, 1982. Mem. Am. Optometric Assn., Calif. Optometric Assn., Phi Kappa Phi. Lodge: Rotary, Elks. Home: 949 Kapareil Dr Tracy CA 95376 Office: Eaton Ave Optometric Group 550 W Eaton Ave Tracy CA 95376

BALKIND, ALVIN LOUIS, curator; b. Balt., Mar. 28, 1921; s. Benjamin and Nessie (Bers) B. Student, Sorbonne U., Paris, 1954-55; BA, Johns Hopkins U., 1953. Curator Fine Arts Gallery U. B.C., Vancouver, Can., 1962-73; curator contemporary art Art Gallery of Ont., Toronto, Can., 1973-75; chief curator Vancouver Art Gallery, 1975-78; head visual art studio Banff (Alta.) Sch. Fine Arts, Can., 1985-87; mem. arts adv. com. Can. Council, Ottawa, Ont., 1971-73; mem. vis. com. Nat. Gallery Can., Ottawa, 1969-71. Served with USN, 1943-46. Avocations: travel, reading, arts. Home: 4177 W 14th Ave, Vancouver Can V6R 2X6 Office: Banff Centre Sch Fine Arts, Visual Art Studio Box 1020, Banff, AB Canada T0L 0C0

BALKWILL, YVETTE JEANNE, radio station executive; b. Gravelbourg, Sask., Can., July 19, 1934; d. Edgard Alvin and Germaine Jeanne (Pouchard) Belhumeur; m. Gilbert Roy Balkwill, May 18, 1958; children—Darrell, Roy, Tami. Interm 1st class, Teacher's Coll., Saskatoon, Sask., 1953; permanent teaching cert., U. Sask., Saskatoon, 1955. Tchr. Rosetown Sch. Milden, Sask., 1953-56; billing clk. Federated Co-op, Saskatoon, 1962-69; receptionist Sta. CFMC-FM, Saskatoon, 1969-73, gen. mgr. 1973-75; gen. mgr. Sta. CJWW, Saskatoon, 1976—. Bd. dirs. Jr. Achievement of Can., Saskatoon, 1984—. Mem. Bus. and Profl. Women, Saskatoon Personnel Assn., Roman Catholic. Club: Saskatoon Press. Office: Sta CJWW Radio, 345 4th Ave S, Saskatoon, SK Canada S7K 5S5

BALL, DOUGLAS SCHELLING, oil, gas and mineral consultant; b. Cheyenne, Wyo., Mar. 5, 1920; s. Max Waite and Amalia (Maeder) B.; P.E., Colo. Sch. Mines, 1943; m. Caroline Marguerite Schmidt, Mar. 12, 1943; children—Richard Neal, Max Waite (dec.), Michael Douglas, Anna Gail. Various positions in refinery constrn. and oil field work, Can. and U.S., 1937-39; geophysics work, Gulf Coast and N. Tex., 1940-42; gas reservoir engr. Phillips Petroleum Co., Panhandle area, 1946-49; mem. firm Max. W. Ball & Douglas Ball, Washington, 1949-55; pres. Ball Assos., Ltd., Washington and Colo., 1955—; co-chmn. tar sands subcom., enhanced recovery com. Interstate Oil Compact Commn., 1969—; chmn. MicroSearch, Inc., 1984—. Mem. Gilpin County (Colo.) Sch. Bd., 1969-73, pres., 1971-73. Served to 1st lt. U.S. Army, 1942-46. Fellow Geol. Soc. Am.; mem. AAAS, Am. Assn. Petroleum Geologists, Soc. Petroleum Engrs. of Am. Inst. Mining and Metall. Engrs. (chmn. petroleum br. econs. com. 1953), Rocky Mountain Assn. Geologists, Israel Inst. Petroleum and Geophysics (hon.). Republican. Episcopalian. Author: (with Daniel S. Turner) This Fascinating Oil Business, 1966; sr. author: U.S. Bur. Mines Monograph 12, Surface and Shallow Oil-Impregnated Rocks and Shallow Oil Fields in the U.S., 1965; contbr. articles to profl. jours. Home and office: 105 Main St PO Box 8 Black Hawk CO 80422

BALL, FRED SHELTON, chamber of commerce executive; b. Ogden, Utah, Sept. 29, 1932; s. Fred S. and Gladys (Thornton) B.; m. Joyce Worsencroft, July 2, 1953; children: Kathryn, Kristine, Kimberly, Karalyn. AS, Weber State Coll., 1952; BS, U. Utah, 1955; MBA, Stanford U., 1966. Gen. sales mgr. IML Freight, San Francisco, 1954-71; pres., gen. mgr. Salt Lake Area C. of C., 1971—; pres. Creative Mgmt., Salt Lake City, 1970—; bd. dirs. Pierson Hosp., Salt Lake City, 1985—. Author: Ten Most Wanted Man, 1973, Authentic Achiever, 1975. Chmn. Cen. Bus. Improvement, Salt Lake City, 1986; mem. Gov.'s Law exec. com., Salt Lake City, 1986. Named Salesman of Yr., Sales Mktg. Execs., 1982, one of Top 10 Speakers in Am., Platform Speakers, 1983. Republican. Mormon. Club: Salt Lake County, Toastmasters (named Speaker of Yr. 1981). Lodge: Rotary. Home: 809 16th Ave Salt Lake City UT 84103 Office: Salt Lake Area C of C 175 E 400 S Salt Lake City UT 84111

BALL, ROBERT JEROME, classics educator; b. N.Y.C., Nov. 4, 1941; s. William and Pauline Ball. BA, Queens Coll., 1962; MA, Tufts U., 1963; PhD, Columbia U., 1971. Asst. prof. classics U. Hawaii, Honolulu, 1971-76, assoc. prof., 1976-83, prof., 1983—. Author: Tibullus the Elegist: A Critical Survey, 1983; editor: The Classical Papers of Gilbert Highet, 1983. Recipient Excellence in Teaching award U. Hawaii, 1979; Presdl. scholar U. Hawaii, 1985. Mem. Am. Philol. Assn. (Excellence in Teaching award 1981). Office: U Hawaii at Manoa Dept European Langs and Lit Honolulu HI 96822

BALL, WILLIAM PAUL, physicist, engineer; b. San Diego, Nov. 16, 1913; s. John and Mary (Kajla) B.; m. Edith Lucile March, June 28, 1941 (dec. 1976); children: Lura Irene Ball Raplee, Roy Ernest. AB, UCLA, 1940; PhD, U. Calif., Berkeley, 1952. Registered profl. engr. Calif. Projectionist, sound technician studios and theatres in Los Angeles, 1932-41; tchr. high sch. Montebello, Calif., 1941-42; instr. math. and physics Santa Ana (Calif.) Army Air Base, 1942-43; physicist U. Calif. Radiation Lab., Berkeley and Livermore, 1943-58; mem. tech. staff Ramo-Wooldridge Corp., Los Angeles, 1958-59; sr. scientist Hughes Aircraft Co., Culver City, Calif., 1959-64; sr. staff engr. TRW-Def. Systems Group, Redondo Beach, Calif., 1964-83, Hughes Aircraft Co., 1983-86; cons. Redondo Beach, 1986—. Contbr. articles to profl. jours.; patentee in field. Bd. dirs. So. Dist. Los Angeles chpt. ARC, 1979-86. Recipient Manhattan Project award for contbn. to 1st atomic bomb, 1945. Mem. Am. Phys. Soc., Am. Nuclear Soc., AAAS, AIAA, N.Y. Acad. Scis., Torrance (Calif.) Area C. of C. (bd. dirs. 1978-84), Sigma Xi. Home and Office: 209 Via El Toro Redondo Beach CA 90277

BALLANTINE, MORLEY COWLES (MRS. ARTHUR ATWOOD BALLANTINE), newspaper publisher; b. Des Moines, May 21, 1925; d. John and Elizabeth (Bates) Cowles; m. Arthur Atwood Ballantine, July 26, 1947 (dec. 1975); children—Richard, Elizabeth Ballantine Leavitt, William, Helen Ballantine Healy. A.B., Ft. Lewis Coll., 1975; L.H.D. (hon.), Simpson Coll., Indianola, Iowa, 1980. Pub. Durango (Colo.) Herald, 1952—, editor, pub., 1975-83, editor, chmn. bd., 1983—; dir. 1st Nat. Bank, Durango, 1976—, Des Moines Register & Tribune, 1977-85, Cowles Media Co., 1982-86. Mem. Colo. Land Use Commn., 1975-81, Supreme Ct. Nominating Comm., 1984—; pres. S.W. Colo. Mental Health Center, 1964-65; bd. dirs. Colo. Nat. Hist. Preservation Act, 1968-78; trustee Choate/Rosemary Hall, Wallingford, Conn., 1973-81, Simpson Coll., Indianola, Iowa, 1981—, U. Denver, 1984—, Fountain Valley Sch., Colorado Springs, 1976—; pres. Four Corners Opera Assn., 1983-86, mem. bd. govs. Mill Reef, Antigua, West Indies. Recipient 1st place award for editorial writing Nat. Fedn. Press Women, 1955, Outstanding Alumna award Rosemary Hall, Greenwich, Conn., 1969, Outstanding Journalism award U. Colo. Sch. Journalism, 1967, Distinguished Service award Ft. Lewis Coll., Durango, 1970; named to Colo. Community Journalism Hall of Fame, 1987. Mem. Nat. Soc. Colonial Dames, Colo. Press Assn. (bd. dirs. 1978-79), Colo. AP Assn. (chmn. 1966-67), Federated Women's Club Durango. Episcopalian. Club: Mill Reef (Antigua, W.I.). Address: care Herald PO Drawer A Durango CO 81302

BALLARD, DEBBI ANN, entrepreneur, management consultant; b. Chgo., July 15, 1949; d. Jordan Joseph and Dorethia Rose (Bartlett) Canzone; m. Dale Earl Ballard, June 10, 1972; 1 child, Dale Phillip. BA, No. Ill. U., 1971, MEd, 1975. Cert. tchr., Ill. Tchr. Ill. Pub. Schs., 1972-79; instr. Mesa

(Ariz.) Community Coll., 1985-86; pres., chief exec. officer Internat. Multi-Level Cons., Inc., Mesa, 1982—; guest speaker SBA, corp. symposiums. Author: Secrets of Multi-Level Fortune Building, 1982; contbr. articles to profl. jours. Sponsor Christian Children's Fund, 1976—. Named one of Am.'s Leading Execs., 1984. Mem. Am. Mktg. Assn., Multi-Level Mktg. Internat. Assn. (bd. dirs. 1985—). Avocations: piano, clarinet. Office: Internat Multi-Level Cons Inc 2051 S Dobson #5-203 Mesa AZ 85202

BALLARD, FLOYD LEON, manufacturing supervisor, engineer; b. Wendell, Idaho, June 2, 1950; s. Leo Arthur Ballard and Lois Mae (Anderson) Stoddard; m. Glenda Rhea Tews, July 11, 1969; children: Brandie Lyn, Casey Leon, Jodie Rhea. BSCE, U. Idaho, 1973, MSCE, 1975. Registered profl. engr., Mo., Idaho. Engr. Monsanto Co., St. Louis, 1975-78, sr. engr., 1978-79; sr. engr. Monsanto Co., Soda Spring, Idaho, 1979-80, process supr., 1980-82, engring. supr., 1982-86, mfg. supr., 1986—; Patentee pollutant removal, 1978. Coach Little League Baseball, Soda Spring, 1986. Mem. ASCE. Avocations: hunting, fishing, basketball, family activities. Home: 730 Hopkins Ln Soda Springs ID 83276 Office: Monsanto Chem Co North Hwy 34 Soda Spring ID 83276

BALLARD, JAMES CURTIS, management company executive; b. Mt. Vernon, Wash., May 10, 1945; s. Alvin Curtis and Emma Berneice (Calkins) B. BA in Econs., BA in History, Seattle U., 1966, BS in Polit. Sci., 1984, PhD in Arts and Letters (hon.), 1981; M in Pub. Adminstrn., U. Md., 1978. Legis. asst. U.S. Senate, Washington, 1965-67; exec. v.p. Ballard & Wood, Inc., San Bernardino, Calif., 1970-75; pres. Ballard & Assocs., Newport Beach, Calif., 1971—; gen. ptnr. B&A Gen. Constrn. Co., San Bernardino, 1979-81; pres. Food Service Co., City of Industry, Calif., 1979-82; cons. Wash. State Senate, Olympia, 1964-66. Author: Management Style and Organizational Behavior, 1980; co-author: Human Relations and the Professional Manager, 1984; contbr. articles to profl. jours. Advisor Calif. Bus. Roundtable, 1983-85; liaison Calif. Post Secondary Edn. Commn., 1983-85; bd. dirs. Crafton Hills Coll. Found., 1978-81; v.p., bd. dirs. Calif. Community Coll. Trustees Assn., 1978-84; trustee San Bernardino Community Colls., pres. 1981-83. Recipient Cert. Achievement Big Bros. Am., Seattle, 1966, Community Service award Mex. C. of C., 1975, Disting. Service award Assn. Governing Bds. Univs. and Colls., 1983; named one of Outstanding Young Men Am. U.S. Jaycees, 1980. Mem. Calif. Bus. Mgrs. Assn. (bd. dirs. 1984-86), Calif. Sch. Bds. Assn. (del. assembly 1978-83). Democrat. Roman Catholic. Club: Balboa Bay (Newport Beach). Avocations: tennis, sailing, swimming. Home: 2739 N F St San Bernardino CA 92405 Office: Ballard and Assocs Inc 710 Lido Park-44 Drake Newport Beach CA 92663

BALLINGER, CHARLES KENNETH, information specialist; b. Johnstown, Pa., July 28, 1950; s. Delores Jean (Cool) B.; m. Deb C. Delger, Sept. 14, 1985. Programmer analyst Cowles Pub. Co., Spokane, Wash., 1975-78; systems analyst Old Nat. Bank, Spokane, 1978-82; software engr. ISC System, Spokane, 1982; micro computer analyst Acme Bus. Computers, Spokane, 1982-85; info. ctr. analyst Wash. Water Power Co., Spokane, 1985—; cons. IDP Co., Spokane, 1978—. Contbr. articles to profl. jours. Served with Signal Corps, U.S. Army, 1968-71. Mem. Assn. Computing Machinery, Spokane Heath Users Group (pres. 1979-83). Avocations: software development, motorcycling, boating, shooting. Home: S 3810 Havana Spokane WA 99223 Office: Wash Water Power Co E 1411 Mission Spokane WA 99202

BALLONOFF, LARRY BRUCE, endocrinologist; b. Cleve., June 4, 1942; s. Irv and Betty Ruth (Cole) B.; m. Margaret Black, June 23, 1969; children: Ahna Beth, Ari Peter. BA, Carleton Coll., 1964; MD, John Hopkins U., 1968. Diplomate Am. Bd. Internal Medicine. Endocrinologist Denver Clinic, 1975-81, Kaiser-Permanente, Denver, 1981—; assoc. clin. prof. medicine U. Colo. Med. Sch., Denver, 1983—. Served to capt. U.S. Army, 1969-71. Mem. ACP, Am. Diabetes Assn., Sigma Xi, Phi Beta Kappa, Alpha Omega Alpha. Jewish. Avocations: skiing, bicycling, reading. Home: 3 Winwood Dr Englewood CO 80110 Office: Kaiser-Permanente 11245 Huron Denver CO 80234

BALSER, ELNORA MARIE, audiologist; b. Cleve., June 9, 1952; d. Charles Joseph and Lucy Ann (Englert) B. BA, Cleve. State U., 1974, MA, 1977; student in elec. engring., Ariz. State U., 1982—. Cert. clin. audiologist. Clerk-cashier LACO Bookstore, Cleve., 1975-77; audiologist George Serbin, M.D., Phoenix, 1977-78, Leon D. Zeitzer, M.D., Phoenix, 1977—; cons. audiologist Phoenix Meml. Hosp., 1978—; pres. Sound Audiologics Inc., Tempe, Ariz., 1984—; Active State Ariz. Never Too Young Project, 1985; audiologist for Community Hearing Aid Program, 1984. Mem. Am. Speech-Language-Hearing Assn. (com. on amplification for hearing impaired 1982-84), Ariz. Speech-Language-Hearing Assn. Democrat. Roman Catholic. Club: Cath. Alumnae (Phoenix). Avocations: reading, Tai Chi Chuan, film. Office: Leon D Zeitzer MD PA 3411 N 32nd St Phoenix AZ 85018

BALTHAZOR, ALBERT, JR., optometrist; b. Fond du Lac, Wis., Jan. 11, 1925; s. Albert Francis and Ernestina Alvina (Smith) B.; m. LaVerne R. Nelson, Aug. 30, 1952; children—Loren, Dean, Michael, Timothy. Student U. Wis., 1942-43, 46-47; O.D., Ill. Coll. Optometry, 1949. Gen. practice optometry, Fond du Lac, 1949-76, Apache Junction, Ariz., 1976-82, Mesa, Ariz., 1982—; cons. Fond du Lac County Mental Health Ctr., 1973-76; vision screening on Seattle Mariners baseball team, U.S. Olympic archery team. Bd. dirs. Fond du Lac County Republican party, 1965-67; county chmn. Wis. Congress Conservatives; mem. sch. bd. Christ the King Sch., Mesa, 1982-85. Served with USAF, 1943-46; to capt. USAFR, 1950-58. Fellow Coll. Optometrists in Vision Devel. (state dir.); mem. Am. Optometric Assn., Central Area Optometric Soc. (pres. 1981-82), Optometric Extension Program, Jaycees (Outstanding Mem. Fond du Lac 1961), VFW, Am. Legion. Roman Catholic. Clubs: Lions; KC (Mesa). Home: 1013 N Barkley St Mesa AZ 85203 Office: 8001 E Apache Trail Mesa AZ 85207

BALZHISER, RICHARD EARL, research and development company executive; b. Wheaton, Ill., May 27, 1932; s. Frank E. and Esther K. (Merrill Werner) B.; m. Christine Karnuth, 1951; children: Gary, Robert, Patricia, Cheryl. B.S. in Chem. Engring., U. Mich., 1955, M.S. in Nuclear Engring., 1956, Ph.D. in Chem. Engring., 1961. Mem. faculty U. Mich., Ann Arbor, 1961-67; White House fellow, spl. asst. to sec. Dept. Def., Washington, 1967-68; chmn. dept. chem. engring. U. Mich., 1970-71; assoc. dir. energy, environ. and natural resources White House Office of Sci. and Tech., Washington, 1971-73; dir. fossil fuel and advanced systems Electric Power Research Inst., Palo Alto, Calif., 1973-79, sr. v.p. research and devel., 1979—; chmn. U.S. Energy R&D Exchange with USSR, 1973-74; mem. adv. bd. Gas Research Inst., Chgo., 1979—, EPCOT Ctr., Orlando, Fla., 1977-80. Editorial bd.: Sci. mag., 1977—; co-author: Chemical Engineering Thermodynamics, 1972, Engineering Thermodynamics, 1977. Mem. Ann Arbor City Council, 1965-67, mayor pro tem, 1967. Charles M. Schwab Meml. lectr. Am. Iron And Steel Inst., 1983. Mem. Am. Inst. Chem. Engrs., AAAS, ASME, Sigma Chi. Republican. Lutheran. Club: Cosmos (Washington). Office: 3412 Hillview Ave Palo Alto CA 94304

BAMBURG, JAMES ROBERT, biochemistry educator; b. Chgo., Aug. 20, 1943; s. Leslie H. and Rose A. (Abrahams) B.; m. Alma Y. Vigo, June 7, 1970 (div. Dec. 1984); children: Eric Gregory, Leslie Ann; m. Laurie S. Minamide, June 22, 1985. BS in Chemistry, U. Ill., 1965; PhD, U. Wis., 1969. Project assoc. U. Wis., Madison, 1968-69; postdoctoral fellow Stanford U., Palo Alto, Calif., 1969-71; from asst. to full prof. Colo. State U., Ft. Collins, 1971—, acad. coordinator cell and molecular biol. program, 1975-78, interim chmn. dept. biochemistry, 1982-85, assoc. dir. neuronal growth and devel., 1986—; vis. prof. MRC Molecular Biol. Lab., Cambridge, Eng., 1978-79, MRC Cell Biophysics Unit, London, 1985-86; mem., chmn. NIH Biomed. Scis. Study Sect., Bethesda, Md., 1980-85. Contbr. articles to sci. jours. Fellow NSF, 1964-65, Nat. Multiple Sclerosis Soc., 1969-71, J.S. Guggenheim Found., 1978-79, Fogarty Ctr., 1985-86. Mem. Am. Chem. Soc., Am. Soc. Cell Biology, Am. Soc. Biol. Chemists, Internat. Neurochem. Soc., Sigma Xi. Home: 2125 Sandstone Dr Fort Collins CO 80524 Office: Colo State U Dept Biochemistry Fort Collins CO 80523

BAME, SAMUEL JARVIS, JR., research scientist; b. Lexington, N.C., Jan. 12, 1924; s. Samuel Jarvis and Stella Blanche (Davis) B.; m. Joyce Carleton Fancher, June 21, 1956; children—Karen, Dorthe, Barbara. B.S., U. N.C., 1947; Ph.D., Rice U., 1951. Mem. staff Los Alamos Nat. Lab., N.Mex., 1951-81, fellow, 1981—; mem. numerous NASA adv. coms. Contbr. articles to profl. jours. Served with AUS, 1943-46. Recipient Disting. Performance award Los Alamos Nat. Lab., 1980. Fellow Am. Phys. Soc., AAAS, Am. Geophys. Union; mem. Am. Astron. Soc. Home: 164 Dos Brazos Los Alamos NM 87544 Office: MS D438 Los Alamos Nat Lab Los Alamos NM 87545

BANAUGH, ROBERT PETER, computer science educator; b. Los Angeles, Oct. 27, 1922; s. Rudolph Otto and Elizabeth (Mantz) B.; m. Catherine Haun, July 6, 1946; children: Elizabeth Anne, Catherine Marie, Robert George, Mary Louise, Laura Jean, Marjorie Theresa, John Gerard, Peter Andrew. AA, Pasadena Jr. Coll., 1942; BA, U. Calif., Berkeley, 1943, MA, 1952, PhD, 1962. Secondary sch. tchr. Richmond (Calif.) Jr. High Sch., 1947-50; instr. math. U. Calif., Berkeley, 1949-72, vis. prof., 1975-76; prof. computer sci. U. Mont., Missoula, 1964-75, 76—; vis. prof. U. Wollongong, Australia, 1985; physicist Boeing Aircraft, Seattle, 1966-72; applied mechanics scientist Appled Theory, Los Angeles, 1968-75; computer scientist U.S. Forest Service, Missoula, 1968-71, engr., 1972—. Contbr. numerous articles to profl. jours. Served to 1st lt. USAAF, 1943-45. Home: Rt 5 Upper Miller Ch Rd Missoula MT 59803 Office: U Mont Dept Computer Sci Missoula MT 59812

BANAVALI, ASHOK DINKAR, scientist; b. Bombay, July 30, 1956; came to U.S., 1979,; s. Dinkar Shivdaas and Usha Dinkar (Kusum Kamath) B.; m. Lata Bhat, Nov. 14, 1984. BS in Chemistry, U. Bombay, 1976; MS in Clin. Biochemistry and Nutrition, Seth G.S. Med. Coll. & K.E.M. Hosp., Bombay, 1978; PhD in Nuclear Radiochemistry, U. Ark., 1983. Sr. lab. instr. dept. biochemistry and nutrition, lectr. Seth G.S. Med. Coll. & K.E.M. Hosp., Bombay, 1979; lectr. K.C. Coll. Arts and Sci., Bombay, 1979; researcher, teaching asst. U. Ark., Fayetteville, 1979-83; staff scientist U.S. Testing Co. Inc., Richland, Wash., 1983—; pvt. tutor in chemistry, Fayetteville, 1980-83, Richland, 1984-85. Sec., treas. Friends of India Soc., Fayetteville, 1979-80. Recipient R.K. Anjaria Meml. prize Seth G.S. Med. Coll. & K.E.M. Hosp., 1978, Merit award U. Bombay, 1976. Mem. AAAS, Am. Chem. Soc., Am. Nuclear Soc., Am. Health Physics Soc. Avocations: reading, music, table tennis. Home: 50 Jadwin Ave Apt #11 Richland WA 99352 Office: U S Testing Co Inc 2800 George Washington Way Richland WA 99352

BANDFIELD, LAWRENCE CHARLES, music director; b. Toledo, Mar. 30, 1933; s. Russel Everett and Helen Mary (Ash) B. BA, Oberlin Coll., 1955; MusM, U. Wis., 1981. Various mgmt. positions to pres. Cameo, Inc., Toledo, 1959-74; music dir. August Chorale, Madison, Wis., 1979-81, Sante Fe Desert Chorale, 1981—; mem. adv. bd. Stewart Awards, Oklahoma City, 1984—. Served with U.S. Army, 1957-59. Mem. Am. Chorale Dirs. Assn. (chmn. minorities com. N.Mex. chpt. 1984-85), Assn. Profl. Vocal Ensembles, Am. Symphony Orchestra League. Episcopalian. Avocation: travel. Home: 1200 Gonzales Ct Sante Fe NM 87501 Office: Sante Fe Desert Chorale PO Box 2813 Sante Fe NM 87504

BANDURRAGA, PETER LOUIS, museum director, historian; b. Los Angeles, Apr. 2, 1944; s. Luis Cipriano and E. Lillian (Slingsby) B.; m. Diane Elizabeth Nassir, Mar. 4 , 1979. B.A., Stanford U., 1966; M.A., U. Calif.-Santa Barbara, 1968; Ph.D., U. Calif.Santa Barbara, 1977. Instr. Chapman Coll., Orange, Calif., 1977-78; research librarian Ventura County Hist. Mus., Ventura, Calif., 1978-81; dir. Nev. Hist. Soc., Reno, 1981—; mem. Nev. State Adv. Council on Libraries, 1981—, State Hist. Records Adv. Bd., 1981—; adj. prof. U. Nev.-Reno, 1981—. Co-author: Ventura County's Yesterdays today, 1980. Mem. Downtown Found., Reno, 1983—. Mem. Am. Assn. State and Local History (state chair); ; Mem. Am. Assn. State and Local History (awards com. 1981). Democrat. Methodist. Club: Stanford (Reno) (v.p. 1983—). Office: 1650 N Virginia St Reno NV 89503 *

BANDY, MARLIN ROBERT, health educator; b. Lancaster, Pa., Feb. 26, 1946; s. Ervin Martin Bandy and Doris May Hilliar; married, Feb. 19, 1966; 1 child, Theresa Ann. BS in Nursing Edn., NYU, 1971; MPHEd, Tulane U., 1977; PhD in Pub. Health, Rosevelt U., 1984. Paramedic instr. City of Los Angeles, 1978-81; community services health edn. specialist Santa Monica (Calif.) Coll., 1981-82; adminstr. Los Angeles Free Clinic, 1982-84; exec. dir. Med. Edn. Service (formerly Med. Ednl. Devel. Assocs.), Los Angeles, 1984—, pres., 1980—; health edn. cons. Med. Edn. Services, Los Angeles, 1980-85. Author: Bilingual Education, 1982; contbr. articles to profl. jours. Bd. dirs. Santa Monica CPR Group, 1986, Aid for AIDS, Los Angeles, 1986, Emergency Disaster Group, Los Angeles, 1986. Named Tchr. of Yr., Assn. Supervision and Curriculum Devel., 1980. Mem. Am. Heart Assn. (Outstanding CPR Trainer 1985), Am. Assn. Physician Assts., Soc. Emergency Medicine Tchrs., Calif. Health Educators Assn. (Outstanding Health Educator 1984), Am. Assn. Trauma Specialists. Avocations: writing, snow skiing, reading. Office: Med Edn Service 1705 Pico Blvd Suite 169 Santa Monica CA 90405

BANERJEE, SANJOY, nuclear and chemical engineering educator; b. Calcutta, India, Nov. 13, 1943; came to U.S., 1979; s. Sidhartha and Kamala (Das) B.; m. Sandhya Denise Roy, June 21, 1964 (div. 1982); children—Anjali, Nobonita. B. Tech., Indian Inst. Tech., Kharagpur, 1964; Ph.D., U. Waterloo, Can., 1968. Head reactor analysis br. Atomic Energy Can., Pinawa, 1972-76, acting dir. applied sci. div., 1975-76; prof. engring. physics McMaster U., Hamilton, Ont., Can., 1976-80, Westinghouse chmn. engring. physics, 1977-80; prof. nuclear engring. U. Calif.-Santa Barbara, 1980—, chmn. dept. chem. and nuclear engring., 1984—; vis. prof. U. Calif.-Berkeley, 1979-81. Contbr. numerous articles to profl. jours. Recipient Acharya P. C. Ray award Indian Inst. Chem. Engrs., 1967. Fellow Am. Nuclear Soc. (chmn. thermohydraulic div. 1983-84); mem. ASME (Melville medal 1983), Am. Inst. Chem. Engrs., Chem. Inst. Can. Office: U Calif Dept Chem/Nuclear Engring Santa Barbara CA 93106

BANGART, GARY LEE, aerospace company executive; b. Billings, Mont., Oct. 1, 1934; s. David Robert and Etta Mae (Straight) B.; B.S.E.E., San Jose State U., 1973; m. Shirley Anne Young, June 8, 1957; children—Kurt Vaughn, Glenn Eric. With Boeing, Seattle, 1957-59, RCA Service Co., 1959-61; with Lockeed Missiles and Space Co., Sunnyvale, Calif., 1961—, successively reliability engr., sr. research engr., group engr., program engring. mgr., chief systems engr. advanced devel. programs, asst. program mgr., 1980-84, program mgr., 1984—; v.p. Beaver Creek Wells, Inc., Sedona, Ariz., 1987—, also bd, dirs. Bd. dirs. Homesteaders 4H Ranch, 1983—. Served with USAF, 1953-57. Recipient award YMCA Leaders Fellowship, 1971, YMCA Youth Leadership, 1975. Mem. IEEE, Nat. Mgmt. Assn., Am. Radio Relay League, San Jose State U. Alumni Assn. Democrat. Baptist. Office: PO Box 3504 Sunnyvale CA 94086-3504

BANGERTER, NORMAN HOWARD, governor, building contractor; b. Granger, Utah, Jan. 4, 1933; s. William Howard and Isabelle (Bawden) B.; m. Colleen Monson, Aug. 18, 1953; children: Garrett, Ann, Jordan, Blair, Alayne, Adam, Erdman (foster son). Student, U. Utah, 1956-57, Brigham Young U., 1951-55. Vice-pres. B and H Real Estate Co., West Valley City, Utah, 1970—; sec. Dixie-Six Land Devel., West Valley City, Utah, 1980—; pres. Bangerter and Hendrickson Co., West Valley City, Utah, 1970—, NHB Construction Co., West Valley City, Utah, 1983—; gov. Utah 1985—. Mem. Utah Ho. of Reps., 1974-85, speaker, 1981-84, majority leader, 1977-78; chmn. task force for alternative forms of govt. West Valley City, 1982. Recipient Outstanding Legislator award VFW, 1981; recipient Disting. Service award Home Bldg. Industry; named Outstanding Businessman West Valley C. of C. Mormon. Home: 4059 Montaia Dr West Valley City UT 84119 Office: Office of Gov 210 State Capital Salt Lake City UT 84114 *

BANK, EVELYN RUTH, retired chemistry educator; b. Bklyn., Sept. 28, 1919; d. Rudolph Andrew and Ruth Selma (Amos) Jastram; m. Walter Bank, May 18, 1942; children: Andrea Ruth Bank Castro, Randolph Edwin, Richard Michael. Cert. profl. tchr. Chemist Feedwaters, Inc., N.Y.C., 1940; research asst., instr. Guggenheim Dental Clinic and Sch. Dental Hygienists, N.Y.C., 1941-42; chemist Pitts. Testing Lab., 1942-43; instr. chemistry Colo. Coll., Colorado Springs, 1943; analytical chemist Foster Dee Snell, Inc., N.Y.C., 1944; instr. chemistry Bklyn. Coll., 1945-46, Davidson Coll. Ctr., Pitts., 1946-47; tchr. math. Highland High Sch., Salt Lake City, 1957-58; tchr. chemistry Westminster (Colo.) High Sch., 1958-84, chmn. dept. sci., 1965-80; presenter chemistry teaching workshops Colo. sect. Am. Chem. Soc., Denver, 1980—. Author: Comprehensive Chemistry, 1981; contbr. articles to profl. jours. Mem. AAAS, Am. Chem. Soc. (chmn. high sch. awards com. 1977-80, chmn.-elect and program chmn. 1980, chmn. Colo. sect. 1981, Outstanding Chemistry Tchr. 1979, James Bryant Conant award 1980), Colo. Alliance Sci., Nat. Retired Tchrs. Assn., Blue Ribbon Commn. on Teaching, Propyaea, Sigma Xi. Home: 6561 Benton Circle Arvada CO 80003

BANK, MILTON HAROLD, II, aviation safety and aeronautical engineering educator; b. Brockton, Mass., Aug. 11, 1935; s. Milton Harold and Fern Elaine (Richey) B.; m. Linda Hollis, Apr. 12, 1958; children—Baynes W., Milton H. B.S., U.S. Naval Acad., 1957; B.S. in Aero. Engring., Naval Postgrad. Sch., 1964; Aero. Engr., Stanford U., 1967; M.S., Ga. Tech., 1970, Ph.D., 1971. Registered profl. engr., Calif. Commd. ensign U.S. Navy, 1957, advanced through grades to lt. comdr., 1965; ret. 1968; assoc. prof. aviation safety and aero. engring. Naval Postgrad. Sch., Monterey, Calif., 1971—; cons. automobile accident reconstructionist. Decorated Air Medal with gold stars (2). Mem. AIAA, Soc. Automotive Engrs., Nat. Fencing Coaches Assn. Am., Soc. Exptl. Stress Analysis, Internat. Assn. Accident Reconstrn. Specialists, Southwestern Assn. Tech. Accident Investigators. Presbyterian. Office: Code 034 BT Naval Postgrad Sch Monterey CA 93940

BANKS, DAVID RUSSELL, health care executive; b. Arcadia, Wis., Feb. 15, 1937; s. J.R. and Cleone B.; married; children: Melissa, Michael. B.A., U. Ark., 1959. Vice pres. Dabbs, Sullivan, Trulock, Ark., 1963-74; chmn., chief exec. officer Leisure Lodges, Ft. Smith, Ark., 1974-77; registered rep. Stephens Inc., Little Rock, 1974-79; pres., chief operating officer Beverly Enterprises, Pasadena, Calif., 1979—; dir. Nat. Council Health Centers, Pulaski Bank, Little Rock. Served with U.S. Army. Office: Beverly Enterprises 873 S Fair Oaks Ave Pasadena CA 91105

BANKS, JAMES ALBERT, teacher educator; b. Marianna, Ark., Sept. 24, 1941; s. Matthew and Lula (Holt) B.; m. Cherry Ann McGee, Feb. 15, 1969; children: Angela Marie, Patricia Ann. A.A., Chgo. City Coll., 1963; B.E., Chgo. State U., 1964; M.A. (NDEA fellow 1966-69), Mich. State U., 1967, Ph.D., 1969. Tchr. elementary sch. Joliet, Ill., 1965, Francis W. Parker Sch., Chgo., 1965-66; asst. prof. edn. U. Wash., Seattle, 1969-71; assoc. prof. U. Wash., 1971-73, prof., 1973—, chmn. curriculum and instrn., 1982-87; vis. prof. edn. U. Mich., 1975, Monash U., Australia, 1985; Disting. scholar lectr. Kent State U., 1978, U. Ariz., 1979, Ind. U., 1983 ; vis. scholar Brit. Acad., June 1983; mem. com. examiners (social studies) Ednl. Testing Service, 1974-77; mem. nat. adv. council on ethnic heritage studies U.S. Office Edn., 1975-78; chmn. Nat. Council for Social Studies Task Force on Ethnic Studies Curriculum Guidelines, 1975-76. Author: Teaching Strategies for Ethnic Studies, 1975, 4th edit., 1987, Teaching Strategies for the Social Studies, 1973, 3d edit., 1985, Black Self-Concept, 1972, Teaching the Black Experience, 1970, Multiethnic Education: Practices and Promises, 1977, (with Cherry Ann Banks) March Toward Freedom: A History of Black Americans, 1970, 2d edit., 1974, rev. 2d edit., 1978, (with others) Curriculum Guidelines for Multiethnic Education, 1976, Multiethnic Education: Theory and Practice, 2d edit., 1988, We Americans: Our History and People, 2 vols., 1982; contbg. author Internat. Ency. of Edn., 1985; editor: Teaching Ethnic Studies: Concepts and Strategies, 1973, (with William W. Joyce) Teaching Social Studies to Culturally Different Children, 1971, Teaching the Language Arts to Culturally Different Children, 1971, Education in the 80's: Multiethnic Education, 1981, (with James Lynch) Multicultural Education in Western Societies, 1986; editorial bd. Jour. of Tch. Edn., 1985—, Council Interracial Books for Children Bull; contbr. articles to profl. jours. Recipient Outstanding Young Man award Wash. State Jaycees, 1975, Outstanding Service in Edn. award Seattle U. Black Student Union, 1985; Spencer fellow Nat. Acad. Edn., 1973-76; Kellogg fellow, 1980-83; Rockefeller Found. fellow, 1980. Mem. Nat. Council Social Studies (dir. 1973-74, 80-85, v.p. 1980, pres.-elect 1981, pres. 1982), Assn. Supervision and Curriculum Devel. (dir. 1976-79, Disting. lectr. 1986), Internat. Assn. Intercultural Edn. (editorial bd.), Social Sci. Edn. Consortium (dir. 1976-79), Am. Ednl. Research Assn. (publs. com. div. G), Disting. Scholar/Researcher on Minority Edn. 1986), Phi Delta Kappa, Phi Kappa Phi, Golden Key Nat. Honor Soc. Home: 1333 NW 200th St Seattle WA 98177

BANKS, LISA JEAN, government official; b. Chelsea, Mass., Dec. 19, 1956; d. Bruce H. and Jean P. (Como) Banks. B.S. in Bus. Adminstrn., Northeastern U., 1979. Coop trainee IRS, Boston, 1975-79, revenue officer, Reno, 1979-81, spl. agt., Houston, 1981-84, Anchorage, 1984—, fed. womens program mgr., 1980-81. Recipient Superior Performance award IRS, 1981. Mem. Nat. Assn. Treasury Agts., Nat. Assn. Female Execs. Democrat. Roman Catholic Office: PO Box 1500 Anchorage AK 99510

BANKS, PETER MORGAN, electrical engineering educator; b. San Diego, May 21, 1937; s. George Willard and Mary Margaret (Morgan) B.; m. Paulett M. Behanna, May 21, 1983; children by previous marriage: Kevin, Michael, Steven, David. M.S. in E.E, Stanford U., 1960; Ph.D. in Physics, Pa. State U., 1965. Postdoctoral fellow Institut d'Aeronomie Spatiale de Belgique, Brussels, Belgium, 1965-66; prof. applied physics U. Calif., San Diego, 1966-76; prof. physics Utah State U., 1976-81, head dept. physics, 1976-81; prof. elec. engring. Stanford U., 1981—, vis. assoc. prof., 1972-73; pres. Earth Data Corp., 1985-86; vis. scientist Max Planck Inst. for Aeronomie, Ger., 1975; pres. La Jolla Scis. Inc., 1973-77, Upper Atmosphere Research Corp., 1978-82; chmn. NASA adv. com on sci. uses of space sta., 1985-87. Author: (with G. Kockarts) Aeronomy, 1973, (with J.R. Doupnik) Introduction to Computer Science, 1976; assoc. editor: Jour. Geophys. Research, 1974-77; assoc. editor: Planetary and Space Sci, 1977-83, regional editor, 1983-86; contbr. numerous articles in field to profl. jours. Mem. space sci. adv. council NASA, 1976-80. Served with U.S. Navy, 1960-63. Recipient Appleton prize Royal Soc. London, 1978, Space Sci. award AIAA, 1981, NASA Disting. Service medal, 1986; Alumni fellow Pa. State U., 1982. Fellow Am. Geophys. Union; mem. Internat. Union Radio Sci. Episcopalian. Club: Cosmos. Home: 928 Casanueva Place Stanford CA 94305 Office: Elec Engring Dept Stanford U Stanford CA 94305

BANKSTON, WILLIAM MARCUS, lawyer; b. San Angelo, Tex., Feb. 16, 1946; s. Wyatt Lester and Mary Alice (Powell) B.; m. Janna Coe Herridge, Aug. 15, 1965 (div.); children—Darla Kae, Kendra Lynne; m. Judith Ann Railsback, Nov. 20, 1981. B.A., Tex. Tech U., 1968, B.S., 1968; J.D., U. Tex., 1971. Bar: Alaska 1971, Tex. 1971, U.S. Tax Ct. 1983, U.S. Ct. Claims 1984, U.S. Supreme Ct. 1986. Assoc. Croft & Bailey, Anchorage, 1971-73; ptnr. Croft, Bailey, Guetschow & Bankston, 1973-74; instr. Anchorage Community Coll., 1972-74; ptnr. Greene & Bankston, Anchorage, 1974—. Mem. ABA, Alaska Bar Assn., State Bar Tex. Methodist. Home: PO Box 102713 Anchorage AK 99510 Office: Bankston McCollum & Fossey PC 550 W 7th Suite 1800 Anchorage AK 99501

BANNER, EARL J, human resources executive; b. Burley, Idaho, May 14, 1937; s. Clarence LeRoy and Olevia Leuanne (Hymas) B.; m. Nyla Wilcock, June 14, 1962; children: Brian, David, Denise, Nathan, Laurel, Rebecca, Kristin. BS in Econs., Brigham Young U., 1962; MS in Indsl. Relations, U. Utah, 1965. Employment interviewer Sperry Rand Co., Salt Lake City, 1962-64; mgr. personnel Ajax Presses, Salt Lake City, 1964-67, Marquardt Corp., Ogden, Utah, 1967-68; v.p. employee relations Macy's Calif., San Francisco, 1968-80; v.p. human resources U I Group Inc., Kennewick, Wash., 1980—. Bd. dirs. Bay Area Urban League, 1974-77; mem. exec. com. United for Wash., 1986—. Mem. Am. Soc. Personnel Adminstrn. (pres. Utah chpt. 1968, sec. Columbia Basin chpt. 1984). Republican. Mormon. Lodge: Rotary, Kiwanis. Avocations: camping, running, gardening, reading. Home: 698 E 650 N Centerville UT 84014 Office: 50 E South Temple Salt Lake City UT 84150

BANNING, JAMES HOWARD, university administrator, clinical psychologist; b. Horton, Kans., Jan. 24, 1938; s. Howard Thomas and Minnie Mae (Carter) B.; m. Carolyn Sue, Oct. 9, 1959; children—Sherri Sue, Michael James. A.B., William Jewell Coll., 1960; M.A., U. Colo., 1965, Ph.D., 1965. Dir., Univ. Counseling Center, U. Colo., 1968-70; project dir. Western Interstate Commn. for Higher Edn., Boulder, Colo., 1970-73; vice chancellor for student affairs U. Mo., Columbia, 1973-78; v.p. student affairs Colo. State U.-Ft. Collins, 1978—, assoc. prof. psychology, 1978—, assoc. prof. edn., 1979—. Bd. dirs. Ft. Collins (Colo.) Area C. of C. Mem. Am.

Psychol. Assn., Nat. Assn. Student Personnel Adminstrn., Environ. Design Research Assn. Co-author monographs; contbr. chpts., numerous articles to profl. publs.; editor Campus Ecology, 1978—. Home: 1901 Bear Ct Fort Collins CO 80525 Office: 108 Adminstrn Colo State U Fort Collins CO 80523

BANSE, KARL, oceanography educator; b. Koenigsberg Pr., East Prussia, Germany, Feb. 20, 1929; came to U.S., 1960, naturalized; s. Karl and Wally (Rumpf) B. Ph.D. in Oceanography, U. Kiel, Fed. Republic Germany, 1955. Postdoctoral fellow in marine sci. U. Kiel, 1955-57; Govt. India scholar Central Marine Fish Research Sta., India, 1958-60; asst. prof. oceanography U. Wash., Seattle, 1960-63, assoc. prof. oceanography, 1963-66, prof. oceanography, 1966—. Co-editor: Biological Oceanography of the Northern North Pacific Ocean, 1972. Office: U Wash Sch Oceanography WB-10 Seattle WA 98195

BANVARD, KRIS, newspaper reporter; b. Los Angeles, Mar. 23, 1957; s. Roger Emil and Mary Elizabeth (Sturgeon) B.; m. Paula Vaadia Deming, June 10, 1978; children: Elaine, Honor. BA in Journalism, U. Oreg., 1978. Reporter, news editor Sun-Enterprise, Monmouth, Oreg., 1978-79; reporter Grants Pass (Oreg.) Daily Courier, 1979, Sacramento Union, 1979—. Avocations: fiction writing, photography. Office: Sacramento Union 301 Capitol Mall Sacramento CA 95812

BAPTIST, OREN CECIL, petroleum engineer, genealogist; b. Uniontown, Kans., Oct. 17, 1912; s. John Oliver and Iva Marie (Jones) B.; m. Ellen Marie Bandy, Mar. 1, 1947; 1 child, Linda Marie Stockton. Grad., Ft. Scott Jr. Coll., 1937; BS, U. Kans., 1940, postgrad., 1941. Registered profl. engr., Wyo., Calif. Asst. engr. U.S.C.E., Albuquerque, 1942-43; geologist-engr. Socony Mobil Oil Co., Bogota, Columbia, 1943-45; petroleum engr. Mobil Oil Co., Casper, Wyo., 1945-47; supr. U.S. Dept. Interior, Laramie, Wyo., 1947-67; dir. San Francisco Energy Research Ctr. U.S. Dept. Energy, 1967-76; sr. petroleum specialist H.K. Van Poollen and Assocs., Littleton, Colo., 1976-81; cons. in petroleum engring. San Rafael, Calif., 1976—; author, pub. Oren C. Baptist & Assocs., 1980—. Author: Oil Production from Permafrost, Umiat, Alaska, The Baptist and Harden Families, The Baptista and Teixeira Families, Madeira and America, 1385-1986; co-author Enhanced Oil Recovery; contbr. 24 articles to sci. jours. Mem. Soc. Petroleum Engrs. (chmn. monograph com. 1969-71, mem. Anthony F. Lucas gold medal award com. 1980-84), NSPE, Am. Assn. Petroleum Geologists, Am. Petroleum Inst., Marin Geneal. Soc., Sigma Xi, Tau Beta Pi. Home and Office: 396 Monticello Rd San Rafael CA 94903

BAPTISTE, CLARENCE BOYSIE, minister; b. Scarborough, Tobago, Trinidad and Tobago, June 8, 1941; came to Can., 1969; s. George and Marjorie Enid (James) B.; m. Beryl Joan Durant, June 13, 1965; children: David J., Peter L., Philip P. AA, Kingsway Coll., Oshawa, Ont., Can., 1971; BA, Andrews U., 1973, MA, 1975, MDiv., 1977. Ordained to ministry Seventh-day Adventist Ch., 1981. Lit. evangelist South Caribbean Conf. Seventh-day Adventsits Ch., Port of Spain, Trinidad and Tobago, 1962-69; minister Man. and Sask. Conf. of Seventh-day Adventists Ch., Saskatoon, 1977-86; pastor, evangelist Yorkton (Sask.) Seventh-day Adventist Ch., 1983-86; pastor West Edmonton (Alta.) Seventh-day Adventist Ch., 1986—; lectr. Brandon (Man., Can.) U., 1979-80. Mem. Edmonton Coralwood Jr. Acad. Sch. Bd.; dir. human relations dept. Alta. Conf. Seventh-day Adventist Chs., chmn. human relations com. Mem. Yorkton Ministerial Assn., Dauphin Ministerial Assn., Saskatoon Ministerial Assn., Edmonton Chs. Ministerial Assn. (pres.). Home: 9 Farmstead Ave, Edmonton, AB Canada T8N 1W1 Office: West Edmonton Seventh-day Adventist Ch, Box 9049 Station E, Edmonton, AB Canada T5P 4K1

BAQUET, RENE PHILIPPE, physician assistant; b. St. Louis, Sept. 16, 1951; s. Harold Anthony and Yvonne Noneka (Barry) B.; m. Beverly Fitzgerald, Aug. 23, 1980 (div. 1983); 1 child, Philippe Rene. BA, St. Louis U., 1975, B in Med. Sci., 1982. Orthopedic physician asst. St. Mary's Health Ctr., St. Louis, 1976-84, instr. practical nursing sch., 1977-84; instr. physician asst. program St. Louis U., 1977-84; pediatric surgery physician asst. City of Hope Med. Ctr., Duarte, Calif., 1984-86; asst. orthopedic physician CIGNA Healthplan of So. Calif., Los Angeles, 1986—. Fellow Am. Coll. Sports Medicine; mem. Calif. Acad. Physician Assts., Mo. Acad. Physician Assts., Am. Acad. Physician Assts., Am. Acad. Surgical Assts., Phi Beta Sigma (Outstanding Service award 1982, asst. dir. S.W. region 1981-82, past pres. local chpt.), Charles R. Drew Physician Asst. Assn., St. Louis Pan-Hellenic Council (vice chmn.). Roman Catholic. Club: Duarte Fitness Ctr. Home: 866 Cinnamon Ln Duarte CA 91010 Office: CIGNA Health Plan of So Calif 1711 W Temple St Los Angeles CA 90026

BARANEK, PAUL PETER, agriculturist; b. Wynn, Pa., Feb. 18, 1914; s. Joseph and Sophia (Koltas) B.; B.S., U. Calif. at Davis, 1936, teaching certificate, 1937, M.Edn., 1946; m. Marie Agatha Herzog, Aug. 18, 1937 (dec. 1974); children—Jeanne Marie Baranek Olmstead, Robert Paul, Barbara May Baranek Plaskett, John Peter. Dir. inst. vocat. agr. Escalon (Calif.) High Sch., 1937-42; mgr., operator Delta Dairy, Courtland, Calif., 1942-45; land use specialist Delta dist., Bur. Reclamation, Sacramento, Stockton, Calif., 1946-50; regional weed specialist Bur. Reclamation, Sacramento 1950-53; farm adviser Agrl. Extension Service U. Calif., Madera, 1953-74, agriculturist emeritus, 1974—; cons. research com. Calif. Raisin Adv. Bd., 1958—, grading com. Fed. Raisin Adv. Bd., 1965—; ofcl. judge vine judging contest Future Farmers of Am., (Fresno Calif.) State, 1955-84. Advancement chmn. Sequoia council Boy Scouts Am., 1953-62, counselor, 1953-62. Mem. Am. Soc. Enologists, Young Men's Inst., Alpha Gamma Rho, Alpha Zeta. Democrat. Roman Catholic. Club: Commonwealth California (San Francisco). Contbr. articles to profl. jours. Address: 511 Barsotti Ave Madera CA 93637

BARASH, ANTHONY HARLAN, lawyer; b. Galesburg, Ill., Mar. 18, 1943; s. Burrel B. and Rosalyne J. (Silver) B.; m. Jean E. Anderson, May 17, 1965; children—Elizabeth, Christopher, Katherine, Andrew. A.B. cum laude, Harvard Coll., 1965; J.D., U. Chgo., 1968. Bar: Calif. 1969. Assoc., Irell & Manella, Los Angeles, 1968-71; assoc. Cox, Castle & Nicholson, Los Angeles, 1971-74, ptnr., 1975-80; ptnr. Barash & Hill, Los Angeles, 1980-84; ptnr. Wildman, Harrold, Allen, Dixon, Barash & Hill, Los Angeles, 1984—; dir. Bank of Beverly Hills, Deauville Restaurants, Inc.; trustee Pitzer Coll., 1981—; nat. adv. bd. Ctr. Nat. Policy, 1981—. Mem. State Bar Calif., ABA, Los Angeles County Bar Assn., Beverly Hills Bar Assn. (bd. dirs. found. 1979—, bd. govs. 1979-81), Pub. Counsel (dir. 1980—). Clubs: Regency (Los Angeles); Harvard of So. Calif. Home: 825 Amalfi Dr Pacific Palisades CA 90272 Office: Wildman Harrold et al 2029 Century Park E Suite 2050 Los Angeles CA 90067

BARASH, DAVID PHILIP, psychology and zoology educator; b. N.Y.C., Jan. 9, 1946; s. Nathan and Anne (Shaposnick) B.; m. Beverly Ann Osband, Jan. 20, 1966 (div. 1975); 1 child, Eva; m. Judith Eve Lipton, Mar. 10, 1977; children: Ilona, Nanelle. BA, Harpur Coll., 1966; MA, U. Wis., 1968, PhD, 1970. Asst. prof. psychology, zoology SUNY Coll., Oneonta, 1970-73; assoc. prof. U. Wash., Seattle, 1973-80, prof., 1980—. Author: Sociobiology and Behavior, 1977, 82, The Whisperings Within, 1979, Stop Nuclear War, 1982, Aging: An Exploration, 1983, The Caveman and the Bomb, 1985, The Hare and the Tortoise, 1986, The Arms Race and Nuclear War, 1987. Fellow NSF, Ctr. Advanced Study in the Behavioral Scis., 1977-78, Bellagio Study and Conf. Ctr., 1984. Fellow AAAS. Democrat. Avocations: hiking, running, cross-country skiing, horseback riding, scuba diving. Home: 6 Bridlewood Circle Kirkland WA 98033 Office: U Wash Psychology Dept Seattle WA 98195

BARATTA-LORTON, ROBERT, educator; b. Fresno, Calif., June 19, 1939; s. Paul Vernon and Jean (Steinbeck) Lorton; B.A. in Econs. with honors, Stanford U., 1961; M.A. in Edn., U. Calif., Berkeley, 1968; widower. Classroom tchr., tchr. educationally handicapped, Calif., 1966-73; instr. Miller Math. State Specialized Tchr. Improvement Program, also Center Improvement Math. Edn., San Diego, 1971-74; co-founder, 1975, since chmn. bd. dirs., dir. Center Innovation in Edn., Saratoga, Calif.; pres., bd. govs. Center Grad. Coll., Saratoga, 1980—. Served to lt. USNR, 1963-66; Vietnam. Mem. Internat. Reading Assn., Nat. Council Tchrs. Math., Assn. Supervision and Curriculum Devel., Nat. Assn. Edn. Young Children, Council Exceptional Children, Calif. Math. Council. Author: Mathematics. . .A Way of Thinking, 1977; Baratta-Lorton Reading Program, 1985. Office: 19225 Vineyard Ln Saratoga CA 95070

BARBEE, JOE E., lawyer; b. Pharr, Tex., Feb. 27, 1934; s. Archie Allen and Concha (Leal) B.; m. Yolanda Margaret Atonna, Feb. 17, 1962; children—Cindy, Adam, Walter. B.S.E.E., U. Ariz., 1961; J.D., Western New Eng. Coll., 1973. Bar: Mass. 1973, U.S. Patent Office 1973, U.S. Ct. Appeals (fed. cir.) 1982. Engr. Gen. Electric Co., Pittsfield, Mass., 1961-73, patent atty., Fort Wayne, Ind., 1973-75; patent atty. Magnavox, Fort Wayne, 1975-76, Motorola, Inc., Phoenix, 1976—. Served to sgt. U.S. Army, 1953-56. Mem. ABA, Am. Patent Law Assn. Republican. Home: 7611 N Mockingbird Ln Paradise Valley AZ 85253 Office: Motorola Inc 4250 E Camelback Rd Phoenix AZ 85018

BARBER, CLIFTON EDWARD, gerontologist, educator; b. Spokane, Washington, Jan. 26, 1947; s. Jack Edward and Ruth Cathrin (Kretzmeier) B.; m. Janet Elaine Carr, Oct. 30, 1971; children: Jennifer, Melanie. BA, Portland (Oreg.) State U., 1972; MS, Brigham Young U., 1974; PhD, Pa. State U., 1978. Asst. prof. Western Ill. U., Macomb, 1977-78; asst. prof. Colo. State U., Ft. Collins, 1978-82, dir. interdisciplinary studies program in gerontology, 1981-86, assoc. prof. gerontology, 1982—. Contbr. articles to profl. jours. Mem. adv. bd. Office on Aging, Ft. Collins, Colo., 1979-82; county del. Gov.'s Conf. on Aging, Denver, 1981. Aging fellowship Nat. Inst. Aging, 1974-77. Mem. Am. Soc. Aging, Gerontol. Soc. Am. (fellowship in applied gerontology 1981), Nat. Council Family Relations. Republican. Mormon. Avocations: pottery, oil painting, tennis, golf. Office: Colo State U Dept Human Devel & Family Studies Fort Collins CO 80523

BARBER, EDWARD R., accountant; b. Ogden, Utah, Apr. 30, 1955; s. Allen and Lorraine (Robinson) B.; m. Pam Westwood, June 2, 1978. B.S., Weber State U., C.P.A., Utah. C.P.A., Utah. Mem. staff John Brough, C.P.A., Layton, Utah, 1977-79, Crouch, Pinnock & Davis, Ogden, Utah, 1979-81; officer Crouch, Davis & Assocs., Ogden, 1981-83, Crouch, Wood & Barber, Ogden, 1984—. Mem. Am. Inst. C.P.A.s, Utah Assn. C.P.A.s, Beta Theta Pi. Office: Crouch Wood & Barber 2485 Grant Ave 103 Ogden UT 84401

BARBER, RUSSELL JEFFREY, anthropology educator, archaeology researcher; b. Bennington, Vt., Aug. 14, 1950; s. Ralph Francis and Hope Louise (Hoctor) B. m. Joanna Ratcliff Roche, Dec. 17, 1983. BA, U. Vt., 1972; AM, Harvard U., 1974, PhD, 1979. Research dir. Inst. Conservation Archaeology Peabody Mus. Harvard U., Cambridge, Mass., 1979-82, dir., 1982-83; vis. asst. prof. Dept. Archaeology Boston U., 1983-84; asst. prof. Dept. Anthropology Calif. State U., San Bernardino, 1984-86, assoc. prof. Dept. Anthropology, 1986—; bd. dirs. San Bernardino County Mus. Assn., Redlands, Calif.; research assoc. San Bernardino County Mus., Redlands, 1986—; dir. mus. studies program Calif. State U., San Bernardino, 1984—; cons. in field. Author: The Wheeler's Site, 1982; author/editor: The Shaw Site, 1982; editor: Quartz Technology in Prehistoric New England, 1981; contbr. articles to profl. jours. Mem. Current Anthropology (assoc.), Am. Anthropol. Assn., Soc. Am. Archaeology, AAAS, Soc. Hist. Archaeology. Democrat. Home: 3324 Genevieve St San Bernardino CA 92405 Office: Calif State U Dept Anthropology 5500 University Pkwy San Bernardino CA 92407

BARBOUR, ALAN GEORGE, microbiologist, physician; b. Los Angeles, Jan. 15, 1946; s. George Johnson and Mary Anita (Jones) B.; m. Ann Wolcott Condon, Dec. 30, 1969; children: Nathan, Evan. MD, Tufts U., 1972; student, U. Calif., Berkeley, 1967. Diplomate Am. Bd. Internal Medicine. Med. resident Dartmouth Coll., Hanover, N.H., 1972-74; epidemic intelligence service officer Ctrs. for Disease Control, Atlanta, 1974-76; chief med. resident LDS Hosp., Salt Lake City, 1976-77; fellow in infectious diseases U. Utah, Salt Lake City, 1977-80; sr. staff fellow Rocky Mountain Labs., Hamilton, Mont., 1980-84, chief arthropod-borne diseases, 1984—; cons. WHO, New Delhi, 1975. Contbr. sci. articles to profl. jours. Served as sr. surgeon USPHS, 1974-76, 1985—. Fellow Infectious Diseases Soc. Am.; mem. ACP, Am. Soc. Microbiology. Office: Rocky Mountain Labs NIH Hamilton MT 59840

BARBOUR, MICHAEL G(EORGE), botany educator, ecological consultant; b. Jackson, Mich., Feb. 24, 1942; s. George Jerome and Mae (Dater) B.; m. Norma Jean Yourist, Sept. 30, 1963 (div. 1981); m. Valerie Ann Whitworth, Jan. 25, 1987; children: Julie Ann, Alan Benjamin. B.S. in Botany, Mich. State U., 1963; Ph.D. in Botany, Duke U., 1967. Asst. prof. botany U. Calif., Davis, 1967-71; assoc. prof. U. Calif., 1971-76, prof., 1976—, chmn., 1982-85; ptnr. Ecolabs Cons., Davis, 1969—; vis. prof. botany dept. Hebrew U., Jerusalem, 1979-81; vis. prof. marine scis. dept. La. State U., Baton Rouge, 1984. Co-author: Coastal Ecology, Bodega Head, 1973, Botany, 6th edit., 1982, Terrestrial Vegetation of California, 1977, Terrestrial Plant Ecology, 1980, North American Terrestrial Vegetation, 1987. Fulbright Found fellow Adelaide, Australia 1964; Guggenheim Found. fellow, 1978; NSF research grantee, 1968-78. Mem. Ecol. Soc. Am. (editorial bd.), Brit. Ecol. Soc., Sigma Xi. Democrat. Jewish. Office: U Calif Botany Dept Davis CA 95616

BARCA, GEORGE GINO, winery executive; b. Sacramento, Jan. 28, 1937; s. Joseph and Annie (Muschetto) B.; m. Maria Sclafani, Nov. 19, 1960; children—Anna, Joseph, Gina and Nina (twins). A.A., Grant Jr. Coll.; student LaSalle U., 1963. With AeroJet Gen. Corp., Sacramento, 1958-65, United Vintners, Inc., San Francisco, 1960-73; pres., gen. mgr. Barcamerica Corp., Sacramento, 1963—; pres., gen. mgr. Barca Wine Cellars, Calif. Wine Cellars, Inc., Calif. Grape Growers, Inc., Calif. Vintage Wines, Inc., Am. Vintners, Inc.; cons. in field. Named Best Producer of Sales, United Vintners, Inc. Mem. Calif. Farm Bur., Met. C. of C., Better Bus. Bur., Roman Catholic. Club: KC. Developer wine trademarks.

BARCHAS, PATRICIA RUTH, sociophysiology educator, researcher; b. Chickasha, Okla., July 26, 1934; d. Bill Doherty and Jimmie Ione (Hendricks) Corbitt; m. Jack David Barchas, Feb. 7, 1957; 1 child, Isaac Doherty. BA, Pomona Coll., 1956; PhD, Stanford U., 1971. Acting asst. prof. dept. sociology Stanford (Calif.) U., 1971-72, asst. prof., 1972-85, asst. research prof. dept. psychiatry, 1975-85, sr. research assoc. dept. psychiatry, 1985—. Author, editor: Social Cohesion: Essays Toward a Sociophysiological Perspective, 1984, Social Hierarchies: Essays Toward A Sociophysiological Perspective, 1984; contbr. articles to profl. jours. Grantee MacArthur Found., 1982-86, NIH, 1971-85, U.S. Office Naval Research, 1977-78, 79-82, 82-86. Mem. Soc. Neurosci., Am. Sociol. Assn., Soc. Study of Social Biology. Home: 669 Mirada Stanford CA 94305 Office: Stanford U Dept Psychiatry Stanford CA 94305

BARCHERS, SUZANNE INEZ, academic administrator; b. Oakland, Calif., July 30, 1946; d. Charles Benjamin and Inez Lorene (Von Ins) Dumville; m. Daniel Emmert Barchers, June 15, 1968; children: Jeffrey Daniel, Joshua Charles. Student, Wesleyan U., Bloomington, Ill., 1964-66; BS in Edn., Eastern Ill. U., 1967; MEd, Oreg. State U., 1973; DEd, U. Colo., 1985; postgrad., Columbia U., 1986. Educator various pub. schs., Peoria, Pekin (Ill.), Augusta (Ga.), Sweet Home (Oreg.), 1967-72; dir. United Meth. Kindergarten, Albany, Oreg., 1972-74; instr. Colo. Women's Coll., Denver., 1981; dir. devel. and reading Janus Wilmont Sch., Wheat Ridge, Colo., 1981-84; dir. curriculum Mountain View Day Sch., Wheat Ridge, 1985-86; tchr. Denver Pub. Schs., 1986—; cons. Colo. Dept. Edn., Denver, 1983, Learning mag., 1987—; lectr. Columbia U. Tchrs. Coll. Folklore Research Ctr., 1986. Contbr. articles to profl. jours. Bd. dirs. and newsletter editor Colo. Parents for All Children, 1978-80; prin. flutist Arvada (Colo.) Ctr. Chamber Orch., 1977-80. Bilingual spl. fellow U. Colo., Boulder, 1983-84. Mem. Nat. Council Tchrs. of English, Assn. Supervision and Curriculum Devel., Internat. Reading Assn., Colo. Council Internat. Reading Assn., Colo. Lang. Arts Soc., Phi Kappa Phi, Alpha Lambda Delta, Delta Omicron. Avocations: performing on flute, piano, gardening, reading. Home: 11417 W 75th Ave Arvada CO 80005 Office: Park Hill Sch 5050 E 19th Ave Denver CO 80220

BARD, GLENIS ELLIS, municipal administrator; b. Foxwarren, Manitoba, Can., Aug. 19, 1925; d. Scott Gwyer and Annie Mae (Lamb) Ellis; m. Charles Flanders Brickenden, June 10, 1950 (div. 1957); m. Milton Thompson Bard, Apr. 16, 1964. Degree in Bus. Adminstrn., Harvard U., 1958; BA in Psychology, San Francisco State U., 1971; MA in Psychology, Calif. State U., San Francisco, 1972. Adminstrv. asst. San Francisco and Canada, 1945-68; instr. human relations in bus., bus. English and math, psychology various colls., San Francisco, 1972-77; instr. San Mateo (Calif.) Coll., 1977-80, Monterey (Calif.) Peninsula Coll., 1981-82; adminstrv. sec., aide Monterey County, Salinas, 1982—. Mem. AAUW (chmn. legis. com. 1985-86, Cen. Coast dist. legis. program 1986—), Harvard Bus. Assn. No. Calif., Phi Delta Kappa. Democrat. Unitarian. Avocations: music, choral singing, cats, legis. advocacy, golf. Home: 345-82 Coleridge Dr Salinas CA 93901 Office: Monterey County Intergovtl Affairs PO Box 180 Salinas CA 93902

BARD, RICHARD H., hardware distributor and executive; b. Irvington, N.J., Nov. 30, 1947; s. Irving and Irene (Pearlman) B.; m. Diane Rose Gibson, Sept. 1984; children by previous marriage: Alison, Jonathan, Adam. B.S.C.E., Pa. State U., 1969; M.B.A., Baruch Coll., N.Y.C., 1973. Asst. v.p. Citibank, N.A., N.Y.C., 1970-74; mgr. Midwest region Citicorp Bus. Credit, Inc., Chgo., 1974-76; chief fin. officer LFV, Inc., Chgo., 1976-77; pres. FoxMeyer Corp., Aurora, Colo., 1977-86; chmn. and chief exec. officer Coast to Coast Stores, Inc., Denver, 1986—; dir. Capital Resource Mgmt., Inc., Denver, 1982—, Prime Home Improvement Ctrs., Inc., 1984—, Prudential Bancshares Inc., 1984—. Bd. dirs. The Denver Children's Mus., 1986—. Mem. Nat. Wholesale Hardware Assn. (chmn. 1982-83), Nat. Intergroup, Inc. (dir. 1986—). Home: 100 Vine St Denver CO 80206 Office: Coast to Coast Stores 501 S Cherry St Suite 1100 Denver CO 80222

BARDACKE, PAUL GREGORY, lawyer, attorney general; b. Oakland, Calif., Dec. 16, 1944; s. Theodore Joseph and Frances (Woodward) B.; m. Lauren Marble, June 21, 1980; children: Julie, Brynn, Francheska. B.A. cum laude, U. Calif.-Santa Barbara, 1966; J.D., U. Calif.-Berkeley, 1969. Bar: Calif. 1969, N.Mex. 1970. Lawyer Legal Aid Soc., Albuquerque, 1969; assoc. firm Sutin, Thayer Browne, Albuquerque, 1970-82; atty. gen. State of N.Mex., Santa Fe, 1982-86; adj. prof. N.Mex. Law Sch., Albuquerque, 1973—; mem. faculty Nat. Inst. Trial Lawyers Advocacy, 1978—. Bd. dirs. All Faiths Receiving Home, Albuquerque; bd. dirs. Friends of Art, 1974, Artspace Mag., 1979-80, Legal Aid Soc., 1970-74. Reginald Heber Smith fellow, 1969. Mem. ABA, Calif. Bar Assn., N.Mex. Bar Assn. Democrat.

BARDEN, KARL ALVIN, minister, dentist; b. Spokane, Wash., Feb. 14, 1940; s. Carl Methner and Hilda Marion (Tessendorf) B.; m. Sherrillann Talbot, Sept. 13, 1958; children—Tamara Karlynne, Karianne Danita, Julianne Victoria. D.D.S., U. Wash., 1962; D. in Ministry, Christian Internat. U., 1986. Gen. practice dentistry Spokane, 1962-64, Pullman, Wash., 1964-84; co-founder Living Faith Fellowship, Pullman, 1971—, sr. pastor, 1975—; founder, pres. Living Faith Fellowship Coll. Ministry Tng., 1987—; lectr. various nat. and internat. seminars and churches. Author: Basic Guidelines to Greater Blessings, 1978; Catechism Training for New Covenant Christian Found., 1980. ALCOA Scholar U. Wash., 1957. Bd. dirs. Pullman Federated Fund, 1966-67, officer, 1968; vestryman Episcopal Ch., 1966-69, diocesan del., 1970; community chmn. Salvation Army, 1974. Recipient Sword of the Spirit Accelerated Christian Edn., 1984. Mem. Spokane Dist. Dental Soc., Wash. State Dental Assn., ADA, Pullman Ministerial Assn., Charismatic Bible Ministries, Network of Christian Ministries. Republican. Lodge: Rotary (pres. 1970-71). Home: SW 700 Fountain Pullman WA 99163 Office: Living Faith Fellowship SW 345 Kimball Pullman WA 99163

BARDIN, MICHAEL D(AVID), public relations executive; b. Berkeley, Calif.; s. David Bardin and Marion Wilma (McConnell) Roller; m. Arlene Carole Greene, Oct. 22, 1966; children—Stephanie Lynn, Laurie Anne. B.A. in Communications and Journalism, Stanford U., 1964; postgrad. in Radio-TV-Film, San Francisco State U., 1964-65. News prodn. asst. sta. KPIX-TV, San Francisco, 1965-66; pub. relations account exec. Phillips-Ramsey, Inc., San Diego, 1969-75, dir. client pub. relations services, 1975-84, v.p. pub. relations, 1977-84; dir. communications and pub. affairs Scripps Meml. Hosp., La Jolla, Calif., 1984—; guest lectr. U. Calif.-San Diego, San Diego State U., Nat. U. Pres. Calif. Ballet Co., 1982, trustee, 1979—; adv. com. San Diego Community Found., 1979-82; trustee Mexican-Am. Found., 1971-79; bd. dirs. Travelers Aid Soc., 1979—. Served to lt. USN, 1966-69. Named Man of Distinction, Mexican-Am. Found., 1977, San Diego Pub. Relations Profl. of Yr., 1980. Mem. Pub. Relations Soc. Am. (accredited, pres. San Diego County chpt. 1983, nat. del., mem. nat. eligibility bd., chmn. South Pacific dist.), Pub. Relations Club of San Diego (pres. 1978, four awards 1974-78), Am. Soc. Hosp. Mktg. and Pub. Relations. Republican. Episcopalian. Club: San Diego Press. Lodge: Rotary. Home: 9989 Bourbon Ct San Diego CA 92131 Office: Scripps Meml Hosp 9888 Genesee Ave La Jolla CA 92137

BARDING, LEWIS DANIEL, stockbroker; b. East Moline, Ill., Mar. 28, 1928; s. Lewis Daniel and Lillian Alice (Braastad) B.; m. Marilyn Marlene Huyett, Mar. 17, 1957; children—Lewis Daniel III, Bradford Huyett. B.A., Tulane U., 1950. Stockbroker Dain, Kalman & Quail, Davenport, Iowa, 1958-73; 1st v.p., resident mgr. Wagenseller & Durst, San Diego, 1973-82; stockbroker, sr. v.p. J. David Securities, La Jolla, Calif., 1982-84, Barding, McCartney & Assocs., 1984—; cons. corp. fin. for mergers and acquisitions. Served with CIC, U.S. Army, 1951-53; Korea. Mem. San Diego Corp. Fin. Council, San Diego Stock and Bond Club (pres. 1977), Stockbroker Soc. (chmn. 1976-82), Coronado Navy League, Assn. Former Intelligence Officers. Republican. Home: 5 The Inlet Coronado CA 92118 Office: 9191 Towne Centre Dr Suite 150 San Diego CA 92122

BAREISS, LYLE EUGENE, aerospace engineer; b. Rawlins, Wyo., Nov. 4, 1945; s. Godfrey Matthew and Vera Edith Bareiss. B.S. in Mech. and Aerospace Engring., Wyo. U., 1969; postgrad. in indsl. mgmt. Colo. State U., 1970. Skylab systems engr. Martin Marietta Aerospace Co., Denver, 1969-73, sr. staff engr. shuttle/spacelab contamination, 1974-79, mgr. tech. unit, contamination and laser effects, from 1980, dep. mgr. materials engring., 1984-85, dep. mgr. systems engring. specialties sect., 1985-87; chmn. Air Force strategic tech. planning panel on survivability/contamination, 1986. Recipient NASA Skylab Achievement award, 1974; NASA New Tech. awards, 1977, 82, 85; Martin Marietta author, performance awardee, 1974, 75, 79, 82, 84. Mem. AIAA (Nat. Thermophysics Com.), Sigma Tau, Omicron Delta Kappa, Sigma Alpha Epsilon. Presbyterian. Lodge: Odd Fellows (Rawlins, Wyo.). Contbr. articles to profl. jours.; architect computer model simulating spacecraft contamination to evaluate US satellite systems; basic research of effects of laser irradiation on satellite/booster systems and materials oxidation/glow of satellites in low earth orbit. Home: 8031 E Phillips Circle Englewood CO 80112 Office: PO Box 179 Denver CO 80201

BARGENQUAST, DOUGLAS WILLIAM, packaged foods marketing executive; b. Maryborough, Australia, Oct. 13, 1946; s. Douglas William and Jean Beryl (Rollwagen) B.; m. Cathy Diane, May 8, 1982; 1 child, Caitlin Marie. B in Commerce, U. Queensland, Australia, 1967, diploma in info. processing, 1968. Mktg. cons. Peat Marwick & Ptnrs., Toronto, Ont., Can., 1977; group product mgr. RJR Foods Can., Montreal, Que., 1978-79; mktg. mgr. Del Monte Can., Hamilton, Ont., 1980-81; group prodn. mgr. Del Monte Corp., San Francisco, 1982, dir. mktg., 1983-86, dir. bus. unit, 1986—. Fund raiser YMCA, Montreal, 1974. Mem. Internat. Foodservice Mfg. Assn. (planning com. 1985-86). Clubs: T.M.R. Rugby (Montreal) (pres. 1974-75, sportsman of yr. 1974); Scottish Rugby (Toronto); Del Monte Golf (San Francisco) (pres. 1986). Office: Del Monte Corp 1 Market Plaza San Francisco CA 94105

BARGER, JAMES DANIEL, physician; b. Bismarck, N.C., May 17, 1917; s. Michael Thomas and Mayte (Donohue) B.; m. Susie Belle Helm, 1945 (dec. 1951); m. Josephine Steiner, 1952 (dec. 1971); m. Jane Ray Regan, Apr. 21, 1980; children: James Daniel, Mary Susan, Michael Thomas, Mary Elizabeth. Student, St. Mary's Coll., Winona, Minn., 1934-35; A.B., U. N.D., 1939, B.S., 1939; M.D., U. Pa., 1941; M.S. in Pathology, U. Minn., 1949. Diplomate: Am. Bd. Pathology; registered quality engr., Calif. Intern. Milw. County Hosp., Wauwatosa, Wis., 1941-42; fellow in pathology Mayo Found., Rochester, Minn., 1941-49; pathologist Pima County Hosp., Tucson, 1949-50, Maricopa County Hosp., Phoenix, 1950-51; chmn. dept. pathology Good Samaritan Hosp., 1951-63; assoc. pathologist Sunrise Hosp., Las Vegas, Nev., 1964-69, chief pathology dept., 1969-81, sr. pathologist, 1981—; former med. dir. S.W. Blood Bank, Blood Services, Ariz. Served to maj. AUS, 1942-46. Recipient Sioux award U. N.D. Alumni Assn., 1975; recipient disting. physician award NSMA, 1983; ASCP-CAP Disting. Service award, 1985. Mem. AAAS, Am. Assn. Pathologists, Am. Assn. Clin. Chemists, Am. Assn. History Medicine, Coll. Am. Pathologists (gov. 1966-72, sec.-treas. 1971-79, v.p. 1979-81, pres. 1980-81 pathologist of yr.), Nev. Soc. Pathologists, Am. Assn. Blood Banks, Am. Soc. Quality Control, Am. Mgmt. Assn., Soc. Advancement Mgmt., Am. Soc. Clin. Pathologists, Am. Cancer Soc. (nat. dir. 1974-80), Am. Pub. Health Assn., Sigma Xi. Lodge: Knights of St. Lazarus (comdr. 1983). Home: 1307 Canosa Ave Las Vegas NV 89104 Office: Humana Sunrise Hosp PO Box 14157 Las Vegas NV 89114

BARGREN, JOHN H., orthopaedic surgeon; b. Rockford, Ill., July 25, 1941; s. Herbert R. and Inga L. (Loy) B.; m. Martha K. Kough, June 13, 1964; children: Jamison, Sarah. BS, U. Wis., 1964, MD, 1967. Residency in medicine Boston City Hosp., 1967-69; research fellow in orthopaedics Columbia U. Coll. Physicians and Surgeons, N.Y.C., 1971-72, resident in orthopaedic surgery, 1972-75; jr. lectr. orthopaedic surgery London Hosp. Med. Coll., 1975-76; practice medicine specializing in orthopedic surgery Tacoma, 1976—; clin. assoc. prof. U. Wash., Seattle, 1976. Contbr. articles to profl. jours. Served to maj. U.S. Army, 1969-71. Berg-Sloat Traveling fellow Orthopaedic Research and Edn. Found., 1975. Fellow Am. Acad. Orthopaedic Surgeons, ACS, Orthopaedic Research Soc., Western Orthopaedic Assn., Knee Soc. Clubs: Tacoma Country and Golf, Lakewood Racquet (Tacoma). Avocations: skiing, golf, tennis, music. Home: Nyanza Rd Tacoma WA 98499 Office: Affliated Bone & Joint Surgeons 1002 South K St Tacoma WA 98405

BARHAM, JESSE WALTER, city official; b. Salem, Oreg., Feb. 22, 1924; s. Jesse Alba and Esther L. (Dewey) B.; m. Marie Frakes, Dec. 27, 1944; children—Terry A., Bruce L. B.S. in C.E., Oreg. State Coll., 1950. Registered profl. engr., Oreg., Calif. Engring. asst. City of Salem, 1951; city engr. City of Coos Bay (Oreg.), 1952-54, dir. pub. works, 1954-58; city mgr., city engr. City of Coalinga (Calif.), 1959-61; city mgr. Coos Bay, 1961-68; city mgr., Longview, Wash., 1968-87; pres. Mcpl. Cons. Services, 1987—. Oreg. chmn. Nat. Library Week, 1967; mem. State Adv. Com. on Library Cooperation; mem. tech. com. Wash. Traffic Safety Commn., 1970-75; chmn. Coalinga Boosters for San Luis Fed. Water Project; mem. Wash. State Solid Waste Com.; pres. Cowlitz-Waukiakum Govt. Conf., 1973, 82. Trustee Seattle Pacific U., 1963—; chmn. bd. dirs. Cowlitz Econ. Devel. Commn., 1987. Served with USMC, 1942-46. Mem. Profl. Engrs. S.W. Oreg. (pres. 1958), Internat. City Mgmt. Assn. (pres. Oreg. 1968, pres. Wash. 1974). Free Meth. (chmn. bd. adminstrn. Oreg. conf. 1963-75), Rotarian. Home: 2938 Madrona Dr Longview WA 98632

BARIDO, MICHAEL RAY, mechanical design engineer; b. Charleston, W.Va., July 26, 1952; s. Charles Nicholas and Ruby Lee (Proffitt) B.; m. Norma Jean Taylor, Aug. 5, 1972 (div. Aug. 1982); children: Michael Ray II, Kelly Nicole; m. Jane Christine Hawkins, June 12, 1983. BSME, W.Va. U., 1983. Mem. tech. staff Rockwell Internat. Space Div., Downey, Calif., 1984—. Served with USAF, 1974-80. Recipient Tech. Utilization award Rockwell Internat., 1985. Mem. ASME (assoc.). Avocations: camping, auto mechanics. Office: Rockwell Internat Space Div 12214 Lakewood Blvd MC FB-18 Downey CA 90241

BARILLA, SAL, management consultant; b. Carle Place, N.Y., Dec. 6, 1932; s. Frank and Maria (Calarco) B.; m. Marie Levett Barilla, Apr. 30, 1959. BA, Adelphi U., 1959. Sales rep. Burroughs Wellcome, Raleigh, N.C., 1959-66, tng. mgr., 1966-70; tng. mgr. Organon, Inc., West Orange, N.J., 1970-75; communications mgr. Searle Radiographics, Des Plaines, Ill., 1975-78, Millipore, Inc., Bedford, Mass., 1978-80; tng., meeting mgr. Beckman Instruments, Inc., Brea, Calif., 1980—; tng., meeting planning cons., Sierra Madre, Calif., 1980—. Served as sgt. U.S. Army, 1953-55. Mem. Nat. Soc. Pharm. Sales Trainers (founder, pres., 1971-73), Clin. Lab. Mgrs. Assn., Am. Assn. Clin. Chemists, Nat. Soc. Sales Tng. Execs. Avocation: boating. Office: Beckman Instruments 200 S Kraemer Blvd Brea CA 92621

BARKAN, ELLIOTT ROBERT, history educator; b. N.Y.C., Dec. 15, 1940; s. Carl and Tessie (Leder) B.; m. Esther Werblud, Nov. 28, 1968 (div. June 1983); children: Ari David, Liana Hillary, Yoni Yehuda; m. Geula Soltz, Aug. 18, 1985; step children: Tal, Gil. BA magna cum laude, Queens Coll., 1962; MA, Harvard U., 1963, PhD, 1969. Instr. Pace U., N.Y.C., 1964-68; asst. prof. history and ethnic studies Calif. State U., San Bernardino, 1968-71, assoc. prof., 1971-76, prof. history, 1976—; vis. prof. U. Hawaii, Honolulu, 1969; cons. MOSAIC Los Angeles Bd. Edn., 1973-74, Balch Inst., Phila., 1985. Book rev. editor Jour. Am. Ethnic History, 1986—; contbr. articles to profl. jours. Bd. dirs. Congregation Emanuel, San Bernardino, 1977-80; advisor Inland Empire Hillel Support Group, San Bernardino, 1983—. Woodrow Wilson Found. fellow, Harvard U., 1962; Fulbright lectureships, 1983, 87; Calif. State U. grantee, 1985-86. Mem. Am. Hist. Assn., Orgn. Am. Historians (film com. 1977-80), Immigration History Soc. (exec. bd. 1985—), Phi Beta Kappa. Democrat. Jewish. Lodge: B'nai Brith. Avocations: bicycling, camping, racquetball. Home: 4704 David Way San Bernardino CA 92404-1922 Office: Calif State U 5500 University Pkwy San Bernardino CA 92407-2397

BARKAN, PHILIP, mech. engr.; b. Boston, Mar. 29, 1925; s. Philip and Blanche (Seifert) B.; m. Hinda Brody, Sept. 5, 1948 (dec. Aug. 1979); children—Ruth, David. B.S.M.E., Tufts U., 1946; M.S.M.E., U. Mich., 1948; Ph.D. in Mech. Engring, Pa. State U., 1953. Asst. prof. engring. research Pa. State U., 1948-51; sect. mgr. applied physics and mech. engring. Gen. Electric Co., Phila., 1953-77; prof. mech. engring. Stanford U., 1977—; vis. prof. Israel Inst. Tech., Haifa, 1971-72; cons. to electric power industry, 1977—. Contbr. numerous articles to profl. publs. Pres. bd. trustees Middletown (Pa.) Free Library, 1959-61; chmn. bd. trustees Sch. in Rose Valley, 1967-68; Democratic candidate for Middletown Twp. Supr., 1959, 61, 63; pres. Middletown Dem. Club, 1960. Served with USN, 1943-46. Recipient 1st Charles P. Steinmetz medal and award Gen. Electric Co., 1973; Electric Power Research Inst. grantee, 1979. Fellow IEEE; mem. ASME, Nat. Acad. Engring., Soc. Mfg. Engrs., Am. Soc. Engring. Educators, Sigma Xi. Patentee in field. Office: Design Div Dept Mech Engring Stanford U Stanford CA 94305

BARKER, JOHN ARTHUR, campus policeman; b. Pitts., Apr. 6, 1947; s. Charles Henry and Edith May (Arlinger) B.; 1 child, Gwendolyn Elizabeth Clinton. AA, Palomar Community Coll.; student, U. Calif., Santa Cruz. Service mgr. Kawasaki Escondido, Calif., 1972-74; campus guard U. Calif., Santa Cruz, 1977-79; police officer Cabrillo Coll., Aptos, Calif., 1979-80; chief police Cabrillo Coll., Aptos, 1980—. Youth com. mem. United Way, Santa Cruz, 1983. Served with USN, 1966-70. Recipient Community Coll. Social Sci. award Bank of Am., 1973. Mem. Calif. Community Coll. Police Chiefs Assn. (pres. 1984-85), Calif. Peace Officers Assn. (mem. campus law enforcement com. 1986—), Santa Cruz County Law Enforcement Chief Assn., Assn. Calif. Community Coll. Adminstrs., Santa Cruz Peace Officers Assn. (bd. dirs. 1984—). Democrat. Avocations: bicycling, aikido, camping. Office: Cabrillo Coll Police 6500 Soguel Dr Aptos CA 95003

BARKER, JOHN MATTHEW, former state senator; b. Twin Falls, Idaho, Nov. 29, 1916; s. John H. and Alice (Scully) B.; B.S. in Bus., U. Idaho, 1938; m. Rose Smith, Jan. 3, 1941; children—John (dec.), Rosemary, James, Marianne. Co-owner John M. Barker Realty, Buhl, Idaho, 1938—; pres. Am. Falls Reservoir Dist., Jerome, Idaho, 1957-87; mem. Idaho Senate, 1967-84; commr. Edn. Commn. States, Denver, 1970-83. Various mil. decorations, WWII; recipient Silver Beaver award, Boy Scouts Am., 1959; named Legislator of Yr., Cable TV, 1981; named to Idaho Water Users Assn. Hall of Fame, 1979, Outstanding Legislator Idaho Rep. Hall of Fame, 1983. C.P.C.U., Idaho. Mem. Buhl C. of C. (pres.), Jr. C. of C. (pres.), Nat. Soc. Pub. Accts. Republican. Presbyterian. Clubs: Rotary (past pres., dist. gov. 1984-85); Masons, Shriners. Office: Box 549 Buhl ID 83316

BARKER, LEROY N., agronomy educator, plant breeder; b. Brigham City, Utah, Oct. 18, 1928; s. Claude Rufus and Iva (Nelson) B.; m. Sara Ann Workman, Aug. 31, 1956; children—Michael, Dennis, LeAnn, Nanette, Amy. B.S., Utah State U., 1953, M.S., 1956; Ph.D., U. Wis., 1960. Plant breeder Asgrow Seed Co., Sun Prairie, Wis., 1960-65; asst. prof. agronomy Calif. State U.-Chico, 1965-68, assoc. prof., 1970-73, prof., 1973—; sr. lectr., plant breeder U. Ife, Ile-Ife, Nigeria, 1968-70; plant breeder U. Wis.-Madison, Rice Researchers, Inc., summers. Active Boy Scouts Am., 1966-68, 70-76; dist. leader, com. chmn. PTO, U. Ife. Served to 1st lt. U.S. Army, 1953-55. Cliff Poole fellow, 1956; U. Wis. research asst., 1956-60. Mem. Am. Soc. Agronomy, Crop Sci. Soc., Calif. Fertilizer Assn., Sigma Xi. Republican. Mormon. Assisted in devel. of two new rice varieties. Home: 2964 Alamo Ave Chico CA 95926 Office: Calif State U Plant & Soil Scis Chico CA 95929

BARKER, NORMAN, JR., banker; b. San Diego, July 30, 1922; s. Norman and Grace (Bolger) B.; m. Sue Keefe, June 27, 1947; children: Peter, Timothy, Michael, Beth. B.A., U. Chgo., 1947, M.B.A., 1953. Asst. cashier Harris Trust & Savs. Bank, Chgo., 1947-55; credit mgr. Am. Can Co., 1955-57; with First Interstate Bank of Calif., Los Angeles, 1957-86, pres., 1968-71, chmn. bd., chief exec. officer, 1973-86; ret. First Interstate Bank of Calif., 1986; bd. dirs. Carter Hawley Hale Stores, Inc., First Interstate Bank Calif., Pacific Am. Income Shares, Inc., Pacific Telesis Group, Southern Calif. Edison Co., Calif. State Tchrs.' Retirement System, Am. Health Properties, Inc. Trustee Occidental Coll., U. Chgo., W.M. Keck Found., Los Angeles County Mus. Art; bd. overseers Henry E. Huntington Library; bd. dirs. Automobile Club of So. Calif. Served to lt. USNR, 1944-46, 50-52. Mem. Delta Kappa Epsilon. Office: 707 Wilshire Blvd Los Angeles CA 90017 Mailing address: PO Box 3666 TA Los Angeles CA 90051

BARKER, RICHARD ALEXANDER, industrial psychologist; b. San Diego, Aug. 11, 1947; s. Alexander Markewich and Donna Lee Barker; A.B. in Psychology, San Diego State U., 1974, M.S. in Indsl. and Organizational Psychology, 1976; m. Julie Ann Akers, Apr. 3, 1971; children—Jaime Lynn, Cory Richard. Statis. analyst U.S. Navy Personnel Research and Devel. Center, San Diego, 1974-75; personnel and testing analyst City of San Diego, 1976; cons. various orgns., 1976-78; employment mgr. Computer Scis. Corp., San Diego, 1978; indsl. psychologist Gen. Dynamics Corp., San Diego, 1978—; instr. music, San Diego City Coll., 1976—; lectr. psychology, mgmt. sci., stats., orgnl. behavior U. Redlands, 1978—. Bd. dirs. San Diego Youth Services, Inc., chmn. personnel com., 1978-81. Served with USNR, 1968-69. Mem. Am. Psychol. Assn. (assoc.), Computer Automated Systems Assn./Soc. Mfg. Engrs., Nat. Mgmt. Assn., Internat. Assn. Applied Psychology (assoc.), Am. Fedn. Musicians, Psi Chi. Home: 5667 C Adobe Falls Rd San Diego CA 92120 Office: General Dynamics Electronics Div 5011 Kearny Villa Rd San Diego CA 92123

BARKER, ROY JEAN, entomologist; b. Norborne, Mo., July 9, 1924; s. Bernard Joseph and Olive Luella (Crockett) B.; m. Ellen Louise Remley, June 10, 1948 (div. Apr. 1970); children: Brian Loyd (dec.), Jeffrey Scott; m. Mary Lou Criss, Nov. 22, 1970. BS in Agr., U. Mo., 1948; PhD, U. Ill., 1953. Registered profl. entomologist. Entomologist E.I. DuPont de Nemours, Wilmington, Del., 1953-55; physiologist USDA, Beltsville, Md., 1955-63; entomologist USDA, Tucson, 1966-79; group leader Rohm and Haas Co., Springhouse, Pa., 1963-66; cons. Pesticide Trouble Shooters, Tucson, 1980—. Scoutmaster Boy Scouts Am.; pilot CAP Served to cpl. U.S. Army, 1943-45. Mem. Am. Chem. Soc., Entomol. Soc. Am., Entomol. Profl. Cons. Lutheran. Home and Office: 4620 E Calle Altivo Tucson AZ 85718

BARKER, STEPHEN MARSHALL, paper company executive; b. Los Angeles, May 26, 1934; s. Percy Morton and Rosalie (Donner) B.; m. Nancy Suzanne Reback, May 22, 1960 (div. 1973); children: Lori Joan, Jonathan Percy. BA, Reed Coll., 1956. Treas. Monogram Co., San Francisco, 1959-62, pres., 1962—; mem. wholesale com. Western Gift Show, San Francisco, 1962—. Mem. editorial adv. bd. Status mag., 1985—. Spl. appointments advisor Pres. Richard M. Nixon, Washington; bd. dirs. San Francisco Community Rehab. Workshop, Jewish Family Service Agy., San Francisco Employers Council. Fellow Am. Guild Organists; Am. Theatre Organ Soc., Internat. Brotherhood Magicians, Soc. Am. Magicians. Clubs: Concordia-Argonaut (San Francisco)(house com.); Tiburon (Calif.) Peninsula. Avocations: organ, magic. Home: 250A Esperanza St Tiburon CA 94920 Office: Monogram of Calif 500 Hampshire St San Francisco CA 94110

BARKLEY, LINDA DOROTHY, engineer; b. San Diego, Dec. 12, 1951; d. James Falls and Helen Patricia (Yoo) B. BA, U. San Diego, 1974; MS, Loyola Marymount U., 1980. Sr. project engr. Hughes Aircraft Co., Los Angeles, 1978—. Recipient Bausch and Lomb Sci. award, 1970, Achievement award YWCA, Los Angeles, 1986. Mem. Soc. Women Engrs., Am. Math. Soc., Assn. Women in Math., Mat./Sci. Interchange of Los Angeles (v.p. 1980—). Office: Hughes Aircraft Co PO Box 92919 S41/A319 Los Angeles CA 90009

BARKLEY, PAUL C., airline holding company executive; b. 1929. BS, San Diego State Coll., 1958. With Arthur Young & Co., 1958-67, with Pacific Southwest Airlines, San Diego, 1967—, formerly pres., chief exec. officer, now pres., chief exec. officer PSA, Inc. Office: PSA Inc 3225 N Harbor Dr San Diego CA 92101 *

BARKLEY, THIERRY VINCENT, lawyer; b. Paris, Mar. 21, 1955; s. Jacques and Michéline Marié (Rossi) B.; came to U.S., 1967, naturalized, 1974; m. Mary Ellen Gamble, June 18, 1983; children: Richard A., Robert V. B.A. in Polit. Sci., UCLA, 1976; J.D., Calif. Western Sch. Law, San Diego, 1979. Bar: Nev. 1980, U.S. Dist. Ct. Nev. 1982, U.S. Supreme Ct. 1986. Intern, Calif. Ct. Appeals 4th Circuit, San Diego, 1978-79; law clk. Nev. Dist. Ct., 7th Jud. Dist., Ely, 1979-81; assoc. firm C.E. Horton, Ely, 1982-83; asst. city atty. Ely, 1982-83; assoc. firm Barker, Gillock & Perry, Reno, 1983—. Assoc. editor Internat. Law Jour., 1979. Mem. Internat. Moot Ct. Team, 1978; recipient Dean's award Calif. Western Sch. Law, 1979. Mem. ABA, Nev. Bar Assn., Washoe Bar Assn., U.S. Jaycees (past pres. White Pine, Nev.). Republican. Roman Catholic. Lodge: Elks (past treas. Ely club). Office: Barker Gillock Perry Koning & Spann 620 Humboldt St Reno NV 89509

BARKLEY-WILEN, PAT, legal executive; b. Los Angeles, Mar. 17, 1951; d. Roy Charleton and Flora Elizabeth (Kennamer) Barkley; m. Daniel Barnett Wilen, Sept. 24, 1981. Degree, Bryan Coll. Ct. Reporting, 1973; MBA, Pepperdine U., 1985. Cert. shorthand reporter, Calif. Pres., owner Pat Barkley Ct. Reporters, Los Angeles, 1975—; ptnr. Barkley Ct. Reporters, Newport Beach, Calif., 1985—; prin. Video-At-Law, Los Angeles, 1987—. Bd. dirs. YWCA, Los Angeles, 1986. Mem. Nat. Shorthand Reporters Assn., Calif. Ct. Reporters Assn., Los Angeles Ct. Reporters Assn. (bd. dirs. 1986), Los Angeles Gen. Shorthand Reporters Assn. (treas. 1987), Orange County Ct. Reporters Assn. (bd. dirs. 1986), Calif. Trial Lawyers Assn., Los Angeles Trial Lawyers Assn. (assoc.), Orange County Women Lawyers (assoc.), Los Angeles Women Lawyers (assoc.), Santa Monica Bar Assn. (assoc.), Nat. Assn. Women Bus. Owners. Republican. Clubs: Profl. Women's Breakfast Group, Key Exec. Investment (pres.) (Los Angeles). Avocations: skiing, golf, tennis, scuba diving. Office: Pat Barkley Ct Reporters 2566 Overland Ave Suite 57 Los Angeles CA 90064 Office: 4000 MacArthur Blvd. Suite 5500 Newport Beach CA 92660

BARKSDALE, ROBERT LEE, military career personnel; b. Emelle, Ala., May 7, 1942; s. Wade and Rosa Etta (Ormond) B.; m. Clara Mae Ruffin, Mar. 19, 1966; children: Michael Robert, Angela Sabrina. BS, Ala. A&M U.; postgrad., Webster U. Enlisted USAF, 1965, advanced through grades to sgt., 1985; control and warning technician USAF, Amarillo, 1965-68, Houston, 1968-69; weapons technician instr. USAF, Okinawa, 1969-73; med. lab. supt. USAF, Wright-Patterson AFB, Ohio, 1974-77; control and warning supt. USAF, Keflavik, Iceland, 1977-79, Tyndall AFB, Fla., 1979-82; space ops. supt. USAF, Peterson AFB, Colo., 1982—. Active Parents-Tchrs. Orgn., Colorado Springs, 1982, Irving Jr. High Accountability Com., Colorado Springs, 1982—; tchr. USAF Chapel Program, Colorado Springs, 1970—; leader Boy Scout Troop, Amarillo, Tex., 1966-68. Mem. AF Assn., AF Sgts. Assn., Sr. NCO Orgn. (publicity officer 1984—), NCO Club. Democrat. Baptist. Avocations: jogging, fishing, golfing, coin collecting, camping. Home: 5640 Lantana Dr Colorado Springs CO 80915

BARLIN, CAROLE ARLENE, educational administrator; b. Oakland, Calif., Nov. 7, 1935; d. Carl Christian and Leona Lillian (Vielhauer) Barlin; B.A., U. Calif., Berkeley, 1958; M.S., U. Redlands, 1971; 1 dau., Lizette Leona Swanson. Tchr., San Francisco Unified Sch. Dist., 1966-69, Los Angeles County Supt. Schs., 1971-74, asst. prin., 1974-76, prin., 1976, personnel coordinator, 1976—; lectr. —The Profl. Woman—. Mem. Assn. of Calif. Sch. Adminstrs. (officer 1976-82), Assn. of Los Angeles County Sch. Adminstrs. (pres. 1981-82), Women in Ednl. Leadership, Am. Speech and Hearing Assn. Office: 9300 E Imperial Hwy Downey CA 90242

BARLOW, HAVEN J., realtor, state legislator; b. Clearfield, Utah, Jan. 4, 1922; s. Jesse and Asdora (Beck) B.; m. Bonnie Rae Ellison, Nov. 23, 1944; children: Jesselie Anderson, Heidi Harris, Rachel, Haven J., Stewart E., Duncan. BS, Utah State U., 1944, postgrad. U. Utah Law Sch., Harvard U. Sch. Bus. Mem. Utah State Senate, 1957—, Utah Ho. of Reps., 1953-57; bd. dirs. Community 1st Bank (formerly Clearfield State Bank), Lockhart Corp. Past pres. Lake Bonniville council Boy Scouts Am.; bd. dirs. Utah State Symphony. Served to lt. (j.g.) USN, 1942-44; PTO, ETO. Recipient Disting. Service award Utah State U., 1986. Republican. Mormon. Home: 552 Elm St Layton UT 84041

BARLOW, LAURIE PATRICIA HILDEBRAND, architect, designer; b. Pasadena, Sept. 9, 1952; d. Robert Adams and Ruth Elsa (Hildebrand) B.; m. James Paul Bochon, Mar. 29, 1980. BA in Environ. Design, U. Wash., 1974; MArch, Calif. Poly. U., San Luis Obispo, 1979. Registered architect, Calif. Lighting designer Sparling & Assocs., Seattle, 1976; draftsperson Ralph D. Anderson, Seattle, 1977; project mgr. Smith & Williams, South Pasadena, 1979-82, Whit Smith FAIA, South Pasadena, 1982-85; architect Neptune & Thomas, Pasadena, 1985-86; project architect, adminstr. Cashon, Horie, Cocke, Gonzalez, Los Angeles, 1986—. Mem. AIA (bd. dirs., chmn. profl. and devel. com., .chmn. bulletin Pasadena chpt., 1985—), Illuminating Engring. Soc., DAR. Avocations: cycling, art illustration, design. Office: Cashon Horie Cocke Gonzalez 825 Colorado Blvd #228 Los Angeles CA 91041

BARLOW, WILLIAM PUSEY, JR., accountant; b. Oakland, Calif., Feb. 11, 1934; s. William P. and Muriel (Block) B.; student Calif. Inst. Tech., 1952-54. AB in Econs., U. Calif.-Berkeley, 1956. CPA, Calif. Acct. Barlow, Davis & Wood, San Francisco, 1960-72, ptnr., 1964-72; ptnr., J.K. Lasser & Co., 1972-77, Touche Ross & Co., San Francisco, 1977-78; self employed acct., 1978—. Co-author: Collectible Books: Some New Paths, 1979, The Grolier Club, 1884-1984, 1984; editor: Book Catalogues: Their Varieties and Uses, 2d edit., 1986; contbr. articles to profl. jours. Fellow Gleeson Library Assos., 1969, pres., 1971-74; mem. Council Friends Bancroft Library, 1971—, chmn., 1974-79; bd. dirs. Oakland Ballet, 1982—, pres. 1986—. Mem. Am. Water Ski Assn. (bd. dirs., regional chmn. 1959-63, pres. 1963-66, chmn. bd. 1966-69, 77-79, hon. v.p. 1969—), World Water Ski Union (exec. bd. 1961-71, 75-78). Clubs: Grolier (N.Y.C.); Roxburghe (San Francisco); Book of Calif. (bd. dirs. 1963-76, pres. 1968-69, treas. 1971-83). Home: 1474 Hampel St Oakland CA 94602 Office: 449 15th St Oakland CA 94612

BARMATZ, MARTIN BRUCE, physicist, consultant; b. Los Angeles, May 25, 1938; s. Hyman and Sylvia Marlene (Weisner) B.; m. Joanne Elaine Love, June 16, 1961 (div. May 1979); children: Laurie Ann, Patricia Lynn; m. Carolyn Darlene Small, May 15, 1983. BA in Physics, UCLA, 1960, MA in Physics, 1962, PhD in Physics, 1966. Asst. prof. in residence UCLA, 1966-67; mem. tech. staff Bell Labs., Murray Hill, N.J., 1967-78; tech. group leader Jet Propulsion Lab., Pasadena, Calif., 1978—; cons., pres. Tech. Unlimited, La Canada, Calif., 1982—. Contbr. articles to profl. jours., patentee in field. Mem. Acoustical Soc. Am., Materials Research Soc. Democrat. Jewish. Home: 3481 Stancrest Dr #210 Glendale CA 91208 Office: Jet Propulsion Lab 4800 Oak Grove Dr 183-401 Pasadena CA 91109

BARNARD, DAVID, marine chemist; b. Rawlings, Wyo., Aug. 20, 1936; s. Patrick and Myrtle Lucile (Salmon) B.; m. Ruth Marianne Handy, Sept. 6, 1957; children: John Patrick, Joy Michelle Barnard Yantis. BS in Chemistry, Whitworth Coll., 1958; postgrad., U. Wash. Med. Sch., 1958-59, Tulane Grad. Sch., 1962-65. Analytical chemist Boeing Co., Seattle, 1961-68; marine chemist JB Kinseley Engring. Corp., Seattle, 1968-70; asst. supr. Job Therapy, Seattle, 1970-71; marine chemist Pacific Chem. Lab., San Francisco, 1971-74; analytical chemist IT Corp., Martinez, Calif., 1974-81; marine chemist Marine Testing Inc., San Diego, 1982—. Vol. book shelver Nat. City (Calif.) Library, 1982—. Served with USNG, 1955-58. Mem. Am. Chem. Soc., Marine Chemists Assn. (sec. treas. 1979-81), Nat. Fire Protection Assn. (cert.). Republican. Mem. Assembly of God. Avocation: gardening. Office: Marine Testing Inc 2146 Main St San Diego CA 92113

BARNARD, FRED, mining geologist, consultant; b. Los Angeles, July 21, 1941; s. Alfred F. and Dorothy D. (Wenning) B.; m. Nancy K. Wagner, Mar. 22, 1969; children: Adam Frederick, Alexandra Alberta. BA in Geology, U. Calif., Berkeley, 1963; PhD in Geology, U. Colo., 1968. Geologist INCO Ltd., Denver, Toronto, Can., and Guatemala, 1968-79; exploration mgr. Anaconda Minerals Co., Denver and Mex., 1980-85; cons. mining geologist Denver, 1985—; adj. prof. U. Colo., Boulder, 1981-84; geol. lectr. People's Republic China, Chile, Mex., Can., and U.S. Contbr. sci. papers to profl. publs. Mem. Geol. Soc. Am., Soc. Mining Engrs., Soc. Econ. Geologists, Assn. Geologists for Internat. Devel. Republican. Methodist. Avocation: numismatics. Home and Office: 1835 Alkire St Golden CO 80401

BARNARD, KATHRYN ELAINE, nursing educator, researcher; b. Omaha, Apr. 16, 1938; d. Paul and Elsa Elizabeth (Anderson) B. B.S. in Nursing, U. Nebr.-Omaha, 1960; M.S. in Nursing, Boston U., 1962; Ph.D., U. Wash., Seattle, 1972. Acting instr. U. Nebr.-Omaha, 1960-61; acting instr. U. Wash., Seattle, 1963-65, asst. prof., 1965-69, prof. nursing, 1972—; cons. Johnson & Johnson, Skillman, N.J., 1975-81; bd. dirs. Nat. Ctr. for Clin. Infant Programs, Washington, 1980—. Mem. program com. Wash. State Council on Child Abuse, 1983-86. Recipient Lucille Petry award Nat. League for Nursing, 1968, Martha Mae Eliot award Am. Assn. Pub. Health, 1983, Professorship award U. Wash., 1985. Fellow Am. Acad. Nursing (bd. dirs. 1980-82); mem. Inst. Medicine; mem. Am. Nurses Assn. (chmn. com. 1980-82, Jessie Scott award 1982, Nurse of Yr. award 1984), Soc. Research in Child Devel. (bd. dirs. 1981-87). Democrat. Presbyterian. Home: 11508 Durland Ave NE Seattle WA 98125 Office: U Wash Mailstop WJ-10 Seattle WA 98195

BARNARD, LLOYD WAYNE, computer systems executive; b. Moline, Ill., July 13, 1940; s. Lee and Helen Mary (Lockwood) B.; A.A., Blackhawk Coll., 1965; postgrad. U. So. Calif., 1978; m. Roberta Lee Fulton, June 1, 1963; children—Todd Lee, Melissa Mary. Engring. aid Bendix, Davenport, Iowa, 1961-66; engr. Univac div. Sperry Rand, Dayton, Ohio, 1966-68; software specialist Emerson Electric, St. Louis, 1968-71; mgr. systems engring. Northrop Data Systems, Carson, Calif., 1971-78; v.p. Mfrs. Resources and Planning, Inc., 1978-80; pres. Technology Support, Inc., Tustin, Calif., 1980—; mgr. devel. Calcomp, Anaheim, Calif., 1980-82; exec. dir. mgmt. info. systems U. So. Calif., Los Angeles, 1982-84; mgr. tech. computer div. Northrop Electronics, Los Angeles, 1984—. Served with U.S. Army, 1958-61. Office: 3175 S Hoover #362 Los Angeles CA 90007

BARNARD, MICHAEL DANA, orthopedic surgeon; b. Denver, Nov. 14, 1946; s. Rollin Dwight and Patricia Reynolds (Bierkamp) B.; m. Susan Carole Bondo, Aug. 3, 1969; children—Alison, Melissa. B.A., Pomona Coll., 1968; M.D., U. Colo.-Denver, 1972. Diplomate Am. Bd. Orthopedic Surgery. Intern U. Oreg., Portland, 1972-73; resident U. Colo., Denver, 1973-77; practice medicine specializing in orthopedic surgery, Canon City, Colo., 1977—; chief of staff St. Thomas More Hosp., Canon City, 1982-84. Fellow Am. Acad. Orthopedic Surgeons; mem. Canon City C. of C. (pres. 1982-83, dir. 1979-82), Fremont County Med. Soc. (pres. 1986—). Republican. Lutheran. Lodge: Rotary (pres. Canon City 1983-84). Home: 654 Van Loo Rd Canon City CO 81212 Office: 616 Yale Pl Canon City CO 81212

BARNARD, ROLLIN DWIGHT, financial executive, retired; b. Denver, Apr. 14, 1922; s. George Cooper and Emma (Riggs) B.; m. Patricia Reynolds Bierkamp, Sept. 15, 1943; children: Michael Dana, Rebecca Susan (Mrs. Paul C. Wulfestieg), Laurie Beth (Mrs. Kenneth J. Kostelecky). B.A., Pomona Coll., 1943. Clk. Morey Merc. Co., Denver, 1937-40; ptnr George C. Barnard & Co. (gen. real estate and ins.), Denver, 1946-47; v.p. Foster &

Barnard, Inc., 1947-53; instr. Denver U., 1949-53; dir. real estate U.S. P.O. Dept., Washington, 1953-55; bur. facilities U.S. P.O. Dept., 1955-59, asst. postmaster gen., 1959-61; pres., dir. Midland Fed. Savs. & Loan Assn., Denver, 1962-84; vice chmn. Bank Western Fed. Savs. Bank, 1984—; vice chmn. Western Capital Investment Corp., 1985—, pres., 1985-87; dir. Verex Assurance Inc., 1983-86. Pres. Denver Area council Boy Scouts Am., 1970-71, mem. exec. bd., 1962-73; adv. bd. Denver Area council Boy Scouts Am, 1973—; chmn. Planning and Zoning Commn. Greenwood Village, Colo., 1969-73; mem. Greenwood Village City Council, 1975-77; mem. nat. council Pomona Coll., 1963—; bd. dirs. Downtown Denver Improvement Assn., pres., 1965; bd. dirs. Bethesda Found., Inc., 1973-82; bd. dirs. Children's Hosp., 1979-84, treas., 1983-84; bd. dirs., Rocky Mountain Child Health Services, Inc., 1982—; trustee Mile High United Fund, 1969-72, Denver Symphony Assn., 1973-74; mem. bd. Colo. Council Econ. Edn., 1971-80, chmn., 1971-76; trustee, v.p., treas. Morris Animal Found., 1969-81, pres., chmn., 1974-78, trustee emeritus, 1981—. Served to capt. AUS, World War II. Nominated One of Ten Outstanding Young Men in Am. U.S. Jaycees, 1955, 57; recipient Distinguished Service award Postmaster Gen. U.S., 1960; Silver Beaver award Boy Scouts Am., 1969; Outstanding Citizen of Year Sertoma, 1982; Colo. Citizen of Year Colo. Assn. Realtors, 1982. Mem. Denver C. of C. (pres. 1966-67), U.S. League Savs. Instns. (bd. dirs. 1972-77, vice chmn. 1979-80, chmn. 1980-81, mem. nat. legis. com., exec. com. 1974-77), Savs. League Colo. (exec. com. 1969-73, pres. 1971-72), Colo. Assn. Commerce and Industry (dir. 1971-76), Fellowship Christian Athletes (Denver area dir. 1963-76), Western Stock Show Assn. (dir. 1971—, exec. com. 1982—, 1st v.p. 1985—), Nu Alpha Phi. Republican. Presbyn. Clubs: 26 (Denver) (pres. 1970), Rotary (Denver) (dir. 1979-81, 2d v.p. 1980); Mountain and Plains Appaloosa Horse (pres. 1970-71), Roundup Riders of the Rockies (dir. 1979—, treas. 1980—, v.p. 1987—). Home: 3151 East Long Rd Littleton CO 80121

BARNEA, URI (NATHAN), music director, conductor, composer, violinist; b. Petah-Tikvah, Israel, May 29, 1943; came to U.S., 1971, naturalized, 1982; s. Shimon and Miriam Burstein; m. Lizbeth A. Lund, Dec. 15, 1977; 1 dau. Teaching cert., Oranim Music Inst., Israel, 1966; postgrad. Hebrew U., Israel, 1969-71; Mus.B., Rubin Acad. Music, Israel, 1971; M.A., U. Minn., 1974, Ph.D., 1977. Mus. dir. Jewish Community Ctr., Mpls. 1971-73; conductor Youval Chamber Orch., Mpls., 1971-73; asst. conductor U. Minn. Orchs., Mpls., 1972-77; music dir., conductor Unitarian Soc., Mpls., 1973-78, Kenwood Chamber Orch., Mpls., 1974-78, Knox-Galesburg Symphony, 1978-83, Billings Symphony Soc., Mont., 1984—; asst. prof. Knox Coll., Galesburg, Ill., 1978-83; violinist, violist Yellowstone Chamber players, Billings, 1984—; violist Tri-City Symphony, Quad-Cities, Ill., Iowa, 1983-84; conductor Cedar Arts Forum String Camp, Cedar Falls, Iowa, 1981, 82; European conducting debut, London, Neuchatel and Fribourg, Switzerland, 1986. Composer of numerous compositions including String Quartet (1st prize Aspen Composition Competition 1976), Sonata for Flute and Piano, 1975 (Diploma of Distinction 26th Viotti Internat. Competition, Italy 1975), Ruth A Ballet, 1974 (1st prize Oberhoffer Composition Contest 1976). Active in music adv. panel Ill. Arts Council, 1980-83; v.p. Community Concert Assn., Galesburg, 1980-83; bd. dirs. Knox Coll. Credit Union, Galesburg, 1982-83, Sta. KEMC Pub. Radio, Billings, 1984—, Fox Theater Corp., Billings, 1984-86 . Recipient Friend of Arts title Sigma Alpha Iota, 1982; Ill. Arts Council grantee, 1979; Hebrew U. Jerusalem scholar, 1972-74, Hebrew U. and Rubin Acad. Mus. scholar, 1969, 70; Individual Artist fellow Mont. Arts Council, 1986. Mem. Minn. Composers Forum, Conductors Guild, ASCAP. Office: Billings Symphony Soc PO Box 602 Billings MT 59103

BARNES, CAROL P., education educator; b. Ann Arbor, Mich., Jan. 21, 1941; d. Reinhold Walter and Ruth Ardillis (McKillen) Pardon; m. Gary Lee Barnes, June 17, 1959; children: Katherine, Erik. BA in Edn., U. Mich., 1962; MEd, Wright State U., 1970; PhD, Claremont Grad. Sch., 1975. Cert. elem. tchr., Mich., Ohio, Calif. Tchr. Plymouth, Mich., 1962-63, Mad River Twp. Schs., Dayton, Ohio, 1963-64, Mad River-Greene Twp. Schs., Enon, Ohio, 1965-67; coll. instr. Wright State U., Dayton, Ohio, 1970-72, Claremont (Calif.) Grad. Sch., 1973-74; prof. Calif. State U., Fullerton, 1975—; cons. to various sch. dists., Calif., Ohio, 1970—, Orange County Grand Jury, Santa ANa, Calif., 1986, various law firms, Calif., 1984—; pres. Programetrics Ltd., Huntington Beach, Calif., 1980—. Co-author: Studies of College Teaching, 1984; contbr. articles to profl. jours. exec. com. mem.-at-large Acad. Senate of Calif. State U., Long Beach, 1984—. Recipient Meritorius Performance award, Calif. State U.-Fullerton, 1984-86; named Outstanding Prof., Sch. Human Devel. and Community Service of Calif. State U.-Fullerton, 1985. Mem. Am. Ednl. Research Assn., Assn. for Supervision and Curriculum Devel. (bd. dirs. 1982-84), Calif. Assn. for Supervision and Curriculum Devel. (bd. dirs. 1982-84), Orange County Reading Assn., Calif. Reading Assn. Republican. Presbyterian. Home: 16472 Grimaud Ln Huntington Harbour CA 92649 Office: Calif State U 800 N St Coll Blvd Fullerton CA 92634

BARNES, CHARLES ANDREW, educator, physicist; b. Toronto, Ont., Can., Dec. 12, 1921; came to U.S., 1953, naturalized, 1961; m. Phyllis Malcolm, Sept. 15, 1950; children—Nancy E., Steven. A. B.A., McMaster U., 1943; M.A., U. Toronto, 1944; Ph.D., Cambridge U., 1950. Physicist Joint Brit.-Canadian Atomic Energy Project, 1944-46; asst. prof. physics U. B.C., 1950-53, 55-56; mem. faculty Calif. Inst. Tech., 1953-55, 56—, prof. physics, 1962—; guest prof. Niels Bohr Inst., Copenhagen, 1973-74. Editor, contbr. to profl. books and jours. NSF sr. fellow Denmark, 1962-63; recipient medal Inst. d'Astrophysique de Paris, 1987, Alexander von Humboldt U.S. Sr. Scientist award, Fed. Republic Germany, 1987—. Fellow Am. Phys. Soc. Office: Calif Inst Tech Pasadena CA 91125

BARNES, CHARLES WINFRED, geology educator, administrator; b. Olkahoma City, Oct. 21, 1934; s. Dewey Lloyd and Enola Florence (Robertson) B.; m. Charlotte Elizabeth Coe, June 15, 1958; children: Kelly Elizabeth, Elizabeth Dawn, Amy Elizabeth, Charlotte Susan. BS in Geology, U. Okla., 1957; MS in Geology, U. Idaho, 1962; PhD in Geology, U. Wis., 1965. Asst. prof. Eastern N.Mex. U., Portales, 1965-68; asst. prof. No. Ariz. U., Flagstaff, 1968-71, assoc. prof. to prof., 1971-74, chmn. geology dept., 1980-84, dean sci., 1984—; cons. U.S. Steel Exploration, Duluth, Minn., 1964-66, Berge Exploration, Salt Lake City, 1978-82. Author: Earth Time and Life, 1980, 2d rev. edit., 1986; also articles. Cons. Flagstaff (Ariz.) Sch. Dist., 1980-82; summer staff mem. Boy Scouts Am., Cimarron, N.Mex., 1966-74. Served to lt. USN, 1957-61. Named Outstanding Faculty mem. Eastern N.Mex. U., 1968, chmn. of faculty No. Ariz. U., 1974-75; recipient Pres. award No. Ariz. U., 1974, 80, Disting. Faculty award No. Ariz. U., 1978. Mem. Geol. Soc. Am., Nat. Assn. Geology Tchrs., Sigma Xi. Democrat. Methodist. Avocations: photography, backpacking, rifle markmanship, writing, choral singing. Home: 250 N Circle Dr Flagstaff AZ 86001 Office: Northern Ariz Univ Box 5621 Flagstaff AZ 86011

BARNES, GORDON D., controller; b. Seattle, Feb. 25, 1933; s. Chester F. and Shirley H. (Melton) B.; m. Shirley M. Walker, Aug. 20, 1954; children: Karen J., Sherri L., Brian D. BA, U. Wash., 1954; MBA, U. Portland, 1986. CPA, Wash.; cert. mgmt. acct. Chief cost acct. Aluminum Co. Am., Davenport, Iowa, 1963-65; corp. cost acct. Aluminum Co. Am., Pitts., 1965-66, mgr. mill products ops. acctg., 1968-77, mgr. systems and services, 1978-79; plant controller Aluminum Co. Am., Evansville, Ind., 1966-68; ops. controller Aluminum Co. Am., Vancouver, Wash., 1979—. Mem. mgmt. task force Vancouver Pub. Schs., 1981—; fin. chmn., treas. S.W. Wash. Hosps., Vancouver, 1984—, trustee, 1984—; bd. dirs. Columbia Pacific council Boy Scouts Am., Portland, Oreg., 1983—. Served to 1st lt. USAF, 1954-57. Recipient Silver Beaver award Boy Scouts Am., 1982. Mem. Nat. Assn. Accts., Exploring Bus. (chmn. 1980—), Vancouver C. of C. (edn. com.), Assn. Wash. Bus. (chmn. econ. devel. and edn. council 1983), Wash. Council Econs. Edn. (trustee 1985—), Phi Beta Kappa. Presbyterian. Lodge: Rotary (local sec. 1985, Paul Harris fellow 1982). Avocations: jogging, kayaking, hiking, boating, camping. Home: 9608 NW 4th Ct Vancouver WA 98665 Office: ALCOA PO Box 120 Vancouver WA 98666

BARNES, HOWARD W., international business educator, management consultant; b. Feb. 9, 1932; married. AB in Gov., Harvard U., 1955; MBA in Mktg., U. So. Calif., 1963; Dr. rer. pol., Technische Universität Braunschweig, Fed. Republic of Germany, 1968. Sales rep. Carnation Co., 1959-60; with mktg. research dept. Carnation Co., Los Angeles, 1960-64; prof. internat. bus. Brigham Young U., Provo, Utah, 1964—; prin. Howard W. Barnes Assocs., 1975—; co-founder and chmn. bd. dirs. Bonneville Bank, 1978—; chmn. faculty adv. council; asst. dean Sch. Mgmt.; dir. MBA Program, Brigham Young U.; condr. mgmt. seminars Mexico City, 1975—. Author: Innovation and Technology Transfer, 1982; co-author: Japanese Management, 1982; contbr. numerous articles to profl. jours. Served with USN, 1955-58. Home: 1180 Mountain Ridge Rd Provo UT 84601

BARNES, JOHN FAYETTE, research scientist; b. Santa Cruz, Calif., Jan. 28, 1930; s. John Fayette and Bertha Henrietta (Youngman) B.; m. Joanne Cecily Lyle, Aug. 28, 1955; children—John Fayette, David Lyle. B.A., U. Calif., Berkeley, 1951; M.S., U. Denver, 1952; Ph.D., U. N.Mex., 1963, M. Mgmt., 1981. Asst. group leader Los Alamos Nat. Lab., N.Mex., 1968-71, dept. group leader, 1971, group leader, 1971-76, asst. theoretical div. leader, 1976-77, assoc. theoretical div. leader, 1977-80, dep. theoretical div. leader, 1980-81, dep. assoc. dir. for energy programs, 1981-82, dep. assoc. dir. for physics and math., 1982-83, applied theoretical physics div. leader, 1983-85, research scientist, group leader, 1985—; mathematician Research Directorate, Air Force Spl. Weapons Ctr., Albuquerque, 1956-57; mem. research adv. bd. Lab. for Laser Energetics U. Rochester, N.Y., 1980—, chmn., 1981, 87. Contbr articles to profl. jours. Active Boy Scouts Am., Los Alamos, 1967-79; precinct chmn. Republican Party, 1968-85; del. state conv. 1972. Mem. Am. Phys. Soc. Home: 13 Village Pl Los Alamos NM 87544 Office: Los Alamos Nat Lab Theoretical Div Group T-1 MS B221 PO Box 1663 Los Alamos NM 87545

BARNES, MARTIN MCRAE, entomologist; b. Calgary, Alta., Can., Aug. 3, 1920; s. Harry Olan and Vida (Killian) B.; m. Julia Butts, Aug. 31, 1946; children—Wayne, Martin, Delia, Brian. B.S., U. Calif., Berkeley, 1941; Ph.D., Cornell U., 1946. Mem. faculty U. Calif., Riverside, 1946—; prof. entomology U. Calif., 1962—, entomologist agrl. research expt. sta., 1946—. Contbr. articles to profl. jours. Fellow AAAS; mem. Entomol. Soc. Am. (pres. Pacific br. 1976-77), Entomol. Soc. Can., Entomol. Soc. Mexico, Sigma Xi. Democrat. Research in deciduous orchard and vineyard entomology. Home: 1946 Prince Albert Dr Riverside CA 92507 Office: Dept Entomology U Calif Riverside CA 92521

BARNES, ROBERT PAUL, college official; b. Minot, N.D., Jan. 16, 1934; s. Richard Neil and Erna Margaret (Broeckel) B.; m. Pamela Kay Frantz, Mar. 13, 1976; children—Claire Margaret, Elizabeth Renee, Christopher Paul. B.A., U. Wash., 1956; M.A., U. Colo., 1963; Ph.D., U. So. Calif., 1967. Tchr. public schs., Calif., Ill., 1960-62; lectr. U. Pacific, 1966; asst. prof. history Western State Coll., Gunnison, Colo., 1966-67; Purdue U., 1967-68; assoc. prof. Central Wash. U., 1968-72; acad. dean N.W. Mo. State U., 1972-75, ednl. cons. and devel. officer, 1975-80; v.p. Rockmont Coll., Denver, 1980-82; v.p. Westmar Coll., LeMars, Iowa, 1982-84; sr. devel. officer Ohio State U., Columbus, 1984-85; exec. dir. univ. devel. Northrop U., Los Angeles, 1985—; mem. Fulbright Selection Com., 1977—. Served with U.S. Army, 1957-58. Contbr. articles to profl. jours. U. So. Calif. scholar, 1964-65; faculty research grantee Cen. Wash. U., 1970-71. Mem. Am. Hist. Assn., Am. Assn. Higher Edn., Conf. Brit. Studies, Faith and History, Christian Stewardship Council, Planned Giving Roundtable, Western Social Sci. Assn., Phi Alpha Theta. Republican. Mem. Christian Ch. Home: 10310 Trabuco Bellflower CA 90706-5054

BARNETT, CHARLES RADCLIFFE, film writer, producer, director, health physicist; b. N.Y.C., Feb. 23, 1934; s. Carlyle Reginald and Anne Nathalie (Mooney) B.; m. Noel Ray Phillips, Feb. 3, 1963 (div. 1963). B.A., Columbia Coll., 1956; Ph.D., Union Grad. Sch., Cin., 1980. Cert. profl. geologist. Health physicist U. Calif., Los Alamos, N.Mex., 1962-69, writer, producer, dir., 1975—, head motion picture prodn., 1977—; pvt. practice geol. cons., Woodstock, N.Y., 1971-73; dir., v.p. Anthrop. Film Found., Santa Fe, 1978—; dir. audio-visuals Albuquerque Mus. Maya Project, 1983-87; Writer, producer, dir. 60 documentary films, 1975—(85 awards); contbr. Smithsonian Mag., Explorers Jour., various jours. Mem. N.Mex. Arts Commn. Media Panel, 1978, chmn., 1979, 80. Served with U.S. Army, 1956-58, W.Ger. Recipient film awards, France, Belgium, Italy, Yugoslavia, Germany, Gt. Brit., Czechoslovakia, Poland, Egypt, Brazil, 1978—, 17 CINE Golden Eagle awards, Council on Internat. Non-theatrical Events, 1978—. Mem. Univ. Film Assn., Am. Film Inst., Rio Grande Producers Assn., Ind. Video and Filmmakers, Am. Inst. Profl. Geologists, Edouard Manet Soc. (Paris, regional v.p. 1967—), Explorers Club of N.Y. Roman Catholic. Club: Quien Sabe. Home: 331 Calle Loma Norte Santa Fe NM 87501 Office: Univ Calif Los Alamos Nat Lab Motion Picture/Video Prodn Unit Mail Stop D-415 Los Alamos NM 87545

BARNETT, CLYDE LANCE, state official; b. Mar. 7, 1946; s. Clyde L. and Eleanor (Pennrich) B.; m. Betty Reed, June 27, 1970; 1 child, Ann Reed. B.A. in Econs., U. Calif.-Santa Barbara, 1971; M.S. in Econs., U. Oreg., 1973, Ph.D. in Econs., 1975. Assoc. economist Rand Corp., Santa Monica, Calif., 1975-77, dep. mgr., 1977-78, mgr., 1979-81, sr. economist, 1981, dir., 1981-83; chief dep. dir. Calif. Dept. Commerce, Sacramento, 1983—; chief economist Calif. Gov.'s Office Planning Research, Sacramento, 1984—; prof. Rand Grad. Inst., 1979—; evaluator NSF, 1983—; vis. lectr. UCLA, 1982—; referee Urban Studies and Policy Scis., 1975—. Co-author: Experimenting with Housing Allowances: Comprehensive Final Report of the Housing Assistance Supply Experiment; Price Effects of Housing Allowances. Contbr. articles to profl. jours. Served with U.S. Army, 1967-70, Vietnam. FDIC fellow, 1974-75. Mem. Sigma Alpha Epsilon. Home: 5421 State Ave Sacramento CA 95819 Office: Calif Dept Commerce Hotel Senator 1121 L St Sacramento CA 95814

BARNETT, KELLY, biophysicist; b. Milw., Nov. 3, 1958; d. Howard John and Muriel Mary (Mongoven) B.; m. Richard Stephen Jany, May 22, 1982. BS, St. Louis U., 1980, MS in Research, 1982. Clin. lab. analyst Colin Campbell MD, San Francisco, 1982-84; staff research assoc. Drug Dependence Unit U. Calif., San Francisco, 1984-86, research assoc. physics, 1986—. Instr. CPR and water safety, ARC, San Francisco, 1982—; intern advisor U.S. Naval Hosp., Oaknoll, Calif., 1983—. Fellow Beta Beta Beta; mem. AAAS. Roman Catholic. Avocations: scuba diving, running, woodworking, traveling. Office: Univ Calif Radiation Oncology Div Physics 501 Parnusus L-75 San Francisco CA 94143

BARNETT, LARRY EUGENE, fire safety specialist, consultant; b. Tucson, Apr. 30, 1954; s. Otis Eugene and Margaret Ellen (Keillor) B.; m. Kim Leslie Bowen, May 28, 1977 (div. Feb. 1986); children: Brooke Ashley, Ryan Michael. AS in Fire Sci., Pima Community Coll., 1981. Fire capt. Flowing Wells Fire Dept., Tucson, 1974-78; fire protection inspector Anamax Mining Co., Sahuarita, Ariz., 1977-85; fire safety coordinator U. Ariz., Tucson, 1985—; cons. in field, 1985—. Editor: University of Arizona Safety Notes, 1985—. Asst. dep. state fire marshal, Ariz., 1986—. Mem. Am. Soc. Safety Engrs. (program chmn. 1983-84), Soc. Fire Protecton Engrs., Internat. Assn. Arson Investigators, Ariz. Emergency Services Assn. Republican. Avocations: bodybuilding, boating, photography. Home: 3271 W Milton Tucson AZ 85746 Office: U Ariz 1143 N Cherry Tucson AZ 85719

BARNHART, DEBORAH MARIE, magazine publisher; b. Columbia, Mo., June 11, 1954; d. Franklin Thomas Barnhart and Marjorie Doris (Schultz) Hargitt; m. Edi Alfred Blatter; 1 child, Berkeley Marie. BA in Urban and Regional Govt., Willamette U., 1976. Clk. Oreg. State Legislature, Salem, 1977; adminstrv. asst. Greyhound Export Fin. Co., San Francisco, 1977-79; planner Zimmer Gunsul Frasca Architects, Portland, Oreg., 1980-81; pub. Metro mag., Portland, 1981—. Bd. dirs. Oreg. Student Pub. Interest Research Group, Salem, 1972-73. Democrat. Avocation: photography.

BARNUM, RANDAL MATTHEW, lawyer; b. N.Y.C., Apr. 30, 1958; s. Clive Anthony and Joan Lenore (Rossi) B.; m. Christine Marie Rodriguez, Sept. 5, 1981; 1 child, Stephanie Elizabeth. BA in Polit. Sci., Stanford U., 1980; JD, U. Calif., San Francisco, 1983. Bar: Calif. 1983, U.S. Dist. Ct. (no. dist.) Calif. 1983. Atty. Bronson, Bronson & McKinnon, San Francisco, 1983-85, Law Offices of Richard T. Bowles, Walnut Creek, Calif., 1985—. Editor: Hastings Constl. Law Quarterly, 1982-83. Bd. dirs. Village Homeowners Assn., Benicia, 1986—. Mem. ABA (torts and litigation com. 1983—), Calif. Bar Assn., Contrs Costa County Bar Assn., Hasting Alumni Assn. (v.p. Contra Costa chpt. 1983—), Stanford U. Alumni Assn., Phi Alpha Delta. Republican. Roman Catholic. Home: 465 Myrtle Ct Benicia CA 44510 Office: Law Offices of Bowles and Verna 2121 N California Blvd Suite 875 Walnut Creek CA 94596

BARNWELL, DAVID RAY, aerospace financial and computer systems analyst, computer programmer; b. Amarillo, Tex., Sept. 9, 1953; s. Jasper Clarence and Mary Evelyn (King) B.; m. Maria Milagrosa Bellido, July 7, 1975; 1 dau., Miriam Louise. Student Army and Navy Acad., Carlsbad, Calif., 1971; A.A. in Bus. Adminstrn., Cerritos Coll., Norwalk, Calif., 1979, AA in Econs., 1986; B.Sc. in Bus. Adminstrn., U. Redlands, 1981. Instr., Cerritos Coll., 1977-79; adjuster Western Thrift and Loan Assn., Long Beach, Calif., 1978-80; prodn. cost analyst, space shuttle orbiter div. Rockwell Internat., Downey, Calif., 1980-85, mem. space shuttle speaker's bur., 1981—, sr. cost analyst space shuttle orbiter div., 1985-86, sr. computer systems analyst, 1986—. Served with USMC, 1970-76. Recipient NASA first shuttle flight achievement award, 1981. Mem. AIAA, Nat. Mgmt. Assn., Am. Legion, Mensa. Club: Am. Philatelic Soc. Office: 12214 Lakewood Blvd Downey CA 90241

BARNWELL, WILLIAM (WOODWARD), geologist, hydrologist; b. New Haven, Aug. 25, 1927; s. Frank Lyon and Theodora Booth (Skinner) B.; m. Audrey Lay, Sept. 3, 1953; children—Charles, Mary, Robert, Theodore. B.S., Harvard U., 1950; M.S. in Geology, U. Wyo., 1955. Exec. officer arctic ops. project U.S. Weather Bur., Mould Bay Sta., Prince Patrick Island, N.W.T., Can., 1951-52; exploration geologist Chevron Oil Co., Wash. and Alaska, 1955-60; geophysicist, geologist Caltex-Amoseas, Tripoli, Libya, 1960-63; sr. geologist Sinclair Oil Co., Anchorage, 1963-65; assoc. dist. chief for Alaska, U.S. Geol. Survey, Anchorage, 1965-75, dist. chief, Madison, Wis., 1975-78, spl. asst. to dir., Reston, Va., 1978-81; dep. dir., dep. state geologist Dept. Natural Resources, Anchorage, 1981-86; commr. Alaska Oil and Gas Conservation Commn., Anchorage, 1986—. Author: Geology of Mendenhall Valley, Alaska, 1969; Water for Anchorage, Alaska, 1972 (Nat. Communication award Dept. Interior 1973); Wisconsin Planning - The Big Picture, 1977; Hydrology for Planning - Anchorage, 1973; Alaska's Resource Inventory, 1984, others. Mem. Solid Waste Commn., Anchorage, 1982—, Hazardous Waste Task Force, Anchorage, 1985-87; vestryman St. Mary's Episcopal Ch., Anchorage, 1969-70. Served with U.S. Army, 1946-47, Japan. Recipient Nat. Achievement award Am. Assn. County Execs., 1973. Mem. Alaska Geol. Soc. (pres. 1973-74), Am. Assn. Petroleum Geologists (nat. del. 1972-73), Geol. Soc. Am., Am. Geophys. Union, AAAS. Clubs: Anchorage Ski (bd. dirs. 1973-75), Seward Yacht (dir. 1982-86).

BARONE, ROBERT MICHAEL, physician; b. Buffalo, Apr. 2, 1941; s. Michael Horace and Antoinette (Buscaglia) B.; m. Mary Margaret Wallis, Mar. 11, 1967; children: Susanne, Julie, Robert. BS, Georgetown U., 1962; MD, SUNY, Buffalo, 1966; MS in Surgery, U. Ill., 1970. Resident in surgery U. Ill., Chgo., 1972, fellowship in surg. oncology, 1974, asst. prof. surgery, 1972-74; chief oncology USN, Oakland, Calif., 1974-76; asst. prof. surgery U. Calif., San Diego, 1976-80, assoc. clin. prof. surgery, 1980—; staff surgeon Oncology Assocs. of San Diego, 1980—; prin. investigator NIH Studies of Hepatic Arterial Therapy, 1983—. Served to commdr. USNR, 1974-76. Recipient Research award Chgo. Surg. Soc., 1971. Fellow: ACS (state chmn. 1983—, mem. commn. cancer, pres. San Diego chpt. 1986—); mem. Soc. Surg. Oncology, Soc. Head and Neck Surgeons, Am. Soc. Clin. Oncology, Warren Cole Soc. Avocations: skiing, golf, tennis, fishing. Office: Oncology Assocs San Diego 3930 4th Ave San Diego CA 92103

BARONE, SHERRY JOY, test engineer; b. Phil., June 23, 1960; s. Leonard and Linda Gwen (Berger) B. BS, U. Md., 1982; MBA suma cum laude, Nat. U., 1985. Registered profl. engr. Computer programmer Office Instl. Studies, U. Md., College Park, 1982; lead software engr. RCA Astro-Electronics, Princeton, N.J., 1982-83; sr. test engr. ITT Gilfillan, Van Nuys, Calif., 1983—; cons. AMJ Acctg. Firm, Los Angeles, 1984-85, IBM, Los Angeles, 1985—. Author: (with others) Children and Computer, 1982. Mem. Am. Computing Machinery Club, IEEE, Soc. Women Engrs., Soc. Test Engrs., Gilfillan Mgmt. Assn. Republican. Jewish. Club: ITT Ski (Van Nuys). Avocations: East Asian history, art, sports. Office: ITT Gilfillan 7821 Orion Ave Van Nuys CA 91409

BAROTH, EDMUND CRAIG, mechanical engineer; b. N.Y.C., Aug. 24, 1952; s. Bernard David and Sylvia (Walder) B.; m. Elaine Ann Boulay, July 9, 1983. BME, CCNY, 1975; MME, U. Calif., Berkeley, 1976, PhDME, 1981. Research asst. U. Calif., Berkeley, 1975-81; mem. tech. staff Jet Propulsion Lab., Pasadena, Calif., 1981—; instr. Calif. State U., Los Angeles, 1984. Recipient Mech. Engring. Alumni award, CCNY, 1975; named Calif. State Regents fellow U. Calif., Berkeley, 1976, N.Y. State Regents scholar, CCNY, 1970-75; grantee NSF, 1974. Mem. AIAA (assoc.), Am. Soc. Mech. Engrs. (assoc.), Calif. Skeptics Soc., AAAS. Avocations: music, computers, photography, model airplanes. Home: 12132 Monogram Ave Granada Hills CA 91344 Office: Jet Propulsion Lab 4800 Oak Grove Dr Mail Stop 125-177 Pasadena CA 91109

BAROVICH, ELI ILIJA, tax consultant; b. Niksic, Yugoslavia, Feb. 16, 1934; came to U.S., 1962, naturalized, 1967; s. Radovan and Zlatana (Maksimovic) B.; m. Anka Radusinovic, Spt. 14, 1973; 2 children: Dennis, Maya. Student, Los Angeles City Coll., 1965-68; BBA, UCLA, 1971, postgrad., 1974-75. Sr. auditor Aetna Life & Casuality, Los Angeles, 1971-76; tax cons. Aetna Icome Tax Service, Woodland Hills, Calif., 1977-79; owner Aetna Income Tax Service, Woodland Hills, 1979—. Mem. Nat. Assn. Bus. and Tax Cons., Nat. Soc. Pub. Accts., Woodland Hills C. of c., UCLA Alumni Assn. Republican. Eastern Orthodox. Home: 5492 Parkmoor Rd Calabasas CA 91302 Office: 22749 Ventura Blvd Woodland Hills CA 91364

BARR, CHARLES MILSTEAD, public relations executive; b. Granville, Mo., Feb. 25, 1915; s. Noel Bland and Loyotte Lee (Arnold) B.; m. Mildred Hoyle, Aug. 16, 1936 (dec. Mar. 1987); 1 child, Robert Noel. Student, Texarkana Coll., 1931-34, U. So. Calif., 1957-58. Pub. relations rep. Northrop Corp., Hawthorne, Calif., 1947-52, pub. relations supr., 1952-54; asst. corp. dir. pub. relations Northrop Corp., Beverly Hills, Calif., 1954-69; corp. dir. pub. relations Northrop Corp., Century City, Calif., 1969-72; pres. CMB Communications Inc., Rancho Palos Verdes, Calif., 1981—. Mem. Pub. Relations Soc. Am. (accredited), Aviation Space Writers Assn. (assoc.), Nat. Assn. Real Estate Editors. Club: Los Angeles Press. Home and Office: CMB Communications Inc 2119 Mendon Dr Rancho Palos Verdes CA 90732

BARR, DONALD WESTWOOD, nuclear chemist; b. Worcester, Mass., May 6, 1932; s. Addison Wilbur and Evelyn (Macfadyen) B.; m. Marilyn Jean Squires, Aug. 28, 1954; children: James, Glenn, Sandra, Brenda. Student, Worcester Jr. Coll., 1950-51; BS, U. Mass., Amherst, 1954; PhD, U. Calif., Berkeley, 1957. Mem. staff Los Alamos (N.Mex.) Nat. Lab., 1957—, leader isotope and nuclear chemistry div. NSF fellow, 1955-56; recipient E.O. Lawrence award Dept. Energy, 1980. Mem. Am. Chem. Soc. Avocations: golf, travel. Office: Los Alamos Nat Lab J515 Los Alamos NM 87545

BARR, KENNETH JOHN, mining company executive; b. Birmingham, Ala., Aug. 25, 1926; s. Archie and Mable Leona (Griffith) B.; m. Jeanne Bonner, Jan. 22, 1951; children: Marsha Jeanne, Kenneth John, Darren Clint. BS in Chem. Engring., Auburn U., 1947; grad., Advanced Mgmt. Inst. Northwestern U., 1964. Jr. petroleum engr. Stanolind Oil & Gas, Hobbs, N.Mex., 1948-49; chief engr. Amoco Prodn. Co., Tulsa, 1962-65; mgr. producing and v.p. producing dept. Amoco Can. Petroleum Co., Calgary, Alta, 1965-70; mgr. producing and v.p., div. mgr. Amoco Prodn. Co., New Orleans, 1970-73; mgr. supply dept. Standard Oil (Ind.), Chgo., 1973-75; exec. v.p. Amoco Internat., Chgo., 1975, Amoco Prodn. Co., Chgo., 1975-79; pres. Cyprus Mines (Std.), Los Angeles, 1979-80, Amoco Minerals Co., Denver, 1980-85; pres., chief exec. officer Cyprus Minerals Co., Denver, 1985—, also bd. dirs. Served with USAAF, 1945. Mem. Am. Mining Congress (bd. dirs. 1983—), AIME. Clubs: Snowmass (Aspen, Colo.); Longboat Key (Fla.). Avocations: skiing; golfing; photography. Office: Cyprus Minerals Co 7200 S Alton Way Englewood CO 80112

BARR, ROBERT DALE, university dean, educator; b. Fort Worth, Nov. 24, 1939; s. Robert Edward and Leota Oleta (Sanders) B.; m. Beryl Lucas, Aug. 26, 1956; children—Bonny, Brady. B.A., Tex. Christian U., 1961;

M.S., North Tex. State U., 1965; Ph.D., Purdue U., 1969. Cert. sch. adminstr. and educator, Oreg. Tchr. social studies, dept. chmn. R.L. Paschal High Sch., Fort Worth, 1961-65; grad. instr. Purdue U., West Lafayette, Ind., 1965-67; asst. prof. edn. U. Tex.-Arlington, 1967-69; staff assoc. Nat. Council for Social Studies, Washington, 1969-70, asst. prof., assoc. prof. social studies edn. and secondary edn., dir. alternative schs. grad. program, 1970-77, prof. edn., dir. tchr. edn. and extended services, 1978; dir. Office Tchr. Edn. and Extended Services, Ind. U., Bloomington, 1980-81; dean Sch. Edn., Oreg. State U., Corvallis, 1982—; vis. prof. Am. Summer Sch., U. Fla., U. New Orleans, U. Innsbruck, Austria, 1979; interim dir. Ctr. for Urban and Multicultural Edn.; co-dir. Nat. Consortium for Options in Pub. Edn., 1971-77; bd. advisors Fielding Inst., Santa Barbara, Calif., 1974—; chmn., mem. publs. bds. Nat. Council for Social Studies, 1970-74; mem. task force on compulsory edn. and transitions for youth, Phi Delta Kappa, 1976-77; mem. research team Project Alternative Edn., 1981; dir. project Nat. Inst. Profl. Devel., Santiago, Chile, 1980-81; co-dir. basic edn. project Lilly Endowment and Indpls. Pub. Schs., 1977-78; cons. and lectr. in field. Author: Optional Alternative Public Schools, 1971 (reprinted as School Violence and Vandalism: Model and Strategies for Change, 1975), Values and Youth, 1971, (with James L. Barth and S. Samuel Shermis) Defining the Social Studies, 1977, The Nature of the S Social Studies, 1978, (with Vernon H. Smith and Daniel J. Burke) Alternatives in Education: Freedom to Choose, 1976 (also Japanese transl.), co-editor: Changing Schools newsletter, Nat. Consortium for Options in Pub. Edn., 1971-77; producer, editor filmstrip To Lead a Profession, 1970; contbr. chpts. to books, reports, monographs, articles, revs., editorials to profl. jours. Recipient Disting. Achievement award Am. Assn. Colls. for Tchr. Edn., 1975; named to Internat. Invitational Colloquium on Adult Edn., U. Nottingham, 1981; Ford Found. Washington fellow, 1969-70. Developer Ind. U. Weekender Inservice Program for Tchrs., 1978; asst. developer tchr. ctr. proposals Indpls. Pub. Schs., Bartholomew Pub. Schs., Columbus, Ind., 1977. Office: Oreg State U Room 215 Edn Hall Corvallis OR 97331

BARRENTINE, CARL DOUGLAS, biology educator, researcher; b. Seattle, Oct. 20, 1952; s. Harold Earl and Delores Jennette (Edwards) B.; m. Shelby Jean Balko, Mar. 17, 1974. BA, Cen. Wash. U., 1974, MS, 1978; ArtsD, Idaho State U., 1983, postgrad., 1984-85. Instr. biology Treasure Valley Coll., Ontario, Oreg., 1978-80; asst. prof. biology Prestonsburg (Ky.) Coll., 1983-84; research coordinator U. Iowa, Iowa City, 1984-85; lectr. biology Calif. State U., Bakersfield, 1985-86, asst. prof. biology, 1986—. Contbr. articles to profl. jours. Mem. Am. Ornithologists Union, Cooper Ornitholog. Soc., Western, Inland and Eastern Bird Banding Socs., Pacific N.W. Bird and Mammal Soc.,Phi Kappa Phi, Phi Delta Kappa, Sigma Xi. Home: 100 Ritter Ct Bakersfield CA 93312 Office: Calif State U Dept Biology 9001 Stockdale Hwy Bakersfield CA 93311

BARRERA, CECILIO RICHARD, research microbiology educator; b. Rio Grande, Tex., Nov. 30, 1942; s. Manuel and Rafaela (Trevino) B.; m. Rosalinda Benavides; children: Marisa, Cristina. BA, U. Tex., 1965, MA, 1967, PhD, 1970. NIH predoctoral trainee U. Tex., Austin, 1966-69; fellow Clayton Found. Biochem. Inst., Austin, 1970-75; asst. prof. biology N.Mex. State U., Las Cruces, 1975-81, assoc. prof., 1981—; vis. asst. prof. U. Tex., San Antonio, 1974; mem. rev. panel NRC, Washington, 1984-87; mem. site visit team NIH, Washington, 1980. Contbr. articles to profl. jours. Mem. AAAS, Am. Soc. Microbiology (pres. N.Mex. br. 1979-81), Sigma Xi (pres. N.Mex. State U. chpt. 1983-84). Office: NMex State U Biology Dept Las Cruces NM 88003

BARRETT, IZADORE, fisheries research administrator; b. Vancouver, B.C., Can., Oct. 4, 1926; came to U.S., 1956; s. Samuel Barrett and Rose (Hyatt) Gordon; m. Fulvia Mercedes Quesada, July 5, 1958; children: Marcus, Byron, Norman, Dora. BA, U. B.C., 1947, MA, 1949; postgrad., U. Toronto, 1949-52; PhD, U. Wash., 1980. Chief hatchery biology B.C. Game Commn., Vancouver, 1952-56; scientist Inter-Am. Tropical Tuna Commn., La Jolla, 1956-67; chief biologist UNDP Fisheries Devel. Project, Santiago, Chile, 1967-69; fisheries advisor FAO, Santiago, 1969-70; dep. dir. S.W. Fisheries Ctr., La Jolla, 1970-77, dir., 1977—; research assoc. Scripps Inst. Oceanography, La Jolla, 1977—; mem. sci. and statis. com. Pacific Fisheries Mgmt. Council, Portland, Oreg., 1977—; chmn. sci. and statis. com. Western Pacific Fisheries Mgmt. Council, Honolulu, 1976-79. Contbr. articles to profl. jours. Bd. govs. San Diego Oceans Found., 1985; chmn. Mayor's San Diego/La Jolla Underwater Park Com., San Diego, 1978—; mem. adv. council Inst. Marine Resources U. Calif., La Jolla, 1979-85, bd. govs. San Diego Sci. Fair, 1984—. Fellow Am. Inst. Fisheries Research Biologists (v.p. 1973-76); mem. AAAS, Am. Soc. Ichthyologists and Herpetologists, Western Soc. Naturalists, Soc. Marine Mammals. Office: SW Fisheries Ctr PO Box 271 La Jolla CA 92038

BARRETT, JAMES E., judge; b. Lusk, Wyo., Apr. 8, 1922; s. Frank A. and Alice C. (Donoghue) B.; m. Carmel Ann Martinez, Oct. 8, 1949; children—Ann Catherine Barrett Sandahl, Richard James, John Donoghue. Student, U. Wyo., 1940-42, LL.B., 1949; student, St. Catherine's Coll., Oxford, Eng., 1945, Cath. U. Am., 1946. Bar: Wyo. 1949. Mem. firm Barrett and Barrett, Lusk, 1949-67; atty. gen. State of Wyo., 1967-71; judge U.S. Circuit Ct. Appeals, 10th Circuit, 1971—; county and pros. atty. Niobrara County, Wyo., 1951-62; atty. Town of Lusk, 1952-64, Niobrara Sch. Dist., 1950-64. Active Boy Scouts Am.; sec.-treas. Niobrara County Republican Central Com.; bd. dirs. St. Joseph's Children's Home, Torrington, Wyo., 1971-85; trustee ch. Served as cpl. AUS, 1942-45, ETO. Recipient Distinguished Alumni award U. Wyo., 1973. Mem. VFW, Am. Legion. Office: US Ct of Appeals PO Box 1288 Cheyenne WY 82001

BARRETT, JAMES LEE, screenwriter; b. Charlotte, N.C., Nov. 19, 1929; s. James Hamlin and Anne (Blake) B.; m. Merete Engelstoft, June 1960; children: Jessica, Penelope, Birgitte, Christian, David. Ed., Furman U., Pa. State U., Columbia U., Art Students League. Screenwriter 1955—. Screenwriter: (motion pictures) D.I. (Marine Corps Combat Corrs. Assn. award), The Greatest Story Ever Told, Bandolero, The Undefeated, Shenandoah, tick...tick...tick, The Cheyenne Social Club, The Green Berets, Something Big, Fools' Parade, Hank, Smokey and the Bandit; (TV films) The Awakening Land (Am. Women in Radio and TV cert. commendation), Belle Starr, Stubby Pringle's Christmas (Humanities nomination), The Day Christ Died, Angel City, Mayflower: The Pilgrim Experience, The Defiant One's, Stagecoach (Award from Nat. Cowboy Hall of Fame and Western Heritage Soc.), Poker Alice, April Morning; creator (TV series) Our House, Vengeance, The Quick and The Dead; playwright: Shenadoah (Tony award for best musical book). Served with USMC, 1950-52. Mem. Writers Guild Am., Dramatists Guild, Acad. Motion Picture Arts and Scis. Address: PO Box 5407 San Luis Obispo CA 93403

BARRETT, MARY HELEN, editor, writer; b. Ozark, Mo., June 8, 1926; d. Paul Watson and Dorothy M. (Bingham) B. AB, Drury Coll., 1948; MA, U. Mo., 1950. Reporter, feature writer Globe-Democrat, St. Louis, 1951-60; book editor Albert Whitman Co., Chgo., 1961-63; encylopedia editor Compton's, Chgo., 1963-67; publs. editor Drury Coll., Springfield, Mo., 1967-70; alumnae quarterly editor Mills Coll., Oakland, Calif., 1972—; freelance writer, 1970—. Contbr. short stories to Ellery Queen Mag., Alfred Hitchcock Mag. Mem. Mystery Writers Am. Republican. Home: Mills Coll PO Box 9941 Oakland CA 94613 Office: Alumnae Assn Reinhardt Alumnae House Oakland CA 94613

BARRETT, PATRICK HARVEY, painter; b. San Jose, Calif., June 26, 1949; s. Harvey Bradford and Marie Louise (Grosslein) B. BFA, Otis Art Inst., 1971, MFA, 1973. Tchr., art Community Services, Morgan Hill, Calif., 1981; tchr. elem., secondary Gilroy (Calif.) Unified Schs., 1981-84; asst. coordinator The Reading Program, Santa Clara County, Calif., 1985—. One-man shows include Kuumbwa Jazz Ctr., Santa Cruz, Calif., 1982, San Jose Art Ctr, 1979; exhibited in group shows at Tapestry in Talent, San Jose, 1980, Santa Clara County Painting Exhibition, San Jose, 1976, Barnsdal Mcpl. Gallery, Los Angeles, 1974, Egg and The Eye Gallery, Los Angeles, 1973. Coordinator Interfaith Task Force on Cen. Am., Santa Clara County, 1985-86; cons. The Neighbors Consortium, Santa Clara County, 1985-86. Mem. Gilroy C. of C. Office: Studio 7421 Dowdy St Gilroy CA 95020

BARRETT, ROBERT MATTHEW, lawyer; b. Bronx, N.Y., Mar. 18, 1948; s. Harry and Rosalind B. AB summa cum laude, Georgetown U., 1976, MS in Fgn. Service, JD, 1980. Bar: Calif. 1981. Assoc. Latham & Watkins, Los Angeles, 1980-82, Morgan, Lewis & Bockius, Los Angeles, 1982-84, Skadden, Arps, Slate, Meagher & Flom, Los Angeles, 1984—. Mem. ABA, Los Angeles Bar Assn. (bd. advisors vols. in parole com. 1981—). Home: 13816 Bora Bora Way #137A Marina del Rey CA 90292 Office: Skadden Arps Slate Meagher Flom 300 S Grand #3400 Los Angeles CA 90071-3144

BARRETT, THOMAS JOSEPH, mental health center executive; b. Elmhurst, Ill., June 15, 1947; s. Francis J. and Hildegarde (Parr) B.; m. Dolores M. Heatherington, July 29, 1972; children—Gregory, Jennifer, Matthew. B.S. in Psychology, U. Ill., 1969; M.A. in Psychology, W.Va. U., 1971, Ph.D. in Clin. Psychology, 1973. Program evaluator Bethesda Community Mental Health Ctr., Denver, 1974-77, exec. dir., 1982—; dir. program evaluation Bethesda Hosp., Denver, 1977—; teaching affiliate U. Denver, 1980—; cons. VA, Denver, 1977-81, various fed. and state grants, Denver, 1974-81. Contbr. articles to profl. jours. Mem. Am. Psychology Assn., Colo. Assn. Community Mental Health Ctrs. and Clinics (pres.-elect 1986—), Denver Mentl Health Consortium (v.p. 1986—). Club: Skyline Soccer Assn. (pres. 1986—). Office: Bethesda Hosp Assn 4400 E Iliff Denver CO 80222

BARRION, MELINDA MANAIG, microbiologist, biochemist, researcher; b. Manila, Nov. 2, 1956; came to U.S., 1981; d. Maximino Albaera and Pascuala Hernandez (Manaig) B.; m. Charles T. Sorensson, May 4, 1985. BS in Sugar Tech., U. Philippines, Laguna, 1979; MS in Soil Microbiology, U. Hawaii, 1986, postgrad in biochemistry, 1986—. Research asst. U. Philippines, Laguna, 1979, Internat. Rice Research, Laguna, 1979-81; research asst. U. Hawaii, Honolulu, 1981-85, researcher, 1986—. Philippines Sugar Tech. scholarship, U. Philippines, 1973. Fellow AAAS. Home: 2918 E Varsity Circle Honolulu HI 96826 Office: U Hawaii Dept Biochemistry Snyder Hall East West Rd Honolulu HI 96822

BARRIOS, MARC, brewing company manager; b. Havana, Cuba, Oct. 1, 1944; came to U.S., 1961; s. Marcos A. and Raquel M. (Rodriguez) B.; A.A., Colo. Inst. Art, 1967; B.A., Loretto Heights Coll., 1973; m. Maria Fuentes, July 12, 1980; children: Alexander, Christopher; 1 son from previous marriage, Kenneth. Art dir. Dacey Wolff & Weir Adv. Agy., Colo., 1967-68; pres., creative dir. Barrios & Assocs., Colo., 1968-69; art dir. Hoflund Graphics, Colo., 1969; group mgr. creative services Adolph Coors Co., Golden, Colo., 1969—; graphic cons. Ken Monfort senatorial campaign, 1968. Adv. bd. Community Coll. Denver. Recipient awards Art Dirs. Club N.Y., 1980-84, Advt. Fedn. of West, 1973, 75 Alfie award, 1973-85, Nikki award, 1976, 78, Ceba award, 1980-85; gold award Packaging Council, 1981. Mem. Denver Advt. Fedn. (bd. dirs.), Art Dirs. Club Denver (award 1973, 74, 80-84), Point of Purchase Inst. Am. (awards 1971-85). Republican. Methodist. Club: Optimist (dir. Golden and Arvada, Colo. 1971-73). Office: Adolph Coors Co Golden CO 80401

BARRON, ROBERT L., broadcasting executive; b. Cleve., Feb. 16, 1955; s. Francis P. and Audrey D. (Lutz) B. BA, U. So. Calif., 1977. Sales rep. Theta Cable TV, Santa Monica, Calif., 1977-78; sales service coordinator Blair TV, Los Angeles, 1978; acct. exec. HRP, N.Y.C. and Los Angeles, 1978-81; nat. sales mgr. Sta. KMGH-TV, Denver, 1981-83, gen. sales mgr., 1983—. Club: Denver Athletic. Home: 1350 Lawrence St Denver CO 80204 Office: Sta KMGH-TV 123 Speer Blvd Denver CO 80203

BARROWS, RUSSELL DEAN, chemistry educator; b. Denver, Apr. 22, 1951; s. Kenneth Dean and Phyllis (Halfner) B.; m. Darcy Louise Rity, Aug. 10, 1974. BS, Met. State Coll., Denver, 1974; MS, U. Idaho, 1976; PhD, U. Denver, 1981. Research scientist Battell Northwest, Richland, Wash., 1981-84; asst. prof. research U. Denver, 1984—; cons. Pasco (Wash.) Sch. Dist., 1983-84, Clayton Coll., Denver, 1985—. Contbr. research articles in organic chemistry to profl. jours. Big brother Big Bros. Inc., Denver, 1985—. Boettcher Found. fellow, 1979-80, Marathon Oil Co. fellow, 1977. Mem. AAAS, Am. Chem. Soc., Nat. Sci. Tchrs. Home: 4695 E Amherst Ave Denver CO 80222 Office: U Denver Dept Chemistry University Park Denver CO 80208

BARRY, ARTHUR JOHN, chemistry educator; b. Buffalo, Mar. 11, 1909; m. Marjorie Hand; 3 children. BS, N.Y.S. Coll. Forestry, 1932, PhD, 1936. Prof. chemistry 1936-37; chemist Dow Chem. Corp., 1937-47, research supr., 1947-50; assoc. dir. research Dow Corning Corp., 1950-65, dir. chem. research, 1965-71; tech. cons. Dow Corning Corp., Midland, Mich., 1971-74; vis. scientist U. Ariz., Tucson, 1974-84, adj. prof. chemistry, 1984—. Contbr. articles to profl. jours., chpts. to textbooks; patentee in field. Mem. AAAS, Am. Chem. Soc., RESA, Sigma Xi. Home: 9102 N Riviera Dr Tucson AZ 85737 Office: U Ariz Dept Chemistry Tucson AZ 85721

BARRY, BYRON ARTHUR, JR., superintendent schools; b. Lockport, N.Y., July 20, 1930; s. Byron Arthur Sr. and Kathryn (Gregg) B.; m. Mary Lou Houser, July 11, 1953 (div. Dec. 1969); children—Greg, Tanya; m. Verla May Gillispie, Feb. 9, 1972; children—Cindi, Kathy, Lew, Sue. A.A., Los Angeles Pacific Coll., 1949; B.S., Seattle Pacific U., 1951; M.S., Oreg. Western, 1955; Ed.D., Ariz. State U., 1965. Cert. sch. adminstr. Tchr. Liberty Sch. Dist., Sweethome, Oreg., 1953-56, Phoenix Christian High, 1956-57, Roosevelt Sch. Dist., Phoenix, 1957-58; supt. Cartwright Sch. Dist. 83, Phoenix, 1958-77, Laramie County Sch. Dist. 1, Cheyenne, Wyo., 1977-86; cons. State of Wyo. Dept. Edn., 1986—. Bd. dirs. United Way, Cheyenne, 1984—, Longs Peak Council Boy Scouts Am., Greeley, Colo., Blue Ribbon com. State Wyo., Cheyenne, 1982-84. Mem. Am. Assn. Sch. Adminstrs., Wyo. Assn. Sch. Adminstrs. (bd. dirs. 1984—), Phi Delta Kappa (pres. 1975). Democrat. Methodist. Club: Chey Music. Lodge: Kiwanis.

BARRY, EDWARD LOUIS, lawyer; b. Greenville, Mich., Mar. 20, 1951; s. Edward H. and Gertrude (Hamper) B.; m. Mary Lynn Berger, Mar. 16, 1974; children—Jane, Laura, Anne Marie. B.A. with high honors, Mich. State U., 1975; postgrad. U. So. Calif., 1977, Oxford U., 1975; J.D., Ariz. State U., 1979. Bar: Ariz. 1979, U.S. Dist. Ct. Ariz. 1979. Sole practice law, Phoenix, 1979—. Recipient Am. Jurisprudence award, 1977. Mem. Assn. Trial Lawyers Am., Ariz. Trial Lawyers Assn., Fed. Bar Assn. Office: 3300 N Central Ave 14th fl Phoenix AZ 85012

BARRY, MICHELLE LYNETTE, television station executive; b. Lynwood, Calif., Feb. 13, 1956; d. Garfield and Marian Lee (Powers) B.; m. Frederick Charles Hoyt, June 19, 1983; 1 child, Justin James-Garfield Hoyt. B.A. in Pub. Relations magna cum laude, Weber State Coll., 1980. Promotion asst. Sta. KIRO-TV, Seattle, 1980-81, writer, producer, 1981-83, mgr. promotion, 1983—. Writer, producer TV promotion: Bad Habits, 1982 (Internat. Film and TV Festival award 1982). Mem. parent policy council Neighborhood House, Seattle, 1985—, Dem. Caucus rep., Seattle, 1984; vol. Spl. Olympics, Seattle, 1980, 82. Recipient Silver award Internat. Film and TV Festival, N.Y., 1982. Mem. Nat. Assn. TV Arts and Scis., Internat. Assn. Bus. Communicators, Broadcast Promotion and Mktg. Execs. Avocations: photography, biking. Home: 7327 23d Ave NW Seattle WA 98117 Office: Sta KIRO-TV 2807 3rd Ave Seattle WA 98121

BARSHAI, RUDOLF BORISOVICH, conductor; b. Labinskaya, USSR, Sept. 28, 1924. Grad., Moscow Conservatory, 1948; student conducting with Ilya Musin, Leningrad; MusD (hon.), U. Southhampton. Organizer Moscow Chamber Orch., 1955; led New Israel Orch., 1977-81; prin. condr., artistic advisor Bournemouth Symphony Orch., Eng., 1982—; music dir., prin. condr. Vancouver Symphony Orch., B.C., Can., 1985—; prin. guest condr. Orchestra National de France, 1987—; guest condr. in Europe, U.S., Japan; compiler, instrumentalist Bach's Art of Fugue, 1972, 85; decoder, instrumentalist Bach's Das Musikalische Opfer, 1970; instrumentalist Shostakovich's Chamber Symphonies No. 1 and 2, 1968, Prokofiev's Visions Fugitive, 1960; numerous recs. for Melodia, Decca, EMI. Office: Vancouver Symphony Orch, 400 E Broadway, Vancouver, BC Canada V5T 1X2

BARTCHY, S(TUART) SCOTT, history educator, theologian; b. Canton, Ohio, Nov. 9, 1936; s. Jacques Robert and Dorothy Elizabeth (Engle) B.; m. Diane Walker, June 13, 1956; children: Beth Bartchy-Smith, Christopher Walker. BA cum laude, Milligan Coll., 1958; MDiv., Harvard U., 1963, PhD, 1971; postgrad., U. Tuebingen, Fed. Republic Germany, 1968-69, Christian Theol. Sem., 1959-60. Inst. Bibl. history Dana Hall Sch., Wellesley, Mass., 1965-68; dir. Inst. Erforschung des Urchristentums, Tuebingen, 1969-74, 77-79; assoc. prof. New Testament Emmanuel Sch. Religion, Johnson City, Tenn., 1974-76, prof. Bibl. Hermeneutics, 1976-77; resident New Testament scholar Westwood Christian Found., Los Angeles, 1979—; adj. assoc. prof. history UCLA, 1982—; vis. assoc. prof. Fuller Theol. Sem., Pasadena, Calif., 1981, 83, 86; lectr. New Testament U. Tuebingen, 1971-74, 77-79, 80, 82, 85, 87. Author: First Century Slavery and First Corinthians, 1973, 2d edition 1986; mem. editorial bd. The Gospel in Context, 1977-79; contbr. articles to profl. jours. Recipient Disting. Scholar award The Staley Found., 1974, 76, Excellence in Hebrew award Indpls. Hebrew Congregation, 1960. Mem. Studiorum Novi Testamenti Soc., Soc. Bibl. Lit., Am. Acad. Religion, Inst. Bibl. Research, Cath. Bibl. Assn., Deutsch-Amerikanisches Inst. (Fed. Republic Germany). Democrat. Avocation: jazz piano. Office: Westwood Found 10808 Le Conte Ave Los Angeles CA 90024

BARTEL, JONATHAN PETER, editor; b. Waltham, Mass., Dec. 2, 1941; s. William Edwin and Mary Elise (Vahey) B.; m. Diane Gay Wall, Dec. 26, 1967; children: Jennifer, Jeremy Michael. BA, Harvard U., 1964. Vol., instr. VISTA, N.Mex., Oreg., Ariz., 1965-69; reporter, editor Gallup (N.Mex.) Independent, 1969-70, Goleta (Calif.) Valley News, 1977-81; freelance writer 1970—; dir. publs., editor Coastlines mag. U. Calif. at Santa Barbara Alumni Assn., 1981—. Author: (booklet) Navajo Nation Statehood or Commonwealth, 1978. bd. dirs. Goleta Valley C. of C.; mem. Devel. Disabilities Adv. Bd., Camarillo State Hosp., Camarillo, Calif., 1977-82. Mem. Council for Advancement and Support of Edn. Democrat. Office: U Calif Santa Barbara Alumni Assn Santa Barbara CA 93106

BARTELL, SELMA DOROTHY CLASSEN, auto distbg. co. exec.; b. Fairview, Okla., Apr. 19, 1906; d. Dietrich John and Helena (Duerksen) Classen; grad. Kern County Jr. Coll., 1924; m. Henry Jacob Bartell, Mar. 1, 1925; children: Lula May, Ruben C., Florence Lucille, Clarence Henry, Lawson Wayne, Henry Lee. Owner, mgr. H.J. Bartell Bardahl Distbrs., Bakersfield, Calif., 1972—. Pres., PTA, 1932, 33, Kern County Home Dept., Rosedale Hy. Bus. Assn., 1985—; v.p. Calif. Farm Bur. Women; Calif. del. Asso. Country Women of the World, 1953; leader 4-H, 1936; pres. Symphony Assos., 1967-68; pianist, Sunday sch. tchr. Mennonite Brethren Ch., 1920-60. Named Woman of Yr., Valley Plaza Mchts. Assn., 1970. Mem. Rosedale Hwy. Bus. Assn. (pres. 1978, treas. 1983), Desk and Derrick Bakersfield (pres. 1966-67). Republican. Home and office: 2001 Calloway Dr Bakersfield CA 93312

BARTELS, JUERGEN E., hotel company executive; b. Swinemuende, Ger., Sept. 14, 1940; s. Herbert and Lilli E. (Wendland) B.; m. Rachel M.P. Villemaire, Mar. 14, 1951. Final, Werner V. Siemens Sch., Hanover, W. Germany, 1956. Vice pres. Commonwealth Holiday Inns Can. Ltd., Can., 1971-76; exec. v.p. Ramada Internat., Brussels, Belgium, 1976-77; pres. Ramada Hotel Group, Phoenix, 1978-83; exec. v.p. Ramada Inns, Inc.; mem. Ramada Mgmt. Com.; pres., chief exec. officer Carlson Hospitality Group, Carlson Cos., Inc., Mpls., 1983—; dir. TGI Friday's Inc. Office: Carlson Cos Inc 12755 State Hwy 55 Minneapolis MN 55441

BARTH, DANIEL STEPHEN, neuroscientist, educator; b. Balt., Jan. 21, 1954; s. John Simmons and Anne (Strickland) B.; m. Lynne E. Albert. Student, Antioch Coll., 1971-73; BA summa cum laude, Boston U., 1977; MA, UCLA, 1980, PhD, 1984. Asst. research psychologist dept. psychology UCLA, 1984-86; co-dir. neuromagnetism lab. Reed Neurological Inst. UCLA, 1985—. Contbr. articles to med. jours. Recipient NSF Travel award, 1982, NSF Presdl. Young Investigator award, 1987, NIH Single Investigator award, 1985—, Joseph A. Gengerelli Disting. Dissertation award, 1985; UCLA fellow 1979-80, UCLA-NIMH fellow, 1980-83, grantee UCLA, 1981-82, NATO Research Conf., 1982, NIH, 1984-86. Mem. AAAS, Am. Epilepsy Soc., Soc. Neurosci., Soc. Psychophysiol. Research, N.Y. Acad. Sci. (James McKeen Cattell award 1986), Phi Beta Kappa, Sigma Xi. Office: UCLA Dept Psychol Los Angeles CA 90024

BARTH, DAVID VICTOR, systems analyst; b. Tulsa, Sept. 23, 1942; s. Vincent David and Norma (Bell) B. BS summa cum laude, Met. State Coll., 1977; MS, U. No. Colo., 1982. Programming mgr. Am. Nat. Bank, Denver, 1967-72; cons. Colo. Farm Bur. Ins. Corp., Denver, 1972; systems analyst Mid-Continent Computer Services, Denver, 1972-73; programming mgr. Bayly Corp., Denver, 1973-75; project leader Cobe Labs. Inc., Denver, 1976-84; systems analyst Affiliated Banks Service Co., Denver, 1985—. Served with USN, 1961-66. Mem. Soc. Info. Mgmt. (editor newsletter 1983), Boulder (Colo.) Area Radio Club, Aurora (Colo.) Repeater Assn., Flying Circus Skating Club. Republican. Avocations: ice skating, amateur radio, flying, creative writing. Home: 509 S Cody St Lakewood CO 80226 Office: Affiliated Banks Service Co 445 E 124th Ave Thornton CO 80241

BARTH, NORMAN KENNETH, hospital administrator, educator; b. Stony Plain, Alta., Can., May 13, 1933; s. Edwin and Leontine (Nickel) B.; children—Lester, Debra. B.S. in Pharmacy, U. Alta., 1957; M.H.A., U. Ottawa, 1967. Staff mem., chief pharmacist Charles Camsell Hosp., Edmonton, Alta., 1958-65; exec. asst. Ottawa Civic Hosp., Ont., 1967-68; asst. adminstr. Foothills Hosp., Calgary, Alta., 1968-70; planning adminstr. Workers Compensation Bd., Vancouver, B.C., 1970-72; planner, dir. hosp. planning Greater Vancouver Regional Dist., 1972-77; pres., chief exec. officer Burnaby Hosp., Burnaby, B.C., 1977—; dir. Health Labour Relations B.C., B.C. Health Assn., B.C. Inst. Tech.; clin. asst. prof. U. B.C., 1977—. Bd. dirs. Burnaby Art Gallery, 1982-84. Mem. Health Adminstrn. Assn. B.C. (pres., bd. dirs. 1979-81), Can. Coll. Health Services Execs. (cert.), Am. Coll. Hosp. Adminstrs., Burnaby C. of C. Progressive Conservative. Mem. United Ch. Lodge: Rotary (bd. dirs. Burnaby chpt. 1980—). Office: Burnaby Hosp, 3935 Kincaid St, Burnaby, BC Canada V5G 2X6 *

BARTHELL, JOLENE HUNTEMAN, business educator; b. Dallas, Oct. 25, 1936; d. Paul Albert and Prunella Aldena (Flowers) Hunteman; m. James G. Jordan, Aug. 31, 1957; 1 dau., Paula; m. 2d, Barry L. Barthell, Aug. 11, 1972; children—Robin, Ben, Gregory. B.S., Oklahoma City U., 1958; postgrad. U. Okla., 1962, Eastern N.Mex. U., 1973-74, Adams State Coll., Alamosa, Colo., 1978-79. Cert. profl. educator, N.Mex. Tchr. bus. edn. Blanchard (Okla.) High Sch., 1960-63; instr. Hill's Bus. U., Oklahoma City, 1963-64; tchr. Los Alamos High Sch., 1964—; coordinator coop. vocat. office edn., 1979—; region II advisor Office Edn. Assn., dir., 1981—; instr. U. N. Mex., Los Alamos, 1987. Mem. LWV, Valle Escondido (N.Mex.) Home Owners Assn., Los Alamos Edn. Assn., N.Mex. Edn. Assn., NEA, N.Mex. Bus. and Office Edn. Assn. (pres., Tchr. of Yr. 1985-86), Am. Vocat. Assn., AAUW. Democrat.

BARTHLOME, RANDIE LEE, law enforcement administrator, consultant; b. Laramie, Wyo., May 4, 1948; d. Ralph Randall and Wilma Lee (Hawk) Benintendi; m. Edward Earl Barthlome, May 5, 1973; children—Sherri Lanee, Lori Lynn, Thomas Arthur, Greg Edward. Student Community Coll. of Denver, 1971-72, Idaho State U. Law Enforcement Acad., 1972-73, Idaho Peace Officer Acad., 1973, Idaho State U., 1977, Duke U., 1985. Advanced law enforcement cert.; cert. law enforcement instr. Advt., pub. relations dir. Consumer Enterprises, Denver, 1969-72; tutor Idaho State U., Pocatello, 1972; officer Blackfoot Police Dept. (Idaho), 1972-73; sec. Idaho Peace Officer Acad., Pocatello, 1973-74; crime prevention officer Pocatello Police Dept., 1974-80, dir., 1980-85; pres. SYNTAX, 1985—; pvt. practice cons., 1983—. Author weekly newspaper column: Police Watch, 1974-85, also articles. Adv. bd. Salvation Army, Pocatello, 1982-85; com. chmn. Mayor's Com. for Handicapped, Pocatello, 1982—; pres. Pocatello Community Services Council, 1975-76; founder Women's Advocates for Battered Women, Pocatello, 1976—. Named Citizen of Yr., Idaho Pros. Attys. Assn., 1982, Idaho Outstanding Supr., Manpower Consortium, 1981, Disting. Young Woman, Pocatello Jay-C-Ettes, 1979; recipient Nat. Award of Merit, Nat. Crime Prevention Coalition, 1981. Mem. Idaho Crime Prevention Assn. (founding, pres. 1981-82), Idaho Peace Officers Assn., Am. Soc. Tng. and Devel., Internat. City Mgmt. Assn., Idaho Press Club, Am. Bus. Women's Assn., Idaho Assn. for Affirmative Action, Am. Mktg. Assn., Centennial C. of C., Denver C. of C. Baptist. Lodge: Zonta. Home: 1170 E Phillips Dr Littleton CO 80122 Office: Syntax 13111 E Briarwood Ave Suite 250 Englewood CO 80112

BARTLEBAUGH, CLYDE ALLAN, III, computer services co. exec.; b. Detroit, Feb. 11, 1943; s. Clyde Allan and Eloise V. Bartlebaugh; B.A., Mich. State U., 1968; m. Marsha C. Strom, June 30, 1979. Mem. mgmt. tng. program Gen. Motors Corp., Pontiac, Mich., 1967-69; with Brit. Am. Yacht Corp., 1969-70; cons. Star Internat., Chgo., 1970-72; cons. Kearney Clark & Assos., Chgo., 1972-77; pres. Western Programmers, Inc., Albuquerque, 1978—. Served with USCG, 1966-67. Mem. Digital Equipment Computer Users Soc., Albuquerque C. of C., N.Mex. Assn. Commerce and Industry, Data Processing Mgmt. Assn. Home: 502 Ashberry Ct SE Rio Rancho NM 87124 Office: 3620 Wyoming NE Albuquerque NM 87111

BARTLETT, DAN REID, county administrative officer; b. Pocatello, Idaho, Mar. 15, 1949; s. Steven N. and Helen L. (Denlinger) B.; m. Susan Margret Mitchell, June 22, 1974; children: Joe, Andy. BS, U. Oreg., 1971. Adminstrv. asst. Benton Linn EOC, Albany, Oreg., 1972-73; adminstrv. asst. Benton County, Corvallis, Oreg., 1974-75, asst. fin. dir., 1975-77, cen. services dir., 1977-79, budget officer, 1977—, exec. asst, 1981-85, adminstrv. officer, 1985—; mem. local budget adv. com. Salem, Oreg., 1985—. Chmn. Corvallis Fed. Emergency Mgmt. Local Bd., 1985-86, Project Hometown Am. Bd., Corvallis, 1986; pres. Willamette Council Camp Fire, Salem, 1986—; past bd. dirs. Benton County United Way. Recipient Sebago Camping award Willamette Council Camp Fire, 1984, Wonderful You award Willamette Council Camp Fire, 1985, United Way Disting. Service award, 1987. Mem. Internat. City Mgmt. Assn. (Oreg. sect.), Internat. Assn. Budget Officers and Program Analysts, Am. Mgmt. Assn., Nat. Assn. County Adminstrs., Tau Kappa Epsilon (sec. 1986). Democrat. Baptist. Lodge: Lions (Corvallis) (pres. 1985-86). Avocations: fly tying, model railroading, gardening, fly fishing. Office: Benton County 180 NW 5th St Corvallis OR 97330

BARTLETT, HALL, motion picture producer, director; b. Kansas City, Mo., Nov. 27, 1929; s. Paul Dana and Alice (Hiest) B.; children: Cathy, Laurie. Grad., Yale U., 1949. Propr. Hall Bartlett Prodn., Los Angeles, 1952—; now pres. Hall Bartlett Films, Inc., Jonathan Livingston Seagull Mcht. Co. Producer, dir. films Navajo, 1953, Crazylegs, 1958, Unchained, 1957, All the Young Men, 1961, Durango, 1959, Zero Hour, 1961, The Caretakers, 1963, A Global Affair, 1968, Changes, 1968, Sandpit Generals, 1971, Jonathan Livingston Seagull, 1973, The Cleo Laine Story, 1978, The Children of Sanchez, 1979, Comeback to Me, 1983, Love is Forever, 1983, Leaving Home, 1985, Catch Me If You Can, 1987, Kis of Fire, 1987; films Zubin Mehta Spl., 1975; author: Body and Soul, 1987. Bd. dirs. Huntington Hartford Theatre; founder Music Ctr. Served with USNR, 1949-56. Recipient 11 Acad. award nominations, Film Festival awards from Cannes 1961, 63, Venice 1959, 65, Edinburgh 1952, San Sebastian 1969, Moscow 1971, NCCJ 1955, Fgn. Press awards. Mem. Motion Picture Acad. Arts and Scis., Acad. TV Arts and Scis., Friends of Library, Cinema Circulus, Phi Beta Kappa. Presbyterian. Club: Bel-Air Country (Los Angeles). Home: 861 Stone Canyon Rd Los Angeles CA 90024 Office: Suite 908 9200 Sunset Blvd Los Angeles CA 90069

BARTLETT, J(AMES) KENNETH, chemist; b. Lynden, Wash., Feb. 2, 1925; s. James Pierce and Hazel Gertrude (Harmelink) B.; m. Patricia Evelyn Curtis, Aug. 21, 1948; 1 dau., Nancy Evelyn. B.S. in Chemistry, Willamette U., 1949; Ph.D., Stanford U., 1954. Instr. U. Santa Clara, Calif., 1953-54; asst. prof. Long Beach (Calif.) State Coll., 1954-56; mem. faculty So. Oreg. State Coll., Ashland, 1956—; prof. chemistry So. Oreg. State Coll., 1963—, chmn. dept., 1976—; cons. in field. Author: General Chemistry Experiments, 1984, Identification of Chemical Substances, 1984. Served with U.S. Army, 1943-46. duPont fellow, 1952-53. Mem. Am. Chem. Soc. Republican. Presbyterian. Home: 1313 Woodland Dr Ashland OR 97520 Office: Chemistry Dept So Oreg State Coll Ashland OR 97520

BARTLETT, THOMAS EDWARD, research exec.; b. Tulsa, Sept. 3, 1920; s. Michael Leo and Elizabeth (Stadden) B.; B.A., U. Okla., 1942; M.S., Columbia U., 1947; postgrad. Purdue U., 1957-59, U. Fla., 1965, Ariz. State U., 1966. Engr., Montgomery Ward & Co., 1947-48; chief indsl. engr. Bank of Am., 1948-50; mem. tech. staff Hughes Research and Devel., 1950-54, Ramo-Wooldridge, 1954; prof. Purdue U., 1955-63; mem. teaching staff Calif. State Poly. Coll., 1964-65; ops. research cons., 1965-67; dir. ops. research Lester Gorstine Assocs., 1967-68; pres., chmn. bd. dirs. Wyvern Research Assos., Inc., Mill Valley, Calif., 1968—; dir. JEBOR, Inc. Served with CIC, U.S. Army, 1942-46. Registered profl. engr., Calif. Mem. Am. Inst. Indsl. Engrs., Inst. Mgmt. Scis., Ops. Research Soc. Am., Fedn. Am. Scientists, Soc. Indsl. and Applied Math., Scis., AAAS, Am. Soc. Personnel Adminstrn., Sigma Xi, Phi Kappa Phi, Phi Kappa Psi. Club: San Francisco Press. Home: 40 W 4th Ave San Mateo CA 94402 Office: 335 Beach Rd Burlingame CA 94010

BARTLETT, THOMAS HENRY, chemist; b. Great Falls, Mont., Jan. 1, 1931; s. Thomas Henry and Sophia (Stenseth) B.; m. Alice Kay Lee, Dec. 29, 1959 (div. Feb. 1962); one child, Brady; m. Iris Elaine Cooper, Aug. 25, 1967; children: Karleen, Elaine. BS, Coll. Great Falls, 1952; postgrad., U. Wash., 1953, LaSalle Extension U., 1958-63. Chemist Anaconda Co., Great Falls, 1954-57, Am. Chrome Co., Nye, Mont., 1957-61; chief chemist Western Nuclear Inc., Jeffery City, Wyo., 1962-67; gen. mgr. Chem. and Geol. Labs., Casper, Wyo., 1967-76; pres., chief exec. officer WAMCO Lab. Inc., Casper, 1977—. Chmn., pres. Winter Meml. Presbyn. Ch., Casper, 1982—. Mem. ASTM. Lodge: Elks. Home: 3301 E 12th St Casper WY 82609 Office: WAMCO Lab Inc PO Box 2953 Casper WY 82602

BARTLEY, DANIEL ROBERT, lawyer; b. Pikeville, Ky., Aug. 21, 1948; s. Robert Earl and Anna Rae (Belcher) B.; m. Pamela Marshane Bethel, Jan. 20, 1973 (div. Dec. 1981). BBA, Eastern Ky. U., 1969; student, Tulane U., 1969-70; JD, U. Ky., 1972. Bar: Ky. 1972, Fla. 1974, Calif. 1978. Sole practice Louisa, Ky., 1972-77; of counsel McKesson Corp., San Francisco, 1977-80; regional counsel Container Corp. Am., Santa Clara, Calif., 1980-86; sole practice San Francisco, 1986—. Mem. Ky. Bar Assn., Fla. Bar Assn., Calif. Bar Assn. Avocations: white water kayaking, snow skiing, motorcycling, photography.

BARTLING, JUDD QUENTON, research corp. exec.; b. Muncie, Ind., July 24, 1936; s. Hubert George and Hildagarde (Good) B.; B.A., U. Calif., 1960, Ph.D., 1969; M.S., Purdue U., 1964; m. Madeline Levesque, June 9, 1973; stepchildren—Mary Johnson, Michael Johnson. Research asst. U. Calif., Riverside, 1965-69; cons. Azak Corp., Chatsworth, Calif., 1969-71, pres., 1971—. Served with U.S. Army, 1960-62. NSF grantee U. Fla., 1969. Research in bus., solid state physics, quantum electronics, electromagnetics and radar. Office: 9738 Nevada St Chatsworth CA 91311

BARTNICKI-GARCIA, SALOMON, microbiologist, educator; b. Mexico City, May 18, 1935; came to U.S., 1957; s. Israel Bartnicki and Refugio Garcia; m. Ildiko Nagy, Aug. 10, 1975; children—Linda Laura, David Daniel. Bacteriological Chemist, Inst. Politecnico Nacional, Mexico City, 1957; Ph.D., Rutgers U., 1961. Research asso. microbiology Rutgers U., 1961-62; mem. faculty U. Calif. at Riverside, 1962—, prof. plant pathology and microbiology, 1971—; vis. prof. Organic Chemistry Inst., U. Stockholm, 1969-70. Author research and rev. papers. Recipient Ruth Allen award Am. Phytopathol. Soc., 1983; grantee NIH, 1963—, NSF, 1971—. Fellow AAAS; mem. Am. Soc. Microbiology, Am. Phytopathol. Soc. (Ruth Allen award), Mycol. Soc. Am., Brit. Soc. Gen. Microbiology, Brit. Mycol. Soc. (hon.), Am. Soc. Biol. Chemists. Home: 1391 Lynridge Riverside CA 92506 Office: U Calif Dept Plant Pathology Riverside CA 92521

BARTON, ANN ELIZABETH, fin. exec.; b. Long Lake, Mich., Sept. 8, 1923; d. John and Inez Mabel (Morse) Seaton; student Mt. San Antonio Coll., 1969-71, Adrian Coll., 1943, Citrus Coll., 1967, Golden Gate U., 1976, Coll. Fin. Planning, 1980-82; m. H. Kenneth Barton, Apr. 3, 1948; children—Michael, John, Nancy. Tax cons., real estate broker, Claremont, Calif., 1967-72, Newport Beach, Calif., 1972-74; v.p., officer Putney, Barton, Assos., Inc., Walnut Creek, Calif., 1975—; bd. dirs., officer Century Fin. Enterprises, Inc., Century Adv. Corp., F.F.A., Inc., SKAIFE & Co. Cert. fin. planner. Mem. Internat. Assn. Fin. Planners, (registered investment advisor), Calif. Soc. Enrolled Agts., Nat. Assn. Enrolled Agts., Nat. Soc. Public Accts., Inst. Cert. Fin. Planners. Office: Putney Barton Assocs Inc 1705 N California Blvd Walnut Creek CA 94596

BARTON, GERALD GAYLORD, land development company executive; b. Oklahoma City, 1931. Student, U. Okla. Pres., dir. Landmark Land Co., Carmel, Calif.; also pres., dir. Barton Theatre Co.; bd. dirs. LSB Industries, Inc. Office: Landmark Land Co Inc 100 Clock Tower Place Carmel CA 93923 *

BARTON, JOHN HAYS, legal educator; b. Chgo., Oct. 27, 1936; s. Jay and Agnes (Heisler) B.; m. Julianne Marie Gunnis, June 13, 1959; children: John II, Robert, Anne, Thomas, David. B.S., Marquette U., 1958; J.D., Stanford U., 1968. Bar: D.C. 1969. Engr., Sylvania Electronic Def. Labs., Mountain View, Calif., 1961-68; assoc. Wilmer, Cutler and Pickering, Washington, 1968-69; prof. Stanford (Calif.) U. Law Sch., 1969—; vis. prof. U. Mich. Law Sch., fall 1981. Served to lt. (j.g.) USN, 1958-61. Rockefeller Found. fellow, 1976-77. Mem. ABA, AAAS, Am. Soc. Internat. Law, Am. Soc. Agrl. Cons. Author: Politics of Peace, 1981, co-author International Trade and Investment, 1986, Law in Radically Different Cultures, 1983 (Am. Soc. Internat. Law award 1984); co-editor: International Arms Control, 1976, Law and High Technology, 1983. Home: 1340 Harwalt Dr Los Altos CA 94022 Office: Stanford U Law Sch Stanford CA 94305

BARTON, NOEL RENEER, records acquisitions manager; b. Salt Lake City, Mar. 22, 1942; s. Harmon Albert and Lillian (Reneer) B.; m. Pamela Parrish, Dec. 13, 1968; children: Brian Parrish, Bret Reneer, Brenda, Brooke, Brad Christopher. AS, Brigham Young U., 1966, BA, 1969. Reference librarian Geneal. Soc. of Salt Lake City, 1965, research specialist, 1969-77, mgr. records extraction, 1977-80, supr. corr., 1980-83, mgr. U.S. records acquisition and geneal. research, 1983—; geneal. research cons., Farmington, 1958—; lectr., instr., Farmington, 1966—. Author: Christopher Layton and ZCMI, 1972, Fun and Names, or How to Dig Your Family History Without Really Prying, 1980; editor: Christopher Layton, 1966; contbr. articles to profl. jours. Served with USNG, 1967-73. Named Hon. Col., Ill. Vols. Reactivated, 1975, Ky. Col., Order of Ky. Cols., 1977. Mem. Soc. Am. Archivists, Am. Assn. State and Local History, Utah Geneal. Assn. (bd. dir. 1985—), Mormon History Assn., Utah Hist. Soc., Midwest Archives Conf., Ill. State Geneal. Soc. (bd. dirs. 1986—), Mid-Atlantic Regional Archives Conf., S.E. Archives & Records Conf., Conf. Intermountain Archives. Republican. Mormon. Avocations: photography, family history, basketball. Home: 410 N Main St Farmington UT 84025 Office: Geneal Soc Utah 50 E N Temple St Salt Lake City UT 84150

BARTON, WILLIAM CLYDE, JR., oil co. exec.; b. Cushing, Okla., Nov. 23, 1931; s. William Clyde and Hazel Jean (Morrow) B.; B.S. in Petroleum Engring., U. Okla., 1954; m. Doris Winnie Casey, Aug. 6, 1951; children—Deborah Sue, Richard Clyde, Charles Wayne. Div. reservoir engr. Pure Oil Co., Houston, 1963-66; with Union Oil Co. Calif., 1966—, regional engring. mgr., Los Angeles, 1968-75, dir. prodn. ops. internat. div., Los Angeles, 1975-83, v.p., Thailand, 1983-86, dir. Overseas Subs., 1986—. Served as officer USAF, 1954-56. Decorated D.S.M.; registered profl. engr., Tex. Mem. Soc. Petroleum Engrs. (pres. 1982). Republican. Clubs: Toastmasters, Petroleum (Los Angeles). Office: 1201 W Fifth Los Angeles CA 90017 *

BARTON-HEYWORTH, SARAH, environmental mediator; b. Columbia, Mo., July 7, 1948; d. Jay Barton and Ann (Taylor) Barton; m. Scott R. Heyworth, May 5, 1982; children by previous marriage—Joshua Barton Feigin, Aaron Taylor Feigin. Student, Swarthmore Coll., 1965-67; B.A., Temple U., 1969, M.A., 1975; postgrad. U. Alaska-Anchorage, 1981. Tech. researcher and writer, Phila., 1969-72, Anchorage, 1972-78; Arctic research historian Arctic Environ. Info. & Data Ctr., Anchorage, 1978-80; faculty Anchorage Community Coll., 1981—, dir. regulatory pub. affairs Ott Water Engrs., Inc., Anchorage, 1981-84; staff mediator Conflict Resolution Ctr., Anchorage, 1983-84; faculty art and art history U. Alaska, 1981-86; pres. Barton-Heyworth Regulatory and Pub. Affairs, Bainbridge Island, Washington, 1986—; dir. regulatory and pub. affairs Capital Projects Office, Municipality of Anchorage, 1984—. Patentee in field. Mem. Am. Arbitration Assn., Am. Planning Assn., Internat. Right of Way Assn., Alaska Hist. Soc., Lindisfarne Soc., N.W. Panel Comml. Arbitrators. Democrat. Mem. Soc. of Friends. Office: PO Box 10063 Bainbridge Island WA 98110

BARTZ, DEBRA ANN, air force pilot; b. Chgo., Jan. 19, 1960; d. Robert Herman and Yvonne Anita (Schwarz) B. BS, U.S. Air Force Acad., 1982. Commd. 2d lt. USAF, 1982, advanced through grades to capt., 1986; copilot USAF, Beale AFB, Calif., 1983-86, pilot, 1986—. Republican. Roman Catholic. Avocations: bike riding, running, swimming, weight training, softball. Office: 350 Air Refueling Sq Beale AFB CA 95903

BARTZ, ROBERT V., association executive, consultant; b. Bremen, Germany, Mar. 1, 1924 (parents U.S. citizens); came to U.S., 1926; s. Carl Frederick and Mary Frances (Plitt) Frederick; m. Rosemary Jean Burghoff, July 24, 1944; children—Mary Jane Bartz Innes, Lauren Lee Bartz Barrett. B.S. in Physics, MIT, 1947; postgrad. in pub. adminstrn., orgnl. behavior U. So. Calif., 1966-67. Exec. aide Lab. for Nuclear Sci. and Engring., MIT, 1947, dir. indsl. liaison program, 1948-52; dir. indsl. assocs. program Calif. Inst. Tech., 1953-56; asst. to v.p. for research Inst. for Def. Analyses, Washington, 1957; v.p. Ednl. Services Inc., Cambridge, Mass., Washington, 1958-59; exec. dir. Associated Rocky Mountain Univs., Inc., Boulder, Colo., 1960-63; dir. univ. relations and profl. devel. Jet Propulsion Lab., Calif. Inst. Tech., 1964-67; dir. program on large orgns. of the future U. So. Calif., 1968-71; dir. BLUEPRINT, 1971—; pres. Corp. for Society, Claremont, Calif., 1981—; cons. NASA Office of Adminstr., 1963, Battelle Meml. Inst., 1972, Calif. State Univ. and Colls., 1976-77. Served with U.S. Army, 1943-46, WWII, 50-52, Korea. Unitarian. Office: Corp for Society 781 W 7th St Claremont CA 91711

BARTZATT, RONALD LEE, research biochemist, consultant; b. Lincoln, Nebr., Dec. 18, 1953; s. Frank Wright and Lorretta (Warta) B.; m. Patricia Ann Dockham, July 30, 1979 (div. Oct. 1983). BS, U. Nebr., 1978, MS, 1980, PhD, 1982. Cert. med. lab. technician. Research biochemist U. Nebr., Lincoln, 1983-84, Eppley Cancer Ctr., Omaha, 1984-85, Theodor Gildore Ctr., San Diego, 1985, U. Calif., San Diego, 1985—; cons. IRCS Med. Sci., Lancaster, Eng., 1985—. Author: Proceedings of ACS Symposia on Computer Data Analysis and Optimization; contbr. articles to profl. jours. Deacon Luth. Ch., San Diego. Served with U.S. Army, 1973-76. Towle Scholar U. Nebr., 1973; NIH fellow, 1984; grantee Nebr. Water Co., 1981. Mem. Am. Soc. Clin. Pathologists, Am. Chem. Soc., AAAS, Planetary Soc., Phi Lambda Upsilon. Republican. Avocations: kayaking, ice skating, skiing, music. Office: U Calif Dept Pediatrics H-814-H San Diego CA 92093

BARUH, MORTON GOLDMAN, liquor company executive; b. San Francisco, Mar. 15, 1923; s. Harold F. and Doris (Goldman) B.; m. Marilyn Felix, Aug. 10, 1944; children: Barry F., Terye Baruh Levy, Randie (dec.). Student, Marin Jr. Coll., 1940-41, San Francisco Inst. Accountancy, 1941-42. Treas., merchandising mgr. Goldman's Store, Oakland, Calif., 1946-53; treas. Goldman's Hayward, Inc., Calif., 1952-53; v.p. Baruh Liquors, Inc., San Jose, Calif., 1953-60, exec. v.p., 1960-69, pres., 1969-70; v.p. E. Martinoni Co., San Francisco, 1954-69, pres., 1969-79, chmn. bd. dirs., 1979-86; v.p. Goldman's Walnut Creek, Inc and Goldman's Alameda, Inc., 1958-79; pres. James A. Robertson of Wash., Seattle, 1969-79, chmn. bd. dirs.; ptnr. Baruh Spirits Co.; chmn. bd. Am. Constrn. Assocs., Menlo Park, Calif., 1962-64. Bd. dirs. Randie Lynn Baruh Research Found. for Leukemia; nat. bd. trustees Leukemia Soc. Am., 1980-84; pres. No. Calif. chpt. Leukemia Soc., 1984-85. Served with USAAF, 1943-45. Decorated Air medal. Mem. Calif. Wholesale Liquor Distbrs. Assn. (pres. 1969), Calif. Distilled Spirits Rectifiers Assn. (pres. 1973—). Club: St. Francis Yacht, Villa Taverna. Lodge: Masons. Office: c/o Baruh Spirits Co 543 Forbes Blvd San Francisco CA 94080

BARUSCH, AMANDA SMITH, social welfare educator, researcher; b. Long Beach, Calif., Sept. 8, 1955; d. Gilbert T. and Helen (Dauphine) Smith; m. Lawrence Roos Barusch, Aug. 7, 1983; 1 child, Nathaniel Morris. BA, Reed Coll., Portland, Oreg., 1977; M in Social Welfare, U. Calif., Berkeley, 1981, D in Social Welfare, 1985. Planner Govt. of Guam, Agana, 1980-82, supr. Title XX, 1983-84; teaching asst. U. Calif., Berkeley, 1982-83; asst. prof. U. Guam, Mangilao, 1984-85; asst. prof. gerontology U. Utah, Salt Lake City, 1985—; chmn. rev. bd. Salt Lake City Alcohol/Drug Abuse Services, 1985—; tng. cons. Sr. Companion Program, Salt Lake City, 1985—; mem. Gov.'s Task Force, Agana, 1984, Gov.'s Commn., Agana, 1984-85. Contbr. articles on social work and psychology to profl. jours. Named Regent's fellow U. Calif., Berkeley, 1982, 83. Mem. Guam Assn. Social Workers (pres. 1984-85), Nat. Assn. Social Workers, Nat. Council on Aging, Am. Soc. on Aging, Gerontol. Soc. Am. Democrat. Office: U Utah Social Work Bldg Salt Lake City UT 84112

BARVICH, BEVERLY JOYCE, graphologist; b. St. Paul, Sept. 26, 1940; d. Harry M. and Crystal Elizabeth (Bevan) Harrold; m. Larry L. Barvich; children: Michelle Marie, Timothy Lawrence. Grad. high sch., Puyallup, Wash. Cert. graphologist. Owner BJB Handwriting Analysis, San Jose, Calif., 1981—; lectr. on graphology, 1984-85; tchr., 1984. Mem. Am. Handwriting Analysis Found. (bd. dirs., hospitality chmn. 1983-86, historian 1986-88), Council Graphol. Socs., Erika Karoh's Inner Circle. Republican. Roman Catholic. Avocations: stream fishing, target shooting, needlepoint. Home and Office: 3400 Sullivan Ct #269 Modesto CA 95356

BASCH, DARLENE CHAKIN, clinical social worker; b. Bklyn., Oct. 12, 1954; s. Samuel Benedict and Vivian (Sidranski) Chakin; m. Loren Bernhardt Basch, May 31, 1982; 1 child, Michael Oswald. BS, Cornell U., 1976; M in Social Welfare, U. Calif., Berkeley, 1979. Lic. clin. social worker, Calif. Child care worker Hathaway Home, Pacoima, Calif., 1976-77; cottage clin. supr. St. Vincent's Sch., San Rafael, Calif., 1979-83; program dir. Jewish Family and Children's Service, San Francisco, 1983-84, therapist, program dir. family life edn., 1985—; pvt. practice therapist Sausalito, Calif., 1982—; workshop leader Unilex, San Francisco, 1985; sch. cons. Learning Assocs., San Francisco, 1985—. Chmn. Generation-to-Generation, San Francisco, 1979—; sec. Holocaust Library and Research Ctr., San Francisco, 1980—; exec. com. mem. World Gathering of Holocaust Survivors, N.Y.C., 1980-81. Mem. Nat. Assn. Social Workers, Am. Orthopsychiat. Assn., Menninger Found. Avocations: singing, guitar, knitting, walking, cooking. Office: Jewish Family & Children's Services 1600 Scott St San Francisco CA 94115

BASEGHI, BEHSHAD, electrical engineer; b. Tehran, Iran, Sept. 18, 1954; came to U.S., 1972; s. Hassan and Behin-Dokht (Navidi-Kasmai) Basseghi; m. Carole Ruth Goyen, Oct. 7, 1983; 1 child, Cyruss David. BSEE, Va. Poly. Inst. and State U., 1976, MSEE, 1978, MS in Applied Math., 1980, PhDEE, 1983. Registered profl engr., Va., Calif. Mem. faculty Ariz. State U., Tempe, 1981-83; sr. design engr. Raytheon Co., Goleta, Calif., 1983-84, tech. dir. digital signal processing, 1983—, mgr. signal processing, 1984—; adj. mem. faculty Calif. Poly. State U., San Luis Obispo, Calif., 1985. Patentee in field. Mem. IEEE, Phi Kappa Phi, Eta Kappa Nu. Republican. Moslem. Office: Raytheon Corp 6380 Hollister Ave Goleta CA 93117

BASHAW, ARDIS EILEEN, educator; b. Moville, Iowa, Mar. 23, 1925; d. Dennis Bryan Countryman and Blossom Eileen (McHenry) Buchanan; m. Deane Orville Bashaw, Dec. 22, 1946; children: Dennis, Thomas, Timothy. BEd, San Francisco State Coll., 1960; postgrad., U. Pacific, 1966, Calif. State U., Stanislaus, 1966. Cert. learning handicapped service adminstr., Calif. Tchr., reading specialist Stanislaus County Dept. Edn., Modesto, Calif., 1976-81, curriculum guide cons., 1968-70, tchr. jr. high, 1981—. Editor Stanislaus County Curriculum Guide, 1966, 68. Active publicity com. Elect John Allard County Supt. of Schs., 1978. Recipient Great Tchr. award Roosevelt Jr. High Sch. Student Council, 1986. Mem. Stanislaus Assn. Cert. Personnel of Calif. Tchr's. Assn. (pres 1980-82), Stanislaus Assn. Retarded Children, 202 Chpt. Council for Exceptional Children (sec. 1960—, Outstanding Service award 1977-78), Delta Kappa Gamma, Phi Delta Kappa(v.p. local chpt. 1985—). Democrat. Seventh Day Adventist. Avocations: bicycle riding, backpacking, boating, baking, writing. Home: 1429 Del Mar Ave Modesto CA 95350

BASILE, PAUL LOUIS, JR., lawyer; b. Oakland, Calif., Dec. 27, 1945; s. Paul Louis and Roma Florence (Paris) B.; m. Linda Lou Paige, June 20, 1970; m. 2d Diane Chierichetti, Sept. 2, 1977. B.A., Occidental Coll., 1968; postgrad. U. Wash., 1969; J.D., UCLA, 1971. Bar: Calif. sup. ct. 1972, U.S. Dist. Ct. (cen. dist.) Calif. 1972, U.S. Sup. Ct. 1978, U.S. Tax Ct. 1977, U.S. Ct. Clms. 1978, U.S. Customs Ct. 1979, U.S. Ct. Customs and Patent Appeals 1979, U.S. Ct. Internat. Trade 1981. Assoc., Parker, Milliken, Kohlmeier, Clark & O'Hara, Los Angeles, 1971-72; corporate counsel TFI Cos., Inc., Irvine, Calif., 1972-73; sole practice, Los Angeles, 1973-80; ptnr., Basile & Siener, Los Angeles, 1980—; ptnr. Clark & Trevithick, Los Angeles, 1986—; sec. J.W. Brown, Inc., Los Angeles, Calif.; sec. Souriau, Inc., Valencia, Calif.; v.p., sec. Pvt. Fin. Assocs., Los Angeles. Trustee, sec. Nat. Repertory Theatre Found., 1975—, mem. exec. com. 1976—; active Los Angeles Olympic Organizing Com.; dir. March Dimes Birth Defects Found., Los Angeles County, 1982—; dir. Canadian Soc. Los Angeles, 1980-83, sec., 1982-83; dist. fin. chmn. Los Angeles Area council Boy Scouts Am., 1982-83. Mem. ABA, State Bar Calif., Los Angeles County Bar Assn., Canada Calif. C. of C. (dir. 1980—, 2d v.p. 1983-84, 1st v.p. 1984-85, pres. 1985-87), French-Am. C. of C. (councilor 1979-84, v.p. 1980, 82-84), Los Angeles Area C. of C. (dir. 1980-81), Grand Peoples Co. (bd. dirs., 1985—, chmn. bd. 1986—). Democrat. Baptist. Home: 3937 Beverly Glen Blvd Sherman Oaks CA 91403 Office: Clark & Trevithick 800 Wilshire Blvd 13th Floor Los Angeles CA 90017

BASINGER, RICHARD LEE, lawyer; b. Canton, Ohio, Nov. 24, 1941; s. Eldon R. and Alice M. (Bartholomew) B.; m. Rita Evelyn Gover, May 14, 1965; children—David A., Darron M. B.A. in Edn., Ariz. State U., 1963; postgrad. Macalester Coll., 1968-69; J.D., U. Ariz., 1973. Bar: Ariz. 1973, U.S. Dist. Ct. Ariz. 1973, U.S. Tax Ct. 1977, U.S. Ct. Appeals (6th cir.) 1975, U.S. Ct. Appeals (9th cir.) 1976, U.S. Supreme Ct. 1977. Assoc. law offices, Phoenix, 1973-74; sole practice, Scottsdale, Ariz. 1974-75; mem., pres. Basinger & Assocs., P.C., Scottsdale, 1975—. Contbr. articles to profl. jours. Bd. dirs. Masters Trail Ventures, Scottsdale, 1984-85, Here's Life, Ariz., Scottsdale, 1976—; precinct committeeman Republican Party, Phoenix, 1983—. NSF grantee, 1968-69. Mem. ABA, Ariz. Bar Assn., Maricopa County Bar Assn., Ariz. State Horseman's Assn. (bd. dirs. 1984-86, 1st up 1986), Scottsdale Bar Assn. Baptist. Clubs: Western Saddle (Phoenix) (bd. dirs. 1983-86, pres. 1985-86), Scottsdale Saddle, Saguaro Saddle. Office: Basinger & Assocs PC 4120 N 70th St Suite 211 Scottsdale AZ 85251

BASISZTA, MARTIN WINSTON, lawyer; b. Antioch, Calif., Jan. 10, 1943; m. Catherine Dawn Czarnecki, Mar. 3, 1978; children—Kelly Jane, Meghan Aileen. B.A. summa cum laude, U. Calif.-Davis, 1968; J.D., U. Calif.-Berkeley, 1972. Bar: Calif. 1973. Assoc., McNamara, Lewis & Craddick, Walnut Creek, Calif., 1973-75, Maloney, Chase, Fisher & Hurst, San Francisco, 1975-76; ptnr. Van Voorhis & Skaggs, Walnut Creek, 1976-78; sole practice law, Walnut Creek, 1978-83; ptnr. Basiszta & Daniels, Hayward, Calif., 1983—. Assoc. editor Calif. Law Rev., 1971-72. Contbr. articles to legal jours. Served with submarine service U.S. Navy, 1960-63. Recipient deptl. citation German studies U. Calif.-Davis, 1968; regents scholar U. Calif., 1966-68; German Govt. grad. grantee, German Govt. Grad. Exchange Program, 1969; John Woodward Ayer fellow in law, 1971-72; Alexander Von Humboldt grad. fellow in law, 1982; hon. Woodrow Wilson fellow, 1968. Mem. Bar Assn. San Francisco, Contra Costa County Bar Assn., Mt. Diablo Bar Assn., Santa Clara Bar Assn., San Mateo Bar Assn., Calif. Trial Lawyers Assn., Contra Costa/Alameda Trial Lawyers Assn., Assn. Def. Counsel, Def. Research Inst., Lawyers Club San Francisco, Barristers Club San Francisco, Phi Beta Kappa, Alpha Gamma Sigma, Phi Kappa Phi. Clubs: Am. Maltese Assn., Bay Area Maltese. *

BASKERVILLE, TIM, publishing executive; b. Burbank, Calif., July 31, 1949; s. David Ross and Roberta Mildred (Hollis) B.; m. Carol Kahler, Jan. 19, 1974 (div. June 1983); 1 child, Robin Ann. BA in Theatre Arts/TV, UCLA, 1971. Assoc. producer Sta. KNXT/CBS News, Hollywood, Calif., 1967-71; reporter Radio News West, Los Angeles, 1972; news producer Sta. KTVU/Cox Broadcasting, Oakland, Calif., 1972-73; dep. bur. chief TV News Inc., Los Angeles, 1973-74; pres. Media Service Corp., Hollywood, 1975-80, video Mktg., Hollywood, 1980—; cons. ABC, CBS, MGM/UA, Eastman Kodak, 20th Century Fox, IBM, Tribune Co., Young & Rubicam, J. Walter Thompson, Grey Advt., and others. Editor Job Leads, 1977; editor, pub. Video Mktg., 1980; writer (TV documentary) Alien and Illegal, 1971; contbr. artilces to Los Angeles Times. Mem. Newsletter Assn. (founder, pres. So. Calif. chpt. 1981-82), Radio TV News Assn. So. Calif., Radio TV News Dirs. Assn., Writers Guild Am. West. Club: Overseas Press of Am. Office: Video Mktg 1680 Vine St Suite 820 Hollywood CA 90028

BASKIN, YVONNE CECILE, science writer; b. Corpus Christi, Tex., Jan. 7, 1948; d. Charles Leroy and Lee Emily (Paine) B. BA, Baylor U., 1969. Staff writer AP, Raleigh, N.C., 1969-72; med. writer Duke U. Med. Ctr., Durham, N.C., 1972-74; sci. writer U. Utah, Salt Lake City, 1974-79, San Diego Union, 1979-81; freelance sci. writer San Diego, 1981—. Author: The Gene Doctors, 1984; co-author Woman of Tomorrow, 1985; contbr. articles to Omni, Sci. Digest, others. Alicia Patterson Found. fellowship winner, 1987. Mem. Nat. Assn. Sci. Writers (exec. com. 1985-87), San Diego Sci. Writers (sec., editor 1985—). Home and Office: PO Box 12339 La Jolla CA 92037

BASLER, RICHARD ALAN, biomedical instruments manufacturer; b. San Francisco, Sept. 12, 1939; s. Henry Edwin and Margaret Henrietta (Cooper) B.; m. Carol Audrey Foster, Aug. 4, 1962; children: Rodney Giles, Eric Richard. BA, U. Calif., Berkeley, 1960; MBA, U. Phoenix, Irvine, Calif., 1983. Indsl. engr., prodn. supr. Standard Register, Oakland and Corcoran, Calif., 1967-72; knitting supt. Duplan Knits West, Carson, Calif., 1972-75; prodn. supr. Am. Edwards Labs., Irvine, 1976-78, chief indsl. engr., 1978-80, supr. mfg. engring., 1980-86, with engring. systems devel., 1986—; owner Internat. Numismatics, Irvine, 1974—. Editor Calif. Engr. mag., 1959; contbr. articles to mags. Bd. dirs. UNCAP, Inc., Los Angeles, 1980-82. Served to lt. USN, 1960-67, Vietnam., with res. 1967-81. Recipient Kenneth Brainard Meml. Literary award, George Bennett Meml. Literary award. Mem. Am. Inst. Indsl. Engrs., U.S. Kerry Blue Terrier Club (gov. 1983-85), Gt. Western Terrier (bd. dirs. 1979—). Republican. Avocations: ancient numismatics, breeding show dogs, racquetball, weight lifting. Office: Am Edwards Labs 17221 Red Hill Ave Irvine CA 92711

BASS, CHARLES MORRIS, financial consultant; b. Miami, Fla., Sept. 21, 1949; s. Benjamin and Ellen Lucille (Williams) B; children—Cheryl Ellen, Benjamin Charles. B.A., U. Md., 1972; M.S., Am. Coll., 1982. C.L.U.; chartered fin. cons. Group rep. Monumental Life Ins. Co., 1972-73; agt. Equitable Life Ins. Co., N.Y., 1973-76; ptnr. Bass, Bridge and Assocs., Columbia, Md., 1976-81; pres. Multi-Fin Service, Inc., Balt., 1981-83; gen. mgr. Mfrs. Fin. Group, Denver, 1983-85; ptnr. Regency Econometrics Group, Denver, 1985—; speaker in field. Chmn. United Way Howard County, 1977-78; mem. Econ. Devel. Adv. Council Howard County, 1979-83. Served with USAF, 1968-71. Mem. Million Dollar Round Table, Nat. Assn. Life Underwriters, Am. Soc. C.L.U.s, Gen. Agts. and Mgrs. Assn., Columbia Life Underwriters Assn. (pres. 1982), Estate Planning Council, Howard County C. of C., Howard County Bus. Club, Columbia Bus. Exchange. Methodist. Home and Office: Regency Econometrics PO Box 61299 Denver CO 80206

BASS, LEWIS, lawyer; b. Bklyn., Oct. 22, 1947; s. Alexander and Doris (Aranowitz) B.; m. Sharon Diane Abdallah; 1 child, Michael. BSME, CCNY, 1969; MS in Indsl. Engring., U. So. Calif., 1971; JD, U. Santa Clara, 1976. Bar: Calif. 1976, U.S. Dist. Ct. (no. dist.) Calif. 1976. Mech. engr. Rockwell Internat., Los Angeles, 1969-70; project engr. Aerospace Corp., Los Angeles, 1970-71; safety engr. Lockheed, Sunnyvale, Calif., 1971-77; assoc. Caputo, Liccardo, Rossi, Sturges & McNeil, San Jose, Calif., 1977-78; corp. counsel Rose Mfg. Co., Englewood, Calif., 1978-79; sole practice Mountain View, Calif., 1979—; pres. Kairos Co. Safety Engring., Mountain View, 1979—; adj. asst. prof. safety sci. U. So. Calif., Los Angeles, 1979—. Author: Products Liability Design and Manufacturing Defects, 1986; contbr. articles to profl. jours. Named Outstanding Teaching award U. So. Calif., 1984. Mem. ABA, Am. Soc. Quality Control, Am. Soc. Safety Engrs., System Safety Soc. Office: 1001 N Rengstroff Ave Suite 100 Mountain View CA 94043-1715

BASSETT, DAVID ARTHUR, municipal building official; b. Grants Pass, Oreg., Oct. 28, 1945; s. James Waddell and Marguerite Marion (Nissen) B.; m. Kathleen Judith Stevens, Dec. 16, 1978. BSME, Oreg. State U., 1968, MSME, 1971. Registered profl. engr., Oreg., Calif. Sr. bldg. inspector City of Medford, Oreg., 1970-72, dir. bldg. safety, 1972-73, dir. community devel., 1973-74; dir. bldg. safety City of Medford, 1977—, Josephine County, Oreg., 1974-76; dep. adminstr. State Bldg. Codes Div., Salem, Oreg., 1976-77. Contbr. articles to profl. jours. Chmn. Oreg. State Structural Codes Bd., Salem, 1973-76; chmn. Gov. Com. on Handicapped, Salem, 1976-78; mem. State Planning Adv. Bd., Salem, 1978-82. Mem. Internat. Conf. Bldg. Officials (pres. chmn. bd. dirs. 1986, mem. ICBO Research Com. 1976-80, pres. So. Oreg. chpt. 1976), Oreg. State Bldg. Officials Assn. (pres. 1980, Outstanding Bldg. Official of Yr., 1980), Profl. Engrs. Oreg. (state v.p. 1975, 83, Outstanding Young Engr., 1975, 76). Republican. Lodge: Elks. Avocations: pilot, skiing, travelling, homebuilding, outdoor sports. Home: 500 Wonder Ln Wilderville OR 97543 Office: City of Medford Bldg Dept 411 W 8th St Medford OR 97501

BASSFORD, FORREST RAYMOND, journalist; b. Canton, Okla., Feb. 2, 1906; s. Horace Albert and Vilura (McGinnis) B.; m. Marian L. Horton, Oct. 12, 1929; children: Marilyn Ann, Karen Lee Bassford Priestly, Dale H. Horton. BS in Animal Husbandry, Colo. Agrl. Coll. (now Colo. State U.), 1929. County agt. Colo. Extension Service, Julesburg, Colo., 1929; editor Brush (Colo.) News, 1929-30; field rep. Denver Daily Record Stockman, 1930-34, Am. Hareford Jour., Kansas City, Mo., 1934-40; editor The Record Stockman, The Westerner mag., Denver, 1940-47; v.p., ptnr. Nelson R. Crow Publs., Inc., Los Angeles and Anaheim (Calif.), then Denver, 1948-77; gen. mgr. Nelson R. Crow Publs., Los Angeles, 1955-57; editor Western Livestock Jour., Denver, 1948-57, exec. editor., 1957-71, pub., 1972-77; founding pub. Charolais Jour., Houston, 1977-78; cons. livestock communications Encinitas, Calif., 1978—; sec., treas. Livestock Publs. Council, 1974-80, exec. dir. 1980—; dir. Western Stock Show Assn., 1941—; trustee Livestock Industry Inst., Kansas City, Mo., adv. council mem. Internat. Stockmen's Sch. San Antonio, 1981-85. Author: Century of Endurance, 1984; contbr. articles to profl. jours. Served with 115th cav. Wyo. N.G., 1920-26, 2d lt. arty. USAR, 1929-40. Named Livestock Marketeer of Yr. The Marketeers, 1972, Father of Yr. Mile Hi CowBelles, 1973; recipient Headliner award Livestock Council. Mem. Colo. Cattlemen's Assn., Am.-Internat. Charolais Assn., Iowa Beef Improvement Assn., Mo. Charolais Breeders Assn., The Marketeers (Livestock Marketeer of Yr., 1972), Mile Hi Cowbelles (Father of Yr. 1973), Am. Polled Hereford Assn., Am. Gelbvieh Assn., Beef Improvement Fedn., Calif. Beef Cattle Improvement Assn., Colo. Cattle Feeders Assn., Am. Soc. Farm Mgrs. Rural Appraisers, Gamma Sigma Delta, Alpha Gamma Rho. Home and Office: 927 Elmview Dr Encinitas CA 92024

BASSO, JOSEPH J., advertising executive; b. Chgo., Oct. 21, 1938; s. Sylvan T. and Agnes (MacMahon) B.; m. Jeannette Louise Wells, Sept. 11, 1978; children: Cory, Randall, Ashley. BA, Northwestern U., 1961. Mktg. salesman Admiral Corp., Chgo., 1961; acctg. supr. Babcock Corp., Costa Mesa, Calif., 1963-69, Durel Advt. Co., Newport Beach, Calif., 1969-72; pres., chief exec. officer Basso & Assocs., Newport Beach, 1972—; mem. internat. mktg. Affiliated Advt. Co.; mem. advt. bd. Agys. Internat. Advisor Golden West Coll., Huntington Beach, Calif.; bd. dirs. Orange County Rescue Mission. Served with USAF, 1956-59. Republican. Clubs: Balboa Bay, John Wayne Tennis (Newport Beach). Office: Basso and Assocs PO Box 8030 3198B Airport Loop Dr Newport Beach CA 92658

BASTIAN, BRUCE WAYNE, software company executive; b. Twin Falls, Idaho, Mar. 23, 1948; s. Arlon Lewis and Una (Davis) B.; m. Melanie Laycock, Apr. 17, 1976; children: C. Richard, Darren B., Jeffrey H., Robert A. BMus, Brigham Young U., 1975, MS in Computer Sci., 1978. Software engr. Eyring Research, Provo, Utah, 1978-79; software developer WordPerfect Corp., Orem, Utah, 1979-81; pres. Satellite Software, Orem, Utah, 1981—. Co-author Word Perfect computer program, 1979. Democrat. Mormon. Office: Word Perfect Corp 288 W Center Orem UT 84057

BASTON, JANET EVELYN, management consultant; b. Laramie, Wyo., Sept. 13, 1941; d. John Sigler and Virginia Ruth (Noell) Ball; m. Virgil Forest Dell Baston, June 7, 1959; children: Patricia, Alan, Linda. BS in Math., U. Wyo., 1960; MS in Math., Idaho State U., 1972, cert. proficiency, 1975, 80; MBA, U. Va., 1986. Programmer Aerojet Nuclear, Idaho Falls, Idaho, 1972-77; staff specialist EG&G Idaho, Idaho Falls, 1977-83; v.p. adminstrn. Phys. Scis. Inc., Sun Valley, Idaho, 1983—, also bd. dirs. Mem. EG&G Retirement and Investment Bd., 1978-83. Mem. The Inst. Mgmt. Sci., Soc. Women Engrs. (sec. southeast Idaho chpt. 1980-81, pres. 1982), Assn. Computing Machinery, Idaho Falls LWV. Home and Office: Phys Scis PO Box 2120 Sun Valley ID 83353

BASU, ASOKE ARIEL, sociologist, educator; b. Calcutta, India, Apr. 28, 1938; came to U.S., 1958; s. Sri Sudhir and Srimati Ila (Dutta) B.; m. Mollie Saine Pope, Nov. 13, 1944; 1 child, Melissa. BA in Sociology, W.Va. U., 1961; MA in Sociology, Okla. U., 1963, PhD in Polit. Sci., 1966. Asst. prof.sociology U. So. Calif., Los Angeles, 1966-68; prof. Calif. State U., Hayward, 1968—; research assoc., Ctr. for S. Asian Studies U. Calif., Berkeley, 1978-79; vis. scholar Harvard U., Boston, 1973, HOover Inst., Stanford, Calif., 1981-83. Author: Elementary Statistical Theory in Society, 1976, Culture, Politics and Critical Academics, 1981; co-author: Poverty in America: The Welfare Dilemma, 1981; contbr. articles to profl. jours. Named Outstanding Immigrant Internat. Inst. of the East Bay, 1972; recipient Scholarly Pub. award, Calif. State U., Northridge, 1981; Sr. Fulbright lectureship Council Internat. Exchange of Scholars, 1984-85; Sr. Smithsonian Research fellow Am. Inst. Indian Studies, 1985. Fellow AAAS; nen. Indian Sociol. Assn. (life), Internat. Soc. Assn. (pres. research com. sociology edn.), Pacific Soc. Assn. (chmn. com. status of minorities inthe profession). Home: 1548 Highland Blvd Hayward CA 94542 Office: Calif State U Dept Sociology Hayward CA 94542

BASYE, JENNIFER BERN, publisher; b. Sacramento, Oct. 16, 1958; d. George Donald and Mary Alice (Johnson) B. BA, Mills Coll., 1981; postgrad., Stanford U., 1983. Pub. Sacramento Women's Yellow Pages, 1983-85; small press buyer Beers Co., Sacramento; co-op. ad dir. Sacramento mag.; circulation dir. Exec. Publs., Sacramento, 1985—; pub. ARCH newspaper, 1986—; v.p. mktg. Am. River Roasters, Inc., Sacramento, 1983-86; publicity cons. Java City, Sacramento. Lobbyist Calif. chpt. NOW, Sacramento; county campaign dir. Proposition 15, Sacramento and Davis, Calif.; commr. Sacramento Mus. and History Commn., 1981—; chmn. Project 2000 Planning Commn., City of Sacramento, 1986. Founding mem. Capitol Pubs. Group (pres.). Democrat. Avocations: traveling, dog raising. Home: 616 47th St Sacramento CA 95819

BATCHELDER, ARTHUR ROLAND, soil scientist; b. Haverhill, Mass., Apr. 17, 1932; s. Arthur Henry and Helen Lee (Macdonald) B.; m. Ruth Merryman Hunt, July 2, 1955; children: Paul, Gary, Cynthia. BS, U. Mass., Amherst, 1954; MS, Va. Poly. Inst. and State U., 1966; PhD, Cornell U., 1971. Soil scientist USDA Agrl. Research Service, Norfolk, Va., 1957-62, Blacksburg, Va., 1962-66, Ithaca, N.Y., 1966-70; soil scientist USDA Agrl. Research Service, Ft. Collins, Colo., 1970-87, safety rep., 1978-87; occupational safety and health cons. Hazard Tng. Assocs., Ft. Collins, 1986—. Contbr. articles to profl. jours. Advisor Order DeMolay 1972-79, asst. exec. officer 1979-84; mem. Ft. Collins Area Safety Council, 1979—, pres. 1983; mem. task force Ft. Collins Model Seat Belt Program, 1985-86. Served to capt. USAR, 1955-57. Mem. Am. Soc. Agronomy, Am. Chem. Soc., Soil Sci. Soc. Am., World Safety Orgn., Western Soc. Soil Sci., Sigma Xi, Gamma Sigma Delta. Lodge: Masons. Avocations: fishing, camping. Home: 3020 Tulane Dr Fort Collins CO 80525

BATCHELDER, WILLIAM HOWARD, psychology educator; b. Columbus, Miss., May 29, 1940; s. Howard Timothy and Mary Lockwood (Sternenberg) B.; m. Marjorie Louise House, Dec. 30, 1962; children; Jennifer Louise, Sarah Marie. BA in Chemistry, Ind. U., 1962; PhD in Psychology, Stanford U., 1966. Asst. prof. psychology U. Ill., Champaign-Urbana, 1966-70; assoc. prof. U. Calif., Irvine, 1970-76, prof., 1977—, chmn. cognitive scis. program, 1976, faculty chmn. Sch. Social Scis., 1973-77, chmn. math. social sci. group, 1984-86; vis. prof. U. Wis., Madison, 1970. Contbr. articles to profl. jours. Grantee NSF, 1984-86, 86—, U. Ill., U. Calif.-Irvine, Nat. Council of Edn., 1966—. Mem. Soc. Math. Psychology (editor jour. 1975-80, ex officio exec. com. 1978-80), Psychonomic Soc., Psychometric Soc., Classification Soc., U.S. Chess Fedn. (chess master 1970—, chess sr. master 1982-83). Avocations: chess, racquetball, mountain climbing. Office: U Calif Sch Social Scis Irvine CA 92717

BATCHELOR, JAMES KENT, lawyer; b. Long Beach, Calif., Oct. 4, 1934; s. Jack Morrell and Edith Marie (Ottinger) B.; m. Jeanette Lou Dyer, Mar. 27, 1959; children—John, Suzanne; m. 2d, Susan Mary Leonard, Dec. 4, 1976. A.A., Sacramento City Coll., 1954; B.A., Long Beach State Coll., 1956; J.D., Hastings Coll. Law, U. Calif., 1959. Bar: Calif. 1960, U.S. Dist. Ct. (cen. dist.) Calif. 1960, U.S. Supreme Ct. 1968. Dept. dist. atty., Orange County, Calif., 1960-62; assoc. Miller, Nisson, Kogler & Wenke, Santa Ana, Calif., 1962-64; ptnr. Batchelor, Cohen & Oster, Santa Ana, 1964-67, Kurilich, Ballard, Batchelor, Fullerton, Calif., 1967-72; pres. James K. Batchelor, Inc., Santa Ana, 1972—; tchr. paralegal sect. Santa Ana City Coll.; judge pro-tem Superior Ct., 1974—. Fellow Acad. Am. Matrimonial Lawyers; mem. ABA, Calif. Trial Lawyers Assn., Calif. State Bar (placque chmn. family law sect. 1975-76, advisor 1976-78), Orange County Barristers (founder, pres., placque 1963), Calif. State Barristers (placque 1965, v.p.), Orange County Bar Assn. (plaque sec. 1977). Republican. Methodist. Office: 1200 N Main Suite 916 Santa Ana CA 92701

BATES, BRYAN COMER, wilderness science educator; b. Cleve., May 19, 1951; s. George Comer and Ida May (Lohman) B. BA in Native Am. Studies, Westminster Coll., 1974; MA in Environ. Sci. and Exptl. Edn., Sangamon State U., 1976. Sci. tchr. Rough Rock (Ariz.) Demonstration Sch., 1976-82; camp dir. Laughing Lakes Camp, Pine Top, Ariz., 1982; sci. tchr., curriculum writer Little Singer Sch., Bird Springs, Ariz., 1982-83; instr. chemistry Yavapai Community Coll., Flagstaff, Ariz., 1983; grad. asst. chemistry dept. No. Ariz. U., Flagstaff, 1983-84; sci. tchr., counselor Rocky Mountain Acad., Bonners Ferry, Idaho, 1984—, soccer coach, 1985—. Writer Flagstaff Non-Nuclear Futures Group, 1982-84, organizer, spokesperson. Mem. Nat. Sci. Tchrs. Assn. Avocations: whitewater rafting, folkmusic, flyfishing, rockclimbing, archeoastronomy. Office: No Ariz Univ Physics Dept Flagstaff AZ 86011

BATES, CHARLES CARPENTER, oceanographer; b. nr. Harrison, Ill., Nov. 4, 1918; s. Carl Albert and Vera Elizabeth (Carpenter) B.; m. Pauline Barta; children: Nancy Ann, Priscilla Jane, Sally Jean. Grad. (Rector scholar 1936-39), DePauw U., 1939; M.A., U. Calif. at Los Angeles, 1944; Ph.D. in Geol. Oceanography, Tex. A. and M. Coll., 1953; student, Cath. U., 1947-48, Johns Hopkins, 1951, George Washington U., 1954. Geophys. trainee Carter Oil Co., 1939-41; spl. asst. to pres. Am. Meteorol. Soc., 1945-46; mem. survey phys. and geol. environment Marshall Is. relative to pending Bikini atomic bomb tests 1946; with div. oceanography U.S. Navy Hydrographic Office, 1946- 57, dept. dir. div., 1953-57; environmental surveillance coordinator Office Devel. Coordinator, Office Naval Research, 1957-60; chief underground nuclear test detection br. Advanced Research Projects Agy., Office Sec. Def., 1960-64; sci. and tech. dir. U.S. Naval Oceanographic Office, 1964-68; sci. adviser to comdt., also chief scientist Office Research and Devel., USCG, 1968-79; environ. cons. 1979—; v.p. Spectrum Internat. Assocs., 1986—; part-time cons. in field and industry, 1946-52; mem. bd. experts Civil Service Examiners, 1954-60; mem. adv. com. postdoctoral awards for Fulbright grants NRC, 1957-60, chmn., 1959-60; vis. geoscientist Am. Geol. Inst., 1959-60; mem. meteorology panel, space sci. bd. Nat. Acad. Sci., 1959-61; mem. Mcht. Marine Council, 1968-71, Nat. Transp. Research Bd., 1968-71; mem. sea grant adv. council La. State U. System, 1968-79; co-chmn. U.S.-Japan panel marine facilities U.S.-Japan Natural Resource Program, 1969-71. Author: Geophysics in Affairs of Man, 1982, America's Weather Warriors, 1814-1985, 1986; numerous articles, reports in field. Served to capt. USAAF, 1941-45, lt. col. USAFR, 1941-65. Decorated Bronze Star; recipient U.S. Navy Meritorious Civilian award, 1962; U.S. Navy Superior Civilian Service award, 1969; U.S. Dept. Transp. Silver medal, 1973. Mem. Am. Geophys. Union (chmn. com. interaction sea and atmosphere 1950, mem. council 1964-67), Soc. Exploration Geophysicists (council 1963-67, v.p. 1965-66, hon. mem. 1981), Am. Meteorol. Soc. (chmn. com. indsl. bus. and agrl. meteorology 1946-48), Am. Assn. Petroleum Geologists (President's award 1954), Am. Mgmt. Assn. (research and devel. council 1970-79), Sigma Xi. Home: 136 W La Pintura Green Valley AZ 85614 Office: PO Box 191 Green Valley AZ 85622

BATES, CHARLES EMERSON, library administrator; b. Los Angeles, Dec. 1, 1946; s. Willard Emerson Bates and Erica (Schmidt) Bates Beckwith; m. Mary Joan Genz, Aug. 7, 1971; children—Christopher, Noah, Colin. B.A., Valparaiso U., 1968; M.Ed., Loyola U., Chgo., 1970; M.L.S., Rosary Coll., 1973. Head of reference Decatur Pub. Library, Ill., 1973-74; cons. Rolling Prairie Library System, Decatur, 1974-76; asst. dir. Fond du Lac Pub. Library, Wis., 1976-81; dir. Pueblo Library Dist., Colo., 1981—. Bd. dirs. Pueblo United Way, 1982-86 ; pres. bd. dirs. Rosemount Victorian House Mus., Pueblo, 1984—. Mem. ALA, Colo. Library Assn., Ark. Valley Library System (pres. 1984-85). Lutheran. Lodge: Rotary (pres. bd. dirs. 1981—). Office: Pueblo Library Dist 100 E Abriendo Ave Pueblo CO 81004

BATES, CHARLES WALTER, personnel executive; b. Detroit, June 28, 1953; s. E. Frederick and Virginia Marion (Nunneley) BA in Psychology and Econs. cum laude, Mich. State U., 1975, M in Labor and Indsl. Relations, 1977; postgrad. DePaul U., 1979-80; JD William Mitchell Coll. Law, 1984. Vista vol., paralegal Legal Aid Assn. Ventura County, Calif., 1975-76; substitute tchr. social studies and history, Lansing, Holt and Okemos, Mich. pub. sch. systems, 1976-77; job analyst Gen. Mills, Inc., Mpls., 1977-78, plant personnel asst., Chgo., 1978-80, asst. plant personnel mgr., Chgo., 1980, personnel mgr., Mpls., 1981, personnel mgr. mktg. divs., Mpls., 1982-84; regional human resource mgr. western div. Godfather's Pizza, Inc., Bellevue, Wash., 1984—, mountain div. 1985—. Candidate lt. gov., 1982. Minn. asst. scoutmaster Boy Scouts of Am., 1971—. Named Eagle Scout, Boy Scouts Am., 1969; recipient God and Country award Boy Scouts Am., 1967, Scouter's Tng. award Boy Scouts Am., 1979. Mem. Nat. Eagle Scout Assn., Nat. Assn. JD/MBA Profls., Pacific N.W. Personnel Mgmt. Assn., Indsl. Relations Research Assn., Am. Soc. Personnel Adminstrn., Mich. State U. Alumni Assn., William Mitchell Coll. Law Alumni Assn., The Nature Conservancy, Sierra Club, Phi Alpha Delta. Libertarian. Unitarian-Universalist. Home: 232 168th Ave NE Bellevue WA 98008-4522 Office: Godfather's Pizza Inc 13434 SE 27th Pl Bellevue WA 98005

BATES, JIM, congressman; b. Denver, July 21, 1941; s. Chester Owen and Asha (East) B.; m. Marilyn Brewer; 1 dau., Jennifer Leigh. B.A., San Diego State U., 1975; L.H.D. (hon.), Nat. U., San Diego, 1983. Loan officer Bank Am., San Diego, 1963-68; adminstr. Rohr, San Diego, 1968, Solar, San Diego, 1969; mktg. analyst Heavenly Donuts, San Diego, 1970; mem. San Diego City Council, 1971-74; supr. County of San Diego, 1975-82; mem. 98th-100th Congresses from 44th Dist. Calif. Mem. com. energy and commerce U.S. Congress, subcom.: telecommunication consumer protection, fin., heath, and environment, mem. ho. adminstrn. com., subcom.: personnel and police, services; chmn. gov. bd. Health Systems Agy.; chmn. mental health adv. bd. City of San Diego. Served with USMC, 1959-63. Recipient Diploma Magistrale and Decoration of Cavaliere nell'ordine al Merito della Repubblica Italiana, 1979, Outstanding Service award Mental Health Assn., cert. appreciation Census Bur., 1980, gavel and holder United Builders Am., 1979, Gary Dores Meml. award, Outstanding Young Citizen award Jaycees; cert. appreciation Mental Health Adv. Bd., Nat. Achievement award Urban League, 1982, Equal Rights award; named '84 San Diegans to Watch, San Diego Mag., 1984, Freshman to Watch, Congl. Insight mag., 1982. Democrat. Office: 1404 Longworth House Office Bldg Washington DC 20515

BATES, JOHN DODD, publishing executive; b. Meadville, Pa., Oct. 10, 1934; s. Edward Irving and Elinor (Van Scoten) B.; m. Louise Murray, Jan. 5, 1957; children: Amy, Laura, Barbara. BA, Duke U., 1956. Asst. to pub. The Tribune, Meadville, 1956-76; pub. Marion (Ohio) Star, 1976-78; gen. mgr. Herald-Mail, Hagerstown, Md., 1980-83; v.p., gen. mgr. Dominion-Post, Morgantown, W.Va., 1978-80, News-Gazette, Champaign, Ill., 1983-85, Sacramento Union, 1985—. Bd. dirs. Sacramento Area C. of C., 1985. Served to sgt. USAR, 1956-61. Republican. Mem. Unitarian Ch. Lodge: Rotary. Home: 3404 N El Macero Dr El Macero CA 95618 Office: The Sacramento Union 301 Capitol Mall Sacramento CA 95812

BATES, J(UNIOR) LAMBERT, ceramic engineer, researcher; b. Ogden, Utah, Mar. 21, 1928; s. A. Parley and Lucille Roene (Lambert) B.; m. Ala Jean Odum, May 28, 1952; children: Steven, Debra, Scott, Roger, Holly. BS, Brigham Young U., 1953; PhD, U. Utah, 1957. Sr. scientist Gen. Electric Co., Richland, Wash., 1957-64; sr. scientist Battelle Meml. Inst., Richland, 1965-68, sect. mgr., 1969-70; staff scientist Pacific Northwest Labs., Richland, 1970-78, sr. staff scientist, program mgr., 1979—. Contbr. articles to profl. jours.; patentee in field. Named Mountain Man Yr. Alumni Assn. U. Utah, 1984. Fellow Am. Ceramic Soc. (v.p. 1979-80, pres. 1983-84). Mormon. Office: Battelle Meml Inst Pacific NW Labs PO Box 999 Richland WA 99352

BATES, KENNETH SCOTT, JR., military officer; b. Jacksonville, Fla., Aug. 5, 1943; s. Kenneth Scott and Mary Louise (Marshall) B.; m. Deborah Ann Quidley; 1 child, Kimberly Anne. Student, Va. Poly. Inst., 1961-65; BS, U.S. Naval Postgrad. Sch., 1972, MS, 1973. Commd. ensign USN, 1965, advanced through grades to capt., 1987; chief engr. T-45 TS program USN, Naval Air Systems Command-Washington, 1981-85; dir. Naval Air Systems Command Detachment Douglas Aircraft Co., Long Beach, Calif., 1985—. Decorated Air medals. Mem. AIAA, Tailhook Assn., Assn. Naval Aviators. Offic: Douglas Aircraft Co Dept NavAir Syscom 3855 Lakewood Blvd Long Beach CA 90846

BATES, RICHARD MATHER, dentist; b. Kalispell, Mont., May 21, 1932; s. Richard Mather and Virginia Susan (Brokaw) B.; m. Jean Frances Delk, June 27, 1959; children—Bruce H., Susan F. B.S., Lewis and Clark Coll., 1954; D.M.D., U. Oreg., 1958. Gen. practice dentistry, Portland, Oreg., 1958—; pres., dir. Dentist Benefit Corp., Portland, 1981—; dir. Beaver State Bank, Beaverton, Oreg., 1980-86; clin. assoc. Oreg. Health Sci. U., Portland, 1976-79; mem. dental staff Physicians and Surgeons Hosp., Portland, 1965-85. Pres., Pub. Affairs Forum of Washington County, Beaverton, 1965-66; bd. dirs. Oreg. Trail chpt. ARC, Portland, 1970-76; pres., co-founder Dental for Children, Hillsboro, Oreg., 1970. Recipient Disting. Service award Beaverton Jaycees, 1965. Fellow Acad. Gen Dentistry (master); mem. ADA, Oreg. Dental Assn. (pres. 1983-84), Washington County Dental Soc. (pres. 1967-68), Acad. Gen. Dentistry (Dentist of Yr. award Oreg. unit 1972), Beaverton Area C. of C. (pres. 1976, J. Arthur Young award 1975). Republican. Presbyterian. Clubs: N.W. Regional Pony of Am. (pres. 1970-72), Oreg. Pony of Am. (pres. 1977-78) (Beaverton). Lodge: Cedar Hills Kiwanis (pres. Beaverton 1970). Office: 1585 SW Marlow Portland OR 97225

BATES, ROBERT THOMAS, consulting engineer; b. Warren, Ohio, Sept. 21, 1947; s. Charles Edward and Jessie Frieda (Putman) B.; m. Susan Mary Carlson, Oct. 14, 1968 (div. Dec. 1984); children: Karin Lynn, Amy Elizabeth; m. Diana Horner, Nov. 23, 1985. BS, U. Wis., Platteville, 1970; postgrad., U. Wis., Madison, 1972-74, U. Denver, 1975-76. Registered profl. engr., Wis., Colo., Wyo., N.Mex., Ariz. Bridge design engr. Wis. Dept. Transp., Madison, 1970-74; project mgr. MSM Inc., Denver, 1974-78; prin. Meurer & Assocs. Inc., Denver, 1974-85; dir. mcpl. engring. JR Engring., Denver, 1986—. Bd. dirs. Lakewood (Colo.) Sister City Internat., 1984—. Mem. ASCE, Am. Concrete Inst. (pres. Rocky Mountain chpt. 1984-85, bd. dirs., 1982—), Am. Cons. Engrs. Council, Cons. Engrs. Council Colo., Am. Inst. Steel Constrn., Am. Waterworks Assn., Post Tensioning Inst. Avocations: athletics, flying. Home: 1979 S Vivian St Lakewood CO 80228 Office: JR Engring Ltd 6857 S Spruce St Englewood CO 80112

BATHEN, KARL HANS, oceanography educator; b. New Haven, Nov. 28, 1934; s. John H. and Jane H. (Koscinski) B.; m. Nancy J., Dec. 29, 1963 (div. 1980); children: Heidi, J., Erik K., Kristin E. BSME cum laude, U. Conn., 1956; postgrad., Orange Coast Coll., 1964, U. Calif., Davis, 1964-65; MS in Oceanography, U. Hawaii, 1968, PhD in Oceanography, 1970. Enlisted USAF, 1956; advanced through grades to capt. USAF, San Francisco, 1963; resigned USAF, 1966; project engr. Colorvision Inc., Glendale, Calif., 1961-57; project research and devel. engr., Philco, Aeronutronic div. Ford Motor Co., Newport Beach, Calif., 1963-64; research asst. in oceanography U. Hawaii, Honolulu, 1966-70, assoc. prof., assoc. researcher, 1971-76, prof., researcher, 1976—; mgr. Dillingham Environ. Co., Honolulu, 1970-71; pres. Sci. Environ. Analyses, Ltd.; cons., lectr. in field. Contbr. numerous articles to profl. jours. Fellow Hawaiian Electric Oceanographic, 1967-68; recipient Internat. Underwater Photographic awards, 1964-66. Mem. Underwater Photographic Soc. Am., Conservation Council for Hawaii, Marine Tech. Soc., Am. Water Resources Assn., Internat. Assn. Water Pollution Research, Am. Geophys. Union, Sigma Xi. Home: PO Box 7224 Honolulu HI 96821 Office: U Hawaii Dept Ocean Engring Honolulu HI 96822

BATHER, HELEN MARIE, lawyer, writer; b. Chgo., Nov. 1, 1955; d. Nick Frank Darras and Mary Ellen (Barkoulies) Fifles; m. William Joseph Bather Jr., Oct. 14, 1983; stepchildren: Charlene, William; children: Phillip Sinclair, Christina Jolie. BA in Pub. Adminstrn., Calif. State U., Long Beach, 1980; JD, Western State U., Fullerton, Calif., 1983. Bar: Calif. 1984. Sole practice Orange, Calif., 1984-85; assoc. Hartford Accident and Indemnity, Brea, Calif., 1985-87, Liebman & Reiner, Los Angeles, 1987—; teaching asst. Western State U., 1984-86. Contbr. articles to Go West mag., 1985, 86. Recipient Am. Jurisprudence award Lawyers Co-op Pub., N.J., 1982. Mem. ABA, Calif. State Bar, Assn. Trial Lawyers Am., Nat. Ind. Contractors Assn. (bd. dirs.). Democrat. Greek Orthodox. Avocations: travel, reading, family activities. Home: 5715 Greenbriar Yorba Linda CA 92686

BATISTE, PEARL THERESA, educator; b. Jeanerette, La., Dec. 9, 1930; d. Erris and Pearl (Armelin) Edgerly; B.A., Calif. State U., San Francisco, 1975; M.A. in Edn., U. San Francisco, 1978; M.S. in Pepperdine U., 1979; m. Berwick Batiste, Sept. 12, 1950; children—Michael, Keith, Ronald, Elissa, Ingrid, Patrick. Dir. counseling tng. dept. Amrick Advt., Oakland, Calif., 1976-77; public relations dir. San Francisco Ednl. Found., Oakland, 1977-78; fashion model, instr., substitute tchr. Barbizon Modeling Sch., 1975-76; program and project coordinator Oakland Pub. Schs., 1976—. Mem. Amway Exec. Women Assts., Profl. Woman Exec. Corp. Am., Black Profl. Bus. Women Assts., Nat. Alliance Black Edn. Democrat. Roman Catholic. Club: Fashionnete Social. Author: The Influence of African on American Fashion, 1980. Home: 2509 Tulare Ave El Cerrito CA 94530

BATTIN, JAMES FRANKLIN, judge, former congressman; b. Wichita, Kans., Feb. 13, 1925; m. Barbara Choate; children: Loyce Battin Peterson, Patricia Battin Pfeiffer, James Franklin. J.D., George Washington U., 1951. Bar: D.C. and Mont. bars. Practice in Washington, 1951-52; now in Billings; past dep. county atty.; past sec.-counsel City-County Planning Bd.; past asst. city atty. Billings; then city atty.; mem. Mont. Ho. of Reps., 1958-59; mem. 87th-91st congresses 2d Dist., Mont.; resigned when apptd. U.S. dist. judge Mont. Dist., 1969; chief judge 1978—. Served with USNR, World War II. Mem. Am. Legion, DeMolay Legion of Honor. Presbyterian. Club: Mason (Shriner). Office: US Dist Ct Mont 5428 Federal Bldg 316 N 26th St PO Box 1476 Billings MT 59103

BATTISTA, ALFRED ANTHONY, nutritionist; b. Newton, Mass., July 29, 1944; s. Alfred and Eleanor B.; m. Ljiljana Krusic, July 30, 1977; children: Anthony Paul, Christian Gerard. Student, U. Mass., 1962-63, Victor Bests Sch. of Broadcasting, 1969, Marquette U., 1975-76. Nat. sales mgr. Standard Process Labs., Milw., 1972-77; owner, operator Nutritional Dynamics, San Carlos, Calif., 1977-81; owner, operator Nutritional Dynamics, Denver, 1984—, real estate cons., 1984—; owner, operator Healthware, Inc., Gilroy, Calif., 1982-84; with Internat. Labs, El Dorado Hills, Calif., 1986—; cons. New Generation/Consumer, Denver and Lake Charles, Colo., 1985—. Author: The Last Diet, 1981, I Lost 13 Pounds in 19 Days, 1983, The Fungus Among Us, 1983; contbr. articles to Let's Live mag., 1982—, Health Freedom News, 1982—. Go-for Republicans, Woodbridge, Va., 1978, Libertarians, San Carlos, 1980, Populists, San Carlos, 1984; coordinator Citizens Emergency Def. System, Gilroy, 1984. Served as sgt. USMC, 1963-66, Vietnam. Mem. Am. Legion, Disabled Am. Vets., Nat. Health Fedn. (bd. govs. 1981—). Lodge: Rotary (Paul Harris fellow, 1981). Avocations: martial arts, horse riding, target shooting, reading, writing. Home: 211 S State Coll Blvd #301 Anaheim CA 92806 Office: Showcase 438 Katella Orange CA 92667 Office: Internat Labs PO Box 5219 El Dorado Hills CA 95630

BATTISTI, PAUL ORESTE, hospital administrator; b. Herkimer, N.Y., Mar. 16, 1922; s. Oreste and Ida (Fiore) B.; m. Constance Muth Drais, May 18, 1985; children—Paul J., Cathy (Mrs. D. Capage), Deborah, Thomas, Daniel, Melora, Stephen. Student, Cornell U., Ithaca, N.Y., 1947-48, U. Neb., 1951-52. With VA, 1946—; dir. VA Hosp., Martinez, Calif., 1969-73; Western region dir. VA Hosp., San Francisco, 1973—; adminstr. State Vets. Home Calif., 1976—; chmn., chief exec. officer Medam., Inc.; dir. Med. Am. Corp.; mem. Contra Costa County Comprehensive Health Planning, Health Facilities Task Force; chmn. adv. com. East Bay Med. Program.; bd. dirs. East Bay Hosp. Conf. Bd. dirs. Easter Seals Contra Costa County. Served with AUS, 1942-46. Fellow Am. Coll. Hosp. Adminstrs.; mem. Hosp. Conf. No. Calif. (pres.), Nat. Assn. State Vets. Homes (pres.). Club: Rotary (Martinez) (dir.). Home: Silverado Country Club 877 Oak Leaf Way Napa CA 94558 Office: Vets Home Calif Yountville CA

BATTISTONE, SAM D., businessman, professional basketball team executive. m. Nan; 6 children. Former owner New Orleans Jazz, now vice-chmn., gov. Utah Jazz, NBA, Salt Lake City. Office: care Utah Jazz 5 Triad Ctr Suite 500 Salt Lake City UT 84180 *

BATZEL, ROGER ELWOOD, chemist; b. Weiser, Idaho, Dec. 1, 1921; s. Walter George and Inez Ruth (Klinefelter) B.; m. Edwina Lorraine Grindstaff, Aug. 18, 1946; children: Stella Lynne, Roger Edward, Stacy Lorraine. B.S., U. Idaho, 1947; Ph.D., U. Calif. at Berkeley, 1951. Mem. staff Lawrence Livermore (Calif.) Lab., 1953—, head chemistry dept., 1959-67, asso. dir. for chemistry, 1961-71, asso. dir. for testing, 1961-64, asso. dir. for space reactors, 1966-68, asso. dir. chem. and bio-med. research, 1969-71, dir. lab., 1971—. Served with USAAF, 1943-45. Named to Alumni Hall of Fame U. Idaho, 1972; recipient disting. assoc. award U.S. Dept. Energy, 1982. Fellow AAAS, Am. Phys. Soc.; mem. Sigma Xi. Club: Commonwealth of Calif. (San Francisco). Office: PO Box 808 Livermore CA 94550

BAUCH, THOMAS JAY, lawyer, apparel company executive; b. Indpls., May 24, 1943; s. Thomas and Violet (Smith) B.; m. Ellen L. Burstein, Oct. 31, 1982; children: Chelsea, Elizabeth. B.S., U. Wis., 1964, J.D., 1966. Bar: Ill. 1966, Calif. 1978. Assoc. Lord, Bissell & Brook, Chgo., 1966-72; lawyer, asst. sec. Marcor-Montgomery Ward, Chgo., 1973-75; spl. asst. to solicitor Dept. Labor, Washington, 1975-77; dep. gen. counsel Levi Strauss & Co., San Francisco, 1977-81, sr. v.p., gen. counsel, 1981—; mem. U. Wis. Law Review, Madison, 1964-66. Bd. dirs. The Urban Sch., San Francisco, 1986. Mem. Am. Assn. Corp. Counsel (dir. 1982—), Order of Coif. Democrat. Clubs: Univ. (San Francisco); Racquet (Chgo.). Office: Levi Strauss & Co Levi's Plaza Box 7215 San Francisco CA 94120

BAUCUS, MAX S., U.S. Senator; b. Helena, Mont., Dec. 11, 1941; s. John and Jean (Sheriff) B.; m. Wanda Minge, Apr. 23, 1983. B.A., Stanford U., 1964, LL.B., 1967. Bar: D.C. 1969, Mont. 1972. Staff atty. CAB, Washington, 1967-69; lawyer SEC, Washington, 1969-71; legal asst. to chmn. SEC, 1970-71; sole practice Missoula, Mont., 1971-74; mem. Mont. Ho. of Reps., 1973-74; mem. 94th-95th congresses from 1st Dist. Mont., 1975-79, mem. com. appropriations; mem. U.S. Senate from Mont., 1979—; mem. fin., small bus. and environ. and pub. works coms. U.S. Senate; acting exec. dir., com. coordinator Mont. Constl. Conv., 1972. Home: Missoula MT 59801 Office: Senate Office Bldg 706 Hart Washington DC 20510

BAUER, A(UGUST) ROBERT, JR., surgeon; b. Phila., Dec. 23, 1928; s. A(ugust) Robert and Jessie Martha-Maynard (Monie) B.; B.S., U. Mich., 1949, M.S., 1950, M.D., 1954; M. Med. Sci.-Surgery, Ohio State U., 1960; m. Charmaine Louise Studer, June 28, 1957; children—Robert, John, William, Anne, Charles, James. Intern Walter Reed Army Med. Center, 1954-55; resident in surgery Univ. Hosp., Ohio State U., Columbus, also instr., 1957-61; individual practice medicine, specializing in surgery, Mt. Pleasant, Mich., 1962-74; chief surgery Central Mich. Community Hosp., Mt. Pleasant, 1964-65, vice chief of staff, 1967, chief of staff, 1968; clin. faculty Mich. State Med. Sch., East Lansing, 1974; mem. staff St. Mark's Hosp., Salt Lake City, 1974—; individual practice surgery, Salt Lake City, 1974—; clin. instr. surgery U. Utah, 1975—. Trustee, Rowland Hall, St. Mark's Sch., Salt Lake City, 1978-84; mem. Utah Health Planning Council, 1979-81. Served with M.C., U.S. Army, 1954-57. Diplomate Am. Bd. Surgery. Fellow ACS, Southwestern Surg. Congress; mem. AMA, Salt Lake County Med. Soc., Utah med. assns., Utah Soc. Certified Surgeons, Salt Lake Surg. Soc., Royal Soc. Medicine (affiliate), Pan Am. Med. Assn. (affiliate), AAAS (affiliate), Sigma Phi Epsilon, Phi Rho Sigma. Episcopalian. Club: Zollinger. Contbr. articles to profl. publs., researcher surg. immunology. Office: PO Box 17533 Salt Lake City UT 84117

BAUER, HENRY LELAND, lawyer; b. Portland, Oreg., June 7, 1928; s. Henry and Emma L. (Peterson) B.; m. Doris Jane Philbrick, May 21; children—Henry Stephen, Thomas Leland. B.S. in Bus., Oreg. State U., 1950; J.D., U. Oreg., 1953. Bar: Oreg. 1953, U.S. Dist. Ct. Oreg., 1956; U.S. Ct. Appeals (9th cir.), 1960. Mem. Bauer & Bauer, Portland, Oreg., 1955-70, Bauer, Murphy, Bayless & Fundingsland, and successor firms, Portland, 1970-75; now sr. mem. Bauer, Hermann, Fountain & Rhoades P.C., Portland. Mem. adv. council Oreg. State U. Coll. Bus.; bd. dirs., vice chmn. St. Vincent Hosp. and Med. Ctr.; mem., vice chmn. council of trustees St. Vincent Med. Found.; bd. dirs., sec. Nat. Interfrat. Conf.; pres. Columbia Pacific council Boy Scouts Am.; past pres. Portland Civic Theatre; bd. visitors U. Oreg. Sch. Law, 1979-83. Served to 1st lt. USAF, 1953-55. Mem. ABA, Oreg. Bar Assn., Multnomah County Bar Assn., Am. Judicature Soc., Oreg. State U. Alumni Assn. (bd. dirs.), Delta Theta Phi, Kappa Sigma (past nat. pres.). Republican. Presbyterian. Clubs: Multnomah Athletic, Arlington, Masons, Rotary. Office: Commonwealth Bldg Suite 1100 Portland OR 97204

BAUER, JAMES LEONARD, architect; b. Council Bluffs, Iowa, Dec. 21, 1949; s. Leonard Eugene and Myrtle Louise (Anderson) B.; m. Mary Elisbeth Stahl, Dec. 27, 1969; children: Hillari Paige, Sloan James, Chase David. BArch, Mont. State U., 1973. Registered profl. architect, Mont., Wyo., N.D., S.D. Architect-in-tng. Moyle & Aanes, Butte, Mont., 1973-74, Johnson Graham Assocs., Billings, Mont., 1974-76; treas. HKM Assocs., Billings, 1976-82; pres. Bauer Group Architects, Billings, 1982—. Mem. streamlining com. City of Billings, 1986, council Good Shepherd Luth. Ch., Billings, 1984-85. Mem. Billings Archtl. Assn. (pres. 1985). Lodge: Elks (trustee 1982—). Avocations: hunting, cross-country skiing, bicycling. Home: 1830 Iris Ln Billings MT 59102 Office: PO Box 2177 Billings MT 59103-2177

BAUER, JEROME LEO, JR., chemical engineer; b. Pitts., Oct. 12, 1938; s. Jerome L. and Anna Mae (Tucker) B.; divorced; children: Lori, Trish, Jeff. BSChemE, U. Dayton, 1960; MSChemE, Pa. State U., 1963; postgrad., Ohio State U., 1969. Registered profl. engr., Ohio. Asst. prof. chem. engring. U. Dayton, Ohio, 1963-67; mgr. advanced composites dept. Ferro Corp., Cleve., 1967-72; engring. material and process specifications mgr. Lockheed Missiles & Space Co., Inc., Sunnyvale, Calif., 1972-74; gen. dynamics design specialist Convair Div., San Diego, 1974-76, project devel. engr., 1976-77; dir. research Furane div. M&T Chems. Inc., Glendale, Calif., 1980-82; mem. tech. staff Jet Propulsion Lab., Calif. Inst. Tech., Pasadena, Calif., 1977-80, 82—. Editor: Materials Sciences for Future, 1986; contbr. articles to profl. jours. Jr. warden St. Luke Episcopal Ch., La Crescenta, Calif., 1980, sr. warden 1981. Mem. Am. Inst. Chem. Engrs. (founder, chmn. Dayton sect. 1964-66, spl. projects chmn. Cleve. sect. 1968-69), Soc. Advancement of Material Process Engring. (membership chmn. no. Calif. sect. 1973-74, sec. San Diego sect. 1974-75, vice chmn. 1975-76, chmn. 1976, chmn. Los Angeles sect. 1977, nat. treas. 1978-82, gen. chmn. 31st internat. symposium exhibition, Las Vegas, Nev., 1986, Meritiorous Achievement award 1983, internat. v.p. 1987-89), Internat. Electronics Packaging Soc. (pres. Los Angeles chpt. 1982), Phi Lambda Upsilon, Delta Sigma Epsilon. Republican. Avocations: carpentry, photography, camping. Home: 1935 E Alpha 205 Glendale CA 91208 Office: Jet Propulsion Lab Calif Inst Tech 4800 Oak Grove Dr Pasadena CA 91109

BAUER, LARRY ALAN, pharmacy educator; b. Wapato, Wash., Aug. 19, 1954; s. George L. and Evelyn M. (Bremer) B.; m. Stephanie Patterson, Aug. 22, 1977. BS in Pharmacy, U. Wash., 1977; PharmD, U. Ky., 1980. Resident U. Ky., Lexington, 1977-80; asst. prof. pharmacy U. Wash., Seattle, 1980-85, assoc. prof., 1985—; cons. pharmacy, Seattle, 1983—. Contbr. articles to profl. jours. Mem. Am. Assn. Colls. of Pharmacy, Am. Coll. Clin. Pharmacy, Am. Soc. Clin. Pharmacology and Therapeutics, Sigma Xi, Rho Chi. Office: U Wash Dept Pharmacy Practice SC-69 Seattle WA 98195

BAUER, RANDY MARK, mgmt. tng. firm exec.; b. Cleve., Sept. 2, 1946; s. Ralph I. and Gloria P. Bauer; B.S. summa cum laude, Ohio State U., 1968; M.B.A., Kent State U., 1971; m. Sue Dellva, July 4, 1975; children—Sherri, Kevin. Mgmt. auditor Peat Marwick Mitchell & Co., Cleve., 1971-72; mgmt. devel. specialist GAO, Denver, 1972-80; adj. prof. mgmt. Columbia Coll., Denver, 1979—; pres. Leadership Tng. Assos., Denver, 1979—; condr. exec. devel. workshops U. Colo., Denver, 1979—. Recipient Best in 1976 award GAO. Mem. Am. Soc. for Tng. and Devel., Beta Gamma Sigma. Address: 16275 E Crestline Pl Aurora CO 80015

BAUER, ROGER DUANE, univ. dean; b. Oxford, Nebr., Jan. 17, 1932; s. Albert Carl and Minnie (Lueking) B.; m. Jacquelyn True, Aug. 10, 1956; children—Lisa, Scott, Robert. B.S., Beloit Coll., 1953; M.S., Kans. State U., 1957, Ph.D., 1959. Asst. prof. chemistry Calif. State U., Long Beach, 1959-64; asso. prof. Calif. State U., 1964-69, prof., 1969—; dean Calif. State U. (Sch. Natural Scis.), 1975—. Served with U.S. Army, 1954-56. USPHS fellow, 1966; Am. Council on Edn. fellow, 1971. Mem. Am. Chem. Soc., Radiation Research Soc., Sigma Xi, Phi Lambda Upsilon. Home: 6320 Colorado St Long Beach CA 90803 Office: Coll Natural Sci Calif State U Long Beach CA 90840

BAUGH, ANN LAWRENCE, physical chemist; b. Freeport, Tex., Sept. 4, 1938; d. Dewey Lawrence and Ruth Elizabeth (Tipton) Baugh. BS, Southwestern U., 1960; MA, U. Tex., 1963, PhD, 1966; MBA, Pepperdine U., 1982. Asst. prof. chemistry Southwestern U., 1964-67; tech. specialist chemistry research dept. Lockheed Propulsion Co., Redlands, Calif., 1969-75; sr. research chemist fuels desulfurization group Occidental Research Corp., Irvine, Calif., 1975-78, group head, 1978-80, sr. research scientist, geothermal energy research, 1980-81, phosphoric acid researcher, 1981-82; program devel. mgr. chem. tech. Rocketdyne div. Rockwell Internat. Corp., Canoga Park, Calif., 1983—; cons. tech. mgmt. 1979—; NSF research asst. U. Tex., Austin, 1961-63. Inventor in field; contbr. articles to profl. jours, World Book Ency. Robert A. Welch postdoctoral fellow in chemistry, 1966-69; named Woman of Achievement, Irvine Bus. and Profl. Women's Club, 1980, Woman of Yr., San Orco Dist. Bus. and Profl. Women's Clubs, 1980. Fellow Am. Inst. Chemists, Assn. for Women in Sci.; mem. AAAS, NOW, Am. Chem. Soc., Am. Inst. Chem. Engrs., Soc. Applied Spectroscopy, Lockheed Propulsion Mgmt. Assn. (treas. 1973-74), Nat. Mgmt. Assn., Am. Phys. Soc., Univ. Law Wives, Bus. and Profl. Women's Club, Iota Sigma Pi, Delta Theta Phi Wives, Delta Delta Delta. Home: 1615 Butternut Way Diamond Bar CA 91765

BAUGH, L. DARRELL, financial executive; b. Prairie Grove, Ark., Oct. 7, 1930; s. Lacey D. and Mary Grace (Brown) B.; BBA, U. Ark., 1954; MBA, U. Colo., 1960; CLU, Am. Coll., 1967, chartered fin. cons., 1983; m. Wileeta Claire Gray, June 15, 1958; children: Adrienne Leigh Calvo, John Grayson. With Penn Mut. Life Ins. Co., 1961-71, gen. agt., Sacramento, 1968-71; pres. Nat. Estate Planning Inst., Boulder, Colo., 1974—; bd. dirs. Sunshower Acres Ltd; faculty estate planning seminars Colo. State U.; cons. U. Colo. Center for Confs. Mgmt./Tech. Programs, 1975-80; sponsor ednl. programs for profl. estate planners and estate owners. Bd. dirs. Stronghold Youth Found. Served with U.S. Army, 1954-56. Mem. Boulder C. of C., Am. Soc. C.L.U.s, Rocky Mountain C.L.U.s (chmn. grad. studies programs), Boulder County Estate Planning Council (pres. 1972-73), Sacramento Estate Planning Council, Nat. Registry Fin. Planners (interview com.), Am. Soc. Agrl. Cons. (cert.). Contbr. articles to profl. jours. Club: Flatirons Country. Home: 92 Caballo Ct Boulder CO 80303 Office: 75 Manhattan Dr Boulder CO 80303

BAUGHMAN, GERALD VAN, tax consultant; b. Jesup, Iowa, Apr. 25, 1931; s. Edward Glen and Florence Pauline (Parker) B.; m. Virginia Ruth Barnes, Apr. 16, 1965. Student San Diego City Coll., 1954-56, San Diego State Coll., 1957-60. Enrolled agt. IRS. With acctg. dept. Gen. Dynamics Convair, 1952-63; pvt. tax cons., La Mesa, Calif., 1963—. Served with U.S. Army, 1951-52. Mem. Nat. Assn. Enrolled Agts., Nat. Assn. Pub. Accts., Nat. Notary Assn. Republican. Lutheran. Clubs: Masons, Shriners. Home: 164 Southern Rd El Cajon CA 92020 Office: 9019 Park Plaza Dr Suite K La Mesa CA 92041

BAUGHMAN, ROBERT A., JR., pharmaceutical researcher; b. Whitehall, Wis., Aug. 12, 1949; s. Robert A. and Charlene C. (Hronek) B.; m. Barbara Ann Neff, July 18, 1982; children: Katharine Neff, Madison Dunn. BS, Loyola U., Los Angeles, 1974; PharmD, U. Calif., San Francisco, 1978, PhD, 1982. Lic. pharmacist, Calif. Research chemist Lederle Labs., Pearl River, N.Y., 1982-83, sr. research scientist, 1983-85, chmn. continuing edn. commn., 1983-85; scientist Genentech Inc., South San Francisco, 1985—; lectr. Community Health Edn., San Francisco, 1975-82. Contbr. chpts. to books, articles to profl. jours. Served as sgt. U.S. Army, 1971-73. Mem. AAAS, Am. Assn. Pharm. Scientists, Am. Chem. Soc., Rho Chi, Phi Sigma Kappa(pres. 1973-74), Phi Pi Phi. Democrat. Roman Catholic. Avocations: family, running, golf, skiing. Office: Genentech Inc 460 Point San Bruno Blvd South San Francisco CA 94080

BAUGHN, ALFRED FAIRHURST, lawyer; b. Florence, Ariz., May 1, 1912; s. Otis James and Mary Holman (Fairhurst) B.; m. Barbara Hobbs, June 17, 1935; children—Brent F., Barbara Hendershot. A.B., U. So. Calif., 1935, J.D., 1938. Bar: Calif. 1938, Ariz. 1959, U.S. Dist. Ct. (so. dist.) Calif. 1939, U.S. Ct. Appeals (9th cir.) 1945, U.S. Dist. Ct. Ariz. 1948, U.S. Supreme Ct. 1967. With Title Guarantee & Trust, Los Angeles, 1937-41; corp. counsel Pacific Western Oil Co., 1942-43; practice, Los Angeles and Hollywood, Calif., 1943-56; Ariz. chief corp. counsel Garrett Corp., 1956-77, ret., 1977; sole practice, Ariz. and Calif., 1959—; Ariz. Assn. Industries spl. counsel utility rate hearings Ariz. Corp. Commn., 1977-80; investment counselor. Bd. dirs. EPI-HAB, Inc., 1974—. Adopted by Hopi Indian Chief Seletstewa and Squaw (2d Mesa), 1967; Pres. U. So. Calif. scholar, 1931-35. Mem. Calif. Bar Assn., Ariz. Bar Assn., Maricopa County Bar Assn., Los Angeles Philanthropic Found., Skull and Scales, Phi Alpha Delta (chpt. pres. 1938), Kappa Sigma (pres. Los Angeles alumni 1945, pres. Phoenix Alumni 1960), Phi Alpha Delta (pres. 1938—). Republican. Mem. Christian Ch. Clubs: Hollywood Exchange (pres. 1947); Kiwanis (Phoenix pres. club 1965); Kachina Klub (organizer, charter v.p. 1974), Hon. Order Ky. Cols. (pres. chpt. 1980—), Phoenix Teocali of Order Quetzalcoatl (pres. 1984), Ariz. Bola Tie Soc., Masons (Master 1953), Shriners (pote 1971), Jesters (bd. dirs. 1969), Internat. Gorillas (chief 1971—). Address: 5530 E Valley Vista Rd Phoenix AZ 85018

BAUGHN, JAMES WESLEY, mechanical engineering educator, flight instructor; b. San Francisco, Mar. 23, 1940; s. Earl G. and Bessie Lorena (Brauner) G.; m. Jo Jeanne Marshall, Dec. 17, 1960; children: Melanie, Lynnette. BS, U. Calif., Berkeley, 1962; MS, Stanford U., 1968, PhD, 1973. Registered profl. mech. engr., Calif. Sr. engr. Atomics Internat., Canoga Park, Calif., 1962-66; thermodynamics engr. Itek Corp., Palo Alto, Calif., 1966-69; teaching asst. Stanford (Calif.) U., 1969-73; prof. U. Calif., Davis, 1973. Co-editor: Proceedings of the 1976 Heat Transfer and Fluid Mechanics Institute, 1976; contbr. articles to profl. jours. Mem. ASME (Outstanding Teaching award, 1980, Outstanding Tchr. in Mech. Engring., 1975). Mem. Univ. Covenant Ch. Avocation: bicycling. Home: 1012 Oeste Dr Davis CA 95616 Office: U Calif Dept Mech Engring Davis CA 95616

BAUM, CARL EDWARD, electromagnetic theorist; b. Binghampton, N.Y., Feb. 6, 1940; s. George Theodore and Evelyn Monica (Bliven) B.; B.S. with honors, Calif. Inst. Tech., 1962, M.S., 1963, Ph.D., 1969. Commd. 2d lt. USAF, 1962, advanced through grades to capt., 1967, resigned, 1971, project officer Air Force Weapons Lab., Kirtland AFB, N.Mex., 1963-71, sr. scientist for electromagnetics, 1971—; U.S. del. to gen. assembly Internat. Union Radio Sci., Lima, Peru, 1975, Helsinki, Finland, 1978, Washington, 1981, Florence, Italy, 1984; mem. Commn. B U.S. Nat. Com., 1982—, Commn. E, 1975—. Commendation medal; recipient research and devel. award USAF, 1970, award Honeywell Corp., 1962. Fellow IEEE (Harry Diamond Meml. award, 1987, Richard R. Stoddart award, 1984); mem. Electromagnetics Soc. (pres. 1983-85), Sigma Xi, Tau Beta Pi. Roman Catholic. Author: (with others) Transient Electromagnetic Fields, 1976; Electromagnetic Scattering, 1978; Acoustic, Electromagnetic and Elastic Wave Scattering, 1980, Advanced Electrical and Optical Diagnostics, 1986; contbr. articles to profl. publs. Home: 5116 Eastern SE Unit D Albuquerque NM 87108 Office: Air Force Weapons Lab Kirtland AFB NM 87117

BAUM, NEAL PATRICK, research scientist; b. Ridley Park, Pa., Aug. 21, 1942; s. George Theodore and Evelyn Monica (Bliven) B.; student Antioch Coll., 1959-60; B.S. in Physics, Lemoyne Coll., 1965; M.S., Syracuse U., 1967, Ph.D., 1970; m. Martha Helen Coleman, June 12, 1971; children—George Patrick, Spencer Earl. Research asso. Syracuse U., 1965-70; postdoctoral research asso. AF Weapons Lab., Nat. Research Council, Kirtland AFB, N.Mex., 1970-71; mgr. instrumentation div. U. N.Mex. Engring. Research Inst., Albuquerque, 1971—; adv. bd. AF, Def. Nuclear Agy. Served with AUS, 1960-62. NSF Research Participation grantee, 1964; recipient invention awards, USAF, 1971. Mem. Laser Inst. Am., Sigma Xi. Republican. Roman Catholic. Research and publs. on solid state theory of metals, optics, instrumentation. Inventor in field. Home: 628 Amherst St SE Albuquerque NM 87106 Office: U NMex Campus PO Box 25 Albuquerque NM 87131

BAUM, WILLIAM ALVIN, astronomer; b. Toledo, Jan. 18, 1924; s. Earle Fayette and Mable (Teachout) B.; m. Ester Bru, June 27, 1961. B.A. summa cum laude, U. Rochester, 1943; Ph.D. magna cum laude, Calif. Inst. Tech., 1950. Physicist U.S. Naval Research Lab., Washington, 1946-49; astronomer Mt. Wilson and Palomar observatories, Pasadena, Calif., 1950-65; dir. Planetary Research Center, Lowell Obs., Flagstaff, Ariz., 1965—; adj. prof. astronomy Ohio State U., 1969—; adj. prof. physics No. Ariz. U., 1973—; cons. physics, astronomy, optics; cons. U.S. Army Research Office, Durham, N.C., 1967-74; vis. prof. Am. Astronomy Soc., 1961—; adv. com. Nat. Acad. Sci., 1958—; mem. optical instrumentation panel adv. Air Force, 1967-76; coms. and panels NSF and NASA Office Space Scis., 1967—; mem. NASA Viking Orbiter Imaging Team, 1970-79, NASA Space Telescope Camera Team, 1977—. Contbr. articles to tech. publs. Served to lt., jr. grade USNR, 1943-46. Guggenheim fellow, 1960-61. Mem. Am. Astron. Soc. (chmn. div. planetary scis. 1976-77), Royal Astron. Soc., Astron. Soc. Pacific, Internat. Astron. Union, Phi Beta Kappa, Sigma Xi, Theta Delta Chi. Home: PO Box 22154 Flagstaff AZ 86002 Office: Lowell Obs Flagstaff AZ 86001

BAUMAN, EARL WILLIAM, accountant, government official; b. Arcadia, Nebr., Jan. 30, 1916; s. William A. and Gracia M. (Jones) B.; B.S. with honors, U. Wyo., 1938; postgrad. Northwestern U., 1938-39; m. Margaret E. Blackman, Oct. 21, 1940 (dec. 1982); children—Carol Ann Bauman Ammerman. Earl William Jr. Acct., Haselmire, Cordle & Co., Casper, Wyo., 1939-42; asst. dir. finance VA, Chgo., 1946-49, chief acctg. group VA, Washington, 1949-52, supr. systems acctg. GAO, Washington, 1952-55; supervising auditor GAO, Washington, 1955-58; dir. finance, asst. dir. Directorate Acctg. and Financial Policy, Office Asst. Sec. Def., Washington, 1958-63; tech. asst. to comdr. AF Acctg. and Finance Ctr., Denver, 1963-73; mem. investigations staff Ho. of Reps. Appropriations Com., 1953-54; prof. acctg. Benjamin Franklin U., 1960-63; mem. exec. council Army Finance, 1963-64; dir. Real Estate Investment Corp., 1962-64; sr. ptnr. EMB Enterprises, 1973—; chmn. Acctg. Careers Council Colo., 1969-71. Chmn. Aurora Citizens Adv. Budget Com., 1975-76; chmn. fin. and taxation com. Denver Met. Study, 1976-78. Served with AUS, 1942-46; col. Res., now ret. C.P.A. Mem. Am. Inst. C.P.A.s, Wyo. Assn. C.P.A.s, Fed. Govt. Accts. Assn. (nat. v.p. 1972-73, pres. Denver 1973-74), Army Finance Assn., Am. Soc. Mil. Comptrollers, Denver Am. Soc. Mil. Comptrollers (pres. 1968-69), Citizens Band Radio Assn. (pres. 1963), Nat. Assn. Ret. Fed. Employees (Aurora 1072 pres. 1986-87), Alpha Kappa Psi, Beta Alpha Psi, Phi Kappa Phi. Club: Columbine Sertoma (pres. 1975-76). Home: 536 Newark Ct Aurora CO 80010

BAUMANN, EUGENE HEINZ, pilot; b. San Francisco, Sept. 2, 1950; s. Eugene Paul and Liane Helga (Lautenschlager) B.; m. Vicki Suzanne Nolan, Apr. 1, 1986. BS, U. Nev., 1976; cer. Cert. flight engr., flight instr., aircraft dispatcher, airline transport pilot. Pilot Golden Gate Airlines, Monterey, Calif., 1979-81, Commuter Airlines, Binghamton, N.Y., 1981-82; pilot and check airman Empire Airlines, Utica, N.Y., 1982-83; pilot Mid Pacific Airlines, Honolulu, 1983-84, Ryan Internat. Airlines, Wichita, Kans., 1984-85, Am. Airlines, San Francisco, 1985—; U.S. rep. Europa Cup Alpine Ski Circuit, 1974-75. Named to 2d Pl. Sr. Nat. Downhill Champion, 4th Place Combined, U.S. Ski Assn., 1977, 2d Nat. Ski Club Champion, U.S. Ski Assn., 1981, Sr. 1 Champion, Far West Ski Competition, 1981, 1st Pl. Internat. Masters Cup Giant Slalom, Squaw Valley, U.S., 1987; finalist 2d Slalom, 3d Overall, 3d Giant Slalom N.Am. Airline Ski Fedn., 1987, 8th Combined, 9th Giant Slalom World Airline Championships, Söll, Austria, 1987. Mem. Allied Pilots Assn., Future Aviation Profls. Am., Am. Airlines

Ski Team. Republican. Roman Catholic. Home: 3151 Shelter Creek Ln San Bruno CA 94066

BAUMBACH, HENRY DALE, psychologist, educator, consultant; b. Lodi, Calif., Sept. 13, 1944; s. Henry C. and Loma D. Baumbach; children: Catherine, Pamela, Christopher, Carrie. BA, U. Calif., Riverside, 1969, MA, 1973, PhD, 1975; MA in Sociology, Loma Linda U., 1970; postgrad. in psychology, U. Mo., 1970-71. Lic. psychologist, Calif. From instr. to asst. prof. psychology Loma Linda U., 1971-75; postdoctoral fellow in neurology Stanford U. Sch. Medicine, 1975-78, research assoc., 1978-79; clin. neuropsychologist Idaho Dept. Health and Welfare, 1979-81; staff psychologist Napa (Calif.) State Hosp. 1981-83; instr. psychology Ohlone Coll., Fremont, Calif., part-time 1978; spl. cons. clin. neuropsychology San Joaquin Gen. Hosp., Stockton, Calif., 1982—, Kentfield (Calif.) Med. Hosp., 1985— ; adj. asst. prof. Chapman Coll., 1982-83; adj. prof. U. Pacific, 1983-84; clin. neuropsychology cons. Los Medanos Community Hosp., Pittsburg, Calif., 1982-83; pvt. practice neuropsychology, Stockton, 1982—, Walnut Creek, Calif., 1986—; pres. Sierra Inst. Med. and Neuropsychology Inc., Walnut Creek, 1986—; cons. neuropsychology and behavioral medicine Kentfield Med. Hosp. and Ctr. for Occupational Health, Kentfield, Calif., 1986—; clin. dir. Pain Mgmt. Ctr., Mt. Diablo Hosp. Med. Ctr., Concord, Calif., 1983—; dir. psychlogy No. Calif. Rehab. Services, Pleasant Hill, 1985-86. Recipient Chancellor's Patent Fund award U. Calif., Riverside, 1974; NSF fellow, 1968. Mem. Am. Psychol. Assn., AAAS. Democrat. Contbr. sci. articles to profl. jours. Home: PO Box 540 Concord CA 94522 Office: 401 Gregory Ln Suite 74 Pleasant Hill CA 94523

BAUMEISTER, DONALD E., social worker; b. Los Angeles, Mar. 15, 1950; s. Arthur Charles and Genevieve Margaret (Moore) B.; m. Toni Starke, Feb. 23, 1974; children: Brandi Elizabeth, Leah Marie. BA in Sociology, Calif. State U., Fullerton, 1971; MSW, U. Hawaii, 1975; JD, Western State U., Fullerton, 1980; MPA, Calif. State U., Long Beach, 1983. Diversion counselor U. Calif., Irvine, 1976-77; social worker, service chief Orange County Calif., 1977-85; pvt. practice specializing in personal and family counseling Pomona, Calif., 1984-85, Pediatric, Adolescent, Adult Psychol. Services, Santa Ana, Calif., 1984—; program dir. Western Youth Services, Fullerton, 1985; instr. Calif. State U., Fullerton, 1981-82; field work and classroom instr. U. So. Calif., Los Angeles, 1984—; cons. Riverside County Calif., 1984, Orange County Calif., 1986—. Contbr. articles to profl. jours. Served to capt. USMC, 1971-74, Vietnam. Mem. Nat. Assn. Social Workers (register of clin. social workers), Am. Soc. Pub. Adminstrn. Roman Catholic. Avocations: reading, marathons, triathlons. Office: Pediatric Adolescent Adult Psych Services Santa Ana CA 92705

BAUMGARTNER, ALLAN RODNEY, computer company executive; b. N.Y.C., May 27, 1938; s. John Herbert and Claire Regina (Strobele) B.; B.S., Carnegie Inst. Tech., 1960; m. Dolores Zalewski, Dec. 4, 1975; children—Yvette Selena, Brendon Allan Hans. Product mgr. Westinghouse Electric Corp., Sunnyvale, Calif., 1966-67, data processing devel. mgr., 1967-71; data communications designer Pacific Telephone Co., San Francisco, 1971-74, internal cons., 1974-78; cons. to advanced communications system AT&T, Morristown, N.J., 1976-77; dir. tech. strategy Nat. Semicondr. Corp., San Diego, 1979-80, dir. software mktg. subs. Nat. Advanced Systems, Inc., Mountain View, Calif., 1980-83, pres. Gyrus Systems Corp., San Diego, 1983-84; v.p. sales and mktg. System Specialists and Cons., 1984-86; pres. Internat. Computer Contracting Corp., San Jose, Calif., 1986—; cons. mgmt. and data processing. Served to capt. C.E., U.S. Army, 1960-65. Mem. Data Processing Mgmt. Assn., IEEE, Assn. Data Processing Service Orgns. Republican. Home: 4221 Quimby Rd San Jose CA 95148 Office: Internat Computer Contracting Corp 4340 Almaden Expressway San Jose CA 95118

BAUMGARTNER, DAVID MICHAEL, forester; b. Pontiac, Mich., June 25, 1943; s. Leo Anthony and Marguerite Marie (Weber) B.; m. Delores Bernice Brandon, Feb. 19, 1965; children: Craig David, Michael James, Patrick John. BS in Forestry, Mich. State U., 1965, MS in Forestry, 1966, PhD in Forestry, 1969. Extension forester Wash State U., Pullman, 1964—, asst. prof., 1969-74, assoc. prof., 1974-81, prof., 1981—; mem. state and pvt. forestry adv. com. USDA, Washington, 1975-79. Editor various symposium proceedings. Mem. Colton (Wash.) Town Council, 1971-85. Recipient cert. USDA Extension Service, 1985, Pres.' Faculty Excellence award Wash. State U., 1986. Mem. Soc. Am. Foresters (chmn. Inland Empire sect. 1978, Outstanding Communicator award Inland Empire sect. 1986), Northwest Sci. Assn., Sigma Xi, Alpha Zeta, Xi Sigma Pi. Roman Catholic. Lodge: KC. Avocations: hunting, photography, youth sports. Home: SE 520 Crestview Pullman WA 99163 Office: Wash State U 131 Johnson Hall Pullman WA 99164-6412

BAUMGARTNER, DONALD JOHN, environmental engineer, researcher; b. Chgo., Aug. 16, 1933; s. Harold Eugene and Catherine (Maher) B.; m. Therese Rita O'Connell; children: Donald, Robert, James, Beth, Thomas, Julie. BS in Sanitary Engring., U. Ill., 1955; MS in Sanitary Engring., MIT, 1958; PhD in Civil Engring., Oreg. State U., 1967. Registered profl. engr., Ill. Commd. ensign USPHS, 1955, advanced through grades to comdr., 1965, resigned, 1967; project engr. research and devel. EPA, Cin., 1962-67; project leader research and devel. EPA, Corvallis, Oreg., 1967-69, chief ecology br. research and devel., 1969-75, dir. marine div. research and devel., 1975-80; dir. Pacific div. research and devel. EPA, Newport, Oreg., 1980—; dir. U.S./USSR Marine Research Project, EPA, Washington and Moscow, 1980-85. Editor: Chemical and Physical Processes of Marine Disposal, 1986. Bd. dirs. Carmel Foulweather Sanitation Dist., Otter Rock, Oreg., 1982-86, Otter Rock Water Dist., 1982-86; chmn. Newport Sch. Com., 1984-85. Recipient Bronze medal EPA, 1975, Silver medal EPA, 1985, Spl. Achievement award EPA, 1985. Mem. AAAS, Water Pollution Control Fedn., Pacific Estuarine Research Soc., Sigma Xi. Club: Toastmasters (Cin. and Fairbanks, Alaska). Avocations: long distance running, white water boating. Office: EPA Marine Sci Ctr Newport OR 97365

BAUMHARDT, ROBERT JAMES, nuclear power executive; b. Fond du Lac, Wis., Aug. 18, 1940; s. Robert Joseph and Grace Charlot (Decker) B.; m. Jean Theres Meyer, Dec. 3, 1966; children: Robert James II, Cara Elizabeth. BS in Math., Marquette U., 1966. Enlisted USN, 1959, advanced through grades to lt. comdr., 1974, ret., 1980; sr. test engr. Westinghouse-Hanford Co., Richland, Wash., 1980-81, mgr. refueling fast flux test facility, 1981-82, mgr. refueling, examination and decontamination services, 1982-83, staff mgr. fast flux test facility ops., 1983-84, mgr. fast flux test facility ops., 1984—. Pres. sch. bd. Christ the King Sch., Richland, 1982-86, sch. bd. Diocese of Yamika, Wash., 1985—; mem. allocation com. United Way of Benton/Franklin Counties, Wash., 1984—. Decorated Legion of Merit. Mem. ASME (assoc.), Am. Nuclear Soc. Roman Catholic. Avocations: skiing, golf, hiking, backpacking, reading. Office: Westinghouse-Hanford Co PO Box 1970 Richland WA 99352

BAWDEN, GARTH LAWRY, museum director; b. Truro, Eng., Dec. 31, 1939; s. Richard Thomas and Susan Elizabeth Olga (Lawry) B.; m. Margaret Ruth Greet, Dec. 21, 1963 (div. Mar. 1978); children: Michael Greet, Teona Mary, Kerenza Elizabeth; m. Elaine Louise Comack, Oct. 26, 1978; children: Jonathan Richard, Rebecca Lawry. Diploma in phys. medicine, West Middlesex Sch. Phys. Medicine, Isleworth, Eng., 1961; BA in Art History, U. Oreg., 1970; PhD in Anthropology, Harvard U., 1977. Assoc. in archaeology Harvard U., Cambridge, Mass., 1977-81, instr., 1980-85, asst., acting dir. Peabody Mus., 1980-85; assoc. prof. U. N.Mex., Albuquerque, 1985—, dir. Maxwell Mus., 1985—; dir. field research project Harvard U., Galindo, Peru, 1971-74, dir. field survey Peabody Mus., Saudi Arabian Archaeol. Survey, 1978-80; field supr. Cuntisuyu Project, Moquegua, Peru, 1983-86. Author: (with C. Conrad) The Andean Heritage, 1982; contbr. articles on archaeology to profl. jours. Fellow Woodrow Wilson, U. Oreg., 1970, Tinker, Harvard U., 1983. Mem. Soc. Am. Archaeology, Assn. Field Archaeology, Assn. Sci. Mus. Dirs., Current Anthropology (assoc.), Phi Beta Kappa, Sigma Xi. Home: 6 Applewood Ln NW Los Ranchos de Albuquerque NM 87107 Office: Univ N M Maxwell Mus Anthropology Albuquerque NM 87131

BAX, RONALD F(RANK), electrical engineer, consultant; b. Niagara Falls, N.Y., Oct. 30, 1941; s. Frank Lou and Margaret (Hallenbeck) B.; m. Gail Ann Barber, Aug. 26, 1961; children: Keith Robert, Bronwyn Lee. BA in Physics, George Mason U., 1977; postgrad., Johns Hopkins. U., 1979. Engring. mgr. Acuity Systems, Reston, Va., 1972-75; prin. engr. Pfizer Med. Systems, Columbia, Md., 1975-81; v.p. Ear Three Systems, Mclean, Va., 1981-86; cons. Diasonics Magnetic Resonance Imaging Inc., South San Francisco, Calif., 1981-82, engring. mgr., 1982-86; dir. Imatron Inc., South San Francisco, 1986—; cons. Elscint, Columbia, 1981-82, in field, 1982—. Inventor jogging computer, laser lensmeter, scanning apparatus, electrocardiographic storage, dark current compensation, method for controlling X-ray tube emissions, gradient power supply. Served with USAF, 1960-64. Mem. Am. Phys. Soc., Packard Club Am., No. Calif. Packards. Republican. Roman Catholic. Avocation: antiques. Home: 554 Forest Ave Palo Alto CA 94301 Office: Imatron Inc 389 Oyster Point Blvd South San Francisco CA 94080

BAXTER, GENE KENNETH, engineering manager; b. Emmett, Idaho, Sept. 4, 1939; s. Glen Wilton and Mable Velhelmina (Casper) B., Sr.; A.A. in Mech. Engring. (scholar), Boise Jr. Coll., 1959; B.S. in Mech. Engring., U. Idaho, 1961; M.S. in Aero. Engring. (NDEA fellow), Syracuse U., 1966, Ph.D. in Mech. Engring., 1971; m. Laraine Marie Mitchell, Jan. 20, 1968; children—Gretchen Lynn, Aaron Gregory. Engr. Pratt & Whitney Aircraft Co., East Hartford, Conn., 1961; teaching and research asst. Syracuse (N.Y.) U., 1962-67; engr. Galson & Galson Cons. Engrs., Syracuse, 1968; sr. mech. engr., staff engr. electronic systems div. Gen. Electric Co., Syracuse, 1968-77, advanced project mgr. mech. design engring. mgr., space div. Daytona Beach, Fla., 1977-82; engring. dept. head Schlumberger Tech. Corp., Rosharon, Tex., 1982-83; mgr. engring., downhole services div. Exploration Logging, Inc. div. Baker Internat. Corp., Sacramento, 1983-85; mgr. handling qualities sect. simulation systems dept. McDonnell Douglas Helicopter Co., Mesa, Ariz., 1985-87, mgr. projects mgmt. engring and tng. simulation dept., 1987—; dir. mech. projects creating visual simulation and tng. systems, nuclear power controls, shipboard digital control systems; dir. elec./mech. projects creating equipment for measurement, analysis and control of wellhead, formation and drilling parameters for oil well services industry; dir. projects creating software models of flight, control and aircraft subsystem performance characteristics for helicopter simulation and training systems; tchr. refresher course N.Y. State Profl. Engrs., Syracuse, 1975-76. Chmn. fin. and stewardship com. United Ch. of Christ, Liverpool, N.Y., 1974-77, chmn. bd. trustees, 1977; ruling elder Ormond Beach (Fla.) Presbyn. Ch., 1979-82, chmn. stewardship com., 1979-80, pres. corp., 1980-82, chmn. fin. com., 1981-82. Recipient design award Machinery Mag., 1961; Raymond J. Briggs award Idaho Bd. Engring. Examiners, 1961; profl. lic. engr., N.Y. Mem. IEEE (sr.; treas. Daytona sect. 1978-79, chmn. 1979-80), ASME, Am. Helicopter Soc., Research Soc. of Am., Sigma Xi, Phi Kappa Phi, Tau Beta Pi. Speaker numerous profl. confs.; contbr. over 30 research papers in field. Home: 1243 N Norwalk Mesa AZ 85205

BAY, BEN, city mayor. m. Eleanor Bay. Formerly with Rockwell Internat., Anaheim, Calif.; mem. city council City of Anaheim, 1979—, mayor, 1986—. Council liaison to fin. audit com., redevel. agy. Anaheim Stadium; chmn. bd. dirs. Eastern/Foothill Transp. Corridor Joint Powers Authority; mem. redevel. commn. City of Anaheim, 1976-79, chmn. charter rev. com., 1978; active community affairs, 1970—. Office: Office of Mayor City of Anaheim PO Box 3222 Anaheim CA 92803

BAYDA, EDWARD DMYTRO, judge; b. Alvena, Sask, Can., Sept. 9, 1931; s. Dmytro Andrew and Mary (Bilinski) B.; m. Marie-Thérèse Yvonne Gagne, May 28, 1953; children: Paula, Christopher, Margot, Marie-Therèse, Sheila, Kathryn. B.A., U. Sask., 1951, LL.B. cum laude, 1953. Bar: Sask. 1954. Barrister, solicitor Regina, Sask., 1953-72; sr. ptnr. Bayda, Halvorson, Scheibel & Thompson, 1966-72; justice Ct. Queen's Bench for Sask., Regina, 1972-74, Ct. Appeal for Sask., Regina, 1974-81; chief justice Sask., Regina, 1981—. Mem. Law Soc. Sask. (past bencher), Can. Bar Assn. (past Sask. chmn. civil justice sect.), Regina Bar Assn. Roman Catholic. Club: Assiniboia (past. bd. dirs.). Home: 9 Turnbull Pl, Regina, SK Canada Office: Ct Appeal for Sask, Court House, 2425 Victoria Ave, Regina, SK Canada S4P 3V7

BAYER, WILLIAM, photgraphy, educator; b. Norwalk, Calif., May 22, 1930; s. Earle Seymoure and Florence (Ebbert) Fitzgerald; m. Jeanette Marie Laverman, Sept. 1, 1951 (div. 1972); children: Cheryl, Arthur, Geoffrey; m. Mary Virginia Fejes, Mar. 27, 1986. BA in Art History with distinction, Ariz. State U., 1959, MFA, 1966; MA, U. Ky., 1964. Prof. photography U. Ky., Lexington, 1966-68; cons. CBS, Hollywood, Calif., 1968; prof. Rio Hondo Coll., Whittier, Calif., 1968—. Author, photographer Victorian Tomb Sculpture, 1967. Bd. dirs. Downey (Calif.) Mus. Art, 1971-73; bd. dirs. Los Angeles Ctr. Photographic Studies, 1973-75. Served with USN, 1948-52. Mem. Friends of Photography, Los Angeles County Mus. Art, San Diego Mus. Photography. Office: Rio Hondo Coll Whittier CA 90608

BAYLES, DANELLA ALICE, dance instructor; b. Red Bluff, Calif., Mar. 31, 1947; d. Daniel George and Elva Rita (Stone) B. BA in Drama and Dance, Calif. State U., Chico, 1974; MA in Theatre Arts, Calif. State U., 1980. Cert. dance instr., Calif. Instr. Mercy Acad., Red Bluff, Calif., 1974-78; dance instr. Shasta Coll., Redding, Calif., 1978—; counselor, instr. Stepping Stones, Redding, 1985—; cons. Victor Orgns., Redding, 1986—; designer Masquerade Costumes, Redding, 1983—. Author: Fancy Free and On the Town, 1980. Dir. Red Bluff Summer Theatre Co., 1975-78. Mem. Dance Masters Am., NEA, Calif. Teacher's Assn., Sta. KIXE Ednl. TV, Phi Kappa Phi. Mem. Eckankar Ch. Avocation: costume design. Office: Shasta Coll PE Dance Dept PO Box 6006 Redding CA 96099

BAYLIFF, WILLIAM HENRY, fishery biologist; b. Annapolis, Md., Aug. 29, 1928; s. William Howard and Nelle (Jones) B.; m. Norma Jean York, Jan. 2, 1969. AB, Western Md. Coll., 1949; MS, U. Wash., 1954, PhD, 1965. Biologist Wash. Dept. Fish, Seattle, 1952-54, 57-58; scientist Inter-Am. Tropical Tuna Commn., Republic of Panama, 1958-63, La Jolla, Calif., 1963-67, 1969—; biologist FAO U.N., Republic of Panama, 1967-68; cons. in field. Contbr. articles to profl. jours. Served with U.S. Army, 1955-56. Fellow Am. Inst. Fishery Research Biologists (W.F. Thompson award, 1969); mem. AAAS, Am. Fisheries Soc., Sigma Xi. Office: Inter-Am Tropical Tuna Commn La Jolla CA 92093

BAYLOR, ELGIN, professional basketball executive; b. Washington, DC, Sept. 16, 1934. Educ., Seattle U. Professional basketball player Los Angeles (formerly Minneapolis) Lakers, 1958-71; now exec. v.p. for basketball operns. Los Angeles Clippers, NBA. Office: care Los Angeles Clippers 3939 S Figueroa St Los Angeles CA 90037 *

BAYM, GORDON ALAN, physicist, educator; b. N.Y.C., July 1, 1935; s. Louis and Lillian B.; m. Lillian Hartmann; children—Nancy, Geoffrey, Michael, Carol. A.B., Cornell U., 1956; A.M., Harvard U., 1957, Ph.D., 1960. Fellow Universitetets Institut for Teoretisk Fysik, Copenhagen, Denmark, 1960-62; lectr. U. Calif., Berkeley, 1962-63; prof. physics U. Ill., Urbana, 1963—; vis. prof. U. Tokyo and U. Kyoto, 1968, Nordita, Copenhagen, 1970, 76, Niels Bohr Inst., Copenhagen, 1976, U. Nagoya, 1979; vis. scientist Academia Sinica, China, 1979; mem. adv. bd. Inst. Theoretical Physics, Santa Barbara, Calif., 1978-83; mem. subcom. theoretical physics, physics adv. com. NSF, 1980-81, mem. phys. adv. com., 1982-85; Mem. nuclear sci. adv. com. Dept. of Energy/NSF, 1982-86. Author: Lectures on Quantum Mechanics, 1969, Neutron Stars, 1970, Neutron Stars and the Properties of Matter at High Density, 1977, (with L.P. Kadanoff) Quantum Statistical Mechanics, 1962; assoc. editor: Nuclear Physics; mem. editorial bd. Procs. Nat. Acad. Scis., 1986—. Recipient Alexander von Humboldt Found. sr. U.S. Scientist award, 1983; fellow Am. Acad. Arts and Scis.; Alfred P. Sloan Found. research fellow, 1965-68; NSF postdoctoral fellow, 1960-62. Fellow Am. Phys. Soc. (exec. com. Div. History of Physics), AAAS; mem. Am. Astron. Soc., Internat. Astron. Union., Nat. Acad. Scis.

BAZILWICH, PAUL, JR., engineering executive; b. Rostraver Twp., Pa., Jan. 21, 1933; s. Paul and Anna (Lastoka) B.; m. LaVerne Madaline Malinchak, July 31, 1955; children: Paul R., Ann E., Lawrence A. BS, U.S. Mil. Acad., 1955; MS, U. Ill., 1961. Registered profl. civil engr. Commd. 2d lt. U.S. Army, 1955, advanced through grades to col., 1976, ret., 1982; v.p. Sverdrup Corp., San Francisco, 1982-87, Hall-Kimbrell Environ. Services, Inc., Oakland, Calif., 1987—. Editor: Engineer Operations, 1976. Mem. ASCE, Soc. Am. Mil. Engrs. (pres. 1976), Am. Def. Preparedness Assn., Am. Cons. Engrs. Councl, Am. Pub. Works Assn., San Francisco C. of C. Club: Ft. Mason (San Francisco). Avocations: golf, hunting, fishing. Home: 2670 Round Hill Dr Alamo CA 94507 Office: Hall-Kimbrell Environ Services 505 14th St Suite 1090 Oakland CA 94612

BAZOVSKY, IGOR, sci. cons.; b. Lucenec, Slovakia, Apr. 13, 1914; s. Louis and Bozena (Fajnor) B.; student Tech. U., Berlin, Germany, 1932-35; Dipl. Ing. in Elec. Engring., German Tech. U., Prague, Czechoslovakia, 1939; m. Drahomira Machacek, Oct. 17, 1939; children—Igor, Eva (Mrs. Donald Booth), John-Louis. Came to U.S., 1957, naturalized, 1962. Engaged in elec. power engring., Europe, 1939-57; research engr. Boeing, Seattle, 1957-59; mgr. reliability engring. United Control Corp., Seattle, 1959-62; chief reliability analyst Raytheon Missile Div., Bedford, Mass., 1962-63; systems reliability mgr. Litton Industries, Woodland Hills, Calif., 1963-66; dir. sci. and cons. div. Genge Industries, Inc., Sherman Oaks, Calif., 1966-69; pres., chief scientist Igor Bazovsky & Assos., Inc., 1969—. Recipient Reliability award IEEE. Am. Soc. for Quality Control, 1963. Registered profl. engr., Wash., Calif. Mem. IEEE Navy League U.S., Am. Nuclear Soc., Am. Def. Preparedness Assn., fellow Inst. Advancement of Engring. Nat. Nat. Soc. Profl. Engrs.; Republican. Lutheran. Author: Reliability Theory and Practice, 1961; co-author, editor: Maintainability Engineering Theory and Practice, 1976. Home: 20305 Oxnard St Woodland Hills CA 91367

BEACH, ARTHUR O'NEAL, lawyer; b. Albuquerque, Feb. 8, 1945; s. William Pearce and Vivian Lucille (Kronig) B.; B.B.A., U. N.Mex., 1967, J.D., 1970; m. Alex Clark Doyle, Sept. 12, 1970; 1 son, Eric Kronig. Admitted to N.Mex. bar, 1970; assoc. firm Smith & Ransom, Albuquerque, 1970-74; assoc. firm Keleher & McLeod, Albuquerque, 1974-75, ptnr., 1976-78, shareholder firm Keleher & McLeod, P.A., Albuquerque, 1978—; teaching asst. U. N. Mex., 1970. Bd. editors Natural Resources Jour., 1968-70. Mem. State Bar N.Mex. (unauthorized practice of law com., adv. opinions com., med.-legal panel, legal-dental-osteo.-podiatry com.), Am., Albuquerque (dir. 1978-82) bar assns., State Bar Specialization Bd. Democrat. Mem. Christian Sci. Ch. Home: 2015 Dietz Pl NW Albuquerque NM 87107 Office: PO Drawer AA Albuquerque NM 87103

BEADLE, CHARLES WILSON, mechanical engineering educator; b. Beverly, Mass., Jan. 24, 1930; s. Thomas and Jean (Wilson) B.; m. Dorothy Elizabeth Struyk, May 5, 1956; children: Steven C., Sara E., Gordon S. BS, Tufts U., 1951; MSE, U. Mich., 1954; PhD, Cornell U., 1961. Registered mech. engr., Calif., Mich. Research engr. Gen. Motors Research Labs., Detroit, 1951-54, RCA Research Labs., Princeton, N.J., 1954-57; prof. mech. engring. U. Calif., Davis, 1961—. Contbr. articles to profl. jours. Fellow ASME. Home: 420 E 12th St Davis CA 95616 Office: U Calif Davis Dept Mech Engring Davis CA 95616

BEADLE, GEORGE WELLS, biologist, emeritus educator; b. Wahoo, Nebr., Oct. 22, 1903; s. Chauncey Elmer and Hattie (Albro) B.; m. Marion Cecile Hill, Aug. 22, 1928 (div. 1953); 1 son, David; m. Muriel Barnett, Aug. 12, 1953; 1 stepson, Redmond James Barnett. B.S., U. Nebr., 1926, M.S., 1927, D.Sc., 1949; Ph.D., Cornell U., 1931; M.A., Oxford (Eng.) U., 1958, D.Sc. (hon.), 1959; D.Sc., Yale U., 1947, Northwestern U., 1952, Rutgers U., 1954, Kenyon Coll., 1955, Wesleyan U., 1956, Birmingham U., 1959, Pomona Coll., 1961, Lake Forest Coll., 1962, U. Rochester, 1963, U. Ill., 1963, Brown U., 1964, Kans. State U., 1964, U. Pa., 1964, Wabash Coll., 1966, Syracuse U., 1967, Loyola U., Chgo., 1970, Hanover Coll., 1971, Eureka Coll., 1972, Butler U., 1973, Gustavus Adolphus Coll., 1975, Ind. State U., 1976; LL.D., U. Calif. at Los Angeles, 1962, U. Miami, 1963, Brandeis U., 1963, Johns Hopkins U., 1966, Beloit Coll., 1966, U. Mich., 1969; D.H.L., Jewish Theol. Sem. Am., 1966, DePaul U., 1969, U. Chgo., 1969, Canisius Coll., 1969, Knox Coll., 1969, Carroll Coll., 1971, Roosevelt U., 1971; D. Pub. Service, Ohio No. U., 1970. Teaching asst. Cornell U., 1926-27, experimentalist, 1927-31; NRC fellow Calif. Inst. Tech., 1931-33, instr., 1933-35; guest investigator Institut de Biologie, physico-chimique, Paris, 1935; asst. prof. genetics Harvard U., 1936-37; prof. biology (genetics) Stanford U., 1937-47; prof. biology and chmn. div. biology Calif. Inst. Tech., 1946-60, acting dean faculty, 1960-61; pres., trustee, prof. biology U. Chgo., 1961-68, pres. emeritus, William E. Wrather Distinguished Service prof., hon. trustee, 1969-75, prof. emeritus, 1975; dir. Inst. Biomed. Research, AMA, Chgo., 1968-70; Eastman vis. prof. Oxford U., 1958-59; mem. Pres.'s Sci. Adv. Council, 1960; hon. pres. 12th Internat. Congress Genetics, 1968. Author: (with Alfred H. Sturtevant) An Introduction to Genetics, 1939, Genetics and Modern Biology, 1963, (with Muriel B. Beadle) The Language of Life, 1966 (Edison award best sci. book for youth 1967). Hon. trustee Mus. Sci. and Industry, Chgo.; trustee Calif. Inst. Tech., 1969-75; adv. bd. Robert A. Welch Found., 1971—. Recipient Lasker award, 1950, Dyer award, 1951, Emil C. Hansen prize Denmark, 1953; Albert Einstein Commemorative award in sci., 1958; Nobel Prize in medicine and physiology (with Edward L. Tatum and Joshua Lederberg), 1958; Am. Cancer Soc. award, 1959; Kimber Genetics award, 1960; Priestley Meml. award, 1967; Donald Forsha Jones medal, 1972; Order St. Olaf. Mem. Nat. Acad. Scis. (council 1969-72), Am. Philos. Soc., Royal Soc., Japan Acad. (hon.), Instituto Lombardo di Scienze e Lettre (Milan), AAAS (pres. 1946), Am. Acad. Arts and Scis., Genetics Soc. Am. (pres. 1955), Genetical Soc. Gt. Britain, Indian Soc. Genetics and Plant Breeding, Indian Nat. Sci. Acad. (hon.), Chgo. Hort. Soc. (pres. 1968-71, trustee 1971-76), Danish Royal Acad. Scis., Phi Beta Kappa (hon.), Sigma Xi. Research on genetics, cytology and origin Indian corn (Zea), genetics and devel. fruit fly Drosophila, biochem. genetics of bread mold Neurospora. Home: 900 E Harrison Apt D-33 Pomona CA 91767

BEADLES, VERNON L., airline pilot, real estate investor, small business executive; b. Huron, S.D., June 24, 1933; s. Harry Ray and Hilda Johnson; m. Bernadine Schoof, Apr. 27, 1957; children—Bruce Allen, David Lawrence. Student pub. schs. Commd. 2d lt. U.S. Air Force, 1955, advanced through grades to lt. col., 1973; fighter pilot, 1955-65; mem. Mich. Air NG, 1965-74; pilot United Airlines, 1965—; pres. Nor Cal Air-Vend, San Francisco, 1986—; pvt. real estate investor, 1971—. Decorated Air Force Commendation medal. Mem. Air Force Assn., Airline Pilots Assn., Tri-County Apt. Assn. Republican. Lutheran. Home: 15768 Hidden Hill Pl Los Gatos CA 95030 Office: United Airlines San Francisco Internat Airport San Francisco CA 94128

BEAKE, JOHN, professional football team executive. m. Marcia Beake; children: Jerilyn, Chip, Christopher. Grad., Trenton (N.J.) State Coll.; M degree, Pa. State U. Asst. coach Pa. State U., 1961-62, Kansas City Chiefs, NFL, 1968-74, New Orleans Saints, NFL, 1976-77; offensive coordinator Colo. State U., 1974-76; dir. profl. personnel Denver Broncos, NFL, 1979-83, dir. football ops., 1983-84, asst. gen. mgr., 1984-85, gen. mgr., 1985—. Office: Denver Broncos 5700 Logan St Denver CO 80216 *

BEAKLEY, GEORGE CARROLL, JR., mechanical engineering educator; b. Marble Falls, Tex., Feb. 3, 1922; s. George Carrol Sr. and Tessielea (Poage) B.; m. Oletha B. Zeh, Aug. 4, 1944; children: George Carroll III, William Don, Martha Ann, David Lee. BSME, Tex. Tech. U., 1947; MSME, U. Tex., 1952; PhD, Okla. State U., 1956. Registered profl. engr. Ariz., Tex., Okla. Assoc. prof. engring. Tarleton State U., Stephenville, Tex., 1947-53; design engr. Bell Helicopter Co., Hurst, Tex., 1953-54; devel. engr. Airesearch Mfg. Co., Phoenix, 1956; prof. and assoc. dean Ariz. State U., Tempe, 1956—; ednl. cons. Tempe, 1960—; mem. bd. accreditation for engring. and tech., N.Y.C., 1972—. Author: (textbooks) Elementary Problems in Engineering, 1949, Design: Serving the Needs of Man, 1974, Architectural Drawing and Design, 1984, Engineering: An Introduction to a Creative Profession, 5th edit., 1986, 25 others. Served with U.S. Army, 1943-45. Recipient Faculty Achievement award Ariz. State U., 1972. Fellow ASME (nat. dir. 1980), Am. Soc. Engring. Edn. (Frank Oppenheimer award 1968, Chester F. Carlson award 1973, Western Electric award 1976); mem. Nat. Soc. Profl. Engrs. (state pres. and nat. v.p. 1964), Inst. Indsl. Engrs. (v.p. chpt. 1957), ASHRAE. Democrat. Baptist. Avocations: fishing, tennis, oil painting. Home: 511 E Concordia Dr Tempe AZ 85282 Office: Ariz State U Coll Engring Tempe AZ 85287

BEAL, BRENDA ULRICH, educator; b. Lockport, N.Y., Nov. 9, 1938; d. Howard Louis and Mary Ruth (Whalen) Ulrich; m. David Russell Beal, Aug. 20, 1960 (div.). Tchr. Newark (N.Y.) Central Sch. Dist., 1960-61, Phelps (N.Y.) Central Sch. Dist., 1961-67; tchr. Union Springs (N.Y.) Central Sch. Dist., 1967-68, coordinator title I, 1968-71; grad. asst. reading ctr.

Ariz. State U., Tempe, 1971-73; prof. dept. edn. Humboldt State U., Arcata, Calif., 1973—; prof. No. Ariz. U., Flagstaff, summers 1980, 81, 83; cons. in field. Mem. Citizens Adv. Bd. for Site Decisions, 1981, 82. Mem. AAUW, Internat. Reading Assn., Humboldt Reading Council, Assn. for Supervision and Curriculum Devel., Phi Delta Kappa. Office: HGH Humboldt State U 202C Arcata CA 95521

BEAL, MERRILL DAVID, conservationist, museum director; b. Richfield, Utah, June 26, 1926; s. Merrill Dee and Bessy (Neill) B.; m. Jean Lorraine Wood, Feb. 24, 1947; children: John David, James Merrill. B.A., Idaho State Coll., 1950; M.S., Utah State U., 1952. Park ranger, naturalist Yellowstone Nat. Park, 1953-60; chief park naturalist Grand Canyon Nat. Park, 1960-69; asst. supt. Great Smoky Mountains Nat. Park, Gatlinburg, Tenn., 1969-72; assoc. regional dir. Midwest region Nat. Park Service, Omaha, 1972-75, regional dir., 1975-78; supt. Gt. Smoky Mountains Nat. Park, Gatlinburg, Tenn., 1978-83; asst. dir. Ariz.-Sonora Desert Mus., Tucson, 1983—. Author: Grand Canyon, the Story Behind the Scenery, 1967. Mem. bd. Grand Canyon Sch., 1964-69. Served with USN, 1944-46. Recipient Meritorious Service award U.S. Dept. Interior, 1975. Mem. AAAS, Wildlife Soc., Southwest Parks and Monument Assn. (bd. dirs. 1975-78), Sigma Xi. Office: Arizona-Sonora Desert Museum Tucson AZ 85743

BEALS, MARK ALLEN, research labortory administrator; b. Amesbury, Mass., Nov. 19, 1961; s. Richard A. and Patricia V. (Clement) B. BSChemE, U. Lowell, 1983. Lab. technician Plasma-Therm, Kresson, N.J., 1982, mem. tech. staff, 1983-84; lab. mgr. Plasma-Therm, San Jose, Calif., 1984-86; engring. supr. Applied Materials, Santa Clara, Calif., 1986—. Mem. Am. Vacuum Soc., Am. Inst. Chem. Engrs., Tau Beta Pi. Republican. Roman Catholic. Avocations: backpacking, skiing, bicycling, rocketry. Office: Applied Materials 3050 Bowers Ave M/S 0807 Santa Clara CA 95052-8039

BEALS, MARK GRADEN, educator; b. Irvona, Pa., Aug. 11, 1936; s. George Bylle and Leila Elzeda (Eidell) B. B.A., Lycoming Coll., 1956; M.A., U. Hawaii, 1958; Ph.D., U. Ariz., 1968. Psychologist Yakima, Wash., 1961-64; instr. psychology Yakima Valley Coll., 1961-64; asst. prof., coordinator program in spl. edn. No. Ariz. U., Flagstaff, 1966-69; prof., dir. undergrad. curricula, coordinator student teaching and programs for gifted U. Nev., Las Vegas, 1969-85, asst. dean Coll. Edn., 1985—; cons. State of Ariz. Dists. 15, 16, 22, 1970-79; founder cons. New Horizons Ctr. for Learning, Las Vegas, 1971—; cons. and lectr. in field. Author: Handbook for Teachers of the Culturally Deprived, 1966, Laughter of Children, 1968 (film); contbr. articles to profl. jours. Pres. So. Nev. Epilepsy Assn., Nev. Epilepsy Assn., 1972-75; mem. Com. on Rehab., 1969; mem. Gov.'s Com. on Gifted, 1975, Com. on Accreditation, 1981—, others. Served with U.S. Army, 1944-47. Recipient Gov.'s award State of Nev., 1968; Epilepsy Found. leadership award, 1975; award for leadership to children Ariz. Assn. Chronic Lung Disease, 1977. Fellow Menninger Found.; mem. Am. Psychol. Assn., Western Psychol. Assn., Council for Exceptional Children, AAAS, Edni. Research Assn., Assn. for Retarded Citizens, Orton Soc. Humanistic Psychology Assn., Mensa. Republican. Office: Univ Nevada Coll of Edn Las Vegas NV 89154

BEAM, TERESA LYNN, municipal specialist, chemist; b. Charleston, S.C., Apr. 12, 1957; d. Arnold Edward and Patricia Anne (Miller) Domke; m. William Cloice Beam, Oct. 10, 1981. Student, Henry Ford Community Coll., 1975-76; BS in Forensic Chemistry, Ohio U., 1979; student, Ohio State U., 1983; MS in chemistry, Calif. State U., Fullerton, 1986. Researcher Battelle Columbus (Ohio) Labs., 1980-83; lectr. Calif. State U., Fullerton, 1983-85, grad. asst., 1984-85, researcher, 1986—; criminalist Orange County (Calif.) Sheriff-Coroner's Office, Santa Ana, 1985-86; tchr. credential studies Calif. State U., Fullerton, 1987—; lectr. health Calif. State U., Fullerton, 1985. Mem. Am. Chem. Soc., Calif. Assn. Criminalists. Avocations: sports, camping, guitar.

BEAMAN, WILLIAM JAMES, stockbroker; b. Missoula, Mont., July 31, 1945; s. Dallas William and Mary Jane (Deegan) B.; m. Vicki Jean Watson, June 29, 1968; children: Derek Michael, Ryan James. BS, U. Mont., 1967, MBA, 1971; cert. fin. planner, Coll. Fin. Planning, Denver, 1977; grad., Commmand and Gen. Staff Coll., Ft. Leavenworth, Kans., 1978. Asst. to pres. D.A. Davidson & Co., Great Falls, Mont., 1972-73; stockbroker, v.p., mgr. D.A. Davidson & Co., Helena, Mont., 1973—; bd. dirs. Helena Fed. Credit Union, treas. 1983—. Pres., bd. dirs. United Way, Helena, 1979-80; pres. St. Peters Hosp. Found., 1984-85. Named an Outstanding Young Man of Am., 1980. Episcopalian. Lodge: Rotary (bd. dirs. Helena club 1985—, pres.-elect 1986). Home: 940 Stuart Helena MT 59601 Office: D A Davidson & Co PO Box 1692 Helena MT 59624

BEAMER, JO ANN JEAN, forging company executive; b. Dedham, Iowa, June 15, 1939; d. William Columbus and Neva Belle (Randolph) Dennis Delzell; m. Michael R. Beamer, July 10, 1973; children—Steven Dean Pease, Donald Lee Newman, Karey Lee (Newman) Davidofsky; stepchildren: Christopher Michael, Shelli. Student Chaffey Jr. College, U. Nev. Exec. sec. Aerojet Gen. Corp., Azusa, Calif., Nuclear Rocket Devel. Sta., Jackass Flats, Nev., 1959-62, 64-68; exec. sec. safety and test ops. Pan Am. World Airways, Nuclear Rocket Devel. Stat., 1962-64; personnel and safety asst. safety and personnel Survival Systems Co., Ontario, Calif., 1968-71; personnel mgr. Hooker Industries, Ontario, 1971-74; asst. terminal mgr. CMD Transp. Co., Vernon, Calif., 1977-80; personnel mgr. Schlosser Forge Co., Cucamonga, Calif., 1980—; guest speaker Ontario Community Hosp. Active Chino (Calif.) High Sch. Band Boosters. Mem. Nat. Assn. Female Execs., Mchts. and Mfrs. Assn., Personnel Indsl. Relations Assn. Home: 5729 Portsmouth St Chino CA 91710 Office: Schlosser Forge Co 11711 Arrow Route St Cucamonga CA 91730

BEAMER, SCOTT, consulting electrical engineer, lecturer; b. Berkeley, Calif., Apr. 2, 1914; s. Joseph H. and Louise (Scott) B.; B.S. in Elec. Engring., U. Calif., 1936; m. Alpha Mae Rogers, Oct. 21, 1939; children—Joan Louise, Scott, Ronald Laurence, Alexander Rogers, Deborah. Jr. elec. engr. Pacific Electric Motor Co., 1938-40; asso. elec. engr. Farm Sect. Adminstrn., U.S. Dept. Agr., 1940-42; cons. engr. with Clyde E. Bentley, 1946-47, Beamer & Tilson, 1949-51; with Beamer/Wilkinson & Assos., 1966-76, Scott Beamer & Assos., 1977—; mem. faculty U. Calif., 1948-63, teaching regular classes architecture and engring. and extension classes at Oakland and San Francisco, 1948-59, also univ. research projects; lighting cons. Bay Area Rapid Transit Dist. Joint Ventures. Former chmn. adv. council Salvation Army Hosp.; former chmn. troop com., mem. exec. council Boy Scouts Am., elected to Order of Arrow; former trustee Children's Hosp. Med. Center Found.; bd. dirs. Oakland Mus. Assn., Heart-Lung Inst. East Bay; mem. adv. bd. Ladies Home Soc., Oakland. Served as maj. AUS, Office Chief of Ordnance, 1942-46, in Washington, France and Germany on Proximity Fuse project; mem. O.R.C., 1937-63. Decorated Bronze Star medal, Distinguished Service Wreath, Army Commendation medal. Registered profl. engr., Calif., Nev., Oreg. Fellow Illuminating Engring. Soc.; mem. IEEE (life), Nat. Acad. Forensic Engrs. (diplomate grade), Nat. Soc. Profl. Engrs. Clubs: Rotary (past pres.), Claremont Country, 100 (past dir.). Contbr. articles to profl. jours. Patentee neon dimming transformer; co-author of patent luminous bodies. Home: 36 King Ave Piedmont CA 94611 Office: Scott Beamer & Assocs 618 Grand Ave Oakland CA 94610

BEAMSLEY, VIRGINIA BACON, speech and language pathologist; b. Corpus Christi, Tex., Jan. 21, 1954; d. Roger Drake and Myrtle Catherine (Hamilton) Bacon; m. Alan Craig Beamsley, July 8, 1985. BS, Elmira Coll., 1976; MS, U. N.Mex., 1983. Speech and lang. pathologist Edni. Assessment Systems, Inc., Albuquerque, 1984-85; pvt. practice speech pathology Gallup, N.Mex., 1985—; cons. Pica/Picac Programs, Albuquerque, 1983—, N.Mex. Sch. for the Deaf, Santa Fe, 1985—, McKinley Area Services for the Handicapped, Gallup, 1985—, Gallup Indian Med. Ctr., 1985—. Mem. Am. Speech-Lang.-Hearing Assn. (cert.), N.Mex. Speech and Hearing Assn., Council for Exceptional Children, Assn. for Edn. and Rehab. of the Blind and Visually Impaired. Avocations: travel, skiing, ballroom dancing. Home: 1706 Kiva Dr Gallup NM 87301

BEAN, GERALD ALAN, publishing executive; b. Peoria, Ill., Mar. 17, 1943; s. Harold Franklin and Shirley Jane (Dreiman) B.; m. Brenda Margreta Carlson, May 28, 1967; children—Scott, Eric. B.S. in Journalism, U. Ill., Urbana, 1966. With Rockford (Ill.) Register Star, 1966-81, gen. mgr., 1978-79, pres., pub., 1979-81; gen. mgr. Gannett Satellite Info. Network, Washington, 1981-82, USA Today, Washington, 1982-83; v.p. Gannett West Newspaper Group, 1983—; pub., pres. San Bernardino (Calif.) County Sun, 1983—. Bd. dirs. Inland Action, Inc., San Bernardino County Mus. Found. St. Bernardine Hosp. Found.; bd. dirs., pres., San Bernardino County Arts Found., Inland Empire Symphony; corp. bd. San Bernardino Hosp. Mem. Am. Newspaper Pubs. Assn., Calif. Newspaper Pubs. Assn., Ind. Colls. of So. Calif. (pres.). Office: 399 N D St San Bernardino CA 92401

BEAN, WILLIAM CARLYSLE, forestry educator; b. Boone, Iowa, July 4, 1938; s. Carlysle and Bettie Ann (Kilborne) B.; children: Deborah, Rebecca, Jennifer. BS, Wash. State U., 1966. Seaman various cos., Seattle and Ketchikan, Alaska, 1956-57, 60-66; forester U.S. Forest Service, Mt. Hebron, Calif., 1966-67; instr. forestry Centralia (Wash.) Coll., 1967—; cons. in field, 1967—; forest warden Wash. Dept. Natural Resources, Chehalis, 1983—. Served as sgt. USMC, 1957-60. Mem. Omicron Delta Kappa, Phi Kappa Phi, Xi Sigma Pi. Republican. Avocation: hunting. Home: 401 Griel Rd Onalaska WA 98570 Office: Centralia Coll 600 W Locust Centralia WA 98531

BEARD, HAROLD FINLEY, JR., insurance broker; b. Spokane, Wash., Apr. 25, 1943; s. Harold Finley and Kathleen Frances (Calkins) B.; m. Nancy Ann Canfield, June 17, 1966; children—Rebecca Kathleen, Malcolm Charles. B.A., U. Wash., 1966. C.L.U. Campus agt. Conn. Mut. Life Ins. Co., Seattle, 1965-66, sales mgmt. trainee, 1968-69; dist. agy. New Eng. Life Ins. Co., Yakima, Wash., 1969-75; sec.-treas. Beard, Bench & Mendenhall, Yakima, Wash., 1975-86, pres., 1986—. Contbr. articles to mags.; speaker profl. convs. Served with U.S. Army Spl. Forces, 1966-69. Life mem. Million Dollar Round Table, New Eng. Life's Hall of Fame, Ten Million Dollar Forum. Mem. Assn. Advanced Life Underwriters, Am. Soc. C.L.U.s, New Eng. Life Leaders Assn. (bd. dirs. 1985-86), U. Wash. Alumni Assn. (bd. dirs., dist. gov. 1978-84). Republican. Episcopalian. Club: Rotary. Office: Beard Bench & Mendenhall 1100 Chinook Tower Box 4044 Yakima WA 98901

BEARD, RODNEY RAU, physician, educator; b. Guinda, Calif., Dec. 27, 1911; s. Aiton Holmes and Mathilda Anne (Rau) B.; m. Marion Lucile Harper, July 3, 1938; children—Julie-Anne, Philip, Marian, Edin. A.B., Stanford U., 1932, M.D., 1938; M.P.H., Harvard U., 1940. Diplomate: Am. Bd. Preventive Medicine (trustee 1961-70), Am. Bd. Indsl. Hygiene. Intern Gorgas Hosp., C.Z., 1937-38; asst. resident Stanford U. Hosps., 1938-39; Rockefeller fellow in med. sci. 1939-40; med. officer Pacific-Alaska div. Pan Am. Airways, 1940-49; instr. med. sch. Stanford U., 1940-42, asst. prof., 1942-45, asso. prof., 1945-49, prof., chmn. dept. preventive medicine, 1949-69, prof. family, community and preventive medicine, 1969-77, prof. emeritus, 1977—; dir. rehab., 1955-60; med. cons. W. P. Fuller & Co., 1952-60; clin. prof. occupational health U. Calif. at Berkeley, 1952-64, lectr., 1964-72; vis. prof. U. Occupational and Environ. Health Sch. Medicine, Japan, 1980; cons. surgeon gen. U.S. Army, 1941-45, 54-75, USAF, 1966-69, Calif. Dept. Pub. Health, 1952—, VA, 1954-67; vis. prof. Clinica del Lavoro, U. di Milano, 1960-61. Author: (with W.P. Shepard et al) Essentials of Public Health, 2d edit, 1952, (with Joseph T. Noe) Patty's Industrial Hygiene and Toxicology, 1981, 2d edit., 1982; contbr. also papers; mem. editorial bd. Archives Environ. Health, 1973-87. Chmn. health council San Francisco Community Chest, 1941-44; pub. health com. San Francisco C. of C., 1951-54, San Francisco Bd. Health, 1954-59; mem. commn. A. com. aviation medicine NRC, 1942-45; mem. commn. environ. hygiene Armed Forces Epidemiol. Bd., 1954-55, dir., 1955-66, 67-73; mem. nat. adv. heart council NIH, HEW, 1957-61; mem. nat. adv. council Nat. Inst. Environ. Health Scis., 1971-74; mem. nat. adv. council pub. health tng. USPHS, 1965-69; mem. hearing bd. San Francisco Bay Area Air Quality Mgmt. Dist., 1973—; mem. tech. adv. com. Calif. Air Resources Bd., 1969-72; mem. subcom. on atherosclerosis of peripheral vascular disease study group Inter-Soc. Comm. for Heart Disease Resources, 1969-76; mem. joint residency rev. com. for preventive medicine AMA-Am. Bd. Preventive Medicine, 1971-76, chmn., 1972-76; mem. biometry and epidemiology contract rev. com. Nat. Cancer Inst., NIH, HEW, 1982-85. Fellow Am. Coll. Preventive Medicine (v.p. 1967), Am. Pub. Health Assn., Am. Occupational Medicine Assn. (sec. 1967), Western sect. 1945-46, pres. 1949), AAAS, Am. Acad. Occupational Medicine; mem. AMA (sec. sect. preventive medicine 1964-69, chmn. 1970-72, mem. com. occupational toxicology 1969-72), Internat Commn. on Occupational Health (hon.), Am. Indsl. Hygiene Assn. (dir. 1956-60), Assn. Tchrs. Preventive Medicine (pres. 1958-59), Am. Heart Assn., Soc. Occupational and Environ. Health, Oceanic Soc., Calif. Acad. Medicine, ACLU, Airline Med. Dirs. Assn. (hon.), Calif. Acad. Preventive Medicine, Sigma Xi, Delta Omega. Unitarian. Home: 511 Gerona Rd Stanford CA 94305 Office: Stanford U Sch Medicine Dept Family Community Preventive Med Stanford CA 94305

BEARDEN, THOMAS EDWARD, petroleum engineer; b. San Angelo, Tex., Apr. 17, 1958; s. Bobby Ray and Lu Ann (Lindley) B.; m. Jacqueline Sue Winter, Oct. 1, 1983; 1 child, Bobby Ray. BSChemE, Tex. A&M U., 1981; M Engring., Colo. Sch. Mines, 1986; postgrad., U. Denver, 1986—. Registered profl. engr. Petroleum engr. Marathon Oil Co., Littleton, Colo., 1981-86; pvt. practice petroleum engring. Littleton, 1986—. Mem. Soc. Petroleum Engrs., Am. Inst. Chem. Engrs. Republican. Avocations: skiing, shooting, investing. Home and Office: 2559 E Geddes Pl Littleton CO 80122

BEARDEN, THOMAS HOWARD, news program producer, correspondent; b. Washington, Feb. 14, 1948; s. Norman C. and Emma Dorothy (Jensen) B.; m. Ruth Ann Harrison, July 12, 1977; children: Jennifer Kate, Emily Jane. BS in Journalism, U. Miss., 1969, MA in Radio and TV, 1971. Reporter, anchorman Sta. WJTV-TV, Jackson, Miss., 1971-72; reporter, anchorman, assignment editor Sta. WHBQ-TV, Memphis, 1972-78; reporter, anchorman Sta. KMGH-TV, Denver, 1978-85; producer, correspondent MacNeil-Lehrer News Hour, Denver, 1985—. Producer/reporter TV news series documentary The Quicksilver Connection, 1984 (Emmy award 1984). Served to 1st lt. U.S. Army, 1971-72. Mem. Sigma Delta Chi. Club: Denver Press (news series award 1983). Avocations: computers, photography. Office: MacNeil-Lehrer News Hour 2480 W 26th Suite 2B Denver CO 80211

BEARDSLEY, JEFFERSON FRANK, industrial psychologist, author; b. Milw., Dec. 25, 1932; s. Daniel Emory and Esther Louise (Harland) B.; m. Rita Jane Bundy, Aug. 27, 1955 (div. Mar. 1972); children—Dawn Marie, Charles Cook, Scott James, Adele Louise. Student Marquette U., 1955-58; B.S., San Jose U., 1968. Cert. tchr., Calif. Machinist, Waukesha Motor Co., Wis., 1951-53; engr. various cos., Wis., Calif., 1955-58, Calif. Interstate Telephone Co., Victorville, 1958-63; tchr., adminstr. Foothill Coll., Palo Alto, Calif., 1968-77; tng. coordinator Lockheed Corp., Sunnyvale, Calif, 1977; pres. Beardsley & Assocs., San Jose, 1977—; founder Internat. Assn. Quality Circles. Author: Quality Circles, 1977; Quality Circles: The Management Process, 1984; also numerous manuals. Contbr. articles to profl. jours. Served as cpl. U.S. Army, 1953-55. Mem. Am. Soc. for Quality Control, Am. Soc. Tng. and Devel. Republican. Lodge: Masons. Home: 4998 Harmony Way San Jose CA 95130 Office: Beardsley & Assocs Inc 4998 Harmony Way San Jose CA 95130

BEARLEY, WILLIAM LEON, consulting company executive; b. Hays, Kans., June 6, 1938; s. William L. and Wilma M. (Sechrist) B.; B.S., U. Wyo., 1969, M.Ed., 1964; Ed.D., U. La Verne, 1983; M.H.R.D., Univ. Assos. Grad. Sch. Human Resource Devel., 1980; also grad. Lab. Edn. Intern Program; m. Diane Lee Kiser, Dec. 15, 1967. Tchr. math. Baldwin Park Unified Sch. Dist., Baldwin Park, Calif., 1961-64, chmn. dept. math, 1962-64; chmn. math. dept. Citrus Coll., Azusa, Calif., 1965-69, chmn. data processing dept., 1969-80, dir. computing and info. systems, 1972-80; pres. Computer Info. Assocs., Inc., Pasadena, Calif., 1980-82; assoc. prof. Sch. Mgmt., U. LaVerne, 1982—; v.p. Organizational Universe Systems, Valley Ctr., Calif., 1985—; cons., trainer info. resource mgmt., 1981—. Mem. Data Processing Mgmt. Assn. (cert.), Am. Soc. Tng. and Devel., Acad. Mgmt., Am. Mgmt. Assn., Am. Guild Organists, Assn. Computing Machinery, Assn. Systems Mgmt. (cert.), Phi Delta Kappa. Author/co-author computer software, books and articles in field. Home: 12665 Cumbres Rd Valley Center CA 92082 Office: U La Verne 1950 3d St La Verne CA 91750

BEASLEY, BRUCE MILLER, sculptor; b. Los Angeles, May 20, 1939; s. Robert Seth and Bernice (Palmer) B.; m. Laurence Leaute, May 21, 1973; children: Julian Bernard, Celia Beranice. Student, Dartmouth Coll., 1957-59; B.A., U. Calif. at Berkeley, 1962. Sculptor in metal and plastic, one man shows at, Everett Ellin Gallery, Los Angeles, Kornblee Gallery, N.Y.C., Hansen-Fuller Gallery, San Francisco, David Stuart Gallery, Los Angeles, Andre Emmerich Gallery, N.Y.C., De Young Mus., San Francisco, Santa Barbara Mus. Art, Fine Arts Gallery, San Diego; exhibited in group shows at, Mus. Modern Art, N.Y.C., Guggenheim Mus., N.Y.C., Albright Knox Gallery, Buffalo, LaJolla (Calif.) Art Mus., Musée d'Art Modern, Paris, San Francisco Mus. Art, Krannert Art Mus. at U. Ill., Jewish Mus., N.Y.C., Luxembourg Gardens, Paris, Calif. Palace of Legion of Honor, De Young Mus., Santa Barbara Art Mus., others; represented in permanent collections, Mus. Modern Art, Guggenheim Mus., Musée d'Art Modern, Paris, Los Angeles County Art Mus., Univ. Art Mus., Berkeley, Oakland (Calif.) Mus., Wichita (Kans.) Art Mus., San Francisco Art Commn., Santa Barbara Art Mus., Dartmouth Coll., others; major sculpture commns. include, State of Calif., 1967, Oakland Mus., 1972, City of San Francisco, 1976, U.S. govt., 1976, City of Eugene, Oreg., 1974, City of Salinas, Calif., 1977, Miami Internat. Airport, Fla., 1978, San Francisco Internat. Airport, 1981, Stanford U., 1982, City of Anchorage, Alaska, Los Angeles Olympic Stadium, 1984. Recipient Andre Malraux purchase award Biennale de Paris, 1961. Home: 322 Lewis St Oakland CA 94607

BEASLEY, MALCOLM ROY, physics educator; b. San Francisco, Jan. 4, 1940; s. Robert Williams and Cora (Miller) B.; m. Jo Anne Horsfall, Sept. 29, 1962; children: Michael, Matthew, Claire. B in Engring. Physics, Cornell U., 1962, PhD in Physics, 1967. Research assoc. Harvard U., Cambridge, Mass., 1967-69, from asst. prof. to assoc. prof. applied physics, 1969-74; from assoc. prof. to prof. Stanford (Calif.) U., 1974—, chmn. dept. applied physics, 1984—. Fellow Am. Phys. Soc.; mem. AAAS. Office: Stanford U Dept Applied Physics Stanford CA 94305

BEASLEY, RULE CURTIS, music educator; b. Texarkana, Ark., Aug. 12, 1931; s. George Herschel and Martha Turrentine (Rule) B.; m. Lida Carolyn Oliver, Dec. 1, 1956; children: John Rule, Paul Timothy. BA, So. Meth. U., 1952; student, Juilliard Sch. Music, 1953-54; MusM, U. Ill., 1958. Assoc. prof. music Centenary Coll., Shreveport, La., 1958-66, North Tex. State U., Denton, 1966-73; prof. Santa Monica (Calif.) Coll., 1973—; prin. bassoonist Ft. Worth Symphony, 1968-73; freelance bassoonist, Los Angeles, 1973—. Composer: Music for Brass Choir, 1965, Symphonic Sketches, 1976, Elegy for Orchestra, 1977, Sonata For Viola, 1985. Served to sgt. U.S. Army, 1953-56. Mem. ASCAP, Am. Soc. Univ. Composers, Phi Beta Kappa. Republican. Episcopalian. Avocations: astronomy, golfing, bicycling. Home: 1127 Pacific St Santa Monica CA 90405 Office: Santa Monica Coll 1900 Pico Blvd Santa Monica CA 90405

BEATTIE, GEORGE CHAPIN, orthopaedic surgeon; b. Bowling Green, Ohio, Sept. 24, 1919; s. George Wilson and Mary Turner (Chapin) B.; m. Nancy U. Fant, Mar. 1, 1947; children: Michael, Suzanne, Eric. BA, Bowling Green U., 1939; MD, U. Chgo., 1943. Diplomate Am. Bd. Orthopaedic Surgery. Commd. lt MC USN, 1943, advanced through grades to lt. comdr., 1951; med. officer, intern U.S. Naval Hosp., Great Lakes, Ill., 1943-44; resident, fellow in orthopaedic surgery Lahey Clinic, Boston, 1944; ward med. officer orthopaedic services Naval Hosp., Guam, 1944-46; sr. med. officer USN, Manus Island, Papua New Guinea, 1947; resident tng. in orthopaedic surgery U.S. Naval Hosp. St. Albans, N.Y.C., 1947-48; resident in orthopaedic surgery Children's Hosp., Boston, 1949; asst. chief orthopaedic surgery U.S. Naval Hosp. Oak Knoll, Oakland, Calif., 1950-52; comdg. officer med. co. 1st Marine Div. Med. Bn., Republic of Korea, 1952-53; chief orthopaedic service Dept. Phys. Medicine and Navy Amputee Ctr. U.S. Naval Hosp., Phila., 1954; resigned USN, 1954; practice medicine specializing in orthopaedic surgery San Francisco, 1954—; co-chmn. handicapping conditions com. Health Action Study San Mateo County, 1965; 1st chmn. orthopaedic sect. surg. dept. Peninsula Hosp. and Med. Ctr., Burlingame, Calif., 1967, chmn. rehab. service, 1967-71, chmn. phys. therapy and rehab. com., 1956—, vice chmn. orthopaedic dept., 1973-76, chmn., 1977-79; med. dir. research and rehab. ctr. San Mateo (Calif.) County Soc. Crippled Children and Adults, 1958-63; mem. exec. com. Harold D. Chope Community Hosp., San Mateo, 1971-76, chief, co-chmn. orthopaedic sect., 1971-76; chief orthopaedic surg. sect. Mills Meml. Hosp., San Mateo, 1976-78; others. Contbr. articles to profl. jours. Active Indian Guides, 1972-77; pres. Calif. Easter Seal Soc., 1969-71. Decorated Bronze Star. Fellow Am. Acad. Orthopaedic Surgeons (exhibit com. 1979—); mem. AMA (Billings Bronze medal 1954), Western Orthopaedic Assn. (pres., bd. dirs. 1986), Leroy Abbott Orthopaedic Soc. U. Calif. San Francisco (asst. clin. prof.), Alpha Omega Alpha. Office: 1515 Trousdale Dr Burlingame CA 94010

BEATTIE, WILLARD HORATIO, research chemist; b. Oak Park, Ill., Mar. 3, 1927; s. John L. and Anna M. (Tonner) B.; m. Virginia L. Kohnke, Aug. 1954; children: Andrea L., Joan B., Cora D. BA, U. Chgo., 1951, MS, 1954; PhD, U. Minn., 1958. Research chemist Shell Chem. Co., Torrance, Calif., 1958-63; asst. prof. chemistry Calif. State Coll., Long Beach, 1962-66; staff mem. Los Alamos (N.Mex.) Nat. Lab., 1966—. Author 35 sci. papers; 5 patents in field. Mem. Am. Chem. Soc. Home: 721 Kris Ct Los Alamos NM 87544 Office: Los Alamos Nat Lab MS-J567 Los Alamos NM 87545

BEAUCAGE, SERGE LAURENT, biochemist; b. St. Hyacinthe, Que., Can., Jan. 11, 1951; came to U.S., 1978; s. Rene and Therese (Bernier) B.; m. Diane Marie Desrosiers, Sept. 6, 1975; 1 child, Brian. BSc in Chemistry, U. du Que., Montreal, 1974; PhD in Chemistry, McGill U., Montreal, 1978. Research assoc. U. Colo., Boulder, 1978-81, U. Mich., Ann Arbor, 1981-82; sr. staff scientist Smith-Kline Beckman, Palo Alto, Calif., 1982—; research assoc. Sch. Medicine Stanford (Calif.) U., 1985—; cons. Genetics Inst., Boston, 1981-84. Patentee in field; contbr. articles to profl. jours. Postdoctoral fellow NRC of Can., 1979-81, Am. Cancer Soc., 1986—. Mem. AAAS, Am. Chem. Soc. Roman Catholic. Office: Beckman Instruments Inc 1050 Page Mill Rd Palo Alto CA 94304

BEAUDET, ROBERT ARTHUR, chemistry educator; b. Woonsocket, R.I., Aug. 18, 1935; s. Ralph Edgar and Blanche L. (Pelchat) B.; m. Julia Marie Hughes, Sept. 14, 1957; children: Susan, Donna, Debra, Stephanie, Michelle, David, Nicole. BS, Worchester Poly. Inst., 1957; MA, Harvard U., 1960, PhD, 1962. Asst. prof. chemistry U. So. Calif., Los Angeles, 1963-66, assoc. prof., 1966-72, prof., 1972—. Served to lt. U.S. Army, 1961-63. Fellow NSF, 1957-61, A.P. Sloan Found., 1966-67, Humboldt, Cologne, Germany, 1974-75. Mem. Am. Chem. Soc., Am. Phys. Soc. Roman Catholic. Home: 887 Vallombrosa Dr Pasadena CA 91107

BEAULAURIER, LARRY ANTHONY, college administrator; b. Yakima, Wash., Feb. 16, 1930; s. Antonio Emil and Louise Veronica (LaBissoniere) B.; divorced; children: Richard, Elizabeth, Robert. B.A., Gonzaga U., 1952; postgrad. Wash. State U., 1954. Advt. mgr. Pendleton Grain Growers, Oreg., 1954-57; advt. mgr., editor Pacific Supply Coop, Walla Walla, Wash., 1957-59; rep. N.Y. Life Ins., Walla Walla, 1959-62; asst. to pres. Whitman Coll., Walla Walla, 1962-77, v.p. fin. devel., 1977—; athletic publicity dir. Gonzaga U., Spokane, Wash., 1950-52; chmn. Am. Alumni Council Dist. VIII, 1965-67. County chmn. Republican Central Com., Walla Walla County, 1967; trustee Walla Walla Community Coll., 1967-71. Served with CIC, U.S. Army, 1953-54. Named Outstanding Young Man of Yr., Nat. Jr. C. of C., Walla Walla, 1966; Disting. Alumnus Gonzaga U., Spokane, 1983. Mem. Council for Advancement and Support Edn. (nat. trustee, dist. chmn. 1975-77, mem. philanthropy and taxation com. 1970-81, mem. govt. relations com. 1976-82, cert. of appreciation 1981). Republican. Clubs: Wash. Athletic (Seattle); Country (Walla Walla). Lodge: Elks. Home: 1206 Lancer Dr Walla Walla WA 99362 Office: Whitman Coll 345 Boyer Ave Walla Walla WA 99362

BEAUMONT, MONA MAGDELEINE, artist; b. Paris, Jan. 1, 1927; came to U.S., 1942, naturalized, 1945; d. Jacques Hippolyte and Elsie M. (Didisheim) Marx; BA, U. Calif., Berkeley, 1945, M.A., 1946; postgrad. Harvard U., Fogg Mus., Cambridge, postgrad. spl. studies Hans Hoffman Studios, N.Y.C., 1946; m. William G. Beaumont; children—Garrett, Kevin. One-woman shows at Galeria Proteo, Mexico City, Gumps Gallery, San Francisco, Palace of Legion of Honor, San Francisco, L'Armitiere Gallery, Rouen, France, Hoover Gallery, San Francisco, San Francisco Mus.

Modern Art, Galeria Van der Voort, San Francisco, William Sawyer Gallery, San Francisco, Palo Alto (Calif.) Cultural Ctr., Galerie Alexandre Monnet, Brussels, Honolulu Acad. Arts, exhibited in group shows at San Francisco Mus. Modern Art, San Francisco Art Inst., DeYoung Meml. Mus., San Francisco, Grey Found. Tour of Asia, Bell Telephone Invitational, Chgo., Richmond Art Ctr., Los Angeles County Mus. Art, Galerie Zodiaque, Geneva, others; represented in permanent collections: Oakland (Calif.) Mus. Art, City and County of San Francisco, Hoover Found., San Francisco, Grey Found., Washington, Bulart Found., San Francisco; also numerous pvt. collections. Recipient Jack London Sq. Ann. Painting award; Purchase award Grey Found.; Ann. awards San Francisco Women Artists (2); Purchase award San Francisco Art Festival; One-Man Show award San Francisco Art Festival; included in Printworld Internat., 1982-86, Internat. Art Diary, N.Y. Art Review, Art in the San Francisco Bay area. Mem. Soc. for Encouragement of Contemporary Art, Bay Area Graphic Arts Council, San Francisco Art Inst., San Francisco Mus. Modern Art, Capp Street Project, Langton Street Ctr., others. Address: 1087 Upper Happy Valley Rd Lafayette CA 94549

BEAUVAIS, MAURICE FIO, chemical engineer, executive; b. New Orleans, Jan. 18, 1934; s. Maurice F. Beauvais and Anna Lewis Martin; m. Crystelle Wallace, Mar. 29, 1956; children: Julie B. Rassell, Jennifer B. Morin. BSChemE, La. State U., 1957, MBA, 1959; postgrad., Miss. State U., 1968, UCLA, 1982. Registered profl. chem. engr., La. Commd. 2d lt. USAF, 1960, advanced through grades to lt. col., 1975; with navigation sch. USAF, Waco, Tex., 1960; standardization electronic warfare officer 55 Strategic Reconnaissance Wing, Topeka, 1960-64; EWO and mission dir. 4157th Strategic Reconnaissance Wing. Det. 1, Shemya, Ala., 1964-65; prof. air force studies Miss. State U., Mississippi State, 1965-68; EWO and adminstrn. officer 55 Tactical Reconnaissance Wing, Thakli, Thailand, 1968-69; wing EWO 97 Bomb Eing, Sault Sainte Marie, Mich., 1969-74; electronic warfare program mgr. F15 Systems Program Office, 1974-79; flight comdr., supr. flying 327th Bonb Wing, Sacramento, 1979-81; chief red force Electronic Warfare Ctr., McClellan AFB, Calif., 1981-83; ret. USAF, 1983; engring. dir. West Halifax Engring., Sacramento, 1983-85; pres. Demain Techs. Inc., Sacramento, 1985—. Decorated D.F.C., Air medal (5). Mem. Air Force Assn., Armed Forces Communication and Electronics Assn., Assn. Old Crows. Methodist. Home: 9070 Thilow Dr Sacramento CA 95826 Office: Demain Techs Inc 1713 Professional Dr Sacramento CA 95826

BECCUE-BROWN, DIANA LYNN, marketing executive, consultant; b. Denver, Sept. 1, 1955; d. Charles Henry and Helen Eileen (Warner) Beccue; m. Robert Edward Brown, Sept. 26, 1981. B.S. in Home Econs., Colo. State U., 1977. Food technologist Keebler Corp. Mfg. Tech. Center, Denver, 1977-78; consumer cons. Colo. Beef Promotion Bd., Denver, 1979-82; mgr. membership promotion Am. Waterworks Assn., Denver, 1982; acct. supr. pub. relations Sam Lusky Assocs. Inc., Denver, 1982-83; pres. Beccue-Brown & Assocs., specializing in food and beverage mktg., 1983—. Bd. dirs. unit Am. Cancer Soc. Home: 5412 Newton St Denver CO 80221 Office: Beccue Brown & Assocs 2204 W 120th Ave Suite A Denver CO 80234

BECERRA, ROSINA MADELINE, social welfare educator; b. San Diego, Mar. 6, 1939; d. Ray and Ruth (Albanez) B. BA, San Diego State U., 1961, MSW, 1971; PhD, Brandeis U., 1975; MBA, Pepperdine U., 1981. Mathematician United Tech. Corp., Sunnyvale, Calif., 1962-63; with Peace Corps, Washington, 1963-65; probation officer San Diego County Probation Office, 1965-69; research assoc. Brandeis U., Waltham, Mass., 1973-75; assoc. prof. UCLA, 1975-81, prof., 1981—, assoc. dean, 1986—. Author: Defending Child Abuse, 1979, Hispanic Veterans Seek Care, 1982, The Hispanic Elderly, 1984 (Choice Mag. Book award 1986); editor: Hispanic Mental Health, 1981; contbr. articles to profl. jours. Ford Found. award, 1980.

BECHTEL, JAMES HARVEY, physicist; b. Bellefontaine, Ohio, Mar. 25, 1945; s. Pearl Conrad and Laura Crystal (Wearly) B.; m. Jean Marie O'Neil, Aug. 20, 1983. BS magna cum laude, Miami U., Oxford, Ohio, 1967; MS, U. Mich., 1968, PhD, 1973. Research asst. U. Mich., Ann Arbor, 1971-73; research fellow Harvard U., Cambridge, Mass., 1973-76; group leader chem. physics Gen. Motors Research Labs., Warren, Mich., 1976-83; v.p. TACAN Corp., Carlsbad, Calif., 1983-85, BBO Enterprises, La Jolla, Calif., 1985—; vis. scientist MIT, Cambridge, 1982-83. Author numerous book chpts.; contbr. articles to profl. jours. Mem. Friendship Force, San Diego, 1984—, Endowment Com. U. Calif. San Diego, 1985—. Fellow Optical Soc. Am. (pres. Detroit sect. 1980); mem. AAAS, Mensa, Am. Phys. Soc., N.Y. Acad. Scis., Sigma Xi, Phi Beta Kappa. Club: Intertel. Office: BBO Enterprises 7910 Ivanhoe Ave La Jolla CA 92037

BECHTEL, STEPHEN DAVISON, JR., engineering company executive; b. Oakland, Cal., May 10, 1925; s. Stephen Davison and Laura (Peart) B.; m. Elizabeth Mead Hogan, June 5, 1946; 5 children. Student, U. Colo., 1943-44; B.S., Purdue U., 1946, Dr. Engring. (hon.), 1972; M.B.A., Stanford, 1948; D.Sc. (hon.), U. Colo., 1981. Registered profl. engr., N.Y., Mich., Alaska, Calif., Md., Hawaii, Ohio, D.C., Va., Ill. Engring. and mgmt. positions Bechtel Corp., San Francisco, 1941-60; pres. Bechtel Corp., 1960-73, chmn. of cos. in Bechtel group, 1973-80; chmn. Bechtel Group, Inc., 1980—; dir. IBM Co.; Mem., former vice chmn. Bus. Council; life councillor, past chmn. Conf. Bd.; mem. policy com. Bus. Roundtable; mem. Labor-Mgmt. Group, Nat. Action Council on Minorities in Engring., from 1974. Trustee, mem., past chmn. bldg. and grounds com. Calif. Inst. Tech.; mem. pres.'s council Purdue U.; mem. adv. council Stanford U. Grad. Sch. Bus. Served with USMC, 1943-46. Decorated officer French Legion of Honor; recipient Disting. Alumnus award Purdue U., 1964, Disting. Alumnus award U. Colo., 1978; Ernest C. Arbuckle Disting. Alumnus award Stanford U. Grad. Sch. Bus., 1974; Man of Yr. Engring. News-Record, 1974; Outstanding Achievement in Constrn. award Moles, 1977; Disting. Engring. Alumnus award U. Colo., 1979; Herbert Hoover medal, 1980; Washington award Western Soc. Engrs., 1985, Chmn.'s award Am. Assn. Engring. Socs., 1982. Fellow ASCE (Engring. Mgmt. award 1979, Pres. award 1985), Instn. Chem. Engrs. (U.K., hon.); mem. AIME, Nat. Acad. Engring. (past chmn.), Calif. Acad. Scis. (hon. trustee), Am. Soc. French Legion of Honor (bd. dirs.), Fellowship of Engring (U.K., fgn. mem.), Chi Epsilon, Tau Beta Pi. Clubs: Pacific Union, Bohemian, San Francisco Golf (San Francisco); Claremont Country (Berkeley, Calif.); Cypress Point (Monterey Peninsula, Calif.); Thunderbird Country (Palm Springs, Calif.); Vancouver (B.C.); Ramada (Houston); Links, Blind Brook (N.Y.C.); Met. (Washington); Augusta (Ga.) National Golf; York (Toronto); Mount Royal (Montreal). Office: Bechtel Group Inc PO Box 3965 San Francisco CA 94119

BECK, ARDIE LAVON, shipyard manager; b. Tulsa, Okla., July 22, 1943; s. Corvis Lavon and Alta Ileane (Carney) B.; m. Phyllis Devora Steckler, Jan. 20, 1964; children—Laura Marcia, Adam Lee. B.S. in Mech. Engring., U. Miss., 1971, M.S. in Engring. Sci., 1971. Commd. ensign U.S. Navy, 1971, advanced through grades to lt., 1977; fin. analysis officer Naval Surface Forces Pacific, 1973-74; project mgr., supr. shipbldg. U.S. Navy, 1977-82; ret., 1982; cons. Contract Adminstrn. Services, San Francisco, 1982; project mgr. S.W. Marine Inc., Terminal Island, Calif., 1982—. Youth soccer coach, Concord, Calif., 1979-81. Decorated Navy Achievement medal. Mem. AIAA, Am. Soc. Naval Engrs., Soc. Port Engrs. Los Angeles/Long Beach, Tau Beta Pi. Republican. Baptist. Home: 526 Sturgeon Dr Costa Mesa CA 92626 Office: Southwest Marine Inc PO Box 3600 Terminal Island CA 90731

BECK, ROD, senator, realtor; b. Rigby, Idaho, May 28, 1951; s. Wayne and Zara (Hendrick) B.; m. Rhonda Beck, July 25, 1974; children: Jeremy, Kirsten, Julie, Tim, Mackenzie. Student, Ricks Coll., Brigham Young U. Senator State of Idaho. Republican. Mormon. Office: 4257 Tattenham Way Boise ID 83704

BECKER, ALEX, geophysical engineering educator; b. Bialystok, Poland, July 27, 1935; came to Can., 1948, to U.S., 1980; m. Sheila Klarberg, Dec. 27, 1960; children: Jeff, Eleanor, Marc. B in Engring. Physics, McGill U., Montreal, Can., 1958, PhD in Physics, 1963. Research scientist Geol. Survey of Can., Ottawa, Ont., Can., 1965-69; prof. geophys. engring. U. Montreal, 1969-79; dir. research Questor Surveys, Toronto, Ont., Can., 1979-80; prof. geophys. engring. U. Calif., Berkeley, 1980—; cons. Geophys. Instrument Industry. Recipient Bell medal Can. Mining Jour., Toronto, 1979. Mem. Soc. Exploration Geophysicists, Can. Inst. Mining and Metall.

BECKER, BORIS WILLIAM, business educator; b. San Francisco, Aug. 30, 1939; s. Henry and Freida (Shmulevsky) B.; m. Joyce Frances Misterka, July 9, 1966; children: William, Holly, David. BS, U. Calif., Berkeley, 1962, MBA, 1967, PhD, 1970. Instr. U. Calif., Berkeley, 1969-70; prof. bus. Oreg. State U., Corvallis, 1970—; cons. Drug Abuse Council, Washington, 1974, First Fed. Savings and Loan, Corvallis, 1972, Siuslaw Nat. Forest, Corvallis, 1972. Author: Economic Aspects of Real Estate Brokerage, 1972; contbr. articles to profl. jours. Coach Olympics of the Mind, Corvallis, 1983-84. Served to 1st lt. USAF, 1962-65. U.S. Steel Found. fellowship, 1967-69. Mem. Am. Mktg. Assn. (editor conf. proceedings 1972), Am. Acad. Advt., Beta Gamma Sigma, Alpha Mu Alpha. Democrat. Buddhist. Avocations: family, gardening, reading. Home: 880 NW Conifer Corvallis OR 97330 Office: Oreg State U Coll Bus Corvallis OR 97331-2603

BECKER, DAVID MANNING, music educator, university band director; b. Corvallis, Oreg., Feb. 6, 1949; s. Manning Henry and Lois Kathleen (Legard) B.; m. Kathryn Jean Brooks, Aug. 29, 1970; children: Allison Christine, Andrew David. B in Mus. Edn., U. Oreg., 1971, M in Mus. Edn., 1975. Tchr. mus., band Lakeview (Oreg.) Jr. and Sr. High Schs., 1971-73; tchr. band, orch. Silverton (Oreg.) Union High Sch., 1973-76, South Salem (Oreg.) High Sch., 1976-81; tchr. band South Eugene (Oreg.) High Sch., 1981-82; dir. bands Lewis & Clark Coll., Portland, Oreg., 1982—; guest conductor and adjudicator numerous band festivals throughout Idaho, Oreg., Wash., Mont., Alaska, Ga. and B.C., Can.; presenter workshops on innovative band adjudication system. Mem. Nat. Band Assn., Coll. Band Dirs. Nat. Assn., Oreg. Band Dirs. Assn. (pres. 1982-84), Oreg. Music Educators Assn. (v.p., other offices, 1980—, Oreg. Sch. Activities Assn. (mus. liaison 1981—), Nat. Assn. Jazz Educators, World Assn. Symphonic Bands and Ensembles, Pi Kappa Lambda. Avocations: fishing, skiing, squash, bassoonist. Home: 14865 Twin Fir Ct Lake Oswego OR 97034 Office: Lewis & Clark Coll Dept Mus Portland OR 97219

BECKER, EDWARD SAMUEL, paper company executive; b. Bisbee, Ariz., Sept. 8, 1929; s. Otto C. and Fanny E. (Hunter) B.; m. Norma Joyce Kloster, Mar. 18, 1951; children: Keith, Kathy. BS, Oreg. State U., 1951, MS, 1953, PhD, 1957. Registered profl. engr., B.C. Can. Mgr. pulping dept. Rayonier Research, Shelton, Wash., 1957-64; group leader pulping dept. Union Co., Princeton, N.J., 1964-66; tech. dir. Columbia Cellulose, Vancouver, B.C., 1966-72; pres. Econotech Services Ltd., New Westminster, B.C., 1972—; Contbr. articles to profl. jours.; patentee in field. Servedas cpl. U.S. Army, 1953-54. Fellow Chem. Inst. Can.; mem. Am. Inst. Chem. Engrs., Tech. Assn. Pulp and Paper Industries (chmn. com. 1973-75), Can. Pulp and Paper Assn., Am. Chem. Soc. Baptist. Avocations: ch. activities, boating. Home: 5243 Uplands, Delta, BC Canada V4M 2G3 Office: Econotech Services Ltd, 852 Derwent Way, New Westminster, BC Canada V3M 5R1

BECKER, GARRY G., physician; b. Jamestown, N.D., Feb. 24, 1945; s. Edward H. and Esther Julia (Buck) B.; m. Margarete Christiane Pajakoff, Aug. 24, 1968; children: Lara, Michael, Matthew. BS, U. N.D., 1966; MD, U. Tex., San Antonio, 1970. Medicine intern Fitzsimmons Army Hosp., Denver, 1970-71; gen. practice medicine Gillette, Wyo., 1974—; clin. instr. family practice U. Utah, 1978—, U. Wyo., 1981—. Mem. Campbell Sherrif's Posse, Gillette, 1981—. Served to maj. M.C., U.S. Army, 1969-74. Fellow Am. Acad. Family Physicians; mem. AMA, Wyo. Med. Soc., Campbell County Med. Soc. Republican. Methodist. Avocations: automobiles, hunting. Office: Family Med Care 720 W 8th St Suite G Gillette WY 82716

BECKER, HENRY WILLIAM, safety director, consultant; b. Bklyn., N.Y., July 29, 1914; s. Henry C. and Elsie C. (Ruthinger) B.; m. Marian A. Brodmerkel, June 21, 1969; children: Lynn, Richard, Deborah. BEE, Poly. Inst. Bklyn., 1937; postgrad., NYU, Pratt Inst. Cert. safety profl., 1971. Safety engr. various locations; mgr. safety Am. Gas Assn.; dir. safety Am. Water Works Assn., 1969-84; safety cons. Littleton, Colo., 1984—; gen. chmn. Colo. Safety Cong. and Exposition; chmn. ANSI Z.16 Com., 1961-84. Chmn. Elec. Examining Bd. Village of Valley Stream, N.Y., 1960-74; bd. dirs. Columbia Knolls Homeowners Assn., Littleton, Nat. Safety Council, 1965-80, Colo. Safety Assn., 1974-83. Recipient Disting. Service to Safety award Nat. Safety Council, 1980. Mem. Am. Soc. Safety Engrs. (profl.), Metro. chpt. Vets. of Safety (pres. 1972), Vets. of Safety (regional v.p. 1978), Nat. Safety Council Pub. Utilities Exec. Commn., AWWA (hon.). Republican. Presbyterian. Lodge: Masons. Avocations: photography, gardening. Home: 6035 W Frost Dr Littleton CO 80123 Office: Am Water Works Assn 6666 W Quincy Denver CO 80235

BECKER, JOHN HOWARD, engineer; b. Balt., Aug. 23, 1954; s. Gene Allen and Diane Mary (Stevenson) B.; m. Robin Kay Myra, May 24, 1980. BSME, U. Idaho, 1980, MSME, 1982. Instr. mech. engring. U. Idaho, Moscow, 1980-82; engr. Gilbert/Commonwealth, Inc., Jackson, Mich., 1982-84; spl. engr. Boeing Comml. Airplane Co., Seattle, 1985—. Vol. USCG Aux., 1985—. Chevron Oil Co. fellow, 1979-80. Mem. ASME (N.W. Regional Paper Contest 1980), Sigma Xi, Tau Beta Pi. Avocations: sailing, camping, reading. Home: 30819 8th Ave SW Federal Way WA 98023 Office: Boeing Comml Airplane Co PO Box 3707 MS 2T-01 Seattle WA 98124

BECKER, MARY LENORE, social worker; b. Seattle, June 11, 1943; d. Thomas Charles and Lenore Elizabeth (Geenen) B. BA, Holy Names Coll., 1961; MSW, San Francisco State U., 1978. Lic. clin. social worker. Educator, youth minister, pvt. schs., San Francisco and Oakland, Calif., 1965-76; sch. social worker Parochial Schs. Diocese of Oakland, 1978-81; therapist Family Service Assn., San Jose, Calif., 1981-85, Monte Villa Hosp., Morgan Hill, Calif., 1985—; staff cons. 3 parochial schs., Oakland, 1978-81; asst. in program devel. Monte Villa Hosp., Morgan Hill, 1985—; adminstr. youth employment program St. Francis De Sales, Oakland, 1974. Community organizer Oakland Tng. Inst., 1974; educator Parochial Schs. Diocese of Oakland, 1965-76. Mem. Nat. Assn. Social Workers, Sisters of the Holy Names. Roman Catholic. Avocations: tennis, running, cooking, sewing. Office: Monte Villa Hosp 17925 Hale Ave Morgan Hill CA 95037

BECKER, RALPH ELIHU, JR., lawyer, planner; b. Washington, May 30, 1952; s. Ralph Elihu and Ann (Watters) B.; m. Nancy Baird Hayworth, June 28, 1980; children: Derek James, William Watters. Student, Lafayette Coll., 1970-71; BA cum laude, U. Pa., 1973; JD, U. Utah, 1977, MS in Geography, 1982. Bar: Utah 1978. V.p. Bonneville Assocs., Salt Lake City, 1978-81; spl. asst. to dir. Utah Dept. Natural Resources, Salt Lake City, 1981-83; dir. dept. Utah Office Planning and Budget, Salt Lake City, 1983-85; chmn. Bear West, Salt Lake City, 1985—; adj. prof. dept. geography U. Utah, Salt Lake City, 1986—. Author, editor: Project Bold: Proposal for Utah Land Consolidation and Exchange, 1985; contbr. numerous articles on clean air, solar energy law to profl. jours. Mem. Greater Avenues Community Council, Salt Lake City, 1980-84; mem. Salt Lake City Housing Appeals and Adv. Bd. Mem. Utah State Bar (natural resources sect., co-chmn. pub. lands com.), Am. Planning Assn. (Outstanding Service to the Planning Profession award), Utah Planning Assn. (chmn. leg. com. 1986—, Outstanding Service to Planning Profession 1986), Am. Inst. Cert. Planners (cert.). Home: 231 Canyon Rd Salt Lake City UT 84103 Office: Bear West 9 Exchange Pl Suite 1000 Salt Lake City UT 84111

BECKER, RAMONA, social worker; b. Bainbridge, Ga., July 16, 1936; d. Roy T. Mock and Margaret Elmyra (Rogers) Benn; m. Norman C. Becker; children: James, Robert. Student, U. Corpus Christi; BA, Western Wash. U.; MSW, U. Wash., 1964. Psychiat. social worker Maple Lane Sch., Centralia, Wash., 1964-68; therapist Wash. Sexual Abuse Program and Fed. Substance Abuse Program, Tacoma, Wash., 1968-70; clin. co-dir. N.W. Inst. Behavioral Scis., Tacoma, 1970—; cons. profl. tng. U.S. Dept. Def., Washington, 1971—; workshop conductor No. Wyo. Comp. Mental Health Ctr., Gillette, 1981-86. Mem. Nat. Assn. Social Workers (cert.), Far East Mgmt. Soc. Internat. (hon. doctorate 1982, Humanitarian award 1984). Avocations: wood-carving, windsurfing, folk-painting, cooking. Office: Northwest Inst 9618 Gravelly Lake Dr SW #204 Tacoma WA 98499

BECKETT, JOHN R., business executive; b. San Francisco, Feb. 26, 1918; s. Ernest J. and Hilda (Hansen) B.; m. Dian Calkin, Nov. 27, 1947 (dec. June 1968); children: Brenda Jean, Belinda Dian; m. Marjorie Abenheim, July 1969. AB, Stanford U., 1939, MA, 1940. Valuator Pacific Gas & Electric Co., 1941-42; utility fin. analyst Duff and Phelps, 1942-43; utility fin. expert SEC, 1943-44; asst. to pres. Seattle Gas Co., 1944-45; investment banker Blyth and Co., 1945-60, v.p., 1955-60; pres. Transam. Corp., 1960-79, chmn. bd. dirs., 1968-82, chief exec. officer, 1965-80, chmn. exec. com., 1982—, also bd. dirs.; bd. dirs. Kaiser Aluminum and Chem. Co., Tex. Eastern Corp., Bank Am., BankAm. Corp., Clorox Co. Clubs: San Francisco Golf, Pacific Union, Bohemian (San Francisco); Cypress Point (Pebble Beach, Calif.). Office: Transamerica Corp 600 Montgomery St San Francisco CA 94111 *

BECKHAM, GEOFFREY SCOTT, designer; b. Glendale, Calif., July 19, 1947; s. Charles Edward and Joan (Nattale) B.; m. Julie Dawn Oswald, July 1, 1972; children Geoffrey Scott, Gerald Edward, Jayme Dawn. AA, Pasadena City Coll., 1968; BA, Calif. State U., Long Beach, 1972. Designer Hatch Bros., Orange, Calif., 1971-74; designer, proprietor G. Beckham & Assocs., Santa Ana, Calif., 1974-75; designer, owner Viejo Trading & Equipment, Santa Ana, 1975-78; designer Beckham/Eisenman, Irvine, Calif., 1979—; also chmn. bd. dirs. Beckham/Eisenman, Irvine. Bd. dirs. N.M.V. Little League, Irvine, 1984—. Recipient Merit award, Restaurant and Instns., 1983, 85, Best Fast Food Restaurant Design award, Restaurant and Hotel Design, 1985, Distinction award, Restaurants and Instns., 1985. Mem. AOPA. Republican. Presbyterian. Avocations: flying, skiing, fishing. Office: Beckham/Eisenman 16811 Milliken Ave Irvine CA 92714

BECKLEY, ALAN PAUL, graphic arts cons.; b. Spencer, Nebr., Nov. 27, 1937; s. Keith Franklin and Aura (Braithwait) B.; student public schs., also various specialized schs.; m. Virginia Evelyn Rowe, Dec. 26, 1974; 1 dau., Valerie Lynn. Mgr. mktg. tech. support Autologic, Inc., 1976; mgr. mktg. tech. support Atex, Inc., Western region, 1977; dir. mktg. for N.Am., Xenotron, Ltd., 1978; sr. cons. Matrix Assos., Portland, Oreg., 1974—, v.p., gen. mgr., 1974—. Served with USAF, 1955-59. Asso. mem. Oreg. Newspaper Publishers Assn. Republican. Devel. hardware tech. to allow no space band composition on Linotype machines, 1st pre-installation survey process for newspaper computer systems. Address: 4140 NE 137th Ave Portland OR 97230

BECKMAN, ARNOLD ORVILLE, chemist, instrument manufacturing company executive; b. Cullom, Ill., Apr. 10, 1900; s. George W. and Elizabeth E. (Jewkes) B.; m. Mabel S. Meinzer, June 10, 1925; children: Gloria Patricia, Arnold Stone. B.S., U. Ill., 1922, M.S., 1923; Ph.D., Calif. Inst. Tech., 1928; D.Sci. (hon.), Chapman Coll., 1965; LL.D. (hon.), U. Calif., Riverside, 1966, Loyola U., Los Angeles, 1969; D.Sci. (hon.), Whittier Coll., 1971, U. Ill., 1982; LL.D. (hon.), Pepperdine U., 1977; D.H.L. (hon.), Calif. State U., 1984. Research asso. Bell Telephone Labs., N.Y.C., 1924-26; chem. staff Calif. Inst. Tech., 1926-39; v.p. Nat. Tech. Lab., Pasadena, Calif., 1935-39; pres. Nat. Tech. Lab., 1939-40, Helipot Corp., 1944-58, Arnold O. Beckman, Inc., South Pasadena, Calif., 1946-58, Beckman Instruments, Inc., Fullerton, Calif., 1940-65; chmn. bd. Beckman Instruments, Inc. (now SmithKline Beckman Corp.), from 1965; vice chmn. SmithKline Beckman Corp., 1984-86; dir. Security Pacific Nat. Bank, 1956-72, adv. dir., 1972-75; dir. Continental Airlines, 1956-71, adv. dir., 1971-73. Author articles in field; inventor. Mem. Pres.'s Air Quality Bd., 1970-74; Chmn. bd. trustees System Devel. Found; chmn. bd. trustees emeritus Calif. Inst. Tech.; hon. trustee Calif. Museum Found.; bd. overseers House Ear Inst., 1981—; trustee Scripps Clinic and Research Found., 1971-83, hon. trustee, 1983—; bd. dirs. Hoag Meml. Hosp. Served as pvt. USMC, 1918-19. Benjamin Franklin fellow Royal Soc. Arts.; named to Nat. Inventors Hall of Fame, 1987. Fellow Assn. Clin. Scientists; mem. Am. Acad. Arts and Scis., Los Angeles C. of C. (dir. 1954-58, pres. 1956), Calif. C. of C. (dir., pres. 1967-68), Nat. Acad. Engring., N.A.M., Am. Inst. Chemists, Instrument Soc. Am. (pres. 1952), Am. Chem. Soc., AAAS, Social Sci. Research Council, Am. Assn. Clin. Chemistry (hon.), Newcomen Soc., Sigma Xi, Delta Upsilon, Alpha Chi Sigma, Phi Lambda Upsilon. Clubs: Jonathan, California, Newport Harbor Yacht, Pacific. Patentee in field. Home: 107 Shorecliff Rd Corona del Mar CA 92625 Office: PO Box C-19600 Irvine CA 92713

BECKMAN, JAMES WALLACE BIM, economist, business executive; b. Mpls., May 2, 1936; s. Wallace Gerald and Mary Louise (Frissell) B. B.A., Princeton U., 1958; Ph.D., U. Calif., 1973. Pvt. practice econ. cons., Berkeley, Calif. 1962-67; cons. Calif. State Assembly, Sacramento, 1967-68; pvt. practice market research and econs. consulting, Laguna Beach, Calif., 1969-77; cons. Calif. State Gov.'s Office, Sacramento 1977-80; pvt. practice real estate cons., Los Angeles 1980-83; v.p. mktg. Gold-Well Investments, Inc., Los Angeles 1982-83; pres. Beckman Analytics Internat., econ. cons. to bus. and govt., Los Angeles and Lake Arrowhead, Calif., 1983—. Served to maj. USMC 1958-67. NIMH fellow 1971-72. Fellow Soc. Applied Anthropology; mem. Am. Econs. Assn., Am. Statis. Assn., Am. Mktg. Assn., Nat. Assn. Bus. Economists (officer). Democrat. Presbyterian. Contbr. articles to profl. jours. Home: Drawer 2350 Crestline CA 92325

BECKMANN, BARBARA EFTING, textile designer; b. Chgo., July 8, 1939; d. Albert W. and Bernice O. (Olsen) Efting; m. Jon Michael Beckmann, June 26, 1965. Student, U. Okla.; BFA, U. Ill., 1962; postgrad., Art Inst. Chgo., 1959-63, Pratt Graphic Ctr., N.Y.C., 1964-67, U. Calif., San Francisco, 1975-76. With Brewster Finishing and Designing Corp., N.Y.C., 1962-67, Children's Book Illustration, N.Y.C., 1964-69; freelance textile designer N.Y.C., 1967-74; pres. Barbara Beckmann Designs, Inc., San Francisco, 1974—; with Fashion Inst. Design and Merchandising, San Francisco, 1974-81. Illustrator children's books. Mem. Nat. Home Furnishing League (nat. officer and chpt. bd. mem. 1977-82), Am. Soc. Interior Designers, Nat. Home Fashions League Ednl. Found. (treas. 1981-82, bd. dirs. San Francisco chpt. 1977-82). Office: Barbara Beckmann Designs Inc 1056 Greenwhich St San Francisco CA 94133

BECKMANN, PETR, electrical engineer, educator; b. Prague, Czechoslovakia, Nov. 13, 1924; came to U.S., 1963, naturalized, 1974; s. Rudolf and Katerina (Fischer) B.; m. Irene Muller, May 31, 1965. M.Sc. in Engring., Prague Tech. U., 1949, Ph.D., 1955; Dr.Sc., Czechoslovak Acad. Scis., 1962. Registered profl. engr., Colo. Research scientist at several Czechoslovak instns. 1949-55; head of wave propagation dept. Inst. Radio Engring. and Electronics, Czechoslovak Acad. Scis., 1955-63; vis. prof. U. Colo., Boulder, 1963-64; prof. elec. engring. U. Colo., 1964-81, prof. emeritus, 1982—; editor, pub. monthly Access to Energy, 1973—. Author: A History of Pi, 1970, The Structure of Language, 1972, The Health Hazards of Not Going Nuclear, 1976, several books on electromagnetic and probability theory.; Contbr. sci. articles to profl. jours. Mem. Ronald Reagan's Energy Task Force, 1980; bd. dirs. Freedom Found., Houston, Assn. for Rational Environ. Alternatives, Center for Free Enterprise, Bellevue, Wash., Accuracy in Academia, Washington, Consumer Alert, Stamford, Conn., Intellectual Activist, N.Y.C. Served with 311 Czechoslovak squadron RAF, 1942-45, Britain. Fellow IEEE; mem. Health Physics Soc., Am. Nuclear Soc. Petr Beckmann scholarship established at Wittenberg U. (Ohio), 1977. Office: Access to Energy Box 2298 Boulder CO 80306

BECKNER, EVERET HESS, diversified research and development laboratory executive; b. Clayton, N.Mex., Feb. 24, 1935; s. Elmer Hess and Ursla (Brown) B.; m. Claudia Lee Garrett, Aug. 12, 1955 (div. Aug. 1983); children: Gregory Mitchell, Lee Elizabeth Strouse, Matthew Hess; m. Mary Caroline Allen, Feb. 16, 1984. BS, Baylor U., 1956; MA, Rice U., 1959, PhD in Physics, 1961. Staff engr. Lockheed Missiles and Space Co., Sunnyvale, Calif., 1956-57; staff mem. Sandia Nat. Labs., Albuquerque, 1961-65, research and device devel. div. supr., 1965-69, plasma research dept. mgr., 1969-74, phys. research dir., 1974-83, energy programs v.p., 1983-86, def. programs v.p., 1986—. Bd. dirs. N.Mex. Dept. Econ. Devel. Tourism, Santa Fe, 1985—, N.Mex. Energy Research and Devel. Inst., 1983-85. Fellow Am. Phys. Soc.; mem. AAAS. Home: 809 Warm Sands Trail SE Albuquerque NM 87123 Office: Sandia Nat Labs Org 5000 Albuquerque NM 87185

BECK-VON-PECCOZ, STEPHEN GEORGE WOLFGANG, artist; b. Munich, Oct. 18, 1933; came to U.S., 1937; s. Wolfgang Anna Marie and Martha Jeanette (Morse) Beck-von-P.; m. Dorothy Ann Freytag, June 16, 1956 (div. 1971); m. Michele Marie Perry, Feb. 8, 1972; children: Stephen Jr., David, Kenneth, Lisa. BEE, Cornell U., 1956; MA in Art, Calif. State U., San Diego, 1974. Electronic engr. Stromberg Carlson Co., San Diego, 1958-60; project mgr. Control Data Corp., San Diego, 1960-65, Digital Devel. Corp., San Diego, 1965-66; project engr. Stromberg Datagraphix, Inc., San Diego, 1966-69; project mgr. Digital Sci. Corp., San Diego, 1969-71; artist San Diego, 1974—; cons. elec. engring., San Diego, 1974-78. Designer

Kinetic Sculptures, 1974-86, Kinetic Sculpture W252, 1980 (Architect's Choice award 1985). Served to 2d lt. USAF, 1956-58. Mem. Artists Equity Assn. (v.p. San Diego chpt. 1981-82), Internat. Sculpture Ctr., Kappa Alpha Soc. Avocations: art, travel. Home: 636 Nardito Ln Solana Beach CA 92075 Office: 11575 Sorrento Valley Rd Suite 201 San Diego CA 92121

BEDAIR, HASSAN MAHMOUD, engineering executive; b. Sayda Zeinb, Cairo, Apr. 25, 1939; came to U.S., 1980; s. Mahmoud Bedair Fayed and Fatma (Aly) Rihan; m. Madeha A. Fateha, Oct. 13, 1975; children: Ghada, Dalia. BSME, Ain Shams U., Cairo, 1961; MSc in Automatic Control, Cairo U., 1974, PhD in Systems Engring., 1978. Cons. to mfr. NICS, Montebello, Calif., 1980-82; project engr. Hydraulic Units Inc., Duarte, Calif., 1982-83; sr. engring. specialist Fairchild Control Systems, Manhattan Beach, Calif., 1983-85; mgr., systems devel. Western Gears Corp., Industry, Calif., 1985—; instr. U. So. Calif., 1982, West Coast U., 1981-83. Contbr. articles to profl. jours. Mem. AIAA, ASME, Soc. Automotive Engrs. Avocations: swimming, walking, reading. Office: Western Gear Corp 14724 E Proctor Ave Industry CA 91749-3299

BEDDOME, JOHN MACDONALD, oil company executive, engineer; b. Vernon, B.C., Can., Sept. 20, 1930; m. Barbara McCarthy; children—Maureen, David. B.Sc. in Chem. Engring., U. B.C., 1952. Various positions Gulf Oil Can., Calgary, Alta., 1952-71; with Dome Petroleum Ltd., Calgary, Alta., 1971—, pres., chief operating officer, 1983—; dir., v.p. IPAC, Calgary, 1980-85; chmn., dir. TransCanada Pipeline Ltd., Calgary, 1979-83; dir. PanArctic Oil Ltd., Calgary, Dome Can. Ltd., Calgary. Mem. Assn. Profl. Engrs., Geologists and Geophysicist Alta. Clubs: Ranchmen's, Calgary Petroleum. Avocations: badminton; reading; skiing. Office: Dome Petroleum Ltd, 333 7th Ave SW, Calgary, AB Canada T2P 2Z1 *

BEDELL, C. BARRIE, advertising executive, publisher; b. Evanston, Ill., Feb. 28, 1931; s. Clyde Orvis and Florence (Evans) B.; m. Nancy Corrine Smoot, Nov. 9, 1958 (div. 1971); children: Evan, Megan. BA, Denison U., 1952. Advt. mgr. Precision Equipment co., Chgo., 1954-56, Wilson-McMahan Stores, Santa Barbara, Calif., 1960-64; acct. exec. Proebsting, August & Harpham, Chgo., 1956-59; v.p. Basic/Bedell Advt. Selling Improvement Corp., Santa Barbara, 1965-71, pres., 1972—, also bd. dirs.; cons., seminar leader, pub. speaker for various corps., media and trade assns. including Nat. Home Furnishings Assn., Millikien, U. Calif. Santa Barbara, So. Furniture Market Ctr.; founding dir. Ctr. for URANTIA Book Synergy, Inc., Santa Barbara, 1983—. Author: Total Selling and Advertising Service, 1975, Profit Proven Ads, 1985; pub. Concordex of The Urantia Book, 3d ed.; mem. adv. bd. Coastlines, 1983-85; contbr. articles to trade mags. Bd. dirs. Child Abuse Listening Mediation, 1971-77; pres., mem. adv. bd. Jesusonian Found., Boulder, 1986—. Served as sgt. USAR, 1950-56. Mem. Direct Mktg. Creative Guild. Republican. Clubs: Channel City, Santa Barbara Sailing. Office: Basic Advt Corp 2040 Alameda Padre Serra PO Box 30571 Santa Barbara CA 93130

BEDELL, JAY DEE, educator, writer; b. Monterey, Calif., Oct. 20, 1946; s. John Dewhirst and Lucille (Huffman) B. BBA, U. Calif.-Davis, 1968. Tchr. Antioch Schs., Calif., 1969-84, v.p., dir. Credit Union, 1979-81; owner Bedell Enterprises, 1986—; pvt. cons., 1985—; mem. Adv. Council for Spl. Edn., Antioch, Calif., 1979-81. Bd. dirs. Storyland Theater, Antioch, 1979. Writer poetry (Golden Poet awards World of Poetry Press, 1985, 86); author: (poems) The Golden Eagle, 1984, Dreams, 1986, Lady Liberty, 1986, Sierra-Nevada, 1986, Grand Canyon, 1986, Mother Teresa, 1987. Served with U.S. Army, 1971-73. Fellow Am. Biog. Assn. (life); mem. Internat. Platform Assn., Delta Upsilon. Democrat. Home: 1020 Claudia Ct Apt 11 Antioch CA 94509

BEDFORD, JANICE LEIGH, physical education educator; b. Blythe, Calif., Dec. 7, 1951; d. Russell Arthur and Roma (Gentry) Duquette; m. Robert Edmund Bedford, May 31, 1975 (div. Dec. 1981). BA with distinction, Ariz. State U., 1974; MA in Phys. Edn., San Diego State U., 1981. Cert. tchr., Ariz.; cert. community coll. instr., Calif. Athletic sec. San Diego City Coll., 1974-77, instr. phys. edn., 1975-77; prof. phys. edn. Saddleback Community Coll., Mission Viejo, Calif., 1977—. Author: Aerobic Dance, 1985. Mem. Am. Assn. Health Phys. Edn. and Recreation, Calif. Assn. Health Phys. Edn. and Recreation (pres. 1980-81), Calif. Tchrs. Assn., NEA, Internat. Dance-Excercise Assn., Women's Profl. Rodeo Assn. Avocations: dirt-biking, water skiing. Former profl. rodeo barrel-racer. Office: Saddleback Community Coll 28000 Marguerite Pkwy Mission Viejo CA 92692

BEDNAR, ERNEST GEORGE, retired industrial arts educator, consultant; b. Lidgerwood, N.D., May 4, 1920; s. Frank F. and Rose (Korbel) B.; m. Rhoene Kelley, Feb. 14, 1948; children: Larry E., Donald F., Kelly M. Hackney. BS, Billings Poly. Inst., 1942; MS, Iowa State U., 1950; EdD, U. Mo., 1955. Tchr. indsl. arts Lincoln Jr. High Sch., Billings, Mont., 1946-53; prof. indsl. arts N. Tex. State U., Denton, 1954-55; prof. indsl. arts and asst. prof. indsl. arts and technology Humboldt State U., Arcata, Calif., 1955-82; pres. Bednar Enterprises, Arcata, 1986—. Contbr. articles to profl. jours; patentee in field. Served with USAAF, 1942-46, ETO. Recipient 1st prize in state and 3d prize in Nat. Air Mail Poster Contest, 1938. Mem. Am. Indsl. Arts Assn., Am. Council Indsl. Arts Tchr. Edn., Calif. Council Indsl. Arts Tchr. Edn. (pres.), Phi Delta Kappa (life), Epsilon Pi Tau (bd. trustees Beta Tau chpt., Laureate Citation). Republican. Roman Catholic. Avocations: inventor, rehab. engring. cons. Home: 2905 Highland Ct Arcata CA 95521

BEDOR, VIRGINIA MILLER, lawyer; b. N.Y.C., July 26, 1949; d. William Henry and Margaret (Malloy) M.; m. Stephen J. Bedor, Sept. 7, 1985. AB in Sociology and Edn., Coll. of William and Mary, 1972; JD magna cum laude, William Mitchell Coll. Law, 1983. Bar: Minn. 1983, Oreg. 1984, Wash. 1986. Inspector J.F. Kennedy Airport U.S. Immigration and Naturalization Service, Jamaica, N.Y., 1972-73; inspector U.S. Immigration and Naturalization Service, Agana, Guam, 1975; examiner U.S. Immigration and Naturalization Service, N.Y.C., 1973-76; regional examiner U.S. Immigration and Naturalization Service, Ft. Snelling, Minn., 1978-83; supervisory examiner U.S. Immigration and Naturalization Service, Honolulu, 1983-85; assoc. McEwen, Gisvold, Rankin & Stewart, Portland, Oreg., 1986—; adj. prof. immigration law NW Sch. Law Lewis & Clark Coll., 1986—. Pihl scholar, 1981. Mem. Am. Immigration Lawyers's Assn. Home: 3107 SW Cascade Dr Portland OR 97201

BEE, ALICE VIRGINIA, librarian; b. Brigham, Utah, Aug. 20, 1918; d. James William and Alice (Berg) Pett; m. Earl Sheldon Bee, Oct. 5, 1940 (dec.); children—Sheldon Wayne, Barbara Ann Bee Hutchason (dec.); m. Reece B. Robertson, Sept. 13, 1986. A.A., San Mateo Jr. Coll., 1940. Statis. clk. Proctor & Gamble Corp., San Francisco, 1939-41; payroll clk. Roberts Pub. Markets, Santa Monica, Calif., 1946-50; sec., treas. Roberts Liquor Stores, Santa Monica, 1953-77, Fred L. Roberts Enterprises, Santa Monica, 1953-77; asst. dir., head librarian Los Angeles Geneal. Library, 1980-83, dir., head librarian, 1983-87; retired 1987. Mem. Daus. Utah Pioneers. Democrat. Mormon. Home: 9027 David Ave Los Angeles CA 90034

BEE, DAVID MERLE, physician; b. Portage, Wis., June 16, 1937; s. Clifford Merle and Emily Seville (Beau) B.; m. Rochelle Soboto, May 1, 1977; children: Cherish, Melissa. BA, Andrews U., 1961; MD, U. So. Calif., 1967. Diplomate Am. Bd. Internal Medicine. Intern. Glendale (Calif.) Adventist Hosp., 1967-68; resident in internal medicine U. So. Calif. Gen. Hosp., Los Angeles, 1970-73; practice medicine specializing in critical care Glendale, 1973—. Active State Bd. Vocational Names, Calif., 1974-79. Served to lt. USNR, 1968-69, Vietnam. Decorated Purple Heart. Mem. AMA, Am. Coll. Physicians, Am. Soc. Internal Medicine, Calif. Med. Rev. Inc. (founding mem. bd. dirs., sec. exec. com.). Republican. Adventist. Avocations: skiing, auto repair, gardening. Home: 1980 Escarpa Dr Los Angeles CA 90041 Office: 435 Arden St Suite 410 Glendale CA 91203

BEEBE, MARY LIVINGSTONE, curator; b. Portland, Oreg., Nov. 5, 1940; d. Robert and Alice Beebe. B.A., Bryn Mawr Coll., 1962; postgrad. Sorbonne, U. Paris, 1962-63. Curatorial asst. Fogg Art Mus., Harvard U., Cambridge, Mass., 1966-67; guard Am. Theater Co., Portland State U., 1969-71; dir. pub. relations Sally Judd Gallery, Catlin Gable Sch., Portland, 1971; exec. dir. Portland Ctr. for Visual Arts, 1973-81; dir. Stuart collection U. Calif.-San Diego, La Jolla, 1981—; cons. in field; bd. dirs. Art Matters Inc., N.Y.C., 1984—. Mem. art steering com. Portland Devel. Commn., 1977-80; bd. dirs. Henry Galley, U. Wash., Seattle, 1977-80; project cons. Nat. Research Ctr. for Arts, N.Y.C., 1978-79; bd. dirs. Art Mus. Assn. San Francisco, 1978-84; bd. dirs., trustee Art Matters Inc., 1985—; trustee Russell Found., 1982—; hon. mem. bd. dirs. Portland Ctr. for Visual Arts, 1984—; mem. arts adv. bd. Centre City Devel. Corp., San Diego, 1982—; arts adv. bd. Port of San Diego; panel mem., cons. Nat. Endowment Arts; juror numerous art shows and exhbns. Nat. Endowment Arts fellow, 1979. Contbr. articles to profl. jours. Office: Stuart Collection U Calif San Diego B-027 La Jolla CA 92093

BEEBE, MORTON PRITCHETT, photographer; b. Oakland, Calif., Jan. 14, 1934; s. Morton Crews and Mary Belle (Pritchett) B.; m. Katia Bojilov, Oct. 1962. BS, U. Calif., Berkeley, 1956. Dir. Globecombers, various international locations, 1959-62; exec. v.p. Ind. Producers, Acquired, 1963-64; prin. Morton Beebe Assocs., San Francisco, 1964—; founder Image Bank West, San Francisco, 1976-80. Author: San Francisco, 1985. Served to lt. (j.g.) USN, 1956-69. Mem. Am. Soc. Mag. Photographers (bd. dirs. 1985—), Advt. Photographers Am. (bd. dirs. 1985—), Explorers Club. Republican. Club: Bohemian (San Francisco). Avocations: skiing, jogging, sports.

BEECHAM, DENISE CARUZZI, construction and engineering company executive; b. Washington, Mar. 16, 1947; d. Theodore Joseph and Fay Lillian (Tabke) Caruzzi; children: John Hunter, Blakely Nichelle, Forest Scott. Student, East Tex. State U., 1965-67, Tex. Tech U., 1967-68; BS in Bus. Mgmt., Boise State U., 1975. Compensation analyst Morrison-Knudsen Co., Inc., Boise, Idaho, 1975-76, supr. internat. adminstrn., 1976-77, mgr. corp. compensation, 1977-78; dir. area office Morrison-Knudsen Internat., Lisbon, Portugal, 1978-79, London, 1979-80; dir. internat. personnel Boise, 1980-82; asst. dir. personnel Morrison-Knudson Co., Inc., Boise, 1982-86; pres. DBW Assocs., Moraga, Calif., 1986—. Bd. dirs. Boise YWCA, 1985—, Community Housing Resource Bd., Boise, 1984—, Hays Shelter Home Bd., Boise, 1985—; pres. Hays Shelter Home Aux., Boise, 1984—; personnel cons. Boise Sr. Ctr., 1985—. Mem. H.R. Assn. Treasure Valley (bd. dirs. 1985—), Am. Soc. Personnel Adminstrs. (v.p., pres.-elect internat. chpt. 1985—, bd. dirs. 1982-86). Avocations: photography, sailing. Office: DBW Assocs 5 Thorndale Pl Moraga CA 94556

BEEHLER, MICHAEL THOMAS, English educator; b. Mpls., Mar. 29, 1950; s. Robert W. and Helen C. (Adler) B.; m. Sharon A. McMurray, Mar. 27, 1976. BA in Math., BA in English, U. Calif., Irvine, 1972; PhD in English, UCLA, 1978. Asst. prof. English U. Tex., Austin, 1978-85; asst. prof. English Mont. State U., Bozeman, 1985-87, assoc. prof. English, 1987—. Author: T.S. Eliot, Wallace Stevens and the Discourses of Difference, 1987; reviewer Tex. Studies for Lang. and Lit., Austin, 1978-85, Bucknell U. Rev., Lewisburg, Pa., 1986—; contbr. articles to profl. jours. Travel grantee NEH, 1985. Mem. MLA, Internat. Assn., Philosophy and Lit., Internat. Assn. Fantastic in the Arts. Democrat. Lutheran. Avocations: handball, softball, racquetball, skiing. Home: 601 W Arnold Bozeman MT 59715 Office: Mont State U Dept English Bozeman MT 59717

BEEKS, GRAYDON FISHER, JR., musicology educator; b. Long Beach, Calif., Oct. 15, 1948; s. Graydon Fisher and Mary Eugene (Swift) B.; m. Serena Elizabeth, July 16, 1978. BA, Pomona Coll., 1969; MA, U. Calif., Berkeley, 1971, PhD, 1981. Editorial asst. Grove's Dictionary, London, 1974-76; dir. music St. Clements Ch., Berkeley, 1976-78; assoc. U. Calif., Berkeley, 1977-78; instr. Vassar Coll., Poughkeepsie, N.Y., 1978-80; vis. instr. Kenyon Coll., Gambier, Ohio, 1980-81; lectr., librarian Pomona Coll., Claremont, Calif., 1983—; dir. music St. Ambrose Ch., Claremont, 1986—. Contbr. article to profl. jours. Alfred Hertz fellow U. Calif., Berkeley, 1973-74; grantee ACLS, 1985. Mem. Am. Musicol. Soc., Am. Guild Organists, Music Library Assoc., Coll. Band Dirs. Nat. Assn., Am. Handel Soc. Democrat. Home: 283 East Green St Claremont CA 91711 Office: Pomona Coll Music Dept Claremont CA 91711

BEELER, FRANK ROBERT, utilities executive, musician; b. Escalon, Calif., Oct. 8, 1953; s. Adolph Joseph Jr. and Mary Theresa (Aufdermaur) B.; m. Diana Fuchs, Nov. 29, 1985. Student, Modesto Jr. Coll., 1971-73; BS in Environ. Health cum laude, Calif. State U., Northridge, 1977. Lab. technician City of Lodi, Calif., 1978-79, lab. dir., 1979—. Composer Swiss Polka music. Calif. State U. scholar, 1973-75, Music Camp scholar U. Pacific, 1971. Mem. Calif. Water Pollution Control Assn. (lab. vice chmn. Calif. chpt., 1987-88, bd. dirs. San Joaquin chpt. 1985—, v.p. No. San Joaquin chpt. 1986—), Mid Valley Water Utilities, No. Calif. Backflow Prevention Assn., West Coast Swiss Wrestling Assn. (pres. 1978—). Republican. Roman Catholic. Club: San Joaquin Valley Swiss (Ripon, Calif.). Avocations: swiss polka music, wrestling, weightlifting. Home: 14250 French Camp Rd Lodi CA 95242 Office: City of Lodi 12751 N Thornton Rd Lodi CA 95240

BEEMAN, MICHAEL JOSEPH, artist, educator; b. Colorado Springs, Colo., Oct. 6, 1946; s. Barney Beeman and Jean (McGinty) Skaggs; m. Barbara J. Connelly, Aug. 26, 1973; children: Brent, Kris. BS, U. Wyo., 1971, MS, 1976. Cert. elem. and secondary tchr., Wyo. Tchr. art Laramie County East High Sch., Cheyenne, Wyo., 1975-81; coord. art Laramie County Sch. Dist. 1, Cheyenne, 1981—. Illustrator mus. manual A Guide to the Plains Indian Gallery for Young People, 1985. Mem. Frontier Days Com., Cheyne, 1984—; cubmaster Cheyenne pack 118 Boy Scouts Am., 1984—; bd. dirs. Very Spl. Arts Festival, 1985—. Served with USN, 1964-68. Mem. Nat. Arts Edn. Assn., Wyo. Watercolor Assn., Wyo. Alliance for Arts Edn., Phi Delta Kappa (historian 1985-86, bd. dirs.). Democrat. Roman Catholic. Avocations: fishing, travel. Home: 5401 Hamilton Cheyenne WY 82009 Office: Laramie County Sch Dist #1 2810 House Ave Cheyenne WY 82001

BEER, FRANCIS ANTHONY, political science educator; b. N.Y.C., Feb. 5, 1939; s. William Joseph and Anne (Benedikt) B.; m. Diana Darnall, June 12, 1965; children: Omar, Marie, Jeremy. BA, Harvard U., 1960; MA, U. Calif., Berkeley, 1963, PhD, 1967. Asst. prof. polit. sci. U. Tex., Austin, 1967-69, assoc. prof., 1969-74; prof. polit. sci. U. Colo., Boulder, 1975—. Author: Integration and Disintegration in NATO, 1969, Peace Against War, 1981. Served to lt. USN, 1960-62. Mem. Am. Polit. Sci. Assn., Internat. Studies. Assn. Office: Polit Sci Dept U Colo Boulder CO 80309

BEERS, RONALD EUGENE, computer systems analyst; b. Visalia, Calif., Jan. 13, 1944; s. Floyd Stanley and Lois Gertrude (Larkins) B.; m. Suzanne Elizabeth Holwick, Aug. 5, 1972; children: Emily Lois and Elizabeth Leigh (twins), Jason Ronald. AA, Coll. of Sequoias, 1963; BS in Criminology, Fresno State Coll., 1966; postgrad., UCLA, 1971, U. LaVerne, 1974-75. Traffic officer State of Calif. Hwy. Patrol, various locations, 1966-78; sgt. State of Calif. Hwy. Patrol, Los Angeles, Ont., 1978-85; systems analyst Modular Computer Systems, Inc., Lakewood, Calif., 1984—. Recipient Outstanding Performance awards, Calif. Hwy. Patrol, 1973, 79, Merit award, State of Calif., 1973. Democrat. Roman Catholic. Avocation: microcomputing. Home: 6758 Grant Ct Chino CA 91710-6217 Office: Modular Computer Systems Inc 1 Center Pointe Dr #360 La Palma CA 90623-1089

BEESLEY, EDWARD MAURICE, mathematician, educator emeritus; b. Belvidere, N.J., Jan. 11, 1915; s. Maurice Edward and Eva Lena (Bair) B.; m. Audrey Champlin Maymon, July 11, 1940; children—Barbara Lyn Beesley Goss, Maurice Edward, Norman Ernest. A.B., Lafayette Coll., 1936; Sc.M., Brown U., 1938, Ph.D., 1943. Instr. math. U. Nev.-Reno, 1940-42, asst. prof., 1942-53, prof., 1954-81, prof. emeritus, 1981—; cons. various gaming clubs, Reno, 1950-60. Contbr. articles to profl. publs. Mem. Am. Math. Soc., Math. Assn. Am., Am. Fedn. Musicians, Sigma Xi, Pi Mu Epsilon (pres. 1980-83). Home: 1940 Royal Dr Reno NV 89503 Office: U Nev Reno NV 89557

BEESLEY, H(ORACE) BRENT, farm credit executive; b. Salt Lake City, Jan. 30, 1946; s. Horace Pratt and Mary (Brazier) B.; m. Bonnie Jean Matheson, Dec. 20, 1980; children—Laura Jean, Sarah Janice, Mary Roslyn. BA, Brigham Young U., 1969; MBA, Harvard U., 1973, J.D., 1973. Bar: Utah 1973. Instr. U. Utah, Salt Lake City, 1973-78; ptnr. Ray, Quinney & Nebeker, Salt Lake City, 1977-81; chmn. bd., chief exec. officer Pioneer Bank, Salt Lake City, 1978-81; dir. Fed. Savs. and Loan Ins. Corp., Washington, 1981-83; chmn., chief exec. officer Charter Savs. Corp., Jacksonville, Fla., 1983-86; pres., chief exec. officer Farm Credit Corp. Am., Denver, 1986—; dir. Bonneville, Inc., Salt Lake City, 1970-84; ptnr. Alpine Hills Co., Salt Lake City, 1974—, Utah Valley Land Co., Salt Lake City, 1977—. Bd. dirs. Utah Heritage Found., 1978-81, Utah Arthritis Found., 1978-81. Mem. Utah State Bar Assn. Club: Alta (Salt Lake City). Home: 5260 S Geneva Way Englewood CO 80111 Office: Farm Credit Corp Am PO Box 5130 Denver CO 80217

BEEZER, ROBERT RENAUT, judge; b. Seattle, July 21, 1928; s. Arnold Roswell and Josephine (May) B.; m. Hazlehurst Plant Smith, June 15, 1957; children—Robert Arnold, John Leighton, Mary Allison. Student, U. Wash., 1946-48, 51; B.A., U. Va., 1951, LL.B, 1956. Bar: Wash. 1956, U.S. Supreme Ct. 1968. Ptnr. Schweppe, Krug, Tausend & Beezer, P.S., Seattle, 1956-84; judge U.S. Ct. Appeals (9th cir.), Seattle, 1984—; alt. mem. Wash. Jud. Qualifications Commn., Olympia, 1981-84. Served to 1st lt. USMCR, 1951-53. Fellow Am. Coll. Probate Counsel, Am. Bar Found.; mem. ABA, Seattle-King County Bar Assn. (pres. 1975-76), Wash. Bar Assn. (bd. govs. 1980-83). Clubs: Rainier, Tennis (Seattle). Office: US Ct Appeals 9th Cir 1010 5th Ave Suite 802 Seattle WA 98104

BEGA, ROBERT VALINO, biology consultant; b. Milford, Mass., Aug. 17, 1928; m. June Wilson, Dec. 31, 1950 (dec. 1970); 1 child, Cyrise; m. Joan Fisher, Mar. 25, 1972. AA, San Diego Jr. Coll., 1950; BS, U. Calif., Berkeley, 1953, PhD, 1957. Research pathologist U.S. Forestry Service, Berkeley, Calif., 1955-84; lectr. U. Calif., Berkeley, 1957—; assoc. Agrl. Expt. Sta., Berkeley, 1957—; vis. prof. U. Hawaii, Honolulu, 1972-73; pvt. cons., Grass Valley, Calif., 1985—. Author: Root Disease and Plant Pathogens, 1972, Diseases of the Pacific Coast, 1978; contbr. articles to profl. jours. Pres. Berkeley Work Council, 1965-78. Served with U.S. Army, 1946-48. Mem. Am. Phytopath. Soc., Am. Forestry Assn. (life), Sigma Xi. Home: 21275 Clydesdale Rd Grass Valley CA 95949 Office: U Calif Berkeley CA 94701

BEGGS, HARRY MARK, lawyer; b. Los Angeles, Nov. 15, 1941; s. John Edgar and Agnes (Kentro) B.; m. Sandra Lynne Mikal, May 25, 1963; children—Brendan, Sean, Corey, Michael. Student, Ariz. State U., 1959-61, Phoenix Coll., 1961; LL.B., U. Ariz., 1964. Bar: Ariz. 1964, U.S. Dist. Ct. Ariz. 1964, U.S. Ct. Appeals (9th cir.) 1973. Assoc. Carson Messinger, Elliott, Laughlin & Ragan, Phoenix, 1964-69, ptnr., 1969—; mem. Civil Practice and Procedure Com., State Bar of Ariz., 1969-80, Fin. Insts. Counsels Com., 1980-83; founding fellow Ariz. Bar Found. Recipient award for highest grade on state bar exam. Atty. Gen. Ariz., 1964; Fegtly Moot Ct. award, 1963, 64; Abner S. Lipscomb scholar U. Ariz. Law Sch., 1963. Mem. State Bar of Ariz., Maricopa County Bar Assn., ABA. (litigation, antitrust sects.), Ariz. Acad. Clubs: Plaza, LaMancha Racquet. Mem. editorial bd. Ariz. Law Rev. 1963-64; contbr. articles to profl. jours. Address: PO Box 33907 Phoenix AZ 85067

BEGOVICH, NICHOLAS ANTHONY, electrical engineer, consultant; b. Oakland, Calif., Nov. 29, 1921; s. Dinko and Anna (Juka) B.; m. Joan Munson Deopker, Apr. 14, 1944. B.S. in Elec. Engring, Calif. Inst. Tech., 1943, M.S., 1944, Ph.D. (Francis J. Cole scholar 1946), 1948. Research physicist, staff cons., lab mgr., dir. engring. Hughes Aircraft Co., Culver City, Calif., 1948-61; corporate v.p. Hughes Aircraft Co., 1961, asst. group exec. ground systems group, 1961-67, group exec., 1967-70; corporate v.p., pres. Data Systems div. Litton Industries, Van Nuys, Calif., 1970-74; mgmt. cons. 1975—; cons. Applied Physics Lab., Johns Hopkins U., 1976—; Cons. weapons system evaluation group Dept. Def., 1952-57; mem. U.S. Army Sci. Bd., 1983—; spl. work devel. electronic-scan radar, free world air def., command and control systems. Fellow IEEE; mem. Am. Phys. Soc., Ops. Research Soc. Am., Sigma Xi. Home: 136 Miramonte Dr Fullerton CA 92635

BEHEN, EDWARD NICHOLAS, podiatrist; b. Evergreen Park, Ill., Apr. 24, 1948; s. Frank Edward and Mary Agne (Witry) B.; m. Katherine Ann Walters, Jan. 5, 1974; children: Jennifer, Edward, Francis, Raymond, Bridget. BS in Biology, Loyola U., 1971; D in Podiat. Medicine, Ill. Coll. Podiat. Medicine, 1975. Resident St. Bernard Hosp., Chgo., 1975-76; pvt. practice podiat. medicine Grand Junction, Colo., 1976—; mem. staff Grand Junction Community Hosp.; pres. Colo. bd. podiatry medicine examiners, 1984-86, pres. 1986—; adj. clin. prof. Ill. Coll. Podiat. Medicine, 1979—. Mem. Am. Podiat. Med. Assn., Colo. Podiat. Med. Assn., Preferred Podiatrists of Colo. (bd. dirs.), Candle Lighters (founder Grand Junction chpt. 1985—). Democrat. Roman Catholic. Lodge: Lions. Avocations: hunting, flying, 4-wheeling. Office: 2217 N 7th St Grand Junction CO 81501

BEHLER, MARTY, sports program administrator. Student, U. Okla., 1968-70, 74, South Plains Coll., 1972; AA in Social Scis. cum laude, De Anza Coll., 1975-76; BA in Am. History and Cultural Anthropology, San Jose State U., 1979. Lic. U.S. Soccer Fedn., Calif. Youth Soccer Assn.; cert. spl. olympics coach. Asst. to coordinator of Title IV-A Santa Clara (Calif.) Unified Sch. Dist., 1977-81, classroom aide, 1978-80; counselor The Foundry Sch., San Jose, Calif., 1979; project coordinator, community liaison specialist for Title IV-A in Am. Indian edn. Milpitas (Calif.) Unified Sch. Dist., 1980—; dir. community relations, coordinator mktg. and sales San Jose Earthquakes Team, 1985-86, camp dir., 1986—; coaching experience includes U.S. Soccer Fedn.-Calif. Youth Soccer Assn.-North, Cen. Coast Sect. Calif. Interscholastic Fedn.; dir. and various other adminstrv. positions in camps and athletic clinics, Calif.; program specialist 'Pros for Kids', San Mateo, Calif.; lectr. grad. seminar on multicultural counseling, San Jose State U., metamorphosis: changes through visualization, Nat. Indian Youth Leadership Conf., San Francisco; cons. San Jose State U. dept. Social Scis. Home: 1136 Starbird Circle #2 San Jose CA 95117

BEHLMER, RUDY H., JR., writer, film educator; b. San Francisco, Oct. 13, 1926; s. Rudy H. and Helen Mae (McDonough) B.; 1 child, Curt. Student, Pasadena Playhouse Coll., 1946-49, Los Angeles City Coll., 1949-50. Dir. Sta. KLAC-TV, Hollywood, Calif., 1952-56; network TV dir. ABC-TV, Hollywood, 1956-57; TV comml. producer-dir., exec. Grant Advt., Hollywood, 1957-60; exec. producer-dir. Sta. KCOP-TV, Hollywood, 1960-63; v.p., TV comml. producer-dir. Hollywood office Leo Burnett USA, 1963-84; lectr. film Art Ctr. Coll. of Design, Pasadena, Calif., 1967—, Calif. State U., Northridge, 1984—; civ. Author: Memo From David O. Selznick, 1972; (with Tony Thomas) Hollywood's Hollywood, 1975; America's Favorite Movies—Behind the Scenes, 1982, Inside Warner Bros., 1985; co-author The Films of Errol Flynn, 1969; text on Warner Bros. Fifty Years of Film Music, 1973; eidtor: The Adventures of Robin Hood,1979, The Sea Hawk, 1982 (Wis./Warner Bros. screenpaly series); various articles on aspects of film history. Served with AC, USNR, 1944-46. Mem. Dirs. Guild Am.

BEHN, PETER WOLFGANG, architect; b. Munich, Germany, Dec. 12, 1936; s. Fritz and Gerda (Schuster) B.; came to U.S., 1951, naturalized, 1956; m. Kathie Carriegan, June 1974; children—Daniel, Kevin. B.Arch., U. Calif.-Berkeley, 1965; With Whiting Assocs., Rome, 1966-67, Ludovico Quaroni, Rome, 1968; project architect Fisher Friedman, San Francisco, 1970; pvt. practice, Berkeley, Calif., 1971-83; visiting assoc. prof. architecture Calif. Polytechnic State U., San Luis Obispo, 1983-85; sr. lectr. in architecture Nat. U. Singapore, 1984—. Served with USN, 1958-60. Recipient 4 AIA-Sunset Western Home awards; Archtl. Record awards, 1973, 79; Calif. Preservation Found. Design award, 1984. Mem. AIA, Nat. Council Archtl. Registration Bds. Cert. Designs include residences of Lozano, Schiro, Kay, Baumrind, Behn. Office: 875 Upham St San Luis Obispo CA 93401 Office: Nat U Singapore, Sch Architecture, Kent Ridge Singapore

BEHNEY, CHARLES AUGUSTUS, JR., veterinarian; b. Bryn Mawr, Pa., Nov. 30, 1929; s. Charles Augustus and Victoria Parks (Wythe) B.; B.S., U. Wyo., D.V.M., Colo. State U., 1961; m. Judith Ann Boggs, May 26, 1979; children—Charles Augustus III, Keenan F. Owner, Cochise Animal Hosp., Bisbee, Ariz., 1961—; veterinarian, dir. S.W. Traildust Zoo, Bisbee, 1966—; owner Kazam Arabians, Bisbee, 1969—; asso. prof. Cochise Coll. Chmn., Comprehensive Health Planning, Cochise County, Ariz., 1968. Mem. Am. Vet. Med. Assn., Soc. for Breeding Soundness. Republican. Episcopalian. Rotarian, Elk. Patentee ultrasound device and eye cover for treating infections, apparatus to alter equine leg conformation, external vein clamp, equine sanitation instrument; developer ear implant instrumentation system. Home and office: PO Box 4337 Bisbee AZ 85603

BEHRENBRUCH, WILLIAM DAVID, filmmaker, educator; b. South Bend, Ind., July 23, 1946; s. Willard Herman and Mildred Kathleen (Steele) B.; m. Ingrid M. Neuschwander, Aug. 16, 1969 (div. 1975). Student, Ind. U., 1970-71; BA, Brooks Inst., 1974. Editor Rex Fleming Prodns., Santa Barbara, Calif., 1974-76, Golden Coast Films, Santa Barbara, 1976; pres. Visual Systems, Santa Barbara, 1976—; adj. instr. Brooks Inst., Santa Barbara, 1978—. Graphic designer (motion picture) Sweat, 1986; spl. effects designer Death Spa, 1986. Served to sgt. USAF, 1966-70. Mem. Soc. Motion Picture and TV Engrs., Aircraft Owners and Pilots Assn. Club: Santa Barbara Flying. Avocations: private pilot, travel, hiking, horseback riding. Office: Visual Systems 2050 Alameda Padre Serra Santa Barbara CA 93103

BEHRENDT, JOHN CHARLES, research geophysicist; b. Stevens Point, Wis., May 18, 1932; s. Allen Charles and Vivian Elaine (Frogner) B.; children: Kurt A. Behrendt, Marc R. BS in Physics, U. Wis., 1954, MS in Geology, 1956; PhD in Geophysics, U. Wisc., 1961. Asst. seismologist Arctic Inst. N.Am., Ellsworth Sta., Antarctica, 1956-58; research assoc. U. Wis., Madison, 1958-64; research geophysicist U.S. Geol. Survey, Denver, 1964-72, research geophysicist, Antarctic coordinator, 1977—; chief br. of Atlantic-Gulf of Mex. marine geology Woods Hole, Mass., 1972-77; advisor to U.S. Depts. State and Interior, Washington, 1977—; mem. U.S. Del. to Antarctic Treaty Meetings, various countries, 1977—, various working groups Nat. Acad. of Sci., 1972; active in Antarctic research, 1956—, in research on earthquakes in Eastern U.S., in research in Gt. Lakes geologic structure. Author more than 100 sci. research papers. Recipient Antarctic Service medal U.S. Dept. Def., 1966. Fellow Geol. Soc. Am.; mem. Am. Geophys. Union, Soc. Exploration Geophysicists, AAAS. Avocations: photography, outdoor activities, music. Office: US Geol Survey MS 903 Denver Fed Ctr Denver CO 80225

BEHRENDT, JOHN THOMAS, lawyer; b. Syracuse, Kans., Oct. 26, 1945; s. Thomas Franklin and Anna Iola (Carrithers) B. m. Martha Jean Montgomery, Dec. 28, 1967 (div.); children—Todd Thomas, Gretchen Jean; m. Theresa Ann Elmore, Oct. 27, 1985. B.A., Sterling Coll.; J.D. cum laude, U. Minn. Bar: Calif. 1971, Tex. 1973. Assoc., then ptnr. Gibson, Dunn & Crutcher, Los Angeles, 1970-71, 1974—. Served to capt. JAGC, U.S. Army, 1971-74. Mem. ABA, Los Angeles County Bar Assn. Republican. Presbyterian. Clubs: Jonathan (Los Angeles); Union League (N.Y.). Office: Gibson Dunn & Crutcher 2029 Century Park East Los Angeles CA 90067 also: 200 Park Ave New York NY 10001

BEHRENS, HENRY WILLIAM, international business educator, financial consulting firm executive; b. Scheessel, Germany, Aug. 4, 1935; came to U.S., 1955, naturalized, 1960; s. Claude William and Sophie Magdalena (Ellmers) B.; m. Eva Paeslack, June 12, 1960; children—Andrew M., Lawrence H. B.S., Columbia U., 1961, M.B.A., 1962; Ph.D., New Sch. for Social Research, 1969. Economist Exxon Internat., Inc., N.Y.C., 1962-65; vis. lectr. econs. Columbia U., N.Y.C., 1965; asst. prof. econs. and fin. Fairleigh Dickinson U., Rutherford, N.J., 1965-68; assoc. prof. econs. and fin. Union Coll. and U., Schenectady, 1968-72; pres. Algonquin Investors Corp., Niskayuna, N.Y., 1972-78; exec. dir. U.S.A.F.E.C., N.Y.C., 1979-81; prof. world bus. Am. Grad. Sch. Internat. Mgmt., Phoenix, 1982-84; prof. fin. and internat. bus. Nat. U., San Diego, 1984-85; mng. dir. The McCormack Group, San Diego, 1985—; pres., fin. cons. to corps. and fgn. govts. Behrens & Assocs., Phoenix and San Diego, 1982—. Author: The Effects of Monetary Policy on Commercial Banks, Thrift Institutions, and the Residential Mortgage Market, 1968; Export Guide, 1985; author research reports. Mem. U.S. Senate Club, Am. Mgmt. Assns., Am. Fin. Assn., Am. Econ. Assn., Acad. Internat. Bus., Alpha Kappa Psi. Club: Columbia U. (N.Y.C.). Office: Nat U 4007 Camino Del Rio S San Diego CA 92108

BEIGHLEY, RUTH VIRGINIA, college official; b. Mercer, Pa., June 18, 1934; s. Conrad Mahan and Helen Leola (Cratty) B. B.S., Bob Jones U., 1956; M.S. in Edn., Westminster Coll., 1961; Ed.D., Ariz. State U., 1977. Cert. tchr., Pa., Ariz. Tchr. 3d grade Slippery Rock Jointure, Portersville, Pa., 1956-57; tchr. high sch. Morgan County, Exel, Ky., 1957-58; tchr. Cranberry Twp., Evans City, Pa., 1958-60, Ray Sch. Dist., Kearney, Ariz., 1960-62, Yuma Dist. No. 1, Ariz., 1962-66; grad. asst. Ariz. State U., Phoenix, 1971-73; coordinator elem. edn., Southwestern Coll., Phoenix, 1966—; mem. accreditation team NATTS, Phoenix, 1983; mem. adj. faculty Ariz. Coll. of the Bible, 1986—; mem. Profl. Standards Cert. Adv. Com. Dept. Edn., Phoenix, 1984—. Mem. Internat. Reading Assn. Republican. Baptist. Home: 4050 E Sharon Dr Phoenix AZ 85032 Office: Southwestern Coll 2625 E Cactus Rd Phoenix AZ 85032

BEIL, DRAKE, management and educational consultant; b. Miami Beach, Fla., Dec. 2, 1949; s. Theodore and Muriel (Feller) B.; m. Judi Iselin, July 2, 1972; children—Joshua Hayden, Dana Malia. B.A. in English, CCNY, 1971; M.Ed., U. Hawaii, 1975, Ed.D. in Curriculm and Instrn., 1981. Coordinator academically talented program Hawaii Dept. Edn., 1978; dir. tng. Survey & Mktg. Services, Inc., Hawaii, 1979-80; assoc. prof., lectr. U. Hawaii, dir. Ednl. Enterprises, 1979—; pres. Drake Beil and Assocs., 1981-86; v.p. Hawaiian Ednl. Council, 1986—. Recipient Presdl. Achievement award, 1982. Mem. Am. Soc. Tng. and Devel. (pres. Hawaii chpt.), Internat. Reading Assn., Am. Chess Fedn. Club: Honolulu. Contbr. articles profl. jours. Office: PO Box 4145 Honolulu HI 96827

BEILBY, ALVIN LESTER, chemistry educator; b. Watsonville, Calif., Sept. 17, 1932; s. Claud Eldred and Elma Fern (Hockabout) B.; m. Ruby Irene Nelson, June 21, 1958; children: Mark Alfred, Lorene Sigrid. BA, San Jose State U., 1954; postgrad., Harvard U., 1954-55; PhD, U. Wash., 1958. Instr. Pomona Coll., Claremont, Calif., 1958-60, asst. prof., 1960-66, assoc. prof., 1966-72, chmn. dept. chemistry, 1972-85, prof. chemistry, 1972—; vis. scholar U. Ill., Urbana, 1964-65; guest worker, research chemist Nat. Bur. Standards, Gaithersburg, Md., 1971-72; guest worker Lockheed Research Lab., Palo Alto, Calif., 1979-80; guest prof. U. Uppsala, Sweden, 1986-87. Co-author: Laboratory Manual for Chemistry: A Quantitative Approach, 1969; editor: Modern Classics in Analytical Chemistry, Vol. I, 1970, Vol. II, 1976; contbr. articles to profl. jours. Moderator Claremont United Ch. of Christ Congl., 1975-77; vice moderator then moderator and bd. dirs. So. Calif. Conf. United Ch. Christ, 1983-85; corp. mem. Congl. Homes, Inc., Pomona, 1985—. Sci. Faculty Profl. Devel. award NSF, 1979-80; Standard Oil Co. Calif. fellow U. Wash., 1957-58. Mem. Am. Chem. Soc. (Faculty award Advanced Study 1964-65), AAAS, Assn. Am. Med. Colls., Western Assn. Advisors for Health Professions (1st chmn. 1970-71), Sigma Xi. Democrat. Avocations: choral singing, Eng. handbell ringing, photography, traveling. Home: 663 Hood Dr Claremont CA 91711 Office: Pomona Coll Seaver Chemistry Lab Claremont CA 91711

BEILENSON, ANTHONY CHARLES, congressman; b. New Rochelle, N.Y., Oct. 26, 1932; s. Peter and Edna (Rudolph) B.; m. Dolores Martin, June 20, 1959; children: Peter, Dayna, Adam. B.A., Harvard Coll., 1954; LL.B., Harvard U., 1957. Bar: Calif. 1957. Mem. Calif. Assmebly from 59th Dist., 1963-66, Calif. Senate from 22d Dist., 1967-76, 97th-100th Congresses from 23d Calif. Dist., 1977—. Democrat. Office: 1025 Longworth Bldg Washington DC 20515 *

BEILIN, BETTY, chemist; b. Moscow, Aug. 16, 1938; came to U.S., 1980; d. Rafail David Shub and Riva Shkolnicov; m. Solomon Isaac Beilin, Sept. 2, 1961; 1 child, Harry Ronald. MSChemE, Inst Cinema-Engrs., Leningrad, USSR, 1962. Technician Film Plan, Moscow, 1956-61; researcher Cinema-Photo Inst., Moscow, 1961-79; chemist Xidex Corp., Sunnyvale, Calif., 1980—. Contbr. articles to profl. jours. Mem. Am. Chem. Soc. Home: 520 Van Buren Ave #303 Oakland CA 94610 Office: Xidex Corp 305 Soquel Sunnyvale CA 94086

BEILIN, SOLOMON ISAAC, chemist; b. Bobruisk, Belorussia, USSR, Mar. 25, 1935; came to U.S., 1980; s. Issac Ilya Aaron and Rachel Beilin; m. Betty Shub, Sept. 2, 1961; 1 child, Harry Ronald. M in Chem. Engring., Inst. Chem. Tech., Moscow, 1956; PhD, Acad. Sci., Moscow, 1966, Diploma sr. scientist, 1968. Shift mgr. Plastic Plan, Moscow, 1956-60; group leader Isolation Inst., Moscow, 1960-62, Acad. Sci. Inst. Petrochem. Synthesis, Moscow, 1962-79; sr. mgr. Exxon Enterprises, San Jose, 1980—; cons. in field. Contbr. articles to jours.; patentee in field. Mem. Am. Chem. Soc. Avocation: chess. Home: 520 Van Buren Ave #303 Oakland CA 94610

BEISCH, HANS R., metal products manufacturing company executive; b. 1927; married. BS, Polytech. Inst., 1950. With SKG Mfg. Co., Ltd., 1951-62, then v.p., plant mgr.; gen. mgr. Rockwell Internat. Corp., 1962-70; gen. mgr. automotive div. Sargent Industries, 1970-73; pres. auto trim div. NI West Inc., 1973-78; sr. v.p. NI West Inc., Long Beach, Calif., 1978-84; pres., chief operating officer NI West Inc., 1984—. Office: NI Industries Inc One Golden Shore Long Beach CA 90802 *

BEITLER, CHLOE ANN, municipal and university administrator; b. Quincy, Ill., Aug. 21, 1935; d. Maxine Davis Elliott; children from previous marriage: Laura, Valerie, Marc; m. Don Rosedale, Dec. 31, 1975. BS in Home Econs. Vocat. Edn., Ill. State U., 1965; postgrad., Claremont Sch. Mgmt., 1978—, U. Calif., Riverside. Tchr. home econs. Danville, Ill., 1965-66; 4-H youth advisor U. Calif. Coop. Extension, San Mateo County, 1966-73; county dir. U. Calif. Coop. Extension, Contra Costa County, 1973-75, Riverside, 1975—; dir. acad. leadership devel. program U. Calif. Coop. Extension, 1979-85, pres. assembly council. Vich-chmn. allocations com. United Way, Riverside, 1985-86. Mem. Am. Home Econs. Assn., Calif. Home Econs. Assn., Am. Mgmt. Assn. Republican. Lodge: Rotary. Home: 38888 Chaparral Dr Temecula CA 92390 Office: U Calif Coop Extension 21150 Box Springs Riverside CA 92507

BEKEMEIER, LUTHER WILLIAM, university administrator, clergyman; b. Berkley, Mich., Mar. 1, 1927; s. Reinhold and Renata M. (Fuelling) B.; m. Lois Esther Huber, Sept. 20, 1952; children—Daniel, Christine, William, Elizabeth, James. Student Concordia Tchrs. Coll., River Forest, Ill., 1941-42, Concordia Coll., Milw., 1942-47; B.A., Concordia Sem., St. Louis, 1952, M.Div., 1973. Ordained to ministry Lutheran Ch., 1952. Vicar Redeemer Luth. Ch., Redwood City, Calif., 1949; pastor Good Shepherd Luth. Ch., Warrenville, Ill., 1950-51, Hope Luth. Ch., Park Forest, Ill., 1952-76; v.p. Pacific Luth. U., Tacoma, 1976—; ptnr. Rickman Assocs., pub. relations, Chgo., 1961-74. Bd. dirs. No. Ill. dist. Luth. Ch.-Mo. Synod, Chgo., 1960-64, chmn. pub. relations dept., 1958-60; pres. Found. for Research on Modification of Behavior, Harvey, Ill., 1967-70; chaplain Park Forest Police Dept., 1960. Mem. Council for Advancement and Support of Edn. Clubs: Tacoma City, Tacoma, Tacoma Country and Golf. Lodge: Lions. Office: Pacific Luth U Tacoma WA 98447

BEKEY, GEORGE ALBERT, computer scientist, engineer, educator; b. Bratislava, Czechoslovakia, June 19, 1928; came to U.S., 1945, naturalized, 1956; s. Andrew and Elizabeth B.; m. Shirley White, June 10, 1951; children: Ronald Steven, Michelle Elaine. B.S. with honors, U. Calif., Berkeley, 1950; M.S., UCLA, 1952, Ph.D., 1962. Research engr. UCLA, 1950-54; mgr. computer center Beckman Instruments, Los Angeles and Berkeley, 1955-58; mem. sr. staff, dir. computer center TRW Systems Group, Redondo Beach, Calif., 1958-62; mem. faculty U. So. Calif., 1962—, prof. elec. and biomed. engring. and computer sci., 1968-82, chmn. dept. elec. engring. systems, 1978-86, dir. Robotics Inst., chmn. computer sci. dept., 1984—; cons. to govt. agys. and indsl. orgns. Author: (with W.J. Karplus) Hybrid Computation, 1968; editor 3 books; mem. editorial bd. 3 profl. jours.; editor IEEE Jour. Robotics and Automation; contbr. over 120 articles to profl. jours. Served with U.S. Army, 1954-56. Recipient Disting. Faculty award Sch. Engring.; Service award U. So. Calif., 1977. Fellow IEEE; mem. Am. Assn. for Artificial Intelligence, Assn. for Computing Machinery, Soc. for Computer Simulation, Biomed. Engring. Soc., AAAS, World Affairs Council, Sigma Xi, Tau Beta Pi, Eta Kappa Nu. Patentee in computer field. Office: Dept Computer Science U So Calif Los Angeles CA 90089

BEKOFF, ANNE C., neurobiologist; b. Denver, May 19, 1947; d. James Gilbert and Jean (Herres) Cox; m. Marc Bekoff, June 28, 1970. BA, Smith Coll., 1969; PhD, Washington U., St. Louis, 1974. Research assoc. U. Colo. Med. Ctr., Denver, 1975-76; asst. prof. neurobiology U. Colo., Boulder, 1976-82, assoc. prof., 1982—. Contbr. articles to profl. jours., chpts. to books. Grantee NSF, 1976-83, NIH, 1983-86; fellow Sloan Found., 1979-81, Guggenheim Meml. Found., 1983-84. Mem. Soc. Neurosci., Soc. Devel. Biology, Animal Behavior Soc., AAAS. Office: U Colo EPO Dept Biology B-334 Boulder CO 80309

BELAN, WILLIAM WELLS, music educator; b. Oakland, Calif., Aug. 31, 1950. BA, UCLA, 1972; MusM, U. Tulsa, 1975; MusD, U. Okla., 1984. Dir. choral activities Calif. State U., Los Angeles, 1981—, acting chmn. dept music, 1985-86; dir. choral activities Home Savs. Am., Los Angeles, 1985—; choral asst. 1984 Olympic Honor Choir, Los Angeles, 1984. Bd. dirs. Pasadena Arts Services, 1987—; mem. arts and culture panel Pasadena (Calif.) Strategic Planning Com., 1985-86. Recipient Meritorious Performance and Promise award Calif. State U., Los Angeles, 1984, 85, 86, Disting. Scholar award Phi Kappa Phi, 1985; research grantee Calif. State U., Los Angeles, 1983. Mem. Am. Choral Dirs. Assn., So. Calif. Vocal Assn., Phi Mu Alpha Sinfonia. Avocations: cooking, travel, reading. Office: Calif State U 5151 State University Dr Dept Music Los Angeles CA 90032

BELCASTRO, JOHN SAMUEL, management consultant; b. Balt., Apr. 26, 1952; s. John James and Sophie Marie (Allevato) B.; m. Margery A. McFadden, Aug. 8, 1981; children: Amy Marie, Anthony James. BA in Psychology cum laude, U. Colo., 1975, MA, 1977. Mgmt. cons. CIBBSA, Boulder, 1977—; research statistician U. Colo., Boulder, 1977-78; registered rep. First Investors Corp., Lakewood, Colo., 1983-85; bd. dirs. Eldorado Trading Co., Boulder, 1982—. Contbr. articles to profl. jours. Bd. dirs. Boulder County Enterprises, 1986—. Named Eagle Scout Boy Scouts of Am., 1968. Mem. Boulder C. of C. (mem. Pres. club, 1984-85). Avocations: gourmet cooking, black powder shooting, scuba diving, cross country skiing. Office: CIBBSA PO Box 4041 Boulder CO 80306

BELCHER, JOHN DAVIS, biochemistry researcher; b. Roanoke, Va., Feb. 28, 1955; s. James Woody and Kathryn Louise (Davis) B. BA in Chemistry, U. Va., 1977; PhD in Biochemistry, Wake Forest U., 1982. Postdoctoral fellow U. Calif Cardiovascular Research Inst., San Francisco, 1982-86; asst. prof. U. Minn. div. Epidemiology, Mpls., 1986—; dir. Lipid Research Lab., Mpls., 1986—. Recipient Mat. and Sci. award Rensselaer Poly. Inst., 1972; Dean's fellow Bowman Gray Sch. Medicine, 1977; NIH fellow Cardiovascular Research Inst., San Francisco, 1982-86. Mem. AAAS, Inst. Econometric Research, Phi Epsilon Pi. Democrat. Methodist. Avocations: camping, fishing, softball, Am. Indian art.

BELDEN, ERNEST, psychologist; b. Vienna, Austria, Oct. 16, 1919; came to U.S., 1938; s. Arthur and Betty (Schmehr) Bellak; m. Elfy K. Kulka, 1942 (div. 1971); children—Gerald A., Claudia G. Sanchez, Michelle A. m. Patricia Ann Prasch, June 12, 1971. A.B., U. Calif.-Berkeley, 1948, M.A., 1953, Ph.D., 1965. Lic. psychologist, Calif. Clin. psychologist U.S. Army, 1950-53; staff psychologist, program dir. Napa State Hosp., Imola, Calif., 1953-83; legal cons., 1984—; instr. U. Calif.-Davis, U. Calif.-Berkeley, 1965-80. Contbr. articles to profl. jours. Served with armed forces, 1942-46. Mem Am. Psychol. Assn. Club: Vallejo Yacht. Address: PO Box 5053 Napa CA 94581

BELDEN, LOUIS DE KEYSER, investment counsel; b. Indpls., July 11, 1926; s. Louis de Keyser and Frances (Pardue) B.; B.A., Harvard U., 1949; M.B.A., Stanford U., 1951. Security analyst Bank of New York, 1951-52; ptnr. Brundage, Story & Rose, N.Y.C., 1961-66; pres. Wentworth, Belden & Dahl, San Francisco, 1966-75, Belden and Assocs. Investment Counsel, San Francisco, 1975—; regent Fin. Analysts Seminar, 1976-80. Community adviser San Francisco Jr. League, 1977—; pres. Internat. Inst. San Francisco, 1970. Served with AUS, 1944-46. Mem. Investment Counsel Assn. Am. (gov. 1976—), World Affairs Council No. Calif. (bd. dirs. 1985—, asst. treas. 1985—, treas. 1987—). Republican. Episcopalian. Clubs: University, Harvard (N.Y.C.); Stock Exchange, St. Francis Yacht (San Francisco). Home: 2298 Pacific Ave San Francisco CA 94115 Office: Aloca Bldg 1 Maritime Plaza Suite 2555 San Francisco CA 94111

BELDEN, ROBERT ADAMS, management consultant; b. Columbus, Ohio, Aug. 18, 1920; s. Charles Lee and Dorothy (Adams) B.; m. Wilanne Emily Schneider, Oct. 14, 1948; 1 child, Leigh Schneider. B.S., U.S. Naval Acad., 1942; M.B.A., Harvard U., 1948; J.D., U. San Diego, 1961. C.P.A., Calif. Budget analyst Convair, San Diego, 1948-54, staff asst., v.p. engring. adminstrn., 1955-56, schedules engr. Astro div., 1956-60; mgr. bid analysis Stromberg Carlson, San Diego, 1960-62; mng. ptnr. Microlabels, San Diego, 1962; mgmt. cons. Robert A. Belden & Assocs., San Diego, 1963—; lectr. bus. Calif. Western U.S. Internat. U., San Diego, 1963-76; lectr. San Diego State U., 1976—; film advisor San Diego United Schs., 1970-75; tchr. U. Calif.-San Diego, 1973; tchr. filmmaking La Jolla Mus. Modern Art, 1974-75. Editor/photographer: (slide-sound publicity film) Schools for Tomorrow, 1972; author (booklet) Strategy Toolkit, 1983. Cons., dir. San Diego Ballet, 1977. Served to lt. USN, 1942-46. Mem. Harvard U. Bus. Sch. Assn. San Diego, Info. Film Producers Assn., Am. Film and Media Educators, Am. Soc. Bus. and Mgmt. Cons., Assn. M.B.A. Execs. Republican. Episcopalian. Home: 1029 Santa Barbara St San Diego CA 92107 Office: Robert A Belden and Assocs PO Box 6344 San Diego CA 92106

BELDEN-POPE, LORI, language-speech-hearing pathologist; b. Hemet, Calif., Jan. 16, 1957; s. Theodore Fowler and Barbara Jean (Vevers) Belden; m. Kevin Lyle Pope, Aug. 10, 1985. BS, Wichita State U., 1979; MS, Calif. State U., Chico, 1981. Speech pathology cons. Sierra Home Health, Susanville, Calif., 1981-83; speech-lang. therapist Lassen Union Sch. Dist., Susanville, 1981-83; lang.-speech-hearing specialist San Bernardino (Calif.) County Schs., 1983-86, Dinuba (Calif.) Pub. Schs., 1986—. Mem. Am. Speech-Hearing Assn., Calif. Speech & Hearing Assn. (cert.), Council of Univ. Suprs. of Practicum in Speech Pathology and Audiology, Am. Morgan Horse Assn., Sports Car Club of Am. Republican. Mem. Evangelical Free Ch. Avocations: show horses, sports car racing, traveling, flower arranging. Home: 7466 S Englehart Reedley CA 93654

BELILLE, RONALD, security executive; b. Portland, Nov. 22, 1947; s. Frank and Geraldine (Kron) B. AA in Law Enforcement, Portland Community Coll., 1970; student, Fed. Law Enforcement Tng. Ctr., Glynco, Ga., 1978; BS in Adminstrn. Justice, Portland State U., 1979; AA in Occupational Safety and Health, Mt. Hood Community Coll., 1985; student, Police Reserve Acad., Oregon City, Oreg., 1985. Cert. emergency med. technician 1. Correctional officer State Penitentiary, Salem, Oreg., 1972; asst. counselor Multiple County Adult Probation, Parole, Portland, Oreg., 1975; fed. protective officer Fed. Protective Services, Portland, 1978; asst. recognizance officer Multiple County Ct., Portland, 1982; safety/security officer Precision Castparts, Portland, 1979-83, security coordinator, 1983—; CPR instr., first aid instr., portable fire extinguishers instr. Precision Castparts, 1983-85. Served with USAF, 1966-68. Mem. Am. Soc. Indsl. Security, Am. Soc. Safety Engrs., Internat. Assn. Quality Circles. Lodge: Elks. Avocations: racquetball, chess, reading. Home: 1238 SE 47th Ave Portland OR 97215

BELJAN, JOHN RICHARD, university administrator, medical educator; b. Detroit, May 26, 1930; s. Joseph and Margaret Anne (Brozovich) B.; m. Bernadette Marie Marenda, Feb. 2, 1952; children: Ann Marie, John Richard, Paul Eric. B.S., U. Mich., 1951, M.D., 1954. Diplomate: Am. Bd. Surgery. Intern U. Mich., 1954-55, resident in gen. surgery, 1955-59; dir. med. services Stuart div. Atlas Chem. Industries, Pasadena, Calif., 1965-66; from asst. prof. to assoc. prof. surgery U. Calif. Med. Sch., Davis, 1966-74; from asst. prof. to assoc. prof. engring. U. Calif. Med. Sch., 1968-74, from asst. dean to assoc. dean, 1971-74; prof. surgery, prof. biol. engring. Wright State U., Dayton, Ohio, 1974-83; dean Sch. Medicine Wright State U., 1974-81, vice provost Sch. Medicine, 1974-78, v.p. health affairs Sch. Medicine, 1978-81, provost, sr. v.p., 1981-83; provost, v.p. acad. affairs, dean Sch. Medicine Hahnemann U., Phila., 1983-85; prof. surgery and biomed. engring. Hahnemann U., 1983-86, spl. adviser to pres., 1985-86; v.p. academic affairs Calif. State U., Long Beach, 1986—, prof. anatomy/physiology and biomed. engring., 1986—; prof. arts and scis., assoc. v.p. med. affairs Central State U., Wilberforce, Ohio, 1976—; trustee Cox Heart Inst., 1975-77, Drew Health Center, 1977-78, Wright State U. Found., 1975-83; trustee, regional v.p. Engring. and Sci. Inst. Hall of Fame, 1983—; bd. dirs. Miami Valley Health Systems Agy., 1975-82; cons. in field. Author articles, revs., chpts. in books. Home 6490 Saddle Dr Long Beach CA 90815 Office Calif State U Long Beach CA 90840. Served with M.C. USAF, 1955-65. Decorated Commendation medal; Braun fellow, 1949; grantee USPHS, 1967—; NASA, 1968—. Fellow A.C.S., Royal Soc. Medicine; mem. Aerospace Med. Assn., AAUP, AMA (council on sci. affairs 1978—), Assn. Acad. Surgery, F.A. Coller Surg. Soc., Biomed. Engring. Soc., IEE, Instrument Soc. Am., Calif. Med. Assn., Los Angeles County Med. Assn., Phi Beta Kappa, Alpha Omega Alpha, Phi Eta Sigma, Phi Kappa Phi, Alpha Kappa Kappa. Clubs: Mich. Alumni (Dayton) (Outstanding Alumnus award 1976), Oakwood Fur, Fin and Feather. Lodge: Rotary. Home: 6490 Saddle Dr Long Beach CA 90815

BELK, JOHN BLANTON, educational and cultural organization executive; b. Orlando, Fla., Feb. 4, 1925; s. John Blanton and Jennie (Wannamaker) B.; m. Elizabeth Jane Wilkes, Dec. 11, 1954; children: Virginia Elizabeth, Katherine Wilkes. Student, Davidson Coll., 1943, U. N.C., 1943-45. Congl. aide U.S. Congress, Washington, 1949-50; with Moral Re-Armament (numerous locations), 1950-68, exec. dir., 1966-68; founder, chmn. bd., pres. Up With People, Tucson, 1968—. Bd. dirs. Internat. Fund Sports Disabled, Arnhem, Netherlands; mem. adv. bd. U. Ariz. Coll. Nursing. Served to lt. (j.g.) USNR, 1943-45. Decorated letter of commendation; decorated Order Vasco Nunez de Balboa Panama. Mem. Zeta Psi. Clubs: Mountain Oyster; Old Pueblo (Tucson); Guaymas Yacht (Mexico). Home: 2920 Cerrado los Palitos Tucson AZ 85718 Office: Up With People 3103 N Campbell Ave Tucson AZ 85719

BELK, JUDITH B(ECKMAN), speech pathologist, clinic director, consultant; b. Bridgeport, Conn., Nov. 4, 1941; d. Stanley Beckman and Lillian (Klein) Schulman; children: Robin, Neil, Corey, Laurie. BS, Syracuse U., 1963, MA, 1964; MS, UCLA, 1969; PhD, U. So. Calif., 1974, postdoctoral studies, 1975. cert. speech lang. pathologist, audiologist, deaf edn. tchr. Asst. dir. research HEAR Ctr., Pasadena, Calif., 1971-73; dir. cranio facial services Rancho Los Amigos Hosp., Downey, Calif., 1974-78; supr. speech pathology U. Ariz., Tucson, 1979-81; pvt. practice speech and lang. pathology Tucson, 1981—; dir. pvt. ctr. Tomatis Method, Tucson and Phoenix, 1985—. Contbr. articles in profl. jours. Mem. Am. Speech, Lang. and Hearing Assn., Ariz. Speech, Lang. and Hearing Assn., Internat. Assn. Oral Myology, Council for Exceptional Children, Pima Council Devel. Disabilities (sec. 1984—). Avocations: gardening, rug-making, cooking. Office: 2204 E Fort Lowell Tucson AZ 85719

BELL, BARBARA FAY, social worker; b. Orlando, Fla., Sept. 22, 1953; d. Walter A. Bell and Rose (Tenniga) Monroe. BA in Psychology, Mercer U., 1975; MSW, U. Md., Balt., 1980. Mail reservationist Disney World, Lake Buena Vista, Fla., 1976-78; psychiat. social worker U. Calif. Ctr. on Deafness, San Francisco, 1980-85; clin. social worker Hearing Soc. for Bay Area, San Francisco, 1983—. Mem. adv. bd. Big Bros. and Sisters. of Am., Inc., San Francisco, 1983—; mem. at large Deaf Services North, San Francisco, 1984—. Mem. Nat. Assn. Social Workers (cert.). Democrat. Avocations: reading, gardening, walking, exploring old archtl. structures. Home: 241 Randall St San Francisco CA 94131 Office: Hearing Soc Bay Area Inc 1428 Bush St San Francisco CA 94109

BELL, DAVID MARTIN, lawyer; b. Cambridge, Ohio, Nov. 12, 1953; s. Robert August and Grace Ann (Cleaveland) B.; m. Janette F. Chavez, Aug. 2, 1986. B.A., U. Iowa, 1976, J.D. with distinction, 1981. Bar: Ariz. 1981, U.S. Dist. Ct. Ariz. 1981, U.S. Ct. Appeals (9th cir.) 1981. Ptnr. O'Connor, Cavanagh, et. al, Phoenix, 1981—. Mem. Sierra Club, 1981—. Recipient U. Iowa Scholarship, Iowa City, 1975. Mem. Maricopa County Bar Assn. (tchr. high sch. teaching program Young Lawyers div. 1982, 84—), Ariz. Bar Assn., ABA (natural resources, torts and ins. practice sects. 1981—), Ariz. Trial Lawyers Assn., Def. Research Inst., Phoenix Assn. of Def. Counsel. Home: 3317 N 47th Pl Phoenix AZ 85018

BELL, DEANE M., medical software executive; b. Mont., 1953. BS in Pharmacy, U. Mont., 1977; MS in Software Engring., Seattle U., 1982. System analyst Pacific Med. Ctr., Seattle, 1982-84; pharmacy product mgr. Phamis Inc., Seattle, 1984—. Served to lt. USPHS, 1976-82. Mem. Seattle Area Soc. Hosp. Pharmacists, Am. Soc. Hosp. Pharmacists. Home: 5229

36th Ave SW Seattle WA 98126-2807 Office: Phamis Inc 419 2d Ave S Seattle WA 98114-3057

BELL, DONALD WILLIAM, experimental psychologist; b. Los Angeles, Apr. 28, 1936; s. Samuel Chamblis and Betty M. (Welz) B. BA, U. So. Calif., 1959, MA, 1963, PhD, 1966. Research assoc. Subcom. on Noise Research Ctr., Los Angeles, 1962-66; postdoctoral fellow Stanford (Calif.) U., 1966-68; research psychologist SRI Internat., Menlo Park, Calif., 1968-76, sr. research psychologist, 1976-82, program mgr., 1982-83, dir. speech research program, 1983—; pres. Digital Voice Corp., 1982—. Contbr. articles to profl. jours. Mem. planning commn. Town of Portola Valley, Calif. Mem. IEEE, Acoustical Soc. Am., Psychonomic Soc., Am. Voice I/O Soc. (dir.). Republican. Home: 15 Peak Ln Portola Valley CA 94025 Office: SRI Internat 333 Ravenswood Menlo Park CA 94025

BELL, GEORGE ALFRED, marketing professional; b. Plattsburgh, N.Y., Mar. 14, 1948; s. George Alfred and Marian (Yersley) B.; AA, Antelope Valley Coll., 1976; BA in Pub. Relations, San Jose State U., 1978. Automobile racing driver, 1964-67, 70-72, 75, 86—; liaison engr., mem. flight test crew Lockheed-Calif. Co., Palmdale, 1972-75; v.p. Bluemenshein & Bell, Leona Valley, Calif., 1975-77; cons. pub. relations, writer, San Jose, Calif., 1977-81; mgr. mktg. communications Dynatel/3M, Sunnyvale, Calif., 1981-83; account exec. Simon Pub. Relations, Sunnyvale, Calif., 1983-84; pub. relations mgr. Imahara & Keep, Sunnyvale, 1984-86; cons. advt., pub. relations agy. mgmt. and ops., 1986—; cons. mktg. communications and research; condr. seminars in high performance driving for law enforcement agys.; designer racing cars and lightweight aircraft, 1964-80. Served with AUS, 1967-70; Vietnam. Decorated Air medal, Army Commendation medal, Purple Heart. Mem. Pub. Relations Soc. Am., Internat. Assn. Bus. Communicators., Bus./Profl. Advt. Assn. (bd. dirs. 1982-85, v.p. fin. 1983-84), Soaring Soc. Am., Exptl. Aircraft Assn., Racing Drivers' Club. Author: Motor Racing' Management, 1975; contbr. numerous articles to mags.

BELL, GEORGE IRVING, laboratory administrator, biophysics researcher; b. Evanston, Ill., Aug. 4, 1926; s. George Irving and Hazel (Seerley) B.; m. Virginia Lotz, Jan. 13, 1956; children—Carolyn Bell Prince, George Irving Jr. B.S. in Physics, Harvard U., 1947; Ph.D. in Theoretical Physics, Cornell U., 1951. Staff mem. Los Alamos Nat. Lab, 1951-70, assoc., alt. or acting div. leader, 1970-80, div. leader, 1980—; Gordon McKay lectr. Harvard U., Cambridge, Mass., 1962-63; mem. Basel Inst. Immunology, Switzerland, 1979-80; scholar in human biology Eleanor Roosevelt Inst. for Cancer Research, Denver, 1977—; mem. bd. sci. counselors Nat. Cancer Inst., Bethesda, 1985—. Author: (with S. (Glasstone) Nuclear Reactor Theory, 1970; editor: Theoretical Immunology, 1978; contbr articles to profl. publs. fellow RCA Corp., 1945-47, AEC, 1948-50. Fellow Am. Phys. Soc., Am. Nuclear Soc. (cert. merit 1966), AAAS; mem. Biophys Soc., N.Y. Acad. Sci. Clubs: Am. Alpine (David A. Sowles medal 1981) (N.Y.); Groupe de Haute Montagne (Paris); Himalayan (India). Avocations: mountaineering; trekking; photography. Office: T-DO MS B210 PO Box 1663 Los Alamos NM 87545

BELL, GREGORY FRANCIS, periodontist; b. Hibbing, Minn., Oct. 11, 1951; s. Orin Russell and Mary Kay (Ivancie) B.; m. Michele Rae Margetts, Aug. 11, 1973; children—Anne, Kate. B.S., U. Minn., 1975, D.D.S., 1976; M.S.D., Mayo Grad. Sch. of Medicine, 1980. Gen. practice dentistry St. Paul, 1976-77; resident in periodontics Mayo Clinic, Rochester, Minn., 1977-80; practice dentistry specializing in periodontics Cheyenne, Wyo., 1980—; mem. adv. bd. Sheridan Coll., Wyo., 1983—. Contbr. articles to profl. jour. Comdr. Cheyenne Sr. Squadron CAP, 1984; col. Wyo. Wing Comdr. CAP, 1986. Recipient Search and Rescue award CAP, 1983, Red Service ribbon, 1984, Recruiter award, 1984; Allan Bluhm Meml. award U. Minn., 1976, CAP Lifesaving award, 1985. Mem. Am. Acad. Periodontology, ADA, Wyo. Dental Assn., Southeast Wyo. Dental Assn., Air Force Assn. (bd. dirs. Cheyenne chpt. 1985), Omicron Kappa Upsilon. Roman Catholic. Office: 3100 Henderson Dr Suite 6 Cheyenne WY 82001

BELL, JACK N., architect; b. Kansas City, Mo., Dec. 22, 1928; s. J.V. and Olive (House) B.; m. Ruth Louise Roberts, Aug. 22, 1953; children: Christopher R., Cozette S., Corwin E., Carla M. BS in Archtl. Engring., U. Colo., 1956. Registered architect, Colo. Architect Ditzen, Rowland, Mueller, Boulder, Colo., 1956-62, James Johnson & Assocs., Lakewood, Colo., 1962-63, Henningston, Durham, Richardson, Denver, 1963-66; ptnr. Roark Assocs., Architects, Denver, 1966-76; mgr. facilities, planning, design Nat. Ctr. Atmospheric Research, Boulder, 1977—. Served with USN, 1951-55, comdr. Res. ret. Recipient awards AIA. Republican. Club: Weimaraner (Colo.)(pres. 1959-60). Avocations: fishing, hunting. Office: Nat Ctr Atmospheric Research PO Box 3000 Boulder CO 80307

BELL, JAYNELLE KHAMILLAH, pharm. mfg. co. mgr.; b. Oakland, Calif., Feb. 26, 1953; d. William Hayes and Genieve Cartwright (Hilton) Jenkins; B.A., U. Calif., Berkeley, 1976; M.B.A. (Basic Edn. Opportunity grantee, Consortium fellow), U. So. Calif., 1979; m. James M. Bell, June 28, 1980; children—Robert, Semaj. Bus. mgr. U. Calif.-Berkeley publ. Blue and Gold, 1975-76; mktg. analyst Oakland Tribune/Gannett Publs., 1976-77; sales rep. Procter & Gamble Co., San Francisco dist., 1979-81; dist. mgr. Drackett Products div. Bristol Myers Corp., Dublin, Calif., 1981-84; sr. account mgr. Block Drug Co., Jersey City, N.J., 1984-86; owner, mgr. In Affairs With Flair!, Benicia, Calif., 1985— Participant Big Sister Program, San Francisco, 1974—; voter registrar for Congressional campaign, 1971—. Mem. Nat. Assn. Female Execs., Women in Advt., Nat. Council Negro Women (publicity dir. asst. 1979), LWV. Republican. Methodist. Club: Profl. and Bus. Women's. Editor United Meth. Women newsletter, 1982. Home: 345 Goheen Circle Vallejo CA 94591 Office: 345 Goheen Circle Vallejo CA 94591

BELL, LARRY STUART, artist; b. Chgo., Dec. 6, 1939; s. Hyman David and Rebecca Ann (Kriegmont) B.; 2 daus. Student, Chouinard Art Inst., Los Angeles, 1957-59. One man exhbns. include Stedelijk Mus., Amsterdam, 1967, Pasadena Art Mus., 1972, Oakland Mus., 1973, Ft. Worth Art Mus., 1975, Santa Barbara Mus. Art, 1976, Washington U., St. Louis, 1976, Art Mus. So. Tex., Corpus Christi, 1976, Hayden Gallery, M.I.T., 1977, Hudson River Mus., Yonkers, N.Y., 1981, Newport Harbor Art Mus., 1982, Marian Goodman Gallery, 1982, Ruth S. Schaffner Gallery, 1982, Erica Williams, Anne Johnson Gallery, 1982, Arco Ctr. Visual Arts, Los Angeles, 1983, Unicorn Gallery, Aspen, Colo., 1983; group exhbns. include Mus. Modern Art, N.Y.C., 1965, 79, Jewish Mus., N.Y.C., 1966, Whitney Mus. Am. Art, 1966, Guggenheim Mus., 1967, Tate Gallery, London, 1970, Hayward Gallery, London, 1971, Detroit Inst. Arts, 1973, Nat. Collections Fine Arts, 1975, San Francisco Mus. Modern Art, 1976, Museo de Arte Contemporaneo de Caracas, Venezuela, 1978, Aspen Center for Visual Arts, 1980, Fruit Market Gallery, Edinburgh, Scotland, 1980, Albuquerque Mus., 1980, Art Inst. Chgo., 1982; represented in permanent collections, Nat. Collection Fine Arts, Mus. Modern Art, N.Y.C., Whitney Mus. Am. Art, Tate Gallery, Gallery New South Wales, Australia, Albright-Knox Gallery, Art Inst., Chgo., Denver Art Mus., Dallas Mus. Fine Arts, Guggenheim Mus., Los Angeles County Mus., Victoria and Albert Mus., London, San Antonio Mus. Art, others; instr. sculpture, U. South Fla., Tampa, U. Calif., Berkeley, Irvine, 1970-73, Copley Found. grantee, 1962, Guggenheim Found. fellow, 1970, Nat. Endowment Arts grantee, 1975. Office: Box 1778 Taos NM 87571 *

BELL, LEO S., retired physician; b. Newark, Nov. 7, 1913; s. Alexander M. and Marie (Saxon) B.; A.B., Syracuse U., 1934; M.D., 1938; m. Edith Lewis, July 3, 1938; children—Jewyl Linn, David Alden. Intern, N.Y.C. Hosp., 1938, Bklyn. Hosp., 1939-40; resident in pediatrics Sea View Hosp., N.Y.C., 1940-41, N.Y.C. Hosp., 1941-42; practice medicine specializing in pediatrics, San Mateo, Calif., 1946-86; mem. staff Mills Meml. Hosp., San Mateo, Peninsula Hosp. & Med. Center, Burlingame, Children's Hosp., San Francisco; assoc. clin. prof. pediatrics U. Calif. Med Sch., San Francisco, Stanford Med. Sch. Palo Alto. Bd. dirs. Mills Hosp. Found., San Mateo, San Mateo County Heart Assn., Hillsborough Schs. Found. (Calif.), 1980-83. Served to capt. as flight surgeon USAAF, 1942-46. Recipient bronze and silver medals Am. Heart Assn.; diplomate Am. Bd. Pediatrics. Fellow Am. Acad. Pediatrics, Am. Pub. Health Assn.; mem. Calif. Fedn. Pediatric Socs. (pres.), Am. Fedn. Pediatric Socs. (pres.), Calif. Med. Assn., Am. Pub. Health Assn., Air Force Assn., AMA (alt. del. to ho. of dels.), Calif. (ho. of dels.), San Mateo County (sec.-treas.) med. assns., Internat., Hong Kong snuff bottle socs., World Affairs Council San Francisco. Clubs: Peninsula Golf and Country (San Mateo); Commonwealth (San Francisco). Contbr. articles to profl. jours. Home: 220 Roblar Ave Hillsborough CA 94010 Office: PO Box 1877 San Mateo CA 94401

BELL, MICHAEL STEVEN, art curator; b. Joplin, Mo., July 4, 1946; s. Vernon L. and Alpha Marie (Russell) B.; children—Shannon, Ororah, Justin, Mercury. B.F.A. (scholar), Calif. Inst. Arts, 1970; M.F.A., U. Ky., 1972. Teaching asst. Calif. Inst. Art, 1970-71, U. Ky., 1971-72; designer Amorphia, Inc., Mill Valley, Calif., 1972; asst. dir. reprodns. dept. Vorpal Gallery, San Francisco, Calif., 1973-74; curatorial asst. Oakland (Calif.) Mus., 1975-76, registrar, 1976-80; dir. Midland (Mich.) Art Council, 1980-81; art curator San Francisco Mus. Modern Art, 1981-84; asst. dir. San Francisco Arts Commn., 1984—. Exhibited in group shows including: Evansville (Ind.) Mus. Art and Sci., 1971, San Francisco Mus. Modern Art, 1978; contbr. poems and articles to various publs. Served with USAF, 1963-67. Mem. Art Mus. Assn., Am. Assn. Mus., Internat. Council Museums. Episcopalian. Home: 685 McAllister #212 San Francisco CA 94102 Office: San Francisco Arts Commn 45 Hyde St San Francisco CA 94102 *

BELL, NORMAN FRANCIS, journalist; b. Troy, N.Y., July 6, 1948; s. Marc E. Bell and Marjorie E. (Francis) Roy; m. Lisa Diane Hayner, Nov. 20, 1971. B. Commerce, McGill U., (Que.), 1970. Copyeditor Troy Record, N.Y., 1970-73; city editor Knickerbocker News, Albany, N.Y., 1973-77; metro editor Detroit News, 1977-78; asst. managing editor Columbus Citizen Jour., Ohio, 1979-81; managing editor Albuquerque Tribune, 1981-85, Tacoma News Tribune, 1985—. Mem. N. Mex. Associated Press Managing Editors (pres. 1982-84). Office: Tacoma News Tribune 1950 S State St Tacoma WA 98411

BELL, PAUL EDWARD, JR., chemist, chemical engineer; b. Verdun, France, Dec. 31, 1955; s. Paul Edward and Helen Marie (Lavin) B. BS, SUNY, 1985. Formulating chemist Inland Speciality Chem. Corp., Costa Mesa, Calif., 1979-82, quality assurance mgr., 1982-83, lab. dir., 1983, product mgr., 1984-85; plant mgr. Flask Chem. Co., Lynwood, Calif., 1986—; pres. Process Automation, Costa Mesa, 1984—. Inventor in field. Mem. Am. Chem. Soc., Instrument Soc. Am. Republican. Roman Catholic. Avocations: skiing, racquetball, running, triathalon. Office: Process Automation PO Box 6100 Costa Mesa CA 92626

BELL, PAULA OBRAY, association executive; b. Paradise, Utah, Aug. 18, 1933; d. Ernest S. and Kate (Hawkes) Obray; m. Charles Connell Bell, June 27, 1952; children—Charles Michael, David Paul, Rodney O., Allison. Student, Utah State U., 1952, 80—. Legal aid Logan, Utah, 1951, 55-65; adminstrv. asst. continuing edn. ctr. Utah State U., 1967-70; exec. v.p. Roosevelt (Utah) C. of C., 1973-86; exec. dir. Cache C. of C., Logan, Utah, 1986—; real estate salesperson Roosevelt area, 1972—; bd. dirs. Cache Valley Health Care Found., Cache Valley United Way, Utah State C. of C., also pres., 1977. Chmn. Roosevelt City Econ. Devel. Com.; chmn. Roosevelt Mcpl. Airport Bd.; bd. dirs. Utah Heart Assn., chmn., 1981-82, regional rep.; mem. bd. commrs. Utah Travel Council; mem. adv. bd. Utah State U. Coll. Bus. Utah Festival Arts, Utah Children's Mus.; mem. Utah State Agenda for 80's steering com.; trustee Utah Council Vols.; past sec.-treas. Republican party, Duchesne County. Named Outstanding Young Woman of Utah, 1976; recipient Total Citizen award Roosevelt Area C. of C. Mem. Utah Airport Ownersand Operators Assn. (sec.-treas., pres., 1986). Mormon. Clubs: Bus. and Profl. Women (Woman of Yr. award 1982, Woman of Achievement 1983), Pilot, Socialette, Fedn. Women's. Home: 300 E 1270 N Logan UT 84321 Office: 332 S 2d St Roosevelt UT 84066

BELL, ROBERT GALEN, university dean, educator; b. Clovis, N.Mex., May 6, 1938; s. Galen Linden and Lillian Vivian (Canipe) B.; m. Elwanda Nicholas, Aug. 19, 1960; 1 child, Robert Harlon. B.A., Eastern N.Mex. U., 1961, M.A., 1964; Ph.D., U. No. Colo., 1973. Prof. history N.Mex. Mil. Inst., Roswell, 1965-73, assoc. acad. dean, 1973-78; dean student services Lamar U., Beaumont, Tex., 1978-80; dean instrn. Eastern N.Mex. U., Clovis, 1980-81; dean instrn. and student devel. Roswell, 1981—. Served with U.S. Army, 1957-59. Mem. Am. Assn. for Counseling and Devel., Am. Personnel and Guidance Assn., Nat. Hist. Soc., Assn. for Supervision and Curriculum Devel., Nat. Council Instrnl. Adminstrs., Phi Delta Kappa, Phi Alpha Theta. Democrat. Baptist. Lodges: Kiwanis (exec. com. 1981—), Rotary. Home: 604 E Vista Pkwy Roswell NM 88201 Office: Eastern N Mex U PO Box 6000 Roswell NM 88202

BELL, ROBERT WILLIAM, lawyer; b. Spokane, Wash., Jan. 12, 1938; s. Harold Edward and Exie Lucille (Harris) B.; m. Bonnie Bell, Jan. 28, 1961; children: Brad, Bruce. BBA, Calif. State U., Sacramento, 1961; JD, McGeorge Sch. Law, 1968. Assoc. atty. Hefner, Stark & Marois, Sacto, Calif., 1968-72, ptnr., 1972—; bd. dirs. Systems Integrators, Sacramento, 1979—; bd. trustees Sutter Community Hosps., Sacto, 1982—. Contbr. articles to monthly mag. Bd. dirs. Citizens Crime Alert, Sacramento, 1984, Sacramento Library Found., Crocker Art Mus., 1984—. Served with USMC, 1955-58. Mem. Sutter Health Systems (bd. dirs. 1983—), Camellia Festival Assn. (bd. dirs. 1980—, past pres.), Air Force Assn. (pres. 1983, Outstanding Performance 1980), Calif. State U. Pres. Club (pres., Outstanding Alumnus, 1980), Del Paso C. of C. (Pres. Spl. award 1979). Republican. Clubs: Downtown (Sacramento) (bd. dirs. 1983), Sutter. Lodge: Rotary. Avocations: snow skiing, golfing. Office: Hefner Stark Marois 555 Capitol Mall #1425 Sacramento CA 95814

BELL, STANLEY JOSEPH, lawyer; b. San Francisco, June 23, 1921; s. Harry James and Rose (Callen) B.; m. Marie S. Morini, Oct. 10, 1942 (div. June 1968); children: Steven, James, Susan, Edward; m. Rita Foegal, June 23, 1979. AB, Stanford U., 1947; LLB, U. So. Calif., 1951. Lic. atty. Calif. Horseracing Bd. Ptnr. Boccardo, Lull, Niland and Bell, San Jose, Calif., 1955-80; sole practice San Francisco, 1980—; lectr. San Francisco Trial Lawyers Assn. Mem. Friends of Filoli, Woodside, Calif., 1986-87. Served with USN, 1942-45. Mem. ABA, Assn. Trial Lawyers Am., Calif. Trial Lawyers Assn., Santa Clara County Trial Lawyers Assn. (pres. 1960), San Francisco Trial Lawyers Assn., Calif. State Bar Assn., Calif. Horseman's Benevolent and Protective Assn., Calif. Thoroughbred Breeder's Assn. Clubs: La Costa (Calif.) Country; San Francisco Bay; Calif. Golf (South San Francisco). Office: 505 Sansome 18th Fl San Francisco CA 94111

BELLER, GERALD STEPHEN, former ins. co. exec.; b. Phila., Aug. 6, 1935; s. Nathan and Adelaide B. (Goldfarb) B.; C.L.U., Am. Coll., Bryn Mawr, Pa., 1972; m. Nancy R. Nelson, June 8, 1968; children—Fay A., Mark S., Royce W., Merrilee A., Marie A., Frank A. Spl. agt. Prudential Ins. Co., San Bernardino, Calif., 1959-62, div. mgr., 1962-66; agy. supr. Aetna Life & Casualty Co., Los Angeles, 1966-69, gen. agt., 1969-77. Active fund-raising drives City of Hope, other charitable orgns. Served with USAF, 1953-57. Recipient Man of Year award, 1961; Manpower Builders award, 1966-69; Agy. Builders award, 1970-72; Pres.'s Trophy award, 1973-74; Nat. Mgmt. award, 1973-76. Mem. Los Angeles Life Underwriters Assn., Am. Soc. C.L.U.s, Calif. Assn. Life Underwriters, Los Angeles County C.L.U.s. Home: 20625 Tonawanda Rd Apple Valley CA 92307

BELLETTO, PETER MICHAEL, school system administrator; b. Lytham, England, Apr. 20, 1945; s. Fred V. and Olive V. (Palmer) B.; m. Patricia S. Belletto, June 18, 1966; children: Jennifer, Rebecca, William. AA, Gavilan Coll., 1966; BA in Social Sci., History, U. Calif., Fresno, 1968; MA in Edn., No. Ariz. U., 1970, MA in Edn. Adminstrn., 1975; postgrad., Nova U., 1986. Cert. elem. tchr., Ariz., secondary tchr., Fla.; cert. elem. prin., high sch. prin., sch. supt., Ariz; cert. jr. coll. tchr., Ariz. Headmaster Navajo Acad., Ganado, Ariz., 1977-78; asst. prof. Coll. Ganado, 1975-76, asst. prof., div. chmn., 1976-79; prin. Ganado High Sch., 1979-80; asst. supt. Ganado Unified Sch. Dist., 1980-84, assoc. supt., 1984—; cons. 1980—; team mem. N. Cen. Assn. Elem. and Secondary Schs., Ariz., 1975—. Contbr. articles to profl. jours. Fire chief Ganado Fire Dist., 1979-85; chairperson Ganado Fire Dist., 1986—, bd. dirs.; Dem. precinct committeeman, Apache County, Ariz., 1984—; voter registrar, Apache County, 1982—; clerk Ganado Children's Village, 1984-86.. Recipient Edn. Service award Ganado Unified Sch. Dist., 1984, Tse Chishi Bi Tsaazi award Rough Rock Demonstation Sch., 1974; named Outstanding Sch. Mgr. The Exec. Educator, 1986. Mem. Ariz. Sch. Adminstrn. Assn., Asm. Assn. Sch. Bus. Offices, Ariz. Sch. Personal Adminstrn. Assn., Phi Delta Kappa. Episcopalian. Lodge: Lions (tail twister 1986). Avocations: piano, photography, chess, hunting and fishing, tennis. Home: PO Box 908 Ganado AZ 86505 Office: care Dist Office Bldg Ganado Unified Sch Dist #20 Ganado AZ 86505

BELLIS, CARROLL JOSEPH, surgeon; b. Shreveport, La.; s. Joseph and Rose (Bloome) B.; m. Mildred Darmody, Dec. 26, 1939; children—Joseph, David. BS, U. Minn., 1930, MS in Physiology, 1932, PhD in Physiology, 1934, MD, 1936, PhD in Surgery, 1941. Diplomate Am. Bd. Surgery. Resident surgery U. Minn. Hosps., 1937-41; pvt. practice surgery Long Beach, Calif., 1945—; mem. staff St. Mary's, Community hosps., Long Beach; cons. surgery Long Beach Gen. Hosp.; prof., chmn. dept. surgery Calif. Coll. Medicine, 1962—; surgical cons. to Surgeon-Gen., U.S. Army. Author: Fundamentals of Human Physiology, 1935, A Critique of Reason, 1938, Lectures in Medical Physiology; contbr. numerous articles in field of surgery, physiology to profl. jours. Served to col. M.C. AUS, 1941-46. Nat. Cancer Inst. fellow, 1934; recipient Charles Lyman Green prize in physiology, 1934; prize Mpls. Surg. Soc., 1938; ann. award Mississippi Valley Med. Soc., 1955. Fellow ACS, Internat. Coll. Surgeons, Am. Coll. Gastroenterology, Am. Med. Writers Assn., Internat. Coll. Angiology (sci. council), Gerontol. Soc., Am. Soc. Abdominal Surgeons, Nat. Cancer Inst., Phlebology Soc. Am., Internat. Acad. Proctology, Peripheral Vascular Soc. Am. (founding); mem. Am. Assn. Study Neoplastic Diseases, Mississippi Valley Med. Soc., N.Y. Acad. Scis., Hollywood Acad. Medicine, Am. Geriatrics Soc., Irish Med. Assn., AAAS, Am. Assn. History Medicine, Pan Pacific Surgical Assn., Indsl. Med. Assn., Los Angeles Musicians Union (hon.), Pan Am. Med. Assn. (diplomate), Internat. Bd. Surgery (cert.), Internat. Bd. Proctology (cert.), Wisdom Soc. (wisdom award of honor), Sigma Xi, Phi Beta Kappa, Alpha Omega Alpha. Home: South Quail Ridge Rd Rolling Hills CA 90274 Office: 1045 Atlantic Ave Long Beach CA 90801

BELLIS, DAVID JAMES, public adminstration educator; b. Nashville, May 1, 1944; s. Carroll Joseph and Helen Louise (Jett) B.; m. Ann S. Seagreaves, Dec. 23, 1972; 1 child, James. BS, UCLA; MA, U. So. Calif., 1969, PhD, 1977. Dir. narcotics prevention project Los Angeles, 1970-72; dir. West End drug abuse control Ontario, Calif., 1972-75; cons. Project Heavy, Los Angeles, 1975-78; dir. econs. Telacu, Los Angeles, 1978-80; asst. dir. Youth Gang Services, Los Angeles, 1980-81; councilman City of Signal Hill, Calif., 1980-86, mayor, 1983-84; assoc. prof. pub. adminstrn. Calif. State U., San Bernardino, 1985—. Author: Heroin and Politicians, 1983. Avocation: flying. Home: PO Box 1064 Cedar Glen CA 92321 Office: Calif State U 5500 University Pkwy San Bernardino CA 92407

BELLUCCI, NANCY ROSINE, psychologist; b. Boston, July 12, 1941; d. Antone Adolph and Dorina Florence (Sartorelli) Bellucci. B.A., U. N.H., 1962; M.S., Calif. State U., 1970; Ph.D., Calif. Sch. Profl. Psychology, 1979. Lic. psychologist, Calif. Tchr., Concord (N.H.) High Sch., 1962-65, Meml. High Sch., Manchester, N.H., 1966-67, Colton (Calif.) Unified Sch. Dist., 1967-69; intern, U. Hosp., San Diego, 1978, Southwood Mental Health Center, Chula Vista, Calif., 1978-79; cons. Applied Personal Dynamics, San Diego, 1979-81; sch. psychologist Chula Vista City Sch. Dist., 1971—; pvt. practice psychology, San Diego, 1979—; acting dir. Calif. Psychol. Services Ctr., 1984-85, assoc. dir., dir. psychol. services, 1985—; affiliate staff mem. Southwood Psychiat. Ctrs., 1981—, Vista Hill Hosp., 1983—, San Diego Ctr. for Children, 1984—; field placement supr. Calif. Sch. Prof. Psychology, San Diego, San Diego State U., U.S. Internat. U.; acting dir. Calif. Psychol. Services Ctr., 1984-85, assoc. dir., dir. psychoednl. services, 1985—. Named Outstanding Sch. Psychologist, Calif. Assn. Sch. Psychologists and Psychometrists, 1976. Mem. Am. Psychol. Assn., Nat. Assn. Sch. Psychologists, Calif. Psychol. Assn., Acad. San Diego Psychologists (legis. rep. 1983—), San Diego Assn. Sch. Psychologists and Psychometrists (treas. 1976-77), S.W. Personnel and Guidance Assn. (treas. pres. 1973-74, 1974-75), Alumni Assn. Calif. Sch. of Professional Psychology-San Diego (sec. 1983-84, pres. 1985-86, past pres. 1986—). Office: 2615 Camino Del Rio S Suite 300 San Diego CA 92108

BELLUOMINI, FRANK STEPHEN, accountant; b. Healdsburg, Calif., May 19, 1934; s. Francesco and Rose (Giorgi) B.; m. Alta Anita Gifford, Sept. 16, 1967; 1 child, Wendy Ann. AA, Santa Rosa Jr. Coll., 1954; BA with honors, San Jose State U., 1956. CPA, Calif. Staff acct. Hood, Gire & Co., C.P.A.'s, San Jose, Calif., 1956-60, ptnr., 1960-66; ptnr. Touche Ross & Co., C.P.A.'s, San Jose, 1967—, ptnr.-in-charge San Jose office, 1971-85, sr. ptnr. San Jose office, 1985—. Mem. adv. bd. Salvation Army, San Jose, 1979-85, San Jose Children's Council, 1982—; trustee Santa Clara County (Calif.) United Way, 1979-83, v.p. planning and allocations, 1981-83, vice chmn., 1985-87, chmn. 1987-89; bd. dirs. San Jose Mus. Art, 1984-86. Named Disting. Alumnus, San Jose State U. Sch. Bus., 1978. Mem. Santa Clara County Estate Planning Council (pres. 1979-80), Calif. Soc. C.P.A.'s (pres. chpt. 1968-69, state v.p. 1976-77), Am. Inst. C.P.A.'s (chmn. state and local govt. com. 1976-79), San Jose State Alumni Assn. (treas. 1960-61, dir. 1961-62, exec. com. 1961-62), San Jose State Acctg. Round Table (bd. dirs., treas. 1982—), Beta Alpha Psi (San Jose State U. Outstanding Alumnus award 1986). Roman Catholic. Club: San Jose Rotary (dir. 1979-81, trustee and treas. San Jose Rotary Endowment 1976-83).

BELOK, MICHAEL VICTOR, educator; b. Whiting, Ind., June 22, 1923; s. Michael and Helen (Dobos) B.; m. Georgina Pilkington, July 31, 1965. B.S., Ind. U., 1948; M.A., Ariz. State U., 1953; Ph.D., U. So. Calif., 1958. Lectr. edn. U. So. Calif., 1958; mem. faculty Ariz. State U., Tempe, 1959—; prof. edn. Ariz. State U., 1968—; editorial cons. Author: Psychological Foundations of Education, 1964, Approaches to Values in Education, 1967, Forming the American Minds: Early Schoolbooks and Their Compilers, 1783-1837, 1973, Explorations in the History and Sociology of Indian Education, 1973, Noah Webster Revisited, 1973, Conflict, Permanency, Change and Education, 1976, Lives in Education, 1984, United States and the Persian Gulf, 1985. Contbg. editor: Internat. Rev. History and Polit. Sci, 1968-73; editor: Rev. Jour. of Philosophy and Social Scis, 1976; guest editor: Parsons and Sociology, 1975; adv. editor: Indian Jour. Social Research, 1965-71, others. Served with AUS, 1943-46. Fellow Nat. Philosophy of Edn. Soc.; mem. History of Edn. Soc., Delta Tau Kappa (region chancellor 1968-80), Phi Delta Kappa, Kappa Delta Pi. Home: 1015 W Fairway Dr Mesa AZ 85201

BELSKY, THEODORE, research public health chemist; b. New Brunswick, N.J., Dec. 24, 1930; s. Wally and Mary Dora (Gross) B.; m. Gloria Ann England, Oct. 5, 1952; 1 child, Elena. AA, City Coll. San Francisco, 1957; BS, U. Calif., Berkeley, 1960, PhD, 1966. Organic geochemist Space Sci. Lab. UCLA, 1966-68; chemist WRRL USDA, Albany, Calif., 1969; pub. health chemist Calif. Dept. Health Services, Berkeley, 1969—. Contbg. author (encyclopedia entry) Precambrian Hydrocarbons, 1972; (book) Guide for Evaluation of Atmospheric Analysis, 1973, Method Air Sampling and Analysis, 1977; contbr. articles to profl. jours. Served with USN, 1951-55. Mem. AAAS, Am. Pub. Health Assn. (intersoc. com. 1971-78), Am. Chem. Soc., Bay Area Mass Spectrometry. Home: 1327 Carlotta Ave Berkeley CA 94703

BELTON, DANIEL JAMES, polymer physicist, researcher; b. Yonkers, N.Y., July 20, 1948; s. Harry James and Anne Maureen (Kupko) B.; m. Kyesook Kim, Oct. 23, 1982; children: Alexndra Kye, Daniel Alan. BS in Ceramic Engring., Ohio State U., 1971, MS, 1973; PhD in Material Sci., Northwestern U., 1980. Registered profl. engr. Ceramic engr. Myerson Corp., Cambridge, Mass., 1973-76; research asst. Northwestern U., Evanston, Ill., 1976-80; mem. then sr. mem. tech. staff Philips Research Labs., Sunnyvale, Calif., 1980—. Contbr. numerous articles to profl jours.; patentee in field. Ferro Corp. fellow, Ohio State U., 1972; research scholar, Northwestern U., 1978. Mem. IEEE, Internat. Soc. Hybrid Microelectronics, Am. Chem. Soc., Sigma Xi. Republican. Roman Catholic. Avocations: skiing, outdoor activities, reading, piano. Home: 3681 Slopeview Dr San Jose CA 95148 Office: Philips Research Labs c/o Signetics Corp 811 E Arques Ave Sunnyvale CA 94088

BELTON, JOHN CLAIR, biology educator, consultant, researcher, administrator; b. Gladstone, Oreg., Dec. 20, 1934; s. Howard Clair and Mae Castle (Brown) B.; m. Carol Marie Inhelder, Aug. 6, 1966; children: Arthur W., Stephen C. BS, Lewis & Clark Coll., 1957; MS, Oreg. State U., 1961, PhD, 1966. Instr. zoology Oreg. State U., Corvallis, 1964-65; asst. prof. biology Calif. State U., Hayward, 1966-69, assoc. prof., 1969-75, prof. biology, 1975—, chmn. dept. biology, 1981—; adj. faculty U. Calif., San

Francisco, 1977—; edn. cons. Am. Inst. Biol. Scis., Washington, 1986—. Contbr. articles to profl. jours; mem. rev. bd. CHEST, 1980—. Recipient Meritorious Teaching award Calif. State U., Hayward, 1986; tng. grantee EPA, 1982-84. Mem. AAAS, Am. Lung Assn. (local exec. bd. dirs. 1981-86), Soc. Electron Microscopy (local pres. 1978-79), Electron Microscopy of Am., Sigma Xi. Avocations: wood working, photography. Home: 1342 Trestle Glen Rd Oakland CA 94610 Office: Calif State U Dept Biol Scis 25800 Carlos Bee Blvd Hayward CA 94542

BELTRÁN, ANTHONY NATALICIO, military officer, deacon; b. Flagstaff, Ariz., Aug. 17, 1938; s. Natalicio Torres and Mary Magdalene (Sandoval) B.; m. Patricia Emily Cañez, Nov. 18, 1962; children: Geralyn P., Bernadette M., Albert A., Catherine M., Elizabeth R., Michael J., Theresa R., Christopher M. AA, Phoenix Jr. Coll., 1971. Ordained deacon Roman Cath. Ch., 1977. Gen. clk. Blue Cross Blue Shield, Phoenix, 1958-61; unit clk. Ariz. Air N.G., Phoenix, 1961, personnel technician, 1962-65, adminstrv. supr., 1965-81, support services supr., 1981—. Bd. dirs. Friendly House, Phoenix, 1982—; mem. Alma de la Gente, Phoenix, 1982—, Chiefs Police Community Adv. Group, Phoenix, 1984—, Mayor's Task Force on Juvenile Crime, Phoenix, 1979-81; pres. IMAGE de Phoenix, 1985-87. Served to staff sgt. USAF, 1961-62. Recipient Community Service award Phoenix C. of C., 1982. Mem. Fed. Exec. Assn. (sec., treas. Phoenix chpt. 1985-86, 1st v.p. 1987—, pres. award for community service 1986), Ariz. Hispanic Personnel Mgmt. Assn. (bd. dirs. 1983-86, sec. 1985), Ariz. Council Hispanic Employment Program Mgrs. (treas. 1980-81, v.p. 1981-82, pres. 1982-84, named Outstanding Mem. of Yr. 1981, 83), Enlisted Assn. N.G. Ariz. Democrat. Avocations: ministry work for the Spanish speaking. Home: 4109 W Monte Vista Rd Phoenix AZ 85009 Office: Ariz Air NG 2001 S 32d St 161 Air Refueling Group Phoenix AZ 85034-6098

BELTRAN, NEIL ALAN, advertising executive; b. San Jose, Calif., Feb. 7, 1958; s. Felix Louis and Gloria Karen (Hansen) B.; m. Pamela Ann Thompson, Feb. 16, 1985. BA in Creative Arts, San Jose State U., 1984. Free-lance advt. artist, writer San Jose, 1978-84; creative dir. Weider Cos., Woodland Hills, Calif., 1984—; advt. and mktg. cons. Jericho Labs., Achievement Plus Inst., RDI Mktg., 1985—. Contbr. articles to mags.; author (short stories) Roomers (1st Place award 1983), The Last Boy in Coulterville (1st Place award 1983); (poems) War Girl (Hon. Mention 1983), The Evangelist (3d Place award 1983); (film) Mostly Ghostly (Ambassador's award Cannes Film Festival 1971, Best Film by a Young Author award Internat. Film Festival 1971). Recipient Best Performance in Artistic Achievement award Weider Cos., Los Angeles, 1985. Republican. Avocations: mil. history, fine art, painting. Office: Weider Health and Fitness 21100 Erwin St Woodland Hills CA 91367

BEMIS, THOMAS BRUCE, civil servant; b. Carlsbad, N.Mex., Oct. 21, 1953; s. Herbert Alva and Joanna Joy (Brenholtz) B.; m. Bobbie Sue Hall, Aug. 15, 1981; children: Melissa Laura, Stephanie Annette. BA, N.Mex. State U., 1978; diploma, Nat. Radio Inst., 1984. Photo journalist Hockley County Free Press, Levelland, Tex., 1978-79; substitute tchr. Carlsbad (N.Mex.) Mcpl. Schs., 1979; pk. aide Nat. Pk. Service, Carlsbad, 1979-80, condr. range expansion, migratory researcher on Cave Swallow, 1979—, electronics worker, 1980-81, electronics technician, 1981—. Author: (short story) The Dollar, 1978 (1st Place award W. Tex. Writers Guild, 1979); editor Southwest Cavers, 1979; an inventor ultrasonic receiver. Recipient Achievement award Nat. Pk. Service, 1980. Mem. Nat. Speleological Soc. (chmn. SW region 1976), Cave Research Found. (joint venturer, 1976—). Republican. Presbyterian. Avocations: caving, climbing, backpacking, snorkeling, amateur radio. Home: 417 Sunnyview Carlsbad NM 88220 Office: Carlsbad Caverns Nat Pk 3225 National Parks Way Carlsbad NM 88220

BENACH, SHARON ANN, physician assistant; b. New Orleans, Aug. 28, 1944; d. Wilbur G. and Freda Helen (Klaas) Cherry; m. Richard Benach, Dec. 6, 1969 (div. Oct. 1976); children: Craig, Rachel. Degree, St. Louis U., 1978. Physician asst. VA Hosp., St. Louis, 1982-84, Maricopa County Health Services, Phoenix, 1984—. Served with USPHS, 1978-82. Recipient Outstanding Performance award Dept. Health and Human Services. Mem. Mensa. Jewish. Avocation: pre-Columbian archaeology. Home: PO Box 1272 Mesa AZ 85201

BENBOW, RICHARD ADDISON, psychological counselor; b. Las Vegas, Dec. 27, 1949; s. Jules Coleman and Bonnie Ray B.; BBA, U. Nev. 1972, M.S. in Counseling, 1974; AAS in Bus. Mgmt. and Real Estate, Clark County Community Coll., 1980; PhD in Clin. Psychology, U. Humanistic Studies, 1986. Cert. tchr., Nev.; cert. clin. mental health counselor. Owner, mgr. Dick's Hardware, Las Vegas, 1981-82; jud. services officer Mcpl. Ct., City of Las Vegas, 1982—, inmate classification technician Detention and Correctional Services, 1982-83; stress mgmt. cons. Mem. Biofeedback Soc. Am., Assn. Humanistic Psychology, Nat. Assn. Psychotherapists, Am. Personnel and Guidance Assn., Am. Mental Health Counselors Assn., Am. Acad. Crisis Interveners, Am. Correctional Assn., U.S. Tai Kung Fu Assn. (black belt), Nev. Marshals Assn. (bd. dirs.), Nat. Assn. Underwater Instrs., So. Nev. Bluegrass Soc., Jr. C. of C., U.S. Jaycees (presdl. award of honor 1978-79), Delta Sigma Phi. Democrat. Christian Scientist. Home: 7131 Pleasant View Ave Las Vegas NV 89117 Office: Mcpl Ct Jud Services City of Las Vegas 400 E Stewart St Las Vegas NV 89101

BENCALA, KENNETH EDWARD, environmental research engineer; b. Detroit, Mar. 26, 1951; married; 2 children. BS in Engring., Harvey Mudd Coll., 1973; MSChemE, Calif. Inst. Tech., 1975, PhDChemE, 1979. Chem. engr. U.S. Geol. Survey, Menlo Park, Calif., 1978—. Contbr. articles to profl. jours. Bd. trustees Hillbrook Sch., Los Gatos, Calif., 1985—, pres. 1986. Mem. Am. Chem. Soc., Am. Geophys. Union, Am. Inst. Chem. Engrs., Sigma Xi. Office: US Geol Survey 345 Middlefield Rd MS496 Menlo Park CA 94025

BENDA, PETER HANS, aeronautical engineer; b. Wytheville, Va., July 17, 1960; s. Rudolf Anton Josef and Gertrude (Beer) B. BS, BA, Wash. and Lee U., 1981; MSAA, U. Wash., 1983. Aeronautical engr. E-Systems, Inc., Fairfax, Va., 1983-85; sr. engr. Alcoa Def. Systems, San Diego, 1985—. Mem. AIAA, Am. Helicopter Soc., Phi Beta Kappa. Lodge: Order of Monocle (chmn. 1979-86). Avocations: flying, biking, sailing. Home: PO Box 261052 San Diego CA 92126 Office: Alcoa Def Systmes 16761 Via Del Campo Ct San Diego CA 92127

BENDER, BETTY WION, librarian; b. Mt. Ayer, Iowa, Feb. 26, 1925; d. John F. and Sadie A. (Guess) Wion; m. Robert F. Bender, Aug. 24, 1946. B.S., N.Tex. State U., Denton, 1946; M.A., U. Denver, 1957. Asst. cataloger N. Tex. State U. Library, 1946-49; from cataloger to head acquisitions So. Meth. U., Dallas, 1949-56; reference asst. Ind. State Library, Indpls., 1951-52; librarian Ark. State Coll., 1958-59, Eastern Wash. Hist. Soc., Spokane, 1960-67; reference librarian, then head circulation dept. Spokane (Wash.) Public Library, 1968-73, library dir., 1973—; vis. instr. U. Denver, summers 1957-60, 63, fall 1959; instr. Whitworth Coll., Spokane, 1962-64; mem. Gov. Wash. Regional Conf. Libraries, 1968, Wash. Statewide Library Devel. Council, 1970-71. Bd. dirs. N.W. Regional Found., 1973-75, Inland Empire Goodwill Industries, 1975-77, Wash. State Library Commn., 1979—, Future Spokane, 1983—, vice chmn., 1986-87. Recipient YMCA Outstanding Achievement award in Govt., 1985. Mem. ALA (mem. library adminstrn. and mgmt. assn. com. on orgn. 1982-83, chmn. nominating com. 1983-85, v.p./pres.-elect. 1985-86, pres. 1986-87), Pacific N.W. Library Assn. (chmn. circulation div. 1972-75, conv. chmn. 1977), Wash. Library Assn. (v.p./pres.-elect 1975-77, pres. 1977-78), AAUW (pres. Spokane br. 1969-71, rec. sec. Wash. br. 1971-73, fellowship named in honor 1972), Spokane and Inland Empire Librarians (dir. 1967-68), Am. Soc. Pub. Adminstrn. Republican. Lutheran. Club: Zonta (pres. Spokane chpt. 1976-77, dist. conf. treas. 1972). Home: 119 N 6th St Cheney WA 99004 Office: Spokane Public Library Comstock Bldg Library W 906 Main Ave Spokane WA 99201

BENDER, BRENDA (ANN), broadcasting company executive; b. Montesano, Wash., May 5, 1956; d. Marion Jr. and Ramona (Cass) Bogdanovich; m. Boyd Joseph Bender Jr., Dec. 18, 1976; children: Tyler Jo, Ronnie Lee, Bobbie Jean. AA in Secretarial Sci., Grays Harbor Community Coll., 1976; student, City U., Seattle, 1981—. With KIRO Inc., Seattle, 1976—, asst. to pres., 1980-81, employee relations coordinator, 1981-83, dir. adminstrv. services, 1983-85, asst. v.p., 1985—. Active King County (Wash.) United Way, 1986—; bd. dirs. Puget Sound chpt. Vols. Am., 1987—. Mem. Adminstrv. Mgmt. Soc. (2d v.p. 1984-85, 1st v.p. 1985-87, pres. 1986-87, Greatest Contbn. award 1984-85). Democrat. Roman Catholic. Avocations: family, music, fitness.

BENDER, BRENDA MARIE, psychiatric nurse, therapist; b. Bethesda, Md., Sept. 26, 1948; d. John Louis and Sue Marie (Wheeler) Carres; m. David Harvey Bender, June 19, 1973; children: Eric, Grant. BS in Nursing, Am. U., 1970; BA in Social Work, Colo. State U., 1979; MA in Social Work, Colo. State Coll., 1986. Registered nurse. Pub. health nurse Montgomery County Health Dept., Silver Spring, Md., 1970-72; sch. nurse Overseas Dependent Schs., Karlsruhe, Fed. Republic Germany, 1972-74; staff nurse Golden Valley (Minn.) Health Ctr., 1975-76; nurse Adams County Juvenile Detention Ctr., Brighton, Colo., 1977-79; psychiat. nurse Mental Health Ctr. Boulder County, Longmont, Colo., 1979—. Mem. Nat. Assn. Social Workers. Democrat. Congregationalist. Home: 2518 Danbury Dr Longmont CO 80501 Office: Longmont Mental Health Ctr 250 Kimbark St Longmont CO 80501

BENDER, GARY LEE, accountant; b. Aberdeen, S.D., Oct. 9, 1948; s. Gideon and Dorothy (Malsom) B.; m. Daena Sue Poynor, Dec. 20, 1971; 1 son, Garrett. B.B.A. magna cum laude, Eastern N.Mex. U., 1974. C.P.A., N.Mex. Acct., Elmer Fox & Co., Colorado Springs, Colo., 1975-76, Williams, Faver, Sudduth & Co., Muleshoe, Tex., 1976-77; bus. mgr. Bender Oldsmobile-Cadillac-Datsun, Inc., Clovis, N.Mex., 1977; ptnr. Hager, McKay, Bender & Co., Portales, N.Mex., 1978; owner Gary L. Bender, C.P.A., Portales, 1978-84; pres. Bender Burnett & Co., Clovis and Portales, N.Mex., 1984—. Pres., Roosevelt County Crimestoppers, 1979-81; bd. dirs. N.Mex. Christian Children's Home, 1980—, sec.-treas., 1983—; mem. Portales Bd. Econ. Devel., 1982—, vice chmn., 1982. Served with USN, 1967-70. Mem. Am. Inst. C.P.A.s, N.Mex. Soc. C.P.A.s, N.Mex. State Bd. Pub. Accts. (dir.), Nat. Assn. State Bds. Accountancy (surveillance and enforcement com.), Roosevelt County C. of C. (dir., v.p. 1982), Sigma Nu (assoc. treas. alumni 1978-80). Republican. Clubs: Rotary (dir., pres. 1982-83). Home: 404 Diamondhead Clovis NM 88101 Office: PO Box 126 Clovis NM 88101 Other: PO Box 570 Portales NM 88130

BENDER, WILLIAM TUCKER, physician; b. San Francisco, Dec. 5, 1926; s. William Lee and Claire Althea (Tucker) B.; m. Joann Heinz, Apr. 4, 1952 (div. 1962); m. Mickie Bender, Oct. 8, 1964; 1 child, Gretchen Ann. B.A., U. Calif.-Berkeley, 1948; M.D., U. Calif.-San Francisco, 1951. Diplomate Am. Bd. Ob-Gyn. Resident in ob-gyn U. Calif.-San Francisco, 1952-54, 56-57; pvt. practice medicine specializing in gynecology and obstetrics, San Francisco, 1957—. Served to capt. USAF, 1954-56. Fellow Am. Coll. Ob-Gyn; mem. AMA, Calif. Med. Soc., San Francisco Med. Soc., Alpha Omega Alpha. Democrat. Club: Mizuri. Office: 490 Post St Suite 1606 San Francisco CA 94102

BENEDETTI, ROBERT L., theatre educator, director, author; b. Chgo., Feb. 27, 1939; s. Dino Rigoletto and Lola (Chiosiri) B.; m. Joan M. Howe, June 5, 1966; children: Kirsten, Benjamin, Nina. BSc, Northwestern U., 1960, MA, 1962, PhD, 1969. Asst. prof. Carnegie-Mellon U., Pitts., 1968-70; chmn. Yale Drama Sch., New Haven, 1970-71, York U., Toronto, Ont., Can., 1971-73; assoc. prof. theater U. Calif., Riverside, 1973-74; dean Calif. Inst. Arts, Valencia, 1974-82, mem. faculty, 1982—; guest dir. at Tyrone Guthrie Theatre, Oreg., Great Lakes and Colo. Shakespeare Festivals, Pacific Conservatory Performing Arts, South Coast Repertory Theatre, Milw. Repertory Theatre, Melbourne Theatre Co.; mem. Second City Theatre, 1963-64. Author: The Actor at Work, 4th rev. edit., 1985, the Director at Work, 1984, Seeming, Being, and Becoming, 1979; dir. (film) Victory Over the Sun, 1984. Recipient Joseph Jefferson award Chgo. Critics, 1981; Named Best Spl. of Yr., Am. Fedn. TV and Radio Artists, 1969. Mem. Nat. Theatre Conf. (v.p. 1982-83). Democrat. Avocations: home bldg., gardening, camping. Office: Calif Inst Arts 24700 McBean Pkwy Valencia CA 91355

BENENATI, THOMAS JOSEPH, podiatrist; b. Rockville Centre, N.Y., Jan. 5, 1950; s. Casper Paul and Mary (McCintyre) B. BS in Biology, Albright Coll., 1972; D in Podiat. Medicine, Ohio Coll. Podiat. Medine. Resident Weirton (W.Va.) Osteo. Hosp., 1976-77, Podiatry Hosp. of Pitts., 1977-78; practice medicine specializing in podiatry Allied Foot & Ankle Clinics of Colo., Denver, 1978—; clin. faculty Highlands Ctr. Hosp., Denver, 1978—; lectr. in field. Contbr. articles to profl. jours. Mem. Am. Podiatry Assn., Colo. Podiatry Assn. Roman Catholic. Avocations: running, weight-lifting, scuba diving, softball, golf. Home: 4110 S Narcissus Way Denver CO 80237 Office: 5401 W Alameda Ave Lakewood CO 80214

BENEŠ, NORMAN STANLEY, meteorologist; b. Detroit, July 1, 1921; s. Stanley and Cecelia (Sereneck) B.; m. Elinor Simson, May 5, 1945 (div. Feb. 1972); children: Gregory, Heather, Michelle, Francine; m. Celia Sereneck, Mar. 3, 1972. BS, U. Wash., 1949; postgrad., U. Calif., Davis, 1963, U. Mich., 1966. Chief meteorologist Hawthorne Sch. of Aero., Moultrie, Ga., 1951-55; meteorologist U.S. Weather Bur., Phoenix, 1955-57, 59-60; meteorologist in charge NSF, Hallett, Antarctica, 1958; sta. sci. leader NSF, Byrd, Antarctica, 1960-61; meteorologist Nat. Weather Service, Sacramento, Calif., 1962-84; mem. exec. com. Benes Peak Range, Antarctica. Contbr. articles to profl. jours. Served with USN, 1943-46, PTO. Mem. PTA (pres. local chpt. 1965), AAAS, Am. Meteorol. Soc., Am. Geophys. Union, Nat. Weather Assn. Lodge: Masons. Avocation: model trains. Home: 7612 Isles Ct Fair Oaks CA 95628 Office: PO Box 2184 Fair Oaks CA 95628

BENET, LESLIE ZACHARY, pharmacokineticist; b. Cin., May 17, 1937; s. Jonas John and Esther Racie (Hirschfeld) B.; m. Carol Ann Levin, Sept. 8, 1960; children: Reed Michael, Gillian Vivia. AB in English, U. Mich., 1959, BS in Pharmacy, 1960, MS in Pharm. Chemistry, 1962; PhD in Pharm. Chemistry, U. Calif., San Francisco, 1965. Asst. prof. pharmacy Wash. State U., Pullman, 1965-69; asst. prof. pharmacy and pharm. chemistry U. Calif., San Francisco, 1969-71, assoc. prof., 1971-76, prof., 1976—, vice chmn. dept. pharmacy, 1973-78, chmn. dept. pharmacy, 1978—, dir. drug studies unit, 1977—, dir. drug kinetics and dynamics ctr., 1979—; cons. to pharm. cos.; mem. pharmacology study sect. NIH, Washington, 1977-81, chmn. 1979-81, mem. pharmacol. scis. rev. com. 1984—, chmn. 1986—. Mem. editorial bd. Pharmacology, 1979—, Pharmacy Internat., 1979-82, Pharmaceutical Research, 1983—; editor: The Effect of Disease States on Drug Pharmacokinetics, 1976, Pharmacokinetic Basis for Drug Treatment, 1984, Pharmacokinetics: A Modern View, 1984; contbr. articles to profl. jours. Fellow Acad. Pharm. Scis. (pres. 1985-86, pres.-elect 1984-85, chmn. basic pharmaceutics sect. 1976-77, mem.-at-large exec. com. 1979-83, Research Achievement award 1982), AAAS (mem.-at-large exec. com. pharm. scis. sect. 1978-81); mem. Am. Assn. Pharm. Scientists (pres. 1986), Internat. Soc. Immunopharmacology, Am. Coll. Clin. Pharmacology, ISSX, Am. Pharm. Assn., Am. Soc. Clin. Pharmacology and Therapeutics, AAUP, N.Y. Acad. Scis., Sigma Xi, Rho Chi. Home: 31 Acacia Ave Belvedere CA 94920 Office: U Calif San Francisco Dept Pharmacy San Francisco CA 94143

BENFIELD, JOHN RICHARD, surgeon; b. Vienna, Austria, June 24, 1931; came to U.S., 1938, naturalized, 1945; s. Richard and Charlotte Lola (Glatter) B.; m. Joyce A. Cohler, Dec. 22, 1963; children: Richard L., Robert E., Nancy J. A.B., Columbia U., 1952; M.D., U. Chgo., 1955. Intern Columbia-Presbyterian Hosp., N.Y.C., 1955-56; E.H. Andrews fellow in thoracic surgery U. Chgo., 1956-57; chief resident and instr. in surgery U. Chgo. Clinics, 1963-64, resident in surgery, 1956-57, 59-63; asst. prof. surgery U. Wis., 1964-67; asst. prof. UCLA, 1967-69, assoc. prof., 1969-72, prof., 1972-76, clin. prof., 1978—; James Utley prof. surgery, chmn. dept. surgery Boston U., 1977; chmn. surgery City of Hope Nat. Med. Ctr., Duarte, Calif., 1978—; cons. U.S. Naval Med. Ctr., San Diego, 1968—; mem. sr. staff VA Wadsworth Med. Ctr., Los Angeles, 1978—; bd. dirs. Am. Bd. Thoracic Surgery, 1982—. Contbr. numerous articles, chpt. to profl. publs.; editor: Current Problems in Cancer, 1975-86; mem. editorial bd.: Annals of Thoracic Surgery, 1979—. Sec., trustee Univ. Synagogue, Los Angeles. Served as capt. M.C. U.S. Army, 1957-59, Korea. Recipient Christopher award Chgo. Surg. Soc., 1958; grantee Life Ins. Med. Research, 1962-66, Am. Heart Assn., 1968-71; USPHS, 1971—. Mem. Am. Surg. Assn., Am. Assn. Thoracic Surgery, Soc. Thoracic Surgeons, Soc. Univ. Surgeons, Pacific Coast Surg. Assn., Soc. Surg. Oncology, Am. Coll. Chest Physicians, ACS (bd. govs. 1982—), Internat. Surg. Soc. Club: Pasadena Athletic. Office: City of Hope Nat Med Center Duarte CA 91010 *

BENFIELD, WILLIAM RICHARD, pharmacy executive; b. San Francisco, May 20, 1946; s. Harold R. and Jean A. (Hurlbert) B.; B.S. in Pharmacy, U. Wash., Seattle, 1969; M.S. in Pharmacy Adminstrn., U. Miss., 1974, Ph.D. in Health Care Adminstrn., 1975; m. Ruth Margaret Fletcher, Aug. 26, 1967; children—Ashley Dawn, Morgan Fletcher. Practicing pharmacist, Seattle, 1969-70, San Francisco, 1970-71; teaching asst. U. Miss. Sch. Pharmacy, 1971-74; guest lectr. U. Tenn. Coll. Nursing, 1972-75; mem. faculty U. Tenn. Ctr. Health Scis., Memphis, 1974-75; sales mgr. drug distbrs. div. Malone and Hyde of Memphis, 1975-77; pres. Diversified Pharm. Interests, Inc., Seattle, 1977—, Downtown Pharmacies, Inc., 1978—, Downtown Delivery, Inc., 1978—. Fellow Royal Philatelic Soc., Am. Soc. Cons. Pharmacists; mem. Am. Pharm. Assn., Am. Mgmt. Assn., Master Resource Council Internat., Postal History Soc., Essay-Proof Soc., Kappa Psi, Rho Chi. Contbr. articles on pharmacy adminstrn. to profl. jours. Office: PO Box 15247 Seattle WA 98115

BENGE, MARY CECELIA RILEY, speech pathologist; b. Tucson, June 9, 1952; d. Joseph Homer and Mary Agnes (Reilly) Riley; m. Ronald Sherman Benge, June 18, 1983. BS, No. Ariz. U., 1975; MS, U. Ariz., 1979. Speech-lang. pathologist Tucson Unified Sch. Dist., 1979-83, Glendale (Ariz.) Union High Sch. Dist., 1983—. Mem. Am. Speech-Lang. Hearing Assn. (cert.), Ariz. Speech Hearing Assn. Home: 7401 W Bloomfield Rd Peoria AZ 85345

BENGTSON, VERN LEROY, sociologist, gerontologist, educator; b. Lindsborg, Kans., May 2, 1941; A.B., North Park Coll., 1963; M.A., U. Chgo., 1965, Ph.D., 1967. Asst. prof. sociology U. So. Calif., Los Angeles, 1967-70, assoc. prof., 1970-77,prof. sociology, 1977—, dir. gerontology research inst., 1982—; vis. assoc. in sociology Calif. Inst. Tech., 1975-76; vis. prof. sociology U. Stockholm (Sweden), 1979. Fellow Am. Psychol. Assn. (mem. council div. 20 adult devel. and aging, 1975-78), Gerontol. Soc. Am. (pres. behavior and social scis. sect. 1983—); mem. Nat. Council Family Relations, Soc. Study Social Problems, Internat. Assn. Gerontology . Assoc. editor Sociology of Education; series editor Brooks-Cole Series in Social Gerontology; mem. exec. bd. Sociology and Social Research; mem. editorial bd. Journal of Marriage and the Family, Journal of Gerontology, Sage Family Studies Abstracts, Research of Aging, NCFR Monographs; contbr. numerous articles to profl. jours. and 5 books. Office: Andrus Gerontology Ctr U Southern Calif Los Angeles CA 90089

BENI, GERARDO, electrical and computer engineering educator, robotics scientist; b. Florence, Italy, Feb. 21, 1946; came to U.S., 1970; s. Edoardo and Tina (Bazzanti) B. Laurea in Physics, U. Firenze, Florence, Italy, 1970; PhD in Physics, UCLA, 1974. Research scientist AT&T Bell Labs., Murray Hill, N.J., 1974-77; research scientist AT&T Bell Labs., Holmdel, N.J., 1977-82, disting. mem. tech. staff, 1982-84; prof. elec. and computer engring. U. Calif., Santa Barbara, 1984—, dir. Ctr. for Robotic Systems in Microelectronics, 1985—. Founder, editor: Jours. Robotic Systems, 1983 (Jour. of Yr. award 1984); editor: Recent Advances in Robotics, 1985; contbr. 100 articles to tech. jours.; 15 patents in field. Fellow Am. Physics Soc.; mem. Robotics Internat., Soc. Mfg. Engrs., Electrochem. Soc. Office: U Calif Ctr Robotic Systems 6740 Cortona Santa Barbara CA 93106

BENICEWICZ, BRIAN CHESTER, chemist; b. Danbury, Conn., June 1, 1954; s. Chester Anthony and Anne (Belorit) B.; m. Pamela King Benicewicz, Aug. 31, 1984. BS, Fla. Inst. Tech., 1976; MS, U. Conn., 1978, PhD, 1980. Research chemist Celanese Research Co., Summit, N.J., 1980-82; sr. scientist Ethicon, Inc., Somerville, N.J., 1982-85; mem. staff Los Alamos (N.Mex.) Nat. Lab., 1985—. Contbr. articles to profl. jours. Fellow Uniroyal Found., U. Conn., 1980. Mem. Am. Chem. Soc., Am. Phys. Soc., Am. Inst. Chemists, N.Y. Acad. Scis. Republican. Lutheran. Avocations: hiking, fishing, camping. Home: 3401 Vereda Alta Santa Fe NM 87505 Office: Los Alamos Nat Lab MS-E549 MST-7 Los Alamos NM 87545

BENJAMIN, ARLIN JAMES, physicist; b. Guthrie, Okla., Oct. 9, 1933; s. Harold Dinsmore and Lula Martha (Black) B.; m. Patricia Ann Crabb, Oct. 10, 1964; children—Arlin James, Cynthia Denise, Deborah Dawn. B.S., Sam Houston State Coll., 1955; M.S., Okla. State U., 1957; postgrad. MIT, 1959, Wichita U., 1959-60. Engr. Boeing Co., Wichita (Kans.), 1956-63; lead nuclear engr. LTV Corp., Dallas, 1963-64; ops. research analyst Research Triangle Inst., Research Triangle Park, N.C., 1964-66; sr. ops. research analyst Gen. Dynamics Corp., Ft. Worth, 1966-68; mgr. Control Data Corp., Honolulu, 1968-70; sr. scientist Southwest Research Inst., San Antonio, 1970-78; mgr., prin. scientist Hittman Assocs. Inc., Sacramento, 1978-81; mgr., sr. staff mem. The BDM Corp., Ft. Lewis, Wash., 1981-86, Northrop Corp., Pico Rivera, Calif., 1986—. Mem. Am. Geophys. Union, Am. Nuclear Soc., Am. Phys. Soc., Inst. Physics (London), Phys. Soc. (London), European Phys. Soc., Inst. Mgmt. Sci., Alpha Chi, Pi Gamma Mu. Author articles and sci. papers for profl. jours. Office: 8900 E Washington Blvd Pico Rivera CA 90660

BENJAMIN, STEPHEN ALFRED, veterinary medicine educator, environmental pathologist, researcher; b. N.Y.C., Mar. 27, 1939; s. Frank Benjamin and Dorothy (Zweighaft) Fabricant; m. Barbara Larson, July 25, 1982; children: Jeffrey, Karen, Susan, Douglas. AB, Brandeis U., 1960; DVM, Cornell U., 1964, PhD, 1968. Diplomate Am. Coll. Vet. Pathologists. Fellow pathology Johns Hopkins U., Balt., 1966-67; asst. prof. comparative medicine M.S. Hershey (Pa.) Med. Ctr. of Pa. State U.; exptl. pathologist Inhalation Toxicology Research Inst., Albuquerque, 1970-77; prof. pathology and radiation biology Colo. State U., Ft. Collins, 1977—, dir. collaborative radiol. health lab., 1977—, assoc. dean grad. sch., 1986—. Contbr. sci. articles to profl. mags. Mem. Am. Assn. Pathologists, Fedn. Am. Soc. for Exptl. Biology, Internat. Acad. Pathology, Radiation Research Soc., Am. Assn. Lab. Animal Sci., Nat. Council Radiation Protection (liver task group). Office: Colo State U Dept Pathology Fort Collins CO 80523

BENJAMIN, SUZANNE F., nurse, consultant; b. Syracuse, N.Y., June 21, 1942; d. Julius and Beatrice (Lichtenstein) Marx; m. Robert Elliot Benjamin, Dec. 16, 1983; children: Julie, John, Lisa, Michael, Michaelyn, Stacey. BS, Queens Coll. CUNY, 1964; diploma, Kings Park Psychiat. Ctr. Sch. Nursing, 1974; M in Health Sci., U. Phoenix, 1984. RN. Head nurse Lakeside Hosp., Copiague, N.Y., 1974-77, South Oaks Hosp., Amityville, N.Y., 1977-78; intravenous therapist Phoenix Gen. Hosp., 1978-81; dir. tng. and devel. Maricopa County Correctional Health Services, Phoenix, 1981—; cons. Robert Benjamin and Assocs., Phoenix, 1980—; Ariz. rep. Nat. Conf. on Correctional Health Care; del. USA-USSR Joint Conf. on Pub. Health Nursing. Author: The Cost Effectiveness of Specialty Nursing in Acute Care Hospitals, 1984. Jewish. Avocations: golf, piano, art collecting. Home: 37 E Boca Raton Rd Phoenix AZ 85022

BENKO, STEPHEN, history educator. Student, U. Budapest, Hungary, 1942-47, U. Zürich and Basel, 1947-51; PhD, U. Basel, 1951. Prof. Temple U., 1954-68, Calif. State Univ., Fresno, 1969—. Author: Sanctorum Communio, 1951, The Meaning of Sanctorum Communio, 1964, Protestants, Catholics and Mary, 1968, My Lord Speaks, 1970, The Early Church, 1972, Pagan Criticism of Christianity during the first Two Centuries, 1980, Pagan Rome and the Early Christians, 1984; contbr. articles and revs. to scholarly jours. and histories. Office: Calif State U Dept History Fresno CA 93740

BENN, FREDERICK JOSEPH, III, fire protection agency executive; b. Boston, Mar. 28, 1947; s. Frederick Joseph Jr. and Lelia Maxine (Buaas) B.; m. Suellen Lee Kohl, Oct. 31, 1970. BSME, Ind. Inst. Tech., 1970; postgrad., U. Dayton, 1970, U. Ky., 1973. Project engr. research and devel. Automatic Sprinkler Corp., Cleve., 1970-74, constrn. mgr., 1974-77; regional design mgr. Automatic Sprinkler Corp., Chgo., 1977-79, dist. mgr., 1979-82; v.p. western region Automatic Sprinkler Corp., San Francisco, 1982-85; pres. Advanced Auto Sprinkler, Inc., Fremont, Calif., 1985—; guest lectr. U. Md., College Park, 1972-74. Author: Automatic Sprinkler Design, 1972. Mem. staff Operation San Francisco, 1983; bd. dirs. Group Four, Lake Forest, Ill., 1980-82. Mem. Nat. Fire Protection Assn., Soc. Fire Protection Engrs. (assoc.), Indsl. Fire Protection Sect., Cleve. Engring. Soc. (cert.). Clubs: Castlewood Country (Pleasanton, Calif.), Bath & Tennis (Lake Forest) (treas.

1981). Office: Advanced Automatic Sprinkler Inc PO Box 14161 Fremont CA 94539

BENNER, DOROTHY SPURLOCK, teacher; b. Greeley, Colo., Dec. 17, 1938; s. Lloyd Elsworth and Helen Rosalee (Pierce) Spurlock; m. Jerry Lee Benner, June 7, 1959; children: Shey Lee, Craig Lloyd. BA, Colo. State Coll., 1962, MA, 1968; EdS, U. No. Colo., 1978. Cert. tchr. elem. and bus. edn., spl. edn. and sch. psychology. Telephone operator Mountain Bell, Greeley, Colo., 1957; sec. Conn. Mut. Life, Greeley, Colo., 1960-61; substitute tchr. Sch. Dist. 6 and Outlying Dists., Greeley, Colo., 1962-67; tchr. Sch. Dist. 6, Greeley, Colo., 1968—; cons. Right to Read, Weld County, Colo., 1980—. Mem. Greeley Tchrs. Assn. (mem. negotiating team 1981—, sec. 1985—), Nat. Edn. Assn. (life), Colo. Edn. Assn., Kappa Delta Pi, Delta Kappa Gamma (pres. 1980-81). Republican. Methodist. Avocations: downhill skiing, piano playing, reading, sewing. Home: 1839 26th St Greeley CO 80631

BENNER, NANCY LEE, speech pathologist; b. Colfax, Wash., Oct. 8, 1955; d. Bernard Dale and Barbara Jean (Pratt) Stover; m. Gregory James Benner, Aug. 19, 1978; children: Erik Gregory, Kyle James. BA in Speech Pathology and Audiology, Eastern Wash. State Coll., 1977, MS in Speech Pathology and Audiology, 1978. Speech therapist Medford (Oreg.) Sch. Dist., 1978-80; communication disorders specialist Mead Sch. Dist., Spokane, Wash., 1980—. Ea. Wash. U. fellow, 1978. Mem. Am. Speech Lang. and Hearing Assn., Wash. Speech and Hearing Assn. Avocations: camping, ballet, gardening. Home: W 2318 Lacrosse Spokane WA 99205 Office: Mead Spl Services W 205 Eddy Spokane WA 99208

BENNETT, ALAN JEROME, electronics executive, physicist; b. Phila., June 13, 1941; s. Leon Martin and Reba (Perry) B.; m. Frances Kitey, June 16, 1963; children: Sarah, Rachel, Daniel. BA, U. Pa, 1962; MS, U. Chgo., 1963, PhD, 1965. Physicist Gen. Electric Research and Devel. Ctr., Schenectady, N.Y., 1966-74, br. mgr., 1975-79; dir. electronics lab. Gould Inc., Rolling Meadows, Ill., 1979-84; v.p. research Varian Assn., Palo Alto, Calif., 1984—. Contbr. articles to profl. jours. Fellow NSF, 1963-65, 66. Mem. AAAS, IEEE (sr.), Am. Phys. Soc., Phi Beta Kappa, Sigma Xi. Avocations: linguistics, amateur radio. Home: 233 Tennyson Ave Palo Alto CA 94301 Office: Varian Assocs 611 Hansen Way Palo Alto CA 94303

BENNETT, CARL MCGHIE, engineering company executive, consultant, national guard officer; b. Salt Lake City, Sept. 11, 1933; s. M. Woodruff and Sybil L. (McGhie) B.; m. Ardel Krantz, Aug. 10, 1954; children: Carlene, Matt, Brent, Dale, Hugh, Caren, Teri. BS, U. Utah, 1956; postgrad., U.S. Army Engr. Sch., 1964; M, Command and Gen. Staff Coll., 1974; postgrad., Indsl. Coll. Armed Forces, 1976. Commd. 2d. lt. ROTC U.S. Army, 1953; treas. and office mgr. Hercules Inc. and Data Source Corp., Salt Lake City and Los Angeles, 1963-70; controller Boise Cascade, Los Angeles, 1970-72; corp. controller Griffin Devel. Co., Los Angeles, 1972-75; controller Dart Industries, Dart Resorts, Los Angeles, 1975-78; chief fin. officer Ford, Bacon & Davis, Salt Lake City, 1978—; cons. Served to lt. col. U.S. Army Res., 1953-79, col. Utah N.G., 1985—. Recipient Meritorious Service medal Pres. of the U.S., 1979. Mem. Controllers Council, Nat. Assn. Accts. (v.p., bd. dirs. 1979-85). Republican. Office: Ford Bacon Davis 375 Chipeta Way Salt Lake City UT 84108

BENNETT, CARLA MARIE, psychotherapist; b. Seattle, Sept. 10, 1955; d. Carl Allen and Myra Elizabeth (Schwan) B. BA in Social Welfare, Pacific Luth. U., 1977; MSW, U. Wash., 1983; postgrad., U. Barcelona, Spain, 1983-84. Bilingual psychotherapist Grant County Mental Health Ctr., Moses Lake, Wash., 1984—; bd. dirs. Nuestro Lugar, Moses Lake, 1985—. Mem. Big Bend Community Coll. Orch. Rotary Internat. scholar, 1983-84. Mem. Nat. Assn. Social Workers, Wash. County Orgn. Designated Mental Health Profls. Lutheran. Home: PO Box 1281 Moses Lake WA 98837-0196 Office: Grant County Mental Health PO Box 1057 Moses Lake WA 98837

BENNETT, CHARLES FRANKLIN, JR., biogeographer, educator; b. Oakland, Calif., Apr. 10, 1926; s. Charles Franklin and Charlotte Louise (Normand) B.; m. Carole Ann Messenger, Nov. 30, 1947; 1 child, Ashley Lynn Bennett-Smith. PhD, UCLA, 1959. Instr. UCLA, 1959-60, asst. prof., 1960-65, assoc. prof., 1965-69, prof. biogeography, 1969—; cons. in field. Author: Human Influence on Zoogeography of Panama, 1968, Man and Earth's Ecosystems, 1976, Conservation of Natural Resources, 1983; contbr. articles to profl. jours. Guggenheim fellow, 1971-71. Mem. AAAS, Ecol. Soc. Am., Brit. Ecol. Soc., Assn. Tropical Biogeography, Assn. Am. Geographers. Avocation: book collecting. Home: 317 S Anita Ave Los Angeles CA 90049 Office: UCLA Dept Geography 405 Hilgard Ave Los Angeles CA 90024

BENNETT, CHARLES LEON, vocational and graphic arts educator; b. Salem, Oreg., Feb. 5, 1951; s. Theodore John and Cora Larena (Rowland) B.; m. Cynthia Alice Hostman, June 12, 1976 (div.); m. Lynn Marie Toland, Aug. 12, 1977 (div.); children: Mizzy Marie, Charles David. AS in Vocat. Tchr. Edn., Clackamas Community Coll., 1977; AS in Gen. Studies, Linn Benton Community Coll., 1979; student SUNY, 1983—. Tchr. printing Tongue Point Job Corps, Astoria, Oreg., 1979-80; tchr., dept. chmn. Portland (Oreg.) pub. schs., 1980—; owner, mgr. printing and pub. co., Portland, 1981—. Served with AUS, 1970-72. Mem. Oreg. Vocat. Trade-Tech. Assn. (dept. chmn., pres. graphic arts div., Indsl. Educator of Year 1981-82), Oreg. Vocat. Assn. (Vocat. Tchr. of Yr. 1982-83), Graphic Arts Tech. Found., In-Plant Printing Mgmt. Assn., Internat. Graphic Arts Edn. Assn. (v.p. N.W. region VI), Oreg. Assn. Manpower Spl. Needs Personnel, Oreg. Indsl. Arts Assn., Nat. Rifle Assn., Internat. Platform Assn. Nat. Assn. Quick Printers, Am. Vocat. Assn., Portland Club Lithographers and Printing House Craftsmen. Republican. Home: 4345 SE 46th Ave Portland OR 97206 Office: 5040 SE Milwaukie Ave Portland OR 97202

BENNETT, CLIFTON FRANCIS, research scientist; b. Tillamook, Oreg., July 27, 1926; s. Lester Nelson and Ida Heloise (Phillips) B.; m. Marvilena Nanette Anderson, Nov. 20, 1956; children: Genevieve, Gretchen, Michelle. BS, Lewis & Clark Coll., 1949; MS, Oreg. State U., 1952; PhD, McGill U., 1956. Research chemist Weyerhaeuser Co., Longview, Wash., 1951-53, CrownZellerbach, Camas, Wash., 1955-81; prin. scientist Container Corp., Carol Stream, Ill., 1981-84; research and devel. scientist Pace Nat. Corp., Kirkland, Wash., 1985—; instr. chemistry Portland (Oreg.) State U., 1963-65; advisor, explorer Scouts Sci. Post, Camas, 1964-72; exchange scientist to eastern Europe Nat. Acad. Scis., Washington, 1972-73, 79, 84. Patentee in field; contbr. articles to profl. jours. Pres. Camas Parent-Tchrs. Assn., 1970; chmn. Camas Schs. Adv. Com., 1972; chmn. State legis. campaign, Camas, 1976. Served as cpl. USMC, 1943-46, PTO. Fellow Allied Corp. McGill U., 1954, Pulp & Paper Inst. of Can., 1955; recipient Presdl. Citation award Harry S. Truman, 1945. Mem. TAPPI, Am. Chem. Soc. (cert., mem. exec. com. 1977-81), Camas-Washougal C. of C. (bd. dirs.), U.S. Jaycees (nat. dir. 1958-60, state of Wash. v.p. 1957-58). Republican. Methodist. Club: Young Life (SW Wash.) (mem. adult com. 1961-81, Distinction award 1981). Avocations: ch. com. work, traveling, camping, bicycling. Office: Pace Nat Corp 500 7th Ave S Kirkland WA 98033

BENNETT, JACQUELINE BEEKMAN, school psychologist; b. Santa Paula, Calif., Sept. 4, 1946; d. Jack Edward and Margaret Blanche (MacPherson) Beekman.; m. Thomas LeRoy Bennett Jr., Aug. 5, 1972; children: Shannon, Brian, Laurie. BA, U. Calif., Davis, 1968; MS, Colo. State U., 1975, PhD, 1984. Histologist Sch. Veterinary Medicine, Davis, 1969-71; sch. psychologist Poudre Sch. Dist. R-1, Ft. Collins, Colo., 1983—. Nominating chmn. United Presbyn. Women, Timnath, Colo., 1982, pres., 1986; com. mem. Women and the Ch. Com., Boulder Presbytery, Colo., 1985-86; elder Timnath Presbyn. Ch., 1985—. Mem. Colo. Soc. Sch. Psychologists (cert.), Nat. Assn. Sch. Psychologists, NEA, Am. Psychol. Assn., Ft. Collins Parents of Twins (pres. 1977-78), Sigma Xi, Phi Kappa Phi. Democrat. Club: Squaredusters (Ft. Collins) (v.p. 1977-78). Avocations: camping, gardening, swimming, cooking. Home: 213 Camino Real Fort Collins CO 80524 Office: Poudre Sch Dist R-1 2407 Laporte Ave Fort Collins CO 80521

BENNETT, JAMES COOPER, business educator; b. Holliday, Tex., Sept. 16, 1934; s. Luther C. and Flora Mae (Carr) B.; m. Judith Ann Swab, Aug. 22, 1964; children: James Lewis, Jennifer Ann. BBA, N. Tex. State U., 1956, M in Bus. Edn., 1957; EdD, UCLA, 1970. Cert. records mgr. Tchr. Sunset High Sch., Dallas, 1957-59, Downey (Calif.) High Sch., 1959-64; prof. Calif. State U., Northridge, 1964-82, 85—, assoc. dean, chmn. dept., 1964-82; prof. U. Tex., Austin, 1982-85; bd. dirs. Great Western Energy, Rolling Hills Estates, Calif.; cons. in field. Co-author: Professional and Personal Typing, 1982, Idlewood College--Simulation for Typewriting, 1985, Professional and Personal Keyboarding and Typewriting; contbr. articles to profl. jours. Recipient Meritorious Performance award Calif. State U., 1986. Mem. Assn. Records Mgrs. and Adminstrs. (Award of Merit 1982), Calif. Bus. Edn. Assn., Nat. Bus. Edn. Assn., Assn. Bus. Communication, Delta Pi Epsilon (pres. research found. 1985), Beta Gamma Sigma, Sigma Phi Epsilon. Democrat. Methodist. Lodge: Kiwanis (chmn. internat. relations com. 1970-82). Avocations: traveling, writing. Office: Calif State U 18111 Nordhoff St Northridge CA 91330

BENNETT, JAMES STARK, television executive; b. N.Y.C., June 1, 1947; s. Rollin Foote and Jane (Williams) B.; m. Carolyn King Doepke, Sept. 17, 1977; children: Katherine Brooks, Lucy Williams, John Brooks. B.A., U. Calif, Berkeley, 1970; M.B.A., Harvard U., 1972. With planning dept. CBS Inc., N.Y.C., 1972-73; dir. adminstr. sta. KCBS, CBS Inc., San Francisco, 1973-74; dir. planning and adminstrn. Sta. WBBM-TV, CBS Inc., Chgo., 1974-76, program dir., 1976-80; gen. mgr., v.p. KCBS-TV, CBS Inc., Los Angeles, 1980-85; v.p. prodn. and programming, domestic TV Walt Disney Co., Burbank, 1985—. Treas. St. Nicholas Theatre, Chgo., 1978-80; bd. dirs. Golden State Minority Found., Los Angeles, 1981-85, ARC, 1982—, W. Alton Jones Found., Charlottesville, Va., 1983—, In the Wings Music Ctr., Los Angeles, 1981-85, Town Hall of Calif., Los Angeles, 1984-87. Recipient Kenneth Priestly award U. Calif.-Berkeley, 1970. Mem. Nat. Acad. TV Arts and Scis. (bd. govs. 1977-80), Calif. Broadcasters Assn. (dir. 1982—), Hollywood Radio and TV Soc., Univ. Calif. Alumni Council (bd. dirs.). Home: 433 S Lucerne Blvd Los Angeles CA 90020 Office: Walt Disney Corp 500 S Buena Vista St Burbank CA 91521

BENNETT, JOHN A., judge; b. Chgo., Apr. 14, 1937; s. John William and Iren (Durnovich) Bocskovits; m. Jeanine Delores Boomgarden, July 23, 1960; children: Martin John, Renea Jean, Denise Lynn, Michelle Ann. AA, Univ. State of N.Y. Regents Coll. Degree, 1975, BS, 1981; AS in Law Enforcement, Blue Mountain Community Coll., Pendleton, Oreg., 1976; LLB, La Salle Extension U., Chgo., 1976; postgrad., Nat. Judicial Coll., Reno, Nev., 1979. Enlisted chief warrant officer U.S. Army, 1955-75; ret., 1975; served intelligence agy., U.S. Army Intelligence Command, 1966-75; judge Mcpl. Ct., Hermiston, Oreg., 1978—, Umatilla, Oreg., 1983—, Echo, Oreg., 1987—; discussion leader Nat. Jud. Coll., Reno, 1984; apptd. adv. and judicial coms. Oreg. Supreme Ct. Bd. dirs. People to People Handicapped Group, Hermiston, Oreg., 1980—; exec. dir. Hermiston Heritage Assn., 1982—; bd. dirs. Oreg. Trail Tourism Council, Hermiston, 1983—, Hist. Preservation League Oreg., 1985—; active Umatilla County Hist. Soc., 1983—. Mem. Nat. Judges Assn. (pres. 1984-85, pub. quar. newspaper 1984, judicial career edn. achievement award, 1985, advanced achievement award in judicial edn., 1985), Oreg. Mcpl. Judges Assn. (bd. dirs. 1980—, v.p. 1987—, editor quar. newspaper 1983—, Meritorious Service award 1982), Assn. Former Intelligence Officers. Roman Catholic. Home: 820 W Highland St Hermiston OR 97838 Office: Mcpl Ct 330 S 1st St Hermiston OR 97838

BENNETT, KEITH ERVIN, civil engineering consulting executive; b. Oklahoma City, Jan. 15, 1948; s. Jack I. and Wilma (Qualls) B.; m. Elizabeth J. Neylon, Nov. 15, 1975; children: Christopher, Rebecca, Matthew. BSCE, USAF Acad., 1970; MSCE, U. Ill., 1971; postgrad., U.S. Air Force Inst. Tech., 1974, U. Denver, 1981. Commd. 2d lt. USAF, 1970, advanced through grades to capt., 1973, civil engineer, 1971-75, resigned, 1975; project mgr. Benham Group, Oklahoma City, 1975-77, Engring. Enterprise, Norman, Okla., 1977-79, Greiner Engring., Denver, 1979-82; prin. Evans, Kuhn and Assocs., Denver, 1982—. Referee Columbine Soccer Assn., South Jefferson County, Colo., 1984-86; skit dir. YMCA Indian Guides, Chatfield, 1984-85; mem. com. Ken Caryl Ranch swim team, South Jefferson County, 1986. Decorated Bronze Star, 1973. Mem. ASCE, NSPE (student chpt. formation com. 1984-85), Colo. Cons. Engrs. Council (pub. relations com. 1985, scholarship com. 1983-85), USAF Acad. Alumni Assn. Office: Evans Kuhn and Assocs Inc 9034 E Easter Pl #202 Englewood CO 80112

BENNETT, LEWIS TILTON, JR., actor, advertising and communications company executive; b. Manchester, N.H., Jan. 14, 1940; s. Lewis Tilton and Elizabeth (Goodwin) B. B.S. in Bus., Babston Inst., 1961; B.A. in Film, San Francisco State U., 1965. Pres., Bennett, Inc., San Francisco, 1967—, Luxembourg, 1967—; actor in films: Petulia, Guess Who's Coming to Dinner, Bullitt, Zabriski Point, Strawberry Statement, Harold and Maude, Magnum Force, Towering Inferno, Time After Time, also TV commls.; tchr. San Francisco Film Clinic, 1968-71, 74—; also stand-in for film actor Steve Mc Queen; stand-in for Jack Warden in TV series Crazy Like A Fox; also photographer. Mem. San Francisco Symphony Found., 1967—; del. sponsor San Francisco Internat. Film Festival, 1967, 68, 69. Mem. SAR. Clubs: Olympic, Lakeside Country, Carmel Beach, Commonwealth, West Coast Yacht, Racket, University, Europe United. Home: 1647 Hyde Park St Sarasota FL 33579 Summer Home: 20 rue des Roses, Luxembourg Luxembourg Office: 1348 Sacramento St San Francisco CA 94109

BENNETT, ROBERT LOUIS, college administrator; b. Winnett, Mont., July 17, 1925; s. William and Florence B.; m. Jean Kathryn Pearson, Oct. 20, 1972; children—Mary, Jean, James, William, Stephen. B.A., Mont. State Coll., 1950; M.S., Eastern Mont. Coll., 1959; Ed.D., U. Calif.-Berkeley, 1967. Tchr., counselor, Billings, Mont., 1951-60; researcher in ednl. devel. San Mateo (Calif.) High Sch. Dist., 1961-67; coll. adminstr. in resource devel. San Mateo Community Coll. Dist.; project dir. Ford Found. Cooperative Edn. Program, Kellogg Found. Community Coll. Mgmt. by Objectives, U.S. Office Edn. Career Edn. Nat. Demonstration, High Tech. Bus. Tng. Ctr. Served with USN, 1945-46. Mem. Am. Soc. Tng. and Devel., Assn. Calif. Community Coll. Adminstrs. (charter), Internat. Platform Assn. Author: Identification of Curriculum Strengths and Weaknesses, 1967, An Improved Urban-Suburban Management Model for Community Colleges, 1977, Careers Through Cooperative Work Experience, 1978, Earning and Learning, 1980, Action Link Industrial Training Systems, 1986. Address: 53 Condon Ct San Mateo CA 94403

BENNETT, THOMAS HUGH, computer specialist; b. Oakland, Calif., Dec. 30, 1935; s. William Cook and Frances (Thompson) B.; m. Marilyn Lois Johansen, Aug. 10, 1963; children: Kristen Louise, Karen Anne, Karl Erik. BS, U. Calif., Berkeley, 1957; MBA, Seattle U., 1973; PhD, U. Wash., 1980. Dist. group mgr. Sun Life of Can., Seattle, 1962-67; mktg. rep. IBM, Seattle, 1967-68, Honeywell Inc., Seattle, 1968-70, Computer Scis. Corp., Seattle, 1970-72; computer specialist U. Wash., Seattle, 1972—, ann. Computer Fair organizer, 1975—; seminar instr. on computing tech. for govt. and non-profit orgns. including Wash. State Legis., Seattle, 1975—. Commnr. Shoreline Park and Recreation Dist., Seattle, 1966-72; chmn. bd. dirs. Olympic Ballet Theatre, Edmonds, Wash., 1979-82; mem. Wash. Office Automation Tech. Com., Olympia, 1982-84, Task Force to Study Statewide Data Communications Network, Olympia, 1978-80. Republican. Lutheran. Home: 824 NW Innis Arden Dr Seattle WA 98177 Office: U Wash Acad Computing Services 3737 Brooklyn Ave NE Seattle WA 98195

BENNETT, THOMAS JERMAN, computer science educator; b. Sioux City, Iowa, Apr. 25, 1940; s. Crane Delbert and Janie (Jerman) B.; m. Carol Ann Gann, Aug. 17, 1962 (div. 1981); children—David, Robert, Michelle, James; m. Mary Ann Padden, Dec. 24, 1982. A.S., Long Beach City Coll., 1960; B.S., UCLA, 1964; M.S., U. Wash., 1967. Registered profl. engr., Wash. Research scientist Hanford Nuclear Project, Richland, Wash., 1964-70; pre-doctoral assoc. Wash. State U., Pullman, 1970-72; instr. Big Bend Coll., Moses Lake, Wash., 1972-79, prof. computer sci., 1982—; sr. engr. Boeing Co., Everett, Wash., 1979-81; tchr. coll. courses to gifted high sch. students, Wash., 1973-79. Contbr. articles on nuclear power to profl. jours., 1964-69. Mem. UCLA Rose Bowl Team, 1962; vice chmn. Democratic Central Com., Grant County, Wash., 1983-84, chmn., 1984—; trustee Free Methodist Ch., Moses Lake, 1975-76. Served with USAF, 1957-63. Recipient Key to City, City of Long Beach, Calif., 1960; AEC fellow, 1967-68; named one of Outstanding Educators of Am., 1974-75. Mem. Faculty Assn. Big Bend Coll. (pres. 1975-76), Tau Beta Pi. Lodge: Elks. Home: Route 4 Box 205 Moses Lake WA 98837 Office: Big Bend Coll 28th at Andrews Moses Lake WA 98837

BENNETT, THOMAS LEROY, JR., clinical neuropsychology educator; b. Norwalk, Conn., Sept. 25, 1942; s. Thomas LeRoy and Gertrude Upson (Richardson) B.; m. Jacqueline Beekman, Aug. 5, 1972; children: Dean, Shannon, Brian, Laurie. B.A., U. N. Mex., 1964, M.S., 1966, Ph.D., 1968. Diplomate: Diplomate Am. Acad. Behavioral Medicine. Lic. psychologist. Asst. prof. Calif. State U., Sacramento, 1968-70; assoc. prof., then prof. psychology and physiology Colo. State U., Ft. Collins, 1970—; pvt. practice, Ctr. for Stress Mgmt. and Personal Growth, 1986—; allied health staff Poudre Valley Hosp., Ft. Collins. Author: Brain and Behavior, 1977, The Sensory World, 1978, The Psychology of Learning and Memory, 1979, Exploring the Sensory World, 1979, Introduction to Physiological Psychology, 1982; contbr. articles to profl. jours. Elder Timnath Presbyterian Ch. Fellow Am. Psychol. Assn.; mem. Psychonomic Soc., Rocky Mountain Psychol Assn., Nat. Acad. Neuropsychologists, Internat. Neuropsychol. Soc., Sigma Xi. Home: 213 Camino Real Fort Collins CO 80524 Office: Dept Psychology Colo State U Fort Collins CO 80523

BENNETT, WILLIAM RICHARDS, former premier British Columbia (Canada); b. Kelowna, B.C., Can., Apr. 14, 1932; s. William Andrew Cecil and Annie Elizabeth May (Richards) B.; m. Audrey Lyne James, April 16, 1955; children: Brad, Kevin, Stephen, Gregory. Grad., Kelowna high sch. Operator, owner furniture and appliance store Kelowna, B.C., Can.; elected Legis. Assembly B.C. from S. Okanagan dist., from 1973; premier Legis. Assembly B.C. from S. Okanagan dist., 1975-86. Mem. Social Credit Party, Kelowna C. of C. (past pres.). Mem. United Ch. *

BENNETTS, DOUGLAS EUGENE, industrial arts teacher; b. Grand Junction, Colo., Sept. 28, 1951; s. William Chris and Dixie Lee (Corbin) B.; m. Mary Jo Hutchcroft, June 18, 1977; children: Dustin Eugene, Matthew Douglas, Blake Thomas. BA in Indsl. Arts Edn., Western State Coll., 1973. Indsl. arts instr. Strasburg (Colo.) Schs., 1973-77, Buena Vista (Colo.) Schs., 1977—; guest speaker Western State Coll., Gunnison, Colo., 1985; guest prof. Colo. State U., Ft. Collins, 1985-86; workshop facilitator for Indsl. Arts around the state of Colo., 1985-86. Presenter papers at Colo. Indsl. Arts Conventions, 1984, 85. Named Citizen of Yr. Buena Vista C. of C., 1984; recipient Disting. Alumni award Western State Coll., 1985. Mem. Colo. Indsl. Arts Assn. (area rep. 1984, pres.-elect 1985, pres.1986), Internat. Technology Edn. Assn. (com. 1986—), Buena Vista Edn. Assn., Colo. Edn. Assn., Nat. Edn. Assn. Democrat. Roman Catholic. Lodge: Optimist. Avocations: camping, fishing, woodworking, hunting. Home: PO Box 411 18410 Rio Hondo Buena Vista CO 81211 Office: Buena vista High Sch PO Box 2027 Railroad and Marquette Ave Buena Vista CO 81211

BENNINGHOFF, DIANE BROWN, director alumni affairs; b. Omaha, Jan. 10, 1946; d. John Dana and Virginia Marcella (Todd) B.; m. Theodore John Benninghoff, Dec. 21, 1969. B.A., Colo. Coll., 1968; M.A., U. No. Colo., 1969; M.B.A., U. Colo., 1984. Dir. advt. and promotion Sta. KKTV, Colorado Springs, Colo., 1970-82; instr. Pikes Peak Community Coll., Colorado Springs, 1973-82, U. Colo., Colorado Springs, 1980-81; exec. dir. Colo. Opera Festival, Colorado Springs, 1982-85; dir. alumni relations Colo. Coll., Colorado Springs, 1985—, speaker career seminars, 1978-85 . Producer, writer TV spots and print advt., TV spl. Adventure of the Arkansas, 1980 (Colo. Broadcasters Assn. 1st. place award). Reader Transcribers for the Visually Impaired, Colorado Springs, 1979-82; bd. dirs. Colo. Opera Festival, Colorado Springs, 1979-82, Pikes Peak Arts Council, Colorado Springs, 1982-86, Opera Council of 500, 1986—; mem. Council for the Advancement and Support of Edn. Boettcher Found. scholar, 1964-68. Mem. Am. Women Radio & T.V. (founder, pres. Pikes Peak chpt. 1978-80), Colorado Springs Exec. Assn. (bd. mem. 1984-85). Club: Pikes Peak Whitewater (Colorado Springs) (treas. 1977-79). Office: The Colo Coll Tutt Alumni House Colorado Springs CO 80903

BENNINGTON, LESLIE ORVILLE, JR., insurance agent; b. Sedalia, Mo., Dec. 29, 1946; s. Leslie Orville Sr. and Eunice May Marguerite (Cole) B.; m. Susan Frances Grotha, June 1, 1968; children: Leslie O. III, Jeremy Lawrence. BSME, U. Mo., Rolla, 1968; postgrad., U. Tenn. Space Inst., 1969; CLU, Am. Coll., 1983. Registered profl. mech. engr., Wash., Wyo. Design engr. Arnold Research Orgn., Tullahoma, Tenn., 1968-70; engr. Pacific Power & Light, Glenrock, Wyo., 1973-75; agt., asst. gen. agt. Am. Nat. Ins. Co., Casper, Wyo., 1975-85; gen. agt. Ins. Sales, Glenrock, 1985—. Pres. Cen. Wyo. Estate Planning Council, Casper, 1985-86; mem. Glenrock Vol. Fire Dept., 1973—, asst. chief, 1982; pres., v.p. Converse County Recreation Bd., Douglas, Wyo., 1980—; judge Dist. High Sch. Speech Contests, Glenrock. Served to 1st lt. USAF, 1971-73. Mem. Nat. Assn. Life Underwriters (Nat. Quality award, Health Ins. Quality award, Nat. Sales Achievement award), Cen. Wyo. Life Underwriters (pres. 1978-80), Wyo. Life Underwriters Assn. (chmn. membership com. 1985—, nat. com. 1982—, v.p. 1986—, bd. dirs. 1980—, Ins. Agt. of Yr., 1980), West Cen. Wyo. CLU's (v.p. 1985—), Million Dollar Round Table, Nat. Pony Express Assn. (pres. Eastern Wyo. div. 1985—). Republican. Roman Catholic. Lodge: KC (grand knight, faithful navigator). Avocations: cattle, livestock. Home: 6 Shannon Dr Glenrock WY 82637 Office: PO Box 2049 217 W Birch Glenrock WY 82637

BENNINGTON, WILLIAM LEWIS, biology and chemistry educator; b. Portland, Oreg., Apr. 19, 1946; s. Elwin Everett Bennington and Marjory Catherine (Whorfield) Byrn; m. Joyce Elaine Hoshour, Mar. 1, 1966; children: Holli R., Shelly L. BS, Met. State Coll., 1970; MS, Eastern Wash. U., 1972; ArtsD, Idaho State U., 1982. Instr. biology Muskegon (Mich.) Community Coll., 1972-76, Coll. Ganado Navajo Reservation, Ariz., 1976-78; chmn. div. math. and sci. Coll. Ganado Navajo Reservation, 1976-78; instr. biology and chemistry Pike's Peak Community Coll., Colorado Springs, Colo., 1980—, pre-med. and math.-sci. advisor. Capt. Ganado Vol. Fire Dept., 1976-78; bd. dirs. Muskegon Planned Parenthood, 1975-76. Fellow Ednl. Profl. Devel. Assistance Dept. Edn., Eastern Wash. U., 1970; named one of Outstanding Young Men. Am. Jaycees, 1978, Outstanding Arts and Scis. Instr. Pikes Peak Community Coll., 1985; grantee Natural Sci. Curriculum ImprovementDept. Edn., 1977. Mem. Colo.-Wyo. Acad. Scis. Democrat. Clubs: Muskegon Skydivers (safety officer 1974-76), Muskegon Community Coll. Ski (faculty advisor 1973-76). Avocations: gardening, carpentry, photography, skydiving, pvt. pilot. Office: Pikes Peak Community Coll 5675 S Academy Blvd Colorado Springs CO 80906

BENNION, DOUGLAS NOEL, chemical engineer, educator; b. Ogden, Utah, Mar. 10, 1935; s. Noel Lindsay and Mildred Amanda (Holmgren) B.; m. Delores Yvonne Wridge, Sept. 15, 1956; children—Debra, Spencer, Donald, Delores, Edwin, Charles, Daniel. B.S. in Chem. Engring, Oreg. State U., 1957; Ph.D. in Chem. Engring, U. Calif., Berkeley, 1964. With Dow Chem., Pittsburg, Calif., 1957-60; mem. faculty dept. chem. engring. UCLA, 1964-80, prof., 1975-80; mem. faculty dept. chem. engring. Brigham Young U., Provo, Utah, 1980—; chmn. dept. Brigham Young U., 1984—. Contbr. articles to profl. jours. Served with U.S. Army, 1958. Mem. Electrochem. Soc. (pres. 1977-78), Am. Inst. Chem. Engrs., Am. Chem. Soc. Mormon. Home: 1742 N Driftwood Dr Provo UT 84604 Office: Brigham Young U Dept Chem Engring 350 CB Provo UT 84602

BENNION, JOHN W., school system administrator; b. Salt Lake City, Nov. 25; s. M. Lynn and Katherine Bennion; m. Sylvia Lustig; children: Philip, Stanford, David, Bryan, Grant, Andrew. BS in Philosophy, English, U. Utah, 1961, MA in Edn. Adminstrn., 1962; PhD in Edn. Adminstrn., Ohio State U., 1966. Tchr. Granite High Sch., Salt Lake City, 1961-63; asst. instr. Ohio State U., Columbus, 1963-64, adminstrv. asst., 1965-66; adminstrv. intern Parma (Ohio) Sch. Dist., 1964-65; asst. supt. Elgin (Ill.) Pub. Schs., 1966-68; asst. prof. edn. adminstrn. Ind. U., Bloomington, 1968-69; supt. Brighton Cen. Schs., Rochester, N.Y., 1969-79, Bloomington (Minn.) Pub. Schs., 1979-80, Provo (Utah) Sch. Dist., 1980-85, Salt Lake City Schs., 1985—. Mem. Assn. Supervision and Curriculum Devel., Assn. Early Childhood Edn., Am. Assn. Sch. Adminstrs., Sch. Mgmt. Study Group, Phi Delta Kappa. Home: 1837 Harvard Ave Salt Lake City UT 84108 Office: Salt Lake City Sch Dist Office of the Supt of Schools 440 E 100 S Salt Lake City UT 84111

BENNION, MARILYN ROBINS, educator; b. Vernal, Utah, June, 1934; d. Stan L. and Lila Lois (Chivers) Robins; m. Enos L. Bennion, Oct. 18, 1956; children—Susan Bennion Johnsen, Annette. B.S., Utah State U., 1972. Cert. tchr. Utah. Sec. Civil Service, White Sands (Utah) Missile Range, 1956-58; sec. Thiokol Corp., Brigham City, Utah, 1958-61; bus. edn. tchr. Box Elder High Sch., Brigham City, Utah, 1972—; student tchr. trainer Utah State U. Organizer, advisor sch. chpt. Future Bus. Leaders Am., Utah No. Valley region advisor; mem. Utah Textbook Com., 1981-83, mem. high sch. accreditation team, Northwest region, 1977-78; bd. dirs. Box Elder Office Occupation Ctr., Brigham City. Recipient Sustained Superior Performance award Civil Service, 1958, Proud award State of Utah, 1986; Outstanding Bus. Student Tchr. award Utah State U., 1972. Mem. NEA, Am. Vocat. Assn., Utah Vocat. Assn., Nat. Bus. Edn. Assn., Utah Bus. Edn. Assn., Box Elder Edn. Assn. (faculty rep.), Future Bus. Leaders Am. (profl., hon.). Republican. Mormon. Club: Civic Improvement. Office: 380 S 600 W Brigham City UT 84302

BENNIS, WARREN, educator, author, consultant; b. N.Y.C., Mar. 8, 1925; s. Philip and Rachel (Landau) B.; m. Clurie Williams, Mar. 30, 1962; children—Katharine, John Leslie, Will Martin. A.B., Antioch Coll., 1951; hon. cert. econs., London Sch. Econs., 1952; Ph.D., MIT, 1955; LL.D. (hon.), Xavier U., Cin., 1972, George Washington U., 1977; L.H.D. (hon.), Hebrew Union Coll., 1974, Kans. State U., 1979; D.Sc. (hon.), U. Louisville, 1977, Pacific Grad. Sch. Psychology, 1987. Diplomate Am. Ed. Profl. Psychology. Asst. prof. psychology MIT, Cambridge, 1953-56, prof., 1959-67; asst. prof. psychology and bus. Boston U., 1956-59; provost SUNY-Buffalo, 1967-68, v.p. acad. devel., 1968-71; pres. U. Cin., 1971-77; U.S. prof. corps. and soc. Centre d'Etudes Industrielles, Geneva, Switzerland, 1978-79; exec.-in-residence Pepperdine U., 1978-79; George Miller Disting. prof.-in-residence U. Ill., Champaign-Urbana, 1978; Disting. prof. research Sch. Bus., U. So. Calif., 1980—; vis. lectr. Harvard U., 1958-59, Indian Mgmt. Inst., Calcutta; vis. prof. U. Lausanne (Switzerland), 1961-62, ISEAD, France, 1983; bd. dirs. First Exec. Corp. Author: Planning of Change, 4th edit., 1985, Interpersonal Dynamics, 1963, 3d edit., 1975, Personal and Organizational Change, 1965, Changing Organizations, 1966, repub. in paperback as Beyond the Bureaucracy, 1974, The Temporary Society, 1968, Organization Development, 1969, American Bureaucracy, 1970, Management of Change and Conflict, 1972, The Leaning Ivory Tower, 1973, The Unconscious Conspiracy: Why Leaders Can't Lead, 1976, Essays in Interpersonal Dynamics, 1979; (with B. Nanus): Leaders, 1985; columnist, chmn. bd. editors New Mgmt.; assoc. editor Jour. Transpersonal Psychology, Community Psychology; cons. editor Jour. Creative Behavior, Jour. Higher Edn., Jour. Occupational Behavior, Ency. of Econs. and Bus., Jour. Humanistic Psychology. Mgmt. Series Jossey-Bass Pubs. Mem. Pres.' White House Task Force on Sci. Policy, 1969-70; mem. FAA study task force U.S. Dept. Transp., 1975; mem. adv. com. N.Y. State Joint Legis. Com. Higher Edn., 1970-71; mem. Ohio Gov.'s Bus. and Employment Council, 1972-74; mem. panel on alt. approaches to grad. edn. Council Grad. Schs. and Grad. Record-Exam Bd., 1971-73; chmn. Nat. Adv. Commn. on Higher Edn. for Police Officers, 1976-78; adv. bd. NIH, 1978-84; trustee Colo. Rocky Mountains Sch.; bd. dirs. Am. Leadership Forum, Foothill Group, Calif. Sch. Profl. Psychology; mem. vis. com. for humanities MIT. Served to capt. AUS, World War II. Decorated Bronze Star, Purple Heart; recipient Dow Jones award, 1987. Fellow Am. Psychol. Assn., AAAS, Am. Sociol. Assn.; mem. Am. Acad. Arts and Scis. (co-chmn. policy council 1969-71), Am. Soc. Pub. Adminstrn. (nat. council), Am. Mgmt. Assn. (dir. 1974-77), U.S. C. of C. (adv. group scholars). Office: Sch of Bus U So Calif University Park Los Angeles CA 90089-1421

BENSINGER, RICHARD EDWARD, physician; b. Milw., Aug. 16, 1943; s. Samuel M. and Jane (Pollak) B.; m. Lenore Cooper, Dec. 14, 1968; children: Kenneth Douglas, Gregory Evan. AB, Johns Hopkins, 1965, MD, 1969. Diplomate Am. Bd. Ophthalmology. Intern Johns Hopkins, Balt., 1969-70; resident in opthalmology Washington U., St. Louis, 1976; instr. in eye surgery Washington U. Med. Sch., St. Louis, 1976-77; staff chief Harborview Hosp., Seattle, 1977-83; U. Wash. Med. Sch., Seattle, 1977—; cons. U. Wash., Seattle, 1983—; bd. dirs. Pacific Eye Found., Seattle. Author numerous sci. pubs. and book chpts. Comdr. USPHS, 1970-73. Recipient Research award Am. Soc. Oculoplastics, 1980. Fellow Am. Acad. Ophthalmology; mem. AAAS, Assn. for Research in Ophthalmology, Alpha Omega Alpha, Phi Beta Kappa. Home: 1221 Madison St 320 Seattle WA 98104

BENSON, ALLEN B., chemist, educator, consultant; b. Sioux Rapids, Iowa, Oct. 1, 1936; s. Bennett and Freda (Smith) B.; m. Marian Richter, Aug. 24, 1959; children: Bradley Gerard, Jill Germaine. BS in Secondary Edn. magna cum laude, Western Mont. U., 1960; postgrad., U. Mont., Missoula, 1960-61, Seattle U., 1962-63; M in Natural Sci., Highlands U., 1965; postgrad., Ill. Inst. Tech., 1969; PhD in Chemistry, U. Idaho, 1970. Chemistry instr. U. Wis., Whitewater, 1968-69, Spokane (Wash.) Falls Community Coll., 1969—; mem. steering com. Handford Edn. Action League, Spokane, 1984-86; energy, nuclear cons., 1970—; mem. Hanford Health Effects Panel, Richland, Wash., 1986; numerous pub. articles on energy and nuclear issues. Active Spokane County Dem. Platform Com., 1980, 84. Served as pvt. U.S. Army, 1955-57. Roman Catholic. Avocations: golf, philosophy. Home: N 4528 Windsor Dr Spokane WA 99205 Office: Spokane Falls Community Coll Spokane WA 99204

BENSON, DAVID BERNARD, computer science educator; b. Seattle, Nov. 18, 1940; s. Allan I. and Martha (White) B.; B.S. in Engring., Calif. Inst. Tech., 1962, M.S. in E.E., 1963, Ph.D. (NASA fellow), 1967; m. Nancy Elaine Dollahite, Sept. 17, 1962 (div. Aug. 1986); children—Megan, Bjorn, Nils, Amy, Kjell, Ingri. Research engr. N. Am. Rockwell, Downey, Calif., 1963-64; asst. prof. U. N.C., Chapel Hill, 1967-70; vis. assoc. prof. U. Colo., Boulder, 1976-77; asst. prof. Wash. State U., Pullman, 1970-72, assoc. prof., 1972-79, prof. computer sci., 1979—; vis. computer scientist U. Edinburgh, Scotland, 1983; pres. Bentec, 1985—. Precinct chmn. 72d Precinct, Whitman County, Wash., 1978-82; Whitman County Dem. Conv. del., 1972, 76. NSF grantee, 1969—. Mem. Assn. Computing Machinery, Am. Math. Soc., Am. Assn. Computational Linguistics, IEEE Computer Soc., AAAS, AAUP, Sigma Xi. Democrat. Mem. Soc. of Friends. Contbr. over 30 articles to profl. jours. Home: NE 615 Campus St Pullman WA 99163 Office: Computer Sci Dept Wash State Univ Pullman WA 99164-1210

BENSON, EZRA TAFT, former secretary agriculture, religious executive; b. Whitney, Idaho, Aug. 4, 1899; s. George Taft and Sarah (Dunkley) B.; m. Flora Smith Amussen, Sept. 10, 1926; children—Reed, Mark, Barbara, Beverly, Bonnie, Flora Beth. Student, Utah State Agrl. Coll., Logan, 1918-21; B.S., Brigham Young U., 1926, Dr. Pub. Service (hon.), 1955; M.S. in Agrl. Econs., Iowa State Coll., 1927, D. Agrl. (hon.), 1953; postgrad., U. Calif., 1937-38; H.H.D., Coll. Osteo. Physicians and Surgeons, 1951; LL.D., U. Utah, 1953, Bowdoin Coll., 1955, U. Maine, 1956; D.Agr. (hon.), Mich. State Coll., 1955; D.Sc. (hon.), Rutgers U., 1955. Mission Ch. Jesus Christ Latter-day Saints, Brit. Isles and Europe; pres. Newcastle dist. Ch. Jesus Christ Latter-day Saints, 1921-23; farm operator 1923-30; county agrl. agt. U. Idaho Extension Service, Preston, 1929-30; extension economist and mktg. specialist in charge econ. and mktg. work State of Idaho, 1930-38; organizer, sec. Idaho Coop. Council, 1933-38; exec. sec. Nat. Council Farmer Coops., 1939-44; mem. exec. com., bd. trustees Am. Inst. Co-op, 1942-52, vice chmn. bd. trustees, 1942-49, chmn., 1952; sec. agr. U.S., Washington, 1953-61; dir. Olson Bros., Inc.; bd. dirs. Farm Found., 1946-50; mem. Nat. Agrl. Adv. Com., World War II; mem. Nat. Farm Credit Com., 1940-43; U.S. del. 1st Internat. Conf. of Farm Orgns., London, 1946. Contbr. to agrl., coop. and church jours. Mem. nat. exec. bd. Boy Scouts Am., 1948-66, awarded Silver Antelope, 1951, Silver Buffalo award, 1954; mem. Boise Stake Presidency, Ch. of Jesus Christ of Latter-day Saints, Idaho, 1935-39, pres. Boise Stake, 1938-39; pres. Wash. Dist. Council, Eastern States Mission, 1939-40, Washington Stake, 1940-44; ordained apostle of Ch., mem. Council of Twelve, 1943, pres. European Mission, 1946, 63-65, mem. Gen. Ch. Bd. Edn.; pres. Ch. Jesus Christ Latter-day Saints, Salt Lake City, 1985—; br. trustees Brigham Young U. Recipient testimonial for disting. service to agr. U. Wis., 1952; scholarship Gamma Sigma Delta, hon. soc. agr. Iowa State Coll.; fellow U. Calif., Berkeley. Mem. Am. Mktg. Assn., Farm Econs. Assn., Delta Nu, Alpha Zeta. Office: Ch of Jesus Christ of Latter-day Saints 50 E North Temple St Salt Lake City UT 84150 *

BENSON, JAMES CARL, accountant; b. Mpls., Aug. 24, 1935; s. Fritz L. and Annie C. (Nordstrom) B.; B.B.S. with distinction, U. Minn., 1960; m. Ruth Ann Backlin, Sept. 10, 1960; 1 dau., Emily Ruthann. Intern, Greyhound Co., 1959, Haskins & Sells, 1960; with Arthur Andersen & Co., San Francisco, Brussels, San Jose, Calif., 1960—, partner, 1970—. Pres., Trinity Luth. Ch., Oakland, Calif., 1966, W. Valley Aquatic Team, 1980; bd. dirs. Family Services Assn., Alexian Bros. Hosp. Found., 1977-82, pres., 1981-82; trustee Alexian Bros. Hosp., 1982; mem. planning and allocations com. United Way of Santa Clara County, 1981-82; mem. council Prince of Peace Luth. Ch., 1977-79, 83—, pres., 1986-87; bd. dirs. San Jose Opera Assn., 1985—. Sloan scholar U. Minn. CPA, Calif. Mem. Am. Inst. CPAs, Nat. Assn. Accts., Calif. CPA Soc., Alliance Francaise of Saratoga (treas.), Beta Alpha Psi, Beta Gamma Sigma. Clubs: West Valley Kiwanis (dir.), Am. Men's (Brussels). Office: 99 Almaden Blvd San Jose CA 95113

BENSON, JOHN ALEXANDER, JR., physician, educator; b. Manchester, Conn., July 23, 1921; s. John A. and Rachel (Patterson) B.; m. Irene Zucker, Sept. 29, 1947; children—Peter M., John Alexander III, Susan Leigh, Jeremy P. B.A., Wesleyan U., 1943; M.D., Harvard U., 1946. Diplomate: Am. Bd. Internal Medicine (mem. bd. 1969—, sec.-treas. 1972-75), and subsplty. bd. gastroenterology (mem. 1961-66, chmn. 1965-66). Intern Univ. Hosps., Cleve., 1946-47; resident Peter Bent Brigham Hosp., Boston, 1949-51; fellow Mass. Gen. Hosp., Boston, 1951-53; research asst. Mayo Clinic, Rochester, Minn., 1953-54; instr. medicine Harvard, 1956-59; prof. medicine, head div. gastroenterology U. Oreg., 1959-75; pres. Am. Bd. Internal Medicine, 1975—; cons. VA Hosps., Madigan Gen. Army Hosp. Editorial bd.: Am. Jour. Digestive Diseases, 1966-73; Contbr. articles to profl. jours. Mem. Oreg. Drug Adv. Council, 1965-73; Dir. Oreg. Med. Ednl. Found., 1967-73, pres., 1969-72. Served with USNR, 1947-49. Mem. Am. Gastroenterol. Assn. (sec. 1970-73, v.p. 1975-76, pres.-elect 1976-77, pres. 1977-78), Am. Clin. and Climatol. Assn., ACP (master), AMA, Am. Soc. Internal Medicine, Western Assn. Physicians, North Pacific Soc. Internal Medicine, Am. Fedn. Clin. Research, Federated Council for Internal Medicine, Am. Assn. Study Liver Disease, Western Soc. Clin. Investigation, Phi Beta Kappa, Sigma Xi, Alpha Omega Alpha. Office: Am Bd Internal Medicine 200 SW Market St Portland OR 97201

BENSON, JOSEPH ARTHUR, librarian, calligrapher; b. Jewett, Tex., May 7, 1947; s. Jerry Edward and Addie Delois (Haynes) B. B.S., Bishop Coll., Dallas, Tex., 1969; M.L.S., Ind. U.-Bloomington, 1974; cert. UCLA, 1974, Los Angeles Community Coll., 1983. Library asst. Bishop Coll., 1965-69; librarian-in-charge St. Louis Pub. Library, 1969-73; counselor House of Uhuru, Los Angeles, 1974-75; librarian-in-charge juvenile Hall Boy's Sch., Los Angeles, 1975-83; librarian govt. documents Los Angeles Pub. Library, 1983—, calligrapher, 1983—; pvt. calligrapher, Los Angeles, 1983—. Coauthor: Community Analysis: The Community College, 1974; Multi-Cultural, Multi-Lingual Resources: A Vendor Directory, 1978. U.S. Office Edn. fellow, 1973; named Eligible Bachelor, Ebony Mag., 1986. Mem. ALA, Calif. Black Librarians Assn. (treas. 1980-81), Mary Wilson and Florence Ballard Internat. Fan Club of the Original Supremes, Soc. for Calligraphy, Friends of Calligraphy, Colleagues of Calligraphy. Democrat. Mem. Ch. of God in Christ. Home: 400 S Hoover St Apt 103 Los Angeles CA 90020 Office: Los Angeles County Pub Library System 23743 W Valencia Blvd Valencia CA 91355

BENSON, KENNETH PETER, forest industry executive; b. Vancouver, B.C., Can., Mar. 1, 1927; s. Lawrence and Clara (Peel) B.; m. Joyce Alice Heino, Nov. 4, 1949; children: David, Sally. Student, U. B.C., Vancouver, chartered acct., 1953. Asst. controller Powell River Co., Vancouver, 1955-62; with B.C. Forest Products Co., Vancouver, 1962, comptroller, 1962, v.p. fin., 1967, dir., 1970, exec. v.p. ops., 1972, sr. exec. v.p., 1974, pres., chief operating officer, 1976-79, pres., chief exec. officer, 1979-84, chmn., chief exec. officer, 1984—; bd. dirs. Pulp & Paper Indsl. Relations Bur., Council Forest Industries, Can. Pulp & Paper Assn., Forest Engring. Research Inst. Can. Office: BC Forest Products Ltd, 1050 W Pender St, Vancouver, BC Canada V6E 2X3

BENSON, NORMAN GUSTAF, research fishery biologist; b. Berlin, Conn., May 7, 1923; s. Olof and Emma Louise (Holmquist) B.; m. Mary Jean Lindenscmidt; children: Nancy J., Norman G. II, Janlee K., Karen L., Carlton L. BS, U. Maine, 1948; MA, U. Mich., 1950, PhD, 1953. Coordinator fed. aid Tenn. Game and Fish Commn., Nashville, 1953-57; chief investigator Rocky Mountain fisheries U.S. Fish and Wildlife Service, Logan, Utah, 1957-61; chief north cen. reservoir investigations U.S. Fish and Wildlife Service, Yankton, S.D., 1961-75; leader nat. stream alteration team U.S. Fish and Wildlife Service, Columbia, Mo., 1975-78; research fisheries biologist U.S. Fish and Wildlife Service, Slidell, La., 1978-84; cons. Soc. Energy Bay James, Montreal, Que., Can., 1976-86, Nat. Audubon Soc., N.Y.C., 1984. Editor: A Century of Fisheries in North America, 1970. Pres. sch. bd. Yankton, 1966-71. Served as staff sgt. inf. U.S. Army, 1943-45. Fellow Am. Inst. Fishery Research Biologists; mem. Am. Fisheries Soc. (pres. So. div. 1954), Ecol. Soc. Am., Sigma Xi. Republican. Lodges: Rotary (pres. Yankton club 1970), Masons (master 1971). Avocations: fishing, travelling, environ. issues. Home: 1330 Northface Ct Colorado Springs CO 80919

BENSON, ROBERT JAMES, communications executive; b. Cortland, N.Y., May 31, 1938; s. Kenneth Raymond and Annie Louise (White) B.; m. Carole Darlene Etchison, June 30, 1963; children: Katherine Michelle, Robert Truman, Stephen Kenneth. BBA, Syracuse U., 1959; MS in Mgmt., U. Ark., 1974. Cert. resources mgr. Lt. col. U.S. Army, 1959-81; chief central communications Baltimore County Govt., Towson, Md., 1977-81; exec. dir. South Bay Regional Pub. Communications Authority, Hawthorne, Calif., 1981—; adj. reviewer U.S. Dept. Commerce Tech. Documents. Contbr. articles to profl. jours. Decorated Bronze Star medal with V, Meritorious Service medal with oak leaf cluster, Army Commendation medal with two oak leaf clusters. Mem. Assn. Pub. Safety Communications, Calif. Law Enforcement Telecommunication System Users Group (1st v.p. 1984-85), Nat. Emergency Number Assn. (pres. 1984-85). Republican. Methodist.

BENSON, SIDNEY WILLIAM, chemistry educator; b. N.Y.C., Sept. 26, 1918; m. Anna Seldis, 1986; 2 children. A.B., Columbia Coll., 1938; A.M., Harvard U., 1941, Ph.D., 1941. Research asst. Gen. Electric Co., 1940; research fellow Harvard U., 1941-42; instr. chemistry CCNY, 1942-43; group leader Manhattan Project Kellex Corp., 1943; asst. prof. U. So. Calif., 1943-48, assoc. prof., 1948-51, prof. chemistry, 1951-64, dir. chem. physics program, 1962-63; dir. dept. kinetics and thermochemistry Stanford Research Inst., 1963-76; sci. dir. Hydrocarbon Research Inst. U. So. Calif., 1977—; research assoc. dept. chemistry and chem. engring. Calif. Inst. Tech., 1957-58; vis. prof. UCLA, 1959, U. Ill., 1959; hon. Glidden lectr. Purdue U., 1961; vis. prof. chemistry Stanford U., 1966-70, 71, 73; mem. adv. panel phys. chemistry Nat. Bur. Standards, 1969-72, chmn., 1970-71; hon. vis. prof. U. Utah, 1971; vis. prof. U. Paris VII and XI, 1971-72, U. St. Andrews, Scotland, 1973, U. Lausanne, Switzerland, 1979; Frank Gucker lectr. U. Ind., 1984; Brotherton prof. in phys. chemistry U. Leeds, 1984; cons. in field. Author: Foundations of Chemical Kinetics, 1960, Thermochemical Kinetics, 1968, 2d edit., 1976, Critical Survey of the Data of the Kinetics of Gas Phase Unimolecular Reactions, 1970, Atoms, Molecules, and Chemical Reactions, 1970, Chemical Calculations, 3d edit., 1971; editor in chief Internat. Jour. Chem. Kinetics, 1967-83; mem. editorial adv. bd. Combustion Sci. and Tech., 1973—; mem. editorial bd. Oxidation Communications, 1978—, Revs. of Chem. Intermediates, 1979—; mem. Hydrocarbon Letters, 1980-81; mem. editorial bd. Jour. Phys. Chemistry, 1981-85. Recipient Polanyi medal Royal Soc. Eng., 1986, Faculty award U. So. Calif., 1984, Presdl. medal U. So. Calif., 1986; Guggenheim fellow, 1950-51; NSF fellow, 1957-58, 71-72. Fellow AAAS, Am. Phys. Soc.; mem. Am. Chem. Soc. (Tolman medal 1977, Hydrocarbon Chem. award 1977, Langmuir award 1986, Orange County award 1986), Faraday Soc., Nat. Acad. Scis., Sigma Xi, Phi Beta Kappa, Pi Mu Epsilon, Phi Lambda Upsilon, Phi Kappa Phi. Home: 1110 N Bundy Dr Los Angeles CA 90049 Office: U So Calif-University Park MC-1661 Los Angeles CA 90089

BENSON, THOMAS QUENTIN, lawyer; b. Grand Forks, N.D., Jan. 9, 1943; s. Theodore Quentin and Helen Marie (Winzenberg) B.; m. Mary Mangelsdorf, Aug. 3, 1968; children: Annemarie C., Thomas Quentin II, Mark W. B.A. U. Notre Dame, 1964; J.D., U. Denver, 1967. Bar: Colo. 1967, N.D. 1967, U.S. Dist. Ct. 1968, U.S. Circuit Ct. Appeals 1974, U.S. Mil. Ct. Appeals 1981. Legal counsel Denver Regional Council Govts., 1968-70; assoc. Schneider, Shoemaker, Wham & Cooke, Denver, 1970-72; prin. Thomas Quentin Benson, Denver, 1972-74, 76—; ptnr. Benson & Vernon, Denver, 1974-76; Mem. bd. Am. Health Planning Assn., 1973-77. Mem. bd. Mayor's Adv. Com. Community Devel., Denver, 1975-78; Republican precinct committeeman, 1972-78; mem. White House Advance for U.S. Pres., 1975; pres. Park Vista-Pine Ridge Homeowners Assn., 1971-73; mem. parish council Ch. of Risen Christ, Roman Catholic, 1978-80, chief lector, 1975-76; pres. M.P.B. Home and Sch. Assn. Served as comdr. JAGC USNR. Cited for Leadership Denver C. of C., 1975-76. Mem. ABA, Colo. Bar Assn. (sect. chmn. 1975-78), Denver Bar Assn., Cath. Lawyers Guild Denver (pres. 1979-80). Republican. Clubs: U. Notre Dame (Denver) (pres. 1980-81), Univ. Hills Rotary (Denver) (dir. 1976-78, program chmn. 1978-81, pres. 1987-88), Eastmoor Swim and Tennis (Denver) (dir. 1973-74, 78-80), Serra Internat. (pres. club 1984-85, dist. gov. 1986-87, internat. membership com. 1985—). Office: 1600 S Albion St Suite 1100 Denver CO 80222

BENSON, WILLIAM THOMAS, contracting/development company executive; b. Topeka, Oct. 19, 1940; s. George William and Emeline Erwin (Phillips) B.; BS, U.S. Naval Acad., 1964; MBA, Columbia U., 1971; m. V. Mary Kr. Mortgage analyst Conn. Gen. Life Ins. Co., Hartford, 1971-73; investment specialist Coldwell Banker Co., San Jose, Calif., 1974-75; div. pres., gen. ptnr. The Koll Co., San Jose, 1976—; dir. First Fin. Savs. Bank, San Jose Trolley Corp.; instr. U. Calif., Santa Cruz, 1979-80. Bd. mgrs. S.W. YMCA, Los Gatos, Calif., also mem. exec. com.; mem. real estate adv. bd. U. Calif., Santa Cruz; bd. dirs. NCCJ. Served with USN, 1964-69. Decorated Air medal. Mem. Assn. South Bay Brokers, Bay Area Exec. Lodge: Rotary. Home: 20433 Montalvo Rd Saratoga CA 95070 Office: 1731 Technology Suite 300 San Jose CA 95110

BENSUASKI, FERNANDO, financial consultant; b. Sao Paulo, Brazil, Oct. 13, 1949; s. Fernando and Luzia Cruz (Oliveira) B.; m. Margaret E. Smith, Nov. 15, 1972; children—Max, Andrea K. B.A. in Physics, Northwest Nazarene Coll., 1972. Asst. v.p. comml. loans Idaho First Nat. Bank, Boise, 1973-80; pres. Bensuaski & Co., Boise, 1980—. Mem. Am. Bankers Assn., Am. Inst. Banking. Mem. Ch. of Nazarene. Office: 250 Bobwhite Ct Suite 200 Boise ID 83706

BENT, MICHAEL WILLIAM, realty company executive, consultant; b. Oakland, Calif., Mar. 7, 1951; s. William Camp and Lorene (Howson) B.; 1 child, J. Donovan; m. Laurie Sue Nelson, Dec. 15, 1984. Student Rutgers U., 1969-72. Lic. real estate broker, Colo. V.p. Century 21 Kato & Co., Denver, 1979-80; broker, mgr. Century 21 Hasz & Assocs., Denver, 1980-81; sec. Metro Brokers, Inc., Denver, 1982-83, v.p., 1983-84; sec., dir. Metro Brokers Fin. Services, Inc., 1984-85, dir., 1984-86, Metro Brokers, Inc., 1982-85 ; broker, owner Metro Broker M. Bent Realty & Mgmt. Co., Aurora, Colo., 1981—; dir. Metro Brokers, Inc.; past pres. Country Club Real Estate, Inc. Mem. Denver Bd. Realtors, Aurora Bd. Realtors, Realtors Nat. Mktg. Inst., Internat. Assn. Fin. Planners. Republican. Roman Catholic. Club: Optimist of Heather Ridge, (pres. 1982-84). Home: 17096 E Dorado Circle Aurora CO 80015 Office: Metro Brokers/M Bent Realty & Mgmt Co 2260 S Xanadu Way Suite 390 Aurora CO 80014

BENTLEY, DONALD LYON, mathematics and statistics educator; b. Los Angeles, Apr. 25, 1935; s. Byron R. and Clara Viola (Lyon) B.; m. Anne P. Alexander, Aug. 28, 1957; children: James, Jillene, Janet. BS, Stanford U., 1956, MS, 1958, PhD, 1961. Asst. prof. math. stats. Colo. State U., Ft. Collins, 1961-64; asst. prof. math. Pomona Coll., Claremont, Calif., 1964-67, assoc. prof., 1967-74, Burkhead prof. maths., 1974—; pres. Claremont Data Research Corp., 1985—; cons. Allergen Pharm., Irvine, Calif., 1968-80, Intermedics IntraOcular, Pasadena, Calif., 1981-86. Co-author: Linear Algebra with Differential Equations, 1973. Fellow Royal Statis. Soc.; mem. Am. Statis. Assn. (pres. elect So. Calif. chpt.), Inst. Math. Stats. Congregationalist. Avocations: music, woodworking, geneaology. Office: Pomona Coll Dept Math Claremont CA 91711

BENTLEY, ROBERT CLYDE, architect; b. Livermore, Calif., July 5, 1926; s. Clyde Edward and Doris Katherin (Taylor) B.; m. Patricia Ann Grant, Sept. 10, 1948 (div. 1974); children—Grant Patrick, Linda, William Clyde; m. Elizabeth Aldrin Hench, June 7, 1974; stepchildren—Anders Hench, Colleen Hench, Carolyn Hench. B.A., U. Calif.-Berkeley, 1950; grad. Anthony Sch. Real Estate, 1982. Registered architect, Calif. Pvt. practice architecture, Los Altos, Calif., 1959—; mng. employee Advanced Interiors, San Jose, 1982-83; interior contractor Red Lion Inn, San Jose, 1982-83, Marriott Hotel, San Jose, 1982-83; architect's rep. San Jose Airport, 1980-81; realtor El Monte Properties, Los Altos, 1980—; asst. city planner Yakima Wash., 1958-59; dir. Bentley Engrs., 1950-75; elec. takeoff estimator of tube Bay Area Rapid Transit, San Francisco, 1967-68. Mem. housing code commn. Yakima City Planning Dept., 1959. Served to lt. (j.g.) USNR, 1944-45. Recipient Spark Plug award, Oakland Jaycees, 1965. Mem. Calif. Council of AIA, Calif. Architects, Los Altos C. of C. Democrat. Unitarian. Clubs: Phi Delta Theta. Home: 595 Jay St Los Altos CA 94022 Office: 745 Distel Dr Los Altos CA 94022

BENTLEY, WILLIAM ARTHUR, electro-optics engineer, consultant; b. Oak Park, Ill., Jan. 21, 1931; s. Garth Ashley and Helen (Dieterle) B.; m. Erika Bernadette Seuthe, Nov. 17, 1956; children—David Garth, Barbara Elizabeth. B.S. in Physics, Northwestern U., 1952; M.S. in Systems Engring., Calif. State U.-Fullerton, 1972. Engr. N. Am. Aircraft, Downey, Calif., 1956-69; chief engr. Fairchild Optical, El Segundo, Calif., 1969-72; project engr. Hughes Aircraft Co., Culver City, Calif., 1972-75; sr. staff engr. Advanced Controls, Irvine, Calif., 1975-80; mgr. mfg. research and devel. Xerox Electro-Optical, Pomona, Calif., 1980-83; prin. Instrument Design Cons., Santa Ana, Calif., 1978—; cons. Kasper Industries, Sunnyvale, Calif., 1977-78, Litton Industries, Woodland Hills, Calif., 1978, Lincoln Laser Co., Phoenix, 1983—, Coopervision, Irvine, 1984—. Patentee in field. Served with U.S. Army, 1952-54. Mem. Soc. Photo-optical Instrumentation Engrs., Optical Soc. Am., Mensa. Democrat. Unitarian. Home: 170 the Masters Circle Costa Mesa CA 92627 Office: Instrument Design Cons PO Box 2203 Santa Ana CA 92707

BENTLY, DONALD EMERY, electrical engineer; b. Cleve., Oct. 18, 1924; s. Oliver E. Bently and Mary Evelyn (Conway) B.; m. Susan Lorraine Pumphrey, Sept. 1961 (div. Sept. 1982); 1 child, Christopher Paul. BSEE with distinction, Iowa State U., 1949, MSEE, 1950. Registered profl. engr., Calif., Nev. Pres. Bently Nev. Corp., Minden, 1961-85, chief exec. officer, 1985—, also chmn. bd. dirs.; chmn. bd. dirs. Gibson Tool Co., Carson City, Nev., 1978—. Contbr. articles to profl. jours.; inventor in field. Served with USN, 1943-46, PTO. Named Inventor or Yr., State of Nev. Invention and Tech. Council, 1983. Mem. IEEE, Am. Petroleum Inst. Episcopalian. Avocations: skiing, racquetball, hiking, biking. Home: Bently Buckeye Ranch Minden NV 89423 Office: Bently Nev Corp 1 Water St Minden NV 89423

BENTON, BRADLEY KEITH, electrical engineer, computer executive; b. Yuma, Ariz., May 21, 1957; s. F. Keith and Margaret Ann (Yarwood) B. Student in ENgring., U. Ariz., 1975-83. Computer programmer, operator Yuma Proving Grounds, 1974-76; ops. mgr. Wood Bros., Tucson, 1977-80; field service engr. Bus. Products Services, Tucson, 1980-81; prodn. mgr. Applied Micro Tech. Inc., Tucson, 1981-82; dir. engring. Tri-Tech. Systems, Inc., Tucson, 1982-83; elec. engr. Hughes Aircraft Co., Tucson, 1983—; prin. Small Computer Systems, Tucson, 1983-86, Carlsbad, Calif., 1986—. Recipient Superior Performance Rating, Yuma Proving Grounds, 1976, Outstanding Achievement award Yuma Proving Grounds, 1976. Mem. IEEE. Republican. Baptist. Club: Hughes Mgmt. (Tucson). Avocations: computers, snow skiing, running, auto racing, surfing. Home: 144 Sequoia Ave #4 Carlsbad CA 92008 Office: Hughes Aircraft Co 6155 El Camino Real Carlsbad CA 92008

BENTON, DOUGLAS GEORGE, government official; b. Denver, Feb. 4, 1946; s. Nicholas and Dorothy Revilla (Sloan) B. B.A. in Journalism, Colo. State U., 1971; M.P.A., U. Colo., 1981. Electronics technician Colo. Engring. Expt. Sta., Nunn, Stanley Aviation, Denver, 1970-72; bldg. mgmt. asst. Gen. Services Adminstrn., Denver, 1973-74, bldgs. mgr., Casper, Wyo., 1974-78, Colorado Springs, Colo., 1978-79, chief maintenance and utilities sect., Denver, 1979-80, dist. mgr., 1980-86; with foreign service U.S. Dept. State, Guinea, 1986—. Chmn., Casper Combined Fed. Campaign, 1976-78; bd.

dirs. Natrona County United Way. Served in USN, 1965-69. Decorated Navy Commendation medal with Combat V. Mem. Casper Fed. Execs., Council (v.p. 1975-76, pres. 1977). Methodist. Home: 13367 W Montana Pl Lakewood CO 80228

BENTON, EDWARD ROWELL, astrophysics and geophysics educator; b. Milw., Jan. 20, 1934; s. Roy Wilmot and Madelon (Chandler) B.; m. Margaret Walker Jennison, Sept. 6, 1958 (div. June 1982); children: Theodore Rowell, Gregory Marshall, Cecilia Pickering. AB cum Laude, Harvard U., 1956, AM, 1957, PhD, 1961. Asst. sr. engr. Arthur D. Little, Inc., Cambridge, Mass., 1960-62; asst. lectr. U. Manchester, Eng., 1962-63; mem. staff Nat. Ctr. Atmospheric Research, Boulder, Colo., 1963-65, asst. dir. advanced studies program, 1967-69; asst. prof. astro-geophysics U. Colo., Boulder, 1965-67, assoc. prof., 1969-71, prof., 1971—, chmn. dept. astro-geophysics, 1969-74; cons. U.S. Geol. Survey, Denver, 1979—; spl. asst. University Corp. Atmospheric Research, Boulder, 1975-77; assoc. dir. Office Space Sci. and Tech. U. Colo., 1986-87. Vestryman St. Aidan's Episcopal Ch., Boulder, 1969-71, St. John's Episcopal Ch., Boulder, 1985—; bd. dirs. Boulder Philharm. Orch., 1972-75. Recipient Group Achievement award NASA, 1983; grantee U.S. Army, USN, U.S. Dept. Commerce, NSF, NASA. Fellow Royal Astron. Soc.; mem. AAAS, Am. Phys. Soc., Am. Geophys. Union, Sigma Xi. Avocations: jogging, skiing, backpacking. Home: 3594 Kirkwood Pl Boulder CO 80302 Office: U Colo Dept Astrophys Planetary and Atmospheric Scis Campus Box 391 Boulder CO 80309-0391

BENTON, ELIZABETH LAQUETTA, real estate marketing company executive, consultant, educator; b. Ozark, Ala., Apr. 1, 1936; d. Horace and Dovie Lee (Gulledge) Pippin; m. Charles Wayne Benton, Dec. 17, 1954; children: Lisa Ann, Charles W. Jr. Diploma Napier Bus. Coll., 1955; student Minot State Coll., 1963-64, U. Md., 1965, 67; grad. Realtors Inst. Cert. residential broker residential specialist. Sec., Aeronca Aircraft Corp., Ft. Rucker, Ala., 1955, Strachan Shipping, Savannah, Ga., 1956, USAF, Savannah, 1956-58; supr. Internal Revenue, Denver, 1959-60; adminstrv. asst. Chrysler Corp., Izmir, Turkey, 1961-63; substitute tchr. Dept. Edn., Honolulu, 1968-71; agt. Naomi Grout Real Estate, Ewa Beach, Hawaii, 1971-77; v.p., ptnr. Benton & Large Realty, Honolulu, 1977; pres., owner Liz Benton, Inc., Aiea, Hawaii, 1977—; dir. Founders Title & Escrow Co., Honolulu, 1983—; resource person, study on agy. Nat. Assn. Real Estate Lic. Law Ofcls., Salt Lake City, 1984, 85; mem. adv. council Hawaii Real Estate Research and Edn. Ctr., 1985—. Contbr. articles to profl. jours. Mem. Small Bus. Council Am., Honolulu, 1977—; mem. Aloha United Way, Honolulu 1974—; bd. dirs. Big Bros., Big Sisters, Honolulu, 1982—; chmn. Easter Seals VIP Panel, Honolulu, 1981—; mem. Realtors Polit. Action Com., Honolulu, 1980—; bd. dirs. Am. Cancer Soc., 1985-86. Recipient Vol. of Yr. award ARC, 1965, Outstanding Service award Dept. of Air Force, 1966, Top Producer award Naomi Grout Real Estate, 1972, 73, 74, 75, 76, Cert. of Excellence award Nat. Research Co., 1980-87. Mem. Hawaii Assn. Realtors (chmn. convention com. 1984, chmn. edn. com. 1979, dir.-at-large 1979, 80, bd. dirs. 1979, chmn. fin. and audit com. 1980, 81, sec. 1981, judge parade of homes 1982, treas. 1982, v.p. 1983, pres. elect 1986, pres. 1987, mem. strategic planning com. 1984, chmn. strategic planning com. 1986, chmn. nominating com. 1986), Honolulu Bd. Realtors (bd. dirs. 1978, chmn. election com. 1979, sec. 1979, chmn. multiple listing service, 1980, 81, pres.-elect 1982, chmn. realtor of yr. selection com. 1983, pres. 1983, chmn. nominating com. 1984, Realtor of Month award June 1981, Realtor of Yr. award 1981, chair strategic planning com. 1986, chair nominating com. 1986, liaison to real estate commn. 1986), Nat. Assn. Realtors (chmn. convention activities subcom. 1984, nat. bd. dirs. 1984-86, prof. standards and arbitration com. 1986, 87, state leadership forum, 1986-87), The Investment Group Realtors, Leeward Regional Group, Realtors Nat. Mktg. Inst. (cert., Hawaii chpt., v.p. 1981, pres. 1982, treas. cert. residential brokers chpt. 1985), C. of C. Office: 98-211 Pali Momi St Suite 411 Aiea HI 96701

BENTON, JOANNE POWERS, educational organization executive; b. Oak Park, Ill., Feb. 1, 1927; d. Frederic E. and Josephine M. Benton; m. Ivan L. Rudnytsky, 1949 (div. 1964); children: Peter L. Rudnytsky, Elizabeth J. Roslosnik. BA, Oberlin Coll., 1948; MEd, Temple U., 1959; postgrad., U. Pa., 1960-68. Tchr. Stetson Jr. High Sch., Phila., 1956-58, Green St. Friends, Phila., 1958-59; tchr., dept. head Germantown Friends, Phila., 1959-65; instructional designer Oreg. Mus. Sci. and Industry, Portland, 1974-79, Educulture, Irvine, Calif., 1974-79; founder, pres. Quality Ednl. Designs, Inc., Portland, Oreg., 1979—; mem. exec. council Internat. Council Computers in Edn., Eugene, Oreg., 1979-81; head math. sect. Ind. Schs. Assn., Phila., 1973-74. Editor EDUSIG newsletter, 1975-76; author computer programs. Mem. Internat. Council Computers in Edn. (hon. life), Nat. Council Tchrs. Math., Math. Assn. Am. Office: Quality Ednl Designs Inc PO Box 12486 Portland OR 97212

BENVENISTE, JACOB, physicist; b. Portland, Oreg., Dec. 21, 1921; s. Nissim Aslan and Boule (Capeluto) B.; m. Lucie Almeleh, Apr. 23, 1944; children: Richard Nissim, David Mark, Daniel Stephen. BA, Reed Coll., 1943; PhD, U. Calif., Berkeley, 1952. Physicist Lawrence Livermore (Calif.) Nat. Lab., 1950-63; dir. nuclear effects subdiv. Aerospace Corp., San Bernardino, Calif., 1963-68; v.p., dir. research Physics Internat. Corp., San Leandro, Calif., 1968-72; sr. staff scientist Aerospace Corp., El Segundo, Calif., 1972-82; chief scientist Northrop Research and Tech. Ctr., Palos Verdes, Calif., 1982—; mem. adv. panel Def. Nuclear Agy., Washington, 1965-68; chmn. adv. tech. panel USAF, El Segundo, 1973-77. Patentee in field; contbr. articles to profl. jours. Chmn. Livermore Joint Union High Sch. Dist., 1955-63. Served with USNR, 1944-45. KERR Scholar, Reed Coll., 1941. Mem. AAAS, Am. Phys. Soc., Phi Beta Kappa, Sigma Xi. Jewish. Avocations: auto mechanics, needlepoint. Home: 4514 Spencer St Torrance CA 90503 Office: Northrop Research and Tech Ctr 1 Research Park Palos Verdes Penninsula CA 90274

BENZER, SEYMOUR, scientist, educator; b. N.Y.C., Oct. 15, 1921; s. Mayer and Eva (Naidorf) B.; m. Dorothy Vlosky, Jan. 10, 1942 (dec. 1978); children: Barbara Ann Benzer Freidin, Martha Jane Benzer Goldberg; m. Carol A. Miller, May 11, 1980; 1 child, Alexander Robin. B.A., Bklyn. Coll., 1942; M.S., Purdue U., 1943, Ph.D., 1947, D.Sc. (hon.), 1968; D.Sc., Columbia U., 1974, Yale U., 1977, Brandeis U., 1978, CUNY, 1978, U. Paris, 1983. Mem. faculty Purdue U., 1945-67, prof. biophysics, 1958-61, Stuart distinguished prof. biology, 1961-67; prof. biology Calif. Inst. Tech., 1967-75, Boswell prof. neurosci., 1975—; biophysicist Oak Ridge Nat. Lab., 1948-49; vis. asso. Calif. Inst. Tech., Pasadena, 1965-67. Contbr. articles to profl. jours. Research fellow Calif. Inst. Tech., 1949-51; Fulbright research fellow Pasteur Inst., Paris, 1951-52; sr. NSF postdoctoral fellow Cambridge, Eng., 1957-58; recipient Award of Honor Bklyn. Coll., 1956; Sigma Xi research award Purdue U., 1957; Ricketts award U. Chgo., 1961; Gold medal N.Y. City Coll. Chemistry Alumni Assn., 1962; Gairdner award of merit, 1964; McCoy award Purdue U., 1965; Lasker award, 1971; T. Duckett Jones award, 1975; Prix Leopold Mayer French Acad. Scis., 1975; Louisa Gross Horwitz award, 1976; Harvey award Israel, 1977; Warren Triennial prize Mass. Gen. Hosp., 1977; Dickson award, 1978; Rosenstiel award, 1986; T.H. Morgan medal Genetics Soc. Am., 1986. Mem. Nat. Acad. Scis., Am. Acad. Arts and Scis., Am. Philos. Soc., Harvey Soc., N.Y. Acad. Scis., AAAS, Royal Soc. London (fgn. mem.). Home: 2075 Robin Rd San Marino CA 91108

BENZING, WALTER CHARLES, materials scientist, consultant; b. N.Y.C., Aug. 28, 1924; s. Frederick Ludwig and Grace Augusta (Engelhart) B.; m. Ruth Elinor McBride, Sept. 11, 1948; children: Steven M., David W., Jefferey C. BS, U. Rochester, 1945; MS, MIT, 1948; PhD, Princeton U., 1964. Mgr. engring. research and devel. Merck & Co., Inc., Rahway, N.J., 1952-63; dir. tech. Union Carbide Corp., Mountain View, Calif., 1964-68; v.p. tech. Applied Materials, Inc., Santa Clara, Calif., 1968-84, also cons. and tech. advisor to pres.; cons. in field Saratoga, Calif., 1984—; bd. dirs. XMR, Inc., Santa Clara, Benzing Techs., San Jose, Calif. Contbr. tech. articles to profl. jours.; patentee in field. Served to lt. USN, 1942-46. Recipient SEMY award Semiconductor Equipment and Materials Inst., Mountain View, 1979. Mem. Electrochem. Soc., Am. Chem. Soc., Am. Assn. Crystal Growth. Republican. Avocations: photography, woodworking, gardening. Home and Office: 20297 Ljepava Dr Saratoga CA 95070

BERARD, PAUL MICHAEL, electrical engineer; b. Portsmouth, N.H., Feb. 10, 1946; s. Paul Emile and Stella Marie (Gosselin) B.; m. Donna May Hill, Oct. 6, 1968; children: Brian Paul, Christine Marie. Assoc. in Engring., N.H. Tech. Inst., 1970; B of Engring. Tech., Northeastern U., 1978, BSEE, 1980; MSEE, U. N.H., 1982. Tech. assoc. Bell Labs., Holmdel, N.J., 1970-72, North Andover, Mass., 1972-80; mem. tech. staff Bell Labs., North Andover, 1980-82; mem. tech. staff GTE Communication Systems, Phoenix, 1982-85, mgr. Siemens Transmission Systems, 1985—. Patentee in field. Mem. Tau Beta Pi, Eta Kappa Nu. Home: 3017 W Kerry Ln Phoenix AZ 85027 Office: Siemens Transmission 2500 W Utopia Rd Phoenix AZ 85027

BERDAHL, PAUL HILLAND, physicist; b. Washington, Aug. 1, 1945; s. Edgar Oliver and Anna Beata (Flansaas) B.; m. Margaret Jane Upson, Feb. 26, 1977; children: Edgar Joseph, Carl Thomas. BA in Math and Physics, Rice U., 1967; MS in Physics, Stanford U., 1968, PhD in Theoretical Physics, 1972. Research assoc. dept. physics Stanford U., Palo Alto, Calif., 1972, U. Wash., Seattle, 1972-74; staff scientist U. Calif. Lawrence Berkeley Lab., 1975—. Co-author: California Solar Data Manaual, 1978; contbr. articles to profl. jours.; inventer solid-state radiative heat pump. Woodrow Wilson fellow, 1967-68. Mem. Am. Solar Energy Soc. (chmn. solar radiation div., 1981), Internat. Solar Energy Soc., Am. Phys. Soc. Avocations: cross-country skiing. Office: U Calif Lawrence Berkeley Lab Bldg 90 Room 2024 Berkeley CA 94720

BERDEL, RICHARD LEE, agricultural researcher; b. San Diego, Sept. 19, 1936; s. Richard Ralph and Grace Eulah (Brower) B.; m. Mable Barbie Kinzie, Dec. 22, 1984. Student, Woodbury U., 1955-56, San Diego City Coll., 1957, U. Ariz., 1984; A in Gen. Studies, Pima Community Coll., 1986. Research aid USDA, Tucson, 1970-72; research asst. Agrl. Research Service USDA, Tucson, 1972-73, research technician, 1973—; cons. statis., Tucson, 1984—. Co-producer documentary on water harvesting, U. Ariz., 1983; contbr. articles to profl. jours. Mem. Tucson Community Cable Corp., 1984—. Recipient Cert. of Merit, USDA, 1972, 78. Mem. Tucson Computer Soc. Democrat. Unitarian. Avocations: hiking, bicycling, handball. Office: USDA Agrl Research Service 2000 E Allen Rd Tucson AZ 85719

BERDROW, STANTON K., power company executive; b. Long Beach, Calif., Oct. 4, 1928; s. Earl Lester and Martha Ann B.; m. Rosa R. Rottger, Feb. 22, 1951; children—Nancy, John, Matthew. B.S., Armstrong Coll., Berkeley, Calif., 1950; postgrad. Sch. Bus. Syracuse U., 1951-52. Dist. advt. and sales promotion mgr. The Pennzoil Co., Los Angeles, 1953-59; v.p., mgmt. supr. Batten, Barton, Durstine & Osborn, Inc., San Francisco, 1960-77; v.p., dir. acctg. services Commart Communications, Santa Clara, Calif., 1978-80; v.p. communications and pub. affairs Sierra Pacific Power Co., Reno, 1980—. Bd. dirs. PBS-TV, Reno. Served with U.S. Army, 1946-48. Mem. Am. Advt. Fedn. (1st award TV nat. competition 1978, Best in the West 1985), Pub. Utility Communicators Assn. (1st award complete campaign 1984, 85, 1st award employee communications 1984), Public Relations Soc. Am., Pacific Coast Electric Assn., Pacific Coast Gas Assn., Assn. Indsl. Advertisers, Pub. Relations Soc. Am. (v.p. Sierra Nev. chpt.), Reno Advt. Club. Republican. Clubs: Innisfree Beach (Lake Tahoe, Calif.); Rotary. Contbr. articles to profl. jours. Home: 3925 Skyline Blvd Reno NV 89509 Office: PO Box 10100 Reno NV 89520

BERDUX, WILLIAM JAMES, JR., optical instruments manufacturing company executive; b. San Diego, Mar. 13, 1947; s. William James and Beatrice Naomi (Martin) B.; m. Barbara Love, Feb. 14, 1976; children—Sabrina M., Chelsie L. B.S. in Bus. Mgmt., San Diego State U., 1973. Mgmt. trainee Union Bank, San Diego, 1973-73, Los Angeles, 1973, comml. loan officer, San Francisco, 1974-76; dir. B.H.R. Fin. Services, Inc. div. Argo Industries, Inc., Los Angeles, 1976-78; v.p. gen. mgr. Argo Trading Co., Inc. div. Argo Industries, inc., Laguna Hills, Calif., 1978-81; v.p., mng. dir. Argo Industries, Inc., Laguna Hills, 1978-81; internat. sales and mktg. mgr., Bausch & Lomb, Inc., Pasadena, Calif., 1981—. Served with USAF, 1965-69. Home: 27382 Celanova Mission Viejo CA 92692-3345

BERELSON, PHILIP P., lawyer; b. N.Y.C., May 22, 1943. AB cum laude and distinction in all subjects, Cornell U., 1964; JD cum laude, Harvard U., 1967. Bar: N.Y., Ariz., Calif. Law clk. to presiding justice U.S. Ct. Appeals, 2d cir., N.Y.C., 1967-68; assoc. Cravath, Swaine & Moore, N.Y.C., 1968-73; assoc. Brown & Bain, Phoenix, 1973-74, ptnr., 1974-81; ptnr. Brown & Bain, Palo Alto, Calif., 1981—. Co-editor: Law Book Guide, 1969-73. Recipient Vedder Prize Cornell U., 1963. Mem. ABA, Santa Clara County Bar Assn. (bench/bar superior ct. com. 1984-85, chmn. bus. litigation com. 1985, chmn. fed. courts com. 1986, dir. Law Found., Inc. 1987—), Am. Arbitration Assn., Phi Beta Kappa, Omicron Delta Epsilon. Office: Brown & Bain 600 Hansen Way Palo Alto CA 94306

BERENBEIM, DAVID MICHAEL, physician; b. Denver, May 29, 1954; s. S. Leonard and Joan Madelon (Goodney) B. BA summa cum laude, Yale U., 1976; MD, Stanford U., 1980. Diplomate Am. Bd. Internal Medicine. Research assoc. Stanford (Calif.) U., 1976-78, resident in medicine, 1980-83; pvt. practice specializing in adult and adolescent internal medicine Englewood, Colo., 1983—; regional med. dir. Parkside Mgmt. Services, Denver, 1985; acting asst. med. dir. Gt. West Life Assurance, Englewood, 1985-86. Contbr. articles to sci. jours. Mem. Am. Coll. Physicians, Am. Med. Assn., N.Y. Acad. Scis., Phi Beta Kappa, Sigma Xi. Lodge: Kiwanis (bd. dirs. Englewood club 1986—). Office: 7180 E Orchard Rd Englewood CO 80111

BERES, JAMES EDWARD, SR., industrial manufacturing engineering consultant; b. Cleve., July 17, 1943; s. John and Mary Elizabeth (Liptak) B.; m. Carol J. Good, July 23, 1966; children: James E. Jr., Christian J., Brian D. Student, Chandler Tech. Inst., 1966-69, U. Calif., Irvine, 1972-73, UCLA, 1974-75. Sr. mfg. engr. ITI Cannon Electric Co., Santa Ana, Calif., 1972-73; mfg. mgr. Calif. Originals Co., Torrance, 1974; plant mgr. Greer Hydraulics, Los Angeles, 1974-75; mfg. mgr. Eskimo Radiatior, Los Angeles, 1976-78; pres. Beres Tech. Service, Huntington Beach, Calif., 1978—. Umpire/coach Seavien Little League, Huntington Beach, 1980—, sponser, 1981; leader Boy Scouts Am., Huntington Beach, 1980; sponser Edison High Sch. Baseball, Huntington Beach, 1986. Served with U.S. Army, 1961-64. Mem. Am. Inst. Indsl. Engrs. (sr.). Avocations: golfing, collecting stamps. Home and Office: 21082 Greenboro Ln Huntington Beach CA 92646

BERG, CLYDE HUET ORVIL, engineer, consultant; b. Mpls., Apr. 12, 1915; s. Hilmar O. and Clara I. (Ellingson) B. BSChemE, U. Minn., 1936, PhD with high distinction, 1940. Registered profl. engr., Calif. Mgr. devel. and exploration of new energy resources Union Oil Co., Los Angeles, 1940-60; owner Clyde Berg & Assocs., Long Beach, 1960-68; pres. Earth Energy, Inc., Long Beach, Calif., 1968—; chmn. energy form oil shale com. U.S. Govt, 1952-56; rep. West USA Petroleum Industry War Council, 1942-46. Contbr. articles to profl. publs.; inventor in field. Mem. pres.' council Chapman Coll., Orange, Calif., 1970—. Served to 2d lt. USCG, 1936—. Hormel Research fellow Minn. Inst. Tech., U. Minn., 1939-40. Mem. ASME (bd. dirs. petroleum div. 1963-65), Am. Chem. Soc., Sigma Xi, Tau Beta Pi, Alpha Chi Sigma. Club: Balboa Bay. Office: 3655 E Ocean Blvd Long Beach CA 90803

BERG, DEBRA KAY, sales professional; b. Washington, Mo., Nov. 5, 1954; d. John Dennis and Dorothy Virginia (Sanders) Mills; m. Charles Robert Berg, Aug. 18, 1974. BS in Chemistry, U. Del., 1976; MBA, Widener U., 1981. Researcher E.I. DuPont de Nemours Co., Wilmington, Del., 1976-83, customer support rep., 1983-84, product specialist, 1984-85; pharm. sales rep. E.I. DuPont de Nemours Co., San Jose, Calif., 1985-87; nuclear magnetic resonance product mgr. Varian Assocs., Inc., Palo Alto, Calif., 1987—. Mem. Am. Chem. Soc. Republican. Lutheran. Avocation: traveling. Office: 611 Hansen Way Palo Alto CA 94303

BERG, LLOYD, chem. engr.; b. Paterson, N.J., Aug. 8, 1914; s. Olav and Anita (Schneider) B.; m. Edna Barrowclough, Jan. 1, 1938; children—Sally, Charles, John, Ann. B.S.Ch.E., Lehigh U., 1936; Ph.D., Purdue U., 1942. Registered profl. engr., Mont., Pa. Tech. service engr. Sherwin-Williams Co., Newark, 1936-39; research engr. Gulf Research and Devel. Co., Pitts., 1942-46; asso. prof. chem. engring. U. Kans., Lawrence, 1946; prof., head dept. chem. engring. Mont. State U., Bozeman, 1946-79; prof. Mont. State U., 1979—; cons. Exxon, Concco, Husky Oil, Phillips Petroleum Co., Champion Internat., U.S. Dept. Energy, Celanese Chem. Co. Contbr. articles in extractive distillation to profl. jours.; 40 recent U.S. patents in extractive distillation. Served with U.S. Army, 1936-42. Fellow Am. Inst. Chem. Engrs.; mem. Am. Soc. Engring. Edn., Am. Chem. Soc. Home: 1314 S 3d Bozeman MT 59715 Office: Dept Chem Engring Mont State U Bozeman MT 59717

BERG, PAUL, biochemist, educator; b. N.Y.C., June 30, 1926; s. Harry and Sarah (Brodsky) B.; m. Mildred Levy, Sept. 13, 1947; 1 son, John. B.S., Pa. State U., 1948; Ph.D. (NIH fellow 1950-52), Western Res. U., 1952; D.Sc. (hon.), U. Rochester, 1978, Yale U., 1978, Wash. U., St. Louis, 1986. Postdoctoral fellow Copenhagen (Denmark) U., 1952-53; postdoctoral fellow Sch. Medicine, Washington U., St. Louis, 1953-54; Am. Cancer Soc. scholar cancer research dept. microbiology Sch. Medicine, Washington U., 1954-57, from asst. to asso. prof. microbiology, 1955-59; prof. biochemistry Stanford Sch. Medicine, 1959—, Sam, Lula and Jack Willson prof. biochemistry, 1970, chmn. dept., 1969-74; dir. Stanford U. Ctr. for Molecular and Genetic Medicine, 1985; non-resident fellow Salk Inst., 1973; adv. bd. NIH, NSF, M.I.T.; vis. com. dept. biochemistry and molecular biology Harvard U.; bd. sci. advisors Jane Coffin Childs Found. Med. Research, 1970-80; chmn. sci. adv. com. Whitehead Inst., 1984; internat. adv. bd. Basel Inst. Immunology. Contbr. profl. jours.; Editor: Biochem. and Biophys. Research Communications, 1959-68; editorial bd.: Molecular Biology, 1966-69. Served to lt. (j.g.) USNR, 1943-46. Recipient Eli Lilly prize biochemistry, 1959; V.D. Mattia award Roche Inst. Molecular Biology, 1972; Henry J. Kaiser award for excellence in teaching, 1972; Disting. Alumnus award Pa. State U., 1972; Sarasota Med. awards for achievement and excellence, 1979; Gairdner Found. annual award, 1980; Lasker Found. award, 1980; Nobel award in chemistry, 1980; N.Y. Acad. Sci. award, 1980; Sci. Freedom and Responsibility award AAAS, 1982; Nat. Library Sci. medal, 1986; named Calif. Scientist of Yr. Calif. Museum Sci. and Industry, 1963; numerous spl. and disting. lectureships including Harvey lectr., 1972, Lynen lectr., 1977, Priestly lectrs. Pa. State u., 1978, Dreyfus Disting. lectrs. Northwestern U., 1979, Lawrence Livermore Dir.'s Disting. lectr., 1983, W.H. Stein Meml. lectr. Rockefeller U., 1984, Charles E. Dohme Meml. lectr. Johns Hopkins U., 1984, Weizmann Inst. Sci. Jubilee lectr., 1984, U. Houston Nobel Prize Winners Series, 1985. Mem. Inst. Medicine, Nat. Acad. Scis. (council 1979—, editorial bd. proc. 1980), Am. Acad. Arts and Scis., Am. Soc. Biol. Chemists (pres. 1974-75), Am. Soc. Microbiology, Am. Philos. Soc. (Nat. Medal of Sci. 1983), Japan Biochem. Soc. (elected fgn. mem. 1978), French Acad. Sci. (elected fng. mem. 1981),. Office: Stanford Sch Medicine 838 Santa Fe Ave Stanford CA 94305

BERGE, DALE LEROY, archaeologist; b. Coalinga, Calif., Sept. 5, 1934; s. William H. and Lucille M. (Provost) B.; B.A., Brigham Young U., Provo, Utah, 1961, M.A., 1964; Ph.D., U. Ariz., 1968; m. Geraldine Mitton, June 30, 1961; children—Kurt W., Tara M., Matt J. Mem. staff Ariz. State Museum, Tucson, 1966-68; mem. faculty Brigham Young U., 1968—, prof. anthropology, 1981—, dir. Mus. Peoples and Cultures, 1968—. Served with AUS, 1957-59. Charles Redd fellow, 1979. Mem. Soc. Hist. Archaeology, Soc. Am. Archaeology, Am. Anthrop. Assn., Sigma Xi. Republican. Mormon. Author articles, monograph in field. Office: Anthropology Dept Brigham Young U Provo UT 84602

BERGENDORFF, FREDERICK L., advertising executive, writer; b. Bremerton, Wash., Feb. 7, 1944; s. Fred R. and Lola M. (Young) B. BA, San Diego State U., 1965; MA, Columbia Pacific U., 1983, PhD, 1983. Publicity mgr. Time-Life Broadcast, San Diego, 1966-68; promotion dir. KABC Radio, Los Angeles, 1968-69; dir. advt., promotion KNX CBS Radio, Los Angeles, 1969—. Author: Broadcast Advertising and Promotion, 1983. Recipient Clio award 1982, Nat. Addy award Am. Advt. Fedn., 1982. Mem. ASCAP, Advt. Club Los Angeles, San Diego State Athletic Fedn. (bd. dirs.), San Diego State Alumni Assn., Columbia Pacific Alumni Assn., Nat. Speakers Assn., Broadcast Promotion Mktg. Execs. (pres. 1984). Home: PO Box 3235 Seal Beach CA 90740 Office: CBS Radio 6121 Sunset Blvd Los Angeles CA 90028

BERGER, AUGUST WALTER, data processing/manufacturing/material systems consultant, educator; b. Los Angeles, June 23, 1937; s. Alfred and Josephine Marie (Obadahl) B.; B.A., Calif. State U., 1971, M.B.A., 1973; m. Camilla Anne Orndorff, Oct. 5, 1957; children—Lisa Ann, Larry Mark, David Andrew, Karen Marie. Dir. purchasing Exec. Industries, Inc., Anaheim, Calif., 1972-73; dir. material Calif. Computer Products, Inc., Anaheim, 1974-76; ind. mgmt., data processing system cons., Yorba Linda, Calif., 1976—; v.p. Mfrs. Resources and Planning, Inc., Santa Ana, Calif., 1977-79; pres. The Gus Berger Group, Inc., educators and cons. mfg./data processing, govt. contractors and comml., Anaheim, 1979—; asst. prof. evenings Calif. State U., Fullerton, 1970-78; lectr. in field. Served with USAF, 1955-59. Mem. Am. Prodn. and Inventory Control Soc. (dir., past pres. Orange County chpt.; participant Internat. Tech. Confs., 1975-79, 81-86, chmn. 1980; cert.), Internat. Material Mgmt. Soc. (cert.), Am. Soc. Tng. and Devel., Soc. Logistical Engrs. Republican. Contbg. editor: Production and Inventory Handbook; contbr. articles to profl. jours. and nat. trade mags. Developer material mgmt. concepts time bucket w.i.p., rotational inventories, flip-flop bills of material, product profile. Office: 5544 E La Palma Ave Suite 2B Anaheim CA 92807

BERGER, BENNETT MAURICE, sociology educator; b. N.Y.C., May 1, 1926; s. Julius and Ethel (King) B.; m. Jean Kirkham, Dec. 9, 1956 (div. 1971); children: Jane, Nora.; m. Chandra Mukerji, Jan. 1981; children—Kenneth, Stephanie. A.B., Hunter Coll., 1950; Ph.D., U. Calif.-Berkeley, 1958. Asst. prof., then assoc. prof. sociology U. Ill., 1959-63; mem. faculty U. Calif.-Davis, 1963-73, prof. sociology, 1965-73, chmn. dept., 1963-66, 67-69; prof. sociology U. Calif.-San Diego, 1973—, chmn. dept., 1979-81. Author: Working-Class Suburb, 1960, Looking For America, 1971, The Survival of A Counterculture, 1981; assoc. editor: Sociometry, 1966-69, Social Problems, 1969-72; editor: Contemporary Sociology, 1974-77; sr. editor: Society, 1983-87. Served with USMCR, 1944-46. Fellow Am. Sociol. Assn.; mem. AAUP. Home: 1410 Luneta Dr Del Mar CA 92014 Office: Univ California San Diego CA 92093

BERGER, GARY JOHN, human resources consultant; b. Toledo, May 15, 1944; s. John Ora and Mary Elizabeth (Bott) B.; m. Miriam Elizabeth Swartz; children: April E., Stephanie A., Christine T. Student, U. Dayton, 1962-63; BS, Defiance Coll., 1972; MEd, U. Toledo, 1975; PhD, Century U., 1985. Dir. human resources Pillsbury Corp., Mpls., 1975-78, Shaklee Corp., San Francisco, 1978-81; human resources div. mgr. Impell Corp., San Francisco, 1981-84; sr. v.p. Am. Savs., Stockton, Calif., 1984-85; dir. Internat. Survey Research, Walnut Creek, Calif., 1985—; cons. L.I. (N.Y.) Lighting Co., 1983-84. Author: Customer Service Practices by California Savings and Loan Employees, 1984, Adult Education Practices in Industry, 1975. Historian Carondelet Parents Bd., Concord, Calif., 1985-86. Mem. Am. Soc. Tng. Devel., Am. Soc. Personnel Adminstrn., Am. Edn. Communications and Tech., Organizational Devel. Network, Tau Kappa Epsilon. Democrat. Roman Catholic. Avocations: model clock builder, photographer, writer. Office: Internat Survey Research 1990 N California Blvd Walnut Creek CA 94596

BERGER, GORDON MARK, historian, educator, consultant, research psychoanalyst; b. New London, Conn., May 10, 1942; s. Julius and Hazel Elinor (Gordon) B.; m. Karen Ann Sommer, Sept. 11, 1966 (div. Sept. 1979); 1 child, Sarah Michelle. A.B., Wesleyan U., Middletown, Conn., 1964; M.A., Yale U., 1966, Ph.D., 1972. Instr. history U. So. Calif., Los Angeles, 1970-72; asst. prof. U. So. Calif., 1972-76, assoc. prof., 1976-83, prof., 1983—; research scholar Japan Fin. Ministry, Tokyo, 1972-74; research clin. assoc. So. Calif. Psychoanalytic Inst., Beverly Hills, 1983—; dir. U. So. Calif. E. Asian Studies Ctr., 1981—, U. So. Calif.-UCLA Joint E. Asian Area and Lang. Studies Nat. Resources Ctr., 1981—; dir. developing internat. bus. skills project U.S. Dept. Edn., 1983-84, 84-85, 85-87; assoc. mem. Inst. Fiscal and Monetary Policy of Japan Ministry of Fin., 1986—. Author: Parties Out of Power in Japan, 1931-1941, 1977; editor, translator: Kenkenroku: A Diplomatic Record of the Sino-Japanese War, 1894-1895, 1982; mem. editorial bd. Pacific Focus: Inha Jour. Internat. Studies, 1986—; contbr. articles to profl. jours. Mem. adv. bd. Pacific Culture Mus., Pasadena, Calif., 1982—; advisor Calif. Econ. Devel. Corp. Research fellow U.S.-Japan Fulbright Commn., 1967-69, 79-80. Mem. Assn. Asian Studies (Disting. lectr. in Japanese studies, N.E. council 1985-86), Internat. House of Japan, So. Calif. Japan Seminar (steering com. 1972—), Korean Studies

Assn. (bd. dirs. 1977—), Found. for Advanced Infor. and Research of Japan (assoc.). Office: Univ So Calif History Dept SOS 252 Los Angeles CA 90089

BERGER, KENNETH JAMES EDWARD, oceanographer, consultant; b. Astoria, N.Y., Mar. 14, 1951; s. Edward Berger and Helen Lucille (Roland) Manfredi. BS, Pace U., 1972; MS, NYU, 1974, postgrad., 1974-78; PhD in Environ. Sci. and Engring., UCLA, 1982; grad. cert., U. San Diego, 1984. Cert. community coll. instr., ESL tchr. Research asst. N.C. State U., Raleigh, 1972, Inst. for Marine and Atmospheric Sci., N.Y.C., 1973-74; oceanographer U.S. Dept. of Interior, N.Y.C., 1975-79; postgrad. reseacher II UCLA, 1979-82; sr. scientist IWG Corp., San Diego, 1980-81; assoc. prof. Chapman Coll., San Diego, 1982—; section mgr., systems scientist Computer Scis. Corp., San Diego, 1984-85; cons. in marine sci., San Diego, 1982—; adj. instr. Cen. Tex. Coll., Clark AFB, Philippines, 1983, U. LaVerne, San Diego, 1985—. Contbr. articles to profl. jours. Served with USCG aux., 1981. Recipient Unit Citation award U.S. Dept. of Interior, 1978, first place San Diego Brit. Car Club Council, 1980, second place San Diego Brit. Car Club Council, 1981; N.Y. State scholar, 1972; Pace U. Sci. scholar, 1972; UCLA fellow. Mem. AAAS, Internat. Oceanographic Found., N.Y. Acad. Scis., Kappa Mu Epsilon. Clubs: San Diego MG (sec. 1983), San Diego MGA's (v.p. 1982), New Eng. MG "T" Register, Ltd. Avocations: numismatics, philately, antique Brit. sports cars.

BERGER, LEV ISAAC, research physics educator; b. Rostov, USSR, June 23, 1929; came to U.S., 1978; s. Isaac Mark and Sara (Poltevsker) B.; m. Ninelle Rossine, July 2, 1956; 1 child, Yuri. MS in Physics, State U., Moscow, 1955; PhD in Physics, State U., Minsk, USSR, 1959; PhD in Tech. Scis., U. Steel Alloys, Moscow, 1968. Lectr. physics U. Nonferrous Metlas, Moscow, 1956-60; docent Physics U. Metallurgy, Moscow, 1960-62; prof. Poly. Inst., Moscow, 1962-77; sr. scientist New Eng. Research Ctr., Sudbury, Mass., 1979-81; lectr. physics Calif. State U., San Diego, 1981—; dir. div. Inst. Spl. Pure Substances, Moscow, 1962-71, Introscopy Research Inst., Moscow, 1971-77. Author: Ternary Diamond-like Semiconductors, 1969; contbr. articles to profl. jours.; patentee in field. San Diego State U. grantee, 1983. Mem. AAAS, Am. Phys. Soc., Am. Assn. Crystal Growth, N.Y. Acad. Scis., Calif. Inst. Electronics and Materials Sci. (pres. 1981—), Inst. Electronics of San Diego State U. (bd. dirs. 1983—). Home: 2115 Flame Tree Way Hemet CA 92343 Office: San Diego State U Dept Physics San Diego CA 92182

BERGER, RALPH JACOB, biology educator; b. Vienna, Austria, Sept. 16, 1937; came to U.K., 1938, came to U.S., 1965; BA, U. Cambridge, Eng., 1960, MA, 1964; PhD, U. Edinburgh, Scotland, 1963. Vis. asst. prof. U. P.R., San Juan, 1963-64; research psychologist NIH, San Juan, 1964-65; asst. research psychologist UCLA, 1965-68; asst. prof. psychology U. Calif., Santa Cruz, 1968-69, assoc. prof. biology, 1969-74, prof. biology, 1974—. Author: Psyclosis: The Circularity of Experience, 1977; contbr. articles to profl jours. Grantee NSF, NIH. Mem. AAAS, Soc. Neurosci., Sleep Research Socs. (exec. com. 1969-71), Internat Hibernation Soc., Internat. Brain Research Orgn. Office: U Calif Santa Cruz CA 95064

BERGER, STEPHEN EDWARD, psychologist, consultant; b. Phila., Oct. 1, 1944; s. Harold Allen and Lilian Eleanor (Loev) B.; m. Diane Marilyn Klein, Dec. 24, 1967; children—Michael Allen, Gary David. Ph.D., U. Miami, 1971. Diplomate in Clin. Psychology, Am. Bd. Profl. Psychology. Asst. prof. psychology U. So. Calif., 1971-78; pvt. practice psychology, Mission Viejo, Calif., 1972—; chief occupational health psychologist Los Angeles County Dept. Health Services, Los Angeles, 1978-82. Contbr. articles to profl. jours. Mem. Am. Psychol. Assn., Western Psychol. Assn., AAAS, Calif. State Psychol. Assn., N.Y. Acad. Scis. Democrat. Jewish. Office: 26302 La Paz Rd #203 Mission Viejo CA 92691

BERGER, STEVEN BARRY, mathematics educator; b. N.Y.C., Dec. 29, 1946; s. Bernard and Sylvia (Reff) B.;. SB, MIT, 1967, PhD, 1973. Sloan Found. fellow MIT, Cambridge, 1973, Fight-for-Sight, Inc. fellow, 1974-76; research physicist Itek Corp., Lexington, Mass., 1976-77, TRW Corp., McLean, Va., 1978-80; systems engr. Redondo Beach, Calif., 1983-85; research physicist Naval Research Lab., Washington, 1981-82; instr. math. Chadwick Sch., Palos Verdes, Calif., 1986—; lectr. George Washington U., Washington, 1981, Loyola Marymount U., Los Angeles, 1985; mem. ednl. council MIT, 1984. Contbr. articles to profl. jours. Mem. Math. Assn. Am., IEEE, Am. Assn. Physics Tchrs., Am. Phys. Soc., Sierra Club, Sigma Xi. Jewish. Club: Toastmasters (Redondo Beach). Avocations: classical piano, sports, chess. Home: 19009 Laurel Park Rd Suite 174 Compton CA 90220 Office: Chadwick Sch 26800 S Academy Dr Palos Verdes CA 90274

BERGER, SUE ANNE, chemist, educator; b. Wichita, Kans., Oct. 8, 1941; d. Oscar Henry and Josephine Mildred (Stucky) B. BE, Kans. State Tchrs. Coll., 1963; MS in Chemistry, U. Miss., 1968; MS in Mineral Econs., Colo. Sch. Mines, 1982. Cert. chemistry and math. tchr., Colo. Tchr. Davy Crockett Jr. High Sch., Amarillo, Tex., 1963-67, Bear Creek Sr. High Sch., Denver, 1968—; dept. chmn. Bear Creek Sr. High Sch., 1980-85. Author: (with others) Element of the Week, 1986. Nominated Presdl. award for Excellence in Sci. Teaching NSF, 1986. Mem. Am. Chem. Soc., Nat. Sci. Tchrs. Assn., Colo. Assn. Sci. Tchrs., Phi Delta Kappa. Democrat. Mennonite. Avocations: cross country skiing, golf, bridge. Home: 6372 S Anapurna Dr Evergreen CO 80439 Office: Bear Creek High Sch 3490 S Kipling St Denver CO 80227

BERGESON, MARIAN, state legislator; m. Garth Bergeson; children; Nancy, Garth Jr., Julie, James. Student UCLA; BA in Edn. Brigham Young U.; postgrad. UCLA. Pres., regional dir. Calif. Sch. Bds. Assn.; officer, dir. Orange County Sch. Bds. Assn.; mem. Newport Beach City Sch. Dist. Bd. Edn., 1964-65; mem. Newport-Mesa Unified Sch. Dist. Bd. Edn., 1965-77; mem. Calif. Assembly, 1978-82, Calif. Senate, 1984—. Past mem. Orange County Juvenile Justice Commn., Riles-Younger Task Force for Prevention of Crime and Violence in the Schs., Com. for Revision State Edn. Code, Joint Com. on Revision Penal Code; mem. Calif. YMCA Model Legislature/Ct.; mem. bd. advisors Calif. Elected Women's Assn. Edn. and Research; bd. dirs. Sta. KBIG Adv. Bd.; mem. govt. relations com. Orange County Arts Alliance. Recipient Marian Bergeson Community Services award Orange County Sch. Bds. Assn., 1975; Anchor award Newport Harbor C. of C., women's div., 1967; Community Services award AAUW, 1976; Disting. Women's award Irvine Soroptimists, 1981; Disting. Service award Brigham Young U., 1980-81; Woman of Achievement award Newport Harbor Zonta Club, 1981; Silver Medallion, YWCA, 1983; Pub. Service award Calif. Speech-Lang.-Hearing Assn., 1983; named Outstanding Pub. Ofcl., Orange County chpt. Am. Soc. Pub. Adminstrn., 1983. Office: 140 Newport Ctr Dr Suite 120 Newport Beach CA 92660 other office address: State Capitol Sacramento CA 95814

BERGIN, BONITA MAE, business executive; b. Port Angeles, Wash., Jan. 22, 1945; d. George Albert and Elaine (Myhr) Bratsberg; m. James Anthony Bergin, Mar. 19, 1967. BA in English, Psychology, Social Sci., Sonoma State U., 1968, MA in Spl. Edn., 1977; postgrad., Nova U., 1982—. Cert. elem., secondary, vocat. and community coll. tchr., Calif. Instr. Shepparton (Australia) Girls High Sch., 1971-73, Konya Maarif Kolleji, Konja, Turkey, 1973-74; founder, exec. dir. Canine Companions for Ind., Santa Rosa, Calif., 1975—; instr. Santa Rosa Adult Edn., 1975-82, Santa Rosa Jr. Coll., 1980—. Founder Friends of Refugees, Santa Rosa, 1977. Recipient Cert. of Merit, City of Santa Rosa, 1983, Disting. Service award Govs. Com. Employment of the Handicapped, Sacramento, 1986. Mem. Calif. Assn. Substitute Tchrs. (founder 1976), Sonoma State U. Almuni Assn., Delta Soc. (bd. dirs. 1986—, Model Program award 1984). Avocations: ranching, animal husbandry, dog training. Home: 4945 Grange Rd Santa Rosa CA 95405 Office: Canine Companions for Ind 1221 Sebastopol Rd Santa Rosa CA 95407

BERGIN, EDWARD PATRICK, physician; b. N.Y.C., June 27, 1946; s. Edward Patrick and Marie Agnes (O'Connell) B.; m. Lila Ann Lokken, June 20, 1981; children: John Joseph, Edward Patrick. BS, U. N.Mex., 1969; MD, N.Y. Med. Coll., 1974. Diplomate Am. Bd. Surgery. Intern Mayo Clinic, Rochester, Minn., 1974-75, resident gen. surgery, 1975-79; staff surgeon Community Meml. Hosp., Sidney, Mont., 1980—, vice chief staff, 1982-83, chief surgeon, 1981—, bd. dirs. 1982-83; med. dir. Region III A Emergency Med. Services, 1982. Fellow ACS, Mont. Med. Assn. (sec.,treas. 1986-87, exec. com. 1984-86); mem. Mont. Malpractice Panel, AMA, Eastern Mont. Med. Soc. (sec. treas. 1981, v.p. 1982). Home: 116 3d Ave SW Sidney MT 59270 Office: 214 14th Ave SW #105 Sidney MT 59270

BERGLUND, MARY FAIR, economist; b. Des Moines, Sept. 11, 1934; d. Richard H. and Mary C. (Porter) Fair; m. James H. Berglund, Feb. 12, 1955; children—Julie, James, Richard. Student Iowa State U., 1952-53, U. Colo., 1953-55; B.S. in Econs. summa cum laude, Pacific U., 1958; M.A., U. Nebr., 1973, Ph.D. in Econs., 1974. Instr., Coll. Bus., Spencer, Iowa, 1967-69; asst. prof. econs. U. Nebr., Lincoln, 1974-77; cons. Fed. R.R. Adminstr./Assn. Am. R.R.s, 1977-80; adj. prof. econs. U. San Diego, 1979-80; research assoc. Inst. Transp. Studies, U. Calif.-Irvine, 1981—; dir. San Diego Transit Corp., 1983—; mem. San Diego Energy Adv. Bd., 1982—, San Diego Paratransit Bd., 1985—. Contbr. articles to profl. jours. Bd. overseers U. Calif.-San Diego, 1982—; bd. dirs. San Diego World Affairs Council, 1981—; chmn. ball Las Patronas, La Jolla, 1984-85, bd. overseers U. Calif.-San Diego, 1986-87; mem. San Diego Symphony Assn., La Jolla Mus. Contemporary Art. M.H. Fling fellow, 1973; Abbott Social Sci. fellow, 1972. Mem. Am. Econ. Assn., Western Econ. Assn., Transp. Research Forum, Beta Gamma Sigma, Omicron Delta Epsilon, Kappa Kappa Gamma. Clubs: City, Charter 100 (San Diego). Home: 6909 Fairway Rd La Jolla CA 92037 Office: U Calif Irvine CA 92717

BERGMAN, DANIEL CHARLES, county official, lawyer, educator; b. Corpus Christi, Tex., Aug. 18, 1943; s. Benjamin and Pearl H. B.; m. Susan Lee Axall, Aug. 15, 1965; children—Erica Catherine, Kelli Lorraine. B.S. in Biology, San Diego State U., 1965, M.S., 1971; J.D., U. San Diego, 1975. Bar: Calif. 1976, U.S. Dist. Ct. (so. dist.) Calif. 1976, U.S. Ct. Appeals (9th cir.) 1977; registered sanitarian, Calif., Ill.; cert. community coll. tchr., Calif. Asst. sanitarian, sanitarian San Diego County (Calif.) Dept. Pub. Health, 1968-71, vector ecologist, 1971-72, supervising sanitarian Dept. Health Services, 1972-79, chief div. sanitation/environ. health protection program mgr., 1979-81; environ. health cons. Contra Costa (Calif.) Dept. Health Services, 1981, asst. health services dir. Div. Environ. Health, 1981—; sole practice law, San Diego and Danville, Calif., 1976—; lectr. in field. Recipient Am. Jurisprudence awards. Mem. Am. Pub. Health Assn., Nat. Environ. Health Assn. (Presdl. citation 1977), Calif. Environ. Health Assn. (Presdl. citation 1977, 78), ABA, Calif. State Bar Assn. Office: 2500 Alhambra Ave Martinez CA 94553

BERGMAN, EDWARD ARTHUR, III, cultural specialist, consultant; b. Newark, Sept. 3, 1946; s. Linden Mouriece and Estelle Elenior (Thomas) B. BA, BS, Boston U., 1975. Real estate broker Grubb & Ellis, San Francisco, 1975-78; spl. project dir. Red Carpet Corp., Walnut Creek, Calif., 1978-79; v.p. mktg. MCI Corp., Tiburon, Calif., 1979-81; pres., chief exec. officer Three Gates Devel. Co., Saulalito, Calif., 1981-86, Am. Accent Programs, Inc., San Francisco, 1986—; chmn., chief exec. officer Pluribus Inc., San Francisco, 1986—; mem. New Eng. Oil Inst., Boston, 1974; bd. dirs. Inst. Lang., San Francisco. Author: Getting Down the Road, 1987. Mem. San Francisco Breakfast Club, Sausalito Rowing Club (projects mgr. 1985-86), Domaine Chandon Club, San Francisco C. of C. Avocations: sailing, backgammon, creative writing, furniture building. Home: 21 Morning Star Corte Madera CA 94925 Office: Pluribus Accents Inc 2140 Pierce San Francisco CA 95155

BERGMAN, GREGORY MARK, lawyer; b. Los Angeles, Sept. 12, 1947; s. Lloyd A. Bergman and Norma Koskoff; m. Leah Schneider Bergman; children: Brian, Alex. BA, UCLA, 1970; JD, S.W. U., Los Angeles, 1975. Bar: Calif. 1975, U.S. Dist. Ct. (cen. dist.) Calif. 1975, U.S. Ct. Appeals (9th cir.) 1975, U.S. Ct. Claims 1977, U.S. Supreme Ct. 1985. Assoc. Fadem, Berger & Norton, Santa Monica, Calif., 1975, Irmas, Simke & Chodos, Los Angeles, 1983; ptnr. Bergman & Wedner, Los Angeles, 1983—. Contbr. articles to profl. jours. Mem. ABA, Assn. Trial Lawyers Am., Assn. Real Estate Attys., Los Angeles County Bar Assn., Chancellor's Assn. Avocation: Tai Kwon Do. Office: Bergman & Wedner Inc 10880 Wilshire Blvd Suite 1011 Los Angeles CA 90024

BERGMANN, DONALD GERALD, biotechnology company executive; b. N.Y.C., Aug. 13, 1949; s. Edgar Frank and Dorothy Bertha (Kurtz) B.; m. Kathy Jeanne Dumont, Sept. 4, 1976; 1 child, Karen Ann. BS, Mich. State U., 1972; PhD, Ohio State U., 1978. Researcher UCLA, 1978-81; project mgr. Burroughs-Wellcome Co., Kansas City, Kans., 1981-83; scientist Genentech, Inc., S. San. Francisco, Calif., 1983, ops. mgr., 1983—. Contbr. articles on cancer research to sci. jours. Fellow Nat. Cancer Inst., 1978-80; grantee Nat. Cancer Inst., Am. Cancer Soc. Avocations: mountaineering, rock climbing, skiing. Home: PO Box 865 Moss Beach CA 94038 Office: Genentech Inc 460 Point San Bruno Blvd South San Francisco CA 94080

BERGMANN, ELIZABETH HELENE, dance educator, arts administrator; b. Evansville, Ind., June 22, 1937; d. Ervin Issac and Frances (Winfield) Weil; m. Klaus Bergmann, July 7, 1965; children: Sasha, Christopher. BS, Juilliard Sch., 1960; MA, U. Mich., 1963. Mem. faculty Jose Limon Dance Studio, N.Y.C., 1959-61; chmn., assoc. prof. U. Mich., Ann Arbor, 1961-82; chmn., prof. Calif. State U., Long Beach, 1982-83; artist in the schs. Calif. Arts Council Torrey Pines High Sch., Del Mar, 1983-85; exec. dir. Found. for Intercultural Edn., Del Mar, 1983—, San Diego Inst. for Arts Edn., 1985—; mem. Council Dance Adminstrs., Los Angeles, 1976-82; cons. Arts Adv. Commn. for Ednl. Testing Service, N.Y.C., 1984—. Choreographer: Moments, 1984, Cycle, 1982, Carmina Burana, 1980, Unicorn, Gorgon and Manticore, 1979 (Internat. Yr. of Child award 1980). Choreographer's grantee Nat. Endowment for Arts, 1975, 80, 83, artist in schs. grantee Calif. Arts Council, 1983-85; recipient Disting. Faculty award U. Mich., 1979, Spl. Achievement award Internat. Women's Yr., 1976. Mem. Am. Coll. Dance Festival Assn. (bd. dirs. 1981-84, adjudicator Tempe, Ariz. 1983), Nat. Assn. Sch. Dance (ethics com. 1981-82). Home: 1630 Landquist Dr Encinitas CA 92024

BERGMANN, JEANNINE ANNE PERSSON, trucking company executive; b. Alameda, Calif., Nov. 11, 1950; d. Ralph Rockwell and Jeannette Jane (Zisa) P.; m. William C. Bergmann. BA, Calif. State U., Hayward, 1972; postgrad. San Jose State U., 1972-73; cert. occupational safety and health Merritt Jr. Coll., 1973; cert. photography Chabot Jr. Coll., 1976. Clk., Kaiser Sand & Gravel, Pleasanton, Calif., 1971-74, clk. dispatcher, 1974-76, dispatcher, 1976-79, coordinator transport ops., 1979-80, mgr. transport ops., 1980; mgr. aggregate transport ops. Miles & Son Trucking Service, Inc., Pleasanton, Calif., 1980-86, ops. mgr., 1987—. Mem. Women in Constrn., Calif. Trucking Assn. (sec. dumptruck conf. 1983, chmn. 1984, 86, sec. cement conf. 1987). Club: Oakland Ski. Home: 543 Ruby Rd Livermore CA 94550 Office: PO Box 40 Pleasanton CA 94566

BERGSTEN, BEBE, business executive; b. New Bedford, Mass.; d. John Carl and Ines (Pietoff) B.; grad. Katharine Gibbs Sch., N.Y.C., 1934. Vice pres. James Brown Assos., N.Y.C., 1955-56, 60-61; dir. Ventures Cons. Corp., N.Y.C., 1957-62, Rochlin & Baran A.I.A. & Assos., Los Angeles; with Locare Research Group, Los Angeles, 1964—; pres. Hist. Films, Los Angeles. Author: The Great Dane; editor: Motion Pictures from the Library of Congress Paper Print Collection, 1894-1912; The First Twenty Years; Mary Pickford, Comedienne; One Reel A Week, Biograph Bulletins; Klaw & Erlanger; D.W. Griffith: His Biograph Films in Perspective, Early Motion Pictures. Home: 8045 Hemet Pl Hollywood CA 90046 Office: 8033 Sunset Blvd Los Angeles CA 90046

BERGUM, CHRISTIAN OLSON, architecture educator; b. Los Angeles, Nov. 3, 1953; s. Jarle Albert and Elna Lucille (Hansen) B.; m. Susan Faye Collins, Mar. 19, 1983; children: Erik, Brian. BA, BArch, U. Oreg., 1976; MArch, U. Wash., 1978; PhD, U. Pa., 1981. Prof. architecture Mont. State U., Bozeman, 1983—; prin., architect Christian Bergum and Assocs., Bozeman, 1985—; vis. fellow Harvard U., Cambridge, Mass., 1984. Fulbright fellow Council Internat. Exchange Scholars, Jordan, 1981, Israel, 198 ; Recipient Cerative Arts fellowship Mont. State U., 1982, Graham Found. fellowship for Research and Writing, 1986. Mem. AIA, Nat. Assn. Home Builders, Gerontol. Soc. Am.

BERKE, JUDIE, publisher, editor; b. Mpls., Apr. 15, 1938; d. Maurice M. and Sue (Supak) Kleyman; student U. Minn., 1956-60, Mpls. Sch. Art, 1945-59. Free lance illustrator and designer, 1959—; pres. Berke-Wood, Inc., N.Y.C., 1971-80, Manhattan Rainbow & Lollipop Co. subs. Berke-Wood, Inc., 1971-80; pres. Get Your Act Together, club act staging, N.Y.C., 1971-80; pres. Coordinator Pubs.,Inc., 1982—; pub., editor Continuing Care Coordinator, Health Watch mags.; pres. Continuing Care Coordinator Convs. and Seminars; cons. to film and ednl. cos.; guest lectr. various colls. and univs. in Calif. and N.Y., 1973—; writer, illustrator, dir. numerous ednl. filmstrips, 1972—, latest being Focus on Professions, 1974, Focus on the Performing Arts, 1974, Focus on the Creative Arts, 1974, Workstyles, 1976, Wonderworm, 1976, Supernut, 1977; author, illustrator film Fat Black Mack (San Francisco Ednl. Film Festival award, part of permanent collection Mus. Modern Art, N.Y.C.), 1970; designer posters and brochures for various entertainment groups, 1963—; composer numerous songs, latest being Time is Relative, 1976, Love Will Live On in My Mind, 1976, My Blue Walk, 1976, You Make Me a Baby, 1982, Let's Go Around Once More, 1983; composer/author off-Broadway musical Street Corner Time, 1978; contbr. children's short stories to various publs., also articles. Trustee The Happy Spot Sch., N.Y.C., 1972-75. Mem. Nat. Fedn. Bus. and Profl. Women, Nat. Assn. Female Execs., Am. Acad. Polit. and Social Sci. Home: 9430 Haskell Ave Sepulveda CA 91343 Office: Pub and Media Services 115 N Hollywood Way #202 Burbank CA 91505

BERKLAND, JAMES OMER, geologist; b. Glendale, Calif., July 31, 1930; s. Joseph Omer and Gertrude Madelyn (Thompson) B.; A.A., Santa Rosa Jr. Coll., 1951; A.B., U. Calif., Berkeley, 1958; M.S., San Jose State U., 1964; postgrad., U. Calif., Davis, 1969-72; m. Janice Lark Keirstead, Dec. 19, 1966; children—Krista Lynn, Jay Olin. With U.S. Geol. Survey, 1958-64; engrng. geologist U.S. Bur. Reclamation, 1964-69; cons. geologist, 1969-72; asst. prof. Appalachian State U., Boone, N.C., 1972-73; county geologist Santa Clara County, San Jose, Calif., 1973—; adj. prof. San Jose State U., 1975-76; mem. evening faculty San Jose City Coll.; West Valley legis. com., 1979; lectr. San Jose real estate bd. annual Deposit Receipt Seminar, 1980-85, San Jose State U. Gen. Edn. Conf.: Sci., Tech., Society, 1985-86-87; numerous TV and radio appearances including PBS, Frontline, Evening Mag., others. Treas. Creekside/Park Place Homeowners Group; v.p. West Coast Aquatics, Creekside/Park Place Swim Team; mem. various city and county adv. bds.; mem. Ctr. for Study Early Man, East Valley YMCA, Route 85 Task Force, Earthquake Watch, 1979-82, New Weather Observer. Registered geologist, Calif.; cert. engrng. geologist, Calif. Fellow Geol. Soc. Am.; mem. Assn. Engring. Geologists (past vice chmn. San Francisco sect.), Seismol. Soc. Am., Chapparal Poets, Sierra Club, Santa Clara County Engrs. and Architects Assn. (v.p.), Mining Lamp, Citizens and Scientists Concerned About Damage to Environment, San Jose Hist. Mus. Assn., Western Council Engrs., Internat. Platform Assn., Nat. Jogging Assn., Nat. Geog. Soc., Calif. State Employees Assn., Calif. State Firemen's Assn., Youth Sci. Inst. Peninsula Geol. Soc. (past treas.), Earthquake Engring. Research Inst., AAAS, Saber Soc. (co-founder, past pres.), Bay Area Reviewing Geologists Assn., Sons of Norway, Sigma Xi. Democrat. Club: King of Clubs Lions (charter, 1st v.p. 1986-87, pres. 1987—) (San Jose). Contbr. numerous articles to profl. jours.; originator seismic window theory for earthquake prediction. Home: 14927 East Hills Dr San Jose CA 95127 Office: Santa Clara County 70 W Hedding St San Jose CA 95110

BERKLEY, GAIL WINNICK, psychotherapist; b. Feb. 21, 1947; d. Lawrence C. and Helen M. (Caner) Winnick. B.A., San Francisco State U., 1970, M.S., 1979, now postgrad. Staff, Work Furlough Program, San Mateo County Jail, Redwood City, Calif., 1978-80; tchr. San Francisco Unified Sch. Dist., 1971-80; couple counselor Mental Health Seminar Tour, No. Council Health Facilities, 1976-79; pvt. practice psychotherapy, San Mateo, Calif., 1982—; self-employed interior designer, 1980—; cons. in field. Active San Mateo Family Services Aux., Mills Meml. Hosp. Aux.; founding sponsor San Francisco Performing Arts Ctr., 1976—; sponsor San Francisco Opera, San Francisco Ballet. Mem. Calif. Assn. Mental Health Counselors, Am. Counselors Mental Health Assn., Am. Personnel and Guidance Assn., Internat. Reading Assn., Am. Soc. Interior Designers, Am. Assn. Marriage, Family and Child Therapists, Am. Arbitration Assn. (panel arbitrators), Internat. Council Sex Edn. and Parenthood. Club: Commonwealth. Office: 36 S El Camino Real Suite 304 San Mateo CA 94401

BERKMAN, CRAIG L., manufacturing company executive; b. Sioux City, Aug. 12, 1941; s. R.B. and Elsie (Schilder) B.; m. Susan Joan Mowat, Aug. 28, 1965; children—Heidi Anne, Jennifer Lynn. B.A., Wheaton Coll., 1963; M.A. in Pub. Adminstrn., U. Calif.-Berkeley, 1967; J.D., Northwestern Sch. Law, Lewis and Clark Coll., 1974. Pres., dir. Cardiac Resuscitator, Portland, Oreg., 1974-80; chmn. bd. Catheter Tech. Corp., Salt Lake City, 1981—; chmn., chief exec. officer Synektron Corp., Portland, 1982—. Del. Oreg. Republican Nat. Conv., 1972, 76, 80, 84; chmn. Pres. Ford Com., 1976; bd. dirs. Bus. and Industry Polit. Action Com., 1983—; trustee Oreg. Rep. Presdl. Trust, Washington, 1984; Oregon fin. chmn. George Bush for Pres. Comm., 1987—; bd. mem. Am. Ctr. for Internat. Leadership. Served to capt. U.S. Army, 1967-69. Recipient Portland Jr. First Citizen award Portland Jaycees, 1971; named one of Ten Outstanding Young Men of Am., U.S. Jaycees, 1971. Office: Synektron Corp 12000 SW Garden Pl Portland OR 97223

BERKMAN, JACK MARTIN, public relations executive; b. San Francisco, Oct. 13, 1946; s. Sidney Allen and Bella (Dworkin) B. B.A., Calif. State U.-Northridge, 1969. Pub. relations staff Gen. Motors, Detroit, 1969-71; acctg. supr. Herbert H. Rozoff Pub. Relations Counsel, Chgo., 1971-73; nat. dir. pub. relations/dir. sales and mktg. Am. Housing Guild, San Diego, 1973-75; v.p., dir. mktg. Rancho La Costa Properties, San Diego, 1975-76; pres. Berkman & Daniels, San Diego, 1976—; pub. relations lectr. univs.; seminar leader; adv. bd. San Diego Bus. Jour. Bd. dirs. San Diego Repertory Theatre, San Diego Symphony Assn.; trustee Combined Arts and Edn. Council of San Diego County; active San Diegans, Inc. Named Most Outstanding Citizen, San Diego Jaycees, 1980; recipient cert. of merit Sr. Citizens Community Med. Clinic, Leukemia Soc. Am., Inc. Mem. Pub. Relations Soc. Am., San Diego Bldg. Contractors Assn., Anti-Defamation League of B'nai Brith, The Cancer Soc., Gas Lamp Quarter Dist. Assn., Sigma Delta Chi. Jewish. Clubs: San Diego Press (past pres.), Boys', Nice Guys. Office: 1717 Kettner Blvd Suite 100 San Diego CA 92101

BERKMAN, JEROME, food service executive, consultant; b. Bronx, N.Y., June 5, 1931; s. Charles and Fanny (Schor) B.; m. Cynthia Gail Lutsky; children—Mark B., David A. B.S. in Bus. Adminstrn., U. Denver, 1953; M.B.A., Pepperdine U., 1973. Registered dietician. Food prodn. mgr. Mountainside Hosp., Montclair, N.J., 1956-59; propr. Beefburger Express Restaurant, Denver, 1959-61; dietary dir. Meml. Hosp., Glendale, Calif., 1961-68; dir. food service Cedars-Sinai Med. Ctr., Los Angeles, 1968—; pres. J. Berkman and Assoc. Food Service Cons. Served with U.S. Army, 1953-56. Recipient Award for Excellence in Food Service, Modern Hosp. Mag., 1963, Ivy award Instns. Mag., 1975, Internat. Silver Plate award Food Mfrs. Assn., 1971, Gold Seal award Nat. Restaurant Assn., 1971. Mem. Am. Dietetic Assn., Silver and Gold Plate Soc, Am. Soc. Food Service Adminstrs., Hosp. Council Dietary Program, Ivy Soc. Contbr. articles to numerous profl. jours. Home: 2003 Manistee Dr La Canada CA 91011

BERKNER, KLAUS HANS, laboratory administrator, physicist; b. Dessau, Anhalt, German Democratic Republic, Mar. 2, 1938; came to U.S., 1948; s. Hans Otto and Sigrid Erika (Kuke) B. SB, MIT, 1960; PhD, U. Calif., Berkeley, 1964. NSF grad. fellowship U. Calif., Berkeley, 1960-61; NSF postdoctoral fellowship Culham, England, 1965-66; physicist Lawrence Berkeley Lab., Calif., 1964-79, sr. physicist, 1979—, deputy div. head, accelerator and fusion research, 1982-84, acting assoc. dir., div. head, 1984-85, assoc. dir., div. head, 1985—. Contbr. over 100 articles on atomic physics and fusion research to profl. jours. NATO research grantee, 1981-83. Fellow Am. Physical Soc.; mem. Am. Vacuum Soc., AAAS. Office: Lawrence Berkeley Lab 1 Cyclotron Rd Berkeley CA 94720

BERKUS, DAVID WILLIAM, computer company executive; b. Los Angeles, Mar. 23, 1941; s. Harry Jay and Clara S. (Widess) B.; m. Kathleen McGuire, Aug. 6, 1966; children: Eric, Matthew, Amy. BA, Occidental Coll., 1962. Pres. Custom Fidelity Inc., Hollywood, Calif., 1958-74, Berkus Compusystems Inc., Los Angeles, 1974-81; pres., chief exec. officer Computerized Lodging Systems Inc., Los Angeles, 1981—. Author: (software) Hotel Compusystem, 1979. Council commr. Boy Scouts Am., San Gabriel Valley, 1986, mem. exec. council. Served to lt. USNR, 1963-72. Recipient

Dist. award of merit Boy Scouts Am., 1986, INC. mag. 500 award, 1986. Mem. Am. Hotel-Motel Assn., Audio Engring. Soc. (chmn. Los Angeles sect. 1973-74). Democrat. Jewish. Avocations: piloting, backpacking. Office: Computerized Lodging Systems Inc 4800 Airport Plaza Dr #160 Long Beach CA 90815

BERLIN, DARYL, city manager; b. Torrance, Calif., Apr. 14, 1941; s. Louis and Zepha Mae (McClurg) B.; m. Anita Berlin, June 3, 1969; children—Dustin, Erin. B.A., Brigham Young U., 1971, M.P.A., 1973. Recreation intern City of Provo (Utah), 1970-71; adminstrv. intern City of Santa Rosa, Calif., 1972-73, adminstrv. asst., 1974-76, asst. city mgr., 1976-80; city mgr. City of Orem (Utah), 1980—. Served with USAF, 1960-64. Mem. Utah City Mgmt. Assn. (pres. 1981-83, dir. 1983—; Adminstr. of Yr. 1981). Office: City of Orem 56 N State St Orem UT 84057

BERLIN, DEBORAH LEE, social worker; b. Bklyn., Aug. 4, 1957. AA in Liberal Arts, San Diego Mesa Coll., 1978; BA in Psychology, Sociology, U. Calif., Berkeley, 1980; MSW, NYU, 1982. Cert. social worker, N.Y. Crisis intervention worker Berkeley Free Clinic, 1978-80; social worker Luth. community Services, Bronx, N.Y., 1980-81; hosp. social worker Huntington (N.Y.) Hosp., 1981-82; tchr. English Carreras, Argentina, 1982-83; sch. social worker N.Y.C. Bd. Edn., 1983-84; program coordinator La Familia Counseling Services, Hayward, Calif., 1984-85; co-dir. San Francisco Peer Resources, 1985-86; pvt. practice social work San Francisco, 1986—. Mem. Nat. Assn. Social Workers, NOW, Sierra Club. Jewish. Avocations: photography, hiking, traveling, langs., dance.

BERLIN, IRVING N., psychiatry, pediatrics educator; b. Chgo., May 31, 1917; m. Deane LaVerne Critchley, June 26, 1975; 3 children. BA, UCLA, 1939; MD, U. Calif., San Francisco, 1943; cert. child psychiatry, Langley Porter N.I., 1948-49, Langley Porter N.I., 1949-50. Mem. Am. Bd. Psychiatry and Neurology. Assoc. clin prof. psychiatry U. Calif. Sch. Medicine, 1960-65, Davis, 1975-78; prof., head div. child psychiatry U. Wash. Sch. Medicine, 1965-75; prof. psychiatry and pediatrics U. N.Mex. Sch. Medicine, Albuquerque, 1978—, dir. div. children and adolescent psychiatry, Children's Psychiat. Hosp., 1978—; cons. Indian Children's Program Indian Health Service, N.Mex., 1979—. Editor: Clinical Studies in Childhood Psychoses, 1973, Advocacy for Child Mental Health, 1975, Basic Text in Child Psychiatry, 1980, Bibliography of Child Psychiatry & Selected Films, 1976. Co-chmn. Task Force on Legis. to build Hosp. for Violent Mentally Ill Adolescents, 1981—. Served to capt. M.C., AUS, 1943-46. Fellow Am. Psychiat. Assn., Am. Orthopsychiat. Assn., AAAS, Am. Acad. Child Psychiatry (ed. bd. jour. 1961—, mem. exec. council 1963-66, pres. elect. 1973-75), Am. Coll. Psychiatrists, Am. Pub. Health Assn., Am. Assn. Social Psychiatry; mem. AMA, Am. Assn. Psychotherapy, Am. Assn. Adolescent Psychiatry, Calif. Med. Soc. Avocation: photography. Home: 4620 Hannett NE Albuquerque NM 87110 Office: U NMex Sch Medicine Dept Psychiatry 2400 Tucker NE Albuquerque NM 87131

BERLIN, MICHAEL IRA, TV, motion picture writer; b. Bklyn., July 21, 1947; s. Philip Berlin and Rita Sylvia (Leff) Labbate; m. Karen Ann Kass, Sept. 1, 1985. BA, CCNY, 1968; PhD, Yeshiva U., 1974. Sch. tchr. Pub. Sch. 164, Bklyn., 1968-70; coordinator in service Research and Devel. Ctr. Mental Retardation, N.Y.C., 1970-72; asst. prof. psychology and edn. Ramapo (N.J.) Coll., 1972-78; staff psychologist Kingbridge Heights Nursing Home and Manor, Bronx, N.Y., 1972-78; dean acac. affairs Coll. Devel. Studies, Los Angeles, 1980-83; freelance writer Los Angeles, 1980—; co-dir. Social Systems Design, Inc., N.Y.C., 1974-78; cons. Rikers Island Prison, N.Y.C., 1974-75, Trenton (N.J.) Bd. Edn., 1977-79, evaluation research ctr. U. Va., 1972-74, Municipality of Tel-Aviv, 1971. Writer: Anguish, 1986, Chips-MGM, 1982, Ultimate Adventure Company-Universal, 1986, (TV shows) Cagney and Lacey, 1986, 87, Miami Vice, 1986, Hunter, 1986, (movie) Mafia Vendetta, Taxman, 1987; co-producer: For Men by Men, 1976. Bd. dirs. Beverlwood Home Owners Assn., Los Angeles, 1984—, Ctr. for Advanced Profl. Edn., 1986. NDEA fellow Yeshiva U., 1970-71. Mem. Assn. Humanistic Psychologists, Media Educators Assocs., Am. Ednl. Research Assn., Writers Guild Am., Phi Delta Kappa. Democrat. Jewish. Avocations: scuba diving, baseball. Home: 2636 Castle Heights Pl Los Angeles CA 90034 Office: Coll Devel Studies 563 N Alfred St Los Angeles CA 90048

BERMAN, HORACE AARON, retired chemist; b. N.Y.C., Nov. 21, 1915; s. Nathan A. and Esther (Warshavsky) B.; m. Florence Levine, June 25, 1939; children: Edward, Eleanor, Carol. BS, Columbia U., 1935, postgrad. in Chem. Engring., 1936. Analytical chemist Union Chem. Corp., Newark, 1936-37, Herstein Labs. Inc., N.Y.C., 1937-40, Nat. Bur. of Standards, San Francisco, 1940-57; research chemist Nat. Bur. of Standards, Washington, 1957-68, Fed. Hwy. Adminstrn., Washington, 1968-76; free lance translator San Bruno, Calif., 1976—; mem. Transp. Research Bd. Com., Nat. Acad. Sci., NRC, 1965-76. Editor: Bulletin of San Francisco Council of Coop. Nursery Schs., 1954-56; co-editor: Calif. Council of Coop. Nursery Schs., 1956. V.p. Miraloma Coop. Nursery Schs., San Francisco, 1953-54. Mem. Am. Chem. Soc. (emeritus). Home and Office: 2741 Plymouth Way San Bruno CA 94066

BERMAN, HOWARD LAWRENCE, congressman; b. Los Angeles, Apr. 15, 1941; s. Joseph M. and Eleanor (Schapiro) B.; m. Janis Schwartz, 1979; children: Brinley Ann, Lindsey Rose. B.A., UCLA, 1962, LL.B., 1965. Bar: Calif. 1966. Vol. VISTA, Balt., San Francisco, 1966-67; assoc. Levy, Van Bourg & Hackler, Los Angeles, 1967-72; mem. Calif. State Assembly from 43d Dist., 1972-82 (majority leader); mem. 98th-100th Congresses from 26th Calif. Dist., freshman rep. steering & policy com., 1983, mem. judiciary com. adminstrv. law & govt. relations, courts, civil liberties & adminstrv. justice liberties, mem. fgn. affairs com. internat. edonomic policy & trade, arms control subcoms. Pres. Calif. Fedn. Young Democrats, 1967-69; mem. exec. bd. Ams. for Democratic Action, Anti-Defamation League B'nai B'rith. Office: Cannon House Office Bldg Room 137 Washington DC 20515

BERMAN, NEIL MARTIN, psychotherapist; b. Bklyn., Oct. 3, 1946; s. Saul and Marion (Dolnick) B.; m. Julie T. Catlin, Dec. 14, 1975. BS in Psychology, U. Md., 1969; MA in Clin. Social Work, U. Chgo., 1976. Vista vol. The Thresholds, Chgo., 1969-71; adminstr. Jewish Children's Bur., Chgo., 1971-74; program dir. Scholarship and Guidance Assn., Chgo., 1976-80; dir. N.Mex. State Employee Assistance Program, Santa Fe, 1980—; psychotherapist, Santa Fe, 1980—; pres. Employee Assistance Program of Santa Fe., 1982—. Julius and Theresa Levy scholar, Jewish Fedn. of Chgo., 1974-76; recipient Exemplary Performance award State of N.Mex. Health and Environment dept., 1982. Fellow Acad. Cert. Social Workers div. Nat. Assn. Social Workers; mem. Assn. Labor and Mgmt. Adminstrs. and Cons. on Alcoholism, Occupational Program Cons. Assn. (nat. v.p. 1984—), Nat. Assn. Social Workers. Democrat. Jewish. Avocations: music, amateur radio. Home: 2232 Calle Alvarado Santa Fe NM 87505 Office: NMex State Employee Assistance Program PO Box 968 Santa Fe NM 87504-0968

BERMAN, SONIA, theatre educator; b. Yedenitz, Romania; came to U.S., 1945; d. Haskell and Miriam (Korman) B. BA, Queens Coll.; MPhil, Columbia U., 1976, PhD, 1980. Prof. Calif. State U, Sacramento. Producer: Bugs/Veronica, Off-Broadway Theater Season, 1965-66. Mem. NEA, Calif. Faculty Assn., Phi Beta Kappa. Democrat. Avocations: writing plays and poetry. home: 230 Central Park W #10A New York NY 10024 Office: Calif State U 6000 J St Sacramento CA 95814

BERMINGHAM, DANIEL FRANCIS, oil company executive; b. Butte, Mont., July 19, 1954; s. William Charles and Helen Louise (Gerry) B.; m. Wendy Patricia Kalafatich, Nov. 26, 1983; 1 child, Kalli Lynn. B.S., U. Mont., 1977. Title examiner, mgr. Mont. Corp., Billings, 1977-80; landman, cons., Denver, 1980-82; land mgr. Mont. Power Co., Butte, 1982-84, Entech Inc., Butte, 1984—. Mem. Am. Assn. Petroleum Landmen, Mont. Assn. Petroleum Landmen, Jaycees (v.p. 1980). Club: Exchange, Big Sky Investment (v.p. 1986, pres. 1987). Office: EnTech 16 E Granite Butte MT 59701

BERMINGHAM, RICHARD P., restaurant and food products company executive; b. Glen Ridge, N.J., 1939. Student, U. Colo. With Arthur Andersen & Co., 1962-67; v.p., sec. fin. Collins Foods Internat., Los Angeles, 1967-73, v.p., sec., gen. mgr. Collins Food Service div., 1973-81, pres., chief operating officer, 1981—; also dir. Collins Foods Internat.; pres. Naugles, Inc., Fullerton, Calif. Office: Collins Foods Internat 5400 Alla Rd Los Angeles CA 90066 Office: Naugles Inc 2932 E Nutwood Ave Fullerton CA 92634 *

BERNACCHI, RICHARD LLOYD, lawyer; b. Los Angeles, Dec. 15, 1938; s. Bernard and Anne (Belluomini) B. B.S. with honors in Commerce (Nat. Merit Found. scholar), U. Santa Clara, 1961; LL.B. with highest honors (Legion Lex scholar, Jerry Geisler Meml. scholar), U. So. Calif., 1964. Bar: Calif. 1964. Since practiced in Los Angeles; partner firm Irell and Manella, 1964—; lectr. Am. Law Inst., 1972-73; lectr. data processing contracts and law U. So. Calif., Los Angeles, 1972, 78, 81; co-chmn. Regional Transp. Com., 1970-72; mem. adv. bd. U. So. Calif. Computer Law Inst., 1979—, Ariz. Law and Tech. Inst., 1982-86; U. Santa Clara Computer and High Tech. Law Jour., 1982—. Author: (with Gerald H. Larsen) Data Processing Contracts and the Law, 1974; (with Frank and Statland) Bernacchi on Computer Law, 1986; editor-in-chief: U. So. Calif. Law Rev, 1962-64; mem. adv. bd. Computer Negotiators Report, 1983—, Computer and Tech. Law Jour., 1984—, Computer Law Strategist, 1984—. Served to capt. AUS, 1964-66, PTO. Mem. Am. Bar Assn. (mem. adv. com. on edn. 1973-74, chmn. subcom. taxation computer systems of sect. sci. and tech. 1976-78), Los Angeles Bar Assn., Computer Law Assn. (bd. dirs. 1973-86, chmn. preconf. symposium on law and computers 1974-75, West Coast v.p. 1976-79, sr. v.p. 1979-81, pres. 1981-83, adv. bd. 1986—), Am. Fedn. Info. Processing Socs. (mem. spl. com. electronic funds transfer systems 1974-78), Order of Coif, Scabbard and Blade, Beta Gamma Sigma, Alpha Sigma Nu. Office: 1800 Ave of Stars Los Angeles CA 90067

BERNAL, ERNESTO MARROQUIN, educational administrator; b. San Antonio, July 9, 1938; s. Ernest M. and Herlinda G. (Marroquin) B.; BA, St. Mary's U., San Antonio, 1960; MEd, Our Lady of Lake U., San Antonio, 1964; PhD, U. Tex., Austin, 1971; m. Carmen Tafolla, June 29, 1979; children: Ann Elizabeth, Sean Michael, Cielos (dec.), Marilinda. Tchr., then asst. prin. Keystone Sch., San Antonio, 1960-66; instr., then asst. prof. edn. St. Mary's U., 1966-71; dir. bilingual early elem. program S.W. Ednl. Devel. Lab., Austin, Tex., 1971-74; assoc. prof. bicultural bilingual studies U. Tex., San Antonio, 1974-78; profl. assoc. Ednl. Testing Service, 1978-79; pres. Creative Ednl. Enterprises, Inc., Austin, 1980-83; coordinator Zone 2 Bilingual Multifunctional Support Ctr., Calif. State U., Fresno, 1983-84; prof. tchr. edn. Calif. State U., San Bernardino, 1984-86; prof., dir. research Ctr. for Excellence in Edn., No. Ariz. U., Flagstaff, 1986—; nat. adv. council Gifted Students Inst. Research and Devel., Nat. Clearinghouse Bilingual Edn., 1980; recipient citation merit Nat./State Leadership Tng. Inst. Gifted and Talented, 1974. Mem. Am. Ednl. Research Assn., Am. Psychol. Assn., Council Exceptional Children, Evaluation Research Soc., Nat. Soc. Study Edn., Nat. Assn. Bilingual Edn. Democrat. Author articles, reports in field.

BERNARD, DEBBIE LYNN, marketing professional; b. Hartford, Conn., June 6, 1957; d. Richard J. and Madelyn M. (Garibaldi) B.; m. Stanley R. Ploof, Apr. 21, 1984. BA in Psychology, U. Conn., 1979. Dir. communications Lakeridge, Inc., Torrington, Conn., 1979-80, mgr. advt. and mktg., 1980; mktg. asst. Kaufman & Broad, Dublin, Calif., 1980-81, coordinator mktg., 1981-83, v.p. mktg., 1983—. Mem. Bldg. and Industry Assn. (Sales award 1982-86), Sales and Mktg. Council. Roman Catholic. Avocations: skiing, hiking, sailing, aerobics. Office: Kaufman & Broad No Calif 6379 Clark Ave Dublin CA 94568

BERNARD, DOUGLAS ALAN, physicist; b. Barrie, Ont., Can., Feb. 1, 1953; came to U.S., 1983; BSc, U. Saskatchewan, Saskatoon, Can., 1975; PhD, Princeton U., 1980. Mem. research staff Xerox Corp., Mississauga, Ont., 1980-83; sr. mem. tech. staff Signetics Corp.-Philips Research, Sunnyvale, Calif., 1983—. Contbr. articles to profl. jours. Mem. Am. Phys. Soc. Home: 5714 McKellar Dr San Jose CA 95129 Office: Signetics Corp 811 E Arques Ave M/S 65 Sunnyvale CA 94088-3409

BERNARD, GEORGE W., anatomy and oral biology educator; b. N.Y.C., Aug. 22, 1925; s. Meyer Welitskin and Helen (Grenadier) Luskin; m. Maxine Shear, Nov. 5, 1947 (div. Feb. 1971); children: Claudia, Nancy; m. Ellie Bragg Schiff, Aug. 24, 1986. AA, U. Fla., 1944; DDS, Wash. U., St. Louis, 1947; BA with honors, UCLA, 1963, PhD, 1967. From assoc. prof. to full prof. anatomy UCLA, 1967—; mem. Dental Research Inst. UCLA, 1974, Cancer Ctr. UCLA, 1977; grad. advisor UCLA Sch. of Dentistry, 1985—; mem. oral biology and med. study sect. NIH, Bethesda, Md., 1978-81; cons. VA Hosp., Long Beach, Calif., 1980—. Contbr. articles to profl. jours., chpts. to books. Served to capt. U.S. Army, 1952-53. NIH fellow, 1964-67. Fellow AAAS; mem. Am. Assn. Anatomists, Electron Microscopy Soc. Am., Am. Assn. Dental Research, Internat. Assn. Dental Research. Avocations: running, skiing. Office: UCLA Dept Anatomy Sch Medicine Los Angeles CA 90024

BERNARD, J. THOMAS, real estate developer; b. Denver, June 26, 1943; s. C.A. and G.I. Bernard; Engr. Mines, Colo. Sch. Mines, 1966; M.B.A., Boston U., 1970; m. Jacqueline J. Ranthum, Feb. 1, 1969; 1 son, James Abbot. With Bechtel Corp., 1966-67; with Cabot, Cabot & Forbes Co., 1970—, v.p., N.W. gen. mgr., Seattle, 1974—. Mem. Republican Exec. Forum, 1978—; bd. dirs. Bellevue Community Coll. Found., 1981-86. Served as officer U.S. Army, 1967-69. Mem. Nat. Assn. Office and Indsl. Parks (pres. Seattle chpt. 1980, bd. dirs. 1982—, chmn. 1983), Bellevue Downtown Assn. (v.p. 1980-81, bd. dirs. 1980—), Bellevue C. of C. (bd. dirs. 1980—), Seattle C. of C. (com. chmn. 1979-80), Soc. Indsl. Realtors (assoc.), South Snohomish C. of C., Lambda Alpha. Clubs: Bellevue Rotary; Seattle Tennis; Bellevue Athletic; Columbia Tower. Home: 1421 Shenandoah Dr E Seattle WA 98112 Office: 3305 160th Ave SE Bellevue WA 98008

BERNARD, JAMES WILLIAM, diversified corporation executive; b. Brainerd, Minn., 1939. BS, U. Oreg., 1960. With Univar Corp., Seattle, 1961—, corp. v.p., 1975-82, sr. v.p., 1982-84, exec. v.p., 1984-86, pres., chief ops. officer, 1986—, also bd. dirs. Mem. Am. Chem. Soc. Office: Univar Corp 1600 Norton Bldg Seattle WA 98104 *

BERNARD, JOHN DAVID, physician, educator; b. Sioux City, Jan. 11, 1932; s. John Baptist and Mabel Elizabeth (Kimmel) B.; m. Anna Franciska Greis, Nov. 22, 1956; children—David, Anne, Mark. B.S., U. S.D., 1954; M.D., U. Calif.-San Francisco, 1957. Diplomate Am. Bd. Internal Medicine, Am. Bd. Nuclear Medicine, Am. Bd. Endocrinology and Metabolism. Resident in internal medicine San Joaquin Gen. Hosp., Stockton, Calif., 1961-64, dir. med. edn., 1965-73; dir. med. edn. St. Joseph's Hosp., Stockton, 1973—; med. staff San Joaquin Hosp., 1965—, St. Joseph's Hosp., 1965—, Dameron Hosp., Stockton, 1965—. Contbr. articles to profl. jours. Served to capt. U.S. Army, 1958-61. Fellow ACP; mem. Endocrine Soc., Soc. Nuclear Medicine, Am. Fedn. Clin. Research, Calif. Med. Assn., Am. Thyroid Assn. Republican. Roman Catholic. Office: 1617 N California St Stockton CA 95204

BERNARD, THELMA RENE, construction company administrator; b. Phila.; d. Michael John and Louise Thelma (Hoffman) Campione; m. Gene Bernard. Grad. high sch. Sec. Penn. Mut. Life Ins. Co., Phila., Suffolk Franklin Savs. Bank, Boston, Holmes and Narver, Inc., Las Vegas; constrn. site office mgr. Miles R. Nay, Inc., Las Vegas; adminstrv. asst to pres. N.W.S. Constrn. Corp., Inc., Las Vegas, 1982-86, corp. sec., 1982-86; gen. mgr., corp. sec. D.A.P., Inc. Author: Blue Marsh, 1972, Winds of Wakefield, 1972, Moonshadow Mansion, 1973, 2d edit., 1976, Spanish transl., 1974, German transl., 1977; contbr. articles to Nat. Doll World, other mags.; also song lyrics; past editor: Cactus Courier; editor/pub. The Hoyer Enthusiastic Ladies Mail Assn. Mem. Nat. League Am. Pen Women (v.p. Red Rock Canyon br. 1986—), Internat. Platform Assn., Nat. Assn. Women in Constrn. (corr. sec. Las Vegas chpt., rec. sec.), Randolph Soc. Quakertown, Antique Valentine Assn., Original Paper Doll Artists Guild, Nat. Orgn. Miniaturists and Dollers, United Fedn. Doll Clubs. Office: PO Box 14002 Las Vegas NV 89114

BERNARDI, MARIO, conductor; b. Kirland Lake, Ont., Can., Aug. 20, 1930; s. Leone and Rina (Onisto) B.; m. Mona Kelly, May 12, 1962; 1 d., Julia. Ed., Coll. Piox, Treviso, Italy, Benedetto Marcello Conservatory, Venice, Italy, Mozarteum, Salzburg, Austria, Royal Conservatory, Toronto. Began career as pianist Italy; music dir. Sadler's Wells Opera Co., 1966-69; music dir., condr. Nat. Arts Centre, Ottawa, Ont., 1969-80; music dir. Calgary Philharm. Orch., 1984—; prin. condr. CBC Vancouver Orch., 1982—; guest condr. with San Francisco Opera Assn., Vancouver Opera, Canadian Broadcasting Co., Canadian Opera Co. Decorated companion Order of Can. Club: Savage. Address: Calgary Philharm Orch, Jack Singer Hall, 205 8th Ave SE, Calgary, AB Canada T2G 0K9 *

BERNASCONI, CLAUDE FRANÇOIS, chemistry educator; b. Zürich, Switzerland, Feb. 17, 1939; came to U.S., 1967; s. Oscar Antonio and Jeanne Marie (Borel) B.; m. Regula Luchsinger, Sept. 15, 1962 (div. Mar. 1979); children: Andrea K., Marc P.; m. Anastassia Kanavarioti, Sept. 10, 1983. MS, Swiss Fed. Inst. Tech., Zürich, 1963, PhD, 1965. Postdoctoral fellow Max Planck Inst. for Phys. Chemistry, Göttingen, Fed. Republic Germany, 1966-67; asst. prof. chemistry U. Calif., Santa Cruz, 1967-72, assoc. prof., 1972-77, prof., 1977—. Author: Relaxation Kinetics, 1976; editor: Investigation of Rates and Mechanisms of Reactions, 1986; contbr. articles to profl. jours. Grantee NSF, 1969—; Alfred P. Sloan fellow, 1971-73. Mem. AAAS, Am. Chem. Soc. (grantee 1970—). Home: 101 Hillcrest Terr Santa Cruz CA 95060 Office: U Calif Dept Chemistry Santa Cruz CA 95064

BERNFIELD, MERTON RONALD, pediatrician, educator; b. Chgo., Apr. 9, 1938; s. Harry B. and Adeline A. (Fischer) B.; m. Audrey A. Rivkin, Aug. 30, 1959; children: Susan, James, Mark. B.S., U. Ill., 1959; M.S.; M.D., U. Ill., Chgo., 1961. Intern U. Ill. Research Hosps., Chgo., 1961-62; asst. resident in pediatrics N.Y. Hosp.-Cornell U. Med. Center, N.Y.C., 1962-63; research assoc. NIH, Bethesda, Md., 1963-65; research investigator Nat. Inst. Child Health and Human Devel., U. Calif., San Diego, 1965-66; chief resident in pediatrics Stanford U. Med. Center, 1967; asst. prof. pediatrics Stanford U., 1967-70, assoc. prof., 1970-75, prof., 1975—, Josephine Knotts Knowles prof. human biology, 1977—, dir. med. scientist tng. program, 1974-77, chmn. program in human biology, 1977-80, dir. fellowship program in membrane pathobiology, 1975-85, dir. fellowship program in neonatal biology, 1982—; mem. research com. Cystic Fibrosis Found., 1972-76; mem. developmental biology panel NSF, 1976-77; mem. physiol. chemistry research com. Am. Heart Assn., 1979-83; mem. craniofacial anomalies evaluation panel Nat. Inst. Dental Research, 1980-81; mem. health adv. com. Calif. Medfly Eradication Project, 1981-82; mem. sci. adv. bd. Collagen Corp., 1981—; chmn. Neonatal Biology Group, 1984—; chmn. Gordon Research Conf. on Basement Membranes, 1986; cons. in field. Contbr. articles to profl. jours.; mem. editorial bd.: Archives Biochemistry and Biophysics, 1974-79, Cell Differentiation, 1980—, Jour. Craniofacial Genetics and Devel. Biology, 1980-83; assoc. editor Developmental Biology, 1981—. Served with USPHS, 1963-66. Guggenheim fellow, 1972-73; Josiah Macy scholar, 1980-81. Mem. Am. Pediatrics Soc., Am. Acad. Pediatrics, Am. Soc. Biol. Chemists, Am. Soc. Cell Biology (chmn. pub. policy com.), Perinatal Research Soc., Soc. Devel. Biology, Soc. Pediatric Research, Teratology Soc., Western Soc. Pediatric Research (Ross award 1973). Home: 1661 Hamilton Ave Palo Alto CA 94303 Office: Dept Pediatrics Stanford Med Center Stanford CA 94305

BERNHARD, HERBERT ASHLEY, lawyer; b. Jersey City, Sept. 24, 1927; s. Richard C. and Amalie (Lobl) B.; m. Nancy Ellen Hirschaut, Aug. 8. 1954; children: Linda, Alison, Jordan, Melissa. Student, Mexico City Coll., 1948; BEE, N.J. Inst. Tech., 1949; MA in Math., Columbia U., 1950; JD cum laude, U. Mich., 1957. Bar: Calif. 1958, U.S. Dist. Ct. (cen. dist.) Calif. 1958, U.S. Dist. Ct. (no., ea. and so. dists.) Calif., U.S. Dist. Ct. (ea. dist.) Wis., U.S. Dist. Ct. (ea. and we. dists.) Ark., U.S. Dist. Ct. Nebr., U.S. Ct. Claims, U.S. Ct. Internat. Trade, U.S. Tax Ct., U.S. Ct. Appeals (2d, 3d, 4th, 5th, 7th, 8th, 9th, 10th, 11th and D.C. cirs.), U.S. Supreme Ct. 1965. Research engr. Curtis-Wright Co., Caldwell, N.J., 1950-52, Boeing Aircraft Co., Cape Canaveral, Fla., 1952-55; assoc. O'Melveny & Myers, Los Angeles, 1957-62; ptnr. Greenberg, Bernhard, et al, Los Angeles, 1962-85, Jeffer, Mangels & Butler, Los Angeles, 1985—; instr. math. U. Fla., Cape Canaveral, 1952-55, elec. engring. U. Mich., Ann Arbor, 1955-57. Contbr. articles to profl. jours. Chmn. adv. com. Skirball Mus.; bd. overseers Hebrew Union Coll.; bd. govs. Am. Jewish Congress, 1986—. Served with USAF, 1946-47. Mem. Jewish Publ. Soc. (trustee 1986—). Club: Mulholland Tennis (Los Angeles). Home: 1105 Tower Rd Beverly Hills CA 90210 Office: Jeffer Mangels & Butler 1900 Ave of Stars 4th Floor Los Angeles CA 90067

BERNHARDT, LINDA LEA, talent management company executive; b. Norfolk, Va., Oct. 29, 1940; d. Robert Allen and Mary Elizabeth (Newsome) Laughbon; m. Robert Budd Bernhardt, Oct. 19, 1967; children: Robert Dirk, Eric Scott, Erika Elizabeth. Student, U. Madrid, 1958-59; BA, U. Md., 1962. Adminstrv. asst. Spanish Embassy, Washington, 1961-63; owner Jolido Agy. Ltd., Anchorage, 1982—. Bd. dirs. Miss Alaska Scholarship Pageant, Anchorage, 1979—; Mrs. Alaska, 1980; advisor Mrs. Alaska Pageant, Anchorage, 1981—. Served to lt. USN, 1963-69. Fellow Anchorage Conv. and Vis. Bur.; mem. Advt. Fedn. (2d v.p. 1983-86), Fashion Adv. Bd. Sch. Dist., Navy League Council (pres. 1980-81). Republican. Avocations: down-hill skiing, fashion tng., cosmetic make-overs, reading. Office: Jolido Agy Ltd 600 W 41st #101 Anchorage AK 99503

BERNHEIMER, MARTIN, music critic; b. Munich, Germany, Sept. 28, 1936; came to U.S., 1940, naturalized, 1946; s. Paul Ernst and Louise (Nassauer) B.; m. Lucinda Pearson, Sept. 30, 1961; children: Mark Richard, Nora Nicoll, Marina and Erika (twins). Mus.B. with honors, Brown U., 1958; student, Munich Conservatory, 1958-59; M.A. in Musicology, N.Y. U., 1962. Free-lance music critic 1958—; mem. music faculty N.Y. U., 1960-62; N.Y. corr. for Brit. publ. Opera 1962-65, Los Angeles corr., 1965—; contbg. critic N.Y. Herald-Tribune, 1959-62; asst. music editor Saturday Rev., 1962-65; mng. editor Philharmonic Hall Program, N.Y.C., 1962-65; music editor, chief critic Los Angeles Times, 1965—; faculty Rockefeller program for tng. music critics at U. So. Calif., 1966-71; mem. music faculty UCLA, 1969-75, Calif. Inst. for the Arts, 1975-82, Calif. State U., Northridge, 1978-81. Contbr. articles newspapers, mags. in field, also liner notes for recordings, radio and TV appearances. Recipient Deems Taylor award ASCAP, 1974, 78, Pulitzer prize for disting. criticism, 1982. Office: Los Angeles Times Times-Mirror Square Los Angeles CA 90053

BERNHEISEL, DONALD PAUL, retail company executive; b. Williamsport, Pa., April 1, 1945; s. Newton Clarance and Lillian Merril (Porte) B.; m. Donna Kay Parrish, Aug. 26, 1967; 1 child, Dana. B.E.E., N.C. State U., 1967; M.B.A., U. Ariz., 1969. Sr. mktg. rep. IBM Corp., Los Angeles, 1969—, Tech., Inc., Tarzana, Calif., 1982—; cons. Lockland Realty, Framingham, Mass., 1980—; v.p., dir. mgmt. info. services, Thrifty Corp., Los Angeles; dir. Nova Technology, Inc., Tarzana, NTI, Inc., Dayton, Ohio, Ergometrics Tech., Inc., 1985—. Office: Thrifty Corp 3424 Wilshire Blvd Los Angeles CA 90010

BERNOTSKI, STEPHEN WALTER, JR., social work administrator; b. Reno, Dec. 16, 1938; s. Stephen Walter and Blanche Rose (Hall) B.; m. Karen Anderson, Dec. 12, 1968; children: Lisa, Erik, Jared. Student, U. Utah, MSW, 1978; BA, Brigham Young U., 1971, postgrad., 1971-73. RN, Utah; cert. social worker, Idaho. Nurse Ch. Jesus Christ Latter Day Saints Hosp., Salt Lake City, 1972-74, assoc. clin. coordinator, 1974-76; house supr. Eastern Idaho Med. Ctr., Idaho Falls, 1978-81, dir. social services, 1982—, acting dir. behavioral unit, 1985—; social worker pub. schs., Idaho Falls, 1978-81; cons. Western Vis. Nurses Assn., Idaho Falls, 1984—. Active Idaho Falls Mental Health Bd., 1984—, Bonneville County (Idaho) Interagy. Council, 1984—, Parkinson's Support Group, Idaho Falls, 1985—, Easy Breathers,Idaho Falls, 1985—, Mended Hearts, Idaho Falls, 1985—. Served with U.S. Army, 1961-63. Grantee NIMH; recipient Exemplary Merit medal Idaho Falls Consol. Hosp., 1981. Mem. Nat. Assn. Social Workers (cert.), Acad. Cert. Social Workers. Mormon. Home: Rt 1 Box 350A Rexburg ID 83440 Office: Eastern Idaho Regional Med Ctr Box 2007 Idaho Falls ID 83403

BERNSTEIN, DIANE, psychotherapist; b. Jacksonville, Fla., Aug. 30, 1957; d. Arthur Harold and Barbara (Ettinger) B. BS in Human Devel., U. Calif., Davis, 1980; MSW, U. So. Calif., 1982. Lic. clin. social worker. Chmn. social work dept. Beverly Palms Rehab. Hosp., Los Angeles, 1982-83; asst. program dir., sr. case mgr. A Touch of Care, West Los Angeles, Calif.,

1983-85; asst. dir. of residential program San Fernando Valley Child Guidance Clinic, Northridge, Calif., 1985—. Vol. NOW, Los Angeles, 1980—. Mem. Nat. Assn. Social Workers, Omicron Nu. Democrat. Jewish. Avocations: tennis, paddle tennis, reading, traveling, sailing. Home: 8109 Raintree Circle Culver City CA 90230 Office: San Fernando Child Guidance Clinic 9650 Zelzah Ave Northridge CA 91325

BERNSTEIN, ELMER, composer, conductor; b. N.Y.C., Apr. 4, 1922; s. Edward and Selma (Feinstein) B.; m. Pearl Glusman, Dec. 21, 1946; children: Peter Matthew, Gregory Eames; m. Eve Adamson, Oct. 25, 1965; children: Emily Adamson, Elizabeth Campbell. Student, NYU. Pres. Young Musicians Found., 1961—. Concert pianist, N.Y.C., Phila., Chgo., 1946-50; composer music for UN radio shows, 1949; composer mus. scores, 1950—, including: Man with the Golden Arm, The Ten Commandments, The Magnificent Seven, Summer and Smoke, Walk on the Wild Side, To Kill a Mockingbird (Golden Globe award Hollywood Fgn. Press 1962), The Great Escape, The Birdman of Alcatraz, Hud, Sudden Fear, God's Little Acre, Sweet Smell of Success, Desire Under the Elm, Some Came Running, From the Terrace, Love With the Proper Stranger, Baby the Rain Must Fall, The Caretakers, The Sons of Katie Elder, Cast a Giant Shadow, Hawaii, Seven Women, True Grit, Thoroughly Modern Millie, The Shootist, National Lampoon's Animal House, Bloodbrothers, Meatballs, Airplane!, Airplane II, Stripes, Heavy Metal, An American Werewolf in London, Honky Tonk Freeway, The Chosen, Genocide, Five Days One Summer, Class, Trading Places, Ghostbusters, The Black Cauldron, Spies Like Us, Legal Eagles; scores for TV include: Serpico, Little Women, The Rookies, Guyana Tragedy: The Story of Jim Jones. Recipient Motion Picture Exhibitor Laurel awards 1956, 57, 62, Emmy award for best music written for TV, Making of a President 1964, Acad. award for best original music score for Thoroughly Modern Millie 1968. Mem. Acad. Motion Picture Arts and Scis. (1st v.p. 1963—), The Thalians (v.p. 1959-62), Screen Composers Assn. (dir.), Composers and Lyricists Guild Am. (pres. 1970—), Nat. Acad. Rec. Arts and Scis. (dir.). Office: care Acad Motion Picture Arts and Scis 8949 Wilshire Blvd Beverly Hills CA 90211 *

BERNSTEIN, GERALD WILLIAM, management consultant, researcher; b. Boston, Nov. 25, 1947; s. Alan Irwin and Anne (Fine) B.; m. Kathleen Ann Chaikin, Jan. 12, 1985. BS in Aero. Engring., Rensselaer Poly. Inst., 1969; MS in Engring., Stanford U., 1978. Transp. engr., dept. transp. State of N.Y., Albany, 1969-70; transp. planner Kennebec Regional Planning Com., Winslow, Me., 1974-77; sr. aviation cons. SRI Internat., Menlo Park, Calif., 1979—; session chmn. aviation workshop NSF, 1985; profl. conf. chmn. Contbr. articles to profl. jours. Chmn. Transp. com. Glenn Park Neighborhood Assn., San Francisco, 1982-85; mem. Balboa Terrace Neighborhood Assn., San Francisco, 1986. Served with U.S. Army, 1970-72. Recipient Cert. Appreciation City of Waterville, Maine, 1977. Mem. Transp. Research Bd. of Nat. Research Council. Democrat. Jewish. Club: Toastmasters (Menlo Park) (pres. 1986—). Avocations: flying, skiing. Office: SRI Internat Menlo Park CA 94025

BERNSTEIN, LAWRENCE ALLEN, architect, industrial designer; York, Pa., Aug. 28, 1932; s. Phillip Gordon and Evelyn (Spielman) B.; m. Susan Hacket, Oct. 8, 1959; m. Johanna Navarro, Feb. 10, 1979; 1 child, Brenda Lena. Student indsl. engring. and architecture MIT, 1951-58. Registered architect, Calif., Va., D.C. Tallesin fellow with Frank Lloyd Wright, 1958; prin. L.A. Bernstein & Assos., Carmel, Calif., 1959-67; pres. Concepts LAB., Inc., N.Y.C., 1968; chief architect, dir. design center new town Linganore, Md., Frederick, Md., 1971-73; pres. bd. chmn., dir. architect and design, prin. The Advanced Design Ctr., San Antonio and Los Angeles, 1973-76, L.A. Bernstein, AIA, 1973-76; dir. design, Diker-Moe Assocs., Los Angeles, 1976-77; prin. Bernstein Assos., Los Angeles, 1977-80; pres., chmn. bd. L.A. Bernstein Assocs., Inc., 1981—; dir. new product devel. Dart Advanced Design Ctr., N.Y.C. and Los Angeles, 1967-71. Contbr. numerous articles to various publs. Recipient awards including 1st award for engring. excellence Cons. Engrs. Council/USA for Lake Linganore Dam and Dams on Twin Lakes Anita, 1972; spl. recognition award Nat. Assn. Home Builders, 1973; 1st award for excellence Environ. Monthly Mag., 1974; 1st Honor award Monterey Bay chpt. AIA for Mira Obs., 1983. Mem. AIA, Soc. Plastics Engrs. Jewish. Lodge: Rotary. Home and Office: 6456 Surfside Way Malibu CA 90265

BERNSTEIN, MORTON IRA, computer research company executive; b. Wilkinsburg, Pa., July 2, 1927; s. Julius Lawrence and Elizabeth Hinda (Schwartz) B.; m. Margaret Maurine Berkstresser, Sept. 1, 1951; children: Robert Scott, Richard Lee. BS, U. Pitts., 1950, MA, 1952. Mathematician Atlantic Research Corp., Alexandria, Va., 1953-54; mathematician, programmer Rand Corp., Santa Monica, Calif., 1954-63; adv. programmer IBM, Los Angeles, 1963-65; mgr. System Devel. Corp., Santa Monica, Calif., 1965-84; pres. Quest Analysis Inc., Los Angeles, 1984—. Co-author: Data Processing: 1980-1985, 1976. Served with USN, 1945-46. Avocations: photography, woodworking. Office: Quest Analysis Inc 11965 Venice Blvd Suite 305 Los Angeles CA 90066

BERNSTEIN, NORRIS STANLEY, management consultant; b. Los Angeles, Nov. 14, 1929; s. Maurice Edward and Sophie Lillian (Borson) B.; m. Irvene Alva Clayton, Sept. 15, 1951; children: Perri Lynn, Robert Clayton. Ptnr. Bernstein Foods Corp., Seal Beach, Calif., 1951-62, pres., 1962-74; head subs. Nalley Foods div. Curtice-Burns, Inc., 1974-76, also head product mktg.; exec. v.p. Funky Foods, Inc., Buena Park, Calif., 1976-77; pres. NSB Corp.; mgmt. cons. Norris Bernstein, Creative Mktg., 1978-86; sr. ptnr. Edgar, Dunn & Co., Inc., Los Angeles, 1986—; ptnr. Mrs. Baker's Calif. Cookies, Munich; mem. adv. bd. Nat. Bank So. Calif.; bd. dirs. Long Beach (Calif.) Family Service. Mem. Assn. Dressings and Sauces (chmn. bd. 1973-75), Pres.'s Roundtable, Internat. Mgmt. Cons. (chpt. dir.), U. Puget Sound Pres. Adv. Com. (chmn. 1978-80), SAG, AFTRA. Lodges: Rotary, Masons. Home: 9309 Marina Pacific Dr N Long Beach CA 90803 Office: Edgar Dunn Co 707 Wilshire Blvd Suite 5555 Los Angeles CA 90017

BERNSTEIN, SOL, physician, med. services adminstr.; b. West New York, N.J., Feb. 3, 1927; s. Morris Irving and Rose (Leibowitz) B.; m. Suzi Maris Sommer, Sept. 15, 1963; 1 son, Paul. A.B. in Bacteriology, U. Southern Calif., 1952, M.D., 1956. Diplomate: Am. Bd. Internal Medicine. Intern Los Angeles County Hosp., 1956-57, resident, 1957-60; practice medicine specializing in cardiology Los Angeles, 1960—; staff physician dept. medicine Los Angeles County Hosp. U. So. Calif. Med. Center, Los Angeles, 1960—; chief cardiology clinics Los Angeles County Hosp. U. So. Calif. Med. Center, 1964, asst. dir. dept. medicine, 1965-72; chief profl. services Gen. Hosp., 1972-74; med. dir. Los Angeles County-U So. Calif. Med. Center, 1974—; med. dir. central region Los Angeles County, 1974-78; dir. Dept. Health Services, Los Angeles County, 1978; assoc. dean Sch. Medicine U. So. Calif., Los Angeles, 1986—; asso. prof. medicine U. Southern Calif. Sch. Medicine, Los Angeles, 1968—; cons. crippled Childrens Ser. Calif., 1965—. Contbr. articles on cardiac surgery, cardiology, diabetes and health care planning to med. jours. Served with AUS, 1946-47, 52-53. Fellow A.C.P., Am. Coll. Cardiology; mem. Am. Fedn. Clin. Research, N.Y. Acad. Sci., Los Angeles, Am. heart assns., Los Angeles Soc. Internal Medicine, Los Angeles Acad. Medicine, Sigma Xi, Phi Beta Phi, Phi Eta Sigma, Alpha Omega Alpha. Home: 4966 Ambrose Ave Los Angeles CA 90027 Office: 1200 State St N Los Angeles CA 90033

BERNTSON, KEVIN ANTON, educational administrator; b. St. Paul, May 18, 1951; s. Wilfred C. and Catherine (Sullivan) B. BA, St. Mary's Coll. of Calif., 1973; MA, U. San Francisco, 1979; MS, Mt. St. Mary's Coll., 1986. Tchr., Sacred Heart High Sch., San Francisco, 1973-76; dean of students Cretin High Sch., St. Paul, 1976-77; guidance counselor Christian Brothers High Sch., Sacramento, 1977-79; asst. prin. Providence High Sch., Burbank, Calif., 1979-82; asst. dir. devel. Mt. St. Mary's Coll., Los Angeles, 1982-83; dean discipline Mater Dei High Sch., Santa Ana, Calif., 1982-85; asst. prin. St. Anthony High Sch., Long Beach, 1985—. Mem. Assn. Supervision and Curriculum Devel., Calif. Personnel and Guidance Assn., Los Angeles Personnel and Guidance Assn., Am.-Scandinavian Found., Nat. Council Tchrs. English, Calif. Assn. Marriage and Family Therapists. Home: 405 E 3rd St #358 Long Beach CA 90802 Office: St Anthony High Sch Fine Arts Dept 670 Olive Ave Long Beach CA 90802

BEROL, EDWARD M., gas company executive. Chmn. bd. Southwest Gas Co., Las Vegas. Office: Southwest Gas Corp 5241 Spring Mountain Rd Las Vegas NV 89102§

BERRES, FRANCES BRANDES, clinical psychologist; b. Chgo., d. Max and Anna (Gould) Brandes; m. George Berres, July 6, 1941 (dec.); 1 dau., Barbara Lo Monaco. B.A., UCLA, 1937, M.A., 1940, Ph.D., 1967. Head remedial instrn., tchr. English, Huntington Beach (Calif.) High Sch., 1940-44; psychologist, tchr. Fernald Sch., psychology dept. UCLA, 1950-52, assoc. dir., acad. adminstr., lectr. learning disabilities, dept. psychology, 1952-71; coordinator child-related programs info. project Neuropsychiat. Inst., 1971-73; pvt. practice clin. psychology, Santa Monica, Calif., 1976—. Past bd. dirs. Los Angeles Philharm. Soc. Women's Com.; past pres., bd. dirs. Marina del Rey Symphony Soc.; sec. bd. dirs. Internat. Children's Sch. Grantee, State of Calif., Dept. Edn., Div. Compensatory Edn., 1966-69, Office Edn., HEW, 1966-70, NIMH, 1970-72, Office Vice Chancellor, UCLA, 1970. Mem. Am. Psychol. Assn. Author: Deep Sea Adventure Series, 1959, 62, 67, 71, 79; A Survey of Child Related Programs, 1975. Office: 2122 Wilshire Blvd Santa Monica CA 90403

BERRETT, LAMAR CECIL, religion educator; b. Riveron, Utah, Mar. 28, 1926; s. John Harold and Stella (Wright) B.; m. Darlene Hamilton, Aug. 3, 1950; children: Marla, Kim, Michael, Susan, LeAnn, Nathan, Evan, Ellen, Jared. BS, U. Utah, 1952; MS, Brigham Young U., 1960, EdD, 1963. Prof. religion Brigham Young U., Provo, chmn. dept. religion, 1968-76, dir. Religious Study Ctr., 1976-82; dir. worldwide tours. Author: The Wilford Wood Collection Vol. 1, 1971, Discovering the World of the Bible, 1973; (family genealogy) Down Berrett Lane 2 Vols., 1980. Served with U.S. Army, 1944-46. Mem. Utah Hist. Soc. (pres. Utah Valley chpt. 1971-72), Sons of Utah Pioneers, Mormon History Assn. Republican. Mormon. Avocations: racquetball, pigeon raising, orchardist. Home: 1032 E 400 S Orem UT 84058 Office: Brigham Young U Dept Religion Office 73JSB Provo UT 84602

BERRIGAN, KAREN LEA, orthodontist; b. Tulsa, May 12, 1958; d. James Harold and Virginia Helen (Lock) B. DMD, Wash. U., 1983, MS in Dental Edn., 1986. Gen. practice dentistry St. Louis, 1983-86; practice dentistry specializing in orthodontics Phoenix, 1986—. Mem. Am. Orthodontic Assn., ADA, Pacific Coast Orthodontic Conss. Group, Ariz. Orthodontic Study Group, Delta Sigma Delta (v.p. 1981-82), Phi Theta Kappa. Republican. Roman Catholic. Club: Westside Study. Home: 3121 W Crocus Phoenix AZ 85023 Office: 4444 W Norhtern Ave Suite B Glendale AZ 85301

BERRING, ROBERT CHARLES, JR., educator, law librarian, dean; b. Canton, Ohio, Nov. 20, 1950; s. Robert Charles and Rita Pauline (Franta) B.; m. Barbara Rust, June 20, 1975; children: Simon Robert, Daniel Fredrick. B.A. cum laude, Harvard U., 1971; J.D., U. Calif.-Berkeley, 1974, M.L.S., 1974. Asst. prof. and reference librarian U. Ill. Law Sch., Champaign, 1974-76; assoc. librarian U. Tex. Law Sch., Austin, 1976-78; dep. librarian Harvard Law Sch., Cambridge, Mass., 1978-81; prof. law, law librarian U. Wash. Law Sch., Seattle, 1981-82; prof. law, law librarian Boalt Hall Law Sch., Berkeley, Calif., 1982—, dean sch. library and info. scis., 1986—; mem. Westlaw Adv. Bd., St. Paul, 1984—; cons. various law firms, Com. on Legal Exchange with China, 1983. Author: How to Find the Law, 8th edit. 1984, Great American Law Reviews, 1985; co-author: Authors Guide, 1981; editor Legal Reference Service Quar., 1981—. Mem. Am. Assn. Law Libraries (pres. 1985-86), Calif. Bar Assn., ABA, ALA. Home: 1969 Marin Ave Berkeley CA 94707 Office: Boalt Hall Law Sch Univ Calif Berkeley CA 94720

BERRY, CAROLYN, artist; b. Sweet Springs, Mo., June 27, 1930; d. Charles Thomas and Florence Valora (Harrison) B.; m. Robert E. Becker, Oct. 13, 1974; m. Benjamin Bishop, Oct. 12, 1952; children—Deborah Rachael, Rebecca. Student Columbia (Mo.) Coll., 1948-49; B.A., U. Mo., 1953; postgrad. in spl. edn. Humboldt U., 1969-71. One person shows include: Monterey Peninsula Mus. Art, 1966, 75, Marist Coll., Poughkeepsie, N.Y., 1969, Studio Performance, Palo Alto, Calif., 1980, Pacific Grove Art Ctr., UCLA, 1985; group exhbns. include: Franklin Furnance, 1980, Sao Paulo Biennale, Brazil, 1981, Women's Caucus For Art, N.Y.C., 1982, Long Beach Mus. Art, 1983, Otis/Parsons, Pratt U., La. World Expn., 1984, Bookworks Washington Project for the Arts, 1982, 85, Clocktower, N.Y.C., 1985, Tex. Women's U., 1986, Nova Scotia Tech. U., 1986; represented in permanent collection: Monterey Peninsula Mus. Art, Brandeis U., Waltham, Mass., Zone, Springfield, Mass., Tweed Mus., Duluth, Minn., Ind. Press Archive, Rochester, N.Y., Internat. Women's Collection, Copenhagen, Portland (Maine) Sch. Art, Art Inst. Chgo., Marvin Sackner Collection; dir. Handicapped Activities Unltd., Pacific Grove, Calif., 1971—. Calif. Arts Council grantee, 1980; recipient Best Small Painting award Pacific Grove Mus. Natural History, 1981. Mem. Womens Caucus for the Arts, Internat. Soc. Copier Arts, Nat. Womens Polit. Caucus. Home: 78 Cuesta Vista Dr Monterey CA 93950 Office: 511 Grand Ave Pacific Grove CA 93950

BERRY, GENE THULI, school system administrator; b. Sewell, Chile, Feb. 5, 1943; d. Alvin J. and Mary Alice (Crippen) Thuli; m. James Gibson Berry, Mar. 14, 1964 (div. Dec. 1985); children: Christine, John, Joanne. BS in Elem. Edn., U. Utah, 1965, MA in Cultural Founds. of Edn., 1981. Cert. elem. sch. tchr., Utah; cert. elem. and secondary adminstr., Utah. Elem. tchr. Salt Lake City Schs., 1965-68, staff devel. responsive edn. program, 1969-77, asst. dir. responsive edn. program, 1977-78, dist. vol. coordinator, 1979—, supr. ednl. support services, 1986—; pres. Nat. Sch. Vol. Program, Alexandria, Va., 1984—. Contbr. articles to profl. jours.; designer (community calendar) Home and Sch. Ptnrs., 1984. Recipient award Community Services Council, 1985, Golden Rule award J.C. Penney Co. Inc., 1985. Mem. Nat. Sch. Vol. Program (nat. pres. 1984-86, Tupperware award 1979-82), Nat. Sch. Pub. Relations Assn., Utah Sch. Pub. Relations Assn., Utah Area Assn. Vol. Dirs., Utah Sch. Vol. Program (bd. dirs.), Utah Community Edn. Assn. (bd. dirs.), Salt Lake City Adminstrs., Phi Delta Kappa. Avocations: tennis, skiing, swimming, the arts, puppeteering. Office: Salt Lake City Bd Edn Vols 440 E 1st S Salt Lake City UT 84111

BERRY, GLENN, educator, artist; b. Glendale, Calif., Feb. 27, 1929; s. B. Franklin and Heloise (Sloan) B.; B.A. magna cum laude, Pomona Coll., 1951; B.F.A. (Honnold fellow), M.F.A., Sch. Art Inst. Chgo., 1956. Faculty, Humboldt State U., Arcata, Calif., 1956-81, prof. art, 1969-81, emeritus, 1981—. Exhibited one-man shows Ingomar Gallery, Eureka, Calif., 1968, Ankrum Gallery, Los Angeles, 1970, Esther Bear Gallery, Santa Barbara, Calif., 1971; exhibited in group shows Palace of Legion of Honor, San Francisco, Pasadena (Calif.) Art Mus., Rockford (Ill.) Coll., Richmond (Calif.) Art Mus., Henry Gallery U. Wash., Seattle; represented in permanent collections at Storm King Art Center, Mountainville, N.Y., Kaiser Aluminum & Chem. Corp., Oakland, Calif., Palm Springs (Calif.) Desert Mus., Hirshhorn Mus., Washington, others; mural Griffith Hall, Humboldt State U., 1978. Mem. Phi Beta Kappa. Home: PO Box 2241 McKinleyville CA 95521

BERRY, JOHN CHARLES, clinical psychologist, educational administrator; b. Modesto, Calif., Nov. 29, 1938; s. John Wesley and Dorothy Evelyn (Harris) B.; A.B., Stanford, 1960; postgrad. Trinity Coll., Dublin, Ireland, 1960-61; Ph.D., Columbia, 1967; m. Arlene Ellen Sossin, Oct. 7, 1978; children—Elise, John Jordan, Kaitlyn. Research asso. Judge Baker Guidance Center, Boston, 1965-66; psychology asso. Napa State Hosp., Imola, Calif., 1966-67, staff psychologist, 1967-75, program asst., 1975-76; program dir. Met. State Hosp., Norwalk, Calif., 1976-77; asst. supt. Empire (Calif.) Union Sch. Dist., 1977—. Mem. Am. Psychol. Assn., Assn. Calif. Sch. Adminstrs., Sigma Xi. Contbg. author: Life History Research in Psychopathology, 1970. Home: 920 Eastridge Dr Modesto CA 95355 Office: Empire Union Sch Dist 200 G St Empire CA 95319

BERRY, KEITH DAVID, micropaleontologist; b. Gladbrook, Iowa, Nov. 18, 1923; s. Fred Gordon and Grace Nadine (Strohm) B.; m. Barbara Ann Wisdom, June 20, 1948; children—David Scott, Ellen Suzanne, Margaret Elaine. B.S., Iowa State U., 1949, M.S. in Geology, 1951. Registered geologist, Calif. Geologist-paleontologist Standard Oil Co. Calif., Taft, 1951-53, Bakersfield, 1953-60, profl. specialist in paleontology, 1960-68, sr. paleontologist, 1968-71; Standard Oil Calif. and Chevron USA, San Francisco, 1971-80; staff paleontologist Chevron USA Inc., San Francisco and Concord, Calif., 1980-85; cons. in field, 1985—; mem. M.S. grad. adv. com. U. Nev., Reno, 1979; mem. Ph.D. grad. adv. com. U. Calif.-Santa Barbara, 1980-85; bd. govs. Calif. Well Sample Adv. Com., Bakersfield, 1980-84; com. mem. Correlation of Stratigraphic Units N.Am., San Francisco, 1979-82. Contbr. articles to profl. jours. Served with U.S. Army, 1943-45. ETO. Mem. Am. Assn. Petroleum Geologists, Soc. Econ. Paleontologists and Mineralogists (sec.-treas. Pacific sect. 1962-63, chmn. conv. program 1976, Best Paper award 1965), San Joaquin Geol. Soc., No. Calif. Geol. Soc., N.Am. Micropaleontol. Soc., Am. Inst. Profl. Geologists, DAV, Phi Delta Theta. Republican. Presbyterian. Home and Office: 745 San Gabriel Ct Concord CA 94518

BERRY, LESLIE ELLIS, public relation executive; b. St. Louis, Aug. 23, 1952; d. John Lindsay and Ruth (Jungmann) Ellis; m. David C. Berry, Sept., 1986. BS, U. Mo., 1974. Writer, editor Today Newspaper, Cocoa, Fla., 1974-77; editor Getty Oil, Los Angeles, 1977-80; communications mgr. AM Internat., Los Angeles, 1980-81; pub. relations dir. The Greyhound Corp., Phoenix, 1981-86, Dial Corp., Phoenix, 1986—. Mem. Pub. Relations Soc. Am. (Award of Excellence 1985, Internat. Assn. Bus. Communicators (Award of Excellence 1985), Council Communications Mgmt., Jr. League. Republican. Home: 6135 N 16th Pl Phoenix AZ 85016 Office: The Dial Corp 111 W Clarendon Phoenix AZ 85077

BERRY, LOGAN IVAN, computer industry executive; b. Wheatland, Iowa, Feb. 27, 1950. BA in Info. Sci., Am. U., 1972; MS in Library Sci., U. Md., Silver Spring, 1976. Info. specialist Dept. of Interior, Washington, 1972-76; mgr. tech. info. Am. Info. Services, Falls Church, Va., 1976-80; dir. info. services Iowa State U., Ames, 1980-85; v.p. info. services MCC Devel., Boulder, Colo., 1985—; mem. adv. bd. Council Info. Scis., Woodbridge, Va., 1977-80. Author: From Words to Riches, 1985; co-author: Libraries: America's Political Time Bomb, 1983. County chmn. Com. to Re-elect Senator Jepson, Ames, 1981-82; treas. Boulder Cen. Am. Peace Coalition, 1985. Mem. Am. Soc. Library Sci. Lodges: Kiwanis, Lions. Avocations: race-walking, etymology. Home: 1300 E Arapahoe Boulder CO 80302 Office: MCC Devel 4775 Walnut St Boulder CO 80301

BERRY, RICHARD DOUGLAS, architectural educator, urban designer; b. Denver, Oct. 28, 1926; s. Howard Thomas and Susie Ann (Ross) B. B.A. in Humanities, U. Denver, 1951; B.Arch., U. Calif-Berkeley, 1957. Scenic artist, lighting designer Univ. Civic Theatre and Central City Opera Festival, Denver, 1948-49; assoc., project dir. Victor Gruen Assocs., Architects and Planners, Los Angeles and N.Y.C., 1957-63; mem. faculty U. So. Calif., Los Angeles, 1963—, prof. architecture, 1976—; coordinator first yr. archtl. design program, 1983-87; planning, programming cons. on new community devel., Gen. Electric Co., 1967-68, U.S. Dept. HUD, 1973-74; cons. Gen. Electric Found., 1967-68, U. N.C., 1971-73; vis. prof. urban design U. Wash., Seattle, 1969. Served with U.S. Army, 1951-53, Korea. Recipient research and ednl. grants from several pub. and pvt. orgns., Urban Design award for downtown Cin. Renewal Plan, editors of Progressive Architecture Mag., 1963. Mem. Am. Inst. Cert. Planners, Am. Planning Assn., AIA (assoc.), AAUP, Urban Land Inst., Nat. Trust for Hist. Preservation. Home: 1081 S Crescent Heights Blvd Los Angeles CA 90035 Office: U So Calif Sch Architecture Los Angeles CA 90089

BERRY, ROBERT EDWARD FRASER, bishop; b. Ottawa, Ont., Can., Jan. 21, 1926; s. Samuel and Clara (Hartley) B.; m. Margaret Joan Trevorrow, May 12, 1951; children—Christopher Fraser, Elisabeth Joan. B.A., Sir George Williams Coll., 1950; B.D., McGill U., 1953; D.D. (hon.), Montreal Diocesan Theol. Coll., 1972. Ordained deacon Anglican Ch. Can., 1953, ordained priest, 1954. Priest St. Margaret's Ch., Hamilton, Ont., 1955-61; priest St. Mark's Ch., Orangeville, Ont., 1961-63, St. Luke's Ch., Winnipeg, Man., Can., 1963-67, St. Michael and All Angels Ch., Kelowna, B.C., Can., 1967; supr. pastor Central Okanagan Region Diocese of Kootenay, Kelowna, 1967-71, bishop, 1971—. Served with RCAF, 1943-45. Avocations: boating; fishing. Home: 1857 Maple St, Kelowna, BC Canada V1Y 1H4 Office: Diocese of Kootenay, PO Box 549, Kelowna, BC Canada V1Y 7P2

BERRY, THOMAS CLAYTON, securities broker, brokerage owner; b. Roswell, N.Mex., May 23, 1948; s. Homer C. and Betty J. (Cronic) B.; m. Bonnie L. Shamas, May 30, 1969; children: Lisa C., Joshua E. AA, N.Mex. Mil. Inst., 1969; Assoc. course in real estate, 1984, NASD DPP rep. and prin. courses, 1983. Farmer Berry Farms, Dexter, N.Mex., 1969-72; sec., dir. Victor & Assoc., Phoenix, 1972-74; dir., foreman Berry Land & Cattle, Dexter, 1974-82; v.p., dir. Trinity Investment Corp., Roswell, 1982-83; pres., dir. Jordache Investments, Roswell, 1982-83; v.p., dir. Diamond Braich Realtors, Roswell, 1982-83; v.p., dir. Tierra Fin. Group, Roswell, 1985-86, pres., dir., 1986—, also bd. dirs.; v.p., dir. Tierra Capital Corp., Roswell, 1984-86, pres., dir., 1986—, also bd. dirs. Deacon North Phoenix Bapt. Ch., Phoenix, 1973-74; bd. dirs. First Assembly of God Ch., Roswell, youth group sponsor, 1978—; coach Roswell Youth Soccer, 1978—. Named one of Outstanding Men of Am., 1982. Mem. Nat. Assn. Securities Dealers, Roswell Realtor Assn., N.Mex. Realtor Assn.,. Republican. Mem. Assembly of God. Avocations: water skiing, racquetball, crafts, church activities. Home: 2010 Brazos Roswell NM 88201 Office: Tierra Fin Group Inc 323 N Virginia Roswell NM 88201

BERRY, WILLIAM BENJAMIN NEWELL, geologist, museum administrator; b. Boston, Sept. 1, 1931; s. John King and Margaret Elizabeth (Newell) B.; m. Suzanne Foster Spaulding, June 10, 1961; 1 child, Bradford Brown. A.B., Harvard U., 1953, A.M., 1955; Ph.D., Yale U., 1957. Asst. prof. geology U. Houston, 1957-58; asst. prof. to prof. paleontology U. Calif., Berkeley, 1958—; curator Mus. of Paleontology U. Calif., Berkeley, 1960-75; dir. Mus. of Paleontology U. Calif., 1975—, chmn. dept. paleontology, 1975—; cons. U.S. Geol. Survey. Author: Growth of a Prehistoric Time Scale, 1968, revised ed., 1987; assoc. editor Paleoceanography; contbr. numerous articles on stratigraphic and paleontol. subjects to profl. jours.; editor publs. in geol. scis. Guggenheim Found. fellow, 1966-67. Fellow Calif. Acad. Scis.; mem. Paleontol. Soc., Geol. Soc. Norway, Internat. Platform Assn., Explorers Club. Home: 1366 Summit Rd Berkeley CA 94708 Office: U Calif Dept Paleontology Berkeley CA 94720

BERS, DONALD MARTIN, physiology educator; b. N.Y.C., Dec. 13, 1953; s. Harold Theodore and Penny (Wall) B.; m. Kathryn Eileen Hammond, July 17, 1976; children: Brian Alexander, Rebecca Ann. BA, U. Colo., 1974; PhD, UCLA, 1978. Postdoctoral research fellow UCLA, 1978-79, asst. research physiologist, 1980-82, adj. asst. prof., 1981-82; postdoctoral research fellow Edinburgh (Scotland) U., 1979-80; asst. prof. U. Calif., Riverside, 1982-86, assoc. prof., 1986—. Contbr. articles to profl. jours. Bd. dirs. Am. Heart Assn., Riverside, 1985—. Fellow Am. Heart Assn., Los Angeles, 1978-80, Brit.-Am., Am. Heart Assn., 1980-81; recipient New Investigator Research award NIH, 1982-85, Research Career Devel. award NIH, 1985—. Mem. AAAS, Am. Physiol. Soc., Biophys. Soc., Internat. Soc. Heart Research. Office: U Calif Div Biomed Scis Riverside CA 92521

BERSHAD, NEIL JEREMY, electrical engineering educator; b. Bklyn., Oct. 20, 1937; s. Milton Frank and Lila (Kaplan) B.; m. Susan Goldman; children: Brian, Melissa. BEE, Rensselaer Poly. Inst., 1958, PhD EE, 1962; MSEE, U. So. Calif., 1960. Mem. tech. staff Hughes Aircraft Co., Culver City, Calif., 1958-62, staff engr., 1964-69; prof. elec. engring. U. Calif., Irvine, 1966—, vice chmn. elec. engring. dept., 1986—; cons. Hughes Aircraft Co., Fullerton, Calif., 1969—. Contbr. over 45 articles on communications theory, signal processing and adaptive filtering to profl. jours. Served to 1st lt. USAF, 1962-65. Sr. mem. IEEE (assoc. editor communications jour., transion acoustics, speech and signal processing jour.). Office: U Calif Irvine Dept Elec Engring Irvine CA 92717

BERSI, ROBERT MARION, university administrator; b. Ark., June 4, 1932; s. Mack M. and Angelina (Perona) B.; m. Ann Brakebill, Nov. 27, 1975; 1 dau., Margaret Ann. B.A., U. of Pacific, 1958; M.A., Stanford U., 1962, Ph.D., 1965. Research assoc. Stanford U., 1964-66; exec. asst. to pres. Calif. State U., Dominguez Hills, 1966-70; prof. edn. Calif. State U., 1970-75, dean innovative programs, 1971-73, v.p. instl. devel., 1973-75; pres. Western Conn. State U., Danbury, 1975-81; chancellor U. Nev. System, 1981-87; mem. exec. com. Conn. Council on Higher Edn. Author: Restructuring the Baccalaureate, 1973; Mem. editorial adv. bd., Coll. Mgmt. mag., 1973-75;

Contbr. articles to profl. publs. Served with U.S. Navy, 1952-54. Recipient award of merit Carson Black Heritage Assn., 1973. Mem. Am. Assn. Sch. Adminstrs., Am. Inst. Pub. Service (bd. nominators), Western Assn. Schs. and Colls., Fed. Edn. Data Acquisition Council, Greater Danbury C. of C. (dir.). Office: U Nev System 405 Marsh Ave Reno NV 89509 *

BERTAIN, G(EORGE) JOSEPH, JR., lawyer; b. Scotia, Calif., Mar. 9, 1929; s. George J. and Ellen Veronica (Canty) B.; m. Bernardine Joy Galli, May 11, 1957; 1 son, Joseph F. A.B., St. Mary's Coll. of Calif., 1951; J.D., Cath. U. Am., 1955. Bar: Calif. Assoc. Joseph L. Alioto, San Francisco, 1955-57, 59-65; asst. U.S. Atty. No. Dist. Calif., 1957-59; pvt. practice of law San Francisco, 1966—. Editor-in-chief, Law Rev. Cath. U. Am. (vol. 5), 1954-55. Chmn. San Francisco Lawyers Com. for Elections of Gov./Pres. Ronald Reagan, 1966, 70, 80, 84; spl. confidential adviser to Gov. Reagan for jud. selection, San Francisco, 1967-74; chmn. San Francisco Lawyers for Better Govt., 1978-87; confidential adv. on jud. selection to Senator Hayakawa, 1981-82, Gov. Deukmejian, 1983—; bd. regents St. Mary's Coll. of Calif., 1980—; mem. civilian adv. com. U.S. 6th Army, Presidio, San Francisco. Recipient De La Salle medal St. Mary's Coll. of Calif., 1951, Signum Fidei award St. Mary's Coll. of Calif., 1976. Mem. ABA, Calif. Bar Assn., Fed. Bar Assn. (del. 9th Circuit Jud. Conf. 1967-76), Am. Judicature Soc., St. Thomas More Soc. San Francisco, Calif. Acad. Scis., Mus. Soc., Assn. Former U.S. Attys. and Asst. U.S. Attys. of No. Calif. (past pres.), Supreme Ct. Hist. Soc., Western Assn. Republican. Roman Catholic. Clubs: Commonwealth, Commercial, Olympic, 1st Friday Group. Lodges: K.C., Order of Knights of Malta. Office: 1250 Alcoa Bldg Suite 1600 One Maritime Plaza San Francisco CA 94111

BERTANI, GIUSEPPE, research scientist; b. Como, Italy, Oct. 23, 1923; came to U.S., 1948; s. Carlo and Armida (Seveso) Bertani; m. L. Elizabeth Teegarden, July 2, 1954; children: Christofer, Niklas. DSc in Natural Scis., State U. of Milano, Italy, 1945; PhD (hon.), U. Uppsala, Sweden, 1983. Research assoc. bacteriology U. Ill., Urbana, 1951-54; sr. research fellow in biology Calif. Inst. Tech., Pasadena, 1954-57; assoc. prof. microbiology U. So. Calif., Los Angeles, 1957-60; prof. microbial genetics Karolinska Inst., Stockholm, 1960-83; sr. research scientist Jet Propulsion Lab., Pasadena, 1981—; Organizer of several internat. symposia on research topics in Molecular biology. Mem. editorial bd. Journal of Gen. Virology, 1967-70, 77-83, Virology, 1958-72, Molecular and Gen. Genetics, 1967-77; contbr. articles to profl. jours. Mem. European Molecular Biology Orgn. (mem. course com. 1972-78), Genetics Soc. Am., Am. Soc. Microbiology. Office: Jet Propulsion Lab 4800 Oak Grove Dr Pasadena CA 91109

BERTHELSDORF, SIEGFRIED, psychoanalyst; b. Shannon County, Mo., June 16, 1911; s. Richard and Amalia (Morschenko) von Berthelsdorf; m. Mildred Friederich, May 13, 1945; children: Richard, Victor, Dianne. BA, U. Oreg., 1934, MA, MD, 1939. Lic. psychiatrist, psychoanalyst. Intern U.S. Marine Hosp., Staten Island, N.Y., 1939-40; psychiat. intern Bellevue Hosp., N.Y.C., 1940-41; psychiat. resident N.Y. State Psychiat. Hosp., N.Y.C., 1941-42; research assoc. Columbia U. Coll. Physicians and Surgeons, N.Y.C., 1942-43; asst. physician Presbyn. Hosp. and Vanderbilt Clinic, N.Y.C., 1942-51; supervising psychiatrist Manhattan (N.Y.) State Hosp., 1946-50; asst. adolescent psychiatrist Mt. Zion Hosp., N.Y.C., 1950-52; psychiat. cons. MacLaren Sch. for Boys, Woodburn, Oreg., 1952-84, Portland (Oreg.) Pub. Schs., 1952-67; clin. prof. U. Oreg. Health Scis. Ctr., 1956—. Author: Treatment of Drug Addiction in Psychoanalytic Study of the Child, Vol. 31, 1976. Bd. dirs., v.p., Portland Opera Assn., 1960-64; bd. dirs., pres., Portland Chamber Orch., 1964-70. Served to major USAF, 1943-46. Recipient Henry Waldo Coe award U. Oreg. Med. Sch., Portland, 1939, citation Parry Ctr. for Children, Portland, 1970. Fellow Am. Psychiat. Assn. (life), Am. Geriatrics Soc. (founding fellow); mem. Am. Psychoanalytic Assn. (life), Portland Psychiatrists in Pvt. Practice (charter, pres. 1958), Mental Health Assn. (bd. dirs., chmn. med. adv. com. 1952-60), Multnomah County Med. Soc. (pres.'s citation 1979), Am. Rhododendron Soc. (bd. dirs., v.p. Portland chpt. 1956—, Bronze medal and citation 1974), Am. Rhododendron Species Found. (bd. dirs. 1960—), Phi Beta Kappa, Sigma Xi, Phi Sigma. Avocations: farming, music. Home and Office: 1125 SW Saint Clair Ave Portland OR 97205

BERTHOLD, JANICE ANNETTE, insurance marketing manager; b. Boulder, Colo., May 10, 1947; d. Maurice A. and Alice O. Notch; m. Thomas R. Berthold, July 21, 1973; children—Timothy Eugene, Alison Marie. B.A. in English, U. San Francisco, 1969. C.L.U. Life specialist Safeco Life, Burlingame, Calif., 1974-77; brokerage supr. Aetna Life, San Jose, Calif., 1977-80, gen. agt., 1980-83, mktg. mgr., 1983—. Mem. Calif. Senate Adv. Com. on Ins. Recipient Pres.'s Trophy, Aetna Life, 1983; Nat. Mgmt. award Gen. Agts. and Mgrs. Conf., 1983-86. Adv. bd. dirs. Hope Rehab. Ctr. Mem. San Jose Gen. Agts. and Mgrs. Assn. (sec.), C.L.U.s Assn. (dir.), Santa Clara County Estate Planning Council, San Jose Life Underwriters Assn., San Jose Ind. Agts. Assn., Nat. Assn. Life Underwriters. Republican. Roman Catholic. Club: San Jose Athletic (bd. dirs.). Office: 1150 N 1st St San Jose CA 95112

BERTIN, IRA LOUIS, manufacturing company executive; b. N.Y.C., May 30, 1939; s. Mannie and Estelle (Cohen) B.; m. Rebecca Perkins, Oct. 28, 1961, Mar. 23, 1976; children: Jeffrey Lee, Andrew David; m. Barbara Bourget, July 4, 1977; 1 child, Isaac Avid. Grad. high sch., N.Y.C. Pres., chief exec. officer Temperature Controllers Inc., Limington, Maine, 1964-73, Bertin Inds., Limington, Maine, 1969-78, Pine Tree Service, Standish, Maine, 1973-76, E3 Corp, Bath, Maine, 1978-80, Geo Trading Corp., Boulder, Colo., 1983—, Golden Energy, Inc., Boulder, Colo., 1980—; state advisor, bd. dir. Win/Win Forums, Denver, 1983-85; co-founder, bd. dirs. GeoFood Project, Boulder, 1985—; founder, chmn. bd. dirs. GeoFood Inc., Denver, 1985—; founder, vice-chmn. The Synergy Found., Denver, 1986; gen. ptnr. Geo One Ltd., Boulder, 1986—. Patentee in field. Notary Pub., Maine, 1970—; chmn. Limington Planning Bd., 1965-71; active York County Regional Plannng Commn., Maine, 1965-71; chmn. Valley Chpt. Internat. Order of Demolay, Limington, 1966-71. Served with USN, 1956-60. Recipient Hat's Off award, Internat. Supreme Council Order of DeMolay, 1967, Zerubbable Key award Internat. Supreme Council Order of Demolay, 1968. Mem. ASHRAE, Internat. Tesia Soc. Lodge: Masons (32 degree), Shriners. Avocations: computers, mountain climbing, inventing systems.

BERTRAMSON, B. RODNEY, agronomist; b. Potter, Nebr., Jan. 25, 1914; s. James W. and Gladys D. (Nelson) B.; m. Eleanor Anne Maloney, Aug. 28, 1938; children: James Leitch, Christina MacPherson, Susan M. B.S., U. Nebr., 1937, M.S., 1938, D.Agr. (hon.), 1978; Ph.D., Oreg. State Coll., 1941. Chemist technician, lab. asst. U. Nebr., 1936-37; soil surveyor U.S. Dept. Agr., 1941; instr. soils Colo. State Coll., 1941; asst. prof. soils U. Wis., 1946; assoc. soil chemist Purdue U., 1946-49; chmn. dept. agronomy Wash. State U., Pullman, 1949-67; dir. resident instruction Coll. Agr., 1967-79, prof. emeritus, cons., 1982—; cons. U.S. Dept. Agr., 1979-80; project leader U. Nebr.-AID Morocco Project, Casablanca, 1981. Editor, Jour. Agron. Edn., 1973; contbr. articles to profl. jours. Entered U.S. Army, 1941; chief of food and agr. for Rheinland, later for Gross Hessen Mil. Govt., 1945; disch. to Research and Devel., U.S. Army Res. as maj. 1946. Fellow AAAS, Am. Soc. Agronomy (v.p. 1959, pres. 1960); mem. Crop Sci. Soc. Am., Soil Sci. Soc. Am., Soil Conservation Soc. Am., Am. Chem. Soc., Sigma Xi, Phi Kappa Phi, Alpha Zeta, Gamma Sigma Delta. Prepared course outlines for soil analysis and soil chemistry. Home: SE 510 Crestview St Pullman WA 99163

BESS, CHARLES WAYNE, lawyer, real estate broker; b. Denver, Mar. 23, 1958; s. Howard Heber and Helen Faye (Esau) B.; m. Jennifer Anne Murray, Feb. 28, 1981; children: Caroline Tempel, Madelaine Kate. BS, Colo. State U., 1980; JD, U. Denver, 1984. Bar: Colo. 1984, U.S. Dist. Ct. Colo. 1985, U.S. Ct. Appeals (10th cir.) 1986. Assoc. Roath & Brega P.C., Denver, 1984-86; sr. assoc. La Salle Ptrns., Denver, 1986—. Mem. ABA (litigation sect.), Colo. Bar Assn., Denver Bar Assn., Assn. Trial Lawyers Am., Colo. Trial Lawyers Assn. Republican. Congregationalist. Club: Denver Athletic. Avocations: hunting, bicycling, tennis, basketball, fishing. Office: La Salle Ptnrs 1225 17th St Suite 2400 Denver CO 80202

BESSE, ROBERT GALE, food technologist; b. Calgary, Alta., Can., Feb. 11, 1923 (parents Am. citizens); s. Rene A. and Doria (Bray) B.; student N.Mex. State Tchrs. Coll., 1941-42; B.S., Oreg. State Coll., 1948; m. Mary A. McKay, Sept. 11, 1948; children—Rene A., Madeleine E., Leon J., Alan G., Michele M., Marc, Angelique. Supt., also in quality control Alderman Farms Frozen Foods, Dayton, Oreg., 1948-50, plant supt., 1950-54; chief food technologist Kuner Empson Co., Brighton, Colo., 1954-60; food technologist Northwest Packing Co., Portland, Oreg., 1960-62; food technologist research and devel. Nat. Can Corp., San Francisco, 1962-67, mgr. Pacific Area tech. research service, 1967-70; mgr. tech. services Western Can Co., 1970-86 ; customer tech. services Continental Can Co., 1986—; dir. Material Metrics. Pres. St. Gregory's Theatre Guild; vol. hunting safety instr. Calif. Fish and Game Dept., 1972—. Served with Signal Corps, AUS, 1942-45. Mem. Soc. Plastic Engrs., Pacific Fish Tech. (pres.), Inst. Food Technologists (sec.-treas. Rocky Mountain sect.; exec. com. Oreg. sect.), Confraternity of Christian Doctrine Cath. (pres.), N.W. Canners and Packers, Packaging Inst. (profl. mem.), Nat. Canners Assn. (mem. western lab. adv. com.), No. Calif. Metal Decorating Assn. (pres.), Western Packaging Assn.; Soc. Mfg. Engrs. Club: Elks. Home: 264 Portola Dr San Mateo CA 94403 Office: Continental Can Co 1849 17th St San Francisco CA 94103

BESSER, PATRICK JAMES, production engineer; b. Santa Monica, Calif., Jan. 4, 1951; s. Nick James and Edna Mae (Patrick) B.; m. Debra Lynne Miller; Mar. 8, 1980; children: Joshua, Amy, Michael. AA in Electronics, El Camino Coll., 1971; BS, Grand Canyon Coll., 1983. Computer technician, prodn. supr. Xerox Corp., El Segundo, Calif., 1972-76; indsl. engr. Honeywell Corp., Phoenix, 1976-83; mfg. engr. Motorola Four Phase, Tempe, Ariz., 1983-85; prodn. engr. Sperry Corp., Phoenix, 1985—. Mem. Soc. Mfg. Engrs. Republican. Lutheran. Avocations: scuba diving, computers, fishing. Home: 5627 W Eva Glendale AZ 85302 Office: Sperry Corp 5260 W Phelps Rd Glendale AZ 85306

BESSLER, URSULA MARTA, management service manager; b. Eberswalde, Germany, Nov. 30, 1938; d. Georg Wilhelm and Maria Anna (Lamparter) Bromann; came to U.S., 1957, naturalized, 1962; children—Joann Ursula, Jacqueline Sue, Michelle Gai. Grad. Hierse Sch. Bus., Frankfurt, Germany, 1956; student Am. Inst. Banking, 1965-70, Am. Mgmt. Assn. Extension Inst., Portland State U., 1980-82. With U.S. Nat. Bank, Portland, Oreg., 1964-72; mktg. analyst, acct. BFG Bank, Frankfurt, Germany, 1972-77; mgr., EEO officer Multnomah-Washington Employment and Tng. Agy., Portland, 1978-82; civil rights investigator State of Oreg., 1982—. Mem. Internat. Personnel Mgrs. Assn., Nat. Assn. Female Execs. Republican.

BEST, RICHARD ALLEN, JR., architect; b. Somers Point, N.J., Apr. 26, 1957; s. Richard Allen Sr. and E. Jeanne (Cunningham).B. BA, U. N.C., 1979, BArch, 1980; MArch, UCLA, 1982. Registered architect, Calif. Intern architect Urban Innovations Group, Los Angeles, 1981; designer, draftsman Charles Moore, Inc., Los Angeles, 1982-84; sr. draftsman WZMH Group, Inc., Los Angeles, 1984-85, project cpt., designer, 1985-87; with Elbasani & Logan Architects, Berkeley, Calif., 1987—; teaching asst. UCLA Sch. Archtecture, 1981-82. Co-author: Un Storico Aldente, 1981; co-designer Mercatale e Albergo, 1981; designer Beverly Hills Civic Ctr., 1982 (1st place 1982); capt., designer Mission Inn, Riverside, Calif., 1986. Fellow UCLA, 1980; scholar UCLA, 1981, Bell Telephone Co., N.J., 1977; named one of Outstanding Young Men Am., Nat. Jaycees, 1982. Mem. AIA. Democrat. Methodist. Avocations: golf, tennis, bridge, guitar, painting and drawing. Home: 9364 Beverlycrest Dr Beverly Hills CA 90210 Office: Elbasani & Logan Architects 2040 Addison St Berkeley CA 94704

BESTWICK, WARREN WILLIAM, construction company executive; b. Missoula, Mont., June 27, 1922; s. William Andrews and Beatrice Anna (Eddy) B.; student Glendale Coll., 1941, U. Mont., 1942; BA, U. Wash., 1949; m. Glenette Haas, Sept. 11, 1949; children: Sharon Kaye, Carol Eddy, Jan Marie. Sr. acct. Frederick & Nelson, Seattle, 1950; controller, bus. mgr. Virginia Mason Hosp., Seattle, 1958-64; controller Bumstead Woolford Co., Seattle, 1964-68; controller, treas. Wash. Asphalt Co., Seattle, 1968-72; exec. v.p., sec. treas. Wilder Constrn. Co., Inc., Bellingham, Wash., 1972-77, pres., 1977—, also dir.; bd. dirs. TRC Thermal Reduction, Ltd., Cost Cutter Foods, Bellingham; treas., dir. Vincent Contracting, Inc., , Vincent Corp.; dir. Mt. Baker Bank, Bellingham; chmn. Area IV advisory bd. Wash. Dept. Commerce and Econ. Devel., 1976-80. Past pres., bd. dirs. Shuckson Found. Whatcom County. Served to col., pilot USMCR, 1942-74. Decorated DFC (3), Air medal (7). Mem. Assn. Wash. Bus., Whatcom County Devel. Council (past dir. and pres.), Bellingham C. of C. (past dir.), Marine Res. Officers Assn. (past dir. Seattle), Res. Officers Assn., Marine Corps League, Associated Gen. Contractors Am., The Beavers Constrn. (hon.), United For Wash., U. Wash. Alumni Assn., Ret. Officers Assn., Marine Aviation Assn. Clubs: Wash. Athletic (Seattle); Bellingham Golf and Country, Bellingham Yacht; Rotary (past pres.). Home: 1000 E Toledo St Bellingham WA 98226 Office: 2006 State St N Bellingham WA 98225 Office: 98225 Lang St Anchorage AK 99515

BETHANY, NORMAN JAMES, financial planner; b. Gorman, Tex., Jan. 23, 1933; s. Elmer Claude and Bessie Lee (Holloway) B.; m. Joyce Gayle Park, Aug. 25, 1952; children—Lagaytha Janell Bethany Yuan, Norma JoLee Bethany Lawrence. B.A., Hardin-Simmons U., 1954; M.R.E., Southwestern Sem., Ft. Worth, 1961; M.A., U. Oreg., 1968. Cert. fin. planner. Tchr. Trent Sch. Dist., Tex., 1954-56, 60-61, Bend Sch. Dist., Oreg., 1961-78; fin. planner Creative Tax Shelters, Bend, Oreg., 1978-82, mng. exec. Integrated Resources, Bend, 1982—; owner Norman J. Bethany, C.F.P., Bend, 1982—; pres. Oreg. Lang. Arts Assn., 1966-67; Mem. Inst. Cert. Fin. Planners (communications com. 1981-84), Internat. Assn. Fin. Planning, Nat. Assn. Life Underwriters, NEA, Nat. Council Tchrs. English, Sigma Tau Delta (pres. 1953-54). Democrat. Baptist. Office: PO Box 5878 Bend OR 97708

BETSON, JOHNNIE RICHARD, JR., gynecologist, banker; b. Ft. Worth, Dec. 6, 1928; s. Johnnie Richard and Prebble Loraine (Lewis) B.; m. Joan Sue Schroeder, June 20, 1956 (div. 1979); children—Kevin, Pamela, Lance; m. 2d, Karen Anne Livoni, Oct. 21, 1980. B.S., East Central U., 1950; M.D., U. Okla., 1955. Diplomate Am. Bd. Ob-Gyn. Intern, Milw. County Hosp., 1955-56; resident in ob-gyn Charity Hosp., New Orleans, 1956-59. Gynecologist, researcher female astronaut program Lovelace Clinic Found., Albuquerque, 1959-62; practice medicine specializing in ob-gyn, Newport Beach, Calif., 1962—; dir. Sunwest Bank, Tustin, Calif., 1970-85, chmn. bd. dirs., 1973-78. Contbr. articles to med. jours.; mem. editorial bd. Jour. Abdominal Surgery, 1964—; developer 3 motion pictures (med.). Bd. dirs. Costa Mesa Med. Ctr. Hosp., 1982—, chmn., 1985—. Served with USMC, 1946-47. Assoc. clin. prof. ob-gyn U. Calif.-Irvine, 1977. Fellow Am. Med. Writers Assn., Am. Coll. Ob-Gyn., Am. Assn. Profs. of Ob-Gyn. Republican. Lodge: Rotary (pres. 1968-69) (Costa Mesa, Calif.). Home: 19 Inverness Ln Newport Beach CA 92660 Office: 1501 Superior #308 Newport Beach CA 92663

BETTENCOURT, LYNN J., industrial health department administrator; b. Nov. 7, 1941. BA, U. Mass., 1964; MS, Cen. Mo. State U., 1976. Cert. Bd. Cert. Safety Profls., Bd. Cert. Hazard Control Mgmt. Air traffic control officer USAF, 1964-75; office mgr. Safety Cons., Inc., Kansas City, Kans., 1976-77; safety mgr. Oak Forest (Ill.) Hosp., 1977-78, Naval Underwater Systems Ctr., New London, Conn., 1978-80; dir. occupational safety and health dept. Long Beach (Calif.) Naval Shipyard, 1980—. Recipient Award of Honor Nat. Safety Council, 1983, Best Safety Performance Award, Nat. Safety Council-Heavy Marine Industry. Mem. Am. Soc. Safety Engrs., Am. Conf. Govtl. Indsl. Hygienists, Navy Field Safety Assn., Assn. Fed. Safety and Health Profls. Home: 2447 Peacock Ln Corona CA 91720 Office: Long Beach Naval Shipyard C106 Occupational Safety Health Dept Long Beach CA 90822

BETTER, JENNIFER REESE, technology marketing executive; b. Sacramento, Feb. 27, 1946; d. Howard Edward and Marion (Meredith) Reese. BA in Spanish, U. Calif., Berkeley, 1967; MEd, U. San Francisco, 1975; postgrad., U. Calif., Berkeley, 1980—. Tchr. San Juan Unified Schs., Sacramento, 1968-75, project adminstr., 1975-80; curriculum dir. Cupertino (Calif.) Union Schs., 1980-84; devel. engr. Hewlett-Packard Co., Palo Alto, Calif., 1984-86, mktg. program mgr., 1986-87, mktg. edn. mgr., 1987—; cons. Goodson & Assocs., Sunnyvale, Calif., 1984—, cons. edn. tech., 1968—; instr. U. Calif., Santa Cruz, 1983—; adj. prof. U. San Francisco, 1986; bd. dirs. PCC, Inc., San Ramon, Calif. 1984—. Co-author: Computer Literacy Curriculum, 1980 (Nat. Difusion Network award 1984); editor: Jour. of Computers Reading and Lang. Arts, 1983—. Mem. adv. bd. Girl Scouts U.S., Santa Clara County, Calif., 1985—; mem. steering com. High Tech. Mus., San Jose, Calif., 1985—. Named Tchr. of Yr., County of Sacramento, 1974, Woman of Yr., Calif. State U., Sacramento, 1976. Mem. Computer Using Educators (legal and ethical issues officer 1983), Commonwealth Club of San Francisco, Am. Mgmt. Assn., Internat. Reading Assn. (tech. cons.), Jr. League Palo Alto and Sacramento (pres., various positions 19796). Avocations: showing horses, gourmet cooking, restoring old homes, golf, skiing. Home: 115 Walter Hays Dr Palo Alto CA 94303 Office: Hewlett-Packard Co 3200 Hillview Ave Palo Alto CA 94304

BETTS, BARBARA LANG (MRS. BERT A. BETTS), lawyer, rancher; b. Anaheim, Calif., Apr. 28, 1926; d. W. Harold and Helen (Thompson) Lang; B.A. magna cum laude, Stanford U., 1948; LL.B., Balboa U., 1951; m. Roby F. Hayes, July 22, 1948 (dec.); children—John Chauncey IV, Frederick Prescott, Roby Francis II; m. Bert A. Betts, July 11, 1962; 1 son, Bruce Harold; stepchildren: Bert Alan, Randy W., Sally Betts Joynt, Terry Betts Marsteller, Linda Betts Hansen, LeAnn Betts Hoffman. Admitted to Calif. bar, 1952, U.S. Supreme Ct. bar, 1978; pvt. practice law, Oceanside, Calif., 1952-68, San Diego, 1960—, Sacramento, 1962—; partner firm Roby F. Hayes & Barbara Lang Hayes, 1952-60; city atty., Carlsbad, Calif., 1959-63; v.p. Isle & Oceans Marinas, Inc., 1970-80, W. H. Lang Corp., 1964-69; sec. Internat. Prodn. Assos., 1968—, Margaret M. McCabe, M.D., Inc., 1977—. Chmn., Traveler's Aid, 1952-53; pres. Oceanside-Carlsbad Jr. Chambrettes, 1955-56; vice chmn. Carlsbad Planning Commn., 1959; mem. San Diego Planning Congress, 1959; v.p. Oceanside Diamond Jubilee Com., 1958; dir. No. San Diego County Chpt. for Retarded Children, 1957-58. Candidate Calif. State Legislature, 77th Dist., 1954; mem. Calif. Dem. State Central Com., 1958-66; co-chmn. 28th Congl. Dist., Dem. State Central Com., 1960-62; alt. del. Dem. Nat. Conv., 1960. Named to Fullerton Union High Sch. Wall of Fame, 1986. Mem. Am. Judicature Soc., Nat. Inst. Mcpl. Officers, ABA, Calif. Bar Assn.,, San Diego County Bar Assn., Oceanside C. of C. (sec. 1957, v.p. 1958, dir. 1953-54, 57-59), AAUW (legis. com. 1958-59); local (pres. 1959-60; asst. state legis. chmn. 1958-59), No. San Diego County Assn. Chambers of Commerce (sec.-treas.), Bus. and Profl. Women's Club (So. dist. legislation chmn. 1958-59), DAR (regent Oceanside chpt. 1960-61), San Diego C. of C., San Diego Hist. Soc., Fullerton Jr. Assistance League, U.S. Supreme Ct. Hist. Soc., Calif. Scholarship Fedn., Loyola Guild of Jesuit High Sch., Phi Beta Kappa. Clubs: Soroptimist Internat. (pres. Oceanside-Carlsbad 1958-59, sec. pub. affairs San Diego, Imperial Counties 1954; pres. of pres.'s council San Diego and Imperial counties and Mexico 1958-59), Barristers, Stanford (Sacramento), Stanford Mothers. Author: (with Bert A. Betts) A Citizen Answers. Office: Betts Ranch PO Box 306 Elverta CA 95626 Office: 3119-A Howard Ave San Diego CA 92104

BETTS, JAMES WILLIAM, JR., financial analyst, consultant; b. Montclair, N.J., Oct. 11, 1923; s. James William and Cora Anna (Banta) B.; m. Barbara Stoke, July 28, 1951; 1 dau., Barbara Susan (dec.). B.A., Rutgers U., 1946; M.A., U. Hawaii, 1957. With Dun & Bradstreet, Inc., 1946-86, service cons., 1963-64, reporting and service mgr., 1964-65, sr. fin. analyst, Honolulu, 1965—; owner, operator Portfolio Cons. of Hawaii, 1979—. Served with AUS, 1942-43. Mem. Am. Econ. Assn., Western Econ. Assn., Atlantic Econ. Soc. Republican. Episcopalian.

BETTS, WILBUR WARD, engineer, author, historian; b. Rockford, Ill., Aug. 28, 1904; s. Fred Grant and Edith Belle (Beach) B.; B.S. with honors in Mech. Engring., U. Ill., 1935; m. Sarah Elizabeth Farrey, June 2, 1928; children—Mary Edith, Sharon Ann; m. Mary Roberta Van DeWalker, Oct. 19, 1970. Design engr. Ingersoll Milling Machine Co., Rockford, 1922-32; asst. sales mgr. Barnes Drill Co., Rockford, 1935-37; sales engr. English & Miller Machinery Co., Detroit, 1937-38; design engr. Farrel Birmingham Gear Corp., Buffalo, 1938-40; group leader Bell Aircraft Corp., Buffalo, 1940-42, W. Coast Engring. rep. B-29 Com., 1942-44; product analyst Webster-Brinkley Co., Seattle, 1944-46; chief engr. Kirsten Pipe Co., Seattle, 1946-48; adminstrn. engr. B47 and Bomarc Functional tests Boeing Co., Seattle, 1948-61; test devel. engr. DynaSoar Gliders, Seattle, 1962, charge test verification saturn booster, New Orleans, 1963-65, adminstrn. engr. 747 airplane, 1965-69; test procedures cons., Seattle, 1969—. Chmn. adv. com. Office of Price Adminstrn., State of Wash., 1944-46. Recipient Bronze Tablet award U. Ill., 1935. Mem. Soc. Automotive Engrs. (25-Yr. Membership award 1969), Am. Indian Profl. Assos., Mayflower Soc., Sons of Union Vets. of Civil War, SAR, Gen. James A. Longstreet Meml. Assn., James Willard Schultz Soc., Jet Pioneers Assn. U.S.A., Phi Eta Sigma, Pi Tau Sigma, Theta Tau, Tau Beta Pi. Methodist. Clubs: Horseless Carriage (pres. 1958), N.W. Intertribal. Author: (with Schultz) Bear Chief's War Shirt, 1983. Contbr. articles to profl. jours., also short story. Home: 1317 44th Ave SW Seattle WA 98116 Office: PO Box 3707 13 59 Seattle WA 98124

BETZ, CECILY LYNN, nursing educator; b. Glendale, Calif., Feb. 26, 1949; d. Cecil Leander and Alda Virginia (Pedersen) B. BS, Calif. State U., Los Angeles, 1976, MS, 1978; PhD, U. So. Calif., 1982. Clin. nurse specialist Children's Hosp., Los Angeles, 1972-77; instr. Pasadena (Calif.) Children'sCtr., 1977-78; asst. clin. prof. nursing UCLA, 1978-85, coordinator nursing tng., 1985—. Editor Jour. Pediat. Nursing, 1985—; contbr. articles to profl. jours. Mem. Mayfield Alumnae Assn. (pres. 1980-82), Sigma Theta Tau (pres. Gamma Tau chpt. 1985—).

BETZ, GEORGE, physician, educator; b. Beloit, Kans., Apr. 27, 1934; s. George and Dudley Beverly (Steahlin) B.; m. Patricia A. Betz; children: George, Carter, Virginia. BS, Kans. State Coll., 1956; MD, U. Kans., 1960, PhD, 1968. Resident physician U. Kans., Kansas City, 1960-65; asst. prof. U. Colo., Denver, 1968-72, assoc. prof., 1972-76, prof., 1976—. Contbr. over 50 articles to profl. jours. Recipient Research Career Devel. award NIH, 1972-77; sr. research fellow NIH, 1981-82. Mem. Soc. for Gynecol. Investigation, Am. Soc. Biol. Chemists, Endocrine Soc., Am. Assn. Obstetricians and Gynecologists. Home: 621 Fairfax Denver CO 80220 Office: U Colo Sch Medicine 4200 E 9th St Denver CO 80262

BETZ, MATHEW JOSEPH, civil engineer educator, researcher; b. Chgo., Jan. 27, 1932; s. Mathew Joseph and Frances (Fleming) B.; m. Judith Feaster, Nov. 27, 1963; 1 child, Alison. BS, Northwestern U., 1955, MS, 1956, PhD, 1961. Prof. civil enginrg. Ariz. State U., Tempe, 1961—, assoc. dean grad. coll., 1969-76, asst. v.p., 1976-83, dir. Ctr. for Advanced Research in Transp., 1983—. Author, editor: Appropriate Technology and Development, 1984 (Choice award 1984); contbr. articles to jours. and chpts. to books. Recipient Engrs. and Scientists Econ. Devel. award NSF, 1973-74. Fellow Inst. Transp. Engrs.; mem. ASCE, African Studies Assn., Am. Planning Assn., Sigma Xi. Office: Ariz State U Ctr Advanced Research Transp Tempe AZ 85287

BEUCK, JULES EDWARD, psychiatric social worker; b. Chgo., July 31, 1950; s. William Frederick and Annette (Weinberg) B.; m. Rose Ann Botkin, June 1, 1980. BA in Psychology, Northeastern Ill. U., 1972; MSW, U. Ill., Chgo., 1983. Cert. social worker, Ill.; lic. clin. social worker, Calif. Dir. activities and rehab. Columbus Manor Ho., Chgo., 1973; alcoholism counselor Martha Washington Hosp., Chgo., 1973-76, Mercy Hosp. and Med. Ctr., Chgo., 1976-77; clin. therapist Northtown Rogers Park Mental Health Ctr., Chgo., 1977-85; psychiat. social worker Patton (Calif.) State Hosp., 1985—; mem. adv. bd. Assn. Ho. Mental Health and Alcoholism Program, Chgo., 1984-85. Dem. vol., Chgo., 1977-84. Mem. Nat. Assn. Social Workers (cert.), Phi Mu Alpha. Democrat. Jewish. Avocations: record collecting, science fiction, mystery reading, bowling, pinochle. Home: 1909 E Garvey Ave N #213 West Covina CA 91791 Office: Patton State Hosp 3102 E Highland Patton CA 92369

BEUERMAN, DAVID DUANE, chemical engineer; b. Hopewell, Va., Nov. 25, 1953; s. Donald Roy and Irma Janice (Lehman) B. BS in Chemistry, Montana Tech., 1978, MS in Geochemistry, 1986; cert. med. tech., St. James Community Hosp., 1979. Med. tech. intern. St. James Community Hosp., Butte, Mont., 1978-79; chemist Mont. Bur. Mines and Geology, Butte, 1979, MHD Task A., Butte, 1979-80; adj. instr. Mont. Tech., Butte, 1980-85; material and process engr. Lockheed Missiles and Space Co., Sunnyvale, Calif., 1985—. Avocations: hiking, camping. Home: 4200 Bay St #236 Fremont CA 94538 Office: Lockheed Missiles and Space Co Org 48-92 PO Box 3405 Sunnyvale CA 94088

BEUERMAN, DONALD ROY, chemistry educator; b. Stanton, Nebr., Mar. 16, 1928; s. Adolph and Mabel (Baumgartner) B.; m. Irma Janice Lehman, Aug. 18, 1950; children: David Duane, Donna Janice, Keith Lehman, Mark Devin. BS, Westmar Coll., 1949; MS, Kansas State U., 1961; PhD, Iowa State U., 1971. Cert. tchr., Iowa, Mo. Process engr. Allied Chem. Co., Hopewell, Va., 1953-59; research chemist Monsanto Corp., St. Louis, 1961-63; prof. chemistry Flat River (Mo.) Jr. Coll., 1963-64; asst. prof. N.W. Mo. State U., Maryville, 1964-71; prof., head dept. Mont. Coll. Mineral Sci. and Tech., Butte, 1971—; cons. in field; pres. Beuerman & Assocs., Butte., 1982—, sec. Fin. Mgmt. Cons. Mont., 1982—. Author: Environmental Science, 1975; contbr. articles to profl. jours.; patentee chem. separation processes. Treas., bd. dirs. ARC, Butte, 1980-86; pres. Aldersgate Found., Butte, 1985—. Served with U.S. Army, 1951-53. Mem. Am. Chem. Soc. (chmn. Mont. sect. 1972-73), Sigma Xi (chmn. local sect. 1975-76), Phi Lambda Upsilon. Home: 1236 W Platinum Butte MT 59701 Office: Mont Coll Mineral Sci and Tech W Park St Butte MT 59701

BEUG, MICHAEL WILLIAM, chemistry educator; b. Austin, Tex., May 18, 1944; s. Leonard Charles and Mildred Carolyn (Nitz) B.; m. Frances Ann Gresham, June 15, 1968; children: Christopher Michael, Benjamin Clayton. BS, Harvey Mudd Coll., 1966; PhD, U. Wash., 1971. Asst. prof.chemistry Harvey Mudd Coll., Claremont, Calif., 1971-72; prof. chemistry Evergreen State Coll., Olympia, Wash., 1972—, acad. dean, 1986—. Mem. AAAS. Home: 3732 Wesley Loop NW Olympia WA 98502 Office: Evergreen State Coll Olympia WA 98505

BEUGELSDIJK, TONY JOHN, chemist; b. Lisse, The Netherlands, Nov. 10, 1949; came to U.S., 1954; s. Leo Jacob and Annie Marie (DeRee) B.; m. Kathryn Argyle MacIvor, June 10, 1972 (div. Sept. 1986); children: Keith Alan, Kirk Hugh. BS, Wichita State U., 1971; MA, U. Ill., 1972, PhD, 1975. Research chemist Shell Devel. Co., Houston, 1975-84; mem. staff Los Alamos (N.Mex.) Nat. Lab., 1984—. Mem. Am. Chem. Soc., Sigma Xi. Republican. Home: 1027 Cedro Ct Los Alamos NM 87544 Office: Los Alamos Nat Lab PO Box 1663 MS E537 Los Alamos NM 87545

BEUTLER, LARRY EDWARD, psychology educator; b. Logan, Utah, Feb. 14, 1941; s. Edward and Beulah (Andrus) B.; m. M. Elena Oró, Feb. 25, 1977; children: Jana, Kelly, Ian David, Gail. BS, Utah State U., 1965, MS, 1966; PhD, U. Nebr., 1970. Diplomate Am. Bd. Clin. Psychology. Asst. prof. psychology Duke U., Ashville, N.C., 1970-71; asst. prof. Stephen F. Austin State U., Nacogdoches, Tex., 1971-73; assoc. prof. Baylor Coll. Medicine, Houston, 1973-79; prof. U. Ariz., Tucson, 1979—. Author: Eclectic Psychotherapy, 1983; assoc. editor Jour. Cons. Clin. Psychology, 1984—. Fellow Am. Psychology Assn., Internat. Acad. Eclectic Psychotherapy; mem. Soc. Psychotherapy Research (pres. 1986—). Home: 2301 E Waverly Tucson AR 85719 Office: U Ariz Dept Psychiatry Tucson AZ 85724

BEVAN, DONALD EDWARD, marine scientist, university dean; b. Seattle, Feb. 23, 1921; s. Arther and Violette B.; m. Tanya L. Potapova, Sept. 8, 1971. B.S., U. Wash., 1948, Ph.D., 1959; postdoctoral student, Moscow U., 1959-60. Sr. fisheries biologist U. Wash., Seattle, 1955-59; lectr., research asst. prof. U. Wash., 1959-61, research assoc. prof, 1961-64, assoc. prof., 1964-66, prof., 1966-86, prof. emeritus, 1986—, asso. dean Coll. Fisheries, 1965-69, dean, 1980-85, dir. Univ. Computer Ctr., 1968-69, asst. v.p. research, 1969-77, adj. prof. Inst. Marine Studies, 1973, acting dean and prof., 1977, assoc. dean and prof. Inst. Marine Studies, 1977-80, adj. prof. Inst. Marine Studies, 1978—, assoc. dean Coll. Ocean and Fishery Scis., 1984-86; pres., dir. Univ. Book Stores, 1977-86, prof. emeritus, 1986—; mem. US-USSR Pacific Fisheries Negotiations. Author articles and pamphlets in field. Served to capt., arty. U.S. Army, World War II. Decorated Purple Heart, Bronze Star. Mem. Pacific Region Fisheries Council (chmn. sci. and statis. com.), N. Pacific Fisheries Council, Marine Tech. Soc., Am. Inst. Fishery Research Biologists, Pacific Fisheries Biologists. Home: 29801 NE Cherry Valley Rd Duvall WA 98019 Office: U Wash Fisheries Center HA40 Seattle WA 98195

BEVAN, MARK HASTINGS, marketing professional; b. Hollywood, Calif., July 24, 1951; s. William Robert and Joanne (Hastings) B. AA in Video, Pasadena City Coll., 1972, AA in Theatre, 1973; BS in Mktg., U. So. Calif., 1976. Stage mgr. Am. Dance Theatre, Hollywood, 1971-73; coordinator, nat. adv. Kaiser/Aetna, Woodland Hills, Calif., 1973-76; dir. Am. Broadcasting Co., Century City, Calif., 1976-79; v.p. Hastings, Clayton & Tucker, Hollywood, 1979—; ptnr. Stiletto, Hollywood, 1979—; cons. C.E. Bent Parade Floats, Pasadena, Calif., 1967—. Big Brother, Big Bros. So. Calif., Glendale, 1982—. Office: Stiletto PO Box 69180 Hollywood CA 90069

BEVERETT, ANDREW JACKSON, merchandising executive; b. Midland City, Ala., Feb. 21, 1917; s. Andrew J. and Ella Levonie (Adams) B.; B.S., Samford U., 1940; M.B.A., Harvard U., 1942; m. Martha Sophia Landgrabe, May 26, 1951; children—Andrew Jackson III, James Edmund, Faye A. Various exec. positions in corporate planning and mgmt. United Air Lines, Chgo., 1946-66; dir. aviation econs., sr. mktg. and econ. cons. Mgmt. and Econs. Research, Inc., Palo Alto, Calif., 1966-71; sr. economist Stanford Research Inst., Menlo Park, 1971-72; pres. Edy's on the Peninsula stores, 1973-78; real estate broker, fin. and tax cons., Saratoga, Calif., 1979—. Served from ensign to lt. USNR, 1942-46. Mem. Nat. Assn. Enrolled Agts., Nat. Assn. Realtors, Pi Gamma Mu, Phi Kappa Phi. Home: 19597 Via Monte Dr Saratoga CA 95070 Office: 12175 Saratoga Sunnyvale Rd Suite A Saratoga CA 95070

BEVOLDEN, CURTIS LYLE, lawyer; b. Havre, Mont., Mar. 17, 1955; s. Alf Leroy and Marie Aileen (Haugo) B.; divorced; children: Kristin Marie, Evan Tyler. BA in History, Pacific Luth. U., 1979; JD, U. Mont., 1984. Bar: Mont. 1984, U.S. Dist. Ct. Mont. 1985, U.S. Ct. Appeals (9th cir.) 1985. Law clk. Mont. Supreme Ct., Helena, 1984; dep. county atty. Yellowstone County, Billings, Mont., 1985—. Bd. dirs. Head Start, Billings, 1985—, Community Day Care and Enrichment Ctr. Mem. ABA, Am. Trial Lawyers Assn. Lutheran. Avocations: swimming, running. Home: 2039 Cook #2 Billings MT 59102 Office: Yellowstone Couty Atty's Office Box 35025 Billings MT 59107

BEYER, EDGAR HERMAN, crop science educator; b. Melrose Park, Ill., Apr. 27, 1931; s. Herman and Martha (Luehrs) B.; m. Carol Lambeth, Apr. 24, 1954; children: Cynthia, Jeanne, Reid. BS, U. Ill., 1958; MS, Purdue U., 1962, PhD, 1964. Asst. prof. agronomy U. Md., College Park, 1963-66; research dir. Farm Seed Research Corp., San Juan Bautista, Calif., 1966-74; prodn. mgr. Ferry Morse Seed Co., Mountain View, Calif., 1974-81; assoc. prof. crop sci. Calif. Poly. State U., San Luis Obispo, 1981—. Contbr. articles to profl. jours. Chmn. bd. Young Life, Monterey County, Calif., 1970. Served to staff sgt. USAF, 1951-55. Mem. Am. Soc. Agronomy, Gideons (meml. chmn.), Sigma Xi, Phi Kappa Phi (sec. 1985-86). Republican. Lutheran. Avocations: photography, woodworking, golf. Home: 1358 Kentwood Dr San Luis Obispo CA 93401 Office: Calif Poly State U Crop Sci Dept San Luis Obispo CA 93407

BEYSTER, JOHN ROBERT, engineering company executive; b. Detroit, July 26, 1924; s. John Frederick and Lillian Edith (Jondro) B.; m. Betty Jean Brock, Sept. 8, 1955; children: James Frederick, Mark Daneil, Mary Ann. B.S. in Engring., U. Mich., 1945, M.S., 1948, Ph.D., 1950. Registered profl. engr., Calif. Mem. staff Los Alamos Sci. Lab., 1951-56; chmn. dept. accelerated physics Gulf Gen. Atomic Co., San Diego, 1957-69; pres., chmn. bd. Sci. Applications, Inc., La Jolla, Calif., 1969—; mem. Joint Strategic Target Planning Staff, Sci. Adv. Group, Omaha, 1978—; panel mem. Nat. Measurement Lab. Evaluation panel for Radiation Research, Washington, 1983—; dir. Scripps Bancorp, La Jolla, 1983. Co-author: Slow Neutron Scattering and Thermalization, 1970. Served to lt. comdr. USN, 1943-46. Fellow Am. Nuclear Soc., Am. Phys. Soc. Republican. Roman Catholic. Home: 9321 La Jolla Farms Rd La Jolla CA 92037 Office: Sci Applications Internat Corp 1200 Prospect St La Jolla CA 92038 *

BEZANSON, LLEWELLYN WELLS, chemical engineering educator, computer applications engineering consultant; b. Sodus, N.Y., Sept. 1, 1956; s. Robert Irving and Priscilla (Hutchinson) B.; m. Carol Susan Burnett, Aug. 23, 1981. BSChemE, U. Fla., 1979; MSChemE, Clarkson U., Potsdam, N.Y., 1981, PhDChemE, 1984. Instr. Clarkson U., 1981-83; asst. prof. Ariz. State U., Tempe, 1983—; cons. Motorola, Mesa, Ariz., 1984; engrng. cons. Honeywell, Phoenix, 1985; vis. prof. Hughes Aircraft, Tucson, 1986. Author: Computer Aided Controller Tuning and Simulation (CACTUS), 1984; contbr. articles to profl. jours. Recipient acad. excellence award, ARCO, Potsdam, 1981; Proctor & Gamble grad. fellow, Potsdam, 1979; engring. scholarship U. Buffalo, N.Y., 1974. Mem. Am. Inst. Chem. Engrs., Internat. Assn. Sci. Tech. Devel., Am. Soc. Engring. Edn., Sigma Xi, Tau Beta Pi. Republican. Clubs: Shotokan Karate (Tempe), Clarkson Outing (Potsdam). Avocations: running, hiking, travel, skiing, cycling. Office: Ariz State U Chem Engring Dept Tempe AZ 85287

BEZAR, GILBERT EDWARD, aerospace company executive; b. Phila., May 24, 1930; s. Abraham Bernard and Leah (Hymowitz) B.; m. Norma Jean Davis, Sept. 4, 1964 (dec. 1968); children—Eric David, Robyn Lisa. B.S. in Acctg., Temple U., 1951; M.B.A. in Fin. and Mgmt., UCLA, 1957. Vice pres. Armco-Hitco, Irvine, Calif., 1972-77; v.p. Armco Nat. Supply Co., Houston, 1977-81; v.p. fin. affairs, treas. Armco Nat. Supply Co., Middletown, Ohio, 1983-84; v.p. adminstrn. OCF Aerospace and Strategic Materials Group, Irvine, 1981-83; v.p. fin. and adminstrn. OCF Aerospace and Strategic Materials Group, Newport Beach, Calif., 1984—; dir. Oreg. Metall. Corp., Albany, 1982—, Hitco, Newport Beach, 1981—; instr. extension program UCLA, 1957-62, U. Calif.-Irvine, 1963-72. Served to lt. USNR, 1952-55. UCLA teaching fellow, 1955-57. Mem. Fin. Execs. Inst. (v.p. 1982-83), NAA Controllers Council, Beta Gamma Sigma. Republican. Jewish. Office: OCF Aerospace Strategic Materials Group PO Box 2140 Newport Beach CA 92658

BEZER, DAVID LEON, real estate appraiser; b. Phila., Nov. 25, 1943; s. Samuel and Frances (Rees) B.; m. Ellen Berkowitz, July 2, 1967; children: Daniel, Adam, Samara, John. Student, NYU, 1962-63, Temple U., 1969-70. Real estate salesman Magnus Internat. Inc., Camden, N.J., 1964-65; right of way agt. St. Davids, Pa., 1965-66; chief real estate appraiser Mfrs. Appraisal Co., Phila., 1966-70; exec. v.p. Enterprise Appraisal, Devon, Pa., 1971-75; pres. David L. Bezer & Co. Inc., Phila., 1975-86; v.p., treas. Valuation Network, Inc., N.Y.C., 1982-83, pres., 1983-84; pres. Valuation Network Inc. of So. Calif., San Diego, 1985-86; ptnr. VNI Rainbow Appraisal Service, San Diego, 1986—. Mem. Am. Inst. Real Estate Appraisers, Am. Soc. Appraisers. Democrat. Jewish. Home: 3844 Radcliffe Ln San Diego CA 92122 Office: VNI Rainbow Appraisal Service 11650 Iberia Pl Suite N San Diego CA 92128

BHAGAT, SANJAI, finance educator; b. India, Mar. 5, 1956. B.Tech. in Mech. Engring., Indian Inst. Tech., 1978; MBA, U. Rochester, 1980; PhD, U. Wash., 1982. Asst. prof. fin. U. Utah, Salt Lake City, 1982-85, assoc. prof., 1985—; vis. asst. prof. fin. and econ. U. Wash., Seattle, 1983-84; fin. economist SEC, Washington, 1983. Contbr. articles to profl. jours. Office: U Utah Grad Sch Bus Salt Lake City UT 84112

BHANDARI, ANIL KUMAR, cardiology educator; b. New Delhi, India, Jan. 26, 1953; came to U.S., 1977; s. Mukand Lal and Pushpa (Vij) B.; m. Eve-Marie Brindak, Mar. 29, 1980. Student, Panjab U., India, 1967-69; MB, BS, All India Inst. Med. Scis., New Delhi, 1975. Lic. physician, N.Y., Calif.; diplomate Am. Bd. Internal Medicine, Am. Bd. Cardiovascular Disease. Intern All India Inst. Med. Scis., New Delhi, 1975, resident in cardiology, 1976; intern in straight internal medicine SUNY, Stony Brook, 1977-78, resident in straight internal medicine, 1978-80; fellow in cardiology U. Rochester Med. Ctr., N.Y., 1980-82; fellow in clin. electrophysiology U. Calif. Med. Ctr., San Francisco, 1982-83; asst. prof. medicine Los Angeles County Med. Ctr. U. So. Calif., 1983—, staff physician, 1983—, dir. Electrophysiology Lab., 1985—; presenter numerous seminars, studies to univs., hosps. and agys., 1981—. Contbr. articles and revs. to profl. jours., chpts. to books. Grantee Am. Heart Assn., 1982-83, Sandoz Labs., 1983-84, 84—, Riker Labs. 1985—; fellow NIH, 1981-82, Am. Heart Assn., 1982. Mem. AAAS, Am. Heart Assn. (Los Angeles chpt.), Am. Coll. Cardiology, N. Am. Soc. Pacing and Electrophysiology, Assn. Physicians of Los Angeles County Hosps., Greater Los Angeles Electrophysiology Soc. Home: 2231 Pelham Ave Los Angeles CA 90024 Office: Los Angeles County U So Calif 2025 Zonal Ave Los Angeles CA 90033

BHANU, BIR, computer information scientist, educator, director university program; b. Etah, India, Jan. 8, 1951; came to U.S., 1975; s. Tameshwar Dayal Saksena and Om Vati; m. Archana Bhanu Bhatnagar, Dec. 21, 1982; 1 child, Shiv Bir. BS with honors, Inst. Tech., BHU, Varanasi, India, 1972; M in Engrng. with distinction, Birla Inst. Tech. and Sci., Pilani, India, 1974; SM and EE, MIT, 1975-77; PhD, U. So. Calif., 1981; MBA, U. Calif., Irvine, 1984. Lectr. in elec. engring. Birla Inst. Tech. and Sci., Pilani, 1974-75; acad. assoc. IBM Research Lab., San Jose, Calif., 1978; research fellow INRIA, Rocquencourt, France, 1980-81; engring. specialist Ford Aerospace and Communications Corp., Newport Beach, Calif., 1981-84; asst. prof. and dir. grad. admissions, dept. computer sci. U. Utah, Salt Lake City, 1984—; cons. U. Calif., Irvine, 1983-84, Evolving Tech. Inst., San Diego, 1983-85, Bonneville Sci. Co., Salt Lake City, 1985—; prin. investigator NSF and other agys., 1985—. Contbr. numerous articles on computer sci. to profl. jours. Recipient Project award for Outstanding Contribution, IBM Corp., 1978; research grantee Ford Aerospace and Communications Corp., 1986, NSF, 1985—. Mem. IEEE, Am. Assn. Artificial Intelligence, Assn. Computing Machinery, Soc. Photo-Optical and Instrumentation Engrs., Pattern Recognition Soc., Sigma Xi. Avocations: swimming, skiing, tennis, writing. Home: 2581 E Lynwood Dr Salt Lake City UT 84109 Office: U Utah 3160 M E B Dept Computer Sci Salt Lake City UT 84112

BHARDWAJA, PREM SAGAR, geophysicist, researcher; b. Rawalpindi, Panjab, Pakistan, Aug. 24, 1937; came to U.S., 1965; d. Haveli Ram and Kaushalya Rani Sharma; m. Kailash Mehta Bhardwaja, July 29, 1963; children: Nand Kishore, Sunita. BS, Agra U., Uttar Pradesh, India, 1957, MS, 1959; MA, Fisk U., 1966; PhD, U. Wash., 1976. Sr. sci. tchr. Khalsa Sch., Delhi, India, 1959-65; teaching and research asst. U. Wash., Seattle, 1969-75; research chemist Lawrence Berkeley Lab. U. Calif., Berkeley, 1976-77; sr. scientist Ill. Inst. Tech. Research Inst., Chgo., 1977-78; sr. staff scientist Salt River Project, Phoenix, 1978—. Mem. Project Polit. Involvement Com., Phoenix, 1982—. Fulbright scholar, 1965: NSF fellow, 1965-66; recipient Eugene Miller award U. Wash., 1969, Elizabeth Gould Meml. award. U. Wash., 1969. Mem. AAAS, Air Pollution Control Assn., Am. Pub. Power Assn. EEI's Utility Air Regulatory Group (co-chmn. visibility com. 1980—), Sigma Xi. Club: East Indian Rel. (treas. 1982-84). Avocations: tennis, golf, badminton. Office: Salt River Project PO Box 52025 Phoenix AZ 85072-2025

BIAETT, HEWITT, lawyer, former railroad exec.; b. Cotton Plant, Ark., Nov. 25, 1914; s. Doddridge Hewitt and Myrtle Louise (Woodruff) B.; student Phoenix Coll., 1934; LL.B., Coll. Law, U. Ariz., 1938; m. Ruthanne Migely, Feb. 8, 1941; children—Doddridge Hewitt III, Julie Jane, Walter M. Admitted to Ariz. bar, 1938, Ill. bar, 1939, Va. bar, 1947; atty. C., B. & Q. R.R., Chgo., 1938-42, commerce atty., 1942-46; gen. atty. C. & O. Ry. Co., 1946-53, gen. solicitor, 1953-58, gen. counsel, 1958-64; gen. atty. P.M. R.R., 1946-47, N.Y.C., & St. L. R.R., 1946-47; v.p. coal traffic and devel. B. & O. R.R., Balt., 1964-70; v.p. Lakefront Dock & R.R. Terminal Co.,1964-70, B. & O. R.R. Co. Chgo. Terminal, 1964-70, S.I. Rapid Transit Ry. Co., 1964-70, Monongahela Ry. Co., 1965-70, Western Pocahontas, Chesapeake Mineral Co., Chesapeake Toledo Corp., Cin. Inter-Terminal R.R. Co., Covington-Cin. Elevated R.R. Transfer & Bridge Co., all 1966-70; pres. Mid-Allegheny Corp., 1965-70, New Gauley Coal Corp., W. Va. & Pitts. Co., Littleton Fuel Co., 1966-70; v.p. Chesapeake and Ohio Railway Co., 1966-69; assoc. Glendale, Phoenix, 1970—; sec., dir. Gemini Pub. Co., 1978—. Served with USNR, 1944-46. Recipient Phi Delta Phi award, 1938. Mem. U. Ariz. Coll. Law Alumni Assn., Order of Coif. Clubs: Rons, Confederate Air Force. Home: 1301 W Townley Phoenix AZ 85021 Office: 1301 W Townley Phoenix AZ 85021

BIALOMIZY-HALE, MARYJANE, speech pathologist; b. Montgomery, Ala., May 27, 1956; s. Stanley Frank and Elizabeth Jane (Gutowski) Bialomizy; m. William Bradford Hale, Aug. 14, 1982. BSEd, SUNY, Fredonia, 1978; MA, San Diego State U., 1986. Speech-lang. specialist San Benito (Tex.) Sch. Dist., 1978-80, Cajon Valley Union Sch. Dist., El Cajon, Calif., 1980-82; tchr. severe lang. disorders Sweetwater Union High Sch. Dist., Chula Vista, Calif., 1984—. Leader Girl Scouts Am., San Diego, 1981—, del., troop organizer. Mem. Nat. Student Speech-Lang. Hearing Assn. (pres. coll. chpt. 1977-78), Am. Speech-Lang. Hearing Assn. (cert.), Council for Exceptional Children (sec. 1985—), Calif. Speech-Lang. Hearing Assn., Kappa Delta Pi. Home: 3979 Montefrio Ct San Diego CA 92130 Office: Sweetwater Union High Sch Dist Granger Jr High 1130 Fifth Ave Chula Vista CA 92010

BIBEL, DEBRA JAN, microbiologist, immunologist; b. San Francisco, Apr. 6, 1945; d. Philip and Bassya (Malzer) B. AB, U. Calif., Berkeley, 1967, PhD, 1972. Research microbiologist Letterman Army Inst. Research, San Francisco, 1972-79; tech. writer Hoefer Sci. Inst., San Francisco, 1979; research assoc. Kaiser Found. Research Inst., San Francisco, 1981-83; product mgr. Tago Inc., Burlingame, Calif., 1983-85; dir. Elie Metchnikoff Meml. Library, Oakland, Calif., 1977—, historian, 1986—; research assoc. U. Calif., San Francisco, 1987—; lectr. U. Calif., Berkeley, 1975, Antioch Coll., West San Francisco, 1975. Columnist Rummagings Along the Dusty Shelf, 1982—; contbr. articles to profl. jours. Mem. Ali Akbar Coll. Music, San Rafael, Calif.; instr. Berkeley Community Health Project, 1971-75. Served to capt. U.S. Army, 1972-76. Mem. ACLU, Am. Soc. Microbiology (archives com. 1986—), AAAS, Fedn. Am. Scientists, Assn. Women in Sci., No. Calif. Soc. Microbiology, Sierra Club. Buddhist. Avocations: painting, Asian philosophy, history of sci., music, rare books. Home and Office: 230 Orange St #6 Oakland CA 94610

BIBLE, PAUL ALFRED, lawyer, state official; b. Reno, Oct. 3, 1940; s. Alan and Loucile Pauline (Jacks) B.; m. Judith Lynn Schmidt, Mar. 21, 1970; children—Chad Alan, Patrick Marshall. Student U. Colo., 1958-59; B.A. in Econs., U. Nev., 1962; J.D., Georgetown U., 1965. Bar: D.C. 1965, Nev. 1965. Assoc. McDonald, Carano, Wilson, Bergin, Bible, Frankovich & Hicks, Reno, 1969-72, ptnr., 1972-83; sole practice, Reno, 1983-84; ptnr. Bible, Santini, Hoy, Miller & Trachok, Reno, 1984—; instr. Old Coll. Sch. Law, Reno, 1983; chmn. Nev. Gaming Commn., Reno, 1983-87. Contbr. articles to law revs. and profl. jours. Pres. DETRAP, Reno, 1971-73; mem. Nev. State Apprenticeship Council, Reno, 1971-83, chmn., 1971-83; mem. Truckee Meadows Community Coll. Found.; chmn. Truckee Meadows Community Coll. Adv. Bd., 1986; mem. Med.-Legal Screening Panel; active Boy Scouts Am., Reno. Served to capt. JAGC, U.S. Army, 1966-68. Recipient Henry Albert Pub. Service award U. Nev., 1962. Decorated Bronze Star medal. Mem. ABA, Assn. Trial Lawyers Am., Calif. Trial Lawyers Assn., Nev. Trial Lawyers Assn., Am. Arbitration Assn., Washoe County Bar Assn., Ducks Unltd. Democrat. Methodist. Club: Greenhead Hunting. Lodge: Rotary (pres. 1980-81). Office: Bible Santini Hoy Miller Trachok 232 Court St Reno NV 89501

BIBLE, WILLIAM ALAN, state government administrator; b. Reno, May 24, 1944; s. Alan H. and Loucille Pauline (Jacks) B.;m. LaVerne Jo McManus, July 30, 1965. BA with distinction, Stanford U., 1967; MBA, U. Nev., 1971. Dep. budget adminstr. State of Nev., Carson City, 1973-77, dir. adminstrn., 1983—; assembly fiscal analyst Legis. Counsel Bur., Carson City, 1977-83, dir. fiscal analysis div., 1981-83. Bd. dirs. Zephyr Cove (Nev.) Property Owners Assn., 1968-75, Carson City YMCA, 1977-81. Mem. Phi Kappa Phi. Democrat. Episcopalian. Home: PO Box 981 Zephyr Cove NV 89449 Office: Dept Adminstrn Blasdel Bldg Room 204 Carson City NV 89710

BICKAR, BETTY ARLENE, business systems executive; b. Plattville, Colo., Nov. 14, 1931; d. Leslie William and Kathryn Mabel (Rutherford) Clawson; children—Patricia J., Andrew L. Bookkeeper, office mgr. Manes Logging Co., Clallam Bay, Wash., 1958-70; lic. ins. agt. life and disability, Wash.; stenographer, prodn. acct. Crown Zellerbach Corp., Sekiu, Wash., 1970-73; bookkeeper, acct., office mgr., A. W. Logging Inc., Corner Bay, Alaska, 1973-79; owner, operator Spectra Northwest, specializing in photo identification and lamination, Bellevue, Wash., 1979—. Mem. Faith, Hope and Love Christian Ctr., Issaquah, Wash.; vol. counselor 700 Club. Mem. NCOA (counselor), Nat. Fedn. Ind. Bus. Home: 140th Ave NE Apt 16 Bellevue WA 98005 Office: Spectra Northwest 18-40 130th Ave NE Suite 6 Bellevue WA 98005

BICKERSTAFF, BERNIE LAVELLE, professional basketball coach; b. Benham, Ky.; m. Eugenia Bickerstaff; children: Tim, Robin, Cyndi, Bernard, John. Student, U. San Diego. Formerly asst. coach U. San Diego; then asst. coach Washington Bullets, Nat. Basketball Assn., Landover, Md.; head coach Seattle SuperSonics, 1985—. Office: care Seattle Supersonics 1980 Queen Anne Ave N Box 900911 Seattle WA 98109 *

BICKETT, JAMES ALAN, loss control administrator, safety consultant; b. Los Angeles, Apr. 30, 1945; s. James Albert and Lorraine Vivian (Muller) B.; m. Nancy Elaine Basil, Feb. 5, 1965; children—Darcel Nanette, Derek Douglas, Nicole Charmaine. A.A., Los Angeles Pierce Coll., 1971; B.A., Calif. State U.-Northridge, 1974. Cert. safety profl. Sr. prodn. planner Whittaker Corp., Northridge, 1968-73; mfg. mgr. Innovative Security Corp., Northridge, 1973-74; safety cons. State Compensation Ins. Fund, Ventura, Calif., 1974-80; loss control mgr. Safeco Ins. Co., Fountain Valley, Calif., 1980-82; safety cons. Unicare Ins. Co., Irvine, Calif., 1982—. Mem. Nat. Safety Council, Am. Soc. Safety Engrs., Democrat. Office: 2361 Campus Dr Irvine CA 92715

BICKNELL, BYRNA DEE, political scientist, educator; b. Norton, Kans., Sept. 12, 1938; d. Lawrence Roth and Thora Helen (Edson) B.; m. Vitus A. Cataldo, Mar. 17, 1955 (div.); children—Larry C., Paul A., Anthony C., Darci M. A.A., Grossmont Coll., 1975; B.A., San Diego State U., 1979. tchr. and vocat. counselor Calif. Adult guidance specialist Grossmont Coll., El Cajon, Calif., 1972-79; research and organizing coordinator San Diego/Imperial Counties Labor Council, San Diego, 1981-83, also coordinator Solidarity Day '81, San Diego; instr. San Diego Community Coll., 1981—; cons. in fin. planning and tax preparation. Mem. YWCA program devel. com.; edn. chmn., treas. Coalition Labor Union Women; charter mem., organizing steering com. CONCORD; founding mem. Networking; mem. coordinating counsel Regional Occupational Program; mem. accreditation com. student personnel services Grossmont Coll., mem. Title IX evaluation, grievance coms.; mem. Calif. Assemblyman Chacon's Com. on Minority and Women Entrepreneurs; mem. adv. com. Womens Ctr. and Studies. Mem. Am. Assn. Women in Community Colls., Indsl. Relations Research Assn. (exec. bd., pres. 1984-85), San Diego Soc. Sex Therapists and Edn. (hon.), Am. Fedn. Tchrs., San Diego Vocat. Guidance Assn., Nat. Ctr. Pub. Service Internship Programs, Nat. Assn. Enrolled Agts., Inland Soc. Tax Preparers, NOW, Nat. Women's Polit. Caucus. Office: 2496 E St San Diego CA 92102

BICKNELL, SUSAN MARCIA HERR, ecology educator; b. Indpls., July 30, 1949; d. George Aloysious and Marcia Louise (Edwards) Herr; m. Donald Wayne Bicknell, Jan. 30, 1971; 1 child, Jeffrey Joseph. AB in English, Ind. U., 1971; M in Forestry Sci., Yale U., 1975, PhD in Forest Ecology, 1978. From asst. prof. to assoc. prof. forestry Calif. State U.-Humboldt, Arcata, 1978—, chmn. dept. forestry, 1983—. Contbr. articles to profl. jours. Bd. dirs. Redwood Region Conservation Council, Santa Rosa, Calif., 1983—. Grantee McIntire-Stennis-Fed., Redwood Nat. Park, 1979-80, Inst. Ecosystem Studies, Redwood Nat. Park, 1985-86, Calif. Air Resources Bd., Calif. Dept. Parks and Recreations, 1985-87. Mem. Soc. Am. foresters, Ecol. Soc. Am. Avocations: woodworking, sewing, electronics, railroads. Office: Calif State U-Humboldt Dept Forestry Arcata CA 95521

BIDDLE, DONALD RAY, aerospace company executive; b. Alton, Mo., June 30, 1936; s. Ernest Everet and Dortha Marie (McGuire) B.; student El Dorado (Kans.) Jr. Coll., 1953-55, Pratt (Kans.) Jr. Coll., 1955-56; B.S. in Mech. Engring., Washington U., St. Louis, 1961; postgrad. computer sci. Pa. State U. Extension, 1963; certificate bus. mgmt. Alexander Hamilton Inst., 1958; m. Nancy Ann Dunham, Mar. 13, 1955; children—Jeanne Kay Biddle Bednosh, Mitchell Lee, Charles Alan. Design group engr. Emerson Elec. Mfg., St. Louis, 1957-61; design specialist Boeing Vertol, Springfield, Pa., 1962; cons. engr. Ewing Tech. Design, Phila., 1962-66; chief engr. rotary wing Gates Learjet, Wichita, Kans., 1967-70; dir. engring. Parsons of Calif. div. HITCO, Stockton, Calif., 1971—. Cons. engr. Scoutmaster, counselor, instl. rep. Boy Scouts Am., St. Ann, Mo., 1958-61; mem. Springfield Sch. Bd., 1964. Mem. Am. Helicopter Soc. (sec.-treas. Wichita chpt. 1969), ASME, Am. Mgmt. Assn., ASTM, Am. Inst. Aeros. and Astronautics,

Exptl. Pilots Assn. Republican. Methodist (trustee, chmn. 1974-76, 84-86). Patentee landing gear designs, inflatable rescue system, glass retention systems, adjustable jack system, cold weather start fluorescent lamp, paper honeycomb core post-process systems. Home: 1140 Stanton Way Stockton CA 95207 Office: 3437 S Airport Way Stockton CA 95206

BIDDLE, WAYNE THOMAS, oil and gas exploration company executive; b. Miller, S.D., May 13, 1924; s. Clifford Henry and Neva Berniece (Rhodes) B.; m. LaFawn H. Hall, Mar. 20, 1952; children—Belinda G., Barbara G. B.S. in Petroleum Engring., U. Okla., 1948. Engr., Stanolind Oil & Gas Co., Ardmore, Okla., 1948-50; sales engr. Dunigan Tool & Supply Co., Abilene, Tex., 1950-53; dir. mgr. Am. Iron & Machine Works, Denver, 1953-56; vice chmn. Exeter Drilling Co., Denver, 1956-83; owner Triple B Co., 1983—; also dir. Named Man of Month, Western Oil Reporter, 1971. Mem. Internat. Assn. Drilling Contractors (dir.), Ind. Petroleum Assn. Am., Am. Petroleum Inst. Republican. Congregationalist. Clubs: Denver Petroleum (Man of Year 1978), Cherry Hills Country (Englewood); Castle Pine (Castle Rock); Old Baldy (Saratoga, Wyo.); Fairbanks Ranch Country (Santa Fe, Calif.). Home: 4001 Nassau Circle Englewood CO 80110 Office: 1801 Broadway Suite 1204 Denver CO 80202

BIDWELL, ROY W., investment company executive, real estate developer and investor. came to U.S., 1958; m. Eileen Bidwell; children: Paul, Mark. Student, Enfield Tech. Coll., Ohio State U.; BA in Comml. Banking, Rutgers U. V.p. First Nat. Bank, Albuquerque, 1958-70; pres., chief exec. officer Rio Grande Title Co., Inc., Albuquerque, 1970—; vice chmn. N.Mex. Internat. Trade and Investment Council; chmn. N.Mex. Bus. and Investment Conv., London, 1984-85. Chmn. Exec. Liaison Com. Albuquerque Bd. Realtors; mem. Mayor's Community Econ. Devel. Action Grant com.; pres. St. Joseph Hosp. and Health Care Found; trustee St. Joseph Health Care Corp.; bd. dirs. Albuquerque Econ. Devel./Indsl. Found. of Ballet West N.Mex.; bd. dirs., chmn. Capital Campaign. Recipient Disting. Community Service award Anti-Defamation League B'nai Brith, 1984, Economic Devel. Achievement award Bus. Expo, 1987. Mem. Am. Inst. Banking (pres. Albuquerque chpt.), Am. Bankers Assn. (ednl. sect.), Albuquerque C. of C. (chmn. Perceptions Albuquerque task force, pres. 1983), New Mex. First Economic Forum. Clubs: Albuquerque Country, Albuquerque Petroleum. Home: 9919 Tanoan Dr NE Albuquerque NM 87111 Office: Rio Grande Title Co Inc PO Box 3565 Albuquerque NM 87190-3565

BIEDERMAN, DONALD ELLIS, lawyer; b. N.Y.C., Aug. 23, 1934; s. William and Sophye (Groll) B.; m. Marna M. Leerburger, Dec. 22, 1962; children: Charles Jefferson, Melissa Anne. AB, Cornell U., 1955; JD, Harvard U., 1958; LLM in Taxation, NYU, 1970. Bar: N.Y. 1959, Calif. 1977, U.S. Dist. Ct. (so. dist.) N.Y. 1967. Assoc. Hale, Russell & Stentzel, N.Y.C., 1962-66; asst. corp. counsel City of N.Y., 1966-68; assoc. Delson & Gordon, N.Y.C., 1968-69; ptnr. Roe, Carman, Clerke, Berkman & Berkman, Jamaica, N.Y., 1969-72; gen. atty. CBS Records, N.Y.C., 1972-76; v.p. legal affairs and adminstrn. ABC Records, Los Angeles, 1977-79; ptnr. Mitchell, Silberberg & Knupp, Los Angeles, 1979-83; v.p. legal and bus. affairs Warner Bros. Music, Los Angeles, 1983—; adj. prof. law Southwestern U., 1982—, Pepperdine U., 1985—. Editor: Legal and Business Problems of the Music Industry, 1980. Bd. dirs. Calif. Chamber Symphony Soc., Los Angeles, 1981—, AMC Med. Ctr., Los Angeles, 1986. Served to 1st lt. U.S. Army, 1959. Recipient Hon. Gold Record, Recording Industry Assn. Am., 1974, Trendsetter award Billboard Mag., 1976. Mem. N.Y. State Bar, State Bar Calif. Democrat. Jewish. Club: Riviera Country (Pacific Palisades, Calif). Avocations: golf, skiing, travel, reading. Home: 2406 Pesquera Dr Los Angeles CA 90049 Office: Warner Bros Music 9000 Sunset Blvd Los Angeles CA 90069

BIELER, CHARLES LINFORD, development director, zoo executive director emeritus; b. East Greenville, Pa., May 19, 1935; s. Frederick William and Emma May (Freed) B.; m. Judith L. Goodwin, Feb. 23, 1963; children: Stewart, Beatriz, Christina. B.A., Gettysburg (Pa.) Coll., 1957. Dir. tng. Gen. Motors Corp., 1962-69; mem. staff Zool. Soc. San Diego, 1969—, exec. asst. to dir., 1972-73, dir., 1973-85; bd. dirs. San Diego Conv. and Visitors Bur., 1983-85. Served with AUS, 1957-62. Recipient Gettysburg Coll. Disting. Alumni award, 1984. Fellow Am. Assn. Zool. Parks and Aquariums (pres. 1983-84). Home: 1915 Sunset Blvd San Diego CA 92103 Office: San Diego Zoo PO Box 551 San Diego CA 92112

BIENENSTOCK, ARTHUR IRWIN, physicist; b. N.Y.C., Mar. 20, 1935; s. Leo and Lena (Senator) B.; m. Roslyn Doris Goldberg, Apr. 14, 1957; children—Eric Lawrence, Amy Elizabeth (dec.), Adam Paul. B.S., Poly. Inst. Bklyn., 1955, M.S., 1957; Ph.D., Harvard U., 1962. Asst. prof. Harvard U., 1963-67; mem. faculty Stanford U., 1967—, prof. applied physics, 1972—, vice provost faculty affairs, 1972-77, dir. synchrotron radiation lab., 1978—; mem. U.S. Nat. Com. for Crystallography, 1983—; lectr., cons. in field. Author papers in field. Bd. dirs. No. Calif. chpt. Cystic Fibrosis Research Found., 1970-73, mem. pres.'s adv. council, 1980—; trustee Cystic Fibrosis Found., 1982—. Recipient Sidhu award Pitts. Diffraction Soc., 1968, Disting. Alumnus award Poly. Inst. N.Y., 1977; NSF fellow, 1962-63. Fellow Am. Phys. Soc.; mem. Am. Crystallographic Assn., AAAS, N.Y. Acad. Scis. Jewish. Home: 967 Mears Ct Stanford CA 94305 Office: Synchrotron Radiation Lab Bin 69 Box 4349 Stanford CA 94305

BIENVENU, ROBERT CHARLES, lawyer; b. Milw., Dec. 3, 1922; s. Harold John and Nellie (Davidson) B.; A.B., U. Calif., Berkeley, 1947; J.D., McGeorge Coll. Law, U. Pacific, 1953; m. Martha Beard, Mar. 28, 1945 (dec. 1969); children—Susan (Mrs. Mitchell Krestan), Nancy (Mrs. Gary Simas), John; m. 2d, Joyce Marlene Holley, Aug. 13, 1971. State parole officer Dept. Corrections, Sacramento, 1947-54; admitted to Calif. bar, 1954; since practiced in Modesto; mem. firm Hoover, Lacy & Bienvenu, 1954-66; individual practice, 1966—. Pres., Stanislaus County Sch. Bds. Assn., 1968-69; mem. Modesto City Schs. Bd. Edn., 1961-81; mem. Calif. Republican Central Com. 1960-70; bd. dirs. Modesto Symphony Orch., 1966-72, Retarded Children's Soc. Stanislaus County, 1965-70, Am. Cancer Soc., 1955-60. Served with AUS, 1942-45. Mem. State Bar Calif., Am., Stanislaus County bar assns., Am. Trial Lawyers Assn. Clubs: Modesto Racquet. Home: 218 Brook Way Modesto CA 95354 Office: 726 10th St Modesto CA 95354

BIER, JOHN L., insurance company executive; b. Pa., Nov. 15, 1936; s. John P. and Ruth P. (Stutzman) B.; m. Lillian M. Dial, Feb. 4, 1967; children: Stephen, James. BS in Geology, Muskingum Coll., 1958. Dept. mgr. Chubb & Son, Inc., Huntington, W.Va., 1964-66; unit mgr. Chubb & Son, Inc., Short Hills, N.J., 1966-68; asst. regional mgr. Chubb & Son, Inc., Chgo., 1968-70, regional mgr., 1970-79; zonal mgr. Chubb & Son, Inc., Sherman Oaks, Calif., 1979—, v.p.; v.p. Pacific Indemnity Co. Served to cpl. U.S. Army, 1959-65. Republican. Presbyterian. Clubs: La Canada Country, La Canada Hunt. Avocations: tennis, golf, cooking. Office: Chubb & Son Inc 15260 Ventura Blvd Sherman Oaks CA 91403

BIERI, CHRISTEL DORIS HESSELSCHWERDT, mfg. co. exec.; b. Karlsruhe, W. Ger., Apr. 29, 1938; came to U.S., 1962; d. Emil and Karolina Hesselschwerdt; m. Jurg H. Bieri, Apr. 21, 1962. B.S. in Langs., U. Geneva (Switzerland); M.A., U. Calif., Berkeley, 1966. Teaching asst. U. Calif., Berkeley, 1964-66, property mgr., 1966-73; bus. co-owner, gen. mgr. Vouvry, Switzerland, 1974-76; co-founder Heliodyne Inc., Richmond, Calif., 1976—, v.p. mktg., 1978—. Mem. No. Calif. Solar Energy Assn. (dir. 1978-80), Internat. Solar Energy Soc. (Am. chpt.), Calif. Solar Energy Industries Assn. Home: 2350 Alva Ave El Cerrito CA 94530 Office: 4910 Seaport Ave Richmond CA 94804

BIERSTEDT, PETER RICHARD, lawyer, film company executive; b. Rhinebeck, N.Y., Jan. 2, 1943; s. Robert Henry and Betty (MacIver) B.; m. Carol Lynn Akiyama, Aug. 23, 1980. A.B., Columbia U., 1965, J.D. cum laude, 1969; cert., Sorbonne, Paris, 1966. Bar: N.Y. bar 1969, Calif. bar 1977. Atty. with firms in N.Y.C., 1969-74; individual practice 1971, 75-76; with Avco Embassy Pictures Corp., Los Angeles, 1977-83; v.p., gen. counsel Avco Embassy Pictures Corp., 1978-80, sr. v.p., 1980-83, dir., 1981-83; gen. counsel New World Pictures, Los Angeles, 1984—, exec. v.p., 1984—; pres. subs. New World Prodns. and New World Advt. New World Pictures, 1985—; bd. dirs. New World Pictures (Australia), Ltd., FilmDallas Pictures, Inc., Cinedco, Inc.; guest lectr. U. Calif., Riverside, 1976, 77, U. So. Calif., 1986, UCLA, 1987. Mem. Motion Picture Assn. Am. (dir. 1980-83), Acad. Motion Picture Arts and Scis. (exec. br.), Am. Film Inst., N.Y. State Bar Assn., Los Angeles County Bar Assn., ACLU., AAAS. Office: New World Prodns 1440 S Sepulveda Blvd Los Angeles CA 90025

BIGGAR, CALVIN HENRY, materials and process engineer; b. San Francisco, May 30, 1920; s. Calvin Schurman and Effie Francis (Busch) B.; m. Christina Elizabeth King, Sept. 13, 1945; 1 child, John Morris. BA, U. B.C., Vancouver, Can. Chem. technician Dow Chem. Co., Pitts., 1940-41, Best Foods Co., San Francisco, 1951-53, W.P. Fuller Paint, South San Francisco, 1953-60; chemist Lockheed Missiles, Sunnyvale, Calif., 1960-68, Lockheed Electronics, Los Angeles, 1968-74; tech. dir. Electrofilm Inc., Valencia, Calif., 1975—. Served to sgt. Can. Army, 1941-45. Mem. Am. Soc. Lubrication Engrs. (program mgr. 1977-78). Home: 26829 Cuatro Milpas St Valencia CA 91355 Office: Electrofilm Inc 27727 Ave Scott Valencia CA 91355

BIGGERS, JOHN ALVIN, automotive and industrial executive; b. Durham, Calif., Oct. 27, 1926; s. Alvin C. and Bessie I. (Green) B.; m. Esther L. Debler, Apr. 20, 1946; children—Curt G., Merlene A. and Marlene J. (twins), Calvin B. Student pub. schs., Chico, Calif. and Sacramento. With Biggers Indsl. Gerlinger (formerly Gerlinger Motor Parts Inc.), Sacramento, 1944—, gen. mgr., 1950—, v.p., 1959-68, pres., 1968—; mem. No. Calif. adv. bd. Calif. Valley Bank; gen. ptnr. Auto Quip Leasing, 1973-83; chief exec. officer Johnny Biggers Video Prodns., Sacramento, 1983—; lectr. in field. Contractor-builder Rail Power Car for 1984 Los Angeles Olympics. Author automotive industries textbooks, also audio and video tape texts. Chmn. automotive sect. United Crusade, 1957-62; mem. dist. fin. com. Boy Scouts Am., 1959-62; bd. dirs., v.p. Sacramento Safety Council; pres. Sacramento Metro Industry Edn. Council, 1978-82, emeritus, 1983—; mem. adv. bd. Los Rios Jr. Coll. Dist.; charter mem. Ronald Reagan Presdl. Task Force; dir. music North Ch. of the Nazarene, 1946—, chmn. bd. stewards, bd. dirs., 1951, chmn. fin. com., 1972-77, 84-85, dir. Laymen's retreat bd., 1970-71, internat. rep. for Sacramento/Nev. dist., 1986—; sec. Sacramento Nazarene Dist. Adv. Bd., 1967-85, mem. internat. side com., internat. del. to Gen. Assembly Internat., 1964, 68, 72, 76, 80; chmn. bd. dirs. rewards council Sacramento Crime Alert, 1986-87; bd. dirs. Sacramento Diabetes Com. Named Hon. Dep. Sheriff, Sacramento, 1967—. Mem. Sacramento Parts Jobbers Assn. (pres.), Sacramento Camelia Soc., Automotive Wholesalers Assn., Eskaton Health Orgn., C. of C. Republican. Lodge: Rotary (chmn. world community service com. 1986-87). Office: Biggers Indsl Gerlinger 555 Sequoia Pacific Blvd Sacramento CA 95814

BIGGS, W(ALTER) GALE, company owner, consultant, meteorologist; b. Ft. Oglethorpe, Ga., May 6, 1935; m. Suzanne Kunkler, Sept. 1, 1956; children: Roxanne, Bruce. BS, Kans. State U., 1959; MS, U. Mich., 1960, PhD, 1966; Diploma, Soc. Soil and Found. Engrs., 1975. Sr. meteorologist Bendix Systems Div., Ann Arbor, Mich., 1960-66; asst. prof. Iowa State U., Ames, 1966-71; prin. Dames & Moore, Denver, 1971-76; sr. meteorologist Geomet, Gaithersburg, Md., 1976-77; environ. programs dir. Sci. Applications Internat. Corp., Boulder, Colo., 1977-82; owner, operator W. Gale Biggs Assocs., Boulder, Colo., 1982—; v.p. Aeroquad, Inc., Boulder, 1979-85; v.p., bd. dirs. Sierra Gulf Flyers, Broomfield, Colo., 1985—; guest speaker Rudarski Inst., Belgrade, Yugoslavia, 1980. Author: Earth Science, 1968; also articles. Chmn. Devils Thumb Townhouse Assn., Boulder, 1972-76; mem. Boulder County Clean Air Resource and Edn. Com., 1985—, People for Eldorado Mountain, 1985—, Colo. Air Quality Control Commn. Subcoms., Denver, 1985—. Served to sgt. N.G., 1953-61. Pub. Health Service fellow, 1961. Mem. AAAS, Air Pollution Control Assn., Am. Meteorol. Soc., Colo. Mining Assn. (air quality com. 1983—), Sigma Xi. Avocations: flying, antiques. Home: 59 Benthaven Pl Boulder CO 80303 Office: W. Gale Biggs Assocs. PO Box 3344 Boulder CO 80307

BIGLIONE, NORMAND JOSEPH, agriculture fertilizer company executive; b. Clovis, Calif., Aug. 12, 1925; s. Fred Julius and Kathryne Margaret (Andreis) B.; m. Shirley Jean Goodwin, Aug. 2, 1952; children—Lisa Normande, Normand Joseph. A.B., Calif. State U., 1949, M.A., 1951; postgrad. U. Okla., 1964. Commd. officer U.S. Army, 1951, advanced through grades to col., 1968, ret., 1970; assigned U.S. Army Command and Gen. Staff Coll., 1960-63, prin. staff asst., to U.S. comdr., West Berlin, W.Ger., 1964-67; chief tng. orgn. and readiness br. Policy and Programs Div., Directorate for Civil Disturbance, Washington, 1967-70; v.p., controller Nat. Bank of Agr., Fresno, Calif., 1971-75; exec. Western Farm Services, Shell Oil Co., Fresno, 1975-81; exec. Agr.-Fertilizer Co., Dos Palos, Calif., 1981—, controller, 1983—. Pres., Clovis Ctr.; pres. Fresno County Farm Bur., 1979-80, bd. dirs., 1981—. Decorated Legion of Merit, Bronze Star medal, Army Commendation medal with oak leaf cluster. Mem. Pacific Coast Quarter Horse Racing Assn., Am. Quarter Horse Assn., Sigma Alpha Epsilon. Democrat. Methodist. Clubs: Fresno Appaloosa (pres. 1974-75), Masons (32 deg.). Home: 12895 Auberry Rd Clovis CA 93612 Office: Agr Fertilizer Co PO Box 1145 Dos Palos CA 93620

BIKLE, DANIEL DAVID, research physician; b. Harrisburg, Pa., Apr. 25, 1944; s. Charles Augustus and Sarah Elizabeth (Yaukey) B.; m. Mary Elizabeth Wanner, June 20, 1965; children: Christine, Hilary. BA, Harvard U., 1965; MD, U. Pa., 1969, PhD, 1974. Diplomate Am. Bd. Internal Medicine; cert. Nat. Bd. Med. Examiners. Research intern Letterman Army Inst. Research, San Francisco, 1974-79; asst. prof. medicine U. Calif., San Francisco, 1979-86, assoc. prof. medicine, 1986—; co-dir. spl. diagnostic and treatment unit VA Med. Ctr., San Francisco, 1979—. Editor: Assay of Calcium Regulating Hormones, 1984; contbr. articles to profl. jours, chpts. to books. Served to col. USAR, 1974—. Research grantee NIH, 1979—, NASA, 1979—, VA, 1979—. Fellow ACP; mem. Endocrine Soc. (mem. editorial bd. 1984—), Am. Soc. Clin. Investigation, Am. Soc. Clin. Nutrition, Am. Fedn. Clin. Research. Republican. Mem. Christian Ch. Clubs: Commonwealth of Calif., Harvard (San Francisco). Avocations: biking, skiing, tennis, sailing. Office: VA Med Ctr 4150 Clement San Francisco CA 94121

BILBRAY, JAMES HUBERT, U.S. congressman, lawyer; b. Las Vegas, May 19, 1938; s. James A. and Ann E. (Miller) B.; student Brigham Young U., 1957-58, U. Nev., 1958-60; B.A., Am. U., 1962; J.D., Wash. U., 1964; m. Michaelene Mercer, Jan. 1960; children—Bridget, Kevin, Erin, Shannon. Admitted to Nev. bar, 1965; staff mem. Senator Howard Cannon, U.S. Senate, 1960-64; dep. dist. atty., Clark County, Nev., 1965-68; mem. firm Fadgen, Lovell, Bilbray & Pottery, Las Vegas, 1969—; mem. Nev. Senate, 1980-86; U.S. Rep. 100th Congress from 1st Nev. dist., 1987—; mem. Fgn. Affairs Com. subcoms. on Africa and on trade, Small Bus. Com., Select Com. on Hunger; chmn. taxation com., 1983-84, chmn. interim com. on pub. broadcasting, 1983; dir. Lenoy Corp., Las Vegas, 1968—, pres., 1979-80; alt. mcpl. judge City of Las Vegas, 1978-80. Bd. regents U. Nev. System, 1968-72; mem. nat. council State Govts. Commn. on Arts and Historic Preservation. Named Outstanding Alumni, U. Nev., Las Vegas, 1979, U. Nev.-Las Vegas Humanitarian of the Year, 1984. Mem. Nev. State Bar Assn., Clark County Bar Assn., Phi Alpha Delta, Sigma Chi. Democrat. Roman Catholic. Lodges: Elks, Rotary. Office: Rm 1431 Longworth House Office Bldg Washington DC 20515

BILBY, RICHARD MANSFIELD, federal judge; b. Tucson, May 29, 1931; s. Ralph Willard and Marguerite (Mansfield) B.; m. Ann Louise Borchert, July 6, 1957; children: Claire Louise, Ellen Markley. B.S., U. Ariz., 1955; J.D., U. Mich., 1958. Bar: Ariz. bar 1959. Since practiced in Tucson; law clk. to Chief Judge Chambers, 9th Circuit Ct. Appeals, San Francisco, 1958-59; mem. firm Bilby, Thompson, Shoenhair & Warnock, 1959-79, partner, 1967-79; judge U.S. Dist. Ct., Dist. Ariz., Tucson, 1979—; chief judge U.S. Dist. Ct., Dist. Ariz., 1985—; conscientious objector hearing officer Dept. Justice, 1959-62; chmn. (Pima County Med.-Legal panel), 1968-70; Mem. Tucson Charter Revision Com., 1965-70. Chmn. United Fund Profl. Div., 1968; chmn. Spl. Gift Div., 1970, St. Joseph Hosp. Devel. Fund Drive, 1970; Republican state chmn. Vols. for Eisenhower, 1956; Rep. county chmn., Pima County, Ariz., 1972-74; Past pres. Tucson Conquistadores; bd. dirs. St. Josephs Hosp., 1969-77, chmn., 1972-75. Served with AUS, 1952-54. Fellow Am. Coll. Trial Lawyers; mem. Ariz. Acad., Town Hall (dir. 1976-79). Home: 4717 Brisa Del Sur Tucson AZ 85718 Office: US Courthouse 55 E Broadway Tucson AZ 85701

BILEZIKJIAN, EDWARD ANDREW, architect; b. Los Angeles, Mar. 29, 1950; s. Andrew and Alice (Dardarian) B. BSArch, U. So. Calif., 1973, MArch, 1977. Registered architect, Calif. Project mgr. RMA Archtl. Group, Inc., Costa Mesa, Calif., 1977-78; dir. architecture Donald De Mars Assocs., Inc., Van Nuys, Calif., 1978-85; prin. architect EAB Architects, Sepulveda, Calif., 1985-86; architect, planner III Trammell Crow Co., Irvine, Calif., 1986—. Mem. AIA, Archtl. Guild U. So. Calif., Triple-X Fraternity of Calif. (corresponding sec. 1984-85), Nat. Council Archtl. Registration Bds. (cert.). Democrat. Mem. Armenia Apostolic Ch.

BILLER, ALAN DAVID, management consultant; b. N.Y.C., Sept. 4, 1944; s. Newman M. and Dorothy (Jacobs) B.; m. Janet E. Burack, Sept. 11, 1966; children: Katherine N., Margaret L. BA, Yale U., 1965; MPhil, U. of London, 1967; PhD, Columbia U., 1970; MBA, Harvard U., 1975. Asst. prof. philosophy Pomona Coll., Claremont, Calif., 1970-72; loan officer Wells Fargo, San Francisco, 1975-78; sr. cons. A.D. Little Inc., San Francisco, 1979; dir. investment industries SRI Internat., Menlo Park, Calif., 1979-82; pres. Alan D. Biller & Assocs., Palo Alto, Calif., 1982—. Contbr. articles to profl. jours. Pres. Childrens Ctr. of Stanford, Calif., 1978-79; bd. dirs. and treas., Peninsula French-Am. Sch., Palo Alto, Calif., 1982—. Fellow NEH 1972, Woodrow Wilson, Eldridge, Yale-Carnegie 1965; Baker scholar, Harvard U. Bus. Sch., 1975. Clubs: Berzelius (New Haven), Century (Cambridge, Mass.), Ladera Oaks (Portola Valley, Calif.) (mem. fin. com. 1985). Home: 121 Fulton St Palo Alto CA 94301 Office: Alan D Biller & Assocs Inc PO Box 879 Palo Alto CA 94302

BILLIGMEIER, ROBERT HENRY, sociologist, educator; b. McClusky, N.D., Jan. 16, 1917; s. Henry and Meta Berta (Masueger) B.; m. Hanny Marie Salvisberg, Jan. 20, 1940; children—Jon Christian, Robin Hanny, Carina. A.B., Stanford U., 1938, Ph.D., 1951; M.A., U. Calif.-Berkeley, 1939. Population analyst U.S. Dept. State, Washington, 1943-45; instr. Stanford U., 1946-50; instr. to prof. sociology U. Calif.-Santa Barbara, 1952—; assoc. dir. U. Calif. Edn. Aboard program, 1964-75. Mem. Am. Hist. Soc., Population Soc. Am., Am. Sociol. Assn. Democrat. Author: Americans from Germany: A Study of Cultural Diversity, 1974; A Crisis in Swiss Pluralism, 1979. Home: 398 Stevens Rd Santa Barbara CA 93105 Office: U Calif Dept Sociology Santa Barbara CA 93106

BILLINGS, BRUCE HADLEY, physicist, aerospace company executive; b. Chgo., July 6, 1915; s. Thomas H. and Grace (Hadley) B.; m. Sarah Winslow, June 23, 1938 (div.); children: Sally Frances, Bruce Randolph, Jane Winslow, Peter Fayssoux; m. Fannie Hu. A.B., Harvard U., 1936, A.M., 1937; Ph.D., Johns Hopkins U., 1943; hon. Ph.D., China Acad. Tchr. math. sci. Am. Community Sch., Beirut, 1937-40; jr. instr. physics Johns Hopkins U., Balt., 1940-41; physicist Polaroid Corp., Cambridge, Mass., 1941-47; mem. radiol. safety sect. atomic bomb test Bikini, 1946; dir. research Baird-Atomic, Inc., Cambridge, 1947-63; exec. v.p. Baird-Atomic, Inc., 1955-59, v.p. and tech. dir., 1960-63; v.p., gen. mgr. labs. operation Aerospace Corp., Los Angeles, 1963-68; v.p. corp. planning Aerospace Corp., 1973-74; v.p. Aerospace Corp., Washington, 1974-76; pres. Thagard Research Corp., 1976-80; chmn. bd. Internat. Tech. Assocs., Inc., 1977—, dir. research, 1980—; commr. Joint Commn. on Rural Reconstrn.; spl. asst. to Am. ambassador for sci. and tech., Taipei, Taiwan, 1968-73; mem. sci. adv. com. Bell & Howell; dir. Ealing Corp., Diffraction, Ltd., Inc., Altovac Tech., Inc.; mem. Air Force Sci. Adv. Bd., 1962-72; asst. dir. def. research and engring. Dept. Def., 1959-60; U.S. del. Marseille Conf. on Thin Films, 1949; U.S. rep. on UN Adv. Com. on Application of Sci. and Tech. to Devel., 1973-78; mem. U.S. nat. com. Internat. Commn. Optics; research asso. Harvard Coll. Obs.; cons. Dept. State, 1973-82; adj. prof. Harvey Mudd Coll., 1986—; fellow East Asian Studies Ctr., U. So. Calif. dir. Laser Sci., Inc., Milco Internat. Inc.; bd. dirs. Physical Optics Corp. Assoc. editor: Inst. Physics Handbook; subject editor: Applied Optics; Contbr. tech. articles to profl. jours. Decorated Order of Brilliant Star Republic of China. Fellow Am. Acad. Arts and Scis. (sec.), Am. Phys. Soc., Optical Soc. Am. (asso. editor jour. 1956-60, pres. 1971, v.p. internat. commn. of optics 1973); mem. Acoustical Soc. Am., AAAS, Sigma Xi. Club: St. Botolph. Office: 7303 N Marina Pacifica Dr Long Beach CA 90803

BILLINGS, DONALD LAWRENCE, motivation company executive; b. Jamaica Plains, Mass., Mar. 25, 1946; s. William Ricker and Marjorie (Gaffney) B.; m. Marilyn Smith, Jan. 16, 1970; children: Heather Nicole, Adam Lawrence. Student, Orange Coast Coll., 1964-66, Calif. State U., Long Beach, 1966-68. Lic. in travel by Mass. Dept. Edn. Various mgmt. positions 1968-76; travel industry specialist Integral Bus. Computing, Los Angeles, 1976-78; v.p. sales. Automated Travel Acctg. Systems, Los Angeles, 1976-78; travel exec. Maritz Travel Co., St. Louis, 1978-81; v.p. mktg. Corp. Resort and Travel, Irvine, Calif., 1981-83, Joint Venture Travel, Orange, Calif., 1983-84; account mgr. Maritz Motivation Co., St. Louis, 1984—. Editorial cons. Fin. Communications in the Travel Industry, 1982-83. Mem. Am. Mktg. Assn., Soc. Incentive Travel Execs., Inst. Cert. Travel. Agts. (cert. travel cons.). Republican. Avocations: reading, tennis, golf, travel. Home and Office: 7620 Cortina Ct Rancho La Costa CA 92009

BILOWITZ, LOUIS I., pensions and insurance consultant; b. N.Y.C., Apr. 22, 1947; s. Herman and Arline (Ochs) B.; m. M. Carol Lingo, Aug. 20, 1972; children: Kyle, Shane. Ptnr. Pension Architects, Los Angeles, 1977—, Ins. Architects, Los Angeles, 1977—; pres. Corporate Pensions Insurance Services, Inc., Los Angeles, 1983—; lectr. on pensions, 1983—. Author: Pension Planning, 1984. Chief regional coach American Youth Soccer Orgn., Pasadena, Calif., 1985; jr. varsity soccer coach La Canada (Calif.) High Sch., 1985—; founding father coach Foothill Flyers Soccer Club, 1986—; active UCLA Coaches' Roundtable, 1986—; nation chief YMCA Indian Guides, La Canada, 1985; active UCLA Sportsman of the South, 1985—. Republican. Avocations: basketball and baseball coaching. Office: Pension Architects 716 S. Olive St 2d Floor Los Angeles CA 91011

BINDER, JAMES KAUFFMAN, computing consultant; b. Reading, Pa., Nov. 20, 1920; s. Paul Burdette and Edna (Kauffman) B.; B.A., Lehigh U., 1941; M.A., Johns Hopkins U., 1952; profl. cert. in systems mgmt. U. Calif.-San Diego, 1976; A.S. in Data Processing, San Diego Evening Coll., 1979, A.A. in Fgn. Lang., 1979; A.A. in Spanish, Mira Costa Coll., Oceanside, Calif., 1981. Instr. English, Notre Dame U., South Bend, Ind., 1948-49; prof. English, Athens (Greece) Coll., 1950-51; CARE rep., Greece, 1951-52; reporter, staff writer Athens News, 1952-53; dir. lang. tng. World Council Chs. Refugee Service, Athens, 1953-54; co-editor Am. Overseas Guide, N.Y., West Berlin, 1957-58; lectr. English, U. Md. Overseas Program, European and Far East divs., 1958-66; successively supr. Cen. Info. Ctr., supt. documents, sr. systems analyst GA Techs., Inc., La Jolla, Calif., 1968-85. Recipient Williams Prize, Lehigh U., 1939, 41; Johns Hopkins U. Grad. Sch. Pres. scholar, 1945-48. Mem. San Diego Opera Assn., Friends of U. Calif.-San Diego Library, IEEE Computer Soc., Assn. Computing Machinery. Roman Catholic. Clubs: Tudor and Stuart, Automobile of So. Calif. Author: The Correct Comedy, 1951; contbg. translator Modern Scandinavian Poetry, 1948; editor: (with Erwin H. Tiebe) American Overseas Guide, 1958.

BINDNER, LOUIS ROBERT, air conditioning executive, mutual fund director; b. Louisville, Sept. 28, 1925; s. Louis Christopher and Bertha Viola (Wernz) B.; divorced; children: Carrie, Eric, Gail, Mark. BSME, Northwestern U., 1946. Registered profl. engr., Colo. Sales engr. Worthington Corp., Chgo., 1947-51, Carrier Corp., Denver, 1954-59, Trane Co., Denver, 1959-62; gen. mgr. Snodgrass & Smith, Denver, 1963-65; owner, pres. Climate Engring., Denver, 1965—; ind. dir. 100/101 Mutual Fund, Denver, 1975—. Mem. Denver Rep. Club. Served with USNR, 1943-46, 52-53. Mem. ASHRAE (pres. local chpt. 1959-60), Air Conditioning Contractors Am. (pres. 1981-82). Avocations: skiing, tennis, handball, bicycling, softball. Home: 9021 E Amherst Dr F Denver CO 80231 Office: Climate Engring Inc 1075 S Fox St Denver CO 80223

BINEGAR, GWENDOLYN ANN, social worker; b. Phoenix, Sept. 23, 1924; d. Glenn Marvin and Mary Lenore (Cartwright) Redington; B.S. in Sociology, Iowa State U., 1948; M.Social Service, Bryn Mawr Coll., 1967; m. Lewis Albert Binegar, Nov. 2, 1951; children—Glen Albert, Birne Thomas, William Lewis, Alan Martin. Coordinator vols. Santa Barbara Mental Health Service, Lompoc, Calif., 1964; psychiat. social worker Child Study Inst., Bryn Mawr (Pa.) Coll., 1967-71; sr. social worker Ruth Sch. for Girls, Seattle, 1972; staff worker Nat. Assn. Social Workers, Los Angeles, 1973;

med. social worker Casa Colina Hosp., Pomona, Calif., 1974; supervising counselor San Gabriel Valley Regional Center, Pomona, 1975-78, program mgr. six Los Angeles County Regional Centers' High Risk Infant Projects, 1978-79; chief case mgmt. services San Diego Regional Center, 1981—. Lic. clin. social worker. Mem. Am. Acad. Certified Social Workers, Am. Assn. on Mental Deficiency (chair region II prevention com. 1983—), Nat. Assn. Social Workers. Republican. Presbyterian. Home: 28809 Lilac Rd Valley Center CA 92082 Office: San Diego Regional Ctr 4355 Ruffin Rd San Diego CA 92123

BINGAMAN, JEFF, senator; b. Silver City, N.Mex., Oct. 3, 1943; s. Jesse and Beth (Ball) B.; m. Anne Kovacovich, Sept. 13, 1968. Ed., Harvard U., 1965; J.D., Stanford U., 1968. Bar: N.Mex. 1968. Partner firm Campbell, Bingaman & Black, Santa Fe, 1972-78; atty. gen. State of N.Mex., from 1979; now U.S. senator from N.Mex. Democrat. Methodist. Home: PO Box 5775 Santa Fe NM 87501 Office: 502 Hart Senate Bldg Washington DC 20510 *

BINGHAM, EDWIN RALPH, history educator; b. Denver, Jan. 21, 1920; s. Guy Edwin and Helen (Hinckley) B.; m. Helen Hopkins, 1943 (div. 1951); children: Susan Kimball, Linda Christine; m. Virginia Wright, Aug. 24, 1952; children: Sheila Jeanne, Sara Lisa. BA, Occidental Coll., 1941, MA, 1942; PhD, UCLA, 1951. Instr. history U. Oreg., Eugene, 1949-51, asst. prof., 1952-57, assoc. prof., 1958-64, prof., 1965—, prof. emeritus, 1982—; Fulbright lectr. Mysore U., India, 1977-78; lectr. U. Shandong, Jinan, Peoples' Republic of China, 1985. Author: Charles F. Lummis, Editor of the Southwest, 1955, Oregon!, 1978; contbr. articles to profl. jours. Mem. Oreg. Geog. Names Bd., Portland, 1965—. Served to 1st lt. USAAF, 1942-46. Grantee Ford Found., Yale U., 1954-55. Mem. Am. Hist. Assn. (pres. Pacific coast br. 1985-86), Oreg. Hist. Soc. Democrat. Avocations: reading, walking, biking, white water canoeing. Home: 118 Tree Hill Loop Eugene OR 97405 Office: U Oreg Dept History Eugene OR 97403

BINNIE, NANCY CATHERINE, nurse, educator; b. Sioux Falls, S.D., Jan. 28, 1937; d. Edward Grant and Jessie May (Martini) Larkin; m. Charles H. Binnie. Diploma, St. Joseph's Hosp. Sch. Nursing, Phoenix, 1965; BS in Nursing, Ariz. State U., 1970, MA, 1974. Intensive care charge nurse Scottsdale (Ariz.) Meml. Hosp., 1968-70, coordinator critical care, 1970-71; coordinator critical care John C. Lincoln Hosp., Phoenix, 1971-73; prof. nursing GateWay Community Coll. (formerly Maricopa Tech. Community Coll.), Phoenix, 1974—; part-time coordinator evening nursing programs Maricopa Tech. Community Coll., 1984—. Named Outstanding Faculty Employee Maricopa Tech. Community Coll., 1986, Innovator of Yr. Maricopa Tech. Community Coll., 1986. Mem. Orgn. Advancement of Assoc. Degree Nursing. Avocations: gardening, golf, sewing. Office: Maricopa Tech Community Coll 104 N 40th St Phoenix AZ 85034

BINTZ, CHARLES THOMAS, stockbroker; b. Salt Lake City, Dec. 9, 1923; s. Charles Carroll and Denise (Karrick) B.; m. Dorothy Cornish, Apr. 28, 1945; children: Dorothy, Martha, Charles, Brian. BA, Cornell U., 1947. Vice pres. sales W. H. Bintz Co., Salt Lake City, 1958-67, chmn. bd., 1970-84; acct. exec. Merrill Lynch, Salt Lake City, 1967-77, v.p., 1977—; chmn. Diversified Investment Corp., Salt Lake City, 1970-84. Mem. bd. dirs. YMCA, Westminster Coll. Found. Served with USNR, 1943-45. Methodist. Clubs: Alta, Salt Lake Tennis, Salt Lake Country. Home: 2550 Elizabeth St Salt Lake City UT 84106 Office: Merrill Lynch Pierce Fenner & Smith 60 East South Temple Salt Lake City UT 84111

BIRCUMSHAW, T(HOMAS) MICHAEL, lecturer, consultant, author; b. Alhambra, Calif., May 18, 1939; s. Thomas Walter and June Rose (McHan) B.; m. Jeannette Ruth Sonder, July 26, 1980; children: Renee, Jamie, Michael, Jaqi, Jeremy. AA, U. Md., 1971, BA with honors, 1972; postgrad., U. No. Colo., 1976-77. Commd. USN, 1956, advanced through grades to chief warrant officer, 1974, ret., 1976; mgr. Stockdale Corp., Salt Lake City, 1978-80; pres. Aspects Unlimited., Hollywood, Calif., 1980-84; cons. The Mgmt. Bus., Hollywood, 1984—; lectr. and author on drug awareness Delta Ednl. Found., Glendale, Calif., 1985—; bd. dirs. Los Angeles Fedn. of Community Coordinating Council. Mem. task force on drug and alcohol abuse City of Los Angeles, 1986. Recipient Outstanding Service award Los Angeles Fedn. of Community Coordinating Council, 1986. Mem. Nat. Speakers Assn., Frazier Park C. of C. Lodge: Lions (Los Angeles University chpt. dep. dist. gov. 1987—, zone chmn. dist. 4L3 1986-87). Avocations: motorcycles, fishing, sailing. Office: The Mgmt Bus 1161 N Highland Hollywood CA 90038-1204

BIRD, BRIAN REX, writer, communications consultant; b. Kewanee, Ill., May 28, 1957; s. Robert Vincent and Rachel Marion (Benson) B.; m. Patricia Ann Richardson, Dec. 13, 1980; children: Benson Daniel, Cameron Joel. BA, Calif. State U., Fullerton, 1980. Sports editor Highlander Publs., Hacienda Heights, Calif., 1975-78; staff writer San Gabriel Valley Tribune, West Covina, Calif., 1978-80; media relations officer World Vision, Monrovia, Calif., 1980—; ind. screen writer, journalist, pub. relations cons. Monrovia, 1982—; cons. Russ Reid Co., Pasadena, Calif., 1986—, Victory Communications Inc., Scottsdale, Ariz., 1986—. Author: Fantasy Island, 1984, Strang Communications, 1985—; screenwriter Final Adieu/Fantasy Island, 1984; (documentaries) Suffer the Children, 1986, The Porn Plague, 1986; contbr. articles to profl. jours. Recipient Best Issue Analysis Series award Press Club of Los Angeles, 1980, Prism award for Internat. Video News Conf. Pub. Relations Soc. Am., 1985. Mem. Fellowship of Christians in the Arts Media and Entertainment, Writer's Guild of Am., Sigma Delta Chi. Baptist. Avocations: fgn. travel, reading, photography, cinema. Home: 2701 Blue Fox Dr Ontario CA 91761 Office: World Vision 919 W Huntington Dr Monrovia CA 91016

BIRD, CHARLOTTE SOETERS, public administration analyst; b. Burley, Idaho, July 15, 1947; d. Harold J. and Dorothy L. (Breakey) Soeters; m. Charles A. Bird, June 28, 1969. B.A. in Anthropology, U. Calif.-Davis; M.A. in Pub. Adminstrn., U. Alaska, 1975. Adminstrv. asst. U. Calif.-Davis, 1970-73; analyst State of Alaska Dept. Labor, Juneau, Alaska, 1973-74, adminstrv. asst. tng. specialist Dept. Human Services, 1975-79, budget analyst Office Mgmt. Budget, 1979-82, mgmt. analyst exec. asst. Office Chief Adminstrn., County of San Diego, 1982-83, personnel officer EDP services dept., 1983-86. Mem. Spl. Fund Devel. Task Force; mem. fund devel. com. San Diego, Imperial Counties Girl Scouts U.S., mediator San Diego Community Mediation Program, 1985—; paricipant LEAD San Diego, Inc., 1985. Mem. Calif. Women in Govt. (program chmn. 1980-81, dir. 1979-83), Am. Soc. Pub. Adminstrn. (chpt. v.p. 1981-83), Women in Mgmt., Children's Home Soc. Calif. (dist. bd. dirs. 1983—, chmn. budget com. 1985, chmn. program com. 1986) Democrat. Author job opportunity information booklets Alaska depts. labor and edn., 1974. Office: County of San Diego Dept EDP Services 1600 Pacific Hwy San Diego CA 92101

BIRD, DAVID A(LBERT), electronics engineer; b. Indpls., July 26, 1941; s. Philip H. and Alberta V. (Davisson) B.; m. Nina Lavena Jane Parks, Nov. 28, 1968; 1 stepchild, B. Randall Bird; 1 child, Deborah E. Bird. BSEE with distinction, Purdue U., 1964; student, Princeton U., 1965; MSEE, Calif. Inst. Tech., 1966. Engr. Info. Systems div. Gen. Elec. Co., Phoenix, 1966-69; sr. engr. Honeywell Info. Systems, Phoenix, 1970-78; mem. devel. staff I Union Carbide Nuclear div., Oak Ridge, Tenn., 1979-83; mem. devel. staff II Martin Marietta Energy Systems, Oak Ridge, 1984; staff engr. II Large Computer div. Honeywell Corp., Phoenix, 1985, staff engr. II Solid-State Electronics div., 1986—; cons. Govt. Can., Union Carbide, Martin Marietta, 1983-84. Patentee in field. Mem. IEEE, Tau Beta Pi, Sigma Pi Sigma. Baha'i. Avocations: telescopes, fishing, family activities. Office: SSED Micro Tech Ctr B176 PO Box 8000 Phoenix AZ 85029

BIRD, JANICE MARIE, educational counselor; b. Pampa, Tex., Mar. 31, 1953; d. Albert and Harriet Frances (Cosgrove) B. B.A. in Edn., Northeastern Okla. State U., 1976, M.Ed., 1979. Tchr., Rattan (Oklan.) Pub. Schs., 1976-78; residence counselor Northeastern Okla. State U., Tahlequah, 1978-79; ednl. counselor Campbell County Sch. Dist., Gillette Wyo., 1979—. Active community choir, 1982-83; choir dir. First Presbyn. Ch., 1985—; musical dir. Community Theater, 1985. Mem. Am. Personnel Guidance Assn., Wyo. Personnel and Guidance Assn., Wyo. Corrections Assn., NEA, Wyo. Edn. Assn. Home: 2210 Wagonhammer Ln Gillette WY 82716 Office: Campbell County School District 7th and Gillette Ave Gillette WY 82716

BIRD, MICHAEL EARL, health science facility administrator; b. Santa Fe, Dec. 7, 1951; s. Earl L. and Petrolena (Archuleta) B. BS, U. Utah, 1976, MSW, 1977; MPH, U. Calif., Berkeley, 1983. Social work supr. USPHS Indian Health, Santa Fe, 1977-81; program analyst USPHS Indian Health, Albuquerque, 1984-86, chief tribal health programs br., 1986—. Chmn. Am. Indian Mental Health Task Force, Santa Fe, 1980-81; bd. dirs. Health Net N.Mex., Albuquerque, 1985-86, N.Mex. Humanities Council, 1985-86. Named Indian Man of Yr., U. Utah, 1976-77, Health Profl., Nat. Indian Health Bd., 1985; Am. Indian fellow, 1982-83; recipient Health Promotion and Disease Prevention in Indian Communities award, 1986. Mem. Am. Pub. Health Assn., N.Mex. Pub. Health Assn. (chmn. 1985-86). Democrat. Roman Catholic. Avocations: running, reading, skiing. Home: 5620 Wingate NW Albuquerque NM 87120 Office: USPHS Indian Health Service 505 Marquette Albuquerque NM 87102-0097

BIRD, ROSE ELIZABETH, former chief justice Calif. Supreme Ct.; b. Tucson, Nov. 2, 1936. B.A. magna cum laude, L.I. U., 1958; J.D., U. Calif., Berkeley, 1965. Bar: Calif. bar 1966. Clk. to chief justice Nev. Supreme Ct., 1965-66; successively dep. public defender, sr. trial dep., chief appellate div. Santa Clara County (Calif.) Pub. Defenders Office, 1966-74; tchr. Stanford U. Law Sch., 1972-74; sec. Calif. Agr. and Services Agy., also mem. governor's cabinet, 1975-77; chief justice Calif. Supreme Ct., 1977-86; chairperson Calif. Jud. Council, Commn. Jud. Appointments; pres. bd. dirs. Hastings Coll. Law, U. Calif.; bd. councilors U. So. Calif. Law Center, 1975-77; Past mem. Western regional selection panel President's Commn. White House Fellowships; bd. assos. San Fernando Valley Youth Found. Named Most Outstanding Sr. L.I. U., 1958; Ford Found. fellow, 1960. Democrat. Address: 350 McAllister St San Francisco CA 94102 *

BIRDLEBOUGH, HAROLD, dentist; b. Yakima, Wash., May 4, 1928; s. Otis Theodore and Elizabeth (Brown) B.; D.D.S., U. Wash., 1959; m. Donna Mae Vensel, June 18, 1977; children: John Michael, Ann Michele, Elizabeth, William Powers, Marcia; stepchildren: Steve Hassenfratz, Nancy Hassenfratz, Keith Fontel. Practice dentistry, Seattle, 1959-61, King County, Wash., 1961—; mem. dental adv. com. Blue Cross Ins. Co. Served with USNR, 1948-52. Mem. ADA, Wash. Dental Assn., Snohomish County Dental Soc., Gen. Acad. Dentistry, U. Wash. Dental Alumni, Soc. Preservation and Encouragement Barbershop Quartet Singing in Am., Delta Sigma Delta, Alpha Delta Phi (1st v.p. local alumni assn., del. nat. constl. conv. 1968). Republican. Episcopalian (sr. warden). Lodge: Kiwanis (v.p. Shoreline chpt.). Home: 16929 Inglewood Rd NE C-105 Bothell WA 98011 Office: 332 NW Richmond Beach Rd Seattle WA 98177

BIRDSALL, CHARLES KENNEDY, electrical engineer; b. N.Y.C., Nov. 19, 1925; s. Charles and Irene (Birdsall); m. Betty Jean Hansen, 1949 (div. 1977); children: Elizabeth (dec.), Anne, Barbara, Thomas, John; m. Virginia Anderson, Aug. 21, 1981. B.S., U. Mich., 1946, M.S., 1948; Ph.D., Stanford U., 1951. Research physicist Hughes Aircraft Co., Culver City, Calif., 1951-55; group leader electron physics group Gen. Electric Co., Palo Alto, Calif., 1955-59; prof. elec. engring. U. Calif., 1959—; founder, 1st chmn. Energy and Resources Com., 1972-74; cons. to industry, Lawrence Livermore Lab. of U. Calif.; prof. Miller Inst. Basic Research in Sci., 1963-64; sr. vis. fellow U. Reading (Eng.), summer 1976; research assoc. Inst. Plasma Physics, Nagoya (Japan) U., winter 1981; Chevron vis. prof. energy Calif. Inst. Tech., 1982; area coordinator phys. electronics/bioelectronics, 1984-86. Author: (with W.B. Bridges) Electron Dynamics of Diode Regions, 1966, (with A.B. Langdon) Plasma Physics via Computer Simulation, 1985; contbr. articles to profl. jours. Served with USNR, 1944-46. U.S.-Japan Coop. Sci. Program grantee, 1966-67. Fellow IEEE, Am. Phys. Soc., AAAS; mem. Sigma Xi, Tau Beta Pi, Eta Kappa Nu. Patentee in field; co-originator many-particle plasma simulations in two and three dimensions using cloud-in-cell methods, 1966. Home: 4050 Valente Ct Lafayette CA 94549 Office: EECS Dept Cory Hall U Calif Berkeley CA 94720

BIRELY, JOHN HORTON, science facility administrator; b. Oct. 17, 1939. BS in Chemistry, Yale U., 1961; MS in Phys. Chemistry, U. Calif., Berkeley, 1963; PhD in Phys. Chemistry, Harvard U., 1966. Alt. group leader Los Alamos (N.Mex.) Nat. Lab., 1975-76, group leader, 1976-80, asst. dir., 1980, dep. div. leader, 1980-81, assoc. dir., 1981-86, dep. dir., 1986—. Mem. Am. Phys. Soc., Am. Chem. Soc., Cosmos Club. Avocation: civil air patrol. Office: Los Alamos Nat Lab PO Box 1663 MS A102 Los Alamos NM 87545

BIRENBAUM, HARVEY, humanities educator; b. Phila., July 8, 1936; s. Samuel and Fanny (Tannenbaum) B.; m. Elizabeth Maya Mandel Mezey, July 21, 1963; children: Tanya A., Joshua D. BA, Antioch Coll., 1958; MA, Yale U., 1959, PhD, 1963. Instr. Queens Coll., N.Y.C., 1964-65; asst. prof. English San Jose (Calif.) State U., 1965-69, assoc. prof., 1969-81, prof., 1981—; vis. lectr. U. East Anglia, Norwich, Eng., 1972-73. Author: Tragedy and Innocence, 1983, Myth and Mind, 1987. Bd. dirs. Northside Theatre Co., San Jose, 1982—. Fellow Woodrow Wilson Found., 1958-62, NEH, 1984-85. Office: San Jose State U English Dept San Jose CA 95192

BIRGENHEIER, HUGH KIRK, lawyer; b. Ellensburg, Wash., May 23, 1958; s. Carl J. and Betty (Kilwein) B. BA, St. Martin's Coll., 1981; D, U. Puget Sound, 1984. Bar: Wash. 1984, U.S. Dist. Ct. (we. dist.) Wash. 1984, U.S. Ct. Appeals (9th cir.) 1984. Assoc. Jeff Robinson, Gig Harber, Wash., 1983-84; dep. pub. defender Pierce County Pub. Defender's Office, Tacoma, 1984-85; dep. prosecuting atty. Lewis County Prosecuting Attys. Office, Chehalis, Wash., 1985—; prof. St. Martin's Coll., Lacey, Wash., 1985-86; instr. Centralia (Wash.) Coll., 1986—. Author: Sports Liability in Washington, 1983. Mem. Wash. State Trial Lawyers Assn., Am. Trial Lawyers Assn. Roman Catholic. Lodges: Kiwanis, Elks. Avocation: athletic officiating. Home: PO Box 772 Chehalis WA 98532 Office: Lewis County Prosecuting Office PO Box 918 Chehalis WA 98532

BIRK, JAMES PETER, chemistry educator; b. Cold Spring, Minn., Aug. 21, 1941; s. Albert Mathew and Christina Marie (Theisen) B.; m. S. Kay Gunter, June 21, 1974; one child, Kara. BA, St. John's U., Collegeville, Minn., 1963; PhD, Iowa State U., 1967. Research asst. U. Chgo., 1967-68; asst. prof. chemistry U. Pa., Phila., 1968-73, Rhodes-Thompson chair chemistry, 1972-73; assoc. prof. chemistry Ariz. State U., Tempe, 1973-79, prof., 1979—, asst. chmn. dept., 1983-86; Bd. dirs. Odyssey Sch. for the Gifted and Talented, Scottsdale, Ariz.; bd. advisors Ctr. for Acad. Precocity, Tempe, 1986—. Author: Laboratory Chemistry, 1983, rev. ed., 1985, Investigations in Chemistry, rev. ed., 1985, Further Investigations in Chemistry, 1983, rev. ed., 1985; also articles. Recipient Distinction in Undergrad. Teaching award, Ariz. State U., 1980, 86; fellow NSF. Fellow Am. Inst. Chemists; mem. Am. Chem. Soc., Assn. Computers in Math. and Sci. Teaching, Soc. Coll. Sci. Tchrs., Sigma Xi, Phi Kappa Phi. Roman Catholic. Home: 10217 E Becker Ln Scottsdale AZ 85260 Office: Ariz State U Dept Chemistry Tempe AZ 85287

BIRKAN, MITHAT AHMET, mechanical engineer, researcher; b. Istanbul, Turkey, Mar. 10, 1952; came to U.S., 1978; s. Halit Ziya and Gulnar Birkan; m. Gonca Muazzez, Sept. 17, 1985. BS, Tech. U. Istanbul, 1973, MS, 1975; PhD, U. Colo., 1984. Research asst. U. Colo., Boulder, 1980-84, lectr., 1982-84, research assoc., 1984; research engr. U. Calif., Davis, 1984—, instr., 1986—. Mem. ASME, Sigma Xi. Avocations: skiing, swimming. Home: 1313 Wake Forest Dr #237 Davis CA 95616 Office: U Calif Davis CA 95616

BIRKBY, WALTER HUDSON, physical anthropologist, curator; b. Gordon, Nebr., Feb. 28, 1931; s. Walter Levy and Margery Hazel (Moss) B.; m. Carmen Sue Gates, Aug. 18, 1955; children: Jeffrey Moss, Julianne. BA, U. Kans., 1961, MA, 1963; PhD, U. Ariz., 1973. Diplomate Am. Bd. Forensic Anthropology. Med. and X-ray technician Graham County (Kans.) Hosp., Hill City, 1955-58; phys. anthropologist Ariz. State Mus., Tucson, 1968-85; lectr. anthropology U. Ariz., Tucson, 1981—; curator phys. anthropology Ariz. State Mus., Tucson, 1985—; forensic anthropologist Pima County Med. Examiner, Tucson, 1981—; dental cons. USAF Hosp., Davis Monthan AFB, Tucson, 1984—; human osteologist, U. Ariz./Republic of Cyprus Archaeol. Expedition, 1985—; dir. dept. Anthropology Masters Program in Forensic Anthropology, 1984—. Co-author video tng. film Identification of Human Remains, 1980; contbr. articles to profl. jours. Served as sgt. USMCR, 1951-52, Korea. NIH fellow, U. Ariz., 1966-68. Fellow Am. Acad. Forensic Scis. (exec. com. 1978-81); mem. Am. Assn. Phys. Anthropologists, Calif. Assn. Criminalists, Internat. Assn. Human biologists, Internat. Assn. for Identification, Am. Bd. Forensic Anthropology (pres. 1985—, exec. com. 1980—), Sigma Xi (pres. local chpt. 1984-85). Democrat. Avocations: photography, hunting, fishing. Home: 7349 E 18th St Tucson AZ 85710 Office: Ariz State Mus Human Identification Lab U. Ariz. Tucson AZ 85721

BIRKENSTEIN, LILLIAN RAY, ornithologist; b. Phila., Oct. 9, 1900; d. Morris and Stella (Schloss) Rosenzweig; B.A. (coll. scholar), Wellesley Coll., 1922; student U. Pa., 1920-21, Northwestern U., 1936-37, Instituto Allende (Mexico), 1951-55, Academia Hispana-Americana (Mexico), 1960-68; m. George Ulman Birkenstein, Sept. 2, 1922; children—Dorothy (Mrs. Jose Vidargas), Jean (Mrs. Atlee Washington). Pres., Anker-Holth Mfg. Co., Port Huron, Mich., 1944-51; researcher local Spanish and tribal Indian names of Mexican birds, 1952—; vol. librarian, San Miguel Allende, 1954-67, tchr. ornithology Institute Allende, San Miguel Allende, 1973. Bd. dirs. Public Library San Miguel Allende, 1954-67, Hot Breakfasts for Sch. Children, San Miguel, 1957-61. Mem. San Miguel Allende Audubon Soc. (founder 1967, pres. 1967-71, dir. 1971—), Am. Soc. Mfg. Engrs. (hon. life), Am. Ornithologists Union, Cooper Ornithol. Soc., Linnaean Soc., Wilson Ornithol. Soc., Cornell Lab. Ornithology, Mexican Natural History Soc. (dir. 1972—), Mexican Ornitholog. Soc. (dir.), Internat. Com. for Bird Preservation (treas. Mexican sect. 1968—), Women's Aux. AIME (hon.). Clubs: San Miguel Allende Garden (1st v.p. 1971—); Golf Malanquin. Author: Native Names of Mexican Birds, 1981. Contbr. articles to various publs. Home: Tenerias 45, San Miguel Allende, Guanajuato Mexico

BIRKITT, JOHN CLAIR, engineer; b. Inglewood, Calif., Aug. 20, 1941; s. Clair Willis and Helene Blanche (Gille) B.; m. Constance Ellen May, June 4, 1966; m. 2d, Linda Ann Aylmer, Sept. 13, 1980; children—Andra, Robert, Danielle. B.S. in Aerospace Engring., Calif. Poly. State U., 1969. Engr., Aerojet Mfg. Co., Fullerton, Calif., 1969-74; with TRW, 1974-83, engr. def. and space systems group, Redondo Beach, Calif., 1974-79, plant mgr. advanced ground systems engring., Long Beach, Calif., 1979-83, test condr. Capistrano test site, San Clemente, Calif., 1975-83; tech. mgr. Ford Aerospace and Communications Corp., Newport Beach, Calif., 1983-86; gen. mgr. White Missile Range Ops., W.J. Schafer Assocs., Inc., Arlington, Va., 1986—. Vice pres., treas., tng. officer El Cariso Vol. Fire Dept., 1978—. Served with USMC, 1959-65. Mem. AIAA, Nat. Assn. Watch and Clock Collectors, Nat. Mgmt. Assn., Nat. Defense Preparedness Assn., Musical Box Soc. Internat. Home: 32536 Ortega Hwy El Cariso Village Lake Elsinore CA 92330 Office: Bldg 23106 High Energy Laser Lab Nike Rd White Sands Missile Range NM 88002

BIRKITT, LINDA ANN AYLMER, physical therapist; b. Oakland, Calif., Feb. 8, 1946; d. William Stanley and Phyllis Jane (King) Aylmer; student U. Md. at Munich, W.Ger., 1967-68; B.S., Calif. State Poly. U., 1963-69; M.A. (HEW scholar), U. So. Calif., 1973; m. John C. Birkitt, Sept. 13, 1980; children: Andra, Robert, Lowell, Daniélle. Staff phys. therapist Valley Presbyn. Hosp., Van Nuys, Calif., 1973-75; chief therapist Ingleside Mental Health Center, Rosemead, Calif., 1975-79; mem. Speakers Bur., 1976-79; lectr. Santa Monica City Coll., 1976-79; asst. chief phys. therapist Alhambra (Calif.) Community Hosp., 1979-81; pvt. practice phys. therapy, San Juan Capistrano, Calif., 1981—; dir. ops. Healthtech Rehab., Inc., 1985—. Vol. fire fighter, El Cariso Village, Calif., 1979—. Contbr. articles to profl. jour. Mem. AAUW, Nat. Assn. Female Execs., Nat. Mgmt. Assn. Episcopalian. Research in motivation as a factor in performance of phys. skill, verticality perception distortion in hemiplegic patients. Home: 32536 Ortega Hwy El Cariso Village Lake Elsinore CA 92330 Office: 14795 Jeffrey Rd Suite 100 Irvine CA 92027

BIRMINGHAM, JOSEPH E., public health administrator; b. Pitts., May 23, 1923; s. Joseph Eugene and Rose Marie (Barzanty) B.; m. Anita L. Loomis, Oct. 25, 1947; children—James P., Thomas E., Richard J.; m. Margaret L. Schell, Oct. 12, 1963; 1 child, Mary E. B.S. in Pharmacy, U. Pitts., 1944, M.S. in Hygiene, 1968; M.S., U. Wash., 1960. Chief pharmacy service VA Hosp., Roanoke, Va., 1946-51, Pitts., 1960-66, chief pharmacy service, Seattle, 1951-60, asst. dir., 1970-72, asst. dir., Amarillo, Tex., 1968-70, Los Angeles, 1972-75; dir. VA Med. Center Albuquerque, 1975—; mem. governing body N.Mex. Health Systems Agy.; mem. N.Mex. State Health Coordinating Council; chmn. Albuquerque-Santa Fe Fed. Exec. Bd., 1983—. Bd. dirs. Albuquerque Vis. Nursing Assn., v.p., 1982-84. Served with AUS, 1944-46; lt. comdr. USNR, 1953-74 (ret.). Recipient Mgr. of Year award Fed. Exec. Bd., 1982; Outstanding Leadership award Am. Pharm. Assn., 1955; Superior Performance award Fed. Exec. Bd. Los Angeles, 1975. Mem. Am. Coll. Hosp. Adminstrn., Am. Pub. Health Assn., N.Mex. Pub. Health Assn., Am. Pharm. Assn. (pres. Puget Sound chpt.), Fed. Hosp. Execs. Alumni Assn., Fed. Exec. Inst. Alumni Assn., AMA, Albuquerque Area Hosp. Council. Roman Catholic. Clubs: K.C., Elks. Home: 4706 Glenwood Hills Dr NE Albuquerque NM 87111 Office: 2100 Ridgecrest Dr SE Albuquerque NM 87108

BIRN, RAYMOND FRANCIS, historian, educator; b. N.Y.C., May 10, 1935; s. Saul Albert and Celia (Markman) B.; m. Randi Ingebrigtsen, July 18, 1960; children—Eric Stephen, Laila Marie. B.A., NYU, 1956; M.A., U. Ill., 1957, Ph.D., 1961. Mem. faculty U. Oreg., Eugene, 1961—; asso. prof. U. Oreg., 1966-72, prof. history, 1972—, head dept., 1971-78. Author: Pierre Rousseau and the Philosophes of Bouillon, 1964, Crisis, Absolutism, Revolution: Europe, 1648-1789/91, 1977; adv. editor Eighteenth-Century Studies, 1974-85, French Hist. Studies, 1977-80; editor: The Printed Word in the Eighteenth Century, 1984; contbr. articles to profl. jours. Mem. adv. screening com. Council for Internat. Exchange of Persons (Fulbright program), 1974-76. Served with AUS, 1959-60. Fulbright research fellow to France, 1968-69; Nat. Endowment for Humanities sr. fellow, 1976-77, 87—. Mem. Am. Hist. Assn., Soc. French Hist. Studies, Am. Soc. 18th Century Studies. Home: 2140 Elk Ave Eugene OR 97403

BIROC, SANDRA LYN, biology educator; b. Los Angeles, Dec. 14, 1947; d. Robert Biroc and Doris Lynell (Haven) Rast; m. Daniel Bernard Unger, Mar. 27, 1982; children: Elizabeth Kaye, Douglas Gustav. BA in Biology, Calif. State U., Northridge, 1970; PhD in Biology, Johns Hopkins U., 1975. Postdoctoral fellow U. Calif., Davis, 1975-78; instr. Calif. State U., Sacramento, 1978-80; lab. coordinator, asst. prof. biology U. Colo., Boulder, 1980—. Author: Developmental Biology, 1986. Dem. del., Boulder, 1986. Mem. AAAS, Am. Assn. Biol. Scis., Sigma Xi, Boulder Internat. Folk Dancers (pres. 1985—). Lodge: Masons (state rep. 1965-66). Avocations: Scrabble tournaments, folk dancing. Office: Univ Colo Dept MCDB Box 347 Boulder CO 80309-0347

BIRREN, JAMES EMMETT, emeritus dean and professor, psychologist; b. Chgo., Apr. 4, 1918; m. Elizabeth S., 1942; children: Barbara Ann, Jeffrey Emmett, Bruce William. Student, Wright Jr. Coll., 1938; B.Ed., Chgo. State U., 1941; M.A., Northwestern U., 1942, Ph.D., 1947, DSc (hon.), 1986; postgrad., U. Chgo., 1950-51; Ph.D. (hon.), U. Gothenberg, Sweden, 1983. Tutorial fellow Northwestern U., 1941-42; research asst. project for study of fatigue Office Sci. Research and Devel., 1942; research fellow NIH, USPHS, 1946-47; research psychologist gerontology unit NIH, 1947-51; research psychologist NIMH, 1951-53, chief sect. on aging, 1953-64; dir. aging program Nat. Inst. Child Health and Human Devel., Bethesda, Md., 1964-65; dir. Gerontology Center; prof. psychology U. So. Calif., 1965—; dean Davis Sch. Gerontology, 1975-86; Brookdale disting. scholar 1986—; dir. Inst. Advanced Study in Gerontology and Geriatrics, 1981—; fellow Center for Advanced Study in Behavioral Scis., Stanford, Calif., 1978-79; Green vis. prof. U. B.C., 1979; vis. scientist Cambridge (Eng.) U., 1960-61; Harold E. Jones meml. lectr. U. Calif., Berkeley, 1965; mem. Los Angeles County Bd. Suprs.' Com. on Aging, 1967—; sr. fellow U. So. Calif. Urban Ecology Inst., 1968-70; mem. Dean's Council, U. So. Calif., 1970—; chmn. aging rev. com. Nat. Inst. Aging, 1974-75; program dir. Integration of Info. on Aging: Handbook Project, 1973-76; mem. steering com. Care of Elderly, Inst. of Medicine, 1976-77; bd. dirs. Sears Roebuck Found., 1977-80; chmn. life course prevention research rev. com. NIMH, 1985-87; cons. Roche Seminars on Aging Series, 1980—. Author: Psychology of Aging, 1964; editor: Handbook of Aging and the Individual, 1959, (with K.W. Schaie) Handbook of the Psychology of Aging, 1977, (with R.B. Sloane) Handbook of Mental Health and Aging; contbr. articles to books, profl. publs.; bd. collaborators:

Gerontologia, 1956—; asst. editor: Jour. Gerontology, 1956-61, assoc. editor 1961-63, editor-in-chief 1968-74, chmn. publs. com., 1975—, adv. editorial bd., 1956-69; bd. adv. editors: Devel. Psychobiology, 1967—; adv. editor: Jour. Human Devel, 1957-58. Served with USNR, 1943-46; to scientist dir. USPHS Scientist Corps, 1947-65. Recipient award for research on problems of aging CIBA Found., 1956, Stratton award Am. Psychopathol. Assn., 1960, Sr. 65er award Dist. 65 Retail Workers and Dept. Store Union, Sr. 65er award AFL-CIO, 1962, medal for meritorious service USPHS, 1965, citation Am. Assn. Ret. Persons, 1970, Am. Pioneers in Aging award U. Mich., 1972, commendation for disting. contbns. to field of gerontology Mayor of Los Angeles, 1968, 74, Merit award Northwestern U. Alumni Assn., 1976, Creative Scholarship and Research award U. So. Calif., 1979, Disting. Educator award Assn. Gerontology in Higher Edn., 1983, Eminent Service award Stovall Found., 1984, Award of Distinction Am. Fedn. for Aging Research, 1986; USPHS research fellow, 1946-47. Fellow AAAS, Am. Geriatrics Soc. (founding fellow Western div.), Am. Psychol. Assn. (Disting. Sci. Contbn. award 1968, chmn. membership com. 1969, Disting. Contbn. award Div. Adult Devel. and Aging 1978, pres. div. 1955-56, editor newsletter 1951-55), Gerontol. Soc. (pres. 1961-62, chmn. publs. com. 1974-77, award for meritorious research 1966, Brookdale award 1980); mem. Am. Physiol. Soc., Internat. Assn. Gerontology (chmn. exec. com. 1966-69, chmn. program com. 1968-69), Psychonomic Soc., Western Gerontol. Soc. (dir. 1965—, pres. 1968-69), Sigma Xi, Phi Kappa Phi. Office: Andrus Gerontology Center U So Calif Univ Park MC 0191 Los Angeles CA 90089

BISCHOFF, ALBERT FREDRICK, telecommunications engineer, consultant; b. Berkeley, Calif., May 2, 1941; s. Albert Fredrick and Emma Geraldine (Rego) B.; m. Marjorie Alice, Oct. 1966 (div. 1969). Grad. high sch., Portland, Oreg. Sr. lab. specialist IBM Corp., San Jose, Calif., 1965-81; chief engr. Vidicom, Westlake Village, Calif., 1981-82; sr. engr. Arco Corp. Telecommunications, Los Angeles, 1982-84; cons. video system engring., 1984—; cons. in field. Contbr. articles to profl. jours. Served with USAF, 1959-63. Recipient Recognition awards IBM Corp., 1970, 73. Mem. Soc. Motion Picture and TV Engrs., Mensa. Home and Office: 3410 Ave Amaranto Thousand Oaks CA 91362

BISCHOFF, ELMER, artist, educator; b. Berkeley, Calif., July 9, 1916; s. John A. and Elna (Nelson) B. B.A., U. Calif.-Berkeley, 1938, M.A., 1939; D.F.A. (hon), Otis Art Inst., Parsons Sch. Design, 1983. Chmn. grad. program San Francisco Art Inst., 1957-63; instr. art dept. U. Calif.-Berkeley, 1963-85. Represented permanent collections, Art Inst. Chgo., Mus. Modern Art, U. Kans. Mus. Art, Whitney Mus. Am. Art, Met. Mus. Art., N.Y.C., Permanent Collections, Rockefeller Inst., permanent collections, New Sch. Art Ctr., N.Y.C., San Francisco Mus. Art, pvt. collections, permanent exhibit, John Berggruen Gallery, San Francisco, Hirschl and Adler-Modern, N.Y.C. Served with USAAF, 1942-46, ETO. Grantee Ford Found., 1959; grantee Nat. Inst. Arts and Letters, 1963; recipient Disting. Teaching award Coll. Art Assn., 1983. Office: 2571 Shattuck Ave Berkeley CA 94704

BISGARD, JAY CRISPIN, physician, retired air force officer; b. Denver, Oct. 26, 1942; s. William Howard and Doris Irene (Carlson) B.; m. Nonja Sherriel Fulsher, June 11, 1964; children: Kirsten Laurel, Erika Lynn. BA, Northwestern U., 1964, MD, 1967; MPH, Harvard U., 1971. Diplomate Am. Bd. Preventive Medicine in Aerospace Medicine. Commd. 2d lt. U.S. Army, 1963; transferred to USAF, 1974, advanced through grades to col., 1980; cons. to surgeon gen. USAF, Washington, 1977—, chief med. readiness, 1978-79; spl. asst. to asst. sec. health affairs Dept. Def., Washington, 1979-81, dep. asst. sec., 1981-84; comdr. USAF Hosp., Robins AFB, Ga., 1984-85; command surgeon Alaskan Air Command, Elmendorf AFB, 1985-86; ret. USAF, 1986; corp. med. dir. Atlantic Richfield Co., Los Angeles, 1986-87, GTE, Stamford, Ct., 1987—. Decorated Bronze Star, Legion of Merit. Fellow Aerospace Med. Assn., Am. Coll. Preventive Medicine; mem. Am. Coll. Physician Execs., Am. Acad. Med. Dirs., Soc. Med. Cons. to Armed Forces.

BISHOP, AMY, marketing and public relations executive; b. Longview, Tex., Apr. 28, 1958; d. Norman Glenn and Barbara (Crockett) B. BS, Ariz. State U., 1981, postgrad., 1983—. With mgmt. devel. program 1st Interstate Bank, Phoenix, 1981-83, pub. relations specialist, 1983-85, mktg. promotions officer, 1986—. Co-author, co-editor Report to Employees mag., 1983 (Internat. Assn. Bus. Communicators Gold Quill award 1983); co-creator NewsHound Communications Program, 1981 (Pub. Relations Soc. Am. Phoenix award 1981). Mem. Pub. Relations Soc. Am. (bd. dirs. Phoenix chpt. 1985—), Direct Mktg. Assn., Pi Beta Phi (v.p. 1978-79, treas. 1979-80). Republican. Presbyterian. Avocations: miniature dollhouse building, sewing, aerobics, stained glass. Office: 1st Interstate Bank #916 PO Box 53456 Phoenix AZ 85072-3456

BISHOP, ARLENE JOYCE, development consultant; b. Oakland, Calif., May 28, 1942; d. Arnold Nicolas and Mildred Carolina (Kwartz) Hamstad; m. Dale Judson Edward Bishop, Sept. 3, 1965 (div.); 1 son, Scott. B.A., U. Calif.-Berkeley, 1963; teaching credential Calif. State U.-Hayward, 1964; postgrad. North Park Theol. Sem., Chgo., 1965-66, Spanish Lang. Inst., San Jose, Costa Rica, 1968-69. Mem. staff Evang. Covenant Ch., Medellín, Colombia, 1969-75; adminstrv. asst. Crown Life Ins. Co., San Francisco, 1976-77; data processing project coordinator Crown Zellerbach Corp., San Francisco, 1977-79; analyst Indsl. Indemnity Ins. Co., San Francisco, 1979-80; adminstr. The Lowell Berry Found., Oakland, 1980-82; dir., pres. The Consol. Capital Found., Emeryville, Calif., 1982-84; v.p. research and bus. devel. Consol. Capital Cos., 1984-85; devel. cons., 1986—. Bd. dirs. Internat. Visitors Ctr., San Fransisco, 1985—, Dunsmuir House, Oakland, 1985—; mem. Coro Found. Women's Adv. Bd., Oakland, 1982—; mem. Bear Boosters Bd., U. Calif., 1984—; mem. Evang. Free Ch., Walnut Creek, Calif., 1979—. Mem. Women and Founds./Corp. Philanthropy, Council on Founds., Bay Area Exec. Women's Forum, World Affairs Council. Republican. Clubs: U. Calif. Alumni, Commonwealth (San Francisco); Last Monday (Oakland). Home: 485 Canyon Oaks #D Oakland CA 94605 Office: 2000 Powell St Emeryville CA 94608

BISHOP, BARRY RHETT, newspaper publisher, rancher; b. Stevens Point, Wis., Aug. 7, 1940; s. Rexford Ernest and Bernice Marie (Whiting) B.; student UCLA, 1960-61; B.S., U. Wis., Madison, 1962; postgrad. U Puget Sound, Tacoma, 1963-64, U. Calif., San Jose, 1973-74; m. Gael Lucette Briggs, Oct. 28, 1966; children—Terri, Steve, Heidi, Barbra, Robert. With Stars and Stripes, 1964; editor Wis. State Farmer, 1965; editor, advt. dir. Manawa (Wis.) Adv., 1965-66, editor, pub., owner, 1966-69; editor The Ariz. Currents, writer/reporter Milw. Jour., also editor, pub. Sierra Vista (Ariz.) Herald-Dispatch, 1969-74; editor, pub., owner The Paper, Sierra Vista, 1974—; pub. Huachuca Scout, 1982—, Desert Airman, 1984—, Friday Times, 1985—; v.p. Sulphur Springs Valley Elec. Coop.; tchr. journalism Cochise Coll. Bd. dirs. Sierra Vista Bd. Edn.; sec.-treas. Sierra Vista Indsl. Devel. Authority. Chmn. Border Relations Commn., Utilities Commn., City of Sierra Vista; fin. chmn. Catalina council Boy Scouts Am.; cubmaster Pack 464, Sierra Vista, also troop chmn. mem. Gov.'s Commn. Ariz.-Mex.; del. Gov.'s Commn. Small Bus. Served to capt. U.S. Army, 1962-64. Recipient Spoke award Wis. Jaycees; winner numerous nat., state awards including editorial award Wis. br. Am. Automobile Assn., Ariz. Dept. Edn.; named Small Businessman of Year, also Citizen of Yr., City of Sierra Vista, 1979. Mem. Nat. Assn. Advt. Publs., Western Pubs. Assn., Western Newspaper Found., Nat. Newspaper Assn., Wis. Newspaper Assn., Ariz. Newspaper Assn., Wis. Press Photographers Assn., Ariz. Interscholastic Assn., Nat. Sch. Bd. Assn., Sierra Vista C. of C. (past pres., bd. dirs.), Full Gospel Businessmen's Internat. Assn. (bd. dirs.), Assn. U.S. Army (dir.), Nat. Guard Employer-Employee Com., Kappa Sigma. Republican. Mormon. Clubs: Sierra Vista Rotary (pres., gov.'s rep. dist. 550), Lions (past mem. Wis. dist. cabinet), U. Wis. Lettermen's, U. Ariz. Wildcat, Masons. Home: 2500 Quail Run Sierra Vista AZ 85635 Office: 200 E Wilcox Dr Sierra Vista AZ 85635

BISHOP, C. DIANE, state agency administrator, educator; b. Elmhurst, Ill., Nov. 23, 1943; d. Louis William and Constance Oleta (Mears) B.; m. Richard Lee Morse, Oct. 20, 1984. BS in Maths., U. Ariz., 1965, MS in Maths., MEd in Secondary Edn., 1972. Lic. secondary educator. Tchr. math. Tucson Unified Sch. Dist., 1966—, mem. curriculum council, 1985-86, mem. maths. curriculum task teams, 1983-86; state supt. of pub. instrn. State of Ariz., 1987—; assoc. faculty Pima Community Coll., Tucson, 1974-84; adj. lectr. U. Ariz., 1983, 85. Mem. Ariz. State Bd. Edn., 1984—, chmn. quality edn. commn., 1986-87, chmn. tchr. cert. subcom. 1984—, outcomes based edn. adv. com. 1986-87, liaison bd. dirs. essential skills subcom. 1985-87, gifted edn. com. liaison 1985—; mem. high sch. task force Ariz. Bd. Regents, 1984-85, com. on preparing for U. Ariz., 1983; mem. Ariz. Stat Bd. Regents, 1987—, Ariz. State Community Coll. Bd., 1987—. Woodrow Wilson fellow Princeton U., 1984; recipient Presdl. Award for Excellence in Teaching of Maths., 1983, Ariz. Citation of Merit, 1983, Maths. Teaching award Nat. Sci. Research Soc., 1984, Distinction in Edn. award Flinn Found., 1986; named Maths. Tchr. of Yr. Ariz. Council of Engring. and Sci. Assns., 1984. Mem. Nat. Council of Tchrs. of Maths. Council of Chief State Sch. Officers, NEA, Ariz. Edn. Assn., Tucson Edn. Assn., Ariz. Assn. Tchrs. of Maths., Women in Maths. Edn., Math. Assn. of Am., NRC (math. scis. edn. bd. 1986), Nat. Tchrs. Forum of Ednl. Commn. of the States, Nat. Forum on Excellence in Edn., Nat. Honors Workshop, Pi Mu Epsilon, Pi Lambda Theta. Democrat. Episcopalian. Office: Ariz State Dept Edn 1535 W Jefferson Phoenix AZ 85007

BISHOP, CRAIG VIRGIL, aerospace manager, physical chemist; b. Eugene, Oreg., Aug. 21, 1948; s. Wallace Myron and Harlon Goddard (Clary) B.; m. Anita Louise Kasson, June 12, 1971 (div. Dec. 1975); 1 child, Ingrid Kristina; m. Deborah Ann Elias, May 3, 1980; 1 child, Morgan Thomas. BS in Biology, Met. State Coll., Denver, 1973, BS in Chemistry, 1974; postgrad., MIT, 1979-80. Miner, tunneler various companies, Clear Creek, Colo., 1966-67, 69-73; plant chemist Thomas Plating Co., Englewood, Colo., 1974-75; tech. rep. RO Hull Co., Chgo., 1975-76; chief analytical chemistry RO Hull Co., Cleve., 1976-80; sr. scientist Lockheed/NASA White Sands Test Facility, Las Cruces, N.Mex., 1980-85, mgr. dept., 1985—; advisor Interagy. Nuclear Safety Review Panel, 1985—; research NASA/51-L Accident Investigation, Houston, 1986—. Co-author Ignition and Thermal Hazards, 1986; inventor and co-inventor in field; contbr. articles to profl. jours. Active in anti-Vietnam war movement, 1969-72; pub. speaker Boy Scouts Am., So. N.Mex., Western Tex., 1983; mem. Ohio City Neighborhood Com., Cleve., 1978-80. Served with USN, 1967-69. Named Employee of Yr., RO Hull Co., Cleve., 1979; recipient Outstanding Achievement award Am. Electroplaters Soc., Phila., 1979, Cert. Appreciation NASA, 1985, Spl. Achievement award NASA, 1982, 83, 84. Mem. AIAA (Tech. com. on Materials), AAAS, Nature Conservancy, Nat. Wildlife Fedn. Republican. Episcopalian. Avocations: environmentalism, commercialization of space, mountaineering, sailing, reading. Home: 497 Cimmaron Ct Las Cruces NM 88001 Office: Lockheed NASA WSTF PO Drawer NM Las Cruces NM 88004

BISHOP, EARLE CARL, electrical engineer; b. Toledo, Dec. 11, 1938; children: Caralynne M., E. Carl Jr. Student, Calif. State U., Sacramento, 1976; BSEE, U. Cen. Calif., 1982, MSME, 1984. Electronics engr. Radio Shack Service, Sacramento, 1975-77; prin. E. Bishop Gen. Contractors, Sacramento, 1977-80; cons. Albuquerque, 1980-84; contract engr. Intel, AT&T, IBM, 1984—; pres. All Cities Engr. Services, Inc., Wilmington, Del., 1985—. Avocations: computers, programming. Home: 3131 Candelaria NE Apt 215 Albuquerque NM 87107

BISHOP, EDWIN BURNETT, real estate executive; b. Haines, Oreg., Mar. 8, 1921; s. Jasper Newton and Vera Leta (Burnett) B.; m. Mary Ellen Mills, Feb. 25, 1953; children: Jeff, Nancy, Kim, Robert. BS, Oreg. State U., 1946. Cert. real estate broker, bldg. contractor. Mgr. Eugene (Oreg.) Sand and Gravel Co., 1954-59; owner Ed Bishop Contractor, Santa Barbara, Calif., 1959-64, Kailua, Hawaii, 1964-65, Lafayette, Calif., 1965-73; prin. Santana Properties, Santa Barbara, 1973—. Served as sgt. AC, U.S. Army, 1943-45. Mem. Calif. Assn. Realtors (bd. dirs. 1983—), Santa Barbara Bd. Realtors (pres. 1985, bd. dirs. 1981—, Realtor of Yr. 1984), Phi Delta Theta. Republican. Avocation: running. Home and Office: 1936 D N Jameson Ln Santa Barbara CA 93108

BISHOP, M(ARLIN) RUSSELL, educational corporation executive, management consultant; b. Alameda, Calif., June 12, 1947; s. Marlin LeRoy and Kathryn Elaine (Van Duzor) B.; m. Carolyn Jane Elbel, Aug. 4, 1973 (div. 1979); m. Sally Kaye Hedges, July 7, 1986. B.A., U. Calif.-Davis, 1970, M.A., 1975. Resident dir. U. Calif.-Davis, 1969-73; dir. tng. Lifespring, San Rafael, Calif., 1974-77; pres. Insight Tng. Seminars, Santa Monica, Calif., 1978—, Time/Design, Santa Monica, 1983—, Insight Cons. Group, Santa Monica, project dir. John Roger Found., Santa Monica, 1983—; cons. Koh-e-Noh U., Santa Monica, 1980—, Movement of Spiritual Inner Awareness, Los Angeles, 1978—, Lockheed Calif., Burbank, 1983—. Co-author: It's Time to Win, 1979; author: Questions for Those in Search of Answers, 1984; author articles. Mem. Task Force on Women in Bus. SBA, Washington, 1979. Recipient Outstanding Service award, Movement of Spiritual Inner Awareness, 1978. Mem. Assn. Humanistic Psychology. Democrat. Office: Insight Cons Group 2101 Wilshire Santa Monica CA 90403

BISI, RONNA JOAN-MICHELLE, mechanical engineer; b. Latrobe, Pa., Feb. 1, 1957; d. Ronald John and Irene Elanor (Slezak) B. Student, Purdue U., 1975-79; BSME, Ariz. State U., 1986. Lic. comml. pilot; cert. flight instr. Clk. Latrobe Airport, 1974-75; pvt. practice flight instrn. Phoenix, 1980-82; vet. technician Mesa (Ariz.) Vet. Hosp., 1982-83; engring. aide Garrett Turbine Engine Co., Phoenix, 1983-86, engr., 1986—; cons. Left Side Enterprises, Mesa, 1976—, Cosoco, Chandler, Ariz., 1974-75. Counselor Crises Intervention Ctr., Lafayette, Ind., 1977-78; troop leader Girl Scouts U.S., Lafayette, 1977-79. Mem. Nat. Computer Graphics Assn., Airplane Owners and Pilots Assn., 99s (editor newsletter 1982-83), Finite-Element Modelers Group (v.p. 1984-86, pres. 1986—). Avocations: flying, water skiing, golfing, restoring antique automobiles, flute. Office: 2303 N 44th St Suite 14-264 Phoenix AZ 85008

BISSELL, JAMES DOUGAL III, motion picture production designer; b. Charleston, S.C., Aug. 6, 1951; s. James Dougal and Elizabeth McPherson (Jones) B.; m. Teresa Ann Atkinson, June 1, 1974; 1 child, James Dougal. BFA in Theatre, U. N.C., 1973. Art dir. various TV movies, Los Angeles, 1976-81; prodn. designer E.T. The Extra-Terrestrial, Los Angeles, 1981, Twilight Zone-The Movie, Los Angeles, 1982, The Falcon and The Snowman, Los Angeles, 1983-84; prodn. designer, 2d unit dir. The Boy Who Could Fly, Los Angeles, 1985, Harry and the Hendersons, Los Angeles, 1986; prodn. mgr. Kentucky Fried Movie, Hollywood, Calif., 1976-77; visual cons. St. Elmo's Fire, Hollywood, 1984; title co-designer Amazing Stories, Hollywood, 1985; art dir. The Last Starfighter, Hollywood, 1983. Nominee Prodn. Design award Brit. Acad. Film Arts, London, 1982. Mem. Acad. TV Arts and Scis. (Emmy award 1980), Soc. Motion Picture and TV Art Dirs., Dir.'s Guild Am., Acad. Motion Picture Arts and Scis.

BISSETT, LESLEY DRUCILLA, financial services company executive; b. Winnipeg, Man., Can., May 26, 1935; d. Richard Rodney and Maybelle Goodwin; m. Frank Weston Bissett, Sept. 30, 1961 (div.) children—John W., Richard L., Thomas. Student pub. schs., Winnipeg. Cert. fin. planner. Featured skater Shipstads & Johnson's Ice Follies, 1957-61; mktg. mgr. University Group, Inc., Long Beach, Calif., 1974-79; regional v.p. Keystone Mass., Inc., Los Angeles, 1979-81; sr. v.p. Integrated Resources Equity Corp., Granada Hills, Calif., 1981—. Mem. Internat. Assn. for Fin. Planning (dir. exec. com.), Bus. and Profl. Womens Club. Methodist. Author: Client Finder, 1982; contbr. articles to fin. jours.

BISSETT, MARJORIE LOUISE, public health microbiologist; b. Miami, Ariz., Sept. 21, 1925; d. Michael Henry and Bessie Lela (Cox) B. AA, Pasadena Jr. Coll., 1944; BA, UCLA, 1949; PhD, U. Mich., 1965. Pub. health bacteriologist Microbiol. Diseases Lab. Calif. State Dept. Health, Berkeley, 1950-55, asst. microbiologist, 1955-61, research microbiologist, 1965—; adv. com. mem. FDA, Washington, 1972-76, cons., 1976-77; guest lectr. U. Calif. Sch. Pub. Health, Berkeley, 1971—; invited participant Internat. Symposium on Yersiniosis, Montreal, Can., 1977. Contbr. chpts. to books and articles to profl. jours. Fellow Am. Acad. Microbiology (Bd. Govs. 1975-78); mem. Am. Soc. Microbiology (council policy com. 1980-83), Am. Pub. Health Assn., Conf. Pub. Health Lab. Dirs., N.Y. Acad. Scis., Soc. Gen. Microbiology, Conf. Pub. Health Lab. Dirs., Sigma Xi, Delta Omega. Office: Microbiol Diseases Lab Calif State Dept Health Services 2151 Berkeley Way Berkeley CA 94704

BISTLINE, STEPHEN, justice; b. Pocatello, Idaho, Mar. 12, 1921; s. Ray D. and Martha (Faber) B.; m. Sharon Mooney; children: Patrick, Paul, Arthur, Claire, Susan, Shelley, Diana, Leslie. LL.B., U. Idaho, 1949. Bar: Idaho bar 1949. Individual practice law Sandpoint, Idaho, 1950-76; justice Idaho Supreme Ct., Boise, 1976—. Served with USN, 1941-45. Office: Supreme Ct Bldg State Capitol Boise ID 83720

BITTAR, DAVID ALBERT, anesthesiologist; b. Bklyn., June 5, 1941; s. Albert Charles and Mabel Nadeema (Naman) B.; m. Phyllis Susan Smith, July 15, 1967 (div. Aug. 1974); m. Susan J. McEachern, May 8, 1976; children: Lisa, Christopher, Alexis, Matthew. BA, NYU, 1962; MD, St. Louis U., 1967. Cert. Am. Bd. Anesthesiologists. Staff anesthesiologist Lahey Clinic Found., Boston, 1971-83; acting chmn. dept. anesthesiology Lahey Clinic Found., Burlington, Mass., 1981-83; mem. anesthesiology service Med. Group Inc., San Diego, 1983—. Contbr. numerous articles to profl. jours. Served to maj. U.S. Army, 1971-73. Fellow Am. Coll. Chest Physicians (assoc.); mem. AMA, Am. coll. Anesthesiologists, Calif. Soc. Anesthesiologists, San Diego County Med. Soc. Avocations: photography, sports, fishing, gardening, music. Home: 1440 Highland Dr Solana Beach CA 92075

BITTER, REED KIRKMAN, oil company executive; b. Twin Falls, Idaho, Jan. 13, 1934; s. Reed Erickson and Phyllis (Kirkman) B.; m. Valeen Buttars, Aug. 26, 1955; children: Rand, Mark, Wade, Julia. BS, Brigham Young U., 1957; postgrad., U. Utah, 1959, MIT, 1981. Geologist Marathon Oil Co., Utah, N.D., Wyo., Tex., Ohio, 1957-75; exploration supr. Marathon Oil Co., Casper, Wyo., 1976-78; dist. exploration mgr. Marathon Oil Co., Casper and Houston, 1979-84; div. exploration mgr. Marathon Oil Co., Casper, 1984-86; mgr. land and contracts Marathon Oil Co., Houston, 1986—; mem. operating com. RMOGA, Denver, 1986—. Contbr. to maj. exhibit Ft. Caspar Interpretive Mus., 1982—. Mem. Am. Assn. Petroleum Geologists (editor jour.), Wyo. Geol. Assn. (editor jour. 1964), Geol. Assn. Am., Rocky Mountain Assn. Geologists, Soc. Exploration Paleontologists and Mineralogists, Geol. Soc. Am. Republican. Mormon. Avocations: golf, geneology, hiking, archeaology, paleontology.

BITTNER, CAROL JEAN, speech, language pathologist; b. Springfield, Mass., Feb. 14, 1946; d. Frederick Warren and Florence (Black) B. BS, Brigham Young U., 1970, MS in Communicative Disorders, 1972. Communicative disorders specialist Alpine Sch. Dist., American Fork, Utah, 1970-85, spl. edn. coordinator, 1986—. Bd. dirs. United Cerebral Palsy, Salt Lake City, 1980. Named Handicapped Employee of Yr., Govs. Com. Employment of Handicapped, 1974. Mem. Am. Speech Hearing Assn. (cert. clin. competence), Nat. Edn. Assn., Alpine Edn. Assn. Avocations: mem. Mormon Tabernacle choir. Home: 605 E 3970 S Salt Lake City UT 84107 Office: Alpine Sch Dist 40 N Center American Fork UT 84003

BITTNER, HARLAN FLETCHER, chemist, researcher; b. Eugene, Oreg., Mar. 26, 1951; s. Francis Winston and Constance (Baxter) B.; m. Rebecca Brittain, Dec. 27, 1981. BA, U. Oreg., 1973; PhD, U. Calif. San Diego, La Jolla, 1977. Mem. research staff Oak Ridge (Tenn.) Nat. Lab., 1978-80; mem. tech. staff The Aerospace Corp., El Segundo, Calif., 1980—. Contbr. articles to profl. jours. Mem. Am. Chem. Soc. (exec. com. 1986—, sec. 1987—), Electrochem. Soc. Office: The Aerospace Corp PO Box 92957 Los Angeles CA 90009

BITTS, TODD MICHAEL, broadcast executive; b. Seattle, Mar. 20, 1946; s. Max Krause and Joye (Kugler) B.; m. Cheryl Whiteman, Dec. 20, 1969 (div. Nov. 1983); children: Kimberly, Craig, Shaun; m. Marcia K. Dion, May 3, 1985. Student, Green River Coll., 1965. Account exec. Sta. KAYO, Seattle, 1967-73; account exec. Golden West Broadcasters Sta. KVI, Seattle, 1973-76; gen. mgr. Sta. KETO, 1974-75; v.p., gen. mgr. Sta. KPLZ, Seattle, 1976-83; pub. Monthly, Seattle, 1984—; Mem. exec. com. Seafair, Inc.; bd. affilates Sta. RKO Radio Network, N.Y.C., 1981-83; bd. dirs. Media Credit Union, Seattle. Mem. Puget Sound Radio Broadcasters Assn. (past pres.). Republican. Lutheran. Clubs: Sahalee Golf & Country (Redmond, Wash.); Washington Athletic (Seattle). Home: 25128 SE 28th St Issaquah WA 98027 Office: Monthly 603 Stewart St Suite 1020 Seattle WA 98027

BIVINS, SUSAN STEINBACH, systems engineer; b. Chgo., June 5, 1941; d. Joseph Bernard and Eleanor Celeste (Mathes) S.; B.S., Northwestern U., 1963; postgrad. U. Colo., 1964, U. Ill., 1965, UCLA, 1971; m. James Herbert Bivins, June 7, 1980. With IBM, 1967—, support mgr. East, White Plains, N.Y., 1977-78, systems support mgr., western region, Los Angeles, 1978-81, br. market support mgr., 1981-84, mgr. IBM ops. and support Los Angeles Summer Olympics, 1984; mgr. IBM office supporting devel. FAA air traffic control system for 1990's, 1984—; pres. Jastech, 1986—. Vol. tchr. computer sci. Calif. Mentally Gifted Minor Programs; vol. Los Angeles Youth Motivation Task Force. Recipient Kranz award Northwestern U., 1963; various engring. and mgmt. awards IBM, 1969—. Mem. Systems Engring. Symposium, Pi Lambda Theta. Developed program to retrieve data via terminal and direct it to any appropriate hardcopy device, 1973. Office: 12501 E Imperial Highway Norwalk CA 90650

BIXLER, OTTO CHAUNCEY, management consultant; b. Morenci, Ariz., May 9, 1916; s. Otto C. and Marie Ophelia (Dominguez) B.; m. Annette Estelle Struck, Sept. 3, 1938; children: Otto C. Jr., Terry Roy. BSEE cum laude, U. So. Calif., 1937; MBA and PhD in Bus. Adminstrn., Kennedy Western U., 1985, PhDEE, 1986. Registered profl. engr., Calif. V.p. Wanlass Elec. Co., Santa Ana, Calif., 1966-67, Rexall Drug Co., Los Angeles, 1967-68, Corp. Exec. Services, Santa Ana, 1968-74; gen. mgr. Waimea (Hawaii) Dispensary & Clinic, 1974-84; adminstr. Hawaiian Eye Ctr., Wahiawa, 1984-85; pres. Comml. Ventures, Inc., Koloa, Hawaii, 1985—; mgr. group activity aeros. div. Ford Motor Co., Newport Beach, Calif., 1958-62, mgr. indsl. systems; asst. gen. mgr. Packard Bell Electronics Corp., Los Angeles, 1962-63, v.p. Univac div. Sperry Rand Corp., St. Paul, 1963-66. Author: Interpersonal Relationship Counseling Program, 1973; designer 1st modern magnetic tape recorder, tape recorder stereo system. Organizer, cons. Island of Kauai Elec. Rates Control com., 1978-82. Recipient Outstanding Service award Am. Lung Assn., 1979-85, Service award, 1976-84. Mem. Hawaii Med. Group Mgmt. Assn. (pres. 1978-79), Sigma Xi, Eta Kappa Nu, Tau Beta Pi. Republican. Presbyterian. Lodge: Rotary (pres. West Kauai club 1977-78). Home: PO Box 633 Koloa HI 96756 Office: Comml Ventures Inc 2827A Poipu Rd Koloa-Kauai HI 96756

BJERKLIE, STEVEN PETERS, publications executive. m. Susan Janson; children: Andrew, Sarah. AA magna cum laude, Coll. of Marin, 1975; BS in Journalism, Mass Communications cum laude, U. Utah, 1977. Exec. producer U. Utah, Sta. KUER-FM Radio, Salt Lake City, 1975-77; editorial asst. Commerce Clearing House, Inc., San Rafael, Calif., 1978-80; asst. to pub. Meat Industry mag. Oman Pub., Inc., Mill Valley, Calif., 1980-85; dir. communication and publ. Western States Meat Assn., Oakland, Calif., 1985-86; editor Meat & Poultry Mag., Oman Pub., Inc., Mill Valley, Calif., 1986—. Office: Meat & Poultry Mag PO Box 1059 Mill Valley CA 94942

BJORHOVDE, REIDAR, civil engineer, educator, researcher, consultant; b. Harstad, Norway, Nov. 6, 1941; s. Reidar Conrad and Rebecca Josefine (Gjertsen) B.; m. Patricia Ellery Ordonez; Oct. 30, 1972; children: Ian Douglas, Heather Leah. MS, Tech. U. of Norway, 1964, PhD in Engring., 1968; PhD, Lehigh U., 1972. Registered profl. engr., Mont., Can. Asst. prof. and govt. scholar Tech. U. of Norway, Trondheim, 1964-68; regional and research engr. Am. Inst. Steel Constrn., Boston and N.Y., 1972-76; prof. civil engring. U. Alta., Edmonton, Can., 1976-81, U. Ariz., Tucson, 1981—; tech. sec. Structural Stability Research Council, Bethlehem, Pa., 1969-71; cons. to indsl. orgna., design firms, contractors, developers and research labs. worldwide. Author: over 70 and papers books in field. Recipient Duggan medal Engring. Inst. Can., 1980, T.R. Higgins Lectureship award, 1987; research fellow NATO, 1969-70; research grantee NATO, 1974; sci. fellow Royal Norwegian Council for Sci. and Indsl. Research, 1970-71; Sr. Guest Scientist fellow NATO, 1987; named Disting. Vis. Prof. Ecole Normale Superiere, Paris, 1987; numerous others, including NSF. Fellow ASCE (numerous coms.); mem. Structural Stability Research Council, Am. Welding Soc., Internat. Assn. for Bridge and Structural Engring., Am. INst. Steel Constrn. (com. chmn.). Democrat. Office: Univ Ariz Dept Civil Engring Tucson AZ 85721

BJORK, ROBERT ALLEN, psychology educator, researcher; b. Hector, Minn., Jan. 30, 1939; s. Oscar and Margaret Josephine (Bjornstad) B.; m.

Tele Boveng, June 10, 1964; m. Elizabeth Ligon, Sept. 13, 1969; children: Olin, Eric. Student, St. Olaf Coll., 1957-58; BA in Math., U. Minn., 1962; PhD in Psychology, Stanford U., 1966. Predoctoral instr. Stanford U., Calif., 1965-66; asst. prof. psychology U. Mich., Ann Arbor, 1966-70, assoc. prof., 1970-74, prof., 1974; prof. dept. psychology UCLA, 1974—; vis. asst. prof. Rockefeller U., N.Y.C., 1969-70; vis. cons. Bell Labs., 1977-78; lectr. Inst. Mgmt. Studies; cons., lectr. in field. Author: (with William Batchelder and John I. Yellott) Problems in Mathematical Learning Theory, 1966. Editor Memory and Cognition, 1981-85. Contbr. articles to profl. jours.; researcher in human memory. Basketball coach Los Angeles Jr. Basketball Program. Evans scholar, U. Minn.; fellow NDEA, 1962-65, NSF, 1965-66. Fellow Am. Psychol. Assn., Soc. Exptl. Psychologists; mem. Psychonomic Soc., Cognitive Sci. Soc., Phi Beta Kappa. Presbyterian. Office: UCLA Dept Psychology Los Angeles CA 90024

BJORKLUND, JANET VINSEN, speech pathologist; b. Seattle, July 31, 1947; d. Vernon Edward and Virginia Lea (Rogers) B.; m. Dan Robert Young, Dec. 04, 1971; children: Emery Allen, Alanna Vinsen, Marisa Rogers. Student, U. Vienna, Austria, 1966-67; BA, Pacific U., 1969; student, U. Wash., 1970-71; MA, San Francisco State U., 1977. Cert. clin. speech pathologist, audiologist. Speech pathologist, audiological cons. USN Hosp., Rota, Spain, 1972-75; traineeship in audiology VA Hosp., San Francisco, 1976; speech pathologist San Lorenzo (Calif.) Unified Schs., 1975-77, 78-81; dir. speech pathology St. Lukes Hosp., San Francisco, 1977-78; audiologist X.O. Barrios, M.D., San Francisco, 1977-81; cons. Visually Impaired Infant Program, Seattle, 1981-82; speech pathologist Everett (Wash.) Schs., 1982—; cons. Madison House, Kirkland, Wash., 1983—, NW Devel. Therapists, Everett, 1985-87, Pediatric Diagnostic and Treatment Ctr., Everett, 1985—. Author: (with others) Screening for Bilingual Preschoolers, 1977, (TV script), Clinical Services in San Francisco, 1978, Developing Better Communication Skills, 1982. Coordinator pre-sch. Christian edn. Kirkland Congl. Ch., Wash., 1983-85; organizer Residents Against Speeding Drivers, Madison Park, Seattle, 1985-87. Mem. Am. Speech and Hearing Assn., Am. Speech and Hearing Found., Wash. Speech and Hearing Assn. (regional rep. 1985-86, chair licensure task force 1986—), Phi Lambda Omicron (pres. Pacific U. chpt. 1968). Congregational. Avocations: numismatics, traveling, needlework, cooking. Office: Everett Sch Dist 2 202 Alder Everett WA 98203

BJORKLUND, LILA B., social services administrator; b. Ogden, Utah, Oct. 28, 1914; d. Michael and Harriet Serepta (Campbell) Burton; m. Russell Eric Bjorklund, Oct. 9, 1936 (dec. May 1977); children: Peter Burton, Jay Russell, Josef Robert, Anne B., Eric Wayne. Student, Weber Coll. Rep. Scholastic Mag. and Book Services, 1962-76; founder, dir. Utah Girls' Village, Salt Lake City, 1969—. Author monthly mags. Monthly Issues, 1962-65 (Nat. award 1965), Community Sch., 1972, Caring, 1986; author article series Critical Issues, 1962-72 (Cup award 1967). Adv. mem. Detention Ctr., Salt Lake City, 1961-68, Juvenile Ct., Salt Lake County, 1969-71, Utah Vocat. Edn. Com., Salt Lake County, 1969-71; pres. Utah State PTA, Salt Lake City, 1970-72; chmn. Utah State Bd. Edn., Salt Lake City, 1973-83; mem. Salt Lake City Commn. on Youth, COY Com. on Child Abuse, Utah Fedn. for Drug Free Youth. Recipient Disting. Service award Utah State Bd. Edn., 1969; named Outstanding Community Leader Eagles, 1984. Mem. Sch. Counselors Assn. (adv. 1969-71), Altrusa (Woman of Yr. 1975), Nat. Assn. Homes for Children (bd. dirs. 1980—), Utah Teaching Family Assn. of Homes (officer, bd. dirs. 1982—), Utah Assn. for Care and Treatment Children and Youth (pres. 1979—), Nat. Teaching Family Assn., Salt Lake Council of Women (pres. 1961-62, Hall of Fame 1978), Alpha Delta Kappa, Delta Kappa Gamma. Republican. Mormon. Club: Aurora (Salt Lake City). Avocations: reading, crafts, needlework. Home: 791 9th Ave Salt Lake City UT 84103 Office: Utah Girls Village 3808 S W Temple Suite 1D Salt Lake City UT 84115

BJORKMAN, DONALD CARL, design educator, consultant; b. Norway, Mich., July 27, 1929; s. Carl Levine and Anna Marie (Herman) J.; m. Gloria Ann Gonser, Oct. 5, 1957; children: Kurt Donald, Karinn Ann. BA, U. Wash., 1963; MFA, Rochester Inst. Tech., 1965. Asst. prof. design Calif. Coll. Art and Design, Oakland, 1965-70, cons., 1968-70; assoc. prof. U. Wis., Menomonie, 1970-73; project coordinator Agostruct Internat., Yakima, Wash., 1973-77; assoc. prof. Calif. Poly. State U., San Luis Obispo, 1977-81, No. Ariz. U., Flagstaff, 1981—; cons. Dependable Furniture, San Francisco, 1967-70, Shell Lake (Wis.) Boat Co., 1972; cooperative furniture mfr. Kirkland, Wash., 1972. One-man shows include Bavier Gallery Rochester Inst. Tech., 1965, Crown Zellerback Bldg., San Francisco, 1966, Art Ctr. Gallery, San Luis Obispo, Calif., 1980, others; group exhbns. include Interiors Pavillion, Seattle World Fair, 1962, 65-66, Mus. Contemporary Crafts, N.Y.C., 1963, 66, Mus. West, San Francisco, 1967, First World Craft Congress, N.Y.C., 1964, No. Ariz. U. Art Gallery, Flagstaff, 1982, Coconino Ctr. for Arts, 1983, others; contbr. chpts. to books and articles on design to profl. jours. Served with USMC, 1947-54. Recipient 3rd prize Fine Hardwood Nat. Design Competition, 1963, 1st, 2d hon. mention, 1964, Best Design of Yr. awards Indsl. Design Annual Rev., 1964-65. Office: No Ariz U Flagstaff AZ 86011

BJURMAN, GEORGE DAVID, investment counselor; b. Pa., Mar. 11, 1906; s. Andrew and Augusta (Bert) B.; B.S., U. Calif., Berkeley, 1930; m. Dorothy Kuhlmeyer, Oct. 10, 1936; children—Susan A., George A. With Wells Fargo Bank, 1930-36; sr. trust investment officer Bank of America, Los Angeles, 1936-46; dir., exec. v.p. fin. Occidental Life Calif., Los Angeles, 1946-70; chmn. bd., chief investment officer George D. Bjurman & Assos., Los Angeles, 1970—. Fellow Fin. Analyst Fedn.; mem. Los Angeles Soc. Fin. Analysts, N.Y. Soc. Fin. Analysts. Republican. Clubs: Los Angeles Country, Calif., Mens Garden of Los Angeles, Chevaliers du Tastevin. Office: 10100 Santa Monica Blvd Suite 2300 Los Angeles CA 90067

BLACIC, JAMES DONALD, geophysicist; b. Hermosa Beach, Calif., Oct. 24, 1942; s. James and Jeannette Lillian (Hamilton) B.; m. Jan Marie Clemens, July 20, 1968; children: Wendy Anne, Tanya Marie, Michael James, David Arthur. AA, El Camino Coll., 1962; BA, UCLA, 1964, PhD, 1971. Asst. prof. U. Wash., Seattle, 1970-78; staff mem. Los Alamos (N.Mex.) Nat. Lab., 1978-85, sect. leader, 1985—. Contbr. articles to profl. jours. Grantee NSF, 1971-78. Mem. Am. Geophys. Union, AAAS. Republican. Roman Catholic. Avocations: astronomy, photography. Office: Los Alamos Nat Lab MS C-335 Los Alamos NM 87545

BLACK, ARTHUR LEO, educator; b. Redlands, Calif., Dec. 1, 1922; s. Leo M. and Marie A. (Burns) B.; m. Trudi E. McCue, Nov. 11, 1945; children—Teresa (Mrs. William Townsend), Janet (Mrs. William Carter), Patti. B.S., U. Calif. at Davis, 1948, Ph.D., 1951. Faculty physiol. chemistry Sch. Vet. Medicine U. Calif. at Davis, 1951—, prof., 1962—, chmn. dept. physiol. scis., 1968-75; cons. NIH, 1970-72, U.S. Dept. Agr., 1977-80; chmn. Nutritional Scis. Tng. Com., 1971-72. Contbr. papers to profl. jours. Served to 1st lt. USAAF, 1943-46. Recipient Sci. Faculty award NSF, 1958; Acad. Senate Disting. Teaching award U. Calif., Davis, 1977; Research grantee NSF; Research grantee NIH, 1952—. Mem. Am. Soc. Biol. Chemists, Am. Physiol. Soc., Am. Inst. Nutrition (Borden award 1963), Sigma Xi, Phi Beta Kappa, Phi Zeta. Home: 891 Linden Ln Davis CA 95616 Office: U Calif Dept Physiol Scis Davis CA 95616

BLACK, ASHLEY VIRGINIA, screenwriter, writer; b. Chgo., Mar. 4, 1947; d. Raymond August and Virginia Josephine (Rogers) Isotta. B.A., DePaul U., 1969, M.A., 1970; postgrad. Georgetown U., 1977. Prin. systems engr. City of Chgo., 1971-74; cons. AEC, Germantown, Md., 1974-76; project mgr. Four Phase Systems Co., Cupertino, Calif., 1977-79; mgr. systems planning VWR, Inc., Brisbane, Calif., 1979-83; screenwriter, course writer, 1983—; cons. long-range planning computer depts.; bus. cons. Am. Honda, Gardena, Calif., 1986; adj. instr. UCLA, 1986—. Mem. San Francisco Zool. Soc., Los Angeles County Mus., Smithsonian Inst. Mem. Nat. Assn. Female Execs., Bay Area Career Women, NOW, Ind. Writers So. Calif., Broadcast Industry Conf. Lodges: Rosicrucian, AMORC. Author screenplays. Office: PO Box 10505 Beverly HIlls CA 90213-3505

BLACK, BRIAN WESTON, executive recruiter; b. Newport, R.I., May 28, 1951; s. John W. and Star R. B.; m. Elizabeth Ann; children: Jonathan Weston, Elizabeth Marion, Julia Star. B.A. in Geography, Colgate U., 1973; M.B.A., St. Mary's Coll., Moraga, Calif., 1979. Systems engr. Electronic Data Systems, San Francisco, 1973-76; project mgr., systems mgr. Decimus Corp., San Francisco; with Source Edp, San Francisco, 1976-78, dir. Mountain View office, 1979-83; owner, operator MTB Video, Inc., Oakland, Calif., 1979-84; owner, producer The Video Gourmet Cooking Sch., Oakland, 1984-86; v.p. The Corp. Service Group, San Francisco, 1985-87, Brian Black Co., 1987. Bd. dirs. Organized People of Elmhurt Neighborhood, Margaret Jenkins Dance Co., Libertarian. Presbyterian. Club: San Francisco Bay. Office: 2063 Landings Dr Mountain View CA 94043

BLACK, COBEY, journalist; b. Washington, June 15, 1922; d. Elwood Alexander and Margaret (Beall) C.; m. Edwin F. Black; children: Star, Christopher, Noel, Nicholas, Brian, Bruce. BA, Wellesley Coll., 1944; postgrad., U. Hawaii. Exec. sec. to Irene, designer Metro-Goldwyn-Mayer, 1944; actress Fed. Republic Germany, 1945-46; women's editor Washington Daily News, 1947-50; columnist Honolulu Star Bull., 1954-65, Honolulu Advertiser, 1972-84; cons. HEW, Peace Corps, 1960-61; v.p. Mandalay Imports Corp. Author: Birth of A Princess, 1962, Iolani Luahine, 1986; travel editor Bangkok World, 1968-69; publicist CBS-TV series Hawaii Five-O, 1978. Mem. Hawaii State Commn. on Status of Women, 1978-86. Democrat. Episcopalian. Clubs: Nat. Press, Royal Bangkok Sports, Outrigger Canoe, Waialae Country. Office: Mandalay Halekulani Hotel 2199 Kalia Rd Honolulu HI 96815

BLACK, CRAIG CALL, museum administrator; b. Peking, China, May 28, 1932; s. Arthur and Mary (Nichols) B.; children—Christopher Arthur, Lorna Varn; m. Mary elizabeth King, Jan. 4, 1986. A.B., Amherst Coll., 1954; M.A. (Simpson fellow), Johns Hopkins U., 1957; Ph.D. (NIH fellow), Harvard U., 1962. Geologist Okla. Geol. Survey, summer 1956; asst. curator Carnegie Inst., Pitts., 1960-62; curator Carnegie Inst., 1962-70; prof. biology U. Kans., 1970-72; dir. Mus. of Tex. Tech. U., Lubbock, 1970-75, Carnegie Inst., 1975-82, Los Angeles Mus. Natural History, 1982—; co-leader John F. Kennedy U. Western Museums Conf. Seminar, 1983; faculty Am. Law Inst.-ABA Course of Study in Legal Problems of Mus. Adminstrn., 1980, 82; co-dir. Mus. Mgmt. Inst., U. Calif., Berkeley, summers, 1979, 80; adj. prof. Univ. Mus. and dept. geology U. Colo., 1965—. Contbr. articles to profl. jours. Presdl. appointee Nat. Mus. Service Bd., Washington, 1982-85; mem. Nat. Sci. Bd., 1985—; rev. panel Inst. of Mus. Services, Washington, 1978-79, policy panel, 1978-80. Simpson fellow, 1954-55; Kellog fellow, 1956-59; NIH precotoral fellow, 1959-60. Fellow AAAS; mem. Am. Assn. Mus. (pres. 1980-82, mem. commn. on mus. for a new century 1982-84, mem. council 1977—). Club: Cosmos (Washington); Calif. (Los Angeles). Home: 777 S Windsor Blvd Los Angeles CA 90007 Office: Los Angeles County Mus of Natural History 900 Exposition Blvd Los Angeles CA 90007

BLACK, DEAN FRANKLIN, infosystems specialist; b. San Diego, Aug. 10, 1958; s. Bruce F. and Margaret B.; married. Student, Occidental Coll., 1976-77; BA in Comparative Lit., San Diego State U., 1982. Programmer San Diego State U. Found., 1978-80; with Pacific Pharmacy Computers, San Diego, 1980-82; project leader Genesis Computer Systems, San Diego, 1983, EDS, San Diego, 1984; v.p. infosystems Calgaro Ins. Services, San Diego, 1984—. Editor: Star Vision mag., 1981; producer Behind The Scenes at PPC, 1982. Mem. Data Processing Mgmt. Assn. Avocations: music, photography. Office: Calgaro Ins Services Inc 6727 Flanders Dr San Diego CA 92121

BLACK, KATHERINE ANDREA, labor union administrator; b. Phila., Nov. 10, 1949; d. Joseph and Marianne Adele (Ingham) B.; m. David St. John, Nov. 10, 1974 (div. 1978); 1 stepchild, Shane Miles. BS, U. Oreg., 1983. Staff rep. Grad. Teaching Fellows Fedn., Am. Fedn. Tchrs., AFL-CIO, Eugene, Oreg., 1982-83; bus. agt. Oreg. Pub. Employees Union, Service Employees Internat. Union, AFL-CIO, Salem and Portland, Oreg., 1983-85, also local sec., conv. del., com. mem. and gen. activist, 1980-83; bus. agt. Engrs. and Scientists of Calif., Marine Engrs Beneficial Assn., AFL-CIO, San Francisco, 1985—. Activist People for So. African Freedom, Eugene, 1980-84, Portlanders Organized for So. African Freedom, 1985, Bay Area Free S. Africa Movement labor com., 1986. Mem. Coalition of Labor Union Women, Alameda County Cen. Labor Council AFL-CIO (del. 1986), Northwest Oreg. Cen. Labor Council AFL-CIO (del. 1984-85), Phi Beta Kappa. Democrat. Office: ESC-MEBA AFL-CIO 340 Fremont St San Francisco CA 94105

BLACK, KEVIN DALE, archaeologist, educator; b. Tiffin, Ohio, Feb. 6, 1955; s. Marlin Jacob and Mary Jane (Gosche) B. BA magna cum laude, U. Colo., 1977, MA, 1979. Staff archaeologist Centuries Research Inc., Montrose, Colo., 1979-81, Metcalf Archaeol. Cons. Inc., Eagle, Colo., 1981—; tchr. Colo. Mountain Coll., Eagle, 1982—. Contbr. articles to profl jours. Mem. Colo. Council Profl. Archaeologists (bd. dirs. 1984-86), Utah Profl. Archaeol. Council, Soc. Am. Archaeology, Phi Beta Kappa, Sigma Xi. Avocations: cross-country skiing, fishing, reading, collecting old books. Office: Metcalf Archaeol Cons Inc PO Box 899 Eagle CO 81631

BLACK, KIRBY SAMUEL, biomedical engineer; b. Salinas, Calif., Mar. 29, 1954; s. Samuel McTarnahan and Rosilind (Strand) B.; m. Christine Mary Sharman, Mar. 5, 1977; children: Matthew, Colin. BSME, UCLA, 1976; postgrad., U. Calif., Irvine, 1984—. Registered profl. engr., Calif. Research asst. dept. surgery UCLA, 1973-77; research assoc. dept. pediatrics U. Calif., Irvine, 1977-78, dir. reconstructive microsurgery labs., assoc. devel. engr., research assoc. div. plastic surgery, 1978-84, co-dir. transplantation labs. and burn reseach labs. divs. plastic surgery and urology, 1981—, dir. reconstructive microsurgery labs., assoc. devel. engr. div. plastic surgery, 1984—; cons. Beckman Instruments, Inc., 1982-83, Am. Edwards, 1982-83; clin. instr. dept. surgery U. Calif., Irvine, 1983—; dir. reconstructive microsurgery demonstration trauma week U. Calif., Irvine Med. Ctr., 1981; co-dir. microsurg. workshop ACS, Newport Beach, Calif., 1982. Contbr. numerous articles to sci. jours., chpts. to books. Bd. dirs. Orange County Burn Assn., Irvine, 1984—. Grantee Am. Assn. Plastic Surgeons, 1980, 81-82, 82-83, U. Calif., Irvine, 1980-82, Am. Soc. for Surgery of Hand, 1981-82, Smart Family Found., 1981-82, 82-83, Plastic Surgery Ednl. Found., 1981, Am. Soc. Aesthetic Plastic Surgery, 1982, NIH, 1984, numerous others. Mem. AAAS, IEEE, Assn. for Advancement Med. Instrumentation, Am. Burn Assn., Assn. Clin. Faculty. Republican. Avocations: family, woodworking. Office: U Calif Dept Surgery Med Scis I Irvine CA 92717

BLACK, WILFORD REX, JR., state senator; b. Salt Lake City, Jan. 31, 1920; s. Wilford Rex and Elsie Isabell (King) B.; m. Helen Shirley Frazer; children—Susan, Janet, Cindy, Joy, Peggy, Vanna, Gayle, Rex. Student schools in Utah. Locomotive engr. Rio Grande R.R., 1941-81; mem. Utah Senate, 1972—, speaker Third House, 1975-76, majority whip, 1977-78, minority leader, 1981—; chmn., vice chmn. United Transp. Union, 1972-78; sec. Utah State Legis. Bd., United Transp. Chmn. bd. Rail Operators Credit Union, 1958—; mission pres. Rose Park Stake Mormon Ch., high priest group leader Rose Park 9th Ward, 1980-83, mem. Rose Park Stake High Council, 1957-63. Served with U.S. Army, 1942-45. Recipient various awards r.r and legis. activities. Democrat. Office: 826 N 13th W Salt Lake City UT 84116

BLACKBURN, JOHN LEWIS, consulting engineer; b. Kansas City, Mo., Oct. 2, 1913; s. John Ealy and Lela (Garnett) B.; m. Margaret Bailey, Sept. 12, 1943; children—Susan T., Joan Blackburn Krist, Margot A. Blackburn Jahns. BSEE with high honors, U. Ill., 1935. With Westinghouse Electric Corp., Newark, 1936-78, cons. engr., 1969-78; pvt. practice as cons. engr., Bothell, Wash., 1979—; adj. prof. Poly. Inst. N.Y., 1949-65, Poly. Inst. N.J., Newark, 1958-71; spl. lectr. IEEE Ednl. Activities, 1952—. Author, editor: Applied Protective Relaying, 1978; author: Protective Relaying Principles and Application, 1987. Trustee, treas. Millington Bapt. Ch., N.J., 1952-69. Recipient Order of Merit award Westinghouse Electric Corp., 1971, Attwood Assocs. award U.S. Nat. Com. Internat. Conf. for Large High Voltage Electric Systems, 1986. Fellow IEEE (chmn. publ. dept. Power Engring. Soc. 1972-76, sec., 1977-79, chmn. power system relaying com. 1969-70, Disting. Service award 1978, Outstanding Service award IEEE ednl. bd. 1979, Centennial medal 1984); mem. Sigma Xi, Tau Beta Pi, Eta Kappa Nu, Phi Kappa Phi. Club: China Stamp Soc., Inc. (pres. 1979—), Am. Soc. Polar Philatelists (dir., treas. 1967—). Home: 21816 8th Pl W Bothell WA 98021

BLACKBURN, ROBERT PARKER, attorney; b. Tacoma, Sept. 24, 1956; s. John Griffin and Dorothy Joan (Parker) B. BS with honors, Case Western Res. U., 1978; JD, Am. U., 1981. Bar: D.C., 1982. Atty. Banner, Birch, McKie and Beckett, Washington, 1981-84; asst. patent counsel Agrigenetics Research Corp., Boulder, Colo., 1984-86; atty. Ciotti and Murashige, Menlo Park, Calif., 1986—. Mem. AAAS, ABA, Am. Chemical Soc., Am. Intellectual Property Law Assn. (biotech. task force mem.). Club: Colo. Mountain (Boulder chpt.) (asst. climbing instr. 1985). Avocation: mountaineering. Office: Ciotti and Murashige 545 Middlefield Rd Menlo Park CA 94025

BLACKMAN, DAVID IRA, health science association administrator, consultant; b. Los Angeles, Mar. 12, 1951; s. Soli and Erika Louise (Ullmann) B. BS, U. So. Calif., 1975; MS, U. LaVerne, 1986. Cert. tchr., Calif. Fin. specialist U. Calif. Med. Ctr., San Francisco, 1975-79; adminstrn. specialist U. Calif. Med. Ctr., Irvine, 1979-80; adminstr. Kaiser Found. Health Plan, Los Angeles, 1980—; cons. health care DIB Group, Glendale, Calif., 1980—. Recipient Gold Achievement award United Way Campaigns, Los Angeles, 1984. Mem. Am. Guild Patient Acct. Mgrs., Health Care Fin. Mgmt. Assocs., Am. Mgmt. Assn., Nat. Right to Work Found., Assn. Western Hosps. Republican. Club: Canyon Shores Country (Palm Springs, Calif.). Avocations: flying, consulting, teaching, tennis. Home: 1203 Viola Ave Glendale CA 91202-1803

BLACKMAN, LAWRENCE DAVID, mechanical and aerospace engineer; b. Wilmington, Del., Sept. 13, 1957; s. Martin Sherman Blackman and Roberta Phyllis (Silver) Altman. BSME cum laude, Poly. Inst. N.Y., 1979; MSME, MIT, 1981. Research asst., engr. magnetohydrodyamic power generation research MIT, Cambridge, 1979-81; MTS-III engr. Rockwell Space div., Downey, Calif., 1981—. Author transient response analysis program, 1982 (NASA-TU award 1983), contbr. tech. articles to profl. jours. Mem. ASME, Soc. Automotive Engrs., Tau Beta Pi. Democrat. Jewish. Avocations: stage and theatre dance, bicycle racing, skiing, volleyball, hiking. Home: 10000 Imperial Hwy F219 Downey CA 90242 Office: Rockwell Space Sta div 12214 Lakewood Blvd AE99 Downey CA 90241

BLACKMAN, MARC CALLAHAN, beverage industry executive; b. Hinsdale, Ill., Aug. 22, 1959; s. John Chadwick and Mary Lee (Bowman) B.; m. Joni Lynn Hirsch, Sept. 5, 1982; 1 child, Ryan Hirsch. BS in Bus. and Econs., U. Ariz., 1982. Fin. analyst Conoco, Houston and Denver, 1982-83; sales rep. Gallo Winery, Denver, 1983-85; state mgr. Bartles and Jaymes brand div., Denver, 1985, Paul Thomas Wines brand div., Denver, 1986—; dist. mgr. Gallo Winery, Denver, 1985-86, area sales mgr., 1986—. Dist. delegate Highlands Ranch (Colo.) Community Assn. 1984, fin. committeeman 1985, mem. tribunal bd. 1986—. Mem. Cyanthos, U. Ariz. Alumni Assn. (bd. dirs.). Republican. Episcopalian. Avocations: skiing, intramural basketball, aerobics. Home: 380 Quail Ridge Circle Highlands Ranch CO 80126

BLACKNER, BOYD ATKINS, architect; b. Salt Lake City, Aug. 29, 1933; s. Lester Armond and Anna (McDonald) B.; m. Elizabeth Ann Castleton, June 4, 1955; children: Catherine Blackner Philpot, David, Elizabeth, Genevieve. B.Arch., U. Utah, 1956, B.F.A., 1956. Registered architect, Fla., Utah, Wyo. Asst. landscape architect Nat. Park Service, Mt. Rainier, Wash., 1956; job capt. Cannon, Smith & Gustavson, Salt Lake City, 1957, Hellmuth, Obata & Kassabaum, St. Louis, 1958-59, Caudill, Rowlett & Scott, Houston, 1959-60; project architect Victor A. Lundy, Sarasota, Fla., N.Y.C., 1960-63; pvt. practice architecture Salt Lake City, 1963—; mem. adv. council, vis. juror, critic Grad. Sch. Architecture U. Utah; grad. program dept. landscape architecture and environ. planning Utah State U., 1977-86; mem. region 8 adv. panel archtl. and engring. services GSA, 1977-78; bd dirs. First Fed. Savs., Salt Lake City. Editorial adv. bd.: Symposia mag, 1977-83; contbr. articles to mags. Vice chmn. Utah Advanced Gift Heart Fund drive, 1964; co-chmn archtl. div. United Fund drive, 1964; mem. Salt Lake City City Walls Com., 1976-77, Salt Lake City Council for Arts, 1977-78, Utah Gov.'s Adv. Com. Low Income Housing, Utah Rev. Panel Emergency Energy Conservation Programs; adv. bd. Utah Citizens for Arts, Utah Soc. Autistic Children.; mem. dinner exec. com. Nat. Jewish Hosp./Nat. Asthma Center, Denver, 1983. Recipient Danforth Honor award, 1951; also numerous AIA awards including regional design awards for U. Utah Library Fountain, 1970; Westminster Coll. Fountain Plaza, 1972; Nat. award for Kearns/Daynes/Alley Annex, 1978; Western Mountain Region Hist. award of merit for Daynes/Kearns/Alley Annex, 1977; Am. Assn. Sch. Adminstrs. Exhibit award for Wilson Elementary Sch. Green River, Wyo., 1974; Award merit Producers' Council, Inc., 1978; award Nat. Lincoln Arc Welding Found., 1978; Urban Design award 3d Ann. Program, 1979; others. Fellow AIA (dir. Utah chpt. 1968, 71, sec. chpt. 1972-73, chmn. regional conf. 1974, pres. Utah soc. 1975-76, chmn. jury for Wyo. chpt. design awards program 1974, regional rep. to housing com., Nat. Honor award jury 1979, recorder nat. conv. 1982); Mem. U. Utah Alumni Assn. (bd. dirs. 1987), Salt Lake Area C. of C. (land use, fine arts, city walls coms.; v.p. 1980-81, chmn. bd. 1982-83). Club: Salt Lake Swim and Tennis. Lodge: Salt Lake Rotary (treas. 1976-77, pres. 1979-80), Alta (bd. dirs.). Home: 1460 Military Way Salt Lake City UT 84103 Office: Kearns Bldg Suite A-400 136 S Main St Salt Lake City UT 84101

BLACKORBY MUELLER, CAROL HILDA, life insurance company executive, educator; b. Helena, Mont., June 23, 1924; d. Stanley Prentice Freeman and Hilda Sophia (Matson) F.; m. Lyle Lee Blackorby, Feb. 18, 1944; children—Richard L., Lynne S., Brian R., Jeffry D. m. Floyd Kenneth Mueller, Oct. 23, 1982. Student Seattle Pacific Coll., 1942-43 U. Wash., Seattle, 1943-44, Am. Coll. 1976. C.L.U.; chartered fin. cons. Brokerage rep., brokerage mgr. Phoenix Mut. Life, 1969-76; brokerage mgr. Mfrs. Life Ins. Co., Spokane, Wash., 1976-83, Gt. West Life Assurance, 1983-84; brokerage mgr. Great West LIfe Assurance, Seattle, 1985—; instr. Spokane Falls Community Coll. Mem. Spokane C.L.U.s (pres. 1979-80), Seattle C.L.U.s, Spokane Assn. Life Underwriters, Spokane Estate Planning Council. Republican. Presbyterian. Club: Am. Contract Bridge League. Office: 3005 112th Ave NE Bellevue WA 98009

BLACKSTOCK, DOROTHY EVELYN LYONS, artist; b. Tacoma, Aug. 4, 1914; d. Frank and Mildred Aubrey (Potts) Lyons; student Whitman Coll., 1931, Coll. Puget Sound, 1932, U. Wash., 1933; m. Carl Mims Blackstock, July 12, 1942; children—Carl Lyons, Gregory Lee. One-man shows State Hist. Mus., Olympia, Wash., Handforth Gallery, Tacoma; exhibited art in group shows at Seattle Art Mus., Woessner Gallery, Kittredge Gallery, U. Puget Sound, Frye Art Mus., Frederick and Nelson Little Gallery and Exhbn. Hall, Puget Sound Area Shows, NW Watercolor Show, Nat. League Am. Pen Women Biennials, Wash. State Hist. Mus.; represented in permanent collections Wash. State Hist. Mus. at Tacoma, Wash. State U. at Pullman; illustrator two covers Tacoma News Tribune Mag. Sect., five covers Seattle Times Mag. Sect. Art chmn. Music and Art Found., Seattle, 1962-64, trustee, 1958-64; mem. Seattle hospitality com. Allied Arts; chaperone Seattle Seafair Princess, 1979-85. Named Woman of Year in art, 1959. Mem. Nat. League Am. Pen Women (br. pres. 1966-68, v.p. Seattle br. 1979-80), Seattle Co-arts and Quad-A Art Club, Fedn. Women's Clubs, Women's Ednl. Club (pres. 1960-61), Women Painters Wash. (pres. 1972-74), Artist's Equity, Seattle Art Mus., Seattle Opera Guild, Assistance League of Seattle. Clubs: Seattle Golf; Sand Point Golf and Country; Wash. Athletic, 200 plus 1. Home: 5520 Coniston Rd NE Seattle WA 98105

BLACKSTOCK, JAMES FIELDING, lawyer; b. Los Angeles, Sept. 19, 1947; s. James Carne and Justine Fielding (Gibson) B.; m. Kathleen Ann Weigand, Dec. 12, 1969; children—Kristin Marie, James Fielding. A.B., U. So. Calif., 1969; J.D., 1976. Bar: Calif. 1976, U.S. Dist. Ct. (cen. dist.) Calif. 1977, U.S. Supreme Ct. 1980. Law clk. Hill Farrer Burrill, Los Angeles, 1975-76, assoc., 1976-80; assoc. Zobrist, Garner, Garrett, Los Angeles, 1980-83; ptnr. Zobrist & Vienna, Los Angeles, 1983; v.p., gen. counsel Tatum Petroleum, La Habra, Calif., 1983; atty. Thorpe, Sullivan, Workman & Thorpe, 1984; ptnr. Sullivan, Workman & Dee, 1985—. Mem. Town Hall, Los Angeles, 1980—. Served to lt. USN, 1969-73, PTO. Mem. ABA, Los Angeles County Bar Assn. Republican. Roman Catholic. Club: Saddle and Sirloin (Glendale, Calif.). Lodge: Elks. Home: 4628 Lasheart Dr La Canada CA 91011 Office: Sullivan Workman & Dee 800 S Figueroa St Suite 1200 Los Angeles CA 90017-2521

BLACKWELDER, KENT GENE, management consultant; b. Alexandria, Minn., Dec. 3, 1955; s. Gene and Greta (Wick) B. BS in Indsl. Mgmt.,

Purdue U., 1977; MBA, Pepperdine U., 1982; postgrad., UCLA, 1983. Cons. Triad Microsystems, El Segundo, Calif., 1982-83; dir. plans and programs Mattel Elec., Hawthorne, Calif., 1983-84; cons. Tecolote Research, El Segundo, 1984-85, Blackbell, Redondo Beach, Calif., 1985—. Liaison officer explorer scouts Boy Scouts Am., Los Angeles, 1977-79; chmn. USAF Space Heritage Program, Los Angeles, 1980-81. Served to capt. USAF, 1977-82. Named one of Outstanding Young Men of Am., U.S. Jaycees, 1983. Mem. Planning Exec. Inst. (Los Angeles chpt.), Project Mgmt. Inst., (Los Angeles chpt.), Air Force Soc. (Los Angeles), Am. Soc. Mil. Comptrollers (Los Angeles chpt.), Kappa Sigma (grand procurator Purdue U. chpt. 1975-76). Baptist. Club: Arnold Air Soc. (West Lafayette, Ind.) (comptroller 1976-77). Avocations: phys. fitness, music, enology.

BLACKWELDER, RON F., engineering educator, consultant, researcher; b. Pratt, Kans., July 16, 1942; s. Forest A. and Evelyn (Meyer) B.; m. Judy P. Tiefel, Sept. 12, 1965; children: Laura, Sherri. BS, U. Colo., 1964; postgrad., Technische Hochschule, Munich, 1964-65; PhD, Johns Hopkins U., 1970. Teaching and research asst. Johns Hopkins U., Balt., 1967-70; asst. prof. engring. U. So. Calif., Los Angeles, 1970-75, assoc. prof., 1975-79, prof., 1980—; vis. scientist Max Planck Inst., Gottingen, Fed. Republic Germany, 1976-77; prof. associé Polytechnique U., Grenoble, France, 1983-84; vis. prof. Inst. Nat. Polytechnique, Grenoble, France, 1983-84; cons. in fluid mechanics, instrumentation and data processing. Author: Methods of Experimental Physics, 1981; contbr. articles to profl. jours.; patentee vorticity probe utilizing strain measurements, hydro-resistance anemometer. Elder St. Matthews Luth. Ch., Harbor City, Calif., 1978-85; pres., v.p. Servant of Christ Luth. Ch., Sepulveda, Calif., 1970-77. Guggenheim fellow, 1976-77; recipient Outstanding Faculty Service award U. So. Calif., 1975. Fellow AIAA (assoc.), Am. Phys. Soc.; mem. AAAS, Sigma Xi, Tau Beta Pi. Office: U So Calif Dept Aerospace Engring Los Angeles CA 90089-0192

BLACKWELL, J.W., purcasing executive; b. Parrish, Ala., Aug. 13, 1932; s. James H. and Effie (Meadows) B.; m. Mary L. Harris, June 4, 1951; children: Kenneth M., Pamela Giesler. BS in Indsl. Mgmt., San Jose State U., 1959. Sr. buyer EIMAC, San Carlos, Calif., 1961-69, IOMEC, Santa Clara, Calif., 1969-71; purchasing mgr. Versatec, Cupertino, Calif., 1971-74, Cobilt, Santa Clara, 1974-77, Advance Electronics Design, Sunnyvale, Calif., 1977—. Bd. dirs. Daybreak Camp Inc., Santa Cruz, Calif. Served with USN, 1951-55, Korea. Mem. Purchasing Mgmt. Assn. Silicon Valley No. Calif. (dir. nat. affairs 1982-83), Purchasing Mgmt. Assn. No. Calif. (dir. nat. affairs 1982-83, pres. 1981-82, 1st v.p. 1980-81). Republican. Clubs: U.S. Bass; West Coast Bass. Avocation: fishing. Office: Advanced Electronics Design 440 Potrero Ave Sunnyvale CA 94086

BLADE, MELINDA KIM, educator, researcher, archaeologist; b. San Diego, Jan. 12, 1952; d. George A. and Arline A. M. (MacLeod) B. BA, U. San Diego, 1974, MA in Teaching, 1975, MA, 1975, EdD, 1986. Cert. secondary tchr., Calif.; cert. community coll. instr., Calif.; registered profl. historian, Calif. Instr. Coronado Unified Sch. Dist., Calif., 1975-76; head coach women's basketball U. San Diego, 1976-78; instr. Acad. of Our Lady of Peace, San Diego, 1976—, chmn. social studies dept., 1983—, counselor, 1984—, co-dir. student activities, 1984—, coordinator advanced placement program, 1986—; mem. archaeol. excavation team U. San Diego, 1975—, hist. researcher, 1975—; lectr., 1981—. Author hist. reports and research papers. Editor U. San Diego pubs. Vol. Am. Diabetes Assn., San Diego, 1975—; coordinator McDonald's Diabetes Bike-a-thon, San Diego, 1977, 78. Mem. Nat. Council Social Studies, Calif. Council Social Studies, Soc. Bibl. Archeology, Assn. Supervision and Curriculum Devel., Assn. Scientists and Scholars Internat. for Shroud of Turin, Medieval Acad. Am., Medieval Assn. Pacific, Am. Hist. Assn., Western Assn. Women Historians, Renaissance Soc. Am., San Diego Hist. Soc., Phi Alpha Theta (sec.-treas. 1975-77), Phi Delta Kappa. Office: Acad Our Lady of Peace 4860 Oregon St San Diego CA 92116

BLAINE, DEVON, public relations executive; b. Lynwood, Calif., Sept. 16, 1947; d. Harold W. and Ruth Mae (Decho) Schulz; m. Robert Beau Baur, Feb. 1970 (div.). Student UCLA, 1965-66. Owner, founder Blaine Group, Los Angeles, 1975—. Mem. exec. com. White House Conf. on Small Bus., 1980, 82, So. Calif. chmn., 1986; mem. exec. com. Calif. State Conf. Small Bus., 1980, 82, 84; mem. blue ribbon planning com. Calif. State Conf. Small Bus., 1984; mem. Gov. Brown's Small Bus. Adv. Council; co-chmn. Calif. Delegation White House Conf. on Small Bus., 1986. Mem. Nat. Small Bus. Assn., Women in Bus., Nat. Assn. Women Bus. Owners (past chpt. pres.), Pub. Relations Soc. Am., Book Publicists So. Calif., Women in Show Bus., Women's Nat. Book Assn., Variety Club, Publicity Club N.Y. Democrat. Lutheran. Office: The Blaine Group 7465 Beverly Blvd Los Angeles CA 90036

BLAINE, DOROTHEA CONSTANCE RAGETTÉ, lawyer, b. N.Y.C., Sept. 23, 1930; d. Robert Raymond and Dorothea Ottilie Ragetté; B.A., Barnard Coll., 1952; M.A., Calif. State U., 1968; Ed.D., UCLA, 1978; J.D., Western State U., 1981; postgrad. in taxation Golden Gate U. Bar: U.S. Dist. Ct. (ea., so. and cen. dists.) Calif., 1986—. Mem. tech. staff Planning Research Corp., Los Angeles, 1964-67; assoc. scientist Holy Cross Hosp., Mission Hills, Calif., 1967-70; career devel. officer and affirmative action officer County of Orange, Santa Ana, Calif., 1970-74, sr. adminstrv. analyst, budget and program coordination, 1974-78; spl. projects asst. CAO/Spl. Programs Office, 1978-80, sr. adminstrv. analyst, 1980-83; admitted to Calif. bar, 1982; sole practice, 1982—; instr. Am. Coll. Law, Brea, Calif., 1987. Bd. dirs. Deerfield Community Assn., 1975-78, Orange YMCA, 1975-77. Mem. Assn. Trial Lawyers Am., Calif. Trial Lawyers Assn., Orange County Trial Lawyers Assn., Calif. Women Lawyers, Nat. Women's Polit. Caucus, ABA, Calif. Bar Assn., Orange County Bar Assn., Orange County Women Lawyers Assn. ACLU, Delta Theta Phi, Phi Delta Kappa. Office: 2121 S Coast Hwy Suite 200 Corona Del Mar CA 92625

BLAIR, CYNTHIA LYNN, nurse, wellness coordinator; b. Riverside, Calif., Apr. 9, 1959; d. Don Harry and Dona Dee (Salisbury) Pritchett; m. Gregory John Blair, Dec. 27, 1980; 1 child, Jenae Marie. AS in Nursing, Yavapai Coll., 1980. RN, Ariz. Sales mgr. Photography Studio, Prescott, Ariz., 1975-80; registered nurse Desert Samaritan Hosp., Mesa, Ariz., 1980-85; health advisor Health Advancement Services, Tempe, Ariz., 1985-86; wellness coordinator City of Glendale, Calif., 1986-87; founder Alive and Well Corp. Health Consultants, Utah., 1987—. Organizer, dir. Am.'s Jr. Miss. Pageant, Prescott, 1978-79, Prescott Jr. Miss Pageant, 1980. Mem. Ariz. Nurses Assn. Republican. Methodist. Club: Keyettes (Prescott) (activity dir. 1976-77). Home and Office: 9141 South Meadow Ct Sandy UT 84092

BLAIR, FREDERICK DAVID, interior designer; b. Denver, June 15, 1946; s. Frederick Edward and Margaret (Whitely) B. BA, U. Colo., 1969; postgrad. in French, U. Denver, 1981-82. Interior designer The Denver, 1969-76, store mgr., 1976-80; v.p. Hartley House Interiors, Ltd., Denver, 1980-83; pvt. practice interior design Denver, 1983—; com. mem. Ice House Design Ctr., Denver, 1985-86, Design Directory Western Region, Denver, 1986. Designs shown in various mags. Mem. Rep. Nat. Com. Mem. Am. Soc. Interior Designers (co-chmn. com. profl. registration 1986), Denver Art Mus., Nat. Trust for Hist. Preservation, Hist. Denver, Inc. Christian Scientist. Avocations: skiing, painting, tennis. Office: 1260 Vine St Suite 1 Denver CO 80206

BLAIR, JACK DONOVAN, steel company executive; b. Estherville, Iowa, Dec. 4, 1951; s. Byron Donovan and Ivy Elizabeth (Hepp) B.; m. Georginna Udink, Mar. 18, 1981, (div. Jan. 1982); 1 child, Misha; m. Edyth Wynn Reddington, Aug. 13, 1983; children: Ora Lee, Kennith, Michael. Student, Iowa Lakes Community Coll., 1970, Coll. Eastern Iowa, 1971. Lab. technician Comml. Testing & Engring. Co., Denver, 1975-79; lab. mgr. Comml. Testing & Engring. Co., Price, Utah, 1979-83, asst. div. mgr., 1983-84; lab. supr. Kaiser Steel, Raton, N.Mex., 1984—. Mem. AIME, Rocky Mountain Coal Mining Inst., Raton Men's Golf Assn. (pres. 1985), Carbon Men's Golf Assn. (statistician 1984, pres. 1983). Methodist. Avocations: investing, computer programming. Home: 220 S 5th St Raton NM 87740 Office: Kaiser Steel PO Box 1107 Raton NM 87740

BLAIR, SIDNEY ROBERT, petroleum company executive; b. Port of Spain, Trinidad, Aug. 13, 1929; s. Sidney Martin and Janet (Gentleman) B.; m. Lois Wedderburn, June 13, 1953; children: Megan, James, Robert, Martin, Charlotte. BS, Queens U., 1951. Field engr., mgr. constrn. of gas and oil pipe lines and refineries 1951-58; dir. gas ops. and purchasing Alta. and So. Gas Co. Ltd. and affiliates, 1959-69; exec. v.p. The Alta. Gas Trunk Line Co. Ltd., 1969-70, pres., chief exec. officer, from 1970; now chmn., chief exec. officer Nova, an Alta. (Can.) Corp., Calgary; former pres., chmn. bd. dirs. Husky Oil Ltd. subs. Calgary. Office: Nova an Alberta Corp, 801 Seventh Ave SW, Calgary, AB Canada T2P 2N6 *

BLAIR, THOMAS EDWARD, cultural association executive; b. Kansas City, Mo., Dec. 18, 1946; s. Thomas Franklin and Martha (Robson) B. Cert. d'Enseignement, U. Poitiers, Tours, France, 1966; BA, U. S. Colo., 1968; MA, PhD, U. Wis., 1976. Researcher U. Wis., Madison, 1975; lectr. French San Francisco State U., 1976-78; dir. European Studies Assn., San Francisco, 1978—. Author: Le Roman de Sade, 1976. Served with U.S. Army, 1969-71. French Gout scholar U. Poitiers, 1965-66; fellow NDEA, 1968-73, Ford Found., 1973-74. Mem. Am. Assn. Tchrs. of French. Republican. Avocations: classical music, opera, theater, travel. Office: European Studies Assn 780 Monterey Suite 203 San Francisco CA 94127

BLAISCH, ILENE MYRA, social worker; b. Los Angeles, July 30, 1953; d. Albert and Sylvia (Nissenson) B. Student, Calif. State U., Northridge, 1971-74; B in Social Work, Humboldt State U., 1979; MSW, U. So. Calif., 1981. Lic. clin. social worker, Calif. Pvt. practice social work Los Angeles, 1979—; intern VA Hosp., Long Beach, Calif., 1979-80, U. So. Calif. Counseling Ctr., Los Angeles, 1980-81; psychiat. social worker Met. State Hosp., Norwalk, Calif., 1981-83; dir. women helping women Nat. Council Jewish Women, Los Angeles, 1983—; supr. Inst. Clin. Social Work, Los Angeles, 1985—; therapist Soc. Work Treatment Ctr., Los Angeles, 1985—. Mem. adv. com. violence project Jewish Family Service. Mem. Nat. Assn. Social Workers (supporting mem. polit. action com.), Soc. Clin. Social Work, So. Calif. Conf. Jewish Communal Workers, Nat. Council Jewish Women (adv. women's issues). Avocations: tennis, piano, hiking, ceramics, sewing.

BLAKE, BENNIE E., social work educator; b. Dallas, Dec. 28, 1943; s. Benjiman R. and Edna Earl (Street) B.; m. Carol Ann Siemers, Sept. 2, 1967; children: Paul A., Julia Lynn. BA with honors, Eastern Wash. U., 1969, MSW, 1977. Social worker Spokane (Wash.) Community Services Office, 1977-79, 85—; psychiat. social worker Eastern State Hosp., Medical Lake, Wash., 1979-85; adj. prof. Eastern Wash. U., Cheney, 1982—; mem. team Western State Hosp. Medicaid audit, 1984; mem. Health Sci. Master's com., Whitworth Coll., 1983; cons.; lectr. to various agys., orgns. and schs. on profl. burn-out. Active Wash. Water Power Citizens Adv. panel (standing com. 1980); participant Wash. State Conf. Advs. for Mentally Ill, 1980; chmn. Gerontology adv. bd. Spokane Falls Community Coll., 1980; mem. Ferry County Mental Health Bd. (budget com.), 1971-75, mem. Area Aging Com. for Stevens, Ferry, Pend Oreille Counties (budget, membership coms.), 1971-75; bd. dirs. Spokane Hospice. Served with U.S. Army, 1962-65. Fellow Dept. Health and Social Services, 1975. Mem. NASW (planning com. 1984—, cert.), Wash. Assn. Social Welfare (state conf. treas. 1979, bd. dirs. 1980, budget com. 1980, Eastern Wash. legis. rep. 1980, chmn. nominating com. 1980, pres. Spokane chpt. 1984), Eastern Wash. U. Alumni Assn. (chmn. organizing com. 1980, bd. dirs., pres. Sch. Social Work chpt. 1985—). Home: West 822 Cascade Way Spokane WA 99208 Office: Spokane Community Services Office N 1425 Washington Spokane WA 99202

BLAKE, GEROLD LYNN, computer systems architect, business executive; b. Lebanon, Mo., Aug. 23, 1950; s. John and Jeraldean (Massey) B.;. Field engr. supr. Ford Aerospace Co., Palo Alto, Calif., 1973-79; computer systems architect Lockheed Missiles and Space Corp., Sunnyvale, Calif., 1979—. Served with USAF, 1970-73. Republican. Baptist. Club: Lera Gun. Avocations: astronomy, home computing. Home: 1613 Diel Dr Milpitas CA 95035

BLAKE, HERBERT, JR., business educator, consultant, researcher; b. Denver, June 1, 1942; s. Herbert and Anna Lou (Morgan) B.; m. Nancy Lee Fiske, July 15, 1972; children: Chelsea Dae, Brook Herbert. BA, U. Colo., 1965; MBA, Calif. State U., Sacramento, 1976; PhD in Bus., U. Santa Clara, 1985. Br. mgr. Washington Inventory Service, Sacramento, 1969-74; lectr. Calif. State U., Sacramento, 1976-77, 1979-84, assoc. prof., 1984—; lectr. U. Santa Clara, Calif., 1977-79; cons. Minority Bus. Devel. Assn., Washington, 1982-85, Regional Transit, Sacramento, 1980. Editor TECLAB Case newsletter, 1982-85. Served with USNR, 1965-69. Mem. Am. Prodn. and Inventory Control Soc. (cert., pres. Sacramento chpt. 1982-83), Tech. Transfer Soc., Inst. Mgmt. Sci. Home: 491 Windward Way Sacramento CA 95831 Office: Calif State U 6000 J St Sacramento CA 95819

BLAKE, LANNY (ORLAND EMERSON), personnel director; b. Brawley, Calif., Oct. 26, 1951; s. Orlando Bud Emerson Sr. and Sybil (Hudson) B.; children from previous marriage: Orlando Andy Emerson III; m. Suzanne Marie Green, Jan. 2, 1983; children: Blaine Michael Prutch, Jennifer Ann Prutch. AA, Fullerton Community Coll., 1974; BA, Calif. State U., Fullerton, 1981; M Pub. Adminstrn., U. So. Calif., 1985. Supr. corp. employment and compensation Knudsen Corp., Los Angeles, 1979-82; supr. personnel Hyland Div. Travenol Labs., Los Angeles, 1982-84; dir. human resources Warner Bros. Inc., Burbank, Calif., 1984—; cons. organizational devel. and career counseling Blake, Green and Hudson. Mem. Am. Soc. Personnel Adminstrn., Am. Compensation Assn., Employment Mgmt. Assn., Am. Psychol. Assn., Assn. Psychol. Type. Republican. Episcopalian. Avocations: reading, writing, music, theater. Home: 1649 Bronze Knoll Rd Diamond Bar CA 91765 Office: Warner Bros Inc 4000 Warner Blvd Bldg 30 Burbank CA 91522

BLAKE, MILTON CLARK, JR., geologist; b. San Francisco, Feb. 20, 1932; s. Milton Clark and Carol (Wilson) B.; m. Dorothy Gordon, Mar. 14, 1959 (div. 1984); 1 child, Emma Cameron. AB, U. Calif., Berkeley, 1958; PhD, Stanford U., 1965. Geologist U.S. Geol. Survey, Menlo Park, Calif., 1958—; vis. prof. Auckland (New Zealand) U., 1970-71, U. Paris, 1978. Contbr. numerous articles to profl. jours. Served as cpl. U.S. Army, 1952-55. Fellow Geol. Soc. Am. (chmn. Cordilleran sect. 1984), Mineralol. Soc. Am.; mem. AAAS, Geol. Soc. France (v.p. 1980), Am. Geophys. Union. Republican. Club: Cosmos (Washington). Avocations: bird watching, geneal. research. Home: PO Box 172 Pescadero CA 94060 Office: US Geol Soc MS 975 345 Middlefield Rd Menlo Park CA 94025

BLAKE, ROBERT WALLACE, aeronautical engineer, consultant; b. Quantico, Va., May 24, 1921; s. Robert and Rosselet Alice (Wallace) B.; m. Ruth Gafney, May 25, 1951. B.S. in Aero. Engring., MIT, 1941; Naval Aviator, U.S. Navy Flight Sch., Pensacola, Fla., 1947; postgrad., Columbia U. Sch. Bus., 1951-52. Engring. exec. Pan Am. World Airways, N.Y.C., 1941-82; exec. v.p., gen. mgr. Ariana Afghan Airlines Pan Am. World Airways, Kabul, Afghanistan, 1962-65; resident rep. Falcon-Concorde programs Pan Am. World Airways, Bordeaux, France, 1965-67; resident rep. 707-737-747-SST programs Pan Am. World Airways, Seattle, 1967-70; staff v.p. Pan Am. World Airways, N.Y.C., 1970-77; mgr. Westchester County Airport Pan Am. World Airways, White Plains, N.Y., 1977-78; resident rep. 727-747 programs Pan Am. World Airways, Seattle, 1978-82; internat. cons. aviation Seattle, 1982—; vis. lectr. NYU, 1942, Princeton U., 1957, MIT, 1974, U. Wash., 1981, Embry-Riddle Aviation U., 1981, Green River Coll., 1986; dir. AID Staff Houses, Afghanistan, 1963-65; mem. ednl. council MIT; cons. Aviation Cons. Inc., Manhasset, N.Y., 1982-84, PRC Aviation, Tucson, 1985—. Contbr. to Wash. Spectator, Seattle Times, Seattle P-I, Naval War Coll. Rev., Naval Inst. Proc., SAE Trans. Served to lt. comdr USNR, 1944-47, ATO. Fellow AIAA (assoc., mem. tech. com.); mem. Soc. Automotive Engrs. (mem. tech. com.), Am. Nuclear Soc., Am. Assn. Airport Execs., Phi Kappa Sigma. Clubs: Army and Navy (Washington); Marines Meml., Commonwealth (San Francisco); Am. Businessmen's (Bordeaux, France). Avocations: photography. Home and Office: 900 Warren Ave N Suite 401 Seattle WA 98109

BLALACK, RUSSELL EDWARD, computer scientist; b. Newport, R.I., Oct. 12, 1946; s. Russell Edward and Joan Stockton (Campbell) B.; m. Jennifer Mary Scott Knight, Mar. 20, 1983; children: Harmony, Juliet, Travis. A Levels, Davies Tutorial, London; BA with honors, Sussex U., Brighton, Eng., 1968; postgrad., Stanford U. Entrepreneur Flash Produx ITC, London, 1971-76; pres. Russell E. Blalack Inc., Cupertino, Calif., 1978—; cons. Nat. Semicondr., Sunnyvale, Calif., 1980-85. Author: (play) Percival, 1971 (Festival Internat. de Jeune Theatre award). Clubs: Decathlon, Naval (London). Avocation: sports. Office: PO Box 893 Cupertino CA 95015

BLAMA, ROBERT JAMES, communications equipment mfg. co. ofcl.; b. Youngstown, Ohio, Oct. 28, 1937; s. Andrew and Ann (Yavorsky) B.; B.S., Youngstown, U., 1961; postgrad. Case Western Res. U. Statistician, U.S. Navy Fin. Ctr., 1962-63; sales rep. IBM, 1963-65; systems analyst/sales rep. Gen. Electric Co., 1965-69; account mgr. Honeywell, Inc., 1969-77; sr. sales rep. Data Gen. Co., 1977-80; dir. Western region Halcyon Communications, Inc., San Jose, Calif., 1980-84, v.p. sales, 1984-86, mgr. west region Precision Image, Redwood City, Calif., 1986—. Office: Precision Image 501 Cheaspeake Dr Rewood City CA 94062

BLANCHARD, JOE LANE, II, naval officer, meteorologist; b. Gainesville, Fla., Nov. 20, 1947; s. Jay Lane and Ethel Louise (Martin) B.; m. Joyce Ann Bostic, Dec. 19, 1967; one child, Jerald Lane. BS in Engring. Tech., U. N.C., Charlotte, 1974; MS in Oceanography/Meteorology, Naval Postgrad. Sch., 1985. Cert. naval oceanographer. Enlisted USN, 1964, commd. ensign, 1975, advanced through grades to lt. comdr., 1984—; research officer USN, Calif., 1976-79; acoustic programs dir. USN Oceanography Ctr., Monterey, Calif., 1979-82; meterol. research officer Naval Research Facility, Monterey, 1984-85; oceanographer USN Oceanography Ctr., Norfolk, Va., 1985—; cons. Sharem 62, Newfoundland, 1985. Inventor in field. Mem. Am. Meteorology Soc., Naval Inst., Am. Geophys. Union, Acoustical Soc. Am., Am. Legion, Non-commd. Officers Assn.,. Republican. Lodge: Moose. Avocations: fishing, scuba diving, sailing.

BLANCHARD, NINA, talent agent; b. Greenwich, Conn., July 21; d. John Dean and Mildred Eleanor (Weakley) Blanchard; m. Benjamin James Tomkins, May 28, 1950 (div.). Student El Camino Coll., 1948, Columbia U., 1950; grad. Burt Reynolds Inst. Theatre Tng. Actress, Los Angeles and N.Y.C., 1948-51; make-up artist NBC-TV, N.Y.C., 1951-58; casting dir., N.Y.C., 1954-55; talent agt., prin. Nina Blanchard Enterprises, Inc. & Nina Blanchard Agy., Los Angeles, 1961—; TV and film faculty UCLA Extension; vis. prof. Fla. State U. lectr. in field. Mem. adv. bd Free Arts Clinic Abused Children, Hathaway Home for Children. Mem. Assn. Talent Agts. (bd. dirs.), Acad. TV Arts and Scis., Women in Film, Com. 200. Author: How to Break Into Motion Pictures, Television, Commercials and Modeling, 1978.

BLANCHARD, WILLIAM STRONG, TV producer; b. Seattle, Feb. 11, 1953; s. William Livingston and Barbara (Strong) B.; m. Joan Marie Dempsey, Sept. 22, 1977; children: Ben, Taylor. BA in Communications, U. Wash., 1980. Producer Sta. KOMO TV, Seattle, 1980-82, Sta. KING TV, Seattle, 1982-83; ind. producer Seattle, 1983-84; producer Kaye-Smith Prodns., Seattle, 1984—. Office: Kaye Smith Prodns 2212 4th Ave Seattle WA 98121

BLANCHETTE, JAMES EDWARD, psychiatrist; b. Syracuse, N.Y., Aug. 28, 1924; s. Joseph M. and Margaret (Vincent) B.; B.A., Syracuse U., 1950; M.D., SUNY-Syracuse Sch. Med., 1953; m. Shirley Ruth Brisco, Sept. 1, 1948 (dec. May 1981). Intern, St. Vincent's Hosp., N.Y.C., 1953-54; resident Patton (Calif.) State Hosp., 1954-55, Met. State Hosp., Norwalk, Calif., 1957-59; pvt. practice psychiatry, Redlands, Calif., 1959—; chief profl. edn. Patton State Hosp., 1960-64, tchg. cons., 1964-69; asst. clin. prof. psychiatry Loma Linda Med. Sch.; mem. staffs San Bernardino Community Hosp., St. Bernadine Hosp. (both San Bernardino); cons. psychiatry Redlands Community Hosp. Served with USAAF, 1945-47. Diplomate Am. Bd. Med. Examiners, Am. Bd. Psychiatry and Neurology. Fellow Am. Psychiat. Assn., AAAS, Pan-Am. Med. Assn.; mem. AMA, Calif. Med. Assn., San Bernardino Med. Soc., Internat. Platform Assn., So. Calif. Psychiat. Soc. (pres. Inland chpt. 1963-64, pres. 1983-84), Royal Soc. Health, Am. Med. Soc. Vienna, Phi Mu Alpha Symphonia, Nu Sigma Nu. Home: 972 W Marshall Blvd San Bernardino CA 92405 Office: 236 Cajon St Redlands CA 92373

BLAND, JOHN C(OOKE), architect; b. Louisville, Apr. 5, 1946; s. Edward Cole and Evelyn Louise (Blakey) b.; m. Janet Lewis (div.); 1 child, Brandi; m. Bonnie Joe Kennedy; 1 child, Julie Anne Butterfield. BFA in Architecture, U. N.Mex., 1974. Registered architect, N.Mex., Colo., Tenn., Tex., Okla., Ariz., Kans. Architect Dean & Hunt, Architects, Albuquerque, 1971-77; prin. John C. Bland. Architect, Albuquerque, 1977-79; prin., pres. Archtl. Concepts, P.C., Albuquerque, 1979-81, Bland & Assocs., P.C., Albuquerque, 1981-84; architect Kirtland AFB, N.Mex., 1984—; Registered architect; cert. Nat. Council Archtl. Registration Bds. Coach Am. Youth Soccer Orgn., Albuquerque, 1981-84. Served with USN, 1967-69. Mem. AIA, Am. Arbitration Assn., Internat. Conf. Bldg. Officials, N.Mex. Soc. Architects (sec.-treas. 1977-78, pres. 1978-80), Circle K Internat.-U. N.Mex. (charter). Club: Coronado (Kirtland AFB). Avocations: snow skiing, racquetball, volleyball. Office: Kirtland Design Ctr 1606 ABW/DEEMCP Kirtland AFB NM 87117

BLAND, MICHAEL FRANK, electrical engineer, consultant; b. Tuba City, Ariz., Feb. 8, 1957; s. Frank and Ruth Ann (Anderson) B.; m. Beth Ann Ripple, Feb. 23, 1985. BS, Harvey Mudd Coll., 1979, ME, 1980. Registered profl. engr., Calif. Engr. Lawrence Livermore (Calif.) Nat. Lab., 1980-84; cons. Lawrence Livermore (Calif.) Lab., 1984—; sr. scientist JAYCOR, Fremont, Calif., 1984—. Club: Livermore Tennis. Avocations: swimming, tennis, cycling, photography. Office: JAYCOR 39650 Liberty St Fremont CA 94538

BLANDIN, SHERMAN WESLEY, JR., educator, academic administrator; b. Racine, Wis., Oct. 1, 1923; s. Sherman Wesley and Edna Mary (Youngs) B.; m. Virginia Ruth Jorgenson, June 24, 1944; children: James S., Susan M., Virginia L., Sara R. BS, U.S. Naval Acad., 1944; B Textile Engring., Ga. Inst. Tech., 1952, MS, 1953; PhD, U. Santa Clara, 1977. Commd. ensign USN, 1944, advanced through grades to capt., 1965, ret., 1967; assoc. prof., asst. dir. Dept. Nat. Security Affairs Naval Post Grad. Sch., Monterey, Calif., 1968-80, prof., chmn., 1980-86. Office: Naval Postgrad Sch Dept Nat Security Affairs Monterey CA 93943

BLANK, LAWRENCE FRANCIS, computer consultant; b. Detroit, Oct. 4, 1932; s. Frank A. and Marcella A. (Pieper) B.; m. Carol Louise Mann, Oct. 12, 1963; children: Ann, Steven, Susan, Lori. BS, Xavier U., 1954. Asst. engr. Gen. Electric Co., Evendale, Ohio, 1956-60; research engr. Gen. Dynamics Corp., San Diego, 1960-62; mem. tech. staff Computer Scis. Corp., El Segundo, Calif., 1962-64; programming mgr. IBM, Los Angeles, 1964-69, Xerox Corp., El Segundo, 1969-74; ind. computer cons., Torrance, Calif., 1974—. Mem. Assn. Computing Machinery, Ind. Computer Cons. Assn. Home: 608 Epping Rd Palos Verdes Estates CA 90274 Office: 3838 Carson St Suite 328 Torrance CA 90503

BLANKENSHIP, EDWARD G., architect; b. Martin, Tenn., June 22, 1943; s. Edward G. and Martha Lucille (Baldridge) B. B.Arch., Columbia U., 1966, M.Sc. in Architecture, 1967; M. Litt. Arch., Cambridge U., 1971. Registered architect, N.Y., Calif. Sr. v.p. Thompson Cons. Internat., Los Angeles. Author: The Airport-Architecture, Urban Integration, Ecological Problems, 1974. William Kinne fellow, 1966; alt. Fulbright fellow to Eng., 1967. Mem. AIA. Episcopalian. Clubs: United Oxford and Cambridge U.; Meadow (Southhampton), Am. Friends of Cambridge U. (sec. Los Angeles chpt.). Lodge: Rotary Internat. Home: 4260 Via Arbolada #207 Monterey Hills CA 90042 Office: 8929 S Sepulveda Blvd Los Angeles CA 90045

BLANKENSHIP, FRANK JAMES, real estate broker, appraiser; b. Dixon, Ky., Nov. 1, 1921; s. Frank Edwin and Lorene (Wilkey) B.; m. Vivian Rosati, July 10, 1945 (div. 1950); 1 child, Thomas Neil; m. Edith Dorene Grider, Feb. 15, 1952; 1 child, James A. B.S., U. Md., 1954; M.B.A., Harvard U., 1956; Ph.D., Calif. Coast U., 1982. Mgr. mktg. Gen. Electric Co., Phila., Huntsville, Ala. and Houston, 1960-68; asst. mgr. Fidelity Mut. Life, Houston, 1968-70; nat. sales mgr. original equipment mfg. dept. Sperry Corp., Phila. and Salt Lake City, 1970-72; pres., owner All Points Inc., Salt Lake City, 1972—; dir. real estate program Westminster Coll., Salt Lake City, 1973-74, adj. prof. fin., 1973-82. Author: The Prentice-Hall Real Estate Appraisal Desk Book, 1986. Contbr. articles to profl. jours. Chmn. adminstrv. bd. Christ United Methodist Ch., Salt Lake City, 1979-82. Served to lt. col. U.S. Army, 1943-60, ETO. Mem. Nat. Assn. Ind. Fee Appraisers (pres. Salt Lake City chpt. 1980), Am. Assn. Cert. Appraisers (cons. mem. 1978), Salt Lake Bd. Realtors (pub. com. 1972). Republican. Lodge: Masons (sr. warden 1958-59), Shriners. Home and Office: 3538 S Suniland Dr Salt Lake City UT 84109

BLANKENSHIP, LUTHER EARL, engineering executive; b. Lebanon, Mo., Oct. 13, 1932; s. William Herbert and Ada Mariah (West) B.; m. Helen Marie Buttram, Aug. 4, 1951; children: Stephen David, Sharon Kaye. BSEE, Ind. Inst. Tech., 1958. Engr. Varian Assocs., Palo Alto, Calif., 1958-66, 1970-78, engring. mgr., 1978—; design engr. Tektronix Inc., Beaverton, Oreg., 1966-70. Patentee in field. Co-founder, chmn. Jack Douglas Youth Found., San Jose, Calif., 1971-82. Served with USAF, 1952-56. Mem. IEEE. Republican. Home: 707 Cardiff Pl Milpitas CA 95035 Office: Varian Assocs 611 Hansen Way Palo Alto CA 94303

BLANKS, HERBERT BEVERLY, pest control co. exec.; b. Cleve., Oct. 27, 1915; s. Anthony Faulkner and Dorothy McGee (Welch) B.; B.S. in Forestry, U. Calif.-Berkeley, 1937; postgrad. Civil Affairs Tng. Sch., U. Chgo., 1944; m. Roxana Caroline Holmes, May 26, 1937; children—George Anthony, Herbert Elliot, Donald Allen. With U.S. Forest Service, Tahoe Nat. Forest, 1936-38; park ranger Sequoia Nat. Park, Calif., 1938-42; co-partner Ailing House Pest Control, Carmel, Calif., 1946-73, pres., 1974-80, chmn. bd., 1980—. Scoutmaster Boy Scouts Am., Carmel, 1949-55. Charter mem. City of Carmel Forestry Commn., 1955; planning commr., Carmel, 1955-62, chmn., 1960-61; councilman, Carmel, 1962-70, mayor, 1964-66; mem. Monterey County (Calif.) Local Agy. Formation Commn., 1967-70, chmn., 1967-68. Bd. dirs. Assn. Monterey Bay Area Govts., 1966-70; trustee Harrison Meml. Library, 1971-77. Served with AUS, 1942-46; lt. col. Res. ret. Decorated Bronze Star, Army Commendation medal. Mem. PTA (hon., life), Pest Control Operators Calif. (dir. 1963-64, sec.-treas. Monterey Bay Area dist. 1974-80), Nat. Pest Control Assn. (committeeman 1962-64), Res. Officers Assn. (life), Ret. Officers Assn. (life). Mem. Community Ch. (pres. bd. govs. 1972, 76). Clubs: Commonwealth, Masons (past master Carmel; knight comdr. Ct. of Honor 1975; 33 deg. 1981; treas. Monterey County Scottish Rite club 1972—); Hi-12. Home: PO Box 241 Carmel CA 93921 Office: PO Box 4977 Carmel CA 93921

BLANTON, JOHN ARTHUR, architect; b. Houston, Jan. 1, 1928; s. Arthur Alva and Caroline (Jeter) B.; B.A., Rice U., 1948, B.S. in Architecture, 1949; m. Marietta Louise Newton, Apr. 10, 1953 (dec. 1976); children—Jill Blanton Lewis, Lynette Blanton Rowe, Elena Diane. With Richard J. Neutra, Los Angeles, 1950-64; pvt. practice architecture, Manhattan Beach, Calif., 1964—; lectr. UCLA Extension, 1967-76, 85, Harbor Coll., Los Angeles, 1970-72. Mem. Capital Improvements Com., Manhattan Beach, 1966, city commr. Bd. of Bldg. Code Appeals. Served with Signal Corps, U.S. Army, 1951-53. Recipient Best House of Year award C. of C., 1969, 70, 71, 83, Preservation of Natural Site award, 1974, design award, 1975, 84. Mem. AIA (contbr. book revs. to jour. 1972—, recipient Red Cedar Shingle/nat. merit award 1979), Soc. Archtl. Historians. Club: Rotary. Six bldgs. included in A Guide to the Architecture of Los Angeles and Southern California. Office: 2100 Sepulveda Blvd Suite 14 Manhattan Beach CA 90266

BLANTON, RICHARD LEWIS, JR., military officer; b. Meridian, Miss., July 23, 1955. Student, Meridian Jr. Coll., 1973-74; BS in Aerospace Engring., Miss. State U., 1978; postgrad., U. So. Calif., 1982-83, Fla. Inst. Tech., 1984—. Commd. 2d lt. Air Force ROTC, 1974; advanced through grades to capt. USAF, 1978; engr. system ops. sect. measurement system div. USAF, Kennedy Space Ctr., Fla., 1974-77; navigator trainee squadron 450/451 USAF, Mather AFB, Calif., 1979; payload test controller USAF, Vandenberg AFB, Calif., 1979-81, flight test integrated mgr., launch controller Ballistic Payloads div., 1981-83; space shuttle test dir. USAF, Kennedy Space Ctr., Fla., 1983-84; space shuttle test dir. USAF, Vandenberg AFB, 1984-86, program supt. mgr. western test range Aerospace Test Mgmt. Br. WSMC, 1986—. Cadet comdr., CAP, Vandenberg AFB, 1978-79, adminstrn. officer, 1980-81, squadron comdr, 1981-83. Mem. AIAA, CAP, Air Force Assn., Co. Grade Officer's Council, Arnold Air Soc. Alumni, Air Force Hist. Found., The Planetary Soc., Aerospace Edn. Assn. Republican. Presbyterian. Avocations: sci. fiction, history, football, softball, baseball. Office: Western Test Range/DOTA Vandenburg AFB CA 93437-6021

BLANZ, ROBERT CARL, telecommunications executive; b. Allegan, Mich., Apr. 22, 1932; s. Christine (Edgerton) B.; m. Ethel Skidmore, Feb. 7, 1959; children: Elizabeth, Jeane, Sarah, Laura, Susanna. B.E.E., Case Inst. Tech., 1954; postgrad. Western Res. U., Princeton U., Carlton Coll., Rutgers U. Asst. v.p. Mountain Bell Telephone Co., subs. US West, Inc., Denver, 1973-76, v.p., gen. mgr., Boise, Idaho, 1977-78, pres., Denver, 1982-87; dir. network adminstrn. AT&T, Basking Ridge, N.J., 1976-77; exec. v.p. South Central Bell Telephone Co., Birmingham, Ala., 1978-82; dir. United Bank of Denver. Mem. exec. bd. Denver Area council Boy Scouts Am., 1985—; campaign chmn. Mile High United Way, Denver, 1985. Served with U.S. Army, 1955-56. Clubs: Petroleum, Athletic, Denver. Lodges: Rotary, Masons. Republican. Episcopalian. Office: Mountain Bell 1801 California St Denver CO 80202 *

BLATT, MORTON BERNARD, medical illustrator; b. Chgo., Jan. 9, 1923; s. Arthur E. and Hazel B. Student Central YMCA Coll., 1940-42, U. Ill., 1943-46. Tchr., Ray-Vogue Art Schs., Chgo., 1946-51; med. illustrator VA Center, Wood, Wis., 1951-57, Swedish Covenant Hosp., Chgo., 1957-76; med. illustrator Laidlaw Bros., River Forest, Ill., 1956-59; cons., artist health textbooks, 1956-59; illustrator Standard Edn. Soc., Chgo., 1960; art editor Covenant Home Altar, 1972-83, Covenant Companion, 1958-82. Served with USAAF, 1943-44. Mem. Art Inst. Chgo. Club: Chgo. Press. Illustrator: Atlas and Demonstration Technique of the Central Nervous System, also numerous med. jours.; illustrator, designer Covenant Hymnal, books, record jackets. Address: PO Box 489 Mill Valley CA 94942

BLATTENBERG, ROBERT JOHN, insurance consultant; b. Des Moines, Iowa, Mar. 22, 1950; s. Robert Charles and Ellen May (Tuttle) B.; m. Cecilia Jane Weiss, July 20, 1978; 1 child, Robert Adam. BS in Bus., U. Kans., 1972; postgrad., Washington U., St. Louis, 1975-77. Mgr. data processing Gen. Am. Life, St. Louis, 1972-80; info. systems supr. Pacific Mut. Life, Newport Beach, Calif., 1980-83; chief operating officer Ringler Assocs, Inc., Newport Beach, 1983—. Fellow Life Office Mgmt. Assn.; mem. Nat. Structured Settlement Trade Assn. Republican. Episcopalian. Office: Ringler Assocs Inc 1300 Quail Suite 201 Newport Beach CA 92660

BLATTNER, ERNEST WILLI, mechanical engineering educator; b. Aarau, Switzerland, Apr. 14, 1929; came to U.S., 1957; naturalized, 1970; s. Ludwig and Martha Blattner; m. Anneke Geurds, May 24, 1958; children: Mark Hermann, Flora Grazia, Elisabeth Rose, Paul Johann. MSME, Swiss Fed. Inst., Zurich, 1953; postgrad., Drexel Inst., 1959-60. Design engr. Brown Boveri Ltd., Baden, Switzerland, 1954-57; engr.-in-charge De Laval Turbine, Inc., Trenton, 1957-65; chief engr. Chicago Pneumatic Tool Co., Franklin, Pa., 1965-73; mgr. advanced design EIMCO div. Envirotech Corp., Salt Lake City, 1973-79; mgr. engring. and mfg. Biphase Energy Systems div. Transam.-De Laval, Santa Monica, Calif., 1979-81; dir. engring. Mafi-Trench Corp., Santa Maria, Calif., 1981-83; prof. mech. engring. Calif. Poly. State U., San Luis Obispo, 1983—; cons. mech. engring. Inventor turbines, compressors. Mem. Franklin Waste and Water Authority, 1963-65. Mem. ASME (chmn. Utah sect. 1976-77, mem. regional policy bd. 1977-79), Am. Soc. for Metals, Am. Soc. Engring. Edn. Home: 490 Miles Ave Santa Maria CA 93455 Office: Calif Poly State U Dept Mech Engring San Luis Obispo CA 93407

BLATTNER, MEERA MCCUAIG, educator; b. Chgo., Aug. 14, 1930; d. William D. McCuaig and Nina (Spertus) Klevs; m. Minao Kamegai, June 22 1985; children: Douglas, Robert, William. B.A., U. Chgo., 1952; M.S., U. So. Calif., 1966; Ph.D., UCLA, 1973 . Research fellow in computer sci. Harvard U., 1973-74; asst. prof. Rice U., 1974-80; asso. prof. applied sci. U. Calif. at Davis, Livermore, 1980—; adj. prof. U. Tex., Houston, 1977—; vis. prof. U. Paris, 1980; program dir. theoretical computer sci. NSF, Washington, 1979-80. NSF grantee, 1977-81. Mem. Soc. Women Engrs., Assn. Computing Machinery, IEEE Computer Soc. Contbr. articles to profl. jours. Office: U Calif Davis/Livermore Dept Applied Sci Livermore CA 94550

BLAUSTEIN, ALAN SCOTT, lawyer, physician; b. Bklyn., Oct. 26, 1953; s. Henry and Grace Blaustein. BA, Northwestern U., 1974, MS, 1975, MD, 1983; JD, U. Ill., 1978. Bar: N.Y. 1978, Ill. 1980, Calif. 1985, U.S. Dist. Ct. (no. and so. dists.) N.Y. 1979, U.S. Dist. Ct. (no. dist.) Ill. 1980, U.S. Ct. Appeals (7th cir.) 1980, U.S. Patent Office 1979. Intern Georgetown U. Hosp., 1983-84; resident in psychiatry Cedars Sinai Hosp., 1984-87; reporter, anchorman Sta. WLRW-FM, Champaign, Ill., 1978; assoc. Pennie Edmonds, N.Y.C., 1978-79, Sonnenschein, Carlin, Nath & Rosenthal, Chgo., 1981-82, Philip H. Corboy & Assocs., Chgo., 1982-83; medical-legal, psychiat. cons. Los Angeles, 1983—. Author: Illinois Special Education Manual, 1977; editor Illinois Consumer Advocacy Manual, 1977; producer radio mag. The Education Strike, 1971 (Evanston Pub. Service award 1971). Mem. AMA, Am. Psychiat. Assn., Ill. Med. Assn., So. Calif. Psychiat. Soc., Calif. Med. Assn., Am. Soc. Law and Medicine, Los Angeles County Bar Assn., BEverly Hills Bar Assn. Democrat. Jewish. Home and Office: 8730 Alden Dr Los Angeles CA 90048

BLAUSTEIN, MARTIN SEYMOUR, lawyer, mental health counselor; b. Bklyn., Mar. 27, 1945; s. Herman and Evelyn (Stein) B.; m. Tamra Sue Scow, July 6, 1974; 1 child, Keston. BA, Tarkio Coll., 1968; MS, U. Utah, 1974; JD, Western State U., Fullerton, Calif., 1980. Bar: Calif. 1982, Utah 1983, U.S. Ct. Appeals (10th cir.) 1985. Dir. treatment Odyssey House, N.Y.C., 1970-76; vet. coordinator Disabled Am. Vets., Salt Lake City, 1980-83; team leader VA, Provo, Utah, 1983—; sole practice law Salt Lake City, 1983—; mem. gov.'s council on vet. issues, 1981—; legal advisor Utah State Dept. Social Service Instl. Rev. Bd., 1983—; chmn. Vet. Problem Action Com., Salt Lake City, 1983-85; vice chmn. Salt Lake City Title 20 Com., 1983-85; legal counsel Vet. Meml. Com., Provo, 1985—. Served with U.S. Army, 1968-70, Vietnam. Decorated Bronze Star with V, Purple Heart. Mem. ABA, Utah Bar Assn., Calif. Bar Assn., Salt Lake County Bar Assn., Assn. Trial Lawyers Am., VA Legal Ethics Com., 1986—. Home and Office: 2944 Imperial St Salt Lake City UT 84601

BLAZ, BEN, government representative; b. Agana, Guam, Feb. 14, 1928; m. Ann Evers; children: Mike, Tom. BS, U. Notre Dame, 1951; MA, George Washington U., 1963; grad., U.S. Naval War Coll., 1971; LLD (hon.), U. Guam, 1974. Commd. 2d lt. USMC, 1951, advanced through grades to brig. gen., ret., 1980; prof. U. Guam, Mangilao, 1983-84; del. from Guam to U.S. Congress, 1985—. Decorated Legion of Merit, Bronze medal with Combat V; Vietnamese Cross of Gallantry; recipient Freedoms Found. Medal of Freedom, 1969. Mem. Guam C. of C., Marine Corps Assn., Young Mens League of Guam. Republican. Lodge: KC. Office: 1130 Longworth Bldg Washington DC 20515 *

BLAZEK, MARY LOUISE, health physicist; b. Boise, Idaho, Mar. 12, 1944. D. Robert Rudolph and Karen Elizabeth (Wennstrom) Bolliger; children—Teresa Marie, Jason Patrick. Student, Bannock Meml. Hosp. Sch. Radiol. Tech., Pocatello, Idaho, 1967-69, Walla Walla Clinic (Wash.), 1969-71, Evergreen State Coll., Olympia, Wash., 1980-81. Cert. nuclear medicine technologist. Tech. services supr., chief nuclear medicine technologist Walla Walla Clinic, 1969-77; health physicist State of Wash. Dept. Health Services, Olympia, 1980-81; radiation specialist State of Oreg. Health Div., Portland, 1981-85; coordinator Hanford program, Oreg. Dept. Energy, 1986—. Mem. Am. Registry Radiol. Technologists, Nuclear, Medicine Technology Cert. Bd., Health Physics Soc., Nat. Honor Soc., Conf. Radiation Control Program Dirs. (assoc., chmn. ad hoc com.). Democrat. Episcopalian. Office: Oreg Dept Energy 625 Marion NE Salem OR 97310

BLECK, EUGENE EDMUND, surgeon, educator; b. Milw., May 2, 1923; s. Henry B. and Edna C. (Kilbert) Bleck; m. Anne M. Blewett, July 7, 1951; children: John, Mary, Patrick, Dan, Jane. Student, Northwestern U., Marquette U.; MD, Marquette U., 1947; postgrad., U. Calif., 1956-57, 60, UCLA, 1960; Docteur Honoris Causa (hon.), U. St.-Etienne, France, 1985. Diplomate Am. Bd. Orthopedic Surgery. Intern St. Francis Hosp., Evanston, Ill., 1947-48; instr. Am. Acad. of Orthopaedic Surgeons, 1964-76, Am. Acad. for Cerebral Palsy, 1967-73; assoc. clin. instr. Stanford U. Sch. of Medicine, 1972-77, assoc. clin. prof. surgery, 1972-77, prof. clin. surgery, 1977—, prof., div. head dept. surgery, 1982—; mem. staff Stanford U. Hosp., 1972; chief pediatric, orthopedic and rehab. services Mills Meml. Hosp., San Mateo, Calif., 1955-72, Peninsula Hosp., Burlingame, Calif., 1955-72; cons. Naval Regional Medical Ctr., Oakland, Calif., 1974-77; medical dir. Motion Analysis Lab., Children's Hosp. at Stanford, 1978—; chmn. Am. Acad. for Cerebral Palsy and Devel. Medicine (chmn. publs. com.), 1980-85. Author: Atlas of Plaster Cast Technique, 1956, (with D.A. Nagel) Physically Handicapped Children: A Medical Atlas for Teachers, 1975, 82, Orthopaedic Management in Cerebral Palsy, 1979, 86; assoc. editor Orthopaedic Survey, 1977—, Devel. Medicine and Child Neurology, 1978-80, Jour. Pediatric Orthopaedics, 1980—; reviewer Jour. Bone and Joint Surgery, 1980—; contbr. articles to profl. jours. Trustee Crescent Porter Hale Found., San Francisco, 1976—; bd. dirs. Notre Dame High Sch., Belmont, Calif., 1970—, pres. 1970-72, United Cerebral Palsy Assn. of San Mateo; mem. adv. com. State of Calif. Dept. of Rehab., 1976-77. Served to lt. USN, 1949-52. Award of Merit in Recognition for Outstanding Pub. Service in Support of the Program of Vocat. Rehab. for the Disabled Calif. Dept. of Rehab., 1983; H. Houston Merrit Clinical fellow United Cerebral Palsy Assn., 1979, Nat. Found. Infantile Paralysis fellow, Duke U., 1948-55. Mem. Am. Acad. for Cerebral Palsy and Devel. Medicine (pres. 1976), Med. Adv. Group State Dept. of Rehab., Calif. (chmn. 1978-82), N.Y. Acad. of Scis., 1984—, Rehab. Engring. Soc. of N.Am., 1979— (charter), Piedmont Orthopedic Soc., Am. Acad. Orthopedic Surgery, Western Orthopedic Assn., Calif. Med. Assn., San Mateo County Med. Assn., Pediatric Orthopaedic Soc. N.Am. (pres. 1984), Am. Orthopedic Assn., Am. Acad. Orthopedic surgeons (com. nat. orthopedic manpower 1970-76). Roman Catholic. Office: Children's Hosp at Stanford 520 Sand Hill Rd Palo Alto CA 94304

BLECKER, MICHAEL JOHN, university president; b. Chgo., May 11, 1931; s. Michael M. and Ida Camille (Witt) B. A.B., Harvard U., 1953; postgrad. St. John's Sem., 1956-60; Ph.D., U. Wis., 1964. Ordained Priest, Roman Catholic Ch., 1960. Instr. dept. history St. John's U., Collegeville, Minn., 1960-61, asst. prof., 1964-70, assoc. prof., 1971, chmn. dept. theology, 1967-79, pres., 1971-82; pres. Grad. Theol. Union, Berkeley, Calif., 1982—. Assoc. editor Am. Benedictine Rev., 1969—. Contbr. articles to Am. Benedictine Rev., Speculum, Liberal Edn., Studi Senesi. Bd. dirs. Holy Names Coll., Oakland, Calif., 1983—; mem. Nat. Conf. Cath. Bishops Commn. on Orthodox/Roman Catholic Dialog, 1969-82. Mem. Nat. Assn. Ind. Colls. and Univs. (bd. dirs. 1979-82). Club: Athenien-Nile (Oakland, Calif.). Office: Grad Theol Union 2400 Ridge Rd Berkeley CA 94709

BLEDSOE, CRAIG VANDERBILT, aviation company executive; b. July 12, 1946. B.A. in English Communications, U. South, 1968; M.S., in Safety Engring., U. So. Calif, 1978. Registered profl. engr.; cert. safety profl. System safety engr., occupational safety health compliance officer Dept. Def., 1976-77; air transport pilot, flight safety engr. Flying Tiger Line, Fairbanks, Alaska, 1978—; dir. aviation and safety. Bur. Land Mgmt, Fairbanks, 1983. Served with USAFR, 1968—. Recipient Air Tng. Command Individual Safety Profl. award, 1972. Mem. NSPE, Alaska Soc. Profl. Engrs., Am. Soc. Safety Engrs., Internat. Soc. Air Safety Investigators, Air Force Assn. Res. Officers, Am. Radio Relay League, Amateur Satellite Corp. Am. Episcopalian. Lodge: Rotary (pres.-elect Fairbanks Sunrisers club, 1986—). Chief pilot Yukon Quest 1,000-mile internat. dog sled race, 1985-86. Office: Flying Tiger Line 7401 World Way West Los Angeles CA 90009

BLEDSOE, MARGARET ANN, occupational therapist, educator, consultant; b. Burbank, Calif., Feb. 18, 1952; d. William Terrell and Doris Ella (Goulding) B. A.A. in Gen. Edn., Pierce Jr. Coll., 1975; B.S. in Occupational Therapy, San Jose State U., 1977; M.S., La. Tech. U., 1984; M.A. in Psychology, Human Relations and Supervision. Registered occupational therapist, La. Occupational therapist Children's Hosp. and Med. Ctr., Oakland, Calif., 1981-82; pvt. practice cons., San Mateo, Calif., 1981-82; instr. N.E. La. U., Monroe, 1982-84; data collector Western Psychol. Services, Los Angeles, 1984; administrv. asst. Ouachita Community Action Program, Monroe, 1984-85; staff occupational therapist Garden Sullivan Rehab. Ctr., San Francisco, 1979-80, Garden Sullivan Learning and Devel. Program, 1979-82; occupational therapist cons. Daniel Webster Elem. Sch., Daley City, Calif., 1981-82. Ednl. scholar Calif. Found. Occupational Therapy, 1981. Mem. Am. Occupational Therapy Assn. (vice chmn. nat. student com. 1977, chmn. 1978-80, sgt.-at-arms rep. assembly 1980—, rep. for Calif. 1985-87), Occupational Therapy Assn. Calif. (sec. Golden Gate chpt. 1979, co-chmn. state conf. 1981), Ctr. for Study of Sensory Integration Dysfunction, Am. Soc. Tng. and Devel., Am. Assn. Counseling and Devel., Gamma Beta Phi. Republican. Avocations: travel; entertaining. Home: 82 Paul Ave Brisbane CA 94005

BLEIBERG, LEON WILLIAM, surgical podiatrist; b. Bklyn., June 9, 1932; s. Paul Pincus and Helen (Epstein) B.; m. Beth Daigle, June 7, 1970; children: Kristina Noel, Kelley Lynn, Kimberly Ann, Paul Joseph. Student, Los Angeles City Coll., 1950-51, U. So. Calif., 1951, Case Western Res. U., 1951-53; DSc with honors, Temple U. Sch. Podiatric Medicine, 1955; PhD, U. Beverly Hills, 1970. Served rotating internship various hosps., Phila., 1954-55; resident Bella Vista Hosp., Montebello, U .So. Calif., Los Angeles, Loma Linda U., Los Angeles, 1956-58; surg. podiatrist So. Calif. Podiatry Group, Westchester (Calif.) and Los Angeles, 1956-75; health care economist, researcher Drs. Home Health Care Services, 1976—; pres. Medica, Totalcare, Cine-Medics Corp., and World-Wide Health Care Services; podiatric cons. U. So. Calif. Athletic Dept., Morningside and Inglewood (Calif.) High Schs., Internet Corp., Royal Naval Assn., Long Beach, Calif. Naval Sta.; lectr. in field UN N.Y., Wash., Jakarta, Indonesia, 1979-80; healthcare affiliate Internat. div. CARE/ASIA, 1987. Producer (films) The Gun Hawk, 1963, Terrified, Day of the Nightmare; contbr. articles to profl. jours. Hon. Sheriff Westchester 1962-64; commd. mem. Rep. Senatorial Inner Circle, 1984-86; lt. comdr. med. services corps Brit.-Am. Cadet Corps, 1984—. Served with USN, 1955-56. Recipient Medal of Merit, U.S. Presdl. Task Force. Mem. Philippine Hosp. Assn. (Cert. of Appreciation 1964, trophy for Outstanding Service 1979), Calif. Podiatry Assn. (hon.), Am. Podiatric Med. Assn. (hon.), Acad. TV Arts and Scis., Royal Soc. Health (Eng.), Western Foot Surgery Assn., Am. Coll. Foot Surgeons, Am. Coll. Podiatric Sports Medicine, Internat. Coll. Preventive Medicine. Clubs: Hollywood Comedy, Sts. and Sinners, Halls Und Beinbruch Ski, Beach Cities Ski, Orange County Stamp, Las Virgenes Track. Logdes: Masons, Shriners. Home: 5871 Lanboard Ln Agoura Hills CA 91301

BLEICH, PAMELA ANN, educator, librarian; b. Glendale, Calif., Oct. 3, 1928; d. Gustav Edward and Mildred Charlotte (Wolford) B.; student Compton Coll., 1947-48, U. Redlands, 1948-50; BA, UCLA, 1951, postgrad., 1951-53; postgrad. U. Md., 1963-64; MLS, U. So. Calif., 1955, MA in History, 1961, postgrad., 1967-77. Tchr., Long Beach (Calif.) Unified Sch. Dist., 1953, Paramount Jr. High Sch., 1953-55; library coordinator library sect. Instructional Materials Center, Los Angeles Unified Sch. Dist., 1955-61; prof. history and library sci., coordinator Instructional Media Ctr., Los Angeles Harbor Coll., 1961—; librarian Mannheim Am. High Sch., 1963-65. Pres. San Pedro Bay Hist. Soc., 1975-76; advisor Los Angeles Maritime Mus. Assn., 1976-79; v.p. Friends of Wilmington Pub. Library, 1980-81, pres., 1984-85, corr. sec., 1986—; Mem. Los Angeles Mayor's Bicentennial History Team, 1979-81; mem. univ. archives com. Calif. State U., Dominguez Hills, 1982-84. Mem. ALA, Calif. Library Assn., Calif. Assn. Ednl. Materials and Tech., Assn. Ednl. Communications Tech., NEA (life), AFT, Calif. Hist. Soc., San Pedro Bay Hist. Soc., So. Calif. Hist. Soc., U. Calif. Los Angeles Alumni Assn., U. So. Calif. Alumni Assn., Beta Phi Mu, Phi Beta Gamma. Democrat. Editor Shoreline, 1974-76; mem. editorial bd. Calif. Librarian, 1958-61; asst. editor, bus. mgr. Calif. Sch. Libraries Quar., 1956-60; contbr. articles to Calif. Hist. Soc. Quar., 1964-66.

BLESCH, ROBERT WILLIAM, lawyer; b. Kansas City, Mo., Feb. 17, 1959; s. William Francis and Barbara Jane (Wolf) B. BBA, Notre Dame U., 1981; JD, U. Iowa, 1984. Bar: Iowa 1984. Commd. U.S. Army, 1981, advanced through grades to capt., 1985; atty. Office of Staff Judge Adv. U.S. Army, Ft. Ord, Calif., 1984-86; atty. U.S. Army Trial Def. Service, Ft. Ord, 1986—. Mem. ABA, Assn. Trial Lawyers Am., Iowa State Bar Assn. Home: 1086 First St #3 Monterey CA 93940 Office: U S Army Trial Def Service AFZW JA D Fort Ord CA 93941

BLETHEN, FRANK A., newspaper publisher; b. Seattle, Apr. 20, 1945. B.S. in Bus., Ariz. State U.; P.M.D., Harvard U. Pub. Walla Walla Union-Bulletin, Wash., 1977-78; asst. circulation mgr. Seattle Times, 1979-80, circulation mgr., 1981, v.p. sales and mktg., 1982-85, pres., chief operating officer, 1985, pub., chief exec. officer, 1985—; v.p. Allied Daily Newspapers, Tacoma, Wash., 1978. Mem. bd., Downtown Seattle Assn., 1985; pres. United Way of Wash., 1978; mem. corp. council arts Seattle Found. Mem. Seattle C. of C. (mem. bd. 1984), Sigma Delta Chi. Clubs: Rainier, Wash. Athletic (Seattle), Bellevue Athletic. Lodge: Rotary. Office: The Seattle Times Fairview Ave N and John PO Box 70 Seattle WA 98111

BLETHEN, HAROLD DAVID, entrepreneur; b. Bristol, Conn., June 26, 1939; s. Kenneth Albion and Margaret Janet (Bickford) B.; m. Sandra May Loux, Nov. 16, 1960 (div. 1965); 1 child, Harold David II; m. Linda Lee Wall, Sept. 30, 1967; 1 child, Scott David. AA, Contra Costa Coll., 1960. Cons. plant security Ford Motor Co., Richmond, Calif., 1959-61; plantman Atlantic Richfield Corp., Richmond, 1963-67; field clk. Pacific Gas & Electric, San Francisco, 1967—; entrepreneur Lindave Bus. Services, San Jose, Calif., 1968—; innovator, designer Harold the Hairman, San Jose, 1973—; v.p. Orbitron Cons. Services, San Francisco, 1983-84; pres. Halstan Cons. Services, San Jose, 1985—, Pacific Service Employees Assn.; chmn. gen. constrn. com. Pacific Gas & Electric, San Francisco, 1979-80. Mem., trustee Rep. Presdl. task force, Washington, 1984. Recipient Presdl. Commn. Rep. Presdl. Task Force, 1986. Mem. Pacific Service Employees Assn. (gen. com. chmn. credit union 1981—, named Mem. of Yr. 1982), Smithsonian Assocs., Travelers Protective Assn. Avocations: people, travel, history. Home: 927 Sapphire Ct San Jose CA 95136 Office: 4960 Almaden Express Way #136 San Jose CA 95118

BLEWETT, ROBERT NOALL, lawyer; b. Stockton, Calif., July 12, 1915; s. Stephen Noall and Bess Errol (Simard) B.; m. Virginia Weston, Mar. 30, 1940; children—Richard Weston, Carolyn Blewett Lawrence. LL.B., Stanford U., 1936, J.D., 1939. Bar: Calif. bar 1939. Dep. dist. atty. San Joaquin County, 1942-46; practice law Stockton, 1946—; mem. firm, pres. Blewett, Garretson & Hachman, Stockton, 1971—. Chmn. San Joaquin County chpt. ARC, 1947-49; v.p. Goodwill Industries, 1967-68; vice chmn. Stockton Sister City Commn., 1969-70; adv. bd. bus. adminstrn. dept. U. Pacific; trustee San Joaquin Pioneer and Haggin Galleries. Fellow Am. Coll. Probate Counsel, Am. Bar Found.; mem. State Bar Calif. (mem. exec. com. of conf. of dels. 1969-72, vice chmn. 1971-72), Am. Bar Assn., Am. Judicature Soc., Am. Law Inst., Stockton C. of C., Delta Theta Phi, Theta Xi. Republican. Clubs: Rotary, Yosemite, San Francisco Comml, Masons, Shriners. Home: 3016 Dwight Way Stockton CA 95203 Office: 141 E Acacia St Stockton CA 95202

BLINDER, MARTIN S., publishing company executive; b. Bklyn., Nov. 18, 1946; s. Meyer and Lillian (Stein) B.; m. Janet Weiss, Dec. 10, 1983. BBA, Adelphi U., 1968. Account exec. Bruns, Nordeman & Co., N.Y.C., 1968-69; v.p. Blinder, Robinson & Co., Westbury, N.Y., 1969-73; treas. BHB Prodns., Los Angeles, 1973-76; pres. Martin Lawrence Ltd. Edits., Van Nuys, Calif., 1976—, also chmn. bd. dirs.; pres., dir. Corp. Art Inc., Visual Artists Mgmt. Corp., Art Consultants Inc.; lectr. bus. symposia. Contbr. articles to mags. and newspapers; appeared on TV and radio. Mem. Dem. Nat. Com.; patron Guggenheim Mus., N.Y.C., Mus. Modern Art, N.Y.C., Los Angeles County Mus. Art, Los Angeles Mus. Contemporary Art (hon. founder), Whitney Mus. Am. Art, Palm Springs Mus. Art, Hirschhorn Mus., Washington, Skirball Mus., Los Angeles, Diabetes Found. of City of Hope, B'nai B'rith Anti-Defamation League; bd. dirs., pres. Research Found. for Crohns Disease. Read into Congl. Record, 1981, 83, 86; recipient resolution of commendation Los Angeles City Council, 1983; State of Calif. resolution for contbn. to arts in Calif., 1983; County of Los Angeles Bd. Suprs. resolution for Contbn. to arts in So. Calif., 1983, Gov. of R.I. resolution for contbns. to arts, 1985. Mem. Citizens for Common Sense; Nov. 18, 1985 declared Martin S. Blinder Day in Los Angeles in his honor by Mayor Tom Bradley. Office: 16250 Stagg St Van Nuys CA 91406

BLINOFF, MARK, radio broadcaster, educator, writer; b. Concord, Calif., Mar. 29, 1939; s. Gennady Nicholas and Olga (Ladd) B.; m. Sherri Gaye Mudd, June 16, 1973; children—Darrick Sean, Kimberly Kay, Nicholas Mark. B.A., U. Pacific, 1957. Program dir. Sta. KTRE-TV, Lufkin, Tex., 1957-59; mgr. KAYS-TV, Hays, Kans., 1959-61; acct. supr. Sta. KWUN, Concord, Calif., 1961-63; asst. program dir. Sta. KSFO, San Francisco, 1963-65; program dir. Sta. KEX, Portland, 1965-68; program dir. Sta. KMPC, Los Angeles, 1968-79; v.p., gen. mgr. Merv Griffin Radio, Hollywood, Calif., 1979-81; pres. Firebird Communications, Salem, Oreg., 1981—; instr. Grad. Sch. Mgmt. UCLA. Respite care parent Los Angeles Children's Home Soc.; child sponsor Los Angeles Maryvale Orphange. Recipient Best Radio Promotion award N.Y. Ad. Club, 1964; Best Radio Comml. award Hollywood Ad Club, 1973; Program Dir. of the Yr. award Billboard Mag., 1978. Author: (with Eric Norberg) Who Put What on the Radio and Why, 1979; Owning and Operating your Own Radio Station, 1982. Office: 1405 E Ellendale St Dallas OR 97338

BLISH, EUGENE SYLVESTER, trade association administrator; b. Denver, Oct. 9, 1912; s. George Joseph and Lillian Lenox (O'Neill) B.; m. Susan M. Monti, Feb. 21, 1950; children—Eugene A., Mary, Susan Blish McCoy, Julia. B.S.C., U. Notre Dame, 1934. Advt. dir. Colo. Milling and Elevator Co., Denver, 1934-45; advt. and mktg. cons., Denver, 1945-57; asst. exec. dir. Am. Sheep Producers Council, Denver, 1957-74; merchandising rep. Nat. Potato Bd., Denver, 1974—. Mem. alumni bd. dirs. U. Notre Dame, 1947-49. Mem. Soc. Mayflower Desc., Barnstable Hist. Soc. (Mass.). Clubs: Denver Athletic, Mt. Vernon Country, Denver Notre Dame. Home and Office: 1370 Madison St Denver CO 80206

BLISS, ANNA CAMPBELL, artist, architect, color consultant; b. Morristown, N.J., July 10, 1925; d. Leo Manning Campbell and Agnes (McManus) Campbell; m. Robert Lewis Bliss, Apr. 2, 1949. BA, Wellesley Coll., 1946; MArch, Harvard U., 1950; postgrad., MIT, 1950, U. Mpls. Sch. of Art, 1954-63, U. Utah. Registered architect, Minn. Ptnr. Bliss & Campbell, Salt Lake City, 1956—; lectr. Utah State U., 1975, U. Md., 1976, Syracuse U., 1976, UCLA, 1977, Yale U., 1979, U. Va., 1982, also various profl. groups and mus.; cons. Peerless Lighting Co., Berkeley, Calif., 1979—, Conoco Oil Co., Ponca City and Wilmington, Del., 1983; pres. Contemporary Arts Group, Salt Lake City, 1984-85. One woman shows include Lowe Art Gallery, Syracuse, N.Y., 1976, Utah Mus. of Fine Arts Traveling Exhibit, 1979-81, Yale U., New Haven, 1979, Ohio State U. Gallery of Fine Art, Columbus, 1980, Focus Gallery, San Diego Mus. of Art, 1981, Salt Lake Art Ctr., 1983; represented in permanent collections Met. Mus. N.Y.C., Art Inst. of Chgo., Minami Gallery, First Nat. Bank, represented in numerous corp. and pvt. collections. Adv. bd. Repertory Dance Theatre, Salt Lake City, 1965-70; Utah Mus. Fine Arts, Salt Lake City, 1972—, Utah Arts Festival, Salt Lake City, 1979-81; mem. Chamber Music Soc., Salt Lake City, 1970—; sec. Salt Lake City Design Bd., 1979-84. Fellow Am. Acad. in Rome, 1984; grantee Graham Found., 1980. Mem. Am. Soc. Interior Designers (presdl. citation 1981, del. chmn. mem. Color Mktg. Group (lectr.), Inter Soc. Color Council (bd. dirs. 1983-86), Color Mktg. Group (lectr.), Artist's Equity. Clubs: New Yorker, Salt Lake Swim and Tennis (Salt Lake City). Avocations: tennis, reading, traveling. Office: Bliss & Campbell Architects 27 University St Salt Lake City UT 84102

BLISS, JEFFREY ROSS, marketing consultant; b. Needham, Mass., Jan. 25, 1953; s. Willard Robinson and Faith Ada (Ross) B. BA, Colgate U.; postgrad., Boston U., UCLA. Sr. mktg. rep. Xerox Corp., Lexington, Mass., 1976-78; asst. product mgr. H.P. Hood, Boston, 1978-80; sr. assoc., product mgr. The Gillette Co., Boston, 1980-82; internat. product mgr. New Balance Athletic Shoe Co., Boston, 1982-83; dir. corp. sponsorship Los Angeles Olympic Com., 1983-84; pres. Creative Corp. Mktg., Santa Monica, Calif., 1984—; cons. City Gardens, Inc., Boston, 1979, Internat. Spl. Olympics Games, South Bend, Ind., 1985—, End Hunger Network, Los Angeles, 1985—, Viet Vets Benefit Concert, Los Angeles, 1986, McLuhan Found., Malibu, Calif., 1986, City of Los Angeles, 1986. Speaker Nat. Jaycees Conv., Newport, R.I., 1975; vol. Navajo Indian Reservation, Delba Sekai Sch., Ariz., 1972, Migrant Workers Assn., 1973. Named one of Outstanding Young Men of Am. Mem. Alpha Tau Omega (pres. 1974-75), Konosioni Honor Soc. (pres. 1974-75). Methodist. Avocations: soccer, skiing, music, sailing. Office: Creative Corp Mktg 2941 Main St #300A Santa Monica CA 90405

BLISS, LAWRENCE CARROLL, botany educator; b. Cleve., Nov. 29, 1929; s. Laurence and Ada May (Peterson) B.; m. Gweneth Ruth Jones, Mar. 15, 1952; children: Dwight I., Karen L. BS, Kent State U., 1951, MS, 1953; PhD, Duke U., 1956. Instr. biology Bowling Green (Ohio) State U., 1956-57; instr. botany U. Ill., Urbana, 1957-58, asst. prof., 1958-61, asso. prof., 1961-66, prof., 1966-68; prof. dept. botany U. Alta., Edmonton, Can., 1968-78, dir. controlled environ. facility, 1968-78; prof. botany U. Wash., Seattle, 1978-87, chmn. dept. botany, 1978-87; cons. in field. Author: (with M. Balbach) Laboratory Manual for General Botany, 6th edit., 1982; editor: Truelove Lowland, Devon Island, Canada: A High Arctic Ecosystem, 1977, (with others) Tundra Ecosystems: A Comparative Analysis, 1981; contbr. articles to profl. jours. Fulbright scholar, 1963-64. Mem. Ecol. Soc. Am. (v.p. 1976-77, treas. 1977-81, pres. 1982-83), Am. Inst. Biol. Sci.; fellow AAAS, Arctic Inst. N. Am.; mem. Can. Bot. Assn., Sigma Xi. Republican. Presbyterian. Home: 1226 NW 175th St Seattle WA 98177 Office: U Wash Dept Botany Seattle WA 98195

BLITZ-WEISZ, SALLY, speech pathologist; b. Buffalo, Nov. 9, 1954; d. Isaac and Paula (Goldstein) Blitz; m. Andrew Weisz, Dec. 16, 1984. BA in Speech Pathology, Audiology, SUNY, Buffalo, 1976, MA in Speech Pathology, 1978. Speech, lang. pathologist Lang. Devel. Program, Tonawanda, N.Y., 1978-82, Bailey and Drown Assocs., La Habra, Calif., 1982-83; speech, lang. specialist, cons. Pasadena (Calif.) Unified Schs., 1983—. Active Anti-Defamation League, San Fernando Valley, 1985-86; mem. 2d Generation Holocaust Survivors, Los Angeles, 1986—. Recipient Excellence in Studies award Temple Shaarey Zedek, Buffalo, 1968. Mem. Am. Speech-Lang.-Hearing Assn. Democrat. Club: Jewish Young Adults. Lodge: B'nai Brith. Avocations: exercise workouts, bicycling. Home: 11671 Amigo Ave Northridge CA 91326 Office: Pasadena Unified Sch Dist 351 S Hudson Ave Pasadena CA 91101

BLIWISE, DONALD LINN, research psychologist; b. Newark, June 14, 1952; s. Daniel and Ruth (Offenkrantz) B.; m. Nancy Gourash, Oct. 12, 1980. BA cum laude, Clark U., 1974; MA, U. Chgo., 1978, PhD, 1982. Clin. research assoc. Stanford (Calif.) Med. Sch., 1982-86, sr. clin. research assoc., 1986—; clin. asst. prof. psychiatry U. Calif., San Francisco, 1984-86; cons. geriatric psychiatry task force Am. Psychiat. Assn., 1984; cons. Discovery Health Cons., Sacramento, 1986—. Contbr. articles to profl. jours. Recipient Clin. Research Trainee award NIMH, 1978-80. Mem. Am. Psychol. Assn., Gerontol. Soc. Am., AAAS, Clin. Sleep Soc. (cert.), Soc. for Neurosci., Phi Beta Kappa. Office: Stanford Med Sch Sleep Disorders Ctr TD 114 Stanford CA 94305

BLIZZARD, ALAN, artist; b. Boston, Mar. 25, 1939; s. Thomas and Elizabeth B. Student, Mass. Coll. Art; M.A., U. Ariz.; M.F.A., U. Iowa, 1963. Instr. in art U. Iowa; vis. asst. prof. art Albion Coll., U. Okla.; asso. prof. UCLA; now prof. painting Scripps Coll. and; Claremont Grad. Sch. Represented in permanent collections, Bklyn. Mus., Met. Mus. Art, N.Y.C., Art Inst. Chgo., Denver Art Mus., La Jolla (Calif.) Mus. Art, Fluor Corp. Office: Scripps Coll Claremont CA 91711

BLOCH, BERNARD JEROME, architect; b. Chgo., Jan. 12, 1927; s. Harry Aaron and Charlotte (Frank) B.; m. Janice May Stern, Apr. 5, 1986; children: Wendy Ann, Lauren Jaye, Deanne Lynn. AA, UCLA, 1948; BA, U. Calif., Berkeley, 1952. Registered architect, Calif. Project job capt. John Carl Warnecke Architects, San Francisco, 1957-59; architect Blanchard & Maher Architects, San Francisco, 1959-65; pvt. practice architecture San Francisco, 1956-70; project mgr. Robert B. Liles Inc. Architects, Corte Madera, Calif., 1970-81; dir. constrn. service, sr. assoc. Whisler & Patri Architects, San Francisco, 1981—. Mem. AIA (chmn. code com. 1984-86), Constrn. Specifications Inst. (chpt. sec. 1986-87), Nat. Fire Protective Assn. Democrat. Jewish. Avocations: painting, photography. Home: 18 Captains Landing Tiburon CA 94920 Office: Whisler & Patri Architects 2 Bryant St San Francisco CA 94120

BLOCH, E. MAURICE, art historian, educator; b. N.Y.C.; s. Leonard and Rose (von Auspitz) B. B.F.A., N.Y.U., 1939; student, Harvard, 1941-42; A.M., N.Y. U., 1942, Ph.D., 1957. With Met. Mus. Art, 1943; instr. art history U. Mo., 1943-44; lectr. art history N.Y.U., 1945-46, U. Minn., 1946-47; Keeper drawings and prints, prof. chalcography Cooper Union, 1949-53; prof. art history, dir., curator Grunwald Center for the Graphic Arts, UCLA, 1956-83; Bd. dirs., v.p. Virginia Steele Scott Found., Pasadena, Calif.; bd. dirs. Tamarind Inst., U. N.Mex., Albuquerque, Print Council Am., Lovis Corinth Meml. Found., N.Y., UCLA Art Council, Am. Art Council, Los Angeles County Mus. Art. Author: Evolution of an Artist, 1967, Catalogue Raisonne, 1967, rev. edit. 1986, The Drawings of George Caleb Bingham, 1975, also articles, revs., mus. and art gallery publns. Recipient Founders Day award of achievement N.Y.U., 1957, Western Heritage Center award, 1968; Belgian Am. Ednl. Found. traveling fellow Belgium, 1951; Am. Council Learned Socs. grant-in-aid, 1962. Mem. Coll. Art Assn. Am., Art Historians So. Calif., Art Students League, Hist. Soc. Mo. Home: 2253 Veteran Ave Los Angeles CA 90064

BLOCH, ERNEST, II, public relations executive; b. Portland, Oreg., Nov. 15, 1938; s. Ivan and Mariana (Troetel) B.; m. Carol Ann Smith, Aug. 18, 1961 (div. June 1970); children: Peter Ernest, Suzanne Margurite; m. Ellen M. Dietz-Dressler, July 24, 1983. BS, U. Oreg., 1961. Mgr. pricing Western Airlines, Los Angeles, 1962-75; dir. pricing Tex. Internat. Airlines, Houston, 1975-77; pres. Bus. Exchange, Inc., Houston, 1977-79; v.p. mktg. Air Oreg., Portland, 1979-80; dir. pub. relations, corp. communications NERCO, Inc., Portland, 1981—. Div. advisor United Way, 1986; co-chmn. Portland Youth Philharmonic Endowment Campaign, 1987; co-chmn. auction Oreg. Mus. Sci. and Industry; bd. dirs. Chamber Music Northwest, 1984; mem. mktg. com. Oreg. Symphony Assn., 1986; co-chmn. youth endowment fund drive com., mem. pub. relations com. Portland Youth Philharmonic. Mem. Pub. Relations Soc. Am., Internat. Assn. Bus. Communicators, Nat. World Affairs Council Oreg., Am. Mining Congress (communication com.), Portland C. of C. (communication com.). Democrat. Jewish. Club: City (Portland). Avocations: photography, boating. Office: NERCO Inc 111 SW Columbia St Portland OR 97201

BLOCH, PAUL DAVID, advt. co. exec.; b. N.Y.C.; s. Max and Albena (Simmons) B.; B.S. in Journalism, Ohio State U.; m. Mary Rose Speziale, Dec. 4, 1965; children—Michael Max, Donna Rose. Vice pres., dir. E.T. Legg & Co., Glendale, Calif., 1967—, Spectacular Sign Corp., Glendale, 1967—; pres. Western Advt., Inc., Paul Bloch. Advt. dir. Freeway Properties, Inc. Pres., Strathmore Village Civic Assn., 1962-64; bd. mem. Greater Manhasset Pres.'s Civic Assn.; mem. bd., col. United Fund Nassau County, N.Y., 1963; bd. dirs. Parents Council, Calif. State U., Northridge. Mem. Nat. Acad. Rec. Arts and Scis., Milline Club of So. Calif., Variety Clubs So. Calif., Nat. Football Found. and Hall of Fame (dir. San Fernando Valley chpt. 1978—). Clubs: Big Ten of So. Calif., Ohio State Alumni of So. Calif. (sec.). Contbr. articles in field to mags. Home: 19620 Los Alimos St Chatsworth CA 91311

BLOCH, RICHARD L., professional basketball team executive. Chmn. Phoenix Suns, Ariz. Address: Phoenix Suns 2910 N Central Phoenix AZ 85012 *

BLOCHBERGER, JOHN CHARLES, communications company executive; b. Kingston, Pa., Jan. 13, 1939; s. Charles H. and Teresa C. (Ketrick) B.; m. Philomena J. Byrne, June 1, 1963; children: Karen, Sean, Donna. BA, William Paterson Coll., 1977. V.p. material mgmt. Singer Communications, Little Falls, N.J., 1965-77; prodn. mgr. Thompson Industries, Phoenix, 1977-80; materials mgr. Revlon Inc., Phoenix, 1980—. Councilman Borough Ogdensburg, N.J., 1967-70. Served to sgt. U.S. Army, 1957-60. Mem. Am. Prodn. and Inventory Control Soc. (v.p. publicity, 1983-84, exec. v.p. 1984-85, pres. 1985—). Republican. Roman Catholic. Avocations: reading, swimming. Home: 5820 W Crocus Dr Glendale AZ 85306 Office: Revlon Inc 4301 W Buckeye Rd Phoenix AZ 85043

BLOCK, JOHN HARVEY, pharmaceutical chemistry educator; b. Yakima, Wash., May 11, 1938; s. Harvey Temple and Gladys Liddel (Spring) B.; m. Alice Lynn McCombe, Dec. 19, 1964; children: Alan, Bonnie, Charlotte. B Pharmacy, Wash. State U., 1961, MS in Pharm. Chemistry, 1963; PhD in Pharm. Chemistry, U. Wis., 1966. Registered pharmacist, Oreg. Asst. prof. Oreg. State U., Corvallis, 1966-72, assoc. prof., 1972-78, prof. medicinal chemistry, 1978—; vis. scholar Stanford U., 1972-73; cons. Bend (Oreg.) Research, 1975-78, Oreg. Bd. Pharmacy, Portland, 1977, 84—. Author: Inorganic and Pharmaceutical Chemistry, 1974 (also co-editor), Solubility and Partition Coefficient, 1986 (also co-editor); contbr. articles to profl. jours. Mem. adv. bd. Corvallis Youth Symphony, 1985—. Grantee in field. Mem. Am. Chem. Soc., Am. Pharm. Assn., AAUP, Sigma Xi, Rho Chi (counselor 1968-70, v.p. 1975-77, pres. 1978-80). Lodge: Kiwanis. Home: 1310 NW 14th St Corvallis OR 97330 Office: Oreg State U Coll Pharmacy Corvallis OR 97331-3507

BLOCK, MICHAEL JOSEPH, oil company executive, research chemist; b. Chgo., June 29, 1942; s. Samuel Albert and Frieda (Kligman) B.; m. Karen Ruth Plotkin, Sept. 19, 1970; children: Laura Miriam, Jeremy Daniel. BS in Chemistry, U. Mich., 1964; MA, Harvard U., 1965, PhD, 1969. With sci. and tech. div. Unocal Corp., Brea, Calif., 1968—, sr. research chemist, 1976-80, supr. carbon and nitrogen chems. research, 1981-86, mgr. chems. research, 1986—. Patentee in field. Mem. AAAS, Am. Chem. Soc. Democrat. Jewish. Home: 757 Toussau Dr Fullerton CA 92631 Office: Unocal sci and tech div 376 S Valencia Ave Brea CA 92621

BLOCK, PAULA MCKENNA, psychiatric social worker; b. Tucson, Nov. 3, 1955; d. Donald Fay and Ann Margaret (Dunning) McKenna; m. Richard Carl Block, Apr. 12, 1980; 1 child, Gregory Donald. Student, U. Ariz., 1973-75; BSWcum laude, Ariz. State U., 1977, MSW, 1978. Ct. liaison Ariz. State U. Law Sch., Tempe, 1976-77; child care worker Brewster Home, Tucson, 1977-78; treatment coordinator Desert Hills, Tucson, 1978-86, dir. admissions, 1986—. Mem. Nat. Assn. Social Workers (cert.), Orthopsychiat. Assn. Democrat. Presbyterian. Avocations: tennis, needlepoint, crocheting. Home: 3675 W Eastham Tucson AZ 85741 Office: Desert Hills 5245 N Camino de Oeste Tucson AZ 85745

BLOCK, RICHARD ALLEN, lawyer; b. St. Louis, Apr. 11, 1940; s. David and Faye (Schneider) B.; m. Nancy McGargel, Jan. 26, 1971 (div. 1980); m. Judith Ann Nelson, Nov. 14, 1981; children—Melissa, Rachelle, Michelle. A.B., Washington U., 1961, J.D., 1963. Bar: Mo. 1963, U.S. Supreme Ct. 1968, Ariz. 1970, U.S. Dist. Ct. Ariz. 1972, U.S. Ct. Appeals (9th cir.) 1982. Staff Counsel Trans World Airlines, N.Y.C., 1968-69; gen. counsel GAC Properties inc. of Ariz., Tucson, 1969-81; sole practice, Tucson, 1981—. Served to capt. USAF, 1964-68. Mem. Ariz. Bar Assn., ABA (Ariz. state chmn. environ. quality com. young lawyers sect. 1971), Pima County Bar Assn., Lawyer-Pilots Assn. Democrat. Jewish. Home: 3350 Morgan Rd Tucson AZ 85745 Office: 215 N Court Ave Tucson AZ 85701

BLOCK, ROBERT JACKSON, investment banker; b. Seattle, Oct. 20, 1922; s. Max Harry and Esther Ida (Parker) B.; m. Dorothy Wolens, Aug. 11, 1946 (dec.); children: Jonathan, Adam, Daniel, Kenan, Susanna, Mary Judith; m. 2d, Mary Lou Moats, Dec. 26, 1972; children: Melinda Mulvaney, Newton Moats, Christina Moats, Tamara Ingle. Student Stanford U., 1940-43, U. Wash., 1943-44. Asst. to pres. Block Shoe Stores, Inc., Seattle, 1946-56, pres., 1956-58; pres. Columbia-Cascade Securities Corp., Seattle, 1958-77; pres. Nat. Securities Corp., Seattle, 1977-80, chmn., chief exec. officer, 1980—; founding dir. North West Bank (merged with Old Nat. Bank); cons. Area Redevel. Adminstrn., 1961-62; exec. reservist policy secretariat Nat. Def. Exec. Res.; GSA, 1968—. Named to Seattle Ctr. Legion of Honor Seattle Ctr. Adv. Commn. and Seattle Ctr. Found., 1987. Pres. Block Found., Inc., Allied Arts Found.; former chmn. Puget Sound chpt. Nat. Found. March of Dimes; mem. nat. exec. council Am. Jewish Com.; former mem. Seattle Bd. Park Commrs.; chmn., dir. Cornish Inst., 1980-82; trustee Pilchuck Sch., Stanwood, Wash.; bd. dirs. Seattle Pub. Library Found.; chmn. King County (Wash.) USO Com., 1950-52; chmn. Civic Ctr. Com., Seattle, 1954; co-chmn. Metro Campaign Com., Seattle, 1958; alt. del. Democratic Nat. Conv., 1956; King County co-chmn. Vols. for Stevenson, 1956; elected King County Freeholder, 1967. Mem. Wash. Bar Assn. (fee arbitration panel, vis. cons.). Clubs: Wash. Athletic; College (Seattle); Rainier. Home: 1617 E Boston Terr Seattle WA 98112 Office: 500 Union St Seattle WA 98101

BLOCK, ROBERT SHELDON, communications exec.; b. Chgo., Nov. 26, 1927; s. Samuel and Revelle (Rose) B.; m. Carol Schlesinger, Dec. 25, 1950; children—Debra Slotnick, David Lee. B.S., U. Wis., 1975; postgrad. U. Ill., 1948-49, Latin Am. Inst., 1949-50, B.A., 1950. Chief exec. officer Robert Block Advt., Milw., 1955-75, InHouse Systems, Inc., Milw., 1955-75; pres. B & F Broadcasting, Inc., Milw., 1973-82; chief exec. officer Telease, Inc., Los Angeles, 1971-85, dir. Harriscope, Los Angeles, 1983—; pres. Nat. Licensing Systems, 1985—; lectr. in field. Served with M.C., U.S. Army, 1945-46. Mem. Western Regional Los Angeles C. of C., Hollywood Radio and TV Soc., World Future Soc., Am. Film Inst., Acad. TV Arts and Scis., Nat. Assn. Broadcasters, U.S. Sports Acad. (past pres., dir. 1973—), Aircraft Owners and Pilots Assn., Nat. Cable TV Assn., Greater Los Angeles C. of C. Clubs: Magic Castle, Masons, Shriners. Patentee in field; author: No Togethers, 1973; 14 Days to Better Faster Reading, 1974; Step-by-Step Cookbook, 1975.

BLOCK, RONALD MARVIN, environmental toxicologist; b. Atlantic City, Dec. 6, 1941; s. Charles and Eleanor Helen (Deutsh) B.; m. Suzanne Brizzolari, Jan. 23, 1967 (div. Mar. 1976); m. Mari Teresa Dolan, Sept. 9, 1982; children: David, Nicole. BA, U. Alaska, 1967; MS, U. N.D., 1972, PhD, 1974. Research prof. U. Md., Solomons, 1973-76; cons. Potomac Research, Panama City, Fla., 1977-78, Kennedy/Jenks Engrs., San Francisco, 1979-84; cons., pres. Aqua Terra Techs., Walnut Creek, Calif., 1984—. Contbr. articles to profl. jours. Atomic Energy Commn. fellow 1971-73. Mem. AAAS, Am. Fisheries Soc., Am. Soc. Zoologists, N.D. Acad. Sci., Soc. Risk Analysis, N.Y. Acad. Scis., Concord (Calif.) C. of C., Sigma Xi. Jewish. Lodge: Elks. Avocations: hunting, fishing. Home: 1221 Thames Dr Concord CA 94518 Office: Aqua Terra Techs 2950 Buskirk Ave Walnut Creek CA 94596

BLODGETT, ELSIE GRACE, association executive; b. Eldorado Springs, Mo., Aug. 2, 1921; d. Charles Ishmal and Naoma Florence (Worthington) Robison; m. Charles Davis Blodgett, Nov. 8, 1940; children: Carolyn Doyel, Charleen Bier, Lyndon Blodgett. Student Warrensburg (Mo.) State Tchrs. Coll., 1939-40; BA, Fresno (Calif.) State Coll., 1953. Tchr. schs. in Mo. and Calif., 1940-42, 47-72; owner, mgr. rental units, 1965—; exec. dir. San Joaquin County (Calif.) Rental Property Assn., Stockton, 1970-81; prin. Delta Rental Property Owners and Assocs., 1981-82; propr. Crystal Springs Health World, Inc., Stockton, 1980-86; bd. dirs. Stockton Better Bus. Bur. Active local PTA, Girl Scouts U.S., Boy Scouts Am.; bd. dirs. Stockton Goodwill Industries. Named (with husband) Mr. and Mrs. Apt. Owner of San Joaquin County, 1977. Mem. Nat. Apt. Assn. (state treas. women's div. 1977-79), Calif. Ret. Tchrs. Assn. Republican. Methodist. Lodge: Stockton Zonta. Home and Office: 2285 W Mendocino Ave Stockton CA 95204

BLODGETT, FORREST CLINTON, economics educator; b. Oregon City, Oreg., Oct. 6, 1927; s. Clinton Alexander and Mabel (Wells) B.; B.S., U. Omaha, 1961; M.A., U. Mo., 1969; Ph.D., Portland State U., 1979; m. Beverley Janice Buchholz, Dec. 21, 1946; children—Cherine (Mrs. Jon R. Klein), Candis Melis (Mrs. Mark A. Schaeffer), Clinton George. Joined C.E., U.S. Army, 1946, commd. 2d lt., 1946, advanced through grades to lt. col., 1965; ret. 1968; engrng. assignments Japan, 1947-49, U.K., 1950-53, Korea, 1955-56, Alaska, 1958-60, Vietnam, 1963; staff engr. 2d Army Air Def. Region, Richards-Gebaur AFB, Mo., 1964-66; base engr. Def. Atomic Support Agy., Sandia Base, N.Mex., 1966-68; bus. mgr., trustee, asst. prof. econs. Linfield Coll., McMinnville, Oreg., 1968-73, assoc. prof., 1973-83, prof., 1983—, also trustee; pres. Blodgett Enterprises, Inc., 1983-85; founder, dir. Valley Community Bank, 1980-86, vice chmn. bd. dirs., 1985-86. Commr., Housing Authority of Yamhill County (Oreg.), chmn., 1980-83; mem. Yamhill County Econ. Devel. Com., 1978-83; bd. dirs. Yamhill County Found., 1983—. Decorated Army Commendation medal with oak leaf cluster; recipient Joint Services Commendation medal Dept. of Def. Mem. Soc. Am. Mil. Engrs. (pres. Albuquerque post 1968), Am. Econ. Assn., Western Econ. Assn. Internat., Nat. Retired Officers Assn., Res. Officers Assn. (pres. Marion chpt. 1976), SAR (pres. Oreg. soc. 1985-86), Pi Sigma Epsilon, Pi Gamma Mu, Omicron Delta Epsilon (Pacific NW regional dir. 1978—). Republican. Episcopalian. Lodge: Rotary (pres. McMinnville club 1983-84). Office: Linfield Coll McMinnville OR 97128

BLODGETT, JAY ALAN, savings and loan executive; b. Ogden, Utah, Nov. 7, 1933; s. Orvil W. Blodgett and Leona (Staley) Wade; m. Eleanor Call Blodgett, July 25, 1956; children: Jeffery A., Michele Blodgett Cockayne, Linda Blodgett Fotheringham, Mark C. BS, Brigham Young U., 1955, MS, 1962. CPA, Utah. Auditor Brigham Young U., Provo, Utah, 1953-60; acct. Deloitte, Haskins, Sells, Portland, Oreg., 1960-61; auditor, acct. Ch. of Latter Day Saints, Salt Lake City, 1962-69, fin. officer, 1969-85; pres., chief exec. officer Am. Savs., Salt Lake City, 1985—, also bd. dirs. Bd. dirs. Salt Lake Airport Authority, 1976—, Utah Symphony, Salt Lake City, 1983-86, Utah State Retirement Bd., Salt Lake City, 1983-85. Served as cpl. U.S. Army, 1956-57. Mormon. Avocations: skiing, running. Office: Am Savings & Loan Assn 77 W 2nd South Salt Lake City UT 84101

BLOEDE, VICTOR CARL, lawyer, university executive; b. Woodwardville, Md., July 17, 1917; s. Carl Schon and Eleanor (Eck) B.; m. Ellen Louise Miller, May 9, 1947; children—Karl Abbott, Pamela Elena. A.B., Dartmouth Coll., 1940; J.D. cum laude, U. Balt., 1950; LL.M. in Pub. Law, Georgetown U., 1967. Bar: Md. 1950, Fed. Hawaii 1958, U.S. Supreme Ct. 1971. Sole practice Balt., 1950-64; mem. Goldman & Bloede, Balt., 1959-64; Md. counsel Seven-Up Bottling Co., Balt., 1958-64; dep. atty. gen. Pacific Trust Ter., Honolulu, 1952-53; asst. solicitor for ters. Office of Solicitor, U.S. Dept. Interior, Washington, 1953-54; atty. U.S. Justice, Honolulu, 1955-58; asst. gen. counsel Dept. Navy, Washington, 1960-61, 63-64; spl. legal cons. Md. Legislature, Legis. Council, 1963-64, 66-67; assoc. prof. U. Hawaii, 1961-63, dir. property mgmt., 1964-67; house counsel, dir. contracts and grants U. Hawaii System, 1967-82; house counsel U. Hawaii Research Corp., 1970-82; legal counsel Law of Sea Inst., 1978-82; legal cons. Research Corp. and research div., U. Hawaii, 1982—; spl. counsel to Holifield Congl. Commn. on Govt. Procurement, 1970-73. Author: Hawaii Legislative Manual, 1962, Maori Affairs, New Zealand, 1964, Oceanographic Research Vessel Operations, and Liabilities, 1972, Hawaiian Archipelago, Legal Effects of a 200 Mile Territorial Sea, 1973, Copyright-Guidelines to the 1976 Act, 1977, Forms Manual, Inventions: Policy, Law and Procedure, 1982; writer, contbr. Coll. Law Digest and other publs. on legislation and pub. law. Mem. Gov.'s Task Force Hawaii and The Sea, 1969, Citizens Housing Com. Balt., 1952-64; bd. govs. Balt. Community YMCA, 1954-64; bd. dirs. U. Hawaii Press, 1964-66, Coll. Housing Found., 1968-80; internat. rev. commn. Canada-France Hawaii Telescope Corp., 1973-82, chmn., 1973, 82; co-founder, incorporator First Unitarian Ch. Honolulu. Served to lt. comdr. USNR, 1942-45, PTO. Grantee ocean law studies NSF and Dept. Energy, 1970-80. Mem. ABA, Balt. Bar Assn., Fed. Bar Assn., Am. Soc. Internat. Law, Nat. Assn. Univ. Attys. (chmn. patents and copyrights sect. 1974-76). Home: 635 Onaha St Honolulu HI 96816

BLOIS, MARSDEN SCOTT, physician, educator; b. San Antonio, Jan. 5, 1919; s. Marsden Scott and Miriam (Eckart) B.; m. Jean McCanna, Dec. 24, 1941; children: Marsden, Byron, Stephen, Philip, Miriam. BS, U.S. Naval Acad., 1941; MS, Stanford U., 1950, PhD, 1952, MD, 1959. Ensign USN, 1941-53, advanced through grades to commdr., 1953; research assoc. Stanford (Calif.) U., 1953-61, assoc. prof., 1961-69; prof. U. Calif., San Francisco, 1969—. Author: Information and Medicine, 1984; editor Free Radicals in Biological Systems, 1959; contbr. articles to sci. jours. Recipient Gold, Silver, Bronze awards for research Am. Acad. Dermatology. Fellow Am. Coll. Med. Informatics (pres. 1984—), N.Y. Acad. Scis., AAAS; mem. Am. Assn. Med. Systems and Infosystems, Am. Phys. Soc. Roman Catholic. Office: U Calif Rm AC4 San Francisco CA 94143

BLOLAND, PAUL ANSON, educator; b. Primrose, Wis., Nov. 15, 1923; s. Arthur George and Sarah (Hustad) B.; m. Ruth Marian Nolte, Apr. 7, 1951; children—Eric Craig, Peter Brian. B.S., U. Wis., 1949, M.S., 1950; Ph.D., U. Minn., 1959. Student activities adviser U. Minn., 1950-51, asso. dir. student activities bur., 1953-55, dir., 1955-60, asst. prof. ednl. psychology, 1959-60; dean of students Drake U., Des Moines, 1960-64; dean of students, asso. prof. edn. U. So. Calif., Los Angeles, 1964-69; v.p. student and alumni affairs U. So. Calif., 1969-72, prof. edn., 1970—, chmn. dept. counseling, 1973—. Author: Student Group Advising in Higher Education; editor: CACD Jour., 1984—editorial bd. Jour. Coll. Student Personnel, 1975-78; contbr. articles to profl. and mountaineering jours. Served with AUS, 1943-46, 1951-52. Mem. Am. Personnel and Guidance Assn. (senate del. 1962-63, mem. com. br. coordination 1963-64, nat. membership com. 1963-65), Am. Coll. Personnel Assn. (program com. 1960-61, commn. advising fgn. students 1963-64, chmn. nat. membership com. 1964-65, mem.-at-large nat. exec. council 1965-66, 67-70, pres. 1970-71), Nat. Assn. Student Personnel Administrs. (mem.-at-large and sec. nat. exec. com.), Am. Psychol. Assn., Coll. Student Personnel Inst. (exec. com. 1965-66, bd. dirs. 1965-69, chmn. acad. council 1967-69), Calif. Coll. Personnel Assn. (pres. 1981-82), Nat. Vocat. Guidance Assn., Educare, Sierra Club, Iron Cross, Skull and Dagger, Blue Key, Alpha Phi Omega, Phi Delta Kappa, Delta Epsilon, Psi Chi, Omicron Delta Kappa. Home: 27128 Fond du Lac Rd Rancho Palos Verdes CA 90274 Office: Univ So Calif Los Angeles CA 90089

BLOMKER, DALE LYNN, correctional service officer; b. Humboldt, Iowa, Aug. 13, 1942; s. Myrl Richard and Bessie Evelyn (Mattoon) B.; m. Donna Jeanne Terwische, Sept. 9, 1967 (div. Nov. 1981); children: Daniel, Melissa; m. Marcia Kay Gross, Dec. 7, 1981. Grad. high sch., Humboldt. Supr. airport services Am. Airlines, Portland, Oreg.; Indpls.; Des Moines; Chgo., 1966-83; owner, operator River City Bowl and Lounge, Mason City, Iowa, 1983-84; correctional services officer Ariz. Dept. Corrections, Goodyear, 1984—; appointed agt. Farmers Ins. Group, 1986—. Asst. cubscout master Boy Scouts Am., Des Moines, 1972-73. Served with U.S. Army, 1963-66, Vietnam. Lodge: Moose. Avocations: model building, radio controlled aircraft. Home: 13-102 2724 W Sahuaro Dr Phoenix AZ 85029 Office: Ariz Dept Corrections Santa Cruz PO Box 3000 Goodyear AZ 85338

BLOMSTEDT, HERBERT THORSON, symphony director, conductor; b. Springfield, Mass., July 11, 1927; s. Adolphe Armintha and Alida (Thorson) B.; m. Waltraud Regina Petersen, May 29, 1955; children—Cecilia, Maria, Elisabet Vivianne, Kristina Ulrika. Diploma in Music Edn., Royal Acad. Music, Stockholm, 1948, Diploma: Organist, 1950, Diploma: Orch. Conductor, 1950; philosophy candidate, U. Uppsala, Sweden, 1952; D.Music (hon.), Andrews U., Mich., 1978. Music dir. Norrköping Symphony, Sweden, 1954-61; prof. conducting Royal Acad. Music, Stockholm, Sweden, 1961-70; permanent conductor Oslo Philharmonic, Norway, 1962-68; music dir. Danish Radio Symphony, Copenhagen, Denmark, 1967-77, Dresden Staatskapelle, German Democratic Republic, 1975-85, Swedish Radio Symphony, Stockholm, Sweden, 1977-82, San Francisco Symphony, San Francisco, 1985—. Author: Till Kämmedomen om J.C. Bach's Symfonier, 1951; Lars Erik Larsson och hans Concertinor, 1957; contbr. articles to profl. jours. Editor: (musical score) Franz Berwald: Sinfonie Singulière, 1965; condr. (hon.) NHK Symphony, Tokyo, 1986—; numerous recordings. Jenny Lind scholar Royal Acad. Music, Stockholm, 1950; recipient Expressen Music prize, 1964; decorated Knight Royal Order North Star, King of Sweden, 1971; Knight Royal Order Dannebrogen, Queen of Denmark, 1978; Litteris et Artibus, Gold medal, King of Sweden, 1979. Mem. Royal Acad. Music (Sweden). Seventh Day Adventist. Office: Interartists, Frans van Mierisstraat 43, 1071 RK, Amsterdam Netherlands NL Office: San Francisco Symphony Orch 201 Van Ness San Francisco CA 94102

BLOOM, FLOYD ELLIOTT, physician, research scientist; b. Mpls., Oct. 8, 1936; s. Jack Aaron and Frieda (Shochman) B.; m. D'Nell Bingham, Aug. 30, 1956 (dec. May 1973); children: Fl'Nell, Evan Russell; m. Jody Patricia Corey, Aug. 9, 1980. A.B. cum laude, So. Meth. U., 1956; M.D. cum laude, Washington U., St. Louis, 1960; D.Sc. (hon.), So. Meth. U., 1983, Hahnemann U., 1985, U. Rochester, 1985. Intern Barnes Hosp., St. Louis, 1960-61; resident internal medicine Barnes Hosp., 1961-62; research asso. NIMH, Washington, 1962-64; fellow depts. pharmacology, psychiatry and anatomy Yale Sch. Medicine, 1964-66, asst. prof., 1966-67, asso. prof., 1968; chief lab. neuropharmacology NIMH, Washington, 1968-75; acting dir. div. spl. mental health NIMH, 1973-75; commd. officer USPHS, 1974-75; dir. Arthur Vining Davis Center for Behavioral Neurobiology; prof. Salk Inst., La Jolla, Calif., 1975-83; dir. div. preclin. neurosci. and endocrinology Research Inst. of Scripps Clinic, La Jolla, 1983—; mem. Commn. on Alcoholism, 1980-81, Nat. Adv. Mental Health Council, 1976-80. Author: (with J.R. Cooper and R.H. Roth) Biochemical Basis of Neuropharmacology, 1971; (with Lazerson and Hofstadter) Brain, Mind, and Behavior, 1984; editor: Peptides: Integrators of Cell and Tissue Function, 1980; co-editor: Regulatory Peptides. Recipient A. Cressy Morrison award N.Y. Acad. Scis., 1971, A.E. Bennett award for basic research Soc. Biol. Psychiatry, 1971, Arthur A. Fleming award Science mag., 1973, Mathilde Solowey award, 1973, Biol. Sci. award Washington Acad. Scis., 1975, Alumni Achievement citation Washington U., 1980, McAlpin Research Achievement award Mental Health Assn., 1980, Lectr.'s medal College de France, 1979, Steven Beering medal, 1985. Fellow AAAS (bd. dirs 1986—), Am. Coll. Neuropsychopharmacology (mem. council 1976-78, chmn. program com. 1987); mem. Nat. Acad. Sci. (chmn. sect. neurobiology 1979-83), Inst. Medicine (mem. council 1986—), Am. Acad. Arts and Scis., Soc. Neurosci. (sec. 1973-74, pres. 1976), Am. Soc. Pharmacology and Exptl. Therapeutics, Am. Soc. Cell Biology, Am. Physiol. Soc., Am. Assn. Anatomists, Research Soc. Alcoholism (chmn. program com. 1985-87). Home: 1145 Pacific Beach Dr Apt B405 San Diego CA 92109 Office: Research Inst of Scripps Clinic La Jolla CA 92037

BLOOM, JOHN PORTER, historian, editor, administrator, archivist; b. Albuquerque, Dec. 30, 1924; s. Lansing Bartlett and Maude Elizabeth (McFie) B.; m. Eva Louise Platt, 1954 (div.); children: Katherine Elizabeth Bloom Jassen, John Lansing, Susan Marie; m. Nancy Jo Tice, July 30, 1968. A.B., U. N.Mex., 1947; A.M., George Washington U., 1949; Ph.D., Emory U., 1956; Cert. Pre-meteorology, Reed Coll., 1944. Mem. faculty No. Ga. Coll., 1950-51, Brenau Coll., 1952-56, U. Tex., El Paso, 1956-60; historian, mus. planner, editor Nat. Park Service, Washington, 1960-64; editor Territorial Papers of the U.S., 1964-80; sr. specialist western history Nat. Archives, Washington, 1964-80; dir. Holt-Atherton Pacific Ctr. Western Studies, Stockton, Calif., 1981-84; editor Pacific Historian, U. Pacific, Stockton, 1981-84; program com. chmn. Conf. History Am. West, Santa Fe, 1961, 71; cons. NEH div. pub. programs Nat. Hist. Publs. and Records Commn., Va. History and Mus. Fedn., 1976-79; mem. adv. bd. Capitol Studies, U.S. Capitol Hist. Soc., 1971-73. Editor: monograph The American Territorial System, 1973, Territorial Papers of the U.S., 1969, 71; editor, co-editor: monograph Soldier and Brave and other vols., 1963; book reviewer, contbr. articles to profl. jours. Chmn. Fairfax County Hist. Commn., 1972-73; active Cultural Heritage Bd., Stockton, Calif., 1982-85 ; bd. dirs. Gateway Inc., Alexandria, Va., 1971-75, Homeowners Assn. Chatham Colony, Reston, Va.; sheriff Potomac Corral of the Westerners Internat., 1974; bd. dirs. Joseph Priestley Chapel Assocs. Inc., 1978-81. Served with USAAF, 1943-45. So. Fellowships Fund fellow, 1955-56. Mem. Western History Assn. (pres. 1974 spl. service award, v.p. 1973, Ray Allen Billington award com. 1979-82), Westerners Internat. Inc. (pres. 1981-83), Nat. Council Pub. History (bd. dirs. 1980-83, co-chmn. program com. 1983-84), Westerners Soc. (Golden Spike award 1969), Council Am.'s Mil. Past (bd. dirs. 1982—), Am. Assn. State and Local History (chmn. Va. awards com. 1976-79), Soc. Am. Archivists, Orgn. Am. Historians, Eastern Nat. Parks and Monuments Assn., Soc. Hist. Archaeology, So. Hist. Assn., Pioneer Am. Soc., Rio Grande Hist. Found., Colonial N.Mex. Found., Mus. N.Mex. Assoc., Unitarian-Universalist Hist. Soc., Commonwealth (San Francisco). Home: 1629 Academy Ct Stockton CA 95207

BLOOM, MICHAEL EUGENE, communications executive; b. Pittsburg, Calif., Jan. 16, 1947; s. Benjamin Bernard and Mildred (Haims) B.; m. Deborah Ann Bresler, Aug. 6, 1977; children—Benjamin Solomon Bresler, Miriam Hannah Bresler. B.A. in Sociology, U. Calif.-Santa Barbara, 1969, postgrad. elec. engring., 1969-71; M.B.A., Stanford U., 1979. Broadcaster, Sta. KCSB-FM, Santa Barbara, 1964-68, gen. mgr., 1968-69; broadcaster KKIS-AM, Pittsburg, Calif., 1965, KMUZ-FM, Santa Barbara, 1965-67, KTMS-AM-FM, Santa Barbara, 1967-69; mem. tech. staff Gen. Research Corp., Santa Barbara, 1970-72; mgmt. scientist, cons. Sci. Applications, Inc., LaJolla, Calif., 1973-74, Planning and Mgmt. Cons. Corp., Cleve., 1974, Bloom Enterprises, Santa Monica, Calif., 1975-77; project team leader, sr. programmer Bendix Field Engring. Corp., Sunnyvale, Calif., 1977; retail product planner Crocker Nat. Bank, San Francisco, 1978; dir. corp. devel. Am. TV & Communications Corp., Englewood, Colo., 1979-82, dir. new bus. devel., 1983-84, dir. bus. and tech. devel., 1984-85; dir. video services devel. Pacific Bell, San Francisco, 1985-86, dir. product strategy and devel., 1986—; chmn. communications bd. U. Calif.-Santa Barbara; v.p., dir. Intercollegiate Broadcasting System, Inc., 1967-70; founder, dir. U. Calif. Radio Network, 1967-69; chmn. systems standards task force on teletext Nat. Cable TV Assn., 1980-81. Adv. council Coll. Info. Studies, U. Denver, 1982-85. Recipient Pres.'s merit award U. Calif., 1965. Mem. IEEE, Assn. MBA Execs., Soc. Cable TV Engrs., Soc. Broadcast Engrs., Nat. Cable TV Assn., U. Calif.-Santa Barbara Alumni Assn. (life), Stanford U. Bus. Sch. Alumni Assn. (program chmn. Rocky Mountain chpt. 1982-85). Author: (with L.A. Sibley) Carrier Current System Design, 1967. Office: Pacific Bell 2600 Camino Ramon Room 4 South 601 San Ramon CA 94583

BLOOMBECKER, JAY JOSEPH, computer crime consultant; b. N.Y.C., Dec. 18, 1944; s. William Samuel and Dorothy (Freeman) Becker; m. Linda Bloom, Sept. 28, 1980. BA, CCNY, 1965; JD, Harvard U., 1968. Dep. dist. atty. Los Angeles Dist. Atty.'s Office, 1970-80; dir. Nat. Ctr. for Computer Crime Data, Los Angeles, 1980—; nat. lectr. Assn. for Computing Machinery, N.Y., 1983—. Mem. editorial bd. Computer Law Strategist, N.Y., 1985—; editor: Computer Crime Law Reporter, 1984, Introduction to Computer Crime, 1985, Computer Crime, Computer Security, Computer Ethics, 1986. Active men's caucus Los Angeles Commn. on Assaults Against Women. Mem. Internat. Fedn. for Info. Processing (chmn.), Working Group on Computer Law (chmn.). Avocation: dancing. Office: Nat Ctr Computer Crime Data 2700 N Cahuenga Blvd Los Angeles CA 90068

BLOSSOM, HERBERT JOHN, medical administrator, physician; b. San Diego, Sept. 22, 1944; s. Herbert Henry Blossom and Grace Elizabeth (Tupper) Licursi; m. Martha McConnell; 1 child, Susanne. AB, U. Calif., Davis, 1966; MD, U. Calif., San Francisco, 1970. Diplomate Am. Bd. Family Practice. Intern Valley Med. Ctr., Fresno, Calif., 1970-71, resident in Family Practice, 1871-73, chief resident, 1972-73, dir. Family Practice Residency, 1976—; med. dir. Firebaugh/Mendota Community Health Ctr., Fresno, 1974-76; assoc. clin. prof. Family and Community Medicine U. Calif., San Francisco; vice-chmn. family and community medicine div. U. Calif., San Francisco. Mem. AMA, Calif. Med. Assn., Fresno/Madera Med. Soc. (sec., v.p.), Fresno Madera Med. Pac (chmn.), Coastal Research Orgn. (chmn.). Home: 708 E Carmen Fresno CA 93728 Office: Valley Med Ctr 445 S Cedar Ave Fresno CA 93702

BLOTTNER, FREDERICK GWYNN, mechanical engineer; b. Richmond, Va., May 27, 1932; s. Herman Eugene and Gwynn Dold (West) B.; m. Myra Ann Manton, Dec. 28, 1957; children: Laura Christine, Cheryl Ann. BS in Aeronautical Engring., Va. Polytech. Inst., 1953, MS in Engring. Mechanics, 1954; student, MIT, 1958; PhD in Engring. Mechanics, Stanford U., 1962. Registered profl. engr., Va. Staff member Sandia Corp., Albuquerque, 1954-59; mem. tech. staff Sanida Nat. Labs., Albuquerque, 1966—; research asst. Stanford (Calif.) U., 1959-62; specialist gas dynamics Gen. Electric Co., Phila., 1962-66; cons. NASA, Washington, 1985—. Contbr. book chpts. and numerous articles to profl. jours. Assoc. fellow AIAA (mem. tech. com. 1970-72, chmn. 3d CFD Conf. 1977, assoc. editor AIAA Jour., 1983-85, service citation 1985); mem. Am. Phys. Soc. Republican. Episcopalian. Avocations: gardening, bicycling. Home: 8510 Harwood NE Albuquerque NM 87111 Office: Div 1636 PO Box 5800 Albuquerque NM 87185

BLOUGH, DOUGLAS DUANE, art director; b. Johnstown, Pa., July 23, 1949; s. S. Duane Blough and Marjorie Romaine (Seese) O'Dell; m. Linda Gay Goldsby, Mar. 1, 1986, 1 stepchild, Justin Lee Maurer. AA, Lorain County Community Coll., 1969; BFA, Bowling Green State U., 1971, postgrad. Graphic designer Walbridge & Bellg Prodns., Toledo, 1971-73; art dir. Sta. WBGU-TV, Bowling Green, Ohio, 1974-75; ptnr., art dir. Barnstorm Studios, Colorado Springs, Colo., 1975—; advisor Pikes Peak Community Coll., Colorado Springs, 1980—. Co-producer (multi-image presentation) Where the Rivers Begin, 1980; writer/producer/dir. (video) Fairfield Pagosa, 1983; writer-co-producer (multi-image presentation) Cuchara Resort, 1984, (multi-image video) An Investment in Fun, 1986. Mem. Pikes Peak Advt. Fedn., Colorado Springs Exec. Assn. (assoc.), Media Producers Guild. Republican. Mem. Ch. of Christ. Club: The Lodge, Western Sportsmans Assn. Avocations: hunting, fishing, racquetball, backpacking, whitewater rafting. Home: PO Box 83 Green Mountain Falls CO 80819 Office: Barnstorm Design/Creative 2502 1/2 W Colorado Suite 301 Colorado Springs CO 80904

BLOUKE, MORLEY MATTHEWS, physicist, consultant; b. Washington, Jan. 9, 1941; s. Pierre and Jessie McConnell (Scott) B.; m. Kay Louise Kisinger, Feb. 5, 1966; children: Jennifer K., Katrina A., Kristen J., Lauri E. BS, Union Coll., 1963; MS, U. Ill., 1965, PhD, 1969. Mem. tech. staff Tex. Instruments, Dallas, 1969-82; sr. engr. Tektronix Inc., Beaverton, Oreg., 1982-83, prin. scientist, 1983—; cons. Jet Propulsion Lab., Pasadena, Calif., 1983—; adj. prof. U. Portland, Oreg., 1986—. Contbr. numerous articles to profl. jours. Mem. IEEE (sr.), Soc. Photo-optical Instrumentation Engrs., Sigma Xi. Avocations: sailing, skiing, reading, astronomy. Home: 14980 NW Oak Hills Dr Beaverton OR 97006 Office: CCD Engring Group PO Box 500 MS 59-567 Beaverton OR 97006

BLOW, JOHN NEEDHAM, social services educator; b. Whitby, Ont., Can., Nov. 30, 1905; came to U.S., 1952; s. Ezekiel Richard and Edith May (Correll) B.; m. Emma Jane White, June 6, 1942; children: Carol Anne, Brenda Jane, Mary Roberta, Elizabeth Diane. BA, McMaster U., 1939; MSW, U. Toronto, Ont., 1948. Cert. elem. tchr., Toronto, community colls. instr., Calif. Exec. sec. Community Welfare Planning Council Ont., Toronto, 1948-52; exec. v.p. Motel Corp., Las Vegas, Nev., 1952-54; exec. dir. Nev. div. Am. Cancer Soc., 1954-56, assoc. exec. dir. Los Angeles County br., 1956-70; program assoc. Am. Heart Assn., Los Angeles, 1970-74; project dir., coordinator sr. community service employment program Orange County, Calif., 1974-75; instr. community service programs for adults North Orange County Community Coll. Dist. and Coastline Coll., 1976-79, Mira Costa and Palomar Community Colls., 1979-85. Author: (poems) New Frontiers, 1984. Vol. Arthritis Found.; asst. commr. tng. Boy Scouts Can., Ottawa, 1934-41; Served to wing comdr. RCAF, 1941-46. Recipient Commendation for Outstanding Service to Srs., Orange County Sr. Citizens Council, 1977, Gold award Orange County United Way, 1977. Mem. Nat. Assn. Social Workers, Acad. Cert. Social Workers, San Luis Rey Officers Club, Valley Sr. Ctr., North County Concert Assn., So. Calif. McMaster U. Alumni Assn. (past pres., inducted Alumni Gallery 1986), Can. Soc. Los Angeles (charter, past pres.), U. Toronto Alumni Assn. (exec. com., past pres. So. Calif. br.). Presbyterian. Lodge: Elks. Home: 3725 Sesame Way Oceanside CA 92056

BLUE, E(MANUEL) MORSE, consulting chemical engineer; b. Spokane, Wash., June 27, 1912; s. Louis and Amelia (Dias) B.; m. Harriet Tieburg, Sept. 2, 1938 (dec. Feb. 1980); children; William A., Bonnie A., Thomas C.; m. Mary Heath Nelson, Aug. 8, 1981. BS, U. Calif., Berkeley, 1935; MS, MIT, 1937. Registered chem. engr., Calif. Sr. engr. assoc. Chevron Research, Richmond, Calif., 1938-66; mgr. invention devel. Chevron Research, San Francisco, 1964-77; cons. chem. engring. Walnut Creek, Calif., 1977-79; pres. E.M. Blue and Assocs., Inc., Walnut Creek, 1979—; lectr. in chem. engring. U. Calif., Berkeley, 1959—. Contbr. articles to profl. jours.; patentee in field. Served to capt. USN, 1941-46. Fellow Am. Inst. Chem. Engring. (held various offices); mem. Am. Chem. Soc., Licensing Execs. Soc. Clubs: San Francisco Engring., Faculty (Berkeley). Avocation: golf. Home and Office: EM Blue and Assocs Inc 2642 Saklan Indian Dr # 2 Walnut Creek CA 94595-3014

BLUE, NANCY ANN, home economics educator; b. Huron, S.D., Aug. 18, 1934; d. Edward Martin and Gladys (Erickson) Rudloff; m. Vernon Wilford Blue, June 3, 1954; children: Debra, David, Diana, Paul, Mark, Ruth. Student, Augustana Coll., Sioux Falls, S.D., 1952-53, Huron Coll., 1953-54, U. Ill., Chgo., 1966-67; BA in Home Econ. Edn., Western Wash. U., 1970. Cert. vocat. home economist. Home econs. tchr. Mt. Vernon (Wash.) High Sch., 1970—. Docent Valley Mus. Art, La Conner, Wash., 1984-85; bd. dirs. Youth Encouragment Service, 1985; sec. to council Immaculate Conception Ch., 1980-83. Mem. AAUW (2d v.p. 1984-86), Mt. Vernon Edn. Assn. (assn. rep. 1983-86), Wash. Home Econs. Assn. (mktg. chmn. 1984-85, recognition chmn. 1986-87), NEA, Am. Vocat. Assn., Am. Home Econs. Assn., Wash. Vocat. Assn., Nat. Assn. Vocat. Home Econs. Tchrs., Wash. Assn. Edn. Young Child, Seattle Art Mus., Valley Art Mus. of Northwest Art. Roman Catholic. Avocations: bridge, travel, gourmet cooking. Home: 521 Shoshone Dr Mount Vernon WA 98273 Office: Mt Vernon High Sch 314 N Ninth Mount Vernon WA 98273

BLUECHEL, ALAN, state senator, wood structural components manufacturing company executive; b. Edmonton, Alta., Can., Aug. 28, 1924; s. Joseph Harold and Edith (Daly) B.; m. Aylene Loughnan, Nov. 2, 1958; children—Gordon, Turner; m. Jeanne Ehrlichman, Aug. 8, 1981. B.A.Sc. in Elec. Engring., B.A., U. B.C.; postgrad. U. Wash. Vice pres. Loctwall Corp., Kirkland, Wash., 1948-64, pres., 1964—; pres. Crystal Mountain Inn Co., developer condominiums, restaurants, hotels, swimming pools, 1968-80; mem. Wash. State Ho. of Reps., 1966-74; mem. Wash. Senate, 1974—, Republican whip, 1979-81, 83—, majority whip, 1981-83, mem. rules, ways and means, parks and ecology coms.; speaker various confs., convs., orgns. Mem. Wash. State Land Planning Commn., 1969-73, Wash. State Women's Council, 1976, Spl. Com. on Office State Actuary, 1983; chmn. Wash. State Winter Recreation Commn., 1983, Wash. State Commn. on Environ. Policy, 1983; mem. arts, tourism and Cultureal faairs com. Nat. Conf. of State Legis., 1976-87; mem. Juanita Citizens Devel. Council, 1975-79, King County Conservation Com., 1967-69, King County Flood Control Adv. Bd., 1968-70, Com. To Save Sch. Trust Lands, 1975—, Edwards Park Adv. Bd., 1977-79, Seattle Symphony Phonathon Fundraisers, 1980, 81, Gov.'s Council on Child Abuse and Neglect, 1983, Wash. State Expo '86 Commn., 1985-87; mem. conservation com. King County Environ. Devel. Commn., 1969-74, numerous other civic orgns. Recipient Outstanding Service award Lake Washington PTSA Council, 1982. Clubs: Mountaineers, Sun Valley Ski, Forelaufer Ski.

BLUEMLE, PAUL EDWARD, college administrator; b. Springfield, Ohio, Sept. 9, 1926; s. Carl Henry and Mary Ann (Wolbert) B.; m. Helen Jean Smain, Sept. 13, 1958; children: Joy, Christine, Jude, Laura, Peter. BBA magna cum laude, Xavier U., 1951; MA, U. Oreg., 1953; postgrad., Mich. State U., 1957-63. Reporter Springfield Daily News, 1943-51; exec. sec. Young Christian Students, Chgo., 1952-54; dir. pub. relations Thomas More Coll., Covington, Ky., 1954-55; bus. mgr. Today mag., Chgo., 1955-56; instr. Mich. State U., East Lansing, 1956-59; editor univ. publs. Bowling Green (Ohio) State U., 1959-60; asst. prof., assoc. prof., exec. sec., asst. dean Monteith Coll., Wayne State U., Detroit, 1960-76; admissions dir., asst. dean U. Detroit, 1976-80; city clk. Pleasant Ridge, Mich., 1980-82; asst. to v.p. academics Northwood Inst., Midland, Mich., 1983; dir. admissions Holy Names Coll., Oakland, CA, 1983—; bd. dirs. Chgo. Research Group Corp., 1956-73. Pres. sch. bd. St. Mary's Parish, Royal Oak, Mich., 1966; mem. Citizen's Adv. Commn., Ferndale (Mich.) Sch. Dist., 1972; chmn. com. on community Archdiocese of Detroit, 1972-74. Served with U.S. Army, 1945-46. Mem. Soc. Profl. Journalists, Am. Newspaper Guild (v.p. Springfield 1945), AAUP (sec. Wayne State U. chpt. 1971-72), Kappa Tau Alpha. Roman Catholic. Home: 2235 Lincoln #207 Alameda CA 94501 Office: 3500 Mountain Blvd Oakland CA 94619

BLUM, JOHN ALAN, urologist, educator; b. Bklyn., Feb. 2, 1933; s. Louis J. and Pauline (Kushner) B.; A.B., Dartmouth, 1954; M.D., N.Y. U., 1958; M.S., U. Minn., 1965; m. Debra Merlin Ackerman, June 30, 1957; children—Louis Jeffrey, Alfred Merlin, Jacqueline. Intern, U. Minn. Hosp., Mpls., 1958-59, resident, 1959-64; practice medicine, specializing in urology, Chgo., 1964-66, Mpls., 1966-67, San Diego, 1969—; chmn. dept. urology Mt. Sinai Hosp., Chgo., 1965-66; asst. prof. urology U. Minn., Mpls., 1967; assoc. clin. prof. urology U. Calif., San Diego, 1969—; mem. staff Mercy, Donald Sharp, Children's hosps., San Diego, 1969—, Scripps Hosp., La Jolla, Calif., 1969—. Bd. dirs. Vietnam Vet. Leadership Program. Served to capt. USNR, 1967—; Vietnam. Diplomate Am. Bd. Urology. Fellow A.C.S.; mem. Am., Calif. med. assns., Am. Urol. Assn., San Diego Urol. Soc., San Diego Surg. Soc. (pres. 1977—), Phi Beta Kappa, Sigma Xi, Alpha Omega Alpha. Club: San Diego Yacht. Research in devel. of silicone rubber for urinary tract. Home: 890 Cornish Dr San Diego CA 92107 Office: 3415 6th Ave San Diego CA 92103

BLUM, RICHARD HOSMER ADAMS, foundation executive; b. Ft. Wayne, Ind., Oct. 7, 1927; s. Hosmer and Imogene (Heino) B.; m. Eva Maria Spitz, July 6, 1957. A.B. with honors magna cum laude, San Jose State Coll., 1949; Ph.D., Stanford U., 1951. Research dir. Calif. Med. Assn., San Francisco, 1956-58, San Mateo County (Calif.) Mental Health Service, San Mateo, 1958-60; lectr. Sch. Criminology, U. Calif., Berkeley, 1960-62; mem. faculty Stanford (Calif.) U., 1962-78, prof. dept. psychology, 1970-75, prof. dept. gynecology and obstetrics, 1982—; mem. faculty Stanford (Calif.) U. Law Sch., 1975-78; chmn. bd. Am. Lives Endowment, Portola Valley, Calif., 1979—; chmn. Internat. Research Group on Drug Legis. and Programs, Geneva, 1969—; pres. Bio-Behavioral Research Group, Inc., Palo Alto 1964—; owner/operator Shingle Mill and Volcano ranches, 1964—; vis. Fellow Wolfson Coll., U. Cambridge, 1984. Author 20 books in field of health, criminology, public policy; author 6 books of Fiction. Served in U.S. Army, 1951-53, Korea. Fellow Am. Psychol. Assn., Am. Sociol. Assn., Am. Public Health Assn., AAAS; mem. Am. Criminol. Assn., Archaeol. Inst. Am., Sigma Xi. Unitarian. Clubs: Cosmos, Athenaeum. Home: PO Box 620066 Woodside CA 94062 Office: Am Lives Endowment PO Box 620482 Woodside CA 94062 also: Stanford U Sch Medicine Stanford CA 94305

BLUM, YIGAL DOV, chemist, researcher; b. Afula, Israel, July 21, 1953; came to U.S., 1984; s. Abraham Andree and Lea Lily (Siegman) B.; m. Shlomit Flum, Sept. 6, 1972; 1 child, Dinur. BS, Tel Aviv U., 1977, MS, 1980, PhD in Chemistry, 1984. Asst. instr. Tel Aviv U., 1977-84; researcher SRI Internat., Menlo Park, Calif., 1984—. Contbr. articles to profl jours.; patentee in field. Mem. Am. Chem. Soc., Israel Chem. Soc., Calif. Catalysis Soc. Home: 1010 Noel Dr #28 Menlo Park CA 94025 Office: SRI Internat 333 Ravenswood Menlo Park CA 94025

BLUMBERG, STEPHEN KAHAN, public administration educator; b. Chgo., Aug. 6, 1935; s. Louis and Kay (Kahan) B.; m. Wendy Wolff, June 17, 1956; children: Daniel, Ronald, Dina, Andrew. BA in Speech and English, Ohio State U., 1958; MA in Urban Studies, Roosevelt U., Chgo., 1970; M in Pub. Adminstrn., U. So. Calif., 1972, PhD, 1975. Mgr. retail furniture J. Blumberg, Inc., Waukegan, Ill., 1958-60; mng. ptnr. and cert. property mgr. Blumberg & Co. Real Estate, Waukegan, 1960-66; dir. community relations Leadership Council Met. Open Communities, Chgo., 1966-70; prof. pub. adminstrn. Calif. State U., Long Beach, 1975—. Author: Win-Win Administration, 1983; contbr. articles to profl. jours. Mayor and City Councilman, City of Manhattan Beach, Calif., 1974-82; founder and pres. bd. Lake County Community Action Project, Waukegan, 1964; pres. bd. North Lake County Family Service Agy., Waukegan, 1965. Fellow Alcoa Found., 1971, Mellon Found., 1971. Mem. Am. Soc. Pub. Adminstrn., Pi Alpha Alpha (Disting. Achievement award 1979). Democrat. Home: 2300 Blance Rd Manhattan Beach CA 90266 Office: Calif State U Grad Ctr Pub Policy 1250 Bellflower Blvd Long Beach CA 90840

BLUME, WALTER MANLEY, software engineer; b. San Bernardino, Calif., Dec. 11, 1958; s. Frank Reinhart and Harriet Manley (Crain) B. BS, U. Calif., Irvine, 1981, MS, 1983. Con. Scanicon Corp., Newport Beach, Calif., 1981; research asst. Mayo Clinic, Rochester, Minn., 1982; software engr. Diasonics, San Francisco, 1983-86; sr. software engr. Siemens Med. Labs., Walnut Creek, Calif., 1987—. Canvasser Peace '84 Rally Dem. Nat. Conv. Mem. IEEE, Phi Beta Kappa, Eta Kappa Nu, Chi Epsilon Mu. Home: 6408 Irwin Ct #2 Oakland CA 94609 Office: Siemens Med Labs 2404 N Main St Walnut Creek CA 94596

BLUMRICH, JOSEF FRANZ, aerospace engineer; b. Steyr, Austria, Mar. 17, 1913; s. Franz and Maria Theresia (Mayr) B.; m. Hildegard Anna Schmidt-Elgers, Nov. 7, 1935; children—Michael Sebastian, Christoph, Stefan. B.S. in Aero. and Mech. Engring., Ingenieurschule Weimar (Germany), 1934. Engr., Gother Waggonfabrik A.G., Gothaer, Germany, 1934-44; ct. interpreter U.S. Mil. Ct., Linz, Austria, 1946-51; dep. chief hydraulics dept. United Austrian Iron and Steel Works, Linz, 1951-59; structural design engr. Army Ballistic Missile Agy., Huntsville, Ala., 1959-61; chief structural engring. br. G.C. Marshall Space Flight Ctr., NASA, Huntsville, 1961-69, chief systems layout br., 1969-74; cons. in field, 1974—. Served with German Army, 1944-45. Recipient Apollo Achievement award NASA, 1969, Exceptional Service medal, 1972. Mem. AAAS. Author: The

Spaceships of Ezekiel, 1974; Kasskara, 1979; editorial cons. on space sci. and rocketry Scribner-Bantan English Dictionary, 1977; contbr. articles to profl. jours. Patentee in field. Home: PO Box 433 Estes Park CO 80517

BLYSTONE, FRANK LYNN, oil and gas company executive; b. La Habra, Calif., Aug. 28, 1935; s. Frank Edgar and Reta Lee Blystone; m. Patricia Louise Baker, Mar. 21, 1964; children: Jon Franklin, Ryan Taylor. AA, Fullerton (Calif.) Community Coll., 1955; BA, Whittier (Calif.) Coll., 1957; postgrad., George Williams Coll., 1958. Pres. Blystone Enterprises, Bakersfield, Calif., 1970-78; mgr. spl. projects Banister Pipelines, Denver, 1974-78; pres., chief exec. officer, bd. dirs. Petro Aviation Corp., Denver, 1979-80, Merit Cos., Denver, 1979-85, Bandera Land Co. Inc., Bakersfield, Calif., 1974—, Tri-Valley Oil and Gas Corp., Bakersfield, 1981—; chmn. bd. Merit Cos., Denver. chmn. Mus. Devel. Com., Bakersfield, 1973; mem. fin. com. Com. to Re-elect Mayor, Denver, 1978, spl. gifts com. YMCA Campaign, Bakersfield, 1986. Mem. Calif. Independent Producers Assn., Petroleum Club of Bakersfield, Whittier Coll. Assocs. (Outstanding Alumnus 1982, 86). Lodges: Masons, Rotary. Home: 2201 Barrington St #11 Bakersfield CA 93309 Office: Tri-Valley Oil and Gas Corp 1801 Oak St Bakersfield CA 93301

BLYTH, LYNN STARKER, psychologist; b. Knoxville, Tenn., May 12, 1951; d. Lee Norman and Judith (Lasky) Starker; m. Daniel Patrick Blyth, Sept. 27, 1981. BS in Psychology, Tufts U., 1973; MS, U. Mass., 1979, PhD, 1982. Intern in clin. psychology U. Colo. Health Scis. Ctr., Denver, 1980-81; clinician Kaiser-Permanente, Denver, 1981-83; pvt. practice specializing in clin. psychology Denver, 1983—; clin. psychologist Denver Mental Health Ctr., 1983—. Alumni interviewer Tufts Univ. Alumni Admissions Com., Denver, 1982-84; mem. West Washington Park Neighborhood Assn., Denver, 1982—. Nat. Merit scholar, 1969; NIMH Clin. Traineeship, 1975-78. Mem. Am. Psychol. Assn., Assn. Women in Psychol., Colo. Women Psychologists, Colo. Psychol. Assn. (chmn. mem. com., 1983-84, bd. dirs. 1984-87, chmn. legis. com.). Home: 785 S Grant St Denver CO 80209 Office: Denver Mental Health Ctr 1760 High St Denver CO 80218

BLYTHE, ELIZ ANN, airline company executive; b. LaFollette, Tenn., Oct. 10, 1947; d. Charles Henry and Allie Annis (Howell) Russell; m. James Raymond Muir Blythe, Dec. 29, 1971 (div.: 1 child, Sayrah Elizabeth Muir; m. Patrick James Ryan, June 1987. BS in Zoology, Philosophy, U. Tenn., 1969; MBA, U. Phoenix, Denver, 1986. Cert. secondary tchr., Tenn.; lic. FAA airframe and power plant mechanic. Head biology dept. Internat. Schole Eerde, Ommen, The Netherlands, 1973-75; mgr. maintenance planning AIR US, Denver, 1982-83; mgr. aircraft records and planning Frontier Horizon and Sky Bus, Denver, 1983-86; mintenance coordinator Continental Airlines, Denver, 1986—. Author: How Hurty Put Humpty Dumpty Back Together Again, 1974; newsletter Women in Mgmt., 1981. Bd. dirs. Theatre Assocs. Group, Denver, 1982-84; dir. youth group Cath. Community, Denver, 1984-87. Mem. Am. Mgmt. Assn., Royal Soc. South Africa, Internat. Aquatic Animal Assn. Medicine. Democrat. Club: Parker Elizabeth Riding (v.p. 1985-86). Avocations: skiing, back packing, horse back riding. Home: 1554 St Paul St Denver CO 80206 Office: Continental Airlines Stapleton Internat Airport Denver CO 80207

BLYTHE, WILLIAM, consulting engineer, retired engineering educator; b. Martinez, Calif., Aug. 8, 1931; s. Alva Vern and Minnie Christine (Torgerson) B.; m. Bonnie Jean Isakson, June 19, 1955; children: Richard, Alison, Kelly. AB, U. Calif., Berkeley, 1955, MS, 1957; PhD, Stanford U., 1962. Registered profl. engr., Calif. Prof. and chmn. engring. dept. San Jose State U., 1957-82; pres. William Blythe, Inc., Palo Alto, Calif., 1982—; bd. dirs. Union Coll., Lincoln, Nebr.; cons. in accident analysis, Palo Alto, 1968—. Contbr. articles to profl. jours. Mem. Am. Acad. Mechanics (founding), Soc. Forensic Engrs. and Scientists (pres. 1981-86).

BOARD, ROBERT ROY, university administrator; b. Lewistown, Mont., Sept. 30, 1922; s. William Charles and Irene Anne (Conners) B.; m. Mary Lu Bush, Feb. 15, 1948; children: Gregory Charles, Bradley Robert. BS, U. Santa Clara, 1947. Systems salesman Nat. Cash Register Co., San Francisco, 1947-51; factory rep. Ames Harris Meville Co., San Francisco and Fresno, Calif., 1951-56; systems and interior office salesman Healey & Popovich Co., Fresno, 1956-64; registrar Calif. State U., Fresno, 1964—; systems cons. Mem. Sierra natural resources com. Three Forests Assn.; research asst. Nat. Park Service, Nat. Forest Service. Served with AUS, 1943-46, PTO. Decorated Purple Heart, Phillipine Liberation medal. Mem. Am. Assn. Coll. Registrars, Student Personnel Assn. Calif. Coll., Pacific Assn. Collegiate Registrars (program dir. 1975, v.p. 1977-78, pres.-elect 1978-79, pres. 1979-80, chmn. nominating com. 1984-85)., Sierra Club (chpt. founder). Republican. Presbyterian. Lodge: Masons. Home: 5494 N Roosevelt St Fresno CA 93704 Office: Calif State U Fresno CA 93740

BOARDMAN, ROSANNE VIRGINIA, military science executive; b. Twin Falls, Idaho, Oct. 4, 1946; d. Gordon Ross and Garnet Othalia (Peterson) Tobin; m. Lowell Jay Boardman, May 12, 1973. BA cum laude, Occidental Coll., 1968; MA with honors, Columbia U., 1969; postgrad., U. Calif., Irvine, 1971-72, U. Calif., Santa Barbara, 1973-74. Cert. jr. coll. tchr., Calif., cert. secondary tchg., Calif. Instr. Ventura (Calif.) Community Coll., 1973-77; engring. analyst John J. McMullen Co., Ventura, 1978-80; sr. logistics specialist Raytheon Co., Ventura, 1977-78, 80-83; civilian tech. writer, editor USN, Port Huerume, Calif., 1983-84; civilian logistics mgr. USN, Port Hueneme, Calif., 1984—. Author numerous manuals and logistics guides. Internat. fellow Occidental Coll., 1967; recipient Outstanding Performance award Naval Ship Weapon Systems Engring. Sta., 1985, 86. Mem. Soc. Logistics Engrs., Phi Beta Kappa. Office: Naval Ship Weapon Systems Engring Sta Code 5C10 Port Hueneme CA 93043

BOBERG, ANNA MARIA, home economics educator; b. Cieszyn, Poland, Feb. 19, 1940; d. William and Emilia J. (Zywczok) Zweck; came to U.S., 1955, naturalized, 1958; m. Walter W. Boberg, June 16, 1962; children—Richard Zweck, Tracy Ann. B.S., Mont. State U., 1963. GED tchr. Army Edn. Ctr., Wildflecken, Germany, 1964-66; tchr. earth sci., home econs. East Jr. High Sch., Casper, Wyo., 1971-84; v.p. Boberg Geotech Internat., Ltd., Casper, 1984—; mem. Natrona County Sch. Dist. Sci. Curriculum Com., Home Econs. Curriculum Com. Mem. Grads. Home Econs. (sec. 1972), Natrona County Classroom Tchrs. Assn., Wyo. Edn. Assn., NEA, Wyo. Sci. Tchrs. Assn. LWV, Our Lady of Fatima Council Catholic Women (St. Joseph's Circle, chmn. 1987—), Casper Geowives (sec. 1987. exec. bd. 1987), Pi Beta Phi Alumni (pres. 1972). Republican. Roman Catholic.

BOBERG, RICHARD WAYNE, computer company executive, electronics engineer; b. Oakland, Calif., Jan. 22, 1948; s. Alvin Arthur and Charlotte Mary (Leedom) B.; m. Jacqueline Shillea, Jan. 1, 1984; 1 child, Ross Owen. B.S.E.E., Calif. State Poly. U., San Luis Obispo, 1970; M.S.E.E., MIT, 1973. Registered profl. engr., Calif. Engr., ISS/Sperry Univac, Cupertino, Calif., 1972-74; engr. Intel Corp., Santa Clara, Calif., 1974-78, engring. mgr., 1977-78; cons. Burkeshire Systems, Mountain View, Calif., 1978; v.p. Microbar Systems, Palo Alto, Calif., 1978-81, pres., Sunnyvale, Calif., 1981—. Patentee in field. Seminar leader Creative Initiative, San Jose, Calif., 1984. Mem. IEEE (chmn. working group 1979-87, Meritorius Service award 1983), Multibus Mfrs. Group (pres. 1983—). Home: 1362 Casa Ct Santa Clara CA 95051 Office: Microbar Systems Inc 785 Lucerne Dr Sunnyvale CA 94086

BOBERG, W(ALTER) WILLIAM, geologist; b. Kalispell, Mont., Jan. 8, 1940; s. Walter Harold and Meva Julia (Lapsley) B.; m. Anna Maria Zweck, June 16, 1962; children: Richard, Tracy Ann. BS in Geology, Mont. State U., 1963; MS, U. Colo., 1970. Exploration geologist Hecla Mining Co., Wallace, Idaho, 1968; teaching asst. U. Colo., Boulder, 1968-70; exploration geologist Gulf Mineral Resources Co., Denver, 1969-70; geologist Anaconda Co., Salt Lake City, 1970; exploration geologist minerals dept. Continental Oil Co., Casper, Wyo., 1970-76, dist. geologist, 1976-77; chief geologist Wold Nuclear Co., Casper, 1977-79; exploration program mgr. Kennecott Exploration, Inc., Casper, 1979-81; ind. geologist Casper, 1981-84; pres. Boberg Geotech Internat., Ltd., Casper, 1984—; mem. adv. com. dept. geology U. Wyo., Laramie, 1979-80; tech. adv. com. dept. geosci. Flathead Valley Community Coll., Kalispell, Mont., 1985—. Author books (5) and maps; contbr. articles to profl. publs. Chmn. sub-com. on water Paradise Valley Civic Com., Casper, 1974-76. Served to capt. AUS, 1963-68. Mem. Soc. Econ. Geologists (publs. com. 1987—), Northwest Mining Assn., Wyo. Geol. Assn. (mineral editor field conf. 1978, 2d v.p. 1978-79, pres. 1979-80, editor field conf. 1983, Frank A. Morgan Jr. award 1981, Best Speaker award 1983, chmn. field conf. trip 1987), Rocky Mountain Assn. Geologists, (2d pl. Best Speaker award 1983), Can. Soc. Petroleum Geologists, Wyo. Mining Assn. (chmn. exploration com. 1978, 80-81, bd. dirs. 1981—), Soc. Geol. Applied to Mineral Deposits, Am. Inst. Profl. Geologists (sec. Wyo. sect. 1987), Mont. Geol. Soc., People to People Internat. (South Africa strategic minerals del. 1983), Casper C. of C. (chmn. subcom. on legis. affairs mineral industry com. 1977-78, chmn. mineral industry com. 1979-81), Sigma Xi. Home and Office: 3810 Plateau Pl Casper WY 82604

BOCK, NANCY DELICH, mental health therapist; b. Riverside, N.J., Dec. 30, 1957; d. Frank Paul and Anne (Spillian) Delich; m. Steven Michael Bock, June 11, 1983. BA in Psychology cum laude, Calif. State U., Northridge, 1981; MSW, San Diego State U., 1983. Office dir. Deaf Counseling Advocacy Referral Agy., San Jose, Calif., 1983-84; counselor Calif. Sch. for the Deaf, Fremont, 1984; mental health therapist, program coordinator for deaf Adult and Child Guidance Ctr., San Jose, 1984—; mem. Coordinating Council on Deaf Services, San Jose, 1983—. Named Deaf Woman of Yr., San Jose Quota Club, 1986. Mem. Nat. Assn. Social Workers, Am. Deafness and Rehab. Assn., Deaf Service Network (v.p. 1985-86). Democrat. Roman Catholic. Avocations: quilting, cross stitching, racquetball, gardening. Office: Adult and Child Guidance Ctr 950 W Julian St San Jose CA 95126

BODANSKY, DAVID, physicist, educator; b. N.Y.C., Mar. 10, 1924; s. Aaron and Marie (Syrkin) B.; m. Beverly Ferne Bronstein, Sept. 7, 1952; children: Joel N., Daniel M. B.S., Harvard U., 1943, M.A., 1948, Ph.D., 1950. Instr. physics Columbia U., N.Y.C., 1950-52, assoc., 1952-54; mem. faculty U. Wash., Seattle, 1954—, assoc. prof. physics, 1958-63, prof., 1963—, chmn. dept., 1976-84. Author: (with Fred H. Schmidt) The Energy Controversy: The Fight over Nuclear Power, 1976; Editorial bd.: Rev. Sci. Instruments, 1967-69. Served with AUS, 1943-46. Sloan Research fellow, 1959-63; Guggenheim fellow, 1966-67, 74-75. Fellow Am. Phys. Soc., AAAS; mem. Am. Assn. Physics Tchrs., Am. Nuclear Soc., Health Physics Soc., Phi Beta Kappa. Research in nuclear physics, nuclear astrophysics and energy policy. Office: U Wash Dept Physics Seattle WA 98195

BODDIE, LEWIS FRANKLIN, SR., obstetrics-gynecology educator; b. Forsyth, Ga., Apr. 4, 1913; s. William F. and Luetta T. (Sams) B.; m. Marian Bernice Clayton, Dec. 27, 1941; children: Roberta Boddie Miles, Lewis Jr., Bernice B. Jackson, Pamela, Kenneth, Fredda, Margaret. BA, Morehouse Coll., 1933; MD, Meharry Med. Sch., 1938. Diplomate Am. Bd. Ob-Gyn (proctor parti exam Los Angeles area 1955-63). Intern Homer-Phillips Hosp., St. Louis, 1938-39, resident in ob-gyn, 1939-42; mem. attending staff Grace Hosp., Detroit, 1944048, Parkside Hosp., Detroit, 1944-48, Los Angeles County Gen. Hosp., 1952-79; sr. mem. attending staff Queen of Angels Hosp., Los Angeles, 1964-86, chmn. dept. ob-gyn, 1968-70; asst. prof. U. So. Calif. Sch. Medicine, Los Angeles, 1953-79, asst. prof. emeritus, 1979—; assoc. prof. U. Calif., Irvine, 1956-81. vice chmn. bd. mgrs. 28th St. YMCA, Los Angeles 1960-75; steward African Meth. Episc. Ch., Los Angeles, 1949—. Fellow ACS (life), Am. Coll. Ob-Gyn (life), Los Angeles Ob-Gyn Soc. (life): mem. Los Angeles United Way (priorities and allocations coms., 1985—), Children's Home Soc. (bd. dirs. 1952—, v.p. 1963-68, pres. 1968-70), Child Welfare League Am. (bd. dirs. 1969-76). Republican. Office: 231 W Vernon Ave Los Angeles CA 90037

BODE, FRANCES LOUISE MAINO (MRS. WILLIAM THEODORE BODE), author, lectr.; b. San Luis Obispo, Calif., Mar. 1, 1920; d. Theodore Michael and Eleanor Elizabeth (Hazard) Maino; B.A., Mills Coll., 1940; postgrad. U. Calif. at Berkeley, 1941; M.A., Sacramento State U., 1958; m. William Theodore Bode, Dec. 25, 1942; children—Eleanor Bode Cauldwell, Catherine Bode Appel, William T. II. Tchr., Ceres Union High Sch., 1941-43, Sacramento State Coll., 1957; free-lance tchr. flower arrangement, 1946—; lectr. on flower arrangements to various orgns. throughout U.S. Teaching specialist Ala. Judges Council, 1971, Ohio Judges Council, 1971, Ga. Judges Council, 1978, Judges Council So. Calif., 1978; dir. Sacramento Garden and Art Center, 1958-68, v.p., 1977-79; floriculture coordinator Calif. State Fair, 1981-84, chmn. Garden Club Day, 1983-85. Recipient Exec. Com. award Calif. Expn., 1969, 82; Community Service award Sacramento Soc. for the Blind, 1976; Design award Calif. State Fair, 1978. Mem. Profl. Arrangers No. Calif. (pres. 1968-69), Am. Horticultural Soc., Calif. Writers Club, Garden Writers Assn. Am., Carmichael Arrangers Guild, Sacramento Arrangers Guild, Kingsley Art Club, Nat. Council State Garden Clubs (Flower Arranger of Yr. 1987), Am. Guild Flower Arrangers, Calif. State Garden Clubs, Inc. (life), Mignonette Garden Club. Author: Creativity in Flower Arrangement, 1967; New Structures in Flower Arrangement, 1968; Dried Flower Designs, 1975; Designing with Flowers, 1976; contbr. author: Brooklyn Botanic Gardens Handbooks. Contbr. pictures of arrangements to various mags, articles on design and color to garden mags. Home: 2800 Huntington Rd Sacramento CA 95864

BODE, GERALD WILLIAM, geologist; b. Bishop, Calif., Aug. 30, 1939; s. Carl Martin and Lydia Bell (Hatley) B.; m. Faith Joy Poch, Nov. 28, 1969; children: Teague Gene, Jason Nathaniel. AB in Chemistry, Calif. State U., Fresno, 1962; postgrad., U. Oreg., 1964-67, 86—. Research chemist Rocketdyne Corp., Canoga Park, Calif., 1967-68; staff research asst. U. Calif.-San Diego, La Jolla, 1968-84; supt. Ocean Drilling Program-Scripps Inst. Oceanography, La Jolla, 1984—; cons., Encinitas, Calif., 1984. Contbr. articles to profl. jours. Active Big. Bros. Corp., Los Angeles, 1968-71. Mem. Sigma Xi. Democrat. Club: Toastmasters. Avocations: outdoor activities, woodworking, photography. Home: PO Box 3041 Olivenhain CA 92024 Office: Scripps Inst Oceanography Ocean Drilling Program La Jolla CA 92093

BODENSIECK, ERNEST JUSTUS, mechanical engineer; b. Dubuque, Iowa, June 1, 1923; s. Julius Henry and Alma Freida (Sommer) B.; B.Sc. in M.E., Iowa State U., 1943; m. Margery Elenore Sande, Sept. 9, 1943; children—Elizabeth Bodensieck Eley, Stephen. Project engr. TRW Inc., Cleve., 1943-57; supr. rocket turbomachinery Rocketydyne div. Rockwell Internat., Canoga Park, Calif., 1957-60, supr. nuclear turbomachinery Rocketydyne div., 1964-70; advance gear engr. Gen. Electric Co., Lynn, 1960-64; asst. mgr. engine components Aerojet Nuclear Systems Co., Sacramento, 1970-71; gear and bearing cons. AiResearch div. Garrett Corp., Phoenix, 1971-81; transmission cons. Bodensieck Engring. Co., Scottsdale, Ariz., 1981—. Registered profl. engr., Ariz. Mem. Soc. Automotive Engrs. (various coms.), Aircraft Industries Assn. (various coms.), Am. Gear Mfrs. Assn. (vice chmn. aerospace and gear rating coms.), ASME, AIAA, Nat. Soc. Profl. Engrs., Pi Tau Sigma. Lutheran. Patentee in field. Home: 7133 N Via De Alegria Scottsdale AZ 85258

BODENSTEIN, KENNETH ALAN, financial executive; b. N.Y.C., Feb. 25, 1937; s. William and Sylvia (Halperin) B.; m. Susan Sims, Sept. 4, 1960; children—Todd, Leslie, A.B., Columbia U., 1957, B.S. in Chem. Engring., 1958, M.B.A., 1960. Asst. to treas. Air Products and Chems. Co., Allentown, Pa., 1960-64; sr. investment analyst Armour & Co., Chgo., 1964-68; mgr. midwest region Goodbody & Co., Chgo., 1968-70; dir. bus. research CNA Fin. Co., Chgo., 1970-74; sr. v.p. Duff & Phelps Inc., Chgo., 1975—. Mem. Assn. Corp. Growth (bd. dirs. 1982-84), Investment Analyst Soc. Chgo. (bd. dirs. 1984-87). Chartered Fin. Analyst. Clubs: University, Midtown Tennis, Fullerton Tennis (Chgo.). Office: Duff & Phelps Inc 640 1801 Ave of Stars Los Angeles CA 90067

BODILY, DAVID MARTIN, chemist, educator; b. Logan, Utah, Dec. 16, 1933; s. Levi Delbert and Norma (Christenson) B.; m. Beth Alene Judy, Aug. 28, 1958; children—Robert David, Rebecca Marie, Timothy Andrew, Christopher Mark. Student, Utah State U., 1952-54; B.A., Brigham Young U., 1959, M.A., 1960; Ph.D., Cornell U., 1964. Postdoctoral fellow Northwestern U., Evanston, Ill., 1964-65; asst. prof. chemistry U. Ariz., Tucson, 1965-67; asst. prof. fuels engring. U. Utah, Salt Lake City, 1967-70, assoc. prof., 1970-77, prof., 1977-83, chmn. dept. mining and fuels engring., 1976-83, assoc. dean Coll. Mines and Mineral Industries, 1983—. Contbr. articles to profl. jours. Mem. Am. Chem. Soc. (chmn. Salt Lake sect. 1975), Am. Inst. Mining and Metall. Engrs., Sigma Xi. Mormon. Home: 2651 Cecil St Salt Lake City UT 84117 Office: 209 WBB U Utah Salt Lake City UT 84112

BODILY, KEVIN RAY, architect; b. Pocatello, Idaho, Apr. 28, 1950; s. Gaylen Leon and Marie Louise (Davis) B.; m. Carol Sue Jorgensen, Mar. 21, 1981; children—Erin Marie, Logan Ray, Kelli Jo. B.Arch. with honors, Idaho State U., 1973. Design architect Alpha Engrs., Inc., Pocatello, 1973-76; architect Call, Nielson, Bodily & Assocs., P.A., Idaho Falls, Idaho, 1976-80, v.p., 1980—, also dir.; works of firm include Ricks Coll. Fine Arts Center, Star Valley Jr. High Sch., Idaho Falls Westside Elem. Sch., Malad City High Sch., Sugar City Thomas D. Kershaw Intermediate Sch. Lic. architect, Idaho, Wyo.; cert. Nat. Council Archtl. Registration Bds. Mem. AIA (Henry Adams Fund cert. of merit 1973; pres. Eastern sect. Idaho chpt. 1981). Mormon. Home: 1439 Fairmont Dr Idaho Falls ID 83401 Office: 990 John Adams Pkwy PO Box 2212 Idaho Falls ID 83403

BODINSON, HOLT, conservationist; b. East Orange, N.J., Nov. 14, 1941; s. Earl Herdien and Hermoine (Holt) B.; B.A., Harvard, 1963; m. Ilse Marie Maier, Feb. 29, 1970. Sr. asso. Am. Conservation Assn., Inc., N.Y.C., 1966-70; dir. Office of Policy Analysis, N.Y. State Dept. Environ. Conservation, Albany, 1970-71, dir. div. ednl. services, 1971-77; dir. Ariz.-Sonora Desert Mus., 1977-78; adminstrv. dir. Safari Club Internat./Safari Club Internat. Conservation Fund, Tucson, 1980—. Committeeman, Montgomery Twp. Conservation Commn., 1967-70. Served with arty. AUS, 1964-66. Mem. Stony Brook-Millstone Watershed Assn. (dir.), Safari Club Internat. (dir. Ariz. chpt.), N.Y. Outdoor Edn. Assn. (dir.), N.Y. State Rifle and Pistol Assn. (dir.). Episcopalian. Club: Harvard of So. Ariz. (pres.). Author: (with Clepper and others) Leaders in American Conservation, 1971. Contbg. editor Jour. Environmental Edn., 1968—; dir. Conservationist mag. 1971-77, N.Y. State Environment newspaper, 1971-74. Home: 4525 Hacienda del Sol Rd Tucson AZ 85718 Office: 5151 E BroadwaySuite 1680 Tucson AZ 85711

BODTKER, DIANA WRIGHT, science educator, college administrator; b. Eugene, Oreg., June 3, 1938; d. Harry James and M. Mildred (Freeman) Wright; m. Egon Paul Bodtker, June 20, 1959; children: Ingrid Marie Baber, Kai Arnold. AA, Cottey Coll., 1957; BS, Oreg. State U., 1964; MA, Drake U., 1970. Lab. instr. Grandview Coll., Des Moines, 1965-67; teaching asst. Drake U., Des Moines, 1969-70; substitute tchr. Salem (Oreg.) Pub. Schs., 1972-73; biology instr. Chemeketa Community Coll., Salem, 1973-84, dir. math., sci., elecs. depts., 1984—; mem. accreditation team N.W. Assn. Schs. and Colls., Seattle, 1986—. HEW fellow, 1967-69. Mem. AAUW, Salem Art Assn., Danish-Am. Heritage Soc., Marion County (Oreg.) Hist. Soc., Am. Women in Sci., AAAS, N.W. Sci. Assn., Oreg. Sci. Math. Equity Network. Democrat. Unitarian. Avocation: gardening. Home: 1132 Newport Dr SE Salem OR 97306 Office: Chemeketa Community Coll 4000 Lancaster Dr NE Salem OR 97309

BOE, THOMAS DANIEL, electrical engineer; b. Seattle, Sept. 21, 1960; s. Lynn Robert and Emilew (Nance) B.; m. Valerie Rae Gutierrez, Nov. 23, 1985. BSEE, DeVry Inst., Phoenix, 1981; MS in Systems Mgmt., U. So. Calif., 1987. Systems design engr. govt. systems group GTE Corp., Mountain View, Calif., 1981-85, program mgr., project engr. Govt. Systems Group, 1985—. Mem. IEEE, Soc. Old Crows. Mem. Kriyaban Ch. Lodge: Masons. Avocations: sports, music, skiing. Office: GTE Govt Systems Group PO Box 7188 MS 6G48 Mountain View CA 94039

BOECKER, BRUCE BERNARD, radiobiologist; b. Aurora, Ill., July 9, 1932; s. Bernard Berthold and Ethel Marion (Smart) B., June 25, 1960; children: Nancy, Brian. BS in Physics, Grinnell Coll., 1954; MS in Radiation Biology, U. Rochester, 1960, PhD in Radiation Biology, 1962. Diplomate Am. Bd. Health Physics. From radiobiologist to asst. dir. Lovelace Inhalation Toxicology Research Inst., Albuquerque, 1961—; cons. div. biology and medicine AEC, Washington, 1970-71. Contbr. numerous articles to profl. jours. Served to capt. USAF, 1956-58. Mem. AAAS, Radiation Research Soc. (assoc. editor 1984—), Health Physics Soc. (bd. dirs. 1985—), Am. Acad. Health Physics. Avocations: travel, woodworking, photography. Home: 8601 La Sala Del Sur NE Albuquerque NM 87111 Office: Lovelace ITRI PO Box 5890 Albuquerque NM 87185

BOEHM, JOSEF FRANZ, wholesale and retail hardware executive; b. Taschwitz, Ger., Jan. 29, 1944; came to U.S., 1956, naturalized, 1963; s. Franz and Cacilia (Boehm) B.; m. Linda Jean Fults, Aug. 3, 1968 (div. Oct. 1985); 1 dau., Brigitte. Student pub. schs., Anchorage. With Anchorage Times, 1957-60, Sears, Roebuck & Co., Anchorage, 1960-63; prin. owner, pres. Alaska Indsl. Hardware, Inc., Anchorage, 1963—. Served with Alaska N.G., 1960-63. Office: 2192 Viking Dr Anchorage AK 99501

BOEHM, KATHLEEN MARY, risk management; b. Eau Claire, Wis., May 12, 1948; d. Harry D. and Rose M. (Luhm) B.; m. Jared W. Dawson, Sept. 22, 1984. BA, U. Wis., 1970; MA, U. Calif., Santa Barbara, 1981. Program planner County of Marin, San Rafael, Calif., 1977-78; escrow asst. Santa Barbara Title Co., 1978-79; with community services City of Santa Barbara, 1979-81, with loss prevention, 1981-85; risk analyst County of Santa Barbara, Santa Barbara, 1985—. Coordinator City of Santa Barbara United Way Campaign, 1985; bd. dirs. Community Tng. Bank, Santa Barbara, 1979-81. Democrat. Unitarian. Club: Goleta Valley Cycling (Santa Barbara) (sec. 1982-84). Avocations: bicycling, swing dancing. Office: County of Santa Barbara Risk Mgmt 1100 Anacapa St Santa Barbara CA 93110

BOEHM, ROBERT FOTY, mechanical engineer, educator, researcher; b. Portland, Oreg., Jan. 16, 1940; s. Charles Frederick and Lufteria (Christie) B.; m. Marcia Kay Pettibone, June 10, 1961; children—Deborah, Robert Christopher. B.S. in Mech. Engring., Wash. State U., Pullman, 1962, M.S., 1964; Ph.D., U. Calif., Berkeley, 1968. Registered profl. engr., Calif. With Westinghouse Corp., Lima, Ohio, 1961; with Lawrence Livermore Lab., Livermore, Calif., 1962, Boeing Aerospace Co., Seattle, 1963, Gen. Electric Co., San Jose, Calif., 1964-66, Jet Propulsion Lab, Pasadena, Calif., 1967; mem. faculty U. Utah, Salt Lake City, 1968—, prof. mech. engring., 1976—, chmn. dept., 1981-84; mem. Utah Solar Adv. Com., Utah Energy Conservation and Devel. Council, 1980—; vis. staff Sandia Nat. Lab., 1984-85. Author: Design Analysis of Thermal Systems; editor: Direct Contact Heat Exchange, 1987; tech. editor Jour. Solar Energy Engring.; contbr. articles to profl. jours. Fellow ASME; mem. Am. Soc. Engring. Edn., Internat. Solar Energy Soc., Bonneville Corvair Club. Congregationalist. Home: 2217 E Bryan Circle Salt Lake City UT 84108 Office: Univ Utah Mech Engring Dept Salt Lake City UT 84112

BOEN, HERBERT PLOWMAN, SR., aeronautics engineer; b. Wadena, Minn., June 1, 1919; s. Harald Edgar and Ena Margaret (Plowman) B.; m. Matsue Suzuki, Jan. 22, 1962; children: Jerry P., Jimmy P., Beth M., Herbert P. Jr., Edgar H. Student, Minn. State Tchr. Coll., 1938-40; A&E lic., War Tng. Service, 1945; BA in Edn., Los Angeles State Coll., 1951; JD cum laude, San Fernando U., 1972. cert. secondary tchr. Tool maker Vega Airplane Co., Burbank, Calif., 1940-43; airplane mechanic Lockheed Aircraft Service, Burbank, 1943-46; flight inspector Lockheed Aircraft Corp., Burbank, 1946-51, tech. instr., 1951-79, service engr., specialist, 1979—; tech. cons. Shin Meiwa Aircraft, Japan, 1958-59, Kawasaki Aircraft Co., Japan, 1959-60, Mitsubishi Aircraft, Japan, 1960-62; instr. pub. schs. Builder full scale replica 1903 Wright Bros. Flyer, exhibited Pioneer Mus., Minden, Nebr. Club: OX-5 of Am. (Pitts.). Lodge: Masons. Home: 9656 Tujunga Caynon Blvd Tujunga CA 92042-3449 Office: Lockheed Aircraft Corp Dept 76-22-03 PO Box 551 Burbank CA 91520

BOERS, TIMOTHY CLARK, architect; b. Peoria, Ill., Oct. 14, 1956; s. Clark Haywood and Jo Ann (Watson) B.; m. Leanna Marie Hoff, June 19, 1982. BS in Archtl. Studies with honors, U. Ill., 1978, MArch., 1980. Registered architect, Colo. Intern architect E.G. Lehmann Assocs., Peoria, 1975-77; teaching asst. U. Ill., Urbana, 1979; intern architect Unteed Scaggs Fritch & Nelson, Ltd., Champaign, Ill., 1979; project mgr. Pouw Outland Murata, Inc., Denver, 1980-81, Murata Outland Assocs., Inc., Denver, 1981-83; assoc. The Hoffmann Ptnrship, Inc., Denver, 1983—; chmn. planning and community devel. com., Highland Neighborhood Housing Service, Inc., Denver, 1985—, com. to protect Scottish Village, Denver, 1984. Prin. works include St. Mary's Acad. Gymnasium, 1985, Cherry Hills Villagi, Colo., Longmont (Colo.) United Hosp. Day Surgery Ctr., 1984, Longmont United Hosp. Therapy Pool, 1985. Mem. Highland Neighborhood Plan Steering Com, Denver, 1984-86, Platte Valley Alliance Neighborhoods, 1986. Francis J. Plym fellow, U. Ill., 1979. Mem. Phi Kappa Phi. Avocations: historic preservation, house renovation, camping, hiking. Office: The Hoffman Ptnrship Inc 1439 Larimer Sq Denver CO 80202

BOGAARD, WILLIAM JOSEPH, lawyer; b. Sioux City, Iowa, Jan. 18, 1938; s. Joseph and Irene Mary (Hensing) B.; B.S., Loyola Marymount U., Los Angeles, 1959; J.D. with honors, U. Mich., 1965; m. Claire Marie Whalen, Jan. 28, 1961; children—Michele, Jeannine, Joseph, Matthew. Bar: Calif. 1966. Ptnr. firm Hufstedler, Miller, Carlson & Beardsley, Los Angeles, 1971-82; exec. v.p., gen. counsel First Interstate Bancorp., Los Angeles, 1982—. Mem. Pasadena (Calif.) City Council, 1978-86; mayor City of Pasadena, 1984-86. Served to capt. USAF, 1959-62. Mem. Am. Bar Assn., Los Angeles County Bar Assn., Pasadena C. of C. Address: First Interstate Bancorp 707 Wilshire Blvd PO Box 54068 Los Angeles CA 90017

BOGARD, DAVID KENNETH, service executive; b. Peoria, Ill., Mar. 6, 1953; s. Dallas Kenneth and Emma Sue (Baker) B.; m. Candietta Ann Dominguez, May 7, 1976; children: Brittney Ann, Preston David. BA, So. Ill. U., 1974. Treas., v.p. Ken Bogard Remodeling, East Peoria, Ill., 1977-82; zone supr. Allright Houston, Inc., 1982-83; ops. auditor western div. Allright Auto Parks, Inc., Houston, 1983-84; city mgr. Allright San Francisco, 1984-86, Bay Park/Oakland, Calif., 1985-86; asst. regional mgr. no. Calif. and Nev. Allright Calif., Inc., 1986; regional mgr. no. Calif. Allright Sierra/ Nev., 1986—. Republican. Avocations: fishing, model building, antique auto restoration. Home: 34857 Skylark Dr Union City CA 94587 Office: Allright Calif Inc 1624 Franklin St #501 Oakland CA 94612

BOGARD-REYNOLDS, CHRISTINE ELIZABETH, stock brokerage executive; b. Aberdeen, Md., Apr. 15, 1954; d. Charles Francis and Donna June (Mosbaugh) Bogard; divorced; 1 child, Zachary Kagan. Student, U. Colo., 1972-73. Adminstrv. asst. Lange Co., Broomfield, Colo., 1973-74; field sales and service rep. Bowman Products Div., Denver, 1974-75; cashier Regency Inn, Denver, 1975-76; gen. mgr., sec.-treas., Edison Agy. Inc., Denver, 1976-81; gen. mgr. Edison Press, Inc., Englewood, Colo., 1979-80, 81; advt. dir. Blinder, Robinson & Co., Englewood, 1981—. Mem. adv. council Contacts for Kids Sake, Denver, 1987—; active fundraising Passages, Inc., Blinder Research Found. for Crohn's Disease (bd. dirs.), Rocky Mountain Multiple Sclerosis Ctr.; mem. Direct Mktg. Assn., Denver Advt. Fedn., Am. Mgmt. Assn. Home: 6860 S Bannock #H Littleton CO 80120 Office: Blinder Robinson & Co 6455 S Yosemite Englewood CO 80111

BOGDAN, LIVIUS SILVIU, real estate developer; b. Bucharest, Romania, Nov. 28, 1932; s. Silviu and Margaret (Laurentzy) B.; m. Florina Tanasescu, Feb. 22, 1955 (div. 1957); m. Margareta Batsu, July 2, 1962. MA, Archtl. Inst., Romania, 1950-55; BArch, Met. Collegiate, London, 1966. Lic. personal property broker, Calif.; cert. registered appraiser. Dir. architecture and engring. Govt. Agy., Romania, 1957-66; v.p., sr. project dir. Welton/Becket, N.Y.C., 1967-78; pres. 1st Regency Devel. Corp., N.Y., Fla., London, 1978-84; v.p. E&E Devel. Corp., Los Angeles, 1985—; mortgage underwriter, Ariz., 1983. Mem. Condo Developers Council of Am., Am. Land Devel. Assn., Am. Hotel and Motel Assn., Merchants-Brokers Exchange, Audobon Soc. Republican. Lodge: Masons.

BOGDANOFF, DAVID WELLS, aerospace research engineer; b. Summit, N.J., Feb. 25, 1941; s. David and Mary Joyce (Wells) B.; m. Sue Ellen Porter, Dec. 26, 1974. BME, McGill U., Montreal, Que.; PhD in Aerospace Engring., Princeton U., 1968. Postdoctoral fellow Plasma Physics Lab., Princeton (N.J.) U., 1968-69, Jet Propulsion Lab., Pasadena, Calif., 1969-71; research engr. UCLA, 1972; research engr. physics dept. U. So. Calif., Los Angeles, 1973-75; research engr. U. Wash., Seattle, 1976—. Contbr. articles to profl. jours. Mem. AIAA, Sigma Xi. Democrat. Avocations: music, folk dancing, mountain climbing, distance running. Home: 1621 108th Ave SE Bellevue WA 98004 Office: U Wash Mail Stop FL-10 Seattle WA 98195

BOGER, DAN CALVIN, economics educator, statistical, economic consultant; b. Salisbury, N.C., July 9, 1946; s. Brady Cashwell and Gertrude Virginia (Hamilton) B.; m. Gail Lorraine Zivna, June 23, 1973; children—Gretchen Zivna, Gregory Zivna. B.S. in Mgmt. Sci., U. Rochester, 1968; M.S. in Mgmt. Sci., Naval Postgrad. Sch., Monterey, Calif., 1969; M.A. in Stats., U. Calif.-Berkeley, 1977, Ph.D. in Econs., 1979. Cert. cost analyst; cert. profl. estimator. Research asst. U. Calif.-Berkeley, 1975-79; asst. prof. econs. Naval Postgrad. Sch., Monterey, Calif., 1979-85, assoc. prof., 1985—; cons. econs. and statis. legal matters CSX Corp, others, 1977—. Assoc. editor The Logistics and Transportation Rev., 1981-85; contbr. articles to profl. jours. Served to lt. USN, 1968-75. Flood fellow Dept. Econs., U. Calif.-Berkeley, 1975-76; dissertation research grantee A.P. Sloan Found., 1978-79. Mem. Am. Econ. Assn., Am. Statis. Assn., Econometric Soc., Math. Assn. Am., Inst. Mgmt. Sci., Sigma Xi. Home: 61 Ave Maria Rd Monterey CA 93940 Office: Naval Postgrad Sch Code 54Bo Monterey CA 93943

BOGGAN, DANIEL, JR., city administrator; b. Albion, Mich., Dec. 9, 1945; s. Daniel and Ruthie Jean (Crum) B.; m. Jacqueline (Boggan,) Oct. 4, 1977 (div.); children—DeVone, Daniel, Dhanthan, Alike. B.A., Albion Coll., 1967; M.S.W., U. Mich., 1968. Clin. supr. West Campus, Starr Commonwealth for Boys, 1968-70; asst. city mgr., Jackson, Mich., 1970-72; dep. city mgr., then city mgr., Flint, Mich.; dir. mgmt. services City of Portland, Oreg., 1976-78; asst. chief adminstrv. officer San Diego County, Calif., 1978-79; adminstr. Essex County, N.J., 1979-81; city mgr., Berkeley, Calif., 1982—; former mem. faculty Jackson Community Coll., Portland State U., Upsala Coll.; assoc. vice chancellor Bus. Adminstrv. Services, U. Calif., Berkeley, 1986, acting vice chancellor, 1986—. Bd. dirs. local United Way 1971-72. Recipient Soc. Afro Am. Police award, 1974; named to Outstanding Young Men Am., U.S. Jaycees, 1974. Mem. Internat. City Mgrs. Assn., Am. Mgmt. Assn., NAACP (Outstanding Youth Services award 1965). Democrat. Baptist. Office: 2180 Milvia Berkeley CA 94708

BOGGIO, DENNIS RAY, architect; b. Detroit, Jan. 28, 1953; s. Michael Anthony and Esther Theresa Boggio; m. Meredith Coleen Ream, June 25, 1983. BArch, Ohio State U., 1975; MArch, U. Colo., 1977. Lic. architect, Colo., Wyo., Utah, N.M. Ptnr. Lantz-Boggio Architects, Denver, 1980—; visiting critic Sch. Architecture, U. Colo., Denver, 1981—. Recipient Design Excellence award USAF Acad., 1985. Mem. AIA, Denver C. of C., Centennial C. of C. Lodge: Rotary. Home: 8101 E Dartmouth #53 Denver CO 80231 Office: Lantz-Boggio Architects 5200 DTC Pkwy #500 Denver CO 80111

BOGGS, GEORGE ROBERT, academic administrator; b. Conneaut, Ohio, Sept. 4, 1944; s. George Robert and Mary (Mullen) B.; m. Ann Holladay, Aug. 8, 1969; children: Kevin Dale, Ian Asher, Micah Benjamin. BS, Ohio State U., 1966; MA, U. Calif., Santa Barbara, 1968; PhD, U. Tex., 1984. Instr. chemistry Butte Coll., Oroville, Calif., 1968-85, div. chmn., 1972-81, assoc. dean, 1981-85; pres. Palomar Coll., San Marcos, Calif., 1985—; speaker SCCCIRA, Calif., 1985; adj. instr. Austin (Tex.) Community Coll., 1982; guest lectr. Calif. State U., Chico, 1970, 83, 84, panelist, 1975; teaching asst. U. Calif., Santa Barbara, 1966-68, Ohio State U., 1965-66; mem. numerous com.'s for coll.'s and univ.'s, Calif., 1968—. Contbr. articles to profl. jours. Presenter Nat. Conf. Teaching Excellence and Conf. of Pres.'s, 1983, presenter, mem. coordinating com., 1984, chmn. steering com., 1985; presenter Profl. and Orgl. Devel. Network, 1984; ad hoc com. CPEC/FIPSE/Chancellor's Office, 1984; mem. steering com. Learning Assessment Retention Com., 1983—, pres.-elect 1985-86; mem. instl. research design team No. Calif. Higher Edn. Council, 1984, mission charrette writing team, 1985. Richardson fellow 1982-83; scholar Gen. Ohio State U., 1963, Stadium Dormitory, 1962-65, Scholastic R., 1962, Nat. Honor Soc., 1962. Mem. Assn. Calif. Coll. Tutorial and Learning Assistance (presenter 1984), Calif. Assn. Community Colls. (conf. presenter 1984, com. on research 1985—), Assn. Calif. Community Coll. Adminstrs. (comm. membership devel. 1985), Am. Chem. Soc., Faculty Assn. Calif. Community Colls., Calif. Tchrs. Assn., NEA, Nat. Faculty Assn., Phi Kappa Phi, Upsilon Pi Upsilon (pres. 1965-66), San Diego and Imperial Counties Community Coll. Assn. Lodge: Rotary (pres. Durham club 1980-81, dist. sec. Calif., 1983-84, various other offices and com. positions held locally and nationally). Home: 255 Rudd Rd Vista CA 92084 Office: Palomar Coll 1140 W Mission Rd San Marcos CA 92069-1487

BOGNAR, CHARLES RALPH, marketing manager; b. Phila., Feb. 2, 1926; s. Charles S. and Anna Bognar. Student Pa. State U., 1957-67; m. Bernadine L. Schantz, Oct. 2, 1948. Tool and model maker in machine shop Franklin Inst. Research Labs., Phila., 1949-55, sr. tech. assoc. friction lubrication div., 1955-70, sr. test engr. utilities services group, 1970-73; mgr. test ops. and cofounder turbo exptl. div. Turbo Research, West Chester, Pa., 1973-75; cofounder Energy Tech., Inc., West Chester, 1975, v.p., dir. mktg., 1975-79; new bus. devel. mktg. spl. services div. Ebasco Services, Inc., N.Y.C., 1979-80, mgr. project devel./mktg. for process indsl. div., Los Angeles, 1980-83, mgr. project devel./mktg. for indsl. bus. devel. for Pacific S.W. and Hawaii, 1983-86; regional sales mgr. Pall Well Tech. Corp. (subs. Pall Corp.), 1986—. Mem. ASME, Research Engrs. Soc. Am., Sigma Xi. Mem. Christian Ch. Home: 817 Dualridge Dr #30 Bakersfield CA 93309 Office: 19448 Colombo St Bakersfield CA 93308 Office: 2200 Northern Blvd East Hills NY 11548

BOGORAD, DENNIS B., video producer; b. Detroit, Sept. 15, 1947; s. Irving and Harriet Ruth (Feld) Bogorad. BA, Wayne State U., 1972. Exec. producer Detroit Inst. Arts, 1981-83; TV producer Dennis Bogorad Prodns., Los Angeles, 1983—. Exec. producer Between Continents/Between Seas: Pre-Columbian Art of Costa Rica, 1982 (Cine Golden Eagle award 1982), From A Mighty Fortress: Prints and Drawings From The Veste Coburg Collection, 1982 (Cine Golden Eagle award 1982). Recipient award of Merit Nation of Costa Rica, 1983. Republican. Jewish. Home: 7245 Hillside Ave Apt 104 Los Angeles CA 90046

BOGUE, BRUCE, insurance agent; b. Los Angeles, Sept. 24, 1924; s. Charles Luther and Viola (Adam) B.; m. Tays Myrl Tarvin, Dec. 18, 1945; children: Tays Elizabeth, Charles Luther II. BA, U. Calif. at Los Angeles, 1947; grad. Inf. Staff and Command Sch. U.S. Army, 1948. Agt. Mut. Benefit Life Ins. Co., Los Angeles, 1948-55, prodn. mgr., 1955-62; gen. agt. Guardian Life Ins. Co., Los Angeles, 1962-85, agt., 1985—; tchr. ins. UCLA. Contbr. articles to profl. jours. Precinct capt., poll watcher, hdqrs. chmn., fund raising chmn., campaign chmn. for Rep. party. Served to capt. inf. AUS, 1942-46, ETO. Recipient Man of Affairs award Los Angeles Wilshire Press, Los Angeles Mirror News, 1958, Nat. Mgmt. award 1980-85. Mem. Million Dollar Round Table (life), Am. Soc. CLUs, Assn. Advanced Life Underwriters, Nat. Assn. Life Underwriters, U. Calif. at Los Angeles Alumni Assn. (life). Congregationalist. Clubs: Annandale Golf (Pasadena, Calif.); Monrovia Tennis, Calif. (Los Angeles). Home: 2200 Homet Rd San Marino CA 91108 Office: 617 S Olive St #1000 Los Angeles CA 90014

BOGUE, DONALD JOSEPH, investment company executive; b. Raymond, Wash., Sept. 11, 1930; s. Joseph A. and Esther M. (Peterson) B.; m. Marian Ann Balderston, Aug. 29, 1952; children: Stephen Paul, Debra Renee. BTh, Cen. Bible Coll., 1951; EdD in Adminstrn., Pacific Western U., 1977, MEd in Curriculum, 1976; PhD, Union U., London, 1977. Ordained to ministry, 1953. Pastor, evangelist Assemblies of God, various cities, Iowa, Wash., Calif., 1953—; founder, pres. Andon Coll., San Jose, Calif., 1970-84; prin. Bogue Enterprises, Stockton, 1984—; with Vocat. Allied Health, Stockton and Modesto, Calif., 1985—; owner, mgr. various office bldgs., San Jose, Stockton and Modesto; commr. Accredited Bur. Health Edn. Schs., Elkhart, Ind., 1975-84; cons. to Colls. and Univs., 1974—; Health Care Ministries Internat., Springfield, Mo., 1984—. Author: Maintaining Student Retention, 1976, How to Teach Teachers to Teach, 1980. Named Outstanding Young Man of Yr., Cedar Rapids (Iowa) C. of C., 1956; recipient Merit of Recognition award, San Juan, Puerto Rico. Mem. Nat. Assn. Health Career Schs. (bd. dirs. 1972-84; recipient Leadership award 1984). Avocations: sports, boating. Office: Bogue Enterprises 2155 W March Ln Suite 1E Stockton CA 95207

BOGUMILL, MICHAEL THOMAS, safety engineer; b. Owen, Wis., Dec. 20, 1938; s. Edward Leonard and Clara Emma (Pierce) B. BS, U. Wis., Eau Claire, 1961; MA in Teaching, U. N.C., 1970. Cert. tchr. Wis., Calif. Tchr. Auburndale (Wis.) Pub. Sch., 1961-63, Neillsville (Wis.) Pub. Sch., 1963-69, Hilmar (Calif.) Unified Sch. Dist., 1969-70; food and drug inspector Bur. Food and Drugs, Berkeley, Calif., 1971-73; food and drug supervising inspector Bur. Food and Drugs, Los Angeles, 1973-78; food and drug program coordinator Bur. Food and Drugs, Sacramento, 1978—. Contbr. articles to profl. jours. Recipient Cert. Appreciation U.S. Consumer Product Safety Commn., 1982. Mem. AAAS, Calif. Assn. Food and Drug Ofcls. (pres. 1978), Assn. Food and Drug Ofcls., Western Assn. Food and Drug Officials, Nat. Council Against Health Fraud, Sacramento Bowling Assn. (bd. dirs. 1984—), River City Bowlers (sec., treas. 1983—). Democrat. Roman Catholic. Lodge: Kiwanis (Neillsville) (pres. 1968-69). Avocations: bowling, personal computing, reading, collecting miniatures. Home: 1332 Wyant Way Sacramento CA 95864-2638 Office: Food and Drug Br 714 P St Room 400 Sacramento CA 95814

BOHAN, MARILYN LAURIS (JACOBS), stress counselor, nurse, educator; b. Bowdle, S.D., Feb. 28, 1935; d. Carl Thomas and Rose Mary (Savelsberg) Jacobs; m. John Francis Bohan, July 30, 1961. B.S., Presentation Sch. Nursing, S.D. Northern State Coll., 1961; M.Ed. in Counseling, Portland State U., 1981. R.N. in S.D., Minn., Wash., Oreg. Program nurse Little Crow Community Council, Willmar, Minn., 1963-72; dir. family planning Interlakes Community Action, Madison, S.D., 1973-74; instr., nurse Shelton (Wash.) Sch. Dist., 1975-76; nurse counselor Community Health, Oregon City, Oreg., 1976-80; dir. Healthwise Stress Counseling Consulting Center, Oregon City, 1981—; cons. Women's Center, 1981—; instr. Clackamas Community Coll., 1981—; tchr. art, choral reading St. Mary's Sch., Willmar, Minn., 1968-70. Chmn., camp nurse Minn. Soc. for Crippled Children & Adults; dir., camp nurse Kandiahi County (Minn.) Assn. for Retarded Children, Willmar, 1965-72; dir. West Central Industries, Willmar, 1968-72; leader Girl Scouts USA, 1967-78; program chmn. Willmar Roundtable Study Club, 1968-72; active Friends of Library, Oregon City, 1982—. Mem. Am. Personnel Guidance Assn., AAUW, Phi Kappa Phi. Author: Psychodrama and the Terminal Patient, 1981.

BOHANNAN, PAUL JAMES, anthropologist, university administrator; b. Lincoln, Nebr., Mar. 5, 1920; s. Hillory and Hazel (Truex) B.; m. Laura Marie Smith, Mar. 15, 1943 (div. 1975); 1 son, Denis Michael; m. Adelyse D'Arcy, Feb. 28, 1981. B.A., U. Ariz., 1947; B.Sc., Oxford U., Eng., 1949, Ph.D., 1951. Lectr. social anthropology Oxford U., 1951-56; asst. prof. Princeton U., 1956-59; prof. Northwestern U., 1959-75, U. Calif.-Santa Barbara, 1976-82; prof., dean social scis. and communications U. So. Calif., 1982—. Author: Justice and Judgement, 1957, Africa and Africans, 1964, Divorce and After, 1970, All the Happy Families, 1985. Served to capt. U.S. Army, 1941-45. Decorated Legion of Merit. Mem. Am. Anthrop. Assn. (pres. 1979-80), Am. Ethnol. Soc. (dir. 1963-66), African Studies Assn. (pres. 1963-64), Social Sci. Research Council (dir. 1962-64). Office: University of Southern California ADM 200 Los Angeles CA 90089

BOHANSKE, ROBERT THOMAS, psychologist; b. Amsterdam, N.Y., June 22, 1953; s. Thomas A. and Nadine K. (Grayson) B.; m. Jacquie C. Scholar, Apr. 20, 1980; 1 child, Michael S. BS, Ariz. State U., 1975; MS, U. So. Calif., 1977; PhD, U. Ariz., 1983. Cert. psychologist, Ariz.; lic. psychologist, Calif. Resident Inst. Behavioral Medicine, Phoenix, 1982-83, postdoctoral fellow, 1983-84, asst. dir. out-patient services, 1985-87; chief psychologist Behavioral Health Inst. Mesa (Ariz.) Luth. Hosp., 1987—. Mem. Am. Psychol. Assn., Am. Congress of Rehab. Medicine. Jewish. Home: 5045 E Redfield Rd Scottsdale AZ 85254 Office: Behavioral Health Inst Mesa Luth Hosp 500 W 10th Pl Mesa AZ 85201

BOHN, DENNIS ALLEN, electronic engineer, consultant, writer; b. San Fernando, Calif., Oct. 5, 1942; s. Raymond Virgil and Iris Elouise (Johnson) B.; 1 dau., Kira Michelle; m. Patricia Tolle, Aug. 12, 1986. B.S.E.E. with honors, U. Calif.-Berkeley, 1972, M.S.E.E. with honors, 1974. Engring. technician Gen. Electric Co., San Leandro, Calif., 1964-72; research and devel. engr. Hewlett-Packard Co., Santa Clara, Calif., 1973; application engr. Nat. Semicondr. Corp., Santa Clara, 1974-76; engring. mgr. Phase Linear Corp., Lynnwood, Wash., 1976-82; v.p. research and devel., ptnr. RANE Corp., Mountlake Terrace, Wash., 1982—; founder TOLECO Systems, Kingston, Wash., 1980. Suicide and crisis ctr. vol., Berkeley, 1972-74, Santa Clara, 1974-76. Served with USAF, 1960-64. Recipient Am. Spirit Honor medal U.S. Air Force, 1961; Math. Achievement award Chem. Rubber Co., 1962-63. Mem. IEEE, Audio Engring. Soc., Tau Beta Pi. Libertarian. Editor: We Are Not Just Daffodils, 1975; contbr. poetry to Reason mag.; tech. editor Audio Handbook, 1976; contbr. articles to tech. jours.; columnist Polyphony mag., 1981-83. Patentee in field. Home: 16429 3d Dr SE Bothell WA 98012 Office: 6510 216th St SW Mountlake Terrace WA 98043

BOHNSACK, KURT KARL, zoologist, educator; b. Stuttgart, Germany, Mar. 23, 1920; came to U.S., 1923, naturalized, 1941; s. Rudolf Otto and Johanna Marie (Mauser) B.; m. Julie Mary Kuhn, June 15, 1946; children: Linda Mae, Richard Carl, Mary Ellen. B.S., Ohio U., 1946; M.S., U. Mich., 1947, Ph.D., 1954. Instr. zoology U. Mich., 1950-51; instr., asst. prof. Swarthmore Coll., 1951-56; from asst. prof. to prof. zoology San Diego State U., 1956—; mem. summer faculty Pa. State U., 1954, 55, Ariz. State U., 1971-73, John Carroll U., 1970, Mich. State U., 1978; researcher Arctic Research Lab., Barrow, Alaska, 1961-64. Mem. editorial bd: Pedobiologia, 1964—; contbr. articles to profl. publs. Trustee San Diego Natural History Soc., 1966-79. Served with U.S. Army, 1942-45. Research grantee Arctic Inst., 1962, 63; research grantee Oak Ridge Nat. Lab, 1956, 57. Fellow AAAS; mem. AAUP, Acarological Soc. Am., Entomol. Soc. Wash., Western Soc. Naturalists, Audobon Soc., Arctic Inst. N. Am., Sigma Xi. Democrat. Unitarian. Office: Biology Dept San Diego State U San Diego CA 92182

BOHOR, BRUCE FORBES, geologist; b. Chgo., May 4, 1932; s. Rudolph Edward and Alexandria (Strain) B.; m. Barbara Ann Stegenga, Aug. 29, 1953 (div. 1974); children: Sue Ann, Jacquelin, Laura, Thomas; m. Leah Joan Barrier, June 19, 1983. BS magna cum laude, Beloit Coll., 1953; MA, Ind. U., 1955; PhD, U. Ill., 1959. Research geologist Continental Oil Co., Ponca City, Okla., 1957-65, Ill. Geol. Survey, Urbana, 1965-74, U.S. Geol. Survey, Denver, 1974—. Patentee in field. Fellow G.K. Gilbert, U.S. Geol. Survey, 1984-86, Ill. Clay Products, U. Ill., 1956-57. Mem. AAAS, Geochem. Soc., Meteoritical Soc. Am., Clay Mineral Soc. (councilor 1981-83), Soc. Econ. Paleontologists and Mineralogists, Sigma Xi. Avocations: squash, bowling, backpacking. Office: US Geol Survey DFC MS 401 PO Box 25046 Denver CO 80225

BOISSONEAU, ROBERT ALLEN, educator; b. Detroit, Sept. 23, 1937; s. Sylvester Napoleon Boissoneau and Dorothea Verjean (DeLamarter) Ball; m. Jo Ellen Marie Fitzgerald, Oct. 15, 1960; children: Mark N., Deborah Jean, Keith Allen. BA, Eastern Mich. U., 1960; MHA, Va. Commonwealth U., 1965; PhD, Ohio State U., 1974; DS (hon.), Ind. No. Grad. Sch. Profl. Mgmt., 1979. Asst. adminstrn. Detroit Meml. Hosp., 1965-67; adminstr. of Means Hall Ohio State U., Columbus, 1967-69, instr., 1969-72; asst. prof. U. Mo., Columbia, 1972-75; dean coll. human services Eastern Mich. U., Ypsilanti, 1975-80; prof. coll. bus. Ariz. State U., Tempe, Ariz., 1980—; cons. Mich. Dept. Mental Health, Lansing, 1978, G.E. Dantona and Assocs., Inc., Phoenix, 1982—, The Health Cen. System, Mpls., 1984—. Author: Continuing Education in the Health Professions, 1980, Health Care Organization and Development, 1986; contbr. articles to profl. jours. Active Planning Com. Community Adv. Bd., St. Joseph Mercy Hosp., Ann Arbor, Mich. 1976-77; chmn. Legis. Com. Adv. Bd., Desert Samaritan Hosp., Mesa, Ariz., 1982-83; judge Profl. Secs. Internat., Phoenix, 1983. Served to 1st lt. U.S. Army, 1960-62. Mem. The Acad. Mgmt., Am. Hosp. Assn., Am. Soc. Allied Health Professions (editorial bd. 1983—). Avocations: running, tennis, reading. Office: Ariz State U Coll Bus Tempe AZ 85287

BOJANOWSKI, CARL, wood products company executive; b. Alpena, Mich., Apr. 11, 1927; s. Carl David and Elli (Bolenz) B.; m. Gertrude A. Zieth, Sept. 18, 1948 (div. Oct. 1985); children: Randy Kent, Ricky Paul, Debra Ann; m. Clara Elizabeth Bojanowski, Feb. 14, 1986. BSME, Mich. Tech. U., 1951. Registered profl. engr., Oreg., Mont., Tex., Ark., La., Miss., Ga. Gen. mgr. Deka Man, Atlanta, 1962-65; sr. project engr. ChM-Hill, Corvallis, Oreg., 1965-72; chief engr. Bonney Bennett Peters, Eugene, Oreg., 1972-80; v.p. engring. Indsl. Mill Inst., Eugene, 1980-85, Evergreen Engring., Inc., Eugene, 1985—; cons. Fundacion Chile, Santiago, 1985—. Patentee in field. Served with USNR, 1946-47, PTO. Mem. ASME, Am. Hardboard Assn. (tech. com. 1957-62), Tech. Assn. Pulp and Paper Industry, Insulation Bd. Inst. (tech. com. 1957-62). Lutheran. Avocations: hunting, fishing, golf. Home: 2599 Terrace View Dr Eugene OR 97405 Office: Evergreen Engring Inc 860 Conger St PO Box 2d Eugene OR 97402-0082

BOKOCH, GARY MICHAEL, immunology research scientist; b. Erie, Pa., Apr. 15, 1954; s. Michael and Pauline Ann (Revak) B.; m. Janet Nicolia, Aug. 20, 1977; 1 child, Jennifer Nicole. BS, Pa. State U., 1976; PhD, Vanderbilt U., 1981. Postdoctoral fellow U. Tex., Dallas, 1981-85; asst. mem. Scripps Clinic Research Fedn., La Jolla, Calif., 1985—. Contbr. articles to profl. jours., chpts. to books. Named Established Investigator, Am. Heart Assn., 1986—. Mem. Pa. Acad. Sci. Democrat. Roman Catholic. Avocations: fishing, hiking, sports. Home: 1426 Peachwood Dr Encinitas CA 92024 Office: Scripps Clinic Dept Immunology 10666 N Torrey Pines Rd La Jolla CA 92037

BOLAK, WILLIAM MICHAEL, dentist; b. Nyack, N.Y., Mar. 29, 1951; s. William J. and Dorothy M. (Rose) B.; m. Diane Robinson, Aug. 14, 1971; children—Kimberly Ann, Lauren Marie, Jason Matthew, Mark Andrew. B.A. in Chemistry, Cornell U., 1972; D.M.D., Fairleigh Dickinson U., 1976. Pvt. practice dentistry, Alamogordo, N.Mex. Served to capt. USAF, 1976-79. Mem. ADA, Acad. Gen. Dentistry. Office: 901 Delaware Ave Alamogordo NM 88310 Office: 880 Telshor Blvd Las Cruces NM 88001

BOLAND, JOHN FRANCIS, JR., lawyer; b. Yonkers, N.Y., July 23, 1915; s. John Francis and Celeste (Kinalley) B.; m. Jean Clayton Smith, Sept. 15, 1942; children: John Francis III, Richard P., Christopher J., Katherine B., Patricia, Anne, Pegeen. B.A., Fordham U., 1935, J.D., 1946. Bar: N.Y. 1946, Ariz. 1949. Practiced in White Plains, N.Y., 1946-48, Tucson, 1949-50, Phoenix, 1951-85; assoc. McCarthy & Gaynor, 1946-48; partner Boland & D'Antonio, 1949-50; partner Evans, Kitchel & Jenckes (P.C.), 1951-85, pres., 1976-85, of counsel, 1985—. Served to capt., Signal Corps AUS, 1941-46. Mem. Am., Ariz., Maricopa County bar assns. Clubs: Ariz. Yacht, University (bd. dirs. 1987) (Phoenix); Southwestern Yacht (San Diego). Home: 1102 E Tapatio Dr Phoenix AZ 85020 Office: 2600 N Central Ave Phoenix AZ 85004-3099

BOLANDER, PETER WARREN, civil and geotechnical engineer; b. Schenectady, N.Y., Aug. 26, 1954; s. Warren Walter and Joan Marie (Scanlan) B. BS, Mich. State U., 1977; MS, Oreg. State U., 1980. Registered profl. engr., Oreg. Geotech. engr. USDA Forest Service, Eugene, Oreg., 1980-82; civil engr. supr. USDA Forest Service, Oakridge, Oreg., 1983-86; geotech engr. ODOT, Salem, Oreg., 1986—. Mem. Sierra Club. Club: Scandia Leikarringen (Eugene). Avocations: Scandinavian folkdancing, fiddling, making beer and wine. Home: 34325 Mathews Rd Eugene OR 97405 Office: ODOT Bridge Sect Rm 329 Transportation Bldg Salem OR 97310

BOLDEN, ROSAMOND, state official; b. Beggs, Okla., May 5, 1938; d. Benjamin James and Mary Crosby; m. James Alan Bolden, Jan. 27, 1963 (dec. Dec. 1973); 1 child, Stacie Lenore. B.S., U. Calif.-Berkeley, 1961, M.A., 1971. Employment counselor to office mgr. Calif. Dept. Employment, Sacramento, 1965-75; asst. civil rights officer Calif. Dept. Health, Sacramento, 1976-77; chief Office Bldg. and Grounds, Calif. Dept. Gen. Services, Sacramento, 1977—; chmn. merit award bd. dept. personnel adminstrn., State of Calif. Sacramento, 1979-84; mem. women's adv. bd. Calif. Personnel Bd., Sacramento, 1980-84. Bd. dirs. Tierra Del Oro council Girl Scouts U.S.A., Sacramento, 1984, Sacramento Urban League, 1986-89; mem. citizen rev. bd., chmn. admission/allocation subcom. United Way, Sacramento, 1984; founding mem. Sacramento Black Women's Network, 1981. Recipient award of appreciation United Calif. State Employee Campaign, 1980; cert. of appreciation Nat. Assn. Retarded Citizens, 1981 United Way, 1984. Mem. Bldg. Owners and Mgrs. Assn. (co-founder Calif. chpt. 1986, mem. govt. bldg. com.), NAACP, Black Advocates in State Service, Alpha Kappa Alpha. Home: PO Box 22457 Sacramento CA 95831 Office: State of Calif 915 Capital Mall Room 106 Sacramento CA 95831

BOLDT, JOHN ROBERT, marketing professional, consultant; b. Ft. Wayne, Ind., Apr. 3, 1948; s. Thayne Robert and Lila Mae (Leppla) B.; m. Beverly Anne Sanders, Sept. 18, 1971 (div. Oct. 1976). BSME, Cornell U., 1970. Sr. engr. Sperry Corp., Blue Bell, Pa., 1970-78; program mgr., technical specialist Diablo/Xerox, Hayward, Calif., 1979-81; product mgr. Dataproducts/Envision, San Jose, 1981-85; product mktg. mgr. Advanced Technologies Internat., Santa Clara, Calif., 1985-86; assoc. dir. Dataquest, San Jose, 1986—; cons. Dataproducts, San Jose, 1984-86, Lear Siegler, Inc., Anaheim, Calif., 1985-86. Patentee in field. Bd. dirs. Alamo (Calif.) Hills Homeowners Assn., 1983-86, also design review bd. Mem. ASME, Diablo Region Porsche Club Am. (charter). Democrat. Methodist. Avocations: auto racing, snow skiing.

BOLEMA, THOMAS WILLIAM, artist, publisher; b. Muskegon, Mich., June 14, 1951; s. William Jay and Grace Helena (Connel); m. Kathleen Marie Gay, Aug. 27, 1980. BA in Literature and Art, Oakland U., 1974. Pres. Notown Records, Hollywood, Calif., 1980—. Author, pub. All Choked Up, 1982, The Beef Goes On, 1984; (for video documentary) Justiceville, 1986 (Emmy award 1986). Leader The Butchers, Los Angeles, 1980—; activist Homeless Organizing Team, Los Angeles, 1986. Mem. Broadcast Music Inc. (pub., writer). Home: 443 S San Pedro #506 Los Angeles CA 90013 Office: Notown Records/Beefbone Music PO Box 38417 Hollywood CA 90038

BOLES, SHAWN MICHAEL, psychologist, computer software developer; b. Grand Rapids, Mich., Nov. 26, 1942; s. Paul Darcy and Dorothy Kathleen (Flory) B.; m. Sandra Beth Klasen, Dec. 22, 1967 (div. July 1976); m. Melva Rhea Jackson, Nov. 20, 1981; 1 child, Darcy Marie. Student, Ga. Inst. Tech., 1960-62, U. Ga., Athens, 1962-63; AB cum laude, Oglethorp U., 1965; PhD in Exptl. Psychology, Ga. State U., 1971. Chmn. dept. psychology Oglethorpe U., Atlanta, 1972-73; service dir. spl. edn. program Ga. Retardation Ctr., Atlanta, 1973-74, dir. unit B, 1974-76; research assoc. specialized tng. program Ctr. Human Devel. div. U. Oreg., Eugene, 1978-85, sr. research assoc. specialized tng. program, 1985—; dir. vocat. opportunities coop., specialized tng. program, U. Oreg., 1978-79; also dir. planning and evaluation, 1981-86; project coordinator Decision Support Systems, Seattle, 1984-84, also dir. microcomputers, 1986—; cons. Ga. Retardation Ctr., 1972-73, Small Scale Hydro Study and Engring. Ctr., Bend, Oreg., 1982, Berkeley (Calif.) Planning Assocs., 1986. Author: (computer software) Brainstormer, 1983; contbr. chpts. to books. V.p. Whitaker Community Council, Eugene, 1980, Neighborhood Econ. Devel. Corp., Eugene, 1985—; mem. budget com. City of Eugene, 1983—, tng. ctr. rev. bd. State of Oreg., 1983. Recipient Mary E. Switzer award, Nat. Inst. Handicapped Research, Washington, 1985; Disting. Research fellow Nat. Inst. Handicapped Research, 1985. Mem. AAAS, Assn. Severely Handicapped, Carrying Capacity. Avocations: sci. fiction, origami, squash. Home: 105 N Adams Eugene OR 97402 Office: U Oreg Micro Support Ctr Coll Edn Eugene OR 97403

BOLIAN, GEORGE CLEMENT, healthcare executive, physician; b. New Orleans, May 24, 1930; s. George William and Effie (McQuaid) B.; m. Patricia Ruth Green, July 27, 1957 (div. 1984); children—Mark Geoffrey, Gregory Wayne; m. Patricia Ann Morrison, Mar. 26, 1984; children—Joshua Sean, Zachary Ryan. B.A., U. Chgo., 1950, Harvard U., 1952; M.D., Tulane U., 1957. Diplomate Am. Bd. Psychiatry and Neurology. Intern Nassau County Med. Ctr., East Meadow, N.Y., 1957-58; resident psychiatry and child psychiatry U. Cin., 1958-62; instr., asst. prof. U. Wash., Seattle, 1965-70; dir. dept. psychiatry Children's Orthopaedic Hosp. and Med. Ctr., Seattle, 1968-70; assoc. prof. U. Hawaii, Honolulu, 1970—; dir. community mental health ctr. Queen's Med. Ctr., Honolulu, 1971-83, sr. v.p., 1976-83, pres., 1983—. Contbr. numerous articles to profl. jours. Served to capt. U.S. Army, 1962-65. Fellow Am. Psychiat. Assn., Am. Acad. Child Psychiatry, Am. Orthopsychiat. Assn.; mem. AMA, Am. Coll. Hosp. Adminstrs. Home: 1248 Kelewina St Kailua HI 96734 Office: Queen's Med Ctr 1301 Punchbowl St Honolulu HI 96813

BOLICH, GREGORY GORDON, religion and history educator; b. Spokane, Wash., July 7, 1953; s. Glenn Gordon and Joanne G. (Stinger) B.; m. Barbara Jo Ransom, Apr. 8, 1976; children: April Louise, Alicia Layne, Amanda Larissa. BA in Philosophy and Religion, Seattle Pacific U., 1974, M of Christian Ministries in Ednl. Psychology, 1975; MA in Religion, Western Evang. Sem., 1977, M Divinity in Christian Thought, 1978; EdD, Gonzaga U., 1983. Mem. faculty Inland Empire Sch. of the Bible, Spokane, 1975-76; adminstr. First Evang. Free Ch., Spokane, 1978-79; pres. Christian Studies Inst., Cheney, 1979—; grad. asst. research Gonzaga U., Spokane, 1981-83, staff mem. Ctr. for Research, 1981-83; mem adj. faculty Eastern Wash. U., Cheney, 1985—; mentor Gonzaga U., 1984-86, Fuller Sem., Pasadena, Calif., 1984; elder Shadle Park Presbyn. Ch., Spokane, 1982; rep. Presbyn. Ch., 1985-86; coordinator Cheney Presbyn. Fellowship, 1986—. Author: The Christian Scholar, 1986, Authority and the Church, 1982, Karl Barth and Evangelicalism, 1980; contbr. religious articles to jours. and mags. Mem. Friends of Seven, Spokane, 1985—; active United Ministries in Higher Edn., Spokane, 1985—; assoc. mem. YWCA, Spokane, 1984-85, Cheney United Ch. Christ, 1986—. Mem. Bibl. Archaeology Soc., Internat. Thespian Soc., Soc. Bibl. Lit., Northwest Soc. Patristic and Koine Studies (v.p. 1986—), Theology Forum (exec. officer 1981-84), Alpha Kappa Sigma. Democrat. Presbyterian. Avocations: basketball, theatre. Home: Rural Rt 2 Box 74 W 1152 Betz Rd Cheney WA 99004 Office: Christian Studies Inst Rural Rt Box 73 Cheney WA 99004

BOLIN, HAROLD ROY, research chemist.; b. Lefors, Tex., Jan. 16, 1930; s. Lloyd D. and Ruth (Langwell) B.; m. Roberta Atkins, Nov. 17, 1952; children: Hal, Pamela. BS in Chemistry, San Jose State U., 1960; PhD, Utah State U., 1970. Lab supr. Dole Corp., 1960-61; chemist Western Regional Res. Ctr., Albany, Calif., 1961—. Contbr. articles to profl. jour.; patnetee in field. Mem. Am. Chem. soc., Inst. Food Tech. Avocation: photography. Office: Western Regional Res Ctr 800 Buchanan St Albany CA 94710

BOLIN, RICHARD LUDDINGTON, industrial development consultant; b. Burlington, Vt., May 13, 1923; s. Axel Birger and Eva Madora (Luddington) B.; m. Jeanne Marie Brown, Dec. 18, 1948; children—Richard Luddington, Jr., Douglas, Judith, Barbara, Elizabeth. B.S. in Chem. Engring., Tex. A&M U., 1947; M.S. in Chem.Engring., MIT, 1950. Jr. research engr. Humble Oil & Refining Co., Baytown, Tex., 1947-49; staff mem. Arthur D. Little, Inc., Cambridge, Mass., 1950-56, Caribbean office mgr. San Juan, 1957-61, gen. mgr., Mex., 1961-72; pres. Internat. Parks, Inc., Flagstaff, Ariz., 1973—; dir. The Flagstaff Inst., 1976—; dir. Parque Indsl. de Nogales, Nogales, Sonora, Mex. Served with U.S. Army, 1942-46. Club: University (Mex.). Office: PO Box 986 Flagstaff AZ 86002

BOLIN, VERNON SPENCER, microbiologist, consultant; b. Parma, Idaho, July 9, 1913; s. Thaddus Bolin and Jennie Bell Harm; m. Helen Epling, Jan. 5, 1948 (div. 1964); children—Rex, Janet, Mark; m. Barbara Sue Chase, Aug. 1965; children—Vladimir, Erik. B.S., U. Wash., 1942; M.S., U. Minn. 1949. Teaching asst. U. Minn.-Mpls., 1943-45; research assoc. U. Utah, Salt Lake City, 1945-50, fellow in surgery, 1950-52; research virologist Jensen-Salsbery Labs., Inc., Kansas City, Mo., 1952-57; research assoc. Wistar Inst. U. Pa., 1957-58; research virologist USPHS, 1958-61; founder Bolin Lab., 1959; dir. Bolin Labs., Inc., Phoenix. Contbr. articles to profl. jours. Served with U.S. Army, 1931-33. Mem. Phi Mu Chi. Home: 4812 W Greenway Rd Glendale AZ 85036

BOLIN, WILLIAM HARVEY, banker; b. Dallas, Dec. 8, 1922; s. William Harvey and Bertha (Dickey) B.; m. Emma Jane Davis, July 9, 1949; children: Teresa Bolin Gonzalez, Patricia Bolin Wade. B.A. in Internat. Relations, U. Calif.-Berkeley, 1947; postgrad., Nat. U. Mexico, 1948. Trainee Bank of Am., N.T. & S.A., San Francisco, 1947-56; asst. v.p. Bank of Am., N.T. & S.A., 1956-57; br. mgr. Bank of Am., N.T. & S.A., Guatemala, 1957-60; asst. v.p. Middle East and Africa div. Bank of Am., N.T. & S.A., 1960, v.p. div., 1961, v.p., head Latin Am. div., 1965-68, sr. v.p., 1968-75, exec. v.p. Latin Am. Caribbean div., 1975-81, exec. v.p. world banking div., 1981, vice chmn., head world banking div., 1982-84; sr. research fellow UCLA, 1984—. Trustee Overseas Devel. Council, World Affairs Council, Caribbean-Cen. Am. Action; mem. San Francisco Com. Fgn. Relations. Served to capt., inf. AUS, 1942-46, to maj. USAR, 1946-59. Decorated Order Francisco de Miranda (Venezuela). Mem. San Francisco World Trade Assn., Am. Bankers Assn. (chmn. internat. div. 1982-83), Pan Am. Soc. Inst. Internat. Fin. (founding dir.). Clubs: Villa Taverna, Commonwealth (San Francisco); Lansdowne (London). Office: Bank of Am PO Box 37000 San Francisco CA 94137

BOLINGER, TRUMAN, sculptor; b. Sheridan, Wyo., Dec. 3, 1944; s. Claude and Cora (Fowler) B.; m. Bonnie Beaucage, Oct. 31, 1966 (div. 1979); children: Kiki Cherie, Travis Justin; m. Sherrie Berry, June 4, 1983 (div.). Student Colo. Inst. Art, Denver, 1964-65, Art Students League, N.Y.C., 1968-69. One man shows: Washington, 1971, Wyo. State Art Gallery, 1971, Hammer Gallery, N.Y.C., 1975, 76, 79, 83, Seaport Village San Diego, 1981; group shows include: Northwestern Nat. Bank, Mpls., 1974, 75, Nat. Cowboy Hall of Fame, 1975; represented in permanent collections: Minn. Hist. Soc., Mpls., First Fed. Savs. Collection, Phoenix. Republican. Contbr. articles to profl. jours. Home: 8600 E San Felipe Dr Scottsdale AZ 85258

BOLLAG, GIDEON EMANUEL, biochemist; b. Safed, Israel, Aug. 17, 1962; Came to U.S., 1965; s. Jean-Marc and Brigitte (Baumgartner) B. BS in Chemistry with honors, Pa. State U., 1984. Research asst. Biozentrum, Basel, Switzerland, 1981; research asst. chemistry dept. Pa. State U., University Park, 1982-84; research asst. Max Planck Inst., Heidelberg, Fed. Republic of Germany, 1983, U. Calif., Berkeley, 1984—. Contbr. articles to profl. jours. Mem. Am. Chem. Soc., Phi Beta Kappa, Phi Lambda Upsilon, Alpha Lambda Delta. Office: U Calif Dept Biochemistry 401 Biochemistry Bldg Berkeley CA 94720

BOLLES, CHARLES AVERY, librarian; b. Pine Island, Minn., Aug. 10, 1940; s. Arthur Marston and Clarice Ione (Figy) B.; B.A., U. Minn., 1962, M.A. in Library Sci., 1963, M.A. in Am. Studies, 1969, Ph.D. in Library Sci., 1975; m. Marjorie Elaine Hancock, May 17, 1964; children—Jason Brice, Justin Brian. Catalog and serials librarian U. Iowa, Iowa City, 1964-67; asst. prof. Emporia (Kans.) State U., 1970-76; dir. library devel. div. Kans. State Library, 1976-78; dir. Sch. Library Sci., Emporia State U., 1978-80; state librarian State of Idaho, Boise, 1980—; network services council Wash. Library Network. Mem. ALA, Chief Officers State Libraries Agys., Western Council State Librarians (chmn. 1985-86), Pacific N.W. Library Assn., Idaho Library Assn. Office: 325 W State St Boise ID 83702

BOLLES, RICHARD NELSON, author, clergyman; b. Milw., Mar. 19, 1927; s. Donald Clinton and Frances Fethers (Fifield) B.; m. Janet Lorraine Price, Dec. 30, 1949 (div. 1971); children: Stephen, Mark, Gary, Sharon; m. Carol Christen, May 19, 1984. Student, M.I.T., 1946-48; B.A. cum laude, Harvard U., 1950; S.T.B., Gen. Theol. Sem., 1955, S.T.M., 1957. Ordained priest Episcopal Ch., 1953; vicar St. James Ch., Ridgefield, N.J., 1955-58; rector St. John's Episcopal Ch., Passaic, N.J., 1958-66; canon pastor Grace Cathedral, San Francisco, 1966-68; provincial sec. for coll. work 8th Province of the Episcopal Ch., 1968-74; dir. Nat. Career Devel. Project, Walnut Creek, Calif., 1974—; fellow, tutor Gen. Theol. Sem., N.Y.C., 1953-55; fellow Coll. Preachers, Washington, 1964. Author: What Color is Your Parachute?: A Practical Manual for Job Hunters and Career Changers, 1972, rev. annually, Where Do I Go From Here With My Life? 1974, The Three Boxes of Life and How to Get Out of Them, 1978; editor: Newsletter about life/work planning, 1974—. Served with USNR, 1945-46. Mem. Mensa. Home: 2135 Londonderry Ct Walnut Creek CA 94596 Office: Nat Career Devel Project PO Box 379 Walnut Creek CA 94597

BOLLINGER, JOHN, architect, planner, consultant; b. London, Apr. 12, 1943; came to U.S., 1948, naturalized 1953.; s. Luzar and Sarah Rosalie (Mayer) B.; m. Paula Jean Carter, Jan. 29, 1947; 1 child, Lara Renee. BArch, U. So. Calif., 1966, MArch, 1968, D in Bldg. Sci., 1971; cert. in pub. adminstrn., Calif. State U., Long Beach,, 1978. Registered architect, Calif.; lic. gen. contractor, Calif. Project coordinator Bank of Am., Los Angeles, 1972-75; sr. planner City of Long Beach, Calif., 1975-84; project mgr. World Trade Ctr., Port of Long Beach, 1979-84; prin. John Bollinger Architect, Fullerton, Calif., 1976—; prin. contractor Bldg. Resources Interface, Fullerton, 1982—; pres. The Mentor Group, Los Angeles, 1984—; lectr. U. So. Calif., Idylwild, Calif., 1970—; teaching asst. architecture U. S. Calif., Los Angeles, 1968-71; cons. for World Trade Ctrs. in Oxnard, Pomona, Santa Ana, San Diego, Fresno, Calif. Co-author: (master plan report) Polb Master Plan, 1979 (E-Star award 1979), feasibility study for World Trade Ctr., (Willy award 1982). Bd. dirs. Forum for Cultural and Ednl. Exchange, Beverly Hills, Calif., 1975; chmn. Jewish Bus. and Profl. Network of Orange Co., 1987; sec. gen. So. Calif. World Trade Ctrs. Council, 1985; mem. Town Hall, Los Angeles, 1978—. Weyerhauser Found. grantee, 1969, AIA fellow, Los Angeles, 1965, U. So. Calif. Archtl. Guild fellow, 1968. Mem. AIA, Am. Inst. of Planners, World Trade Ctrs. Assn., Internat. Bus. Assn., Long Beach C. of C., U. So. Calif. Alumni Assn. Democrat. Jewish. Lodge: Lions. Avocations: computer, stamps, art, skiing, swimming. Home: 717 N Carhart Ave Suite 64 Fullerton CA 92633 Office: The Mentor Group 9200 Sunset Blvd Los Angeles CA 90069

BOLLINGER, RICHARD AMSEY, minister; b. Blacksburg, Va., Apr. 10, 1928; s. Amsey Floyd and Florence (Moyer) B.; m. Anna Mae Enrmin, June 10, 1950; children: Virginia Kaye, Rebecca Jane. BA cum laude, Manchester Coll., 1949; DivM cum laude, Union Theol. Sem., 1958; D in Ministry, Princeton Theol. Sem., 1979. Ordained to ministry Ch. of the Brethren, 1958. Tchr. instrumental music Ft. Wayne (Ind.) Pub. Schs., 1949-51, Woodstock Sch., Landour, Mussourie, India, 1951-54; asst. pastor Union Congl. Ch., Richmond Hill, N.Y., 1956-58; pastor Ch. of the Brethren, Topeka, 1958-64; staff, dir. of div. Religion and Psychiatry The Menninger Found., Topeka, 1964-86; assoc. dir. The Samaritan Inst., Denver, 1986—; ch. cons. Menninger Found., Topeka, 1975-86; moderator Dist. of Kans., Ch. of the Brethren, 1962-63. Author: The Church in a Changing World, 1965; contbr. numerous articles to profl. jours. Concertmaster Topeka Civic Symphony, 1964-86; bd. dirs. Topeka Youth Project, 1983-86, Multiple Sclerosis Soc., Topeka, 1985-86. Fellow Fund for Theol. Edn., Princeton U., 1955-56; recipient Hope Chest award Multiple Sclerosis Soc., 1968. Fellow Am. Assn. for Marriage and Family Therapy (clin., approved supr., bd. dirs. 1984-86, Cert. of Appreciation 1982), Assn. for Clin. Pastoral Edn. (inactive supr., mem. coms. 1967-75). Democrat. Avocations: music (violinist symphony orch. and string quartet), photography, hiking. Home: 7141 S Olive Way Englewood CO 80112 Office: The Samaritan Inst 1805 S Bellaire St Suite 205 Denver CO 80222

BOLT, ROBERT O'CONNOR, oil company executive; b. Detroit, Aug. 31, 1917; s. Ellswoth Lewis and Rose Elizabeth (Phillips) B.; m. Martha Anne Anthony, Apr. 27, 1943 (dec. Nov. 1981); children: Sandra Jean Bolt Berry, Patricia Anne, Barbara Anthony Bolt Almeida. BS, Millikin U., 1939; MS, Purdue U., 1942, PhD, 1944. Research chemist Chevron Research Co., Richmond, Calif., 1946-63, supr. research chemist, 1963-66, sr. research assoc., unit leader ind. oils, 1966-69, mgr. mktg. services, 1969-85; cons. in field, San Rafael, Calif., 1985—. Co-author, co-editor Radiation Effects on Organic Materials, 1963; contbr. articles to profl. jours. Mem. Am. Soc. Lubrication Engrs., Am. Chem. Soc. (bd. dirs. Calif. sect. 1986—, mem. chmn. 1970—), Sigma Xi. Republican. Presbyterian. Home and Office: 55 Culloden Park Rd San Rafael CA 94901

BOLTE, KATHY, personnel director. Area v.p. Thomas Services, Riverside, Calif. Mem. staff 1984 Olympic Transp. Program, Los Angeles Olympic Organizing Com.; mem. adv. com. regional occupational program Riverside County Supt. Schs., 1984—; mem. steering com. women of achievement luncheon YWCA, Riverside, 1985—. Recipient Award of Merit, Los Angeles Olympic Organizing Com., 1984. Mem. Am. Assn. Med. Transcription (co-founder Orange Empire chpt., 1980—, exec. com., pres. 1980-81), Greater Riverside C. of C. (bd. dirs. 1982—, exec. com., v.p. internal affairs 1984—, pres.-elect 1986—, named Ambassador of Yr. 1982-83, recipient Outstanding Service award 1982-84). Club: 2%. Address: 117 E Campus View Dr Riverside CA 92507

BOLVIN, BOYD MICAEL, educational administrator, library-media consultant, media producer; b. Chehalis, Wash., Aug. 4, 1924; s. Thomas Micael and Norma Nadieda (Nelson) B.; m. Virginia Isabel (Reed), June 7, 1952; children: Debra Ann, Shari Ann. BA, U. Puget Sound, 1950, BEd, 1951; MA in Librarianship, U. Wash., 1960; PhD, U. So. Calif., 1970. Music dir. Moses Lake High Sch., Wash., 1950-53, Shelton Jr. High Sch., Shelton, Wash., 1953-54; librarian, English instr. Mojave High Sch., Calif., 1955-56; coordinator instructional materials Bellevue Pub. Sch., Wash., 1956-65; assoc. dean instrn. Bellevue Community Coll., 1965-82; library-media cons., media producer, Media Prodn. Assocs., Tacoma, Wash., 1982-84; dir. library media ctr. Highline Community Coll., Midway, Wash, 1984-85; pres. U. Wash. Grad. Sch. Library and Info. Sci, 1985-86; retired; media cons. Pierce County Library System, Tacoma, Wash., 1972-73; evaluator library/media N.W. Assn. Schs. and Colls., Seattle, 1976-82; mem. NEH Adv. Com., Seattle Pub. Library, 1978-81; chmn. AV com. Wash. State Gov.'s Conf. on Library and Info. Services, Olympia, Wash., 1979. Contbr. articles to profl. jours. Served with U.S. Army, 1943-46, PTO. Council on Library Resources fellow, 1975; recipient Spl. Service awards Wash. Dept. AV Instr., 1967-68, Outstanding Service award Wash. Dept. AV Instr., 1969, 70, 71, Disting. Service award Region IX, 1983, Disting. Alumnus award U. Wash. Grad. Sch. Library and Info. Sci., 1985. Mem. ALA, Assn. for Edn. Communications and Tech., Community Coll. Library and Media Specialists (pres. 1978-79). Lodge: Kiwanis (pres. 1978-79). Home: 2603 175th St NE Redmond WA 98052 Office: Media Prodn Assocs 10506 Wauna St SW Tacoma WA 98498

BOMBEN, KENNETH DAVID, chemist; b. Concord, Calif., Aug. 12, 1949; s. Americo Edward and Lillian Marie (McKinnon) B.; m. Carol Johnson, June 14, 1975; children: Valerie, Victoria, Elizabeth. BS, Sonoma State U., 1972; PhD, Oreg. State U., 1981. Postdoctoral chemist U. Calif., Berkeley, 1980-81, Lawrence Berkeley (Calif.) Lab., 1981-82; research chemist Conoco, Ponca City, Okla., 1982-83; sr. lab. scientist Perkin-Elmer, Mountain View, Calif., 1983—; sci. cons. Bay Area Skeptics, 1982—. Mem. Am. Chem. Soc., Calif. Acad. Scis., Sigma Xi, Phi Lambda Upsilon. Libertarian. Office: Perkin-Elmer Phys Electronics div 1161C San Antonio Rd Mountain View CA 94043

BOMMER, JERRY CHARLES, chemical company manager, researcher; b. Ogden, Utah, Sept. 29, 1948; s. Theodore John Bommer and Afton Lenore Wayment. BS, Weber State U., 1970; PhD, Utah State U., 1977; sabbatical, U. Calif., Davis, 1980. Analysis technologist Lithium Corp. Am., 1968-69; head chemist Porphyrin Products, Logan, Utah, 1976-80, v.p. research and devel., 1980-85, gen. mgr., 1985—. Contbr. numerous articles to profl. jours. Served to capt. USAR. Mem. Am. Chem. Soc. Avocations: hunting, fishing. Office: Porphyrin Products Inc 195 South 7th West PO Box 31 Logan UT 84321

BOMZE, F(ERN) BARBARA, clinical social worker; b. N.Y.C., May 12, 1934; d. Philip and Estelle Mildred (Rothnagel) Stein; m. Marc Raymond Bomze, Feb. 12, 1956 (div. Jan. 1985); children: Rhonda Jarema, Jay Bomze, Michelle Bomze. BA, U. Miami, Coral Gables, Fla., 1954; MSW, Wayne State U., 1976. Cert. social worker, marriage counselor, Mich.; lic. social worker, marriage and family counselor, Calif. Psychiat. social worker Henry Ford Hosp., West Bloomfield, Mich., 1976-83; clin. social worker, ptnr. Saddleback Counseling and Psychotherapy Assocs., Laguna Hills, Calif., 1984—; cons. Saddleback Women's Ctr., Laguna Hills, 1985—, Saddleback Hosp. Cardiac Rehab., 1986—; mem. faculty eating disorder program U. Calif.-Irvine. Mem. Saddleback Bus. and Profl. Women (sec. 1986), Saddleback C. of C., Nat. Assn. Social Workers (cert., diplomate, bd. dirs. referral service 1985—), Calif. Assn. Marriage and Family Therapists, Am. Group Psycotherapy Assn. Democrat. Jewish. Avocations: tennis, travel. Office: Saddleback Counseling Assocs 23521 Paseo de Valencia #302A Laguna Hills CA 92653

BONACINA, JOSEPH ANDREW, retired lawyer, writer; b. Gravedona, Italy, Oct. 30, 1903; s. Antonio and Annunciata (Riella) B.; Ph.B., U. Santa Clara, 1927, J.D., 1931; student Humboldt State Coll., 1926; m. Clare M. Valle, Nov. 28, 1928 (dec. May 1981); m. Eileen S. Stark, Dec. 5, 1981. Newspaper reporter San Jose (Calif.) Mercury Herald, San Jose News, San Francisco Examiner, 1923-36; dep. county clk., ct. clk. Santa Clara County, 1935-41; city atty. City of Sunnyvale (Calif.), 1942-48; practice, San Jose, 1951—; city atty. City of Campbell (Calif.), 1952-71, emeritus, 1971—; now writer. Active numerous civic orgns. Clubs: Rinconada Country, KC (4 deg.), St. Thomas More, others. Home: 15215 Sobey Rd Saratoga CA 95070

BONAR, ROBERT WAYNE, pediatrician; b. Wendell, Idaho, Sept. 30, 1944; s. Ivan Lee and Mary Elizabeth (Fulkerson) B.; m. Jean Ann Houston, July 13, 1968; children: Andrew, Alison. BS, Coll. Idaho, 1966; MD, George Washington U., 1970. Diplomate Am. Bd. Pediatrics. Intern UCLA, 1970-71, resident in pediatrics, 1973-75; asst. clin. prof. U. So. Calif., Los Angeles, 1976-79; asst. prof. U. Nev., Reno, 1979-85, acting chmn. dept. pediatrics Sch. Medicine, 1983-85; med. dir. Reno Nev. Jobs Corps Ctr., 1979-85; practice medicine specializing in pediatrics The Permanent Med Group, Inc., Sacramento, Calif., 1985—. Author: Seminars in Family Medicine, vol. 2, 1981; contbr. articles to profl. jours. Bd. dirs. Planned Parenthood, No. Nev., Physicians for Social Responsibility. Served to capt. U.S. Army, 1971-73. Mem. Am. Acad. Pediatrics, Soc. Adolescent Medicine. Office: The Permanent Med Group Inc PO Box 254999 2025 Morse Ave Sacramento CA 95825

BONAR, ROLAND BIRT, educational administrator; b. El Paso, Tex., Jan. 24, 1934; s. Bernard E. and Dorothy L. (Birt) B.; student Calif. Inst. Tech., 1951-54, U. Tex. at El Paso, 1957-62; L.H.D., Lincoln Meml. U., 1968; Ph.D., Columbia U., 1972; m. Charlotte Ronning; children—Robert James, Marla Lynn, Michael G. Vice-pres., gen. mgr. Western GMC Truck Co., El Paso, 1955-60; tchr. Dale Carnegie courses N.Mex. and W. Tex., 1960-66; prin. Roland B. Bonar & Assos., presenting Dale Carnegie courses, Balt., 1966-73, Denver, 1973—; past pres. Dale Carnegie Internat. Sponsors Assn.; guest lectr. U. Md., 1968-74; chmn. bd. Explorex Oil Co., Houston, 1975—; past chmn. First Savs. & Loan of Orland Park, Chgo.; dir. Transportes de Ref de Mex. S.A., Bombas Turbinas de Mex. S.A., B & M Oil Co., N.Mex. Vice-pres. Denver area Boy Scouts Am., 1973—; chmn. fin. Denver area council Cancer Soc., 1964-83, fin. dir., 1974-75; mem. Pres. Johnson's Council on Mental Retardation, 1965-68; mem. cabinet Mile Hi United Way, 1978—; bd. dirs. Colo. Boys Ranch, 1976—, Balt. Cystic Fibrosis Found., 1966-70; trustee Lincoln Meml. U., 1969-80, Luth. Social Services Colo. Served with USAF, 1950-54; Korea. Decorated D.F.C., Air medal; named outstanding citizen Albuquerque, 1972; Group Pres.'s awardee Dale Carnegie & Assos., 1974-76. Mem. Am. Soc. Tng. Dirs., Am. Mgmt. Assn., U. Tex., Columbia, Lincoln Meml. U. alumni assns., Denver C. of C., Colo. Assn. Commerce and Industry (chmn. fin.), Civil War Round Table. Republican. Lutheran. Clubs: Rolling Hills Country; University (N.Y.C.); Lawyers (Washington); Denver Rotary, Masons. Office: 210 University Blvd Suite 820 Denver CO 80206

BOND, RICHARD MILTON, utility company executive; b. Spokane, Wash., Apr. 23, 1924; s. Joseph McKinley and Ethel (Campbell) B.; m. Pat Hendrickson, June 30, 1946; children: David Preston, Marc Douglas, Andrew Joseph. Student, Calif. Inst. Tech., 1942-43; BA, BS, U. Calif., Berkeley, 1946; student, U. So. Calif., 1945-46. Sales engr. Ingersoll Rand Corp., N.Y.C. and Phila., 1947-48; adminstrv. asst. Bendix Aviation, North Hollywood, Calif., 1949-50; v.p. sales Calor Gas Co., San Francisco, 1950-57; v.p., mng. dir. Vancouver Island Gas Co., Nanaimo, B.C., Can., 1957-65; pres. Solar Gas Co., Spokane, 1955-87, Solar Gas Ltd., Nanaimo, 1958—; mem. Wash. Ho. Reps., Olympia, 1974-86. Named Legislator of Yr., Young Ams. for Freedom, 1977, Legislator of Yr., Wash. Conservative Union and Wash. Taxpayers Assn., 1977. Mem. Nat. LP Gas Assn. (bd. dirs. 1972—), Am. Legis. Exchange Council (bd. dirs. 1985—, named Outstanding Legislator, 1985). Republican. Office: Solar Gas Ltd N 411 Havana Spokane WA 99202

BOND, THOMAS MOORE, JR., labor mediation and arbitration executive; b. Louisville, Dec. 17, 1930; s. Thomas Moore and Louise Elizabeth (Jones) B.; m. Kathryn Keith, Apr. 10, 1950 (dec.); children: Gilbert, Louise, Lela; m. Ethel Ayako Kuramitsu, Aug. 15, 1965; children: Richard, Jane, Julian Horace. BS in Econs., Ind. U., 1953. Bus. agt. organizer Hosp. Workers, San Francisco, 1961-65; internat. rep. organizer Service Employees' AFL-CIO, Louisville, 1965-70; exec. dir. Union Am. Physicians, San Francisco, 1973-78; owner Thomas Moore Bond & Assocs., Berkeley, Calif., 1979—; pvt. practice labor mediator and arbitrator, Berkeley, 1981—. Editor: The Negro Conservative, 1981. Bd. dirs. adv. com. for paralegal tng. Merritt Coll., Oakland, Calif., 1983; mem. labor commn. City of Berkeley, 1986—. Served to 1st lt. inf., U.S. Army, 1946-48. Mem Indsl. Relations Research Assn., Soc. Fed. Labor Relations Profls., Inst. Advanced Law Study. Republican. Congregationalist. Office: Thomas Moore Bond & Assocs 2123 1/2 5th St Berkeley CA 94710

BONDAREFF, WILLIAM, psychiatry educator; b. Washington, Apr. 29, 1930; s. Leon and Gertrude Bondareff; m. Winifred Vanderwalker, Sept. 28,

1958 (div. Oct. 1976); children: Hyla, Sarah. BS in Zoology, George Washington U., 1951, MS in Zoology, 1952; PhD in Anatomy, U. Chgo., 1954; MD, Georgetown U., 1962. Lic. physician, Calif., Ill., Md. Research assoc., instr. anatomy U. Chgo., 1955; rotating intern USPHS Hosp., Balt., 1962-63; resident in psychiatry Northwestern Meml. Hosp. Inst. Psychiatry, Chgo., 1978-80; asst. prof. anatomy Northwestern U., Evanston, Ill., 1963-65, assoc. prof., 1965-69, prof., 1969-78, chmn. dept. anatomy, 1970-78; prof. psychiatry and gerontology U. So. Calif., Los Angeles, 1981—; mem. staff Hosp. Good Samaritan, Los Angeles, 1981—, St. John's Hosp. and Health Ctr., Los Angeles, 1981—; physician/cons. VA Hosp., Downey, Ill., 1969-80, Jewish Home for Aged, Reseda, Calif., 1981—; vis. staff mem. medicine Passavant Pavilion Northwestern Meml. Hosp., 1972-80; dir. div. geriat. psychiatry U. So. Calif., 1981—; dir. U. So. Calif.-St. Barnabas Alzheimer Disease Ctr., 1985—; acting dir. dept. Gerontology Research Inst. Andrus Gerontology Ctr.-U. So. Calif., 1982; staff psychiatrist Los Angeles County Hosp., 1981—; past holder various com. offices Northwestern U. Editor Mechanisms of Aging and Devel., 1970—; assoc. editor Am. Jour. Anatomy, 1970-76; mem. editorial Bd. Alzheimer Disease and Associated Disorders-An Internat. Jour., 1985—, Neurbiology of Aging, 1980—; The Jour. of Gerontology, 1981-84; contbr. articles to profl. jours. Served with USPHS, 1955-63. USPHS fellow, 1955; scholar Allergy Found., 1960, U. Chgo., 1953; recipient Career Devel. award Nat. Inst. Neurol. Disease and Blindness, 1966-69, Sesquicentennial award Hobart and William Smith Colls., 1972, Sandoz prize Internat. Assn. Gerontology, 1983, Alzheimer Disease and Related Disorders Assn. award, 1984; Fulbright Lectr., U. Goteborg, Sweden, 1967-68. Fellow AAAS (councilor 1970-74), Gerontol. Soc.; mem. Am. Assn. Anatomists (chmn. local com. ann. meeting 1969), Electron Microscope Soc. Am., Am. Soc. Cell Biology, Am. Acad. Neurology (chmn. neuroanatomical scis. sect. 1971-77), Soc. Neurosci., Assn. Anatomy Chmn. (councilor 1975-77), Am. Psychiat. Assn. (geriatrics task force 1981), Am. Geriat. Soc., Am. Assn. Geriat. Psychiatry (program com. 1984—, bd. dirs. 1985—), So. Calif. Psychiat. Soc., Internat. Psychogeriat. Assn., Cajal Club, Sigma Xi. Home: 11814 Kiowa Ave #101 Los Angeles CA 90049

BONDI, BERT ROGER, accountant, financial planner; b. Portland, Oreg., Oct. 2, 1945; s. Gene L. and Elizabeth (Poynter) B. BBA, U. Notre Dame, 1967. CPA, Colo., Calif., Wyo. Sr. tax acct. Price Waterhouse, Los Angeles, 1970-73; ptnr. Valentine Adducci & Bondi, Denver, 1973-76; sr. ptnr. Bondi & Co., Englewood, Colo., 1977—; dir. Citizens Bank. Bd. govs. Met. State Coll. Found. Served with U.S. Army, 1968-70. Mem. C. of C., Community Assns. Inst., Govt. Fin. Officers Assn., Home Builders Assn., Am. Inst. CPAs, Colo. Soc. CPAs, Wyo. Soc. CPAs. Roman Catholic. Clubs: Notre Dame, Metropolitan (Denver); Castle Pines Country. Home: 6765 S Magnolia Ct Englewood CO 80112 Office: Bondi & Co 44 Inverness Dr E Bldg B Englewood CO 80112

BONDURANT, CECIL WILLIAM, emeritus educator; b. Grass Creek, Wyo., June 26, 1918; s. Perle Oscar and Mary Lucile (Williams) B.; B.S., Am. TV Inst. Tech., 1952; m. Doris Mae Box; children by previous marriage—Curtis Dean, Gary Michael, Laura Marie. TV engr. WENR-TV, Chgo., 1952; engring. supr. KBTV, Denver, 1953-60; engr. and instr. Washington State U., 1961; instr., dir. radio TV engring. U. Idaho, Moscow, 1962-81, emeritus, 1981—; learning lab cons. for sch. dists. in No. Idaho; vol. exec. Internat. Exec. Service Corps., Ecuador TV, 1981. Pres. Idaho chpt. Am. Junior Bowlers Congress, 1968-81. Served with AUS, USAF, 1939-47. Decorated Bronze Star medal. Mem. IEEE, Soc. Broadcast Engrs., Internat. Platform Assn., AAUP, Alpha Epsilon Rho. Mason. Moose. Mem. Order Eastern Star. Home: 3300 E Broadway #102 Mesa AZ 85204

BONE, LUCIEN ARMINT, JR., advertising company executive; b. Los Angeles, Sept. 28, 1937; s. Lucien Armint and Rose Erma (Bernard) B.; m. Carol Leta Smale, June 20, 1969. A.A., Compton Jr. Coll., 1957; student Long Beach State Coll., (Calif.) 1957. Store mgr. Albertson's, Long Beach, 1961-66; Gardena, Calif., 1966-68; with PIA Merchandising Co., Los Angeles, 1969-86, exec. v.p., chief operating officer, 1981-82, pres., 1983-86; pres. In-Store Directory; pres. Pivotal Mktg. Services; v.p. sales service Gannett Outdoor Advt. Co., 1986—. Mem. East Los Angeles (Calif.) Library Com., 1982; mem. State Senate Food Industry Spl. Task Force; bd. dirs. Rams Boosters Club, 1984—; mem. World Affairs Council of Orange County. Recipient award of appreciation Bd. Trustees North Orange County Regional Occupational Program and Calif. Dept. Edn., 1976. Mem. Sales and Mktg. Execs. Los Angeles (dir. 1982-84, 85-86, v.p. 1985-86, Disting. sales award 1971, Merit award 1980, honor award 1983, Pres.'s award 1984), Illuminators (bd. dirs. 1985—), Calif. Grocers Assn. (assoc.). Republican. Clubs: Capitol (exec. com. 1982-84) (Sacramento); Shriners, Masons. Office: 1731 Workman St Los Angeles CA 90031

BONFIELD, ANDREW JOSEPH, tax practitioner; b. London, Jan. 26, 1924; s. George William and Elizabeth Agnes B.; came to U.S., 1946, naturalized, 1954; m. Eleanor Ackerman, Oct. 16, 1955; children—Bruce Ian, Sandra Karen. Gen. mgr. Am. Cushion Co., Los Angeles, 1948-50, Monson Calif. Co., Redwood City, 1951-58; mfrs. mktg. rep., San Francisco, 1958-62; tax practitioner, bus. cons., Redwood City, San Jose, Los Gatos, Calif., 1963—. Past treas., dir. Northwood Park Improvement Assn.; mem. exec. bd. Santa Clara County council Boy Scouts Am., 1971—, past council pres., mem. Nat. council; mem. Santa Clara County Parks and Recreation Commn., 1975-81, 82-86; mem. County Assessment Appeals Bd., 1978-86. Served with Brit. Royal Navy, 1940-46. Decorated King George VI Silver Badge; recipient Silver Beaver award, Vigil honor award Boy Scouts Am.; enrolled to practice before IRS. Mem. Nat. Soc. Public Accts., Nat. Assn. Enrolled Agts., Calif. Soc. Enrolled Agts., Royal Can. Legion (past state parliamentarian, past state 1st vice comdr.). Club: Rotary (pres. San Jose E. 1977-78). Home: 760 S Kihei Rd #215 Kihei Maui HI 96753

BONGIANNI, WAYNE L., physicist; b. Chgo., June 25, 1940; s. Leo Joseph and Irene Clementine (Populaski) B.; m. Mary Kay Flynn, May 2i, 1966; children: Juliet Kay, Nicholas Wayne. BS in Physics, Ill. Inst. Physics, 1963. Physicist N. Am. Aviation, El Segundo, Calif., 1963-64, Ground Systems div. Hughes Aircraft Corp., Fullerton, Calif., 1964-69, Autonetics div. Rockwell Internat., Anaheim, Calif., 1965-78, Materials Sci. div. Los Alamos (N.Mex.) Nat. Lab., 1978-87; prin. Bongianni Tech. Assocs., 1987—. Patentee in field. Recipient Disting. Service award, 1984. Avocation: ultralight aviation. Home: 408 Kolleen Ct Los Alamos NM 87545 Office: Los Alamos Nat Lab E545 Los Alamos NM 87545

BONHAM, TERRENCE JAMES, lawyer, hearing officer; b. Richmond, Calif., June 8, 1938; s. Harry L. and Helen G. (Gately) B.; m. Joyce E. Trout, July 28, 1968; 1 dau., Teresa J. B.A. in Econs., St. Mary's Coll., 1960; J.D., U. Calif., Hastings Coll. Law, San Francisco, 1963. Bar: Calif. 1964, U.S. Dist. Ct. (no. dist.) Calif. 1964, U.S. Ct. Mil. Appeals 1964, U.S. Ct. Appeals (9th cir.) 1964, U.S. Supreme Ct. 1983. Assoc. Halde, Battin, Barrymore & Stevens, Santa Barbara, Calif., 1968-73; ptnr. Barrymore, Stevens & Bonham, Santa Barbara, 1973-74; mem. Riley, Holzhauer, Denver & McClain, Santa Barbara, 1974-80; ptnr. Lawler & Ellis, Ventura, Calif., 1980-85, ptnr. Lawler, Bonham & Walsh, 1985—; judge protem Santa Barbara-Goleta Mcpl. Ct., Ventura County Superior Ct.; hearing officer County of Santa Barbara Civil Service Com., Santa Barbara Bd. Retirement; lectr. Bridging the Gap, Ventura County; lectr. to assns. Mem. Civil Arbitration Panel Ventura County, 1979—; mem. Republican Presdl. Task Force, Nat. Rep. Senatorial Com. Served to capt. U.S. Army, 1964-68. Decorated Bronze Star. Mem. Assn. So. Calif. Def. Counsel, Am. Bd. Trial Advs. (pres. 1984-85), Ventura County Bar Assn. (formerly exec. com., co-chmn. atty./client com.), ABA, Am. Soc. Law and Medicine. Roman Catholic. Clubs: KC (past faithful navigator) (Santa Barbara); Elks (Ventura). Home: 2851 Seahorse Ave Ventura CA 93001 Office: PO Box 1269 Ventura CA 93002

BONKER, DON L., congressman; b. Denver, Mar. 7, 1937; m. Carolyn Jo Ekern, 1971. A.A., Clark Coll., Vancouver, Wash., 1962; B.A., Lewis and Clark Coll, 1964; postgrad., Am. U., Washington, 1964-66. Research asst. to Senator Maurine B. Neuberger of Oreg., 1964-66; auditor Clark County, Wash., 1966-74; mem. 94th-100th Congresses from 3d Wash. Dist., 1975—, mem. fgn. affairs com., chmn. internat. econ. policy and trade subcom., mem. select com. on aging, chmn. subcom. housing and consumer interest, mem. merchant marine com., chmn. house export task force, chmn. demonstration task force. Office: 434 Cannon House Office Bldg Washington DC 20515

BONKOWSKI, MICHAEL STEVEN, geologist, educator; b. Ann Arbor, Mich., Dec. 12, 1954; s. Ralph Raymond Bonkowski and Marilyn Rita (Mayette) Hartson. BA, U. Calif., Santa Barbara, 1978, MA, 1981. Geologist Chevroc USA Inc., San Francisco, 1980-83; project geologist, mktg. mgr. J.H. Kleinfelder & Assocs., Walnut Creek, Calif., 1983-86; prin. Mike Bonkowski & Co., Lafayette, Calif., 1986—; instr. U. Calif., Berkeley, 1984—. Contbr. articles to profl. jours. Mem. Nat. Water Well Assn., Geol. Soc. Am. Republican. Roman Catholic. Avocations: fly fishing, camping. Home: 1076 Carol Ln #63 Lafayette CA 94549

BONN, ETHEL MAY, psychiatric administrator; b. Cin., Oct. 14, 1925; d. Stanley Ervin and Ethel May (Cliffe) B. BA, U. Cin., 1947; MD, U. Chgo., 1951. Asst. chief VA Hosp., Topeka, 1956-57, chief women's neuro-psychiat. services, 1957-61, chief north service, 1961-62; assoc. dir. for clin. services Ft. Logan Mental Health Ctr., Denver, 1962-67, dir., 1967-76; field rep. Joint Commn. on Accreditation of Hosps., Chgo., 1976-78, cons., 1978-81; quality assurance chief Brentwood VA Med. Ctr., Los Angeles, 1978-81; chief psychiatry service VA Med. Ctr., Albuquerque, 1981—; cons. Fitzsimons Army Hosp., Denver, 1963-67, U. Calif. Dept Biobehavioral Scis., Los Angeles, 1978-81, VA Hosps., Ft. Lyon, Colo., Sheridan, Wyo., Tuscaloosa, Ala., 1963-67. Contbr. chpts. to books, articles to profl. jours. Recipient Commendation, VA, 1962, 81, Psychiat. Administrs. award Am. Assn. Psychiat. Administrs, 1976. Fellow Am. Coll. Psychiatrists, Am. Psychiat. Assn. (program com. 1977-81), Am. Coll. Mental Health Administrs. (founding fellow 1975—), Am. Coll. Utilization Rev. Physicians; mem. Am. Hosp. Assn. (chmn. psychiat. sect. 1974-76), AMA. Avocations: travel, gardening, fishing. Office: VA Med Ctr116A 2100 Ridgecrest Dr SE Albuquerque NM 87108

BONNELL, VICTORIA EILEEN, sociologist; b. N.Y.C., June 15, 1942; d. Samuel S. and Frances (Nassau) B.; m. Gregory Freidin, May 4, 1971. B.A. Brandeis U., 1964; M.A., Harvard U., 1966, Ph.D., 1975. Lectr. politics U. Calif.-Santa Cruz, 1972-73, 74-76; asst. prof. sociology U. Calif.-Berkeley, 1976-82, assoc. prof., 1982—. AAUW fellow, 1979; Regents faculty fellow, 1978; Fulbright Hays faculty fellow, 1977; Internat. Research and Exchanges Bd. fellow, 1977; Stanford U. Hoover Instn. nat. fellow, 1973-74; Guggenheim fellow, 1985; fellow Ctr. for Advanced Study in Behavioral Scis., 1986-87; grantee Am. Philos. Soc., 1979, Am. Council Learned Socs., 1976. Mem. Am. Sociol. Assn., Am. Assn. Advancement Slavic Studies. Author: Roots of Rebellion: Workers' Politics and Organizations in St. Petersburg and Moscow, 1900-1914, 1983; editor: The Russian Worker: Life and Labor under the Tsarist Regime, 1983; contbr. articles to profl. jours. Office: Dept Sociology U Calif Berkeley CA 94720

BONNER, FREDRIC ALDEN, oil company executive; b. Beverly, Mass., Mar. 1, 1939; s. George Frederick and Virginia Alice (Blanchard) B.; m. Marjorie Amy Heydt, Aug. 11, 1962 (div. Sept. 1984); children: Fredric Lee, Andrea Ellis. BA, Colby Coll.; MBA, NYU. Asst. v.p. Mfrs. Hanover, N.Y.C., 1965-73; v.p. First Interstate Bank, Los Angeles, 1973-77; mgr. shareholder relations Unocal Corp., Los Angeles, 1977—. Served as sgt. U.S. Army, 1962-65. Mem. Corp. Transfer Agts. Assn., Stock Transfer Assn. (bd. dirs. 1983—, Man of Yr. in West 1985), Western Securities Transfer Assn. (pres. 1984-85), Corp. Shareholder System User Group (chmn. 1983-84). Republican. Presbyterian. Avocations: tennis, camping, hiking. Office: Unocal Corp 1201 W 5th St Los Angeles CA 90017

BONNER, JAMES FREDERICK, biology educator, genetic engineering researcher; b. Ansley, Nebr., Sept. 1, 1910; s. Walter Daniel and Grace (Gaylord) B.; m. Ingelore Silberbach, Nov. 11, 1967; children—Joey, James Jose, Pamela, Terry. A.B., U. Utah, 1931; Ph.D., Calif. Inst. Tech., 1934; M.S. (hon.), Oxford U., Eng., 1963; hon. degree, Westminster Coll., Salt Lake City, 1970. Postdoctoral fellow U. Leiden, Netherlands, 1934; postdoctoral fellow Swiss Fed. Inst., Zurich, 1935; instr. to prof. biology Calif. Inst. Tech., Pasadena, 1936-81, prof. emeritus, 1981—; chmn. bd. Phytogen Corp., Pasadena, 1981—; Eastman prof. Oxford U., Eng., 1963-64; cons. Malaysian Rubber Bd., Kuala Lumpur, 1960—; mem. biology panel Pres.'s Sci. Adv. Com., Washington, 1957-62; mem. adv. coms. NIH, Bethesda, Md., 1960-70. Author 11 books, numerous articles. Mem. Nat. Acad. Scis., Am. Chem. Soc. (Tolman prize 1974), Am. Soc. Plant Physiologists (pres. 1949-50), Am. Soc. Biol. Chemists. Club: Am. Alpine (N.Y.C.). Avocations: skiing; mountain climbing. Home: 1914 Edgewood Dr South Pasadena CA 91030

BONNY, MARY ANN, real estate company executive; b. Bremerton, Wash., Mar. 10, 1942; d. Clinton Clifford Culbertson and Caroline Fay St. John; m. Roland Lyle Bonny, Nov. 29, 1958; children: Bradley J., M. Teresa, Rosemarie B., Carol C., Sharon A. Notary Pub., Wash.; Lic. Real Estate Agt., Wash. Co-owner, co-mgr. Bonny's Valley Air Service, Sunnyside, Wash., 1976-77, Bonny Farms, Grandview, Wash., 1978—; sec. Lower Valley Realtors Exchange Club, 1979-80. Mem. Grandview High Sch. agrl. adv. com., 1977-78; past bd. dirs., home econs. bldg. supt., sheep div. supt. Lower Valley Jr. Fair; bd. dirs., treas. Campfire Inc., 1976-77, advisor, 1976; advisor Grandview Jr. High Sch. Rally Squad; council sec. Lower Valley 4-H Leaders, 1974-75; Lower Yakima Valley 4-H leader; active St. Joseph's Cath. Sch.; religious edn. instr. Blessed Sacrament Parish, Grandview, 1972-78; mem. Allied Arts Council, Farm Bur., Yakima Valley Mus. and Hist. Soc., Yakima County Dem. Cen. Com.; del. Wash. Dem Conv., 1986. Recipient Award of the Silver Clover, USDA and Wash. State U., 1977; named Hon. Chpt. Farmer, Future Farmers Am., 1978. Mem. Nat. Assn. Realtors, Wash. Assn. Realtors, Lower Valley Bd. Realtors, Am. Quarter Horse Assn., Wash. 4-H Internat. Assn., Wash. Women for the Survival of Agr. (govt. relations com.), Am. Agri-Women, Nat. Soc. Colonial Dames XVII Century, Bus. and Profl. Women's Club, Back Country Horseman. Roman Catholic. Clubs: St. Joseph's Women's, Antique (Lower Yakima Valley). Home: Bonny Farms Forsell Rd Box 7 Grandview WA 98930 Office: Lower Valley Realty 708 Hwy 12 Grandview WA 98930

BONO, PHILIP, aerospace consultant; b. Bklyn., Jan. 14, 1921; s. Julius and Marianna (Culcasi) B.; m. Gertrude Camille King, Dec. 15, 1950; children: Richard Philip, Patricia Marianna, Kathryn Camille. B.E., U. So. Calif., 1947; postgrad., 1948-49. Research and systems analyst N.Am. Aviation, Inglewood, Calif., 1947; engring. design specialist Douglas Aircraft Co., Long Beach, Calif., 1948-49; preliminary design engr. Boeing Airplane Co., Seattle, 1950-59; dep. program mgr. Douglas Aircraft Co., Santa Monica, Calif., 1960-62; tech. asst. to dir. advanced launch vehicles and space stas. Douglas Aircraft Co., Huntington Beach, Calif., 1963-65; br. mgr. advanced studies, sr. staff engr. advanced tech. McDonnell Douglas Astronautics Co., Huntington Beach, 1966-73; sr. engr.-scientist Douglas Aircraft Co., Long Beach, 1973-83; engring. specialist Northrop Advanced Systems Div., Pico Rivera, Calif., 1984-86; mgr. Cal-Pro Engring. Cons., Costa Mesa, 1986—; lectr. seminars, univs. and insts. including Soviet Acad. Scis., 1965. Author: Destination Mars, 1961, (with K. Gatland) Frontiers of Space, 1969; contbr. articles to profl. jours., chpts. in books. Served with USNR, 1943-46. Recipient Golden Eagle award Council Internat. Events, 1964, A.T. Colwell merit award Soc. Automotive Engrs., 1968, M.N. Golovine award Brit. Interplanetary Soc., 1969, cert. of recognition NASA, 1983; named engr. of distinction Engrs. Joint Council, 1971, Knight of Mark Twain, 1979. Fellow AAAS, Royal Aero. Soc., Brit. Interplanetary Soc. (editorial adv. bd.), AIAA (assoc.); sr. mem. Am. Astronautical Soc.; mem. N.Y. Acad. Scis., Internat. Acad. Astronautics, (academician), ASME, Soc. Automotive Engrs. (chmn. space vehicle com.). Inventor recoverable single-stage space shuttle for NASA. Home: 1951 Sanderling Circle Costa Mesa CA 92626

BONSER, ERNEST LEE, academic administrator; b. Sterling, Colo., June 27, 1952; s. Bernard Clayton and LaVerna (Roth) B.; m. Deborah Elaine Leonard; children: Candice Sommer, Jarrod Michael. AS, U. State of N.Y., Albany, 1981. Computer operator City of Ft. Collins, Colo., 1977-79, programmer, analyst, 1979-81; programmer, analyst Littleton (Colo.) Schs., 1981-82; dir. data processing Cannons Bus. Coll., Honolulu, 1982—. Served with USN, 1972-76. Mem. Data Processing Mgmt. Assn., Nat. Bus. Edn. Assn., Hawaii Bus. Edn. Assn., Am. Univac Users Assn. (co-coordinator 1985-86, co-dir. OS/3 group, dir. edn. group). Avocations: reading, photography, golf. Office: Cannons Internat Bus Coll 1500 Kapiolani Blvd Honolulu HI 96814

BONSER, QUENTIN, surgeon; b. Sedro Wooley, Wash., Nov. 1, 1920; s. George Wayne and Kathleen Imogene (Lynch) B.; B.A. in Zoology, UCLA, 1943; M.D., U. Calif., San Francisco, 1947; m. Loellen Rocca, Oct. 20, 1945; children—Wayne, Gordon, Carol, Patricia Adams (Mrs. Terry Adams). Intern U. Calif. Hosp., San Francisco, 1947-49, resident gen. surgery, 1949-56; practice gen. surgery, Placerville, Calif., 1956—; surgeon King Faisal Splty. Hosp., Saudi Arabia, Sept.-Oct., 1984; vis. prof. surgery U. Calif., San Francisco, 1968. Served to capt. M.C., USAF, 1950-51. Vol. physician, tchr. surgery Vietnam, 1971, 72, 73. Diplomate Am. Bd. Surgery. Fellow A.C.S.; mem. H.C. Naffziger Surg. Soc. (pres. 1974-75). Home: 2590 Northridge Dr Placerville CA 95667 Office: 1108 Corker Dr Placerville CA 95667

BONTING, SJOERD LIEUWE, biochemist; b. Amsterdam, The Netherlands, Oct. 6, 1924; came to U.S., 1952; s. Sjoerd L. and Johanna H.M. (Hagedoorn) B.; m. Suzanne Maarsen, Jan. 10, 1951 (dec. Jan. 1986); children: Marion S., Paul S., Elizabeth J., Peter J.; m. Erica J.M. Schotman, Feb. 27, 1987. BSc in Chemistry, U. Amsterdam, 1944, MSc in Biochemistry cum laude, 1950, PhD in Biochemistry, 1952; lic. in theology (hon.), St. Mark's Inst. Theology, London, 1975. Ordained priest Episcopal Ch., 1964. Instr. U. Amsterdam, 1947-52; research assoc. State U. Iowa, Iowa City, 1952-55; asst. prof. biochemistry U. Minn., Mpls., 1955-56; asst. prof. U. Ill., Chgo., 1956-60; sect. chief NIH, Bethesda, Md., 1960-65; prof., chmn. dept. biochemistry U. Nymegen, The Netherlands, 1965-85; research assoc. NASA Ames Research Ctr., Moffett Field, Calif., 1985—. Editor: Transmitters in the Visual Process, 1976, Evolution and Creation, 1978, Membrane Transport, 1981; also articles. Bd. dirs. Multidisciplinary Ctr for Ch. and Soc., Driebergen, The Netherlands, 1981-85; curate St. Luke's Episc. Ch., Bethesda, 1963-65; Anglican chaplain Ch. of Eng., various cities, The Netherlands, 1965-85; asst. priest St. Thomas' Episc. Ch., Sunnyvale, Calif., 1985—. Postdoctoral fellow USPHS, Iowa City, 1952-54; Rudolf Lehmann Fund scholar, Amsterdam, 1941-46; recipient Fight for Sight citation Nat. Council to Combat Blindness and Assn. for Research in Ophthalmology, N.Y., 1961, 62, Arthur S. Flemming award, Jaycees, Washington, 1964, 1st prize Competition on Enzymology of Leucocytes Karger Found., Basel, Switzerland, 1984. Fellow AAAS; mem. Am. Soc. Biol. Chemists, The Netherlands Biochem. Soc. (officer 1973-76, v.p. 1976-79, pres. 1979-81), Sigma Xi. Democrat. Home: 1006 E Evelyn Ave Sunnyvale CA 94086 Office: NASA Ames Research Ctr Moffett Field CA 94035 Office: St Thomas Episc Ch Sunnyvale CA 94086

BONUTTI, ALEXANDER CARL, architect, urban designer; b. Cleve., June 25, 1951; s. Karl Borromeo and Hermina (Rijavec) B. BArch, Ill. Inst. Tech., 1974; MSArch in Urban Design, Columbia U., 1978. Registered architect Ohio, W.Va. With William B. Morris, AIA, Shaker Heights, Ohio, 1973; designer Stouffer's Hotels, Cleve., 1974, Ellerbe, Dalton, Dalton and Newport, Bethesda, Md., 1975-76; designer, asst. project mgr. Dalton, Dalton and Newport, Shaker Heights, 1976-79; prin. ACB Design, Cleve., 1980; studio dir. Kaplan, McLaughlin and Diaz, San Francisco, 1981—; mem. San Francisco Planning and Urban Research Council, 1981—. Contbr. articles to profl. jours. Recipient Honor award Architects Soc. Ohio, Bay Village, 1979. Mem. AIA (Hon. awards U.S. Univ. Health Sci., Naval Facilities Command), Calif. Council AIA (bd. dirs. 1986—), San Francisco chpt. AIA (chair urban design com. 1986—), Urban Land Inst. (assoc.), Nat. Trust Hist. Preservation, Inst. Urban Design, Phi Kappa Sigma (sec. 1970-71). Democrat. Avocations: jogging, cycling. Office: Kaplan McLaughlin and Diaz 222 Vallejo St San Francisco CA 94111

BOOCHEVER, ROBERT, federal judge; b. N.Y.C., Oct. 2, 1917; s. Louis C. and Miriam (Cohen) B.; m. Lois Colleen Maddox, Apr. 22, 1943; children: Barbara K., Linda Lou, Ann Paula, Miriam Deon. A.B., Cornell U., 1939, LL.B., 1941; HHD (hon.), U. Alaska, 1981. Bar: N.Y. 1944, Alaska 1947. Asst. U.S. atty. Juneau, 1946-47; partner firm Faulkner, Banfield, Boochever & Doogan, Juneau, 1947-72; asso. justice Alaska Supreme Ct., 1972-75, 78-80, chief justice, 1975-78; judge U.S. Ct. Appeals for 9th Circuit, 1980—; chmn. Alaska Jud. Council, 1975-78; mem. appellate judges seminar N.Y.U. Sch. Law, 1975; mem. Conf. Chief Justices, 1975-79, vice chmn., 1978-79; mem. adv. bd. Nat. Bank of Alaska, 1968-72. Chmn. Juneau chpt. ARC, 1949-51, Juneau Planning Commn., 1956-61; mem. Alaska Devel. Bd., 1949-52, Alaska Jud. Qualification Commn., 1972-75; mem. adv. bd. Juneau-Douglas Community Coll. Served to capt. inf. AUS, 1941-45. Named Juneau Man of Year, 1974. Fellow Am. Coll. Trial Attys.; mem. ABA, Alaska Bar Assn. (pres. 1961-62), Juneau Bar Assn. (pres. 1971-72), Am. Judicature Soc. (dir. 1970-74), Am. Law Inst., Juneau C. of C. (pres. 1952, 55), Alaskans United (chmn. 1962). Clubs: Marine Meml, Wash. Athletic, Juneau Racket, Altadena Town and Country. Home: 336 Orange Grove Blvd Pasadena CA 91105 Office: US Ct Appeals 9th Cir 125 S Grand Ave Pasadena CA 91109-1510

BOOKMAN, PHILIP, newspaper editor; b. N.Y.C., July 11, 1936; s. Henry and Anne (Mandel) B.; children—Jonathan, Charles; m. H. Mary (Bookman,) Oct. 25, 1975. B.A. in English Lit., U. Buffalo, 1957. Assoc. editor Lebhar-Friedman Publs., N.Y.C., 1959-63; regional editor Evening Press, Binghamton, N.Y., 1964-71; asst. mng. editor Sun-Bull., Binghamton, 1971-74; mng. editor Camden (N.J.) Courier-Post, 1975-80; exec. editor The Record, Stockton, Calif., 1980—. Served with U.S. Army, 1959, U.S. N.G., 1959-61. Mem. AP Mng. Editors Assn. (bd. dirs.), Calif. Freedom of Info. Com. (chmn., exec. com.), Sigma Delta Chi. Office: Stockton Record 530 E Market St Stockton CA 95202

BOONE, CHARLES DANIEL, computer programmer; b. Cheyenne, Wyo., June 21, 1949; s. Grady Henry and Eileen (Gustafson) B.; m. Sally Butcher, Sept. 29, 1979; 1 child, Michael Charles. BSChemE, Washington U., St. Louis, 1971; cert. in computer programming, Community Coll. Denver, 1986. Engr. Emerson Electric Co., St. Louis, 1971-73; research and devel. engr. 3M Co., St. Paul, 1973-77; tech. service engr. Gen. Electric Co., Pittsfield, Mass., 1977-81; project mgr. Plastic Tooling Aids, Boulder, Colo., 1981-84; computer programmer IBM, Boulder, 1986—. Avocations: reading, classical music, sailing. Home: 2412 Tulip St Longmont CO 80501 Office: IBM PO Box 1900 Boulder CO 80306

BOONE, DANIEL RICHARD, speech disorders educator; b. Chgo., Oct. 30, 1927; s. Claude Benjamin and Pearl Lillian (Richardson) B.; m. Mary Augusta Mosenthal, Dec. 28, 1954; children: Mary P., James R., Robert T., Rebecca A. BA, U. Redlands, 1951; MA, Case Western Res. U., 1954, PhD, 1958. Chief speech pathology Highland View Hosp., Cleve., 1956-60; asst. prof. speech disorders Case Western Res. U., Cleve., 1960-63; assoc. prof. U. Kans. Med. Ctr., Kansas City, 1963-66; prof. U. Denver, 1966-73, U. Ariz., Tucson, 1973—; cons. U.S. Office Edn., Washington, 1967-75, NIH, Bethesda, Md., 1975-85, Prentice-Hall, Englewood Cliffs, N.J., 1973—. Author: The Voice and Voice Therapy, 1971, 3d rev. edit. 1983, Cerebral Palsy, 1973, Human Communication and Its Disorders, 1987; also articles to profl. jours. Served as cpl. U.S. Army, 1945-47, Korea. Recipient Disting. Service award U. Redlands, Calif., 1978. Fellow Am. Speech Lang. and Hearing Assn. (v.p. 1969, pres. 1975-77); mem. Colo. Speech and Hearing Assn. (pres. 1971), Ariz. Speech and Hearing Assn., Acad. Aphasia (treas. 1969-72), Sigma Xi. Democrat. Avocations: tennis, fiction writing, hiking, jazz. Home: 5715 N Genematas Dr Tucson AZ 85704

BOONE, DAVID RIDGWAY, microbial ecology educator; b. Lewes, Del., Jan. 19, 1952; s. Daniel Herbert and Grace (Bradley) B.; m. Jane Emslie, Sept. 4, 1976; 1 child, Michael David. BS in Microbiology, U. Fla., 1973, PhD in Microbiology and Cell Sci., 1977. Postdoctoral fellow U. Ill., Urbana, 1978-79; asst. research officer Alta. Research Council, Edmonton, Can., 1979-82, assoc. research officer, 1982-84; asst. prof. environ. microbiology UCLA Sch. Pub. Health, 1984—. Contbr. articles to profl. jours.; chpts. to books. Mem. Am. Soc. Microbiology, Soc. Indsl. Microbiology, AAAS, Sigma Xi. Democrat. Avocations: mountaineering, bridge, botany. Home: 5335 Village Green Los Angeles CA 90016 Office: UCLA Sch Pub Health Los Angeles CA 90024

BOONE, JAMES VIRGIL, engineering executive; b. Little Rock, Sept. 1, 1933; s. Virgil Bennett and Dorothy Bliss (Dorough) B.; m. Gloria Marjorie Gieseler, June 5, 1955; children—Clifford B., Sandra J. Smyser, Steven B. B.S. in Elec. Engring., Tulane U., 1955; M.S.E.E., Air Force Inst. Tech., Ohio, 1959. Assoc. elec. engr. Martin Co., Balt., 1955; research and develop. engr. U.S. Air Force, 1955-62; electronics engr. Nat. Security Agy., Ft.

Meade, Md., 1962-77, dep. dir. for research and engring., 1978-81; spl. asst. to gen. mgr. Mil. Electronics div. TRW, Inc., San Diego, 1981-83, asst. gen. mgr., 1983-85, dir. program mgmt. and group devel. TRW Electronic Systems Group, 1985-86, v.p., dir. program mgmt. and group devel, 1986-87; v.p., gen. mgr. Defense Communications div. TRW Electronic Systems Group, 1987; Served to capt. USAF, 1955-62. Recipient Nat. Security Agy. Exceptional Civilian Service award, 1975. Mem. IEEE (sr.), AIAA. Republican. Presbyterian (elder). Contbr. articles to profl. jours. Home: 3030 Deluna Dr Rancho Palos Verdes CA 90274 Office: One Space Park Redondo Beach CA 90278

BOONE, SHARON LARAE, aerospace company chemist; b. Rapid City, S.D., Sept. 5, 1959; d. Raymond Edward and Mary (Deisz) Wagner; m. Robert Dale Boone, May 16, 1981; 1 child, Rachel Larae. BS in Chemistry, S.D. Sch. Mines and Tech., 1981, MS in Chemistry, 1982. Chemist Dow Chem. Co., Midland, Mich., 1982-85, Hercules Aerospace Co., Magna, Utah, 1985—. Mem. Am. Chem. Soc. Office: Hercules Aerospace Co PO Box 98 Magna UT 84044

BOONE, TIMOTHY ALLEN, organization development consultant; b. Watsonville, Calif., June 14, 1945; s. Arthur Merle and Lillian Margaret (Rudolph) B.; m. Marabee Kay Rush, Feb. 14, 1965 (div. Dec. 1974); m. Linda Lee Snyder, Jan. 10, 1975; children: Jennifer Susan, Conor Patrick. BA in Psychology, Chapman Coll., 1974; MA in Human Resource Mgmt., Pepperdine U., 1975; PhD in Human Behavior, U.S. Internat. U., 1981. Lectr. orgn. devel. Monterey (Calif.) Inst. Fgn. Studies, 1974; commd. U.S. Army, 1965, advanced through grades to capt., 1968, resigned, 1976; staff trainer, cons. University Assocs., Inc., La Jolla, Calif., 1976-80, v.p. ops., 1978-79, v.p. profl. services, chief ops. officer, sr. cons., grad. sch. faculty mem., 1979-80; gen. mgr. NTL/Learning Resources Corp., San Diego, Calif., 1976-78; dir. orgn. devel. services Ctr. Leadership Studies, Escondido, Calif., 1980-81; ptnr., cons. Keilty, Goldsmith & Boone, La Jolla, 1981-87; dir. human resource devel. Coca-Cola U.S.A., Atlanta, 1987—. Contbr. articles to profl. jours. Chmn. Community Goals Monitoring com., Poway Unified Sch. Dist., 1977; youth dir. Monterey Peninsula Jaycees, 1974. Decorated Bronze Star (2), Air medal (3), Purple Heart. Mem. Am. Acad. Mgmt., Orgn. Devel. Network. Republican. Mem. Chs. of Christ.

BOOTH, CHARLES BENNY, computer systems company executive; b. Memphis, Sept. 1, 1948; s. Elza Lathe and Mary Nadine (Johnson) B.; B.S., Ariz. State U., 1971; m. Sylvia Kay Pickett, June 10, 1967; children—Charles David, Dennis Wayne. Acct., Sol G. Oxford, C.P.A., Odessa, Tex., 1965-68, Grand's Plumbing Co., Phoenix, 1969-70; partner Raymond & Booth, C.P.A.s, Scottsdale, Ariz., 1971-78; pres. R & B Computer Systems, Inc., Tempe, Ariz., 1978-83, dir., 1981-83; dir. DIMIS, Inc., Ocean Twp., N.J. Computer Systems House, 1982-83; controller Transform Logic Corp., 1983-86, sec. and treas., 1985-86, owner Transfirst Bus. Brokers, 1986—. C.P.A., Ariz. Mem. Am. Inst. C.P.A.s, Ariz. Soc. C.P.A.s. Democrat. Baptist. Office: 1108 E Greenway Mesa AZ 85203

BOOTH, WALLACE WRAY, electrical distribution and aerospace executive; b. Nashville, Sept. 30, 1922; s. Wallace Wray Booth and Josephine England; m. Donna Cameron Voss, Mar. 22, 1947; children: Ann Conley (Mrs. F. Brian Cox), John England. BA, U. Chgo., 1948, MBA, 1948. Various positions Ford Motor Co., Dearborn, Mich., 1948-59; v.p. fin., treas. dir. Ford Motor Co., Toronto, Ont., 1959-63; mng. dir., chief exec. officer Ford Motor Co. Australia, Melbourne, 1963-67; v.p. corp. staffs, indsl. products Philco-Ford Corp., Phila., 1967-68; sr. v.p. corp. staffs, mem. exec. com. Rockwell Internat. Corp., El Segundo, Calif., 1968-75; pres., chief exec. officer United Brands Co., Boston, 1975-77, also dir.; chmn., chief exec. officer Ducommon, Inc., Los Angeles, 1977—, pres., 1987—; dir. First Interstate Bank of Calif., Rohr Industries, Litton Industries, Inc., Navistar Internat. Corp., Chgo. Past pres. United Way, Los Angeles; pres. Children's Bur. Los Angeles. Served to 1st lt. USAAF, 1943-46. Office: Ducommon Inc 611 W Sixth St Los Angeles CA 90017 *

BOOTHE, JAMES STEVEN, chemical engineer; b. Portales, N.Mex., Nov. 6, 1948; s. James Elmer and Sammie Elizabeth (Sparks) B.; m. Barbara Ann Wise, Nov. 27, 1982; 1 child, Carrie Dee. BSChemE, N.Mex. State U., 1971. Research engr. Tex. Eastman, Longview, 1971-74; prodn. mgr. Merichem Co., Houston, 1974-81; assoc. Purvin & Gertz, Dallas, 1981-82; plant engr. Mountain Devel., Portales, N.Mex., 1984; engr. Howe-Baker Engrs., Portales, 1985; plant engr. Energy Fuels Devel. Corp., Portales, 1985—. V.p. Portales Council Camp Fire, 1985-86; chmn. bd. 1st Christian Ch., Pasadena, Tex., 1978-79; local sec. Salvation Army, 1984—. Served with USNG, 1972-80. Republican. Lodge: Lions (pres. Portales club 1986—). Avocations: hunting, shooting, woodworking, bicycling, gardening. Office: Energy Fuels Devel Corp PO Box 892 Portales NM 88130

BOOTHE, JAY BRIAN, architect; b. Glendale, Calif., Apr. 28, 1951; s. William Howard Boothe and Marjorie Jan (Martin) Johnson; m. Phyllis Ann Runner, Feb. 11, 1979. BArch, Calif. State U., Pomona, 1975. Registered architect, Calif. Archtl. designer Robert Englekirk Inc., Honolulu, 1977-80; sr. project architect, assoc. Gruen Assocs. Architects and Planners, Los Angeles, 1980—. Prin. works include Regent Hotel, Costa Mesa, Calif., Beverly Wilshire Hotel (renovation), Beverly Hills, Calif., Montebello (Calif.) Town Ctr., Beverly Square, Los Angeles, Koreatown Plaza, Los Angeles. Served with USN, 1970-77. Named one of Outstanding Young Men of Am., 1985. Mem. AIA (pub. relations com. 1985-86), Nat. Trust for Hist. Preservation, Nat. Wildlife Fedn. Republican. Avocations: travelling, fishing, hunting, golfing, tennis. Office: Gruen Assocs 6330 San Vicente Blvd Los Angeles CA 90048

BOOZE, THOMAS FRANKLIN, toxicologist; b. Denver, Mar. 4, 1955; s. Ralph Walker and Ann (McNatt) B.; m. Patricia Jude Bullock, Aug. 8, 1981; 1 child, Heather N. BS, U. Calif., Davis, 1978; MS, Kans. State U., 1981, PhD, 1985. Asst. instr. Kans. State U., Manhattan, 1979-85; toxicologist Chevron Environ. Health Ctr., Richmond, Calif., 1985—; cons. in field, Manhattan, Kans., 1981-83. contbr. articles to profl. jours. Vol. Amigos de las Americas, Marin County, Calif., 1973, Hospice Care, Manhattan, 1985. Mem. AAAS, N.Y. Acad. Sci., Soc. of Toxicology, Sigma Xi. Home: 233 Oriole Ct Hercules CA 94547 Office: Chevron Environ Health Ctr PO Box 4054 Richmond CA 94804

BORANE, RAY ANTHONY, JR., school superintendent; b. Douglas, Ariz., June 18, 1938; s. Ray Anthony and Alyce (Salem) B.; m. Mary L. Bourdo, June 7, 1969; children—Joseph Bourdo, Michael Bourdo. B.A., Ariz. State U., 1961, M.A., 1968; postgrad. Universidad Libre de Colombia, Bogota, 1963, Universidad de Guadalajara, Mex., 1967. Spanish tchr. Douglas High Sch., Ariz., 1960-72, athletic dir., 1966, chmn. lang. dept., 1966-72, basketball coach, 1968-72, vice prin., 1972-74, asst. supt. Douglas Unified Sch. Dist. 27, 1974-77, supt., 1977—; spl. agt. FBI, Washington, 1964; coach Ariz. High Sch. All Stars South Basketball Team, 1968; mem. Ariz. Bd. Edn., Phoenix, 1984—, Ariz. Bd. Vocat. Edn., Phoenix, 1984—. Mem. exec. bd. Cochise County Fair Assn., Douglas., mem. citizens' adv. council Ariz. Dept. Corrections, 1984—, So. Ariz. Affirmative Action Council; spl. FBI agt., Washington, 1963. Active Ariz. Nat. Guard, 1955-63. Recipient Youth award VFW, Douglas, 1981, Meritorious and Disting. Service award, 1982; Community Service award Ariz. dept. Am. Legion, 1983. Mem. So. Ariz. Sch. Supts. (pres. 1983-84), Ariz. Sch. Adminstrs., Pinal County Sch. Adminstrs. (hon.), Mem. Ariz. Bd. Edn. (v.p. 1986, pres. 1987), Cochise County Sch. Adminstrs., Pinal County Sch. Adminstrs. (hon.), Cochise County Hist. and Archaeol. Soc., Nat. Assn. State Bds. Edn., Douglas C. of C., Future Farmers Am. (hon. chpt. farmer), Sigma Delta Mu, Phi Delta Kappa. Democrat. Roman Catholic. Home: 2408 9th St Douglas AZ 85607 Office: Douglas Unified Sch Dist 27 11 1132 12th St PO Drawer 1237 Douglas AZ 85067

BORCHARDT, DONALD RICHARD, mechanical engineer; b. Manitowoc, Wis., May 22, 1934; s. Richard Albert and Arleen Viola (Erickson) B.; m. Suzanne Joy Stutzke, Apr. 7, 1956; children: Ellen Suzanne, Mark Donald, Matthew Richard. BSME, Mich. State U., 1959; cert. Man in the Sea program, UCLA, 1963. Mem. tech. staff Martin Marietta, Denver, 1959-61; project engr. TRW Systems, Redondo Beach, Calif., 1961-71; dept. mgr. Global Marine Devel., Inc., Los Angeles, Irvine (Calif.) and Houston, 1971-85; mgr. program Lockeed Calif. Co., Burbank, 1985—. Contbr. articles to profl. jours. Leader YMCA, Indian Guides, Boy Scouts Am., Fountain Valley, Calif., 1970-73; holder various offices Grace Luth. Ch., Huntington Beach, Calif. Recipient Disting. Service award YMCA, Fountain Valley, 1973. Mem. ASME, Nat. Mgmt. Assn., Pi Tau Sigma. Avocations: woodworking, traveling, WWI aircraft models, radio control aircraft. Home: 7780 Via Rosa Maria Burbank CA 91504 Office: Lockheed Calif Co PO Box 551 Burbank CA 91520

BORCHARDT, GLENN A., soil mineralogist; b. Watertown, Wis.; s. Arnold William and Marjorie Ellen B.; m. Marilyn Gerbig, June 12, 1965; children: Nina, Natalie. BS in Soil Sci., U. Wis., 1964, MS in Soil Clay Mineralogy, 1966; PhD in Soil Mineralogy, Oreg. State U., 1969. Postdoctoral research associate NRC U.S. Geol. Survey, Denver, 1969-71; soil mineralogist Calif. Div. Mines and Geology, Pleasant Hill, 1972—; cons. Merrill, Seely, Mullen & Sandefur, Pleasanton, Calif., 1984—. Contbr. articles to profl. jours.; author: Clay Minerals and Slope Stability, 1977, Stabilization of Landslides, 1984. Recipient Herfurth Efficiency award; Louis Ware Scholar. Mem. Soil Sci. Soc. Am., Clay Minerals Soc., Geol. Soc. Am. (assoc. editor 1972-82), AAAS, Philosophy of Sci. Assn., Sigma Xi, Alpha Zeta, Phi Kappa Phi. Home: PO Box 5335 Berkeley CA 94705 Office: Calif Div Mines and Geology 380 Civic Dr Pleasant Hill CA 94523

BORCHARDT, JAMES GERALD, safety engineer; b. Racine, Wis., Feb. 18, 1947; s. Harold William and Anne Emma (Kloss) B.; m. Lois Ann Dennis, May 6, 1972; children: Julia Andrea, James Dennis, Christopher Andrew. BA in Math., Ill. State U., 1970. Cert. product safety mgr., safety profl. Loss prevention rep. Liberty Mut. Ins. Co., Detroit, 1970-72; loss prevention cons. Liberty Mut. Ins. Co., Rockford, Ill., 1972-75; asst. loss prevention mgr. Liberty Mut. Ins. Co., Chgo., 1975-79; loss prevention mgr. Liberty Mut. Ins. Co., San Francisco, 1979-83, tech. cons., 1983—. Safety commr. Town of Moraga, Calif., 1980-82. Mem. Am. Soc. Safety Engrs. (Bay area dir. National Safety in Workplace 1985, mem. public relations com. 1983-85, program com. 1977-79, mgmt. div. 1983—), Vets. of Safety. Home: 11 Gloria Ct Moraga CA 94556-1905 Office: Liberty Mut Ins Co 216 Pine St San Francisco CA 94104

BORCHARDT, KENNETH ANDREW, microbiology consultant, educator; b. Chgo., Sept. 20, 1928; s. Leo Andrew and Edith R. (Peterson) B.; m. C. Joyce Truitt, Feb. 6, 1954; children: Gregory David, Kimberly Jo, Jeffrey Andrew. BS, Loyola U., Chgo., 1950; MS, Miami U., Oxford, Ohio, 1951; PhD, Tulane U., 1961. Chief clin. microbiologist Fitzsimmons Army Hosp., Denver, 1957-58, Letterman Army Hosp., San Francisco, 1961-65; commd. USPHS, 1965, advanced through grades to capt., 1983, resigned, 1982; prof., cons. microbiology San Francisco State U., 1982—. Contbr. articles to med. jours. Fellow in Tropical Medicine, La. State U., 1970. Fellow Am. Acad. Microbiology, Royal Acad. Tropical Medicine and Hygiene (London); mem. N.Y. Acad. Scis., Sigma Xi. Republican. Lutheran. Avocation: organ. Home: 15 Capilano Dr Novato CA 94947 Office: San Francisco State U 1600 Holloway Ave San Francisco CA 94132

BORCHERDT, EDWARD RAHR, JR., foreign trade company executive; b. Butte, Mont., July 12, 1930; s. Edward Rahr and Martha (Youlden) B.; m. Wendy Hawley, July 6, 1958; children: Kimberley, Edward Rahr. AB in History, Stanford U., 1953, MBA, 1957. With Pope & Talbot, Inc., San Francisco, 1957-59, Crown Zellerbach Corp., Los Angeles, 1959-60; sr. staff cons. George Fry & Assocs., Los Angeles, 1960-66; founder, chmn. Calif. Small Bus. Devel. Co., Los Angeles, 1966—; fgn. trade cons. Brocherdt & Co., Los Angeles, Washington and Seoul, Republic of Korea, 1966—; pres. Western Video Industries, Inc., Los Angeles, 1968-71, Korean War Meml., Inc., Washington, 1984-86; chmn. Monterey Vineyards, Gonzales, Calif., 1974-75, West Bay Fin. Corp., Newport Beach, Calif, 1972-74, E. Africa Fisheries Co., Ltd., Dar es Salaam. Bd. visitors (Presdl. appointment) U.S. Naval Acad., 1981—; Taft Sch. rep. Los Angeles area, 1965-80; mem. Los Angeles World Affairs Council; sr. warden and Sunday sch. tchr. All Sts. Episcopal Ch., Beverly Hills, Calif., 1972-81; trustee Devil Pups, Inc. Served as officer, inf. USMC, 1953-55. Mem. The Asia Soc., U.S.-Korea Soc., Capitol Marines, Am. Legion, Marine Corps. League. Republican. Clubs: Beach (Los Angeles); Rancheros Vistadores (Santa Barbara, Calif.); Marines Meml. (San Francisco). Home: 400 S Bentley Ave Los Angeles CA 90049 Office: 10960 Wilshire Blvd Suite 500 Los Angeles CA 90049 Office: 2000 M St NW Suite 200 Washington DC 20036

BORDALLO, RICARDO JEROME, governor of Guam; b. Sumay, Guam, Dec. 11, 1927; s. Baltazar Jerome and Josephine Torres (Pangelinan) B.; m. Madeleine Zeien, June 20, 1953; 1 child, Deborah Bordallo Gerber. Student U. San Francisco, 1948-50. Owner, operator Toyota dealership, Guam, 1956-1974, Ricky's Enterprises, 1956-1975; pub. Pacific Jour., Guam, 1966; chmn., dir. Family Fin. Co., 1959-74; mem. Guam Legislature, 1956-70, elected minority leader 8th Guam Legislature, 1964, chmn. Democratic Party of Guam, 1960-63, 1971-73, del. to Nat. Dem. Conv., 1964, 68, gov. of Guam, 1974-78, 1982-86. Bd. dirs. Marianas Assn. for Retarded Children, 1962-64, Navy League of Guam, 1965-73; vice chmn., bd. dirs. ARC; active Guam Tourist Commn., 1963-65, Guam Spl. Olympics orgn. Mem. Guam C. of C., 1960-73. Lodge: Lions (pres. 1956). Office: Executive Chambers PO Box 2950 Agana GU 96910

BORDEN, GAIL JOHNSON, human factors engineering executive; b. Los Angeles, July 16, 1935; s. Lewie Colona and Lillian James (Snyder) B.; m. Dorothy Alison Dalgetty, Jan. 4, 1960; children: Todd William, Jonathan Gail. BA, U. So. Calif., 1962. V.p. Human Factors Research, Inc., Santa Barbara, Calif., 1961-76; pres. Human Performance Research, Inc., Goleta, Calif., 1976—. Contbr. artilces to profl. publs. Served to lt. USN, 1956-60. Office: Human Performance Research Inc 616 Carlo Dr Goleta CA 93117

BOREK, MARY BURNS, psychologist; b. Pitts. Sept. 6, 1916; s. Joseph Anthony and Myral (Anderson) Burns; m. Theodore Borek, Mar. 3, 1943; 1 son, Theodore B. A.B., West Liberty Coll., 1942; M.A., Columbia U., 1953; Ed.D., Ariz. State U., 1970. Lic. psychologist, Ariz. Instr. chemistry West Liberty (W.Va.) Coll., 1945-48; counselor Phoenix Union High Sch. Dist., 1953-75, psychologist, 1975-82; pvt. practice psychology, Phoenix, 1982—; co-dir. human relations workshops. Mem. Am. Psychol. Assn., Ariz. Psychol. Assn. Mem. United Ch. Christ. Author: Problem Solving, 1977. Address: 1526 W Avalon Dr Phoenix AZ 85015

BOREL, JAMES DAVID, physician; b. Chgo., Nov. 15, 1951; s. James Albert and Nancy Ann (Sieverson) B. BS, U. Wis., 1973; MD, Med. Coll. of Wis., 1977. Diplomate Am. Bd. Anesthesiology, Nat. Bd. Med. Examiners, Am. Coll. Anesthesiologists. Research asst. McArdle Lab. for Cancer Research, Madison, Wis., 1972-73, Stanford U. and VA Hosp., Palo Alto, 1976-77; intern. The Cambridge (Mass.) Hosp., 1977-78; clin. fellow in medicine Harvard Med. Sch., Boston, 1977-78, clin. fellow in anaesthesia, 1978-80, clin. instr. in anaesthesia, 1980; resident in anesthesiology Peter Bent Brigham Hosp., Boston, 1978-80; anesthesiologist Mt. Auburn Hosp., Cambridge, 1980; fellow in anesthesiology Ariz. Health Scis. Ctr., Tucson, 1980-81; research assoc. U. Ariz. Coll. Medicine, Tucson, 1980-81, assoc. in anesthesiology, 1981—; active staff Mesa (Ariz.) Luth. Hosp., 1981—; courtesy staff Scottsdale (Ariz.) Meml. Hosp., 1982—; vis. anaesthetist St. Joseph's Hosp., Cambridge, 1980. Contbr. numerous articles to profl. jours. Mem. AMA, AAAS, Mass. Anesthesia Council on Edn., Ariz. Anesthesia Alumni Assn., Ariz. Soc. Anesthesiologists, Am. Soc. Regional Anesthesia, Can. Anesthestists' Soc., Internat. Anesthesia Research Soc., Am. Soc. Anesthesiologists. Office: Valley Anesthesia Cons 2000 N 7th St Phoenix AZ 85006

BORENSTEIN, DANIEL BERNARD, physician, educator; b. Silver City, N.Mex., Mar. 31, 1935; s. Jack and Marjorie Elizabeth (Kerr) B.; B.Ch.E., MIT, 1957; M.D., U. Colo., 1962; m. Bonnie Denice Ulland, June 11, 1967; 1 son, Jay Brian. Intern, U. Hosp., U. Ky., 1962-63; resident psychiatry U. Colo. Med. Center, 1963-66, chief resident, instr. dept. psychiatry U. Colo. Sch. Medicine, 1965-66; instr. dept. psychiatry U. So. Calif. Sch. Medicine, 1966-67, asst. clin. prof. dept. psychiatry UCLA Sch. Medicine, 1972-84, assoc. clin. prof., 1984—, founder, dir. Mental Health Program for Physicians in Tng., 1980-84; clin. assoc. Los Angeles Psychoanalytic Soc. and Inst., 1967-71, pres. clin. assocs., 1970-71, faculty, 1973-83, sr. faculty, 1983—; pvt. practice medicine specializing in psychoanalysis and psychiatry, West Los Angeles, 1966—; assoc. vis. psychiatrist UCLA Ctr. Health Scis., 1973—. Served to lt. AUS, 1957-58. Diplomate Am. Bd. Psychiatry and Neurology. Fellow Am. Psychiat. Assn. (council Area VI 1977-79, 81—, dep. rep. assembly of dist. brs. 1981-82, rep. 1982—, com. to rev. psychiat. news 1979-81, nominating com. 1982-83, assembly liaison to peer rev. com. 1982-86, assembly liaison to fin. and mktg. com. 1986—, med. student edn. com. 1987—); mem. So. Calif. Psychiat. Soc. (outstanding service citation 1975, chmn. peer rev. com. 1974-77, exec. council 1976—, mem. ethics com. 1977-85, pres. 1978-79, chmn. fellowship and awards com. 1979-85, chmn. Commn. on Psychiatry and the Law 1980-81, 1st recipient Disting. Service award 1984, Appreciation award 1979), Los Angeles County Med. Assn. (chmn. Bay dist. mental health com. 1979-85, 87—, bd. dirs. 1981—, com. on substance abuse 1981-86, v.p. 1985-86, pres. elect 1986-87, com. on well-being, 1986—), Calif. Med. Assn. (rep. for psychiat. specialty to Ho. of Dels. 1979-86, com. on mental health and mental disabilities 1979-85, del. 1986—), Calif. Psychiat. Assn. (chmn. legal and judicial com.), Los Angeles Psychoanalytic Soc. and Inst. (co-chmn. extension div. 1973-74, chmn. peer rev. com. 1975-78, mem. curriculum com. 1980-84), Am. Psychoanalytic Assn. (com. on confidentiality 1983—, com. on govt. relations and ins. 1983—), Internat. Psychoanalytic Assn. Author: Manual of Psychiatric Peer Review, 3d rev. edit., 1985, Psychiatric Peer Review: Prelude and Promise, 1985; contbr. articles to profl. publs. Office: 151 N Canyon View Dr Los Angeles CA 90049

BORER-SKOV, LONDA LOU, chemistry educator; b. Windom, Minn., Mar. 7, 1942; d. Archie and Charlotte Eliza (Roesner) Borer; m. Luther Jǿrgen Skov, June 20, 1976. AA, Concordia Coll., St. Paul, 1961; BS, Concordia Coll., Seward, Nebr., 1963; PhD, Wayne State U., 1972. Tchr. Luth. High Sch., Harper Woods, Mich., 1963-67; sci. tchr. Luth. High Sch., Mayer, Minn., 1967-68; assoc. prof. chem. Calif. State U., Sacramento, 1973-85, prof. chem., 1985—; research chemist Naval Weapons Ctr., Crane, Ind., 1981; vis. scholar U. Va., Charlottesville, 1986. Author: (lab. manual) Chemistry for Liberal Studies Majors, 1975, rev. eds., 1976—; contbr. articles to profl. jours. Grantee Calif. State U. Found, 1978—. Mem. Am. Chem. Soc. (local soc. treas. 1983-85). Republican. Lutheran. Avocations: traveling, cooking, skiing, walking. Office: Calif State U 6000 J St Sacramento CA 95819

BORESI, ARTHUR PETER, educator, author; b. Toluca, Ill.; s. John Peter and Eva (Grotti) B.; m. Clara Jean Gordon, Dec. 28, 1946; children—Jennifer Ann Boresi Hill, Annette Boresi Pueschel, Nancy Jean. Student, Kenyon Coll., 1943-44; B.S. in Elec. Engring, U. Ill., 1948, M.S., 1949, Ph.D., 1953. Research engr. N. Am. Aviation, 1950; materials engr. Nat. Bur. Standards, 1951; mem. faculty U. Ill. at Urbana, 1953—, prof. theoretical and applied mechanics and nuclear engring., 1959-79; Disting. vis. prof. Clarkson Coll. Tech., Potsdam, N.Y., 1968-69; NAVSEA research prof. Naval Postgrad. Sch., Monterey, Calif., 1978-79; prof. civil engring. U. Wyo., Laramie, 1979—; head U. Wyo., 1980—; cons. in field. Author: Engineering Mechanics, 1959, Elasticity in Engineering Mechanics, 1987, Advanced Mechanics of Materials, 1987, also articles. Served with USAAF, 1943-44; Served with AUS, 1944-46. Founding mem. Am. Acad. Mechanics (treas.); mem. ASME, ASCE, Am. Soc. Engring. Edn., Engring. Sci. Soc., Sigma Xi. Office: Box 3295 Univ Station U Wyo Laramie WY 82071

BORISSOFF, ROBERT ALEXANDER, security company executive, educator; b. Vladivostok, Siberia, Russia, Nov. 4, 1927; came to U.S., 1947, naturalized, 1953; m. Gail V. Pochaeff, Feb. 15, 1952; children: Nicholas, Maria, Boris. B.A., Aurora U., Shanghai, China, 1947; A.A. in Criminology, City Coll. San Francisco, 1961; B.A., Diablo Coll., 1963; grad. Concord Police Acad., 1963. Adminstrv. asst. U.S. Purchasing and Fiscal Office for Calif., San Francisco, 1951-61; police officer Pacifica (Calif.) Police Dept., 1961-65; security cons. Citywide Investigations Co., San Francisco, 1965—; dir. Nor-Cal Security, San Francisco, 1965-81, Nor-Cal. Tng. Acad., San Francisco, 1981—, Master Alarm Co., 1981—; sr. instr. U.S. Army Res. Sch., San Francisco, 1970—; dir. Security Travel Internat., 1978—; hon. del. Am. Police Conf., 1980; cons. in field. Served with U.S. Army, 1945-48; with USAR, 1948—. Recipient commendation Gov. Reagan Calif., 1969, Internat. Security Conf., 1973, U.S. Army, 1981; Mem. Acad. Security Educators and Trainers (cert. security trainer), World Assn. Detectives, Calif. Assn. Lic. Investigators (gov. 1974-75), Nat. Assn. Federally Lic. Fire-Arms Dealers, Nat. Assn. Chiefs of Police, Am. Soc. Indsl. Security, Calif. Security Mgrs. Assn. (v.p. 1984—). Club: Russian-Am. (master-at-arms San Francisco). Author publs. in field. Office: Nor-Cal Tng Acad 2016 Oakdale Ave San Francisco CA 94124

BORJAS, GEORGE J(ESUS), economics educator; b. Havana, Cuba, Oct. 15, 1950; came to U.S., 1962; s. Juan V. Borjas and Edita F. Diaz. BS, St. Peter's Coll., Jersey City, 1971; MA, M in Philosophy, PhD, Columbia U., 1975. Asst. prof. Queens Coll., Flushing, N.Y., 1975-77; research assoc. Nat. Bur. Econ. Research, Cambridge, Mass., 1983—; prof. econs. U. Calif., Santa Barbara, 1978—; cons. Unicon Research Corp., Santa Monica, Calif., 1982—. Editor: Hispanics in the United States, 1985; contbr. articles to profl. jours. Fellow Columbia U. Alumni Fund, 1973, NIHM U. Chgo., 1977; grantee Rockefeller Found., 1983-85. Mem. Am. Econ. Assn., Western Econ. Assn., NAS (mem. panel 1984-85). Roman Catholic. Home: 469 Barker Pass Rd Montecito CA 93108 Office: U Calif Dept Econs Santa Barbara CA 93106

BORN, TED J(AY), mathematics educator; b. Chgo., Sept. 17, 1938; s. Johannes Conrad and Blanda (Newman) B.; m. Dixie Joanne Lee, June 18, 1965; children: Jon-Lee, Jay, Todd, Lea-Ann. BA, Northwestern U., 1960, MA, 1961; MS, U. Ariz., 1972, PhD, 1974. Staff sociologist Dames and Moore, Lakewood, Colo., 1974-75; assoc. prof. George Williams Coll., Downers Grove, Ill., 1975-77; asst. prof. Iowa State U., Ames, 1977-80; ednl. cons. Keystone Area Edn. Assn., Dubuque, Iowa, 1980-81; dir. communications Striker Petroleum, Englewood, Colo., 1982; math. tchr. Cherry Creek Schs., Englewood, 1984-86; instr. math. Arapahoe Community Coll., Littleton, Colo., 1986—; socio-econ. cons. Dames and Moore, 1976. Contbr. articles to profl. jours. Fellow NDEA Title IV, 1966-67, 72-74; Tchr. Interchange fellow U. Hawaii, 1965-66. Mem. Sigma Xi (research grantee 1973), Phi Kappa Phi, Xi Sigma Pi, Gamma Sigma Delta. Avocations: tennis, running.

BOROUGH, HOWARD COLSON, physicist; b. Klamath Falls, Oreg., Mar. 28, 1930; s. Lionel Lincoln and Lorena Helen (Colson) B.; B.S., U. Wash., 1952, M.S., 1956; cert. Inst. Optics, U. Rochester, 1964, U. So. Calif. Image Processing Inst., 1974; children from previous marriage—David, Mark, Brita. Supr. optics group Boeing Aerospace, Seattle, 1956-67; mgr. optics research sect. IIT Research Inst., Chgo., 1967-69; sensor systems mgr. Mil. Spacecraft br. Boeing Aerospace Co., Seattle, 1969-73, mgr. spl. projects Info. Systems div., 1973-79, prin. engr. MX phys. security program, 1980-81, acting mgr. IR optics product devel., 1982—. cons., 1969—; freelance photographer, 1952—. Safety chmn. Wash. State Sports Diving Council. Mem. Am. Soc. Photogrammetry, Soc. Photo Optical Instrumentation Engrs., Underwater Soc. Am. (v.p. N. Pacific area 1983—), Discovery South (pres. 1982-83), Infrared Info. Symposium. Patentee in field; contbr. articles to profl. jours. Club: Wash. State Sports Diving Council (past pres.). Home: 12715 Shorewood Dr SW Seattle WA 98146 Office: PO Box 3999 Seattle WA 98124

BOROVOY, ROGER STUART, lawyer; b. Milw., Apr. 13, 1935; s. Sam and Anne D. (Finkler) B.; m. Brenda Ruth Gordon, June 7, 1959; children: Amy, Richard. B.S., M.I.T., 1956; J.D., Harvard U., 1959. Bar: Mass. 1960, Calif. 1961. Patent atty. Chevron Research Corp., San Francisco, 1960-62; asso. Lippincott, Ralls & Hendricson, San Francisco, 1962-63; patent counsel Fairchild Camera & Instrument Corp., Mountain View, Calif., 1963-74; v.p., gen. counsel, sec. Intel Corp., Santa Clara, 1974-83; ptnr. Sevin Rosen Mgmt., 1983—; dir. Ansa Corp., Palantir Corp., Proteon, Inc., SiScan Corp., Tech. Ctr. Silicon Valley. Served with U.S. Army, 1959. Mem. IEEE. Clubs: M.I.T. of No. Calif, Los Altos Golf and Country. Office: 1245 Oakmead Pky Suite 101 Sunnyvale CA 94086

BORRELL, JERRY, magazine editor; b. El Paso, Tex., May 23, 1952; s. Gerald Joseph and Harriet (Green) B.; divorced; children: Sean, Allistair. BA, U. Miami, 1975; MS, Cath. U., 1981. Researcher U.S. Congress, Washington, 1976-79; sr. editor Computer Graphics, San Francisco, 1979-81; editor in chief Digital Design, Boston, 1981-83; sr. editor MiniMicro Systems, Boston and San Jose, Calif., 1983-85; editor Macworld, San Francisco, 1985—. Contbr. numerous articles to profl. publs. Mem. Assn. Computing Machinery, Soc. Info. Display, Sigma Delta Chi. Home: 2000 Broadway #712 San Francisco CA 94115 Office: PC World Communications 501 2d St Suite 600 San Francisco CA 94107

BORRUP, RONALD JAMES, manufacturer's representative; b. New Brunswick, N.J., Apr. 19, 1920; s. John Jensen and Margaret Elizabeth Addison (Jack) B.; B.S., Worcester Poly. Inst., 1942; m. Margo Vivian Peterson, Aug. 25, 1979; children by previous marriage—David Hollister, Carol Elizabeth, Beth Tracy, John William. Test engr. Hamilton Standard div. United Aircraft Corp., 1946-48; chief design, devel. engr. Safeway Heat Elements Co., 1948-54; founder, pres., chmn. bd. Electro-Flex Heat Inc., 1954-63; founder, dir. Electro-Flex Calif., 1958-61; market devel. engr. Pratt & Whitney Aircraft div. United Aircraft Corp., 1963-67; project engr. Hamilton Standard div., Windsor Locks, Conn., 1967-70; sales mgr. Kaman Automation div. Kaman Aerospace Corp., Bloomfield, Conn., 1970-73; chief engr. Thermal Systems div. Sierracin Corp. (formerly Electroflex Corp. Calif.), Los Angeles, 1974-81; founder Rongo Co., South Pasadena, Calif., 1981—. Pres. congregation Congregational Ch., South Glastonbury, Conn., 1959-60. Served from ensign to lt. USNR, 1942-46. Mem. Lambda Chi Alpha. Republican. Patentee in field. Home: 1311 Lyndon St South Pasadena CA 91030 Office: Rongo Co PO Box 1472 South Pasadena CA 91030

BORSAY, ALEC STEPHEN, safety engineer; b. Ungvar, Hungary, Oct. 9, 1924; came to U.S., 1956, naturalized, 1962; s. Geza Victor and Clementine (Csapo De Ecsed) B.; m. Gabriella Margaret Tasnady, Apr. 20, 1963; 1 child, Gabriella Clementine. BA in Math., Los Angeles City Coll.; BSME, Calif. State U., Los Angeles, 1979. Design engr. Purolator Products, Newbury Park, Calif., 1958-62, Ralph M. Parsons Co., Los Angeles, 1962-64, W.C. Dillon Co., Van Nuys, Calif., 1964-70; material testing engr. City of Los Angeles, 1970-75; safety engr. State of Calif. Indsl. Relations, Santa Fe Springs, 1975—. Mem. Nat. Bd. of Boiler and Pressure Vessel Inspectors, Calif. Cert. Boiler and Elevator Inspectors. Avocation: tennis. Home: 12826 Halkirk St Studio City CA 91604 Office: Calif Dept Indsl Relations 14111 E Freeway Dr Santa Fe Springs CA 90670

BORSHCHEVSKY, ALEXANDER, materials scientist, educator; b. Leningrad, USSR, Jan. 4, 1933; came to U.S., 1978; s. Simon and Ida (Lanzat) B.; m. Lia Meisel, Sept. 11, 1954; 1 child, Misha Lanzat. M in Engring., Poly. Inst., Leningrad, 1956; PhD, Physico-Tech. Inst., Leningrad, 1962; DSc, Inst. Chemistry, Moscow, 1972. Technician, research assoc. Physico-Tech. Inst. Acad. Scis., 1956-77; sr. research assoc. Stanford (Calif.) U., 1978-80; sr. devel. engr. Gen. Instrument, Palo Alto, Calif., 1980-86; with Jet Propulsion Lab., Calif. Inst. Tech., Pasadena, 1986—; instr. Poly. Inst., Leningrad, 1960-62, Leningrad U., 1963-64, San Francisco State U., 1979-80, Cogswell Poly. Coll., San Fransicso, 1981-86. Contbr. articles to sci. jours.; patentee in field. Mem. Am. Assn. Crystal Growth, N. Calif. Crystal Growers. Home: 355 S Marengo Ave #203 Pasadena CA 91101 Office: Calif Inst Tech Jet Propulsion Lab 4800 Oak Grove Dr Pasadena CA 91109

BORTON, WILLIAM MONROE, mgmt. cons.; b. Cambridge, Ohio, Nov. 26, 1914; s. Grover Cleveland and Estella Corinne (Monroe) B.; B.Sc. with honors in Mktg., Ohio State U., Columbus, 1938, M.B.A., 1944; Ph.D. (grantee Sales Execs. Club Los Angeles), U. So. Calif., 1956. Advt. mgr., gen. mgr. J.G. Bair Co., Cambridge, 1939-44; market analyst, sales mgr. Van Tuyl Engring. Corp., Los Angeles, 1944-45; market analyst Lane-Wells Co., Los Angeles, 1945-46; market, product research mgr. Weber Showcase & Fixture Co., Los Angeles, 1946-47; mgmt. cons., Los Angeles, 1947—; instr. bus. Ohio State U., 1944, U. So. Calif., 1946-49, Calif. State U. at Los Angeles, 1949-51, UCLA, 1957-59, 77. Licensed psychologist, Calif. Mem. Am. Psychol. Assn., Am. Mktg. Assn., AAAS, Phi Delta Theta, Phi Eta Sigma, Beta Gamma Sigma. Club: Sports Connection. Contbg. editor So. Calif. Yachting News, 1968-69. Contbr. articles on bus., social sci. to profl. jours. Address: 8400 De Longpre Ave Suite 411 Los Angeles CA 90069

BORUM, WILLIAM DONALD, retired military officer, construction company executive; b. St. Louis, Dec. 26, 1932; s. William Doris and Lura Mae (Jackson) B.; m. Mary Margaret Bullard, Nov. 29, 1952; children—Mary Bradly, Patricia Elaine, Kimberly Anne. B.A. U. Nebr., 1967; M.A., U. So. Calif., 1971; postgrad. U.S. Army Staff Coll., 1968, NATO Defense Coll., 1975-76. Commd. 2d lt. U.S. Army, 1954, advanced through grades to col., 1975; various assignments in Fed. Republic Germany, Iran, Lebanon, Socialist Republic of Vietnam, Rome, London, The Netherlands, 1954-72; with Office Dep. Chief of Staff for Ops., Pentagon, 1972-75; served at NATO Hdqrs., Netherlands, 1976-79; dep. commdr. Engrs. Div., South Pacific, 1979-84; ret., 1984; constrn. exec. Williams and Burrows, Belmont, Calif., 1984—. Editor, project mgr. plan for constrn. of deployment facilities for MX missile system, 1980. Active Republican Nat. Com., 1982—. Decorated Legion of Merit with one oak leaf cluster, Bronze Star with one oak leaf cluster, Air medal, Purple Heart, others. Mem. Soc. Am. Mil. Engrs., Assn. U.S. Army, Acad. Polit. Sci., Calif. Acad. Sci. Episcopalian. Clubs: California, Commonwealth, Queens (San Francisco). Home: 1805 Alderwood Ct San Mateo CA 94403 Office: Williams and Burrows Inc 500 Harbor Blvd Belmont CA 94402

BORYLA, VINCE, professional basketball team executive; b. East Chicago, Ind., Mar. 11, 1927; m. Cappie Boryla; children: Karen, Mike, Mark, Matt, Vinnie. Student, Notre Dame U., Denver U. Profl. basketball player Nat. Basketball Assn.; with N.Y. Knicks, 1950-54, coach, 1956-58, then gen. mgr.; businessman, pres. Utah Stars, Am. Basketball Assn., 1970-74; pres., gen. mgr. Denver Nuggets, 1984—. Served with USAF, 1941-46. Office: Denver Nuggets McNichols Sports Arena 1635 Clay St PO Box 4658 Denver CO 80204 *

BOSCH, RICHARD LAWRENCE, manufacturing company executive; b. Bklyn., Sept. 21, 1956; s. Francis Lorenzo and Elly (Bobbe) B.; m. Stacy McLoughlin, Jan. 6, 1984. BS in Biology, Chile U., S.Am., 1978; BS in Chemistry, BS in Computer Sci., Adelphi U., 1982; BS in Chem. Engring., Calif. State Long Beach, 1986. Molecular research asst. Adelphi U., Garden City, N.Y., 1979-81; nuclear reactor supr. engr. Mich. State U., East Lansing, 1982-83; staff engr. thermodynamic div. RotoFlow Corp., Santa Monica, Calif., 1983-84; asst. product mgr. Fuller Co., Compton, Calif., 1984—. Mem. Am. Chem. Soc., Am. Inst. Chem. Engrs., Am. Mgmt. Assn. Democrat. Avocations: water skiing, wind surfing, hang gliding. Office: Fuller Co 2966 E Victoria St Compton CA 90225

BOSCH, SAMUEL HENRY, electronics company executive; b. Waupun, Wis., Dec. 24, 1934; s. Henry Samuel and Emma (Elgersma) B.; m. Corinne Marilyn Aardema, June 21, 1958; children—Michelle, Jonathan, David, Sara. B.S. in Physics, San Diego State U., 1961; M.S. in Physics, UCLA, 1962. Mgr. mktg. Digital Equipment Corp., Maynard, Mass., 1969-77; dir. mktg. System Engring. Lab., Ft. Lauderdale, Fla., 1977-79; mgr. mktg. Intel, Hillsboro, Oreg., 1979-81; dir. mktg. Metheus, Hillsboro, 1981-82; pres. ATM Techs., Beaverton, Oreg., 1982-86; pres. Peregrin Data, Beaverton, 1986—. Contbr. articles to profl. jours. Served with U.S. Army, 1955-57. Mem. Am. Electronics Assn., Nat. Petroleum Inst. Republican. Mem. Christian Ref. Ch. Home: 20055 NW Nestucca Dr Portland OR 97229 Office: Peregrin Data 1600 NW Compton Dr Beaverton OR 97006

BOSCO, DOUGLAS H., congressman; b. N.Y.C., July 28, 1946. B.A. in English, Willamette U., 1968, J.D., 1971. Bar: Calif. Practiced la; mem. 98th-100th Congresses from 1st Dist. Calif. Bd. dirs. Marin County Housing Authority; bd. dirs. Marin County Consumer Protection Agy., Sonoma County Fair; fundraiser hosp. ship S.S. Hope; co-founder No. Calif. Emeritus Coll. for Sr. Citizens; mem. Calif. Wildlife Conservation Bd.; mem. Calif. State Assembly, 1978-81, Democratic caucas chmn., 1981. Office: 408 Cannon House Office Bldg Washington DC 20515

BOSE, ANJAN, electrical engineering educator, researcher, consultant; b. Calcutta, India, June 2, 1946; s. Amal Nath and Anima (Guha) B.; m. Frances Magdelen Pavlas, Oct. 30, 1976; children: Rajesh Paul, Shonali Marie, Jahar Robert. B Tech with honors, Indian Inst. Tech., Kharagpur, 1967; MS, U. Calif., Berkeley, 1968; PhD, Iowa State U., 1974. Systems planning engr. Con Edison Co., N.Y.C., 1968-70; instr., research assoc. Iowa State U., Ames, 1970-74; postdoctoral fellow IBM Sci. Ctr., Palo Alto, Calif., 1974-75; asst. prof. elec. engring. Clarkson U., Potsdam, N.Y., 1975-76; mgr. EMSD, Control Data Corp., Mpls., 1976-81; prof. elec. engring. Ariz. State U., Tempe, 1981—; v.p. Power Math Assocs., Tempe, 1981-84. Contbr. over 30 articles to engring. jours.

BOSEKER, EDWARD HERBERT, orthopedic surgeon; b. Fort Wayne, Ind., Feb. 16, 1936; s. Herbert W. and Helen M. (Mueller) B.; B.S. with honors, U. Mich., 1958; M.D., Ind. U., 1962; M.S. in Orthopedic Surgery, 1967; m. Yvonne Jean Park, June 9, 1962; children—Andrea, Susan, Resa. Intern, Lutheran Hosp., Ft. Wayne, Ind., 1962-63; resident Mayo Clinic, Rochester, Minn., 1963-67; practice medicine, specializing in orthopedic surgery, Santa Ana, Calif., 1967—; asst. clin. prof. U. Calif., Irvine, 1970—. Pres. Tustin (Calif.) Unified Sch. Dist., 1980-81, 83-84. Diplomate Am. Bd. Orthopedic Surgeons. Fellow ACS; mem. Am. Acad. Orthopedic Surgeons. Office: 801 N Tustin Santa Ana CA 92705

BOSHEARS, GARY L., utilities executive; b. Medford, Oreg., Mar. 2, 1933; s. Miner Templeton and Myrtle Irene (Beelby) B.; m. Fidelia Janet Boone, June 17, 1956; children: Jeffrey, Mark, Christopher, Nicholas. B in Engring., Yale U., 1956. Registered profl. engr., 1964; cert. purchasing mgr. 1971. With tech. mktg. dept. Gen. Electric Co., San Francisco and Palo Alto, Calif., 1959; test devel. atomic engr. Gen. Electric Co., San Jose, Calif., 1960; engr. Pacific Power & Light Co., Medford, Oreg., 1960-64; asst. to v.p., treas. Pacific Power and Light Co., Portland, Oreg., 1971-73; dir. purchasing and stores Pacific Power and Light Co., Portland, 1973-80, dir. procurement and office services, 1980-84; instr. adult edn. Jackson County, Medford, Oreg., 1962-64; dir. elec. utility City of Ashland, Oreg., 1964-67, city adminstr., 1967-70; dir. local govt. div. Assn. Oreg. Industries, Portland, 1970-71; v.p., gen. mgr. Western Distbn. Service, Inc., Wilsonville, Oreg., 1984-86, pres., 1986—. Contbr. articles to profl. jours. V.p. bd. dirs. Shakespeare Festival Assn., Ashland, 1964-70; pres. Sch. of Hope for Mentally Retarded, Medford, 1966-70, bd. dirs.; bd. dirs. United Fund of Jackson County, Medford, 1967-70, campaign chmn. 1967; bd. dirs. United Way of Oreg., Portland, 1974-83, chmn. 1978-80. Served to lt. (j.g.) USN, 1956-59. Recipient United Fund award United Way, 1963, 67, Disting. Service award City of Ashland, 1967, One of Ten Outstanding Men of Oreg. award, 1967. Mem. Utility Purchasing Mgmt. Group (mem. exec. com. 1984—, vice chmn. 1986-87), Edison Electric Inst. (chmn. exec. com. 1985), N.W. Electric Light & Power Assn. (chmn. 1982-83). Club: Multnomah Athletic (Portland). Lodge: Rotary (found. chmn. East Portland club 1984-85). Home: 3672 SW Tempest Dr Lake Oswego OR 97035 Office: Western Distbn Service Inc 9450 SW Commerce Circle Suite 400 Wilsonville OR 97070

BOSL, GORDON E., architect, specification consultant; b. Milw., May 17, 1927; s. Max J. and Edna C. (Meyer) B.; children: Susan B. Bosl Tangeman, Gail L. Bosl Garver; m. Rita M. Benson Haus, May 22, 1981; stepchildren—Michael, Mary, David, Cathrine Benson. Student Mich. State U.; B.S., U. Wis., Madison, 1951; postgrad. U. N.Mex. Lic. and registered architect, N.Mex.; cert. constrn. specifier. Architect, Bur. Indian Affairs, Albuquerque, 1969-74; asst. chief engr. VA Hosp., Albuquerque, 1974-77; state architect Farmers Home Adminstrn., U.S. Dept. Agr., Albuquerque, 1977-81, State of N.Mex., Santa Fe, 1981-82; ind. practice, 1971—. Served with USAF, 1945-46, ETO. Fellow Constnr. Specification Inst. (cert. com. 1982—, long range planning com. 1980, jury of fellows 1979, chmn. tech. documents com. 1974-76; chpt. bd. dirs. 1971-74, chpt. pres. 1974, chmn. chpt. nominating com. 1975-81, chmn. chpt. tech. com. 1978-80, chmn. SW region conf. 1980, chmn. chpt. bylaws com. 1980-86, nat. bd. dirs. 1984-87; Spl. Chpt. Presdl. award 1974, Region 8 Dir.'s award 1976, Inst. Bd. Dirs. Spl. award 1977, Inst. Pres.'s plaque 1977, Chpt. Outstanding Profl. Mem. award 1980); mem. AIA, Am. Arbitration Assn. (arbitrator 1976—), Mensa. Club: N.Mex. Mountain (Albuquerque). Home: #1 Pool NW Albuquerque NM 87120 Office: 1806 Cardenas Dr NE Albuquerque NM 87110

BOSLER, LAWRENCE M., III, manufacturing engineer; b. Phila., Nov. 21, 1940; s. Lawrence M. Jr. and Emma M. (Weber) B.; m. Carol M. Rankin, Dec. 4, 1965; children: John Lawrence, Robert Lawrence. Diploma, Cleve. Inst. Electronics, 1964. Engring. tech. Philco-Ford Corp., Phila., 1958-71, Optical Scanning Corp., Newtown, Pa., 1971-73, Terak Corp., Scottsdale, Ariz., 1979-81; mgr. ops. Micor Internat., Inc., Tempe, Ariz., 1974-79; mfg. engr. Sundstrand Aviation, Phoenix, 1981—; gen. mgr. Ponderosa, Inc., Warminster, Pa., 1962-76; cons. Computer Consoles, Syracuse, N.Y., 1969. Coach YMCA Soccer Program, Tempe, 1977-82, 86—. Mem. Am. Vecturist Assn. Mem. United Ch. Christ. Avocations: model tractioneering. Office: Sundstrand Aviation 18008-B N Black Canyon Hwy Phoenix AZ 85023

BOSLEY, GARY OSCAR, civic organization administrator; b. Oakland, Calif., Apr. 11, 1944; s. Allen Eugene and Eva Marie Bosley; AB in Econs., U. Calif., Berkeley, 1966. Agrl. specialist, analyst Merrill Lynch, Pierce, Fenner & Smith, Winnipeg, Man., Can., 1971-72, stockbroker, commodity broker, Houston, 1972-74; stockbroker, commodity broker Dean Witter & Co., Hayward, Calif., 1975-84; pvt. investor, 1984-85; exec. v.p. Hawthorne (Calif.) C. of C., 1986—. Rep. candidate for Calif. Assembly, 1976; mem. Alameda County Rep. Cen. Com., 1977-78; mem. Calif. State Rep. Cen. Com., 1977-78; past bd. dirs. Regional Citizens Forum, San Francisco Bay Area; past deacon, past mem. council, past moderator Broadmoor Congregational Ch., San Leandro, Calif. Served to capt. USAF, 1967-71. Decorated Commendation medal. Mem. Rep. Bus. and Profl. Club of Hayward (past pres.), Delta Tau Delta. Clubs: Commonwealth (San Francisco). Lodge: Rotary (past dir. Castro Valley, Calif. club). Address: 17887 Trenton Dr Castro Valley CA 94546

BOSMAJIAN, HAIG ARAM, speech communication educator; b. Fresno, Calif., Mar. 26, 1928; s. Aram and Aurora (Keosheyan) B.; m. Hamida Just, Feb. 27, 1957; 1 child, Harlan. BA, U. Calif., Berkeley, 1949; MA, U. of Pacific, 1951; PhD, Stanford U., 1960. Instr. U. Idaho, Moscow, 1959-61; asst. prof. U. Conn., Storrs, 1961-65; prof. speech communication U. Wash., Seattle, 1965—. Author: Language of Oppression (Orwell award), 1983; editor: Censorship, Libraries and the Law, 1983; Justice Douglas, 1980, Freedom of Speech, 1983, First Amendment in the Classroom Series, 1987. Bd. dirs. Am. Civil Liberties Union, Washington, 1984—. Mem. Nat. Council Tchrs. of English, Speech Communication Assn., AAUP. Office: U Wash Seattle WA 98195

BOSMAJIAN, HAMIDA, English educator; b. Hamburg, Fed. Republic Germany, Apr. 7, 1936; came to U.S., 1952; d. Gerhart and Doris (Becker) Just; m. Haig Bosmajian, Feb. 27, 1957; 1 child, Harlan. BA, U. Idaho, 1960; MA, U. Conn., 1962, PhD, 1968. Prof. English Seattle U., 1966—, Pigott-McCone Humanities chair, 1986—. Editor: This Great Argument the Rights of Women, 1971, Metaphors of Evil: Contemporary German Literature and the Shadow of Nazism, 1979; contbr. articles to children's and contemporary lit. Younger Humanists fellow NEH, 1973-74. Mem. MLA, Nat. Council Tchrs. English, Children's Lit. Assn. Home: 4820 Purdue NE Seattle WA 98105 Office: Seattle U Dept English Seattle WA 98122

BOSS, BRUCE DAVID, wood product manufacturer, photographer; b. Bklyn., Aug. 17, 1940; s. Phillip and Leonora (Rubenstein) B.; m. Dorris Thompson, Dec. 21, 1960 (div. June 1969); children: Deborah Phyllis, Phillip P.; m. Peggy Hawbecker, Aug. 8, 1969; 1 child, Sarah Elizabeth. BS, St. Lawrence U., 1962; PhD in Chemistry, U. Wis., 1966. instr. Modesto (Calif.) Jr. Coll., 1976-77. Contbr. articles to profl. jours. Pres. Toastmasters at NRL, 1973. Recipient Am. Inst. Chemists award 1962, Disting. Civilian Service award FEA, 1974, 76. Mem. Am. Chem. Soc., Phi Beta Kappa, Gamma Sigma Epsilon, Pi Mu Epsilon, Sigma Pi. Democrat. Avocations: photography, bowling, golf. Home and Office: 16223 Lower Colfax Rd Grass Valley CA 95945

BOSS, CLARA MARION, court administrator; b. Chelsea, Mass., Aug. 16, 1943; d. John William and Clara Marguarita (Gormley) Rupe; m. Frederick Allen Boss, May 3, 1965; children: Edward, Thomas, Brian, Kevin, Martha, Katherine. AS, Mt. San Jacinto Coll., 1976; BA in Polit. Sci., Social Sci., Calif. State U., San Bernardino, 1978. Program analyst Inland Manpower Assn., San Bernardino, 1978-81, supr. audit contract property, 1981-83; adminstrv. services officer Riverside (Calif.) Superior Ct., 1983-86, acting ct. exec. officer, 1986-87; sr. mgmt. analyst Riverside (Calif.) Superior Ct., Vista, Calif., 1987—. Mem. juvenile delinquency prevention commn., Riverside County, 1980-81; mem. com. to elect Carver Honne, 1984. Mem. Inland Area Personnel Assn. Baptist. Lodge: Rotary (Rulon Jones award 1976). Avocations: camping, ceramics, needle work. Office: City Hall 600 Eucalyptus Ave Vista CA 92501

BOSSERT, STEVEN THOMAS, education educator; b. San Diego, July 22, 1948; s. Thomas Richard and Evelyn Mae (Harris) B.; m. Linda Gay Gelvin, Oct. 20, 1978; children: Kathleen Ann, Christopher Steven. BA in Sociology, U. Calif., San Diego, 1970; PhD in Edn., U. Chgo., 1975. Asst. prof. sociology U. Mich., Ann Arbor, 1974-80; dir. research Far West Lab., San Francisco, 1980-83; prof., chmn. dept. ednl. adminstrn. U. Utah, Salt Lake City, 1983—. Author: Tasks and Social Relationships in Classrooms, 1979; mem. editorial bd. Sociology of Edn., 1982-84; advisory editor Elem. Sch. Jour., 1983—; sr. assoc. editor Ednl. Adminstrn. Quar., 1986—; contbr. articles to profl. jours. Nat. Inst. Edn. grantee, 1978-84. Mem. Am. Sociol. Assn., Am. Ednl. Research Assn. Presbyterian. Avocations: sailing, skiing. Home: 8499 S Gad Way Sandy UT 84092 Office: U Utah 339 Milton Bennion Hall Salt Lake City UT 84112

BOSSON, CHELL ERIC, mechanical engineer; b. Cannon Falls, Minn., Oct. 31, 1924; s. Nils Evert and Asta Viola (Ahnfors) B.; m. Doris Richards, Mar. 23, 1951 (div. 1976); children—Darryl Winslow, Charles Elliott, Karin Lynne. Diploma in engring., Inst. Tech., Stockholm, Sweden, 1946; B.S. with distinction in M.E., U. Minn., 1950. Registered profl. engr., Wis. Project engr. Calif. Ordnance Research Corp., Altadena, 1953-54; sr. research engr. N.Am. Aviation, Downey, Calif., 1954-60; supr. research engring. N.Am. Rockwell, Anaheim, Calif., 1962-72; sr. engring. specialist Rockwell Internat., Anaheim, 1973—; pres. Chell of Calif. City pub. works commr. La Mirada, Calif. Served with AUS, Honor Guard SHAEF, 1946-48. Mem. Nat. Mgmt. Assn., ASME, IEEE (gyro and accelerometer tech. panel), Vasa Order Am., Pi Tau Sigma. Home: 14209 Jalisco Rd La Mirada CA 90638 Office: 3370 Miraloma Ave Anaheim CA 92803

BOSSUYT, COLETTE MARIE, speech pathologist, educator; b. Mesa, Ariz., Nov. 24, 1957; d. Maurice John and Kathryn May (Knobloch) B. BS, Ariz. State U., 1979, M in Natural Sci., 1983. cert. clin. competent, ESL tchr., lang. tchr. Speech lang. pathologist Gomper's Rehab. Ctr., Phoenix, 1979-80; speech lang. pathologist Chandler (Ariz.) Pub. Schs., 1980-85, lang. disorders specialist, 1985—; ESL adult educator Rio Salado Community Coll., Phoenix, 1985—. Mem. NEA, Ariz. Edn. Assn., Chandler Edn. Assn., Am. Speech Hearing-Lang. Assn. Republican. Roman Catholic. Home: 1650 S Arizona Ave #240 Chandler AZ 85224 Office: Chandler Pub Schs Dist #80 500 W Galveston Chandler AZ 85224

BOSTED, RICHARD JOHN, fire chief; b. Bklyn., May 11, 1931; s. John Reinholt and Helen Mary (DuMolin) B.; A.A., San Jose City Coll., 1969; m. Saundra Sue Payne, Oct. 10, 1957; Fire fighter, engr. Compton (Calif.) Fire Dept., 1955-65; fire capt. Brea (Calif.) Fire Dept., 1965-69; tng. officer Campbell City (Calif.) Fire Dept., 1969-73; fire chief San Carlos (Calif.) Fire Dept., 1973-77, Riverside (Calif.) City Fire Dept., 1977-87; fire protection officer U.S. Dept. State, Washington, 1987—; fire sci. tchr. Santa Ana City Coll., San Jose Community Coll., Coll. San Mateo. Vice pres. We Turn in Pushers, Calif., 1978—. Served with U.S. Army, 1953-55. Recipient Gold award United Way Riverside, 1980; named Man of Year, We Turn In Pushers, 1979-80. Mem. Internat. Assn. Fire Chiefs, Citrus Belt Fire Chiefs (pres. 1983—), Calif. Fire Chiefs Assn. (dir., v.p. 1984—, pres. 1985-86), Assn. Mexican Fire Chief's, Calif. Firemen's Assn., Riverside County Fire Chiefs Assn. (pres. 1984—). Republican. Roman Catholic. Club: Exchange (pres. 1980). Contbr. articles to profl. jours. Home: 909 Le Conte St Riverside CA 92507 Office: 3900 Main St Riverside CA 92522

BOSTICK, LORRAINE, director non-profit organization; b. Buffalo, Dec. 11, 1946; d. Arthur Frederick Wilhelm and Ethel Louise (Wallin) Moll; m. Thomas Durrell Bostick, May 3, 1968 (div. 1987); children: Jason Durrell, Michelle Kathleen. BA in Social Welfare, Calif. State U., Long Beach, 1973; MA in Spl. Edn., Calif. State U., Los Angeles, 1981. Founder, dir. Pegasus Programs, Garden Grove, Calif., 1979-84; ednl. cons. Pegasus Programs, Irvine, Calif., 1979—, pres., 1984—. Author: (book chpt.) Parent Advocacy, 1980; contbr. articles to profl. jours. legis. intern assemblyman for Dennis Mangers, Huntington Beach, Calif., 1979-80; active Gifted and Talented Adv. Com., Garden Grove, Calif., 1981-82; phone counselor New Hope Crystal Cathedral, Garden Grove, 1986—. Recipient Outstanding Service award Orange County Council for Gifted Educators, 1979; Recognition award Gifted Children's Assn., 1979, Calif. Assn. for the Gifted, 1980; Traineeship Gifted Edn. Office of Gifted and Talented, 1980-81. Mem. AAUW (legis. chairperson 1981), Am. Assn. Ednl. Research, Calif. Assn. Counseling Devel., Assn. Calif. Sch. Adminstrs., Newport Beach Area C. of C., Calif. Assn. Gifted, Nat. Assn. Gifted. Democrat. Avocations: humanistic psychology, theatre, traveling. Home: 875 Village Creek Costa Mesa CA 92626 Office: 2900 S Bristol #B-306 Costa Mesa CA 92626

BOSTOCK, RICHARD MATTHEW, plant pathologist, educator; b. Rochester, N.Y., Sept. 23, 1952; s. William Thomas and Virginia Marie (Weaver) B.; m. Katherine Eugenia Bruce, Sept. 14, 1974.; BS, Rhodes Coll., 1974; PhD, U. Ky., 1981. Environ. assoc. Harland Bartholomew & Assocs., Memphis, 1974-75; research asst. U. Ky., Lexington, 1976-81; asst. prof. plant pathology U. Calif., Davis, 1981—. Contbr. numerous articles to profl. jours. Grantee NSF, 1984. Mem. AAAS, Am. Phytopathol. Soc., Am. Chem. soc., Am. Soc. Plant Physiology, Internat. Soc. Plant Molecular Biology. Avocations: tennis, guitar. Office: U Calif Dept Plant Pathology Davis CA 95616

BOSTON, (O.E.) ERNIE, real estate broker; b. New Haven, W. Va.; s. Wilbur Joseph B.; m. Betty Roach, Oct. 11, 1952; children: Brian R., Kerry A. BA, Ohio U., 1949; MBA, Ohio State U., 1950. Cert. real estate broker. Various mgmt. positions in pub. and employee relations Gen. Electric Co., 1952-65; mgr. employee relations Battelle N.W., Richland, Wash., 1965-70; mng. broker Keith Adams & Assocs., Richland, 1970-81; pres., broker Boston Real Estate Assocs., Richland, 1981—; chmn. profl. conduct Tri-City Bd. Realtors, Kennewick, Wash., 1980-85. Columnist Tri-Cities Bus. Rev., 1985-86. Past mem. Franklin County Boundary Rev. Bd.; mem. Wash. State Community Econ. Revitalization Bd., Olympia, 1983—; bd. dirs. Mid-Columbia Symphony, Tri-Cities, Wash., 1986; mem. Region X SBA adv. council, Spokane, Wash., 1986—; pres. Tri-Cities C. of C., 1983-84; chmn. bd. dirs. Tri-Cities Regional Research Bur., 1986; bd. dirs. Southeastern Wash. Devel. Assn. (1982—), Tri-Cities Visitor and Conv. Bur., also v.p.; Served with USN, 1944-46, 50-52. Mem. Realtor's Nat. Mktg. Inst. (cert. residential broker), Nat. Assn. Realtors, Wash. Assn. Realtors, Nat. Inst. Real Estate Cons. (master real estate cons.), Soc. Profls. in Dispute Resolution (assoc.), Am. Arbitration Assn. (comml. panel), Better Bus. Bur. (arbitrator). Lodge: Rotary (pres. Richland club 1970-71, Paul Harris fellow 1983, Tri-Citian of Yr. award 1986). Home: 420 Rd 39 Pasco WA 99301 Office: Boston Real Estate Assocs 511 Lee Blvd Richland WA 99532

BOSTWICK, RICHARD RAYMOND, lawyer; b. Billings, Mont., Mar. 17, 1918; s. Leslie H. and Maude (Worthington) B.; m. Margaret Florence Brooks, Jan. 17, 1944; children: Michael, Patricia, Ed, Dick. Student, U. Colo., 1937-38; A.B., U. Wyo., 1943, J.D., 1947. Bar: Wyo. 1947. Claim atty. Hawkeye Casualty Co., Casper, Wyo., 1948-49; partner Murane & Bostwick, Casper, 1949—; Lectr. U. Wyo. Coll. Law; mem. 10th Cir. Jud. Adv. Com. Contbr. articles profl. jours. Past trustee Casper YMCA; dep. dir. Civil Def., 1954-58; chmn. local SSS, 1952-70; mem. curriculum coordinating com. Natrona Co. Sch. Dist. 2, High Sch. Dist. Served to capt. AUS, 1943-46. Decorated Bronze Star medal; recipient Silver Merit awards Am. Legion. Mem. ABA, Wyo. Bar Assn. (pres. 1964-65), Natrona County Bar Assn. (pres. 1956), Am. Judicature Soc. (exec. com. 1973-75, sec. 1975-77 Herbert Harley award), Internat. Assn. Def. Counsel, Fedn. Ins. and Corp. Counsel, Nat. Conf. Bar Pres. (exec. council 1970-72), Internat. Soc. of Barristers (dir. 1971-76, pres. 1975), Am. Legion (dir. 1951-58, post comdr. 1953-54), Wyo. Alumni Assn. (trustee 1955-57), Casper C. of C. (chmn. legis. com. 1955-57, dir. 1959-62, v.p.). Presbyn. Club: Mason (Shriner, KT). Home: 1137 Granada Ave Casper WY 82601 Office: Wyoming Bldg 350 West A St Suite 100 Casper WY 82601

BOSWELL, CHRISTOPHER ORR, broadcast journalist; b. Milan, Oct. 4, 1957; came to U.S., 1958; s. William Osgood and Janine (Werner) B. BA in Broadcasting, U. Wyo., 1980, postgrad., 1983-87. Press asst. Senator Malcolm Wallop, Washington, 1980-81; news dir. Sta. KUGR Radio, Green River, Wyo., 1981-83; freelance reporter Wagonwheel Broadcasting, Green River, 1983—; pres. Embassy Bar, Inc., Green River, 1985—. Interview judge Wyo. Acad. Decathlon, Laramie, 1986. Recipient Disting. Service award Sta. KUWR Radio, Laramie, Wyo., 1978-79, 79-80; named Broadcaster of Month, AP, Cheyenne, Wyo., 1982, 83. Mem. Soc. Profl. Journalists, Wyo. Assn. Broadcasters (bd. dirs. 1985-86). Democrat. Presbyterian. Avocations: softball, bicycling, audio electronics. Home: 635 Evers St PO Box 134 Green River WY 82935 Office: Sta KUGR Radio 157 E Railroad PO Box 970 Green River WY 82935

BOSWORTH, BRUCE LEIGHTON, educator, consultant; b. Buffalo, Mar. 22, 1942; s. John Wayman and Alice Elizabeth Rodgers; children—David, Timothy, Paul, Reuben, Sheri, Roy. B.A., U. Denver, 1964; M.A., U. No. Colo., 1970; Ed.D., Walden U., 1984. Elem. tchr. Littleton (Colo.) Pub. Schs., 1964-67, 70-81; bldg. prin. East Smoky Sch. Div. 54, Valleyview, Alta., Can., 1967-70; pres., tchr. Chatfield Sch., Littleton, 1981—; mem. research bd. advisors Am. Biog. Inst.; adoption cons. hard-to-place children; ednl. cons. spl. needs children. Dir. Christian Edn.; mem. adminstrn. bd. Warren United Meth. Ch.; Mem. Council Exceptional Children, Assn. Supervision and Curriculum Devel., Englewood C. of C. Republican. Methodist. Clubs: Masons, Shriners. Home: 6170 S Bemis St Littleton CO 80120 Office: Chatfield School PO Box 1039 Littleton CO 80160

BOTKIN, DANIEL BENJAMIN, biologist, educator; b. Oklahoma City, Okla., Aug. 19, 1937; s. Benjamin Albert and Gertrude (Fritz) B.; m. Ellen Chase, Dec. 22, 1962 (div. 1976); children: Nancy, Jonathan; m. Erene Victoria Youngberg, Apr. 7, 1978. BA, U. Rochester, 1959; MA, U. Wis., 1962; PhD, Rutgers U., 1968. From asst. to assoc. prof. Yale U., New Haven, 1968-76; assoc. scientist Marine Biol. Lab., Woods Hole, Mass., 1976-78; prof. biology U. Calif., Santa Barbara, 1978—, chmn. environ. studies program, 1978-85, dir. global environ. research orgn., 1986. Co-author: Environmental Studies, 1982, 87 (software) JABOWA model of forest growth, 1970; contbr. articles to profl. jours. Fellow Rockefeller Bellagio (Italy) Inst., 1985, East-West Ctr., Honolulu, 1985—, Woodrow Wilson Internat. Ctr. for Scholars, Washington, 1977-78; grantee NSF, NASA, NOAA, Mellon Found., World Wildlife Fund, SOHIO Alaska Corp. Mem. AAAS, Ecol. Soc. Am., Am. Soc. Naturalists, Brit. Ecol. Soc. Avocations: aircraft piloting, photography, hiking. Office: U Calif Dept Biology Santa Barbara CA 93106

BOTNARESCUE, HELEN CHASE, education educator; b. Medford, Mass., June 22, 1927; d. Elton Fletcher and Eleanor Marden (Jones) Chase; m. Kenneth W. Meyer, Aug. 28, 1948 (div. 1972); children: Cynthia Anne Carter, Karl Frederick, Richard Werner, Thomas Alan, Mary Katharine; m. Vlad Vladus Botnarescue-Lenskey, July 23, 1983. BA, Denison U., 1949; MA, U. Ala., 1965, PhD, 1970. Dir., tchr. Granville (Ohio) Coop. Nursery Sch., 1952-55; tchr. sci. Tuscaloosa (Ala.) High Sch., 1963-65; grad. teaching asst. U. Ala., Tuscaloosa, 1966-67; supr. counseling lab. U. Ala., 1967-68; prof. edn. Calif. State U., Hayward, 1968—; cons. in edn., Redwood City, Calif., 1968—. Co-author: Early Childhood Practicum Guide, 1984. Mem. bd. mgrs. Carlmont YMCA, San Carlos, Calif., 1972-80. Mem. Nat. Assn. Edn. of Young Children, Calif. Assn. Edn. of Young Children (conf. program com. mem. 1982), Peninsula Assn. Edn. of Young children, Nat. Assn. Early Childhood Tchr. Educators (bd. dirs. 1982-84, 86—), Calif. Profs. of Early Chldhood Edn. (bd. dirs. 1981-84, chmn. membership com. 1982-84). Lutheran. Club: Redwood City Aquatic (bd. dirs. 1973-77, sec. bd. dirs. 1974-76, pres. bd. dirs. 1976-77). Avocations: traveling, reading, gardening, music. Home: 824 Canyon Rd Redwood City CA 94062 Office: Calif State U Dept Tchr Edn Hayward CA 94542

BOTTARI, MARIANNA TERESA, public relations executive, fund raiser, editor; b. Phila., Nov. 17, 1941; d. Guido Albert and Malvina Rose (Seccia) B. Student U. Pa., 1962-64, Charles Morris Price Sch. Journalism and Advt., 1964-66. News relations asst. Smith Kline & French Labs., Phila., 1952-64; pub. relations asst. St. Luke's and Children's Med. Ctr., Phila., 1964-66, Thomas Jefferson U. Hosp., Phila., 1969-71; pub. relations dir. Albert Einstein Med. Ctr., Phila., 1971-74, John Muir Meml. Hosp., Walnut Creek, Calif., 1974-77, Peralta Hosp., Oakland, Calif., 1977-80; community relations and devel. dir. Sequoia Hosp., Redwood City, Calif., 1980-82; community relations and mktg. dir. Valley Meml. Hosp., Livermore, Calif., 1982-84; owner PR Woman & Co. Bd. dirs. Coop. Center Council, 1976-77; v.p. Sun Country Homeowners Assn., 1977-79. bd. dirs. Yqnacu Terr. Homeowners Assn., 1986—. Served with USNR, 1979-81. Recipient MacEachern nat. citation, 1973, MacEachern cert. of merit, 1976. Mem. Acad. Hosp. Pub. Relations, Hosp. Pub. Relations Assn. No. Calif., Internat. Assn. Bus. Communicators, Nat. Assn. Hosp. Devel., Nat. Assn. Female Execs. Office: 101 Kinross Dr #4 Walnut Creek CA 94598

BOTTENBERG, JOYCE HARVEY, social services executive; b. Melrose, Mass., June 29, 1945; d. Robert Willis and Amy Sheppard (Wood) Harvey; 1 child, Joanne Harvey; m. Norman G. Bottenberg, 1985. BA, U. Mass., 1967, diploma grad. journalism program, 1969; diploma, Simmons Coll. Grad. Sch. Mgmt., 1984. Lic. social worker. Sr. tech. writer Itek Corp., Lexington, Mass., 1967-70; dir. pub. info. Walla Walla (Wash.) Community Coll., 1970; profl. interviewer McGraw Hill Research, N.Y.C., 1971-73; coordinator pub. relations James B. Rendle Assocs., Malden, Mass., 1973-76; exec. dir. ARC, Melrose, Mass., 1976-80, regional mgr., 1980-84; regional mgr. ARC, Lynn, Mass., 1984-85; tech. writer Municipality of Met. Seattle, 1985-86; exec. dir. Epilepsy Assn. Western Wash., Seattle, 1986—. Chmn. adv. bd. Mass. Dept. Pub. Welfare Community Service Area; mem. Melrose Mayor's Energy Commn.; civic adv. bd. Met. Bank and Trust; instr. 1st aid, CPR, ARC; merit badge counselor Boy Scouts Am. New Eng. Newspaper fellow, 1969; Cert. of merit ARC, 1981. Mem. AAUW, DAR, Nat. Conf. Social Welfare, Soc. Mayflower Descendents, Nat. Assn. Female Execs., Soc. Tech. Communications, Nat. Ski Patrol System, Alpha Phi Gamma. Episcopalian. Lodge: Zonta. Avocations: amateur radio operating. Home: 2205 197th Ave SE Issaquah WA 98027 Office: 8511 15th Ave NE Seattle WA 98115

BOTTI, RICHARD CHARLES, association executive; b. Brockton, Mass., May 1, 1939; s. Alfred Benecchi and Elizabeth Savini; stepson Ernest Botti; student Pierce Jr. Coll., 1959, Orange Coast Coll., 1964; m. Gwen Botti; children—Randolph K., Douglas S., Richard II. Pres., Legis. Info. Services Hawaii, Inc., Honolulu, 1971—; exec. dir., profl. lobbyist Hawaii Food Industry Assn., Honolulu, Hawaii Automotive & Retail Gasoline Dealers Assn., Inc., Honolulu, Hawaii Bus. League, Retail Liquor Dealers Assn. Hawaii, Liquor Dispensers of Hawaii, Honolulu. Mem. Food Industry Assn. Execs., Am. Soc. Assn. Execs., Aloha Soc. Assn. Execs. Address: Legis Info Services 677 Ala Moana Blvd Suite 815 Honolulu HI 96813

BOTTOMS, WILLIAM CLAY, JR., aviation company executive; b. Atlanta, June 13, 1946; s. William Clay and Alice Elizabeth (Walker) B.; m. Nancy Lou Snodgrass, Mar. 16, 1968; children: Janet Elizabeth, Sharon Suzanne. B in Aerospace Engring., Ga. Inst. Tech., 1969. Aerodyn. engr. McDonnell Aircraft Co., St. Louis, 1969-73; dir. engring. and quality control Southern Airways, Atlanta, 1973-78; staff v.p. maintenance Tex. Internat. Airlines, Houston, 1978-80; v.p. tech. services N.Y. Air, N.Y.C., 1980-83; sr. v.p. ops. Rocky Mountain Airways, Denver, 1983-85; exec. dir. Colo. Aero Tech., Broomfield, 1985—; regional cons. Robert Jameson Assocs., Denver, 1985. Pres. Golden Meadows Homeowners Assn., Morrison, Colo., 1983—; del. Regional Homeowners Assn., Aspen Park, Colo., 1985-86. Republican. Baptist. Home: 8244 Wagon Wheel Rd Morrison CO 80465 Office: Colo Aero Tech 10851 120th Ave Broomfield CO 80020

BOUCHÉ, BRUCE RAYMOND, chiropractor; b. Appleton, Wis., Aug. 31, 1950; s. Rayomond Richard and Shirley Marilyn (White) B.; m. Mary Jane Moses, Sept. 24, 1983. BA in Pscyhology, U. Ariz., 1972; D chiropractic cum laude, Cleve. Chiropractic Coll., 1984. Asst. dir. Spectrum Photographic Gallery, Tucson, 1976-77; photographic lab. technician Pima Community Coll., Tucson, 1977-79, photography instr., 1979; practice medicine specializing in chiropractic San Diego, 1985-86, Los Angeles, 1986—. Sec. Sathya Sai Baba Ctr. of Los Angeles, 1980-82, v.p., 1982-84, mem. ctr. adv. com., Los Angeles, 1982-86, v.p., San Diego, 1985-86. Recipient Cert. Appreciation Student Body Council Cleve. Chiropractic Coll., 1983, Clin. Proficiency award Cleve. Chiropractic Coll., 1984. Mem. Am. Chiropractic Assn., Calif. Chiropractic Assn. Club: Toastmasters. Avocations: reading, walking, outdoors, sculpting, art. Home: 834 S Orange Grove Ave #6 Los Angeles CA 90036 Office: 12331 Washington Blvd Los Angeles CA 90066

BOUCHER, MAYO TERRY, lawyer, judge; b. Stephenville, Tex., July 15, 1918; s. Terry S. and Henryetta (Turley) B.; m. Mary Catherine Lake, July 31, 1942; children: Phillip Larry, Terri Sue. Student, Tex. Tech, 1937-41; LLB, U. N.Mex., 1952, JD, 1969. Bar: N.Mex.; ordained deacon Bapt. Ch. With Atchison, Topeka & Santa Fe Ry., Belen, N.Mex., 1946-52; sole practice Belen, 1952-80; dist. judge 13th Jud. Dist. 1980—; mem. ho. of reps. State of N.Mex., 1957-64; bd. dirs., v.p. Belen Broadcasting Co., 1963-64; atty. City of Belen, 1956-57; sec.-treas. First Belen Escrow Co., 1986—; bd. dirs. First Nat. Bank, Belen, 1956-81. Served with USNR, 1942-45. Mem. C. of C. (dir. 1954-57, pres. 1955), Pi Sigma Alpha. Lodges: Masons (past master), Order Eastern Star (past patron Jessamine chpt., 1954, 78, past grand patron, grand jurisdiction N.Mex., 1984-85), Rotary (pres. 1961-62). Home: 1620 Velta Dr Belen NM 87002 Office: 700 Dalies Ave Belen NM 87002

BOUDART, MICHEL, chemical engineering educator; b. Belgium, June 18, 1924; came to U.S., 1947, naturalized, 1957; s. Francois and Marguerite (Swolfs) B.; m. Marina D'Haese, Dec. 27, 1948; children: Mark, Baudouin, Iris, Philip. B.S., U. Louvain, Belgium, 1944, M.S., 1947; Ph.D., Princeton U., 1950. Research asso. James Forrestal Research Ctr., Princeton, 1950-54; mem. faculty Princeton U., 1954-61; prof. chem. engring. U. Calif. - Berkeley, 1961-64; prof. chem. engring. and chemistry Stanford U., 1964-80, William J. Keck prof. chem. engring., 1980—; cons. to industry, 1955—; dir. Catalytica Assos., Inc.; Humble Oil Co. lectr., 1958, Am. Inst. Chem. Engrs. lectr., 1961, Sigma Xi nat. lectr., 1965; chmn. Gordon Research Conf. Catalysis, 1962. Author: Kinetics of Chemical Processes, 1968, (with A. Djéga-Mariadassou) Kinetics of Heterogeneous Catalytic Reactions, 1983; editor: (with J.R. Anderson) Catalysis: Science and Technology, 1981; adv. editorial bd. Jour. Catalysis 1964-86, Internat. Chem. Engring., 1964—, Advances in Catalysis, 1968—, Catalysis Rev., 1968—, Accounts Chem. Research, 1978—. Belgium-Am. Ednl. Found. fellow, 1948; Procter fellow, 1949; recipient Curtis-McGraw research award Am. Soc. Engring. Edn., 1962, R.H. Wilhelm award in chem. reaction engring., 1974. Fellow AAAS; mem. Am. Chem. Soc. (Kendall award 1977, E.V. Murphee award in Indsl. & Engring. Chemistry 1985), Catalysis Soc., Am. Inst. Chem. Engrs., Chem. Soc., Nat. Acad. Sci., Nat. Acad. Engring.; fgn. assoc. Académie Royale de Belgique. Home: 512 Gerona Rd Stanford CA 94305 Office: Dept Chem Engring Stanford Univ Stanford CA 94305

BOUDREAU, ROBERT DONALD, meteorology educator; b. North Adams, Mass., Mar. 9, 1931; s. Lucien Albert and Rose Elizabeth (Franceschini) B. BS with honors, Tex. A&M U., 1962, MS, 1964, PhD, 1968. Cert. cons. meteorologist; cert. instrument and multi engine flight instr., airline transport pilot. Research meteorologist Atmospheric Scis. Lab., Ft. Huachuca, Ariz., 1965-68, Deseret Test Ctr., Salt Lake City, 1968-70, Meteorol. Satellite Lab., Washington, 1970-71; sr. atmospheric scientist Earth Resources Lab. NASA, St. Louis, Mo., 1971-75; prof., chmn. meteorology dept. Metro. State Coll., Denver, 1976—. Contbr. articles to profl. jours. Mem. Am. Meteorol. Soc., Nat. Weather Assn., U.S. Pilots Assn., Pilots Internat. Assn., Internat. Meteorology Aviation and Electronics Inst. (pres. 1982—), Sigma Xi. Republican. Mem. Unitarian Ch. Office: Metro State Coll Meteorology 22 1006 11th St Denver CO 80204

BOUHER, MARGARET ANN, clinical social worker; b. Phoenix, July 19, 1955; d. Russell I. and Caroline L. (Poole) B. BSW, Ariz. State U., 1977, MSW, 1978. Lic. clin. social worker, Calif. Social worker St. Joseph's Hosp., Phoenix, 1977-82, Grossmont Dist Hosp., La Mesa, Calif., 1982-86; pvt. practice psychotherapy La Mesa, 1983—; group facilitator USN Family Advocacy Program; group counselor Daughters United, La Mesa, 1985. Newspaper columnist The Daily California Newspaper. Active Nat. Kidney Found. (cert. recognition 1984). Mem. Soc. Clin. Social Workers (San Diego membership com. chmn.), Nat. Assn. Social Workers (cert.), Council Nephrology Social Workers (pres. Ariz. chpt. 1981), Sierra Club, ACLU, Physicians for Social Responsibility, Alpha Eta. Democrat. Lodge: Soroptimists Internat. (judge for outstanding women of service, 1983-84). Home: 6202 Friars Rd 322 San Diego CA 92108 Office: 237 Avocado Ave Suite 110 El Cajon CA 92020

BOULDIN, DANNY LEE, electrical engineer; b. Fyffe, Ala., Oct. 31, 1953; s. Virgil Dee and Johnnie Mag (Gibson) B.; m. Brenda Gale Wooten, Apr. 13, 1974; children: Kelly, Stacey. BSEE, Auburn U., 1978; MSEE, Fla. Inst. Tech., 1983. Sr. engr. Harris Corp., Ft. Walton Beach, Fla., 1978-80, Martin Marietta Aerospace Div., Orlando, Fla., 1980-83, ITT Corp., Roanoke, Va., 1983-85; devel. engr. Hewlett Packard Corp., Palo Alto, Calif., 1985—. Republican. Home: PO Box 51477 Palo Alto CA 94303 Office: Hewlett Packard Corp 640 Page Mill Rd Palo Alto CA 94304

BOULET, ROGER HENRI, art gallery director; b. Winnipeg, Man., Can., Feb. 15, 1944; s. Henri Elzear and Jeanne (Bourget) B. B.F.A. with honors, U. Man., 1970. Dir. curator Burnaby Art Gallery, B.C., 1981—. Author: F.M. Bell-Smith, 1978, The Silent Thunder, 1981, The Tranquility and the Turbulence, 1981, The Canadian Earth, 1982. Can. Council grantee, 1970. Office: Burnaby Art Gallery, 6344 Gilpin St, Burnaby, BC Canada V5G 2J3

BOULET, TAMI LEE, social worker; b. Lawton, Okla., Sept. 12, 1958; d. Aristide Ferdinand and Sharon Ann (Adeline) B.; m. Gary Wade Verboon, May 17, 1980 (div. Nov. 1985). BA in Religion, B in Social Work, Azusa Pacific U., 1980; MSW, UCLA, 1984. Licensed clin. social worker, Calif. Social work intern East Los Angeles Regional Ctr. for Developmentally Disabled, Alhambra, Calif., 1979-80; social worker United Cerebral Palsy, Sylmar, Calif., 1980-82; social work intern St. John's Hosp., Santa Monica, Calif., 1982-83, Didi Hirsch Community Mental Health Ctr., Culver City, Calif., 1983-84; social worker Hollygrove Residential Treatment Ctr. for Children, Hollywood, Calif., 1984—; dir. clin. services Hollygrove Residential Treatment Ctr. for Children, Hollywood, 1987—. Participant South American Mission, Columbia, 1978, Latin American Mission, Mexico City, 1979, travel seminar on world religions, Inter-Religious Found., 1985; group coordinator Amnesty Internat. group 96, Santa Monica, 1982—; mem. vestry St. Augustine's Episcopal Ch., Santa Monica, 1987—. Mem. Nat. Assn. Social Workers, UCLA Sch. Social Welfare Alumni Assn. Democrat. Episcopalian. Avocations: snow skiing, bicycling, travelling, ceramics, dance. Home: 1626 Armacost #5 West Los Angeles CA 90025 Office: Hollygrove 815 N El Centro Ave Los Angeles CA 90038

BOULTON, LYNDIE MCHENRY, professional society administrator; b. Corvallis, Oreg.; d. W.B. Jim and Lillian (Hosken) McHenry; m. Roger Boulton. BA in Anthropology, U. Calif., Santa Barbara, 1974. Ops. mgr. C. Brent Scoh & Assocs., Sacramento, 1979-81; exec. dir. Am. Soc. Enology and Viticulture, Davis, Calif., 1981—; bd. dirs. Am. Vineyard Found., San Francisco. Mem. Nat. Assn. Expn. Mgrs., Am. Soc. Assn. Execs. Office: Am Soc Enology & Viticulture PO Box 1855 Davis CA 95617

BOULTON, SHAUNA DEE, educator; b. Salt Lake City, May 29, 1949; d. Melvin and Afton Lillie (Davidson) Boulton. B.S., U. Utah, 1971, M.Ed., 1981. Cert. elem., severely handicapped, spl. resource tchr., Utah. Tchr. Habilitation Ctr. for Multiple Handicapped, Salt Lake City, 1971-73, Hartvigsen Sch. for Multiple Handicapped, Salt Lake City, 1973-79, William Penn Elem. Sch., Salt Lake City, 1979-83, East Mill Creek Elem. Sch., 1983—. Vol., Spl. Olympics. Mem. NEA, Utah Edn. Assn., Granite Edn. Assn., Assn. Supervision and Curriculum Devel., Internat. Platform Assn. Home: 1516 Glen Arbor St Salt Lake City UT 84105 Office: East Mill Creek Elem Sch 2965 E 3435 S Salt Lake City UT 84109

BOUNDS, DORIS SWAYZE, banker; b. Muskogee, Olka., Oct. 26, 1904; d. Frank B. and Anna Abby (Miller) Swayze; m. Roger Jackson Bounds, 1931 (dec. 1960); 1 child, Roger Swayze. B.A., Stanford U., 1926; M.A., Columbia U., 1927. Adminstrv. asst. U.S. Senate, 1927-39; to Gen. L. Clay, Washington, 1940-41, to asst. sec. Dept. Commerce, 1941-42; specialist Nat. Housing Agy., Washington, 1943-45; D.C. rep. Stanford U., 1945-47; corp. sec., dir. First Nat. Bank Hermiston, Oreg., 1947-53; dir. Inland Empire Bank, Hermiston, 1953—, chmn. bd., 1960—, chief adminstrv. officer, exec. v.p., 1960-72, sr. v.p., 1972—; mem. Oreg. State Banking Bd., 1983—. Bd. dirs. Oreg. Arts Found., 1977-81; mem. Oreg. Arts Commn., 1969-71, 81—; bd. overseers Lewis and Clark Coll., Portland, Oreg., 1974—; pres. Roger J. Bounds Found., Hermiston, 1965—; trustee Umatilla County Library, 1950-79, Mus. Native Am. Cultures, 1966-83; bd. dirs. Indian Festival of Arts, 1966—; mem. Oreg. Rural Devel. Com., 1968-72, Pendleton Round-Up Assn., 1960—, Hermiston Devel. Corp., 1965—, Oreg. Lewis and Clark Trail Com., 1977—, Gov.'s Listening Post Adv. Bd., 1980-81; mem. hon. council Oreg. Hist. Soc., 1981—. Recipient Disting. Service award Hermiston C. of C., 1978; award Altrusa Club, 1983, Gov.'s Art award, 1986. Mem. Nat. Assn. Bank Women (bd. dirs. 1963-64), Oreg. Bankers Assn. (treas. 1962-63, exec. council 1965-66), Ind. Bankers Oreg. (bd. dirs. 1972-74, treas. 1973-74), Western Ind. Bankers, State Chartered Banks Oreg., PEO, AAUW, Bus. and Profl. Women, Chi Omega. Republican. Episcopalian. Clubs: McNary Yacht; Portland University; Pendleton Country. Office: Inland Empire Bank PO Box 1170 Hermiston OR 97838

BOUQUET, FRANCIS LESTER, physicist; b. Enterprise, Oreg., Feb. 1, 1926; s. Francis Lester and Esther (Johnson) B.; m. Betty Jane Davis, Sept. 26, 1979; children: Tim, Jeffrey, Janet; stepchildren: John Perry, Peggy Korv. AA, U. Calif., Berkeley, 1948, BA, 1950; MA, UCLA, 1953. Physicist U.S. Radiol. Def. Lab., San Francisco, 1953-55; engr., mgr. Lockheed Aircraft Co., Burbank, Calif., 1955-74; physicist Jet Propulsion Lab., Pasadena, Calif., 1974—; cons. in field. Author: Solar Energy Simplified, 1984, Radiation Damage in Materials, 1985, Radiation Effects on Electronics, 1986, Introduction to Materials Engineering, 1986; writer numerous govt. and industry reports; contbr. articles to sci. jours. Elder 1st Presbyn. Ch., Van Nuys, Calif. 1970-81. Served with U.S. Army, 1944-465, with Signal Corps U.S. Army, 1951-52, PTO. Recipient Eagle Scout Award Boy Scouts Am., 1940, Performance commendations Lockheed Aircraft Co., 1964, 66, Mgmt. Achievement Program award, 1973, 12 NASA awards, 1980-86; named to Honor Roll of Inventors, 1966. Mem. N.Y. Acad. Sci., Calif. Soc. Profl. Engrs., Nat. Soc. Profl. Engrs., IEEE (chmn. Los Angeles chpt. Nuclear and Plasma Scis. Soc. 1973-74), Am. Inst. Physics, AIAA, Nat. Mgmt. Assn., Air Force Assn., Lockheed Mgmt. Club, Caltech Mgmt. Club. Republican. Office: Jet Propulsion Lab 4800 Oak Grove Dr Mail Stop 157-507 Pasadena CA 91109

BOURGEOIS, PAMELA CHEVREAUX, speech therapistt, communication disorders administrator; b. Tulsa, Sept. 25, 1955; d. Heiman Chevreaux and Geraldine (Alley) Heibucher; m. Alan Michael Bourgeois, Jan. 19, 1981; 1 child, Lauren. BA in Speech Pathology and Audiology, U. Denver, 1977, MA in Speech Pathology, 1979. Speech and lang. pathologist Mt. Diablo Rehab. Ctr., Pleasant Hill, Calif., 1979; speech and lang. pathologist, specialist neuropsychology service Casa Colina Hosp. for Rehabilitative Medicine, Pomona, Calif., 1980-83; mgr. communication disorders Queen of the Valley Hosp., West Covina, Calif., 1983-86, v.p. diagnostic and Therapeudic services, 1986—. Contbr. articles to profl. jours. Named one of Outstanding Young Women in Am., 1983. Mem. Am. Speech, Lang. and Hearing Assn. (cert. clin. competence in speech), Calif. Speech, Lang. and Hearing Assn., Am. Congress Rehab. Medicine, Dir.'s Council So. Calif. Office: Queen of the Valley Hosp 1115 S Sunset West Covina CA 91790

BOURKE, ROBERT HATHAWAY, oceanographer; b. Portsmouth, Va., June 23, 1938; s. Robert Emmet and Frances Helen (Hathaway) B.; m. Portia Ann Hilton, Nov. 14, 1964; children: Robert Kyle, Christopher Hilton. BS in Gen. Engring., U.S. Naval Acad., 1960; MS in Phys. Oceanography, Oreg. State U., 1969, PhD in Phys. Oceanography, 1972. Commd. ensign USN, 1960, advanced through grades to capt., 1968; prof. of oceanography Naval Postgrad. Sch., Monterey, Calif., 1971—; as arctic oceanographer has led 10 major oceanographic cruises to Atlantic and Pacific ice margins. Assoc. editor USN Jour. Underwater Acoustics, 1986—; contbr. articles to profl. jours. Info. officer U.S. Naval Acad., Monterey, 1978—. Overseas fellow Churchill Coll. Cambridge U., Eng., 1981. Mem. Am. Geophys. Union, Sigma Xi. Republican. Roman Catholic. Avocation: tennis. Office: Naval Postgrad Sch Dept Oceanography Monterey CA 93943

BOURLA, JACK MARTIN, scientific corporation executive; b. San Francisco, Mar. 4, 1955; s. Albert Maurice and Jacqueline Jane (Assoun) B.; m. Arnette Alice Bonzani, June 23, 1978; stepchildren: James J.A. Hoskins, William P. Hoskins. AA, Coll. San Mateo, 1975; BA, Calif. State U., San Francisco, 1977, postgrad., 1977-80. Adminstr. Stanford (Calif.) U., 1979-81; lab. mgr. CETUS Immune Corp., Palo Alto, Calif., 1981-84, mgr. ops. and adminstrn., 1984-85, assoc. dir., 1985-86; dir. CETUS Corp., Emeryville, Calif., 1986—; cons. in field, 1983—. Vol. Los Amigos de las Americas, Nicaragua, 1973, Planned Parenthood, San Mateo County, Calif., 1978-80. Mem. AAAS, Am. Soc. Microbiologists, Am. Assn. Lab. Animal Sci. Democrat. Jewish. Avocations: sports, music, cooking, refinishing antique furniture. Home: 631 Dartmouth Ave San Carlos CA 94070 Office: CETUS Corp 1400 53d St Emeryville CA 94608

BOURNE, LYLE EUGENE, JR., psychology educator; b. Boston, Apr. 12, 1932; s. Lyle E. and Blanche (White) B. B.A., Brown U., 1953; M.S., U. Wis., 1955, Ph.D., 1956. Asst. prof. psychology U. Utah, 1956-61, assoc. prof., 1961-63; vis. assoc. prof. U. Calif.-Berkeley, 1961-62, vis. prof., 1968-69; assoc. prof. psychology U. Colo., Boulder, 1963-65, prof., 1965—, chmn. dept. psychology, 1982—, dir. Inst. Cognitive Sci., 1979-83; clin. prof. psychiatry U. Kans. Med. Ctr., 1967—; vis. prof. U. Wis., 1966, U. Mont., 1967, U. Hawaii, 1969; cons. in exptl. psychology, VA, 1965—. Author: Human Conceptual Behavior, 1966, Psychology of Thinking, 1971, Psychology: Its Principles and Meanings, 1973, Psychology: Its Principles and Meanings, rev. edits., 1976, 79, 82, 85, Cognitive Processes, 1979, rev. edit., 1986; acad. editor: Basic Concept Series, Learning-Cognition Series, Scott, Foresman Pub. Co., 1970-76, Charles Merrill Co., 1980-86; editor: Jour. Exptl. Psychology: Human Learning and Memory, 1975-80; cons. editor: Jour. Clin. Psychology, 1975—; Jour. Exptl. Psychology: Learning, Memory and Cognition, 1984—; Memory and Cognition, 1984—. Recipient Research Scientist award NIHM, 1969-74. Mem. Am. Psychol. Assn. (council editors 1975-80, bd. sci. affairs, 1978-84, chmn. early awards com. 1978-79), Psychonomic Soc. (governing bd. 1976-81, chmn. 1980-81), Sigma Xi. Home: 785 Northstar Ct Boulder CO 80302

BOURNE, SAMUEL G., mathematician, consultant, educator; b. Liverpool, Eng., Apr. 29, 1916; came to U.S., 1931, naturalized, 1939; s. William and Fanny (Gilford) B. B.S., Rutgers U., 1938; A.M., The John Hopkins, 1944, Ph.D., 1950. Instr. U. Conn., Storrs, 1950-52; asst. prof. math. Temple U., Phila., 1952-54, Lehigh U., Bethlehem, Pa., 1954-56; research assoc. Calif. Inst. Tech., Pasadena, 1958-59; visiting scholar U. Calif.-Berkeley, 1959-63, sr. research mathemation, 1964—; prof. math. U. Fla., Gainesville, 1963-64; lectr. Hungarian Acad. of Scis., Budapest, 1975, 1981; Einstein lectr. Yugoslav Acad. Scis., Belgrade, 1985. Author: Einstein in Princeton, 1950-55, 1982. Recipient Bogart math. prize Rutgers U., 1938; Johns Hopkins U. fellow, scholar, 1945-50; Einstein lectr. Hellenic Am. Found., Athens, Greece, 1980. Fellow AAAS; mem. Am. Math Soc., Math Assn. Am., Internat. Platform Assn., Inst. Advanced Study, Phi Beta Kappa, Sigma Xi. Mem. Unified Ch. Clubs: Faculty (The Johns Hopkins, U. Calif.-Berkeley). Home: PO Box 4583 Berkeley CA 94704 Office: U Calif Dept Math Evans Hall Berkeley CA 94720

BOURQUE, LINDA ANNE BROOKOVER, public health educator; b. Indpls., Aug. 25, 1941; d. Wilbur Bone and Edna Mae (Eberhart) B.; m. Don Philippe Bourque, June 3, 1966 (div. Nov. 1974). BA, Ind. U., 1963; MA, Duke U., 1964, PhD, 1968. Postdoctoral researcher Duke U., Durham, N.C., 1968-69; asst. prof. sociology Calif. State U., Los Angeles, 1969-72; asst. to assoc. prof. pub. health UCLA, 1972-86, prof. pub. health, 1986—, acting assoc. dir. Inst. for Social Sci. Research, 1981-82. Contbr. articles to profl. jours. Violon cellist with Santa Monica (Calif.) Symphony Orch., 1978—. Mem. Am. Sociol. Assn. (mem. med. sociology sect. council 1975-78, co-chmn. com. freedom research and teaching, 1975-78, cert. recognition 1980), Pacific Sociol. Assn. (co-chmn. program com. 1982, v.p. 1983), Am. Pub. Health Assn. (mem. standing com. on status of women 1974-76), Sociologists for Women in Society, Am. Assn. Pub. Opinion Research, Assn.

Research in Vision and Ophthalmology, Delta Omega, Phi Alpha Theta. Avocation: playing the violoncello. Home: 817 Venezia Ave Venice CA 90291 Office: UCLA Sch Pub Health Los Angeles CA 90024

BOURQUE, PHILIP JOHN, business economist, educator; b. Holyoke, Mass., Aug. 16, 1922; s. Oliver H. and Emma G. (Tremblay) B.; m. Dorothea A. Lohmann, June 18, 1949; children: Cynthia, Diane, Nancy, Alison, Constance. BS, U. Mass., 1949; MA in Econs., U. Pa., 1950, Ph.D., 1956. Instr. econs. U. Pa., Phila., 1952-54; asst. prof. econs. Muhlenberg Coll., Allentown, Pa., 1954-55, Lehigh (Pa.) U., 1955-57; prof. bus. econs. U. Wash., Seattle, 1957—; bd. govs. Wash. State Council Econ. Advisors, 1978—. Contbr. articles to profl. jours. Served to USAF, 1943-46. Mem. Am. Econ. Assn., Regional Sci. Assn., Nat. Assn. Bus. Economists, Western Regional Sci. Assn., Pacific N.W. Regional Econ. Conf., Seattle Economists Club. Home: 19604 53d Ave NE Seattle WA 98155-3030 Office: U Wash Grad Sch Bus Adminstrn Seattle WA 98195

BOUWER, HERMAN, laboratory executive; b. Haarlem, Netherlands, July 11, 1927; came to U.S., 1952, naturalized, 1959; s. Eduard and Trinette (Dusschoten) B.; m. Agnes N. Temminck, Mar. 29, 1952; children: Edward John, Herman (Archie) Gerard, Annette Nancy. B.S., Nat. Agr. U., Wageningen, The Netherlands, 1949, M.S., 1952; Ph.D., Cornell U., 1955. Assoc. agr. engr. Auburn U., 1955-59; research hydraulic engr. U.S. Water Conservation Lab., Phoenix, 1959-72, dir., 1972—; lectr. groundwater hydrology Ariz. State U.; cons. in field. Author: Groundwater Hydrology, 1978; Contbr. articles in field to profl. jours. OECD fellow, 1964; recipient Superior Service awards U.S. Dept., Agr., 1963, 73, Scientist of Yr. 1985. Mem. ASCE (Walter Huber Research prize 1966, Royce J. Tipton award 1984), Am. Soc. Agr. Engrs., Am. Soc. Agronomy, Nat. Water Well Assn., Dutch Inst. Agr. Engrs. Club: Tempe Racquet and Swim. Home: 338 La Diosa St Tempe AZ 85282 Office: US Water Conservation Lab 4331 E Broadway Rd Phoenix AZ 85040

BOVERIE, ROBERT LOUIS, campground owner; b. Lubbock, Tex., Oct. 15, 1939; s. Clem Benjamin and A. Estelle (Griffin) B.; m. A. Diane Penny, Mar. 10, 1961 (div. 1982); children: Michele Lynn, Robert Louis Jr., James Noel, Annette Nicole; m. Phyllis Gwen Fuquay, Jan. 1, 1986. BBA, Tex. Tech. U., 1963; BA, Am. Grad. Sch. Internat. Mgmt., 1971. Div. mgr. Furr's, Inc., Lubbock, Tex., Albuquerque, 1963-70; v.p. Furr's, Inc., Lubbock, 1975-79; pres. Internat. Basic Econ. Corp., San Salvador, El Salvador, 1971-75, Boverie Investments, Inc., Ruidoso, N.Mex., 1980—. Bd. dirs. Spirit of Ruidoso; vice chmn. County Lodgers Tax. Com., Carrizozo, N.Mex., 1986—; vestry mem. Holy Mount Episcopal Ch., Ruidoso, 1983—; v.p. Ruidoso C. of C., 1985—. Republican. Episcopalian. Lodge: Rotary (bd. dirs. 1986—). Avocation: travel. Home: PO Box 2946 Ruidoso NM 88345 Office: Boverie Investments Inc PO Box 146 Ruidoso Downs NM 88346

BOVEY, TERRY ROBINSON, insurance executive, sports official; b. Oregon, Ill., May 13, 1948; s. John Franklin and Frances (Robinson) B.; m. Diana Carmen Rodriguez, Aug. 29, 1970 (div. July 1980); 1 child, Joshua; m. Kathy Jo Johnson, Sept. 14, 1985: stepchildren: Lara, Mickey, Keri. Student, Ariz. Western Coll., 1966-68, Grand Canyon Coll., 1968-69; BBA, U. Ariz., 1972. Salesman All-Am. Dist. Co., Yuma, Ariz., 1972-76; dist. asst. mgr. Equitable Life Ins., Yuma, 1976-81; gen. sales mgr. Ins. Counselors, Yuma, 1981-83; mng. gen. agt. Hutton Life Ins. Co., Yuma, 1983—; regional commnr. Ariz. Interscholastic Assn., Yuma, 1972—. mem. Century Club, Boy's Club of Yuma. Mem. Nat. Assn. Life Underwriters (nat. sales achievement award 1979, 82, 84, 86), Life Underwriters Political Action Com., Million Dollar Round Table, Yuma City Assn. Republican. Presbyterian. Club: Yuma Golf and Country. Avocations: golf, officiating. Office: Hutton Life Ins PO Box 29 Yuma AZ 85364

BOWA, LAWRENCE ROBERT (LARRY), professional baseball manager; b. Sacramento, Dec. 6, 1945; m. Sheena Bowa; 1 child, Tori. Student, Sacramento City Coll. Player various minor league teams, 1966-69; player with Phila. Phillies, Nat. League, 1970-81, Chgo. Cubs, Nat. League, 1982-85, N.Y. Mets, 1985; mgr. Las Vegas Stars, 1986, San Diego Padres, 1986—; player All-Star games, 1974-76, 78, 79, World Series, 1980. Holder major league record for highest lifetime fielding percentage for shortstop; winner Gold Glove, 1972, 78. Avocations: golf, racquetball, billiards. Address: care San Diego Padres PO Box 2000 San Diego CA 92120 *

BOWDEN, JAMES ALVIN, construction company financial executive; b. Vernal, Utah, Mar. 19, 1948; s. Alvin George and Erva (Kirk) B.; m. Jane Ruth Taylor, May 31, 1973; children—Scott James, Julie, Jeffrey Taylor, Camille, Timothy Kirk. B.S. in Civil Engring., Brigham Young U., 1972, M.B.A., 1974. Planning analyst Morrison Knudsen Corp., Boise, 1974, asst. mgr. corp. planning, 1974-75, mgr. fin. analysis, 1975-78, asst. treas., 1978-83, v.p. fin. real estate subs., 1983-84, treas., 1984-86; v.p. and treas., 1986—; spl. instr. Boise State U., 1977-78. Bd. dirs. Boise chapter ARC, 1982—, treas., 1984-86, vice chmn. 1986—; mem. United Way, Boise, 1980-85. Mem. Beta Gamma Sigma. Republican. Mormon. Home: 10058 W Ironclad Ct Boise ID 83704 Office: Morrison Knudsen Corp Morrison Knudsen Plaza Boise ID 83729

BOWEN, CHARLES HUGH, JR., lawyer, electronics engineer, retired naval officer; b. Belle Ellen, Ala., Jan. 8, 1923; s. Charles Hugh and Lavada (Lawley) B.; m. Nina Gwen Stevens, July 29, 1945 (div.); children: David Hugh, Charles Hugh III; m. Joan H. Steffens, Mar. 18, 1978. Student, U. Ariz., 1939-40, 46, U. So. Calif., 1946-47; B.S. in Engring. Electronics, Naval Postgrad. Sch., 1953, M.S., 1954; grad., Naval War Coll., 1961; J.D., U. Santa Clara, 1977. Bar: Calif. Commd. ensign U.S. Navy, 1943, advanced through grades to capt., 1965; flight tng. 1942-43; pilot and flight officer PTO, 1944-45; flight instr. Aviation Tng. Unit 5, 1947-49; radar projects supr. VX-1 Key West, Fla., 1949-51; operations officer Attack Squadron 55, 1954-55; aviation electronics engring. officer, staff Comdr. Naval Air Force Pacific Fleet, 1956-58; assigned spl. studies sect. Spl. Projects Office, Bur. Weapons, 1958-60; student replace air tng. group Attack Squadron 122, 1961; comdg. officer Attack Squadron 115, 1962-63; navigator U.S.S. Kitty Hawk, 1963-64, exec. officer, 1964; tchr. elec. sci. U.S. Naval Acad., also head sci. dept., 1965-67; command U.S.S. Vesuvius, 1967-68; advanced devel. engr. Sylvania Electronics Systems, Mountain View, Calif., 1968-72; mktg. mgr. Sylvania Electronics Systems, 1972-74; jud. extern with Justice Calif. Supreme Ct., 1976; individual practice law Campbell, Calif., 1978-81; ptnr. Finch & Bowen, Campbell, Calif., 1981—. Decorated D.F.C. with gold star, Air medal with silver star. Mem. IEEE, Naval Inst., Internat. Platform Assn. Democrat. Home: 5941 Drytown Pl San Jose CA 95120

BOWEN, CLOTILDE DENT, retired army officer, psychiatrist; b. Chgo., Mar. 20, 1923; d. William Marion Dent and Clotilde (Tynes) D.; m. William N. Bowen, Dec. 29, 1945 (dec.). B.A., Ohio State U., 1943, M.D., 1947. Intern, Harlem Hosp., N.Y.C., 1947-48, resident and fellow in pulmonary resident in psychiatry VA Hosp., Albany, N.Y., 1969-62; private practice, N.Y.C. 1950-55; chief pulmonary disease clinic, N.Y.C. 1950-55; chief psychiatry VA Hosp., Roseburg, Oreg., 1962-66, acting chief of staff, 1964-66; commd. capt. U.S. Army, 1955, advanced through ranks to col., 1968; neuropsychiat. cons. U.S. Army Vietnam, 1970-71; chief dept. psychiatry Fitzsimmons Army Med. Ctr., 1971-74; chief dept. psychiatry. Tripler Gen. Hosp. Fitzsimons Army Med. Center, 1974-75, chief dept. primary care and community medicine, 1979-83, chief psychiat. consultation service, 1983-85; psychiat. cons., surveyor Joint Commn. Accreditation Hosps., 1985—; assoc. prof. psychiatry U. Colo. Med. Center, Denver, 1970-83. Decorated Legion of Merit, several other medals. Fellow Menninger Found. Fellow Am. Psychiat. Assn., Acad. Psychosomatic Medicine; mem. AMA. Home: 1020 Tari Dr Colorado Springs CO 80908

BOWEN, FRANCIS LEE, elec. engr.; b. Lincoln, Nebr., Jan. 17, 1932; s. Earl and Besse B.; B.E.E., U. Nebr., 1958; M.B.A., Calif. Luth. Coll., 1977; m. Bonnie Jean Yentes, June 5, 1951; children—Sandra Fern, Scott LeMar. With Pacific Missile Test Center, Point Mugu, Calif., 1958—, head communications engring. br., from 1970, now head inservice engring. div. Design and Fabrication Dept. Mem. Camarillo (Calif.) Planning Commn., 1970-82, chmn., 1971-75, 78-79; mem. Camarillo City Council, 1982-86, vice mayor, 1983-84, mayor, 1984-85; trustee Camarillo Meth. Ch., 1976-79, chmn., 1977. Served in USN, 1952-54. Republican. Clubs: Masons, Shriners, Order of DeMolay. Office: Code 3510 Point Mugu CA 93042

BOWEN, JAMES CURTIS, food products executive; b. Evanston, Ill., Mar. 18, 1945; s. James Curtis Bowen and Bernice (Kraft) Knoernschild; m. Patricia Collins, Sept. 2, 1980. Student, U. Wis., LaCrosse, 1963-64; BA, Lakeland Coll., 1968. Div. sales mgr. Beatrice Grocery Group, Fullerton, Calif., 1978-82, mktg. mgr., Peter Pan, 1982-84, sr. mktg. mgr., Hunt's, 1984, group mktg. mgr., 1984-85; v.p. mktg. Van de Kamp's Bakery, Los Angeles, 1985—. Republican. Roman Catholic. Avocations: golf, travel. Home: 11 Blacksmith Circle Phillips Ranch CA 91766 Office: Van de Kamp's Holland Dutch Bakers Inc 2930 Fletcher Dr Los Angeles CA 90065

BOWEN, JAMES ROSS, weapons design engineer; b. Wooster, Ohio, Feb. 20, 1935; s. James W.R. and Gayle L. (Altland) B.; m. Glada Roberts, Sept. 2, 1958; children: Michael D. (stepson), James R., Jason M. Project engr. guidance systemfor air-to-air missiles system Naval Weapons Ctr., China Lake, Calif., 1958-59, program mgr. weapons system, 1969-72, line supr. design groups, mgr. weapon systems, div. head, 1972-78, mgr. spl. facilities and equipment study, 1978-81, dep. support dir., 1981—. Safety dir. Ridgecrest (Calif.) Little League, 1975—; mem. Am. Def. Preparedmess Assn., 1982-87; bldg. com. Calvary Assembly of God Ch., Ridgecrest, 1975—; pres. Indian Wells Valley chpt. Full Gospel Bus. Men's Fellowship Internat., 1978-81, field rep., 1980-85, internat. dir., 1985-87; v.p. Sierra Breeze Mobil Home Estates, 1980, pres., 1981. Recipient Michelson Lab. award Naval Weapons Ctr., 1985. Mem. Nat. Contract Mgmt. Assn., Internat. Footprinters Assn. (chpt. bd. dirs. 1986-87), Tech. Mktg. Soc. Am. Republican. Home: 5233 Ocotillo Ave Ridgecrest CA 93555 Office: Naval Weapons Ctr Comdr Code 02A China Lake CA 93555

BOWEN, J(EAN) DONALD, educator; b. Malad, Idaho, Mar. 19, 1922; s. John David and Lillian (Larson) B.; m. Catherine Holley, May 27, 1948; children: David James, Douglas Ray, Dale Eugene, Christina Lee, Karen Lucy. A.B., Brigham Young U., 1944; M.A., Columbia U., 1949; Ph.D., U. N.Mex., 1952. Instr. Duke U., Durham, N.C., 1952-53; sci. linguist Fgn. Service Inst., Washington, 1953-58; prof. English UCLA, 1958—; co-dir. UCLA (Philippine Center for Lang. Study), 1958-63; field dir. (Survey of Lang. Use and Lang. Teaching in Eastern Africa), 1968-70; vis. prof. Am. U. Cairo, 1974-77, Ain Shams U., 1976-77. Author: Patterns of English Pronunciation, 1975, (with others) Adaptation in Language Teaching, 1978, Patterns of Spanish Pronunciation, 1960, The Sounds of English and Spanish, 1965, The Grammatical Structures of English and Spanish, 1965, English Usage, 1983, TESOL Techniques and Procedures, 1985; author, editor: (with others) Studies in Southwest Spanish, 1976, Linguistics in Oceania, 1971, Language in Ethiopia, 1976; contbr. articles to profl. jours. Served with U.S. Army, 1943-46. Mem. Linguistic Soc. Am., MLA, TESOL. Mormon. Home: 3055 Corda Dr Los Angeles CA 90049 Office: UCLA Dept Applied Linguistics/TESL Los Angeles CA 90024

BOWEN, JEWELL RAY, chemical engineering educator; b. Duck Hill, Miss., Jan. 9, 1934; s. Hugh and Myrtle Louise (Stevens) B.; m. Priscilla Joan Spooner, Feb. 4, 1956; children: Jewell Ray, Sandra L., Susan E. B.S., MIT, 1956, M.S., 1957; Ph.D., U. Calif.-Berkeley, 1963. Asst. prof. U. Wis., Madison, 1963-67; assoc. prof. U. Wis.-Madison, 1967-70, prof. chem. engring., 1970-81; chmn. U. Wis.-Madison (Dept. Chem. Engring.), 1971-73, 78-81, asso. vice chancellor, 1972-76; prof. chem. engring. U. Wash., Seattle, 1981—; dean U. Wash. (Coll. Engring.), 1981—; cons. in field; adviser NSF, Dept. Def. Contbr. articles to profl. jours.; editor: 7th-10th Internat. Colloquia on Dynamics of Explosions and Reactive Systems, 1979, 81, 83. Bd. dirs. Wash. Tech. Ctr.; mem. Wash. High Tech. Coordinating Bd. NATO-NSF postdoctoral fellow, 1962-63; sr. postdoctoral fellow, 1968; Deutsche Forschungsgemeinschaft prof., 1976-77. Mem. Am. Inst. Chem. Engrs., Am. Phys. Soc., Combustion Inst., NSPE, Sigma Xi, Tau Beta Pi, Beta Theta Pi. Lodge: Rotary. Home: 5324 NE 86th St Seattle WA 98115 Office: Coll of Engring FH-10 Univ of Wash Seattle WA 98195

BOWEN, MARY FRANCES, biologist; b. Hazleton, Pa., May 17, 1951; d. Richard Edward and Frances Aldona (Wierbowski) B.; m. James Otha Burke, Feb. 15, 1986. BS, Pa. State U., 1973; MS, U. Del., 1976, PhD, 1981. Reasearch assoc. Northwestern U., 1981; NIH postdoctoral fellow U. N.C., 1981-84; sr. biologist SRI Internat., Menlo Park, Calif., 1984—. Contbr. articles to profl. jour. and books. NIH grantee, 1986-89. Mem. AAAS. Avocations: music, ethnic foods. Office: SRI Internat 333 Ravenswood Ave Menlo Park CA 94025

BOWEN, PETER GEOFFREY, real estate investment advisor; b. Iowa City, Iowa, July 10, 1939; s. Howard Rothmann and Lois Berntine (Schilling) B.; m. Shirley Johns Carlson, Sept. 14, 1968; children—Douglas Howard, Leslie Johns. B.A. in Govt. and Econs., Lawrence Coll., 1960; postgrad. U. Wis., 1960-61, U. Denver, 1965. Dir. devel. Mobile Home Communities, Denver, 1969-71; v.p. Perry & Butler, Denver, 1972-73; exec. v.p., dir. Little & Co., Denver, 1973; pres. Builders Agy. Ltd., Denver, 1974-75; pres. The Investment Mgmt. Group Ltd., Denver, 1975—; gen. ptnr. 8 real estate ltd. ptnrships.; lectr. on real estate syndications; bd. dirs. Colo. Plan for Apportionment, 1966. Contbr. articles to profl. pubs. Vice-chmn. Greenwood Village (Colo.) Planning and Zoning Commn., 1983-85; elected mem. City Council Greenwood Village, 1985-86, also mayor pro tem, 1985-86; bd. dirs. Colo. Plan for Apportionment, 1966; speaker Forward Metro Denver, 1966-67. Mem. Lawrence U. Alumni Assn. (bd. dirs. 1966-72, 82-86). Home: 4950 S Beeler Greenwood Village Englewood CO 80111 Office: 1562 S Parker Rd Suite 208 Denver CO 80231

BOWEN, RICHARD L., academic administrator; b. Avoca, Iowa, Aug. 31, 1933; s. Howard L. and Donna (Milburn) B.; m. Connie Smith Bowen, 1976; children: James, Robert, Elizabeth, Christopher; children by previous marriage—Catherine, David, Thomas. B.A., Augustana Coll., 1957; M.A., Harvard, 1959, Ph.D., 1967. Fgn. service officer State Dept., 1959-60; research asst. to U.S. Senator Francis Case, 1960-62; legis. asst. to U.S. Senator Karl Mundt, 1962-65; minority cons. sub-com. exec. reorgn. U.S. Senate, 1966-67; asst. to pres., assoc. prof. polit. sci. U. S.D., Vermillion, 1967-69, pres., 1969-76, disting. prof., 1980-85; commr. higher edn. Bd. Regents State S.D., Pierre, 1976-80; prof. polit. sci. Idaho State U., Pocatello, 1985, pres., 1986—. Served with USN, 1951-54. Recipient Outstanding Alumnus award Augustana Coll., 1970; Woodrow Wilson fellow, 1957, Congl. Staff fellow, 1965; Fulbright scholar, 1957. Office: Idaho State U Office of Pres Campus Box 8310 Pocatello ID 83209

BOWEN, SCOTT MICHAEL, chemist; b. Santa Fe, Dec. 7, 1956; s. Benjamin Scott and Lee (Langspekt) B. BS, U. N.MEx., 1978, MS, 1981, PhD, 1983. Postdoctoral fellow EG&G Idaho Inc., Idaho Falls, 1983-85; mem. staff Los Alamos (N.Mex.) Nat. Lab., 1985—. Mem. AAAS, Am. Chem. Soc., Phi Beta Kappa. Democrat. Avocation: computers. Home: 1424B 40th St Los Alamos NM 87544 Office: Los Alamos Nat Lab INC-11 Los Alamos NM 87545

BOWER, DONALD EDWARD, author; b. Lockport, N.Y., July 19, 1920; B.A., U. Nebr., 1942. Pres., D.E. Bower & Co., Inc., Denver, 1945-60; editor, pub. Arapahoe Tribune, 1960-62; editor Adams County Almanac, Adams County Dispatch, Jefferson County Herald, 1962-65; editor, pub. Buyer's Showcase mag. and FURN Club News 1965-66; exec. editor Colo. mag., 1966-69; editor-in-chief, v.p., dir. Am. West Pub. Co., editor Am. West mag., 1970-74; pres. Colo. Authors League, 1975-76; dir. Nat. Writers Club, Denver, 1974-86; dir. Assoc. Bus. Writers Am., 1978-86, also pres. Assn. Hdqrs., 1978-86; editorial dir. Nat. Writers Press, 1982-86; freelance staff Writer Fawcett Publs., 1962-64; lit. cons., 1962-67. Mem. Soc. Authors and Journalists, Authors Guild Am., Denver Posse, The Westerners (dir. 1976), Outdoor Writers Assn. Am., Western Writers Assn. Am., Friends of Denver Pub. Library, Denver Press Club, Sigma Delta Chi. Author: Roaming the American West, 1970; Ghost Towns and Back Roads, 1972; intro. to The Magnificent Rockies, 1972; Fred Rosenstock: A Legend in Books and Art, 1976; The Professional Writers' Guide, 1984;Ten Keys to Writing Success, 1987; also 4 paperback detective novels, 1960-64; editor: Living Water, Living Earth, 1971; Anasazi: Ancient People of the Rock, 1973; The Great Southwest, 1972; Edge of a Continent, 1970; The Mighty Sierra, 1972; The Magnificent Rockies, 1972; The Great Northwest, 1973; Gold and Silver in the West, 1973; Steinbeck Country, 1973; contbr. articles to mags. Address: 15087 E Radcliff Dr Aurora CO 80015

BOWER, FAY LOUISE, nurse; b. San Francisco, Sept. 10, 1929; d. James Joseph and Emily Clare (Andrews) Saitta; B.S. with honors, San Jose State Coll., 1965; M.S.N., U. Calif., 1966, D.N.Sc., 1978; children—R. David, Carol Bower Tomei, Dennis James, Thomas John. Office nurse Dr. William Grannis, Palo Alto, Calif., 1950-55; staff nurse Stanford Hosp., 1964-72; asst. prof. San Jose State U., 1966-70, asso. prof., 1970-74, prof., 1974-82, coordinator grad. program in nursing, 1977-78, chairperson dept. nursing, 1978-82; dean U. San Francisco, 1982—; speaker; cons. univs.; vis. prof. Harding Coll., 1977, U. Miss., 1976; lectr. U. Calif., San Francisco, 1975. Cert. public health nurse, sch. nurse, Calif. Fellow Am. Acad. Nursing; mem. Calif. Nurses Assn., Nurses Assn. Coll. Ob-Gyn, Calif. Tchrs. Assn., AAUP, Public Health Assn. Calif., Nat. League Nursing (bd. dirs.), Calif. League for Nursing (pres.), Western Gerontol. Assn., Sigma Theta Tau (pres. Beta Gamma chpt.), Jesuit Deans in Nursing (chair). Democrat. Roman Catholic. Club: Commonwealth (San Francisco). Author: (with Em O. Bevis) Fundamentals of Nursing Practice: Concepts, Roles and Functions, 1978; (with Margaret Jacobson) Community Health Nursing, 1978; The Process of Planning Nursing Care, 3d edit., 1982; Theoretical Foundations of Nursing I, II, and III, 1972; editor: Normal Development of Body Image, 1977; Distortions in Body Image in Illness and Disability, 1977; Foundations of Pharmacologic Therapy, 1977; Nursing Assessment, 1977. Home: 1820 Portola Rd Woodside CA 94062 Office: U San Francisco Sch Nursing San Francisco CA

BOWER, MICHAEL O'BANNON, communications exec.; b. Los Angeles, June 13, 1949; s. David F. and Barbara Jeanne (O'Bannon) B.; m. Jennifer Louise Robison, Aug. 23, 1975; children—Timothy, Jonathan. A.A., Cerritos Coll., 1970; B.A. in Communications, Calif. State U., 1972; M. Pub. Relations, U. So. Calif., 1979. Interscholastic press corr. Los Angeles Herald Examiner and Long Beach (Calif.) Press-Telegram, 1966-67; recreation and sports specialist S.E. Recreation and Parks dist., 1967-70; sports editor Daily S.E. News, Downey, Calif., 1969-71; asst. sports info. dir. Cerritos Coll., Norwalk, Calif., 1968-71; sports dir., show host "Sports Mike," RETV, Laguna Hills, Calif., 1971; sports editor, Saddleback Valley News, Mission Viejo, Calif., Leisure World News, Laguna Hills, 1970-71; dir. pub. info. Orange County unit Am. Cancer Soc., 1972-73; pres. Sports Specialties, Norwalk, 1973; dir. pub. relations Orange County Youth Christ/Campus Life, 1973-74; dir. pub. info. Azusa Pacific Coll., 1973-74; info. specialist Norwalk-La Mirada Unified Sch. Dist., 1974-78; pres. chief exec. officer Bower Communications, Inc., Huntington Beach, Calif., 1981-84; pres., chief exec. officer Golden West Communications, Huntington Beach, 1984—; pres. Michael Bower and Assocs., 1976—; guest lectr., instr. area colls., univs. and adult edn. classes. Statistician state jr. coll. basketball playoffs, 1969;dir. Orange County "Up with People"; mem.Los Angeles Area Council communications com. Boy Scouts Am., La Mirada Fiesta de Artes Assn., Boys Clubs of Orange County; Interscholastic Press Assn. scholar, 1967; Rotary scholar, 1967; recipient Freedoms Found. Schoolman medal, 1977, award of excellence internal communications, Jour. Ednl. Communication, 1977; Mem. Pub. Relations Soc. Am. (30 awards), Nat. Sch. Pub. Relations Assn., Publicity Club Los Angeles, Bldg. Industry Assn. (sales and mktg. council), U. So. Calif Alumni Assn. Democrat. Clubs: U. So. Calif. Trojan Fourth Estate (bd. dirs.), U. So. Calif. Trojan Club (bd. dirs.), U. So. Calif. Cardinal and Gold, Orange County Press. Lodge: Kiwanis (bd. dirs.). Contbr. articles to profl. jours. Office: 7400 Center Ave #208 Huntington Beach CA 92617

BOWERS, ALBERT, pharmaceutical company executive; b. Manchester, Eng., July 16, 1930; came to U.S., 1954; s. Albert and Mary (Munn) B.; m. Eileen Easthope, Sept. 26, 1953 (div. May 1985); children—Anita, Karen, Deborah; m. Gwynn C. Akin, Dec. 23, 1985. BS in Chemistry, U. London, 1951; PhD in Organic Chemistry, U. Manchester, 1954. Group leader research Syntex S.A., Mexico City, 1956, v.p., dir. research, 1963; v.p. internat. Syntex, 1964; dir. Syntex Corp., Palo Alto, Calif., 1968; pres. Syntex Corp., 1976-82, 86, also bd. dirs., chief exec. officer, 1980—, chmn., 1981—; pres. Syntex Labs., 1967-73, Syntex USA, 1967-82; dir. U.S. Leasing Internat.; former mem. adv. com. N.Y. Stock Exchange. Contbr. articles to profl. jours.; patentee in selective fluorination of steroids, corticoid compounds synthesis, norethindrone synthesis. Active Calif. Bus. Roundtable, Bus. Higher Edn. Forum, Rockefeller U. Council, U. Calif.-San Francisco Found.; external adv. bd. U. Calif.-San Francisco Cancer Research Inst.; adv. bd. Ctr. for History of Chemistry. Recipient Sci. prize Mex. Acad. Sci., 1964; Fulbright fellow Wayne State U., 1954-55. Mem. Pharm. Mfrs. Assn. (bd. dirs., former chmn.). Office: Syntex Corp 3401 Hillview Ave Palo Alto CA 94304

BOWERS, CHARLES EDWARD, aerospace company executive; b. Crestview, Fla., Feb. 15, 1933; s. Michael Alexander and Lillian Lobelia (Searcy) B.; m. Joan Austin, June 25, 1969; children—Charles, Andrea, Randy, Michele. B.S., Morehead State U., 1956; M.S. in Nuclear Engring., U. Wash., 1965. Reactor physicist Gen. Electric Corp., Richland, Wash., 1956-65; quality control mgr., Wilmington, N.C., 1971-73; mfg. mgr. UNC Resources, Richland, 1965-71, engring. mgr., Montville, Conn., 1973-74, gen. mgr. fuel recovery ops., Wood River Junction, R.I., 1974-79, pres. recovery systems div., 1979-80; pres. Nickel Battery div. Yardney Electric Corp., Pawcatuck, Conn., 1980-81; v.p. ops. Burns Internat. Security Systems, Atlanta, 1980-81; project dir. Hercules Aerospace, Salt Lake City, 1983—; cons. AEC, Oak Ridge, 1967-68; dir. U.S. Nuclear Corp., Oak Ridge. Trustee, United Methodist Ch. Mem. Am. Nuclear Soc., Am. Mgmt. Assn. Republican. Clubs: Oak Ridge Country, Masons, Elks; New Yorker. Home: 1861 E Dimple Dell Rd Sandy UT 84092 Office: Hercules Aerospace PO Box 27408 Salt Lake City UT 84127

BOWERS, JOHN C., association executive; b. Plattsburg, Mo., Dec. 18, 1939; s. Raymond and Ruth Charlotte (Anderson) B.; m. Shirley Kathleen Tucker, Feb. 16, 1962; children—John Bradford, Craig Andrew, Beth Anne. B.S., S.W. Mo. State U., 1961. Mgr. Augusta C. of C., Kans., 1964-66; exec. v.p. Newton C. of C., Kans., 1966-70; pres., gen. mgr. Lakewood-South Jeffco C. of C., Colo., 1970—; dir. Jefferson Econ. Council, Golden, Colo., 1976—. Bd. dirs. Lakewood on Parade, 1977—. Served to 1st lt. U.S. Army, 1962-64. Mem. Colo. C. of C. Execs. (pres. 1976-77), Kansas Jaycees (v.p. 1966, Outstanding State Vice-pres. award 1966), Colo. Assn. Commerce and Industry (dir. 1976-77), Mountain States Assn. (pres. 1983-84), Am. C. of C. Execs. (com. chmn. 1973-74, cert. chamber exec. 1985), C. of C. of U.S. Republican. Home: 918 S Swadley St Lakewood CO 80228 Office: Lakewood/South Jeffco C of C 55 Wadsworth Blvd Lakewood CO 80226

BOWERS, WILLIAM EUGENE, geologist; b. Big Run, Pa., Sept. 28, 1927; s. Arnold Goodrich and Mabel Lucille (Payne) B.; B.S., U. Wash., 1956; M.S., U. N.Mex., 1960. Geologist, U.S. Geol. Survey, Denver, 1961-82, Minerals Mgmt. Service, Denver, 1982-83, U.S. Geol. Survey, 1986—; geologist, researcher geol. map of Bryce Canyon Nat. Park, Utah. Served with USAAF (became USAF 1947), 1946-49; ETO. Mem. Geol. Soc. Am., Colo. Sci. Soc., N.Mex. Geol. Soc. Club: Appaloosa Horse Club (Moscow, Idaho). Research on geology So. Utah. Home: 1605 Iris St Lakewood CO 80215

BOWERS, ZELLA ZANE, real estate broker; b. Liberal, Kans., May 24, 1929; d. Rex and Esther (Neff) Powelson; m. James Clarence Bowers, Aug. 12, 1949; (div. 1977); 1 child: Dara Zane. B.A., Colo. Coll., 1951. Cert. real estate brokerage mgr. Sec. Bowers Ins. Agy., Colorado Springs, Colo., 1955-59, Central Colo. Claims Service, Colorado Springs, 1959-63; pres. Premium Budgeting Co., Colorado Springs, 1962-67; pres., owner Monument Valley Realty, Inc., Colorado Springs, 1981—. Hon. trustee The Palmer Found., Colorado Springs, 1980—, pres., 1983-84; pres. Vis. Nurse Assn., Colorado Springs, 1966-67, 74; dir. Colo. League Nurses, Denver, 1968; advisor Found. of the Robin, Colorado Springs, 1985—; sec. Care & Share, Colorado Springs, 1984; chmn. McAllister House Mus., Colorado Springs, 1973-74; docent chmn. Colorado Springs Fine Arts Ctr., 1969-70; pres. Friends of the Library, 1971-72; pres. Woman's Ednl. Soc. Colo. Coll., 1974-77; civil adminstrv. staff asst. Air Def. Filter Ctr., 1956-57, ground observer, 1956, others. Named State Regent for Life, Daus. of Am. Colonists, 1973. Recipient Women's Trade Fair Recognition award, 1987. Mem. Nat. Assn. Realtors, Colo. Assn. Realtors, Colorado Springs Bd. Realtors (dir., v.p. pres.-elect), Children of the Am. Revolution (pres. 1956-57), Daus. of Am. Colonists (state regent 1970-73), Nat. Soc. Colonial Dames of Am., DAR,

Gamma Phi Beta. Avocations: geneology; travel. Home: 11 W Caramillo St Colorado Springs CO 80907 Office: Monument Valley Realty Inc 219 E Yampa St Colorado Springs CO 80903

BOWES, FLORENCE (MRS. WILLIAM DAVID BOWES), writer; b. Salt Lake City, Nov. 19, 1925; d. John Albreckt Elias and Alma Wilhelmina (Jonasson) Norborg; student U. Utah, 1941-42, Columbia, 1945-46, N.Y. U., 1954-55; grad. N.Y. TV Workshop, 1950; m. Samuel Ellis Levine, July 15, 1944 (dec. July 1953); m. 2d, William David Bowes, Mar. 15, 1958 (dec. 1976); 1 son, Alan Richard. Actress, writer Hearst Radio Network, WINS, N.Y.C., 1944-45; personnel and adminstrv. exec. Mut. Broadcasting System, N.Y.C., 1946-49, free-lance editor, writer, 1948-49; freelance writer NBC and ABC, 1949-53; script editor, writer Robert A. Monroe Prodns., N.Y.C., Hollywood, Calif., 1953-56; script and comml. dir. KUTV-TV, Salt Lake City, 1956-58; spl. editor, writer pub. relations dept. U. Utah, Salt Lake City, 1966-68, editor, writer U. Utah Rev., 1968-75; author: Web of Solitude, 1979; The MacOrvan Curse, 1980; Interlude in Venice, 1981; Beauchamp, 1983. Mem. Beta Sigma Phi. Home: 338-K St Salt Lake City UT 84103

BOWIE, GEORGE HENRY, university official, public relations consultant; b. Aberdeen, Scotland, Nov. 25, 1945; came to U.S., 1971; s. Joseph and Florence (Patterson) B.; m. Lorna A. Andrew, June 15, 1968; children—Mark George, Lisa Ann. B.A., Brigham Young U., 1976. Income tax officer Inland Revenue Service, Aberdeen, Scotland, 1962-67; officer Aberdeen City Police, 1967-71; dir. pub. affairs Brigham Young U., 1976-82, mng. dir. pub. relations, 1982-85; exec. dir. pub. affairs, 1985—; ptnr. Darais, Bowie & McIlroy, Provo, 1983-85. Bd. dirs. Utah Valley Indsl. Devel. Assn., Provo, 1976-79; v.p. pub. relations United Way of Utah County, Provo, 1984. Recipient Outstanding Achievement award Utah Valley Indsl. Devel. Assn., 1977, 78; Exec. of Yr. award Profl. Secs. Internat., 1983. Mem. Pub. Relations Soc. Am. (accredited), Internat. Pub. Relations Assn., Council for Advancement and Support of Edn., Provo Area C. of C. (bd. dirs. 1985—). Mem. Ch. of Jesus Christ of Latter-day Saints. Home: 2843 Apache Ln Provo UT 84604 Office: C-389 Brigham Young Univ Provo UT 84602

BOWLEN, PATRICK DENNIS, holding company executive, lawyer; b. Prairie du Chien, Wis., Feb. 18, 1944; s. Paul Dennis and Arvella (Woods) B. B.B.A., U. Okla., 1966, J.D., 1968. Bar: Alta. 1969. Read law Saucier, Jones, Calgary, Alta., Can., assoc., 1969-70; asst. to pres. Regent Drilling Ltd., 1970-71; pres. Batoni-Bowlen Enterprises Ltd., 1971-79, Bowlen Holdings Ltd., Edmonton, Alta., Can., 1979—; pres., chief exec. officer, owner Denver Broncos, 1984—. Mem. Law Soc. Alta., Can. Bar Assn., Young Presidents Orgn. Roman Catholic. Clubs: Mayfair Golf and Country; Edmonton Petroleum; Outrigger Canoe (Honolulu). Avocations: golf; skiing; surfing. Office: Denver Broncos 5700 Logan St Denver CO 80216 *

BOWLER, MICHAEL LEE, lawyer; b. San Diego, Aug. 3, 1949; s. Leo Francis and Elizabeth Anne (Shepperd) B.; m. Julie Ann St. Jacques, Mar. 8, 1969; children: Shawna, Lee Matthew, Ryan. BA, San Diego State U., 1976; JD, U. San Diego, 1983. Bar: Calif. 1983, U.S. Dist. Ct. (so. dist.) Calif. 1983. Assoc. editor San Diego mag., 1977-83; assoc. Miller & Gibbs, San Diego, 1983-84, Higgs, Fletcher & Mack, San Diego, 1984-86; sole practice San Diego, 1986—; exec. dir. Inst. Quality Constrn., San Diego, 1986; mktg. cons., San Diego, 1983—. Mem. editorial bd. Attorneys Marketing Report, 1987; contbr. articles to profl. jours. Served as sgt. USAF, 1968-72. Mem. ABA, San Diego Bar Assn., Calif. State Bar Assn., San Diego Trial Lawyers Assn., Soc. Profl. Journalists, Phi Beta Kappa, Phi Kappa Phi. Democrat. Roman Catholic. Club: San Diego Press. Office: 530 B St Suite 910 San Diego CA 92101

BOWLES, CHERYL LEE, nursing educator; b. Waukegan, Ill., July 26, 1945; d. Paul Edwin Bowles and Shirley Jean (Waldorf) Stefanic. BS in Nursing, U. Ill., Chgo., 1968, MS in Psychiat. Mental Health Nursing, 1972; EdD, No. Ill. U., 1984. Registered nurse, Ill., Ariz., Nev. Research project coordinator Inst. Clin. Toxicology, Houston, 1972-74; asst. prof. Coll. Nursing U. Okla., Oklahoma City, 1974-77; lectr. Coll. Nursing U. Ariz., Tucson, 1977-79; clin. specialist adolescent psychiat. unit Mercy Ctr. for Health Care, Aurora, Ill., 1979-80; instr. No. Ill. U., DeKalb, 1980-84; assoc. prof. nursing U. Nev., Las Vegas, 1984—; research cons. State Nev. Dept. Edn., Las Vegas, 1986—. Vol. Las Vegas Health Fair, 1985, 86; vol. counselor Domestic Crisis Shelter, Las Vegas, 1986; speaker Las Vegas Speakers' Bur., 1986. Mem. Am. Nurses Assn. (mem. council of nurse researchers), Nev. Nurses Assn., Soc. for Menstrual Cycle Research, Western Soc. Research in Nursing, Sigma Xi, Sigma Theta Tau (counselor 1986—, grantee 1983-84,). Democrat. Club: Las Vegas Track. Avocations: running, skiing, photography. Office: U Nev Dept Nursing 4505 Maryland Pkwy Las Vegas NV 89154

BOWLES, RICHARD JOSEPH, church administrator; b. Evanston, Ill., Mar. 2, 1944; s. Richard Joseph and Virginia (Minger) B.; m. Mary Ann Singer, July 16, 1966; children—Richard S., Brian E. AB with honors, Regis Coll., 1966; MA, Cath. U. Am., 1970. Dir. religious edn. St. John's Parish, Clinton, Md., 1969-70; asst. prof. religious studies Regis Coll., Denver, 1970-75, assoc. dir. campus ministry, 1975-78; dir. liturgy Archdiocese of Denver, 1978—; deacon Basilica of the Immaculate Conception, Denver; archbishop's rep. Living the Good News, v.p., 1984-85. Mem. planning com. Holocaust Awareness Week, 1982-83; mem. Holocaust Inst., Bd. Judaic Studies Program, Denver U., 1985—, Jewish-Cath. Dialogue, 1982—, Lutheran-Cath. Dialogue, 1975—; mem. planning com. Cath. Charities Run, 1982-83, Denver Symphony Marathon; mem. steering com. Denver Area Interfaith Clergy Conf., 1985—, bishop's com. Nat. Conf. Cath. Bishops, 1985, sub-com. on Book of Blessings, 1985—. Recipient Faculty of Yr. award Regis Coll., 1974; Service award Denver Liturg. Commn., 1982. Mem. S.W. Liturg. Conf. Bd., Fedn. Diocesan Liturg. Commns., Alpha Sigma Nu. Office: Denver Archdiocese 200 Josephine St Suite 525 Denver CO 80206

BOWLING, LANCE CHRISTOPHER, record producer, publisher; b. San Pedro, Calif., May 17, 1948; s. Dan Parker and Sylvia Lois (Van Devander) B. BA in Polit. Sci. and History, Pepperdine U., 1966-70, M in Pub. Adminstrn., 1973. Owner, founder Cambria Records and Pub., Palos Verdes, Calif., 1972—. Editor: Joseph Wanger: A Retrospective of Composer-Conductor 1900-1974, 1976, Harzards Pavilion, Journal of Society for Preservation of South California' Musical Heritage, 1985—; author: Eugene Hemmer: Composer-Pianist, 1983; produced over 30 Am. classical records including works by Charles W. Cadman, Madeleine Dring, Mary Carr Moore, John Crown, Ed Bland, and Florence Price, also produced classical music for Sta. KPFK-Radio and Sta. KFAC-Radio. Ative allocation com. region V. United Way, Los Angeles, 1978-85. Mem. ASCAP, Assn. Recorded Sound Collections, Music. Library Assn., Sonneck Soc. Republican. Episcopalian. Clubs: Variety Arts (Los Angeles); Mus. Arts (Long Beach). Avocations: collecting early Calif. books and ephemera, restoration of 1978 RPM recordings and antique automobiles. Home: 2625 Colt Rd Rancho Palos Verdes CA 90274 Office: Cambria Records and Pub Box 374 Lomita CA 90717

BOWMAN, BRUCE, writer, artist, educator; b. Dayton, Ohio, Nov. 23, 1938; s. Murray Edgar Bowman and Mildred May (Moler) Elleman; m. Julie Ann Gosselin, 1970 (div. 1980); 1 child, Carrie Lynn. A.A., San Diego City Coll., 1962; B.A., Calif. State U.-Los Angeles, 1964, M.A., 1968. Tchr. art North Hollywood Adult Sch., Calif., 1966-68; instr. art Cypress Coll., Calif., 1976-78, West Los Angeles Coll., 1969—; tchr. art Los Angeles City Schs., 1966—; seminar leader So. Calif., 1986—. Author: Shaped Canvas, 1976; Toothpick Sculpture and Ice Cream Stick Art, 1976; Ideas: How to Get Them, 1985, (cassette tape) Develop Winning Willpower, 1986. Contbr. articles to profl. jours. One-man shows include Calif. State U.-Los Angeles, 1968, Pepperdine U., Malibu, Calif., 1978; exhibited in group shows McKenzie Gallery, Los Angeles, 1968, Trebor Gallery, Los Angeles, 1970, Cypress Coll., Calif., 1977, Design Recycled Gallery, Fullerton, Calif., 1977, Pierce Coll., Woodland Hills, Calif., 1978, Leopold/Gold Gallery, Santa Monica, Calif., 1980. Served with USN, 1957-61. Home: 28322 Rey De Copas Malibu CA 90265

BOWMAN, GARY MARTIN, social worker; b. Chatham, Ont., Can., July 13, 1943; came to U.S., 1960; s. John Martin and Hilda Ruth (Shaw) B.; m. Gwendolyn Yit-Wah Lee, July 3, 1970 (div. Dec. 1982); m. Jacqueline Custis Miller Lien, Mar. 17, 1984. BA, Graceland Coll., 1965; MSW, U. Hawaii, 1972. Lic. clin. social worker, Calif. Pub. social service worker Linn County Dept. Social Services, Cedar Rapids, Iowa, 1965-67; dir. Joint Services Recreation Assn. for Handicapped, Honolulu, 1967-69, 71-72; social group worker Adolescent Unit Hawaii State Hosp., Kaneohe, 1970-73, 81-83; coordinator adolescent mental health services St. Joseph's Hosp. Health Ctr., Syracuse, N.Y., 1973-74; community services coordinator Elmcrest Children's Services, Syracuse, 1974-75; psychiat. social worker Santa Rosa County Mental Health ctr., Milton, Fla., 1975-80, St. Francis Hosp. Health Care, Honolulu, 1980-81, Los Angeles County Coastal Community Mental Health Ctr., Carson, Calif., 1984-86, West-Cen. Family Mental Health Services, Los Angeles, 1986—; pvt. practice cons., therapy and tng. Burbank, 1986—; adj. faculty mem. U. Syracuse, Western Fla. U. at Pensacola, U. Hawaii, 1976-83; trainer crisis mgmt. Syracuse Police Dept., 1974; presentor Hawaii-Pacific Gerontology Conf., 1981. Author: Joys, Fears, Tears, 1968; editor (newsletter) The Javelin, 1967-69. Bd. dirs., program chmn. Summer Action Vol. Youth Program, Honolulu, 1972-73, 80-83; pres. Friends of Library Santa Rosa County, Milton, 1979-80; founder singles separated divorced support group Reorganized Ch. Jesus Christ Latter-day Saints, Burbank, Calif., 1985—; founder Camp In Search Of, 1978-80. Named Citizen for Day Sta. KGU, Honolulu, 1972; recipient Unheralded Humanitarianism, Dist. 1 Mental Health Bd., 1980. Mem. Nat. Assn. Social Workers (cert., steering com. region H&I Calif., 1983—, alt. dir. region H, Calif., 1984-85, chmn. licensing com. 1979-80, mem. program and continuing edn. coms. 1980-83, Loyal and Dedicated Leadership award 1980), Assn. Labor Mgmt. Adminstrs. and Cons. on Alcoholism, Inc. Lodges: Kiwanis, Optimist (youth ctr. dir. Hiawatha, Iowa club 1966-67). Avocations: tennis, jogging, poetry, gardening, camping. Home: 4433 E Sinova St Los Angeles CA 90032

BOWMAN, JEAN LOUISE, lawyer, civic worker; b. Albuquerque, Apr. 3, 1938; d. David Livingstone and Charlotte Louise (Smith) McArthur; student U. N.Mex., 1956-57, U. Pa., 1957-58, Rocky Mountain Coll., 1972-74; B.A. in Polit. Sci. with high honors, U. Mont., 1982, J.D., 1985; children—Carolyn Louise, Joan Emily, Amy Elizabeth, Eric Daniel. Dir. Christian edn. St. Luke's Episcopal Ch., 1979-80; law clk. to assoc. justice Mont. Supreme Ct., 1985-87; dir. 1st Bank West. Bd. trustees Rocky Mountain Coll., 1972-80; bd. dirs. Billings (Mont.) Area C. of C., 1977-80; mem. City-County Air Pollution Control Bd., 1969-74, chmn., 1970-71; del. Mont. State Constnl. Conv., 1971-72, sec. conv., 1971-72; chmn. County Local Govt. Study Commn., 1973-76; mem. Billings Sch. Dist. Long Range Planning Com., 1978-79; former pres. Billings LWV, dir., 1987—; former pres. Silver Run Ski Club. Named one of Billings' most influential citizens, Billings Gazette, 1977; Bertha Morton Scholar, 1982. Republican. Home: 481 South Park Ave Helena MT 59601

BOWMAN, MICHAEL JOHN, academic administrator; b. Inglewood, Calif., Jan. 11, 1947; s. Charles Andrew Bowman and Bette Lou (Scott) Smith; m. Sherri Lyn Novak, Feb. 3, 1968; 1 child, Jonathan Michael. BA with distinction, U. Redlands, 1968; BA summa cum laude, San Jose Bible Coll., 1970; BA, MA, San Jose State U., 1971. Cert. history tchr., Calif.; ordained to ministry, Christian Ch., 1970. Teaching asst. San Jose (Calif.) Bible Coll., 1968-72, prof. history, 1973-81, dean students, 1979-81, v.p. acad. affairs, 1981—; instr. Pacific Christian Coll., Long Beach, Calif., 1972-73, Chapman Coll., Garden Grove, Calif., 1972-73. Tchr. Los Gatos (Calif.) Christian Ch., 1978—. Named one of Outstanding Young Men of Am., U.S. Jaycees, 1977. Mem. Am. Hist. Assn., Am. Assn. Collegiate Registrars and Admissions Officers, Pacific Assn. Collegiate Registrars and Admissions Officers, Assn. Christian Schs. Internat., Delta Epsilon Chi. Republican. Avocations: antique restoration, coaching youth athletics. Home: 6734 Mt Leneve Dr San Jose CA 95120 Office: San Jose Bible Coll 790 S 12th St San Jose CA 95112

BOWMAN, RICHARD WOOD, health care management consultant; b. Jacksonville, Ill., Dec. 2, 1939; s. Harold Samuel and Nellie Elizabeth B.; B.B.A., U. Wichita, 1962; M.S. in Bus. Adminstrn. (Univ. teaching fellow), Wichita State U., 1965; m. Angela Bowman; children—Jennifer Nicole, Guy Joseph. Teaching fellow Wichita State U., 1963-65; sr. health care cons., project mgr. Cresap McCormick & Paget, Inc., N.Y.C., 1965-71; prin., partner, health care cons. Peat, Marwick Mitchell & Co., N.Y.C., 1971-76, prin. partner. Midwest Regional dir. health cons. services, Chgo., 1977-81, prin. partner, Western regional dir. health cons. services, Los Angeles, 1975-85 ; prin. partner Peat Marwick Internat., 1975-85; sr. v.p., Amicare Nat. Health Network System, Am. Med. Internat., Group Health Services, Beverly Hills, Calif. 1985— ; pres. Am. Health Cons. Group, Rolling Hills Estates, Calif., 1986—; tchr. health care adminstrn. U. Wis.; nat. lectr. Am. Hosp. Assn., Healthcare Fin. Mgmt. Assn., Am. Coll. Hosp. Adminstrs.; spl. advisor fed. Health Care Fin. Adminstrn., HEW; mem. tech. com. Chgo. Health Systems Agy., 1984. Mem. Health Fin. Mgmt. Assn., Am. Hosp. Assn., Young Adminstrs. Calif., Health Care Execs. So. Calif., Assn. Western Hosps. Monthly contbr. to Modern Healthcare Mag., 1977-81, contbg. editor, 1982—; contbg. editor Dimensions in Health Care Quar. Home: 28103 Ella Rd Rancho Palos Verdes CA 90274 Office: Ami/Group Health Services 414 N Camden Dr Beverly Hills CA 90210 Office: Am Health Cons Group Peninsula Pointe 27520 Hawthorne Blvd Rolling Hills Estates CA 90274

BOWMAN, ROBERT DALE, architect; b. Mount Sterling, Ohio, May 30, 1947; s. Avery Elton and Ruby Mildred (Boyd) B.; 1 child, Marc Anthony. BArch, Ohio State U., 1970; postgrad, Memphis State U., 1974-75; opera studies, N.C. Sch. Arts, 1977. Architect George Kontogiannis & Assocs., Columbus, Ohio, 1970-72, Heery & Heery, Atlanta, 1972-73; univ. architect Memphis State U., 1974-75; project mgr., archtl. designer, ptnr. Environ. Designers Collaborative, Bradenton, Fla., 1977-82; asst. project architect DMMJ/Kidde, Cairo, 1982; project mgr., architect Gee & Jenson, Bradenton, 1982-84; architect Sarasota-Bradenton Airport, 1984-85; project mgr., aviation architect Phoenix, 1985—. Author: Solar Energy in South Florida, 1981; operatic debut as Sid el Kar in Desert Song, Springfield (Ohio) Civic Opera, 1971; appeared with Internat. Opera Ctr., Zurich, 1975; several others. Artistic advisor, bd. dirs. Inter-City Opera. Recipient Civic Beautification award City of Sarasota, 1976, design award Alcoa Aluminium, 1965. Mem. AIA, Constrn. Specifications Inst., Urban Land Inst. Home: 888 E Clinton #1064 Promontory Pointe Phoenix AZ 85020

BOWNE, ELISE MARIE, anaytical chemist; b. Hillsboro, Oreg., Oct. 26, 1961; d. John Clarence and Kathryn Estelle (Kroeger) B. BA in Chemistry, U. Colo., 1983. Chemist Rockwell Internat., Golden, Colo., 1983-86, analytical chemist, 1986—. Instr. Eldora Handicapped Recreation Program, Nederland, Colo., 1980-81, supr., 1981-84, asst. dir., 1984-86, program dir. 1986—. Touff scholar, 1981. Mem. Am. Chem. Soc. (cert.), Profl. Ski Instrs. Am. (assoc., cert.), Mortar Bd, Phi Beta Kappa. Club: Rocky Mountain Handicapped Sportsman's Assn. Avocations: skiing, swimming, hiking, camping, bicycling.

BOWSER, DANIEL ROBERT, JR., business, tax, financial consultant; b. Brookville, Pa., Jan. 3, 1941; s. Daniel Robert Sr. and Jean (Ewing) B.; m. Nova Mae Wolfe, Sept. 28, 1963; 1 child, Robert. BA, Grove City Coll., 1962. CLU; chartered fin. cons. Dist. sales mgr. Mut. Benefit Life, Chgo., 1969-70; spl. agt. Northwestern Mut. Life, Chgo., 1970-72; Tenn. rep. Gardner & White, Nashville, 1972-74; nat. sales mgr. Gardner & White, Indpls., 1974-83; owner Gen. Bus. Services, Durango, Colo., 1983—; mem. Score/Ace, Durango, 1984—; bus. columnist Durango Herald, 1984—; founding mem. Bus. Cons. Study Group, Denver, 1984—. Mem. exec. com. S.W. Colo. Econ. Devel. Dist., Durango, 1986. Mem. Am. Soc. CLU's, Am. Soc. Chartered Fin. Cons., Nat. Soc. Pub. Accts., Nat. Fedn. Ind. Bus., Durango C. of C. (membership chmn. 1986, treas. 1987). Republican. Presbyterian. Lodges: Rotary (bd. dirs. Durango club 1984-86), Masons, Shriners. Avocations: motorcycle touring, camping, skiing, hiking, reading. Home: 18 Oak Dr DWII Durango CO 81301 Office: Gen Bus Services 813 Main Ave Suite 301 Durango CO 81301

BOWSHER, ARTHUR LEROY, geologist, researcher, petroleum company executive; b. Wapakoneta, Ohio, Apr. 29, 1917; s. Dallas and Sally Loraine (Fox) B.; m. Lanorah Jane Higgins, Oct. 17, 1943 (div. Dec. 1965); m. Ruth E. Webber, Aug. 29, 1967; children: Sally Jane Drake, Arthur L. Jr., Anne Lorraine Atkinson, Dale C. BS in Petroleum Engring., U. Tulsa, 1941; postgrad., U. Kans., 1941-42, 46-47. Cert. geologist. Assoc. curator U.S. Nat. Mus., Washington, 1947-52; geologist U.S. Geol. Survey, Fairbanks, Alaska, 1952-57; chief exploration strategist U.S. Geol. Survey, Menlo Park, Calif., 1978-81; explorationist Arco and Sinclair Oil and Gas Co., Tulsa, Dallas, 1957-70; staff geologist Arabian Am. Oil Co., Dhahran, Saudi Arabia, 1970-78; sr. geologist Yates Petroleum Corp., Artesia, N.Mex., 1981-86, cons., 1986—; instr. U. Tulsa, 1938-41; instr. and geologist U. Kans., Lawrence, 1941-42, 46-47. Contbr. articles to profl. jours. Served to capt. U.S. Army C.E. Mem. Am. Assn. Petroleum Geologists (emeritis), Roswell Geol. Soc., Paleontologic Soc. Republican. Methodist. Avocations: photography, fishing. Home and Office: 2707 Gaye Dr Roswell NM 88201

BOWYER, JANE BAKER, science educator, academic director; b. Dayton, Ohio, Mar. 16, 1934; d. Homer Kenneth and Helen Elizabeth (Brown) Baker; m. Charles Stuart Bowyer, Feb. 27, 1957; children: William Stuart, Robert Baker, Elizabeth Ann. BA, Miami U., Oxford, Ohio, 1956; MA, U. Calif., Berkeley, 1972; PhD, U. Calif., 1974. Cert. tchr., Ohio, Calif. Prof. Mills Coll., Oakland, Calif., 1975—, head dept. edn., 1986—; cons. Lawrence Hall Sci., U. Calif., Berkeley, 1975—, Nat. Assn. Ednl. Progress, 1975-78, Utah State Bd. Edn., 1985-86; mem. Calif. Round Table's Math/Sci. Task Force, 1983-85; dir. ednl. research Industry Initiatives in Sci. and Math Edn., 1985-86, bd. dirs., 1985—. Author: Science and Society, 1984, Science and Societies Activity Book, 1984; contbr. articles to profl. jours. Bd. dirs. Oakland Sci. and Art Sch., 1979-82, Eric Erickson Sch., San Francisco, 1983-85; Calif. coordinator Nat. Sci. Week Activities, 1986. Fullbright Research fellow, 1982-83. Mem. Nat. Assn. Research in Sci. Teaching (mem. editorial bd. 1980-82, bd. dirs. 1985—, Outstanding Paper award, 1979, 81), Am. Ednl. Research Orgn. Home: 147 Overhill Rd Orinda CA 94563

BOXBERGER, MATTHEW DEAN, electric company executive; b. Russell, Kans., Feb. 19, 1959; s. Dean H. and Betty A. (Balloon) B. BSEE, U. Kans., 1982. Buyer Gen. Electric Co., San Jose, Calif., 1983; with mfg. mgmt. program Gen. Electric Co., Fairfield, Conn., 1983-85; quality engr. Gen. Electric Co., San Jose, Calif., 1983-84; mfg. engr. Gen. Electric Co., Willoughby, Ohio, 1984, shop ops. supr., 1984-85; OEM purchasing agt. Gen. Electric Co., Milpitas, Calif., 1985-86, supplier quality engr., 1986—. Mem. IEEE, Mensa. Republican. Lutheran. Avocations: skiing, bicycling. Home: 3591 Flint Creek Dr San Jose CA 95148 Office: Gen Electric Calma 501 Sycamore Dr MS C51R Milpitas CA 95035

BOXER, BARBARA, congresswoman; b. Bklyn., Nov. 11, 1940; d. Ira and Sophie (Silvershein) Levy; m. Stewart Boxer, 1962; children: Doug, Nicole. B.A., Bklyn. Coll., 1962. Stockbroker Merrill Lynch, N.Y.C., 1962-65; journalist, assoc. editor Pacific Sun, 1972-74; congl. aide to rep. 5th Congl. Dist. San Francisco, 1974-76; mem. Marin County Bd. Suprs., San Rafael, Calif., 1976-82; mem. Budget Com., Com. Govt. Ops., Select Com. Children, Youth and Familie, majority whip at large. Pres. Marin County Bd. Suprs., 1980-81; mem. Bay Area Air Quality Mgmt. Bd., San Francisco, 1977-82, pres., 1979-81; bd. dirs. Golden Gate Bridge Hwy. and Transport Dist., San Francisco, 1978-82; founding mem. Marin Nat. Women's Polit. Caucus, Marin Community Video; pres. Democratic New Mems. Caucus, 1983; elected to U.S. Ho. of Reps. for 98th, 99th and 100th Congresses from 6th Dist. Calif. Recipient Open Govt. award Common Cause, 1980. Jewish. Office: 307 Cannon House Office Bldg Washington DC 20515

BOXER, JEROME HARVEY, accountant; b. Chgo., Nov. 27, 1930; s. Ben Avrum and Edith (Lyman) B.; A.A. magna cum laude, East Los Angeles Coll., 1952; A.B. with honors, Calif. State U., Los Angeles, 1954; m. Sandra Schaffner, June 17, 1980; children by previous marriage—Michael, Jodi. Lab. instr. Calif. State U., Los Angeles, 1953-54; staff accountant Dolman, Freeman & Buchalter, Los Angeles, 1955-57; sr. accountant Neiman, Sanger, Miller & Beress, Los Angeles, 1957-63; partner firm Glynn and Boxer, C.P.A.s, Los Angeles, 1964-68; v.p., sec. Glynn, Boxer & Phillips Accountancy Corp., Los Angeles, 1968—; pres. Echo Data Services, Inc., 1978—; instr. data processing Los Angeles City Adult Schs.; tchr. lectr., cons. wines and wine-tasting; instr. photography. Mem. ops. bd. Everywoman's Village; co-founder Open Space Theatre; past post adviser Explorer Scouts, Boy Scouts Am., also Eagle Scout. Recipient Youth Service award Mid-Valley YMCA, 1972-73; C.P.A., Calif., cert. systems profl. Mem. Am. Inst. C.P.A.s, Calif. Soc. C.P.A.s, Assn. for Systems Mgmt., Data Processing Mgmt. Assn., Am. Fedn. Musicians, Friends of Photography, Los Angeles Photog. Ctr., Acad. Model Aeros., Nat. Model Railroad Assn., Maltese Falcons Home Brewing Soc., San Fernando Valley Silent Flyers, San Fernando Valley Radio Control Flyers, Associated Students Calif. State U., Los Angeles (hon. life), Acad. Magical Arts, Internal Brotherhood of Magicians, Soc. Preservation of Variety Arts, Les Amis du Vin, Knights of the Vine, Soc. Wine Educators, Soc. Bacchus Am., German Shepherd Dog Club Am., German Shepherd Dog Club Los Angeles County, Blue Key, Alpha Phi Omega. Clubs: Kiwanis (pres. Sunset-Echo Park 1968), Braemar Country, Pacific Mariners Yacht, S.Coast Corinthian Yacht (Former dir., officer), B'nai B'rith. Cons., contbr. Wine World Mag., 1974—. Home: 15534 Morrison St Sherman Oaks CA 91403 Office: 1824 Sunset Blvd Los Angeles CA 90026

BOXER, SANDOR THEODORE, lawyer; b. Chgo., Dec. 23, 1939; s. Oscar Ben and Dorothye (Stein) B.; m. Edith G. Boxer, Dec. 22, 1963; children: Jeffrey, Susan, Steven. AB, UCLA, 1961, LLB, 1964. Law clk. to assoc. justice Calif. Supreme Ct., San Francisco, 1964-65; assoc. then ptnr. Coskey, Coskey and Boxer, Los Angeles, 1966—. Bd. dirs. San Fernando Region of Jewish Fedn. Council, Canoga Park, Calif., 1984-86; v.p., bd. dirs. Jewish Family Service, Los Angeles, 1985-87. Mem. ABA, Calif. State Bar Assn., Assn. Bus. Trial Lawyers, Los Angeles County Bar Assn. (vice chmn. arbitration com. 1985-86). Democrat. Office: Coskey Coskey and Boxer 11601 Wilshire Blvd #1960 Los Angeles CA 90025

BOYAJIAN, CAROL LOUISE, graphics designer, interior designer; b. Fresno, Calif., Jan. 6, 1948; d. Armon K. Boyajian and Louise (Josephine) Miroyan. BFA cum laude, The Art Ctr. Coll. Design, 1969. Typographical liaison Doyle Dane Bernbach Advt., N.Y.C., 1969-70; prin. The Enchanted Nook Co., Pasadena, Calif., 1972-78; cons., pvt. practice pub. relations developer Ajijic, Jalisco, Mex., 1978-80; sales assoc. Forbes Monselle Inc., Los Angeles, 1980-84; prin. Carol Boyajian & Assocs., Beverly Hills, Calif., 1980—; co-owner ZERO, Los Angeles, 1968-69; co-ordinator Nat. Resource Council, Los Angeles, 1982; rep. Empire West. Cons. Los Angeles Theater Ctr., 1985. Recipient Cert. Merit, Nat. Fedn. Music Tchrs., Fresno, Calif., 1965. Mem. AIA (profl. affiliate Los Angeles chpt.), Nat. Fedn. Music, Network Exec. Women in Hospitality. Republican. Home and Office: PO Box 663 Beverly Hills CA 90213

BOYCE, RONALD REED, social and behavioral sciences educator, academic administrator; b. Los Angeles, Jan. 7, 1931; s. Reed S. and Martha Fern (Pusey) B.; m. Norma Rae Loraas, May 6, 1955; children: Renee Noreen, Susan Annette. BS, U. Utah, 1956, MS, 1957; PhD, U. Wash., 1960; BS, Seattle Pacific U., 1982, Seattle Pacific U., 1986. Instr. Western Wash. U., Bellingham, 1959; research assoc. Washington U., St. Louis, 1960-62; asst. prof. planning U. Ill., Urbana, 1962-64; assoc. prof. bus. and geography U. Iowa, Iowa City, 1964-65; prof. geography U. Wash., Seattle, 1965-76; dean social, behavioral scis. Seattle Pacific U., 1976—. Author: Economic Geography, 1978, Geography Perspectives on Global Problems, 1982, The Nature of Cities, 1985, Regional Development and the Wabash Basin, 1964; co-author: The United States and Canada, 1970, Seattle, Tacoma and the Southern Sound, 1986 and others. Councilman City of Woodway, 1969-74; chmn., farmland pres. Seattle C. of C., 1979-80; co-pres. Seattle-Beersheva Sister City com., 1985—; mem. tech. II com. City of Redmond, Wash., 1984-85; pres. Allied Arts Orch., Seattle, 1975-78. Served to capt. U.S. Army, 1952-54. Recipient Service award Beersheva, Israel, 1978, Quadrenniel award Congress of South African Geographers, 1981; Nat. scholar Nat. Council of Social Sci., 1969; Am. Council Edn. fellow, 1978-79. Mem. Assn. Am. Geographers (pres. Bible speciality group 1981-84), Assn. Wash. Geographers (pres. 1976-78), Regional Sci. Assn., Sigma Xi. Democrat. Presbyterian. Avocations: trumpet playing. Home: 23606 112th Pl W Edmonds WA 98020 Office: Seattle Pacific U Sch Social & Behavioral Scis 3rd and W Nickerson Seattle WA 98119

BOYD, AYLETTE MARLOWE, art educator; b. Oakland, Calif., July 13, 1939; s. Everett Charles and Cornelia Helen (Lippert) B.; m. Barbara Jane Taylor, June 30, 1968; 1 child, Ryan Marshall. AA, Diablo Valley Coll., 1958; BA, Calif. State U., Chico, 1961; postgrad., U. Calif., Berkeley, 1971-

84. Cert. gen. secondary tchr. (life), spl. art secondary tchr., Calif. Tchr. art Sequoia Middle Sch., Pleasant Hill, Calif., 1963—; cons. art Magic Threads, Clayton, Calif., 1985—. Painter celebrity portraits (Las Juntas 1st award 1981, Pleasanton 2d award 1984, Las Juntas Most Popular award 1985). Juror San Francisco Film Festival, 1981—. Phelan award Phelan Com., San Francisco, 1966. Mem. NEA, Mt. Diablo Edn. Assn., Calif. Tchrs. Assn., Calif. Art Educators Assn., Las Juntas Art Assn. (judge 1983). Avocations: film studies, travel, bowling, weight-tng., video. Home: 19 Darian Ln Pleasant Hill CA 94523 Office: Mt Diablo Sch Dist 1936 Carlotta Dr Concord CA 94523

BOYD, GERALD WILLIAM, police chief; b. Long Beach, Calif., Feb. 3, 1946; s. William E. and Mary (Boyer) B.; m. Patricia M. Hood, May 13, 1967 (dec. May 1985); children: Christopher, Kevin, Brian; m. Elizabeth H. Sedlacek, July 5, 1986. B.A. cum laude, Loyola U., 1967; M.S., Calif. State U., 1977. Dep. sheriff Los Angeles County Sheriff's Dept., 1968-73, sgt., 1973-75; lt. Irvine Police Dept., Calif., 1975-79, capt., 1979-81; chief of police Coronado Police Dept., Calif., 1981—. Author: The Will to Live, 1980. Contbr. articles to profl. jours. Pub. info. officer Am. Radio Relay League, Newington, Conn., 1982—; bd. dirs. U. San Diego High Sch., 1984; adv. bd. Southwestern Community Coll., Chula Vista, 1984. Named Law Enforcement Newsmaker of Year, San Diego Press Club, 1981; Medal of Valor, Am. Legion, 1981. Mem. Calif. Peace Officers Assn., Calif. Police Chief's Assn., San Diego County Chiefs of Police/Sheriff's Assn. Republican. Roman Catholic. Office: Coronado Police Dept 578 Orange Ave Coronado CA 92118

BOYD, JOSEPHINE WATSON, microbiology writer, editor; b. St. Paul, Feb. 19, 1927; d. Leonard Edward and Mae (Watson) Daubney; m. William Lee Boyd, Jan. 6, 1956; children: Victoria Leonard, Samantha Daubney, Laurence Samuel. BChemE, BBA, U. Minn., 1948, MS, 1953; PhD, U Minn., 1955. Cert. wastewater and water treatment operator, Colo. Arctic research scientist Arctic Inst. N.Am., Port Barrow, Alaska, and Tromso, Norway, 1956-65, 70, 72; postdoctoral fellow Colo. State U., Ft. Collins, 1968-72; chemist City of Ft. Collins, 1974-78; sr. tech. editor Hach Co., Loveland, Colo., 1978—. Contbr. articles to profl. jours. Recipient Excellence award Colo. Tech. Writer's Assn. Mem. AAAS, Colo. Water Pollution Control Fedn., Sigma Xi. Avocations: knitting, quilting, bicycle riding.

BOYD, LEONA POTTER, former social worker; b. Creekside, Pa., Aug. 31, 1907; d. Joseph M. and Belle (McHenry) Johnston; grad. Ind. Normal Sch., 1927; student Las Vegas Normal U., N.Mex., summer 1933; postgrad. Carnegie Inst. Tech. Sch. Social Work, summer 1945, U. Pitts. Sch. Social Work, 1956-57; m. Edgar D. Potter, July 16, 1932 (div.); m. Harold Lee Boyd, Oct. 1972. Tchr., Creekside (Pa.) pub. schs., 1927-30, Papago Indian Reservation, Sells, Ariz., 1931-33; caseworker, supr. Indiana County (Pa.) Bd. Assistance, 1934-54, exec. dir., 1954-68, ret. Bd. dirs. Indiana County Tourist Promotion; cons. asso. Community Research Assos., Inc.; mem. Counseling Center Aux., Lake Havasu City, Ariz., 1978-80; mem. Western Welcome Club, Lake Havasu City, Sierra Vista Hosp. Aux., Truth or Consequences, N.Mex. Recipient Jr. C. of C. Disting. Service award, 1966, Business and Profl. Women's Club award, Indiana, Pa., 1965. Mem. Am. Assn. Ret. Persons, Daus. Am. Colonists, Internat. Platform Assn., Sierra County hist. socs. Lutheran. Club: Hot Springs Women's. Home: 507 N Foch St Truth or Consequences NM 87901

BOYD, MARTIN JOSE, emergency physician; b. Albuquerque, Nov. 22, 1948; s. Edward Lewellyn Boyd and Mattie Belle (Smith) Boyd Webb; m. Rita Mae Suina, May 29, 1982; children: Holly Marie, José Edward. B.S., U. N.Mex., 1974, M.D., 1978. Diplomate Am. Bd. Emergency Medicine. Intern Henry Ford Hosp., Detroit, 1978-79, resident in emergency medicine, 1978-81; emergency physician Gallup Indian Med. Ctr., N.Mex., 1981—, chief dept. emergency medicine, 1983—; med. dir. Gallup Ambulance Service, Inc., 1983—, Thoreau Emergency Med. Services, N.Mex., 1983-86. Served as sgt. U.S. Army, 1968-71. Fellow Am. Coll. Emergency Physicians. Democrat. Home: 3714 Zia Dr Gallup NM 87301 Office: Gallup Indian Med Ctr PO Box 1337 Gallup NM 87301

BOYD, MARY H. (MERRILL), assn. exec.; b. Winnetka, Ill., Sept. 11, 1929; d. Harold Gatton and Martha Emily (Lawson) Heberling; student Long Beach City Coll., 1956, UCLA, 1973; cert. in human services U. Calif.-Riverside, 1973-74; B.S. with honors, LaVerne U., 1982; children—Constance Anne Boyd, Richard Parker Boyd Jr. Exec. sec. Ontario-Pomona Assn. for Retarded Citizens, Montclair, Calif., 1962-65, exec. dir., 1965—; instr. Chaffey Coll., Alta Loma, Calif., 1972-76, coordinator classes for disabled, 1972-76; instr. weekend series LaVerne U., 1974, vis. lectr., 1969-74; vis. lectr. Mt. San Antonio Coll., 1976, U. Calif. at Riverside, 1972, UCLA, 1981-82; trainer various subjects Kellogg Found., OPARC Aux. Found., 1969; lectr. in field. Founder, Mental Retardation Service Council of San Gabriel Valley, 1965; mem. Calif. Developmental Disabilities Area planning bd., Area 12, Inyo, Mono, Riverside, San Bernardino counties, 1970-76, chmn. profl. adv. counsel, 1977-80; mem. steering com. for development of Regional Ctrs. Inland Counties, 1969-70, San Gabriel Valley, 1973; active Girl Scouts U.S.A., 1960-68; leader, advisor Tri-Hi-Y, 1968-71; bd. dirs. PTA, 1958-62; chmn. Mt. Baldy United Way Conf. Execs., 1983, 86-87; adv. bd. Mt. San Antonio Coll. Allied Health Adv. Bd., 1975—, Los Angeles United Way, 1966—, Calif. Inst. for Men, 1968-72, San Bernardino County Child Health and Disability Prevention, 1975-78, chmn., 1977-78; adv. bd. Chaffey Coll., 1972-78. Recipient Award of Merit, San Bernardino County Council of Community Services, 1966; Hon. Service award Ontario Montclair Sch. Dist., 1971; Humanitarian award, San Bernardino County, 1976; Chaffey Community Rep. Women Federated Recognition award, 1977; Community Service, Lioness awards U. LaVerne, 1982, Service award ARC, 1983, Calif. CCE Leadership award ARC, 1983, 85; HEW grantee, 1968, 69, 70, 72, 73, 74, 75, 76, 79; Calif. Community Found. grantee, 1968; Price Found. grantee, 1969, 72; Calif. Dept. Rehab. grantee, 1972, 73, 74, 75, 79, 81; Calif. Dept. Health grantee, 1976, 77. Mem. Assn. for Retarded-U.S. (pres. SW chpt. 1987), Assn. for Retarded-Calif. (v.p. 1979-81, pres. 1981-82), Conf. of Execs. of Assns. for Retarded U.S. (charter), Conf. Execs.-Calif. (chmn. 1982-83), Council Agy. Execs. Republican. Baptist. Author: (with J.Cook, J. Travers) Parents as Natural Helpers to Physicians at Time of Diagnosis of Developmental Disability, 1979. Home: 940 W 5th St Ontario CA 91762 Office: 5405 Arrow Hwy Suite 102 Montclair CA 91763

BOYD, NEVA FAYE, manufacturing company executive; b. Amherst, Colo., Nov. 21, 1937; f. Selmar Willard and Edna May (Helms) Deden; m. Melvin Eugene Boyd, Dec. 4, 1955; s. Wayne Eugene, Debra Faye. Cert. chiropractic asst. Chiropractic asst. Fair Chiropractic, Walnut Creek, Calif., 1970-75; head cashier U.S. Dept. Def., Dhahran, Saudi Arabia, 1980-83; pres. Melva Engring. Corp., Boise, Idaho, 1983—; also bd. dirs. Melva Engring. Corp. Com. chmn. Cub Scouts Am., Mossyrock, Wash., 1967. Republican. Lutheran. Avocations: bowling, fishing, golf, reading. Home: 11965 Goldenrod Dr Boise ID 83704

BOYD, ROBERT ANDREW, state agency administrator; b. Phila., Apr. 6, 1945; s. Andrew and Edma Mae (Gruitt) B.; m. Kathleen Lois Turner, Feb. 19, 1967; children: Rebecca Mae-Lois, Amanda Lewellyn. AA, AAS, Matanuska Susitna Community Coll., 1983. Mgr. airport, chief controller Pompano Beach (Fla.) Airport, 1970-74; air traffic controller FAA, Fla., Alaska, 1974-81; supt. transp. maintenance State of Alaska, Kodiak, 1983—. Served with USAF, 1964-69. Mem. VFW. Republican. Methodist. Lodge: Rotary (bd. dirs. Kodiak club 1985-86). Avocations: flying, fishing, hunting, reading. Home: PO Box 3043 Kodiak AK 99615

BOYD, THOMAS EDGAR, chemistry lab supervisor; b. Colorado Springs, Colo., June 1, 1946; Joseph Ivan and Oba Geraldine (Garside) B.; m. Margaret Lynn Atkinson, Jan. 20, 1973; children: Ann Carissa, Lynne Margaret, Jenny Renee. BS, Colo. Coll., 1968; PhD, U. Ill., 1973. Sr. research chemist Mobay Chem. Co., New Martinsville, W.Va., 1974-81; research specialist I Rockwell Internat., Golden, Colo., 1981-84, lab. mgr. I, 1984-87, systems engr., 1987—. Co-author numerous articles. Active Steelton Meth. Adult Choir, New Martinsville, W.Va., 1974-81; chmn. administrv. bd. Steelton Meth. Ch., 1978-80; active Mountain View Meth. Chancel Choir, Boulder, Colo., 1981-83, Boulder First Presbyn. Chancel Choir, 1983—, Boulder Messiah Choral and Orchestra, 1983—; pres., treas. Men's Softball League, New Martinsville, 1977-80. Recipient IR-100 award Indsl. Research Mag., 1985. Mem. Nat. Mgmt. Assn., Am. Chem. Soc., Automobile Lic. Plate Collectors Assn. (regional sec. treas. 1983—). Presbyterian. Avocations: license plate collecting, sports, numismatics, geneology. Home: 838 Rockway Pl Boulder CO 80303 Office: Rockwell Internat PO Box 464 Golden CO 80401

BOYD, WILLIAM ELKINS, lawyer; b. San Mateo, Calif., Oct. 13, 1947; s. William Sprott and Katherine (Elkins) Boyd; m. Elizabeth Johnston Kroeber, May 19, 1984. BA, Stanford U., 1969; JD, Hastings Coll. of Law, 1974. Admitted to Calif. bar, 1975; ptnr. firm Boyd and McKay, San Francisco, 1980—; v.p. Boyd Bros., investments, San Francisco, 1980—; pres. Trio I Assocs. Investments, San Francisco, 1985—. Spl. asst. to chmn. Calif. Republican Com., 1968; bd. dirs. San Mateo County Planned Parenthood, 1971-73, Hastings Child Care Center, 1974-76. Mem. Am. Bar Assn., State Bar Calif. Assn. (bus. law sect.), Stanford U. Alumni Assn., Hastings Alumni Assn. Episcopalian. Clubs: Burlingame Country, Hastings 1066 Club. Home: 590 Remillard Dr Hillsborough CA 94010 Office: 601 Montgomery St Suite 1900 San Francisco CA 94111

BOYD, WILLIAM HARLAND, historian; b. Boise, Idaho, Jan. 7, 1912; s. Harland D. and Cordelia (Crumley) B.; A.B., U. Calif.-Berkeley, 1935, M.A., 1936, Ph.D., 1942; m. Mary Kathryn Drake, June 25, 1939; children—Barbara A. Boyd Voltmer, William Harland, Kathryn L. Tchr. Fall River High Sch., McArthur, Calif., 1937-38, Watsonville (Calif.) High Sch., 1941-42, San Mateo (Calif.) High Sch., 1942-44; prof. history Bakersfield Coll., 1946-73, chmn. social sci. dept., 1967-73. Pres., Kern County Hist. Soc., 1950-52; adv. com. Kern County Mus., 1955-60; chmn. Fort Tejon Restoration Com. Bakersfield, 1952-55, sec., 1955-60; mem. Kern County Hist. Records Commn., 1977—, Bakersfield Hist. Preservation Commn., 1984-87. Recipient Merit award Kern County Bd. Trade, 1960; commendation Kern County Bd. Supvrs., 1952, 76, 78. Mem. Calif. Tchrs. Assn., Am. Hist. Assn., Phi Alpha Theta. Republican. Baptist. Author: Land of Havilah, 1952, (with G.J. Rogers) San Joaquin Vignettes, 1955, (with others) Spanish Trailblazers in the South San Joaquin, 1957; A Centennial Bibliography on the History Kern County, California, 1966; A California Middle Border, 1972; A Climb Through History, 1973; Bakersfield's First Bapt. Church, 1975; Kern Country Wayfarers, 1977; Kern County Tall Tales, 1980; The Shasta Route, 1981; Stagecoach Heyday in the San Joaquin Valley, 1983. Contbr. to Ency. Brit. Home: 339 Cypress St Bakersfield CA 93304

BOYD, WILLIAM LEE, educator, researcher, consultant; b. Kingsport, Tenn., Apr. 20, 1926; s. Samuel Niel and Sarah Mauveline (Dukes) B.; m. Josephine Watson Daubney, Jan. 6, 1956; children: Victoria, Samantha, Laurence. BA, U. Tenn., 1950; MS, U. Minn., 1952, PhD, 1954. Asst. prof. U. Ga., Athens, 1954-55; prin. investigator Arctic Research Lab., Barrow, Alaska, 1955-57; assoc. prof. Ohio State U., Columbus, 1958-64; prof. Colo. State U., Ft. Collins, 1964—; field scientist various orgns. Alaska, Can., Norway, Iceland, Greenland, Antarctica, 1954—; dir. water quality lab. Colo. State U., 1983—. Contbr. numerous articles to profl. jours. Served with USN, 1943-46, PTO. Fellow AAAS, Arctic Inst. N.Am.; mem. Am. Soc. Microbiology, Water Pollution Control Fedn., Sigma Xi. Avocations: mountain climbing, polar philately, polar history. Home: 1313 Stover St Fort Collins CO 80524 Office: Colo State U Dept Environ Health Fort Collins CO 80523

BOYD A., VANDER HOUWEN, bank executive; b. Yakima, Wash., Jan. 17, 1946; s. John W. and Elsie W. (Lanfear) V.; m. Loma Alene Madsen, June 27, 1970; children: Garth John, Dana Madsen. BA in Journalism, U. Mont., 1968; BA in Econs., U. Wash., 1971, MA in Communications/Bus., 1978; grad., NW Intermediate Banking Sch., Portland, Oreg., 1985. Reporter city hall Idaho Falls Post Register, 1971-72; writer farm bus. Tri City Herald, Kennewick, Wash., 1973-74; bus. mgr., editor Yakima Valley Tri City Herald, Sunnyside, Wash., 1974-76; editor Jour. Contemporary Bus.; mgr. bus. publs. Grad. Sch. Bus. Adminstrn. U. Wash., Seattle, 1978-81; v.p., mgr. employee communications Rainier Nat. Bank, Seattle, 1981—. Mem. publs. redesign commn. Hist. Seattle, 1982; mem. Rainier Bancorp. United Way Cabinet, 1983—; mem. selection commn. Nat. Merit Scholarship Program, Rainier Nat. Bank, 1984; mem. mktg. commn. United Way King County, 1985—, chmn. communications commn., 1986—. Served with U.S. Army, 1969-71. NEH grantee, 1979; recipient Gold award United Way Am., 1985. Mem. Pub. Relations Soc. Am. (Totem award NW chpt. 1985), Internat. Assn. Bus. Communicators (named Communicator Yr., Pacific NW chpt. 1985, two awards excellence 1983, Silver 6 award 1982, 83, 85), Sigma Delta Chi. Home: 8575 SE 76th Pl Mercer Island WA 98040 Office: Rainier Nat Bank PO Box 3966 Seattle WA 98124

BOYDSTUN, JAMES ALLEN, psychiatrist; b. LaRue, Ark., Sept. 13, 1940; s. Raymond Dennis and Mary Helen (Bland) Boydstun-Anderson; m. Myrna Louise McCool (div. Jan. 1965); 1 child, Barry Allen; m. Shelley Jean Hudson, Mar. 12, 1966; 1 child, Wendy Lynn. BA, U. Ark., 1962, BS, MD, 1966. Cert. Am. Bd. Neurology and Psychiatry. Commd. 2d lt. USAF, 1965, advanced through grades to col., 1979; chief neuropsychiatry br. USAF, Brooks AFB, Tex., 1974-76, dep. chief clin. scis. div., 1976-79; comdr. USAF Hosp., Fairchild AFB, Wash., 1979-81; vice-comdr. USAF Sch. Aerospace Medicine, Brooks AFB, 1981-83; asst. dep. chief staff USAF Systems Command, Andrews AFB, Washington, 1983-85; ret. USAF, 1985; med. dir. Chelan (Wash.) Pavillion, 1985—; instr. Sch. Aerospace Medicine, San Antonio, 1974-79; from asst. to assoc. clin. prof. U. Tex. U. Health Scis., San Antonio, 1974-79; clin. prof. psychiatry Uniformed Services U. Health Scis., Bethesda, Md., 1983—. Contbr. articles to profl. jours. Decorated Legion of Merit with oak leaf cluster. Fellow Am. Psychiat. Assn., Aerospace Med. Assn.; mem. AMA, Am. Psychosomatic Soc., Sigma Xi. Republican. Lodge: Masons (master mason). Avocations: fly fishing, skiing, music, photography, gun dogs. Home: PO Box 1647 Chelan WA 98816 Office: Chelan Pavilion 503 E Highland Dr Chelan WA 98816

BOYER, DAVID ALAN, finance manager; b. Worthington, Minn., Sept. 16, 1949; s. Floyd Ralph and Fern Charlotte (Hurley) B.; m. Sandra Rae Heeren, Sept. 19, 1968; children: Jeffrey, Kristine. BA, Calif. State U., Fullerton, 1977. Acct. City of Riverside, Calif., 1977-78; acctg. supr. City of Chino, Calif., 1979-82; gen. ledger supr. Multnomah County, Portland, Oreg., 1979-82, fin. mgr., 1982—. Treas. Vols. Am., Portland, 1982—. Democrat. Avocations: golf, tennis, snow skiing, reading. Office: Multnomah County 1120 SW Fifth Room 1430 Portland OR 97204

BOYER, LAURA MERCEDES, librarian; b. Madison, Ind., Aug. 3, 1934; d. Clyde C. and Dorcas H. (Willyard) Boyer. A.B., George Washington U., 1956; A.M., U. Denver, 1959; M.L.S., George Peabody U., 1961. Pub. sch. tchr., Kankakee, Ill., 1957-58; asst. circulation librarian U. Kans., Lawrence, 1961-63; asst. reference librarian U. of Pacific Library, Stockton, Calif., 1963-65, head reference dept., 1965-84, coordinator reference services, 1984-86. Compiler of Play Anthologies Union List, 1976. Author article in profl. jour. Mem. Am. Soc. Info. Sci., ALA, Calif. Library Assn., AAUP, Nat. Assn. Female Execs., Nat. Assn. Vietnamese Am. Educators, DAR, Daughters of the Am. Colonists, Phi Beta Kappa, Kappa Delta Pi, Beta Phi Mu. Republican. Episcopalian. Home: 5650 Stratford Circle Apt 29 Stockton CA 95207 Office: U of Pacific Library Stockton CA 95211

BOYER, MELVIN ALTON, data processing executive; b. Filmore, Calif., Apr. 22, 1938; s. Marvin Alfred and Lulu Marie (Hinkle) B.; m. Nancy Jean Walters, July 25, 1959; children—John Michael, Mark Allen. Unit record operator Boeing Airplane Co., Seattle, 1960-62; programmer Tektronix Inc., Beaverton, Oreg., 1962-65; sr. programmer, analyst Longview Fibre Co. (Wash.), 1965-78; dir. data processing La. Pacific Corp., Portland, Oreg., 1978—. Served with USMC, 1956-58. Mem. Soc. Info. Mgmt., Assn. System Mgmt. (cert. systems profl.), Beaverton Area C. of C. Republican. Roman Catholic. Club: K.C. Home: 1875 NE Lincoln St Hillsboro OR 97123 Office: 111 SW 5th Ave Portland OR 97204

BOYKIN, JAMES LESTER, retired aerospace company engineer, consultant; b. Clarendon, Tex., Jan. 6, 1928; s. Garland Lester and Lucy Edna (Matthews) B.; m. Dulcie Mildred Ligon, Sept. 2, 1958; children—Tracy Lynette, Leslie Dee, James Russell, Robin Elisa. B.S.M.E., N.Mex. State U., 1951, B.S.E.E., 1959. Comml. pilot rating. With Hughes Aircraft Co., 1951-54; fighter pilot U. S. Air Force, 1954-58; flight test engr., test ops. supr. N.Am. Aviation div. Rockwell Internat., Los Angeles, 1959-63, Las Cruces, N.Mex., 1963-69; test ops. supr. LTV (Ling Temco Vaught), Las Cruces, 1969-71, Dynalectron Corp., Las Cruces, 1971-74; with Rockwell Internat., Las Cruces, 1974-85, ops. supr., 1978-85, project engr., 1981, sr. project engr., 1981-85; cons.; charter flying, instr., 1985—. Served to capt. USAF, 1946-48, 54-58; with USAFR, 1969. (ret.). Mem. Nat. Rifle Assn. (life), Air Force Assn., Res. Officers Assn. Democrat. Methodist. Club: Lions (pres. 1975-76) (Las Cruces). Home: 2390 Rosedale Dr Las Cruces NM 88005

BOYLAN, AMY COOPER, academic administrator; b. N.Y.C., Mar. 20, 1959; d. Leonard and Carole Rae (Holzer) Cooper; m. Thomas Michael Boylan, Sept. 4, 1982. BSW summa cum laude, Ariz. State U., 1981. Social worker Cath. Social Services, Mesa, Ariz., 1981-83; caseworker Valley Big Bros. and Big Sisters, Inc., Phoenix, 1983-86, 87—; student services counselor U. Phoenix, 1986; acad. advisor coll. bus. Ariz. State U., Tempe, 1986—; researcher, freelance writer, Tempe, 1986—. Mem. Nat. Assn. Social Workers, Ariz. Ctr. to Reverse the Arms Race, Phi Kappa Phi. Democrat. Avocations: reading, writing, bicycle riding, camping, doll collecting. Home: 4540 S Rural Rd #J-8 Tempe AZ 85282 Office: Ariz State Univ College of Business Tempe AZ 85287

BOYLAN, RICHARD JOHN, psychologist, educator; b. Hollywood, Calif., Oct. 15, 1939; s. John Alfred and Rowena Margaret (Devine) B.; m. Charnette Marie Blackburn, Oct. 26, 1968 (div. June 1983); children: Jennifer April, Stephanie August. BA, St. John's Coll., 1961; MEd, Fordham U., 1966; MSW, U. Calif., Berkeley, 1971; PhD in Psychology, U. Calif., Davis, 1984. Lic. clin. social worker; lic. marriage, family and child counselor. Asst. dir. Berkeley (Calif.) Free Ch., 1970-71; psychiat. social worker Marin Mental Health Dept., San Rafael, Calif., 1971-77; dir. Calaveras Mental Health Dept., San Andreas, Calif., 1977-85; prof., coordinator Nat. U., Sacramento, 1985—; instr. Calif. State U., Sacramento, 1985—, U. Calif., Davis, 1986—; pvt. practice psychotherapy, Sacramento, 1974—. Cons. Calif. State Legis., Sacramento, 1979-80; chmn. Calaveras County Bd. Edn., Angels Camp, Calif., 1981-84. Recipient Geriatric Medicine Acad. award NIH, 1984, Experiment Station grant USDA, Calif., 1983. Mem. Am. Psychol. Assn., Am. Anthropol. Assn., Nat. Assn. Social Workers, AAUP, Sierra Club. Democrat. Taoist. Avocations: hiking, racquetball, swimming, biking, camping. Home: 6724 Trudy Way Sacramento CA 95831 Office: 2222 Sierra Blvd D-19 Sacramento CA 95825

BOYLE, BRIAN J., state agency administrator; b. Butte, Mont., Apr. 23, 1941; s. Albert J. and Yvonne (Chevigny) B.; m. Susan Whittington, Apr. 16, 1982; children: Stephen, Karen. BS, Mont. Sch. Mines, 1964; postgrad., U. Chgo., 1966; MBA, U. Portland, 1973. Mgr., engr. Reynolds Aluminum, Longview, Wash., 1967-79; county commr. Cowlitz County, Longview, 1975-79; dir. Pacific NW Innovation Group, Vancouver, Wash., 1980; commr. pub. lands State of Wash., Olympia, 1981—; chmn. Bd. Natural Resources, Olympia, 1981—, Forest Practices Bd., Olympia, 1981—, Harbor Lines Commn., Olympia, 1981—; Wash. state rep. Inter Oil Compact Com., Oklahoma City, 1981—. Candidate lands commr., Wash., 1980, 84, county commr., Cowlitz County, 1974. Mem. Western States Lands Com. Assn. (v.p. 1985—), China Relations Council (bd. dirs. 1985—), Internat. Trade Ctr. U. Wash. (bd. dirs. 1984—), Wash. Export council (bd. dirs. 1983—), Wash. Council Internat. Trade (bd. dirs. 1984—). Republican. Avocations: reading, running, hiking, travel. Office: Office of Commr John A Cherberg Bldg Olympia WA 98504

BOYLE, CAROLYN MOORE, public relations practitioner, marketing communications manager; b. Los Angeles, Jan. 29, 1937; d. Cory Orlando Moore and Violet (Brennan) Baldock; m. Robert J. Ruppelt, Oct. 8, 1954 (div. Aug. 1964); children—Cory Robert, Traci Lynn; m. 2d, Jerry Ray Boyle, June 1, 1970 (div. 1975). A.A., Orange Coast Coll., 1966; B.A., Calif. State U.-Fullerton, 1970; student U. Calif.-Irvine, 1970-71. Program coordinator Newport Beach Cablevision (Calif.), 1968-70; pub. relations dir. Fish Communications Co., Newport Beach, 1970-74; mktg. rep. Dow Pharm. div. Dow Chem. Co., Orange County, Calif., 1974-77, Las Vegas, Nev., 1980-81; product publicity mgr. Dow Agrl. Products div. Dow Chem. Co., Midland, Mich., 1977-80; mgr. mktg. communications Dowell Fluid Services Region div. Dow Chem. Co. Houston, 1981-84; mktg. communications adminstr. Swedlow, Inc., Garden Grove, Calif., 1984-85; mktg. communications cons., 1985-86; mktg. communications mgr. Am. Convertors Div. Am. Hosp. Supply, 1986— ; guest lectr. Calif. State U., Long Beach, 1970; seminar coordinator U. Calif., Irvine, 1972; mem. Western White House Press Corps, 1972; pub. relations cons. BASF Wyandotte, Phila., 1981-82. Author: Agricultural Public Relations/Publicity, 1981. Editor Big Mean AG Machine (internal mag.), 1977. Contbr. numerous articles to trade publs. Contbg. editor Dowell Mktg. Newsletter, 1983. Creator/designer Novahistine DMX Trial Size nat. mktg. program, 1977. Com. mem. Dow Employees for Polit. Action, Midland, Mich., 1978-80; bd. dirs. Dowell Employees for Polit. Action Com., Houston, 1983-84. Named Salesman of Yr. Pharm. div. Dow Chem. Co., 1975; scholar World Campus Afloat (U. Seven Seas), 1966-67; recipient PROTOS in video prodn., 1985. Mem. Pub. Relations Soc. Am. (cert.), Soc. Petroleum Engrs., Internat. Assn. Bus. Communicators. Episcopalian. Recipient first rights to televise President Nixon in Western White House. Address: 26259 Rainbow Glen Dr Newhall CA 91321

BOYLE-LOPEZ, BARBARA, advertising executive; b. Detroit, Mar. 28, 1943; d. James Joseph and Daisy Irene (Porter) Boyle; div.; 1 dau., Yvette Emma. Account exec. various Los Angeles advt. agys., 1969-74; pres., co-creative dir. Cozad & Lopez Advt., Los Angeles, 1974-77; chief exec. officer Boyle/Lopez Advt., Inc. Corp. advt., Los Angeles, 1977—; lectr. in field. Mem. Los Angeles Advt. Women (past pres.), Western States Advt. Agys. Assn. (bd. dirs., 1979-81), Am. Advt. Fedn. (dir. 1979). Club: Los Angeles Athletic. Home: 12021 Wilshire Blvd Suite 500 Los Angeles CA 90025 Office: Boyle/Lopez Advt Inc 10845 Lindbrook Dr Suite 201 Westwood Village CA 90024

BOYLLS, JOHN CHARLES, electronic engineer; b. Memphis, Sept. 16, 1942; s. Stanley Smith and Kathryn Ann (Anderson) B.; m. Virginia Wright, July 15, 1967. Devel. engr. U. Calif. San Diego, La Jolla, 1970-82; engring. mgr. Access Research, Encinitas, Calif., 1983—; cons. Sea Systems Encinitas, 1976—, Exec. Aviation, Carlsbad, Calif., 1976—. Author: Flight Tng. Manuals, 1978-83; contbr. articles to profl. jours. Accident Prevention Counselor FAA, San Diego, 1982—. Served with USN, 1964-68. Mem. IEEE, Am. Mgmt. Assn., Nat. Assoc. Flight Instrs., Assn. Old Crows, AAAS, Alpha Phi Omega. Republican. Methodist. Avocations: flying, flight instrn., reading.

BOYNTON, BUCK WILLIAM, physician; b. Houston, Feb. 27, 1920; s. George Wesley and Mabel (Palmer) B.; B.A., U. Tex., 1950, M.D., 1954; m. Maryanna Craig, Sept. 3, 1947 (div. Jan., 1965); children—Buck William, Suzanne; m. 2d, Donna Carlisle, Apr. 22, 1978. Intern, Riverside County Gen. Hosp., 1954-55, resident, 1955-56; gen. practice of medicine, Riverside, Calif., 1954-82; physician Riverside County Jail, 1971-83; staff physician and surgeon Folsom State Prison, Represa, Calif., 1983-86. Served with USNR, 1942-45. Lodges: Masons, Shriners. Home: PO Box 699 Gualala CA 95445

BOYNTON, ROBERT MERRILL, psychology educator; b. Evanston, Ill., Oct. 28, 1924; s. Merrill Holmes and Eleanor (Matthews) B.; m. Alice Neiley, Apr. 9, 1947; children: Sherry, Michael, Neiley, Geoffrey. Student, Antioch Coll., 1942-43, U. Ill., 1943-45; A.B., Amherst Coll., 1948; Ph.D., Brown U., 1952. Asst. prof. psychology and optics U. Rochester, N.Y., 1952-57; asso. prof. U. Rochester, 1957-61, prof., 1961-74, dir. Center for Visual Sci., 1963-71, chmn. dept. psychology, 1971-74; prof. psychology U. Calif., San Diego, 1974—, assoc. dean grad. studies and research, 1987—; guest researcher Nat. Phys. Lab., Teddington, Eng., 1960-61; vis. prof. physiology U. Calif. Med. Center, San Francisco, 1969-70. Author: Human Color Vision, 1979; chmn. bd. editors Vision Research, 1982-86; contbr. articles to profl. jours. Served with USNR, 1943-45. Fellow AAAS, Optical Soc. Am. dir.-at-large 1966-69), Am. Psychol. Assn., Nat. Acad. Scis., Assn. for Research in Vision and Ophthalmology (trustee 1984—). Home: 376 Bellaire St Del Mar CA 92014

BOYNTON, WILLIAM LEWIS, electronic mfg. co. ofcl.; b. Kalamazoo, May 31, 1928; s. James Woodbury and Cyretta (Gunther) B.; ed. pub. schs.; m. Kei Ouchi, Oct. 8, 1953. Asst. mgr. Speigel J & R, Kalamazoo, 1947-48; served with U.S. Army, 1948-74, ret., 1974; with Rockwell/Collins div.,

Newport Beach, Calif., 1974—, supr. material, 1978-81, coordinator, 1981—; supr. coordinator Rockwell/CDC, Santa Ana, Calif., 1981—, coordinator investment recovery, 1982-86; mem. faculty Western Mich. U., 1955-58. Trustee Orange County Vector Control Dist., 1980—; mem. adv. panel for bus./econ. devel. Calif. State Legislature, 1979-86. Decorated Bronze Star. Mem. Assn. U.S. Army, Assn. U.S. Army. Non-Commd. Officers Assn., Nat. Mgmt. Assn., Nat. Geog. Soc., Smithsonian Inst. (assoc.). Republican. Roman Catholic. Home: 5314 Lucky Way Santa Ana CA 92704 Office: PO Box 11963 Santa Ana CA 92704-1048

BOYSEN, LARS, bank executive; b. Vejle, Denmark, Aug. 23, 1948; came to U.S., 1975; s. Svenn and Erna (Thomsen) B.; m. Mary E. Arnold, June 7, 1986. BS in Bus. Adminstrn., The Aarhus Sch. Bus., Denmark, 1973, MS in Econs., 1975; postgrad., U. Wash., 1981-82. Mktg. research analyst Santa Fe Fed., San Bernardino, Calif., 1975-77, mktg. research mgr., 1977-79, v.p., mktg. dir., 1979-81; v.p., office adminstrn. mgr. Pacific Fed. Savs. & Loan Assn., Costa Mesa, Calif., 1981-82; v.p., human resources and corp. research dir. Pacific Savs. Bank, Costa Mesa, 1982-86, sr. v.p. corp. services, 1986—. Recipient First award The Advt. Club, Los Angeles, 1979, Andy award of merit The Advt. Club, N.Y.C., 1980. Mem. Calif. League Savs. and Loan Assns. (human resources, indsl. devel. coms.). Office: Pacific Savs Bank 1901 Newport Blvd Costa Mesa CA 92927

BOYTER, SCOTT M., business manager; b. Cedar City, Utah, June 19, 1947; s. Neil K. and Mae (Macfarlane) B.; m. Sherrie L. Bowen, Aug. 2, 1974; children: Laura Michelle, Tonia Leigh, Diana Lynn. BS, Brigham Young U., 1973, MS, 1987. Adminstrv. asst. coll. fine arts and communications Brigham Young U., Provo, Utah, 1973-76, bus. mgr. dept. music, 1976-82, bus. mgr. Coll. Fine Arts and Communications, 1982—. Missionary Ch. Jesus Christ of Latter-day Saints, Ohio and W.Va., 1967-69. Served with USAR, 1971—. Recipient Adminstrv. Excellence award Coll. Fine Arts and Communications, Brigham Young U., 1985. Mem. Adminstrv. Mgmt. Soc., Am. Mgmt. Assn., Am. Philatelic Soc., Postal Commemorative Soc. Republican. Mormon. Club: Key Internat. Avocations: Philately. Home: 331 North 875 East Orem UT 84057-5075 Office: Brigham Young U A-410 HFAC Coll Fine Arts & Communications Provo UT 84602

BOZDECH, MAREK JIRI, physician; b. Wildflecken, Bavaria, Federal Republic Germany, Oct. 12, 1946; s. Jiri Josef and Zofia Jadwiga (Swiatecka) B.; m. Frances Barclay Craig, Dec. 22, 1967; children: Elizabeth, Andrew, Matthew. AB, U. Mich., 1967; MD, Wayne State U., 1972. Diplomate Am. Bd. Internal Medicine, Am. Bd. Med. Oncology, Am. Bd. Hematology. Intern and resident in internal medicine U. Wis. Hosps., Madison, 1972-75, dir. clin. hematology lab., 1978-82, dir. bone marrow transplantation, 1984-85; asst. prof. medicine U. Wis., Madison, 1978-84, assoc. prof. medicine, 1984-85; clin. fellow in hematology Moffitt Hosp. U. Calif., San Francisco, 1975-76, postdoctoral fellow in hematology Cancer Research Inst., 1976-78, research assoc. Cancer Research Inst., 1977-78, assoc. prof., 1985—; dir. adult bone marrow transplantation U. Calif. Med. Ctr., San Francisco, 1985—. Contbr. articles to profl. jours. Scout leader Boy Scouts Am., Novato, Calif., 1985. Recipient Nat. Research Service award NIH, 1977-78; Wayne State U. scholar, 1971. Mem. ACP, AAAS, Am. Fedn. Clin. Research, Am. Soc. Hematology. Avocations: skiing, gardening, hiking, tennis, theatre. Home: 50 La Placita Novato CA 94947 Office: U Calif Med Ctr 1282 M 505 Parnassus Ave San Francisco CA 94143

BOZZA, KELLY LYNN, entrepreneur; b. Newport Beach, Calif., June 26, 1963; d. Charles McDonald and JoAnn Marie (Varilek) B. AA in Mktg. Mgmt., Orange Coast Coll., 1983; BA in Econs., UCLA, 1986. Fin. cons. Beneficial Calif., Costa Mesa, 1979-83; prin. Balboa Pedal Boats, Newport Beach, 1986—; bd. dirs. Westwood Student Fed. Credit Union, Los Angeles, 1984-86. Vol. Children's Hosp. Orange County, Calif., 1980; site coordinator Project MAC, Los Angeles, 1984-85. Mem. Newport Harbor Panhellenic, Alpha Gamma Sigma, Phi Mu (treas. 1985-86). Republican. Home: 3315 Florida Circle Costa Mesa CA 92626 Office: Balboa Pedal Boats 400 Main St Newport Beach CA 92626

BRAATELIEN, EDWIN HAROLD, JR., environmental engineer; b. Phoenix, Feb. 7, 1934; s. Edwin Harold and Leila Estelle (Linville) B.; m. Susan Swan Emmons, Oct. 25, 1958; children: Thomas Oliver, Martin Robert. BA in Chemistry, Ariz. St. U., 1961; MSCE, Ariz. State U., 1969. Registered profl. engr., Ariz., Calif., Ky., Tenn., Wis. Sewage treatment supr. City of Phoenix, 1963-67, asst. supt. sewers, 1967-68, supt. sewers, 1968-71, asst. water and sewers dir., 1971-78; sr. engr. Camp, Dresser & McKee Inc., Boston, 1978-81; dir. water pollution control City of San Jose, Calif., 1981—; faculty assoc. Ariz. State U., 1968, 70, 75. Fellow Am. Acad. of Environ. Engrs. (diplomate), ASCE; mem. Am. Water Work Assn. (George Warren Fuller award 1976), Soc. of Am. Mil. Engrs., Water Pollution Control Fedn. (William D. Hatfield award 1966, Arthur Sidney Bedell award 1971). Avocations: model ships, metalworking. Home: 6457 Camelia Dr San Jose CA 95120 Office: Dept of Water Pollution Control 700 Los Esteros Rd San Jose CA 95134

BRABSTON, DONALD CAMPBELL, aerospace engineer; b. Birmingham, Ala., Nov. 5, 1945; s. Donald Campbell and Mary Jane Brabston; m. Janis Susan Forman, June 24, 1984. BS, Ga. Inst. Tech., 1967; MS, Calif. Inst. Tech., 1968, PhD, 1974. Mem. tech. staff TRW Systems, Redondo Beach, Calif., 1974-77, sect. head, 1977-80, project mgr., 1980-81, dept. mgr., 1981-83, sr. systems engr., 1983—. Served to lt. USNR, 1969-72. Mem. IEEE, Assn. Computing Machinery. Avocations: personal computers, sci. fiction, cats. Home: 15573 Briarwood Dr Sherman Oaks CA 91403

BRABY, LESLIE ALAN, biophysicist, researcher; b. Kelso, Wash., Jan. 12, 1941; s. Leslie Arthur Edward and Wilma Josie (Cooper) B.; m. Barbara Evelyn Shearer, May 1, 1966; children: Kevin, Joel, Ryan. BA in Physics, Linfield Coll., 1963; PhD in Radiation Physics, Oreg. State U., 1972. Scientist Battelle Labs.-Northwest, Richland, Wash., 1963-69, sr. research scientist, 1971—; research scientist Oreg. State U., Corvallis, 1969-71. Contbr. numerous articles on radiation and biophysics to profl. jours. Mem. AAAS, Radiation Research Soc., Health Physics Soc., Am. Phys. Soc., Sigma Xi, Sigma Pi Sigma. Methodist. Avocations: hiking, woodworking, photography. Home: 1527 Johnston Ave Richland WA 99352 Office: Battelle NW PO Box 999 Richland WA 99352

BRACHER, KATHERINE, astronomy educator; b. San Francisco, Oct. 26, 1938; d. Frederick G. and Agnes Hargreaves (Nuttall) B. AB cum laude, Mt. Holyoke Coll., 1960; AM, Ind. U., 1962, PhD, 1966. Instr. astronomy U. So. Calif., Los Angeles, 1965-66, asst. prof., 1966-67; asst. prof. Whitman Coll., Walla Walla, Wash., 1967-72, assoc. prof., 1972-81, prof., 1981—. Column editor Mercury, 1983—; contbr. articles to profl. jours. Recipient Town and Gown award Whitman Coll., 1980. Mem. Am. Astron. Soc., Hist. Astronomy Div. (council mem. 1985—, vice-chair, 1987—), Astron. Soc. Pacific, AAUP. Avocation: music. Home: 20 Merriam Walla Walla WA 99362 Office: Whitman Coll Dept Astronomy Walla Walla WA 99362

BRACK, O.M.JR., English language educator; b. Houston, Nov. 30, 1938; s. O. M. and Olivia Mae (Rice) B.; m. Christine Yvonne Ferdinand, July 5, 1983; 1 child, Matthew Rice. Student, U. Houston, 1956-57; B.A., Baylor U., 1960, M.A., 1961; Ph.D., U. Tex., Austin, 1965. Asst. prof. William Woods Coll., 1964-65; asst. prof. English lit. U. Iowa, Iowa City, 1965-68; assoc. prof. U. Iowa, 1968-73, dir. center textual studies, 1967-73; prof. English lit. Ariz. State U., Tempe, 1973—; chmn. 18th Century Short Title Catalogue Com., 1970-73; pres. Arete Publs., Ltd., 1976-81; Albert H. Smith Meml. lectr. bibliography Birmingham (Eng.) Bibliog. Soc., 1983 vis. fellow U. Oxford Wolfson Coll., 1986-87. Author: Bibliography and Textual Criticism, 1969, Samuel Johnson's Early Biographers, 1971, Hoole's Death of Johnson, 1972, Henry Fielding's Pasquin, 1973, A Catalogue of the Leigh Hunt Manuscripts, 1973, The Early Biographies of Samuel Johnson, 1974, American Humor, 1977, Shorter Prose Writings of Samuel Johnson, 1987; textual editor: Works of Tobias Smollett, 1966—; gen. editor: Works of Tobias Smollett, 1973-86; editor: English Literature in Transition, 1981-82, mem. editorial com., 1982—; editor: Studies in Eighteenth Century Culture, 1981-86; mem. editorial com.: Yale edit. Works of Samuel Johnson, 1977—; editorial cons.: The Literature of England, Scott, Foresman & Co., 1977-79; asst. editor: Eighteenth-Century Bibliography, 1964-73, Books at Iowa, 1966-73; editor Eighteenth Century: A Current Bibliography, 1983—; mem. editorial com.: Age of Johnson, 1985—, Rocky Mountain Rev. of Lang. and Lit., 1980—. Am. Philos. Soc. grantee, 1967; Phi Kappa Phi. disting. scholar, 1975; Huntington Library fellow, 1978; Am. Council Learned Socs. fellow, 1979-80; fellow Newberry Library, 1982; recipient Grad. Coll. Disting. Research award, 1981-82; Rocky Mountain MLA Huntington Library award, 1986. Mem. Am. Soc. 18th Century Studies, South Central 18th Century Soc. (pres. 1982-83), Rocky Mountain MLA, Bibliog. Soc. Am., Bibliog. Soc. U. Va., Bibliog. Soc. (London), Printing Hist. Soc., Am. Printing History Assn. Roman Catholic. Club: The Johnsonians. Office: Dept English Ariz State U Tempe AZ 85281

BRACKETT, MICHAEL HOWARD, univeristy administrator; b. Waynesboro, Pa., Sept. 10, 1939; s. George Sylvester and Betty Lou (Murdock) B.; m. Joann Camille Lindahl, July 3, 1963 (div. Apr. 1984); children: Marc Tyson, Sean Galen, Kevin Lloyd. BS in Forestry, U. Wash., 1961, MS in Forestry, 1964; MS in Soils, Wash. State U., 1966. Sr. research and devel. analyst Wash. Dept. Natural Resources, Olympia, 1966-74, asst. data processing mgr., 1974-76; data processing mgr. Wash. Dept. Fisheries, Olympia, 1976-81; data adminstr. Wash. Employment Security Dept., Olympia, 1981-84, Wash. State U., Pullman, 1984—; instr. first aid and emergency med. technician, Olympia, 1965-80. Author: Developing Data Structured Information Systems, 1983, Developing Data Structured Databases, 1986. Pres., mem. Delphi Planning Assn., Olympia, 1970-74; commr. Thurston County (Wash.) Fire Dist. 5, 1970-76; mem. bd. dirs. Skyway Youth Home, Olympia, 1972-74. Served with U.S. Army, 1961, with Res. 1961-67. Mem. Wash. State Assn. Data Processing Mgrs. (chmn. 1980), Data Adminstrn. Mgmt. Assn. Lodge: Moose,. Avocations: hiking, climbing, camping, skiing, sailing. Home: PO Box 2285 CS Pullman WA 99165 Office: Wash State U Adminstrv Computing Pullman WA 99164

BRADBURY, JOHN FREDERICK, utility exec.; b. Boise, Idaho, Sept. 10, 1929; s. Frederick Carroll and Jeannette Frances (Plunkett) B.; student pub. schs., Oreg.; m. Hazel E. Weyer, 1984; children: Kim, Ray, Carol, Ross. Salesman, Bradbury Motor Co., Astoria, Oreg., 1955-58; clk. E.W. Hendrickson Inc., Warrenton, Oreg., 1959-60; with Pacific Power & Light Co., 1960, sales and mktg. exec., Riverton, Wyo., 1970-77, mgr. Arlington (Oreg.) office, 1977-82, Seaside, Oreg., 1982-87, Clatsop Ops. Ctr. Line Extension supr., 1987—. Dist. chmn. Freemont County council Boy Scouts Am., 1972. Served with USAF, 1951-55. Mem. Nat. Rifle Assn. (life), Ducks Unltd. Republican. Clubs: Lions, Elks, Shriners (past pres. Riverton). Home: 1227 Ave D Seaside OR 97138 Office: 2860 Dolphin Warrenton OR 97138

BRADEN, VERLON PATRICK, author, automotive writer, producer, photographer; b. Flint, Mich., July 8, 1934; s. Verlon Lee and Mary Virginia (Presson) B.; m. Marie Elsie Kobrehel, June 30, 1956 (dec.); children—Mark Patrick, Leslie Marie; m. 2d, Cheryl Marie Olson, Oct. 5, 1980; 1 dau., Mary Kathryn. B.A., Western Mich. U., 1956; M.A., U. Mich., 1957; postgrad. U. Iowa, 1959. Cert. secondary tchr., Mich. Tchr., prison social worker, probation officer State of Mich., 1959-67; writer Bill Sandy Co., Communico, and Maritz Communications, Bob Thomas & Assocs., Dancer Fitzgerald Sample, Inc., Torrance, Calif., 1969—; editor The Alfa Owner. Mem. Am. Soc. Tng. and Devel., Am. Alfa Romeo Owners Club, Am. Abarth Register, Scuderia del Portello. Author: The 365 GTB/4 Daytona Ferrari, 1982; Abarth, 1983; Weber Carburetors, 1986.

BRADFORD, DAVID GALEN, air force officer; b. Graham, Tex., July 20, 1948; s. Leo Galen and Elizabeth Arline (Younger) B.; m. Irene Carol Boehning, June 2, 1972; children: Emily Neumann, Scott Galen. AA, Howard Coll., 1968; BA, S.W. Tex. State U., 1970; MA, U. No. Colo., 1974; diploma, U.S. Army Comdr. and Gen. Staff Coll., 1985. Commd. 2d lt. USAF, 1972, advanced through grades to maj., 1984; logistics plans officer USAF, Vandenberg AFB, Calif., 1980-82; exec. officer dep. chief of staff Logistics of Strategic Air Command, USAF, 1982-83, exec. officer dep. chief of staff plans Strategic Air Command,, 1983; staff officer long range planning staff Strategic Air Command, USAF, Omaha, 1983-84; plans officer N.E. Asia div. Comdr. in Chief Pacific Command, USAF, Hawaii, 1985—; mem. adj. faculty English, History and Bus., Wayland Bapt. U., Honolulu, 1986—. Mem. USAF Assn., East-West Ctr. Hawaii, World Future Soc. Republican. Baptist. Avocation: collecting books. Home: 302-A Travis Ave Honolulu HI 96818 Office: USCINCPAC Staff Box 15 Camp HM Smith HI 96861

BRADFORD, GORDON RICHARD, soil chemist; b. Spanish Fork, Utah, Nov. 30, 1918; s. Granville and Daisy (Pye) B.; m. Virginia Wright, Oct. 24, 1949; children: Sandra, Dennis, Connie, Karen, Brian, Scott, Paul. MS, Brigham Young U., 1947. Meteorologist U.S. Weather Bur., Fresno, Calif., 1948; soil chemist dept. soils and environ. scis. U. Calif., Riverside, 1949—. Baseball coach Sr. League, Riverside, 1980. Served to lt. col. USAF, 1942-45, ETO. Grantee NIH, 1962, So. Calif. Edison Co., 1980—, U. Calif., 1985. Mem. Sigma Xi. Republican. Mormon. Avocations: gardening, bicycling, jogging. Home: 260 Green Oaks Riverside CA 92507 Office: U Calif Dept Soils and Environ Scis Riverside CA 92507

BRADFORD, ROBERT GRANT, management consultant; b. Los Angeles, Oct. 22, 1936; s. Raymond William and Martha (Boyle) B.; m. Kay Morse Bradford, Mar. 27, 1964; children: Brooke Easton, Blair Andrew, Carrie. Student, Harvard U., 1954-56, Harvard U., 1961-62; BA, U. Utah, 1961; MA, Stanford U., 1963; PhD, Ariz. State U., 1969. Cert. secondary tchr. Asst. dean students Ariz. State U., Tempe, 1963-69; dir. pub. affairs Utah Symphony, Salt Lake City, 1969-72; dean of students Tenn. Tech. U., Ferrum Coll., 1972-76; exec. v.p., gen. mgr. Ballet West, Salt Lake City, 1976-79; pres. Crossroads Mgmt. Assocs., Salt Lake City, 1979—; cons. Jerome Barnum Assn., N.Y.C., 1972-74; adj. assoc. prof. U. Utah, Salt Lake City, 1977-80, v.p. devel. Salt Lake Symphony, 1985—; pres. Youth Arts Consortium, Salt Lake City, 1982-84. Lobbyist Utah Trial Lawyers Assn., Salt Lake City, 1985—. Mormon. Avocations: traveling, writing, sports, choral music. Home: 6779 Olivet Dr Salt Lake City UT 84121

BRADLEY, ABRAM ALLEN, chemical engineer; b. Arlington, Va., Sept. 6, 1955; s. Benjamin Lewis and Anna Lou (Steele) B.; m. Denita Sue Hyler, Dec. 27, 1981; 1 child, Rebecca Anne. BS in Chemistry, Campbell U., 1977; MS in Chem. Enging., N.C. State U., 1983. Chem. engr. cons. Woodward-Clyde Cons., Walnut Creek, Calif., 1983—. Mem. Am. Chem. Soc., Am. Nuclear Soc. Republican. Baptist. Avocations: skiing, jogging, bicycling. Home: 1766-C Camino Verde Walnut Creek CA 94596 Office: Woodward-Clyde Cons 100 Pringle Ave Walnut Creek CA 94596

BRADLEY, CHARLES WILLIAM, podiatrist; b. Fife, Tex., July 23, 1923; s. Tom and Mary Ada (Cheatham) B.; student Tex. Tech., 1940-42; D. Podiatry, Calif. Podiatry Coll., 1949; D.Sc. (hon.), Calif. Coll. Podiatric Medicine; m. Marilyn A. Brown, Apr. 3, 1948 (dec. Mar. 1973); children—Steven, Gregory, Jeffrey, Elizabeth, Gerald. Practice podiatry, Beaumont, Tex., 1950-51, Brownwood, Tex., 1951-52, San Francisco, San Bruno, Calif., 1952—; chief of staff Calif. Podiatry Hosp., San Francisco; mem. surg. staff Sequoia Hosp., Redwood City, Calif.; mem. podiatry staff Peninsula Hosp., Burlingame, Calif.; chief podiatry staff St. Luke's Hosp., San Francisco; pres. Podiatry Ins. Co. Am.; cons. VA. Mem. San Francisco Symphony Found.; mem. adv. com. Health Policy Agenda for the Am. People, AMA. Chmn. trustees Calif. Coll. Podiatric Medicine, Calif. Podiatry Coll., Calif. Podiatry Hosp. Mem. Am. Podiatric Med. Assn. (trustee, pres. 1983-84), Calif. Podiatry Assn. (pres. No. div. 1964-66, state bd. dirs., pres. 1975-76, Podiatrist of Yr. award 1983), Nat. Council Edn. (vice chmn.), Nat. Acads. Practice, Am. Legion, San Bruno C. of C. (dir. 1978—). Clubs: Elks, Lions, Commonwealth of Calif. Served with USNR, 1942-45. Home: 2965 Trousdale Dr Burlingame CA 94010 Office: 560 Jenevein Ave San Bruno CA 94066 Office: 2469 Mission St San Francisco CA 94110

BRADLEY, DUNCAN LEE, lawyer; b. Chgo., Apr. 2, 1939; s. Maurice Edmond and Ethel Virginia (Carroll) B.; m. Renné Colette Angel, Aug. 29, 1970; children: Parker Edmond Carroll, Esther Elizabeth Sandra. BA, So. Ill. U., 1963, MA, 1966, PhD, 1972; JD, U. Denver, 1984. Bar: Colo. 1985, U.S. Dist. Ct., Colo., 1985. Grad. asst. So. Ill. U., Carbondale, 1961-66, 68-72; with Am. Peace Corps, Tehran, Iran, 1966-68; dep. Sheriff Jefferson County Sheriff's Dept., Golden, Colo., 1974-82; ptnr. Duncan Bradley & Assocs. (formerly Bradley, Maurier & Assocs.), Denver, 1985—; lectr. philosophy law Met. State Coll., Denver, 1976-79. Mem. Citizens Adv. com. Colo. United Way, 1977-79. Recipient award for Excellence in Advocacy Am. Coll. Trial Lawyers, 1984; named Regional Champion ABA Moot Ct. Competition Tex. Young Lawyers Assn., 1984. Mem. ABA, Assn. Trial Lawyers Am., Colo. Trial Lawyers Assn., Denver Bar Assn., Colo. Bar Assn., Aircraft Pilots and Owners Assn. Republican. Club: Jeffro Men's. Lodge: Masons. Avocations: flying, writing, Persian poetry. Home: Box 777 Arvada CO 80001 Office: Duncan Bradley & Assocs 5805 Carr St Suite 2 Arvada CO 80004-5401

BRADLEY, EMMETT HUGHES, corporate executive; b. Hampton, Va., Dec. 8, 1927; s. Alfred Thomas and Bessie Margaret (Patrick) B.; m. Linda Alice Frolen; children—Warren Hughes, Mark Harris, Todd Hamilton. B.S. in Elec. Enging. summa cum laude, Duke, 1949; M.S. in Elec. Enging, Mass. Inst. Tech., 1950. With Melpar, Inc., Falls Church, Va., 1950-62; gen. mgr. spl. products div. Melpar, Inc., 1960-62; v.p., gen. mgr. missile systems div. Atlantic Research Corp., 1962-67, pres., 1967-70; chief operating officer Susquehanna Corp., 1968-72, exec. v.p., 1970-72; also mem. exec. com., dir.; sr. exec. v.p. Pan Am. Sulphur Co., 1970-71; mem. exec. com. 1970-71, bd. dirs., 1969-71; chief exec. officer, pres., mem. exec. com., dir. Airtronics, Inc., Chatsworth, Calif., 1973-81; chief exec. officer, mem. exec. com., pres., dir. Powertec, Inc., Chatsworth, Calif., 1976—; chmn., chief exec. officer, dir. Semicondr. Circuits, Inc., Windham, N.H., 1985—; dir. Azufrera Panamericana, S.A., Fertilizantes Fosfatados Mexicanos, S.A., Greendale Power, Ltd., Chesterfield, Eng. Author. Mem. exec. bd. Nat. Capital area council Boy Scouts Am., 1967-69; Orange Empire area council Boy Scouts Am., 1965-67; chmn. United Fund Duarte-Bradbury, 1964; Bd. dirs. Orange County Safety Council, 1967; mem. president's adv. council Calif. Bapt. Theol. Sem., 1966-68, now bd. trustees. Mem. Nat. Security Indsl. Assn. (exec. com. 1965-67, v.p. 1968, bd. trustees 1969-72), I.E.E.E., Phi Beta Kappa, Sigma Xi, Tau Beta Pi. Patentee in field. Home: 6028 Little Oak Ln Woodland Hills CA 91367 Office: Powertec Inc 20550 Nordhoff St Chatsworth CA 91311

BRADLEY, MARION ZIMMER, novelist, educator; b. Albany, N.Y., June 3, 1930; d. Leslie Raymond and Evelyn Parkhurst (Conklin) Zimmer; m. Robert Alden Bradley, Oct. 1949; 1 son, David Robert; m. Walter H. Breen, Feb. 14, 1964; children: Patrick Russell Donald, Moira Evelyn Dorothy. B.A., Hardin Simmons U., 1964; postgrad., U. Calif.-Berkeley, 1965-67. Author: (Darkover novels) Planet Savers, 1962, The Sword of Aldones, 1962, The Bloody Sun, 1964, The Winds of Darkover, 1970, The World Wreckers, 1971, Darkover Landfall, 1972, The Spell Sword, 1972, The Heritage of Hastur, 1975, The Shattered Chain, 1976, The Forbidden Tower, 1977, Stormqueen, 1978, The Bloody Sun (rewritten) 1979, Two to Conquer, 1980, The Keeper's Price, 1980, Sharra's Exile, 1981, Sword of Chaos, 1982, Hawkmistress, 1982, Thendara House, 1983, City of Sorcery, 1984, (other sci. fiction, anthologies, gothics, mainstream novels), (mainstream novels) The Catch Trap, 1979, The Mists of Avalon, 1983. Home: PO Box 352 Berkeley CA 94701

BRADLEY, SISTER MYRA JAMES, health science facility executive; b. Cin., Feb. 1, 1924; d. John Joseph and Mary (McMannus) B. BS in Edn., Atheneum Ohio, 1950; BS in Nursing, Mt. St. Joseph Hosp., 1954; MHA, St. Louis U., 1959. RN. Mem. faculty U. Dayton, Ohio, 1955-57, Good Samaritan Hosp., Dayton, 1955-57; asst. adminstr. St. Mary-Corwin Hosp., Pueblo, Colo., 1960; adminstr. St. Joseph Hosp., Mt. Clemens, Mich., 1960-65; pres. Penrose Hosp., Colorado Springs, Colo., 1965—; trustee Mercy Hosp., Denver; preceptor St. Louis U. Mem. adv. council Pikes Peak Vocat. Edn., Colorado Springs; mem. Womens Forum, Colorado Springs, Gov. Lamm's Data Commn., Colorado Springs; com. mem. C. of C. Pub. Services, Colorado Springs. Recipient Disting. Service award U. Colo., 1983. Mem. Cath. Hosp. Assn. (trustee, sec.), Am. Hosp. Assn. (mem. adv. bd.), Colo. Hosp. Assn. (trustee), Colo. Found. Med. Care (regional council), Nat. Com. Health Care Costs (trustee). Home: 2417 N Cascade Ave Colorado Springs CO 80907 Office: Penrose Hosp 2215 N Cascade Ave PO Box 7021 Colorado Springs CO 80907

BRADLEY, ROSALEE, psychologist, horse breeder and trainer; b. Calhoun, Mo., Sept. 20, 1939; d. Wayne Beecher and Alice Maureen (Shrout) B. B.S., U. Kansas City, 1961; M.A., Hollins Coll., 1963; Ph.D., Wash. State U., 1969. Lic. psychologist, Calif., Wash. Staff psychologist No. State Hosp., Sedro-Woolley, Wash., 1968-74; staff psychologist Calif. Correctional Ctr., Susanville, Calif., 1974-78, adminstrv. asst. to supt., 1975-78, EEO officer, 1975-78, women's liaison rep., 1975-78; pvt. practice clin. psychology, Susanville, 1978—; cons. Right Way Homes, boy's ranch; tchr. in field; horse breeder, trainer, 19—. Mem. Lassen County Women Democrats. Recipient numerous awards in horse show circuit, 1981, 82. Mem. Am. Psychol. Assn., Mortar Bd., Psi Chi. Democrat. Clubs: Appaloosa Horse (Bronze Medallion award 1975), Honey Lake Valley Riders. Exhibited photography: Lassen Community Coll. (Merit award), 1982, Lassen County Fair (2 First place awards and 2d place award), 1981. Avocation: cribbage (numerous tournament awards). Home: PO Box 88 Janesville CA 96114 Office: 617 Main Suite 204 Susanville CA 96130

BRADLEY, THOMAS (TOM BRADLEY), mayor of Los Angeles; b. Calvert, Tex., Dec. 29, 1917; s. Lee Thomas and Crenner (Hawkins) B.; m. Ethel Mae Arnold, May 4, 1941; children: Lorraine, Phyllis. Student, UCLA, 1937-40; LL.B., Southwestern U., 1956, LL.D., 1980; LL.D., Brandeis U., 1974, Oral Roberts U., 1974, Pepperdine U., 1974, Loyola Marymount U., 1974, Calif. Lutheran U., 1974, Wilberforce U., 1974, Whittier Coll., 1976, Yale U., 1979, U. So. Calif., 1979, Princeton U., 1979, Bus Nat. U., Korea, 1979, Antioch U., 1983, N.C. Central U., 1983; Ph.D. (hon.), Humanity Research Ctr. Beverly Hills, 1976. Bar: Calif. 1956. Police officer Los Angeles, 1940-62; practiced in Los Angeles, 1956-73; mem. Los Angeles City Council, 1963-73; mayor of Los Angeles, 1973—; founder, dir. Bank of Fin., Nat. Urban Coalition Pres. Nat. League Cities, 1974, also mem. nat. bd. dirs.; pres. League of Calif. Cities, 1979, So. Calif. Assn. Govts., 1968-69, Nat. Assn. Regional Councils, 1969-71; mem. Nat. Energy Adv. Council, Nat. Commn. on Productivity and Work Quality; mem. advisory bd., vice chmn. transp. com. U.S. Conf. Mayors; former mem. Council Intergovt. Relations; chmn. State, County and Fed. Affairs Com.; former chmn. Pub. Works Priority Com., Com. for Proposed Legis. bd. dirs. Nat. Urban Fellows. Mem. Calif. Democratic Central Com.; del. Dem. Nat. Mid-Term Conf., 1974; co-chmn. Dem. Nat. Conv., 1976; former mem. bd. dirs. Joint Com. Mental Health for Children; former mem. adv. council Peace Corps. Named African Methodist Episcopal Man of Yr., 1974; recipient Dr. Martin L. King, Jr. award, 1974, Pub. Ofcl. of Yr. award Los Angeles Trial Lawyers Assn., 1974, award CORO Found., 1978, award of merit Nat. Council Negro Women, 1978, John F. Kennedy Fellowship award Govt. of N.Z., 1978, Internat. Humanitarian award M.E.D.I.C., 1978, City Employee of Yr. award All City Employees Benefits Service Assn., 1983, Magnin award, 1984. Mem. Los Angeles Urban League, NAACP (Spingarn medal 1985), So. Calif. Conf. on Community Relations, Los Angeles Conf. Negro Elected Ofcls., UN Assn. Los Angeles (bd. dirs.), Kappa Alpha Psi. Democrat. Mem. African Methodist Episcopal Ch. (trustee). Office: Office of Mayor City Hall Los Angeles CA 90012 *

BRADSHAW, JERALD SHERWIN, chemistry educator, researcher; b. Cedar City, Utah, Nov. 28, 1932; s. Sherwin H. and Maree (Wood) B.; m. Karen Lee, Aug. 6, 1954; children: Donna M. Webster, Melinda C. BS, U. Utah, 1955; PhD, UCLA, 1963. Postdoctoral Calif. Inst. Tech., Pasadena, 1962-63; chemist Chevron Research, Richmond, Calif., 1963-66; asst. prof. chemistry Brigham Young U., Provo, Utah, 1966-69, assoc. prof., 1969-74, prof., 1974—, asst. chmn. chemistry dept., 1980-86; vis. prof. Nat. Acad. Sci., U. Ljubljana, Yugoslavia, 1972-73, U. Sheffield, England, 1978. Contbr. 156 sci. articles to profl. jours.; patentee in field. Served with USNR, 1955-59. Named Prof. of Yr., Brigham Young U., 1974; recipient Maeser Research award, Brigham Young U., 1978, Maeser Teaching award, 1982. Mem. Am. Chem Soc., Internat. Soc. Heterocyclic Chemistry (bd. advisors 1980-82), Utah Acad. Sci., Sigma Xi. Republican. Mormon. Lodge: Kiwanis (local pres. 1978). Avocations: stamp collecting, church activities. Office: Brigham Young U Provo UT 84602

BRADSHAW, RALPH ALDEN, biochemistry educator; b. Boston, Feb. 14, 1941; s. Donald Bertram and Eleanor (Dodd) B.; m. Roberta Perry Wheeler, Dec. 29, 1961; children: Christopher Evan, Amy Dodd. BA in Chemistry, Colby Coll., 1962; PhD, Duke U., 1966. Asst. prof. Washington U., St. Louis, 1969-72, assoc. prof., 1972-74, prof., 1974-82; prof., chair dept. U. Calif., Irvine, 1982—; study sect. chmn. NIH, 1979, mem., 1975-79, 80-85;

mem. sci. advisory bd. Hereditary Disease Found., 1983—, ICN Nucleic Acids Research Inst., 1986—; program com. Am. Soc. for Neurochemistry, 1983; research study com. physiol. chem. Am. Heart Assn., 1984-86, mem. Council on Thrombosis, 1976—; fellowship screening com. Am. Cancer Soc. Calif., 1984—; external advisory bd. Program in Hypertension Cleve. Clinic, 1985—; chmn. adv. com. Western Winter Workshops, 1984—; dir., chmn., mem. organizing com. numerous symposia, confs. in field including Proteins in Biology and Medicine, Shanghai, Peoples Republic China, 1981, Symposium Am. Protein Chemists, San Diego, 1985. Mem. edit. bd. Archives Biochemistry and Biophysics, 1972—, Jour. Biological Chemistry, 1973-77, 78-79, 81-86, Jour. Supramolecular Structure/Cellular Biochemistry, 1980—, Bioscience Reports, 1980—, Peptide and Protein Reviews, 1980—, Jour. Protein Chemistry, 1980—, IN VITRO Rapid Communication in Cell Biology, 1984—; editor Trends in Biochemical Sciences, 1975—, editor-in-chief, 1986—; contbr. numerous articles to scientific jours. Recipient Young Scientist award Passano Found., 1976. Mem. Am. Chem. Soc. (Sect. award 1979), AAAS, Am. Soc. Biol. Chemists, N.Y. Acad. Scis., Protein Soc. (acting pres. 1986-87), Am. Soc. for Neurochemistry, Am. Soc. for Cell Biology, Soc. for Neuroscience, The Endocrine Soc., Sigma Xi. Home: 25135 Rivendell Dr El Toro CA 92630 Office: Univ Calif Calif Coll Medicine Dept Biol Chemistry Irvine CA 92717

BRADSHAW, RICHARD JAMES, conductor; b. Rugby, Eng., Apr. 26, 1944; s. Alfred James and Florence Mary B.; m. Diana Hepburne-Scott, June 30, 1977; children—Jenny Alexandra, James Edward Merton. B.A. with honors, U. London, 1965. Condr., chorus dir. Glyndebourne Festival Opera, 1975-77; dir. New London Ensemble, 1972—; condr., chorus dir. San Francisco Opera; freelance symphony and operatic condr. Calouste Gulbenkian conducting fellow, 1972. Home: 957 The Alameda Berkeley CA 94707 Office: San Francisco Opera San Francisco CA 94102

BRADSHAW, ROBERT V. (BRAD), police chief, educator; b. Upland, Calif., Apr. 17, 1938; s. Charles B. and Alys P. (Dickinson) B.; m. Dixie L. Bradshaw, Aug. 16, 1960; children—Deborah A., Kelly L., Kimberly D. A.A. in Bus., Pasadena City Coll., 1959; B.A. in Criminal Justice, San Jose State Coll., 1964; M.P.A., Golden Gate U., 1980. Cert. secondary tchr., Calif. Successively police officer, sgt., lt., capt., dep. chief, asst. chief of police San Jose (Calif.) Police Dept., 1960-80; police chief Reno (Nev.) Police Dept., 1981—; instr. police adminstrn. Truckee Meadows Community Coll., Reno. Served with USAR. Mem. Internat. Assn. Chiefs of Police, Police Exec. Research Forum. Republican. Club: Rotary (Reno). Office: PO Box 1900 Reno NV 89505 *

BRADSHAW, ROXANNE ELIZABETH, educator; b. Pueblo, Colo., Oct. 31, 1943; d. Foster Costin and Martha M. (Moore) Moore. BA, Western State Coll., 1965, MA, 1969; m. David Lee Reinke, Dec. 15, 1974; stepchildren—Lisa Ann, Alison Lee. Advisor, Dean of Women's office Western State Coll., Gunnison, Colo., 1963-64; tchr., Pueblo, 1965-68; kindergarten tchr., Monument, Colo., 1968-69; women's counselor Rangely (Colo.) Coll., 1969-70; instr./coordinator tchr. aid program Pikes Peak Community Coll., Colorado Springs, Colo., 1970-74, instr. psychology, 1974—; developer grad. level tchr. aide course and workshop So. Colo. State Coll., 1970-73; bd. dirs. Tchrs. Services Corp. Bd. dirs. Joint Council Econ. Edn.; commr. Nat. Coalition on Working Women. W.G. Carr Profl. Study scholar, 1981. Mem. NEA (sec.-treas., exec. com., bd. dirs., program and budget com., mem. Employee Retirement Bd., PAC steering com. and council, sec. Mems. Ins. Trust, mem. spl. com. structure and services, rep. UN regional seminar Venezuela 1983, del. World Confedn. Orgns., Togo 1984 and Sask., Human Relations award 1986), Pikes Peak Community Coll. Faculty Assn., Colo. Edn. Assn., NOW, Alpha Delta Kappa (Beta chpt., Outstanding Woman in Edn. 1981-82). Democrat. Presbyterian. Office: 1201 16th St NW Washington DC 20036

BRADSHAW, WILLIAM NEWMAN, environmental scientist; b. Louisville, Nov. 2, 1928; s. Hugh Elmer and Rachel Elizabeth (Lundy) B.; m. Joyce Elaine Austin, Sept. 14, 1956; children: David N., Kathryn E. BA, Austin Coll., 1951; MA, U. Tex., 1956, PhD, 1962. Asst. prof. biology McMurry Coll., Abilene, Tex., 1956-61; asst. prof. biology W.Va. U., Morgantown, 1962-67, assoc. prof., 1967-73, prof., 1973-76; project mgr. Stearns-Roger, Inc., Denver, 1976-84; prin. environ. scientist Stearns Catalytic Corp., Denver, 1984-86, Stearns-Roger div. United Engrs. and Constructors, Inc., Denver, 1986—; lectr. Stephen F. Austin U., Nacogdoches, Tex., 1956, U. Tex., Austin, 1961-62; vis. assoc. prof. M.D. Anderson, Tumor Inst., Houston, 1970-71; sec., treas. Acad. Assocs., Inc., Morgantown, 1973-76. Contbr. articles to profl. jours. Team leader blue chip div. United Way, Morgantown, 1972; chmn. Rep. Precinct, Morgantown, 1969. Served to capt. USMC, 1952-54. Grantee NSF, 1968, 74, NIH, 1970-71; Southern Fellowship Fund fellow, 1961-62. Mem. Nat. Assn. Environ. Profls., Am. Inst. Biol. Sci., Ecol. Soc. Am., Am. Soc. Mammalogists, Sigma Xi. Republican. Presbyterian. Lodge: Rotary (1st v.p. Morgantown club 1975-76) (bd. dirs. Denver club 1980-82). Home: 6175 Ponderosa Way Parker CO 80134 Office: United Engrs and Contructors Inc Stearns-Roger Div 700 S Ash St PO Box 5888 Denver CO 80217

BRADY, BARBARA C., psychologist; b. Burbank, Calif., May 29, 1946; d. Roger Ralph and Lespith (Albright) Crist; 1 son, Scott Thomas Bauer. B.A. in Psychology, San Jose State U., 1969; M.S. in Home Econs., Calif. Poly. State U., 1974, M.A. in Counseling, 1976; Ph.D. in Ednl. Psychology, Brigham Young U., 1981. Instr. psychology Cuesta Coll., San Luis Obispo, Calif., 1974-76, counselor, 1976-80; counselor Brigham Young U., Provo, Utah, 1980-81, lectr., 1981; psychol. asst. Pacific Profl. Assocs., San Luis Obispo, 1981-83; pvt. practice psychology, San Luis Obispo, 1983—; lectr. in field, 1976—; cons. San Luis Obispo County Mental Health Services. Bd. dirs. Family Services, San Luis Obispo, 1984-86; active Boy Scouts Am., San Luis Obispo, 1976-78. Mem. San Luis Obispo County Psychol. Assn. (pres. 1984-85), Calif. Psychol. Assn., Am. Psychol. Assn., Western Psychol. Assn., Am. Personnel and Guidance Assn., Women's Network San Luis Obispo (membership chmn. 1983), San Luis Obispo C. of C. (bd. dirs. 1986—, chmn. profl. devel. com.), Phi Kappa Phi, Psi Chi, Phi Upsilon Omicron, Kappa Alpha Theta. Club: Toastmasters (pres. 1984). Office: 1461 Higuera San Luis Obispo CA 93401

BRADY, DORSEY RAY, hotel executive; b. Long Beach, Calif., Apr. 20, 1942; s. Arnold Ray and Dora Della (Helzer) B.; m. Patricia Dip Sheong Hoo, Aug. 25, 1968; children: Diana, Dawn, Dane. Student, UCLA, 1959-63. Cert. hotel adminstr. Asst. mgr. Deauville Country Club, Tarzana, Calif., 1963-65, Playboy Club, Hollywood, Calif., 1965-66; mgr. Hawaii Kai Golf Course, Honolulu, 1966—; asst. Kauai Surf, Lihue, Hawaii, 1966-70, resident mgr., 1972-75; gen. mgr. Kaanapali Beach Hotel, Lahaina, Hawaii, 1970-71, Kona Inn, Kailua-Kona, Hawaii, 1971-72, The Whaler, Kaanapali Beach, Hawaii, 1975; various positions Del Webb Hotels, various cities, 1975-83; sr. v.p., staff ops. Del Webb Hotels, Las Vegas, Nev., 1981, v.p. hotel ops., 1981-83; v.p. western region Quality Hotels and Resorts, Anaheim, Calif., 1983-84; gen. mgr. Surf and Sand Hotel, Laguna Beach, Calif., 1985; exec. v.p. ops. Continental Inns Inc., La Jolla, Calif., 1985—; lectr. Kauai Community Coll., Lihue, 1968, mem. adv. bd., 1974, Maui Community Coll., Kahului, Hawaii, 1970-71. Bd. dirs. Kauai Visitor Industry Orgn., Lihue, 1973. Served with USMC, 1960-62. Mem. Confrerie De La Chaine Des Rotisseurs, Calif. Hotel Assn., Hawaii Hotel Assn. (bd. dirs. 1974), Skal (exec. com. 1984), Am. Hotel and Motel Assn., Kailua Kona C. of C. (bd. dirs. 1971), UCLA Alumni Assn. (life). Republican. Avocations: cooking, coin and medal collecting, photography, computers. Office: Continental Inn Inc 4180 La Jolla Village Dr #330 La Jolla CA 92037

BRADY, JOHN PATRICK, JR., electronics educator, consultant; b. Newark, Mar. 20, 1929; s. John Patrick and Madeleine Mary (Atno) B.; m. Mary Coop, May 1, 1954; children—Peter, John P., Madeleine, Dennis, Mary G. B.S. in E.E., MIT, 1952, M.S. in E.E., 1953. Registered profl. engr., Mass. Sect. mgr. Hewlett-Packard Co., Waltham, Mass., 1956-67; v.p. engring. John Fluke Mfg. Co., Inc., Mountlake Terrace, Wash., 1967-73; v.p. engring. Dana Labs., Irvine, Calif., 1973-77; engring. mgr., tech. advisor to gen. mgr. Metron Corp., Upland, Calif., 1977-78; ptnr. Resource Assocs., Newport Beach, Calif., 1978—; prof. electronics Orange Coast Coll., Costa Mesa, Calif., 1977-83, dean technology, 1983-84; instr. computers and electronic engring. Calif. State U., Long Beach, 1982-84. Mem. evaluation team Accrediting Commn. for Community and Jr. Colls., 1982—. Served with USN, 1946-48. Mem. Measurement Sci. Conf. (dir. 1982-83). Club: MIT (Los Angeles). Contbr. articles in field to profl. jours. Office: Orange Coast College Costa Mesa CA 92626

BRADY, JOSEPH WILLIAM, real estate development executive; b. Los Angeles, Oct. 22, 1956; s. Donald Sheridan and Mary (Rolfes) B. BS, Calif. Poly. Inst., 1979. Lic. real estate broker, Calif.; ins. solicitor, Calif. Pres. Santa Barbara (Calif.) Mgmt. Corp., 1979-80; adminstrv. officer Islay Investments, Santa Barbara, 1980-83; dir. ops. Suntree Co., Santa Barbara, 1983-85; v.p. Pegasus Devel. Corp., Santa Barbara, 1985—. Mem. Bldg. Industry Assn. (bd. dirs.). Republican. Roman Catholic. Home: 175 A North Kellogg Ave Santa Barbara CA 93111-1663

BRADY, KATHLEEN ANN, word processing supervisor; b. Des Moines, Sept. 12, 1949; d. James Patrick and Marian Ruth (Feik) O'Byrne. Grad. high sch., Orlando, Fla., 1967. Supr. word processing and mailing services Continental Holding Corp., Concord, Calif., 1983—. Mem. Assn. Info. System Profls., Internat. Soc. Wang Users. Office: Continental Holding Corp 1333 Willow Pass Rd #206 Concord CA 94524

BRADY, KEVIN TIMOTHY, research chemist; b. Lynwood, Calif., Mar. 1, 1955; s. Thomas Leland and Loretta Jean (Leonard) B.; m. Judith Anne Gathmann, Dec. 16, 1978; children: Pamela, Scott. BA, Whittier Coll., 1977; PhD, U. So. Calif., 1982. Jr. chemist Magna Corp., Santa Fe Springs, Calif., 1976-77; research chemist Amvac Chem. Corp., Los Angeles, 1982-85, sr. chemist, dir. organic chemistry lab., 1986—. Mem. Am. Chem. Soc., Sigma Xi. Baptist. Avocations: woodworking, swimming. Office: Amvac Chem Corp 4100 E Washington Blvd Los Angeles CA 90023

BRADY, RODNEY HOWARD, business executive, former college president and government official; b. Sandy, Utah, Jan. 31, 1933; s. Kenneth A. and Jessie (Madsen) B.; m. Carolyn Ann Hansen, Oct. 25, 1960; children: Howard Riley, Bruce Ryan, Brooks Alan. B.S. in Accounting with high honors; M.B.A. with high honors, U. Utah, 1957; D.Bus. Adminstrn., Harvard U., 1966; postgrad., UCLA, 1969-70. Missionary Ch. Jesus Christ of Latter-day Saints, Great Britain, 1953-55; teaching assoc. Harvard U. Bus. Sch., Cambridge, Mass., 1957-59; v.p. Mgmt. Systems Corp., Cambridge, 1962-65, Center Exec. Devel., Cambridge, 1963-64; v.p., dir. Center Exec. Devel., Boston, 1964-65; v.p. Tamerand Reef Corp., Christiansted, St. Croix, V.I., 1963-65; v.p., dir. Am. Inst. Execs., N.Y.C., 1963-65; v.p., mem. exec. com. aircraft div. Hughes Tool Co., Culver City, Calif., 1966-70; asst. sec. adminstrn. and mgmt. Dept. HEW, Washington, 1970-72; chmn. subcabinet exec. officers group Dept. HEW, 1971-72; exec. v.p., chmn. exec. com., dir. Bergen Brunswig Corp., Los Angeles, 1972-78; chmn. bd. Uni-mgrs. Internat., Los Angeles, 1974-78; pres. Weber State Coll., Ogden, Utah, 1978-85; pres., chief exec. officer Bonneville Internat. Corp., Salt Lake City, 1985—, also dir.; dir. Bergen Brunswig Corp., Western Mortgage Loan Corp., Flying J Oil Co., Inc., 1st Security Bank Corp., Smith's Mgmt. Corp., Intermountain Health Care Corp.; bd. advisors Mountain Bell Telephone; chmn. Nat. Adv. Com. on Accreditation and Instl. Eligibility; chmn. Utah Gov.'s Blue Ribbon Com. on Tax Recodification; cons. Dept. Def., Dept. State, Dept. Commerce, HEW, NASA, Govt. of Can., Govt. of India (and indsl. firms), 1962—. Author: An Approach to Equipment Replacement Analysis, 1957, Survey of Management Planning and Control Systems, 1962, The Impact of Computers on Top Management Decision Making in the Aerospace and Defense Industry, 1966, (with others) How To Structure Incentive Contracts—A Programmed Text, 1965, My Missionary Years in Great Britain, 1976, An Exciting Start Along an Upward Path, 1978; contbr. (with others) articles to profl. jours. Mem. exec. com. nat. exec. bd. Boy Scouts Am., 1977—; chmn. nat. Cub Scout commn., 1977-81, pres. Western region, 1981-83, chmn. nat. ct. of honor; mem. adv. com. program for health systems mgmt. Harvard U.; mem. adv. council U. Utah, 1971—; mem. adv. com. Brigham Young U. Bus. Sch., 1972—; mem. dean's round table UCLA Grad. Sch. Mgmt., 1973-78; trustee Ettie Lee Homes for Boys, 1973-79; mem. governing bd. McKay Dee Hosp., Ogden, Utah, 1979—; bd. dirs. Utah Endowment for Humanities, 1978-80. Served to 1st lt. USAF, 1959-62. Recipient Silver Antelope award Boy Scouts Am., 1976; recipient Silver Beaver award Boy Scouts Am., 1979, Silver Buffalo award Boy Scouts Am., 1982. Mem. Am. Mgmt. Assn. (award 1969), Am. Def. Preparedness Assn., Nat. Indsl. Security Assn., U.S. Army Assn., Air Force Assn., Am. Helicopter Soc., Los Angeles C. of C. (tax structure com. 1969-70), Ogden C. of C. (dir. 1978), Salt Lake Area C. of C. (dir. 1985—), SAR (pres. Utah chpt. 1986-87), Sons of Utah Pioneers, Phi Kappa Phi, Tau Kappa Alpha, Beta Gamma Sigma. Mormon (pres. Los Angeles stake). Clubs: Los Angeles Country (Los Angeles); Rotary; Harvard (Cambridge, Mass.); Alta (Salt Lake City). Office: Bonneville Internat Corp Broadcast House Salt Lake City UT 84180

BRAGA, DEBRA A., laywer; b. San Diego, Jan. 10, 1957; d. Alfred August and Mary (Pereira) B. BA, U. Calif., San Diego, 1978; JD, U. San Diego, 1982. Bar: Alaska 1984, U.S. Dist. Ct. Alaska 1985. Law clk. to presiding justice Anchorage, 1983, U.S. Dist. Ct., Anchorage, 1983-85; assoc. Laurel J. Peterson P.C., Anchorage, 1985—; vol. arbitrator Conflict Resolution Ctr., Anchorage, 1985. Pres. Eastridge IV Condominium Assn., Anchorage, 1985. Mem. ABA, Alaska Bar Assn., Anchorage Bar Assn., Am. Trial Lawyers Assn. Avocations: travel, racquetball. Office: Laurel J Peterson 805 W 3d Ave Suite 200 Anchorage AK 99501

BRAGDON, PAUL ERROL, college president; b. Portland, Maine, Apr. 19, 1927; s. Errol Freemont and Edith Lillian (Somerville) B.; m. Nancy Ellen Horton, Aug. 14, 1954; children: David Lincoln, Susan Horton, Peter Jefferson. B.A. magna cum laude, Amherst Coll., 1950, D.H.L., 1980; J.D., Yale U., 1953; LL.D., Whitman Coll., 1985. Bar: N.Y. 1954. With firm Dewey, Ballantine, Bushby, Palmer & Wood, N.Y.C., 1953-58, Javits, Trubin, Sillcocks, Edelman & Purcell, N.Y.C., 1961-64; counsel Tchrs. Ins. and Annuity Assn. Coll. Retirement Equities Fund, N.Y.C., 1958-61; asst. to mayor City of N.Y., 1964-65, exec. sec. to mayor, 1965, exec. asst. to pres. City Council, 1966-67; v.p. NYU, 1967-71; pres. Reed Coll., Portland, Oreg., 1971—; dir. Pres.'s Task Force on Priorities in Higher Edn., 1969-70, N.Y. State Commn. on Powers of Local Govt., 1970-71; mem. commn. on fed. relations Am. Council on Edn., 1972-74, 78—; chmn. Gov.'s Council Econ. Advisers, 1984—; dir. Tektronix, Inc.; chmn. bd. Portland br. Fed. Res. Bank of San Francisco. Mem. Oreg. Environ. Quality Commn., 1973-74; chmn. Oreg. Select Com. on Conflict of Interest Legis., 1973-74; trustee Amherst Coll., 1972-78. Served with USMCR, 1945-46. Mem. N.W. Assn. Schs. and Colls. (com. on colls. 1974-81), Nat. Assn. Ind. Colls. and Univs. (vice chmn.), ABA, Phi Beta Kappa, Beta Theta Pi. Clubs: Century (N.Y.C.), Univ. (N.Y.C.); City (Portland, Oreg.), Univ. (Portland, Oreg.).

BRAGG, CLARENCE CORDER, elec. products mfg. co. exec.; b. Duffy, W.Va., Apr. 13, 1915; s. George William and Arcelia Mitilda (Pickens) B.; B.S. in Elec. Engring., W.Va. U., 1947; m. Mary Barbara McLain, July 1, 1938; children—Douglas M., Michael J., Steven M. With Westinghouse Electric Corp., 1936-39, 42-46, gen. foreman, Emeryville, Calif., 1945-46; gen. mgr. Indsl. Electric Co., Clarksburg, W.Va., 1947-51; prodn. supt. Lear, Inc., Grand Rapids, Mich., 1951-52; dept. supt. top secret security clearance Dow Chem. Co., Denver, 1952-53; mgr. mfg. Schwager-Wood Corp., Portland, Oreg., 1953-60; founder, dir., v.p. mfg. Powerdyne, Inc., Lake Oswego, Oreg., 1960-65; exec. v.p., gen. mgr. Portland Chain Co. (Oreg.), 1965-67; gen. mgr., dir. Williams Air Control, Portland, 1967-68; pres., chief exec. officer, chmn. bd. Eltec, Inc., Portland, 1968-76; regional mgr. elec. sales Willamina Lumber Co., Portland, 1974-81; pres., owner Gus Gragg & Assos., 1981—. Dist. advancement chmn. Pioneer Dist., Portland Area council Boy Scouts Am. Mem. citizens budget com. Lake Oswego Pub. Schs. Recipient Golden Hammer award Mechanix Illus. Registered profl. engr., W.Va., Oreg. Mem. IEEE (life), Eta Kappa Nu, Kappa Mu Alpha, Phi Sigma Kappa. Methodist (trustee). Mason (Shriner). Patentee garage door operator. Home: 15695 SW 114th Ct #7 Tigard OR 97224 Office: 16330 SW 72d Ave Portland OR 97223

BRAGG, ROBERT HENRY, physicist; b. Jacksonville, Fla., Aug. 11, 1919; s. Robert Henry and Lilly Camille (McFarland) B.; m. Violette Mattie McDonald, June 14, 1947; children: Robert Henry, Pamela. B.S., Ill. Inst. Tech., 1949, M.S., 1951, Ph.D., 1960. Asso. physicist research lab. Portland Cement Assn., Skokie, Ill., 1951-56; sr. physicist physics div. Armour Research Found., Ill. Inst. Tech., Chgo., 1956-61; sr. mem., mgr. phys. metallurgy dept. Lockheed Palo Alto Research Lab., Palo Alto,, Calif., 1961-69; prof. materials sci. U. Calif., Berkeley, 1969—, chmn. dept. materials sci. and mineral engring., 1978-81; faculty sr. scientist Lawrence Berkeley Lab., 1969—; mem. materials research adv. com. NSF, 1982-86; cons. IBM, Siemens-Allis, NASA, NIH, NSF. Contbr. articles to profl. jours. Pres. Palo Alto NAACP, 1967-68. Served with U.S. Army, 1943-46. Decorated Bronze star (2); Recipient Disting. award No. Calif. sect. Am. Inst. Mining and Metall. Engrs., 1970. Mem. Am. Phys. Soc., Am. Ceramics Soc. (chmn. No. Calif. sect. 1980), AIME (chmn. No. Calif. sect. 1970), Am. Carbon Soc., Am. Soc. Metals, AAUP, AAAS, No. Calif. Council Black Profl. Engrs., Sigma Xi, Tau Beta Pi, Sigma Pi Sigma., Am. Crystallographic Assn. Democrat. Home: 2 Admiral Dr 373 Emeryville CA 94608 Office: Dept Materials Sci and Mineral Engring Univ of Calif Berkeley CA 94720

BRAIN, GEORGE BERNARD, university dean; b. Thorp, Wash., Apr. 25, 1920; s. George and Alice Pearl (Ellison) B.; m. Harriet Gardinier, Sept. 28, 1940; children—George Calvin, Marylou. B.A., Central Wash. State U., Ellensburg, 1946, M.A., 1949; Ed.D., Columbia Tchrs. Coll., 1957; postgrad., U. Wash., Wash. State U., Harvard U., U. Colo., Stanford U. Tchr. math. and sci. Yakima (Wash.) secondary schs., 1946-49; instr. Central Wash. State Coll., 1949-50; elementary sch. prin. Ellensburg, 1950-51; successively elementary sch. prin., asst. supt. schs., supt. schs. Bellevue, Wash., 1951-59; vis. prof. Central Wash. State Coll., 1953, Wash. State U., 1959, U. Md., 1964; supt. schs. Balt., 1959-66; dean Coll. Edn., also dir. summer schs. Wash. State U., Pullman, 1965-85; lectr. Columbia, U. Conn., Harvard, U. Ga., U. Del., Johns Hopkins, Morgan U., U. Okla., Towson State U., Stanford, Wash. U.; chmn. Fulbright Group Western European Seminar Comparative Edn., 1959; chmn. ednl. policies commn. N.E.A.; ednl. cons. (Office Edn.), 1962—; cons. Ednl. Testing Service, Princeton, N.J., 1964-67; dir. Intext Pub. Inc., Scranton, Pa., Worldbook-Childcraft (Scott-Fetzer); bd. dirs. Md. Acad. Sci., 1960-65, Nat. Edn. Found., Field Enterprises Ednl. Corp., 1970—, Pacific Am. Inst., 1977—. Mem. editorial adv. bd.: Scholastics Publs, 1963—, Am. Sch. and Univ, 1960-64, Education, USA, 1964-71; mem. editorial bd.: World Book, 1966—, Jour. Tchr. Edn, 1966—. Served with USNR, 1941- 42; Served with USMCR, 1942-46; maj. Res. Recipient Disting. Service award Wash. State Jr. Assn. Commerce, 1956; named Man of Year Met. Civic Assn. Balt., 1962; Disting. Service award in edn. NCCJ, 1963; Fulbright scholar, 1959. Life mem. Am. Assn. Sch. Adminstrs. (exec. com. 1964-66, pres. 1965), NEA; hon. life mem. Wash. State Assn. Sch. Adminstrs. (pres. 1959), Md. Assn. Sch. Adminstrs., Nat. Congress P.T.A.; mem. Wash. Edn. Assn. (pres. dept. adminstrn. and supervision 1957), AAAS (exec. com. commn. elementary and secondary sci. 1963-66), Assn. Supervision and Curriculum Devel., Univ. Council Ednl. Adminstrn., Nat. Joint Council Econ. Edn. (exec. com. 1963—), Nat. Conf. Profs. Ednl. Adminstrn., AAUP, Internat. Platform Assn., Nat. Council for Edn. in Health Professions, Nat. Acad. Sch. Execs., Nat. Council Fgn. Study League, Exec. Hall Fame, Phi Delta Kappa, Kappa Delta Pi. Presbyterian. Lodge: Rotary (dir. Balt. 1964-65).

BRAINARD, MARYTHELMA, counselor, educator; b. Quiriqua, Guatemala, July 31, 1933; came to U.S., 1937, naturalized, 1954; d. Cecil Rhodes and Margaret Rebecca (Miller) Bryant; children—Margaret Renee Brainard-Gentz, Robert Lyle, James Edward. B.A. in English, San Jose State U., 1966; M.A. in Counseling Psychology, U. Santa Clara, 1976; Ph.D. in Counseling Psychology, U. N.Mex., 1984. Tchr. English, Sonora (Calif.) Union High Sch., 1966-68; Title I reading specialist Live Oak Sch. Dist., Santa Cruz, Calif., 1968-72, Title I coordinator, 1972-75, staff devel. specialist/counselor, 1975-76; coordinator-counselor Albuquerque Transactional Analysis Assn., 1976-77; instr. N. Mex. State U.-Grants, 1977-79; cons. counselor Laguna (N. Mex.) Indian Services Ctr., 1977-82; pvt. practice counseling, Albuquerque, 1977—; tchr. transactional analysis seminars; condr. workshops in field; moderator Multi-ethnic Conf.; condr. tng. programs for vols. in reading instrn.; vol. asst. instr. U. Calif.-Santa Cruz, 1974; vol. instr. on group process U. N.Mex., Albuquerque; vol. trainer Hogares staff, Albuquerque, 1979. Named Outstanding Sophomore Woman, U. N. Mex., 1952-53. Mem. Internat. Transactional Analysis Assn., Nat. Acad. Cert. Clin. Mental Health Counselors, Am. Psychol. Assn., Mortar Bd. Democrat. Home: PO Box 1021 Corrales NM 87048 Office: 9412 Indian School Rd NE Albuquerque NM 87112

BRAINARD-SMITH, WARREN B., pharmaceutical executive; b. Lincoln, Nebr., Aug. 8, 1943; s. Dale Wilfred and Marian Joy (Brainard) Smith; m. Joan McDaniel Reining, Aug. 15, 1971; children: Darren Jay, Hilary Ann, Ryan Thomas. BS, U. Wis., 1966; MS, U. Ariz., 1970; M in Internat. Mgmt., Am. Grad. Sch. Internat. Mgmt., 1971. Salesman Sci. Products div. Am. Hosp. Supplies, Evanston, Ill., 1972-75; gen. mgr. Am. Hosp. Supplies, San Juan, Puerto Rico, 1975-78; mng. dir. Am. Hosp. Supplies, Mex. City, 1978-83; regional dir. Latin Am. Allergan Pharms., Irvine, Calif., 1983-85, v.p. Am. region, 1985—; bd. dirs. America Medica y Assn., Mex. City, 1983—, Allergan Pharms., Argentina, Can., Mex., Colombia, Brazil; research asst. Immuno Supressant Drug Research. Research asst., editor Bacteriophageasan Indicator of Viral Pollution, 1969. Recipient Eagle Scout award Boy Scouts Am., 1957. Mem. Am. Soc. Microbiology, Argentine C. of C. Republican. Presbyterian. Avocations: antique car restoration, fgn. langs. Office: Allergan Pharms 2525 Dupont Dr Irvine CA 92715

BRAINERD, CHARLES J(ON), experimental psychologist, applied mathematician, educator; b. Lansing, Mich., July 30, 1944; emigrated to Can., 1971; s. Charles Donald and Geraldine Elaine (Leffler) B.; m. Susan Haske, Jan. 18, 1964 (div.); 1 dau., Tereasa Gail; m. Valerie Reyna, Oct. 5, 1985; 1 son, Bertrand. B.S., Mich. State U., 1966, M.A., 1968, Ph.D., 1970. Asst. prof. psychology U. Alta., Edmonton, Can., 1971-73, assoc. prof., 1973-76, H.M. Tory prof. social sci., 1983-86; prof. U. Western Ont., London, 1976-83, U. Ariz., Tucson, 1987—; vis. prof. U. Minn., Mpls., 1980-81, So. Meth. U., Dallas, 1986-87. Author: Piaget's Theory of Intelligence, 1978, Origins of the Number Concept, 1979; editor: Alternatives to Piaget, 1978, Recent Advances in Cognitive-Developmental Theory, 1983, Springer-Verlag Series in Cognitive Development, 1979—; assoc. editor: Behavioral and Brain Scis., 1980—. Fellow Am. Psychol. Assn., Can. Psychol. Assn.; mem. Psychonomic Soc., Soc. for Research in Child Devel. (assoc. editor Child Devel. 1977-80). Republican. Office: U Ariz Coll Edn Tucson AZ 85715

BRAITHWAITE, ERNEST M., oil and gas company executive. Pres. Epoch Capital Corp., Calgary, Alta., Can. Office: Epoch Capital Corp, 340 12th Ave SW, Calgary, AB Canada T25 1L5 *

BRALEY, JESSIE E., banker; b. Upton, Wyo., July 23, 1927; d. Raymond Paul and Maggie Sophia (George) McAulay; m. Earl W. Braley, Oct. 14, 1956 (dec. July 1967); 1 foster child, Dwayne E. Secretarial student U. Wyo., 1945-47; grad. Colo. Sch. Banking, 1971. Sec., bookkeeper Union State Bank, Upton, Wyo., 1947-56; bookkeeper, teller Stockmen's Bank & Trust, Gillette, Wyo., 1958-67, asst. cashier, auditor, 1967-80, v.p., cashier, 1980—. Mem. Pioneer Manor Adv. Bd., 1980—, pres., 1984; elder, fin. sec. 1st Presbyn. Ch., 1969—. Named Gillette Woman of Yr., 1980. Mem. Nat. Assn. Bank Women (state chmn. 1968), Wyo. Bankers Assn. (25 yr. plaque 1983), Bank Adminstrn. Inst. (Wyo. group chmn. 1980-81), Bus. and Profl. Women Gillette (pres. 1974-75). Republican. Lodge: Order Eastern Star. Home: Box 234 Gillette WY 82716 Office: Stockmen's Bank & Trust 222 Gillette Ave Gillette WY 82716

BRAMBLE, JOHN MYLES, city manager; b. Vancouver, Wash., May 3, 1946; s. Paul Eugene and Beulah Elizabeth (Henderson) B.; m. JoAnn Tolle, May 2, 1980; children: Scott Byron, Steven Tolle. BS, Oreg. State U., 1969; MPA, U. Nev., Las Vegas, 1978. Adminstrv. asst. City of Salem (Oreg.), 1969-73; research analyst Abt Assocs., Inc., Cambridge, Mass., 1973-74; dir. budget and mgmt. City of Las Vegas (Nev.), 1975-79; asst. city mgr., fin. dir. City of Belmont (Calif.), 1979-81; city mgr. City of Commerce City (Colo.), 1981-84, City of Pueblo (Colo.), 1984-87. Mem. exec. bd. Colo. Mcpl. League, 1982-83. Mem. Internat. City Mgmt. Assn., Denver Met. Mgrs. Assn. (chmn. 1983), Colo. City Mgmt. Assn. (pres-elect 1986-87). Lodge Rotary (Pueblo). Home: 13 Amaranth Ct Pueblo CO 81001 Office: 1 City Hall Pl Pueblo CO 81002

BRAME, ARDEN HOWELL, II, herpetologist, genealogist; b. Los Angeles, Mar. 19, 1934; s. Arden Howe and Marguerite Lucile (Adams) B.; m. Susan Diane Bronn, Aug. 23, 1964 (div. June 1969); m. Patricia Louise Verret Reinholtz, Apr. 19, 1970. BA, U. So. Calif., 1957, MS, 1967; student, UCLA, 1956-57. Grad. teaching asst. U. So. Calif., Los Angeles, 1959-65; also student profl. worker in ichthyology-herpetology and vertebrate paleontology Los Angeles County Mus., 1959-65, later research asst. in herpetology; supr. Eaton Canyon Nature Ctr., 1965-68, 70-78; asst. curator sect. herpetology Los Angeles County Mus. of Natural History, 1968-70; instr. genealogy Pasadena (Calif.) City Coll. and Calif. State U., Northridge, 1977—; mem. citizen nongame adv. com. Calif. Dept. Fish and Game, 1975-79; herpetol. group advisor Survival Service Commn., Internat. Union for Conservation Nature and Natural Resources, Morges, Switzerland, 1974-82. Author: (with Dr. D.B. Wake) The Salamanders of South America, 1963; Systematics and Evolution of the Mesoamerican Salamander Genus Oedipina, 1968; contbr. articles to scholarly and profl. jours.; assoc. pub. TV Facts of Pasadena and Altadena, 1978-79. Served with AUS, 1958. Fellow Herpetologists' League, Augustan Soc. (registered genealogist, pres. 1980-81); mem. Soc. Study Amphibians and Reptiles (bd. dirs. 1967-70, chmn. 1973), Southwestern Herpetologists Soc. (pres. 1971-74), Am. Soc. Ichthyologists and Herpetologists, Brit. Herpetol. Soc., Phila. Herpetol. Soc., N.Y. Herpetol. Soc., Ariz. Herpetol. Soc., N.Mex. Herpetol. Soc., Conn. Herpetol. Soc., Chgo. Herpetol. Soc., Soc. Study of Evolution, Soc. Systematic Zoologists, Ecol. Soc. Am., Western Soc. Naturalists, Biol. Soc. Wash., So. Calif. Acad. Scis., Soc. Tropical Biologists, Pasadena Audubon Soc. (pres. 1971-76), SAR (pres. Pasadena chpt. 1977-83, genealogist Calif. Soc.), S.R., SCV (camp comdr. 1979-83), Gen. Soc. War of 1812, Descendants of the Illegitimate Sons and Daus. of the Kings of Britain, Plantagenet Soc., Sovereign Colonial Soc. Ams. Royal Descent, Soc. Descendanta Knights of the Garter, Colonial Order of Crown, Magna Charta Barons, Order of Washington, Sons of Union Vets. of Civil War, Mil. Order Loyal Legion of U.S., Mil. Order of Stars and Bars (comdr. Calif. chpt.), Dames of Guild of St. Margaret of Scotland (protector), Order of Augustan Eagle, Descents From Antiquity, Order of Armigerous Augustans, Hospitaller Order of St. John of Jerusalem (companion of honor), Noble Co. of Rose, Jamestowne Soc., St. JOhn's Vol. Corps, Sigma Xi, Phi Sigma. Home: 9545 E Guess St Rosemead CA 91770

BRAMHAM, DAVID LEROY, sand and rock products company executive; b. Sebastopol, Calif., July 18, 1938; s. Norman William and Marjorie (Layton) B.; m. Grace Rebecca Anderson, Nov. 30, 1969; children: Norma Jane, Michael David. BBA, Pacific Union Coll., 1961. Asst. mgr. NW Bramham Co., Sebastopol, 1961-66; prin. Dave Bramham Trucking Co., Sebastopol, 1966-70, Dry Creek Sand and Gravel Co., Healdsburg, Calif., 1970-77; pres., gen. mgr. Bramham Sand and Rock Products, Forestville, Calif., 1975—; sec.-treas. Don Wesner Inc.-Blue Rock Co., Forestville, 1978—. Ch. soloist, gospel singer weddings and funerals. Treas. Redwood Chordsmen Barbershop, Santa Rosa, 1966-67; mem. Redwood Four Barbershop Quartet, 1968-76; treas. Sebastopol Seventh Day Adventist Ch., 1962-65 youth dir., asst. dir., 1961-77; sec.-treas., pres. elect Redwood Regional Youth, 1965-69; youth dir. Sebastopol Pathfinder Club, 1966; mem. sch. bd. Redwood Acad., Santa Rosa, 1972—, fin. chmn., 1978-80, 84-85, vice-chmn., 1984—. Mem. Nat. Fedn. Ind. Bus.'s, Calif. C. of C. Republican. Home: 4550 Gravenstein Hwy N Sebastopol CA 95472

BRANCA, JOHN GREGORY, lawyer, consultant; b. Bronxville, N.Y., Dec. 11, 1950; s. John Ralph and Barbara (Werle) B. AB in Polit. Sci. cum laude, Occidental Coll., 1972; JD, UCLA, 1975. Bar: Calif. 1975. Assoc. Kindel & Anderson, Los Angeles, 1975-76, Hardee, Barovick, Konecky & Braun, Beverly Hills, Calif., 1977-81; ptnr. Ziffren, Brittenham & Branca, Los Angeles, 1981—; bd. dirs. Brother Records, Los Angeles, MJJ Prodns., Los Angeles. Editor-in-Chief UCLA Law Rev., 1974-75; contbr. articles to profl. jours. Cons. United Negro Coll. Fund; bd. dirs. Michael Jackson Burn Ctr., UCLA Law Com. Recipient Bancroft-Whitney award; named Entertainment Lawyer of Yr. Am. Lawyer Mag. Mem. ABA (patent trademark and copyright law sect.), Calif. Bar Assn., Beverly Hills Bar Assn. (entertainment law sect.), Phi Alpha Delta, Sigma Tau Sigma. Avocations: art, antiques, music, real estate. Office: Ziffren Brittenham & Branca 2049 Century Park E #2350 Los Angeles CA 90067

BRANCH, CHARLES VERNON, college dean; b. Newton, Kans., May 15, 1929; s. Charles Holaday and Ruth Eileen (Reffner) B.; m. Janet Sue Smith, 1972 (div. 1981); m. Lucille Loraine Sandoval, Mar. 11, 1983; 1 child, Francheska. Student Bethany Coll., Lindsborg, Kans., 1947-50; B.S. in Music Edn., Kans. State U., 1952; M.Ed. in Ednl. Adminstrn., U. West Fla., 1972; Ed.D., U. Fla., 1974. Tchr. music pub. schs., Fla., Kans., 1952-68; dir. humanities ctr. Escambia Sch. System, Pensacola, Fla., 1968-72; research asst. U. Fla., Gainesville, 1972-73, instr., 1973-74; assoc. prof. edn., head dept. Lab. Sch., Ball State U., Muncie, Ind., 1974-78; dean Sch. Edn., Met. State Coll., Denver, 1978-85, dean Sch. Profl. Studies, 1985—; mgr. band instrument dept. Keyboard Music Ctr., Pensacola, 1959-61. Mem. accountability com. Denver Pub. Schs., 1982-84; mem. Colo. Basic Skills Assessment Com., Denver, 1982-83; mem. adv. bd. Ctr. for Employment Tng., Denver, 1982-83; mem. bd. govs. Colo. Partnership for Ednl. Renewal; mem. governing adv. com. Edn. Block Grants; chmn. NCA Outcomes Accreditation Team, Denver. Mem. Tchr. Edn. Council of State Colls. and Univs. (bd. dirs. 1982-84), Am. Assn. Colls. for Tchr. Edn. (chief instl. rep. 1978—), Assn. Humanistic Edn. (pres. 1982-83), Colo. Council Deans of Edn., Nat. Assn. Lab. Schs. (rec. sec. 1972-78), Kappa Delta Pi, Phi Delta Kappa, Alpha Eta Rho, Delta Lambda Epsilon. Democrat. Methodist. Home: 3005 S Xeric Ct Denver CO 80231 Office: Met State Coll Sch Profl Studies Box 8 1006 11th St Denver CO 80204

BRANCH, MELVYN CLINTON, mechanical engineering educator; b. Charlotte, N.C., June 13, 1944; s. Milton Clark and Georgia (McLurkin) B.; m. Noelle Ann Bergstrom, June 13, 1970; children: Miles, Nicole. BSE, Princton U., 1966; MS, U. Calif., Berkeley, 1968, PhD, 1971. Postdoctoral fellow Imperial Coll., London, 1971-72; asst. prof. mechanical engring. U. Calif., Berkeley, 1972-76; from assoc. prof. to prof. mechanical engring. U. Colo., Boulder, 1976—, assoc. dean grad. sch., 1981-82, 87—; cons. Sandia Nat. Labs., Livermore, Calif., 1974—; program com. mem. Combustion Inst., Pitts., 1978—; grad. fellowship panel mem. Nat. Research Council, Washington, 1981-85. Contbr. articles to profl. jours. Active Colo. Air Quality Control Com., Denver, 1979—. Fulbright fellow, 1982-83; recipient Tchr. Rec. award, U. Colo., 1981, Ralph Teetor award, Soc. of Automotive Engrs., 1974. Mem. ASME (Gustus Larson award, 1983), Sigma Xi, Pi Tau Sigma, Tau Beta Pi. Avocations: running, skiing, equestrian. Home: 2899 S Lakeridge Trail Boulder CO 80309 Office: U Colo Mechanical Engring Dept Boulder CO 80309-0427

BRANCHAUD, BRUCE PAUL, chemistry educator; b. New Bedford, Mass.; s. Paul Martin and Marion Edith (Shurtleff) B.; m. Mary Elizabeth Smith. BS, Southeastern Mass. U., 1976; MA, PhD, Harvard U., 1981. Postdoctoral research fellow MIT, Cambridge, 1981-83; asst. prof. chemistry U. Oreg., Eugene, 1983—. Contbr. articles to profl. jours. Fellow NIH, 1981-83, Alfred P. Sloan Found., 1987—; grantee Research Corp., Petroleum Research Fund, Am. Heart Assn., Med. Research Found. of Oreg., NSF, 1983—. Mem. Am. Chem. Soc. Home: 2182 Hilyard St Eugene OR 97405 Office: U Oreg Dept Chemistry Eugene OR 97403-1210

BRANCHFLOWER, LYLE, business executive; b. Seattle, Sept. 25, 1940; s. Norman H. and Edith R. (Williams) B.; m. Nancy Wildermuth; children: Hillary, Christine. BA, U. Pa., 1962, MBA, 1968. Cost analyst Kimberly-Clark Corp., Anderson, Calif., 1969-70; mergers and acquisitions analyst Pacific Lighting Corp., Los Angeles, 1970-73; pres. RG Mfg. Co., San Pedro, Calif., 1973-75, dir., 1973-77; project mgr. TRW, Redondo Beach, Calif., 1976-77; instr. Fed. Correctional Inst., Terminal Island, 1975; cons. Spl. Offender Ctr. Wash. State Reformatory; spl. cons. TCA Films, Palos Verdes Estates, Calif., 1976-85; ptnr. Conley-Branchflower Stables, 1980-81, Branchflower-Carr Prodns., 1982-85, B.F. Leasing, 1982-85; pres. Branchflower Investment Co., 1980—; v.p. H.E.S., Inc., 1981; pres. LWBCo., 1985—; mem. exec. com. Corp. Interviewing Network, 1985—. Contbr. articles to profl. jours.; patentee in field of mechs. Assoc. vestryman St. Peter's Episcopal Ch., San Pedro, 1975-76; adv. bd. Salvation Army, San Pedro, 1975-78; active fund raising YMCA, San Pedro, 1976-78; vestryman St. Aidan's Episcopal Ch., Camano Island, Wash., 1980; mem. adv. com. Marysville (Wash.) Pub. Schs., 1987—. Served to lt. USN, 1961-65. Mem. U. Pa. Alumni Club of Wash. (bd. dirs.). Republican. Clubs: Seattle Tennis, Wharton MBA. Lodge: Kiwanis. Home: 13614 56th Ave NE Marysville WA 98270

BRANDIN, ALF ELVIN, retired mining and shipping company executive; b. Newton, Kans., July 1, 1912; s. Oscar E. and Agnes (Larsen) B.; m. Marie Eck, June 15, 1936 (dec. 1980); children: Alf R., Jon, Erik, Mark.; m. Pamela J. Brandin, Jan. 28, 1983. A.B., Stanford U., 1936. With Standard Accident of Detroit, 1936-42; bus. mgr. Stanford U., Calif., 1946-52; bus. mgr., exec. officer for land devel. Stanford U., 1952-59, v.p. for bus. affairs, 1959-70; sr. v.p. Utah Internat. Inc., San Francisco, from 1970; pres., mem. exec. com. Richardson-Brandin, 1964-86; bd. dirs. Hershey Oil Co.; vice chmn. bd. dirs. Doric Devel. Inc. Bd. govs. San Francisco Bay Area Council; trustee Reclamation Dist. 2087, Alameda, Calif.; bd. overseers Hoover Instn. on War, Revolution and Peace, Stanford. Served as comdr. USNR, 1942-46. Mem. Zeta Psi. Clubs: Elk, Stanford Golf, Bohemian, Pauma Valley Country, Silverado Country; Royal Lahaina. Mem. VIII Olympic Winter Games Organizing Com., 1960. Home: 668 Salvatierra St Stanford CA 94305 Office: 550 California St San Francisco CA 94104

BRANDL, ROBERT JOHN, service executive, church administrator; b. Portland, Oreg., Jan. 26, 1937; s. Raymond John and Mabel (Davis) B.; 1 stepchild, Aaron Michael Morrison (dec.). Maitre 'D Paul Shank Assocs., Scottsdale, Ariz., 1961-65; exec. chef N.Am. Hotel Corp., Phoenix, 1965-67; v.p. Gradco Corp., Tempe, Ariz., 1986—; dir. N. Phoenix Bapt. Ch., 1986—; owner Branson & Assocs., Phoenix, 1979—; pres. Branson Cons. Corp., Phonenix, 1979—; pres., founder Sound Communications Co., 1986; profl. pub. speaker in field. Composer classical music; lyricist Christian Gospel music. Mem. Nat. Trust for Hist. Preservation, Nat. Restaurant Assn. (conductor of nat. seminars). Avocations: Christian Gospel music. Home: 2417 W Calavar Rd Phoenix AZ 85023 Office: Branson & Assocs 1533 E McDowell Phoenix AZ 85006

BRANDLEY, REINARD W., airport engineer; b. Stirling, Alberta, Can., Apr. 2, 1923; came to U.S., 1946; s. Albert and Luella (Wilcox) B.; m. Doreen H., June 15, 1947 (div. 1973); children: R. Dirk; m. Suzanne T. Brandley, Dec. 3, 1973; children: R. Damon, Melissa Suzanne. BCE, U. Alta., Edmonton, 1945; MCE, U. Alta., 1946; SM, Harvard U., 1948. Research engr. dept. transp. Can. Govt., 1945; instr. Harvard U., Cambridge, Mass., 1946-48; asst. prof. U. Saskatchewan, 1948-49; chief engr. O.J. Porter Co., Sacramento, Calif., 1949-53; owner, chief engr. Reinard W. Brandley Co., Sacramento, 1953—. Patentee in field. Fellow Am. Soc. Civil Engrs.; mem. Am. Assn. Airport Execs., Calif. Assn. Airport Execs. Republican. Mormon. Avocations: boating, fishing. Home: 3855 Oak Vista Way Loomis CA 95650 Office: 2041 Hallmark Dr Sacramento CA 95825

BRANDMEYER, DONALD WAYNE, maritime consultant, retired foreign service officer; b. New London, Iowa, Aug. 22, 1919; s. Frederick Theodore, Jr. and Viola Jane (Wright) B.; m. Esther Delle Noss, Mar. 22, 1941 (div. Nov. 1953); children—Donna Delle, David Wayne, Dennis Ray, Debra Sue; m. Elizabeth Louise Hansen, Nov. 25, 1953. Student Burlington Coll. Commerce, 1936-37; B.A. in World Bus. and Econs. cum laude, San Francisco State U., 1951; postgrad. U. Calif.-Berkeley, 1952. Calif. State U.-Long Beach, 1958-61, U. Pitts., 1969. Registered marine surveyor; pvt. pilot; unltd. master mariner. Transp. officer Ft. MacArthur, Calif., 1940-43, transp. officer, exec. asst. to comdg. officer spl. services U.S. War Dept., 1942-44; from mate to master large vessels in fgn. service, 1944-46; marine supt. San Francisco Port of Embark, 1946-51, Naval Supply Ctr., Oakland, Calif., 1951-52; head terminal ops. br. U.S. Navy, Washington, 1952-54; sr. civilian advisor Army Transp. Bd., 1954-57; pres. Brandmeyer Internat., Rancho Palos Verdes, Calif., 1957—; sr. maritime advisor AID, Vietnam and UN, 1967-71; Cons. Internat. Maritime Orgn., 1978-79; U.S. rep. UN Conf. on Internat. Intermodal Transport of Container Cargo, Bangkok, 1972. Contbr. articles to periodicals. Pres. Mira Costa Terr. Homeowners Assn., 1979-80. Served with USN, 1937-40. Recipient commendation AID, Vietnam, 1969, Outstanding Service award and medal, Govt. of Vietnam, 1971. Mem. Masters, Mates and Pilots Internat., Internat. Assn. Marine Surveyors (charter), World Affairs Council, Master Mariners Council. Republican. Club: Toastmasters.

BRANDNER, MARGARET ANNE SHAW, polygraph examiner; b. Denver, Sept. 4, 1937; d. Bertram James and Bessie (Syme) Shaw; m. Kenneth LeRoy Brandner, Dec. 26, 1970. B.A. in Elem. Edn., Loretto Heights Coll., 1959; polygraph examiner Rocky Mountain Security Inst., 1978; grad. Famous Writer's Sch., 1964, Inst. Forensic and Investigative Hypnosis, 1980; A.A.S. in Polygraph Tech., Pikes Peak Community Coll., 1982. Lic. polygraphist, Nebr., Utah.Acct., Denver Children's Home, 1970; acct.Keny's Equip., Inc., Green River, Wyo., 1971-78; polygraph examiner, sec.-treas. The Brandner Corp., Green River, Wyo., 1978—; founder AccuComp, 1986—. Mem. Green River Planning Commn., 1971-79; bd. dirs. Green River Co-op Pre-Sch., Inc., 1977-79; trustee Sweetwater County Sch. Dist. #2, 1986—; vol. chmn. Arthritis Found., Sweetwater County, 1986—. Mem. Am. Acad. Forensic Hypnotists, Am. Mensa Ltd., Am. Polygraph Assn.,Utah Polygraph Assn., Wyo. Polygraph Assn. (charter, editor newsletter). Roman Catholic. Home: 60 W Railroad Ave Green River WY 82935 Office: 78 W Railroad Ave PO Box 1147 Green River WY 82935

BRANDON, BURT (ALF G. JACOBSEN), actor; b. Tonsberg, Norway, Mar. 15, 1937; came to U.S., 1957, naturalized, 1964; s. Lauritz Arne and Gunvor (Johnsen) J.; student Theater of Arts U., 1957-60; m. Inga-Lill Nordstrom, July 9, 1966; 1 son, Mikael Arne. Starred stage plays including The Skyscraper, 1957; The Fourposter, 1958; Home Of The Brave, 1959; Ghosts, 1960; featured in various movies including: Summer and Smoke, 1960; Torn Curtain, 1964, Seconds, 1965; played four different parts in TV show Village of Guilt, series Voyage to the Bottom of the Sea, 1964; guest star segments of Batman, 1964; various other TV appearances since; tech. adviser in filming airplane sequences for most films and TV shows in Hollywood. Served with Royal Norwegian Air Force, 1955-57. Mem. Internat. Platform Assn., Sons of Norway.

BRANDON, KATHRYN ELIZABETH BECK, pediatrician; b. Salt Lake City, Sept. 10, 1916; d. Clarence M. and Hazel A. (Cutler) Beck; M.D., U. Chgo., 1941; B.A., U. Utah, 1937; M.P.H., U. Calif., Berkeley, 1967; children—John William, Kathleen Brandon McEnulty, Karen. Intern, Grace Hosp., Detroit, 1941-42; resident Children's Hosp. Med. Center No. Calif., Oakland, 1953-55, Children's Hosp., Los Angeles, 1951-53; practice medicine, specializing in pediatrics, La Crescentia, Calif., 1946-51, Salt Lake City, 1960-65; med. dir. Salt Lake City public schs., 1957-60; dir. Ogden City-Weber County (Utah) Health Dept., 1965-67; pediatrician Fitzsimmons Army Hosp., 1967-68; coll. health physician U. Colo., Boulder, 1968-71; student health physician U. Utah, Salt Lake City, 1971-81; occupational health physician Hill AFB, Utah, 1981-85; practice medicine specializing in pediatrics and occupational medicine, Salt Lake City, 1986—; child health physician Salt Lake City-County Health Dept., 1971—; cons. in field; clin. asst. U. Utah Coll. Medicine, Salt Lake City, 1958-64; clin. asst. pediatrics U. Colo. Coll. Medicine, Denver, 1958-72; active staff Primary Children's Hosp., Latter Day Saints Hosp., and Cottonwood Hosp., 1960-67. Diplomate Am. Bd. Pediatrics. Fellow Am. Pediatric Acad., Am. Pediatric Health Assn., Am. Sch. Health Assn.; mem. Utah Coll. Health Assn. (pres. 1978-80), Pacific Coast Coll. Health Assn., AMA, Utah Med. Assn., Salt Lake County Med. Soc., Utah Public Health Assn. (sec.-treas. 1960-66), Intermountain Pediatric Soc. Address: PO Box 8482 Salt Lake City UT 84108 Office: 3236 E 3300 S Salt Lake City UT 84109

BRANDT, GEORGE, electronics executive; b. N.Y.C., Jan. 12, 1934; s. George and Pauline Marie (Mueller) B.; m. Ann Katherine Brandt, Sept. 13, 1953; children: Kathleen, Cynthia, George, Alice. BSEE, U. Colo., 1966. Assoc. engr. Martin Marietta Corp., Denver, 1958-63; mfg. engr. Ball Bros. Research Co., Boulder, Colo., 1963-65; staff engr. product analysis IBM Corp., Boulder, 1966-78; staff engr. reliability dept. IBM Corp., Tucson, 1978-83, staff engr., product assurance dept., 1983-84, adv. engr., storage products dept., 1984—; owner/operator Raggedy Ann Presch./Day Care Ctr., Boulder, 1970-76. Mem. council Dove of Peace Luth. Ch., Tucson, 1977-84; advisor Boulder Valley Sch. Bd., 1963-65; mem. Rep. Presdl. task force, Washington, 1985-86. Mem. Soc. Reliability Engrs., Tex. Instruments Computer Group (sec. Tucson chpt. 1983-85). Republican. Lodge: Masons. Home and Office: 1115 W San Martin Dr Tucson AZ 85704

BRANDT, SUSAN LORAE, social worker; b. Washington, June 26, 1950; d. Lloyd Adrian and Rachel DeSpang (Miller) N.; m. James S. Brandt, May 31, 1986. Student, W.Va. Wesleyan, Buckhannon, 1968-69, Montgomery Coll., 1970, U. Md., 1971, Art Inst. Miami, 1971-73; BA, U. Mont., 1976. Layout, paste-up artist LithoComp, Bethesda, Md., 1973-74; receptionist Real Log Homes, Inc., Missoula, Mont., 1976-77, sec., bookkeeper, 1978, mktg. sec., 1978-79; gen. office clk. State of Montana, Missoula, 1979-80; social worker Mont. Social and Rehab. Services, Shelby, 1980—; rep. social and rehab. services 9th Jud. Foster Care Rev. Com., Choteau, Mont. 1982-86. Active Big Sister Big Bros. and Sisters Program, Shelby, 1980-84, Missoula, 1977-80; chairperson Mental Health Adv. Bd., Shelby, 1981-83, 86; bd. dirs. Triangle Transition, Shelby, 1981-83. Mem. Nat. Assn. Social Workers. Avocations: reading, cross country skiing, gardening. Home: 649 N Teton Ave Shelby MT 59474 Office: Toole County Office Human Services Courthouse Shelby MT 59474

BRANDT, WARREN HERMAN, civil engineer, telecommunications researcher, consultant; b. Chgo., June 1, 1924; s. Fred William and Amanda (Voelz) B. BSCE, U. Ill., 1954; postgrad., Colo. State U., 1965-70, Colo. Sch. Mines, 1977. Registered profl. engr., Ill., Colo. Asst. to traffic engr. Ill. Div. Highways, Elgin, 1954-61; traffic engr. City of Racine, Wis., 1961-65, Inter-County Regional Planning Commn., Denver, 1965-68; instr. Community Coll. of Denver, 1968-79; founder, chief engr. Brandt Telecommunications, Rye, Colo., 1979—; engring. cons. Air Tech. Internat., Tucson, 1979—, Rye Telephone Co., Colorado City, Colo., 1981—, J.K. Smith and Assocs., Denver, 1980—, Pueblo (Colo.) Community Coll., 1985—. Author: Vehicular Speed Manual, 1966, Transportation--Its Role in the Denver Metropolitan Area, 1967, Apparent Trends in Subscriber Station Apparatus, 1980. Colo. Petroleum Assn. scholar, 1977. Mem. Beta Sigma Psi. Avocation: computer research. Home: 10001 Scenic View Dr Rye CO 81069 Office: Brandt Telecommunications Box 68 Rye CO 81069

BRANN, DONALD LEWIS, JR., superintendent schools; b. Los Angeles, Nov. 1, 1945; s. Donald Lewis and Shirley June (Scott) B.; m. Sari Ellen Donohoe, June 17, 1967; children—Shanonn, Rebecca. A.A. in Bus. Adminstrn. El Camino Coll., 1966; B.S. in Bus. Adminstrn. U. So. Calif.-Los Angeles, 1968, Ed.D. in Ednl. Adminstrn., 1982; M.A. in Elem. Edn., Calif. State U.-Los Angeles, 1972. Cert. tchr., sch. adminstr., Calif. Tchr. El Segundo Unified Sch. Dist., Calif., 1970-72, reading specialist, 1972-76, program coordinator, 1976-79; prin. Wilsona Sch. Dist., Lancaster, Calif., 1979-81, supt., 1981-84; supt. Old Adobe Union Sch. Dist., Petaluma, Calif., 1984—; bd. dirs. Schs. Committed To Reducing Utility Bills, Sacramento, 1983—; mem. State Supts. Small Sch. Adv. Com.; coordinator El Segundo Jr. Olympics, 1972; bd. dirs. Antelope Valley Fedn. Tchrs. Credit Union, Lancaster, 1983; v.p., bd. dirs. Friends of Antelope Valley Indian Mus., Lancaster, 1982. Named One of Top 100 Sch. Execs. in N.Am., Exec. Educator, 1985. Mem. Am. Assn. Sch. Adminstrs., Sonoma County Supts. Harbinger Club , Assn. Calif. Sch. Adminstrs., Small Sch. Dist. Assn. (founder; treas. 1983—), Alpha Kappa Psi. Home: 18 Weatherby Ct Petaluma CA 94952 Office: Old Adobe Union Sch Dist 845 Crinella Dr Petaluma CA 94952

BRANSFORD, JAMES CHRISTIAN, petroleum geologist; b. Galveston, Tex., Aug. 7, 1900; s. Charles Dean and Carrie Martie (Whiteside) B.; m. Martie Elizabeth Wilkes, Aug. 20, 1975. Student Colo. Sch. Mines, 1918-19, U. Tex.-El Paso, 1921. With Calif. Petroleum Corp. and Texas Co., Los Angeles, 1923-29; petroleum geologist, Los Angeles, 1929-50, Palm Springs, Calif., 1950—. Author oil maps. Mem. Am. Assn. Petroleum Geologists, Soc. Petroleum Engrs. Republican. Presbyterian. Address: 360 Monte Vista Dr Palm Springs CA 92262

BRANSON, MARGARET ABER, businesswoman, former state legislator; b. Sheridan, Wyo., May 12, 1927; d. Seth Perry and Fannie Mary (Hults) Aber; B.A., U. Denver, 1949; postgrad. U. Oreg., 1972; m. Ralph B. Branson, July 16, 1959; children—Melissa, Malcolm, Seth, Alec. Columnist, Seward (Alaska) Phoenix Log, 1966-78; employment specialist Alaska Skill Ctr., Seward, 1969-74; owner, mgr. Turquoise Barrabora, Cooper Landing, 1974—; owner, pub. Celebrations Pub. Co., Alaska, 1987—; mng. gen. ptnr. McElb Group. mem. Alaska Ho. of Reps., Juneau, 1979-81. Pres., Cooper Landing Adv. Sch. Bd., 1975-76; v.p. Kenai Peninsula Borough Assembly, 1976-77; mem. Alaska Regional Manpower Tng. Bd., 1977-78, Kenai Peninsula Arbitration Bd., 1977—, Alaska Vocat. Tech. Center Adv. Bd., 1981-81; chmn. New Capitol Site Planning Commn., State of Alaska, 1981-82, Kenai Peninsula Sch. Dist. Vocat. Edn. Com.; commr. Seward Planning and Zoning Commn., Alaska, 1983—. Recipient President's award Alaska Jaycees, 1964. Mem. Alaska Press Women, Nat. Fedn. Press Women, Nat. Order Women Legislators, Anchorage Rep. Women. Home: 500 4th Ave Seward AK 99664 Office: Box 271 Seward AK 99664

BRANTINGHAM, CHARLES ROSS, podiatrist; b. Long Beach, Calif., Feb. 14, 1917; m. Lila Carolyn Price; children: Paul Jeffery, John Price, Charles Ross, James William. Student, Long Beach City Coll., 1935; D in Podiatric Medicine, Calif. Coll. Podiatric Medicine, 1939, cert. foot surgery, 1947. Resident in podiatry San Francisco, 1939-40; pvt. practice podiatry Long Beach, 1946-56; podiatrist, dir. Podiatric Group, Long Beach, 1956-71, Los Alamitos (Calif.) Podiatric Group, 1971-86; chmn. podiatry dept. orthopedics Los Alamitos Med. Ctr., 1983—; clin. asst. prof. medicine U. So. Calif., Los Angeles, 1965—; adj. prof. Calif. State U., Long Beach, 1972—; cons. Specified Products Co., El Monte, Calif., 1968—, Armstrong World Industries, Lancaster, Pa., 1983—. Contbr. articles to profl. jours., chpts. to books. Bd. dirs. Diabetes Assn. of So. Calif., Los Angeles, 1964-67; cons., bd. dirs. Comprehensive Health Planning Assn., Los Angeles, 1969-72; pub. improvement and adv. cons. Long Beach City Council and Office of Mayor, 1957-67. Served to lt. comdr. USN, 1941-46. Named Disting. Practitioner in Podiatry Nat. Acad. Practice, 1982. Fellow Am. Assn. Hosp. Podiatrists (pres. 1958-60), Am. Pub. Health Assn. (council 1986—, Steven Toth award 1982), Am. Soc. Podiatric Medicine, Internat. Acad. for Standing and Walking Fitness (pres. 1963—); mem. Am. Podiatric Med. Assn. (exec. council 1957-59, Hall of Sci. award 1973), Assn. Mil. Surgeons of U.S. (life), Res. Officers Assn. of U.S. Republican. Mormon. Clubs: Exchange (Long Beach) (pres. 1948-49), Ind. Bus. (pres. 1958). Avocations: history, swimming. Home: 11386 Holder St Cypress CA 90630 Office: 3791 Katella Ave Suite 207 Los Alamitos CA 90720

BRANTLEY, ROBERT LEE, real estate executive; b. Goodrich, Colo., Aug. 21, 1919; s. Roscoe L. and Dora B. (Rupe) B.; m. Jewelene Snider Turcotte, Nov. 11, 1973; m. Edith Todd, Aug. 21, 1940 (dec. Dec. 1971); children: Carolee Brantley Jones, Bonnie Brantley Murphy. BS, U. Calif., Berkeley, 1946. CPA, Alaska, N.Mex., Tex. Pres., Jewelene Corp., Anchorage, 1970-78, ABC Bus. Corp., Las Cruces, N.Mex., 1978-82, Brantley & Assocs., Inc., Las Cruces, 1978—; mng. ptnr. Jewelene II, Ltd., Las Cruces, 1982—, Jewelene Properties, Las Cruces, 1978— ; cons. KASK-TV, Las Cruces, 1980—, Dooley Corp., Anchorage, 1975-82; sec. Waste Mgmt., Inc., Las Cruces, 1983—; dir. MGB Corp., Las Cruces. Mem., officer Anchorage Budget Commn., 1976; mem. Oreg. Gov.'s Com. on Employment, 1967. Mem. Am. Inst. C.P.A.s, Alaska Soc. C.P.A.s, Fed. Govt. Accts., Mil. Controllers Assn., Exec. Sales Club Las Cruces (officer). Republican. Presbyterian. Office: PO Box 277 Las Cruces NM 88004

BRASEL, JO ANNE, physician; b. Salem, Ill., Feb. 15, 1934; d. Gerald Nolan and Ruby Rachel (Rich) B. B.A., U. Colo., 1956; M.D., U. Colo., 1959. Diplomate Am. Bd. Pediatrics, Am. Bd. Pediatric-Endocrinology. Pediatric intern, resident Cornell Med. Coll.-N.Y. Hosp., N.Y.C., 1959-62; pediatric endocrine fellow Johns Hopkins U. Sch. Medicine, Balt., 1962-65, asst. prof. pediatrics, 1965-68; asst. prof. then assoc. prof. pediatrics Cornell U. Med. Coll., N.Y.C., 1969-72; assoc. prof. then prof. pediatrics Columbia U. Coll. Physicians and Surgeons, N.Y.C., 1972-79, asst. dir. Inst. Human Nutrition, 1972-79; prof. pediatrics Harbor-UCLA Med. Ctr., UCLA Sch. Medicine, 1979—, program dir. Gen. Clin. Research Ctr., 1979—, prof. medicine, 1980—; mem. adv. com. FDA, Rockville, Md., 1971-75; mem. nutrition study sect. NIH, Bethesda, Md., 1974-78; mem. select panel for promotion of child health HEW, Washington, 1979-80; mem. life scis. D adv. screening com. Fulbright-Hays program, Washington, 1981—. Recipient

Research Career Devel. award NIH, 1973-77, Irma T. Hirschl Trust Career Scientist award, 1974-79, Sr. Fulbright Sabbatical Research award, 1980. Mem. Soc. Pediatric Research (pres. 1978-79), Am. Fed. Clin. Research, Endocrine Soc., Am. Soc. Clin. Nutrition, Am. Inst. Nutrition, Lawson Wilkins Pediatric Endocrine Soc. (dir., mem. bd. 1972-74), Am. Pediatric Soc., Assn. Program Dirs. for Gen. Clin. Research Ctrs. (pres. 1982-83), N.Am. Assn. for Study Obesity, Internat. Orgn. for Study Human Devel., Western Soc. Pediatric Research, Phi Beta Kappa, Alpha Omega Alpha. Office: Harbor-UCLA Med Ctr 1000 W Carson St Torrance CA 90509 *

BRASELL, HAROLD KEARY, educator; b. Fort Sumner, N.Mex., Mar. 1, 1922; s. Hugh T. and Dora (Keary) B.; B.A., Eastern N.Mex. U., 1947; M.A., U. Denver, 1952, Ph.D., 1956; children—Sherrie Lou, Meriam Lynette, Hugh Keary. Sci. and lang. arts remedial tchr. Tatum (N.Mex) Pub. Schs., 1949-51; exec. asst. dir., class demonstration tchr. U. Denver Children's Speech Clinic, 1951-53; spl. edn. dir.-speech therapist Odessa (Tex.) Pub. Schs., 1954-56; coordinator psychology, speech and hearing, dir. Sch. Psychology and Spl. Edn. Programs, U. Denver Clin. Services, 1956-60; sch. psychologist Ch. Study Services, Phoenix, 1968-69; dir., prin. spl. edn. Jefferson County Schs., Lakewood, Colo., 1960-62; instr., asst. prof. spl. edn. U. Denver, 1953-54, 1956-60; asso. prof. spl. edn. Ariz. U., 1961-68; asso. prof. Eastern N.Mex. U., Portales, 1969—, chmn. spl. edn. dept., 1969-77. Diagnostic cons. Navajo Nation. Served with USMC, 1944-45; PTO. Decorated Bronze Star medal, Purple Heart medal. Recipient certificates of Commendation, Gov. Ariz. for Outstanding Services to Handicapped, 1964, 65. Mem. NEA, Council for Exceptional Children, Am. Assn. for Mentally Deficient, VFW, DAV. Lodges: Masons, Elks. Home: 213 W 3d St Portales NM 88130

BRASSELL, ROSELYN STRAUSS, lawyer; b. Shreveport, La., Feb. 19, 1930; d. Herman Carl and Etelka (McMullan) Strauss. BA, La. State U., 1949; JD, UCLA, 1962. Bar: Calif. 1963. Legal sec. Welton P. Mouton, Lafayette, La., 1949-50; office sec. Leake, Henry, Golden & Burrow, Dallas, 1950-57; atty. CBS, Los Angeles, 1962-68, sr. atty., 1968-76, asst. gen. atty., 1976-83, broadcast counsel, 1983—. Co-writer: Life After Death for the California Celebrity, 1985; bd. editors U. Calif. Law Rev., 1960-62. Named Angel of Distinction Los Angeles Cen. City Assn., 1975. Mem. Calif. Bar Assn., Los Angeles County Bar Assn. (exec. com. 1970—, sect. chmn. 1980-81), Beverly Hills Bar Assn., Los Angeles Copyright Soc. (treas. 1977-78, sec. 1978-79, pres. 1981-82), Am. Women in Radio and TV (nat. dir.-at-large 1971-73, nat. pub. affairs chmn. 1977-78), Nat. Acad. TV Arts and Scis., Women in Film, Los Angeles World Affairs Council, U. Calif. Law Alumni Assn. (dir. 1971-74), Order of Coif, Alpha Xi Delta, Phi Alpha Delta. Republican. Home: 631 N Wilcox Ave Los Angeles CA 90004 Office: 7800 Beverly Blvd Los Angeles CA 90036

BRATT, C. GRIFFITH, organist, composer; b. Balt., Nov. 21, 1914; s. George Augustus and Emilie Holtzman (Gettier) B.; m. Mary E. Wallis, Sept. 8, 1937; children—Barbara, J. Wallis, Gary G., C. Stephan. Cert., Peabody Conservatory of Music, Balt., 1936, artist's diploma in organ, 1939, M.Mus., 1943; D.Mus. (hon.), Northwest Nazarene Coll., Nampa, Idaho, 1970. Organist, choirmaster St. John's and Grace Lutheran chs., Balt., 1935-43; minister of music Luther Pl. Meml. Ch., Washington, 1943-44, 46; prof. music Boise State U., Idaho, 1946-76, chmn. dept., 1946-70, composer-in-residence, 1963-76; organist, choirmaster St. Michael's Episcopal Cathedral, Boise, 1946—; recitalist. Composer 4 operas, 2 symphonies, numerous choral, organ, chamber and orchestral works; commd. composer Academic Rhapsody, Boise State U.'s 50th Anniversary, 1982 author: Harmony Text, 1965. Served with USN, 1944-45. Recipient Gov. Idaho's Silver medal, 1972, Disting. Alumni award Peabody Conservatory Music, 1971, Disting. Citizen Recognition award Idaho Statesman, 1971, Boise City Arts Council award, 1972, Cert. Recognition, State of Idaho, 1976, Disting. Service award Boise State U., 1976, award for outstanding service to music Idaho Fedn Music. Mem. Am. Guild Organists (assoc.) (chpt. dean 1947-52), Nat. Fedn. Music Clubs. Episcopalian. Home: 1020 N 17th St Boise ID 83702

BRATTAIN, WALTER HOUSER, physics educator; b. Amoy, China (parents Am. citizens), Feb. 10, 1902; s. Ross R. and Ottilie (Houser) B.; m. Keren Gilmore, July 5, 1935 (dec. Apr. 1957); 1 child, William G.; m. Emma Jane Miller, May 10, 1958. B.S., Whitman Coll., 1924, D.Sc. (hon.), 1955; M.A., U. Oreg., 1926; Ph.D., U. Minn., 1929; D.Sc. (hon.), U. Portland, 1952, Union Coll., 1955, U. Minn., 1957, Gustavus Adolphus Coll., 1963; L.H.D. (hon.), Hartwick Coll., 1964. With radio sect. Bur. Standards, 1928-29; research physicist Bell Telephone Labs., Murray Hill, N.J., 1929-67; with div. war research Columbia U., N.Y.C., 1942-43; vis. lectr. Harvard U., 1952-53; vis. prof. Whitman Coll., Walla Walla, Wash., 1962-72; overseer emeritus Whitman Coll., 1972—. Recipient Stuart Ballantine medal Franklin Inst., 1952; John Scott award City of Phila., 1955; (with William Shockley and John Bardeen) Nobel prize in Physics, 1956; named to Nat. Inventors Hall of Fame, 1974, Disting. Alumnus, U. Oreg., 1976. Fellow Am. Phys. Soc., AAAS, Am. Acad. Arts and Scis., Explorers Club; mem. Swedish Royal Acad., IEEE (hon.), Franklin Inst., Nat. Acad. Scis., Phi Beta Kappa, Sigma Xi. Club: Walla Walla Country. Co-inventor of semiconductor. Office: Whitman Coll Walla Walla WA 99362

BRATTON, HOWARD CALVIN, judge; b. Clovis, N.Mex., Feb. 4, 1922; s. Sam Gilbert and Vivian (Rogers) B. B.A., U. N.Mex., 1941, LL.D., 1971; LL.B., Yale U., 1947. Bar: N.Mex. 1948. Law clk. U.S. Circuit Ct. Appeals, 1948; mem. Grantham & Bratton, Albuquerque, 1949-52; spl. asst. U.S. atty. charge litigation OPS, 1951-52; assoc., then ptnr. Hervy, Dow & Hinkle, Roswell, N.Mex., 1952-64; judge U.S. Dist. Ct. N.Mex., 1964—, chief judge, 1978-87, sr. judge, 1987—; chmn. N.Mex. Jr. Bar Assn., 1952; pres. Chaves County (N.Mex.) Bar Assn., 1962; chmn. pub. lands com. N.Mex. Oil and Gas Assn., 1961-64, Interstate Oil Compact Commn., 1963-64; mem. N.Mex. Commn. Higher Edn., 1962-64, Jud. Conf. of U.S. Com. on operation of jury system, 1966-72, 79—. Bd. regents U. N.Mex., 1958-68, pres., 1963-64; bd. dirs. Fed. Jud. Ctr., 1983-87. Served to capt. AUS, 1942-45. Mem. Trial Judges Assn. 10th Circuit (pres. 1976-78), Nat. Conf. Fed. Trial Judges (exec. com. 1977-79), Sigma Chi. Home: 1117 Salamanca NW Albuquerque NM 87107 Office: PO Box 38 Albuquerque NM 87103

BRATTSTROM, BAYARD HOLMES, biology educator; b. Chgo., July 3, 1929; s. Wilber LeRoy and Violet (Holmes) B.; m. Cecile D. Funk, June 15, 1952 (div. May 1975); children: Theodore Allen, David Arthur.; m. Martha Isaacs Marsh, July 8, 1982. B.S., San Diego State Coll., 1951; M.A., UCLA, 1953, Ph.D., 1959. Dir. edn. Natural History Mus., San Diego, 1949-51; asst. curator herpetology Natural History Mus., 1949-51; assoc. zoology UCLA, 1954-56; research fellow paleoecology Calif. Inst. Tech., Pasadena, 1955; instr. biology Adelphi U., Garden City, N.Y., 1956-60; asst. prof. Calif. State U., Fullerton, 1960-61; assoc. prof. Calif. State U., 1961-66, prof., 1966—; assoc. prof. zoology UCLA, summers 1962-63; hon. research assoc. herpetology, vertebrate paleontology Los Angeles County Mus., Los Angeles, 1961—; pres. Fullerton Youth Mus. and Natural Sci. Center, 1962-64, dir., 1962-66; vis. prof. zoology Sydney U., Australia, 1978, U. Queensland, Brisbane, Australia, 1984. Author: poetry The Talon Digs Deeply into My Heart, 1974; Contbr. chpts. to books. Research grantee Am. Philos. Soc., Mex., 1958; Research grantee Am. Philos. Soc., Panama, 1959; NSF, 1964-66; NSF Sr. Postdoctoral fellow Monash U., Australia, 1966-67; recipient Distinguished Teaching award Calif. State U., Fullerton, 1968. Fellow AAAS (mem. council 1965—), Herpetological League; mem. Am. Soc. Ichthyologists and Herpetologists (bd. govs. 1962-66, v.p. western div. 1965), Orange County Zool. Soc. (mem. bd. 1962-65, pres. 1962-64), So. Calif. Acad. Sci. (dir. 1964-67), Ecol. Soc. Am., Soc. for Study Evolution, Soc. Systematic Zoology, San Diego Soc. Natural History, Soc. Vertebrate Paleontology, Am. Soc. Mammalogists, Cooper, Am. ornithol. socs., Am. Soc. Zoologists, Sigma Xi. Research and publs. in osteology, paleontology, systematics, behavior, ecology, physiology especially temperature regulation, zoogeography of vertebrates especially amphibians and reptiles, repopulation of volcanic islands, social behavior. Office: Dept Biology Calif State U Fullerton CA 92634

BRATZ, ROBERT DAVIS, retired biology educator; b. Sherman, Tex., Dec. 14, 1920; s. Lee Harrison and Gladys Claudius (Lisenby) B.; m. Dorothy Arleen Davis, Sept. 5, 1947; children: Barbara Lee, Cynthia Lin, Kenneth Gordon. BS, Sam Houston State Coll., 1941; postgrad., Manchester Coll., 1943; MS, Oreg. State U., 1950, PhD, 1952. Asst. prof. biology The Coll. Idaho, Caldwell, 1953-58, assoc. prof., 1958-63, prof., 1963-85, emeritus, 1985—; plant survey of Reynolds Watershed Agrl. Research Service USDA, Boise, Idaho, 1964-74; with expeditions in U.S. and Mex., 1955-80. Fellow AAAS; mem. Idaho Acad. Sci. (life, Nat. Assn. Acad. of Sci. rep. 1970-82), Danforth Assocs. N.W. Inc. (hon.), Danforth Found. (assoc. N.W. region). Home: 1400 Willow St Caldwell ID 83605 Office: Coll Idaho Mus Natural History Caldwell ID 83605

BRAULT, JAMES WILLIAM, physicist; b. New London, Wis., Feb. 10, 1932; s. Lucian Joseph and Alvina Lucy (Boville) B.; m. Marguerite Elaine Bryan, June 29, 1952 (div. May 1986); children: Stephen Michael, Lisa Lynn, Jennifer Elaine. BS in Physics, U. Wis., 1953; student, Cornell U., 1953-55; PhD in Physics, Princeton U., 1962. Research staff member project Matterhorn Princeton U., N.J., 1955-57, instr., 1961-64; asst. physicist Kitt Peak Nat. Obs., Tucson, 1964-68, assoc. physicist, 1969-70; physicist Nat. Solar Obs., Tucson, 1971—. Conbtr. articles to profl. jours. Recipient Alexander von Humboldt award (Rep. of Germany), 1986—. Fellow Optical Soc. Am., mem. Am. Phys. Soc., Internat. Astron. Union, Am. Astron. Soc. (affiliate solar physics div.). Democrat. Office: Nat Solar Obs PO Box 26732 Tucson AZ 85726

BRAUMAN, JOHN I., chemist, educator; b. Pitts., Sept. 7, 1937; s. Milton and Freda E. (Schlitt) B.; m. Sharon Lea Kruse, Aug. 22, 1964; 1 dau., Kate Andrea. B.S., Mass. Inst. Tech., 1959; Ph.D. (NSF fellow), U. Calif., Berkeley, 1963. NSF postdoctoral fellow U. Calif., Los Angeles, 1962-63; asst. prof. chemistry Stanford (Calif.) U., 1963-69, asso. prof., 1969-72, prof., 1972-80, J.G. Jackson-C.J. Wood prof. chemistry, 1980—, chmn. dept., 1979-83; cons. in phys. organic chemistry; adv. panel chemistry div. NSF, 1974-78; adv. panel NASA, AEC, ERDA, Research Corp., Office Chemistry and Chem. Tech., NRC. Mem. editorial adv. bd. Jour. Am. Chem. Soc, 1976-83, Jour. Organic Chemistry, 1974-78, Nouveau Jour. de Chimie, 1977-85, Chem. Revs, 1978-80, Chem. Physics Letters, 1982-85, Jour. Phys. Chemistry, 1985—; dep. editor for phys. scis. Science, 1985—. Fellow Alfred P. Sloan, 1968-70, Guggenheim, 1978-79; Christensen, Oxford U., 1983-84. Fellow AAAS; mem. Nat. Acad. Scis., Am. Acad. Arts Scis., Am. Chem. Soc. (award in pure chemistry 1973, Harrison Howe award 1976, James Flack Norris award 1986, Arthur C. Cope scholar award 1986, exec. com. phys. chemistry div.), Brit. Chem. Soc., Sigma Xi, Phi Lambda Upsilon. Home: 849 Tolman Dr Stanford CA 94305 Office: Dept Chemistry Stanford U Stanford CA 94305

BRAUN, BARBARA ILENE, advertising executive; b. Charleston, W.Va., May 8, 1944; d. Arthur Goodman and Charlotte C. Braun; BS, Northwestern U., 1966; MBA, Pepperdine U., 1982. Supr., Leo Burnett Advt., Chgo., 1966-67; account coordinator Lake Public Relations, London, Eng., 1967-68; account exec. Beneficial Standard Corp., Los Angeles, 1968-70; asso. Argosy Group, Los Angeles, 1970-73; owner Braun & Assos., Los Angeles, 1973—, Charleston Tent Awning Co. (W.Va.), 1984—; lectr., cons. in field. Mem. Nat. Assn. Women Bus. Owners, Nat. Assn. Female Execs., Internat. Platform Assn., Phi Beta. Democrat. Office: 515 Ocean Avenue Santa Monica CA 90402

BRAUN, STANLEY, insurance company executive; b. N.Y.C., July 2, 1937; s. Herman and Gussie (Cigler) B.; m. Madeline Joan Littman, Dec. 25, 1959 (div. Jan. 1984); children: Cindy Karen, Dina Jill, Suzanne Alyse; m. Ardis Nadine Knoppel, May 11, 1985. BS in Banking and Fin., NYU, 1959. V.p. CNA Ins. Co., N.Y.C., Chgo., Los Angeles, 1959-74; sr. v.p. Harbor Ins. Co., Los Angeles, 1974-76; pres. Mission Ins. Co., Los Angeles, 1976-84; exec. v.p. Fairmont Fin., Inc. and Fairmont Ins., Burbank, Calif., 1984-86; pres., chief exec. officer Fairmont Ins. Co., Burbank, Calif., 1986—; bd. dirs. Am. Capitol Ins. Co., Los Angeles, Chase World Info. Corp., Los Angeles, Fairmont Ins. Co., Chiltar Ins. Co., Centinental Surety and Fidelity Ins. Co. Founder Raritan Valley Civic Assn., Hazlet, N.J., 1965. Served as sgt. U.S. Army, 1961-67. Mem. Calif. Workers' Compensation Inst. (bd. dirs. 1983-84). Republican. Jewish. Clubs: Los Angeles Athletic; Calabasas Golf and Country (Calabasas Park, Calif.). Avocations: hiking, camping, tennis, golf, travel. Home: 3417 Coy Dr Sherman Oaks CA 91423

BRAUN, STEPHEN HUGHES, clinical and consulting psychologist; b. St. Louis, Nov. 20, 1942; s. William Lafon and Jane Louise B.; B.A., Washington U., St. Louis, 1964, M.A., 1965; Ph.D. (USPHS fellow in Clin. Psychology), U. Mo., Columbia, 1970; m. Penny Lee Prada, Aug. 28, 1965; 1 son, Damian Hughes. Asst. prof. psychology Calif. State U., Chico, 1970-71; dir. social learning div. Ariz. State Hosp., Phoenix, 1971-74; chief bur. planning and evaluation Ariz. Dept. Health Services, Phoenix, 1974-79; pres. Braun and Assocs., human service program cons.'s, Scottsdale, Ariz., 1979—; also pvt. clin. practice; asst. prof. psychology Ariz. State U., 1971-79, vis. asst. prof. Ctr. of Criminal Justice, 1974-79, Ctr. for Public Affairs, 1979-81; cons. Law Enforcement Assistance Adminstrn., NIMH, Alcohol, Drug Abuse, and Mental Health Adminstrn., Ariz. Dept. Health Services, Ariz. Dept. Corrections, Ariz. Dept. Econ. Security, local and regional human service agys. NIMH research grantee, 1971-74; State of Calif. research grantee, 1971; cert. clin. psychologist, Ariz. Mem. Am. Psychol. Assn., Sigma Xi. Editorial cons.; contbr. articles to profl. publs. Home: 6122 E Calle Tuberia Scottsdale AZ 85251 Office: 7125 E Second St Scottsdale AZ 85251

BRAUN, SUZANNE SANDRA, registered nurse; b. Santa Ana, Calif., July 20, 1947; d. Raymond Frank and Betty Irene (Sorenson) B.; m. Randall Gordon Craig, July 9, 1966 (div. Mar. 1970); children: Randall Gordon Jr., John Scott; m. Philip Edward Nicholas Lemaster. AA, Santa Ana Coll., 1977; teaching cert., U. Calif., Irvine, 1980. Staff nurse Childrens Hosp., Orange, Calif., 1972-74, Canyon Gen. Hosp., Anaheim, 1974-78; staff nurse, childbirth educator U. Calif. Med. Ctr., Irvine, 1978-85; dir. surgery Covina Valley Community Hosp., West Covina, Calif., 1985—. Author: Policies of the Adolescent Psychiatric Patient, 1976, Policies for Ambulatory Care, 1986. Mem. Assn. Operating Room Nurses, Internat. Childbirth Educators Assn. (childbirth educator), Assn. Operating Room Nurses, Ambulatory Care (chairperson 1986—). Republican. Avocations: Am. Indian history, hiking, fishing. Home: 8741 Holly Ln Riverside CA 92503

BRAUNSTEIN, HERBERT, pathologist, educator; b. N.Y.C., Jan. 10, 1926; s. Max and Ida (Meyerson) B.; m. Frances Toomey, Aug. 1, 1954; children: Sheila, Mary, John, Anne. BS, CCNY and CUNY, 1944; MD, Hahnemann Med. Coll., 1950. Intern Montefiore Hosp., N.Y.C., 1950-51; resident in pathology U. Mich., Ann Arbor, 1951-52; resident in pathology U. Cin., 1952-55, from asst. prof. to assoc. prof. pathology, 1956-64; chmn. dept. pathology Michael Reese Hosp., Chgo.; also prof. pathology Chgo. Med. Sch., 1964-65; from assoc. prof. to prof. pathology U. Ky., Lexington, 1965-70; chmn. dept. labs. San Bernardino (Calif.) County Med. Ctr., 1970—, also dir. sch. med. tech.; clin. prof. pathology Loma Linda (Calif.) U., 1970—, UCLA, 1980-83; prof. in residence biomed. scis. U. Calif., Riverside, 1979-83. Contbr. articles to sci. jours., chpts. to books. Served with USNR, 1944-46, PTO. Recipient numerous research grants, Career devel. award USPHS, 1958-64. Mem. AMA, Calif. Med. Assn., San Bernardino County Med. Soc., Am. Soc. Clin. Pathologists, Coll. Am. Pathologists, Internat. Acad. Pathology, Am. Assn. Pathologists, Histochem. Soc., Phi Beta Kappa, Sigma Xi, Alpha Omega Alpha. Republican. Home: 30524 Los Altos Dr Redlands CA 92373 Office: 780 E Gilbert St San Bernardino CA 92404

BRAUTBAR, NACHMAN, physician, educator; b. Haifa, Israel, Oct. 22, 1943; came to U.S., 1975; s. Pinhas and Sabine (Lohite) B.; m. Ronit Aboutboul, Mar. 25, 1968; children—Sigalit, Shirley, Jaques. M.D., Med. Sch. Jerusalem, 1968. Diplomate Am. Bd. Internal Medicine, Am. Bd. Nephrology. Intern, Rambam Hosp., Haifa, 1968-69; resident in internal medicine Hadassah Med. Center, Jerusalem, 1972-75; fellow in nephrology UCLA Med. Sch., 1975-77, asst. prof. medicine, 1977-78; asst. prof. medicine U. So. Calif., Los Angeles, 1978-80, assoc. prof. medicine, pharmacology and nutrition, 1980—, dir. Ctr. for Toxicology and Chem. Exposure; chmn. nephrology sect. Hollywood Presbyn. Med. Center, 1980—. Author: Cellular Bioenergetics, 1985. Contbr. numerous articles, papers to scientific publs. Chmn. research com., pub. relations com. Kidney Foundation Los Angeles, 1980—. Named Hon. Citizen, Los Angeles City Council, 1984; Grantee Am. Heart Assn., 1980—, NIH, 1983. Mem. Am. Soc. Nephrology, Am. Soc. Bone and Mineral Research, Am. Physiol. Soc., Am. Chem. Soc., Am. Soc. Parenteral Nutrition, Am. Coll. Nutrition, Israeli Soc. Nephrology (hon.). Office: U So Calif 2025 Zonal Ave Los Angeles CA 90023

BRAVER, MICHAEL BRUCE, clinical psychologist, educator; b. N.Y.C., Sept. 25, 1946; s. Solomon Wolf and Sylvia (Gruber) B.; m. Ricki Marsha Ellis, June 15, 1969 (div. Apr. 1973); m. Angela Robin Polansky, Sept. 9, 1979; children: Joshua Stanton, Andrew Emerson. AB, MA, UCLA, 1969; MSW, U. So. Calif., 1978; PhD, Calif. Sch. Profl. Psychology, 1983. Lic. clin. psychologist, clin. social worker, marriage and family counselor. Asst. prof. Cen. Wash. U., Ellensburg, 1969-71; field dir. Inst. Cultural N.Am., Puebla, Mex., 1970-71; psychologist Comprehensive Care Adolescent Treatment Program, Glendale, Calif., 1983-84; program dir. Children's Home Soc., Los Angeles, 1984-85; pvt. practice clin. psychology Toluca Lake, Calif., 1980—; vis. asst. prof. State U., Tempe, 1974-75, psychiat. social worker, 1978-82; bd. dirs. Valley Counseling Clinic, Sherman Oaks, Calif., 1984-86, Mt. San Antonio Coll., Walnut, Calif., 1985—; clin. supr. San Fernando Valley Counseling Ctr., Van Nuys, Calif., 1978-83, Calif. Family Studies Inst., 1986—. Cons. Students for Dem. Soc., Ellensburg, Wash., 1971, E.L.F., Ellensburg, 1970. Recipient Meritorious Teaching award Cen. Wash. U., 1969. Mem. Am. Psychol. Assn., Calif. State Psychol. Assn., Los Angeles Psychol. Assn., San Fernando Valley Psychol. Assn., Nat. Assn. Social Workers, Phi Beta Kappa, Pi Gamma Mu. Avocations: table tennis, aquaria culture, gardening. Office: 4444 Riverside Dr Suite 206 Toluca Lake CA 91505

BRAVERMAN, DONNA CARYN, fiber artist; b. Chgo., Apr. 4, 1947; d. Samuel and Pearl (Leen) B. Student, U. Mo., 1965-68; BFA in Interior Design, Chgo. Acad. Fine Arts, 1970. Interior designer Ascher Dental Supply-Healthco, Chgo., 1970-72, Clarence Krusinski & Assocs. Ltd., Chgo., 1972-74, Perkins & Will Architects, Chgo., 1974-77; fiber artist Fiber Co-op Fibrecations, Chgo., 1977, Scottsdale, Ariz., 1977—. Exhibited in group shows at Mus. Contemporary Crafts, N.Y.C., 1977, James Prendergast Library Art Gallery, Jamestown, N.Y., 1981, Grover M. Herman Fine Arts Ctr., Marietta, Ohio, 1982, Okla. Art Ctr., 1982, Middle Tenn. State U., Murfreesboro, 1982, Redding (Calif.) Mus., 1983, Tucson Mus. Art, 1984, 86, The Arts Ctr., Iowa City, 1985, The Wichita Nat., 1986; in traveling exhibitions Ariz. Archtl. Crafts, 1983, Clouds, Mountains, Fibers, 1983; represented in permanent collections Phillips Petroleum, Houston, Metro. Life, Tulsa, Directory Hotel, Tulsa, Keys Estate Ariz. Biltmore Estates, Phoenix, Sohio Petroleum, Dallas, Reichold Chem., White Plains, N.Y., Rolm Telecommunications, Colorado Springs, Colo., Mesirow & Co., Chgo.; contbr. articles to profl. jours. Avocation: photography. Home and Office: 7920 E Camelback Rd #511 Scottsdale AZ 85251

BRAXTON-BROWN, GREG, management consultant, educator; b. Vincennes, Ind., Sept. 30, 1953; s. Bobby Ray and Ramona (Stoval) Brown; m. Ruth Ann Thompson, Apr. 17, 1978; children: Jonah, Jeremy, Justin. BS, U. Redlands, 1980; MBA, Pepperdine U., 1983; BA, SUNY, Albany, 1985; D in Bus. Adminstrn., U.S. Internat. U., 1985. Paramedic Los Angeles County, 1971-75; sales rep. Med. Research Lab., Niles, Ill., 1975-77; mgr. western region IPCO Med. Electronics, White Plains, N.Y., 1977-81; mgmt. cons. Mission Viejo, Calif., 1981—; prof. bus. U. Redlands, Calif., 1983—; assoc. prof. mktg. Pepperdine U., Malibu, Calif., 1986—. Contbr. articles to profl. jours. Adult leader Boy Scouts Am., Mission Viejo, 1982—. Mem. AAUP, Acad. Mgmt., U. Redlands Alumni Bd. (bd. dirs. 1985). Republican. Mem. Ch. Religious Sci. Avocation: water polo. Home: 28186 Amable Mission Viejo CA 92692

BRAY, ABSALOM FRANCIS, JR., lawyer; b. San Francisco, Nov. 24, 1918; s. Absalom Francis and Leila Elizabeth (Veale) B.; m. Lorraine Cerena Paule, June 25, 1949; children—Oliver, Brian, Margot. B.A., Stanford U., 1940; J.D., U. So. Calif., 1949. Bar: Calif. 1949, U.S. Supreme Ct. 1960. Sr. ptnr. Bray & Baldwin and successive firms to Bray, Egan, Breitwieser & Costanza, Martinez, Walnut Creek & Moraga, Calif., 1949—, now pres. Bray, Egan, Breitwieser & Costanza, P.C., Martinez, Walnut Creek & Moraga; founder, dir. John Muir Nat. Bank, Martinez, 1983—. Chmn. Martinez Recreation Commn., 1949-54; chmn. nat. bd. dirs. Camp Fire Girls, 1959-61, 1969-71; pres. Contra Costa County (Calif.) Devel. Assn., 1959-60. Mem. State Bar Calif. (chmn. adoption com. 1955-56), Martinez Hist. Soc. (pres. 1894), Navy League U.S. (pres. Contra Costa Council 1981-83). Republican. Episcopalian. Served to lt. USNR, 1942-46. Club: Masons. Home: 600 Flora St Martinez CA 94553 Office: Ward & Ferry Sts Martinez CA 94553

BRAY, ARTHUR PHILIP, corporation executive; b. San Francisco, Sept. 23, 1933; s. Arthur T. and Anna F. (Nevin) B.; m. Grace McCarthy, June 16, 1956; children: Bernard, Peter, Erin, Eileen, Mary, Florence. A.A., San Francisco City Coll., 1953; B.S.M.E. with highest honors, U. Calif., Berkeley, 1955. With Gen. Electric Co., 1955-84; v.p., gen. mgr. nuclear power systems div. Gen. Electric Co., San Jose, Calif., 1978-84; exec. v.p. Mgmt. Analysis Co., San Diego, 1984-86; chmn. Mgmt. Analysis Co. Internat., San Diego, 1986; pres., chief exec. officer Renewable Resources Systems, Inc., Menlo Park, Calif., 1986—; mem. dean's adv. council Sch. Engring., San Jose State U. Co-author: Nuclear Power and the Public, 1970. Bd. fellows, regent Bellarmine Coll. Prep., San Jose., U. Santa Clara, Calif. Recipient Ernest O. Lawrence Meml. award U.S. Dept. Energy, 1977. Mem. Nat. Acad. Engring., Am. Nuclear Soc., ASME, Phi Beta Kappa, Tau Beta Pi, Pi Tau Sigma. Republican. Roman Catholic. Patentee in field. Home: 21459 Saratoga Hills Rd Saratoga CA 95070 Office: Renewable Resources Systems Inc 3000 Sand Hill Rd Bldg 3 Suite 285 Menlo Park CA 94025

BRAY, GEORGE AUGUST, physician, scientist, educator; b. Evanston, Ill., July 25, 1931; s. George A. and Mary H. B.; m. Martha, Aug. 8, 1959 (div. July 1981); children: George, Thomas, Susan, Nancy; m. Marilyn Rice, Jan. 1, 1983. BA summa cum laude, Brown U., 1953; MD magna cum laude, Harvard U., 1957. Diplomate Am. Bd. Internal Medicine; cert. Nat. Bd. Med. Examiners, Mass. Bd. Registration Medicine, Calif. Bd. Med. Examiners. Intern Johns Hopkins Hosp., Baltimore, Md., 1957-58; research assoc. NIH, Bethesda, Md., 1958-60; resident U. Rochester, N.Y., 1960-61; research assoc. Mill Hill Med. Research Ctr., London, 1961-62; asst. prof. Medicine Tufts U., Boston, 1964-69, assoc. prof., 1969-70; assoc. prof. UCLA, 1970-72, prof., 1972-81; prof. U. So. Calif., Los Angeles, 1981—, prof. medicine and physiology, 1983, chief of Diabetes and Nutrition Los Angeles County USC Med. Ctr., 1981; cons. FDA, 1971, Can. Dept. of Health and Welfare, Ottawa, 1974, Nat. Inst. on Aging, 1982, Swedish Dept. of Health and Social Services, Stockholm, 1982, Nat. Diabetes Adv. Bd. , Reston, Va., 1983, Brit. Broadcasting Corp., 1985; nutrition coordinator HEW office asst. sec., Washington, 1978-79. Author: Obese Patient, 1976; editor: Obesity in America, 1979, Obesity in Perspective, 1976, Treatment of Obesity, 1985, profl. jours. Recipient Travel award Am. Thyroid Assn., 1970, Sam E. Roberts award Kans. Nutrition Soc., 1977; Wellcome Vis. Prof. award Mich. State U., 1978, U. Ill., 1981, Alumni Day speaker Harvard Medical Sch., Boston, 1982; grantee NIH, 1965-70, 1970-81, 1973, 1977, 1981-86, 1981-89, Weight Watchers Found., 1979-81, Kroc Found., 1980-81; fellow NSF, 1961-62, NIH, 1962-64. Fellow ACP; mem. Am. Soc. for Clin. Nutrition (councillor 1982-84, v.p. 1985-86, pres.-elect 1986-87, pres. 1987—), Assn. of Am. Physicians (hon.), The Endocrine Soc., AAAS (council del. for med. scis. 1985-88), Am. Diabetes Assn. (bd. dirs. So. Calif. 1984-87), Am. Fedn. for Clin. Research, Peripatetic Club (hon.), Am. Soc. Clin. Investigation (hon.), Am. Inst. of Nutrition, N.Am. Assn. for the Study of Obesity (pres. 1982-84, councillor 1984—, editor Intern Jour. Obesity), Nat. Inst. Arthritis Diabetes and Digestive and Kidney Diseases (adv. council 1986—) Sigma Xi, Alpha Omega Alpha. Avocations: medical history, travel. Office: Sect Diabetes Nutrition 2025 Zonal Ave Los Angeles CA 90033

BRAY, HAROLD VINCENT, JR., psychologist; b. Independence, Mo., Aug. 28, 1946; s. Harold Vincent and Marie Lucille B.; m. Suzanne Joy Couch, June 21, 1980. A.B., Westminster Coll., 1971; M.Ed., U. Mo., 1973; postgrad. U. Kans., 1974-75, Chapman Coll., 1977, U. Calif.-Berkeley, 1978; Ph.D., U.S. Internat. U., 1981; postgrad. McGeorge Sch. Law, U. Pacific, 1981, Harvard Med. Sch., 1983. Recreation dir./counselor Midwest Children's Ctr., 1970; clin. caseworker Mo. Dept. Mental Health, 1973-74; counselor Job Corps Tng. Ctr., Excelsior Springs, Mo., 1975; vocat. rehab. specialist VA, San Francisco, 1975-78; counselor Alcohol and Drug Abuse Div., Fort Ord, Calif., 1980; counseling psychologist VA, San Francisco,

1980-82, regional chmn. vocat. rehab. bd., 1981-82; clin. dir. U.S. Mil. Clinic, W.Ger., 1982—; instr. U. Md.-Europe, 1983—. Legis. asst. Mo. State Legislature, 1970-72; active Archtl. and Heritage Found., Vallejo, Calif.; mem. Republican Presdl. Task Force, 1981-83; mem. U.S. Congl. Adv. Bd., 1983—; mem. Rep. Senatorial Com., 1983—. Served with U.S. Army, 1966-68. Recipient Award for Research, Midwest Sociol. Soc., 1971, Mo. Soc. Sociology and Anthropology, 1970. Mem. ABA, Am. Psychol. Assn., AAAS, Psi Chi, Phi Alpha Delta. Republican. Presbyterian.

BRAY, MAUREEN ELIZABETH, clergy; b. Medford, Oreg., Nov. 23, 1946; d. Jouett Philip and Edith Pearl (Cape) Bray. B.A., Trinity Bible Inst., Jamestown, N.D., 1970; B.A., Northwest Coll., Kirkland, Wash., 1971. Ordained to ministry Assemblies of God, 1972; assoc. pastor Lake City Tabernacle, Seattle, 1970—, youth dir., 1972—, Christian edn. dir., 1972—, asst. dir., 1970—, trustee, 1970—. Mem. Alumni Assn. Northwest Coll., Alumni Assn. Trinity Bible Inst. Democrat. Home: 529 Taylor Pl NW Renton WA 98055 Office: Lake City Tabernacle 3001 NE 127th St Seattle WA 98125

BRAY, WILLIAM OTIS, IV, diversified electronics company executive; b. Santa Monica, Calif., Sept. 2, 1949; s. Willliam Otis III and Nadine Hope (Sauer) B.; m. Gerda Smit, Aug. 22, 1982; children: William V, Patricia, Alida, Veronica. BS in Computer Sci., Calif. Poly. State U., San Luis Obispo, 1974; MS in Bus. Adminstrn., San Diego State U., 1985. Cert. computer sci. tchr., Calif. Communications developer spl. systems div. NCR Corp., San Diego, 1975-76, communications cons. spl. systems div., 1976-77, modular lodging systems mgr. Systems Engring./Torrey Pines div., 1978-84, system software products mgr. Systems Engring./San Diego div., 1984-86; exec. asst. exec. office NCR Corp., Dayton, Ohio, 1986—; adj. instr. Palomar Coll, San Marcos, Calif., 1976-82, San Diego State U., 1982-84; adj. prof. Nat. U., San Diego, 1984—. Served with USAF, 1968-72. Republican. Lutheran. Avocations: racquetball, tennis. Office: NCR 1700 S Patterson Blvd Dayton OH 45479

BRAYTON, SANDRA KING, advertising agency executive; b. Torrance, Calif. Mar. 6, 1944; d. Walter Raymond and Eleanor Christina (Mehlhoff) King; m. George Brayton, Dec. 31, 1974 (div.); 1 son, Beau King. B.B.A., U. Miami, 1966. Sales rep. Chart Pak, N.Y.C., 1966-67; mem. acctg. staff Air Calif., Newport Beach, 1967-69; mktg. rep. U.S. Fin., Sandiego and Santa Ana, Calif., 1969-70, dir. advt. and pub. relations, 1970-72, regional sales mgr., 1972-73; account exec. Hubbert Advt., Tustin, Calif., 1973-74; pres. King Advt. and Pub. Relations, Inc., Newport Beach, Calif., 1974—; lectr. career counseling advt. Vol. worker Orangewood Home of Dependent Children, Arthritis Telethon. Designer logo for America's Cup. Recipient 11 Mame awards. Mem. Bldg. Industry Assn. Orange County Advt. Fedn. (Golden Orange award, 3 awards of excellence), Indsl. League Orange County, Sales and Mktg. Council, Bldg. Industry Assn., Home Builders Council. Republican.

BRAZELL, MILDRED JEANETTE, health science educator; b. Conway, Ark., Mar. 30, 1925; d. Troy C. and Wilma M. (Miller) Hill; m. David B. Brazell, May 1, 1946; children: Diane Lee Brazell Corley, Donald Fred. BA, Ark. State U., 1957; MA, EdD, Ariz. State U., 1967. Tchr. Omaha (Ark.) High Sch., 1944-45, Lead Hill (Ark.) High Sch., 1945-46; psychometrist VA, Conway, 1947-50; tchr. Bentonville (Ark.) High Sch., 1950-52; prof. health sci. Grand Canyon Coll., Phoenix, 1952—; cons. Glendale (Ariz.) Recreation Dept. North Cen. Accreditation Teams, 1960—. Danforth fellow. Mem. Am. Alliance Health, Phys. Edn. and Recreation, Delta Kappa Gamma, Kappa Delta Pi. Baptist. Avocation: golf. Office: Grand Canyon Coll 3300 W Camelback Phoenix AZ 85017

BRAZELTON, FRANK ALEXANDER, optometry educator; b. Chgo., May 22, 1926; s. Frank Alexander and Katharine (Keating) B.; m. Margaret Bernice Shean, Aug. 15, 1948 (div. 1971); children: Stephen, Martin, Claire, Kathleen. B in Vision Sci., Los Angeles Coll. Optometry, 1950, OD, 1951; MS in Edn., U. So. Calif., 1975. Asst. prof. So. Calif. Coll. Optometry, Fullerton, 1955-58, assoc. prof., 1958-65, prof. optometry, 1965—, dean acad. affairs, 1984-85, assoc. dean faculty affairs, 1985—. Author: Handbook for Optometric Educators, 1978; also articles. Served with USNR, 1943-46, PTO. Fellow Am. Acad. Optometry (diplomate in low vision, sec.-treas. 1982-84, pres.-elect 1984—); mem. AAAS, AAUP. Democrat. Roman Catholic. Avocations: golf, bridge. Home: 1505 Sherwood Village Circle Placentia CA 92670 Office: So Calif Coll Optemetry 2575 Yorba Linda Blvd Fullerton CA 92631

BRAZER, WYNONA MARIE, accountant; b. Seattle, Mar. 6, 1937; d. Perry Henry and Katherine Emma (Bjordal) Moler; m. Henry Brazer, Dec. 1, 1955 (div.); children—Ronald, Kenneth, Gregory, Jeffory, Samuel, Nancy. A.A., Olympic Community Coll., 1971. Gen. clk. GN and NP Laureland, Billings, Mont., 1955-63; office mgr. Denny's Music Co., Portland, Oreg., 1971-72; bookkeeper GAM Distbg. Co., Portland, 1972; Acme Signs Inc., Portland, 1972-73; acct. Old Spaghetti Factory Inc., Portland, 1973-74; close-down mgr., lead acct. Portland Met. Steering Com., 1973-78; asst. controller Harsh Investment Inc., Portland, 1979; acctg. mgr. United Cerebral Palsy Assn., Portland, 1980-83; acct. San Francisco Housing Authority, 1983—. Mem. Am. Bus. Women Assn., Nat. Assn. Female Execs., Nat. C. of C. for Women. Democrat. Roman Catholic. Home: 240 Dolores St Apt 236 San Francisco CA 94103

BRAZIER, ROBERT G., transportation executive. Student, Stanford U. With Airbone Aircraft Service Inc., 1953-63; v.p. ops. Pacific Air Freight Inc., 1963-68; sr. v.p. ops. Airbone Freight Corp., Seattle, 1968-73, exec. v.p., chief operating officer, 1973-78, pres., chief operating officer, dir., 1978—. Office: Airborne Freight Corp PO Box 662 Seattle WA 98111 *

BRAZIL, ELIZABETH ANNE, educator, consultant, social worker, psychotherapist, businesswoman; b. Visalia, Calif., Feb. 5, 1941; d. Byron William and Mary Wallace (Fisher) Jennings; m. Ernest William Brazil, July 4, 1970 (div. 1975); 1 adopted child, Robert Dale. BA, Calif. State U.-San Jose, 1963; MSW, Calif. State U.-Fresno, 1979. Music tchr. Earlimart Sch. Dist., Calif., 1963-64, 64-65, Dept. Def., Naha, Okinawa, 1965-67, Wiesbaden, Germany, 1967-69; Visalia Unified Sch. Dist., Calif., 1969-85, San Luis Unified Sch. Dist., Sunnyside Elem., Los Osos, Calif., 1986—; owner, proprietor Superstarter Music Classes for Keybd. and Voice, 1987—; travel agt. Calif. Internat. Travel, Fresno, 1986—; mgr. Personal Investment Portfolio, Visalia, 1980—; owner Better Scents by Anne, Visalia, 1981—; owner, mgr. Mommy and Me Superstarter Music Classes, 1987—; cons. Dinuba Pub. Schs., Calif., 1984; prof. Pacific Coll., Fresno, 1982-84. Creator game: Hysteria, 1978; author play: Monday Morning Live, 1979; author cassette tape and manual: Self Esteem through Music, 1982; inventor: Knowledge of Results Meter. Organizer Toastmastress Internat., 1970-74; facilitator Turning Point Drug Diversion Group, 1971-75; active YMCA, Beyond War. Mem. Nat. Assn. Female Execs., NEA, Nas. Assn. Social Workers, Music Educators Nat. Conf., Soc. Lic. Clin. Social Workers. Democrat. Avocations: computers, basset hounds, travel, sewing, reading. Home: 2117 Inyo Los Osos CA 93402 Office: Sunny Side Sch Los Osos CA 93402

BRAZILL, NANCY LOUISE, bookkeeper; b. Pittsfield, Mass., Feb. 10, 1946; d. David Vosburg and Christine Elizabeth (Parker) R.; m. Stephen Cabot Hunt, June 13, 1964 (div. Mar. 1974); 1 child, Matthew; m. William Robert Brazill, Sept. 19, 1976. Grad. high sch., Pittsfield. Adminstrv. clk. U.S. Army, Ft. Huachuca, Ariz., 1966-69; order clk. Mountain Bell, Tucson, 1970-74; prodn. control clk. Crane & Co., Dalton, Mass., 1974-75; ind. sales agt. Tucson, 1975-77; bookkeeper Globe Supply, Las Vegas, Nev., 1977-81; ind. bookkeeper Las Vegas, 1981—. Treas. Nellis Officers Mixed Bowling League, Las Vegas, 1983, v.p. 1986-87; treas. Boy Scout Troop 206, Las Vegas, 1984—, com. mem. 1986. Home: 5203 W Golden Spring Las Vegas NV 89102

BREAKEY, LISA KATHERINE, speech pathologist; b. Los Angeles, Oct. 25, 1945; d. Melvin Harvey and Inez (Rey) Smith. BA in Speech Pathology and Audiology, U. Calif., Santa Barbara, 1967; MA in Speech Pathology, San Jose State U., 1975. Cert. community coll. spl. edn. tchr., Calif. Speech pathologist Manitoba (Can.) Rehab. Hosp., 1968-69; speech pathologist Kingston (Ont.) Health Unit, Can., 1969-70, dir. speech therapy, 1970-73; pvt. practice San Jose, Calif., 1975—; cons. Atari Inc., Sunnyvale, Calif., 1977-79, Evergreen Valley Community Coll., San Jose, 1977-80, Los Gatos (Calif.) Rehab. Hosp., 1977—, VA Med. Ctr., Livermore, Calif., 1979-83, Irwin Lehrhoff and Assocs., Beverly Hills, Calif., 1985—; profl. staff priviledges Santa Teresa Hosp., San Jose, 1981—, Valley West Hosp., San Jose, 1982—, Good Samaritan Hosp., San Jose, 1983—; presenter numerous seminars, workshops in adult communication disorders, 1979—; guest lectr. San Jose State U., 1975-85. Contbr. articles to profl. jours. Mem. Am. Speech Lang. and Hearing Assn. (cert., Found. Founders Club 1981—, legis. counselor 1986—, congl. action contact 1985, cert. appreciation 1983, 84), Calif. Speech Lang. Hearing Assn. (chmn. printing com. 1977, mem. conf. commn. 1982-84, task force on occupational therapy, 1983-84, hospitality com. 1984, legis. handbook com. 1985, state nominating com. 1986-88, editor newsletter 1985, Outstanding Achievement award 1986), Calif. Speech Pathologists and Audiologists in Pvt. Practice (v.p. 1979-81, pres. 1983-85, chmn. speakers bur. 1981, 82, current trends workshop 1980, pvt. practice workship 1978-80, rev. cource in preparation com. 1978-81, 83, 85-86, govt. affairs com. 1983—, nomination com. 1985—, cert. appreciation 1982), Calif. Assn. Post Seconary Educators of Disabled, Profl. Group for Adult Communication Disorders (1st pres. 1977), Bay Area Group for Non-Oral, Bay Area Neurolinguistic Group, Bay Area Pvt. Practitioners Speech Pathology and Audiology (1st pres. 1977), Washington Sq. Soc.-San Jose State U., Phi Kappa Phi. Democrat. Roman Catholic. Avocations: tennis, ballet, sculpture. Office: 2444 Moorpark Ave Suite 300 San Jose CA 95128

BREAM, BERT RICHARD, municipal court administrator; b. Covina, Calif., Dec. 10, 1945; s. Robert O. and Mary Vera (Richardson) B.; m. Virginia Ann Stamper, June 13, 1970 (div. Sept. 9, 1983); children: Brendan Richardson, Mary Rebecca, Elizabeth Ann. BA, U. Redlands, 1967; MA, Chapman Coll., 1975. Social worker San Bernardino (Calif.) County, 1967-68; probation officer Sonoma County Probation, Santa Rosa, Calif., 1970-75; asst. dir. Cen. Calif. Planning, Tulare, 1975-80, exec. dir., 1980-82; asst. adminstr. West Kern Mcpl. Ct., Bakersfield, Calif., 1982-83, San Bernardino Mcpl. Ct., 1983—. Author (criminal justice plan) Kings County Criminal Assessment, 1982; co-author (criminal justice plan) Kern County Criminal Justice Needs, 1979. Served as sgt. U.S. Army, 1968-69, Vietnam. Decorated Bronze Star. Mem. Mcpl. Ct. Clk.'s Assn. (bd. dirs. 1982—), Inst. Ct. Mgmt. Methodist. Lodge: Kiwanis. Avocations: reading, boating. Home: 2551 Serrano Rd San Bernardino CA 92410 Office: San Bernardino County Mcpl Ct Dist 468 W 5th St Suite 120 San Bernardino CA 92415-0520

BREAZEAL-SIMAS, MARGARET JEAN, corporate professional, registered nurse; b. Little Rock, Dec. 22, 1936; d. James Curtis Jones and Leona Beatrice (Holt) Jones-De Souza; m. Bill W. Wilhite, July 22, 1952 (annuled 1957); children: Linda-Jean Hollingsworth, William Bruce Wilhite; m. Franklin Henry Breazeal, Apr. 6, 1959 (div. Nov. 1970); 1 child, Mark Henry; m. Francisco José Rueda, Dec. 19, 1970 (dec. July 1976); m. Walter John Simas, Oct. 8, 1977. Student, St. Joseph's Nursing Sch., 1958-60; AA in Nursing, Harford Coll., 1969; student, Johns Hopkins U., 1970; BS in Nursing, U. Md., 1971. RN, Md., Va., Calif. Dir. nurses Rosewood Hosp. Inc., Hot Springs, Ark., 1965-66; adminstr. nursing Greater Balt. Med. Ctr., Towson, Md., 1967-69; supr. nursing Franklin Square Hosp., Essex, Md., 1969-71; supr. nursing in operating and recovery rms. Richmond (Va.) Meml. Hosp., 1973-74; sec., treas. Simas Bros. Properties, Diablo, Calif., 1975—; sec., treas., co-owner Simas Bros. Properties and Simas Service Stas.div. Ashland Oil Co., Diablo, 1977—. Tutor Calif. Literacy campaign, Alameda and Contra Costa Counties, 1984—. Mem. Am. Nurses Assn. (registered). Democrat. Presbyterian. Clubs: Diablo Country, Danville (Calif.) Women's (chmn. logo com.), Danville Women's Christian. Lodges: Order Eastern Star (various offices), Order White Shrine Jerusalem. Avocations: voice, world travel, gourmet cooking, interior design, crochet/knitting/dress designing. Home: Diablo Country Club Diablo CA 94528 Office: Simas Properties div Ashland Oil Calif. PO Box 403 Diablo CA 94528

BRECHBILL, SUSAN REYNOLDS, government official; b. Washington, Aug. 22, 1943; d. Irving and Isabell Doyle (Reynolds) Levine; B.A., Coll. William and Mary, 1965; J.D., Marshall-Wythe Sch. Law, 1968; m. Raymond A. Brechbill, June 29, 1973; children—Jennifer Rae, Heather Lea. Admitted to Va. bar, 1969, Fed. bar, 1970; atty. AEC, Berkeley, Calif., 1968-73, indsl. relations specialist AEC, Las Vegas, 1974-75; atty. ERDA, Oakland, Calif., 1976-77; atty. Dept. Energy, Oakland, 1977-78, dir. procurement div. San Francisco Ops. Office, 1978-85, asst. chief counsel, 1985—; mem. faculty U. Calif. Extension; speaker Nat. Contract Mgmt. Assn. Ann. Symposiums, 1980, 81, 83, 84; speaker on doing bus. with govt. Leader Girl Scouts U.S.A., San Francisco area. Named Outstanding Young Woman Nev., 1974. Mem. Va. State Bar Assn., Fed. Bar Assn., Nat. Contract Mgmt. Assn. (pres. Golden Gate chpt. 1983-84, N.W. regional v.p. elect 1984-86), Nat. Assn. Female Execs. Republican. Contbr. articles to profl. jours. Home: 67 Scenic Dr Orinda CA 94563

BRECK, ALLEN DU PONT, historian, educator; b. Denver, May 21, 1914; s. Chesney Yales and Isabelle Estelle (Lee) B.; m. Alice Rose Wolfe, Sept. 7, 1944 (dec. June 1973); 1 dau., Anne Rose Breck Peterson; m. Salome Ripley Hansen, Dec. 19, 1974. B.A., U. Denver, 1936, L.H.D. (hon.), 1973; M.A., U. Colo., 1939, Ph.D., 1950; D.Litt. (hon.), Regis Coll., 1974. Tchr. public schs. Denver, 1936-42; prof. history U. Denver, 1946—; Danforth lectr. 1949-61; mem. commn. on coll. student Am. Council on Edn., 1958-61; Mem. Colo. Commn. on Ednl. Standards, 1962-65; v.p. Colo. Commn. on Social Studies, 1964-68; regional program chmn. Danforth Found., 1960-63. Author: A Centennial History of the Jews of Colorado, 1960, Johannis Wyclyf Tractatus de Trinitate, 1962, Episcopal Church in Colorado, 1860-1963, 1963, William Gray Evans, Western Business Executive, 1964, John Evans of Denver, 1971, Episcopal Church in Colorado, 1960-78, 1978, Johannis Wyclyf, Tractatus de Tempore, 1981, (with Salome J. Breck) The Episcopal Church in Colorado since 1963, 1981; editor: (with Wolfgang Yourgrau) Internat. Colloquium I: Physical Science, History, Philosophy, 1968, II: Biological Science, History, Natural Philosophy, 1971, III: Cosmology, History Theology, 1975, The West in America series, 1960—, Colorado Ethnic History series, 1977—; contbr. articles to profl. jours. Served with field arty. U.S. Army, 1942-46. Danforth asso., 1946—. Fellow Royal Hist. Soc. Gt. Britain; mem. Am. Hist. Assn., Medieval Acad. Am., Rocky Mountain Renaissance and Medieval Assn. (pres. 1968-76), Far Western Slavic Conv., Western Social Sci. Assn., Western History Assn., Phi Beta Kappa, Lambda Chi Alpha, Phi Alpha Theta, Omicron Delta Kappa. Republican. Episcopalian. Home: 2060 S Saint Paul St Denver CO 80210 : Dept History U Denver Denver CO 80208

BRECKENRIDGE, H. LEON, energy economic services executive; b. Beloit, Kans., Sept. 10, 1933; s. Harold Ezra and Esther Mattie (Atchison) B.; m. Virginia Marie Boulanger, Nov. 23, 1952; children: Cathy Yvonne Calhoun, H. Kent. BS in Physics and Math, Colo. State U., 1969; MS Mgmt. of Waste and Energy, Cen. Wash. U., 1974. Campus engr. Cen. Wash. U., Ellensburg, 1969-74; systems mgr. energy conservation Am. Can Copr., Fair Lawn, N.J., 1974-76; sr. project engr. EG&G Idaho, Inc., Idaho Falls, 1976-79; energy mgmt. cons. The Foxboro Co., Lynnwood, Wash., 1979-82; pres. Integrated Energy Econ. Services, Inc., Yakima, Wash., 1982—; cons. ANCO Engring., Los Angeles, 1981-84, Power Recovery Systems, Cambridge, Mass., 1978-85; bd. dirs. Bio-Energy Enterprises, Inc., Copr., Yakima. Contbr. articles to profl. publs. Alternative Energy grantee U.S. Dept. Energy, 1979. Mem. Assn. Phys. Plant Dirs., Assn. Energy Engrs., Instrument Soc. Am., Am. Flame Inst., Cryogenic Soc. Am., Assn. Finishing Processes of Soc. Mech. Engrs. Avocations: skiing, camping, fishing, golf, woodworking. Home: 1310 S 16th Ave Yakima WA 98902 Office: Integrated Energy Econ Services Inc 1224 1/2 N 1st St Yakima WA 98901

BRECKENRIDGE, KLINDT DUNCAN, architect; b. Iowa City, Apr. 24, 1957; s. Jack Duncan and Florence (Kmiecik) B.; m. Nancy Ann Dernier, Apr. 19, 1986. BArch, U. Ariz., 1981. Registered architect, Ariz. Architect Finical & Dombrowski, Tucson, 1981-84; assoc. The IEF Group, Inc., Tucson, 1984—. Bd. dirs. Lighthouse YMCA; mem. Tucson Mus. Art., 1981—. Recipient cert. Nat. Council Archtl. Review Bds. Mem. AIA. Democrat. Episcopalian. Avocations: running, rugby. Home: 6001 E Pima St #15 Tucson AZ 85712 Office: The IEF Group 705 N Seventh Ave Tucson AZ 85705

BRECKINRIDGE, JAMES BERNARD, research physicist; b. Cleve., May 27, 1939; s. Albert Coles and Catherine Rose (Wengler) B.; m. Ann Marie Yoder, July 24, 1965; children: Douglass E., John Brian. B.S. in Physics, Case Inst. Tech., 1961; M.S. in Optical Sci, U. Ariz., 1970, Ph.D. in Optical Sci, 1976. Research asst. Lick Obs., Mt. Hamilton, Calif., 1961-64; electron tube engr. Rauland Corp., Chgo., 1967; research asst. Kitt Peak Nat. Obs., Tucson, full time, 1964-66, 68, 75-76, part time, 1969-74; mem. tech. staff Jet Propulsion Lab., Calif. Inst. Tech., 1976—, part-time faculty, 1981—, mgr. optics sect., 1981—; also co-investigator NASA Spacelab 3; author, lectr. Scoutmaster Boy Scouts Am. Mem. Am. Astron. Soc., IEEE, Internat. Astron. Union, Optical Soc. Am., Astron. Soc. of Pacific. Research in remote optical and infrared sensing instrumentation, interferometry, solar spectroscopy, image intensifiers and image analysis. Home: 4565 Viro Rd La Canada CA 91011 Office: JPL CaltechMS 169-314 4800 Oak Grove Dr Pasadena CA 91109

BREDDAN, JOE, systems engineer; b. N.Y.C., Sept. 18, 1950; s. Hyman and Sylvia (Hauser) B. BA in Math. and Psychology, SUNY, Binghamton, 1972; MS in Ops. Research, U. Calif., Berkeley, 1975; PhD in Systems Engring., U. Ariz., 1978. Teaching and research assoc. Dept. Systems and Indsl. Engring. U. Ariz., Tucson, 1975-79; project engr. B.D.M. Services Co., Tucson, 1979-80; mem. tech. staff Bell Labs., Am. Bell, AT&T Info. Systems, Denver, 1980-86; staff mgr. AT&T, Denver, 1986—. Patentee in field. Regents scholar N.Y. State Bd. Regents, 1968. Home: 3455 Table Mesa Dr #147E Boulder CO 80303 Office: AT&T 11900 N Pecos St Denver CO 80234

BREDEMEIER, LORENZ FRIEDRICH, conservationist, consultant; b. Mayberry, Nebr., Apr. 2, 1911; s. Friedrich Wilhelm and Louisa (Gottula) B.; m. Audrey White, June 25, 1938; children—Linda Kay Bredemeier Holloway, Lana Loumeda Bredemeier McWilliams, Brenda Jean Bredemeier Kuehner. BS, U. Nebr., 1934, MS, 1938, postgrad. in planning and devel., U. Okla., 1967; postgrad. in advanced plant scis., U. Nebr., 1970. Asst. agr. agt. Nebr. Agr. Extension, Lincoln, 1934-36, adminstrv. asst., 1936-38; jr. agronomist Soil Conservation Service, U.S. Dept. Agr., Centerville, Iowa, 1938-39, Corydon, Iowa, 1939-41, soil conservationist, Auburn, Nebr., 1941-42, dist. conservationist, Hebron, Nebr., 1942-44, O'Neill, Nebr., 1944-48, Valentine, Nebr., 1948-49, area conservationist, Valentine, 1949-51, range conservationist, Valentine, 1951-52, North Platte, Nebr., 1952-63, Milw., 1963-64, resource devel. specialist, Madison, 1964-69, range conservationist, Ft. Worth, 1969-73; agrl. research officer, Maseru, Lesotho, 1974-78; cons. in range mgmt., resource conservation, land and resource use, 1978—. Recipient Superior Accomplishment award U.S. Dept. Agr., 1948, Outstanding Performance award, 1962; Nebr. Range Mgmt. award, 1965; Nebr. Centennial Grassland Mgmt. award, 1966. Mem. Am. Inst. Biol. Sci., AAAS, Ecol. Soc. Am., Soc. Range Mgmt. (presentor papers ann. meetings), Soil Conservation Soc. Am., Tech. and Sci. Soc. Range Mgmt. (pres. 1971), Alpha Zeta, Gamma Sigma Delta, Alpha Gamma Rho. Methodist. Clubs: Masons, Shriners, Lions, Toastmaster. Contbr. articles to profl. jours. Home and office: 6507 S Pike Dr Larkspur CO 80118

BREECE, JENANNE NELSON, lawyer; b. Evanston, Ill., Dec. 30, 1941; d. Oscar William and Anne L. (Moll) Nelson. B.S. magna cum laude, U. So. Calif., 1967, J.D., 1976. Admitted to D.C. bar, 1977, Calif. bar, 1983; sec., corp. officer Sta. KUPD-AM-FM, Phoenix, 1959-61; media dir. West, Weir & Bartel, Los Angeles, 1962-65; asso. media dir. Eisaman, Johns & Laws, Los Angeles, 1966-68; media supr. Ogilvy & Mathers, N.Y.C., 1968-69; v.p. media and mktg. services Smith-Gent Advt. Co., N.Y.C., 1969-71; media supr. The Media Dept., N.Y.C., 1971-72; v.p. media Perkal Advt. Co., Los Angeles, 1972-74; research asst. U. So. Calif. Law Center, 1975-76; atty. advisor Broadcast Bur. FCC, Washington, 1977-80; gen. atty. Nev. Ops. Office, Office Chief Counsel, U.S. Dept. Energy, Las Vegas, 1980—; pro bono atty. Friends of Animals, N.Y.C. Mem. ABA, Calif. Bar Assn., D.C. Bar Assn., Fed. Bar Assn., Los Angeles Advt. Women, U. So. Calif. Alumni, Presbyterian. Mensa, Cactus and Succulent Soc., Sierra Club, North Shore Animal League, Phi Beta Kappa, Beta Gamma Sigma. Office: US Dept Energy PO Box 14100 Las Vegas NV 89114

BREED, MICHAEL DALLAM, environmental, population, organismic biology educator; b. Kansas City, Mo., Sept. 2, 1951; s. Laurence W. and Loree (Dallam) B.; m. Cheryl A. Ristig, Aug. 9, 1975. BA, Grinnell Coll., 1973; MA, U. Kans., 1975, PhD, 1977. Asst. prof. environ., population, organismic biology U. Colo., Boulder, 1977-83, assoc. prof., 1983—, chmn. dept., 1986—. Contbr. articles to sci. jours. Mem. Internat. Union for Study of Social Insects (pres. N.Am. sect. 1984), Animal Behavior Soc., Internat. Bee Research Assn., Entomol. Soc. Am. Home: 700 Dahlia Denver CO 80220 Office: U Colo Dept Biology #102 Boulder CO 80309-0334

BREEN, TIMOTHY ALAN, software executive; b. Pitts., June 21, 1951; s. John Francis and Mildred (Miles) B.; m. Caroline Louise Lapp, Aug. 26, 1984. BS in Econs., U. Pa., 1973; MBA, Stanford U., 1978. Fin. analyst Standard Brands Foods, N.Y.C., 1973-76; assoc. McKinsey & Co., N.Y.C., 1978-82; mng. dir. Breen Enterprises, Miami, Fla., 1983-84; chief exec. officer Micro Planning Internat., San Francisco, 1985—. Author: Micro Manager, 1986. Roman Catholic. Avocation: skiing. Home: 154 Lombard St # 49 San Francisco CA 94111 Office: Micro Planning Internat 235 Montgomery St Suite 840 San Francisco CA 94104

BREEN, WALTER HENRY, numismatic writer; b. San Antonio, Sept. 5, 1928; m. Marion Zimmer Bradley, Feb. 14, 1964; children: Patrick Russell Donald, Moira Evelyn Dorothy. AB, John Hopkins, 1952; MA, U. Calif., Berkeley, 1966. Researcher Wayte Raymond, Inc., N.Y.C., 1951-52; cataloguer New Netherlands Coin Co., Inc., N.Y.C, 1952-60, Lester Merkin, Inc., N.Y.C, 1968-72; mng. editor Twin Worlds Publs., N.Y.C, 1970-71; sr. v.p. research First Coinvestors, Inc., Albertson, N.Y., 1973—; contbrg. editor Guidebook of U.S. Coins, 1953—; cons. Smithsonian Inst., U.S. Secret Service, U.S. Treasury, 1961—; trustee New Eng. Jour. Numis. Author: A Coiner's Caviar: Walter Breen's Encyclopedia of U.S. and Colonial Proof Coins, 1722-1977, 1977, The Darkover Concordance: A Reader's Guide, 1979, Encyclopedia of U.S. Gold and Silver Commemorative Coins, 1981 (Book of Yr. award Numis. Lit. Guild 1982), (with Ron Gillio) California Pioneer Fractional Gold, 1983, Walter Breen's Encyclopedia of United States Half Cents, 1793-1857, 1984 (Book of Yr. award Numis. Lit. Guild, 1985), Walter Breen's Comprehensive Encyclopedia of United States Coins, 1987; also articles, essays, monographs and revs. Recipient Silver Medal of Honor Roosevelt U., 1966, Order of the Laurel Soc. for Creative Anachronism, 1969. Mem. Am. Numis. Assn. (life, mem., Heath award 1952), Am. Numis. Soc., AAAS, Numis. Lit. Guild (Clemy award 1985). Democrat. Home: Box 245A Berkeley CA 94701

BREER, LAWRENCE LEE, writer, educator; b. Salina, Kans., Feb. 5, 1936; s. George Joseph Breer and Lila Iona (Armbruster) Fierro; m. Ardith Mary Grimmett, June 6, 1959 (div. Sept. 1975); children: Melinda, Cassandra, Laura, Michael; m. Carmen Eileen Fenn Barton, Sept. 18, 1977. BJ, Cen. Wash. U., 1980. Enlisted USAF, 1956, advanced through grades to sgt., ret., 1976; editor Selah (Wash.) Valley Optimist, 1980-81; corr. The Packer Newspaper, Shawnee Mission, Kans., 1982-86; freelance writer Cen. Wash. Agr. News, Selah, 1981—; prof. English/journalism Heritage Coll., Toppenish, Wash., 1986—. Contbr. poetry various anthologies, 1978. Photographic contbr. Yakima (Wash.) River Greenway Assn., 1985-86. Democrat. Avocations: photography, reading, writing, research. Home and Office: 1013 Goodlander Dr #1 Selah WA 98942

BREGAR, JOHN FRANCIS, college dean; b. Scott Haven, Pa., Nov. 20, 1923; s. William Wencel and Anna Mathilde (Spang) B.; m. Marjorie Jean Lanning, Sept. 23, 1946; children: John Ellis, Diana Elizabeth Bregar Vincent, Leigh Elaine Bregar Payne. Student, Syracuse U., 1944; BEE, Pa. State U., 1948; PhD in Nuclear Engring., U. Ariz., 1966. Registered profl. engr., Ariz. Engr. USN, Newport News, Va., 1953-57, Newport News Ship Bldg. & Dry Dock Co., 1957-62; prof. engring. Ariz. State U., Tempe, 1965-77; engr. Puget Sound Naval Shipyard, Bremerton, Wash., 1980-83; prof., dean sch. engring. Walla Walla Coll., College Place, Wash., 1983—; pub. info. speaker AEC, Phoenix, 1966-77, mem. adv. com. 1970-77. Contbr.

articles to profl. jours. Bd. dirs. Tempe Community Hosp., 1976-77. Served to cpl. U.S. Army, 1943-46. Named Boss of Yr., Am. Bus. Women's Assn., 1978-79; AEC fellow, 1964. Mem. Am. Soc. for Engring. Edn., Sigma Xi, Eta Kappa Nu, Pi Mu Epsilon. Republican. Adventist. Avocations: sailing, flying, amateur radio. Home: 801 Southeast Date College Place WA 99324 Office: Walla Walla Coll College Place WA 99324

BREIDENBACH, STEVEN THEODORE, research psychologist; b. Oakes, N.D., June 30, 1953; s. Theodore Michael and Elizabeth Catherine (Ackerman) B.; m. Cherie Elizabeth Johnson, Aug. 9, 1975. B.A., U. S.D., 1975, M.A. in Human Factors/Applied Exptl. Psychology, 1977, Ph.D., 1979. Research asst. Human Factors Lab., U. S.D., 1975-77, 78-79; personnel mgmt. specialist State of Wyo., 1977-78; assoc. scientist Dunlap and Assocs., Inc., La Jolla, Calif., 1979-83; research psychologist U.S. Navy Personnel Research and Devel. Ctr., San Diego, 1983-84; tech. specialist Cubic Corp., 1984—; computer software cons., 1983—; tech. adv. Tng. Tech. Jour. Mem. Am. Psychol. Assn., Human Factors Soc., Soc. Applied Learning Tech., Soc. Engring. Psychologists, Alpha Tau Omega. Republican. Roman Catholic. Contbr. articles to profl. jours. Home: 4858 Tinasa Way San Diego CA 92124 Office: Cubic Corp 9233 Balboa Ave San Diego CA 92123

BREITHAUPT, BRENT HENRY, museum curator; b. Milw., Jan. 11, 1956; s. Henry G. Breithaupt and Ann M. (Kluge) Catalano; m. Vicki Ann Burton, Aug. 2, 1980. BS in Geology, U. Wis., Milw., 1978; MS in Geology, U. Wyo., 1981. Mus. asst. Milw. Pub. Mus., 1975-78; curatorial asst. Geol. Mus. U. Wyo., Laramie, 1980-81, curator Geol. Mus., 1981—, instr. correspondence study, 1983—. Contbr. articles to profl. jours. Mem. Paleontol. Soc., Soc. for Study of Amphibians and Reptiles, Am. Soc. Ichthyologists and Herpetologists, Herpetologists League, Colo.-Wyo. Acad. Scis., Colo.-Wyo. Assn. Mus., Soc. Vertebrate Paleontology (regional editor news bulletin 1985—), Wis. Geol. Soc. (v.p. 1976). Avocations: fencing, running, skiing, rock climbing, caving, soccer. Office: U Wyo The Geol Mus Laramie WY 82071-3006

BREITHAUPT, STEPHEN ALLAN, environmental scientist; b. Dallas, June 29, 1954; s. Joe Jefferson and Andrea Jean (McCallum) B.; m. LouAnn Fleming, June 2, 1976 (div. Sept. 1979). BS in Zoology, Aquatic Biology, S.W. Tex. State U., 1976; MS in Environ. Sci., Wash. State U., 1979. Aquatic biologist Mountain View Sanitary Dist., Martinez, Calif., 1979-80; environ. specialist M.A. Kennedy Cons. Engrs., Spokane, Wash., 1980—. Mem. AAAS, N.W. Sci. Assn., Sierra Club (chmn. toxic and radioactive waste subcom. No. Rockies chpt. 1983). Avocations: canoeing, bicycling, photography, backpacking, skiing. Office: MA Kennedy Cons Engrs W 1720 4th Ave Spokane WA 99204

BREMER, DONALD DUANE, school administrator; b. Sioux City, Iowa, June 19, 1934; s. Donald Forbes and Irma Marjorie (Schaller) B.; m. Carol Louise Rankin, May 3, 1955; children—Douglas Duane, Robert Alan, Kevin Ray. B.A., Nebr. State U., 1958; M.A. sch. adminstr., Los Angeles State U., 1962; postgrad., U. Iowa, 1966, U. Calif., Riverside, 1967. Cert. tchr., Calif. Math. tchr. Chino Unified Sch. Dist., Calif., 1958-66; tchr. Chaffey Jr. Coll., Alta Loma, Calif., 1961-63; prin. summer sch., Chino Schs., 1966-67; vice prin. Ramona Jr. High Sch., Chino, 1967-77; prin. Boys Republic High Sch., Chino, 1978—, chmn. accreditation com., 1981-82. Com. chmn., asst. cubmaster Mt. Baldy council Boy Scouts Am., 1966-68. Grantee NSF, 1964. Served with U.S. Army, 1954-56. Mem. NEA, Calif. Tchrs. Assn., Assn. Calif. Sch. Adminstrs., Chino Adminstrs. Assn. (treas. 1971-73, pres. 1973-74, Am. Legion, Chino C. of C., Republican Senatorial Com. Club: Toastmasters. Lodges: Rotary Internat., Masons, Elks. Home: 12183 Dunlap Pl Chino CA 91710 Office: Boys Republic High Sch Chino CA 91709

BREMER, RONALD ALLAN, genealogist, editor; b. South Gate, Calif., May 2, 1937; s. Carl Leonard and Lena Evelyn (Jury) B.; m. Dorothy Louise Pinegar, May 12, 1958 (div.); Joan Ellen Brenner, Apr. 30, 1967 (div.); children—Ron, Trina, Rebecca, Serena, Lorrie, Jennie, Elizabeth, Hans, Adam, Rachel. Student Los Angeles Trade Tech., Cerritos Coll., Am. U., Brigham Young U. Research specialist Geneal. Soc., Salt Lake City, 1969-72; profl. lectr. on genealogy, Salt Lake City, 1973—; editor Genealogy Digest mag., Salt Lake City, 1983—, Roots Digest, 1984—; lectr. in field. Mem. German Harmony Choir. Mem. Fedn. Geneal. Socs. (founder), Wholistic Soc. (founder), Assn. Geneal. Editors (founder). Republican. Mormon. Author: World's Funniest Epitaphs, 1983; Compendium of Historical Sources, 1983. Office: PO Box 16422 Salt Lake City UT 84116

BREMERMANN, HANS J., mathematics educator, biophysicist; b. Bremen, Ger., Sept. 14, 1926; m. 1954. M.A., U. Munster, Ger.; Ph.D. in Math., U. Munster, 1951. Instr. math. U. Munster, 1952, asst. prof., 1954-55; research assoc. Stanford U., 1952-53, vis. asst. prof., 1953-54; mem. staff Inst. Advanced Study, 1955-57, 58-59; asst. prof. U. Wash., 1957-58; assoc. prof. math. U. Calif.-Berkeley, 1959-64, assoc. prof. math. and biophysics, 1964-66, prof. math. and biophysics, 1966—; research fellow Harvard U., 1953; indsl. cons.; mem. exec. com. grad. group biophysics and med. physics U. Calif.-Berkeley, 1964-82. Mem. Am. Math. Soc., Austrian Math. Soc., German Math Soc., Biophys. Soc. Office: Dept Biophysics U Calif Berkeley CA 94720

BREMNER, JAMES DOUGLAS, psychiatrist; b. Lynden, Wash., Aug. 9, 1932; s. George Adelbert and Marian Alica (Bay) B.; m. Linnea Marie Leonardson, June 4, 1966; children: Steven, Lynn, Anne, James Douglas. Student, U. Puget Sound, 1949-52; MD, U. Wash., 1956. Intern USPHS Hosp., N.Y.C., 1956-57; resident Menninger Sch. Psychiatry and Topeka VA Hosp., 1959-62; practice medicine specializing in psychiatry Olympia, Wash., 1962—; clin. assoc. prof. psychiatry U. Wash., 1968—; pharm. research Hoechst-Roussel Pharms., Hoffman-LaRoche Pharms., Eli Lilly and Co., Sandoz Pharms., Shering Plough, Beecham Labs., Glaxo Labs., Organon, Inc.; staff mem. St. Peter Hosp.; cons. Madigan Army Hosp. Chmn. bd. dirs. Thurston County Guidance Assn., 1965-66; bd. dirs. Wash. Capital Hist. Assn., 1963-64. Served with USPHS, 1956-59. Fellow Am. Psychiat. Assn. (pres. Tacoma chpt. 1968-69, pres. North Pacific br. 1972-73); mem. AMA, Wash. Med. Assn., Fellows Assn. Menninger Sch. Psychiatry (past pres.), Thurston-Mason Med. Soc. (pres. 1972), PSRO (mem. state bd.), Thurston County Med. Bur. (v.p. 1981—). Home: 3422 Country Club Dr NW Olympia WA 98502 Office: 1021 W 4th St Olympia WA 98502

BREMNER, WILLIAM JOHN, physician; b. Bellingham, Wash., July 5, 1943; s. George Adelbert and Marian (Bay) B.; m. Jane Belden Stimpson, June 18, 1965; children: Jennifer, Andrew, Sara, Tim. BA, Harvard U., 1964; MD, U. Wash., 1969; PhD, Monash U., 1978. Diplomate Am. Bd. Internal Medicine; Nat. Bd. Med. Examiners. Med. intern Vanderbilt U. Hosp., Nashville, 1969-70; resident in internal medicine U. Wash., Seattle, 1970-72; sr. fellow in Endocrinology U. Wash. Sch. Medicine, Seattle, 1972-74; sr. research officer Australian Nat. Health and Med. Research Council, Melbourne, Australia, 1974-77; asst. prof. medicine U. Wash., Seattle, 1977-82; chief of endocrinology V.A. Med. Ctr., Seattle, 1979-87, chief. med. service, 1987—; assoc. prof. medicine U. Wash., Seattle, 1982-87, prof., vice chmn. dept. medicine, 1987—; mem. steering com. WHO, Geneva, 1984-87; cons. NIH, Bethesda, Md., 1985—. Mem. Editorial Bd. Jour. Clin. Endocrinology and Metabolism, 1983—, assoc. editor Internat. Jour. of Andrology, 1983-87; contbr. articles and book chpts. to numerous profl. jours. Mem. The Endocrine Soc., Am. Fedn. Clin. Research Am. Soc. Clin. Investigation, Western Soc. Clin. Investigations (chmn. West Coast Endocrine Club Meeting, 1982), The Am. Soc. Andrology (mem. council 1981-84, nominating com. 1983-86, program com. 1986-87), Soc. for Study Reproduction (publ. com. 1983-85, chmn. 1984-85), Pacific Cost Fertility Soc. (Wyeth award 1974), Am. Fertility Soc., Western Assn. Physicians, Alpha Omega Alpha. Office: Veteran Adminstrn Med Ctr 1660 S Columbian Way Seattle WA 98108

BREMS, DAVID PAUL, architect; b. Lehi, Utah, Aug. 10, 1950; s. D. Orlo and Geraldine (Hitchcock) B. B.S., U. Utah, 1973, M.Arch., 1975. Registered architect, Utah, Calif., Colo., Ariz., Wyo., N.Mex., Idaho. Draftsman, Environ. Assoc., Salt Lake City, 1971-73; draftsman/architect Environ. Design, Salt Lake City, 1973-76; architect Frank Fuller AIA, Salt Lake City, 1976-77; prin. Edwards & Daniels, Salt Lake City, 1978-83; prin. David Brems & Assocs., Salt Lake City, 1983-86; prin. Gillies, Stransky & Brems, Salt Lake City, 1986—; mem. urban design com. Assist, Inc., Salt Lake City, 1982—. Prin. works include solar twinhomes Utah Holiday, (Best Solar Design award), Sun Builder, Daily Jour., Brian Head Day Lodge, Kirkwood Hotel, Four Seasons Hotel, residences. Del. Utah Democratic Conv., Salt Lake City, 1972; chmn. Dem. Voting Dist., Salt Lake City, 1974. Mem. AIA (pres. Salt Lake chpt. 1983-84, pres. Utah Soc. 1987, chmn. Western Mountain Region conf., 1986, 3 Honor awards 1983). Home: 161 Young Oak Dr Salt Lake City UT 84108

BRENDEL, KLAUS, pharmacology and toxicology educator, research chemist; b. Berlin, June 14, 1933; came to U.S., 1963; s. Erich Rudolf and Eva (Keysselitz) B.; m. Barbara Brigitte Luge, Nov. 2, 1957; children: Sabine, Katrin, Caroline. BS in Chemistry, Free U. Berlin, 1955, MS in Chemistry, 1959, PhD in Chemistry, 1962. Research assoc. Free U. Berlin, 1962-63, U. Pacific, Stockton, Calif., 1963-64; research assoc. Duke U., Durham, N.C., 1964-67, asst. prof. pharmacology and toxicology, 1967-70; assoc. prof. U. Ariz., Tucson, 1970-76, prof. pharmacology, 1976—. Contbr. numerous articles to profl. jours.; mem. editorial bd. Life Scis., Internat. Jour. Biol. Research Pregnancy, Internat. Jour. Clin. Pharmacology. Grantee and fellow NIH, NSF, NATO, Studien Stiftung Des Deutschen Volkes. Fellow Am. Heart Assn. (atherosclerosis council, grantee); mem. Am. Soc. Pharmacology and Exptl. Therapeutics, Gesellschaft Dentscher Chemiker, Am. Chem. Soc., Sigma Xi. Avocations: gourmet cooking, sailing. Home: 3213 N Manor Tucson AZ 85715 Office: U Ariz Coll Medicine Dept Pharmacology Tucson AZ 85724

BRENEMAN, WILLIAM C(ALVIN), chemical engineer; b. Braddock, Pa., July 9, 1941; s. Calvin N. and Mary E. (Morrow) B.; m. Gracie E. Craig, May 25, 1968; 1 child, William C. BSChemE, Carnegie-Mellon U., 1963; MSChemE, Ohio U., 1971, MBA, 1975. Registered profl. chem. engr., Wash., W.Va. Engr. research and development Silicones div. Union Carbide Corp., Sisterville, W.Va., 1963-81, lead process engr., 1981-84; chief design engr. electronics div Union Carbide Corp., Washougal, Wash., 1984-86; mgr. silicone fluids and emulsions process tech. electronics div Union Carbide Corp., Sisterville, W.Va., 1987—. Inventor and patentee in field. Recipient Tech. Achievement award Union Carbide Corp., 1985. Fellow Am. Inst. Chemists (Chem. Pioneer award 1985); mem. AAAS, Am. Inst. Chem. Engrs. Avocation: aviation. Home: 809 Main St Sisterville WV 26175 Office: Union Carbide Corp PO Box 180 Sisterville WV 26175

BRENGLE, KENNETH GORDON, JR., chamber of commerce executive; b. Perry, Okla., June 3, 1954; s. Kenneth Gordon and Donna Ernistine (Spillman) B.; m. Carol Sue James, May 19, 1979; children: James Kenneth, Christine Carol. BA in Polit. Sci., Fort Lewis Coll., 1976; grad. Inst. Orgn. Mgmt. U. Colo. and C. of C. of U.S. Mgr. Cortez Area C. of C., Colo., 1976-77; asst. mgr. Ft. Collins C. of C., Colo., 1977-79; exec. v.p. Greater Cheyenne C. of C., Wyo., 1979-86; chief exec. officer Durango (Colo.) C. of C. Resort Assn., 1986—; legis. intern Colo. State Senate, Denver, 1975; spl. investigator Dist. Atty.'s Office Dist. 22, Cortez, Colo., 1975. Republican del. for Colo. State Conv., 1976; asst. treas. St. Lukes Episcopal Ch., 1978; treas. St. Christopher Episc. Ch., Cheyenne, 1982; bd. dirs. Silent Witness, Cheyenne, 1984; trustee Laramie County United Way; bd. dirs. Cheyenne Family YMCA, 1984-86. Named Outstanding Young Man Am., 1984. Mem. Cortez Jaycees (charter pres. 1977-78) (Ft. Collins v.p. 1978-79), Am. C. of C. Execs., Colo. C. of C. Execs. (bd. dirs. 1976-79), Wyo. C. of C. Execs. (pres. 84-85), Mountain States Assn. (bd. dirs. 1983—), Southeast Wyo. Tourism Council (pres. 1984-85). Republican. Lodges: Optimists (bd. dirs. 1981-83), Elks, Rotary. Avocations: golf, skow skiing, running.

BRENMAN, ALBERT, lawyer; b. Batavia, N.Y., Mar. 28, 1926; s. Joseph M. and Helen (Shapiro) B.; m. Rosalie Rhea Feldman, Oct. 23, 1952; children—Jeffrey M., Cynthia Sue, David W. B.S., B.A., Denver U., 1950, J.D., 1953. Bar: Colo., 1953. Pres., dir., stockholder Brenman, Raskin , Friedlob & Tenenbaum P.C., Denver, 1961—. Pres., trustee Temple Micah, Denver. Served as 1st lt. U.S. Army, 1945-48. Mem. Denver U. Law Sch. Alumni Council (chmn. 1981-83, chmn. Alumni Fund Drive 1978-81). Beta Alpha Psi (pres. 1950), Beta Gamma Sigma, Phi Delta Phi. Democrat. Jewish. Clubs: Town, Denver Athletic. Home: 4300 E 6th Avenue Pkwy Denver CO 80220 Office: Brenman Raskin Friedlob & Tenenbaum P C 1400 Glenarm Pl Denver CO 80220

BRENNA, TERRANCE RICHARD, health services executive; b. Grand Forks, N.D., Aug. 1, 1944; s. Willard and Ione (Block) B.; m. Christina H. Lauks; 1 child, Bruce L. PhB, U. N.D., 1966. Cert. tchr. jr. colls., Calif. (life). Dir. social recreation Boys Club Am., Mpls., 1967-68; health educator Mpls. Health Dept., 1968-71; dep. dir. Fresno (Calif.) County Health Dept., 1971-79; adminstr. Kingsview Corp., Madera, Calif., 1981—; prin. Devel. Assocs., Fresno, 1979—. Producer weekly radio program, 1969, one-hour broadcast, 1970; pub. Internat. Jour. of the Addictions, 1981. Avocations: running in 10-K races, gardening, reading novels. Home: 2642 W San Madele Fresno CA 93711

BRENNAN, JAMES THOMAS, educational administrator, educator; b. Evergreen Park, Ill., Apr. 30, 1947; s. Thomas J. and Sheila Ann (McFee) B. AA, St. Bede Jr. Coll., 1967; BA, Loras Coll., 1969; MSEd, Chgo. State U., 1977; EdD, U. San Francisco, 1983. Credentials community coll. service, community coll. chief exec. officer, community coll. counselor, tchr. K-12 social scis., pupil personnel services K-12, Calif. Tchr., Chgo. parochial schs., 1969-74, St. Mary's Sch., Lake Forest, Ill., 1974-75; co-prin. St. Joseph's Sch., Libertyville, Ill., 1975-79; prin. St. Paul's Sch., San Pablo, Calif., 1979-83; adminstr. Salesian High Sch., Richmond, Calif., 1983-1985; adj. prof. dept. grad. edn. St. Mary's Coll., 1982—; instr. dept. mgmt. and supervision Contra Costra Community Coll., 1980—; assoc. dir. student leadership program Diocese of Oakland, 1981—; cons. communication arts program St. Theresa Sch., Woodland, Calif., 1985, student leadership devel. St. Leo Sch., Oakland, 1985, Sacred Heart Sch., Oakland, 1985, renewal in edn. Fitch Mt. Sch., Healdsburg, 1985, developing a mission statement St. Paul Parish, San Pablo, Calif., 1986, staff devel. Emergency dept. Providence Hosp., 1985-86, sch. mgmt., curriculum devel., long-range planning St. John Sch., Healdsburg, 1985—, student leadership devel. St. Bernard Sch., Oakland, 1986, conflict mgmt. Pacific Gas and Electric Co., 1986; speaker DePaul U., Chgo., 1978, Archdiocese of Chgo., 1978, Diocese of Oakland, 1981, Diocese of Sacramento, 1985, 86, Mustard Seed, 1985, St. Thomas Coll., St. Paul, 1986, U. Calif., Berkeley, 1986; com. mem. Diocese Oakland Sch. Bd.; mem. doctoral proposal com. St. Mary's Coll., Moraga, Calif., 1985-86, mem. adv. bd. ctr. study edn. and leadership, 1982-83; mem. WASC sch. accreditation team St. Mary's High Sch., Berkeley, 1983; mem. diocesan athletic council Diocese of Oakland, 1981-82; del. Title I Tech. Assistance Inst., Los Angeles, 1980; mem. com. pub. relations Diocese Oakland Sch. Bd., 190-83, com. on personnel, 1980-83, assoc. dir. student leadership program 1980—; mem. bd. conciliators Cath. Schs. Office, Chgo., 1974-76; archdiocese Chgo. rep. Cath. Assn. Student Councils, 1977-78. Mem. Nat. Cath. Edn. Assn. (assoc. dir. vision and value leadership tng. program, speaker 1982, 83, 84), Assn. Supervision and Curriculum Devel., Calif. Assn. Supervision and Curriculum Devel., U. San Francisco Edn. Alumni, Phi Delta Kappa. Democrat. Roman Catholic. Club: K.C. (San Pablo). Editor Chgo. Archiocesan Tchrs. Assn. Monthly, 1970-74. Home: 405 Del Valle Circle El Sobrante CA 94803

BRENNAN, JERRY MICHAEL, economics educator, statistician, reseacher, clinical psychologist; b. Grosse Pointe, Mich., July 17, 1944; s. Walter X. and Aretta May (Gempler) B. Student Kalamazoo (Mich.) Coll., 1962-64, Pasadena (Calif.) City Coll., 1966-67; B.A., UCLA, 1969; M.A., U. Hawaii, 1973, Ph.D., 1978. Researcher, UCLA, 1968-69; researcher U. Hawaii, 1972, 74-78, cons., 1975, 77, 78, data analyst and statis. cons., 1979-80, lectr., 1976-80, asst. prof. econs., 1980—; cons. WHO; v.p. Hawaii Sch. Profl. Psychology. Light scholar, 1964-66. Mem. Am. Psychol. Assn., Soc. Multivariate Exptl. Psychology, Psychometric Soc., Western Psychol. Assn., AAUP, Hawaii Ednl. Research Assn. Contbr. psychol. articles to profl. jours. Address: U Hawaii 2424 Maile Way Porteus 247 Honolulu HI 96822

BRENNAN, PAMELA F., corporate training executive; b. Indpls., Mar. 19, 1945; d. Stanley Valinet and Estelle (Sider) Bahre; m. Michael Brennan, Oct. 8, 1967 (div. Mar. 1970); 1 child, Kelley Brennan. Student, Cornell Coll., Mt. Vernon, Iowa, 1962-64; BA, U. Ariz., 1966; MS in Systems Mgmt., U. So. Calif., 1979. Cert. secondary tchr., Calif. From instr. to staff devel. specialist Project Step-Up, San Diego, 1970-72; coordinator S.E. Learning Ctr. Community Coll. Dist., San Diego, 1972; ednl. dir. Am. Cancer Soc., San Diego, 1972-76; ednl. dir. Calif. div. Am. Cancer Soc., Riverside, 1976-79; corp. tng. mgr. Gt. Am. First Savs. Bank, San Diego, 1979—; bd. dirs. San Diego Fed. Credit Union; mem. adv. bd. basic edn. and ESL San Diego Community Coll. Dist.; cons. Inst. Urban and Human Devel., San Diego, 1976—. Democrat. Avocations: jogging, aerobic dancing, interpretive dance, piano, guitar.

BRENNAN, ROBERT GILBERT, librarian; b. Mount Vernon, N.Y., Mar. 26, 1927; s. Robert Gilbert Sr. and Lydia Gertrude (Jost) B.; m. Dawn Hazel Tolson, June 11, 1952 (dec. 1979); children: Margaret L. Selkirk, Thomas L., Lawrence A., Amy E. Rash. BA, Mount Union, 1951; MLS, Pratt Inst., 1952. Reference librarian Dayton (Ohio) Montgomery County Library, 1952-54; dir. library Howard Whittemore Meml. Library, Naugatuck, Conn., 1954-62; head librarian social sci. and bus. div. Calif. State U., Chico, 1962-66, head librarian pub. services, 1966-81, asst. library dir., 1981-83, reference librarian, 1983—. Mem. NEA, AAUP, Calif. Tchrs. Assn., Calif. Faculty Assn. Republican. Methodist. Home: 11 Woodside Ln Chico CA 95926 Office: Calif State U Chico CA 95929

BRENNEMAN, JOHN, design and graphic arts marketing executive; b. Phoenix, June 22, 1945; s. Leroy John and Euta (Adams) B. BFA, Ariz. State U., 1968, MFA, 1971. Prin. John Brenneman Studios, Tempe, Ariz., 1972-78; mgr. Durst, U.S., Phoenix, 1978-79; pres. John Brenneman & Assocs., Tempe, 1979—; bd. dirs. GrafTek, Phoenix. Author: Documents, 1975. Served to sgt. U.S. Air N.G., 1968-73. Mem. Photo Mktg. Assn., Assn. Multi-Image, Assn. Profl. Color Labs., Soc. Motion Picture and TV Engrs. Republican. Episcopalian. Avocations: trap and skeet shooting, fly fishing.

BRENNEMAN, JOHN DAVID, optometrist, state senator; b. Corvallis, Oreg., Mar. 18, 1942; s. John Mark and Ruth Elvira (Gingrich) B.; m. Janet Kay Roper, Feb. 1, 1964; children—Tracey Leanne, Shannon Rae. B.S., Pacific U., 1964, O.D., 1965. Self-employed optometrist, Reedsport, Oreg., 1965-67, Newport, Oreg., 1967—. City planner Newport Planning Commn., Oreg., 1968; councilman City of Newport, 1970-74, mayor, 1974-78, 80-84; mem. Oreg. Senate, 1984—. Mem. Newport C. of C., Newport Jaycees (recipient Disting. Service award 1972). Republican. Presbyterian. Lodges: Rotary (bd. dirs. 1970-72). Elks. Home: 2780 NE Jackson Pl Newport OR 97365 Office: 14 SW Nye Newport OR 97365

BRENNER YOUNGGREN, ELIZABETH FORD, geologist, cattle rancher, consultant; b. Butte, Mont., Jan. 8, 1941; d. John Skoning and Frances Marshall (Ford) Brenner; m. Harry A. Tourtelot, Sept. 24, 1964 (div. 1976); children: John Brenner, Frances Grace; m. Thomas Charles Younggren, Aug. 20, 1983. BA in Geology, Wellesley (Mass.) Coll., 1962. Technician U.S. Geol. Survey, Denver, 1962-67, geologist, 1967-77; pres. X-Min Co., Billings, Mont., 1978—. Contbr. articles to profl. jours. Fellow Geol. Soc. Am.; mem. Beaverhead C. of C. (resource com. 1979-84), Tobacco Root Geol. Soc. (bd. dirs.), Am. Geol. Inst. (women geoscientists com. 1974-77), Am. Inst. Profl. Geologists (cert.) (past v.p. Mont. east), Soc. Econ. Geologists, Rocky Mountain Assoc. Geologists (past assoc. editor), AAAS, Mont. Geol. Soc. (pub. affairs com.), Wyo. Geol. Soc., Colo. Sci. Soc., Mont. Mining Assn. (past pres. local chpt.), Assn. Women Geoscientists, Montana Stockgrowers Assn., Nat. Cattlemans Assn., Denver Region Exploration Geologists Soc. Home and Office: 3201 LeeAnn Blvd Billings MT 59102

BRENT, JASON G., lawyer; b. N.Y.C., Apr. 9, 1936; s. Alex and Jeanne (Heitel) Perkovitch; m. Linda R. Polinger, May 7, 1957; children: Lorri J., Tracy. BS in Indsl. Engring., Lehigh U., 1956; MS in Bus., Columbia U., 1957, LLB, 1960. Bar: N.Y., Calif.; CPA, N.Y., Calif. Mgmt. cons. Touche Ross & Co., N.Y.C., 1960-62; asst. to sr. v.p. REA Express, N.Y.C., 1962-66; div. controller Paramount Pictures, Hollywood, Calif., 1967-70; ptnr. Donnenfeld & Brent, Los Angeles, 1970-84, Shea & Gould, Los Angeles, 1985—. Pres. Stallion Springs Community Services Dist., Tehachapi, Calif., 1982—. Mem. San Fernando Valley Bar Assn., Los Angeles County Bar Assn., Kern County Bar Assn. Republican. Jewish. Club: Horse Thief Country (Tehachapi). Lodge: Knights of Pythias. Avocation: World War II memorabilia. Home: Star Route 1 Box 2800-111 Tehachapi CA 93561 Office: Shea & Gould 1800 Ave of the Stars Los Angeles CA 90067

BRENT, PAUL LESLIE, educator; b. Douglass, Okla., July 3, 1916; s. Paul Leslie and Ruth (McKee) B.; m. Aledo Render, May 29, 1938; children: Carolyn J., Paul Richard; m. E. Ferne McCoy, Nov. 19, 1984. B.S., Central State U., 1938; M.Ed., U. Okla., 1949, Ed.D., 1959. Tchr. math. and sci. public schs. Adair, Okla., 1938-40; prin. Alden Public Schs., Carnegie, Okla., 1940-43; supt. Alden Public Schs., 1950-58; tchr. public schs. Cooperton, Okla., 1946-47; prin. high sch., public schs. Washita, Okla., 1947-48; supt. 1948-50; asst. prof. Calif. State U., Long Beach, 1959-63, assoc. prof. edn., 1963-72, asst. to chmn. div. edn., 1961-67, prof. instructional media, 1972-86, coordinator graphics support sect. dept. mech. engring., 1981-86; mem. Baptist Edn. Study Task, 1966-67; trustee Calif. Bapt. Coll., 1969-74. Co-Author: Point, Line, Plane and Solid, 1984. Trustee Calif. Bapt. Coll., 1969-74. Served with USNR, 1943-46. Mem. Calif. Faculty Assn. (pres. elect), NEA, Calif. Media and Library Educators Assn., Am. Assn. Sch. Adminstrs., Congress of Faculty Assns., Phi Delta Kappa, Kappa Delta Pi, Phi Kappa Phi, Phi Beta Delta. Democrat. Baptist. Home: 11112 Bos Pl Cerritos CA 90701 Office: 1250 Bellflower Blvd Long Beach CA 90840

BRESCIA, ANTHONY JOSEPH, customer service executive; b. Jersey City, Sept. 26, 1950; s. Anthony Joseph and Josephine (Russo) B.; m. Donna Mae Kremers, Apr. 5, 1974; children: Anthony Joseph, Brandon Michael. AA, Coll. of Sequoias, 1972; student, Calif. State U., Fresno, 1975-78, Ariz. State U., 1981-82. Supr. U.S. Postal Service, Hanford, Calif., 1973-78; station mgr. U.S. Postal Service, Bakersfield, Calif., 1978-80; mgr. stations and brs. U.S. Postal Service, Phoenix, 1980-83; dir. customer services U.S. Postal Service, Fresno, Calif., 1983—. Bd. dirs. Woodward Park Homeowner Assn., Fresno, 1985—. Served with USN, 1968-72. Mem. Fed. Exec. Assn., Am. Legion, U.S. Jaycees (external dir. 1975-76). Republican. Roman Catholic. Avocations: golfing, stamp collecting, penny stock investing. Office: US Postal Service 1900 E St Fresno CA 93706-9996

BRESEE, INA FAY, trucking company executive; b. Protem, Mo., Sept. 22, 1934; d. C.F. and Willa L. (Blakey) Wood; m. Charles Gross, Aug. 30, 1951 (div. 1954); 1 child, Ronald G.; m. Elbert Davis Bresee, Aug. 7, 1962; 1 child, Darren S. Degree, Crow's Beauty Sch., 1954. Pvt. practice beautician Las Vegas, Nev. and Springfield, Mo., 1954-65; chmn. bd. dirs. D&N Delivery Corp., Las Vegas; pres. Air Truck express Inc., Las Vegas, 1985—, Air and Ocean Cons. Inc., Las Vegas, 1985—. Republican. Avocations: tennis, swimming, reading.

BRESHEARS, ROBERT BRUCE, government engineer; b. Spokane, Wash., Sept. 16, 1951; s. Robert Griffith Breshears and Dorothy Lidell (Thames) Emert; m. Josephine Belle McLain, Jan. 12, 1980; children: Marie Allison, Marcie Ann. AAS, Spokane Community Coll., 1972. Cert. engring. technician. Engr. technician Lincoln County, Wash., Davenport, 1972-80, asst. county engr., 1980—. Named one of Outstanding Young Men of Am., 1977. Mem. Am. Pub. Works Assn., Nat. Assn. County Engrs., Wash. State Assn. County Engrs. (assoc.), Jaycees (pres. Davenport 1976-77). Office: Lincoln County Hwy Dept 509 Morgan Davenport WA 99122

BRESNOCK, ANNE ELIZABETH, economics educator; b. Belfonte, Pa., Mar. 22, 1951; d. Edward and Dorothy Catherine Ann (Geffert) B. B.A. in Econs., Russell Sage Coll., 1973, M.A. in Econs., U. Colo., Boulder, 1976, Ph.D., 1981. Research asst. Econs. Inst., Boulder, 1974; research asst. Ctr. for Energy and Econ. Devel., 1974-76; teaching asst. dept. econs. U. Colo., 1976-77, instr., 1978-79; research asst. Bur. Econ. Research, 1977-78; asst. prof. dept. econs. San Diego State U., 1979-83; lectr. Sch. Bus., U. San Diego, 1980-83; asst. prof. econs. U. Redlands, 1983—. Mem. Am. Econ. Assn., Am. Environ. and Resource Econs. Assn., Com. on Status of Women in Econs., Acad. Ind. Scholars. Democrat. Roman Catholic. Club: Sierra. Office: U Redlands Dept Econs Redlands CA 92373

BRESSLER, RICHARD MAIN, railroad executive; b. Wayne, Nebr., Oct. 8, 1930; s. John T. and Helen (Main) B.; m. Dianne G. Pearson, Apr. 17,

1981; children: Kristin M., Alan L. B.A., Dartmouth Coll., 1952. With Gen. Electric Co., 1952-68; v.p., treas. Am. Airlines Inc., 1968-72, sr. v.p., 1972-73; v.p. finance Atlantic Richfield Co., Los Angeles, 1973-75; sr. v.p. fin. Atlantic Richfield Co., 1975-77; pres. Arco Chem. Co., 1977-78, exec. v.p., 1978-80; pres., chief exec. officer, dir. Burlington No., Inc., St. Paul, 1980—; chmn. Burlington No., Inc., Seattle, 1982—; dir. Baker Internat., El Paso Co., Seafirst Corp., Honeywell Inc., Gen. Mills, Inc.; trustee Penn Mut. Life Ins. Co. Office: Burlington Northern Inc 999 3d Ave Seattle WA 98104 *

BRETERNITZ, DAVID ALAN, archaeologist, researcher; b. Fremont, Nebr., Nov. 12, 1929; s. Louis Alexander and Gretchen Frances (Yost) B.; m. Barbara Blair Myers, Dec. 26, 1952; children: Cory Dale, Susan Lee, Nancy Jane. BA, U. Denver, 1952; MA, U. Ariz., 1956, PhD, 1963. Curator of anthropology Mus. No. Ariz., Flagstaff, 1956-59; prof. anthropology U. Colo., Boulder, 1962-86; field dir. Kainji Rescue Archeol., Ibadan, Nigeria, 1968-72; dir. Mesa Verde Research Ctr., Dove Creek, Colo., 1969—; sr. prin. investigator Dolores (Colo.) Archeol. Project, 1978-85; chmn. bd. dirs. Woods Can. Archeol. Cons., Yellow Jacket, Colo., 1982—; bd. dirs. Soil Systems Inc., Phoenix, 1984—. Contbr. articles to profl. jours. Served to 2d lt. U.S. Army, 1952-54, Korea. Recipient State Archaeologists award, Colo., 1980, Robert L. Stearns award U. Colo., 1986. Fellow Soc. Am. Archaeology (exec. com. 1979-81); mem. Colo. Council Profl. Archaeologists (adv. com. 1978-79), Colo. Archeol. Soc. (editor 1963-72), Plains Anthrop. Soc. (exec. com. 1971-73), Ariz. Archeol. and Hist. Soc. Home and Office: PO Box 592 Dove Creek CO 81324

BRETT-ELSPAS, JANIS E., public relations executive; b. Hackensack, N.J., Sept. 6, 1956; d. Charles and Jean Estelle (Hawrey) B. BA, U. Ariz., 1978; pub. relations cert., UCLA, 1983. Pub. relations traffic and prodn. mgr. D'Arcy-MacManus & Masius, Los Angeles; then asst. pub. relations dir. SSC&B Advt., Los Angeles; then pub. relations mgr. Informatics Gen. Corp., Woodland Hills, Calif.; then account exec. Hill & Knowlton Inc., San Jose, Calif., Rogers & Cowan, Los Angeles; now pres. and cons. in mktg. communications Rachel P. R. Services, Santa Monica, Calif. Mem. Pub. Relations Soc. Am., Independent Writers So. Calif., Delta Zeta. Office: Rachel P R Services 513 Wilshire Blvd Suite 238 Santa Monica CA 90401

BRETTSCHNEIDER, EDMUND ALBERT, journalist; b. Buenos Aires, Argentina, July 4, 1936; came to U.S., 1971; s. Johannes and Lydia (Knuth) B.; m. Kiki Kachrimani, Aug. 28, 1969; 1 dau., Nadja. Law diplom Humboldt-U., Berlin, 1961. Assoc. editor Radio Deutsche Welle, Cologne, Germany, 1966-68; fgn. affairs editor Stern mag., Hamburg, Germany, 1967-69; news editor Bauer Publs., Hamburg, 1969-71; U.S.A. corr. Bauer Pub. Co., Hamburg, 1971—; pres. Inter Contact, Inc., Interlens Products, Inc.; pub. (German weekly) Neue Presse, Los Angeles. Mem. Fgn. Press Center USIA, Hollywood Fgn. Press Assn., Meadow Lark. Social Democrat. Home: 4085 Meadow Lark Dr Calabasas CA 91302 Office: 23987 Craftsman Rd Calabasas CA 90302

BRETZ, THOMAS EDWARD, geologist, state official; b. Carson City, Mich., Oct. 19, 1919; s. Paul V. and Mildred Elizabeth (Davy) B.; m. Muriel Corine Nederbo, Jan. 29, 1944; children—Thomas Edward, Paul Torbjorn. B.A., U. Minn., 1949. Geologist U.S. Geol. Survey, 1949-51; surveyor Nat. Geophys. Co., 1951-53, party mgr., 1953-54; pvt. practice geology, 1954-55; geologist Knox Bergman Shearer, 1955-57; with Geophoto Services, Inc., 1957-70, resident mgr., Bogota, Colombia, 1966-67, chief photogeologist, geomorphologist, Managua, Nicaragua, 1968-69, sr. geologist, Denver, 1969-70; sr. geologist King Resources Co., various locations, 1970-71; pvt. cons. geologist, Denver, 1971-73; mineral dir. Colo. Bd. Land Commrs., Denver, 1973—. Served with USCG, 1941-45; ETO. Mem. Rocky Mountain Assn. Geologists, Am. Assn. Petroleum Geologists, Am. Inst. Profl. Geologists, Colo. Mining Assn., Denver Assn. Petroleum Landmen (hon.), Soc. Mining Engrs., Clear Creek County Metal Mining Assn. Republican. Clubs: Denver Coal; Rocky Mountain Petroleum Pioneers; Denver Petroleum (hon.). Home: 1955 Glen Shiel Dr Lakewood CO 80215 Office: State Land Bd 1313 Sherman St Room 620 Denver CO 80203

BREUER, STEPHEN ERNEST, temple adminstrator; b. Vienna, Austria, July 14, 1936; s. John Howard and Olga Marion (Haar) B.; came to U.S., 1938, naturalized, 1945; B.A. cum laude, UCLA, 1959, gen. secondary credential, 1960; m. Gail Fern Breitbart, Sept. 4, 1960 (div. 1986); children—Jared Noah, Rachel Elise. Tchr. pub. high schs., Los Angeles, 1960-62; dir. Wilshire Blvd. Temple Camps, Los Angeles, 1962—; exec. dir. Wilshire Blvd. Temple, 1980—; dir. Edgar F. Magnin Religious Sch., Los Angeles, 1970-80. Instr. edn. Hebrew Union Coll., Los Angeles, 1965-76; field instr. San Francisco State U., 1970-80, Calif. State U., San Diego, Hebrew Union Coll., 1977-81. Vice pres. Los Angeles Youth Programs Inc., 1967-77; youth adviser Los Angeles County Commn. Human Relations, 1969-72. Bd. dirs. Community Relations Conf. So. Calif., 1965—, Union Am. Hebrew Congregations, Alzheimer's Disease and Related Disorders Assn., 1984—, v.p. Los Angeles County chpt., 1984-86, pres., 1986—; mem. golas program City of Beverly Hills, Calif., 1985-86; active United Way. Recipient Service awards Los Angeles YWCA, 1974, Los Angeles County Bd. Suprs., 1982, Ventura County Bd. Suprs., 1982, Weinberg Chai Achievement award Jewish Fed. Council Los Angeles, 1986. Mem. So. Calif. Camping Assn. (dir. 1964-82), Nat. Assn. Temple Adminstrs., Nat. Assn. Temple Educators (br. mem. 1987—), Los Angeles Assn. Jewish Edn. (dir.), Profl. Assn. Temple Adminstrs. (pres. 1985—), Assn. Supervision and Curriculum Devel., Am. Mgmt. Assn., So. Calif. Conf. Jewish Communal Workers, Jewish Profl. Network, Amnesty Internat., Jewish Resident Camping Assn. (pres. 1976-82), UCLA Alumni Assn., Wilderness Soc., Center for Environ. Edn., Wildlife Fedn., Los Angeles County Art Mus., People for the Am. Way, Assn. Reform Zionists Am. Jewish. Office: Wilshire Blvd Temple 3663 Wilshire Blvd Los Angeles CA 90010

BREWER, ALEXANDER FREDERICK, electronic systems consultant; b. Geneva, Dec. 18, 1917; s. Louis L. and Elise (Breuer) B.; m. Barbara C. Gustafson, May 12, 1945 (dec. Jan. 1983); children: Gregory J., Pamela L., Douglas A. BS, Calif. Inst. Tech., 1940; MA, Stanford U., 1942; postgrad., UCLA, 1947-55. Mgr. systems research Hughes Aircraft Co., Culver City, Calif., 1946-53; exec. v.p., dir. Electronic Control Systems, Los Angeles, 1953-59; bus. mgr. Hughes Aircraft Co. Component Group, El Segundo, Calif., 1959-61; dir. market planning TRW Space Tech. Labs., El Segundo, 1962-68; electronic systems cons. The Rand Corp., Santa Monica, Calif., 1968—. Inventor, patentee in field. Bd. dirs. Malibu Twp. (Calif.) Council, v.p.; chmn. Malibu Incorp. Com.; elder Malibu Presbyn. Ch. Recipient Honor Key Calif. Inst. Tech., Pasadena, 1940. Mem. AIEE (life, chmn. automation com. 1956). Republican. Avocations: golf, tennis. Home: 21511 Deerpath Ln Malibu CA 90265 Office: The Rand Corp 1700 Main St Santa Monica CA 90406-2138

BREWER, CHRISTOPHER D., historic preservation consultant; b. Bakersfield, Calif., June 20, 1950; s. Harold Baker and Anne (Grothaus) B.; m. Sally M. Botkin, July 10, 1977. A.A., Bakersfield Coll., 1979; B.A. in Pub. Adminstrn., Calif. State U.-Bakersfield, 1982, M.A. in Pub. Adminstrn., 1983. Registered profl. historian, Calif. Musician, U.S. Navy Band, 1968-72, profl. musical orgns., 1972-77; mgmt. positions Kern County Mus., Bakersfield, 1978-82; owner, cons. Brewer's Hist. Cons., Bakersfield, 1982—; cons. City of Bakersfield, 1983—; owner, dir. Redford Gallery, Bakersfield, 1984—. Mem. Bakersfield Hist. Preservation Commn., 1982-83, Com. for Preservation of History. Author: Kern's Historic Landmarks, 1987; Bakersfield Picture Album, 1986, Bakersfield and Kern County Picture Album II, 1987; editor of history articles. Mem. Calif. Hist. Socs. (active conf., regional v.p. 1980-83), Soc. Calif. Pioneers, E Clampus Vitus (pres. Peter Lebeck chpt. 1980), Calif. Preservation Found. Office: 3204 Perry Pl Bakersfield CA 93306

BREWER, DAVID AUGUSTINE, project manager, civil engineer; b. Portland, Oreg., Apr. 29, 1940; s. Myron L. and Ellen (Shade) B. BCE, Ga. Inst. Tech., 1964; MCE, Stanford U., 1976. Registered civil engr., Calif.; lic. gen. engring. contractor, Calif. Asst. project mgr., chief engr. McGuire & Hester, Oakland, Calif., 1971-74, 81-82; cons. D.A. Brewer, Santa Cruz, Calif., 1974-76; asst. project mgr. Huber Hunt & Nichols, Indpls., 1976-81; chief estimator Rosewall & Son, Watsonville, Calif., 1982-83; project mgr. Rudolph & Sletten, Foster City, Calif., 1983—; Instr. civil engring. Sacramento State U., 1977-80. Served to lt. USNR, 1963-68. Mem. Am. Arbitration Assn. (arbiter 1981—), Assn. Gen. Contractors (edn. com. 1976-77). Democrat. Roman Catholic. Avocations: photography, backpacking, travel. Home: 21550 Madrone Dr Los Gatos CA 95030

BREWER, KENNETH WAYNE, English educator; b. Indpls., Nov. 28, 1941; s. Ulyss and Edna Juanita (Virt) B.; m. Carol Ann Hayton, Aug. 22, 1964 (div. July 1977); children: Kimberley Diane Marsing, Jonathan Keith; m. Roberta Stearman, Sept. 22, 1978 (div. Nov. 1986). BA, Wester N.Mex. U., 1965; MA, N.Mex. State U., 1967; PhD, U. Utah, 1973. Tchr. English Las Cruces (N.Mex.) High Sch., 1967-68; assoc. prof. English Utah State U., Logan, Utah, 1968—. Author: Sum of Accidents, 1977, Round Again, 1980, Collected Poems of Mongrel, 1981, To Remember What Is Lost, 1982. Panel mem. literary bd. Utah Arts Council, Salt Lake City, 1981-85; bd. dirs. Planned Parenthood, Logan. Recipient 1st pl. prize for Long Poem Utah Arts Council, 1978, Creative Activity award Coll. of HA&SS Utah State U., 1983. Mem. Nat. Writers Union, Western Lit. Assn., Associated Writing Programs. Avocations: hunting, fishing, stamp collecting. Home: PO BOx 3393 Logan UT 84321 Office: Utah State U English Dept Logan UT 84322-3200

BREWER, LEO, physical chemist, educator; b. St. Louis, June 13, 1919; s. Abraham and Hanna (Resnik) B.; m. Rose Strugo, Aug. 22, 1945; children: Beth A., Roger M., Gail L. BS, Calif. Inst. Tech., 1940; PhD, U. Calif., Berkeley, 1943. Mem. faculty U. Calif., Berkeley, 1946—; prof. phys. chemistry U. Calif., 1955—; research assoc. Lawrence Berkeley Lab. (formerly Radiation Lab.), 1943-61, head inorganic materials div., 1961-75, prin. investigator, 1961—, assoc. dir. lab., 1967-75; Huffman Meml. lectr. Calorimetry Conf., 1966; Coover lectr. Am. Chem. Soc., 1967; Robert W. Williams lectr. MIT, 1963; Henry Werner lectr. U. Kans., 1963; O.M. Smith lectr. Okla State U., 1964; G.N. Lewis lectr. U. Calif., 1964, faculty lectr., 1966; Corn Products lectr. Pa. State U., 1970; W.D. Harkins lectr. U. Chgo., 1974; Frontiers in Chem. Research lectr. Texas A & M U., 1981; research scholar lectr., Drew U., 1983; 10th Louis J. Bircher lectr., Vanderbilt U., 1985; mem.rev. com. reactor chem. div. Oak Ridge Nat. Lab.; research assoc. Manhattan Dist. U. Calif., Berkeley, 1943-45; sec. gas subcom. high temperature commn. Internat. Union Pure and Applied Chemistry, 1957-60; assoc. mem. commn. on thermodynamics and thermochemistry, 1973—; chmn. materials adv. bd. Com. Investigation Application Plasma Phenomena, 1959-60. Author: (with others) Thermodynamics, 1961; assoc. editor: Jour. Chem. Physics, 1959-63; mem. editorial adv. bd.: Jour. Physics and Chemistry Solids, Progress Inorganic Chemistry, Jour. Chem. Thermodynamics, 1968-77, Jour. High Temperature Sci., Jour. Solid State Chemistry, Jour. Chem. Engring. Data, 1977—, Jour. Phys. Chemistry Reference Data, 1978-81; divisional editor high temperature sci and tech. div.: Jour. Electrochem. Soc., 1977-84. Fellow Great Western Dow, 1942, Guggenheim, 1950; recipient Ernest Orlando Lawrence Meml. award, 1961; Disting. Alumni award Calif. Inst. Tech., 1974. Mem. Nat. Acad. Scis. (exec com. Office Critical Tables 1961-66, com. on Data Needs, 1975-78, com. on High Temperatures, 1975-85), AAUP, AAAS, Am. Acad. Arts and Scis., Am. Chem. Soc. (Leo H. Baekeland award 1953), Electrochem. Soc. (lectr. 1970, Palladium Medallist 1971), Am. Plant Life Soc., ACLU, Cobletz Soc., Combustion Inst., Faraday Soc., Fedn. Am. Scientist, Calif. Assn. Chemistry Tchrs., Internat. Plansee Soc. Powder Metallurgy, Am. Optical Soc., Metall. Soc. (William Hume-Rothery award 1983), Am. Phys. Soc., Am. Soc. for Metals Internat. council on Alloy Phase Diagrams, Calif. Acad. Sci., Calif. Native Plant Soc., Calif. Botanic Soc., Lawrence Hall of Sci., Save Redwoods League, Sierra Club, Sigma Xi, Alpha Chi Sigma, Tau Beta Pi. Home: 15 Vista del Orinda Orinda CA 94563 Office: U Calif Dept Chemistry Berkeley CA 94720

BREWER, LISA MARIE, criminalist; b. Beaumont, Tex., Oct. 12, 1958; d. Ronald Ernest Brewer and Sharon Lee (Abbors) Cowen. BS in Chemistry, U. Nev., 1983; postgrad., San Jose State U. Teaching fellow U. Nev., Reno, 1983-84; lab. aid U.S. Geol. Survey, Menlo Park, Calif., 1984; criminalist Calif. Dept. Justice, Salinas, 1984—; lectr. Gavilan Coll., Gilroy, Calif., 1986—; workshop leader Math-Sci. Network, San Francisco, 1985—. Mem. Monterey (Calif.) Bay Aquarium, 1985. Mem. Calif. Assn. Criminalists, Am. Chem. Soc., Mothers Against Drunk Drivers (Monterey chpt.). Republican. Methodist. Office: Calif Dept Justice 745 Airport Rd Salinas CA 93901

BREWER, MARION ALYCE, lawyer; b. Brownfield, Tex., Dec. 28, 1949; d. Deral Henry and Marion Thomas (Magee) B. BA, Stanford U., 1972; JD, Georgetown U., 1980. Bar: Colo. 1982, D.C. 1983, U.S. Dist. Ct. (Colo.), 1982, U.S. Ct. Appeals (10th cir.), U.S. Tax Ct., 1984. Reporter, anchor woman Sta. KMGH-TV CBS, Denver, 1972-76; TV corr. Ind. TV News Assn., Washington, 1976-78; asst. dir. Law Sch. Admission Council, Washington, 1978-79; asst. dean admissions Georgetown U. Law Ctr., Washington, 1979-80; law clk. to judge U.S. Dist. Ct. D.C., 1981-83; assoc. Ireland, Stapleton, Pryor & Pascoe, Washington, 1983-87; gen. counsel Colo. Counties, Inc., Denver, 1987—; mem. coms. Women in Communications, Inc., Denver, 1972-76. Mem. fin. com. Schoettler for Treas., Denver, 1986; co-chmn. Lawyers for Wirth Com., Denver, 1986; mem. Big Sisters Support Group, Denver, 1986—. Recipient Outstanding Service award United Vets. Council Colo., 1976, Outstanding Service award Optimists, Aurora, Colo., 1975. Mem. ABA, Colo. Trial Lawyers Assn., Alliance Profl. Women, Colo. Women's Bar Assn. (bd. dirs. 1984-86), Colo. Bar Assn. (bd. govs. 1985-87), Denver Bar Assn. (mem. coms. 1980—), Stanford Alumni Assn., Georgetown Law Alumni Assn. (inaugural nat. bd. dirs. 1986—), Am. Trial Lawyers Assn. Episcopalian. Clubs: Denver Press, Rocky Mountain Stanford (Denver) (pres., chmn. bd. dirs. 1973-75, treas. 1983—); Nat. Press (Washington). Office: Colo Counties Inc 1177 Grant Denver CO 80202

BREWSTER, HENRY HODGE, psychiatrist; b. Boston, Oct. 20, 1912; s. George W.W. and Ellen (Hodge) B.; M.D., Harvard U., 1938; children by previous marriage—Rodman Peabody, Ellen Hodge, Henry Hodge; m. 3d, Judy M. Jacobsen, Aug. 24, 1970; stepchildren—Penny Robben, Daryl Ray Jacobsen. Intern, Mass. Gen. Hosp., Boston, 1938-40; resident in medicine Boston City Hosp., 1940-42; practice medicine specializing in psychiatry and psychoanalysis; asst. prof. psychiatry Western Res. Sch. Medicine, Cleve., 1954-60, Harvard U. Med. Sch., 1962-65; assoc. prof. psychiatry Colo. Med. Center, Denver, 1960-62; chief profl. edn. Stockton (Calif.) State Hosp., 1967-78; asst. clin. prof. psychiatry U. Calif. at Davis, 1968-73, assoc. clin. prof., 1973-83. Bd. dirs. Stockton Symphony Assn. Served with M.C., U.S. Army, 1942-45; ETO. Mem. AMA, San Francisco, Am. psychoanalytic assns., Am. Psychiat. Assn., Calif. Med. Assn., San Joaquin County Med. Soc., Soc. Mayflower Desc. Republican. Episcopalian. Clubs: Delphic (Harvard); Masons, Stockton Golf and Country, N. Stockton Rotary. Contbr. chpt. Psychiatry and Religion, 1948. Home and Office: 3414 Quail Lakes Dr Stockton CA 95207

BREWSTER, RUDI MILTON, judge; b. Sioux Falls, S.D., May 18, 1932; s. Charles Edwin and Wilhemina Therese (Rud) B.; m. Gloria Jane Nanson, June 27, 1954; children: Scot Alan, Lauri Diane, Alan Lee, Julie Lynn. AB in Pub. Affairs, Princeton U., 1954; JD, Stanford U., 1960. Bar: Calif. 1960. From assoc. to ptnr. Gray, Cary, Ames & Frye, San Diego, 1960-84; judge U.S. Dist. Ct. (so. dist.) Calif., San Diego, 1984—. Served to capt. USNR, 1954-82. Fellow Am. Coll. Trial Lawyers; mem. Am. Bd. Trial Advs., Internat. Assn. Ins. Counsel. Republican. Lutheran. Lodge: Rotary (pres. San Diego club 1980-81). Avocations: skiing, hunting, gardening. Office: US Dist Ct 940 Front St San Diego CA 92189

BREZZO, STEVEN LOUIS, museum director; b. Woodbury, N.J., June 18, 1949; s. Louis and Ella Marie (Savage) B.; m. Dagmar Grimm, Aug. 10, 1975. B.A., Clarion State Coll., 1969; M.F.A., U. Conn., 1973. Chief curator La Jolla Mus. Contemporary Art, Calif., 1974-76; asst. dir. San Diego Mus. Art, 1976-78, dir., 1978—. Mem. Am. Assn. Mus. (del. to China 1981, to Italian mus. study trip 1982), La Jolla Library Assn. (pres. 1980). Club: University (San Diego). Lodge: Rotary. Office: San Diego Mus Art PO Box 2107 Balboa Park San Diego CA 92112 *

BRICK, DEAN CLARK, ophthalmologist, physician; b. Phila., Aug. 17, 1946; s. Robert Maynard and Dorothy (Smith) B.; married, July 5, 1980; children: Patrick, Ashley, Aubrey. BA, Northwestern U., 1968; MD, Chgo. Med. Sch., 1972. Resident Med. Coll. Va., Richmond, 1974-77; fellow U. Calif., San Francisco, 1977-79, Bascom Palmer Eye Inst., Miami, Fla., 1979-80; asst. prof. U. Ariz., Tucson, 1980-83, asst. clin. prof., 1983—; practice medicine specializing in ophthalmology Tucson, 1983—. Contbr. articles to profl. jours. Recipient Pfizer award for scholarship 1969, Lange award for scholarship 1970. Fellow Am. Acad. Ophthalmology; mem. Assn. Research in Vision and Ophthalmology, Ocular Microbiology and Immunology Group, Am. Uveitis Soc., Pima county Med. Soc., Alpha Omega Alpha. Avocations: skiing, hiking, diving. Office: 490 N Alvernon Way Tucson AZ 85711

BRICKER, RUTH, national foundation administrator, real estate developer; b. Oak Park, Ill., Mar. 23, 1930; m. Neal S. Bricker; children—Daniel Baker, Cary, Dusty, Suzanne. B.A. in Urban Planning, postgrad. in pub. adminstrn. 1987—, Antioch U. Staff writer Artforum Mag., Los Angeles, 1966-69; western dir. Expts. in Art and Tech., Los Angeles, 1969-75; owner Empire Real Estate and Property Mgmt., Los Angeles, 1975—; designer Trade-Off, a computer simulation for use in urban planning; developed programs in art and technology for Calif. State Coll.-Long Beach, U. So. Calif., UCLA; designer laser light wall Calif. Inst. Tech.; lectr. and cons. in field. Mem. Mayor's Housing Task Force, Los Angeles; bd. councillors Internat. Inst. Kidney Diseases UCLA, mem. exec. com. Savings and Preserving Archtl. and Cultural Environ.; mem. Am. Found. for Pompidou Mus., Paris. Author: Getting Rich-Investing in Real Estate Partnerships, 1982; editor, contbg. author: Experiments in Art and Technology/Los Angeles jour., 1974-79.

BRICKNER, CYNTHIA, advertising professional; b. Des Moines, Nov. 14, 1957; d. John R. and Marlyn Kay B. Advt. mgr. Soaring Soc. Am., Los Angeles, 1981-84, membership dir., 1985, promotions and advt. exec., 1985-86; exec. dir. U.S. Hang Gliding Assn., Los Angeles, 1986—. Recipient Exceptional Service award Sailplane Homebuilders Assn., 1985. Mem. Soaring Soc. Am., So. Calif. Soaring Assn. (pres. 1982). Avocations: volleyball, horseback riding, motorcycling. Office: US Hang Gliding Assn 11423 Washington Blvd PO Box 66306 Los Angeles CA 90066

BRIDGE, HERBERT MARVIN, jewelry executive; b. Seattle, Mar. 14, 1925; s. Ben and Sally (Silverman) B.; m. Shirley Selesnick, Jan. 25, 1948; children—Jonathan J., Daniel E. B.A. in Polit. Sci., U. Wash., 1947. Pres. Ben Bridge Jeweler Inc., Seattle, 1955-76, chmn., 1977—; dir. Wash. Mut. Savs. Bank. Past pres. Downtown Seattle Assn., Am. Jewish Com.; bd. dirs. March of Dimes, Naval Acad. Found. Served to rear adm. USNR, 1942-83; World War II, Korea. Decorated Legion of Merit with Gold Star; recipient Israel Bonds Masada award, 1974; Am. Jewish Com. human relations award, 1976; NCCJ brotherhood award, 1978; Navy League scroll honor, 1980. Mem. Pacific N.W. Jewelers (past pres.), Greater Seattle C. of C. (past pres., mem. pres. club, chmn. 1986-87), Naval Res. Assn. (past pres.), Assn. Wash. Bus. Democrat. Clubs: Wash. Athletic (dir.), City (dir.), Rotary (dir. found.), Shriners. Home: 2125 1st Ave Seattle WA 98121 Office: Box 1908 Seattle WA 98111

BRIDGES, ROBERT MCSTEEN, mechanical engineer; b. Oakland, Calif., Apr. 17, 1914; s. Robert and Josephine (Hite) B.; B.S. cum laude in Mech. Engring., U. So. Calif., 1940; postgrad. UCLA; m. Edith Brownwood, Oct. 26, 1945; children—Ann, Lawrence, Robert. Engr. Nat. Supply Co., Torrance, Calif., 1940-41; design engr. landing gear and hydraulics Lockheed Aircraft Corp., Burbank, Calif., 1941-46; missile hydraulic controls design engr. Convair, San Diego, 1946-48; sr. staff engr. oceanic systems mech. design Bendix Corp., Sylmar, Calif., 1948—; adv. ocean engring. U.S. Congress. Com. chmn. Boy Scouts Am., 1961. Recipient award of Service Am. Inst. Aero. Engrs., 1965. Mem. Marine Tech. Soc. (charter; com. cables, connectors 1969), Tau Beta Pi. Republican. Patentee in field of undersea devices (53 internat., 14 U.S.), including deep ocean rubber band moor; inventor U.S. Navy sonobuoy rotochute; contbr. articles to profl. jours. and confs. Home: 10314 Vanalden Ave Northridge CA 91326 Office: Bendix Corp 15825 Roxford St Sylmar CA 91342

BRIDGFORTH, ROBERT MOORE, JR., research specialist; b. Lexington, Miss., Oct. 21, 1918; s. Robert Moore and Theresa (Holder) B.; student Miss. State Coll., 1935-37; B.S., Iowa State Coll., 1940; M.S., M.I.T., 1948; postgrad. Harvard U., 1949; m. Florence Jarnberg, November 7, 1943; children—Robert Moore, Alice Theresa. Asst. engr. Standard Oil Co., of Ohio, 1940; teaching fellow M.I.T., 1940-41, instr. chemistry, 1941-43, research asst., 1943-44, mem. staff div. indsl. cooperation, 1944-47; asso. prof. physics and chemistry Emory and Henry Coll., 1949-51; research engr. Boeing Airplane Co., Seattle, 1951-54, research specialist 1954-55, sr. group engr., 1955-58, chief propulsion systems sect. Systems Mgmt. Office, 1958-59, chief propulsion research unit, 1959-60; chmn. bd. Rocket Research Corp. (name now Rockcor, Inc.), 1960-69, Explosives Corp. Am., 1966-69. Fellow Brit. Interplanetary Soc., AIAA (asso.), Am. Inst. Chemists; mem. Am. Astronautical Soc. (dir.), AAAS, Am. Chem. Soc., Am. Rocket Soc. (pres. Pacific NW 1955), Am. Ordnance Assn., Am. Inst. Physics, Am. Assn. Physics Tchrs., Tissue Culture Assn., Reticuloendothelial Soc., N.Y. Acad. Scis., Combustion Inst., Sigma Xi. Home: 4325 87th Ave SE Mercer Island WA 98040

BRIEGER, STEPHEN GUSTAVE, mfg. co. ofcl.; b. Marburg, Ger., Sept. 7, 1935; came to U.S., naturalized, 1945; s. Heinrich and Kate L. (Steitz) B.; B.Sc., Springfield (Mass.) Coll., 1955; M.S., Fla. State U., 1970, Ph.D., 1972; m. Karen L. Jentes, Nov. 27, 1968; children—Jennifer B., Benjamin A. Tchr., Calif. schs., 1954-69; indsl. cons. mgmt. tng., 1960-70; mgmt. cons. Nebr. Criminal Justice System, 1972; research criminologist Stanford Research Inst., 1972-74; evaluation cons. Office Gov. Calif., 1974-76; mgmt. devel. assoc. Am. Electronics Assn., 1976-80; mgr. employee and mgmt. devel. ISS Sperry Univac, Santa Clara, Calif., 1980-83; mgr. tng. and devel. Lawrence Livermore Nat. Lab., U. Calif., 1983—; mem. faculty U.S. Internat. U., St. Mary's Coll., U. San Francisco. Mem. Am. Soc. Tng. and Devel., Am. Mgmt. Assn., Am. Electronics Assn. Author studies, reports in field. Home: 1665 Fairorchard Ave San Jose CA 95125 Office: PO Box 5508 L-490 Livermore CA 94550

BRIERLEY, JAMES ALAN, research administrator; b. Denver, Dec. 22, 1938; s. Everette and Carrie (Berg) B.; m. Corale Louise Beer, Dec. 21, 1965. BS in Bacteriology, Colo. State U., 1961; MS in Microbiology, Mont. State U., 1963, PhD, 1966. Research scientist Martin Marietta Corp., Denver, 1968-69; asst. prof. biology N.Mex. Inst. Mining and Tech., Socorro, 1966-68, from asst. prof. to prof. biology, chmn. dept. biology, 1969-83; research dir. Advanced Mineral Techs., Golden, Colo., 1983—; vis. fellow U. Warwick, Coventry, Eng., 1976, vis. prof. Catholic U., Santiago, Chile, 1983; cons. Mountain States Mineral Enterprises, Tucson, 1980, Sandia Nat. Lab., Albuquerque, 1976, Bechtel Civil and Minerals, Scottsdale, Ariz., 1984. Contbr. numerous articles to profl. jours.; patentee bacterial metal leaching process. Served to staff sgt. Air N.G., 1956-61. Recipient 28 research grants. Fellow AAAS; mem. Am. Soc. Microbiology, Soc. Gen. Microbiology, Sigma Xi. Avocations: travel, model railroading, gardening. Home: 3611 Vivian Ct Wheat Ridge CO 80033 Office: Advanced Mineral Techs 5920 McIntyre St Golden CO 80403

BRIERLY, KEPPEL, investment executive; b. Denver, Mar. 9, 1909; s. Justin Keppel and Pearl A. (Walters) B.; Engr. Mines, Colo. Sch. Mines, 1934; student, Denver U., 1936-37, U. Colo., 1939-41; m. Ruth E. Davis, Nov. 4, 1934; 1 child, Barbara Brierly Brann. Engr., Pub. Service Co. of Colo., Denver, 1930-38; coordinator, tchr. Denver pub. schs., 1938-41; pres. J & K Constrn. Co., Denver, 1945-68; investment exec.; v.p. Disputes Settlement Inc. Trustee, mayor pro tem Town of Bow Mar.; pres. Denver Lions Found., 1967-68; bd. dirs. Colo. Leukemia Soc. Served to lt. col. AUS, 1941-45; lt. col. Res. ret. Decorated Bronze Star Medal; also VI Haakon (Norway); award (France). Registered profl. engr., Colo.; real estate license, Colo. Mem. Denver Assn. Home Builders (pres. 1949, hon. life mem.), Asso. Bldg. Contractors Colo. (pres. 1956-57, Asso. Gen. Contractors Am. (dir. 1956-65), hon. life mem.), Am. Arbitration Assn., Theta Tau, Kappa Sigma, Blue Key. Presbyterian. Clubs: Denver Press (life), Denver Athletic (life), Pinehurst Country (life), Mount Vernon Country, Lions (pres. 1963-64), Masons, Shriners, Royal Order Jesters. Home: 5151 Juniper Rd Bow Mar Littleton CO 80123 Office: 601 Broadway Suite 206 Denver CO 80203

BRIËT, RICHARD, electrical engineer; b. Temanggoeng, Indonesia, June 18, 1942; s. Fernand A. and Amelia B. (Hofdijk) B.; B.S. in Physics, Math.

(Long Beach scholar), Calif. State U., 1968; Ph.D. in Physics, U. Utah, 1974; children—Rosewita, Paul, Pierre. Research specialist, cons. Asso. Food Stores, Mchts., Inc., Salt Lake City, 1974-77; sr. engr. nuclear survivability and vulnerability Boeing Wichita Co. (Kans.), 1977-79; design specialist electromagnetic and nuclear radiation effects Gen. Dynamics, San Diego, 1979-81; staff engr. TRW, Redondo Beach, Calif., 1981-84; mem. tech. staff The Aerospace Corp., El Segundo, Calif., 1984—. NDEA fellow, 1972. Mem. IEEE. Club: Toastmasters.

BRIGGS, CARLYLE WILKE, civil engineer; b. Boise, Idaho, July 1, 1922; s. Raymond Joel and Weltha (Wilkie) B.; m. Maxine Roberts, Aug. 6, 1943; children: Carlye, Paul, Molly. AA, Boise Jr. Coll., 1941; BS, U. Idaho, 1943, Degree in Civil Engring., 1957; postgrad., U. Wash., 1944. Registered profl. engr. and land surveyor, Idaho, Oreg., Wash., Utah, Nev. Engr. Pan Am. World Airways Inc., Seattle, 1943, Miami, Fla., 1943-46; engr. N.Am. Aviation, Los Angeles, 1946-48; prin. Briggs & Assocs., Boise, 1948-79; pres. B&A Engrs. Inc., Boise, 1979-85, chief engr., 1985—; engr. City of Garden City, Idaho, 1950—, Nampa (Idaho) Mcpl. Airport, 1972—, Boise County, Idaho, 1981—. Mem. Boise Airport Tech. Com., 1986, Ada County Devel. Adv. Com., Boise, 1986, Boise Future Found., 1986. Mem. NSPE, ASCE, Nat. Fedn. Ind. Bus., Water Pollution Control Fedn., Northwest Aviation Council, Idaho Pilots Assn., Am. Arbitration Assn. (cert.), Greater Boise C. of C., Delta Tau Delta Alumnae. Republican. Congregationalist. Avocations: antique cars, flying. Home: 204 S EAgleson Rd Boise ID 83705 Office: B & A Engrs Inc 619 Grove St Boise ID 83702

BRIGGS, CARROLL GREY, plant breeder; b. Glendale, Calif., June 27, 1928; s. Carroll Carlton and Ruby Elisabeth (Gray); m. Ardith Morrisseau, Nov. 22, 1953; children: Carroll Morrisseau, Chandler Carlton, Cymry Baranduin, Rowan Christopher. AA in Chemistry, Hartnell Coll., 1948; BS in Agrl. Edn., U. Calif., Davis, 1951, PhD in Genetics, 1962. Dir. Asgrow Research Ctr., Milpitas, Calif., 1967-72, br. mgr., 1972-74; facility designer Asgrow Research Ctr., San Juan Bautista, Calif., 1974-80; plant breeder Nickerson-Zwaan, Gilroy, Calif., 1980—. Author: (play) Wicked Enchantment, 1980; patentee tomato plants. Trustee Gavilan Coll., pres. bd. trustees 1981-82. Served with USN, 1951-52, with Res. 1952-55. Mem. Am. Name Soc., Sigma Xi. Club: Naval Inst. Introduced (with others) over 40 varieties of vegetables. Avocations: watercolors, poetry, theater. Home: 120 Hillside Rd San Juan Bautista CA 95045-1318 Office: Nickerson-Zwaan 40 Hornlein Gilroy CA 95021-1787

BRIGGS, CHANNING MATTHEW, former association executive; b. Fitchburg, Mass., Jan. 24, 1915; m. Virginia Boys; children—Jeffrey Lee, John Channing, Craig Matthew, Dean Rupert. B.S., George Williams Coll., 1948; M.A., U. Chgo., 1952, A.B.D., 1958. Instr., then asst. prof. social psychology and group work George Williams Coll., 1949-54, dir. group work and recreation div., 1954-56; assoc. gen. sec. YMCA, San Francisco, 1958-61; prof. sociology and anthropology Chabot Coll., San Leandro, Calif., 1961-62; dean of students, Portland State U., Oreg., 1962-70, dean admissions and records, 1970-74; controller Nat. Assn. Student Personnel Adminstrs., Portland, 1970-74, exec. dir., 1974-81, chmn., dir. Inst. Research and Devel., 1981-83; cons. Canisius Coll., Buffalo, 1979-82, Niagara U., N.Y., 1980-83, Broward Community Coll., Ft. Lauderdale, Fla., 1986. Author: (with Appleton, and Rhatigan) Pieces of Eight, 1978. Active San Mateo boundaries com., 1960-62, Portland United Way, 1972—; bd. dirs. Portland YMCA, 1964-71. Service to country as conscientious objector in civilian pub. service, 1942-46. Recipient Fred Turner award for service Nat. Assn. Student Personnel Adminstrs., 1981; Danforth grantee, 1956. Mem. Portland State U. Emeritii Profs. Orgn. (pres. 1986-87), Am. Assn. Univ. Adminstrs. (v.p. 1979-80, bd. dirs. 1978-81, 1970-76), Am. Soc. Social Workers, Adult Edn. Assn., Oreg. Deans Assn., Northwest Coll. Personnel Assn., Kappa Delta Pi. Democrat.

BRIGGS, CHARLES WESLEY, state official; b. Missoula, Mont., Sept. 26, 1948; s. Edwin Wesley and Bonnie Mae (Kratz) B.; m. K. Laurie Bernatz, 1971 (div. 1979); children—Elisabeth Ann, Amber Louise, Kevin Anthony. B.A., U. Mont., 1970, M.A., 1978. Communication liaison U.S. Senate, Washington, 1967; ref. librarian Pub. Library, Missoula, 1972-75; assoc. pastor Covenant Ch., Missoula, 1975-79; exec. dir. Missoula Advocacy, 1979-82; dir. Missoula Aging Services, 1982-83; aging coordinator Mont. Gov.'s Office, Helena, 1983—. Trustee Dist. No.1 Elem. Schs., Missoula, 1982-84; mem. State Foodbank Network Bd., Helena, 1984-87, Mont. Med. Care Adv. Council, Helena, 1984—; co-chmn. Internat. Yr. Disabled, Missoula, 1981; mem. Gov.'s Alcohol and Drug Commn., Helena, 1969-71; chmn. Mont. Energy Assistance Adv. Council, 1986—; chmn. commn. on aging and accessibility Mont. Episcopal Diocese; pres. bd. dirs. Poverello Ctr., Missoula, 1979; candidate for Missoula City Council, 1981; chmn. Mont. Episcopal Diocese Commn. on Aging & Accessibilty, 1986—; chmn., adv. council Mont. Low Income Energy Program, 1986—. Assn. Recipient Mont. Jefferson award Mont. TV Network, 1981; Silent Sentinel fellow U. Mont., 1969. Mem. Mont. Gerontology Soc., Am. Soc. Aging, Nat. Council on Aging, Mont. Sch. Bds. Assn. (mcpl. dir. 1982-84). Democrat. Office: Office of Gov Capitol Sta Helena MT 59620

BRIGGS, DAVID GEORGE, wood science educator; b. North Brookfield, Mass., July 3, 1943; s. Urban George and Georgia Kent (Linton) B.; m. Laurie Jane Mayer, Mar. 20, 1971; one child, Jeremy. BS, U. Mass., 1966; MF, Yale U., 1968; PhD, U. Wash., 1980. Market analyst Wash. Iron Works, Seattle, 1971-73; spl. asst. to dean Coll. Forest Resources, U. Wash., Seattle, 1973-80; asst. prof. wood sci. U. Wash., Seattle, 1980-85, assoc. prof., 1986—; staff officer Nat. Acad. Scis., Seattle, 1975-76; data mgr. Ctr. Internat. Trade in Forest Products, U. Wash., 1984—. Contbr. articles in profl. jours. Mem. Inst. Mgmt. Sci., Forest Products Research Soc., Soc. Wood Sci. and Tech., Sigma Xi, Xi Sigma Pi. Clubs: Am. Alpine (N.Y.C.); Mountaineers (Seattle). Avocations: mountaineering, malacology, running. Home: 25325 SE 133 Issaquah WA 98027 Office: U Wash Coll Forest Resources AR-10 Seattle WA 98195

BRIGGS, DINUS MARSHALL, agriculturist; b. Stillwater, Okla., Mar. 5, 1940; s. Hilton Marshall and Lillian (Dinusson) B.; m. June Elaine Wolf, Sept. 2, 1962; children: Denise, Deborah. BS, S.D. State U., 1962; MS, Iowa State U., 1969, PhD, 1971. Asst. pastor Stroudsburg (Pa.) Meth. Ch., 1962-64; grad. asst. Iowa State U., Ames, 1964-66, research assoc., 1966-70; asst. prof. N.C. State U., Raleigh, 1970-75; asst. dir. Ark. Agrl. Expt. Sta., Fayetteville, 1976-82; assoc. dir. N.Mex. Agrl. Expt. Sta., Las Cruces, 1982—. Co-author: Modern Breeds of Livestock, 1980. Mem. Poultry Sci. Assn. (resolutions com. 1972-73), Am. Assn. Animal Sci., World's Poultry Sci., Sigma Xi. Lodge: Rotary. Avocation: horses. Home: 1927 Francine Ct Las Cruces NM 88005 Office: NMex Agrl Experiment Sta PO Box 3BF Las Cruces NM 88003

BRIGGS, DONALD CLIFFORD, engingeering manager; b. Los Angeles, Sept. 19, 1932; s. Clifford Russell and Mildred Louise (Wainscott) B.; m. Sonja Louise Schwab, May 10, 1963; children: Robin, Tammie, Linda. BSME/MSME, Stanford U., 1960; MBA, U. Santa Clara, 1965, MSEE, 1973. Design engr. A. Research, Los Angeles, 1959-60; sr. engr. ITEK, Palo Alto, Calif., 1960-65; mgr. Ford Aerospace, Palo Alto, 1965—. Contbr. articles to profl. jours.; patentee in field. Committeeman Boy Scouts Am., Mountain View, Calif., 1965-72; bd. dirs. Stanford Hist. Soc., Palo Alto, 1981—. Served with USN, 1953-55. Fellow AIAA (assoc., committeeman tech. coms.), Early Dodge Club. Republican. Methodist. Lodges: Elks, Masons (Grand Master 1979). Avocations: antique autos, fishing, reading. Home: 2713 Doverton Sq Mountain View CA 94040 Office: Ford Aerospace & Communications 3939 Fabian Way Palo Alto CA 94303

BRIGGS, GEORGE SCOTT, lawyer; b. Amesbury, Mass., Jan. 10, 1944; s. Richard Clark and Marjorie (Lloyd) B.; m. Karen Lee Henry, Aug. 24, 1968; children: Amy Christine and Richard Clark. AB, Brown U., 1966; JD, Vanderbilt U., 1969. Bar: Colo. 1971, U.S. Dist. Ct. Colo. 1971, U.S. Ct. Appeals (10th cir.) 1974, U.S. Supreme Ct. 1975. Assoc. Evans, Peterson & Torbet, Colorado Springs, Colo., 1971; ptnr. Evans, Peterson, Torbet & Briggs, Colorado Springs, 1972-75, Evans & Briggs, Colorado Springs, 1975—. Organizer North Am. Def. Command Cans. Media Hockey Game, Colo. Springs, 1982. Served with U.S. Army, 1969-71. Mem. ABA, Assn. Trial Lawyers Am., Colo. Trial Lawyers Assn., Colo. Bar Assn., El Paso County Bar Assn. (trustee 1978-79, pres. elect 1986-87), Hort. Art Soc. (pres. 1983-84). Republican. Lodge: Lions (pres. 1978-79). Home: 1415 N Nevada Ave Colorado Springs CO 80907-7430 Office: Evans & Briggs 532 S Weber St Colorado Springs CO 80903-3906

BRIGGS, GERALD GREGORY, clinical pharmacist, consultant; b. Sacramento, Nov. 29, 1937; s. Clarence G. and Carol (Skemp) B.; m. Susan A. McLennan, Aug. 30, 1963; 1 child, Leslee Anne. AB in Chemistry, Calif. State U., Chico, 1964; B in Pharmacy, Wash. State U., 1968. Registered pharmacist, Calif., Alaska. Pharmacist Seward (Alaska) Drug, 1968-69; clin. pharmacist Meml. Hosp., Long Beach, Calif., 1969-77, 1979—; dir. clin. pharm. services Alcon Labs., Ft. Worth, 1977-79; v.p. Pharmacy Cons. Services, Huntington Beach, Calif., 1984-85, pres., 1985—; mem. sci. adv. bd. Amherst Med. Research Ctr., Newport Beach, Calif., 1985—. Author: Drugs in Pregnancy and Lactation, 1983, 2d rev. edit., 1986; contbr. chpts. to books, articles to profl. jours. Served with USNR, 1954-62. Recipient Hosp. Pharmacy award Hoffmann-La Roche, Inc., 1970. Mem. Sigma Xi. Republican. Lodges: Masons, Shriners. Avocations: hunting, fishing. Office: Meml Med Ctr Long Beach 2801 Atlantic Ave Long Beach CA 90801

BRIGGS, JAMES BERNARD, electronics manufacturing company executive, consulting engineer; b. Kewanee, Ill., Aug. 11, 1933; s. Bart Wayne and Eileen Katherine (Carney) B.; m. Barbara Lea Catton, Sept. 11, 1954; children—Patrick, Steven, Katherine, Teresa. B.S.E.E., U. Ill., 1955; M.S.E.E., U. So. Calif.-Los Angeles, 1957. Design engr. Lockheed Aircraft, Los Angeles, 1955-57; staff engr. Jet Propulsion Labs., Pasadena, Calif., 1960-63; head tech. staff Hoffman Electronics, El Monte, Calif., 1964-69; owner, mgr. J.B. Briggs & Assocs., Pasadena, 1969-82; pres., chief exec. officer TPL Communications, Inc., Gardena, Calif., 1982—; dir. 3dbm, Inc., Westlake Village, Calif. Patentee in electronic systems. Served to capt. USAF, 1957-60. Mem. IEEE. Lodge: Rotary Internat (pres. 1983-84). Home: 1722 La Barranca Rd La Canada CA 91011

BRIGGS, RICHARD JULIAN, research physicist; b. Shanghai, China, May 26, 1937; s. Julian Rosser and Olive May (Harris) B.; m. Kathleen Francis Malloy, Sept. 3, 1960; children: Susan Marie, Richard Julian Jr., Carolyn Elizabeth. BS, MS, MIT, 1961, PhD, 1964. Controlled fusion physicist Lawrence Livermore (Calif.) Nat. Lab., 1964-66, beam research program leader, 1972-84, dep. assoc. dir. beam research program, 1983-86, program dir., 1986—; from asst. prof. to assoc. prof. elec. engring. MIT, Cambridge, 1966-72; cons. Microwave Assocs., Burlington, Mass., 1967-70, AVCO Everett (Mass.) Research Lab., 1968-72, Energy Scis. Inc., 1969-72. Author: Electron Stream Interaction with Plasma, 1964; assoc. editor Physics of Fluids, 1973-76. Recipient Tech. Achievement award Strategic Def. Initiative Orgn., 1986. Fellow Am. Phys. Soc.; mem. Sigma Xi, Eta Kappa Nu, Tau Beta Pi. Democrat. Roman Catholic. Avocation: snow skiing. Home: 179 Town & Country Dr Danville CA 94526 Office: Lawrence Livermore Nat Lab PO Box 808 L-626 Livermore CA 94550

BRIGGS, WILLIAM MORSE, ski instructor; b. Augusta, Maine, Dec. 21, 1931; s. Henry Adie and Mary (Morse) B.; m. Julie Griffin, Nov. 25, 1963 (div. July 1968); m. Sabra Jean Palmer, Sept. 7, 1969 (div. Dec. 1979); 1 child, Berg Shanessa. Student, Dartmouth Coll., 1951-53; D in Religious Philosophy, Advanced Orgn., Los Angeles, 1979. Ski instr. Cannon Mountain Ski Area, Franconia, N.H., 1955-56; dir. ski sch. Sugarloaf Mountain Ski Area, Kingfield, Maine, 1957; prin., dir. Suicide Six Ski Sch., Woodstock, Vt., 1958-60; ski instr. Sugar Bowl Ski Area, Norden, Calif., 1961-65, Jackson Hole Ski Area, Teton Village, Wyo., 1966; prin., dir. Snow King Ski Sch., Jackson, Wyo., 1967—; Exum mountain guide Sch. Am. Mountaineering, Moose, Wyo., 1958-80; founder Great Am. Ski Sch., Jackson, 1971—; ski area mgr. Snow King Mountain, Jackson, 1981. Author/pub. The Skier's Manual I & II, 1976, 79, The Ski Dictionary, 1978; editor/pub. Crud and Corruption, 1961; contbr. articles to profl. jours. Originator Teton Tea Party, Grand Teton Nat. Park, 1958, co-originator Climber's Campground, 1959, Episcople Horizons Folk Festival, Jackson, 1966-69, Stagecoach Band, 1969—. Mem. Profl. Ski Instrs. Am. (founding), Internat. Assn. Scientologists (founding), Flag Artists Assn. (founding), Am. Mountain Guide Assn. (chmn. 1974-75). Republican. Mem. Ch. Scientology. Clubs: Dartmouth Mountaineering (Bugaboos, B.C., Can.) (explorer/surveyor 1951-54); Alpine Skiing (Jackson Hole) (founder/expedition leader 1955-61); Am. Alpine (N.Y.C.) (guide cert. 1974-75). Avocations: pioneering first ascents, ski descents, ski traverses, computerizing ski sch., playing country/western and folk music. Home: 295 E Snow King Ave Mail Box 427 Jackson WY 83001 Office: Great Am Ski Sch 350 E Snow King Box SKI Jackson WY 83001

BRIGGS, WINSLOW RUSSELL, plant physiologist; b. St. Paul, Apr. 29, 1928; s. John DeQuedville and Marjorie (Winslow) B.; m. Ann Morrill, June 30, 1955; children: Caroline, Lucia, Marion. B.A., Harvard U., 1951, M.A., 1952, Ph.D., 1956. Instr. biol. scis. Stanford (Calif.) U., 1955-57, asst. prof., 1957-62, asso. prof., 1962-66, prof., 1966-67; prof. biology Harvard U., 1967-73; dir. dept. plant biology Carnegie Instn. of Washington, Stanford, 1973—. Author: (with others) Life on Earth, 1973; Asso. editor: (with others) Annual Review of Plant Physiology, 1961-72; editor (with others), 1972—; Contbr. (with others) articles on plant growth and devel. and photobiology to profl. jours. Recipient Alexander von Humboldt U.S. sr. scientist award, 1984-85; John Simon Guggenheim fellow, 1973-74, Deutsche Akademie der Naturforscher Leopoldina, 1986. Fellow AAAS; mem. Am. Soc. Plant Physiologists (pres. 1975-76), Calif. Bot. Soc. (pres. 1976-77), Nat. Acad. Scis., Am. Acad. Arts and Scis., Am. Inst. Biol. Scis. (pres. 1980-81), Am. Soc. Photbiology, Bot. Soc. Am., Nature Conservancy, Deutsche Akademie der Naturforscher Leopoldina, Sigma Xi. Home: 480 Hale St Palo Alto CA 94301 Office: Carnegie Inst Wash Dept of Plant Biology 290 Panama St Stanford CA 94305

BRIGHAM, LANCE NATALE, orthopedic surgeon. BA in Chemistry, U. Wash., 1968, MD, 1972. Diplomate Am. Bd. Orthopedic Surgery. Resident in gen. surgery N.Y. Hosp. Cornell Med. Ctr., N.Y.C., 1972-74; resident in orthopedic surgery Hosp. Spl. Surgery, N.Y.C., 1974-76; orthopedic surgeon Seattle Orthopedic and Fracture Clinic, 1976—; cons. Family Practice Clinic, Providence Hosp., Seattle; clin. instr. family practice U. Wash., Seattle, Dept. Orthopedics, U. Wash., Seattle; resident teaching orthopedic dept. Swedish Hosp., Seattle. Fellow ACS, Am. Acad. Orthopedic Surgeons; mem. King County Med. Soc., Wash. State Med. Assn., Wash. State Orthopedic Assn., Western Orthopedic Assn., Am. Coll. Sports Medicine, Arthroscopy Assn. N.Am., Internat. Arthroscopy Assn., Seattle Surgical Soc. Office: Seattle Orthopedic and Fracture 801 Broadway 10th Floor Seattle WA 98122

BRIGHT, DONALD BOLTON, environmental consultant; b. Ventura, Calif., Nov. 28, 1930; s. Claude Wilson and Ruby Thelma (Bolton) B.; m. Patricia Jean McLaughlin, Nov. 25, 1955; children: Debra Ann, Steven Allan. BA in Zoology, U. So. Calif., 1952, MS in Biology, 1957, PhD in Biology, 1967; postdoctoral studies, Ariz. State U., 1974. Instr. Fullerton (Calif.) Coll., 1960-67; prof., chmn. dept. biol. scis. Calif. State U., Fullerton, 1967-77; dir. commerce Port of Long Beach, Calif., 1977-78, dir. environ. affairs, 1975-78; exec. v.p. EFS, Inc., Los Angeles, 1978-79; pres. Bright & Assocs., Anaheim, Calif., 1979—; Mem. Marine Sci. Coast Guard Adv. Com., Washington, 1977-80. Editor: Proc. National Magazine Science Edmc., 1970, Proc. Southern California Coastal Zone Supervisor, 1972; sci. advisor Am. Scientist mag., 1975-77; contbr. articles to profl. jours. Chmn. Calif. Regulatory Coastal Commn., Long Beach, 1973-75. Served to 1st lt. U.S. Army, 1952-55. Grantee NSF, 1969-75. Mem. Am. Inst. Planners, So. Calif. Acad. Sci. (v.p. 1975-78, fellow 1975), Western Soc. Naturalists, Sierra Club, Sigma Xi, Phi Sigma. Democrat. Presbyterian. Avocations: photography, golf, woodwork, rare books, traveling. Home: 921 Finnell Way Placentia CA 92670 Office: Bright & Assocs 1200 N Jefferson Suite B Anaheim CA 92807

BRIGHT, JAMES HUNTER, mining corporation executive; b. Webster, S.D., Sept. 15, 1927; s. Hunter Edwin and Malvida Sofia (Gustavson) B.; children—Jenni Sue Bright Smith, Marin June. Geol. Engr., Colo. Sch. Mines, 1952. Geologist, Anaconda Corp., Salt Lake City, 1952-54, Kennecott Corp., Spokane, Wash., 1954-55, Union Carbide Corp., Reno, 1956-62; exploration mgr. Asbestos Corp. Ltd., Vancouver, B.C., Can., 1963-67; U.S. exploration mgr. Noranda Mines Ltd., Reno, 1967-68; pres. Nev. Resources Inc., Reno, 1968-87, mining cons. and investor, Reno, 1987— . Served to 1st lt. AUS, 1944-48, PTO. Mem. Soc. Econ. Geologists, AIME. Republican. Lodges: Masons, Shriners. Home: 2875 Idlewild Dr #114 Reno NV 89509

BRIGHT, LYN EDWARD, packaging machinery manufacturing company executive; b. Sacramento, Apr. 7, 1947; s. Calvin Edward and Marjorie O. (Hensley) B.; BS, Brigham Young U., 1969; MBA, U. So. Calif., 1971; m. Cheryl Ann Varone, Aug. 22, 1974; children: Parker Hensley, Lyndsay Varone. Prodn. asst. Bright Foods, Inc., Turlock, Calif., 1963-69; project mgr. F.M. Stamper Co., Turlock, 1969-70; with Wilson & Co., Buenos Aires, Argentina, 1968; asst. to pres., dir. A G I, Modesto, Calif., 1971-72; gen. mgr., cons. Woodside Properties, Turlock, 1972-75; gen. mgr., dir. B & H Mfg., Ceres, Calif., 1975—; pres., dir. B & H Europe; dir. Valley Sales, Inc.; cons. CLS Investment. Dir. Yosmite Council Boy Scouts Am., 1984—. Republican. Mormon.

BRIGHT, PETER BOWMAN, engineer, researcher; b. Gallipolis, Ohio, Dec. 27, 1937; s. Warren Harris and Elizabeth (Bowman) B.; divorced; children: Alicia Laurel, Debra Elaine, Michael Murray. BS, Antioch Coll., Yellow Springs, Ohio, 1960; PhD, U. Chgo., 1966. Asst. research biomathematician UCLA, 1973-75; cons. The Aerospace Corp., Los Angeles, 1975-79, mem. tech. staff, 1980-84, project engr., 1984—; asst. prof. math. U. Calif., Northridge, 1977-79; project dir. U. So. Calif., Los Angeles, 1979-80. Contbr. numerous articles to profl. jours. Mem. AIAA, Computer and Reliability Socs. of IEEE (vice chmn. seminars 1983-86, spl. recognition 1985), Soc. Math. Biology, Computer Soc. (software reliability measurement working group, steering com.), Sigma Xi. Home: 39 Sunset Ave Apt 405 Venice CA 90291 Office: The Aerospace Corp 2350 El Segundo Blvd El Segundo CA 90245

BRIGHTUP, JOY ARLEEN, clinical psychologist; b. Los Angeles, Mar. 19, 1952; d. John Anthony and Margaret Ann (Ledwinka) Sielen; m. Vern Eugene Brightup II, May 22, 1982; 1 child, Steven John. B.A. in Psychol., Pitzer Coll., Claremont, Calif., 1973; M.A. in Theology, Fuller Theol. Sem., Pasadena, Calif., 1978, Ph.D. in Psychology, 1980. Lic. psychologist, Calif. Psychology intern Pasadena Community Counseling Clinic, 1978-79, VA Hosp., Loma Linda, Calif., 1979-80; clin. psychologist Live Oak Counseling Ctr., Glendora, Calif., 1980-85, Imperial Counseling Ctr., Fullerton, Calif., 1982-85, Birchbrook Counseling Services, Brea, Calif., 1985—. Author: Increasing Self-Esteem Through Assertiveness Training in a Management Population, 1980. Co-dir., counseling ministry 1st Evangelical Free Ch., Fullerton, 1983—. Mem. Am. Psychol. Assn., Calif. Psychol. Assn. Office: Birchbrook Counseling Services 3000 Birch St Suite 101 Brea CA 92621

BRILL, LESLEY W., literature and film studies educator; b. Chgo., Sept. 3, 1943; s. Walter Henry and Fay (Trolander) B.; m. Megan Parry, Jan. 18, 1970; children: Benjamin, Calista. BA, U. Chgo., 1965; MA, SUNY, Binghamton, 1967; Ph.D., Rutgers U., 1971. Asst. prof. English U. Colo., Boulder, 1970-80, assoc. prof., 1981—, chmn. dept. English, 1981-85, grad. dir., 1985—; vis. lectr. U. Kent, Canterbury, Eng., 1978-79; vis. prof. U. Paul Valery, Montpellier, France, 1984. Contbr. articles on lit. and film to profl. jours. Rockefeller Found. fellow, 1977-78. Mem. MLA, Soc. Cinema Studies. Office: U Colo Dept English Box 226 Boulder CO 80309-0226

BRILLA, LORRAINE R., physiology educator; b. Scranton, Pa., Oct. 10, 1955; d. Henry Vincent Brilla and Rosemary Angela (Ross) Gaffrey. BS, Pa. State U., 1976, MS, 1978; PhD, U. Oreg., 1983. Exercise physiologist St. Francis Heart Ctr., Port Washington, N.Y., 1977-78; dir. cardiac services Lewistown (Pa.) Hosp., 1978-80; echocardiographer McKenzie-Willamette Hosp., Springfield, Oreg., 1980-84; instr. U. Oreg., Eugene, 1980-83; asst. prof. Western Wash. U., Bellingham, 1985—; lectr. Ballarat (Australia) Coll. A. Edn., 1984-85; dir. adult fitness program, Bellingham, 1985—; dir. Ctr. for Fitness Evaluation, Bellingham, 1985—. Contbr. articles to profl. jours. Grantee NSF, 1976, Australian Dept. Sports, Tourism, and Recreation, 1984, Australian Nat. Rowing Team, 1985; named Most Valuable Forward Eugene Women's Rugby Club, 1983-84. Mem. Am. Coll. Sport Medicine, Australian Sport Medicine Fedn., Am. Alliance for Health, Phys. Edn., Recreation and Dance, Assn. Fitness in Bus. Clubs: Eugene Women's RFU (pres. 1982-83); WWU Women's RFU (Bellingham) (union rep. 1986—). Avocations: sporting endeavors, jogging, hiking, rugby, traveling. Office: Western Wash U 26 Carver Bellingham WA 98225

BRILLIANT, ASHLEIGH ELLWOOD, writer, cartoonist, publisher, educator; b. London, Dec. 9, 1933; s. Victor and Amelia (Adler) B.; came to U.S., 1956, naturalized, 1969; B.A. with honors, Univ. Coll., London, 1955; M.A. in Edn., Claremont Grad. Sch., 1957; Ph.D. in Am. History, U. Calif., Berkeley, 1964; m. Dorothy Low Tucker, June 28, 1968. Tchr. English, Hollywood High Sch., Los Angeles, 1956-57; teaching asst., reader in history U. Calif., Berkeley, 1960-63; asst. prof. history Central Oreg. Coll., Bend, 1964-65, Floating Campus div. Chapman Coll., Orange, Calif., 1965-67; entertainer in coffeehouses, outdoor speaker San Francisco, 1967-68; syndicated cartoonist, dir. Brilliant Enterprises, pub. and licensing, San Francisco, also Santa Barbara, Calif., 1967—; creator Pot-Shots postcards, T-shirts, cocktail napkins, tote-bags, other items; mem. faculty Sonoma State U., Santa Barbara City Coll. Claremont Grad. Sch. scholar, 1956, Haynes fellow, 1962, Panama-Pacific fellow, 1963. Recipient Raymond B. Bragg award, 1987. Mem. Newspaper Comics Council, No. Calif. Cartoonists Assn., Mensa. Jewish. Author: I May Not Be Totally Perfect, But Parts of Me Are Excellent, And Other Brilliant Thoughts, 1979; I Have Abandoned My Search for Truth and Am Now Looking for a Good Fantasy, 1980; Appreciate Me Now and Avoid the Rush, 1981; I Feel Much Better Now That I've Given Up Hope, 1984; All I Want Is A Warm Bed and A Kind Word, and Unlimited Power, 1985, Just When I Was Getting Used to Yesterday, Along Came Today, 1987. Home and office: 117 W Valerio St Santa Barbara CA 93101

BRIMHALL, JOHN CLARK, editor, composer, arranger; b. Huntington Park, Calif., Nov. 22, 1928; s. John Clark and Nora Louise (Baffa) B.; m. Virgin Mae Ravain, Apr. 1, 1951; children—James, Mary, Anthony. Mus.B. cum laude, Loyola U., 1950; M.A., Calif. State U.-San Francisco, 1952. Tchr., Corcoran (Calif.) High Sch., 1953-55; supr. music Corcoran Union Sch. Dists., 1955-56; instr. Porterville (Calif.) Coll., 1956-59, Orange Coast Coll., Costa Mesa, Calif., 1959-61; chief editor Hansen Publs., Inc., Miami Beach, Fla., 1962-78; pres. Brimhall Publs., Inc., Las Vegas, 1978—; creative dir. Columbia Pictures Publs., Miami, 1986—; composer, arranger, numerous books, sheet music; composer primary series John Brimhall Piano Method, John Brimhall Organ Method. Recipient La Croix de Commandeur, Merite et Devouement Francais (France), 1973. Mem. ASCAP, Am. Coll. Musicians, Am. Fedn. Musicians, Music Educators Nat. Conf. Home: 7205 Mira Vista St Las Vegas NV 89120

BRIMMER, CLARENCE ADDISON, judge; b. Rawlins, Wyo., July 11, 1922; s. Clarence Addison and Geraldine (Zingsheim) B.; m. Emily O. Docken, Aug. 2, 1953; children: Geraldine Ann, Philip Andrew, Andrew Howard, Elizabeth Ann. B.A., U. Mich., 1944, J.D., 1947. Bar: Wyo. 1948. Practice in Rawlins, 1948-71, mcpl. judge, 1948-54; U.S. commr., magistrate 1963-71; atty. gen. Wyo. Cheyenne, 1971-74; U.S. atty. 1975; chief U.S. dist. judge Wyo. Dist. Cheyenne, 1975—. Sec. Rawlins Bd. Pub. Utilities, 1954-66, Gov.'s Com. on Wyo. Water, 1963-65; del. Rep. Nat. Conv., 1956; chmn. Wyo. Rep. Platform Com., 1966; sec. Wyo. Rep. Com., 1966, chmn., 1967-71, Rep. gubernatorial candidate, 1974; Trustee Rocky Mountain Mineral Law Found., 1963-75. Served with USAAF, 1945-46. Mem. ABA, Wyo. Bar Assn., Am. Judicature Soc., Laramie County Bar Assn., Carbon County Bar Assn. Episcopalian. Clubs: Masons, Shriners. Office: US District Court PO Box 985 Cheyenne WY 82003

BRINKMAN, CORNELIUS MARIA, project engineer; b. Amsterdam, The Netherlands, July 5, 1951; came to U.S., 1976; s. Jacobus Franciscus and Lucie Eulalie (De Meurichy) B. BSME, U. Pretoria, South Africa, 1973; MSME, U. Ill., 1978. Registered profl. engr., Calif., Ill. Project engr. Assoc. Air, Durban, South Africa, 1973-75; research asst. U. Ill., Champaign, 1976-77; mech. engr. Enercom, Ltd., Evanston, Ill., 1977-79; project mgr. Schmidt, Garden & Erickson, Chgo., 1979-83; project engr. LSW Engrs., San Diego, 1983—. Mem. ASHRAE. Avocations: running, backpacking, mountaineering, fgn. travel, sailing. Home: 4730 Noyes St Apt 413 San Diego CA 92109 Office: LSW Engrs 5560 Ruffin Rd 1 San Diego CA 92123

BRINKMAN, WILLIAM FRANK, physicist, research executive; b. Washington, Mo., July 20, 1938; s. William F. Sr. and Mildred A. (Bocklege) B.; m. B. Carol, Aug. 27, 1960; children: David, Curtis. BS, U. Mo., 1960, PhD, 1966. Postdoctoral fellow Oxford U., 1966; mem. staff Bell Labs., Murray Hill, N.J., 1966-72, dept. head, 1972-74, dir., 1974-84; v.p. research Sandia Nat. Labs., Albuquerque, 1984—. Contbr. numerous articles on theoretical physics to sci. jours. Fellow Am. Phys. Soc., AAAS; mem. Nat. Acad. Sci. (chmn. 8-vol. report Physics Through the 1990's). Home: 5007 Calle de Luna NE Albuquerque NM 87111 Office: Sandia Nat Lab PO Box 5800 Albuquerque NM 87185

BRINKS, KENNETH JOHN HENRY, milling company executive; b. Quincy, Ill., May 18, 1935; s. William Michael and Grace Marie (Bergman) B.; m. Sharon Lee DeWitt, Dec. 27, 1957 (div. 1972); m. Darlene Mary Ann Ghelfi, Apr. 7, 1973; children—Vonnie, Danney, Sheri, Bradley. Student U. Ill., 1953-55; B.A., Quincy Coll., 1958. Purchasing agt. Electric Wheel div. Firestone Tire, Quincy, 1959-60; credit corr. Moorman Mfg. Co., Quincy, 1959-63; office mgr. Bell Grain & Milling Inc. Subs. Moorman Mfg. Co., Pomona, Calif., 1963-64; sec., 1964-65, dir., 1965—; treas., sec., 1965-73, v.p. and treas., 1973-83, exec. v.p. and treas., 1983—; sec. Bellmilling Corp. (subs.), Escondido, Calif., 1964-65, treas., sec., 1965-73, pres., chief exec. officer, 1973—; div., chmn. Marshall's Pullets Inc.. Bd. dirs., former treas. Nehi-Kai Villas Homeowners Assn., pres. 1986—. Served to sgt. 1st class U.S. Army. Mem. Toastmasters (treas., v.p., pres.). Lodge: Lions (treas., div.). Office: Bell Grain & Milling 17771 Highway 215 Perris CA 92370

BRINTON, RICHARD KIRK, marketing executive; b. Hanover, Pa., Apr. 21, 1946; s. James Henry and Mabel (Adelung) B.; m. Joan Marita Ayo, Mar. 21, 1970; children: Katherine, Mark, Michael. BA in Liberal Arts, Pa. State U., 1968, BS in Indsl. Engring., 1968. Lic. profl. engr., Ohio. From systems engr. to dir. mktg. Accuray Corp., Columbus, Ohio, 1968-82; group systems engr. to dir. mktg. Accuray Corp., London, 1982-84; internat. sales mgr. Flow Systems, Seattle, 1984, v.p. mktg., 1985—. Home: 18137 149th Ave SE Renton WA 98058 Office: Flow Systems Inc 21440 68th Ave S Kent WA 98032

BRISBIN, ROBERT EDWARD, insurance company executive; b. Bklyn., Feb. 13, 1946. BSBA, San Fancisco State U., 1968. Cert. safety exec. Field rep. Index Research, San Mateo, Calif., 1969-82; mgr. loss control Homeland Ins. Co., San Jose, Calif., 1982-87; ins. exec. Morris and Dee Ins. Agy., San Luis Obispo, Calif., 1987—; prin., cons. San Francisco, 1975—; mgt. cons. Robert E. Brisbin & Assoc., Foster City, Calif., 1972—. Author: A Guide to Optimal Health, 1986; composer: Country Songs and Broken Dreams, 1978, America the Land of Liberty, 1986. Mem. Am. Soc. Safety Engrs. Republican. Avocations: photography, flying, scuba diving, hiking. Address: PO Box 4386 Foster City CA 94404

BRISTOL, ROBERT LEONARD, dentist; b. Silverton, Oreg., June 26, 1923; s. Ny Orin and Marie (Jones) B.; m. Vivian Marie Pearson, Feb. 20, 1949; children—Ann Marie, Roger, Karen. B.S., U. Oreg., 1948; D.M.D., U. Oreg. Dental Sch., 1953. Pvt. practice dentistry, Bend, Oreg., 1953-87. Mayor, City of Bend, 1969; mem. Bend City Commn., 1967-74, Bend Urban Area Planning Commn., 1974—. Served with USNR, 1942-45. Named Outstanding Citizen, Bend Jaycees, 1965. Fellow Am. Coll. Dentists; mem. Pierre Fauchard Acad., Acad. Gen. Dentistry (master), Bend C of C (pres. 1965), Delta Sigma Delta. Republican. Episcopalian. Lodges: Rotary (pres. 1963-64), Masons. Address: 63281 Cherokee Ln Bend OR 97701

BRISTOL, WANDA (JUNE) MASON, nurse, therapist; b. Ft. Cobb, Okla., Jan. 26, 1931; d. Alva Albert and Clara Belle (Bowman) Mason; A.A. diploma of nursing San Bernardino Valley Coll., 1951; B.S. (Polio Fund scholar), Calif. State U., Los Angeles, 1961, M.A., 1968; M.S. (USPHS grantee), Loma Linda U., 1964; M.S.Ed., U. So. Calif., 1976, postgrad., 1976—; m. Carl Eugene Bristol, Nov. 18, 1951 (div.); children—Bruce Edward, Brian Keith, Barry Lee. Staff nurse San Bernardino County Hosp., 1951-52, head nurse, 1952-59; staff nurse San Bernardino Community Hosp., 1954; spl. staff nurse Riverside (Calif.) Health Nurse, 1959-60; instr. Mt. San Antonio Coll., 1961-62; sch. nurse Bloomington (Calif.) Sch. Dist. unified with Colton Joint Unified Sch. Dist., 1963—; pvt. practice marriage, family, and child counseling, Rialto, Calif., 1979—; also pvt. practice hypnotherapy; psychodrama practitioner; vol. counselor. Health clinic. Bloomington Community Services Council, including establishment dental clinic, 1964-67; mem. Colton Children's Services Council, 1967—; mem. mental health task force Los Angeles chpt. Calif. NOW, 1978-79; bd. dirs. Widowed Persons Service. Mem. Am. Nurses Assn., Calif., Nurses Assn., Colton Educators, Calif. Tchrs. Assn., Nat. Tchrs. Assn., Am. Assn. Marriage and Family Therapists, Calif. Assn. Marriage and Family Therapists, Am. Psychol. Assn., Calif. State Psychol. Assn., Am. Soc. Group Psychotherapy and Psychodrama. Republican. Methodist. Contbr. articles to profl. jours. Home and office: 1485 N Mulberry Rialto CA 92376

BRITT, JAMES DOUGLAS, photographer; b. San Francisco, Oct. 5, 1937; s. James J. and Helen Elisabeth (Congdon) B.; m. Harriet Mirka Melendy, June 2, 1964 (div. Feb. 1985); children: Jody Elisa, Melendy Anne. BA, U. Wash., 1959. Singer, entertainer Los Angeles, 1959-72; asst. art dir. Motown Records, Los Angeles, 1972-75; chief photographer ABC TV, Los Angeles, N.Y.C., 1975-79; freelance photographer specializing in entertainment industry and advt. Los Angeles, 1979—; cons. E. Leitz Inc., Rockleigh, N.J., 1982—, Wetzlar, Germany, 1982—. Contbr. photographs to mags. Recipient Key Arts award The Reporter, Los Angeles, 1979. Mem. Am. Soc. Mag. Photographers. Democrat. Roman Catholic. Avocation: tennis. Home and Office: 140 N La Brea Los Angeles CA 90036

BRITTAIN, JERRY LEE, clinical psychologist, naval officer; b. Bossier City, La., Aug. 4, 1947; s. Melvin Houston and Reba Cleo (Eaves) B.; B.A. in Psychology, Villanova U., 1972; B.S. in Biology, Centenary Meth. Coll., 1974; M.A. in Counseling Psychology, La. Tech., 1975; Ph.D. in Clin. Psychology, Calif. Sch. Profl. Psychology, 1978; lic. clin. psychologist, Calif. Psychologist, medic U.S. Army, Valley Forge, Pa., 1969-72; med. intern Mental Health Ctr., Shreveport, La., 1975; pre-doctoral intern Calif. Mens Colony, San Luis Obispo, 1975-76; doctoral intern Visalia (Calif.) Community Counseling Ctr., 1976-77, Fresno County (Calif.) Mental Health Ctr., 1977-78; commd. lt. U.S. Navy, 1979; chief psychologist Naval Drug Rehab. Ctr., San Diego, 1979-83, Naval Hosp., Naples, Italy, 1983—; instr., pvt. practice psychology, San Diego. Mem. Am. Psychol. Assn. Republican. Mem. Ch. of Nazarene. Contbr. articles to profl. jours.

BRITTAN, PATRICK JOHN, chemical engineer; b. Alliance, Neb., June 18, 1958; s. John J. and Edith (Reidy) B. BS in Chemistry, St. John's U., 1980; BS in Chem. Engring., U. Wyo., 1982. Process engr. Western Filter Co., Denver, 1983—. Office: Western Filter Co PO Box 16323 Denver CO 80216

BRITTEN, ROY JOHN, biophysicist; b. Washington, Oct. 1, 1919; s. Rollo Herbert and Marion (Hale) B.; m. Jacqueline Reid, 1986; children: Gregory, Kenneth. BS, U. Va., 1941; PhD, Princeton U., 1951. Staff mem. dept. terrestrial magnetism Carnegie Instn., Washington, 1951—; sr. research assoc. Calif. Inst. Tech., Corona del Mar, 1973-81. Inventor in field. Named Disting. Carnegie Sr. Research Assoc. in Biology, 1981—. Fellow Am. Acad. Arts and Scis., Nat. Acad. Arts and Scis.; mem. Nat. Acad. Scis. Discoverer repeated DNA Sequences in genomes of higher organisms. Office: Calif Inst of Tech Div Biol Kerchhoff Marine Lab 101 Dahlia Ave Corona del Mar CA 92625

BRITTON, DAVID CARL, hotel executive; b. Dallas, Oreg., Aug. 7, 1946; s. Robert Elwin and Corinne Ana (Applequist) B.; m. Rosalind Kathryn Thomas, Nov. 30, 1947; 1 dau., Tara Marie. Student San Diego State U., 1964-65. Cert. hotel adminstr. Asst. mgr. Las Vegas Marina Hotel, Fred Harvey, Inc., 1974-75; gen. mgr. The Inn at the Park, Wrather Hotels div., Anaheim, Calif., 1975-80, v.p. hotel ops. RMS Queen Mary, Long Beach, Calif., 1980-81; gen. mgr. Ramada Hotel, Beverly Hills, Calif., 1981-82; resort and club mgr. Coto de Caza Resort, Tracubo Canyon, Calif., 1982-83; exec. v.p. Gateway Mgmt., Inc., Riverside, Calif., 1983—. Served with USAF, 1965-68. Mem. Am. Hotel and Motel Assn., Nat. Tour Assn., Calif. Hotel and Motel Assn. Hotel Sales Mgmt. Assn. (past territorial dir. internat.), Single Action Shooting Soc., NRA, Calif. Rifle and Pistol Assn.,

Nat. Assn. Lic. Firearms Dealers, Cousteau Soc., Sierra Club. Democrat. Office: Gateway Mgmt Inc 6865 Airport Dr Riverside CA 92504

BRITTON, M(ELVIN) C(REED), JR., physician, rheumatologist; b. San Francisco, Apr. 11, 1935; s. Melvin Creed and Mathilda Carolyn (Epeneter) B.; m. Mary Elizabeth Phillips, Nov. 2, 1957; children: Elizabeth Carolynne, Lisa Marie. AB, Dartmouth Coll., 1957, MS, 1958; MD, Harvard U., 1960. Diplomate Am. Bd. Internal Medicine, Am. Bd. Rheumatology, Am. Bd. Quality Assurance. Resident Dartmouth Coll. Sch. Medicine, Hanover, N.H., 1964-67; fellow Harvard U. Sch. Medicine, Boston, 1967-69; ptnr. Palo Alto (Calif.) Med. Clinic, 1969—; Pres. med. staff Stanford (Calif.) U. Med. Ctr., 1985-87, mem. med. staff bd., 1969—. Contbr. articles to med. jours. Pres. Found. for Med. Care Santa Clara County, Campbell, 1983—. Fellow ACP, Am. Rheumatism Assn. (bd.dirs. 1986); mem. AMA, Calif. Med. Assn., Santa Clara County Med. Soc. (pres. 1980-81, Board Service award 1981), Arthritis Found. No. Calif. (chmn. bd. dirs 1984-87, Disting. Service award 1985). Republican. Presbyterian. Clubs: Vintners (San Francisco), Commonwealth (San Francisco). Avocations: skiing, (v.p. 1975-78), traveling, enology. Office: Palo Alto Med Clinic 300 Homer Ave Palo Alto CA 94301-2794

BRITTON, THOMAS WARREN, JR., management consultant; b. Pawhuska, Okla., June 16, 1944; s. Thomas Warren and Helen Viola (Haynes) B.; B.S. in Mech. Engring., Okla. State U., 1966, M.S. in Indsl. Engring. and Mgmt., 1968; m. Deborah Ann Mansour, Oct. 20, 1973; children—Natalie Dawn, Kimberly Ann. Cons., Arthur Young & Co., Los Angeles, 1968-72, mgr., 1972-76, prin., 1976-79, partner, 1979—; office dir. mgmt. services dept., Orange County, Calif., 1980—; lectr. in field. Mem. City of San Dimas Creative Growth Bd., 1976-77, chmn. planning commn., 1977-83; trustee World Affairs Council of Orange County, 1980; benefactor, founders com., trustee South Coast Repertory Theater; trustee Providence Speech and Hearing Ctr.; mem. devel. com. U. Calif.-Irvine Med. Sch.; chmn. Costa Mesa Arts Council. Served to capt. USAR, 1971—. Cert. mgmt. cons. Mem. Los Angeles Inst C.P.A.s, Mgmt. Adv. Services Com., Pacific Coast Electric Assn., Pacific Coast Gas Assn., Am. Inst. Indsl. Engrs., Greater Irvine Indsl. League, Okla. State Alumni Assn. Clubs: Univ. of Los Angeles, Via Verde Country, Jonathan, Ridgeline Country, Santa Ana Country. Home: 18982 Wildwood Circle Villa Park CA 92667

BRIXNER, MYRON JOSEPH, real estate firm executive; b. Seattle, Mar. 26, 1948; s. Myron Raymond and Alvina Anne (Krininger) B.; m. Renee Marie Petrut, Aug. 21, 1976; children: Michael Christian, Nicholas Paul. B.A. in Polit. Sci., Seattle U., 1970; J.D., Gonzaga U., 1974; licensed realtor, Wash. Quality control mgr. Petschl's Quality Meats, Seattle, 1978-80, owner-ptnr., v.p.; property mgr. Ewing and Clark, Inc., Seattle, 1978-80, owner-ptnr., v.p.; sr. v.p., 1983-86; with Martin Selig Real Estate, 1987—. Actor numerous TV commls. and indsl. films; voice-over work in TV and radio. Coach, agt. Magnolia Youth Assn., Seattle. Mem. Seattle Bd. Realtors, AFTRA, Seattle U. Alumni Assn. Roman Catholic. Clubs: Washington Athletic, Seattle Mariners, RBI (Seattle).

BRKLJACK, MARY KAY, interior designer; b. Savanna, Ill., Oct. 19, 1961; d. Stephen and Marie B. BFA, No. Ill. U., 1983. Designer IDG Inc., Palo Alto, Calif., 1984-85, C.A.L., Santa Clara, Calif., 1985—. Mem. Inst. Bus. Designers, Nat. Trust Hist. Soc. Home: 21 Willow Rd 25 Menlo Park CA 94025

BROAD, ELI, housing and insurance company executive; b. N.Y.C., June 6, 1933; s. Leon and Rebecca (Jacobson) B.; m. Edythe Lois Lawson, Dec. 19, 1954; children: Jeffrey Alan, Gary Steven. B.A. cum laude in Bus. Adminstrn, Mich. State U., 1954. Acct. 1954-56; asst. prof. Detroit Inst. Tech. 1956-57; co-founder Kaufman & Broad, Inc., Los Angeles, 1957; pres., chmn. Kaufman & Broad, Inc., 1957-72, part-time chmn., 1973-75, chmn., chief exec. officer, 1976—; chmn., chief exec. officer Sun Life Ins. Co. Am., Balt., 1976-79; dir. Sun Life Ins. Co. Am., 1979—; chmn. Sun Life Group Am., Atlanta, 1978—; dir. Fed. Nat. Mortgage Assn., 1984—, Anchor Nat. Life Ins. Co., 1986—; past dir. Verex Corp.; real estate adv. bd. Citibank, N.Y.C. Dir. devel. bd. Mich. State U., 1969-72; mem. Nat. Indsl. Pollution Control Council, 1970-73; co-founder Council Housing Producers; chmn. Los Angeles Mayor's Housing Policy Com., 1974-75; del. Democratic Nat. Conv., 1968; pres. Calif. Non-Partisan Voter Registration Found., 1971; bd. dirs. Nat. Energy Found., 1979—, NCCJ, YMCA, Los Angeles United Way, Haifa U.; bd. dirs., trustee Windward Sch.; mem. acquisition com. Los Angeles County Mus. Art, 1979-81; exec. com. Internat. Forum for Los Angeles World Affairs Council; exec. com., bd. fellows Claremont Colls.; adv. bd. Inst. Internat. Edn.; chmn. founding bd. trustees Mus. Contemporary Art, Los Angeles, 1980—; vis. com. U. Calif. at Los Angeles Grad. Sch. Mgmt.; trustee City of Hope, Calif. State Univs. and Colls.; trustee Pitzer Coll., 1979—, chmn. bd. trustees, 1972-79. Recipient Man of Year award City of Hope, 1965; Golden Plate award Am. Acad. Achievement, 1971; Humanitarian award NCCJ, 1977; Housing Man of Yr. Nat. Housing Conf., 1979; Am. Heritage award Anti-Defamation League, 1984. Mem. Beta Alpha Psi. Clubs: Regency, Hillcrest Country (Los Angeles). Home: 1 Oakmont Dr Los Angeles CA 90049 Office: Kaufman & Broad 11601 Wilshire Blvd Los Angeles CA 90025

BROADBENT, H. SMITH, chemistry educator, retired; b. Snowflake, Ariz., July 21, 1920; s. Hyrum Broadbent and Lorana Smith; m. Katherine Mary Miller, Sept. 9, 1942; children: Karen, David S., Justin M., Camille, Nathan E., Thomas A., Marla, Daniel H. BS, Brigham Young U., 1942; PhD, Iowa State U., 1946. Postdoctoral fellow Harvard U., Cambridge, Mass., 1946-47; asst. prof. chemistry Brigham Young U., Provo, Utah, 1947-49, assoc. prof., 1949-52, prof., 1952-85, prof. emeritus, 1985—; group leader med. chemistry div. Schering Corp., Bloomfield, N.J., 1958-59; vis. scientist Kettering Labs., Yellow Springs, Ohio, 1962-63, Eastman Kodak, Rochester, N.Y., 1970-71, Kuwait U., 1980, Konstanz U., Fed. Republic Germany, 1980. Contbr. articles to profl. jours.; patentee in field. Recipient Karl G. Maeser Teaching Excellence award Brigham Young U., Karl G. Maeser Research award Brigham Young U. Mem. Am. Chem. Soc. (pres. Salt Lake City chpt.), Royal Soc. Chemists, Internat. Soc. Heterocyclic Chemistry, Sigma Xi (pres. Brigham Young U. chpt.). Republican. Mormon. Avocations: backpacking, gardening, woodworking, photography. Home: 1147 Aspen Ave Provo UT 84604 Office: Brigham Young U 310G Engring Sci Ctr Provo UT 84602

BROADHURST, NORMAN NEIL, foods company executive; b. Chico, Calif., Dec. 17, 1946; s. Frank Spencer and Dorothy Mae (Conrad) B.; B.S., Calif. State U., 1969; M.B.A., Golden Gate U., 1975; m. Victoria Rose Thomson, Aug. 7, 1976; 1 son, Scott Andrew. With Del Monte Corp., San Francisco, 1969-76, product mgr., 1973-76; product mgr. Riviana Foods, Inc., div. Colgate Palmolive, Houston, 1976-78; new products brand devel. mgr. foods div. Coca Cola Co., Houston, 1978-79, brand mgr., 1979-82, mktg. dir., 1982-83; v.p. mktg. Beatrice Foods Co., Chgo., 1983-86; pres., chief operating officer Famous Amos Chocolate Chip Cookie Co., 1986—; pres. Ross-Broadhurst & Assocs., 1986—; bd. dirs. Arcana Producsts, Inc., 1986—, Tevele N.Am., Inc. Chmn. youth soccer program Cystic Fibrosis; pres., chmn. South Coast Symphony, 1985—. Recipient Cystic Fibrosis Community Services award, 1982. Mem. Am. Mgmt. Assn., Am. Mktg. Assn. Clubs: Toastmasters Internat. (past chpt. pres.). Home: 31152 Monterey St South Laguna CA 92677 Office: Famous Amos 14553 Delano Van Nuys CA 91411

BROBERG, JAMES, management company executive; b. Pueblo, Colo., Mar. 8, 1934; s. Carl Oscar and Dorothy Mae (Hartman) B.; m. Lotte Beck, Aug. 28, 1962; children—Ronald, Kimberly Ann. B.S. in Biochemistry, U. Colo., 1960, B.S. in Computer Sci., 1985; M.H.A., U. Minn., 1970. Adminstr. Plum City Community Hosp., Wis., 1965-67, Tri-County Meml. Hosp., Whitehall, Wis. 1967-75, Illini Community Hosp., Pittsfield, Ill., 1975-78, Weisbrod Meml. Hosp., Eads, Colo., 1978-81; pres., chief exec. officer St. Joseph Hosp., Florence, Colo., 1981-84; pres. Eureka Mgmt., Inc., Colorado Springs, Colo., 1984—; dir. Sisters of Charity Health Care Systems, Cin., Eastern Colo. Health Care Assn., Lamar; adminstrv. cons. La Crosse Hosp, Inc., Wis., 1971-72. Pres. Whitehall Ind. Devel. Corp., 1967-75. Served with USAF, 1951-56. Mem. Am. Acad. Health Care Adminstrs., Am. Acad. Nursing Home Adminstrs., Colo. Hosp. Assn., Colo. Health Care Assn., Western Wis. Health Care Assn. (bd. dirs. 1969-75). Republican.

Club: Shadow Hills (Canon City, Colo.). Lodge: Lions. Home: 231 W 4th St Florence CO 81226 Office: Eureka Mgmt Inc 1715 N Weber St Suite 170 Colorado Springs CO 80907

BROCA, LAURENT ANTOINE, aerospace scientist; b. Arthez-de-Bearn, France, Nov. 30, 1928; came to U.S., 1957, naturalized, 1963; s. Paul L. and Paule Jeanne (Ferrand) B.; B.S. in Math., U. Bordeaux, France, 1949; Lic. es Scis. in Math. and Physics, U. Toulouse (France), 1957; grad. Inst. Technique Professionnel, France, 1960; Ph.D. in Elec. Engring., Calif. Western U., 1979; postgrad. Boston U., 1958, MIT, 1961, Harvard U., 1961; m. Leticia Garcia Guerra, Dec. 18, 1962; 1 dau., Marie-There Yvonne. Teaching fellow physics dept. Boston U., 1957-58; spl. instr. dept. physics N.J. Inst. Tech., Newark, 1959-60; sr. staff engr. advanced research group ITT, Nutley, N.J., 1959-60; examiner math. and phys. scis. univs. Paris (France) and Caen, Exam. Center, N.Y.C., 1959-69; sr. engr. surface radar div. Raytheon Co., Waltham, Mass., 1960-62, Hughes Aircraft Co., Culver City, Calif., 1962-64; asst. prof. math. Calif. State U., Northridge, 1963-64; prin. engr. astrionics lab. NASA, Huntsville, Ala., 1964-65; fellow engr. Def. and Space Center, Westinghouse Electric Corp., Balt., 1965-69; cons. and sci. adv. electronics, phys. scis. and math. to indsl. firms and broadcasting stations, 1969-80; head engring. dept. Videocraft Mfg. Co., Laredo, Tex., 1974-75; asst. prof. math. Laredo State U., summer, 1975; engring. specialist dept. systems performance analysis ITT Fed. Electric Corp., Vandenberg AFB, Calif., 1982-82; engring. mgr. Ford Aerospace and Communications Corp., Nellis AFB, Nev., 1982-84; engring. mgr. Arcata Assocs., Inc. Las Vegas, Nev., 1984-85; sr. scientific specialist engring. and devel. EG&G Spl. Projects, Inc., Las Vegas, 1985—. Served with French Army, 1951-52. Recipient Published Paper award Hughes Aircraft Co., 1966; Fulbright scholar, 1957. Mem. IEEE, Am. Nuclear Soc. (vice chmn. Nev. sect. 1982-83, chmn. 1983-84), Am. Def. Preparedness Assn.; Armed Forces Communications and Electronics Assn., Air Force Assn. Home: 5040 Lancaster Dr Las Vegas NV 89120 Office: EG&G Spl Projects Inc PO Box 15110 Las Vegas NV 89114-5110

BROCCOLI, ALBERT ROMOLO, motion picture producer; b. N.Y.C., Apr. 5, 1909; s. Giovanni and Cristina (Vence) B.; m. Dana Natol Wilson, June 21, 1959; children: Michael Wilson, Anthony, Christina, Barbara. Student pub. schs., N.Y.C. Asst. dir. 20th Century Fox, 1941-42; RKO under Howard Hughes, 1947-48; theatrical agt. Charles Feldman, 1948-51; producer Warwick Films, 1951-60, Eon Prodns., Inc., from 1960. Producer: Red Beret, 1952, Hell Below Zero, 1953, Black Knight, 1954, Prize of Gold, 1955, Cockleshell Heroes, 1956, Safari, 1956, April in Portugal, 1956, Fire Down Below, 1956, Odongo, 1956, Pickup Alley, 1957, Arrivederci Roma, 1957, Interpol, 1957, How to Murder a Rich Uncle, 1957, High Flight, 1958, No Time to Die, 1958, The Man Inside, 1958, Killers of Kilimanjaro, 1958, Bandit of Zhobe, 1958, In The Nick, 1959, Jazz Boat, 1960, Let's Get Married, 1960, The Trials of Oscar Wilde, 1960, Idol on Parade, 1960, Johnny Nobody, 1961, Call Me Bwana, 1963, Chitty Chitty Bang Bang, 1967 (Family Film award So. Calif. Motion Picture Council 1968); James Bond films Dr. No, 1962, From Russia With Love, 1963 (Screen Producers Guild certificate of nomination as best picture 1964), Goldfinger, 1963 (Screen Producers Guild cert. of nomination as best picture 1964), Thunderball, 1964 (Mkkin Kogyo Tsushin cert. of award 1966), You Only Live Twice, 1966 (Mkkin Kogyo Tsushin cert. of award 1967), On Her Majesty's Secret Service, 1969, Diamonds Are Forever, 1971, Live and Let Die, 1972, The Man With the Golden Gun, 1974, The Spy Who Loved Me, 1977, Moonraker, 1979, For Your Eyes Only, 1981, Octopussy, 1983, A View to a Kill, 1985, The Living Daylights, 1987. Bd. Dirs. Boys Club of Queens, Inc., 1968, recipient Man of the Yr. award. Served to lt. (j.g.) USN, 1942-47, PTO. Decorated grand officer Order of Crown (Italy), Order St. Constantine (Italy); recipient Irving G. Thalberg Meml. award 54th ann. Acad. Awards, 1982. Mem. Producers Guild, Am. Film Inst. Roman Catholic. Club: Metropolitan (N.Y.C.). Office: care GS Davis 1900 Ave of the Stars Suite 535 Los Angeles CA 90067

BROCK, ERNEST GEORGE, physicist; b. Detroit, Apr. 7, 1926; s. Ernest Guy and Ethel A. (Baugh) B.; m. Alice Muriel Cook, June 10, 1950; children: Ernest Allen, Philip Lawton, Cynthia Alice. BS in Physics, U. Notre Dame, 1946, BS in Math., 1946, PhD, 1951. Research assoc. Gen. Electric Research Inst., Schenectady, N.Y., 1951-56; group leader research projects Linfield Research Inst., McMinnville, Oreg., 1956-58; lab. mgr. research and engring. div. Gen. Dynamics/Electronics, Rochester, N.Y., 1958-66; sr. staff engr. The Aerospace Corp., El Segundo, Calif., 1966-71, head quantum electronics dept., 1966-68, project dir. tech. application studies of high power laser systems, 1969-71; sr. engr. N.Am. Rockwell, Downey, Calif., 1972; sr. engring. specialist Garrett Corp., Torrance, Calif., 1973-74; mem. staff laser research and tech. div. Los Alamos (N.Mex.) Sci. Lab., 1974—; assoc. mem. spl. group on optical masers of Adv. Group on Electron Devices, Dept. Def. Research and Engring., 1967-69. Contbr. articles on quantum electronics and laser systems to profl. jours. Served to lt. (j.g.) USNR, 1944-54. Mem. AAAS, IEEE, Am. Phys. Soc., Optical Soc. Am., N.Y. Acad. Scis., Sigma Xi. Republican. Methodist. Home: 1880 Camino Redondo Los Alamos NM 87544 Office: Los Alamos Nat Sci Lab Los Alamos NM 87545

BROCK, JOHN HENRY, ecologist, educator; b. Beloit, Kans., June 12, 1944; s. Frank Fredrick and Elizabeth (Brant) B.; m. Cathleen Ann Beckman, Dec. 29, 1964; children: Christopher John, Amy Ann. BS in Agr., Ft. Hays (Kans.) State U., 1966, MS in Botany, 1968; PhD in Range Sci., Texas A&M U., 1978. Research assoc. Tex. Agrl. Exptl. Sta., Lubbock, 1969-72, Vernon, 1972-77; asst. prof. Ariz. State U., Tempe, 1977-82, assoc. prof. rangeland ecology, 1982—; range ecology cons. U.S. Forest Service, Montrose, Colo., 1978, Hopi Tribe, Oraibi, Ariz., 1980; riparian ecology cons. Bur. of Reclamation, Phoenix, 1985-86. Contbr. articles to profl. jours. Mem. Soc. Range Mgmt. (chmn. adv. council), Ariz. Soc. Range Mgmt. (sec., treas. 1980, pres. 1986). Avocations: camping, fishing, leaded glass artwork. Home: 5319 S Holbrook Ln Tempe AZ 85283 Office: Ariz State U Div Agr Tempe AZ 85297

BROCK, KENNETH GLENN, medical media executive; b. Glendale, Calif., Oct. 27, 1951; s. Harold Glenn and Marvel Lou (Hoffman) B.; m. Holly R. Hewitt, Aug. 24, 1980. BA in Communications, Calif. State U., Fullerton, 1974. Asst. producer Western Instructional TV, Hollywood, Calif., 1977-79; producer, dir. KB Videotape Production, Madison and Whitewater, Wis., 1979-81; prod. asst. spl. projects Sta. KOCE-TV, Huntington Beach, Calif., 1981-82; mgr. media services Queen of the Valley Hosp., West Covina, Calif., 1982—. Producer-dir.: (videotape) Reconstruction of Left Cruciate Ligament, Left Knee, 1985 (Angel award 1985). Named in Innovators Catalog, Hosp. Forum Mag., 1985. Mem. Internat. TV Assn. (communications dir. Los Angeles 1985-86, v.p. Los Angeles 1986—. Home: 643 Crown St Glendora CA 91740 Office: Queen of the Valley Hosp 115 S Sunset West Covina CA 91790

BROCK, RICHARD EUGENE, marine biologist, researcher; b. Astoria, Oreg., July 1, 1943; s. Vernon Eugene and Rosemary Faye (Hannemann) B.; m. Julie Helen Bailey, Dec. 26, 1970; children: Vernon, Mika. MS, U. Hawaii, 1972; PhD, U. Wash., 1979. Research assoc. Hawaii Inst. Marine Biology U. Hawaii, Kaneohe, 1975—; fisheries specialist Sea Grant U. Hawaii, Honolulu, 1982—; cons. Honolulu, 1965—. Contbr. articles to profl. jours. Office: U Hawaii Sea Grant MSB210 1000 Pope Rd Honolulu HI 96822

BROCK, WILLIAM GEORGE, real estate investor, developer, financial consultant; b. Dallas, Oreg., Dec. 6, 1928; s. Guy Glen and Sarah Jennie (Schriver) B.; m. Carol June Sharp, Aug. 19, 1950; children—Geoffrey Stuart, Gregory Philip. Student Linfield Coll., 1946-48; B.A. in Bus. Adminstrn., U. Wash., 1950; cert. bank mgmt., U. Calif.-Berkeley, 1960; cert. Grad. Sch. Credit and Fin. Mgmt., 1963. Trust adminstrn. Nat. Bank Commerce, Seattle, 1950-53; asst. trust officer Alaska Nat. Bank, Fairbanks, 1953-56; credit analyst to sr. v.p. Wells Fargo Bank, San Francisco and Los Angeles, 1956-74; pres. Security Bank Corp., Portland, 1974; exec. v.p., pres. B.M. Behrends Bank, Juneau, Alaska, 1974-78; prin. William Brock & Assocs., Juneau, 1978—; bd. govs. Med. Indemnity Corp. Alaska, Anchorage, 1976—. Bd. dirs. Juneau Lyric Opera Assn., 1980-84, pres. 1982-83. Mem. Alaska Bankers Assn. (bd. dirs. 1975-78, pres. 1978), Juneau C. of C. (pres. 1977), Phi Beta Kappa, Beta Gamma Sigma. Clubs: Washington Athletic (Seattle), Juneau Yacht. Home: 300 Hermit St #9 Juneau AK 99801 Office: 311 N Franklin St Suite 202 Juneau AK 99801

BROCKMAN, MICHAEL STEPHEN, broadcasting company executive; b. Bklyn., Nov. 19, 1938; s. Gustave and Sonya (Schechter) B.; m. Wendy Kaltman, Nov. 26, 1965; children: Laura, David. B.S., Ithaca Coll., 1963. With ABC-TV, 1963-77; mgr. daytime programming ABC-TV, N.Y.C., 1970-72; dir. ABC-TV, 1972-74; dir. daytime programming ABC Entertainment, N.Y.C., 1974; v.p. ABC Entertainment, 1974-77, v.p. tape prodn. and ops., 1977; v.p. daytime and children's programs NBC-TV, Burbank, Calif., 1977-80; v.p. programs Lorimar Prodns., Culver City, Calif., 1980-82; v.p. daytime and children's programs CBS Entertainment, Los Angeles, 1982-86, v.p. daytime, children's and late night programs, 1986—. Mem. Nat. Acad. TV Arts and Scis., Acad. TV Arts and Scis., Alpha Epsilon Rho. Home: 22455 Dardenne St Woodland Hills CA 91364 Office: CBS Entertainment Co Office VP Daytime/Childrens TV 7800 Beverly Blvd Los Angeles CA 90036

BROCK-NELSON, LINDA VOSS, retail executive; b. Austin, Tex., Mar. 14, 1942; d. William Bruce and Sara Louise V.; children by previous marriage: Catherine Louise, Deborah Elizabeth, Stephen Lawrence, Richard Keith. Student U. Tex., Austin, 1959-62; BS, Oklahoma City U., 1963, postgrad., 1964-66; MC, Ariz. State U., 1975. Dispatcher Xerox Corp., Oklahoma City, 1963-64; acct., bookkeeper Star Constrn. Co., Oklahoma City, 1964-66; counselor, tchr., lectr., retreatmaster Franciscan Renewal Ctr., Scottsdale, 1975-85; v.p. Linda Brock BMW-Volkswagen, Scottsdale, 1969-79, owner, pres., 1979-86; owner, pres. Linda Brock Oldsmobile, Scottsdale, 1986—. Pres. Lucky 13 Ednl. Ctr., 1977-79; sec. council St. Maria Goretti Cath. Ch., 1978-79; bd. dirs., past. v.p. Scottsdale Symphony; bd. dirs., v.p. pub. relations Ariz. Bus. and Industry Edn. Council, 1982-82; bd. dirs. Nat. Council on Alcoholism; pres. Brock Haus; active Scottsdale Sch. Bd., 1987—. Recipient Disting. Woman's award Northwood Inst., 1986; named Entrepreneur of Yr., 1986. Mem. Am. Internat. Automobile Dealers Assn. (state chmn.), Nat. Auto Dealers Assn., Ariz. Auto Dealers Assn., Scottsdale Auto Dealers Assn. (pres. 1980—), Scottsdale C. of C. (bd. dirs. 1986-88), Ariz. C. of C., Ariz. Safety Assn. (bd. dirs. 1981—), Beta Sigma Gamma. Republican. Club: Scottsdale Exec. Office: 3230 N Scottsdale Rd Scottsdale AZ 85252

BROCKWAY, RONALD GEORGE, geologist; b. Fairview, Mont., Jan. 11, 1926; s. George Arden and Velma Gertrude (Hawley) B.; m. Mary Ann Kocar, Nov. 23, 1957; children: Thomas Allen, Risa Ann, Janine Marie. BA, U. Mont., 1957. Geologist Sinclair Oil & Gas Co., Billings, Mont., 1957-60, Am. Stratigraphic Co., Denver, 1960-67; mgr., geologist Am. Can. Stratigraphic Co., Anchorage, 1967—; cons. Husky Oil, Anchorage, 1976-80. Pack leader Boy Scouts Am., Anchorage, 1970; baseball coach Anchorage Little League, 1970-73. Served as cpl. U.S. Army, 1950-52. Mem. Am. Assn. Petroleum Geologists (province coordinator 1980-83), Alaska Geol. Soc. (sec. 1971-72, stratigraphic com. chmn. 1975). Roman Catholic. Office: Am Can Stratigraphic Co 6280 E 39th Ave Denver CO 80207

BRODERICK, CARLFRED BARTHOLOMEW, sociology educator; b. Salt Lake City, Apr. 7, 1932; s. Frederick Anthony and Napina (Bartholomew) B.; m. Kathleen Adelle State, July 3, 1952; children: Katherine, Carlfred Bartholomew, Victor, Wendi, Jenifer, Frank, Beverly, Benjamin. A.B. magna cum laude, Harvard, 1953; Ph.D., Cornell U., 1956; postgrad., U. Minn., 1966-67. Assoc. prof. family devel. U. Ga., 1956-60; assoc. prof. family relations Pa. State U., 1960-69, prof., 1969-71; prof. sociology, dir. marriage and family therapy program U. So. Calif., Los Angeles, 1971—; sr. ptnr., clin. dir. Broderick, Langlois and Assocs., San Gabriel, Calif., 1981—; ptnr. Broderick-Wood Marriage and Family Therapy, Cypress, Calif., 1984—. Author: Sexuelle Entwickland in Kindheit und Jungend, 1970, Couples: How to Confront Problems and Maintain Loving Relationships, 1979, Marriage and the Family, 1979, Marriage and the Family, 2d edit., 1983, The Therapeutic Triangle, 1983, One Flesh, One Heart, 1986; editor: (with Jessie Bernard) The Individual, Sex and Society, 1969, A Decade of Research and Action on the Family, 1971, Jour. Marriage and The Family, 1970-75; contbr. articles to profl. jours. Pres. Cerritos (Calif.) stake Ch. Jesus Christ Latter-day Saints., 1976-82. Fellow Am. Assn. Marriage and Family Therapists (supr.), So. Calif. Assn. Marriage and Family Therapists (pres. 1974), Nat. Council Family Relations (pres. 1976), Assn. Mormon Counselors and Psychotherapists (pres. 1982). Home: 18902 Alfred Ave Cerritos CA 90701 Office: U So Calif Dept Sociology University Park Los Angeles CA 90089-0032 Office: Broderick Langlois & Assocs Family Counseling 7220 Rosemead Blvd #204 San Gabriel CA 91775 Office: Broderick-Wood Marriage and Family Therapy 5252 Orange Ave #110 Cypress CA 90630

BRODERICK, HAROLD CHRISTIAN, interior designer; b. Oakland, Calif., Apr. 8, 1925; s. Harold Christian and Laura Jane (Lloyd) B. BA, U. Tex., 1947. A founder Arthur Elrod Assos., Inc., Palm Springs, Calif., 1954, now pres. Mem. Planning Commn., City of Palm Springs, 1972-74; trust Palm Springs Desert Mus.; mem. devel. com. Barbara Sinatra Children's Ctr. Mem. Am. Soc. Interior Designers. Republican. Office: Arthur Elrod Associates Inc 850 N Palm Canyon Dr Palm Springs CA 92262

BRODIAN, LAURA, broadcasting executive; b. Newark, Oct. 16, 1947; d. Sol and Jean Dolores (Posner) Brodian. BA, Kean Coll., 1972; M in Music Edn., Ind. U., 1974, D in Mus. Edn., 1982. Lic. radio and TV operator. Tchr. various schs., N.J., 1967-72; assoc. instr. Ind. U., Bloomington, 1973-74; edn. dir. Ind. Arts Commn., Indpls., 1975-76; announcer, engr. Sta. WFIU-FM, Bloomington, 1979-80; announcer, producer Sta. KQED-FM, San Francisco, 1982-87; exec. producer, announcer Sta. KUSC-FM, Los Angeles, 1987—. Mem. Am. Women in Radio and TV, Bay Area English Regency Soc. (founder). Jewish. Avocations: reading, history, dancing, costumes, music. Office: KUSC-FM PO Box 77913 Los Angeles CA 90007

BRODNAX-WATSON, SHIRLEY JEAN, microbiologist; b. Norfolk, Va.; d. John B. and Louise (Booker) Holloway; m. Jack Leon Brodnax, July 31, 1976; children: Melodie, Tracey, Maisha. AA, Contra Costa Coll., 1978; BS in Cell and Molecular Biology, San Francisco State U., 1985. Jr. accountant Philco Corp., Phila.; sec., supr. U.S. Govt., Phila. and San Francisco, 1968-76; research asst., microbiologist Kelly Tech. Services, Oakland, Calif., 1986; microbiologist Nabisco Brands, Inc., Oakland, 1986—. Kennedy King scholar Contra Costa Coll., 1978-80. Roman Catholic. Avocations: tennis, horseback riding, reading. Home: 1537 Hellings Ave Richmond CA 94801 Office: Nabisco Brands Inc 98th Ave Oakland CA 94630

BRODSKY, ROBERT FOX, aerospace engineer; b. Phila., May 16, 1925; s. Samuel H. and Sylvia (Fox) B.; m. Patricia Wess, Jan. 24, 1959; children: Bette W., Robert D., David V., Jeffrey M. B.M.E., Cornell U., 1947; M.Aero. Engring., N.Y. U., 1948, D.Sc. in Engring, 1950; M.S. in Math, U. N.Mex., 1957. Registered profl. engr., Calif., Iowa. Instr. N.Y. U., 1948-50; supr. theoretical aerodynamics Sandia Corp., Albuquerque, 1950-56; chief aerodynamics Convair/Pomona, 1956-59; with Aerojet-Gen. Corp., 1959-71; chief engr. Space-Gen., El Monte, Calif., 1963-67; corp. mgr. European ops. Space-Gen., Paris, 1969-70; mgr. systems test Aerojet Electrosystems Co., 1970-71; prof., head dept. aerospace engring. Iowa State U., Ames, 1971-80; on faculty improvement leave with space and communications group Hughes Aircraft Co., 1978-79; sr. systems engr. TRW Space and Tech. Group, Redondo Beach, Calif., 1980-83, dir. technol. planning, 1982-86, program mgr., 1986—; adj. prof. aerospace engring. U. So. Calif., 1983—; cons. in field. Served with USN, 1944-46. Recipient Ednl. Achievement award AIAA/Am. Soc. Engring. Edn. Aerospace Div., 1978; NSF/NATO sr. fellow in sci., 1973. Fellow AIAA, Inst. Advancement Engring.; mem. Am. Astronautical Soc., Nat. Soc. Profl. Engrs., AIAA (ednl. activities com. 1972—, spacecraft systems tech. com. 1978-82, space transp. tech. com. 1985—, editorial adv. bd. A&A 1977-81, chmn. Los Angeles sect. 1986-87), Am. Soc. Engring. Edn. (chmn. aerospace div., chmn. tech. assessment com.), Am. Soc. Aerospace Edn. (v.p. 1979-80, Univ. Educator of Yr. 1979), Sigma Xi. Lodge: Rotary. Inventor space lifeboat. Home: 401 2d St Hermosa Beach CA 90254 Office: TRW One Space Park Redondo Beach CA 90278

BRODY, ARTHUR WILLIAM, artist, educator; b. N.Y.C., Mar. 2, 1943; s. Joshua and Evelyn Charlotte (Edleberg) B.; m. Anne Loring Sullivan, Aug. 1964 (dec. Feb. 1968); m. Bonnie Ann Mechlowe, June 22, 1969. BS, Harvey Mudd Coll., 1965; MFA, Claremont Grad. Sch., 1967. Instr. U. Alaska, Fairbanks, 1967-69, from asst. to assoc. prof., 1977-83, prof., 1985—; from instr. to asst. prof. Ripon (Wis.) Coll., 1970-75; vis. prof. Harvey Mudd Coll., Claremont, Calif., 1983-84; lectr. Scripps Coll., Claremont, 1983-84. Author (computer program) Edpaint, 1986. Individual Artist grantee Alaska State Arts Council, 1985. Mem. Fairbanks ARts Assn. (bd. dirs. 1985—), Coll. Art Assn., The Print Club, N.W. Printmakers, World Print Council. Club: Running Club North (Fairbanks). Avocation: running. Home: 1548 Heather Dr Fairbanks AK 99709 Office: U Alaska Fairbanks AK 99701

BRODY, JACOB JEROME, art history educator; b. Bklyn., Apr. 24, 1929; s. Aladar and Esther (Kraiman) B.; m. Jean Lindsey, Feb. 13, 1956; children: Jefferson, Jonathan, Allison. Cert. fine arts, Cooper Union, 1950; B.A., U. N.Mex., 1956, M.A., 1964, Ph.D., 1970. Curator of art Everhart Mus., Scranton, Pa., 1957-58; curator collections Isaac Delgado Mus. Art, New Orleans, 1958-60; Mus. Internat. Folk Art, Santa Fe, 1960-61; prof. art history U. N.Mex., 1964—; curator Maxwell Mus., U. N.Mex., Albuquerque, 1962-72; dir. Maxwell Mus., U. N.Mex., 1972-84; mem. adv. bd. Ghost Ranch Mus., N.Mex. Mus. Natural History, 1981-84; mem. fine arts bd., City of Albuquerque, vice chmn., 1970-74; mem. Gov. N.Mex. Task Force Paleontol. Resources, 1978-79. Author: Indian Painters and White Patrons, 1971, Mimbres Painted Pottery, 1977. Recipient Tom L. Popejoy Dissertation award U. N.Mex., 1970, Conservation award N.Mex. Hist. Commn., 1979; Non-Fiction award Border-Regional Library Assn., 1972; Art Book award, 1979; resident scholar Sch. Am. Research, 1980-81. Mem. Am. Assn. Museums, Soc. Am. Archaeology, Mountain Plains Mus. Conf., Council Mus. Anthropology, N.Mex. Mus. Assn., N.Mex. Cactus and Succulent Soc. Office: Maxwell Museum Univ New Mexico Albuquerque NM 87131

BROFMAN, WOODY, astronautical engineer, educator; b. N.Y.C., Mar. 5, 1935; s. Harold and Dorothy Brofman; divorced; children: Marie Louise, Brett Karen, Tara Lynn, David Paul. BS in Aero. Engring., Poly. U. N.Y.C., 1957, PhD in Astronautics, 1964; MS in Aeronautics, Calif. Inst. Tech., 1960. Sr. engr. Jet Propulsion Lab., Pasadena, Calif., 1957-64, mem. tech. staff, 1970-74; mem. tech. staff Aerospace Corp., San Bernardino, Calif., 1964-65; sr. engr. McDonnell Douglas Corp., Santa Monica, Calif., 1965-69; staff engr. Interstate Elecs. Corp., Anaheim, Calif., 1974-78; sr. engring. specialist Rockwell Internat., Downey, Calif., 1978—; lectr. astronautics West Coast U., Los Angeles, 1983—. Advisor local post Boy Scouts Am., 1971-74. Named Eagle Scout. Fellow AIAA (assoc., chmn. career devel com. 1971); mem. Sigma Xi, Sigma Gamma Tau (student chpt. pres. 1956-57). Avocations: reading, photography, model airplanes, model rocketry, swimming. Home: 1919 E Romneya Dr #307 Anaheim CA 92805 Office: Rockwell Internat Space Transp Systems Div 12214 Lakewood Blvd Downey CA 90241

BROGGI, MICHAEL, marketing executive; b. Los Angeles, June 19, 1942; s. Roger Edward and Thelma Cecile (Marshal) B.; children: Michael Jr., Stephen. AA in Journalism, Los Angeles Valley Coll., 1961; grad., USAF Sch. Medicine, Montgomery, Ala., 1962; BA in Mktg. and Communications, Calif. State U., Northridge, 1967; cert. bus. and real estate, San Bernardino Coll., 1975; postgrad., Lincoln U. Law Sch., San Jose, Calif., 1975-76, Calif. Pacific U., 1984—. Newswriter, reporter Sta. KGIL, San Fernando, Calif., 1963-67; mem. corp. mktg. staff Walt Disney Prodns., Burbank, Calif., 1967-70; mgr. pub. relations Magic Mountain Amusement Park, Valencia, Calif., 1970-72; exec. v.p., gen. mgr. Lake Arrowhead, Calif., 1972-75; dir. adminstrv. services Marriott Corp. Gt. Am. Theme Park, Santa Clara, Calif., 1975-78; v.p., dir. mktg. Mktg. and Fin. Mgmt. Engerprises, Inc., Encino, Calif., 1978—; lectr. Calif. Poly. State U., Pomona, Calif. State U., Northridge, Moorpark (Calif.) Community Coll., Los Angeles Valley Coll., U. So. Calif., Acad. Ambulatory Surgery, Scottsdale, Ariz., Los Angeles Publicity Club, San Francisco Advt. Club, Orange County Advt. Club. Mem. Fire Commn., Spl. Dep. Commn., San Bernardino County. Mem. Am. Mktg. Assn., Cultural Found., Internat. Platform Assn., Am. Soc. Profl. Cosn., Journalism Alumni Assn. Avocations: sailing, tennis, golf, photography, etching. Office: Mktg and Fin Mgmt 16055 Ventura Blvd #700 Encino CA 91436

BROGLIATTI, BARBARA SPENCER, television and motion picture executive; b. Los Angeles, Jan. 8, 1946; d. Robert and Lottie (Goldstein) Spencer; m. Raymond Haley Brogliatti, Sept. 19, 1970. B.A. in Social Scis. and English, UCLA, 1968. Asst. press. info. dept. CBS TV, 1968-69, sr. publicist, 1969-74; dir. publicity Tandem Prodns. and T.A.T. Communications (now Embassy Communications), 1974-76, corp. v.p., 1977-82, sr. v.p. worldwide publicity, promotion and advt. Embassy Communications, 1982-85; sr. v.p. corp. communications Lorimar-Telepictures Corp., 1985—. Mem. Dirs. Guild Am., Publicists Guild, Acad. TV Arts and Scis. Office: Lorimar-Telepictures Corp Office Sr VP Corp Communications 10202 W Washington Blvd Culver City CA 90232

BROHM, LYNETTE HARRIS, social services administrator; b. Ft. Riley, Kans.; d. Cleo Knox and Wilma Irene (Baumgartner) Harris; m. Robert Jay Brohm, July 21, 1979; step-children: Suzanne, Laura (dec.), Martin. BS, Fla. State U., 1960; MSW with honors, Wash. U., 1963. Assoc. dir. Consol. Neighborhood Services, Inc., St. Louis, 1963-76; dir. in-home care system Peninsula Hosp., Burlingame, Calif., 1977-84; exec. dir. Meml. Hosp. HomeCare, Modesto, Calif., 1985—; charter mem., chmn. Home Care Agys. Network San Mateo County, Burlingame, 1977-84; charter mem. San Mateo County Elder Abuse Steering Com., 1983-84. Contbr. articles to profl. jours. Mem. Services to Older Adults Adv. Council, Modesto, 1985—; sub-com. chmn. San Mateo County United Way Planning Com. 1978-83; drive team leader Via Agy., Modesto, 1986; active Stanislaus Community AIDS Project, 1987—. Mem. Nat. Assn. Social Workers (sec. St. Louis chpt. 1975-76), Calif. Assn. Health Services at Home (mem. ethics com. 1979, membership com. 1987—). Democrat. Lutheran. Avocations: gardening, ballet, choir. Office: Meml Hosp HomeCare 1329 Spanos Ct C-4 Modesto CA 95355

BROM, LIBOR, educator; b. Ostrava, Czechoslovakia, Dec. 17, 1923; came to U.S., 1958, naturalized, 1964; s. Ladislav and Bozena (Bromova) B.; m. Gloria S. Mena, Aug. 31, 1961; 1 son, Rafael Brom. Ing., Czech Inst. Tech., 1948; J.U.C., Charles U. Prague, 1951; postgrad., San Francisco State Coll.; M.A., U. Colo., 1962, Ph.D., 1970. Vice pres. Brom, Inc., Ostrava, Czechoslovakia, 1942-48; economist Slovak Magnesite Works, Prague, Czechoslovakia, 1948-49; economist, chief planner Vodostavba, Navika, Prague, 1951-56; tchr. Jefferson County Schs., Colo., 1958-67; prof., dir. Russian area studies program U. Denver, 1967—; journalist, mem. editorial staff Denni Hlasatel-Daily Herald, Chgo., 1978—; Pres. Colo. Nationalities Council, 1970-72; comptroller Exec. Bd. Nat. Heritage Groups Council, 1970-72; mem. adv. bd. Nat. Security Council, 1980—; acad. bank participant Heritage Found; adv. bd. Independence Inst. Author: Ivan Bunin's Proteges, Leonid Zurov, 1973, in Czech, In the Windstorms of Anger, 1976, On Restoring the Moral Order, 1980, Time and Duty, 1981, Teacher of Nations and Our Times, 1983, The Way of Light, 1983, On the Attack, 1983, Between the Currents, 1985; translator: Problems of Geography, 1955. V.p. Colo. Citizenship Day, 1968-69; v.p. Comenius World Council, 1976-85, World Representation of Czechoslovak Exiles, 1976-85; pres. Czeck World Union, 1985—; acting gen. sec. Czechoslovak Republican Movement. Recipient Americanism medal DAR, 1969, Disting. Service award Am. by Choice, 1968; named Tchr. with Superlative Performance MLA, 1961, Outstanding Faculty mem. Omicron Delta Kappa, 1972. Mem. Econ. Inst. Research and Edn., Am. Assn. Tchrs. Slavic and Eastern European Langs. (v.p. 1973-75), Am. Assn. Advancement Slavic Studies, Intercollegiate Studies Inst., Western Social Sci. Assn., Rocky Mountain Assn. Slavic Studies (sec. treas. 1975-78, v.p. 1978-81, pres. 1982-83), Czechoslovak Nat. Council of Am., Czechoslovak Christian Democratic Movement in Exile (central com. 1970-79), Dobro Slovo (hon.), Slava (hon.), Aleksandr Solzhenitsyn Soc., Shavano Inst. Nat. Leadership, Nat. Republican Nationalities Council (co-chmn. human rights com. 1979-81), Lincoln Ednl. Found. Republican. Roman Catholic. Home: 39 Hillside Dr Wheat Ridge CO 80215 Office: Univ Denver Denver CO 80208-0293

BROMAN, BARRY MICHAEL, diplomat; b. Louisville, Oct. 13, 1943; s. Harry Frank and Hilda (Foley) B.; m. Betty Jane Apilado, Nov. 30, 1968; children: Seth Timothy, Brendan Clay. BA in Polit. Sci., U. Wash., 1967, MA in Asian Studies, 1968. Fgn. service officer U.S. Dept. State, Washington, 1972—. Author: The Old Homes of Bangkok: Fragile Link, 1984; contbr. articles to profl. jours. Served to capt. USMC, 1968-71, Vietnam. Decorated Cross of Gallantry (South Vietnam), Civil Affairs medal (South Vietnam). Club: Royal Bangkok Sports. Avocations: photography, fine arts, writing. Home: 4325 105th Ave NE Kirkland WA 98033

BROMMER, JERE JOSEPH, banker; b. Lancaster, Pa., Sept. 8, 1929; s. Phillip Harold and Margaret Rose (Gigl) B.; m. Mary Roseann Rhoads, Oct. 15, 1949; children: Susan Brommer Kieborz, Sharon, Jeffrey, Michael, Eric, Lisa Brommer Neitz. Grad., Am. Inst. Banking, Phoenix, 1958, Pacific Coast Sch. Banking, U. Wash., 1974, Mgmt. Sch. Bank Mktg. and Strategic Planning, U. Wis., 1978. With Farmers Bank and Trust Co., Lancaster, Pa., 1948-56; br. mgr., comml. loan officer First Nat. Bank Ariz., Phoenix, 1957-63; br. mgr. Valley Nat. Bank Ariz., Phoenix, 1963-67, computer service mgr., 1968-72, v.p. mktg., sales mgr., 1973-82; corp. strategic planner Valley Nat. Corp., Phoenix, 1982—; v.p., dir. Christian Communications, Inc., Phoenix, 1980—; Mem. Ariz. State Bus. and Edn. Adv. Council; lectr. various grad. schs. banking. Author: (with others) Pricing Financial Services, 1981. Mem. The Planning Forum, Bank Mktg. Assn., Am. Bankers Assn. Avocations: water skiing, golf, gardening. Office: Valley Nat Corp 241 N Central Ave Phoenix AZ 85004

BRONDOS, GREGORY ALAN, pathologist; b. West Frankfort, Ill., Jan. 7, 1938; s. Stephen and Margaret (Palic) B.; m. Sharon Elaine Hardy, May 7, 1966; children: Gregory A. Jr., Thomas Edward, Pamala Margaret. Student, U. Ill., 1958; BA, Milligan Coll., 1960; MD, Bowman Gray, 1964. Diplomate Am. Bd. Pathology, Anatomic Pathology, Clin. Pathology. Intern, resident N.C. Bapt. Hosp., Winston-Salem, 1964-66; resident New England Deaconess, Boston, 1966-69; pathologist Meml. Hosp. Natrona County, Wyo. Med. Ctr., Casper, Wyo., 1971—; cons. Converse County Meml. Hosp., Douglas, Wyo., 1981—; adj. prof. U. Wyo., Casper, 1976—. Contbr. articles to profl. jours. Pres., bd. dirs. YMCA, Casper, 1978-81; pres. Grace Luth. Ch. Council, Casper, 1982-85; mem. Ft. Caspar Commn., 1981—; mem. Natrona County Sch. Bd., Casper, 1982—, chmn., 1985-86. Served to maj. USAF, 1969-71. Fellow Am. Cancer Soc., Boston, 1967-68, Harvard Med. Sch., Boston, 1967-69. Fellow Am. Soc. Clin. Pathologists, Coll. Am. Pathologists; mem. Wyo. Soc. Pathologists (sec. treas. 1976-82), Colo. Soc. Clin. Pathologists. Republican. Lodge: Lions. Avocations: archaeology, skiing, fishing, golf, travel. Home: Box 9057 Casper WY 82609 Office: Wyo Med Ctr 1233 E Second St Casper WY 82601

BRONSON, BRENDA LOU, safety engineer; b. Independence, Mo., Aug. 31, 1948; d. Cecil Lester and Virginia Ruth (Frazier) B.; m. John Lee Pyatt, June 16, 1976 (div. Feb. 1980); 1 child, Nathan Stuart Pyatt; m. Thomas Walker, Oct. 26, 1986. BSChemE, U. Mo., Rolla, 1970. Cert. engr. in tng. Loss prevention engr. Factory Mut. Engring., St. Louis, 1970-74; chem. engr. Amoco Sugar Creek (Mo.) Refinery, 1975-76; masterplanning engr., safety mgr. U.S. Army Mil. Community, Heilbronn, Fed. Republic of Germany, 1976-77; safety engr. Lake City Army Ammunition Plant, Independence, 1978-80, Tooele (Utah) Army Depot, 1980-82, Naval Air Rework Facility, Alameda, Calif., 1982-85, Navy Pub. Works Ctr., Oakland, Calif., 1985—. Contbr. articles to profl. jours. Sec. Paden Sch. PTA, Alameda, 1983-84; den leader Cub Scouts Am., Alameda, 1984-86. Recipient Outstanding Performance award, Naval Air Rework Racility, 1983, 84, 85. Mem. Am. Soc. Safety Engrs., Alameda Naval Air Sta. Engrs. Assn. (sec. 1985—). Democrat. Methodist. Avocations: reading, swimming, dancing, singing, pool. Home: 424 Callan Ave #128 San Leandro CA 94577 Office: Navy Pub Works Ctr PO Box 24003 Code 20A Oakland CA 94623

BROOK, JOHN LORD, management consultant; b. Chgo., Oct. 31, 1943; s. Herbert Cecil and Jane Crowell (Lord) B.; m. Sheryn Prideaux, Sept. 1964 (div. Aug. 1971); children: Michelle, James. BS, U. Wis., 1968; MBA, Harvard U., 1971. V.p. M. Hoffman & Co., Inc., Boston, 1971-79; exec. v.p. Eastrock Internat., Los Angeles, 1979-81; gen. mgr. Electronics Internat., Woodside, Calif., 1981-82; ptnr. Southland Assocs., Foster City, Calif., 1982—; cons. Univ. Synagogue, Los Angeles, 1985; mem. legis. com., city chmn. San Mateo/Burlingame Bd. Realtors, Foster City, Calif. Administrv. advisor Friends of Reconstructive Surgery, Los Angeles, 1984-85. Presbyterian. Club: Harvard (com. chmn. 1975-79); Harvard Bus. Sch. (San Francisco). Office: Southland Assocs 655 Sky Way Suite 207 San Carlos CA 94070

BROOKBANK, JOHN W(ARREN), professor emeritus microbiology; b. Seattle, Apr. 3, 1927; s. Earl Bruce and Louise Sophia (Stoecker) B.; m. Marcia Ireland, Sept. 16, 1950 (div. 1978); children: Ursula Ireland, John W. Jr., Phoebe Bruce; m. Sally Satterberg Cahill, Aug. 6, 1983. BA, U. Wash., 1950, MS, 1953; PhD, Calif. Inst. Tech., 1955. Asst. prof. U. Fla., Gainesville, 1955-58, assoc. prof., 1958-68, prof. microbiology and cell sci., 1968-85, prof. emeritus, 1985—; vis. assoc. prof. U. Fla. Coll. Medicine, Gainesville, 1961-63, U. Wash., Seattle, 1965; cons. in field, Friday Harbor, Wash. 1986—. Author: Developmental Biology, 1978; editor Improving Quality of Health Care for the Elderly, 1977; contbr. articles to profl. jours. Pres. Griffin Bay Preservation Com., Friday Harbor, 1985—, Bridge Council on Narcotics Addiction, Gainesville, 1974; founding pres. Gainesville Regional Council on Alcoholism, 1976. Research grantee NIH, 1957-80, NSF, 1972-73. Mem. Am. Soc. Zoologists, Soc. Devel. Biology, The Gerontol. Soc. Am., Sigma Xi. Republican. Episcopalian. Club: Seattle Tennis. Avocations: fishing, boating, tennis. Home: 1061 Pear Point Rd Friday Harbor WA 98250

BROOKE, EDNA MAE, business educator; b. Las Vegas, Nev., Feb. 10, 1923; d. Alma Lyman and Leah Mae (Ketcham) Shurtliff; m. Bill T. Brooke, Dec. 22, 1949; 1 child, John C. BS in Acctg., Ariz. State U., 1965, MA in Edn., 1967, EdD, 1975. Grad. teaching asst. Ariz. State U., Tempe, 1968-69; prof. bus. Maricopa Tech. Coll., Phoenix, 1967-72, assoc. dean instl. services, 1972-74; prof. bus. and acctg. Scottsdale (Ariz.) Community Coll., 1974—; cons. in field. Author: The Effectiveness of Three Techniques Used in Teaching First Semester Accounting Principles to Tech. Jr. College Students, 1974. Mem. Nat. Bus. Edn. Assn., Western Bus. Edn. Assn., Ariz. Bus. Edn. Assn., Am. Acctg. Assn., Delta Pi Epsilon. Home: 2139 E Solano Dr Phoenix AZ 85016 Office: Scottsdale Community Coll 9000 E Chaparral Scottsdale AZ 85252

BROOKE, ROBERT J., social worker; b. Iola, Kans., Nov. 3, 1946; s. Joseph R. and Barbara Joyce (Works) B.; m. Francene Ann Hess, May 29, 1969; children: Candice Ann, Robert A. BA in Psychology, Southwestern Coll., Winfield, Kans., 1968; MSW, U. Okla., Norman, 1974. Social worker Southeast Kans. Mental Health Ctr., Humboldt, 1974-78; treatment leader Colo. Boys Ranch, La Junta, 1978-86; program dir. Southeast Colo. Family Guidance and Mental Health Ctr., Lamar, 1986—. Served with U.S. Army, 1968-72. Mem. Nat. Assn. Social Workers (cert.). Avocations: running, fishing, hunting. Home: 201 Country Village Lamar CO 81050 Office: Southeast Colo Family Guidance Mental Health Ctr PO Box 824 Lamar CO 81052

BROOKER, ALAN EDWARD, clinical neuropsychologist, air force officer; b. Madison, Wis., Jan. 26, 1949; s. Russell Alan and Margaret Gorman (Simpson) B.; m. Mary Naglee, Apr. 15, 1972; children: Jeffrey Alan, Jarrod Russell. B.A. in Psychology, Chapman Coll., Orange, Calif., 1971; M.S. in Rehab. Counseling, Calif. State U., Sacramento, 1975; Ph.D. in Counseling Psychology, Kans. State U., Manhattan, 1977. Diplomate in clin. neuropsychology Am. Bd. Clin. Neuropsychology; diplomate Am. Bd. Profl. Psychology; cert. rehab. counselor; lic. psychologist, Calif., Colo., Pa., Tex. Rehab. counselor Auburn office State of Calif., 1973-75; commd. 2d lt. U.S. Air Force, 1968; advanced through grades to maj. 1973; intern clin. psychology Wright-Patterson AFB Med. Ctr., Ohio, 1977-78; clin. psychologist, chief psychol. testing USAF Hosp., Wiesbaden, W. Ger., 1978-81; resident in med. psychology specializing in neuropsychology U. Oreg. Med. Sch., Oreg. Health Scis. U., Portland, 1981-82; clin. neuropsychology officer dept. mental health Travis AFB, Calif., 1982-85, chief mental health clinic and psychol. services, 1985—; vocat. expert Bur. Hearings and Appeals, Social Security Adminstrn.; mil. cons. neuropsychology Surgeon Gen. USAF. Vice pres. Central Sierra chpt. Calif. Human Services Orgn., 1974-75; v.p. Voluntary Action Ctr., South Lake Tahoe, Calif., 1976-77. Decorated Meritorious Service medal, Humanitarian Service medal, Air Force Achievement medal, recipient award of merit Calif. Dept. Rehab. Fellow Pa.

Psychol. Assn. (Div. 19 mil. psychology award, 1981), Soc. Air Force Clin. Psychologists (Europe rep.); mem. Affiliated Bd. Examiners, Am. Bd. Profl. Psychology, Internat. Neuropsychol. Soc. Democrat. Roman Catholic. Club: Wiesbaden-Am. Ski. Contbr. articles to profl. jours. Home: 206 Emory Dr Vacaville CA 95688 Office: David Grant USAF Med Ctr SGHAC Travis AFB CA 94535

BROOKES, CRITTENDEN EDWARDS, psychiatrist; b. Oakland, Calif., May 8, 1931; s. Arthur Blayne and Ruth Delilah (Crittenden) B.; m. Mauna Berkov; children—Lisa, Aaron, Jedidiah, Jesse. A.B., Calif. State U.-Chico, 1952; M.A., Stanford U., 1953, Ph.D., 1956, M.D. (J. Kaiser Family, USPHS, John D. Nappert scholars, USPHS, Univ., Russell Sage Found. fellows), 1960. Diplomate Am. Bd. Psychiatry and Neurology. Psychoanalytic tng. C.G. Jung Inst., San Francisco; intern, USPHS Hosp., S.I., N.Y., 1960-61; resident U. Calif., San Francisco, 1961-63, clin. instr., 1964-67, asst. clin. prof., 1967-75, assoc. clin. prof., 1979—; resident Mt. Zion Hosp., San Francisco, 1963-64, asst. clin. prof. psychology, 1964-67, adj. prof., and supr., 1967—, asst. chief, 1966—; cons. Letterman Gen. Hosp., San Francisco, 1976—, Family Service Agy., San Francisco, 1979—; pvt. practice psychiatry, 1964—. Served with USPHS, 1960-64. Fellow Am. Psychiat. Assn. (mem. bd. trustees), Am. Acad. Psychoanalysis; mem. Am. Psychol. Assn., AMA, No. Calif. Psychiat. Soc. Contbr. articles to profl. lit. Office: 407 Locust St San Francisco CA 94118

BROOKES, VALENTINE, lawyer; b. Red Bluff, Calif., May 30, 1913; s. Langley and Ethel (Valentine) B.; m. Virginia Stovall Cunningham, Feb. 11, 1939; children—Langley (Mrs. Jerrold B. Brandt), Lawrence Valentine, Alan Cunningham. A.B., U. Calif., Berkeley, 1934, J.D., 1937. Bar: Calif. bar 1937, U.S. Supreme Ct. bar 1942. Asst. franchise tax counsel State of Calif., 1937-40; dep. atty. gen. Calif., 1940-42; spl. asst. to U.S. atty. gen., asst. to solicitor gen. U.S., 1942-44; partner firm Kent & Brookes, San Francisco, 1944-70, Alvord & Alvord, Washington, 1944-50, Lee, Toomey & Kent, Washington, 1950-79, Brookes and Brookes, San Francisco, 1971—; lectr. Hastings Coll. Law, U. Calif., 1941-48, U. Calif. Law Sch., Berkeley, 1948-70. Author: The Continuity of Interest Test in Reorganizations, 1946, The Partnership Under the Income Tax Laws, 1949, The Tax Consequences of Widows Elections in Community Property States, 1951, Corporate Trasactions Involving Its Own Stock, 1954, Litigation Expenses and the Income Tax, 1957. Bd. dirs. Childrens Hosp. Med. Center of N.Calif., 1963-74, v.p., 1968-70; trustee Oakes Found., 1957-70; regent St. Mary's Coll., Calif., 1968—, pres. bd., 1970-72. Fellow Am. Bar Found. (life); mem. Am. Law Inst., ABA (chmn. com. on statute of limitations 1954-57, mem. council, tax sect. 1960-63), Calif. Bar Assn. (chmn. com. on taxation 1950-52, 60-61), Soc. Calif. Pioneers (v.p. 1964, 1975-86), Am. Coll. Tax Lawyers, Phi Kappa Sigma, Phi Delta Phi. Republican. Clubs: Pacific Union, Orinda Country, Bankers, World Trade. Home: 7 Sycamore Rd Orinda CA 94563 Office: Brookes and Brookes 300 Montgomery St San Francisco CA 94104

BROOKIE, DEAN ROBERT, architect; b. Bozeman, Mont., June 3, 1953; s. Robert Hill and Edna Clara (Bryant) B.; m. Cyn Myer; 1 child, Drew Myer. B in Environ. Design, U. Colo., 1975, MArch, 1977. Designer, Key-Fletemeyer, Landscape Architects, Boulder, Colo., 1975-77; project architect, designer Everett, Zeigel, Tumpes and Hand, Architects, Boulder, 1977-80; prin., owner Brookie Architecture and Planning, Durango, Colo., 1980—; v.p. Appanage Inc., 1986—; instr. U. Colo. Grad. Sch. Planning and Community Devel., 1980-81; art dir. Appanage Catalog of Contemporary Art-to-Wear. Designer urban housing complexes and adobe housing projects; graphic designer, art dir. for three publs. Mem. Colo. Soc. Architects (bd. dirs. 1975-76). Democrat. Methodist. Office: 2703 W 2nd Ave PO Box 714 Durango CO 81301

BROOKINS, DOUGLAS GRIDLEY, geochemist, educator; b. Healdsburg, Calif., Sept. 27, 1936; s. Rex McKain and Ellyn Caroline (Hitt) B.; m. Barbara Flashman, Sept. 16, 1961; children: Laura Beth, Rachel Sarah. A.A., Santa Rosa Jr. Coll., 1956; A.B., U. Calif.-Berkeley, 1958; Ph.D., MIT, 1963. Geologist Bear Creek Co., San Francisco, 1957-59; research asst. MIT, Cambridge, 1958-63; physicist Avco Corp., Wilmington, Mass., 1961; asst. prof. geology Kans. State U., Manhattan, 1963-65; assoc. prof. Kans. State U., 1965-70; prof. geology U. N.Mex., Albuquerque, 1971—; acting chmn. U. N.Mex., 1972, chmn. dept., 1976-79. Author: Earth Resources, Energy and the Environment, 1980, Geochemical Aspects of Radioactive Waste Disposal, Physical Geology, Eh-ph Diagrams for Geochemists, Earth and Energy Resources and Their Environmental Impact; contbr. 500 articles to profl. jours. Bd. dirs. Jewish Community Council Albuquerque, 1974; trustee Congregation Albert, 1975-81 , v.p., 1983-84, pres., 1985—. Named Researcher-Tchr. of Year, 1971. Fellow Geol. Soc. Am., Am. Inst. Chemists, Mineral Soc. Am., Explorers Club; mem. Geochem. Soc., Meteoritical Soc., Am. Geophys. Union, N.Y. Acad. Sci., AAAS, AAUP, Albuquerque Geol. Soc. (pres. 1973), N.Mex. Geol. Soc., N.Mex. Inst. Chemists (councillor 1974-75), Am. Assn. Petroleum Geologists, Internat. Assn. Geochemistry and Cosmochemistry, Mineral Soc. Am., Soc. Economic Geologists, Soc. Exploration Geochemists, Materials Research Soc., Am. Chem. Soc., Am. Nuclear Soc., Phi Beta Kappa (pres. Alpha Assn. Kans. 1967-68), Sigma Xi. Mem. B'nai B'rith faith (fin. sec. 1974-75). Address: Dept Geology Univ NMex Albuquerque NM 87131

BROOKMAN, ANTHONY RAYMOND, lawyer; b. Chgo., Mar. 23, 1922; s. Raymond Charles and Marie Clara (Alberg) B.; m. Marilyn Joyce Brookman, June 5, 1982; children—Meribeth Brookman Patrick, Anthony Raymond, Lindsay Logan. Student Ripon Coll., 1940-41; B.S., Northwestern U., 1947; J.D., U. Calif.-San Francisco, 1953. Bar: Calif. 1954. Law clk. Calif. Supreme Ct., 1953-54; ptnr. Nichols, Williams, Morgan, Digardi & Brookman, 1954-68; sr. ptnr. Brookman & Hoffman, Inc., San Francisco, 1968—. Pres., Young Republicans Calif., San Mateo County, 1953-54. Served to 1st lt. USAF. Mem. ABA, Alameda County Bar Assn., State Bar Calif., Lawyers Club Alameda County, Alameda-Contra Costa County Trial Lawyers Assn., Assn. Trial Lawyers Am., Calif. Trial Lawyers Assn. Republican. Clubs: Masons, Athenian Nile, Crow Canyon Country, Shriners. Pub. Contra Costa New Register. Office: Brookman and Hoffman 901 H St Suite 200 Sacramento CA 95814 Office: 1990 N California Blvd Walnut Creek CA 94596 Office: Court Plaza Bldg Sacramento CA 95814

BROOKS, AL, city mayor. Mayor City of Mesa, Ariz. Office: Office of the Mayor City of Mesa PO Box 1466 Mesa AZ 85201 *

BROOKS, DAVID BOGEN, photographer, magazine editor, writer; b. Regina, Sask., Can., May 7, 1933; s. Roy David and Florence Pauline (Bogen) B.; m. Jean Marjorie Lister, 1959 (div. 1967) m. Constance Rice; 1 child, Marjean Rich. BA, Calif. State U., Northridge, 1960; postgrad., Brooks Inst. Photography, Santa Barbara, Calif., 1956-58. Freelance writer, photographer Los Angeles, 1962—; feature editor Petersen's Photographic mag., Los Angeles, 1975-78, sr. editor, 1982—. Author various textbooks on photography. Served with USAF, 1951-55. Mem. Am. Soc. Mag. Photographers (pres. Los Angeles chpt. 1972-74). Avocations: audiophile, epicurean. Office: Petersen's Photog Mag 8490 Sunset Blvd Los Angeles CA 90069

BROOKS, EDWARD HOWARD, retired college administrator; b. Salt Lake City, Mar. 2, 1921; s. Charles Campbell and Margery (Howard) B.; m. Courtaney June Perren, May 18, 1946; children: Merrillee Brooks Runyan, Robin Anne (Mrs. R. Bruce Pollock). B.A., Stanford U., 1942, M.A., 1947, Ph.D., 1950. Mem. faculty, adminstrn. Stanford, 1949-71; provost Claremont (Calif.) Colls., 1971-81; v.p. Claremont U. Center, 1979-81; sr. v.p. Claremont McKenna Coll., 1981-84. Trustee EDUCOM, 1978-80, Webb Sch. of Calif., 1979—, Menlo Sch. and Coll., 1985—; bd. overseers Hoover Instn., 1972-78; bd. dirs. Student Loan Mktg. Assn., 1973-77; mem. Calif. Student Aid Commn., 1984—, chmn., 1986—. Served with AUS, 1942-45. Clubs: University (Los Angeles); Bohemian (San Francisco). Home: 800 High Point Dr Claremont CA 91711 Office: Claremont McKenna Coll 321 Bauer Ctr Claremont CA 91711

BROOKS, ELWOOD RALPH, geology educator, academic director; b. Charlevoix, Mich., Aug. 10, 1934; s. Ralph Elwood and Lois Louise (Vogg) B.; m. Norma Gene Kvool, July 25, 1986; children: Eric Devin, Katherine Jean. BS in Geol. Engring., Mich. Coll. Mining and Tech., 1956; MS in Geology, U. Calif., Berkeley, 1958; PhD, U. Wis., 1964. Mine geologist White Pine (Mich.) Copper Co., 1959-60, field geologist, 1962, 67-69; sr. field asst. Dept. Mineral Resources, Sask., Can., 1963; lectr. in geology U. Calif., Riverside, 1964-65; acting asst. prof. geology Stanford (Calif.) U., 1965; prof., chmn. dept. geol. sci. Calif. State U., Hayward, 1965—. Contbr. articles to profl. jours. Served to 1st lt. C.E., U.S. Army, 1958-59. Grantee Calif. State U., Hayward. Fellow Geol. Soc. Am. (Penrose conf. com. 1981-83); mem. Am. Geophys. Union, Nat. Assn. Geology Tchrs., Sigma Xi. Democrat. Home: 2060 Quail Canyon Ct Hayward CA 94542 Office: Calif State U Dept Geol Scis Hayward CA 94542

BROOKS, FILOMENA MATIA, early childhood educator; b. N.Y.C., June 3, 1940; d. Albert and Frances Bena Jurlin; m. Roger W. Brooks, Nov. 23, 1963; children—Andrew, Jason, Stephanie. B.A., U. Ariz., 1962, M.Ed., 1966. Cert. tchr., Ariz. Tchr. primary grades Wheeler Elem. Sch. and Erickson Elem. Sch., 1962-71; owner Young Explorers, Tucson, 1971—, developer new sch., 1976, ednl. dir. 2 locations Young Explorers, 1983—; chmn. Gov.'s Day Care Adv. Bd.; mem. Tucson Trade Bur., 1986. Mem. Tucson Assn. Edn. Young Children (v.p.), Nat. Assn. Edn. Young Children, Ariz. Assn. Child Devel. Edn. (v.p.), Assn. Supervision and Curriculum Devel., Assn. Childhood Edn. Internat., Adlerian Soc. Ariz., Resources for Women Networking Orgn., Phi Delta Kappa, Alpha Delta Kappa. Democrat. Methodist. Contbr. article to publ. in field.

BROOKS, FOREST CLYDE, civil engineer; b. Seattle, Sept. 13, 1947; s. Clyde N. and Angela Teresa (Kennedy) B.; m. Catherine Susan Burns, Oct. 15, 1977. BSCE, Seattle U., 1970; water resources planner cert., Bd. Engrs. for Rivers and Harbors, Ft. Belvoir, Va., 1980. Survey crew mem. C.E., U.S. Army, Eureka, Mont., 1969; engr. trainee C.E., U.S. Army, Seattle, 1969-71, hydraulic engr., 1971-72, study mgr. asst., 1972-73, study mgr., 1973-84, project mgr., 1984—. Co-editor, author: (monthly newsletter) Unltd. News Jour., 1981—. basketball statistician Seattle U., 1965—; asst. cross country coach Seattle Prep High Sch., 1966—; youth sport coach Cath. Youth Orgn., Seattle, 1967-79; survey and pit tour Seattle Seafair Hydroplane Race, 1972—. Recipient Commendation award Wash. Second. Sch. Athletic Adminstrs. Assn., 1982, Outstanding Achievement and Contbn. award, Seattle U., 1985. Mem. Soc. Am. Mil. Engrs., Steamship Hist. Soc. Am., Nat. Bldg. Mus., Wash. Environ. Council., Sierra Club, The Nature Conservancy, Am. Forestry Assn., Pacific N.W. Masters Swimming, Pacific NW Writers Conf., Masters Aquatics Coaches Assn., Tau Beta Pi, Pi Mu Epsilon, Alpha Sigma Nu. Republican. Roman Catholic. Clubs: Unltds. Unanimous (Seattle); Unlmtds. (Detroit). Avocations: photography, swimming, history. Home: 6917 S 131 St Seattle WA 98178 Office: Seattle Dist CE US Army 4735 E Marginal Way S Seattle WA 98124

BROOKS, JOHN ROSCOE, architectural draftsman; b. Berkeley, Calif., Nov. 10, 1961; s. Roscoe Harris and Jean Ann (Peterson) B. BArch, U. Calif., Berkeley, 1983. With Dahlin Group, San Ramon, Calif., 1984-86; project mgr., architect in tng. Arete, Walnut Creek, Calif., 1986—. Recipient Eagle Scout award Boy Scouts Am., 1976. Republican. Avocations: photography, music, camping, fishing, skiing. Office: Arretê 2211 Olympic Blvd Suite B Walnut Creek CA 94545

BROOKS, LARRY L(EROY), geologist, consultant; b. Albuquerque, Dec. 31, 1952; s. Jerry R. and Ruth N. (Burkholder) B.; m. Barbara A. Travland, June 26, 1985; 1 child, Jim Ray. AS, N.Mex. Highlands U., 1977, BS, 1978. Emergency room technician Las Vegas, Hosp. (N.Mex.), 1973-74; hydrologic technician U.S. Geol. Survey, Albuquerque, 1976-78; engr. technician State Engrs. Office, Albuquerque, 1978-79; dist. geologist N.Mex. Oil Commn., Artesia, 1979-86; exploration geologist Harvey E. Yates Co., Artesia, 1985—; guest lectr. Eastern N.Mex. U. Oil Field Tng. Ctr., Roswell, 1984—. Author jour. Geology of the Pecos Slope, 1982; contbr. articles to mags., profl. jours. Colonel-aide de camp Democratic Party, Santa Fe, 1978—; sci. fair judge N.Mex. Highlands U., 1978-83; staff loss control officer Energy and Minerals Dept., Santa Fe, 1984. Served with U.S. Army, 1970-72. Recipient Exemplary Performance award N.Mex. Energy and Minerals Dept., 1983; named hon. sec. of state N.Mex., 1984. Mem. Artesia C. of C. (bd. dirs. 1984—), Artesia Jaycees (pres. 1984), Am. Assn. Petroleum Geologists, Roswell Geol. Soc., N.Mex. Geol. Soc., N.Mex. Waterflood Assn., Sigma Gamma Epsilon, Tau Kappa Epsilon. Democrat. Mem. Society of Friends. Lodge: Moose. Office: HEY Co 324 W Main St 109 Artesia NM 88210

BROOKS, MILO RALPH, career military officer; b. Lake Odessa, Mich., May 3, 1944; s. Melvin Charles and Yvonne Fern (Haney) B.; m. Bonita Louise Thorpe, Dec. 1, 1962; children: Milo Jr., Steven, Marcella. BS in Bus. and Personnel Mgmt., Culver-Stockton Coll., 1974; MS in Mgmt., U. La Verne, 1981. Enlisted USAF, Rickenbacker AFB, Ohio, 1963; advanced through grades to capt. USAF, March AFB, Calif., 1978; chief, base adminstrn. USAF, Rickenbacker AFB, Ohio, 1977-78, commdr. Hdqrs. squadron, 1978-79; exec. officer, 71st Air Rescue and Recovery Service USAF, Elmendorf AFB, Alaska, 1979-82; exec. officer 379 Bomb Wing USAF, Wurtsmith AFB, Mich., 1982-86; commdr. Hdqrs. Squadron, 22d Air Refueling Squadron USAF, March AFB, Calif., 1985-86, chief base adminstrn. 22d combat support group, 1986—. Named Adminstrv. Officer of Yr. Air Rescue and Recovery Service, Elmendorf AFB, 1979, Adminstrv. Officer of Yr. BMW, Wurtsmith AFB, 1982-84. Mem. Air Force Assn. Home: 13135 Peacock A-155 Moreno Valley CA 92388 Office: USAF 22 CSG/DA March AFB CA 92518

BROOKS, PATTON MARTIN, food products merchandiser; b. Comanche, Okla., Dec. 24, 1939; s. Cecil Bryant and Murrel (Bounds) B.; m. Patricia McMahan, June 1, 1963; children: Gary, Lynn. Student, Draughns Bus. Sch., 1958-59, Modesto Jr. Coll., 1961, Delta Jr. Coll., 1979-80. From clk. to asst. mgr. Safeway Stores, various locations, 1956-61, Save Mart Stores, Modesto, Calif., 1962-67; buyer, merchandiser Save Mart Stores, Modesto, 1981—; store mgr. Save Mart Stores, Manteca, Calif., 1967-80. Bd. dirs. Manteca C. of C., 1970-71, 77-78. Served with USAR, 1963-66. Mem. Frozen Food Council No. Calif. (charter, treas. 1985, sec. 1986). Democrat. Lodge: Kiwanis. Avocations: golf, fishing. Home: 136 Hintze Ave Modesto CA 95354 Office: Save Mart Supermarkets 1800 Standiford Ave PO Box 4278 Modesto CA 95352-4278

BROOKS, RITA JANE, leasing company executive; b. Plainfield, N.J., Jan. 7, 1936; d. Robert Edward and Barbara Ann (Kowalak) Vanderweg; m. Donald Jerry Brooks, Mar. 28, 1959 (div. Jan. 1981); children: Gregory Paul, Terri Laine, Jana Deanne, Steven Donald. Student, Los Angeles City Coll., 1953-54; AA, Glendale (Calif.) Jr. Coll., 1955; BBA, UCLA, 1957. Expediter Statham Instruments, West Los Angeles, Calif., 1958-61; ops. asst. FMC Fin. Corp., San Jose, Calif., 1971-72, ops. supr., 1973-75, ops. mgr., 1976-77; nat. ops. mgr. FMC Fin. Corp., Santa Clara, Calif., 1977-83, v.p. nat. ops., 1983-86; v.p. Crossland Credit Corp., Santa Clara, 1986—. Area coordinator Bluebirds of Am., San Jose, 1969-71. Democrat. Roman Catholic. Avocations: handicrafts, culinary arts, investment studies, rose enthusiast, bowling.

BROOKS, ROBERT EUGENE, computer software executive; b. Chgo., June 13, 1946; s. Robert Eugene and Shirley Mae (Kunkel) B.; m. Tonya Thompson, Aug. 19, 1969; children: Shannon, Gabriel, Cyrus, Aleisha, Aaron, Ethan. AB, U. Calif., Berkeley, 1968; MA in Physics, U. Tex., 1972; PhD in Mgmt., MIT, 1975. Asst. prof. bus. U. So. Calif., Los Angeles, 1975-76; prin. Robert Brooks & Assocs., Norwalk, Calif., 1976-79; v.p. Transportation and Econ. Research Assocs., Washington, 1979-82; pres. RBA Cons., Los Angeles, 1982-84; v.p. Profit Mgmt. Devel. Inc., Barrington, Ill., 1984—; v.p. software devel. Profit Mgmt. Devel. Inc., Los Angeles and Barrington, 1984—; Cons. Arthur D. Little, Inc., Cambridge, Mass., 1972-75, Chase Econometrics, Bala Cynwyd, Pa., 1976, Mathematica, Inc., Princeton, N.J., 1977-78, 82, McDonald-Douglas Corp., 1987, fed. and state govts., Washington, Sacramento, Austin, Tex., 1976-83. Author: (computer models) GASNET, 1976, GASNET2, 1977, NETS, 1981, CMOTSIM, 1982; (books) Profit Maker, 1986. Mem. Inst. Mgmt. Scis. Mem. Ch. Scientology. Avocations: basketball, guitar, recorder. Home: 2150 Micheltorena St Los Angeles CA 90039 Office: PMD Inc 4209 Santa Monica Blvd Los Angeles CA 90029

BROOKS, STEVEN WESLEY, safety and loss control administrator; b. Spokane, Wash., Aug. 22, 1946; s. Jess Severian and Edith Irene (Benson) B.; A.A. in Police Sci. and Adminstrn., Spokane Community Coll., 1972, A.A. in Lab. Sci., 1973; B.A. in Gen. Studies, B.S. in Occupational Safety and Health, 1977; cert. safety exec. Gov.'s Safety Conf.; m. Doris Nancy Strom, June 19, 1971; children—Jody Ann, John Severian Bradford, Stefanie Doris. Personnel dir., safety officer Hygrade Food Product Corp., Spokane, 1977-78, safety dir., asst. personnel dir., Tacoma, 1978-79; safety edn. rep. Wash. State Dept. Social and Health Services, Medical Lake, 1979-86, safety loss control dir. Eastern State Hosp., 1986—; mem. panel Gov.'s Safety Conf. Food and Beverage Industries, 1977-79; active Boy Scouts Am.; Cubmaster with Cub Scouts. Served with U.S. Army, 1967-70. Mem. Am. Soc. Safety Engrs., World Safety Orgn., Nat. Fire Protection Assn., Profl. Safety Officers Assn., Inland Empire Infection Control Assn. Methodist. Clubs: Kiwanis, Eagles, Masons. Home: 3022 N Girard St Spokane WA 99212 Office: PO Box A Medical Lake WA 99022

BROOKS, TOM D., interior designer; b. Mangum, Okla., Oct. 6, 1930; s. Joe West and Lucille Marie (Kite) B.; m. Bessie Lee Norberg, Sept. 4, 1956; children: John Welsford, Katherine Marie. AA, U. Calif., Berkeley, 1951; BS in Fine Arts, Brigham Young U., 1959, postgrad., 1960; MS in Deaf Edn., Eastern N.Mex. U., 1970. Tchr. arts and crafts Liberty Union High Sch., Brentwood, Calif., 1960-62; office mgr. Fibreboard Paper Products Corp., San Francisco, 1962-65; display mgr. Montgomery Ward, Pleasant Hill, Calif., 1965-69; deaf edn. tchr. Napa (Calif.) Valley Sch. Dist., 1970-78; owner Gourmet Food and Cookware, St. Helena, Calif., 1978-84; pvt. practice interior design St. Helena, 1984—. Mem. archtl. rev. bd., Pleasant Hill, 1967-69. Served to cpl. U.S. Army, 1952-54. Office: Westwind Designs 1238 Spring St Saint Helena CA 94574

BROOKS, WAHNER EMALUS, government agency engineer; b. Portland, Oreg., Oct. 14, 1938; s. Raymond Emalus and Lorna Martha (Wahner) B.; m. Carol Louise Houghton, Apr. 15, 1966; children: Lorna Margaret, Susan Heather, Deborah Elise. BS in Gen. Engring., U. Portland, 1960. Materials engr. U.S. Bur. Reclamation, Sacramento, 1960-61; test engr. U.S. Army Yuma (Ariz.) Proving Ground, 1961-66, devel. engr., 1966-75, chief devel., 1975-81, dep. dir. testing, 1981—, acting tech. dir., 1981-86. Patentee in field. Chmn. Yuma Proving Ground Hist. Presevation com., 1984—; exec. sec. Yuma Proving Ground Hist. Soc., 1986. Served with U.S. Army, 1961-64. Mem. Inst. Environ. Scis. (sr.). Republican. Roman Catholic. Home: 2855 S Madison Ave Yuma AZ 85364 Office: US Army Yuma Proving Ground STEYP-MT Yuma AZ 85365

BROOM, GLEN MARTIN, communication educator; b. Anna, Ill., Nov. 2, 1940; s. Ralph Curvella and Wanda Audrey (Broadway) B.; m. Betty Lou Bollinger, Aug. 31, 1963. BS in Agrl. Communication, U. Ill., 1963, MS in Advt., 1967; PhD in Mass Communication, U. Wis., 1977. Asst. extension editor U. Ill. Coop. Extension Service, Urbana, 1963-68; v.p., dir. pub. relations Applied Behavioral Sci., Inc., Chgo., 1969-72; asst. prof. communications U. Wis., Madison, 1975-79; from assoc. prof. to prof. San Diego State U., 1979—; vis. prof. U. Tex., Austin, 1985-86. Author: (with others) Effective Public Relations, 1985; contbr. articles to profl. jours. Served with USAR, 1960-66. Mem. Pub. Relations Soc. Am., Assn. Edn. in Journalism and Mass Communication, Arthur W. Page Soc. Avocation: stained glass artisan. Office: San Diego State U Dept Journalism San Diego CA 92182-0116

BROOMFIELD, ANN LOUISE, heavy construction company executive; b. Portland, Oreg., June 2, 1943; d. Harold Eugene and Betty Anne (Applegate) Sanders; m. Robert William Broomfield, July 1, 1978; 1 child, Mary Louise. AA, Pima Coll., Tucson, 1978, postgrad., 1978—. Cert. constrn. assoc. Civil engring. technician, maintenance analyst Ariz. Dept. Transp., 1975-82; office mgr., comptroller Borderland Constrn. Co., Inc., 1982-86; office adminstr. Prodn. Concrete Constrn. Inc., Tucson, 1987—. Bd. dirs. Big Bros./Big Sisters; life mem. Girl Scouts U.S.; active United Way. Mem. Nat. Assn. Women in Constrn. (chpt. pres. 1983-85, cert. constrn. assoc. coordinator for edn. found., 1986—, nat. occupation research and referral com. chmn., 1985-86, nat. nominating com. 1985-86, coordinator nat. com. 1987-88), Profl. Secs. Internat., Nat. Rifle Assn., Nat. Wildlife Fedn. (life), Am. Biog. Inst. (hon.), Nat. C. of C. for Women, Nat. Assn. Female Execs., Nat. Fedn. Bus. and Profl. Women's Club, Phi Theta Kappa. Republican. Episcopalian.

BROPHY, JAMES JOHN, physicist, university official; b. Chgo., June 6, 1926; s. James J. and Ella Helen (Nerad) B.; m. Muriel Ann Johnson, Aug. 26, 1949; children: James J., John R., Thomas C. B.S. in Elec. Engring, Ill. Inst. Tech., 1947, M.S. in Physics, 1949, Ph.D. in Physics, 1951. Research physicist Armour Research Found. of Ill. Inst. Tech., 1951-53, supr. solid state physics, 1953-56, asst. dir. physics div., 1956-61, dir. tech. devel. of Found., 1961-63, v.p. for tech. devel., 1963-66; acad. v.p. Ill. Inst. Tech., 1967-76; sr. v.p. Inst. Gas Tech., Chgo., 1976-80; v.p. research U. Utah, Salt Lake City, 1980—; trustee Underwriters Labs., Inc. Author: Semiconductor Devices, 1965, Basic Electronics for Scientists, 1966, 4th edit., 1983; co-author: Electronic Processes in Materials, 1963; Co-editor: Organic Semiconductors; Contbr. articles to profl. jours. Fellow Am. Phys. Soc.; mem. AAAS, Western Soc. Engrs., Sigma Xi. Patentee on semiconductors, magnetic devices. Home: 2592 Elizabeth St Salt Lake City UT 84106 Office: 304 Park U Utah Salt Lake City UT 84112

BROSE, DAVID A., state folk arts coordinator; b. Columbus, Ohio, May 17, 1951; s. Albert R. and Betty (Van Schoyck) B.; m. Phyllis Harrison, Oct. 23, 1982. B.A., Ohio State U., 1978; M.A., Ind. U., 1982. Dir., Folklife Ctr., Columbus, Ohio, 1973-80; dir. Ohio Folklife Inc., Columbus, 1975-80; assoc. instr. Ind. U., Bloomington, 1980-82; coordinator folk arts Colo. Council on Arts, Denver, 1982—; cons. Mayor's Commn. on Arts, Denver, 1984—, Colo. Folk Arts Council, 1983—, Mus. N.Mex., Santa Fe, 1983—. Nat. Folk Festival, Washington, 1976—. Dir. Folk Arts Celebration, Denver Mayor's Office, 1984. Nat. Endowment Arts grantee, 1979, 82, 83, 84, 85, 86, 87. Mem. Am. Folklore Soc., Ohio Folklore Soc., Ind. Folklore Soc. Democrat. Lutheran. Home: 4865 Stuart St Denver CO 80212 Office: Colo Council on Arts and Humanities 770 Pennsylvania St Denver CO 80203

BROTMAN, RICHARD DENNIS, marriage, family and child counselor; Detroit, Nov. 2, 1952; s. Alfred David and Dorothy G. (Mansfield) B.; m. Debra Louise Hobold, Sept. 9, 1979. A.A., E. Los Angeles Jr. Coll., 1972; A.B., U. So. Calif., 1974, M.S., 1976. Instructional media coordinator Audio-Visual Div., Pub. Library, City of Alhambra, Calif., 1971-78; clin. supr. Hollywood-Sunset Community Clinic, Los Angeles, 1976—; client program coordinator N. Los Angeles County Regional Center for Developmentally Disabled, 1978-81; sr. counselor Eastern Los Angeles Regional Ctr. for Developmentally Disabled, 1981-85; dir. community services Almansor Edn. Ctr., 1985-87; counselor youth services City of Bell Gardens Police Dept., Calif., 1987—; intern U. So. Calif. Student Affairs Div., 1976. Corp. dir. San Gabriel Mission Players, 1973-75. Lic. marriage, family and child counselor, Calif.; cert. counselor Calif. Community Coll. Bd. Mem. Calif. Personnel and Guidance Assn. (conv. participant, 1976, 77, 79), Calif. Rehab. Counselors Assn. (officer), San Fernando Valley Consortium of Agys. Serving Developmentally Disabled Citizens (chmn. recreation subcom.), Los Angeles Aquarium Soc. Democrat. Home: 3515 Brandon St Pasadena CA 91107 Office: City Bell Gardens Police Dept 7100 S Garfield Ave Bell Gardens CA 90201

BROTO, VICTOR, testing laboratory administrator; b. Aquilue, Spain, July 26, 1924; came to U.S., 1948; s. Miguel and Maria (Llorens) B.; m. Ann Cloutier, June 16, 1952; children: Jose, Abigail, Jan. Baccalaureate, Barcelona U., Spain, 1946; BA in Chemistry, NYU, 1950, MS in Phys. and Organic Chemistry, 1954. Research chemist Aerojet Gen., Sacramento, Calif., 1959-65; mgr. research and prodn. Soundcraft, Danbury, Conn., 1966-68; research specialist Boeing, Seattle, 1968-74; pres. B&P Labs. Inc., Seattle, 1970—. Mem. Am. Chem. Soc. Home and Office: B & P Labs Inc 5635 Delridge Way SW Seattle WA 98106

BROUELETTE, JAMES ARTHUR, personnel director; b. Missoula, Mont., Mar. 25, 1941; s. Walter A. and Frances A. (Curran) B.; married; children: Heather, Justin. Grad. high sch., Missoula, 1959. Mgr. field office Wash. Corps., Missoula, 1971-76, equal opportunity officer, safety officer, 1977-84, mgr. personnel, 1984—. Served with USAF, 1959-63. Mem. Am. Soc. Safety Engrs., Mont. Contractors Assn. (chmn. equal opportunity/safety com. 1982—). Avocations: hunting, motorcycling, snowcatting.

Home: 3434 Mountain Dr Turah MT 59825 Office: Wash Corps 101 International Way Missoula MT 59807

BROUGH, THEODORE GORDON, statistician; b. Congress Park, Ill., Mar. 4, 1924; s. John Capen and Helen Merle (McFadden) B.; student Lyons Town Jr. Coll., 1945-46; A.B., UCLA, 1953; M.A., N.Mex. State U., 1966, Ph.D., 1974; m. Martha W. Johnson, July 4, 1964. Asst. to curator reptiles and invertebrates Brookfield Zoo, Chgo., 1947-48; lit. editor Inland Journalist, Congress Park, 1949-51; editor Sears Catalog, Chgo., 1950-52; sci. editor U.S. Naval Radiol. Def. Lab., San Francisco, 1953-59, publ. br. head, 1955-59, research physicist, 1959-61, sr. physicist, 1961-65; teaching asst. English dept. N.Mex. State U., Las Cruces, 1966, ednl. research tng. fellow Office of Edn., 1966-69; research specialist Western Nev. Regional Edn. Center, Lovelock, 1969-71; project supr. Pupil Personnel Center, Fallon, Nev., 1971-72; dir. Western Research and Evaluation Center, Las Cruces, 1972—; environ. scientist in radiation N.Mex. Environ. Improvement Div., Milan, 1977-86; cons. Bi-Lingual Migrant Student Project, Pasco, Wash., 1975-76. Co-dir., co-founder Mt. Taylor Wilderness Forum, Grants, N.Mex., 1978. Served with USNR, 1942-46. Recipient award for outstanding research in Nev., Office of Edn., 1970, HEW award for outstanding bilingual project, 1976. Mem. Am. Phys. Soc., Health Physics Soc., AAAS, Sigma Xi, Phi Delta Kappa, Beta Beta Beta, Sigma Pi Sigma, Psi Chi. Methodist. Club: Lions. Editor: Principles of Radiation Contamination and Control, 3 vols., 1959; contbr. chpt. to book, Effects of Nuclear Weapons, 1962, articles to sci. and edn. publs. Home: 1513 Andrews Dr Las Cruces NM 88001 Office: 1513 Andrews Dr Las Cruces NM 88001

BROUGHAM, WILLIAM POWERS, resource, land management and brokerage executive; b. Joilet, Ill., Jan. 16, 1942; s. Erwin Roy and Ann (Powers) B.; B.S. in Community Recreation and Bus. Mgmt., So. Ill. U., 1966; M.S., Ind. U., 1968; m. Sandra Elaine Schechter, Nov. 30, 1968 (div. 1974); children—Calburn Powers, Brandy Ayn; m. Ineke Minke Boorsma, Oct. 15, 1983; 1 child, William Powers II. Asst. dir. parks and recreation Village of Park Forest (Ill.), 1966-67; teaching assoc. Ind. U., Bloomington, 1967-68; regional parks dir. Colo. Div. Games, Fish & Parks, Southeast region, 1968-72; met. regional dir. Colo. Div. Parks and Outdoor Recreation, Denver, 1972-78; founder, pres. Colo. Gold Consulting, Inc., Denver, 1978—; recreation land and property specialist, broker-assoc. Fuller & Co. Comml. and Ind. Investments, 1978—; registered lobbyist Colo. Legislature, 1978—; cons. on park devel. and recreation programming; cons. on environ. ecology Pikes Peak Area Council of Govts., also Denver Regional Council Govts.; guest lectr. U. Colo., Met. State Coll. Founder, trustee Colo. State Park Found. Named to Hall of Fame, Denver Post Newspapers, 1976; named Man of Yr., Colo. Div. Parks and Outdoor Recreation, 1976. Mem. Nat. Recreation and Park Assn. (nat. membership chmn. 1974-78), Nat. Soc. for Park Resources (dir.), Colo. Park and Recreation Soc. (dir.), Colo. Regional Park Assn., Denver Bd. Realtors, Million Dollar Round Table, Colo. Assn. Realtors, Nat. Assn. Realtors, Realtor Land Inst. (met. regional v.p., nat. membership com., chmn. nat. edn. com.), Grad. Realtor Inst. (accredited land cons.), Alumni Tau Kappa Epsilon. Mem. Calvary Temple Ch. Home: 4517 S Lowell Blvd Denver CO 80236 Office: Fuller & Co One Park Central Suite 1600 Denver CO 80202

BROUGHTON, RAY MONROE, banker; b. Seattle, Mar. 2, 1922; s. Arthur Charles and Elizabeth C. (Young) B.; B.A., U. Wash., 1947, M.B.A., 1960; m. Margret Ellen Ryno, July 10, 1944 (dec.); children—Linda Rae Broughton Hellenthal, Mary Catherine Broughton Boutin; m. 2d, Carole Jean Packer, 1980. Mgr. communications and managerial devel. Gen. Electric Co., Hanford Atomic Products Ops., Richland, Wash., 1948-59; mktg. mgr., asst. to pres. Smyth Enterprises, Seattle, 1960-62; dir. research Seattle Area Indsl. Council, 1962-65; v.p., economist (mgr. econ. research dept.) First Interstate Bank of Oreg., N.A., Portland, 1965—; mem. econ. adv. com. to Am. Bankers Assn., 1980-83; mem. Gov.'s Econ. Adv. Council, 1981—; instr. bus. communications U. Wash., Richland, 1956-57. Treas., dir. Oreg. affiliate Am. Heart Assn., 1972-78, chmn., 1980-81, dir., 1980-84. Served to 1st lt. U.S. Army, 1943-46; ETO. Mem. Western Econ. Assn., Pacific N.W. Regional Econ. Conf. (dir. 1967—), Nat. Assn. Bus. Economists (co-founder chpt. 1971), Am. Mktg. Assn. (pres. chpt. 1971-72), Alpha Delta Sigma. Episcopalian. Author: Trends and Forces of Change in the Payments System and the Impact on Commercial Banking, 1972; contbg. editor Pacific Banker and Bus. mag., 1974-80. Office: First Interstate Bank Oreg 1300 SW 5th Ave PO Box 3131 Portland OR 97208

BROUGHTON-SORMAN, RUSTY EVELYN, personal and management counselor; b. Holdrege, Nebr., Apr. 22, 1944; s. Mitchell Woodrow and Aline G. McCain; m. James Michael Broughton, Nov. 13, 1970 (div.); children: Stephen Edward, Eric Sean, Kirsten Lee; m. Karl Lewis Sorman, May 28, 1983. AA, Northeastern Colo. Coll., 1964; BA, Western Colo. Coll., 1966; postgrad. Tulane U., 1968; MA, Idaho State U., 1977. Supr. in child protection Colo. Dept. Health and Welfare, 1968-70; coordinator aftercare Boise (Idaho) Mental Health, 1970-73; coordinator, psychologist, mgr. mental health services Idaho Falls (Idaho) Dept. Health and Welfare, 1973-77; initiator, mgr., indsl. psychologist Idaho Nat. Engring. Lab., Employee Assistance Program Idaho, Idaho Falls, 1977-81; sr. facilitator, dir. Learning Dynamics, Inc., Boston and Idaho Falls, 1980—, cons., 1983—; assoc. Caditz & Assocs., Mercer Island, Wash., 1986—; mgr. Employee Assistance Program Hosp. Corp. of Am., Idaho Falls, Idaho; pres. Interpersonal Dynamics, Inc., Idaho Falls, 1980; v.p. ASM Interchange, Profl. Travelers Network, Inc. Contbr. articles to profl. jours. Past bd. dirs. YMCA, Women Against Violence, Christian Family Services; bd. dirs. United Way, 1984—, campaign chmn., 1985—, Rockwood Growth Fund, Inc. Recipient Outstanding Achievement award Nat. United Way Am., 1986; Idaho Gov.'s Outstanding Achievement award; appreciation awards from various local orgns.; Northeastern Colo. Coll. scholar; Western Colo. Coll. scholar; Tulane U. scholar. Mem. Am. Soc. for Tng. and Devel., Am. Soc. for Personnel Adminstrn., Idaho Falls C. of C. (Wayne C. Hammond award for outstanding service), Am. Assn. Counseling Devel.

BROUILLETTE, JOSEPH EDWARD, telecommunications company executive, consultant, lecturer; b. Ft. Thomas, Ky., Aug. 28, 1946; s. Edward Joseph and Mary Agnes (Kunkler) B.; m. Madlyn Cheryl DeWolf, Nov. 17, 1973; children—Kristin, Joshua, Logan. B.S. in Fin., Econs., Psychology, San Diego State U., 1969. Cons. Pacific Telephone Co., Los Angeles, 1969-73, industry mgr., 1978-80; chmn., pres. Joseph Brouillette Co., Inc., Newport Beach, Calif., 1973-80; exec. v.p. Retrievers Corp., Boulder, Colo., 1980-82; group v.p. fin., adminstrn. and data processing TMC, Inc., Denver, 1982-84; pres. TMC/Am., Inc., 1984—; pres. Securities, Inc., TMC Network Services, Inc., TelAmerica, Inc., Men's W.C. Martin Ch., Bedford, Tex.; cons., lectr. in field; motivational speaker; dir. Retrievers Corp., Pacific Bio-Med. Corp., Irvine, Calif. Trustee St. Andrew's Found., Newport Beach, Calif.; mem. Christian Businessmen's Com., Tampa, Fla.; trustee Carrollwood Presbyn. Ch. Mem. Smithsonian Inst. Assocs. Lodge: Elks. Home: 2208 Pine Thicket Ln Bedford TX 76021

BROUSSARD, ALLEN E., state supreme court justice; b. Lake Charles, La., Apr. 13, 1929; m. Odessa Broussard; children: Eric, Craig, Keith. A.B. in Polit. Sci., U. Calif.-Berkeley, 1950, J.D., 1953. Bar: Calif. 1954. Sole practice San Francisco and Oakland, Calif., 1954-56; research atty. for presiding justice Dist. Ct. Appeals 1st Appellate Dist., 1st Div., 1953-54; sole practice 1956-59; assoc. Wilson, Metoyer & Sweeney, 1959-61; mem. firm Metoyer, Sweeney & Broussard, 1961-64; judge Oakland-Piedmont dist. Mcpl. Ct., 1964-75, Alameda County Superior Ct., Oakland, 1975-81; justice Calif. Supreme Ct., San Francisco, 1981—; mem. faculty Golden Gate Coll., San Francisco, 1971, U. San Francisco, 1972, Calif. Coll. Trial Judges, 1969-72, 74; advisor to exec. com. Jud. Council Calif.; v.p. governing com. Ctr. Jud. Edn. and Research; mem. council judges Nat. Council Crime and Delinquency. Vice pres. East Bay Big Bros. Am.; bd. dirs. Alameda County Community Found.; bd. dirs., past chmn. Oakland Men of Tomorrow, Black Bus. and Profl. Men's Service Orgn. Served with U.S. Army, 1954-56. Arthur Newhouse, Arthur Gold Tashiera scholar. Mem. Conf. Calif. Judges (exec. bd. 1970-71, pres. 1972-73), Nat. Bar Assn. (exec. bd. jud. council), Alameda County Bar Assn. (v.p.), Alameda County Criminal Cts. Bar Assn., Boalt Hall Alumni Assn. (past dir.), State Bar Calif., Phi Alpha Delta. Club: Charles Houston Law. Office: Calif Supreme Ct 4050 State Bldg 350 McAllister St San Francisco CA 94102 *

BROWER, MYRON RIGGS, architect, interior designer, educator; b. Muscatine, Iowa, Dec. 8, 1949; s. Myron Orson and Marcene P. (Shafnett) B. BArch, Ariz. State U., 1973, BA in Edn., 1977. Registered architect, Ariz., Calif. Architect in tng. Fenlason Assocs., Architects, Tempe, Ariz., 1975-77; pres. Myron Riggs Brower, Architect, Inc., Scottsdale, Ariz., 1977—; v.p. Herges Brower Corp. Gen. Contractors, Scottsdale, 1985—; ptnr. R.A.M. Devel. Group., Scottsdale, 1986—; prof. Scottsdale Community Coll., 1982—. Mem. AIA, Am. Soc. Interior Designers (assoc.). Republican. Avocations: sports, music.

BROWN, ALBERT CLARENCE, city official; b. Los Angeles, Oct. 25, 1918; s. Albert C. and Wanda (Albright) B.; m. Virginia Little, 1941; children—Cheryl Kinsman, Susan Baltagi, Becky Westerdahl. A.A., Riverside City Coll., 1939. Owner, mgr. Brown's Engine, Riverside, Calif., 1948-84; mayor City of Riverside, 1978—. Trustee Riverside City Coll., 1964-78. Served with USN, 1940-45, PTO. Recipient Alumnus of Yr. award Riverside City Coll., 1977, Outstanding Service award Catholic Athletic League, Riverside. Republican. Lodges: Elks, Masons, Shriners, Lions (past pres.). Home: 2330 Prince Albert Dr Riverside CA 92507 Office: Office of Mayor 3900 Main St Riverside CA 92522

BROWN, ALBERTA MAE, respiratory clinician; b. Columbus, Ohio, Nov. 11, 1932; d. Sylvester Clarence and Malinda (Mason) Angel; grad. Antelope Valley Coll., 1961; A.A., Los Angeles Valley Coll., 1975; B.S., Calif. State U., Dominguez Hills, 1981; m. Norman Brown, Dec. 29, 1967; children—Charon, Charles, Stevan, Carole. Nurses aid, vocat. nurse, respiratory therapist St. Bernardines Hosp., 1965-69, Good Samaritan Hosp., Los Angeles, 1969-70, Midway Hosp., Los Angeles, 1973-81; allergy nurse, instr. respiratory therapy VA Hosp., Los Angeles, 1970—, also acting dept. head; nurse, respiratory splty. unit Jerry L. Pettis Meml. Hosp., Loma Linda, Calif., 1984—; instr. Los Angeles Valley Med. Technologists Sch., Compton Coll. seminar instr., 1979. Active Arrowhead Allied Arts Council of San Bernardino; CPR instr. Am. Heart Assn. Lic. vocat. nurse; R.N. Mem. Am. Assn. Respiratory Therapy, Nat. Honor Soc., Eta Phi Beta. Democrat. Baptist. Clubs: Social-Lites, Inc. of San Bernardino, (pres.) Order Eastern Star. Patentee disposable/replaceable tubing for stethoscope. Home: 1545 N Hancock St Orangewood Estates San Bernardino CA 92411 Office: Jerry L Pettis VA Hospital Wilshire and Sawtelle Blvds Loma Linda CA 92357

BROWN, ANN CAROL, business consultant, psychologist; b. Beech Grove, Ind., May 6, 1946; d. Irmel Nelson and Margaret Pauline (Harmon) B.; m. Richard Tanner Pascale, June 14, 1975. B.A. summa cum laude with honors in Psychology, Tulane U., 1968; M.A. in Social Psychology, U. Rochester, 1969, Ph.D., 1973. Cons. Boston Consulting Group, 1970-71, Olympus Research, San Francisco, 1971-72; gen. mgr. Wells Fargo Bank, San Francisco, 1973-80; cons. bus. mgmt. and mktg., San Francisco, 1980—; exec. com. mem. Coca-Cola USA, Atlanta, 1983-86; sr. v.p. Fed. Asset Disposition Assn ., 1986—. Pres. Women's Forum-West, San Francisco, 1982-84. Mem. Am. Psychol. Assn., Am. Bankers Assn. (chmn. mktg. research div. 1977-79), Sierra Club (chmn. fin. adv. adminstrn. and investment com. 1973-76, Outstanding Vol. 1973), Phi Beta Kappa, Psi Chi, Pi Delta Phi. Republican. Office: Fed Asset Disposition Assn 2203 Divisadero St San Francisco CA 94115

BROWN, ANTHONY B., aerospace executive; b. Mpls., Apr. 5, 1922; s. Wayland Hoyt and Adele (Birdsall) B.; m. Mary Alice Ann Anderson, July 28, 1956. BS, Rutgers U., 1949; postgrad. U. So. Calif., 1968-69; PhD, U. Beverly Hills, 1986. Cert. data processor, systems profl. Sr. system analyst Thrifty Corp., Los Angeles, 1957-69; system engr. Informatics Gen., Inc., Los Angeles, 1969-73; contract instr. computer software York U., 1970, McGill U., U. Victoria, 1971, USMC, Boston U., W.Va. U., U. Guelph, 1972; sr. system engr. Jet Propulsion Lab., La Canada, Calif., 1974-76; sr. system engr. Informatics Gen., Inc., Anchorage, Los Angeles, Washington, 1976-78; supr. project control Hughes Aircraft Co., Los Angeles, 1978-81; mgr. fin. Contel Corp., Redondo Beach, Calif., 1981— . Author: A Century of Blunders--America's China Policy 1844-1949. Rep. precinct capt., presdl. election, 1964; chmn. bd. govs. La Brea Vista Townhouses, 1967-68; active numerous animal welfare orgns. Served with Finance Corps, U.S. Army, 1951-57. Decorated Bronze Star. Fellow Brit. Interplanetary Soc.; mem. AAAS, The Planetary Soc., Nature Conservancy, Town Hall of Calif., Assn. Computer Machinery (chpt. sec. 1973-74), Assn. Systems Mgmt., Mensa, Intertel, Armed Forces Communications and Electronics Assn., Assn. Inst. Cert. Computer Profls., Am. Assn. Fin. Profls., Am. Def. Preparedness Assn., Washington Legal Found., Am. Security Council (mem. nat. adv. bd.), Calif. Soc., SAR, Mil. Order World Wars, Aircraft Owners and Pilots Assn., Internat. Platform Assn., Theodore Roosevelt Assn., Res. Officers Assn., Delta Phi Epsilon. Republican. Club: Los Angeles Athletic. Lodges: Masons, Shriners, Nat. Sojourners. Home: 4333 Redwood Ave Marina del Rey CA 90292 Office: Contel Corp 2411 Santa Fe Ave Redondo Beach CA 90278

BROWN, ARCHIBALD MANNING, JR., magazine publisher; b. Burlington, Vt., Sept. 2, 1942; s. Archibald Manning and Mary Marshall (Canfield) B.; m. Laura Havemeyer Webb, July 12, 1969; children: Brewster, Hope, Alexander. BA, Boston U., 1965; MBA, U. Ariz., 1967. Account exec. Merrill Lynch, Tucson, 1972-79; advt. dir. Am. West Mag., Tucson, 1980-83, pub., 1983—; pres. Monterey (Calif.) Life Mags. Inc., 1984-85. Devel. dir. Green Fields Sch., Tucson, 1984-85; bd. dirs. Tucson Mus. Art., 1984-85, Ariz. Sonora Desert Mus., Tucson, 1976-78, nominating chmn., 1978; pres. Big Bros. of Tucson, 1978-79. Served to capt. USAF, 1967-72. Rebublican. Episcopalian. Avocations: skiing, jogging, hiking. Home: 6161 E Miramar Dr Tucson AZ 85715 Office: Am West Mag 7000 E Tanque Verde Rd #30 Tucson AZ 85715

BROWN, BARBARA BLACK, publishing company executive; b. Eureka, Calif., Dec. 11, 1928; d. William Marion and Letitia (Brunia) Black; m. Vinson Brown, June 18, 1950; children—Tamara Pinn, Roxana Hodges, Keven. B.A., Western State Coll., Gunnison, Colo. Owner, mgr. Naturegraph Pubs., Inc., Los Altos, Calif., 1950-53, San Martin, Calif., 1953-60, Healdsburg, Calif., 1960-76, Happy Camp, Calif., 1976—. Mem. Baha'i World Faith. Office: Naturegraph Pubs Inc 3543 Indian Creek Rd Happy Camp CA 96039

BROWN, BERT MAHLON, state legislator; b. Shreveport, La., Jan. 21, 1914; s. Bert Mahlon and Perle (Sells) B.; student UCLA, 1931-34; LL.B., George Washington U., 1937; m. Lucille Cummings, Apr. 20, 1938; children—Bert Mahlon III, Stephen Cummings. Admitted to Nev. bar, 1947, sole practice, Las Vegas, ret. 1985; mem. Nev. Senate from Clark County Dist., 1950-77, minority leader, 1955-64, majority leader, 1965-77, pres. pro tem, 1967-68, ret., 1977. Mem. Nev. Legis. Commn., 1953-73, chmn., 1959; mem. Adv. Commn. on Intergovt. Relations, 1969-74; adv. council Nat. Legis. Found., 1977; mem. exec. com. Nat. Conf. State Legis. Leaders, 1971-74, Nat. Legis. Conf., 1970-74, Nat. Conf. State Legislatures, 1975-76; trustee Nat. Legis. Leaders Found., 1975-76, Nev. Law Found., 1985—; named to Nev. Commn. on Aging, 1986—. Served to lt. USNR, 1943-46. Named Disting. Nevadan, U. Nev.-Las Vegas, 1978; B. Mahlon Brown Jr. High Sch. named in his honor, Henderson, Nev., 1983. Democrat. Home: 60 Country Club Ln Las Vegas NV 89109 Office: Valley Bank Plaza 300 S 4th St Suite 600 Las Vegas NV 89101

BROWN, BRUCE LEONARD, psychology educator; b. Am. Fork, Utah, May 10, 1941; s. Marvin Erwin and Ruby Marie (Harrington) B.; m. Susan Brinton, June 6, 1966; children: Catherine, Suzanne, Jennifer, Robert Bruce, Rebecca, Barbara, Elizabeth, Kristina, Annette, Michelle. BS with honors, Brigham Young U., 1965, MS, 1968; PhD, McGill U., Montreal, Can., 1969. Instr. psychology Brigham Young U., Provo, Utah, 1968-69, asst. prof., 1969-72, assoc. prof., 1972-79, prof. psychology, 1979—; cons. quantitative methods Behavioral Sci. Resources, Inc., 1984—, Loveland Constrn. Co., 1986—; rep. faculty adv. council Brigham Young U., 1985—. Author: Statistics for Behavioral Scis., 1983; contbr. articles to profl. jours.; assoc. editor Jour. Assn. Mormon Counselors and Psychotherapists, 1984—. Utah County Rep. del., 1972, 86; advisor Explorer Pres.'s Assn. Boy Scouts Am., Cascade Dist., 1985, dist. chmn. 1985—. Served with Utah Air N.G., 1960. Fellow NSF, Brigham Young U., 1965, U. Mich., Ann Arbor, 1969; grantee NIMH, Washington, 1970-74. Mem. Acoustical Soc. Am., Psychometric Soc., Rocky Mountain Psychol. Assn., Jaycees (one of Outstanding Young Men of Am. 1972), Sigma Xi, Phi Kappa Phi, Phi Eta Sigma. Mormon. Avocations: sports, woodworking, wilderness survival. Home: 4061 Devonshire Dr Provo UT 84604 Office: Brigham Young U Psychology Dept 1126SWKT Provo UT 84602

BROWN, BURNELL ROLAND, JR., anesthesiology educator, biomedical researcher; b. Dallas, May 9, 1933; s. Burnell R. Sr. and Josephine Elizabeth Brown; m. Helen Diane Guilbault, Dec. 24, 1959; children: Monica, Michelle, Gregory, Philip. BS, Springhill Coll., 1954; MD, Tulane U., 1958; PhD in Pharmacology, U. Tex., 1969. Diplomate Am. Bd. Anesthesiology. Asst. prof. medicine U. Tex., Dallas, 1968-69, Harvard U., Boston, 1969-71; prof. anesthesiology U. Ariz., Tucson, 1971—; head FDA Com. on Anesthetic and Respiratory Drugs, 1977-79. Editor Anesthesiology Journal, 1973-82; contbr. articles to profl. jours. Served to capt. U.S. Army, 1959-62. Named Plenary Speaker World Congress Anesthesiologists, Manila, Philipines, 1983. Mem. Assn. Univ. Anesthetists (pres. 1980-82). Republican. Roman Catholic. Avocations: astronomy, jogging, music. Home: 3562 Placita Vistosa Tucson AZ 85715 Office: U Ariz Dept Anesthesiology Tucson AZ 85721

BROWN, BYRON WILLIAM, JR., biostatistician, educator; b. Chgo., Apr. 21, 1930; s. Byron William and Ruth (Munson) B.; m. Janet Louise Hyde, July 30, 1949; children: Byron William III, Eric Paul, Alan Thomas, Nancy Ellen, Mark Andrew, Lisa Anne. B.A. in Math., U. Minn., 1952, M.S. in Stats., 1955, Ph.D. in Biostats., 1959. Asst. prof. biostats. La. State U. Med. Sch., New Orleans, 1956-57; from lectr. to assoc. prof. Sch. Pub. Health, U. Minn., 1957-65, prof., head biostats., 1965-68; prof. biostats., head div. Stanford U., Calif., 1968—; cons. govt. and industry. Co-author: Statistics: A Biomedical Introduction; Contbr. articles to profl. jours., books, encys. Served with USAF, 1949. Fellow Am. Statis. Assn. (sect. pres., asso. editor Jour.), Am. Heart Assn., AAAS; mem. Biometrics Soc. (pres. Western N.Am. region 1978), Inst. Math. Statistics, Phi Beta Kappa, Sigma Xi. Democrat. Lutheran. Home: 981 Cottrell Way Stanford CA 94305

BROWN, CAROL NAPIER SUTTON, financial planning company executive; b. Atlanta, Dec. 2, 1943; d. Homer Bates and Eulalia (Napier) Sutton; m. W. Hilory Brown, June 11, 1977. BA, Agnes Scott Coll., 1965; student, Peabody Coll., 1966-67; teaching cert., U. Chattanooga, 1967; student, Golden Gate U., 1983—. Cert. fin. planner. Sales agt. Lincoln Nat. Life Ins., Atlanta and San Francisco, 1975-77; pension rep. Crown Life Ins. Co., San Francisco, 1977-79; group health and pension rep. Mutual of N.Y., San Francisco, 1979-80; registered rep. Judith Briles & Co., Palo Alto, Calif., 1980-81; registered prin. Pvt. Ledger Fin. Services, Inc., Los Altos, Calif., 1981—. Contbr. articles to profl. jours. Mem. AAUW, Santa Clara County Chpt. Internat. Assn. Fin. Planners (v.p. programs 1985-86, v.p. mem. 1984-85, sec. 1983-84, pres.-elect 1986-87, pres., 1987—), Fin. Planning Forum, Western Pension Conf., Peninsula Life Underwriters, Peninsula Profl. Women's Network. Republican. Methodist. Avocations: reading, music, cooking. Home: 2323 Sharon Rd #137 Menlo Park CA 94025 Office: Fin Resource Team Inc 199 First St #300 Los Altos CA 94022

BROWN, CAROLYN SMITH, communications educator, consultant; b. Salt Lake City, Aug. 12, 1946; d. Andrew Delbert and Olive (Crane) Smith; m. David Scott Brown, Sept. 10, 1982. BA magna cum laude, U. Utah, 1968, MA, 1972, PhD, 1974. Instr. Salt Lake Ctr., Brigham Young U., Salt Lake City, 1976-78; vis. asst. prof. Brigham Young U., Provo, 1978; asst. prof. Am. Inst. Banking, Salt Lake City, 1977—; prof., chmn. English, communication and gen. edn. depts. Latter Day Saints Bus. Coll., Salt Lake City, 1973—, acad. dean, 1986—; founder, pres. Career Devel. Tng., Salt Lake City, 1979—; field mktg. dir. Personal Dynamics/Performax Inc., Mpls., 1978—; cons. inhouse seminars First Security Realty Services, USDA Soil Conservation Service, Utah Power & Light, Utah State Social Services, Utah State Dept. Corrections, Intermountain Health Care, Continental Bank; chmn. centennial coordination com. Latter Day Saints Bus. Coll., 1986-87, N.W. accreditation self-study com. 1980-82, 87, Title IX self-evaluation com., 1977, 79, grievance com., 1979—. Author: Writing Letters & Reports That Communicate, 6 ed., 1985; contbr. articles to profl. jours. Demi-soloist Utah Civic Ballet (now Ballet West), Salt Lake City, 1964-68; active Mormon Ch. Named Outstanding Alumnus in Literature, Kappa Kappa Gamma, Salt Lake City, 1974, Tchr. of Month, Salt Lake City Kiwanis, 1981; NDEA fellow, U. Utah, 1972. Mem. Am. Bus. Communications Assn. (lectr. West/N.W. Regional mtg., 1987), Phi Kappa Phi, Delta Kappa Gamma Soc. for Educators (2d v.p. 1977-79). Republican. Clubs: Alice Louise Reynolds Literary (Salt Lake City) (v.p. 1978-79, sec. 1985-86). Avocations: racquetball, swimming, hiking, slide lectures on Israel and literary topics. Office: LDS Bus Coll 411 E South Temple Salt Lake City UT 84111

BROWN, CHARLES STUART, state supreme court justice; b. Freedom, Wyo., June 30, 1918; s. Charles William and Julia Teola (Rainey) B.; m. Jane Hurst, Aug. 6, 1941; children: Ann (Mrs. Paul Christensen), Julia (Mrs. Dan Gibson), James Stuart, Colleen (Mrs. Rick Perkins), Patricia (Mrs. John Evans), Robert William, Helen (Mrs. Timothy Curry), Virginia (Mrs. John Evans). B.S., Utah State U., 1943; J.D., U. Utah, 1950. Bar: Wyo. 1950, Utah 1950. Prin. Freedom Elem. Sch., 1946-47; individual practice law Kemmerer, Wyo., 1950-59; pros. atty. Lincoln County, 1959-65; judge 3d Jud. Dist. Wyo. Dist. Ct., Kemmerer, 1965-81; chief justice Wyo. State Supreme Ct., Cheyenne, 1981—; asso. solicitor Dept. Interior, Washington, 1961-62. Author: Wyoming Ranch and Farm Law, 1959. Served to col. AUS, 1942-46. Office: Supreme Ct Bldg Cheyenne WY 82001 *

BROWN, CHET (CHESTER ARTHUR), JR., sales executive; b. Boston, Oct. 14, 1938; s. Chester Arthur and Anna Hilda (Smith) B.; m. Marcie K. Brown; children—Patricia, Lind, Stephen, Christopher, Laura, Edward. B.A. in Chemistry, Boston U., 1960; M.B.A. in Mktg., Northeastern U., 1962. Vice pres., sales and mktg. High Voltage Engring. Corp., Burlington, Calif., 1961-72; founder/ptnr. Ferro Fluidics Corp., Burlington, 1972-75; mgr. West Coast Office, Alpha Industries, San Jose, Calif., 1976-78; internat. mktg. mgr. Network Products Operation, Beckman Instruments, Fullerton, Calif., 78-80; group v.p. communications and subsystems Western Digital Corp., Irvine, Calif., 1980—. Mem. IEEE, Am. Mgmt. Assn., Assn. Old Crows. Republican. Recipient Assn. Indsl. Advertisers award, 1967; Bus. Press Assn. awards; patentee in field. Office: Western Digital Corp 2445 McCabe Way Irvine CA 92714

BROWN, DANIEL CARLING, physician; b. Berkeley, Calif., Nov. 16, 1941; s. Irving C. and Helen G. (Garber) B.; m. Joan Lynn DeBakcsy, July 6, 1968; children: Christopher, Alex. BSME, U. Mich., 1963; MD, U. Calif., Irvine, 1973. Diplomat Am. Bd. Internal Medicine and Cardiology. Intern U. So. Calif.-Los Angeles County Med. Ctr., 1973-74, resident in internal medicine, 1974-76; cardiology fellowship UCLA-Harbor Geneva Hosp., 1976-78; physician Bellingham, Wash., 1978—; pres. Cons. in Internal Medicine, Bellingham, 1986—; dir. coronary care unit, St. Luke Hosp., Bellingham, 1978—. Pres. Whatcom County div. Wash. chpt. Am. Heart Assn. Served to lt. USN, 1965-68. Fellow Am. Coll. Cardiology, Am. Heart Assn. (clin. council). Republican. Episcopalian. Lodge: Rotary (pres.-elect 1986). Home: 638 Fieldston Bellingham WA 98225

BROWN, DENNIS EDWARD, journalism educator; b. Marshalltown, Iowa, Feb. 4, 1933; s. Theodore Thomas and Pauline Evangeline (Bootjer) B.; m. Maureen Ann Cavanaugh, Sept. 7, 1963; children: Katherine Ann, Douglas Edward, Laura Elizabeth. A.B. magna cum laude; A.B. (Coll. scholar), Harvard U., 1955; postgrad. (Rockefeller Theol. fellow), Union Theol. Sem., 1955-56; M.A., U. Iowa, 1961; Ph.D. (U.S. Steel Found. fellow), U. Mo., 1970. Reporter Des Moines Register, 1959-60; editor-writer Office Public Info., U. Iowa, Iowa City, 1960-65; assoc. dir. Office Public Info., U. Mo., Columbia, 1966-67; asst. dir. Freedom of Info. Center, 1967-68; mem. faculty dept. journalism and mass communications San Jose State U., 1968—, prof. journalism, 1971—, chmn. dept., 1970—. Editorial bd.: Harvard Crimson, 1954-55; Contbr. articles to profl. jours. Served to 2d lt. U.S. Army, 1957-58. Mem. Assn. Schs. Journalism and Mass Communications, Assn. Edn. in Journalism and Mass Communications, Soc. Profl. Journalists, Sigma Delta Chi, Kappa Tau Alpha. Home: 7008 Elmsdale Dr San Jose CA 95120

BROWN, DOUGLAS HAZEN, II, manufacturing executive; b. Salt Lake City, Nov. 29, 1951; s. Douglas H. Sr. and Joy (Wooley) B.; m. Judy Bess, Apr. 17, 1984. BS, Westminster Coll., Salt Lake City, 1974; MBA, U. Utah, 1976. Mgr. Capitol Tempering, Salt Lake City, 1976-80; mgr. glass fabrication Capitol Glass & Aluminum Corp., Salt Lake City, 1980-82, v.p. ops., 1982-84, pres., 1984—. Mem. Porsche Club (local pres. 1982-83, nat. chmn.). Avocations: flying, scuba, auto racing, motorcycling, biking. Office: Capitol Glass and Aluminum Corp 3515 S 300 W Salt Lake City UT 84115

BROWN, DUART VINSON, publisher, author, biologist; b. Reno, Nev., Dec. 7, 1912; s. Henry Alexander and Bertha (Bender) B.; m. Elisabeth Bragden (div. 1945); children: Kirby, Jerrold; m. Barbara Ann Black, June 18, 1950; children: Tamara Duncan, Roxana Vanderhoof, Keven Alexander. BA in Zoology, U. Calif., Berkeley, 1939; MA in Biology, Stanford U., 1947. Dir. Boy Naturalists' Club, Berkeley, Calif., 1935-41; asst. scout dir. Boy Scouts Am., Olympia, Wash., 1942; writer Office War Info., San Francisco, 1943-44; founder, pres., co-owner Naturegraph Pubs., Inc., Los Altos, Calif., 1946-85, Happy Camp, Calif., 1985—; lectr. Nat. Sch. Assemblies, 1949-50; columnist weekly newspapers Calif., Gilroy Dispatch, Los Altos News, Los Gatos Times Observer, Sebastopol Times, Santa Rosa News, Healdsburg Tribune, Sonoma Index-Tribune, 1950-85. Author: Amateur Naturalists Handbook, 1947, revised edit., 1980, Russian edit., 1986, John Paul Jones, a School Reader, 1950, Black Treasure, 1951, Sea Mammals and Reptiles of Pacific Coast, 1972, The Explorer Naturalist, 1978, Peoples of the Sea Wind, 1978, Reading the Outdoors at Night, 1982, The Amateur Naturalist's Diary, 1982, Investigating Nature Through Outdoor Projects, 1983, Native Americans of Pacific Coast, 1985, Tracking the Glorious Lord, 1986; (with Willoya) Warriors of the Rainbow, German edit., 1980; others. Served with U.S. Army, 1945-46. Baha'i. Home: 3633 Indian Creek Rd PO Box 1045 Happy Camp CA 96039 Office: Naturegraph Pubs Inc PO Box 1075 Happy Camp CA 96039

BROWN, ERIC WARREN, mechanical engineer; b. Bklyn., Aug. 8, 1959; s. Morris and Hannah Brown;. BSME, MIT, 1981, MS, 1982. Mem. tech. staff Hughes Aircraft Co., El Segundo, Calif., 1982-84; gen. ptnr. I-FLOW Biomed. Co., Redondo Beach, Calif., 1983-86; pres., bd. dirs. I-FLOW Corp., Torrance, Calif., 1985—; prin. OFFSITE Product Devel. Group, Redondo Beach, 1983—, OFFSITE Computers, Torrance, 1985—. Patentee medical instruments. Mem. ASME, Assn. Advancement Med. Instrumentation, Pi Lambda Phi. Office: I-Flow Corp 3302 Sepulveda Blvd Suite D Torrance CA 90505

BROWN, GARY ROSS, lawyer, magistrate; b. Denver, Nov. 11, 1947; s. F. Ross and Leona R. (Temple) B.; m. Kelly Ann Simms, May 31, 1969; children—Julie Marie, Phillip Ross. B.A., Lewis and Clark Coll., 1969; J.D., U. Denver, 1973. Bar: Colo. 1973, U.S. Dist. Ct. Colo. 1973. Assoc. Clarence L. Bartholic, Denver, 1973-75; sole practice, Denver and Estes Park, Colo., 1975—; U.S. magistrate U.S. Dist. Ct. Colo. with specific jurisdiction over Rocky Mountain Nat. Park, 1980—; judge adv. gen. Colo. Dept. Military Affairs. Served with Army N.G., 1969—. Named Soldier of Yr., Army N.G., 1975. Mem. ABA, Colo. Bar Assn., Denver County Bar Assn., Larimer County Bar Assn. Presbyterian. Club: Masons (presiding officer Rocky Mountain Consistory).

BROWN, GEORGE EDWARD, JR., congressman; b. Holtville, Calif., Mar. 6, 1920; s. George Edward and Bird Alma (Kilgore) B.; m. Rowena Somerindyke (dec. Feb. 1987); 4 children. B.A., UCLA, 1946; grad. fellow, Fund Adult Edn., 1954. Mgmt. cons. Calif., 1957-61; v.p. Monarch Savs. & Loan Assn., Los Angeles, 1960-68; mem. Calif. Assembly from 45th Dist., 1959-62, 88th-91st congresses from 29th Dist. Calif., 93d Congress from 38th Dist. Calif., 94th-99th Congresses from 36th Dist. Calif.; mem. standing com. on agr., sci. space and tech. com., permanent select com. on intelligence, 94th-100th Congresses from 36th Dist. Calif., chmn. dept. ops., research and fgn. agriculture; apptd. to Office of Tech. Assessment; coll. lectr., radio commentator, 1971. Mem. Calif. Gov.'s Adv. Com. on Housing Problems, 1961-62; mem. Mayor Los Angeles Labor-Mgmt. Com., 1961-62, Councilman, Monterey Park, Calif., 1954-58, mayor, 1955-56; candidate for U.S. Senate, 1970. Served to 2d lt., inf. AUS, World War II. Mem. Am. Legion, Colton C. of C., Urban League, Internat. Brotherhood Elec. Workers, AFL-CIO, Friends Com. Legislation, Ams. for Dem. Action. Democrat. Methodist. Lodge: Kiwanis. Home: Colton CA 92324 Office: 2256 Rayburn House Office Bldg Washington DC 20515

BROWN, GEORGE STEPHEN, physicist; b. Santa Monica, Calif., June 28, 1945; s. Paul Gordon and Frances Ruth (Moore) B.; m. Nohema Fernandez, Aug. 8, 1981; 1 child, Sonya. BS, Calif. Inst. Tech., 1967; MS, Cornell U., 1968, PhD, 1973. Mem. tech. staff Bell Labs., Murray Hill, N.J., 1973-77; sr. research assoc. Stanford (Calif.) U., 1977-82, research prof. physics, 1982—; assoc. dir. Stanford Synchrotron Radiation Lab., Stanford, 1980—. Mem. editorial bd. Rev. Sci. Instruments, 1983—; contbr. articles to profl. jours. Fellow Am. Phys. Soc. Avocation: music performance. Home: 740 Alameda Redwood City CA 94061 Office: SSRL Bin 69 PO Box 4349 Stanford CA 94305

BROWN, GILES TYLER, educator, lecturer; b. Marshall, Mich., Apr. 21, 1916; s. A. Watson and Ettroile (Kent) B.; m. Crysta Beth Cosner, Nov. 21, 1951. A.B., San Diego State Coll., 1937; M.A., U. Calif.-Berkeley, 1941; Ph.D., Claremont Grad. Sch., 1948; post-doctoral seminar, U. Edinburgh, Scotland, 1949. Tchr., counselor, binet intelligence tester San Diego City Schs., 1937-46; chmn. social sci. div. Orange Coast Coll., Newport Beach, Calif., 1948-60; prof. history, chmn. social sci. div. Calif. State U., Fullerton, 1961-66; also chmn. history dept., dean grad. studies Calif. State U., 1967-83, assoc. v.p. acad. programs, 1979-83; pub. lectr. nat., internat. affairs, 1951—; also cons. gerontology; participant Wilton Park Conf., Eng., 1976; mem. instl. research bd. So. Calif. Coll. Optometry, 1980—; moderator Behind the Headlines Forum, Orange Coast Coll.; lectr. Laguna Hills Leisure World Forum; past chmn. Hist. Landmarks Com. Orange County; mem. nat. task force Assement Quality Masters' Degree, Council Grad. Schs., 1981-83. Author: Ships That Sail No More, 1966; Contbr. to: Help in Troubled Times, 1962; contbr. articles, book reviews to profl. jours. Trustee, past pres. and chmn. bd. World Affairs Council Orange County; past pres. U. Calif.-Irvine Friends Library; nat. bd. dirs., past nat. pres. Travelers Century Club; mem. grad. fellowship adv. com., State of Calif., 1980, Orange County Bd. NCCJ, 1984—; bd. dirs. Pacific Symphony Orch., NCCJ, Orange County. Served to lt. USNR, 1942-46. Recipient Pacific History award Pacific Coast br. Am. Hist. Assn., 1950; hon. medal DAR, 1977; named Outstanding Prof. Calif. State U., 1966, Hon. Citizen of Orange County, 1969; hon. medal Nat. Soc. Daus. Colonial Wars, 1984. Mem. AAAS, Am. Hist. Assn., Western Grad. Schs. (exec. com. 1981-83), SAR, Phi Beta Kappa, Phi Delta Kappa, Phi Alpha Theta, Kappa Delta Pi. Baptist. Clubs: Explorers, Masons. Home: 413 Catalina Dr Newport Beach CA 92663

BROWN, HANK, congressman; b. Denver, Feb. 12, 1940; s. Harry W. and Anna M. (Hanks) B.; m. Nana Morrison, Aug. 27, 1967; children: Harry, Christy, Lori. BS, U. Colo., 1961, JD, 1969; LLM, George Washington U., 1986, M in Tax Law, 1986. Bar: Colo. 1969. Tax acct. Arthur Andersen, 1967-68; asst. pres. Monfort of Colo., Inc., Greeley, 1969-70; corp. counsel Monfort of Colo., Inc., 1970-71; v.p. Monfort Food Distbg., 1971-72, v.p. corp. devel., 1973-75, v.p. internat. ops., 1975-78, v.p. lamb div., 1978-80; mem. 97th-100th Congresses from Colo. 4th dist.; mem. Colo. State Senate, 1972-76, asst. majority leader, 1974-76. Served with U.S. Navy, 1962-66. Decorated Air Medal. Mem. Colo. Bar Assn. Republican. Congregationalist. Office: US Ho of Reps 1424 Longworth Washington DC 20515

BROWN, HAROLD JESS, chemistry educator; b. Kemmerer, Wyo., June 5, 1924; s. Willard Harold and Esta Beulah (Hight) B.; m. Norma Rae Long, Mar. 3, 1944 (dec.); children: Stan, Jan, Dwight. BS, Utah State U., 1947, MS, 1948, EdD, 1965. Tchr., prin. Minidokan County Schs., Rupert, Idaho, 1948-52; chem. tchr., sci. supr. Salt Lake City Schs., 1952-69; prin. Jordan Jr. High Salt Lake City Schs., Salt Lake City, 1970-71; tchr. chemistry Salt Lake City Schs., 1971—; asst. prof. Lesley Coll., Cambridge, Mass., 1965-66; sci. expert UNESCO, Uganda, 1969-70; dir. Salt Lake Met. Sci. Fair, 1972—; dir. Salt Lake City Schs. Credit Union, 1980—; instr. U. Utah, Salt Lake City, 1972-85; radiation specialist USPHS, Winchester, Mass., 1966. Fellow NSF, 1957-58, Utah State U., 1964-65. Fellow AAAS; mem. Utah Sci. Tchrs. Assocs. (pres. 1983), Am. Chem. Soc. Republican. Avocations: flying small planes, trout fishing, hunting, photography. Home: 465 N 1150 E Bountiful UT 84010

BROWN, HAROLD MACVANE, lawyer; b. Colon, Panama, Oct. 2, 1940; s. Harold MacVane and Geraldine (Lynch) B.; m. Susan Murphy, June 20, 1970; children—Molly Curran, Katy Bradford. B.A., U. N.H., 1963; LL.M., Boston U., 1968. Bar: Mass. 1968, Alaska 1972, U.S. Dist. Ct. Mass. 1968, U.S. Dist. Ct. Alaska 1972. Assoc., Mahoney, McGrath, Atwood, Piper & Goldings, Boston, 1968-69; mem. atty.'s gen.'s office criminal div. Commonwealth of Mass., Boston, 1969-71; dist. atty. State of Alaska, 1971-73; ptnr. Ziegler, Cloudy, King, Brown & Peterson, Ketchikan, Alaska, 1974-85; Atty. Gen., State of Alaska, 1985-87. Mem. ABA, Alaska Bar Assn. (bd. govs. 1981—, pres., 1984). Mass. Bar Assn. Democrat. Episcopalian. Home: 1670 Evergreen Ave Juneau AK 99801 *

BROWN, IONA, violinist, orchestra director; b. Salisbury, Siltshire, England, Jan. 7, 1941. Studied w. Hugh Maguire, London, Remy Principe, Rome, Henryk Szeryng, France. Violinist Nat. Youth Orch. of Gt. Britain, 1955-60, Philharmonia Orch. of London, 1963-66; violinist Acad. of St. Martin-in-the-fields, 1964—, concertmaster, 1974-87; artistic dir. Norwegian Chamber Orch., Oslo; prin. guest dir. City of Birmingham Symphony Orch., Birmingham, England; music dir. Los Angeles Chamber Orch., Los Angeles, 1987—. Office: Los Angeles Chamber Orch 285 W Green St Suite 204 Pasadena CA 91105 *

BROWN, JAMES DOUGLAS (J.D.), occupational safety engineer; b. Idaho Falls, Idaho, Sept. 22, 1947; s. Harold Joshua Brown and Edith (Myers) Pinto; m. Myra Lou Watson, June 7, 1975. BS in Civil Engring cum laude, Utah State U., 1977; MS in Safety Engring., U. So. Calif., 1982. Cert. safety profl., Bd. Cert. Safety Profls. Ams.; registered profl. engr., Calif. Safety engr. Rockwell Internat., Richland, Wash., 1977-80, Lawrence Livermore Nat. Lab., Livermore, Calif., 1980-85; safety program adminstr. Sacramento Mcpl. Utility Dist., 1985—; cons. in field, Livermore, 1983—. Served to sgt. USMC, 1970-73. Mem. Am. Soc. Safety Engrs. (del. 1985), System Safety Soc., Laser Inst. Am., Am. Nat. Standards Inst., Tau Beta Pi. Republican. Club: Christian Businessmen's Com. (Livermore). Avocations: hunting, fishing. Office: Sacramento Mcpl Utility Dist Box 15830 Sacramento CA 95852

BROWN, JAMES MARSTON, lawyer; b. Aberdeen, Wash., Feb. 5, 1950; s. Donald Matthew and Jeanette Marie (Phillips) B.; m. Coleen Tina Chin, July 6, 1974; children—William Lester, Peter James. Student U. Wash., 1968-72, Calif. State U.-Fullerton, 1975-76; B.S. in Laws, Western State U., Fullerton, 1977, J.D., 1978. Bar: Calif. 1979, U.S. Dist. Ct. (no. dist.) Calif. 1979, Wash. 1981, U.S. Dist. Ct. (we. dist.) Wash. 1982. Law clk. Orange County Superior Ct., Santa Ana, Calif., 1977-78; assoc. Gladys & Phillips, Aberdeen, 1979-81; ptnr. Phillips & Brown, Aberdeen, 1981—; lectr. Grays Harbor Coll., Aberdeen, 1983—. Bd. dirs. Channel 10 Ministries, Aberdeen, 1980-83; trustee Aberdeen Pub. Library Bd., 1979—. Mem. ABA, Wash. Bar Assn. (bar examiner 1982-83), Wash. State Trial Lawyers Assn. (chmn. Grays Harbor round table 1984-85), Assn. Trial Lawyers Am., Christian Legal Soc., Delta Theta Phi. Republican. Baptist. Home: 527 W 6th St Aberdeen WA 98520 Office: Phillips & Brown 525 Seattle First Nat Bank Bldg Aberdeen WA 98520

BROWN, JEAN BUSH, speech and language pathologist, audiologist; b. Springfield, Mo., Jan. 22, 1947; d. Denzil Lee and Betty Jean (Smith) Bush; 1 child, Larry G. Brown II. BA, Memphis State U., 1973, MA, 1974, PhD, 1981. Cert. speech and lang. pathologist, audiologist, counselor. Instr., coordinator audiol. services U. Minn., Duluth, 1981-82, instr., dir. audiol. programs, 1981-83, coordinator coop. tng. program, Duluth component, 1981-83, asst. prof., dir. audiology programs, 1981-83; clin. group practice and direct patient care Albuquerque Aphasia and Speech Consultants, 1983-86; pvt. practice direct patient care Communication and Cognitive Treatment Ctr., Inc., Albuquerque, 1986—. Grantee U. Minn., 1980, 81, Blandin, Inc., 1981. Mem. Am. Speech-Lang.-Hearing Assn., N.Mex. Speech-Lang.-Hearing Assn., Cen. Registry Translators, others. Home: 11901 El Dorado Pl NE Albuquerque NM 87111 Office: Communication/Cognitive Treatment Ctr Inc 3900 Juan Tabo NE Suite 17 Albuquerque NM 87111

BROWN, JOHN FRANCIS, social worker; b. Stockton, Calif., Jan. 26, 1950; s. John Francis and Loise Louise (Baird) B.; m. Catherine Hall, July 10, 1971 (div. 1982); 1 child, Jennie M. AA, Coll. Marin, 1971; AB, U. Calif., Berkeley, 1973, M in Social Welfare, 1983. Eligibility worker County of Marin, Point Reyes, Calif., 1973-81, social service worker, 1981-85; social services practitioner County of Marine, Point Reyes, Calif., 1986; psychiat. social worker County of Alameda, Oakland, Calif., 1986—; cons. Pacific Bell, 1986—. Participant in Anit-Aparteid Demonstration, Berkeley, 1985. Served with USAF, 1968. U.S. Dept. Health and Health Services grantee, 1985. Mem. Nat. Assn. Social Workers, Phi Beta Kappa. Avocations: tennis, softball, fiction writing. Home: PO Box 521 Stinson Beach CA 94970 Office: East Oakland Mental Health 10 Eastmont Mall Suite 400 Oakland CA 94612

BROWN, JOHN WEBSTER, civil engineer; b. Reno, July 17, 1926; s. Ernest S. and Edna Louise (Bonner) B.; m. Estella Marie Hicks, Dec. 23, 1949; children: Ernest C., Curtis Webster, Denise Gail. BSCE, U. Nev., 1950. Registered profl. engr., Nev., Calif., Idaho. Bridge design engr. Nev. Dept. Hwys., 1950-51; civil engr. Kaiser Engrs. Corp., Oakland, Calif., 1951-53; structural designer H.M. O'Neil Co., Oakland, 1953; pres. John Webster Brown Civil and Structural Engrs., Reno, 1953—. Mem. Washoe County (Nev.) Pub. Works Commn., 1961-66; mem. Gov.'s Hwy. Safety Com., 1968-70; mem. cub pack com. Reno council Boy Scouts Am., 1967-68, chmn. activities troop com. 1967-74; mem. SSS, Nev. State Appeals Bd., 1969-76. Served with USNR, 1944-46. Mem. Nev. Soc. Profl. Engrs. (univ. com. 1957-60, state pres. 1960-61, Engr. of Yr. award 1969), NSPE (awards com. 1970-71), ASCE (pres. Nev. br. 1961-62, bldg. code com. 1963-65), Structural Engrs. Assn. Calif., Am. Assn. Engring. Socs., Sigma Tau, Tau Beta Pi. Home: 387 Chevy Chase Dr Reno NV 89509 Office: 1135 Terminal Way Suite 108 Reno NV 89502

BROWN, JONATHAN MARK, agronomist; b. Lebanon, Oreg., Feb. 9, 1956; s. Stanley Edward and Becky (Ketchum) B.; m. Victoria Anne Wood, Aug. 10, 1980. BS, Oreg. State U., 1979. Agronomist Oreg. Dept. Agr., Salem, 1979-85; field rep. Norpac Foods, Inc. (formerly Stayton Canning Co.), Stayton, Oreg., 1985—. Mem. Western Soc. Weed Sci., Oreg. Weed Sci. Soc., Oreg. Vegitation Mgmt. Assn. (advisor 1983-84), Oreg. Agrl. Chem. Assn., Willamette Valley Fieldman's Assn., U.S. Jaycees (charter, pres. local chpt.). Republican. Avocations: hunting, golf, fishing. Home: 630 S 3d PO Box 399 Jefferson OR 97352 Office: Norpac Foods Inc 4755 Brooklake Rd Salem OR 97305

BROWN, JONATHAN MEEKER, financial consulting firm executive, investment advisor; b. Chgo., Mar. 27, 1942; s. Hugh Osborne and Raymonde Elizabeth (McGary) B.; m. Vicki Peterson, Nov. 9, 1975 (div. Feb. 1977). B.A. in Polit. Sci., B.S. in Bus., U. Utah, 1964; M.B.A., U. Calif.-Berkeley, 1968; C.F.A., U. Va., 1972. Ptnr., mgr. Physicians' Econ. Pub. Co., Salt Lake City, 1958-66; sr. security analyst Bank of Am., San Francisco, 1966-69; v.p. Eaton & Howard, Inc., San Francisco, 1969-75; v.p. fund raising Nestle/Hershey Cos., San Francisco to Salt Lake City, 1977-79; pres., founder The Nine-J Corp., Salt Lake City, 1979—; pres. The Owl Pub. Corp., Salt Lake City, 1986—, The Lucky Nine-J Mining Corp., Salt Lake City, 1986—, Pamela-Browning, Ltd., Salt Lake City, 1986—; cons. Rocky Ridge Properties, Tahoe City, Calif., 1972-76, State of Utah, Salt Lake City, 1983, Salt Lake County, Salt Lake City, 1983. Editor, pub. The Owl Report, SEC registered investment newsletter, 1984—. Served to staff sgt. U.S. Army, 1966-72. Recipient Mut. Funds Sales Achievement award Nat. Assn. Securities Dealers, 1972-73. Fellow Inst. Chartered Fin. Analysts, Fin. Analysts Soc. Salt Lake City; mem. Fin. Analysts Fedn. N.Y.C. Republican. Episcopalian. Club: Freelance Photographers Assn. Am. (Los Angeles). Home: PO Box 11904 Salt Lake City UT 84147 Office: The Nine-J Corp PO Box 11904 Salt Lake City UT 84147

BROWN, JUNE DIANNE, interior design executive, educator; b. L.I., N.Y., July 8, 1934; s. Walter Joseph and Marie Ann (Wolf) Scherer; m. Robert Neil Brown, July 19, 1954; children: Robert Lee, Todd Craig, Scott Louis. Diploma, Chgo. Sch. Interior Decorating, 1969; BS, Woodbury U., 1973. Prin. Coast Surgical Co., Los Angeles, 1973-74; instr. in interior design Barker Bros., Los Angeles, 1971-72, Sears, Los Angeles, 1968-71; owner Brown & Co., Glendora, Calif., 1969-83, J.S. Brown Co., Diamond Bar, Calif., 1983—; educator community colls. Covina, Calif., 1976-79, Anaheim, Calif., 1981-82; educator Fashion Inst. of Los Angeles, 1978-79. Recipient Hon. Citation Children's Hosp., Santa Ana, Calif., 1982. Fellow Nat. Home Fashions League (nat. sec., chpt. pres. 1986, bd. mem. 1975-81); mem. Jaycees (coordinator house of design Newport Harbor chpt. 1982, 84, 86; commendations 1981, 84). Republican. Christian Scientist. Avocations: dress designing, camping, teaching. Home: 839 San Remo Irvine CA 92714 Office: JS Brown Design 2500 S Fairview Suite S Santa Ana CA 92704

BROWN, KEITH LAPHAM, political party official, former U.S. ambassador to Lesotho, investor; b. Sterling, Ill., June 18, 1925; s. Lloyd Heman and Marguerite (Briggs) B.; m. Carol Louise Liebmann, Oct. 1, 1949; children: Susan, Briggs (dec.), Linda, Benjamin. Student, U. Ill., 1943-44, Northwestern U., 1946-47; LL.B., U. Tex., 1949. Bar: Tex., Okla., Colo. Assoc. Lang, Byrd, Cross & Ladon, San Antonio, 1949-55; v.p., gen. counsel Caulkins Oil Co., Oklahoma City, 1955-70, Denver, 1955-70; pres. Brown Investment Corp., Denver, 1970—; U.S. ambassador to Kingdom of Lesotho, 1982-84; chmn. Republican Nat. Fin. Com., 1985—; founder, developer Vail Assocs., Colo., 1962; developer Colo. State Bank Bldg., Denver, 1971; dir. Colo. State Bank, Pub. Service Co. of Colo. Trustee Soil Sci. Found. of U. Denver, 1981—; mem. Council Fgn. Relations, Denver, 1981—; dir. Nat. Western Stock Show, Boys Club, 1980—; trustee, past pres. Colo. Acad., 1975-80; past pres. Mile-Hi Club, Denver, 1981; nat. committeeman Republican Party, 1975-82. Mem. Tex. Bar Assn., Okla. Bar Assn., Colo. Bar Assn. Presbyterian. Clubs: Denver Country; Univ. (Denver). Office: Republican National Committee 310 First St SE Washington DC 20003 also: 1600 Broadway Suite 2100 Denver CO 80202

BROWN, LEE FRANCIS, chemical engineer; b. Elmhurst, Ill., Feb. 23, 1929; s. Walter I. and Hazel G. (Dutton) B.; m. Monica J. Walsh, Aug. 26, 1967; children: Eric, Cecilia, Timothy. BSChemE, U. Notre Dame, 1951; MChemE, U. Del., 1955, PhDChemE, 1963. Chem. engr. Houdry Process Corp., Marcus Hook, Pa., 1951-54; research assoc. U. Colo., Boulder, 1963-64, from asst. prof. to prof., 1964-81; staff mem. Los Alamos (N.Mex.) Nat. Lab., 1981—. Contbr. articles to profl. jours. Served with U.S. Army, 1954-56. Roman Catholic. Office: Los Alamos Nat Lab MS F665 Los Alamos NM 87545

BROWN, LESLIE WEARN, construction company executive; b. Sonora, Calif., May 29, 1944; s. Leslie and Genevieve (Evans) B.; m. Kay I. Davis, June 28, 1980; children: Leslie W. III, Charlotte. BA, Stanford U., 1966; postgrad., Claremont (Calif.) Grad. Sch. Supr. Pacific Mut. Life Ins. Co., Los Angeles, 1967-69, Allstate Ins. Cos., Menlo Park, Calif., 1969-73; contract compliance mgr. Granite Constrn. Co., Watsonville, Calif., 1973-80; dir. indsl. relations J.F. Shea Co., Walnut, Calif., 1981-86, v.p., 1986—; bd. dirs. Madison Capital, Inc. Mem. Associated Gen. Contractors (mem. collective bargaining com.), Risk and Ins. Mgrs. Soc. (assoc.). Republican. Presbyterian. Avocations: sailing, gardening. Home: 2696 Shady Ridge Diamond Bar CA 91765 Office: J F Shea 655 Brea Canyon Walnut CA 91789

BROWN, LOWELL SEVERT, physicist, educator; b. Visalia, Calif., Feb. 15, 1934; s. Volney Clifford and Anna Marie Evelyn (Jacobson) B.; m. Shirley Isabel Mitchell, June 23, 1956; 1 son, Stephen Clifford. A.B., U. Calif., Berkeley, 1956; Ph.D. (NSF predoctoral fellow 1956-61), Harvard U., 1961; postgrad., U. Rome, 1961-62, Imperial Coll., London, 1962-63. From research asso. to asso. prof. physics Yale U., 1963-68; mem. faculty U. Wash., Seattle, 1968—; prof. physics U. Wash., 1970—; vis. prof. Imperial Coll., London, 1971-72; summer vis. scientist Brookhaven Nat. Lab., 1965-68, Lawrence Berkeley Lab., 1966, Stanford Accelerator Ctr., 1967, CERN, Geneva, 1979; mem. Inst. Advanced study, Princeton, N.J., 1979-80; cons. Los Alamos Sci. Lab.; vis. physicist Deutsches Elektronen-Synchrotron, Hamburg, 1986; trustee Aspen Ctr. for Physics, 1982—. Mem. editorial bd. Phys. Rev., 1978-81; editor Phys. Rev. D, 1987—; contbr. articles to profl. publs. Trustee Seattle Youth Symphony Orch., 1986—. Postdoctoral fellow NSF, 1961-63; sr. post-doctoral fellow, 1971-72; Guggenheim fellow, 1979-80. Fellow Am. Phys. Soc. (exec. com. div. particles and fields 1982-84, publs. com. 1984-86), AAAS; mem. Phi Beta Kappa, Sigma Xi. Home: 1157 Federal Ave E Seattle WA 98102 Office: Physics Dept Univ Wash Seattle WA 98195

BROWN, MARGARET DEBEERS, lawyer; b. Washington, Sept. 24, 1943; d. John Sterling and Marianna Hurd (Hill) deBeers; m. Timothy Nils, Aug. 28, 1965; children—Emeline Susan, Eric Franklin. B.A. magna cum laude, Radcliffe Coll., 1965; postgrad. Harvard U. Law Sch., 1965-67; J.D., U. Calif.-Berkeley, 1968. Bar: Calif. 1969, U.S. Ct. Appeals (9th cir.) 1971, U.S. Supreme Ct. 1972, U.S. Ct. Appeals (D.C. cir.) 1986. Assoc. White, Hamilton, Wyche, Shell & Pollard, Petersburg, Va., 1968-70, Heller, Ehrman, White & McAuliffe, San Francisco, 1970-73; sole practice, San Francisco, 1973-77; atty. Pacific Telephone (name changed to Pacific Bell 1984), San Francisco, 1977-83, sr. atty., 1983-85; sr. atty. Pacific Telesis Group, 1985—; speaker McGeorge Law Sch., Sacramento, 1983. Mem. ABA, San Francisco Bar Assn., Phi Beta Kappa. Office: Pacific Telesis Group 140 New Montgomery San Francisco CA 94105

BROWN, MARIANNE PARKER, university program coordinator; b. Yreka, Calif., Mar. 19, 1943; d. Edwin Bruce and Iris (LaPraik) P.; m. Eugene Richard Brown, June 19, 1966; children: Delia Mara, Adrienne Elana. BA, U. Calif., Berkeley, 1965, elem. credential, 1968, MPH, 1977. Asst. coordinator Emergency Med. Services Contra Costa County, Martinez, Calif., 1979; lectr. UCLA Pub. Health Sch., 1980-82; project dir. Am. Cancer Soc., Los Angeles, 1982-84; coordinator occupational health program UCLA Inst. Indsl. Relations, 1984—. Co-author: Preventing Lung Cancer in the Los Angeles Basin, 1981, Occupational Health Eduation: A Review of Perspectives and Current Status, 1981; also articles. Mem. Mayor's adv. com. on Hazardous Wastes, Los Angeles, 1985-86, Los Angeles County Fedn. Labor's Health and Safety Com., 1984-86. Mem. Am. Lung Assn. (chmn. subcom. 1982-86), Soc. Pub. Health Ed. (chmn. advocacy com. 1985-86), Am. Pub. Health Assn. Office: UCLA Inst Indsl Relations 1001 Gayley Ave Los Angeles CA 90024

BROWN, MARK KINGSLEY, advertising company executive, cartoonist; b. Berkeley, Calif., Dec. 2, 1952; s. Robert Malcolm and Mildred (Kingsley) B. AA, Orange Coast Coll., 1974; student, San Diego State U., 1974-76. Freelance designer R.K. Evans Graphic Design, San Diego, 1975-77; graphic designer First Impressions Design, San Diego, 1977-79; freelance cartoonist San Diego, 1979-82; owner, creative dir. The Kingsley Group, Leucadia, Calif., 1982—. Creator (greeting cards) Duck Cards, 1981, billbd. competition Olympia Beer, 1975 (1st place), logo competition Sta. KPRI Radio, 1976 (1st place), illustration Casteel Pens, 1978 (merit award 1978). Mem. governing bd. Community Resource Ctr., San Dieguito, 1983-86. Mem. San Diego Assn. Advt. Agys., Better Bus. Bur., San Diego Cartoonists Soc. Office: The Kingsley Group 1400 N Hwy 101 Leucadia CA 92024

BROWN, MARY ALICE BUNYARD, community services executive officer, consultant, author; b. Chgo., Aug. 3, 1945; d. Prince William and Stella D. (Broderson) Bunyard; m. David Basel, Apr. 1, 1987. B.A. in Design, U. Ill.-Chgo., 1969; M.S. in Counseling Psychology, U. Oreg., 1974, postgrad. in Counseling Psychology. Research asst. Batten, Barton, Durstine & Osborn, Chgo., 1965-66; counselor Pritzker Ctr. and Hosp., Chgo., 1967-68; writer Coronet Instructional Films, Chgo., 1970-71; student adviser Community Services and Pub. Affairs, U. Oreg., Eugene, 1972-74, grad. teaching fellow, 1974-75; exec. dir. Laurel Hill Ctr., Eugene, 1975—; cons. in field. Mem. planning com. United Way of Lane County, 1981-82; mem. Gov.'s Task Force on Mental Health, 1980-81; mem. United Way Agy. Dirs.' Orgn., 1978—, pres., 1981; mem. Lane County Employment and Tng. Council, 1979-81, Mental Health Assn., 1976—, pres., 1976. Research grantee Boston U., 1982-83, 84-87; Ind. Living Program grantee Oreg. Vocat. Rehab. Div., 1981-88. Mem. Nat. Rehab. Assn., Nat. Assn. Female Execs. Author: Training Manual for the Development of Community Centers and Work Programs for the Psychiatrically Disabled, 1981, rev., 1982, 83, 84, 86.

Home: 33481 Bloomberg Rd Eugene OR 97405 Office: Laurel Hill Ctr 2621 Augusta St Eugene OR 97403

BROWN, NATHANIEL ALFRED, virologist, physician; b. New Haven, Mar. 17, 1948; s. Raymond Lester and Joan (Rich) B. Student, Yale U., 1966-68, 71-72; MD, Georgetown U., 1972-76. Diplomate Am. Bd. Med. Examiners; cert. Am. Bd. Pediatrics. Intern, then resident Cornell Med. Ctr., N.Y.C., 1976-78; postdoctoral fellow Yale U. Sch. Medicine, New Haven, 1978-81, instr. pediatrics, 1981-82; asst. prof. UCLA Sch. Medicine, Los Angeles, 1982—; grant reviewer NIH/Nat. Cancer Inst., Bethesda, Md., 1985—. Contbr. articles on virology and infectious diseases to profl. jours. prin. investigator grantee Nat. Cancer Inst., 1983—. Mem. AAAS, Am. Soc. Virology, Western Soc. Pediatric Research, Philoptochos Soc. (faculty scholar award Los Angeles chpt. 1985), Morey's Assn., Alpha Omeg Alpha. Office: UCLA Sch Medicine Dept Pediatrics 405 Hilgard Ave Los Angeles CA 90024

BROWN, OGDEN, JR., psychologist, educator; b. Evanston, Ill., Apr. 1, 1927; s. Ogden and Frances Louise (Falck) B.; A.B. in Psychology, Am. U., 1950, M.A. in Psychology, 1951; Ph.D. in Indsl./Orgnl. Psychology, Purdue U., 1965; m. Alyce Marie Whitesides, May 1, 1953; children—Marsha Marie Brown Akse, Lynda Lou Brown Dunne, Ogden III, Tarleton II. Psychometrician, U.S. Employment Service, Washington, 1950-51; commd. 2d lt. USAF, 1951, advanced through grades to col., 1971; from instr. to assoc. prof. U.S. Air Force Acad., 1961-68; asst. for edn. and tng. Office of Sec. of Air Force, Washington, 1968-71; comdr. 3415 Spl. Tng. Group, Lowry AFB, Colo., 1971-73; ret., 1973; exec. v.p. Am. West Enterprises, Colorado Springs, Colo., 1973-78; from asst. prof. to prof. human factors Inst. Safety and Systems Mgmt., U. So. Calif., Los Angeles, 1978—; pres. Mgmt. Devel. Assocs., Colorado Springs, 1973—. Decorated Legion of Merit, Meritorious Service medal, Commendation medal. Mem. Acad. of Mgmt., Am. Psychol. Assn., Assn. Human Resources Mgmt. and Organizational Behavior, Human Factors Soc., Internat. Ergonomics Assn., Rocky Mountain Psychol. Assn., Sigma Xi, Psi Chi, Omicron Delta Kappa, Delta Phi Alpha. Republican. Episcopalian. Club: Elks, Contbr. articles to profl. jours. Home: 2 Belle Aire Rd Colorado Springs CO 80906 Office: U So Calif Human Factors Dept ISSM Los Angeles CA 90089

BROWN, OUIDA MILDRED, academic dean, counselor; b. Sweatman, Miss., July 23, 1945; d. Raphael Sanzio and Frances Rebecca (Hapman) McCuiston; m. Thomas Brown, June 14, 1964; children: Tony Christopher, Angela Khristin. BS, Alcorn U., 1966; MEd in Counseling, U. Nev., 1980, MEd Adminstrn., 1982. Elem. tchr. Nev. Pub. Schs., 1966-67, home econs. tchr., 1967-68, 70-74, 80-84, dean of students, 1983-86, adminstrv. asst., 1986-87; counselor Clark County Religious Edn. Ctr. Del. Dem. Nat. Conv., 1978-86; mem. state and county cen. coms.; vol. for registration of voters, 1975-86. Alcorn U. scholar, 1962. Mem. Secondary and Elem. Prins. Assn., Nev. Assn. Sch. Adminstrn., Assn. for Supervision and Curricululm Devel., Nat. Home Econs. Assn., Clark County Classroom Tchrs. Assn. (past pres., v.p., exec. bd., dir. religious edn.), Alpha Kappa Alpha. Roman Catholic. Home: 320 Lance Ave North Las Vegas NV 89030 Office: Nev Pub Schs 1900 East Owens North Las Vegas NV 89030

BROWN, PAUL FREMONT, aerospace engineer, educator; b. Osage, Iowa, Mar. 10, 1921; s. Charles Fremont and Florence Alma (Olson) B.; m. Alice Marie Culver, Dec. 5, 1943; children—Diane, Darrell, Judith, Jana. B.A. in Edn. and Natural Sci., Dickinson State Coll., 1942; B.S. in Mech. Engring., U. Wash., 1948; M.S. in Cybernetic Systems, San Jose State U., 1971. Profl. quality engr., Calif., 1978; cert. reliability engr., Am. Soc. Quality Control, 1976. Test engr., supr. Boeing Aircraft Corp., Seattle, 1948-56; design specialist, propulsion systems, Lockheed Missiles and Space Co., Sunnyvale, Calif., 1956-59; supr. system effectiveness, 1959-66, staff engr., 1966-76, mgr. product assurance, 1976-83; v.p. research, devel. Gen. Agriponics Inc. of Hawaii, 1971-76; pres. Diversatek Engring. and Product Assurance Conss., 1983—; coll. instr., lectr., San Jose State U. Active in United Presbyn. Ch., 1965—; scoutmaster, Boy Scouts Am., 1963-65. Served to 1st lt., USAF, 1943-46. Recipient awards for tech. papers, Lockheed Missiles and Space Co., 1973-75. Mem. Am. Soc. Quality Control, AIAA. Clubs: Toastmasters (Sunnyvale, Calif.). Contbr. articles to profl. jours. Home and Office: 19608 Braemar Dr Saratoga CA 95070

BROWN, RAYMOND DUTSON, state agency administrator; b. Phila., Feb. 3, 1933; s. Allen Webster and Helen Ruth (Belshaw) B.; m. Joyce Marie Floor, Feb. 10, 1978; children: Nicholas, Samual; children by previous marriage: Raymond D., Timothy R., Katherine E., Lura A. Ordained to ministry Episcopal Ch., 1962. Curate Episcopal Ch., Schenectady, N.Y., 1962-63; vicar Whitefish (Mont.) Mission Field, 1963-66; dean St. Peter'sCathedral, Helena, Mont., 1966-75; adminstr. Mont. Human Rights div., Helena, 1975-83; chief civil rights Mont. Highway Dept., Helena, 1985—; chaplain Mont. Ho. of Reps., 1967, 69. Mem. Helena Sch. Bd., 1973-76; pres. Lewis and Clark Search & Rescue, 1973-77; bd. dirs. St. Peter's Hosp., United Way. Served to sgt. USMC, 1951-54. Mem. Nat. Assn. Human Rights Workers, Internat. Assn. Ofcl. Human Rights Agys., EMT, Mont. Assn. Chs. (pres. 1973-74), Mont. Council Chs. (chmn. Indian task force 1968-70). Democrat. Office: Mont Dept Highways 2701 Prospect Ave Helena MT 59620

BROWN, RAYMOND WARREN, engineering and construction executive; b. Oakland, Calif., Sept. 3, 1937; s. Harry Warren and Dorothy Hazel (Frienzi) B.; m. Ana Rosa Alcaide de Rodriguez, July 27, 1964; children: Josephine M., Harry R., Anna D. Student, Automation Inst., 1970, Cerritos Coll., 1980; cert. ops., Bechtel Internat., 1982. Project expediter Bechtel Corp. subs. Bechtel Group, Inc., San Francisco, 1974-77; expediting supr. Bechtel Power Corp. subs. Bechtel Group, Inc., Los Angeles, 1977-81; procurement mgr. Bechtel Power Corp. subs. Bechtel Group, Inc., San Francisco, 1981-84; expediting mgr. Bechtel Petroleum, Inc., subs. Bechtel Power Group, San Francisco, 1984-85, Bechtel Nat., Inc., San Francisco, 1985—; presenter, developer, instr. expediting tng. programs, 1980, 82. Rep. promotion bd., CSC City of Los Angeles. Served with Calif. N.G., 1970-74. Mem. Expediting Mgmt. Assn., Inc., (chmn. profl. devel. com, 1983-85, nat. pres. 1985—, cert.), Calif. Waterfowl Assn. Republican. Roman Catholic. Avocations: hunting, fishing. Office: Bechtel Nat Inc 50 Beale St PO Box 3965 San Francisco CA 94119

BROWN, RICHARD ALLEN, horticulturist, consultant; b. Seattle, Feb. 15, 1943; s. Cecil Clifford and Barbara Katherine (Richards) B.; m. Sue Ann Geerling, Oct. 01, 1970; children: Karl Clifford, Carey James. BA, BS, U. Wash., 1966; MS, U. Del., 1970. Cert. computer profl. Commd. ensign USN, 1967, advanced through grades to lt. comdr., 1977; asst. dir. Plant Scis. Data Ctr., Mt. Vernon, Va., 1970-72, dir., 1972-76; curator The Bloedel Res., Bainbridge Island, Wash., 1976—. Contbr. articles to profl. jours. Sec. Bainbridge Island Water Coordinating Com., 1980-84, co-chmn., 1985—; sec. Bainbridge Island Planning and Adv. Counsel, 1982-85; bd. dirs. N. Kitsap High Sch. Vocat. Adv. Bd., 1983—. Fellow Royal Hort. Soc.; mem. Am. Assn. Bot. Gardens, Am. Rock Garden Soc. (northwest chpt. vice chmn.), Naval Res. Assn., Profl. Ground Maintenance Assn. Republican. Lutheran. Club: Bainbridge Island Sportsman's. Lodges: Renton (master 1984-85), Masons. Avocations: fishing, woodworking, hiking, photography. Office: The Bloedel Reserve 7571 NE Dolphin Dr Bainbridge Island WA 98110

BROWN, ROBERT ALLEN, physicist; b. Calif., 1955; married. BS, Humboldt State U., 1979; MS, U. Calif., Davis, 1982, PhD, 1984. Physicist Lawrence Livermore Nat. Lab., Livermore, Calif., 1979-80; research engr. SRI Internat., Menlo Park, Calif., 1984—. U. Calif. fellow, 1980-84. Mem. Am. Phys. Soc., Optical Soc. Am., Soc. Photo-optical Instrumentation Engrs. (fellowship 1984). Office: SRI Internat 333 Ravenswood Menlo Park CA 94025

BROWN, ROBERT EDWIN, logistics manager; b. Terre Haute, Ind., Sept. 7, 1931; s. Elmer D. and Jennie L. (Swimm) B.; children from previous marriage: Edward, Kathleen, Brian, Sean; m. Lee Irene Applebaum, Mar. 19, 1978. BBA, Ind. State U., Terre Haute, 1957, MS in Econs., 1962. Systems mgr. Nissan Motor Corp., Compton, Calif., 1970-76; project mgr. McDonnell Douglas, Cypress, Calif., 1976-82, logistics mgr., 1982—; pres. Los Angeles chpt. Council of Logistics, 1980-81. Served to cpl. U.S. Army, 1951-53. Democrat. Avocation: tennis. Home: 8404 Leeward Dr Huntington Beach CA 92646 Office: McDonnell Douglas 5701 Katelca K34-2W Cypress CA 90630

BROWN, ROBERT R., grocer; b. Yakima, Wash., Nov. 10, 1942; s. Wray R. and Rosella S. (Bragstad) B.; m. L. Sharon Brown, Mar. 21, 1964; children: Stephanie, Jeffrey, Christopher. Student, U. Wash., 1961-64; BA, Mich. State U., 1967. Pres., chief exec. officer Wray's Inc., Yakima, 1971—. Pres. Yakima Valley Visitors and Conv. Bur., 1977-78. Mem. Wash. State Food Dealers Assn. (bd. dirs. 1970—, pres. 1977-78, Grocer of Yr. 1981), Nat. Grocers Assn. (bd. dirs. 1980—). Methodist. Lodges: Kiwanis (local bd. dirs., past local pres.), Elks. Office: Wray's Inc 5635 Summitview Yakima WA 98908

BROWN, RONALD DEAN, accountant; b. Moscow, Idaho, July 18, 1950; s. Donald Dean and Molly Christine (Cox) B.; m. Marilyn Louise Meyer, Aug. 31, 1975 (div. Nov. 1982); m. Lynn Anne Marek, Feb. 9, 1985. BA in Polit. Sci., U. Wash., 1972; BA in Bus., Eastern Wash. U., 1975, MBA, 1982. CPA, Wash. Gen. acctg. mgr. Nat. Music Service, Spokane, Wash., 1977-78; cost acct. Welk Bros. Metal Products, Spokane, 1978-80; asst. controller Am. Sign & Indicator, Spokane, 1980-83; div. controller Warn Industries, Milwaukie, Oreg., 1983—. Mem. Am. Inst. CPA's, Nat. Assn. Accts. Avocations: running, snow skiing, golfing, reading. Office: Warn Industries 13270 SE Pheasant Ct Portland OR 97222

BROWN, RONALD MALCOLM, industrial engineer; b. Hot Springs, S.D., Feb. 21, 1938; s. George Malcolm and Cleo Lavonne (Plumb) B.; m. Sharon Ida Brown, Nov. 14, 1964 (div. Apr. 1974); children: Michael, Troy, George, Curtis, Lisa, Brittney. AA, Southwestern Coll., 1970; BA, Chapman Coll., 1978. Commd. USN, 1956, advanced through grades to master chief, 1973, ret., 1978; engring. mgr. Beckman Inst., Fullerton, Calif., 1978-82; mech. engring. br. mgr. Northrop Corp., Hawthorne, Calif., 1982-83; dir. of ops. Transco, Marina Del Rey, Calif., 1983-85; v.p. ops. Decor Concepts, Arcadia, Calif., 1985—. Mem. Soc. Mfg. Engrs., Inst. Indsl. Engrs., Nat. Trust for Hist. Preservation, Fleet Res. Assn. Avocations: golf, running, racquetball. Office: Decor Concepts 5611 N Peck Rd Arcadia CA 91006

BROWN, SHARON SHELTON, government official; b. Washington, Oct. 10, 1948; d. James William and Shirley (Herrity) Shelton. BS, U. Md., 1978. Pub. service dir. Sta. WPGC/AM/FM, Washington, 1969-71; office mgr. Sta. KJAZ/FM, Alameda, Calif., 1972; asst. ops. mgr. Sta. KPIX-TV, San Francisco, 1972-73; copywriter William D. Murdock Advt., Alexandria, Va., 1973-75; dir. pub. affairs Naval Security Group Activity, Fort Meade, Md., 1976-78; photojournalist NAS Alameda Pub. Affairs Office, 1978-79; asst. pub. affairs officer Mil. Sealift Comand, Pacific, Oakland, Calif., 1979-81, dir. legis. and pub. affairs, 1981-83; dir. pub. affairs Mil. Traffic Mgmt. Command, Western Area, Oakland, 1983—; publicity chair Combined Fed. Campaign, San Francisco Bay Area, 1985—. Mem. Oakland World Trade and Maritime Day Com., 1983-86, Oakland Olympic Torch Com., 1984; maritime queen Port of Golden Gate, 1984-85; chmn. community affairs Fed. Exec. Bd., San Francisco, 1985-87. Recipient Outstanding Performance awards Dept. Navy, U.S. Army. Mem. Pub. Relations Soc. Am., East Bay Press Club, NOW, Oakland C. of C. Clubs: Propeller of U.S. (bd. govs. 1986-87). Office: Mil Traffic Mgmt Command Oakland Army Base Western Area Oakland CA 94626-5000

BROWN, SID A., materials manager; b. Osceola, Iowa, May 22, 1941; s. Millard L. and Lois R. (Mayfield) B.; m. Brenda E. Clements, Apr. 23, 1960; children: Rebecca Lynn, Cynthia Sue, Todd Mathew. Student, William Penn Coll., 1959-60, Portland State U., 1960-68; AA, Golden West Coll., 1976; BA, Calif. State U., Fullerton, 1979. Purchasing clk. Gen. Electric Supply Co., Portland, Oreg., 1960-64; buyer Sawyer's Inc., Portland, 1964-68; sr. buyer GAF Corp., Portland, 1968-74; purchasing agt. GAF Corp., Long Beach, Calif., 1974-79; sr. purchasing agt. BASF Video Corp., Fountain Valley, Calif., 1979-80; purchasing mgr. Siltec Silicon, Salem, Oreg., 1980-83, materials mgr., 1983—. Mem. Adv. Council Oreg. Assn. Rehab. Facilities, Salem, 1985—. Named one of 1985's Top 10 Purchasing Profls., Electronic Buyer's News, Manhasset, N.Y., 1985. Mem. Oreg. Mid-Valley Purchasing Mgmt. Assn. (pres. 1981-83, 86-87), dir. nat. affairs, 1982-84, 87-88, Founder's award renamed the Sid Brown award 1983), Nat. Assn. Purchasing Mgmt. (cert., exec. com. 1986—, chmn. dist. XI internat. com. 1986—, asst. v.p. dist. XI 1984-85, dir. nat. bd. 1985-86, v.p., chief exec. officer 1985-86, treas. dist. XI 1986—, chmn. dist. XI internat. com., mem. exec. com. MRO group), Purchasing Mgmt. Assn. Oreg. (Gavalier's award 1982). Republican. Methodist. Avocations: recreational athletics, hiking, travelling. Home: 1725 Scotch Ave SE Salem OR 97306-1404 Office: Siltec Silicon PO Box 7748 1351 Tandem Ave NE Salem OR 97303

BROWN, STEVEN MICHAEL, educational foundation director, computer consultant; b. Los Angeles, Aug. 5, 1947; s. Harold and Roslyn (Bigman) B.; B.S., U. Fla., 1969; M.A., U. South Fla., 1973; Ph.D., Iowa State U., 1977; m. Deborah Levine, Aug. 15, 1971. Lang. arts instr., media dir. Hillsborough County Schs., Tampa, Fla., 1970-75; instr. coll. of edn. Iowa State U., Ames, 1975-77; high sch. prin. North Hills Schs., Pitts., 1977-78; high sch. asst. prin. for curriculum, Sierra Vista (Ariz.) Pub. Schs., 1978-80; high sch. asst. prin. for student services Scottsdale (Ariz.) Pub. Schs., 1980-81; dir. funded and enrichment programs Madison Pub. Schs., Phoenix, 1981-83; exec. dir. Horizons Cons. Unltd., 1983—; exec. dir. Howard kale Ednl. Found., Scottsdale, Ariz., 1985—; exec. dir. Kale Ednl. Found. Scottsdale, 1985—; cons. Vice pres. Young Democrats, Tampa, 1973; com. chmn. troop 423, Cochise County council Boy Scouts Am., Sierra Vista, 1979—. Served with USAR, 1970-76. Recipient PACE award Iowa State U., 1976-77; named Outstanding Young Educator, Cochise County, Ariz., 1979-80. Mem. Nat. Assn. Secondary Sch. Prins., Assn. Supervision and Curriculum Devel., Ariz. Assn. for Gifted and Talented (dir. 1982-84), Am. Assn. Sch. Adminstrs., Scottsdale Affiliated Adminstrs., Nat. Soc. Fund Raising Execs., Phi Delta Kappa (pres. Cochise County chpt. 1979—, state coordinator 1982-84, named One of 10 Outstanding Young Educators Ariz. 1979-80). Democrat. Contbr. articles to profl. publs. Home: 1239 N Nevada Way Mesa AZ 85203 Office: 10900 N Scottsdale Rd #502 Scottsdale AZ 85254

BROWN, SYLVIA, public relations executive, advertising executive; b. Watsonville, Calif., Nov. 28, 1946. BA, U. Calif., Berkeley, 1968; postgrad., Cen. Sch. Arts and Design, London, 1968-70. Asst. dir. Vorpal Gallery, San Francisco, 1972-73; editor, critic City Mag., San Francisco, 1973-75; dir. Braunstein/Quay Gallery, San Francisco, 1973-77; ptnr. Quay Ceramics Gallery, San Francisco, 1974-77; pub. relations dir. San Francisco Art Inst., 1977-79; ptnr. Brown and Collins, San Francisco, 1979—; co-founder, editor Art Dealers Assn., San Francisco, 1973-79; co-founder, pres. bd. dirs. 80 Langton St., San Francisco, 1975-77; co-founder, bd. dirs. Zyzzyva, San Francisco, 1984—. Contbg. editor: Images & Issues, 1979-81; critic: Art in America, 1974-78; Author: (catalogue essay) Ron Nagle, 1978. Mem. Pub. Relations Soc. Am., Internat. Sculpture Ctr. Home: 306 Lombard St San Francisco CA 94133 Office: Brown & Collins 1045 Sansome Suite 219 San Francisco CA 94111

BROWN, THOMAS HUNTINGTON, neuroscientist; b. N.Y.C., June 13, 1945; s. Thomas Huntington and Elvira C. (Crandall) R.; m. Patricia Ann Carson, Aug. 10, 1968. BA in Molecular Biology, Calif. State U.-San Jose, 1972; MA in Psychology, 1972; PhD in Neurosci., Stanford U., 1977. Postdoctoral fellow Stanford U., Calif., 1977-79; asst. research scientist Beckman Research Inst., City of Hope, Duarte, Calif., 1979-82, assoc. research scientist, 1982-86, research scientist, 1986—; adviser NIH, NIMH study sections, 1982-83; Mem. editorial bd. Behavioral Neurosci. jour., 1983—. Contbr. articles to sci. jours., 1976—. Recipient Epilepsy Found. Am. award, 1980, McKnight Found. Scholar's award, 1981; McKnight Found. Career Devel. award, 1984; Muscular Dystrophy Found. fellow, 1978, NIH fellow, 1979; grantee in field, 1980—. Mem. AAAS, Soc. Neurosci. Office: 1500 E Duarte Rd Beckman Research Inst of the City of Hope Div Neurosciences Duarte CA 91010

BROWN, WALTER CREIGHTON, biologist; b. Butte, Mont., Aug. 18, 1913; s. D. Frank and Isabella (Creighton) B.; m. Jeanette Snyder, Aug. 20, 1950; children: Pamela Hawley, James, Julia Elizabeth. AB, Coll. Puget Sound, 1935, MA, 1938; PhD, Stanford U., 1950. Chmn. dept. Clover Park High Sch., Tacoma, Wash., 1938-42; acting. instr. Stanford U., Calif., 1949-50; instr. Northwestern U., Evanston, Ill., 1950-53; dean sci. Menlo Coll., Menlo Park, Calif., 1955-66, dean instrn., 1966-75; research assoc., fellow Calif. Acad. Sci., San Francisco, 1978—; lectr. Sillman U., Philippines, 1954-55, dir. research Program on Ecology and Systematics of Philippine Amphibians and Reptiles, 1958-74; ; vis. prof. biology Stanford U., 1962, 64, 66, 68, Harvard U., Cambridge, Mass., 1969, 72. Author: Philippine Lizards of the Family Gekkonidae, 1978, Philippine Lizards of the Family Scincidae, 1980. Served to sgt. U.S. Army, 1942-46. Fellow AAAS, Calif. Acad. Sci.; mem. Am. Soc. Ichthyologists and Herpetologists, Sigma Xi. Office: Calif Acad Scis Dept Herpetology Golden Gate Park San Francisco CA 94118

BROWN, WALTER FREDERICK, senator; b. Los Angeles, July 28, 1926; s. Walter Andrew and Emily Anna (Weber) B.; m. Barbara Mae Porter Stahmann, Aug. 6, 1950; children: Jeffrey David, Kendall Paul, David Walter. BA, U. So. Calif., 1949, JD, 1952; MA, Boston U., 1961; MLS, U. Oreg., 1975. Bar: Calif. 1952, Oreg. 1981, U.S. Tax Ct. 1974, U.S. Supreme Ct. 1975; cert. Am. Assn. Law Librarians. Assoc. prof. and law librarian Northwestern U. Sch. Law, Evanston, Ill., Lewis and Clark Coll., Portland, Oreg., 1970-80; senator Oreg. Legis. Assembly, Salem, 1975—; bd. dirs. Oreg. Consumer League, 1972—; chmn. Senate Agrl. and Forestry Com., 1985, Senate Task Force Vet.'s Home Loans, 1985-87; chmn. capitol constrn. subcom. Joint Ways and Means Com., 1983; chmn. Senate Bus. and Consumer Affairs Com., 1981; senate co-chmn. Joint Legis. Counsel Com., 1979-87; mem. Legis. Emergency Bd., 1983-84; senate co-vice chmn. Joint Trade and Econ. Devel. Com., 1985-87; commr. Gov.'s Commn. Sr. Services, 1985-87; vice chmn. Judiciary Com., 1975, 79, 81, 83, 85, Labor Com., 1983, Elections, 1981. Contbr. articles to law jours. Pres. Clackamas County Citizens Assn., Oreg., 1971-74. Served to comdr. JAGC, USNR, 1944-70. Recipient Oreg. Civil Liberties Union award, 1983, Oreg. Environ. Council award, 1975, 79, 81, 83, 85, Trout Unltd. award Oregon City, 1975, Liberty award Oreg. Conf. Seventh-day Adventists, 1985. Mem. Crime Prevention Assn. Oreg., Citizens Utility Bd. Oreg., Citizens for Tax Justice, Oreg. UN Assn., Oreg. Common Cause, Nat. Eagle Scout Assn., Oreg. Meml. Assn., Am. Legion (award 1981, 82), VFW, Oreg. Small Woodlands Assn., Oreg. Wildlife Fedn., Sierra Club, Oreg. State Rifle and Pistol Assn., Mazamas, Farmers Union. Democrat. Unitarian-Universalist. Lodges: Kiwanis, Masons. Avocations: sailing, hiking, skiing, farming, reforestation. Home: 3710 SE Concord Rd # 95 Milwaukie OR 97267 Office: Room S211 Oreg State Senate Oreg State Capitol Salem OR 97310

BROWN, WILBUR KNIGHT, physicist, astrophysicist; b. Oakland, Calif., July 6, 1932; s. Herbert Walter and Donna Louise (Anderson) B.; m. Kathryn Lomilla Lind, June 27, 1954; children: Walter Anderson, Craig Alexander. AB, U. Calif., Berkeley, 1954, MS, 1957, PhD, 1962. Registered profl. engr., Calif. Physicist Research Establishment Risö, Roskilde, Denmark, 1962-64, Los Alamos (N.Mex.) Nat. Lab., 1964-70, 1972—; assoc. prof. U. Wyo., Laramie, 1970-72. Contbr. articles to profl. jours. Served to lt. (j.g.) USN, 1954-56. Mem. Am. Phys. Soc., Am. Nuclear Soc., Am. Astron. Soc., Astron. Soc. of Pacific, Sigma Xi, Phi Beta Kappa. Republican. Home: 3232 Woodland Rd Los Alamos NM 87544 Office: Los Alamos Nat Lab Physics Div Los Alamos NM 87545

BROWN, WILLIAM DUANE, contracting company executive; b. Dec. 19, 1937; s. Floyd and Evelyn Brown; m. Karen A. Mattson, May 31, 1959 (div. 1978); children: Lari Anctil, Duane Brown; m. Pamela Jean Brown, June 12, 1982; 1 child. Calif. Trade Cert., State Calif. Dept. Indsl. Relations; various contract licenses, State Calif. Apprentice sheet metal worker 1955-60; founder NCI, Inc., Eureka, Calif., 1968, chief exec. officer, pres. Avocation: game hunting. Office: NCI Inc 242 Manzanita Ave Eureka CA 95501

BROWN (HARDEN), LENORA MARIE, speech and language pathologist; b. Cleve., Oct. 16, 1949; d. Edward Eugene and Edith May (Byrd) Harden; m. Joel Timothy Brown, Nov. 27, 1981; 1 child, Jarrett Edward. BFA, Lake Erie Coll., 1973; MA, Cleve. State U., 1980. Cert. speech pathologist. Speech pathologist Cleve. Pub. Schs., 1980-81, Parent Vol. Assn., Cleve., 1980-81, Mesa (Ariz.) Unified Schs., 1981—; speech pathologist Mesa Luth. Hosp., 1986—. Mem. Am. Speech and Hearing Assn., Mesa Ednl. Assn. Democrat. Roman Catholic. Avocations: jogging, bicycling, sewing.

BROWNE, ALAN KINGSTON, bank consultant; b. Alameda, Calif., Nov. 12, 1909; s. Ralph Stuart and Etta E. (Bouve) B.; m. Elisabeth Leone Henrotte, Feb. 7, 1942. Student, U. Calif., 1929. With Bankamerica Co. (formerly securities div. Nat. Bank Italy Co.), 1929-41; successively clk., mgr. mcpl. bond dept., asst. v.p.; with Bank of Am. Nat. Trust & Savs. Assn., 1941-71, asst. cashier, 1941-42, asst., v.p., mgr. mcpl. bond dept., 1946-52, v.p., 1952-65, sr. v.p., 1965-71, head investments, 1964-71; cons. 1971-72; sr. v.p., dir. Drexel Firestone Inc., N.Y.C., 1972-73; dir. Drexel Burnham & Co., Inc., 1973; cons. 1974—; past pres., dir. San Francisco Stadium, Inc., Candlestick Park; trustee Calif. Muni Fund, Calif. Tax Free Money Fund; mem. arbitration panel N.Y. Stock Exchange, Inc., Nat. Assn. Securities Dealers. Contbr. articles to profl. jours. Mem. San Francisco Mus. Art, The Museum Soc.; past chmn. bd., past pres. Friends of San Francisco Pub. Library; chmn. adv. bd. on financing San Francisco Bay Area Rapid Transit Dist.; chmn. San Francisco Bay Area Rapid Transit Commn.; bd. dirs. Adminstrv. Bldg. Corp., Calif. Alumni Berkeley Found.; past dir. Golden Rain Found., Rossmoor and Walnut Creek, Calif.; past mem. Presdl. Adv. Com. Fed. Debt Mgmt. Served from pvt. to maj. AUS, 1942-46. Recipient Disting. Citizens award Nat. Mcpl. League, 1964; recipient Wheeler Oak award U. Calif.-Berkeley, 1984. Mem. San Francisco C. of C. (past pres.; chmn. sr. council), Mcpl. Fin. Forum Washington, San Francisco Mcpl. Forum, Air Force Assn., Calif. Alumni Assn., Calif. Geneal. Soc., Calif. Hist. Soc., Friends Bancroft Library, Investment Bankers Assn. Am. (now Securities Industry Assn.) (past gov., v.p. mcpl. div.), SAR, Navy League, Mechanics Inst., Am. Legion, Phi Kappa Sigma. Clubs: Bond (San Francisco) (past pres.; named outstanding investment banker of yr. 1958), Olympic (San Francisco) (50-year Mem.), Merchants Exchange (San Francisco), Commonwealth (San Francisco), Stock Exchange (San Francisco), Municipal Bond (San Francisco); Faculty (Berkeley). Lodge: Rotary. Home: 1113 Singingwood Ct 6 Walnut Creek CA 94595

BROWNE, JOSEPH PETER, librarian; b. Detroit, June 12, 1929; s. George and Mary Bridget (Fahy) B.; A.B., U. Notre Dame, 1951; S.T.L., Pontificium Athenaeum Angelicum, Rome, 1957, S.T.D., 1960; M.S. in L.S., Cath. U. Am., 1965. Joined Congregation of Holy Cross, Roman Cath. Ch., 1947, ordained priest, 1955; asst. pastor Holy Cross Ch., South Bend, Ind., 1955-56; librarian, prof. moral theology Holy Cross Coll., Washington, 1959-64; mem. faculty U. Portland (Oreg.), 1964-73, 75—, dir. library, 1966-70, 76—, dean Coll. Arts and Scis., 1970-73, asso. prof. library sci. 1967—, regent, 1969-70, 77-81; prof., head dept. library sci. Our Lady of Lake Coll., San Antonio, 1973-75; chmn. Interstate Library Planning Council, 1977-79. Mem. Columbia River chpt. Huntington's Disease Soc. Am., 1975—, pres., 1979-82. Recipient Culligan award U. Portland, 1979. Mem. Cath. Library Assn. (pres. 1971-73), ALA, Cath. Theol. Soc. Am., Pacific N.W. Library Assn. (pres. 1985-86), Oreg. Library Assn. (pres. 1967-68), Nat. Assn. Parliamentarians, Oreg. Assn. Parliamentarians (pres. 1985-87), Mensa Internat., All-Ireland Cultural Soc. Oreg. (pres. 1984-85). Democrat. Club: KC. Home: 5410 N Strong St Apt 8 Portland OR 97203 Office: U Portland 5000 N Willamette Blvd Portland OR 97203

BROWNE, LEE F(RANKE), academic administrator; b. N.C., Dec. 18, 1922; m. Doroghy G.; children: Gail, Daryl Alice, Adriene, Scott (dec.). BS in Chemistry and Biology, W.Va. State Coll., 1944; postgrad., UCLA, 1946-48; MS, NYU, 1950, postgrad., 1950-53. Chemist, asst. to pathologist N.Y. Dept. Hosps., 1953-55; asst. prof. Langston (Okla.) U., 1955; chemistry instr. Valley Jr. Coll., Van Nuys, Calif., 1956-57, John Muir High Sch., Pasadena, Calif., 1958-64; chemistry instr., dept. chmn. Blair High Sch., Pasadena, 1964-70; sci. coordinator Pasadena Schs., 1970; dir. secondary sch. relations Calif. Inst. Tech., Pasadena, 1971—, dir. spl. student projects, 1977—; mem. grading team for chemistry, Advanced Placement Program Coll. Entrance Examination Bd. and Ednl. Testing Service, 1971-72, 74, 75, 76, 78; lectr. radio stas.; mem. monitoring com. Los Angeles Bd. Edn., mem. Multicultural Edn. Resource Bd.; bd. dirs. NACME, Inc. Founding editor Pasadena Eagle newspaper, 1968-73. Chmn. CORE, 1963-64, Pasadena Commn. on Human Need and Opportunity, 1973-74, Pasadena Community Services Ctr., 1974, Ad-Hoc Integration Com., 1970, Northwest Community Convention,

1969, vice chmn., 1970; vice chmn. Calif. Assn. Afro-Am. Tchrs., 1970-72; bd. dirs., chmn. Monrovia (Calif.) Job Resources Bd., 1973, 75, 76; bd. dirs. Pasadena Hall of Sci., Westside Study Ctr. Bd., Co-op Village, Pasadena, Help Invest in People; council mem. ESSA adv. council Pasadena Urban Coalition, Parent Policy council Project Head-Start, Pasadena; vol. advisor Pasadena Urban League, Turner Sch. ESSA Project. Named Tchr. of Yr., Industry And Ednl. Council, 1968; recipient Raymond Pitts Human Relations award Pasadena Star-News, 1970, 76. Mem. Am. Chem. Soc., AAAS, AAUP, Nat. Sci. Teachers Assn., Nat. Assn. Curriculum Specialists, Calif. Chemistry Teachers Assn., Am. Inst. Chemists. Office: Calif Inst Tech 10-63 Cal Tech Pasadena CA 91125

BROWNE, MIRANDA CONSTANCE, interior designer; b. New Bedford, Mass., Feb. 15, 1949; d. John H. and Dorothy (Fuller) B. Diploma, Boston Mus. Fine Arts Sch., 1971. Project coordinator Tropicana Enterprises, Las Vegas, Nev., 1978-79; project mgr. Doubletree Inc., Phoenix, 1979-80; project adminstr. D.S. Assocs. Inc., Encino, Calif., 1980-81; project mgr. Western Contract Internat., San Francisco, 1981-82; dir. purchasing Granada Royale Hometels, Newport Beach, Calif., 1983-84; interior designer, project mgr. Trust House Ft. Hotels, Travelodge Internat. Inc., El Cajon, Calif., 1984-86; free-lance interior design Long Beach, Calif. Office: Travelodge Internat Inc 1973 Friendship Dr El Cajon CA 92020

BROWNE, ROBERT MCCORMICK, psychiatrist; b. Bklyn., Apr. 12, 1926; s. Robert Davis and Kathryn Cecelia (McCormick) B.; m. Mieko Gayle Morimoto, Aug. 8, 1952; children—Kevin, Sean, Kathleen, Sharon. B.A., U. Rochester, 1946; M.D., Johns Hopkins U., 1950. Intern, then psychiat. resident Queen's Med. Ctr., 1950-55; founding dir. Territorial Convalescent Ctr., Honolulu, 1957-59, Child Devel. Ctr., Honolulu, 1968-76; dir. psychiat. clinic St. Francis Hosp., Honolulu, 1959-81; psychiat. cons. Kamehameha Schs., 1959-82. Art works exhibited: Honolulu Acad. Arts, 1967, Art Inst. Chgo., 1967, 71, Mus. Primitive Art, New York, 1968, Dallas Mus. Fine Arts, 1970, U. Hawaii Art Gallery, 1976, Nat. Gallery Art, 1979-80. Founding bd. dirs. ACLU Hawaii, Honolulu, 1965-71; participant Civil Rights March, Selma, Ala., 1965, Martin Luther King rally, Montgomery, Ala., 1965; founder Contemporary Art Ctr., Honolulu. Served with USNR, 1944-46; capt. M.C., U.S. Army, 1955-57, Korea. Recipient citation Hawaii State Senate, 1965, Honolulu City Council, 1965, United Pub. Workers, 1965. Mem. Am. Psychiat. Assn. Hawaii Psychiat. Soc., Contemporary Arts Ctr. (founder), Honolulu Acad. Arts (life), Bishop Mus. Assn. Anthropol. Soc. Hawaii, Arts Council Hawaii. Democrat. Home: 3625 Anela Pl Honolulu HI 96822

BROWNELL, GAIL DELZELL, environmental engineer; b. New Haven, Nov. 13, 1957; d. Richard Miller and Elizabeth (Darrow) B. BS in Environ. Engring., Northwestern U., 1980. Cert. engr.-in-tng. Environ. engr. Varian Assocs., Palo Alto, Calif., 1980-84; supr. environ. engring. components group Hewlett-Packard Co., San Jose, Calif., 1984—. Mem. Am. Electronics Assn. (chmn. environ. subcom. 1982), Peninsula Indsl. and Bus. Assn., Am. Water Well Assn., Women in Waste Mgmt. Professions (founder, editor newletter 1983—), LWV. Unitarian. Avocations: bicycling, swimming, studying, upholstering, windsurfing. Home: 1765 Shamrock Ave Santa Clara CA 95051 Office: Hewlett Packard Co 350 W Trimble Bldg 91 San Jose CA 95131

BROWNELL, PHILIP HARRY, research biologist, educator; b. Castro Valley, Calif., Aug. 2, 1947; s. Harry Brownell and Eva (Cole) Brown; m. Kathy Greathouse, Sept. 20, 1969; children: Benjamin, Emily. AB, U. Calif., Berkeley, 1970; PhD, U. Calif., Riverside, 1976. Teaching assoc. U. Calif., Riverside, 1971-75; postdoctoral fellow U. Calif., San Francisco, 1976-79; asst. prof. Oreg. State U., Corvallis, 1979-85, assoc. prof. biology, 1985—. Contbr. articles to profl. jours. NIH research grantee, 1982—. Mem. AAAS, Soc. Neurosci., Am. Heart Assn., Union of Concerned Scientists, Sigma Xi. Avocations: youth soccer, hiking, basketball, canoeing. Office: Oreg State U Dept Zoology Corvallis OR 97331

BROWNER, CAROLE H., research anthropology educator; b. N.Y.C., May 23, 1947; s. Alfred H. and Shirley (Kapp) B.; m. Lawrence Howard Mintz, June 22, 1969 (div. Sept. 1976). BA, New Sch. Social Research, 1969; MA, U. Calif., Berkeley, 1972, PhD, 1976, MPH, 1977. Asst. prof. anthropology Wayne State U., Detroit, 1977-83, assoc. prof., 1983-84; asst. prof. UCLA, 1983—; cons. Xerox Corp., Palo Alto, Calif., 1977-78, Detroit Dept. Health, 1979-80, Nat. Inst. Edn., Washington, 1979, WHO, Geneva, 1980, Planned Parenthood, Tulsa, 1985, Social Sci. Research Council, N.Y.C., 1985, NSF, Washington, 1987;mem. steering com. So. Calif. Applied Anthropology Network, Los Angeles, 1983—. Editor: (jour.) Practicing Anthropology, 1983; contbr. articles to profl. jours. Research grantee Nat. Inst. Gen. Med. Scis., Washington, 1972-75, NSF, Washington, 1980-83, Wenner-Gren Found., N.Y.C., 1980-83, U. Calif. Mexus, Riverside, 1985-86. Fellow Am. Anthropol. Assn., Soc. Applied Anthropology; mem. Soc. Med. Anthropology, Latin Am. Studies Assn., Sigma Xi. Office: U Calif. 760 Westwood Plaza Los Angeles CA 90024

BROWNING, IBEN, biophysicist, climatologist, inventor; b. Vanderbilt, Tex., Jan. 9, 1918; s. Bede and Lugilla (McCormick) B.; m. Florence A. Pinto, July 30, 1945; 1 dau., Evelyn. B.S., S.W. Tex. State Tchrs. Coll., 1937; M.A., U. Tex., 1947, Ph.D. in Physiology, Genetics and Bacteriology, 1948. Tutor in physiology U. Tex., Austin, 1937-38; technician U. Tex., 1938-39, instr. biology, 1946-47; pres. Tex. Cedar Products Co., 1940-41; Nat. Research fellow in biophysics U. Pa., Phila., 1948-49; asst. biologist M.D. Anderson Hosp., Houston, 1949-52, asst. prof., 1950-52; devel. physicist Am. Optical Co., 1952-54; supr. optics div. Bell Aircraft Corp., 1954-57; staff mem., scientist Sandia Lab., Albuquerque, 1957-60; prin. investigator Panoramic Research Co., Palo Alto, Calif., 1960-64; exec. dir. Thomas Bede Found., Los Altos, Calif. and Albuquerque, 1963—; pres. Sydnor-Barent Scanner Corp., Albuquerque, 1971—; cons. in various fields to numerous bus. and fin. instns. and research orgns. Author: (with N. Winkless) Climate and the Affairs of Men, 1975, Robots on Your Doorstep, 1978, (with Evelyn Garriss) Past and Future History: A Planner's Guide, 1982; editor The Browning Newsletter, 1977—; holder numerous U.S. and fgn. patents. Served with USAAF, 1941-45. Mem. AAAS. Researcher and inventor in field of optical engring., info. theory, brain physiology, enzymes, climatology, and others. Home and Office: PO Drawer 130 Sandia Park NM 87047

BROWNING, JAMES ROBERT, U.S. judge; b. Great Falls, Mont., Oct. 1, 1918; s. Nicholas Henry and Minnie Sally (Foley) B.; m. Marie Rose Chapell, Aug. 14, 1941. LL.B. with honors, Mont. State U., 1941; LL.D. (hon.), U. Mont., 1978. Bar: Mont. bar 1941, D.C. bar 1950, U.S. Supreme Ct. bar 1952. Spl. atty. antitrust div. Dept. Justice, 1941-46; chief Dept. Justice (N.W. regional office), 1948-49, asst. chief gen. litigation sect. antitrust div., 1949-51, 1st asst. civil div., 1951-52; exec. asst. to atty. gen. U.S., 1952-53; chief U.S. (Exec. Office for U.S. Attys.), 1953; pvt. practice Washington, 1953-58; lectr. N.Y.U. Sch. Law, 1953, Georgetown U. Law Center, 1957-58; clk. Supreme Ct. U.S., 1958-61; judge U.S. Ct. Appeals 9th Circuit, 1961—, chief judge, 1976—. Mem. Am. Law Inst., Am., Mont., Fed. bar assns., Inst. Jud. Adminstrn., Am. Judicature Soc., Am. Soc. Legal History (adv. bd. jour.). Office: US Court of Appeals and Post Office Bldg San Francisco CA 94101

BROWNING, JESSE HARRISON, manufacturing company executive; b. Kingsville, Mo., July 27, 1935; s. Jesse Harrison and Anna Love (Swank) B.; m. Vicki Carol Thompson, Dec. 21, 1957; children: Caroline Kaye, Marcia Lynn, Nanci Ann, Susan Louise. Student, U. Wash., 1955-61. Cert. mfg. engr. Field engr. The Boeing Co., Los Angeles, 1961-64; gen. mgr. SPI, Los Angeles, 1964-70; chmn. Browning Inc., Los Angeles, 1970—, Indsl. Systems, Los Angeles, 1979—, Vapor Engring., Los Angeles, 1979—. Patentee in field. Mem. Palos Verdes Breakfast Club, Los Angeles C. of C., Am. Helicopter Soc., Am. Electroplaters Soc., Soc. Mfg. Engrs. Republican. Lutheran. Avocations: snow skiing, flying helicopters and airplanes, traveling, working out. Home: 4217 Via Pinzon Palos Verdes Estates CA 90274 Office: Indsl Systems Inc 5631 Leeds St South Gate CA 90280

BROWNING, WILLIAM DOCKER, judge; b. Tucson, May 19, 1931; s. Horace Benjamin and Mary Louise (Docker) B.; m. Courteny Browning (div.); children: Christopher, Logan, Courtenay; m. Zerilda Sinclair, Dec. 17, 1974; 1 child, Benjamin. BBA, U. Ariz., 1954, LLB, 1960. Bar: Ariz., U.S. Dist. Ct. Ariz., U.S. Ct. Appeals (9th cir.), U.S. Supreme Ct. Sole practice Tucson, 1960-84; judge U.S. Dist. Ct., Tucson, 1984—; mem. jud. nominating comm. appellate ct. appointments, 1975-79. Del. 9th Cir. Jud. Conf., 1968-77, 79-82. Served to 1st lt. USAF, 1954-57, capt. USNG, 1958-61. Fellow Am. Coll. Trial Lawyers, Am. Bar Found.; mem. ABA (spl. com. housing andurban devel. law 1973-78, com. urban problems and human affairs 1978-80), State Bar Ariz. (securities regulation com. 1964-66, chmn. uniform jury instructions com. 1962-66, chmn. merit selection of judges com. 1973-76, bd. govs., 1968-74, pres.-elect 1971-72, pres. 1972-73, named Outstanding Mem. 1980), Pima County Bar Assn. (exec. com. 1964-68, med.-legal screening panel 1965-75, pres. 1967-68), Am. Bd. Trial Advocates, Am. Judicature Soc. (bd. dirs. 1975-77, Herbert Lincoln Harley award 1978), Inst. Ct. Mgmt. (trustee 1978—). Office: US Dist Ct 55 E Broadway #301 Tucson AZ 85701

BROWNLEE, DON ROBERT, speech communication educator; b. Corpus Christi, Tex., Mar. 21, 1951; s. Robert Ned and Esther Mae (Tarver) B.; m. Suzan Lynn Bennett, June 30, 1975. BA, Tex. Christian U., 1973; MS, North Tex. State U., 1974; PhD, U. Tex., 1982. Lectr. North Tex. State U., Denton, 1975-80; asst. prof. speech communication Wingate (N.C.) Coll., 1980-82; asst. prof. Calif. State U., Northridge, 1982—; cons. Value Systems Analysis, Dallas, 1978-80. Polit. debate advisor Daily News, Los Angeles. Mem. So. Forensic Assn. (v.p. 1982, pres. 1982-83, Pres.'s award 1986), Cross-Exam Debate Assn., Phi Beta Kappa, Pi Kappa Delta (gov. 1982-85). Methodist. Avocation: golfing. Home: 18739 Sunburst Northridge CA 91324 Office: Calif State U Dept Speech Communications 18111 Nordhoff St Northridge CA 91330

BROWN, LORI ELLEN LIPMAN, lawyer; b. Bklyn., June 17, 1958; d. Melvin S. and Anita (Orlen) L.; m. Paul R. Brown, June 7, 1986. BA, U. Nev., 1981; JD, Southwestern U., Los Angeles, 1983. Bar: Calif. 1983, Nev. 1984, Ariz. 1985, U.S. Dist. Ct. (cen. dist.) Calif. 1983, U.S. Dist. Ct. Nev. 1984. Assoc. Rawlings, Olson & Cannon, Las Vegas, Nev., 1984-85, Phillip S. Aurbach, Ltd., Las Vegas, 1985-86; sole practice Las Vegas, 1987—. Trustee Theatre Arts Group, Las Vegas, 1985-86; sec., bd. dirs. Unitarian Fellowship Las Vegas, 1985-86, v.p., 1986—; mem., dep. registrar of voters Dem. State and County com., Clark County, Nev., 1984—. Mem. Calif. Bar Assn., Nev. Bar Assn., Ariz. Bar Assn., Am. Trail Lawyers Assn., Phi Lamda Alpha. Office: 101 E Charleston #7 Las Vegas NV 89104

BRUBAKER, MARIAN M., dermatologist; b. Salina, Utah, Nov. 8, 1926; d. Don Clatyon and LaVerne (Larson) M.; m. Rowan C. Ward, Aug. 24, 1975; children from previous marriage; Anne, David. BA, Stanford U., 1948, MA, 1951, MD, 1954. Diplomate Am. Bd. Dermatology. Postgrad. U. So. Calif., Los Angeles; mem. staff Glendale (Calif.) Meml. Hosp., Verdugo Hills (Calif.) Hosp., Children's Hosp. Los Angeles; practice medicine specializing in dermatology La Canada, Calif., 1957—; from asst. clin. prof. to clin. prof. dermatology U. So. Calif., 1963-81, interviewer office admissions Sch. Medicine, 1970-80, admissions com. 1976-79, coordinator postgrad. dermatology courses, 1959-60; supr., tchr. Pediat. Clinic, Los Angeles County-U. So. Calif., 1960—, chmn. dermatology profl. staff, 1974-76; initiator dermatology services Adolescent Unit Children's Hosp. Los Angeles, 1960; vice chmn. Dept. Medicine Verdugo Hills Hosp.; mem. rev. com. Bd. Med. Quality Assurance, Dist. XI, Calif.; lectr. dermatology local hosps. Contbr. articles to profl. jours. Scholar Henry Newell, Stanford U., 1950-51, Anna B. Eyre, Stanford U., 1951-52, Jessie B. Langford, Stanford U., 1952-53; recipient C.V. Mosby Co. award, Stanford U., 1953. Mem. AMA, Am. Med. Women's Assn., Calif. State Med. Assn. (sec. sect. dermatology 1974-75, chmn. 1975-76), Los Angeles County Women Physicians Assn., Los Angeles County Med. Assn., Los Angeles Dermatol. Soc. (asst. sec. 1974-75, sec. 1975-76, pres. 1976-77, recorder and editor 1976-77), Am. Acad. Dermatology, Soc. Investigative Dermatology, Soc. Adolescent Medicine, Los Angeles Acad. Medicine, Pediat. Dermatology Soc., Sigma Xi (assoc.), Iota Sigma Pi, Alpha Omega Alpha. Mormon. Avocations: family, gardening. Home: 1788 N Pepper Dr Altadena CA 91001 Office: Foothill Dermatology Med Group Inc 1346 Foothill Blvd La Canada-Flintridge CA 91011

BRUCE, CHERYL LYNN, optometric technician, educator; b. Spokane, Wash., Feb. 17, 1954; d. Ralph Eugene and Margaret Louise (Berrong) B.; m. M. Gibson, Mar. 10, 1977 (div.); children: Megan Christan, Melissa Mary. A.A., So. Calif. Coll. Optometry, 1975; A.A., Spokane Falls Community Coll., 1976; B.A., Eastern Wash. U., 1984. Cert. vocat. tchr., Wash. Optometric asst., office mgr. Dr. Ralph E. Bruce, Spokane, Wash., 1969-73; optometric technician Dr. Robert Kettenhofen, Pomona, Calif., 1975-76; optician Lund Optical, Provo, Utah, 1976-77; program coordinator, instr., optometric technician Spokane Community Coll., 1978—. Mem. Am. Optometric Assn., Assn. Higher Edn., Wash. Edn. Assn., Assn. Paraoptometric Edn. Programs, Optometric Extension Program, Am. Bd. Opticians (cert.). Home: 3018 Marquerite Spokane WA 99212 Office: Spokane Community Coll Health Sci Bldg 9 1810 N Greene St Spokane WA 99207

BRUCE, CYNTHIA SUE, city planning official; b. Oak Park, Ill., Aug. 6, 1948; d. Roy Alford and Henrietta H. (Denk) B.; m. Christopher Moody Davis, Jan. 9, 1982. B.A., Univ. N.Mex., 1972, M. Arch., 1982. Presentation draftsman City of Albuquerque, 1979-80, assoc. planner, 1980-82, planner, 1982-84, sr. planner, 1984-85, chief of advance palnning, 1985—. Grantee State of N.Mex., 1980. Mem. Am. Inst. Planners, AIA. Office: City of Albuquerque PO Box 1293 Albuquerque NM 87103

BRUCE, GORDON JAMES, information services administrator; b. Toronto, Ont., Can., June 10, 1949; came to U.S., 1979; s. Gordon L.L. and Mary (FitzPatrick) B.; m. Barbara Marie McKenna, Oct. 18, 1968; 1 child, Lauri Anne. BS in Computer Sci., Ryerson Poly. Inst., Toronto, 1977. With Corp. N City of Toronto, 1967-79; sr. systems programmer Bank of Hawaii, Honolulu, 1979-81; mgr. systems programming Queen's Med. Ctr., Honolulu, 1980-81, dir. info. services, 1981—; pres. integrated healthcare techs. Travenol Labs, Haugpaug, N.Y., 1983—. Mem. Am. Mgmt. Assn., Electronic Computing Health Oriented Assn., Data Processing Mgmt. Assn. Home: 967 Wainiha St Honolulu HI 96825 Office: Queens Med Ctr 1301 Punchbowl St Honolulu HI 96813

BRUCE, JAMES EDMUND, utility company executive; b. Boise, Idaho, June 23, 1920; s. James E. and Bessie (Barcus) B.; m. Lois I. Stevens, Aug. 24, 1946; children: James E., IV, Steven, Robert, David. Student, Coll. Idaho, 1937-39; B.A., Portland U., 1941; postgrad., Georgetown U., 1941-42; LL.B., U. Idaho, 1949. Bar: Idaho bar 1948. Asst. atty. gen. State of Idaho, 1948-49; dep. pros. atty. Ada County (Idaho), 1949-51; with Idaho Power Co., Boise, 1951—, v.p., 1968-74, pres., chief operating officer, 1974-76, pres., chief exec. officer, 1976-85, chmn., 1985—, also dir.; dir. Albertson's Inc., First Security Corp., Fuel Cell User Group; vice chmn. Blue Cross of Idaho, 1986—. Bd. dirs. United Fund, Boise, 1976-84, Mountain States Legal Found.; mem. Boise Park Bd., 1958-78; Idaho chmn. U.S. Savs. Bonds, 1976-85; chmn. bd. trustees St. Alphonsos, 1985-86; trustee Coll. Idaho. Served with U.S. Army, 1942-46. Mem. Boise Execs. Assn., YMCA, Bishop Kelly Found., Am. Bar Assn., Edison Electric Assn. (dir. 1978—), Northwest Electric Light and Power Assn. (pres. 1982), Boise C. of C. Roman Catholic. Clubs: Arid, Crane Creek Country, Rotary, Elks, K.C. Office: Idaho Power Co 1220 Idaho St Boise ID 83707

BRUCE, JOHN CLAYTON, JR., educator, clergyman; b. Warrensburg, Mo., Mar. 31, 1918; s. John Clayton and Maybelle (Warnick) B.; B.S., Central Mo. State Coll., Warrensburg, 1939; B.Div., San Francisco Theol. Sem., San Anselmo, Calif., 1950, M.Div., 1971; M.A., San Francisco State U., 1962; postgrad. State U. Iowa, Iowa City, 1940-41, U. Calif., Berkeley, 1962-63, Sonoma State Coll., Cotati, Calif., 1972-73; m. Eleanor Mortensen, May 25, 1941. Tchr. bus. and English, Alma (Mo.) High Sch., 1939-41; tchr. bus. Naperville (Ill.) High Sch., 1941-46; psychologist VA Regional Office, Kansas City, Mo., 1946-47; ordained to ministry Presbyn. Ch., 1950; minister St. Marks Presbyn. Ch., Van Nuys, Calif., 1950-54, Sleepy Hollow Presbyn. Ch., San Anselmo, Calif., 1954-61; prof. bus. and econs. dept. Coll. of Marin, Kentfield, Calif., 1961—; chmn. candidates com. Presbytery of Redwoods, United Presbyn. Ch. in U.S.A., 1958-63; elder First Presbyn. Ch., San Anselmo, 1971-74. Served with AUS, 1942-46. Recipient Hon. plaque for 25th Anniversary, St. Marks Presbyn. Ch., 1976. Mem. Kappa Delta Pi, Phi Sigma Pi. Contbr. articles to religious publs. Home: 9 Bay Tree Ln San Anselmo CA 94960 Office: Coll Marin Arcade Bldg Dept of Bus and Econs Kentfield CA 94904

BRUCH, CAROL SOPHIE, lawyer, educator; b. Rockford, Ill., June 11, 1941; d. Ernest and Margarete (Willstätter) B.; m. Jack E. Myers, 1960 (div. 1973); children: Margarete Louise Myers, Kurt Randall Myers. A.B., Shimer Coll., 1960; J.D., U. Calif.-Berkeley, 1972. Bar: Calif. 1973, U.S. Supreme Ct. 1980. Law clk. to Justice William O. Douglas U.S. Supreme Ct., 1972-73; acting prof. law U. Calif.-Davis, 1973-78, prof., 1978—; vis. prof. U. Calif., Berkeley, 1983, Columbia U., 1986; cons. to Ctr. for Family in Transition, 1981, Calif. Law Revision Commn., 1979-82, NOW Legal Def. and Edn. Fund, 1980-81; lectr., legis. drafting and testimony, 1976—. Contbr. articles to legal jours. Editor Calif. Law Rev., 1971; editorial Bd. Family Law Quar., 1980—. Mem. adv. com. child support and child custody Calif. Commn. on Status of Women, 1981-83; host parent Am. Field Service, Davis, 1977-78. Max Rheinstein sr. research fellow Alexander von Humboldt Found., Fed. Republic Germany, 1978-79. Mem. ABA, Calif. State Bar Assn., Am. Law Inst., Order of Coif. Democrat. Jewish. Office: Sch of Law U Calif Davis CA 95616

BRUCH, JOHN CLARENCE, JR., engineer, educator; b. Kenosha, Wis., Oct. 11, 1940; m. Susan Jane Tippett, Aug. 19, 1967. BCE, U. Notre Dame, 1962; MCE, Stanford U., 1963, PhD in Civil Engring., 1966. Acting instr. engring. Stanford (Calif.) U., 1966; asst. prof. engring. U. Calif., Santa Barbara, 1966-74, assoc. prof. engring., 1974-78, prof. engring., 1978—. NSF grantee, 1977-78; U. Calif. Santa Barbara faculty grantee, 1968. Mem. Am. Soc. Civil Engrs., Internat. Assn. Computational Mechanics, Sigma Xi, Tau Beta Pi. Avocations: golf, jogging. Office: U Calif Dept Mech Engring Santa Barbara CA 93106

BRUCH, REINHARD FRANK, physics educator; b. Berlin, Nov. 28, 1941; came to U.S., 1984; s. Walter Heinz and Ruth Hildegard (Jeskulke) B.; m. Karin Siglinde Falge, Aug. 1, 1980 (div. Dec. 1983); one child, Jan Frederik. Vordiplom, Technische U., Hanover, Fed. Republic Germany, 1966, Diplom, 1970; Dr. Rer. Nat., Freie U., West Berlin, 1976. Lectr. Medizinische Hochschule, Hanover, 1969-70; research assoc. Freie U., West Berlin, 1970-76; research scientist Arhus (Denmark) U., 1976-77; group leader U. Freiburg, Fed. Republic Germany, 1978-83; assoc. prof. physics U. Nev., Reno, 1984—; research scientist Argonne (Ill.) Nat. Lab., 1982. Contbr. articles to profl. jours. Grantee Deutsche Forschungs Gemeinschaft, 1970-83, Land Baden-Württemberg Wissenschaftliche Gesellschaft, 1978-83, Research Corp., 1986. Mem. Am. Phys. Soc., Deutsche Physikalische Gesellschaft, Sigma Xi, Sigma Pi Sigma. Lutheran. Avocations: painting, music, theatre, opera, skiing. Home: 685 College Dr Reno NV 89503 Office: U Nev-Reno Dept Physics Reno NV 89557

BRUCK, HENRY WOLFGANG, policy and strategic analyst, writer; b. Berlin, Sept. 1, 1926; came to U.S., 1938; s. Ernest Alfred and Beatrice (Asarch) B.; m. Eugenie Tourison, Dec. 31, 1951. AB, UCLA, 1948; AM, Princeton U., 1952. Dir. regional planning Penn Jersey Transp. Study, Phila., 1959-64, N.E. Corridor Transp. Study, U.S. depts. Commerce and Transp., Washington, 1964-67; lectr. dept. civil engring., assoc. dir. Urban Systems Lab. MIT, Cambridge, 1967-74; research planner U. Calif., Berkeley, 1974-82; free-lance writer 1982—. Co-author: Foreign Policy Decision-Making, 1962, Getting It Off the Shelf, 1977; contbr. numerous articles to jours. Served with U.S. Army, 1944-46. Mem. AAAS, Am. Sociol. Assn., World Future Soc. Home: 600 Cragmont Ave Berkeley CA 94708

BRUCKNER, ADAM PETER, aerospace educator; b. Istanbul, Turkey, Mar. 21, 1943; s. Peter Eugene and Agnes (Csiki) B.; m. Rebecca Jean Ginnings, July 22, 1972; 1 child, Elizabeth. BS in Engring., McGill U., Montreal, Que., Can., 1966; MA, Princeton U., 1968, PhD, 1972. Research assoc. U. Wash., Seattle, 1972-75, research asst. prof. aerospace sci., 1975-78, research assoc. prof., 1978—; cons. Spectra-Tech., Bellevue, Wash., 1978—, United Techs., East Hartford, Conn., 1984—. Contbr. articles to profl. jours. Recipient Brit. Assn. medal, Montreal, 1966, Cert. of Recognition, NASA, Seattle, 1983, Cert. Appreciation, NASA, Kennedy Space Ctr., 1985. Mem. AIAA (Outstanding Contrbn. award 1973), Optical Soc. Am., Sigma Xi. Avocations: music, model railroads, travelling, reading. Office: U Wash Seattle WA 98195

BRUCKNER, ANDREW MICHAEL, educator; b. Berlin, Germany, Dec. 17, 1932; s. Ferdinand and Bettina (Pollack) B.; m. Judith Brostoff, Jan. 27, 1957; children—Theodore, Michael. B.A., U. Calif. at Los Angeles, 1955, Ph.D., 1959. Mem. faculty U. Calif. at Santa Barbara, 1959—, asst. prof., 1959-64, asso. prof., 1964-68, prof. math., 1968—; acting dean grad. div., 1966-69. Recipient NSF grants, 1962—. Mem. Am. Math. Soc., Math Assn. Am. Home: 910 Mission Canyon Rd Santa Barbara CA 93105

BRUDER, DAVID M., mechanical engineer, energy management consultant; b. Monterey Park, Calif., Jan. 16, 1957; s. Wilbert E. Jr. and Maryanne (Berger) B. BS in Environ. Engring., Calif. Poly. State U., 1982. Mech. engr. Pullman Power Products, Avila Beach, Calif., 1983-84, Naval Energy and Environ. Support Activity, USN, Port Hueneme, Calif., 1984—; cons. energy mgmt., Oxnard, Calif., 1984—. Mem. ASHRAE (assoc.). Roman Catholic. Avocations: boating, golf, tennis. Home: 1430 San Marino Ave San Marino CA 91108 Office: Naval Energy Environ Support Activity Code 1111E Port Hueneme CA 93043

BRUENING, REIMAR CASPAR, chemistry educator, marine bio-organic chemistry researcher; b. Munich, Dec. 31, 1948; came to U.S., 1981; s. Hans and Elizabeth (Gerlach) B. BS, U. Munich, 1970, MS, 1973, PhD, 1979. Research asst. U. Munich, 1978-79; research fellow U. Nagoya, Japan, 1979-81; research assoc. Columbia U., N.Y.C., 1981-85; asst. prof. U. Hawaii, Honolulu, 1985—. Co-author: Centrifugal Partition Chromatography, 1987. Recipient Eisai award NAITO Found, Japan. Mem. Gesellschaft Deutscher Chemiker, Phytochemical Soc. Europe, Am. Chem. Soc. Office: U. Hawaii Dept Chemistry 2545 The Mall Honolulu HI 96822

BRUGGE, DAVID MARTIN, anthropologist, curator; b. Jamestown, N.Y., Sept. 3, 1927; s. Oswald Adolph and Frances Margaret (Jones) B.; m. Ruth Virginia Sherlog, Feb. 22, 1959; children: Douglas Martin, Steven Paul, Janet Esther. BA, U. N.Mex., 1950. Mem. staff Unitarian Service Com., Gallup, N.Mex., 1955-57; archeologist Four Corners Pipeline Co., Houston, 1957-58; anthropologist The Navajo Tribe, Window Rock, Ariz., 1958-68; curator Nat. Park Service, Ganado, Ariz., 1968-73; anthropologist Nat. Park Service, Albuquerque, 1973-77; regional curator Nat. Park Service, Santa Fe, 1979—; seminar participant Sch. Am. Research, Santa Fe, 1979, 85; chmn. Navajo Studies Conf., Albuquerque, 1985-86. Author: Navajos in the Catholic Church 1694-1875, 1968, 2d rev. edit., 1986, Navajo Pottery and Ethnohistory, 1963, 2d rev. edit., 1981, A History of the Chaco Navajos, 1980, Tsegai: An Archeological Ethnohistory, 1986; co-editor: Navajo Religion and Culture, 1982. Bd. dirs. Navajo Nation Health Found., Ganado, 1972-73, Title I Ganado Pub. Sch.Bd., 1972-73. Served with U.S. Army, 1945-47. Recipient Cert. Recognition Project Hope, Ganado, 1973, Unit award Dept. Interior, Santa Fe, 1982. Mem. AAAS, Am. Anthrop. Assn., Soc. Am Archaelogy, Am. Soc. Ethnohistory (sec.-treas. 1966-67, nominating com. 1986), N.Mex. Assn. Mus. (treas. 1977-79). Democrat. Home: 601 Arizona SE Albuquerque NM 87108

BRUHN, JOHN AUDOLPH, JR., finance executive, writer; b. Indpls., Oct. 13, 1935; s. John Audolph Bruhn and Rachell (Hull) Bruhn Ruddell; m. Joene Marie Cline, Dec. 28, 1957; children: John Allan III, Jeffrey Cline. BA in Econs. and Math., DePauw U., 1957; MBA in Mgmt., San Diego State U., 1961; attended, U. So. Calif., 1963-64; PhD in Communications, U.S. Internat. U., 1971. Cert. assessment evaluator. Asst. bus. mgr. U. Calif., San Diego, 1961-66; chief dep. assessor County San Diego, 1966-72, dir. fin., 1972-75, asst. county mgr., 1975-79; gen. mgr. Marine Corps Credit Union, San Diego, 1979-80; pres. and chief exec. officer Fin. Fed. Credit Union, San Diego, 1980—; instr. U. Calif., San Diego, 1963-75; trustee Consumer Credit Counselors, San Diego, 1983—; pres. chpt. Calif. League, 1983-84; chmn. bd. WesCorp, Pomona, Calif., 1984—. Author-editor: CUNA Management, 1981; editor and contbr. to numerous profl. and sci. jours. Bd. dirs. San Diego YMCA, 1967-71. Served to maj. USMC, 1957-60. Recipient Internat. award in Govtl. Adminstrn., Internat. Assn. Assessing Officers, 1971; named Nat. Exec. of Yr., Credit Union Exec. Soc., 1983; nominated Outstanding Young Man, City of San Diego, 1973. Mem. Credit Union Mgrs. Assn. (pres. 1982-84), Am. Soc. Pub. Adminstrs. (pres. 1969-72), Credit Union Exec. Soc. (awards judge 1983-84), Calif. Credit Union League Coop. (founding trustee 1980-82), San Diego Jr. C. of C. (bd. dirs. 1971-73), Eagle Scout Alumni Assn. (founding chmn. 1971-81), DePauw U. Alumni Assn. (pres. 1966). Republican. Home: 4102 Point Loma Ave San Diego CA 92107 Office: Fin Fed Credit Union 440 Beech St San Diego CA 92101-3281

BRUMBAUGH, JANA JO, social worker; b. Seattle, Mar. 30, 1959; d. Fredrick LaVerne and Jean Marie (Sundquist) B. BA in Social Welfare summa cum laude, U. Wash., 1981, postgrad. Therapist Community Psychiat. Clinic, Seattle, 1981-82; program mgr. Keystone Resources, Seattle, 1982—. Mem. Nat. Assn. Social Workers, Internat. Assn. Psychosocial Rehab., Wash. Community Mental Health Assn., Phi Beta Kappa. Avocation: running. Office: Keystone Resources 3515 Woodland Park Ave N Seattle WA 98103

BRUMMEL, STEVEN WILLIAM, foundation administrator; b. Los Angeles, Feb. 17, 1946; s. Henry William and Claudia (Borja) B.; m. Shari Marie Reville; children—Michael, Christopher, John William; stepson Netha Olive (Barlow) B.; B.A. in Govt. and Journalism with honors, Calif. State U., Sacramento, 1972, M.A. in Govt., 1975. Newsman, Sta. KNTV-TV, San Jose, Calif., 1969-71, Sta. KCRA-TV, Sacramento, 1971-73; cons. Calif. Assembly, 1973; dist. rep. U.S. Congressman Leo J. Ryan, 1973-75; pres. Pacific Cons., San Francisco, 1975, ELS, Inc., Santa Cruz, Calif., 1975-82; tchr., counselor Operation SHARE, 1970-71; pres., Elvirita Lewis Found. Geriatric Health and Nutrition, Palm Springs, Calif., 1976—; v.p. San Jose Ecology Action, 1970-71; pres., chmn. bd. dirs. Verde-Mar, Ltd., La Quinta, Calif., 1978—. Publicity chmn. Santa Clara County Easter Seals, 1970-71; mem. Rep. Nat. Com., Senatorial Inner Circle, Calif. Rep. Golden Circle; mem. Gov.'s Adv. Task Force on Long Term Care; mem. Santa Cruz County Housing Adv. Commn., 1976-81. Served with USN, 1964-67; Vietnam. Mem. Am. Acad. Polit. and Social Scientists, Nat. Council on Aging, Am. Soc. Aging (chmn. communications com., editorial bd., bd. dirs. 1986—), World Affairs Council San Francisco, Calif. Council on Internat. Trade, Calif. Farm Bur., Export Mgrs. Assn., Nat. Rifle Assn., Am. Assn. Internat. Aging (bd. dirs., treas.), Acad. Polit. Sci., East Riverside County Young Reps. (bd. dirs.), Smithsonian Instn., Am. Mus. Natural History, Gerontol. Soc., Internat. Council Nat. Founds. on Aging (bd. dirs.), Nat. Hispanic Council on Aging (bd. dirs. 1986—), Sigma Delta Chi (Journalism award 1972, 73), Pi Sigma Alpha. Clubs: Commonwealth (San Francisco); La Quinta Tennis; Los Angeles. : Elvirita Lewis Found Suite 144 255 N El Cielo Rd Palm Springs CA 92262

BRUMMET, ANTHONY J., Canadian provincial official; b. Mar. 31, 1931. BEd, U. B.C. Formerly sch. tchr., adminstr.; mem. B.C. Legis Assembly; minister edn., Province of B.C., Can. Office: Parliament Bldgs, Victoria, BC Canada V8V 1X4

BRUMMETT, ROBERT EDDIE, pharmacology educator, researcher; b. Concordia, Kans., Feb. 11, 1934; s. Gordon Legonia and Gladys Leona (Anderson) B.; m. Naomi Deen Weaver, Dec. 19, 1955; children: Randall, Wendy, Robin, Philip. BS, Oreg. State U., 1959, MS, 1960; PhD, U. Oreg., 1964. Registered pharmacist, Oreg. Asst. prof. pharmacology Oreg. State U., Corvallis, 1961-62; asst. prof. otolaryngology Oreg. Health Scis. U., Portland, 1964-70, assoc. prof. otolaryngology and pharmacology, 1970-80, prof. otolaryngology and Pharmacology, 1981—; mem. Oreg. Council on Alcohol and Drug Problems, Salem, 1979-85; instr. Am. Acad. Otolaryngology, Washington, 1964—; cons. in field, 1969—;. Patentee in field; contbr. 100 articles to profl. jours. Ednl. officer U.S. Power Squadron, Portland, 1982-86, adminstrv. officer 1986—. Grantee NIH, 1969—, Deafness Research Found., 1970, Med. Research Found., 1979, 83. Mem. AAAS, Am. Acad. Otolaryngology (instr. 1964—), Head and Neck Surgery, Associated Researchers in Otolaryngology, Sigma Xi. Republican. Club: Hayden Island Yacht (Portland) Lodge: Elks. Avocations: sailing, celestial navigation, fishing, wood carving. Home: 505 NE Bridgeton Rd Portland OR 97211 Office: Oreg Health Scis Univ 3181 SW Sam Jackson Park Rd Portland OR 97201

BRUMMUND, FRANCINE ANN, public relations specialist; b. Tacoma, Apr. 7, 1960; d. Arnold Raymond Brummund and Georgia Lenore (Fischer) Holmstrom. B in Univ. Studies, N.D. State U., 1985. Seminar coordinator YMCA of N.D. State U., Fargo, 1980-83; coordinator Knorr for U.S. Senate campaign, Fargo, N.D., 1982; intern U.S. Senator Mark Andrews, Washington, 1983; interviewer Job Service of N.D., Fargo, 1983-84; pub. relations vol. coordinator Altenburg for Cong., Fargo, 1984; with pub. relations GTE-Sylvania Corp., Orange, Calif., 1985—. Youth mem. Gov.'s Employment and Tng. Forum, Bismarck, N.D., 1980-82. Republican. Roman Catholic. Avocations: biking, swimming. Home: 2307 E Ball Rd Anaheim CA 92806 Office: GTE Sylvania Cons Services 1483 N Main Orange CA 92667

BRUNACINI, ALAN VINCENT, fire chief; b. Jamestown, N.Y., Apr. 18, 1937; s. John N. and Mary T. Brunacini; B.S., Ariz. State U., 1970, M.P.A., 1975; m. Rita McDaugh, Feb. 14, 1959; children—Robert Nicholas, John Nicholas, Mary Candice. Mem. Phoenix Fire Dept., 1959—, bn. chief, then asst. fire chief, 1971-78, fire chief, 1978—; condr. nat. seminar on fire dept. mgmt., 1970—. Redford scholar, 1968. Mem. Am. Soc. Public Adminstrn. (Superior Service award 1980), Nat. Fire Protection Assn. (chmn. fire service sect. 1974-78, dir. 1978), Internat. Assn. Fire Chiefs, Soc. Fire Service Instrs. Author: Fireground Command; also articles in field. Office: Office of Fire Chief 520 W Van Buren Phoenix AZ 85003 *

BRUNDAGE, ANTHONY LEON, history educator; b. Glendale, Calif., Jan. 17, 1938; s. John Vincent and Marguerite Mary (Hayes) B.; m. Martha L. Donaldson, Aug. 14, 1964; 1 child, Catherine. BA, UCLA, 1964, MA, 1966, PhD, 1970. From asst. to assoc. prof. history Calif. State Poly. U., Pomona, 1968-76, prof., 1976—, chmn. dept. history, 1979-81. Author: The Making of the New Poor Law, 1978; contbr. articles to profl. jours. Served with U.S. Army, 1957-60. Mem. Am. Hist. Assn., Am. Soc. Legal History, North Am. Conf. Brit. Studies, Pacific Coast Conf. on Brit. Studies (membership sec. 1978-80, program chmn. 1983, pres. 1984—). Democrat. Avocation: running. Office: Calif State Poly U History Dept Pomona CA 91768

BRUNDAGE, ARTHUR LAIN, animal science educator, dog breeder; b. Wallkill, N.Y., Dec. 19, 1927; s. David E. And Caroline M. (Boyce) B.; m. Helen E. Harvey, June 23, 1951; children: William H., Caroline E. (dec.), Richard T., Rodney A. BS with distinction, Cornell U., 1950; MS, U. Minn., 1952, PhD, 1955. Research scientist USDA U. Alaska, Fairbanks, 1952-68, prof. animal sci., 1968-85, prof. emeritus, 1985—; dog breeder Boreadae Kennel, Palmer, Alaska, 1985—. Contbr. articles to profl. jours. Mem. Am. Dairy Sci. Assn. (life), AAAS, Am. Inst. Biol. Sci., Am. Registry Profl. Animal Scientists (companion animals and dairy cattle), Old English Sheepdog Club Am., Bearded Collie Club Am., Cook Inlet Kennel Club (bd. dirs. 1986, v.p. 1987), Old English Sheepdog Club Alaska (v.p. 1985, treas. 1986), N.W. Bearded Collie Club. Home: PO Box 616 Palmer AK 99645

BRUNE, JAMES NEIL, geophysics educator; b. Modesto, Calif., Nov. 23, 1934; s. Alphonse Frank and Margie Jean (Whitmore) B.; m. Karla Sue Whitney, June 5, 1957. B.Sc., U. Nev., 1956; Ph.D., Columbia U., 1961. Exploration in geophysics and research Chevron Oil Co., Calif. and Tex., 1956-57; research scientist Columbia U., N.Y.C., 1958-63; adj. prof. geology Columbia U., N.Y.C., 1964; assoc. prof. geophysics Calif. Inst. Tech., Pasadena, 1965-69; prof. U. Calif.-San Diego, La Jolla, 1969—. Fellow Seismological Soc. Am., Geol. Soc. Am., Geophys. Union. Quaker. Office: University of California-San Diego Scripps Institute of Oceanography A-025 La Jolla CA 92093

BRUNER, CHARLES PHILLIP, JR., engineer; b. St. Louis, Apr. 27, 1948; s. Charles Phillip Sr. and Virginia Mae (Willoughby) B.; m. Glenda Marie Lopez, July 11, 1981. AAS, Florissart Valley Coll., 1969; BSE, So. Ill. U., Edwardsville, 1971. Avionic engr. McDonnell Aircraft Co., St. Louis, 1971-78; system engr. Litton Guidance and Control, Woodland Hills, Calif., 1978-85, mgr. system design, 1985—. Mem. IEEE, Exptl. Aircraft Assn. Avocations: pilot, homebuilt aircraft, aerobatics, skiing, travel. Office: Litton Guidance and Control 5500 Canoga Woodland Hills CA 91365

BRUNNER, EARL CHESTER, JR., school administrator; b. Los Angeles, Dec. 13, 1924; s. Earl Chester and Louise Esther (Jones) B.; m. Laurine Adams, July 28, 1948; children—Earl Claude, David Arnold, Michael Bruce, Karl Martin, Kurt Lafi, Laurine Louise. B.S., Brigham Young U., 1950, M.Ed., 1957. Tchr., Las Vegas Sch. Dist., Nev., 1950-52, biology Las Vegas High Sch., 1953-57, sci. and math. Ch. Coll. W. Samoa, Apia, Western Samoa, 1958-60; tchr. Las Vegas pub. schs., 1960-63, elementary prin., 1963-82; chief librarian Branch Genealogical Library, Las Vegas, Nev., 1980—. Committeeman, Republican Central Com., Las Vegas, 1974-82; scoutmaster, dist. commr. Boy Scouts Am., Las Vegas, 1960-82. Recipient Scout award Boy Scouts Am. 1975. Republican. Mormon. Home: 330 N 9th St Las Vegas NV 89101 Office: Las Vegas Br Geneal Library PO Box 1360 Las Vegas NV 89101

BRUNO, THOMAS JOSEPH, research scientist; b. N.Y.C., Oct. 12, 1954; s. Pat and Kay (Barrett) B. BS in Chemistry, Poly. Inst. N.Y., 1976; MS in Chem. Physics, Georgetown U., 1978, PhD in Physical Chemistry, 1981. Cons. statistician Harbison & Bruno, Washington, 1979-81; research assoc. Nat. Bur. Standards, Boulder, Colo., 1981-83, research scientist, 1983—; adj. assoc. prof. chem. engring. Colo. Sch. Mines. Contbr. articles to profl. jours.; inventor. Active Broomfield (Colo.) Emergency Preparedness Team, 1985—; hazardous materials advisor Adams County Fire Dept. Hercules Corp. fellow, 1976-78, Eugene Hult fellow Constrn. Industry, 1976-77; Nat. Research Council associateship Nat. Acad. Sci., 1981-83; recipient Dept. Commerce Bronze Medal, 1986. Mem. Am. Inst. Chem. Engrs., Am. Chem. Soc. Republican. Avocations: carpentry, fishing. Office: Nat Bur Standards Thermophysics Mail Stop 774-03 325 Broadway Boulder CO 80303

BRUNO, VICTOR SALVATORE, real estate executive, broker; b. Gary, Ind., Sept. 24, 1950; s. Salvatore Patrick and Jane Florence (Vasile) B.; m. Barbara Ann Lockwood, Feb. 21, 1951; children: Justin Everett, Wesley Salvatore. BA in Univ. Studies, U. N.Mex., 1973. Sales and deliveryperson Black's Office Furniture, Albuquerque, 1968-73; real estate and comml. salesperson Bud Lewis Co., Albuquerque, 1973-79; real estate, indsl. and comml. salesperson Vic Bruno Co., Albuquerque, 1979—. Sponsor and team mgr. Roadrunner Little League, Albuquerque, 1984—. Mem. Soc. Indsl. Realtors (chpt. pres. 1984), Exec.'s Assn. of Greater Albuquerque, Soc. Real Property Adminstrs. (candidate mem.), Albuquerque Bd. Realtors, Nat. Assn. Realtors, N.Mex. Assn. Realtors, Execs. Assn. Greater Albuquerque (pres. 1984). Republican. Methodist. Clubs: Midtown Exchange (v.p. 1975), Tanoan Country (Albuquerque). Avocations: sports, woodworking, landscape gardening. Office: 4300 San Mateo NE #B-275 Albuquerque NM 87110

BRUNSON, HAROLD RYAN, retired federal agency administrator, technical writer; b. Sumter, S.C., Apr. 16, 1939; s. Bennie Ryan and Thelma (Pierce) B.; m. Jeri Brunson, July 5, 1961 (div. 1975); children: Gregory, Mark Randall. BA in Fin., San Francisco State U., MBA; postgrad., U. Va., FBI Acad. Commd. spl. agt., FBI U.S. Dept. Justice, Washington, 1961, ret., 1981; internal auditor Great Western Savings, Beverly Hills, Calif., 1982-84; product liability litigator Carl Warren & Assocs., Glendale, Calif., 1984—; Writer liability, reconstruction, environmental guides; contbr. adventure and photojournalism articles to profl. pubs. Mem. Assn. Retired FBI Spl. Agts. Republican. Lutheran. Avocations: sailing, snow skiing, municipal league softball. Home: 28155 Oaklar Dr Saugus CA 91350 Office: Carl Warren & Assocs 320 Arden Ave Suite 110 Glendale CA 91203

BRUNT, DAVID CRAIG, economist; b. Canton, Ohio, Jan. 22, 1947; s. Albert Edward and Dorothy Naome (Gamble) B. B.S. in Econs., No. Ariz. U., 1972; M.S. in Econs., U. Ariz., 1975, M.S. in Urban Planning, 1975. Prin., economist Socio-Economic Research Assocs., Denver, 1975-77; budget dir. Navajo Tribe, Window Rock, Ariz., 1977-79; gen. mgr. Dee Bee Enterprises, Denver, 1979-80; economist Mountain Bell, Denver, 1980-86, Bell Tri-Co. Services, 1986—; fin. assurance mgr. U.S. West Carrier Mktg., Denver, 1986—; cons. TOSCO, Boulder, Colo., 1976—; pub. speaker Mountain Bell, 1980—; pres. Advanced Tele Response, Inc., 1987—. Author articles in field. Active Voter Registration Drive, Colo., 1983; vol. Service to Am., 1969-71; bd. dirs. Opportunities Industrialization Ctr., Flagstaff, Ariz., 1971-72. Urban Planning fellow HUD, 1973. Mem. ACLU, Am. Planning Assn., Denver Assn. Bus. Economists, Western Economists Assn., Navajo Nation Tax Commn., Associated Photographers Internat. Democrat. Roman Catholic. Club: Clarkson Street Mens (Denver) (pres. 1983—). Home: 909 Clarkson St Denver CO 80218 Office: Bell Tri-Co Services 1999 Broadway HG1110 Denver CO 80202

BRUSCA, RICHARD C., zoologist, museum curator, researcher; b. Los Angeles, Jan. 25, 1945; s. Finny John and Ellenora C. (McDonald) B.; m. Caren Irene Spencer, 1964 (div. 1971); children: Alec Matthew, Carlene Anne; m. Anna Mary Mackey, Jan. 1, 1983. BS, Calif. Poly. State U., 1967; MS, Calif. State U., 1970; PhD, U. Ariz., 1975. Curator and researcher Aquatic Insects Lab., Calif. State U., Los Angeles, 1969-70; resident dir. U. Ariz. and U. Sonora (Mex.) Cooperative Marine Lab., Sonora, 1970-72; prof. biology U. So. Calif., Los Angeles, 1975-86; acting chmn. Dept. Marine Invertebrates San Diego Natural Hist. Mus., 1982-83; head Invertebrate Zoology sect. Los Angeles County Mus. Natural Hist., 1984—; dir. acad. programs, Catalina Marine Sci. Ctr. U. So. Calif.; field researcher North, Central and South Americas, Antarctica, New Zealand, Europe; bd. dirs. Internat. Orgn. for Tropical Studies. Author: Common Intertidal Invertebrates of the Gulf of California, 1980; co-author: A Naturalist's Seashore Guide, 1978; contbr. numerous articles to profl. jours. Recipient Presdl. Medal Service U.S. Govt., 1965. Mem. Crustacean Soc., Soc. Systematic Zoology, Willi Hennig Soc., AAAS, U. Edinburgh Biog. Study Group, Sigma Xi. Avocations: photography, Mesoamerican Indian art and culture, Latin American politics. Office: Los Angeles County Mus Natural History 900 Exposition Blvd Los Angeles CA 90007

BRUSSARD, PETER FRANS, biologist, educator; b. Reno, June 20, 1938; s. William and Evelyn (Anderson) B.; Janet E. McDonald, Oct. 1962 (div. Dec. 1969); 1 child, William R.; m. Trudy Elizabeth Byers, Dec. 20, 1969; 1 child, Peter H. AB, Stanford U., 1960, PhD, 1969; MS, U. Nevada, 1965. Asst. prof. Cornell U., 1969-75, assoc. prof., 1975-85; prof., head biology dept. Montana State U., Bozeman, 1985—; trustee Rocky Mountain Biol. Lab, Crested Butte, Colo., 1985—. Editor: Ecological Genetics, 1978; contbr. articles and book revs. to profl. publ. Served to lt. USNR. NSF Research grantee, 1971-75, 77-78, 81-85; NIH Research grantee, 1971-74. Mem. Soc. Study Evolution (council mem. 1978-80), Am. Soc. Naturalists (treas. 1980-83), Soc. Conservation Biology (sec., treas. 1985—), Soc. Sci. Exploration (council mem. 1983-85). Democrat. Episcopalian. Avocations: antique automobiles, camping, fishing. Home: 3408 Wagon Wheel Rd Bozeman MT 59715 Office: Biology Dept Montana State U 310 Lewis Hall Bozeman MT 59717

BRUST, DAVID, physicist; b. Chgo., Aug. 24, 1935; s. Clifford and Ruth (Klapman) B.; B.S., Calif. Inst. Tech., 1957; M.S., U. Chgo., 1958, Ph.D., 1964. Research assoc. Purdue U., Lafayette, Ind., 1963-64; research assoc. Northwestern U., Evanston, Ill., 1964-65, asst. prof. physics, 1965-68; theoretical research physicist U. Calif., Lawrence Radiation Lab., Livermore, Calif., 1968-73; cons. Bell Telephone Lab., Murray Hill, N.J., 1966. Campaign co-ordinator No. Calif. Scientists and Engrs. for McGovern, 1972. NSF travel grantee, 1964; NSF research grantee, 1966-68. Mem. Am. Phys. Soc., Am. Assn. Coll. Profs., Internat. Solar Energy Soc., Pacific Assn. of AAU, Sierra Club, Sigma Xi. Office: PO Box 13130 Oakland CA 94661

BRUSTAD, WESLEY O., symphony executive, theater and opera director; b. Fergus Falls, Minn., Aug. 16, 1943; s. Otto Waldemar and Doris Mina (Holoien) B.; m. Sharon D. Culbertson, Aug., 1963; m. Karla Kay Stratford, Dec. 23, 1970; children—Robert W., Jason M., Stephanie B., Jessica A. B.A., Sch. of Drama, U. Wash., 1965, M.A., 1970. Asst. dir. Ohio Arts Council, Columbus, 1970-71; exec. dir. S.C. Arts Commn., Columbia, 1971-73; v.p. Guthrie Theater, Mpls., 1974-75; mng. dir. Tenn. Performing Arts Ctr., 1975-77; artistic dir., producer Advent Theater, Nashville, 1978-79; exec. producer Creative Factory, Deer Park, Wash., 1979-80; exec. dir., gen. mgr. Spokane (Wash.) Symphony Orch., 1980-85; exec. dir. Los Angeles Chamber Orch., 1985-86, San Diego Symphony Orch., 1986—; founder, pres. Phoenix Entertainment, 1974-80; producer records, TV spls., films; theater director; cons. in field. Bd. dirs. Friends of Seven/KSPS-TV, 1982-84, Deer Park Community Ch., 1982-85, Wash. Arts Alliance, 1981-83. Served to capt. USAF, 1965-69. NSF scholar, 1960; Alcoa Aluminum scholar, 1961-65. Mem. Am. Symphony Orch. League. Author play, TV spl.: Fat Tuesday (And All That Jazz!), 1977; author: Community Arts Councils: Reason for Being, 1972.

BRUTON, ALPHEUS COSBY, II, resort executive; b. Atlanta, Sept. 30, 1946; s. Alpheus Cosby and Johanna (Schouten) B.; m. Marjorie Gayle McDaniel, Apr. 11, 1976; children: Johanna, Alpheus, Jené. BBA, Angelo State U., 1971. With Hilton Hotels, Las Vegas, Nev., 1971-73, Continental Hotels, Clearlake, Calif., 1973-77, Village Green Corp., Cottage Grove, Oreg., 1977-79; gen. mgr. Furnace Creek Inn and Ranch Resort, Death Valley, Calif., 1979—. Home and Office: Furnace Creek Inn & Ranch Resort PO Box 1 Death Valley CA 92328

BRUZEWSKI, JAMES ROBERT, vocational rehabilitation counselor; b. Dubuque, Iowa, Sept. 20, 1946; s. Robert F. and Ann M. (McGovern) B. B.A. U. Mo., 1969, postgrad., 1972-77; M.S. Okla. State U., 1979. Cert. rehab. counselor, 1979. Vocat. rehab. counselor State of Ariz., Mesa, 1979-86. Chmn. housing accessibility com. Mesa Community Council, Mesa Mayor's Handicap Awareness Com.; active Gov.'s Com. on Employment of Handicapped. Bd. dirs. Copperstate 4-Wheelers. Served to 1st lt. USAF, 1969-74. Decorated Silver Star, DFC, Bronze Star, Air medal. Mem. Nat. Rehab. Assn. Am. Personnel and Guidance Assn., Nat. Rehab. Counselors Assn., Ariz. Rehab. Assn., Am. Rehab. Counselors Assn.

BRYAN, A(LONZO) J(AY), service club official; b. Washington, N.J., Sept. 17, 1917; s. Alonzo J. and Anna Belle (Babcock) B.; student pub. schs.; m. Elizabeth Elfreida Koehler, June 25, 1941 (div. 1961); children: Donna Elizabeth, Alonzo Jay, Nadine; m. Janet Dorothy Onstad, Mar. 15, 1962 (div. 1977); children: Brenda Joyce, Marlowe Francis, Marilyn Janet. Engaged as retail florist, Washington, N.J., 1941-64; now spl. asst. adminstrv. services Kiwanis Internat., Indpls. Fund drive chmn. ARC, 1952; bd. dirs. Washington YMCA, 1945-55, N.J. Taxpayers Assn., 1947-52; mem. Washington Bd. Edn., 1948-55. Mem. Washington Grange, Sons and Daus. of Liberty, Soc. Am. Florists, Nat. Fedn. Ind. Businessmen, Florists Telegraph Delivery Assn., C. of C. Methodist. Clubs: Masons, Tall Cedars of Lebanon, Jr. Order United Am. Mechanics, Kiwanis (pres. Washington (N.J.) 1952, lt. gov. internat. 1953-54, gov. N.J. dist. 1955, sec. N.J. dist. 1957-64, sec. S.E. area Chgo. 1965-74; editor The Jersey Kiwanian 1958-64); Breakfast (pres. 1981-82) (Chgo.). Home and Office: Fox Ridge Apts #203 8115 S Poplar Way Englewood CO 80112-3137

BRYAN, DAVID BARCLAY, lawyer; b. Los Angeles, Aug. 30, 1933; s. Frederick Conger and Florence Evelyn (Hamburger) B.; m. Jeanne Yvonne Wo, May 17, 1959 (div.); children—Michael David, Jon Frederic. B.A., Duke U., 1955; J.D., U. Calif.-Berkeley, 1958. Bar: Hawaii 1964, U.S. Supreme Ct. 1968. Labor relations mgr. Hawaiian Airlines, Honolulu, 1960-61; dir. personnel Civil Air Transport, Air Asia and Air Am., Taipei, Taiwan, 1961-63; employment and tng. mgr. Hawaiian Electric Co., Honolulu, 1963-65; dep. pros. atty. City and County of Honolulu, 1965-68; ptnr. Kai & Dodge, and predecessor firms, Honolulu, 1968-79; sole practice, Honolulu, 1979—. Active Muscular Dystrophy Assn., Honolulu, pres., 1980-82; bd. dirs., trustee Alliance Francaise, Honolulu; bd. dirs. Iaorana Tahiti, Young Republicans. Recipient awards from civic organizations. Mem. Am. Assn. Trial Lawyers, Assn. Imigration Lawyers Am., ABA, Hawaii Bar Assn., Am. Tng. Dirs. Assn., Indsl. Relations Assn. Hawaii. Episcopalian. Clubs: Honolulu, Outrigger Canoe (Honolulu), Oahu Country. Office: Suite 1657 Pioneer Plaza 900 Fort St Mall Honolulu HI 96813

BRYAN, JACK YEAMAN, former diplomat, photographer, author; b. Peoria, Ill., Sept. 24, 1907; s. James Yeaman and Regina (Gibson) B.; m. Margaret Gardner, June 21, 1934; children: Joel Yeaman, Guy Kelsey, Donna Gardner, Kirsten Stuart (Mrs. Winkle-Bryan). Student, U. Chgo., 1925-27; B.A. with high distinction, U. Ariz., 1932, M.A., 1933; postgrad. (fellow philosophy), Duke U., 1933-35; Ph.D., U. Iowa, 1939. Research analyst Fed. Emergency Relief Adminstrn., Washington, 1935-36; from instr. English to prof., head dept. journalism U. Md., 1936-48; pub. relations adviser OCD, 1942-43; dir. pub. relations Welfare Fedn. Cleve., 1943-45; pub. info. officer UNRRA, 1945-46; cultural attaché Am. Embassy, Manila, 1948-51; chief program planning Internat. Exchange Service, State Dept., 1951-53; pub. affairs officer USIS, Bombay, India, 1953-54, Bangalore, India., 1954-55; cultural affairs officer embassy Cairo, Egypt, 1956, Tehran, Iran, 1956-58; cultural attaché, chief cultural affairs officer embassy Karachi, Pakistan, 1958-63; personnel officer for Africa USIA, 1964-65; officer in charge Project AIM, U.S. Dept. State, Washington, 1965; officer-in-charge spl. recruitment program Bur. Edn. and Cultural Affairs, 1965-67; chief cultural affairs adviser USIA, 1968; ret. 1968; lectr. creative photography U. Calif. at Riverside, 1968-80. Author: novel Come to the Bower, 1963, 1986, Cameras in the Quest for Meaning, 1986; contbr. short stories, articles, photographs to numerous mags.; Photog. exhibits one man shows, Pakistan, 1961-62, U.S., 1964, 66, Perspectives Eastward on tour U.S., 1968-71. Chmn. publs. bd. U. Md., 1946-48; chmn. bd. dirs. U.S. Ednl. Founds, Philippines, 1949-51, Pakistan, 1958-63; exec. dir. Iran Am. Soc. in Tehran, 1956-58; founder, exec. dir. Pakistan-Am. Cultural Center, 1959-60, 62-63. Recipient ann. prize for best novel Tex. Inst. Letters, 1964, Summerfield Roberts award, 1964, award for best short story, 1974. Mem. Am. Soc. Mag. Photographers, Friends of Ctr. for Tex. Studies, Tex. Inst. Letters, Tex. Hist. Assn., Am. Mus. Natural History, Am. Fgn. Service Assn., Nat. Parks and Conservation Assn., Nature Conservancy, Audubon Soc., Sierra Club, Phi Delta Theta, Delta Sigma Rho, Phi Gamma Mu. Home: 3594 Ramona Dr Riverside CA 92506

BRYAN, JOYCE BEVERLY, gerontologist; b. Los Angeles, Jan. 12, 1938; d. David Chasen and Belle (Greenberg) Davis; m. David Marvin Galfond, June 23, 1957 (div. Oct. 1964); m. Edgar Coleman Bryan Jr., Nov. 15, 1968; children: Lauren Szukalski, Adam Bryan. BA in Hebrew summa cum laude., UCLA, 1979; MSW, MS in Gerontology, U. So. Calif., 1981. Instr. Mt. St. Mary's Coll., Los Angeles, 1981-82; site dir. Long Beach (Calif.) Sr. Day Treatment Ctr., 1981-84; instr. Saddleback Community Coll., Mission Viejo, Calif., 1984; dir. vols. Everhealth Hospice, La Mirada, Calif., 1983-84; social worker Meml. Home Health, Long Beach, 1984-86; project dir. Sr. Connection div. St. Francis Med. Ctr., Lynwood, Calif., 1986—. Vol. vis. to shut-ins Jewish Family Service, Los Angeles, 1972-77. Mem. Am. Soc. on Aging., Nat. Assn. Social Workers, Gerontol. Soc. of Am. Democrat. Jewish. Avocations: swimming, jogging, backpacking, classical music. Office: St Francis Med Ctr Sr Connection 3630 E Imperial Hwy Lynwood CA 90262

BRYAN, RICHARD H., governor Nevada; b. Washington, July 16, 1937; married; 3 children. B.A., U. Nev., 1959; LL.B., U. Calif.-San Francisco, 1963. Bar: Nev. 1963, U.S. Supreme Ct. 1967. Dep. dist. atty. Clark County, Nev., 1964-66; public defender Clark County, 1966-68; counsel Clark County Juvenile Ct., 1968-69; mem. Nev. Assembly, 1969-71, Nev. Senate, 1973-77; atty. gen. State of Nev. 1979-82, gov. Nev., 1982—. Bd. dirs. March of Dimes; former v.p. Nev. Easter Seal Soc.; former pres. Clark County Legal Aid Soc. Served with U.S. Army. Mem. ABA, Clark County Bar Assn., Am. Judicature Soc., Nat. Gov.'s Assn. (com. econ. devel. and technol. innovation, com. internat. trade and fgn. relations, task force on adult literacy, task force on jobs growth and competitiveness, chmn. subcom. tourism), Council of State Govts. (pres.), Phi Alpha Delta, Phi Alpha Theta. Democrat. Clubs: Masons, Lions, Elks. Office: Office of Gov Capitol Complex Carson City NV 89710

BRYANT, BRENDA, management coordinator, educator, consultant; b. Rome, Ga., Apr. 12, 1948; d. O.M. Hoover and Mary (Bryant) Jennings. B.S. cum laude in Fin. and Stats., Central State U., 1971; M. in Human Resources and Orgn. Devel., U. San Francisco, 1985. Asst. analyst Ohio Bell Telephone Co., Brecksville, 1971-73; mgr. Army/Air Force Exchange Service, Dallas, 1973-74; sec. St. Joseph Med. Ctr., Burbank, Calif., 1977-82;

engr. outside plant Pacific Tel. & Tel. Co., Riverside, Calif., 1977-78, market adminstr., Los Angeles and San Francisco, 1978-85; pvt. practice mgmt. devel., North Hollywood, Calif., 1986—; instr. Golden Gate U., The Learning Tree; advisor various TV prodns., 1986—. Vocalist Burbank Civic Light Opera, 1978-82, Paul Laurence Dunbar Choir, Columbus, Ohio, 1971-76. Mem. Am. Soc. Tng. Devel., AAUW, Nat. Assn. Female Execs., Nat. Assn. Negro Musicians, Alpha Kappa Mu, Phi Gamma Nu. Office: 5706 Fair Ave 204 North Hollywood CA 91601-1963

BRYANT, MARY HELEN, advertising executive; b. Chgo., June 3, 1955; d. Thomas George and Helen Jane (Flaherty) B.; m. Michael Cameron, Feb. 18, 1980 (div. June 1982). BA, So. Ill. U., 1977. Cert. substance abuse counselor, Nev. Supr. prodn. Daily Egyptian Newspaper, Carbondale, Ill., 1974-77; supr. printing plates Sweetheart Cup Corp., Chgo., 1977-78; bus. mgr. Leo Graphic, Chgo., 1978-80; counselor, adv. Temorary Assistance for Domestic Crisis, Las Vegas, Nev., 1980-84; account exec. Valley Graphics, Las Vegas, 1984-85; dir. publicity and advt. Flamingo Hilton Hotel, Las Vegas, 1985—. Bd. dirs. Temporary Assistance Domestic Crisis, Las Vegas, 1985—; mem. Nev. Network against Domestic Violence, Las Vegas, 1982—. Mem. Women in Communication. Democrat. Avocations: hiking, camping. Home: 1813 Wengert Las Vegas NV 89104 Office: Flamingo Hilton 3555 Las Vegas Blvd S Las Vegas NV 89109

BRYANT, STEVEN HARRY, design engineer; b. Des Moines, Nov. 28, 1946; s. Harry Kenneth and Hannah Levey B. AA in Engring., Fullerton Coll., 1968; BA in History, Calif. State U., Long Beach, 1970. Practice design engr. So. Calif., 1966—; pres. Hawkeye Enterprises, Cathedral City, Calif., 1986—. Contbr. polit. commentary to local newspapers, 1979-82. Commr. San Bernardino County, Calif.; mem. Calif. Dem. State Cen. Com., 1979-85, county sec. 1985; alt. del. Dem. Nat. Conv., 1984; 39th Congl. dist. campaign coordinator Jimmy Carter Dem. Presdl. campaign, 1976; 35th Congl. dist. campaign coordinator Gary Hart Dem. Presdl. campaign, 1984; fin. contbr. Calif. Dems., Dem. Nat. Com.; charter mem. Statue of Liberty Ellis Island Found., 1984—; service area com. for area 19, Chino Hills, 1979-82. Avocations: dancing, skiing, swimming, poetry writing.

BRYCE, MURRAY DAVIDSON, real estate development and management corporation executive, international economic development economist; b. Keeler, Sask, Can., Sept. 25, 1917; s. David Henry and Evelyn Margaret (Morgan) B.; m. Anna-Maria Sophia De la Cour, May 15, 1975; children by previous marriage—Karen L. Bryce Funt, Lisa K. B.A., U. B.C., 1949; M.A., Am. U., 1956. Ops. officer World Bank, Washington, 1951-57; sr. internat. economist A.D. Little Inc., Cambridge, Mass., 1959-64; pres. Projects Internat. Inc., Winchester, Mass., 1964-68, Can. Projects Ltd., Vancouver, B.C., Can., 1968—; vis. prof. U. B.C., Vancouver, 1974-75. Chmn. edn. com. Bd. of Trade, Vancouver, 1971-72. Served with RCAF, 1940-45. Mem. Soc. for Internat. Devel. Author: Industrial Development, 1960, Policies and Methods for Industrial Development, 1965. Address: Apt 701, 845 Chilco St, Vancouver, BC Canada V6G 2R2

BRYDON, HAROLD WESLEY, entomologist; b. Hayward, Calif., Dec. 6, 1923; s. Thomas Wesley and Hermione (McHenry) B.; m. Ruth Bacon Vickery, Mar. 28, 1951 (div.); children: Carol Ruth, Marilyn Jeanette, Kenneth Wesley. AB, San Jose State Coll., 1948; MA, Stanford U., 1950. Insecticide sales Calif. Spray Chem. Corp., San Jose, 1951-52; entomologist, fieldman, buyer Beech-Nut Packing Co., 1952-53; mgr., entomologist Lake County Mosquito Abatement Dist., Lakeport, Calif., 1954-58; entomologist, adviser Malaria Eradication Programs ICA (name changed to AID), Kathmandu, Nepal, 1958-61, Washington, 1961-62, Port-au-Prince, Haiti, 1962-63; dir. fly control research Orange County Health Dept. Santa Ana, Calif., 1963-66; free-lance writer in field, 1966—; research entomologist U. N.D. Sch. Medicine, 1968; developer, owner Casierra Resort, Lake Almanor, Calif., 1975-79; owner Westwood (Calif.) Sport Shop, 1979-84; instr. Lassen Community Coll., Susanville, Calif., 1975—; mem. entomology and plant pathology del. People to People Citizen Ambassador Program, China, 1986. Research and publs. on insecticides, mech. methods for dispersing insecticides, biol. control parasites of houseflies. Served with USNR, 1943-46. Recipient Meritorious Honor award for work in Nepal, AID, U.S. Dept. State, 1972. Mem. Entomol. Soc. Am., Am. Mosquito Control Assn., Pacific Coast Entomol. Soc., Am. Legion. Republican. Methodist. Club: Commonwealth of California. Lodges: Masons, Rotary. Home: PO Box 312 Westwood CA 96137

BRYDON, RUTH VICKERY, educator; b. San Jose, Calif., June 2, 1930; d. Robert Kingston and Ruth (Bacon) Vickery; m. Harold Wesley Brydon, Mar. 28, 1951 (div.); children—Carol Ruth Brydon Koford, Marilyn Jeanette, Kenneth Wesley. B.A., Stanford U., 1952; student San Jose State Coll., 1964-65, Calif. State Coll.-Chico, 1979—. Cert. tchr., Calif., cert. sch. adminstr. Tchr., Lincoln Sch., Kathmandu, Nepal, 1959-60; tchr. Am. Sch., Port-au-Prince, Haiti, 1962-63; tchr. social studies Norte Vista High Sch., Riverside, Calif., 1965-67, chmn. social studies dept., 1966-67; tchr. home econs. Westwood (Calif.) High Sch., 1967—, mentor tchr., 1984-85; coordinator extended day classes Lassen Coll., 1977-84. Co-chairperson Almanor Art Show, 1980—. NDEA grantee, 1967. Mem. Assn. Calif. Sch. Adminstrs., Am. Home Econs. Assn., Calif. Home Econs. Assn., Home Econs. Tchrs. Assn. Calif., NEA, Calif. Edn. Assn. United Methodist. Club: Commonwealth of Calif. Home: 3454 Hill Crest Dr Hamilton Br Lake Almanor CA 96137 Office: Westwood High Sch PO Box H Westwood CA 96137

BRYND, SCOTT RICHARD, screen writer, artist management executive; b. Chgo., Oct. 29, 1954; s. Richard J. and Betty L. (Schluraff) B. B.F.A. in Communications, Pacific Lutheran U.; M.F.A. in Theatre Mgmt., UCLA. Formerly pres. Am. Theatrical Prodns., Los Angeles, fin. v.p. Hollywood's New View (Calif.), producing mgr. UCLA's Resident Theatre Co.; former mgr. Los Angeles Ballet; exec. dir. Circuit Network; actor, dir., theatrical producer, screen writer. Recipient Amoco Oil award of Excellence, John F. Kennedy Ctr., Hollywood Wall of Fame award. Mem. Wilshire C. of C. Republican. Lutheran. Office: 101 The Embarcadero Suite 105 San Francisco CA 94105

BRYNGELSON, JIM, educational administrator; b. Billings, Mont., Mar. 8, 1941; s. Ivan Carl and Clarie (Ellingwood) B.; m. Judy Bryngelson, June 29, 1969; children—Joy, Nick. B.S., U. Mont., 1959; M.S., Purdue U., 1967; Ed.S., U. No. Colo., 1974, Ed.D., 1976. Tchr. sci. Littleton Pub. Schs., Colo., 1964-66, sch. counselor, 1967-73, sch. psychologist, 1974-75; spl. edn. cons., Steamboat Springs, Colo., 1975-78; asst. prin. pub. sch., Steamboat Springs, 1977-78; dir. edn. Yellowstone Boys and Girls Ranch, Billings, Mont., 1978—; pres. Self Esteem Assocs., Billings, 1980—. Bd. dirs. Tumbleweed Foster Homes, Billings, 1980-84, Rocky Mountain Little League, Billings, 1982, Mental Health Assn., Billings, v.p., 1986, pres. 1987—. Recipient Disting. Educator award Charles Kettering Found., 1983; named U.S. Cultural Exchange Delegate to Republic of China, 1986. Fellow Assn. Supervision and Curriculum Devel., Sch. Adminstrs. Mont., Council Exceptional Children, Council for Children with Behavior Disorders, Council for Adminstrs. Spl. Edn., Albert Schweitzer Soc., John Dewey Soc., Phi Delta Kappa (v.p. 1984-85, pres 1985-86); mem. Mont. Educators Emotionally Disturbed (charter). Democrat. Roman Catholic. Home: 1144 Henry Rd Billings MT 59102 Office: Sch Dist 58 Route 1 Box 212 Billings MT 59106

BRYSON, KENNETH DONALD, speech communication educator; b. Woodbine, Ill., Apr. 3, 1924; s. Donald LeRoy and Mary Elizabeth (Williams) B.; m. Mary Elizabeth Moore, Apr. 25, 1944; children: Patricia E. Henry, Thomas J., Julia A. BS, So. Ill. U., 1947; MA, Northwestern U., 1949, PhD, 1952. Instr. Mont. State U., Bozeman, 1950-53, asst. prof., 1953-57, assoc. prof., 1957-64, prof., 1964—, dept. head, 1970-79, acting head dept., 1985—; dir. tng. Peace Corps./Equador, Bozeman, 1966-68; dep. and acting dir. Peace Corps./Guyana, Georgetown, 1968-70; tng. cons. Mont. State Dept. of Adminstrn., Helena, 1972-78; exec. bd. Mont. Arbitrators Assn., Helena, 1983—. Author: Peace Corps. Country Plan for Guyana, 1970; co-author Effective Communication; dir. videotape for Intercultural Commn. Tng., 1984; contbr. articles on mediation and intercultural communications to profl. jours. Mem. Mont. State Democratic Exec. Bd., Helena, 1974-78. Served with U.S. Army, 1942-45. Mem. Western Speech Communication Assn., Speech Communication Assn., Fed. Mediation and Conciliation Service (bd. of arbitrators 1984—), Mont. Arbitrator's Assn. (mem. exec. bd. 1982-85). Avocations: canoeing, fishing. Home: 716 S Black Bozeman MT 59715 Office: Dept Speech Communication Mont State Univ Bozeman MT 59717

BRYSON, VERN ELRICK, nuclear engineer; b. Woodruff, Utah, May 28, 1920; s. David Hyrum and Luella May (Eastman) B.; m. Esther Sybil de St Jeor, Oct. 14, 1942; children: Britt William, Forrest Lee, Craig Lewis, Nadine, Elaine. Commd. 2d lt. USAAF, 1941; advanced through grades to lt. col. USAF, 1960, ret., 1961; pilot, safety engr., civil engr., electronic engr., nuclear engr., chief aeronaut. Systems div., Aircraft Nuclear Propulsion Program, Wright-Patterson AFB, Ohio, 1960-61; chiefRadiation Effects Lab., also chief Radiation Effects Group Boeing Airplane Co., Seattle, 1961-65; nuclear engr. Aerospace Corp., San Bernardino, Calif., 1965-68; service engr., also head instrumentation lab., Sacramento Air Logistic Ctr. USAF, McClellan AFB, Calif., 1968-77; owner, mgr. Sylvern Valley Ranch, Calif., 1977—; Mem. panel Transient Radiation Effects on Electronics Weapons Effects Bd., 1959-61. Contbr. research articles on radiation problems to profl. pubs. Decorated D.F.C. with oak leaf cluster, Air medal with 12 oak leaf clusters. Mem. IEEE. Mem. Ch. Jesus Christ of Latter-day Saints. Home: 1426 Caperton St Penryn CA 95663

BUBB, HARRY GEIPLE, insurance company executive; b. Trinidad, Colo., Dec. 16, 1924; s. Harry H. and Grace Alleine (Geiple) B.; June 9, 1951; children—Melinda, Howard, Susan, John, Mary. BA in Econs, Stanford U., 1946, MBA, 1949; grad., Advanced Mgmt. Program, Harvard U., 1973. With Pacific Mut. Life Ins. Co., 1949—, asst. v.p., 1966-68, then v.p., 1968-72, sr. v.p. group ins., 1972-75, pres., 1975—, chief exec. officer, 1986—. Bd. dirs. Orange County Bus. Com. for Arts, United Way of Orange County; trustee U.S. Acad. Decathlon, Calif. Mus. Found.; adv. bd. Town Hall of Calif. Served as pilot USNR, World War II. Mem. World Affairs Council Orange County, Calif. Med. Assn. Health Care Commn., Calif. C. of C. (bd. dirs.), Los Angeles C. of C. (bd. dirs.). Clubs: Lincoln of Orange County, Balboa Yacht, California, Center. Home: 27 Beacon Bay Newport Beach CA 92660 Office: Pacific Mutual Life Ins Co 700 Newport Center Dr Newport Beach CA 92663

BUBE, RICHARD HOWARD, materials scientist; b. Providence, Aug. 10, 1927; s. Edward Neser and Ella Elvira (Baltteim) B.; m. Betty Jane Meeker, Oct. 9, 1948; children: Mark Timothy, Kenneth Paul, Sharon Elizabeth, Meryl Lee. Sc.B., Brown U., 1946, M.A., Princeton U., 1948, Ph.D., 1950. Mem. sr. research staff RCA Labs., Princeton, N.J., 1948-62; prof. materials sci. and elec. engring. Stanford U., 1962—, chmn. dept., 1975-86; cons. to industry and govt. Author: A Textbook of Christian Doctrine, 1955, Photoconductivity of Solids, 1960, The Encounter Between Christianity and Science, 1968, The Human Quest: A New Look at Science and Christian Faith, 1971, Electronic Properties of Crystalline Solids, 1974, Electrons in Solids, 1981, Fundamentals of Solar Cells, 1983, Science and the Whole Person, 1985; also articles; editor: Jour. Am. Sci. Affiliation, 1969-83; editorial bd.: Solid State Electronics; assoc. editor: Ann. Rev. Materials Sci., 1969-83, Materials Letters. Fellow Am. Phys. Soc., AAAS, Am. Sci. Affiliation; mem. Am. Soc. Engring. Edn., Internat. Solar Energy Soc., Sigma Xi. Evangelical. Home: 753 Mayfield Ave Stanford CA 94305 Office: Dept Materials Sci and Engring Stanford Univ Stanford CA 94305

BUBENIK, PATRICIA JEAN HADLE, school principal; b. Denver, Jan. 12, 1947; d. H. Paul and Allie Hadle; B.A., Colo. State U., 1969; M.A., U. Calif., Santa Cruz, 1970; Ed.D., U. San Francisco, 1981; m. David M. Bubenik, June 21, 1969. Tchr. Madrone Sch., Sunnyvale Sch. Dist. (Calif.), 1970-77; tchr. Demonstration Sch. for Gifted, San Jose State U., 1977; lang. arts specialist Sunnyvale Sch. Dist., 1977-78, vice prin., Madrone Sch., 1978-79, prin. summer sch., 1979, prin. Lakewood Sch., 1979-82; prin. Columbia Community Sch., Sunnyvale, 1982—; ednl. cons., Calif., 1977—; established Kids Can Write Project; founder Jr. Scribe, dist. wide student mag. Bd. dirs. Calif. Young People's Theatre, Umbrella House; founder Mayor's Youth Council, 1964. Fellow, Bay Area Writing Project, U. Calif., Berkeley, 1978; Boettcher Found. scholar, 1965. Recipient Vol. award Calif. Parks and Recreation Assn., 1983. Mem. Assn. Calif. Adminstrs., Assn. Curriculum and Supervision Devel., Santa Clara Reading Council (exec. bd.), Calif. Reading Assn., Nat. Council Tchrs. English, Calif. Assn. Gifted, Calif. Assn. Tchrs. English, Internat. Reading Assn., Am. Assn. Sch. Adminstrs., Phi Delta Kappa, Phi Beta Kappa, Phi Kappa Phi, Phi Sigma Iota. Club: Women Leaders in Edn. Author: A New Direction: Focusing on the Whole Person Through the Affective Domain, 1977; Effects of Principal-Delivered Written Positive Reinforcement on Teacher and Class Behavior, 1981. Office: Columbia Community Sch 739 Morse Ave Sunnyvale CA 94086

BUCCIGROSSI, DAVID ERIC, physician, chemistry educator; b. Riverside, Calif., Sept. 12, 1956; s. Sam Anthony and Geraldien (Ligman) B.; m. Debbie Lee Winkelbauer, Sept. 7, 1985. BA, U. Calif., San Diego, 1979; MD, U. Calif., 1984. Chemistry researcher San Diego, 1978-80, guitar instr., 1973-78, chemistry instr., 1978-81; resident Seattle, 1984—, practice medicine specializing in internal medicine. Family Practice Preceptorship grantee U. Calif., San Diego, 1981. Mem. AAAS, Internat. Physicians for Prevention Nuclear War, Physcians Soc. Responsibility Speakers Bur., A. Baird Hasting Soc. Democrat. Roman Catholic. Avocations: photography, backpacking, musician, space sciences. Home: 1957 8th Ave W Seattle WA 98119 Office: Harborview Med Ctr 325 9th Ave Seattle WA 98104

BUCHANAN, BARBARA VAALER, interior designer; b. Kansas City, Kans., July 31, 1951; d. Raymond Alden and Ann Irene (Hansen) Vaaler; m. Gary David Greegard, Nov. 4, 1972 (div. May 1981); m. John Lynn Buchanan II, Jan. 21, 1984. BFA, Ariz. State U., 1973. Prin. designer Estrella Designs, Phoenix, 1975-83; dir. design Plaza Three Acad., Phoenix, 1982-83; pres. Designs Two Inc., Scottsdale, Ariz., 1983—; mem. faculty Maricopa Community Coll. Dist., Phoenix, 1979—. Democrat. Lutheran. Avocations: cooking, gardening. Office: Designs Two Inc PO Box 10428 Scottsdale AZ 85271

BUCHANAN, BEN F(RANKLIN), food science and technology consultant; b. Fontana, Kans., Aug. 12, 1908; s. William Johnson and Margaret Irene (Erps) B.; m. Edith Cornelia Ross, Sept. 9, 1934; children—Fredrick Earl, Margaret Lynn. A.B., U. Kans., 1933; Ph.D., Iowa State U., 1938. Dir. tech. service lab. Am. Maize Products Co., N.Y.C., 1938-45, dir. research, 1945-46; dir. tech. service, mgr. pharm. dept. Internat. Mineral & Chem. Corp., Chgo., 1946-57; dir. product devel. and engring. research Gen. Foods Corp., Tarrytown, N.Y., 1957-60, dir. tech. applications, 1960-73; cons. food sci. and tech., Santa Rosa, Calif., 1973—; dir. APPL, Inc., Fresno, Calif. Fellow Inst. Food Technologists (pres. 1972-73), Am. Inst. Chemists; mem. Am. Chem. Soc., Am. Assn. Cereal Chemists, N.Y. Acad. Scis., AAAS. Club: Chemists of N.Y. Author profl. publs. and patentee in food formulations and processing concerning starches, sugars, proteins, monosodium glutamate, sodium lactate, and meat and poultry processing. Home: 7326 Oakleaf Dr Santa Rosa CA 95405

BUCHANAN, CHARLES CALVIN, educational technology professional, consultant; b. Murray, Utah, Apr. 23, 1937; s. Elby Leon Buchanan and Pauline Esther (Mundell) Martin; m. Judith Ann Mathis, July 20, 1957; children: Mark Kevin, Scott Charles. BA, U. Colo., 1961. Tng. devel. specialist United Airlines, Denver, 1960-84; ednl. tech. cons. Northglenn, Colo., 1984—; tech. cons. Buchanan & Assocs., 1984—; ptnr. devel. CompuTrends, Inc., Boulder, Colo., 1986—, also bd. dirs.; bd. dirs. Inst. Personal Competency, Kansas City, Mo., Rocky Mountain Assn. Ednl. Data Systems. Editor Assn. Devel. Computer-based Instrnl. Systems newsletter, 1981-83. Pres. accountability com. Adams County Sch. Dist., Northglenn, 1976-79, mem. bd. edn., 1979—. Mem. Nat. Sch. Bd. Assn., Colo. Sch. Bd. Assn., Nat. Staff Devel. Council. Methodist. Avocations: bicycling, Southwest history, photography. Home: 10683 Sperry St Northglenn CO 80234 Office: Computrends Inc 637-B S Broadway Suite 129 Boulder CO 80303

BUCHANAN, FLOYD B., school superintendent; b. Dale, Ark., Feb. 2, 1924; s. Millard Brison and Laura Ella (DuPriest) B.; m. Myrlee DaVee Strain, June 9, 1945; children—Larry, Randy, Deborah, Laurie, John. B.A., U. Denver, 1948, M.A., 1950; Ed.D., U. Calif., Berkeley, 1957. Cert. tchr., adminstr., Calif. Tchr. Arvada Pub. Schs., Colo., 1948-49, prin., 1949-50; tchr. Alamo Sch. Dist., Calif., 1950-52; prin. Walnut Creek Sch. Dist., Calif., 1952-57; supt. Jefferson Unified Sch. Dist., Clovis, Calif., 1957-60; supt. Clovis United Sch. Dist., 1960—. Named Clovis Citizens Hall of Fame, 1976; recipient Am. Educators medal Freedom Found., Valley Forge, Pa., 1979. Mem. Assn. of Calif. Sch. Adminstrs., Am. Assn. Sch. Adminstrs. (past pres. Region IX), Clovis C. of C. Democrat. Lodge: Scottish Rite (Pub. Schs. Educator of Yr. award 1978). *

BUCHANAN, JOHN ANDREW, advertising executive; b. Dayton, Ohio, Feb. 17, 1951; s. Charles Andrew and Lois Eileen (Foust) B. BA, Cooper Union; BA (hon.), U. Dayton, 1976, Wright State U., 1979. Advt. mgr. Systems Research Inc., Dayton, Ohio, 1973-76; art dir. Franklin Creation Group, Dayton, 1976-78; v.p. Philip Office Assn., 1978-82; pres. Advt. Group Inc., Canoga Park, Calif., 1982; bd. dirs. Los Angeles Advt. and Communications Network, 1985-86. Mem. LAACN, Graphic Artist Guild of Los Angeles. Democrat. Avocations: photography, painting. Home: 4187 Sarah St Toluca Lake CA 91505 Office: Advt Group Inc 6940 Owensmouth Ave Canoga Park CA 91303

BUCHANAN, TERRY LEE, electronics engineer; b. Hastings, Nebr., Sept. 5, 1951; s. Burt Waldean and Mary Margaret (Andrews) B.; m. Karen Dorothy White, June 22, 1974; children: Sean Robert, James Michael, Lisa Anne. AAS, Met. State Coll., Denver, 1980, BSEET, 1985; postgrad. in Mgmt. Tech., Regis Coll., 1986—. Tech. ops. mgr. Tech. Services, Inc., Denver, 1982-83; sales engr. Tech. Mktg. Mfg., Inc., Lakewood, Colo., 1984-85; engr. Martin Mariette Corp., Denver, 1985—. Layminister Fellowship of Christian Inmates, Golden, Colo. 1983-84; chmn. Christian Boys Brigade, Aurora, 1984. Served to sgt. USAF, 1971-76. Mem. IEEE (br. chmn. 1981-82, student sect. br. vice-chmn. 1980-81). Episcopalian. Avocation: reading. Office: Martin Marietta Corp PO Box 179 M/S D6511 Denver CO 80201

BUCHANAN, WILLIAM JESSE, author, educator; b. Morganfield, Ky., Jan. 30, 1926; s. William Jesse and Margaret Evelyn (Kagy) B.; m. Mildred Berniece Sites, Dec. 15, 1950; children: William J. III, Steven, James, Rebecca. BS, U. Louisville, 1950. Enlisted USAF, 1943, advanced through grades to lt. col., ret., 1970; features editor Grant County Press, Petersburg, W.Va., 1971-72; tchr. creative writing U. N.Mex., Albuquerque, 1983—. Author: A Shining Season, 1978 (Scholastic Book Club selection), Present Danger, 1986; (films) John Baker's Last Race, 1976 (entrant Internat. Youth Peace Festival), Moscow, 1970, Spirit of the Wind, 1979, A Shining Season, 1979; contbr. to books. Recipient Freedoms Found. award 1966, Reader's Digest First Person award 1967, S.C. Young Adult Book award 1981, Christopher award 1980, Gold Camera award 1980, CHRIS Statuette 1980, Nat. Council Family Relations award 1980, Silver CINDY award 1981. Mem. N.Mex. First Friday Forum, Mystery Writers Am., Buchanan Soc. (Glasgow, Scotland). Home: 11421 Key West Dr NE Albuquerque NM 87111 Office: U NMex Albuquerque NM 87131

BUCHER, CHARLES AUGUSTUS, physical education educator; b. Conesus, N.Y., Oct. 2, 1912; s. Grover C. and Elizabeth (Barr) B.; m. Jacqueline N. Dubois, Aug. 24, 1941; children: Diana, Richard, Nancy, Gerald. B.A., Ohio Wesleyan U., 1937; M.A., Columbia, 1941; Ed.D., N.Y. U., 1948; post-grad., Yale, 1948-49. Tchr. pub. schs. N.Y., 1937-41; asso. prof. New Haven State Coll., 1946-50; prof. edn. N.Y. U., 1950-79, dir. Sch. Health, Phys. Edn., Recreation and Dance, 1981-86; prof. U. Nev., Las Vegas, 1980—; editor Appleton-Century-Crofts, N.Y.C.; Am. specialist U.S. State Dept., 1962; del. Pres. Eisenhower's White House Conf. on Youth Fitness, 1956; cons. Pres.'s Council on Phys. Fitness and Sports, 1972—, Nat. Fitness Found.; chmn. nat. adv. bd. Am. Fitness Club; pres. Nat. Fitness Leaders Assn. Author: Methods and Materials in Physical Education and Recreation, 1954, Foundations of Physical Education, rev. edit, 1983, Recreation for Today's Society, 1984, Methods and Materials Secondary School Physical Education, rev. edit, 1983, Physical Education in Modern Elementary School, rev, 1971, College Ahead, rev. edit, 1961, Athletics in Schools and Colleges, 1965, Guiding Your Child toward College, 1967, Physical Education for Life, 1969, Dimensions of Physical Education, 2d edit, 1974, Administration of Health and Physical Education Programs, 1983, Administrative Dimensions of Health and Physical Education Programs, 1971, The Foundations of Health, 1976, Physical Education for Children: Movement Foundations and Experiences, 1979, Physical Education: Change and Challenge, 1981, Health, 1981, Fitness for College and Life, 1985, Foundations of Physical Education and Sport, 1987, Management of Physical Education and Athletic Programs, 1987; columnist and contbr. articles to profl. jours.; columnist Los Angeles Times Syndicate. Trustee, chmn. scholarship com. Coll. Scholarship Plan, Inc., 1959—. Served to capt. USAAF, 1941-46. Recipient Sch. Bell award, 1960; named One of 10 Ams. who have contributed most to nation's health and fitness Jaycees, 1982. Fellow A.A.H.P.E.R., Am. Coll. Sports Medicine, Am. Sch. Health Assn.; mem. N.E.A. Home: 4239 Pinecrest Circle W Las Vegas NV 89121 Office: U Nev 4505 Maryland Pkwy Las Vegas NV 89154

BUCHSBAUM, RALPH, publishing company executive, biologist; b. Chickasha, Okla., Jan. 2, 1907; s. Maurice and Mabel (Roberts) B.; m. Mildred Shaffer, June 14, 1933; children: Monte, Vicki (Mrs. John Pearse). B.S., U. Chgo., 1928, Ph.D., 1932. Mem. faculty U. Chgo., 1932-50; prof. biology U. Pitts., 1950-72; dir. Inst. for Edn. Research, Palo Alto, Calif., 1962-63; cons. UNESCO; pres., editor Boxwood Press, Pacific Grove, 1956—; assoc. curator of invertebrates Carnegie Mus., Pitts., 1950-72. Author: Animals Without Backbones, (with Lorus Milne) The Lower Animals, (with Mildred Buchsbaum) Basic Ecology, (with Vicki Pearse, John Pearse, and Mildred Buchsbaum) Living Invertebrates. Served to capt. USAAF, 1942-46. Fulbright prof. Thailand, 1959-60. Mem. Ecol Soc. Am., Am. Soc. Zoology, Biol. Photographers Assn. Unitarian. Home and Office: 183 Ocean View Blvd Pacific Grove CA 93950

BUCHWALD, JENNIFER SULLIVAN, neurophysiologist; b. Okmulgee, Okla., Oct. 20, 1930. AB, Lindenwood Coll., 1951, LLD (hon.), 1970; PhD, Tulane U., 1959. Asst. prof. pediatrics UCLA, 1963-66, asst. prof. physiology, 1966-67, assoc. prof. physiology, 1967-73, prof. physiology, 1973—, assoc. dir. Brian Research Inst., 1978—; mem. programs adv. NIH, 1982-86, counselor, 1977-81. Recipient Career Devel. award NIH, 1965-69, Parkinson Found. award USPHS, 1963-69, Women of Sci. award U. Calif., Los Angeles, 1969. Mem. Neurosci. Soc. (treas. 1975-77). Office: UCLA Med Ctr Dept Physiology Los Angeles CA 90024

BUCK, CAROLYN BURRELL, learning skills administrator, counselor; b. Benham, Ky., Oct. 12, 1948; d. Rumiller and Ola Mae (Norwood) Burrell; children: Patricia Ayodele, Roland Ade Kule. BS, Bennett Coll., 1971, MS in Counselor Edn., N.C. Agrl. and Tech. State U., 1976, San Diego State U., 1983; postgrad. Claremont Coll., 1985-87; Cert. Class A tchr., counselor, N.C.; pupil personnel service, Calif. Resident counselor N.C. Sch. Arts, Winston-Salem, 1973-76; asst. dir., tchr. United Day Care Services, Greensboro, N.C., 1972-77; counseling intern Greensboro City Schs., 1976; residence hall dir. SUNY-Stony Brook, 1977-79; asst. coordinator acad. success program Office Acad. Support and Instructional Services U. Calif.-San Diego, 1980-81, coordinator Acad. Success and Summer Bridge programs, 1981-83, asst. dir. Office Acad. Support and Instructional Services, Ednl. Opportunity and Student Affirmative Action Programs, 1983-84, coordinator Summer Bridge programs, 1984-85 , group facilitator orientation and student devel. impacting students of color, 1979—, facilitator/trainer peer cong. and personal growth and develop. workshops, 1981—, intern student fin. aid service Acad. Services, 1986—, coordinator tutorial program, 1987—. Author: Summer Bridge: A Residential Learning Experience for High Risk Freshman at the University of California San Diego, 1985; co-author: A Peer Counseling Training Module, 1985. Action Community Ctr., La Jolla, Calif., 1983-86; 2d v.p. Albirda Green Missionary Soc., 1982—. Mem. Nat. Assn. Employment Counselors, Calif. Assn. Third World Counselors, Nat. Assn. Employment Counselors, Assn. Non-White Concerns, Bennett Coll. Alumni Assn. (bus. mgr. co-chmn. recruitment com. 1978-79, pres. chpt. 1979-80). Office: U Calif B-036 Oasis 1254 Humanities Library La Jolla CA 92093

BUCK, CHRISTIAN BREVOORT ZABRISKIE, ind. oil operator; b. San Francisco, Oct. 18, 1914; s. Frank Henry and Zayda Justine (Zabriskie) B.; student U. Calif., Berkeley, 1931-33; m. Natalie Leontine Smith, Sept. 12, 1948; children—Warren Zabriskie, Barbara Anne. Mem. engring. dept. U.S. Potash Co., Carlsbad, N.Mex., 1933-39; ind. oil operator, producer, Calif., 1939-79, N.Mex., 1939—; owner, operator farm, ranch, Eddy County, N.Mex., 1951-79; dir. Belridge Oil Co. until 1979; dir. Buck Ranch Co. (Calif.). Served with RAF, 1942-45. Democrat. Episcopalian. Club: Riverside

Country (Carlsbad). Home: 108 W Alicante Rd Santa Fe NM 87501 Office: PO Box 2183 Santa Fe NM 87504

BUCK, DAVID LAWRENCE, business executive, consultant, lecturer; b. Lexington, Ky., Nov. 1, 1951; s. William Lawrence Buck and Wilda Lois (Heath) Tanner; m. Lois Jean Lawrie, July 14, 1979; children: Alexander David, Sarah Ruth. B.S. with honors, U. Ky., 1973; M.Math., U. Waterloo (Can.), 1975; postgrad. Imperial Coll., London, 1974, U. Waterloo, 1976-78. Sr. systems programmer U. Ky., Lexington, 1972-75; dir. product devel. Norango Computer Systems, Ltd., Toronto, Ont., Can., 1977-79; dir. product devel. Telecom Network Tech., Toronto, 1977-79; pres. DKL Innovative Cons., Inc., Toronto, 1979-84; sr. mgr. Durango Systems, Inc., San Jose, Calif., 1980-82; chmn. D.L. Buck & Assocs., Inc., San Jose, 1982—; mem. faculty Northeastern U., Santa Clara, Calif.. Contbr. computer articles to profl. lit. Recipient Oswald award U. Ky., 1973. Mem. Assn. Computing Machinery, USR Group (chmn. subcom. on systems interface 1982-85, vice chmn. standards com. 1984-85, standards editor 1983-85, chmn. networking and DFS com. 1985-87). Club: Bus. Aircraft Flying.

BUCK, DONALD FREDERICK, JR., soil scientist; b. Foxboro, Mass., Apr. 21, 1934; s. Donald F. and Dora P. (Engle) B.; children—Edmond, G. Myron, Jeffrey, Heather, Amber. B.S., U. Maine-Orono, 1977. Soil scientist, U.S. Dept. Interior, Las Vegas, 1977-79; mem. planning staff Environ. Protection for Soil, Air and Water of Western Oreg., Bur. of Land Mgmt., Portland, 1980-82, area soil scientist, Tillamook, Oreg., 1982—. Contbr. articles to profl. jours. Served with U.S. Navy, 1951-55, USAF, 1955-71. Decorated D.F.C., Air medal with 11 oak leaf clusters; recipient Dept. Interior Group award, 1979; Bur. Land Mgmt. Letter of Commendation, 1980. Mem. Soil Sci. Soc. Am., Soil Conservation Soc. Am. Home: 1785 Maxwell Ave PO Box 177 Oceanside OR 97134 Office: Bur Land Mgmt 6615 Officers Row Tillamook OR 97041

BUCK, LINDA DEE, executive recruiting company executive; b. San Francisco, Nov. 8, 1946; d. Sol and Shirley D. (Setterberg) Press; student Coll. San Mateo (Calif.), 1969-70; divorced. Head hearing and appeals br. Dept. Navy Employee Relations Service, Philippines, 1974-75; dir. personnel Homestead Savs. & Loan Assn., Burlingame, Calif., 1976-77; mgr. fin. placement VIP Agy., Inc., Palo Alto, Calif., 1977-78; exec. v.p., dir. Sequent Personnel Services, Inc., Mountain View, Calif., 1978-83; Founder, pres. Buck & Co., San Mateo, 1983—. Publicity mgr. for No. Calif., Osteogenesis Imperfecta Found. Inc., 1970-72; cons. Am. Brittle Bone Soc., 1979—. Mem. Nat. Assn. Personnel Cons., Calif. Assn. Personnel Cons. Jewish. Office: Buck and Co 100 S Ellsworth Ave 9th Floor San Mateo CA 94401

BUCK, NATALIE SMITH, former state ofcl.; b. Carlsbad, N.Mex., Jan. 10, 1923; d. Milton R. and Rosa Adele (Binford) Smith; student Coll. William and Mary, 1940-41; B.B.S., U. Colo., 1943; postgrad. U. Tex., 1945-46; m. C. B. Buck, Sept. 12, 1948; children—Warren Z., Barbara Anne. Chief clk., State Senate, N.Mex., 1951-53; sec. of state, N.Mex., 1955-59; chief personnel adminstr. N.Mex. Health and Social Services Dept., 1959-73. Democrat. Home: 108 W Alicante Rd Santa Fe NM 87501

BUCK, STEVEN LOUIS, experimental psychologist; b. Urbana, Ill., July 7, 1949; s. Warren L. and Bernice (Francis) B.; m. Jeanette Norris, Sept. 11, 1982. BA, Reed Coll., 1971; MA, U. Calif., San Diego, 1974; PhD, U. Calif., 1976. Postdoctoral sr. fellow U. Wash., Seattle, 1976-79, acting asst. prof. dept. psychology, 1979-84, research asst. prof., 1984-86, research assoc. prof., 1986—. NIH research grantee, 1979—. Mem. AAAS, Am. Psychol. Assn., Optical Soc. Am., Assn. Research in Vision and Ophthalmology. Office: U Wash Dept Psychology NI 25 Seattle WA 98195

BUCK, STEVEN MERRIMEN, speech communication educator; b. Bozeman, Mont., Sept. 11, 1926; s. Edwin Reynolds and Marie Catherine (Stevens) B.; m. Jeanne Talbot, Dec. 27, 1952; children: Steven, Bruce, Byron, Tracey. BA, Wash. State U., 1954, MA, 1955; PhD, Purdue U., 1960. Program dir. Stas. KOPR, KOPR-TV, Butte, Mont., 1948-50, 52-53; instr. Purdue U., West Lafayette, Ind., 1958-59; asst. prof. speech, radio Eastern Ill. U., Charleston, 1959-61; from asst. prof. to prof. Calif. State U., Long Beach, 1961—. Author: (textbook) Oral Interpretation: A Guide to Oral Interpretation, 1985; contbr. articles to profl. jours. Served as sgt. U.S. Army, 1950-52, Korea. Nominated Outstanding Young Prof., Cen. States Speech Assn., 1960. Mem. Western States Speech Assn., Speech Communicators Assn. Democrat. Avocations: flying, photography. Office: Calif State U 1250 Bellflower Blvd Long Beach CA 90840

BUCK, WILLIAM FRASER, II, university bookstore administrator; b. Salt Lake City, May 6, 1944; s. William Fraser and Ada (Dabling) B.; m. Lynette Riding, Jan. 27, 1967; children: Kimberly, Arienne, Tamara, Joshua Fraser, Zackary Erne, Gabriel Robert, Bethany, Emily, Cassandra. BS, Brigham Young U., 1977, postgrad. Clk. Clark Drugs Inc., Hawthorne, Calif., 1962-63; gen. mdse. clk. Albertson's Inc., Orem, Utah, 1967-68, grocery mgr., Utah div., 1976-81; asst. mgr. Allen's Markets, Orem, 1968-72; mgr. Quality Market, Delta, Utah, 1972-76; gen. mdse. mgr. BYU Bookstore, Brigham Young U., Provo, Utah, 1981—. Troop leader Boy Scouts Am., Provo, 1969-85, dist. pub. chmn., Delta, 1973-76; mem. Delta Planning and Zoning Bd., 1974-76; sec.-treas. West Millard Golf Com., Delta, 1973-76; pres. Sunset ward elders quorum Ch. Jesus Christ of Latter-day Saints, Provo, 1971-72, ward exec. sec., 1976-77. Mem. Nat. Assn. Coll. Stores (cert.), Western Coll. Bookstore Assn., Mountain States Coll. Store Assn. (instr. seminars 1983-85), Provo C. of C. (com. chmn. 1981-83). Avocations: hiking, camping, reading. Office: Brigham Young U BYU Bookstore Provo UT 84602

BUCKEL, JOHN J., aerospace company executive; b. Berlin, Feb. 8, 1935; came to U.S., 1947, naturalized, 1953; s. Alexander Buckel and Ursula (Camnitzer) Buckel Levell; m. Elizabeth Regina Lawlor, Oct. 3, 1959; children—Deborah, Deanna, Brian. B.S. in Marine Engring., U.S. Mcht. Marine Acad., 1959; M.B.A., U. Santa Clara, 1965. Lic. marine engr. Engring. officer S.S. Constitution, American Export Lines, N.J., 1958-59; various ops. mgmt. positions Lockheed Missiles & Space Co., Sunnyvale, Calif., 1959-86, dir. mfg., 1985—; mem. indsl. adv. bd. Calif. Poly. State U., San Luis Obispo, 1982—; frequent lectr. in quality engring. and mgmt. Calif. State U. campuses, 1975—. Served to lt. USNR, 1957-58. Mem. Nat. Mgmt. Assn. Home: 7558 Heatherwood Dr Cupertino CA 95014 Office: Lockheed Missiles & Space Co Dept 86-01/B181 PO Box 3504 Sunnyvale CA 94088-3504

BUCKELEW, DEBORAH LYNN, civic association executive; b. Memphis, Dec. 10, 1951; d. Clyde Truman and Helen Jean (Jackson) B. B.A., Calif. State U.-Los Angeles, 1976. Editor, Discover monthly theme supplement, Los Angeles Civic Ctr. Newspapers, 1977-79; promotion mgr. Los Angeles Knapp Communications, 1979-81; mem. corp. pub. relations staff Vidal Sassoon, Century City, Calif., 1981; dir. pub. relations ARC Santa Ana, 1981—, dir. nat. disasters, 1982-83, Los Angeles Children's Mus., 1985—. KNBC scholar, 1975. Mem. Pub. Relations Soc. Am., Orange County Press Club, Internat. Assn. Bus. Communicators, United Way Communications Com. Club: Zonta. Editor: Bon Appetit Social Planner, 1980, 81, Wine Jour., 1980, Archtl. Digest Engagement Calendar, 1980, 81, Metalsource Directory, 1981. Office: ARC 601 N Golden Circle Dr Santa Ana CA 92711

BUCKLAND, MICHAEL KEEBLE, librarian, educator; b. Wantage, Eng., Nov. 23, 1941; came to U.S., 1972; s. Walter Basil and Norah Elaine (Rudd) B.; m. Waltraud Leeb, July 11, 1964; children: Anne Margaret, Anthony Francis. B.A., Oxford U., 1963; postgrad. diploma in librarianship, Sheffield U., 1965, Ph.D., 1972. Grad. trainee Bodleian Library, Oxford, Eng., 1963-64; asst. librarian U. Lancaster (Eng.) Library, 1965-72; asst. dir. for tech. services Purdue U. Libraries, West Lafayette, Ind., 1972-75; dean Sch. Library and Info. Studies, U. Calif., Berkeley, 1976-84; asst. v.p. library plans and policies Sch. Library and Info. Studies, U. Calif., 1983—; v.p. Ind. Coop. Library Services Authority, 1974-75; vis. scholar Western Mich. U., 1979; vis. prof. U. Klagenfurt, Austria, 1980. Author: Book Availability and the Library User, 1975, (with others) The Uses of Gaming in Education for Library Management, 1976; co-author: (with others) Reader in Operations Research for Libraries, 1976, Library Services in Theory and Context, 1983. Mem. ALA, Am. Soc. for Info. Sci., Assn. Library and Info. Sci. Edn., Calif. Library Assn. Office: Sch Library and Info Studies U Calif Berkeley CA 94720

BUCKLES, KRISTI RACHELLE, diversified electronics company executive; b. Dumas, Tex., Dec. 15, 1960; d. Richard Milton and Doris Helen (Ohlenbusch) B. BA, U. Ariz., 1983; MA in Internat. Mgmt., Am. Grad. Sch. Internat. Mgmt., 1985. Mktg. dir. Dynacomp Inc., Phoenix, 1985; mgr. mkt. devel. and sales TRW, Inc., Phoenix, 1986—; bd. dirs. Tex. Cornerstone Corp., Aledo, S.W. Glazing Supply, Dallas. Adminstrv. asst. U.S. Rep. for Ariz., Tucson, 1982; dir. Girl Scouts U.S., Tucson, 1981. Named one of Outstanding Young Women of Am., 1984-85. Mem. Am. Mktg. Assn., Kappa Kappa Gamma. Republican. Club: Toastmasters. Avocations: skiing, antiques, music, basketball, swimming.

BUCKLEY, CHRISTINE, personnel administrator; b. Cheyenne, Wyo., July 30, 1952; d. Daniel and Angela (Canepa) B. BA in Psychology and Sociology, Trinity U., 1974; MS in Indsl. Organizational Psychology, San Diego State U., 1977. Adminstrv. asst. The Broadway, San Diego, 1978-80; adminstrv. mgr. Ceramic Systems, San Diego, 1980-81; mgr. personnel Cox Cable, San Diego, 1982-86; sr. employee relations rep. Rohr Industries, Chula Vista, Calif., 1986—. Cons. project bus. Jr. Achievement, San Diego, 1985-86. Mem. Internat. Assn. Personnel Women, Personnel Mgmt. Assn. Roman Catholic. Avocations: distance running, bicycling, theater, ballet, movies. Home: 1145 Woodlake Dr Cardiff-by-the-Sea CA 92007 Office: Rohr Industries PO Box 878 Chula Vista CA 92078

BUCKLEY, FRANCIS JOSEPH, priest, educator; b. Los Angeles, Aug. 31, 1928; s. Francis Joseph and Elizabeth Agnes (Haiss) B. Student, U. Notre Dame, 1944-45, U. Santa Clara, 1945-49; MST, U. Santa Clara, 1959; BA, Gonzaga U., 1951, MA in Philosophy, 1952; Licentiate in Sacred Theology, Alma Coll., 1959; STD, Gregorian U., Rome, 1964. Joined S.J., 1945, ordained priest Roman Cath. Ch., 1958. Instr. classics, religion Bellarmine Coll. Prepatory Sch., San Jose, Calif., 1952-55; instr. theology U. San Francisco, 1960-61, asst. prof. theology, 1963-68, assoc. prof. theology, 1968-72, prof. theology, 1972—, acting chmn. dept. theology, 1971-73, chmn. dept. theology, 1978-79, dir. grad. programs in religious edn., 1974-75, 79-81, 86-87; chaplain St. Elizabeth Infant Hosp., San Francisco, 1963—; trustee Loyola Marymount U., Los Angeles, 1974—, Jesuit Community U. San Francisco, 1969-76, 78-82; theol. advisor to U.S. Bishops Synod of Bishops, Rome, 1977; del. to Asian Catechetical and Liturgical Conf., Manila, 1967, Latin Am. Catechetical Conf., Medellin, Colombia, 1968, Internat. Catechetical Congress, Rome, 1971; vis. scholar Ctr. for Research in Learning and Teaching U. Mich., Ann Arbor, 1973-74; bd. dirs. Paul Wattson Ecumenical Lecture Series, San Francisco; mem. Nat. Council Nat. Christian Leadership Conf. for Israel, 1979—. Author: Christ and the Church according to Gregory of Elvira, 1964, Children and God: Communion, Confession, Confirmation, 1970, I Confess: The Sacrament of Penance Today, 1972, Reconciling, 1981, Come Worship with US, 1987, (with Johannes Hofinger) The Good News and Its Proclamation, 1968; (with Sister Maria de la Cruz Aymes) (series) With Christ to the Father, 1966, Christ's Life in Us, 1967, Jesus, 1968, Spirit, 1968, Jesus in the Gospels and the Eucharist, 1969, In the Spirit of Jesus, 1969, One in Christ, 1970, God's People, 1970; (series) Our Father, 1971, Christ Our Life, 1971, Jesus Our Lord, 1971, Spirit of God, 1972, One in the Lord, 1973, God Among Us, 1973, Jesus Forgives, 1974, (series) Jesus Gives Joy, 1978, Jesus is with Us, 1978, Jesus and His Friends, 1978, Living God's Word, 1979, Celebrating God's Life, Sharing God's Promises, 1979, God Loves Me, 1980, We Share Forgiveness, 1980, We Share Reconciliation, 1980, Compartimos el Perdon, 1981, Fe Y Cultura, 1985; (with Sister Maria de la Cruz Aymes and Thomas H. Groome) (series) Growing with God, 1982, Growing with Jesus, 1982, Growing with the Church, 1982, Growing with God's Love, 1983, Growing with God's Life, 1983, Growing with God's Word, 1984, (with Donald Sharp) Deepening Christian Life: Integrating Faith and Maturity, 1987; contbr. articles to numerous jours. Trustee Pacific Grad. Sch. Psychology, Menlo Park, Calif., 1984-86, pres. bd. trustees, 1986. Mem. Coll. Theology Soc. (pres. 1972-74, bd. dirs. 1969-76, regional chmn. 1966-72), Cath. Theological Soc. Am., Cath. Bibl. Assn., Assn. Profs. and Researchers in Religious Edn., Religious Edn. Assn., Assn. Dirs. Grad. Religious Edn. Programs, Internat. Assn. Jesuit Ecumenists, Am. Soc. Ch. History, U. San Francisco Faculty Assn. (sec. 1980—).

BUCKLEY, GAIL GEARY, health adminstrator; b. Providence, Jan. 18, 1951; d. Thomas Francis and Marianne (Stauble) Geary; m. Glenn William Buckley, Feb. 5, 1972; children: Eric W., Aaron W. BA, U. R.I., 1972; MS in Health Adminstrn., U. Colo., 1983. Adminstrv. asst. Yale-New Haven Hosp., 1973-78, Rose Med. Ctr., Denver, 1978-81; staff analyst Colo. Dept. Health, Denver, 1982; mgr. utilization Blue Cross/Blue Shield Co., Cheyenne, Wyo., 1984-85; health services coordinator ConnectiCare, Inc., Hartford, 1985-86, data adminstr., 1986—. Avocations: bicycling, weaving, personal computers. Home: 179 Brentwood Dr Newington CT 06111

BUCKLEY, JAMES W., librarian; b. Los Angeles, Aug. 16, 1933; s. George W. and Alta L. (Hale) B.; m. Margaret Ann Wall, Aug. 7, 1965; children: Kathleen Ann, James William, John Whitney. AA, Los Angeles Harbor Coll., 1953; BA, Calif. State U., Long Beach, 1960; MLS, U. So. Calif., 1961, M in Pub. Adminstrn., 1974. Cert. tchr., Calif. Librarian West Gardena br. Los Angeles County Pub. Library, 1961-62, librarian Carson br., 1962-63; librarian Montebello (Calif.) Regional Library, 1963-68; regional librarian Orange County (Calif.) Pub. Library, 1968, dir. pub. services, 1969-74; county librarian San Mateo County (Calif.) Library, 1974-77, Marin County (Calif.) Library, 1978; city librarian Torrance (Calif.) Pub. Library, 1979—; exec. dir. Calif. Nat. Library Week, 1970; tchr. pub. service Coll. San Mateo, 1975. Served with U.S. Army, 1955-57. Mem. ALA, Am. Soc. Pub. Adminstrn., Calif. Library Assn., Pub. Library Execs. of So. Calif. Lodge: Rotary. Office: Torrance Pub Library 3301 Torrance Blvd Torrance CA 90503 *

BUCKLEY, JOHN JOSEPH, JR., healthcare executive; b. Evanston, Ill., Oct. 5, 1944; s. John Joseph and Mary Ruth (Smith) B.; m. Sarah Amelia Puceloski, May 16, 1970; children—Ruth Mary, Patricia Kimberly, John Joseph III. A.B., Kenyon Coll., 1966; M.B.A., George Washington U., 1969. Asst. adminstr. Maricopa County Gen. Hosp., Phoenix, 1969-71; asst. adminstr. St. Joseph's Hosp. and Med. Ctr., Phoenix, 1971-74, assoc. adminstr., 1974-76, v.p., 1976-79, pres., 1984—; pres. St. Anthony's Hosp., Amarillo, Tex., 1979-84, St. Anthony's Devel. Corp., Amarillo, 1982-84; chief operating officer Harrington Cancer Ctr., Amarillo, 1982-84. Active Amarillo Alliance of Community Service Execs., Amarillo Area Acad. Health Ctr. Corp., Amarillo Area Hosp. Home Care, Amarillo Found. Health and Sci., Panhandle chpt. Tex. Soc. to Prevent Blindness, Amarillo Jr. League, Children's Oncology Services of Tex. Panhandle; Amarillo diocesan coordinator health affairs; mem. adminstrv. com. Amarillo; pres. Mercy Services Corp., 1984—; bd. dirs. Greater Phoenix Affordable Health Care Found. Fellow Am. Coll. Healthcare Execs. (regent Ariz. 1984—); mem. Tex. Hosp. Assn. (trustee 1983-84), Phoenix C. of C. (bd. dirs. 1985—), Cath. Health Assn. U.S. (bd. dirs., services com., trustee 1985-88), Ariz. Kidney Found. (bd. dirs. 1984—). Republican. Roman Catholic. Home: 6834 E Belmont Circle Paradise Valley AZ 85253 Office: St Joseph's Hosp and Med Ctr PO Box 2071 Phoenix AZ 85001

BUCKLEY, RICHARD EDWARD, conductor; b. N.Y.C., Sept. 1, 1953; s. Emerson and Mary (Henderson) B. B.M., N.C. Sch. of Arts, 1973; M.Mus., Cath. U. Am., 1974; student, Aspen Sch. of Music, 1974, Mozarteum, Salzburg, Austria, 1977. Asst. condr., chorus master Opera Soc. Washington, 1973-74; asst. condr., music adminstr., Seattle Opera, 1974-75; mus. asst., asst. condr., assoc. condr., resident condr. and prin. concert condr., Seattle Symphony, 1974-84; music dir., Oakland Symphony, Calif., 1983-86; guest condr., Ft. Lauderdale Symphony, Oreg. Symphony, Alaska Festival Music, N.Y. Philharmonic, 1978-81, BBC Symphony, Winnipeg Symphony, Nashville Symphony, Oakland Symphony, Pasadena Symphony, Houston Symphony, Syracuse Symphony, Phila. Orch., San Antonio Symphony, Royal Philharm., opera cos., N.Y.C., Seattle, Houston, St. Louis, Santa Fe, Miami, Anchorage, Washington, Milw., B.H., Ft. Worth, Balt., Columbus, Chgo., Netherlands, Canada. Home: 12 Starview Dr Oakland CA 94618

BUCKLIN, ROBERT VAN ZANDT, forensic pathologist, lawyer; b. Chgo., June 25, 1916; s. James VanZandt and Lucy Monica (Dunderdale) B.; m. Patricia Lynch. BS in Medicine, Loyola U., Chgo., 1937, MD, 1941; JD, So. Tex. Coll. Law, 1969. Diplomate Am. Bd. Pathology, Am. Bd. Law In Medicine. Intern St. Joseph's Hosp., Tacoma, 1940-41; resident in pathology Tacoma Gen. Hosp., 1941-42, U.S. Army Hosps., 1942-45; dep. chief med. examiner Harris County (Tex.) Med. Examiner, Houston, 1964-69, 78-80; chief med. examiner Galveston County (Tex.) Med. Examiner, Galveston, 1969-71; dep. med. examiner Los Angeles County Med. Examiner, 1974-77, 80-83; chief med. examiner Travis County (Tex.) Med. Examiner, Austin, 1977-78; supervising pathologist San Diego County Coroner's Office, 1983—. Fellow ACP, Am. Coll. Legal Medicine, Am. Soc. Clin. Pathologists, Am. Acad. Forensic Scis. Republican. Avocation: Shroud of Turin research. Home and Office: 2528 Katherine St El Cajon CA 92020

BUCKMAN, ALAN HOWARD, communications company executive; b. Richmond, Va., Apr. 22, 1949; s. Herman and Miriam (Osmalov) B.; m. Marilyn I. Joseph, June 24, 1978; children: Philip, Rachael. BS in Mktg., Va. Commonwealth U., 1971; postgrad., Northeastern U., 1981. Account exec. Jefferson Pilot Broadcasting, Charlotte, N.C., 1970-73, Group W TV, Chgo. and N.Y.C., 1973-79; sales mgr. sta. WJZ-TV, Balt., 1979; nat. sales mgr. sta. WBZ-TV, Boston, 1979-83; v.p. Group W TV, Los Angeles, 1983—, western sales mgr., 1986—. Home: 19800 Greenbriar Dr Tarzana CA 91356 Office: Group W TV 6420 Wilshire Blvd Los Angeles CA 90048

BUCKNER, PAUL EUGENE, sculptor, educator; b. Seattle, June 16, 1933; s. Martin Monroe and Edna Laurel (Olson) B.; B.A., U. Wash., 1959; M.F.A., Claremont Grad. Sch., 1961; postgrad Slade Sch., Univ. Coll. London, 1961-62; m. Kay Lamoreaux, Aug. 15, 1959; children—Matthew, Nathan. Studio asst., sculptor Albert Stewart, Claremont, 1959-61; one man shows Oreg. Mus. Art, Eugene, 1964, 86; Gallery West, Portland, Oreg., 1977; Frye Art Mus., Seattle, 1979; exhibited in group shows Seattle Art Mus., 1964, 67; Oreg. Sculpture, Portland, 1968; Mainstreams Internat. Exhbns., Marietta, Ohio, 1971, 76, 77; Portland Art Mus., 1976, Clark Art Ctr. Rockford (Ill.) Coll., 1985; represented in permanent collections Salem (Oreg.) Civic Center, Olympic Coll., Bremerton, Wash., Oreg. Mus. Art, Mt. Angel Abbey, St. Benedict, Oreg., St. Paul's Cath. Ch., Silverton, Oreg., St. Mary's Cath. Ch., Hood River, Oreg., Leighton Pool, U. Oreg., Eugene, Sacred Heart Gen. Hosp., Eugene, Multnomah Athletic Club, Portland, United Ch. of Christ, Forest Grove, Oreg.; instr. sculpture U. Wash., Seattle, summer 1959, 62, San Bernardino Valley Coll., 1961; mem. faculty Oreg., 1962—, prof., 1972—. Served with USCG, 1953-57. Avery fellow, 1959-61; Fulbright grantee, 1961-62; Oreg. U. faculty grantee, 1965; recipient prize Nat. Sculpture Rev., N.Y.C., 1977. Home: 2332 Rockwood Ave Eugene OR 97405 Office: Sch Architecture and Allied Arts U Oreg Eugene OR 97403

BUCY, RICHARD SNOWDEN, aerospace engineering and mathematics educator, consultant; b. Washington, July 20, 1935; s. Edmond Howard and Marie (Glinke) B.; m. Ofelia Teresa Rivva, Aug. 25, 1961; children: Phillip Gustav, Richard Erwin. B.S. in Math., MIT, 1957; Ph.D. in Math. Stats., U. Calif.-Berkeley, 1963. Researcher in math. Research Inst. Advanced Studies, Towson, Md., 1960-61, 63-64; research asst. U. Calif.-Berkeley, 1961-63; asst. prof. math. U. Md., College Park, 1964-65; assoc. prof. aerospace engring. U. Colo., Boulder, 1965-66; prof. aerospace engring. and math. U. So. Calif., Los Angeles, 1966—; professeur associe French Govt., Toulouse, 1973-74, Nice, 1983-84; vis. prof. Technische Universität Berlin, 1975-76; cons. to industry. Author: Filtering for Stochastic Processes, 1968, Nonlinear Stochastic Problems, 1984; editor Jour. Info. Scis.; contbr. numerous articles to profl. publs. Recipient Humboldt prize Govt. W.Ger., Berlin, 1975-76; recipient grant Air Force Office Sci. Research, 1965-81. Fellow IEEE; mem. Am. Math. Soc. Republican. Home: 240 South Juanita Redondo Beach CA 90277 Office: U So Calif Aerospace Engring Dept Los Angeles CA 90089-1191

BUDAGHER, JOHN ADALBERTO, lawyer, state senator; b. Albuquerque, June 13, 1946; s. John and Frances Dolores (Ramirez-Rodriguez) B.; m. Sandra K. C'DeBaca, July 28, 1979; children—John A., Joseph C. B.U.S., U. N.Mex., 1969; J.D., U. Tulsa, 1973; LL.M. in Estate Planning, U. Miami, 1976. Bar: N.Mex. 1974, U.S. Dist. Ct. N.Mex. 1974, U.S. Tax Ct. 1981. Assoc. Johnson Paulantis & Lanphere, Albuquerque, 1974-75; asst. dist. atty. Dist. Atty.'s Office, Santa Fe, 1975-76; sole practice John Budagher Law Offices, Albuquerque, 1976—; instr. bar revs. Bay Area Rev., Albuquerque, 1976-78; mem. N.Mex. Senate, 1980—; mem. Commn. Uniform State Laws, 1983—. Served with USAF, 1969-71, Vietnam. Mem. Am. Legion, VFW, DAV. Republican. Roman Catholic. Lodge: Elks. Home: 5804 Pauline Rd NW Albuquerque NM 87107 Office: 1115 3d St NW Albuquerque NM 87102

BUDDENBOHM, HAROLD WILLIAM, aerospace project engineer; b. Wellington, Kans., Aug. 8, 1959; s. Dorothy Ruth (Webber) B. BSMechE, U Ill, 1981; MBA, Pepperdine U., 1984; postgrad., West Coast U., 1986. Registered engr. in tng. Design engr. Rockwell Internat., Canoga Park, Calif., 1981-84, devel. engr., 1984-85, project engr., 1985—. Patentee turbine tip sealing. Mem. ASME, Am. Mgmt. Assn. Republican. Presbyterian. Avocations: golf, volleyball. Home: 18419 Delano St Reseda CA 91335 Office: Rockwell Internat 6633 Canoga Ave Canoga Park CA 91304

BUDDINGH, JAMES LEROY, publications manager; b. Paris Twp., Mich., Mar. 24, 1934; s. Fredrick Rudolph and Carol Evelyn (VanZee) B.; m. Delhia Contraras, Sept. 17, 1955 (div. Jan. 1984); children: Carla Jean, Dahlia Ann, Mark Wade, Pamila Lynn, James Mathew; m. Jean McCombs. Graduated, Acme Sch. of Tool and Die Engring., 1962; AA, Orange Coast Coll., 1972. Engring. illustrator Volt Tech. Corp., San Diego, 1957-60; tech. art dir. Volt Tech. Corp., Anaheim, Calif., 1961-65, cons., 1960-65; engring. illustrator Jules Fielding & Assocs., San Diego, 1960-61; staff illustrator McDonnel Douglas Corp., Huntington Beach, Calif., 1965-78; publs. adminstr. Argosystems Inc., Los Angeles, 1978-82; publs. mgr. Ultrasystems Def. and Space Systems Inc., Irvine, Calif., 1982—; freelance artist, Calif., 1953—; proprietor, artist Buddingh Enterprises, Westminster, Calif., 1980-82. Pub./author Yahweh's News, 1985. Served as cpl. U.S. Army, 1953-55. Democrat. Roman Catholic. Home: PO Box 6234 Crestline CA 92325 Office: Ultrasystems Def & Space Systems Inc 16775 Von Karman Ave Irvine CA 92714

BUDESINSKY, BRET WENCESLAS, chemist, educator; b. Prague, Czechoslovakia, Apr. 10, 1928; came to U.S., 1971; BCE, Tech. U., Prague, 1951; PhD in Chemistry, Tech. U., 1957. Research chemist Research Inst. Pharmacology and Biochemistry, Prague, 1957-60; head analytical chemistry dept. Czechoslovakian Acad. Sci., Prague, 1960-68; assoc. prof. U. Waterloo, Ont., Can., 1968-71; sr. chemist Phelps Dodge Corp., Morenci, Ariz., 1972-85; research assoc. Imperial Coll., London, 1967-68, U. Ariz., Tucson, 1971-72. Author: Chelates in Analytical Chemistry, vols. 1, 2, 5, 1966, 69, 75; patentee metallochromic reagents. Chemical Inst. Can. grantee, 1969, 70, 71. Mem. Am. Chem. Soc. Democrat. Roman Catholic. Avocations: travel, photography, chess. Home: 2000 E Roger Rd #129-356 Tucson AZ 85719

BUDINGER, WILLIAM GEORGE, investment brokerage company executive; b. Chgo., Oct. 6, 1909; s. John Peter and Margaret Agnes (Birong) B.; m. Mariette Alice McGrew, Aug. 21, 1937; children—William, Donald, Jean, Mary. Student U. Ill., 1931. Vice pres. Harris-Hall, Chgo., 1948-53; gen. ptnr. Dean Witter & Co., Chgo., 1958-65, Dewar, Robertson & Pancoast, San Antonio, 1965-67, Hornblower & Weeks, Dallas, 1967-72; v.p. investments Prudential-Bache, Tucson, 1979—; with investment bankers' assocs. program Wharton Sch. Commerce, U. Pa., Phila. Bd. dirs. Community Orgn. Drug Abuse, Tucson, 1974-76. Served to maj. USAAF, 1942-46. Mem. Securities Industry Assn. Republican. Roman Catholic. Club: Tucson Country. Home: 2581 N Camino Valle Verde Tucson AZ 85715 Office: Prudential-Bache Securities Inc 5255 E Williams Circle Suite 2050 Tucson AZ 85711

BUDLONG, DUDLEY WEBSTER, engineering company executive; b. Mount Prospect, Ill., May 9, 1922; s. Dudley W. and Louise B. (Schiller) B.; m. DeLores M. Boppre, Jan. 16, 1943; children: Gerald M., Steven C., Bruce E., Roger D.; m. Gladys M. Lacerda, Dec. 15, 1979. BS, Ill. Inst. Tech., 1948, postgrad., 1951-53; postgrad., U. So. Calif., 1953-54. Registered profl. engr., Calif., N.J., N.Y., Nev., Va., Fla., Mich., Minn., Alaska. Asst. staff engr. Standard Oil Co. of Ind. (now AMOCO), Whiting, 1948-51; plant engr. Argonne (Ill.) Nat. Lab., 1951-53; sr. job engr. Bechtel Corp., Los Angeles,

1953-54; chief engr. May Engring. Co., Van Nuys, Calif., 1954-58; pres., chief engr. Budlong and Assocs., Sherman Oaks, Calif., 1958-69; exec. v.p. Quinton-Budlong Architects, Engrs. and Planners, Los Angeles, 1969-73; pvt. practice cons. Northridge, Calif., 1973; pres. Killian Assocs. West Inc., Northridge, 1973-78; v.p. facilities systems group Boyle Engring. Corp., Northridge, 1974-81; pres. Dudley W. Budlong Cons., Woodland Hills, Calif., 1981-86, Budlong & Moore Assocs., Woodland Hills, 1986—; mem. planning cabinet Am. Cons. Engrs. Council U.S., 1970-76, chmn., 1975; mem. engring. profl. adv. council Sch. Engring. Calif. State U., Northridge, 1976—. Served to 2d lt. USAF, 1943-45. Recipient Disting. Achievement award Los Angeles Council Engrs. and Scientists, 1986, Disting. Internat. Engring. Achievements award Calif. Council Indsl. and Bus. Assocs., Los Angeles, 1986. Fellow Inst. Advancement Engring.; mem. Am. Inst. Plant Engrs. (cert.), Assn. Energy Engrs. (charter), Cons. Engrs. Assn. Calif. (past bd. dirs.), Calif. Soc. Profl. Engrs. (past pres., state dir.), Cons. Elec. Engrs. So. Calif. (past pres., bd. dirs.), Illuminating Engring. Soc., Mech.-Elec. Engrs. Council Calif. (past state chmn.), Indsl. Assn. San Fernando Valley, Tau Beta Pi, Eta Kappa Nu, Alpha Phi Omega. Presbyterian. Club: Pres.'s of Calif. State U. (Northridge). Office: Budlong & Moore Assocs Inc 21241 Ventura Blvd #169 Woodland Hills CA 91364

BUDNER, DIANE FRANKLIN, clinical social worker; b. Milw., Mar. 12, 1940; d. Sol and Minnie Dora (Gold) F.; m. Alan Budner, Jan. 29, 1961; children: Deborah, Miriam, Rebecca. BA, U. Wis., Milw., 1961; MA, U. Wis., Madison, 1963; MSW, Portland State U., 1981. Registered clin. social worker, Oreg. Social worker Jewish Family and Child Service, Portland, Oreg., 1981-84, PACT Sr. Ctr., Portland, 1984-85, Veterans Hosp., Portland, 1985—. Bd. dirs. Jewish Community Ctr., Portland, 1980-82; adv. bd. Multnomah Pub. Sch., Portland, 1975-77. Detling fellow U. Wis., Madison, 1962-63. Mem. Acad. Clin. Social Workers (clin.), Nat. Assn. Social Workers, Registry Clin. Social Workers. Democrat. Lodge: Hadassah. Avocations: knitting, canoeing, cross-country skiing, swimming, gardening.

BUDZINSKI, JAMES EDWARD, interior designer; b. Gary, Ind., Jan. 4, 1953; s. Edward Michael and Virginia (Caliman) B.; student U. Cin., 1971-76. Mem. design staff Perkins & Wills Architects, Inc., Chgo., 1973-75, Med. Architectonics, Inc., Chgo., 1975-76; v.p. interior design Interior Environs., Inc., Chgo., 1976-78; pres. Jim Budzinski Design, Inc., Chgo., 1978-80; dir. interior design Robinson, Mills & Williams, San Francisco, 1980—; instr. design Harrington Inst. Design, Chgo.; cons. Chgo. Art Inst., Storwal Internat., Inc.; speaker at profl. confs. Designs include 1st Chgo. Corp. Pvt. Banking Ctr., 1st Nat. Bank Chgo. Monroe and Wabash Banking Ctr., 1978, IBM Corp., San Jose, Deutsch Bank, Frankfort, Crowley Maritime Corp., San Francisco, offices for Brobeck, Phleger and Harrison, offices for chmn. bd. Fireman's Fund Ins. Cos., Nob Hill Club, Fairmont Hotel, San Francisco, offices for Cooley, Godword, Castro, Huddleson, and Tatum, Palo Alto, Calif, offices for Pacific Bell Acctg. div., San Francisco, showroom for Knoll Internat., San Francisco, lobby, lounge TransAm. Corp. Hdqrts, San Fransisco. Pres. No. Calif. chpt. Design and Interior Furnishings Found. for AIDS. Office: Robinson Mills & Williams 153 Kearny St San Francisco CA 94108

BUEHRING, GERTRUDE CASE, tumor biology educator; b. Chgo., May 28, 1940; d. Theodore Johnston and Rosemary (Lawrence) Case; m. William Richard Buehring, Aug. 24, 1962; children: Anna, Jessica. BA in Biology, Stanford U., 1962; PhD in Genetics, U. Calif., Berkeley, 1972. Postdoctoral fellow U. Calif., Berkeley, 1972-73, asst. prof., 1973-80, assoc. prof. medical microbiology and tumor biology, 1980—; vis. prof. U. Innsbruck, Austria, 1981-82. Research grantee Nat. Cancer Inst., 1974-77, U. Calif. Cancer Research Coordinating Com., 1983-84, Pardee Found., 1985-86. Mem. AAAS, Am. Assn. Cancer Research, Tissue Culture Assn., Sigma Xi. Office: U Calif Sch Pub Health Berkeley CA 94720

BUERK, GUNTHER WILLIE, management consulting company executive, business consultant; b. Milw., Sept. 27, 1935; s. Eugene Johannes and Kaethe Hildegard (Hoferichter) B.; m. Michele Yvonne Cauvin, Dec. 19, 1967; children: Axel Henry, Cecile Katja. BSME, Tech. U. Munich, Fed. Republic Germany, 1957, MSChemE, 1959, MBA, 1964, PhDChemE magna cum laude, 1965. Research engr. Siemens A.G., Berlin, 1960-62; head econ. analysis Garrett-Airesearch, Torrance, Calif., 1966-69; asst. coordinator overseas div. Union Oil Co., Los Angeles, 1969-73, sr. corp. planner, 1973-79, mgr. econs., 1979-83; pres. Am. Cons. Co., Rancho Palos Verdes, Calif., 1983—; adj. prof. U. So. Calif., Los Angeles, 1985—; bd. dirs. Fail-Safe Tech. Corp., Kiesel Mktg., Inc. Co-author: Operations Research and Data Processing for Maintenance Planning, 1969. Patentee plastic foam processing, 1960-62. Founding councilman City of Rancho Palos Verdes, 1973-80, mayor, 1976-77; mem. Los Angeles County Economy and Efficiency Commn., 1981—, Los Angeles County Pub. Adminstr. Pub. Guardian Adv. Commn., 1982—. Siemens A.G. scholar, 1954; NATO postdoctoral fellow, 1965-66. Mem. Inst. Mgmt. Sci. (exec. com. 1972-75), German Am. C. of C., So. Calif. Corp. Planners Assn., Internat. Assn. Energy Economists. Republican. Lutheran. Club: Rancho Verde Racquet. Home and Office: 19 Stirrup Rd Rancho Palos Verdes CA 90274

BUFFINGTON, ANDREW, physicist, astronomer; b. Fall River, Mass., Dec. 25, 1938; s. James and Lois (Chapman) B.; m. Sally Woodworth, June 26, 1968; children: Katherine, Anne. BS, MIT, 1961, PhD, 1966. Research assoc. MIT, Cambridge, 1967-68; research physicist U. Calif., Berkeley, 1968-79; sr. research assoc. Calif. Inst. Tech., Pasadena, 1979-84; research physicist U. Calif., La Jolla, 1984—; cons. U. Ariz., Tucson, 1985—. Contbr. articles to profl. jours. Mem. Am. Phys. Soc. (sec. astrophysics div. 1976-80, vice chmn. 1981-82, chmn. 1982-83), Am. Astron. Soc., Sigma Xi. Avocations: music, photography. Home: 3166 Bremerton Pl La Jolla CA 92037 Office: U Calif San Diego CASS C-011 La Jolla CA 92093

BUFFINGTON, LINDA BRICE, interior designer; b. Long Beach, Calif., June 21, 1936; d. Harry Bryce and Marguerite Leonora (Tucciarone) Van Bellehem; student El Camino Jr. Coll., 1955-58, U. Calif., Irvine, 1973—; children—Lisa Ann, Phillip Lynn. with Public Finance, Torrance, Calif., 1954-55, Beneficial Finance, Torrance and Hollywood, Calif., 1955-61; interior designer Vee Nisley Interiors, Newport Beach, Calif., 1964-65, Leon's Interiors, Newport Beach, 1965-69; partner Marlind Interiors, Tustin, Calif., 1969-70; owner, designer Linda Buffington Interiors, Villa Park, Calif., 1970—; cons. builders, housing developments. Mem. Bldg. Industry Assn., Internat. Soc. Interior Designers, Sales and Mktg. Council, Home Builders Council, Nat. Assn. Home Builders. Republican. Club: POCA. Office: 17767 Santiago Blvd Villa Park CA 92667

BUFFORD, RODGER KEITH, psychologist, educator; b. Santa Rosa, Calif., Dec. 23, 1944; s. John Samuel and Evelyn A. (Rude) B.; m. Kathleen A. Parson; children—Heather, Brett. B.A., King's Coll., 1966; M.A., U. Ill., 1970; Ph.D., 1971. Lic. psychologist, Oreg., Va. Psychologist, Adolph Meyer Zone Ctr., Decatur, Ill., 1969-70; asst. prof. psychology Am. U., Washington, 1971-76; asst. prof., chmn. dept. psychology Huntington (Ind.) Coll., 1976-77; assoc. prof. Psychol. Studies Inst., Atlanta, 1977-81; psychologist Atlanta Counseling Ctr., 1980-82; assoc. prof., chmn. dept. psychology Western Baptist Sem., Portland, Oreg., 1982-86, prof. and chmn., 1986—; pvt. practice psychology, 1973—; dir. Mental Health Assn., Huntington, Ind., 1976-77. Elder, Chapel Woods Presbyterian Ch., 1983. USPHS trainee, 1967-68, 70-71; Am. U. Faculty Research grantee, 1972. Mem. Am. Psychol. Assn., Western Psychol. Assn., Christian Assn. Psychol. Studies, Am. Sci. Affiliation, Oreg. Psychol. Assn. Author: The Human Reflex: Behavioral Psychology in Biblical Perspective, 1981; contbg. editor Jour. Psychology and Theology, Jour. Psychology and Christianity; contbr. chpts. to texts, numerous articles to profl. jours. Home: 19505 Hidden Springs Rd West Linn OR 97068 Office: 5511 SE Hawthorne Blvd Portland OR 97215

BUFORD, JACK WILLIAM, consultant; b. Topeka, July 22, 1912; s. Charles Homer and Bess (Thomas) B.; m. Helen Malott, Dec. 27, 1934; children: Anne Ludwin, Thomas. BSCE, U. Wash., 1933; MS in Engring., Harvard U., 1934. Various positions Pa. RR, 1934-50; sr. v.p. internat. ops. Hanna Mining Co., Cleve., 1950-77; dir. MAPCO Inc., cons., 1977—. Served to lt. col. U.S. Army, 1941-46. Mem. Am. Iron and Steel Inst., AIME. Republican. Clubs: Union (Cleve.); Rolling Rock (Ligonier, Pa.); Paradise Valley Country (Ariz.); Westwood Country (Rocky River, Ohio). Lodges: Masons, Shriners. Home and Office: 7337 E Echo Ln Scottsdale AZ 85258

BUHL, KARL FRANZ, communications executive; b. Crystal Lake, Ill., Feb. 27, 1953; s. Otto Franz and Lucille H. (Schutman) B.; m. Jackie Lynn Newville, Aug. 24, 1974; 1 child: Erica Lynn. BA, Mich. State U., 1975; MSJ, Northwestern U., 1976. Media planner, buyer Leo Burnett U.S.A., Chgo., 1976-77; account exec. Needham Harper & Steers, Chgo., 1977-79, 81-82; sales assoc. Real Estate One, Traverse City, Mich., 1979-81; sr. account exec. Chiat Day, Seattle, 1982-85; account supr. Borders, Perrin & Norrander, Seattle, 1985-86; dir. U.S. corp. communications Mannesmann Tally Corp., Kent, Wash., 1986—. Mem. Mktg. Communications Execs. Internat. Avocations: photography, mountaineering. Home: 13644 178th Ave NE Redmond WA 98052 Office: Mannesmann Tally Corp 8301 S 180th St Kent WA 98032

BULKLEY, DWIGHT HATFIELD, biologist; b. Bangkok, May 15, 1919; s. Lucius Constant and Edna (Bruner) B.; m. Miriam Wilson, Aug. 1, 1953 (div. 1972); 1 child: Brian David. BA, Pomona Coll., 1941. Cert. clin. hypnotherapist. Vice consul U.S. Embassy, Bangkok, 1945-48; research assoc. Psychol. Research Found., Phoenix, 1952-54; chemist Nat. Distillers, Cin., 1955-59; aerospace sr. engr. Autonetics div., Anaheim, Calif., 1959-66; owner printing bus. Calif. and Oreg., 1967-72; founder, dir. Seattle Inst. Life Sci., 1975—. Author: Psycles: Psychogenesis of Accidents/Diseases, 1981; (newsletter) A New Physics of Life, 1987. Served to sgt. OSS, 1942-45. Decorated Order of White Elephant 3d Class (Royal Thai Govt.); recipient 3rd prize Writer's Digest Contest. Mem. AAAS, Internat. Soc. for Study of Origins of Life. Home and Office: 6519 40th Ave NE Seattle WA 98115

BULL, BRIAN STANLEY, physician, educator; b. Watford, Hertfordshire, Eng., Sept. 14, 1937; came to U.S., 1954, naturalized, 1960; s. Stanley and Agnes Mary (Murdoch) B.; m. Maureen Hannah Huse, June 3, 1963; children: Beverly Velda, Beryl Heather. B.S. in Zoology, Walla Walla Coll., 1957; M.D., Loma Linda (Calif.) U., 1961. Diplomate: Am. Bd. Pathology. Intern Yale U., 1961-62, resident in anat. pathology, 1962-63; resident in clin. pathology NIH, Bethesda, Md., 1963-65; fellow in hematology and electron microscopy NIH, 1965-66, staff hematologist, 1966-67; research assoc. dept. anatomy Loma Linda U., 1958, dept. microbiology, 1959, asst. prof. pathology, 1968-71, assoc. prof., 1971-73, prof., 1973—, chmn. dept. pathology, 1973—; vis. prof. Institut de Pathologie Cellulaire, Paris, 1972, 74, Royal Postgrad. Med. Sch., London, 1972, U. Wis.-Madison, 1973, U. Ohio, Columbus, 1974, U. Minn., Mpls., 1979, U. Hawaii, 1981, St. Thomas Hosp. and Med. Sch., 1981, Mayo Clinic, 1985. Bd. editors Jour. Clin. and Lab. Haematology, U.K.; editor-in-chief Blood Cells U.S.; contbr. chpts. to books and numerous articles to med. jours. Served with USPHS, 1963-67. Nat. Inst. Arthritis and Metabolic Diseases fellow, 1967-68; recipient Daniel D. Comstock Meml. award Loma Linda U., 1961, Merck Manual award, 1961, Mosby Scholarship Book award, 1961; Ernest B. Cotlove Meml. lectr. Acad. Clin. Lab. Physicians and Scientists, 1972. Fellow Am. Soc. Clin. Pathologists, Am. Soc. Hematology, Coll. Am. Pathologists, N.Y. Acad. Scis.; mem. AMA, Assn. Pathology Chmn., Calif. Soc. Pathologists, San Bernardino County Med. Soc., Acad. Clin. Lab. Physicians and Scientists, Am. Assn. Pathologists, Sigma Xi, Alpha Omega Alpha. Seventh-day Adventist. Patentee in field. Home: 24489 Barton Rd Loma Linda CA 92354 Office: Loma Linda U Sch Medicine Department of Pathology and Laboratory Medicine Loma Linda CA 92350

BULL, STANLEY RAYMOND, energy company executive; b. Montezuma, Iowa, May 15, 1941; s. Raymond Wayne and Neola Arlene (Stanley) B.; m. Diana Lee Maxwell, Sept. 7, 1963; children: Melanie J., Julia D., Jeffrey D. BS, U. Mo., 1963; MS, Stanford U., 1964, PhD, 1967. Registered profl. engr., Mo. From asst. to full prof. U. Mo., Columbia, 1967-80; sr. engr. Solar Energy Research Inst., Golden, Colo., 1980-81, sr. sci. advisor, 1981-82, mgr. planning and evaluation, 1982-84, dep. dir. solar fuel, 1984-86, dir. solar fuel, 1986—; cons. Argonne (Ill.) Nat. Lab., 1967-73, Ellis Fischel State Hosp., Columbia, 1972-80, U. Louisville Health Sci., 1978, Boone County Hosp., Columbia, 1979-80. Contbr. articles to jours. Bd. dirs. Columbine Soccer Assn., Littleton, Colo., 1985; commr. Club Columbine Competitive Soccer, Littleton, 1986; chmn. policy and prodecures, Ken Caryl Ranch, Littleton, 1986. Fulbright-Hays vis. prof., France, 1972. Mem. Am. Inst. Chem. Engrs., Am. Solar Energy Soc., ASME. Home: 7577 Parkview Mountain Littleton CO 80127 Office: Solar Energy Research Inst 1617 Cole Blvd Golden CO 80401

BULLARD, EDWARD DICKINSON, manufacturing executive; b. San Francisco, Nov. 9, 1948; s. Edward Wheatley Jr. and Marion Elizabeth (Kelly) B.; m. Sharon Clarke Smith, June 21, 1972; children: Edward W., Victoria K. BS, U. Calif., Berkeley, 1971; MBA, Harvard U., 1975. Staff acct. Price Waterhouse, San Francisco, 1975-77; br. mgr. Averill Equipment Co. subs. E.D. Bullard Co., Troy, Mich., 1977-81; v.p. fin. E.D. Bullard Co., Sausalito, Calif., 1981-83, pres., chief exec. officer, 1983—. Office: E D Bullard Co 2680 Bridgeway Sausalito CA 94965

BULLARD, GILDA, state official; b. Chicago Heights, Ill., Dec. 12, 1927; d. Pietro Antonio and Philomena D'Antonoli; B.S., Calif. State U., Sacramento, 1967, M.B.A., 1973; 1 son, David L. Gard. With Pacific Telephone Co., 1945-61; with State of Calif., 1961—, fiscal specialist in state welfare programs, 1966-74, staff mgr. licensing div., Sacramento, 1974-76, San Jose, 1975, citation hearing officer on appeals by nursing homes Dept. Health, Berkeley, 1976-78, mgr., fed. audits specialist audits and investigations div. Dept. Health Services, 1978-84, appeals unit, 1984-86, mgr. audits, 1986-87, State Dept. Indsl. Relations, 1987—; part-time instr. Am. River Coll., 1976-77, Cosumnes River Coll., 1980-86, Sacramento City Coll., 1985-86 . Mem. Nat. Assn. Accts. (asst. treas. 1971, editor 1971), AAUW, Calif. State Employees Assn. (editor 1971, 72, chpt. pres. 1977, 81-86). Presbyterian. Home: State Calif Dept Indsl Relations 2833 Danube Ave Davis CA 95616 Office: 525 Golden Gate Ave San Francisco CA 94101

BULLAS, LEONARD RAYMOND, microbiology educator; b. Lismore, New South Wales, Australia, Dec. 8, 1929; came to U.S., 1959; s. Raymond and Arum Adelaide (Semmens) B.; widowed; children: Roslyn, Graham. BSc, U. Adelaide, Australia, 1953, MSc, 1957; Phd, Mont. State U., 1963. Instr. bacteriology U. Adelaide, 1953-58; research asst. Mont. State U., Bozeman, 1959-62; instr. microbiology Loma Linda (Calif.) U., 1962-64, asst. prof., 1964-70, assoc. prof., 1970-80, prof. microbiology, 1980—; vis. prof. U. Louvain, Belgium, 1973-74, European Molecular Biology Lab., Heidelberg, Fed. Republic Germany, 1981-82. Contbr. articles to sci. jours. Recipient Basic Sci. Investigator of Yr. award MacPherson Soc., 1975, 81; Basic Sci. fellow MacPherson Soc., 1981. Mem. Am. Soc. Microbiology, Genetics Soc. Am., Sigma Xi. Adventist. Office: Loma Linda U Anderson St Loma Linda CA 92350

BULLIN, CHRISTINE NEVA, arts administrator; b. New Plymouth, N.Z., Apr. 13, 1948; d. Kenneth and Hazel Iris B. B.A., Wellesley Coll., 1969; M.L.A., Simmons Coll., 1973. Dir., Opera New England, Boston, 1974-78; with San Francisco Opera, 1978-81; mgr. San Francisco Opera Ctr., 1981—. Office: War Memorial Opera House San Francisco CA 94102

BULLOCK, JOSEPH DANIEL, physician, pediatrician, educator; b. Cin., Jan. 23, 1942; s. Joseph Craven and Emilie (Woide) B.; m. Martha Foss, June 20, 1964; children: Jennifer Zane, Sarah Harrison. BA, Wittenberg U., 1963; MD, Ohio State U., 1967, degree in pediatrics, 1969; degree in immunology, allergy, U. Calif., San Francisco, 1971. Diplomate Am. Bd. Pediatrics, Am. Bd. Allergy and Immunology. Clin. prof. pediatrics Ohio State U., Columbus, 1971—; v.p. Midwest Allergy Assocs., Inc., Worthington, Ohio, 1971—. Contbr. articles to profl. jours. Active fund raising Wittenberg U., Springfield, Ohio, 1980-83, Columbus Sch. for Girls, 1977-86. Served to capt. USAF, 1967-71. Recipient Mead Johnson award, 1965. Fellow Am. Acad. Pediatrics, Am. Acad. Allergy, Am. Coll. Allergists (Bd. Regents 1979-82, Clemens von Pirquet award 1968, 69, 70, 71), Am. Thoracic Soc., Interasma, Ohio Soc. Allergy and Immunology (pres. 1985-87). Republican. Lutheran. Clubs: Columbus Country; The Golf (New Albany, Ohio); Indian Creek Country (Miami Beach, Fla.), The Surf (Surfside, Fla.). Home: 189 N Parkview Columbus OH 43209 Office: Midwest Allergy Assocs Inc 85 E Wilson Bridge Rd Worthington OH 43085

BULLOCK, RONALD ELVIN, nuclear physicist, materials scientist; b. Camden, Ark., June 17, 1934; s. Elvin Clingan and Essie Lee (Naron) B.; m. Jewell Faye Zuber, Aug. 30, 1964. BS in Physics, La. Poly. Inst., 1956; MS in Math., Tex. Christian U., 1963, MA in Physics, 1969. Registered profl. engr., Calif. Nuclear engr. Gen. Dynamics Corp., Ft. Worth, 1956-62, sr. nuclear engr., 1962-74; sr. staff scientist GA Techs., Inc., San Diego, 1974—; reviewer Tech. Jours., 1975—; guest lectr. various univs., 1970—. Contbr. more than 30 articles to tech. jours.; patentee in field. Mem. Am. Nuclear Soc., Am. Carbon Soc. Baptist. Home: 1127 Sea Village Dr Cardiff-By-The-Sea CA 92007

BULLOCK, THOMAS EUGENE, consulting engineer; b. Twin Falls, Idaho, Oct. 6, 1927; s. Thomas Elias and Mabel Edna (Howard) B.; m. Claudia McGregor, Dec. 1, 1956; 1 child, Belinda. AA in Engring., Sacramento Coll., 1951; BSE, Idaho Mines, 1953; MSCE, U. So. Calif., 1958; postgrad. in modern bus., Alexander Hamilton, 1960-62; postgrad. in engring. mgmt., UCLA, 1965-66. With United Geophys. Corp., Morgan City, La., 1954; project engr. Dames & Moore, Los Angeles, 1959, assoc., 1970; cons. Dames & Moore, Burbank, Calif., 1961; head civil engring. dept. Davidson & Maurer, Los Angeles, 1962; project engr. Rocketdyne, Los Angeles, 1963; specialist adv. engring. Ocean Systems Ops. Rockwell Internat., Long Beach, Calif., 1966; v.p. Converse Cons., Pasadena, Calif., 1976, also bd. dirs.; cons. in field., La Canada, Calif., 1983. Author: Sonic Soil Testing, 1958. Served to capt. C.E., USAR, 1944-62. Recipient Pride award NASA, 1965. Fellow ASCE; mem. Seismol. Soc. Am., Am. Inst. Mining Engrs., Soc. Am. Mil. Engrs., ASTM, Tau Beta Pi, Chi Epsilon, Sigma Tau, Sigma Gamma Epsilon. Republican. Avocations: camping, fishing, electronics, photography. Home: 4451 St Francis Pl La Canada-Flintridge CA 91011 Office: 4529 Angeles Crest Hwy PO Box 1083 La Canada-Flintridge CA 91011

BULTMANN, PHYLLIS WETHERELL, journalist; b. Ottumwa, Iowa, Aug. 21, 1923; d. Harry Gillette and Venice B. (Lewis) Wetherell; B.A., UCLA, 1944, M.A., 1945, Ph.D., 1950; m. William Arnold Bultmann, Dec. 28, 1949; 1 dau., Janice. Instr. Ark. State U., Conway, 1950-58, Ohio Wesleyan U., Delaware, 1958-64, Western Wash. U., Bellingham, 1966-71, 80-86; profl. writer columnist SEA Mag., Newport Beach, Calif., 1973—; columnist Everett (Wash.) Herald, 1981-84; pub. relations officer Press Boat, PITCH Regatta, Bellingham, 1976-78; sr. Fulbright lectr., East Pakistan, 1960-61; dir. Maritime Heritage Found., Bellingham, 1980-84. Mem. Conf. Brit. Studies. Episcopalian. Clubs: Bellingham Yacht; Squalicum Yacht (commodore 1981-82). Author: Two Burners and An Ice Chest, 1977; (with Bill Bultmann) Border Boating, 1979; Editor: (with W.A. Bultmann) Current Research in British Studies, 1975; (with Leroy Dresbeck) British Studies Intelligencer, 1972-77. Home and office: 1600 43d Ave E #101 Seattle WA 98112

BULTMANN, WILLIAM ARNOLD, historian; b. Monrovia, Calif., Apr. 10, 1922; s. Paul Gerhardt and Elsa (Johnson) B.; AB, UCLA, 1943, PhD, 1950; m. Phyllis Jane Wetherell, Dec. 28, 1949; 1 child, Janice Jane. Assoc. prof. history Central Ark. U., Conway, 1949-52, prof., 1954-57; assoc. prof. Ohio Wesleyan U., Delaware, 1957-61, prof., 1961-65; prof. Western Wash. U., Bellingham, 1965-87, chmn. dept., 1968-70, dean arts and scis., 1970-72, provost, 1971-73; vis. assoc. prof. U. Tex., Austin, 1952-53; vis. prof. U. N.H., summers 1965, 66; acad. cons. Wash. Commn. for Humanities, 1973-87, Nat. Endowment for Humanities, 1976-87; reader Ednl. Testing Service Princeton, 1973-85. Bd. dirs. Bellingham Maritime Heritage Found., 1980-85; adminstrv. officer Bellingham Power Squadron, 1981-82, comdr., 1982-84. Fulbight sr. lectr. Dacca (Bangladesh) U., 1960-61; Ohio Wesleyan U. research fellow, 1964; Fund for Advancement Edn. fellow for fgn. study, 1953-54; recipient research award Social Sci. Research Council, 1957. Mem. Am. Hist. Assn., Ch. Hist. Soc., Conf. Brit. Studies, Pacific, Pacific N.W. confs. Brit. studies, AAUP, Mystery Writers of Am., Nat. Boating Fedn., Interclub Boating Assn. Washington, Phi Beta Kappa, Phi Delta Kappa, Pi Gamma Mu. Episcopalian. Clubs: Park Athletic Recreation, Bellingham Yacht (chmn. public relations com. 1981-86), Squalicum Yacht (trustee 1979-82), Birch Bay Yacht; Wash. Athletic. Co-author: Border Boating, 1978; cofounder, mem. editorial bd. Albion, 1968-84; mng. editor Brit. Studies Intelligencer, 1973-80; co-editor Current Research in British Studies, 1975; editor Jib Sheet, 1981-86; feature writer, columnist Sea mag., 1974—; feature writer Venture mag., 1981-85. Home: 1600 43d Ave E Suite 101 Seattle WA 98112

BUMGARDNER, LARRY GAYNOR, academic administrator; b. Chattanooga, June 10, 1957; s. Walter G. and Kathryn (Hamrick) B. BA, David Lipscomb Coll., 1977; JD, Vanderbilt U., 1981. Bar: Tenn. 1981, U.S. Dist. Ct. (cen. dist.) Tenn. 1982, Calif. 1984, U.S. Dist. Ct. (cen. dist.) Calif. 1985. From reporter to copy editor Nashville (Tenn.) Banner, 1975-79; editor Tenn. Attorneys' Memo, Tenn. Jour., Nashville, 1979-83; dir. founds. Pepperdine U., Malibu, Calif., 1983-85, asst. v.p. for communications and grants, asst. prof. communications, 1986—. Contbr. numerous articles to various pubs. ABA, Calif. Bar Assn., Tenn. Bar Assn. Home: 50 Maegan Pl #8 Thousand Oaks CA 91362 Office: Pepperdine U 24255 Pacific Coast Hwy Malibu CA 90265

BUMSTED, MARY PAMELA, anthropologist; b. Wilmington, Del., Feb. 21, 1950; d. Alexander R. and Lydia (Green) B. BA cum laude, Beloit Coll., 1972; Diploma in Human Biology, Oxford U., 1975; PhD, U. Mass., 1984. Asst. archaeologist U. Vt., Burlington, 1978-79; vis. scholar, geoscis. U. Ariz., Tucson, 1980-83; staff research asst. Lab. of Tree-Ring Research, U. Ariz., Tucson, 1981; postdoctoral fellow Los Alamos (N.Mex.) Nat. Lab., 1983-86, cons. in analytical, isotope and nuclear chemistry, 1986—. Contbr. articles to profl. jours. Grantee NSF, 1980, Ruggles-Gates Fund, 1981, Wenner-Gren Fund, 1982. Fellow Royal Anthrop. Inst.; mem. AAAS, Am. Assn. Phys. Anthropologists, Am. Anthrop. Assn., Soc. Am. Archaeology, Soc. Environ. Geochemistry and Health, Sigma Xi. Office: Los Alamos Nat Lab MS G740 Los Alamos NM 87545

BUNCH, DONALD LEROY, physician; b. Sedgwick, Colo., Jan. 12, 1938; s. Leonard P. and Helen (Hallock) B.; m. Cindee Ruth Ellett, May 26, 1979; 1 child, Kristen. B.A., Union Coll., 1960; M.D., Loma Linda U., 1964. Diplomate Am. Bd. Thoracic Surgery, Am. Bd. Surgery, Nat. Bd. Med. Examiners. Rotating intern Porter Meml. Hosp., Denver, 1964-65; resident in surgery U. Colo. Med. Ctr., 1965-66, 68-69, resident research fellow in transplant surgery, 1969-70; sr. resident in surgery, 1970-71; jr. resident in cardiopulmonary surgery U. Oreg. Hosps., 1971-72, sr., chief resident in cardiopulmonary surgery, 1972-73; practice medicine specializing in cardiovascular and thoracic surgery, Denver, 1973-74, Las Vegas, 1974—; chief cardiovascular surgery So. Nev. Meml. Hosp., 1976-77; mem. surgery com., 1975-77; mem. critical care com. Sunrise Hosp., 1977-78, cardiovascular surgery advisor to critical care com., 1983; mem. critical care com. Valley Hosp., 1979—, mem. emergency room com., 1979-84. Served with USAF, 1966-68. Fellow Internat. Coll. Surgeons; mem. AMA, Clark County Med. Soc., Nev. State Med. Assn. (mem. com. on med. practice 1979—), Am. Heart Assn. (bd. dirs. Nev. affiliate 1981—, v.p. affiliate, program dir. So. div. 1983, Most Outstanding Profl. Vol. award So. Div. 1983, so. div. pres.). Office: 1090 E Desert Inn Rd 202 Las Vegas NV 89109

BUNCHMAN, HERBERT HARRY, II, plastic surgeon; b. Washington, Feb. 23, 1942; s. Herbert H. and Mary (Halleran) B.; m. Marguerite Fransioli, Mar. 21, 1963; children: Herbert H. III., Angela K., Christopher. BA, Vanderbilt U., 1964; MD, U. Tenn., 1967. Diplomate Am. Bd. Surgery, Am. bd. Plastic Surgery. Resident in surgery U. Tex., Galveston, 1967-72, resident in plastic surgery, 1972-75; practice medicine specializing in plastic surgery Mesa, Ariz., 1975—; chief surgery Desert Samaritan Hosp., 1978-80. Contbr. articles to profl. jours. Eaton Clin. fellow, 1975. Mem. AMA, Am. Soc. Plastic and Reconstructive Surgery, Am. Soc. Aesthetic Plastic Surgery, Singleton Surgical Soc., Tex. Med. Assn., So. Med. Assn. (grantee 1974), Ariz. Med. Assn. Office: Plastic Surgery Cons PC 1520 S Dobson #314 Mesa AZ 85202

BUNDESEN, FAYE STIMERS, educator, investment/management company owner; b. Cedarville, Calif., Sept. 16, 1932; d. Floyd Walker and Ermina Elizabeth (Roberts) Stimers; m. Allen Eugene Bundesen, Dec. 27, 1972; children—William, David, Edward Silvius; Ted, Eric Bundesen. B.A., Calif. State U.-Sacramento, 1955; M.A., Calif. State U.-San Jose, 1972. Licensed real estate broker, Calif. Elem. sch. tchr. San Francisco Pub. Schs.,

1955-60; elem. and jr. high sch. tchr., lang. arts specialist Sunnyvale (Calif.) Schs., 1978-83; cons. Santa Clara County Office of Edn. and Sunnyvale Sch. Dist., 1983—; v.p. Bundesen Enterprises, San Jose, Calif., 1975-81, pres., 1981—. Bd. dirs. Sunnyvale Sch. Employees' Credit Union, 1983—, v.p., 1984-86; mem. City of San Jose Tenant/Landlord Hearing Com., 1983—, v.p., 1984-85. Mem. Internat. Reading Assn., Santa Clara County Reading Assn., Nat. Council Tchrs. English, Calif. Assn. Tchrs. English, Assn. Supervision and Curriculum Devel., Calif. Personnel and Guidance Assn., Tri-County Apt. Assn., Calif. Scholarship Fedn. (life), AAUW, Nat. Apt. Assn., Nat. Assn. Female Execs. Presbyterian. Author, editor numerous dist. publs. Office: 1334 Randol Ave San Jose CA 95126

BUNDY, HALLIE FLOWERS, biochemist, educator; b. Santa Monica, Calif., Apr. 2, 1925; d. Douglas and Phyllis (Flowers) B. BA in Chemistry, Mt. St. Mary's Coll., Los Angeles, 1947; MS in Biochemistry, U. So. Calif., 1955, PhD in Biochemistry, 1958. Instr. sch. medicine U. So. Calif., Los Angeles, 1959-60; asst. prof. Mt. St. Mary's Coll., 1960-63, assoc. prof., 1963-66, prof. biochemistry, 1966—; asst. program dir. Undergrad. Research Participation NSF, Washington, 1965-66. Contbr. research articles to profl. jours. Predoctoral fellow USPHS, 1955-57, Sci. Faculty fellow NSF, 1969-70; grantee NIH, 1960-66, NSF, 1961-78, Grad. Women in Sci., 1974. Mem. Am. Chem. Soc., Pacific Slope Biochem. Conf., Internat. Soc. Plant Molecular Biology, N.Y. Acad. Scis., Sigma Xi. Avocations: philately, tennis, golf. Office: Mt St Mary's Coll 12001 Chalon Rd Los Angeles CA 90049

BUNGER, JAMES WALTER, fuels engineering educator, engineering consultant; b. Orange City, Iowa, Apr. 7, 1945; s. C. Walter; m. Brenda Bernhisel. BSc in Chemistry, U. Wyo., 1968; PhD in Fuels Engring., U. Utah, 1979. Chemist U.S. Dept. Energy, Laramie, Wyo., 1968-75; research assoc. U. Utah, Salt Lake City, 1975-79, asst. prof. research, 1979—; sci. advisor State of Utah, 1979-81; prin. investigator research grants U.S. Dept. Energy, 1975—. Editor: Chemistry of Asphaltenes, 1981; contbr. articles to profl. jours. Mem. Am. Chem. Soc. (chmn. div. petroleum chemistry, 1985-86, treas., 1979-83), Am. Inst. Chem. Engring. Avocations: music, sailing, skiing, basketball. Office: U Utah Dept Fuels Engring Salt Lake City UT 84112-1183

BUNKER, JOHN BIRKBECK, sugar company executive; b. Yonkers, N.Y., Mar. 28, 1926; s. Ellsworth and Harriet (Butler) B.; m. Emma Cadwalader, Feb. 27, 1954; children: Emma, Jeanie, Harriet, John C., Lambert C. BA, Yale U., 1950. With Nat. Sugar Refining Co., 1953-62; pres. Gt. Western Sugar Co., Denver, 1966; pres. Holly Sugar Co., Colorado Springs, Colo., 1967-81, chmn., 1971-81, chief exec. officer, 1971-81; pres., chief exec. officer Calif. and Hawaiian Sugar Co., San Francisco, 1981—, also bd. dirs.; bd. dirs., mem. exec. com., past chmn. The Sugar Assn., Inc., Washington; bd. dirs., mem. exec. com. World Sugar Research Orgn., London. Bd. dirs. Bay Area Council, San Francisco, World Affairs Council, San Francisco, Japan Soc. of No. Calif., World Affairs Council of Calif.; adv. bd. Leavey Sch. Bus. and Adminstrn., Santa Clara U.; trustee, mem. exec. com. Colo. Coll.; trustee Asia Found. Served to 1st lt., inf. AUS, 1951-52. Office: One California St Room 2000 San Francisco CA 94111

BUNN, CHARLES NIXON, strategic bus. planning cons.; b. Springfield, Ill., Feb. 8, 1926; s. Joseph Forman and Helen Anna Frieda (Link) B.; student U. Ill., 1943-44; B.S. in Engring., U.S. Mil. Acad., 1949; M.B.A., Xavier U., Cin., 1958; m. Cecine Elizabeth Cole, Dec. 26, 1951; children—Sisene, Charles. Flight test engr. Gen. Electric Co., Cin., also Edwards AFB, Calif., 1953-59; sr. missile test engr., space systems div. Lockheed Aircraft Corp., USAF Satellite Test Center, Sunnyvale, Calif., 1959-60, 63-70, economist, advanced planning dept., 1961-63; economic and long-range planning cons., Los Altos, Calif., 1970-73; head systems planning, economist, strategic bus. planning, Western Regional hdqrs. U.S. Postal Service, San Bruno, Calif., 1973-78; strategic bus. planning cons., investment analysis cons., 1978-79; strategic bus. planning Advanced Reactor Systems dept. Gen. Electric Co., Sunnyvale, Calif., 1979-84; strategic planning cons., 1984—. Served with inf. paratroops U.S. Army, 1944-45, with inf. and rangers, 1949-53; Korea. Decorated Battle Star (5). Mem. Nat. Assn. Bus. Economists, World Future Soc., Sigma Nu. Episcopalian. Home and Office: 870 E El Camino Real #143 Mountain View CA 94040

BUNN, DOROTHY IRONS, court reporter; b. Trinidad, Colo., Apr. 30, 1948; d. Russell and Pauline Anna (Langowski) Irons; m. Peter Lynn Bunn; children—Kristy Lynn, Wade Allen, Russell Ahearn. Student No. Va. Community Coll., 1970-71, U. Va., Fairfax, 1971-72. Registered profl. reporter; cert. shorthand reporter. Pres., chief exec. officer Ahearn Ltd., Springfield, Va., 1970-81, Bunn & Assocs., Glenrock, Wyo., 1981—. Cons., Bixby Hereford Co., Glenrock, 1981—. Del., White House Conf. on Small Bus., Washington, 1986. Mem. Nat. Shorthand Reporters Assn., Wyo. Shorthand Reporters Assn. (chmn. com. 1984—), Nat. Assn. Female Execs., Nat. Fedn. Ind. Businesses, Am. Indian Soc. Avocations: art; music. Home: PO Box 1602 Bixby Hereford Co Glenrock WY 82637 Office: Bunn & Assocs 506 W Birch St Glenrock WY 82637

BUNN, ROBERT BURGESS, lawyer; b. Boise, Idaho, May 31, 1933; s. Marion Roy and Lois Lucile (Burgess) Bunn; m. Frances Patten Bull, Sept. 12, 1959; children—Carolyn B., F. Robin, Andrew R., Kathryn B. A.B., Harvard U., 1955, LL.B., 1961. Bar: Hawaii 1961, U.S. Dist. Ct. Hawaii 1961, U.S. Ct. Appeals (9th cir.) 1968, U.S. Supreme Ct. 1973. Ptnr., Cades, Schutte, Fleming & Wright, Honolulu, 1961—. Counsel, Honolulu Symphony Soc., 1974-80; counsel Hawaii Opera Theatre, Honolulu, 1980-82, pres., 1982-86 . Served to lt. USN, 1958-61. Mem. ABA, Hawaii Bar Assn. Club: Pacific (Honolulu). Home: 2493 Makiki Heights Dr Honolulu HI 96822 Office: Cades Schutte Fleming & Wright PO Box 939 Honolulu HI 96808

BUNNETT, JOSEPH FREDERICK, chemist, educator; b. Portland, Oreg., Nov. 26, 1921; s. Joseph and Louise Helen (Boulan) B.; m. Sara Anne Telfer, Aug. 22, 1942; children—Alfred Boulan, David Telfer, Peter Sylvester (dec. Sept. 1972). B.A., Reed Coll., 1942; Ph.D., U. Rochester, 1945. Mem. faculty Reed Coll., 1946-52, U. N.C., 1952-58; mem. faculty Brown U., 1958-66, prof. chemistry, 1959-66, chmn. dept., 1961-64; prof. chemistry U. Calif. at Santa Cruz, 1966—; Erskine vis. fellow U. Canterbury, N.Z., 1967; vis. prof. U. Wash., 1956, U. Würzburg, Germany, 1974; research fellow Japan Soc. for Promotion of Sci., 1979; Lady Davis vis. prof. Hebrew U., Jerusalem, Israel, 1981; mem. adv. council chemistry dept. Princeton U. Contbr. articles to profl. jours. Trustee Reed Coll., Societá Chimica Italiana (hon.). Fulbright scholar Univ. Coll., London, Eng., 1949-50; Guggenheim fellow, Fulbright scholar U. Munich, Germany, 1960-61. Fellow AAAS; mem. Am. Acad. Arts and Scis., Am. Chem. Soc. (editor jour. Accounts of Chem. Research 1966-86), Chem. Soc. (London), Internat. Union Pure and Applied Chemistry (chmn. commn. on phys. organic chemistry 1978-83, sec. organic chemistry div. 1981-83, v.p. 1983-85, pres. 1985-87; mem. Bur.), Pharm. Soc. Japan (hon.). Home: 608 Arroyo Seco Santa Cruz CA 95060 Office: U of California Santa Cruz CA 95064

BUNTING, DAVID RABE, real estate broker, civil engineer, land surveyor; b. Quincy, Ill., Nov. 3, 1938; s. Robert Russell and Lydia Frederika (Rabe) B.; m. Gloria May Poole, June 2, 1976. Student U. Ill., 1956-59, U. Wash., 1960-63. Registered profl. land surveyor, Wash., Oreg.; registered profl. engr., Wash. Oreg.; lic. real estate broker, Wash. Project engr. U.S. Forest Service, Gifford Pinchot Nat. Forest, Packwood and Randle, Wash., 1959-72; owner and prin. engr. and surveyor D. R. Bunting & Assocs., Cons. Engrs. & Land Surveyors, Packwood, 1969—; designated broker Ethel White Real Estate, Packwood, 1973-85; owner, broker Dave Bunting Realty, 1985—. Mem. Wash. Senate ad hoc com. on geol. hazards in State of Wash., 1974; past pres., sec., treas., and chmn. bd. Packwood Improvement Club; chmn. Lewis County Planning Com.; coordinator Boy Scouts Am., 1980—. Served with Army N.G., 1962-64. Mem. Land Surveyors Assn. of Wash., Sigma Phi Delta. Republican. Presbyterian (elder). Office: PO Box 435 13053 US Hwy 12 Packwood WA 98361

BUNTING, SUSAN, audiologist, speech pathologist; b. Wilmington, Del., Mar. 22, 1957; d. William Wallar and Marjorie Mae (Flores) B. BA, U. Mont., 1979, MA, 1982. Dir. Camp Horizons program U. Mont., Missoula, 1977-79; pediatric audiologist, speech pathologist Children's Hosp., Denver, 1981-82; audioloist, counselor rehab. Aurora (Colo.) Sch. Dist., 1982-83; speech pathologist, audiologist, coordinator infant learning Northwest Arctic Dist., Kotzebue, Alaska, 1983-84; SE regional audiologist State of Alaska, Sitka, 1984—; instr. Islands Community Coll., Sitka, 1986—; cons. Sitka Community Hosp., 1985—, Com. High Risk Infants, Anchorage, 1985—, Vision/Hearing State Program, Anchorage, 1984-85. Author (manual) Identification Audiometry, 1985. Cons. Alaska Senate Fin. Com., Juneau, 1985-86; active Parents Assn. for Children in Need, Sitka. Epilepsy Found. scholar, Missoula, 1978. Mem. Am. Speech Lang. Hearing Assn. (cert.), Am. Auditory Soc., Alaska Speech Lang. Hearing Assn. (sec. 1984—, chmn. ethics and practices com. 1984—, continuing edn. com. 1983-85), Kappa Kappa Gamma (chmn. by-lays com. 1978, social com. 1978, fraternity edn. com. 1979). Avocations: classical ballet, dance, collecting Native Am. art and artifacts, fly fishing. Office: Alaska Regional Audiology Program 222 Tongass Ave Sitka AK 99835

BUNTON, CLIFFORD ALLEN, chemist, educator; b. Chesterfield, Eng., Jan. 4, 1920; came to U.S., 1963, naturalized, 1978; s. Arthur and Edith (Kirk) B.; m. Ethel Clayton, July 28, 1945; children—Julia Margaret, Claire Jennifer. B.Sc., Univ. Coll., London, 1941, Ph.D., 1945; hon. degree, U. Perugia, Italy, 1986. Successively asst. lectr., lectr., reader Univ. Coll., 1944-63; prof. chemistry U. Calif. at Santa Barbara, 1963—, chmn. dept., 1967-72; Commonwealth Fund fellow U. Columbia, 1948-49; Brit. Council vis. lectr., Chile and Argentina, 1960; vis. prof. U. Calif. at Los Angeles, 1961, U. Toronto, 1962, U. Sao Paolo, Brazil, 1973, U. Lausanne, Switzerland, 1976, 79; Mem. policy com. U. Chile-U. Calif. Coop. Program, chmn. sci. and engring. sub-com., 1969—. Contbr. articles to profl. jours. Fellow AAAS; mem. N.Y. Acad. Sci., Am. Chem. Soc., Chem. Soc. (London); corr. mem. Chilean Acad. Scis. (1974). Home: 935 Cocopah Dr Santa Barbara CA 93110

BUNTON, JACK HOWARD, automotive executive; b. Havre, Mont., Sept. 18, 1941; s. June (Whipple) B.; m. Carol Annett House, Oct. 10, 1959 (div. Feb. 1982); children: Greg, Cindy, Scott, Stacy. Apprentice mechanic Olsen's Garage, Havre, 1953-59; apprentice machinist Vally Motors, Havre, 1959-65; machinist Auto Parts Co., Spokane, Wash., 1965-75; pres. Ram Remanufacturing and Distbg. Inc., Spokane, 1975—. Mem. Spokane C. of C., Nat. Fedn. of Ind. Bus., Automotive Engine Rebuilders Methods Com., Prodn. Engine Rebuilders Mktg. Com., Washington Assn. Rebuilders Mktg. Com., Pacific N.W. Speakers Assn., Nat. Speakers Assn., Wash. Automotive Wholesalers Assn., U.S. C. of C., Ind. Bus. Assn. Wash., Assn. Builders and Contractors. Clubs: Newcomers (Exton, Pa.), Police Guild, Toastmasters. Lodge: Elks, Eagles. Avocations: speaking, flying.

BURAS, NATHAN, hydrology and water resources educator; b. Barlad, Romania, Aug. 23, 1921; came to U.S., 1947; s. Boris and Ethel (Weiser) B.; m. Netty Stivel, Apr. 13, 1951; 1 child, Nir H. BS with highest honors, U. Calif., Berkeley, 1949; MS, Technion, Haifa, Israel, 1957; PhD, UCLA, 1962. Registered profl. engr., Israel. Prof. hydrology and water resources Technion, 1962-80, dean, 1966-68; vis. prof. Stanford (Calif.) U., 1976-81; prof., head dept. hydrology and water resources U. Ariz., Tucson, 1981—; cons. Tahal, Ltd., Tel Aviv, 1963-73, World Bank, Washington, 1972-76, 79-81. Author: Scientific Allocation of Water Resources, 1972; editor: Control of Water Resources Systems, 1976. Mem. Israel-Mex. Mixed Commn. on Sci. Cooperation, 1976, So. Ariz. Water Resource Assn., 1982—. Named Laureat du Congres, Internat. Assn. Agrl. Engring., 1964; recipient Cert. of Appreciation, USDA., 1970. Fellow ASCE; mem. Am. Geophys. Union, Am. Water Resources Assn. (charter). Jewish. Avocations: music, hiking. Home: 625 N Van Buren Ave #216 Tucson AZ 85711 Office: U Ariz Dept Hydrology & Water Resources Tucson AZ 85721

BURBIDGE, GEOFFREY, astrophysicist, educator; b. Chipping Norton, Oxon, Eng., Sept. 24, 1925; s. Leslie and Eveline B.; m. Margaret Peachey, 1948; 1 dau. B.Sc. with spl. honors in Physics, Bristol U., 1946; Ph.D., U. Coll., London, 1951. Asst. lectr. U. Coll., London, 1950-51; Agassiz fellow Harvard, 1951-52; research fellow U. Chgo., 1952-53, Cavendish Lab., Cambridge, Eng., 1953-55; Carnegie fellow Mt. Wilson and Palomar Obs., Calif. Inst. Tech., 1955-57; asst. prof. dept. astronomy U. Chgo., 1957-58, assoc. prof., 1958-62; assoc. prof. U. Calif.-San Diego, La Jolla, 1962-63; prof. physics U. Calif.-San Diego, 1963-83; dir. Kitt Peak Nat. Obs., Tucson, 1978-84; Phillips vis. prof. Harvard U., 1968; bd. dirs. Associated Univs. Research in Astronomy, 1971-74; trustee Associated Univs., Inc., 1973-82. Author: (with Margaret Burbidge) Quasi-Stellar Objects, 1967; Contbr. (with Margaret Burbidge) articles to sci. jours. Fellow Royal Soc. London, Am. Acad. Arts and Scis., Royal Astron. Soc.; mem. Am. Phys. Soc., Am. Astron. Soc., Internat. Astron. Union, Astron. Soc. of Pacific (pres. 1974-76). Office: Ctr for Astrophys Space Scis C-011 Univ of Calif San Diego La Jolla CA 92093

BURCAW, GEORGE ELLIS, museum director, educator; b. Houston, July 13, 1921; s. George Henry and Mary Elizabeth (Ellis) B.; m. Susan Straight, June 24, 1961 (div.); children—Geordi Elizabeth, Geoffrey George; B.A., Maryville Coll., 1943; M.A., U. Idaho, 1973; postgrad. U. Chgo., 1946-48, U. Ariz., 1949-50, U. Paris, 1951-52, U. Wis., 1956—, U. Pa., 1960—. Mus. dir. Neville Pub. Mus., Green Bay, Wis., 1952-58; chief curator Comml. Mus., Phila., 1958-62; curator State Museums Colo., Denver, 1962-66; dir. mus., chmn. mus. studies, prof. museology, prof. anthropology U. Idaho, Moscow, 1966—; archaeologist Smithsonian Instn., 1950, Am. Found. Study of Man, 1950-51, New World Archaeol. Found., 1956. Bd. dirs. Appaloosa Horse Club Mus., 1979—. Served to 1st lt. USMC, 1942-46. Mem. Internat. Council Mus. (mus. tng. com., museology com.), Am. Assn. Mus. (sr. examiner accreditation commn.), Am. Assn. State and Local History (mem. consultation bd.), Western Museums Conf., Sigma Xi, Phi Alpha Theta, Beta Theta Pi, Phi Kappa Phi. Author: Directory of Museum Training, 1971; Introduction to Museum Work, 1975; The Saxon House: A Cultural Index in European Ethnography, 1979; mem. editorial bd. Mus. Studies Jour., 1982—; contbr. articles in field to mus. jours. Office: U Idaho Mus Moscow ID 83843

BURCH, JAY DORRANCE, physics research; b. Modesto, Calif., Aug. 25, 1944; s. Hamlin Doughty and Bernia (Ingers) B.; m. Glenda Marie Russel, Aug. 11, 1968 (div. 1972); 1 child, Shana. BS in Physics, St. Mary's Coll. of Calif., 1967; PhD, U. Colo., 1977. Instr. physics Colo. Sch. Mines, Golden, 1979-80; physicist Solar Energy Researh Inst., Golden, 1980—. Mem. Am. Phys. Soc., Am. Solar Energy Soc. Home: 620 S 46th St Boulder CO 80303 Office: Solar Energy Research Inst 1617 Cole Blvd Golden CO 80401

BURCH, KARL DOUGLAS, organization development and training consultant; b. Lorain, Ohio, Nov. 28, 1948; s. Kenneth Edward and Gloria Lorraine (Wilson) B.; m. Marilyn Cleary, June 23, 1972; children—Merideth, Jessica. Student Bowling Green State U., 1967-70; B.S. cum laude, Ohio State U., 1974, M.S., 1976. Researcher Ohio Biol. Survey, Columbus 1975-76; county extension agt. Coop. Extension Service, Canton, Ohio, 1976-79; community relations mgr. Weyerhaeuser Co., Chehalis, Wash., 1979-82, region tng. cons., Federal Way, 1982-84; orgn. devel. cons. Wash. Water Power, Spokane, 1984—. Campaign co-chmn., v.p. United Way Lewis County, 1980-82. Recipient Leadership award United Way, 1980, 81, 4-H, 1978; grantee Ohio Biol. Survey, 1975; Outstanding Hawaii Outrigger Canoe paddler, 1971. Mem. Am. Soc. Tng. and Devel., Chehalis C. of C. (dir. 1981-82). Club: Rotary.

BURCH, PAUL GILSON, mechanical engineer; b. Queens, N.Y., Sept. 30, 1954; s. Wesley Parker and Patricia Moana (Smythe) B.; m. Ann Stuart Herrmann, June 24, 1977; children: Stephen Wesley, Emily Stuart. BS in Marine Engring., U.S. Mcht. Marine Acad., 1976. Field service engr. Babcock & Wilcox Co., Chgo., 1976-80; contract mgr. Barberton, Ohio, 1980-83; product mgr. Babcock & Wilcox Constrn. Co., Barberton, Ohio, 1984-86; resident engr. San Francisco, 1984-85, Walnut Creek, Calif., 1986—; cons. B&W/Pacific G&E, San Francisco, 1983-84; devel. engr. cyclone fired furnace redesign. Mem. Am. Soc. Mech. Engrs. Republican. Lutheran. Avocations: computer programming, sailing, golf.

BURCHAM, LEVI TURNER, ecologist, geographer; b. Ronda, N.C., May 30, 1912; s. James Avery and Della (Smoot) B.; m. Miriam Lee Parsons, Jan. 7, 1942; children: Arthur Forrest, Charles Lee. BS, U. Calif., Berkeley, 1941, PhD, 1956; MS, U. Nebr., 1950. Range examiner U.S. Dept. Interior, Reno, Nev., 1941-42; forester Calif. Dept. Forestry, Fresno, 1947-48; forester Calif. Dept. Forestry, Sacramento, 1948-56, asst. dep. state forester, 1956-64, 66-75; cons. forestry, ecology and geography, 1976, also cons. and lectr. in field; environ. scis. adviser Office of Sec. Def., Advanced Research Projects Agy., Wash., 1964-66. Contbr. articles to profl. pubs. Served with USMC, 1933-37, to capt. USMCR, 1942-46. Mem. AAAS, Am. Geog. Soc., Calif. Acad. Scis. (life), Ecol. Soc. Am., Soc. Am. Foresters, Soc. Range Mgmt. (life), Wildlife Soc. Home: 4701 Crestwood Way Sacramento CA 95822

BURCK, PATRICIA ANN, metallurgical engineer; b. Houston, June 18, 1953; d. Elza Vance and Norma Patricia (Wilson) Bullock. BS in Zoology, Tex. A&M U., 1975; BS in Welding Engring., Letourneau Coll., 1980; MSMetE, Colo. Sch. Mines, 1984. Research, teaching asst. Colo. Sch. Mines, Golden, 1981-83; mfg. engr. Storage Tech. Corp., Louisville, Colo., 1983-85; metall. engr. Spectra-Physics, Eugene, Oreg., 1985—. Recipient Nat. Welding Design award James F. Lincoln Arc Welding Found., 1980; Research fellow Army Research Office, 1981-83. Mem. Am. Welding Soc. (speaker, 1982), Am. Soc. Metals (speaker 1981), Soc. Mfg. Engrs. (sr.). Avocations: gardening, bicycling, motorcycling. Home: 1420 Santa Rosa Eugene OR 97404 Office: Spectra-Physics 959 Terry St Eugene OR 97402

BURDETT, BENJAMIN WILLIAM, mining company executive; b. Salt Lake City, July 14, 1939; s. Benjamin and Wilma Maria (Salisbury) B.; m. Barbara Mae Hepworth, June 10, 1964; children: Brooke An, Barbi Lyn, Britta Kim, Brady Benjamin. BSEE, U. Utah, 1964, postgrad., 1975-76. Registered profl. engr., Calif. Process control engr. Inland Steel Co., East Chicago, Ind., 1964-69; sr. programmer Kennecott Computing Ctr., Salt Lake City, 1969-75; sr. prin. inst. engr. Kennecott Process Tech., Salt Lake City, 1975-86; supt. process control Utah Copper div. Kennecott, Bingham Canyon, Utah, 1986—; cons. Colmek Engring., Salt Lake City, 1977. Editor: Instruments in the Mining and Metallurgical Industry, 1981; contbr. articles to profl. jours. Dist. chmn. Utah Youth Soccer Assn., Salt Lake City, 1982-83; mem. Utah Youth Soccer Referee Assn./U.S. Soccer Fedn., 1983—. Served with USAR, 1957-64. Mem. Instrument Soc. Am. (bd. dirs. mining and metall. div. 1978—, dir. 1983-85), Soc. Mining Engrs. of AIME (ops. controls com. mem. 1985—). Mormon. Avocations: photography, jogging, soccer refereeing. Office: Kennecott Utah Copper Div 8362 W 10200 S Bingham Canyon UT 84006-0525

BURDITT, ARTHUR KENDALL, JR., entomologist; b. Elizabeth, N.J., Feb. 12, 1928; s. Arthur Kendall and Hazel (Howard) B.; m. Jeane Josephine McComber, Oct. 18, 1952; children: Arthur, Janet, Nancy, Betty. BS in Agriculture, Rutgers U., 1950; MS in Entomology, U. Minn., 1953, PhD, 1955. Asst. prof. entomology U. Mo., Columbia, 1955-57; research entomologist USDA, Honolulu, 1957-60, Orlando, Fla., 1960-64, Beltsville, Md., 1964-72, Miami, Fla., 1972-80, Yakima, Wash., 1980—; adj. prof. U. Fla., 1972-81; courtesy entomologist Wash. State U., 1981—; cons. IAEA, Vienna, Austria, 1981—, AID, Washington, 1984-85. Recipient Outstanding Performance award USDA, 1958, Certs. Merit, USDA, 1980, 82, Resolution Appreciation award Fla. Citrus Commn., 1975. Fellow AAAS, Entomol. Soc. Am., Sigma Xi. Home: 5607 Englewood Ave Yakima WA 98908 Office: Yakima Agrl Research Lab 3706 W Nob Hill Blvd Yakima WA 98902

BURG, GERALD WILLIAM, temple administrator; b. Pitts., Oct. 16, 1923; s. Julius Samuel and Anna (Shapiro) B.; student Walsh Inst., 1940-43; m. Flavia Kafton, Aug. 12, 1945; children—Cindy, Melinda, Andrew. Engring. rep. U.S. Rubber Co., 1943-45; adminstr. Beverly Hills (Calif.) B'nai B'rith, 1945-52, Univ. Synagogue, Brentwood, 1952-55; exec. dir. Wilshire Blvd. Temple, Los Angeles, 1956-80; mgmt. and fin. cons., 1980-85; admisntr. Sinai Temple, 1985—. Mem. Jewish relations com. Los Angeles council Boy Scouts Am., 1959-85; mem. Mayor's Adv. Com. on Community Activities, Los Angeles, 1963-73; chmn. Crime Prevention Fifth Councilmanic Dist., Los Angeles, 1968-73. Bd. dirs. McCobb Home for Boys, Los Angeles Psychiat. Service, Maple Ctr. for Crises Intervention, Save a Heart Found., Didi Hirsch Community Mental Health Services, pres., 1975-77; bd. dirs., chmn. finances, chmn. adminstrv. com. Community Care and Devel. Services, 1975—. Mem. Nat. (bd. dir., pres. 1975-77), Western (pres. 1969-71, bd. dirs.), So. Calif. (pres. 1958-60) assns. temple adminstrs., NCCJ (bd. dirs. brotherhood anytown 1966-82), Los Angeles Jewish Communal Execs. (dir.). Mem. B'nai B'rith (youth dir. 1945-82, Akiba award 1950, Beverly Hills pres. 1953-54). Club: Sertoma (v.p. 1973-82). Home: 141 N La Peer Dr Beverly Hills CA 90011 Office: Sinai Temple 427 N Canon Dr Beverly Hills CA 90210

BURG, MACLYN PHILIP, historian, educator; b. Hoquiam, Wash., Jan. 30, 1927; s. LeRoy Peter and Beatrice Norma (McKay) B.; m. Patricia Ann Kelsey, Aug. 26, 1950; children—Jacquelyn, Kerry, Alan, Scott. B.A., U. Wash., 1951, M.A., 1967, Ph.D., 1971. Tchr., Longview pub. schs., Wash., 1951-65, instr. U. Wash., Seattle, 1966-70; oral historian Dwight D. Eisenhower Library, Abilene, Kans., 1970-80; spl. asst. to chmn. dept. history U. Wash., Seattle, 1980—; lectr. Am. sect. Inst. Gen. History, Acad. of Scis., USSR, 1973; asst. dir. NDEA Summer Inst., U. Wash., 1966, 68; rapporteur gen. oral history session XV Internat. Congress Hist. Scis., Bucharest, 1980. Contbr. articles to profl. jours.; mem. editorial bd. Oral History Rev., 1974-78. Served with U.S. Army, 1945-46. Mem. Orgn. Am. Historians, Am. Hist. Assn., Oral History Assn. (bd. cons. 1977—), Assn. Wash. Historians (bd. dirs. 1984—), Royal Norfolk Regiment Assn. (hon.), Japanese Sword Soc. U.S. (bd. dirs. 1984—), Soc. for Preservation Japanese Art Sword, Phi Alpha Theta. Home: 10120 NE 68th St Apt D-202 Kirkland WA 98033 Office: Dept History DP-20 U Wash Seattle WA 98195

BURGE, DR. JOHN H., criminology researcher, educator; b. Glendale, Calif., Jan. 13, 1949; s. Eugene Field Burge and Elizabeth Ada (Johnson) Greenman; m. Anja Laitinew, Aug. 15, 1970; children: Anna Maria, Erika Michele. AA, Pasadena City Coll., 1972; BS, U. Calif., Fresno, 1975, MS, 1979; EdD, U. of the Pacific, 1984. Recording artist Dot, Decca and LHI records, Hollywood, Calif., 1964-69; dep. sheriff Fresno County, Calif., 1972-84; prof. criminology Calif. State U., Fresno, 1984—; asst. dir. Criminal Justice Ctr., Fresno, 1984; research adv. Calif. Commn. of Peace Officers Standards and Tng., Sacramento, 1985; cons. Royal Hong King Police, 1986, Thammiset U., Bangkok, 1986. Author: Occupational Stress in Policing, 1984; artist, producer numerous records, 1964-69. Recipient Randolph Lovelace Meml. award Air Force Assn., Washington, 1975. Mem. Retired Peace Officers Assn., Nat. Acad. of Recording Arts and Scis., Nat. Mil. Intelligence Assn. Avocations: camping, travel. Office: Calif State U Dept Criminology Fresno CA 93740

BURGES, STEPHEN JOHN, civil engineer; b. Newcastle, Australia, Aug. 26, 1944. BS, BE with honors, U. Newcastle, Australia, 1967; MS, Stanford U., 1968, PhD, 1970. Registered profl. engr., Wash. Asst. prof. U. Wash., Seattle, 1970-75, assoc. prof., 1975-79, prof. civil engring., 1979—. Contbr. articles to profl. jours. Fulbright-Hays Travel grantee, 1967. Mem. AAAS, Am. Soc. Civil Engrs., Am. Geophys. Union (editor Water Resources Research jour. 1981-84, editor Water Resources Monographs 1984-86), Am. Water Resources Assn., U.S. Nat. Research Council (water sci. tech. bd. 1985—), Internat. Assn. Hydraulic Research, Sigma Xi. Home: 4306 54th Ave NE Seattle WA 98105 Office: U Wash Dept Civil Engring FX-10 Seattle WA 98195

BURGESS, JOSEPH WESLEY, metall. engr., photographer; b. St. Louis, Nov. 27, 1910; s. Joseph Francis and Amanda (Woodrome) B.; B.S. in Civil Engring., Washington U., St. Louis, 1932; m. Dorothea Ines Nelson, Mar. 5, 1941; children—Joseph Wesley, Sarah Jane. Trainee, Shell Pipe Line Corp., Kilgore, Tex., 1933-35, asst. div. supt., Tex., N.Mex., St. Louis, 1935-39; mgr. products pipe line dept. Shell Oil Co., N.Y.C., 1939-41; chief engr., gen. supt. Am. Zinc Co. of Ill., Dumas, Tex., 1941-59; gen. mgr. constrn. Uranium Reduction Co., Salt Lake City, Moab, Utah, 1955-59; chief engr. Am. Zinc Co., St. Louis, 1959-71; mgr. project engring. Fluor Utah, Inc., San Mateo, Calif. 1971-73, v.p. engring., 1973, v.p. project mgmt., 1974-76; ret., 1976; cons., 1976—, photographer, 1977—; photographs exhibited in one-man shows including: San Jose (Calif.) Mus. Art, 1980, Stanford U. Faculty Club, Palo Alto, Calif., 1981; group shows include: Olive Hyde Art Gallery, Fremont, Calif., 1977, Atkinson Art Gallery, Santa Barbara, Calif., 1978, Tower Art Gallery, Berkeley, Calif., 1979, Internat. Exhbn. of Photography, Adelaide, Australia, 1980, Westwood Arts Nat. Photog.

Exhbn., Los Angeles, 1980, others. Registered profl. engr., Tex. Mem. Am. Inst. Mining, Metall. and Petroleum Engrs., Nat., Calif. socs. profl. engrs., Mo. Hist. Soc., Calif. Hist. Soc., Am. Rose Soc., Sigma Xi, Tau Beta Pi. Co-author: European Zinc Smelters, 1964; contbr. articles to profl. jours. Home: 1178 Hamilton Ave Palo Alto CA 94301

BURGESS, KIMBERLY GORDON, social worker, consultant; b. Santa Monica, Calif., June 29, 1957; d. Austin Pierre and Dorothy Evelyn (Jackson) Gordon; m. Thomas Burgess, Nov. 12 , 1980. AA, Santa Barbara City Coll., 1977; BA, San Jose State U., 1979; MSW, Portland State U., 1983. Registered clin. social worker, Oreg. Clin. social worker, mental health specialistin treatment of co-existing psychiat. and chemically dependent disorders Benton County Mental Health, Corvallis, Oreg., 1983—; trainer Wash. County Mental Health, Hillsboro, Oreg., 1985, Ethnic Minorities Conf., Portland, 1985, Mental Health Dirs. Spring Conf., Salishan, Oreg., 1986. Pres.'s scholar San Jose State U., 1979, Dean's scholar, 1978. Mem. Nat. Assn. Social Workers. Democrat. Avocations: gardening, camping, travel, skiing, softball. Office: Benton County Mental Health 530 NW 27th Corvallis OR 97330

BURGESS, LEONARD RANDOLPH, business administration and economics educator, writer; b. Washington, Mar. 8, 1919; s. W. Randolph and May Ayres B.; m. Virginia Frost, May 26, 1946 (dec. Feb. 1978); m. Marga Minnick, Dec. 26, 1979 (div. 1983); m. Hyon Suk Kim, Dec. 30, 1983. B.A., Brown U., 1942; M.B.A., Harvard U., 1947; Ph.D., Columbia U., 1961. Chief statistician W.Va. Pulp and Paper Co., N.Y.C., 1947-52; sr. staff assoc. Nat. Indsl. Conf. Bd., N.Y.C., 1952-57; lectr., instr. CCNY, N.Y.C., 1958-59; asst. prof. N. Tex. State U., Denton, 1961-64; assoc. prof. Tex. A & M U., College Station, 1964-68; prof. Tex. A & M U., 1968-73, Temple U., Phila., 1973-74, U. Del., Wilmington, 1974-75; lectr. San Francisco State U., 1975-78; prof. Lincoln U., San Francisco, 1978—; head dept. bus. adminstrn. and econs. Lincoln U., 1981—; mem. Lang Research Inc., Cambridge, Mass., 1961-76; pres. Su-Len Corp., 1984—. Author: (with Malcolm C. Neuhoff) Managing Company Airplanes, 1954, Top Executive Pay Package, 1963, Wage and Salary Administration in a Dynamic Economy, 1968, Wage and Salary Administration: Pay and Benefits, 1984; contbr. articles to profl. jours. Staff asst. Brazos County Community Action Com., Tex., 1966-72, Brazos Valley Community Action Program, 1972-73. Served with U.S. Army, 1941-45 lt col. Res. Decorated Purple Heart. Mem. Acad. Mgmt., Acad. Polit. Sci., AAUP, Am. Compensation Assn., Harvard Bus. Sch. Assn. No. Calif. (Writer's Connection No. Calif. chpt.), Delta Upsilon. Club: Presidio Officers. Home: 899 Crestview Dr San Carlos CA 94070 Office: Lincoln U Coll of Grad/Undergrad Studies 281 Masonic Ave San Francisco CA 94118

BURGESS, MARTHA AMES, naturalist, ethnobotanist, writer; b. Washington, Nov. 27, 1945; d. Robert Hyde and Virginia Dunbar (Wade) Ames; m. Tony Lambard Burgess, Aug. 4, 1979; 1 child, Beauregard Ames. BA in Geology, Brown U., 1967; MS in Dendrochronology, U. Ariz., 1972. Archaeologist U. Ariz. and Mus. No. Ariz., Tucson and Flagstaff, Ariz., summers 1967-71; dendrochronologist Lab. Tree-Ring Research, U. Ariz., Tucson, 1967-75; expedition leader Ariz.-Sonora Desert Mus., Tucson, 1975-85; freelance writer on natural history Tucson, 1985—. Edn. dir., bd. dirs. Native Seeds/SEARCH, Tucson, 1984—; vol. Ariz.-Sonora Desert Mus., 1985—. Mem. Tree-Ring Soc., Ariz. Native Plant Soc. (bd. dirs. 1983-84, 86—), Boyce Thompson Southwest Arboretum, Desert Bot. Garden, Tucson Bot. Garden (vol. 1985—), Mus. No. Ariz. Republican. Episcopalian. Avocations: plant photography, whale watching, camping, exploration.

BURGESS, MICHAEL, librarian, author; b. Fukuoka, Kyushu, Japan, Feb. 11, 1948; came to U.S., 1949; s. Roy Walter and Betty Jane (Kapel) B.; m. Mary Alice Wickizer, Oct. 15, 1976; stepchildren—Richard Albert Rogers, Mary Louise Reynnells. AB with honors, Gonzaga U., 1969; MS in Library Sci., U. So. Calif., 1970. Periodicals librarian Calif. State U.-San Bernardino, 1970-81, chief cataloger, 1981-86, prof. and head collectiondevel., 1986—; editor Newcastle Pub. Co., North Hollywood, Calif., 1971—, publisher Borgo Press, San Bernardino, 1975—; adv. editor Arno Press, N.Y.C., 1975-78. Author 50 books, including: Cumulative Paperback Index, 1973, Things to Come, 1977, Science Fiction and Fantasy Literature, 1979, Tempest in a Teapot, 1984, Lords Temporal & Lords Spiritual, 1985, Futurevisions, 1985; editor 15 sholarly series, including Milford Series: Popular Writers of Today (40 vols.), Science Fiction (63 vols.), Stokvis Studies in Historical Chronology and Thought (10 vols.), editor 6 reprint series, 2 jours.; author over 100 articles. Named Title II fellow U. So. Calif., 1969-70. Mem. NEA, AAUP, Calif. Tchrs. Assn., Kent Hist. Soc., Sci. Fiction Writers Am., Calif. Faculty Assn., Sci. Fiction Research Assn. Home: PO Box 2845 San Bernardino CA 92407 Office: Calif State U Library 5500 University Pkwy San Bernardino CA 92407

BURGESS, NORMAN ELVIN, conservatory administrator, educator, musician; b. Spiritwood, Sask., Can., Dec. 31, 1946; s. Peter Robert and Mary Elizabeth (Gingara) B.; m. Joan Elizabeth Barrett, Feb. 20, 1971; 1 child, Gordon Robert. BEd with distinction, U. Sask., 1966; MusMEd, Ind. U., 1969, MusDEd with high distinction, 1974. Cert. tchr., Sask. Dir. music Sheldon-Williams Collegiate, Regina, Sask., 1969-71; asst. prof. Empria State U., Kans., 1973-75; coordinator strings Conservatory of Music and Speech Arts, Mt. Royal Coll., Calgary, Alta., 1975-76, asst. dir., 1976-77, dir., 1977—; asst. concertmaster Regina Symphony, 1969-71; clinician String Pedagogy, Fiddling Instructional Tech. Workshops, 1974—; condr. Jr. Orch., 1986-87, Calgary Fiddlers, 1981—; cons. in field. Bd. dirs. Calgary Philharmon. Orch., 1978—; mem. 1988 Olympics Music Subcom.; pilot Civil Aviation Rescue and Emergency Services, Calgary, 1983—. Mem. Can. String Tchrs. Assn. (v.p. region 1977—), Assn. Colls. and Conservatories of Music (v.p. 1981—), Am. String Tchrs. Assn., Music Educators Nat. Conf., Can. Registered Music Tchrs. Assn., Can. Music Educators Assn. Club: Calgary Flying. Office: Mount Royal Coll, Conservatory of Music and Speech Arts, 4825 Richard Rd SW, Calgary, AB Canada T3E 6K6

BURGESS, WILLIAM VANDER, education educator; b. Brownfield, Ill., June 5, 1934; s. Felix Siegfried and Verna Gertrude (Stockdale) B.; m. Mary Etta Layman, Aug. 20, 1961; children: Eric, Sara, Brian. BS, U. Ill., 1955; MS, So. Ill. U., 1962; PhD, U. Calif., Berkeley, 1970. Cert. nurseryman, Calif. Tchr. agr. Rosiclare (Ill.) High Sch., 1955-56, St. Francisville (Ill.) High Sch., 1960-63, Mt. Auburn (Ill.) High Sch., 1963-64; supt. schs. Mt. Auburn Unit Dist., 1964-65; prof. edn. U. San Francisco, 1968—, dir. secondary tchr. internship, 1971-73, dean summer session and spl. programs, 1973-75, chmn. dept. orgn. and leadership, 1984-86, chmn. faculty council Sch. Edn., 1978-80, 84-86; pres. William V. Burgess & Assocs., San Ramon, Calif., 1983—. Editor: Current Issues in Organizational Leadership, 1983; co-editor: Handbook of High Speed Machining Technology, 1985. Arbitrator Better Bus. Bur., San Francisco, 1983—; docent Strybing Arboretum, San Francisco, 1982—. Served with U.S. Army, 1956-59. Grantee NSF, Washington, 1978, Calif. Community Colls., Sacramento, 1979. Mem. Phi Delta Kappa (pres. 1985-86, Service award 1986). Democrat. Avocations: piano, camping. Home: 9593 Davona Dr San Ramon CA 94583 Office: U San Francisco Dept Edn Ignatiam Heights CA 94117

BURGHARDT, KURT JOSEF, marketing professional, infosystems specialist; b. Mainz, Fed. Republic of Germany, June 8, 1935; came to U.S., 1957; s. Karl Franz and Aenne Elizabeth (Lohr) B.; m. Alison Gertrude Koch, Dec. 9, 1980; children: Lars, Kristina. Student, U. Frankfurt, Fed. Republic of Germany, 1956-57; BBA, U. Wis., 1957, MBA, 1960. Mgmt. trainee A.C. Nielsen, Chgo., 1960-62, asst. to pres., 1962-66; nat. sales mgr., v.p. Neodata Services, Boulder, Colo., 1966-76, exec. v.p., div. mgr., 1976-77, pres., 1977—; also chmn. bd. dirs., exec. v.p. Neodata Services, Boulder and Louisville, Colo.; bd. dirs. 1st Nat. Bank, Boulder. Pres. and tenure mem. Philharm. Soc., Boulder; mem. endowment bd. dirs. Arts and Humanities Assembly of Boulder; active Boulder Econ. Council. Served with U.S. Army, 1960. Mem. Audit Bur. Circulation, Direct Mail Mktg. Assn., XYZ Club, City and Regional Mag. Assn., Boulder C. of C. (bd. dirs.), U. Colo. Relations Assn. (bd. dirs.), U. Colo. Accord Assn. (bd. dirs.), Phi Beta Kappa. Club: Boulder Country. Office: Neodata Services PO Box 4586 Boulder CO 80306

BURGIN, GEORGE HANS, computer scientist, educator; b. Liestal, Switzerland, Feb. 13, 1930; s. Jakob and Fanny B.; m. Ulrike Franziska, July 8, 1960; children: Bernard, Claudia, Paul. Diplom ingenieur, Swiss Fed. Inst. Tech., Zurich, 1953, PhD, 1961. Registered profl. engr., Calif. Design specialist Gen. Dynamics Corp., San Diego, 1962-64; sr. scientist Decision Sci., San Diego, 1964-82; chief scientist Titan Systems, San Diego, 1982—; lectr. San Diego State U., 1979—. Contbg. author: Simulation, 1968. Served to 1st lt. Swiss Army. Mem. IEEE, Assn. Computing Machinery, Soc. for Computer Simulation. Home: 6284 Avenida Cresta La Jolla CA 92037 Office: Titan Systems 9191 Towne Centre Dr San Diego CA 92122

BURK, JACK ANDREW, investment co. exec.; b. Springfield, Tenn., Mar. 19, 1935; s. Andrew Jackson and Elizabeth Ethelyne (Revels) B.; student Central Bible Inst., Springfield, Mo., 1953-54, So. Calif. Coll., Costa Mesa, 1955; student San Fernando Valley Coll., 1956; m. Alice Jean Jackson, Apr. 24, 1965; children—Teresa Lynn, Cheryl Ninette, Loren Dwayne. With Rocketdyne div. N. Am. Aviation Santa Susana Rocket Test sect., 1959-65; with Equity Funding Corp., 1965-73, area. v.p. So. Calif., Century City, 1970-71, v.p., resident mgr., Tarzana, Calif., 1972-73; founder, pres. Preferred Exec. Programs Inc., Woodland Hills, Calif., 1973-76; mem. adv. com. Am. Pacific Life Ins. Co., San Rafael, Calif., 1973-77; dir. bus. affairs Peoples Found., Fresno, Calif., 1977-84; gen. mgr. PF Communications Inc., Fresno, 1979-84; mgmt. cons. TV stas. and prodn. facilities, 1984-85; dist. sales mgr., Omega Video, Inc., Lawndale, Calif., 1985—. Mem. Nat. Assn. Securities Dealers, Nat. Assn. Life Underwriters, Internat. Assn. Fin. Planners. Republican. Home: 9391 E Ellery Clovis CA 93612

BURKE, ARTHUR THOMAS, engineering consultant; b. Pueblo, Colo., Nov. 26, 1919; s. Daniel Michael and Naomi Edith (Brashear) B.; B.S., U.S. Naval Acad., 1941; postgrad. UCLA; m. Regina Ahlgren Malone, June 15, 1972; children—Arthur Thomas, Craig Timothy, Laura Ahlgren, Scott Ahlgren. With USN Electronics Lab. Center, San Diego, 1947-72, sr. satellite communications cons., 1964-72, satellite communications engrng. cons., 1974—. Judge, San Diego Sci. Fair, 1960—. Served with USN, 1938-46; comdr. Res., ret. Recipient Superior Performance award USN Electronics Lab. Center, 1967. Mem. IEEE (mem. San Diego membership com. 1958-68), AAAS, San Diego Astronomy Assn., San Diego Computer Assn., Am. Radio Relay League. Patentee electronic bathythermograph. Home and Office: 4011 College Ave San Diego CA 92115

BURKE, DAVID JAMES, biochemist; b. McAllen, Tex., July 18, 1946; s. Cletus Reilly and Margaret Ann (Tallman) B.; m. Rae Lyn Conrad, June 23, 1972 (div. 1979); m. Paula Chi-Ting Li, Oct. 7, 1984. BS, U. Iowa, 1968; MS, U. Colo., 1974; PhD, SUNY, Stony Brook, 1976. Postdoctoral U. Calif., Berkeley, 1977-79, Lawrence Berkeley (Calif.) Lab., 1980-82; biochemist Bio-Rad Labs., Richmond, Calif., 1982-85, Xoma Corp., Berkeley, 1985—. Patentee in field; contbr. articles to profl. jours. Mem. AAAS, Phi Beta Kappa. Democrat. Avocations: skiing, windsurfing, jogging. Office: Xoma Corp 2910 Seventh St Berkeley CA 94710

BURKE, E. JAMES, lawyer; b. Wilmington, Del., June 26, 1949; s. Earl J. Burke and Elizabeth M. (Glenn) Jones; m. Michele C. Haney, Aug. 16, 1975 (div. May 1981); 1 child, Erick; m. Linda G. Matthew, Apr. 15, 1982; children: Matthew, Leanna. BS in Psychology, St. Joseph's U., Phila., 1971; JD, U. Wyo., 1977. Bar: Wyo. 1977, U.S. Dist. Ct. Wyo. 1977, U.S. Ct. Appeals (10th cir.) 1981. Ptnr. Hanes & Burke P.C., Cheyenne, Wyo., 1977—. Served to 1st lt. USAF, 1971-74. Mem. Wyo. Bar Assn., Laramie County Bar Assn., Assn. Trial Lawyers Am. (state del. 1985—), Wyo. Trial Lawyers Assn. (bd. dirs. 1977—, pres. 1980), Western Trial Lawyers Assn. (bd. dirs. 1979—, pres. 1986—), Cheyenne C. of C. (leadership award 1986). Home: 7032 Valley View Pl Cheyenne WY 82009 Office: Hanes & Burke PC 1720 Carey Ave Cheyenne WY 82001

BURKE, JOHN JAMES, utility executive; b. Butte, Mont., July 25, 1928; m. Nancy M. Calvert, July 12, 1952; children: Cheryl Burke Harris, Mary Burke Orizotti, Kathleen, John James, III, Elisabeth. BS in Bus., BA in Law, U. Mont., 1950, J.D., 1952. Bar: Mont. 1952, U.S. Supreme Ct. 1957. Ptnr. Weir, Gough, Booth and Burke, Helena, 1954-59; atty. Mont. Power Co., Butte, 1959-67, v.p., 1967-78, exec. v.p., 1979-84, vice chmn. bd. dirs., 1984—; bd. dirs. Blue Cross/Blue Shield Mont. Trustee U. Mont. Found., Carroll Coll. Mont.; pres City-County Planning Bd., 1966078; past dir. Vigilante council Boy Scouts Am., Shining Mountains council Girl Scouts U.S.. Served to capt. JAGC, USAF, 1952-54, with Res. 1954-61. Mem. ABA (mem. council pub. utility law sect.), Silver Bow County Bar Assn., Mountain States Legal Found. (bd. dirs), Lazard Freres Spl. Equity Fund (bd. dirs.), Nat. Assn. Mfrs. (bd. dirs), Edison Electric Inst. (exec. adv. com. on planning), Butte C. of C. (v.p. 1965-72), U. Mont. Alumni Assn. (past bd. dirs.), Phi Delta Phi. Roman Catholic. Clubs: Montana, Butte Country, Elks, Rotary (sec. Helena 1955-58); 116 (Washington). Home: 50 Burning Tree Ln Butte MT 59701 Office: Mont Power Co 40 E Broadway Butte MT 59701

BURKE, JOHN PATRICK, internist, educator; b. Marshalltown, Iowa, Jan. 19, 1940; s. Raphael Eggleston and Marjorie N. (Busch) B.; m. Andrea Marie Keane, May 9, 1970; children—Paul, Matthew, Edward, Erin. B.A., U. Iowa, 1961, M.D., 1964. Diplomate Am. Bd. Internal Medicine. Intern Yale-New Haven Hosp., 1964-65, resident in medicine, 1965-67; research fellow Harvard med. unit Boston City Hosp., 1968-70; chief infectious disease sect. Latter-day Saints Hosp., Salt Lake City, 1970—; asst. prof. medicine U. Utah, Salt Lake City, 1970-75, assoc. prof., 1975-83, prof., 1983—; spl. reviewer NIH, Bethesda, Md., 1978, 80. Mem. editorial bd. Am. Jour. Infection Control, 1980—, Infection Control, 1979—. Contbr. numerous articles to med. jours., chpts. to books. Surgeon USPHS, 1967-70. NIH-Nat. Inst. Allergy and Infectious Disease grantee, 1974-79, 79-82, 83—. Fellow Infectious Disease Soc. Am., ACP; mem. Soc. Hosp. Epidemiologists Am. (councillor 1981-82, treas. 1985—), Utah Med. Assn. (del. 1975-77). Mem. Disciples of Christ Ch. Home: 1966 Yale Ave Salt Lake City UT 84108 Office: LDS Hosp Salt Lake City UT 84143

BURKE, KENNETH IBER, nutrition educator, researcher; b. Covert, Mich., Aug. 21, 1933; s. Lloyd Ernest and Nora Francis (McNeal) B.; m. Theresa Ann Cunningham, Aug. 14, 1960; children: Thomas Edward, Sabrina Kay, Susan Marie, Daniel Edward. BS in Chem., So. Missionary Coll., 1959; MEd in Natural Sci., Clemson U., 1963; PhD, Fla. State U., 1973. Assoc. prof. So. Missionary Coll., Collegedale, Tenn., 1972-74; chemist dept. agriculture State of Fla., Tallahassee, 1968-72; instr. So. Missionary Coll., Collegedale, Tenn., 1963-66; assoc. prof. Loma Linda (Calif.) U., 1974-83, prof. nutrition and dietetics, 1983—, assoc. chmn. dept. nutrition and dietetics, 1985—; cons. food industries, 1978—; chmn. mgmt. com. 1st Internat. Congress on Vegetarian Nutrition, Washington, 1987. Contbr. health and nutrition articles to profl. jours. Served as cpl. U.S. Army, 1953-55. Mem. Am. Dietetic Assn. (registered dietitian), Inst. Food Technologists (profl.), Calif. Dietetic Assn. (treas. Inland dist. 1979-82, rep. 1981-82, nominating com. 1982), Sigma Xi. Adventist. Avocations: running, swimming, cooking. Office: Loma Linda U Dept Nutrition Dietetics Loma Linda CA 92350

BURKE, LLOYD HUDSON, judge; b. Oakland, Calif., Apr. 1, 1916; s. James H. and Edna L. (Taylor) B.; m. Virginia Joan Kerchum, Apr. 27, 1941; children—Brian Hudson, Bruce Thomas. A.B., St. Mary's Coll., 1937; LL.B., U. Calif., 1940, J.D., 1972; LL.D., St. Mary's Coll. of Calif. Dep. dist. atty. Alameda County, Calif., 1940-53; sr. criminal trial dep. 1950-53, U.S. atty., 1953-58; U.S. dist. judge Northern Dist. Calif., 1958—. Served with U.S. Army, 1942-46; capt. Res., to 1951. Mem. Phi Delta Phi. Office: US Court House 450 Golden Gate Ave San Francisco CA 94102

BURKE, MICHAEL JOHN, academic dean, director of academic programs; b. Chgo., July 7, 1942; s. John J. and Rejean P. (Ough) B.; m. Mary Ellen Mueller, Aug. 4, 1964; children: Mara Jean, John Edmund. BA, Blackburn Coll., 1964; PhD, Iowa State U., 1969. Asst. prof. U. Minn., St. Paul, 1972-76; assoc. prof. Colo. State U., Ft. Collins, 1976-79; prof., chairperson U. Fla., Gainesville, 1979-84; assoc. dean Oreg. State U., Corvallis, 1984—; bd. dirs. E.R. Jackman Found., Agrl. Research Found. Recipient Hon. State Farmer degree Oreg. Future Farmers of Am., Salem, 1986. Mem. Am. Chem. Soc., Am. Soc. Hort. Sci. (Darrow award 1979), Am. Soc. Plant Physiologists, AAAS, Cryobiology Soc. Avocations: sailing, mountain climbing, hiking. Home: 3510 NW Dimple Hill Corvallis OR 97330 Office: Oreg State U Coll Agrl Sci Ag Hall 137 Corvallis OR 97331-2202

BURKE, RICHARD JAMES, legal administrator; b. Mpls., June 4, 1949; s. George Ivan and BettyJo (Balcom) B.; m. Paulette Louise Sheets, Nov. 27, 1978; children: Danielle René. Student, U. Oreg., Calif. State U., Fullerton; AA, Fullerton Community Coll., 1970; cert., Paralegal Inst., Phoenix. cert. law office mgr. Dir. gen. services Rutan & Tucker, Santa Ana, Calif., 1968-71; owner, mgr. Barristers' Aide, Eugene, Oreg., 1974-80; adminstrv. asst. Warner & Angle, Phoenix, 1981-83; adminstr. Murphy & Posner, Phoenix, 1983—. Author: (instrn. manual) Fencing: Ancient Art-Modern Sport. Mem. ABA, Assn. Legal Adminstrs. Avocation: fencing. Office: Murphy & Posner 3200 E Camelback Phoenix AZ 85018

BURKE, ROBERT EUGENE, history educator; b. Chico, Calif., July 22, 1921; s. Ralph Ambrose and Frieda (Rupp) B.; m. Helen Blom, Oct. 31, 1952 (dec. 1976); m. Edith Baras, 1978. A.B., Chico State Coll., 1946; M.A., U. Calif. at Berkeley, 1947, Ph.D., 1950. Dir. Bancroft Library research project, Eng., 1950-51; head manuscript div. Bancroft Library, U. Calif. at Berkeley, 1951-56; asst. prof. history U. Hawaii, 1956-57; faculty U. Wash., Seattle, 1957—; prof. history U. Wash., 1965—, chmn. dept. 1962-67; summer vis. prof. Columbia U., 1960, Stanford, 1968, U. Wyo., 1969, U. Oreg., 1971, Yugoslav-Am. Seminar, Novi Sad, 1965. Author: Olson's New Deal for California, 1953, (with J.D. Hicks and G.E. Mowry) The American Nation, 5th edit, 1971, The Federal Union, 5th edit, 1970, A History of American Democracy, 4th edit, 1970, (with Richard Lowitt) The New Era and the New Deal, 1920-1940, 1981; editor: The Diary Letters of Hiram Johnson, 1917-1945, 1983; co-editor: Modern American History series; mng. editor: Pacific N.W. Quar.; gen. editor: Americana Library Series. Served with AUS, 1942-45, PTO. Mem. Orgn. Am. Historians (exec. bd. 1967-70), Western History Assn., Am. Assn. State and Local History (award of merit 1978). Home: 7336 19th Ave NE Seattle WA 98115

BURKE, TIMOTHY JOSEPH, tax mgr.; b. Davenport, Iowa, Jan. 9, 1951; s. Edward R. and Dorothy A. (Brophy) B.; m. Kathleen M. Bielser, Aug. 20, 1973; children: Christine M., Stephen T. BBA in acctg., U. Iowa, 1973, JD, 1976. CPA. Tax mgr. Arthur Andersen and Co., Milw. and Denver, 1976-82; v.p., tax mgr. Jones Intercable, Inc., Englewood, Colo., 1982. Mem. Iowa Bar Assn., Am. Inst. CPA's, Colo. Inst. CPA's. Office: Jones Intercable Inc 9697 E Mineral Ave Englewood CO 80112

BURKE, WILLIAM JAMES, chemist, educator, consultant; b. Lowellville, Ohio, May 24, 1912; s. Sylvester L. and M. Catherine (Saltzman) B.; m. Katharine M. King, June 21, 1940; children: Mary Katharine (Mrs. Frank Noyes), Susan E. (Mrs. Victor Burke), Thomas W.J., D. Kevin. A.B., Ohio U., Athens, 1934; Ph.D., Ohio State U., 1937. Research chemist central chem. dept. E.I. duPont de Nemours & Co., Henry Clay, Del., 1937-46; assoc. prof. Ohio U., Athens, 1946-47; assoc. prof. U. Utah, 1947-50, dept. head, 1949-62, prof., 1950-62; v.p. Ariz. State U., Tempe, 1962-76; prof. chemistry Ariz. State U., 1962-83, prof. emeritus, 1983—, dean Grad. Coll., 1963-76; cons. U.S. Army, 1956-62, 72-75, Monsanto Co.; Mem. ICA team to survey higher edn. in Ethiopia U.S. State Dept., 1959-60; past pres. Western Assn. Grad. Schs; mem. exec. com. Nat. Assn. State Univs. and Land Grant Colls., 1969-71; mem. Grad. Record Exam. Bd., 1972-74; chmn. editorial bd. Grad. Programs and Admissions Manual; generalist cons. Nat. Council Archtl. Registration Bd., 1969-72; mem. Nat. Archtl. Accrediting Bd., 1973-78. Contbr. articles to profl. jours. Past pres., dir. Catholic Charities Salt Lake City. Fellow AAAS; mem. Am. Chem. Soc. (vis. assoc. com. on profl. tng. 1959—, councilor for Central Ariz. sect. 1967-70), Australian Rock Art Research Assn., Am. Rock Art Research Assn., Midwest Conf. on Grad. Study and Research (past chmn.), Phi Beta Kappa, Sigma Xi, Phi Lambda Upsilon, Gamma Alpha, Alpha Chi Sigma, Phi Kappa Phi (pres. Ariz. State U. chpt. 1977-78). Patentee in field. Home: 501 E Bishop Dr Tempe AZ 85282

BURKE, YVONNE WATSON BRATHWAITE (MRS. WILLIAM A. BURKE), lawyer; b. Los Angeles, Oct. 5, 1932; d. James A. and Lola (Moore) Watson; m. William A. Burke, June 14, 1972; 1 dau., Autumn Roxanne. A.A., U. Calif., 1951; B.A., UCLA, 1953; J.D., U. So. Calif., 1956. Bar: Calif. bar 1956. Mem. Calif. Assembly, 1966-72, chmn. urban devel. and housing com., 1971, 72; mem. 93d Congress from 37th Dist. Calif., 94th-95th Congresses from 28th Dist. Calif., House Appropriations Com.; chmn. Congl. Black Caucus, 1976; now ptnr. Burke, Robinson & Pearman, Los Angeles; Dep. corp. commr., hearing officer Police Commn., 1964-66; atty., staff McCone Commn. (investigation Watts riot), 1965; bd. dirs. Ednl. Testing Service, 2A br. Fed. Res. Bank. vice chmn. 1984 U.S. Olympics Organizing Com.; bd. dirs. or bd. advisers numerous orgns.; regent U. Calif., Bd. Ednl. Testing Service, Amateur Athletic Found. Recipient Profl. Achievement award UCLA, 1974, 84; named one of 200 Future Leaders Time mag., 1974; recipient Achievement awards C.M.E. Chs.; numerous other awards, citations.; fellow Inst. Politics John F. Kennedy Sch. Govt. Harvard, 1971-72; Chubb fellow Yale, 1972. Office: Burke Robinson & Pearman Suite 350 1925 Century Park E Los Angeles CA 90067

BURKEE, IRVIN, artist; b. Kenosha, Wis., Feb. 6, 1918; s. Omar Lars and Emily (Quardokas) B.; diploma Sch. of Art Inst. Chgo., 1945; m. Bonnie May Ness, Apr. 12, 1945; children—Brynn, Jill, Peter (dec.), Ian. Owner, silversmith, goldsmith Burkee Jewelry, Blackhawk, Colo., 1950-57; painter, sculptor, Aspen, Colo., 1957-78, Cottonwood, Ariz., Pietrasanta, Italy, 1978—; instr. art U. Colo., 1946, 50-53, Stephens Coll., Columbia, Mo., 1947-49. John Quincy Adams travel fellow, Mex., 1945. Executed copper mural of human history of Colo. for First Nat. Bank, Englewood, Colo., 1970, copper mural of wild birds of Kans. for Ranchmart State Bank, Overland Park, Kans., 1974; exhibited Art Inst. Chgo., Smithsonian Instn. (award 1957), Milw. Art Inst., Krannert Mus., William Rockhill Nelson Gallery, St. Louis Art Mus., Denver Art Mus.; represented in permanent collections several southwestern galleries, also pvt. collections throughout U.S.; work illustrated in books Design and Creation of Jewelry, Design through Discovery, Walls. Address: Box 2071 Rio Verde Acres Cottonwood AZ 86326

BURKET, PAUL EDWARD, state aeronautics official; b. Hollidaysburg, Pa., June 19, 1924; s. Charles Vinton and Naomi Grace (Folk) B.; m. Joyce L. Walker, Apr. 14, 1944; children—Charles R., Phillip E. B.Ed., Omaha U., 1966. Commd. 2d lt. USAAC, 1943, advanced through grades to lt. col. USAF, 1963; B-47 crew comdr. and staff officer, Lincoln, Nebr., 1954-65; ret., 1965; supt. ops. Lincoln Airport Authority, 1965-69; dir. Nebr. Dept. Aeros., 1969-71; adminstr., chief exec. officer Oreg. Div. Aeros., Salem, 1972—. Recipient Pres.'s award Am. Assn. State Hwy. and Transp. Ofcls., 1983. Mem. Am. Assn. Airport Execs. (accredited exec. mem.), Nat. Assn. State Aviation Ofcls. (pres. 1977-78). Baptist. Home: 545 Joseph St SE Salem OR 97302 Office: Oreg State Aeros Div 3040 25th St SE Salem OR 97310

BURKETT, FRANK ELLIS, surgeon; b. Syracuse, N.Y., Aug. 21, 1947; s. Vernon Thomson and Elizabeth (Ellis) B.; m. Anita Nadine Newman, Dec. 30, 1978; children: Justin, Chelsea, Andrew. BS, Yale U., 1969; MD, Northwestern U., 1973. Diplomate Am. Bd. Surgery. Clin. asst. prof. surgery U. So. Calif., Los Angeles, 1980—; Bd. dirs N.E. Los Angeles County unit Am. Cancer Soc., Pasadena. Contbr. med. articles to profl. jours. Fellow Am. Coll. Surgeons, Soc. Surgical Oncology, Soc. Head and Neck Surgeons; mem. AMA, Calif. Med. Assn., Pasadena Med. Soc., Am. Cancer Soc. Home: 127 S Citrus Ave Los Angeles CA 90036 Office: Tumor Clinic Med Group 635 E Union Pasadena CA 91101

BURKETT, WILLIAM CLEVELAND, management consultant; b. San Mateo, Calif., June 3, 1956; s. William Andrew and Juliet Ruth (Johnson) B. BA with honors, Stanford U., 1978; postgrad., Stanford U., Clivenden, Eng., 1976; MBA with honors, Yale U., 1983. Fin. analyst dept. merger and acquisitions First Boston Corp., N.Y.C., 1978-80; assoc. internat. coordinator fin. dept. Credit Suisse First Boston, Ltd., London, 1980-81; assoc. mgmt. cons. McKinsey and Co., San Francisco, 1983—; pres. Security Properties, Inc., San Francisco, 1981—. V.p. Mt. Rushmore Hall of Records Commn., Pebble Beach, Calif., 1987. Recipient Spl. Achievement medal U.S. Geol. Survey. Mem. Nat. Hist. Found. (pres. 1986), Mt. Rushmore Nat. Meml. Soc. (life), The Soc. Calif. Pioneers (life), Stanford U. Alumni Assn. (life), Yale U. Alulmni Assn. Clubs: N.Y. Athletic, Yale; Commonwealth

(San Francisco); Beach (Pebble Beach, Calif.). Home: 1901 Pacific St San Francisco CA 94109 Office: McKinsey and Co 555 California St Suite 4800 San Francisco CA 94104

BURKHARDT, ROBERT EDWARD, military construction manager, former army officer; b. Ann Arbor, Mich., July 11, 1927; s. Paul Fred and Ella Amm (Byfuss) B.; m. Lois Jeane Ordway, Aug. 30, 1947; children—Ronald Robert, Christopher Todd, Douglas Craig. Grad. U.S. Army Command and Gen. Staff Coll., 1971; A.A., Jackson Community Coll., 1972; B.A., Mich. State U., 1975, M.A., 1977. Served as enlisted man U.S. Army, 1945-50; with War Crimes Group, Germany, 1946; commd. 2d lt., 1950, advanced through grades to maj., 1968; served with 987th Armored Arty. Bn., 8th U.S. Army, Korea; comdr. Co. A 979th Engr. Constrn. Bn., 1960, 323d M.P. CID, 1963-67, provost marshal 5064th U.S. Army Garrison, Detroit, 1968-73, comdr. 406 Maintenance Bn., Ann Arbor, 1974, ret., 1974; mgr. maintenance and shipping Hancock Industries, Jackson, Mich., 1965-71; asst. dir. plant ops. Foote Hosp., Jackson, 1972-79, also instr. safety, fire and disaster seminars; purchasing agt. Addison Products, Jonesville, Mich., 1980-83; dir. purchasing Linden Tree, Jackson, Mich., 1983-84; MCA program mgr. Directorate Engring. and Housing, Nat. Tng. Ctr., Ft. Irwin, Calif., 1984—; instr. polit. sci., sociology and geography Jackson Community Coll., 1978-81. Contbr. articles to Nat. Geog. Jour. of India. Fin. sec. Redeemer Lutheran Ch., 1961-62, 65-66, treas., 1969-73, 75-76, 78-79; past pres. chpt. 4299, Aid Assn. for Lutherans; treas. Concordia Luth. Ch., 1987; active Republican Nat. Com. Decorated Air medal with oak leaf cluster. Mem. NAM, So. Calif. Assn. Mil. Planners (sec.), Indsl. Execs. Club, Res. Officers Assn., Mich. State U. Alumni Assn., M.P. Assn., Nat. Geog. Soc. Home: 1513 Solana Ct Barstow CA 92311 Office: Directorate Engring and Housing Bldg 365 Nat Tng Ctr Fort Irwin CA 92310

BURKHOLDER, GRACE ELEANOR, educator, archeologist; b. Sumas, Wash., Sept. 21, 1920; d. George Lewis and Leah (Benke) Welch; m. Warren Stanford Burkholder, June 4, 1938 (div. Apr. 1957); children—Warren Stanford, Carol Joyce Van Dyke. B.Ed. cum laude, U. Miami, Fla., 1956; M.Ed., U. Okla., 1980. Tchr., Laurel Sch., Oceanside, Calif., 1956-58; elem. tchr. U.S. Navy, Kwajalein, M.I., 1958-59, Transport Co. Tex., Kwajalein, 1959-60, Arabian Am. Oil Co., Dhahran, Saudi Arabia, 1960-80. Author: An Arabian Collection: Artifacts from the Eastern Province, 1984; research, publs. on Ubaid sites and pottery in Saudi Arabia. Mem. Archeol. Inst. Am., Smithsonian Instn., Audubon Soc. Republican.

BURKHOLDER, JAMES ALFRED, JR., air force officer; b. Bonners Ferry, Idaho, June 23, 1944; s. James Alfred and Valdie Virginia (White) B.; m. Karen Ann Simmons, May 30, 1968 (div.); 1 son, James Alfred III; m. Ruth Ann Meyer, Mar. 17, 1987. B.S. in English, Speech and Secondary Edn., U. Idaho, 1967; M.A. in Bus. Adminstrn., Boise State U., 1977. Commd. 2d lt U.S. Air Force, 1967; advanced through grades to lt. col., 1983; pilot Vance AFB, Okla, 1967-68, Vietnam, 1969, Holloman AFB, N.Mex., 1969-71; chief Standarization and Evaluation Div., Shaw AFB, S.C., 1971-74; chief Tng. Support Div., Mountain Home AFB, Idaho, 1974-77; chief ops. and tng., Lakenheath, Eng., 1977-79, Air Command and Staff Coll., Maxwell AFB, Ala., 1979-80; Cadet Squadron comdr. U.S. Air Force Acad., Colorado Springs, 1980-82, chief mil. tng., 1982-84, asst. dep. comdt. cadet wing, 1985—; chief contingency plans Air Component Command, Osan AFB, Republic of Korea, 1984-85; mem. base Speakers Bur. Decorated D.F.C., 13 Air medals, 3 Meritorious Service medals, Air Force Commendation medal, Dept. Def. Meritorious Service medal. Mem. Air Force Assn., Am. Soc. Tng. and Devel., Orders and Medals Soc. Am., Orders and Medals Soc. Eng., Am. Soc. Mil. Insignia Collectors, Am. Legion, Theta Chi. Methodist. Author: Concepts of Airforce Leadership, 1983; contbr. articles to profl. publs. Home: 5620 Old Farm Terr Colorado Springs CO 80917 Office: USAF Acad Asst Dep Comdt for Cadet Wing Colorado Springs CO 80840

BURKLIN, RALPH W(ALDO)., protective services official; b. Alameda, Calif., Sept. 21, 1946; s. Ralph Waldo and Barbara Francis (Morse) B.; m. Paula Rene Choitz, July 1, 1967; children: Sarah Rene, Erin Elizabeth. AA, Chabot Jr. Coll., 1974; BA in Pub. Mmgt., St. Mary's Coll., Moraga, Calif., 1976. Cert. fire officer I, cert. fire investigator I. Fire capt. Lawrence Livermore (Calif.) Lab., 1976—. Co-author: Fire Terms and a Guide to Their Meaning and Use, 1980. Mem. Nat. Fire Protection Assn., Santa Cruz Grand Jury Assn. Republican. Lutheran. Avocations: jogging. Home: 615 Burlingame Ave Capitola CA 95010 Office: U Calif Lawrence Livermore Lab 7000 East Ave PO Box 5505 Livermore CA 94550

BURLEIGH, ALLISON CURTIS, psychologist; b. Portland, Oreg., Apr. 12, 1920; d. Francis Day and Edith (Clements) C.; m. Charles LeMoyne Burleigh, June 19, 1940 (div. 1967); children: Charles LeMoyne, Catherine Burleigh Rickert; m. Edward G. Esty, Nov. 24, 1984. B.A. with distinction, U. Mich., 1954; M.A.Ed., UCLA, 1969. Ednl. psychologist Gateways Hosp. Ctr. of Hyperkinetic Children, Los Angeles, 1969-73; program analyst, health systems planner, health systems specialist VA Med. Ctr., Brentwood, Los Angeles, 1973-82; EEO specialist VA Med. Ctr., Wadsworth, Los Angeles, 1982-83, employee devel. specialist, 1983-86; ind. cons. mgmt. and behavioral scis., Los Angeles, 1986—. Fed. women's program mgr., Brentwood, 1979-81; chmn. VA Med. Dist. #26 Com. for Study of Violence and Suicide, 1976-79; earthquake cons. Med. Center Disaster Com., 1981—; condr. workshops, cons. in field. Recipient Teaching Faculty award, VA Med. Ctr. Brentwood, 1976; Fed. Women's Program Mgr. of Yr. award Los Angeles Fed. Exec. Bd., 1981; Superior Performance award, VA Med. Ctr. Wadsworth, 1982. Mem. Am. Assn. Tng. and Devel., Am. Psychol. Assn., Calif. Psychol. Assn., NOW, Researchers for Action, Western Psychol. Assn. Contbr. articles to profl. jours. Home and Office: 15907 Asilomar Blvd Pacific Palisades CA 90272

BURLEIGH, JOAN BILLGER, audiologist; b. Rochester, N.Y., June 2, 1949; d. D. Ross and Harriet (Melander) Billger; m. Andrew James Burleigh, Aug. 6, 1983. BS, U. Tulsa, 1971; MA, Northwestern U., 1973. Clin. audiologist U. Hosp., London, Ontario, Can., 1973-74; lectr. U. Western Ontario, London, Ontario, Can., 1973-74; coordinator audiological services Colo. State U., Ft. Collins, 1974-80, instr. audiology, 1974-85, dir. hearing clin., 1980-85; asst. dir. Cen. Auditory Disorders Research Ctr., Ft. Collins, 1985—; cons. Colo. Sch. for Deaf and Blind, Colo. Springs, 1977-81, Purdue U., 1980-81, U. Wyo., 1982-84, Tex. Tech U. Health Scis. Ctr., 1984. Co-author: Handbook of Central Auditory Processing Disorders in Children, 1985; assoc. producer movie Silent World-Lonely World, 1980 (Bronze award 1980, Freedoms Found. award 1981); co-designer Ipsilateral/Contralateral Competing Sentences, 1979. Recipient Colo. State U. Faculty Service Award, Communication Disorders Colo. State U., 1983. Mem. Am. Speech and Hearing Assn., Kappa Alpha Theta. Home: 718 Larkbunting Dr Fort Collins CO 80526 Office: Colo State U 18 Humanities Bldg Fort Collins CO 80523

BURMAN, ALDEN HAYWARD, nursing home exec.; b. Bellingham, Wash., Nov. 18, 1919; s. John A. and Winifred C. (Larson) B.; student health care adminstrn. U. Wash., 1967-68; m. Miriam Rodriguez, July 10, 1983; children from previous marriage: Ronald Alden, Richard, James David, Shirley Ann. Pres., Federal Way Convalescent Center, Inc., 1968—; pres., Parklane Convalescent Center, Inc., Aberdeen, Wash., 1969—; owner The Gallery gift and antique store, Ocean Shores, Wash., 1962—; owner AFCO Personnel Services, Buffalo and Seattle, 1973—; v.p. Western Farms, Inc., Moses Lake, Wash., 1974—; Fellow Am. Coll. Health Care Adminstrs., Internat. Biog. Assn. (life); mem. Wash. Health Facilities Assn. (state pres. 1962, bd. govs. 1961-65), Am. Health Care Assn. (bd. govs. 1962), Nat. Employment Assn. Home: 424 N D St Tacoma WA 98403 Office: PO Box 3260 Federal Way WA 98063

BURNASH, ROBERT JOHN CHARLES, hydrologist; b. Bklyn., Aug. 17, 1931; s. James Francis and Marion Josephine (Olifiers) B.; B.S., Bucknell U., 1953; postgrad. Naval Postgrad. Sch., 1954; m. Jeanne Carolyn Mack, July 11, 1953; children—Charles, Kathleen, Mary, Elizabeth, David, Daniel. Hydrologist, Nat. Weather Service River Forecast Center, Cin., 1957-62, prin. asst., Sacramento River Forecast Center, 1963-71, hydrologist in charge Calif.-Nev. River Forecast Center, 1972-87, retired 1987—; guest lectr. hydrologic systems Australian Water Resources Council, Melbourne, Perth, Brisbane, Sydney, 1984; World Meteorological Orgn. lectr. U. Calif., Davis, 1983-86; prin. organizer Internat. Tech. Conf. on Mitigation of Natural Hazards through Real-Time Data Collection and Hydrological Forecasting, World Meteorol. Orgn., Sacramento, 1983; cons. Hydrologic Services, 1987—. Served with USNR, 1953-56. Recipient Bronze medal Dept. Commerce, 1970, Silver medal, 1975, Gold medal, 1980; Outstanding Public Service award NOAA, 1978. Fellow Am. Meteorol. Soc. (Outstanding Forecaster award 1979, Robert E. Horton meml. lectr. 1983); mem. Am. Geophys. Union, AAAS, N.Y. Acad. Scis., Western Snow Conf., Delta Mu Delta, Phi Lambda Theta. Author: (with others) The Sacramento Model. Contbr. articles to profl. jours. Originator real time event reporting telemetering systems and ALERT flood warning system. Home: 3539 Ridgeview Dr El Dorado Hills CA 95630

BURNER, LAVERNE CAROLYN, retired nursing administrator; b. St. Louis, Apr. 15, 1923; d. Herman Frank and Caroline Mary (Spreckelmier) B.; R.N., DePaul Hosp. Sch. Nursing, 1948; B.S.N. (scholar 1948, 50), St. Louis U., 1952; M.S. in Hosp. Adminstrn., Northwestern U., 1957; postgrad. No. Ill. U., 1973. Instr., DePaul Hosp. Sch. Nursing, St. Louis, 1950-52; clin. coordinator St. Francis Sch. Nursing, Evanston, Ill., 1952-56; adminstr. Sandwich (Ill.) Community Hosp., 1957-61; bus. mgr. Victory Meml. Hosp., Waukegan, Ill., 1961-65; asst. adminstr. Rockford (Ill.) Meml. Hosp., 1966-74; v.p. Bergan-Mercy Hosp., Omaha, 1974-77; asst. adminstr. patient services St. Joseph's Hosp., Tucson, 1978-83; faculty No. Ill. U., DeKalb, 1972-74; clin. asso. U. Nebr., Omaha, 1974-77; guest lectr. U. Ariz., Tucson, 1979-81. Mem. task force Rockford Sch. Medicine, 1972-74, task force on nursing State of Ariz., 1980-83; steering com. Crusader's Clinic, Rockford, 1971-73; pres. Hidden Valley Townhomes Assn., 1980, 84-86. Recipient award for acad. and clin. performance Class of '48, DePaul Hosp., 1948. Mem. Ariz. Orgn. Nurse Execs. (hon.). Democrat. Roman Catholic. Home: 7887 N Lacholla Blvd #2183 Tucson AZ 85741

BURNETT, ANNE L., marketing executive, journalist; b. Ogden, Utah, Apr. 6, 1944; d. Louis Steven and Anne (Bernardi) Patrick; m. Ronald Wesley Burnett, Aug. 31, 1963; children: Stephanie, Matthew, Heidi, Juliet. Student, Mt. San Antonio Coll., 1962-63, Calif. State U., Fullerton, 1965-68, Calif. State U., Long Beach, 1969-72, UCLA, 1972-76, U. Utah., 1979. Media buyer Foote, Cone, Belding, Hoenig, Los Angeles, 1972-73; asst. pub. relations dir. Volvo Western Distbg., 1973-74; adminstrv. asst. Diener, Hauser, Bates Advt. Agy., Los Angeles, 1974, mktg. account exec., media buyer, officer mgr., 1975-79; asst. advt. dir. Taylor-Laughlin Distbg., 1974-75; news reporter Sta. KLUB/KISN Radio, Salt Lake City, 1979-81, The Park Record, Park City, Utah, 1981-82; news reporter, anchorwoman Sta. KSL Radio, Salt Lake City, 1981—, news corr., 1981—; mktg. account exec. corp. promotions U.S. Ski Team, Park City, 1982-84; asst. dir. 1985 Internat. Winter Spl. Olympics Games, Park City, 1984; co-founder Athletes Unltd. Inc., 1984, Intermountain Actors Ensemble Inc., Park City, 1980-81, bd. dirs., publicity chmn.; speaker Barnes-Hind/Hydrocurve, 1984. Casting dir. Ronick Prodns., 1974; producer news program Sta. KPFK, 1975-77; producer, dir. photographer, editor Mad Dog Summer, 1976; co-film editor The Inheritor, 1976; script editor Richard's Mountain, 1977; choreographer Here's Love, 1971-73; actress Kimball Art Ctr., 1979-80; co-dir. Prospector Theatre, 1981, 82. Recipient Best News Story in its Class award Utah Press Assn., 1981. Mem. Soc. Profl. Journalists (hon. mention 1983). Democrat. Roman Catholic. Avocations: pub. speaking, theatre, sewing, skiing, aerobics. Office: Athletes Unltd Inc 2952 Arabian Dr Park City UT 84060

BURNETT, BRENDA BULLOCK, government agency official; b. Red Mountain, Calif., Apr. 12, 1941; d. Miles Wallace and Harriet Jane (Wittmeyer) Bullock; student U. Redlands, 1959-60, 61-62; B.A., U. Md., 1967; m. Daniel George Burnett, Oct. 3, 1970. With U.S. Navy, various locations, 1969—, asso. head budget div. Naval Weapons Center Office Fin. and Mgmt., China Lake, Calif., 1975-77, head reports and analysis br., 1977-78, head fin. mgmt. Br. A, 1978-81, mem. staff Hdqrs. Dept. Def. Schs. Ger., 1982-84, head plans and programs br., 1984—. Mem. Ridgecrest City Council, 1980-81; instr. Stop Smoking Clinic, Am. Cancer Soc.; founding mem. Maturango Mus., Ridgecrest. Mem. Am. Soc. Public Adminstrn., Am. Soc. Mil. Comptrollers (ins. pres., China Lake chpt., 1987), NAACP. Democrat. Home: 735 Sonja St Ridgecrest CA 93555 Office: Code 0825 Naval Weapons Center China Lake CA 93555

BURNETT, ERIC STEPHEN, environmental engineer; b. Manchester, Eng., Apr. 5, 1924; s. William Louis and Edith Winifred (Gates) B.; came to U.S., 1963; naturalized, 1974; B.Sc. in Physics (with honors), London U., 1954; M.S. in Environ. Studies, Calif. State, Dominguez Hills, 1976; Ph.D. in Environ. Engring., Calif. Coast U., 1982; children—Diana, Ian, Brenda, Keith. Program mgr. Brit. Aircraft Corp., Stevenage, Eng., 1953-63; sr. systems engr. RCA, Princeton, N.J., 1963-66; project mgr. Gen. Electric Co., Valley Forge, Pa., 1966-67; dept. head TRW systems Group, Redondo Beach, Calif., 1967-72; dir. energy and pollution control ARATEX Services, Inc., Calif., 1974-81, dir. tech. devel., 1981-83, staff cons., 1983—; cons., lectr. in energy conservation, environ. and contamination controls. Served with Royal Air Force, 1942-47. Asso. fellow AIAA; mem. Water Pollution Control Fedn., Air Pollution Control Assn., AAAS, Inst. Environ. Scis. (sr.). Contbr. articles in field to profl. jours. Home: 22901 Leadwell Ave Canoga Park CA 91307 Office: PO Box 3000 Encino CA 91316

BURNETT, LOWELL JAY, physicist, educator; b. Portland, Oreg., June 15, 1941; s. Jay Duffy and Barbara Montana (Blair) B.; m. Joan Susan Merk, June 17, 1961; children—David Alan, Craig Michael. B.S., Portland State U., 1964; Ph.D. (NSF predoctoral trainee), U. Wyo., 1970. Instr. physics U. Wyo., Laramie, 1970; presdl. fellow chemistry div. Los Alamos (N.Mex.) Sci. Lab., 1971-72; prof. physics San Diego State U., 1972—, chmn. physics dept., 1979—, dir. applied sci. research lab., 1981—; cons. energy conservation utilization, environ. monitoring and control, sci. instrumentation design; Assoc. Western Univs. faculty fellow, 1973-74; cons. energy office tech. assessment U.S. Congress, UOP, Inc., Nat. Inst. for Petroleum and Energy Research, Sci. Applications, Inc., IRT Corp., Gillette Corp., Control Data Corp., Los Alamos Nat. Lab., Quantum Design; mem. internat. adv. panel Electronics, McGraw-Hill. Contbr. articles to profl. jours. Am. Chem. Soc. petroleum research grantee, 1974—. Co-developer membrane for oxygen enrichment of air. Home: 8696 Jackie Dr San Diego CA 92119

BURNETT, LYNN BARKLEY, health science educator; b. Reedley, Calif., Oct. 20, 1948; s. Charles Erbin and Ruth Clarice (Erickson) B. B.S., Columbia Pacific U., 1979, M.Sc., 1980; diploma candidate in nat. security mgmt. Nat. Def. U. of U.S., 1985; postgrad. Columbia Pacific U., Nova U. Ctr. Higher Edn. Cert. community coll. tchr., Calif. Assoc. dir. Cen. Valley Emergency Med. Services System, Fresno, Calif., 1974-75; faculty Calif. State U.-Fresno, 1977—, prof. health sci., dir. continuing edn. in health, 1981—; lectr., cons. in field; co-dir. conjoint research program of Stanford U. Sch. Medicine and Dept. Health Sci. Calif. State U., Fresno, 1986. Chmn. Fresno County steering com. The Chem. People, 1983-86, Generation at Risk, 1987—; mem. Emergency Med. Care Com. Fresno County, 1979-85, vice chmn., 1984-85; mem. Calif. State Commn. Emergency Med. Services, 1974-75; mem. Fresno County Adv. Bd. on Drug Abuse, 1984, chmn. drug adv. bd., 1985—; bd. dirs., chmn. pub. edn. Fresno County unit Am. Cancer Soc., 1984—, v.p., 1985—, pub. edn. com.; pres. Fresno County Safety Council, 1985—. Recipient State Service medal Calif. Mil. Dept., 1980; Bronze medal Am. Heart Assn., 1974, Appreciation award Am. Cancer Soc., 1985. Mem. Am. Coll. Preventive Medicine, Am. Acad. Forensic Scis. (alt. del. People's Republic of China, citizen ambassador program People to People Internat. 1986), Am. Assn. Suicidology, N.Y. Acad. Scis., AAAS, Internat. Platform Assn. Democrat. Baptist. Home: PO Box 4512 Fresno CA 93744 Office: Calif State U Fresno CA 93740-0026

BURNETT, M(ELVIN) DALLAS, journalism, communications educator; b. Ogden, Utah, Jan. 25, 1931; m. Patricia MacArthur; 4 children. BS, Brigham Young U., 1954; MS in Journalism, Northwestern U., 1958, PhD, 1967. Reporter Indl. Post, Bell, Calif., 1947-50, United Press, Salt Lake City, 1953, Daily Signal, Huntington Park, Calif., 1954, Desert News, Salt Lake City, 1957-58; adviser Daily Universe, 1958-59, pub., 1974-79, mng. dir., 1980-82; chmn. dept. journalism Brigham Young U., Provo, Utah, 1961-62, chmn. dept. communications, 1974-79, assoc. dean Coll. Fine Arts and Communications; mng. editor Brigham Young Alumnus; assoc. editor The Ensign, Salt Lake City, 1970-71; pub., editor Better Living Bank Notes; dir. BYU Study Abroad, London, 1979; mem. faculty adv. council, 1970's, tchr. devel. com., 1970's, BYU Today adv. com. 1970's. Author: Mass Communications and the Law: Resource Materials, 1983, (with Wayne Pace and Brent Peterson) Techniques for Effective Communication, 1979; contbr. numerous articles to profl. publs. Served with CIC, U.S. Army, 1954-56. Mem. Assn. Edn. Journalism and Mass Communication, Sigma Delta Chi, Phi Kappa Phi. Office: Brigham Young U Coll Fine Arts Communications Provo UT 84602

BURNETTE, MICHAEL JACKSON, broadcasting executive; b. Fresno, Calif., Aug. 31, 1951; s. Woodrow Jackson and Ruth Marjorie (Loeffel) B.; m. Sarah Marx, June 10, 1977. Grad., U. N.H., 1984. Announcer Sta. KFIG Radio, Fresno, 1969-70; announcer and prodn. dir. Sta. KMAK Radio, Fresno, 1970-77; program dir. Sta. KJQY Radio, San Diego, 1977-82; group ops. mgr. Group W Radio, N.Y.C., 1982-86; v.p., gen. mgr. Sta. KMEO Radio, Phoenix, 1986—. Bd. dirs. Phoenix Symphony Orch., 1986—, Hope: Ctr. for Head Injury, Phoenix, 1986—. Mem. Met. Phoenix Broadcasters (bd. dirs. 1986—). Mem. Zen Baptist Ch. Club: Magic Castle (Los Angeles).

BURNEY, VICTORIA KALGAARD, management consulting and training company executive; b. Los Angeles, Apr. 12, 1943; d. Oscar Albert and Dorothy Elizabeth (Peterson) Kalgaard; children—Kim Elizabeth, J. Hewett. B.A. with honors, U. Mont., 1965; M.A., U. No. Colo., 1980; postgrad. Webster U., St. Louis, 1983-84. Exec. dir. Hill County Community Action, Havre, Mont., 1966-67; community orgn. specialist ACCESS, Escondido, Calif., 1967-68; program devel. and community orgn. specialist Community Action Programs, Inc., Pensacola, Fla., 1968-69; cons. Escambia County Sch. Bd., Fla., 1969-71; pres. Kal Kreations, Kailua, Hawaii, 1974-77; instr., dir. office human resources devel. Palomar Coll., San Marcos, Calif., 1978-81; chief exec. officer IDET Corp., San Marcos, 1981—; cons. County of Riverside, Calif., 1983. Mem. San Diego County Com. on Handicapped, San Diego, 1979; cons. tribal resource devel., Escondido, Calif., 1979; mem. exec. com. Social Services Coordinating Council, San Diego, 1982-83; mem. pvt. sector com. and planning and rev. com. Calif. Employment and Tng. Adv. Council, Sacramento, 1982-83; bd. mgrs. Santa Margarita Family YMCA, Vista, Calif., 1984-85; bd. dirs. North County Community Action Program, Escondido, 1978, Casa de Amparo, San Luis Rey, Calif., 1980-83; mem. San Diego County Pub. Welfare Adv. Bd., 1979-83, chairperson, 1981; assoc. mem. Calif. Republican Central Com., Sacramento, 1984-85; ofcl. San Diego County Rep. Central Com., 1985. Mem. Nat. Assn. County Employment and Tng. Adminstrs. (chairperson econ. resources com. 1983-84), Calif. Assn. Local Econ. Devel., San Diego Econ. Devel. Corp., Oceanside Econ. devel. Council (bd. dirs. 1982-85), Oceanside C. of C., San Marcos C. of C. (bd. dirs. 1982-85), Carlsbad C. of C. (indsl. council 1982-85), Escondido C. of C. (comml. and indsl. devel. council 1982-85), Vista C. of C. (vice chairperson econ. devel. com. 1983-84), Vista Econ. Devel. Assn., Nat. Mgmt. Assn. (charter mem. North County chpt.), Nat. Job Tng. Partnership, Job Tng. Assn. San Diego, Am. Mgmt. Assns., San Diego County Golden Eagle Club, Oceanside Rep. Women's Club Federated. Office: IDET Corp 1125 Linda Vista Dr Suite 101 San Marcos CA 92069

BURNISON, BOYD EDWARD, lawyer; b. Arnolds Park, Iowa, Dec. 12, 1934; s. Boyd William and Lucile (Harnden) B.; m. Mari Amaral; children—Erica Lafore, Alison Katherine. B.S., Iowa State U., 1957; J.D., U. Calif.-Berkeley, 1961. Bar: Calif. 1962, U.S. Supreme Ct. 1971, U.S. Dist. Ct. (no. dist.) Calif. 1962, U.S. Dist. Ct. (ea. dist.) Calif. 1970, U.S. Ct. Appeals (9th cir.) 1962. Dep. country counsel Yolo County, Calif., 1962-65; counsel Davis and Woodland (Calif.) Unified Sch. Dists., 1962-65; assoc. Steel & Arostegui, Marysville, Calif., 1965-66, St. Sure, Moore & Hoyt, Oakland, 1966-70; ptnr. St. Sure, Moore, Hoyt & Sizoo, Oakland and San Francisco, 1970-75; v.p., dir. Crosby, Heafey, Roach & May, P.C., Oakland, 1975—; mem. labor and employment law sect. State Bar Calif., 1982—, spl. labor counsel, 1981-84. Adviser Berkeley YMCA, 1971—, Yolo County YMCA, 1962-65; bd. dirs. Easter Seal Soc. Crippled Children and Adults of Alameda County, Calif., 1972-75, Yolo County YMCA, 1965, Moot Ct. Bd., U. Calif., 1960-61; trustee, sec., legal counsel Easter Seal Found., Alameda County, 1974-79, hon. trustee, 1979—. Fellow ABA Found.; mem. ABA (labor relations and employment law sect.; equal employment law com. 1972—), Alameda County Bar Assn. (chmn. memberships and directory com. 1973-74, 80, chmn. law office econs. com. 1975-77, assn. dir. 1981-85, pres.-elect, 1983, pres., 1984, vice chmn. bench bar liaison com. 1983, chmn. 1984, Disting. Service award 1987), Yolo County Bar Assn. (sec. 1965), Yuba Sutter Bar Assn., Bar Assn. San Francisco (labor law sect.), Sproul Assoc. Boalt Hall Law Sch. U. Calif. Berkeley, Iowa State Alumni Assn., Order Knoll, Pi Kappa Alpha, Phi Delta Phi. Democrat. Club: Round Hill Country. Lodge: Rotary. Home: 2500 Caballo Ranchero Dr PO Box 743 Diablo CA 94528 Office: Crosby Heafey Roach and May 2300 Lake Merritt Plaza Bldg 1999 Harrison St Oakland CA 94612

BURNS, ALEXANDRA (SANDRA) DARROW, rehabilitation program supervisor; b. West Point, Ky., Mar. 28, 1946; d. Eugene Alexander and Phyllis Anna (Kedroski) D.; m. Maurice Edward Burns Jr., Sept. 8, 1966 (div. May 1985); 1 child, Megan Alexandra. BS in Journalism, U. Colo., 1967, MA in Guidance and Counseling, 1974. Cert. ins. rehab. specialist. Probation and parole officer Office of Probation and Parole, Olympia, Wash., 1969-70; employment counselor Div. Employment, Denver, 1971-73; rehab. counselor Colo. Div. Rehab.-Blind Services, Denver, 1973-77; rehab. supr. Colo. Div. Rehab., Denver, 1978-81, program supr. Rehab. Ins. Services for Employment,, 1981—. vice chmn. Juvenile Parole Bd., Denver, 1982-87, chmn. 1987—; del. Dem. County Caucus, Aurora, Colo., 1986; mem. adv. bd. Indsl. Commn., 1983-86. Mem. Nat. Rehab. Assoc., Nat. Rehab. Adminstrn. Assn., Colo. Rehab. Adminstrn. Assn. (bd. dirs. 1985—). Episcopalian. Lodge: Zonta (corr. sec. 1984-86). Avocations: skiing, do-it-yourself projects. Home: 16299 E Nassau Dr Aurora CO 80013 Office: RISE Colo Div Rehab 6000 E Evans # 3-201 Denver CO 80222

BURNS, DAN, manufacturing company executive; b. Auburn, Calif., Sept. 10, 1925; s. William and Edith Lynn (Johnston) B.; 1 son, Dan. Dir. materials Menasco Mfg. Co., 1951-56; v.p., gen. mgr. Hufford Corp., 1956-58; pres. Hufford div. Siegler Corp., 1958-61; v.p. Siegler Corp., 1961-62, Lear Siegler, Inc., 1962-64; pres., dir. Electrada Corp., Culver City, Calif., from 1964; now chmn. Sargent Industries and related cos.; chmn., chief exec. officer Arlington Industries, Inc.; dir. Gen. Automotive Corp., Dover Tech. Internat., Inc., Monitor Techs., Inc. Bd. dirs. San Diego Aerospace Mus. Served to capt. U.S. Army, 1941-47; prisoner of war Japan; asst. mil. attache 1946, China; a.d.c. to Gen. George C. Marshall 1946-47. Mem. Orgn. Am. States Sports Com. (dir.). Clubs: Los Angeles Country, St. Francis Yacht, Calif, Conquistadores del Cielo, Garden of the Gods. Home: 10851 Chalon Rd Bel Air Los Angeles CA 90077 Office: Sargent Industries 1901 Bldg Suite 1251 Century City Los Angeles CA 90067

BURNS, JAMES M., judge; b. Nov. 24, 1924. BA in Bus. Adminstrn., U. Portland, 1947; JD cum laude, Loyola U., Chgo., 1950. Sole pracitce Portland, 1950-52; dist. atty. Harney County, Oreg., 1952-56; ptnr. Black, Kendall, Tremaine, Booth & Higgins, Portland, 1956-66; judge Oreg. Cir. Ct., Multnomah County, 1966-72; mem. faculty Nat. Jud. Coll., 1972—; judge U.S. Dist. Ct. Oreg., Portland, 1972—, chief judge, 1979-84; Mem. Oreg. Criminal Law Revision Commn., 1967-72; chmn. continuing legal edn. com. Oreg. State Bar, 1965-66; faculty advisor Nat. Jud. Coll., 1971. Mem. Oreg. Cir. Judges Assn. (pres. 1969-70), U.S. Jud. Conf. (com. on adminstrn. of probation system 1978—). Office: US Dist Ct 702 US Courthouse 620 SW Main St Portland OR 97205 *

BURNS, JOHN EDWARD, forester; b. Lexington, Ky., Aug. 20, 1939; s. Foster S. and Mary E. (Johnson) B.; m. Ruth Catharine Fenton, July 22, 1972. B.S. in Forestry, U. Mont., 1961. Dist. ranger White River Nat. Forest, Aspen, Colo., 1968-73; info. officer U.S. Forest Service, Denver, 1973-75, mem. staff, Washington, 1975-76; dist. ranger Shasta-Trinity Nat. Forest, Redding, Calif., 1976-78; regional staff U.S. Forest Service, San Francisco, 1978-80; supr. Targhee Nat. Forest, St. Anthony, Idaho, 1980—. Contbr. articles to profl. jours. Mem. Soc. Am. Foresters, Rocky Mountain Outdoor Writers, Greater Yellowstone Area Mgmt. Group, Yellowstone Ecosystem Grizzly Bear Mgmt. Com., Fremont County C. of C., Xi Sigma Pi. Roman Catholic. Lodge: Rotary. Home: Rt 1 Box 147 A Saint Anthony ID 83445 Office: Targhee Nat Forest 420 N Bridge St Saint Anthony ID 83445

BURNS, JOHN FRANCIS, state official, archivist; b. Joliet, Ill., Sept. 13, 1945; s. Francis J. and Agnes A. (Vidmar) B.; m. Jacqueline Honora Patterson, Oct. 11, 1980. BA in History, Lewis Coll., 1967; MA in History, Wash. State U., 1972; Cert., Western Wash. U., 1977. Instr., Skagit Valley Coll., Mt. Vernon, Wash., 1972-75; Pace prof. Chapman Coll., Orange, Calif., 1975-76; instr. Western Wash. U., Bellingham, 1976; project adminstr. Wash. State Records Bd., Olympia, 1977-81; chief of archives State of Calif., Sacramento, 1981—; cons. and lectr. in field. Editor: Historical Records of Washington State, 3 vols., 1980-81, co-editor Washington State Guide to Governor's Papers, 1977. Contbr. articles to profl. jours. Sec. Calif. Heritage Preservation Commn., Sacramento, 1981—; coordinator Calif. Hist. Records Adv. Bd., Sacramento, 1981—; chmn. Nat. Steering Com. of State Records Coordinators, Sacramento, 1983-85; mem. Calif. Hist. State Capitol Commn., Sacramento, 1984—. Served as lt. USN, 1967-70, Vietnam. Grantee Nat. Hist. Publ. and Records Commn., Washington, 1977-86. Mem. Nat. Assn. Govt. Archives and Records Adminstrs. (v.p. 1986—, bd. dirs. 1983-85), Soc. Am. Archivists, Calif. Com. for Promotion of History (steering com. 1984—), Spindex Users Network (chmn. 1979-81), Orgn. Am. Historians, Soc. Calif. Archivists, Western History Assn. Office: Calif State Archives 1020 O St Sacramento CA 95814

BURNS, KENNETH DARRYL, financial company executive; b. Redwood City, Calif., Oct. 18, 1955; s. Phillip Arthur and Ruth (Pomerantz) B.; m. Michele Celine Mueller, May 26, 1984. BBA, San Jose State U., 1979. Cert. credit union exec. Sr. auditor O'Rourk & Clark Accountancy, Brisbane, Calif., 1979-81; controller San Mateo Employees Credit Union, Redwood City, 1981-83; v.p. Bay Fed. Credit Union, Scotts Valley, Calif., 1983—; cons. credit unions, Calif., 1982-83; v.p. Ultradata User's Group, Hayward, Calif., 1985—, Credit Union Chpt., Monterey, Calif., 1986—; lectr. Credit Union Regional Learning Ctr., Santa Clara, Calif., 1986—. Mem. Credit Union Execs. Soc., Cert. Credit Union Execs. Republican. Avocations: skiing, camping, raquetball, golf, meditation. Office: Bay Fed Credit Union PO Box 66999 Scotts Valley CA 95066 Home: Campbell CA 95008

BURNS, KENNETH MAX, safety engineer; b. Tulare, Calif., Mar. 20, 1937; s. Fred Ray Burns and Jewel (Groves) Rogers; m. Diane Virginia Cassel, Apr. 28, 1963 (deceased); children: Robert Daniel, Paris Denise Dau, Catherine Diane. Student, U. Md., 1956-57, Tanana Valley Community Coll., 1976-77, Community Coll. of Air Force, 1978—, U. Alaska Community Coll. of the Air Force, 1984—. Commd. USAF, 1955-68, advanced through grades to sgt.; pub. safety advisor U.S. State Dept., Vietnam, 1968-73; area mgr. The Wackenhut Corp., Phoenix, 1973-74; ops. mgr. The Wackenhut Corp., Fairbanks, Alaska, 1974-75; safety engr. H.C. Price Co., Fairbanks, 1975-78; sr. safety engr. Alaska Nat. Ins. Co., Anchorage, 1980—; chmn. Alaska Safety Adv. Council, Anchorage, 1980-85, Gov's. Safety and Health Conf., Alaska, 1983-85. Mem. Crane Safety Com., Anchorage, Council on Safety Edn., Anchorage. Served with Alaska Air N.G., 1978—. Mem. Am. Soc. Safety Engrs. (pres. 1982-83, Profl. of Yr.), Alaska Chpt. Am. Soc. Safety Engrs. (editor newsletter 1984, Engr. Yr. 1983, Safety Profl. Yr., 1983, Regional Safety Profl., 1984), World Safety Orgn., Soc. Mil. Engrs. Republican. Mem. Assemblies of God. Avocations: big game hunting, boating, slow pitch softball. Home: 3160 W 71st Ave Anchorage AK 99502 Office: Alaska Nat Ins Co 7001 Jewel Lake Rd Anchorage AK 99502

BURNSIDE, WALDO HOWARD, department store executive; b. Washington, Nov. 5, 1928; s. Waldo and Eleanor B.; m. Jean Mae Culbert, June 24, 1950; children: Diane Louise, Leslie Ann, Arlene Kay, William Howard. B.S., U. Md., 1949. With Woodward & Lothrop, Washington, 1949-80; divisional mdse. mgr. Woodward & Lothrop, 1957-65, v.p., gen. mdse. mgr., 1965-74, exec. v.p., 1974-78, pres., 1978-80; also dir.; vice chmn., chief operating officer Carter Hawley Hale Stores, Inc., Los Angeles, 1980-83, pres., chief operating officer, 1983—; dir. Security Pacific Corp. Trustee Md. Edni. Found.; trustee St. John's Hosp. and Health Ctr. Found.; trustee, past chmn. U. Md. Alumni Internat.; bd. dirs. Ind. Colls. Mem. Ind. Colls. So. Calif. (bd. dirs.), Los Angeles Area C. of C. (bd. dirs.), Automobile Club So. Calif. (bd. dirs.), Phi Kappa Phi, Sigma Chi. Episcopalian. Clubs: California, Los Angeles Country, N.Y. Athletic. Office: Carter Hawley Hale Stores Inc 550 S Flower St Los Angeles CA 90071

BURPEAU-DI GREGORIO, MICHELE YOUNG, educator; b. Danville, Va., July 9, 1952; d. George Oscar and Marie Davis (Young) Burpeau; m. Silvio Harold Di Gregorio, Feb. 14, 1982. BS in Elem. Edn. magna cum laude, U. Va., 1974; MEd in Ednl. Psychology, U. Ariz., 1980, PhD in Ednl. Psychology and Bus. Mgmt., 1982. Cert. elem. and secondary tchr., Ariz. Tchr. various elem. and secondary schs. and colls. throughout U.S., 1974-82; faculty mem. U. Phoenix, Tucson, 1983—, U. Arix. Coll. Medicine, Tucson, 1985—; cons. Burpeau-Di Gregorio, Inc., Tucson, 1981—, pres. 1985—; indsl. psychologist Duval Corp., Tucson, 1981; mem. edn. curriculum devel. adv. com. U. Phoenix, 1985—; cons., trainer Performax Products; mem. Community Cable Corp. Author: Communication Concepts: Tools for Teamwork, 1985, Interpersonal Communications, 1985. Assessment ctr. evaluator Tucson Fire Dept., 1985. Named Young Career Woman, Renton Wash. Bus. and Profl. Women, 1975. Mem. Am. Soc. Tng. and Devel. (publicity dir. 1982), Inst. for Renewal of Family and Community Unity (bd. dirs. 1982-84). Republican. Methodist. Home: 9310 E Vallarta Dr Tucson AZ 85749 Office: U Ariz Coll Medicine Office Med Edn 1501 N Campbell Ave Tucson AZ 85724

BURPEE, JON CHARLES, ophthalmologist; b. Alexandria, Va., Nov. 14, 1941; s. William and Margaret Jane (Evans) B; m. Jean Louise Davis, Aug. 22, 1964; children—John Evans, Mark Davis, Heather Jean. B.A. in Biology cum laude, Whitman Coll., 1964; M.D. cum laude, U. Oreg., 1968. Diplomate Am. Bd. Ophthalmology. Intern Fitzsimons Army Hosp., Denver, 1968-69, resident in ophthalmology, 1969-72; practice medicine specializing in ophthalmology, Roseburg, Oreg., 1975—; mem. staff Mercy Med. Ctr., Roseburg, 1975—, sec. staff, 1980, v.p. staff, 1981, chief staff, 1982. Bd. dirs., safety chmn. Oregon Trail council Boy Scouts Am., 1983-86, chmn. Douglas Fir dist., 1984-86. Served to maj. M.C., U.S. Army, 1967-75. Paul Harris fellow, 1982. Mem. Am. Acad. Ophthalmology, AMA, Oreg. Med. Assn., Oreg. Acad. Ophthalmology, Order of Waiilatpu, Phi Beta Kappa, Alpha Omega Alpha, Beta Theta Pi. Republican. Episcopalian. Lodge: Rotary (bd. dirs. Roseburg 1978-80, pres. 1981). Home: 1435 Quail Ln Roseburg OR 97470 Office: Mercy Med Ctr 341 Medical Loop Roseburg OR 97470

BURR, ALEXANDER FULLER, physics educator; b. Cambridge, Mass., July 18, 1931; s. Alexander Carothers and Lillie (Fuller) B.; m. Marjorie McKinstry, Aug. 18, 1962; children: Margaret, Catherine, Susan. BS, Jamestown Coll., 1953; MA, U. Edinburgh, Scotland, 1958; PhD, Johns Hopkins U., 1966. Physicist Ballistic Research Lab., Aberdeen, Md., 1954; reseach asst. Johns Hopkins U., Balt., 1958-65; solid state physicist Naval Reseach Lab., Washington, 1965-66; instr. physics N.Mex State U., Las Cruces, 1966-69, assoc. prof., 1969-77, prof., 1977—; sr. vis. fellow U. Strathclyde, Glasgow, Scotland, 1973; chief scientist Duntech Industries, Las Cruces, N.Mex., 1979-80; cons. IAEA, Sri Lanka, 1981, Bangladesh, 1983, 85. Co-Author: Atomic Energy Levels, 1965; contbr. articles to profl. jours. and popular mags. Bd. dirs. Common Cause, N.Mex., 1985—. Served with U.S. Army, 1954-56. Fellow AAAS, N.Mex. Acad. Scis. (editor N.Mex. Jour. Scis. 1983-86); mem. Am. Phys. Soc., Am. Assn. Physics Tchrs. (councillor 1978—, 2d prize apparatus competition 1973), Sigma Xi. Republican. Presbyterian. Avocations: amateur radio, photography, camping. Home: 2025 O'Donnell Dr Las Cruces NM 88001 Office: NMex State U Dept Physics Las Cruces NM 88003

BURR, EDWARD BENJAMIN, life insurance company executive, financial executive; b. Worcester, Mass., Dec. 19, 1923; s. Guy Weatherbee and Bertha Mary (Clark) B.; m. Mary Elizabeth Hayes, Sept. 2, 1944 (div. Sept. 1970); children—Susan Jean Burr Williams, Nancy Carol Burr Montanaro; m. Kay Frances Flanagan, Nov. 1, 1970; children—Kristine Kay, Kelly Anne. B.A., Bowdoin Coll., 1945; M.B.A., U. Pa., 1948; grad., Am. Coll. Life Underwriters, 1951. C.L.U. Dir. Inst. Life Ins., N.Y.C., 1948-54; exec. dir. Investment Co. Inst., N.Y.C., 1954-58; exec. v.p., dir. One William Street Fund, N.Y.C., 1958-62; pres., dir. William Street Sales, Inc., N.Y.C., 1958-62; pres., vice chmn. Anchor Corp., Elizabeth, N.J., 1964-78; chmn. bd. Anchor Nat. Life, Phoenix, 1965-85, hon. chmn., 1985—; chmn. bd. Anchor Nat. Fin. Services, Phoenix, 1971-75, hon. chmn., 1986—; dir. United Bancorp, Phoenix. Pres. Phoenix Bus. Action Resources Council, 1985—; trustee Scottsdale Meml. Hosp., Ariz., 1985—; dir. Ariz. Community Found., 1985—. Served with U.S. Army, 1943-46, ETO. Decorated Bronze Star, Silver Star. Mem. Am. Soc. C.L.U.s, Nat. Assn. Life Underwriters, Phoenix Met. C. of C. (bd. dirs. 1982—). Clubs: Plaza (bd. govs. 1979—), Kiva (Phoenix). Home: 8317 N 75th St Scottsdale AZ 85259 Office: Anchor Nat'l Life Ins Co 2201 E Camelback Rd Phoenix AZ 85016

BURR, IRVING WINGATE, statistician, educator; b. Fallon, Nev., Apr. 9, 1908; s. Eugene Wyllys and Mary Hopper (Jennings) B.; m. Elsie Darrington Haney, Mar. 26, 1966; children by previous marriage—John T., Mary Kate, Peter S.; 1 stepchild, John D. Haney. B.S., Antioch Coll., 1930; M.S., U. Chgo., 1935; Ph.D., U. Mich., 1941. Assoc. prof. math, chmn. dept. Antioch Coll., Yellow Springs, Ohio, 1930-41; mem. faculty statistics Purdue U., West Lafayette, Ind., 1941-74; prof. Purdue U., 1949—, head dept. statistics, 1962-64; cons. Ocean Park, Wash., 1974—. Author: Engineering Statistics and Quality Control, 1953; Applied Statistical Methods, 1974; Statistical Quality Control Methods, 1976; Elementary Statistical Quality Control, 1979. Editor: Industrial Quality Control, 1961-65. Fellow Am. Statis. Assn., Am. Soc. Quality Control (Shewhart medal 1959, Brumbaugh award 1950, Edward J. Oakley citation 1971), Ind. Acad. Sci.; mem. Am. Math. Soc., Math. Assn. Am., Biometric Soc., Inst. Math. Statistics. Home: PO Box 527 Ocean Park WA 98640 Office: c/o Sherwood Manor PO Box 1630 Sequim WA 98382

BURR, ROBERT KENDALL, ski binding company executive; b. Salina, Utah, July 13, 1943; s. Gene Morse and Zelma (Willardsen) B.; B.S. in Acctg., Brigham Young U., 1965; m. Melanee Violet Mickelsen, Feb. 1, 1964; children—Monique, RK, Travis, Chandler, Teylor, Azure. Audit mgr. Arthur Andersen & Co., Los Angeles, 1965-73; mgr. mgmt. services CED, Inc., Los Angeles, 1973-74; chief audit mgr. Office State Auditor, State of Utah, Salt Lake City, 1974-81; controller IVIE Electronics, Inc., Orem, Utah, 1981, Fields Petroleum, Park City, Utah, 1981-82; v.p. Marker U.S.A., also treas. Marker Internat., Salt Lake City, 1982—. C.P.A., Calif., Utah. Mem. Am. Inst. C.P.A.s, Utah Assn. C.P.A.s (chmn com. for mems. in industry, govt. and edn.). Home: 963 Green Oaks Dr Bountiful UT 84010 Office: Marker USA 2250 S 1300 W Salt Lake City UT 84119

BURRI, BETTY JANE, research chemist; b. San Francisco, Jan. 23, 1955; d. Paul Gene and Carleen Georgette (Meyers) B.; m. Kurt Randall Annweiler, Dec. 1, 1984. BA, San Francisco State U., 1976; MS, Calif. State U., Long Beach, 1978; PhD, U. Calif. San Diego, La Jolla, 1982. Research asst. Scripps Clinic, La Jolla, 1982-83, research assoc., 1983-85; research chemist Western Human Nutrition Research Ctr., USDA, San Francisco, 1985—. Contbr. articles to profl. jours. Affiliate fellow Am. Heart Assn., 1983, 84; grantee NIH, 1982, 85. Mem. AAAS, Assn. Women in Sci. (founding dir. San Diego chpt.). Democrat. Lutheran. Avocations: photography, swimming, reading. Office: Western Human Nutrition Research Ctr PO Box 29997 Presidio San Francisco CA 94129

BURRILL, GEORGE STEVEN, accounting firm executive; b. Madison, Wis., Sept. 15, 1944; s. George T. and Frances Louise (Gump) B.; m. Kelli Susan Fitzpatrick; children—Jeffrey P., Peter C., Thomas C., Joel S. Student U. Ariz, 1962-64; B.B.A., U. Wis.-Madison, 1966. CPA, Calif. With Arthur Young and Co., San Francisco, 1966-69, mgr. 1970-74, prin. 1974-77, ptnr. 1977—, chmn. nat. high tech. group; lectr. internat. bus., acctg., fin.; seminar leader high tech. and SEC-related topics; instr. grad. programs on Fgn. Corrupt Practices Act and entrepreneurship Golden Gate U., San Francisco. Host TV series Prime Time High Tech, 1985. Bd. dirs. Exploratorium, Am. Social Health Assn., No. Calif. Rehab. Found. Mem. Am. Inst. CPAs, Calif. Soc. CPAs, Pan Am. Soc., Am. Electronics Assn., No. Calif. Rehab. Found. (pres.), Am. Social Health Assn. (pres., bd. dirs.). Republican. Presbyterian. Office: Arthur Young and Co 1 Sansome St Suite 3500 San Francisco CA 94104

BURRILL, MELINDA JANE, animal science educator; b. Washington, Mar. 31, 1947; d. Richard William and Virginia (Jones) B. BS, U. Ariz., 1969; PhD, Oreg. State U., 1974. Cert. prof. animal scientist in genetics and breeding. Lab. tech. Bio-test Inc., Northbrook, Ill., 1969; teaching asst. Oreg. State U., Corvallis, 1970-74; research fellow U. Minn., St. Paul, 1975-76; from asst. to full prof. Calif. State Poly. U., Pomona, 1976—; cons. in field. Contbr. articles to profl. jours. Women in Devel. USAID fellow, 1984. Mem. Am. Soc. Animal Sci., Can. Soc. Animal Sci., Brit. Soc. Animal Sci., Am. Genetics Assn., Phi Beta Kappa, Sigma Xi (bd. dirs. 1981,86), Phi Kappa Phi, Gamma Sigma Delta, Alpha Omicron Pi (treas. 1968-69). Club: Richard III Soc. (pres. so. Calif. chpt. 1985-86). Office: Dept Animal Sci Calif Poly U 3801 W Temple Ave Pomona CA 91768

BURRIS, STEVEN MICHAEL, lawyer; b. Los Angeles, Dec. 30, 1952; s. Michael Victor and Patricia (McNeer) B.; m. Melanie Schultz, Oct. 29, 1983; 1 son by previous marriage, Michael Steven. A.B. with distinction, Stanford U., 1975; J.D. with honors, U. So. Calif., 1978. Bar: Nev. 1978, Calif. 1978, Nev. Fed. Dist. Ct. 1978, U.S. Ct. Appeals (9th cir.) 1982. Assoc. firm Rogers, Monsey, Woodbury et al, Las Vegas, Nev., 1978-81; ptnr. Sacco & Burris, Las Vegas, 1981-84; pres. Burris & Thomas, Las Vegas, 1984—; tchr. Clark County Community Coll., Las Vegas, 1979-80. Author: Your Personal Injury Case, 1982 (booklet). Bd. dirs. Sr. Citizens Mobile Home Park Found., Las Vegas, 1981-84. Recipient Pres.'s award U.S. Jaycees, 1981; Am. Jurisprudence award Bancroft Whitney' Pubs., 1977. Mem. Nev. Trial Lawyers Assn., Assn. Trial Lawyers Am., Nev. Bar Assn., Clark County Bar Assn. Democrat. Mem. Christian Ch. Office: Burris & Thomas 1605 S Maryland Pkwy Las Vegas NV 89104

BURROUGH, LARRY, newspaper editor. City editor Los Angeles Herald Examiner. Office: Los Angeles Herald Examiner City Desk 1111 S Broadway Los Angeles CA 90015 *

BURROUGHS, ROBERT CLARK, theatre educator, designer; b. Milw., Mar. 1, 1923; s. S. Dillon and Matta (Smith) B.; m. Patricia Yvon Genematas, Dec. 29, 1951; children: Robert Clark II, Christopher Dillon. BA, Hanover Coll., 1943; MA, Iowa U., 1947; postgrad., Cornell U., 1951-53. Art dir. Tucson Children's Theatre, 1950-70; prof. drama U. Ariz., Tucson, 1947—, head dept. drama, 1978—; chmn. theatre program Nat. Music Camp, Interlochen, Mich., 1958-78; guest dir. Ariz. Theatre Co., Tucson, 1969, 74, 75. Exhibited in group show titled Design Reflections, 1974-75; dir. Imperial Players, Cripple Creek, Colo., 1968-81. Narrator Ann. San Xavier Festival, Tucson, 1958—; designer Tucson Festival Soc., 1950-54; bd. dirs. Jr. League Children's Series, Tucson, 1952-54, Tucson Med. Ctr. Fund Raiser, 1968. Served to sgt. U.S. Army, 1943-46. Recipient Directing and Design prize Am. Coll. Theatre Festival, 1969, Citation of Merit, Am. Coll. Theatre Festival, 1977; Research grantee U. Ariz. Found., Eng., 1986, Humanities Grants Com., 1986. Mem. Ariz. Theatre Assn., Dramatist Guild Inc., Assn. Communications Adminstrs., Am. Theatre Assn., Ariz. Alliance for Arts Edn. Democrat. Methodist. Avocations: swimming, travel, reading. Home: 5810 N Williams Dr Tucson AZ 85704 Office: U Ariz Dept Drama Tucson AZ 85721

BURROUGHS, WALTER LAUGHLIN, journalist, editor; b. Bridgewater, S.D., Aug. 21, 1901; s. William S. and Bertha (Laughlin) B.; B.A., U. Wash., 1924; postgrad. U. Calif. at Berkeley, 1925-28; m. Hazel Georgia Sexsmith, June 1, 1925 (dec. Oct. 1970); 1 dau., Toni (Mrs. Philip Schuyler Doane); m. 2d, Lucy Bell, Feb. 28, 1972. Dir. publs. U. Calif. at Berkeley, 1925-28; gen. mgr. North Pacific Gravure Co., Seattle, 1928-30; gen. mgr. Crocker Union Lithograph and Publishing Co., Los Angeles, 1930-41; co-founder Bantam Books, Los Angeles, 1938; ind. book pub. with Merle Armitage, 1938-42; Pacific coast rep. H.W. Kaster & Sons, advt. agy., Los Angeles, 1941-42; exec. v.p. Eldon Industries Los Angeles, 1946-62; corp. pres., pub. Orange Coast Daily Pilot, Newport Beach, Costa Mesa, Huntington Beach, Calif., 1948-65, chmn. bd., 1965-68; pres. Orion Mgmt. Corp., Constellation ORION Corp. Chmn. bd. dirs. emeritus Children's Hosp. Orange County; trustee Jefferson Trust, Western World Med. Found., Irvine, Calif. Served to col. U.S. Army, 1942-45. Honored (with late E.J. Power) for role in bringing U. Calif. to Irvine with dedication of Founders Ct. on campus, 1978. Mem. Sigma Delta Chi (nat. pres.). Clubs: Bohemian (San Francisco); Jonathan (Los Angeles); Newport Harbor Yacht, Newport Beach Country; Ctr. Performing Arts Ctr. Lodge: Rotary. Home: 260 Cagney Ln Apt 313 Newport Beach CA 92663 Office: 1670 Westminster Ave Costa Mesa CA 92627

BURROW, BARBARA KATHERINE, speech pathologist; b. Troy, Ohio, Apr. 24, 1953; d. Robert Moore and Lena Lucille (VanCleve) B. BA, U. Redlands, 1975, MS, 1977. Lang. speech specialist Los Angeles County Office Edn., Downey, Calif., 1977—, tchr. on spl. assignment, 1987—; tchr. ABC Unified Sch. Dist., Cerritos, Calif., 1980, Downey Unified Sch. Dist., Adult Sch., 1982; lang. speech pathologist Marina Profl. Services, Long Beach, Calif., 1984, 85; chmn. resource file Parent Info. Research File for Tchrs., 1982. Mem. Am. Speech Lang. Hearing Assn., Calif. Speech and Hearing Assn., Calif. Assn. Bilingual Lang./Speech Specialists (editor newsletter 1984—), Sorority Alumni Assn. (pres. 1979), Delta Exec. Council (v.p. 1986). Republican. Avocations: skiing, tennis, cooking, sewing, crafts. Home: 22995 Caminito Brisa Laguna Hills CA 92653 Office: Los Angeles County Office Edn 9300 E Imperial Hwy Downey CA 90059

BURROW, CLAUDE HOKE, plastic surgeon, educator; b. Toledo, Oct. 5, 1947. BA, Vanderbilt U., 1969; MD, U. Miss., 1973. Diplomate Am. Bd. Plastic Surgery, Am. Bd. Surgery. Practice medicine specializing in plastic surgery Boulder, Colo., 1980—; clin. instr. surgery U. Colo. Health Scis. Ctr., Denver, 1981—. Fellow ACS; mem. Am. Soc. Plastic and Reconstructive Surgeons, Rocky Mountain Assn. Plastic Surgeons, Colo. State Soc. Plastic Surgeons. Avocations: flying, golf, sports, computers. Office: 2617 Broadway Boulder CO 80302

BURROW, HAROLD, gas company executive; b. Navasota, Tex., Dec. 1, 1914; s. Benjamin Donald and Minnie (Weaver) B.; m. Vassa Woodley; children: Larry W., Harry W., Janice K. Grad., Advanced Mgmt. Program, Harvard U. With Tenneco, Inc., Houston, 1943-66, pres., mem. exec. com., 1960-66; chmn. bd., chief exec. officer Colo. Interstate Gas Co., Colorado Springs, 1974—, also bd. dirs.; vice chmn. bd. Coastal Corp. (formerly Coastal States Gas Corp.), Houston, 1974-82, also mem. exec. com., until 1982; chmn. bd., chief exec. officer Colo. Interstate Corp., Colorado Springs, 1982—, also bd. dirs.; Mem. Petroleum Club Houston. Methodist. Club: Ramada (Houston). *

BURROW, JOHN CLENDENEN, marketing professional; b. Amarillo, Tex., Jan. 31, 1937; s. John H. and Bertie (Clendenen) B.; m. Carla A. Maffei, June 1, 1962; children: Tina Elizabeth, Toni Lynne. BA in Mktg., U. Tex., El Paso, 1962. With Gen. Motors Corp., El Paso, 1963-65; asst. mgr. regional process ctr. Gen. Motors Corp., Denver, 1966; spl. clk. passenger schedule Gen. Motors Corp., Dallas, 1966; dist. mgr. Gen. Motors Corp., Corsicana, Tex., 1967-69, Waco, Tex., 1969; asst. zone merchandising mgr. Gen. Motors Corp., Dallas, 1970-72, mgr. zone distbn., 1972-73, mgr. zone bus., 1973; adminstr. field ops. Gen. Motors Corp., Memphis, 1973-74; asst. nat. merchandising mgr. Chevrolet div. Gen. Motors Corp., Detroit, 1974-76; asst. zone mgr. Gen. Motors Corp., Louisville, 1976-78, N.Y.C., 1978-80; zone mgr. Chevrolet div. Gen. Motors Corp., Omaha, 1980-81; zone mgr. Gen. Motors Corp., Boston, 1981-85, Los Angeles, 1985; mgr. west area mktg. Chevrolet div. Gen. Motors Corp., Thousand Oaks, Calif., 1985—. Served with U.S. Army, 1956-59. Mem. Phi Kappa Tau (pres., treas.). Lodge: Elks. Office: Chevrolet Motor Div 515 Marin St Suite 212 Thousand Oaks CA 91360

BURROWS, BENJAMIN, educator, physician; b. N.Y.C., Dec. 16, 1927; s. Samuel and Theresa Helen (Handelsman) B.; m. Nancy Kreiter, June 14, 1949; children—Jan C., Susan K., Lynn A., Steven M. M.D., Johns Hopkins, 1949. Intern Johns Hopkins Hosp., 1949-50; resident King County Hosp., Seattle, 1950-51; resident U. Chgo., 1953-55, instr. to asso. prof. medicine, 1955-68; prof. internal medicine U. Ariz. Coll. Medicine, Tucson, 1968—, head section pulmonary diseases, 1968-87, Chalfant-Moore prof. of medicine, 1987—; cons. Tucson VA Hosp.; dir. div. respiratory scis. Nat. Heart Lung and Blood Inst. Specialized Ctr. Research in Pulmonary Diseases, U. Ariz. Coll. Medicine, 1971—. Mem. editorial bd.: Am. Rev. Respiratory Disease, 1967-71, 74-80, Chest, 1971-76, Annals Internal Medicine, 1973-76, Archives of Environ. Health, 1976—; contbr. articles to profl. jours., chpts. to books. Served to capt. USAF, 1951-53. Research grantee USPHS, 1958—. Fellow Am. Coll. Chest Physicians (regent dist. 11 1970-75), A.C.P.; mem. Am. Thoracic Soc. (counsilor), Ariz. Thoracic Soc. (pres.), Assn. Am. Physicians, Am. Soc. Clin. Investigation (emeritus), Am. Physiol. Soc. Home: 6840 Table Mountain Rd Tucson AZ 85718 Office: U Ariz Health Scis Ctr Tucson AZ 85724

BURROWS, LARRY EUGENE, controller; b. Cedar Rapids, Iowa, July 5, 1944; s. Leonard Eugene Burrows and Leona Bernice (Candler) Tincher; m. Lorene Marie Stenerson, June 7, 1953; 1 child, Lee Eugene. BS, Calif. State U., Los Angeles, 1966; MS, Woodbury U., 1972; cert. exec. program, UCLA, 1977. Mgr. cost acctg. Products Research and Chem. Co., Glendale, Calif., 1961-66; supr. project adminstrs. electro-optical systems group Xerox Corp., Pasadena, Calif., 1966-74; group mgr. fin. ops. energy products group TRW Inc., Los Angeles, 1974-77; div. controller Container div. Carnation Co., Los Angeles, 1977-79; asst. corp. controller Kerr Glass Mfg. Corp., Los Angeles, 1979—; cons. computer installations and mgmt., Los Angeles, 1985—; freelance photographer, Los Angeles, 1980—. Author: Mergers and Acquisitions, Financial Aspects, 1972. Coach Little League Baseball, Glendale, 1976-78, Babe Ruth Baseball, Glendale, 1979-81, Glendale Bears Youth Football Teams, 1976-79. Served with U.S. Army. Recipient Dora E. Kirby award Woodbury U., Los Angeles, 1977, McDonnell Douglas award, 1974, Award for Fin. Controls, Jet Propulsion Lab., 1971, Mgmt. Team Contbn. award Boeing Corp., 1973. Mem. Am. Mgmt. Assn., Nat. Assn. Accts (v.p. 1974), UCLA Alumni Assn. Republican. Avocations: photography, hiking, painting, tennis, travelling. Home: 2246 El Arbolita Dr Glendale CA 91208 Office: Kerr Glass Mfg Corp 501 S Shatto Pl Los Angeles CA 90020

BURSTEIN, DAVID, astronomer, educator; b. Englewood, N.J., May 19, 1947; s. Bernard and Mildred (Mindlin) B.; m. Gail Maureen Kelly, June 19, 1971; children: Jonathan, Elizabeth. BA in Physics, Wesleyan U., Middletown, Conn., 1969; PhD in Astronomy and Physics, U. Calif., Santa Cruz, 1978. Postdoctoral fellow Carnegie Instn. Washington, dept. terrestrial magnetism, 1977-79; research assoc. Nat. Radio Astronomy Obs., Charlottesville, Va., 1979-82; asst. prof. dept. physics Ariz. State U., Tempe, 1982—; adj. asst. astronomer Steward Obs., Tucson, 1984—; vis. asst. astronomer Lick Obs. U. Calif., Santa Cruz, 1983-86. Contbr. articles to profl. jours. Mem. Am. Astron. Soc., Sigma Xi. Democrat. Jewish. Office: Ariz State U Dept Physics Tempe AZ 85287

BURSTEIN, PAUL, sociology educator; b. Chgo., Dec. 24, 1946; s. Hymen and Rebecca (Soifer) B.; m. Florence Gertrude Katz, Dec. 22, 1976; children: Nathan Katz, Anna Katz. BA, U. Chgo., 1968; PhD, Harvard U., 1974. Asst. prof. Yale U., New Haven, 1973-80; assoc. program dir. NSF, Washington, 1980-81; assoc. prof. sociology Vanderbilt U., Nashville, 1981-85, U. Washington, 1985—; mem. adv. panel NSF, Washington, 1983—. Author: Discrimination, Jobs and Politics, 1985, Basic Research Methods, 1985; cons. editor Am. Jour. Sociology, 1984-86; assoc. editor Am. Sociol. Rev., 1980-83; contbr. articles to profl. jours. Vice chmn. community relations com. Jewish Fedn., Nashville, 1984-85. Howard Found. fellow, 1984; NSF grantee, 1979-80. Mem. Am. Sociol. Assn. (mem. council polit. sociology sect. 1984—), Am. Polit. Sci. Assn., So. Sociol. Soc., Law & Society Assn., Phi Beta Kappa. Office: U Wash Dept Sociology Seattle WA 98195

BURT, ROBERT NORCROSS, diversified manufacturing company executive; b. Lakewood, Ohio, May 24, 1937; s. Vernon Robert and Mary (Norcross) B.; m. Lynn Chilton, Apr. 19, 1969; children: Tracy, Randy, Charlie. BSChemE, Princeton U., 1959; MBA, Harvard U., 1964. With Mobil Oil Corp., N.Y.C. and Tokyo, 1964-68; dir. corp. planning and acquisitions Chemetron Corp., Chgo., 1968-70, mgr. internat. div., 1970-73; dir. corp. planning FMC Corp., Chgo., 1973-76; v.p. agrl. chems. group FMC Corp., Phila., 1976-83; v.p. def. group FMC Corp., San Jose, Calif., 1983—; Bd. dirs. Silicon Valley Tech. Ctr. Co-chmn. San Jose Mus. Art Fund Drive. Served to lt. USMC, 1959-62. Mem. Calif. Bus. Round Table, Santa Clara Mfg. Group (bd. dirs. 1983—), Am. Def. Preparedness Assn. (bd. dirs. 1983), San Jose C. of C. (bd. dirs. 1985—). Club: La Rinconda Country (Los Gatos, Calif.). Avocations: reading, golfing, spectator sports. Home:

730 Bicknell Rd Los Gatos CA 95030 Office: Def Group FMC Corp 881 Martin Ave Santa Clara CA 95050

BURTNER, ROGER LEE, research geologist; b. Hershey, Pa., Mar. 31, 1936; s. Bruce Lemmuel and Bernetta Viola (Quigle) B.; m. Carol Ann Spitzer, Aug. 1, 1965; 1 child, Pamela Sue. BS cum laude, Franklin and Marshall Coll., 1958; MS, Stanford U., 1959; PhD, Harvard U., 1965. Assoc. research geologist Calif. Research Corp. div. Standard Oil Co. of Calif., La Habra, 1963-64, research geologist, 1964-68; exploration geologist Tex. div. Standard Oil Co. of Calif., Corpus Christi, Houston, 1968-69; research geologist Chevron Oil Field Research Co. (formerly Calif. Research Corp.), La Habra, 1969-74, sr. research geologist, 1974-77; sr. research assoc. Chevron Oil Field Research Co., La Habra, 1977—, petrology group project leader, 1975-80, supr. electron microscopy lab., 1977-82. Contbr. articles to profl. jours. Founder Christ Coll. Irvine, 1976, Orange County Permorming Arts Ctr., Costa Mesa, Calif., 1979; mem. Friends of Christ Coll. Irvine, Fullerton (Calif.) Arboretum, 1983—, Orange County Master Chorale, 1978-81; bd. dirs. Luth. High Sch. Assn. Orange County, Orange, Calif., 1975-81, pres., 1977-79, v.p. 1979-81; v.p. Prince of Peace Luth. Ch., Anaheim, Calif., 1980-86, pres. 1986—. NSF fellow, 1958-60. Fellow Geol. Soc. Am.; mem. Am. Assn. Petroleum Geologists, Soc. Econ. Paleontologists and Mineralogists, Clay Minerals Soc. (councilor 1981-84), Geochem. Soc., Los Angeles Basin Geol. Soc., Sierra Club, Sigma Xi, Phi Beta Kappa. Republican. Club: Orange County Wheelmen. Avocations: chorale singing, backpacking, bicycling, tennis, gardening. Home: 721 E Harmony Ln Fullerton CA 92631 Office: Chevron Oil Field Research Co PO Box 446 La Habra CA 90631

BURTNETT, STEVEN CHARLES, municipal judge; b. Hollywood, Calif., July 29, 1942; s. Joseph Mark and Mildred (Walker) B.; m. Judith Jean Lambert, June 29, 1968 (div. Nov. 1985); 1 child, Steven Christian Jr. BS, Iowa State U. Sci. and Tech., 1964; JD, U. Calif., Hastings, 1967; postgrad., U. Calif., Berkeley, 1975. Bar: Calif. 1967. Intern in pub. affairs Coro Found., Los Angeles; dep. dist. atty. Los Angeles County, 1968-74; commr., judge pro tem Los Cerritos Mcpl. Ct., Bellflower, Calif., 1974—. Editor-in-chief law student newspaper Voir Dire, 1967. Chmn. bd. mgrs. Los Cerritos YMCA, Bellflower, 1981-83; mem. speakers' bur. Gov. Deukmejian campaign, 1982; coach Am. Youth Soccer Orgn., Huntington Beach, 1979—, Robinwood Little League, Huntington Beach, 1979—; mem. organizing com. Los Angeles Olympics, 1982-84; host parent Am. Field Service Fgn. Exchange Program, 1985—. Served with USMC, 1968. Mem. Los Angeles County Bar Assn., Southeast (Calif.) Dist. Bar Assn., Am. Judiciary Soc., Calif. Ct. Commrs. Assn. (v.p., co-founder), SAR, Sons of Union Vets. of Civil War, Sigma Alpha Epsilon, Phi Delta Phi. Republican. Methodist. Club: Commonwealth (San Francisco). Avocations: geneaolgy, sailing, fishing, white-water rafting. Home: 16911 Coral Cay Huntington Beach CA 92649 Office: Los Cerritos Mcpl Ct 10025 E Flower St Bellflower CA 90706

BURTON, AL, producer, director, writer; b. Chgo., Apr. 9, 1928; s. D. Chester and Isabelle (Olenick) G.; m. Sally Lou Lewis, Jan. 8, 1956; 1 dau., Jennifer. B.S. cum laude, Northwestern U., 1948. Exec. v.p. creative affairs Norman Lear-Embassy Communications, Inc., 1973-83; exec. producer-cons. Universal TV, 1983—; bd. dirs. Pilgrim Group Funds; mem. Second Decade council Am. Film Inst., adv. bd. Samantha Smith Found. Producer various youth-oriented TV series, 1949-52; producer Johnny Mercer's Mus. Chairs, 1952-55, Oscar Levant Show, 1955-61; creative producer Teen-Age Fair, 1962-72; exec. producer Charles in Charge, CBS-TV, 1984-85, Tribune Entertainment, 1986—, Together We Stand, CBS-TV, 1986-87, Nothing Is Easy, 1987—; creative supr. Mary Hartman, Mary Hartman; prodn. supr. One Day At a Time, Facts of Life, Silver Spoons, The Jeffersons, Square Pegs, Diff'rent Strokes. Composer-lyricist theme songs for Facts of Life, Diff'rent Strokes, Charles in Charge, Together We Stand, Nothing Is Easy; Cons. Domestic Life, CBS-TV, 1983-84, Alan King Show, 1986—. Recipient Emmy award for outstanding comedy series All in the Family, 1978-79, Producers award Nat. Council for Families and TV, 1984; honored for Diff'rent Strokes, NCCJ, 1979-80, honored for Facts of Life, Calif. Gov's. Com. for the Employment of the Handicapped, 1981-82. Mem. Caucus for Producers, Writers and Dirs., Dirs. Guild Am., Writers Guild Am., AFTRA, Acad. of TV Arts and Scis., Acad. Magical Arts. Home: 2300 Coldwater Canyon Beverly Hills CA 90210 Office: Universal Studio Universal City CA 91608

BURTON, CHARLES EDWARD, electrical engineer, systems engineer; b. Colorado Springs, Colo., Jan. 4, 1946; s. Charles Richard and Easter Drees (Kuettner) B.; m. Linda Ruth Robinson, Jan. 27, 1969; children: Heather Marie, Stephanie Anne. BSEE, Tex. Tech. U., 1969; MSEE, Tex Tech U., 1971, PhD EE, 1973. Sr. research engr. S.W. Research Inst., San Antonio, 1973-75; research engr. NCR Corp., Dayton, Ohio, 1975-76; sr. systems engr. Systems Research Labs., Dayton, 1976-81; chief engr. Profl. Geophysics Inc., Denver, 1981-84; sr. staff engr. Hughes Aircraft Co., Denver, 1984—; adj. prof. U. Tex., San Antonio, 1974-75, Wright State U., Dayton, 1976-78, U. Colo., Denver, 1984—; cons. various orgns. Designer copyrighted software; contbr. over 16 articles to profl. jours. Asst. coach Lakewood Soccer Assn., Denver, 1982; judge U.S. Swimming Assn., Denver, 1984-86. Sr. mem. IEEE (various offices); mem. Assn. Computing Machinery, Am. Assn. Artificial Intelligence, Sigma Alpha Epsilon. Club: Heather Ridge Country. Avocations: consulting, personal computing, racquetball, cross-country skiing. Home: 13284 W Utah Circle Denver CO 80228

BURTON, DANNY WAYNE, lawyer; b. Plainview, Nebr., Oct. 27, 1952; s. Wayne Eugene and Vivian LaRose (Hollander) B.; m. Debra Joy Peldo, Sept. 19, 1980; 1 child, William Delbert. BA, U. Alaska, 1975; JD, U. Colo., 1978. Sole practice atty. Wasilla, Alaska, 1978-83, 85—; spl. asst. to commr. Alaska Dept. Health and Social Services, Juneau, 1983-85. Rep. Precinct Committeeman, 1986. Mem. ABA, Am. Trial Lawyers Assn., Alaska Bar Assn., Matanuska Bar Assn. (v.p. 1983, pres. 1984). Lutheran. Office: 390 B Railroad Ave Wasilla AK 99687

BURTON, GENE EARLE, university administrator, educator; b. Coffeyville, Kans., May 8, 1929; s. Floyd Earle and Pauline Ellen (Williams) B.; m. Phyllis Celestine Wisner, Sept. 4, 1948; children: Rebecca, David, Vicki, Judy. AA, Antelope Valley Coll., 1968; BBA, U. Tex., Arlington, 1970, MBA, 1972; PhD in Mgmt., North Tex. State U., 1974. Various mgmt. positions Rockwell Internat., Los Angeles, 1948-70; fin. mgr. Gen. Electric Co., Dallas, 1970-72; teaching fellow North Tex. State U., Denton, 1972-74; lectr. U. Tex., Arlington, 1972-74; assoc. prof. Appalachian State U., Boone, N.C., 1974-76; chmn. dept. bus. adminstrn. Eastern Ky. State U., Richmond, 1976-79; dean sch. bus. Calif. State U., Fresno, 1979-85, prof. mgmt. and mktg., 1985—; mem. adv. bd. Fresno County Econ. Devel. Corp., 1980, bd. dirs. Bashford Travel, Fresno. Contbr. numerous articles to profl. jours. Mem. Market Fresno Project Task Force, 1980, adv. council U.S. SBA, Fresno, 1980—. Mem. Am. Inst. Decision Sci. (v.p. 1978-79), Ops. Research Soc. Am., Am. Mktg. Assn. (bd. dirs. 1984—), Acad. Mgmt. Lodge: Rotary. Home: 5701 N Callisch St Fresno CA 93710 Office: Calif State U Sch Bus Fresno CA 93740

BURTON, HILARY D., technical information specialist; b. Pitts., June 26, 1943; d. Paul and Esther (Kizlaitis) De Pace. BA, U. Calif., Berkeley, 1965, MLS, 1966, PhD, 1972. Computer specialist USDA, Berkeley, 1966-70, Beltsville, Md., 1970-78; tech. info. specialist USDA, Oakland, Calif., 1978-84, Lawrence Livermore (Calif.) Nat. Lab., 1984—; cons. UNESCO, India, 1984—, IDRC, Can., India, Africa, 1980—, Brazilian Dept. Agr., Brasilia, 1972-82. Contbr. articles, book revs. to profl. jours. Mem. AAAS (chmn. nomination com. 1985-86), Am. Soc. Info. Sci., Assn. Computing Machinery. Avocations: antique glass collecting, orchid raising. Home: 5700 Sonoma Mountain Rd Santa Rosa CA 95404 Office: Lawrence Livermore Nat Lab PO Box 808 L-542 Livermore CA 94550

BURTON, JOHN PAUL, lawyer; b. New Orleans, Feb. 26, 1943; s. John Paul and Nancy (Key) B.; children: Jennifer, Susanna, Derek, Catherine. BBA magna cum laude, La. Tech. U., 1965; LLB, Harvard U., 1968. Bar: N.Mex. 1968, U.S. Dist. Ct. N.Mex. 1968, U.S. Ct. Appeals (10th cir.) 1973, U.S. Supreme Ct. 1979. Assoc., Rodey, Dickason, Sloan, Akin & Robb, Albuquerque, 1968-74, dir., 1974—, chmn. comml. dept., 1980-81; lectr. workshops, seminars. Contbr. articles to legal pubs. Packleader, Greater Southwest council Boy Scouts Am., 1976-77; mem. Mus. N.Mex. Found., N.Mex. Mus. Natural History Found.; fellow State Bar Found., Santa Fe Symphony Assn.; vice chmn. St. Simeon's Retirement Complex; chmn. com. N.Mex. Harvard Law Sch. Fund; bd. dirs. Brunn Sch. Mem. N.Mex. State Bar Assn. (dir., budget officer 1983, chmn. uniform comml. code study and legis. com., sect. corp. bus. and banking 1984), Albuquerque Bar Assn., Santa Fe Bar Assn., Am. Arbitration Assn. (panel arbitrators, regional adv. com.). Republican. Episcopalian (vestry 1977-80; lay reader 1982-84, chmn. evaluation commn., mem. constn. and canons com. Diocese of Rio Grande). Club: Harvard-Radcliffe of N.Mex. (dir. 1981-84). Office: Rodey Dickason Sloan Akin & Robb PA PO Box 1888 Albuquerque NM 87103 Office: PO Box 1357 Santa Fe NM 87504

BURTON, PAUL FLOYD, social worker; b. Seattle, May 24, 1939; s. Floyd James and Mary Teresa (Chovanak) B.; B.A., U. Wash., 1961, M.S.W., 1967; m. Roxanne Maude Johnson, July 21, 1961; children—Russell Floyd, Joan Teresa. Juvenile parole counselor Div. Juvenile Rehab. State of Wash., 1961-66; social worker VA, Seattle, 1967-72, social worker, cons. Work Release program King County, Wash., 1967-72; supr., chief psychiatry sect. Social Work Service VA, Topeka, Kans., 1972-73; pvt. practice social work, Topeka and Los Angeles, 1972—; chief social work service VA, Sepulveda, Calif., 1974—, Equal Employment Opportunity coordinator Med. center, 1974-77. Mem. Nat. Assn. Social Workers (newsletter editor Puget Sound chpt. 1970-71), Acad. Cert. Social Workers, Am. Group Psychotherapy Assn., Internat. Transactional Analysis Assn., Center for Studies in Social Functioning, Am. Sociol. Assn., Am. Public Health Assn., Am. Hosp. Assn., Soc. Hosp. Social Work Dirs., Assn. VA Social Work Chiefs (founder 1979, charter mem. and pres. 1980-81, newsletter editor 1982-83), Am. Assn. Sex Educators, Counselors, and Therapists. Home: 14063 Remington St Arleta CA 91331 Office: 16111 Plummer St Sepulveda CA 91343

BURUD, SANDRA LEE, child care benefit executive; b. Crosby, Minn., Oct. 23, 1948; d. Arnold James and Marilyn Elizabeth (Morrison) B.; m. Larry Allen Remlinger, May 20, 1975. AA, Bakersfield Coll., 1971; BA, Pacific Oaks Coll., 1973, MA, 1976; PhD, Claremont Grad. Sch., 1986. Dir. Creative Ptnrships. for Child Care, Pasadena, Calif., 1979-81; prin. investigator, child care project Nat. Employer, Pasadena, 1981-84; pres. Burud & Assocs., Inc., Pasadena, 1984—; chmn. Summa Assocs., Inc., 1986—; cons. Office of Pvt. Sector Initiatives, Washington, 1984, Women's Bur. Dept. Labor, Washington, 1984. Co-author: Employer-Supported Child Care: Investing in Human Resources, 1984; contbr. articles to profl. jours. HHS grantee, 1981-84. Mem. Nat. Assn. for Edn. Young Children. Office: Burud and Assocs Inc 553 S Marengo Suite 102 Pasadena CA 91101

BURWEN, MICHAEL P., computer industry executive, consultant; b. Winthrop, Mass., Mar. 15, 1938; s. Charles B. and Charlotte (Freedman) B.; children—Marcy, Jill; m. 2d, Margaret March Ross, Nov. 8, 1976; 1 son, Ross. B.A.E., Rensselaer Poly. Inst., 1959; M.S.E., UCLA, 1964. With Gen. Dynamics, Pomona, Calif., 1959-63; mgr. Electronic Assocs., Palo Alto, Calif., 1963-68; pres. Basic Computing Arts, Mountain View, Calif., 1968-70; sr. v.p. Quantum Sci. Corp., Palo Alto, 1970-75; pres. Mackintosh Research, 1975-77; pres., dir. Input, Palo Alto, 1977-81; founder, pres. Palo Alto Mgmt. Group, 1981—; lectr. Home: 611 Teresi Ln Los Altos CA 94022 Office: 2685 Marine Way Suite 1212 Mountain View CA 94043

BUSA, PAULINE ROSE, podiatrist; b. Seattle, Feb. 1, 1957; d. Santiago and Engracia (Beato) B. BS in Pre-Med, U. San Francisco, 1978; BS in Biol. Scis., Calif. Coll. Podiatric Medicine, 1983, D of Podiatric Medicine. Podiatric preceptor Monterey (Calif.) Podiatry Group, 1983-84; gen. practice podiatric medicine Merced, Calif., 1984—. Bd. dirs. Merced Mariposa Chpt. ARC. Mem. Am. Podiatric Med. Assn., Calif. Podiatry Assn., Acad. Ambulatory Foot Surgeons, Calif. Coll. Podiatric Medicine Alumni Assn., Bus. and Profl. WOmen's Club (Young Career Woman award 1985). Lodge: Soroptimists. Avocations: running, golf, graphic printing and design, travel. Home: 30 W 23d St #A Merced CA 95340 Office: 3071 College Green Dr Suite B Merced CA 95348

BUSECK, PETER ROBERT, geochemistry educator. s. Paul M. and Edith G. (Stern) B.; m. Alice E. Buseck, June 20, 1960; children—Lori, David, Susan, Paul. A.B., Antioch Coll., 1957; M.A., Columbia U., 1959, Ph.D., 1962. Fellow geophysics lab. Carnegie Inst., Washington, 1961-63; mem. faculty depts. chemistry and geology Ariz. State U., Tempe, 1963—, now prof.; vis. prof. dept. geology Oxford U., Eng., 1970-71, Stanford U., Calif., 1979-80; vis. prof. U. Paris, 1986-87. Contbr. articles to profl. jours. NSF fellow, 1970-71; recipient Corning award, 1975, JEOL award Microbeam Analysis Soc., 1981. Fellow AAAS, Geol. Soc. Am., Mineral Soc. Am.; mem. Am. Geophys. Union, Geochem. Soc., Microbeam Soc., Soc. Econ. Geologists, Can. Mineral Soc., Air Pollution Control Assn., Am. Assn. Aerosol Research, Electron Microscope Soc. Am. Office: Ariz State U Dept Geology Tempe AZ 85287

BUSH, BERNARD JOSEPH, JR., clergyman, religious organization administrator; b. Garberville, Calif., Sept. 13, 1934; s. Bernard Joseph and Anne Josephine (Kelly). MA in Philosophy, Gonzaga U., 1957; MA in Theology, St. Mary's U., Halifax, N.S., Can., 1967; STL in Theology, St. Mary's U., 1967; PhD in Human Sci., Saybrook Inst., 1985. Joined S.J., 1951; ordained priest Roman Catholic Ch., 1965. With campus ministry U. San Francisco, 1967-69; spiritual dir. Grad. Theol. Union, Berkeley, Calif., 1969-71; chaplain, psychology intern Boston State Hosp., 1971-74; dir. House of Affirmation, Boston, 1974-77, Montara, Calif., 1977—; cons. Saybrook Inst., 1985-86. Author: Living in His Love; contbr. articles to profl. mags. Mem. Internat. Fedn. for Systems Research. Democrat. Avocations: sculpting, private piloting. Home: 589 Kanoff Ave PO Box 437 Montara CA 94037 Office: House of Affirmation 1185 Acacia St Montara CA 94037

BUSH, MARJORIE AMABEL, accountant; b. Honolulu, Feb. 26, 1949; d. William Oscar and Marjorie Kasumi (Yokoyama) B. BBA, U. Hawaii, 1978, MBA, 1980. CPA, Hawaii. Systems analyst U. Hawaii, 1980; acct., tax specialist Deloitte, Haskins & Sells, Honolulu, 1981-84; customer service rep. Control Data Bus. Ctrs., Inc., Honolulu, 1984-85; prin. M.A. Bush, CPA, Kailua, Hawaii, 1984—. Mem. budget rev. panel Aloha United Way, Honolulu, 1979-85. Mem. Am. Inst. CPA's, Hawaii Soc. CPA's, Am. Women's Soc. CPA's, Assn. Govt. Accts. (dir. 1981-83), U. Hawaii MBA Alumni Group, Beta Alpha Psi, Beta Gamma Sigma. Democrat. Episcopalian.

BUSH, SPENCER HARRISON, metallurgist; b. Flint, Mich., Apr. 4, 1920; s. Edward Charles and Rachel Beatrice (Roser) B.; m. Roberta Lee Warren, Aug. 28, 1948; children: David Spencer, Carl Edward. Student, Flint Jr. Coll., 1938-40, Ohio State U., 1943-44, U. Mich., 1946-53. Registered profl. engr., Calif. Asst. chemist Dow Chem. Co., 1940-42, 46; asso. Engring. Research Inst., U. Mich., 1947-53; research asst. Office Naval Research, 1950-53, instr. dental materials, 1951-53; metallurgist Hanford Atomic Products Operation, Gen. Electric Co., 1953-54, supr. phys. metallurgy, 1954-57, supr. fuels fabrication devel., 1957-60, metall. specialist, 1960-63, cons. metallurgist, 1963-65; cons. to dir. Battelle N.W. Labs., Richland, Wash., 1965-70; sr. staff cons. Battelle N.W. Labs., 1970-83; pres. Rev. & Synthesis Assocs., cons., 1983—; lectr. metall. engring. Center for Grad. Study, U. Wash., 1953-67, affiliate prof., 1967-78; chmn., com. study group on pressure vessel materials Electric Power Research Inst., 1974-78; cons. U. Calif. Lawrence Berkeley Labs., 1975-79; chmn. com. on reactor safeguards U.S. AEC, 1971; mem. Wash. Bd. Boiler Rules, 1972-85; Gillett lectr. ASTM, 1975; Mehl lectr., 1981, mem. Bd. Nuclear Codes and Standards, 1983—. Contbr. tech. articles to profl. jours. Served with U.S. Army, 1942-46. Recipient Silver Beaver award Boy Scouts Am.; Am. Foundrymens Soc. fellow, 1948-50; Regents prof. U. Calif., Berkeley, 1973-74. Fellow Am. Nuclear Soc. (adv. editorial bd. nuclear applications 1965-77, bd. dirs. 1984—, Thompson award 1987), ASME (chmn. sect. XI 1985—, exec. bd. NDE div. 1984—, Langer award 1983); mem. AIME (chmn. ann. seminar com. 1967-68), ASTM, Am. Soc. Metals (life, chmn. program council 1966-67, trustee 1967-69, chmn. fellow com. 1968), Nat. Acad. Engring., Sigma Xi, Tau Beta Pi, Phi Kappa Phi. Home: 630 Cedar Ave Richland WA 99352 Office: Battelle Pacific NW Labs PO Box 999 Richland WA 99352

BUSHING, WILLIAM WALTER, electronic publishing company executive; b. Oak Park, Ill., June 12, 1947; s. William Henry and Barbara Ann (Gallond) B. AB cum laude, Harvard U., 1969. Asst. headmaster Catalina Island Sch., Toyon Bay Santa Catalina Island, Calif., 1969-77; energy engr. Northrop Corp., Anaheim, Calif., 1977-78; gen. mgr. Catalina Island Odyssey, Avalon Santa Catalina Island, Calif., 1978-80; pres. Tamar Triad Group, Glenview, Ill., 1980-83, Starthrower Pubs., Avalon, 1984—; bd. dirs. Catalina Design Ctr., Avalon; cons. Cousteau Soc., Los Angeles, 1976—, BBDO Inc., Avalon, 1985—, USS Constitution Mus., Boston, 1983—, Santa Catalina Island Co., Avalon, 1986—. Author: The Changing Lake, 1982, Not Quite the Whole Universe Catalogue, 1985, AWEstronomy, 1986. Bd. dirs. Northbrook (Ill.) YMCA, 1981-82, Catalina Island Film Festival, Avalon, 1978-79; vice chmn. Mayor's Select Com. Water Conservation, Avalon, 1977; chmn. Nature Ctr.-Evanston (Ill.) Environ. Assn., 1981-82. Mem. Astron. Soc. Pacific, Catalina Conservancy, Catalina Island Sch. Alumni Assn. (bd. dirs. 1979—). Avocations: nature photography, astronomy, ocean kayaking, scuba diving, channel islands. Home: 330 Descanso Ave Avalon Catalina CA 90704 Office: Starthrower PO Box 849 Avalon Catalina CA 90704

BUSHMAN, EDWIN FRANCIS ARTHUR, engineer, plastics consultant, rancher; b. Aurora, Ill., Mar. 16, 1919; s. George J. and Emma (Gengler) B.; B.S., U. Ill., 1941, postgrad., 1941-42, Calif. Inst. Tech., 1941; m. Louise Kathryn Peterson, Jan. 3, 1946; children—Bruce Edwin, Gary Robert, Joan Louise, Karen Rose, Mary Elisabeth, Paul George. Jr. engr. Gulf Refining Co. Gulf Oil Corp., Mattoon, Ill., 1940-41; engr. radio and sound lab. war research, div. U. Calif. at Navy Electronics Lab., Pt. Loma, San Diego, 1942-45; project engr. Bell and Howell Co., Lincolnwood, Ill., 1945-46; research cons., Scholl Mfg. Co., Inc., Chgo., 1946-48; project engr. deepfreeze div. Motor Products Corp., North Chicago, Ill., 1948-50; research and product design engr. Bushman Co., Aurora, Ill. also Mundelein, Ill., 1946-55; with Plastics div. Gen. Am. Transp. Corp., Chgo., 1950-68, tech. dir., 1950-55, mgr. sales and sales engring. Western states, Compton, Calif., 1955-68, sales and sales engring. research and devel. div., 1962-64; with USS Chems., 1968-70; plastics cons. E.F. Bushman Co., 1970—, Tech. Conf. Assos., 1974—. Program mgr. Agriplastics Symposium Nat. Agrl. Plastics Conf., 1966; program mgr. Plastics in Hydrospace, 1967; originator Huisman Plastics awards, 1970, Un-Carbon Polymer prize and Polymer Pool Preserve Plan, 1975, Polymer Independence award, 1977, 78. Bd. dirs. Coastal Area Protective League, 1958-66, Lagunita Community Assn., 1959-66 (pres. 1964-65), Calif. Marine Parks and Harbors Assn., 1959-69. Recipient Western Plastics Man of Yr. award, 1972. Mem. Soc. Plastics Industry Inc. (chpt. pres. 1971-72), Soc. Plastic Engrs. (Lundberg award 1981), Western Plastics Engrs., Western Plastics Mus. and Pioneers, Plastics Pioneers Assn., ASTM, Sunkist Growers, Calif. Avocado Soc., Cal. Citrus Nurserymen's Soc., Calif. Farm Bur. Fedn. U. Ill. Alumni Assn., Lemon Men's Club, Soc. for Advancement Materials and Process Engring., Geopolymers Inst. Roman Catholic. Moose. Author various profl. and strategic resource papers. Patentee in field of plastics, carbon and colored glass fibers, process, and applications. Home: 19 Lagunita Laguna Beach CA 92651 Office: PO Box 581 Laguna Beach CA 92652

BUSHNELL, T(ED) DARRELL, real estate brokerage executive; b. Meadow, Utah, Mar. 7, 1934; s. Daniel Deardon and Melba Ellen (Stott) B.; m. Marjorie Gay Killpack, Aug. 19, 1953; children: Mikel, Debra, Sherri, Sandra. BS, Brigham Young U., 1958; grad., Realtor Inst. Pres., prin. broker Bushnell Real Estate, Provo, Utah, 1956—, also bd. dirs. Charter mem. City Council, Woodland Hills, Utah, 1980-81. Named Outstanding Young Man Yr. Jr. C. of C., Provo, 1962. Mem. Realtors Nat. Mktg. Inst., Nat. Assn. Realtors (cert. residential specialist, Utah Assn. Realtors (pres.-elect 1983-84, pres. 1984-85, bd. dirs., Realtor of Yr. 1975), Innovative Bus. Assn. (pres., chmn. bd. 1980—), Utah County Bd. Realtors (Realtor of Yr. 1969), Realtors Nat. Mktg. Inst. (cert. real estate brokerage mgr., cert. commercial investment mem.). Republican. Mormon. Lodge: Sertoma. (held past offices). Office: Bushnell Real Estate PO Box 1404 Prove UT 84603

BUSIG, RICK HAROLD, mining company executive; b. Vancouver, Wash., June 21, 1952; s. Harold Wayne and Ramona (Riley) B. A.A., Clark Coll., Vancouver, 1972; B.A. in Econs., U. Wash., 1974. C.P.A., Wash. Acct., Universal Services, Seattle, 1975-78; acct., acctg. mgr., controller Landura Corp., Woodburn, Oreg., 1978-80; asst. controller Pulte Home Corp., Laramie, Wyo., 1980-81; treas., controller Orcal Cable, Inc., Sparks, Nev., 1981-82; controller Saga Exploration Co., Reno, Nev., 1982—; acct. Sterling Mine Joint Venture, Beatty, Nev., 1982—. Del. Nev. State Dem. Conv., Reno, 1984. Recipient Spaatz award CAP. Mem. Am. Inst. CPAs, Wash. Soc. CPAs, Oreg. Soc. CPAs. Home: 2500 Dickerson Rd #147 Reno NV 89503 Office: Saga Exploration Co 2660 Tyner Reno NV 89503

BUSKIRK, RICHARD HOBART, marketing educator; b. Bloomington, Ind., Jan. 24, 1927; s. Cyrus Hobart and Aimee Ruth (Borland) B.; m. Barbara Jean Lusk, June 14, 1947; children: Bruce David, Carol Ann. BBA with distinction, Ind. U., 1948, MBA, 1949; PhD, U. Wash., 1955. Instr. mktg. U. Kans., Lawrence, 1949-53; instr. mktg. U. Wash., Seattle, 1953-55; asst. prof. mktg. U. Okla., Norman, 1955-57; prof. mktg. U. Colo., Boulder, 1957-70, Calif. State U., Fullerton, 1970-73; prof. bus. adminstrn. U. So. Calif., Los Angeles, 1973-74, prof. mktg., dir. entrepreneur program, 1980—; Herman W. Lay chair mktg. So. Meth. U., Dallas, 1974-80; dir. Staar Surg., Inc.; cons. Delta Drilling Co., Tyler, Tex., 1978-79, Weyerhaeuser Co., Tacoma, 1962-64. Author: Cases in Marketing, 1970, 74, Concepts of Business, 1970, Business and Administrative Policy, 1970, Retail Selling, 1974, Machiavelli and Modern Management, 1974, Your Career, 1975, Principles of Marketing, 4th edit., 1975, Handbook of Managerial Tactics, 1975, Retailing, 1979, Management of the Sales Force, 7th edit., 1986, Textbook of Salesmanship, 11th edit., 1982, How to Beat Men at Their Own Game, 1980, Handbook of Entrepreneurship, 1984. Mem. minority bus. opportunity com. Fed. Exec. Bd. Served with USN, 1944-46. Mem. Assn. Bus. Simulation and Exptl. Learning (past pres.), Am. Mktg. Assn. Home: One Cornell Rancho Mirage CA 92270 Office: U So Calif Sch Bus Los Angeles CA 90007

BUSS, JERRY HATTEN, real estate co. exec., sports team owner. children: John, Jim, Jeanie, Jane. BS in Chemistry, U. Wyo.; MS, PhD in Chemistry, U. So. Calif., 1957. Chemist Bur. Mines; past mem. faculty dept. chemistry U. So. Calif.; mem. missile div. McDonnell Douglas, Los Angeles; partner Mariani-Buss Assos.; former owner Los Angeles Strings; chmn. bd., owner Los Angeles Lakers (Nat. Basketball Assn.); owner Los Angeles Kings (Nat. Hockey League.). Office: care Los Angeles Lakers PO Box 10 The Forum Inglewood CA 90306 *

BUSSINGER, ROBERT E., service executive; b. Dayton, Ohio, Jan. 26, 1932; s. Albert G. and Louise B. (Hoffman) B.; m. Doreen L. Fine, Jan. 25, 1957 (div. 1968); children: Leslie E., Daniel M., David M. Student, U. Dayton, 1955-56, U. Redlands, 1957-59. Broker Bussinger Ins., Carmel, Calif., 1962-69; broker, dealer Esper Corp., Carmel, 1969-72; owner Esperanto Coffee House, Carmel, 1972-76; gen. mgr. Gen. Store Restaurant, Carmel, 1976-77; food service dir. Lodge at Pebble Beach (Calif.), 1977-79; resort v.p., gen. mgr. TransAm. Corp., Big Sur, Calif., 1979—, Ventana Inn Resort, Big Sur, 1979—. Pres. Big Sur C. of C., 1984—; bd. dirs. Monterey Penninsula C. of C., 1984—. Served with USN, 1951-55, Korea. Mem. Nat. Restaurant Assn., Calif. Hotel Assn., Monterey Penninsula Hotel Restaurant Assn., Carmel Bus. Assn., Calif. Hotel Sales Mktg. Assn., Monterey Advt. Club (v.p. 1985—). Avocations: reading and writing, photography, piano, snorkeling, dancing. Home and Office: Ventana Big Sur CA 93920

BUSSMAN, JOHN WOOD, physician, health care administrator; b. Mankato, Minn., July 4, 1924; s. A.M. and Myrtle E. (Wood) B.; m. Muriel J. Koenck, June 17, 1950; children: David, John, Sarah, James, Rebecca, Penelope. BSc, U. Minn., 1946, MB, 1947, MD, 1948. Diplomate Am. Bd. Pediatrics, Am. Bd. Pediatric Cariology. Intern Sioux Valley Hosp., Sioux Falls, S.D., 1948; residency in pediatrics U. Minn. Hosp., Mpls., 1949-50, pediatric cardiology feoow, 1951; gen. practice medicine The Children's Clinic-Sylvan Med. Services, Inc., Portland, Oreg., 1953—; clin. prof. pediatrics U. Oreg. Med. Sch.; cons. in pediatric cardiology; chief pediatrics Emanuel Hosp., 1966-69, health maintenance orgn. com. 1972; bd. dirs. Health Choice, Inc., 1983-86; chmn. Physicians' Health Network, 1982-83. Chmn. health services adv. com. Multnomah County Commrs., 1973-77; mem. Multnomah County Health Care Commn. 1977-82. Fellow Am. Acad. Pediatrics, Am. Coll. Chest Physicians (sec. com. myopathy in childhood 1976), Am. Coll. Cardiology (Oreg. gov. 1974-77); mem. Nat. Acad. Sci.

(Inst. of Medicine), Portland Acad. Pediatrics (pres. 1963), Portland Acad. Medicine, Portland Heart Club, Oreg. Heart Assn. (chmn. 1976-77, exec. com., bd. dirs. 1960-81, chmn. community service com. 1972-74, chmn. rheumatic fever commn. 1954-77, del. Am. Heart Assn. regional heart com. 1973-80, budget com., chmn. program rev. council, 1985), Oreg. Thoracic Soc. (chmn. research com. 1966), Multnomah Found. Med. Care (pres. 1970-80, med. dir. 1972-83, treas. 1980-83), Multnomah County Med. Soc. (pres. 1970, trustee 1963-71, treas .1965, sec. 1966, v.p. 1967, pres.-elect 1969, chmn. bd. censors 1971, chmn. peer rev. commn. 1971, chmn. Portland Council Hosps. liaison com. 1971), Oreg. Med. Assn. (v.p. 1972, chmn. health manpower 1972, ad hoc com. peer rev. 1972, long-range planning com. 1972, trustee 1969-80), Oreg. Found. Med. Care (bd. dirs. 1972-77), Oreg. Comprehensive Health Planning Authority (health manpower com.), Comprehensive Health Planning Assn. (chmn. project rev. com., chmn. profl. health service com., bd. dirs. 1970-77, exec. com. 1970-74), N.W. Oreg. Health Systems (health planning com. 1978-80, diagnosis and treatment subcom. 1978-80, chmn. health care tech. assessment com. 1983), HEW (Exptl. Med. Care Rev. Orgns. 1972-73), and others. Clubs: Portland City, Multnomah Athletic. Lodge: Rotary. Office: Sylvan Med Service Inc 5415 SW Westgate Dr Portland OR 97221

BUSSOLINI, PETER LOUIS, engineer, science laboratory administrator; b. Westfield, Mass., Nov. 29, 1937; s. Peter J. and Romilda (Ruffo) B.; m. Lee Oakes, June 29, 1968; children: Jeffrey, Wendy, Angela. BSCE, U. N.Mex., 1968, MSCE, 1969. Registered profl. engr., Tex., Calif. Engr. Pacific Gas & Electric Co., San Luis Obispo, Calif., 1969-71, mgr. quality control, 1971-74; mgr. quality assurance Brown & Root, Inc., Granbury, Tex., 1974-78; engr., group leader robotics, mech. engring., induction heating, plasma physics, quality assurance Los Alamos (N.Mex.) Nat. Lab., 1978—; cons. Los Alamos, 1979—. Contbr. articles to profl. jours. Served as sgt. U.S. Army, 1960-66. Avocations: running, karate, fishing. Home: 248 Canada Way Los Alamos NM 87544 Office: Los Alamos Nat Lab PO Box 1663 Los Alamos NM 87545

BUSTER, JOHN EDMOND, physician, gynecologist, medical researcher; b. Oxnard, Calif., July 18, 1941; s. Edmound B. and Beatrice (Keller) B.; m. Frances Bunn. Student, Stanford U., 1959-62; M.D., UCLA, 1966. Diplomate Am. Bd. Gynecology. Intern., Harbor UCLA Med. Ctr., Torrance, 1966-67, resident, 1967-71, research fellow, 1971-73, faculty, 1975—; prof. obstetrics and gynecology UCLA Sch. Medicine, 1983. dir. research group human embryo transplants UCLA; examiner Am. Bd. Obstetrics and Gynecology. Contbr. articles to profl. jours. Served to lt., U.S. Army, 1973-75. Mem. Soc. for Gynecologic Investigation. Presbyterian. Office: Harbor UCLA Med Ctr 1000 W Carson St Torrance CA 90509

BUSWELL, ARTHUR WILCOX, physician, surgeon; b. Oklahoma City, Jan. 6, 1926; s. Albert Currier and Enid May (Scott) B.; B.Sc., U. Okla., 1950, M.D., 1952; m. Loleta JoAnn Sherrill, June 11, 1950; children—Arthur Lee, Robert Joseph, Barbara JoAnn, Brian A., Gayla, Richard; m. 2d, Jane Marie Fuksa, Mar. 1, 1969. Intern. Fitzsimons Army Hosp. Aurora, Colo., 1952-53; surg. resident Wesley Hosp., Oklahoma City, 1954-55; practice medicine and surgery, Hennessey, Okla., 1955-63; dep. surgeon, Fort Wainwright and Yukon Command, 1963-65; chief staff Kingfisher (Okla.) Community Hosp., 1956-57; supt. health Kingfisher County, 1960-61; chief profl. service Bassett Army Hosp., 1963-65; div. surgeon 1st Armored Div., Ft. Hood, Tex., 1965-67, 1st Inf. Div., 1967-68; med. project officer U.S. Army Combat Devels. Command, Experimentation Command, Ft. Ord, Calif., 1968-72, also chief human factors div. and chief experimentation div. of experimentation command; chief profl. services Reynolds Army Hosp., Ft. Sill, Okla., 1972-73; comdr. med. dept. activities Ft. Stewart, Ga., 1973-77; chief profl. services Kenner Army Hosp., Ft. Lee, Va., 1977-78; comdr. med. dept. activities, Alaska, 1979-83; adj. asst. prof. med. scis. Baylor U., 1973—. Pres., Ft. Stewart Sch. Bd., 1977; bd. dirs. Ft. Stewart Fed. Credit Union, 1977, Chisholm Trail Mus., 1986—; pres. Friends of Library for Kingfisher County, 1984—. Served with AUS, 1944-46, 1st lt. U.S. Army, 1952-54, maj. to col., 1961-83. Decorated Legion of Merit with 2 oak leaf cluster, Soldier's medal, Bronze Star for Valor with oak leaf cluster, Meritorious Service medal, Air medal with 3 oak leaf clusters, Army Commendation medal; Gallantry cross with palm, Honor medal 1st class (both Vietnam). Fellow Royal Soc. Health; mem. Am., Okla. State (mem. no. dels.), Aerospace, Army Aviation (charter) med. assns., Assn. Mil. Surgeons U.S., Garfield-Kingfisher County Med. Soc. Home: PO Box 703 Kingfisher OK 73750

BUTH, DONALD GEORGE, biology educator; b. Chgo., Feb. 23, 1949; s. Werner George and Arlene Dolores (Kreier) B. BS in Zoology, U. Ill., 1971, AB in Anthropology, 1972, MS in Zoology, 1974, PhD in Ecology, Ethol. and Evolution, 1978. Research asst. U. Ill., Urbana, 1971-78; postdoctoral researcher UCLA, 1978-79, instr. biology, 1980, asst. prof., 1980—. Contbr. articles to profl. jours. Fellow AAAS, Willi Hennig Soc. (councilor 1981-82); mem. Am. Soc. Ichthyologists and Herpetologists (bd. govs. 1984—, exec. com. 1983-86, assoc. editor COPEIA 1985—). Office: UCLA Dept Biology Los Angeles CA 90024-1606

BUTIGAN, WILLIAM CLAY, lawyer; b. Seattle, Mar. 25, 1957; s. Kenneth Leo and Beverly Jean (Cate) B. BA, U. Chgo., 1977, MA, 1978; JD, U. Ill., 1983. Bar: Wash. 1983, Alaska 1984, U.S. Dist. Ct. (we. dist.) Wash. 1983, U.S. Dist. Ct. Alaska 1986, U.S. Ct. Appeals (9th cir.) 1984. Assoc. Cable, Barrett et Al, Seattle, 1983-84; prin. Butigan Legal Services, Seattle, 1985—. Mem. Pioneer Sq. Preservation Bd., Seattle, 1986. Mem. Wash. State Bar Assn. Alaska State Bar Assn., Wash. State Trial Lawyers Assn., Seattle-King County Bar Assn., ABA, Am. Trial Lawyers Assn., U. Chgo. Alumni Assn. Avocation: sailing. Home and Office: 318 1st Ave S #601 Seattle WA 98104

BUTLER, BYRON CLINTON, physician, gemologist; b. Carroll, Iowa, Aug. 10, 1918; s. Clinton John and Blance (Prall) B.; m. Jo Ann Nicolls; children: Marilyn, John Byron, Barbara, Denise; 1 stepdau., Marrianne. MD, Columbia Coll. Physicians and Surgeons, 1953; grad., Gemol. Inst. Am., 1986. Intern Columbia Presbyn. Med. Ctr.; resident Sloane Hosp. for Women; instr. Columbia Coll. Physicians and Surgeons, 1950-53; dir. Butler Research Found., Phoenix, 1953-86, pres., 1970—; mem. staff St. Luke's Hosp., St. Joseph's Hosp., Humana Hosp. of Phoenix; pres. GSG, Inc./World Gems. Bd. dirs. Heard Mus., Phoenix, 1965-74; founder Dr. Byron C. Butler, G.G., Fund Inclusion Research, Santa Monica, Calif., 1987. Served to capt. M.C. AUS, 1944-46. Grantee Am. Cancer Soc., 1946-50, NIH, 1946-50. Fellow AAAS; mem. Am. Gemstones Trader Assn., Internat. Gemstone Assn. Home: 6302 N 38th St Paradise Valley AZ 85253 Office: 550 W Thomas Rd Phoenix AZ 85013

BUTLER, DAVID ALLEN, typesetting company executive; b. Pasadena, Calif., Mar. 13, 1944; s. Franklin Pierce and Leora Ruby (Westbrook) B. B.A., Pasadena Coll. (name changed to Point Loma Nazarene Coll.), 1966. Proofreader, Los Angeles Times, 1967-68, 71-72; tchr. Pasadena City Schs., 1968; typesetter Freedmen's Orgn., Los Angeles, 1972—, small bus. pres., 1977—. Served with U.S. Army, 1968-71, ETO. Republican. Mem. Ch. of Nazarene. Office: Freedmens Orgn 3311 Beverly Blvd Los Angeles CA 90004

BUTLER, GARY GUY, oil company executive, marketing executive; b. Napa, Calif., Oct. 18, 1955; s. Myles Milton and Martha Marie (Borchers) B. AA in Nat. Sci., Napa Jr. Coll., 1976; BA in Chemistry, Sonoma State Coll., 1978; MBA, St. Mary's Coll. Calif., 1984. Lab. tech. Chevron USA Inc., Emeryville, Calif., 1978-80; chemist Chevron USA Inc., San Francisco, 1980-82, sales rep., 1982-84; tech. rep. Chevron USA Inc., Chgo., 1984-85; mktg. rep. Chevron USA Inc., Portland, Oreg., 1985—. Mem. Am. Chem. Soc., Am. Soc. Lubrication Engrs., Nat. Rifle Assn. Republican. Lutheran. Avocations: hunting, fishing, water skiing, photography. Office: Chevron USA Inc PO Box 4168 Portland OR 97208

BUTLER, JEFFREY SHERIDAN, publisher; b. Christopher, Ill., June 19, 1939; s. Jefferson Macklin and Veneita May (Slinger) B.; B.S. in Mktg., U. Ill., 1961; m. Erin Clarke; children—Drew Sheridan, Emily Louise. With UARCO Bus. Systems Sales, Chgo., 1961-62; dir. public relations Pacific S.W. Airlines, San Diego, 1965-68; chmn. bd., chief exec. officer, founder, pub. East/West Network Inc., Los Angeles, 1968—; pub. mags. N.W. Airlines, Pan Am. Airlines, PSA, United Airlines, Eastern Airlines, TWA, S.W. Airlines, also Dial mags. Bd. dirs. So. Calif. Visitors Council, United Service Orgn. met. N.Y. Served with M.C., AUS, 1962-65. Mem. Sigma Nu. Clubs: Regency (Los Angeles); Doubles Internat., Westchester Country (N.Y.); Annabel's (London). Office: East/West Network Inc 5900 Wilshire Blvd 8th Floor Los Angeles CA 90036

BUTLER, LESLIE ANN, creative director advertising agency; b. Salem, Oreg., Nov. 19, 1945; d. Marlow Dole and Lala Ann (Erlandson) Butler. Student Lewis and Clark Coll., 1963-64; B.S., U. Oreg., 1969; postgrad. Portland State U. 1972-73. Creative trainee Ketchum Advt., San Francisco, 1970-71; asst. advt. dir. Mktg. Systems, Inc., Portland, Oreg., 1971-74; copywriter prodn. mgr., art dir., copywriter Finzer-Smith, Portland, 1974-76; copywriter Gerber Advt., Portland, 1976-78; freelance copywriter, Portland, 1978-80, 83-85; copywriter McCann-Erickson, Portland, 1980-81; copy chief Brookstone Co., Peterborough, N.H., 1981-83. Co-founder, v.p., newsletter editor Animal Rescue and Care Fund, 1972-81. Recipient Internat. Film and TV Festival N.Y. Finalist award, 1985, 86, Internat. Radio Festival of N.Y. award, 1984, 85, Hollywood Radio and TV Soc. Internat. Broadcasting award, 1981, TV Comml. Festival Silver Telly award, 1985, TV Comml. Festival Bronze Telly, 1986, AVC Silver Cindy, 1986, Los Angeles Advt. Women LULU, 1986, 87, Ad Week What's New Portfolio, 1986, N.W. Addy award Seattle Advt. Fedn., 1985, Best of N.W. award N.W. Seminar Film and Video, 1985, numerous others. Mem. Portland Advt. Fedn. (Rosey Finalist award 1986), Portland Art Assn., Assn. Research and Enlightenment. Address: 6005 SE 21st Ave Portland OR 97202

BUTLER, OCTAVIA ESTELLE, free-lance writer; b. Pasadena, Calif., June 22, 1947; d. Laurice and Octavia Margaret (Guy) B. AA, Pasadena City Coll., 1968; student, Calif. State U., Los Angeles, 1969—. Free-lance writer Los Angeles, 1975—. Author: Patternmaster, 1976, Mind of my Mind, 1977, Survivor, 1978, Kindred, 1979, Wild Seed, 1980, Clay's Ark, 1984, Dawn, 1987; also sci. fiction short stories. Recipient fifth prize Writer's Digest Short Story Contest, 1967, Creative Arts Achievement award Los Angeles YWCA, 1980, Sci. Fiction (Hugo) Best Noveletteaward Sci. Fiction Writers Am., 1985, Best Short Story award Sci. Fiction Writers Am., 1984, Nebula Best Novelette award Sci. Fiction Writers Am., 1985, Locus Best Novelette award World Sci. Fiction Conv., 1985, Best Novelette award Sci. Fiction Chronicle Reader, 1985. Mem. Sci. Fiction Writers Am. Address: PO Box 6604 Los Angeles CA 90055

BUTLER, PARLEY NARVIN, metal products manufacturing company executive; b. Ogden, Utah, Dec. 22, 1928; s. Parley A. and Louisa Ardelia (Thompson) B.; grad. Weber Coll., 1950; grad. indsl. engr., 1958; m. Wilma Johansen, Sept. 11, 1950; children—Susan, Curtis, Paul, Julie, Mary. Crew foreman Ogden Union Ry. & Depot Co. (Utah), 1944-50; office mgr. Quaker Oats Co., Ogden, 1950-55, Joplin, Mo., 1955-59, Marion, Ohio, 1959-62, Chattanooga, Tenn., 1962-65, St. Joseph, Mo., 1965-73; controller Magic Pan Inc. subs. of Quaker Oats Co., San Francisco, 1973-74; asst. gen. mgr., controller Powder River Enterprises, Provo, Utah, 1974-81; asst. sec., treas. Powder River Enterprises, Inc., Provo, 1975-83, sec., 1983-85; v.p. Provo Aviation, 1978-80, sec. 1983-85; v.p. Am. West Advt., 1978-82; sec.-treas. Powder River Motor Transport, Inc., 1977-85; sec.-treas. Stout Corp., 1981-84; pres. Quaker Oats Employees Credit Union, St. Joseph, 1971-73; trustee, adminstr. Powder River Enterprises Profit Sharing Plan, 1974-85; v.p., bd. dirs. Certa Fin. Group, Inc., Provo, 1986—. Curator St. Joseph Archeaol. Soc., 1965-73. Served with U.S. Army, 1946-48. Mem. Nat. Assn. Accts. (v.p. 1972-73), Adminstrv. Mgmt. Assn. (v.p. 1964-65), Utah Taxpayers Assn. (dir. 1982-85). Republican. Mormon. Club: Lions (past pres. 1971-72). Home: 625 E 60 N Circle St Orem UT 84057 Office: PO Box 758 Provo UT 84601

BUTLER, REX LAMONT, lawyer; b. New Brunswick, N.J., Mar. 24, 1951; s. Ekker and Beatrice (Curry) B.; m. Willie Ruth Harris; children: Nijel Jaibrun, Vikteria Lamontra. AA, Fla. Jr. Coll., 1975; BA, U. North Fla., 1977; JD, Howard U., 1983. Bar: Alaska, U.S. Dist. Ct. Alaska, U.S. Ct. Appeals (9th cir.). Assoc. M. Ashley Dickerson, Inc., Anchorage, 1983-84; project legis. asst. State of Alaska, Juneau, 1984; asst. atty. gen. %, Anchorage, 1984-85; sole practice Anchorage, 1985—; adj. prof. law Anchorage Community Coll., 1985. Pres. Alaska Black Caucus, Anchorage, 1986, bd. dirs. 1987—; gen. counsel NAACP, Anchorage, 1985—; commr. Anchorage Telephone Utility, 1985—; trustee Anchorage Sr. Ctr., Inc., 1985—, Shiloh Missionary Bapt. Ch., Anchorage, 1985—; bd. dirs. Ctr. for Drug Problems, Anchorage, 1985-86, Alaska Civil Liberties Union, 1987—. Served with USN, 1969-73. Named one of Outstanding Young Men Am., 1984; recipient Cert. Appreciation, African Relief Campaign, 1985. Mem. ABA, Nat. Bar Assn., Alaska Bar Assn., Assn. Trial Lawyers Am., Anchorage Bar Assn., Alaska Trial Lawyers Assn., Omega Psi Phi. Democrat. Home: PO Box 200025 Anchorage AK 99520 Office: 1016 W 6th Ave Suite 440 Anchorage AK 99501

BUTLER, WILLIAM DAVID, state agency administrator; b. Manhattan, N.Y., May 15, 1938; s. William and Margaret Butler. BA in Psychology, Long Island U.-C.W. Post Ctr., 1968; MA in Clin. Psychology, Ball State U., 1970; EdD in Rehab., U. Ariz., 1984. Social worker State of Ariz., Phoenix, 1972-74; counselor in vocat. rehab. Dept. Econ. Security, State of Ariz., Phoenix, 1978-80, rehab. supr. Good Samaritan Med. Ctr., 1980—. Editor/author (manual) Community Resources Learning Disabled Adults, 1985; contbr. articles to profl. jours. Mem. adv. council disabled student services, Scottsdale Community Coll. Served with U.S. Army, 1955-62. Mem. Nat. Rehab. Assn., Cert. Rehab. Counselors (cert.), Ariz. Assn. Counselors of Learning Disabled (adv. bd.), Nat. Network of Learning Disabled Adults (steering com. 1981-82, pres. 1981-83, editor newsletter 1984—). Avocations: real estate, skiing. Office: Samaritan Rehab Inst 1111 E McDowell Rd 1B Phoenix AZ 85062

BUTT, THOMAS KING, architect, real estate broker; b. Albuquerque, Mar. 23, 1944; s. Thomas Franklin and Cecilia (King) B.; m. Shirley Ann Ryland, Nov. 26, 1971; children: Andrew Martin, Daniel Ryland. BA, BArch, U. Ark., 1967; MArch, UCLA, 1973. Registered architect, Calif., Nev., Ark.; lic. real estate broker, Calif.; lic. gen. contractor, Calif. Architect, Edward Durrell Stone, Inc., N.Y.C. and Palo Alto, Calif., 1968-70; design architect Mayhew & Thiederman, Architects, San Francisco, 1971; founder, pres. Interactive Resources, Inc., Richmond, Calif., 1973—; pres. Rainbow Enterprises, Inc., Richmond, 1978—; lectr. in field. Contbr. articles to profl. jours. Pres., East Bro. Light Sta., Inc., San Francisco, 1979-87; chmn. Richmond Econ. Devel. Commn., West Contra Costa Bayshore Council. Served with C.E., U.S. Army, 1968-70. Decorated Bronze Star, Army Commendation medal; recipient Pres.'s Cert. for Outstanding Community Achievement of Vietnam-Era Vets., 1979, Pub. Service award U.S. Coast Guard, 1982. Mem. AIA, Nat. Assn. Realtors, Am. Arbitration Inst., Constrn. Specifications Inst., Richmond C. of C. (bd. dirs. 1987), Nat. Trust for Historic Preservation (honor award 1982), Sigma Nu. Club: Rotary (bd. dirs.). Office: 117 Park Pl Richmond CA 94801

BUTTERFIELD, DONALD GENE, physician, gastroenterologist; b. Bloomfield, Iowa, Dec. 20, 1937; s. James Delbert and Sada Larue (Beckly) B.; m. Beverly Bebe Butters, June 12, 1960 (dec. Oct. 1974); children: Bradley James, Andrew Edward, Matthew Willard; m. Cynthia Wentworth Strickland, June 28, 1975; stepchildren: Geoffry H. Manning, Meredith S. Manning. BA in Biology, Cornell Coll., Mt. Vernon, Iowa, 1960; MD, Iowa State U., 1963. Diplomate Am. Bd. Internal Medicine, Am. Bd. Gastroenterology. Intern Phila. Gen. Hosp., 1963-64; resident U. Colo. Med. Ctr., Denver, 1966-68, fellow in gastroenterology, 1968-70; practice medicine specializing in gastroenterology Denver and Aurora, Colo., 1970—; mem. staff, chmn. div. gastroenterology, dir. gastrointestinal lab. Presbyn. Med. Ctr., 1970—, chief of staff, 1981-84, chief of medicine, 1977-79; pres. consol. med. bd. Presbyn./St. Luke's Hosps., 1985, also bd. dirs.; mem. staff St. Joseph Hosp., 1970—, St. Luke's Hosp., 1970—, Mercy Hosp., 1970—; asst. clin. prof. internal medicine U. Colo. Health Scis. Ctr., Denver, 1978-86, assoc. clin. prof., 1986—; bd. fellows U. Denver, 1985—; bd. dirs. Denver Presbyn. Hosp., physician Nat. Advisory bd. Am. Med. Internat., Beverly Hills, Calif., 1986—, bd. dirs.; founding mem., sec. Colo. Trust, Denver, 1985—. Contbr. articles to profl. jours. Served to capt. USAF, 1964-66. Mem. ACP, Am. Soc. Internal Medicine, Colo. Soc. Internal Medicine, Denver Med. Soc., Colo. Med. Soc., AMA, Am. Soc. Gastrointestinal Endoscopy, Am. Gastroenterology Assn., Denver Symphony Orch. Assn., Denver Mus. Natural History, Denver Bot. Gardens, Denver Art Mus., Denver Mus. Western Art, Phi Beta Kappa, Alpha Omega Alpha. Republican. Congregationalist. Clubs: Racquet World (Denver), Snowmass Country (Colo.). Avocations: skiing, tennis, golf, gardening. Home: Denver/Aurora Gastroenterologist 1721 E 19th Ave Suite 260 Denver CO 80218

BUTTERFIELD, SETH JAMES, small business owner, consultant; b. Murray, UT, Nov. 12, 1933; s. Thomas Ralph and Cornelia Jane (Crane) B.; m. Shirley Joyce Henshaw, July 30, 1955; children: Seth Lee, Ronda Suzanne Caywood. BS in Acctg. and Mgmt., Weber State Coll., 1976. Enlisted USAF, Parks AFB, Calif., 1952; commd. 2d lt. USAF, Kessler AFB, Miss., 1954; advanced through grades to lt. col. USAF, Kincheloe AFB, Mich., 1971, ret., 1973; dir. community devel. City of Ogden, Utah, 1973-77; pres. Butterfield & Assocs., Inc., Ogden, 1977-86; owner Butterfield Lines Antiques, Ogden, 1985—. Capt. voting dist. Reps. Weber County, Ogden, 1978, also dist. chmn., 1980. Decorated Air medal USAF, 1970. Mem. Nat. Assn. Housing Redevel. (state chmn. 1975). Republican. Mormon. Lodge: Lions (pres. Roswell, N.Mex. Club 1966-67). Avocations: square dancing, bowling. Home: 1413 Marilyn Dr Ogden UT 84403

BUTTERWORTH, EDWARD LIVINGSTON, distributing company executive, lawyer; b. Los Angeles, May 24, 1914; s. Esther (Livingston) B.; m. Shirley Townsend, Oct. 12, 1946; children—Edward, Lynne, Kenneth, David, Lorell. BA, Stanford U., 1936, LLB, 1939. Ptnr. Butterworth & Waller, Los Angeles, 1946-77; pres., chief exec. officer, dir. Fedco Inc., Santa Fe Springs, Calif., 1977—. Mayor City of Arcadia, Calif., 1968-72; pres. San Gabriel Valley council Boy Scouts Am., 1980; mem. Arcadia Arboretum Commn.; U.S. del. Internat. Conf. of Local Authorities, Am. Mcpl. Assn., 1963. Felix Frankfurter scholar Harvard U., 1936-37. Mem. Order of Coif, Phi Beta Kappa. Methodist. Office: Fedco Inc 9300 Santa Fe Springs Rd Santa Fe Springs CA 90670

BUTTERWORTH, ROBERT ROMAN, psychologist, psychoanalytic psychotherapist; b. Pittsfield, Mass., June 24, 1946; s. John Leon and Martha Helen (Roman) B. BA, SUNY, 1972; MA, Marist Coll., 1975; PhD in Clin. Psychology, Calif. Grad. Inst., 1983; postgrad., Am. Inst. for Psychotherapy and Psychoanalysis, 1978. Counselor intern Community Mental Health Ctr., Albany, N.Y., 1971, SUNY Coll., New Paltz, 1974-75; asst. clin. psychologist N.Y. State Dept. Mental Hygiene, Wassaic, 1972-75; pvt. practice clin. psychology Encino and Westwood, Calif., 1976—; psychometrist SAFA Med. Ctr., Hollywood, Calif., 1976-77; staff counselor Friends of the Famly Counseling Ctr., Van Nuys, Calif., 1977-78; dir. clin. alcohol services Los Angeles County Dept. Health Services, 1977-78; psychologist Acad. Guidance Services, Los Angeles, 1977-78; psychol. cons., Los Angeles, 1977-78; dir. Famliy Service Agy., 1981-82; clin psychologist Sir Thomas More Clinic, 1982—; staff clinician San Bernardino County Dept. Mental Health, 1983—; pres. Contemporary Psychology Assocs., Inc. 1976—. Past mem. Los Angeles County Drug Commn. Served with USAF, 1965-69. Mem. Am. Personnel and Guidance Assn., Am. Psychol Assn., Calif. State Psychol. Assn., Am. Assn. Marriage and Family Counselors, Assn. Humanistic Psychology, Nat. Accreditation Assn. of Psychoanalysis. Office: 431 S Kingsley Suite 308 Los Angeles CA 90020

BUTTERY, RONALD GORDON, research chemist; b. Terowie, Australia, Dec. 4, 1930; came to U.S., 1955; s. Percy Shelton and Dora (Jose) B.; m. Marie Amato, Sept. 7, 1957; children: Christopher J., Mark J., Margaret A. BS, U. Adelaide, Australia, 1953, PhD, 1956. Postdoctoral fellow Hickrill Research Found. Yale U., Katonah, N.Y., 1955-56; postdoctoral fellow U. Adelaide, Australia, 1956-57, U. Western Ontario and Laval U., Ontario and Quebec, Can., 1957-58; research chemist western regional research lab. USDA, Albany, Calif., 1958—. Contbr. articles to profl. jours.; patentee in field. Recipient USDA award for Superior Service, 1967. Fellow Am. Chem. Soc., Royal Soc. Chemistry. Democrat. Office: USDA Western Region Research Ctr 800 Buchanan St Albany CA 94710

BUTTRY, DANIEL ALAN, chemistry educator; b. Fairborn, Ohio, Apr. 4, 1955; s. Royal Hinus and Cleta Mae (Parker) B.; m. Kathie Marie Cuomo, June 5, 1982; 1 child, Clare Elaine. BA in Chemistry magna cum laude, U. Colo., Colorado Springs, 1979; PhD in Electrochemistry, Calif. Inst. Tech., 1983. Cons. Kaman Scis., Colorado Springs, 1979; teaching asst. Calif. Inst. Tech., Pasadena, 1979-83; research chemist IBM San Jose (Calif.) Research lab., 1983-85; asst. prof. chemistry U. Wyo., Laramie, 1985—. Contbr. articles to profl. jours.; inventor new etch bath for alumina. Recipient Herbert Newby McCoy award Calif. Inst. Tech., 1982; fellow ARCS Found., Los Angeles, 1981-83; grantee Research Corp., Phoenix, 1985, Calif. Inst. Tech., 1982-83. Mem. Am. Chem. Soc. (grantee 1985), Electrochem. Soc. Inc. Office: Dept Chemistry U Wyo Laramie WY 82071

BUTTS, DAVID SALM, chemical company executive, chemical engineer, consultant; b. Salt Lake City, Feb. 14, 1935; s. Curtis John and Flora (Salm) B.; m. Patricia Labrum, Nov. 1, 1957; children: Kemy Pyper, Paul, Alan, Desmon, Scott, Jamie. BSChemE, U. Utah, 1960. Tech. asst. Hercules Powder Co., Magna, Utah, 1960-65; project engr. Lithium Corp. of Am., Ogden, Utah, 1965-68; supt. Gr. Salt Lake Minerals and Chem. Corp., Ogden, 1968-72, mgr., 1972-80, asst. v.p., 1980-84; v.p. GSL Solar Cons. and Advs., Inc., Ogden, 1984—. Editor: (book) Theory and Practice of Extracting Minerals from Brine, 1984; contbr. articles to profl. jours. Treas. Jaycees State of Utah, 1969; commr. Ogden council Boy Scouts Am., 1970—; Bishopric Ch. Jesus Christ of Latter-day Saints, Ogden, 1983—. Recipient Kilpatric award Chemical Engring pub., 1970, Silver Beaver award Boy Scouts Am. Bonniville Council, 1985, Pres. award Ogden Jaycees, 1968. Mem. AIME, Am. Chem. Soc., Am. Inst. Chemists, Royal Chem. Soc. (London). Republican. Home: 4232 Porter Ave Ogden UT 84403 Office: GSL Solar Cons and Advs Inc PO Box 1190 Ogden UT 84402

BUXTON, RICHARD MILLARD, financial executive; b. Denver, July 8, 1948; s. Charles Roberts and Janet (Millard) B.; m. Consuelo Gonzalez, June 15, 1974; children—Richard Fernando. B.A. with distinction, Stanford U., 1970; M.B.A., Harvard U., 1975. Mgr. ops. planning Western Fed. Savs., Denver, 1975-78; sr. fin. analyst Rocky Mountain Energy Co., Denver, 1978-83; dir. fin. analysis, treas. Frontier Devel. Group, Inc., Denver, 1983-85; treas. Frontier Holdings, Inc., Denver, 1985-86; dir. fin. services K N Energy, Inc., Denver, 1986—. Mem. Colo. Harvard Bus. Sch. Club, Rocky Mountain Stanford Club (bd. dirs. 1982-84). Presbyterian. Club: Columbine Country. Home: 17 Wedge Way Littleton CO 80123 Office: K N Energy Inc PO Box 15265 Lakewood CO 80215

BUYERS, JOHN WILLIAM AMERMAN, agribusiness and specialty foods company executive; b. Coatesville, Pa., July 17, 1928; s. William Buchanan and Rebecca (Watson) B.; m. Elsie Palmer Parkhurst, Apr. 11, 1953; children: Elsie Buyers Viehman, Rebecca Watson Buyers-Basso, Jane Palmer Buyers-Russo. B.A. cum laude in History, Princeton U., 1952; M.S. in Indsl. Mgmt., MIT, 1963. Div. ops. mgr. Bell Telephone Co. Pa., 1964-66; dir. ops. and personnel Gen. Waterworks Corp., Phila., 1966-68; pres., chief exec. officer Gen. Waterworks Corp., Phila, 1971-75; v.p. adminstrn. Internat. Utilities Corp., Phila., 1968-71; pres., chief exec. officer, dir. C. Brewer and Co., Ltd., Honolulu, 1975—, chmn. bd., 1982—; chmn. Calif. and Hawaiian Sugar Co., 1982-84; dir. First Hawaiian Bank, IU Investment Corp.; mem. Gov.'s Adv. Council on China Affairs, U.S. Army Civilian Adv. Group, Hawaii Joint Council Econ. Edn., Japan-Hawaii Econ. Council, Commn. on Jud. Discipline. Pres., trustee U. Hawaii Found.; bd. dirs. Research Corp. U. Hawaii, Pacific Aerospace Mus. Served with USMC, 1946-48. Sloan fellow, 1963. Mem. Hawaiian Sugar Planters Assn. (chmn. bd. dirs. 1980-82, dir.), C. of C. Hawaii (chmn. bd. dirs. 1981-82), Nat. Alliance Bus. (chmn. Hawaii Pacific Metro chpt. 1978), Newcomen Soc. N.Am. Presbyterian. Clubs: Cap and Gown (Princeton); Hilo Yacht, Oahu Country, Pacific, Waialae Country, Prouts Neck (Maine) Country. Home: 148 Poipu Dr Honolulu HI 96825 Office: C Brewer & Co Ltd 827 Fort St Honolulu HI 96813 *

BUYSSE, JAMES LESTER, college official; b. Geneseo, Ill., Mar. 9, 1946; s. Lester Henry and Mabel Helen (Kemmis) B.; m. Mary Jane Wells, July 14, 1973; children: Heather Maureen, Jeremy Wade. B.S., U. Ill., 1969, M.Acctg. Sci., 1970, Ph.D. in Edn., 1978. C.P.A., Ill. Coordinator fiscal services Colo. Commn. on Higher Edn., Denver, 1972-74, assoc. exec. dir., 1979-80; coordinator fiscal research and planning Colo. State Bd. for Community Colls. and Occupational Edn., Denver, 1974-79; v.p. for adminstrv. and planning Colo. Mountain Coll., Glenwood Springs, 1980—, instr., 1981, 84; cons. Arapahoe Community Coll., Littleton, Colo., 1976; guest lectr. Colo. Ednl. Assn., Denver, 1977. Author: The Definitive Guide on How Not To Quit Smoking, 1982. Contbr. articles to newspaper. Mem. City Fin. Com., Glenwood Springs, 1983-84; basketball coach YMCA, Littleton, 1979-80; coach Youth Soccer League, Englewood, Colo., 1979. Recipient resolution of appreciation Colo. Commn. on Higher Edn., 1980. Mem. Nat. Assn. Coll. and Univ. Bus. Officers, Colo. Assn. Planners and Instnl. Researchers, Colo. Assn. Community Coll. Bus. Officers. Republican. Roman Catholic. Office: Colo Mountain Coll PO Box 10001 Glenwood Springs CO 81602

BUZZO, MARGARET MINNIE WALKER (MARGE), artist; b. San Diego, Nov. 28, 1927; d. Harold Styles and Mollie (Whittman) Walker; m. Frank Ross Buzzo, Mar. 4, 1946; children—Yvonne, Marie, Wayne Bennette. A.A., Long Beach City Coll., 1952; postgrad. Los Angeles Art Ctr. Sch. Design, 1956-58. Artist, owner Marge Buzzo Art Service, Woodland Hills, Calif., 1972—; owner Margie Ditto Creations; lectr. in field. Exhibitions include Burbank (Calif.) Pub. Library, 1977, Independence Bank, Canoga Park, Calif., 1975; invitational shows include KCET Art Auction, Hollywood, Calif., 1971, Descanso Gardens, La Canada, Calif., 1972, ARC Nat. Hdqrs., 1982, Le Salon Des Nations, Paris, 1983; group exhibits include Lemon Tree Art Gallery, 1974, Soc. Security Office (Canoga Park), 1975, Happy Eye Gallery, 1976, Shirley Meyers Art Gallery, 1977; represented in permanent collections Burbank Pub. Lib., others. Recipient Flier Prodns. Desi award, 1980. Mem. Zonta Internat. (charter), Nat. Mus. and Gallery Registration Assn. (life), San Fernando Valley Arts Council. Roman Catholic. Juror numerous art shows and lectr. in field; illustrator numerous children's books, including: The Story of Grandma Water, 1977, The Wee River, 1979. Home: 4620 Santa Lucia Dr Woodland Hills CA 91364 Office: 21500 Wyandotte St Suite 101 Canoga Park CA 91303

BYBEE, DAVID WILLIAM, industrial electronic design consultant; b. Salt Lake City, Sept. 12, 1957; s. Don Leroy Bybee and Barbara Ann (Selby) Olsen; m. Pamela Bradley, Sept. 21, 1978 (div.); children: Michael David, Amy Catherine; m. Gaynell Ruth Anderson, June 27, 1982 (div. Apr. 1986); m. Martha Teresa Soto, July 3, 1986. Student, Utah State U., 1977. Aerial photographer, pilot Aerial Surveys, Ltd., Salt Lake City, 1977-78; photographer, drafting supr. ENH Mapping, Inc., Salt Lake City, 1978-79; CAD printed circuit designer Evans and Sutherland, Salt Lake City, 1979-83; mgr. computer aided design Wicat Systems, Inc., Orem, Utah, 1983—, dir. product devel., 1986—; v.p. MCR Records, Inc., Alpine, Utah, 1986—; pres., chief exec. officer Hytek CAD, Inc., Orem, 1985—, also chmn. bd.; treas. Racal-Redac Users Group, Inc., Boulder, 1981-82, v.p. 1984-85, pres. and chmn. bd. dirs. Contbr. articles on fine line design techniques to profl. jours. Mem. Fedn. Fly Fishermen. Republican. Club: Bonneville Knife and Fork (Salt Lake City). Avocation: ski instr. Home: PO Box 485 Orem UT 84057 Office: Wicat Systems Inc 1875 S State Orem UT 84058

BYE, ROSEANNE MARIE, marketing professional; b. Chgo., Nov. 27, 1946; d. Paul David and Gwendalynn Luciell (Hipp) Forrester; B.S. in Foods and Nutrition, Western Ill. U., 1969; m. Richard Wayne Bye, June 14, 1969. Banquet mgr. Western Ill. U., 1967-69; new product home economist Hunt/Wesson Foods, Fullerton, Calif., 1969-73; retail and restaurant home economist Lawry's Foods, Los Angeles, 1973-74; mgr. product devel. Carl Karcher Enterprises, Anaheim, Calif., 1974-81; v.p. research and devel. Denny's Restaurants, La Mirada, Calif., 1981—; mem. speakers bur. mktg. fast food Industry/Edn. Council. Mem. food service adv. com., Calif. State U., Long Beach, Chapman Coll., adv. com. Santa Ana Jr. Coll., Garden Grove Sch. Dist. Recipient Nat. Mktg. award for devel. of Charbroiler Steak Sandwich, 1975-76, serve-yourself salad bar, 1978-79. Mem. Am. Home Econs. Assn., Calif. Home Econs. Assn. (Outstanding Economist in Bus. 1977, 79, pres. 1977-79), Home Economists in Bus. (award of excellence, Western regional adv. 1976-78, nat. pub. relations chmn. 1983-85), Women in Mgmt., Nat. Restaurant Assn. (chmn. mktg. research div.), NOW, Anaheim C. of C. (publicity chmn. 1977-78), Soc. Advancement Food Service Research (bd. dirs. 1986—), Internat. Food Service Editorial Council, Internat. Platform Assn. Republican. Presbyterian. Clubs: Tennis and Swim; Gourmet/Wine; Teddy Bear; Literary Guild; Newport Harbor Art Mus.; Bower's Art Mus.; Gem Theatre Guild. Office: Denny's Restaurants 16700 Valley View Ave La Mirada CA 90637

BYER, DOROTHY ELAINE, artist, designer craftsman, botanist; b. Watkins Glen, N.Y., May 22, 1925; d. Clinton and Edna (Randall) VanVleet; m. Marshall Byer, June 13, 1949; children: Deborah and Judith (twins), Linda. BA, SUNY, Binghamton, 1984. Designer Corning Glass Works, N.Y.C., 1941-43; profl. potter, designer, craftsman, sculptor 1953—; Bd. dirs. Roberson Mus. Fine Arts Soc., 1959, N.Y. State Craftsmen, 1958-61, 64-67, asst. mgr. fair 1960, mgr. fair 1961, pres. 1964, bd. advisors, 1975. Exhibited shows include Roberson Mus. (award for pottery), Binghamton, 1959, Design Ctr. for Interiors, N.Y.C., 1959, Cooper Union Mus. for Arts of Decoration, 1959, N.Y. State Craft Fair, 1959, 60, Lowe Gallery, 1960, Rundell Gallery, 1960, SUNY-Binghamton, 1961, Cortland, 1961; represented in Sculpture Courtyard, SUNY-Binghamton, 1981. Mem. Am. Fern Soc., Internat. Palm Soc. Address: 2076 Warmlands Ave Vista CA 92084

BYER, MARSHALL, mechanical engineer; b. Boston, Sept. 16, 1924; s. Selik Jacob and Flora (Goldsmith) B.; m. Dorothy Elaine Van Vleet, June 13, 1949; children: Deborah E. Byer McLaren, Judith Y. Byer Freeman, Linda D. SB in Naval Architecture and Marine Engring., MIT, 1947. Registered profl. engr., N.Y., Fla., Calif. Test engr. Foster Wheeler Corp., Dansville, N.Y., 1947-48; sr. product engr. Corning Glass Works, N.Y., 1948-58; mgr. analytical design engring. IBM Corp., Owego, N.Y., 1958-69; sr. engr. IBM Corp., Endicott, N.Y., 1970-84; cons., tax preparer on bus. mgmt. and computer applications Byer Cons., Vista, Calif., 1984—. Contbr. articles to profl. jours.; patentee making of composite glaceramic articles. Active Broome County United Way, 1978-80. Served to lt. comdr. USNR, 1943-46, 51-53. Charles Hayden Meml. scholar MIT. Mem. ASME, NSPE. Jewish. Home: 2076 Warmlands Ave Vista CA 92084 Office: Byer Consultants 2076 Warmlands AVe Vista CA 92084

BYERS, EDWARD W., library director; b. Pitts., Jan. 2, 1948. B.A. in History, Lawrence U., 1971; M.A.L.S., U. Denver, 1972. Sci. ref. librarian Pub. Library of Cin. and Hamilton County, 1972-73; head of reference Warder Pub. Library, Springfield, Ohio, 1973, head main library, 1974-77; dir. Laramie County Library System, Cheyenne, Wyo., 1977—. Bd. dirs. Bibliog. Ctr. for Research, Denver. Mem. Wyo. Library Assn. (exec. bd., pres. pub. library sect. 1984), ALA (mem. council 1980-83), PLA, LAMA, Mountain Plains Library Assn. (v.p. pub. library sect. 1987), Am Soc. Info. Sci., Bd. editors Miami Valley List of University Serials, 1973-77. Office: Laramie County Library System 2800 Central Ave Cheyenne WY 82001

BYNAGLE, HANS EDWARD, library director, philosophy educator; b. Ruurlo, The Netherlands, Feb. 24, 1946; came to U.S., 1956; s. Cornelius Adrian and Maria (Kalfsbeek) B.; m. Janet Mae Monsma, June 27, 1969; children: Maria Elizabeth, Derek Johannes. BA, Calvin Coll., 1968; PhD, Columbia U., 1973; MLS, Kent State U., 1976. Asst. prof. philosophy Union Coll., Schenectady, N.Y., 1972-73, Coll. Wooster, Ohio, 1974-75; dir. learning resources Friends U., Wichita, Kans., 1976-82; dir. library Eckerd Coll., St. Petersburg, Fla., 1982-83; dir. library, assoc. prof. Whitworth Coll., Spokane, Wash., 1983—. Author: Philosophy: A Guide to the Reference Literature, 1986; numerous rev. to profl. jours. Named one of Outstanding Young Men of Am., 1982. Mem. ALA, Kans. Library Assn. (chmn. Coll. and Univ. Library sect. 1980-81), Assn. Coll. and Research Libraries (chmn. Kans. chpt. 1980-81), Wash. Library Assn. Presbyterian. Avocation: music. Home: W 1122 Bellwood Dr Spokane WA 99218 Office: Whitworth Coll Spokane WA 99251

BYNUM, RANDY JON, sales manager; b. Camden, N.J., Dec. 17, 1950; s. E. Earl and Betty M. (Boyer) B.; m. Della M. Tinney, June 19, 1971; children: Kathryn M., Virginia L. AS, Ryder Inst., 1971. Product mgr. Plasma-Therm, Inc., Kresson, N.J., 1973-80; western region mgr. Plasma-Therm, Inc., San Jose, Calif., 1980-83; nat. sales mgr. ITP Inc., Sunnyvale, Calif., 1983-85; product sales mgr. Prometrix Corp., Santa Clara, Calif., 1985-86; Western regional mgr. GCA Tropel, Sunnyvale, 1986—; RF design cons. DR Enterprises, San Jose, Calif., 1986—, clean room cons. Gilbert Techs., Shrewsburg, Mass., 1986. Vol. communications ARC, Santa Cruz, Calif., 1981. Mem. Am. Vacuum Soc., Semicondr. Equipment Mfrs. Inc. (editor 1983). Methodist. Home: 3634 Deedham Dr San Jose CA 95148

BYRD, BARBARA JEAN, gerontological social worker, writer; b. Oak Park, Ill., Mar. 28, 1946; d. Milford Arthur and Carolyn Louise (Heflin) Bergsten. BS, Iowa State U., 1968; MSW, U. Calif., Berkeley, 1978. Lic. cert. social worker, 1982. Tchr. pub. schs. N.J. and Va., 1968-73; coordinator outreach and supportive services Services for Srs., San Francisco, 1973-76; asst. dir. Retired Sr. Vol. Program, San Francisco, 1975, S. San Francisco Sr. Ctr., 1975-76; dir. projects S. San Francisco Sr. Outreach, 1975-76; intern Family Service Agys., Palo Alto, Calif., 1976-77, Marin, Calif., 1977-78; dir. social and resident services The Redwoods retirement community, Mill Valley, Calif., 1978—; lectr. Sch. Social Welfare U. Calif., Berkeley, 1980, various community groups, 1978—; supr. grad. student interns, Depts. Social Welfare, Psychology, U. Calif. Berkeley, San Francisco State U., and San Francisco Theol. Sem., 1978—. Mem. Am. Soc. on Aging, Calif. Specialists on Aging, Bay Area Social Workers in Health Care (exec. com. 1983—), Marin County Sect. Aging (co-chmn. exec. com.), Connections Western Gerontol. Soc. (editorial bd. Connections newsletter), Case Mgmt. Adv. Com., Marin County Long Term Care Com. (chmn. assessment subcom.), Nat. Assn. Social Workers. Democrat. Avocations: hiking, reading, attending movies and theatre. Home: 134 Granada Dr Corte Madera CA 94925 Office: Redwoods Retirement Community 40 Camino Alto Mill Valley CA 94941

BYRD, JOANN KATHLEEN, newspaper editor; b. Baker, Oreg., Jan. 5, 1943; d. Joe Bryant and Anne Bradford (Dickson) Green; m. James Douglas Byrd, Mar. 11, 1978; 1 child by previous marriage—Drew Joseph Gibbs. B.S. in Journalism, U. Oreg., 1964. Student reporter East Oregonian, Pendleton, 1956-64; reporter Spokane Daily Chronicle, 1964-69, 72-74, asst. city editor, 1974-78; city editor The Herald, Everett, Wash., 1978-81, mng. editor, 1981, exec. editor, 1981—. Bd. visitors John S. Knight Fellowships, Stanford U., 1983-84, program com., 1984—; continuing studies chmn. Wash. AP News Execs., 1984-85, v.p. 1986-87; judge Ernie Pyle awards, 1984. Mem. Am. Soc. Newspaper Editors. Home: 7930 53d Ave W #203 Mukilteo WA 98275 Office: The Herald Grand and California Sts Everett WA 98206

BYRD, RONALD DALLAS, civil engineer, consultant; b. Reno, Nov. 30, 1934; s. Eugene Richard and Helen Madelyn (Hursh) B.; m. Irene Josephine Phenix, Sept. 19, 1953; children: Kevin Gregory, Helen Christine, Stephanie Irene. BSCE, U. Nev., 1960. Registered profl. engr., Nev., Calif., Oreg., Wash., Idaho., Wyo. Staff engr. Sprout Engrs., Sparks, Nev., 1960-64, design engr., 1964-67; office mgr. Sprout Engrs., Seattle, 1967-70; v.p. SE&A Engrs., Seattle, 1970-72; exec. v.p. SE&A Engrs., Sparks, 1972—; also bd. dirs. SE&A Engrs.; bd. dirs. ABS Land Co. Fellow ASCE (sec. 1966-67); mem. NSPE (bd. dirs. 1983-86), Am. Pub. Works Assn., U. Nev. Reno Engring. Alumni Assn. (sec. 1985-86). Republican. Methodist. Lodges: Kiwanis (pres. Sparks club 1965-66), Rotary (pres. Federal Way, Wash. club 1971-72), Elks, Masons. Home: 50 Rancho Manor Dr Reno NV 89509 Office: SE&A Inc 950 Industrial Way Sparks NV 89431

BYRNE, GEORGE MELVIN, physician; b. San Francisco, Aug. 1, 1933; s. Carlton and Esther (Smith) B.; B.A., Occidental Coll., 1958; M.D., U. So. Calif., 1962; m. Joan Stecher, July 14, 1956; children—Kathryne, Michael, David; m. 2d, Margaret C. Smith, Dec. 18, 1982. Intern, Huntington Meml. Hosp., Pasadena, Calif., 1962-63, resident, 1963-64; family practice So. Calif. Permanente Med. Group, 1964-82, physician-in-charge Pasadena Clinic, 1966-81; asst. dir. Family Practice residency Kaiser Found. Hosp., Los Angeles, 1971-73; clin. instr. emergency medicine Sch. Medicine, U. So. Calif., 1973-80; v.p. East Ridge Co., 1983-84, sec., 1984; dir. Alan Johnson Porsche Audi, Inc., 1974-82, sec., 1974-77, v.p., 1978-82. Bd. dirs. Kaiser-Permante Mgmt. Assn., 1976-77; mem. regional mgmt. com. So. Calif. Lung Assn., 1976-77; patron Los Angeles County Mus. Art; mem. pres.'s circle Occidental Coll. Diplomate Am. Bd. Family Practice. Fellow Am. Acad. Family Physicians (charter); mem. Am., Calif., Los Angeles County med. assns., Calif. Acad. Family Physicians, Nat. Rifle Assn. (life), Internat. Horn Soc., Friends of Photography, Am. Radio Relay League (Pub. Service award). Clubs: Sierra (life mem.). Home: 528 Meadowview Dr La Canada Flintridge CA 91011

BYRNE, JOHN PATRICK, state official, retired army officer; b. Detroit, May 25, 1929; s. George Arnold and Opal Vere (Cooper) B.; B.S., Johns Hopkins U., 1958; M.B.A. with high distinction, U. Mich., 1961; grad. Army War Coll., 1971; m. Dolores Ann Meyer, Aug. 11, 1951; children—John Patrick, David Michael, Richard Terrence, Kevin Francis. Commd. 2d lt. Chem. Corps, U.S. Army, 1950, advanced through grades to col., 1970; served with Far East Command in Japan, 1951-54; various logistic assignments Army Chem. Center, Md., 1954-58; assigned to Chem. Corps Hdqrs. and Dept. of Army, The Pentagon, Washington, 1961-65; U.S. Army exchange officer to Brit. Army, Eng., 1965-68; comdr. 2d chem. bn. Ft. McClellan, Ala., 1968-70; chief of staff Cam Ranh Support Command in Vietnam, 1970-71, dep. comdr., 1971-72; dep. comdr. Bayern Support Dist., Germany, 1972-73, exec. to comdg. gen. of Theater Army Support Command, 1973-74, dep. comdr. of 1st. Support Brigade, 1974-75; comdr. Rocky Mountain Arsenal, Denver, 1975-78; dir. emergency preparedness Denver County, 1978-79; dir. disaster emergency services State of Colo., Golden, 1979—; dir. St. Vincent DePaul Stores, Denver, 1979—. Pres. Brookland Estates Citizens Assn., Alexandria, Va., 1963-65; bd. advisors Natural Hazards Research and Applications Info. Ctr., U. Colo., 1984—; bd. visitors Emergency Mgmt. Inst. at Nat. Emergency Tng. Ctr., 1987—, chmn., 1987—; hon. bd. dirs. Mile High chpt. ARC. Decorated Legion of Merit, Bronze Star; Vietnam Cross of Gallantry with palm. Mem. Nat. Emergency Mgmt. Assn. (pres. 1983-84), Assn. of U.S. Army (sec. Gallant Pelham chpt. 1969-70), Nat. Def. Preparedness Assn., Nat. Ret. Officers Assn., Denver C. of C. (mil. affairs com. 1975—), Colo. Emergency Mgmt. Assn. (sec.-treas. 1978-80), Emergency Med. Technicians Assn. of Colo. (adv. 1980—), Beta Gamma Sigma, Delta Sigma Pi, Phi Kappa Phi. Roman Catholic. Clubs: Rotary, Denver Execs. Home: 7679 Waverly Mountain Littleton CO 80127 Office: State of Colorado Div Disaster Emergency Services Camp George West Golden CO 80401

BYRNE, JOHN VINCENT, academic administrator; b. Hempstead, N.Y., May 9, 1928; s. Frank E. and Kathleen (Barry) B.; m. Shirley O'Connor, Nov. 26, 1954; children: Donna, Lisa, Karen, Steven. AB, Hamilton Coll., 1951; MA, Columbia U., 1953; PhD, U. So. Calif., 1957. Research geologist Humble Oil & Refinery Co., Houston, 1957-60; assoc. prof. Oreg. State U., Corvallis, 1960-66, prof. oceanography, 1966—, chmn. dept., 1968-72, dean Sch. Oceanography, 1972-76, acting dean research, 1976-77, dean research, 1977-80, v.p. for research and grad. studies, 1980-81, pres., 1984—; adminstr. NOAA, Washington, 1981-84; Program dir. oceanography NSF, 1966-67. Recipient Carter teaching award Oreg. State U., 1964. Fellow AAAS, Geol. Soc. Am., Am. Meteorol. Soc.; mem. Am. Assn. Petroleum Geologists, Am. Geophys. Union, Sigma Xi, Chi Psi. Club: Arlington (Portland, Oreg.). Avocations: research on oceanography and marine geology, skiing, music. Home: 3520 NW Hayes Ave Corvallis OR 97330 Office: Oreg State U Office of the Pres Corvallis OR 97331

BYRNE, NOEL THOMAS, sociologist, educator; b. San Francisco, May 11, 1943; s. Joseph Joshua and Naomi Pearl (Denison) B.; m. Elizabeth Carla Rowlin, Nov. 5, 1966 (div.); 1 child, Ginger Butler. BA in Sociology, Sonoma State Coll., 1971; MA in Sociology, Rutgers U., 1975, PhD in Sociology, 1986. Instr. sociology Douglass Coll., Rutgers U., New Brunswick, N.J., 1974-76, Hartnell Coll., Salinas, Calif., 1977-78; research dir. mgmt. grads. survey projects Sonoma State U., Rohnert Park, Calif., 1983-86; lectr. depts. sociology and mgmt. Sonoma State U., 1978—. Contbr. articles and revs. to profl. lit. Recipient Dell Pub. award Rutgers U. Grad. Sociology Program, 1976, Louis Bevier fellow, 1977-78. Mem. Am. Sociol. Assn., Pacific Sociol. Assn., AAAS, Soc. for Study Symbolic Interaction (rev. editor Jour. 1980-83), Soc. for Study Social Problems. Democrat. Home: 330 W Sierra Ave Cotati CA 94928 Office: Dept Mgmt and Econs Sonoma State U Rohnert Park CA 94928

BYRNE, WILLIAM MATTHEW, JR., federal judge; b. Los Angeles, Sept. 3, 1930; s. William Matthew and Julia Ann (Lamb) B. B.S., U. So. Calif., 1953, LL.B., 1956; LL.D., Loyola U., 1971. Bar: Calif. Mem. firm Dryden, Harrington & Schwartz, 1960-67; asst. U.S. atty So. (now Cen. Dist. Calif., 1958-60; U.S. atty. Cen. Dist. Calif., 1967-70; exec. dir. Pres. Nixon's Commn. Campus Unrest, 1970; judge U.S. Dist. Ct. (cen. dist.) Calif., Los Angeles, 1971—; instr. Loyola Law Sch., Harvard U., Whittier Coll. Served with USAF, 1956-58. Mem. ABA, Fed. Bar Assn., Calif. Bar Assn., Los Angeles County Bar Assn. (vice chmn. human rights sect.), Am. Judicature Soc. Address: US District Court US Courthouse 312 N Spring St Los Angeles CA 90012

BYRON, JUDITH ANNE, art director; b. Phila., Oct. 13, 1941; d. Joseph M. and Elizabeth (Maguiness) B.; m. Cesare M. Olivieri, Feb. 5, 1967 (div. July 1984); children: Adriana C., Stephanie L. BFA in Illustration, Moore Coll. Art, 1963. Art supr. Pa. Mut. Ins. Co., Phila., 1963-67; freelance artist Bennington, Vt., 1967-81; art dir. Sun Graphics, Tucson, 1981-84, Tucson Lifestyle Mag., 1984—. Recipient Addy award Tucson Ad Club, 1985, 86. Republican. Home: 1170 W Las Lomitas Tucson AZ 85704 Office: Tucson Lifestye Mag 7000 E Tanque Verde Tucson AZ 85715

BYRUM, DAVID LAWRENCE, chemistry and physics educator; b. Chgo., Nov. 1, 1948; s. Gloria Elizabeth (DeLyle) B.; m. Sylvia Gallegos Silvas, Sept. 13, 1969 (div. Jan. 1987); 1 child, Raymond David. BA in Edn., Ariz. State U., 1972; MEd, U. Ariz., 1978. Cert. tchr., Ariz., cert. community coll. tchr., Ariz. Instr. chemistry, track coach Salpointe High Sch., Tucson, 1972-77; instr. chemistry and physics, track coach Globe (Ariz.) High Sch., 1977-85; instr. chemistry Eastern Ariz. Coll., Thatcher, 1977-85; instr. chemistry and physics Flowing Wells High Sch., Tucson, 1985—; adj. instr. sci. edn. U. Ariz., 1986—; workshop leader NSF. Co-author BASIC Program Conversions, 1984. Recipient Golden Bell award Ariz. Sch. Bd. Assn., 1983. Mem. Nat. Sci. Tchrs. Assn. (publ. com. 1983—, speaker various locations 1979—, Search for Excellence in Sci. Edn. award 1984), Ariz. Sci. Tchrs. Assn. (regional dir. 1978-80, Search for Excellence in Sci. Edn. award 1984), Ariz. Edn. Assn., Catalina Commodore Computer Club. Republican. Roman Catholic. Avocations: tennis, golf, reading, woodworking, snow skiing. Home: 3301 E Fort Lowell Rd Tucson AZ 85716 Office: Flowing Wells High Sch 3725 N Flowing Wells Rd Tucson AZ 85705

BYWATER, MURRAY ALSTON, airport dir.; b. Salt Lake City, Feb. 7, 1915; s. Murry Mowry and Annie (Alston) B.; B.S. in Bus. Adminstrn., U. Utah, 1936; postgrad. George Washington U.; m. Frankie Lale Galloway, July 2, 1941; 1 dau., Teresa Kaye. Commd. 2d lt. USAAF, 1937, advanced through grades to brig. gen. USAF, 1960; service in Europe, Africa, Pacific, Philippines; ret., 1968; mgr. Salt Lake City Internat. Airport, 1969-76; dir. Riverside (Calif.) Mcpl. Airport, 1979—. Decorated Legion of Merit with 2 oak leaf clusters, D.F.C., Air medal with 3 oak leaf clusters, Purple Heart; accredited airport exec. Mem. U.S. Congl. Adv. Bd., Am. Security Council, Armed Services Mut. Benefit Assn. (advisor), Fifteenth Air Force Assn. (pres.), Am. Theatre Organ Soc. Mem. Ch. of Jesus Christ of Latter-day Saints. Author: Island Hopping to Kyushu, Airport Report. Office: Riverside Mcpl Airport 6951 Flight Rd Riverside CA 92504

CABARET, JOSEPH RONALD, transtechnology corporation executive; b. Astoria, N.Y., Dec. 26, 1934; s. Joseph Henry and Henrietta (Nevejans) C.; m. Giovanna Longhitano, Dec. 26, 1960; children: Grace, Joseph, Corinne. BSME, Stevens Inst. Tech., 1957; MBA, Pepperdine U., 1980. Chief engr. Space Ordnance Systems, Canyon Country, Calif., 1962-67, sales rep., 1968-76, program mgr., 1977-79, asst. gen. mgr., 1980, gen. mgr., 1981, pres., 1982-85; v.p. corp. devel. Transtech., Sherman Oaks, Calif., 1985—. Office: Trans Tech Corp 15303 Ventura Blvd 12th Fl Sherman Oaks CA 91403

CABLE, DOUGLAS CHARLES, physician; b. Glendale, Calif., June 27, 1951; s. Donovan Chambers and Edith (Smith) C. BS in Zoology, U. Okla., 1972; MD, Wayne State U., 1977; postgrad., U. So. Calif. Diplomate Nat. Bd. Med. Examiners, Am. Bd. Internal Medicine, Am. Bd. Infectious Diseases. Intern Cleve. Met. Gen. Hosp., 1977-78, jr. asst. resident in straight medicine, 1978-79; sr. resident in internal medicine Los Angeles County-U. So. Calif. Med. Ctr., Los Angeles, 1979-80, supr. residents and jr. fellow infectious diseases, 1980-81, sr. clin. research fellow infectious diseases, 1981-82, asst. clin. dir. communicable disease service, 1981-82; clin. instr. medicine and pediatrics U. So. Calif., Los Angeles, 1981-82, clin. asst. prof., 1982; dir. med. edn. Los Angeles County div. CDC, STD Model Clinic Program, 1982-83; practice medicine specializing in adult and pediatric infectious diseases Fountain Valley, Calif., 1983—. Contbr. articles to profl. jours. Bd. dirs. Los Angeles Peace and Justice Ctr. Nat. Merit scholar. Mem. Orange County Med. Assn., Am. Soc. Microbiology, ACP, Mensa, SAR, Mayflower Soc., Infectious Disease Soc. Am. Mem. Soc. of Friends.

CABLE, RICHARD ALBERT, manufacturing executive; b. Port Townsend, Wash., Apr. 22, 1950; s. Anton and Josephine Elizabeth (Kiesel) C.; m. Glenda Gaye Swain, Aug. 12, 1972; children: Emily Serena, Grant Michael. B in Mgmt. Sci. and Mktg., U. Wash., 1972; MBA, U. Nev., 1974. Cert. mgmt. acct. Sr. acct. Crown Zellerbach Co., Camas, Wash., 1974-77, mgr. acctg., 1977-79; asst. controller Crown Zellerbach Co., West Linn, Oreg., 1979-82; controller Crown Zellerbach Co., Los Angeles, 1982-83; corp. controller Grant and Roth Plastics, Hillsboro, Oreg., 1983-84, corp. gen. mgr., 1984—, also sec. bd. dirs.; proprietor Yo Plus, West Linn, Oreg., 1986—; market researcher Swain's Gen. Store, Port Angeles, Wash., 1972, co-dir., 1980—. Cub master Boy Scouts Am., Camas, 1977-79, West Linn, 1986, asst. scoutmaster, Oreg. City, Oreg., 1982; mem. exec. adv. com. Clackamas Community Coll. Named Eagle Scout Boy Scouts Am., 1965. Mem. Am. Mgmt. Assn., Assn. MBA Execs., Nat. Assn. Accts. (bd. dirs. Portland chpt.), Soc. Plastics Engrs., Am. Soc. Quality Control, Beta Gamma Sigma. Republican. Mormon. Clubs: Clark County Kennel (Vancouver, Wash.) (bd. dirs. 1977-79), Portland Borzoi (treas. 1977-80). Lodge: Elks. Avocations: hiking, skiing, horseback riding, showing dogs, traveling. Office: Grant & Roth Plastics 1600 NE 25th Ave Hillsboro OR 97124

CABOT, HUGH, III, painter-sculptor; b. Boston, Mar. 22, 1930; s. Hugh and Louise (Melanson) C.; m. Olivia P. Taylor, Sept. 8, 1967; student Boston Museum, 1948, Ashmolean Mus., Oxford, Eng., 1960, Coll. Ams., Mexico City, 1956, San Carlos Acad., Mexico City. Portrait, landscape painter; sculptor in bronze; one-man shows: U.S. Navy Hist. and Recreation Dept., U.S. Navy Art Gallery, The Pentagon, Nat. War Mus., Washington, La Muse de la Marine, Paris; group shows include: Tex. Tri-state, 1969 (1st, 2d, 3d prizes). Served as ofcl. artist USN, Korean War. Named Artist of Yr., Scottsdale, Ariz., 1978. Clubs: Salmagundi (N.Y.C.). Author, illustrator: Korea I (Globe).

CACUCI, GABRIEL D., physician, surgeon; b. Beznea, Romania, Nov. 22, 1921; came to U.S., 1970, naturalized, 1976; s. Dimitrie and Irina (Sturz) C.; div.; 1 child, Dan. Baccalaureate Lyceum (Romania) 1942; M.D., King Ferdinand U. Sch. Medicine (Romania), 1948. Resident in surgery Univ. Hosp., Romania, 1948-52, Lenox Hill Hosp., French and Polyclinic, A. Logan Hosps., N.Y.C., 1972-75; attending surgeon Univ. Hosp., Cluj, Romania, 1952-60, asst. prof. surgery, 1954; attending surgeon Railways Hosp., Oradea, Romania, 1964-69, Tg. Mures U. Hosp., Romania, 1969-70, N.Y.C. and Ft. Lauderdale hosps., 1975-78; practice medicine, Las Vegas, 1978—. Co-author: Surgery, 1952; contbr. articles to profl. jours. Mem. AMA, N.Y. Med. Soc., Passaic County Med. Soc., Broward Country-Ft. Lauderdale Med. Soc., Nev. State Med. Soc., Clark County Med. Soc. Republican. Greek Orthodox. Home: PO Box 60246 Las Vegas NV 89160 Office: 3163 S Eastern Las Vegas NV 89109

CADDELL, HAROLD LEWIS, business educator, retired career military officer; b. Effingham, Ill., Mar. 15, 1934; s. Harold Lavergne and Mary Lou (Winkelman) C.; m. Wauneta Ann Hazlett, May 29, 1959; children: Harold Lynn, David Paul. BS in Aero. Engring., Okla. State U., 1957, MS in Aero. Engring., 1966; PhD in Leadership and Human Behavior, U.S. Internat. U., 1979. Ordained to ministry Bapt. Ch., 1982. Design engr. Goodyear (Ariz.) Aircraft, 1957-58; commd. aircraft maintenance officer USAF, Ellsworth AFB, S.D., 1958; adv. through grades to lt. col. USAF, 1974; project engr. Gemini Target Vehicle Program Office USAF, Los Angeles, 1964-66, project engr. Titan III Manned Orbiting Lab. program, 1966-68; with 6595th Aero. Test Wing USAF, Vandenberg AFB, Calif., 1968, commdr., dir. energy squadron, 1972-74, from chief maintenance to dep. commdr. and dir. 6595th Instrumentation Squadron, 1974-79, shuttle liaison officer satellite control facility, 1979, from chief devel. test div., 1st Strategic Aero. div. to dir. test programs, 1979-82, dir. ops. 6595th Aero. Test Group, Western Space and Missile Ctr., 1982-83, retired, 1983; assoc. prof. bus. adminstrn. Calif. Bapt. Coll., Riverside, 1983—; speaker leadership and motivation seminars, Riverside, 1974—. Fellow Nat. Assn. Ch. Bus. Adminstrn. (dir. West coast tng. ctr. 1984—); mem. Am. Mgmt. Assn., Christian Ministries Mgmt. Assn., U.S. Tennis Club. Club: Toastmasters (Vandenberg AFB chpt.). Avocations: advanced license ham radio operator, tennis coach. Home: 7885 Big Rock Dr Riverside CA 92509 Office: Calif Bapt Coll 8431 Magnolia Ave Riverside CA 92504

CADDY, EDMUND HARRINGTON HOMER, JR., architect; b. N.Y.C., Apr. 17, 1928; s. Edmund Harrington Homer and Glenna Corinne (Garratt) C.; m. Mary Audrey Ortiz, Dec. 22, 1951; children—Edmund Harrington Homer III, Mary Elizabeth. B.A., Princeton, 1952, M.F.A. (grad. sch. fellow), 1955. With firm Louis E. Jallade (architect), N.Y.C., 1949; Eggers & Higgins (architects), N.Y.C., 1953; dir. design Dalton-Dalton Assos. (architects and engineers), Cleve., 1955-60; asso. mem. firm Raymond & Rado (architects), N.Y.C., 1960-68; gen. partner Raymond & Rado and Partners (architects), N.Y.C., 1968-72, Raymond, Rado, Caddy & Bonington (P.C.), N.Y.C., 1972-80; pres. Raymond, Rado, Caddy & Bonington (P.C.), 1980—; Mem. adv. com. arts John F. Kennedy Center Performing Arts, 1963-70; mem. archtl. adv. commn. N.Y.C. Community Coll., City U. N.Y., 1979—. Works include Suburban Hosp, Cleve., 1957, J.M. Smucker Co, Salinas, Cal., 1957, Brookpark (Ohio) City Hall, 1959; Cleve. Transit System addition, 1959, administrn. bldg., Met. Water Treatment System, Saigon, 1960, Franklin D. Roosevelt High Sch, N.Y.C., 1963, Crown Heights Intermediate Sch, N.Y.C., 1966, engrng. complex, Stony Brook Campus, State U. N.Y., 1970, Sibley's dept. stores, Syracuse, N.Y., 1973, Rochester Downtown Devel. Study, 1975, R.H. Macy & Co. dept. store, Stamford, Conn., 1979. Pres. bd. trustees Montclair (N.J.) Community Hosp., 1973-80. Served with USMC, 1946-48; Served with USMCR, 52-53. Mem. AIA, Architects Soc. Calif., N.J., Ohio, N.Y. State Architects Assn. Clubs: Tower (Princeton); Racquet and Tennis (N.Y.C.). Home: 550 Battery St San Francisco CA 94111 Office: Robinson Mills & Williams 153 Kearny St San Francisco CA 94108

CADY, PATRICIA MAE (PATRICIA MAE FLORY), speech pathologist, health facility director; b. Belle Fourche, S.D., Jan. 10, 1944; d. William Arthur and Hannah Marie (Ollila) Turpen; m. Jim Cady, June 7, 1964 (div. Oct. 1972); children: John, Scott. BA, San Diego State U., 1968, MA, 1970. Intern San Diego State U., 1970-71; co-founder Barefoot Sch. for Neurologically Handicapped Children, Point Loma, Calif., 1971-73; psychomotrist North Park (Calif.) Children's Sch., 1973-74; assoc. dir. Del Mar (Calif.) Counseling and Speech Ctr., 1973-74; dir. spl. edn. Sch. Dist. 25, Riverton, Wyo., 1974-76; ednl. diagnostician and speech therapist Sch. Dist. 1, Lander, Wyo., 1976-78; dir., pvt. practice in aphasiology and speech pathology Fremont County (Wyo.) Speech Pathology Services, 1977—; ednl. diagnostician Wyo. Indian Sch. Dist. 14, Ethete, 1984-85; dir. spl. edn., speech therapist Fremont County (Wyo.) Sch. Dist. 38, Riverton, 1985—. Hearing judge State Wyo., Cheyenne, 1982-85; mem. adv. panel handicapped children Wyo. State Dept. Edn., Cheyenne, 1981-85; organized first Fremont County Health Faire, 1982; bd. dirs. N.Am. Indian Heritage Ctr., Riverton, 1985—; lay rep. Am. Luth. Ch., Wyo., 1984. Fellow U.S. Office of Edn., Washington, 1970. Mem. Am. Speech and Hearing Assn., Calif. Assn. for Neurologically Handicapped Children (treas. 1973), Wyo. Speech and Hearing Assn., Council for Exceptional Children, Council for Adminstrs. in Spl. Edn., C. of C., Phi Kappa Phi. Republican. Lodge: Order Eastern Star. Avocations: sports, private pilot, travel. Home: 803 Vance Dr Lander WY 82520

CADY, WALLACE MARTIN, research geologist; b. Middlebury, Vt.; s. Frank William and Alice Marian (Kingsbury) C.; m. Helen Johanna Raitanen, Jan. 1, 1942; children—John Wallace, Nancy Helen, Norma Louise. B.S., Middlebury Coll., Vt., 1934; M.S., Northwestern U., 1936; Ph.D., Columbia U., 1944. Registered geologist, Colo., Vt., D.C. Research geologist U.S. Geol. Survey, Washington, 1939-45, Montpelier, Vt., 1945-61, Denver, 1961-85. Author: New England and Quebec, 1969; (with others) geol. maps. Fulbright lectureship, USSR, 1975; recipient Meritorious award U.S. Dept. Interior. Fellow Geol. Soc. Am.; Am. Geophys. Union; mem. Colo. Sci. Soc., (pres. 1975), Soc. Econ. Geologists, Vt. Geol. Soc. Home: 348 S Moore St Lakewood CO 80226 Office: US Geol Survey Fed Ctr Box 25046 Denver CO 80225

CAESAR, RICHARD CORNELIUS, dentist; b. Lake Village, Ark., Apr. 12, 1918; s. Robert C. and Lenora (Campbell) C.; B.S., Morehouse Coll., 1940; postgrad. Atlanta U., 1946-47; D.D.S., Meharry Med. Coll., 1951; m. Lois Towles, June 6, 1956. Pvt. practice dentistry, San Francisco, 1951—. Pres., bd. dirs. San Francisco YMCA, 1978-80; v.p. Pacific region bd. Nat. Council YMCA, 1974-77; trustee United Way Bay Area, 1973-77; chmn. San Francisco Subarea Adv. Council, West Bay Health System Agy., 1977-78; bd. govs. San Francisco Symphony Assn. Served to lt. col. USAF, 1941-46. Recipient Bay Area Vol. Activist award, 1977; Humanitarian of Yr. award YMCA San Francisco, 1984. Fellow Am. Coll. Dentistry, Acad. Dentistry Internat. (trustee, pres. Pacific Coast area, mem. alumnae resources adv. bd., 1986), Internat. Coll. Dentists; mem. ADA (life; alt. del. 1970-74), Calif. Dental Assn. (life; del. house 1970-77, state council for membership 1975-82), Acad. Gen. Dentistry, Pierre Fauchar Acad. (chmn. No. Calif. sect.), San Francisco Dental Soc. (pres. 1974-75), NAACP (life), Res. Officers Assn. (life), Kappa Alpha Psi (life, chmn. West Province's achievement com. 1958-83, mem. nat. achievement com. 1969—). Republican. Episcopalian. Club: Commonwealth (Calif.). Lodge: Rotary (A. Paul Harris fellow, 1984). Home: 150 Topeka Ave San Francisco CA 94124 Office: 2340 Sutter St Suite 208 San Francisco CA 94115

CAESAR, VANCE ROY, newspaper executive; b. Pa., Dec. 22, 1944; s. Jack Raymond and Norma Norine (Wiles) C.; m. Carol Ann Richards, Apr. 22, 1967; 1 son, Eric. B.S. in Bus. Adminstrn., The Citadel, 1966; M.B.A., Fla. Atlantic U., 1969; grad., Stanford U. Exec. Program, 1982. From asst. to gen. mgr. to consumer mktg. dir. Miami Herald, Fla., 1970-77; assoc. editor Detroit Free Press, 1977-78; sr. v.p., gen. mgr. Long Beach Press-Telegram, Calif., 1978—. Bd. dirs. Meml. Med. Ctr., Long Beach, Downtown Long Beach Assocs., Region III, United Way; adviser Extended Edn. Dept. Calif. State U.-Long Beach, mem. bus. sch. adv. bd., vice chmn. Bus. Roundtable; exec. com. Am. Cancer Soc.; mem. Long Beach promotion com.; mem. Long Beach Area Conv. and Tourism Bur. Mem. Long Beach Area C. of C., Stanford Bus. Sch. Alumni, Am. Newspaper Pubs. Assn., The Citadel Alumni Assn. Club: Rotary (Long Beach). Home: 110 Ocean Ave Seal Beach CA 90740 Office: Long Beach Pess-Telegram 604 Pine Ave Long Beach CA 90844

CAFFERATA, PATRICIA DILLON, former state treasurer; b. Albany, N.Y., Nov. 24, 1940; d. Kenneth P. and Barbara Vucanovich (Farrell) Dillon; m. H. Treat Cafferata, June 17, 1961; children—Elisa, Janet, Reynolds. Student Mills Coll., 1958-61; B.A., Lewis and Clark Coll., 1963. Mem. Nev. Assembly, 1980-82; treas. state of Nev., Carson City, 1982-86; nominee for gov. of Nev., 1986 . Mem. Nev. Republican Central Com.; past pres. Doctor's Wives Washoe County, St. Mary's Hosp. Guild. Named outstanding freshman legislator Nev. State Med. Assn., 1981. Mem. Nat. Assn. State Auditors, Controllers and Treasurers, Western State Treasurers, Carson City C. of C. Episcopalian. Office: 205 Urban Rd Reno NV 89509

CAHAN, LESLIE DARYLL, neurosurgeon, educator; b. Los Angeles, Oct. 12, 1946; s. Aaron and Ruth (Weiner) C.; m. Melinda Bodbar; children: Benjamin, Molly. BS in Chemistry, UCLA, 1967, MD, 1971. Intern Mass. Gen. Hosp., Boston, 1971-72; resident UCLA Hosp., 1972-73, 75-80; clin. assoc. NIH, Bethesda, Md., 1973-75; house physician Nat. Hosp., London, 1976; asst. prof. UCLA Med. Sch., 1985-86; assoc. prof. surgery U. Calif., Irvine, 1986—. Served to surgeon USPHS, 1973-75. Fellow ACS; mem. Cong. Neurol. Surgeons, Am. Assn. Neurol. Surgeons, Phi Beta Kappa, Sigma Xi. Office: U Calif-Irving Med Ctr Div Neurosurgery 101 City Dr S Orange CA 92668

CAHILL, THOMAS ANDREW, physicist; b. Paterson, N.J., Mar. 4, 1937; s. Thomas Vincent and Margery (Groesbeck) C.; m. Virginia Ann Arnoldy, June 26, 1965; children: Catherine Frances, Thomas Michael. B.A., Holy Cross Coll., Worcester, Mass., 1959; Ph.D. in Physics; NDEA fellow, U. Calif., Los Angeles, 1965. Asst. prof. in residence U. Calif., Los Angeles, 1965-66; NATO fellow, research physicist Centre d'Etudes Nucleaires de Saclay, France, 1966-67; prof. physics U. Calif., Davis, 1967—; acting dir. Crocker Nuclear Lab., 1972, dir., 1980—; dir. Inst. of Ecology, 1972-75; cons. NRC of Can., Louvre Mus.; mem. Internat. Com. on PIXE and Its Application. Author: (with J. McCray) Electronic Circuit Analysis for Scientists, 1973; Contbr. articles to profl. jours. on physics, applied physics, hist. analyses and air pollution. OAS fellow, 1968. Mem. Am. Phys. Soc., Air Pollution Control Assn., Am. Chem. Soc., Sigma Xi. Democrat. Roman Catholic. Club: Sierra. Home: 1813 Amador Ave Davis CA 95616 Office: Dept Physics U Calif Davis CA 95616

CAHN, HAROLD A(RCHAMBO), biologist, consultant; b. Mpls., July 1, 1922; s. Robert Reinholt and Maybell (Archambo) C.; m. Winifred Schnacke, Aug. 1, 1953; children: Helen, Steven, Fred. BA in Sci., U. Minn., 1947; MA in Physiology and Vertebrate Paleontology, U. Wyo., 1949; PhD in Psychophysiology, U. Iowa, 1961. Research asst. physiology U. Wyo., Laramie, 1948-49; instr. biology Dickinson Coll., Carlisle, Pa., 1953-56, U. Colo., Boulder, 1956-59; asst. prof. biology Utica (N.Y.) Coll. of Syracuse U., 1961-65, dir. computer ctr., 1966, assoc. prof., 1967-71; prof. No. Ariz. U., Flagstaff, 1971-75; dir. research Potential Research Found., 1976-80; prin. Wellness Research Assocs., 1980-81; cons. in biomed. sci. 1982—; sec. bd. dirs. Potential Research Found. Contbr. articles to profl. jours. Recipient Silver Anniversary award Utica Coll. of Syracuse U., 1971; 1st pl. award art show, Utica Coll. of Syracuse U., 1971; grantee NSF, 1962, Utica Coll. of Syracuse U., 1964. Mem. Electronics Assocs. Inc. (cert.), Am. Assn. Profl. Hypnotists (cert. profl.), Sigma Xi. Avocations: painting, harmonica playing. Office: 5033 N 66th Ave Glendale AZ 85301

CAIN, BRUCE EDWARD, political science educator, consultant; b. Boston, Nov. 28, 1948; s. Arthur James and Ruth Elizabeth (Osterberg) C.; m. Anne Henley, June 5, 1976; children: Timothy, Andrew. BA, Bowdoin U., 1970; BPhil, Oxford (Eng.) U., 1972; PhD in Polit. Sci., Harvard U., 1976. Asst. prof. Calif. Inst. Tech., Pasadena, 1976=82, assoc. prof., 1983-86, prof. polit. sci., 1986—; cons. Calif. State Assembly, 1981-82, Los Angeles City Council, 1986—, Fairbank and Co., Los Angeles, 1985—, Los Angeles Times, 1986. Author: The Reapportionment Puzzle, 1984; contbr. articles to profl. jours. Rhodes scholar Oxford U., 1970-72. Mem. Am. Polit. Sci. Assn. Democrat. Avocations: tennis, softball, squash, jogging. Office: Calif Inst Tech Div Humanities & Social Scis Pasadena CA 91125

CAIN, ELVIS VERNON, furniture retailer, civic worker; b. Bison, S.D., Feb. 16, 1915; s. Harvey Edward and Ada Pearl (McKim) C.; m. Florence Marie Brennen, Sept. 28, 1940; children: Dennis Lee, Candice Ann, Allan Ross. Student, U. Oreg., 1938-39. Dept. mgr. Allied Stores, Nampa, Idaho, 1934-38; dept. mgr., buyer Allied Stores, Twin Falls, Idaho, 1940-44; owner Cain's Home Furnishings, Twin Falls, 1946-56, also chmn. bd. dirs., 1956—; county chmn. Johnny Horizon's Clean Up Event, 1958—. Active 1st Christian Ch., Twin Falls, 1948-87, numerous offices; chmn. Twin Falls United Way, 1950; mem. Twin Falls Sch. Bd., 1954-62, clk., 1957-62; active Twin Falls council Boy Scouts Am., 1956-62, dist. fin. chmn., 1962-65; council bd. dirs., 1966-67, v.p. fin., 1968-72, council pres., 1973-75, hon. trustee, 1982-87; active mcpl. govt. City of Twin Falls. Served alt. mil. duty as procurment and expediting supr. for USN, Willamette Iron and Steel Works, Portland, Oreg., 1938-39. Recipient Silver Beaver award Twin Falls council Boy Scouts Am., 1975. Mem. Nat. Assn. Retail Dealers Am. (conv. speaker 1982), Service Corp. Ret. Execs., Snake River Valley Elec. Assn. (pres. 1975), Twin Falls C. of C. (bd. dirs. 1952). Republican. Club: Blue Lakes Country (Twin Falls). Lodge: Kiwanis. Avocations: travel, golfing, civic and church activities. Home: 174 Larkspur Dr Twin Falls ID 83301 Office: Cain's Home Furnishings 204 Main Ave N Twin Falls ID 83303-0427

CAIN, JAMES DOUGLAS, JR., government official; b. Oakland, Calif., July 4, 1946; s. James Douglas and Daisy Doris (DeBerry) C.; m. Joyce Mae Dilworth, Aug. 12, 1967. B.S., SUNY-Albany, 1980; postgrad. Troy State U., 1980-81; B.A. in History cum laude, U. Md., 1982. Fgn. service staff officer Office Def. Attache, Saigon, Vietnam, 1973-74; counter-intelligence ops. specialist Dept. Army, various locations, 1974-87; intelligence ops. specialist, vice counter-intelligence ops. specialist, Dept. Army, 1987—. Active Minn. Chippewa Tribe, Nat. Congress Am. Indians; mem. Ramstein Council on Internat. Relations (W.Ger.). Served from 2d lt. to capt., M.I., U.S. Army, 1967-73. Fellow Internat. Ctr. for Asian Studies, 1984. Mem. Internat. Polit. Sci. Assn., Am. Polit. Sci. Assn., Am. Econs. Assn., Nat. Geog. Soc., Middle East Inst., VFW, Vietnam Vets. Am., Alpha Sigma Lambda, Pi Alpha Theta, Pi Sigma Alpha. Democrat. Club: Masons. Office: PO Box 1702 APO New York NY 09021

CAIN, VIRGINIA HARTIGAN, judicial educator; b. Bklyn., May 1, 1922; d. James Gerard and H. Virginia (Williams) Hartigan; m. Edmund Joseph Cain, Dec. 3, 1944; children: Edmund Joseph III, Mary Ellen McMullen, James Michael. AB, NYU, 1943; MEd, U. Del., 1963; postgrad., U. Nev., 1972. Personnel counselor Research and Devel. Labs., Ft. Monmouth, N.J., 1943-47; elem. and secondary tchr. and counselor Reno, 1968-73; dir. children in placement project Nat. Council Juvenile and Family Ct. Judges, Reno, 1974-76; asst. tng. dir. Nat. Coll. Juvenile Justice, Reno, 1976-80, curriculum dir., 1980-83, child support enforcement project dir., 1983—; adj. asst. prof. U. Nev., Reno; mem. adv. bd. Com. To Aid Abused Women, Nat. Assn. Family Counselors in Juvenile Ct., 1981-82; del.-at-large White House Conf. on Families, 1980. Mem. Nev. Gov.'s Commn. on Status of Women, 1966-70, 72-81; del. Nat. Dem. Convs., 1970, 72, 80; Dem. chmn. Nev. chpt. ERA, 1980-82; mem. Dem. Nat. Com., 1980-82; mem. platform accountability commn., 1982; 1st vice chmn. Nev. Dem. Com., 1980-82; mem. adv. bd. Mental Health Assn. Nev., 1966-72; mem. Nev. Gov.'s Commn. on Girl's Tng. Sch., 1972-76; mem. exec. com. Washoe County Dem. Central Com., 1966-80; Nev. mem. Compliance Rev. Commn., 1972-76; mem. Nev. Charter Com., 1972-74; No. Nev. Coordinator for Senator Edward Kennedy, 1979-80; active campaign worker for Adlai Stevenson, John F. Kennedy, Jimmy Carter; bd. dirs. United Way No. Nev., Planned Parenthood Nev.; mem. Nat. Com. for Support Pub. Schs.; mem. Sr. Citizens Adv. Bd. Washoe County; former chmn. early childhood edn. and legis. com. Del. PTA Bd.; former mem. adv. bd. Washoe Assn. For Mentally Retarded; co-program chmn. 21st Ann. South Pacific Regional Conf., Child Welfare League Am.-Nat. Council Juvenile Ct. Judges, 1976; numerous other civic polit. activities. Recipient various service and profl. awards. Mem. Internat. Soc. Family Law, Children's Def. Fund, Women's Polit. Caucus, Nat. Women's Polit. Caucus, Nat. Assn. Counsel for Children, AAUW, LWV, Reno Bus. and Profl. Women (legis. chmn.), Nev. Art Gallery, Croesus Corp. Investment Club (pres.), Nat. Jud. Educators Assn. Roman Catholic. Club: U. Nev. Faculty Wives. Home: 3710 Clover Way Reno NV 89509 Office: U Nev Box 8978 Reno NV 89507

CAINE, STEPHEN HOWARD, computer software co. exec.; b. Washington, Feb. 11, 1941; s. Walter E. and Jeanette (Wenborne) C.; student Calif. Inst. Tech., 1958-62. Sr. programmer Calif. Inst. Tech., Pasadena, 1962-65, mgr. systems programming, 1965-69, mgr. programming, 1969-70; pres. Caine, Farber & Gordon, Inc., Pasadena, 1970—; lectr. applied sci. Calif. Inst. Tech., Pasadena, 1965-71, vis. asso. elec. engring., 1976, vis. asso. computer sci., 1976—. Mem. Pasadena Tournament of Roses Assn., 1976—. Mem. Assn. Computing Machinery, Nat. Assn. Corrosion Engrs., AAAS, Am. Ordnance Assn. Clubs: Athenaeum (Pasadena); Engrs. (N.Y.C.). Home: 77 Patrician Way Pasadena CA 91105

CAINES, KENNETH L.D., management consulting company executive; b. N.Y.C., 1926; s. Clarence and Monica C.; B.S. in Psychology and Sociology, N.Y. U., 1954; postgrad. Calif. State Coll., 1965-67; m. Josephine A. Robinson, July 17, 1950. pres. People Oriented Systems, Santa Ana, Calif., 1969—; v.p. Band Aide, 1984—; dir. Joken Human Factors Assocs. lectr. civil and social systems U. Calif.-Irvine, 1970-71. Vice pres. tech. adv. com. on testing Calif. Fair Employment Practices Commn., 1967-71; mem. U. Calif. at Irvine-Project 21 Com. on Population Growth, 1971-72; pres. Orange YMCA, 1973; mem. adv. bd. Orange County council Boy Scouts Am., 1970—; mem. Orange County Grand Jury, 1980-81. Mem. Orange Planning Commn., 1973-76. Bd. dirs. Orange County United Way, 1971-73, Orange County Community Housing Corp., 1986—. Served with USAAF, 1944-46. Named Citizen of Year Orange YMCA, 1972. Mem. IEEE, Am. Mgmt. Assn., Human Factors Soc. Orange County, Assn. Profl. Cons. Office: People Oriented Systems 2060 N Tustin Ave Santa Ana CA 92701

CAIRNS, ELTON JAMES, chemical engineering educator; b. Chgo., Nov. 7, 1932; s. James Edward and Claire Angele (Larzelere) C.; m. Miriam Esther Citron, Dec. 26, 1974; 1 dau., Valerie Helen; stepchildren: Benjamin David, Joshua Aaron. B.S. in Chemistry, Mich. Tech. U., Houghton, 1955; B.S. in Chem. Engring, 1955; Ph.D. in Chem. Engring. (Dow Chem. Co. fellow, univ. fellow, Standard Oil Co. Calif. grantee, NSF fellow), U. Calif., Berkeley, 1959. Phys. chemist Gen. Electric Co. Research Lab., Schenectady, 1959-66; group leader, then sect. head chem. engring. div. Argonne (Ill.) Nat. Lab., 1966-73; asst. head electrochemistry dept. Gen. Motors Corp. Research Labs., 1973-78; assoc. lab. dir., head applied sci. div. Lawrence Berkeley (Calif.) Lab., 1978—; prof. chem. engring. U. Calif., Berkeley, 1978—; Croft lectr. U. Mo., 1979; cons. in field, mem. numerous govt. panels. Author: (with H.A. Liebhafsky) Fuel Cells and Fuel Batteries, 1968; editorial bd.: Advances in Electrochemistry and Electrochem. Engring, 1974—; div. editor: Jour. Electrochem. Soc, 1970—; regional editor Electrochimica Acta, 1984-86; contbr. articles to profl. jours. Recipient IR-100 award, 1968; Case Centennial medal Case Western Res. U., 1980; grantee duPont Co., 1956. Fellow Am. Inst. Chemists; mem. Electrochem. Soc. (chmn. phys. electrochem. div. 1981-84, v.p. 1986—, Francis Mills Turner award 1963), Am. Chem. Soc., Am. Inst. Chem. Engrs. (chmn. energy conversion com. 1970—), Internat, Soc. Electrochemistry (chmn. electrochem. energy conversion div. 1977-85, U.S.A. nat. sec. 1983—, v.p. 1984—), AAAS, Intersoc. Energy Conversion Engring. Conf. (gen. chmn. 1976, program chmn. 1983—). Patentee in field. Home: 239 Langlie Ct Walnut Creek CA 94598 Office: Lawrence Berkeley Lab Berkeley CA 94720

CAIRNS, JOHN J(OSEPH), retail executive; b. Detroit, Dec. 7, 1927; s. John Joseph and Agatha Bertha (Krebs) C.; m. Jean Elizabeth Wise, Aug. 21, 1948; children—John Joseph, Linda Cairns Morrow. Ph.B., U. Detroit, 1950, M.B.A., 1959. Nat. sales dir. Gt. Atlantic & Pacific Tea Co., N.Y.C., 1968-70, v.p. merchandising, corp. officer, 1970-76, regional pres., 1976-78; v.p. planning and devel., v.p. sales, corp. dir. Smith Mgmt. Co., Salt Lake City, 1978-81; chief operating officer, exec. v.p., gen. mgr. Carr's Quality Ctrs., Anchorage, 1981—; bd. dirs., v.p., sec. Carr-Gottstein Co., Inc.; bd. dirs. Topco Assocs., Inc. Mem. adv. bd. Providence Hosp.; bd. dirs. United Way of Alaska. Served with U.S. Army, 1945-47. Recipient speakers award Sales Exec. Club N.Y., 1968. Mem. Food Mktg. Inst., Western Assn. Food Chains, Commonwealth North (dir.), Beta Gamma Sigma. Republican. Roman Catholic. Club: Anchorage Racquet. Office: Carrs Quality Centers 1341 Fairbanks St Anchorage AK 99501

CAIRNS, SHIRLEY ANN, financial planner; b. Hundred, W.Va., Sept. 26, 1937; d. John Martin and Thelma Irene Stiles; children: John Michael, Lyle Dennis, Glynis Ann. BS, W.Va. U., 1959, MA, 1964. Cert. fin. planner. Tchr. public schs., Alliance, Ohio, 1958-60, Morgantown, W.Va., 1960-61; receptionist Strand Realty, Coronado, Calif., 1962-63; tchr., head bus. edn. dept. Sutherlin (Oreg.) High Sch., 1964-80; registered rep. IDS, 1980-83; prin. Shirley A. Cairns & Assocs., 1983—. Active Oreg. State Dem. 4th dist. Cen. Com., Oreg. Dem. Rules Com., Oreg. Dem. Exec. Com., Douglas County Tourist Adv. Com.; mem. Roseburg dist. adv. com. Bur. Land Mgmt., 1987-90; bd. dirs. Calapooia Water Dist., March of Dimes. Mem. Nat. Women's Polit. Caucus, So. Oreg. Women's Polit. Caucus (v.p.). Oreg. Women's Polit. Caucus, Nat. Assn. Female Execs., Internat. Assn. Fin. Planners, Inst. Cert. Fin. Planners, Am. Bus. Women's Assn., Roseburg C. of C., Douglas County C. of C., AAUW. Lodge: Lioness. Home: 2460 Hwy 138W PO Box 76 Oakland OR 97462 Office: 1012 SE Oak Suite 330 Roseburg OR 97470

CAKSTE, ANASTASIJA, librarian, educator; b. Riga, Latvia, Feb. 24, 1909; came to U.S., 1951; d. Antons Stipnieks and Anete Strupkajs; married 1932, widowed 1945; children: Anna Justine, Katrina Konstance. Attended, Latin Sch., Riga, 1927; student, University L.V.U., Riga, 1932, LLB, 1941; lic., Inst. Library Sci., Paris, 1934. Librarian, periodical jurist LLS pubs., Riga, 1936-41; archivist Meteorologiska Instit. Kungi Univ., Uppsala, Sweden, 1945-51; librarian, research asst. Harvard U. and Blue Hill (Mass.) Met. Obs., Cambridge, 1954-57; reference librarian L.F.E. Electronics, Boston, 1958-65; librarian and cataloguer, reference dept. Northeastern U., Boston, 1966-82; translator Nordisk Ekuminiske Institut, Sigtuna, Sweden, 1945, State Archive Uppsala, Sweden, 1945-46. Author: New Hampshire Snowstorms, 1956, World Hot-Wet Ground Temperature, 1957. Recipient Electronics award Internat. Advisory Panel, Mass., 1974. Mem. Am. Meteorol. Soc., Am. Library Assn., Mass. Library Assn., AAUP, Nat. Goeg. Soc., A.L.A., Baltic Women's Council, Baltic Freedom League. Lutheran. Avocations: painting, history, gymnastics, music. Home: 1930 Encinitas Rd Apt #42 San Marcos CA 92069

CALABRETTA, MARTI A., senator; b. Sandusky, Ohio, Dec. 14, 1940; d. Wilfred and Ida (Gerding) Beutler; m. Joseph Miller, Feb. 2, 1963 (div. Mar. 1976); m. Bennie G. Calabretta, Dec. 18, 1976; children: Jospeh, Patrick, Rebeca, Debora, John, Ben, Lisa. Student, Case Western Res. U., 1961-63; BA, U. Utah, 1963, MSW, 1966; cert. mental health mgmt., U. Wash., 1981. Mental health specialist 4 Corners Mental Health Services, Moab, Utah, 1972-75, Idaho Mental Health Services, Coeur d'Alene, Idaho, 1975-81; sch. social worker Wallace (Idaho) Sch. Dist., 1981—; state senator Boise, Idaho, 1984—. Pres. Valley Coordinating Corp., Kellogg, Idaho, 1982—; mem. Pvt. Industry Council, Coeur d'Alene, 1984—; vice chmn. Silver Valley Human Resources task force, Kellogg, 1982—. Mem. Idaho Edn. Assn. (del. 1983-84), Nat. Conf. State Legis. (health and welfare com.). Democrat. Episcopalian. Avocation: quilting. Home: Nichols Gulch Box 784 Osburn ID 83849 Office: Wallace Sch Dist 393 Wallace ID 83849

CALABRO, ANTHONY DOMINIC, educational administrator, consultant; b. Denver, Aug. 21, 1938; s. Anthony F. and Amelia (Molaske) C.; m. Claudia Ann Persichette, July 12, 1958; children—Michael E. and Melissa A. B.A. U. Colo., 1961; M.A., U. No. Colo., 1966; Ed.D., 1973. Tchr. social sci. Arvada (Colo.) High Sch., 1961-65; counselor Golden (Colo.) High Sch., 1965-68; mgr. Manpower Skill Ctr. Community Coll. Denver, 1968-72; dir. spl. programs, 1972-75; adminstrv. asst. to pres. Community Coll. Div., U. Nev. System, Reno, 1975-77; assoc. dean ednl. and instructional services Western Nev. Community Coll., Carson City, 1977-78, asst. to pres. institutional studies and planning, 1978-79; asst. pres. Truckee Meadows Community Coll., Reno, 1979-83; pres. Western Nev. Community Coll., Carson City, 1983—; instr. U. Nev.-Reno, Community Coll.; ednl. cons. in community coll. curriculum, textbooks, adminstrv. organ. chmn. bd. selective service appeals State of Nev. Served to capt. Air Force N.G., 1961-68. Mem. Am. Assn. Community and Jr. Colls. (commn. on small and/or rural colls.), NW Assn. Schs. and Colls. (evaluator), Carson City C. of C. Lodge: Rotary (Carson City). Office: Western Nev Community Coll 2201 W Nye Ln Carson City NV 89701

CALCAGNO, THERESA MARIE, math and science resource specialist; b. Phila., Nov. 3, 1956; d. Francis Anthony and Mary Louise (Gorman) Hughes; m. Frank Calcagno, Oct. 3, 1981; 1 child, Marissa. BA, Case Western Res. U., 1979; MS, Rutgers U., 1982. Research asst. Rutgers U., New Brunswick, N.J., 1980-81; personnel co-ordinator Target Stores, Inc., Billings, Mont., 1982-83; resource specialist Eastern Mont. Coll., Billings, 1983-86, program coordinator, 1986—, 1986—; com. mem. Shell Scholarship, Billings, 1984—. Vol. Valley Nursing Home, Billings, 1982; bd. dirs. Natural Family Planning Program, St. Vincent Hosp., Billings, 1982-85. Named one of Outstanding Young Women in Am., 1986, 87. Mem. AAAS, Am. Indian Sci. and Engring. Soc., Sigma Xi., Native Am. Sci. Edn. Assn., Soc. Econ. Paleontologists and Mineralogists. Roman Catholic. Avocations: photography, gardening, hiking. Home: 2224 Lyndale Ln Billings MT 59102 Office: Eastern Mont Coll Indian Career Services 1500 N 30th St Billings MT 59101-0298

CALDER, BRETT ALAN, insurance company executive; b. Inglewood, Calif., Sept. 26, 1960; s. William Richard C.; m. Margo Lee Clapper, Feb. 14, 1981. Dog handler Calif. Police K-9 Patrol, Garden Grove, 1978-80; pvt. investigator Dillahunty Investigative Services, Huntington Beach, Calif.,

1980-81; sales rep. JC Penney Ins. Co., Industry, Calif., 1982; area sales mgr. JC Penney Ins. Co., Glendale, Calif., 1983-86, market mgr., 1986—. Recipient Eagle Scout Gold and Bronze Palms, Boy Scouts Am., 1973. Lodge: Optimists. Avocations: computers, photography. Office: JC Penney Ins Co 3800 La Crescenta 103 Glendale CA 91710

CALDER, ROBERT MAC, aerospace engineer; b. Vernal, Utah, Oct. 16, 1932; s. Edwin Harold and Sydney (Goodrich) C.; m. Yoshiko Iemura, Feb. 14, 1959; children—Suzanne, Alex, Irene, John. B.S. in Chem. Engring., U. Utah, 1956, M.S. in Math. and Geology (NSF grantee), 1967; postgrad. U. Wash., 1964, Utah State U., 1965, U. Iowa, 1966. Cert. secondary tchr., Utah. Tchr. Utah Pub. Schs., 1958-79; v.p. Sydney Corp., Bountiful, Utah, 1958-82; sr. engr. aero. div., Hercules Inc., Magna, Utah, 1979—; owner RMC Enterprises, Nations Imports; cons. in field, 1960—. Active Boy Scouts Am., 1945-75, instr., Philmont Scout Ranch, 1972, asst. scoutmaster Nat. Jamboree Troop, 1973; instr. hunter safety and survival, Utah Dept. Fish and Game, 1964-74; state advisor U.S. Congl. Adv. Bd., 1982—. Served to capt. USAF, 1956-70. Mem. AIAA, Nat. Rifle Assn. (life), Am. Quarter Horse Assn., Internat. Platform Assn., Oratorio Soc. Utah, Republican Nat. Com. Mormon. Club: Hercules Toastmasters (treas. 1980, v.p. edn. 1981, pres. 1982). Home: 594 Calder Ct Kaysville UT 84037 Office: PO Box 98 Magna UT 84044

CALDERONE, JAMES JOSEPH, dentist; b. Conneaut, Ohio, Aug. 1, 1934; s. James Paul and August Cecilia (Polito) C.; m. Mary Louise Halbruegger, Dec. 28, 1957; children: Dominic J., James J., Theresa M., Martina M., Gina M., Camille M., Christina M., Anthony J. D.D.S., St. Louis U., 1959; M.P.H., U. Mich., 1974, DrPH, 1979. Diplomate Am. Bd. Dental Pub. Health. Pvt. practice dentistry, Belen, N.M., 1961-63, Albuquerque, 1963-73, Westland, Mich., 1974-75; pub. health dentist State of N.Mex., Santa Fe, 1975—; chmn. dental staff Bernalillo County Hosp., 1968-71; mem. N.Mex. Bd. Dentistry, 1972-74, v.p., 1974; cons. U.S. Indian Health Service, N.Mex. and Ariz., 1974—, Head Start, N.Mex., 1975—; adj. prof. U. N.Mex., Albuquerque, 1980—; bur. chief N.Mex. Health Dept., Santa Fe, 1980-84. Contbr. articles to profl. publs. Weblows leader Boy Scouts Am., Albuquerque, 1972; bd. dirs. St. Pius High Sch., Albuquerque, 1979-82. Served to lt. Dental Corps, USNR, 1959-61. Recipient Exemplary Performance award N.Mex. Health and Environ. Dept., 1981. Fellow Internat. Coll. Dentists; mem. Pierre Fauchard Acad., N.Mex. Dental Assn. (legis. chmn. 1972), Albuquerque Dist. Dental Soc. (bd. dirs. 1969-72). Roman Catholic. Home: 7613 Comanche Rd NE Albuquerque NM 87110 Office: NMex Health and Environment Dept PO Box 968 Santa Fe NM 87504

CALDERONE, JOHN AUGUST, healthcare executive; b. Pitts., Jan. 4, 1948; s. James and Mary Theresa (Rossi) C. B.A., Edinboro State Coll., 1970, M. Counselor Edn., 1971, postgrad. 1982; Ph.D., U. Pitts., 1978. Program coordinator Spencer Hosp. Counseling Ctr., Meadville, Pa., 1972-73; assoc. dir. Counseling Ctr. Drug and Alcohol Abuse, Meadville, 1973-75; treatment dir. Serenity Hall, Inc., Erie, Pa., 1975-77, exec. dir., 1977-81; psychologist Gen. Electric Co., Erie, 1981-83; adj. prof. Gannon U., Erie, 1981-83; v.p. clin. services Westworld Community Healthcare, Inc., Lake Forest, Calif., 1983-85; corp. dir. Devel. Med. Mgmt. Devel. Assocs., Arcadia, Calif., 1980-86; with Calderone Healthcare Services, Laguna Beach, Calif., 1986—; cons. Crawford County Adult Probation Dept. and Driving Under the Influence Program, 1980—, Erie County Driving while Intoxicated Program, 1977—; mem. adv. com. rehab. counseling dept. Edinboro State Coll., 1980-85. Bd. dirs. health Systems, Inc. Recipient Cert. Appreciation, Bd. Probation and parole, Commonwealth of Pa., 1977, Cert. Recognition, Health Systems, Inc. Northwestern Pa., 1981; Exemplary Work and Achievement award U.S. Adminstrn. on Aging, 1981. Mem. Assn. labor/Mgmt. Adminstrs. and Cons. Alcoholism, Soc. Advancement Mgmt., Inst. Advanced Study Rational Psychotherapy, Am. Pub. health Assn., Citizen Vols. Pa. for State Parolees, Pa. Driving Under Influence Assn., Nat. Assn. Alcoholism Treatment Programs. Home: 185 Roycroft Ave Long Beach CA 90803 Office: Calderone Healthcare Services 500 N First Ave Suite 7 Arcadia CA 91006

CALDERWOOD, WILLIAM ARTHUR, physician; b. Wichita, Kans., Feb. 3, 1941; s. Ralph Bailey and Janet Denise (Christ) C.; m. Nancy Jo Crawford, Mar. 31, 1979; children: Lisa Beth, William Arthur, Christopher Robert, Adam J.W. MD, U. Kans., 1968. Diplomate Am. Bd. Family Practice. Intern Wesley Med. Ctr., Wichita, 1968-69; gen. practice family medicine Salina, Kans., 1972-80, Peoria, Ariz., 1980—; pres. staff St. John's Hosp., Salina, 1976; dist. coroner, Salina, 1973-80; clins. instr. U. Kans., Wichita, 1978-80. Served to lt., M.C., USN, 1969-70. Fellow Am. Acad. Family Physicians; mem. AMA, Ariz. Med. Soc., Maricopa County Med. Soc. Lodge: Shriners. Home: 7015 W Calavar Peoria AZ 85345 Office: 13660 N 94th Dr Peoria AZ 85345

CALDWELL, CHARLES DEWEY, history educator; b. Del Norte, Colo., June 13, 1925; s. Ralph Dewey and Anna (Ydren) C.; m. Geraldine Delores Showalter, June 15, 1947. AA, Mt. San Antonio Coll., 1965; BA, La Verne U., 1967; MA, Claremont Grad. Sch., 1969. Cert. jr. coll. tchr., Calif. Instr. history La Verne (Calif.) U., 1968-69, Kapiolani Community Coll., Honolulu, 1969-71, Honolulu Community Coll., 1970—; asst. dir. field study on Oreg. Trail and Colonial Am. La Verne U., 1967; mem. State Hawaii Found. History and Humanities com., 1971-72, Hawaii Bicentennial Commn. Publs. com., 1975-76; instr. Hoomana Sch., Honolulu, 1975-76, Lanikila Sr. Ctr., Honolulu, 1976-78. Mem. Nat. Hist. Soc., Community Coll. Soc. Sci. Assn., Hawaiian Hist. Soc., Bishop Mus. Assn., Honolulu Acad. Arts. Republican. Mem. Christian Ch. Club: Queen Emma Hawaiian Civic. Avocations: Hawaiian music and dance, travel. Home: 1325 Wilder Ave mauka 6 Honolulu HI 96822 Office: U Hawaii Honolulu Community Coll 874 Dillingham Blvd Honolulu HI 96822

CALDWELL, DAVID ORVILLE, physics professor; b. Los Angeles, Jan. 5, 1925; s. Orville Robert and Audrey Norton (Anderson) C.; m. Miriam Ann Planck, Nov. 4, 1950 (div. Apr. 1978); children: Bruce David, Diana Miriam; m. Edie Helen Anderson, Dec. 29, 1984. BS in Physics, Calif. Inst. Tech., 1947; postgrad., Stanford U., 1947-48; MA in Physics, UCLA, 1949, PhD in Physics, 1953. From instr. to assoc. prof. physics MIT, Cambridge, 1954-63; vis. assoc. prof. physics Princeton U., N.J., 1963-64; lectr. physics dept. U. Calif., Berkeley, 1964-65; prof. physics U. Calif., Santa Barbara, 1965—; cons. U. Calif. Radiation Lab., Berkeley, 1957-58, 64-67, Am. Sci. and Engring., Boston, 1959-60, Inst. Def. Analysis, Washington, 1060-67, U.S. Dept. Def., Washington, 1966-70; dir. U. Calif. Inst. for Research at Particle Acceleration, 1984—. Contbr. numerous articles to profl. jours. Served to 2d lt. USAAF, 1943-46. Research grantee Dept. Energy, 1966—; Ford Found. fellow, 1961-62, NSF fellow, 1953-54, 1960-61, Guggenheim fellow, 1971-72; recipient Sr. Disting. Sci. award, 1987. Fellow Am. Phys. Soc.; mem. Phys. Soc. (exec. com. 1976-78). Democrat. Avocations: tennis, skiing. Office: U Calif Physics Dept Santa Barbara CA 93106

CALDWELL, GLYN GORDON, epidemiologist, physician; b. St. Louis, Jan. 14, 1934; s. Cecil Gordon and Zelma Mae (Peeler) C.; m. Mary Jean Pandolfo, Aug. 13, 1960; children: Michael Gordon, Elizabeth Ann, Thomas Gordon. BS, St. Louis U., 1960; MS, Mo. U., 1962, MD, 1966. Diplomate Nat. Bd. Med. Examiners. Intern, USPHS Hosp., Brighton, Mass., 1966-67; resident in internal medicine Cleve. Met. Gen. Hosp., 1969-71; grad. instr. microbiology U. Mo., 1960-62; with USPHS, 1966-85, med. virologist-epidemiologist Ecol. Investigations Program, Ctr. Disease Control, Kansas City, Kans., 1967-69, chief leukemia and oncogenic virus activities, 1968-69, acting chief virus disease sect., 1968-69, chief oncology and teratology activities, 1969-71, biohazards cons., 1972-73, asst. to chief leukemia sect. cancer and birth defects br. Bur. Epidemiology, Atlanta, 1973-74, dep. chief, 1974-77, chief cancer br. chronic diseases div., 1977-81, chief cancer br. chronic diseases div. Ctr. Environ. Health, 1981-82, dep. dir. chronic diseases div., 1982-85; asst. dir. disease prevention Ariz. Dept. Health Services, Phoenix, 1985-87, state epidemiologist, 1985-87; dep. dir. Ariz. Dept. Health Services, Phoenix, 1987—; asst. prof. microbiology U. Kans., 1968-70; docent Kansas City Gen. Hosp., 1972-73; clin. asst. prof. medicine U. Mo., Kansas City, 1972-73; clin. asst. prof. preventive medicine and community health Emory U., Atlanta, 1975-85, asst. prof. community medicine U. Ariz., 1986—; dir. Atlanta Cancer Surveillance Ctr., 1976-77; mem. adv. bd. Ctr. for Disease Control, 1979-84; mem. subcom. on Three Mile Island, Interagy. Radiation Research Com., 1980-84; mem. com. on health research initiatives on radiation research HHS, 1980-85; mem. fed. interagy. cen. coordinating com. for radiation planning and preparedness Fed. Emergency Mgmt. Agy., 1980-85, mem. subcom. on fed. response, 1982-85; mem. dosimetry assessment adv. com. Dept. Energy, 1980—; chmn. Hanford Health Effects Radiation Rev. Panel, 1986. Served with Signal Corps, U.S. Army, 1954-60. St. Louis U. scholar, 1952-53; recipient McComas History of Medicine prize U. Mo., 1966, Commendation medal USPHS, 1980. Fellow Am. Coll. Epidemiology; mem. Internat. Assn. Comparative Research on Leukemia and Related Diseases, Am. Soc. Preventive Oncology, Am. Soc. Microbiology, Commd. Officers Assn. USPHS (pres. Atlanta br. 1976), Soc. Epidemiologic Research, N.Y. Acad. Scis., Sigma Xi. Roman Catholic. Lodge: K.C. Contbg. editor Internat. Jour. Cancer Control and Prevention, 1979-84. Contbr. articles to profl. jours. Home: 2201 E Lawrence Rdano Phoenix AZ 85016

CALDWELL, MARY ALICE, medical venture capital executive; b. Los Angeles, Nov. 21, 1949; d. Jack B. and Patricia A. (Towey) C.; m. Steven N. Weiss, May 28, 1984. BS, U. San Francisco, 1971; MBA, Pepperdine U., 1984. RN, Calif.; cert. cardiovascular nurse specialist, cert. critical care nurse. Mgr. edn. Stanford (Calif.) U. Hosp., 1976-79; mgr. clin. research Oximetrix, Inc., Mountain View, Calif., 1979-80; mgr. products Am. Edwards Labs., Irvine, Calif., 1980-83; sr. cons. SRI Internat., Menlo Park, Calif., 1984-86; v.p. Telos Devel., San Francisco, 1986—. Contbr. articles to profl. jours. Mem. Am. Inst. Ultrasound in Medicine, Am. Assn. Critical Care Nurses (chpt. pres. 1979—), Am. Heart Assn. Cardiovascular Nursing Council. Avocations: tennis, travel, reading. Office: Telos Devel Corp 655 Montgomery St San Francisco CA 94111

CALDWELL, RICHARD LLOYD, mechanical engineer; b. Los Angeles, May 12, 1939; s. Ernest Brocket and Laura Fern (Blanchard) C. BME, Calif. Poly. State U., San Luis Obispo, 1962. Cert. plumbing engr. Gen. bldg. contractor Nevada City, Calif., 1970-80; cons. engr. Caldwell Engring., 1980-84; project engr. CDI, Inc., San Jose, Calif., 1984—; cons. engr. Standard Oil, San Francisco, 1982-83, Bechtol Corp., 1983-84. Author: (software package) Cost Estimating, 1985. Am. Soc. Plumbing Engrs., ASHRAE. Democrat. Unitarian. Home: 1617 Whitton Ave San Jose CA 95116 Office: CDI Inc 911 Bern Ct San Jose CA 95112

CALE, CHARLES GRIFFIN, lawyer; b. St. Louis, Aug. 19, 1940; s. Julian Dutro and Judith Hadley (Griffin) C.; B.A., Principia Coll., Elsah, Ill., 1961; LL.B., Stanford U., 1964; LL.M., U. So. Calif., 1966; m. Jessie Leete Rawn, Dec. 30, 1978; children—Whitney Rawn, Walter Griffin, Elizabeth Judith. Bar: Calif. 1965. Practice law, Los Angeles, 1965—; ptnr. firm Adams, Duque & Hazeltine, 1970-81, firm Morgan, Lewis & Bockius, Los Angeles, 1981—. Group v.p. sports Los Angeles Olympic Organizing Com., 1982-84; assoc. counselor U.S. Olympic Com., 1985, spl. asst. to pres., 1985—; bd. dirs. Hallum Prevention Child Abuse Fund, Los Angeles, Harvard Sch., Los Angeles, Big Bros. of Greater Los Angeles. Recipient Gold medal of Youth and Sports, France, 1984. Mem. ABA, State Bar Calif., Calif. Thoroughbred Breeders Assn. Clubs: California, Los Angeles Country, The Beach. Office: Morgan Lewis Bockius 801 S Grand Ave Los Angeles CA 90017

CALE, LETTIE BEASLEY, educational program administrator; b. Lyon County, Minn., May 7, 1935; d. William Leonard and Emma Ingeborg (Anderson) Beasley; m. Robert C. Noe, Jan. 22, 1955; m. 2d, Charles Ellison Cale, Oct. 24, 1971. B.S., Ariz. State U., 1957; M.S. in Home Econs. Edn., U. Ariz., 1969. Cert. supervisory, standard vocat. and secondary tchr., Ariz. Tchr. pub. schs., Ariz., 1957-61; kindergarten tchr., Tucson, 1962-63; tchr. home econs., biology, phys. edn. Pinetop-Lakeside High Sch., Lakeside, Ariz., 1963-67; asst. supr. home econs. edn. and state adviser Future Homemakers Am., Ariz. Dept. Edn. Phoenix, 1968-77, specialist adult vocat., community edn., 1977-80, coordinator schs. and community resource programs, 1983—. Recipient Nat. Disting. Service award Future Homemakers Am.; speech contest winner Toastmasters Internat., 1978, 82, 85; Disting. Service award State Toastmasters, 1983; Ariz. Community Educator of Yr. award, 1983; named Employee of Month, Ariz. Dept. Edn., 1986. Mem. Future Homemakers Am. (chmn. bd. dirs.), Ariz. Assn. Supervision and Curriculum Devel., Ariz. Community Edn. Assn. (pres.), Ariz. Sch. Adminstrs. Inc., Nat. Community Edn. Assn., Ariz. Adult Edn. Assn., Nat. Council State Edn. Agy. Community Educators. Clubs: Toastmasters Internat., Norseman's Forbundet. Author: Guidelines for Training Volunteers in Community Education, 1980; Reaching the Hard-to-Reach Parent, 1981; Administrative Perspectives, 1981; Directory of Educational Resources, 1982; editor: Displaced Workers Program: Guidelines for Instruction and Operation, 1983; co-editor: Arizona's Best Bet: Effective Schools. Home: 1924 W Ashland Phoenix AZ 85009 Office: Ariz Dept Edn Phoenix AZ 85007

CALER, WILLIAM ERNEST, research and development engineer; b. Berea, Ohio, Sept. 30, 1955; s. William Eugene and Alice Felicia (Frew) C. BS, U. Wash., 1978; MS, Stanford U., 1984. Research asst. dept. orthopaedics U. Wash., Seattle, 1977-79; research engr. biomechanics, dept. orthopaedics Mass. Gen. Hosp., Boston, 1979-82; research and devel. engr., rehab. research and devel. ctr. Stanford (Calif.) U. and Palo Alto (Calif.) VA Med. Ctr., 1982—. Contbr. articles to profl. jours. Asst. coach Stanford Area Youth Basketball, Palo Alto, 1985, Palo Alto Little League, 1987. Mem. ASME, Am. Soc. Biomechanics, Sigma Xi. Avocation: ind. animation. Office: Stanford U Design Div Dept Mech Engring Stanford CA 94305

CALFEE, ROBERT CHILTON, educational researcher, psychologist; b. Lexington, Ky., Jan. 26, 1933; s. Robert Klair and Nancy Bernice (Stipp) C.; m. Kathryn Ann McOsker, Dec. 26, 1975; children: Adele, LeeAnn, Janet, Jeffrey, Robert, Elise. B.A., UCLA, 1959, M.A., 1960, Ph.D., 1963. Asst. prof. psychology U. Wis., 1964-66, assoc. prof., 1966-69; assoc. prof. edn. Stanford U., 1969-71, prof., 1971—; assoc. dean research and devel., dir. Center for Ednl. Research, 1976-80; cons and speaker in field. Author: Human Experimental Psychology, 1975, Cognitive Psychology and Educational Practice, 1982, Experimental Methods in Psychology, 1985; editor: (with P.A. Drum) Teaching Reading In Compensatory Classes, 1979, Jour. Ednl. Psychology, 1984—. Trustee Palo Alto (Calif.) Sch. Dist., 1984—. Guggenheim Meml. fellow, 1972; fellow Center for Advanced Study in Behavioral Scis., 1981-82. Mem. AAAS, Am. Psychol. Assn., Am. Ednl. Research Assn., Internat. Reading Assn., Nat. Conf. Research in English, Psychonomic Soc., Soc. Research in Child Devel., Nat. Council Tchrs. English, Sigma Xi. Home: 995 Wing Pl Stanford CA 94305 Office: Sch Edn Stanford U Stanford CA 94305

CALHOUN, JILL SHAVER, software company executive; b. Akron, Ohio, June 8, 1954; d. Richard Conway and Joy Eileen (Aikey) Shaver; m. William Paul Steffy, Oct. 16, 1976 (div. June 1977); m. David Johnston Calhoun, Nov. 25, 1982. Student, North Tex. State U., 1972-73. Sec. Mgmt. Sci. Am. Inc., Marina del Rey, Calif., 1978-79, account mgr., 1979-82; edn. mgr. Mgmt. Sci. Am. Inc., Santa Monica, Calif., 1982-83, support mgr., 1983-85; regional adminstr. Mgmt. Sci. Am. Inc., Los Angeles, 1985—. Served with U.S. Army, 1976-77. Mem. Nat. Assn. Female Execs. Office: Mgmt Sci Am Inc 12121 Wilshire Blvd Suite 700 Los Angeles CA 90025

CALHOUN, ROBERT MILTON, real estate developer; b. Bakersfield, Calif., Nov. 25, 1918; s. David and Miriam (Kamp) C.; student UCLA, 1937-41; Ph.D. (hon.), Los Angeles U. Arts and Scis., 1944; m. Elaine Zazueta, Nov. 20, 1971; 1 dau., Heather June. Real estate developer and investor, Beverly Hills, Calif., 1946—. West Coast chmn. Nat. Audience Bd.; bd. govs. Women's Aux. Internat. Fedn.; chmn. Calif. Rehab. Center of Kaiser Found. Served with USN, 1942-45. Mem. Ind. Consultants Am., Am. Mgmt. Assn., Nat. Inst. Fin. Planners. Episcopalian. Clubs: Beverly Hills Tennis, The Cellar, Beverly Hills Health, Rotary. Author: The Power Profane, 1979. Home: 818 N Doheny Dr Los Angeles CA 90069 Office: 9701 Wilshire Blvd Beverly Hills CA 90212

CALICA, ARNOLD BARRY, neurological surgeon; b. Bklyn., Sept. 6, 1938; s. Bencion and Edith (Feldrais) C.; m. Diana Winifred Krakower, Dec. 20, 1974; children—Bencion, Emily, David; m. Patricia Ruth Uchill, June 20, 1959 (div. June 1974). B.A., U. Mich., 1959; S.M., U. Chgo., 1961; Ph.D., Johns Hopkins U., 1970; M.D., U. Chgo., 1975. Intern, U. Chgo., 1975-76, resident in neurosurgery, 1976-81; asst. prof. U.S. Naval Acad., 1968-71, U. Hawaii, 1971-72; practice medicine specializing in neurosurgery, Phoenix, 1981—.; assoc. staff Barrow Neurol. Inst., Phoenix, Good Samaritan Hosp., Phoenix Children's Hosp., Ariz. Children's Hosp. Contbr. articles to profl. jours. Fellow ACS; mem. N.Y. Acad. Sci., AAAS, Am. Math. Soc., Congress Neurol. Surgeons, Am. Assn. Neurol. Surgeons. Home: 4139 E Sandy Mountain Rd Scottsdale AZ 85253 Office: 345 E Virginia St Phoenix AZ 85004

CALKINS, CARL JEROME, real estate broker, rancher; b. Riverside, Calif., Oct. 4, 1933; s. Leslie Burton Calkins and Anna Francis (Porietz) Fischbeck; m. Yvonne Marie Harrison, Nov. 19, 1955; children: Mark J., Colette M. Macbeth, Kristina M. Hart. BS, Calif. State U., 1960; M of Criminology, U. Calif., Berkeley, 1969; M of Pub. Adminstrn., U. So. Calif., 1973. Capt. Los Angeles Police Dept., 1954-74; pub. safety dir. City of Carson, Calif., 1974-76; chief of police Long Beach Police Dept., Calif., 1976-79; mng. gen. ptnr. Tule Valley Ranch, Long Beach, 1979—. Bd. dirs. Long Beach Community Hosp. Found., 1979-85, Long Beach Y.M.C.A., 1977-81, Long Beach Boy Scouts Am., 1977-81. Served to sgt. U.S. Army, 1951-54. Mem. Internat. Assn. Police Chiefs, Calif. Peace Officers Assn., FBI Nat. Exec. Inst., Long Beach Bd. Realtors, Phi Kappa Phi. Democrat. Roman Catholic. Clubs: Mounted Police (Long Beach) (hon. pres. 1977-79), Long Beach Yacht. Lodge: Rotary (pres. Long Beach club 1982-83). Avocations: photography, sailing, shooting, fine art collecting. Home: 5980 The Toledo Long Beach CA 90803 Office: Tule Valley Ranch Partnership care 5980 The Toledo Long Beach CA 90803

CALL, DWIGHT VINCENT, accountant, educator; b. Chgo., Mar. 19, 1934; s. Jerome V. and Ruth E. (Wright) C.; m. Claudia Louise Hand, July 13, 1956; children—Jeanene Lee, Victoria Irene, Doreen Ann, Carrie Leann, Dwayne Vincent, Michelle Antoinette. m. Christine Gail Fox, Dec. 30, 1976. B.S., UCLA, 1957, M.B.A., 1959, Ph.D., 1966. C.P.A., Calif. Prof. acctg. Calif. State U.-Northridge, 1959—; staff acct. Anderson, Gursky & Maccallum, Los Angeles, 1959-62; ptnr. Call & Call, Sherman Oaks Calif., 1962-76; owner Dwight V. Call, C.P.A., Sherman Oaks, 1976-81; ptnr. Call & Trapani, Van Nuys, Calif., 1981-83; pres. Call & Call, Van Nuys, 1983—; instr. UCLA, 1964-69; lectr. in field. Recipient Outstanding Prof. award from acctg. students Calif. State U., 1968. Mem. Nat. Assn. Accts., Calif. Soc. C.P.A.s, Am. Inst. C.P.A.s, Beta Gamma Sigma. Clubs: Lakeside Golf, Desert Island Country, Jonathan Club. Office: Call and Call 5900 Sepulveda Blvd Suite 431 Van Nuys CA 91411

CALL, JOSEPH RUDD, accountant; b. Pensacola, Fla., Oct. 18, 1950; s. Melvin Eliason and Doris Mae (Rudd) C.; m. Nola Jean Pack, Dec. 20, 1973; children—Benjamin, Jeremy, Joshua, Rebecca, Jacob. BS, Brigham Young U., 1974. CPA, Calif., Idaho; cert. fin. planner, 1986. Small bus. specialist Deloitte, Haskins & Sells, Los Angeles, 1974-78; audit mgr. Rudd, DaBell & Hill, Rexburg, Idaho, 1978-80, audit ptnr. Rudd & Co., 1980-82, ptnr. in charge Idaho Falls office, 1982—. Mem. task force Small Bus. High Tech. Devel. State of Idaho, 1983; pres. Bonneville-Idaho Falls Crimestoppers, Inc., 1984-85. Mem. Am. Inst. CPAs (hon. mention on CPA exam 1975), Calif. Soc. CPAs., Idaho Soc. CPAs (pres. S.E. Idaho chpt. 1983-84, state bd. dirs., 1984—), Internat. Assn. Fin. Planners Mcpl. Fin. Officers Assn., Healthcare Fin. Mgmt. Assn., Idaho Falls C. of C. (bd. dirs. 1984—, chmn. bd. dirs. 1986—), Rexburg C. of C. (dir. 1981-82), MENSA, Eastern Idaho Sailing Assn. (rear commodore 1983—). Mormon. Office: Rudd & Co/Chartered 1820 E 17th St Suite 310 Idaho Falls ID 83401

CALL, OSBORNE JAY, bus. exec.; b. Afton, Wyo., June 4, 1941; s. Osborne and Janice C.; m. Tamra Compton, Dec. 16, 1977; children—Thad, Crystal. Student, Ricks Coll., Rexburg, Idaho, Brigham Young U., Provo, Utah. Engaged in petroleum mktg. 1960-68; v.p. Caribou Four Corners, Afton, 1964-68; pres. Flying J Inc. (retail and wholesale gasoline and real estate devel. co.), Brigham City, Utah, 1968—; dir. No. div. First Security Bank, Brigham City. Address: Flying J Inc 770 W 2250 S Perry Brigham City UT 84302

CALLAGY, FLORENCE MAE, accounting executive; b. Canton, Ohio, May 6, 1920; d. Charles J. and Pearl M. (Sadler) Brown; m. Francis Henry Callagy, Sept. 14, 1940 (dec.), children—Larry Francis, Richard Michael. Student San Diego State Coll., 1937-39; U. Calif.-San Diego, 1951, 1966-67. Jr. acct. Kramer and Zucker C.P.A.s, San Diego, 1951-53; office mgr., auditor, Town and Country Devel. Inc., San Diego, 1953-59, sec., treas., 1953-68; sec., treas., comptroller, Atlas Hotels, Inc., San Diego, 1959-70, dir., 1959—, cons., 1981—; ptnr. Callagy Snyder and Assocs., San Diego, 1971-81; owner, mgr. FMC Cons., San Diego, 1981—; sec., dir. Electra Corp., Crest Advt., Inc., Mut. Hotel Supply Co., OmniVideo, Inc., Mission Valley Inn, Inc., Mission Valley Devel., Inc., Med. Impact, Inc. Sustaining mem., capital fund com. YMCA, 1978-79; active United Community Services; adv. bd. Traveler's Aid Soc., San Diego; bd. dirs. San Diego Pres. Council, 1982-83, Freedom Found., Monteverdi Chamber Orch. Mem. Nat. Hotel Accts. (dir. 1972-73), San Diego Advt. Club, San Diego Assn. Advt. Agys., Nat. Mgmt. Assn. (past dir. San Diego chpt.), La Mesa C. of C., San Diego C. of C. Clubs: Altrusa (holder numerous offices, dist. gov. 1983-85); Toastmistress, Calif. Staters. Home: 6349-1 Rancho Mission Rd San Diego CA 92108

CALLAHAN, MARILYN JOY, social worker; b. Portland, Oreg., Oct. 11, 1934; s. Douglas Quinlin and Anona Helen (Bergemann) Maynard; m. Lynn James Callahan, Feb. 27, 1960 (dec. June 1979); children: Barbara Erin, Susan Dana and Jeffrey Lynn (twins). BA, Mills Coll., 1955; degree secondary teaching, Portland State U., 1963, MSW, 1971. Cert. secondary tchr., Oreg.; registered clin. social worker, Oreg. Child welfare counselor Clackamas County Pub. Welfare, Oregon City, Oreg., 1955-58; med. social worker U. Oreg. Med. Sch., Portland, 1958-59; counselor Multnomah County Juvenile Ct., Portland, 1959-62, Marion County Juvenile Ct., Salem, Oreg., 1965-69; devel., adminstrn. 1st ednl. program Oreg. Women's Correctional Ctr., Salem, 1966-67; mental health counselor Benton County Mental Health Clinic, Corvallis, Oreg., 1970-71; tchr. inst. Hillcrest Sch., Salem, 1975-81; social worker Mid Will Valley Sr. Service Agy., Salem, 1981—; bd. dirs. Vols. for Srs., Devel. of Tri County Area Conservator-Guardian Program, 1985 conf. on Age Discrimination. Mem. exec. bd. South Salem Neighborhood Assn., 1982—, sch. bd. Sacred Heart Acad., 1977-81, Boys and Girls Aid Soc., past dist. v.p.; bd. dirs. Camp Fire Girls, 1971-81. Mem. Nat. Assn. Social Workers (cert., diplomate, registered clin. social worker), AAUW (past v.p., past bd. dirs., directed study on family ct. bill 1967), Salem City Club (directed and published research study), U.S. Power Squadron, Catalina 22 Nat. Sailing Assn. Republican. Methodist. Club: Eugene Yacht (Oreg.). Avocations: sailing, downhill skiing, travel, reading, camping. Home: 2880 Mountain View Dr S Salem OR 97302 Office: Mid Willamette Valley Sr Services Agy 410 Senator Bldg 220 High St NE Salem OR 97301

CALLAN, COLLEEN, interior architect; b. Winona, Minn., Mar. 23, 1957; d. John and Rosemarie (Neumann) Callan; m. Kenneth Stein, Apr. 2, 1983. BFA, U. Idaho, 1980. Ski enthusiast Mt. Hood (Oreg.) Meadows, 1980-83; swimming instr. various locations, Portland, Oreg., 1975-83; owner, interior designer Alpine Interiors, Whitefish, Mont., 1983—. Mem. Am. Soc. Interior Designers. Democrat. Roman Catholic. Avocations: skiing, aerobics, travelling by car. Home: PO Box 10 Whitefish MT 59937 Office: Alpine Interiors 100 E Second St Whitefish MT 59937

CALLANT, MARCEL ALPHONSE, supermarket executive; b. Winifred, Mont., Oct. 31, 1919; s. Gustav Joseph and Emma Matilda (Schram) C.; m. Eleanor Mary Gaetze (dec.); children: Lawrence Gustav and Mary Anne. Grad. high sch., Harlowton, Mont. Switchman Milw. R.R., Harlowton, 1945-48; ptnr. Wheatland Grocery, Harlowton, 1949-57; ptnr. A-G Supermarket, Harlowton, 1957-68, owner, 1968-82; ret.; vice chmn. Assn. Food Stores, Inc., Salt Lake City, 1977-82; acting gen. mgr. Winnecook Ranch Co., Inc., Harlowton, 1986. Mem. Harlowton City Council, 1975, pres., 1979. Served as sgt. AUS, 1940-45, PTO.

CALLAO, MAXIMO JOSE, psychologist, educator; b. San Jose, Calif., Feb. 18, 1941; s. Juan Alfonso and Marta (Pinaroc) C.; m. Denise Naomi Inafuku, Mar. 29, 1969; children: Aaron Mark, Jenny Alia. BA in Psychology, San Jose State Coll., 1962; PhD in Counseling Psychology, Purdue U., 1971. Lic., psychologist, Idaho. Tchr., U.S. Peace Corps, Philippines, 1962-64; tchr. Baker Sch., San Jose, Calif., 1965-66; counselor Maili Sch., Waianae, Hawaii, 1967-69; adminstrv. intern State of Hawaii Dept.

Edn., 1969; counselor Psychol. Services Clinic Purdue U., Lafayette, Ind., 1969-71; counseling psychologist, prof. psychology Boise State U., Idaho, 1971-83, also dir. Counseling and Testing Ctr.; pvt. practice psychology, Boise, 1983—; adj. prof. Coll. of Idaho, 1983—, San Francisco Theol. Sem., San Anselmo, Calif., 1985—; mem. adj. faculty San Francisco Theol. Sem., 1985—. Mem. Am. Mental Health Counselors Assn., Idaho Psychol. Assn., Assn. Asian-Am. Psychologists. Democrat. Presbyterian. Clubs: Highlanders Bagpipe Band (Boise), Boise State U. Fencing Assn. Home: 5680 Kriscliffe Ct Boise ID 83704

CALLAWAY, ENOCH, psychiatrist, educator; b. LaGrange, Ga., July 12, 1924; s. Enoch and Jennie L. (Crowell) C.; m. Dorothy Campbell, July 3, 1948; children: Rebecca, Deborah. AB, Columbia U., 1944, MD, 1947. Diplomate Am. Bd. Psychiatry and Neurology. Instr. U. Md., Balt., 1952-55, asst. prof., 1955-58; assoc. prof. U. Calif., San Francisco, 1958-65, prof., 1965—; mem. rev. com. on psychopharmacology NIMH, 1963-67, rev. com. on alcohol, 1968-72, rev. com. on research scientists, 1975-76, adv. bd. EEG Systems Lab., San Francisco, 1985—. Author: Brain Electrical Potential and Individual Psychological Differences, 1975; editor: Event Related Brain Potentials in Man, 1978, Human Evoked Potentials, 1978, assoc. editor Biol. Psychiatry, 1983—, mem. editorial bd. AMA Archives Gen. Psychiatry, 1970-83; contbr. numerous articles to sci. jours. Served to comdr. USN, 1950-52. Recipient Career Devel. award NIMH, 1954-58; research prize Md. Assn. Pvt. Practicing Psychiatrists, 1956; Royer award U. Calif., San Francisco, 1981. Fellow Am. Coll. Neuropsychopharmacology; mem. Soc. Biol. Psychiatry (pres. 1982-83), Soc. Psychophysiol. Research (pres. 1982), Calif. Med. Assn. (exec. com. sci. bd. 1977-83)., Marin Recorder Soc. Democrat. Club: Tiburon Peninsula. Avocations: tennis, recorder playing. Home: 1 Mt Tiburon Tiburon CA 94920 Office: U Calif 401 Parnassus Ave San Francisco CA 94920

CALLAWAY, JAMES ALBERT, dentist; b. Las Vegas, Apr. 24, 1947; s. Albert Moore and Kathlyn Lilythe (Peck) C.; B.S., U. Nev., 1969; D.D.S., U. Detroit, 1972; m. Pamela Maria Luczynski, Oct. 27, 1972; children—Casey James, Bonnie Rebecca, Daniel Albert. Gen. practice dentistry, Troy, Mich., 1973, Las Vegas, Nev., 1973—; dentist to Las Vegas Stars Baseball Team; owner Griffith Callaway Gallery, Las Vegas, 1978—. Mem. Am. Orthodontic Assn., Am. Endodontic Soc., ADA, Nev. Dental Assn., Acupuncture Research Inst., Freeman Inst., Portrait Inst., Am. Portrait Soc., Clark County Dental Soc., Sigma Alpha Epsilon. Democrat. Mormon. Clubs: Las Vegas Gem, Lions. Exhibitor Las Vegas Art Mus. Home: 6225 Shadywood Las Vegas NV 89102 Office: 3100 W Sahara St Las Vegas NV 89102

CALLEN, LON EDWARD, county ofcl.; b. Kingman, Kans., Mar. 31, 1929; s. Cleo Paul and Josephine Nell (Mease) C.; B.A. in Math. and Physics, U. Wichita (Kans.), 1951; m. Barbara Jean Sallee, Oct. 12, 1954; children—Lon Edward, Lynnette J. Commd. 2d lt. USAF, 1951, advanced through grades to lt. col., 1968; comdr. Tuslog Detachment 93, Erhac, Turkey, 1966-67; sr. scientist Def. Atomic Support Agy., Washington, 1967-71; ret., 1971; dir. emergency preparedness City-County of Boulder, Colo., 1976—; bd. dirs. Boulder County Emergency Med. Services Council, 1977, Boulder County Amateur Radio Emergency Services, 1978—. Mem. hon. awards com. Nat. Capital Area council Boy Scouts Am., 1971; chmn. Boulder County United Fund, 1976-82; mem. asst. staff Indian Princesses and Trailblazer programs Boulder YMCA, 1974-78. Decorated Joint Service Commendation medal; recipient cert. achievement Def. Atomic Support Agy., 1970. Mem. AASA, Am. Ordnance Soc., Am. Soc. Cybernetics, Planetary Soc., Math. Assn. Am., N.Y. Acad. Scis., Fedn. Am. Scientists, U.S. Civil Def. Council, Nat. Assn. Atomic Vets., Union Concerned Scientists, Colo. Civil Def. Assn., Boulder County Fire Fighters Assn., Ret. Officers Assn., Colo. Front Range Protective Assn., Mensa, Sigma Xi, Pi Alpha Pi. Clubs: Boulder Knife and Fork, Boulder Gunbarrel Optimists, Denver Matrix, U. Colo. Ski, U. Wichita. Author articles in field. Home: 4739 Berkshire Ct Boulder CO 80301 Office: Box 471 County Courthouse Boulder CO 80306

CALLIHAN, C. MICHAEL, lt. gov., former state senator, broadcaster; b. Spokane, Wash., Aug. 7, 1947; s. Cal and Dorothy C.; m. Ann L. Duckett, 1973. B.A., Western State Coll., 1973. Owner, Callihan Broadcasting Group; county assessor, 1975-78; mem. Colo. Ho. of Reps., 1979-80; mem. Colo. Senate, 1982-86; lt. gov. State of Colo., 1986—. Served with USN. Mem. Am. Legion. Democrat. Club: Lions. Office: 130 State Capitol Denver CO 80203

CALLISON, ANTHONY, architectural executive; b. Seattle, May 21, 1932; s. Henry Sheldon and Margaret (Dilling) C.; m. Shirley Sires, Aug. 25, 1961; children: Katherine Anne, Kirk Dilling. BArch, U. Wash., 1956. Registered architect, Wash., Alaska, Calif., Colo., Idaho, Oreg., Utah, Tex., Nev., Miss., Ohio, N.J., Ind. Pres. Callison Assocs., Seattle, 1970-72, Callison, Erickson, Hobble, Seattle, 1972-75, The Callison Partnership, Ltd., Seattle, 1975—; bd. dirs. Continental Savs. Bank, Seattle, 1986—, Seattle Repertory Theater, 1986—; mem. council of The Corp. Arts. Mem. Mcpl. League, Seattle, 1980—. Mem. AIA (bd. dirs. 1985-86, treas. 1986—), Urban Land Inst., Internat. Council Shopping Ctrs. Republican. Episcopalian. Clubs: Seattle Yacht, Seattle Tennis, Seattle Golf, Down Town (Seattle), Columbia Tower. Lodge: Rotary (bd. dirs. Seattle club). Avocations: skiing, golfing, boating. Home: 1121 38th Ave E Seattle WA 98112 Office: The Callison Partnership Ltd 1423 Third Ave Suite 300 Seattle WA 98101

CALLISON, NANCY FOWLER, nurse; b. Milw., July 16, 1931; d. George Fenwick and Irma Esther (Wenzel) Fowler; m. B.G. Callison, Sept. 25, 1954 (dec. Feb. 1964); children: Robert, Leslie, Linda. Diploma, Evanston (Ill.) Hosp. Sch. Nursing, 1952; BS, Northwestern U., 1954. RN, Calif. Staff nurse, psychiat. dept. Downey VA Hosp., 1954-55; staff nurse Camp Lejeune Naval Hosp., 1955, 59-61; obstet. supr. Tri-City Hosp., Oceanside, Calif., 1961-62; pub. health nurse San Diego County, 1962-66; sch. nurse Rich-Mar Union Sch. Dist., San Marcos, Calif., 1966-68; head nurse San Diego County Community Mental Health, 1968-73; dir. patient care services Southwood Mental Health Ctr., Chula Vista, Calif., 1973-75; program cons. Comprehensive Care Corp., Newport Beach, Calif., 1975-79; dir. Manpower Health Care, Culver City, Calif., 1979-80; dir. nursing services Peninsula Rehab. Ctr., Lomita, Calif., 1980-81; clinic supr., coordinator utilization and authorizations, acting dir. provider relations Hawthorne (Calif.) Community Med. Group, 1981-86; mgr. Health Care Delivery Physicians of Greater Long Beach, Calif., 1986—; clinic coordinator, translator Flying Samaritans, 1965—, mem. internat. bd. dirs., 1975-77, 79—, pres. South Bay chpt., 1975-81. Mem. Am. Nurses Assn., Nat. Assn. Female Execs., Aircraft Owners and Pilots Assn., U.S.-Mex. Border Health Assn., Cruz Roja Mexicana (Delegacion Rosarito 1986—). Office: Health Care Delivery Physicians of Greater Long Beach 1045 Atlantic Blvd Long Beach CA 90813

CALLISTER, LOUIS HENRY, JR., lawyer; b. Salt Lake City, Aug. 11, 1935; s. Louis Henry and Isabel (Barton) C.; B.S., U. Utah, 1958, J.D., 1961; m. Ellen Gunnell, Nov. 27, 1957; children—Mark, Isabel, Jane, Edward, David, John Andrew, Ann. Admitted to Utah bar, 1961; asst. atty. gen. Utah, 1961; sr. ptnr. Callister, Duncan & Nebeker, Salt Lake City, 1961—; pres. Callister Devel. Corp.; bd. dirs. Am. Stores Co., Premium Oil Co., Quality Oil Co. Vice chmn. Salt Lake City Zoning Bd. Adjustment, 1979-84; bd. govs. Latter Day Saints Hosp., 1983—; treas. exec. com. Utah Rep. Com., 1965-69; chmn. Utah chpt. Rockefeller for Pres. Com., 1964-68; sec., trustee Salt Lake City Police Hon. Cols., 1982—. Mormon. Home: 1454 Tomahawk Dr Salt Lake City UT 84103 Office: Callister Duncan Nebeker 800 Kennecott Bldg Salt Lake City UT 84133

CALLISTER, MARION JONES, federal judge; b. Moreland, Idaho, June 6, 1921; m. Nina Lynn Hayes, June 7, 1946; children—Nona Lynn Callister Haddock, Lana Sue Callister Meredith, Jenny Ann Callister Thomas, Tamara Callister Banks, Idonna Ruth Callister Andersen, Betty Patricia Callister Jacobs, Deborah Jean Hansen, Mary Clarice Fowler, David Marion, Nancy Irene, Michelle, Kimberly Jane. Student, Utah State U., 1940-41; B.S.L., U. Utah, 1950, J.D., 1951. Bar: Idaho 1951. Dep. pros. atty. Bingham County, Utah, 1951-52; asst. U.S. atty. Dist. of Idaho, 1953-57, U.S. atty., 1975-76; sole practice 1958-69; judge Idaho Dist. Ct. 4th Jud. Dist., 1970-75, U.S. Dist. Ct. Idaho, Boise, 1976—; now chief judge U.S. Dist. Ct. Idaho. Served with U.S. Army, 1944-46. Decorated Purple Heart. Republican. Mormon. Office: US Courthouse PO Box 040 550 W Fort St Boise ID 83724

CALLOW, KEITH MCLEAN, judge; b. Seattle, Jan. 11, 1925; s. Russell Stanley and Dollie (McLean) C.; m. Evelyn Case, July 9, 1949; children: Andrea, Douglas, Kerry. Student, Alfred U., 1943, CCNY, 1944, Biarritz Am. U., 1945; B.A., U. Wash., 1949, J.D., 1952. Bar: Wash. 1952. Asst. atty. gen. Wash., 1952; law clk. Wash. Supreme Ct., 1953; dep. pros. atty. King County, 1954-56; partner firm Little, LeSourd, Palmer, Scott & Slemmons, Seattle, 1957-62, Barker, Day, Callow & Taylor, 1964-68; judge King County Superior Ct., 1969-71, Wash. State Ct. of Appeals, Seattle, 1972-84; presiding chief judge Wash. State Ct. of Appeals, 1980; justice Wash. State Supreme Ct., Olympia, 1985—; lectr. bus. law U. Wash., 1956-62; faculty Nat. Jud. Coll., 1980; co-organizer, sec. Council of Chief Judges, 1980. Editor works in field. Bd. dirs. Evergreen Safety Council; pres. Young Men's Republican Club, 1957, chief Seattle Council Boy Scouts Am. Served with AUS, 1943-46. Decorated Purple Heart.; recipient Brandeis award Wash. State Trial Lawyers Assn., 1981. Mem. ABA (chmn. com. on judiciary 1984—), Wash. State Bar Assn., D.C. Bar Assn., Seattle-King County Bar Assn., Estate Planning Council, Navy League, Psi Upsilon, Phi Delta Phi. Clubs: Rainier (sec. 1978), Harbor, Forty Nine (pres. 1972); Harbor. Lodges: Masons, Rotary. Office: Temple of Justice Olympia WA 98504

CALLOWAY, DORIS HOWES, university provost; b. Canton, Ohio, Feb. 14, 1923; d. Earl John and Lillian Ann (Roberts) Howes; m. Nathaniel O. Calloway, Feb. 14, 1946 (div. 1956); children: David Karl, Candace; m. Robert O. Nesheim, July 4, 1981. B.S., Ohio State U., 1943; Ph.D., U. Chgo., 1947. Head metabolism lab., nutritionist, chief div. QM Food and Container Inst., Chgo., 1951-61; chmn. dept. food sci. and nutrition Stanford Research Inst., Menlo Park, Calif., 1961-63; prof. U. Calif., Berkeley, 1963—, provost profl. schs. and colls., 1981—; mem. expert adv. panel nutrition WHO, Geneva, 1972—; trustee Internat. Maize and Wheat Improvement Ctr., 1983—; trustee Winrock Internat. Inst., 1986—; cons. FAO, UN, Rome, 1971,74-75,81-83; adv. council NIH, Nat. Inst. Arthritis, Metabolic and Digestive Diseases, Nat. Inst. Aging, Bethesda, Md., 1974-77, 78-82. Author: Nutrition and Health, 1981, Nutrition and Physical Fitness 11th edit., 1984. Recipient Meritorious Civilian Service Dept. Army, 1959; named Disting. Alumna Ohio State U., 1974, Wellcome vis. prof. Fedn. Am. Soc. Exptl. Biol., U. Mo., 1980. Mem. Am. Inst. Nutrition (pres. 1982-83, sec. 1969-72, editorial bd. 1967-72; Conrad A. Elvehjem award 1986), Am. Dietetic Assn. (editorial bd. 1974-77, Cooper Meml. lectr. 1983), Sigma Xi. Office: U Calif California Hall Berkeley CA 94720 *

CALOF, DAVID LORNE, family hypnotherapist; b. Seattle, Dec. 12, 1949; s. Jacob and Thea (Golden) C.; m. Cindy Salazar, Nov. 14, 1974 (div.). Coordinator Office Coop. Edn., asst. to Dean Devel. Services, Evergreen State Coll., 1971-72; dir. mgmt. services, mgr. personnel staff devel. Seattle Opportunities Industrialization Ctr., 1974-77; family hypnotherapist, cofounder Seattle Family Inst., pvt. practice specializing in hypnotherapy and treatment of multiple personality, as well as adult survivors of incest and child abuse, 1973—; clin. cons. and lectr. Mem. Wash. Gov.'s Youth Commn., state chmn. Wash. Assn. Student Govts., 1970-71; exec. dir. Citizens Conf. on Wash. State Legislature, 1972-73. Mem. Am. Mental Health Counselors Assn., Am. Assn. Counseling and Devel., Assn. Advance Ethical Hypnosis, Am. Counsel Hypnotist Examiners (cert. hypnotherapist), Northwest Family Tng. Inst., Internat. Soc. Study of Multiple Personality and Dissociation, Internat. Platform Assn. Contbr. to various profl. publs.; spl. cons. Wash. State Council Higher Edn. "State Report on Campus Unrest." Office: Seattle Family Inst 2722 Eastlake Ave E Seattle WA 98102

CALVERT, DAVID L., non-profit foundation executive, public relations consultant; b. Artesia, N.Mex., Dec. 11, 1958; s. Donald L. and Linda R. (Siegenthaler) C.; m. Gaye Ellen Williams, Nov. 24, 1979; children: Daniel Asher, Dathan Andrew. Student, Lubbock Christian Coll., 1977-78, Tex. Tech U., 1978-79, U. N.Mex., 1986. With Currier Abstract Co., Artesia, 1979-80; area dir. March of Dimes Birth Defects Found., Las Cruces, N.Mex., 1980-81; exec. dir. March of Dimes, Albuquerque, 1981—; dir. Nat. Health Agys., Albuquerque, 1981—, chmn. 1985—. Producer March of Dimes Telethon Against Birth Defects, 1983-85, Born Am., 1986; editor Vista newspaper, 1985. Lobbyist N.Mex. Bill for Medically Fragile Children, Santa Fe, 1984; organizer N.Mex. Parents Reaching Out Conf., Albuquerque, 1986, Healthy Mothers Healthy Babies Coalition, Santa Fe, 1986; advisor Parentcraft, Albuquerque, 1982-84. Mem. Meeting Planners Internat., Albuquerque Hispano Chamber, Greater Albuquerque C. of C., Las Cruces C. of C. Republican. Avocations: gardening, swimming, reading, backpacking. Home: 3508 Parsifal NE Albuquerque NM 87111 Office: March of Dimes Birth Defects Found 3705 Westerfeld Dr NE Albuquerque NM 87111

CALVERT, MARSHALL ALAN, financial services manager, substance abuse counselor; b. Kansas City, Mo., Aug. 15, 1952; s. Wesley Dale and Maxine Leona C.; m. Darcy Lou Berline, Dec. 28, 1974; 1 child, Cara Lynne. Lic. in ins., Alaska; lic. in securities series 6, 63, and 26 Nat. Assn. Securities Dealers, registerd prin. 1st Am. Nat. Securities, Inc.. Grad. in Geology, Wichita State U., 1974; MBA Webster Coll., 1977; grad. USAF Squadron Officers Sch., 1978. Cert. substance abuse counselor, Alaska. Dept. mgr. Gibson Discount Ctr., Wellington, Kans., 1972-74; commd. 2d lt. U.S. Air Force, 1974, advanced through grades to capt., 1978; assignments in Tex., Calif., Kans., Ala., Alaska, 1974-82; exec. dir. Alaska Native Tng. Inst., Anchorage, 1982; coordinator Brother Francis Shelter, Anchorage, 1982-83; regional mgr. A.L. Williams Corp., and First Am. Nat. Securities, Inc., Anchorage, 1983—; pvt. practice substance abuse counseling; primary trainer Alaska Dept. Military and Vets. Affairs, Employee Assistance program and Human Resource Specialists; contract prospector; mineral evaluator; instrument pilot Gen. Aviation Aircraft. Past pres. bd. dirs. Alaska Council for Prevention of Alcohol and Drug Abuse, 1983. Served to maj. Air N.G., 1983—. Recipient God and Country award First Christian Ch., Wellington, Kans., 1964, Eagle Scout award Boy Scouts Am., Wellington, 1966, Nat. Exploration award Explorers Club, N.Y.C., 1970, Nat. Sojourners medal AFROTC, 1973; Tasch geology scholar, 1972. Mem. Alaska Council for Prevention of Alcoholism and Drug Abuse (life), Am. Soc. for Counseling and Devel., Mil. Educators and Counselors Assn., Nat. Rifle Assn. (life), AIME, Soc. Mining Engrs., Soc. Petroleum Engrs., Alaska Miners Assn., Alaska Geol. Soc., Res. Officers Assn., Air Force Assn., Am. Personnel and Guidance Assn., Soc. for Specialists in Group Work, Alaska Airmen's Assn., Wellington Gem and Mineral Soc., Aircraft Owners and Pilots Assn., Alaska Air N.G. Officers Assn., Chugach Gem. and Mineral Soc. Clubs: Elmendorf AFB Aero. Avocations: flying, hunting, prospecting and gold dredging, glacier climbing, biking. Office: 3400 Spenard Rd Suite 7 Anchorage AK 99503

CALVERT, TERRY LYNN, systems analyst, programmer, computer executive; b. Indpls., July 11, 1950; s. Victor Junior and Annie May (Skaggs) C.; m. Cynthia Ann Matzka, Aug. 29, 1970; children: Derek, Sean, Marc, Ryan. BS, Ill. State U., 1973, MS in Exptl. Psychology, 1977. Mental health specialist Lincoln (Ill.) State Sch., 1974-77; research asst. Western CArolina Ctr., Morgantown, N.C., 1977-78; unit dir. Eastern Oreg. State Hosp., Pendleton, 1978-79, psychologist, 1980-81; salesman Comrie Olds, Pendleton, 1981-82; pres. Calvert Computer Systems, Athena, Oreg., 1982—. Mayor City of Athena, 1984-85. Republican. Office: Calvert Compter Systems Inc 240 E Main St PO Box 95 Athena OR 97813

CALVIN, ALLEN DAVID, psychologist, educator; b. St. Paul, Feb. 17, 1928; s. Carl and Zelda (Engelson) C.; m. Dorothy VerStrate, Oct. 5, 1953; children—Jamie, Kris, David, Scott. B.A. in Psychology cum laude, U. Minn., 1950; M.A. in Psychology, U. Tex., 1951, Ph.D. in Exptl. Psychology, 1953. Instr. Mich. State U., East Lansing, 1953-55; asst. prof. Hollins Coll., 1955-59, assoc. prof., 1959-61; dir. Britannica Center for Studies in Learning and Motivation, Menlo Park, Calif., 1961; prin. investigator grant for automated teaching fgn. langs. Carnegie Found., 1960; USPHS grantee, 1960; pres. Behavioral Research Labs., 1962-74; prof., dean Sch. Edn., U., San Francisco, 1974-78; Henry Clay Hall prof. Orgn. and leadership, 1978—; pres. Pacific Grad. Sch. Psychology, 1984—. Author textbooks. Served with USNR, 1946-47. Mem. Am. Psychol. Assn., AAAS, Sigma Xi, Psi Chi. Home: 1645 15th Ave San Francisco CA 94122 Office: U San Francisco San Francisco CA 94117

CALVIN, DOROTHY VER STRATE, computer company executive; b. Grand Rapids, Mich., Dec. 22, 1929; d. Herman and Christina (Plakmyer) Ver Strate; m. Allen D. Calvin, Oct. 5, 1953; children—Jamie, Kris, Bufo, Scott. B.S. magna cum laude, Mich. State U., 1951. Mgr. data processing. Behavioral Research Labs., Menlo Park, Calif., 1972-75; dir. Mgmt. Info. Systems Inst. for Prof. Devel., San Jose, Calif. 1975-76; systems analyst, programmer Pacific Bell Info. Systems, San Francisco, 1976-81; staff mgr., 1981-84; mgr. applications devel. Data Architects Inc., San Francisco, 1984-86; pres. Ver Strate Press, San Francisco, 1986—. Instr., Downtown Community Coll., San Francisco, 1980-84; mem. computer curriculum adv. council San Francisco City Coll., 1982-84. Vice pres. LWV, Roanoke, Va., 1956-58; pres. Bulliss Purissima Parents Group, Los Altos, Calif., 1962-64; bd. dirs. Vols. for Israel, 1986—. Mem. Nat. Assn. Female Execs., Assn. Systems Mgmt., Assn. Women in Computing. Democrat. Avocations: computing; gardening; jogging; reading. Office: Ver Strate Press 1645 15th Ave San Francisco CA 94122

CALVIN, DOUGLAS WAYNE, corporate executive, energy engineer; b. San Diego, Calif., Jan. 28, 1942; s. Wayne Calvin and Delores Platz; m. Lena Lorraine Lee, Feb. 6, 1965; 1 child, Christina. BSBA, U. Phoenix, 1984; postgrad., Golden Gate U., 1986—. Plant engr. Northern Telecom, Nashville, 1978-80; mgr. maintenance, plant engring. Lindsay (Nebr.) Mfg. Co., 1980-81; mgr. plant engring. Kaiser Electronics Co., San Jose, 1981-84; dir. cen. services Ultratech Stepper, Santa Clara, Calif., 1984—. Pres. Glenmoor Meadows Homeowners Assn., San Jose, 1986. Served with USN, 1960-67. Mem. Assn. Plant Engrs., Planning Forum, Risk and Ins. Mgmt. Soc., Am. Soc. Indsl. Security, Telecommunications Assn. Club: Toastmasters (San Jose). Home: 6467 Matthew Ct San Jose CA 95123 Office: Ultratech Stepper Inc 3230 Scott Blvd Santa Clara CA 95054

CALVIN, LYLE DAVID, statistician, educator; b. Dannebrog, Nebr., Apr. 12, 1923; s. David A. and Muriel (Harvey) C.; m. Shirley Jeanne Schmidt, Apr. 19, 1952; children—James Arthur, Ronald David, Janet Lee. Grad., Parsons (Kans.) Jr. Coll., 1943; B.S. in Meteorology, U. Chgo., 1948; B.S., N.C. State U., 1947, Ph.D., 1953. Biometrician G.D. Searle & Co., Chgo., 1950-52; asst. statistician N.C. State U., Raleigh, 1952-53; statistician (Agrl. Expt. Sta.); asso. prof. Oreg. State U., 1953-57, prof., 1957—, chmn. dept. statistics, 1962-81; dir. Survey Research Center, 1973-85; dean Grad. Sch., 1981—; vis. prof. U. Edinburgh, 1967, Inst. Stat. Studies and Research, U. Cairo, 1971-72; chmn. Com. of Pres. of Statis. Socs., 1985—. Served from pvt. to 1st lt. USAAF, 1943-46. Fellow AAAS, Am. Statis. Assn.; mem. Internat. Statis. Inst., Biometric Soc. (pres. WNAR 1964-65, gen. sec. 1980-84), Am. Statis. Assn., Internat. Assn. Survey Statisticians. Home: 3463 NW Crest Dr Corvallis OR 97330

CALVIN, MELVIN, chemist, educator; b. St. Paul, Apr. 8, 1911; s. Elias and Rose I. (Hervitz) C.; m. Marie G. Jemtegaard, 1942; children: Elin, Karole, Noel. B.S., Mich. Coll. Mining and Tech., 1931, D.Sc., 1955; Ph.D., U. Minn., 1935, D.Sc., 1969; hon research fellow, U. Manchester, Eng., 1935-37; Guggenheim fellow, 1967; D.Sc., Nottingham U., 1958, Oxford (Eng.) U., 1959, Northwestern U., 1961, Wayne State U., 1962, Gustavus Adolphus Coll., 1963, Poly. Inst. Bklyn., 1962, U. Notre Dame, 1965, U. Gent, Belgium, 1970, Whittier Coll., 1971, Clarkson Coll., 1976, U. Paris Val-de-Marne, 1977, Columbia U., 1979. With U. Calif., Berkeley, 1937—; successively instr. chemistry, asst. prof., prof., Univ. prof., dir. Lab. Chem. Biodynamics U. Calif., 1963-80, assoc. dir. Lawrence Berkeley Lab., 1967-80; Peter Reilly lectr. U. Notre Dame, 1949; Harvey lectr. N.Y. Acad. Medicine, 1951; Harrison Howe lectr. Rochester sect. Am. Chem. Soc., 1954; Falk-Plaut lectr. Columbia U., 1954; Edgar Fahs Smith Meml. lectr. U. Pa. and Phila. sect. Am. Chem. Soc., 1955; Donegani Found. lectr. Italian Nat. Acad. Sci., 1955; Max Tishler lectr. Harvard U., 1956; Karl Folkers lectr. U. Wis., 1956; Baker lectr. Cornell U., 1958; London lectr., 1961, Willard lectr., 1982; Vanuxem lectr. Princeton U., 1969; Disting. lectr. Mich. State U., 1977; Prather lectr. Harvard U., 1980; Dreyfus lectr. Dartmouth Coll., 1981, Berea Coll., 1982; Barnes lectr. Colo. Coll., 1982; Nobel lectr. U. Md., 1982; Abbott lectr. U. N.D., 1983; Gunning lectr. U. Alta., 1983; O'Leary disting. lectr. Gonzaga U., 1984; Danforth lectr. Dartmouth Coll., 1984, Grinnell Coll., 1984; R.P. Scherer lectr. U. S. Fla., 1984; Imperial Oil lectr. U. Western Ont., Can., 1985; disting. lectr. dept. chemistry U. Calgary, Can., 1986; Melvin Calvin lectr. Mich. Tech. U., 1986; Eastman prof. Oxford (Eng.) U., 1967-68. Author: (with G. E. K. Branch) The Theory of Organic Chemistry, 1940, Isotopic Carbon, (with others), 1949, Chemistry of Metal Chelate Compounds, (with Martell), 1952, Path of Carbon in Photosynthesis, (with Bassham), 1957, Photosynthesis of Carbon Compounds, 1962, Chemical Evolution, 1969; contbr. articles to chem. and sci. jours. Recipient prize Sugar Research Found., 1950, Flintoff medal prize Brit. Chem. Soc., 1953, Stephen Hales award Am. Soc. Plant Physiologists, 1956, Nobel prize in chemistry, 1961; Davy medal Royal Soc., 1964; Virtanen medal, 1975; Priestley medal, 1978; Am. Inst. Chemists medal, 1979; Feodor Lynen medal, 1983; Sterling B. Hendricks medal, 1983, Melvin Calvin Medal of Distinction Mich. Tech. U., 1985. Mem. Britain's Royal Soc. London (fgn. mem.), Am. Chem. Soc. (Richards medal N.E. sect. 1956, Chem. Soc. Nichols medal N.Y. sect. 1958, award for nuclear applications in chemistry, pres. 1971, Gibbs medal Chgo. sect. 1977, Priestley medal 1978, Oesper award Cin. sect., 1981), Am. Acad. Arts and Scis., Nat. Acad. Scis., Royal Dutch Acad. Scis., Japan Acad., Am. Philos. Soc., Sigma Xi, Tau Beta Pi, Phi Lambda Upsilon. Office: Univ of Calif Lawrence Radiation Lab Berkeley CA 94720

CAMACHO, EFRAIN FLORES, civil engineer; b. Saipan, Mariana Islands, Dec. 17, 1949; s. Vicente Sablan and Estefania (Flores) C. BS in Engring., Tex. A&M U., 1974, BCE, 1976. Grad. engr. I Turner, Collie & Branden, Houston, 1977-78; project engr. Juan C. Tenorio & Assoc., Tamuning, Guam, 1978-79; resident engr. M&E Pacific Inc, Saipan, 1979—; sec. Profl. Licensing Bd., Saipan, 1979-85. Vice-chmn. Planning and Budget Affairs Office, Saipan, 1979. Mem. Soc. Am. Mil. Engrs. Roman Catholic. Avocation: golf. Home: PO Box 233, Saipan Northern Mariana Islands

CAMACHO, LUIS GUILLERMO, physician; b. Bolivia, Nov. 6, 1939; came to U.S., 1965, naturalized, 1969; s. Juan J. and Angela M. (Parrilla) C.; M.D., Nat. U. Cordoba (Argentina), 1963; m. Nov. 7, 1970; children—William Andrew, Ana Maria. Intern, Christ Community Hosp., Oaklawn, Ill., 1967-68; resident Mayo Clinic, Rochester, Minn., 1968-72, chief resident, 1972; cons. Riverside Clinic, Menasha, Wis., 1973-74; pvt. practice medicine, specializing in gen. and vascular surgery, Concord, Calif., 1974—; pres. Luis G. Camacho MD, Inc, Concord, 1974—; mem. staff Mt. Diablo Med. Center, John Muir Meml. Hosp., Walnut Creek Calif., Los Medanos Hosp., Pittsburg, Calif. Mem. AMA (Physician Recognition award 1972-83), A.C.S., Royal Soc. Health (London), Am. Coll. Angiology, Internat. Acad. Proctology, Inter-Am. Coll. Physicians and Surgeons, Priestley Soc., Am. Soc. Abdominal Surgeons, Mayo Clinic Alumni Assn. Office: 2211 East St Concord CA 94520 Office: 2260 Gladstone Dr Pittsburg CA 94565

CAMARDELLA, LEE O., municipal transit administrator; b. N.Y.C., Aug. 8, 1938; s. Olindo and Letizia (Della Torre) C.; m. Maria Pia Frascatani; children: Monique, Daniel. BS, Nova U., 1979. With Mil. Sea Transport Service, Bklyn., 1956-62, Dept. Marine and Aviation, N.Y., 1962-67; sgt., comdr. traffic div. Boynton Beach (Fla.) Police Dept., 1967-80; chief transit safety Municipality Metro. Seattle, 1981—; cons., lectr. various orgns., Seattle, 1981—; accident reconstrn. expert witness, Seattle. Author tng. manual Accident Investigation, 1982; co-author policy manual Non-Revenue Guide, 1986. Tchr. Palm Beach County Hwy. Safety, West Palm Beach, Fla., 1974-80, Evergreen Safety Council, Seattle, 1982—. Named Officer of Yr. Boynton Beach Police Dept., 1973-74; recipient Lifesaving awards, Boynton Beach Police Dept., 1973, 74, Citation bar Dept. Commerce Maritime Adminstrn., 1956. Mem. Nat. Com. Motor Fleet Supr. Tng., Nat. Assn. Fleet Suprs. (bd. dirs. 1981-87, instr. 1982—), Am. Soc. Safety Engrs. (bd. dirs. 1986—), Gov.'s Indsl. Safety and Health Com., Gov.'s Vehicle and Fleet Safety Com. (chmn. 1982, 86). Republican. Roman Catholic. Avocations: swimming, hiking. Home: 8520 E Mercer Way Mercer Island WA 98040 Office: Municipality Metro Seattle 821 2d Ave MS/SA Seattle WA 98104

CAMARGO, RAFAEL ENRIQUE, chemical engineer; b. Pereira, Colombia, June 15, 1952; came to U.S., 1978; s. Rafael Francisco and Marcela (Ramirez) C.; m. Cecilia Garcia, Jan. 14, 1977; children: Nicolas,

Felipe, Esteban. BSChemE, Universidad Pontificia, Medellin, Colombia, 1976; PhDChemE, U. Minn., 1983. Asst. faculty UPB, Medellin, 1976-77; process engr. Enka de Colombia, Medellin, 1977-78; instr. U. Minn., Mpls., 1982-83; staff engr. Raychem Corp., Menlo Park, Calif., 1983—, sr. engr., 1986—. Contbr. articles to profl. jours. Mem. Am. Chem. Soc., Soc. Plastics Engrs., Am. Soc. Metals, Am. Vacuum Soc. Avocation: bicycling.

CAMARILLO, ALBERT MICHAEL, history educator; b. Compton, Calif., Feb. 2, 1948; s. Benjamin Trinidad and Rose Ynez (Lopez) C.; m. Susan Diane Garb, June 25, 1972; children: Jeffrey, Gregory. BA, UCLA, 1970, PhD, 1975. Asst. prof. history Stanford (Calif.) U., 1975-80, assoc. prof., 1980—; dir. Stanford U. Ctr. for Chicano Research, 1980-85; exec. dir. inter-Univ. program for Latino Research, 1985—. Co-author: The Southwest: Myth and Reality, 1979; author: Chicanos in a Changing Soc., 1979, Chicanos in Calif., 1984. Mem. adv. bd. Mid-Peninsula Family Living Ctr. Shelter, Menlo Park, Calif., 1985—. Fellow NEH, 1977-78, Rockefeller Found., 1982-83, Ctr. for Advanced Studies in Behavioral Sci., 1982-83, Urban Studies Program, 1984-86. Mem. Nat. Assn. Chicano Studies (program com. 1979), Am. Hist. Assn., Pacific Coast Br. Am. Hist. Assn. (mem. council 1982-84), Orgn. Am. Historians (mem. nominating bd. 1982-84). Democrat. Avocations: basketball, running, woodworking. Office: Stanford U Dept History Bldg 200 Stanford CA 94305-2027

CAMERON, ALISON STILWELL, artist, author, illustrator; b. Beijing, China, Feb. 5, 1921; d. Joseph Warren and Winifred Alison (Smith) Stilwell; m. William Roderick Cameron, Dec. 27, 1947; children—Catherine, Laurie, Bruce. Grad. high sch., Beijing, China, 1937. Studied Chinese traditional painting under Prince P'u Ju, Beijing, China, 1936-39; exhibited in China, U.S. and S.Am., 1940—; prin. Stilwell Studio, Carmel, Calif., 1974—; tchr. Chinese Painting, Hawaii, Calif. and Ecuador, 1956—. Author: Chinese Painting Techniques, 1967; author, illustrator: ChinLing, the Chinese Cricket, 1947, 1981. Bd. dirs. Nat. Com. U.S.-China Relations, N.Y.C., 1976—, Planned Parenthood Monterey County, Calif., 1983—; trustee Monterey Inst. Internat. Studies, 1984—. Recipient Disting. Women of 1984 award Northwood Inst. Mem. Am. Women for Internat. Understanding, Soc. Women Geographers. Office: Stilwell Studio 6th Ave at Dolores PO Box 50 Carmel CA 93921

CAMERON, COLIN CAMPBELL, pineapple co. and land devel. exec.; b. Paia, Maui, Hawaii, Feb. 2, 1927; s. J. Walter and Frances (Baldwin) C.; m. Margaret Hartley, Aug. 25, 1951 (dec. Apr. 1986); children—Douglas, Richard, Margaret, Frances. A.B., Harvard U., 1950, M.B.A., 1953. Chmn., pres. Maui Land & Pineapple Co., Inc., 1969—; chmn. Kapalua Land Co., Ltd., 1974—, Maui Pineapple Co. Ltd.; v.p., dir. Haleakala Ranch Co., Ltd.; pres., dir. Maui Pub. Co. Ltd. (publishers Maui News); dir. Bank of Hawaii, Hawaiian Air Lines, Inc., Maui Electric Co., Ltd., High Tech. Devel. Corp. Vice pres. J. Walter Cameron Ctr., also chmn. long-range planning com.; bd. dirs., mem. exec. com. Lahaina Restoration Found.; bd. dirs. Hawaii Resort Developers Conf., Maui Philharmonic Soc., Found. 21st Century; exec. group Recreation Developers council Urban Land Inst.; mem. vis. com. East Asian Studies, Harvard U.; bd. visitors Fletcher Sch. Law and Diplomacy, East Asian Studies Harvard U.; mem. adv. bd. Travel Industry Mgmt. Sch. and Sch. Architecture, both U. Hawaii; chmn. Maui Econ. Devel. Bd.. Served with USNR, 1945-46. Mem. Japan-Western States Assn., Pacific Basin Economic Council, North Pacific Assn., Honolulu Council Fgn. Relations. Clubs: Pacific, Plaza. Office: PO Box 187 Kahului HI 96732

CAMERON, DONALD KENZIE, JR., oil company palynology coordinator; b. Trenton, N.J., Aug. 20, 1930; s. Donald Kenzie and Rachael (Allen) C.; m. Barbara J. Cross, June 19, 1954; children: Donald K. III, Dorothy C. Sheppard. BS, McGill U., 1952; AM, Ind. U., 1954. Paleontologist Chevron USA, New Orleans, 1954-61, palynology coordinator, 1980-85; palynologist Chevron USA, Jackson, Miss., 1961-69; palynologist Aramco, Dhahran, Saudi Arabia, 1969-74, supr. biostratigraphy, 1974-78; supr. biostratigraphy Aramco Overseas Co., Croydon, Eng., 1978-80; supr. stratigraphic services Chevron Overseas Co., San Francisco, 1985—. Mem. Am. Assn. Petroleum Geologists, Am. Assn. Stratigraphic Palynologists, New Orleans Geol. Soc., Soc. Organic Petrologists, Soc. Econ. Paleontology and Mineralogy (Gulf Coast sect.). Meth. Home: 1519 Gilboa Dr Walnut Creek CA 94598 Office: Chevron Overseas Co PO Box 5046 San Ramon CA 94583

CAMERON, DUNCAN FERGUSON, museum dir.; b. Toronto, Ont., Can., Feb. 1, 1930; s. Charles Gordon and Winnifred Petrie (Peppderdene) C.; m. Nancy Tousley, Apr. 24, 1975. Chief info. services Royal Ont. Museum, Toronto, 1956-61; pres. Janus Ltd., Toronto, 1961-70; nat. dir. Can. Conf. Arts, Toronto, 1968-70; dir. Bklyn. Mus., 1971-73; prin. P.S. Ross & Partners, Toronto, 1974-77; dir. Glenbow-Alta. Inst., Calgary, 1977—. Author articles in field. Mem. Internat. Council Museums, Museums Assn., Am. Assn. Museums, Can. Museums Assn., Can. Art Mus. Dirs. Orgn. (pres.), Commonwealth Assn. Museums (pres.), Royal Can. Mil. Inst. Anglican. Club: Ranchmen's (Calgary). Home: 3438 6th St SW, Calgary, AB Canada T2T 0H8 Office: Glenbow Museum, 130 9th Ave SE, Calgary, AB Canada T2G 0P3

CAMERON, EWAN, health science facility administration; b. Glasgow, Scotland, July 31, 1922; came to U.S., 1978; s. Neil Black and Mary Black (Carmichael) C.; m. Lillias Phemie Easton, Sept. 25, 1956; children: Fiona Margaret, Neil Easton. MBChB, Glasgow U., 1944; FRFPS, Royal Coll. Physicians and Surgeons, Glasgow, 1949; FRCS, Royal Coll. Surgeons, Edinburgh, 1950, Royal Coll. Surgeons, Glasgow, 1963. Registered Med. Practitioner. Intern Royal Infirmary, Falkirk, Scotland, 1944-45; trainee surgeon Western Infirmary, Glasgow, 1948-56; cons. surgeon Vale of Leven Hosp., Alexandria, Scotland, 1956-82; med. dir. Linus Pauling Inst., Palo Alto, Calif., 1978—; cons. to Royal Navy in Scotland, 1976—. Author: Hyaluronidase and Cancer, 1966; co-author Cancer and Vitamin C, 1979; contbr. articles to profl. jours. Served to lt. col. Brit. Army Med. Corps, 1945-48. Mem. AAAS, Brit. Med. Assn., Internat. Orgn. for Advancement of Human Potential. Presbyterian. Avocations: cine-photography, stock markets. Office: Linus Pauling Inst Sci and Medicine 440 Page Mill Rd Palo Alto CA 94306 Office: 47 Colquhoun St, Helensburgh Scotland G849LQ

CAMERON, FRANKLIN DANE, magazine editor; b. Los Angeles, Jan. 30, 1947; s. James B. Cameron and Evangeline C. (Booth) Hixson. BA, U. Calif., Berkeley, 1968. Mng. editor Photographic mag., Los Angeles, 1979-83; mng. editor Small Bus. Mag. Bus. Research and Monitoring Co., Monterey, Calif., 1983-84; mng. editor Petersen's Photographic mag., Los Angeles, 1984—; pres. Beauty Mgmt., Los Angeles, 1985—. Contbr. numerous articles to popular mags. Archaelogist York (Eng.) Archeol. Trust, 1973. Mem. Wilderness Soc., World Wildlife Fund. Pantheist. Office: Photographic Mag 8490 Sunset Blvd Los Angeles CA 90069

CAMERON, J. ELLIOT, parochial educational system administrator; b. Panguitch, Utah, Feb. 9, 1923; s. B.A. and Leonia (Sargent) C.; m. Maxine Petty, Dec. 23, 1942; children—Bruce, Kim, Kerry Lynn, Preston. B.S., M.A., Brigham Young U., 1946-49; Ed. D., 1966. Former high sch. prin., supt. schs. Duchesne, Sevier, Utah; later pres. Snow Coll., Ephraim, Utah; then dean students Utah State U.; former dean of student life, prof. edn. Brigham Young U., Provo, Utah; v.p. student services, then pres. Hawaii campus Brigham Young U.; commr. ch. ednl. system Ch. of Jesus Christ of Latter-day Saints. Served with AUS, World War II. Mem. NEA, Nat. Assn. Student Personnel Adminstrs., Phi Delta. Kappa. Mem. Ch. of Jesus Christ of Latter-day Saints. Home: 1057 E 5000 S Salt Lake City UT 84117

CAMERON, JAMES DUKE, state justice; b. Richmond, Calif., Mar. 25, 1925; s. Charles Lee and Ruth M. (Mabry) C.; m. Suzanne Jane Pratt, Aug. 16, 1952 (div. 1982); children: Alison Valerie, Craig Charles, Jennifer Elaine. A.B., U. Calif. at Berkeley, 1950; J.D., U. Ariz., 1954; LL.M., U. Va., 1982. Bar: Ariz. 1954. Practice in Yuma, 1954-60, 61-65; judge Superior Ct. Yuma County, 1960, Ariz. Ct. Appeals, 1965-70; justice Ariz. Supreme Ct., 1970—, vice chief justice, 1971-75, chief justice, 1975-80; mem. faculty appellate judges seminar Inst. Jud. Adminstrn., 1968-80; bd. dirs. Ariz. State Justice Inst., 1986—. Author: Arizona Appellate Forms and Procedures, 1968, also article. Mem. Ariz. Bd. Pub. Welfare, 1961-64, chmn., 1963-64; Mem. Eagle Scout bd. rev. Theodore Roosevelt council Boy Scouts Am., 1968—; Alternate del. Republican Nat. Conv., 1952; treas. Ariz. Rep. Party, 1958-60; Trustee Yuma City-County Library, 1958-67. Served with AUS, World War II. Mem. ABA (chmn. appellate judges conf. Judicial Adminstrn. div. 1977-78, jud. mem.-at-large 1986-88), Yuma County Bar Assn. (past pres.), State Bar Ariz., Ariz. Acad., Inst. Jud. Adminstrn., Nat. Inst. Justice (adv. com. 1984-86), Conf. Chief Justices U.S. (chmn. 1978-79), Am. Judicature Soc., Am. Law Inst., Lambda Chi Alpha, Phi Alpha Delta, Delta Theta Phi. Clubs: Mason, Shriner, Arizona. Home: 5812 N 12th St #20 Phoenix AZ 85014 Office: State Capitol Bldg Phoenix AZ 85007

CAMERON, JOHN STUART, economics educator, university administrator; b. Lincoln, Nebr., June 2, 1934; s. John Gunn and Dorothea (Kaiser) C.; m. Janet Ann Nielsen, Nov. 10, 1962; 1 child, Jill Lyn. B. Gen. Studies, U. Nebr.-Omaha, 1967; M.A., U. Nebr., 1971, Ph.D., 1979. Sales mgr. Midwest Utilities Service, Omaha, 1960-63, Arcs Inc., Omaha, 1964-65; instr. Midland Coll., Fremont, Nebr., 1971; chmn. dept. bus. and econs. McPherson Coll., Kans., 1972-78; asst. prof. Rockhurst Coll., Kansas City, Mo., 1978-81; chmn. div. bus. and econs. N.Mex. Highlands U., Las Vegas, 1981-86, dir. Internat. Bilingual M.B.A., 1982-86, dir. Tech. Innovative Ctr., 1983-86; chmn. dept. Bus. and Agribus./Hotel, Restaurant and Instl. Mgmt., Southwest State U., Marshall, Minn., 1986—. Author: United States Professional Manpower, 1979. Served to cpl. U.S. Army, 1954-57. Mem. Internat. Council Small Bus., Am. Assembly Collegiate Schs. of Bus., Western Econs. Assn. Republican. Lutheran. Home: 607 Camden Dr Marshall MN 56258 Office: Southwest State U Dept Bus/Agribus Hotel Restaurant Instl Mgmt Marshall MN 56258

CAMERON, JUDY LEA, business educator; b. Waco, Tex., Jan. 2, 1948; d. Earl Henry and Martha Elizabeth (Truman) Helphrey; m. Alexander Brian Cameron, June 7, 1969; children: Michelle Lea, Michael David. BA, Eastern Wash. U., 1970, MEd, 1978. File clk. Columbia Lighting, Spokane, Wash., 1970, field sales sec., 1970-74, purchasing clk., sec., 1974-76; instr. bus. Spokane Community Coll., 1976—; part time instr. U. Utah, Salt Lake City, 1979-80; instr. Hewlett Packard, Spokane, 1986; facilitator Utah Army, Toele, 1980. Recipient Semi-finalist Faculty Achievement award Burlington Northern, Spokane, 1986. Mem. Wash. Vocat. Assn. (sec. 1981-83), Wash. State Bus. Edn. Assn., Ea. Wash. State Bus. Edn. Assn., Nat. Bus. Edn. Assn. Avocations: skiing, reading, travelling. Home: 24415 Tumtum Dr Liberty Lake WA 99019 Office: Spokane Community Coll N 1810 Greene St Spokane WA 99207

CAMERON, ROBERT GEORGE, utilities executive; b. North Bergen, N.J., July 9, 1931; s. Robert William Cameron and Frieda (Nungesser) Mory; m. Florence G. Reilly, Dec. 17, 1955 (div. Apr. 1978); children: Florence F., Robert William; m. Gwendolyn Hackett, July 26, 1978; 1 child, Elizabeth. BS in Indsl. Mgmt., Fairleigh Dickinson U., 1963, MBA, 1967. Registered profl. engr., N.J. Engr. Bell Telephone Labs., N.Y.C., 1954-62; prin. engr. N.J. Bell, Newark, 1962-72, pub. utilities mgr., 1972-75; asst. to v.p. AT&T Corp. Hdqrs., N.Y.C., 1975-77, mgr. legal dept., 1977-80; mgr. legal dept. AT&T Communications, N.Y.C., 1980-86; cons. AT&T Hdqrs., N.Y.C., 1985-86. Author: Performance Rating, 1967; contbr. articles in telephony; designer Bell Labs. switchboards and pvt. br. exchanges. Dem. chmn. Hudson County, N.J., 1970. Served to cpl. USMC, 1952-54, Korea. Named Man of Yr., Luth. Ch. in Am., 1975. Mem. N.J. Profl. Engrs. Assn., State of N.J. Pub. Utilities Assn. Democrat. Lodge: Order of Turtles (Imperial Turtle 1970—). Home: 1209 Hupmobile Dr NE Albuquerque NM 87112

CAMERON, WINIFRED SAWTELL, astronomer; b. Oak Park, Ill., Dec. 3, 1918; d. Amos Alexander and Mildred Winifred (Shields) S.; m. Robert Curry Cameron, Oct. 17, 1953 (dec. Dec 1972); children: Selene Jean, Sheri Carina. BE, No. Ill. U., 1940; MA in Astronomy, Ind. U., 1952. Researcher Weather Forecasts, Inc., Chgo., 1942-46; instr. Mount Holyoke Coll., South Hadley, Mass., 1950-51; solar researcher U.S. Naval Observatory, Washington, 1951-58; planetologist NASA-Goddard Space Flight Ctr., Greenbelt, Md., 1959-84; lectr. NASA, Greenbelt and Sedona, Ariz., 1960-84. Mem. Internat. Astron. Union, Internat. Assn. Planetology (v.p. 1985—), Am. Astron. Soc., Am. Geophys. Union, Assn. Lunar and Planetary Observers, British Astron. Assn. (hon.), Lunar Transient Phenomena Lunar Recorder. Club: Goddard Astronomy (v.p. Greenbelt chpt. 1972-74, pres. 1974-76). Home and Office: 200 Rojo Dr Sedona AZ 86336

CAMMACK, RICHARD LEWIS, ballet school administrator; b. Knoxville, Tenn., Oct. 24, 1945; s. Owen Floyd and Glenna (Begley) C.; m. Zola Dishong, Aug. 1976; 1 stepchild, Charles David Anderson. BA, Butler U., 1968. Dancer Harkness Youth Ballet, N.Y.C., 1968-69, Am. Ballet Theatre, N.Y.C., 1969-73; ballet master San Francisco Ballet, 1973-75; dir. San Francisco Ballet Sch., 1975-86, Contra Costa Ballet Ctr., Walnut Creek, Calif., 1987—; master tchr. several ballet festivals; jury mem., U.S.A. rep. Prix de Lausanne (Switzerland), 1982, 84. Choreographer: (musical) Stephen Foster Story, 1967-68, (San Francisco Ballet 50th Anniversary Gala) Polonaise, 1983. Mem. Nat. Assn. Sch. Dance (bd. dirs. 1982-86). Office: Contra Costa Ballet Ctr 2040 N Broadway Walnut Creek CA 94596

CAMMACK, SHARON (GRACE) MCCALL, writer; b. San Francisco, Mar. 13, 1949; d. Thomas James and Grace Courtney McCall; m. Nathan A. Cammack III, Aug. 28, 1985. BA, U. Portland, 1971; postgrad., Golden Gate U., 1980-82. Purser Alaska State Ferry, Juneau, 1975-79; coop. advt. coordinator Levi Strauss, San Francisco, 1979-80; sales asst. Katz Communications, San Francisco, 1980-82; asst. mgr. promotional planning Atari, Inc., Sunnyvale, Calif., 1982-84; product mktg. mgr. Computerland Corp., Hayward, Calif., 1984-85; freelance writer AMG Enterprises, San Jose, Calif., 1985—. Mem. Sierra Club, Writer's Connection. Democrat. Roman Catholic. Avocation: photography.

CAMMALLERI, JOSEPH ANTHONY, university administrator, retired air force officer; b. Bronx, N.Y., Feb. 2, 1935; s. Leo Anthony and Angela Marie (Mirandi) C.; B.S., Manhattan Coll., 1956; M.S., Okla. State U., 1966; postgrad. Golden Gate U., 1974—; children—Anthony R., Aaron L., Thomas K., Jeffrey A. Commd. 2d lt. USAF, 1956, advanced through grades to lt. col., 1973; trainee flight crew, 1956-58; crew mem. B-52, 1958-64; behavioral scientist Aerospace Med. Research Labs., Wright-Patterson AFB, Ohio, 1966-68; EB-66 crew mem. Tahkli AFB, Thailand, 1968-69; faculty mem. dept. life and behavioral scis. USAF Acad. (Colo.), 1969-74, assoc. prof., dir. operational psychology div., 1972-74, B-1 human factors engring. mgr. Air Force Flight Test Center, Edwards AFB, Calif., 1974-76, chief handbook devel., 1976-77; ret., 1977; account exec. Merrill Lynch, Pierce, Fenner & Smith, Sherman Oaks, Calif., 1977-80; acad. program rep. U. Redlands (Calif.), 1980-84, regional dir. admissions assessment, 1984—, assoc. dean admissions Whitehead Ctr., 1986—, mem. faculty, 1979—; faculty Golden Gate U., 1975-80; sec., 7th Ann. Narrow Gauge Com., Pasadena, Calif., 1986. Decorated D.F.C., Air medal (5), Meritorious Service medal. Mem. Nat. Ry. Hist. Soc., Ry. and Locomotive Hist. Soc., Rocky Mountain R.R. Club, Los Angeles Live Steamers, Nat. Model R.R. Assn., Colo. R.R. Hist. Found. (life), Santa Fe Ry. Hist. Soc., USAF Acad. Athletic Assn. (life), DAV, Psi Chi. Home: 3093 Charlotte St Newbury Park CA 91320 Office: U Redlands Redlands CA 92373

CAMP, JOAN CAROLYN, home economist; b. Greeley, Colo., May 4, 1945; d. Melvin James and Ruth Carol (Bowman) C. BA in Home Econs. Edn. (award), U. No. Colo., 1969; EdM, Colo. State U., 1976. Home econs. tchr., Walsenburg, Colo., 1969-70, Lamar, Colo., 1971-73; extension agt., Lamar Colo., Prowers County, 1973-75, Boulder County, 1975-85; internat. 4-H youth exchange del. to Ireland, Colo. State U., 1970. Active Zonta Internat. (treas. Boulder County), PEO Sisterhood. Mem. Am. Home Econs. Assn. Republican. Methodist.

CAMP, LOUISE PHIFER (MRS. WOFFORD BENJAMIN CAMP), farmer, musician; b. Winston-Salem, N.C., Mar. 22, 1912; d. Charles McKnight and Louisa (Williams) Phifer; B.A. in Mus., Limestone Coll., 1933, H.H.D. (hon.), 1977; postgrad. in music Converse Coll., 1933-34; m. George William Wise, June 7, 1934 (dec. 1945); children—Addie Louise, George William, Sarah Emily; m. Wofford Benjamin Camp, Jan. 18, 1956 (dec. Aug. 1986). Minister of music Baptist evang. meetings in N.C., S.C., Ga., summers 1930-34; tchr. voice Limestone Coll., Gaffney, S.C., summer 1932, trustee, 1960—; tchr. elementary sch., Gaffney, 1933-34; farmer, Edgefield County, S.C., 1945-77; dir. Bank of Trenton (S.C.), 1945-78; dir., sec. W.B. Camp, Inc., Bakersfield, Calif., 1956—. Organizer, dir. numerous choral groups, N.C., S.C., Ga., 1935-55; soloist St. John's Methodist Ch., Augusta, Ga., 1953-55; soloist Presbyn. Ch., Trenton, S.C., 1934-55, organist, 1946-53. Co-founder Trenton Devel. Corp., 1950; pres. Pro-Am., Bakersfield, 1958-59; dir. Kern County (Calif.) Music Assn., 1957-59, program chmn., 1958-59; co-founder Louise Phifer Camp Found., Limestone Coll., 1957; mem. Bakersfield Woman's Club, Bakersfield Garden Club, Farm Bur.; co-founder, dir. Kern County Free Enterprise Assn., 1960; mem. hospitality com. Philharmonic Assn., Bakersfield, 1958-61; organizer, pres. Kern County Women's chpt. Freedom's Found. at Valley Forge, 1969; pres. Symphony Assos. of Kern County, 1972-73, life mem. bd. trustees Limestone Coll., chmn. bd. trustees, 1973-83. Trustee Freedoms Found. at Valley Forge; bd. dirs. John and Beverly Stauffer Found.; mem. exec. bd., nat. treas. Religious Heritage Am.; mem. nat. exec. bd. Gospel Music Assn., 1978-81, nat. campaign chmn. Gospel Music Hall of Fame Research Library and Mus. Recipient award as outstanding cotton grower S.C., S.C. Agrl. Extension Service, 1954, Outstanding Alumna award Limestone Coll., 1956, Freedom Founds. award, 1973; named hon. alumnus Clemson U., 1982; mem. Order Knights Hospitallers St. John. Mem. D.A.R., UDC, AAUW, P.E.O. Democrat. Presbyterian. Home: 701 Oleander Ave Bakersfield CA 93304

CAMP, WOFFORD BENJAMIN, JR., financial planning and investment consultant; b. Bakersfield, Calif., Sept. 3, 1923; s. Wofford Benjamin and Georgia Anna (App) C.; m. Anita Jana King, Sept. 3, 1944; children: Wofford B. III, Carl J., Bruce K., David C. BS, Clemson U., 1947; MA, Biola U., 1975. Cert. fin. planner; registered investment adviser. Co-owner, v.p. W.B. Camp & Sons, Bakersfield, 1944-63; sr. v.p. The Agribus. Council, Inc., N.Y.C., 1971-72; v.p. bus. and fin. affairs Biola U., La Mirada, Ca., 1975-79; assoc. broker McGarvey Clark Realty, Inc., Fullerton, Calif., 1980-83; owner, pres. W.B. Camp Jr., Inc., Fullerton, 1960—, Eclectic Assocs., Inc., Fullerton, 1984—; Mem. Nat. Ctr. for Fin. Edn., Inc. Mem. World Affairs Council of Orange County; participant USDA Sec. Hardin's Agrl. Mission to Turkey, 1971. Served with U.S. Army, 1942-44. Mem. Inst. Cert. Fin. Planners, Nat. Assn. Personal Fin. Advisors, Internat. Assn. Fin. Planning, Am. Assn. Individual Investors, Nat. Assn. Realtors, Fullerton C. of C. Republican. Mem. First Evang. Free Ch. Home: 2630 N Harbor Blvd Fullerton CA 92635 Office: Eclectic Assocs Inc 1021 W Bastanchury Rd Suite 120 Fullerton CA 92633

CAMPANA, JOSEPH E., research facility administrator; b. Buffalo, Aug. 19, 1952; s. Frank Joseph and Angela (Balone) C. BS in Chemistry, Canisius Coll., 1974; PhD in Chemistry, Pa. State U., 1979. Lab. asst. Canisius Coll., Buffalo, 1973-75; research asst. Pa. State U., University Park, 1975-79; postdoctoral fellow Johns Hopkins U. Sch. Medicine, Balt., 1979; research assoc. NRC, Washington, 1980; sect. head Naval Research Lab., Washington, 1981-85; dir. Quality Assurance Lab. Environ. Research Ctr. U. Nev., Las Vegas, 1985—; cons. in field. Contbr. articles to profl. jours.; patentee in field. Mem. AAAS, N.Y. Acad. Scis., Soc. Applied Spectroscopy, Am. Chem. Soc., Am. Soc. Mass Spectrometry (chmn. ion physical instrumentation com 1984—), Phi Lambda Upsilon. Office: U Nev Environ Research Ctr Las Vegas NV 89154

CAMPBELL, ALICE DEL CAMPILLO, biochemist, researcher; b. Santurce, Puerto Rico, May 30, 1928; d. José Adrian and Julia Pilar (Rivera) del Campillo; m. Allan McCulloch Campbell, Sept. 5, 1958; children: Wendy Alice, Joseph Lindsay. AB, Columbia U., 1947; MS, NYU, 1953; PhD, U. Mich., 1960. Research asst. Pub. Health Research Inst., N.Y.C., 1947-48, NYU, 1948-54; instr. biochemistry Sch. Medicine, San Juan, Puerto Rico, 1954-56; research assoc. U. Rochester, N.Y., 1960-68; sr. research assoc. Stanford U., Calif., 1968—. Contbr. articles to sci. jours. Fellow Am. Inst. Chemists; mem. Am. Chem. Soc., Sigma Xi (sec., treas. 1985-86, v.p. Stanford chpt. 1986-87). Avocations: prehistoric art, pictographs, petroglyphs. Home: 947 Mears Ct Stanford CA 94305 Office: Dept Biological Scis Stanford U Stanford CA 94305

CAMPBELL, ALLAN MCCULLOCH, educator; b. Berkeley, Calif., Apr. 27, 1929; s. Lindsay and Virginia Margaret (Henning) C.; m. Alice Del Campillo, Sept. 5, 1958; children—Wendy, Joseph. B.S. in Chemistry, U. Calif. at Berkeley, 1950; M.S. in Bacteriology, U. Ill., 1951; Ph.D., 1953; Ph.D. hon. degree, U. Chgo., 1978, U. Rochester, 1981. Instr. bacteriology U. Mich., 1953-57; research asso. Carnegie Inst., Cold Spring Harbor, N.Y., 1957-58; asst. prof. biology U. Rochester, N.Y., 1958-61; assoc. prof. U. Rochester, 1961-63, prof., 1963-68; prof. biol. sci. Stanford, 1968—; mem. genetics study sect. NIH, 1964-69, mem. DNA recombinant adv. com., 1977-81; mem. genetics panel NSF, 1973-76. Author: Episomes, 1969; co-author: General Virology, 1978; Editor: Gene, 1980—; assoc. editor: Virology, 1963-69, Ann. Rev. Genetics, 1969-84, editor, 1984—; editorial bd.: Jour. Bacteriology, 1966-72, Jour. Virology, 1967-75. Served with AUS, 1953-55. Recipient Research Career award USPHS, 1962-68. Mem. Nat. Acad. Scis., Am. Acad. Arts and Scis., Am. Soc. Microbiology, Soc. Am. Naturalists, Am. Soc. Virology, AAAS. Democrat. Home: 947 Mears Ct Stanford CA 94305 Office: Dept Biol Scis Stanford U Stanford CA 94305

CAMPBELL, ALTON GAILEY, JR., educator; b. Pittsboro, N.C., May 21, 1949; s. Alton Gailey and Elizabeth (Porter) C.; m. Janet Cheek, Nov. 24, 1978. BS, U. N.C., 1971; MA, Duke U., 1977; PhD, N.C. State U., 1983. Chemistry tchr. Spartanburg (S.C.) High Sch., 1977-78; chemistry instr. Campbell U., Buies Creek, N.C., 1978-80; asst. prof. pulp and paper sci. U. Idaho, Moscow, 1983—; cons. Potlatch Corp., Lewiston, Idaho, 1985—. Contbr. articles to profl. jours. Mem. Phi Beta Kappa, Phi Lambda Upsilon, Xi Sigma Pi. Avocations: fishing, hunting, racquetball. Office: U Idaho Dept Forest Products Moscow ID 83843

CAMPBELL, BEN NIGHTHORSE, congressman; b. Auburn, Calif., Apr. 13, 1933; m. Linda Price; children: Colin, Shanan. BA, U. Calif., San Jose. Educator Sacramento Law Enforcement Agy.; mem. Colo. Gen. Assembly, 1983-86, U.S. Ho. Reps., 1987—; owner, trainer horse ranch, Ignacio, Colo.; designer jewelry, Ignacio. Chief No. Cheyenne Tribe. Named Outstanding Legislator Colo. Bankers Assn., 1984, Man of Yr. LaPlata Farm Bur., Durango, Colo., 1984; named one of Ten Best Legislators Denver Post/Channel 4, 1986. Mem. Am. Quarter Horse Assn., Am. Brangus Assn., Am. Paint Horse Assn., Am. Indian Edn. Assn., Colo. Pilots Assn. Democrat. Office: US House of Reps 1724 Longworth House Office Bldg Washington DC 20515

CAMPBELL, BETTY LOUISE, university administrator, educator; b. Greeley, Colo., Jan. 6, 1935; d. Lawrence Edwin and Doris Marie (Herrick) Kime; m. John Monroe Campbell, Aug. 1, 1954 (div. Sept. 1983); children: Gail Louise Campbell, John Duane. BA, U. No. Colo., 1967, MA, 1979; PhD, Tex. Tech U., 1984. Home econs. tchr. Sch. Dist. Re-1, LaSalle, Colo., 1967-71; home econs. instr. U. No. Colo., Greeley, 1978-80; dir. pilot program Colo. State Bd. Community Colls. and Occupational Edn., Denver, 1979; workshop coordinator Tex. Tech U., Lubbock, 1981; dir. Meals on Wheels, Lubbock, 1982-84; dir. sch. tech. Eastern N.Mex. U., Portales, 1984—; cons. Sta. KENW-TV, Portales, 1984—, N.Mex. State U., Las Cruces, 1986. Grantee Eastern N.Mex. U., 1984, N.Mex. State Dept. Edn. Spl. Needs and Entrepreneurship 1986; Boeer-Wolf Endowed fellow Tex. Tech. U., 1986. Mem. N.Mex. Home Econs. (adv. bd. mem. 1984—), Assn. Coll. Prof. Clothing and Textiles (research reviewer 1985). Republican. Avocations: horseback riding, breeding and showing horses. Home: 1505 S Main Portales NM 88130 Office: Eastern NMex U Station #11 Portales NM 88130

CAMPBELL, BILLY WILMON, librarian; b. Los Angeles, Sept. 14, 1927; s. Joe Carson and Claire Ellen (Wilmon) C.; m. Patricia Jean Cowan, Apr. 20, 1951 (div. 1971); children: Frederick William, Bruce Duane, Aisha Ellen, Cameron Clay; m. Judith Weinberg Stang, Feb. 14, 1973. AA, UCLA, 1950, BA, 1952; BLS, U. Calif., Berkeley, 1954. Periodicals and films librarian Library of Hawaii, Honolulu, 1954-56; asst. acquistions librarian Los Angeles State Coll., 1956-57; serials librarian San Fernando Valley State Coll., Northridge, Calif., 1957-63; from cataloguer to head tech. documents ctr. Hughes Aircraft Co., El Segundo, Calif., 1963-85, mgr. info. services dept., electro-optical and data systems group, 1985—. Contbr. articles to profl. jours. Served as pvt. USAAF, 1945-46. Mem. Spl. Libraries Assn., Los Angeles Regional Tech. Info. Users Council, Alpha Mu Gamma.

Democrat. Presbyterian. Avocations: folk dancing, running, reading, gardening. Office: Hughes Aircraft Co Electro Optical and Data Systems Group MS E1/J145 El Segundo CA 90245

CAMPBELL, CAROL NOWELL, lawyer; b. Phoenix, Dec. 16, 1944; d. Richard Converse Nowell and Nancy (Newcomb) Olson; m. Robert Norman Campbell, Jan. 2, 1965 (div. 1968); 1 child, Kelly Christine; m. Harding Briggs Cure, June 28, 1984. B.A., Ariz. State U.-Tempe, 1972, J.D., 1978. Bar: Ariz. 1979, Calif. 1979, U.S. Dist. Ct. Ariz. 1979, U.S. Dist. Ct. (cen. dist.) Calif. 1984, U.S. Ct. Apls. (9th cir.) 1981. Ptnr. O'Connor, Cavanagh, Anderson, Westover, Killingsworth & Beshears, Phoenix, 1978—; faculty mem. Pacific regional chpt. Nat. Inst. Trial Advocacy, 1985-86. Bd. dirs. Ariz. Council of the Blind, Social Services and Rehab. Inc., 1980-85, sec., 1980-82, v.p. ops. 1983-84; bd. dirs. Phoenix Childrens Theatre, 1981-83, v.p. ops., 1982-83; bd. dirs. Ariz. Cen. Credit Union, 1985-87; judge pro tem Ariz. Ct. Appeals. 1985. Mem. ABA (vice-chmn. rules and procedures com. 1983-87, chair-elect, 1987, co-chmn. long range planning subcom. 1984-85, chmn. ann. mtg. arrangements TIPS rules and procedures com. 1986-87, chmn.-elect rules and procedure com. 1987, publ. subcom. for The Brief 1987, chmn. use of expert witness subcom. of com. trial practice), State Bar Ariz. (com. on rules of civil practice and procedure), Maricopa County Bar Assn. (bd. dirs. 1983—), Maricopa County Bar Found. (trustee 1984—, sec. 1986—), Nucleus (chmn. membership com. 1984-85, chmn. 1986-87), AAUW (parliamentarian, bd. dirs. Ariz. State div. 1980-82), Ariz. State U. Alumni Assn. (bd. dirs. 1980-83), Kappa Delta Pi, Assn. Trial Lawyers Am., Phoenix Assn. Def. Counsel, Ariz. Women Lawyers Assn., Def. Research Inst. (practice and procedure com.). Democrat. Episcopalian. Office: O'Connor Cavanagh et al 1 E Camelback Rd Phoenix AZ 85012

CAMPBELL, CAROLINE KRAUSE, drug company executive; b. Praha, Tex., May 5, 1926; d. Charles Joseph and Mary Victoria (Havrde) Krause; student, U. N.Mex., 1958-63; diploma Alexander Hamilton Inst., 1966-69; m. Richard E. Campbell, Dec. 30, 1946; children—Richard E., Don Michael, Scott Gary, Jonathan Miles, Candace Kay. Survey researcher Winona Research Co., Mpls., 1953-54; merchandiser, buyer Campbell Drug Inc., Albuquerque, 1961-77, gen. mgr., 1978—, pres., 1978—, dir., 1978—. Mem. Nat. Assn. Corp. Dirs., Assn. Commerce and Industry of N.Mex., C. of C. Albuquerque (bd. dirs.), Small Business Roundtable, Nat. Assn. Retail Druggists, Medicine/Bus. Coalition, N.Mex. Pharm. Assn., Internat. Platform Assn., Albuquerque Symphony Women's Assn. Republican. Clubs: Albuquerque Rose Soc., Italian Cultural. Lodge: Elks. Office: Campbell Drug Inc 8252 Menaul Blvd NE Albuquerque NM 87110

CAMPBELL, COLIN HERALD, mayor, former management consultant; b. Winnipeg, Man., Can., Jan. 18, 1911; s. Colin Charles and Aimee Florence (Herald) C.; B.A., Reed Coll., 1933; m. Virginia Paris, July 20, 1935; children—Susanna Herald, Corinna Buford, Virginia Wallace. Exec. sec. City Club of Portland, 1934-39; alumni sec., dir. endowment adminstrn. Reed Coll., 1939-42, exec. sec. N.W. Inst. Internat. Relations. 1940-42, instr. photography, 1941-42; contract engr. Kaiser Co., Inc., 1942-45; asst. personnel dir. Portland Gas & Coke Co., 1945-48; dir. indsl. relations Pacific Power & Light Co., Portland, 1948-76. Mem. Oreg. Advisory Com. on Fair Employment Practices Act, 1949-55; trustee, chmn., pres. Portland Symphonic Choir, 1950-54; trustee Portland Civic Theater, 1951-54; bd. dirs. Portland Symphony Soc., 1957-60, Community Child Guidance Clinic, 1966-68; active United Way, 1945-75; bd. dirs. Contemporary Crafts Assn., 1972-76, treas., 1975-76; bd. dirs. Lake Oswego Corp., 1961-65, 71-73, 74-76, corporate sec., 1964, pres., 1973-74, treas., 1975-76; mem. Com. on Citizen Involvement, City of Lake Oswego, 1975-77; chmn. Bicentennial Com., Lake Oswego; sec.-treas. Met. Area Communications Comm., 1980-85; treas. Clackamas County Community Action Agy., 1980-82, chmn., 1982-85; mem. fin. adv. com. W. Clackamas County LWV, 1974-76, 78-80; councilman City of Lake Oswego, 1977-78, mayor, 1979-85; chmn. energy adv. com. League of Oreg. Cities, 1982-84. Mem. Edison Electric Inst. (exec. com.), NW Electric Light and Power Assn., Lake Oswego C. of C. (v.p. 1986-87), Portland Art Assn., Pacific NW Personnel Mgmt. Assn. (past regional v.p.), St. Andrews Soc., Oreg. Hist. Soc. Republican. Presbyterian. Lodge: Rotary. Home: 1219 Maple St Lake Oswego OR 97034

CAMPBELL, DIANE HOYE, psychiatrist; b. Waltham, Mass., Sept. 2, 1942; d. Robert Golden and Priscilla (Davis) Hoye; m. Gordon Campbell, Apr. 23, 1983; 1 child, Elizabeth Anne. BA, Wellesley Coll., 1964; MD, Tufts U., 1975. Diplomate Am. Bd. Med. Examiners, Am. Bd. Psychiatry and Neurology. Intern, then resident in psychiatry U. Calif. San Diego, La Jolla, 1975-78, fellow in child psychiatry, 1977-79; supervising psychiatrist Child Guidance Clinics, San Diego, 1979-80; staff child psychiatrist County Mental Health, San Diego, 1980-82; private practice specializing in adult and child psychiatry 1979—. Bd. dirs. Three's Co. and Dancers, San Diego, 1979-84. Mem. Am. Acad. Child Psychiatry, Am. Psychoanalytic Assn., Am. Psychiat. Assn., San Diego Psychiat. Soc., San Diego Child Psychiatry Council, San Diego Women Physicians. Office: 1011 Camino del Mar #270 Del Mar CA 92014

CAMPBELL, DOUGLAS ALDEN, ski outerwear manufacturing company executive; b. Los Angeles, Mar. 8, 1935; s. Ray Maurice and Olga (Wiksell) C.; m. Roberta Congdon, Sept. 7, 1957; children—Leslie Diane, Barbara Ann. BA in Mktg., U. Wash., 1957. Acount exec. Robert L. Rogers Co., Seattle, 1957-64; dir. mktg. Jo-Lock Fabricators, Seattle, 1964-69; dir. sales and mktg. Roffe, Inc., Seattle, 1969-77, v.p. mktg., 1977—. Bd. dirs. Big Bros. of Seattle-King County, 1977—, v.p. 1982-86, pres. 1987—. Served to capt. USAF, 1957-62. Mem. Ski Industries Am. (bd. dirs. 1973—, chmn. 1983-85, hon. chmn. 1986—), Am. Ski Fedn. (bd. dirs. 1982—, vice chmn. 1983-85, chmn. 1986—), Wash. State Ski Industries (chmn. 1986—). Republican. Presbyterian. Clubs: Seattle Golf, Wash. Athletic (Seattle). Home: The Highlands Seattle WA 98177 Office: Roffe Inc 808 Howell St Seattle WA 98101

CAMPBELL, ELSIE GEE, nursing educator; b. Bakersfield, Calif., Dec. 24, 1928; d. James Wong and Agnes (Lum) Gee; m. Joseph Campbell, June 12, 1960 (div. 1974); children: George, Stuart, Joseph. Student, Bakersfield Coll., 1946-47, U. Calif., Berkeley, 1947-48; BS, U. Calif., San Francisco, 1951; MA, Columbia U. Tchrs. Coll., 1959. Nurse Mercy Hosp., Bakersfield, 1951-52, Queen's Hosp., Honolulu, 1952-53, U. Calif. Hosp., San Francisco, 1953-55; instr. Middletown (N.Y.) State Hosp., 1955-59; prof. nursing Bakersfield Coll., 1959-60, 65—; instr. Auburn (N.Y.) Hosp. Sch. Nursing, 1960-61, Ithaca (N.Y.) Sch. Practical Nursing, 1961-64. Active PTA, Bakersfield, 1967-84; mem. sch. site council Fruitvale Sch., Bakersfield, 1974-80, sec. 1977-80. Mem. Calif. Tchrs. Assn., Am. Nurses Assn. (sec. 1961-62), Calif. Alumni Assn., U. Calif. San Francisco Nurses Alumni Assn. Republican. Office: Bakersfield Coll 1801 Panorama Dr Bakersfield CA 93305

CAMPBELL, FREDERICK HOLLISTER, lawyer; b. Somerville, Mass., June 14, 1923; s. George Murray and Irene Ivers (Smith) C.; A.B., Dartmouth, 1944; J.D., Northwestern U., 1949; postgrad. Indsl. Coll. Armed Forces, 1961-62; M.A. in History, U. Colo., 1984; m. Amy Holding Strohm, Apr. 14, 1951; 1 dau., Susan Hollister. Served with USMCR, 1944-46; joined USMC, 1950, advanced through grades to lt. col., 1962; admitted to Ill. bar, 1950, U.S. Supreme Ct. bar, 1967, Colo. bar, 1968; judge adv. USMC, Camp Lejeune, N.C., Korea, Parris Island, S.C., El Toro, Calif., Vietnam, Washington, 1950-67; asso. editor Callaghan and Co., Chgo., 1949-50; practice law, Colorado Springs, Colo., 1968—, partner firm Gibson, Gerdes and Campbell, 1969-79, Frederick H. Campbell, P.C., 1980—; hon. instr. history U. Colo., Colorado Springs, 1986—. Mem. Estate Planning Council, Colorado Springs, 1971-81, v.p., 1977-78. Republican precinct committeeman, 1971-86; del. Colo. Rep. State Conv., 1972, 74, 76, 80, alt., 1978; trustee Frontier Village Found., 1971-77; bd. dirs. Rocky Mountain Nature Assn., 1975—, pres., 1979—. Mem. Colo. Bar Assn., El Paso County Bar Assn., Am. Arbitration Assn., Marines Meml. Club, Phi Alpha Theta. Congregationalist. Club: Kiwanis (lt. gov. Rocky Mountain Dist. 1973-74, pres. Rampart Range Club 1970-71). Author: John's American Notary and Commissioner of Deeds Manual, 1950. Contbr. articles to profl. jours. Home and Office: 2707 Holiday Ln Colorado Springs CO 80909

CAMPBELL, GARY HOLT, real estate developer, consultant; b. Hanover, N.H., Sept. 5, 1946; s. Gavin Frederick Hendry and Grace Irene (Holt) C.; m. Lucretia Hope Bonner, June 11, 1966 (div. Mar. 1975); children: Melany Elizabeth, Gavin Frederick Hendry II. Student, San Antonio Coll., 1964-66, 68, Amarillo Coll., 1967, Anchorage Community Coll., 1969. Profl. golfer The Olympic Club, San Francisco, 1970-75; dir. golf Kaanapali Beach Resort, Maui, Hawaii, 1975-80; v.p. Amfac Property Corp., Kaanapali, Hawaii, 1980—. Pres. Lahaina Restoration Found., 1979—, Maui County Visitors Bur., 1982-83, Kaanapali Beach Operators Assn., 1978; bd. dirs. Maui United Way; commr. county bd. variances and appeals, 1983-85. Served to staff sgt. USAF, 1966-70. Recipient KOA Anvil award Pub. Relations Soc. Am., 1984. Mem. Profl. Golf Assn. Am. (cert. Class A, Profl. Medal Play Champion award Hawaii chpt. 1977), Alaska Golf Assn. (State Amateur Champion award 1969). Democrat. Roman Catholic. Club: Plaza (Honolulu). Avocation: sports. Office: Amfac Property Investment Corp 2530 Kekaa Dr Lahaina HI 96761

CAMPBELL, GORDON MUIR, mayor; b. Vancouver, B.C., Can., Jan. 12, 1948; s. Charles Gordon and Margaret Janet (Muir) C.; m. Nancy J. Chipperfield, July 4, 1970; children: Geoffrey Gordon, Nicholas James. AB, Dartmouth Coll., 1970; MBA, Simon Fraser U., 1978. Tchr. Can. Univ. Service Overseas, Yola, Nigeria, 1970-72; exec. asst. to mayor City of Vancouver, 1972-76, mayor, 1986—; gen. mgr. Marathon Realty Devel. Co., Vancouver, 1976-81; pres. Citycore Devel. Corp., Vancouver, 1981-86. Alderman City of Vancouver, 1984-86. Mem. Downtown Vancouver Assn. (bd. dirs.). Office: City of Vancouver, 453 W 12th Ave, Vancouver, BC Canada V5Y 1V4

CAMPBELL, HARRY MEIKLE, consulting civil engineer; b. Los Angeles, Feb. 4, 1922; s. Harry Meikle Sr. and Grace (Alward) C.; m. Karen E. Hose, Apr. 3, 1964; children: Tyrra Jo, Nancy June, Martin James. BSCE, U. Calif., Berkeley, 1943; MS in Bus., UCLA, 1964. Registered profl civil engr., Calif.; cert. tchr., Calif. Resident engr., project engr. Am. Bridge div. U.S. Steel Corp., San Francisco and Pitts., 1946-50; structural engr. Fluor Corp., Los Angeles, 1950-54; transp. engr. Calif. Div. Hwys., Los Angeles, Ventura and Orange Counties, 1955-73; practice civil engring. Los Angeles, 1973—; seminar leader Calif. Div. Hwys., 1958-73. Active Doves program Los Angeles Unified Sch. Dist.; instr. 1st aid ARC. Served to capt. USAF, 1942-46. Mem. Am. Soc. Civil Engrs. (chmn. integration of engring. edn. and practice nat. com. 1974-78), Am. Soc. Engring. Edn., VFW, DAV, Marines Meml. Club San Francisco, Native Sons of the Golden West, Calif. Dept. Transp. 25-Yr. Club. Republican. Baptist. Home: 15912 Chanera Ave Gardena CA 90249 Office: Campbell Engring Co 1052 W 6th St Los Angeles CA 90017

CAMPBELL, HARRY WOODSON, gelogist, mining engineer; b. Carthage, Mo., Jan. 14, 1946; s. William Hampton and Elizabeth Verle (Legrand) C. BSEE, Kans. State U., 1969; MBA, U. Oreg., 1973, BS in Geology, 1975; MS in Geology, Brown U., 1978. Registered profl. engr., Wash.; cert. profl. geologist, Va. Geologist, mining engr. and phys. scientist U.S. Br. Mines, Spokane, 1980—. Served with U.S. Army, 1969-71. Recipient Spl. Achievement award U.S. Bur. Mines, 1983, 86. Mem. Geol. Soc. Am., Soc. Mining Engrs., Am. Soc. Safety Engrs. Avocation: genealogy. Office: US Bur Mines E 360 3d Ave Spokane WA 99202

CAMPBELL, IAN DAVID, banker; b. Bloomington, Ind., Sept. 3, 1953; s. Sam L. Campbell and Ruth M. (Englehardt) MacLean; m. Nancy Jean Alires, June 2, 1984; 1 child, Walter Lee II. BA in Govt. magna cum laude, Pomona Coll., 1975; MA in Urban Studies, Occidental Coll., 1980. Reporter Santa Monica (Calif.) Evening Outlook, 1975-76; account exec. Braun & Co., Los Angeles, 1978-81, v.p., 1981-83; dep. dir. Calif. Dept. Commerce, Sacramento, 1983-85; sr. v.p. Gt. Western Fin. Corp., Beverly Hills, Calif., 1985—. Contbr. articles on politics and pub. affairs to jours. Bd. dirs. Calif. Rep. League, 1978-85, treas., 1979-81. Winner nat. championship impromptu speaking, Nat. Forensic League, 1971; CORO found. fellow 1976-77. Mem. Nat. Investor Relations Inst., Pub. Relations Soc. Am., Calif. Mus. Found., Calif. C. of C. (regulatory affairs com. 1986—), Los Angeles Pub. Affairs Officers Assn., Los Angeles LWV Edn. Fund. (bd. dirs.). Mem. Disciples of Christ. Avocations: hiking, camping, jazz trombone. Office: Gt Western Fin Corp 8484 Wilshire Blvd Beverly Hills CA 90211

CAMPBELL, IAN DAVID, opera company director; b. Brisbane, Australia, Dec. 21, 1945; came to U.S., 1982; BA, U. Sydney, Australia, 1966. Prin. tenor singer The Australian Opera, Sydney, 1967-74; sr. music officer The Australia Council, Sydney, 1974-76; gen. mgr. The State Opera of South Australia, Adelaide, 1976-82; asst. artistic adminstr. Met. Opera, N.Y.C., 1982-83; gen. dir. San Diego Opera, 1983—; guest lectr. U. Adelaide, 1978; guest prof. San Diego State U., 1986—; cons. Lyric Opera Queensland, Australia, 1980-81; bd. dirs. Opera Am., Washington, 1986—. Recipient Peri award Opera Guild So. Calif., 1984. Mem. Australian Inst. Mgmt. (assoc.). Club: University (San Diego). Lodge: Rotary. Avocations: squash, golf, tennis. Office: San Diego Opera PO Box 988 San Diego CA 92112-0988

CAMPBELL, JAMES ARTHUR, chemistry educator; b. Elyria, Ohio, Oct. 1, 1916; s. James Allen and Helen (Metcalf) C.; m. Dorothy Carnell, Nov. 12, 1938; children: Kathleen Annette Campbell Fischer, Christine (Mrs. Richard North). A.B., Oberlin Coll., 1938; M.Sc., Purdue U., 1939; Ph.D., U. Calif., Berkeley, 1942; D.Sc., Beaver Coll., 1972. Instr. U. Calif., Berkeley, 1942-45; prof. Oberlin Coll., 1945-57; program dir. NSF, 1956-57; prof. chemistry Harvey Mudd Coll., Claremont, Calif., 1957—; dir. chem. edn. material study Harvey Mudd Coll., 1960-63, dean faculty, 1974-75; Sci. adviser UNESCO, Asia, 1969-70; adviser Ford, Sloan, Danforth founds.; Research Corp.; lectr. AAAS-Znaniye (USSR) Exchange, 1973; vis. prof. U. Nairobi, 1983; Fulbright lectr. Punjab U., India; AAAS exchange prof. People's Republic China. Author: (with L.E. Steiner) General Chemistry, 1955, Why Do Chemical Reactions Occur?, 1965, Chemical Systems, 1970, Teacher's Guide to Chemical Systems, 1970, (with Barbara Burke) Chemistry, The Unending Frontier, 1978; Columnist Jour. Chem. Edn., 1972-79. Recipient James Flack Norris award N.E. sect. Am. Chem. Soc., 1963; Mfg. Chemists award, 1963; So. Calif. Industry award, 1965; Fund for Advancement Edn. fellow Cambridge U., 1952-53; Guggenheim fellow Kyoto U., also Cambridge U., 1963-64; Nat. Sci. Faculty fellow Harvard, 1970-71; resident scholar Villa Serbelloni, 1972; vis. prof. Chinese U., Hong Kong, 1975-76. Mem. AAAS, AAUP, Am. Chem. Soc. (scientific apparatus makers award 1972), Chem. Soc. Mem. Soc. of Friends. Home: 4326 Via Padova Claremont CA 91711

CAMPBELL, JUDITH LYNN, molecular biology educator; b. New Haven, Mar. 24, 1943; d. John Campbell. B.A., Wellesley Coll., 1965; Ph.D., Harvard U., 1974; postgrad. Harvard Med. Sch., 1969-74. Postdoctoral fellow Harvard Med. Sch., 1974-77; asst. prof. dept. chemistry Calif. Inst. Tech., Pasadena, Calif., 1977-83, assoc. prof., 1983—, assoc. prof. biology div., 1984—. Reciepient Research Career Devel. award NIH, 1979-84; Bavarian State scholar U. Munich, 1966-67, Wellesley Coll. Pendleton scholar, 1965. Mem. Am. Soc. Biol. Chemists. Home: 625 Sierra Meadow Dr Sierra Madre CA 91024 Office: Calif Inst Tech Dept Biology and Chemistry 147-75 Pasadena CA 91125

CAMPBELL, MARTHA JEAN (JEAN F.), public relations consultant; b. Indpls., Oct. 13, 1926; d. Matthew Stanley and Rachel Nell (Campbell) Farson; m. Donald Guy Campbell, Oct. 15, 1949; children: Scott Guy, Jennifer Lee. BA, Butler U., 1962. Dir. media relations St. Joseph Med. Ctr., Phoenix, 1970-72; feature writer N.Am. Newspaper Alliance, N.Y.C., 1972-74; communications specialist Samaritan Health Service, Phoenix, 1974-77; sr. v.p. Ralph Jackson Assocs., Los Angeles, 1979-82; prin. Jean Campbell Pub. Relations, Phoenix, 1977-79, Los Angeles, 1982—; press sec., cons. senator Barry Goldwater, Phoenix, 1968, mayor John Driggs, Phoenix. 1969; media cons. Scottsdale (Ariz.) Pub. Schs., 1969-70, Ariz. Commn. Arts/Humanities, Phoenix, 1971-74. Recipient 1st Pl. "Lulu" award Los Angeles Advt. Women, 1978. Mem. Pub. Relations Soc. Am. (Los Angeles newsletter editor 1980, reception chmn. 1985), Publicity Club Los Angeles, LWV (dir. publs. Ind. chpt. 1960, founder, pres. Brownsburg, Ind. chpt. 1959). Republican. Presbyterian. Avocation: oil painting. Home and Office: 2236 Micheltorena St Los Angeles CA 90039

CAMPBELL, MARY KATHLEEN, mortgage banker; b. Torrance, Calif., Aug. 5, 1944; d. David F. and Katherine I. (Norton) Shields; m. John Alan Campbell, Aug. 19, 1963; children—Lisa Marie Campbell Mitchell, John Andrew. B.B.A. in Acctg., Nat. U., San Diego, 1984. Head cashier Navy Exchange, San Diego, 1968-69; customer relations mgr. J.M. Fields, Norfolk, Va., 1970-72; acct. Hart Enterprises, San Diego, 1973-76; asst. treas. Midwest Pacific Fin., Inc., San Diego, 1976-80, treas., 1980-84, v.p., treas., 1984—; asst. sec. Midwest Fed. Savs. of Eastern Iowa, Burlington, 1978—, asst. v.p., 1985—; treas., dir. Burlington Fin., San Diego, 1984—. Vol. worker Girl Scouts U.S.A., San Diego, 1970-77, Boy Scouts Am., San Diego, 1972-79, Am. Cancer Soc., San Diego, 1978-82; student-family liaison Am. Field Service, Poway, Calif., 1983—. Mem. Fin. Mgrs. Soc., Assn. for Profl. Mortgage Women, Am. Bus. Women's Assn. (treas. 1980-81, Woman of Yr. Poway 1982). Office: Midwest Pacific Financial Inc 7720 Cardinal Ct San Diego CA 92123

CAMPBELL, MAYNARD THOMAS, English language educator; b. Atlanta, Ohio, Mar. 23, 1917; s. James Wiley and Florence (Thomas) C.; cert. Capital U., 1937; B.S., Ohio State U., 1942; M. Ed., U. Ariz. at Tucson, 1952, Ed.D., 1967; m. Shirley I. Hare, July 14, 1960; stepchildren—Michael R. Hare, Kathleen D. Rogers, Kevin S. Hare. Tchr., Salt Creek Twp. Schs., Pickaway County, Ohio, 1937-40; tchr.-prin. Venice (Ohio) Elem. Sch., 1942-44, Sasebo (Japan) Dependents Sch., 1954-55, Upper Secondary Comml. Japanese High Sch., Sasebo, 1954-55; tchr., counselor Tucson Pub. Schs., 1944-81; tutor in English for speakers of other langs., 1981—. Mem. NEA (life), Am. Assn. for Counseling and Devel., Ariz. Counselors Assn., George Washington Masonic Nat. Meml. Assn. (life), Ariz. State Geneal. Soc. (life), Pickaway County (Ohio) Hist. Soc., Internat. Platform Assn., Phi Delta Kappa (life, pres. chpt. 1965-66). Unitarian Universalist. Club: Masons. Author: Campbell, Evans, Hosler and Thomas Family Trees of Ohio, 1973. Home: 1310 Avenida Sirio Tucson AZ 85710

CAMPBELL, MILDRED WASSON, health care executive; b. Muskogee, Okla., May 1, 1926; d. Clement W. and Goldie Sybil (Jones) Wasson; student Northeastern State U., Tahlequah, Okla., 1944-46; children—Linda A. Trujillo, Carl W. Lagoni. Gen. mgr. claims dept. Blue Shield Calif., 1970-73; exec. sec. inservice dept. and infection control dept. Bannock Meml. Hosp., Pocatello, Idaho, 1975-77; profl. relations rep., mktg. rep., officer mgr. Southeastern Idaho region Blue Shield Idaho, Pocatello, 1977—; lectr. S. Idaho Coll.; artist, owner Serenity Studio; mem. orientation staff Idaho State U.; mem. adv. bd. Lic. Practical Nurse program Idaho State U.; mem. adv. bd. Non Traditional Students, Idaho State U.; chmn. Idaho State Commn. for Women. Mem. Nat. Assn. Female Execs., Profl. Women's Network, Twin Falls Networking, Greater Pocatello C. of C., Zonta, Ninety-Nines (membership chmn.). Seventh-day Adventist. Author Grandma Puddin children's books. Home: 2128 Marigold #1 Pocatello ID 83201 Office: PO Box 4504 Blue Shield Idaho Pocatello ID 83205

CAMPBELL, RICHARD ALDEN, electronics executive; b. Bend, Oreg., July 31, 1926; s. Corlis Eugene and Lydia Amney (Peck) C.; m. Edna Mary Seaman, June 12, 1948; children: Stephen Alden, Douglas Niall (dec.), Carolyn Joyce. B.S. in Elec. Engring., U. Ill., 1949, M.S. in Elec. Engring., 1950. With TRW Inc., Redondo Beach, Calif., 1954—; exec. v.p. TRW Inc., 1979—; ptnr. Calif. Investment Assos.; dir. Tylan Corp., Cetec Corp. Trustee Nat. Multiple Sclerosis Soc.; bd. dirs. U. Ill. Found., Hugh O'Brien Youth Found. Served with USN, 1944-46. Recipient Alumni Honor award U. Ill. Coll. Engring. Mem. Am. Electronics Assn. (pres. 1969, dir. 1970), IEEE (sr.), Sigma Xi, Phi Kappa Phi, Tau Beta Pi, Eta Kappa Nu, Sigma Tau, Pi Mu Epsilon, Phi Eta Sigma. Republican. Clubs: Kiwanis (Palos Verdes, Calif.); Rolling Hills Country, Rancheros Visitadores, Los Caballeros. Patentee in radio communications. Office: TRW Inc 1 Space Park Bldg E-2 Redondo Beach CA 90278

CAMPBELL, ROBERT ALLEN, computer scientist, consultant; b. Afton, Lincoln, Wyo., Dec. 27, 1942; s. Allen Ernest and Ellen (Pearson) C.; m. Susan Vanilleer Shafer, Jan. 27, 1967; children—Cristine, Robert Glen, Cindalee, Scott O'Brian, Dustin Troy. B.S. in Stats., Brigham Young U., 1968, M.S. in Stats., 1970; Ph.D. in Stats. and Computer Sci., Kans. State U., 1973. Cert. computer programmer Inst. Cert. Computer Profls. Actuarial programmer Pacific Mut. Life, Los Angeles, 1968; statistician Hill AFB, Utah, 1969; environ. data analyst Kennecott Copper Corp., Salt Lake City, 1970; programmer Great Western Sugar, Longmont, Colo., 1971; asst. prof. computer sci., Kearney (Nebr.) State Coll., 1973-75; asst. prof. stats., No. Ariz. U., Flagstaff, 1975-81; software engr. Abacus Programming Corp., Los Angeles, 1981; assoc. prof. computer sci. Montana State U., Bozeman, 1981-83; assoc. prof. computer sci. Utah State U., Logan, 1983—; pres. Computer Software Cons., cons. Superior Info. Services, Idaho Falls, Idaho, NSF grantee, 1978. Mem. Mont. Acad. Sci. (sect. v.p.), Statis. Assn. (com. on coms. 1980-83) Assn. Computing Machinery, Assn., Sunstone Found., B.H. Roberts Soc., Sigma Xi. Republican. Mormon. Author numerous manuals on computer simulation and data analysis. Office: Utah State U Dept Computer Sci Logan UT 84322

CAMPBELL, ROBERT BRAUN, management systems analyst; b. Battle Creek, Mich., July 15, 1917; s. Thomas Dewitt and Maria Sophia (Braun) C.; student Ventura Coll., 1959-60, Orange Coast Coll., 1972-73, U. Calif.-Fullerton, 1975; m. Beulah Mae Landis, June 25, 1937 (dec.); children—David Rolland, Susan Marie, Bruce Allan; m. 2d, Jane Ann Boulware, Oct. 10, 1963. Material mgmt. analyst and tng. supr. Ford Motor Co., Dearborn, Mich., 1937-48; mem. staff to exec. mgmt. McCulloch Corp., Los Angeles, 1949-55; ordained to ministry Methodist Ch., 1958; minister edn., Santa Paula, pastor Shandon and San Miguel, Calif. in the So. Calif., Nev. Conf., 1958-62; nat. mgmt. systems coordinator R.J. Reynolds, Inc., N.Y.C., 1964-70; methods engring. analyst nuclear ops. So. Calif. Edison Co., Los Angeles, 1971-77, research and devel. methods analyst, 1977-79, sr. staff analyst systems planning and research, 1980—; cons., speaker indsl. cos., univs., profl. assns.; condr. tng. courses. Commr. Boy Scouts Am., Detroit, 1942-48; chaplain Ventura County (Calif.) Fire Dept., 1958-59, San Luis Obispo County (Calif.) Fire Dept., 1961-62. Served with U.S. Army, 1945-46. Mem. Assn. for Systems Mgmt. (pres. Orange County chpt. 1967, dir. western systems conf. 1968, 69, div. dir. 1970, 71, 72, gen. chmn. western systems conf. 1971, internat. committeman 1970, 73; merit award 1971, achievement award 1973, Disting. Service award as Man of Year, Atlanta 1978). Author: The Secretary's Handbook, 1974; The Forms Control Function, 1975; Analyzing Systems Analysts, 1976; Standardizing Procedure Documentation, 1976. Home: 453 Baywood Dr Newport Beach CA 92660 Office: PO Box 800 Room 497 Rosemead CA 91770

CAMPBELL, ROBERT W., transportation executive; b. Valentine, Nebr., Oct. 22, 1922; s. Harry Lee and Margaret (Haley) C. Grad., Creighton U., 1948, grad. in law, 1950. Chmn. Can. Pacific Enterprises, Calgary, Alta.; chmn. Can. Pacific Ltd., Calgary, 1986—; dir. Algoma Steel Corp. Ltd., AMCA Internat. Ltd., Can. Pacific Ltd., Can. Pacific Enterprises Ltd., Great Lakes Forest Products Ltd., Westinghouse Electronic Corp., Royal Bank Can., Pan Can. Petroleum Ltd. (also chmn.), Westinghouse Electric Corp. Served to capt. U.S. Army, World War II. Roman Catholic. Office: Can Pacific Enterprises, 125 9th Ave SE Suite 2300, Calgary, AB Canada T2G 0P6 *

CAMPBELL, TAMMY DIANNE, advertising executive; b. Sewickley, Pa., June 28, 1958; d. Michael H. and Gloria (Gueirrieri) Sumko; m. Marc B. Campbell, Apr. 27, 1979; 1 child, Marc B. Jr. Student, Brigham Young U., 1976-79. Jr. account exec. Henry J. Kaufman & Assoc., Washington, 1979-81; account exec. S. Thompson & Assoc., Salt Lake City, 1981-82; advt. dir. Peoples Jewellers, Salt Lake City, 1981-82; account supr. Everett Lewis & Assoc., Salt Lake City, 1982-83; pres. Campbell & Assoc., Salt Lake City, 1983-86; sr. account mgr. Goldberg/Marchesand, Washington, 1986—. Creative dir. (radio comml.) Game Show, 1984 (CLIO award 1984), (direct mail offer) Holiday Checking, 1984 (cert. of excellence 1984), (point-of-purchase) Money Market Display, 1984 (cert. of excellence 1984), (In A Time Crunch, 1984 (cert. of excellence 1984). Recipient Medal of Honor FIMA, 1986. Mem. Utah Advt. Fedn. (Gold award 1984), Utah Assn. Women Bus. Owners. Republican. Mormon. Avocations: gourmet cooking, gardening, tennis, skiing, antiques. Office: Goldberg/Marchesand 927 15th St NW Washington DC 20005

CAMPBELL, W(ALLACE) SHERWOOD, III, import-export company executive, engineering, marketing and finance consultant. BE, Stevens Inst. Tech., 1964; MBA, U. Denver, 1977. Registered profl. engr., N.J., N.Y.,

Pa., Colo. Pres. Balios, Inc., Littleton, Colo., 1981—. Contbr. numerous articles to profl. jours.; patentee in field. Mem. IEEE, Nat. Soc. Prof. Engrs. Home and Office: 6948 W Nova Dr Littleton CO 80123

CAMPBELL, WESLEY GLENN, economist, educator; b. Komoka, Ont., Can., Apr. 29, 1924; s. Alfred E and Delia (O'Brien) C.; m. Rita Ricardo, Sept. 15, 1946; children: Barbara Campbell Bizewski, Diane Campbell Porter, Nancy. B.A., U. Western Ont., 1944; M.A., Harvard, 1946, Ph.D., 1948. Instr. econs. Harvard, 1948-51; research economist U.S. C. of C., 1951-54; dir. research Am. Enterprise Assn., 1954-60; dir. Hoover Instn. War, Revolution and Peace, Stanford, Calif., 1960—; Co-dir. project on Am. competitive enterprise, fgn. econ. devel. and aid program, spl. com. to study fgn. aid program U.S. Senate, 1956-57; mem. Pres.'s Commn. on White House Fellows, 1969-74, President's Com. on Sci. and Tech., 1976; mem. personnel adv. com. to Pres., 1980-81; mem. adv. bd. Ctr. for Strategic and Internat. Studies, 1980-85; dir. Hutchins Ctr. for Study Dem. Instns., 1981—; bd. dirs. NSF, 1972-78, Com. on Present Danger, 1976—; chmn. Pres.'s Intelligence Oversight Bd., 1981—; mem. Pres.'s Fgn. Intelligence Adv. Bd., 1981—; chmn. Am. panel Joint Com. Japan-U.S. Cultural and Ednl. Coop., 1983—; chmn. Japan-U.S. Friendship Commn., 1983—; mem. UNESCO Monitoring Panel, 1984; chmn. bd. trustees Ronald Reagan Presdl. Found., 1985—. Co-author: The American Competitive Enterprise Economy, 1952; Editor, prin. author: The Economics of Mobilization and War, 1952; contbr. articles to profl. jours. Trustee Herbert Hoover Presdl. Library Assn.; mem. bd. visitors Bernice P. Bishop Mus.; regent U. Calif., 1968—. Fellow Royal Econ. Soc.; mem. Am. Econ. Assn., Phila. Soc. (pres. 1965-67), Mont Pelerin Soc. (dir. 1980—). Clubs: Bohemian (Cal.), Cosmos (Cal.), Commonwealth (Cal.). Home: 26915 Alejandro Dr Los Altos Hills CA 94022 Office: Hoover Instn Stanford Stanford CA 94305

CAMPBELL, WILLIAM V., computer company executive; b. Pitts.; married; 1 son. B.S. in Econs., M.S. in Econs., Columbia U. Former football coach Columbia U.; past v.p. J. Walter Thompson; past dir. mktg. communications film div. Eastman Kodak Co.; exec. v.p. U.S. Sales div. Apple Computer Inc., Cupertino, Calif., 1983—. Bd. dirs. Nat. Football Found. and Hall of Fame. Office: Apple Computer Inc 20525 Mariana Ave 36 S Cupertino CA 95014 *

CAMPER, JOHN SAXTON, public relations and marketing executive; b. Trenton, N.J., Apr. 24, 1929; s. Thomas Emory and Mildred Ruth (Burke) C.; m. Ferne Arlene Clanton; children: Susan Jennifer, John Saxton III. BS in History and Econs., U. Nebr., 1968. Enlisted U.S. Army, 1948, commd. to 1st lt., advanced through ranks to maj., 1972, ret., 1972; regional mktg. officer First Bank System, Mont., 1982—; mng. dir. R.A. Howard U Assocs., Helena, Mont., 1983; lectr., instr. mktg. and advt., pub. relations; pres. Camper Communications, Helena, 1983. Decorated Legion of Merit. Mem. Helena Advt. Fedn. (1st pres., founder). Republican. Methodist. Lodge: Rotary.

CAMPHAUSEN, FRED HOWARD, physicist; b. Los Angeles, Aug. 23, 1933; s. Fred Henry and Eloise (Ingebretsen) C.; B.A. in Physics, U. Calif., 1961; m. Martina Simon, Apr. 2, 1956 (div.); children—Raymond Thomas, Karin Maria; m. 2d, Marianna P. Dembinski, Aug. 2, 1980. With Naval Weapons Center, China Lake, Calif., 1961—, physicist, project mgr. electronic warfare test and evaluation, 1980—; owner, mgr., Mountain High, Ltd., 1980—. Served with U.S. Army, 1953-56. Mem. Naval Aviation Execs. Inst., Assn. of Old Crows, Am. Alpine Club, Sierra Club. Republican. Roman Catholic. Club: Vägmarken, Eastern Sierra Mountaineers. Contbr. tech. writings to publs. Home: 2765 Sierra Vista Way Bishop CA 93514 Office: Naval Weapons Center China Lake CA 93555

CAMPO, FRANK PHILIP, composer, educator; b. N.Y.C., Feb. 4, 1927; s. Philip and Charlotte (Rothe) C.; Mus.B., U. So. Calif., 1950, Mus.M., 1953, D. Mus. Arts, 1968; m. Leda LaPeyre, July 10, 1955; 1 son, Darius. Arranger, performer clarinet, 1943—; mem. faculty U. So. Calif., Los Angeles, 1966-68, mem. faculty Calif. State U., Fullerton, 1967-68, prof. composition, chmn. composition-theory dept., 1968—. Served with AUS, 1945-47. Recipient Composers award Broadcast Music Inc., 1958, Screen Composers Assn. award, 1966. Fulbright scholar, 1957. Mem. Internat. Soc. Contemporary Music, Nat. Assn. Am. Composers and Condrs., A.S.C.A.P., Pi Kappa Lambda. Composer: Bassoon Concerto, 1966; Madrigals for Brass Quintet, 1970; Dialogues II for Orchestra, 1971; Cantata No. 3, 1972; Sinfonia Sacra, 1974. Home: 12336 Milbank St Studio City CA 91604 Office: Calif State U Dept Music 18111 Nordhoff St Northridge CA 91324

CAMPOS, SANTIAGO E., federal judge; b. Santa Rosa, N.Mex., Dec. 25, 1926; s. Ramon and Miquela Campos; m. Patsy Campos, Jan. 27, 1947; children: Teresa, Rebecca, Christina, Miquela Feliz. J.D., U. N.Mex., 1953. Bar: N.Mex. 1953. Asst., 1st asst. atty gen. State of N.Mex., 1955-57; judge N.Mex. Dist. Ct.; 1st Jud. Dist., 1971-78; now judge U.S. Dist. Ct. for Dist. N.Mex. Served as seaman USN, 1944-46. Mem. State Bar N.Mex., First Jud. Dist. Bar Assn., Order of Coif. Office: US Dist Ct PO Box 2244 Santa Fe NM 87504

CANBY, WILLIAM CAMERON, JR., U.S. judge; b. St. Paul, May 22, 1931; s. William Cameron and Margaret Leah (Lewis) C.; m. Jane Adams, June 18, 1954; children—William Nathan, John Adams, Margaret Lewis. A.B., Yale U., 1953; LL.B., U. Minn., 1956. Bar: Minn. bar 1956, Ariz. bar 1972. Law clk. U.S. Supreme Ct. Justice Charles E. Whittaker, 1958-59; asso. firm Oppenheimer, Hodgson, Brown, Baer & Wolff, St. Paul, 1959-62; asso., then dep. dir. Peace Corps, Ethiopia, 1962-64; dir. Peace Corps, Uganda, 1964-66; asst. to U.S. Senator Walter Mondale, 1966; asst. to pres. SUNY, 1967; prof. law Ariz. State U., 1967-80; judge U.S. Ct. Appeals 9th Circuit, Phoenix, 1980—; bd. dirs. Ariz. Center Law in Public Interest, 1974-80, Maricopa County Legal Aid Soc., 1972-78, D.N.A.-People's Legal Services, 1978-80; Fulbright prof. Makerere U. Faculty Law, Kampala, Uganda, 1970-71. Author: American Indian Law, 1981; also articles.; Note editor: Minn. Law Rev, 1955-56. Precinct and state committeeman Democratic Party Ariz., 1972-80; bd. dirs. Central Ariz. Coalition for Right to Choose, 1976-80. Served with USAF, 1956-58. Mem. State Bar Ariz., Minn. Bar Assn., Maricopa County Bar Assn., Phi Beta Kappa, Order of Coif. Office: US Courthouse 230 N 1st Ave Phoenix AZ 85025

CANCINO, KAREN, social worker; b. St. Louis, Sept. 18, 1940; d. John and Edna (Rosemann) Tomasovic; m. Charles Zuzich (dec. 1968); m. Rodolfo Cancino, Dec. 11, 1976; children: Juan Carlos, Miguel David. BA in Sociology, Colo. U., 1962; MSW, U. Mich., 1966. Social worker East Lansing (Mich.) Pub. Sch., 1968-69; dir. Info. and Referral Ctr. for Pregnant Girls, San Mateo, Calif., 1969-77; social worker Children's Protective Services, San Mateo, 1977-81; sex edn. trainer Sex Edn. for Foster Parents, Oakland, Calif., 1981-84; case mgr. Teen Parent Assistance Program, Oakland, 1981—; adv. bd. Friends to Parents, San Bruno, Calif., 1980—; ptnr. Golden Gate Tng. Cons., 1985. Author: What Will I Say? 1983, Am I Doing it Right? 1982. Pres. Beideman Area Neighborhood Group, San Francisco, 1977; founder Parents United, Daus. United, Chpts., San Mateo, 1977; mem. Tree Adv. Bd., San Francisco, 1985—; sec. Women's Action for Nuclear Disarmament, San Francisco, 1985-86; treas., bd. dirs. Claire Lilienthal After Sch. Program, San Francisco, 1985-86. Recipient Achievement award Nat. Alliance Concerned with Sch. Age Parents, 1976. Mem. Calif. Alliance Concerned with Sch. Age Parents (founder, bd. dirs. 1983-85, network cons. 1985—, cert. appreciation), Nat. Assn. Social Workers, Calif. Assn. Sch. Social Workers. Avocations: tennis, reading, knitting. Home: 1927 Ellis St San Francisco CA 94115

CANFIELD, GRANT WELLINGTON, JR., orgn. exec.; b. Los Angeles, Nov. 28, 1923; s. Grant Wellington and Phyllis Marie (Westland) C.; B.S., U. So. Calif., 1949, M.B.A., 1958; m. Virginia Louise Bellinger, June 17, 1945; 1 dau., Julie Marie. Personnel and indsl. relations exec., Los Angeles area, 1949-55; employee relations cons., regional mgr. Mchts. and Mfrs. Assn. Los Angeles, 1955-60; v.p., orgnl. devel. cons. Hawaii Employers Council, Honolulu, 1960-75; pres., dir. Hawaiian Ednl. Council, 1969—; exec. v.p. Hawaii Garment Mfrs. Assn., 1965-75, Assn. Hawaii Restaurant Employers, 1966-75; exec. dir. Hawaii League Savs. Assns., 1971-78; exec. dir. Pan-Pacific Surg. Assn., 1980-81, exec. v.p., 1982-83; exec. dir. Hawaii Bus. Roundtable, 1983—; sec., treas. Econ. Devel. Corp. Honolulu, 1984-85; sec., treas. Hawaii Conv. Park Council, Inc., 1984-86, hon. dir., 1986—; lectr. orgn. devel. and human resources mgmt. Bd. dirs. Hawaii Restaurant Assn., 1974-76, bd. dirs. Hawaii chpt. Nat. Assn. Accountants, 1963-67, nat. dir., 1965-66; bd. dirs. Vol. Service Bur. Honolulu, 1965-66, pres., 1966-68; bd. dirs. Vol. Info. and Referral Service Honolulu, 1972-75, Goodwill Vocat. Tng. Centers of Hawaii, 1973-81, Girl Scout council Pacific, 1961-65, 71-72; bd. dirs. Hawaii Com. Alcoholism, 1962-71, co-chmn., 1964-68; pres., dir. Friends of Punahou Sch., 1972-75; mem. community adv. bd. Jr. League Hawaii, 1968-70; exec. bd. Aloha council Boys Scouts Am., 1962-65; bd. regents Chaminade U., 1983-85. Served to 1st lt. inf. AUS, 1943-46. Decorated Bronze Star, Purple Heart, Combat Inf. badge. Mem. Am. Soc. Assn. Execs. (cert. assn. exec.), Am. Soc. Tng. and Devel., Am. Agrl. Econs. Assn., Am. Soc. Personnel Adminstrn., Rotarian, Mason. Clubs: Pacific (Honolulu) Kaneohe Yacht; Plaza (Honolulu). Co-author: Resource Manual for Public Collective Bargaining, 1973. Home: 1605 Mokulua Dr Kailua HI 96734 Office: PO Box 4145 Honolulu HI 96812-4145

CANNON, BARBARA EVELYN MARIE, academic administrator; b. Big Sandy, Tex., Jan. 17, 1936; d. Archie and Jimmie (Jones) C.; m. Bookert T. Anderson, May 8, 1982 (dec. Nov. 1982). BA, San Francisco State U., 1957, MA, 1965; certs., U. Paris, 1966-67; cert. in administrn., U. Calif., Berkeley, 1973; MA, Stanford U., 1975, EdD, 1977. Cert. spl. secondary and jr. high tchr. Tchr., staff developer, adminstr. Berkeley Pub. Schs., 1958-74; administrv. asst. U.S. Office of Edn., Washington, 1975-76, cons., 1978; teaching fellow, coordinator Stanford (Calif.) U., 1974-75, research asst., 1976-77, research assoc., 1977-78; asst. dean Peralta Colls., Oakland, Calif., 1978—; cons. Far West Edn. Lab., San Francisco, 1978;. Exec. bd. dirs., v.p. Mozart Festival of Alameda, Calif., 1979-81. Ednl. Policy fellow Inst. for Edn. Leadership, 1975-76. Mem. Assn. Calif. Community Coll. Adminstrs. (commn. mem. 1979-81), Bus. Profl. Women, Phi Delta Kappa, Pi Lambda Theta, Mu Phi Epsilon (named Outstanding Sr. 1957). Lodge: Soroptimist Internat. Alameda. Avocation: photography. Office: Merritt Coll 12500 Campus Dr Oakland CA 95619

CANNON, EARL NELSON, lawyer; b. Delavan, Wis., Jan. 20, 1900; s. Dan E. and Lenora (Nelson) C.; B.S., U. Wis., 1924, LL.B., 1927, J.D., 1966; m. Helen Gibson, July 23, 1926. Atty., law firm Stephens, Cannon & Cooper (now Stephens, Cannon, Bieberstein & Cooper), 1928-53; pres. Yellow Truck Lines, Inc., 1930-45; exec. dir., legal counsel Central States Area Employers Assn., 1940-53; labor counsel Central Motor Freight Assn., 1940-53; v.p. charge personnel and labor relations Greyhound Corp., Chgo., 1952-65. Pres. Idyllwild Property Owners Assn.; dir. Idyllwild County Water Dist. Industry mem. War Labor Bd., 1944-45; industry mem. Nat. WSB, 1946; v.p. Am. Trucking Assn., 1936-46 commr. Riverside County Flood Control and Water Conservation Dist.; mem. adv. com. Hemet-San Jacinto YMCA; bd. dirs. Idyllwild (Calif.) Arts Found., Hemet-San Jacinto YMCA. Mem. Theta Chi, Phi Alpha Delta. Clubs: Executive, Union League (Chgo.); Madison; Indian Wells Country (Palm Desert, Calif.); Palm Springs Country, Tennis (Palm Springs, Calif.); Idyllwild Lions (pres.); Ojai (Calif.) Country; San Jacinto Lions (Zone A chmn.), Sobobe Springs Country Soboba Springs Mens (chmn. membership com.) (San Jacinto, Calif.). Home: 42701 Main St #116 San Jacinto CA 92383 Office: Greyhound Towers 111 W Clarendon Ave Phoenix AZ 85013

CANNON, JACK ARLO, surgeon; b. Salina, Kans., July 17, 1919; s. Charles Heaton and Bess May (Beadle) C.; m. Helen Stacia Snieszko, Feb. 15, 1949; children—Susan Martus, Patricia B., Jack C., Michael G., Deborah Cushing. B.A., UCLA, 1940; M.D., Harvard U., 1943. Diplomate Nat. Bd. Med. Examiners, Am. Bd. Surgery. Intern, resident Mass. Gen. Hosp., 1944-46; resident in surgery Los Angeles County Gen. Hosp., 1948-49, sr. resident surgery, instr. surgery U. So. Calif. Med. Sch.-Los Angeles County Gen. Hosp., 1949-50; research assoc. dept. surgery UCLA Med. Ctr., 1950-51, instr. surgery, 1951-54, asst. prof., 1954-58, assoc. prof., 1958-63, prof., 1963-69; staff surgeon Wadsworth VA, Los Angeles, 1950-51, 52-60; attending surgeon Maricopa County Hosp., Phoenix, 1969—; practice medicine specializing in gen. and vascular surgery, Phoenix, 1969-76; chief dept. surgery VA Hosp., Phoenix, 1976-78; cons. W.L. Gore & Assocs., Inc., Flagstaff, Ariz., 1978—. Contbr. articles to profl. jours. Served to capt. USMC, 1946-47, USAF, 1953. Mem. AMA (Physicians Recognition award), Calif. Med. Assn., Los Angeles County Med. Assn., Ariz. Med. Assn., Maricopa County Med. Assn., ACS, Am. Surg. Assn., Soc. Univ. Surgeons, Soc. Vascular Surgery, Internat. Cardiovascular Soc., Western Surg. Assn. Republican. Home: 3142 N Tam O'Shanter Flagstaff AZ 86001 Office: WL Gore & Assocs Inc 1505 N 4th St PO Box 800 Flagstaff AZ 86002

CANNON, JONATHAN H., Mayor, City of Garden Grove, Calif. Office: Office of the Mayor City of Garden Grove PO Box 3070 Garden Grove CA 92642 *

CANNON, PETER, electric and aerospace company executive; b. Chatham, Eng., Apr. 20, 1932; came to U.S., 1956, naturalized, 1958; s. William Douglas and Ena (Bennett) C.; m. Elaine Moosdorf, Aug. 5, 1955; children—Ian Douglas, Adrienne Louise, Eric Milton, Peter Andrew. BSc in Math. and Chemistry with honors, U. London, 1952, PhD in Phys. Chemistry, 1955. Chem. engr. Procter & Gamble, Cin., 1955-56; mem. tech. staff Gen. Electric Research Lab., Schenectady, N.Y., 1956-64; liaison scientist Gen. Electric Research Lab., 1964-65; mgr. ops. analysis-info. systems bus. Gen. Electric Research Lab., Charlottesville, Va., 1965-67; mgr. sensors and microelectronics automation bus. systems Gen. Electric Research Lab., 1967-72; mgr. strategic devel. Gen. Electric Research Lab., West Lynn, Mass., 1972-73; v.p. bus. devel. utility and indsl. ops. Rockwell Internat., Pitts., 1973-76; corp. staff v.p. research, v.p. Sci. Center, Thousand Oaks, Calif., 1976-84; v.p. research, chief scientist of corp. Sci. Ctr., 1984—; adj. prof. physics Bklyn. Poly. Inst., 1962-67; lectr. U. Va., 1967, Royal Soc. London, 1978; mem. U.S. Nat. Acad. Sci. vis. team U. Alexandria, Egypt, 1980; mem. visiting com. to Div. of Physical Scis. U. Chgo., 1983—; chmn. Nat. Bur. of Standards Panel for Nondestructive Evaluation, 1983-85, Inst. for Materials Sci. and Engring., 1984—, Fed. Sci. & Tech. com., 1985; adv. panel on robotics and microelectronics U. Calif., Santa Barbara, 1985—; vice chmn. Indsl. Research Inst., 1984; chmn. Fec. Sci. and Tech. com., 1985-86. Author: (with others) Vacuum Technique, 1961, Reactivity of Solids, 1968; contbr. (with others) articles to profl. jours.; patentee in field. Bd. dirs. Ventura County (Calif.) United Way, 1978-79, 84, chmn. bd. trustees, 1985; campaign chmn. Ventura County Jr. Achievement Program, 1979; program chmn. White House Advisory com. for Historically Black Colls. and Univs, 1986, co-chmn. 1987. Fellow Royal Soc. Chemistry; mem. Nat. Mgmt. Assn. (recipient Silver Knight of Mgmt. award 1980), Am. Phys. Soc., Am. Chem. Soc., Am. Mgmt. Assn. Patentee in field. Office: Rockwell Internat Corp 1049 Camino Dos Rios Thousand Oaks CA 91360

CANON, JOHN LAWRENCE, safety engineer; b. El Reno, Okla., Feb. 19, 1922; s. John A. and Carrie M. (Coburn) C.; m. Christine G. Prater, Sept. 11, 1943; 1 child, Judith Ann. BBA, North Tex. State Coll., 1957. Safety engr. Temco Aircraft Co., Grand Prairie, Tex., 1953-60, Samuels Meat Co., Dallas, 1960-62, USF&G Ins. Co., Dallas, 1962-66; supt. IEA USF&G Ins. Co., Sacramento, 1966-83; supr. IEA USF&G Ins. Co., Sacramtento, 1983—. Served as tech. sgt. USAAF, 1942-46. Mem. Am. Soc. Safety Engrs. (pres. Sacramento chpt. 1969-70), Vets. of Safety, Profl. Engrs. of Calif., Nat. Fire Protection Assn., No. Calif. Audit Assn., Audit Assn. of West, Am. Assn. Retired Persons. Democrat. Lodge: Masons. Avocations: reading, gardening, fishing, traveling, woodwork.

CANOVA-DAVIS, ELEANOR, biochemist, researcher; b. San Francisco, Jan. 18, 1938; d. Gaudenzio Enzio and Catherine (Bordisso) Canova; m. Kenneth Roy Davis, Feb. 10, 1957; children: Kenneth Roy Jr., Jeffrey Stephen. BA, San Francisco State U., 1968, MS, 1971; PhD, U. Calif., San Francisco, 1977. Research, teaching asst. U. Calif., San Francisco, 1972-77, asst. research biochemist, 1980-84; NIH postdoctoral fellow U. Calif., Berkeley, 1977-80; sr. scientist Liposome Tech., Menlo Park, Calif., 1984-85; scientist Genentech, Inc., South San Francisco, 1985—. Contbr. articles to profl. jours. Recipient Nat. Research Service award NIH, 1977-80; grantee Chancellor's Patent Fund, U. Calif., San Francisco, 1976, Earl C. Anthony Trust, U. Calif., San Francisco, 1975. Mem. Am. Chem. Soc., Calif. Scholarship Fedn. Roman Catholic. Club: Sequoia Woods County (Arnold, Calif.). Avocations: reading, sewing, bridge. Home: 2305 Bourbon Ct South San Francisco CA 94080 Office: Genentech Inc 460 Point San Bruno Blvd South San Francisco CA 94080

CANTOR, ROBERT FRANK, computer company executive; b. N.Y.C., Apr. 29, 1943; s. Myron David and Phyllis Jane (Singerman) C.; m. Nancy Marie Carpenter, May 3, 1970 (div.); 1 child, Michelle; m. Brenda Lee Cousins, May 5, 1984; children: Anthony, Samuel. BSBA, Pa. State U., 1965, MSBA, 1967. Mem. faculty loan program Xavier U., New Orleans, 1972-73; adv. planner banking and security IBM Corp., Kingston, N.Y., 1973-78; program mgr. strategy bus. practices at div. hdqrs. Harrison, N.Y., 1978-80; mgr. tech. products planning Boulder, Colo., 1980-83; program mgr. OEM supplies 1983—; bd. dirs. and pres. Colo. Neurodiagnostic Inst., Boulder. Inventor in field. Mem. Beta Gamma Sigma. Republican. Mem. Bahai Faith. Avocations: basketball, tennis, investments. Home: 745 Linden Ave Boulder CO 80302 Office: IBM 80H 935 6300 Diagonal Hwy Boulder CO 80301

CANTWELL, THOMAS CALVIN, JR., electrical engineer; b. Pomona, Calif., Mar. 30, 1942; s. Thomas Calvin and Jewell Dean (Ellis) C.; m. Carol Jean Flanagan, Nov. 20, 1977; children: Christina, Colleen. AA, Chaffey Jr. Coll., 1962; BSEE with honors, Calif. State U., Los Angeles, 1966; MSEE, U. So. Calif., 1968. Mem. tech. staff Hughes Aircraft Co., Fullerton, Calif., 1966-72, staff engr., 1972-78, tech. supr., 1978-79, sr. staff engr., 1979-80, tech. sect. head, 1980-84, sr. scientist, 1984—. Patentee in field. Mem. Country Riders, Phi Kappa Phi, Eta Kappa Nu, Tau Beta Pi. Republican. Avocations: horsemanship, sailing, home computing. Office: Hughes Aircraft Co 7000 Village Dr BP 691/P218 Buena Park CA 92601

CAPE, ROBERT LEE, plastics design consultant; b. Desloge, Mo., Mar. 8, 1943; s. Farrel Woodrow and Mildred Eloise Smith; m. Elizabeth Florence Grimm, Apr. 20, 1963 (div.); 1 son, Matthew Kenyon (dec.). Student, U. Colo., 1960-61, Washington U., St. Louis, 1963-71, evening colls. NYU. Various design positions 1963-72; primary project engr. Gen-Tire Automotive Plastics, Detroit, 1972-74; process devel. engr. Raychem Corp., Calif., 1974-76; project engr. Glastic Corp. Cleve., 1976-79; sr. prodn. engr., design engr. computers TRIAD, Sunnyvale, Calif., 1979-86, Cape Design, San Jose, Calif., 1986—; lectr. indsl. design program San Jose State U. Served with USN, 1961-62. Mem. Soc. Plastics Engrs., Am. Soc. Cert. Engring. Technicians. Home: 1681 Peachwood Dr San Jose CA 95132 Office: Cape Design 1681 Peachwood Dr San Jose CA 95132

CAPELLI, CAROL ANNE, psychologist, educator; b. Paterson, N.J., Apr. 16, 1956; d. Francis John and Margaret Anne (McAlevey) C. ScB, Brown U., 1978; PhD, Stanford U., 1984. Tchg. asst. Stanford (Calif.) U., 1979-84; asst. prof. Lewis & Clark Coll., Portland, 1984—; cons. SRI Internat., Menlo Park, Calif., 1982. Contbr. articles to profl. jours. Undergrad. research fellow NSF, 1977, grad. fellow Stanford U., 1979-81, predoctoral fellow NIMH, 1981-83. Mem. Soc. for Research in Child Devel., Am. Ednl. Research Assn., Sigma Xi. Office: Lewis and Clark Univ Dept Psychology Portland OR 97219

CAPERS, GINA, real estate lending company executive; b. San Francisco, Mar. 5, 1938; d. Anthony and Esther (Duncan) C. Exec. v.p. Western States Funding, Walnut Creek, Calif., 1979—; sec. Nat. Wrap Servicing, Walnut Creek, 1981—, Bethom Corp., Walnut Creek, 1983—. Mem. Assn. Profl. Mortgage Woman (East Bay charter rec. sec. 1964, Mt. Diable charter rec. sec. 1977), East Bay Escrow Assn. (pres. 1981). Episcopalian. Club: Zonta Internat. (Mt. Diablo area dir. 1984). Office: Western States Funding Corp 710 S Broadway Suite 208 Walnut Creek CA 94596

CAPIAUX, RAYMOND, aerospace company executive; b. Lille, France, Aug. 19, 1927; came to U.S., 1953, naturalized, 1959; s. Lucien and Aimee (Maucourt) C.; m. Aimee Cook, Aug. 20, 1960; children—Claude, Frank, Philip, Corinne, Sean; m. 2d, Etienne Ledbetter, Nov. 20, 1983. B.S. in Aero. Engring, Swiss Inst. Tech., 1950, M.S., 1951. Research engr. Sulzer Bros., Winterthur, Switzerland, 1950-53; sr. propulsion-aerodynamics engr. Convair, Fort Worth, 1953-56; supr. aerodynamic design Curtiss Wright Corp., Princeton, N.J., 1956-57; staff engr. Fairchild Engring. & Airplane Corp., Deerpark, N.Y., 1957-58; research specialist, staff scientist, sr. mem. for aerophysics, mgr. aerospace scis. lab., dir. engring. scis., asst. gen. mgr., dir. research, v.p. r Lockheed Missiles & Space Co., Inc., Sunnyvale, Calif., 1958—, v.p. Strategic Def. Orgn. astronautics div., 1983-86, v.p., asst. gen. mgr. astronautics div., 1987—. Mem. Am. Def. Preparedness Assn., Am. Inst. Aeros. and Astronautics, Assn. U.S. Army. Home: 12610 Via Ventana Los Altos Hills CA 94022 Office: PO Box 3504 Sunnyvale CA 94088

CAPICE, PHILIP CHARLES, television production executive; b. Bernardsville, N.J., June 24, 1931; s. Philip Joseph and Angelina Mary (Togno) C.; B.A., Dickinson Coll., 1952; M.F.A., Columbia U., 1954. Production supr., assoc. program dir. Benton & Bowles Inc., N.Y.C., 1954-64, Vice pres. in charge program devel., 1965-69; dir. spl. programs CBS-TV Network, N.Y.C., 1969-74; sr. v.p. creative affairs Lorimar Prodns., Burbank, Calif., 1974-78; pres. Lorimar TV, Burbank, Calif., 1978-79; ind. producer Lorimar Productions, Culver City, Calif., from 1979; pres., chief exec. officer Raven's Claw Productions, Studio City, Calif. Since 1974, exec. producer Dallas, Eight Is Enough, The Blue Knight, Two Marriages, Helter Skelter, Sybil (Emmy Award, 1977, Peabody Award, 1977), Green Eyes (Peabody Award, 1978, Humanitas Prize, 1978), Eric, Widow, Studs Lonigan, A Man Called Intrepid, The Runaways, The Prince of Central Park, A Question of Guilt, Some Kind of Miracle (Christopher Award, 1978), Returning Home, Conspiracy of Terror, Hunter, Married: The First Year, The Rivermen, Mary and Joseph: A Love Story, The Stranger Within, A Matter of Life and Death, Bunco, Some People Like Us, Private Sessions, others. Recipient Emmy award, 1977, Peabody award, 1977, 78. Mem. Acad. TV Arts and Scis., The Caucus for Producers, Writers and Directors, Dickinson Coll. Alumni Advisory Bd.

CAPIEL/COLLIN, SUSAN, satellite services executive; b. Van Nuys, Calif., Oct. 4, 1952; d. Joe A. and Josie (Toler) Capiel; m. Steve Collin, July 7, 1984. Student La. State U., 1973. Legal sec. Austin & Jordan, Aspen, Colo., 1978-82; ptnr., broker satellite services SAT TIME, Inc., Aspen, 1982—. Democrat. Roman Catholic. Home and office: SAT TIME Inc Box 3057 Aspen CO 81612

CAPLES, JERRY LAUREN, oral and maxillofacial surgeon; b. Portland, Oreg., Aug. 12, 1936; s. Ralph Francis and Edna Fay (Webster) C.; m. Darlene Marie Passut, Feb. 1, 1958; children: Miles, Peter, Michael, Suzanne, Patrick. BS, Oreg. State U., 1960; DMD, U. Oreg., 1964. Diplomate Am. Bd. Oral and Maxillofacial Surgery. Oral surgeon Oral Surgery Assocs., Corvallis, Oreg., 1964—. Served to lt. col. U.S. Army, 1967-69, Vietnam. Fellow Am. Assn. Oral and Maxillofacial Surgeons (regional info. rep., 1980—), Internat. Assn. Oral and Maxillofacial Surgeons; mem. Oreg. Assn. Oral and Maxillofacial Surgeons (pres. 1980). Republican. Lodge: Rotary. Avocations: basketball coaching, fishing. Office: Oral Surgery Assocs 3640 NW Samaritan Dr Corvallis OR 97330

CAPLES, WILLIAM GOFF, IV, marketing executive; b. Chgo., Nov. 23, 1946; s. William Goff III and Jean Coburn (Dunbar) C.; m. Regina Marie Cummings, Dec. 22, 1973. BSBA, Lakeland Coll., 1970. With Carson Pirie Scott, Chgo., 1970-73; sales rep. Mohasco, Chgo., 1973-78; nat. sales mgr. Barcalounger, Chgo., 1978-80, dir. mktg. administr. and budgets, 1980-81; regional mgr. Baker Knapp & Tubbs, Seattle, 1981—. Served as sgt. U.S. Army, 1965-67. Clubs: Union League (Chgo.), Tavern. Avocations: boating, riding, books, history. Home: 2805 First Ave N Seattle WA 98109 Office: Baker Knapp & Tubbs 5701 Sixth Ave S Seattle WA 98108

CAPPS, ANTHONY THOMAS (CAPOZZOLO), international public relations executive; b. Pueblo, Colo.; s. Nicolo and Anna (Solomone) Capozzolo; m. Theresa Cecelia Harmon, Nov. 12, 1945. Student, Los Angeles Bus. Coll., Pueblo Bus. Coll., 1929-33; pvt. studies in arts, music. Dance dir., choreographer, producer motion pictures for TV and radio; featured profl. dance team Biltmore Bowl, Cocoanut Grove, Los Angeles, St. Catherine Hotel, Catalina, Calif., 1939-42; dance dir., producer NBC, ABC, Sta. KCOP-TV, Columbia Pictures, 20th Century Fox, Calif. Studios, 1940-60; exec. dir. activities Lockheed and Vega Aircraft Co., various locations, 1942-44; internat. pub. relations dir. Howard Manor, Palm Springs Key Club, 1960—, Country Club Hotel, Palm Springs Ranch Club, 1970-71, Kedes Radio, Cameron Ctr., 1971-73, Cameron Enterprises, Murietta Hot Springs

Hotel, Health and Beauty Spa, 1972-73; numeruos TV interviews on religion and politics, history of ballet and opera of last 500 yrs.; founder, pres., dir. Tony Capps Enterprises, Inc., Palm Springs, Calif., 1959—, chmn., exec. dir. golf and tennis tournaments, benefit dinners, govt. ofcls., various fund-raising events; mem. research council Scripps Clinic and Research Found. Columnist Desert Sun Newspapers, 1959—. Founder, co-chmn. Nat. Football Found. and Hall of Fame Golf Classic, Palm Springs; founder, pres. Capps-Cappazzolo Art Gallery, City of Hope, Duarte, Calif.; exec. dir. Alan Cranston for Senator Dinner, 1963, Edmund G. (Pat) Brown Testimonial Dinner, 1964, Progressive Jet Set Party-Nat.Cystic Fibrosis Research Found. fund raising, 1968, United Fund Gala Premier Ball, 1971; mem. Assistance League Palm Springs Desert Area, Desert Hosp., Palm Springs Desert Mus., Desert Art Ctr. of Coachella Valley, Mary and Joseph League, Eisenhower Med. Ctr, Women's Aux. Internat. Found., Boys Club of Palm Springs, Children Charity of the Desert; founder, pres. City of Hope Duarte. Mem. Nat. Artists and Art Patrons Soc., Am. Film Inst., Nat. Cystic Fibrosis Found. and Hall of Fame in Calif. (founder, pres. Tri-county chpt., founder, co-chmn. golf classic at Palm Springs), Internat. Platform Assn., Nat. Hist. Soc. Gettysburg, Nat. Trust for Historic Preservation, Smithsonian Instn., Jacques Cousteau Soc., Palm Springs Pathfinders (life), Internationale Philanthropique Societe de Gourmet (founder). Clubs: Balboa Bay; Newport Beach; Century. Home: 2715 Junipero Ave Palm Springs CA 92262

CAPRON, ALEXANDER MORGAN, lawyer, educator; b. Hartford, Conn., Aug. 16, 1944; s. William Mosher and Margaret (Morgan) C.; m. Barbara A. Brown, Nov. 9, 1969 (div. Dec. 1985); 1 child, Jared Capron-Brown. B.A., Swarthmore Coll., 1966; LL.B., Yale U., 1969; M.A. (hon.), U. Pa., 1975. Bar: D.C. 1970, Pa. 1978. Law clk. to presiding justice U.S. Ct. Appeals, Washington, 1969-70; lectr., research assoc. Yale U., 1970-72; asst. prof. law U. Pa., 1972-75, vice dean, 1976, assoc. prof., 1975-78, prof. law and human genetics, 1978-82; exec. dir. Pres.'s Commn. for Study of Ethical Problems in Med., Biomed. and Behavioral Research, Washington, 1980-83; prof. law, ethics and pub. policy Law Ctr. Georgetown U., Washington, 1983-84, inst. fellow Kennedy Inst. Ethics, 1983-84; Topping prof. law, medicine and pub. policy U. So. Calif., Los Angeles, 1985—; mem. policy adv. com. Joint Commn. Accreditation of Hosps., 1984-85; cons. NIH, Office Tech. Assessment; bd. advisors Am. Bd. Internal Medicine, 1985—; trustee 20th Century Fund, 1985—; mem. working group on human gene therapy NIH, 1984-85. Author: (with Katz) Catastrophic Diseases: Who Decides What?, 1976, (with others) Genetic Counseling: Facts, Values and Norms, 1979, Law, Science and Medicine, 1984; contbr. articles to profl. jours. Bd. mgrs. Swarthmore Coll., 1982-85. Fellow Hastings Ctr. (Inst. Soc. Ethics and the Life Scis., dir.), Am. Coll. Legal Medicine (hon.); mem. Inst. of Medicine of Nat. Acad. Sci. (bd. dirs.), Soc. Am. Law Tchrs., AAUP (mem. exec. com. Pa. chpt.), Am. Soc. Law and Medicine (sec., dir.), Am. Coll. Legal Medicine (hon. fellow), Swarthmore Coll. Alumni Soc. (v.p. 1974-77). Club: Cosmos (Washington). Office: U So Calif Law Ctr of Univ Park Los Angeles CA 90089-0071

CARACENA, FERNANDO, research physicist; b. El Paso, Tex., Mar. 13, 1936; s. Fernando Caracena and Herminia (Samaniego) Alva; m. Leila Rich, May 2, 1969; children: Stephanie, Michael David. BS, U. Tex., El Paso, 1958; MA, Case Western Res. U., 1966, PhD, 1968. Physicist White Sands (N.Mex.) Missile Range, 1959-61; postdoctoral fellow Case Western Res. U., Cleve., 1968-69; asst. prof. physics Met. State Coll., Denver, 1969-74; advanced studies fellow Nat. Ctr. Atmospheric Research, Boulder, Colo., 1974; physicist NOAA, Boulder, 1975—. Contbr. numerous articles to profl. jours. Served with U.S. Army, 1959-61. Recipient Disting. Authorship award Nat. Oceanic and Atmospheric Admnstrn., Boulder, 1978, Adminstr.'s award, Washington, 1984. Mem. Am. Phys. Soc., Sigma Xi. Avocations: landscape painting, home computers, gardening, fly fishing. Home: 4412 Pali Way Boulder CO 80301 Office: Nat Oceanic and Atmospheric Adminstrn ERL R-E22 325 Broadway Boulder CO 80303

CARAS, ALAN MEYER, personnel consultant; b. Lawrence, Mass., Apr. 18, 1939; s. Mitchell Ralph and Gertrude (Zuckerman) C.; B.S. in Bus. Adminstrn., Suffolk U., Boston, 1961; m. Selma Sattin, Apr. 12, 1964; children—Daani-Ruth, Samuel, Benjamin. Mgmt. trainee Merrimack Valley Nat. Bank, Andover, Mass., 1962; budget mgr. J.M. Fields, Inc., Boston, 1962-65; acctg. mgr. Zayre Corp., Framingham, Mass., 1965-66; budget mgr. Rust Craft Greeting Cards, Dedham, Mass., 1966-67; controller Caceres Johnson Corp., Hato Rey, P.R., 1967-68; div. controller Computing & Software, Inc., Los Angeles, 1968-70; ind. cons. mktg. search, 1970-71; acctg. mgr. Jewish Fedn. Council Los Angeles, 1971-73; owner, operator Corp. Dimensions, Inc., Los Angeles, 1973-87; pres. Integrations, Redondo Beach, Calif., 1987—; bd. dirs. Colan Corp.; speaker in field. Served with U.S. Army, 1961-62. Office: Integrations 113 W Torrance Blvd Redondo Beach CA 90277-3633

CARDELLA, KENNETH CHARLES, real estate executive; b. Los Angeles, Jan. 3, 1932; s. Ben and Lucy (Colletta) C.; B.S. in Indsl. Mgmt., U. Ariz., 1955; m. Sharon Townsdin, Aug. 24, 1963; children—Kynn, Kenneth Charles, Marisa. Mgmt. trainee Union Oil Calif., 1955; pilot Am. Airlines, N.Y.C., 1959-60; mgr. Bankers Life Iowa, Tucson, 1964-67; mem. Ariz. Senate, 1967-71; founder, pres., chief exec. officer Cochise Airlines, Inc., Tucson, 1971-82; with Coldwell Banker, 1984—. Served with USAF, 1955-59. Recipient Disting. Citizen award Alumni Assn. U. Ariz., 1978. Office: Coldwell Banker 3901 E Broadway Tucson AZ 85711

CARDELLINA, JOHN HENRY, II, chemistry educator; b. Washington, Oct. 18, 1947; s. John H. and Gertrude P. (Grote) C. BA in Russian, BS in Chemistry, Pa. State U., 1968; PhD, U. Hawaii, 1979. Analytical chemist McNeil Labs., Ft. Washington, Pa., 1973-74; from asst. prof. to assoc. prof. chemistry Mont. State U., Bozeman, 1980—. Served to lt. USN, 1968-72. Mem. Am. Chem. Soc., Am. Soc. Pharmacognosy, Mont. Acad. Sci. Office: Mont State U Dept Chemistry Bozeman MT 59717

CARDEN, ROBERT CLINTON, III, electrical engineer; b. Phila., Mar. 26, 1933; s. Robert Clinton and Mary Alice (Blanton) C.; B.E.E., Ga. Inst. Tech., 1955, M.S. in Elec. Engring., Ga. Inst. Tech., 1959; postgrad. UCLA, 1961-74, U. Calif.-Irvine, 1980-81; m. Mary Eleanore Clapp, Aug. 15, 1959; children—Robert Clinton IV, Linda Warren. Project engr. Bendix Radio div. Bendix Aviation, Towson, Md., 1950-57; mem. tech. staff Space Tech. Labs. TRW, 1959-62, El Segundo, Calif.; mem. tech. staff Marshall Labs., Torrance, Calif., 1962-68; founder, dir. Time Zero Corp., Torrance, 1968-71; founder, dir., mgr. engring. Comtec Data Systems div. Am. Micro Systems, Cupertino, Calif., 1971-75; engring. mgr., prin. engr. Ball Corp., Gardena, Calif., 1975-80, staff cons. Ball Corp., Huntington Beach, Calif., 1980-83; sr. staff engr. TRW Inc., Redondo Beach, Calif., 1983—; cons. engr. digital systems, 1980—; instr. in field. Served with AUS, 1957. Mem. Am. Rocket Soc., IEEE, Computer Soc., Ga. Tech. Alumni Assn., Tau Beta Pi, Eta Kappa Nu, Scabbard and Blade, Chi Phi. Republican. Presbyterian. Research in digital space systems. Author, producer: Space for the Everday Man, 1978; contbr. articles to profl. jours. Home: 1217 N Kennymead St Orange CA 92669 Office: TRW Inc 1 Space Park 105/2810 Redondo Beach CA 90278

CÁRDENAS, RENÉ, television executive, demographer; b. San Francisco, Feb. 13, 1928; s. Lauro and Maria (Ball) C.; m. Doris F. Marino, June 7, 1952; children—Rene, Kevin, Gregory. Ph.D. in Cultural Anthropology, U. Calif.-Berkeley, 1970. Producer, writer Villa Alegre, Oakland, Calif., 1970-81; mgr. Kingston Trio, 1959-69; with Stanford Research, Inc., 1956, Ampex Corp., San Juan, P.R., 1957-59; pres. BCTV, San Leandro, Calif., 1969—; adj. prof. sch. edn. U. Mass., Amherst, 1986—; cons. U.S. Office Edn., 1971-72, Office Mgmt. and Budget, 1972-73, White House, 1974-75, also fed. govt. agys. Served with USNR, 1941-48. Grantee Exxon USA Found., 1973-76, Ford Found., 1972, Lilly Endowment Found., 1975-76, HUD, 1978, Dept. Labor, 1972-73, Levi Strauss Corp., 1975; named Hon. Col. N.Mex.; Hon. Citizen Okla.; recipient Tex. Silver Spur award, 1975; NEA Humanitarian award, 1974; recognition Calif. State Legislature for outstanding ednl. achievement in broadcasting; 4 Emmys, 1977, 79, 80, 81. Mem. Nat. Acad. TV Arts and Scis. Democrat. Club: Oakland Athletic. Author: Parenting in a Multi Cultural Society, 1980; contbr. numerous articles on edn. of culturally disadvantaged child to profl. jours. Home: 4265 Bemis St Oakland CA 94605 Office: BCTV 155 Callan Ave San Leandro CA 94605

CARDIEL, JAVIER MARTINEZ, controller; b. Ciudad Juarez, Chihuahua, Mexico, Aug. 21, 1954; came to U.S., 1962; s. Francisco Martinez and Maria Del Refugio Cardiel; m. Rosa Martinez, June 26, 1982; 1 child, Marcco. BBA in Acctg., Idaho State U., 1978. CPA, Idaho. Social service worker Idaho Migrant Council, Burley, 1976-77, mem. health aid com., 1977-78; auditor Boise (Idaho) Cascade Corp., 1978-80, sr. fin. auditor, 1980-81, sr. electronic data processing auditor, 1981-83, plant controller, 1983—; cons. electronic data processing, Boise Cascade Corp., 1981-83, fin. cons., 1978-81. Officer Mex.-Am. Student Orgn., Pocatello, Idaho, 1974-78; mem. Idaho Migrant Council, Burley, 1976-78. Recipient Pres.'s Outstanding award Idaho State U, Pocatello, 1975; Nat. Hispanic Orgn. Calif. scholar, 1977, Crawford Moore scholar, 1977, Presdl. Grant scholar, 1974-76. Mem. Idaho Soc. CPA's, Beta Gamma Sigma. Democrat. Lodge: Elks. Avocations: sports, photography, stamp collecting, personal computers. Office: Boise Cascade Corp 1544 W 27th St Burley CA 83318

CARDIFF, ROBERT DARRELL, pathology educator; b. San Francisco, Dec. 5, 1935; s. George Darrell and Helen (Kohfield) C.; m. Sally Joan Bounds, June 23, 1962; children: Darrell, Todd, Shelley. BS, U. Calif., Berkeley, 1958, PhD, 1968; MD, U. Calif., San Francisco, 1962. Intern King's County Hosp., Bklyn., 1962-63; resident in pathology U. Oreg., Portland, 1963-66; NIH fellow U. Calif., Berkeley, 1966-68; mem. faculty U. Calif. Med. Sch., Davis, 1971—, prof. pathology, 1977—; mem. sci. adv. bd. John Muir Cancer Inst., Walnut Creek, Calif., 1985—; mem. Univ-Wide AIDS task force, Berkeley, 1984—; vis. prof. People's Republic of China, Zhongshan Med. Coll., 1985. Contbr. articles to profl. jours. Served to lt. col. U.S. Army, 1968-71. Recipient Triton Research award Triton Bioscis., Inc., 1985, Kaiser Found. Teaching award U. Calif. Med. Sch., Davis, 1985, Disting. Teaching award U. Calif., Davis, 1985, Sadusk award Peralta Cancer Inst., 1986. Mem. AAUP (exec. com. 1983-85), Pluto Soc., Internat. Acad. Pathology, Internat. Assn. Breast Cancer (bd. dirs. 1984—), Sacramento Pathology Soc. (bd. dirs. 1985—), Sigma Xi. Avocations: basketball, skiing, jogging. Office: U Calif Med Sch Dept Pathology MSIA Davis CA 95616

CARDINE, GODFREY JOSEPH, state supreme court justice; b. Prairie Du Chien, Wis., July 6, 1924; s. Joseph Frederick and Mary (Kasparek) C.; m. Janice Irene Brown, Sept. 14, 1946; children—Susan, John, Lisa. B.S. in Engring., U. Ill., 1948; J.D. with honors, U. Wyo., 1954. Bar: Wyo. 1954, U.S. Dist. Ct. Wyo. 1954, U.S. Ct. Appeals (10th cir.) 1954. Assoc. Schwartz, Bon & McCrary, Casper, Wyo., 1954-66; dist. atty. Natrona County, Wyo., 1966-70; ptnr. Cardine, Vlastos & Reeves, Casper, 1966-77; prof. law U. Wyo., Laramie, 1977-83; justice Wyo. Supreme Ct., Cheyenne, 1983—; mem. Wyo. State Bd. Law Examiners, 1973-77; faculty, dir. Western Trial Advocacy Inst., Laramie, 1981—; bd. advisors Land and Water Law Rev., 1985—. Contbr. articles to profl. jours. Active Little League Baseball, Casper, 1960-62; mem. Gov.'s Com. on Dangerous Drugs, 1968-69. Served to 1st lt. USAF, 1943-46, PTO. Fellow Internat. Soc. Barristers; mem. Assn. Trial Lawyers Am., Wyo. State Bar (pres. 1977-78), Chi Epsilon, Phi Alpha Delta. Club: Potter Law (pres. 1953-54). Lodge: Rotary. Home: PO Box 223 Cheyenne WY 82003 Office: Wyo Supreme Ct Supreme Ct Bldg Cheyenne WY 82002

CARDNO, DONALD BARRY, personnel director; b. Winnipeg, Manitoba, Can., Jan. 5, 1936; s. Frederick Noble and Pearl Lillian (Bloxham) C.; m. Sallie Ann Waterman, Feb. 12, 1955; children: Scott G., Ross A. BA, Calif. State U., San Francisco, 1959, Calif. State U., Sacramento, 1964. Personnel analyst State of Calif., Sacramento, 1959-64; employee relations mgr. Calif. State Employees Assn., Sacramento, 1964-74; dir. personnel Oakland (Calif.) Housing Authority, 1977-80; dir. personnel and labor relations City of Vallejo (Calif.), 1980—. Served with USMC, 1959. Mem. Internat. Personnel Mgmt. Assn., N. Calif. Mcpl. Personnel Mgrs. Group. Democrat. Lodge: Rotary. Avocation: sailing. Home: 311 Bluebell Pl Vallejo CA 94591 Office: City of Vallejo City Hall Vallejo CA 94590

CARETTO, LAURENCE STEPHEN, engineering educator; b. Los Angeles, Oct. 5, 1939; s. Bert and Katherine (Gaudino) C. B.S. in Engring, UCLA, 1960, M.S., 1963, Ph.D., 1965. Technologist Shell Chem. Co., 1960-61; asst. prof. U. Calif., Berkeley, 1965-70; sr. vis. fellow Imperial Coll. Sci. and Tech., London, 1970; mem. faculty Calif. State U., Northridge, 1971—; prof. engring. Calif. State U., 1974—, chmn. dept. mech. and chem. engring., 1974-79; mem. Calif. Air Resource Bd., 1978-83; cons. air pollution, combustion and energy. Author articles in field. Mem. Air Pollution Control Assn., Soc. Automotive Engrs., AAAS, Combustion Inst. Office: Dept Mech and Chem Engring Calif State U Northridge CA 91330

CAREY, ANDREW GALBRAITH, JR., research biological oceanographer; b. Balt., Apr. 11, 1932; s. Andrew Galbraith Carey and Lorna (Underwood) Sagendorph; m. Elizabeth Menges, Aug. 24, 1957; children: Todd L., Arianne V.K. AB, Princeton U., 1955; PhD, Yale U., 1962. From asst. prof. Oreg. State U., Corvallis, 1961-82, prof. biol. oceangraphy, 1982—; vis. prof. Japan Soc. Promotion Sci., Tokyo, 1977. Contbr. articles to profl. jours. Recipient Lindbergh Fund award, 1984; George C. Marshall Meml. fellow U. Copenhagen, 1970. Mem. Am. Soc. Limnology and Oceanography (v.p., pres. Western div. 1976-78), Ecol. Soc. Am., Marine Biol. Assn. U.K., Sigma Xi. Democrat. Home: 3225 NW Deer Run Corvallis OR 97330 Office: Oreg State U Coll Oceanography Corvallis OR 97331

CAREY, AUDREY LANE, interior designer, educator; b. Spokane, Wash., Sept. 26, 1936; d. Glen Howard and Beatrice M. (Olsen) L.; m. Willard Keith Carey, July 4, 1959; children—Natalie Kay, Robert Lane, Willard Arthur. B.S. with honors in Home Econs., Wash. State U., 1958; postgrad. U. Wash., 1958, Eastern Oreg. State Coll., 1960—. High sch. home econs. tchr. Coulee City, Wash., 1958, Reardan, Wash., 1958-59; substitute tchr. LaGrande pub. schs. (Oreg.), 1960-65; nutrition instr. Eastern Oreg. State Coll., 1968-71; owner, mgr. Audrey Lane Carey Studio of Interior Design, LaGrande, 1973—; speaker in field. Active local Episcopal Ch., 1960—; youth activities dir. City of LaGrande, 1959-60; v.p., bd. dirs. Grande Ronde Symphony, 1960-64; den mother Blue Mountain council Boy Scouts Am., 1970; leader 4-H Clubs, 1971-73; pres. DeMolay Mothers Club, 1983; advisor EOSC Canterbury Club, 1961-65; campaign chmn. Union County, Sec. State, 1976, 80; pres. Union County Rep. Women, 1968; advisor Rainbow Girls, 1974-78; sponsor S.E. Asian Family, 1980—; mem. Gov.'s Higher Edn. Mission, 1985; Eastern Oreg. chmn. Employer Support of Guard and Res. Family Readiness Program, 1985; mem. bd. trustees Oreg. State Library. Viola Coulter scholar, 1957. Mem. Am. Soc. Interior Designers, Eastern Oreg. Regional Arts Council, Wash. State U. Alumni Assn., Wash. State U. Home Econs. Assn., N.G. Assn. U.S. (rep. task force western states), Kappa Alpha Theta (rush bd. chmn. 1960-84), Phi Kappa Phi, Pi Lambda Theta, Omicron Nu. Republican. Episcopalian. Club: PEO (past pres., charter mem. 1962—) (La Grande).

CAREY, CYNTHIA, physiology educator; b. Denver, July 17, 1947; d. Raymond Giddens and Faye Vivian (Kingsbury) C. AB, Occidental Coll., 1969, MA, 1970; PhD, U. Mich., 1976. Teaching fellow U. Mich., Ann Arbor, 1970-74, research asst., 1974-76; asst. prof. physiology U. Colo., Boulder, 1976-82, assoc. prof., 1982—; cons. NASA, Washington, 1984, NSF, Washington, 1983-86; bd. dirs. Rocky Mountain Biology Lab., Crested Butte, Colo., 1979—. Contbr. articles to profl. jours. Fellow AAAS; mem. Am. Ornithologists Union, Am. Soc. Zoologists, Am. Soc. Ichthyologists and Herpetologists, Am. Physiol. Soc., Cooper Ornithol. Soc. (bd. dirs.). Avocations: mountain climbing, bike touring. Home: 3335 Chisholm Trail #301 Boulder CO 80309 Office: U Colo Dept EPO Biology Boulder CO 80309

CAREY, GERT, manufacturing company executive; b. Leith, N.D., Nov. 18, 1931; d. Daniel and Matilda (Brodehl) Beirwagen; divorced; children: Daniel, Barbara, Pam, Cathy. Computer operator Pipco Inc., Portland, Oreg., 1968-73; instr. Portland Community Coll., 1968-72; computer cons. Computer Knowledge Corp., Wenatchee, Wash., 1973-75; mgr. computer ops. Gilmore Steel Corp., Portland, 1975—; advisor Occupational Skills Ctr., Milwaukie, Oreg., 1968—. Mem. Computer Ops. Mgrs. Assn. (pres. 1983-84). Democrat. Lutheran. Lodge: Grange. Avocation: pvt. pilot. Office: Gilmore Steel Corp 14400 N Rivergate Blvd Portland OR 97203

CAREY, KATHRYN ANN, corporate philanthropy, advertising and public relations executive, editor, consultant; b. Los Angeles, Oct. 18, 1949; d. Frank Randall and Evelyn Mae (Walmsley) C.; m. Richard Kenneth Sundt, Dec. 28, 1980. B.A. in Am. Studies with honors, Calif. State U.-Los Angeles, 1971. Tutor Calif. Dept. Vocat. Rehab., Los Angeles, 1970; teaching asst. U. So. Calif., 1974-75, UCLA, 1974-75; claims adjuster Auto Club So. Calif., San Gabriel, 1971-73; corp. pub. relations cons. Carnation Co., Los Angeles, 1973-78; cons., adminstr. Carnation Community Service Award Program, 1973-78; pub. relations cons. Vivitar Corp.; sr. advt. asst. Am. Honda Motor Co., Gardena, Calif., 1978-84; exec. dir. Am. Honda Found., 1984—; mgr. Honda Dealer Advt. Assns.; cons. advt., pub. relations, promotions. Editor: Vivitar Voice, Santa Monica, Calif., 1978, Honda Views, 1978-84, Found. Focus, 1984—; asst. editor Friskies Research Digest; contbg. editor Momentum, Am. Honda Motor Co., Inc. employees mag.; Calif. Life Scholarship Found. scholar, 1967. Mem. Advt. Club Los Angeles, Pub. Relations Soc. Am., So. Calif. Assn. Philanthropy, Council Founds. of Washington, Los Angeles Soc. for Prevention Cruelty to Animals, Green Peace, German Shepherd Dog Club Am., Ocicats Internat., Am. Humane Assn., Elsa Wild Animal Appeal. Democrat. Methodist. Office: PO Box 2205 Torrance CA 90509-2205

CAREY, MARCIA J., medical transcription service executive; b. Willmar, Minn., Feb. 13, 1941; d. Franklin N. and Thelma L (Portinga) F.; m. Donald L. Carey, June 23, 1962 (div. May 1976); children: Michelle C., Matthew S. Student, Trinity Coll., 1959-61, Calif. State U., Chico., 1961-62. Cert. med. transcriptionist; accredited record technician. Med. transcriptionist Hillcrest Hosp., Petaluma, Calif., 1972-73; med. care evaluation coordinator Santa Teresa Community Hosp., San Jose, Calif., 1973-79; med. transcriptionist San Jose, 1979-84; dir. pub. relations Dictation West, South San Francisco, Calif., 1984-85, dir. ops., 1985—. Mem. Am. Assn. Med. Transcription, (treas. 1981, v.p. 1982, bd. dirs. 1979-82, pres. South Bay chpt. 1979-81, 85-86), Am. Med. Record Assn. Avocations: music, needlework. Home: 6283 Channel Dr San Jose CA 95123 Office: Dictation West 1177 Mission Rd South San Francisco CA 94080

CAREY, PETER KEVIN, reporter; b. San Francisco, Apr. 2, 1940; s. Paul Twohig and Stanleigh M. (White) C.; m. Joanne Dayl Barker, Jan. 7, 1978; children: Brendan Patrick, Nadia Marguerite. BS in Econs., U. Calif., Berkeley, 1964. Reporter San Francisco Examiner, 1964; reporter Livermore (Calif.) Ind., 1965-67, editor, 1967; aerospace writer, spl. projects and investigative reporter San Jose (Calif.) Mercury, 1967—. Recipient Pulitzer Prize for Internat. Reporting, Columbia U., 1986, George Polk award L.I. U., 1986, Investigative Reporters and Editors award, 1986, Jessie Meriton White Service award Friends World Coll., 1986, Calif.-Nev. UPI Editors Assn. Newspaper award, 1985, Mark Twain award Calif.-Nev. AP, 1983, Best Bus. Story award San Francisco Press Club, 1984, Best Daily News Story award San Francisco Press Club, 1982; profl. journalism fellow NEH, 1983-84. Mem. Soc. Profl. Journalists, Sigma Delta Chi. Avocation: classical piano. Office: San Jose Mercury-News 750 Ridder Park Dr San Jose CA 95190

CAREY, RICHARD GWYNN, principal; b. Jacksonville, Fla., Dec. 18, 1945; s. John Dick and Betty (Marshall) C.; m. Bonnie Lou Richardson, June 8, 1970; children—Merrilyn, Allison. B.S. in Community Services, So. Coll., 1969; M.A. in Ednl. Adminstrn., Andrews U., 1980. Cert. tchr., Kans. Tchr. Louisville Jr. Acad., 1969-70; prin. Ridgetop Sch., Nashville, 1970-72; tchr. H.J. Detwiler Sch., Washington, 1972-75; prin. Columbia Jr. Acad., S.C., 1975-79, Midland Adventist Sch., Shawnee, Kans., 1980, Redding Adventist Sch., Calif., 1980—; computer cons. Mem. Assn. Supervision and Curriculum Devel., Redding Commodore Computer Group (pres.), No. Calif. Seventh-day Adventist Educator's Computer Group (pres.). Republican. Seventh-day Adventist. Club: Kansas City Pet Users Group. Home: 4020 Cirrus Redding CA 96002 Office: Redding Adventist Sch 1356 E Cypress St Redding CA 96002

CAREY, THOMAS CARL, educational association manager, consultant; b. Port Huron, Mich., Oct. 30, 1944; s. Lewis Marshall and Iva Marie (Daines) C.; m. Susan Jean Boomgarden, June 24, 1967 (div. July 1977); 1 child, Thomas Michael; m. Patricia Francis Pescatore, Jan. 27, 1979; children: Lena Marie, Patrick Thomas. BA, Western Mich. U., 1966. Cert. profl. educator. Tchr. pub. schs. East Detroit, Mich., 1966-67, Warren, Mich., 1967-71; exec. dir. Scottsdale (Ariz.) Edn. Assn., 1971-73, Phoenix Metro. United Tchrs. Assn., 1973-79; field services staff mem. Ariz. Edn. Assn., Phoenix, 1979-85, field services mgr., 1985—; owner, cons. specialist, Play and Learn Schs. Inc., Scottsdale, 1985—. Contbr. edn. articles to profl. jours. Mem. governing bd. dirs. Scottsdale Pub. Schs., 1976-80; candidate Scottsdale City Council, 1982; legis. com. mem. Scottsdale C. of C., 1983; pres. Phoenix com. UNICEF, 1977-78. Recipient Cert. Merit, Houston Tchrs. Assn., 1973, Disting. Service award, Scottsdale Sch. Dist. #48, 1980. Mem. NEA. Republican. Avocations: furniture refinishing and upholstering, golf, Western saddle riding, home improvement. Office: Ariz Edn Assn 2102 W Indian School Rd Phoenix AZ 85015

CAREY, THOMAS PATRICK, data processing executive; b. Geneva, Ill., Feb. 7, 1954; s. William Frederick and Mary Jane (Tatara) C.; divorced; children: Pamela Anne, Julie Marie. Student, Coll. San Mateo, 1971-73. Mgr. applications Data Node, Inc., Sunnyvale, Calif., 1980-82; dir. data processing Health Services, Santa Clara, Calif., 1982-84, ReadiCare, Inc., Sunnyvale, Calif., 1984-85; v.p. ReadiCare, Inc., Sunnyvale, 1985—. Served as sgt. U.S. Army, 1973-77. Mem. Digital Equipment Users Soc. Republican. Office: ReadiCare Inc 446 Oakmead Pkwy Sunnyvale CA 94086

CAREY, VAN PATRICK, mechanical engineering educator; b. Syracuse, N.Y., May 18, 1952; s. Lee Francis and Marylyn Jane (Palgrave) C.; m. Judith Anne Reichert, July 12, 1975; children: Elizabeth Megan, Sean Wesley. BS, Cornell U., 1974; MS, SUNY, Buffalo, 1976, PhD, 1981. Project engr. Gen. Motors Corp., Lockport, N.Y., 1976-78, sr. project engr., 1980-82; asst. prof. mech. engring. U. Calif., Berkeley, 1982-85, assoc. prof., 1985—; cons. Gen. Motors, Lockport, N.Y., 1985—, Westinghouse Corp., Sunnyvale, Calif., 1985—; mem. assoc. faculty Lawrence Berkeley (Calif.) Lab., 1984—. Contbr. articles to profl. jours.; patentee in field. Recipient Excellence in Teaching award Pi Tau Sigma , 1985, Pres. Young Investigator award NSF, 1985; research grantee U. Calif., 1982-83, NSF, 1983-85, 1985-86, Lawrence Berkeley Lab., 1984-85, Solar Energy Research Inst., 1984-85, IBM, 1984-85, Gen. Motors Corp., 1985-86, S. Levy, Inc., 1985-86. Mem. ASME, Soc. Automotive Engrs. (Teetor award 1984), AAAS, ASHRAE, AIAA. Avocations: tennis, jogging, photography. Office: U Calif Dept Mech Engring 6169 Etcheverry Hall Berkeley CA 94720

CAREY, WILLIAM LAWRENCE, coast guard officer; b. Boston, Dec. 31, 1950; s. William Alfred and Ina Lucretia (Bean) C.; m. Elizabeth Ann Zirbes, Sept. 17, 1983; 1 child, Moira Kathleen. BA, Holy Cross Coll., 1973; postgrad., Am. U.; MA, Wash. State U., 1976; postgrad., U. Alaska, Juneau. Commd. ensign USCG, Washington, 1977; advanced through grades to lt. USCG; staff officer USCG, Washington, 1977-81; asst. chief port ops. dept. USCG, Portland, Oreg., 1981-82, chief investigations dept., 1982-83, chief small passenger vessel br., 1983-85; asst. chief marine environ. protection br. USCG, Juneau, 1985—. Mem. U.S. Naval Inst. Democrat. Roman Catholic. Avocations: skiing, sailing, hiking. Office: Comdr 17th Coast Guard Dist PO Box 3-5000 Juneau AK 99801

CARGILL, MARTHA, publishing co. ofcl.; b. Munich, W. Ger., Jan. 2, 1954 (parents Am. citizens); d. Everett Leslie and Elizabeth Cecelia (Vercuski) C.; m. David Hal Schwartz, 1981. B.S. in Anthropology, Ariz. State U., 1978. Proofencoder, Valley Nat. Bank Mesa (Ariz.) Ops. Ctr., 1972-74; reconciler Continental Bank Ops. Ctr., Phoenix, 1974-75; records clk. Admissions Office, Ariz. State U., Tempe, 1977-79; editorial asst. Jaques Cattell Press, Tempe, Ariz., 1980, asst. editor, 1981, editor Biog. div., 1981-84; asst. mgr. Mitchell Sweet & Assocs., 1985; prodn. control coordinator Xerox Reprodn. Ctr., 1985-86; supr. micrographics dept. Prudential Life Ins., Scottsdale, Ariz., 1986—. Active Scottsdale Ctr. for Arts Assn. Mem. Jersey Wildlife Assn., Ariz. Humane Soc. Republican. Home: 2101 E Fairview Ave Mesa AZ 85204

CARLAND, JAMES FRANK, III, pediatrician; b. St. Louis, Mar. 24, 1941; s. James Frank and Winifred (Miller) C.; B.A. cum laude in Psychology, U. Colo., 1963, M.D. cum laude 1967; m. Jane Hopp, Sept. 23, 1978; children—Patrick N., Liesl R., Jill M., Julie M. Lic. instrument-rated comml. pilot. Intern in pediatrics, U. Colo Sch. Medicine, Colo. Gen. Hosp., 1967-68; resident in pediatrics, U. Wash., Children's Orthopedic Hosp., Seattle, 1968-69, chief resident, 1969-70; fellow in pediatric respiratory disease, 1969-70; pediatrician, Mesa Pediatrics Profl. Assn., Mesa, Ariz., 1970-72; practice medicine specializing in pediatrics, Mesa and Tempe, Ariz., 1972—; chmn. pediatrics Southside Dist. Hosp., 1972-73; chmn. pediatrics Mesa Luth. Hosp., 1974-75, sec. med. staff, 1976; chmn. pediatrics Desert Samaritan Hosp., 1978-81, chmn. pediatric critical care, 1979-81, pres.-elect med. staff, 1984-85; chmn. pharmacy and therapeutics Phoenix Children's Hosp., 1984-85; mem. long-range planning com. Samaritan Health Service, 1984-85, also mem. program and planning com. on bd. trustees; pres. and chief of staff Desert Samaritan Hosp., 1985-86, active various other hosp. coms.; chmn., founding bd. dirs. The Samaritan Group, Inc., 1985, Desert Physician Assn., 1985, Health Care Alternatives, Inc., 1985—, also pres.; founder Delta Health Systems, Inc.; mem. adv. bd. and animal care and use com. The Primate Foundn., Mesa; cons. in field. Pres., Yesterday's Wings, Ltd., Mesa, 1976-80; cert. provider and instr. advanced cardiac life support Am. Heart Assn., 1984; mem. profl. adv. com. Ariz. chpt. March of Dimes. Served with USNR, 1967-73. Recipient A. Gordon Meml. award, 1965; F.E. Gengenbach award, 1966; W.A. Robb award, 1967; Gottesfield Meml. Prize, 1965, 67 (all from U. Colo. Sch. Medicine), U.S. Pub. Health Service grantee. Mem. Am. Acad. Pediatrics (sec. Ariz. chpt.), Maricopa County (exec. com.), Ariz. pediatric socs., AMA, Maricopa County, Ariz. med. socs., Flying Physician's Assn., Alpha Omega Alpha, Waring Soc., Desert Physician Assn. (pres., chmn. founding bd. dirs.). Contbr. articles in field to profl. jours. Patentee in field. Home: 2434 S Catarina St Mesa AZ 85202

CARLE, HARRY LLOYD, social worker, career devel. specialist; b. Chgo., Oct. 26, 1927; s. Lloyd Benjamin and Clara Bell (Lee) C.; B.S.S., Seattle U., 1952; M.S.W., U. Wash., 1966; m. Elva Diana Ulrich, Dec. 29, 1951; children—Joseph Francis, Catherine Marie; m. 2d, Karlen Elizabeth Howe, Oct. 14, 1967; children—Kristen Elizabeth and Sylvia Ann (twins), Eric Lloyd. Indsl. placement and employer relations rep. State of Wash., Seattle, 1955-57, parole and probation officer, Seattle and Tacoma, 1957-61, parole employment specialist, 1961-63, vocat. rehab. officer, 1963-64; clin. social worker Western State Hosp., Ft. Steilacoom, Washington and U.S. Penitentiary, McNeil Island, Wash., 1964-66; exec. dir. Community Action Council/Social Planning Council, Everett, Wash., 1966-77; career devel. counselor, 1962—; employment and edn. counselor Pierce County Jail Social Services, Tacoma, 1979-81; dir. employment devel. clinic North Rehab. Facility, King County Div. Alcoholism and Substance Abuse, Seattle, 1981—; community orgn./agy. problems mgmt. cons., 1968—; mem. social service project staff Pacific Luth. U., Tacoma, 1979-81. Cons. to pres. Geneal. Inst., Salt Lake City, 1974-78. Served with USN, 1944-46. U.S. Office Vocat. Rehab. scholar, 1965-66. Mem. Seattle Geneal. Soc. (pres. 1974-76), Soc. Advancement Mgmt. (chpt. exec. v.p. 1970-71), Acad. Cert. Social Workers, Nat. Assn. Social Workers, Pa. German Soc., Henckel Family Nat. Assn., various hist. and geneal. socs. in Cumberland, Perry and Lancaster counties, Pa., Peoria and Fulton Counties, Ill., Seattle. Roman Catholic. Home: 1425 10th Pl N Edmonds WA 98020-2629 Office: North Rehab Facility 2002 NE 150th St Seattle WA 98155-7399

CARLEONE, JOSEPH, administrative mechanical engineer; b. Phila., Jan. 30, 1946; s. Frank Anthony and Amelia (Ciaccia) C.; m. Shirley Elizabeth Atwell, June 29, 1968; children—Gia Maria, Joan Marie. B.S., Drexel U., 1968, M.S., 1970, Ph.D., 1972. Civilian engring. trainee, mech. engr. Phila. Naval Shipyard, 1963-68; grad. asst. in applied mechanics Drexel U., Phila., 1968-72, postdoctoral research assoc., 1972-73, NDEA fellow, 1968-71, adj. prof. mechanics, 1974-75, 77-82; chief research engr. Dyna East Corp., Phila., 1973-82; chief scientist warhead tech. Aerojet Ordnance Co., Tustin, Calif., 1982—. Mem. ASME, Sigma Xi, Tau Beta Pi, Pi Tau Sigma, Phi Kappa Phi. Contbr. articles to profl. jours.; researcher explosive and metal interaction, ballistics, projectile penetration, impact of plates. Home: 19741 Marsala Dr Yorba Linda CA 92686 Office: Aerojet Ordnance Co 2521 Michelle Dr Tustin CA 92680

CARLEY, JAMES FRENCH, chemical and plastics engineer; b. N.Y.C., July 16, 1923; s. Benjamin Lambert and Helen Jeanne (French) C.; m. E. Lucille Heitz, June 6, 1947 (div. Apr. 1955); children: James French, Ben Lewis; m. Marilyn Jo Mullens, July 29, 1955 (div. Apr. 1976); 1 dau., Katherine Jeanne; m. Nancy Kay Paquette, Nov. 7, 1981 (div. June 1987). B.S. in Chem. Engring., Cornell U., 1944, B.Ch.E. (now M.Ch.E.), 1947, Ph.D., 1951. Research chem. engr. DuPont Co., Wilmington, Del., 1950-55; engring. editor Modern Plastics, N.Y.C., 1955-59; asso. prof. chem. engring. U. Ariz., Tucson, 1959-62; tech. dir. Prodex Corp., Fords, N.J., 1962-64; devel. asso. Celanese Plastics Co., Clark, N.J., 1964; prof. chem. engring. and engring. design and econ. evaluation U. Colo. at Boulder, 1964-76; research engr. oil shale project Lawrence Livermore Nat. Lab. (Calif.), 1976-83, research engr. composites and polymers tech., 1983—; Instr. Cornell U., Ithaca, N.Y., 1949-50; lectr. U. Del. extension at Wilmington, 1952-54. Contbr. articles to profl. jours., books; tech. editor Modern Plastics mag., 1982—. Served to ensign USNR, 1943-46. Fellow Soc. Plastics Engrs. (pres. Rocky Mt. chpt. 1968-69); mem. Am. Inst. Chem. Engrs., Sigma Xi, Tau Beta Pi. Home: 579 Ruby Rd Livermore CA 94550 Office: Chem and Materials Sci Dept Lawrence Livermore Lab PO Box 808 Livermore CA 94550

CARLEY, JOHN BLYTHE, retail grocery executive; b. Spokane, Wash., Jan. 4, 1934; s. John Lewis and Freida June (Stiles) C.; m. Joan Marie Hohenleitner, Aug. 6, 1960; children: Christopher, Kathryn, Peter, Scott. AA, Boise Jr. Coll., 1955; student, U. Wash., 1956-57, Stanford U. Exec. Program, 1973. Store dir. Albertson's Inc., Boise, Idaho, 1961-65, grocery merchandiser, 1965-70, dist. mgr., 1970-73, v.p. gen. mdse., 1973, v.p. corp. merchandising, 1973-75, v.p. retail ops., 1975-76, sr. v.p. retail ops., 1976-77, exec. v.p. retail ops., 1977-84, pres., 1984—, also dir. Active fund-raising drives United Way. Served with U.S. Army, 1957-59. Mem. Am. Mgmt. Assn., Food Mktg. Inst. Republican. Roman Catholic. Clubs: Arid (Boise), Hillcrest Country (Boise). Office: Albertsons Inc 250 Park Center Blvd Boise ID 83726 *

CARLINGTON, GARY ALLEN, accountant; b. Puyallup, Wash., Feb. 25, 1947; s. Harry Arthur and Frances Lucille (Rosin) C.; B.A., U. Puget Sound, 1969; M.S. in Taxation, Golden Gate U., 1978; m. Sara Ann Martinson, Dec. 4, 1976; children: Rachel Amber, Courtney Ann, Melanie Amanda. Acct., Knight, Vale & Gregory, C.P.A.s, Tacoma, 1969-76, Moreland, Phillips, Carlington & McCutcheon, C.P.A.s, Tacoma, 1976-78; acct., v.p., mng. dir. Phillips, Carlington & Co., C.P.A.s, Tacoma, 1978-83; owner Gary A. Carlington, C.P.A., Puyallup, Wash., 1983-84; ptnr. Carlington, Gismervig & Co., CPAs, Puyallup, 1984—. C.P.A., Wash. Mem. Am. Inst. C.P.A.s, Wash. Soc. C.P.A.s, Tacoma Estate Planning Council. Republican. Lutheran. Home: 8402 68th Ave Ct E Puyallup WA 98371 Office: 317 4th St NW Puyallup WA 98371

CARLISLE, KEVIN BRUCE, choreographer, director, producer; b. Bklyn., Dec. 24, 1935; s. Theodore Daily and Ruth (Bardell) C. Degree, Juilliard Sch. Music, N.Y.C., 1956. Choreographer Garry Moore Show, Dean Martin Show, Bell Telephone Hour; producer, dir., choreographer numerous TV series and variety spls. including Barry Manilow, Rich Little, Dionne Warwick, Michael Landon, Herb Alpert, Doris Day, Bea Arthur, Bob Hope, Bill Cosby, Sha Na Na, Mother/Daughter Pageant, 1987, John Sebastian Special, 1986, Barry Manilow in Japan, 1985; dir., choreographer live shows including Paul Anka, Shaun Cassidy, Melissa Manchester, Barry Manilow, Shields and Yarnell, Liberace, George Burns, Judy Garland, Barry Manilow Tour 1979, 86, Robert Guillaume, 1985-87, Marilyn McCoo, 1984-87, Cathy Rigby, 1985-86, Solid Gold in Vegas, 1984, 85; creator Solid Gold Dancers, 1979; pres. Kevin Carlisle and Assocs., Hollywood, Calif.; choreographer, dir. Broadway, Barry Manilow on Broadway, 1983, Harry Blackstone Jr. On Broadway, 1980, Hallelujah Baby, Happy Time, Tammy Wynette, 1984, Melissa Manchester, 1984, Marilyn McCoo, 1984, Solid Gold Las Vegas Riviera, 1984, Videos, Debbie Reynolds Exercise Video, 1983, Barry Manilow, 1983, Solid Gold Dancers 5 Day Workout, 1984, Exercise in the Flesh, 1984, Suzanne Somers Exercise Video, 1987, Joe Tremaine's Dance, 1985, 86, 87; dir., choreographer stage and TV in Can., Belgium, Germany, France, Eng., Italy, Mex., Spain, Bora Bora; dir., choreographer various comml. and indsl. shows. Recipient Emmy award for Third Barry Manilow TV Spl., 1979. Home and Office: 1647 Woods Dr Los Angeles CA 90069

CARLISLE, RODNEY TURNER, medical products executive; b. Red Bluff, Calif., Aug. 7, 1941; s. Jason Joseph and Helen (Turner) C.; m. Maureen Anne Herold, Aug. 17, 1978; children: Megan, Cary. BSEE, Tex. A&M U., 1965. Registered profl. engr., Calif. Design engr. Westinghouse Corp., Balt., 1965-68; site mgr. Gen. Environments, Springfield, Va., 1968-71; sr. engr. Puritan-Bennett, Los Angeles, 1972-78; adminstr. Advanced Tech., Bellevue, Wash., 1980-82; ops. dir. Lawrence Med., Redmond, Wash., 1982—; tech. cons., Los Angeles, 1972-79, Seattle, 1980—. Contbr. articles to profl. jours. Mem. Am. Soc. Quality Control (cert.), Broadcast Music Inc., Eta Kappa Nu. Home: 20355 170th Ave NE Woodinville WA 98072 Office: Lawrence Med Systems 14910 NE 31 Circle Redmond WA 98052

CARLSON, DALE ARVID, university dean; b. Aberdeen, Wash., Jan. 10, 1925; s. Edwin C.G. and Anna A. (Anderson) C.; m. Jean M. Stanton, Nov. 11, 1948; children—Dale Ronald, Gail L. Carlson Manahan Joan M. Carlson Lee, Gwen D. Carlson Elliott. A.A., Grays Harbor Coll., 1947; B.S. in Civil Engring, U. Wash., 1950, M.S., 1951; Ph.D., U. Wis., 1960. Registered profl. engr., Wash. Water engr. City of Aberdeen, 1951-55; asst. prof., assoc. prof., prof., chmn. dept. civil engring. U. Wash., Seattle, 1955-76; dean (Coll Engring.) U. Wash., 1976-80, dean emeritus, 1980—, dir. Valle Scandinavian Exchange Program, 1980—; chmn. dept. civil engring. Seattle U., 1983—; vis. prof. Tech. U. Denmark, Copenhagen, 1970, Royal Coll. Agr., Uppsala, Sweden, 1976, 78. Contbr. articles to profl. jours. Mem. exec. bd. Pacific N.W. Synod Luth. Ch. in Am., chmn. fin. com., 1980-84, treas., 1986—; mem. exec. bd. Nordic Heritage Mus., 1981-86; bd. dirs. Evergreen Safety Council, 1980-86. Served with AUS, 1943-45. Named Outstanding Grad. Weatherwax High Sch., Aberdeen, 1972, Outstanding Grad. Grays Harbor Coll., 1947; guest of honor Soppeldagene, Trondheim, 1978. Mem. Water Pollution Control Fedn., ASCE, Am. Water Works Assn., Am. Scandinavian Found., Swedish Water Hygiene Assn. Club: Rotary. Home: 9235 41st St NE Seattle WA 98115 Office: 335 More Hall U Wash Seattle WA 98195

CARLSON, GARY, infosystems educator, consultant; b. Los Angeles, Mar. 6, 1928; s. Alvin W. and Jennie (Mann) C.; m. Barbara Lyn West, Aug. 24, 1954; children: Reginald, Nancy, Tom, Elizabeth, Jane. AA, BA, UCLA, 1956, MA, 1958, PhD, 1962. Pres. CTI, Provo, Utah, 1979-81; v.p. computers MSC, Salt Lake City, 1981-83; pres. and cons. Internat. Computer Monitors, Provo, 1971—; prof. info. mgmt. Brigham Young U., Provo, 1985—. Contbr. articles to profl. jours. Rep. dist. chmn., Los Angeles, 1958, Provo, 1978. Served with U.S. Army, 1953-55. Mem. Assn. Computer Machinery (reviewer books and articles 1963—), AAAS (reviewer books and articles 1963—). Republican. Mormon. Avocations: computers, history, gardening. Home: 3289 Mohawk Cir Provo UT 84604 Office: Brigham Young U 590 TNRB Provo UT 84602

CARLSON, GARY LEE, public relations executive; b. Yakima, Wash., Oct. 15, 1954; s. Glenn Elmer and Helen Mary (McLean) Carlson. AA, Yakima Community Coll., 1975; BA in Communications, U. Wash., 1977. Dir. pub. affairs Sta. KCMU Radio, Seattle, 1976-77; dir. programming and promotions Sta. KAPP TV, Yakima, 1978-80; dir. promotions Sta. WBZ TV, Boston, 1980-84; producer Sta. KCBS TV, Los Angeles, 1985; dir. creative services Metromedia Producers, Los Angeles, 1985-86; dir. promotion publicity 20th Century Fox, Los Angeles, 1986—. Recipient Internat. Film and TV Festival of N.Y. award, Houston Internat. Film and TV award, producer, writer, dir., Consumer Reports, 1983. Mem. Broadcast Promotion and Mktg. Execs., Nat. Assn. TV Program Execs., Beta Theta Pi. Avocations: photography, scuba diving, history, traveling. Home: 1510 Rockglen Ave Glendale CA 91205 Office: 20th Century Fox Film Corp 10201 W Pico Century City CA 90038

CARLSON, GEORGE LEWIS, anesthesiologist; b. Aberdeen, Wash., Oct. 29, 1946; s. Darrell Kurt and Barbara Eileen (Lewis) C.; m. Kathy Dawn Snyder, Dec. 9, 1980; children: Alicia Kauna Snyder, Theodore Keoki Lewis. BA, U. Wash., 1968; MS, U. Hawaii, 1972, MD, 1977. Diplomate Am. Bd. Anesthesiology. Intern U. Ariz., Tucson, 1977-78, resident in anesthesia, 1978-80; anesthesiologist Maui Meml. Hosp., Wailuku, Hawaii, 1980—, chmn. dept. anesthesia, 1984—. Contbr. articles to profl. jours. Mem. AMA, Am. Soc. Anesthesiology, Undersea Med. Soc., South Pacific Underwater Medicine Soc., Am. Soc. Regional Anesthesia, Small Bus. Council Am., Hawaiian Malacologic Soc. Club: Lahaina (Hawaii) Yacht. Avocations: jogging, fishing, scuba diving, shell collecting. Home: 3505 Hookipa Pl Kihei HI 96753 Office: PO Box 888 Wailuku HI 96793

CARLSON, HELEN MARIE, health care administrator; b. St. Paul, Oct. 3, 1950; d. Paul Arnold and Eleanor (Jacobson) C. BA in Psychology, San Diego State U., 1976; MBA, Nat. U., 1984. Analyst U. Calif., San Diego, 1980-82; dir. outpatient services U. Calif. Med. Ctr., San Diego, 1982-85; dir. immediate care Eisenhower Med. Ctr., Rancho Mirage, Calif., 1985—. Mem. La Quinta C. of C., Assn. Western Hosps., Med. Group Mgmt. Assn. Republican. Avocation: photography. Office: Eisenhower Med Ctr 39000 Bob Hope Dr Rancho Mirage CA 92270

CARLSON, JERRY STUART, educational psychology educator; b. Seattle, May 4, 1936; s. John and Svea Alexandria (Larsson) C.; m. Johanna Ellen Berry, Aug. 20, 1960 (div. Dec. 1964); children: Mathieu, Wendy; m. Ingrid Anita Schultz, June 4, 1965; 1 child, Kirsten. BA, U. Wash., 1958; MS, U. S.D., 1963; PhD, U. Calif., Berkeley, 1966. Cert. elem. tchr., Wash. Tchr. Mercer Island (Wash.) Sch. Dist., 1959-62; asst. prof. edn. U. Calif., Riverside, 1966-70, assoc. prof. edn., 1970-76, prof. edn., 1976—; assoc. dir. research Edn. Abroad program U. Calif., Santa Barbara, 1983—; assoc. dir. Edn. Abroad program Goettingen, Fed. Republic of Germany, 1977-79. Contbr. articles to profl. jours. Recipient sr. lectureship Fulbright-Hays Found., 1970-71; Woodrow Wilson fellow, 1964-65, NSF fellow, 1965-66, Alexander von Humboldt fellow, 1974-75. Mem. Am. Ednl. Research Assn., Am. Psychol. Assn., Internat. Soc. for Ednl., Sci. and Cultural Interchange. Democrat. Lutheran. Home: 219 Nisbet Way Riverside CA 92507 Office: U Calif Sch Edn Riverside CA 92521

CARLSON, LEE EDWIN, TV station executive; b. Chgo., Mar. 7, 1937; s. Edwin Axel and Evelyn Louise (Sunder) C.; m. Helen Geri Joseph, Nov. 10, 1961 (div. Feb. 1971); 1 child, Jay; m. Annemarie Rita Shotzbarger, May 1, 1971 (div. Sept. 1981); children: Brett, Todd; m. Linda Kamalaehua Reynolds, Aug. 23, 1986. BJ, Northwestern U., 1959. Media buyer North Advt., Chgo., 1959-61; account exec. ABC TV spot sales, Chgo., N.Y.C., 1961-67; sales mgr. Sta. KYW-TV, Phila., 1968-73, Sta. KOIN-TV, Portland, Oreg., 1973-83; sta. mgr. Sta. KGMB-TV, Honolulu, 1983-85, gen. mgr., 1985—. Bd. dirs. Portland Advt. Fedn., 1977-81, Assn. for Portland Progress, 1982, Aloha United Way, Honolulu, 1985-86, Honolulu Symphony, 1985-86. Served with USAR, 1959-65. Mem. Hawaiian Assn. Broadcasters (pres. 1986-87), Hawaii Advt. Fedn. Methodist. Avocation: golf. Office: Sta KGMB-TV 1534 Kapiolani Blvd Honolulu HI 96814

CARLSON, LESLIE GAIL, clinical social worker; b. Juneau, Alaska, May 18, 1954; d. Bill Howard and Carol Jean (Karnes) C. BA in Psychology, U. Wash., 1975, MSW, 1982. Crisis line supr. Crisis Clinic, Seattle, 1982-83; staff therapist Eastside Mental Health Ctr., Bellevue, Wash., 1982-84; pvt. practice social work Bellevue, 1984—; adj. faculty Seattle Cen. Community Coll. and Antioch U., 1985; workshop leader U. Wash., 1985; leader Group Health Coop., Seattle, 1984. Bd. dirs. Eastside Domestic Violence Program, Bellevue, 1986—. Mem. Acad. Cert. Social Workers (cert.), Nat. Assn. Social Workers, Assn. Women in Social Work. Democrat. Unitarian Universalist. Lodge: Soroptimists. Avocations: cross-country skiing, foreign films, cross stitch, creative writing. Office: 700 112th NE #200 Bellevue WA 98004

CARLSON, LINDA CHRISTINE, marketing professional; b. Tacoma, Dec. 11, 1950; d. Bruce E. and Georgiana (Stedman) C.; m. James R. Beaty, June 15, 1984. BA, Wash. State U., 1973; MBA, Harvard U., 1980. Editor Davenport (Wash.) Times, 1972-75; mgr. pub. relations Am. Plywood Assn., Tacoma, 1976-78; dir. mktg. Auto-Chlor, Seattle, 1980-82; div. mgr. The Exchange, Bellevue, Wash., 1982-83; mgr. mktg. Prudential Bank, Seattle, 1983-84, U. Wash. Extension, Seattle, 1984—. Author: The Publicity and Promotion Handbook, 1981. Mem. City Planning Commn., Davenport, 1974-75. Office: U Wash Extension GH-24 Seattle WA 98195

CARLSON, MARIANNE RIRIE, speech pathologist; b. Hamilton, New Zealand, Oct. 7, 1957; s. David and Ruth Joanne (Irwin) Ririe; m. David Martin Carlson, June 18, 1982; children: Elizabeth Melissa, David Wayne. BS in Communications Disorders, Brigham Young U., 1980; MS in Speech Pathology, U. Utah, 1983. Cert. clin. competence in speech pathology. Speech language pathologist Jordan Sch. Dist., Sandy, Utah, 1983—, mem. social and inservice coms. Mem. Am. Speech and Hearing Assn., Utah Speech and Hearing Assn. Avocations: reading, sewing, running, classical music, ballet. Home: 2848 Adams Salt Lake City UT 84115

CARLSON, PAUL EDWIN, real estate developer and manager; b. San Francisco, June 29, 1944; s. Carl John and Marguerite Eutha (Kovatch) C.; m. Sharon Raye Hammond, Nov. 14, 1964; children: Kimberly, Davin, Christina. AA, Yosemite Coll., 1964; BA, Calif. State U., Long Beach, 1971; cert. shopping ctr. mgr., Internat. Council of Shopping Ctrs. Mgmt. Sch., 1981. Cert. shopping ctr. mgr. Vice and narcotics officer Modesto and Los Angeles Police Depts., Calif., 1964-69; owner Universal Prodns., N.Y.C. and Modesto, 1963-73; gen. mgr. City Investing Co., N.C.Y. and Beverly Hills, Calif., 1973-75; v.p. The Koll Co., Newport Beach, Calif., 1975-79, Irvine Co., Newport Beach, 1979-80; owner Willows Shopping Ctr., Concord, Calif., 1980-83; sr. v.p. Lee Sammis Co., Irvine, 1983-85; pres. Am. Devel. Co., Costa Mesa, Calif., 1985-86; chmn. bd. The Carlson Co., Huntington Beach, Calif., 1986—; guest lectr. U. So. Cal., U. Calif., Los Angeles, Orange Coast Coll.; real estate cons. Bank of Am., Union Bank, Chevron U.S.A., Aetna Life Ins. Co., James Lang Wooten, Eng., Peoples Republic of China. Author three screen plays for Police Story; comedy contbr. to The Tonight Show and Sat. Night Live; pub. Property Mgrs. Handbook. mem. Calif. State Juvenile Justice Commn.; past chmn. City of Newport Beach Traffic Commn.; pres. bd. trustees Mt. Diablo Hosp.; v.p., bd. dirs. City of Concord Pavillion; bd. dirs. Concord Visitors and Conv. Bur. Mem. Am. Cancer Soc. (bd. dirs. Contra Costa Co.). Republican. Avocation: youth couseling. Home: 1830 Port Barmouth Pl Newport Beach CA 92660 Office: The Carlson Co 19900 Beach Blvd Suite C Huntington Beach CA 92646

CARLSON, PHILIP JAY, aerospace engineering company executive; b. Fergus Falls, Minn., Aug. 9, 1946; s. Walter Joseph and Alice Lenora (Olson) C.; m. Nancy Darlene Cheney, Aug. 30, 1969; children: Patricia, Kathleen. BEE with honors, U. Minn., 1968; MSEE, U. Santa Clara, 1974. From engr. to sr. engr. GTE Govt. Systems, Mountain View, Calif., 1968-71; from research and devel. engr. to systems engr. to engring. specialist Ford Aerospace and Communications Corp., Palo Alto, Calif., 1971-81, program mgr., 1981—. Mem. Model A Restorers Club (bd. dirs. San Francisco Bay region 1982-83), Tau Beta Pi, Eta Kappa Nu. Republican. Baptist. Avocations: antique car restoration, personal computers. Home: 586 Smokey Ct Campbell CA 95008 Office: Ford Aerospace Communications Corp 3939 Fabian Way MS X60 Palo Alto CA 94303

CARLSON, RALPH WILLIAM, JR., food products company executive; b. Oak Park, Ill., Dec. 28, 1936; s. Ralph W. and Evelyn Marie (Benson) C.; m. Donna Drevs, Feb. 9, 1963; children—Daniel, Karen, Susan, Robert, Kathleen. B.A., Mich. State U., 1958; M.B.A., U. Chgo., 1965; J.D., De Paul U., 1976. Bar: Ill. Group product mgr. The Kendall Co., Chgo., 1966-70; dir. mktg. Ovaltine Products Co. div. Sandoz, Inc., Chgo., 1970-76; mgr. new products Arco Polymers, Inc. subs. Atlantic Richfield Co., Chgo., 1976-78; mgr. internat. fleet ops. Arco Transp. Co., Long Beach, Calif., 1978-81; mgr. mktg. planning Arco Solar Industries, Woodland Hills, Calif., 1981-85; mgr. licensee mktg. Sunkist Growers Assn., Inc., Ontario, Calif., 1986—. Mem. Oak Park Sch. Bd., 1976-78; bd. dirs. Phila. Maritime Exchange, 1978-79. Served to lt. USNR, 1958-63. Mem. ABA, Am. Mktg. Assn., Calif. Solar Energy Soc. (dir. 1983-85), U.S. Naval Inst., Delta Chi. Republican. Roman Catholic. Club: Economic (Chgo.); Newfoundland of So. Calif. (bd. dirs. 1985—). Home: 9117 Wagner River Circle Fountain Valley CA 92708 Office: Sunkist Growers Assn 720 E Sunkist St Ontario CA 91761

CARLSON, RIA MARIE, public relations executive, writer; b. Los Angeles, Apr. 8, 1961; d. Erick Gustaf and Roberta Rae (Bandelin) C.; m. James Bradley Gerdts, May 19, 1985. BA cum laude, U. So. Calif., 1983. Assoc. producer NBC, Burbank, Calif., 1982-85; account exec. Kerr & Assocs. Pub. Relations, Huntington Beach, Calif., 1985-86; pub. relations mgr. Orange County Performing Arts Ctr., Costa Mesa, Calif., 1986—; free lance writer, 1985—. Scriptwriter award ceremony Latin Bus. Assn., 1985; author, editor newsletter Am. Sch. Food Service Assn. Bus. Report, 1985-86; contbr. articles to publs; cast mem. Disneyland, Anaheim, Calif. Prodn. asst. Profiles in Pride, Black History Month, Burbank, 1985. Named one of Outstanding Young Women in Am., 1985. Mem. Nat. Assn. Female Execs., Am. Film Inst., U. So. Calif. Alumni Assn., Blackstonians Pre-Law Hon. Soc. (life), Calif. Scholarship Fedn. (sealbearer, life). Republican. Roman Catholic. Avocations: writing short stories, reading, skiing, softball, travel. Office: Orange County Performing Arts Ctr 600 Town Ctr Dr Costa Mesa CA 92626

CARLSON, RICHARD CARL, economist, consultant; b. Mpls., Apr. 1, 1942; s. Carl Edward and Clara (Finsveen) C.; m. Patricia Jane Kiichli, Jan. 4, 1964; children—Christopher Scott, Allegra Lyn. B.A., Harvard U., 1964; M.A., U. Md., 1969; postgrad. Stanford U., 1969-76. Planning analyst HEW, Washington, 1964-65; budget analyst Office Mgmt. and Budget, Washington, 1965-71; planning dir. U.S. Office Edn., Washington, 1971-73; asst. dir. Ill. Bur. of Budget, Springfield, 1973-75; sr. economist SRI Internat., Menlo Park, Calif., 1976-84; v.p. QED Research Palo Alto, Calif., 1984—; cons. in field. Author: Energy Futures, 1982; California Work Force, 1982; Choosing A Future, 1984. Guest editor: Sunset Market Almanac, 1984. Mem. Palo Alto Sch. Closure Com., Calif., 1982; trip chmn. troop 51 Stanford council Boy Scouts Am., 1983-84. Nat. Merit scholar, 1960. Mem. Nat. Economists Club, Nat. Assn. Bus. Economists (Santa Clara County chpt.), Audubon Soc. (bd. dirs. local chpt. 1970-71). Republican. Methodist. Office: QED Research 125 California Palo Alto CA 94306

CARLSON, ROBERT CODNER, industrial engineering educator; b. Granite Falls, Minn., Jan. 17, 1939; s. Robert Ledin and Ada Louis (Codner) C.; children: Brian William, Andrew Robert, Christina Louise. BSME, Cornell U., 1962; MS, Johns Hopkins U., 1963, PhD, 1976. Mem. tech. staff Bell Telephone Labs., Holmdel, N.J., 1962-70; asst. prof. Stanford U., Stanford, Calif., 1970-77, assoc. prof., 1977-82, prof. indsl. engring., 1982—; vis. prof. Dartmouth Coll., Hanover, N.H., 1978-79; vis. faculty Internat. Mgmt. Inst., Geneva, 1984; program dir., lectr., cons. various spl. programs U.S., Japan, France, 1971—. Contbr. articles to profl. jours. Recipient Maxwell Upson award in Mech. Engring. Cornell U., 1962; Bell Labs. Systems Engring. fellow, 1962-63, Bell Labs. Doctoral Support fellow, 1966-67. Mem. Ops. Research Soc. Am. (chmn. membership com. 1981-83), Inst. Mgmt. Scis., Inst. Indsl. Engrs., Am. Soc. Engring. Edn., Am. Prodn. and Inventory Control Soc. (bd. dirs. 1975-81), Internat. Material Mgmt. Soc., Tau Beta Pi, Phi Kappa Phi, Pi Tau Sigma. Club: Soc. of Enophiles (Woodside, Calif.). Avocations: wine tasting, travelling. Office: Stanford U Dept Indsl Engring & Engring Mgmt Stanford CA 94305

CARLSON, ROBERT MARTIN KULHONEN, petroleum research chemist; b. Elmhurst, Ill., May 20, 1949; s. Herbert Martin and Lucille Gladys (Woolum) C.; m. Elaine Joyce Walker, Sept. 28, 1968; children: Eric, Ian. BS in Chemistry, U. Redlands, 1971; PhD in Biochemistry, Stanford U., 1977. Postdoctoral fellow Syntex Research Co., Palo Alto, Calif., 1978; sr. research chemist Chevron Oil Field Research, La Habra, Calif., 1979—. Co-editor: 2D NMR for Chemists and Biochemists, 1986; contbr. articles to profl. jours. Recipient E.C. Jaeger Naturalists award; named J. Clarence Karcher Lectr. in Geochemistry. Mem. AAAS, Am. Chem. Soc. (treas. Orange County sect. 1982-83), Geochem. Soc. Avocation: scuba diving. Office: Chevron Oil Field Research PO Box 446 La Habra CA 90631

CARLSON, TIMOTHY POWYS, financial executive; b. Chgo., Feb. 9, 1938; s. Leland H. and LaVerne S. (Larson) C.; m. Jeana Hurst, Aug. 29, 1980; children: Jeffrey, Brian. BS, Northwestern U., 1959; MBA with honors, Stanford U., 1968. Various mfg. mgmt. positions Procter & Gamble, Chgo., Balt., Cin., 1959-64; tech. sales rep., product mgr., mktg. mgr. Monsanto Co., San Ramon, Calif., St. Louis, Kalamazoo, 1964-69; controller, treas. U.S. Nat. Resources, Inc., Menlo Park, Calif., 1969-73; v.p. fin. Acurex Corp., Mountain View, Calif., 1973-83, Tech. for Communications Internat., Mountain View, 1983-85, Laserpath Corp., Sunnyvale, Calif., 1985—; tchr. personal fin. mgmt. courses; cons. Project Bus. Mem. Peninsula Fin. Forum (pres. 1976-77), Fin. Execs. Inst. Republican. Avocations: travel, backpacking, kayaking, mountain climbing. Home: 522 Sand Hill Circle Menlo Park CA 94025 Office: Laserpath Corp 160 Sobrante Way Sunnyvale CA 94086

CARLSON, WAYNE EDWARD, insurance and risk management consultant; b. Altadena, Calif., June 9, 1946; s. Charles A. and P. Lovene (McNew) C.; m. Carol J. Gibbons; children: Mark B., Amy L. BA, Pepperdine U., 1967; teaching credential, Calif. State U., Long Beach, 1969; MBA, Grad. Sch. Bus., U. Nev., 1987. Property, package mgr. The Hartford Ins. Group, Reno, Nev., 1971-79; v.p. comml. lines Bayly, Martin & Fay, Reno, 1979-80; pvt. practice ins. agt. Reno, 1980-81; sr. risk mgmt. analyst Washoe County, Reno, 1981-83; risk mgmt. cons. Reno, 1983-85; propr., risk mgr. Pub. Agy. Risk Mgmt. Services, Carson City, Nev., 1985—; exec. dir. Nev. Pub. Agy. Ins. Pool, Carson City, 1987—; instr. ins. U. Nev., Reno, 1981—; bd. dirs. Nev. Ins. Edn. Found. Author: Property and Casualty Insurance in Brief, 1980. Area dir. Am. Youth Soccer Orgn., Hawthorne, Calif., 1980—. Served to sgt. U.S. Army, 1969-71. Mem. Soc. Chartered Property and Casualty Underwriter (cert.), Am. Soc. Safety Engrs., Pub. Risk Ins. Mgmt. Assn., Pub. Agy. Risk Mgrs. Assn. Republican. Avocation: soccer coaching. Home: 731 Desert View Sparks NV 89431 Office: Pub Agy Risk Mgmt Services 308 N Curry Suite 205 Carson City NV 89701

CARLSTROM, R. WILLIAM, special education educator; b. Seattle, Oct. 22, 1944; s. Roy Albert Carlstrom and Dorothy (Anderson) Hart; m. Ann Scheffer, July 29, 1967; children: Trina Anderson, Paul Scheffer. BA, Lewis & Clark Coll., 1967; MA, U. Wash., 1970. Tchr. Shoreline Pub. Schs., Seattle, 1968-71; program coordinator fo adult handicapped City of Seattle, 1971-72; spl. edn. tchr. South Shore Middle Sch., Seattle, 1972-75, Sharples Jr. High, Seattle, 1975-78, Ryther Child Ctr., Seattle, 1978—; sec., treas., bd. dirs. Glaser Found., Inc., Edmonds, Wash., 1974-86, exec. dir., 1983—; adv. com. mem. U. of Wash. Dentistry for Handicapped, Seattle, 1979; pres., cons. R. William Carlstrom & Assocs., Edmonds, 1984—. Council mem. U. Wash. Grad. Sch. for Dentistry, 1979—; trustee Edmonds Unitarian Ch., 1980-81, Pub. Edn. Fund, Dist. 15, Edmonds, 1986—; pres. Madrona Middle Sch. PTA, Edmonds, 1983-84. Grantee Seattle Masonic Temple, 1974-75, Fed. Govt., 1970-71. Mem. Seattle Tchrs. Assn., Pacific N.W. Grantmakers Forum, Nat. Council on Founds. Democrat. Club: Harbor Square Athletic. Avocations: computers, camping, fishing, guitar, singing. Office: Glaser Found Inc PO Box N Edmonds WA 98020

CARMAN, MICHAEL DENNIS, museum director; b. Monahans, Tex., Nov. 6, 1938; s. Herbert Charles and Marie Noelie (Watkins) C.; m. Malica Jean Brunet, Jan. 27, 1967 (div. June 1984); m. Sharon Ruth Morrisson, Nov. 29, 1985. BA in History, San Diego State U., 1970, MA in History, 1973. Commd. USN, 1956, advanced through grades to petty officer I, resigned, 1966; curator San Diego Hist. Soc., 1973-77, Pioneers Mus., Colorado Springs, Colo., 1978-82; chief curator Network Curatorial Services, Colorado Springs, 1982-84; dir. Ariz. State Capitol Mus., Phoenix, 1984—. Author: United States Customs and the Madero Revolution, 1975; contbr. articles to profl. jours. Mem. Am. Assn. Mus. (MAP evaluator 1980—, curator com., sec. 1982-83), Am. Assn. State and Local History (rep. 1974-77, cons. 1975—), Mus. Assn. Ariz., Cen. Ariz. Mus. Assn. (v.p. 1985—). Club: Phoenix City. Avocations: woodwork, hiking, photography. Office: Ariz State Capitol Mus 1700 W Washington Phoenix AZ 85007

CARMICHAEL, MARIE S., biopsychology educator; b. Indpls., Dec. 28, 1957; d. Mary Ellen (Hayden) Hock. AB, U. Calif., Berkeley, 1977, MA with honors, 1979, PhD, 1981. Research affiliate Stanford (Calif.) U., 1981-82; vis. lectr. psychology U. Calif., Riverside, 1985—. Co-author: Circadian Rhthyms, Brain Peptides and Reproduction, 1981; contbr. articles to profl. jours. Grantee USPHS, 1979-81; research scholar NIH, Stanford U., 1982-85. Mem. AAAS, Sigma Xi, Phi Beta Kappa. Office: U Calif Dept Psychology Riverside CA 92521

CARMODY, KERRY LEE, clinical biochemist; b. N.Y.C., Feb. 28, 1951; s. Everett Leo and Norma Jane (Whelan) C.; m. Kristie Lin Pouliot, June 9, 1973. BA in Chemistry cum laude, Linfield Coll., 1973; MS, Calif. State U., Dominguez Hills, 1978. Cert. med. technologist, Calif. Clin. lab. technologist St. Joseph Med. Ctr., Burbank, Calif., 1974-79, supr. chemistry and immunology, 1979—. Linfield Research Inst. grantee, McMinnville, Oreg., 1969. Mem. Coll. Am. Pathologists (inspector), Am. Soc. Clin. Pathologists (cert. med. technician, inspector 1984, 86), Am. Assn. Clin. Chemistry, Delorean Owners Assn. (bd. dirs., editor Delorean World mag. 1986). Democrat. Roman Catholic. Avocations: Delorean auto rallies, jogging, weight tng., travelling, classic films. Home: 13963 Breger Ave Sylmar CA 91342 Office: St Joseph Med Ctr 501 S Buena Vista Burbank CA 91505

CARNAHAN, CHALON LUCIUS, hydrogeologist, environmental consultant; b. Beverly, Mass., Sept. 17, 1933; s. C. Wesley and Vina (Hinton) C.; m. Mardel Maynard, Dec. 25, 1960; children: Kim A., Lee W. BS, Calif. Inst. Tech., 1955; MS, U. Calif., Berkeley, 1958; PhD, U. Nev., 1975. Research asst. Lawrence Berkeley Lab., 1957-62, staff scientist III, 1978—; radiol. chemist U.S. Naval Radiol. Def. Lab., San Francisco, 1957-62; group leader Teledyne Isotopes, Palo Alto, Calif., 1962-71; research assoc. Desert Research Inst., Reno, 1971-76; supervisory assoc. Environ. Sci. Assocs., Foster City, Calif., 1976-78; ind. environ. cons., Orinda, Calif., 1978—. Contbr. articles to sci. jours. Mem. Am. Geophys. Union, AAAS, Materials Research Soc., Amer. Inst. Hydrology (cert.), Sigma Xi. Avocations: hiking, skiing, photography, reading. Office: Lawrence Berkeley Lab 50E 1 Cyclotron Rd Berkeley CA 94702

CARNEY, ANTHONY JOHN, city planner; b. Phila., Oct. 16, 1941; s. Anthony John and Catherine Carney. BA in Sociology, San Jose State U., 1966, M in Urban Planning, 1972. Exec. dir. San Jose (Calif.) Housing Ctr., 1975-79; community devel. coordinator City of Campbell, Calif., 1979-82; asst. planning dir. City of Watsonville, Calif., 1982-84, planning dir., 1984—; guest lectr. Stanford (Calif.) U., 1977-79; temp. prof. San Jose State U., 1981; guest speaker ABA, Washington, 1979. Served to capt. U.S. Army. Mem. Am. Planning Assn., Nat. Assn. Housing and Redevel. Officials, Am. Inst. Cert. Planners. Roman Catholic. Avocations: golf, restoring old corvettes. Home: 347 Arthur Ave Aptos CA 95003 Office: City of Watsonville 250 Main St Watsonville CA 95076

CARNEY, CHERYL ANN, psychotherapist; b. Denver, Apr. 20, 1945; d. Herbert P. and Audrey P. (Chappell) Sims; m. Robert Forman, Oct. 19, 1980 (dec. Aug. 1983); children: Keely Carney, Tarryn Carney. BA, Ft. Lewis Coll., 1967; MSW, U. Denver, 1971. Prin. social worker Adams County Social Service, Commerce City, Colo., 1971-77; pvt. practice psychotherapy Denver, 1977—; instr. Dale Carnegie courses, Denver, 1979—. Fin. edn. grantee NIMH, 1970-71. Mem. Nat. Assn. Social Workers, Acad. Cert. Social Workers. Roman Catholic. Avocations: skiing, cat showing and breeding, aerobics. Office: 2343 E Evans Denver CO 80210

CARNEY, HEATH JOSEPH, aquatic ecologist; b. Lyon, France, Aug. 7, 1955; s. Stephen McLure and June (Kempf) C. BS, Coll. William and Mary, 1979; MS, U. Mich., 1981; PhD, U. Calif., Davis, 1987. Research asst. U. Mich., Ann Arbor, 1979-82; aquatic ecology fellow U. Calif., Davis, 1982—; cons. U. Mich., 1980-81. Contbr. articles to profl. jours. Grantee EPA, NOAA, NSF. Mem. AAAS, Am. Soc. Limnology and Oceanography, Ecol. Soc. Am., Phycol. Soc. Am., Soc. Internat. Limnologiae, Internat. Assn. Ecology, Union Concerned Scientists, Sierra Club, Sigma Xi, Phi Beta Kappa. Avocations: music, swimming, gardening. Office: U Calif Inst Ecology Davis CA 95616

CARNEY, JAMES F., archbishop; b. Vancouver, B.C., Can., June 28, 1915; s. John and Ethel (Crook) C. Ed., Vancouver Coll., Jr. Sem. of Christ the King, 1930-38, St. Joseph's Sem., Alta., Can., 1938-42. Ordained priest Roman Catholic Ch., 1942; pastor Corpus Christi Ch., Vancouver; later vicar gen., domestic prelate; consecrated bishop Corpus Christi Ch., 1966; ordained titular bishop of Obori and aux. bishop of Vancouver, 1966-69, installed as archbishop, 1969—. Office: 150 Robson St, Vancouver, BC Canada V6B 2A7

CARNEY, PATRICIA, Canadian minister of international trade; b. Shanghai, China, May 26, 1935; d. John James and Dora (Sanders) C. B.A. in Econs. and Polit. Sci., U. B.C., Can., 1960, M.A. in Regional Planning, 1977. Econ. journalist various publs., including Vancouver Sun, Toronto Star, N.Y. Times, Times of London, 1955-70; owner, cons. Gemini North Ltd., Vancouver, B.C., Can., 1970-80, Yellowknife, Alta., Can., 1970-80; mem. Can. Ho. of Commons, Ottawa, Ont., 1980—, minister of state, 1981, minister of fin., 1983, minister energy, mines and resources, 1984-86, minister of internat. trade, 1986—; project mgr. B.C. Ministry Edn., 1977-78; project dir. B.C. govt., 1978-79; designer Can. Satellite Communications, Inc., 1979; asst. dir. gen. UN Human Settlements (HABITAT), 1976; writer TV spls. on fin. and econs. CBC. Progressive Conservative critic of sec. of state Can., 1980. Recipient Can. Women's Press award, 1968, 3 MacMillan Bloedel Ltd. awards. Mem. Assn. Profl. Economists B.C., Can. Inst. Planners. Club: Rideau (Ottawa, Ont., Can.). Office: Ho of Commons, Room 440-n Centre Block, Parliament Bldgs, Ottawa, ON Canada K1A 0A6 *

CARNEY, PHILLITA TOYIA, marketing communications management company executive; b. Chgo., Apr. 18, 1952; d. Phillip Leon Carney and Margaret Clarice (Ewing) Brown. Student, U. Utah, 1971-74; BS in Bus., Westminster Coll., 1976. Corp. tng. dir. U&I Sugar Corp., Salt Lake City, 1974-76; program coordinator Div. on Aging, also Moses Lake, Wash., 1976-77; program coordinator Div. on Aging, Seattle, 1977-78; bus. devel. officer Del Green Assoc., Foster City, Calif., 1978-79; regional v.p. Equitec Fin. Group, San Francisco, Irvine and Oakland, Calif., 1979-84, United Resources, Oakland, San Francisco, Nev., 1984-86; owner, mgr. Carney & Assocs., Oakland, 1986; regional v.p. Eastcoast Ops. Benefits Communications Corp. div. Great West Life Assurance Co., Washington, 1986—; dir. Total One, San Francisco; corp. cons., advisor Am. Intermediation Services, San Francisco, 1986; sr. bus. cons., ptnr. Performance Strategies Inc., San Diego, 1986. Moderator, creator pub. affairs radio program, 1975-76 (Best Pub. Affairs Program award Nat. Pub. Radio 1976). Del., White House Conf. on Small Bus., Washington, 1986. Recipient award Am. Legion, 1970, DAR, 1970. Mem. Internat. Assn. Fin. Planning, Women Entrepreneurs, Bus. and Profl. Women, Sales Mktg. Exec. Assn., Zonta Internat. (pres. 1985—). Avocations: jogging, swimming, reading, writing. Home: 1200 N Nash St Apt #1155 Arlington VA 22209

CARNEY, RAYMOND, author, English educator; b. Pitts., Mar. 1, 1950; s. Raymond and Priscilla (McDaniel) C.; m. Mary Emerson Dunsmore, Aug. 3, 1972; 1 child, Daniel. BA magna cum laude, Harvard U., 1969; PhD with distinction, Rutgers U., 1978. Asst. prof. English, Middlebury Coll., Vt., 1978-86; prof., Stanford (Calif.) U., 1986—; cons. on art and film Whitney Mus. of Am. Art, N.Y.C., 1984—. Author: American Dreaming, 1985, Figures of Desire, 1985, American Vision, 1986. Editor: Mont-Saint Michel and Chartres (Henry Adams), 1985, Kim (Rudyard Kipling), 1984, Spoils of Poynton (Henry James), 1985. Contbr. articles to profl. publs. Chair schs. and scholarship com. Harvard U., Cambridge, Mass., 1980—. Served to lt. USN, 1969-72. Recipient Harvard Club Book award, John Harvard award (both Harvard U.); Fellow NEH, 1983-84, Louis J. Bevier, William Rice Kimball, 1986—; grantee NSF, NIMH, Gov. of Pa., NEH, Nat. Endowment for Arts, Vt. Council on Arts. Avocations: squash; bicycle racing; gardening; cultivation of roses. Home: 4252 Newberry Ct Palo Alto CA 94306 Office: Stanford U Humanities Ctr Mariposa House Stanford CA 94305

CARNICOM, GENE E., health services administrator; b. Miami, Fla., Nov. 13, 1944; s. Francis Eugene and Kathleen (Kitchens) C.; m. Sharon Boisseau Brown, 1966; m. Lillian Helen Baehr, Mar. 22, 1970; children: Patrick Dylan, Danielle Brooke; m. Clare Helminiak, Nov. 1, 1984; children: Whitney Alexis, Heath Britten. B.A. in Social Welfare, San Diego State U., 1971, M.S.S.W., 1972; Ph.D., Southeastern U., 1981. Cert., Acad. Cert. Social Workers. Coordinator, Beach Area Free Clinic, San Diego, 1970-72; program cons. Balt. City Dept. Social Services, 1973; chief of social work Balt. City Jail, 1974-76; hosp. social work dir. Pine Ridge (S.D.) Indian Health Service Hosp., 1980-81; dir. mental health and social service USPHS Indian Health Service Hosp., Mescalero, N.Mex., 1981-84; health ins. coordinator Alaska Native Med. Ctr., Anchorage, 1984—; mem. faculty U. Md., 1972-76, Community Coll. Balt., 1973-76, Morgan State U., 1974-76, Webster Coll., 1977-80, Oglala Sioux Community Coll., 1980-81, Park Coll., 1982-84, Golden Gate U., 1982-84, N.Mex. State U., 1982-84. Steering com. Community Congress San Diego, 1980-82; bd. dirs. Innercity N.W. Neighborhood Corp., 1970-72; exec. dir. RETIRED, Inc., 1971-72; site selection task force Community Corrections Program of Md. Dept. Corrections, 1973-74; grad. council Webster Coll., San Antonio, 1978-80; coordinator child protection team Pine Ridge Indian Reservation, 1980-81, coordinator Mescalero Apache Indian Reservation Child Protection Team, 1981-84; comdr. Sierra Blanca CAP Cadet Squadron, 1982-84; mem. CAP. Served with USNR, 1962-68, to capt. U.S. Army, 1976-80. Decorated Army Commendation medal; recipient Isolated Hardship Duty award USPHS, 1981, Hazardous Duty award, 1981. Mem. Nat. Assn. Social Workers, Am. Anthrop. Assn., Soc. Med. Anthropology, Assn. Mil. Surgeons U.S., Found. Exceptional Children, Am. Soc. Circumpolar Health, Am. Assn. Med. Systems and Informatics, Am. Pub. Health Assn., Profl. Assn. Commd. Corps of USPHS, Indian Health Service Computer Users Group, Mensa. Democrat. Contbr. articles profl. jours.

CAROSELLI, PATRICIA ANN, film production executive; b. Rochester, N.Y., Feb. 21, 1954; d. Patrick R. and Elvira J. (Ciaccia) Caroselli. B.A., SUNY-Buffalo, 1975; M.B.A., U. Conn., 1977; student at European Arts Workshop, summer 1971. Asst. project dir. mktg. research dept. Grey Advt., Los Angeles, 1977-79; prodn. assoc. on films "10", S.O.B., Victor/Victoria, Trail of the Pink Panther, Curse of the Pink Panther, The Man Who Loved Women, 1979—; v.p. prodn. Blake Edwards Entertainment, Los Angeles, 1982—, assoc. producer Micki and Maude, 1984, A Fine Mess, 1985, That's Life, 1985, Blind Date, 1986. Vol., Operation Calif.'s world disaster relief program, 1979—; mem. Conn. Commn. on the Arts, 1976. U. Conn. scholar, 1976-77. Mem. Assn. M.B.A. Execs., Women in Film, Am. Film Inst. Contbr. articles to profl. jours.

CAROTHERS, STEVEN WARREN, natural scientist, environmental consultant; b. Prescott, Ariz., Dec. 19, 1943; m. Marion M. Sharp, Dec. 20, 1981; children: Carol A., Kenneth R., Cooper H. BS, No. Ariz. U., 1966, MS, 1969; PhD, U. Ill., 1974. Curator, dept. head Mus. No. Ariz., Flagstaff, 1966-80; prin. S.W.C. Assocs., Flagstaff, 1980-84; pres. SWCA, Inc., Flagstaff, 1984—, also bd. dirs. Author: Enchanted Light, 1979; co-author: Grand Canyon: Up Close and Personal, 1980, Grand Canyon Birds, 1987. Recipient award Gov.'s Commn. on Ariz. Environment, 1984. Fellow Ariz./Nev. Acad. Sci.; mem. Soc. Wetland Scientists, N. Am. Riparian Council, Bald Eagle Recovery Team. Home: Rt 4 PO Box 878 Flagstaff AZ 86001 Office: SWCA Inc PO Box 96 Flagstaff AZ 86002

CAROUSO, NICHOLAS HARRY, mining executive; b. Oakland, Calif., Mar. 25, 1920; s. Victor Harry and Nina (Mitchell) C.: student St. Mary's Coll., 1946-47; B.A., U. Calif., 1950, M.S., 1959; postgrad. U. Nev., 1956-57, U. Ariz., 1968—; m. Barbara Elizabeth Stephenson, Feb. 2, 1952; children—Mark Nicholas, Joan Patricia, Valerie Elizabeth. Sr. research engr. Berkeley Research Co. (Calif.), 1957-59; geophys. engr. Phelps Dodge Corp., Douglas, Ariz., 1959; plant prodn. engr. Eitel-McCullough, Inc., San Bruno, Calif., 1959-61; concentrator, metall. engr. Kennecott Copper Corp., Hayden, Ariz., 1961-65; mgmt. supr., cons. Bonanza-MJV, Superior, Ariz., 1969-70; pres. Geo-Processing, Inc., Prescott, Ariz., 1971—, also bd. dirs.; v.p. mining Cherry Creek Gold Corp., 1985-86; mining cons. Ibex Keystone Mine, Nev., Gold Star, Inc., Ariz., 1985—, Specific Products Devel., Ariz., 1986—; mineral exploration cons. Capt. Kearny (Ariz.) Vol. Fire Dept., 1964-65. Served with USNR, World War II. Mem. Am. Inst. Mining, Metall. and Petroleum Engrs., Ariz. Geol. Soc., Am. Radio Relay League. Republican. Episcopalian. Inventor distance calculator, 1955. Home: 2106 Nolte Dr Prescott AZ 86301

CARPENTER, ADELAIDE TROWBRIDGE CLARK, geneticist; b. Athens, Ga., June 24, 1944. BS, N.C. State U., 1966; MS, U. Wash., 1969, PhD, 1972. Postdoctoral fellow U. Wis., Madison, 1972-74; research assoc. Duke U., Durham, N.C., 1974-75, adj. asst. prof. anatomy, 1975-76; asst. prof. biology U. Calif. at San Diego, La Jolla, 1976-79, assoc. prof. biology, 1979-85, prof. biology, 1985—; ad hoc mem. genetics study sect. NIH, NSF. Assoc. editor Genetics jour., 1980—; contbr. articles to profl. jours. NIH grantee, 1975—. Mem. Genetics Soc. Am., AAAS, Am. Soc. Naturalists, Am. Soc. Cell Biology, Genetics Soc. Can., Sigma Xi. Office: U Calif at San Diego Dept Biology B-022 La Jolla CA 92093

CARPENTER, CLAYTON ARNOLD, electrical engineering consultant; b. Tonopah, Nev., Jan. 18, 1916; s. Jay Arnold and Florence Fassett (Bender) C.; m. Virginia Lillian Petit, Apr. 12, 1941 (div. Jan. 1951); children: David Caldwell, Bonnie, Peter Bender, Daniel Edwin, Sally; m. Mary Elizabeth Cooper, Jan. 1952; children: Jay Edwin, Thomas Charles. BSEE, U. Nev., 1939, postgrad., 1966; postgrad., Cornell U., 1939-40. Registered profl. engr., Nev. Resident engr. Calif. Inst. Tech., Pasadena, 1941-43; instr. U. Redlands, Calif., 1943-45; owner citrus groves Redlands, 1943-47; elec. engr. Union Oil Co. Calif. Research Dept., Brea, 1947-55; engring. chief U. Nev., Reno, 1961-71; emeritus faculty U. Nev., 1971—; cons. engr. Carpenter Engring., Reno, 1971—; elec. engr. Dinter Engring., Reno, 1985—; cons. in field, Reno, 1973—; forensic engr., Reno, 1970—. Inventor in field. Mem. City Elec. Code Com., Reno, 1965-83. Mem. IEEE (Prodn. and Application of Light 1985—), NSPE, Illuminating Engring. Soc., Assn. Energy Engrs., Nat. Acad. Forensic Engrs. Club: U. Nev. Faculty (Reno). Avocation: organic gardening. Home and Office: 1175 Yates Ln Reno NV 89509-5237

CARPENTER, CYRIL HILARY, farm organization officer; b. Stearns County, Minn., Dec. 21, 1922; s. Dwight Waldo and Bertha Olive (Robertson) C.; m. Frances Elaine Stauning, Oct. 11, 1958; children—Richard Carpenter, Kris. Farmer, Sauk Centre, Minn., 1940-56; field rep. Farmers Union Mktg. and Processing Assn., S. St. Paul, 1956-65; with Minn. Farmers Union, St. Paul, 1965-84; pres. Nat. Farmers Union, Denver, 1984—. Chmn., Pennington County DFL Party, Thief River Falls, Minn., 1960-64; pres. KIDS, Inc., St. Paul, 1971; mem. Fed. Council Aging, Washington, 1979; pres. Nat. Farmers Union Green Thumb, Washington, 1984—; trustee CARE, 1984—; mem. econ. policy council United Nations Assn. of the U.S.A., 1984—; bd. dirs. Agrl. Coop. Devel. Internat., 1984—; chmn. Minn. Gov.'s Citizens Bd. on Aging, 1974-70; mem. exec. com. Internat. Fedn. Agrl. Producers, 1986—. Recipient John Carroll award, Minn. Voc. Edn. Assn., 1982; Cert. Spl. Recognition, Congressman Bruce Vento, 1984. Democrat. Lutheran. Home: 8200 Portland Minneapolis MN 55420 Office: Nat Farmers Union 10065 E Harvard Ave Denver CO 80251

CARPENTER, DAVID ROLAND, life insurance executive; b. Fort Wayne, Ind., Mar. 24, 1939; s. Geary W. and Rita (Ueber) C.; m. Karen Woodard, Oct. 20, 1963 (div. Apr. 1975); children: Kimberly, Clayton; m. Leila E.M. Sjogren, Sept. 20, 1980; 1 dau., Michelle. B.B.A., U. Mich., 1961, M.S., 1962. Sr. v.p. Booz, Allen Cons., Newport Beach, Calif., 1976-77; v.p. Tillinghast, Nelson & Warren, Newport Beach, Calif., 1977-80; chief mktg. officer Transamerica Occidental Life Ins. Co., Los Angeles, 1980-81, exec. v.p., chief mktg. officer, 1981-82, pres., from 1982, chief operating officer, 1982-83, chief exec. officer, 1983—, now also chmn., dir.; dir. Transam. Life & Annuity Co., Transam. Assurance Co., Transam. Ins. Corp., Transam. Internat. Ins. Services. Mem. exec. com. Steve Garvey Sports Classic-So. Calif. Multiple Sclerosis Soc., Los Angeles, 1981; trustee Griffith Found., Columbus Ohio, 1982; bd. govs. Arthritis found., Los Angeles, 1983; trustee Calif. Hosp., 1983. Fellow Soc. Actuaries (bd. dirs. 1978-81); mem. Am. Acad. Actuaries (v.p. 1981-83). Presbyterian. Home: 346 Poppy Ave Corona del Mar CA 92625 Office: Transamerica Occidental Life Ins Co Hill and Olive at 12th St Los Angeles CA 90015 *

CARPENTER, FRANK CHARLES, JR., retired electronics engineer; b. Los Angeles, June 1, 1917; s. Frank Charles and Isobel (Crump) C.; A.A., Pasadena City Coll., 1961; B.S. in Elec. Engring. cum laude, Calif. State U.-Long Beach, 1975, M.S. in Elec. Engring., 1981; m. Beatrice Josephine Jolly, Nov. 3, 1951; children—Robert Douglas, Gail Susan, Carol Ann. Self-employed design and mfgr. aircraft test equipment, Los Angeles, 1946-51; engr. Hoffman Electronics Corp., Los Angeles, 1951-56, sr. engr., 1956-59, project mgr., 1959-63; engr.-scientist McDonnell-Douglas Astronautics Corp., Huntington Beach, Calif., 1963-69, spacecraft telemetry, 1963-67, biomed. electronics, 1967-69, flight test instrumentation, 1969-76; lab. test engr. Northrop Corp., Hawthorne, Calif., 1976-82, spl. engr., 1982-83; mgr. transducer calibration lab. Northrop Corp., Pico-Rivera, Calif., 1983-86. Served with USNR, 1941-47. Mem. IEEE (sr.), Amateur Radio Relay League. Contbr. articles to profl. jours. Patentee transistor squelch circuit; helicaland whip antenna. Home: 2037 Balearic Dr Costa Mesa CA 92626 Office: 8900 E Washington Blvd Pico Rivera CA 90660

CARPENTER, JOHN EVERETT, former educator; b. Tarrytown, N.Y., Nov. 27, 1923; s. Everett Birch and Mary (Avery) C.; student Union Coll., 1943; B.A., Iona Coll., 1946; M.A., Columbia, 1949, profl. diploma, 1961; m. Marie F. McCarthy, Nov. 14, 1944; 1 son, Dennis Everett. Tchr., Blessed Sacrament High Sch., New Rochelle, N.Y., 1946-50; tchr., adminstr. Armonk (N.Y.) pub. schs., 1950-62; dir. guidance Ridge Street Sch., Port Chester, N.Y., 1962-64; counselor Rye (N.Y.) High Sch., 1964-66, prin., 1966-78, ret.; guest lectr. Served to lt. USNR; now lt. comdr. ret. Res. Decorated Bronze Star medal. Mem. Middle States Assn. Colls. and Schs. (commn. on secondary schs.), Am. (life), Westchester-Putnam-Rockland (past pres.) personnel and guidance assns., NEA, Am. Legion (past comdr.), Phi Delta Kappa, Kappa Delta Pi. Rotarian (past pres., Paul Harris fellow). Clubs: Tarrytown Boat (past commodore), Green Valley Elks. Home: 321 Paseo de los Conquistadores Green Valley AZ 85614

CARPENTER, PETER ROCKEFELLER, trust company executive; b. Sunbury, Pa., Apr. 18, 1939; s. Alvin Witmer and Katherine (Rockefeller) C.; m. Janet Ross Buck, Aug. 24, 1963; children—Karen Louise, Jean Ellen, Peter Alvin. B.A., Pa. State U., 1962. Mgr. J.C. Penney Co., Menlo Park, N.J., 1964-67; ops. mgr. Allstate Ins. Co., Summit, N.J., 1967-73; adminstrv. mgr. Prudential Property & Casualty, Scottsdale, Ariz., 1973-75; v.p. Fortune Properties, Scottsdale, 1975-76; life underwriter Conn. Mutual Life, Phoenix, 1976-81; v.p. and dir. sales and mktg. No. Trust Bank, Phoenix, 1981—; Sec. exec. bd. Samuel Gompers Rehab. Ctr., 1981-84, chmn. bd., 1984—. Chmn. Phoenix div. United Way, 1981, 82, 86—. Rep. committeeman, Phoenix, 1978-86 . Served with USN, 1962-64. Mem. Nat. Assn. Life Underwriters, Am. Inst. Banking, Internat. Platform Assn., Pa. State U. Alumni Assn. (dir. 1979-86), Sigma Alpha Epsilon. Lutheran. Clubs: Ariz., LaCamarilla, Mansion. Lodges: Kiwanis (Disting. lt. gov.), Masons. Home: 5817 E Cochise Rd Scottsdale AZ 85253 Office: No Trust Bank Ariz 4350 E Camelback Rd Suite G-100 Phoenix AZ 85018

CARPENTER, RAY WARREN, materials scientist and engineer, educator; b. Berkeley, Calif., 1934; s. Fritz Josh and Ethel Thordis (Davisson) C.; m. Ann Louise Leavitt, July 10, 1955; children: Shannon R., Sheila A., Matthew L. BSE, U. Calif., 1958; MS in Metallurgy, U. Calif., Berkeley, 1959, PhD in Metallurgy, 1966. Registered profl. engr., Calif. Sr. engr. Aerojet-Gen. Nucleonics, San Ramon, Calif., 1959-64; sr. metallurgist Stanford Research Inst., Menlo Park, Calif., 1966-67; mem. sr. research staff Oak Ridge (Tenn.) Nat. Lab., 1967-80; prof. Solid State Sci. & Engring. Ariz. State U., Tempe, 1980—, dir. Facility for High Resolution Electron Microscopy, 1980-83, dir. Ctr. for Solid State Sci., 1985—; bd. dirs. Ctr. Solid State Sci.; chmn. sci. and engring. of materials doctoral program Ariz. State U., 1987—; adj. prof. Vanderbilt U., Nashville, 1979-81. Author and contbr. to prof. research jour., symposia, books. Recipient awards, Internat. Metellographic Soc. and Am. Soc. for Metals competition, 1976, 77. Mem. Electron Microscopy Soc. Am. (dir. phys. sci. 1980-83), Metall. Soc. of AIME, Materials Research Soc., Materials Resources Soc., Sigma Xi. Office: Ariz State U Ctr for Solid State Sci Tempe AZ 85287

CARPENTER, RONALD JOHN, police officer, realtor; b. Orange, Calif., Aug. 21, 1941; s. John Orin and Cora Elizabeth (Barton) C.; m. Sheila Gail Wimsatt, May 15, 1965; 1 child, Eric Scott. AA, Long Beach City Coll., 1969; BS, Calif. State U., Long Beach, 1975. Cert. peace officer, Calif.; cert. tchr., Calif. Dep. sheriff UN, Kwajalein Atoll, Marshall Islands, 1963-64; indsl. police officer Douglas Aircraft (now McDonnell Douglas Corp.), Long Beach, 1964-66; sgt., juvenile detective Long Beach Police Dept., 1967—; realtor Coldwell Banker, Yorba Linda, Calif., 1985—; part-time tchr. pub. schs., Calif., 1975—; juvenile officer, State of Calif., 1976—. Served with

USAF, 1958-62. Mem. Internat. Union Police Assns. of AFL-CIO, Calif. Orgn. Police and Sheriffs, Long Beach Police Officers Assn., North Orange County Bd. Realtors. Republican. Lodge: Elks. Avocations: geneal. research, gardening, flying, computers. Home: 765 Carhart Ave Fullerton CA 92633 Office: Long Beach Police Dept 400 W Broadway Ave Long Beach CA 92802

CARPENTER, SAMUEL CLYDE, podiatrist; b. Farmington, N.Mex., Dec. 12, 1950; s. James Warden and Helen Agnes (Burroughs) C.; m. Loretta Karen Lee, Jan. 22, 1970; children: Samuel, Eric, Jared, Jacob, Zachary. BS, U. N.Mex., 1975; D in Podiatric Medicine, Calif. Coll. Podiatric Medicine, 1983. Lab. technician Presbyn. Hosp., Albuquerque, 1972-75; lab. supr. Med. Investigators, Albuquerque, 1975-77; lab. technician Pvt. Pathology, Roswell, N.Mex., 1977-79; research asst. Calif. Coll. Podiatric Medicine, San Francisco, 1979-83; resident in podiatry Vets. Hosp., Albuquerque, 1983-84; practice podiatry Farmington, 1984—; cons. podiatrist Good Samaritan Nursing Home, Aztec, N.Mex., 1984—, San Juan Manor Nursing Home, Farmington, 1985—; surg. staff mem. Sam Juan Regional Med. Ctr., Farmington, 1984—. Named one of Outstanding Young Men of Am., 1983. Mem. N.Mex. Podiatric Med. Assn., Am. Podiatric Med. Assn. Republican. Mormon. Avocations: woodworking, fishing, backpacking, gardening. Home: 1416 Camino Monte Farmington NM 87401 Office: 204 N Auburn Farmington NM 87401

CARR, ALLAN, film producer, celebrity representative; b. Chgo., May 27, 1941; s. Albert and Ann (Neimitz) Solomon. BA, Lake Forest Coll., 1962. Reopened Civic Theater, Chgo., 1959; formed Rogallan Prodns., 1966; became mgr. Ann-Margret's career, 1966; formed Allan Carr Enterprises, 1971; mgr. careers of Peter Sellers, Marvin Hamlisch, Rosalind Russell, Paul Anka, Mama Cass, others, producer nightclub extravaganzas, TV spls., motion pictures; creative cons. to Robert Stigwood Orgn. for motion picture and TV prodn. including Tommy, 1975, Bugsy Malone, also Deer Hunter; producer: The First Time, 1969, C.C. & Company, 1970, Can't Stop the Music, 1980; co-writer, producer motion picture Grease; producer Broadway show La Cage Aux Folles, 1983; producer motion pictures: Survive, 1976, Grease II, 1982, Where the Boys Are, 1984, Cloak and Dagger, 1984. Office: Allan Carr Enterprises PO Box 691670 Los Angeles CA 90069 *

CARR, CHARLES DAVID, marketing director; b. Phoenix, Feb. 26, 1945; s. Niles Lorence and Alma (Tanner) C.; m. Janice Lynn Steed, Sept. 16, 1967; children: Deborah, David, Christopher, Rebecca, Jennifer. BA in Chemistry with honors, U. Calif., Berkeley, 1968. Flavor chemist Carnation Co., Van Nuys, Calif., 1970; applications chemist Varian Assocs., Walnut Creek, Calif., 1971-75; lab. mgr. ARL, Sunland, Calif., 1975-83; mktg. mgr. Angstrom, Bellevue, Mich., 1983-84, Vydac, Hesperia, Calif., 1984—. Contbr. articles to sci. jours. Mem. Am. Chem. Soc., Soc. for Applied Spectroscopy, Phi Beta Kappa. Republican. Mormon. Avocations: computer programming, music, tennis. Home: 6140 Acorn PO Box 952 Wrightwood CA 92397 Office: Vydac 17434 Mojave Hesperia CA 92345

CARR, FRED, insurance company executive; b. 1931; married. Student, UCLA. Former pres. Shareholders Mgmt. Corp., Los Angeles; fin. advisor Cons. Assocs. Inc., Los Angeles, 1970-71; pres. Carr Mgmt. & Research Corp., Los Angeles, 1971-74; with First Exec. Corp., Los Angeles, 1974—, chmn., 1974—; pres., chmn. Exec. Life Ins. Co. (subs. First Exec. Corp.), Los Angeles. Office: First Exec Corp 11444 W Olympic Los Angeles CA 90064 *

CARR, KENNETH GERALD, manufacturing company executive; b. Iowa Falls, Iowa, May 30, 1937; s. Gerald and De Loris Arlene (Stone) C.; m. Joan Victoria Vallely, Nov. 8, 1978; children: Kurt Kenneth, Canda Joy, Kevin Dean, Christa Jean. Student, Carlsbad Jr. Coll., 1957-58, Santa Ana Coll., 1962-63, Golden West Coll., 1968; BS in Bus. Mgmt., Pacific Western U., 1979. With Ford Aerospace Communications Corp., Newport Beach, Calif., 1962, sect. supr., 1972-76, mgr. program mfg., 1976-77, mgr. prodn. control dept., 1977-83, prodn. mgr., 1983—. Chmn. bd. Gloria Dei Luth. Ch.; bd. dirs. Orange County Indsl. Ctr., 1980. Served with USMC, 1956-58. Recipient Community Service citation Ford Motor Co., 1974, 78, South Coast YMCA,San Juan Capistrano Jaycees. Mem. Am. Inventory and Prodn. Control Soc., Am. Mgmt. Assn. (bd. dirs. 1980-81). Republican. Club: Newport Beach Country. Home: 1038 Sea Ln Corona del Mar CA 92625 Office: Ford Aerospace Communications Corp Bldg 15 Ford Rd Newport Beach CA 92660

CARR, MICHAEL ALAN, design engineer; b. Wichita, Kans., Feb. 28, 1947; s. Joseph Ellsworth and Juanita Opal (Doris) C.; student Pasadena (Calif.) City Coll., 1971-72; m. Robin Ruth Margosian, May 26, 1979; children: Ethan Michael, Trevor Brook. Lens grinder Teledyne Optics, Monrovia, Calif., 1964-65; apprentice forging shop Calif. Drop Forge Co., Los Angeles, 1965-67; machinist central engring. services Calif. Inst. Tech., 1972-73, tech. instrument specialist geology div., 1973—; propr. Carr Instrumentation, cons. engring. of mass spectrometry; participant lunar neutron probe expt. of Apollo 17, 1972, space telescope wide field/planetary camera project, 1978-83; chief technician 4-Shooter Camera Project, Palomar Obs., 1983, now design engr. Served with U.S. Army, 1967-69. Recipient award for black and white exptl. photograph U.S. Army, 1969. Inventor V filament jig, borehole camera, carbon dioxide reaction heads; co-inventor bubble tilt meters. Home: 3622 Montrose Ave La Crescenta CA 91214 Office: Calif Inst Tech 1201 E California Blvd Pasadena CA 91109

CARR, MICHAEL HAROLD, geologist; b. Leeds, Eng., May 26, 1935; came to U.S., 1956, naturalized, 1965; s. Harry and Monica Mary (Burn) C.; m. Rachel F. Harvey, Apr. 14, 1961; son, Ian M. B.Sc., London U., 1956; M.S., Yale U., 1957, Ph.D., 1960. Research asso. U. Western Ont., 1960-62; with U.S. Geol. Survey, 1962—; chief astrogeologic studies br. U. Geol. Survey, Menlo Park, Calif., 1973-79; mem. Mariner Mars Imaging Team, 1969-73; leader Viking Mars Orbiter Imaging Team, 1969-80; mem. Voyager and Galileo Jupiter Imaging Teams, 1978—; Interdisciplinary scientist, Mars observer. Author: The Surface of Mars, The Geology of the Terrestrial Planets. Recipient Exceptional Sci. Achievement medal NASA, 1977; Meritorious Service award Dept. Interior, 1979. Mem. Geol. Soc. Am., AAAS, Am. Geophys. Union. Home: 1389 Canada Rd Woodside CA 94062 Office: US Geological Survey Menlo Park CA 94025

CARR, PETER JAMES, publishing executive; b. N.Y.C., June 19, 1917; s. John J. and Mary A. (Finn) C.; m. Dorothy Anne Healey, Jan. 23, 1954; children: Kevin, Brian, Michael, Kelly Anne, Colin. Student, CCNY Sch. Commerce. Sales mgr. Life mag. Time Inc., N.Y.C., 1952-53, sales mgr. Sports Illustrated, 1953-83; pub's rep. Time Inc., 1983—; cons. Lorillard Corp. Served with USN, 1941-45. Republican. Roman Catholic. Club: RSF Golf. Avocations: golf, swimming. Home: PO Box 3194 Rancho Santa Fe CA 92067

CARR, ROBERTA MARION, librarian; b. Mandan, N.D., Oct. 4, 1940; d. William Benjamin and Marion (Morgan) Conitz; m. Thomas Calvin Carr, Apr. 29, 1961; 1 child, Jane Marion. Student, Concordia Coll., Moorhead, Minn., 1958-61; BA, Calif. State U., Sacramento, 1973; MA, San Jose State U., 1976. Head catalog div. McGeorge Law Library, Sacramento, 1976-80; catalog librarian Sacramento Pub. Lib., 1980-81; head. bibliographic control Naval Postgrad. Sch., Monterey, Calif., 1981—. Mem. No. Calif. Tech. Processes Group (pres., 1980-81), Calif. Library Assn. (tech. processes sect.), Phi Kappa Phi, Beta Phi Mu. Home: 789 Jessie St Monterey CA 93940

CARRANZA, FERMIN ALBERT, periodontology educator; b. Buenos Aires, Argentina, Feb. 28, 1926; came to U.S., 1974; s. Fermin Alberto and Olga Ernestina (Falco) C.; m. Rita Maria Ostivar, Dec. 12, 1953; children: Fermin A., Patricia I., Laura V. DDS, U. Buenos Aires, 1948; cert. periodontics, Tufts U., 1952. Asst. prof. periodontology Tufts U., Boston, 1955-56; adj. prof. pathology U. Buenos Aires, 1961-65, prof., chmn. periodontics, 1966-74; dir. postdoctoral periodontics program UCLA Sch. Dentistry, 1976-80, prof., chmn. periodontology, 1974—; attending dentist UCLA Hosp, 1974—; dir. UCLA Clin Research Ctr. for Periodontal Disease, 1974—. Author: Glickman's Clinical Periodontology, 6th edit., 1984; contbr. articles to profl. jours. Recipient Sci. award Internat. Assn. Dental Research, W.G. Gies Found. award. for Latin-Am. Scientists, 1977. Fellow AAAS; mem. ADA, Am. Acad. Periodontology, Western Soc. Periodontology, Calif. Soc. Periodontists, Internat. Assn. Dental Research, Pan Am. Assn. Periodontology, Calif. Dental Assn., Assn. Odontologica Argentina, Soc. Argentina de Periodontologia, Acad. de Estomatologia del Peru (hon.), Soc. Espanola de Parodoncia (hon), Soc. Colombiana de Periodoncia (hon.), Soc. Chilena de Parodontologia (hon.), Sigma Xi, Omicron Kappa Upsilon. Home: 10577 Eastborne Ave Los Angeles CA 90024 Office: UCLA 405 Hilgard Ave Los Angeles CA 90024

CARRARA, PIER LUIGI, engineer; b. Lucca, Italy, Sept. 17, 1943; came to U.S., 1958; s. Giovanni Sabatino and Corradina (Nieri) C.; m. Barbara K. Garcia, Oct. 4, 1969; 1 child, Amy Catherine. BS in Math. and Statistics, U. N.Mex., 1974. Sr. engr. Computer Tech. Assocs., Albuquerque, 1985—. Served with U.S. Army, 1966-68. Mem. Trinity Sect. Am. Nuclear Soc. Avocations: fishing, woodworking. Office: Computer Tech Assocs 1650 University Blvd NE Albuquerque NM 87102

CARREY, NEIL, lawyer, educator; b. Bronx, N.Y., Nov. 19, 1942; s. David L. and Betty (Kurtzburg) C.; m. Karen Krysher, Apr. 9, 1980; children—Jana, Christopher; children by previous marriage—Scott, Douglas, Dana. B.S. in Econs., U. Pa., 1964; J.D., Stanford U., 1967. Bar: Calif. 1968. Mem. firm, v.p. corp. DeCastro, West, Chodorow & Burns, Inc., Los Angeles, 1967—; instr. program for legal paraprofls. U. So. Calif., 1977—. Author: Nonqualified Deffered Compensation Plans-The Wave of the Future, 1985. Officer, Vista Del Mar Child Care Center, Los Angeles, 1968-84; treas. Nat. Little League of Santa Monica, 1984-85, pres., 1985-86, coach Bobby Sox Team, Santa Monica, 1987—; curriculum com. Santa Monica Sch. Dist., 1983-84. Mem. ABA, Western Pension Conf., U. Pa. Alumni Soc. So. Calif. (pres. 1971-79, dir. 1979—), The Group, Alpha Kappa Psi (disting. life). Republican. Jewish. Club: Mountaingate Tennis Los Angeles). Home: 616 23d St Santa Monica CA 90402 Office: 10960 Wilshire Blvd Suite 1800 Los Angeles CA 90024

CARRIGAN, JIM RICHARD, judge; b. Mobridge, S.D., Aug. 24, 1929; s. Leo Michael and Mildred Ione (Jaycox) C.; m. Beverly Jean Halpin, June 2, 1956; children: Sheila, Maura, Patrick, Kathleen, Andrew, Michael. Ph.B., J.D., U. N.D., 1953; LL.M. in Taxation, NYU, 1956. Bar: N.D. 1953, Colo. 1956. Assoc. firm Long & Smart, Denver, 1956; asst. prof. law U. Denver, 1956-59; vis. assoc. prof. NYU Law Sch., 1958, U. Wash. Law Sch., 1959-60; jud. adminstr. State of Colo., 1960-61; individual practice law Denver, 1961-62; prof. law U. Colo., 1961-67; partner firm Carrigan & Bragg (and predecessors); (predecessors), Boulder, Colo., Denver, 1967-76; justice Colo. Supreme Ct., 1976-79; judge U.S. Dist. Ct. for Colo., 1979—; mem. Colo. Bd. Bar Examiners, 1969-71; lectr. Nat. Coll. State Judiciary, 1964-77; bd. dirs., mem. exec. com. Nat. Bd. Trial Advocacy, 1978—; bd. dirs., mem. faculty, mem. exec. com. Nat. Inst. Trial Advocacy. Editor-in-chief: N.D. Law Rev., 1952-53; editor: DICTA, 1957-59, Internat. Soc. Barristers Quar, 1972-79; contbr. numerous articles to profl. jours. Chmn. Boulder County Democratic Party, 1967-68; bd. regents U. Colo., 1975-76; bd. visitors U. N.D. Coll. Law, 1983—. Recipient Disting. Service award Nat. Coll. State Judiciary, 1969, Outstanding Alumnus award U. N.D., 1973, Regent Emeritus award U. Colo., 1977. Fellow Colo. Bar Found., Boulder County Bar Found.; mem. ABA (action com. on tort system improvement 1985—, TIPS sect. long range planning council 1986—), Colo., Boulder, Denver County bar assns., Cath. Lawyers Guild, Internat. Soc. Barristers, Internat. Acad. Trial Lawyers, Fed. Judges Assn. (bd. dirs. 1985—), Am. Judicature Soc. (bd. dirs. 1985—), Order of Coif, Phi Beta Kappa. Roman Catholic. Club: Denver Athletic. Lodge: Rotary. Office: US Dist Ct C-236 1929 Stout St Denver CO 80294

CARROLL, DAVID WILLIAM, computer consultant, author; b. Portland, Oreg., May 16, 1949; s. Cecil Thomas and Florence Emily (Grant) C.; m. Carol Lynne Cantando, Nov. 17, 1984; step-children—Theresa Marie, Georgia Bahia, Nicholas Joshua. Student Pomona Coll., 1967-68. System design cons. Calif. Microwave, Sunnyvale, 1977-80; tech. mgr. Vector Communications, Sunnyvale, 1978-80; sales mgr. Fulcrum Computer Systems, San Jose, Calif., 1980-82; computer cons. Harris Electronics, Santa Clara, Calif., 1982; game programmer Videosoft Corp., Santa Clara, 1983; author, free-lance writer, Volcano, Calif., 1983—; cons. Multitech Electronics, Sunnyvale, 1984—, Jilchris Devel. Co., 1986—, Gold Country Computers, 1986—; dir. World Videovend Inc., Sunnyvale, 1984—; tech. reviewer Scott Foresman & Co., Chgo., 1984—, Dow Jones-Irwin, Homewood, Ill., 1984—. Editor Newsletter, 1985; author: Telecommunications With the IBM PCjr, 1985, Programming with Turbo Pascal, 1985, Assembly Language Programming for the IBM PC, 1986, Modula 2 Programming for the IBM PC, 1986; contbr. numerous computer-related articles to mags. Leader 4H, Volcano, 1984—; capt. Calif. Wing, CAP, 1980-83. Recipient Space Communications and Electronics award NASA, 1964. Mem. IEEE, Assn. Computing Machinery, Am. Inst. Indsl. Engrs., Mensa. Democrat. Home: 23522 Shakeridge Rd Volcano CA 95689 Office: Amador Computer PO Box 699 Pine Grove CA 95665

CARROLL, JAMES RAYMOND, marketing professional; b. Chgo., Nov. 13, 1934; s. Daniel James and Jennie Ann (Michels) C.; m. Phyllis A., Feb. 4, 1967; children: Daniel James, Melanie Ann. AA in Applied Sci., DeVry Inst. Tech., Chgo., 1962. Programmer IBM Corp., San Francisco, 1962-63; field engring. specialist RCA Corp., Cherry Hill, N.J., 1963-73; systems analyst Litton Industries, New Orleans, 1973-74; dist. services mgr. ITEL Inc., San Francisco, 1974-79; peripheral product mgr. Tandem Computers, Cupertino, Calif., 1979-85; product mktg. mgr. Spectra Logic Corp., Mountain View, Calif., 1985—; ptnr. Azary Inc., Scott Valley, Calif., 1983—, Rugged Digital Computers, Mountain View, 1983—. Lodge: Rotary (sec. San Jose, Calif. club 1985-86, v.p. 1986-87). Home: 1725 Seville Way San Jose CA 95131 Office: Spectra Logic Corp 297 N Bernardo Ave Mountain View CA 94043

CARROLL, JOHN JOSEPH, III, atmospheric science educator; b. N.Y.C., Sept. 2, 1940; s. John J. Jr. and Irene Cathrine (Lenz); m. Ingeborg Wiese, June 2, 1966; children: Andrea, Nicholas. BS in Geology, CCNY, Bklyn., 1962; M in Atmospheric Scis., UCLA, 1966, PhD in Atmospheric Scis., 1971. Cons. McDonnell-Douglas Corp., Santa Monica, Calif., 1967-69; asst. prof. atmospheric scis. U. Calif., Davis, 1969-75, assoc. prof., 1976-84, prof., 1985—; cons., Davis, 1975—; corp. and govtl. research contracter, 1972—. Contbr. articles to profl. jours. Recipient various grants NSF, 1973-84. Mem. Am. Geophys. Union, Am. Meteorol. Soc., Cal Aggie Flying Farmers, Nat. Atmospheric Sci. Assn., Sigma Xi. Clubs: Stonegate Country (Davis) (bd. dirs. 1983-85). Avocations: sailing, aviation. Office: U Calif Dept Land Air Water Resources Davis CA 95616

CARROLL, JOSEPH BARRY, professional basketball player; b. Pine Bluff, AR, July 24, 1958. BA in Business Economics, Purdue U. Player Golden State Warriors, Nat. Basketball Assn., Oakland, Calif., 1980-84, 85—, team SIMAC, Milan, Italy, 1984-85; Selected to NBA All-Star team, 1987. Office: care Golden State Warriors Oakland Coliseum Arena Oakland CA 94621 *

CARROLL, LON DAY, dentist; b. Cambridge, Nebr., Feb. 7, 1934; s. Charles Worth and Lola May (Gutzman) C.; m. Linda Anne Reese, Oct. 2, 1954; children—Denise Anne, Brian Rees, Suzanne, Stacie. Grad., Jr. Coll. of Eastern Oreg., 1954; D.M.D., U. Oreg., 1961; M in Acad. Gen. Dentistry, 1985. Gen. practice dentistry, Portland, 1961—; asst. prof. crown and bridge dept. Dental Sch., U. Oreg., 1961-63; mem. dental staff Woodland Park Hosp., 1973-79. Chmn. United Good Neighbors, Portland, 1971-72; asst. scoutmaster Boy Scouts Am., 1973-75; coach Barlow Babe Ruth Baseball, Gresham, Oreg., 1973-75, Gresham Girls Little League, 1977-78. Served with USAF, 1954-57; capt. USNR, 1967—. Named Oreg. Gen. Dentist of Yr., 1985. Fellow Internat. Coll. Dentists (vice-regent 11th dist. 1982-84, dist. regent 1985—), Acad. Gen. Dentistry (editor Recall 1983, 84, Most Improved Jour. award 1983, 84), Am. Coll. Dentists, Pierre Fauchard Acad.; mem. Multnomah County Dental Soc. (pres. 1974-75), Alumni Assn. U. Oreg. Dental Sch. (pres. 1978-79), Oreg. State Dental Assn. (editor 1978-81), Delta Sigma Delta (supreme grand master 1983-84, chmn. nominating, budget and awards coms. 1984-85). Democrat. Mormon. Lodge: Elks. Home: 10301 SE Eastmont Dr Gresham OR 97030 Office: 1234 SE 122d Ave Portland OR 97233

CARROLL, THOMAS WILLIAM, plant pathology educator; b. Los Angeles, Aug. 22, 1932; s. William Joseph and Moneta Emma (Dwight) C.; m. Earlene L. Carroll, Aug. 24, 1952; children: Vickie, Lori, Jenifer, Amy. BS, Calif. State Poly. U., Pomona, 1954; MS, U. Calif., Davis, 1962, PhD, 1965. Postdoctoral research plant pathologist U. Calif., Davis, 1965-66; asst. prof. botany Mont. State U., Bozeman, 1966-69, assoc. prof., 1969-74, prof. plant pathology, 1974—; cons. Carroll & Zaske Cons. Plant Pathologists, Bozeman, 1985—. Served as sgt. U.S. Army, 1955-58. Research grantee NSF, Bozeman, 1968-80, Am. Malting Barley Assn., Bozeman, 1983-86, Mont. Wheat Research and Mktg. Commn., Bozeman, 1984-85, USDA, GAM, OGPS, Bozeman, 1985—. Mem. AAAS, Am. Phytopathol. Soc., Am. Soc. Virology, Sigma Xi. Republican. Presbyterian. Avocations: travelling, fishing, hunting, cross-country skiing. Home: 412 W Grant St Bozeman MT 59715 Office: Mont State U Bozeman MT 59717

CARRUTHERS, GARREY E., state governor; b. Alamosa, Colo., Aug. 29, 1939; m. Katherine Carruthers; children: Deborah, Carol, Steven. BS in Agr., N.Mex. State U., MS in Agrl. Econs.; PhD in Econs., Iowa State U. From assst. prof. to assoc. prof. dept. agrl. econs. and agrl. bus. N.Mex. State U., Las Cruces, 1968-71; spl. asst. U.S. Sec. of Agr., Washington, 1974-75; acting dir. N.Mex. Water Resources Research Inst., 1976-78; asst. sec. interior for land and water resources Dept. Interior, Washington, 1981-85; Gov. State of N.Mex., 1987—. Contbr. articles to profl. jours. Mem. Am. Agrl. Econs. Assn., Western Agrl. Econs. Assn., Am. Acad. Polit. and Social Services, Sigma Xi, Omicron Delta Kappa. Office: State Capitol Office of Gov Santa Fe NM 87503 *

CARRUTHERS, PETER AMBLER, physicist, educator; b. Lafayette, Ind., Oct. 7, 1935; s. Maurice Earl and Nila (Ambler) C.; m. Jean Ann Breitenbecher, Feb. 26, 1955; children: Peter, Debra, Kathryn; m. Lucy J. Marston, July 10, 1969; m. Cornelia B. Dobrovolsky, June 20, 1981. B.S., Carnegie Inst. Tech., 1957, M.S., 1957; Ph.D., Cornell U., 1960. Asst. prof. Cornell U., N.Y., 1961-63, assoc. prof., 1963-67, prof. physics, atomic and solid state physics, nuclear studies, 1967-73; div. leader, theoretical div. Los Alamos (N.Mex.) Sci. Lab., 1973-80, group leader of elem. particles and field theory, 1980-85, sr. fellow, 1980-86; prof., dept. head physics U. Ariz., Tucson, 1986—; vis. asso. prof. Calif. Inst. Tech., 1965, vis. prof., 1969-70, 77-78; mem. physics adv. panel NSF, 1975-80, chmn., 1978-80; trustee Aspen Center for Physics, 1976-82, chmn. exec. com., 1977-79, chmn. bd. trustees, 1979-82, advisor, 1982—; mem. High Energy Physics Adv. Panel, 1978-82; mem. com. on U.S.-USSR cooperation in physics Nat. Acad. Scis., 1978-82; cons. SRI Internat., 1976-81, MacArthur Found., 1981-82, 84—, Inst. for Def. Analysis, 1985—. Author: (with R. Brout) Lectures on the Many-Electron Problem, 1963, Introduction to Unitary Symmetry, 1966, Spin and Isospin in Particle Physics, 1971; editor: (with D. Strottman) Hadronic Matter in Collision, 1986; cons. editor Soviet Physics Series; editorial advisor World Sci. Trustee Santa Fe Inst., 1984—, v.p., 1986-87. Recipient Merit award Carnegie Mellon U., 1980; Alfred P. Sloan research fellow, 1963-65; NSF sr. postdoctoral fellow U. Rome, 1967-68; Alexander von Humboldt sr. fellow, 1987—. Fellow Am. Phys. Soc. (panel on pub. affairs 1984-86), AAAS. Home: 2220 E Camino Miraval Tucscon AZ 85718 Office: U Ariz Dept Physics Tucson AZ 85721

CARSON, EDWARD MANSFIELD, banker; b. Tucson, Nov. 6, 1929; s. Ernest Lee and Earline M. (Mansfield) C.; m. Nadine Anne Severns, Dec. 13, 1952; children: Dawn, Tod. B.S. in Bus. Adminstrn., Ariz. State U., 1951; grad., Stonier Sch. Banking, Rutgers U., 1963. With First Interstate Bank of Ariz., Phoenix, 1951-85; exec. v.p. First Interstate Bank of Ariz., 1969-72, chief adminstrv. officer, 1972-75, vice chmn. bd., 1975-77, pres., chief exec. officer, 1977-85, also dir.; pres., dir. First Interstate Bancorp, Los Angeles, 1985—; bd. dirs. Inspiration Resources Corp., Ramada Inns, Inc., First Interstate Bank of Oreg. Bd. fellows Am. Grad. Sch. Internat. Mgmt. Recipient Service award Ariz. State U. Alumni Assn., 1968, named to Hall of Fame, 1977. Mem. Assn. Res. City Bankers, Assn. Bank Holding Cos. (bd. dirs.). Clubs: Kiva, Paradise Valley Country, Phoenix Country, Thunderbirds. Address: First Interstate Bancorp 707 Wilshire Blvd Los Angeles CA 90017

CARSON, MARY LOUISE, social worker; b. Long Beach, Calif., Nov. 29, 1944; d. William Wallace and Emma Louise (Dell) Busby; m. James Arthur Carson, Jan. 1976. BA, U. Oreg., 1966; MSW, U. Calif., 1981. Lic. clin. social worker. From social worker II to child welfare worker Alameda County Dept. Social Services, Oakland, Calif., 1966-74; dep. probation officer Alameda County Probation Dept., Oakland, Calif., 1974-77; tng. cons. San Francisco Child Abuse Council, 1978-79; coordinator profl. parent program Children's Garden, San Rafael, Calif., 1981-82, supr. social work, 1982-83, clin. dir., 1983—; instr. Peralta Community Coll. Dist., Oakland, 1978-79, South county Community Coll. Dist., Hayward, Calif., 1975-81; coleader of child abuse workshop Chabot Coll., 1977; tng. officer in child abuse Hayward Police Dept., 1981; field worker instr. grad. sch. social welfare program U. Calif., Berkeley, 1983-84. Mem. exec. com. Marin county Community Mental Health Child and Youth Com., 1985-86; com. chmn. Community Mental Health Outpatient Task Force, 1985; v.p. bd. dirs. Pacific Children's Ctr., Oakland, 1977-79. Mem. Calif. Assn. Services for Children (peer reviewer 1984). Home: 2900 Redwood Rd Napa CA 94558 Office: Children's Garden 7 Mt Lassen Dr Suite B256 San Rafael CA 94903

CARSON, ROBERT DOUGLAS, financial consultant, brokerage house executive; b. Phila., July 30, 1945; s. William Edward Carson and Mary Theres (Allen) Jones; m. Sheryl Jean Stroup, Feb. 21, 1970; children: Stephen, William, Timothy. Engr. of Mines degree, Colo. Sch. Mines, 1967; MS, Pitts. State U., 1969. Registered profl. engr., Colo., Ky., W.Va., Utah, Wyo. Gen. mgr. Pontiki Coal Corp., Lovely, Ky., 1974-78; v.p. Mapco Inc., Tulsa, 1978-79; pres. Natomas Coal Co., Englewood, Colo., 1979-81, West Appa Coal Co., Aurora, Colo., 1981-85; fin. cons. Merrill Lynch, Denver, 1986—; cons. in field, 1985-86. Com. mem. Parent-Tchrs. Orgn. Cottonwood Creek Elem. Sch., Englewood, 1986—. Mem. Soc. Mining Engrs., Am. Inst. Mine Engrs. Republican. Roman Catholic. Avocations: tennis, fishing, traveling. Office: Merrill Lynch 1700 Lincoln 46th Floor Denver CO 80203-4599

CARSTEN, MARY E., biochemist, educator; b. Berlin, Germany, Mar. 2, 1922; came to U.S., 1940, naturalized, 1946; d. Paul and Frida (Born) C.; m. Don Marlin, Apr. 23, 1964. A.B., N.Y. U., 1946, M.S., 1948, Ph.D., 1951. Instr. N.Y. U., 1951-53; research asso. microbiology Columbia Coll. Physicians and Surgeons, 1953-55; mem. faculty U. Calif. at Los Angeles Med. Sch., 1956—, prof. obstetrics and gynecology, 1970—; established investigator Los Angeles County Heart Assn., 1961-64. Contbg. author: Ion Exchangers in Organic and Biochemistry, 1957, Thyrotropin, 1963, Biology of Gestation, 1968, The Prostaglandins, Clinical Applications in Human Reproduction, 1972, The Biochemistry of Smooth Muscle, 1976, Excitation-Contraction Coupling in Smooth Muscle, 1977, Uterine Physiology, 1979, Initiation of Parturition: Prevention of Prematurity, 1983, Essentials of Obstetrics and Gynecology, 1986; contbr. articles to profl. jours. Nat. Found. Infantile Paralysis fellow, 1954-55; Am. Cancer Soc. fellow, 1955-57; recipient award cardiovascular research Los Angeles County Heart Assn., 1962, 63, 64, Research Career Devel. award USPHS, 1964-74. Mem. Am. Soc. Biol. Chemists, Am. Chem. Soc., N.Y. Acad. Scis., Am. Physiol. Soc., Soc. for Gynecol. Investigation, Sigma Xi. Home: 624 N Highland Ave Los Angeles CA 90036

CARTÉ, GEORGE WAYNE, geophysicist, mayor; b. Buhl, Idaho, Sept. 8, 1940; s. Harold D. Carte and Reba E. (Lammert) Magoon; m. Katherine I. Williams, Sept. 8, 1962; children: Charles M., Theresa L., Jeannette M., Suzanne I. AAS, Columbia Basin Coll., Wash., 1962; BS in Geol. Engring., U. Idaho, 1964; postgrad. U. Hawaii, 1978-79. Hydraulic engr. U.S. Geol. Survey, Anchorage, 1964-66; seismologist AK Tsunami Warning Ctr., Palmer, Alaska, 1966—; instr. Mat-Su Community Coll., Palmer, 1971-72, 81. Mayor City of Palmer, 1981—; chmn. Palmer Planning and Zoning Commn., 1968-78; mem. Mat-Su Borough Planning Commn., 1975-78. Recipient cert. of achievement Anchorage Fed. Exec. Assocs., 1981, 87. Mem. Alaska Mcpl. League (bd. dirs. 1983-86, pres. 1986-87), Earthquake Engring. Research Inst., Seismol. Soc. Am., Am. Geophys. Union, Tsunami Soc., Alaska Geol. Soc. Mem. Pentecostal Ch. Home: 367 N Valley Way Palmer AK 99645 Office: 910 S Felton St Palmer AK 99645

CARTER, AARON LOUIS, aerospace company executive; b. Center, Tex., Dec. 6, 1944; s. John Robert and Mary (Dupree) C.; m. Mary Alice Jones, Aug. 20, 1967; children: Carol, Cheryl, Candice. BSME, Calif. State U., Fullerton, 1968, MSME, 1971; EDCE, U. So. Calif., 1978, PhDME, 1981. Mem. tech. staff Rockwell Internat. Inc., Anaheim, Calif., 1968-72; mgr. engring. div. Holmes & Narver Inc., Orange, Calif., 1972-83; lctr. UCLA, 1981-83, Calif. State U., Fullerton, 1982—. Mem. ASME. Avocations: fishing, skiing, backpacking. Office: Hughes Aircraft Co 1610 Forbes Way Long Beach CA 90810

CARTER, ARTHUR H., infosystems specialist, paramedic; b. Bklyn., Jan. 21, 1945; m. Linda L. Bryson, Feb. 1, 1984; 1 child, Adam. BA in Communications, Evergreen State Coll., 1973, BS in Computer Sci., 1986. Ins. sales rep. N.Y. Life Ins. Co., Olympia, Wash., 1969-71; firefighter McLane Fire Dept., Olympia, 1972-74; paramedic Lacey (Wash.) Fire Dept., 1974—, info. mgmt. officer, 1984—, mgmt. info. systems project engr., 1985—. Mem. Lacey Energy Adv. Bd., 1983—. Mem. Soc. Info. Mgmt. Avocations: photography, astronomy. Office: Lacey Fire Dept PO Box 3366 Lacey WA 98503

CARTER, CLAYTON CHESTER, insurance loss control executive, consultant; b. Portland, Oreg., Sept. 4, 1942; s. Chester Boyd and Margaret (Brady) C.; m. Carolyn Jean Arvin, July 31, 1965; children: Stephen C., Jeffrey M. BBA, U. Portland, 1964. Underwriter comml. lines Fireman's Fund Ins. Co., Portland, 1965-68, tech. advisor loss control dept., 1968-76; tech. advisor loss control dept. Fireman's Fund Ins. Co., Boise, Idaho, 1976-82; mgr. loss control dept. Fireman's Fund Ins. Co., Portland, 1982—; instr. defensive driving Portland Traffic Safety Commn., 1973-76, 82—. Recipient Spoke award U.S. Jaycees, Portland chpt. Fellow Am. Soc. Safety Engrs. (sec. 1980-81, treas. 1981-82), Oreg. Defensive Driving Instrs. Assn. (treas. 1983-84, pres. 1984-86); mem. Nat. Safety Council (cert. defensive driving instr., instr. achievement award 1985). Republican. Roman Catholic. Avocations: stamp collecting, fishing, backpacking, tennis. Home: 1695 NW 131st Portland OR 97229 Office: Fireman's Fund Ins Co 121 SW Salmon St Suite 830 Portland OR 97204

CARTER, DAVID LAVERE, soil scientist, researcher, consultant; b. Tremonton, Utah, June 10, 1933; s. Gordon Ray and Mary Eldora (Hirschi) C.; m. Virginia Beutler, June 1, 1953; children: Allen David, Roger Gordon, Brent Ryan. BS, Utah State U., 1955, MS, 1957; PhD, Oreg. State U., 1961. Soil scientist USDA Agrl. Research Service, Corvallis, Oreg., 1956-60; research soil scientist, line project leader USDA Agrl. Research Service, Weslaco, Tex., 1960-65; research soil scientist USDA Agrl. Research Service, Kimberly, Idaho, 1965-68, supervisory soil scientist, research leader, 1968—. Contbr. sci. articles to profl. jours. Recipient Emmett J. Culligan award World Water Soc. Fellow Am. Soc. Agronomy (cert.), Soil Sci. Soc. Am. (cert., soil conservation award 1985); mem. Soil Conservation Soc. Am., AAAS, Internat. Soc. Soil Sci., Western Soc. Soil Sci. Mormon. Office: Snake River Conservation Research Ctr Rt 1 Box 186 Kimberly ID 83341

CARTER, DENNIS ROBERT, biomechanical engineer, educator; b. Santa Monica, Calif., Aug. 9, 1949; s. Garth Benaire and Betty Jacqueline (Saderup) C.; m. Alice Amanda Eisenstat, Aug. 16, 1969; children: Amanda, Todd. BS, U. Mich., 1971; MS, Stanford U., 1973, PhD, 1976. Asst. prof. biomech. engring. U. Wash., Seattle, 1976-79, Harvard U. Sch. Medicine, Boston, 1979-82; lectr. MIT, Cambridge, 1979-82; biomed. engr. VA Med. Ctr., Palo Alto, Calif., 1982—; assoc. prof. Stanford (Calif.) U., 1982—. Bd. assoc. editors Jour. Orthopaedic Research, 1983—; assoc. editor Jour. Biomech. Engring., 1987—; mem. editorial cons. panel Jour. Biomechs., 1984—; contbr. numerous articles to profl. and scholarly jours. Recipient Research Career Devel. award NIH, 1981-86. Mem. Am. Soc. Biomechs., European Soc. Biomechs., Orthopaedic Research Soc. (pres 1988—, bd. dirs. 1986—), Hip Soc., Tau Beta Pi. Democrat. Mormon. Avocations: cooking, coaching children's soccer and basketball. Office: Stanford U Dept Mech Engring div Design Stanford CA 94305

CARTER, EDWARD WILLIAM, retail executive. m. Hannah Locke Caldwell, 1963; children: William Dailey, Ann Carter Huneke. AB, UCLA, 1932; MBA cum laude, Harvard, 1937; LLD (hon.), Occidental Coll., 1962. Chmn. emeritus bd. dirs. Carter Hawley Hale Stores, Inc., Los Angeles. Trustee Occidental Coll., Brookings Instn., Los Angeles County Mus. Art, Nat. Humanities Ctr. Com. Econ. Devel.; bd. dirs. Assocs. Harvard Grad. Sch. Bus., Stanford Research Inst., James Irvine Found., Santa Anita Found., Los Angeles Philharm. Assn.; mem. vis. com. UCLA Grad. Sch. Mgmt.; mem. Woodrow Wilson Internat. Center Council, Harvard Bd. Overseers Com. Depts. Econs., Art Mus. and Univ. Resources, Council on Fgn. Relations. Mem. Bus. Council, Conf. Bd., Council on Fgn. Relations. Clubs: Calif. (Los Angeles), Los Angeles Country; Pacific Union, Bohemian, Burlingame Country (San Francisco); Cypress Point (Pebble Beach). Office: Carter Hawley Hale Stores 550 S Flower St Los Angeles CA 90071

CARTER, GARRY, entrepreneur; b. Fayetteville, Ark., Jan. 20, 1948; s. S. Russell and Elma I. (Dotson) C.; m. Wendy Scott Neustrup, Feb. 14, 1981; children: Joshua Andrew, Zoë Nicole. Student, U. Ark., 1966-71, Undergrad. Pilot Tng., Willow AFB, 1972. Commd. 2d lt. USAF, 1972, advanced through grades to 1st lt.; tactical fighter pilot U.S. Air Force, Europe, 1972-75; resigned U.S. Air Force, 1975; owner The Flite Suit Co., Pope Valley, Calif., 1976—; owner, chief cons. Advise & Compute, Angwin, Calif., 1984—. Mem. U.S Parachute Assn. (bd. dirs. 1980-84, named World Champion 1973, 77, 79). Republican. Avocations: skydiving, computers, gardening, sports. Home: 1065 Summit Lake Dr Angwin CA 94508

CARTER, GRACE MURRAY, infosystems specialist; b. N.Y.C., Aug. 18, 1940; d. Francis Joseph and Madge (O'Donnell) Murray; m. Robert H. Carter. BA, Duke U., 1962; MS, Stevens Inst. Tech., 1966; PhD, Rand Grad. Inst., 1974. Staff mem. Bell Telephone Labs., Holmdel, N.J., 1962-68; asst. dept. head, info. scientist The Rand Corp., Santa Monica, Calif., 1975-76, sr. info. scientist, 1976—; cons. NSF, 1975-86, NIH, 1985. Contbr. numerous articles to profl. jours. Mem. AAAS. Home: 2002 Las Flores Canyon Rd Malibu CA 90265 Office: The Rand Corp 1700 Main St Santa Monica CA 90401

CARTER, JOEL WILLIAM, parks and recreation educator; b. Americus, Ga., Nov. 26, 1932; s. Xury Bernard and Lizzie May (Gammage) C.; m. Doris Gail Higby, Feb. 2, 1959 (div. Aug. 1970); children: Shirley Lynn, Bonnie Jean, Michael Joel; m. Louise Wester, Aug. 14, 1971. AA, Ga. Southwestern Coll., 1952; BS, Fla. State U., 1954; MS, U. Tenn., 1955; PhD, Tex. A&M U., 1980. Supt. recreation Arlington Heights (Ill.) Park Dist., 1959-60; dir. parks and recreation Dundee (Ill.) Twp. Park Dist., 1960-68; prof. Calif. State Poly. U., Pomona, 1968—. Author: How to Make Athletic Equipment, 1960; contbr. articles to profl. jours. Commr. Archtl. Commn., Upland, Calif., 1974-84. Served to lt. (j.g.) USN, 1955-59. Mem. Calif. Park and Recreation Soc. (v.p. educators sect.), Nat. Recreation and Parks Assn. Republican. Mem. Brethern Ch. Avocations: classic cars, gardening, travel. Home: 882 Notre Dame Upland CA 91786 Office: Calif Poly State U Ornamental Horticulture Bldg 94 Pomona CA 91768

CARTER, JOY EATON, electrical engineer, consultant; b. Comanche, Tex., Feb. 8, 1923; d. Robert Lee and Carrie (Knudson) Eaton; m. Clarence J. Carter, Aug. 22, 1959; 1 child, Kathy Jean. Student, John Tarleton Agrl. Coll., 1939-40; B Music cum laude, N. Tex. State Tchrs. Coll., 1943, postgrad., 1944-45; postgrad., U. Tex., 1945; MSEE, Ohio State U., 1949, PhDEE and Radio Astronomy, 1957. Engr. aide Civil Service Wright Field, Dayton, Ohio, 1945-46; instr. math. Ohio State U., Columbus, 1946-48, research asst., assoc.Research Found., 1947-49, from instr. to asst. prof. elec. engring., 1949-58; research engr. N. Am. Aviation, Columbus, 1955-56; mem. tech. staff Space Tech. Labs. (later TRW Inc.), Redondo Beach, Calif., 1958-68; sect. head, staff engr. electronics research labs. The Aerospace Corp., El Segundo, 1968-72, staff engr. and mgr. system and terminals, USAF Satellite Communications System Program Office, 1972-77, mgr. communications subsystem Def. Satellite Communications System III Program Office, 1978-79; cons. Mayhill, N.Mex., 1979—. Mem. Am. Astron. Soc., IEEE (sr.), Soc. Women Engrs. (sr.), Am. Nat. Cattle Women (sec. Otero CowBelles chpt. 1986—), Sacramento Mountains Hist. Soc. (bd. dirs. 1986—), Pacific Coast Walking Horse Assn., Sun Country Walking Horse Assn., Nat. Pleasure Walking Horse Assn., Calif. Rare Fruit Growers, Native Plant Soc. N.Mex., Sigma Xi (life), Eta Kappa Nu (life), Sigma Alpha Iota (life), Alpha Chi, Kappa Delta Pi, Pi Mu Epsilon, Sigma Delta Epsilon. Avocations: breeding Tenn. Walking Horses, photography, sculpture, local history, gardening with unusual plants. Home and Office: PO Box 23 Mayhill NM 88339

CARTER, KELLY ARTHUR, air force officer; b. Omaha, Oct. 13, 1958; s. Victor Samuel and Marie Ann (Majek) C. Degree in phys. sci., U. Nebr., Omaha, 1981; degree in aero. engring., Air Force Inst. Tech., 1984. Commd. 2d lt. USAF, 1982, advanced through grades to capt., 1984; project officer USAF, Los Angeles Air Force Sta., 1984—. Editor Tiger Tales newsletter, 1982. Mem. AAAS, N.Y. Acad. Scis., Ohio Acad. Scis., Air Force Assn., Nature Conservancy Club. Avocations: photography, writng, reading. Office: Space Div/CLNCC Los Angeles AFS CA 90009

CARTER, MARTHA ELIZABETH, educator; b. Fayetteville, N.C., Nov. 20, 1935; d. Charlie David and Emma (Dawson) Spell; m. Donald Claython Fuller, Apr. 4, 1954 (div. Apr. 1972); children: Deborah Johnson, Sharon Holmes, Donald C., Anthony Craig; m. Ronald A. Carter, June 14, 1974. BS in Sci. Edn., SUNY, Old Westbury, 1975; MS, Calif. State U., Fullerton, 1979; postgrad., U.S. Internat. U. Cert. community coll. tchr., ednl. adminstr., Calif. Tchr. Willard Intermediate Sch., Santa Ana, 1976—, coordinator Univ. Calif. at Irvine Partnership Program, 1980-81, adminstrv. asst., 1981-82; adminstrv. intern Valley High Sch., 1978-79; panel mem. Fulbright Tchr. Exchange Interviewing Com., Santa Ana Unified Sch. Dist. Reading Com., supt. forum; v.p. sch. improvement program Willard Intermediate Sch.; coordinator coop. teaching for thinking adv. council Orange County Dept. Edn. representing Santa Ana (Calif.) Unified Sch., 1984. Mem. Assn. Supervision and Curriculum Devel., Santa Ana Educator Assn., Irvine C. of C., Black Cultural Council of Bowers Mus., Calif. Teaching Assn. Democrat. Avocations: golf, tennis, cooking.

CARTER, RICHARD BERT, church official, retired government official; b. Spokane, Wash., Dec. 2, 1916; s. Richard B. and Lula Selena (Jones) C.; B.A. in Polit. Sci., Wash. State U., 1939; postgrad. Georgetown U. Law Sch., 1941, Brown U., 1944, Brigham Young U. Extension, 1975-76; m. Mildred Brown, Sept. 6, 1952; children—Paul, Mark, Janis, David. Advt. credit mgr. Elec. Products Consol., Omaha, 1939-40; pub. communications ofcl., investigator FBI, Washington, 1940-41, Huntington, W.Va., 1941, Houston, 1942, Boston, 1943, S. Am., 1943, Providence, 1944-45, N.Y.C., 1945, Salt Lake City, 1945, P.R., 1946-48, Phoenix, 1948-50, Washington, 1950-51, Cleve., 1952-55, Seattle, 1955-75, ret., 1975; assoc. dir. stake and mission pub. communications dept. Ch. Hdqrs., Ch. of Jesus Christ of Latter-day Saints, Salt Lake City, 1975-77. Dist. chmn. Chief Seattle council Boy Scouts Am., 1967-68, Council v.p., 1971-72, council commr., 1973-74, nat. council rep., 1962-64, 72-74, dir. pub. relations, area II, Eagle Scout Assn., 1984—. Bd. dirs. Salvation Army, 1963, United Good Neighbors, 1962-63, mem. allocations com., 1962. Served to 1st lt., Intelligence Corps, U.S. Army, 1954. Recipient Silver Beaver award Boy Scouts Am., 1964, Vigil Honor, 1971; named Nat. Media Man-of-Month, Morality in Media, Inc., N.Y.C., 1976. Mem. Profl. Photographers Am., Internat. Assn. Bus. Communicators, Am. Security Council (nat. adv. bd.), Internat. Platform Assn., Sons Utah Pioneers (pres. 1982), SAR (bd. mgrs. Utah Soc., pres. Salt Lake City chpt.), William Carter Family Orgn. (nat. pres.), Nat. Assn. Chiefs of Police, Scabbard and Blade, Am. Media Network (nat. adv. bd.), Assn. Former Intelligence Officers, Alpha Phi Omega, Pi Sigma Alpha, Sigma Delta Chi, Phi Delta Theta. Mormon (coordinator pub. communications council Seattle area 1973-75, br. pres. 1944-45, dist. pres. 1954-55, high priest 1958—, pres. stake 1959-64, stake Sunday Sch. pres. 1980-81). Clubs: Bonneville Knife and Fork (bd. dirs. 1982—), Rotary (dir., editor The Rotary Bee, 1982-83, Paul Harris fellow 1982, award for best newsletter in dist. 1983). Author: The Sunbeam Years--an Autobiography, 1986; assoc. editor FBI Investigator, 1965-75; contbg. author, editor: Biographies of Sons of Utah Pioneers, 1982. Home: 2180 S Elaine Dr Bountiful UT 84010

CARTER, ROBERTA ECCLESTON, educator, therapist; b. Pitts.; d. Robert E. and Emily B. (Bucar) Carter; (div.); children—David Michael, Daniel Michael. Student Edinboro State U., 1962-63; B.S., California State U. of Pa., 1966; M.Ed., U. Pitts., 1969; postgrad. Rosebridge Grad. Sch., Walnut Creek, Calif., 1985—. Tchr., Bethel Park Sch. Dist., Pa., 1966-69; writer, media asst. Field Ednl. Pub., San Francisco, 1969-70; educator, counselor, specialist Alameda Unified Sch. Dist., Calif., 1970—; master trainer Calif. State Dept. Edn., Sacramento, 1984—; personal growth cons., Alameda, 1983—. Author: People, Places and Products, 1970, Teaching/Learning Units, 1969; co-author: Teacher's Manual Let's Read, 1968. Mem. AAUW, Calif. Fedn. Bus. and Profl. Women (legis. chair Alameda br. 1984-85, membership chair 1985), NEA, Calif. Edn. Assn., Alameda Edn. Assn., Charter Planetary Soc., Oakland Mus., Exploratorium, Big Bros. of East Bay, Alameda C. of C. (service award 1985). Republican. Avocations: aerobics, gardening, travel, tennis. Home: 1516 E Shore Dr Alameda CA 94501

CARTER, SHERMAN FLOYD, university administrator, retired army officer; b. American Fork, Utah, Mar. 27, 1926; s. Floyd and Florence (Nelson) C.; m. Lois Redington, July 7, 1950 (div. June 1978); children: Carrie Cail Schulman, Martha Joan Hays, Susan Cay Coffland, Jeffrey David, Kathryn Ann, Daniel Edward; m. Sharon Y. Anderson, Oct. 19, 1978 (dec. July 1986); m. Nina Bradfield, May 1, 1987. BS, U. Ga., 1955; grad., U.S. Army Command and Gen. Staff Coll., 1956; MBA, Syracuse U., 1957; grad., Armed Forces Staff Coll., 1961, Indsl. Coll. of the Armed Forces, 1967; PhD, Am. U., 1968. Enlisted U.S. Army, 1945, advanced through grades to col., 1968, ret., 1969; v.p. fin. and adminstrn. U. Idaho, Moscow, 1969-78; v.p. fin. U. Alaska, Fairbanks, 1978-80, exec. v.p., 1980—. Treas. U. Alaska Found. Inc., Fairbanks, 1978—, U. Idaho Found. Inc., Moscow, 1969-78. Decorated Legion of Merit. Mem. Nat. Assn. Univ. and Coll. Bus. Officers, Western Assn. Univ. and Coll. Bus. Officers, Sigma Chi. Republican. Lodge: Rotary. Avocation: outdoor sports. Home: 709 Colville Fairbanks AK 99775 Office: U Alaska 101 Bunnell Bldg 303 Tanana Dr Fairbanks AK 99775-5260

CARTER, SUSAN MONTGOMERY, actress, business woman; b. Great Falls, Mont.; d. A. Raymond and Jean (Anderson) Montgomery; m. George Robert Carter, III, July 15, 1961 (div.), children—George Robert, Anne Strong. B.A., UCLA, 1961; postgrad. Stanford U. Bus. Sch. Profl. model Vogue mag., 1969-75, Harper's Bazaar mag., 1976-79; actress stage and screen, 1969—, commls., 1970—; mktg. and adminstrv. dir. Landor Assocs., Los Angeles and Hawaii, 1979-82; personal fin. mgr., 1982—; exec. bd. dirs. Olympic Five Ring Club. Trustee Strong Carter Dental Clinic, Honolulu, 1963-69; bd. dirs. Hawaii Child and Family Service, 1963-69, Big Bros. Chgo., 1973-75, Northwestern U. Med. Ctr., 1973-75; dir. Hawaii Air/Water Pollution Campaign, 1967; bd. govs. Burlington House, N.Y.C., 1969-75; active Los Angeles Olympic Com., UCLA Chancellors Assocs., Royce 270, Los Angeles Jr. League; bd. govs. Jeffrey Found., 1985—; patron Vatican Art, Nat. Charity League. Mem. Prytanean Soc. Clubs: San Francisco Met.; Hawaii Outrigger Canoe; Beach (Santa Monica); Beverly Hills Country.

CARTER, VICTOR M., private investor; b. Rostov, Russia, Aug. 21, 1910; s. Mark and Fanya (Rudnick) C.; m. Adrea Zucker, July 15, 1928; 1 dau., Fanya. Dir., 1st Interstate Bank, Hamburger Hamlets, Inc., Nat. Lumber, Ampal-Am. Israel Corp.; mem. exec. com. IDB Bankholding Co.; v.p., dir. So. Calif. Theatre Assn. Past pres. United Way, City of Hope, Japan Am. Soc., Japanese Philharmonic Soc. Bd. dirs. Fedn. Jewish Welfare Orgns., World Affairs Council, Century City Cultural Commn.; hon. chmn. bd. Israel Devel. Corp., CLAL (Israel) Ltd. (exec. com.), Teva Pharm.; bd. govs. Jewish Agy., Inc. Democrat. Mason; mem. B'nai B'rith. Club: Hillcrest Country. Home and Office: 10375 Wilshire Blvd 2A Los Angeles CA 90024

CARTERETTE, EDWARD CALVIN HAYES, psychologist; b. Mt. Tabor, N.C., July 10, 1921; s. John Calvin and Alma Olivia (Fowler) C.; m. Patricia Spidel Blum, Jan. 18, 1955 (dec. Jan. 1977); 1 son, Christopher Edward; m. Noël McSherry, Sept. 27, 1980. Diploma, U.S. Army Command and Gen. Staff Coll., 1943; A.B., U. Chgo., 1949; A.B. cum laude, Harvard U., 1952; M.A., Ind. U., 1954, Ph.D. (NSF predoctoral fellow), 1956. Served as enlisted man U.S. Army, 1937-42; commd. 2d lt. 1942, advanced through grades to lt. col., 1946; served in Hawaii, 1937-41; dep. dir. personnel Hampton Roads Port of Embarcation, Newport News, Va., 1942-45; adj. gen. 32d Inf. Div., Philippines and Japan, 1945-46; ret. 1946; mem. research staff acoustics lab. M.I.T., 1952; instr. UCLA, 1956-58, asst. prof. psychology, 1958-63, asso. prof., 1963-68, prof., 1968—; vis. asso. prof. U. Calif., Berkeley, 1966; NSF postdoctoral fellow in physics Royal Inst. Tech., Stockholm and Cambridge (Eng.) U., 1960-61; NSF sr. postdoctoral fellow Inst. Math. Studies in Social Scis., Stanford U., 1965-66; cons. neuropsychology VA Wadsworth Hosp. Center, 1978—; chmn. selection com. Woodrow Wilson Nat. Fellowship Found., 1963-72, chmn., 1966-72; mem. editorial com. U. Calif. Press, 1970-77, co-chmn., 1973-77, mem. bd. control, 1973-77; Disting. visitor Am. Psychol. Assn., 1979—; bd. dirs. Packard Humanities Inst., 1987—. Author: Brain Function: Speech, Language and Communication, 1966, (with Margaret Hubbard Jones) Informal Speech, 1974; editor: (with M.P. Friedman) Handbook of Perception, 11 vols, 1973-78, Academic Press Series in Cognition and Perception, 1973—; asso. editor: Perception and Psychophysics, 1972—, Music Perception, 1981—. Fellow Acoustical Soc. Am., AAAS (electorate nominating com. 1981-84, chmn. 1984), Am. Psychol. Assn., Soc. Exptl. Psychologists (sec.-treas., mem. exec. com. 1982-87, co-chmn. 1977); mem. IEEE, Psychonomic Soc., Internat. Neuropsychol. Soc., Soc. Math. Psychology, Sigma Xi (sec. 1983-86). Club: Harvard Radcliffe of So. Calif. (bd. dirs. 1982-85, v.p. 1985-87, pres. 1987—). Home: 456 Greencraig Rd Los Angeles CA 90049 Office: U Calif Dept Psychology Los Angeles CA 90024

CARTY, WILLIAM E., moving services company executive. Chmn. U-Haul Internat., Inc., Phoenix. Office: Office of the Chmn U-Haul Internat Inc 2727 N Central Ave Phoenix AZ 85004 *

CARUANA, EDWARD JOHN, architectural technologist, consultant; b. St. Julian's, Malta, May 13, 1947; s. Andrew and Edwidge (Portanier) C.; divorced; children: Bryan, Kimberly; m. Yoko Arizumi, Oct. 11, 1985; 1 stepchild: Ryuhei. Diploma in archtl. tech., Centennial Coll. Applied Arts and Tech., Toronto, Ont., Can., 1973. Intermediate and sr. draftsman W.Z.M.H., Toronto, Ont., Can., 1971-78; job capt. Edward Lutman, Toronto, Ont., Can., 1978, Joseph Bognan, Toronto, Ont., Can., 1978-79; sr. job. capt. Crang & Boake, Toronto, Ont., Can., 1979-81; job capt. Gensler & Assocs., Los Angeles, 1981—. Mem. AIA (assoc.), Am. Hypnosis Assn., Photographers Soc. Am. Democrat. Methodist. Avocations: photography, travelling, reading, hypnotherapy. Office: Gensler & Assocs 2049 Century Park E Suite 570 Los Angeles CA 90067

CARUSO, WILLIAM JOSEPH, food service management consultant; b. Summit, N.J., July 25, 1948; s. Joseph R. and Mary (Crane) C.; m. Linda Ann Renn, Apr. 26, 1972; children: Kristin Ann, Tara Lee. BS, Cornell U., 1970; MBA, U. Colo., 1974. Prin. The LFL Cons. Group, Toronto, Ont., Can., 1974-82, The Ricca, Colburn & Caruso Group, Englewood, Colo., 1982—; dir. Clin. Industries, Aurora, Co., 1985—; dir. CLN Industries, Aurora, Colo., 1985—. Contbr. articles to profl. jours. Served as sgt. USAR, 1970-76. Fellow Foodservice Cons. Soc. Internat. (bd. dirs. 1980-86, pres. 1985-86, pres.-elect 1984-85, treas. 1983-84, sec. 1982-83), Cornell Soc. Hotelmen (2d v.p. 1987—, award of service 1986), Sigma Chi Alumni Assn. (bd. dirs. 1983—). Republican. Roman Catholic. Avocations: sports, motor touring, automobiles. Home: 7819 Waverly Mountain Littleton CO 80127 Office: Thomas Ricca Assocs 6087 S Quebec #200 Englewood CO 80111

CARUTHERS, MARVIN HARRY, biochemistry educator; b. Des Moines, Feb. 11, 1940; s. Harry A. and Eva D. (Schultz) C.; m. Jennie Mary Smoly, Oct. 9, 1971; children: Jonathan, Andrew. BS, Iowa State U., 1962; PhD, Northwestern U., 1968. Postdoctoral fellow U. Wis., Madison, 1968-70; sr. research scientist MIT, Cambridge, 1970-72; from asst. prof. to prof. biochemistry U. Colo., Boulder, 1973—; mem. sci. adv. bd. Amgen, Thousand Oaks, Calif., and Boulder, 1980—; cons. Applied Biosystems, 1981—. Contbr. articles to profl. jours.; patentee in field. Recipient career devel. award USPHS, 1975-80; Guggenheim fellow, 1981. Mem. AAAS, Am. Chem. Soc., Am. Soc. Biol. Chemists. Home: 2450 Cragmore Rd Boulder CO 80303 Office: U Colo Dept Chemistry and Biochemistry Boulder CO 80309

CARVER, BEVERLY ANN, educational software company executive, consultant; b. Douglas, Wyo., Sept. 17, 1934; d. John Emmett and Lillian Beryl (Russell) Carver; m. Raymond Pergeau, July 12, 1958; (div.); children—Natalie Alayne, Raymond James. B.A. (scholar), MacMurray Coll., 1956; Ed.M., Harvard U., 1957; Ph.D. (Charles F. Mott fellow), Ariz. State U., 1980. Cert. tchr., supt., reading specialist, Ariz. Tchr., Anchorage, Alaska, 1957-60, Roseville, Minn., 1960-63; instr. elem. edn. Hamline U., St. Paul, 1963-66; tchr., Scottsdale, Ariz., 1966-70; sch. adminstr. Scottsdale Unified Sch. Dist. 48, 1970-81; v.p. mktg. and product devel. Computing Adventures, Ltd., Phoenix, 1981-84; pres. Computing Adventures, Ltd., Phoenix, 1985—; cons. editorial, small bus. Parent adv. with mentally retarded; precinct committeewoman dist. 28, Scottsdale, 1975-76, sec., 1976; v.p. Monterosa Homeowners' Assn., 1984; mem. Dist. 1 Human Rights Com. for Developmentally Disabled, Ariz. Mem. Am. Assn. Sch. Adminstrs., Computer Users in Edn., Phi Delta Kappa, Pi Lambda Theta. Unitarian. Author poems; developer ednl. software. Office: Computing Adventures Ltd PO Box 15565 Phoenix AZ 53060

CARVER, DONALD STANLEY, university administrator, consultant; b. Colfax, Wash., Feb. 22, 1928; s. John Stuart and Martha Jane (Buck) C.; m. Barbara Bristol, Apr. 2, 1949; children—David, John, Steven, Joan, Jane, Beth, Scott. B.S., Wash. State U., 1950; Ph.D., Iowa State U., 1953. With Swift & Co., 1953-54, Gen. Mills, Inc., 1956-63; pres. Ovaltine Food Products Co., Villa Park, Ill., 1963-70; v.p. planning Standard Brands, Inc., N.Y.C., 1971-72; pres. Cracker Jack Co., Chgo., 1972-74; dean Sch. Mgmt. and Bus. Nat. U., San Diego, 1974—. Served to 1st lt. USAF, 1954-56. Recipient Packaging award of Yr., Packaging Inst., 1967, 69. Mem. Grocery Mfrs. Am., Pet Food Inst., Animal Nutrition Research Council, Sales and Mktg. Execs. San Diego, Small Bus. Assn. (dir.), Am. Assembly Schs. Bus., Phi Kappa Phi, Sigma Xi, Phi Delta Theta. Republican. Presbyterian. Club: Executives (Chgo.). Contbr. articles to popular mags., profl. jours. Home: 12102 Rancho Bernardo Rd San Diego CA 92128 Office: Sch Mgmt and Bus Nat U 4141 Camino Del Rio S San Diego CA 92108

CARVER, DOROTHY LEE ESKEW (MRS. JOHN JAMES CARVER), educator; b. Brady, Tex., July 10, 1926; d. Clyde Albert and A. Maurine (Meadows) Eskew; student So. Ore. Coll., 1942-43, Coll. Eastern Utah, 1965-67; B.A., U. Utah, 1968; M.A., Cal. State Coll. at Hayward, 1970; postgrad. Mills Coll., 1971; m. John James Carver, Feb. 26, 1944; children—John James, Sheila Carver Bentley, Chuck, David. Instr., Rutherford Bus. Coll., Dallas, 1944-45; sec. Adolph Coors Co., Golden, Colo., 1945-47; instr. English, Coll. Eastern Utah, Price, 1968-69; instr. speech Modesto (Calif.) Jr. Coll., 1970-71; instr. personal devel. men and women Heald Bus. Colls., Oakland, Calif., 1972-74, dean curricula, Walnut Creek, Calif., 1974-86; instr. Diablo Valley Coll., Pleasant Hill, Calif., 1986—; communications cons. Oakland Army Base, Crocker Bank, U.S. Steel, I. Magnin, Artec Internat. Author: Developing Listening Skills. Mem. Gov.'s. Conf. on Higher Edn. in Utah, 1968; mem. finance com. Coll. Eastern Utah, 1967-69; active various community drives. Judge election Republican party, 1960, 64. Bd. dirs. Opportunity Center, Symphony of the Mountain. Mem. AAUW, Bus. and Profl. Womens Club, Nat. Assn. Deans and Women Administrs., Delta Kappa Gamma. Episcopalian (supt. Sunday Sch. 1967-69). Clubs: Soroptimist Internat. (pres. Walnut Creek 1979-80); Order Eastern Star. Home: 20 Coronado Ct Walnut Creek CA 94596 Office: Diablo Valley Coll 2085 N Broadway Walnut Creek CA 94596

CARVER, JUANITA, plastic company executive; b. Indpls., Apr. 8, 1929; d. Willard H. and Golda M. Ashe; children—Daniel Charles, Robin Lewis, Scott Alan. Treas. and chmn. bd. dirs. MOBIUS, 1983—; pres. Carver Corp., Phoenix, 1977—. Bd. dirs. Scottsdale Meml. Hosp. Aux., 1964-65, now assoc. Republican. Methodist. Patentee latch hook rug yarn organizer. Home: 6255 E Avalon St Scottsdale AZ 85251

CARVER, PHILIP HOWARD, state agency economist; b. Cheyenne, Wyo., Sept. 30, 1950; s. Harold Issac and Charlotte Ann (Wolfer) C.; m. Jane Ann Conover, July 27, 1973 (div. Dec. 1984); children: Laura G., Jason H. BA with honors, Revelle Coll., 1972; PhD, Johns Hopkins U., 1978. Asst. prof. Dartmouth Coll., Hanover, NH, 1978-80; sr. economist dept. energy State of Oreg., Salem, 1980—; policy cons. utilities and other groups Balt. and Hanover, 1974-80. Contbr. articles to profl. jours. Mem. Citizen Action for Lasting Security, Salem, 1983-86, also bd. dirs. Mem. AAAS, Sierra Club, Quest (group leader Portland, Oreg. chpt. 1984-85). Democrat. Avocations: jogging, cross-country skiing, hiking, bicycling, tennis. Home: 1049 Cynthia St N Salem OR 97303 Office: Oreg Dept Energy 625 Marion St NE Salem OR 97310

CARVER, RONALD ELLIS, physician; b. Emmett, Idaho, Sept. 27, 1941; s. C. Ellis and Eleanor (Wright) C.; m. Mary Virginia Bates, Apr. 17, 1971; children: Jonathan Wright, Christopher Ronald. Student, Pasadena City Coll., 1959-61; BA, UCLA, 1963; MD with honors, Baylor Coll. Medicine, 1967. Diplomate Am. Bd. Ob-Gyn. Intern Oreg. Health Scis. U., Portland, 1967-68, resident in ob-gyn, 1970-74, asst. clin. prof., 1978—; mem. staff St. Charles Med. Ctr., Bend, Oreg., 1974—, chief of staff, 1981; practice medicine specializing in ob-gyn Mt. View Women's Clinic P.C., Bend, 1974—; mem. vis. staff Cen. Oreg. Dist. Hosp., Redmond, 1974—. Pres. Cen. Oreg. Health Planning Council, 1976-78; bd. dirs. Sunriver (Oreg.) Music Festival, 1986; served as elder in Presbyn. Ch., 1986—. Served to lt. M.C., USAR, 1968-70, Vietnam. Decorated Bronze Star with Combat V device. Fellow Am. Coll. Ob-Gyns, Am. Fertility Soc., Am. Soc. Cervical Dysplasia and Colposcopy; mem. AMA, Cen. Oreg. Med. Soc., Oreg. Med. Assn., Physicians for Social Responsibility, Sierra Club. Republican. Clubs: Bend Golf and Country, Bend Swim (v.p., bd. dirs. 1985—). Avocations: gardening, hiking, backpacking. Home: 60345 Woodside Rd Bend OR 97702 Office: Mt View Women's Clinic PC 2381 NE Conners Ave Bend OR 97701

CARY, JOHN ROBERT, physics educator; b. Livermore, Calif., Mar. 15, 1953; s. John Robert and Helen Cramer (Harris) C.; m. Christine Lettie Graham, June 11, 1972; children: Jeremy, Colleen, Cathryn. BA, U. Calif., Irvine, 1973; MA, U. Calif., Berkeley, 1975, PhD, 1979. Staff mem. Los Alamos (N.Mex.) Nat. Lab., 1978-80; research scientist Inst. for Fusion Studies, Austin, Tex., 1980-84; assoc. prof. physics U. Colo., Boulder, 1984—; cons. Oakridge (Tenn.) Nat. Lab., 1985—. Contbr. articles to profl. jours. Pres.' scholar U. Calif., Irvine, 1970; Regent's fellow U. Calif., Berkeley, 1975. Mem. Am. Phys. Soc. Office: U Colo Dept Astrophysics Planetary Atmospheric Scis Campus Box 391 Boulder CO 80309

CARY, SHARON L., accountant, computer installation consultant, fruit and poultry farmer; b. San Francisco, Nov. 5, 1950. Office mgr. Shamrock Motors, Mill Valley, Calif., 1975-77; acctg. clk. Sonoma Lifestyle Furniture, Rohnert Park, Calif., 1977-80; acct. Living Earth Crafts, Santa Rosa, Calif., 1980-83; controller Santa Rosa Golf and Country Club, 1983—; cons. in field, Santa Rosa, 1970—; research dir. The Great Egg, Petaluma, Calif., 1979—. Author: Smooth Transition: A Guide to Your Small Business's First Computer, 1985. Avocations: cooking, dancing, painting.

CASALE, GERALD VINCENT, music-video artist, director, entertainer; b. Kent, Ohio, July 28, 1948. BFA, Kent State U., 1970, MFA, 1974; post-grad., U. Mich., 1971. Instr. Akron (Ohio) U., 1975; counselor, therapist Ohio Mental Health Service Ctr., Akron, 1975-77; graphic designer Unit Prodns., Akron, 1977-78; recording artist and singer, songwriter with group Devo Los Angeles, 1978—; chmn. Devo, Inc., Los Angeles, 1978—; creative cons. Digital Prodns., Los Angeles, 1982-83. Albums include Are We Not Men? We are Devo!, 1978 (cert. gold album), Freedom of Choice, 1980 (cert. platinum album), Duty Now for the Future, 1979, New Traditionalists, 1981, O No It's Devo, 1982, Shout, 1984; dir. film shorts, videos Whip It, Freedom of Choice, Girl U Want, Through Being Cool, Love Without Anger, Beautiful World (A.F.I Short Subject award, Mus. Modern Art Collection), That's Good, Peek-a-Boo, Time Out for Fun, Shout, We're All Devo (1984 Video Internat. Recognition award); dir. Touch and Go, Panorama (performed by Cars, Electra Asylum Recording Artists), Mystic Rhythms (performed by Rush, Polydor Recording Artists), I Can See It (performed by Blancmange, London Records), One More Colour (performed by Jane Siberry, A&M Records), Love is the Strangest Way (performed by Andy Summers). Mem. Musician's Union, AFTRA, Screen Actors Guild, Dirs. Guild, Nat. Acad. Video Arts Soc., Am. Film Inst. Avocations: printmaking, photography, tennis, running. Home: 2714 4th St Santa Monica CA 90405 Office: DEVO Inc c/o Neal Levin CPA 9595 Wilshire Blvd Beverly Hills CA 90212

CASANI, EDWARD KANE, aerospace research and development manager; b. Phila., June 17, 1935; s. John C. and Julia J. (Bateman) C.; children—Anita, Aundrea. C.E., U. Pa., 1959; postgrad. U. So. Calif., UCLA. With Jet Propulsion Lab., Pasadena, Calif., 1958—, mgr. spacecraft system design and integration sect., 1973-76, project mgr. infrared astron. satellite, 1976-80, dep. mgr. Observational Systems div., 1980-81, div. mgr., 1981—; tchr. various univs., guest lectr., cons.; cons. movie Andromeda Strain; v.p. JETS, Ltd.; active design and devel. of Ranger, Mariner, Viking, Voyager and Galileo spacecraft. Mem. YMCA. Recipient Exceptional Service medal NASA. Mem. AIAA, Sigma Xi. Contbr. articles profl. jours.

CASANOVA, ALDO JOHN, sculptor; b. San Francisco, Feb. 8, 1929; s. Felice and Teresa (Papini) C.; children: Aviva, Liana, Anabelle. B.A., San Francisco State U., 1950, M.A., 1951; Ph.D., Ohio State U., 1957. Asst. prof. art San Francisco State U., 1951-53; asst. prof. Antioch (Ohio) Coll., 1956-58; asst. prof. art Tyler Sch. Art, Temple U., Phila., 1961-64, Tyler Sch. Art, Temple U. (Italy campus), Rome, 1968-70; prof. art Scripps Coll., Claremont, Calif., 1966—; chmn. art dept. Scripps Coll., 1971-73; vis. prof. SUNY, 1981; faculty mem. Skowhegan Sch. Painting and Sculpture, Maine, summers 1973-74. One-man shows include, Esther Robles Gallery, Los Angeles, 1967, Santa Barbara (Calif.) Mus., 1967, Calif. Inst. Tech., 1972, Carl Schlosberg Fine Arts, Los Angeles, 1977, SUNY, 1981; represented in permanent collections, Whitney Mus., San Francisco Mus. Art, Hirshhorn Collection, Cornell U., Columbus (Ohio) Mus., UCLA Sculpture Garden, Calif. Inst. Tech., Pasadena, Univ. Judaism, Los Angeles, Air and Space Mus., Washington. Recipient Prix-de-Rome Am. Acad. in Rome, 1958-61; Louis Comfort Tiffany award, 1970. Fellow Am. Acad. in Rome; mem. Sculptors Guild. Democrat. Roman Catholic. Office: Scripps Coll Claremont CA 91711

CASAZZA, RALPH ANTHONY, architect; b. Reno, May 12, 1926; s. Anthony T. and Rena Katherine (Lagomarsino) C.; m. Eileen Kathryn Cole, Feb. 4, 1954; children: Thomas, Richard, Kathryn, Marianne, Susan, Elizabeth. Student, U. Nev., Calif. State U., San Francisco. Pvt. practice architecture Reno, 1948-49; ptnr. Lockard & Casazza, Reno, 1949-72; pres. Casazza, Peetz & Assocs., Reno, 1972—; owner, v.p., mgr. Tore & Casa, Ltd., Reno, 1963-86; pres. Triangle Devel. Co., Reno, 1982-86. Mem. Boosters Club U. Nev., 1984—, U. Nev. Found., 1984—, Econ. Devel. Authority Western Nev., 1984—; del. to Rep. Nat. Conv., San Francisco, 1956; Nev. state chmn. Young Reps., 1956-58. Mem. AIA (legis. com. 1986), Nev. Inst. Architects (pres.1960-62, pres. N. Nev. chpt. 1956-58, Bradley B. Kidder award 1965), Associated Gen. Contractors, Inter Council Shopping Ctrs. (state dir. 1972-74, legis. dir. 1986—), Western Indsl. Nev. Roman Catholic. Club: Prospectors (Reno). Lodges: KC (dep. grand knight 1965-67), Italian Benevolent Soc. (v.p. 1962-65). Home: 2395 Crescent Circle Reno NV 89509 Office: Casazza Peetz & Hancock Architects 480 Casazza Dr Reno NV 89502

CASCOS, PATRICIA VILLARREAL, hydrologist; b. Mexico City, Mar. 19, 1944; came to U.S., 1949; d. Isauro Barte Villarreal and Elena Cascos Tilley; m. David Holmen Peterson, June 21, 1981; children: Erik Michael, Sabrina Elena. BA, San Francisco State U., 1978, MA, 1985. Chemist Trapelo-West, Richmond, Calif., 1974-75; oceanographer Frederic Burk Found., San Francisco, 1976-79; hydrologist, geographic info. system specialist U.S. Geol. Survey, Menlo Park, Calif., 1979—; guest lectr. Mills Coll., Oakland, 1980, Hayward State Coll., 1985, San Jose State U., 1982, 83; presenter workshops, seminars at high schs. Recipient Meritorious Service award U.S. Geol. Survey, 1985. Mem. Math. Sci. Resource Network. Club: Commonwealth (San Francisco). Office: Water Resources U S Geol Survey 345 Middlefield Rd Menlo Park CA 94025

CASE, DONALD OWEN, information science educator; b. Bellingham, Wash., May 20, 1953; s. Oliver Maxwell and Esther Mary (Earlandson) C. BA, Evergreen State Coll., 1976; MLS, Syracuse U., 1977; PhD in Communication Research, Stanford U., 1984. Systems analyst N.Y.S. Housing Authority, 1978-79; research asst. Stanford (Calif.) U., 1979-82; statis. cons. Ctr. Advanced Study, Stanford, 1982-83; asst. prof. info. sci. UCLAGrad. Sch. Library Info. Sci., 1983—. Co-editor: Visual Display Terminals, 1984; contbr. articles to profl. jours. Fellow Stanford U., 1979-80; Retail Clarks Internat. scholar, 1971-75. Mem. AAAS, Internat. Communication Assn., Am. Soc. Info. Sci. (treas. Los Angeles County chpt. 1985—), ALA. Office: GSLIS UCLA 405 Hilgard Ave Los Angeles CA 90024

CASE, JAMES HUGHSON, mathematics educator; b. Franklinville, N.Y., May 25, 1928; s. Hughson Lester and Ella Jane (Maxwell) C.; m. Joanna Elsie Hogue, Sept. 15, 1951; children: Judith, Thomas, Eliot. BS, Auburn U., 1950; PhD, Tulane U., 1954. Asst. prof. U. Rochester, N.Y., 1959-61; asst. prof. U. Utah, Salt Lake City, 1954-59, assoc. prof., 1961-69, prof., 1969—; cons. Gen. Dynamics Corp., Rochester, 1960-61, CIS Corp., Manhattan, Kans., 1983—. Patentee in field. Served with U.S. Army, 1955-56. Mem. Am. Math. Soc., AAAS. Home: 2286 Preston St Salt Lake City UT 84106 Office: U Utah Dept Math Salt Lake City UT 84112

CASE, LEE OWEN, JR., college official; b. Ann Arbor, Mich., Nov. 5, 1925; s. Lee Owen and Ava (Comin) C.; m. Dolores Anne DeLoof, July 1950 (div. Feb. 1958); children—Lee Douglas, John Bradford; m. Maria Theresia Breninger, Feb. 27, 1960; 1 adopted dau., Ingrid Case Dunlap. A.B., U. Mich., 1949. Editor Washtenaw Post-Trib, Ann Arbor, 1949; dir. pub. relations Edison Inst., Dearborn, Mich., 1951-54; field rep. Kersting, Brown, N.Y.C., 1954-58; campaign dir. Cumerford Corp., Kansas City, Mo., 1958-59; v.p. devel., pub. relations U. Santa Clara, 1959-69; v.p. planning, devel., Occidental Coll., Los Angeles, 1969—; bd. visitors South Western U. Law Sch., Los Angeles, 1981—. Chmn. Santa Clara City Proposition A, 1966; mem. Santa Clara County Planning Com. on Taxation and Legis., Santa Clara, 1968. Served to 1st lt. USAAF, 1943-46. Mem. Am. Coll. Pub. Relations Assn. (bd. dirs. 1968-74), Council for Advancement and Support Edn. (founding bd. dirs. 1974-75), 1st Tribute for Distinction in Advancement, Dist. VII, 1985), Santa Clara C. of C. (pres. 1967), Santa Clara County C. of C. (founding bd. dirs. 1968), Town Hall. Republican. Club: University (Los Angeles). Lodge: Rotary. Home: 2633 Risa Dr Glendale CA 91208 Office: Occidental Coll 1600 Campus Rd Los Angeles CA 90041

CASE, PAUL WATSON, JR., cable television company executive; b. Elmira, N.Y., Dec. 4, 1949; s. Paul Watson and Josephine Pharr (Pollock) C.; m. Laura Lee Moseley, Dec. 12, 1972; 1 child, Brian M. BA, U. Colo., 1971. Cert. computer programming Inst. Cert. Computer Profls., data processing Inst. Cert. Computer Profls. Programmer analyst Boulder (Colo.) Daily Camera, 1968-73; v.p. Mr. Steak Inc., Denver, 73-83, United Cable TV Corp., Denver, 1983—. Mem. Assn. Computer Machinery, Data Processing Mgmt. Assn. (cert.), Cable Data User Com. (chmn. 1986—). Home: 4672 S Kittredge Way Aurora CO 80015 Office: United Cable TV Corp 4700 S Syracuse Pkwy Denver CO 80237

CASE, ROBERT WILLIAM, geophysicist; b. Akron, Ohio, Nov. 3, 1952; s. Charles Roy and Marjorie (Hazlett) C.; m. Sarah Elizabeth Bentley, Nov. 21, 1981; children—Amy, Christen, Lee, Ben. B.S. in Geology, Allegheny Coll., 1975; M.S. in Geophysics, U. Utah, 1977. Geophysicist, Gulf Oil Corp., Casper, Wyo., 1977-80, Skyline Oil Co., Salt Lake City, 1980-86; cons. Denver, 1986—. Grad. fellow U. Utah, 1975; recipient W.M. Small Meml. award, Allegheny Coll., 1975. Mem. Soc. Exploration Geophysicists, Am. Assn. Petroleum Geologists, Wyo. Geol. Assn., Utah Geophys. Soc. (v.p. 1982-84). Episcopalian. Home: 4511 Homestead Littleton CO 80123 Office: Skyline Oil Co 1775 Sherman St Suite 1200 Denver CO 80203

CASE, STEPHEN SHEVLIN, lawyer; b. Mpls., Nov. 16, 1943; s. George Price and Helen (Beckwith) C.; m. Judy Elizabeth Everett, Apr. 5, 1969 (div. Feb. 1979); children—Mackenzie Beckwith, Julia Lee; m. 2d, Pamela Ellen Hansen, Aug. 26, 1949. B.A., Washington and Lee U., 1966, LL.B. with honors, 1969. Bar: Ariz. 1969. Assoc., Fennemore, Craig, von Ammon & Udall, Phoenix, 1969-73; majority atty. (Republican) Ariz. State Senate, 1973; trust counsel First Interstate Bank of Ariz., Phoenix, 1973-76; ptnr. Norris & Case, P.C., Sun City, Ariz., 1976-85, Case and Bennett, Sun City and Scottsdale, Ariz., 1985—; sec., dir. The Camel Bank, Inc.; instr. Golden Gate U., Phoenix Campus. Bd. dirs. Central Ariz. Estate Planning Council, 1978-81. Fellow Am. Coll. Probate Counsel; mem. ABA, State Bar Ariz. (chmn. sect. real property, probate and trust law 1981-82, chmn. sect. taxation 1983-84), Delta Theta Phi. Clubs: Paradise Valley Country; Rotary (dir. 1977-81) (Sun City, Ariz.). Contbr. articles in field to profl. jours. Office: 10032 W Bell Rd Sun City AZ 85351

CASE, WILLIAM B., sugar company executive; b. Lihue, Hawaii, Aug. 30, 1922; s. A. Hebbard and Elizabeth (McConnell) C.; m. Anne Goldsmith, July 12, 1952; children: Catherine, William Jr., Peter, Deborah, Mary Elizabeth, Patricia Anne. B.A., Williams Coll., 1947. Vice pres. C. Brewer & Co., Honolulu, 1971-75, sr. v.p., 1975—; pres., chmn. Hawaiian Agronomics, Honolulu, 1975-77; pres., chief exec. officer Hilo Coast Processing Co., Pekeekeo, Hawaii, 1982—; pres., dir. Olokele Sugar Co., Kauai, Hawaii, 1977—; pres., dir., chmn. bd. Ka'u Sugar Co., Hawaii, 1977—; pres., chief exec. officer, dir. Hilo Coast Processing Co., Hawaii, 1977—; pres. chmn. bd., dir. Wailuku Sugar Co., Maui, 1977—, Mauna Kea Sugar Co., Hilo, 1977—. Chmn. U.S. Dept. Agr. Hawaiian Agr. Stabilization, 1975; mem. exec. bd. Kilauea council Boy Scouts Am., 1972-76; pres. Brantley Rehab. Ctr., 1967-70. Served with USNR, 1943-46. Mem. Internat. Sugar Cane Tech., Hawaiian Sugar Planters Assn. (dir. 1971-81), Hawaiian Sugar Technologists. Clubs: Honolulu, Pacific, Hilo Yacht. Home: PO Box 18 Pekeekeo HI 96783 Office: Hilo Coast Processing Co PO Box 18 Pekeekeo HI 96783

CASEBEER, ROBERT (SCOTT), automobile dealer; b. Portland, Oreg., Feb. 20, 1955; s. Richard Roy and Marcia Jane (Wyland) C.; m. Leslie Diane Green, Aug. 7, 1977; children: Matthew McKay, Alexander James. Student, U. Oreg., 1973-77; grad., Gen. Motors Sch. Mgmt., 1981. Sales rep. Blitz-Weinhard Co. subs. G. Heileman Brewing Co., Portland, 1976-77, Joe Romania Chevrolet, Eugene, Oreg., 1976-77; pres. Capitol Chevrolet Cadillac Inc./Capitol Toyota Inc., Salem, Oreg., 1977—. Chmn. YMCA Youth Dr., Salem, 1983; fin. chmn. Com. to Re-Elect Sue Harris Mayor, Salem, 1984; mem. Salem Econ. Devel. Commn., 1985; vice chmn. Marion County (Oreg.) Jail Constrn. Project, 1986; bd. dirs. Salem Art Assn., chmn. art fair, 1986-87; bd. dirs. United Way Willamette Valley. Recipient Service Supremacy dealer award Chevrolet div. Gen. Motors, 1984, 85, Service Mgmt. award Gen. Motors, 1985. Mem. Salem C. of C., Salem Home Builders Assn., Willamette U. Cardinal Roundtable, Nat. Automobile Dealers Assn., Oreg. Auto Dealers Assn. (chmn. polit. action com. 1986). Republican. Episcopalian. Club: Illahe Hills Country (Salem). Lodge: Rotary (bd.dirs.). Avocations: running, snowskiing, golf, tennis. Home: 1866 Merritt St S Salem OR 97302 Office: Capitol Chevrolet Cadillac Capitol Toyota 2575 Mission St S Salem OR 97309

CASEBIER, RONALD LEROY, paper company executive; b. Topeka, Oct. 11, 1933; s. Louis Roy and Ada Augusta (Behm) C.; m. Beverly Ann Barber, Dec. 5, 1959; children: Joel K., David S. BS, Wash. State U., 1955; PhD, U. Minn., 1959. Research supr. ITT Rayonier, Shelton, Wash., 1974-78, mgr. research programs, 1978-80, asst. dir., 1980-83, sr. tech. advisor, 1983-86, dir., 1986—; bd. dirs. Wash. Pulp and Paper Found. Contbr. articles to profl. jours.; patentee in field. Mem. Am. Chem. Soc. Office: ITT Rayonier Rayonier Research Ctr Shelton WA 98584

CASEY, J. JOSEPH, heavy construction and manufacturing company executive; b. 1921; married. Grad. Georgetown U.; postgrad NYU Law Sch. With Dillingham Corp., 1967—, v.p., controller, 1967-70, exec. v.p. Dillingham Corp. of Australia Ltd., 1970-72, pres., chief exec. officer, now chmn. subs., beginning 1972, then asst. to group v.p.-constrn. and pres., group v.p.-constrn., 1981-82, corp. pres. Honolulu, 1982—, also dir., now chief exec. officer, dir. Office: Dillingham Corp Box 3468 Honolulu HI 96801 *

CASEY, J(ESS) GREGORY, lawyer; b. Spokane, Wash., Feb. 22, 1946; s. Jess Garret and Marguerite (Schoenberg) C.; m. Candyce Roleen Buckingham, Apr. 5, 1968; children—Heidi Denise, Shaloma Annette, Brandon Reid, Marshall Wade. B.B.S., Gonzaga U., 1968, J.D., 1971. Bar: Wash. 1971, U.S. Dist. Ct. (ea. dist.) Wash., 1971. Legal intern, then assoc. Richter, Wimberley, & Ericson, Spokane, 1968-73, ptnr., 1973-77; sole practice, Spokane, 1977-83; ptnr. Casey & Ecton, Spokane, 1983-86; pres. Casey & Ecton, 1986—. Mem. Wash. State Bar Assn., Wash. State Trial Lawyers Assn. (trustee 1980-83, eastern v.p. 1984), Assn. Trial Lawyers Am. Office: Casey & Ecton W 1402 Broadway Spokane WA 99201

CASEY, JOSEPH T., corporate executive; b. 1931; married. B.S., Fordham U. With Arrow Surgical Supply Co., 1947-51, Am. Lumberman's Mutual Casualty Co. of Ill., 1951-52, Thoroughbred Racing Protective Bur. Inc., 1952-55; mgr. audits Touche, Ross, Bailey & Smart, 1955-63; controller Litton Industries Inc., Beverly Hills, Calif., 1963-67, v.p. fin., 1967-69, sr. v.p. fin., 1969-76, exec. v.p. fin., 1976—. Office: Litton Industries Inc 360 N Crescent Dr Beverly Hills CA 90210 *

CASEY, STEPHEN JAMES, administrative electrical engineer; b. Hanford, Calif., Aug. 20, 1948; s. James Alfred and Juanita Alice (Spanke) C.; m. Maureen Patricia Kearney, May 26, 1985. AA, Southwestern Coll., Chula Vista, Calif., 1968; BSEE, San Diego State U., 1972; MBA, Pepperdine U., 1985. Assoc. elec. engr. Lockheed Calif. Co., Burbank, 1973-74, mgmt. trainee, mfg. br., 1974-75, engr., functional test, 1975, supr. mgr. test equipment engring., 1975-84, supr. and group engr., mfg. research automation technology dept., 1984—. Mem. Nat. Mgmt. Assn., Pepperdine Alumni Assn. Republican. Home: 1304 N Sparks St Burbank CA 91506

CASEY, WILLIAM JOSEPH, ophthalmologist; b. Balt., Feb. 9, 1936; s. Harry J. and Florence H. (McDivit) C. A.B., Johns Hopkins U., 1958, M.D., 1962. Intern Kaiser Found. Hosp., San Francisco, 1962-63; resident ophthalmology U. Calif. Med. Center-San Francisco, 1963-64, 65-67; postdoctoral fellow NIH, Uppsala, Sweden, 1964-65; lectr. anatomy Makerere U. Coll., Kampala, Uganda, 1965; Heed Ophthalmic fellow Yale, New Haven, 1967; dir. eye bank St. John Ophthalmic Hosp., Jerusalem, Jordan, 1967-69, dir. Eye Bank Fellowship Program, 1969—; prin. investigator for research grant NIH for Glaucoma Research, San Francisco, 1969-77; practice medicine specializing in ophthalmology, San Francisco, 1969—; cons. ophthalmology San Francisco Gen. Hosp., 1969—; assoc. prof. ophthalmology U. Calif.-San Francisco, 1969—; mem. adv. bd. Visual Scis. Info. Center, U. Calif.-Berkeley, 1970-76; expert civilian cons. in ophthalmology, U.S. Army, Letterman Gen. Hosp., Presidio San Francisco, 1972; owner St. Clement Winery, St. Helena, Calif., 1976—. Vice-chmn. Bay Area Graphic Arts Council, Calif. Palace Legion of Honor, San Francisco, 1971-72. Knighted Order Hosp. St. John Jerusalem (Eng.). Diplomate Am. Bd. Ophthalmology. Mem. AMA, Assn. Research Vision and Ophthalmology, Am. Acad. Ophthalmology and Otolaryngology, Pacific Coast Oto-Ophthalmol. Soc., Calif. Med. Assn. Home: 3584 Pierce St San Francisco CA 94123 Office: 490 Post St Suite 934 San Francisco CA 94102

CASH, BARBARA LEWIS, interior designer; b. Ft. Bragg, N.C., Sept. 21, 1952; s. Leroy Herman and Margaret Jean (Nofcier) Lewis; m. Larry Stephen Cash, June 22, 1979; children: Allison Leia, Jordan Lewis. BFA in Interior Design, N. Tex. State U., 1974. Cert. Nat. Council Interior Design Qualification. Interior designer Louis Owen, Inc., Anchorage, 1976-78; owner, prin. Interior Space Design, Anchorage, 1978—; exam proctor Nat. Council Interior Design Qualification, 1986. Interior design com. chair Anchorage Hist. and Fine Arts Mus. "Architecture for Children" exhibit, 1985; mem. Anchorage Community Coll. Interior Design Adv. Council. Mem. Am. Soc. Interior Designers (profl., treas. Alaska chpt. 1986), Interior Designers Alaska. Methodist. Avocation: snow skiing. Home: 2265 Arcadia Dr Anchorage AK 99517 Office: Interior Space Design 3111 C St Suite 202 Anchorage AK 99503

CASH, LARRY STEPHEN, architect; b. Mentone, Ala., May 24, 1951; s. Max Gerome and Roberta (Galloway) C.; m. Barbara Jean Lewis, June 22, 1979; children: Allison Leah, Jordan Lewis. B.Arch. with honors, Auburn U. Intern architect/designer Hoover & Assocs., Palo Alto, Calif., 1973-76, Foug & Assocs., Palo Alto, 1976-77, architect, 1977; design architect Harold Wirum & Assocs., Anchorage, 1977-78; assoc. and project architect, Wirum & Cash, 1978-81, assoc., project mgr., 1981-83, ptnr., 1983-86; prin. Larry S. Cash Architects, Anchorage, 1986—. Recipient Design Excellence Medal and hon. mention Nat. Inst. Archtl. Edn., 1972. Mem. AIA (chmn. south central sect. Alaska chpt. 1984). Methodist.

CASH, ROY DON, gas and petroleum company executive; b. Shamrock, Tex., June 27, 1942; s. Bill R. and Billie Mae (Lisle) C.; m. Sondra Kay Burleson, Feb. 20, 1966; 1 child, Clay Collin. BSIndslE, Tex. Tech U., 1966. Registered profl. engr., Utah. Former engr. Amoco Prodn. Co.; v.p. Mountain Fuel Supply, Salt Lake City, 1976-79; pres. Wexpro Co., Salt Lake City, 1979-80; pres., chief exec. officer Mountain Fuel Supply Co., Salt Lake City, 1980-84; pres., chief exec. officer Questar Corp., Salt Lake City, 1984-85, pres., chmn., chief exec. officer, 1985—, also bd. dirs.; bd. dirs. Zions First Nat. Bank, Salt Lake City; trustee Inst. Gas Technology, Chgo., 1986—. Mem. Higher Edn. Master Planning Bd., Salt Lake City, 1986—; bd. dirs. Utah Symphony Orch., Salt Lake City, 1983-86. Mem. Soc. Petroleum Engrs., Rocky Mountain Oil and Gas Assn. (bd. dirs., pres. 1982-84), Utah Mfrs. Assn. (bd. dirs., chmn. 1986), Pacific Coast Gas Assn. (bd. dirs. 1981-85), Am. Gas Assn. Club: Alta (Salt Lake City), Fort Douglas Country. Avocations: boating, skiing, tennis, fishing, hunting. Office: Questar Corp 180 E First South St Salt Lake City UT 84147

CASHATT, CHARLES ALVIN, hydro-electric power generation company executive; b. Jamestown, N.C., Nov. 14, 1929; s. Charles Austin and Ethel Buren (Brady) C.; m. Wilma Jean O'Hagan, July 10, 1954; children—Jerry Dale, Nancy Jean. Grad. high sch., Jamestown. Bldg. contractor, Jamestown, 1949-50; 1954-58; powerhouse foreman Tri-Dam Project, Strawberry, Calif., 1958-66; power project mgr. Merced Irrigation Dist., Calif., 1966—. Contbr. article to ASCE pub.,1985. Pres. Merced County Credit Union, 1981-82. Served with USAF, 1950-54. Mem. Am. Legion. Republican. Lodge: Elks, Odd Fellows. Office: Merced Irrigation Dist 9188 Village Dr Snelling CA 95369

CASHEN, JOSEPH LAWRENCE, real estate broker; b. Kansas City, Mo., May 10, 1931; s. John Lawrence and Anna May (Sutcliffe) C.; m. Michele Ann Hayes, June 15, 1960; children: Michael, Patricia, Kelly. Student real estate U. Calif. at Los Angeles, 1965-66. Sales cons. chems. Economics Lab., Los Angeles, 1954-64; broker Forest E. Olsen Realtors, Canoga Park, Calif., 1964-67; pres. Property World, Inc., Woodland Hills, Calif., 1967-71; pres. Century 21 Real Estate #1, Inc., Woodland Hills, 1971—. Inventor in field. Pres. Police Activity League, Woodland Hills, 1975-80; dir., mem. adv. council Pierce Coll. Rotoract, 1974-75. Served with USMC, 1950-54. Mem. San Fernando Valley Bd. Realtors, Calif. Assn. Realtors, Nat. Assn. Realtors, Nat. Inst. Farm and Land Brokers, Nat. Assn. Home Builders, Aircraft Owners and Pilots Assn., Woodland Hills C. of C. (pres. 1976). Lodges: K.C., Rotary (pres. 1974-75). Office: 5959 Topanga Canyon Woodland Hills CA 91367

CASHIN, CONSTANCE ELIZABETH, marketing executive; b. Lynwood, Calif., Feb. 21, 1953; d. Albert Harris and Maryanna (Shigley) C. BA in Pub. Relations, U. So. Calif., 1975, MA in Journalism, 1978. Mktg. asst. Hahn Property Mgmt., Los Angeles, 1975-77, mktg. dir., 1977-79; mktg. dir. Nu-West Devel., Los Angeles, 1979-82, LA City Tower, Los Angeles, 1982-84, Draper and Kramer, Sherman Oaks, Calif., 1984-85, City Freeholds, Sherman Oaks, 1985—. Advisor North Univ. Park Assn., Los Angeles, 1982-84; mem. Los Angeles Olympic Organizing Com. Community Relations, 1983-84; chmn. KIDS Safety Week, So. Calif., 1986. Mem. So. Calif. Mktg. Dirs. Assn., (pres. 1984-85), Internat. Council of Shopping Ctrs. (cert., merit award 1985), U. So. Calif. Trojan Fourth Estate (pres. 1985—), Trojan Affiliates (publicity com. 1986-87), Trojan Jr. Aux. (2d v.p. 1982-83), Sherman Oaks C. of C. (bd. dirs. 1984—), Zeta Phi Eta (v.p., 1981-85, disting. service award 1985). Lodge: Order Eastern Star. Avocations: tap dancing, gardening, needlepoint, decorating. Office: City Freeholds Inc 13760 Riverside Dr Sherman Oaks CA 91423

CASIAS, DANIEL LAWRENCE, clinical psychologist; b. Dawson, N.Mex., Dec. 19, 1944; s. Maximilliano and Ignacita (Trujillo) C. BA in Secondary

Edn., U. N.Mex., 1972, MA in Counseling, 1974; PhD, Wash. State U., 1978. Dir. Adelante Youth Ctr., Santa Fe, 1978-79; county coordinator Sangre de Cristo Mental Health Ctr., Santa Fe, 1979-81; dir. mental health services Los Lunas (N.Mex.) Correctional Ctr., 1981—; pres. community bd.dirs. Valencia Counseling Services, Los Lunas, Estancia and Socorro, N.Mex., 1984—. Mem. Am. Psychol. Assn., Am. Correctional Assn. Roman Catholic. Lodge: Elks. Avocations: jogging, hiking, backpacking, boating, fishing. Home: Rt 1 Box 1107 Los Lunas NM 87031 Office: Los Lunas Correctional Ctr 3201 Hwy 85 SW Los Lunas NM 87031

CASKIE, WILLIAM WIRT, accountant, securities broker; b. N.Y.C., May 9, 1945; s. John Minor and Rosa Maria (Marchese) C.; B.S. in Physics, Georgetown U., 1967; M.B.A. in Ops. Research, N.Y.U., 1970; B.S. magna cum laude in Acctg., Golden Gate U., 1976. Tchr. math. N.Y.C. pub. schs., 1968-71; statistician Fed. Res. Bank of San Francisco, 1972-74; pvt. practice acctg., Marina Del Rey, Calif., 1977—; registered rep. Am. Pacific Securities Corp., 1986—. Mem. Assn. Bus. and Tax Cons., Nat. Assn. Enrolled Agts., Calif. Soc. Enrolled Agts., Mensa, Am. Pacific Securities Corp. (registered rep.). Home and Office: 557 1/2 Washington St Marina Del Rey CA 90292

CASMIR, FRED LUTZ, communication educator, consultant; b. Berlin, Germany, Dec. 30, 1928; came to U.S., 1954; s. Arthur and Gertrude (Wolter) C.; m. Mina G. Halliday, Dec. 12, 1986; children: Karen Anne Casmir Safian, Fred Otis. B.A. in Speech, David Lipscomb Coll., 1950; M.A., Ohio State U., 1955, Ph.D., 1961. Instr. speech Pepperdine Coll., Los Angeles, 1956-57, asst. prof. dept. of speech, 1957-62, assoc. prof., 1962-70, marshal of coll., 1959-70, of univ., 1970—, prof. Seaver Coll., Div. of Communication, Pepperdine U., 1970—; part-time instr. San Fernando Valley (Calif.) State Coll., 1961-64, asst. prof., 1965-69; assoc. prof. speech Calif. State U.-Northridge, 1970-73; assoc. prof. East Los Angeles Coll., 1973-74; cons. for oral communication Mgmt. Tng. Corp., 1968-70; radio spokesman Sta. KTYM, Los Angeles, 1969-70; pres. Nat. Edn. Inst., 1972, cons., 1972-74; mgmt. cons., 1975—; presenter numerous seminars, workshops and symposiums, 1962—; lectr. on communication for numerous internat. insts. and groups. Chmn. citizens by choice com. Los Angeles Republican Central Com., 1961-64, state nationalities dir., 1964-65, chmn. 31st congl. dist. com., mem. central com., 1970-72, treas. central com., 1971-72; mem. Calif. State Scholarship and Loan Commn., 1968-76; co-chmn. Citizens Com. for Welfare Reform Los Angeles County, 1971; mem. bicentennial com. Los Angeles City Schools, 1975-76, citizens mgmt. rev. com., 1976-77; sr. advisor to U.S. del. UNESCO, 2d World Confs. on Cultural Policies, Mexico City, 1982; elder Ch. of Christ, Arcadia, Calif., 1979-81; forum developer Pepperdine Ann. Bible Lectureships; U.S. del. Internat. Program Devel. Communication, Paris, 1984. Served with German Air Force, World War II. Recipient numerous civic and polit. awards; named Outstanding Tchr. Pepperdine U., 1973, 85. Mem. Speech Communication Assn. (founding editor Internat. and Intercultural Communication ann. 1973-76, chmn. publs. com. mass communications div. 1980-81), Internat. Soc. Phonetics, Western Speech-Communication Assn., World Communication Assn., (hon. dir., sponsor, advisor), Internat. Communication Assn., Soc. for Intercultural Edn., Tgn., Research (coordinating v.p. for N.Am., 1982-83). Author: Interaction: An Introduction to Speech Communication, 1974; Intercultural and International Communication, 1978; Contbr. numerous articles to profl. jours. and books. Home: 20139 Leadwell St #3 Canoga Park CA 91306 Office: Pepperdine U Div Communication Malibu CA 90265

CASPER, JEFFREY ELLIOT, research engineer, physics educator; b. N.Y.C., July 23, 1956; s. Herman and Betty (Rappaport) C. BS, MIT, 1977; MS, U. Chgo., 1978. Aerospace engr. NASA Johnson Space Ctr., Houston, 1978; mem. tech. staff Hughes Aircraft Co., Culver City, Calif., 1979-81; research engr. SRI Internat., Menlo Park, Calif., 1981—; physics educator Mission Coll., Santa Clara, Calif., 1983—. Mem. Soc. Photo-optical Instrumentation Soc., Sigma Xi. Home: 2449 Betlo Ave Mountain View CA 94043 Office: SRI Internat 333 Ravenwood Ave Menlo Park CA 94025

CASPERSON, KERRY LEE, health care clinic administrator; b. Preston, Idaho, July 4, 1956; d. Owen and Dottie (Wilde) C.; m. Deanne Porter, May 25, 1979; children: Cole, Brock, McKay. AS, Ricks Coll., 1978; BS in Health Care Adminstrn., Idaho State U., 1980, MBA, 1984. Lectr. Idaho State U., Pocatello, 1983—; adminstr. Pocatello Adolescent and Children's Clinic, 1980—. Mem. Med. Group Mgmt. Assn. Avocations: hunting, woodworking, fishing. Home: 15187 W Lacey Rd Pocatello ID 83202 Office: Pocatello Adolescent Children's Clinic 527 S 12th Pocatello ID 83201

CASSENS, NICHOLAS, JR., ceramics engineer; b. Sigourney, Iowa, Sept. 8, 1948; s. Nicholas and Wanda Fern (Lancaster) C.; B.S., Iowa State U., 1971, B.S. in Chem. Engring., 1971; M.S. in Material Sci. and Engring., U. Calif., Berkeley, 1979; m. Linda Joyce Morrow, Aug. 30, 1969; 1 son, Randall Scott, Jr. research engr. Nat. Refractories and Minerals Corp., Kaiser Pleasanton, Calif., 1971-72, research engr., 1972-74, sr. research engr., 1974-77, staff research engr., 1977-84, sr. staff research engr., 1984—. Mem. Am. Ceramic Soc. Democrat. Patentee in field, U.S., Australia, S.Am., Japan, Europe. Home: 4082 Suffolk Way Pleasanton CA 94566 Office: PO Box 877 Pleasanton CA 94566

CASSER, CONRAD VERNON, automobile executive; b. Kew Gardens, N.Y., Sept. 10, 1947; s. Constantine and June V. (Vernon) C.; children: Noah, Meghan. BA, Denison U., 1969; MBA, U. Pitts., 1970. Ski patrolman Sun Valley Idaho Co., 1974-75; mng. dir. Smith Goggle, Ketchum, Idaho, 1975-85; owner, pres. Sun Valley Motors, Inc., Ketchum, 1985—. Mem. Nat. Assn. Auto Dealers. Avocations: skiing, tennis, sailboarding, bicycling.

CASSIDY, RICHARD ARTHUR, environmental engineer, governmental water resources specialist; b. Manchester, N.H., Nov. 15, 1944; s. Arthur Joseph and Alice Ethuliette (Gregoire) C.; m. Judith Diane Maine, Aug. 14, 1971; children—Matthew, Amanda, Michael. B.A., St. Anselm's Coll., 1966; M.S., U. N.H., 1969, Tufts U., 1972. Field biologist Pub. Service Co. of N.H., Manchester, 1968; jr. san. engr. Mass. Div. Water Pollution Control, Boston, 1968-69; aquatic biologist Normandeau Assocs., Bedford, N.H., 1969-70; hydraulic engr. New Eng. div. U.S. Army C.E., Waltham, Mass., 1972-77, environ. engr., Portland Dist., Oreg., 1977-81, supr. environ. engring., 1981—. Contbr. articles to profl. jours. Den leader Pack 164 Columbia Pacific council Cub Scouts Am., Beaverton, Oreg., 1982-83, Webelos leader, 1984-85, troup 764 committeeman, 1985—, Columbia Pacific council Boy Scouts Am., 1985—; mem. Planning Commn. Hudson, N.H., 1976-77. Recipient commendation for exemplary performance Mo.-Miss. flood, 1973, commendation for litigation defense, 1986. Mem. Am. Inst. Hydrology (cert., profl. ethics com. 1986), Am. Soc. Limnology and Oceanography. Democrat. Roman Catholic. Home: 7655 SW Belmont Dr Beaverton OR 97005 Office: Portland Dist COE Chief Reservoir Reg & Water Quality Services PO Box 2946 Portland OR 82946

CASSUTO, ALEXANDER ELIO, university official; b. Chgo., Jan. 4, 1944; s. Arnold Caesare and Nelda (Gentilli) C.; m. Barbara Jill Silvern, Mar. 28, 1970; children—Denise, Kira, Arnold. B.A., Queens Coll., 1965, M.A., 1967; Ph.D., UCLA, 1973. Economist IMF, Washington, 1969; prof. econs. Calif. State U.-Hayward, 1971—, chmn. dept., 1978-83, asst. v.p., 1983-85; vis. prof. U. Calif.-Berkeley, 1981, U. Rome, 1983, 86, AMPART, U.S. Info. Service, 1986; cons. Calif. State U. Chancellor's Office, Long Beach, 1982-83, Far West Labs., San Francisco, 1982, Diablo Systems, Inc., Hayward, 1980-82, R. Beck and Assocs., Seattle, 1976-77. Co-author: Macroeconomics: Monetary, Search and Income Theories, 1981; The Impact of the California State University on the California Economy, 1983; (jour.) Productivity and the Schools, 1983. Contbr. articles to profl. jours. Grantee Invest-in-Am., Nat. Council Inc., 1981, 83-86, No. Calif. Council, 1976-81, Clorox Corp., 1977-80, Container Corp. Am., 1976-77. Republican. Office: Calif State U Dept Econs Hayward CA 94542

CASTANEDA, ROBERT E., investment banker, financial planning executive; b. Los Angeles, 1932; s. Robert S. and Antonia Dora Castaneda; student Fordham U., 1950-51, Loyola Coll., 1951-52; B.S. in Fin., U. Santa Clara, 1957; m. Pierangela Figini, Jan. 30, 1960; 1 dau., Gabrielle Ann. Account exec. Shearson Hamill & Co., Inc., Beverly Hills, Calif., 1967-73; asst. v.p. Sutro & Co., Inc., Beverly Hills, 1973-76; with Shearson Am. Express (formerly Loeb Rhoades Hornblower), Los Angeles, 1976-82, 2d v.p., 1980-82; exec. v.p. Calif. R & J, Inc., 1980-82; with Smith, Barney, Harris, Upham & Co., Inc., Los Angeles, 1982-86; with Paine Webber, Los Angeles, 1986—. Bd. dirs. Am. Rehab., Portland, Oreg. Named Outstanding Toastmaster of Yr., 1968. Mem. U. Santa Clara Alumni Assn., Los Angeles Stockbrokers Soc., Am. Stock Exchange, Chgo. Bd. Trade, Chgo. Merc. Exchange, Chgo. Bd. Options Trading, N.Y. Stock Exchange, Delta Sigma Pi. Republican. Roman Catholic. Office: Paine-Webber Inc 700 S Flower St Suite 2000 Los Angeles CA 90017

CASTELLANO, VIRGINIA HELEN, historical foundation and museum executive; b. Santa Fe, Jan. 22, 1953; d. Roberto and Felipa Castellano. A.Secretarial Adminstrn., N.Mex. State U., 1973; B.B.A., Coll. Santa Fe, 1981. Sec./bookkeeper N.Mex. Investment Council, Santa Fe, 1975-78; sales asst. to investment firms, Denver, 1978-79; market researcher Leach Research, Santa Fe, 1979-81; exec. dir. Guadalupe Hist. Found., Santa Fe, 1981-87; mem. Santa Fe Arts Bd., 1983-87; orgnl. rep. Santa Fe Fiesta Council, 1982-82; sole juror N.Mex. Women's Art Show, 1987. Sec. Democratic Ward C, Santa Fe, 1983-84. Nat. Endowment for Arts fellow Sagamon State U., Springfield, Ill., 1982. Roman Catholic. Office: Guadalupe Historic Found 100 Guadalupe Santa Fe NM 87501

CASTELLINO, RONALD AUGUSTUS DIETRICH, radiologist; b. N.Y.C., Feb. 18, 1938; s. Leonard Vincent and Henrietta Wilhelmina (Geffken) C.; m. Joyce Cuneo, Jan. 26, 1963; children: Jeffrey Charles, Robin Leonard, Anthony James. Student, Creighton U., Omaha, 1955-58, M.D., 1962. Diplomate: Am. Bd. Radiology. Rotating intern Highland Alameda County Hosp., Oakland, Calif., 1962-63; USPHS/Peace Corps physician Brazil, 1963-65; resident in radiology Stanford U. Hosp., 1965-68, chief resident, 1967-68; asst. prof. radiology Stanford U. Med. Sch., 1968-74, assoc. prof., 1974-81, prof., 1981—, chief diagnostic oncologic radiology, 1970—, chief CT body scanning, 1979—, dir. div. diagnostic radiology and assoc. chmn. dept. radiology, 1981-86, acting chmn. dept. diagnostic radiology and nuclear medicine, 1986—; mem. U.S. Cancer del., People's Republic China, 1977. Co-editor: Pediatric Oncologic Radiology, 1977; assoc. editor: Lymphology, 1973—, Investigative Radiology, 1985—, Radiology, 1986—, Postgraduate Radiology, 1986—; contbr. over 125 research papers to profl. publs. Recipient T.F. Eckstrom Fund award, 1978; Guggenheim fellow, 1974-75. Mem. Internat. Soc. Lymphology (exec. com. 1975-83), Am. Coll. Radiology, Assn. U. Radiologists (exec. com. 1984-86), Radiol. Soc. N.Am., Soc. Cardiovascular Radiology (charter), Am. Roentgen Ray Soc., Western Angiography Soc. (charter, pres. 1980-81), Calif. Med. Assn. (adv. panel sect. radiology 1972—), Calif. Radiol. Soc., Calif. Acad. Medicine, Alpha Omega Alpha. Office: Stanford U Sch Medicine Dept Diagnostic Radiology Nuclear Med S-078 Stanford CA 94305

CASTEN, CAROLE MARILYNN SOKOLOW, physical education and dance educator; b. Los Angeles, May 24, 1949; d. Gordon and Frances (Hartstein) Sokolow; m. Richard Guy Casten, June 22, 1969; 1 child, Kimberly Sheree. Student, UCLA, Westwood, Calif., 1967-70; BS in Phys. Edn., Purdue U., 1972, MS in Phys. Edn., 1976; PhD in Phys. Edn. Adminstrn., U. So. Calif., 1983. Cert. tchr., Ind., community coll., Calif. Elem. phys. edn. specialist West Lafayette (Ind.) Schs., 1972-73; tchr. phys. edn., driver's edn. West Lafayette High Sch., 1972-77, coach volleyball, gymnastics, 1972-77; tchr. phys. edn. Redondo (Calif.) Union High Sch., 1977-79; instr. health El Camino Coll., Torrance, Calif., 1978-79; prof. dance, phys. edn. Calif. State U. Dominguez Hills, Carson, 1979—, coordinator dance program, 1979-84, coordinator grad. program, 1984—; cons. Niecies's Dance Excercise, Manhattan Beach, Calif., 1984—, Los Angeles County Office of Edn., 1987. Contbr. articles to profl. jours. Affirmative Action grantee Calif. State U. Dominguez Hills, 1982, 84, 86. Mem. Calif. Assn. Health-Phys. Edn. and Dance (chmn. profl. edn. 1983-84, pres. Unit 401 1983-86, Profl. Excellence award 1986), Calif. Faculty Assn. (v.p. 1985—), AAAPERD (chmn. S.W. dist. 1982—, faculty advisor 1983-84), Phi Delta Kappa (sec. 1982-83, 84-85). Democrat. Jewish. Avocations: country western and ballroom dancing, skiing, swimming, sailing. Office: Calif State U Dominguez Hills 1000 E Victoria Carson CA 90747

CASTETTER, SANDRA LEA, nursing executive; b. Seymour, Ind., Jan. 24, 1950; d. Bruno Frank and Viola Mae (Gray) Browalski; 1 son, Alan Lowell. B.S., Ball State U., 1971; M.S., U. Colo., 1979. R.N., Ind., Colo., Calif. Staff nurse Ball Meml. Hosp., Muncie, Ind., 1971, Mesa Meml. Hosp., Grand Junction, Colo., 1971-72; charge nurse Rose Med. Center, Denver, 1972-73; staff nurse to dept. head St. Luke's Hosp., Denver, 1974-79; clin. instr. U. Colo., Denver, 1978-79; asst. dir. nursing St. Joseph Hosp., Denver, 1979-81; assoc. adminstr. patient care services, St. Francis Meml. Hosp., San Francisco, 1981-84; v.p. Mills-Peninsula Hosps., San Mateo and Burlingame, Calif., 1984—. Mem. Calif. Soc. Nursing Service Adminstrs., Am. Orgn. Nurse Execs., Nat. League for Nursing, Assn. Western Hosps., Nat. Forum for Adminstrs. of Nursing Services. Lutheran. Office: 1783 El Camino Real Burlingame CA 94010

CASTILLO, MARIO ENRIQUE, artist, educator; b. Rio Bravo, Mexico, Sept. 19, 1945; came to U.S., 1955, naturalized, 1965; s. Manuel Castillo and Maria Enriquez de Allen; cert. Ill. Inst. Design, 1964; B.F.A., Sch. of Art Inst. Chgo., 1969; M.F.A., Calif. Inst. of Arts, 1972; postgrad. U. So. Calif., 1969-70, Pasadena City Coll., 1977, Calif. State U. at Los Angeles, 1980-81, East Los Angeles City Coll., 1982. Designer J.M. Pateros Studios, Inc., Chgo., 1965, Lukas & Assocs., Chgo., 1966; instr. Pilsen Settlement House, Chgo., 1967; comml. artist Chgo. Bd. Edn., 1968; mural dir. City of Chgo., 1968; instr. United Christian Community Service, Chgo., 1968-69; mural dir. Halsted Urban Progress Ctr., 1968, Dept. Human Resources, Chgo., 1969; teaching asst. Calif. Inst. Arts, Valencia, 1970-72, instr., 1972-73; instr. Santa Monica (Calif.) City Coll., 1973; mem. faculty dept. art U. Ill., Champaign, Ill., 1973-76; commercial artist, Los Angeles, 1977; instr. art Immaculate Heart Coll., Hollywood, Calif., 1979-80, Pacific Asian consortium in edn., 1980-81, E.C.F. Art Ctr., Los Angeles, 1985-86, Los Angeles Unified Sch. Dist., 1986-87, Instituto Comercial Artistico, Maywood, Calif., 1987; guest lectr. workshop Corpus Christi (Tex.) State U., 1978; interior designer El Mercado Co., Los Angeles, 1981-83; regular performer musical program Noches Rancheras, East Los Angeles, Calif., 1981-83. One-man shows of drawings, paintings and/or photographs include: Scholarship and Guidance Assn., Chgo., 1968, Calif. Inst. of the Arts, Burbank, 1971, Valencia, Calif., 1972, Latino Cultural House, U. Ill., Champaign, 1976; numerous group shows including: Coll. Lake County, Grayslake, Ill., 1987, Northeastern Ill. U., Chgo., 1974, Mus. of Sci. and Industry, Chgo., 1975, Krannert Art Mus., Champaign, Ill., 1975, Truman Coll., Chgo., 1977, Chgo. Pub. Library Cultural Ctr., 1978 Immaculate Heart Coll., 1979; also film screenings U.S., Europe and Mexico; commd. muralist in public locations and pvt. residences; represented in permanent collections: Bell Telephone Co., Chgo., Lake Meadows Assn., Chgo., Scholarship and Guidance Assn., Chgo., City of Chgo., also numerous pvt. collections. Recipient numerous awards including: nat. gold medal, gold keys and certs. Scholastic Mag., 1963-65, cert. of merit N.Y. Times, 1965, 1st Prize award, Chgo. Police Dept., 1964, Homewood (Ill.) C. of C., 1967, Fiesta del Quinto Sol, Chgo., 1974, Mus. Sci. and Industry, Chgo., 1975, Am. Film Inst. grantee, 1972; Oakley Fellow U. So. Calif., 1970; Scholarship and Guidance Assn. grantee, 1965-68, Ford Found. grantee, 1975. Composer numerous songs. Residence and Studio: 1153 W 65th Pl Los Angeles CA 90044 Represented By: Orlando Gallery 14553 Ventura Blvd Sherman Oaks CA 91403

CASTLE, FREDERICK HOWARD, telecommunications company executive; b. Denver, Nov. 19, 1940; s. Bruce Leroy and Margaret (Howard) C.; m. Brenda Jo Egelston, Mar. 2, 1983; children—Kathleen Marie, Jennifer Jo, Brandee Leigh. Student U. Philippines, 1961, Visalia Jr. Coll., Calif., 1965, Ednl. Inst. Am. Hotel and Motel Assn., 1986—. Commd. Enlisted U.S. Navy, 1958, served in Vietnam, staff comdr. Patrol Wing Two, Hawaii, 1976; ret., 1981; sales mgr. Montgomery Ward, Aurora, Colo., 1981-82; salesman Handy Dan, Denver, 1982-83; dist. mgr. Am. Phone Ctrs., Littleton, Colo., 1983-84; founder, v.p. Internat. Bus. Communications Inc., Aurora, 1984—. Office: Internat Bus Communications Inc 14150 E Alameda Ave Aurora CO 80012

CASTLEBERRY, ARLINE ALRICK, architect; b. Mpls., Sept. 19, 1919; d. Bannona Gerhardt and Meta Emily (Veit) Alrick; m. Donald Montgomery Castleberry, Dec. 25, 1941; children: Karen, Marvin. B in Interior Architecture, U. Minn., 1941; postgrad., U. Tex., 1947-48. Designer, draftsman Elizabeth & Winston Close, Architects, Mpls., 1940-41, Northwest Airlines, Mpls., 1942-43, Cerny & Assocs., Mpls., 1944-46; archtl. draftsman Dominick and Van Benscotten, Washington, 1946-47; ptnr. Castleberry & Davis Bldg. Designers, Burlingame, Calif., 1960-65; prin. Burlingame, 1965—. Smith Coll. scholar, Cambridge, Mass., 1941. Mem. AIA, Am. Inst. Bldg. Designers (chpt. pres. 1971-72), Commaisini, Alpha Alpha Gamma, Chi Omega. Democrat. Lutheran. Home and Office: 3004 Canyon Rd Burlingame CA 94010

CASTNER, MYRA HAHN, educational administrator; b. Cleve., Nov. 5, 1929; d. Edgar A. and Margaret Ellen (Ward) Hahn; m. Thomas J. Castner, Aug. 30, 1952; children—Sarah Lynn, Margaret Jo. B.A. in Edn., U. Mich., 1951; M.S. in Edn. Psychology and Linguistics. Elem. teaching credential, Calif., Mich., Pa.; reading specialist, supervision, jr. coll. teaching credentials, Calif. Mem. research staff Exemplary Ctr. Reading Instrn., Salt Lake City, 1965-67; dist. master tchr., coordinator Early Childhood Edn./Title I/Bilingual Edn., Campbell (Calif.) Union Sch. Dist., 1972-75, prin., 1976—; lectr. lang. arts; participant curriculum devel. Founder, chmn. Bountiful Young People's Theater (Utah), 1964-67; active LWV, 1955-67; bd. dirs. Girl Scouts Santa Clara County. Recipient Gold medallion Calif. Reading Assn., 1976. Mem. Calif. Reading Assn., Internat. Reading Assn., Nat. Council Tchrs. English, Assn. Supervision and Curriculum Devel., Assn. Calif. Sch. Adminstrs, Nat. Assn. Elem. Sch. Prins. Republican. Home: 6390 Janary Way San Jose CA 95129 Office: Campbell Union Sch Dist 155 N 3d St Campbell CA 95008

CASTOR, WILBUR WRIGHT, marketing executive; b. Harrison Twp., Pa., Feb. 3, 1932; s. Wilbur Wright and Margaret (Grubbs) C.; m. Donna Ruth Schwartz, Feb. 9, 1963; children: Amy, Julia, Marnie. BA, St. Vincent Coll., 1959; postgrad., Calif. U. Advanced Studies, 1986—. Sales rep. IBM, Pitts. and Cleve., 1959-62; v.p. data processing ops. Honeywell, Waltham, Mass., 1962-80; pres., chief exec. officer Aviation Simulation Tech., Lexington, Mass., 1980-82; sr. v.p. Xerox Corp., El Segundo, Calif., 1982—. Author: (play) Un Certaine Soirire, 1958, (mus. comedy) Breaking Up, 1960; contbr. articles to profl. jours. Mem. Presdl. Rep. Task Force; trustee Info. Inst., Santa Barbara, Calif.; pres. bd. dirs. Internat. Acad., Santa Barbara. Served to capt. USN, 1953-58. Clubs: Manhattan Country (Manhattan Beach, Calif.); Caballeros, Rolling Hills (Calif.) Tennis; U.S. Senator's. Avocations: flying, scuba diving, music, reading, writing. Home: 19 Georgeff Rd Rolling Hills CA 90274 Office: Xerox Corp ESXC-15B 101 Continental Blvd El Segundo CA 90245

CASTRO, DONALD STEVEN, academic administrator, history educator; b. Bakersfield, Calif., June 27, 1940; s. Emilio Castro-Galvez and Lilia (Mayer) Castro; m. Constance Lee Picella, June 12, 1971; children: Antonia Carolina, Daniela Emilia. AB, UCLA, 1962, MA, 1964, PhD, 1970. Asst. prof. history Calif. State Poly. U., Pomona, 1967-69, assoc. prof., 1969-72, prof., 1978—, dir. Ctr. Chicano and Am. Indian Studies, 1969-72, dean undergrad. studies, 1978-80, dean instrn. Office grad., undergrad. studies, 1980—; assoc. dir. office internat. programs Chancellor's office, Calif. State U. Hdqrs., Long Beach, 1972-78; presenter numerous confs. on Latin Am. studies; mem. gen. edn. rev. com. Calif. State U. system, 1980—; steering com. Calif. State U. NEXA consortium, 1982—, outside evaluator Univ. Honors Program, Chico, 1985-86; cons. Office Internat. Edn. Am. Assn. State Colls. and Univs., 1972-76, on minority edn., Calif. sch. dists., 1969—; mem. social sci. adv. com. Ryan Commn. Calif. Dept. Edn., 1972-74; faculty senate rep. Sch. of Arts on Campus, 1969-72; guest lectr. Instituto Ricardo Levene, Facultad de Filosofia y Letras, U. Nacional de Buenos Aires, 1965-66. Contbr. articles to profl. jours. Community rep. Bilingual Edn. Com. Pomona Unified Sch. Dist., 1980-83; commnr. City of Claremont (Calif.) Environ. Quality Commn., 1982—; bd. govs. Fund for Pub. Edn., Claremont, 1981—; mem. Claremont Unified Sch. Dist. adv. council, 1983—, chmn., 1985—. Fulbright fellow, 1965-67; grantee Kellogg Found., 1971. Mem. Pacific Coast Council Latin Am. Studies (bd. govs. 1976-80, 1983-85), Council on Latin Am. Studies (founding pres. 1979-82, bd. dirs. 1982—), So. Calif. Consortium on Internat. Studies (bd. govs. 1980—, com. Latin Am. Studies 1972—, chmn. 1984—, chmn. subcom. Latin Am. Studies Coop. program 1972-79, chmn. subcom. Latin Am. Studies Outreach 1979—), Am. Hist. Assn. (conf. Latin Am. History Rio de la Plata Area studies com. 1970—), Latin Am. Studies Assn. (membership com. 1977-79), Nat. Assn. Fgn. Student Advisors, Calif. State U. Assn. Deans of Undergrad. Studies, Acad. Planning, Calif. State U. Assn. Deans of Grad. studies (chmn. com. improving grad. studies), Calif. State U. Assn. undergrad. advisors (founding mem.), Calif. State U. Consortium on Desert Studies (bd. govs. 1979—, chmn. 1983—, interim dir. 1983-84), Golden Key, Phi Alpha Theta, Pi Gamma Mu. Office: Calif State Poly U Dean Instrn Office Undergrad/Grad Studies 3801 W Temple Ave Pomona CA 91768

CASTRO, GEORGE, research scientist; b. Los Angeles, Feb. 23, 1939; s. Peter Melendez and Carmen (Chavez) C.; m. Beatrice Alice Melendez, Feb. 23, 1963; children: Gerald M., Sylvia Ann., Valerie Jean, Cynthia Marie. BS in Chemistry, UCLA, 1960; PhD in Phys. Chemistry, U. Calif., Riverside, 1965. Research fellow Dartmouth Coll., Hanover, N.H., 1962-65; postdoctoral fellow U. Pa., Phila., 1965-67, Calif. Tech. U., Pasadena, 1967-68; staff mem. IBM Research, San Jose, Calif., 1968-71; mgr. IBM Almaden Research Ctr., San Jose, Calif., 1971-75; mgr. phys. sci. IBM Research, San Jose, Calif., 1975—. Mem. Santa Clara County Grand Jury, San Jose, 1976-77; bd. dirs. GI Forum Scholarship Found., San Jose, 1980-84, Notre Dame High Sch., San Jose, 1985—. Named Outstanding Citizen, Mexican-Am. Community Services Agy., 1979, Outstanding profl. Mexican-Am. C. of C., 1982. Mem. AAAS, Am. Chem. Soc., Am. Phys. Soc. Soc. Hispanic Profl. Engrs. (Hispanic Tech. award 1986), Soc. Adv. Chicanos & Native Ams. in Sci. (sec. 1986). Democrat. Roman Catholic. Home: 789 E William St San Jose CA 95112 Office: IBM Almaden Research Ctr 650 Harry Rd San Jose CA 95120-6099

CASTRO, LEONARD EDWARD, lawyer; b. Los Angeles, Mar. 18, 1934; s. Emil Galvez and Lily (Meyers) C.; 1 son, Stephen Paul. A.B., UCLA, 1959, J.D., 1962. Bar: Calif. 1963, U.S. Supreme Ct. 1970. Assoc. Musick, Peeler & Garrett, Los Angeles, 1962-68, ptnr., 1968—. Mem. ABA, Internat. Bar Assn., Los Angeles County Bar Assn. Office: Musick Peeler & Garrett 1 Wilshire Blvd Suite 2000 Los Angeles CA 90017

CASTRO, RODOLFO HADER, county official., community services adminstr.; b. Riverside, Calif., May 31, 1942; A.A. with honors, Riverside City Coll., 1967; B.S. with honors in Bus. Adminstrn., Calif. Poly. Coll., 1970; M.B.A., Harvard U., 1973. Dep. dir. Econ. Opportunity Bd., Riverside, 1970; dir. program ops. LULAC Nat. Edn. Center, Washington, 1973-74, asst. dir., 1975, exec. dir., 1975; exec. dir. community services dept. San Bernardino County (Calif.), 1976—; pres. Rodolfo H. Castro & Assos., 1977—. Mem. Calif. Republican Hispanic Assembly, sustaining mem. Calif. Rep. Com.; mem. adv. bd. Calif. State Social Services, 1985—; primary candidate for U.S. Ho. of Reps. from 37th dist. Calif. Mem. Harvard U. Bus. Sch. Alumni Assn., Am. Soc. for Pub. Adminstrn. Club: Palm Springs Harvard (treas. 1982-83). Home: 250 N Phillips Ave Banning CA 92220 Office: 602 S Tippecanoe Ave San Bernardino CA 92314

CASTRUP, JACQUELINE RAE, speech pathologist; b. Cambridge, Nebr., June 12, 1956; d. Richard Dean and Shirley Ann (Miller) Wright; m. Larry Ray Castrup, Nov. 24, 1983; one child, Kevin Robert. BA, U. No. Colo., 1978, MA, 1979. Cert. tchr., Colo. Speech/lang. pathologist Ft. Morgan (Colo.) Pub. Schs., 1979—. Mem. NEA, Colo. Edn. Assn., Am. Speech-Lang.-Hearing Assn. (cert. clin. competent). Avocations: softball, sewing, knitting. Home: 1215 Edmunds Brush CO 80723 Office: Fort Morgan Pub Schs 230 Walnut Fort Morgan CO 80701

CATE, FLOYD MILLS, electronic components executive; b. Norfolk, Va., Aug. 2, 1917; s. Floyd Mills and Ellen (Lewis) C.; m. Ann Willis, Jan. 31, 1943; 1 child Carol Cate Webster. B.A. U. Tenn., 1940; student exec. program UCLA, 1958; B.A. (hon.) Calif. Inst. Tech., 1947. With special sales dept. Cannon Electric Co., Los Angeles, 1930-46, western sales mgr., 1946-50, with internat. sales dept., 1950-57, v.p. sales, mktg., 1957-62, pres. internat. sales, 1958-62; v.p. sales, mktg. Zemco, Irvine, Calif., 1968-77-80, cons., 1977-80; pres., owner F.E.S. Cons., San Clemente, Calif., 1968—. Co-chmn. Ron Packard for Congress, San Clemente, 1984; chmn. adhoc com. Seascape Village, 1986—; v.p. community liason Assn. Shorecliffs Residence, San

Clemente, 1982—. Mem. Internat. Electric Electronic Engrs., IEEE. Democrat. Roman Catholic. Club: Shorecliff Golf (bd. dirs. San Clemente). Office: 205 Via Montego San Clemente CA 92672

CATE, RODNEY MICHAEL, educator; b. Sudan, Tex., Mar. 9, 1942; s. Tommy Archie and Elsie Pearl (Cherry) C.; m. Patricia Maelene Weaver, Dec. 31, 1961; children: Brandi Carol, Shani Lee. BS in Pharmacy, U. Tex., 1965; MS, Tex. Tech U., 1975; PhD, Pa. State U., 1979. Predoctoral trainee NIMH, Washington, 1977-78; asst. prof. human devel. and family studies Tex. Tech U., Lubbock, 1978-79; asst. prof. human devel. and family studies Oreg. State U., Corvallis, 1979-83, assoc. prof. human devel. and family services, asst. dean, 1983-85; prof. and chmn. dept. child and family studies Wash. State U., Pullman, 1985—. Assoc. editor Jour. Family Issues, 1983—; reviewer Jour. Personal and Social Relationships, 1983—; contbr. articles to profl. jours. Served to lt. USN, 1965-69. Mem. Am. Psychol. Assn., Internat. Soc. Study of Personal Relationships, Nat. Council Family Relations, Am. Home Econs. Assn. Democrat. Avocations: reading, golf. Home: SE 1315 Earthtone Ct Pullman WA 99163 Office: Wash State U 101 White Hall Pullman WA 99164-2010

CATE, WILLIAM BURKE, religious organization administrator; b. Itasca, Tex., Mar. 25, 1924; s. Emmet Cate and Irene N. (Kincaid) Moberly; m. Janice McLeod Patterson, Aug. 20, 1946; children: Lucy, Nancy, Michael, Sara, Rebecca, Mary. BA, Willamette U., 1945; STB, Boston U., 1948, PhD, 1953; DD (hon.), Lewis and Clark U., 1965. Ordained minister United Meth. Ch., 1952. Exec. dir. Interchurch Council of Greater New Bedford, Mass., 1953-58, Greater Portland (Oreg.) Council of Chs., 1958-70; pres., dir. Ch. Council of Greater Seattle, 1970—; v.p. Nat. Council of Chs., N.Y.C., 1970-73; pres. Nat. Assn. of Ecumenical Staff, 1972-73. Served with USN, 1943-46. Recipient Disting. Alumni award Boston U. Sch. Theology, 1968. Lodge: Rotary. Home: 12642 NE 5th Bellevue WA 98005 Office: Ch Council Greater Seattle 4759 15th Ave NE Seattle WA 98105

CATE, WILLIAM CYRUS, mining investment consultant; b. San Pedro, Calif., June 1, 1938; s. William Cyrus and Isabelle Marie (Casey) C. B.A., St. Louis U., 1965, M.A., 1967; postgrad. Washington U., St. Louis, 1967-69, So. Ill. U., 1968. Explorer, developer, cons. gold mining ventures, N.Am. and Europe, 1970—; presenter seminars on mining investments; instr. Miami-Dade Jr. Coll., Miami, Fla., 1969-70, U. Mo., St. Louis, 1967-68, Forest Park Community Coll., St. Louis, 1967-69. Author: Finding California Gold, 1981; Prospector's Guide, 1982. Served with U.S. Army, 1961-63; Korea. Mem. Nat. Speological Soc., Calif. Cave Diving Group (pres. 1974-76), South Am. Explorer's Club. Club: Press of San Francisco. Home: 101 Peralta St Pacifica CA 94044 Office: PO Box 1160 Pacifica CA 94044

CATER, JACK ERNEST, underwater acoustician; b. N.Y.C., Apr. 28, 1950; s. Ernest Everett, Jr., and June Mary (Sohigian) C.; S.B.E.E., M.I.T., 1972, S.M. in Ocean Engring., 1974; m. Judy Jerstad, Nov. 24, 1973; children: Joanne Jerstad, Jennifer Jerstad. Cons., Lincoln Lab., Lexington, Mass., 1972-73, also research employee M.I.T., 1972-74; sr. engr. BBN Labs. Inc., San Diego, 1977—. Asst. scoutmaster Boy Scouts Am., 1976—. Served to lt. USNR, 1974-77. Named Eagle Scout Boy Scouts Am., recipient Silver Beaver award. Mem. Acoustical Soc. Am., AAAS, IEEE, N.Y. Acad. Scis., Sigma Xi. Home: 2386 Botella Pl Carlsbad CA 92009 Office: BBN Labs Inc 4015 Hancock St Suite 101 San Diego CA 92110

CATES, GILBERT, director-producer; b. N.Y.C., June 6, 1934; s. Nathan and Nina (Peltzman) Katz; m. Jane Betty Dubin, Feb. 9, 1957 (div.); children: Melissa Beth, Jonathan Michael, David Sawyer, Gilbert Lewis; m. Judith Reichman, Jan. 25, 1987. B.S., Syracuse U., 1955, M.A., 1965. Bd. dirs. Childville, Inc., N.Y.C., 1966-73; mem. com. 1 Syracuse U. Drama Dept., 1969-73. TV producer, dir.: Haggis Baggis, NBC-TV, 1959, Camouflage, ABC-TV, 1961-62, Internat. Showtime, 1962-64; producer-dir.: Hootenanny, ABC-TV, 1962, To All My Friends on Shore, CBS-TV, 1972, The Affair, ABC-TV, 1974, After the Fall, NBC-TV, 1974, Johnny, We Hardly Knew Ye, NBC-TV, 1977, The Kid From Nowhere, NBC-TV, 1982, Country Gold, CBS-TV, 1982, Faiere Tale Theatre, 1982, Hobson's Choice CBS-TV, 1983, Consenting Adult, ABC-TV, 1984, Who Hears the Child's Cry?, CBS-TV, 1986; film producer, dir.: The Painting, 1962, Rings Around the World, 1967, I Never Sang for My Father, 1970, Summer Wishes, Winter Dreams, 1973, Dragonfly, 1976, The Promise, 1978, The Last Married Couple in America, 1979, Oh God, Book II, 1980, Backfire, 1986; theatrical producer: You Know I Can't Hear You When the Water's Running, 1967, I Never Sang for my Father, 1968, The Chinese and Doctor Fish, 1970, Solitaire-Double Solitaire, 1971; dir.: Voices, 1972, Tricks of the Trade, 1980; film Jamel, Inc, Los Angeles, 1977—. Recipient Best Short Film award Internat. Film Importers and Distbrs., 1962; Chancellor's medal Syracuse U., 1974. Mem. Dirs. Guild Am. (v.p. Eastern region 1965, Western region 1980—, pres. 1984-87), Acad. Motion Picture Arts and Scis. (bd. govs., chmn. bd. dirs.), League N.Y. Theaters. Club: Friars (Los Angeles) (gov. 1980—). Office: 195 S Beverly Dr Ste 414 Beverly Hills CA 90212

CATHCART, (GUY) RICHARD, research biochemist; b. Laurel, Miss., Oct. 10, 1950; s. Guy Henry and Kate (Pennington) C.; m. Patricia Soltis, June 23, 1979. BS in Chemistry, Kent State U., 1973, MS in Chemistry, 1975; PhD in Biochemistry, Case Western Res. U., 1980. Postdoctoral researcher U. Calif., Berkeley, 1980-84; biochemist research and devel. Applied Biosystems, Foster City, Calif., 1984—. Patentee in field; contbr. articles to profl. jours. Fellow NIH, 1980-82, Am. Heart Assn., 1982-84. Mem. AAAS. Republican. Episcopalian. Avocations: classical music, wine, gardening, travel. Home: 523 Nottingham Ln Foster City CA 94404 Office: Applied Biosystems 850 Lincoln Ctr Dr Foster City CA 94404

CATHEY, WADE THOMAS, electrical engineering educator; b. Greer, S.C., Nov. 26, 1937; s. Wade Thomas Sr. and Ruby Evelyn (Waters) C.; children: Susan Elaine, Cheryl Ann. BS, U. S.C., 1959, MS, 1961; PhD, Yale U., 1963. Group scientist Rockwell Internat., Anaheim, Calif., 1962-68; from assoc. prof. to prof. elec. engring. U. Colo., Denver, 1968-85, chmn. dept. elec. engring. and c.s., 1984-85; prof. U. Colo., Boulder, 1985—; chmn. faculty senate U. Colo., Denver, 1982-83; cons. in field, 1968—; dir. ctr. Optoelectronic Computing Systems, Boulder, 1985—. Author: Optical Information Processing and Holography, 1978; contbr. articles to profl. jours.; inventor in field. Fellow Crft, U. Colo., 1982, Faculty, U. Colo., 1972-73. Fellow Optical Soc. Am. (topical editor 1977-79); mem. IEEE (sr.), Soc. Photo-optic Instrumentation Engrs. Avocations: skiing, hiking, reading, writing. Home: 228 Alpine Way (PBH) Boulder CO 80302-0406 Office: U Colo Dept Elec Engring Boulder CO 80309-0425

CATO, GLORIA MAXINE, educator, school program administrator; b. Covington, La., Mar. 22, 1942; d. Dan and Roxieana (Washington) Smith; widowed; 1 child, Mark. BS, Southern U., 1965; MS, Pepperdine U., 1974. Tchr. Los Angeles Unified Sch. Dist., 1965-81, counselor, magnet program coordinator, 1981—, PUSH for Excellence program coordinator, 1978-80, student activities coordinator, 1982-84, coll. advisor, 1984-85, personnel specialist, tchr. advisor, 1986—. Recipient Community-Sch. Service award City of Los Angeles, 1978. Charter mem. NEA, Nat. Assn. Biology Tchrs., Magnet Coordinator Assn., Los Angeles Counselors Assn., United Tchrs. Los Angeles, Phi Delta Kappa. Democrat. Baptist. Home: 3661 Kensley Dr Inglewood CA 90305 Office: Los Angeles Unified Sch Dist 450 N Grand Ave Los Angeles CA 90814

CATRON, NORMAN RAY, professional association administrator; b. Denver, Nov. 28, 1928; s. John Frank and Marie Thelma (Graham) C.; m. Lucille Josephine Urbanus, Nov. 25, 1950; children: Linda Marie Catron Delano, Russell Paul, Andrea Diane Catron Wiedman, Michael Paul. Grad., Am. Inst. Banking, San Francisco. Chief note teller Bank Am., San Francisco, 1949-52; office mgr. Morf & Morf, San Mateo, Calif., 1952-58; exec. dir Calif. Soc. Anesthesiologists, San Mateo, 1959—. Grand juror San Mateo County, Calif., 1961. Served as chief warrant officer U.S. Army, 1945-48, ETO. Recipient Service Recognition award Calif. Soc. Anesthesiologists Ho. Dels., 1984. Mem. Am. Assn. Med. Soc. Execs., Am. Soc. Assn. Execs., Gtr. Anesthesia Service and Polit. Action Com. (treas. 1976—). Democrat. Roman Catholic. Lodge: Lions (local pres. 1968-69). Avocations: golf, fishing, travel. Home: 291 Spinnaker St Foster City CA 94404 Office: Calif Soc Anesthesiologists Inc 100 S Ellsworth Ave Suite 806 San Mateo CA 94401

CATTANEO, JACQUELYN ANNETTE KAMMERER, artist, educator; b. Gallup, N.Mex., June 1, 1944; d. Ralph John and Gladys Agnes (O'Sullivan) Kammer; m. John Leo Cattaneo, Apr. 25, 1964; children: John Auro, Paul Anthony. Student Tex. Woman's U., 1962-64. Portrait artist, Gallup, N. Mex., 1972; one-man shows: Gallup Pub. Library, 1963, 66, 77, 78, 81, 87, Gallup Lovelace Med. Clinic, Santa Fe Station Open House, 1981, Gallery 20, Farmington, N.Mex., 1985—; group shows include: Navajo Nation Library Invitational, 1978, Santa Fe Festival of the Arts Invitational, 1979, N.Mex. State Fair, 1978, 79, 80, Catharine Lorillard Wolfe, N.Y.C., 1980, 81, 84, 85, 86, 4th ann. exhbn. Salmagundi Club, 1984, 3d ann. Palm Beach Internat., New Orleans, 1984, Fine Arts Ctr. Taos, 1984, The Best and the Brightest O'Brien's Art Emporium, Scottsdale, Ariz., 1986; represented in permanent collections: Zuni Arts and Crafts Ednl. Bldg., U. N.Mex., C.J. Wiemar Collection, McKinley Manor, Gov.'s Office, State Capitol Bldg., Santa Fe, Sunwest Bank. represented by Rosequist Galleries, Tucson, also Scott Roseborough Gallery, Farmington, N.Mex., Fine Arts Ctr., En Taos, N.Mex. Mem. Internat. Fine Arts Guild, Am. Portrait Soc. (cert.), Pastel Soc. of W. Coast, Mus. N.Mex. Found., Mus. Women in the Arts, Fechin Inst., Gallup C. of C., Gallup area Arts and Crafts Council, Catharine Lorillard Wolfe Art Club of N.Y.C. Lodge: Soroptimists. Address: 210 E Green St Gallup NM 87301

CATTERTON, MARIANNE ROSE, occupational therapist; b. St. Paul, Feb. 3, 1922; d. Melvin Joseph and Katherine Marion (Bole) Maas; m. Elmer John Wood, Jan. 16, 1943 (dec.); m. Robert Lee Catterton, Nov. 20, 1951 (div. 1981); children: Jenifer Ann Dawson, Cynthia Lea. Student, Carleton Coll., 1939-41, U. Md., 1941-42; BA in English, U. Wis., 1944; MA in Counseling Psychology, Bowie State Coll., 1980; postgrad., No. Ariz. U., 1987—. Registered occupational therapist. Occupational therapist VA, N.Y.C., 1946-50, Anne Arundel County Health Dept., Annapolis, Md., 1967-78; cons. occupational therapist Fondo del Seguro del Estado, Puerto Rico, 1950-51, Kachina Point Health Ctr., Sedona, Ariz., 1986; dir. rehab. therapies Spring Grove State Hosp., Catonsville, Md., 1953-56; dir. occupational therapy Eastern Shore Hosp. Ctr., Cambridge, Md., 1979-85; regional chmn. Conf. on revising Psychiat. Occupational Therapy Edn., 1958-59; instr. report writing Anne Arundel Community Coll., Annapolis, 1974-78. Editor Am. Jour. Occupational Therapy, 1962-67. Active Md. Heart Assn., 1959-60; mem. task force on occupational therapy Md. Dept. of Health, 1971-72; chmn. Anne Arundel Gov. Com. on Employment of Handicapped, 1959-63; mem. gov.'s com. to study vocat. rehab., Md., 1960; com. mem. Annapolis Youth Ctr., 1976-78; mem. ministerial search com. Unitarian Ch. Anne Arundel County, 1962; curator Dorchester County Heritage Mus., Cambridge, 1982-83. Mem. Puerto Rico Occupational Therapy Assn. (co-founder 1950), Am. Occupational Therapy Assn. (chmn. history com. 1958-61), Md. Occupational Therapy Assn. (del. 1953-59), Dorchester County Mental Health Assn. (pres. 1981-84), Delta Delta Delta. Republican. Clubs: Severn Town (treas. 1965), International (publicity chmn. 1966) (Annapolis); Toastmasters, Newcomers (pres. 1986) (Sedona). Home: 100 Canyon Circle Dr #4 Sedona AZ 86336

CATTON, WILLIAM ROBERT, JR., sociology educator; b. Mpls., Jan. 15, 1926; s. William Robert and Helen Carpenter (Willard) C.; m. Nancy Lewis, Sept. 3, 1949; children: Stephen Lewis, Philip Ellery, Theodore Randolph, Jonathan Muir. Student, Millikin U., 1946-47; AB, Oberlin Coll., 1950; MA, U. Wash., 1952, PhD, 1954. Intern Reed Coll., Portland, Oreg., 1954-55; asst. prof. sociology U. N.C., Chapel Hill, 1956-57; from asst. prof. to prof. U. Wash., Seattle, 1957-70; prof. U. Canterbury, Christchurch, New Zealand, 1970-72, Wash. State U., Pullman, 1973—; tng. specialist The Rand Corp., Santa Monica, Calif., 1955-56. Author: From Animistic to Naturalistic Sociology, 1966, Overshoot, 1980; co-author: Sociology, 4th rev. edit., 1968. Served with USN, 1943-46, PTO. Recipient Award of Merit Rural Sociol. Soc. Natural Resources Research Group, 1985. Mem. AAAS, Am. Sociol. Assn., Pacific Sociol. Assn. (pres. 1984-85, Disting. Scholar 1985), Sociol. Assn. Australia and New Zealand (v.p. 1972), Soc. Human Ecology. Avocations: hiking, travel, photography. Home: SE 500 Crestview Pullman WA 99163 Office: Wash State U Dept Sociology Pullman WA 99164

CATZ, BORIS, physician; b. Troyanov, Russia, Feb. 15, 1923; s. Jacobo and Esther (Galbmilion) C.; came to U.S., 1950, naturalized, 1955; B.S., Nat. U. Mexico, 1941, M.D., 1947; M.S. in Medicine, U. So. Calif., 1951; m. Rebecca Schechter; children—Judith, Dinah, Sarah Lea, Robert. Intern, Gen. Hosp., Mexico City, 1945-46; prof. adj., sch. medicine U. Mexico, 1947-48; research fellow medicine U. So. Calif., 1949-51, instr. medicine, 1952-54, asst. clin. prof., 1954-59, assoc. clin. prof., 1959-83, clin. prof., 1983—; pvt. practice, Los Angeles, 1951-55, Beverly Hills, Calif., 1957—; chief Thyroid Clinic Los Angeles County Gen. Hosp., 1955-70; sr. cons. thyroid clin. U. So. Calif.-Los Angeles Med. Center, 1970—; clin. chief endocrinology Cedars-Sinai Med. Ctr., 1983-87. Served to capt. U.S. Army, 1955-57. Boris Catz lectureship named in his honor Thyroid Research Endowment Fund, Cedars Sinai Med. Ctr., 1985. Fellow ACP, Am. Coll. Nuclear Medicine (pres. elect 1982); mem. AMA, Soc. for History of Medicine (chmn.), Los Angeles County Med. Soc., Calif. Med. Assn., Endocrine Soc., Am. Thyroid Assn., Soc. Exptl. Biology and Medicine, Western Soc. Clin. Research, Am. Fedn. Clin. Research, Soc. Nuclear Medicine, So. Calif. Soc. Nuclear Medicine, AAAS, N.Y. Acad. Scis., Los Angeles Soc. Internal Medicine, Am. Soc. Internat. Medicine, Calif. Soc. Internal Medicine, The Royal Soc. Medicine (affiliate), Collegium Salerni, Cedar Sinai Soc. of History of Medicine, Beverly Hills C. of C., Phi Lambda Kappa. Jewish. Mem. B'nai B'rith. Club: The Profl. Man's (past pres.). Author: Thyroid Case Studies, 1975, 2d edit., 1981. Contbr. numerous articles on thyroidology to med. jours. Home: 300 El Camino Dr Beverly Hills CA 90212 Office: 435 N Roxbury Dr Beverly Hills CA 90210

CAUCHI, GARY STEVEN, clarinetist, educator; b. London, Can., July 17, 1952; s. Francis Xavier and Mary Agnes (Toth) C. BMus, U. Western Ont., 1976, BE, 1978; MMus, Mich. State U., 1977; D in Musical Arts, U. Mich., 1984. Tchr. music Denis Morris High Sch., St. Catherines, Ont., Can., 1978-82; instr. Calif. State U., Fresno, 1983—; clarinetist Orch. London, 1973-76; instr. clarinet Brock U., St. Catherines, 1979-80; prin. clarinetist McMaster Symph. Orch., Hamilton, Ont., 1979-82; woodwind coach Niagra Youth Orch., St. Catherines, 1981-82. Contbr. articles to profl. jour. Henry Lewis Calkins scholar, U. Mich., 1982; recipient scholarship London Music Scholarship Found., 1975. Mem. Internat. Clarinet Soc., Coll. Music Soc., Am. Fedn. Musicians, Fresno-Madera Counties Music Educators Assn. Roman Catholic. Avocations: liturgical and folk music, table tennis, travel, hockey. Home: 89 Santa Ana Ave #104 Clovis CA 93612 Office: Calif State U Music Dept Fresno CA 93740

CAUDRON, JOHN ARMAND, safety engineer, technical forensic investigator; b. Compton, Calif., Sept. 26, 1944; s. Armand Robert and Evelyn Emma (Hoyt) C.; m. Marilyn Edith Fairfield, Mar. 16, 1968; children—Melita, Rochelle. A.A., Ventura Coll., 1965; B.A., Calif. State U.-Fullerton, 1967; postgrad., U. Nev., 1975-78; M.S., U. So. Calif., 1980. Dist. rep. Gen. Motors Corp., Reno, 1969-75; mgr. Snyder Research Lab., Reno, 1976-78, v.p., El Monte, Calif., 1978-82, pres., 1982-85; prin. Fire and Accident Reconstruction, Rowland Heights, Calif., 1985—. Pub. accident reconstrn. newsletter. Served with U.S. Army, 1967-69. Mem. ASCE, Am. Soc. Safety Engrs., Nat. Fire Protection Assn., Geol. Soc. Am., Firearms Research and Identification Assn. (pres. 1978—), Am. Soc. Metals, Nat. Safety Council, Ft. Tejon Hist. Assn. (info. adviser 1983—). Republican. Baptist. Avocations: hiking, traveling, photography. Office: Fire & Accident Reconstruction 1608 Nogales St Suite 360 Rowland Heights CA 91748

CAUGHLIN, STEPHENIE JANE, futures company executive, metals company executive; b. McAllen, Tex., July 23, 1948; d. James Daniel and Betty Jane (Warnock) C. BA in Family Econs., San Diego State U., 1972, MEd, 1973; M. in Psychology, U.S. Internat. U., San Diego, 1979. Cert. secondary life tchr., Calif. Owner, mgr. Minute Maid Service, San Diego, 1970-75; prin. Rainbow Fin. Services, San Diego, 1975-78; tchr. San Diego Unified Sch. Dist., 1973-80; mortgage broker Santa Fe Mortgage Co., San Diego, 1980-81; commodity broker Premex Commodities, San Diego, 1981-84; pres., owner Nationwide Futures Corp., San Diego, 1984—; owner, sec. Nationwide Metals Corp.; owner gen. mgr. Nationwide Farms, 1984—; owner, officer Nationwide Broker's Resources, 1987—, Nationwide Brokers Revolution. Sec. Arroyo Sorrento Assn., Del Mar, Calif., 1978—. Mem. Nat. Futures Assn., Greenpeace Nature Conservancy, DAR, Sierra Club. Republican. Avocations: horseback riding, swimming, skiing, gardening, raising domestic and exotic birds. Lodge: Jobs Daughters. Home: 3909 Arroyo Sorrento Rd San Diego CA 92130 Office: Nationwide Futures Corp 11230 Sorrento Valley Rd Suite 100 San Diego CA 91121

CAVALLI-SFORZA, LUIGI LUCA, educator; b. Genoa, Italy, Jan. 25, 1922; s. Pio and Attilia (Manacorda) C.; M.D., U. Pavia (Italy), 1944; M.A., Cambridge U. (Eng.), 1950; D.Sc. (hon.), Columbia U., 1980; m. Albamaria Ramazzotti, Jan. 12, 1946; children—Matteo, Francesco, Tommaso, Violetta. Came to U.S., 1970. Asst. research Istituto Sieroterapico Milanese, Milan, Italy, 1945-48, dir. research, 1950-57; prof. genetics U. Parma, 1958-62; prof. genetics, dir. Istituto di Genetica, U. Pavia, 1962-70; prof. genetics Stanford, 1970—. Vice-pres. Internat. Congress Genetics, Tokyo, Japan, 1968. Served as med. officer, Italian Army, 1947-48. Recipient T.H. Huxley award in anthropology, 1972, Weldon award in biometry, 1975. Fellow AAAS; mem. Am. Assn. Phys. Anthropology, Am. Soc. Human Genetics, Associazione Genetica Italiana, Behavioral Genetic Assn., Biometric Soc. (pres. 1967-68), Genetical Soc. Gt. Britain, Institut Internat. de Statistique, Soc. for Study Evolution, Union Internat. pour L'Etude Scientifique de la Population, Royal Statis. Soc., Am. Acad. Arts and Scis. (fgn. hon.), Japanese Soc. Human Genetics (fgn. hon.), U.S. Nat. Acad. Sci. (fgn. hon.). Author: (with W. Bodmer) The Genetics of Human Populations, 1971; Genetics, Evolution and Man, 1976; (with M. Feldman) Cultural Transmission and Evolution, 1981. Office: Dept Genetics Stanford U Med Sch Stanford CA 94305 *

CAVELL, GEORGE ROBERT CIAVARELLA, government administrator, consultant; b. Marlborough, N.Y., Aug. 19, 1926; s. Matthew Ciavarella and Jean Sarah (Moore) C.; m. Doris Mae Wade, Apr. 19, 1952 (div. 1973); children: Christian Moore, Scott Wade, Mark Douglas, 1 step daughter, Cheryl Ann Stahl; m. Phyllis Esther Parry, Oct. 20, 1973; stepchildren: Barton Parry Spencer, Sherra Ford Spencer, Wendra Whitman Spencer. BS, Yale U., 1947; MEA, George Washington U., 1970. Registered mech. and industrial engr., D.C., Calif. vice pres. engring. CF Butz Engring., Azusa, Calif., 1968-69; program dir. nat. bulk mail system, nat. hdgrs. U.S. Postal Service, Washington, 1969-73, gen. mgr. N.Y. bulk and fgn. mail ctr., Jersey City, 1973-74, spl. projects mgr. N.E. region, N.Y.C., 1974-75, mgr. ops programs br., So. region, Memphis, 1975-81, gen. mgr. engring. Western regional office, San Bruno, Calif., 1981-86; program mgr. facilities maintenance, Maintenance Overhaul and Tech. Service Ctr., U.S. Postal Service, Santa Ana, Calif., 1986—; pres., cons. materials handling Cavell Assocs., Escandido, Calif., 1969—. John Speed Murphy scholar, Yale U., 1944-46. Mem. Inst. Indsl. Engrs. (sr. mem., program chmn. 1960-61), Evansville Jr. C. of C. (program com. and derby day com.). Presbyterian. Club: Mt. Vernon Yacht (Alexandria, Va.) (vice commodore 1967-68). Lodge: Masons (Chaplain 1957-58). Home: 3342 Avenida Hacienda Escondido CA 92025-7244 Office: US Postal Service Hdqrs Maintenance Overhaul and Tech Service Office Maintenance Mgmt 1400 E Santa Clara Ave Santa Ana CA 92711-1962

CAVIGGA, MARGARET MADDOX, quilt collector, art consultant, quilt historian; b. Poplar Bluff, Mo., Oct. 31, 1924; d. Thomas Clarence and Octabelle (Peterson) Maddox; m. Albert Anthony Cavigga, Jan. 19, 1952; Student So. Meth. U., 1943, U. Mo., Columbia, 1945; B.A. in Art, Psychology and Sociology, La. State U., 1946; postgrad. in art and edn. UCLA, 1949-53, Calif. State U.-Northridge, 1953-60. Tchr. pub. schs., Los Angeles, 1953-72, master tchr., tchr. tng. program, 1954-72; tour condr. Club Universe Unitours, Los Angeles, 1960-73; owner, operator Margaret Cavigga Quilt Collection, Los Angeles, 1973—; appraiser Am. quilts and collectibles; lectr. on collecting textiles and Americana; curator numerous hist. quilt exhbns. U.S., abroad; TV and radio appearances; bd. dirs. Women In Design, Los Angeles; mem. Decorative Arts Council, Los Angeles County Mus.; mem. Costume and Textile Council, Los Angeles County Mus. Recipient Civic award Los Angeles County Supr., 1981, Mayor of Los Angeles, 1981, Mayor of Santa Monica, 1982, Gov. of Calif., 1982; Senate Resolution, Calif. Senate, 1982. Mem. Am. Soc. Interior Designers (design affiliate), Internat. Soc. Interior Designers (trade mem.), Craft and Folk Art Mus., N.Y. Folk Art Mus., Hancock Park Hist. Soc., Smithsonian Inst., Nat. Trust Hist. Preservation, Los Angeles State U. Alumnae. Methodist. Author: American Antique Quilts, Japanese and English edits., 1981, Quilt Connoisseurship, 1982, Antique Quilts: American Legacy, 1984. Established the Margaret Cavigga Quilt Found. at N.Y. Am. Mus. of Folk Art, N.Y.C., 1985. Office: 8648 Melrose Ave Los Angeles CA 90069

CAVNAR, SAMUEL MELMON, author, publisher, activist; Denver, Nov. 10, 1925; s. Samuel Edward and Helen Anita (Johnston) C.; student public schs., Denver; m. Peggy Nightengale, Aug. 14, 1977; children by previous marriage—Dona Cavnar Hambly, Judy Cavnar Bentrim; children—Heather Anne, Heide Lynn. Dist. mgr. U.S. C. of C., various locations, 1953-58; owner Cavnar & Assos., mgmt. cons., Washington, Las Vegas, Nev., Denver and Reseda Calif., 1958—; v.p. Lenz Asso. Advt., Inc., Van Nuys, Calif., 1960—; dist. mgr. Western States Nu-Orm Plans, Inc., Los Angeles, 1947-52; cons. to architect and contractor 1st U.S. Missile Site, Wyo., 1957-58; prin. organizer Westway Corp. and subsidiaries, So. Calif. Devel. Co., 1958—; chmn. bd. Boy Sponsors, Inc., Denver, 1957-59; pres. Continental Am. Video Network Assn. Registry, Inc., Hollywood, Calif., 1967—; pres. United Sales Am., Las Vegas and Denver, 1969—; sr. mgmt. cons. Broadcast Mgmt. Cons. Service, Hollywood, Las Vegas, Denver, Washington, 1970—; pres., dir., exec. com. Am. Center for Edn., 1968—; pub. Nat. Ind., Washington, 1970—, Nat. Rep. Statesman, Washington, 1969—, Nat. Labor Reform Leader, 1970—, Nat. Conservative Statesman, 1975—; owner Ran Vac Pub., Las Vegas and Los Angeles, 1976—; partner P.S. Computer Services, Las Vegas, 1978—, C & A Mgmt., Las Vegas, 1978—, Westway Internat., 1983—; lectr. in field; spl. cons. various U.S. senators, congressmen, 1952—. Nat. gen. chmn. Operation Houseclean, 1966-81; nat. candidate chmn. Citizens Com. To Elect Rep. Legislators, 1966, 68, 70, 72-74, 85—; mem. Calif. and Los Angeles County Rep. Central Coms., 1964-70; nat. gen. chmn. Project Prayer, 1962—; exec. dir. Project Alert, 1961—; nat. chmn. Nat. Labor Reform Com., 1969—; sustaining mem. Rep. Nat. Com., 1964—; Western states chmn. and nat. co-chmn. Am. Taxpayers Army, 1959—; area II chmn. Calif. Gov.'s Welfare Reform Com., 1970; chmn. Com. Law and Order in Am., 1975; mem. Nev. State Rep. Com., 1972—; mem. Clark County Rep. Com., 1972—; bd. dirs. Conservative Caucus, Las Vegas, 1980—; Rep. candidate for U.S. Senate from Nev., 1976, 82; nat. chmn. Return Pueblo Crew, 1968, Citizens League for Labor Reform, 1984—; nat. co-chmn. U.S. Taxpayers Forces, 1985—; pres., trustee Community Youth Activities Found., 1977—; nat. chmn. Operation Bus Stop, 1970—, P.R.I.D.E. Com., 1981—, Positivics Program, 1982—; co-chmn. Question 8 Com., 1980-82, S.H.A.F.T.E.D. Tax Repeal Com., 1982 C.H.I.C. Polit. Edn. Com., 1977—, People Against Tax Hikes Com., 1983—. Served with USN, 1942-45, USAF, 1950-53; Korea; comdr. USCG Aux., 1959-60. Recipient Silver medal SAR. Mem. Am. Legion (comdr. 1947-48, mem. nat. conv. disting. guest com. 1947-52), DAV, VFW, Am. Security Council (nat. adviser 1966—). Author: Run, Big Sam, Run, 1976; The Girls on Top, 1978; Big Brother Bureaucracy, The Cause and the Cure, 1979; Kiddieland West, 1980; Games Politicians Play: How to Clean Up Their Act, 1981; A Very C.H.I.C. President, 1981; How to Clean Up Our Act, 1982; Assassination By Suicide, 1984; How to Get Limited Government, Limited Taxes, 1985; Tax Reform or Bust, 1985. Home: 301A Misty Isle Ln Las Vegas NV 89107 Office: PO Box 26073 Las Vegas NV 89126

CAWLEY, CHARLES NASH, enviromental scientist; b. Shreveport, La., Aug. 21, 1937; s. Charles Preston and Carnall (Nash) C. BA, U. Okla., 1960, MA, 1970; MS, U. Tex.-Dallas, Richardson, 1976, PhD, 1978. Project leader Tex. Woman's U. Research Inst., Denton, 1964-73; gen. ptnr. Southwest Textile Lab., Denton, 1973-77; research assoc. U. Tex.-Dallas, 1978; asst. prof. Cornell U., Ithaca, N.Y., 1979-83; staff scientist Hanford Ops. div. Rockwell Internat., Richland, Wash., 1983-87, Westinghouse Corp., Richland, 1987—; cons. Saint St. Cons., Richland, 1984—. Contbr. articles on tritium and air pollution to profl. jours. Served with U.S. Army, 1962-64. Mem. AAAS, Soc. Risk Analysis, Soc. Computer Simulation, Am. Nuclear Soc., Health Physics Soc., Sigma Xi, Delta Upsilon. Home: 515 Saint St Richland WA 99352 Office: Westinghouse Hanford Co PO Box 1970 Richland WA 99352

CAWLEY, ROBERT M., motion pictures and television executive; b. Columbus, Ohio, Jan. 24, 1925; s. Robert and Kathryn (Fry) C.; m. Dixie Shamblee, Sept. 16, 1950 (div. 1964); children: Robert, Sharon Cawley Morse, Sean Patrick; m. Rena Fletcher, Mar. 17, 1966; 1 child, Dana Koch. Ed. Ohio State U., 1950. Child actor Our Gang Comedies, 1928-29, weekly radio program, 1934-36; actor TV show KPHO, Ariz., 1950-51, KOTV, Okla., 1951-52; with Kate Smith Hour, NBC-TV, 1952, Kathy Godfrey Show, ABC-TV, 1953, TV show WUSN, S.C., 1954, KTVK, Ariz., 1954-55; NBC-TV producer, dir., writer, 1955-61; with Westinghouse Broadcasting Co., San Francisco, 1961-62; dir. Dance Party; producer, dir., writer Frankie Carle Show series, 1962; ABC-TV producer dir., writer, 1962-64; own show group to maj. hotels, casinos including Las Vegas, Lake Tahoe, Reno, Chgo., Miami, 1964-70; pres. Reina Prodns., Phoenix, 1970-72; pres., dir. mktg. Multi-Media Internat., Las Vegas and Hollywood, Calif., 1972-78; ind. producer, 1979; pres. Bob Cawley Prodns., Northridge, Calif., 1980—, CCW Prodns., Northridge, 1985—; producer (feature) This Is Not A Test, 1986; cons. Ohio State U., Red Carpet Realtors Am., Republic of Bophuthatswana, Stanley Mfg. Co., Fin. News Network; lectr. TV prodn. U. So. Calif.; lectr. TV prodn., direction, creative writing Los Angeles div. Columbia Coll. Recipient Golden Globe award. Mem. Acad. TV Arts and Scis., ASCAP, Greenbrier Mil. Acad. Alumni Assn., Ohio State U. Alumni Assn., Big Band Acad. Am. Republican. Episcopalian. Club: Hollywood Press. Office: CCW Prodns Inc 8915 Yolanda Ave Northridge CA 91324

CAWOOD, ELIZABETH JEAN, public relations executive; b. Santa Maria, Calif., Jan. 6, 1947; d. John Stephen and Gertrude Margaret (Shelton) Dille; m. Neil F. Cawood, Jan. 4, 1975; 1 child, Nathan Patrick. BA, Whitworth Coll., 1964-68. Dir. pub. info. Inland Empire Goodwill, Spokane, Wash., 1967-72; adminstrv. asst. Northwest Assn. Rehab. Industries, Seattle, 1973-74; pres., counselor Cawood Communications, Eugene, Oreg., 1974—; pres. Women in Communications, Inc., 1981-83. Editor: Dictionary of Rehabilitation Acronyms, (newsletters) INTERCOM, Family Communicator, Oreg. Focus, (dictionary) Work-Oriented Rehabilitation Dictionary and Synonyms, 1st and 2nd edits. Bd. dirs. Eugene Action Forum, 1981—, Birth-to-Three, 1982-85, Lane County ARC, 1982-83, Lane County Unit Am. Cancer Soc., 1984—, Eugene Opera, 1985—, Joint Com. Econ. Diversification, 1985—, Lane County United Way, 1987—; bd. dirs. So. Willamette Pvt. Industry Council, 1985—, v.p., 1987—; chmn. Eugene Pvt. Industries Council, 1981-83, vice chmn. 1981-84, chmn. Bus. Owner's Network, Eugene, 1980-81. Mem. LWV (bd. dirs. 1979), Pub. Relations Soc. Am. (bd. dirs. Columbia River chpt. 1987—), Nat. Rehab. Assn. (pres. 1980-81), Profl. Women's Network (bd. dir. Oreg. chpt. 1982), Eugene C. of C. (econ. devel. chair 1982-83, ambassador com. chair 1984, bd. dirs. exec. com. 1984—, v.p. 1987), Mid-Oreg. Advt. Club (bd. dirs. 1985—), Oreg. Sales and Mktg. Execs. (bd. dirs. 1985—). Office: Cawood Communications 1200 High St Suite 21 Eugene CO 97401

CAWOOD, JAMES SCOTT, security professional; b. Lansing, Mich., May 6, 1956; s. James Humes and Joan Patricia Cawood; m. Anne Virginia Capron, Aug. 28, 1982. BA, U. Calif., Berkeley, 1978. Cert. protection profl. Security officer St. Francis Hotel, San Francisco, 1980-82; investigator W.J. Weaver Co., Hayward, Calif., 1982; dir. corp. security IMI, San Francisco, 1983; security ops. mgr. BankAmerica Data Ctr., San Francisco, 1984; pres. Factor One Security and Investigative Service, Inc., San Leandro, Calif., 1985—. Spl. asst. U.S. delegation UN, N.Y.C., 1977. Mem. Am. Soc. Indsl. Security, Calif. Assn. Licensed Investigators, Commonwealth Club of Calif., Internat. Assn. Arson Investigators. Republican. Mem. Taoist faith. Avocations: shooting, martial arts, reading, new technology. Office: Factor One Security and Investigative Service Inc PO Box 1772 San Leandro CA 94577

CAYETANO, BENJAMIN JEROME, lieutenant governor, former state senator; b. Honolulu, Nov. 14, 1939; s. Bonifacio Marcos and Eleanor (Infante) C.; B.A., UCLA, 1968; J.D., Loyola U., 1971; m. Lorraine Gueco, Sept. 20, 1958; children—Brandon, Janeen, Samantha. Admitted to Hawaii bar, 1971; practiced in, Honolulu, 1971—; mem. Hawaii Senate, 1978-86; lt. gov., state of Hawaii, 1987—; bar examiner Supreme Ct. State Hawaii, 1976-80; adv. U. Hawaii Law Rev., 1981—; mem. Hawaii Ho. of Reps., 1974-78, Hawaii State Senate, 1978-86. Mem. bd. regents Chaminade U., 1981—. Democrat. Office: 1835 Palamoi St Pearl City HI 96782

CAYETANO, DAVID MATA, safety engineer, consultant; b. Laoag, Philippines, Dec. 22, 1909; came to U.S., 1930; s. Pascual Hernando (Cayetano) and Teodora (Cid) Mata; m. Felipa Kihano, Nov. 23, 1933; children: Gloriana Cayetano Castillo, Lorna, Fay Cayetano Vazquez, Esther Cayetano Bieda. Diploma in engring., Internat. Correspondence Sch., Scranton, Pa., 1944; B in Pub. Adminstrn., U. Hawaii, 1981. Registered profl. engr., Calif. Safety dir., engr. Oahu Sugar Co., Waipahu, Hawaii, 1956-72; cons. Honolulu, 1972—; liquor commr. City of Honolulu, 1964-72; bd. dirs. Internat. Cooperation Ctr. hawaii, 1958. Active Gov.'s Commn. Fgn. Aid, Honolulu, 1956. Named Engr. of Yr., Hawaii Dept. Labor, 1961, Man of Week, Honolulu C. of C., 1949; recipient War Service award Office of Price Adminstrn., 1945, Honor award Hawaii chpt. ARC, 1962. Mem. NSPE, Hawaii Soc. of NSPE, Am. Soc. Safety Engrs. Home: 91-623C Pohakupuna Rd Ewa Beach HI 96706

CAYWOOD, JOHN MILLARD, electronics company executive; b. Chico, Calif., Oct. 27, 1941; s. John Marion and Doris Bernice (Mackey) C.; m. Pamela Ann Marlow, Dec. 17, 1967; children: Lisa, Carolyn. BS, Calif. Inst. Tech., 1963, MS, 1964, PhD, 1969. Research fellow Calif. Inst. Tech., Pasadena, 1970-72; mem. tech. staff Tex. Instruments, Dallas, Tex., 1972-75; process devel. mgr. Fairchild Semiconductor, Palo Alto, 1975-76; mgr. reliability engr. Intel Corp., Santa Clara, Calif., 1976-80; v.p., tech., reliability, quality assurance Xicor, Inc., Milpitas, Calif., 1981—. Contbr. articles to profl. jours. Mem. IEEE, Böhmische Physickalische Gesellschaft, Sigma Xi. Home: 1410 Wright Ave Sunnyvale CA 94087 Office: Xicor Inc 851 Buckeye Ct Milpitas CA 95035

CAZIER, BARRY JAMES, electrical engineer, software developer; b. Phoenix, May 10, 1943; s. James Henry and Dorothy Marie (Lynton) C.; m. Susan Arline Shewey, June 13, 1964 (dec. July 1979); children: Suzanne, Bryan. Student, Colo. Sch. Mines, 1961-62; BSEE, U. Colo., 1965; student advanced bus. adminstrn., Ariz. State U., 1974-77. Mfg. mgmt. Gen. Electric, Richland, Wash., 1965-66, Warren, Ohio, 1966-67; system engr. Gen. Electric, Schenectady, N.Y., 1967-69; project mgr. Honeywell, Phoenix, 1970-80, dir. field ops., 1980—; prin. Cazier Software Designs, Scottsdale, Ariz., 1985—. adv. Jr. Achievement, Phoenix, 1972. Club: IBM PC Users (Phoenix). Avocations: music, jogging, camping, fishing, reading. Home: 6616 E Desert Cove Scottsdale AZ 85028 Office: Honeywell 16404 N Black Canyon Wwy Phoenix AZ 85023

CAZIER, STANFORD, university president; b. Nephi, Utah, June 11, 1930; m. Shirley Anderson, 1952; children: David, John, Paul. B.S. in Philosophy, U. Utah, 1952, M.A. in History, 1956; Ph.D. in History, U. Wis., 1964. Reader, U. Utah, 1954-56; teaching asst. U. Wis., 1957-58, research asst., 1959; instr. Bronx Community Coll., 1959-60; mem. faculty Utah State U., 1960-71, instr., 1960-62, asst. prof. history, 1962-67, asso. prof., 1968-69, prof., 1969-71, asst. to pres., 1968-69, chmn. dept. history, 1969, vice provost, 1969-71; Am. Council on Edn. fellow in acad. adminstrn. NYU, 1967-68; pres. Calif. State U., Chico, 1971-79, Utah State U., Logan, 1979—; chmn. council of pres. Calif. State Univs. and Colls., 1978-79, mem. exec. com. council pres., 1976-79; chmn. Utah Rhodes scholars com., 1980-86. Contbr. articles to profl. publs.; author: Student Discipline in Higher Education, 1973; also articles; bibliography editor history div.: Am. Quar., 1968-71. Served as ensign USN, 1952-53. Named Tchr. of Year, Robin's award, 1966; Danforth Found. asso., 1966—. Mem. Am. Assn. Higher Edn., Nat. Assn. Colls. and Univs., Soc. Coll. and Univ. Planning, Phi Kappa Phi, Phi Alpha Theta. Office: Office of Pres Utah State U Logan UT 84322

C. DE BACA, FRANCES, bank executive; b. Alamogordo, N. Mex., Jan. 29, 1937; d. Lalie L. and Refugio (Sarmiento) Sanchez; m. Richard F.C. de Baca, Sept. 14, 1957 (div. 1981); children—Richard Allen, Ronald Wayne. Grad. degree in banking Colo. Sch. Banking, 1980. Loan sec. Otero County State Bank, Alamogordo, 1954-59; sec. Merchants Bank, Gallup, N.Mex., 1959-61; loan sec. Santa Fe Nat. Bank, 1961-62; exec. sec. First Nat. Bank of Santa Fe, 1962-63, trust officer, 1964-73, asst. v.p. investment dept., 1974-83, asst. v.p. custom banking office, 1983—, asst. v.p., trust officer, 1985-86, v.p., trust officer, 1986-87; panelist Women in State Govt. Seminars, Santa Fe, 1981-83, Investment Seminars, Coll. Santa Fe. Active Democratic Women's Club, Santa Fe, 1979—; bd. dirs. Santa Fe Council Internat. Relations, 1980—, Sangre de Cristo Council, Girl Scouts U.S.A., Santa Fe, 1975-78; trustee St. Vincent Hosp., 1983; active Santa Fe C. of C., 1982—. Mem. N.Mex. Bus. and Profl. Women's Club (pres. 1975-78, state dir. 1979, state sec. 1980), Nat. Assn. Bank Women, Bank Adminstrn. Inst., Am. Inst. Banking (pres., dir. 1979-82). Roman Catholic. Home: 134 La Placita Circle Santa Fe NM 87501 Office: Banquest/1st Nat Bank Santa Fe PO Box 609 Santa Fe NM 87504-0609

CEASE, JANE HARDY, state senator; b. Columbus, Miss., Jan. 23, 1936; m. Ron Cease, 1960; children—Allison, Abigail. B.F.A., Tulane U. State rep. Oreg. Legislature, Salem, 1979-85, state senator, 1985-89. Pres. Portland League Women Voters, 1971-73; chair Portland Area Women's Polit. Caucus, 1977-78, Met. Govts. Subcom. Local Govt. Com., Portland, 1979-83, Portland-Multnomah Commn. Aging Transp. Com., 1983-85; active Nat. Hwy. Safety Adv. Commn., 1980-83, Transp. and Communications Com. of Nat. Council State Legislatures, 1983-85, Oreg. Commn. Women, 1985—. Democrat. Clubs: Phoenix Rising, Parents United. Home: 2625 NE Hancock St Portland OR 07212 Office: State Capitol Salem OR 97310

CECH, THOMAS R., chemistry and biochemistry educator; b. Chgo., Dec. 8, 1947; m. Carol Lynn Cech; children: Allison E., Jennifer N. BA in Chem., Grinnell Coll., 1970; PhD in Chem., U. Calif., Berkeley, 1975. Postdoctoral fellow dept. biology MIT, Cambridge, Mass., 1975-77; from asst. prof. to assoc. prof. chemistry U. Colo., Boulder, 1978-83, prof. chemistry and biochemistry also cellular and devel. biology, 1983—; research prof. Am. Cancer Soc., 1987; Phillips disting. visitor Haverford Coll., 1984; Vivian Ernst meml. lectr. Brandeis U., 1984; mem. Welch Found. Symposium, 1985; Danforth lectr. Grinnell Coll, 1986; Pfizer lectr. Harvard U., 1986; Verna and Marrs McLean lectr. Baylor Coll. Medicine, 1987; Harvey lectr., 1987; co-chmn. Nucleic Acids Gordon Conf., 1984. Assoc. editor Cell; mem. editorial bd. Genes and Development. NSF fellow, 1970-75, Pub. Health Servcie research fellow Nat. Cancer Inst. 1975-77, Guggenheim fellow, 1985-86; recipient medal Am. Inst. Chemists, 1970, Research Career Devel. award Nat. Cancer Inst., 1980-85, Young Sci. award Passano Found., 1984, Harrison Howe award, 1984, Pfizer award, 1985, U.S. Steel award, 1987; named to Esquire Mag. Register, 1985, Westerner of Yr. Denver Post, 1986. Mem. Am. Soc. Biol. Chemists. Office: Univ of Colorado Dept of Chemistry Boulder CO 80309 *

CEDAR, PAUL ARNOLD, congregational minister; b. Mpls., Nov. 4, 1938; s. C. Benjamin and Bernice P. Cedar; m. Jean Helen Lier; children: Daniel Paul, Mark John, Deborah Jean. BS, No. State Coll., S.D., 1960; postgrad., Trinity Div. Sch., 1962, Wheaton Grad. Sch., 1962, U. Iowa Grad. Sch. of Religion, 1965; M Div., No. Baptist Theol. Sem., 1968; postgrad., Calif. State U., Fullerton, 1971; D Ministry, Am. Baptist Sem., 1973. Ordained to ministry Congl. Ch., 1966. Crusade dir. Leighton Ford Team, 1967-69; sr. pastor Evang. Free Ch. of Yorba Linda, Calif., 1969-73; exec. pastor of evangelism 1st Presbyn. Ch. of Hollywood, Calif., 1975-80; sr. pastor Lake Ave. Congl. Ch., Pasadena, Calif., 1981—; pres. Dynamic Communications, Pasadena, Calif., 1973—; mem. adv. bd. World Wide Pictures, Mpls., 1982-86; guest dean Billy Graham Sch. Evangelism, Mpls., 1983—; adj. prof. Fuller Theol. Sem., Pasadena, 1978—, Talbot Theol. Sem., LaHabra, Calif., 1978—. Author: Seven Keys to Maximum Communication, 1980, Servant Leadership in The Church, 1986. Vice chmn. Billy Graham So. Calif. Crusade, 1984-85. Mem. Lausanne Com. for World Evangelization, Phi Kappa Delta (life). Club: University. Avocations: athletics, music, writing, carpentry. Home: 1771 East Orange Grove Pasadena CA 91104 Office: Lake Ave Congl Ch 393 North Lake Ave Pasadena CA 91101

CEDERBERG, GAIL ANNE, hydrogeologist, researcher; b. St. Paul, Feb. 5, 1955; d. Allan Gunnar and May Burrows (Hofacker) C.; m. Nicholas E. Schlotter, Aug. 2, 1980. BA in Physics, Carleton Coll., 1977; MSCE, Stanford U., 1978, Engr. degree, 1981, PhD in Civil Engring., 1985. Research scientist Los Alamos (N.Mex.) Nat. Lab., 1979, staff member, 1984—. EPA fellow, 1977. Mem. Am. Geophys. Union, Women in Sci. and Engring., Sigma Xi. Avocations: backpacking, hiking, photography. Office: Los Alamos Nat Lab MS F655 Los Alamos NM 87545

CEDZO, KAREN LUCILLE, public relations executive; b. Milw., Dec. 10, 1950; d. Joseph Martin and Florence Lucille (Lonski) C.; m. J. Harvey Wieler, June 5, 1979. B.A., U. Wis.-Milw., 1973, M.A., 1975. Ins. agt. Equitable Life Assurance Soc., Milw., 1973-74; reporter, anchor, news dir. No. TV Inc., Fairbanks, Alaska, 1976-78; co-owner, prin. No. Info. Services, Fairbanks, 1978-81; dir. pub. affairs U. Alaska—Fairbanks, 1979-85, dir. univ. relations, 1985—; cons. in field. Co-chmn. pub. relations com. Arctic Winter Games, 1981-82; bd. dirs. Citizens for Mgmt. of Alaska's Lands, 1978-79; mem. Alaska Statehood Day Com., Fairbanks Festival '84, co-chmn. Park and Statue Celebration. Mem. Pub. Relations Soc. Am., Greater Fairbanks C. of C.; Fairbanks First Family Statue Dedication. Home: PO Box 60316 Fairbanks AK 99706 Office: U Alaska Fairbanks Signers Hall Suite 210 Fairbanks AK 99775

CEFKIN, J. LEO, political scientist, educator; b. Rochester, N.Y., Mar. 16, 1916; s. Mischa and Bluma (Jacobson) C.; m. Rose MacKanick, Aug. 13, 1949 (div. Oct. 1975); children: Judith, Barbara, Jonathan, Melissa, Carol, Danny; m. Susan West Funess, Dec. 27, 1976. AA, Los Angeles City Coll., 1939; BA, U. So. Calif., 1948; MA, Columbia U., 1949, PhD, 1954. Lectr., instr. Bklyn. Coll., 1949-53, Hunter Coll., N.Y.C., 1953-55; from asst. to full prof. Colo. State U., Ft. Collins, 1956-86, prof. emeritus, 1986—; vis. prof. and dept. head Rockefeller Found., U. Coll. of Rhodesia and Nyasaland, 1965-66.; Del. Dem. Nat. Convs., Chgo., N.Y.C., 1968, 76; chmn. 4th Dem. Congl. Dist., 1972-77; chmn. Larimer County Dems., Ft. Collins, 1961-63. Named Harris T. Gaurd disting. prof., Colo. State U., 1969, Top Prof. Colo. State U., 1965; Fulbright scholar, USIA, Washington, 1985; J. Leo Cefkin Day named at Colo. Race Tracks, Mar. 16, 1986, in honor of his 70th birthday. Fellow African Studies Assn.; mem. Western Assn. Africanists, (pres. 1975-77, 1982-83), Am. Profs. for Peace in Middle East, Internat. Studies Program, Colo. Racing Commn. (vice chmn. and chmn. 1976—). Jewish. Avocations: classical music, baseball, track, football. swimming. Home: 1901 Mohawk Fort Collins CO 80525 Office: Colo State U Dept Polit Sci Fort Collins CO 80523

CELIC, RICHARD ALBERT, technical writer; b. Glen Ridge, N.J., Mar. 31, 1946; s. Alexander and Marion Ethel (Schmidt) C.; m. Lillian Schellhase, Sept. 2, 1967 (div. July 1974); m. Margaret Marie McGreevey, Aug. 2, 1980; 1 child, Michael. BS, Ill. Inst. Tech., 1968. Tech. writer Schwinn Bicycle Co., Chgo., 1976-78; sales tng. specialist Teletype Corp., Skokie, Ill., 1978-79; mgr. tech. writer Vector Graphic, Inc., Thousand Oaks, Calif., 1979-83; mgr. publs. Protype Corp., Sun Valley, Calif., 1983-84; sr. tech. writer Micom Systems, Inc., Simi Valley, Calif., 1984-87; cons. Vector Graphic, Inc., Thousand Oaks, 1984, Teradyne Corp., 1987. Author: Repair Your TRS-80 Model III, 1987; contbr. articles to profl. publs. Ill. Inst. Tech. Alumni Club scholar, 1964. Mem. Intertel, Triple Nine Soc., Internat. Soc. Philos. Enquiry, Personal Programming Ctr., Council of Hand-Held Users, The Planetary Soc., Mensa. Avocations: sailing, digital electronics, photography, computer bldg. Office: CDI Corp 15760 Ventura Blvd Suite 1110 Encino CA 91436

CELMER, DAVID ALVIN, construction engineer, real estate developer; b. Kingston, Pa., Jan. 31, 1958; s. Alvin Ronald and Irene (Lechak) C.; m. Miriam Judith Weigel, Aug. 2, 1983; 1 child, Jennifer Ashley. B in Archtl. Engring., Pa. State U., 1980; postgrad., U. So. Calif., 1984—. Registered profl. mech. engr., Calif.; lic. elec. and mech. contractor, Calif. Design engr. Honeywell Inc., Los Angeles, 1981-83; project engr. Carrier Corp., Los Angeles, 1983-84; constrn. engr. Tishman Constrn., Los Angeles, 1984-85, Dinwiddie Constrn., Los Angeles, 1985—; prin. EquitySpec Cons. Engrs. Inc., Huntington Beach, Calif., 1982—; pres. EquitySpec Capital Sourcing Group Inc., Huntington Beach, 1985—, The EquitySpec Group Inc., Huntington Beach, 1984—; prin. EquitySpec Devel. Co., Huntington Beach, 1982—. Contbr. articles to profl. jours. Served with C.E., U.S. Army, 1977-78. Recipient Tech. Excellence award Honeywell Inc., Mpls., 1982. Mem. NSPE, Nat. Soc. Archtl. Engrs. (founding), Constrn. Specifications Inst., Sierra Club, Mensa. Avocations: family field trips, sailing, computers, German automobiles. Office: EquitySpec Cons Engrs INc 5901 Warner Suite 492 Huntington Beach CA 92649

CENARRUSA, PETE T., sec. state Idaho; b. Carey, Idaho, Dec. 16, 1917; s. Joseph and Ramona (Gardoqui) C.; m. Freda B. Coates, Oct. 25, 1947; 1 son, Joey Earl. B.S. in Agr, U. Idaho, 1940. Tchr. high sch. Cambridge, Idaho, 1940-41, Carey and Glenns Ferry, Idaho, 1946; tchr. vocat. agr. VA, Blaine County, Idaho, 1946-51; farmer, woolgrower, nr. Carey, 1946—; mem. Idaho Ho. of Reps., 1951-67, speaker, 1963-67; sec. state Idaho, 1967—; mem. Idaho Bd. Land Commrs., Idaho Bd. Examiners; pres. Idaho Flying Legislators, 1953-63; chmn. Idaho Legis. Council, 1964—, Idaho Govt. Reorgn. Com.; Idaho del. Council State Govts., 1963—. Republican adminstr. Hall of Fame, 978. Served to maj. USMCR, 1942-46, 52-58. Named Hon. Farmer Future Farmers Am., 1955; named to Agrl. Hall of Fame, 1973; Idaho Athletic Hall of Fame, 1976, Basque Hall of Fame, 1983. Mem. Blaine County Livestock Mktg. Assn., Blaine County Woolgrowers Assn. (chmn. 1954), Carey C. of C. (pres. 1952), U. Idaho Alumni Assn., Gamma Sigma Delta. Republican. Office: Office of Sec State State Capitol Room 203 Boise ID 83720 *

CENTANNI, RUSSELL JOSEPH, microbiology educator; b. Cleve., Feb. 24, 1942; s. Joseph Michael and Mary Louise (Maenza) C.; divorced; children: Joseph W., Michele L.; m. Ginny Gannon, Mar. 20, 1987. BS, John Carroll U., 1964, MS, 1966; PhD, U. Mont., 1971; postdoctoral, U. B.C., Can., 1981-82. Instr. Laredo (Tex.) Jr. Coll., 1971-73; asst. prof. biology Boise (Idaho) State U., 1973-76, assoc. prof., 1976-83, prof. microbiology, 1983—; vis. asst. prof. Idaho State U., Pocatello, 1975, vis. prof. U. B.C., Vancouver, 1981-82; edn. dir. Idaho AIDS Found., Boise, 1985—. Mem. Am. Soc. Microbiology, Idaho Acad. Sci., Sigma Xi (sec., treas. 1975—), Phi Kappa Phi (v.p. 1985-86). Democrat. Roman Catholic. Avocations: stamp collecting, photography, cross country skiing. Home: 5959 Elkhorn Ave Boise ID 83709-3112 Office: Boise State U Dept Biology Boise ID 83725

CERKO, EUGENE ANDREW, metallurgist, chemist, researcher; b. Freeport, N.Y., Dec. 11, 1950; s. Stanley Benedict and Helen Magdalyn (Walko) C.; m. Paula Cooper, Feb. 10, 1969 (div. Sept. 1971). Ed. U. So. Calif., 1971. Pres., Continental Industries, Los Angeles, 1971—; pres. Cerko Corp., Huntington Beach, Calif., 1976—. Patentee in field. Recipient Zero Defects award U.S. Dept. Def., 1984. Mem. Republican Senatorial and Congl. Coms., Nat. Rifle Assn. Home: 2515 Bamboo St Newport Beach CA 92660 Office: Cerko Corp 5939 Sycamore Ct Chino CA 91710

CERMAK, JACK EDWARD, engineer, educator; b. Hastings, Colo., Sept. 8, 1922; s. Joseph and Helen (Herman) C.; m. Helen Jane Carlson, Dec. 17, 1949; children: Douglas Karl, Jonathan Joel. B.S., Colo. State U., 1947, M.S., 1948; Ph.D., Cornell U., 1959; NATO postdoctoral fellow, Cambridge U., Eng., 1961-62. Mem. faculty Colo. State U., Ft. Collins, 1948—; prof. charge fluid mechanics and wind engring. program, also dir. Fluid Dynamics and Diffusion Lab. Colo. State U., 1960-85, disting. prof., 1986—, chmn. engring. sci. maj. program, 1963-72; pres., dir. Colo. State U. (Research Found.), 1965-72; pres. Cermak/Peterka and Assocs, Inc., 1982—; cons. in field. Mem. bd. mems. Univ. Corp. Atmospheric Research, 1966-67; pres., chmn. 10th Midwestern Mechanics Conf., 1966-67; dir. summer inst. fluid mechanics NSF, 1963, 65, 68, 72; chmn. 2d U.S. Nat. Conf. Wind Engring. Research, 1975, 5th Internat. Conf. Wind Engring., 1979; pres. Wind Engring. Research Council, Inc., 1979-85; co-chmn. U.S.-Japan Seminar Lab. Simulation of Stratified Shear Flows; mem. Colo. Gov.'s Sci. and Tech. Adv. Council, Com. on Army Basic Research, NRC, 1979-83. Mem. editorial adv. bd. Indsl. Aerodynamics Abstracts, Mechanics Research Communications; regional editor for U.S., Internat. Jour. Wind Engring; mem. editorial bd. Meteorology and Atmospheric Physics; contbr. articles to profl. jours. Fellow ASCE (chmn. engring. mechanics div. 1965), Am. Acad. Mechanics, AIAA (assoc.); mem. Am. Soc. Engring. Edn. (chmn. mechanics div.), Nat. Acad. Engring. (chmn. com. natural disasters, chmn. panel on wind engring. research), Internat. Assn. Wind Engring. (chmn. bd. 1975-79, regional sec. North and S.Am. 1983—), Am. Meteorol. Soc., Am. Geophys. Union, ASME (Freeman scholar 1974, disting. lectr. 1987—), AAAS, ASHRAE (mem. com. flow around bldgs.), Air Pollution Control Assn., N.Y. Acad. Scis., Sigma Xi (nat. lectr. 1976-77). Home: 407 E Prospect St Fort Collins CO 80525

CERULLO, MORRIS, evangelist, educator, religious magazine publisher; b. Passaic, N.J., Oct. 2, 1931; s. Joseph and Bertha (Rosenblatt) C.; m. Vivian Theresa LePari, July 28, 1951; children: Charles David, Susan Darlene Gilhuis, Mark Stephen. Graduate, New England Bible Coll., 1951. Ordained Assembly of God, 1952, Evangelism Church Alliance. Pastor Clairmont (N.H.) Assembly of God Ch., 1951-52; internat., domestic evangelistic crusade organizer various locations, 1952-59; pastor Calvary Temple, South Bend, Ind., 1959-61; pres. Morris Cerullo World Evangelism, Inc., San Diego, 1961—; found., pub. Victory mag., San Diego, 1961—; organizer internat. and domestic evangelistic crusades, Jewish World Outreach, radio and TV appearances, prayer ministry; participant Global Satellite Network programming. Author 42 books on evangelism. Named one of Community Leaders and Noteworthy Americans, 1973-76. Office: Morris Cerullo World Evangelism PO Box 700 San Diego CA 92138

CETTI, WILLIAM CHARLES, utility manager; b. Phoenix, June 5, 1945; s. Fred Robert and Mary Elizabeth (Baker) C.; B.S. in Advt., Ariz. State U., 1972, M.B.A., 1978; m. Mary Jane Stone, Oct. 11, 1963; children—Sherri Kay, William Robert. Mgt. trainee Gen. Electric Co., Phoenix, 1967-72; customer service rep. Ariz. Pub. Service Co., Globe, 1972-74, sr. pub. safety rep., Phoenix, 1974-79, Sedona Area mgr., 1979-82, Prescott customer service supr., 1982-83, Payson dist. mgr., 1983-86, Coconimo dist. mgr., 1986—. Active Authority. Chmn. Citizens Against a Nat. Monument in Sedona, Payson Sch. Citizen Adv. Com., Econ. Devel. Steering Com.; adv. bd. No. Ariz. U. Safety Programs; bd. dirs. Keep Sedona Beautiful; Yavapai Coll. dist. adv. bd.; pres. Rim County Healthcare Found.; past pres., charter mem. Payson Indsl. Authority; past pres. Rural Country Health Found. Cert. safety profl. and hazard control mgr. Named outstanding loss control profl. S.W. Safety Congress, 1979. Mem. Am. Soc. Safety Engrs. (profl.; pres. Ariz. chpt. 1978-79), Cert. Safety Profls. of the Americas (dir.). Republican. Club: Sedona-Oak Creek. Lodges: Rotary (dir. Sedona club), Kiwanis. Home: 2020 N Rio de Flag Flagstaff AZ 86004

CHABOT-FENCE, DENE, engineer; b. Long Beach, Calif., Dec. 20, 1932; s. Marvin Carl and Jessica May Castelberry (Albrecht) Fence. AA, Am. River Coll., Sacramento, 1965; BS, Calif. Inst. Tech., 1966, U. San Francisco, 1983; MS, U. San Francisco, 1985. Research technician Calif. Inst. Tech., Pasadena, 1960-66; engr. various firms, Calif., 1966-80; design engr. J.R. Simplot, Helm, Calif., 1980-85; project engr. J. Oakley & Assocs., Fresno, Calif., 1985-86; prin. engr. Handypersons, Fresno, 1986-87; design engr. Heublein Wines, Madera, Calif., 1987—. Patentee in field. Mission pilot Airlifeline, Sacramento. Served with USAF, 1950-54, Korea. Mem. Am. Assn. Indsl. Hygiene (cert.), 99's (chmn. local chpt. 1985-86). Democrat. Avocations: flying, singing, painting, song writing. Home: 1037 N Fruit Ave Fresno CA 93728

CHABRE, STEPHEN WILLIAM, marketing executive; b. Los Angeles, Dec. 12, 1943; s. Pierre and Mildred (Pflugh) C.; m. Holly Ellen Hoffine, Aug. 28, 1973; 1 child, Nicole. BS, U. Ariz., 1966; Grad. Sch. Mgmt., UCLA. Acctg. trainee McCann-Erickson, Los Angeles, 1967; account supr. Grey Advt., Los Angeles, 1967-72; ptnr. Sanders White Assocs., Los Angeles, 1972-73; with Benton & Bowles, N.Y.C., Los Angeles, 1973-76; chief operating officer Dailey & Assocs., Los Angeles, 1976—. Bd. dirs. Am. Heart Assn., Los Angeles. Recipient Marsy award Am. Mktg. Assn., N.Y.C., 1983. Republican. Club: Advertising (Los Angeles) (treas. 1984). Avocations: golf, tennis. Office: Dailey & Assocs 3055 Wilshire Blvd Los Angeles CA 90010

CHADHA, KIDAR NATH, structural engineer, administrator; b. India, Sept. 29, 1945; came to U.S., 1967; s. Ram Lal and Raj Kumari (Kohli) C.; m. Nita Chopra, Sept. 26, 1950; children: Rima Chadha, Mala Chadha. BSCE, Tech. Inst. Engring. and Tech., Patiala, India, 1966; MS in Structural Engring., Stanford U., 1968; MBA, UCLA, 1972. Engring. specialist Douglas Aircraft Corp., Long Beach, Calif., 1968-74; dir. Atma

Ram Constrn. Co., New Delhi, 1974-75; tech. mgr. Northrop Corp., Hawthorne, Calif., 1975—. Named Engr. of Month Douglas Aircraft Corp., 1969, Northrop Corp., 1979. Mem. AIAA (interactive computer graphics tech. com. 1985—). Home: 12759 Alconbury St Cerritos CA 90701 Office: Northrop Corp 1 Northrop Ave Hawthorne CA 90250

CHADWICK, SHARON STEVENS, librarian; b. Syracuse, N.Y., June 1, 1951; d. Robert Harold and Melba Frances (Hurlburt) Stevens; m. Gary Robert Chadwick, May 27, 1972. BS in Chemistry, Clarkson Coll. Tech., 1973; MSLS, Syracuse U., 1975; MS in Chemistry, SUNY, Oswego, 1980. Asst. librarian SUNY, Oswego, 1977-78; chemistry, physics bibliographer Syracuse U., 1978-79; sci. librarian Humboldt State U., Arcata, Calif., 1980—. Mem. AAAS, Am. Chem. Soc., ALA, Calif. Library Assn., Med. Library Assn. Avocations: swimming, aerobics, reading mysteries, white-water canoeing. Home: 190 Willow Ln Arcata CA 95521 Office: Humboldt State U The Library Arcata CA 95521

CHAFFART, ROBBY GHISLAIN, French language educator; b. Oostende, Belgium, Aug. 5, 1958; came to U.S., 1981; s. Achille Jimmy and Regine Irene (Germonprez) C.; m. Lynona Ann Gordon, June 3, 1984. BA, Faculté du Salève, Collonges, France, 1981; MA, Andrews U., 1983; postgrad., U. Ariz., 1986—. Instr. French Walla Walla Coll, College Place, Wash., 1983—; tchr. French Walla Walla Valley Acad., College Place, Wash., 1984—; sponsor, counselor French Club, College Place, 1984—; leader French Sabbath Sch., College Place, 1983—. Mem. Modern Lang. Assn., Alpha Mu Gamma. Republican. Adventist. Avocations: playing guitar, computer programming, studying lit. Home: 31 W Los Reales Lot #58 Tucson AZ 85706 Office: Walla Walla Coll College Place WA 99324

CHAFFEE, PAUL STANLEY, veterinarian, zoo administrator; b. Port Huron, Mich., Jan. 23, 1928; s. Walter Henry and Leland Elizabeth (Green) C.; children: David P., Daniel P., Richard P., Denise J. AS, Port Huron Jr. Coll., 1949; BS, DVM with honors, Mich. State U., 1953. Asst. veterinarian Peigh Animal Hosp., 1953-54; owner, veterinarian McKinley Pet Hosp., Fresno, Calif., 1955-65; veterinarian Fresno Zoo, 1960—, zoo dir., 1965—. Contbr. numerous articles to profl. publs. Served as cpl. U.S. Army, 1946-48. Mem. Am. Assn. Zoo Veterinarians (pres. 1972), Zoo Act (pres.), Am. Assn. Zool. Parks and Aquariums (pres. 1980-81, past chmn. ethics com.), Fresno Zool. Soc., Calif. Acad. Vet. Medicine, Phi Zeta. Republican. Lodge: Rotary (pres. Fresno club 1978-79). Office: Fresno Zoo 894 W Belmont Ave Fresno CA 93728

CHAIRES, ROBERT HAROLD, JR., police officer, lawyer; b. South Bend, Ind., July 22, 1948; s. Robert Harold Chaires Sr. and Betty Teresa (Cross) C.; children: Nicole, William. BS, Loyola U., Chgo., 1974; MCJ, U. Colo., 1978, DPA, 1987; JD, U. Denver, 1982. Bar: Colo. 1983, U.S. Dist. Ct. Colo. 1983. Officer, Denver Police Dept., 1975—; ptnr. Lentz & Chaires, Denver, 1983—. Author column Streets, 1983-85. Mem. The Brotherhood, Denver, 1975—; adj. prof. Met. State Coll., Denver, 1986—. Served to pvt. E-2 Airborne Inf., U.S. Army, 1965-69. Recipient 11 commendation awards Denver Police Dept. Mem. U.S. Parachute Assn. (jumpmaster award), Am. Motorcyclist Assn., Am. Soc. Pub. Adminstrn., ABA, Assn. Trial Lawyers Am., Soc. Colo. Attys. in Law Enforcement (charter), Police Involved in Grad. Studies (charter). Home: 2856 W Warren Ave Denver CO 80219 Office: Lentz & Chaires 1321 Delaware St Denver CO 80204

CHAITIN, RAYMOND MORRIS, psychiatrist; b. N.Y.C., July 27, 1915; s. Morris Joseph and Yetta (Horowitz) C.; m. Jeannette Rita Weisberg, Apr. 7, 1940; children: Barry Frederick, Ellen Laurie. BS, L.I. U., 1935; DO, Phila. Coll. Osteopathic Medicine, 1939; MD, Chgo. Coll. Medicine and Surgery, 1946; JD, Bklyn. Law Sch., 1952. Diplomate Am. Bd. Psychiat. Medicine. Intern Harbor Hosp., Bklyn., 1939-40; resident Bklyn. State Hosp., 1968-71; epidemiologist N.Y.C. Dept. Health, 1940-46; assoc. prof. Downstate Med. Sch., Bklyn., 1968-78; med. cons. State of Calif., Los Angeles, 1980-82; mem. hosp. staff Los Robles Hosp., Calif., 1979—; panelist Am. Arbitration Assn., Calif., 1955—; prin. Bryant Fisebler & Co., N.Y.C., 1952-55. Fellow Am. Coll. Legal Medicine, N.Y. Acad. Scis., Am. Assn. Psychoanalytic Physicians. Avocation: economics.

CHAKRAPANI, DURGAM G., engineer; b. Salem, India, Nov. 28, 1940; came to U.S., 1969; s. Govinda Rajulu and Suseela Chakrapani.; m. Subha Chakrapani, May 29, 1967; children: Sri Jayanth, Sanjay. BE with honors, U. Madras, India, 1962; ME, Indian Inst. Sci., 1964; PhD, U. Ill., 1974. Registered profl. engr. Oreg., Wash., Calif. Tech. mgr. Gokul Industries, 1964-69; research assoc. U. Ill., Urbana, 1969-74; research scientist U. Ill., Champaign, 1974-76; prof. engring., v.p. MEI Charlton, Portland, Oreg., 1976—. Contbr. tech. articles to profl. publs. Mem. Nat. Assn. Corrosion Engrs., TAPPI, Am. Soc. Metals, Am. Chem. Soc., Am. Cons. Engrs. Council Oreg. Club: City (Portland).

CHAKRAVARTI, DIPTIMAN, chemist, biotechnologist; b. Sylhet, India, Sept. 19, 1928; came to U.S., 1949; s. Nagendra Nath and Usah Rani (Choudhuri) C.; m. Susan Bertha Johnson, Sept. 10, 1955; children: Devdas, Ava. BSc, Calcutta U., India, 1948; MS, U. Mass., 1951; PhD, Wash. State U., 1955. Planning supt. Eraligool Tea Estates, Cachar, India, 1955-56; asst. prof. radiation biology U. Wash., Seattle, 1957-61, assoc. prof., head radio-chemistry lab., 1961-66; sr. mgr. Life Sci. Dept. Corning (N.Y.) Glass Works, 1966-69; pres. Innova Corp., Seattle, 1969-83, chmn., 1974-84; cons. tech. transfer Newport Beach, Calif., Seattle, 1985-86; internat. fin. cons., San Francisco, 1987—. Contbr. articles to profl. jours.; patentee in field. Founder, bd. dirs. N.W. Sch. of Arts, Humanities and Environment, Seattle, 1981-83; bd. regents Wash. State U., Pullman, 1977-83, pres. bd. regents, 1982-83. Mem. Am. Chem. Soc. (chmn. Puget Sound sect. 1960-61, centennial chmn. 1966), Pacific Sci. Ctr. Found. (trustee 1966-80), Phila. String Quartet Found. (founder, trustee 1985—). Avocations: travel, jazz, classical music, polit. reading. Address: 107 Schmidt Ln San Rafael CA 94903

CHALFIN, NORMAN LEONARD, electronics engineer, patent and trademark practitioner; b. Phila., Oct. 13, 1913; s. Nathan M. and Katherine M. (Tinkelman) C.; m. Ethel Friedman, Jan. 22, 1937; 1 son, Gregory Thomas. Student, NYU, 1931-33; BS, U. Ga., 1936; postgrad., Columbia U., 1936-41; JD, Southwestern U., 1960. Bar: U.S. Patent Office 1955, Can. Patent Office 1955. Instr. communications tng. project Nat. Youth Adminstrn., 1941-42; sr. elec. engr. Western Electric Co., Clifton, N.J., 1942-43; chief radio engring. Crystal Research Labs., Hartford, Conn., 1943; project engr. Am. Type Founders, N.Y.C., 1944; sr. applications engr. N.Am. Phillips Co., Dobbs Ferry, N.J., 1945; sr. devel. engr. Daven Co., Newark, 1946; chief engr. Eastern Ed. Radio News, N.Y.C., 1947-48, Eastern Ed. radio and TV maintenance, 1950; chief engr. Crystal Devices Corp., Freeport, N.Y., 1949-51; tech. editor Hughes Aircraft Corp., Culver City, Calif., 1951-52, patent engr., 1952-57; tech. editor Litton Industries, Beverly Hills, Calif., 1957-58, Hughes Aircraft Co., Fullerton, Calif., 1958-61; sole practice 1961-63; instr. Manpower Devel. and Tng. Act courses Solar Electronics Schs., Monrovia, Calif., 1963-64; patent agt. Aerojet Gen. Corp., Azusa, Calif., 1964; instr., coordinator Agy. for Internat. Devel. communications tng. project Pasadena (Calif.) City Coll., 1964-66; mem. staff Office of Patent Counsel Jet Propulsion Lab., Pasadena, 1966-77; mem. staff Office of Patents and Tech. Utilization Calif. Inst. Tech., Pasadena, 1977—, mgr. Office Tech. Utilization, 1985—; lectr. UCLA, Calif. Inst. Tech. Contbr. articles to profl. jours. Fellow Radio Club Am.; mem. Los Angeles Patent Law Assn. (historian 1966—), IEEE (life), Audio Engring. Soc. (life, chmn. Los Angeles sect. 1959, 69), Am. Radio Relay League, Radio Amateur Satellite Corp. (life). Avocations: photography, video, amateur radio. Office: Calif Inst Tech-Jet Propulsion Lab 4800 Oak Grove Dr Pasadena CA 91109

CHALLET, GILBERT LYLE, entomology executive; b. San Diego, Sept. 19, 1940; s. Gilbert Frank and Velma Grace (Henry) C.; m. Linda Ellen Cleator, June 27, 1965; children: Laurel, Lisa. BS, San Diego State U., 1963, MS, 1965. Registered profl. entomologist. Research assoc. U. Calif., Riverside, 1965-67; entomologist Los Angeles County Agriculture Dept., 1967-69; vector ecologist Orange County (Calif.) Vector Control Dist., Garden Grove, 1969-73, asst. mgr., 1973-74, mgr., 1974—; cons. U. So. Calif., 1969-73; bd. dirs. Orange County Solid Waste Enforcement Agy., Santa Ana. Contbr. articles on vector control to profl. jours. Commr. City of Irvine (Calif.) Community Service Com., 1973-74; bd. dirs. Irvine Hist. Soc., 1978-83; chmn. Fullerton (Calif.) Coll. Horticulture Adv. Com., 1985-86, Ranch Homeowners Assn., Irvine, 1971-72. Mem. Am. Mosquito Control Assn. (pres. 1984, Meritorious Service award 1981), Soc. Vector Ecologists (pres. 1978, disting. service award 1986), Entomol. Soc. Am. (com. chmn. 1983), Calif. Mosquito and Vector Control Assn. (pres. 1978-79), Am. Registry Profl. Entomologists (outstanding med. entomologist 1986), WHO (expert com. on vector control in urban areas, 1987). Republican. Avocations: taxonomy, collection of Dytiscidae (Coleoptera Insecta). Home: 5262 Royale Ave Irvine CA 92714 Office: Orange County Vector Control Dist 13001 Garden Grove Blvd Garden Grove CA 92643

CHAMBERLAIN, ADRIAN RAMOND, corporate executive; b. Detroit, Nov. 11, 1929; s. Adrian and Leila (Swisher) C.; m. Melanie F. Stevens, May 19, 1979; children: Curtis (dec.), Tracy, Thomas (dec.). B.S., Mich. State U., 1951, D.Engring., 1971; M.S., Wash. State U., 1952; Ph.D., Colo. State U., 1955; Litt.D., Denver U., 1974. Registered profl. engr., Colo. lic. real estate broker, Colo. Research engr. Phillips Petroleum Co., 1955; research coordinator, civil engr. Colo. State U., 1956-57, chief civil engr. sect., 1957-61, dean engring., 1959-61, v.p., 1960-66, exec. v.p., treas., governing bd., 1966-69, pres., 1969-80; chmn. bd. dirs. Univ. Nat. Bank, 1964-69, dir., 1964-74; pres., dir. Mitchell & Co., Inc., 1981-85; exec. v.p. Simons, Li & Assocs., Inc., 1985-87; pres., chief exec. officer Chemognitics, Inc., 1987—; bd. dirs. Solaron Corp.; chmn. NSF Commn. Weather Modification, 1964-66; mem. Nat. Air Quality Criteria Adv. Com., 1967-70. Colo. commr. Western Interstate Commn. on Higher Edn., 1974-78; pres. State Bd. Agr. System, 1978-80; trustee Cystic Fibrosis Found., 1971-84; trustee Univ. Corp. for Atmospheric Research, 1967-72, 74-81, chmn. bd. trustees, 1977-79; bd. dirs. Nat. Center for Higher Edn. Mgmt. Systems, 1975-80, chmn. bd. dirs., 1977-78; bd. visitors Air U., USAF, 1973-76, chmn., 1975-76; exec. com. Nat. Assn. State Univs. and Land Grant Colls., 1976-81, pres.-elect, 1978-79, chmn., 1979-80; mem. adv. council to dir. NSF, 1978-81; chmn. Ft. Collins-Loveland Airport Authority, 1983-86; bd. dirs. Food Prodn. Found., 1985—. Fulbright student U. Grenoble, 1955-56. Mem. ASCE, Ft. Collins C. of C. (bd. dirs.), Sigma Xi, Tau Beta Pi, Phi Kappa Phi, Chi Epsilon. Lodges: Rotary, Order of Aztec Eagles (Mex.). Home: 4200 Westshore Way Fort Collins CO 80525 Office: Chemognitics Inc 208 Commerce Dr Fort Collins CO 80524

CHAMBERLAIN, DAVID M., consumer products company executive; b. 1943; married. B.S., U. Pa., 1965; M.B.A., Harvard U., 1969. With Quaker Oats Co., Chgo., 1969-80, former pres. Frozen Foods div.; pres. Standard Brands Foods, N.Y.C., 1980-82; sr. v.p. and group exec. Nabisco Brands, Inc., Toronto, Ont., Can., 1980-83; pres., chief operating officer Shaklee Corp., San Francisco, 1983—, chief exec. officer, 1986—. Served to 1st lt. U.S. Army, 1965-67. Office: Shaklee Corp 444 Market St San Francisco CA 94111 *

CHAMBERLAIN, JAMES HERBERT, marketing executive; b. Riverside, N.J., Dec. 12, 1947; s. Herbert Bryce and Helen Francis C.; m. Barbara A. Baker, Dec. 27, 1969 (div. Jan. 1980). AS, Beckley Coll.; BS, W.Va. U.; student, U. Pitts.; MBA, Pepperdine U., 1984. Research chemist W.H. Rorer, Inc., Ft. Washington, Pa., 1972-74; sales rep. Amersham Corp., Arlington Heights, Ill., 1974-77, regional mgr., 1977-81; nat. sales mgr. Amersham Corp., Oakville, Ont., Can., 1981-83, BFI, Houston, 1983-84; mktg. mgr. Am Gen, Thousand Oaks, Calif., 1984—. NIH fellow U. Pitts., 1971-72. Mem. Biomed. Mktg. Assn., Med. Mktg. Assn. Avocations: tennis, theater. Home: 2998 Parkview Dr Thousand Oaks CA 91362 Office: AmGen 1900 Oak Terrace Ln Thousand Oaks CA 91320

CHAMBERLAIN, JOHN HAROLD, JR., county official; b. Omaha, Oct. 20, 1929; s. John Harold and Geneva Mildred (Roland) C.; m. Mary Elizabeth Mendietta, July 3, 1950; children—Cecilia Marie, John Nicholas, Mary Francis. Student in acctg. Ranger Jr. Coll., Tex., 1953-57; student in criminal justice Los Medanos Coll., 1978; student in math. San Diego Jr. Coll., 1950. Cert. disaster planner. Vice pres. Geneva Petroleum Co., Eastland, Tex., 1953-59, Chamberlain Lithographing & Direct Advt., Oakland, Calif., 1959-71; mgr. dispatching services Alameda County Sheriff's Dept., San Leandro, Calif., 1971—; mem. disaster planning com. Oakland Internat. Airport, 1977—; mem. prehosp. ops. com. Alameda County Health Care, Oakland, 1983—. Regional campaign dir. Eastland March of Dimes, 1957. Served with USN, 1948-53. Recipient award for lithographic excellence Crown Zellerback Corp., Oakland, 1969. Fellow Am. Biographical Inst. (Medal of Honor 1987); mem. Assn. Pub. Safety Communications Officers, Dublin Fire Fighters Assn. (pres. 1974-75, award for outstanding accomplishments 1975), Nat. Acad. TV Arts and Scis. Democrat. Roman Catholic. Club: Lone Cedar Country (pres. 1957-58) (Eastland). Lodge: K.C. (3d degree). Office: OES Consol Dispatch 2000 150th Ave San Leandro CA 94578

CHAMBERLAIN, OWEN, nuclear physicist; b. San Francisco, July 10, 1920; divorced 1978; 4 children; m. June Steingart, 1980. A.B. (Cramer fellow), Dartmouth Coll., 1941; Ph.D., U. Chgo., 1949. Instr. physics U. Calif., Berkeley, 1948-50; asst. prof. U. Calif., 1950-54, assoc. prof., 1954-58, prof., 1958—; civilian physicist Manhattan Dist., Berkeley, Los Alamos, 1942-46. Guggenheim fellow, 1957-58; Loeb lectr. at Harvard U., 1959; Recipient Nobel prize (with Emilio Segrè) for physics, for discovery antiproton, 1959. Fellow Am. Phys. Soc., Am. Acad. Arts and Scis.; mem. Nat. Acad. Scis. Address: Univ of Calif Physics Dept Berkeley CA 94720 *

CHAMBERLAIN, RICHARD DENNIS, retail company executive; b. Oroville, Calif., July 8, 1940; s. Ellis Arthur and Addie Vesta (Stiles) C.; m. Ann Burden Thomas, Jan. 25, 1969; children—John, Susan. B.S., Calif. State U., 1963. Retail trainee Emporium-Capwell Co., Oakland, Calif., 1963-66, mgr., N.Y.C., 1967-68, buyer, Oakland, 1968-70; mgr. Morris Dept. Store, Delano, Calif., 1970-75; owner, mgr. City of Paris Dept. Store, Oroville, 1976—. Mem. bus. adv. com. Calif. State U., Chico, 1982—; trustee Oroville Hosp., 1983—. Mem. Jr. Dept. Stores of Calif., Oroville C. of C. Republican. Congregationalist. Club: Commonwealth (San Francisco). Lodges: Masons, Rotary. Office: City of Paris Dept Store PO Box 1511 Oroville CA 95965

CHAMBERLAIN, ROBERT GLENN, mechanical engineer, systems analyst; b. Atascadero, Calif., May 8, 1939; s. Glenn John and Portia May Chamberlain; m. Elene Marie Roen, Dec. 17, 1960; children: Brandt Oliver, David Glenn, Mary Elizabeth, Charles Robert. BS in Engring., Calif. Inst. Tech., 1960, MS, 1961. Registered profl. mech. engr., Calif. Spacecraft engr. USAF, Pasadena, Calif., 1961-64; sr. engr. Jet Propulsion Lab., Pasadena, 1964-67, mem. tech. staff, 1967-73, 1975—, acting supr., 1973-75. Author numerous math. models. Served to capt. USAF, 1961-64. Mem. Ops. Research Soc. Am. (jour. editor 1983—), Inst. Mgmt. Scis. (jour. editor 1983—), AAAS, Sigma Xi (assoc.). Avocation: square dancing. Office: Jet Propulsion Lab 4800 Oak Grove Dr Pasadena CA 91109

CHAMBERLAIN, ROBERT WAYNE, financial planner; b. Flint, Mich., Feb. 28, 1951; s. Wayne J. and Elaine E. (Scheidler) C.; m. Sue Ann S. H. Lee, June 29, 1974 (div. 1987). Student, Flint Jr. Coll., 1969, Honolulu Community Coll., 1975, N.Y. Inst. Fin., 1976, Coll. Fin. Planning, 1981. Cert. fin. planner. Registered rep. Blyth Eastman Dillon & Co., Inc., Honolulu, 1976-78; registered rep., regional dir. personal fin. mgmt. E.F. Hutton & Co., Inc., Honolulu, 1978-81; pres. Chamberlain & Assocs., Inc., Honolulu, 1981—; dir. securities prin. Associated Planners Securities Corp., Los Angeles, 1983—; adj. faculty Coll Fin. Planning, Denver, 1981—. Served to staff sgt. USAF, 1970-74. Mem. Internat. Assn. Fin. Planning (bd. dirs. 1985—, registry appeals bd. 1985—, legis. liaison Honolulu chpt. 1984—), Inst. Cert. Fin. Planners (ethics com. 1985—, legis. liaison Honolulu chpt. 1984—), Am. Arbitration Assn. (panel mem. 1983—), Hawaii C. of C. (chmn. Small Bus. Council 1983—, v.p. 1984—). Republican. Office: Chamberlain & Assocs 737 Bishop St Suite 2770 Honolulu HI 96813

CHAMBERLIN, EUGENE KEITH, historian, educator; b. Gustine, Calif., Feb. 15, 1916; s. Charles Eugene and Anina Marguerite (Williams) C.; B.A. in History, U. Calif. at Berkeley, 1939, M.A., 1940, Ph.D., 1949; m. Margaret Rae Jackson, Sept. 1, 1940; children—Linda, Thomas, Rebecca, Adrienne (dec.), Eric. Tchr. Spanish, Latin, Lassen Union High Sch. and Jr. Coll., Susanville, Calif., 1941-43; tchr. history Elk Grove (Calif.) Joint Union High Sch., 1943-45; teaching asst. history U. Calif., Berkeley, 1946-48; instr. history Mont. State U., Missoula, 1948-51, asst. prof., 1951-54; asst. prof. to prof. San Diego City Coll., 1954-78; cab driver San Diego Yellow Cab Co., 1955-74, 79, 86; vis. prof. history Mont. State Coll., Bozeman, summer 1951, U. Calif. Extension, 1965-68, San Diego State Coll., 1965-68, others; instr., coordinator history lectures San Diego Community Colls.-TV, 1969-77; prof. San Diego Miramar Coll., 1978-83; prof. history San Diego Mesa Coll., 1983-86. Huntington Library-Rockefeller Found. grantee, 1952; Fulbright-Hays grantee, Peru, 1982; recipient merit award Congress of History San Diego County, 1978; Outstanding Educator award, San Diego City Coll., 1970. Mem. AAUP (various coms., nat. council 1967-70, pres. Calif. conf. 1968-70, acting exec. sec. 1970-72), San Diego County Congress of History (pres. 1976-77, newsletter editor 1977-78), Am. Hist. Assn. (Beveridge-Dunning com. 1982-84, chmn. 1984), Pacific Coast Council on Latin-Am. Studies, Cultural Assn. of the Californias, The Westerners (Calafia chpt.), E Clampus Vitus (historian 1970—, chpt. pres. 1972-73, dir. 1983—, grand council mem. 1972—, dir. T.R.A.S.H 1979—, pres. 1983-84), Phi Alpha Theta (sec. U. Calif. Berkeley chpt. 1947-48, organizer and faculty adv., Mont. State U. chpt. 1948-54). Democrat. Mem. Ch. of the Brethren (del. 200th Annual Conf. 1986). Author numerous booklets on SW Am. history and numerous articles on Mexican NW to profl. jours. Home: 3033 Dale St San Diego CA 92104

CHAMBERLIN, MARGARET JEAN, association executive; b. Fairport Harbor, Ohio, Apr. 15, 1937; d. Oscar Wilho and Lillian Irene (Ahlberg) Pasanen; m. John D. Chamberlin, Aug. 19, 1961; 1 child, Robert John. B.A. in Econs., Hiram Coll., 1959; postgrad. Baldwin-Wallace Coll., 1961, Grand Canyon Coll., 1964, Ariz. State U., 1964, 76. Instr. tng. div. Cleve. Trust Co. subs. Ameritrust Co., 1959-62; elem. sch. tchr., Parma, Ohio, 1962-63, Phoenix, 1964-66; asst. buyer Webb's Dept. Store, Glendale, Calif., 1963-64; bookkeeper for atty., Phoenix, 1974-76; with Am. Inst. Banking, Phoenix, 1977—, program developer, 1979-80, exec. dir., corp. sec. Ariz. chpt., 1980—. Mem. early childhood edn. com., Pasadena, Calif., 1973-74; mem. adv. bd. on banking and fin. Rio Salado Community Coll.; clk. to vestry All. Sts. Episcopal Ch., Pasadena, 1972-74. Mem. Nat. Assn. Bank Women, Am. Assn. Tng. Devel., Am. Bankers Assn. (execs. adv. com. 1986). Democrat. Episcopalian. Office: Ariz Chpt Am Inst Banking 3003 N Central Ave Trader Bldg Suite 109 Phoenix AZ 85012

CHAMBERS, DOROTHY ROSE, educator; b. Yakima, Wash., May 8, 1941; d. George Milford and Blance Mary (McCarthy) Hollenbeck; B.S. in Speech and Lang. Therapy, Marquette U., 1964; M.A. in Spl. Edn., San Francisco State U., 1969; m. Thomas M. Chambers, Aug. 14, 1971; adopted children—David, Monique, Christopher, George, Elizabeth. Speech pathologist Mpls. Pub. Schs., 1964-65, Milbrae (Calif.) Sch. Dist., 1965-68; reading specialist Dept. Def., Landstuhl, Germany, 1970-71; tchr. children with extreme learning problems Portland (Oreg.) Public Schs., 1971-80, dept. chmn. spl. edn., 1980-84, program specialist program devel., 1984—; cert. instr. develop. therapy U. Ga., 1982; instr. Portland State U., D.C.E., 1982, 83. HEW Dept. Rehab. fellow, 1969. Mem. Am. Speech and Hearing Assn. (cert. in clin. competence), Common Cause, Cousteau Soc., NEA, Oreg. Edn. Assn., Nat. Council Exceptional Children (presenter nat. conv. 1984). Democrat. Roman Catholic. Author: PEACHES (Pre-Sch. Ednl. Adaptation for Children Who Are Handicapped), 1978. Home: 12414 SE Oatfield Rd Milwaukie OR 97222 Office: Portland Pub Schs 501 N Dixon St Portland OR 97227

CHAMBERS, JAMES RICHARD, retired chemistry educator, consultant; b. Birmingham, Ala., Aug. 20, 1914; s. James Richard and Eddie Clyde (Garrett) C.; m. Alice Helen Gates, Aug. 27, 1939; 1 child, Harry Donald. BA, Columbia Union Coll., 1939; MS, Case Western Res. U., 1949; PhD, Tex. A&M U., 1958. Instr. Columbia Union Coll., Takoma Park, Md., 1939-41; prin. Nashville Jr. Acad., 1941-42; chief chemist, aviation gasoline plant Pennzoil Co., Oil City, Pa., 1942-46; head dept. chemistry Atlantic Union Coll., South Lancaster, Mass., 1946-54; head sci. dept. Southwestern Union Coll., Keene, Tex., 1954-60; assoc. prof. chemistry Walla Walla Coll., College Place, Wash., 1960-61, prof., 1961-80, prof. emeritus, 1980—; cons. Bionostics Inc., Lisle, Ill., 1981—. Mem. Internat. Union Pure and Applied Chemistry, Am. Chem. Soc. (chmn. local sect. 1980), Northwest Sci. Assn. (pres. 1980), Sigma Xi (pres. local chpt.), Phi Lambda Upsilon. Adventist. Home: 22 Tremont College Place WA 99324

CHAMBERS, KENTON LEE, botany educator; b. Los Angeles, Sept. 27, 1929; s. Maynard Macy and Edna Georgia (Miller) C.; m. Henrietta Laing, June 21, 1958; children—Elaine Patricia, David Macy. A.B. with highest honors, Whittier Coll., 1950; Ph.D. (NSF fellow), Stanford U., 1955. Instr. biol. scis. Stanford U., 1954-55; instr. botany, Yale U. 1956-58, asst. prof., 1958-60; assoc. prof. botany Oreg. State U., Corvallis, 1960-65, prof., 1965—, curator Herbarium, 1960—; program dir. systematic biology NSF, Washington, 1967-68. NSF fellow, 1955-56. Mem. Bot. Soc. Am., Am. Soc. Plant Taxonomists, Soc. Study Evolution, AAAS, Am. Inst. Biol. Scis., Calif. Bot. Soc., Soc. Systematic Zoology, Western Soc. Naturalists, Democrat. Presbyterian. Clubs: Triad, Oreg. State U. Contbr. articles in field to profl. jours. Home: 3220 NW Lynwood Circle Corvallis OR 97330 Office: Oreg State U Herbarium Botany Dept Corvallis OR 97331

CHAMBERS, LOIS I., ins. agent and exec.; b. Omaha, Nov. 24, 1935; d. Edward J. and Evelyn B. (Davidson) Morrison; m. Frederick G. Chambers, Apr. 17, 1981; 1 son, Peter Edward. Ins. clk. Gross-Wilson Ins. Agy., 1955-57; ins. sec., bookkeeper Reed-Paulsen Ins. Agy., 1957-58; office mgr., asst. sec., agent Don Biggs & Assocs., Vancouver, Wash., 1958—; prin. Chambers & Assocs., ins. agy. automation cons. Mem. Citizens Com. Task Force, City of Vancouver, 1976, Block Grant Rev. Task Force, 1978—; chmn. adv. com. Clark Community Coll.; mem. agts. adv. council Safecom Mgmt. Systems, Inc. Mem. Ins. Women of S.W. Wash., Nat. Assn. Ins. Women, Nat. Users Agena Systems (pres.). Roman Catholic. Club: Soroptimist (Vancouver). Office: 916 Main St PO Box 189 Vancouver WA 98666

CHAMBERS, PETER R., psychologist; b. Los Angeles, Aug. 23, 1953; s. Ralph James and Eileen Lucy (Allsworth) C. Student U. Calif., Riverside, 1975-77; B.A., Chapman Coll., 1978; M.A., U.S. Internat. U., 1980, Ph.D., 1982. Researcher, Rancho Los Amigos Hosp., Downey, Calif., 1972-76; counselor educator Free Clinic of Orange County, Anaheim, Calif., 1976-78; psychotherapist Care Manor Hosp., Orange, Calif., 1978-80; asst. adminstr. Cabrillo Med. Center, San Diego, 1980-81, psychologist Cabrillo Mental Health Group, 1982, prof. Nat. U.; evaluation and guidance unit Orange County Mental Health, Orange, 1982—; instr. Calif. Community Coll. Mem. Am. Psychol. Assn. Republican.

CHAMBERS, ROBERT ROOD, biomedical instrument executive; b. Lincoln, Nebr., May 23, 1923; s. Guy Cleveland and Grace (Rood) C.; m. Martha Wayne, May, 1948 (div. 1965); children: Anne, Guy, Carl; m. Clytia Capraro, May 28, 1965. AB, U. Nebr., 1944; PhD, U. Ill., 1947; JD, De Paul U., 1951. Bar: Ill. Research chemist to v.p. Atlantic Richfield (merged Sinclair Oil), 1947-82; pres. Sandhill Sci., Burbank, Calif., 1982—; chmn. bd. dirs. Montedoro-Whitney, San Luis Obispo, Calif. Patentee in field of petrochemistry. Mem. Am. Chem. Soc., Royal Soc. Chemistry. Club: California (Los Angeles). Avocations: fruit trees, philosophy. Home: 11439 Laurelcrest Dr Studio City CA 91604 Office: Sandhill Sci 224 E Olive Ave Suite 210 Burbank CA 91502

CHAMBERS, THOMAS DOANE, professional basketball player; b. Ogden, UT, June 21, 1959; m. Erin C.; children: Ericka, Skylar. Attended, U. Utah. Player San Diego Clippers, Nat. Basketball Assn., 1981-83, Seattle SuperSonics, 1983-; Selected to NBA All-Star team, 1987. Office: care Seattle SuperSonics 190 Queen Anne Ave North 2nd Floor Seattle WA 98109 *

CHAMBERS, THOMAS MACK, social work administrator; b. Seattle, Jan. 11, 1945; s. Thomas Maclellan and Vivian Elizabeth (Finnell) C.; m. Dorothy Rose Hollenbeck, Aug. 14, 1971; children: David Leonard, Monique Dorothy, Christopher Ronald, George Henry, Elizabeth Ruth. BA in Psychology, Stanford U., 1967; MSW, Portland State U., 1973. Staff social worker Rehab. Inst. of Oreg., Portland, 1973-74, lead social worker, 1974-76; staff social worker Good Samaritan Hosp., Portland, 1976-84, asst. dir. social work, 1984—; instr. sch. nursing U. Wash., Seattle, 1977; adj. prof. social work Portland State U., 1977-78, 81-82. Chmn. bd. dirs. Northwest Pilot Project, Portland, 1982-84 (mem. 1980—). Served with U.S. Army, 1968-71. Mem. Nat. Assn. Social Workers, Acad. of Cert. Social Workers (cert.), Registry of Clin. Social Workers (cert.). Democrat. Roman Catholic. Avocations: sailing, backpacking, running, reading. Home: 12414 SE Oatfield Rd Milwaukee OR 97222 Office: Good Samaritan Hosp Social Work 1015 NW 22d Ave Portland OR 97210

CHAMBERS-MEYERS, TRESSA, consultant, writer; b. Lyon, Miss., Apr. 26, 1942; d. James W. and Anna L. (Dorsey) Chambers; m. Joseph R. Meyers, Mar. 18, 1961 (div. Apr. 1983); children—Monica Denise Meyers, Jon Raymond Meyers. B.A., Eastern Wash. U., 1965. Cert. sch. tchr., Calif. Tchr., San Francisco Unified Schs., 1969-75; freelance writer, San Francisco, 1975-81; writer-cons., 1981-83; founder, pres. Thought Motivation Inst., San Francisco, 1983—. Author: Balanced Living Program 1986; contbg. author: The Stress Strategists, 1986. Mem. Mayor's San Francisco Host Com., 1979—; mem. host. com. 1984 Democratic Conv., 1983; mem. Dem. Women's Forum, 1978—. Mem. Bus. Execs. for Nat. Security (charter), World Affairs Council No. Calif. (membership com.), Nat. Assn. Female Execs., Nat. Speakers Assn., Internat. Platform Assn., Assn. Continuing Higher Edn. Roman Catholic. Club: Circlets (v.p. 1978-84). Office: Thought Motivation Inst 2966 Diamond St Suite 151 San Francisco CA 94131

CHAMPIE, ELLMORE ALFRED, historian, writer; b. Eden, Tex., Sept. 11, 1916; s. Sam Houston and Nora Louise (Sorrell) C.; student Tex. Coll. Mines and Metallurgy, 1941-42; B.A. with highest honors, U. Tex, Austin, 1947, M.A. (Univ. Scholar), 1948; Ph.D. in History (Bayard Cutting Scholar), Harvard U., 1967; m. Rosemary Erter, Sept. 7, 1947 (dec. Nov. 1962); children—Ellmore Alfred, Nora Beatrice; m. 2d, Miriam Helene Boysen Mann, Aug. 28, 1971 (div. Oct. 1974). Archivist, Nat. Archives, 1952-55; historian U.S. Marine Corps Hdqrs., 1955-56, Joint Chiefs of Staff, U.S. Dept. Def., 1956-61; asso. agy. historian Fed. Aviation Agy., 1961-67; agy. historian FAA, Dept. of Transp., 1967-72; hist. researcher and writer, 1972—; mem. tech. com. on history U.S. Inst. of Aeros. and Astronautics, 1970-72; editorial cons. history of FAA and predecessor agys., 4 vols. Served with U.S. Navy, 1936-40; served to 1st lt. USAAF, 1942-45. Mem. Am. Hist. Assn., Am. Acad. Polit. and Social Sci., Am. Soc. for Eighteenth-Century Studies, Am. Soc. for Pub. Adminstrn., Phi Beta Kappa. Democrat. Clubs: Masons, Harvard (So. Ariz.). Author: The Federal Turnaround on Aid to Airports, 1926-38, 1973. Home: 7480 E Rio Verde Dr Tucson AZ 85715

CHAMPINE, DENNIS, mayor, investment real estate broker; b. Detroit, Mar. 29, 1942; s. Earl and Margaret (Keigher) C.; m. Joanna D'Angelo, Jan. 6, 1961; children—Jeff, Brett, Dana, Earl. Bus. mgr. Am. Motor Sales Corp., Seattle and San Francisco, 1963-69; dist. mgr. Toyota Motor Distbrs., Denver, 1969-73; now dir. instnl. equities group Marcus & Millichap, Inc., Denver; mayor City of Aurora (Colo.), 1979—, councilman, 1974-79. Served with USMC, 1960-63. Mem. U.S. Conf. Mayors, Nat. Assn. Republican Mayors. Republican. Office: Office of Mayor City Hall 1470 S Havana St Aurora CO 80012 *

CHAMPION, JAY FREDERIC, social worker; b. Portland, Oreg., Nov. 5, 1942; s. Wilfred Leethorpe and Ella Mae (Hagen) C.; m. Geraldine Annette Hobbs, July 25, 1968 (div. Nov. 1985); children: Crystal Ann, Michelle Lynn. BA in Social Work, U. Mont., 1975; MSW, U. Wash., 1978. Cert. social worker. Vocat. counselor Wash. State Dept. Employment Security, Seattle, 1964-66, 68; minister, social worker The Salvation Army, San Luis Obispo, Calif., 1968, Kalispell, Mont., 1968-70, Missoula, Mont., 1970-74, Kelso, Wash., 1974-75, Seattle, 1975-78, 82-85, Denver, 1978-79, Oakland, Calif., 1982; dir., planner Lewis-Mason-Therston Area Agy. Aging, Olympia, Wash., 1979-81; mgr. evangeline residence Salvation Army, Seattle, 1985-86, social service planner, music dir. N.W. div., 1986-87; dir. community services Salvation Army, Olympia, Washington, 1987—. Served with U.S. Army, 1965. Mem. Nat. Assn. Social Workers, N.Am. Assn. Christians in Social Work, Nat. Conf. Social Welfare, Wesleyan Theol. Soc., Wash. Assn. Social Welfare, Christian Holiness Assn. Democrat. Avocations: reading, music, chess, table tennis, swimming. Home: 600 Black Lake Blvd SW #184 Seattle WA 98502

CHAMPOUX, PEGGY MARIE, mental health administrator; b. Yakima, Wash., Sept. 25, 1953; s. Alan Carroll and Mary Ann (Bailey) C. BS in Sociology, Cen. Wash. U., 1979; MSW, Eastern Wash. U., 1982. Dir. social services Cen. Meml. Hosp., Toppenish, Wash., 1982-83; county designated mental health profl. Cen. Wash. Comprehensive Mental Health, Yakima, 1983—, sexual assault adv., 1982-83. Named one of Outstanding Young Women of Am., 1985. Mem. Nat. Assn. Social Workers. Roman Catholic. Avocations: guitar, music ministry. Home: 904 S 1st Avenue Yakima WA 98902 Office: Cen Wash Comprehensive Mental Health 321 E Yakima Ave Yakima WA 98901

CHAN, FLORENCE MAY HARN, librarian; b. Victoria, B.C., Can., Sept. 29, 1929; d. Jack Nam and Eva (Lowe) Yipp; children: Jonathan Hoyt, Barry Alan. Student Victoria Coll., 1949-51; BA, U. B.C., 1953; MLS, U. Calif., Berkeley, 1956; MA, San Jose State U., 1976. Circulation, reference asst. Victoria Pub. Library, 1953-54; cataloger Golden Gate Coll., San Francisco, 1956-57, Coll. San Mateo, Calif., 1957-60; catalog, reference librarian Canada Coll., Redwood City, Calif., 1968-75, coordinator library services, 1975—. Author: Using Library Resources, 1976, Using Library Resources: A Skills Building Worktext, 1986; contbr. article to profl. jour. Pres. Asian Am. Community Council, San Mateo, Calif., 1983—; mem. San Mateo County Hist. Assn., Kodenkan Inst. Adv. Com., San Carlos, Calif., 1982—; mem. San Mateo County Project READ Council, 1986—. Mem. Assn. Coll. and Research Libraries, ALA, Calif. Library Assn., Community Coll. Media Assn. Phi Kappa Phi. Democrat. Episcopalian. Office: Canada Coll 4200 Farm Hill Blvd Redwood City CA 94061

CHAN, FRANKLIN JACK, environmental horticulturist; b. Grass Valley, Calif., May 15, 1941; s. Sherman B.K. and Lily (Fore) C.; m. Suzanne Fong, Aug. 4, 1963; children—Christine Dianne, Gregory Alexis. B.S., U. Calif.-Davis, 1964, M.S., 1967. Research specialist U. Calif.-Davis, 1965-72; cons. in pvt. practice, Davis, 1972-74; instr. Foothill Coll., Los Altos Hills, Calif., 1974-75, U. Calif.-Davis, summer 1975; arborist City of Sacramento, 1975-78; environ. horticulturist Pacific Gas & Electric Co., San Francisco, 1978—; mem. Horticultural Adv. Council for Jepson Manual, 1987—; contbr. to book World of Trees, 1977, also reports and papers on various revegetation subjects. Grantee (with Harris and Leiser) for revegetation studies U.S. Forest Service, Cal-Trans. and U.S. Army C.E., at U. Calif.-Davis, 1968-73. Mem. Internat. Erosion Control Assn. Democrat. Club: Kiwanis. Office: Pacific Gas & Electric Co 77 Beale St San Francisco CA 94106

CHAN, FREDERICK MAN-HIN, architect, developer; b. Hong Kong, June 17, 1947; s. William Chak-Yan and Nancy Sui-Yin (Tse) C.; B.Arch., U. Calif., Berkeley, 1969; M.Arch., Harvard U., 1974. Architect, N.Y. State Urban Devel. Corp., N.Y.C., 1973-74; devel. mgr. community land devel. Ministry of Housing, Toronto, Ont., Can., 1974-78; pres. Nu West Cos., Los Angeles, 1978—; project dir. North Broadway Mall Devel. Corp., Los Angeles, 1981—. Mem. Am. Planning Assn., Ont. Assn. Architects, Urban Devel. Inst., Chinese C. of C. Los Angeles (dir.), Internat. Council Shopping Centers, Am. Mgmt. Assn., Los Angeles Jaycees, Urban Land Inst. Clubs: Marina City, Los Angeles Racquet, Internat. Office: 350 S Figueroa St Suite 555 Los Angeles CA 90071

CHAN, HARVEY THOMAS, JR., food technology researcher; b. Astoria, Oreg., Mar. 5, 1940; s. Harvey Thomas Sr. and Flora Mae (Lum) C.; m. Doreen Eiko Yoshizumi, Dec. 26, 1964; children: Baron D., Dwight D., Teruko M. BS, Oreg. State U., 1963, PhD, 1968; MS, U. Hawaii, 1965. Food technologist Agrl. Research Service USDA, Honolulu, 1968-79, Hilo, Hawaii, 1979—; cons. Internat. Exec. Service Corp., Guatamala, 1986—. Editor: Handbook of Tropical Foods, 1983; contbr. articles to profl. jours.; inventor device for removal of Papaya seeds. Cubmaster Boy Scouts Am., Hilo, 1980-83. Mem. Inst. Food Technologists (chmn. Hawaii sect. 1977-78, chmn.-elect, 1976-77, sec.-treas. 1973-75), Am. Chem. Soc., Am. Hort. Soc., Sigma Xi. Home: 932 Komomala Dr Hilo HI 96720 Office: USDA PO Box 4459 Hilo HI 96720

CHAN, JOSEPH P.H., system integration engineer; b. Hong Kong, Feb. 1, 1959; s. Chak and Siu-Ping (Chung) C. BS, U. Calif., Berkeley, 1982; MS, Stanford U., 1984. Research asst. Stanford (Calif.) U., 1982-83; system integration and project engr. Newport Corp., Fountain Valley, Calif., 1983—. Designer video instruction system, 1983. Mem. ASME, Soc. Automotive Engrs., Pi Tau Sigma. Home: 41 Hillgrass Irvine CA 92715 Office: Newport Corp 18235 Mt Baldy Circle Fountain Valley CA 92708

CHAN, KELVIN WING-SHUI, analytical chemist, researcher; b. Hong Kong, June 1, 1957; came to U.S., 1974; s. Chak-Yan and Bo-San (Law) C. BS, U. Nev., 1978; PhD, U. Ill., 1983. Postdoctoral assoc. Cornell U., Ithaca, N.Y., 1983-84; staff researcher Syntex Research, Palo Alto, Calif., 1984—. Contbr. articles to profl. jours. Mem. AAAS, Am. Chem. Soc. (Travel award 1981), Am. Soc. Mass Spectrometry, Sigma Xi, Phi Kappa Phi, Phi Lambda Upsilon, Sigma Sigma Chi. Avocations: volleyball, hang gliding. Home: 73 Cliffside Dr Daly City CA 94015

CHAN, LAURENCE KWONG-FAI, physician, educator, scientist. came to U.S., 1977; m. Cynthia Cheung, July 19, 1977; 1 child, Joseph. Pre-med. student, Queen Elizabeth Sch., 1967; MD, U. Hong Kong, 1972; MRCP, Royal Coll. Physicians, London, 1976; PhD, Oxford (Eng.) U., 1982. Lectr. Oxford U., 1977-83; fellow Green Coll., Oxford, 1977-83; asst. prof. U. Colo., Denver, 1983—; dir. dialysis unit Univ. Hosp., Denver, 1985—; bd. dirs. NMR Lab., U. Colo. Health Scis. Ctr., 1985—. Mem. Royal Coll. Physicians, Am. Soc. Transplant Physicians. Office: U Colo Health Scis Ctr Dept Medicine Denver CO 80262

CHAN, LINDA SIM YING, research analyst, biostatistical and research consultant; b. Hong Kong, Aug. 17, 1942; d. Chung Hon Cheung and Kwan (Chan) C.; m. Kenneth Hung-Yip Chan, Sept. 17, 1967; children—Andrew, Kevin, Michael, Stephanie. B.S., U. Calif.-Berkeley, 1966, M.S., Los Angeles, 1967, Ph.D., 1970. Research analyst Los Angeles County/U. So. Calif. Med. Ctr., 1970-79, Instr. dept. community and family medicine, 1970-74, asst. clin. prof., 1974-82, dir. research, planning and evaluation unit, chief research analyst, 1979—; assoc. prof. research pediatrics U. So. Calif. Sch. Medicine, 1984—; cons. health related areas. Mem. Am. Statis. Assn., Biometric Soc., Am. Pub. Health Assn., Evaluation Research Soc., UCLA Alumni Assn. Contbr. numerous articles to profl. jours. Office: LAC-USC-MC Room 12-900 1200 N State St Los Angeles CA 90033

CHAN, LOREN BRIGGS, telecommunications analyst; b. Palo Alto, Calif., Sept. 10, 1943; s. Shau Wing and Anna Mae (Chin) C.; m. Frances Anastasia Chow, Apr. 19, 1975; children: Karen Monique, Pierre Bénédict, Marc Henri. BA, Stanford U., 1965, MA, 1966; PhD, UCLA, 1971. Assoc. prof. history San Jose (Calif.) State U., 1971-80; lectr. history Calif. State U., Hayward, 1980-81; prodn. test technician Nicolet Paratronics Corp., Fremont, Calif., 1982; computer service technician Bell-Northern Research, Mountain View, Calif., 1982-83; research analyst Bell-No. Research, Mountain View, Calif., 1984-85, tech. writer, 1985—. Author: Sagebrush Statesman, 1973; editor: Chinese-American History Reader, 1976; contbr. articles to profl. jours. Radio sta. trustee ARC, Menlo Park, Calif., 1975-80. Recipient Presdl. Sports award Pres.' Council on Phys. Fitness and Sports, 1973. Mem. Nat. Geographic Soc., Soc. Tech. Communication, Chinese Inst. of Engrs., Am. Radio Relay League, Buick Club of Am., SJA Masters Swim Club. Republican. Christian Scientist. Avocations: masters swimming, amateur radio, philately. Home: 6182 Ocho Rios Dr San Jose CA 95123-4637

CHAN, MARGARET MAY-SHENG, marketing and applications specialist, biochemist; b. N.Y.C., June 28, 1951; d. Chan, Shu-Kang and Tsang, Chui-Kwan. B.Sc., U. Santa Clara, 1972; M.A., U. Calif.-Berkeley, 1976, Ph.D., 1978. Research assoc. U. Calif.-Berkeley, 1978-80; sr. biochemist Beckman Instruments, Berkeley, 1981-83, mktg. specialist, 1984—, tech. cons., 1981—; speaker at seminars. Contbr. articles to tech. jours. Mem. AAAS, Am. Chem. Soc., Gamma Pi Epsilon. Home: PO Box 1154 San Leandro CA 94577 Office: Beckman Instruments PO Box 5101 San Ramon CA 94583-0701

CHAN, MARJORIE A., geology educator; b. Fort Ord, Calif., May 6, 1955; d. Gordon Luke and Maxine (Wong) C. BS, U. Calif., Davis, 1977; PhD, U. Wis., 1982. Geologist Lawrence Livermore (Calif.) Nat. Lab., 1977-78; asst. prof. geology U. Utah, Salt Lake City, 1982—; cons. Tera Corp., Berkeley, Calif., 1983, Arco Oil and Gas Co., Dallas, 1983-85, State of Utah Oil and Gas Mining Div., Salt Lake City, 1984-85. Tchr. 1st Baptist Ch., Salt Lake City, 1985—. Mem. Internat. Assn. Sedimentologists, Am. Assn. Petroleum Geologists, Soc. Econ. Paleontologists and Mineralogists, Am. Sci. Affiliation, Sigma Xi. Democrat. Avocations: hiking, tennis, biking, music, photography. Office: U Utah Dept Geology WC Browning Bldg Salt Lake City UT 84112

CHAN, PETER WING KWONG, pharmacist; b. Los Angeles, Feb. 3, 1949; s. Sherwin T.S. and Shirley W. (Lee) C.; BS, U. So. Calif., 1970, D in Pharmacy, 1974; m. Patricia Jean Uyeno, June 8, 1974; children: Kristina Dionne, Kelly Alison, David Shoichi. Clin. instr. U. So. Calif., 1974-76; staff clin. pharmacist Cedars-Sinai Med. Ctr., Los Angeles, 1974-76; 1st clin. pharmacist in ophthalmology Alcon Labs., Inc., Ft. Worth, 1977—, formerly in Phila. monitoring patient drug therapy, teaching residents, nurses, pharmacy students, then assigned to Tumu Tumu Hosp., Karatina, Kenya, also lectr. clin. ocular pharmacology tng. course, Nairobi, Cairo, Athens, formerly dist. sales mgr. Alcon/BP, ophthal. products div. Alcon Labs., Inc., Denver; v.p., gen. mgr. Optikem Internat., Sereine Products Div., Optacryl, Inc., Denver; formerly product mgr. hosp. pharmacy products Am. McGaw div. Am. Hosp. Supply Corp.; past internat. market mgr. IOLAB subs. Johnson & Johnson, past dir. new bus. devel. Iolab Pharms. div., dir. Internat. Mktg.; bd dirs. SUDCO Internat., Los Angeles; del. Am. Pharm. Assn. House of Dels., 1976-78; bd. dirs. Calif. Youth Theatre. Recipient Hollywood-Wilshire Pharm. Assn. spl. award for outstanding service, 1974; licensed pharmacist, Calif. Mem. Am. Pharm. Assn., Calif. Pharm. Assn., Hollywood-Wilshire Pharm. Assn. (bd. dirs. 1972-76), Am. Soc. Hosp. Pharmacists, Am. Pharm. Assn. Acad. of Pharmacy Practice, U. So. Calif. Gen. Alumni Assn., OSAD Centurions. Democrat. Home: 1005 W Idaho Ct Claremont CA 91711 Office: IOLAB 500 Iolab Dr Claremont CA 91711

CHAN, RAYMOND YUEN-FONG, ophthalmologist; b. Shanghai, China, Nov. 2, 1948; came to U.S., 1968; s. Joy Ka-on and So-Ying (Cheung) C.; m. Helen Yuk-yu Chang, Feb. 25, 1982; children: Stephen, Christina. BSAE and BSME, Calif. Poly. State U., 1971; MS, Calif. Inst. Tech., 1972, PhD, 1975; MD, U. Miami, Fla., 1977. Diplomate Am. Bd. Ophthalmology, Nat. Bd. Med. Examiners. Intern, Baylor Coll. Medicine affiliated hosps., Houston, 1977-78; resident, instr. Cullen Eye Inst., Houston, 1978-81; practice medicine, specializing in ophthalmology Scripps Clinic, LaJolla, Calif., 1981—; clin. instr. U. Calif., San Diego, 1983—; lectr. in field. Patentee in field. Contbr. articles to profl. jours. Active San Diego Eye Bank, Research to Prevent Blindness, Inc. Recipient Goar Research award in ophthalmology Baylor Coll. Medicine, 1979, 80; First place research paper award Tex. Ophthal. Assn., 1980; Farris Research Found. grantee, 1981—. Fellow Internat. Coll. Surgeons, Am. Acad. Ophthalmology, ACS; mem. Assn. for Research in Vision and Ophthalmology, Baylor Ophthalmology Alumni Assn., Sigma Xi, Tau Beta Pi, Phi Kappa Phi. Office: 9333 Genesee Ave Suite 180 San Diego CA 92121

CHAN, SHU-WING, physician; b. Hong Kong, Sept. 6, 1944; came to U.S., 1970; s. Kwong-Ying and Yee-Lan (Yip) C.; M.B., B.S., U. Hong Kong, 1968; m. Flora Yu-Big Yau, May 19, 1973; children: Mai-Sie, Mai-San, Ming-Jeung, Mai-King. Intern, Northwestern Hosp. of Mpls., 1970-71, in internal medicine, 1972-75; fellow in cardiology U. Minn. Hosps., Mpls., 1975-76; practice medicine specializing in internal medicine and cardiology, San Francisco, 1976—; attending physician St. Frances Meml. Hosp., Chinese Hosp., chmn. cardiopulmonary unit com., 1983—, mem.-at-large exec. com., 1983-86; pres. Shu-Wing Chan M.D., Inc., San Francisco, 1979—; asst. clin. prof. medicine U. Calif., San Francisco, 1985—; med. adv. to YMCA, San Francisco, 1978. Bd. dirs. Chinese Newcomers Service Center, San Francisco, 1980. Diplomate Am. Bd. Internal Medicine. Mem. Am. Heart Assn., San Francisco Med. Soc., AMA, Calif. Med. Assn., Chinese C. of C. (bd. dirs. 1985—). Office: 929 Clay St Suite 303 San Francisco CA 94108

CHAN, STEVEN RODERICK, federal agency officer; b. Berkeley, Calif., May 29, 1959; s. John and Lily (Wong) C.; 1 child, Chip. BS in Biochemistry, U. Pacific, 1981, BS in Mgmt. Info. Sci., 1983; MBA, Stanford U., 1985. Registered profl. engr., Calif. Ops. officer Del Monte Corp., San Francisco, 1979-82; strategic analyst Amdahl Corp., Sunnyvale, Calif., 1983-85; tech. ops. officer CIA, Sunnyvale, 1985—. NSF grantee, 1976, Nat. Security Agy. grantee, 1984. Fellow MENSA; mem. Digital Equipment Computer Users Soc., IEEE. Republican. Avocations: microcomputers, shooting, high tech. innovations.

CHAN, SUCHENG, history educator, academic administrator; b. Peoples Republic of China, Apr. 16, 1941; came to U.S., 1957; d. Kock K. and Dora K.W. (Chen) C.; m. Mark K. Juergensmeyer, Sept. 21, 1969. BA, Swarthmore Coll., 1963; MA, U. Hawaii, 1965; PhD, U. Calif., Berkeley, 1973. Asst. prof. Sonoma State U., Cotati, Calif., 1971-72; from asst. to assoc. prof. U. Calif., Berkeley, 1974-84; prof. history, univ. provost Oakes Coll. U. Calif., Santa Cruz, 1984-87. Author: This Bittersweet Soil, 1986, Asians in California History, 1987; also articles. Recipient Disting. Teaching award U. Calif., Berkeley, 1978. Mem. Assn. Asian Am. Studies (pres. 1980-83), Am. Hist. Assn. (Louis Knott Koontz prize 1985), Orgn. Am. Historians, Immigration History Soc., Calif. History Soc., Agrl. Hist. Soc. (Theodore Saloutos prize 1987). Democrat. Office: U Calif Dept History Santa Cruz CA 95064

CHAN, WAN HOR, physician; b. Batu Gajah, Malaysia, Dec. 13, 1939; came to U.S., 1971, naturalized, 1979; s. Tong Thye and Seow Ying (Ng) C.; M.B.B.S., U. Singapore, 1964; m. Amy Chan, June 29, 1967; children—Evelyn, Jennifer, Donald. Intern, Loma Linda U., 1971; resident Royal Maternity Hosp., Belfast, No. Ireland, 1967-70; asst. lectr. ob-gyn U. Singapore, 1966; tutor, fellow ob-gyn Queen's U. Belfast, 1967-71; asst. prof. ob-gyn U. So. Calif., 1972-74, Charles Drew Postgrad. Med. Sch., 1972-74; practice medicine specializing in ob-gyn, Los Banos, Calif., 1974—; asst. clin. prof. family practice U. Calif., Davis, 1976-80. William Blair Bell Meml. Research fellow, 1970. Fellow Royal Coll. Surgeons Can., Am. Coll. Obstetricians and Gynecologists, Royal Coll. Obstetricians and Gynecologists (Eng.), Methodist. Club: Rotary. Author: Outline of Obstetrics and Gynecology, 1971. Internat. Coll. Surgeons, Am. Soc. Abdominal Surgeons; mem. Am. Fertility Soc., AMA, N.Y. Acad. Scis. Office: 600 W I St Los Banos CA 93635

CHANCE, GAILYA MONROE, educational administrator, educator, consultant; b. Pearl River County, Miss., May 2, 1937; d. John Thomas and Frankie Dee (Clark) Monroe; m. Jay Paul Chance, Sept. 30, 1934; children: Jay, Jeffrey. B.S., Miss. U. Women (formerly Miss. State Coll. Women), 1959; M.A., Southwestern Baptist Theol. Sem., 1972; Ed.D., in Edni. Adminstrn., Miss. State U., 1979. Adminstrv. services credential; community coll. teaching credential. Children's center teaching permit, Calif. Dir., Child Enrichment Center, Memphis, 1964-75; dir. Creative Learning Center, Starkville, Miss., 1975-78; instr. bus. mgmt. Miss. State U., Starkville, 1978-80; chmn. dept. early childhood studies, coordinator tchr. tng. lab. Riverside (Calif.) City Coll., 1981-84, dean Bus. and Office Adminstrn., 1984—; regional cons. church adminstrn. dept., So. Bapt. Sunday Sch. Bd. Active Friends Mission Inn, Cultural Heritage Bd.; trustee Magnolia Ave. Baptist Ch.; mem. fin. devel. com. Calvary-Arrowhead Assn. Calif. So. Baptist Conv.; mem. citizens adv. com. Calif. Baptist Coll. Mem. Acad. Mgmt., Calif. Community Coll. Early Childhood Educators, Calif. Tchrs. Assn., Nat. Tchrs. Assn., Nat. Assn. Edn. Young Children, Phi Delta Kappa. Republican. Author: Church Weekday Early Education Teacher's Guide, Birth-Three, 1977; (with Jean Kirk Reynolds) How to Choose and Use Day Care, 1980; contbr. articles in field to ednl. and religious publs. Home: 2141 Westminster Dr Riverside CA 92506 Office: Riverside City Coll 4800 Magnolia Ave Riverside CA 92506

CHANCE, JAY PAUL, college administrator; b. Chickasha, Okla., Sept. 30, 1934; s. Russell Jay and Mary Beale (Roberts) C.; m. Gailya LaDelle Monroe, Feb. 26, 1961; children—Jay Frank, Jeffrey Shay. B.S., Okla. Bapt. U., 1956; M.A., Southwestern Bapt. Sem., Ft. Worth, 1961; Ed.D., Miss. State U., 1980. Edn. dir. First Baptist Ch., San Angelo, Tex., 1961-64; nat. dir. Royal Ambassadors, Memphis, 1964-75; assoc. dir. So. Rural Devel. Ctr., Starkville, Miss., 1975-80; v.p. Calif. Bapt. Coll., Riverside, 1980—; dir. Bold Venture Campaign, Riverside, 1982—. Author: Boys in Missions, 1970; Editor: Rural Development, 1978. Mem. Riverside Community Relations Commn., 1980-84; mem. community council Mission Inn, Riverside, 1982—; mem. San Gorgonio council Girl Scouts U.S.A., Riverside, 1983—; pres. Starkville Swim Team, 1978-79, Tchr./Parent Fellowship, Memphis, 1974-75. Served with U.S. Army, 1956-58. Named Trainer of Yr., Brotherhood Commn., Memphis, 1973. Fellow Nat. Recreation and Park Assn.; mem. Phi Delta Kappa. Republican. Baptist. Club: Optimists (v.p. 1977-78). Lodge: Rotary. Home: 5940 Intervale Dr Riverside CA 92506 Office: Calif Baptist College 8432 Magnolia Ave Riverside CA 92504

CHANDLER, COLSTON, physics educator; b. Boston, June 7, 1939; s. William Knox and Margaret Belle (Colston) C.; m. Seeley Dole, Jan. 30, 1965 (div. Feb. 1987); children: Andrew, Martin, Thomas. BS in Applied Math., Brown U., 1961; PhD in Physics, U. Calif., Berkeley, 1967. Asst. prof. U. N.Mex., Albuquerque, 1966-68, 70-73, assoc. prof., 1973-78, prof. physics, 1978—; vis. prof. U. Bonn, Fed. Republic Germany, 1978. Contbr. articles to profl. publs. Mem. AAUP, AAAS, Am. Phys. Soc., Internat. Assn. Math. Physics, Sigma Xi. Office: U NMex Dept Physics and Astronomy Albuquerque NM 87131

CHANDLER, DOROTHY BUFFUM, civic worker; b. Lafayette, Ill.; d. Charles Abel and Fern (Smith) Buffum; m. Norman Chandler, Aug. 30, 1922; children: Camilla (Mrs. F. Daniel Frost), Otis. Student, Stanford U., 1919-22; LHD (hon.), U. Calif., U. Judaism, U. Redlands, Hebrew Union Coll.; LLD (hon.), Occidental Coll., Mt. St. Mary's Coll., U. So. Calif.; DFA (hon.), U. Portland, Pepperdine Coll., Loyola Marymount U.; D of Arts (hon.), Art Inst. Los Angeles County. Hon. life chmn. Los Angeles Philharmonic Assn.; chmn. bd. govs. Performing Arts Council, Music Ctr. Los Angeles County; chmn. The Amazing Blue Ribbon of Music Ctr., Music Ctr. Found.; former regent U. Calif.; hon. life trustee Occidental Coll., Calif. Inst. Tech. Recipient Herbert Hoover medal Stanford Alumni Assn., Humanitarian award Variety Clubs Internat., 1974. Address: care Los Angeles Philharm Assn 135 N Grand AveBlvd Los Angeles CA 90012 *

CHANDLER, GEORGE DENNIS, electrical engineer; b. Port Jervis, N.Y., Apr. 15, 1943; s. George Eugene and Doris Elanor (Talcott) C.; m. Ruth Estelle Edwards, July 13, 1974 (dec. Oct. 1976); m. Marie Carolyn Fairchild, Nov. 4, 1977; 1 child, Nicholas George. BSEE, Syracuse U., 1970; MSEE, Calif. State U., Fullerton, 1984. Elec. engr. Westinghouse Corp., Balt., 1971-76; chief engr. Magnetic Pulse Tech., Riverside, Calif., 1976-81; mem. tech. staff Rockwell Internat., Anaheim, Calif., 1981—. Served with U.S. Army, 1965-67. Mem. Tau Beta Pi, Eta Kappa Nu. Avocations: music, golf. Home: 400 W Patwood Dr La Habra CA 90631 Office: Rockwell Internat 3370 Miraloma Ave MS DC 25 Anaheim CA 92803

CHANDLER, JOHN HERRICK, college president; b. San Francisco, Aug. 7, 1928; s. Ralph William and Gwen Thornton (Herrick) C.; m. Nancy Gordon Phillips, Dec. 10, 1955; children: John, Seth, Will. A.B., U. Calif., Los Angeles, 1952; B.D. (Danforth fellow), U. Chgo., 1958, Ph.D. (fellow),

1963. Instr. English Dartmouth Coll., 1961-63; asst. prof. U. Calif., Los Angeles, 1963-64; asso. prof., dean spl. programs Ohio U., 1964-67; v.p. Danforth Found., St. Louis, 1967-71; pres. Salem Coll. and Acad., Winston-Salem, N.C., 1971-76, Scripps Coll., Claremont, Calif., 1976—; ordained to ministry Episcopal Ch., 1960. Trustee Newton Coll. Sacred Heart, 1970-75, Thacher Sch., 1977-85; bd. dirs. Clayton (Mo.) Bd. Edn., 1970-71, Ctr. Theater Group, 1985—. Clubs: University (Los Angeles); Twilight, Bohemian. Office: Scripps College Balch Hall Claremont CA 91711

CHANDLER, JOHN PARSONS, anatomy educator; b. Washington, Mar. 13, 1948; s. James Greenough and Barbara (Dunlap) C.; m. Nancy Blankshine, Apr. 2, 1977. AB, Transylvania U., 1970; MA, East Carolina U., 1974; PhD, Pa. State U., Hershey, 1981. Postdoctoral fellow dept. anatomy U. Utah, Salt Lake City, 1981-84, asst. prof. pathology, 1985—; instr. anatomy U. Rochester, N.Y., 1984-85; dir. electron microscopy lab. VA Med. Ctr., Salt Lake City, 1985—. Mem. AAAS, Am. Assn. Anatomists, Soc. for Neurosci., Electron Microscopy Soc. Am. Office: EM Lab (113) VA Med Ctr 500 Foothill Blvd Salt Lake City UT 84148-0001

CHANDLER, KRISTIAN, computer consultant, educator; b. Cleveland Heights, Ohio, June 26, 1948; d. Gerhard A. and Hanna R. (Rittmeyer) Hoffmann; m. William D. Chandler, July 1, 1982; children—Karen, Heidi. Postgrad. U. So. Colo., 1984-85; MBA, U. Ark., 1987. Owner, mgr. V&W Fgn. Car Service, Canon City, Colo., 1970-80; prin. The Chandlers, Computer Cons., Pueblo, Colo., 1982—; faculty U. So. Colo., also mgr. Sch. Bus. microcomputer lab. Bd. dirs. Canon City Community Service Ctr., 1978-80, Canon City chpt. ARC, 1978-81. Mem. Student Programmers-Operators of Computers, Data Processing Mgmt. Assn., U. So. Colo. Honors Soc. (pres.), U. So. Colo. Grad. Assn. (founder), Alpha Chi. Home and Office: 42 MacNaughton Rd Pueblo CO 81001

CHANDLER, LINDA CLINE, investment broker; b. Sioux Falls, S.D.; d. Lawrence Alphonse and Wilba Nell (Leatherwood) Dhaemers; m. Terence E. Chandler, Oct. 16, 1976. BS, Iowa State U., 1968, MA, 1972. Registered investment advisor. With Sutro & Co., San Jose, Calif., 1974—, assoc. v.p., 1977-78, v.p. investments, 1978—; pres. Chandler Roberts, Inc., Santa Clara, Calif., 1983—, Pacific Integrated Group, 1987—; sr. v.p. Morgan, Olmstead, Kennedy & Gardner, 1985—; assoc. gen. ptnr. Brichard Properties; bd. advisors Rancon Securities; contbg. personal fin. editor Sta. KCSM-TV; fin. commentator Sta. KPEN; speaker in field. Contbr. articles to profl. jours. Bd. dirs. League of Women Friends. Named Fin. Planner of Yr., Am. Home Properties, 1981, 83, one of nations leading brokers Wall Street Transcript, 1982, Nation's Outstanding Fin. Planners, Consol. Capital, 1983, Number One Sales Performance Rancho Cons. Realty, 1983, Fin. Planner of Yr., Brichard & Co., 1985-86, Outstanding Broker of Yr., Brichard & Co., 1986, Fin. Planner of Yr., Rancon Fin., 1986. UN fellow. Mem. Santa Clara County Profl. Brokers Assn., Santa Clara County Profl. Young Women, AAUW, Phi Kappa Phi, Phi Delta Theta, Alpha Delta Pi. Methodist. Clubs: Sutro Century (pres.'s council 1978-81), Sutro Second Century, Sutro Pres. Office: 2900 Gordon Ave Suite 101 Santa Clara CA 95051 *

CHANDLER, OTIS, publisher; b. Los Angeles, Nov. 23, 1927; s. Norman and Dorothy (Buffum) C.; m. Marilyn Brant, June 18, 1951 (div.); children: Norman, Harry, Cathleen, Michael, Carolyn; m. Bettina Whitaker, Aug. 15, 1981. Grad., Andover Acad., 1946; B.A., Stanford U., 1950. Joined Times Mirror Co., 1953; pub. Los Angeles Times, 1960-80; chmn. bd., editor-in-chief Mirror Times Mirror Co., Los Angeles, 1980-86, chmn. exec. com., 1986—. Served to 1st lt. USAAF, 1951-53. Mem. Am. Soc. Newspaper Editors, Am. Newspaper Pubs. Assn. Club: California. Office: The Times Mirror Co Times Mirror Sq Los Angeles CA 90053

CHANDLER, ROD DENNIS, congressman; b. La Grande, Oreg., July 13, 1942; s. Robert John and Edna Pearl (Hagey) C.; m. Joyce Elaine Laremore, Aug. 3, 1963; children: John Gifford, Amanda Joy. B.S.in history, Oreg. State U., 1968. News corr. Sta. KOMO-TV News, Seattle, 1968-73; mktg. officer Wash. Mut. Savs. Bank, Seattle, 1973-77; mem. Wash. State Ho. of Reps., 1975-82, 98th, 99th and 100th Congresses from 8th Wash. Dist., 1983—; mem. King County Metro Council 1973-75; ptnr. Chandler & Corcoran Communications Inc., Seattle, 1977-82. Recipient Sigma Delta Chi award, 1972, Guardian of Small Business award (Nat. Fedn. Ind. Business), 1984, 1986, Excellence in Public Service award (Am. Acad. Pediatrics), 1984, Humanitarian of the Year award (Seattle-King Co. Humane Soc.), 1984, Golden Bulldog award (Watchdogs of Treas. Inc.), 1984, 86, Legislator of Yr. award (Washington Vocat. Assn.), 1984, 85. Republican. Lodge: Rotary. Office: 223 Cannon House Office Bldg Washington DC 20515

CHANDLER, STEPHEN RAY, musical instrument company executive; b. Berkeley, Calif., Feb. 8, 1949; s. Allen Stephen and Edna (Erickson) C.; m. Barbara Louise Gunn, Jan. 28, 1972; children: Jane, David. BA magna cum laude, Utah State U., 1979. Pres. R. Chandler & Co., Salt Lake City, 1979-84; tech. dir. Young Chang Piano Co., Cerritos, Calif., 1984—; chief technician Utah Symphony, Salt Lake City, 1979-84, Internat. Bachauer Piano Competition, Salt Lake City, 1982; founder, dir. Friends and Music Concerts, Salt Lake City, 1979-82. Mem. Am. Guild Organists, Royal Sch. Ch. Music, Am. Choral Dirs. Assn., Piano Technicians Guild (craftsman). Republican. Mormon. Avocations: water-skiing, squash, tennis. Home: 9822 Kite Dr Huntington Beach CA 92646 Office: Young Chang Am Inc 13336 Alondra Blvd Cerritos CA 90701

CHANDRAKASAN, GOWRI W., dental educator, medical researcher; b. Cochin, India, Mar. 1, 1942; came to U.S., 1983; d. K.R. and Seethalakshmi Balachandran; m. Nagappa Chandrakasan, May 6, 1963; children: Nagarajan C., Anantha P. BSc, U. Madras, India, 1961, MSc, 1966, PhD, 1971. Scientist Cen. Health Research Inst., Madras, 1966—; vis. fellow Nat. Inst. Dental Research div. NIH, Md., 1972-75; vis. assoc. prof. med. ctr. U. Calif., San Francisco, 1984—; mem. protein research unit Loyola Coll., Madras, 1980—, nutrition dept. Women's Christian Coll., Madras, 1982-83, doctoral com. U. Madras, 1977-83. Contbr. articles to profl. jours. Sr. Fulbright Scholar health ctr. U. Conn., 1983-84, med. ctr. U. Calif., San Francisco, 1984—. Mem. AAAS, Indian Women Scientists Assn., Indian Assn. Biomed. Scientists, Soc. Biol. Chemists, India, Altrusa Internat. (pres. Madras chpt. 1982-83), Sri Satya Sai Baba, Am. Soc. Cell Biology. Avocations: social service, gardening, music. Home: 200 Parnassus Ave #204 San Francisco CA 94117 Office: U Calif Med Ctr San Francisco CA 94143

CHANDRAMOULI, RAMAMURTI, electrical engineer; b. Sholinghur, Madras, India, Oct. 2, 1947; s. Ramamurti and Rajalakshmi (Ramamurti) Krishnamurti; B.Sc., Mysore U., 1965, B.E., 1970; M.E.E., Pratt Inst., 1972; Ph.D., Oreg. State U., 1978; m. Ranjani, Dec. 4, 1980. Instr., Oreg. State U., Corvallis, 1978; sr. engr. research and devel. group, mem. tech. staff spacecraft datasystems sect. Jet Propulsion Lab., Pasadena, Calif., 1978-81; staff engr., design automation group Am. Microsystems Inc., Santa Clara, Calif., 1982-83; staff software engr. corp. computer-aided design Intel, Santa Clara, 1983-86; project leader computer-aided design Sun Microsystems, Mountain View, Calif., 1985—; adj. lectr. Calif. State U.-Fullerton, 1987—. Sec., South India Cultural Assn., Los Angeles, 1980-81; bd. dirs. Am. Assn. East Indians. Mem. IEEE, IEEE Computer Soc., Sigma Xi, Eta Kappa Nu. Home: 205 W Red Oak Dr Apt P Sunnyvale CA 94086 Office: Sun Microsystems 2550 Garcia Ave Mountain View CA 94043

CHANDRASEKARAN, SANTOSH KUMAR, chemical engineer, researcher; b. Delhi, India, July 8, 1942; came to U.S., 1964, naturalized, 1985; s. Chidambara and Lakshmi (Venkatram) C.; m. Uma Anant, July 2, 1967; children: Rajiv, Ravi. B Tech. in Chem. Engring., Indian Inst. Tech., 1964, MS in Chem. Engring., 1964; MS in Chem. Engring., U. Calif., Berkeley, 1965, PhD, 1971. Research asst. U. Calif., Berkeley, 1964-65, 1967-71, teaching asst. in mass transfer, 1968, teaching asst. polymer sci., 1969, teaching asst. process design, 1970; sr. engr. E.I. DuPont de Nemours & Co., Gibbstown, N.J., 1965-67; devel. engr. ALZA Corp., Palo Alto, Calif., 1971-76, prin. scientist, 1976-81; assoc. project leader, transdermal delivery program ALZA Research div. ALZA Corp., Palo Alto, 1972-78, dir. engring. sci., 1974-78; project leader, transdermal delivery program Sandoz, Inc., 1977-79, dir. phys. sci., 1979-81; teaching asst. applied chemistry and chem. engring. Stanford (Calif.) U., 1974; dir. research and devel. Abcor, Inc., Wilmington, Mass., 1981-82; v.p. tech. affairs Sola Syntex Opthalmics, Phoenix, 1982—; mem. panel on controlled release theory, U. Akron, Ohio, 1975, program con. 28th ann. conf. on engring. in medicine and biology, 1975; vis. prof. U. Utah, Salt Lake City, 1981. Mem. edit. bd. Food, Pharms. and Bioengring. div. quar., 1984. J.N. Tata scholar Tata Endowment, 1964; research fellow U. Calif., Berkeley, 1964-65, 1967-71. Mem. Am. Inst. Chem. Engrs. (vice-chmn. program com. 1979, session chmn. 1980, publ. chmn. food, pharm. and bioengring. div. 1980—), N.Y. Acad. Sci., Am. Pharm. Assn., Am. Chem. Soc., Sigma Xi. Home: 9501 N 52d St Paradise Valley AZ 85253 Office: Sola Syntex Opthalmics 1100 E Bell Rd PO Box 39600 Phoenix AZ 85069-9600

CHANEY, FREDERICK BENNETT, management education company executive; b. Boulder, Colo., Sept. 8, 1936; s. Marjorie (Elliott) Hendrickson; m. Linda S. Spearman; children: Melanie, Andrew, Kira, Ari. BS in Psychology, Purdue U., 1959, MS in Exptl. Psychology, 1960, PhD in Managerial Psychology, 1962. Research asst. The Boeing Co., Seattle, 1962-63, N.Am. Ops. div. Rockwell Internat. Corp., 1964-68; pres. Continuing Edn. Corp., 1968-81; pres., chief exec. officer successor firm Vedax Scis. Corp., Santa Ana, Calif., 1981—; instr. managerial psychology U. So. Calif., 1969-70; adj. prof. mgmt. Pepperdine U., 1970-74; cons. Xerox Corp., Collins Radio, Lockheed Corp., State of Calif., 1969—. Author: (with D.H. Harris) Human Factors in Quality Assurance, 1969; contbr. articles to profl. jours. NSF fellow, 1964. Office: Vedax Scis Corp 5000 Birch #6200 Newport Beach CA 92660

CHANEY, ROBERT GALEN, religious organization executive; b. LaPorte, Ind., Oct. 27, 1913; s. Clyde Galen and Maree (Francis) C.; student Miami U., Ohio, 1931-33; D.D., Coll. Universal Truth, 1954; m. Earlyne Cantrell, Oct. 4, 1947; 1 dau., Sita. Ordained to non-denominational ministry, 1939; pastor various parishes, Eaton Rapids and Lansing Mich., 1938-50; founder, pres. Astara, Los Angeles, 1956-76, Upland, Calif., 1976—. Republican. Lodges: Mason, Kiwanis. Author: The Inner Way, 1962; Adventures in ESP, 1975; Mysticism: The Journey Within, 1979. Office: Astara 800 W Arrow Hwy Upland CA 91786

CHANG, ANNIE CHUAN-YUEN, molecular biologist; b. Shanghai, Republic of China, Oct. 6, 1944; came to U.S., 1967; d. Shang-Tze Chang and I-Tan New. BS, McGill U., 1967; PhD, Stanford U., 1980. Molecular biologist Stanford (Calif.) U., 1967—; cons. Cetus Palo Alto, Calif., 1980-84; research dir. RDNA Systems Inc., Palo Alto, 1981—. Contbr. articles to profl. jours.; patentee in field. Mem. AAAS. Avocations: gardening, traveling, art. Office: Stanford U Med Ctr Pasteur Dr Stanford CA 94305

CHANG, CHIOU-HSIUNG (BEAR), accounting educator, financial consultant; b. Taipei, Republic of China, Oct. 15, 1940; came to U.S., 1967; s. Peaceful and Chuan (Lee) C.; m. Eleanor Man-Ying Hung, Sept. 17, 1967; children: Patrick, Liesl. BA, Tam Kiang U., Taipei, 1964; MBA, Calif. State U., Long Beach, 1969; PhD in Acctg., La. State U., 1973. Cert. mgmt. acct. Asst. prof. mgmt. acctg. So. U., Baton Rouge, 1970-72; asst. prof. U. Ill., Chgo., 1972-77; assoc. prof. U. Cen. Fla., Orlando, 1977-78; assoc. prof. Calif. State U., Long Beach, 1978-83, Dominique Hills, 1983—; pres. 1st Irvine (Calif.) Corp., 1984—, Bear Chang & Co., Irvine, 1973-84, also founder. Bd. dirs. Chineses-Am. Council, Santa Ana, Calif. 1983—. Mem. Am. Acctg. Assn., Nat. Assn. Accts. Democrat. Home: 5 Sandpebble Irvine CA 92715 Office: Calif State U Dominique Hills Sch Mgmt 1000 Victoria Blvd Carson CA 90747

CHANG, DONALD AWO, physician's assistant, medical society executive; b. Hilo, Hawaii, May 11, 1948; s. Anthony Ah Wo and Margaret C.; B.S. in Med. Sci., Emory U., 1975; A.A., Community Coll. Denver, 1973; m. Karen Toshiko Isemoto, July 28, 1973; 1 dau., Jennifer Lianne. Cert. fitness instr. Am. Coll. Sports Medicine. Asst. clin. instr. respiratory therapy Mercy Hosp., Denver, 1973; physician's asst. Hilo (Hawaii) Med. Group, 1976-83; exec. dir. Hawaii Unit Am. Cancer Soc., 1983—; basic cardiac life support instr. Am. Heart Assn. Mem. Hilo Hosp. Home Health Adv. Bd., Big Island Interagy. Council, Human Services Council, Health Fair Adv. Com.; mem. Hawaii County First Lady's Outstanding Vol. Awards Com.; bd. dirs. Big Island Ednl. Fed. Credit Union. Mem. Am. Acad. Physician's Assts., Hawaii Island C. of C., Japanese C. of C. (bd. dirs.), Hawaii Acad. Physician's Assts. Club: Lehua Jaycees (sec. 1977-78, individual devel. v.p. 1978-79, dist. dir. 1979-80, dir. awards and competition, 1980-81, exec. v.p. 1981-82, regional dir. 1982-83). Office: Hawaii Unit Am Cancer Soc 614 Kilanea Ave Suite 2 Hilo HI 96720

CHANG, DONALD MARK, law and economics educator, consultant; b. Honolulu, Nov. 30, 1927; s. Y.K. and L.K. (Leong) C.; m. Mildred Sachiko Matsunaga, July 6, 1957. B.A. cum laude, U. Nebr., 1950; J.D., Yale U., 1953; Ph.D. in Econs. and Ethics and Law, U. Chgo. and Claremont Sch. Theology, U. So. Calif., 1961; student U. Hawaii, 1945-46, 47-48. Jr. exec. Castle & Cooke Co., Honolulu, 1953-54; gen. counsel Hawaii AFL-CIO, Honolulu, 1954-56; spl. asst. to chmn. NLRB, Washington, 1961-62; minority, gen. counsel Com. on Judiciary, U.S. Senate, Washington, 1962-71; prof. law and econs. U. Hawaii, Honolulu, 1971—; cons. Calif. Western Sch. Law, San Diego, 1978-81, Patton, Boggs & Blow, Washington, 1978-80. Bd. dirs. Honolulu Symphony Soc., 1973-78; chmn. United Charities, Honolulu, 1976; chmn. Gubernatorial Candidacy Com., Honolulu, 1972; pres. Waialee Nui Assn., Honolulu, 1972-79. Recipient Outstanding Accomplishment award Moot Ct. Program, U. Hawaii, 1983. Fellow Ethics and Society Colloquium (dir. 1976-85; gold award 1984); mem. Am. Bus. Law Assn., Am. Econ. Assn., Am. Indsl. and Labor Relations Assn., Am. Immigration and Nationality Conf. Democrat. Methodist. Mem. Phi Alpha Delta (pres. 1972-73), Acacia. Lodge: Lancers (pres. 1972-76). Home: 1803 Halekoa Dr Honolulu HI 96821 Office: U of Hawaii 96-045 Ala Ike Pearl City HI 96782

CHANG, ERNEST SUN-MEI, endocrinology and aquaculture educator; b. Berkeley, Calif., Dec. 7, 1950; s. Shu-Chi and Helen (Fong) C. BA, U. Calif., Berkeley, 1973; PhD, UCLA, 1978. Postdoctoral fellow U. Chgo., 1978; asst. prof. endocrinology U. Calif., Davis, 1978-85, assoc. prof., 1985—. Contbr. numerous articles to profl. jours. Chief Jenner (Calif.) Fire Dept., 1986—. Recipient Research medal, UCLA, 1978; grantee Am. Cancer Soc., 1979-81, Sea Grant Coll. Program grantee, 1978—. Mem. Am. Soc. Zoologists, Tissue Culture Assn., World Aquaculture Soc., Nat. Shellfisheries Assn. Office: Bodega Marine Lab PO Box 247 Bodega Bay CA 94923

CHANG, GARY KINGTON, computer music composer, consultant; b. Mpls., Feb. 22, 1953; s. Melvin C. and Diana (Lee) C.; m. Margaret Ann Craig, Feb. 14, 1982. BFA in Music Composition, Carnegie-Mellon U., 1975; MFA in Music Composition, Calif. Inst. Arts, 1977. Product specialist Fairlight Instruments, West Los Angeles, Calif., 1980-82; freelance composer, studio musician Gary Chang Co., Newhall, Calif., 1982-85; prin. Gary Chang Music Co., Inc., Newhall, Calif., 1985—; cons. Roland Corp., USA, Los Angeles, 1985—. Composed music soundtrack for the motion picture The Breakfast Club, 1984 (Gold Record). Grantee NEA, 1977. Mem. Am. Fedn. Musicians. Avocation: cooking.

CHANG, SIDNEY HSU-HSIN, history educator; b. Wuchang, China, Jan. 1, 1934; s. Chung Ning and Wen Jane (Hwang) C.; B.A., Nat. Taiwan U., 1956; M.A., U. Mo., 1959; M.S., Fla. State U., 1961; Ph.D., U. Wis., 1966; postdoctoral research Harvard U., 1969-70; m. Elaine Pardue, Sept. 15, 1962; children—Walter Gerald Chi-chung, Gregory Eugene Chi-tung. Asst. prof. history Calif. State U. at Fresno, 1966-69, assoc. prof., 1969-73, prof., 1973—; chmn. Asian studies, 1967-69; chmn. bd. dirs. Chinese Culture & Arts Co., Inc., San Francisco, 1975-77; chmn. bd. trustees C.C.Y. Corp., 1972-77; pres. Am. Chinese Hua Hui Co., 1976-79; chmn. bd. dirs. Am. Chinese Culture and Arts Co., 1977—; vis. prof. Nat. Chengchi U., 1975-76. Mem. Republican Presdl. Task Force, 1983—; dir. Far East Trade Service in Ger., 1983-85. Research grantee Am. Philos. Soc., summers 1967, 69, Sun Yat-Sen Found., 1986-88; Wis. Ford Area fellow, 1963-65. Mem. Am. Hist. Assn., Assn. for Asian Studies, Oral History Assn., Asian Studies on Pacific Coast, Asia Sci. Research Assocs. Author: Method and Form for Paperwriting: A Manual, 1977. Mem. editorial bd. Am. Asian Rev., 1983-84. Contbr. articles to various scholarly jours. Home: 4526 E Santa Ana Fresno CA 93726 Office: Calif State U Dept History Fresno CA 93740 Office: 241 Columbus Ave San Francisco CA 94133

CHANG, TSU-SHUAN, electrical engineering educator; b. Republic of China, Feb. 10, 1950; came to U.S., 1976; s. Tao-Ming and Erh-Chun (Teng) C.; m. Yu-Hwa Mary King, Aug. 21, 1976. BS, Nat. Chiao Tung U., Taiwan, Republic of China, 1971, MS, 1973; SM, PhD, Harvard U., 1981. Instr. Chinese Navy Communication and Electronic Sch., Taiwan, 1974-75, Nat. Chiao Tung U., Hsinchu, Taiwan, 1975-76; research asst. IBM T.J. Watson Research Ctr., Yorktown Heights, N.Y., 1977; asst. prof. elec. engring. SUNY, Stony Brook, 1981-84, U. Calif., Davis, 1984—; cons. Harvard U., Cambridge, 1981, 82. Contbr. articles to profl. jours. Served to 1st lt. Chinese Navy, 1973-75. Fellow Harvard U., 1977, NSF, 1984, 85, U. Calif. and FMC Corp., 1985, 86. Mem. Control Systems Soc. of IEEE, Computer Soc. of IEEE, Communications Soc. of IEEE, Phi Tau Phi. Avocations: gardening, hiking, Tai-Chi Chuan, travel. Office: U Calif Electrical and Computer Engring Dept Davis CA 95616

CHANIOT, GEORGE EDWARD JR., educator; b. Decatur, Ill., July 9, 1939; s. George E. and Betty (Mannering) C.; m. Janet Lorraine Trautwein, June 30, 1962; children: Gregory Edward, Maria Isabel. BA, U. Mich., 1961; postgrad., U. Calif., Berkeley, 1969. Prin. Potter Valley (Calif.) Community High Sch., 1971-75; sci. tchr. Colegio F.D. Roosevelt, Lima, Peru, 1975-78, Potter Valley High Sch., 1978-86. Mem. AAAS, Nat. Sci. Tchrs. Assn., Calif. Sci. Tchrs. Assn., Ecol. Soc. Am., Cooper Ornithol. Soc.

CHANNAPRAGADA, RAO SATYANARAYAN, electronics company executive; b. Hyderabad, India, June 3, 1928; came to U.S., 1949; s. Hanumanth Rao and Leelavati (Yelluri) C.; divorced; children: Kishan, Leela Kiran. BCE, Gsmania U., Hyderabad, 1948; BS in Aero. Engring., U. Ill., 1956, MS in Applied Math., 1957, PhD in Math., Physics, 1961. Chief applied scis. United Techs. Inc., Sunnyvale, Calif., 1961-65; pres. Consolidated Engring. Tech. Corp., Mountain View, Calif., 1965-68, Consolidated Engring. Research Corp., Sunnyvale, 1968-75, Elec. Mech. Prods. Inc., Santa Clara, Calif., 1975-81; chmn., chief exec. officer Media Tech. Internat. Inc., Sunnyvale, 1981—. Contbr. articles to profl. jours. Mem. Sigma Xi, Pi Mu Epsilon. Avocations: tennis, photography. Home: 707 Continental Circle Apt 631 Mountain View CA 94040 Office: Media Tech Internat 243 S Mathilda Suite 501 Sunnyvale CA 94086

CHAO, CHIH HSU, research mechanical engineer; b. Shantung, China, Aug. 2, 1939; s. Ching Fung and Ching Chih (Lin) C.; B.S., Nat. Taiwan U., 1962; M.S., U. Calif.-Berkeley, 1965, Ph.D., 1972; m. Grace Yng Chu, Apr. 15, 1967; children—Henry Shaw, Lily Yuin. Research asst., applied mechanics U. Calif.-Berkeley, 1965-72; research engr. Boeing Co., Seattle, 1966-67; research scientist, mgr. engring. analysis, chief engr. Physics Internat. Co., San Leandro, Calif., 1969—; cons. engr. Registered profl. engr., Calif. Mem. ASME (sect. chmn.), Nat. Soc. Profl. Engrs., Calif. Soc. Profl. Engrs., Nat. Apt. and Property Owners Assn. Democrat. Roman Catholic. Contbr. research papers in field to profl. jours. Home: 1018 Contra Costa Dr El Cerrito CA 94530

CHAO, GEORGE YAO TUNG, electronics company executive; b. Shanghai, China, July 4, 1946; came to U.S., 1950; s. S. Di Wha and Polly (Lee) C. B.S., Rensselaer Poly. Inst., 1970; M.B.A., SUNY-Albany, 1972. Asst. v.p. Bank of Canton of Calif., San Francisco, 1972-77; dir. microprocessor mktg. Nat. Semicondr., Santa Clara, Calif., 1977-80; v.p. mktg./sales Cermetek Microelectric, Sunnyvale, Calif., 1980-81; pres. Liberty Electronics, San Francisco, 1981-85; pres. Sigmaguest, Inc., Sausalito, Calif., 1985—. Address: Liberty Electronics 625 3d St San Francisco CA 94107

CHAO, JAMES MIN-TZU, architect; b. Dairen, China, Feb. 27, 1940; s. T. C. and Lin Fan (Wong) C.; came to U.S., 1949, naturalized, 1962; m. Kirsti Helena Lehtonen, May 15, 1968. BArch, U. Calif., Berkeley, 1965. Cert. architect, Calif.; cert. instr. real estate, Calif. Intermediate draftsman Spencer, Lee & Busse, Architects, San Francisco, 1966-67; asst. to pres. Import Plus Inc., Santa Clara, Calif., 1967-69; job capt. Hammaberg and Herman, Architects, Oakland, Calif., 1969-71; project mgr. B A Premises Corp., San Francisco, 1971-79; constrn. mgr. The Straw Hat Restaurant Corp., 1979-81, mem. sr. mgmt., dir. real estate and constrn., 1981—; lectr. comml. real estate site analysis and selection for profl. real estate seminars; coordinator minority vending program, solar application program Bank of Am.; guest faculty mem. Northwest Ctr. for Profl. Edn. Patentee tidal electric generating system; author first comprehensive consumer orientated performance specification for remote banking transaction. Recipient honorable mention Future Scientists Am., 1955. Mem. AIA. Republican. Clubs: Encinal Yacht (dir. 1977-78).

CHAO, STELLA TZU-YUN, pharmacology consultant; b. N.Y.C., Apr. 14; d. Shou-Ting and Anna Shiao-Man (Wen) C. BS, U. Md., 1972; MA, Stanford U., 1973; PhD, U. Wash., 1980. Zoologist NIH, Bethesda, Md., 1973-74; postdoctoral fellow U. Calif., San Francisco, 1980-82; research investigator Am. Critical Care, McGaw Park, Ill., 1982-83; research scientist ALZA Corp., Palo Alto, Calif., 1983—; cons. Environ. Toxicology Internat. Inc., Seattle, 1986—. Contbr. numerous articles to profl. jours., chpts. to books. Recipient Young Pharmacologist award IUPhar Congress, Tokyo, 1981; Senatorial scholar State of Md., Annapolis, 1968-72. Mem. AAAS, Am. Chem. Soc., Am. Pharm. Assn., Am. Assn. Pharm. Scientists, N.Y. Acad. Scis. Republican. Avocations: swimming, sailing, theatre. Office: ALZA Corp 950 Page Mill Rd Palo Alto CA 94304

CHAPDELAINE, ROLAND JOSEPH, academic administrator; b. Springfield, Mass., Aug. 23, 1946; s. Roland George and Therese Rose (LaRose) C.; m. Pamela Jeanne Mearns, Aug. 24, 1968; children: Eric Roland, Denise Elizabeth. BA, Providence Coll., 1968; MS, Ball State U., 1969, EdD, 1976. Instr. biology Ball State U., Muncie, Ind., 1969-72; assoc. prof. Howard Community Coll., Columbia, Md., 1972-78, div. chmn., 1975-80, coordinator faculty devel., 1978-80, acting dean students, 1983-84, dean instrn., 1980-86; v.p. acad. affairs Mohave Community Coll., Kingman, Ariz., 1986—; co-chmn. adv. com. Columbia Assn. Urban Lake Water Quality Project, 1976-86; advisor Solar Energy Ednl. Project State of Md., 1977; cons. various community colls., Md., Pa., N.J., 1974—; lectr. Md. Acad. Scis., Balt., 1976-80. Contbr. articles to profl. jours. Vice-chmn. AYRA Youth Baseball, Howard County, Md., 1982; bd. dirs. St. John's Parish, Howard County, 1980-84; co-chmn. Citizens Adv. Com. Critical Areas Planning, Howard County, 1976-77; edn. coordinator Middle Patuxent Environ. Assn., Howard County, 1974-78; appointed State Commn. for Study of Future of Md. Community Coll., 1985-86; bd. dirs. Industry Edn. Alliance Council, Howard County, 1984-86, Hist. Savage Mill Mus., 1985-86. Recipient Cert. Appreciation, Md. Dept. Vocat. Edn., 1982, Spl. Achievement award Howard Community Coll., 1986; grantee NSF, 1981, FIPSE, 1984, 85. Mem. Nat. Council Staff Program and Orgnl. Devel. (regional dir. 1984-85, Cert. Appreciation 1985), Nat. Council Instructional Adminstrs. (regional dir. 1980-85, dir. nat. issues 1985-86, sec. 1986—), Council Md. Deans (pres. 1983-84), Nat. Council for Staff, Program and Orgnl. Devel. (regional dir.), Md. Consortium of Biol. Scientists (steering com. 1973-80), Howard County C. of C. (leadership tng. program 1986). Democrat. Roman Catholic. Home: 3705 Martingdale Dr Kingman AZ 86401 Office: Mohave Community Coll Kingman AZ 86401

CHAPIN, HELEN GERACIMOS, college official, educator; b. Honolulu, Oct. 6, 1929; d. George Nicholas and Pota (Demetrak) Geracimos; m. Henry B. Chapin, Oct. 1, 1960; children: Georganne, Julia, Henry E., Nicholas. BA, U. Hawaii, 1958, MA, 1959; PhD, Ohio State U., 1975. Assoc. prof. English, Wilmington (Ohio) Coll., 1965-78; assoc. v.p. Hawaii Pacific Coll., Honolulu, 1978—, dean for spl. programs, 1978—. Editor: Hawaiian Jour. History, 1985—. Bd. dirs. Hawaii Heritage Com., 1980—, Hawaiian Hist. Soc., 1985—, Hawaiian Com. for Humanities, Honolulu, 1985—. Mem. Am. Council Edn., Women in Higher Acad. Adminstrn. Democrat. Greek Orthodox. Home: 2052 Mott-Smith Dr Honolulu HI 96822 Office: Hawaii Pacific Coll 1166 Fort Honolulu HI 96813

CHAPIN, NED, data processing consultant; b. Port Gamble, Wash., Aug. 8, 1927; s. M.C. and Rose A. (Smallwood) C.; m. June Roediger, June, 12, 1954; children: Suzanne, Elaine. MBA, U. Chgo., 1949; PhD, Ill. Inst. Tech., 1959. Registered profl. engr., Calif. From lectr. to asst. prof. various schs., Chgo., 1953-56; systems analyst SRI Internat., Menlo Park, Calif., 1956-61; assoc. prof. San Francisco State U., 1961-64; data processing cons. InfoSci Inc., Menlo Park, 1965—; session chmn. Nat. Computer Conf.; bd.

dirs. CTS Time Sharing Corp., Palo Alto, Calif., 1967-69. Author: Computers: A Systems Approach, 1971; editor, computer sci. series Van Nostrand Reinhold Co., N.Y.C., 1967—; researcher for invention; contbr. articles to profl. jours. Officer Home Owners Assn., Menlo Park. Served with U.S. Army, 1951-53. Mem. Software Maintenance Assn. (pres. 1986—), Inst. Indsl. Engrs., EDP Auditors Assn. (cert.), Soc. Gen. Systems Research, Ops. Research Soc. Am., Assn. Ednl. Data Systems, Assn. Computing Machinery, Data Processing Mgmt. Assn., Soc. Info. Mgmt., Assn. Computers and Humanities, Am. Econ. Assn., Sigma Xi, Delta Sigma Rho. Home: 1190 Bellair Way Menlo Park CA 94025-6611 Office: InfoSci Inc Box 7117 Menlo Park CA 94026-7117

CHAPLIN, GEORGE, editor; b. Columbia, S.C., Apr. 28, 1914; s. Morris and Netty (Brown) C.; m. Esta Lillian Solomon, Jan. 26, 1937; children—Stephen Michael, Jerry Gay. B.S., Clemson Coll., 1935; Nieman fellow, Harvard U., 1940-41. Reporter, later city editor Greenville (S.C.) Piedmont, 1935-42; mng. editor Camden (N.J.) Courier-Post, 1946-47, San Diego Jour., 1948-49; mng. editor, then editor New Orleans Item, 1949-58; asso. editor Honolulu Advertiser, 1958-59, editor, 1959-86, editor at large, 1986—; Pulitzer prize juror, 1969, 83; mem. selection com. Jefferson fellowships East-West Ctr.; Chmn. Gov.'s Conf. on Year 2000, 1970; chmn. Hawaii Commn. on Year 2000, 1971-74; co-chmn. Conf. on Alt. Econ. Future for Hawaii, 1973-75; charter mem. Goals for Hawaii, 1979—; alt. U.S. rep. South Pacific Commn., 1978-81; chmn. search com. for pres. U. Hawaii, 1983; chmn. Hawaii Gov.'s Adv. Council on Fgn. Lang. and Internat. Studies, 1983—; bd. dirs. Econ. Corp. Honolulu, 1984—. Editor, officer-in-charge: Mid-Pacific edit. Stars and Stripes World War II; Editor: (with Glenn Paige) Hawaii 2000, 1973. Bd. dirs. U. Hawaii Research Corp., 1970-72, Inst. for Religion and Social Change, Hawaii Jewish Welfare Fund; bd. govs. East-West Center, Honolulu, 1980—, chmn., 1983—, Pacific Health Research Inst., 1984, Hawaii Pub. Schs. Found., 1986— ; Am. media chmn. U.S.-Japan Conf. on Cultural and Ednl. Interchange, 1978-86. Served as capt. AUS, 1942-46. Decorated Star Solidarity (Italy), Order Rising Sun (Japan), Prime Minister's medal (Israel); recipient citations Overseas Press Club, 1961, 72, Headliners award, 1962, John Hancock award, 1972, 74, Distinguished Alumni award Clemson U., 1974, E.W. Scripps award Scripps-Howard Found., 1976, Champion Media award for Econ. Understanding, 1981. Mem. Soc. Nieman Fellows, Honolulu Symphony Soc., Pacific and Asian Affairs Council (dir.), Internat. Press Inst., World Future Soc., Am. Soc. Newspaper Editors (dir., treas. 1973, sec. 1974, v.p. 1975, pres. 1976), Nat. Conf. Editorial Writers, Friends of East-West Center, Sigma Delta Chi. Clubs: Pacific, Waialae Country. Home: 4437 Kolohala St Honolulu HI 96816 Office: care Honolulu Advertiser PO Box 3110 Honolulu HI 96802

CHAPMAN, ARTHUR JOSEPH, computer science educator; b. Vallejo, Calif., May 27, 1946; s. Arthur B. and Josephine M. (Tafoya) C.; m. Mary Danielle Wise, Sept. 7, 1968; children: Jennifer Joy, Karen Ann. BS in Math., Calif. Poly. State U., 1969, BArch, 1969; MS in Computer Sci., Penn. State U., 1971. Prodn. scheduler URS Systems, N.Y.C., 1971-72; prof. Calif. Poly State U., San Luis Obispo, 1972—. Author books; contbr. articles to profl. jours. Recipient Research award Porgressive Architecture mag., 1980, Meritorious Teaching award Calif. Poly Sch. Architecture, 1985, 87. Office: Calif Poly State U Sch Architecture San Luis Obispo CA 93407

CHAPMAN, JEFFREY IAN, educator; b. Milw., Jan. 16, 1946; s. Philip and Sophia (Shachnov) C.; m. Elaine Jonas, June 22, 1969; children—Michael Aaron, Allison Beth. A.B., Occidental Coll., 1967; M.A., U. Calif.-Berkeley, 1968, Ph.D., 1971. Research economist Inst. of Govt. and Pub. Affairs, UCLA, 1971-73; prof. U. So. Calif., Los Angeles, 1973-79, assoc. prof. sch. pub. adminstrn., 1979-86, prof. 1986—, dir. grad. ednl. instn., 1983—; cons. HRS, Inc., Los Angeles, 1981-83, Kirlin & Assocs., 1982-83. Author: Proposition 13 and Land Use, 1981, Long Term Fin. Planning, 1987; contbr. articles to profl. jours. Lincoln Inst. grantee, 1979; HUD grantee, 1978; NSF grantee, 1983. Mem. Am. Soc. Pub. Adminstrn. (regional bd.), Am. Econ. Assn., Nat. Tax Assn. Democrat. Jewish. Club: Comstock. Lodge: Rotary. Office: U So Calif Sch Pub Adminstrn Los Angeles CA 90007 Home: 4841 Sherlock Way Carmichael CA 95608

CHAPMAN, JOHN BRENT, tool engineer; b. Evansville, Ind., Apr. 21, 1955; s. John Lewis and Irma Joyce (Woolsey) C.; m. Terrie Lee Ott, Mar. 20, 1976. BS in Mfg. Engring. Tech., Calif. State Poly. U., Pomona, 1985. Tool draftsman Rail system Inc., Mira Loma, Calif., 1975-77; tool designer Smith Tool, Irvine, Calif., 1977-79; tool engr. Bourns Inc., Riverside, Calif., 1979—. Republican. Avocations: music, weight tng., bldg. cars. Home: 960 W Morgan Rialto CA 92376 Office: Bourns Inc 1200 Columbia Ave MS 169 Riverside CA 92501

CHAPMAN, LORING, psychologist, neuroscientist; b. Los Angeles, Oct. 4, 1929; s. Lee E. and Elinore E. (Gundry) Scott; children: Robert, Antony, Pandora. B.S., U. Nev., 1950; Ph.D., U. Chgo., 1955. Lic. psychologist, Oreg., N.Y., Calif. Research fellow U. Chgo., 1952-54; research asso., asst. prof. Cornell U. Med. Coll., N.Y.C., 1955-61; asso. prof. in residence, mem. Neuropsychiat. Inst., UCLA, 1961-65; research prof. U. Oreg., Portland, 1965; br. chief NIH, Bethesda, Md., 1966-67; prof., chmn. dept. behavioral biology Sch. Medicine U. Calif., Davis, 1967-79; prof. psychiatry Sch. Medicine U. Calif., 1977—, prof. neurology, 1977-81, prof. human physiology, 1977-81; vice chmn. div. of sci. basic to medicine 1976-79; vis. prof. U. Sao Paulo, Brazil, 1959, 77, Univ. Coll., London, 1969-70, U. Florence, Italy, 1979-80; clin. prof. Georgetown U., 1966-67; mem. Calif. Primate Research Center, 1967—; dir. research Fairview Hosp., 1965-66; cons. Nat. Inst. Neurol. Disease and Stroke, 1961—, Nat. Cancer Inst., 1977—, Nat. Inst. Child Health Devel., 1967—, mem. research and tng. com., 1968-72. Author: Pain and Suffering, 3 vols, 1967, Head and Brain 2 vols, 1971, (with E.A. Dunlap) The Eye, 1981; contbr. sci. articles to publs. Recipient Thornton Wilson prize, 1958, Career award USPHS, 1964, Commonwealth Fund award, 1970; grantee NASA, 1969—; grantee NIH, 1956—; grantee Nat. Inst. Drug Abuse, 1971—; Forgarty Sr. Internat. fellow, 1980. Mem. Am. Acad. Neurology, Am. Physiol. Soc., Am. Psychol. Assn., Royal Soc. Medicine (London), Am. Neurol. Assn., Am. Assn. Mental Deficiency, Aerospace Med. Assn., Soc. for Neurosci. Condr. research in field of behavioral and sensory physiology, brain function, neuropharmacology, psychopharmacology. Home: 205 Country Place Sacramento CA 95831 Office: Dept Psychiatry U Calif Med Ctr 2315 Stockton Blvd Sacramento CA 95817

CHAPMAN, RICHARD FISKE, psychiatrist, educator; b. Colorado Springs, Colo., Feb. 18, 1933; s. Edward Northrop and Janet (Johnson) C.; m. Carol Shirley Carlson, Dec. 26, 1956 (div. 1970); stepchildren—James Q. Collins III, Charles L. Collins, William R. Collins; m. 2d, Nancy Whisnant Collins, May 29, 1982; children by previous marriage—Karen Kay, Eric Robert. B.A., Yale U., 1955; M.D., Northwestern U., 1959. Diplomate Am. Bd. Neurology and Psychiatry; cert. Menninger Sch. Psychiatry, 1963; cert. psychoanalysis San Francisco Psychoanalytic Inst., 1972. Intern, Highland-Alameda County Hosp., Oakland, Calif., 1959-60; fellow in psychiatry Menninger Sch. Psychiatry, Topeka, Kans., 1960-63; resident in psychiatry VA Hosp., Topeka, 1960-63; practice medicine specializing in psychiatry, Palo Alto, Calif., staff psychiatrist Adult Psychiat. Clinic, San Mateo County Mental Health Services Div. (Calif.), 1965-66, asst. dir. psychiat. tng., 1966-68; mem. faculty San Francisco Psychoanalytic Inst., 1978—, pres., 1981-82; dep. chief psychiatry Stanford U. Hosp. (Calif.), 1972-74; v.p. for planning and dean faculty Pacific Grad. Sch. Psychology, 1977—, adj. prof., 1977—; clin. prof. psychiatry Stanford U. Med. Sch., 1982—. Contbr. articles to med. jours. Pres. Chapman Research Fund, Carmel Valley, Calif., 1972—, trustee, 1968—. Served to capt. M.C., U.S. Army, 1963-65. Fellow Am. Psychiat. Assn.; mem. Am. Psychoanalytic Assn., Internat. Psychoanalytic Assn., AAAS (life mem.), No. Calif. Psychiat. Soc. (fellow, councillor 1977-80), Mid-Peninsula Psychiat. Soc. (pres. 1971-72). Office: 780 Welch Rd Suite 201 Palo Alto CA 94304

CHAPMAN, RICHARD LEROY, public policy researcher; b. Yankton, S.D., Feb. 4, 1932; s. Raymond Young and Vera Everette (Trimble) C.; m. Marilyn Jean Nicholson, Aug. 14, 1955; children: Catherine Ruth, Robert Matthew, Michael David, Stephen Raymond, Amy Jean. BS, S.D. State U., 1954; postgrad., Cambridge (Eng.) U., 1954-55; MPA, Syracuse U., 1958, PhD, 1967. Profl. staff mem. com. govt. ops. U.S. Ho. Reps., Washington, 1966-67; program dir. NIH, Bethesda, Md., 1967-68; sr. research assoc. Nat. Acad. Pub. Adminstrn., Washington, 1968-72, dep. exec. dir., 1973-76, v.p., dir. research, 1976-81; sr. research scientist Denver Research Inst., 1982-86, mem. adv. com., 1984-86; ptnr. Milliken Chapman Research Group Inc., Denver, 1986—; cons. U.S. Office Personnel Mgmt., Washington, 1977-81, Denver, 1986; cons. CIA, Washington, 1979, 80, 81, Arthur S. Fleming Awards, Washington, 1977-81. Contbr. articles to profl. jours. Mem. aerospace com. Colo. Commn. Higher Edn., Denver, 1982-83; chmn. rules com. U. Denver Senate, 1984-85; bd. dirs. S.E. Englewood Water Dist., Littleton, 1984—, pres. 1986—. Brookings fellow, 1964-65. Mem. Tech. Transfer Soc., Am. Soc. Pub. Adminstrn., AAAS, Order of DeMolay (Cross of Honor 1982). Republican. Lodges: Masons, Commandery. Avocations: hunting, fishing, golf, reading, gardening. Home: 6129 S Elizabeth Way Littleton CO 80121 Office: U Denver Denver Research Inst Denver CO 80208

CHAPMAN, ROBERT DALE, research chemist; b. Glendale, Calif., June 4, 1955; s. Forrest Dale and Berta (Jäger) C.; m. Debra Jay Cullen, Dec. 5, 1981. BA in Chemistry, U. Calif., Irvine, 1977, PhD, 1980. Research assoc. U. Colo., Boulder, 1981; research chemist Naval Weapons Ctr., China Lake, Calif., 1981-82, Astronautics Lab., Edwards AFB, Calif., 1982—. NRC fellow, 1981. Mem. Am. Chem. Soc., Sigma Xi. Methodist. Office: Air Force Rocket Propulsion Lab LKL Edwards AFB CA 93523

CHAPMAN, ROBERT GALBRAITH, hematologist, administrator; b. Colorado Springs, Colo., Sept. 29, 1926; s. Edward Northrop and Janet Galbraith (Johnson) C.; m. Virginia Irene Potts, July 6, 1956; children: Lucia Tully Chapman Chatzky, Sarah Northrop, Robert Bostwick. Student, Westminster Coll., 1944-45; BA, Yale U., 1947; MD, Harvard U., 1951; MS, U. Colo., 1958. Diplomate Am. Bd. Internal Medicine and Pathology. Intern Hartford (Conn.) Hosp., 1951-52; resident in hematology U. Colo. Med. Ctr., Denver, 1955-58; fellow in hematology U. Wash., Seattle, 1958-60; chief resident in medicine U. Colo., Denver, 1957-58, instr. medicine, 1960-62, asst. prof. medicine, 1962-68, assoc. prof., 1968—; chief staff VA Hosp., Denver, 1968-70; dir. Belle Bonfils Meml. Blood Ctr., Denver, 1977—; mem. regionalization com. Am. Blood Commn., Washington, 1985—, Colo. hemophilia com., Denver, Colo. sickle cell com., Denver; mem. adv. com. Colo. AIDS Project, Denver; trustee Council Community Blood Ctrs. (v.p. 1979-81), Chapman Research Fund. Contbr. articles to profl. jours. Served as capt. USAF, 1953-55. USPHS fellow, 1958-60. Fellow ACP; mem. Am. Assn. Blood Banks, Denver Med. Soc., Colo. Med. Soc., Western Soc. Clin. Research, Am. Soc. Hematology, Am. Radio Relay League, Denver Heath User Group (sec. treas. 1985-87). Mem. United Ch. Christ. Avocations: amateur radio, computers. Home: 250 S Eudora St Denver CO 80222 Office: Belle Bonfils Meml Blood Ctr 4200 E Ninth Ave Denver CO 80262

CHAPMAN, ROGER GREEN, manufacturing company executive; b. Salt Lake City, June 27, 1952; s. Lowell Welcome and Gloria (Green) C.; m. Julianne Winkler, Dec. 19, 1975; children: Camille, Natalie, Richard, Jakob. BS, Brigham Young U., 1977. Mgr. quality assurance Poly Seal Inc., Salt Lake City, 1978, Am. Laser Inc., Salt Lake City, 1979; quality engr. Deseret Med./Warner-Lambert, Sandy, Utah, 1980-84; mgr. quality assurance Deseret/Becton-Dickenson, Sandy, 1985—. Area commr. Boy Scouts Am., Kearns, Utah, 1985—. John Einer Anderson Grad. scholar, 1977. Mem. AAAS, Am. Soc. Quality Control. Republican. Mormon. Avocations: watercolor, karate, basketball, camping. Home: 4535 Twilight Dr Kearns UT 84118 Office: Deseret Med Inc 9450 S State St Sandy UT 84070

CHAPPELL, DUNCAN, criminology educator; b. Blandford, Dorset, Eng., Aug. 1, 1939; came to Can., 1980; s. Francis Roy and Dorothy M. (Lardner) C.; m. Susan Fenn Parsons, Apr. 29, 1962 (div. Sept. 1976); children—Hamish, Kirstin; m. Rhonda Dorothea Moore, Apr. 9, 1982. B.A., U. Tasmania, 1962, LL.B. with 1st class honors, 1962; Ph.D., U. Cambridge, 1965. Barrister and solicitor, Tasmania. Sr. lectr. Faculty of Law, U. Sydney, Australia, 1966-70; assoc. prof. Sch. Criminal Justice, SUNY-Albany, 1971-73; dir. Law and Justice Study Ctr., Battelle Meml. Inst., Seattle, 1973-77; vis. prof. legal studies La Trobe U., Melbourne, Australia, 1977-78; mem. Australian Law Reform Commn., Sydney, 1978-79; prof. Sch. Criminology Simon Fraser U., Burnaby, B.C., Can., 1980—, chair dept., 1982-84; adv. criminal procedure project Law Reform Commn. Can., sentencing reform project Ministry of Justice Can., Ottawa, 1983; cons. B.C. Law Found., 1982, U.S. Senate Select Com. on Small Bus., 1973-74; mem. working group Australian Criminal Scis. Com., 1979. Editorial cons. Jour. Criminal Law and Criminology, 1973—; author: From Sawdust to Toxic Blobs: A Consideration of Sanctioning Strategies: Combat Pollution in Canada, 1987; co-author: The Police and the Public in Australia and New Zealand, 1969, The Police Use of Deadly Force: Canadian Perspectives, 1985; co-editor: The Australian Criminal Justice System, 1972, 77, 87—; Violence and Criminal Justice, 1975; Forcible Rape: The Crime, the Victim and the Offender, 1977; contbr. chpts. to books, articles to profl. jours., encys. Bd. mgmt. No. Conf., Vancouver, 1983-84; mem. rape edn. com. Premier's Dept., Melbourne, Australia, 1978. Brit. Commonwealth scholar, 1962-65; Harkness fellow, 1969. Mem. Am. Soc. Criminology (exec. com. 1976-78, 83-84), Australian Acad. Forensic Sci., Australian Assn. Cultural Freedom. Home: 1934 Barclay St #9, Vancouver, BC Canada V6G 1L4 Office: Simon Fraser U, Sch Criminology, Burnaby, BC Canada V5A 1S6

CHAPPIE, EUGENE A., former congressman; b. Sacramento, 1920. Supr., El Dorado County, 1950-64; mem. Calif. State Assembly, 1964-80, chmn. com. on rules, 1968-70, chmn. com. on social welfare, 1966-68; mem. 97th-99th Congresses from Calif. 1st dist. Served with U.S. Army, World War II, Korean conflict. Decorated Bronze Star. Republican.

CHAPPLE, PERSIS MARTHA, speech, hearing, language specialist; b. Billings, Mont., Feb. 16, 1930; d. Henry Alexander and Dorothy Ann (Massee) C.; m. William F. Anderson, Dec. 22, 1948; children: Michael W. Anderson, Cherie C. Anderson, Karin L. Ramsey, Leeann Hendrickson; m. Robert Charles Donaldson, Jan 4, 1975. BA, Calif. State U., Sacramento, 1964, MA, 1973. Tchr. educationally handicapped Grant Sr. High Sch., Sacramento, 1964-66; speech therapist Grant Sch. Dist., Sacramento, 1966-79, Las Palmas Jr. High Sch., Sacramento, 1979-82; speech therapist Norte Jr. High Sch., Sacramento, 1982—, chmn. spl. edn., 1985—. Mem. Am. Speech Hearing Assn., Sacramento Speech Hearing Assn. (program chmn. 1981-82), Calif. Credentials Adv. Com. Speech Pathologists. Democrat. Avocations: travel, theatre, symphony concerts, opera, swimming. Home: 1516 Little Ct Carmichael CA 95608

CHAR, CARLENE MAE, publisher, editor, systems developer; b. Honolulu, Oct. 21, 1954; d. Richard Y. and Betty S.M. (Fo) C. B.A. in Econs., U. Hawaii, 1977; M.A. in Bus. Adminstrn., Columbia Pacific U., 1984, Ph.D. in Journalism, 1985, B. Gen. Sci. in Computer Sci., Roosevelt U., 1986, cert. in mgmt. systems analysis and computer sci., 1986. Freelance writer, Honolulu, 1982—; editor Computer Book Rev., Honolulu, 1983—, Maeventec Software Review, Honolulu, 1985—; dir. Maeventec, Honolulu, 1983—. Office: Maeventec PO Box 37127 Honolulu HI 96837

CHAR, DONALD FOOK BIAU, pediatrics educator; b. Honolulu, Mar. 25, 1925; s. Charles A. and Annie Y. (Ching) C.; m. Agnes Hazel Taylor, Dec. 15, 1951; children: Donna Lynn, Brenda Jill, Linda Sue, John Taylor, Matthew Charles. MD, Temple U., 1950. Diplomate Am. Bd. Pediatrics. Intern Atlantic City (N.J.) Hosp., 1950-51; resident in pediatrics St. Christopher's Hosp., Phila., 1953-56; practice medicine specializing in pediatrics Honolulu, 1956; dir. edn. Children's Hosp., Honolulu, 1956-59; mem. faculty U. Wash., Seattle, 1959-63; prof. pediatrics, dir. student health service dept. U. Hawaii, Honolulu, 1965—; vis. med. faculty to Samoa, U. Hawaii East-West Ctr., 1965; vis. faculty Chinese U. Hong Kong, Shatin, 1973-74; teaching cons. Hong Kong U., 1973-74; univ. physician Australian Nat. U., Canberra, 1974. Contbr. articles to profl. jours. Mem. tech. adv. com. Hawaii Health Planning and Devel. Agy., 1977-80; mem. Hawaii Bd. Health, 1980-85, chmn., 1983-85. Served to capt. M.C., U.S. Army, 1951-53. Grantee Hawaii Dept. Health, 1976—. Fellow Am. Acad. Pediatrics; mem. Am. Coll. Health Assn., Am. Acad. Sci. (pres. 1980-81), Pacific Coast Health Assn. (pres. 1975-76). Home: 5650 Halepa Pl Honolulu HI 96821 Office: U Hawaii Student Health Service 1710 East-West Rd Honolulu HI 96822

CHAR, WASHINGTON TIENTSIN, structural engineer, consultant; b. Honolulu, Aug. 26, 1924; s. Yew and Helen Mow C.; m. Rose Lum, Aug. 1, 1948; children—Karen, Dexter, Jill, Orrin. B.S.C.E., Washington U., St. Louis, 1949; M.S.C.E., Ga. Inst. Tech., 1950; M.B.A., St. Louis U., 1961. Registered profl. engr., Hawaii. Chief structural engr. U.S. Army C.E., Honolulu, 1951-54, gen. engr., Liverno, Italy, 1954-59; project mgr. Lublin, McGaughy and Assocs., Honolulu, 1961-63; dep. Air Force regional engr. USAF, Taiwan, Thailand, 1963-70; chief structural engr. U.S. Army C.E., Huntsville, Ala., 1970-84; cons. State Farm Ins., 1983-85; lectr. U. Ala., 1983-85. Served to lt. USAF, 1950. Named Engr. of Yr., Nat. Soc. Profl. Engrs. and ASCE, 1978; Achievement award Soc. Am. Mil. Engrs., 1977. Mem. ASCE (past pres.), Am. Concrete Inst., Soc. Am. Mil. Engrs. (past pres.). Republican. Methodist. Club: Huntsville (Ala.) Athletic. Home: 204 Makee Rd Apt 304 Honolulu HI 96815

CHARACKLIS, WILLIAM GREGORY, research institute administrator, engineering educator; b. Annapolis, Md., Aug. 21, 1941; s. Gregory A. and Artemis Characklis; m. Nancy Crowley; children: Gregory William, Erin Elizabeth. BS, Johns Hopkins U., 1964, PhD, 1970; MS, U. Toledo, 1967. Prof. Rice U., Houston, 1970-80; dir. Inst. Process Analysis, Bozeman, Mont., 1980—; pres. CCE Inc.; mem. Karl Marx Cardinal Distbg. Contbr. articles to profl. jours. Fellow NSF; recipient Faculty Research award Stone & Webster Enging. Corp., Denver, 1984. Mem. Am. Inst. Chem. Engrs., Assn. Environ. Enging. Profs., Am. Soc. Microbiology. Greek Orthodox. Office: Inst Process Analysis 407 Cobleigh Hall Bozeman MT 59717

CHARBONNEL, RENAY DELANE, accountant, controller; b. Hebron, Nebr., July 21, 1951; d. Leroy and Willa Mae (Kegans) Matheson; m. David James Charbonnel, Feb. 29, 1972 (div. Sept. 1982). Student, U. Md., 1978-80. Acct. Nat. Farmers Orgn., Clarksville, Tenn., 1974-76, U.S. Dept. Def., Kaiserslautern, Fed. Republic Germany, 1976-80, O Bee Credit Union, Colorado Springs, Colo., 1980-82; comptroller H.P. Colo. Fed. Credit Union, Colorado Springs, 1982—; instr. Colo. Credit Union League, Colorado Springs, 1986—; tutor local univs., Colorado Springs, 1986—. Mem. VFW Aux. Democrat. Baptist. Avocations: reading, cooking. Office: HP Colorado Fed Credit Union 1900 Garden of Gods Rd Colorado Springs CO 80907

CHAREAU, KENET EDWARD, lawyer; b. East Cleveland, Ohio, Feb. 13, 1945; s. Walter J. and Dorothy C.; m. Margo Chareau, Dec. 19, 1970; 1 son, Sean Louis. A.B., John Carroll U., 1967; J.D., Cleve. State U., 1970. Bar: Ohio 1970, Ariz. 1973, U.S. Ct. Mil. Appeals 1970. Mem. firm Leonard & Felker, Tucson; guest lectr. real estate, various bds. off realtors, insts.; registered rep. Univs. Securities Group, 1980-82, Design Capital Securities, 1982-87. Served to capt. JAGC, U.S. Army, 1970-75. Mem. Ariz. Bar Assn., ABA, Ohio Bar Assn., Cochise County Bar Assn., Pima County Bar Assn., Nat. Assn. Securities Dealers, Real Estate Securities and Syndication Inst. (sec.-treas. Ariz. chpt., pres. 1987). Home: 5961 E San Mateo Pl Tucson AZ 85715 Office: 155 W Council Tucson AZ 85701

CHARLEY, PHILIP JAMES, testing lab. executive; b. Melbourne, Australia, Aug. 18, 1921; came to U.S., 1940, naturalized; 1948; s. Walter George and Constance Mary (Macdonald) C.; B.S., U. Wis., 1943; M.S. in Mech. Engring., U. So. Calif., 1947, Ph.D. in Biochemistry, 1960; m. Katherine Truesdail, Jan. 31, 1948; children—James Alan, Linda Kay, William John. Test engr. Gen. Electric Co., Schenectady, 1943-44; lectr. in engring. U. So. Calif., Los Angeles, 1947-49; project engr. Standard Oil of Calif., El Segundo, 1948-55; v.p. Truesdail Labs., Los Angeles, 1955-70, pres., 1970—. Served to lt. Royal Can. Elec. and Mech. Engrs., 1943-45. Recipient Dueul award U. So. Calif., 1960, research asso., 1960-65; registered profl. engr., Calif. Mem. AAAS, Am. Soc. Metals, ASTM, ASME, Am. Soc. Safety Engrs., Am. Chem. Soc., Sigma Xi, Tau Beta Pi, Beta Theta Pi. Republican. Club: Rotary. Home: 1906 Calle de los Alamos San Clemente CA 92672 Office: 14201 Franklin Ave Tustin CA 92680

CHARLIE, WAYNE ALEXANDER, civil engineering educator; b. Toronto, Mar. 4, 1945; s. Jack C. and Ellen (Whitenham) C.; m. Deanna Durnford, Oct. 21, 1984. BSCE, BA in Social Scis., Mich. State U., 1971, MSCE, 1972, PhDCE, 1975. Registered profl. engineer, Maine, Colo. Vol. U.S. Peace Corps., Ethiopia, 1966-68; asst. prof. U. Maine, Orono, 1975-76; asst. prof. Colo. State U., Ft. Collins, 1976-82, assoc. prof., 1982—; Fulbright prof. Univ. Khartoum, Sudan, 1980; vis. prof. U. Auckland, New Zealand, 1983-84, Cornell U., Ithaca U., 1983-84; cons. Tasman Paper Co., Kawerau, New Zealand, 1984-85, Bur. Reclamation, Denver, Colo., 1981, D'Appolonia Cons. Engrs., Denver, 1980, Climax (Colo.) Molybdenum Co., 1978. Contbr. articles to profl. jours. Mem. ASCE, Soc. Explosive Engrs., Internat Soc. Soil Mechanics and Found. Engrs., Phi Kappa Phi. Avocations: camping, outdoor sports. Office: Colo State U Dept Civil Engring A319 ERC Fort Collins CO 80523

CHARLTON, IRENE K. ZIMMERS, watercolorist; b. Charleston, Ill., Aug. 7, 1902; d. Edward Lee King and Nettie Mae (Money) K.; m. Charles Philip Zimmers, June 1932 (dec.); children—Philip Hays, Hugh Morley. Student Eastern Ill. State Tchrs. Coll., 1922. Exhibited watercolorist juried shows; artists of the S.W. Los Angeles County Mus., 1954; represented Calif. Group Art Tour, 1982, 83; judge Watercolor shows; demonstrator pure transparent watercolor. Past pres. Morongo Valley Republican Club. Recipient honorable mention Palm Springs Civic Art Assn. award, 1977; Date Festival Indio Calif. award, 1964; N. Mex. Watercolor Soc. Purchase Prize award, 1981. Mem. Watercolor West (assoc.), N.Mex. Watercolor Soc., Old Bergen Art Guild. Episcopalian.

CHARLTON, JAMES WILLIAM MARK, cable TV executive; b. Klamath Falls, Oreg., Feb. 9, 1948; s. James William Herbert and Ruth Estelle (Richardson) C.; m. Dawn Cecelia Tibus; children: Robert Carl, John William. Student, Calif. State U., Northridge. Founder, co-owner HFU Mfg., North Hollywood, Calif., 1972-82; HFU TV, Coleville, Calif., 1979—, Sierra Pines Apts., Coleville, 1979—; founder, owner New Dawn Electric Co., Westlake Village, Calif., 1985—; founder, pres. HFU Investments, Inc., Reno, Nev., 1983—. Chmn. Buhs High Sch. Class Reunion Com., Bishop, Calif., 1986. Served with U.S. Army, 1968-70, Vietnam. Mem. VFW, Nat. Rifle Assn. Avocations: chess, world travel, motor cycling, flying. Office: New Dawn Electric Co 30941 Agoura Rd #314 Westlake Village CA 91361

CHARLTON, JOHN KIPP, pediatrician; b. Omaha, Jan. 26, 1937; s. George Paul and Mildred (Kipp) C.; A.B., Amherst Coll., 1958; M.D., Cornell U., 1962; m. Susan S. Young, Aug. 15, 1959; children—Paul, Cynthia, Daphne. Intern, Ohio State U. Hosp., Columbus, 1962-63; resident in pediatrics Children's Hosp., Dallas, 1966-68, chief pediatric resident, 1968-69; nephrology fellow U. Tex. Southwestern Med. Sch., Dallas, 1969-70; practice medicine specializing in pediatrics, Phoenix, 1970; chmn. dept. pediatrics Maricopa County Gen. Hosp., Phoenix, 1971-78, 84—, assoc. chmn. dept. pediatrics, 1979-84; med. dir., bd. dirs. Crisis Nursery, Inc., 1977—. Pres. Maricopa County Child Abuse Council, 1977-81; bd. dirs. Florence Critenton Services, 1980-83; mem. Gov.'s Council on Children, Youth and Families, 1984-86. Served as officer M.C., USAF, 1963-65. Recipient Hon Kachina award for volunteerism, 1980, Jefferson award for volunteerism, 1980. Mem. Am. Acad. Pediatrics, Ariz. Pediatric Soc., Maricopa County Pediatric Soc. (past pres.). Author articles, book rev. in field. Home: 6230 E Exeter St Scottsdale AZ 85251 Office: Maricopa County Gen Hosp 2601 E Roosevelt St Phoenix AZ 85008

CHARLTON, SAMUEL GEORGE, research psychology educator; b. Loma Linda, Calif., Sept. 9, 1956; s. Samuel George and Loretta Bee (Grim) C.; m. Jean Ellen Newman, Aug. 7, 1981; 1 child, Colin Peter. BA in Psychology, San Jose State U., 1977; MA in Psychology, U. N.Mex., 1979, PhD in Psychology, 1983. Research assoc. NASA-Ames Research Ctr., Moffett Field, Calif., 1977; lectr., research assoc. U. N.Mex., Albuquerque, 1977-83, adj. prof., 1985—; asst. prof. psychology U. Albuquerque, 1983-84; research assoc. neuropsychology VA Med. Ctr., Albuquerque, 1983-84; research psychologist The BDM Corp., Albuquerque, 1984—; statis. cons. Ednl. Research and Evaluation Ctr., Albuquerque, 1980; project coordinator BDM-U.N.Mex. joint Cognitive Sci. Internship program, 1985—. Contbr. articles to profl. jours. Judge N.Mex. sci. fairs, Albuquerque and Bernalillo, 1980, 83, 86; sec., editor Silver Hill Homeowners Assn., Albuquerque, 1984—. Mem. Animal Behavior Soc. (guest reviewer jour. 1983), Assn. for

Behavior Analysis, Southwestern Comparative Psychology Assn. (founding mem.), Psychonomic Soc. (assoc.), Human Factors Soc. (assoc.), Sigma Xi (Outstanding Doctoral Candidate 1983). Democrat. Avocation: hist. preservation. Office: The BDM Corp 1801 Randolph Rd SE Albuquerque NM 87106

CHARNEY, MICHAEL, science laboratory administrator; b. N.Y.C., Aug. 6, 1911; s. Jacob Louis and Sonja (Barnhard) C.; m. Helen Ricci, Mar. 2, 1941 (div. 1963); children: Elena Diane, Danielle; m. Jean Ellen Ormsbee, Sept. 7, 1966; children: Jacob Mattson, Alexandra Ormsbee, Jared Kirk. BA, U. Tex., 1934; postgrad., Columbia U., 1950-55; PhD, U. Colo., 1969. Diplomate Am. Bd. Forensic Anthropology. Forensic scientist Tex. State Police, Austin, 1938-39; bioassayist Hormone Prodn., N.Y.C., 1941-42; chief bacteriologist Longevity Research, N.Y.C., 1946-47; dir. Bio-chem. Lab., Hackensack, N.J., 1947-65; prof. anthropology Colo. State U., Ft. Collins, 1971-77, dir. forensic sci. lab., 1973—; dep. coroner Larimer County, Colo., 1974—; spl.investigator forensic scis., Larimer County Sheriff Ft. Collins and Colo. State U. Police, 1976—; cons. Gen. Hosp., Saddle Brook, N.J., 1947-65, Colo. Bur. Investigation, Denver, 1976—; researcher Shoshone Reservation, Pocatello, Idaho, 1969-71. Author: Forensic Anthropology, 1973; contbr. chpts. to books; articles to profl. jours. Mem. Victims Compensation Bd., Ft. Collins, 1986—. Served to maj. U.S. Army, 1942-46, ETO. Recipient Letter of Appreciation, Gov. Colo., Ft. Collins, 1976. Fellow Am. Acad. Forensic Scis (Cert. Appreciation, 1977); mem. Sigma Xi. Mem. Soc. Friends. Avocations: sailing, fencing. Home: 635 Peterson Fort Collins CO 80524 Office: Colo State U Forensic Sci Lab Fort Collins CO 80523

CHARTIER, ROBERT ARMAND, academic principal; b. Putnam, Conn., July 6, 1939; s. Gerard Marcel and Lenore Rubia (Lavigne) C.; m. Eleanor Eischet, Jan. 11, 1964 (div. 1984); children: Robert C., Renee L. BS, Cen. Conn. U., 1964; MA, U. Conn., 1966, Edn. Specialist, 1972, EdD, 1984. Tchr. Plainfield (Conn.) Bd. Edn., 1964-65, prin., 1967-72; tchr. Brooklyn (Conn.) Bd. Edn., 1965-67; prin. Oxford (Conn.) Bd. Edn., 1972-77, Madison Sch. Dist., Phoenix, 1977—; bd. dirs. Head Start Program, Brooklyn, 1965-68; cons. Communicators, Pomfret, Conn., 1965-72. Elected mem. Killingly Town Council, Danielson, Conn., 1970-72; tchr. St. James Cath. Youth Orgn., Danielson. Mem. Nat. Assn. Elem. Sch. Prins., Ariz. Sch. Adminstrs., Assn. Supervision and Curriculum Devel., Elem. Sch. Prins. Assn. Conn. (county dir. 1967-75), Plainfield Prins. Ass . (pres. 1967-72). Republican. Roman Catholic. Avocations: skiing, camping, auto restoration, golfing. Home: 12023 N 27th Pl Phoenix AZ 85028 Office: Madison Sch 1 5525 N 16th St Phoenix AZ 85016

CHARTIER, VERNON LEE, electrical engineer; b. Ft. Morgan, Colo., Feb. 14, 1939; s. Raymond Earl and Margaret Clara (Winegar) C.; m. Lois Marie Schwartz, May 20, 1967; 1 child, Neal Raymond. B.S. in Elec. Engring., U. Colo., 1963, B.S. Bus., 1963. Registered profl. engr., Pa. Research engr., cons. Westinghouse Electric Co., East Pittsburgh, Pa., 1963-75; chief high voltage engr. Bonneville Power Adminstrn., Vancouver, Wash., 1975—. Contbr. articles to profl. jours. Fellow IEEE (chmn. transmission and distbn. com.); mem. Internat. Conf. Large High Voltage Electric Systems, Acoustical Soc. Am., Internat. Electrotech. Commn., Club: Chartier Family Assn. Baptist. Home: 5190 SW Dover Ln Portland OR 97225 Office: Bonneville Power Adminstrn PO Box 491 Vancouver WA 98666

CHARTOCK, MICHAEL ANDREW, science facility administrator; b. Palo Alto, Calif., May 25, 1943; s. Samuel and Emma Jane (Granucci) C. AB, U. Calif., Berkeley, 1965; MA, San Jose State U., 1971; PhD, U. So. Calif., 1972. Jr. engr. Pacific Gas & Electric, Emeryville, Calif., 1967; instr. San Jose (Calif.) State U., 1970; asst. prof. U. Okla., Norman, 1971-78, assoc. prof. sci., 1978-85; sr. planner Lawrence Berkeley (Calif.) Lab., 1985—; vis. scientist Ctr. Energy and Environ. Research, Mayaguez, Puerto Rico, 1980; cons. Mitre Corp., McClean, Va., 1980, U.S. Synthetic Fuels Corp., Washington, 1982, NSF, Washington, 1983. NSF grantee, 1974, 76, 78; NSF fellow, 1970. Mem. AAAS, Am. Geophys. Union, Soc. Research Adminstrs., Ecol. Assn. Am. Office: Lawrence Berkeley Lab One Cyclotron Rd 50A-4112 Berkeley CA 94720

CHARTRAND, MARK RAY, III, astronomer; b. Miami, Fla., Aug. 2, 1943; s. Mark Ray, Jr. and Barbara Dunaway (Wilkins) C. B.S. in Astronomy, Case Inst. Tech., Cleve., 1965; Ph.D., Case Western Res. U., 1970. Asst. to dir. Mueller Planetarium, Cleve., 1965-66; research asst. Warner and Swasey Obs., Cleve., 1966-70; edn. coordinator, asst. astronomer Am. Museum-Hayden Planetarium, N.Y.C., 1970-74; chmn., asso. astronomer Am. Museum-Hayden Planetarium, 1974-80; exec. dir. Nat. Space Inst., Washington, 1980-84, v.p., dir., 1984—; dir. Scientia, Inc.; speaker colls., public groups; cons., lectr. satellite telecommunications, 1984—. Co-author: Astronomy, 1975; author: Skyguide, 1982; columnist: Omni mag, 1979-81; contbr. articles to mags., newspapers; host, producer: radio program What's Up?, 1977-78. Fellow Brit. Interplanetary Soc.; mem. AAAS, Am. Astron. Soc., Am. Astronautical Soc., Explorers Club, N.Y. Acad. Scis., Soc. Satellite Profls., Internat. Planetarium Soc., AIAA, Nat. Space Club, Sigma Xi. Home and Office: 12564 E Bates Circle Aurora CO 80014

CHASE, CHARLES ANTHONY, executive engineer; b. Detroit, June 27, 1939; s. Joseph Leon and Marion Katherine (Lukowiak) C.; m. Carole Ann Chaikin, June 10, 1961; children—Carlton, William. B.S.A.E., U. Mich., 1961, M.S.A.E., 1962; D.Engring. A.E., Stanford U., 1968. Design engr. Chem. Systems div. United Technologies Corp., San Jose, Calif., 1962-68, project engr., 1968-71, chief solid propulsion advanced design, 1971-74, chief engr. space motor programs, 1974-86, chief engr. space transp. systems, 1986—; guest lectr. Stanford U., Naval Postgrad. Sch. Mem. Monte Sereno Sch. Bd., 1972-77. Recipient Outstanding Service award United Techs. Corp., 1981. Assoc. fellow AIAA (solid rocket com.); mem. AAAS, ASME. Republican. Roman Catholic. Club: Courtside Racquet (Los Gatos, Calif.). Contbr. numerous articles to profl. jours. Patentee in field.

CHASE, C(HARLES) WARD, independent petroleum landman; b. Hartford, Conn., Feb. 28, 1908; s. Warren D. and Elizabeth S. (Ward) C.; B.A., Princeton U., 1928; m. Olga Memi, Feb. 12, 1966. Drama critic, asst. dramatic editor Billboard mag., 1930-31; ins. editor Real Estate Record and Guide, N.Y., 1940-43; v.p. Butler and Baldwin, Inc., 1931-41; account exec. Johnson & Higgins, 1942, dept. mgr., 1950, v.p., 1953-69, dir., 1956-69; pres., dir. Johnson & Higgins (Can.), Ltd., 1955-63; chmn. bd. Johnson & Higgins Calif., 1964-65; pres. Chase Resources Co., 1970—. Served with USNR, 1943-46. Mem. Soc. Mayflower Descs. Clubs: Eldorado, Indian Wells (Calif.). Home: 1189 Kaimoku Pl Honolulu HI 96815 Office: PO Box 88586 Honolulu HI 96830-8586

CHASE, COCHRANE, advertising agency executive; b. Berwyn, Ill., Feb. 6, 1932; s. Henry Cochrane and Roselyn (Scott) C.; m. Janis Valeria Kueber, June 19, 1954; children—Katherine Ann, Anthony Scott, Lisa Marie. B.A., Wesleyan U., 1954. With steel warehousing div. Jessop Steel Co., Broadview, Ill., 1956-62; mgr. sales Jessop Steel Co., 1961-62; with Jessop Steel Calif., Santa Fe Springs, 1963-64; asst. mgr. market research Ducommun Metals & Supply Co., Los Angeles, 1964-65; v.p. Newport Advt. Inc., Newport Beach, Calif., 1965; pres. Cochrane Chase, Livingston & Co., Inc., Irvine, Calif., 1966; chmn. bd., chief exec. officer Cochrane Chase, Livingston & Co., Inc., 1966—. Co-author: Marketing Problem Solver, 1973, Newport Financial Planner, 1985. Served with USNR, 1954-56. Mem. Am. Assn. Advt. Agys., Western States Assn. Advt. Agys. (Advt. Leader of Yr 1982). Home: 2162 Papya Dr La Habra CA 90631 Office: #5 Civic Plaza Newport Beach CA 92658

CHASE, DONALD DWIGHT, park administrator; b. Seattle, Jan. 31, 1942; s. Dwight B. and Lola L. (William) Chase. AA in Phys. Sci., Cerritos Coll., 1962; BS in Park Adminstrn., Calif. Poly. U., 1966. Park ranger Lake Mead Nat. Recreation Area, Boulder City, Nev., 1966-70, Sequoia and Kings Canyon Nat. Park, Three Rivers, Calif., 1970-74; unit mgr. Grand Canyon (Ariz.) Nat. Park, 1974-78; chief ranger Glacier Bay Nat. Park, Gustavus, Alaska, 1978-85; park supt. Yukon Charley Rivers Nat. Preserve, Eagle, Alaska, 1985—; instr. mountain climbing, search and rescue technique, 1971. Com. chmn. Eastside, Bishop, Calif., 1973; vol. fireman, community emergency med. technician, Eagle. Served to sgt. U.S. Army, 1967-69, Vietnam. Recipient Quality Increase award Nat. Park Service, 1974. Mem. Alaska Hist. Soc., Assn. Nat. Park Rangers, Nat. Assn. Search and Rescue Corrdinators, Sierra Club, Wilderness Soc., Alpha Zeta. Democrat. Avocations: travel, mountain climbing, cross country skiing, photography, music appreciation. Home: PO Box 64 Eagle AK 99738 Office: Yukon Charley Rivers Nat Preserve Eagle AK 99738

CHASE, JULIA P., public relations and advertising company executive, editor; b. Riverside, Calif., May 21, 1942; d. Harold W. Peebles and Jean M. Smith. BA, San Francisco State U., 1965; postgrad. Calif. State U., Long Beach, U. Calif., Berkeley, U. Calif., Irvine, U. So. Calif. Tchr. English, Calif. high schs., 1966-70; assoc. editor Videorecord World mag., Newport Beach, Calif., 1970-71; advt. promotion dir. Technicolor, Inc., 1971-72; pub. relations account exec. Cochrane Chase & Co., Inc., Orange County, Calif., 1973; community relations dir. McGaw Labs., Irvine, 1976-77; pres. J.P. Chase & Co., Inc. Advt. & Pub. Relations, Newport Beach, 1977-83; pres. Medcomm Mktg., Newport Beach, 1984—. Rep. council agys., allocations and communications United Way, 1976-83; bd. dirs. United Way North/South, 1980-81; mem. devel. dirs. So. Calif. Hosp. Recipient award Am. Advt. Fedn., 1978; award of merit Western Art Dirs.; award of excellence Creative Arts mag., N.Y. Art Dirs.; award of merit/communication excellence So. Calif. Bus. Communicators; Mem. Orange County Ad Club, Orange County Sportswriters, Newport Harbor Art Mus., Laguna Beach Mus. Art. Democrat. Presbyterian. Clubs: Orange County Press (life mem.; dir. 1979), Newport Beach Tennis. Editor, pub.: Newport Set mag.; art editor Orange County Illustrated; editor: Add One, 1983, 84. Office: PO Box 8343 Newport Beach CA 92658

CHASE, LORIENE ECK, psychologist; b. Sacramento; d. Walter and Genevieve (Bennetts) Eck; A.B., U. So. Calif., 1948, M.A., 1949, Ph.D., 1953; m. Leo Goodman-Malamuth, 1946 (div. 1951); 1 son, Leo; m. 2d, Allen Chase, Mar. 4, 1960 (div.); m. 3d, Clifton W. King, 1974. Psychologist, Spastic Children's Found., Los Angeles, 1952-55, Inst. Group Psychotherapy, Beverly Hills, Calif., 1957-59; pvt. practice, 1953—; v.p. VSP Exec. Relocation Consultants. Condr., Dr. Loriene Chase Show, ABC-TV, Hollywood, Calif. 1966—. Cons., Camarillo State Hosp.; bd. dirs., pres.'s circle U. So. Calif.; founding mem. Achievement Rewards for Coll. Scientists; bd. dirs. Chase-King Personal Devel. Center, Los Angeles; exec. bd. Cancer Research Center, Los Angeles. Writer syndicated newspaper column Casebook of Dr. Chase. Served with Waves World War II. Recipient Woman of Year in Psychology award Am. Mothers Com. Mem. Diadames, Assn. Media Psychologists, Les Dames de Champagne, Dame de Rotisseur, Nat. Art Assn., AFTRA, Screen Actors Guild, Internat. Platform Assn. Clubs: Regency, Lakeside Country. Author: The Human Miracle; columnist Westways mag. Address: 4925 Tarzana Woods Dr Tarzana CA 91356 also: 375 Palomar Shell Beach CA 93449

CHASTAIN, GARVIN, psychology educator, research director; b. Fort Worth, Feb. 23, 1945; s. Garvin Dunn and Bertha Pearl (Parrish) C.; m. Patricia Jean Ritter, Dec. 16, 1967; m. 2d, Gloria Jean Pollard, Nov. 21, 1975; 1 son, Ross Calvert. Ph.D. in Human Exptl. Psychology, U. Tex., Austin, 1976. Head, computer instn. Durhams Coll., Austin, Tex., 1976-77; research scientist Human Resources Research Orgn., Fort Hood, Tex., 1977-78; asst. prof. psychology Boise State U. (Idaho), 1978-82, assoc. prof., 1982-86, prof., 1986—, dir. Perceptual Research Labs., 1982—; sci. cons. Northwest Skeptics. Cons. editor Jour. Gen. Psychology, 1986—; contbr. articles to profl. jours. Mem. Idaho com. of correspondance on creation/evolution, 1982—. Recipient Boise State U. Alumni Assn. award, 1979; Summer fellow USAF Office of Scientific Research, 1986. Mem. Psychonomic Soc., Am. Psychol. Assn. (exptl. and philos. divs.), AAAS, Freedom from Religion Found. (bd. rep. from Idaho), Am Humanist Assn., Psi Chi, Phi Kappa Phi. Libertarian. Home: 3500 Tulara Dr Boise ID 83706 Office: Boise State U Dept Psychology Boise ID 83706

CHATFIELD, CHERYL ANN, stock brokerage firm executive, writer; b. King's Park, N.Y., Jan. 24, 1946; d. William David and Mildred Ruth (King) C.; m. Gene Allen Chasser, Feb. 17, 1968 (div. 1979); m. James Bernard Arkebauer, Apr. 16, 1983. BS, Cen. Conn. Coll., 1968, MS, 1972; PhD, U. Conn., 1976. Cert. gen. prin. securities. Tchr. Bristol East High Sch., Conn., 1968-77; adminstr. New Britain Schs., Conn., 1977-79; prof. Ariz. State U., Phoenix, 1979; stockbroker J. Daniel Bell, Denver, 1980-83, Hyder and Co., Denver, 1983-84; stockbroker, pres. Denari Securities, Denver, 1984—; tchr. investment seminars Front Range Community Coll., Denver, 1984-86; speaker women's groups, Denver, 1983-86. Author: Low-Priced Riches, 1985, Selling Low-Priced Riches, 1986, (newspaper columns) For Women Investors, 1982-84, Commentary, 1985-86. Project bus. cons. Jr. Achievement, Denver, 1986. Mem. Nat. Assn. Female Execs., Aircraft Owners and Pilots Assn., Colo. Assn. Securities Dealers (bd. dirs., v.p.), Denver Security Traders Assn., Women in Securities (founder, pres.), AAUW, Colo. Venture Group (founding), Kappa Delta Pi. Republican. Roman Catholic. Avocation: flying. Office: Denari Securities Inc 1812 Market St Denver CO 80202

CHAULS, ROBERT NATHAN, musician, educator; b. Port Chester, N.Y., July 18, 1942; s. Reuben and Lillian (Segall) C.; m. Sylvia Jane Whyte, May 20, 1967; 1 child, Jessica. ARCM, Royal Coll. Music, 1963; BA, Antioch Coll., 1964; MMus., U. Mich., 1966; DMA, U. So. Calif., Los Angeles, 1972. Asst. prof. music Willamette U., Salem, Oreg., 1966-70; prof. Los Angeles Valley Coll., 1973—; Lake George Opera, Glens Falls, N.Y., 1984-85, Am. Inst. Mus. Studies, Graz, Austria, staff pianist 1979-80; gen. dir. Valley Opera, Los Angeles, 1977—; mus. dir. Los Angeles Valley Coll. Concert Choir 1975-78, Los Angeles Met. Opera Co., 1970, City of the Angels Opera, 1974, Valley Inst. for Mus. Theater, 1983; chorusmaster Portland Opera Assn., 1972; asst. conductor Oberlin (Ohio) Opera Theater, 1969; coach, conductor U. So. Calif. Opera, 1970-72; coach, accompanist U. Mich. Opera, 1965-66; assoc. conductor Salem Community Symphony 1967-68. Author: Piano for Adults, An Aural Approach, 1984; composer: (instrumental works) Requiem for a Peaceful Man for string orchestra, trumpet and oboe, Sonata-Fantasy for piano trio, Something for violin and piano, Wind Quintet, Piano Sonata; (operas) Alice in Wonderland, The Thirteen Clocks, The Magic Rhyme; (vocal works) Nicholas Christmas, This is L.A., The Bells, Sing Unto the Lord, Nasherei, The Sunne Rising; concert appearances as pianist: Antioch Symphony Orchestra, 1961-64, Salem (Oreg.) Community Symphony, 1966, Peter Britt Festival Orch., 1967, Portland Chamber Orch., 1969, Royal Coll. Music Orch., 1963, asst. conductor 1962-63; solo and chamber performances, various cities, 1961-82. Bd. dirs. Opera for Youth, 1985—. Recipient North Bavarian Critics award, Fed. Republic of Germany, 1962, Eugene O'Neill Theatre award, 1983. Mem. Nat. Opera Assn. (bd. dirs. 1985—, dir. New Opera Competition 1984—). Home: 3451 Valley Meadow Rd Sherman Oaks CA 91403 Office: Los Angeles Valley Coll 5800 Fulton Ave Van Nuys CA 91401

CHAUNCEY, TOM, retired radio and TV executive.; b. Houston, Jan. 20, 1913; s. Brinkley and Lucille Dunn (Weber) C.; 6 children; student pub. schs.; LHD (hon.) Ariz. State U., 1983. Owner, Tom Chauncey Jeweler, 1940-61; v.p., gen. mgr. Sta KPHO, 1941-48; pres. Sta. KOPO, Tucson, 1947-76; v.p., mng. dir. KOOL Radio-TV, Inc., 1948-55, exec. v.p., gen. mgr., 1955-57, pres., gen. mgr., 1957-61, pres., 1961-81, chmn. bd., pres., chief exec. officer, 1981-82, owner, chief exec. officer Sta. KOOL-AM-FM, 1982-86; owner H Lazy A Ranches, Tom Chauncey Arabians, Tom Chauncey Properties; pres., mng. dir. Old Pueblo Broadcasting Co., (KOLD-TV), Tucson, 1957-69; daily columnist TV Views, Ariz. Republic, Phoenix Gazette, (weekly) Broadcasting mag., 1960-61; former chmn. bd. CBS TV Network Affiliates 1961-62; dir. Valley Nat. Bank; mem. nat. com. Support Free Broadcasting; rep. of pres. U.S., ambassador, Nigeria, 1960. Grand marshal J.C. World Championship Rodeo and Parade, 1963; former nat. trustee City of Hope; former mem. Ariz. Nat. Livestock Show; past Ariz. chmn. Radio Free Europe; former mem. bd. Phoenix Symphony Assn., Phoenix Art Mus., Muscular Dystrophy Assn. Am.; gen. campaign. chmn. Greater Phoenix-Scottsdale United Fund Campaign; former mem. bd., v.p., pres. Phoenix Better Bus. Bur.; mem. Citizen's Action Com.; voting mem. Ariz. State U. Found.; former mem. Phoenix Baseball Stadium Com., U. Ariz. Found., chmn. Ariz. com. A.R.C.; past dir. at large for Ariz. Am. Cancer Soc.; past dir. and pres. Community Council; exec. v.p., mem. bd., Incorporator, co-founder Barrow Neurol. Inst.; mem. Com. for Phoenix Civic Plaza Dedication Ceremonies, 1972, Ariz. Commn. on Nat. and Internat. Commerce; past nat. chmn. Broadcaster's adv. com. U.S. Savs. Bonds; past dir. United Cerebral Palsey Assn. Central Ariz.; past mem. Phoenix All-Am. City Com.; chmn. Ariz. Motion Picture Adv. Bd.; past chmn. adv. bd. on radio and TV, Ariz. State U.; bd. dirs. Central Ariz. Water Conservation Dist.; Nat. Cowboy Hall of Fame bd. dir. 1979—; pres., bd. dirs. Ariz. Children's Found. Named Man of Yr., City of Hope, 1962, NCCJ, 1967, B'nai B'rith Anti-Defamation League, 1975; Citizen of Yr., Phoenix Real Estate Bd., 1965; recipient Nat. Sch. Bell award, 1961; award U.S. Treasury Dept., 1961; Tom Chauncey award United Fund, 1962; Jesse Owens award; George Foster Peabody award, Disting. Achievement award Coll. Pub. Programs Ariz. State U., 1984. Mem. Ariz. (past pres., past dir., past mem. legis. com.), Met. Phoenix (past pres., dir.) broadcasters assns., Nat. Assn. Broadcasters, Nat. Acad. TV Arts and Scis. (Bd. Govs. award Phoenix chpt. 1962, past Ariz. bd. gov.), Mus. Broadcasting (hon.), Nat. Retail Jewelers Assn. (past dir.), Phoenix C. of C., Ariz. Quarterhorse Breeders Assn., Ariz. State Horseman's Assn., Ariz. Heart Inst. 1974—, Arabian Horse Assn. Ariz. (dir. 1972), Ariz. Hereford Assn., Ariz. Retail Jewelers Assn., Am. Gem Soc., TV Pioneers, Phoenix Press Box Assn. (life), Phoenix Thunderbirds, Navy League, Newcomen Soc. N. Am., Sigma Delta Chi. Elk. Clubs: Phoenix Country, Phoenix Execs.; Paradise Valley Country; Rancheros Vistacores; Cowman's. Author: Educational Contributions of Commercial Television, 1960. Tom and Dorothy Chauncey Student Loan Fund established at Ariz. State U. Home: 18000 N Scottsdale Rd Scottsdale AZ 85255

CHAUNCEY, TOM WEBSTER, II, lawyer; b. Phoenix, May 30, 1947; s. Tom Webster and Kathryn (Geare) C.; m. Mary Kathleen LaCroix, Dec. 28, 1972. BA with departmental honors in Sociology, Northwestern U., 1970; JD, Ariz. State U., 1973. Bar: Ariz. 1973, U.S. Dist. Ct. Ariz. 1973. Assoc. Gust, Rosenfeld, Divelbess & Henderson, Phoenix, 1972-76; exec. v.p., counsel KOOL Radio-TV, Inc., Phoenix, 1972-82; gen. counsel, sta. mgr. KOOL-AM-FM, Phoenix, 1982-86; chmn. Cameras in the Courtroom Com., 1979-86; mem. bd. CBS RadioRadio Network Affiliates, 1984-86. V.p. 1st Amendment Coalition, 1981-83, pres., 1984-85; bd. dirs. Park Found. of Phoenix, 1980-84, NCCJ, 1978—, nat. exec. bd. 1986—; bd. dirs. Ariz. Bus.-Industry-Edn. Council, Inc., 1979-83, Friendly House, 1983-84, Ariz. Community Found., 1981-85, Sands North Townhouse Homeowners Assn., 1973-77; mem. met. fin. com. YMCA Phoenix and Valley of Sun, 1974-80, mem. camp com., 1978-80; bd. dirs., mem. Project Pool It, Valley Forward Assn., 1977-83; mem. media adv. bd. Traffic Accident Reduction Task Force, 1980; bd. dirs. Meml. Hosp. Found., 1978-83, planning com., 1980-83, community relations com., 1982-83; bd. dirs. Barrow Neurol. Found., 1979—, mem. exec. com., 1980—, v.p., 1983-85, pres., 1986—, mem. investment com. 1985—; bd. dirs. Ariz. Hist. Soc., 1982-84, mem. bldg. com., 1983, bylaws com., 1983, bd. dirs. Central Ariz. Mus. chpt., 1979-84; mem. Walter Cronkite Found. for Journalism and Telecommunications, Ariz. State U., 1982—; mem. Maricopa City voter awareness com. 1986—. Fellow Ariz. State Bar Found.; mem. ABA, Ariz. Bar Assn. (pub. relations com. 1975-86, fee arbitration com. 1976-86), FCC Bar Assn., Maricopa County Bar Assn. (past dir. Young Lawyers sect.), Ariz. Trial Lawyers Assn., Assn. Trial Lawyers Am., Phoenix Assn. Def. Counsel, Orme Sch. Alumni Assn., Northwestern U. Alumni Assn. Phoenix (pres. 1975-76), Ariz. State U. Alumni Assn., Ariz. State U. Law Alumni Assn., Phoenix Press Club, Nat. Assn. Broadcasters, Ariz. Broadcasters Assn. (bd. dirs. 1985-86), Met. Phoenix Broadcasters (bd. dirs. 1976-86, pres. 1985-86), Phi Delta Phi, Phi Gamma Delta. Office: Gust Rosenfeld Divelbess & Henderson 3300 Valley Bank Ctr Phoenix AZ 85073

CHAUVIN, RICHARD LUCIEN, software company executive; b. Manchester N.H., Apr. 6, 1949; s. Lucien F. and Violette G. (LeMay) C.; m. Theresa Ann Pachtner, June 20, 1977; children—Christopher Scott, Michael Andrew. Computer supr. Nat. CSS, San Francsico 1974-76, tech. rep., 1976-77, computer systems programmer, 1977-78, sr. systems programmer, 1978-79; with Fireman's Fund Ins. Co., San Rafael, Calif., 1979-80; with Magnuson Computer Systems, San Jose, Calif., 1979-80, systems software specialist, 1980, mgr. systems software, 1980-82; owner Chauvin Cons., 1982—; chmn. bd., chief fin. officer, sr. exec. v.p. Dovetail Systems, Inc., Sunnyvale, Calif., 1982-85; pres. Software Assistance, Sunnyvale, 1984-85. Served with U.S. Air Force, 1968-74. Mem. Assn. Computing Machinery, Aircraft Owners and Pilots Assn. Home and Office: 418 Ridge Rd San Carlos CA 94070

CHAVE, KEITH ERNEST, oceanographer, educator; b. Chgo., Jan. 18, 1928; s. Ernest John and Winnifred (Carruthers) C.; m. Edith Hunter, May 19, 1969; children: Alan D., Warren T. PhB, U. Chgo., 1948, SM, 1951, PhD, 1952. Research geochemist Chevron Research, La Habra, Calif., 1952-59; prof. geology Lehigh U., Bethlehem, Pa., 1959-67; prof. oceanography U. Hawaii, Honolulu, 1967—; pres. Palau Marine Research Inst., Koror, Palau, 1979—. Contbr. articles to profl. jours. Grantee NSF, 1960-80, ONR, 1960-80, NOAA Sea, 1970-86, ACS-PRF, 1960-88. Fellow AAAS; mem. Alex. Von Humboldt Stiftung (sr. U.S. Scientist), Geochem. Soc., Am. Geophys. Union, Am. Soc. Limnology and Oceanography, Sigma Xi. Home: 4935 Mana Pl Honolulu HI 96816 Office: U Hawaii 1000 Pope Rd Honolulu HI 96822

CHAVELLE, ANNA HENDERSON, physician; b. Seattle, Jan. 28, 1933; s. Joseph Edmonds and Evelyn (Colpitts) Henderson; m. Dennis Chipman, 1954 (div.); 1 child, Judith Colpitts Chipman; m. C.C. Chavelle, 1970 (div.). BA, U. Wash., 1953, MD, 1957. Diplomate Am. Bd. Family Practice. Gen. practice medicine Seattle, 1960—; dir. 1st Choice Health Plan, Bellevue, Wash., 1985—. Pres. Physicians Bur., King County Med. Blue Shield, Seattle, 1980-82; trustee Blue Shield of King County, 1982-85, Northwest Hosp., Seattle, 1980—; bd. dirs. Wash. Physician Service, 1983-85. Mem. AMA, Wash. State Med. Assn. (asst. sec.-treas 1981—), King County Med. Soc., Wash. Acad. Family Physics (pres. 1979), Am. Acad. Family Physicians. Home: 2256 38th Pl E Seattle WA 98112 Office: 2501 N 45th Seattle WA 98103

CHAVEZ, CESAR ESTRADA, union official; b. nr. Yuma, Ariz., Mar. 31, 1927; married; 8 children. Mem. staff Community Service Orgn., Calif., 1952-58; gen. dir. Community Service Orgn., 1958-62; organized Nat. Farm Workers Assn., 1962; merged 1966 with Agrl. Workers Organizing Com. of AFL-CIO to form United Farm Workers Organizing Com., dir. 1966-73, Delano, Calif.; now pres. United Farm Workers Am. AFL-CIO, Keene, Calif. Served with USNR, 1944-45. Roman Catholic. Address: United Farm Workers of Am La Paz Keene CA 93531 *

CHAVEZ, CHRISTINA LINDA GARCIA, lawyer, state official; b. El Paso, Tex., Mar. 6, 1953; d. Raymond D. and Emma M. (Garcia) C. BA, N.Mex. State U., 1975; JD, Cath. U. Am., 1978. Bar: N.Mex. 1978, U.S. Dist. Ct. (N.Mex. dist.) 1978, U.S. Ct. Appeals (10th cir.) 1978. Equal employment opportunity specialist trainee Office Human Rights OEO, 1972-73; govt. intern equal employment div. N.Mex. State Planning Office, 1974; tutor, counselor Spl. Student Services, N.Mex. State U., 1973-75; summer intern The White House, Exec. Office of Pres., Washington, 1975, Dept. Labor, 1976; legal intern AYUDA para el Consumidor, Washington, 1977, Senator Pete Domenici, N.Mex., 1977; law clk. Dept. Labor, 1978; law clk., N.Mex. Supreme Ct., 1978-79; ptnr. Mitchell, Alley & Rubin, Santa Fe, 1979-83; supt. State N.Mex. Regulation and Licensing Dept., Santa Fe, 1983-86; sole practice, Santa Fe, 1987—. Trustee No. N.Mex. Legal Services, Santa Fe, 1980-81, St. Vincent's Hosp. Bd., Santa Fe, 1982-83, Santa Fe Group Homes, Inc., 1982-83, 85-86; mem. N.Mex. Women's Polit. Caucus, 1975—. Recipient Spl. Achievement and Merit award Dept. of Labor, 1976, Gov.'s award for Outstanding N.Mex. Women, 1986; named Woman in 80's, N.Mex. Women's Polit. Caucus, 1980, other honors. Mem. Internat. Fedn. Women Lawyers, NOW, Mexican Am. Women Nat. Assn., LWV, Women Execs. in State Govt., Bus. and Profl. Women, N.Mex. Bar Assn. (mem. young lawyers div., women's legal rights sect.), First Judicial Dist. Bar Assn. (pres. 1984). Democrat. Roman Catholic.

CHÁVEZ, DANIEL, minister, educator; b. Chgo., Apr. 19, 1929; s. Ricardo and Ruth Elaine (Larson) C.; m. Ana María Rodríguez, May 18, 1952; children: Daniel, David Pedro (dec.), Duel Netzahualcóyotl. BA, So. Miss. Coll., 1950; MA, Seventh-day Adventist Theol. Sem., 1955, BDiv., 1956; PhD, Claremont Sch. Theology, 1980. Ordained to ministry Seventh-day Adventist Ch., 1957. Pastor Tex. Conf. Seventh-day Adventists, Corpus Christi and Laredo, 1964-74; chaplain, pastor Bella Vista Hosp., Mayagüex,

Puerto Rico, 1972-74; prof. Universidad de Montemorelos, Mex., 1974-75; assoc. prof. Loma Linda U., Riverside, Calif., 1978-84; pastor S.E. Calif. Conf. Seventh-day Adventists, Costa Mesa, 1984—; tchr. Santa Ana (Calif.) Unified Sch. Dist., 1985—; cons. bibl. translation Bapt. Pubs. House., El Paso, Tex., 1983—, United Bible Soc., Mexico City, 1983—, Gen. Conf. Seventh-day Adventists, Washington, 1981—. Translator: Jeremiah, 1969-71, Greek-Spanish Interlinear NT. Mem. Soc. Bibl. Lit.

CHAVEZ, GILBERT ESPINOZA, bishop Roman Catholic Church. Educated St. Francis Sem., El Cajon, Calif., Immaculate Heart Sem., San Diego, U. Calif., San Diego. Ordained priest Roman Cath. Ch., 1960; later consecrated bishop. Aux. bishop Diocese of San Diego, 1974—. Office: 2020 Alaquinas Dr Ysidro CA 92703 *

CHAVEZ, JOSE GUADALUPE, aerospace company executive; b. Chihuahua, Mex., Dec. 14, 1950; s. Alfredo and Petra (Flores) C.; m. Lilia Irene Mena, June 4, 1976; children: Miguel Alberto, Laura Irene. BSEE, U. Tex.; MA in Mgmt., Redlands U.; postgrad., Western State U. Sr. staff engr. Hughes Aircraft Corp., Fullerton, Calif., 1978-80, head acctg. sect., 1980-81; pres., chief engr. Guaranteed Energy Mgmt. Corp., Fullerton, 1981-83; cons. Tech. Devel. Systems, Fullerton, 1983-84, pres., 1985—; cons. U.S. Energy Mgmt. Corp., Encino, Calif., 1984-85; pres. Facilities Automation, Orange, Calif., 1985—; cons. Hughes Aircraft, 1982-83, IBM, Tucson, 1982, Power Efficiency Mgmt. Cor., 1983-84, Infotec, Costa Mesa, Calif., 1984-86. State Dem. rep., El Paso, Tex., 1972; mem. YMCA, Orange County Indian Guides. Recipient Outstanding Performance award Enlog of Calif., 1985, Achievement award U.S. Energy Corp. of Nev., 1986. Mem. IEEE, Assn. Energy Engring., ASHRAE, Orange County C. of C. Libertarian. Roman Catholic. Avocations: racquetball, flying. Home: 161 La Paz Anaheim Hills CA 92807

CHAVEZ, KARREN VICTORIA, advertising executive; b. Denver, Dec. 5, 1954; d. Rudolfo and Lucille (Portales) C. BA in Elem. Edn., U. No. Colo., 1975, MA in Curriculum and Instrn., 1979. Cert. tchr., Colo. Educator Denver Pub. Schs., 1975-81; account exec. Mountain Bell, Denver, 1981-84; advt. exec. AT&T, San Francisco, 1984—. Active Great Books Found., Denver, 1978-81, Congress of Hispanic Educators, Denver, 1976-81; rep. for AT&T The Nat. Conf. for Christians and Jews, San Francisco, 1986. Avocations: reading, skiing, photography, art. Office: AT&T 795 Folsom San Francisco CA 94107

CHAVEZ, LAWRENCE ANDREW, biologist; b. Albuquerque, Nov. 13, 1949; s. Feliz Anaya and Martha (Garcia) C.; m. Kathleen Ann Fitzgerald, Aug. 28, 1976 (div. Feb. 1986). B. of Univ. Studies, U. N.Mex., 1972; PhD, U. Calif., Berkeley, 1981. Postdoctoral fellow U. N.Mex., Albuquerque, 1981-83; investigator U.S. FDA, San Francisco, 1983-84; research zoologist U. Calif., Berkeley, 1984-85; asst. supr. Cetus Corp., Emeryville, Calif., 1985-86; research fellow NFID Tropical Disease Research U. Calif. Sch. Pub. Health, Berkeley, 1986—. Fellow Ford Found.; E.E. Just fellow; recipient honorarium U. Calif., 1985. Mem. Am. Soc. Parasitologists, Soc. of Protozoologists, Sigma Xi. Republican. Roman Catholic. Avocations: skiing, jogging, tennis. Office: U Calif Sch Pub Health NFID Tropical Disease Research Berkeley CA 94720

CHAVEZ, TERESA L., bank operations officer; b. Los Angeles, Jan. 10, 1935; d. Flavio F. and Marie S. Chavez. A.A., East Los Angeles Coll., 1975; B.A. in Liberal Studies, Calif. State U.-Los Angeles, 1982. Various banking positions Union Bank, Los Angeles, 1960—, trainer courses, 1960—, ops. officer, 1979—. Mem. Palm Springs Property Owners Assn., Mt. Washington Homeowners Assn., Sacred Heart Alumnae Assn. (pres.), Mexican Am. Polit. Assn. Clubs: Union Bank Toastmistresses (sec.), Union Bank Bowling League (sec.-treas.). Office: 1980 Saturn St Monterey Park CA 91754

CHAVIS-BUTLER, GRACE LEE, educator; b. Charleston, S.C., Aug. 26, 1916; d. Thomas and Sarah (Lafayette) Chavis; m. E. Hardy Butler, June 15, 1974 (div. Feb. 1984); remarried, Sept. 17, 1985. Diploma in Teaching, Avery Normal Inst., 1937; BA, Am. U., 1954, MA, 1955; PhD, U. Beverly Hills, 1982. Educator Washington high schs., 1955-73; chmn. history dept. Western High Sch., Washington, 1971-73; substitute tchr. Oakland (Calif.) Pub. Schs., 1973-74; substitute instr. Los Angeles Community Coll. Dist., 1974-80, 82—. Author: Reflections on Africa, 1975; contbr. articles to newspapers, profl. jours. Mem. Friends of Vernon Br. Library, Los Angeles, 1978—; vol. asst. mgr. The Mankind Ctr., Los Angeles, 1978-79. Served as sgt. WAC, 1943-46. Recipient Cert. of Merit Human Relations Commn., Los Angeles, 1982, Martin Luther King award So. Christian Leadership Conf. West, 1978, Annual Fin. Support award Am. U. John Fletcher Hurst Soc., Washington, 1981-82. Mem. AAUW (life mem., 1st v.p. Los Angeles br. 1978-80, Recognition of Service award Los Angeles chpt. 1979, Significant Contbn. to Edn. Found. award State div. 1984), Am. Inst. Parliamentarians (adminstrv. lt. gov. region 7 1984-85, pres. El Camino Real chpt., Los Angeles, 1982-84), Nat. Council of Negro Women (life, chmn. ann. festival com. 1976-77), Seeds of Sequoia (v.p. 1983—), Am. U. Alumni Assn. (Recognition award 1987). Democrat. Roman Catholic. Avocations: writing poems, collecting epigrams, sewing, knitting, playing bridge. Home: 3465 W 54 St Los Angeles CA 90043

CHAYKIN, STERLING, biochemistry educator; b. N.Y.C., Sept. 18, 1929; s. Frank David and Ruth (Berman) C.; m. Elaine Loeb, June 13, 1954; children: Ronald Scott, William Lawrence, Janet Gail, Nancy Elizabeth. AB, NYU, 1950; PhD, U. Wash., 1954. Postdoctoral fellow Harvard U., Cambridge, Mass., 1956-59; prof. U. Calif., Davis, 1959—; bd. dirs. Knowledge Devel. Found. Contbr. articles to profl. jours. Served with U.S. Army, 1954-56. Damon Runyon Found. fellow, 1956-59; Fulbright fellow, 1966-67; Guggenheim fellow, 1966-67. Mem. AAAS, Am. Soc. Biol. Soc., Am. Chem. Soc. Office: U Calif Dept Biochemistry and Biophysics Davis CA 95216

CHEAL, MARYLOU, psychobiologist; b. St. Clair County, Mich.; d. Marion Louis Fast and Leda Eleanor (Shaw) M.; m. James Cheal, Apr. 13, 1946; children: Thomas James, Catheryn Leda, Robert David. BA in Psychology with honors, Oakland U., Rochester, Mich., 1969; PhD in Psychology, U. Mich., 1973. Research investigator dept. zoology U. Mich., Ann Arbor, 1973-75, research investigator dept. oral biology, 1975-76, lectr. dept. psychology, 1973-76; Charles A. King research fellow Harvard U. Med. Sch., Boston, 1976-77; asst. psychologist McLean Hosp., Belmont, Mass., 1977-81, assoc. psychologist, 1981-83; lectr. dept. psychology/psychiatry Harvrd U. Sch. Medicine, Boston, 1977-83; faculty research assoc. dept. psychology Ariz. State U., Tempe, 1983—, mem. faculty Women's Studies program, 1986; research psychologist U. Dayton Research Inst.-Williams AFB, Higley, Ariz., 1986—; vis. prof. Air Force Systems Command U. Resident Research Program appointment, Williams AFP, Ariz.; reviewer CUNY, NIMH, NSF, Ont. Mental Health Found., Tufts U. Sch. Medicine. Referee Internat. Jour. Aging and Human Devel., Pharmacology Biochemistry and Behavior, Jour. Experimental Psychology: Animal Behavioral Processes, Jour. Comparative Psychology, Animal Behaviour, Physiology and Behavior, Science, Behavioral Research; contbr. articles to profl. jours. Recipient numerous research awards. Fellow AAAS; mem. Am. Psychol. Assn. (program com. 1985, chmn. symposium 1985, fellow physiol. and comparative psychology and psychopharmacology 1986, mems. and fellows com.), Assn. Chemoreception Scis., Soc. Neurosci., Southwestern Comparative Psychology Assn. (governing bd. 1984-85), Women in Neurosci. (steering com. 1982-85), Sigma Xi. Avocations: reading, gardening, traveling. Home: 127 E Loma Vista Tempe AZ 85282 Office: U Dayton Research Inst PO Box 44 Higley AZ 85236

CHEBUL, CHARLES RAY, safety engineer, nuclear engineer; b. Butte, Mont., Mar. 6, 1954; s. Joseph Robert and Melodie (Heffern) C.; m. Vicki Henry, July 30, 1977; children: Zachary Charles, Joshua Michael. BS in Occupational Safety and Health, Mont. Coll. of Mineral Sci. and Tech., 1979. Cert. safety profl., Bd. Cert. Safety Profls. Indsl. hygienist Inspiration Copper, Claypool, Ariz., 1979-80; safety advisor Thunder Basin Coal, Wright, Wyo., 1980-81; safety rep. Cyprus Mining Co., Challis, Idaho, 1981-84; sr. safety engr. E.G.& G. Idaho, Inc., Idaho Falls, 1984—. Mem. Am. Soc. Safety Engrs. Roman Catholic. Avocations: fishing, rafting, skiing. Home: 1615 Parkwood Idaho Falls ID 83401 Office: EG&G Idaho Inc Box 1625 Idaho Falls ID 83415

CHECKETTS, DAVID WAYNE, professional sports team executive; b. Salt Lake City, Sept. 16, 1955; s. Clyde Alvin and Edith (Jones) C.; m. Deb Leishman, June 2, 1977; children: Spencer, Katie, Nathaniel, Andrew. BS., U. Utah; MBA, Brigham Young U. Mgmt. cons. Bain and Co., Boston, 1980-83; exec. v.p. Utah Jazz, Nat. Basketball Assn., Salt Lake City, 1983-84, pres., 1984—. Trustee Salt Lake Visitor and Conv. Bur., 1986. Mormon. Lodge: Rotary. Avocations: basketball, golf, water sports, photography. Office: Utah Jazz 5 Triad Center Suite 500 Salt Lake City UT 84180

CHEDID, JOHN G., bishop Roman Catholic Church; b. July 4, 1923. Ordained priest Roman Cath. Ch., 1951, later consecrated bishop. Bishop Maronite Diocese, Los Angeles, 1981—. Office: Our Lady of Mount Lebanon Church 333 S San Vicente Blvd Los Angeles CA 90048 *

CHEE, PERCIVAL HON YIN, ophthalmologist; b. Honolulu, Aug. 29, 1936; s. Young Sing and Den Kyau (Ching) C.; B.A., U. Hawaii, 1958; M.D., U. Rochester, 1962; m. Carolyn Siu Lin Tong, Jan. 27, 1966; children—Lara Wai Lung, Shera Wai Sum. Intern, Travis AFB Hosp., Fairfield, Calif., 1962-63; resident Bascom Palmer Eye Inst., Miami, Fla., 1965-68, Jackson Meml. Hosp., Miami, 1965-68; partner Straub Clinic, Inc., Honolulu, 1968-71; practice medicine specializing in ophthalmology, Honolulu, 1972—; mem. staffs Queen's Med. Center, St. Francis Hosp., Kapiolani Children's Med. Center, Honolulu; clin. assoc. prof. surgery U. Hawaii Sch. Medicine, 1971—; cons. Tripler Army Med. Center. Mem. adv. bd. Services to Blind; bd. dirs. Lions Eye Bank and Makana Found. (organ bank), Multiple Sclerosis Soc. Served to capt. USAF, 1962-65. Fellow Am. Acad. Ophthalmology, ACS; mem. AMA, Pan Am. Med. Assn., Pan Pacific Surg. Assn., Am. Assn. Ophthalmology, Soc. Eye Surgeons, Hawaii Ophthal. Soc. Pacific Coast Ophthal. Soc., Am. Assn. for Study Headache, Pan Am. Ophthal. Found. Contbr. articles to profl. pubs. Home: 3755 Poka Pl Honolulu HI 96816 Office: Kukui Plaza 50 S Beretania St Honolulu HI 96513

CHELAPATI, CHUNDURI VENKATA, civil engineering educator; b. Eluru, India, Mar. 11, 1933; came to U.S., 1957, naturalized, 1971; s. Lakshminarayana and Anjamma (Kanumuri) Chunduri. B.E. with honors, Andhra U., India, 1954; M.S., U. Ill., 1959, Ph.D., 1962. Jr. engr. Office of Chief Engr., State of Andhra, India, 1954-55; asst. prof. structural engring. Birla Coll. Engring., Pilani, India, 1956-57; research asst. dept. civil engring. U. Ill., 1957-62; asst. prof. engring. Calif. State U., Los Angeles, 1962-65; asso. prof. Calif. State U., 1965-70, prof. civil engring., 1970—, vice chmn. dept., 1971-73, chmn. dept., 1973-79, coordinator profl. engring. rev. programs, 1972-81, dir. continuing engring. edn., 1982-86, dir. CADDS/AEC Research Ctr., 1986—; pres. C.V. Chelapati & Assos., Inc., Huntington Beach, Calif., 1979—; cons. U.S. Navy Civil Engring. Lab., 1962-68, 75—, Holmes & Narver, Inc., Anaheim, Calif., 1968-73. Contbr. articles to profl. jours. Mem. ASCE, Am. Soc. Engring. Edn., Structural Engrs. Assn. So. Calif., Earthquake Engring. Research Inst., Seismol. Soc. Am., Am. Concrete Inst., Am. Inst. Steel Constrn., Sigma Xi, Chi Epsilon, Tau Beta Pi, Phi Kappa Phi. Home: 16292 Mandalay Circle Huntington Beach CA 92649 Office: Dept Civil Engring Calif State U Long Beach CA 90840

CHELLAPPA, RAMALINGAM, electrical engineering educator; b. Tanjore, India, Apr. 8, 1953; came to U.S., 1977; s. Munthukrishnan and Kamakshi (Rajagopalan) R.; m. Vishnu P. Chellappa, June 16, 1983. BE with honors, Madras U., India, 1975; ME with distinction, Indian Inst. Sci., Bangalore, 1977; MSEE, Purdue U., 1978, PhD, 1981. Research asst. Purdue U., West Lafayette, Ind., 1979-81; faculty research asst. U. Md., College Park, 1979-81; asst. prof. electrical engring. U. So. Calif., Los Angeles, 1981-86, assoc. prof., 1986—; cons. Northrop Corp., Anaheim, Calif., 1985—, Hughes Aircraft Co., 1986—. Editor: Digital Image Processing Vols. I, II, 1985; contbr. articles to profl. jours., chpts. to books. Mem. IEEE (sr.), Am. Assn. Artificial Intelligence. Avocations: tennis, music. Office: U So Calif Dept EE-Systems University Park MC-0272 Los Angeles CA 90089

CHEN, CHARLES HSIN, obstetrician, gynecologist; b. Lo-Tong, I-Lan, Taiwan, Jan. 30, 1942; came to U.S., 1973; s. Jong-Song and Jen-Chu (Lin) C. M.D., Taipei Medical Sch., 1969. Diplomate Am. Bd. Obstetrics and Gynecology. Intern, Albert Einstein Med. Center, Phila., 1973-74; resident N.J. Med. Sch., 1974-77; attending physician New Jersey Medical Sch. Martland Hosp., Newark, 1977-78; clinical instr. New Jersey Medical Sch., Newark, 1977-78; mem. medical staff Humana Hosp., Huntington Beach, Calif., 1979—, Fountain Valley Hosp., Calif., 1979—; practice medicine specializing in obstetrics and gynecology, Fountain Valley, 1979—. Fellow Am. Coll. Obstetricians and Gynecologists; mem. Am. Fertility Soc., Orange County Med. Assn., Calif. Med. Assn., Orange County OB-GYN Soc. Home: 9067 Wagner River Circle Fountain Valley CA 92708 Office: Charles H Chen MD Inc 11160 Warner Ave #111 Fountain Valley CA 92708

CHEN, CHUAN FANG, educator; b. Tientsin, China, Nov. 15, 1932; came to U.S., 1950, naturalized, 1963; s. Kwang Yuan and Chin Han (Wang) C.; m. Frances Ya-Kieng Liu, Aug. 10, 1957; children: Peter Peishan, Paul Peichuan, Philip Peihai. B.Sc., U. Ill., 1953, M.Sc., 1954; Ph.D., Brown U., 1960. Asst. to chief engr. Hydronautics, Inc., Laurel, Md., 1960-63; asst. prof. mech. and aerospace engring. Rutgers U., New Brunswick, N.J., 1963-66; asso. prof. Rutgers U., 1966-69, prof., 1969—, chmn. dept., 1976-80; prof., head aerospace and mech. engring. dept. U. Ariz., Tucson, 1980—; cons. Vitro Labs., Silver Spring, Md., Hydronautics, Inc., Laurel, C.R. Bard, Inc., Murray Hill, N.J.; Am. Soc. Engring. Edn.-NASA fellow, summers 1968, 69, Rutgers Research Council Faculty fellow, 1971-72; sr. visitor DAMTP, Cambridge (Eng.) U.; vis. fellow Research Sch. Earth Scis., Australian Nat. U., Canberra, summer 1978. Contbr. articles to profl. jours. Fellow Am. Inst. Aeros. and Astronautics (asso.), ASME; mem. AAAS, Am. Phys. Soc., Am. Soc. Engring. Edn., Sigma Xi, Tau Beta Pi, Pi Tau Sigma. Home: 4266 E Coronado Dr Tucson AZ 85718 Office: U Ariz Dept Aero and Mech Engring Tucson AZ 85721

CHEN, GA-LANE, mechanical enginner; b. Chia-I, Taiwan, Mar. 26, 1953; came to U.S., 1979; s. Li and Chiu-Kuei (Tseng) C.; m. Chao-Ling Hsu, Mar. 29, 1979; 1 child, George. BSME, Nat. Taiwan U., Taipei, 1976; PhD in Metallurgy and Materials Sci., U. Minn., 1985. Mech. engr. China Steel Corp., Kaoshiung, Taiwan, 1978-79; lab. supr., research and devel. engr. Varian Assocs., Santa Clara, Calif., 1985; sr. engr. Varian Vacuum Systems, Santa Clara, 1985-86; research and devel. engring. mgr. Komag, Inc., Milpitas, Calif., 1986—. Contbr. articles to profl. jours. Mem. IEEE, Electron Devices Soc. of IEEE, Components, Hybrids and Mfg. Tech. Soc. of IEEE, Magnetics Soc. of IEEE, Computer Soc. of IEEE, Metall. Soc. of AIME, Am. Soc. Metals, Am. Phys. Soc., Am. Vacuum Soc. Home: 43064 Grimmer Terr Fremont CA 94538 Office: Komag Inc 591 Yosemite Dr Milpitas CA 95035

CHEN, HERBERT HWA-SEN, physics educator; b. Chung-King, Peoples Republic of China, Mar. 16, 1942; m. Catherine C. Li, May 25, 1969; 1 child, Christine H. BA, Calif. Inst. Tech., 1964; MA, PhD, Princeton U., 1968. Asst. research physicist U. Calif., Irvine, 1968-71, asst. prof., 1971-74, assoc. prof., 1974-79, prof., 1979—. Contbr. articles to profl. jours. Mem. AAAS, DOE and NSF (instrumentation subcom. 1982, nuclear sci. adv. com. 1983-86, chmn. computers and computing subcom. 1984-85, grantee NSF 1972—, DOE 1976—), Am. Phys. Soc. Home: 11 Rustling Wind Irvine CA 92715 Office: U Calif Dept Physics Irvine CA 92717

CHEN, MARJORIE WONG, aviation and marketing consultant; b. Los Angeles, Oct. 28, 1940; d. Thomas A. and Mayme M. (Moe) Wong; children: Barbara Joanne, Cynthia Anne. BA, Goucher Coll., 1962; MA, U. Calif. at Berkeley, 1965. Research economist Fed. Reserve Bank San Francisco, 1964-65; bus. cons., travel industry, 1968-74; marketing analyst The Flying Tiger Line Inc., Los Angeles, 1974-76, systems analyst, 1976-77, mgr. mgmt. reporting and performance analysis, 1977-78; dir. passenger pricing and fare devel. Continental Airlines, 1978-80, dir. internat. pricing, 1980-83; aviation and mktg. cons. Chen and Assocs., 1983—; dir. Continental Fed. Credit Union. Mem. Calif. Republican Assembly, 1976; trustee Marlborough Sch., Los Angeles Library Assn.; trustee, deacon 1st Congl. Ch. of Los Angeles; mem. evaluation com. Am. Heart Assn. Danforth Found. assoc., 1968-79. Mem. Nat. Mgmt. Assn. (membership chmn.), World Affairs Council Los Angeles, Town Hall Calif., U. Calif., Marlborough alumni assns. Republican. Conglist. Club: Goucher. Home: 640 N June St Los Angeles CA 90004

CHEN, TUAN WU, physics educator; b. Chia-yi, Republic of China, Mar. 26, 1936; came to U.S., 1961; s. Cheng Chong and Li-yu (Lin) C.; m. Laura F. Lin, June 22, 1963; children: Christopher T., Richard T. BS, Nat. Taiwan U., Taipei, Republic China, 1958; MS, Nat. Tsing Hua U., Hsinchu, Republic China, 1960; PhD, Syracuse U., 1966. Research assoc. U. Toronto, Ont., Can., 1966-68; asst. prof. physics N.Mex. State U., Las Cruces, 1968-73, assoc. prof., 1973-79, prof., 1979—; vis. scientist Los Alamos (N.Mex.) Nat. Lab., 1974-75, Calif. Inst. Tech., Pasadena, 1982-83. Contbr. articles to profl. jours. Mem. Am. Phys. Soc. Avocations: traveling, fishing. Home: 4835 Ocotilla Rd Las Cruces NM 88001 Office: NMex State U Dept Physics Las Cruces NM 88003

CHEN, TUNG-SHAN, food science educator; b. Chungking, China, Apr. 17, 1939; s. Sze-Chen Lin and Mary M. Chen; came to U.S. 1962, naturalized, 1976; m. Yolanda Chu, Dec. 26, 1964; children—Andy, Lynn. B.S., Nat. Taiwan U., 1960; M.S., U. Calif.-Berkeley, 1964, Ph.D., 1969. Research chemist Food Tech. Ctr., Taipei, Taiwan, 1961-62; research and teaching asst. U. Calif.-Berkeley, 1962-69; asst. prof. food sci. Calif. State U.-Northridge, 1969-73, assoc. prof., 1973-78, prof., 1978—; vis. assoc. prof. UCLA, 1974; cons. to food industry and govt. agys. Pres. San Fernando Valley Chinese Cultural Assn., 1974-75, bd. dirs., 1975-78; food engring. specialist Chinese U. Devel. Project, Nat. Acad. Scis., 1985. Earl Antony fellow, 1965-69; Nat. Acad. Sci. NRC research fellow, 1969; NSF/Calif. State U., Northridge research grantee, 1971, 74-76, 81, 84, 86; Joseph Drown Found. research equipment grantee, 1983, Nat. Dairy Promotion and Research Bd. grantee, 1986; sr. research fellow Ctr. for Cancer and Developmental Biology, Calif. State U., Northridge. Fellow Am. Inst. Chemists; mem. AAAS, Am. Chem. Soc., Am. Dietetic Assn., Am. Home Econ. Assn., Inst. Food Technologists, Greater Los Angeles Nutrition Council (bd. dirs. 1978-81), Sigma Xi, Phi Tau Sigma. Contbr. numerous articles to profl. jours. Office: Calif State U Northridge CA 91330

CHEN, WILLIAM KEH, aerospace engineer; b. Foochow, Fukien, China, Aug. 14, 1936; came to U.S., 1967; s. Hang-min and So-lang (Chiang) C.; m. Hermenegilda A. Ablan, Sept. 30, 1967; children: Michael W., Cindy A. BSME, Taiwan U., 1961; MSBA, St. Francis Coll., 1969; postgrad., Purdue U., 1974, Pierce Coll., 1983. Lic. real estate broker. Application engr. Dana Corp., Ft. Wayne, Ind., 1969-71; account supr. Pekins House, Ft. Wayne, 1971-76; product engr. Internat. Harvester Co., Ft. Wayne, 1976-81; standards engr. Rocketdyne div. Rockwell Internat. Corp., Canoga Park, Calif., 1981-84; sr. engr. aircraft div. Northrop Corp., Hawthorne, Calif., 1984—; engring. cons. Tinhong Internat., Canoga Park, 1982-85. Served to 2d lt. C.E., Chinese Army, 1961-63. Mem. Chinese-Am. Engrs. and Scientists Assn. of So. Calif., Soc. Automotive Engrs. Republican. Avocations: astronomy, model building, fishing, shooting. Home: 6335 Jumilla Ave Woodland Hills CA 91367 Office: Northrop Corp Aircraft Div One Northrop Ave Hawthorne CA 90250

CHEN, YUNG-GANN, pulsed power scientist, educator; b. Hsin-Chu, Taiwan, Feb. 2, 1935; came to U.S., 1963, naturalized, 1975; s. Chin-Hsing and Chu-Huan (Cheng) C.; m. Ing-Mei Lin, Oct. 1, 1966; children—Chia-Lin, Eugene. B.S.E.E., Nat. Taiwan U., 1957; M.S.E.E., Chaio-Tung U., 1960; D.Eng., Columbia U., 1966. Registered profl. engr., Taiwan. Dept. chmn. Chiao-Tung U., Hsin-Chu, Taiwan, 1966-69; sr. research assoc. Columbia U., N.Y.C., 1969-73; asst. prof. U. Md., College Park, 1974-77; staff physicist and dept. mgr. Physics Internat. Co., San Leandro, Calif., 1978-80; tech. dir. Maxwell Lab., Inc., San Diego, 1980—; vis. prof. UNICAMP, Campinas, Brazil, summer 1975, 1976. NASA Internat. fellow 1963; presdl. chair prof. President Chiang Kai-Sek Found. 1968. Mem. Am. Phys. Soc., U. Alumni Assn. (exec. sec. nat. com. 1971). Democrat. Buddhist. Office: Maxwell Lab Inc 9244 Balboa Ave San Diego CA 92123

CHENEY, ERIC SWENSON, geology educator; b. New Haven, Nov. 17, 1934; s. Kimberly and Margreta Curtis (Swenson) C.; m. Olga Marie Campaigne, Sept. 20, 1958 (div. Nov. 1983); children: Eric, Kathryn, Jamison, Luis. BS in Geology, Yale U., 1956, PhD in Geology, 1964. Asst. prof. U. Wash., Seattle, 1964-69, assoc. prof., 1969—; pres. Cambria Corp., Seattle, 1981—; vis. assoc. prof. Stanford (Calif.) U., 1974; vis. research prof. U. Pretoria, South Africa, 1984-85; cons. in field., 1963—. Contbr. articles to profl. jours. Served with USNR, 1956-58. Grantee Am. CHem. Soc., 1967-70, Wash. Mining Mineral Inst., 1980; recipient Best Paper award Mining Engrs. of AIME, 1971. Fellow Geol. Soc. Am.; mem. Soc. Econ. Geologists (councilor 1984-87), N.W. Mining Assn., Am. Soc. Mining. Engrs., AAAS. Avocations: traveling, hiking. Office: U Wash Dept Geol Scis Seattle WA 98195

CHENEY, RICHARD BRUCE, Congressman; b. Lincoln, Nebr., Jan. 30, 1941; s. Richard Hebert and Marjorie Lauraine (Dickey) C.; m. Lynne Anne Vincent, Aug. 29, 1964; children—Elizabeth, Mary Claire. B.A., U. Wyo., 1965, M.A., 1966; postgrad., U. Wis., 1966-68. Staff aide to Gov. Warren Knowles, Wis., 1966; mem. staff Congressman William A. Steiger, 1969; spl. asst. to dir. OEO, Washington, 1969-70; dep. to counsellor to Pres. 1970-71; asst. dir. Cost of Living Council, 1971-73; partner Bradley, Woods and Co., 1973-74; dep. asst. to Pres. 1974-75, asst. to Pres., 1975-77; mem. 96th-100th Congresses from Wyo. at large; chmn. Republican policy com. Named One of 10 outstanding young men in Am., U.S. Jaycees, 1976; Congl. fellow Am. Polit. Sci. Assn., 1968-69. Mem. Am. Polit. Sci. Assn. Republican. Office: US Ho of Reps 104 Cannon House Office Bldg Washington DC 20515

CHENG, DAVID, experimental physicist; b. Chungking, Peoples Republic of China, July 21, 1941; came to U.S., 1958; s. Elbert CY and Emma Cheng; m. Jennifer Jung, Dec. 24, 1984; children: Denise, Daniel. BS, U. Calif., Berkeley, 1962, MA, 1963, PhD, 1965. Physicist Lawrence Berkeley (Calif.) Nat. Lab., 1962-67, Brookhaven Nat. Lab., Upton, N.Y., 1967-69; mem. tech. staff Bell Labs., Murray Hill, N.J., 1969-74; mem. research staff Xerox PARC, Palo Alto, Calif., 1974-83; pres. Computer Machine Control Inc., Mountain View, Calif., 1982—; dir. engring. Applied Materials, Santa Clara, Calif., 1983—. Patentee in field. Mem. ASME (sr.), IEEE, Optical Soc. Am., Am. Phys. Soc., Phi Beta Kappa, Sigma Xi. Home: 974 Sherman Oaks Dr San Jose CA 95128 Office: Computer Machine Control Inc 831-H Sierra Vista Ave Mountain View CA 94043

CHENG, EDWARD TEH-CHANG, nuclear engineer; b. Pingtung, Taiwan, Nov. 23, 1946; came to U.S., 1972; s. Sui Ping and Tsai Yin (Li) C.; m. Shu-Ching Lai, June 4, 1973; children: Eric, Wendy. BS, Nat. Tsing Hua U., Hsinchu, Taiwan, 1969, MS, 1971; MS, U. Wis., 1974, PhD, 1976. Asst. scientist U. Wis., Madison, 1976-78; staff engr. GA Technologies, Inc., San Diego, 1978—. Mem. Am. Nuclear Soc. (sec., treas. fusion energy div. 1980-82). Office: GA Technologies Inc PO Box 85608 San Diego CA 92138

CHENG, H(WEI) H(SIEN), agriculture science educator; b. Shanghai, China, Aug. 13, 1932; came to U.S., 1951, naturalized, 1961; s. Chi-Pao and Anna (Lan) C.; m. Jo Yuan, Dec. 15, 1962; children: Edwin, Antony. BA, Berea Coll., 1956; MS, U. Ill., 1958, PhD, 1961. Research assoc. Iowa State U., Ames, 1962-64, asst. prof. agronomy, 1964-65; asst. prof. dept. agronomy and soils Wash. State U., Pullman, 1965-71, assoc. prof., 1971-77, prof., 1977—, chmn., 1986—, chmn. program environ. sci. and regional planning, 1977-79, assoc. dean Grad. Sch., 1982-86; vis. scientist Julich Nuclear Research Ctr., Fed. Republic Germany, 1971-73, 79-80, Academia Sinica, Taipei, Republic of China, 1978, Fed. Agrl. Research Ctr., Braunschweig, Fed. Republic Germany, 1980. Assoc. editor Jour. Environ. Quality, 1983—. Fulbright scholar, 1962-63. Fellow Am. Soc. Agronomy, Soil Sci. Soc. Am.; mem. AAAS, Am. Chem. Soc., Soc. Environ. Toxicology and Chemistry. Methodist. Home: NW 305 Joe St Pullman WA 99163 Office: Wash State U Dept Agronomy and Soils Pullman WA 99164

CHENG, KENNETH TAT-CHIU, pharmacy educator; b. Hong Kong, Feb. 24, 1954; came to U.S., 1972; s. Shiu Fun and Alice Shiu-Wing (Leung) C.; m. Ying Hsu, Aug. 11, 1984; 1 child, Jonathan Yee-Hang. BS in Pharmacy, SUNY, Buffalo, 1977; PhD, Purdue U., 1985. Lic. pharmacist N.Y., Ind., Kans., N.Mex. Resident in hosp. pharmacy U. Kans. Med. Ctr., Kansas City, 1978-79; research/teaching asst. Purdue U., West Lafayette, Ind., 1980-

84; research fellow Harvard U. Med. Sch., Boston, 1984-85; asst. prof. pharmacy U. N.Mex., Albuquerque, 1985—. Recipient Donald E. Francke award Drug Info. Assn., 1981, Glenn E. Jenkins Qualifying Research award Purdue U., 1984; Research fellow Am. Cancer Soc., 1984-85; named one of Outstanding Young Men of Am., 1986. Mem. AAAS, Soc. Nuclear Medicine, Am. Soc. Hosp. Pharmacists, Am. Chem. Soc., Soc. Magnetic Resonance Imaging, Sigma Xi, Rho Chi, Eta Sigma Gamma. Avocations: music, fishing, swimming. Office: U NMex Coll Pharmacy Albuquerque NM 87131

CHENG, PETER YU-HUNG, electronics engineer; b. Hong Kong, Feb. 4, 1952; came to U.S., 1970, naturalized, 1984; s. Yuk Kwan and Sussy Shui-Wan (Kao) C.; m. Pearl Po-Yee Li, Mar. 21, 1981. BSEE summa cum laude, Wash. State U., 1974; MSEE, U. Pa., 1976; postgrad., Stanford U., 1982. Design engr. Tex. Instruments, Houston, 1977-78; design engr. Intel, Santa Clara, Calif., 1978-79, sr. design engr., 1980-81; sr. design engr. Intersil, Cupertino, Calif., 1979-80; devel. engr. Hewlett Packard, Cupertino, Calif., 1981-82, project mgr., 1982—, chmn. design tech. conf., 1983—. Contbr. tech. articles to profl. confs. S. Town Stephenson scholar Wash. State U., Pullman, 1974; fellow U. Pa., Phila., 1975-76. Mem. IEEE, AAAS, Am. Mgmt. Assn., Am. Assn. Artificial Intelligence, Stanford Alumni Assn. (life), Tau Beta Pi (treas. 1973-74), Phi Kappa Phi. Republican. Avocations: tennis, fine arts, classical music, reading, bridge games. Home: 10229 Palo Vista Rd Cupertino CA 95014 Office: Hewlett Packard 5301 Stevens Creek Blvd Santa Clara CA 95051

CHENG, SABRINA SIU-WOON, social worker; b. Kowloon, Hong Kong, Mar. 5, 1949; came to U.S., 1977; d. Koon Lok and Yee Wan (Wong) Siu; m. Paul Sai-Ho Cheng, Jan. 11, 1975; 1 child, Luke Yun-Lo. B in Social Scis. (hon.), Chinese U. of Hong Kong, 1973; MSW, Portland State U., 1985. Asst. social welfare officer Social Welfare Dept., Hong Kong, 1973-77; bilingual asst. ESL/Bilingual Program, Portland (Oreg.) Pub. Schs., 1980-82, asst. area coordinator, 1982-84, sch. social worker, 1985—; advisor to Chinese Social Service Ctr. Portland, 1982—. Mem. Oreg. State Migrant Spl. Edn. Com.; elder Chinese Presbyn. Ch. Mem. Nat. Assn. Social Workers, Council Sch. Social Workers (Oreg. chpt.), Oreg. Tchrs. of English to Speakers of Other Languages. Office: ESL/Bilingual Program 531 SE 14th Ave Portland OR 97214

CHENG, WILLIAM WAI LING, electrical engineer; b. Hong Kong, Jan. 8, 1961; s. David Leung and Pui Sheung (Chan) C. BS, U. Calif., Berkeley, 1983; MS, UCLA, 1984. Mem. tech. staff Gen. Motors Hughes Electronics, El Segundo, Calif., 1983—. Contbr. articles to profl. jours. Fellow Hughes Full Staff, 1983, Calif. Microelectronics, 1984. Mem. IEEE, Electrochem. Soc. Avocation: photography.

CHENHALLS, ANNE MARIE, nurse, educator; b. Detroit, May 26, 1929; d. Peter and Beatrice Mary (Elliston) McLeod; m. Horacio Chenhalls, 1953 (dec.); children—Mark, Anne Marie Chenhalls Delamater. Student Detroit Conservatory Music, 1946-47; B. Vocat. Edn., Calif. State U.-Los Angeles, 1967, B.S. in Nursing, 1968; M.A., Calif. State U.-Long Beach, 1985. R.N., Calif. Nurse, Grace Hosp., Detroit, 1951-52; pvt. duty nurse, Mexico City, 1953-54; nurse St. Francis Hosp., Lynwood, Calif., 1957-63; assoc. prof. nursing Compton Coll. (Calif.), 1964-72; health educator, sch. nurse Santa Ana Unified Sch. Dist. (Calif.), 1972-76, 79—; med. coordinator, internat. health cons. Agape Movement, San Bernardino, Calif., 1976-79; instr. community health, Uganda, 1982; med. evaluator Athletes in Action, 1979. Assoc. staff mem. Campus Crusade for Christ. Solo vocalist, Santa Ana and Seal Beach, Calif. U.S. govt. grantee, 1968. Mem. Calif. Sch. Nurses Assn., Nat. Educators Assn., Calif. Assn. Vocat. Educators, Internat. Platform Assn. Democrat. Home: 12092-69 Sylvan River Fountain Valley CA 92708 Office: Santa Ana Unified Sch Dist 1405 French St Santa Ana CA 92701

CHENOY, SOHRAB YADGAR, speech pathologist; b. Secunderabad, India, Sept. 16, 1952; came to U.S., 1974; s. Yadgar Faridoon and Goolbanoo Chenoy. BA in English Lit., U. Utah, 1975; MS in Communicative Disorders, Utah State U., 1982. Lang. and speech specialist Riverside (Calif.) County Supt. Schs., 1980-81; cons. lang. and speech program Profl. Med. Software, La Cañada, Calif., 1981-83; lang. and speech specialist San Bernardino County Schs., Calif., 1983-85, Imperial County Office of Edn., El Centro, Calif., 1985—. Mem. Am. Speech-Lang.-Hearing Assn., Calif. Speech-Lang.-Hearing Assn. Lodge: Noashir 'Chenoy GLI. Avocations: health, fitness, opera, fashion, tennis. Office: Imperial County Office Edn 1398 Sperber Rd El Centro CA 92243

CHEOROS, PETER JOSEPH, history educator; b. Chgo., Dec. 14, 1941; s. Peter William and Virginia Grace (Gordon) C.; m. Edith Marie Fuchs, June 20, 1966; 1 child, Lisa Maria. AA, Long Beach City Coll., 1961; BA, Calif. State U., Long Beach, 1965; MA, La Verne Coll., 1976; postgrad., U. London, 1986. Cert. tchr., Calif. Tchr. history Lynnwood (Calif.) High Sch., 1964—; lectr. econs. Calif. State U., Long Beach, 1977-78. Pres. Long Beach State Young Reps., 1962-63; mem. cen. com. Los Angeles County Young Reps., 1961-64. NEH fellow, 1984; named Tchr. of Yr., Lynwood C. of C., 1975. Mem. NEA (del. 1977-83), Lynwood Tchrs. Assn. (pres., v.p., exec. bd. idrs. 1973—), Calif. Council Edn. (negotiation com. 1982—), South Eastern Service Ctr., Archaeol. Inst. Am. Republican. Lutheran. Avocations: traveling, reading, stamp and coin collecting. Home: 1226 Jackson St Long Beach CA 90805 Office: Lynwood High Sch 12124 Bullis Rd Lynwood CA 90262

CHERBERG, JOHN ANDREW, lieutenant governor Washington; b. Pensacola, Fla., Oct. 17, 1910; s. Fortunato and Annie (R) C.; m. Elizabeth Ann Walker, Aug. 17, 1935; children—Kay Elizabeth (Mrs. Ray Cohrs), Barbara Jean (Mrs. Dean Tonkin), James Walker. B.A., U. Wash., 1933. High sch. tchr., athletic coach 1934-46; football coach U. Wash., 1946-56; lt. gov. Wash., 1957—; Chmn. Nat. Conf. Lt. Govs., 1968-69. Mem. NEA, AFTRA, Nat. Acad. TV Arts and Scis., Wash. State Assn. Broadcasters (hon. life), Sigma Nu. Club: Variety. Home: 515 Howe St Seattle WA 98109 Office: Office of the Lt Gov 304 Legislative Bldg AS-31 Olympia WA 98504 *

CHERMAK, GAIL DONNA, communications disorders educator; b. N.Y.C., Sept. 30, 1950; d. Martin I. Chermak and Zelda (Kessler) Lax. BA in Communication Disorders, SUNY, Buffalo, 1972; MA in Speech and Hearing Sci., Ohio State U., 1973, PhD in Speech and Hearing Sci., 1975. Asst. prof. speech So. Ill. U., Edwardsville, 1975-77; assoc. prof. and dir., communication disorders program Wash. State U., Pullman, 1977—, coordinator grad. program, dept. speech, 1983—; editorial cons. Ear and Hearing pub., Cinn., 1984, profl. advisor Palowe chpt. Self-Help for Hard of Hearing, Moscow, Idaho, 1984—. Author: Handbook of Audiological Rehabilitation, 1981; contbr. articles to profl. jours. Kellogg Nat. fellow, 1986—. Mem. Am. Speech-Lang.-Hearing Assn. (cert. clin. competence), Acoustical Soc. Am., Am. Auditory Soc., Internat. Soc. Audiology, NOW (v.p. Moscow chpt. 1985-86), Phi Beta Kappa. Avocations: gardening, opera, orinthology, skiing. Office: Wash State U Dept Speech Pullman WA 99164-2420

CHERNEGA, JACK OLIVER, manufacturing company executive; b. Bellefonte, Pa., Dec. 29, 1957; s. John and Joan O. (Jenkins) C.; m. Michele Iannelli, Apr. 23, 1983. BS, Pa. State U., 1980. Geologist EXLOG, La.; ski instructor Taos (N.Mex.) Ski Valley Inc.; pres. DP Skis, Taos, 1983—. Mem. Ski Industries Am. Club: Taos Racquetball. Avocations: skiing, soccer, racquetball, bowling, fishing. Home: 1007 La Lomita PO Box 1094 Taos NM 87571 Office: DP Skis 211 Cruz Alta PO Box 1094 Taos NM 87571

CHERNICK, MICHAEL ROSS, mathematical statistician; b. Havre de Grace, Md., Mar. 11, 1947; s. Jack and Norma Leonia (Weiner) C. B.S., SUNY-Stony Brook, 1969; M.A., U. Md., 1973; M.S., Stanford U., 1976, Ph.D., 1978. Mathematician, Army Materiel System Analysis Activity, Aberdeen Proving Ground, Md., 1969-74; math. statistician Oak Ridge Nat. Lab., 1978-80; mem. tech. staff Aerospace Corp., Los Angeles, 1980—. Stanford U. Sch. Engring. fellow, 1974. Mem. Am. Statis. Assn., Inst. Math. Stats., Soc. Indsl. and Applied Math., Bernoulli Soc. Democrat. Jewish. Contbr. articles to math. and statis. jour.

CHERNY, ROBERT WALLACE, history educator; b. Marysville, Kans., Apr. 4, 1943; s. Clarence L. and Lena M. (Hobbs) C.; m. Rebecca Ellen Marshall, June 11, 1967; 1 child, Sarah Catherine. BA with distinction, U. Nebr., 1965; MA, Columbia U., 1967, PhD, 1972. Instr. history San Francisco State U., 1971-72, asst. prof., 1972-77, assoc. prof., 1977-81, prof., 1981—; assoc. dean behavioral and social scis. Sam Francisco State U., 1984, acting dean behavioral and social scis., 1985, chair history dept., 1987—; cons. in field. Author: A Righteous Cause: The Life of William Jennings Bryan, 1985, Populism, Progressivism and the Transformation of Nebraska Politics, 1981; (with William Issel) San Francisco, 1865-1932, 1986, San Francisco: Presidio, Port, and Pacific Metropolis, 1981. Bd. dirs. San Francisco Labor Found., 1984—. Woodrow Wilson fellow, 1965-66; Woodrow Wilson dissertation fellow, 1969. Mem. Am. Hist. Assn., Orgn. Am. Historians, Southwest Labor Studies Assn. (pres. 1982-86), Calif. Hist. Soc., Inst. His. Study, Nebr. State Hist. Soc. Democrat. Home: 1462 9th Ave San Francisco CA 94122 Office: San Francisco State U Dept Hist 1600 Holloway Ave San Francisco CA 94132

CHERRY, JAMES DONALD, physician; b. Summit, N.J., June 10, 1930; s. Robert Newton and Beatrice (Wheeler) C.; m. Jeanne M. Fischer, June 19, 1954; children—James S., Jeffrey D., Susan J., Kenneth C. B.S., Springfield (Mass.) Coll., 1953; M.D., U. Vt., 1957; M.Sc. in Epidemiology, London Sch. Hygiene and Tropical Medicine, 1983. Diplomate: Am. Bd. Pediatrics. Intern, then resident in pediatrics Boston City Hosp., 1957-59; resident in pediatrics Kings County Hosp., Bklyn., 1959-60; research fellow in medicine Harvard U. Med. Sch.-Thorndike Meml. Lab., Boston City Hosp., 1961-62; instr. pediatrics U. Vt. Coll. Medicine, also asst. attending physician Mary Fletcher DeCoesbriand Meml. hosps., Burlington, Vt., 1960-61; asst. prof., then assoc. prof. pediatrics U. Wis. Med. Sch., Madison, 1963-66; assoc. attending physician Madison Gen., U. Wis. hosps., 1963-66; dir. John A. Hartford Research Lab., Madison Gen. Hosp., 1963-66; mem. faculty St. Louis U. Med. Sch., 1966-73, prof. pediatrics, 1969-73, vice chmn. dept., 1970-73; mem. staff Cardinal Glennon Meml. Hosp. Children, St. Louis U. Hosp., 1966-73; prof. pediatrics, chief div. infectious diseases center Health Scis. UCLA Sch. Medicine, 1973—; acting chmn. dept. pediatrics center for Health Scis., 1977-79; attending physician, chmn. asepsis com. UCLA Med. Ctr.; cons. Project Head Start; vis. worker dept. community medicine Middlesex Hosp. and Med. Sch., London, 1982-83; vis. worker Common Cold Research Unit, 1969-70; mem. immunization adv. com. Los Angeles County Dept. Health Services, 1978—. Co-editor Textbook of: Pediatric Infectious Diseases, 1981, 2d edit., 1987; author numerous papers in field; editorial reviewer profl. jours. Bd. govs. Alexander Graham Bell Internat. Parents Orgn., 1967-69. Served with USAR, 1958-64. John and Mary R. Markle scholar acad. medicine, 1964. Mem. Am. Acad. Pediatrics (exec. com. Calif. chpt. 2 1975-77, mem. com. infectious diseases 1977-83, assoc. editor 19th Red Book 1982), Am. Soc. Microbiology, Am. Fedn. Clin. Research, AAAS, Soc. Pediatric Research, Infectious Diseases Soc. Am., Am. Epidemiological Soc., Am. Pediatric Soc., Los Angeles Pediatric Soc., Assn. Practitioners in Infection Control, Soc. Exptl. Biology and Medicine, Internat. Orgn. Mycoplasmologists, Am. Soc. Virology, Soc. Hosp. Epidemiologists Am., Am. Pub. Health Assn., Alpha Omega Alpha. Home: 1402 San Vicente Blvd Santa Monica CA 90402 Office: UCLA Sch Medicine Los Angeles CA 90024

CHERRY, JOHN THOMAS, chemist; b. Houston, Mar. 18, 1951; s. Roy Wilson and Francis (Johns) C.; m. Anne Janette Kemp (dec. Dec. 1977). 1 child, Tressa Anne. BA in Biology, U. Houston, 1976, BS in Chemistry, 1981. Head extracorporeal tech./surgery M.D. Anderson Hosp., Houston, 1970-73, 75-76, 80; microbiologist Baylor Coll. Medicine, Houston, 1977-79; chemist Tex. City (Tex.) Refining, 1980-82; sr. chemist Unocal-Oil Shale Ops., Parachute, Colo., 1982—. Mem. Am. Chem. Soc., Petroleum div. Am. Chem. Soc. Republican. Baptist. Avocations: skiing, fishing, archery hunting, scuba diving, backpacking. Home: 361 Tamarisk Parachute CO 81635 Office: Unocal 2717 County Rd 215 Parachute CO 81635

CHERRY, PETER DENHAM, electrical engineer; b. London, Aug. 19, 1942; came to U.S., 1974; s. Denham Walter and Wendy (Hartley) C.; m. Sandra Lenore Lubin, Feb. 15, 1975; 1 child, Denham J. BS, Leeds U., Eng., 1964. Dir. engring. Wordplex Corp., Westlake, Calif., 1978-83, gen. mgr., v.p. ops., 1983-86; program mgr. TRW Technar, Irwindale, Calif., 1987—; bd. dirs., Wordplex Tech. Ltd., London, 1983-86. Mem. IEEE, Inst. Elec. Engrs. Home: 2817 Parkview Dr Thousand Oaks CA 91362 Office: TRW Technar 5462 N Irwindale Ave Irwindale CA 91706

CHESADA, DAN V., financial trader; b. Bangkok, July 31, 1952; came to U.S., 1971; s. Mueng and Suprattra (Pankoncheen) Vuthanavisit; m. Susan J. Wakefield, Feb. 27, 1980; children: Brendon Lee Wakefield, Jennifer Susan Wafefield. Student, UCLA, 1972-74, U. So. Calif., 1976; BA in Biochemistry, Calif. State U., Northridge, 1978. Owner Chatsworth Metal Fabrication, Chatsworth, Calif., 1980—; ptnr. Calif. Trading Co., Chatsworth, 1986—. Democrat. Buddhist. Avocations: flying, painting. Office: CMF Co 9601 Cozycroft Avce #6 Chatsworth CA 91311

CHESLEY, MARY KAY, speech pathologist; b. Grand Island, Nebr., Sept. 23, 1952; d. Robert Leo and Phyllis Gene (Daberkow) Dryer; m. Steven Dale Chesley, Aug. 11, 1979; children: Tara Lea, Stefanie Kay (dec.). BS, U. Nebr., 1974, MA, 1976. Cert. speech pathologist, Colo. Speech therapist Henderson (Nebr.) Community Schs., 1975-78; speech and lang. specialist Poudre Sch. Dist., Ft. Collins, Colo., 1978-79; child find coordinator Mountain Bd. Coop. Services, Leadville, Colo., 1979-80, speech pathologist, 1985—; speech pathologist Glenwood Hearing and Speech Assn., Glenwood Springs, Colo., 1981-83, Mountain Valley Devel. Services, Glenwood Springs, 1982-85. Mem. Am. Speech, Lang., and Hearing Assn., Colo. Speech, Lang., and Hearing Assn. Democrat. Roman Catholic. Home: 1217 Fir Ave Rifle CO 81650 Office: Mountain Bd Coop Services 110 W 10th Leadville CO 80631

CHESNUT, CAROL FITTING, economist; b. Pecos, Tex., June 17, 1937; d. Ralph Ulf and Carol (Lowe) Fitting; BA magna cum laude, U. Colo., 1971; m. Dwayne A. Chesnut, Dec. 27, 1955; children: Carol Marie, Michelle, Mark Steven. Research asst. U. Colo., 1972; head quality controller Mathematica, Inc., Denver, 1973-74; cons. Mincome Man. (Can.), Winnipeg, 1974; cons. economist Energy Cons. Assocs. Inc., Denver, 1974-79, also dir.; exec. v.p. tng. ECA Intercomp, 1980-81; gen. ptnr. Chestnut Consortium, 1981—; sec., dir. Critical Resources, Inc., 1981-83; staff aide Senator Gary Hart, 1978. Rep., Lakehurst Civic Assn., 1968; precinct capt. Democratic Party, 1982—. Mem. Am. Mgmt. Assn., Soc. Petroleum Engrs., Assn. Women Geoscientists (treas. Denver 1983-85), ACLU, NOW, Colo. Assn. Commerce and Industry, Phi Beta Kappa, Phi Chi Theta. Unitarian. Clubs: City (Denver), Century. Office: 419-A St Paul Denver CO 80206

CHESTER, ARTHUR NOBLE, physicist; b. Seattle, Aug. 5, 1940; s. Arthur Malbridge and Marjorie (Stenberg) C.; m. Cynthia Anne Ashford, Sept. 6, 1961 (div. June 1968); m. Catherine Rogers Buchanan, Aug. 10, 1969. B.S. in Physics, U. Tex., 1961; Ph.D. in Theoretical Physics, Calif. Inst. Tech., 1965. Mem. tech staff Bell Labs., Murray Hill, N.J., 1965-69; mem. tech. staff Hughes Research Labs., Malibu, Calif., 1969-73, mgr. laser dept., 1973-75, assoc. dir., 1975-80; program mgr. very high speed integrated circuits Hughes Aircraft Co., El Segundo, Calif., 1980-83, mgr. tactical engring. div., 1984-85; group v.p., mgr. space and strategic systems div. Hughes Aircraft Co., 1985—; cons. U.S. Dept. Def., Washington, 1975-79; co-dir. Internat. Sch. Quantum Electronics, Erice, Sicily, Italy, 1980—; bd. dirs., chmn. exhbn. comm. Fellows Contemporary Art, Los Angeles. Co-editor: Integrated Optics: Physics and Applications, 1983, Free Electron Lasers, 1983, Analytical Laser Spectroscopy, 1985, Laser Photobiology and Photomedicine, 1985, Optical Fiber Sensors, 1986; contbr. articles to publs. Pres. Masterwork Chorus, Morristown, N.J., 1968-69; bd. dirs. Fellows Contemporary Art, Los Angeles. Recipient A.A. Bennett Calculus prize U. Tex., 1959; recipient Nat. Merit scholar, 1957; NSF fellow, 1961; Howard Hughes doctoral fellow, 1963. Fellow IEEE (chmn. com. 1982—, Centennial Medal 1984); mem. IEEE Lasers and Electro-Optics Soc. (pres. 1980), Optical Soc. Am., Am. Phys. Soc., AAAS, Sigma Xi. Office: Hughes Aircraft Co PO Box 902 E55/G200 El Segundo CA 90245

CHESTER, JOHN E., medical supplies company executive; b. N.Y.C., Nov. 9, 1932; s. John E. and Helen (Burns) C.; m. Arden J. Chester, Sept. 20, 1952. Grad., USN Sch. Nursing, 1953; BA, Queens Coll., 1957; postgrad., Columbia U., Advance Mgmt. Program, Internat. Sch. Mgmt. Registered Nurse. V.p. corp devel. E.R. Squibb Corp., Lawrenceville, N.J., 1959-75; mktg. dir. Am. Hosp Supply Corp., Evanston, Ill., 1954-79; v.p., gen. mgr. G.D. Searle Corp., Skokie, Ill., 1979-81; v.p., then pres. Unitek Corp. Div. Bristol-Myers Co., N.Y.C., 1981-85; pres., chief operating officer Thoratec Labs. Corp., Berkeley, Calif., 1985—; pres., chief exec. officer Thoratec Med. Inc., Berkeley, Calif., 1985—; guest lectr. Claremont Grad. Sch. Bus., St. Mary's Coll. Grad. Sch. Bus., Peter Drucker/Reed Powell Seminars; profl. papers presented in Australia, People's Rep. of China, U.K. and U.S. Contbr. articles to profl. jours.; 3 patents of surg. instruments. Served with USN, 1951-55. Office: Thoratec Labs Corp 2023 8th St Berkeley CA 94710 *

CHESTER, SHARON ROSE, photographer, natural history educator; b. Chgo., July 12, 1942; d. Joseph Thomas and Lucia Barbara (Urban) C. BA, U. Wis., 1964; postgrad., Coll. San Mateo, 1972-74, U. Calif., Berkeley, 1977. Flight attendant Pan Am. World Airways Inc., San Francisco, 1965; free lance photographer San Mateo, Calif., 1983—; stock photographer Comstock, N.Y.C., 1987—; lectr. Soc. Expdns., Seattle, 1985—. Author (checklist) Birds of the Antarctic and Sub-Antarctic, 1986; photographer mag. cover King Penguin and Chick for Internat. Wildlife mag., 1985, Sierra Club Calendar, 1986; exhibited photos at Royal Geog. Soc., London, 1985. Mem. Audubon Soc., Am. Soc. Mag. Photographers, Calif. Acad. Sci. Avocations: wandering, writing, birdwatching. Home: 724 Laurel Ave #121 San Mateo CA 94401

CHESTER, THOMAS JAY, astrophysicist; b. Topeka, Oct. 6, 1951; s. Z.P. and Esther (Meyer) C.; m. Deborah Ann Welch, Sept. 18, 1976; 1 child, Scott. BA, U. Kans., 1969-72, 73; MA, Princeton U., 1975, PhD, 1977. Postdoctoral research Calif. Inst. Tech., Pasadena, 1979, mem. evaluation team, 1979-82; mem. tech. staff Jet Propulsion Lab., Pasadena, 1979-85; supr. new products IPAC/Calif. Inst. Tech., 1985—; Infrared Astron. Satellite sci. support team chief 1982-85. Editor: IRAS Explanatory Supplement, 1984; contbr. articles to profl. jours. Recipient Exceptional Service medal NASA, 1984, Disting. Citizen award Topeka, 1984; Nat. Merit scholar, 1969, Summerfield scholar Kans. U., 1969-73; Proctor fellow Princeton U., 1973-76, NSF fellow, 1973-76. Mem. Am. Astron. Soc., Am. Geophys. Union, Am. Phys. Soc., Sea Satellite Scanning Multichannel Microwave Radiometer (evaluation team), Phi Beta Kappa, Sigma Xi. Home: 1169 Meadowbrook Rd Altadena CA 91001 Office: IPAC Calif Inst Tech 100-22 1201 E California Blvd Pasadena CA 91125

CHESTERFIELD, RHYDONIA RUTH EPPERSON, financial company executive; b. Dallas, Tex., Apr. 23, 1919; d. Leonard Lee and Sally E. (Stevenson) Griswold; m. Chad Chesterfield, Apr. 21, 1979. BS Southwestern U., 1952; BS, N. Tex. U., 1954, ME, 1956; PhD, Bernardean U., 1974, Calif. Christian U., 1974, LLD (hon.), 1974. Evangelist with Griswold Trio, 1940-58; tchr., counselor Dallas public schs., 1952-58, Los Angeles public schs., 1958-74; pres. Griswold-Epperson Fin. Enterprise, Los Angeles, 1974—; pres. GEC Enterprises, 1979—; guest speaker various schs., chs. and civic orgns. in U.S. and Can. Author: Little Citizens series, Cathedral Films; contbr. articles on bus. to profl. publs. Fellow Internat. Naturopathic Assn.; mem. Los Angeles Inst. Fine Arts, Assn. of Women in Edn. (hon.), Internat. Bus. and Profl. Women, Calif. C. of C., Los Angeles C. of C., Pi Lambda Theta (hon.), Kappa Delta Pi (hon.). Office: 10790 Wilshire Blvd 202 Los Angeles CA 90024

CHEUNG, RUDOLF LAP-TUNG, electrical engineer; b. Guangdong, Peoples Republic of China, Oct. 27, 1954; came to U.S., 1972; s. See-Yee Cheung and Gek-Ken Choo. BSEE, U. Wash., 1976, MSEE, 1978, PhD, 1982. Research assoc. U. Wash., Seattle, 1976-82; staff engr. Transco Products, Inc., Marina Del Rey, Calif., 1982-85; mem. tech. staff Jet Propulsion Lab., Pasadena, Calif., 1985—. Contbr. articles to profl. jours. Mem. IEEE, Optical Soc. Am., Tau Beta Pi. Avocation: classical music. Home: 198 N Marguerita Ave Alhambra CA 91801 Office: Jet Propulsion Lab 4800 Oak Grove Dr Pasadena CA 91109

CHEVALIER, PAUL EDWARD, retail executive, lawyer; b. N.Y.C., Jan. 30, 1939; s. Arthur and Grace (Eaton) C.; m. Anne-Marie Leitner, May 4, 1963; 1 child, Marc. B.A., Columbia U., 1960, LL.B., 1966, M.B.A., 1966, A.M.P., Harvard U., 1979. Bar: Ill., 1968, U.S. Supreme Ct. 1974. Employee relations program staff Gen. Electric Co., 1966-67; Western regional mgr. labor relations Montgomery Ward & Co., Chgo. and Oakland, Calif., 1967-72; dir. labor relations Carter Hawley Hale Stores, Inc., Los Angeles, 1972-74, v.p. employee relations, 1974-86, sr. v.p. human relations, 1986—. Pres. Jonathan Art Found.; mem. employee relations com. Bus. Roundtable, Washington; sec., bd. dirs. Calif. Employment Law Council. Served to lt. USN, 1960. Mem. ABA, Am. Retail Fedn. (chmn. employee relations com. 1979-82), Calif. Retail Assn., Harvard Bus. Sch. Assn. (bd. dirs. 1980-87, pres. 1984-85, council 1987—), Harvard Bus. Sch. Alumni Council, Jonathan Art Found. (chmn. miscellaneous com. 1984, pres.). Republican. Roman Catholic. Home: 2405 Glendower Ave Los Angeles CA 90027

CHEW, DENNIS W., fund raising consultant, arbitrator; b. Hong Kong, Jan. 1, 1941; s. Stephen and Wai (Mui) C.; B.S., U. Redlands, 1963; postgrad. U. Calif.-Riverside, 1965; m. Linda Lee Olson, July 23, 1965; children—Stephanie L.S., Erica L.S. Tchr., Riverside (Calif.) Unified Sch. Dist., 1965-71; asst. exec. dir. Sacramento City Tchrs. Assn., 1971-73; negotiations cons. Calif. Tchrs. Assn., Burlingame, 1973-77, asst. exec. dir., 1977-78, assoc. exec. dir., 1979-82, cons., 1982—; instr. U. Calif. Extension. Bd. dirs. Redlands Winter Concerts, 1969-71, San Francisco council Girl Scouts Am., 1986—. Mem. AAAS, Am. Arbitration Assn., Nat. Soc. Fund Raising Execs.

CHEW, LINDA LEE, fund raising and management consultant, public relations executive; b. Riverside, Calif., Mar. 3, 1941; d. LeRoy S. and Grace (Ham) Olson; m. Dennis W. Chew, July 23, 1965; children—Stephanie, Erica. B.Mus., U. Redlands, 1962. Cert. fund raising exec. Dir. pub. events U. Redlands (Calif.), 1962-69; dir. fin. and communications San Gorgonio council Girl Scouts U.S.A., Colton, Calif., 1969-71; exec. dir. United Cerebral Palsy Assn. Sacramento-Yolo Counties, 1972-73; fin. devel. dir. San Francisco Bay council Girl Scouts U.S.A., 1973-76; chief devel. and pub. info. East Bay Regional Park Dist., Oakland, Calif., 1976-86; cons. Chew & Assocs., San Ramon, Calif., 1986—. Bd. dirs. Planned Parenthood Contra Costa County, 1980-82, San Ramon Valley Edn. Found., 1984—. Mem. Nat. Soc. Fund Raising Execs. (nat. bd. dirs. 1981—, nat. vice chmn. 1982-84, pres. Golden Gate chpt. 1979-80, Abel Hanson Meml. award 1977, bd. mem. 1987—), Pub. Relations Soc. Am., Calif. Park and Recreation Soc., AAUW (pres. Redlands br. 1968-69), Am. Guild Organists (dean Riverside-San Bernardino chpt. 1969-71), Nat. Assn. Hosp. Devel., 1986—. Office: 3211 Crow Canyon Pl Suite A-29 San Ramon CA 94583

CHEW, SOO HONG, economics educator; b. Singapore, Apr. 26, 1954; came to U.S., 1980; s. Choo Keng and Pek Hup (Loh) C. Ph.D., U. B.C., 1980. Asst. prof. econs. U. Ariz., Tucson, 1980-84, Johns Hopkins U., Balt., 1984—. Served with Singapore Armed Forces, 1972-75. Recipient Leonard J. Savage thesis award, 1982, dissertation award Am. Inst. for Decision Scis., 1982, theoretical empirical research paper award, 1982; grantee Decision and Mgmt. Sci. program NSF, 1982-84. Mem. The Econometric Soc., Am. Econ. Assn., Ops. Research Soc. Am., Sci. Research Soc., Math. Assn. Am., Sigma Xi.

CHHIBBER, RAJESHWAR CHANDER, physicist, consultant; b. Chhokran, India, June 2, 1960; came to U.S., 1983; s. Badri Nath and Shakuntla (Devi) C.; m. Seema Mohan, Dec. 30, 1985. HNC in Applied Physics, Slough Coll., Eng., 1979; BS, MS in Physics (hon.), Essex (Eng.) U., 1983. Research and devel. engr. Kodak Ltd., U.K., London, 1979-83; staff engr. NSC Datachecker/DTS, Santa Clara, Calif., 1983—; chief exec. officer, internat. coordinator ATC Overseas Enterprises, Ltd., Douglas, Isle of Man, 1985—. Mem. Optical Soc. Am., Internat. Soc. Optical Engring., Laser Inst. Am. Home: 3009 D'Amico Dr San Jose CA 95148 Office: NSC Datachecker/DTS 800 Central Expressway Santa Clara CA 95052

CHI, TSU-TSAIR OLIVER, pharmaceutical laboratory administrator; b. Chang-Su, Republic of China, Jan. 15, 1949; s. K.C. and C.C. (An) C.; m. Weijia Deng, Dec. 29, 1949; children: Shirley, Jennifer. BSc, Chung-Yuan U., Taiwan, Republic of China, 1971; MS, CCNY, 1975; PhD, Rutgers U., 1978. Research investigator E.R. Squibb & Sons, Princeton, N.J., 1978-79; group leader Park-Davis Co., Ann Arbor, Mich., 1979-83; lab. dir. Omicron Inc., Redlands, Calif., 1983—. Mem. Am. Soc. Microbiology, Am. Chem. Soc., AAAS. Home: 5465 E Estate Ridge Rd Anaheim CA 92807 Office: Seven W Enterprises Inc PO Box 111 Redlands CA 92373

CHIANG, ALBERT CHIN-LIANG, electrical engineer; b. Putai, Taiwan, Jan. 25, 1937; s. San Chi and Chiu (Hsu) C.; B.S. in E.E., Nat. Taiwan U., 1959; M.S. in E.E., Chiaotung U., Taiwan, 1963; Ph.D., U. So. Calif., 1968; m. Steffie F.L. Huang, Dec. 24, 1967; children—Margaret, Stacy, Kathy, George. Came to U.S., 1963, naturalized, 1973. Research asst. U. So. Calif., Los Angeles, 1963-68; engr. specialist Litton Industries, Woodland Hills, Calif., 1968-70; dir. internat. sales Macrodata Co., Woodland Hills, Calif., 1970-77; pres. Tritek Internat. Co., Northridge, Calif., 1977—. Mem. IEEE, Sigma Xi, Eta Kappa Nu. Home: 24132 Lupin Hill Rd Hidden Hills CA 91302 Office: Tritek Internat Co 8345 Reseda Blvd Northridge CA 91324

CHIANG, HENRY KUOLIANG, electrical engineer; b. Yeh, Peoples Republic of China, Sept. 23, 1937; came to U.S., 1961; s. Shu-Sheng and Wang-Shih (Wang) C.; m. Teri Yunhwa Tsao, June 17, 1967; children: Ray Lon, Lilian, Victor Lon. BSEE, Hanyang U., Seoul, Republic of Korea, 1960; MSEE, U. Nev., 1963; PhDEE, U. Wash., 1970. Devel. engr. Research and Devel. div. Fairchild Corp., Palo Alto, Calif., 1963-65; devel. engr. Microwave div. Fairchild Research and Devel. Labs., Palo Alto, Calif., 1970-72, sr. devel. engr. research and devel. div., 1972-75; teaching and research asst. U. Wash., Seattle, 1965-70; mem. tech. staff Hewlett-Packard Lab., Palo Alto, 1976—. Contbr. articles to profl. jours. Chmn. bd. dirs. Palo Alto Chinese Sch., 1982-83. Mem. IEEE. Democrat. Roman Catholic. Home: 923 Lundy Ln Los Altos CA 94022 Office: Hewlett Packard Co 3500 Deer Creek Rd Palo Alto CA 94304

CHIANG, WEN-LI, civil engineer; b. Choulan, Republic of China, Apr. 14, 1946; came to U.S., 1972; naturalized, 1985; s. Pen-Hsiu and Yanagi (Shizuko) C.; m. Hsiu-lan Wang, Dec. 26, 1974; children: Dean Tsung, Charles. BS, Nat. Taiwan U., Taipei, Republic of China, 1969; MS, Nat. Cen. U., Chungli, Republic of China, 1972, U. Kans., Lawrence, 1977; PhD, U. So. Calif., 1980. Registered civil engr., Calif. Prin. engr. Tetra Tech Inc., Pasadena, Calif., 1979—. Contbr. numerous articles to profl. jours. Recipient Sea grant NOAAt, 1976-79; NSF grantee, 1982-83. Mem. ASCE (tech. council computer practices pubs. com. 1986—), Nat. Cen. Univ. Alumni Assn. So. Calif. (pres. 1986), Sigma Xi, Tau Beta Pi. Avocations: reading, dancing. Home: 1139 Calle Malaga Duarte CA 91010 Office: Tetra Tech Inc 630 N Rosemead Blvd Pasadena CA 91170

CHIANG, YAWEN LEE, research molecular biologist; b. Taipei, Taiwan, Republic of China, May 26, 1950; came to U.S., 1971; d. Stanley Y.C. and Chieh Fang (Ou) L.; m. Nelson N.C. Chiang, Aug. 10, 1972; children: David, Andrew. BS, U. Md., 1974; MS, George Washington U., 1979, PhD, 1983; MA, Cen. Mich. U., 1981. Clin. chemist, med. technician Holy Cross Hosp., Silver Spring, Md., 1974-84; chemist NIH/George Washington U., Bethesda, Md., 1978-83; chemist, postdoctoral fellow Uniform Service Univ. of Health Scis., Bethesda, 1983-84; assoc. scientist Cetus, Palo Alto, Calif., 1984—. Mem. AAAS, Am. Soc. Med. Technologists, Am. Soc. Clin. Pathologists, Clin. Lab. Technologists Calif., Columbian Women Assn. (corr. sec. 1983-85).

CHIAPPELLI, FREDI, literary critic, educator; b. Florence, Italy, Jan. 24, 1921; came to U.S., 1969; s. Francesco and Maria (Von Zdekauer) C.; m. Aymerica Bollati, Dec. 1 1945 (div. Aug. 1970); children: Marina, Francesco; m. Gabriella R. Carboneschi, June 10, 1980. LittD, U. Florence, 1945; postdoctoral, U. Zurich, Switzerland, 1948; LittD (hon.), McGill U., Montreal, Can., 1978, Ariz. State U., 1982. Asst. prof. U. Florence, 1945-46; lectr. U. Zurich, 1946-49; prof. Italian U. Lausanne and Neuchatel, Switzerland, 1950-59; prof. Italian, dean Coll. Letters U. Lausanne, 1959-69; prof. Italian UCLA, 1969—; dir. Ctr. Medieval And Renaissance Studies UCLA, 1972—. Author: Niccoló Machiavelli: Legazioni Commissarie, 1971, 73, 84, 1985, Il Legame Musaico, 1984. Served as 2d lt. Italian Army, WWII. Decorated Grand Officer Order of Merit (Italy), Comdr. Palmes Académiques (France), Officer Order of Orange-Nassau (The Netherlands), Officer Order of Merit (Germany); Guggenheim fellow, 1972. Fellow Academia della Crusca (Italy), Real Academia de Buenas Letras (Barcelona, Spain), Academia das Ciencias (Lisbon, Portugal), Accademia Ligure di Scienze e Lettere (hon., Italy). Roman Catholic. Avocations: gardening, cooking, print collecting, travelling. Home: 600 N Kenter Ave Los Angeles CA 90049 Office: UCLA Ctr Medieval Renaissance Studies 11365 Bunche Hall Los Angeles CA 90024

CHIAVERINI, JOHN EDWARD, construction company executive; b. Providence, Feb. 6, 1924; s. John and Sadie (Ginsberg) C.; m. Cecile Corey, Mar. 31, 1951; children—Caryl Marie, John Michael. Cert. advanced san. engring. U. Ill., 1945; B.S., U. R.I., 1947. Registered profl. engr., Mass., R.I., Calif. Project engr. Perini Corp., Hartford, Conn., 1950-51, project mgr., 1951-55, asst. project mgr., Pitts. and Que., 1955-61, v.p., Framingham, Mass., 1965-84, sr. v.p., San Francisco, 1984—; pres., dir. Compania Perini S.A., Colombia, 1961—; v.p., exec. mgr. Perini Yuba Assocs., Marysville, Calif., 1966-70, v.p. Western ops., 1970-78, 79-84, group v.p., 1978-79; sr. v.p. spl. projects Perini Corp., 1984—; dir. Perini Corp.; mem. U.S. com. Internat. Commn. on Large Dams. Served to 2d lt. USAAF, 1944-46. Fellow ASCE; mem. Nat. Soc. Profl. Engrs., Calif. Soc. Profl. Engrs., Soc. Am. Mil. Engrs. (bd. dirs.), Beavers (bd. dirs.). Democrat. Roman Catholic. Lodges: K.C., Rotary. Home: 37 Dutch Valley Ln San Anselmo CA 94960 Office: Perini Corp 75 Broadway San Francisco CA 94111 *

CHIDLEY, THOMAS HOWARD, architect, structural engineer; b. Dublin, Ireland, Sept. 3, 1948 (parents Am. citizens); s. Henry Walter and Jeannette (Bell) C.; m. Carol Joy Gerk, Jan. 24, 1974 (div. Oct. 1981). B.Arch., U. Colo., 1972, B.S. in Archtl. Engring., 1972. Registered architect, Calif.; registered engr., Calif. Architect CTA Architects/Engrs., Billings, Mont., 1973-76; engr. Pregnoff & Matheu, San Francisco, 1976-79, Skidmore, Owings, Merrill, San Francisco, 1979-82, Martin Cagley & Nishkian, San Francisco, 1982-83; prin. T.H. Chidley, San Francisco, 1983—. Mem. AIA, Structural Engrs. Assn. No. Calif., Am. Concrete Inst. Democrat. Office: 750 Church St San Francisco CA 94114-3033

CHIGOS, DAVID, university president; b. Scranton, Pa., Mar. 29, 1933; s. Andrew D. and Emma (Kossmann) C.; m. Ruth Elizabeth Chamberlain, May 22, 1954; children: Catherine Mary Chigos Bradley, Carla Jane Chigos Sotelo, Lisa Anne, Laura Elizabeth. B.S. in Chemistry, W.Va. Wesleyan Coll., 1954, LL.D., 1980; M.A. in Counseling and Guidance, U.S. Internat. U., 1968, Ph.D., 1972. Teaching asst. U. Tex., 1954-56; commd. ensign USN, 1957, advanced through grades to lt. comdr., 1967, capt. Res., 1983; indsl. relations Convair Aerospace div. Gen. Dynamics Corp., San Diego, 1967-70; faculty U. Calif. Extension at San Diego, 1967—, San Diego State U. Extension, 1968-71, San Diego Evening Coll., 1967-71; pres. Nat. U., San Diego, 1971—. Bd. dirs. Nat. Def. U. Found., San Diego council Boy Scouts Am. Mem. Nat. Mgmt. Assn. (exec. adv. com., Golden Knight award 1979), Convair Nat. Mgmt. Assn. (hon. life), Am. Assn. of Presidents of Ind. Colls. and Univs., Naval Res. Assn. (life), Navy League U.S. (life, nat. dir.; Scroll of Honor 1979), Res. Officers Assn. (life, mem. pvt. sector council Washington). Clubs: San Diego Yacht, Kona Kai, Cuyamaca, University (San Diego); Army-Navy, Capitol Hill (Washington). Office: Nat Univ University Park San Diego CA 92108-4194

CHIKALLA, THOMAS DAVID, science facility administrator; b. Milw., Sept. 9, 1935; s. Paul Joseph and Margaret Ann (Dittrich) C.; m. Ruth Janet Laun, June 20, 1960; children: Paul, Mark, Karyn. BS in Metallurgy, U. Wis., 1957, PhD in Metallurgy, 1966; MS in Metallurgy, U. Idaho, 1960. Research scientist Gen. Electric Co., Richland, Wash., 1957-62; sr. research scientist Battelle Pacific N.W. Labs., Richland, 1964-72, sect. mgr., 1972-80, programs mgr., 1980-83, dept. mgr., 1983-86, assoc. dir., 1986—; tchr. U. Wis., Madison, 1962-64. Contbr. articles to profl. jours. Fellow AEC. Fellow Am. Ceramic Soc. (counselor 1974-80); mem. AAAS, Am. Nuclear Soc., Sigma Xi. Republican. Roman Catholic. Clubs: Desert Ski (pres. 1958-59), Alpine. Avocations: skiing, golfing, woodworking, mountain climbing. Home: 2108 Harris Richland WA 99352 Office: Battelle Pacific NW Labs Battelle Blvd Richland WA 99352

CHILCOTE, ROBERT RALPH, pediatrician, educator; b. Cleve., Oct. 8, 1941; s. Ralph E. and Margaret A. (Fisher) C.; m. Denise Buckley; children: Kelly, Krista, Ryan. AB, Cornell U., 1963; MD, U. Rochester, 1969. Diplomate Am. Bd. Pediatrics. Intern in pediatrics Strong Meml. Hosp. U. Rochester, N.Y., 1969-70, resident in pediatrics, 1970-71, chief resident in pediatrics, 1971-72; fellow in pediatric hematology James Whitcomb Riley Hosp. for Children Ind. U. Sch. Medicine, Indpls., 1972-75; practice medicine specializing in pediatric hematology and oncology Chgo., 1975-84; dir. div. pediatric hematology Michael Reese Hosp. and Med. Ctr., Chgo., 1975-77; co-dir. div. pediatric hematology-oncology Wyler Children's Hosp., Chgo., 1977-84; asst. prof. dept. pediatrics Pritzker Sch. Medicine U. Chgo., 1975-84; dir. pediatric oncology, assoc. prof. pediatrics U. Calif., Irvine, 1984—. Contbr. articles to profl. jours. Mem. Am. Acad. Pediatrics (sect. on oncology-hematology), Am. Cancer Soc., Am. Soc. Clin. Oncology, Am. Soc. Hematology. Office: U Calif Med Sci C237 Irvine CA 92715

CHILCOTE, RONALD HODELL, political science educator, author; b. Cleve., Feb. 20, 1935; s. Lee Alfred and Katherine (Hodell) C.; m. Frances Tubby, Jan. 6, 1961; children: Stephen, Edward. BA, Dartmouth Coll., 1957; MBA, Stanford U., 1957, MA, 1963, PhD, 1965; Diploma Superior, U. Lisbon, Portugal, 1960; Diploma Estudios Hispanicos, U. Madrid, 1961. Instr. polit. sci. Stanford (Calif.) U., 1961-63, asst. prof., 1963-70, assoc. prof., 1970-75; prof. polit. sci. U. Calif., Riverside, 1975—. Author: Brazilian Communist Party, 1974, Theories of Comparative Politics, 1981, Theories of Development, 1984; editor: Protest and Resist in Angola and Brazil, 1972; mng. editor Latin Am. Perspectives, 1974—. Pres. Temple Hills Community Assn., Laguna Beach, Calif., 1974—; trustee Laguna Beach Unified Sch. Dist., 1975-83, pres. bd. trustees, 1978-80, 82-83; bd. dirs. Laguna Greenbelt Inc., Laguna Beach, 1978—. Recipient Fulbright Sr. Lectureship, 1983, 84; grantee N.Y. Social Sci. Research Council, OAS. Mem. Am. Polit. Sci. Assn., Latin Am. Studies Assn. Democrat. Home: 1940 San Remo Dr Laguna Beach CA 92651 Office: U Calif Dept Polit Sci Riverside CA 92521

CHILD, ARTHUR JAMES EDWARD, food company executive; b. Guildford, Eng., May 19, 1910; s. William Arthur and Helena (Wilson) C.; m. Mary Gordon, Dec. 10, 1955. B.Commerce, Queen's U., 1931, LL.D., 1983; grad., Advanced Mgmt. Program, Harvard, 1956; M.A., U. Toronto, 1960, LL.D., 1984; LL.D., U. Calgary, 1984. Chief auditor Can. Packers Ltd., 1938-52, v.p., 1952-60; pres. Intercontinental Packers Ltd., 1960-66; chmn., chief exec. officer, dir. Burns Foods Ltd., Calgary, Alta., 1966—; chmn. bd., dir. Can. West Found. A.R. Clarke & Co. Ltd.; chmn. bd., dir. Scott Nat. Co., Ltd.; chmn. Ajex Investments Ltd.; pres. Jamar Inc.; chmn. ACF Grew Inc., bd. dirs. Newsco Investments Ltd., Nova, an Alta., Corp., Canoe Cove Mfg. Ltd., Grove Valve & Regulator Co., Nova Energy Systems Inc., Imperial Trust Co.; asso. prof. U. Sask., 1964-65. Author: Economics and Politics in United States Banking, 1965, (with B. Cadmus) Internal Control, 1953. chmn. Can. West Found.; pres. RHW Found. Decorated Order of Can. Fellow Chartered Inst. Secs.; mem. Can. Meat Council (past pres.), Inst. Internal Auditors (past pres.), Am. Mgmt. Assn., Inst. for Strategic Studies. Office: PO Box 2520 Sta M, Calgary, AB Canada T2P 3X4

CHILD, PAUL LORIN, dentist; b. Clinton, Utah, Sept. 14, 1940; s. John Theodore and A. Katherine Child; m. Mary Margaret Ginn, June 7, 1963; children—Michael D., John T., David S., Mark B., Melissia A., Paul Lorin, Cassandra, Jennifer, Thomas. Cert. completion Weber Jr. Coll., 1960; B.S., Brigham Young U., 1966; D.D.S., Northwestern U., 1967. Gen. practice dentistry, Ogden, Utah, 1970—; dental health rep. Weber County Dental Assn., Ogden, 1975-77; lectr. continuing edn. U. Utah, Salt Lake City, 1972, Ogden City Schs., 1970—, civic groups, 1970—. Author: John L. Child, 1978; co-author: Genealogy of Child, Childe, Childs, 1980, Childe and Bradshawe Genealogy, 1986. Contbr. articles to profl. jours. Explorer chmn. Boy Scouts Am.; voting dist. chmn., county del., state del., 1974—; presdl. elector Utah; mem. Utah Rep. Com. 1974—, Rep. Nat. Com., 1980—. Served to capt. U.S. Army, 1967-70. Recipient Scouters Key, Scouters Tng. award, Explorers Tng. award, Explorers Key, Commrs. Arrowhead award, 25 Yrs. Vets. award, award of merit Boy Scouts Am. Mem. ADA, Acad. Gen. Dentistry (continuing edn. com. 1973—), Am. Profl. Practice Assn., Am. Preventive Dentistry Assn., Weber Dist. Dental Soc., Utah Dental Assn. (ho. of dels. 1978-83). Mormon. Home: 3787 Jackson Ave Ogden UT 84403 Office: 3785 Harrison Blvd Suite 1 Ogden UT 84403

CHILDRESS, DENNIS ROBERT, municipal protective service administrator; b. South Gate, Calif., Oct. 3, 1945; s. Robert Wier and Janice Alicia (Sayles) C.; m. Suzanne Dietrich, Dec. 12, 1970; children: Bryan, Scott, Lara. AA in Fire Sci., Long Beach City Coll., 1975; BS in Indsl. Tech.-Fire Protection Adminstrn., Calif. State U., Los Angeles, 1978. Cert. fire officer, tchr., Calif. Firefighter Lynwood (Calif.) Fire Dept., 1967-76, apparatus engr., 1976-79, fire capt., battalion chief, 1970-85; dir. tng. and safety Buena Park (Calif.) Fire Dept., 1985—; instr. Rancho Community Coll., Santa Ana, Calif., 1981—, State Fire Marshal, Santa Ana, 1984—; cons., 1979—. Author articles in field. Coach Am. Youth Soccer Orgn., Orange County, 1979-85; vice chmn. Orange County Tng. and Edn. com., 1986—; instr. CPR Orange County ARC; developer, coordinator Smoke Detector Program for Sr. Citizens, Lynwood, Fire Flow Research Program, Lynwood. Mem. So. Calif. Tng. Officers Assn., Orange County Fire Chief's Tng. Officers Assn. (sec. treas. bd. dirs. 1987—), Calif. State Firefighter's Assn., Lynwood Firefighters Assn. (bd.dirs. 1979-82, v.p. 1980, pres. and chmn. bd. dirs. 1981), Epsilon Pi Tau. Republican. Avocations: outdoor activities, camping, fishing, sports. Office: Buena Park Fire Dept 8081 Western Ave Buena Park CA 90622

CHILDRESS, PHYLLIS ANN, construction executive; b. Fort Wayne, Ind., Feb. 28, 1937; d. Paschal J. and Pietrina M. (Ceccanese) Pallone; m. Kelly W. Childress, Aug. 24, 1973; children: Patricia, William, Jeffrey. B.S. in Commerce, Internat. Coll., 1955; postgrad. Pima Community Coll., 1978-80. Cert. constrn. assoc. Sec. to v.p. trust dept. Lincoln Nat. Bank, Ft. Wayne, Ind., 1955-57; sec. to pres. adminstrn. dept. Internat. Coll., Ft. Wayne, 1957-60; dir., sec. Lightning Homes, Inc., Homebuilders and Developers, Ft. Wayne, 1960-63; sec. to v.p., fin. dept., office mgr. fleet maintenance dept. N.Am. Van Lines, Inc., Ft. Wayne, 1963-71; asst. mktg. dir. ITT Electro-Optical Products, Ft. Wayne, 1972-76; asst. v.p. Empire West Builders, Inc., Tucson, 1977-80; staff constrn. mgmt. Akins Co., Tucson, 1981-82; constrn. mgr. Archtl. Div., City of Tucson, 1982-85; pres. Construction Techniques, Inc., Tucson, 1985—. Recipient Appreciation Cert. Nat. Assn. Women Constrn., 1978; named Sec. of yr. Tawasi chpt. Nat. Secs. Assn., 1967, Woman of Yr., 1986; recipient plaque for outstanding service, 1977. Mem. Bus. and Profl. Women (past chpt. pres.), Nat. Assn. Women Constrn. (past pres.). Democrat. Baptist. Contbr. articles to various publs. Home: 2833 N Laurel Ave Tucson AZ 85712 Office: Constrn Techniques Inc 2833 N Laurel Ave Tucson AZ 85712

CHILDS, ALLAN HAROLD, chemistry educator; b. Manchester, Iowa, June 20, 1948; s. Harold Wilbert and Gladys Caroline (Woeste) C.; m. Cynthia Ann Newbury, May 25, 1975; children: Graham, Dana. BS, Iowa State U., 1970; MS, Kans. State U., 1973, PhD, 1980. Asst. prof. Ripon (Wis.) Coll., 1980-85; asst. prof. chemistry N.W. Community Coll., Powell, Wyo., 1985—; vis. asst. prof. U. Wis., Milw., 1983, Kans. State U., Manhattan, 1984. Grantee Kans. Agrl. Experiment Sta., Manhattan, 1976-78, Ripon Coll., 1984-85. Mem. Am. Chem. Soc., Sigma Xi., Alpha Chi Sigma, Phi Lambda Upsilon. Methodist. Avocations: woodworking, refinishing antique furniture. Office: Northwest Community Coll 231 W 6th St Powell WY 82435

CHILDS, JOHN DAVID, computer hardware and services company executive; b. Washington, Apr. 26, 1939; s. Edwin Carlton and Catherine Dorothea (Angerman) C.; m. Margaret Rae Olsen, Mar. 4, 1966 (div.); 1 child, John-David; m. Carole Mae Albert, July 21, 1984. Student Principia Coll., 1957-58, 59-60; BA, Am. U., 1963. Jr. adminstr. Page Communications, Washington, 1962-65; account rep. Frieden Inc., Washington, 1965-67; Western sales dir. Data Inc., Arlington, Va., 1967-70; v.p. mktg. Rayda, Inc., Los Angeles, 1970-73, pres., 1973-76, chmn. bd., 1976-84; sr. v.p. sales Exec. Bus. Systems, Encino, Calif., 1981—; sr. assoc. World Trade Assocs., Inc., 1976—. Pres. Coll. Youth for Nixon-Lodge, 1959-60, dir. state fedn.; mem. OHSHA policy formulation com. Dept. Labor, 1967. Served with USAFR, 1960-66. Mem. Assn. Data Ctr. Owners and Mgrs. (chmn. privacy com. 1975, sec. 1972-74, v.p. 1974). Democrat. Christian Scientist. Office: 15760 Ventura Blvd #900 Encino CA 91436

CHILDS, MARJORIE M., lawyer; b. N.Y.C., July 13, 1918; d. Charles W. and Eva M. (Tarrant) C. Student Hunter Coll., 1942-46; BA in Econs., U. Calif., Berkeley, 1948; JD, U. San Francisco, 1956; LLD (hon.), Iowa Wesleyan Coll., 1973. Bar: Calif. 1957, U.S. Supreme Ct. 1969. With Office of Regional Counsel, U.S. Navy, Ft. Mason, Calif., 1957-60; asst. county counsel Humboldt County, Calif., 1960-62; sole practice, San Francisco, 1962-64, 79—; referee, commr. Juvenile dept. Superior Ct., San Francisco, 1964-79. Pres. Diamond Heights Community Assn., 1983-84. Recipient James A. Harlan award Iowa Wesleyan Coll., 1969. Fellow Am. Bar Found.; mem. ABA, Internat. Bar Assn., Lawyers Club San Francisco, Queen's Bench (pres. 1967), Bar Assn. San Francisco, Internat. Fedn. Women Lawyers (pres. 1974-75), Nat. Assn. Women Lawyers (pres. 1974-75). Democrat. Episcopalian. Club: Metropolitan (San Francisco). Contbr. articles to profl. jours. Address: 64 Turquoise Way San Francisco CA 94131 Office: 301 Junipero Serra Blvd #260 San Francisco CA 94127

CHILLINSKY, SANDRA JEAN, trucking co. exec.; b. Houston, Aug. 6, 1935; d. Laurence Vernon and Winnie Mae (Pace) Butler; student U. Houston, 1953-54, S. Tex. Law Sch., 1955; m. John Chillinsky, Oct. 12, 1974; children by previous marriage—Claud V. Sherrill, Catherine L. Sherrill. With San Jacinto Fin. Corp., Houston, 1953-54, Guns, Inc., Houston, 1955, Magcobar, Southwestern Indsl. Electronics, Houston, 1956-57; acct. Durban G. Ford, C.P.A., Barstow, Calif., 1960, Dept. Def., Barstow, 1960-61; sec. U.S. Marine Corps Exchange Contracts Div., San Diego, 1961-65; computer analyst, stenographer Rohr Corp., Chula Vista, Calif., 1966-68; office mgr. Mesa Motors, DBA Honda, Lemon Grove, Calif., 1968-72; office mgr. Sky Trucking Co., San Diego 1972—, sec.-treas., 1976—. Trustee, Mark IV Equipment Trust, Alpine Trust, 1978-81. Recipient Cert. of Commendation, Rohr Corp., 1968, 69; Cert. of Recognition, Nat. Republican Congressional Com., 1980. Mem. Cal-West Tariff Bur., Hwy. Carriers Assn., Nat. Right to Work Com., VFW Aux. (trustee, publicity chmn. 1982—). Republican. Lutheran. Office: 187 Mace St Chula Vista CA 92011

CHILTON, MICHAEL WILLIAM, agriculturist, agronomist; b. Iowa City, Iowa, July 31, 1937; s. Allen Ralph and Verna Louise (long) C.; m. Simone Anne-Marie Minh Chau thi Phan, May 31, 1961; 1 child, Richard Paul. BS in Gen. Sci., Iowa State U., 1958, MS in Seed Tech. and Econ. Botany, 1960. Cert. profl. agronomist, pesticide research consultant, Oreg. Team leader, project officer Internat. Vol. Services U.S. Agy for Internat. Devel., Saigon, Republic Vietnam, 1960-65; regional officer DEVCON U.S. Agy for Internat. Devel., Bangkok, 1966-71; gen. mgr. Trade Assocs., Inc., Saigon, 1972-75; v.p. Agriculture Services Corp., Salem, Oreg., 1976-85; pres. Agrl. Alternatives, Turner, Oreg., 1985—; team leader, agronomist, Devel. Alternatives U.S. Agy. Internat. Devel., Maruoa, Cameroon, 1978, cons. Niger, Pakistan; mem. invitational bus. devel. com. China Nat. Seed Corp., Beijing, 1983. Mem. Am. Soc. Agrl. Cons., Am. Soc. Agronomy, Am. Soc. Horticultural Scis., Native Plant Soc. Republican. Club: Willamette Hen House (Salem) (pres. 1984-86). Avocations: collecting old agrl. books, raising exhibition poultry, gardening. Home and Office: 3533 Ridgeway Dr SE Turner OR 97392

CHILTON, SHIRLEY R., state offical. Sec. State and Consumer Services Agy., State of Calif. Office: Office of Sec State and Consumer Services Agy 915 Capitol Mall Suite 200 Sacramento CA 95814 *

CHIMY, JEROME ISIDORE, bishop; b. Radway, Alta., Can., Mar. 12, 1919; s. Stanley and Anna (Yahnij) C. J.C.D., Lateran U., Rome, 1966. Ordained priest Ukrainian Cath. Ch., 1944; consecrated bishop 1974; consultor to Provincial Superior, 1958-61; sec. to Superior Gen. of Basilian Order, Rome, 1961-63; consultor Superior Gen. of Basilian Order, 1963-74; rector St. Josaphat Ukrainian Pontifical Coll., Rome, 1966-74; former consultor to Sacred Congregation for Eastern Chs.; former commissario for matrimonial cases at Sacred Congregation for Doctrine of Faith; bishop of New Westminster B.C., Can., 1974—; consultor to Pontifical Comm. for Revision Oriental Canon Law. Author: De Figura Luridica Archiepiscopi Maioris in Iure Canonico Orientali Vigenti, 1968. Home and office: 502 5th Ave, New Westminister, BC Canada V3L 1S2

CHIN, ARK GEOW, civil engineering executive; b. Toishan, Republic of China, Feb. 9, 1924; came to U.S., 1934; s. Jing Teung and Yu Sung (Lim) C.; m. Winifred Chung, May 6, 1948; children: Candace, Curtis, Patrick, Phoebe, Colin, Wilson. BSCE, U. Wash., 1950, MSCE, 1952. Registered profl. engr., Wash., Oreg., Alaska, Mich., Wis., Iowa, Ill., N.Y., S.C., Kans. Design engr. Richardson Assocs., 1951-52; design engr. Carey & Kramer, Seattle, 1953-61, ptnr., 1961-72; pres. Kramer, Chin & Mayo, Inc., Seattle, 1972—; vis. com. mem. U. Wash. Coll. Engring., 1976-79. Contbr. articles to profl. jours. Mem. Am. Cons. Engrs. Council's Minority Affairs Com., 1979-81. Served to sft. U.S. Army, 1943-46. Named Engr. of Yr., Seattle Chinese Engrs. Soc., 1984. Fellow Am. Concrete Inst.; mem. ASCE, Nat. Panel Am. Arbitration Assn., Structural Engrs. Assoc. Wash., Pre-Stress Concrete Inst., Am. Pub. Works. Assn., Cons. Engring. Council Wash. (pres. 1982-83), Gee How Oak Tin Assn. (pres. 1960—). Mem. Christian Ch. Club: Wash. Athletic. Avocations: golf, reading, investments. Office: Kramer Chin May Inc 1917 First Ave Seattle WA 98101

CHIN, EDWARD JIN-HUNG, physician; b. Hong Kong, Sept. 3, 1930; m. Mary Lo-Van; children—Holman Edward, Elaine Mary. B.Sc., McGill U., 1955, M.D., C.M., 1959. Diplomate Am. Bd. Ob-Gyn. Intern St. Michael Hosp., Toronto, Ont., Can., 1959-60; resident Bethany Meth. Hosp., Chgo., 1960; ob-gyn officer Queen Mary Hosp., Hong Kong, 1961; Kwong Wah Hosps., Hong Kong, 1968-69; ob-gyn resident Kapiolani Ob-Gyn Hosp., Honolulu, 1961-62, Kaiser Hosp., Oakland, Calif., 1962-64; instr. children's Hosp., San Francisco, 1964-65; surgery resident East Toronto Gen. Hosp., 1965-66; staff physician Raxlen Clinic, Toronto, 1966; chief emergency room dept. Fairmont Hosp., San Leandro, Calif, 1969; practice medicine specializing in ob-gyn, San Leandro, 1969-71, Oakland, Calif., 1971. Fellow Am. Coll. Ob-Gyn. Club: Lakeview. Office: 320 8th St Suite 1D Oakland CA 94607 Address: 320 8th St Suite 1-D Oakland CA 94607

CHIN, JANET SAU-YING, data processing executive, consultant; b. Hong Kong, July 27, 1949; came to U.S., 1959; d. Arthur Quock-Ming and Jenny (Loo) C. BS in Math, U. Ill., Chgo., 1970; MS in Computer Sci., U. Ill., Urbana, 1972. System programmer Lawrence Livermore (Calif.) Lab., 1972-79; sect. mgr. Tymshare Inc., Cupertino, Calif., 1979-83, Fortune Systems, Redwood City, Calif., 1983-85; div. mgr. Impell Corp, Berkeley, Calif., 1985; pres. Chin Assocs., Oakland, Calif., 1985—; Vice-chmn. Am. Nat. Standards Inst. X3H3, N.Y.C., 1979-82, internat. rep. X3H3, 1982—. Author tech. papers to profl. publs. Mem. Assn. Computing Machinery, Nat. Computer Graphics Assn., World Computer Graphics Assn., Eurographics Assn., Sigma Xi. Avocations: piano, karate, iaido, racquetball, tennis.

CHIN, KIM HOCK, public relations consultant; b. Singapore, Mar. 25, 1957; came to U.S., 1979; s. Richard K.H. and Bobbie J.E. (Ou) C.; m. Virginia Marie Rentschler, June 19, 1984. BJ, U. Oreg., 1983. Account exec. Cawood Communications, Eugene, Oreg., 1983; gen. mgr. King Design Inc., Eugene, 1983-85; mktg. coordinator C-Tran, Vancouver, Wash., 1986—; cons. mktg. communications, Portland, Oreg., 1985—. Author: Singaporean Literature in Perspective, 1980. Vol. fundraiser Tualatin (Oreg.) Valley Bod Ctr., 1986. Mem. Internat. Trade and Communications Inst. (chmn. pub. relations com. 1985—), Chartered Inst. Secs. and Adminstrs. (assoc.), Pub. Relations Soc. Am., Ad 2, Portland Advt. Fedn., Met. Ethnic Minority Execs. Coalition, Chinese C. of C. Club: Singapore Island Country. Avocations: automobiles, haute cuisine, body building, reading. Home and Office: 2316 NW Quimby Portland OR 97210

CHIN, PENNY, interior designer; b. N.Y.C., Feb. 29, 1948; d. Peter and Celia (Goon) Chu; m. Chester Chin, May 1967 (div.); children: Wendy, Michelle, Kenneth, Cynthia, Karina. AS in Interior Design with honors, Canada Coll., 1984. New accounts teller Lincoln Savs., Bklyn., 1965-66; exec. sec. Stauffer chem. Co., N.Y.C., 1966-69; kitchen sales designer KBA Design, Palo Alto, Calif., 1982-84; designer, planner PC Design Assocs., Hillsborough, Calif., 1984—. Dir. health edn. San Francisco Med. Soc., 1980-81; coordinator health lectrs. Am. Cancer Soc., San Mateo, Calif., 1981. Named Miss N.Y. Chinatown, 1965, Miss Congeniality Miss USA Chinatown, 1966. Fellow Am. Soc. Interior Designers (sec. student chpt. 1982), Internat. Soc. Interior Designers. Avocation: tennis. Home and Office: 1060 Crystal Springs Rd Hillsborough CA 94010

CHIN, SUE S. (SUCHIN), artist, photographer, community affairs activist; b. San Francisco; d. William W. and Soo-Up (Swebe) Chin; grad. Calif. Coll. Art, Mpls. Art Inst., (scholar) Schaeffer Design Center; student Yasuo Kuniyoshi, Louis Hamon, Rico LeBrun. Photojournalist, All Together Now show, 1973, East-West News, Third World Newscasting, 1975-78, KNBC Sunday Show, Los Angeles, 1975, 76, Live on 4, 1981, Bay Area Scene, 1981; graphics printer, exhbns. include Kaiser Center, Zellerbach Plaza, Chinese Culture Center Galleries, Chinese Culture Center Galleries, Capricorn Asunder Art Commn. Gallery (all San Francisco), Newspace Galleries, New Coll. of Calif., Los Angeles County Mus. Art, Peace Plaza Japan Center, Calif. Mus. Sci. and Industry, Lucien Labaudt Gallery, Sacramento State Fair, AFL-CIO Labor Studies Center, Washington, Asian Women Artists (1st prize for conceptual painting, 1st prize photography), 1978; represented in permanent collections Los Angeles County Fedn. Labor, Calif. Mus. Sci. and Industry, AFL-CIO Labor Studies Center, Australian Trades Council, Hazeland and Co., also pvt. collections. Del. nat., state convs. Nat. Women's Polit. Caucus, 1977-83, San Francisco chpt. affirmative action chairperson, 1978-82, nat. conv. del., 1978-81, Calif. del., 1976-81. Recipient Honorarium AFL-CIO Labor Studies Center, Washington, 1975-76; award Centro Studi Ricerche delle Nazioni, Italy, 1985; bd. advisors Psycho Neurology Found. Bicentennial award Los Angeles County Mus. Art, 1976, 77, 78. Mem. Asian Women Artists (founding v.p., award 1978-79, 1st award in photography of Orient 1978-79), Calif. Chinese Artists (sec.-treas. 1978-81), Japanese Am. Art Council (chairperson 1978-84, dir.), San Francisco Women Artists, San Francisco Graphics Guild, Pacific/Asian Women Coalition Bay Area, Chinatown Council Performing and Visual Arts. Chmn., Full Moon Products; pres., dir. Aumni Oracle Inc. Featured in Calif. Living Mag., 1981; subject of documentary KGO-TV, 1982. Address: PO Box 1415 San Francisco CA 94101

CHING, ALAN S.L., media director; b. Honolulu, Aug. 23, 1953; s. Anthony D.K. and Amy K.C. (Chong) C. AB with honors, Stanford U., 1975; MBA, U. Chgo., 1977. Asst. media planner Foote Cone & Belding, San Francisco, 1977-78, media planner, 1978-82; media supr. Ogilvy & Mather, San Francisco, 1982-83; assoc. media dir., media research dir. Hal Riney & Ptnrs. (formerly Ogilvy & Mather), San Francisco, 1983—. Prin. flautist with San Francisco Park and Recreation Symphony and Peninsula Symphonic Band. Office: Hal Riney & Ptnrs 735 Battery St San Francisco CA 94111

CHING, CHAUNCEY TAI KIN, agriculture and human resources organization administrator; b. Honolulu, July 25, 1940; m. Theodora Lam, July 7, 1962; children: Donna, Cory. AB in Econs., U. Calif., Berkeley, 1962; MS in Agrl. Econs., U. Calif., Davis, 1965, PhD in Agrl. Econ., 1967. Assoc. prof. U. N.H., Durham, 1968-72; asst. prof. U. Nev., Reno, 1969-72, assoc. prof., 1972-77, prof., head div. agrl. and resource econs., 1972-80; prof., chmn. dept. agrl. and resource econs. U. Hawaii, Honolulu, 1980-84; dir. Hawaii Inst. Tropical Agrl. and Human Resources, Honolulu, 1984—. Recipient Charles H. Seurferle award U. Nev., Reno, 1977. Office: Hawaii Inst Tropical Agriculture 3050 Maile Way Gilmore 202 Honolulu HI 96822

CHING, ERIC SAN HING, health care and insurance administrator; b. Honolulu, Aug. 13, 1951; s. Anthony D.K. and Amy K.C. (Chong) C. BS, Stanford U., 1973, MS, MBA, 1977. Fin. analyst Mid Peninsula Health Service, Palo Alto, Calif., 1977; acting dep. exec. dir. Santa Clara County Health Systems Agy., San Jose, Calif., 1977-78; program officer Henry J. Kaiser Family Found., Menlo Park, Calif., 1978-84; dir. strategic planning Lifeguard Health Maintenance Orgn., Campbell, Calif., 1984—; dir. ops. Found. Life Ins. Co., Calif., 1986—; cons. El Camino Dialysis Service, Mountain View, Calif., 1984. Mem. vol. staff Los Angeles Olympic Organizing Com., 1984; mem. panel United Way of Santa Clara County, 1985, panel chmn., 1986-87. Mem. Stanford U. Alumni Assn., Stanford U. Bus. Sch. Alumni Assn., Stanford U. Swordmasters (pres. 1980—). Avocations: fencing, volleyball, piano playing and composition, photography, travel. Office: Lifeguard HMO Inc 1715 S Bascom Ave Campbell CA 95008

CHING, FRANCIS F. T., horticulturist; b. Honolulu, May 30, 1930; s. Akui C. and Ruth C.; m. Elaine Young., Dec. 27, 1958; children—Byron Alan, Daryl Lane. B.S., Mich. State U., 1951, M.S., 1956. Mem. staff Los Angeles State and County Arboretum, 1956-70, supt., 1967-70; dir. Los Angeles County Dept. Arboreta and Bot. Gardens, 1970—; Mem. U.S. Nat. Arboretum Adv. Council. Mem. sci. adv. council Calif. Poly. State U.; panelist Sunset Mag. and Book Co. Served with USAR, 1953-55. Mem. Am. Assn. Bot. Gardens and Arboreta (pres. 1979-81, hon. life), Am. Hort. Soc., Am. Soc. Hort. Scis., Zool. Soc. San Diego, Los Angeles Beautiful. Clubs: Men's Garden (Los Angeles); Arcadia Rotary. Home: 821 St John Pl Claremont CA 91711 Office: Los Angeles State & Co Arboretum 301 N Baldwin Ave Arcadia CA 91006 *

CHING, LARRY FONG CHOW, constrn. co. exec.; b. Honolulu, Mar. 15, 1912; s. Dung Sen and Dai (Chong) C.; B.C.E., U. Hawaii, 1935; postgrad. U. Utah Sch. Mining Engring., 1938-39; m. Beatrice Jook Yee Fong, Aug. 6, 1944; children—Randall Ming-Yu, Thalia Ping-Hsia. Instr. math. and engring. U. Yunan, Kunming, China, 1935-37; engr. Moses Akiona, Contractor, 1939-42, 45; supr. roads and airport constrn. U.S. Corps Engrs., 1942-44; mgr. Universal Contracting Co., 1945-47; constrn. supt. Associated Builders, 1948-49; pres., gen. mgr. Hwy. Constrn. Co., Ltd., Honolulu, 1949—; dir. Hawaii Franchise No-Joint Concrete Pipe, Hawaii Contractor's License Bd., 1960-63; pres., dir. Constrn. Industry Legis. Orgn., 1977-78; sub-chmn. design constrn. and maintenance Hawaii Hwy. Safety Council. Pres., Larry and Beatrice Ching Found; pres., dir. Hawaii Chinese History Center, 1971; pres. Hawaii Heritage Center, 1982-83. Registered profl. engr., Hawaii. Mem. Asso. Gen. Contractors Am. (dir., treas. 1983), Gen. Contractors Assn. Hawaii (pres. 1968, dir.), Soc. Am. Mil. Engrs., Honolulu, Chinese (dir., pres. 1971-72), Hawaii (dir.) chambers commerce, Honolulu Better Bus. Bur., Friends of East-West Center, United Chinese Soc. (pres. 1980—), Tu Chiang Sheh (pres.). Home: 18 Kimo Dr Honolulu HI 96817 Office: 720 Umi St Honolulu HI 96819 *

CHINN, THOMAS WAYNE, typographic company executive; b. Marshfield, Oreg., July 28, 1909; s. Wing Chin and Shee Lee; student U. Calif.; m. Daisy Lorraine Wong, June 8, 1930; 1 son, Walter Wayne Chinn. Propr., Chinn Linotype Co., San Francisco, 1937-42; owner Calif. Typesetting Co., 1949-56; typographer, 1956-71; pres. Gollan Typography, Inc., San Francisco, 1971-80. Mem. San Francisco Mayor's Citizens Com., 1958—; mem. San Francisco Twin Bicentennial History Com., 1974-76; mem. Nat. Am. Revolution Bicentennial Advisory Com. on Racial, Ethnic and Native Am. Participation, 1974-76; governing mem. San Francisco YMCA, 1972-82; founding pres., Chinese Hist. Soc. Am., San Francisco, 1963, pres., 1964-66, 75; foreman Civil Grand Jury, City and County of San Francisco, 1983-84. Recipient awards of merit Conf. Calif. Socs., 1976, 81, Am. Assn. State and Local History, 1976. Mem. Calif. Hist. Soc. (award of merit 1970, trustee 1981-83), E Clampus Vitus, The Westerners. Clubs: Masons (32 deg.) (past master lodge), Shriners. Editor: A History of the Chinese in California-A Syllabus, 1969; editor, co-pub. 1st newspaper in English for Chinese-Ams., 1935-37; contbr. articles to hist. jours.

CHIOU, CARY TSAIR, environmental scientist, hydrologist; b. Miaoli, Taiwan, Nov. 22, 1940; came to U.S. 1968, naturalized 1977; s. Jen-Wen and Shih-Mei (Hsu) C.; m. Chao-Chih Ho, Aug. 1, 1968; children—Lisa A, Brenda K. B.S. in Engring., Cheng Kung U., Taiwan, 1965; M.S., Kent State U., 1970, Ph.D., 1973. Research Assoc. Brown U., Providence, 1973-74, U. Ky., Lexington, 1974-75; sr. research assoc. Oreg. State U., Corvallis, 1975-78; asst. prof., 1978-81, assoc. prof., 1981-83; research hydrologist U.S. Geol. Survey, Denver, 1983—; cons. on environ. guidelines FDA, Washington, 1983; lecturer, cons. UN devel. programs in China, Nanjing, 1983. Contbr. articles to profl. jours. Grantee NSF, EPA, Nat. Inst. Environ. Health Sci. Mem. AAAS, Am. Chem. Soc., Internat. Humic Substances Soc., Sigma Xi. Home: 5260 Tabor St Arvada CO 80002 Office: US Geological Survey 5293 Ward Rd Arvada CO 80002

CHIS, JOHN EDWARD, sales executive; b. Cleve., Aug. 15, 1956; s. John Joseph and Vivian (Embrecia) C.; m. Julie Ann Quilter, Aug. 23, 1980; children: John Joseph, Jaimie Ann. BA, U. Akron, 1978. Sr. sales rep. Telxon Corp., Akron, Ohio, 1980-82, regional sales mgr., 1982-84; v.p. sales, western div. Telxon Corp., Akron and Buena Park (Calif.), 1984—. Named Number 1 Salesman Telxon Corp., 1982, Man of Yr., Telxon Corp., 1983. Mem. Sorin Soc. U. Notre Dame, Jonathan Jacques Cancer Soc. Republican. Roman Catholic. Office: Telxon Corp 6556 Caballero Blvd Buena Park CA 90620

CHISHOLM, DONALD WILLIAM, political science educator; b. Coronado, Calif., July 16, 1953; s. William Kaiser and Mary Katherine (Carmichael) C. AB, U. Calif., Berkeley, 1975, MA, 1977, PhD, 1984. Instr. Mich. State U., East Lansing, 1983-84; vis. lectr. U. Calif. San Diego, La Jolla, 1984-86; asst. prof. Ohio State U., Columbus, 1986—; vis. asst. prof. U. Calif., Berkeley, 1986-87. Contbr. articles to profl jours. Recipient Leonard D. White award Am. Polit. Sci. Assn., 1985. Mem. Am. Soc. Pub. Adminstrn., Am. Polit. Sci. Assn., Phi Beta Kappa. Avocations: surfing, backpacking, car restoration, gardening. Home: 206 Purdue Ave Kensington CA 94708 Office: U Calif Inst Govtl Studies Berkeley CA 94720

CHITTICK, DONALD ERNEST, chemist, consultant; b. Salem, Oreg., May 3, 1932; s. Ernest Stanley and Laura Martina (Jorgensen) C.; m. Donna May Wright, Aug. 25, 1957; children: Anna Laurene, Peter Stanley (dec.). BS, Willamette U., 1954; PhD, Oreg. State U., 1960. From instr. to asst. prof. U. Puget Sound, Tacoma, 1958-68; prof. chemistry George Fox Coll., Newberg, Oreg., 1968-79; dir. research and devel. Pyrenco Inc., Prossor, Wash., 1979-82; cons. Chittick and Assocs., Newberg, 1982—. Author: The Controversy, 1985; patentee chem. waste disposal, and programmed instruction chem. edn., alt. fuels. Republican. Avocations: fishing, outdoors.

CHITTUM, ROGER DEAN, lawyer, consultant; b. Millersburg, Ohio, Mar. 21, 1939; s. John William and Alma Pearl (Spencer) C.; m. Elizabeth Ann Johnson, July 6, 1963 (div. 1970); m. Susan Frances Kovacs, Dec. 10, 1978. A.B. in Chemistry, Coll. Wooster, 1962; LL.B., Stanford U., 1966. Bar: D.C. 1967, Calif. 1973, U.S. Supreme Ct. 1971. Assoc. Cleary, Gottlieb, Steen & Hamilton, Washington, 1966-71; asst. to pres. Tosco Corp., Los Angeles, 1972-73, v.p., 1973-80, sr. v.p., 1981-83; sole practice, Los Angeles, 1984-85; ptnr. Rosenberg, Chittum & Hobbet, 1985—; lawyer, cons. mgmt. environ. affairs, govt. relations. Office: 10951 W Pico Blvd Suite 300 Los Angeles CA 90064

CHIU, ARTHUR NANG LICK, engineering educator; b. Singapore, Mar. 9, 1929; came to U.S., 1948; s. S.J. and Y.N. (Wong) C.; m. Katherine N. Chang, June 12, 1952; children: Vicky, Gregory. BSCE, BA, Oreg. State U., 1952; MSCE, MIT, 1953; PhD in Structural Engring., U. Fla., 1961. Instr. U. Hawaii, Honolulu, 1953-54, asst. prof., 1954-59, assoc. prof., 1959-64, chmn. dept. civil engring., 1963-66; prof. structural engring. Colo. State U. (on assignment to Asian Inst. Tech., Bangkok, Thailand), 1966-68; acting assoc. dean research, tng. and fellowships grad. div. U. Hawaii, Monoa, 1968; assoc. dean research, tng. and fellowships grad. div. U. Hawaii, Manoa, 1972-76, prof. civil engring., 1964—; research specialist Space and Info. Systems div. N.Am. Aviation, Inc. (now Rockwell Internat.), Downey, Calif.; vis. scholar UCLA and vis. assoc. Calif. Inst. Tech., Pasadena, 1970; vis. research scientist Naval Civil Engring. Lab., Port Hueneme, Calif., 1976-77; mem. several univ. coms., U. Hawaii. Contbr. articles to profl. jours. NSF research grantee 1970—. Fellow ASCE (mem. team that surveyed damage caused by Kaoiki earthquake, 1983, mem. task com. on turbulence, past. pres. Hawaii sect.); mem. NSPE, NRC (leader of team that surveyed and reported damage caused by Hurricane Iwa 1982, mem. com. on natural disasters 1985-88, com. vice-chmn. 1986-87), Am. Concrete Inst. (assoc. mem. Response of bldgs. to lateral forces com.), Structural Engrs. Assn. of Hawaii (coordinator, lectr. Wind Engring. Design Seminar 1984, co-chmn. annual state convs. 1983, 84, Conv. of Western State Council of Structural Engrs. Assns. 1979, v.p. 1981, pres. 1982), Am. Soc. Engring. Edn., Earthquake Engring. Research Inst., Wind Engring. Research Council Inc., Internat. Conf. on Engring. for Protection Against Natural Disasters (mem. internat. steering com. 1980), Pan-Pacific Tall Bldgs. Conf. (gen. chmn. 1975), Hawaii State Dept. Transp. Research Com., Sigma Xi (mem. com. internat. membership 1978-85), Chi Epsilon (nat. pres. 1986-88, Pacific dist. councilor 1982—, faculty advisor to U. Hawaii chpt.), Pi Mu Epsilon, Phi Eta Sigma, Tau Beta Pi, Phi Kappa Phi. Home: 1654 Paula Dr Honolulu HI 96816 Office: U Hawaii Monoa Dept Civil Engring 2540 Dole St Honolulu HI 96822

CHIU, JOHN TANG, physician; b. Macao, Jan. 8, 1938; s. Lan Cheong and Yau Hoon C.; m. Bonnie Doolan, Aug. 28, 1965 (div. Apr. 1986); children: Lisa, Mark, Heather. Student, Harvard U., 1959; BA, U. Vermont, 1960, MD, 1964. Diplomate Am. Bd. Allergy & Immunology. Pres. Allergy Med. Group, Inc., Newport Beach, Calif., 1969-72, 1972—; asst. clin. prof. med. U. Calif., Irvine, 1975—. Contbr. articles to profl. jours. Active Santa Ana Heights Adv. Commn., 1982-83. Recipient Freshman Chem. Achievement award, Am. Chem. Soc., 1958. Fellow Am. Acad. Allergy and Immunology, Am. Coll. Allergists, Am. Coll. Chest Physicians (sec. steering com. allergy 1977-81), Am. Assn. Allergy and Clin. Immunology, Orange County Med. Assn. (chmn. mktg. sect. 1985—, communications task force), Newport Med. Plaza Assn. (bd. dirs.). Avocations: snow skiing, swimming, aerobics, travels, windsurfing. Office: Allergy Med Group Inc 400 Newport Ctr Dr Newport Beach CA 92660

CHIU, PETER YEE-CHEW, physician; b. Republic of China, May 12, 1948; came to U.S., 1965; s. Man Chee and Yiu Ying (Cheng) C. BS, U. Calif., Berkeley, 1969, MPH, 1970, DrPH, 1975; MD, Stanford U., 1983. Diplomate Am. Bd. Family Practice; registered profl. engr., Calif.; registered sanitarian, Calif. Asst. civil engr. City of Oakland, Calif., 1970-72; assoc. water quality engr. Bay Area Sewage Services Agy., Berkeley, 1974-76; prin. environ. engr. Assn. Bay Area Govts., Berkeley, 1976-79; resident physician San Jose (Calif.) Hosp., 1983-86; ptnr. Chiu and Crawford, San Jose, 1986—; adj. prof. U. San Francisco, 1979—. Contbr. articles to profl. publs. Mem. Chinese for Affirmative Action, San Francisco, 1975—; bd. dirs. Calif. Regional Water Quality Control Bd., Oakland, 1979-84, Bay Area Comprehensive Health Planning Council, San Francisco, 1972-76. Recipient Resident Tchr. award Soc. Tchrs. Family Medicine, 1986, Resolution of Appreciation award Calif. Regional Water Quality Control Bd., 1985. Mem. Am. Acad. Family Physicians, Am. Pub. Health Assn. Democrat. Avocations: song writing, recording. Office: Chiu and Crawford 1610 Westwood Dr San Jose CA 95125

CHOA, RICHARD CHAN, civil engineer; b. Rangoon, Burma, June 8, 1946; came to U.S., 1971; s. Keng Hong and Kim Tee (Tan) C.; m. Agnes Lee, Aug. 11, 1977; one child, Paul. BEngring., Rangoon Inst. Tech., 1970; MCE, Calif. State U., Los Angeles, 1977. Registered profl. engr., Calif., N.Y. Asst. engr. Kaiser Engrs., Oakland, Calif., 1974-75; sr. engr. C.F. Braun, Alhambra, Calif., 1975-78; design supr. Lockman & Assocs., Monterey Park, Calif., 1978-79; sr. engr. Ralph M. Parsons, Pasadena, Calif., 1979-80; prin. engr. Singmaster & Breyer, N.Y.C., 1980-81; sr. civil engr. Jacobs engring. Group, Pasadena, 1981—. Mem. ASCE. Avocations: tennis, photography, sight seeing. Home: 724 Topacio Dr Monterey Park CA 91754 Office: Jacobs Engring Group 251 S Lake Ave Pasadena CA 91101

CHOATE, EMILY TERESA, theater educator; b. Nashville, May 16, 1953; d. J.E. and Florence Marie (Jones) C.; m. D. Cliff Jewell, Sept. 1983. BA in Communications magna cum laude, David Lipscomb Coll., 1975; student, U. London, 1974; studies with Tony Church, 1975, studies with Patrick Tucker, 1976; MA in Theater, Denver U., 1976; MFA in Directing, Cath. U. Am., Washington, 1981; studies with Cecily Berry, 1982. Assoc. prof., dir. theater dept. Rockmont Coll., Denver, 1977-85, Colo. Christian Coll., Denver, 1985—; mem. Gen. Assembly, Rockmont Coll., 1981-86; chair Artist Lecture Series Selection Com., Rockmont Coll., 1981-83, 85; chair Faculty Senate, Rockmont Coll., 1982-83; mem. Presdl. Search Com., 1982-83; artistic dir. Theatre Parthenos, Nashville, 1983—; dir. Improvisational Players, Denver. Dir. various plays including Fiddler on the Roof and Taming of the Shrew, Lambotte Performance Ctr., Denver, 1977-81; Streamers and Lu Ann Hampton Laverty Oberlander, Callan Theater, Washington, 1979-80; Mark Twain: The Truth Mostly and The Maids, Source Theater, Washington, 1980-81; Antigone, Medea and Oedipus the King, Theatre Parthenos, Nashville, 1983-85; Murder in the Cathedral, St. John's Cath., Denver, 1986. Democrat. Avocation: skiing. Office: Colo Christian Coll 1805 S Garrison Denver CO 80226

CHOCK, ERNEST PHAYNAN, physical chemist; b. Medan, Indonesia, Oct. 27, 1937; came to U.S., 1957; m. Margaret I. Brown, June 18, 1965; children: Diana L., Michael C. BS in Chemistry, Ohio No. U., 1961; MS in Polymer Chemistry, U. Calif., Santa Barbara, 1964, PhD in Phys. Chemistry, 1967. Postdoctoral fellow U. Calif., Santa Barbara, 1967-68; postdoctoral fellow UCLA, 1968-69, from asst. research prof. to research prof. physics, 1970-82; cons. Hughes Aircraft Co., El Segundo, Calif., 1983; staff scientist TRW Corp., Redondo Beach, Calif., 1983—. Contbr. articles to profl. jours. Mem. Chinese-Am. Engring. and Sci. Assn. So. Calif. (program com.), TRW Asian Employees Assn. (v.p. 1986—), Am. Chem. Soc., Am. Phys. Soc., So. Calif. Crystal Growers Assn. Presbyterian. Home: 1048 24th St Santa Monica CA 90403-4528 Office: TRW Corp One Space Park 01/1240 Redondo Beach CA 90278

CHOCK, JAY RICHARD, lawyer; b. York, Pa., Feb. 24, 1955; s. Robert Lee and Ione Nancy (Serata) C. BA in History, Pa. State U., 1977; JD, Lewis & Clark U., 1982. Bar: Oreg. 1983, U.S. Dist. Ct. (Oreg.) 1986. Assoc. Columbia County Dist. Atty's. Office, St. Helen's, Oreg., 1983, Zikes, Kayser, Freed, Smith & Heald, P.C., Portland, Oreg., 1983—. Vol. Big Brother Family Program, York, Pa., 1972-73; active Portland chpt. YMCA. Recipient photography award Kodak Internat. Contest, 1978, Hon. Mention award Kodak Internat. Contest, 1978. Mem. Assn. Trial Lawyers Am., Oreg. Assn. Def. Lawyers. Democrat. Jewish. Avocations: skiing, whitewater rafting, fishing, photography. Office: Zikes Kayser Freed et al 621 SW Morrison St Portland OR 97205

CHODOROW, NANCY JULIA, sociology educator; b. N.Y.C., Jan. 20, 1944; d. Marvin and Leah (Turitz) C.; m. Michael Reich, June 19, 1977; children: Rachel Esther Chodorow-Reich, Gabriel Issac Chodorow-Reich. BA, Radcliffe Coll., 1966; PhD, Brandeis U., 1975. From lectr. to assoc. prof. U. Calif., Santa Cruz, 1974-86; assoc. prof. sociology U. Calif., Berkeley, 1986—. Author: The Reproduction of Mothering, 1978 (Jessie Bernard award 1979); contbr. articles to profl. jours. Fellow Russell Sage Found., NEH, Ctr. Advanced Study Behavioral Scis. Mem. Am. Sociol. Assn., Nat. Women's Studies Assn. Office: U Calif Dept Sociology Barrows Hall Berkeley CA 94720

CHOE, WON-GIL, high tech electronic executive; b. Gang-Nung, Korea, Apr. 24, 1932; s. Chan-Jang and Sook-Ja (Shim) C.; came to U.S., 1957, naturalized, 1970; B.S., Ariz. State U., 1960; M.S., Stanford U., 1962, Ph.D., 1975; m. Mirang Wonne. children: Iliad, Christopher, Charlotte, Scott. Engr. Fairchild Semiconductor, 1962-64; project mgr. Memorex Corp., 1966; mgr. indsl. engring. Internat. Video Corp., 1967-68; v.p. ops. Dole Electro-Systems, Inc., Palo Alto, Calif., 1968-70; v.p. ops. Intellex Corp., Palo Alto, 1970-72; v.p. fin. Vacu-Blast Corp., Belmont, Calif., 1972-74, exec. v.p., 1977-79; pres. Tronic Corp., Belmont, 1973-79; v.p. Applied Implant Tech, Santa Clara, Calif., 1979-81; pres., chief exec. officer Video Logic Corp., Sunnyvale, Calif., 1982—; dir. EEI, Inc., TRI, Inc., Visidata, Inc., Adivan Tech. Inc., Chexel Internat., Inc., Gold Tech., Inc., PSI, Inc., Video Logic Corp. Mem. Am. Mgmt. Assn., Inst. Indsl. Engring. Assn. Republican. Presbyterian. Author: Quality of Profit in Non-Financial Companies, 1975. Home: 11 Cowell Ln Atherton CA 94025 Office: Video Logic Corp 597 N Mathilda Ave Sunnyvale CA 94086

CHOLEWA, ELLEN KAY, advertising executive; b. Highland Park, Ill., June 21, 1944. Student, Lakeland Coll., 1963-66, Chgo. Acad. of Fine Art, 1966-68. Owner Ellen Cholewa Design, Chgo., 1971-78; owner, ptnr. Graphic Resource, Medford, 1978-83; pres. Laurel Communications, Medford, Oreg., 1983—; mktg. cons. Nat. Pub. Radio Sta. KSOR, Asland, Oreg., 1980—; pub. relations cons. Winema Girl Scout Council, Medford, 1982-84. Regional council mem. Am. Lung Assn. of Oreg., Medford, 1984—, bd. dirs., Portland, 1986—. Mem. Financial Instns. Mktg. Assn. Avocations: gardening, skiing. Office: Laurel Communications 724 S Central Medford OR 97501

CHONG, MARY DRUZILLEA, nurse; b. Fairview, Okla., Mar. 8, 1930; d. Charles Dewey and Viola Haddie (Ford) Crawford; A.A. (Bells scholarship), El Camino Jr. Coll., 1950; R.N., Los Angeles County Hosp. Sch. Nursing, 1953; B.S. in Nursing, Calif. State U., 1968; M. Nyuk Choy Chong, Aug. 24, 1952 (div. 1968); children—Anthony, Dorlinda. Staff nurse neurosurgery Los Angeles County Gen. Hosp., Los Angeles, 1957-58; staff nurse Harbor Gen. Hosp., Torrance, Calif., 1958-59, emergency room staff nurse, 1959-61, asst. head nurse, 1963-64, supr. neurosurgery intensive care unit, 1964-67, part-time relief nurse, 1967-69, head nurse chest medicine, 1969-72; emergency room staff nurse mobile intensive care nurse Victor Valley Hosp., Victorville, Calif., 1974-79; dir. nursing San Vicente Hosp., Los Angeles, 1980-82, Upjohn Healthcare Services, Los Angeles, 1983-85; dir. home health services Bear Valley Community Hosp. Home Health Agy., Big Bear Lake, Calif., 1986—. Leader, South Bay council Girl Scouts Am., 1968; tchr. YWCA Job Corps, 1972-74. Mem. AAUW, Nat. Assn. Female Execs., Calif. State U. Los Angeles Alumni Assn., Internat. Platform Assn., Assn. for Continuity of Care. Home: PO Box 697 Lucerne Valley CA 92356 Office: PO Box 6586 Big Bear Lake CA 92315

CHONG, RICHARD DAVID, architect; b. Los Angeles, June 1, 1946; s. George and Mabel Dorothy (Chan) C.; m. Roze Gutierrez, July 5, 1969; children: David Gregory, Michelle Elizabeth. BArch, U. So. Calif., 1969; MArch, UCLA, 1974. Registered architect, Utah, Calif., Wyo. Assoc. Pulliam, Matthews & Assocs., Los Angeles, 1969-76; dir. Asst. Community Design Ctr., Salt Lake City, 1976-77; prin. Richard D. Chong & Assocs., Salt Lake City, 1977—; planning cons. Los Angeles Harbor Dept., 1974-76; asst. instr. So. Calif. Inst. Architecture, Santa Monica, 1973-74; vis. design critic Calif. State Poly. U., Pamona, 1975, U. Utah, Salt Lake City, 1976-78; design instr. Calif. State Poly. U., 1975-76; adj. asst. prof. urban design, U. Utah, 1980-84; bd. dirs. Utah Housing Coalition, Salt Lake City; Salt Lake City Housing Adv. and Appeals Bd., 1976-80. Author: Design of Flexible Housing, 1974 (Lighting award 1986); prin. works include Airmen's Dining Hall, 1985 (1st Pl. Mil. Facility 1986), Oddfellows Hall, 1984 (Heritage Found. award 1986). Mem. Task Force for the Aged Housing Com. Salt Lake County, Salt Lake City, 1976-77; Salt Lake City Mortgage Loan Instns. Rev. Com., 1978; bd. dirs. Neighborhood Housing Services of Fed. Home Loan Bank Bd., Salt Lake City, 1979-81, devel. com.; vice chmn. Water Quality Adv. Council, Salt Lake City, 1981-83; mem. adv. bd. Pub. Utilities Commn., Salt Lake City, 1986-87. Served as staff sgt. N.G., 1969-75. Mem. AIA (jury mem. Am. Soc. Interior Designers Annual awards 1981-82), Am. Inst. Planning (juror Annual Planning award 1984-85), Am. Planning Assn., Salt Lake City C. of C. (mem. housing com. 1977). Democrat. Club: Ft. Douglas Country (Salt Lake City). Avocations: tennis, sailing, fgn. travel. Office: Richard D Chong & Assocs 248 Edison St Salt Lake City UT 84111

CHONG, SANDRA G.H., speech pathologist; b. Hilo, Hawaii; d. Richard J.K. and Maile (Yamada) C. BS, U. Hawaii, MS. Speech and hearing specialist Hawaii Sch. Deaf and Blind, Honolulu, 1978-79; speech pathologist, Leeward Dist. Dept. Edn. State of Hawaii, Waipahu, 1979—. Youth coach canoe paddling McKinley High Sch., Honolulu, 1981-83. Mem. Am. Speech-Hearing Assn. (cert. clin. competence), Hawaii Speech-Hearing Assn., Lokahi Canoe Club (women's canoe paddlingcoach 1983—). Democrat. Congregationalist. Avocations: long-distance canoe paddling, biathlons.

CHONG, THOMAS, comedian, writer, director, musician; b. Edmonton, Alta., Can., May 24, 1938; s. Stanley and Lorna Jean (Gilchrist) C. Ed. public schs. Co-founder: rhythm and blues band The Shades; mem.: group

Bobby Taylor and the Vancouvers, until, 1968; founder: improvisational theater troupe City Works; formed: comedy duo with Cheech Marin called Cheech and Chong; appeared in nightclubs, Can., Los Angeles; recs. include Sleeping Beauty; co-writer, co-star: film Up in Smoke, 1978, Things Are Tough All Over, 1982; writer, actor, dir.: film Cheech & Chong's Next Movie, 1979, Cheech & Chong's Nice Dreams, 1981, Still Smokin, 1983, Cheech & Chong's Corsican Bros., 1984; co-writer: title song Up in Smoke. Recipient with Cheech Grammy award for Best Comedy recording Los Cochinos 1973.

CHORNOBOY, MAURICE, real estate executive; b. Mossey River, Man., Can., Aug. 14, 1925; s. William and Telka (Michaluk) C.; m. Dagney Margaret Kristiansen, Dec. 29, 1952; children: Gregory, Rinde. BS, U. Man., 1950. Rural mcpl. adminstr. City of Lawrence, Man., 1951-56; v.p., dir. Qualico Devel. Ltd., Winnipeg, Man. then Calgary, Alta., Can., 1956-84; pres., dir. Carma Developers, Calgary, 1984—. Exec. dir. Grace Luth. Ch., Calgary, 1983-84. Mem. New Home Warranty Program, Calgary Real Estate Bd., So. Alta. Ins. Inst. Home: 2926 Lathom Crescent SW, Calgary Can T3E 5W7 Office: Carma Developers Ltd, 6715 8th St NE, Calgary, AB Canada T2E 7H7

CHOTINER, KENNETH LEE, judge; b. Los Angeles, Aug. 14, 1937; s. Murray M. and Phyllis Sylvia (Levenson) C.; m. Florence Helene Penney, May 29, 1964; children—Dana Lynne, Cara Lee. B.A. in Polit. Sci. with honors, UCLA, 1959; J.D. with honors, Loyola U., Los Angeles, 1969; grad. Hastings Coll. Law Coll. Criminal Advocacy, San Francisco, 1980, Calif. Jud. Coll., U. Calif.-Berkeley, 1981. Bar: Calif. 1970, U.S. Ct. Customs and Patent Appeals 1971, U.S. Ct. Mil. Appeals 1974, U.S. Sup. Ct. 1975. Instr. Am. govt. U. Alaska, 1962; dep. city atty., Los Angeles, 1970-71; sole practice, Santa Monica, Calif., 1971-81; spl. counsel City of Hawthorne (Calif.), 1973-80; judge pro tem Los Angeles Mcpl. Ct., 1975-81, Santa Monica Mcpl. Ct., 1977-81; judge Los Angeles Mcpl. Ct., 1981—, supervising judge valley div., 1983, Van Nuys-Encino br., 1983-84; justice pro tem Calif. Ct. Appeal, 1982; adj. prof. U. West Los Angeles Sch. Law, 1981-82; faculty Calif. Jud. Coll., Earl Warren Legal Inst., U. Calif., Berkeley, 1982, Calif. Ctr. Jud. Edn. and Research, Berkeley, 1982—, Media Workshop on Calif. Cts., 1982—; chmn. Media Conf. on Calif. Cts., 1986; conf. del. State Bar Calif., 1972, 73, 76-80. Mem. exec. com. Los Angeles Mcpl. Ct., 1975. Bd. dirs. So. Calif. ACLU, 1972-81, v.p., 1978-81; dir. ex-officio Legal Aid Soc. Santa Monica, 1979-80; bd. dirs. Friends of the Santa Monica Mountains, Parks and Seashore, 1979-81; mem. dean's council UCLA Coll. Letters and Sci.; mem. wildlife adv. com. Los Angeles County Fish and Game Commn., 1973-75, chmn., 1974; mem. Los Angeles County Interdepartmental Drinking Driver Program, Task Force, 1985—; mem. PTA, 1973-81, Los Angeles Olympic Organizing Com. Criminal Justice System Subcom., 1983-84. Served to capt. USAF, 1961-66. Recipient recognition awards Calif. Trial Lawyers Assn. (trial lawyer and criminal def.), 1980, U. W. Los Angeles Sch. Law award for Outstanding Service, 1984, Nat. Council on Alcoholism award of Appreciation, 1984, Eagle Scout award Boy Scouts Am., Order of the Arrow. Mem. Nat. Conf. State Trial Judges, Nat. Conf. Spl. Ct. Judges (del. 1985), Calif. Judges Assn., Nat. Conf. Bar Pres., ABA (presdl. showcase program, Washington 1985), Am. Arbitration Assn. (panel 1970-81), Santa Monica Bay Dist. Bar Assn. (pres. 1979), Assn. Trial Lawyers Am., Women's Lawyers Assn. Los Angeles, Criminal Ct. Bar Assn., Los Angeles County Bar Assn., St. Thomas More Law Soc., UCLA Alumni Assn. (Blue and Gold Circle), U. Calif. Santa Cruz Fiat Lux Soc., Am. Judicature Soc., Ephebian Soc., Quill and Scroll Soc., Sealbearer Soc., Phi Alpha Delta. Lodge: Lions (zone chmn. 1975-76). Author: Restricting Handguns, 1979; contbr. articles to legal jours. Office: Los Angeles Mcpl Ct 110 N Grand Ave Los Angeles CA 90012-3055

CHOU, RICHARD CHI-CHANG, mechanical engineer; b. Peking, China, Feb. 7, 1934; s. Kuan-Shih and Chi-Chung (Chang) C.; m. Ming Hsu, Sept. 3, 1958; children: Henry, Jerry, Karol. BME, Purdue U., 1959; BS in Applied Math., Milton Coll., 1961; postgrad. in mech. engring., U. Pa. Prin. engr. Franklin Inst., Phila., 1961-85; sr. mem. tech. staff ITT-Gilfillan, Van Nuys, Calif., 1985—. Inventor motion systems. Mem. Am. Def. Preparedness Assn., Sigma Xi. Home: 136 S Atlantic Blvd Monterey Park CA 91754 Office: ITT-Gilfillan 7821 Orion Ave Van Nuys CA 91409

CHOULES, JOHN MAYNARD, civil engineer, contract administrator; b. Salt Lake City, May 28, 1934; s. George and Esther Rosella (Anderson) C.; m. Doris Anne Johnson, Sept. 1, 1952 (div. May 1976); children—Jack Mark, David Victor, Karen Diane, Dale William, Nancy Carol, Stacy Lynn, Grant Alden, Ryan Trent. B.S.C.E., Utah State U., 1956; postgrad. LaSalle Extension U., 1969, Cleve. Inst. Electronics, 1982-85. Registered profl. engr., Calif., Utah. With Pacific Soils Engring. Co., Los Angeles, 1957-60; civil engr. Fresno County, Calif., 1960; dam safety engr., resident engr. State of Calif., 1960-72; engr. Fulton Constrn. Co., 1972; office engr., contract adminstr. Rancho Seco Nuclear Power Sta., Bechtel Power Co., 1972-78; builder fruit juice processing plant and villa Dadco Co., Saudi Arabia, 1979-80; cons. Utah fed. aid projects, 1980-81; site constrn. mgr. Prowswood/ Caldwell, Richard & Sorensen, 1981-83; developer apt. housing projects Choules Devel. Co., Inc., Salt Lake City, 1983—; chief engr. Hawthorne Aviation, Dugway Proving Grounds, Utah, 1983-84; tchr. engring. Bakersfield (Calif.) Jr. Coll. Active nuclear campaign in Calif., 1976. Recipient award for pub. service Bechtel Corp., 1976. Mormon. Club: Orange County Toastmasters (dist. lt. gov.). Home: 4456 E Earll Dr Phoenix AZ 85018-7234 Office: PO Box 187 Bldg 5474 Dugway UT 84022

CHOUTEAU, WALTER C(HRISTY), utility company executive, researcher; b. San Francisco, Mar. 3, 1950; s. Walter Cerre and Francesca (Young) C. Student, Dartmouth Coll., 1969, U. Wash., 1970-73; AB in Biology, U. Calif., Berkeley, 1974, MS in Resource Science, 1975. Biologist Pacific Gas & Electric Co., San Ramon, Calif., 1977-80, research advisor, 1980-81, sr. research advisor, 1981-83, supr. research, 1983, acting dir. research and devel., 1984-86; asst. to v.p., elec. resource planning and devel. Pacific Gas & Electric Co., San Francisco, 1986—. Myers scholar U. Wash., 1971-72; Needham fellow U. Calif. Berkeley, 1975; grantee U. Calif., Berkeley, 1972-73. Mem. AAAS, Electric Power Research Inst. (utility advisor task force on environment, 1984-86, chmn. ecol. studies program com. 1986), Sigma Xi (research honor soc. 1975). Club: Olympic (San Francisco). Avocations: hiking, rowing, sailing, travel, theater. Office: Pacific Gas and Electric 77 Beale St San Francisco CA 94106

CHOW, EILEEN SIU-HA, computer retailing, investment company executive; b. Hong Kong, Jan. 18, 1951; d. Hin To and Oi (Kuen) Choi; came to U.S., 1969, naturalized, 1983; m. Chun Ping Chow, Aug. 25, 1973; children—Connie, Sandra, Eugene. B.A. cum laude, UCLA, 1972, M.S., 1973. Systems analyst Gen. Motors Research Lab., Warren, Mich., 1973-77; v.p. Cougar of Calif., Inc., South San Francisco, 1977-85, Choice Investment Co. N.V., Netherlands Antilles, 1978—, Computer Selection, Inc., 1983—. Mem. Soc. Women Engrs., ACM. Office: 201 Mission St San Francisco CA 94105

CHOW, FRANKLIN SZU-CHIEN, physician; b. Hong Kong, Apr. 15, 1956; came to U.S., 1967; s. Walter Wen-Tsao and Jane Ju-Hsien (Tang) C. BS, CCNY, 1977; MD, U. Rochester, 1979. Diplomate Am. Bd. Ob-Gyn. Intern Wilmington (Del.) Med. Ctr., 1979-80, resident in ob-gyn, 1980-83; practice medicine specializing in ob-gyn Vail (Colo.) Valley Med. Ctr., 1983—, chmn. obstetrics com., 1984-85, 86—. Named to Athletic Hall of Fame, CCNY, 1983. Fellow Am. Coll. Ob-Gyn's; mem. AMA, Colo. Med. Soc., Intermountain Med. Soc. (pres. 1985-86), Internat. Fedn. Gynecol. Endoscopists, Am. Assn. Gynecol. Laparoscopists. Avocations: skiing, swimming, photography. Home: 0746 N Deer Blvd PO Box 3257 Vail CO 81658 Office: Vail Valley Med Ctr 181 W Meadow Dr Suite 600 Vail CO 81657

CHOW, KAO LIANG, neurobiologist, educator; b. Tientsin, China, Apr. 21, 1918; came to U.S., 1946, naturalized, 1963; s. Su Tau and Tau Yu (Tsau) C.; m. Margaret W.C. Zee, May 2, 1964. B.S., Yenching U., China, 1943; Ph.D., Harvard, 1950. Staff Yerkes Lab. Primate Biology, Orange Park, Fla., 1947-54; research asso. Yerkes Lab. Primate Biology, 1947-54; faculty U. Chgo., 1954-61; mem. faculty Stanford Med. Sch., Palo Alto, Calif., 1961—; prof. neurology Stanford Med. Sch., 1965-84, prof. emeritus, 1984—. Contbr. articles profl. jours. Mem. Internat. Brain Research Orgn., Am. Physiol. Assn., AAAS, Sigma Xi. Home: 101 Alma St Apt 805 Palo Alto CA 94301

CHOW, KAY (KAROLYN) MARGARET, interior and fashion designer; b. Pullman, Wash., Apr. 22, 1918; d. Ray Alan and Edna Mabel (Ringer) Wagner; m. Norman Charles Wallace, Aug. 22, 1943 (div. 1952); 1 child, Richard; m. David Chow, Aug. 25, 1957. BA cum laude, Wash. State U., 1936; postgrad., Art Students' League, N.Y.C., 1936-37; MFA, Kans. State U., 1942. Cert. tchr., Calif. Fashion illustrator Womens' Wear Daily, N.Y.C., 1936; designer S. Doree, N.Y.C., 1937; instr. art dept. Mills Coll., Oakland, Calif., 1938, Kans. State U., Manhattan, 1939-43; designer Gump's, San Francisco, 1943-45, Warren O. Wagner & Assocs., Pasadena, Calif., 1951-65; dir. home planning ctr. Harbour-Longmire, Oklahoma City, 1946-47; coordinator tech. illustration Jet Propulsion Lab, Calif. Inst. Tech., Pasadena, 1965-66; prof. profl. arts Woodbury U., Los Angeles, 1967-81; designer David Chow & instr. interior design Pasadena City Coll., 1971-72; designer David Chow & Assocs., South Pasadena, 1968—; co-chmn. fine arts Woodbury U., Los Angeles, 1976-78. Mem. Los Angeles Regional Occupational Council Program, 1977. Recipient Spl. award Pasadena Festival of the Arts, 1978. Mem. Inst. Bus. Designers' (treas. 1974-78, v.p. edn. 1979-80), Am. Soc. Interior Designers (edn. mem.), Interior Design Educators Council (copr. mem.). Lodge: Order Eastern Star. Home and Office: 1643 Indiana Ave South Pasadena CA 91030

CHOW, TSAIHWA JAMES, chemist; b. Shanghai, Republic of China, Oct. 13, 1924; came to U.S., 1947, naturalized, 1960; s. Ma Son and Tze (Hsu) C. BS, Nat. Chiao-tung U., Shanghai, 1946; MS, Wash. State U., Pullman, 1949; PhD, U. Wash., 1953; postgrad., Stanford U., 1954. Research assoc. oceanography U. Wash., Seattle, 1953-55; research fellow geochemistry Calif. Inst. Tech., Pasadena, 1955-60; asst. research chemist Scripps Inst. Oceanography, U. Calif., San Diego, 1960-65, assoc. research chemist, 1966-71, research chemist, 1971—; vis. researcher Royal Inst. Tech., Stockholm, 1962-63; vis. scientist Acad. Sci. People's Republic of China, 1979, Nat. Bur. Oceanography, People's Republic of China, 1981, 83, 85; mem. trace metal subcom. of safe drinking water com. Assembly of Life Sci., NRC, 1976-77; adv. marine productivity project Instituto del Mar del Peru, Lima, OAS, 1976. Contbr. numerous articles to profl. jours. Mem. Am. Soc. Limnology and Oceanography, Am. Geophys. Union, Geochem. Soc., AAAS, Japan Oceanographic Soc., Sigma Xi. Office: U Calif Scripps Inst Oceanography La Jolla CA 92093

CHOW, WINSTON, chemical engineer, research and development executive; b. San Francisco, Dec. 21, 1946; s. Raymond and Pearl C.; m. Lilly Fah, Aug. 15, 1971; children: Stephen, Kathryn. BSChemE, U. Calif., Berkeley, 1968; MSChemE, Calif. State U., San Jose, 1972; MBA with honors, Calif. State U., San Francisco, 1985. Registered profl. chem. and mech. engr.; instr.'s credential Calif. Community Coll. Chem. engr. Sondell Sci. Instruments, Inc., Mountain View, Calif., 1971; mem. research and devel. staff Raychem Corp., Menlo Park, Calif., 1971-72; with Bechtel Power Corp., San Francisco, 1972-79, engr., 1972-76, sr. engr., 1976-77, engring. mech. supr., 1977-79; sr. project mgr. water quality and toxic substances control program Electric Power Research Inst., Palo Alto, Calif., 1979—. Contbr. author Water Chlorination, vol. 4; contbr. articles to profl. publs. Pres., chief exec. officer Directions, Inc., San Francisco, 1985-86, bd. dirs. 1984-87, chmn. strategic planning com., 1984-85. Recipient Grad. Disting. Achievement award, 1985; Calif. Gov.'s Exec. fellow. Mem. Am. Inst. Chem. Engrs. (Profl. Devel. Recognition cert.), NSPE, Calif. Soc. Profl. Engrs. (pres. Golden Gate chpt. 1983-84, v.p. 1982-83, state dir.), Water Pollution Control Fedn., Calif. Water Pollution Control Assn., ASME, Calif. Alumni Assn., Beta Gamma Sigma. Democrat. Presbyterian. Office: Electric Power Research Inst 3412 Hillview Ave Palo Alto CA 94303

CHOW-HOY, DIANE MICHIKO, speech and language pathologist, educator; b. Waialua, Hawaii; d. Charles Waichi and Edna Fumiko (Takata) Sakuma; m. Douglas Yun Wah Chow-Hoy, June 21, 1969; children: Todd Kalani, Robyn Lei. BA, Pacific U., 1967; MS, U. Hawaii, 1969. Cert. clin. competence speech pathology, cert. speech hearing specialist, Hawaii. Speech-lang. pathologist Dept. Edn., Honolulu, 1969—, tchr. hearing impaired, summers 1976, 1980. Mem. Am. Speech, Lang. and Hearing Assn., Hawaii Speech and Hearing Assn. Democrat. Avocations: tennis, swimming. Home: 94-306 Kiilani Pl Mililani Town HI 96789 Office: Dept Edn 94-366 Pupupani St Waipahu HI 96797

CHOY, HERBERT YOUNG CHO, judge; b. Makaweli, Kauai, Hawaii, Jan. 6, 1916; s. Doo Wook and Helen (Nahm) C.; m. Dorothy Helen Shular, June 16, 1945. B.A., U. Hawaii, 1938; J.D., Harvard U., 1941. Bar: Hawaii bar 1941. Practiced in Honolulu, 1946-57, 58-71; atty. gen. Ter. Hawaii, 1957-58; judge U.S. Ct. Appeals, 9th circuit, Honolulu, 1971—. Trustee Hawaii Loa Coll., 1963-79. Served with AUS, 1942-46. Decorated Order Civil Merit Korea). Fellow Am. Bar Found.; mem. Am., Hawaii bar assns., World Peace Through Law Center. Home: 3964 Monterey Pl Honolulu HI 96816 Office: US Courthouse Honolulu HI 96850

CHOY, KOON HIN, pension and estate planning executive; b. Honolulu, Mar. 12, 1925; s. Yin and Wong S. Choy; student La. State U., 1973; m. Kazuko Tsuchiya, Feb. 19, 1950; children—Roberta Lee Choy Quenzer, Isaac William. Dist. mgr. Honolulu Star Bull., 1942; asst. circulation mgr. Pacific Stars & Stripes, Far East, 1946-60; life ins. agt. West Coast Life, Honolulu, 1961-63; estate and retirement planning cons. Manulife, Honolulu, 1963-73; pres. K.H. Choy & Associates, Inc., Honolulu, 1973—; state chmn. Life Underwriters Polit. Action Com., 1975-76. Served with U.S. Army, 1946-48. Mem. Nat. Assn. Life Underwriters (Nat. Quality award, Sales Achievement award), Hawaii Assn. Life Underwriters (dir.), Assn. for Advanced Life Underwriting, Nat. Assn. Pension Consultants, Am. Soc. of Chartered Life Underwriters, Nat. Fedn. Ind. Bus., Am. Soc. Pension Actuaries (state chmn. 1976—). Mem. Congregational Ch. Club: Mid-Pacific Country. Lodge: Elks. Home: 3421-A Woodlawn Dr Honolulu HI 96822 Office: Suite 948 Pacific Tower 1001 Bishop St Honolulu HI 96813

CHOY, TERENCE TIN-HO, artist, art educator; b. Hong Kong, Nov. 26, 1941; s. Yang Fai and Yin Chen (Ng) C.; B.A., San Francisco State U., 1965; M.A., U. Calif.-Berkeley, 1967; m. Carol Eastland, Oct. 10, 1975. Instr. art deYoung Mus. Art Sch., San Francisco, 1969-70; assoc. prof. art U. Alaska, Fairbanks, 1970-81, prof., 1981—; hon. vis. prof. Chinese U. of Hong Kong; vis. prof. U. Minn., Murray (Ky.) State U., 1986; one-man shows Richmond (Calif.) Art Center, 1968, Coll. Holy Names, Oakland, Calif., 1969, Valley Art Gallery, Walnut Creek, Calif., 1970, Alaska State Mus., Juneau, 1972, Anchorage Hist. and Fine Arts Mus., 1974, 81, U. Alaska, Fairbanks, 1975, U. Minn., 1982, Murray (Ky.) State U., 1982, Alma (Mich.) Coll., 1982, Am. Library, Hong Kong, 1984, Musée Luis de Camoes, Macau, 1984, U. Alaska Mus., Fairbanks, 1987; exhibited in group shows Massillon (Ohio) Mus., 1975, Honolulu Acad. Art, 1977, Woodson Art Mus., Wausau, Wis., 1977, Nat. Collection Fine Arts, Washington, 1978, Columbus (Ga.) Mus. Arts and Crafts, 1978; represented in permanent collection Alaska State Council Arts, Alaska State Mus., U. Alaska. Mem. art in public place com. Alaska State Council Arts. Rockefeller/Nat. Endowment Arts fellow, 1977-78; Nat. Endowment Humanities grantee, 1979; Andrew W. Mellon Found. grantee, 1980, 81, 85, 86; Alaska State Council Arts travel grantee, 1979, 86. Mem. AAUP, Coll. Art Assn. Am., Am. Assn. Mus., Visual Arts Center Alaska, Fairbanks Art Assn. Home: 4820 Palo Verde Ave Fairbanks AK 99709 Office: U Alaska Dept Art Fairbanks AK 99701

CHOY, WILLIAM, chemistry educator; b. Phila., Apr. 17, 1950; s. George and Kwan (To) C. BS, U. Calif., Berkeley, 1972, PhD, 1980. Asst. research chemist U. Calif., Santa Cruz, 1976-79; assoc. research chemist MIT, Cambridge, 1980-82; asst. prof. chemistry U. Denver, 1984—. Author: Strategies and Tactics in Organic Synthesis, 1984; contbr. articles to profl. jours.; patentee in field. Mem. AAAS, Am. Chem. Soc. Office: U Denver Dept Chemistry University Park Denver CO 80208

CHRISLIP, LAURA JEAN, speech pathologist, educator; b. St. Louis, Apr. 12, 1957; d. Robert Arthur and Bernice Dorothy (Smith) Oberjuerge. BA, Calif. State U., Fullerton, 1979, MA, 1983. Cert. speech and lang. pathologist. Speech, lang. pathologist Rehab. Inst. of Orange County, Orange, Calif., 1982, Craig and Ford Rehab. Services, Anaheim, Calif., 1982-83; pvt. practice speech and lang. pathology San Clemente, Calif., 1983-84; speech, lang. pathologist Newport Lang., Speech and Audiology Ctr., Laguna Hills, Calif., 1984-85; dir. speech pathology and audiology Healthtech Rehab. Inc., Irvine, Calif., 1985—; prof. speech pathology Coastline Community Coll., Westminster, Calif., 1986—. Mem. Calif. Scholastic Fedn. (life), Am. Speech, Lang. and Hearing Assn., Calif. Speech, Lang. and Hearing Assn., Nat. Student Speech and Hearing Assn., Departmental Assns. Council, Phi Kappa Phi. Republican. Lutheran. Avocations: singing, tennis, bicycling, weight-lifting. Office: Healthtech Rehab Inc 14795 Jeffrey Rd Suite 100 Irvine CA 92720

CHRISS, JAMES MICHAEL, manufacturing company executive, marketing professional; b. North Tonawanda, N.Y., Oct. 14, 1942; s. Walter and Stephanie (Wegrzyn) C.; m. Keven Price, Dec. 21, 1975; children: J. Alexander, Erica Leigh. BA, U. Dayton, 1964. Mgr. quality control Levi Strauss and Co., Amarillo Tex. and Albuquerque, 1967-68; product mgr. men's sportswear Levi Strauss and Co., San Francisco, 1968-70, mdse. mgr. youthwear, 1971-72; account exec. sales youthwear Levi Strauss and Co., Washington, 1972-74; merchandising dir. Levi Strauss Can., Toronto, 1974-77; mktg. dir. Levi Strauss Australia, Sydney, 1977-78, gen. mgr., 1979; v.p., gen. mgr. women's wear Levi Strauss Europe, London, 1980-83; v.p. mktg. Levi Strauss and Co. Internat., San Francisco, 1983—. Mgr. Ross Valley (Calif.) Little League. Served to capt. U.S. Army, 1965-67. Club: Bay (San Francisco); Ross Valley Tennis (Kentfield, Calif.). Avocations: running, reading, tennis. Office: Levi Strauss and Co 1155 Battery St San Francisco CA 94160

CHRISS, MICHAEL, astronomer, educator; b. N.Y.C., Dec. 6, 1934; s. Samuel David and Mollie (Weissman) C.; m. Hazel Einarson; children: Sabrina, John, Julie. BS, U. Ariz., 1957, MS, 1959; postgrad., U. Calif., Berkeley, 1964-66, Stanford U., 1979-82. Asst. astronomer Steward Obs. of U. Ariz., Tucson, 1957-59; astronomer Smithsonian Inst., Cambridge, Mass., 1959-60; satellite engr. Lockhead Missiles and Space, Sunnyvale, Calif., 1960-64; prof. astronomy Coll. of San Mateo, Calif., 1966—, dir. honors program, dir. CSM Planetarium, 1985—; lectr./leader U. Calif. Berkeley Extension Eclipse Expedition, 1972, Nature Expeditions, Palo Alto, Calif., 1978; lectr. Royal Viking Lines, San Francisco, 1986; chmn. honors program com. Coll. San Mateo, 1985—, instrn. com., 1982-83, profl. personnel com., 1983-86. Author: Physical Science Today, 1979; producer planetarium shows, 1966-76; author/actor (play) Galileo Tonight, 1975—; TV instr. Dimension Universe, 1967-68, San Francisco State Edn. TV award. Bd. dirs. ACLU, Palo Alto, 1961. Faculty fellow NSF, 1979; recipient 1st Prize sci. writing contest, Griffith Obs., 1980. Mem. Community Coll. Humanities Assn., Community Coll. Honors Assn., Pacific Planetarium Assn. (pres. 1976-77), Internat. Planetarium Soc. Office: Coll San Mateo San Mateo CA 94402

CHRISTAINSEN, GREGORY BRUCE, economist, consultant; b. Newton, Mass., Aug. 30, 1953; s. Philip Lucian and Sylvia (Ballard) C. BA, U. Wis., 1974, MA, 1977, PhD, 1981. Asst. prof. economics Colby Coll., Waterville, Maine, 1981-83; lectr. Calif. State U., Hayward, 1983-84, assoc. prof., 1984—; sr. economist Pacific Research Inst. Pub. Policy, San Francisco, 1984—; cons. U.S. Congress, Washington, 1979-80, Resources for the Future, Washington, 1980, Orgn. Econ. Cooperation and Devel., Paris, 1982, Atlas Econ. Research Found., San Francisco, 1984. Contbr. articles to profl. jours. Henry Vilas fellow U. Wis., 1977-78, Olive Garvey fellow Mont Pelerin Soc., 1984, Eisenhower scholar Eisenhower Meml. Scholarship Found., 1979, fellow U. Wis., 1979-80. Mem. Am. Econ. Assn., Western Econ. Assn., David Hume Soc., Colo. Chautauqua Assn. Home: 815 N Humboldt St San Mateo CA 94401 Office: Pacific Research Inst Pub Policy 177 Post St San Francisco CA 94108

CHRISTE, KARL OTTO, research chemist; b. Ulm, Fed. Republic Germany, July 24, 1936; s. Eugen A. and Elsa M. (Heller) C.; m. Brigitte F. Fischer, Jan. 27, 1962; children: Ralf, Mark, Tina. BS, Tech. U., Stuttgart, Fed. Republic Germany, 1957, MS, 1960, PhD, 1961; postgrad., U. Vienna, Austria, 1957-58. Sr. research chemist Stauffer Chem. Co., Richmond, Calif., 1962-67; mem. tech. staff Rocketdyne Div. Rockwell Internat., Canoga Park, Calif., 1967-78, mgr. research, 1978—. Contbr. articles to profl. jours.; patentee in field. Mem. Am. Chem. Soc. (Creative Work in Fluorine Chemistry award 1986). Avocations: tennis, fencing. Home: 5645 Parkmor Rd Calabasas CA 91302 Office: Rockeydyne div Rockwell Internat 6633 Canoga Ave Canoga Park CA 91304

CHRISTENSEN, ALLEN CLARE, agricultural educator, university dean, administrator, consultant; b. Lehi, Utah, Apr. 14, 1935; s. Clare Bernard and Relia Sarah (Allen) C.; m. Kathleen Ruth Atwater, Dec. 19, 1958; children—Ann Marie, Allen Clare Jr., James Lynn, Niel Daniel, Eric Wayne. B.S. with honors, Brigham Young U., 1957; M.S., U. Calif.-Davis, 1960; Ph.D., Utah State U. 1979. Cert. Am. Registry Profl. Animal Scientists. Vocat. agr. tchr. White Pine County Schs., Lund, Nev., 1961-64; from asst. to assoc. prof. agr. Calif. State Poly. U., Pomona, 1964-73, prof., 1973—, dean coll. agr., 1980-85, 87—; acting provost and acad. v.p., 1985-87; cons. Agrl. Edn. Found., Davis, Calif., 1971-85, AID, Washington, 1983—, W.K. Kellogg Found., Battle Creek, Mich., 1984; trustee Consortium for Internat. Devel., Tucson, Ariz., 1980—; mem. deans' council Calif. Agr. Leadership Program, Davis, 1980-85; mem. joint com. on agr. research and devel., AID, 1982—, chmn. strengthening grant panel bd. internat. food and agrl. devel., 1983—. Author: (with others) Working in Animal Science, 1978. Contbr. articles to profl. jours. Pres. Chino, Calif Latter-day Saint Stake, 1979—. Recipient Hon. State Farmer Degree, Calif. Assn. Future Farmers Am., 1983. Mem. Am. Soc. Animal Scis., Poultry Sci. Assn., Phi Kappa Phi, Gamma Sigma Delta (Outstanding Faculty award of Merit, 1976, pres. 1969-70), Alpha Zeta. Republican. Mormon. Office: Calif State Poly U Sch Agr 3801 W Temple Ave Pomona CA 91768

CHRISTENSEN, ARNOLD, state senator, electrical contractor; b. Salt Lake City, July 26, 1936; s. Walter A. and Joyce (Pierce) C.; m. Necia Ann Larsen, May 10, 1956; children—Valerie Ann, Cheryl Ann, Kathy Ann, Bruce Arnold. Student, U. Utah, 1954-56; D in Vocat. Tech. (hon.), Utah Tech. Coll., 1986. Mem. Utah Senate, Salt Lake City, 1978—, majority whip, 1980-84, pres., 1985—; owner, pres. Christensen Electric. Leader Boy Scouts Am., Salt Lake City; mem. adv. bd. Utah Symphony; bd. dirs. Cottonwood Hosp., Salt Lake City; leader Latter Day Saints Ch., Salt Lake City. Named Legislator of Yr., Assoc. Builders and Contractors of Utah, 1982. Republican. Avocations: hunting, horses, fishing, water skiing. Home: 891 E 8600 S Sandy UT 84070

CHRISTENSEN, C. LEWIS, real estate developer; b. Laramie, Wyo., June 3, 1936; s. Raymond H. and Elizabeth C. (Cady) C.; B.S. in Indsl. Engring., U. Wyo., 1959; m. Sandra Stadheim, June 11, 1960; children—Kim, Brett. Mgmt. trainee Gen. Mills Chgo., 1959, Mountain Bell, Helena, Mont., 1962-63; data communications mgr. Mountain Bell, Phoenix, 1964-66, dist. mktg. mgr., So. Colo., 1970-73; seminar leader AT&T Co., Chgo., 1966-68, mktg. supr., N.Y.C., 1968-70; land planner and developer Village Assocs., Colorado Springs, Colo., 1973, exec. v.p., 1975-77; v.p. Cimarron Corp., Colorado Springs, 1974-75; pres. Lew Christensen & Assocs., Inc.; ptnr., gen. mgr. Briargate Devel. Group, 1977—. Mem. Chancellor's adv. bd. U. Colo., Colorado Springs; bd. dirs. Pikes Peak council Boy Scouts Am., Citizens Goals, Colo. Council on Econ. Edn. Served with USAF, 1959-62. Mem. Colorado Springs Home Builders Assn. (bd. dirs.), Urban Land Inst., Colorado Springs C. of C. (bd. dirs. chmn. bd.), Republican. Presbyterian. Clubs: Broadmoor Golf, Colorado Springs Country (bd. dirs.). Developer of 10,000-acre New Town area, east of USAF Acad., Colorado. Home: 2948 Country Club Dr Colorado Springs CO 80909 Office: Lew Christensen & Assocs Inc 7710 N Union Blvd Colorado Springs CO 80918

CHRISTENSEN, CARL WILLIAM, social service agency director; b. Indpls., Mar. 25, 1946; s. William Carl and Helen (Thuesen) C.; m. Sonya Marie Hruschka, Sept. 22, 1977; children: Candace Marie, Benjamin Ray, Michael Andrew, Sally Helen. BA, Antioch Coll., 1969; MSW, Portland State U., 1983. Reg. clin. social worker. Vol. U.S. Peace Corps, Jamaica, 1969-71; community organizer Southwest Oreg. Community Action, North Bend, Oreg., 1971-73; clin. dir. Southwest Oreg. Community Action, North Bend, 1983—; supr. Coos County Juvenile, Coquille, Oreg., 1973-81; prin. clinician Coastal Ctr. for Counseling, North Bend, 1984—; bd. dirs. Ctr. Systemic Research, North Bend, 1984—. Mem. Northwest Steelheaders, Acad. Cert. Social Workers, Nat. Assn. Social Workers (dist. chmn. 1985-

86), Am. Assn. Marriage and Family Therapists (clin.), Am. Orthopsychiat. Assn., ACLU. Democrat. Roman Catholic. Lodge: KC. Avocations: golf, photography, fishing. Home: 3783 Spruce North Bend OR 97459 Office: Coastal Ctr Counseling/Research 1931 Meade PO Box 215 North Bend OR 97459

CHRISTENSEN, CAROLINE, educator; b. Lehi, Utah, Oct. 5, 1936; d. Byam Heber and Ruth (Gardner) Curtis; m. Marvin Christensen, June 16, 1961; children—Ronald, Roger, Robert, Corlyn, Richard, Chad. B.S., Brigham Young U., 1958, M.S., 1964. Sec. Brigham Young U., Provo, Utah, 1954-58; instr. bus. Sevier Valley Area Vocat. Ctr., Richfield, Utah, 1970—. Historian, Sevier Sch. Dist. PTA, 1968, 69; chmn. Heart Fund Dist., 1983. Mem. Utah Edn. Assn., Am. Vocat. Assn., Utah Vocat. Assn., Nat. Bus. Edn. Utah Bus. Edn. Assn. (sec. 1986-87), NEA, Western Bus. Edn. Assn., Sevier Valley Tech. Tchrs. Assn. (sec. 1971—, pres. 1986-87), Delta Pi Epsilon, Delta Kappa Gamma (treas. 1975—).

CHRISTENSEN, DON M., general contractor, realtor; b. Hinckley, Utah, Jan. 3, 1929; s. Joseph M. and Lula (Payne) C.; m. Arda Jean Warnock, Oct. 8, 1953; children—Jean Larie, Jolene, Mary Kaye, Martin Don, Evan Warnock, Rachel, Glenn Leroy, Ruth Angela. Student agr. Utah State U., 1951-53, student bldg. Brigham Young U., 1955-56. Ptnr. Christensen Bros. Constrn. Co., Salt Lake City, 1956-59; pres. Constrn. Realty, Inc., Salt Lake City, 1959—, Don M. Christensen Constrn. Co., Salt Lake City, 1965—, Bountiful Constrn. Co., Salt Lake City, 1960-65, Advanced Reprodns., Inc., Salt Lake City, 1960-61, Land Investors, Inc., Salt Lake City, 1960-63. Co-author: Yours Can Be a Happy Marriage, 1983. Co-editor: Precious Testimonies, 1976. Bishop's counselor Ch. of Jesus Christ of Latter Day Saints, Salt Lake City, 1960-66, bishop, 1966-76, high councilman, 1976-85, counselor to stake pres., 1985—. Served with U.S. Army, 1954-55. Named Missionary of Yr., Mormon Finland Mission, 1951. Mem. Home Builders Assn. Republican. Home: 1630 Olive Dr Salt Lake City UT 84124 Office: Constrn Realty Inc 345 E 33d S Salt Lake City UT 84115

CHRISTENSEN, DONN WAYNE, insurance and management executive; b. Atlantic City, Apr. 9, 1941; s. Donald Frazier and Dorothy (Ewing) C.; B.S., U. Santa Clara, 1964; m. Mei Ling Fill, June 18, 1976; children—Donn Wayne, Lisa Shawn; m. 3d Susan Kim, Feb. 14, 1987; stepchildren: Don Kim, Stella Kim. West Coast div. mgr. Ford Motor Co., 1964-65; agt. Conn. Mut. Life Ins. Co., 1965-68, Christensen & Jones, Mgmt. and Ins. Services, Los Angeles, 1968—; v.p. Research Devel. Systems Inc. Pres. Duarte Community Drug Abuse Council, 1972-75; pres. Woodlyn Property Owners Assn., 1972-73; mem. L'ermitage Found., 1985-86, instl. rev. bd. White Meml. Hosp., Los Angeles, 1975—. Recipient Man of Yr. award Los Angeles Gen. Agts. and Mgrs. Assn., 1969, 72, 73. Mem. Nat. Life Underwriters Assn., Calif. State Life Underwriters Assn., Nat. Assn. Music Mchts. and Mfrs., Soc. Pension Actuaries, Foothill Community Concert Assn. (pres. 1970-73). Office: 709 E Colorado Blvd Suite 270 Pasadena CA 91101

CHRISTENSEN, ROBERT WAYNE, JR., financial and leasing company executive; b. Chester, Calif., Nov. 11, 1948; s. Robert Wayne and Ann (Forsyth) C.; 1 dau., Heather. B.A. with honors, Coll. Gt. Falls, 1976; M.B.A., U. Puget Sound, 1978. Cert. flight instr. Corp. pilot Buttrey Food Stores, Gt. Falls, Mont., 1972-74; asst. to pres. Pacific Hide & Fur, Gt. Falls, 1974-76; fin. analyst Olympia Brewing Co., Olympia, Wash., 1977; pres., chief exec. officer Republic Leasing, Olympia, 1978—; pres. PacWest Fin. Corp., Olympia, 1984—; dir. Republic Leasing, Olympia, 1978—, Wash. Independent Bancshares, Olympia, 1982, Nat. Vehicle Leasing Assn., Los Angeles, 1982—, also pres., 1985-86, PacWest Fin. Corp., Olympia, 1984—. Served to sgt. USAF, 1969-72. Mem. Nat. Vehicle Leasing Assn. (2d. v.p. 1984), Western Assn. Equipment Lessors, Western Leasing Conf., Heritage Fed. Savs. Loan Assn. (bd. dirs. 1987—), Mensa. Lodge: Rotary (dir. 1982—, v.p. 1986—). Office: Republic Leasing The Republic Bldg PO Box 737 Olympia WA 98507

CHRISTIAENS, (BERNARD F.) CHRIS, financial analyst, senator; b. Conrad, Mont., Mar. 7, 1940; s. Marcel Jules and Virgie Jeanette (Van Spyk) C. BA in Chemistry, Coll. Gt. Falls, 1962, postgrad., 1984—. Fin. and industry mgr. Rice Motors, Gt. Falls, Mont., 1978-84; senator State of Mont., 1983—, majority whip 49th legis., 1985-86; fin. planner Jack Stevens CPA, Gt. Falls, 1984-85; adminstr., fin. analyst Gt. Falls Pre-Release, 1986—. Chmn. Balance of State Pvt. Industry Council, Mont. 1984—; mem. Mont. Human Rights commn., Mont. 1981-84; bd. dirs. St. Thomas Child and Family Ctr., Gt. Falls, 1983—, Coll. Gt. Falls, 1984—; bd. dirs., treas. Gt. Falls Community Food Bank, 1984-86; Dem. committeeman, Cascade County, Mont., 1976-82; Mont. del. to Nat. Rules Conv., 1980; pub. chmn. Cascade County chpt. ARC, 1986; mem. adv. bd. Cambridge Court Sr. Citizen Apt. Complex, 1986; bd. dirs. Cascade County Mental Health Assn., 1986—. Named one of Outstanding Young Men of Am., Jaycees, 1976; recipient Outstanding Young Alumni award Coll. Gt. Falls, 1979. Roman Catholic. Clubs: Gt. Falls Ski, Toastmasters. Lodge: Optimists. Avocations: skiing, tennis, fishing, reading, hiking. Home: 210 36th St N Great Falls MT 59401 Office: Great Falls Pre-Release Services Inc 1019 15 St N Great Falls MT 59401

CHRISTIAN, C(HARLES) RUSSELL, art director, artist; b. Louisville, Oct. 27, 1949; s. Russell O. and Mary Elizabeth Christian. BFA, U. Cin., 1974. Cert. set designer, art dir. Prin. works include asst. art dir. Another World, N.Y.C., 1980-81, Sophie's Choice, N.Y.C., 1981, Invaders From Mars, Los Angeles, 1985; art director O'Neill Playwright's Conf., New London, Conn., 1983, 52 Pick-Up, Los Angeles, 1986. Mem. United Scenic Artists. Democrat. Avocations: air brush rendering, traveling, photography. Home: 1829 Lucile Ave Los Angeles CA 90026

CHRISTIAN, DAVID LYNN, architect; b. Clovis, N.Mex., Nov. 28, 1946; s. Orphane Eugene and Nola Maxine Christian; student N.Mex. State U., 1964-65; B.Arch., Tex. Tech. U., 1970. Project designer D. A. Wexler Assocs., Palm Springs, Calif., 1970-72; head project architect Kaptur & Lapham, Palm Springs, 1972-76; founder, since pres. Christian Assocs., Palm Springs, 1976. Mem. Palm Springs Archtl. Adv. Bd., 1979—; mem. Com. for Palm Springs Cultural Center, 1979—, Palm Springs Desert Mus., 1976—, Palm Springs Planning Commn., 1980-82. Recipient various local and nat. archtl. awards including Instns. mag. award of Merit, 1979. Mem. AIA, Nat. Council Archtl. Registration Bds. (cert.). Office: 1000 S Palm Canyon Dr Palm Springs CA 92264

CHRISTIAN, GARY DALE, chemistry educator; b. Eugene, Oreg., Nov. 25, 1937; s. Roy C. and Edna Alberta (Trout) Gonier; m. Suanne Byrd Coulbourne, June 17, 1961; children: Dale Brian, Carol Jean. B.S., U. Oreg., 1959; M.S., U. Md., 1962, Ph.D., 1964. Research analytical chemist Walter Reed Army Inst. Research, Washington, 1961-67; asst. prof. U. Md., College Park, 1965-66; asst. prof. U. Ky., Lexington, 1967-70, assoc. prof., 1970-72; prof. chemistry U. Wash., Seattle, 1972—; vis. prof. Universite Libre de Bruxelles, Brussels, 1978-79; invited prof. U. Geneva, 1979; cons. Ames Co., 1968-72, Beckman Instruments, Inc., 1972-84, Westinghouse Hanford Co., 1977-83, Tech. Dynamics, Inc., 1983-85, Instrumentation Lab., Inc., 1984—; examiner Grad. Record Exam., 1985-88. Author: Analytical Chemistry, 4th edit., 1986, Instrumental Analysis, 1978, 2d edit., 1986, Atomic Absorption Spectroscopy, 1970, Trace Analysis, 1986; contbr. articles to profl. jours.; editorial bd. Analytical Letters, 1971—, Can. Jour. Spectroscopy, 1974—, Analytical Instrumentation, 1974—, Talanta, 1980—, Analytical Chemistry, 1984-87, Critical Revs. in Analytical Chemistry, 1985—, The Analyst, 1986—. Fulbright Hays scholar, 1978-79; recipient Medal U. Brussels, 1978. Mem. Am. Chem. Soc. (sect. chmn.), Soc. Applied Spectroscopy (sect. chmn. 1982), Spectroscopy Soc. Can., Am. Inst. Chemists (cert.). Republican. Home: 7827 NE 12th St Medina WA 98039 Office: U Wash Dept Chemistry BG-10 Seattle WA 98195

CHRISTIAN, ROLAND CARL (BUD), English and speech communications educator; b. LaSalle, Colo., June 7, 1938; s. Roland Clyde and Ethel Mae (Lattimer) C.; m. Joyce Ann Kincel, Feb. 15, 1959; children: Kathleen Marie Christian-Davis, Kristine May Sweet. BA in English and Speech, U. No. Colo., 1962, MA, 1966. Cert. tchr., N.Y., Colo. Tchr. Southside Jr. High Sch., Rockeville Ctr., N.Y., 1962-63, Plateau Valley High Sch., Collbran, Colo., 1963-67; prof. English Northeastern Jr. coll., Sterling, Colo., 1967—; presenter seminars, workshops, Sterling, 1967—; emcee/host Town Meeting of Am., Sterling, 1976. Author: Be Bright! Be Brief! Be Gone! A Speaker's Guide, 1983, The Family Treasury of Great Poems, 1982, Our Twentieth Century's Greatest Poems, 1982, Anti-War Poems: Vol. II, 1985, Potpourrivia, A Digest of Curious Words, Phrases and Trivial Information, 1986, Nicknames in Sports: A Quiz book, 1986, Impressions, 1986; lit. adv. New Voices mag., 1983—; contbr. Ways We Write, 1964, World Poetry Anthology, 1986, American Poetry Anthology, 1986. Served with U.S. Army, 1956-59. Recipient Colo. Recognition of Merit scholarship, 1956, Merit cert. Poets Anonymous, 1983, Award of Merit (9), 1985, 86, Golden Poet of Yr. award World of Poetry Press, 1985, 86, Joel Mack Tchr. of Yr. award Northeastern Jr. Coll., 1986; Jr. Coll. Found. grantee, 1986. Mem. NEA, AAUP, Jr. Coll. Faculty Assn. (sec./treas. 1970-72), Colo. Edn. Assn., Nat. Council Tchrs. of English, Poets of Foothills. Roman Catholic. Avocations: fishing, hunting, sports, trivia, music. Home: 1027 Park St Sterling CO 80751 Office: Northeastern Jr Coll Dept Gen Studies Sterling CO 80751

CHRISTIAN, WAYNE GILLESPIE, environmental consultant; b. King City, Mo., Oct. 28, 1918; s. Elza Orval and Maude Amelia (Gillespie) C.; m. Kara Lorraine Groom, Oct. 29, 1943; children: Kara, Karl. BS, West Tex. State U., 1939; MS, U. Denver, 1948, DSc Edn., 1951. Hist. geology lab. supr. and mus. technician West Tex. State U., Canyon, 1936-39; supr. groundwater surveys and mineral survey U.S. Dept. Interior and State Tex., 1937-39; field and lab. supr. Plains Hist. Mus., Canyon, 1939-40; chief computer Western Geophys. Co., Houston, 1940-44; supt. schs. Darlington, Mo., 1943-44; sci. and social studies tchr., Pickering, Mo., 1944-45; prin. jr.-sr. high sch., Tarkio, Mo., 1945-46; supr. schs., Pickering, 1946-48; dep. dir. Colo. State Home for Children, 1951-52; instr. U. Denver, 1948-57; geophysicist Sun Co., Denver and Dallas, 1952-77; environ. coordinator Sunedco Energy Devel. Co., Dallas, 1977-78, mgr. environ. affairs, 1978-82; sr. environ. specialist Sunedco Coal Co., Lakewood, Colo., 1982-84, retired, 1984. Contbr. articles to profl. jours. Bd. dirs. Am. Bapt. Chs. U.S.A., Rocky Mountain Ctr. on Environment, 1968-70, Byers Home for Boys, Denver, 1969-70; bd. dirs. Denver Bot. Gardens, 1965-70, chmn. edn. com.; chmn. steering com. Balarat Sci. Edn. Ctr., 1969-70; bd. dirs., part-time dir. Plains Conservation Ctr., Denver, 1969-70; pres. Rocky Mountain Bapt. Assn., Denver, 1963-70; bd. dirs. Denver's War on Poverty, 1967-69, one yr. chmn. city-wide Head Start Program; bd. dirs. Met. Council, Denver, 1967-69; exec. com. Bapt. Home Assn. Colo., chmn. bd. 1967-70; bd. dirs. Curtis Park Community Ctr., Denver, 1962— , pres., 1965-70. Mem. Soc. Vertebrate Paleontologists. Republican. Home and Office: 1360 Monaco St Pkwy Denver CO 80220

CHRISTIANSEN, EDWARD KRISTIAN, wholesaler; b. Seattle, Feb. 29, 1928; s. Sigvald and Ingeborg C. (Scheldrup) C.; m. Alene Ruth Hubbard, June 10, 1949; children: Claudia Jo Christiansen Herrick, Karen Louise. Student U. Wash. With Riches & Adams, Seattle, 1950-59; with Fairbanks (Alaska) News, 1959—, pres., gen. mgr., 1969—; sec. Denali State Bank, Fairbanks, 1986—. Bd. dirs. Alaska Kidney Found.; pres. operating bd. and found. Fairbanks Meml. Hosp. Served with U.S. Army. Republican. Lutheran.

CHRISTIANSEN, ERNEST BERT, educator; b. Richfield, Utah, July 31, 1910; s. Ernest C. and Sarah (Nielsen) C.; m. Susan Mann, Sept. 6, 1935; children—David Ernest, Susan Catherine, Gale Ann, Alan Grant, Philip Arne, Richard Lee, Lisa Beth. B.S., U. Utah, 1937; M.S., U. Mich., 1939, Ph.D., 1945. Registered profl. engr., Utah. Chem. engr. E.I. DuPont de Nemours Co., 1941-46; prof. chem. engring. U. Idaho, 1946-47; prof. chem. engring. U. Utah, 1947—, head dept., 1947-75, distinguished research prof., 1977-78. Contbr. articles to profl. jours. Fellow Am. Inst. Chem. Engrs. (nat. dir. 1966-68, Founders award), Utah Acad. Sci., Arts and Letters; mem. Am. Chem. Soc., Am. Soc. Engring. Edn., Am. Soc. Rheology, Tau Beta Pi, Sigma Xi, Phi Kappa Phi. Home: 3025 S 1935 E St Salt Lake City UT 84106 Office: U Utah Salt Lake City UT 84112

CHRISTIANSEN, JOHN REES, educator, sociologist; b. Wales, Utah, Aug. 17, 1927; s. ElRay Lavar and Lewella (Rees) C.; m. Lucele Kartchner, Sept. 18, 1951; children: David, Steven, ElRay, Carol, Daniel. B.S., Utah State U., 1949, M.S., 1952; Ph.D., U. Wis., 1955. Asst. rural sociologist U. Ky., 1954-55; social sci. analyst Dept. Agr., 1955-57; mem. faculty Brigham Young U., 1957—, prof. social work and sociology, 1963—; vis. prof. Tex. A. and M. U., 1963-64, Mich. State U., 1969; U. Wis., 1970-71; collaborator Dept. Agr., 1963-65; cons. Teamwork Found., 1967-69, Rivkin/Carson, 1973, Center for Planning and Research, 1978, Far West Labs., 1978-83. Author: Introductory Sociology, 1963, Disaster Preparedness, 1984, Emergency Preparedness: A Handbook for Families, 1984; also monographs, articles.; Bull. index editor: Rural Sociology, 1969-76. Served with USNR, 1945-47. Fellow Am. Sociol. Assn.; mem. Nat. Council Family Relations, Rural Sociol. Soc., Sigma Xi, Phi Kappa Phi, Pi Kappa Alpha, Alpha Kappa Delta. Home: 1161 Holly Circle Provo UT 84604 Office: Sch Social Work Brigham Young Univ Provo UT 84602

CHRISTIANSEN, JOYCE L. SOELBERG, newspaper editor; b. Salt Lake City, May 25, 1924; d. Lloyd LeRoy and Irene (Lindberg) Soelberg; student public schs.; m. Ernald Christiansen, Sept. 7, 1947; children: Melodie Joyce, Lynda Lee, Lloyd Randall, Catherine Jill. Sec., COBUSCO Steel, Salt Lake City, 1941-42, Universal Film, Inc., Salt Lake City, 1942-43, Delivery Service Co., Salt Lake City, 1946-47; legal sec. Clearfield Naval Supply (Utah), 1943-45; editor Sunset News, Bountiful, Utah, 1972-75; religion writer Deseret News, Salt Lake City, 1976-82, photographer, feature writer, 1976—; editor, writer, photographer South Salt Lake Bugle, Salt Lake City, 1982-83. Pres., Backman Elem. Sch. PTA, 1958-60; 2 v.p. N.W. Jr. High Sch. PTA, 1961-62; active Girl Scouts U.S.A., 1965—, originator Girl Scout Baby award, Utah, 1980; mem. adv. bd. N.W. Multi-Purpose Ctr., 1972-82, sec., 1973-82, substitute day care tchr., 1982—; host radio show Get Me to the Church on Time, 1977; mem. Utah Rose Park Latter-day Saint Stake, 1986, pub. relations specialist, 1986—; mem. Salt Lake Library Bd., 1980-86, sec. bd. 1982, mem. ops., bldgs. and grounds coms.; appointed by gov. Utah State Bldg. Bd., Utah State Bldg. ownership Authority. Recipient 3rd place award Nat. Fedn. Press Women Communication Contest, 1977; numerous first and second place awards Utah Press Women. Mem. Nat. Fedn. Press Women, Utah Press Women (sec. 1978-82, corr. sec. 1982—, 2d v.p. 1980-82, 1st v.p. 1986—, pres.-elect 1987—). Mem. Ch. Jesus Christ of Latter-day Saints (mem. Sunday sch. bd. Riverside Stake 1955). Clubs: Women's Dem., Jane Jefferson, Lady Lions (2d v.p. 1979-80). Contbr. articles to Utah Life mag. Home: 755 N 1400 W Salt Lake City UT 84116 Office: Deseret News 30 E First South Salt Lake City UT 84110

CHRISTIANSEN, ROBERT M., engineering consultant; b. Chgo., Nov. 5, 1924; s. Milton John and Lillian Marion (Donat) C.; m. Lois Elinor Todd, July 12, 1952; children—Eric Todd, Dana Scott, Lois Martha. B.S., Northwestern U., 1947, M.S., 1949; Ph.D. in Chem. Engring. (Allied Chem. Fellow), U. Pa., 1955. Lic. profl. engr., Colo. Pilot plant engr. Universal Oil Products, Riverside, Ill., 1947-48; jr. engr. Shell Devel. Co., Emeryville, Calif., 1949-52; dir. physics research lab. Owens Corning Fiberglas, Granville, Ohio, 1955-59; chief process engr. (now Stearns Roger Corp.), Denver, 1959-70, mgr. environ. scis. div., 1970-83, mgr. new tech., 1983-86; ind. tech. cons., Englewood, Colo., 1986—; instr. U. Pa., 1952-54, Ohio State U., 1955-56. Mem. home owners assn., Cherry Hills Village, Colo., 1982-83. Mem. Am. Inst. Chem. Engrs., Am. Chem. Soc., Sigma Xi, Phi Lambda Upsilon. United Ch. of Christ. Club: Denver Athletic. Home and Office: 4081 S Holly St Englewood CO 80111

CHRISTIANSEN-ENGLERT, KAYE, interior designer, space planner; b. Ft. Collins, Colo., Apr. 2, 1955; d. Dale and Pauline (Winget) Christiansen; m. Robert Anthony Englert; May 14, 1983. BFA in Interior Design, Advt. Design, Utah State U., 1977. Cert. interior designer Nat. Council Interior Design. Interior designer Interior Systems, Midvale, Utah, 1977-78; interior designer, space planner McEntire Anderson Assn., Salt Lake City, 1978-79; dir. interior design and space planning Swenson Assocs., Salt Lake City, 1979-81; design dir. Richard L. Peterson, Salt Lake City, 1981-86; owner, bd. dirs., chief exec. officer purchasing Design Plus, Salt Lake City, 1979—; owner, chief exec. officer interior design Kaye Christiansen-Englert, ASID Interior Design, Salt Lake City, 1979—; mem. exec. residence com. State of Utah, 1986—. Prin. works include restaurants Wildflower Restaurant and Lounge, SNowbird, Ft. Douglas-Hidden Valley Country Club, Iron Blosam Lodge, The Lodge at Snowbird, Turramurra Lodge, Cliff Lodge, conv. ctrs. Salt Palace Exhbn. Hall Expansion, Dixie Ctr., condominuims Turramurra Lodge, Cliff Lodge, Dragolovich Residence, Courtyard Condominiums, offices Del E. Webb Realty and Mgmt. Co., Watkiss & Campbell Law offices, 1st Nat. Bank Chgo. John Madden & Co., health care ctrs., Beesley Youth Ctr., VA Med. Ctr., Grand Junction, Colo., Multi-Purpose and Adminsrn. Bldg. and Div. Orthopedic Surgery, Utah State Mental Hosp. Recipient Merit award Utah Soc. AIA, 1984. Mem. Am. Soc. Interior Designers (Intermountain chpt. publicity chairperson 1981-83, v.p. 1984, pres. 1985, 86, nat. bd. dirs. 1986, Rocky Mountain regional v.p. 1987-88), Salt Lake City C. of C. Avocations: downhill skiing. Home: 2370 Kensington Ave Salt Lake City UT 84108 Office: 323 S 600 E Suite 100 Salt Lake City UT 84102

CHRISTIANSON, LEE EDWARD, biology educator, department chairman; b. Dayton, Ohio, May 5, 1940; s. Orlando and Johanna (Lutness) C.; m. Deann Eliason, Apr. 5, 1963; children: Leann, Elizabeth. BS, U. N.D., 1963; MA, So. Ill. U., 1965; PhD, U. Ariz., 1967. Asst. prof. biol. sci. U. Pacific, Stockton, Calif., 1967-72, assoc. prof., 1972-78, prof., 1978—, chmn. dept., 1984—. Mem. AAAS, AAUP, Am. Soc. Mammalogists, Am. Inst. Biol. Sci., Sierra Club, Wilderness Soc. Office: U Pacific Dept Biol Sci Stockton CA 95211

CHRISTIANSON, ROGER GORDON, biology educator; b. Santa Monica, Calif., Oct. 31, 1947; s. Kyle C. and Ruby (Parker) C.; m. Angela Diane Rey, Mar. 3, 1967; children: Lisa Marie, David Scott, Stephen Peter. BA in Cell and Organismal Biology, U. Calif., Santa Barbara, 1969, MA in Biology, 1971, PhD in Biology, 1976. Faculty assoc. U. Calif., Santa Barbara, 1973-79, staff research assoc., 1979-80; assoc. prof. So. Oreg. State Coll., Ashland, 1980—. Contbr. articles to profl. jours. Active Oreg. Shakespeare Festival Assn., Ashland, 1983—; mem. bikeway com. Ashland City Council, 1986—; coordinator youth program First Bapt. Ch. Ashland, 1981-85, mem. Frontline staff, 1985—. Mem. AAAS (coordinator Pacific div. edn. sect. 1985—), Am. Mus. Natural History, Oreg. Sci. Teacher's Assn., Oreg. Acad. Scis. Republican. Avocations: youth work, sports, photography, multimedia presentations. Home: 430 Reiten Dr Ashland OR 97520 Office: So Oreg State Coll Dept Biology Ashland OR 97520

CHRISTIE, H. FREDERICK, utility company executive; b. Alhambra, Calif., July 10, 1933; s. Andreas B. and Sigrid (Falk-Jorgensen) C.; m. Susan Earley, June 14, 1957; children—Brenda Lynn, Laura Jean. B.S. in Fin., U. So. Calif., 1957, M.B.A., 1964. Treas. So. Calif. Edison Co., Rosemead, 1970-75, v.p., 1975-76, sr. v.p., 1976-80, exec. v.p., 1980-84, pres., dir., 1984—; dir. Gt. Western Fin. Corp., Beverly Hills, Calif., Ducommun Inc., Los Angeles, Am. Mut. Fund, Inc., Los Angeles, Bond Fund Am., Inc., Los Angeles, Tax-Exempt Bond Fund Am., Los Angeles, Los Angeles, Assoc. Electric and Gas Ins. Services Ltd., Jersey City; trustee Cash Mgmt. Trust Am., New Economy Fund, Am. Funds Income Series, Los Angeles, The Am. Funds Tax-Exempt Series II. Trustee Occidental Coll., Los Angeles, Nat. History Mus. Los Angeles County; bd. dirs. United Way, Los Angeles; bd. govs. Music Ctr. Los Angeles. Served with U.S. Army, 1953-55. Named Outstanding mem. Arthritis Found., Los Angeles, 1975, Outstanding Trustee, Multiple Sclerosis Soc. So. Calif., 1979. Mem. Pacific Coast Elec. Assn. (bd. dirs. 1981—, treas. 1975—), Los Angeles C. of C. (bd. dirs. 1983—). Republican. Club: California. Avocations: swimming; horseback riding; jogging. Home: 548 Paseo Del Mar Palos Verdes Est CA 90274 Office: So Calif Edison Co 2244 Walnut Grove Ave Rosemead CA 91770 *

CHRISTISON, PAUL KIMBERLY (KIM), theater arts educator; b. Payson, Utah, May 10, 1948; s. Paul Merritt and Donna Olive (Garbett) C.; m. Mary Ann Parson, Mar. 20, 1970; 1 child, Cameron. AS, Snow Coll., 1968; BFA, Utah State U., 1970, MFA, 1977; PhD, U. Utah, 1985. Assoc. prof. theater arts Snow Coll., Ephraim, Utah, 1978—, chmn. div. humanities and arts, 1986—. Author plays. Served with USN, 1970-74. Floyd T. Morgan scholar, Utah State U., 1969. Mem. Utah Theater Assn. (pres. 1985-87), Rocky Mountain Theater Assn. (local rep. 1983-85). Democrat. Avocations: fishing, gardening. Home: 310 N 550 E 23-1 Ephraim UT 84627 Office: Snow Coll 150 College Ave Ephraim UT 84627

CHRISTMAN, HELEN DOROTHY NELSON, resort executive; b. Denver, Nov. 25, 1922; d. Hector C. and Dorothy C. (Hansen) Russell; m. James Ray Christman, Aug. 7, 1942; children: J. Randol, Linda Rae. Student, Colo. U., 1940-42. Producer Sta. KRMA-TV, Denver, 1960-62; resident mgr. Mana Kai Maui, Maui, Hawaii, 1974-76, exec. coordinator, 1976-78; pres. Resort Apts., Inc., 1986—. Pres. Stephen Knight PTA, Denver, 1957; radio and TV chmn. Colo. PTA, 1958-59; producer ednl. TV programs for PTA, Denver County, 1960-61; bd. dirs. Maui United Way, 1983—. Mem. Delta Delta Delta. Club: Maui Country (chmn. women's golf assn.). Address: 3448 Hookipa Kihei-Maui HI 96753

CHRISTMAS, JANICE JEAN, multimedia producer; b. Monroe, Wis., Apr. 4, 1946; s. Walter Dean and Helen Isabel (Lanz) Lavasseur; divorced; children: Ianthe Ingham, Anna Elissa. BS in Art Edn., U. Wis., 1974. Guest fashion editor Mademoiselle mag., N.Y.C., 1967; fashion designer N.Y.C., 1967-69; broadcast prodn. coordinator McCann-Erickson, Chgo., 1975-77; prodn. mgr. Laurence Deutsch Design, Los Angeles, 1978-80; producer, v.p. Kevin Biles Design, Venice, Calif., 1980—. Author, producer, dir. videotape Wood Heat, 1975. Troop leader Girl Scouts, Los Angeles U.S., Los Angeles, 1979-80. Mem. Venice C. of C. Home: 12922 Stanwood Dr Los Angeles CA 90066 Office: Kevin Biles Design 358 Hampton Dr Venice CA 90291 Office: 5 E 16th St 8th Floor New York NY 10003

CHRISTOFFERSEN, RALPH EARL, chemist; b. Elgin, Ill., Dec. 4, 1937; s. Arthur Henry and Mary C.; m. Barbara Hibbard, June 10, 1961; children: Kirk Alan, Rachel Anne. B.S., Cornell Coll., 1959; Ph.D., Ind. U., 1963. Asst. prof. chemistry U. Kans., Lawrence, 1966-69; assoc. prof. U. Kans., 1967-72, prof., 1972-81, asst. vice chancellor for acad. affairs, 1974-75, assoc. vice chancellor for acad. affairs, 1976-79, vice chancellor for acad. affairs, 1979-81; pres. Colo. State U., Ft. Collins, 1981-83; exec. dir. Upjohn Co., 1983-85, v.p. biotech. and basic research support, 1985—; mem. sci. adv. bd. U.S. Solar Energy Research Inst., 1981—, chmn., 1981-86; chmn. bd. dirs. Mich. Biotech Inst., Kalamazoo Area Math and Sci. Ctr. Adv. Bd.; bd. trustees Kendall Sch. Design; bd. dirs. UCLA Symposia, Indsl. Biotech. Assn. Contbr. articles to profl. jours. Trustee Kalamazoo Symphony Orch. NIH fellow, 1962-63, 64-66. Fellow Am. Inst. Chemists; mem. Am. Chem. Soc., Am. Phys. Soc. (v.p. theoretical div. 1981), AAUP, Internat. Soc. Quantum Biology (pres. 1977-79), Pharm. Mfrs. Assn. (chmn. biotech. adv. com.), Sigma Xi, Phi Lambda Upsilon.

CHRISTOPHER, F. SCOTT, family psychology educator; b. Lincoln, Nebr., Apr. 8, 1952; s. Francis and Carol Lee (Campbell) C.; m. Fonda Lynn Kravin, June 2, 1985. BS, U. Nebr., 1975, MS, 1979; PhD, Oreg. State U., 1982. Intern in psychology Omsorgstyrelson, Gothenburg, Sweden, 1973-74; program coordinator Lancaster Office Mental Retardation, Lincoln, 1976-79; asst. prof. U. Nev., Reno, 1982-86, Ariz. State U., Tempe, 1986—; cons. Community Cooperative Services, Inc., Reno, 1983-85, Northern Nev. Fertility Clinic, Reno, 1985—. Assoc. editor Family Relations, St. Paul, Minn., 1985—; contbr. articles to profl. jours. Adv. bd. mem. Lancaster County Welfare-Child Abuse, Lincoln, 1978, Com. to Aid to Aid Abused Women, Reno, 1986. Sperry Hutchison Co. scholar, 1975; Dean's research award Oreg. State U., 1981; U. Nev. research grantee, 1985. Mem. Internat. Soc. for the Study of Personal Relationships, Am. Home Econs. Assn., Nat. Council on Family Relations, Phi Kappa Nu, Omicron Nu. Avocation: nature study. Home: 914 E Vaughn Gilbert AZ 85234 Office: Ariz State Univ Dept Family Resources Tempe AZ 85287

CHRISTOPHER, RICHARD SCOTT, journalist, editor, marketing executive; b. Chgo., May 21, 1953; s. James J. and Geraldine A. (Kaulback) C. B.J., U. Mo.-Columbia, 1975. Gen. assignment reporter Salem (Mo.) News, 1975; news editor, tech. writer AVMA Schaumburg, Ill., 1975-77; sports reporter Paddock Publs., Arlington Heights, Ill., 1977-78; assoc. editor, mktg. coordinator Farm and Land Inst/Nat. Assn. Realtors, Chgo., 1978-80; mgr. project services Kiwanis Internat., Chgo., 1980-82; acct. exec. Eckis Advt. & Design, Irvine, Calif., 1982-83; advt., pub. relations exec. R.S. Christopher & Assoc., Newport Beach, Calif., 1983-86; pub. relations acct. mgr., Basso & Assocs. Advt. Pub. Relations, 1986—; editor, advt. mgr. Nat. Assn. Ind. Ins. Adjusters, Chgo., 1982—. Recipient Bronze award Internat.

Film & TV Festival of N.Y., 1981, 82. Mem. Internat. Assn. Bus. Communicators, Pub. Relations Soc. Am. Roman Catholic. Club: Kiwanis.

CHRISTY, LARRY DEE, military officer; b. Christopher, Ill., Mar. 31, 1949; s. Howard Wilmont and Dorothy Virginia (Payne) C.; m. Linda Kay Glenski, May 10, 1968; children: Lorri Dee, Erick Shawn. AA in Aviation and Indsl. Tech., So. Ill. U., 1984. Commd. USAF, 1972, advanced through grades to tech. sgt., master instr., aircraft technician, 1972-78; metrologist USAF, Little Rock, 1978-81; metrology instr. USAF, Denver, 1981—, master instr., 1982—; cons. Concept Engring., Aurora, Colo., 1983—. Author: (Tech. manuals) Optical Measurement, 1984, Physical Measurement, 1986. mem. Soc. Mfg. Engrs. Club: Colo. Commodore (librarian 1986—), Condor. Avocations: computers, computer edn., tech. writing. Home: 403 S Royal St Royalton IL 62983 Office: 48 CRS/MABM, RAF Laken Heath England

CHRISTY, THOMAS PATRICK, bank executive; b. Urbana, Ill., May 18, 1943; s. Edward Michael and Iona Theresa (Rogers) C.; m. Marjorie Anne McIntyre, June 1966 (div. May 1973); children: Thomas Patrick Jr., Derek Edward; m. Sandra Allen Stern, May 19, 1984; 1 child, Patrick Edward. BA in Psychology, Adams State Coll., 1965. Tchr. Colorado Springs Pub. Sch., 1965-69; regional personnel dir. Forest Service USDA, Washington, 1969-81; sr. account exec. Mgmt. Recuriters Inc., Costa Mesa, Calif., 1981-84; v.p. Coleman & Assoc. Inc., Santa Monica, Calif., 1984; asst. v.p. Union Bank, Los Angeles, 1984—; adj. prof. grad. sch. bus. Northrop U., Los Angeles. Arbitrator Bus. and Consumer Arbitrator program Better Bus. Bur., Los Angeles and Orange County; mem. Pasadena Area Young Reps. Mem. Personnel and Indsl. Relations Assn. (chmn. fed. issues com, govtl. affairs com.), Employment Mgrs. Assn. (co-chmn. regional com.), Am. Soc. of Personnel Adminstrs., Soc. of Profls. in Dispute Resolution, Sigma Pi Alumni Assn., Adams State Coll. Alumni Assn. (Calif. state pres.), AAUP. Episcopalian. Clubs: Athletic (Los Angeles), Beach (Santa Monica). Avocations: squash, golf, skiing, collecting antiques, gardening. Home: 1444 Wellington Ave Pasadena CA 91103-2320 Office: Union Bank Corp Staffing Dept 445 S. Figuroa St Los Angeles CA 90071

CHRISTY, WILLIAM O., food products company executive; b. 1931. With Certified Grocers of Calif. Ltd., 1952-60; owner Rancho Mirage, Calif., 1960-62; with Certified Grocers of Calif., 1962—, asst. treas., 1971-72, treas., 1972-74, sr. v.p., 1974-75, exec. v.p. ops., 1975-77, chief exec. officer, 1977—, dir. Office: Certified Grocers of Calif 2601 S Eastern Ave Los Angeles CA 90040 *

CHRYSOSTOMOS OF OREOI, BISHOP GONZÁLEZ-ALEXOPOULOS, bishop, educator; b. Calif., Apr. 6, 1945; s. A.E. and J. (Rothmann) González-Alexopoulos. BA, U. Calif., Riverside, Calif. State U.; MA, U. Calif., Davis; MA, PhD, Princeton U. Ordained bishop True Orthodox Ch. Greece. Preceptor psychology Princeton (N.J.) U., 1972-75; asst. prof. psychology U. Calif., Riverside, 1975; adj. asst. prof. Christian thought Ashland Theol. Sem., 1981-83; asst. prof. then assoc. prof. psychology Ashland Coll., 1980-83; dir. Ctr. for Traditional Orthodox Studies, 1981-85, scholar-in-residence, 1986, acad. dir., 1986—; vis. scholar Harvard U. Divinity Sch., 1981. Marsden research fellow Oxford U., 1985. Office: Ctr Traditionalist Orthodox Studies PO Box 398 Etna CA 96027

CHU, CHARLES R., podiatrist; b. Kaoshiung, Republic of China, Mar. 4, 1953; came to U.S., 1962; s. David C.M. and Sue (Hsieh) C.; m. Helen Wang. BA in Biochemistry, U. Calif., Berkeley, 1976; D in Podiat. Medicine, Calif. Coll. Podiat. Medicine, 1979. Diplomate Am. Bd. Podiat. Orthopedics. Resident So. Calif. Podiat. Med. Ctr., Los Angeles, 1980; pvt. practice podiat. medicine Bellevue, Wash., 1981—. Mem. Am. Coll. Foot Surgeons. Avocations: fishing, golfing, camping. Home: 18708 132d Pl SE Renton WA 98058 Office: 4317 128th SE Bellevue WA 98006

CHU, DANIEL YUE MAN, project engineer; b. Canton, Republic of China, Dec. 30, 1954; s. Kong and Chui (Ming) C.; m. Sunnie So Fun, Dec. 19, 1983. Assoc. of Poly., Hong Kong Poly., 1980. Registered profl. engr., Calif. Engring. apprentice U. of Hong Kong, 1972-75, from technician to sr. technician, 1975-81; from technician to engring. assoc. Bio Rad Labs., Richmond, Calif., 1982-84, engr., 1985—. Inventor electrophoresis equipment. Recipient Research award of Yr. Bio-Rad Labs., 1984. Mem. Instn. of Mech. Engrs. (grad.). Home: 1331 47th Ave San Francisco CA 94122 Office: Bio Rad Labs 1414 Harbour Ways Richmond CA 94801

CHU, ERNEST HSIAO-YING, human genetics and toxicology educator; b. Haining, Chekiang, China, June 3, 1927; came to U.S., 1949; s. Homing and Si-Tseng (Tang) C.; m. Nien-Si Liu, Aug. 14, 1954; children: Clara, David, Wellington. BS, St. John's University, Shanghai, China, 1947; postgrad., Nat. Chekiang U., Hang Chow, China, 1947-48; MS, U. Calif., 1951, PhD, 1954. Research assoc. in botany Yale U., New Haven, 1954-59, lectr. in anatomy, 1958-59; prof. of zoology U. Tenn., Knoxville, 1967-72; biologist Oak Ridge (Tenn.) Nat. Lab., 1959-72, prof. of toxicology, 1985—; prof. human genetics U. Mich., Ann Arbor, 1972—; cons. FDA, EPA. Fellow AAAS, N.Y. Acad. Sci.; mem. Genetics Soc. Am., Soc. Cell Biology, Am. Soc. Human Genetics, Tissue Culture Assn., Am. Genetics Assn., Am. Soc. Microbiology, Am. Soc. Photobiology, Radiation Research Soc.

CHU, FONG-FONG, biomedical research scientist; b. Taipei, Taiwan, Sept. 30, 1951; came to U.S., 1974; d. Yun-Ting and Wen-Mei (Shen) C.; m. Robert Steven Esworthy, Sept. 30, 1981; 1 child, Sean Robert. BS, Nat. Taiwan U., Taipei, 1973; MS, So. Ill. U., Edwardsville, 1976; PhD, SUNY, Buffalo, 1983. Research asst. Academia Sinica, Taipei, 1973-74; teaching asst. SUNY, Buffalo, 1976-78; research asst. Roswell Park Meml. Inst., Buffalo, 1978-82; postdoctoral fellow Howard U. Cancer Ctr., Washington, 1982-84, UCLA, 1985—. Mem. AAAS. Avocation: stamp collecting. Office: UCLA Lab Biomed & Environ Scis 900 Veteran Ave Los Angeles CA 90024

CHU, MORGAN, lawyer; b. N.Y.C., Dec. 27, 1950; m. Helen M. Wong, Dec. 29, 1970. AB, UCLA, 1971, MA, 1972, PhD, 1973; postdoctoral studies in library sci., Yale U., 1974; JD, Harvard U., 1976. Bar: Calif. 1976, U.S. Dist. Ct. (cen. dist.) Calif. 1977, U.S. Ct. Appeals (9th cir.) 1976, 77, U.S. Dist. Ct. (no. dist.) Calif. 1980, U.S. Dist. Ct. (so dist.) Calif. 1984, U.S. Dist. Ct. (ea. dist.) Calif. 1986. Law clk. to presiding judge U.S. Ct. Appeals (9th cir.) Calif., San Francisco, 1976-77; assoc. Irell & Manella, Los Angeles, 1977-82, ptnr., 1982—; adj. prof. UCLA Sch. Law, 1979-82; judge pro tem Los Angeles Mcpl. Ct., 1980—. Assoc. editor Litigation News, 1981-84. Fellow, Yale U., 1974. Mem. ABA (chmn. high tech. intellectual property and patent trials subcom. 1986—, trial practice com., litigation sect.), Calif. Bar Assn., Los Angeles County Bar Assn. (judiciary com.). Office: Irell & Manella 1800 Ave of Stars Suite 900 Los Angeles CA 90067

CHU, YEE-YEEN, computer company executive; b. Taoyuan, Republic of China, Mar. 7, 1949; s. Shen and Chu (Hwang) C.; m. Yueh-Sung Hsieh, Sept. 26, 1983; 1 child, Jennifer. MS, Clemson U., 1974; PhD, U. Ill., 1978. Vis. assoc. prof. NTIT, Taipei, Republic of China, 1981; sr. scientist Perceptronics Inc., Woodland Hills, Calif., 1978-84, dir., 1984—; guest speaker UCLA short course on Battle Field Robotics and Intelligent Interfaces for Advanced Man-Machine Systems, 1983-85. Author 20 papers on expert systems, intelligent automation, decision support systems. Mem. IEEE, Am. Assn. Artificial Intelligence. Home: 808 Springwood St Thousand Oaks CA 91320 Office: Perceptronics Inc 21111 Erwin St Woodland Hills CA 91367

CHUANG, RONALD YAN-LI, biochemistry educator; b. Chen-Tu, Szechwan, China, Feb. 12, 1940; came to U.S., 1965; s. Shao-In and Chingwha (Chang) C.; m. Linda L. Fang, Aug. 7, 1967; children: Ann, Katherine, Ted. BS in Agrl. Chemistry, Nat. Taiwan U., Taipei, 1961; MS in Food Sci. and Tech., U. Calif., Davis, 1966, PhD in Biochemistry, 1971. Research assoc. Columbia U., N.Y.C., 1971-72; asst. prof. pharmacology Duke U., Durham, N.C., 1972-76; asst. prof. biochemistry Oral Roberts U., Tulsa, 1978-81; asst. research biochemist Primate Ctr. U. Calif., Davis, 1976-78, asst. prof. pharmacology, 1981-85; assoc. prof. U. Calif., 1985—. Contbr. articles to profl. jours. Recipient Christine Landgraf award U. Calif. Med. Sch., Davis, 1984, Research Career Devel. award NIH, 1984. Mem. Am. Soc. Biol. Chemists, Am. Assn. Cancer Research, Am. Assn. Pharm. and Exptl. Therapeutics, Soc. Chinese Bioscientists in Am. (symposium organizer 1985—). Avocation: fishing. Home: 1521 Brown Dr Davis CA 95616 Office: U Calif Dept Pharmacology Davis CA 95616

CHUANG, TUNG JUNG, chemist; b. Chiayi, Taiwan, Apr. 25, 1940; came to U.S., 1964; s. King T. and Kuei-Li (Chang) C.; m. Betty Y. Chiang, Dec. 30, 1969; 1 child, Henry H. BS, Nat. Taiwan U., 1963; MS, U. Ill., 1966; PhD, U. Calif., Berkeley, 1970. Postdoctoral fellow IBM Research Lab., San Jose, Calif., 1970-71, mem. research staff, 1971—; adj. prof. San Diego State U., 1984—; vis. prof. U. Munich, 1985-86. Contbr. articles to profl. jours.; patentee in field. Grantee NSF, 1985; recipient IBM Outstanding Innovation award, 1982, Alexander Von Humbold Sr. U.S. Scientist award Alexander Von Humboldt Found., 1985. Mem. Am. Chem. Soc., Am. Vacuum Soc. Democrat. Office: IBM Almaden Research Ctr K33/801 650 Harry Rd San Jose CA 95120-6099

CHUCK, WALTER G(OONSUN), lawyer; b. Wailuku, Maui, Hawaii, Sept. 10, 1920; s. Hong Yee and Aoe (Ting) C.; m. Marian Chun, Sept. 11, 1943; children: Jamie Allison, Walter Gregory, Meredith Jayne. Ed.B., U. Hawaii, 1941; J.D., Harvard U., 1948. Bar: Hawaii 1948. Navy auditor Pearl Harbor, 1941; field agt. Social Security Bd., 1942; labor law insp. Terr. Dept. Labor, 1943; law clk. firm Ropes, Gray, Best, Coolidge & Rugg, 1948; asst. pub. prosecutor City and County of Honolulu, 1949; with Fong, Miho & Choy, 1950-53; ptnr. Fong, Miho, Choy & Chuck, 1953-58; pvt. practice law Honolulu, 1958-65; ptnr. Chuck & Fujiyama, Honolulu, 1965-74; ptnr. firm Chuck, Wong & Tonaki, Honolulu, 1974-76, Chuck & Pai, Honolulu, 1976-78; sole practice Honolulu, 1978-80; pres. Walter G. Chuck Law Corp., Honolulu, 1980—; dist. magistrate Dist. Ct. Honolulu, 1956-63; mem. ad hoc specialization of lawyers com. Superior Ct. Hawaii; treas., dir. M & W, Inc.; gen. ptnr. Tripler Warehousing Co., Kapalama Investment Co.; dir. Pacific Resources, Inc., Gasco, Inc., Aloha Airlines, Inc., Hawaiian Ind. Refinery, Inc., Honolulu Painting Co., Ltd., Enerco, Inc. Chmn. Hawaii Employment Relations Bd., 1955-59; bd. dirs. Nat. Assn. State Labor Relations Bd., 1957-58, Honolulu Theatre for Youth, 1977-80; chief clk. Ho. of Reps., 1951, 53; chief clk. Hawaii senate, 1959-61; govt. appeal agt. SSS, 1953-72; mem. jud. council, State of Hawaii; exec. com. Hawaiian Open; mem. Friends of Judiciary Mus., ad hoc com. for Supreme Ct. of Hawaii on Specialization of Lawyers; former bd. dirs. YMCA. Served as capt. inf. Hawaii Territorial Guard. Fellow Internat. Acad. Trial Lawyers (dir.); mem. ABA (chmn. Hawaii sr. lawyers div.), Hawaii Bar Assn. (pres. 1963), Am. Trial Lawyers Assn. (editor), U. Hawaii Alumni Assn. (Distinguished Service award 1967, dir., bd. govs.), Law Sci. Inst., Assoc. Students U. Hawaii, Am. Judicature Soc., Internat. Soc. Barristers, Am. Inst. Banking, Chinese C. of C. Republican. Clubs: Harvard of Hawaii, Waialae Country (pres. 1975), Pacific, Oahu Country. Home: 2691 Aaliamanu Pl Honolulu HI 96813 Office: Suite 1814 745 Fort St Honolulu HI 96813

CHUDD, JAMES MICHAEL, science administrator; b. Fond du Lac, Wis., Sept. 5, 1949; s. John Anthony and Domicell Dorothy (Silke) C.; m. Darryl Yvonne Schumpert, Dec. 31, 1976; 1 child, Jean Michelle. BS in Chemistry, U. Wis., Oshkosh, 1971; MS in Chemistry, U. Ill., 1975. Analytical chemist Eastman Kodak Co., Rochester, N.Y., 1976-80, electrochemistry group leader, 1980-82; acting unit supr. Colo. div. Eastman Kodak Co., Windsor, 1982-86, unit dir., 1986—; environ. cons. Larimer-Weld Regional Council of Govts., Loveland, Colo., 1984-85. Served with U.S. Army, 1971-74. Mem. Am. Chem. Soc., Ft. Collins Coin Club, No. Colo. Philatelic Soc. Republican. Avocations: numismatics, philately. Home: 1406 Independence Rd Fort Collins CO 80526 Office: Kodak Colo Div C-42 Analytical Services Windsor CO 80551

CHUGHTAI, ABDUL REHMAN, research scientist; b. Sialkot, Pakistan, Dec. 8, 1934; came to U.S., 1962; s. Allah Abdul Karim Rekha and Ahmad Bibi Chughtai; m. Marla S. Tuck, Nov. 2, 1966; children: Joseph Rehman, Shirin Marla, Mariam L.W. BSc with honors, U. Panjab, Lahore, Pakistan, 1957, MSc with honors, 1958; PhD, U. Colo., 1967. Assoc. prof. chemistry U. Mosul, Iraq, 1971-73; sr. research scientist, vis. assoc. prof. U. Denver, 1973—. Author textbooks; contbr. articles to profl. jours. Mem. Am. Chem. Soc. Moslem. Avocations: walking, jogging. Home: 3071 W 134th Ave Broomfield CO 80020 Office: U Denver Dept Chem 2101 E Wasely Denver CO 80208

CHUN, LOWELL KOON WA, architect; b. Honolulu, Sept. 2, 1944; s. Kwai Wood and Sara Lau C. BA in Eng., U. Hawaii, 1967; BArch, Cornell U., 1971. Registered profl. architect, Hawaii. Archtl. designer Wilson, Okamoto & Assocs., Honolulu, 1972-74; architect, planner Aotani & Assocs., Inc., Honolulu, 1974-82; design planner Daniel, Mann, Johnson & Mendenhall, Manila and Honolulu, 1982-84; architect, planner Alfred A. Yee div. Leo A. Daly Co., Honolulu, 1984—. Prin. author: Kauai Parks and Recreation Master Plan, 1978, Hawaii State Recreation Plan (Maximum Federal Eligibility award, 1980), Maui Community Plans, 1981. Advisor, locations officer Maitreya Inst., Honolulu, 1983-84; v.p., treas. Kagyu Theg Chen Ling Tibetan Ctr., Honolulu, 1982, 84; rep. Environ. Coalition to Hawaii State Legislature, 1974. Recipient Master Plan award Nat. Assn. Counties, 1975. Mem. Am. Planning Assn., Sierra Club (local vice-chmn. 1974-76). Buddhist. Club: Cornell of Hawaii (Honolulu). Avocations: creative writing, photography, hiking. Home: 456 N Judd St Honolulu HI 96817 Office: Leo A Daly Alfred A Yee Div 1441 Kapiolani Blvd Suite 810 Honolulu HI 96814

CHUN, WENDY SAU WAN, investment company executive; b. China, Oct. 17, 1951; came to U.S., 1975; d. Siu Kee and Lai Ching (Wong) C.; m. Wing Chiu Ng, Aug. 12, 1976. B.S., Hong Kong Bapt. Coll., 1973; postgrad. U. Hawaii-Manoa, 1975-77. Real estate saleswoman Tropic Shores Realty Co., Honolulu, 1977-80; pres., prin., broker Advance Realty Investment Co., Honolulu, 1980—; owner Video Fun Centre, Honolulu, 1981-83; v.p., immigration/fin. cons. Asia-Am. Investment, Inc., Honolulu, 1983—, pres, Asia-Am. Bus Cons., Inc., Canada, 1986—; co-owner, dir. H & N Tax, Honolulu, 1983—; internat. cons. Capital Investment of Hawaii, 1983—; bd. dirs. B.P.D. Internat., Ltd., Hong Kong. Mem. Nat. Assn. Realtors. Avocations: singing; dancing; swimming; dramatic performances. Home: Apt 3302 2333 Kapiolani Blvd Honolulu HI 96826

CHUNG, ALICE PO YING, civil engineer; b. Hong Kong, Apr. 27, 1956; came to U.S., 1975; d. Kue Suen and Yuk (Ching) Chung. BA, UCLA, 1979, MS, 1982. Registered profl. engr., Calif. Postgrad. research engr. UCLA, 1980-81; civil engring. asst. Los Angeles County, 1982-83, sr. civil engring. asst., 1983-84, profl. civil engring. asst., 1984-85, civil engr. I, 1985—. Contbr. articles to profl. jours. Mem. ASCE, Water Pollution Control Fedn., Tau Beta Pi. Home: 249 Alpine St #50 Pasadena CA 91106 Office: Los Angeles County Dept Pub Works PO Box 4089 Terminal Annex Los Angeles CA 90051

CHUNG, DAVID SHIN, podiatrist; b. Busan, Republic of Korea, Apr. 10, 1957; came to U.S., 1972; s. Richard Dukhwan and Rose Sangun (Han) C.; m. Elise Sungran Kim, Aug. 4, 1984. Student, Portland State U., 1975-79; BS, Scholl Coll. Podiatric Medicine, 1983, D in Podiatric Medicine, 1983. Diplomate Am. Bd. Podiatric Medicine. Practice medicine specializing in podiatry Beaverton, Oreg., 1983—; staff mem. Med. Ctr. Hosp., Portland, Oreg., 1985—. Youth leader Cen. Ch., Beaverton, 1984—. Mem. Am. Podiatric Med. Assn., Oreg. Podiatric Med. Assn. Avocations: bowling, calligraphy, table tennis, singing. Office: 12400 SW Allen Blvd #B Beaverton OR 97005 Office: 2734 19th Ave Forest Grove OR 97116

CHUNG, JIN SOO, ocean mining and offshore engineer; b. Seoul, Korea, Jan. 27, 1937; s. Hyun Mo and Soon Mo (Yoo) C.; B.S.E. in Naval Architecture, Seoul Nat. U., 1961; M.S., U. Calif., Berkeley, 1964; Ph.D. in Engring. Mechanics, U. Mich., 1969; m. Yang Ja Park, Aug. 11, 1967; children—Claude H., Christine M. Sr. research engr. Exxon Prodn. Research Co., Houston, 1969-73; staff engr. Lockheed Missiles & Space Co., Sunnyvale, Calif., 1973-80; prof. Colo. Sch. Mines, Golden, 1980—; cons. in hydrodynamics to Inter-Govtl. Maritime Consultative Orgn., UN, 1981; chmn., editor Proceedings of 1st Offshore Mechanics/Arctic Engring. Symposium, New Orleans, 1982, chmn., editor 2d Internat. Symposium, Houston, 1983, 3d Internat. Symposium, New Orleans, 1984, 4th Internat. Symposium, Dallas, 1985, 5th Internat. Symposium and Exhibit, Tokyo, 1986. Recipient Eugene W. Jacobson award Energy Tech. Conf., Houston, 1978. Mem. ASME (Ralph James award 1980, policy bd. communication 1981-85, chmn. offshore mechanics com., 1982-84, paper revs. chmn. Petroleum Div. 1980-84, 1st chmn. offshore mechanics and arctic engring. div. 1984-86, Outstanding Achievement award 1987, editor various publications 1987—), Internat. Council on Offshore Mechanics and Arctic Engring. (founder, chmn. 1986—), Soc. Petroleum Engrs., Soc. Naval Architects Japan, Sigma Xi. Sr. editor Transactions Jour. of Energy Resources Tech., 1980-85; assoc. editor Applied Mechanics Rev., 1985—; pioneer in advanced tech. devel. and position control simulation of deep ocean mining system. Home: 12757 W 57th Dr Arvada CO 80002 Office: Colo Sch Mines Golden CO 80401

CHUNG, STEWART, architect; b. Hong Kong, Sept. 2, 1956; came to U.S., 1973; s. Shek-Chuen and Alice (Wong) C. BArch, U. So. Calif., 1979; MArch, UCLA, 1981. Architect Jarvis & Murray AIA, Newport Beach, Calif., 1979-81; prin. Chung & Assocs., South Pasadena, Calif., 1981—; chmn. Com. to Rebuild South Pasadena, 1984-85; mem. adv. com. Cerritos Coll., Norwalk, Calif., 1985—. Served to lt. USNR, 1985—. Named Bachelor of Yr., Man-Watchers of Los Angeles, 1985. Mem. AIA. Republican. Club: Nice Guys Am. (award 1985). Avocations: skiing, traveling, flying, sky diving, scuba diving. Home and Office: 2000 Hanscom Dr South Pasadena CA 91030

CHURCH, BROOKS DAVIS, microbiologist; b. Youngstown, Ohio, May 6, 1918; s. Brooks Davis and Clara (Santorius) C.; m. Jean Marie Church, Nov. 26, 1965; children: Elizabeth, Stephen, Heather, Heidi. BS, U. Mich., 1947, MS, 1953, PhD, 1956. Sr. research assoc. Warner-Lambert, Morris Plains, N.J., 1955-60; asst. prof. microbiology U. Wash., Seattle, 1960-63; assoc. prof. U. Minn., Mpls., 1963-67; sr. research assoc. Northern Star Research Ctr., Mpls., 1967-72; prof. U. Denver, 1972-77; pres. BioSearch Assocs., Littleton, Colo., 1981—; cons. WACON, Denver, 1983—, PennWalt, Phila., 1985, Allied Mills, Sydney, Austrailia, 1983-84, Marion Labs, Kansas City, Mo., 1982-83. Contbr. numerous articles to profl. jours.; patentee in field. Vol. Am. Heart Assn., Denver, 1985—. Served as sgt. U.S. Army, 1942-46. Fellow Am. Soc. Microbiology (pres. Rocky Mountain chpt. 1973); mem. AAAS, N.Y. Acad. Sci., Sigma Xi, Phi Sigma. Democrat. Methodist. Avocations: tennis, music, travel. Home: 329 W Caley Dr Littleton CO 80120 Office: BioSearch Assocs Inc PO Box 2988 Littleton CO 80161

CHURCH, CHANDLER BERNARD, bank executive; b. Sacramento, Mar. 2, 1935; s. Chandler B. and Genevieve (Prisk) Bryant Church; children—Carol Lynn, Kathryn Mary, Chandler B. B.S. in Animal Sci., U. Wyo., 1960. Asst. cashier Bank Tulare, Calif., 1968-69, asst. mgr., Chowchilla, Calif., 1969-70, asst. mgr. loans, Merced, Calif., 1970-80, v.p., mgr. Yuba City, Calif., 1980-82, v.p., head corp. agribus. fin., 1983—. Bd. dirs. United Way, Yuba-Sutter, Calif., 1982-84; chmn. Salvation Army Service Extension 1981—; bd. dirs. Bicounty Econ. Devel. Commn., Marysville, Calif., 1984; mem. Rideout Hosp. Inst., Marysville, 1983-84. Mem. Phi Epsilon Phi, Alpha Zeta. Republican. Lodges: Rotary, Kiwanis, Elks. Home: 1570 Spencer Ln Yuba City CA 95991 Office: Bank of America 1100 Butte House Rd Yuba City CA 95991

CHURCH, JOHN BRADFORD, data processing executive; b. Denver, Oct. 3, 1949; s. Harry Bradford and Marcelle Clotilde (Koller) C.; m. Geraldine Lee Uhl, Sept. 27, 1968; 1 child, Jeremy Bradford. Student, Platte Valley Bible Coll., 1967-68, Community Coll. Denver, 1972-74, Aurora Tech. Ctr., 1974. Computer operator Wilhelm Foods Inc., Denver, 1974; computer programmer CPS Distbrs. Inc., Denver, 1974-75; mgr. data processing Friendly Markets Inc., Arvada, Colo., 1975-77, Allied Carriers Exchange Inc., Denver, 1976—. Served with U.S. Army, 1969-72. Mem. Data Processing Mgmt. Assn., N.Am. Honeywell Users Assn. Republican. Avocations: camping, fishing, swimming, gardening, sports. Home: 3069 S Quintero Way Aurora CO 80013 Office: Allied Carriers Exchange Inc 4242 Delaware Denver CO 80216

CHURCHILL, WILLIAM DELEE, retired educator, psychologist; b. Buffalo, Nov. 4, 1919; s. Glenn Luman and Ethel (Smith) C.; A.B., Colgate U., 1941; M.Ed., Alfred U., 1951; Ed.D., U. Rochester, 1969; m. Beulah Coleman, Apr. 5, 1943; children—Cherylee, Christie. Tchr. secondary sci., Canaseraga, N.Y., 1947-56; dir. guidance Alfred-Almond Sch., Almond, N.Y., 1956-63; grad. asst. U. Rochester, 1963-65; asst. prof. psychology Alfred (N.Y.) U., 1965-66; assoc. prof. edn. Ariz. State U., Tempe, 1966-86. Served to lt. col. USAAF, 1942-46; PTO. Mem. Am., Western, Ariz. psychol. assns., Am. Ednl. Research Assn. Author: Career Survey of Graduates, 1973. Home: 11454 N 85th St Scottsdale AZ 85260

CHUTE, DONALD DEAN, leasing company executive; b. Creston, Iowa, Dec. 25, 1944; s. Paul Clifford and Harriet Ann (Lawrence) S.; m. Helen Elaine Hogan, Aug. 27, 1966; children: Dawn M., Robin A. BA in Bus. Mgmt., Sonoma State U., 1974. Spl. asst. So. Pacific Transp. Co., San Francisco, 1974, car hire acctg. mgr., 1975-78; car hire acctg. mgr. Itel Rail Corp., San Francisco, 1978-80; car hire acctg. dir. Itel Rail Corp. div. Itel Corp., San Francisco, 1981, car hire & system services dir., 1982-83, car hire, bus. systems planning and ops. dir., 1983, dir. ops., 1983—. Mem. Nat. and Southwestern Care Hire and Car Service Assns., Am. Short Line Assn. Republican. Roman Catholic. Avocations: carpentry, mechanics, coin collecting. Office: Itel Rail Corp 55 Francisco San Francisco CA 94133

CHYKALIUK, PETER BOHDAN, product development representative; b. Newark, Sept. 12, 1955; s. John and Oxana (Federuk) C.; m. Amanda Brigman, Jan. 6, 1979. BS, Rutgers U., 1977; MS Tex. Tech. U., 1979; PhD, Okla. State U., 1981. Technician, Tex. A&M Exptl. Sta., Lubbock, Tex., 1977; research asst. Tex. Tech. U., Lubbock, 1978-79; technician Monsanto Co., Lubbock, 1979; research asst. Okla. State U., Stillwater, 1979-81; product devel. rep. III, Monsanto Co., 1981-84, product devel. assoc., 1984-86; pres. Kansagra Farm Supplies, Inc, KC Land Co., Inc., 1986—. Recipient Wimberly Small Grains Grad. Achievement award Agronomy Dept., Okla. U., 1981; Monsanto Product Devel. Achievement award, 1984. Mem. Council Agrl. Sci. and Tech., Weed Sci. Soc. Am., North Cen. Weed Control Conf., Ellis county Wheat Growers (chmn. 1986—), Western Weed Sci. Soc., Soil Conservation Soc., Wyo. Pest Council. Baptist. Contbr. articles to profl. jours.

CICHORZ, ROGER STANLEY, research chemist; b. Chgo., Nov. 5, 1942; s. Stanley Joseph and Pauline Elizabeth (Stupca) C.; m. Norma Jean Sattler, July 19, 1975; children: Christopher, Alyssa Ann. BA, Rockford Coll., 1964; MA, So. Ill. U., 1966. Analytical chemist Rockwell Internat., Golden, Colo., 1967-79, lab. mgr., 1979—; cons. CDC Assocs., Boulder, Colo., 1974-79. Mem. AAAS, Am. Chem. Soc., Nat. Mgmt. Assn., Am. Philatelic Soc., Lundy Collectors Club (bd. dirs. 1980—, editor quar. jour., exhibition awards for jour. 1985, 86), Sigma Xi. Democrat. Unitarian-Universalist. Avocation: philately. Home: 3925 Longwood Ave Boulder CO 80303 Office: Rockwell Internat Bldg 559 Rocky Flats Plant PO Box 464 Golden CO 80401

CIKAN, FRANTISEK, architect; b. Chomutov, Czechoslovakia, Mar. 9, 1948; came to U.S., 1969; s. Jaroslav Cikan and Emilie (Bustova) Cikanova. Student, Charles U., Prague, Czechoslovakia, 1967-69, Brandywine Jr. Coll., 1969-71; BA, Mont. State U., 1977. Registered profl. architect, Mont. Architect State of Mont., Helena, 1979-85; prin. Archiczech, East Helena, Mont., 1985-86, Cikan Architects P.C., East Helena, 1986—. Mem. AIA. Avocations: basketball, handball. Home and Office: 205 W Main St PO Box CC East Helena MT 59635

CIMINO, RICHARD ANGELO, broadcasting personality, actor; b. Gilroy, Calif., Dec. 17, 1929; s. Angelo and Laura Maria (Macchione) C.; student Hartnell Coll., 1948-50; m. Enid Lucile Kilburn, Dec. 9, 1962. Program mgr. Sta. KCRA, Sacramento, 1966-68; morning program host Sta. KNEW, Oakland, 1968-72; afternoon program host Sta. KSFO, San Francisco, 1974-77; ptnr. Charles Jewelry; pres. Rick Cimino, Inc.; developer and chief exec. officer Compu-Cast; owner comml. fishing vessel African Queen; instr. voice, acting; freelance advt. voice. Served with U.S. Army, 1951-53. Recipient Best Radio Personality award TV-Radio Mirror mag., 1969; 9 CLIO awards, 1976-83, Gold Clio award, 1985; 2 Nat. Acad. TV Arts and Scis. awards,

1981; Gold medal 1982 Internat. Film Festival; Addy award, 1983. Mem. Am. Advt. Fedn. (radio div. chmn. Am. Advt. Best in West awards), AFTRA, Screen Actors Guild, Il Cenacolo, Cousteau Soc., Oceanic Soc., Internat. Platform Assn. Home: 7352 Stockton Ave El Cerrito CA 94530

CIPRIANO, PATRICIA ANN, educator, consultant; b. San Francisco, Apr. 24, 1946; d. Ernest Peter and Claire Patricia (Croak) C. B.A. in English, Holy Names Coll., Oakland, Calif., 1967; M.A. in Edn. of Gifted, Calif. State U.-Los Angeles, 1980. Cert. tchr., tchr. spl. edn., adminstrv. service, Calif. Tchr. English, math. and bus. Bancroft Jr. High Sch., San Leandro, Calif., 1968-79, 83-85, coordinator gifted edn., 1971-79; tchr. English, math. San Leandro High Sch., 1979-83, 85—, coordinator gifted and talented edn., 1981-83; cons. Calif. State Dept. Edn., various Calif. sch. dists. Recipient Hon. Service award Tchr. of Yr., Bancroft Jr. High Sch. PTA, 1973. Mem. Calif. Assn. for Gifted (rep. Region 3 tchr. com.), Assn. for Gifted, Nat. Assn. for Gifted, World Council Gifted and Talented, Central Calif. Council of Tchrs. English (pres.), Calif. Assn. Tchrs. English (bd. dirs., treas.), Nat. Council Tchr. English, San Leandro Tchrs. Assn., Calif. Tchrs. Assn., NEA, Delta Kappa Gamma. Roman Catholic. Contbr. articles to profl. jours. Office: San Leandro High Sch 2200 Bancroft Ave San Leandro CA 94577

CIRONE, WILLIAM JOSEPH, educational administrator; b. Bklyn., Dec. 27, 1937; s. Joseph Nicholas and Marie Ann (Basile) C.; m. Barbara Jane Skirkie, Dec. 22, 1962; 1 son, Peter Craig. B.A., Providence Coll., 1959; M.A., NYU, 1960; adminstrv. cert. U. Calif.-Santa Barbara, 1977. Tchr., N.Y.C. Pub. Schs., 1960-68; dir. product devel. ednl. div. Mead Corp., Atlanta, 1968-70, dir. mktg., 1970-73; founder/dir. Ctr. Community Edn. and Citizen Participation, Santa Barbara, Calif., 1973-82; supt. schs. Santa Barbara County, 1983—; vis. fellow Chisholm Inst. Technology, Melbourne, Australia, 1986; vis. scholar Ctr. for Excellence Tenn. State U., 1986. Contbg. editor New Designs for Youth Development, 1984—. Bd. dirs. Community Action Commn., 1973-81, Community Resource Info Service, 1978-82, Community Housing Corp., 1980-82; bd. dirs., sec. Pvt. Industry Council, Santa Barbara, 1983—; bd. dirs. Industry Edn. Council, Santa Barbara, 1983—, Santa Barbara Lung Assn., 1983—, Community Devel. Assistance Corp., 1980—; hon. bd. dirs. So. Coast Spl. Olympics; mem. Gov.'s Commn. on Earthquake Hazards, 1981; mem. state bd. Common Cause, 1974-77, organizer and 1st state chmn., Ga., 1970-73; mem. voter accessibility adv. bd. Santa Barbara County, 1986—; mem. adv. bd. CALM, Peace Resource Ctr., Marymount Sch., Women's Community Bldg., Jodi House, commdrs. community liasion com. Vandenburg AFB. Recipient Smallheiser award United Fedn. Tchrs., 1968; Meritorious Service award Community Action Com., Santa Barbara, 1981, Ind. Living Resource Ctr., 1985; named Calif. Community Educator Yr., Calif. Community Edn. Assn., 1984, Pub. Servant of Yr., Santa Barbara County, 1987; Hon. Service award 15th Dist. PTA, 1979. Mem. World Future Soc. (life), Am. Assn. Sch. Adminstrs., Assn. Calif. Sch. Adminstrs., So. Coast Coordinating Council (past chmn., past exec. com.), Nat. Soc. Fundraising Execs., Phi Delta Kappa. Democrat. Unitarian. Home: 953 Elk Grove Ln Solvang CA 93463-9608 Office: PO Box 6307 Santa Barbara CA 93160

CITTADIN, LENELLE UNDERWOOD, academic administrator, lawyer; b. Davenport, Okla., Oct. 28, 1926; d. Wayne Shurlock and Erma (Holmquist) Underwood; m. Joseph Francis Cittadin, Dec. 12, 1948; 1 child, Kyle Wayne. BS, BA, Tex. Women's U., 1947; MA, Calif. State U., Long Beach, 1952; JD, Western State U., 1982. Bar: Calif. Instr. chemistry Tex. Women's U., Denton, 1947-48; chemist Glidden Paint Co., Buena Park, Calif., 1950-54; tchr. sci. Fullerton (Calif.) Sch. Dist., 1954-77, vice prin., 1977-80, prin., 1980—; labor negotiator Fullerton Sch. Dist., 1981—. Bd. dirs. Muckenthaler Cultural Ctr., Fullerton, 1985—. Recipient Hon. Service award Wilshire Jr. High Sch. PTA, 1980, Hon. Service award Parks Jr. High Sch. PTA, 1983, Disting. Sch. award Orange County Dept. Edn., 1986. Mem. Calif. Bar Assn., NEA, Assn. Calif. Sch. Adminstrs., Calif. Tchrs. Assn. (Award of Merit 1976), Fullerton Elem. Tchrs. Assn. (pres. 1975-76), No. Orange County United Tchrs. Assn. (bd. dirs. 1975-78), Delta Kappa Gamma, Alpha Gamma (pres. 1986—). Republican. Lutheran. Avocations: traveling, photography, lectures, musical instrument (recorder). Home: 672 E Dorothy Ln Fullerton CA 92631 Office: D Russell Parks Jr High Sch 1710 Rosecrans Fullerton CA 92633

CIVILIKAS, ROBERT GEORGE, naval officer; b. Needham, Mass., Dec. 30, 1959; s. Frank J. and Alice M. (Hampshire) C. BS in Aerospace Engring., U.S. Naval Acad., 1982. Ensign USN, 1982—, advanced through grades to lt., 1986. Mem. Assn. Naval Aviation, Tailhook Assn., Sigma Xi. Avocation: pilot. Office: Fighter Squadron One Fleet Post Office San Francisco CA 92145

CLAES, DANIEL JOHN, physician; b. Glendale, Calif., Dec. 3, 1931; s. John Vernon and Claribel (Fleming) C.; A.B. magna cum laude, Harvard U., 1953, M.D. cum laude, 1957; m. Gayla Christine Blasdel, Jan. 19, 1974. Intern, UCLA, 1957-58; Bowyer Found. fellow for research in medicine, Los Angeles, 1958-61; practice medicine specializing in internal medicine, Los Angeles, 1962—; v.p. Am. Eye Bank Found., 1978-83, pres., 1983—, dir. research, 1980—; pres. Heuristic Corp., 1981—. Mem. Los Angeles Mus. Art, 1960—. Mem. AMA, Calif. Med. Assn., Los Angeles County Med. Assn. Clubs: Harvard and Harvard Med. Sch. of So. Calif. Contbr. papers on diabetes mellitus, computers in medicine to profl. lit. Office: 845 Via de la Paz Suite A236 Pacific Palisades CA 90272

CLAGETT, LESLIE PLUMMER, editor; b. Providence, Apr. 30, 1956; d. Robert Eugene and Peg (Hassett) Plummer; m. John Stephen Clagett, June 10, 1982. BA in English, Denison U., 1978. Mng. editor N.Y. Arts Jour., N.Y.C., 1978-81, Arts & Architecture, Los Angeles, 1981-85; assoc. editor architecture Home mag., Los Angeles, 1985—. Mem. Archtl. League, Nat. Trust for Hist. Preservation. Office: Home Mag Box 92000 Los Angeles CA 90009

CLAGETT, VIRGINIA MARIE, manufacturing company executive; b. Mesa, Ariz., Aug. 3, 1938; d. Westall Irwin and Elna Jeanne (Smith) Harmon; B.A., U. Ariz., 1959. Engring. aide numerical analysis lab. U. Ariz., Tucson, 1959-61; systems analyst Gen. Electric Co., Phoenix, 1961-70; project leader Honeywell Info. Systems, Inc., Phoenix, 1970-73, project engr., 1973-78, mgr. comml. compiler, 1978-81, mgr. software editing and control, 1982—. Mem. Am. Bus. Women's Assn., Nat. Assn. Female Execs., Epsilon Sigma Alpha (pres. Ariz. council 1979-80, corr. sec. internat. council 1984-85), credentials chmn. internat. council). Republican. Episcopalian. Home: 3044 E Cannon Dr Phoenix AZ 85028 Office: PO Box 8000 Phoenix AZ 85066

CLAIR, THEODORE NAT, ednl. adminstr.; b. Stockton, Calif., Apr. 19, 1929; s. Peter David and Sara Renee (Silverman) C.; A.A., U. Calif. at Berkeley, 1949, A.B., 1950; M.S., U. So. Calif., 1953, M.Ed., 1963, Ed.D., 1969; m. Laura Gold, June 19, 1961; children—Shari, Judith. Tchr., counselor Los Angeles City Schs., 1957-63; psychologist Alamitos Sch. Dist., Garden Grove, Calif., 1963-64, Arcadia (Calif.) Unified Sch. Dist., 1964-65; head psychologist Wiseburn Sch. Dist., Hawthorne, Calif., 1966-69; asst. prof. spl. edn., coordinator sch. psychology program U. Iowa, Iowa City, 1969-72; dir. pupil personnel services Orcutt (Calif.) Union Sch. Dist., 1972-73; adminstr. Mt. Diablo Unified Sch. Dist., 1973-77; program dir., psychologist San Mateo County Office of Edn., Redwood City, 1977—; assoc. prof. John F. Kennedy U. Sch. Mgmt., 1975-77; pvt. practice as ednl. psychologist and marriage and family counselor, Concord, Calif., 1972-77, Menlo Park, Calif., 1977—; dir. Peninsula Vocat. Rehab. Inst., 1978—. Served with USNR, 1952-54. Mem. Calif., San Francisco Bay Area assns. for spl. edn. adminstrs., Calif. Assn. Marriage and Family Counselors, Am. Psychol. Assn., Nat. Rehab. Assn., Phi Delta Kappa. Club: Palo Alto B'nai B'rith (pres.). Author: Phenylketonuria and Some Other Inborn Errors of Amino Acid Metabolism, 1971; mem. editorial adv. bd. Psychology in Schs., 1972—; contbr. articles to profl. jours. Home and office: 56 Willow Rd Menlo Park CA 94025

CLAIRE, FRED, professional baseball team executive. A.A., Mt. San. Antonio Coll.; B.A. in Journalism, San Jose State Coll., 1957. Formerly sports writer and columnist Long Beach Ind. Press Telegram and Whittier News; sports editor Pomo Progress-Bull, Calif., until 1969; dir. publicity Los Angeles Dodgers, Nat. League, 1969-75, v.p. pub. relations and promotions, 1975-82, exec. v.p., from 1982, gen. mgr., 1987—; bd. dirs. Major League Baseball Promotion Corp. Bd. dirs. Greater Los Angeles Vistors and Conv. Bur. Mem. Echo Park C. of C. Lodge: Los Angeles Rotary. Office: Los Angeles Dodgers 1000 Elysian Park Ave Los Angeles CA 90012 *

CLANCEY, PATRICK KEVIN, chemical engineer; b. Grand Rapids, Mich., Oct. 25, 1962; s. Francis Joseph and Delores Marie (Gallo) C. BS in Chem. Engring., U. Calif., Berkeley, 1984. Internat. prodn. mgr. Chemcrete Internat., San Mateo, Calif., 1984—; prodn. cons. Adhesive Coatings Co. Inc., San Mateo, 1985—. Patentee in field. Mem. Am. Chem. Soc., Am. Inst. Chem. Engrs., U. Calif. Alumni Assn. (scholar 1980). Republican. Roman Catholic. Avocations: tennis, running, golf, reading.

CLANCY, GARY JAMES, manufacturing company executive; b. Flushing, N.Y., Feb. 23, 1945; s. Michael J. and Jessie B. (Austin) C.; m. Doris M. Janning, Sept. 30, 1969; children: Sean G., Nicole S. BS, St. John's U., Jamaica, N.Y., 1968; postgrad., Syracuse U., 1977-78. Sales mgr. Allied Chem. Co., Morristown, N.J., 1977-79, mgr. sales, 1979-80, mgr. mktg., 1980-82; dir. mktg. Gyrex Co., Santa Barbara, Calif., 1982-84, gen. mgr., 1984—, pres., 1986—. Served as sgt. USNG, 1968-74. Mem. Semiconductor Equipment Mfrs. Inst., Inst. Hybrid Mfrs. Roman Catholic. Avocations: marathons, youth ch. work. Home: 5454 San Patricio Dr Santa Barbara CA 93111 Office: Gyrex Corp 436 E Gutierrez Santa Barbara CA 93101

CLANTON, GORDON, sociologist educator, consultant; b. Bayonne, N.J., Mar. 25, 1942; s. Robert Gordon and Vivian (Singletary) C. BA, La. State U., 1964; MDiv, Austin (Tex.) Presbyn. Theol. Sem., 1967; PhD, U. Calif., Berkeley, 1973. Asst. prof. religion Rutgers U., New Brunswick, N.J., 1970-73; asst. prof. sociology and anthropology Trenton (N.J.) State Coll., 1973-74; lectr. in sociology San Diego State U., 1975—; lectr., cons. AT&T, U.S. Info. Agy., Planned Parenthood, Jewish Family Services, San Diego Police Dept., Inst. Advanced Study of Human Sexuality, UCLA, others. Co-editor: Face to Face to Face: An Experiment in Intimacy, 1975, Jealousy, 1977; recorded Love and Jealousy cassette, 1985; contbr. articles to profl. jours.; numerous pub. interviews, radio and tv appeareances; newspaper columnist Del Mar (Calif.) Citizen. Mem. Am. Sociol. Assn. (sects. emotion, social psychology, orgns. and occupations, polit. economy of world systems), Pacific Sociol. Assn., Nat. Council on Family Relations, Soc. Sci. Study of Religion, Groves Conf. Marriage and Family, Soc. Values in Higher Edn., San Diego Soc. for Sex Therapy and Edn. (pres. 1979-80), Calif. Faculty Assn., AAUP, Ctr. for Studies Person. Office: San Diego State U Dept Sociology San Diego CA 92182

CLAPP, NORTON, building materials company executive; b. Pasadena, Calif., Apr. 15, 1906; s. Eben Pratt and Mary Bell (Norton) C.; m. Mary Cordelia Davis, July 8, 1929 (dec.); children: James Hayes (dec.), Matthew, Ralph (dec.), Roger (dec.); m. Evelyn Beatrice Booth, Jan. 15, 1941 (dec.); children—William Hayes, Stephen Gilbert; m. Jane Bumiller, Apr. 19, 1952 (div. 1980); m. Jacquline Hazen, Apr. 14, 1984. A.B., Occidental Coll., 1928, LL.D., 1958; Ph.B., U. Chgo., 1928, J.D., 1929; D.C.L., U. Puget Sound, 1958. Bar: Calif., Wash. bars 1929. Practiced in Tacoma, 1929-42; chmn. Met. Bldg. Corp., Seattle, 1954-75; pres. Pelican (Alaska) Cold Storage Co., 1947-60, chmn., 1960-77; pres. Boise (Idaho) Payette Lumber Co., 1949-55, Laird Norton Co., bldg. materials, Winona, Minn., 1950-60; chmn. Laird Norton Co., bldg. materials, 1960—; v.p. Weyerhaeuser Co., 1956-57, chmn. bd., 1957-60, 66-76, pres., 1960-66. Mem. nat. adv. bd., hon. v.p. Boy Scouts Am., nat. pres., 1971-73; trustee U. Puget Sound, Tacoma; life trustee U. Chgo.; trustee Menninger Found., Episcopal Ch. Found. Served as lt. comdr. USNR, 1942-46. Mem. Seattle C. of C. (pres. 1970-71). Republican. Episcopalian. Clubs: Harbor (Seattle), Rainier (Seattle), University (Seattle), Overlake Golf and Country (Seattle), Yacht (Seattle), Tennis (Seattle); Tacoma (Tacoma), Country and Golf (Tacoma), Yacht (Tacoma). Home: PO Box 99 Medina WA 98039 Office: Norton Bldg Seattle WA 98104

CLARK, ALAN B., library director. Dir. Albuquerque Pub. Library. Office: Albuquerque Pub Library 501 Copper Ave NW Albuquerque NM 87102 *

CLARK, ARTHUR JOSEPH, JR., mech. and elec. engr.; b. West Orange, N.J., June 10, 1921; s. Arthur Joseph and Marjorie May (Courter) C.; B.S. in Mech. Engring., Cornell U., 1943; M.S., Poly. Inst. Bklyn., 1948; M.S. in Elec. Engring., U. N.Mex., 1955; m. Caroline Katherine Badgley, June 12, 1943; children—Arthur Joseph, III, Durward S., David P. Design engr. Ranger Aircraft Engines Co., Farmingdale, N.Y., 1943-46; sr. structures engr. propeller div. Curtis Wright Co., Caldwell, N.J., 1946-51; mgr. space isotope power dept., also aerospace nuclear safety dept. Sandia Labs., Albuquerque, 1951-71, mgr. environ. systems test lab., 1971-79, mgr. mil. liaison dept., 1979—; mem. faculty U. N.Mex., 1971-75; invited lectr. Am. Mgmt. Assn. Pres. Sandia Base Sch. PTA, 1960-61; chmn. finance com. Albuquerque chpt. Am. Field Service, 1964-66; chmn. Sandia Labs. div. U.S. Savs. Bond drive, 1972-74, chmn. employee contbn. drive, 1973-75; active local Boy Scouts Am., 1958-66. Recipient Order Arrow, Boy Scouts Am., 1961, Order St. Andrew, 1962, Scouters Key award, 1964; cert. outstanding service Sandia Base, 1964. Fellow ASME (nat. v.p. 1975-79, past chmn. N.Mex. sect.); mem. IEEE (sr.), Cornell Engring. Soc., Theta Xi. Clubs: Kirtland Officers, Four Hills Country. Home: 905 Warm Sands Trail Albuquerque NM 87123 Office: Sandia Labs Dept 7210 Albuquerque NM 87185

CLARK, BILLY RAY, insurance executive; b. Little Falls, Minn., Mar. 18, 1928; s. William Edward and Cora Esther (Crabtree) C.; B.A. in Bus. Adminstrn., Bemidji State U., 1953; m. Elsie Helen Torgerson, Oct. 28, 1951; children—Nancy Jo, Kathryn Jean, Julie Rae, Janice Renee. Field supr., supt. Fidelity and Surety Lines, Travelers Ins. Co., Mpls., Denver, 1953-63; account exec. Talbert Corp., Denver, 1963-65, v.p. sales, 1965-73, pres., chmn. bd., 1973—; lectr. engring. dept. U. Colo., 1972-79; lectr. constrn. mgmt. Colo. State U., 1972-79. Mem. panel of arbitrators Am. Arbitration Assn.; adv. com. Indsl. Constrn. Mgmt. Program, Colo. State U., also mem. constrn. com. Bus.-Econ. Outlook Forum. Served with USN, 1946-48, 51-53. Named Agt. of Yr., Travelers Ins. Co., 1981. Mem. Nat. Assn. Surety Bond Producers (past pres.), Nat., Colo. assns. ins. agts., Profls. for Colo. Contractors Council (past pres.), Colo. Transp. Assn. Republican. Lutheran. Club: Columbine Country (Littleton, Colo.). Home: 5186 Tule Lake Dr Littleton CO 80123 Office: Talbert Corp 1001 Lincoln St Denver CO 80203

CLARK, BRIAN THOMAS, mathematical statistician, operations research analyst; b. Rockford, Ill., Apr. 7, 1951; s. Paul Herbert and Martha Lou (Schlensker) C. B.S. cum laude, No. Ariz. U., 1973; postgrad. Ariz. State U., 1980-82. Math. aide Center for Disease Control, Phoenix, 1973-74, math. statistician, 1979-83; math. Statistician Ctrs. for Disease Control, Atlanta, 1983-84 ops. research analyst U.S. Army Info. Systems Command, Ft. Huachuca, Ariz., 1984—; math. statistician U.S. Navy Metrology Engring. Center, Pomona, Calif., 1974-79. Mem. Am. Stats. Assn., Biometric Soc. Republican. Lutheran. Office: US Army Info Systems Command Dep Chief Staff Resource Mgmt Systems Econ Analysis Div Fort Huachuca AZ 85613

CLARK, BRUCE ROBERT, geology consultant; b. Pitts., June 17, 1941; s. Harold Thomas and Florence (Miller) C.; m. Karen Pelton Heath, Dec. 30, 1967; children: Adam, Andrea. BS, Yale U., 1963; PhD, Stanford U., 1967. Asst. prof. U. Mich., Ann Arbor, 1968-73, assoc. prof., 1973-77; v.p. Leighton and Assocs., Inc., Irvine, Calif., 1977-85, pres., 1986—. Contbr. articles to profl. jours. Fellow Geological Soc. Am.; mem. U.S. Nat. Com. for Rock Mechanics, Am. Geophysical Union, Assn. Engring. Geologists, Sigma Xi. Home: 1127 Goldenrod Ave Corona del Mar CA 92625 Office: Leighton and Assocs Inc 1151 Duryea Ave Irvine CA 92625

CLARK, BURNILL FRED, TV executive; b. Horton, Kans., Nov. 8, 1941; s. Fred Charles and Mildred Anna (Magner) C.; m. Diane Rae Oswald, Aug. 25, 1963; children: Michelle Rae, Marcie Diane, Melissa Esther. BA, U. Denver, 1963, MA, 1964; postgrad., Mich. State U., 1964, Harvard U., 1981. Prodn. dir., mgr. Nebr. Ednl. TV Network, Lincoln, 1965-73, asst. network program mgr., 1973-75; asst. gen. mgr., dir. programming Sta. KCTS-TV, Seattle, 1975-82, gen. mgr., 1982-87; exec. dir. KCTS Assn., Seattle, 1983-87, pres., chief exec. officer, 1987—; chmn. PBS Border Consortium, Vancouver, B.C., Can., 1984-86; chmn., bd. govs. Pacific Mountain Network, Denver, 1984-86; bd. dirs. Internat. Pub. TV Bd., London, 1985—, Pub. TV Outreach Alliance, 1985—; mem. PBS program mgr. adv. com., 1978-82, PBS program adv. com., 1982-85, Frontline mgmt. bd. and editorial adv. bd., 1983—. Mem. TV and Radio Commn., Lincoln, 1966-69; bd. dirs. N.W. Ctr. for the Retarded, Seattle, 1983-85. Methodist. Lodge: Rotary. Office: Station KCTS-TV 401 Mercer St Seattle WA 98109

CLARK, CALEB MORGAN, political scientist, educator; b. Washington, June 6, 1945; s. Tanner Morgan and Grace Amanda (Kautzmann) C.; B.A., Beloit Coll., 1966; Ph.D., U. Ill., 1973; m. Janet Morrissey Sentz, Sept. 28, 1968; children—Emily Claire, Grace Ellen, Evelyn Adair. Lectr., N.Mex. State U., Las Cruces, 1972-75, asst. prof., 1975-78, assoc. prof. govt., 1978-81; assoc. prof. polit. sci. U. Wyo., Laramie, 1981-84, prof., 1984—. NDEA fellow, 1966-69; Woodrow Wilson dissertation fellow, 1969-70; grantee N.Mex. Humanities Council, 1975, Wyo. Council for Humanities, 1982, U.S. Dept. Edn., 1983-85, Pacific Cultural Found., 1984-86. Am. Council Learned Socs., 1976, Met. Life Edn., 1978-80, NEH, 1978, NSF, 1981. Mem. Am. Polit. Sci. Assn., Am. Assn. Advancement Slavic Studies, Rocky Mountain Assn. Slavic Studies, Western Polit. Sci. Assn., Western Social Sci. Assn., Internat. Studies Assn. (exec. dir. West 1981-84), Phi Beta Kappa (treas. 1983—), Pi Eta Sigma, Phi Kappa Phi. Author: (with Robert L. Farlow) Comparative Patterns of Foreign Policy and Trade, 1976; (with Karl F. Johnson) Development's Influence on Yugoslav Political Values, 1976; mng. editor IS Notes, 1984—; co-editor: North/South Relations, 1983, Polit. Stability and Economic Development, 1987; cons., assoc. editor Soviet Union, 1974-77, World Affairs, 1975-84, Social Sci. Jour., 1978-80; contbr. articles to profl. jours. Home: 519 S 12th St Laramie WY 82070 Office: U Wyo Dept Polit Sci Laramie WY 82071

CLARK, CAROL LOIS, state government agency administrator, consumer advocate, consultant; b. Salt Lake City, May 23, 1948; d. Norman W. and Lois Amanda (Colt) C. B.A. in English cum laude, U. Utah, 1970; M.Ed. in Secondary Edn., 1972, Ph.D. in Cultural Founds. of Edn., 1979; postgrad. Columbia U., summer 1980. Cert. profl. tchr., Utah, Mass. Tchr. Jordan Sch. dist., Sandy, Utah, 1972-78, 81-82; curriculum cons. Brigham Young U., Provo, 1978-79, cons., lectr., 1978—; program specialist Utah System Approach to Individualized Learning, Salt Lake City, 1980-81; consumer edn. specialist Utah Atty. Gen.'s Office, Salt Lake City, 1982-84; free-lance editor, curriculum developer Utah Office Edn., Salt Lake City, 1981-82; free-lance editor, cons. Dian Thomas Enterprises, Provo, 1981—; gov.'s adminstrv. asst. for edn. and communication; bd. dirs. Deseret Gymnasium, Salt Lake City, 1982—; mem. Fund for Improvement of Post-Secondary Edn., 1986—; mem. unproven med. practices com. Utah State Med. Assn., 1983-84; mem. Utah Ins. Consumer Action Com., 1983-84; mem. Utah Records Com., 1983-84; mem. Utah Gov.'s Securities Fraud Task Force, 1984; chmn. Utah Atty. Gen.'s Consumer Adv. Com., 1984; state del. U.S. Consumer Product Safety Commn., 1985—; mem. Utah Higher Edn. Work group for Integrating Women into Work Force, 1985—; bd. dirs. Salt Lake City Sch. Vols., 1985—. Author: A Singular Life, 1974; How to Avoid Getting Ripped Off: Essential But Hard-to-Find Consumer Facts for Women, 1985; co-author: Principles of Learning, 1981; contbr.: Consumer's Resource Handbook, 1986; consumer columnist Deseret News, 1982-84, Standard-Examiner, 1983-84, Golden Age, 1983-84, Cache County Citizen, 1984, Park Record, 1984, Sun Advocate, 1984, Richfield Reaper, 1984, Vernal Express, 1984, Color County Spectrum, 1984, Provo Daily Herald, 1984; contbr. articles, poetry to various publs.; editor: The Relief Society Magazine: A Legacy Remembered, 1914-1970, 1982. Mem. gen. bd. Relief Soc., Ch. of Jesus Christ of Latter-day Saints, Salt Lake City, 1973-84, state del., 1986; acting chmn. Republican Party Voting Dist., Salt Lake City, 1977, dist. vice chmn., 1984; mem. Utah Women's Legis. Council, 1977-79; mem. Denver region Ford Consumer Appeals Bd., 1983-84; mem. planning com. Utah Ednl. Seminar, 1985—. Recipient Tchr. of Yr. award Utah State Hist. Soc., 1975, Ann. Achievement award for best consumer publ. Nat. Assn. Consumer Agy. Adminstrs., 1983; named Outstanding Young Woman from Utah, 1982, Young Woman of Achievement, Nat. Council Women, 1984; Ch. of Jesus Christ of Latter-day Saints Historian's Office fellow, 1976. Mem. Salt Lake C. of C. (bus. in edn. com.), Nat. Futures Assn. (edn. adv. com. 1984—), Nat. Assn. Consumer Agy. Adminstrs. (Best Book award 1985), Profl. Rep. Women, Utah Women's Forum (founding mem.), Home Econs. Assn. (bd. dirs. 1985—), Phi Kappa Phi, Alpha Xi Delta, Lambda Delta Sigma. Office: Utah Gov's Office 210 State Capital Bldg Salt Lake City UT 84114

CLARK, CHARLES JOSEPH (JOE CLARK), Canadian government official, former prime minister; b. High River, Alta., Can., June 5, 1939; s. Charles A. and Grace R. (Welch) C.; m. Maureen McTeer, June 30, 1973; 1 dau., Catherine Jane. B.A. in History, U. Alta., 1960, M.A. in Polit. Sci., 1973; LL.D. (hon.), U. N.B., 1976, U. Calgary, 1984. Lectr. polit. sci. U. Alta., 1965-67; journalist CBC Radio and TV, Calgary Herald, Edmonton Jour., 1966; exec. asst. in Ottawa to Robert L. Stanfield, 1967-70; M.P. for Rocky Mountain 1972-79, M.P. for Yellowhead, 1979—; leader Progressive Conservative Party, 1976-83; prime minister Can., 1979-80; leader of opposition 1976-79, 80-83, sec. of state for external affairs, 1984—. Roman Catholic. Office: House of Commons Room 448-N, Ottawa, ON Canada K1A 0A6 *

CLARK, CHARLES RICHARD, toxicologist; b. Burbank, Calif., Jan. 22, 1947; married. BS in Biology, U. Calif., Davis, 1973, PhD in Toxicology, 1977. Diplomate Am. Bd. Toxicology. Research toxicologist Lovelace Research Inst., Albuquerque, 1977-82; mgr. toxicology and product safety Union Oil Co., Los Angeles, 1982—. Contbr. numerous articles to profl. publs. Served to sgt. U.S. Army, 1966-69. Mem. Soc. Toxicology, Environ. Mutagen Soc., Soc. Environ. Toxicology and Chemistry. Office: Union Oil Co Med Dept 461 S Boylston Los Angeles CA 90017

CLARK, CHARLES SUTTER, interior designer; b. Venice, Calif., Dec. 21, 1927; s. William Sutter and Lodema Ersell (Fleeman) C. Student Chouinard Art Inst., Los Angeles, 1950-51. Interior designer LM.H. Co., Gt. Falls, Mont., 1956-62, Andreason's Interiors, Oakland, Calif., 1962-66, Western Contact Furnishers Internat., Oakland, 1966-70, Design Five Assocs., Lafayette, Calif., 1972-73; owner, interior designer Charles Sutter Clark Interiors, Greenbrae, Calif., 1973—. Served with USAF, 1951-55. Recipient prizes Mont. State Fair, 1953-55. Mem. Am. Soc. Interior Designers. Home: 61 Via Belardo #11 Greenbrae CA 94904

CLARK, CHASE GORDON, JR., commercial flooring consulting executive; b. Chgo., Apr. 21, 1928; s. Chase Gordon and Eleanor Marie C.; m. Mary Jo Ann Woolsey, Nov. 29, 1952; children—Brenda, Diane. Student Kansas City Jr. Coll., 1945-47, U. Mo., 1947-49. With Fibreboard Paper Products, various locations, 1954-65; dist. sales mgr. Comml. Carpet Corp., Los Angeles, 1965-78; contract mgr. Westwood Carpet, Los Angeles, 1978-80; pres. Chase Clark & Assocs., Inc., Beverly Hills, Calif., 1980—. Served with U.S. Army, 1950-52. Republican. Methodist. Clubs: Mercedes Benz, Masons, Shriners.

CLARK, DARLA MAE, personnel director; b. Sioux Falls, S.D., Feb. 15, 1954; d. Gordon Vance and Charlotte Laurine (Johnson) Ustrud; m. Douglas Lee Clark, Dec. 31, 1979. BS in Psychology, Utah State U., 1977. Biofeedback asst. Problems-in-Living Ctr., Sioux Falls, S.D., 1977; personnel asst., word processing specialist Blood Systems Inc., Scottsdale, Ariz., 1978-80; office systems mgr., word processing specialist Cella Barr Assocs., Tucson, 1980-87, personnel dir., 1987—. Chmn. United Way campaign, 1986. Recipient Model Campaign United Way, 1986. Mem. Assn. Info. Systems Profls. (bd. dirs. 1984—). Republican. Avocations: golf, racquetball, aerobics, reading. Home: 7912 E Colette Circle #40 Tucson AZ 85710 Office: Cella Barr Assocs 2075 N 6th Ave Tucson AZ 85705

CLARK, DAVID HOWARD, ruminant nutritionist, researcher; b. Evanston, Wyo., Sept. 22, 1950; s. Terrance D. and Lois Elizabeth (Bond) C.; m. Sandra Gale Singer, Dec. 18, 1971; 1 child, J. Justin. BS, U. Wyo., 1977, MS, 1979; PhD, Utah State U., 1985. Asst. mgr. dairy plant U. Wyo., Laramie, 1975-77; research technician Utah State U., Logan, 1983-84; research animal scientist USDA Agrl. Research Service, Logan, 1984—; adj. prof. Utah State U., 1986—, instr. 1980-83, 86—; chmn. Forage Network, 1985—. Author: Near Infrared Reflectance, 1985; contbr. articles to profl. jours. Mem. Am. Soc. Animal Scientists, Am. Agronomy Soc., AAAS, Cache Valley Cyclists (v.p. Logan chpt. 1985—), Am. Dairy Sci. Assn.,

Gamma Sigma Delta, Alpha Zeta. Lodge: Royal Order Yellow Dogs. Avocations: restoring cars, motorcycle racing, reading. Home: 1521 E 1200 N Logan UT 84321 Office: USDA Argl Research Service Utah State U Logan UT 84322-9463

CLARK, DONALD CHARLES, chemical engineer; b. Los Angeles, Jan. 8, 1950; s. Walter McCary and Inez Virginia (Aldridge) C.; m. Glenda Sue Nielsen, Apr. 10, 1976. AA in Chemistry, El Camino Coll., 1970; BS in Chemistry, Calif. State U., Fullerton, 1973; MSChemE, U. Houston, 1975. Process engr. research Rohm & Haas Co., Phila., 1975-77; process engr. 3M Co., White City, OR, 1977—. Bd. dirs. Barnstormers Community Theater, Grants Pass, Oreg., 1982-84; bd. elders First Bapt. Ch., Grants Pass, 1984—. Grantee NATO, 1974; named Process Engr. of Yr., 3M Co., 1983. Republican. Avocations: classical music, world philosophies. Home: 1059 NE Pepperwood Grants Pass OR 97526 Office: 3M Co 8124 Pacific Ave White City OR 97503

CLARK, DONALD EDWARD, social service administrator; b. Silverton, Oreg., Apr. 25, 1933; s. Harold and Vera Clark; m. Shirley Paulus Clark; children: Rick, Donald Jr., Kim. AB, San Francisco State U.; postgrad., Portland State U. Prison guard San Quentin (Calif.) State Penitentary, 1954-56; dep. sheriff Multnomah County, Oreg., 1956-62, sheriff, 1963-66, commr., 1969-75, county exec., 1979-83, chmn., 1975-79; exec. dir. Cen. City Concern, Portland, Oreg., 1984—; adj. prof. urban affairs Portland State U., 1983; cons. Cogan and Assocs., Portland, 1983-84. Author: Educational Standards for Police, 1966; contbr. articles to profl. jours. Mem. regional commn. Columbia River Gorge Nat. Scenic Area. Recipient Achievement award Portland Observer, 1982, Wayne Morse Tiger award Dem. Party of Oreg., 1983, Martin Luther King Merit award Skanner Publs., 1984, Russell E. Peyton Human Relations award, 1985, Founders award Friends of the Columbia River Gorge, 1987. Mem. Nat. Assn. Counties, Nat. Corrections Assn., Nat. Sheriff's Assn. (life). . Democrat. Office: Central City Concern 222 NW Couch St Portland OR 97209

CLARK, DONALD STEPHEN, pharmaceutical company executive; b. New Orleans, Nov. 29, 1949; s. Max Warren and Audry (Segari) C.; m. Andrea Jeanette Moser, Nov. 6, 1976; children: Arie Elizabeth Moser-Clark, Kira Nicole Moser-Clark, Mikaela Lynn Moser-Clark. BS in Biochemistry and Chemistry, La. State U., 1972, PhD in Phys. Biochemistry, 1976; postgrad., Fla. State U., 1976-78, U. Calif., Irvine, 1978-79. Sr. research chemist Rohm and Haas Co., Spring House, Pa., 1979-81; mgr. pharm. devel. Allergan Pharms. Inc., Irvine, 1981—. Contbr. articles to profl. jours. Bd. dirs. Ridgefield Homeowners Assn., Laguna Hills, Calif., 1986—. Mem. Am. Pharm. Assn., Acad. Pharm. Scis., Am. Chem. Soc., Sigma Xi. Republican. Home: 24761 San Pedro Laguna Hills CA 92653 Office: Allergan Pharms Inc 2525 Dupont Dr Irvine CA 92715

CLARK, EARNEST HUBERT, JR., tool company executive; b. Birmingham, Ala., Sept. 8, 1926; s. Earnest Hubert and Grace May (Smith) C.; m. Patricia Margaret Hamilton, June 22, 1947; children: Stephen D., Kenneth A., Timothy R., Daniel S., Scott H., Rebecca G. B.S. in Mech. Engring, Calif. Inst. Tech., 1946, M.S., 1947. With Baker Hughes, Inc. (formerly Baker Oil Tools, Inc.), Los Angeles, 1947—, v.p., asst. gen. mgr., 1958-62, pres., chief exec. officer, 1962-69, 75-79, chmn. bd., 1969-75, 79—, chief exec. officer, 1979-87; bd. dirs. CBI Industries, Inc., Honeywell Inc., Am. Petroleum Inst.; mem. Nat. Petroleum Council. Bd. dirs. Downey (Calif.) YMCA, YMCA for Met. Los Angeles; mem. nat. council YMCA; chmn. bd. trustees Harvey Mudd Coll. Served with USNR, 1944-46, 51-52. Mem. Am. Inst. M.E., Am. Petroleum Inst. (bd. dirs.), Petroleum Equipment Suppliers Assn. (bd. dirs.), Calif. C. of C. (mem. exec. com.), Tau Beta Pi. Office: Baker Hughes Inc Koll Ctr Newport W Tower #3000 5000 Birch St Newport Beach CA 92660

CLARK, EDGAR SANDERFORD, insurance broker, consultant; b. N.Y.C., Nov. 17, 1933; s. Edgar Edmund, Jr., and Katharine Lee (Jarman) C.; student U. Pa., 1952-54; B.S., Georgetown U., 1956, J.D., 1958; postgrad. INSEAD, Fountainbleau, France, 1969, Golden Gate Coll., 1973, U. Calif., Berkeley, 1974; m. Nancy E. Hill, Sept. 13, 1975; 1 dau., Schuyler; children by previous marriages—Colin, Alexandra, Pamela. Staff asst. U.S. Senate select com. to investigate improper activities in labor and mgmt. field, Washington, 1958-59; underwriter Ocean Marine Dept., Fireman's Fund Ins. Co., San Francisco, 1959-62; mgr. Am. Fgn. Ins. Assn., San Francisco, 1962-66; with Marsh & McLennan, 1966-72, mgr. for Europe, resident dir. Brussels, Belgium, 1966-70, asst. v.p., mgr. captive and internat. div., San Francisco, 1970-72; v.p., dir. Risk Planning Group, Inc., San Francisco, 1972-75; sr. v.p. internat. div. Alexander & Alexander Internat. Inc., San Francisco, 1975—; lectr. profl. orgns.; guest lectr. U. Calif., Berkeley, 1973, Am. Grad. Sch. Internat. Mgmt., 1981, 82. Served with USAF, 1956-58. Mem. Am. Mgmt. Assn., Am. Risk and Ins. Assn., Chartered Ins. Inst., Am. Soc. Internat. Law. Episcopalian. Clubs: Meadow (Fairfax, Calif.); World Trade (San Francisco). Editorial adv. bd. Risk Mgmt. Reports, 1973-76. Home: 72 Millay Pl Mill Valley CA 94941 Office: Alexander & Alexander Internat Inc Suite 1700 Three Embarcadero Ctr San Francisco CA 94111

CLARK, EDYTHE MIDDLETON, religious executive; b. Queen, N.Mex., Apr. 18, 1912; d. John Reagan and Rhoda J. (Tulk) M.; student Coll. Indsl. Arts, 1928-30; LHD, Inst. Religious Scis., 1967, DD, 1974; m. Alton Herbert Clark, Feb. 17, 1936; children: Carolynn, Farris. Rancher, N.Mex., 1936-56; farmer, Tex., 1939—; oil operator, Roswell, N.Mex., 1952—; ordained to ministry United Ch. Religious Sci., 1960; pres. bd. dirs. Pala Dura Uranium, Amarillo, Tex., 1955-56; ptnr. Alton H. Clark Royalty Co., Roswell, 1952-74; part-owner Clark & Clark Oil & Uranium, Roswell, 1954-58; asst. minister Founder's Ch. of United Ch. Religious Sci., Los Angeles, 1960-73, first exec. sec., 1973-74, corp. sec., sec. bd. trustees, 1974-76, v.p. in charge adminstrn., 1975, adminstrv. exec. of bd. trustees, 1977—, nat. and internat. dir. dept. member chs., 1977-82; faculty Inst. Religious Sci. of United Ch. of Religious Sci. Sch. Ministry, 1960-82, Independent oil producer, Montecito, Calif., 1984. Recipient Meritorious Service award United Ch. of Religious Sci., 1976, Ernest Holmes award, 1981. Mem. United Clergy Religious Sci., Internat. New Thought Alliance. Compiler, editor, pub. eight volumes Jr. Ch. material for United Church Religious Sci. Home: 1304 Plaza de Sonadores Montecito CA 93108 Office: 1187 Coast Village Rd Montecito CA 93108

CLARK, FRANK JACKSON, electronic systems engineer; b. Muncie, Ind., Apr. 2, 1922; s. Ray Wallace and Sarah Rebecca (Jackson) C.; m. Patricia M. Van Hoos, Mar. 11, 1944 (div. Mar. 1966); 1 child, Richard Van; m. Mary Elizabeth Adams, May 14, 1966 (div. Mar. 1978); m. Wilma Evelyn Arms, July 25, 1981. BSEE, Purdue U., 1943, MSEE, 1948. Instr. U. So. Calif., Los Angeles, 1948-50; tech. staff mem. Hughes Aircraft, Culver City, Calif., 1950-55; research and devel. engr. Lockheed Aircraft Corp., Burbank, Calif., 1955-84; sr. tech. specialist Northrop Corp., Pico Rivera, Calif., 1984—. Treas. San Fernando Valley Symphony Assn., Van Nuys, Calif., 1965-81. Served to 1st. lt. U.S. Army, 1943-46. Mem. IEEE, AIAA, Inst. Navigation. Republican. Episcopalian. Avocations: square dancing, bicycling, hiking, swimming. Home: 143 N Alabama St San Gabriel CA 91775 Office: Northrop Advanced Systems Div 8900 E Washington Blvd Pico Rivera CA 90660

CLARK, GEOFFREY GEORGE ANDERSON, archaeology educator; b. Phila., Aug. 17, 1944; s. Parker George and Elinor Mosby (Anderson) C.; m. Valerie Jackson, Mar. 17, 1967 (div. 1977); m. Barbara Louise Stark, Jan. 9, 1981. BA in Anthropology magna cum laude, U. Ariz., 1966, MA in Anthropology, 1967; PhD in Anthropology, U. Chgo., 1971. Asst. prof. Ariz. State U., Tempe, 1971-75, assoc. prof., 1975-82, prof. dept. anthropology, 1982—. Editor: Ariz. State U. Anthropol. Research Papers, 1974—, (assoc. editor) Anthropology, 1985—; contbr. articles to profl. jours. NSF grantee, 1966-70, 76-81, 84-87, Nat. Geographic Soc. grantee, 1983; NSF fellow, 1967-71. Fellow AAAS, Am. Anthropol. Assn. (mem. exec. bd. 1986-88); mem. Soc. Am. Archaeology, Royal Anthropol. Inst., Phi Beta Kappa, Sigma Xi, Phi Kappa Phi. Democrat. Avocation: restoring Austin-Healey Roadsters. Home: 2025 E Woodman Dr Tempe AZ 85283 Office: Ariz State U Dept Anthropology Tempe AZ 85287

CLARK, GLEN EDWARD, judge; b. Cedar Rapids, Iowa, Nov. 23, 1943; s. Robert M. and Georgia L. (Welch) C.; m. Deanna D. Thomas, July 16, 1966; children: Andrew Curtis, Carissa Jane. BA, U. Iowa, 1966; JD, U. Utah, 1971. Bar: Utah 1971, U.S. Dist. Ct. Utah 1971, U.S. Ct. Appeals (10th cir.) 1972. Assoc., Fabian & Clendenin, 1971-74, ptnr., 1975-81, dir., chmn. banking and comml. law sect., 1981-82; judge U.S. Bankruptcy Ct. Dist. Utah, Salt Lake City, 1982—; vis. prof. U. Utah, Salt Lake City, 1977-79, 83. Served with U.S. Army, 1966-68. Finkbine fellow U. Iowa. Mem. Utah Bar Assn., Order of Coif. Presbyterian. Office: US Bankruptcy Ct US Cthouse Room 361 350 S Main St Salt Lake City UT 84101

CLARK, JAMES CHARLES, publishing executive; b. Olney, Ill., May 30, 1939; s. Harry Delmis and Martha Marguerite (DeVore) C. BS, U. Ill., 1961. Asst. advt. dir. Automatic Electric, Northlake, Ill., 1965-66; account exec. Barnes, Champ Advt., San Diego, 1966-68; exec. v.p., assoc. pub. East/West Network, Los Angeles, 1968-78; pres. Clark Calif. Corp., Los Angeles, 1976—; pub., pres. San Francisco Mag., 1978-81; exec. v.p., pub. Exec. Publs., Beverly Hills, 1984—. Served with U.S. Army, 1961-64. Democrat. Roman Catholic. Avocations: internat. travel, writing, swimming, running. Home: 2113 Mt Olympus Dr Los Angeles CA 90046 Office: Exec Publs Inc 1888 Century Park E Suite #830 Los Angeles CA 90067

CLARK, JAMES DOUGLAS, computer company executive; b. San Diego, Apr. 30, 1948; s. James W. and Eva I. (Russell) C.; m. Marion Y. Davis, May 5, 1972; children: Marcella S., Ryan C., Carissa R. Profl. musician various locations, Las Vegas, 1968-74; owner James Clark Co., San Diego, 1974-80; pres. Pacific Infosystems, Inc., San Diego, 1980-86, Clarkware, San Diego, 1986—. Com. mem. Mid-City Revitalization Task Force, San Diego, 1983-84, San Diego Hospice Corp.; bd. dirs. El Cajon Blvd. Bus. Improvement Dist., San Diego, 1985—. Named Small Bus. Person of Yr., State Select Com. under Senator Jim Ellis, 1985. Mem. Mid-City C. of C. (bd. dirs. 1981—, v.p. 1984—). Avocations: golf, billiards. Office: Pacific Infosystems Inc 2855 El Cajon Blvd San Diego CA 92104

CLARK, JAMES GILBERT, pharmacist; b. Duluth, Minn., Aug. 27, 1927; s. Gilbert Rolph and Edith (Briggs) C.; student U. Minn., 1946-50; B.S. in Pharmacy, U. So. Calif., 1951; m. Betty Marie Larson, 1949 (div. 1966) children—Lor-Anne, Paula. Pharmacist, Cameron Pharmacy, Huntington Park, Calif., 1951-57; pharmacist, owner Clark Pharmacy, Long Beach, Calif., 1957-69, Abrams and Clark Pharmacy, Long Beach, 1969-77. Licensed pharmacist, Calif., Nev. Mem. Nat. Assn. Retail Druggists, Calif., Palm Springs-Coachella Valley pharm. assns., Pacific R.R. Soc. Home: 2235 Los Patos Dr Palm Springs CA 92264

CLARK, JAMES HOWARD, environmental engineer; b. Vancouver, Wash., Sept. 22, 1953; s. Robert Wallace and Florence Inez (Krein) C. BSCE cum laude, Wash. State U., 1975, MS in Environ. Engring., 1976. Registered profl. engr., Wash., Calif., Oreg. Lectr., research assoc. Wash. State U., Pullman, 1976-77; research san. engr. Pentech Houdaille, Cedar Falls, Iowa, 1977-78; regional san. engr. Pentech Houdaille, Napa, Calif., 1979-80; v.p. Treatment Equipment Co., Lake Oswego, Oreg., 1980-85; project engr. Black & Veatch Engrs.-Architects, Los Angeles, 1985—. Contbr. articles to profl. publs. Recipient Disting. Alumni Lectr. award Wash. State U., 1985. Mem. ASCE, Calif. Water Pollution Control Assn., Nat. Wildlife Fedn., Water Pollution Control Fedn., Pacific N.W. Pollution Control Assn., Tau Beta Pi. Presbyterian.

CLARK, JAMES MARTIN, hotel corporation executive; b. Chincoteague, Va., Apr. 6, 1953; s. Martin and Josephine Teresa (Gabarro) C.; married; children: Michele A. Madeleine E., James M. Jr., Marshall M. BS, Univ. State of N.Y., 1979; MBA, Columbia Pacific U., 1980, PhD, 1981. Accredited genealogist. Pres., chief exec. officer Island Spice Hotels, Inc., Salt Lake City, Bridgetown, Barbados; chmn. Ginger Bay Beach Club, St. Philip, Barbados; dir., pres. Bajan Devel. Co., Bridgetown, Barbados; past pres. Bajan Resorts, Inc., also bd. dirs. Compiler (nomagraph) Nanaimo BC Pioneer Cemetery, 1972. Treas. Profl. Genealogist Soc., Utah, 1976-77; Republican rep. to state conv., Utah, 1980, 84; life patron, ABI; mem. nat. bd. advisers, exec. com. Sunstone Found., Utah, 1983. Served with USN, 1970-76. Recipient Naval Acad. award, 1970. Mem. SAR (v.p. Salt Lake City chpt. 1975), Phi Kappa Phi, Tau Beta Pi. Home: Saint Philip Barbados Office: Island Spice Hotels 215 S State St Suite 275 Salt Lake City UT 84111

CLARK, JANET EILEEN, political scientist, educator; b. Kansas City, Kans., June 5, 1940; d. Edward Francis and Mildred Lois (Mack) Morrissey; A.A., Kansas City Jr. Coll., 1960; A.B., George Washington U., Washington, 1962, M.A., 1964; Ph.D., U. Ill., 1973; m. Caleb M. Clark, Sept. 28, 1968; children—Emily Claire, Grace Ellen, Evelyn Adair. Staff, U.S. Dept. Labor, Washington, 1962-64; instr. social sci. Kansas City (Kans.) Jr. Coll., 1964-67; instr. polit. sci. Parkland Coll., 1970-71; asst. prof. govt., N.Mex. State U., Las Cruces, 1971-77, assoc. prof., 1977-80; assoc. prof. polit. sci. U. Wyo., 1981-84, prof., 1984—. Wolcott fellow, 1963-64, NDEA Title IV fellow, 1967-69. Mem. NEA (pres. chpt. 1978-79), Western Social Sci. Assn. (exec. council 1978-81, pres.-elect 1983-84), Am. Polit. Sci. Assn., Western Polit. Sci. Assn. (exec. council 1984—), Western Social Sci. Assn. (exec. council 1978-81, v.p. 1982, pres. 1985), Women's Caucus for Polit. Sci. (treas. 1982, pres. 1987), LWV (exec. bd. 1980-83), Women's Polit. Caucus, Beta Sigma Phi (v.p. chpt. 1978-79), Phi Beta Kappa, Chi Omega (prize 1962), Phi Kappa Phi. Democrat. Lutheran. Book rev. editor Social Sci. Jour., 1982—. Contbr. articles to profl. jours. Home: 519 S 12th St Laramie WY 82070

CLARK, JEFFRY RUSSELL, counseling psychologist, consultant, researcher; b. Wareham, Mass., Oct. 12, 1950; s. John Russell and Barbara Jean (Roberts) C.; children—Stephen Russell, Jeffry John Taylor. B.S., Trinity Coll., 1975; M. Ed., Am. U., 1979; Ph.D., Stanford U., 1987. Social worker Monmouth Family Ctr., Middletown, N.J., 1975-76; counselor Annandale Correctional Ctr., Annandale, N.J., 1977, Temple Hills Counseling (Md.) Ctr., 1977-79; adminstrv. dir. Stanford (Calif.) Counseling Inst., 1979-82, counselor Emergency Treatment Ctr., Palo Alto, Calif., 1981-87, dir. tng., 1985-86; dir. adolescent and family services Mid Peninsula, Palo Alto, 1986—; pvt. practice family counseling, Palo Alto, 1986—; cons. Peninsula Children's Ctr. Served with USMC, 1969-71. Mem. Am. Psychol. Assn., Am. Assn. for Counseling and Devel., Assn. Advancement Behavior Therapy, Western Psychol. Assn., Annandale Jaycees (pres. 1978-79). Democrat. Research on children of divorce, stress, insomnia. Home: 114D Escondido Village Stanford CA 94305

CLARK, JERRY HOLLIS, psychologist; b. Albany, Tex., Oct. 25, 1912; s. John Quincy and Alice Bret (King) C.; B.A., So. Meth. U., 1933; M.A., So. Meth. U., 1936; Ph.D., U. Tex., 1948; m. Edith Mattiat, Aug. 8, 1959; 1 son, Jon Edmond. Served with U.S. Army, 1942-46, 50-52, 57-71; registrar, dir. admissions U. Calif., Santa Barbara, 1948-50, 52-54, asst. prof., 1954-57; commd. 2d lt. U.S. Army, 1943, advanced through grades to col., 1967, ret., 1971; psychologist, chief of service, various Army hosps., 1957-71; psychology cons. Sansum Med. Clinic, Santa Barbara, 1973—. Decorated Legion of Merit, Army Commendation medal. Fellow Am. Psychol. Assn.; mem. Calif. State Psychol. Assn. (pres. 1983, 87), Western Psychol. Assn. Democrat. Contbr. articles to psychology jours. Home: 3211 Beach Club Rd Carpinteria CA 93013

CLARK, JOANNA MICHELLE, computer executive; b. Pontiac, Mich., June 16, 1938; d. Edwin Forbes and Roberta Louise (Kinsey) C.; divorced; 1 child, Jon Michael. AA, Saddleback Community Coll., 1979; AS, SUNY, Albany, 1979, BA, 1980; postgrad., Pepperdine U., 1980. Enlisted USN, 1955, avionics technician, 1957-61; avionics instr. Naval Air Tech. Tng. Ctr., Memphis, 1961-65; instr., evaluator Naval Air Tng. Operating Procedures Standardization, 1966-69; with USNR, 1969-74; ocean systems technician Makai Undersea Test Range, Waimanelo, Hawaii, 1969-71; project coordinator, engr. Kentron Hawaii, Ltd., 1971-72; office supr. Environment Mgmt. Agy., Santa Ana, Calif., 1975-76; staff tng. asst., acting supr. Ft. MacArthur USAR Ctr., San Pedro, Calif., 1976-77; pres. Joanna M. Clark & Assocs., San Juan Capistrano, Calif., 1978—, Advanced Systems Group, San Juan Capistrano, 1985—; cons. Joseph Feury Productions, 1984, South Australian Parliament, 1983. Bd. dirs. Orange County (Calif.) Elections Com., 1985—, John Augustus Found., 1980—; mem. profl. adv. bd. CONFIDE Personal Counseling Services, Inc.; mem. Sisters in Gay Ministry Associated, Gender Dysphoria Program of Orange County. Recipient Merit award Orange County, 1975-76, Hawaii Heart Assn., Honolulu, 1969. Republican. Episcopalian. Avocations: scuba diving. Office: 31815 Camino Capistrano San Juan Capistrano CA 92675-3212

CLARK, JOE See CLARK, CHARLES JOSEPH

CLARK, JOHN ELWOOD, mayor of Portland, Oregon; b. Nampa, Idaho, Dec. 19, 1931; m. Sigrid Fehrenbacher; 4 children. Student, Oreg. State Coll., 1950, Reed Coll., 1954, Portland State U., 1984. Owner, operator Aardvark Pest Control, 1959; owner, operator Goose Hollow Inn, 1961—, Mother Goose Antiques, 1974—; founder, operator local newspaper The Neighbor, 1974—; co-owner, operator Forsstrom & Clark Waterfowl Spltys. and Duck Stuff, Portland, 1982—; mayor City of Portland, 1985—; mem. Portland Waterways Adv. Com., 1978, Portland Central Precinct Police Adv. Com., 1975-76. Bd. dirs. Goose Hollow Neighborhood Assn., 1977-81, Planned Parenthood, 1979-80, Restaurants of Oreg. Assn., 1977-78; mem. planning com. Portland-Multnomah Area Agy. on Aging, 1974-76; mem. United Good Neighbor Policy and Devel. Com., 1975-76; mem. Multnomah County Venereal Disease Action Com., 1973-77; treas. N.W. Dist. Assn., 1972-75; vol. Meals-On-Wheels, 1971-82. Served with USMC, 1951-54. Office: Mayor's Office 1220 SW 5th Ave Portland OR 97204

CLARK, JOHN FRANCIS, software development company executive; b. Phila., Feb. 27, 1940; s. John Francis and Mary Louise (Burghardt) C.; m. Sally Ann Spangler, June 18, 1960; children: John, Eric, Kevin, Kara. BSEE, Drexel U., 1963; MSE, Johns Hopkins U., 1968. Coop. engr. Philco Corp., Phila., 1958-63; sr. staff engr. Applied Physics Lab, Laurel, Md., 1963-69; various engring. and mgmt. positions Magnavox, Torrance, Calif., 1969-81; pres. Cast, Los Alamitos, Calif., 1981—. Active Cypress (Calif.) Little League, 1970-81, Cypress Indian Guides, 1970-76; coach Am. Youth Soccer Orgn., Cypress, 1976-81. Mem. IEEE, Inst. Navigation, Am. Def. Preparedness Assn., Navy League. Republican. Mem. Reformed Christian Ch. Avocations: sports, home computing. Office: Cast 5450 Katella Ave Los Alamitos CA 90720

CLARK, KENNETH COURTRIGHT, physics and geophysics educator; b. Austin, Tex., Sept. 30, 1919; s. Evert Mordecai and Grace (Courtright) C.; m. Eleanor Lorraine McKenna, June 10, 1947; children: David Templeton, Gracia Courtright. B.A., U. Tex., 1940; A.M., Harvard U., 1941, Ph.D., 1947. Spl. research assoc. nat. def. research project Electro-Acoustic Lab., Harvard, 1942-45, instr. physics, 1947-48; mem. faculty U. Wash., Seattle, 1948—; asso. prof. U. Wash., 1955-60, prof., 1960—, chmn. geophysics, 1967-69; research asso. prof. Geophys. Inst., U. Alaska, Fairbanks, 1957-58; mem. sci. adv. bd. Geophys. Inst., U. Alaska, 1972-76; vis. prof. div. theoretical and space physics LaTrobe U., Melbourne, Australia, 1979-80; cons. AID, State Dept. and Ministry Edn. India, Varanasi, 1964, Udaipur, 1966; dir. aeronomy program NSF, Washington, 1969-70; cons. Boeing Co., Seattle, 1964, Los Alamos (N.Mex.) Sci. Labs., 1961, Aerospace Corp., Los Angeles, 1964, Battelle Meml. Inst., Richland, Wash., 1965—. Fellow Am. Phys. Soc., Optical Soc. Am.; mem. Am. Geophys. Union, Am. Assn. Physics Tchrs., Phi Beta Kappa, Sigma Xi. Methodist. Home: 5211 17th Ave NE Seattle WA 98105

CLARK, KENNETH SEARS, architect; b. Lamont, Okla., Jan. 21, 1909; s. Allen Sears and Alice (Lumsden) C.; m. Betty M. Cullen, Jan. 25, 1936; children: Kay Melicent, William K., Susan Sears; m. Ellen Montgomery, Feb. 15, 1964; children—Bridget Sharon, John Brion. B.Arch., Okla. State U., 1932, M.A., 1933. With U.S. Coast and Geodetic Survey, 1933-35; asst. state architect N.Mex. W.P.A., 1935-38; pvt. archtl. practice Santa Fe, 1938—. Works include missile research structures, White Sands Missile Range, N.Mex. Pres. Santa Fe United Fund, 1959. Served to capt. C.E. AUS, 1942-45. Recipient civilian service award Dept. Army, 1960. Fellow AIA; mem. Am. Arbitration Assn., ASTM, Soc. Am. Mil. Engrs., Bd. Examiners Architects N.Mex., N.Mex. Soc. Architects (pres. 1968), Santa Fe C. of C. (dir. 1953-54). Methodist (trustee). Club: Santa Fe Kiwanis (lt. gov. SW dist. 1957). Office: 208 Delgado St Santa Fe NM 87501

CLARK, LANA LOUISE, social worker; b. Spokane, Wash., June 21, 1941; d. Charles William Bergen and Magdalene Louise (Gehrke) Schrecengost; m. Francis Warren Clark; July 29, 1960; children: Christopher Kenneth, Matthew Charles, Leah Marlene. Student, U. Calgary, Alta., Can., 1970-74, U. Tex., 1982-83; BA with high honors, U. Mont., 1984. Adminstrv. sec. various cos., Wash., Oreg., Mont. and Alta., 1960-81; psychometrist Community Hosp., Missoula, Mont., 1984-85, med. social worker, 1985—. Mem. edn. com. Planned Parenthood, Missoula. Mem. Nat. Assn. Social Workers, Mont. Gerontology Soc., Golden Key. Democrat. Congregationalist. Avocations: reading, sewing, needlework. Home: 3916 Timberlane Missoula MT 59802 Office: Missoula Community Med Ctr 2827 Fort Missoula Rd Missoula MT 59801

CLARK, LLOYD, historian, educator; b. Belton, Tex., Aug. 4, 1923; s. Lloyd C. and Hattie May (Taylor) C.; B.S. in Journalism, So. Meth. U., 1948; B. Fgn. Trade, Am. Grad. Sch. Internat. Mgmt., 1949; M. Pub. Adminstrn., Ariz. State U., 1972; m. Jean Reeves, June 17, 1950; children—Roger, Cynthia, Candyce. String corr. A.P., Dallas, 1941-42; editor, pub. Ex-Press, Arlington, Tex., 1945-48; publicity mgr. Advt. Counselors Ariz., Phoenix, 1949; reporter Phoenix Gazette, 1949-65; asst. pub. Ariz. Weekly Gazette, 1965-66; founder Council on Abandoned Mil. Posts-U.S.A., 1966; project cons. City of Prescott, Ariz., 1971-72; dep. dir. adminstrv. services No. Ariz. Council Govts., Flagstaff, 1972-73; regional adminstr. South Eastern Ariz. Govts. Orgn., Bisbee, 1973-75; local govt. assistance coordinator Ariz. Dept. Transp., Phoenix, 1975-80, program adminstr., 1980-83; history instr. Rio Salado Community Coll., Phoenix, 1983—; editor and pub. Clark Biog. Reference, 1956-62. Bd. dirs. Friends of Channel 8, 1984-86; Phoenix del. Papago Park Prisoner of War Camp Commn., 1985. Served to lt. AUS, 1942-46; maj., 1966-70; col. Res. Recipient Ariz. exemplary gen. news coverage award, 1960, outstanding news reporting, 1961. Mem. Am. Grad. Sch. Internat. Mgmt. Alumni Assn. (pres. Phoenix chpt. 1965), Ariz. Hist. Soc., Sharlot Hall Hist. Soc. (life mem.), Res. Officers Assn., Ex-Students Assn. U. Tex. at Arlington (life mem., pres. 1946-48), The Westerners (sheriff Phoenix Corral 1986-87), Sigma Delta Chi (pres. Valley of Sun chpt. 1964). Club: University (Phoenix). Author: Lloyd Clark's Scrapbook, Vol. 1, 1958, Vol. 2, 1960. Address: PO Box 13344 Phoenix AZ 85002

CLARK, MALCOLM MALLORY, research geologist; b. Palo Alto, Calif., Sept. 21, 1931; s. Birge Malcolm and Lucile (Townley) C.; children from previous marriage: Dean, Dana, Douglas, Andrew, Mallory; m. Laurie D. Hodgen, Sept. 1, 1979. BSChemE with highest honors, U. Calif., Berkeley, 1957; PhD in Geology, Stanford U., 1967. Engr. Temescal Metallurgical, Richmond, Calif., 1957-60; mgr. lab. Dumont Mfg. Co., San Rafael, Calif., 1960-61; mgr. mfg. Monitor Plastics Co., San Rafael, 1961-63; geologist U.S. Geol. Survey, Menlo Park, Calif., 1967—; acting asst. prof. Stanford U., 1968; lectr. De Anza Coll., Cupertino, Calif., 1976, Foothill Coll., Los Altos Hills, Calif., 1977-80. Contbr. articles to profl. jours. Served to 2d lt. USAF, 1953-55. Grad. fellow NSF, 1964-67. Fellow Geol. Soc. Am.; mem. Am. Quaternary Assn., Am. Geophys. Union, Seismol. Soc. Am., Internat. Glaciol. Soc., Sierra Club, Sigma Xi, Phi Beta Kappa. Office: US Geol Survey 345 Middlefield M/S 977 Menlo Park CA 94025

CLARK, MARY ELLON, historian, writer; b. Norton, N.Mex., Dec. 22, 1934; d. Edward and Delia (Kingston) Brown; m. Donald G. Clark, June 11, 1981; children: Elaine, Terry, Johnny, Joe. Society editor Tucumcari (N.Mex.) News, 1969-70, correspondent, 1970-75, editor, 1975-76; anchorwoman Sta. KTNM Radio, Tucumcari, 1975-80, reporter, history program hostess, 1976-80; news correspondent Amarillo (Tex.) Globe & TV, 1976-80. Author: El Chaparito, 1976 (DAR Bicentennial award), A Mark of Time, 1984; author numerous poems; contbr. articles to mags. Mem. Dem. Campaign Com., Tucumcari, 1979; active with Tucumcari Hist. Mus., 1974-75. Recipient N.Mex. N.G. cert. 1976, Col. Aide-de-Camp award Exec. Staff of State of N.Mex. bestowed by the gov. Bruce King and lt. gov. Roberto Mondragon, 1979. Baptist. Home: PO Box 946 Tucumcari NM 88401

CLARK, MARY KATHERINE, range conservationist; b. TachiKowa AFB, Japan, Mar. 11, 1953; (parents Am. citizens); d. Peter A. and Mary Ellen (Wallace) Foley; m. Henry William Clark, July 23, 1977; children: Wendy Michele, Peter William. AA, Am. River Coll., 1973; BS in Range and Wildlands Sci., U. Calif., Davis, 1975. Range technician U.S. Forest Service, Adin, Calif., 1974-76; range conservationist U.S. Forest Services, Union, Oreg., 1980-85, Duchesne, Utah, 1985—; range conservationist Bur. Land Mgmt., Bakersfield, Calif., 1976-77, Las Cruces, N.Mex., 1977-80. 10 Yr. Cert. U.S. Forest Service, 1985. Mem. Soc. Range Mgmt. Republican. Avocations: crocheting, tole painting, camping, water skiing, cooking. Home: PO Box 321 Duchesne UT 84021-0321 Office: US Forest Service PO Box I Duchesne UT 84021

CLARK, PAMELA ELIZABETH, planetary geologist; b. Troy, N.Y., Apr. 26, 1951; d. Frederick Earl and Elizabeth Cecilia (Smyth) C. BS, St. Joseph Coll., West Hartford, Conn., 1973; PhD, U. Md., 1979. Research asst. NASA, Goddard, U. Md., Greenbelt, 1974-70; geologist U.S. Geol. Survey, Flagstaff, Ariz., 1977-78; Nat. Acad. Scis. research assoc. Jet Propulsion Lab. div. NASA, Pasadena, Calif., 1980-82, cons., research fellow, 1983-84, mem. tech. staff, 1984—; asst. prof. geoscis. Murray (Ky.) State U., 1982-84; faculty advisor undergrad. and grad. students Geoscis. Club Murray State U., 1982-84; prin. investigator NASA Planetary Geology and Pioneer Venus Programs, 1983—; mem. organizing com. First Mercury Workshop, 1985-86; advisor/colleague summer faculty fellowship program Jet Propulsion Lab. NASA, 1986-87, interdisciplinary sci. experiment rep. Mars Observer Project, 1987—, mission interface team sci. rep. Planetary Data SYstem Project, 1987—. Contbr. numerous articles to profl. jours. Recipient Disting. Alumna award St. Joseph's Coll., 1985; NASA/Am. Soc. Elec. Engring. Summer Faculty Research fellow, Pasadena, 1983. Mem. AAAS, Am. Chem. Soc. (cert.), Am. Geophys. Union, Geol. Soc. Am., Am. Astron. Union (div. Planetary Scis.), Sierra Club, Wilderness Soc. Democrat. Roman Catholic. Avocations: writing, singing, soft sculpture, hiking, sailing.

CLARK, PAULINE AGNES VIRGINIA, trust executive, fund raiser, educator; b. Jersey City, Oct. 11, 1940; d. Nicholas F. and Helen A. (Lamb) Novak; m. Noel A. Clark, Dec. 17, 1940; children—Caitlin, Ian, Maura. B.A. cum laude, Immaculata Coll., 1962; M.A. in English Lit., John Carroll U., 1966. English instr. Fisher Jr. Coll., Andover Inst. Bus., U. Mass., Northeastern U., 1968-75; acting dir. devel. Channel 12 Pub. TV, Broomfield, Colo., 1978-80; diploma cons. adult diploma program Cambridge Pub. Schs., 1975-77; exec. dir. Hall of Life Health Edn. Ctr., Denver, 1980-84; officer regional devel. Mountains-Plains regional office Nat. Trust Historic Preservation, Denver, 1984-85; pres., bd. dirs. San Juan Children's Learning Ctr., Boulder, 1986—; fund raiser, program adminstr., bd. liaison. Co-author: A Guide to the Asssessment of Life Experience for High School Credit, 1977; contbr. articles in field to profl. jours. Bd. dirs. Boulder County United Way, 1979-80, mem. NOW, 1982-83. Teaching fellow John Carroll U., 1964-66. Mem. Colo. Assn. Fund Raisers. Home: 3106 Kittrell Ct Boulder CO 80303 Office: Chew Design 1523 18th St Kittrell CO 80202

CLARK, RAYMOND OAKES, banker; b. Ft. Bragg, N.C., Nov. 9, 1944; s. Raymond Shelton and Nancy Lee (McCormick) C.; children: Matthew Patrick, Geoffry Charles. BBA, U. Ariz., 1966; postgrad., U. Wash., 1984-86. Mgmt. trainee First Interstate Bank, Phoenix, 1966, credit analyst, 1968-69, asst. br. mgr., Scottsdale, Ariz., 1969-72, asst. v.p., br. mgr., Tempe, Ariz., 1972—. V.p. bd. dirs. Sun Devil Club, Tempe, 1975—; pres. Tempe Diplomats, 1979—; pres. Tempe Diablos, 1975—; major chmn. Fiesta Bowl, Tempe, 1975-79; bd. dirs. Maricopa County Bd. Mgrs., Phoenix, 1973, YMCA, Tempe, 1974, Tempe Design Rev. Bd., 1983—. Named Outstanding Young Man Am., Tempe Jaycees, 1977, Outstanding Young Man, Ariz. Jaycees, 1978, U.S. Jaycees, 1979. Served with U.S. Army, 1966-68. Mem. Tempe C. of C. (pres. 1979-80). Republican. Episcopalian. Lodge: Kiwanis (dist. lt. gov. 1980).

CLARK, RICHARD JAMES, advertising and marketing executive, designer, artist; b. Attica, N.Y., Aug. 19, 1945; s. Claude Jonas and Rita Elizabeth (McKernan) C.; m. Joy Lynne, Dec. 22, 1966. B.S., SUNY-Buffalo, 1964, B.A., 1969; postgrad. Yale U., summer 1965; M.A., SUNY-Buffalo, 1970. Designer, Calspan Corp., Buffalo, 1966-69; mktg. exec. Erie Bank, Buffalo, 1969-71; designer Design for Industry, Buffalo, 1972-77; v.p. creative dir., 1978—; ptnr. Design Graphics, Buffalo, 1977—; pres., chmn. bd. Nat. Design Concepts, Huntington Beach, Calif., 1979-84; pres., chmn. Clark Meyer Charters & Howell, 1984—; chmn. bd. Design for Industry, 1985—; cons., tchr. SUNY. Recipient Western N.Y. Communicators award, 1981, 82, 83; Clio award. Mem. Orange County Advt. Fedn., Bus. and Profl. Advt. Assn., Western N.Y. Communicators, Huntington Beach C. of C. Art editor Scene Mag.; exhibited several one-man shows. Office: Clark Meyer Charters & Howell Suite 263 North 16052 Beach Blvd Huntington Beach CA 92647

CLARK, RICHARD LEFORS, systems research scientist; b. Aberdeen, S.D., Oct. 29, 1936; s. Robert Montgomery and Marion (Shook) C.; m. Barbara Louise Battersby, Mar. 28, 1980; 1 child, Robert James. BA, Pacific Western U., 1974, MS, 1975, PhD, 1978; BS in Engring. and Applied Sci., Jackson State Coll., 1968, MA in Bus. Mgmt., 1972. Technician Honeywell Co., 1957-58; quality assurance Martin Co., 1958-59, Remington Rand, 1959; engr. Gen. Dynamics/Electronics, 1959-68; supr. Graco, Inc., 1971-74; with Internat. Harvester, 1975-81, Caterpiller Tractor Co., 1981—, Solar Turbines subs. Caterpiller Tractor Co.; systems research in fusion power, parapsychology and physics, over unity elec. generators and gravity research, San Diego, 1975—; lectr. gravity/Maxwell-Faraday physics systems and devices. Inventor vortex fusion engine; author tech. papers. Served with U.S. Army, 1954-57.

CLARK, ROBERT EDWARD HOLMES, atomic physicist; b. Washington, July 8, 1947; s. Austin Bryant Jackson and Barbara (McClenon) C.; m. Charlsea Dee Shipp, July 18, 1970; children: Robin Ann, Victoria Gayle. BS, Frostburg State Coll., 1969; MS, Pa. State U., 1978, PhD, 1980. Tchr. physics Prince Georges County High Sch., Oxon Hill, Md., 1969-75; research asst. Sacramento Peak Obs., Sunspot, N.Mex., 1978; postdoctoral researcher Los Alamos (N.Mex.) Nat. Lab, 1980-82, staff scientist, 1982—. Contbr. articles to profl. jours. Mem. Am. Physical Soc., Sigma Xi, Phi Kappa Phi. Republican. Home: 110 Yosemite Dr Los Alamos NM 87544 Office: Los Alamos Nat Lab Group X-6 MS B226 Los Alamos NM 87545

CLARK, ROBERT MARC, social worker; b. Richland, Wash., July 13, 1957; s. Beverly Earl and Mary Kay (Booth) C. AA, Yakima Valley Coll., 1978; BA in Social Work, Eastern Wash. U., 1980, MSW, 1982. Registered clin. social worker, Oreg. Social worker II Stress Ctr., St. Anthony Hosp., Pendleton, Oreg., 1983-85; pvt. practice counseling Pendleton, 1983—; proctor program counselor Homestead Youth Lodge, Pendleton, 1985—, coordinator Proctor Program, 1986—; dir. social work Pioneer Meml. Hosp., Heppner, Oreg., 1985—; dir. Satellite Referral Service, 1985—; cons. Murphy Assn. Vocat., 1987—. Vol. Spokane Health Dept. Mem. Nat. Assn. Social Workers. Avocations: songwriting, writing poetry, jogging. Office: 17 SW Emigrant Suite 6 Pendleton OR 97801

CLARK, RONALD DUANE, chemistry educator; b. Hollywood, Calif., Nov. 21, 1938; s. Marvin Ansel and Elsie Susanna (Appel) C.; m. Rosalind Estelle Proell, Sept. 9, 1967; children: Jennifer, Roger, Kenneth, Stephanie. BS, UCLA, 1960; PhD, U. Calif., Riverside, 1964. Postdoctoral researcher Mich. State U., East Lansing, 1964-65; research chemist Standard Oil Co. Ohio, Warrensville, 1965-69; prof. chemistry N.Mex. Highlands U., Las Vegas, 1969—; pres. Cycad Products, Las Vegas, 1983—. Author: Chemistry-The Science and the Scene, 1975; contbr. articles to profl. jours. Grantee NSF, Dept. of Energy, NASA. Mem. Am. Chem. Soc. (holder offices local chpts.). Republican. Home: 509 Dora Celeste Dr Las Vegas NM 87701 Office: NMex Highlands U Las Vegas NM 87701

CLARK, R(UFUS) BRADBURY, lawyer; b. Des Moines, May 11, 1924; s. Rufus Bradbury and Gertrude Martha (Burns) C.; m. Polly Ann King, Sept. 6, 1949; children: Cynthia Clark Maxwell, Rufus Bradbury, John Atherton. B.A., Harvard U., 1948, J.D., 1951; diploma in law, Oxford U., Eng., 1952; D.H.L., Ch. Div. Sch. Pacific, San Francisco, 1983. Bar: Calif. Assoc. firm O'Melveny & Myers, Los Angeles, 1952-62, sr. ptnr., 1961—, mem. mgmt. com., 1983—; dir. So. Calif. Water Co., Econ. Resources Corp., Brown Internat. Corp., Automatic Machinery & Electronics Corp. Editor: California Corporation Laws, 6 vols, 1976—. Pres. John Tracy Clinic, Los Angeles; chancellor Episcopal Diocese of Los Angeles, 1967—, hon. canon, 1983—. Served to capt. U.S. Army, 1943-46. Decorated Bronze star with oak leaf cluster; decorated Purple Heart with oak leaf cluster; Fulbright grantee, 1952. Mem. ABA (subcom. on audit letter responses, com. on law and acctg.), State Bar Calif. (chmn. drafting com. on gen. corp. law 1973-81, chmn. drafting com. on nonprofit corp. law 1980-84, mem. exec. com. bus. law sect. 1984-87, sec. 1986-87), Los Angeles County Bar Assn. Republican. Clubs: California (Los Angeles), Harvard (Los Angeles), Chancery (Los Angeles); Alamitos Bay Yacht (Long Beach). Office: O'Melveny & Myers 400 S Hope St Los Angeles CA 90071

CLARK, THOMAS LLOYD, English linguistics educator; b. Havre, Mont., July 10, 1939; s. Lloyd Thomas and Loretta Margaret (LaPlante) C.; m. H. Jeanne Wilson, Apr. 8, 1960; children—Tim, Helen-Margaret, Kristin. B.A., U. Utah, 1964, M.A., 1966; Ph.D., Ohio U., 1970. Prof. U. Nev., Las Vegas, 1970—; dir. Nev. Lang. Survey, 1974-84; cons. Lexik House Pubs., Barnhart Books, Prentice-Hall Pubs., U. Nev. Press; lectr. lang., names, lexicography, Am. English. Author: Language: Structure and Use, 1981; (monograph) Marietta, Ohio; Erosion of a Speech Island, 1972; contbr. articles to Am. Speech, Names, Dictionaries, Jour. of English Linguistics, Conn. English Jour., Verbatim, Halcyon, Language and Speech, Elem. English jours., others. Active Nev. Humanities Com. Programs, Sta. KNPR shows, Credit Com. for Silver State Schs. Fed. Credit Union. Served with USN, 1959-61. NDEA, 1966-70, Dictionary of Am. Regional English, 1967-68; NEA grantee. Mem. Am. Dialect Soc. (pres. 1985-87), Nat Council Tchrs. English. (dir. Commn. on English Lang. 1974-78), Dictionary Soc. N.Am., Am. Name Soc. (bd. mgrs. 1977-80), MLA, Rocky Mountain MLA, Internat. Conf. on Methods in Dialectology (mem. steering com. 1974-84), So. Nev. Tchrs. English (pres. 1974). Roman Catholic. *

CLARK, THOMAS RYAN, federal agency executive; b. Aberdeen, Wash., Sept. 16, 1925; s. George O. and Gladys (Ryan) C.; m. Barbara Ann Thiele, June 14, 1948; children: Thomas R. III, Kathleen A., Christopher J.T. Student, U. Kans., 1943-44; BS, U.S. Mil. Acad., 1948; MSEE, Purdue U., 1955; cert., U.S. Army Command and Gen. Staff Coll., 1960, Harvard U., 1979. Commd. C.E., U.S. Army, 1948, advanced through grades to col., 1968; ret. U.S. Army, 1968; program mgr. U.S. AEC, Washington, 1968-75; dep. mgr. Dept. of Energy, Albuquerque, 1976-83; mgr. Nev. ops. Dept. of Energy, Las Vegas, 1983—; mem. adv. bd. Dept. Chem. and Nuclear Engring., U. N.Mex., 1984—; mem. statewide adv. bd. Desert Research Inst., U. Nev., 1985—. Editor, co-author: Nuclear Fuel Cycle, 1975. Trustee Nev. Devel. Authority, Las Vegas, 1984—. Decorated Legion of Merit, Bronze Star; named Disting. Exec., Pres. of U.S., 1982. Mem. Las Vegas C. of C. (bd. dirs. 1983—), Sigma Xi, Tau Beta Pi, Eta Kappa Nu. Episcopalian. Lodge: Rotary. Office: US Dept Energy PO Box 14100 Las Vegas NV 89114

CLARK, WENDELINE DIANE, nurse; b. Wichita, Kans., Jan. 9, 1951; s. Henry Lee Wofford and Blanche Deloris (Neely) Jackson; m Marvin Max Lawton, Nov. 7, 1969 (div. Jan. 1977); children: Cyndrya Dawn, Marvin Max, II; m. William Taft Clark, Jan.12, 1980. Grad., Wesley Sch. Nursing, Wichita, 1973; BS, Calif. State U., Carson, 1986. R.N., Calif., Kans. Allergy nurse Dr. J.A. Budetti, Wichita, 1974; charge nurse Wesley Med. Ctr., Wichita, 1973-77; unit supr. Daniel Freeman Hosp., Inglewood, Calif., 1977—; adj. faculty Mt. St. Mary's Coll., Los Angeles, 1985—; facilitator Carondelet Health Care Corp., Inglewood, 1985—; mem. faculty dept. edn. Daniel Freeman Hosp., 1983, 86. Vol. nurse ARC, Wichita, 1973; mem. PTA, Los Angeles, 1980—; mem. Fontbonne Guild St. Mary's Acad., Inglewood, 1985—; v.p. nurses unit Triedstone Revival Ctr. Ch. of God in Christ, Watts, Calif., 1985. Named one of Outstanding Young Women Am., 1984. Mem. Alpha Kappa Alpha (debutante 1969). Pentecostal. Avocations: music, sewing, sports, community activities, fishing. Home: 2030 W 108th St Los Angeles CA 90047 Office: PO Box 2321 Inglewood CA 90305

CLARK, WILLIAM HILTON, biology educator, water scientist; b. Caldwell, Idaho, Dec. 17, 1944; s. Hilton Montrose and Margaet Lucille (Bales) C.; m. Mary Elizabeth Clark, June 8, 1968; children: Ellen Mary, Cynthia Jane, Karen Diana. BS in Biology, Coll. Idaho, 1967; MS in Biology, U. Nev., 1971. Research asst. U. Nev., Reno, 1968, 72-73; research asst. Coll. Idaho, Caldwell, 1967, 76, expdn. leader, 1977—, asst. dir. Mus. Natural History, 1978—, adj. prof. biology, 1979—; sr. water quality specialist Idaho Dept. Health, Welfare and Environment, Boise, 1974-85, sr. water quality analyst, 1985—; cons. Nev. Archeol. Survey, Reno, 1972; bd. dirs. Coll. Idaho Alumni Assn. Contbr. articles to profl. jours. Served with U.S. Army, 1969-71, Vietnam. Decorated Bronze Star; recipient Disting. Alumni award Coll. Idaho, 1985; named Employee of Yr., Idaho Div. Environment, Boise, 1984; grantee Earthwatch, Am. Philos. Soc. Mem. Ecol. Soc. Am. (cert.), Idaho Acad. Sci. (rep. to Nat. Acad. Sci. and AAAS 1984—) Am. Fisheries Soc. (cert. fisheries scientist), Idaho Entomology Group (pres., editor 1976-79, pres.-elect 1987, pres. 1988), Sigma Xi. Club: Boise State U. (v.p. 1986—). Avocations: exploring in Baja Calif., Mex., entomology, natural history. Home: 6305 Kirkwood Rd Boise ID 83709 Office: Idaho Dept Health Welfare Div Environment 450 W State St Boise ID 83720

CLARK, WILLIAM PHILIP, television network executive; b. N.Y.C., Apr. 20, 1954; m. Sharon Carlock; B.S. cum laude in Acctg., Fordham U., 1976; M.B.A., USC, 1986. Auditor Arthur Young & Co., N.Y.C., 1975-76; sr. auditor Hurdman & Cranstoun, N.Y.C., 1976-79; mgr. data processing audit CBS, Inc., N.Y.C., 1979-80; mgr. ops. CBS Records Internat., N.Y.C., 1980-82; dir. systems planning CBS Entertainment, Los Angeles, 1982-85, dir. MIS and systems planning, 1985—. Mem. Am. Inst. C.P.A.s, N.Y. State Soc. C.P.A.s, Calif. State Soc. C.P.A.s, AMA, Calif. Realty Bd. Office: 7800 Beverly Blvd Los Angeles CA 90036

CLARKE, DAVID MARSHALL, college president; b. Chewalah, Wash., Nov. 28, 1927; s. Melvin L. and Louise M. (Van Bibber) C. B.S., Gonzaga U., 1949, M.S. in Organic Chemistry, 1949, Licentiate in Philosophy, 1958; Ph.D. in Phys. Chemistry, Northwestern U., 1953; Licentiate in Sacred Theology, Weston Coll., 1965. Instr., asst. prof. chemistry and math. Gonzaga U., Spokane, Wash., 1949-50, 56-61; asst. prof. chemistry Gonzaga U., 1966-68, assoc. prof., 1968-70, acad. v.p., 1968-69, exec. v.p., 1969-70; research scientist Weston Obs., Boston Coll., 1961-65; provost, acad. v.p. St. Francis Coll., Joliet, Ill., 1970-72; pres. Regis Coll., Denver, 1972—; mem. Commn. on Edn. Credits and Credentials, Washington, 1981-85, Commn. on Higher Edn. and Adult Learner, 1986—; bd. dirs. Midwest Research Inst., 1982—; mem. exec. com. Ind. Coll. Funds Am., 1985—. Mem. Denver Commn. Community Relations, 1975-83; trustee, mem. exec. com. N.W. Assn. Pvt. Colls. and Univs., 1968-70; trustee Gonzaga U., 1968-70, Coll. Holy Cross, 1969-78, Regis Coll., 1972—, Inst. Health, Denver; trustee, chmn. acad. com. Loyola U., Chgo., 1971-80, trustee, New Orleans, 1982-85; bd. dirs. Assn. Jesuit Colls. and Univs., 1973—; mem. adv. bd. Colo. Youth Leadership Seminar. Named 1 of 10 most disting. Denver Bus. Mag., 1985. Mem. Am. Chem. Soc., Pres.'s Assn., Sigma Xi, Delta Epsilon Sigma, Phi Lambda Upsilon, Alpha Sigma Nu. Research and publs. in field. Address: 3539 W 50th Pkwy Denver CO 80221

CLARKE, DENNIS FRANCIS, electrical engineer; b. Plymouth, Eng., Sept. 13, 1945; came to U.S., 1946; s. Leonard Francis and Barbara Ellen (Fowler) C.; m. Donna Jean Bayhouse, Dec. 21, 1968; children: Darlene, David. BEE, Gonzaga U., 1967. Design engr. Bettis Atomic Power Lab., Pitts., 1967-73; constrn. elec. engr. Stearns-Catalytic, Denver, 1973-75; staff elec. engr. Kaiser Aluminum, Spokane, Wash., 1975-86; elec. engr. Pacific Test and Design, Idaho Falls, Idaho, 1986—. Pres. Glenrose Assn., Spokane, 1981. Mem. IEEE, Am. Nuclear Soc., NSPE. Roman Catholic. Clubs: Spokane Rugby, Football. Avocations: flying, scuba diving, chess. Home: E 6121 32nd Ave Spokane WA 99223 Office: Pacific Test and Design Services 567 W 19th St Idaho Falls ID 83402

CLARKE, FRANK, family physician, medical educator; b. Blythe, Calif., Nov. 11, 1921; s. Francis Dodsworth; grad. cum laude Los Angeles City Coll., 1942; B.S., UCLA, 1946; M.D., St. Louis U., 1950; postgrad. U.S. Naval Med. Sch., 1951-52; MPH, U. Calif.-Berkeley; m. Pearl Tucker, children—Michael A., Timothy L., Stephen, Teressa, M. Robert, Sha-ni. Diplomate Am. Bd. Family Practice. Intern, USN Hosp., Oakland, Calif., 1950-51; resident Tulare County Gen. Hosp., Tulare, Calif., 1953-54; practice medicine and surgery, Woodlake, Calif., 1974-75; mem. staff Kaweah Delta Dist. Hosp.; chief staff Exeter Meml. Hosp., 1954-56; team physician Coll. of Sequoias, 1968-75; med. dir. USPHS (ret. 1986); clin. dir. Albuquerque Indian Hosp., 1975—; lecturer U. Calif. at Santa Cruz, 1971-73; asst. clin. prof. dept. family and community medicine Georgetown U., 1980—; adj. faculty Sch. Allied Health Profls. Idaho State U. Trustee, Woodlake Union Elementary Sch. Dist., 1956-60, pres. bd. trustees, 1958-60; chmn. Citizens Adv. Com., Title I Funds, 1969-73. Bd. dirs. D-Q. U., 1971. Served with USN, 1942-46, 50-53. Recipient fellowship and grant John Hay Whitney Found., 1950; Indian achievement award Indian Council Fire Chgo., 1961; named Man of Year, City of Woodlake, 1962. Charter fellow Am. Acad. Family Physicians; mem. Assn. Am. Indian Physicians (pres. 1973-74), Nat. Council Clin. Dirs. (chmn. 1977-79), Phi Chi, Tau Alpha Epsilon. Episcopalian (del. 1969-73). Home: PO Box 309 Woodlake CA 93286

CLARKE, IAN CAMERON, mechanical engineer, researcher educator; b. Kilmarnock, Scotland, Mar. 17, 1946; came to U.S., 1972, s. Donald L. and Elizabeth Clarke, m. Anne Clarke, June 30, 1967; children—Lynne C., Alan C. B.Sc. in Mech. Engring., U. Strathclyde, Glasgow, Scotland, 1968, Ph.D., in Bioengring., 1972. Bioengring. research tech. U. Strathclyde, 1968, bioengring. research asst., 1971-72; asst. research bioengr. UCLA, 1972-73, asst. adj. prof., 1973-79; assoc. prof. mech. engring. and orthopaedics U. So. Calif., Los Angeles, 1979-83, dir. Orthopaedic Biomechanics Lab., Orthopaedic Hosp., 1979-83; pres. Bioengring. Research Inst., Los Angeles, 1983—. Contbr. articles to profl. jours., also reviewer various jours; mem. arthroplasty editorial bd. Techniques in Orthopaedics, 1982—; mem. editorial bd. Anns. Biomed. Engring., 1975—; mem. U.S. bd. editors Biomaterials Jour., 1982—. Numerous research grants including NIH, NASA, NSF. Mem. Inst. Mech. Engrs. (grad. mem.), ASME, Biomed. Engring. Soc., Orthopaedic Research Soc., ASTM (F-4 com. on med. devices), Biomaterials Soc., Hip Soc. (John Charnley award for paper 1977, Otto AuFrance award for paper 1979). Home: 2215 23d St Santa Monica CA 90405 Office: Bioengring Research Inst 10780 Santa Monica Blvd Suite #100 Westwood CA 90025

CLARKE, JOHN, physics educator; b. Cambridge, Eng., Feb. 10, 1942; came to U.S., 1968; s. Victor Patrick and Ethel May (Blowers) C.; m. Grethe Fog Pedersen, Sept. 15, 1979; 1 child, Elizabeth Jane. B.A., Cambridge U., 1964, M.A., 1968, Ph.D., 1968. Postdoctoral scholar U. Calif.-Berkeley, 1968-69, asst. prof. physics, 1969-71, assoc. prof., 1971-73, prof., 1973—. Contbr. numerous articles to profl. jours. Recipient Charles Vernon Boys prize Brit. Inst. Physics, 1977, award Soc. Exploration Geophysics, 1979, Outstanding Teaching award U. Calif., 1983; fellow Sloan Found., 1970-72, Miller Inst. for Basic Research, 1975-76; Guggenheim fellow, 1977-78; named Calif. Scientist Yr., 1987. Fellow AAAS, Royal Soc. London, Am. Phys. Soc. Office: U Calif Dept Physics Berkeley CA 94720

CLARKE, JOHN EDWARD, mgmt. recruitment co. exec.; b. Vancouver, B.C., Can., Dec. 13, 1937; s. William James and Laura Mackay C.; BA cum laude, Oberlin Coll., 1960; m. Joanne Saltsman, June 10, 1958; children: Sheryl, Lynn, Bill. Comml. mgr. Ohio Bell Telephone Co., Cleve., 1960-66; mgr. staff recruiting Booz, Allen & Hamilton, Inc., N.Y.C., 1966-69; spl. asst. to postmaster gen. U.S. Post Office Dept., Washington, 1969-70; exec. asst. to dir. OEO, Washington, 1970-71; staff asst. to Pres., White House, Washington, 1971-73; v.p. S.E. Banking Corp., Miami, Fla., 1973-74; mng. dir. nat. splty., mem. exec. com., sr. officer Korn/Ferry Internat., Los Angeles, 1974-81; pres. Clarke & Assos., mgmt. recruiters, Woodland Hills, Calif. and Jackson Hole, Wyo., 1981—; adv. com. West Valley Bank. Mem. Calif. Exec. Recruiters Assn., Westlake Village C. of C., Los Angeles Town Hall. Republican. Clubs: Jonathan, North Ranch Country.

CLARKE, KAY PALMER, corporate communications director; b. San Diego; d. A. John Palmer and Lilliam E. Venero; m. Jon E. Clarke, 1966 (dec.); children: Jon Scott, Anne; m. Herbert Lechner, Sept. 11, 1982. BS, Coll. of Mt. St. Vincent; MA, Columbia U. R.N., Calif. Nurse supr. St. Vincent's Med. Ctr., N.Y.C., 1963-65; mktg. officer First Nat. City Bank, N.Y.C., 1965-70; corp. communications dir. SRI Internat., Menlo Park, Calif., 1978—; bd. dirs. Interplast (vol. pub. relations dir). Sec. Civic Assn., Mt. Sinai, N.Y., 1971-72. Named Nurse of Yr. Mayor of N.Y.C., 1961. Mem. Pub. Relations Soc. Am. (accredited, Pub. Service award 1986), AAUW, Women In Communications, Am. Bus. Women's Assn., Issues Mgmt. Assn., Bay Area Pub. Affairs Council, Internat. Assn. Bus. Communications, Menlo Park C. of C. (bd. dirs., chmn. various coms.). Republican. Avocations: piano playing, tennis, walking. Office: SRI Internat 333 Ravenswood Ave Menlo Park CA 94025

CLARKE, RICHARD ALAN, lawyer, electric and gas utility company executive; b. San Francisco, May 18, 1930; s. Chauncey Frederick and Carolyn (Shannon) C.; m. Mary Dell Fisher, Feb. 5, 1955; children: Suzanne, Nancy C. Stephen, Douglas Alan. AB cum laude, U. Calif.-Berkeley, 1952, JD, 1955. Bar: Calif. 1955. Atty. Pacific Gas and Electric Co., San Francisco, 1955-60, 69, sr. counsel, 1970-74, asst. gen. counsel, 1974-79, v.p., asst. to chmn., 1979-82, exec. v.p., gen. mgr. utility ops., 1982-85, exec. v.p., pres., 1985-86, chmn. bd., chief exec. officer, 1986—; ptnr. Rockwell, Fulkerson and Clarke, San Rafael, Calif., 1960-69; bd. dirs. Potlach Corp. Bd. dirs. Ind. Colls. No. Calif., San Francisco, 1980—, Invest-in-Am., 1986—; chmn. active budget study com. United Way of the Bay area, profl. div. Marin United Way campaign. Served to capt. USAR, 1952-60. Mem. Calif. Bar Assn., Pacific Coast Elec. Assn., Pacific Coast Gas Assn., Edison Electric Inst. (bd. dirs. 1986—), Calif. Bus. Roundtable (bd. dirs. 1986—), Calif. C. of C. (bd. dirs. 1986—). Clubs: Marin Tennis (San Rafael); Pacific Union (San Francisco). Office: Pacific Gas and Electric Co 77 Beale St San Francisco CA 94106

CLARKE, ROBERT EMMETT, writer, poet; b. Cleve., May 28, 1906; s. Robert Emmett and Mary Bernadette (Paquette) C. Student schs. Lakewood, Ohio. Reporter, Cleve. Times, 1925; asst. mgr. UP, Cleve., 1925-26; police reporter Canton Daily News (Ohio), 1926-27; courthouse and police reporter, asst. sports editor Akron Times-Press (Ohio), 1927-30; with Thompson Products, 1943-45, Erie R.R., 1945-46; hotel cashier, 1937-38; with Grant Photo Products, 1946-55. Author: polit. satire: Charley Horse, 1944, 4 line poetry: Rhyming Robert, 1966, Violets, Tulips, Rosebuds, Buttercups, 1971; works included in World of Poetry Anthology, 1984, Am. Poetry Anthology, Vol. III, No. 3-4, 1984, Ashes to Ashes, Vol. V, 1985, The Art of Poetry, 1985, The National Poetry Anthology, 1985, Masterpieces of Modern Verse, 1985, Our World's Most Beloved Poems, 1984, Our Western World's Most Beautiful Poems, 1985, Moods and Mysteries (Poetry Press vol. 3), Pauses in Time, 1986, American Poetry Anthology, 1986, 87, numerous editions of Am. Poetry Assn. and Poetry Press, 1986, Words of Praise Vol. II, 1986, Peace on Earth Poetry Anthology, 1986, World of Poetry--American Poetry Anthology, vol. 6, no. 1, 1986, Pleasant Journeys, 1986, Riders of the Rainbow, 1986, The New York Poetry Foundation Anthology, 1986, The World's Most Cherished Poems, 1986, Celebrations of Life, 1987, The Poet's Hand, 1987. Precinct committeeman Democratic Party, Ohio, Cuyahoga County, 1944-48; candidate Ohio Senate Primary, 1944. Recipient Golden Poetry award World of Poetry, 1986. Roman Catholic. Home: 212 S 6th St Apt B Alhambra CA 91801

CLARKE, ROBERT FRANCIS, metallic ore processing research executive; b. Mpls., Mar. 20, 1915: s. Charles Patrick and Maurine Elizabeth (Clark) C.; B.S. with honors, U. Fla., 1948; M.S., U. Ariz., 1971; m. Charlotte Adele Radwill, July 24, 1966; children—Robert, Carol, David. Meteorologist, U.S. Weather Bur., 1940-42, 48-50, 52-55; supervisory electronics engr., chief navigation br. aviation dept. U.S. Army Electronics Proving Ground, 1956-58, nuclear physicist, chief scientist nuclear surveillance div., 1958-62; aerospace engr. NASA, Lewis Research Ctr., 1962-66; physicist Hughes Aircraft Co., 1966-68; instr. Math. Pima Community Coll., and San Juan campus N.Mex. State U., 1974-75; instr. math. Am. Internat. Sch., Kabul, Afghanistan, 1976-78; dir. Polaris Internat. Metals Corp., Tucson. Radiol. def. officer Fed. Emergency Mgmt. Agy., CAP. Trustee Rep. Presdl. Task Force. Served with U.S. Army, 1942-46, USAF, 1950-52; res. ret. as col., 1975. Recipient nat. award for best articles in Officer Rev.; honor cert. for excellence in published works Freedoms Found. of Valley Forge; recipient Presdl. Medal of Merit. Sr. mem. IEEE (plasma physics and computer sects.), AIAA; mem. Am. Nuclear Soc. (fusion power and reactor physics sect.), Space Studies Inst., Internat. Platform Assn., Fusion Power Assocs., Soc. Photo-Optical Instrumentation Engrs., Am. Meteorol. Soc., Am. Optical Soc., Soc. Unmanned Vehicle Systems, Arctic Inst. N.Am., AAUP, Assn. Former Intelligence Officers, Am. Def. Preparedness Assn., Scientists and Engrs. for Secure Energy, N.Y. Acad. Scis., Ariz.-Nev. Acad. Scis., Navy League, Am. Legion, VFW, (pres. 1986, honor degree), AMVETS, Ret. Officers Assn., U.S. Naval Inst., Assn. U.S. Army (chpt. pres. 1982-83), Air Force Assn., Mil. Order World Wars (chpt. commdr. 1987—), Am. Security Council, Vets. Affairs Tucson (com. chmn. 1956), Inst. Polit. Sci. Club: Army and Navy. Lodges: Odd Fellows, Kiwanis. Contbr. articles in aerospace and nat. def. to mags., jours. Home: 5846 E South Wilshire Dr Tucson AZ 85711 Office: 1745 E Factory Ave Tucson AZ 85719

CLARKE, SHEILA RISE, marketing professional; b. Buffalo, Feb. 14, 1942; d. Harry Niesen and May (Idels) Bordignon; m. George Rogers Clarke, Mar. 4, 1961 (div. 1971); m. Arthur William Childs, Nov. 22, 1984. Student, Choinard Art Inst., 1958, Los Angeles Valley Coll., 1959, 61, 64, Los Angeles City Coll., 1972. Prin. Cybergrafix Advt. Agy., Los Angeles, 1976-80; dir. advt. Info World, Palo Alto, Calif., 1980-82; v.p. mktg. Adscope, Inc., Goldendale, Wash., 1982—. Mem. U.S. C. of C., Goldendale C. of C. Avocations: music, gardening, learning. Home: PO Box 226 Goldendale WA 98620 Office: Adscope PO Box 226 Goldendale WA 98620

CLARKE, URANA, musician, writer, educator; b. Wickliffe-on-the-Lake, Ohio, Sept. 8, 1902; d. Graham Warren and Grace Urana (Olsaver) C.; artists and tchrs. diploma Mannes Music Sch., N.Y.C., 1925; certificate Dalcroze Sch. Music, N.Y.C., 1950; student Pembroke Coll., Brown U.; B.S., Mont. State U., 1967, M.Applied Sci., 1970. Mem. faculty Mannes Music Sch., 1922-49, Dalcroze Sch. Music, 1949-54; adv. editor in music The Book of Knowledge, 1949-65; v.p., dir. Saugatuck Circle Housing Devel.; guest lectr. Hayden Planetarium, 1945; guest lectr., bd. dirs. Roger Williams Park Planetarium, Providence; radio show New Eng. Skies, Providence, 1961-64, Skies Over the Big Sky Country, Livingston, Mont., 1964-79, Birds of the Big Sky Country, 1972-79, Great Music of Religion, 1974-79; mem. adv. com. Nat. Rivers and Harbors Congress, 1947-58; instr. continuing edn. Mont. State U. Chmn., Park County chpt. ARC, co-chmn. county blood program, first aid instr. trainer, 1941—; instr. ARC cardio-pulmonary resuscitation, 1976—; mem. Mont. Commn. Nursing and Nursing Edn., 1974-76; mem. Park County Local Govt. Study Commn., 1974-76, chmn., 1984-86. Mem. Am. Acad. Polit. Sci., Am. Musicol. Soc., Royal Astron. Soc. Can., Inst. Nav., Maria Mitchell Soc. Nantucket, N.Am. Yacht Racing Union, AAAS, Meteoritical Soc., Internat. Soc. Mus. Research, Skyscrapers (sec.-treas. 1960-63), Am. Guild Organists, Park County Wilderness Assn. (treas.), Trout Unlimited, Nature Conservancy, Big Sky Astron. Soc. (dir. 1965—), Sierra Club. Lutheran. Club: Cedar Point Yacht. Author: The Heavens are Telling (astronomy), 1951; Skies Over the Big Sky Country, 1965; also astron. news-letter, View It Yourself, weekly column Big Skies; contbr. to mags, on music, nav. and astronomy. Pub. Five Chorale Preludes for Organ, 1975; also elem. two-piano pieces. Inventor, builder of Clarke Adjustable Piano Stool. Address: Log-A-Rhythm 9th St Island Livingston MT 59047

CLARKE-CRICHTON, MELISSA BROTHERTON, psychotherapist, medical and psychiatric social worker; b. Omaha, June 2, 1955; d. Robert Louis and Sally Lou (Searle) Clarke; m. Keith Renold Crichton, June 23, 1984. BA in Psychology and Sociology, Colo. Women's Coll., 1977; MA in Guidance and Counseling, U. Mich., 1978; MSW in Treatment, U. Denver, 1985. Lic. social worker in applied psychotherapy, Colo. Counselor Colo. Upward Bound, La Junta, 1976; with Toledo Mental Health Ctr., 1979-80; med. and psychiat. social worker St. Anthony's Hosp., Denver, 1980-83; caseworker, family employment project Adams County Social Services, Commerce City, Colo., 1983; team psychotherapist Cath. Community Services, Aurora, Colo., 1985-86; pvt. practice psychotherapy Denver, 1983—. Mem. Nat. Assn. Social Workers, Colo. Soc. Clin. Social Work (assoc.). Republican. Avocation: skiing. Office: 8000 E Girard Suite 606 Denver CO 80231

CLAUS, CLYDE ROBERT, banker; b. East Orange, N.J., June 21, 1931; s. Clyde Emil and Ruth Ida (Hanks) C.; m. Eleanor Louise Graham, Aug. 22, 1956. Student, Dartmouth Coll., 1949-52, postgrad. Amos Tuck Sch., 1963-65; B.A., Boston U., 1956; M.B.A., Babson Coll., 1958. With Marine Midland Bank-N.Y., N.Y.C., 1958-77; v.p. Marine Midland Bank-N.Y., 1967, v.p. exec. devel., 1969-71, sr. v.p. human resources, 1971-72, sr. adminstrv. officer, 1974-77; exec. v.p., dir. Dreyfus-Marine Midland, Inc., N.Y.C., 1972-74; dir. Marine Midland, Ltd., London; exec. v.p., chief adminstrv. officer BA Investment Mgmt. Corp., San Francisco, 1978-82, dir., 1982—; v.p. Montgomery Street Income Securities, San Francisco, 1978-82; sr. v.p. adminstrn. and mktg./trust Bank of Am., 1981-82, exec. v.p. trust/worldwide, from 1982, exec. v.p. pvt. banking/worldwide, 1985—; dir. Pacific Clearing Corp., Pacific Trust Co., TemPositions, N.Y. Bd. dirs., vice chmn. YMCA; pres., bd. dirs. Clear Water Children's Ranch; trustee Boston U., St. Paul's Sch., Oakland, Calif. Served with U.S. Army, 1952-55. Mem. Phi Sigma Kappa. Clubs: Metropolitan (N.Y.C.); Commonwealth of Calif. Bankers. Home: 6301 Bullard Dr Oakland CA 94611 Office: Bank of Am 555 California St San Francisco CA 94104

CLAUSEN, ALDEN WINSHIP, banker; b. Hamilton, Ill., Feb. 17, 1923; s. Morton and Elsie (Kroll) C.; m. Mary Margaret Crassweller, Feb. 11, 1950; children: Eric David, Mark Winship. B.A., Carthage Coll., 1944, LL.D., 1970; LL.B., U. Minn., 1949; grad., Advanced Mgmt. Program, Harvard U., 1966. Bar: Minn. bar 1949, Calif. bar 1950. With Bank Am. (NT & SA), San Francisco, 1949-81, 1986—; v.p. Bank Am. (NT & SA), 1961-65, sr. v.p., 1965-68, exec. v.p., 1968-69, vice chmn. bd., 1969, pres., chief exec. officer, 1970-81, chmn., chief exec. officer, 1986—; pres. World Bank, 1981-86; chmn., chief exec. officer Bank Am. (NT & SA), San Francisco, 1986—; past pres. Internat. Monetary Conf., San Francisco; Clearing House Assn. Past pres. Fed. Adv. Council, 1972; past chmn. Bay Area Council; past bd. govs. United Way of Am.; past chmn. United Way of Bay Area; past mem. Bus. Roundtable; mem. Bus. Council; past mem. Japan-U.S. Adv. Council; past bd. dirs. Conf. Bd., San Francisco Opera; past bd. dirs., mem. adv. council SRI Internat.; mem. adv. council Stanford U. Grad. Sch. Bus.; bd. dirs. Harvard Bus. Sch.; trustee Carthage Coll., Brookings Instn. Mem. Res. City Bankers Assn. (hon.), Calif. Bar Assn. Clubs: Bankers of San Francisco, Pacific Union, Burlingame Country; Bohemian (N.Y.C.), Links (N.Y.C.); Metropolitan (Washington); Chevy Chase (Md.). Office: Bank of Am Nat Trust Savs Assn Office of Chmn 555 California St San Francisco CA 94104 *

CLAUSEN, BRET MARK, loss prevention specialist; b. Hayward, Calif., Aug. 1, 1958; s. Norman E. and Barbara Ann (Wagner) C.; m. Cheryl Elaine Carlson, May 24, 1980; children: Katherine, Eric, Emily. BS, Colo. State U., 1980, MS, 1983. Diplomate Am. Acad. Indsl. Hygiene; cert. hazard control mgr., safety profl.; assoc. in risk mgmt. Indsl. hygienist, safety rep. Samsonite Corp., Denver, 1980-83, mgr. loss prevention, 1984—; health, safety and environment rep. Storage Tech., Longmont, Colo., 1984. Mem. Am. Indsl. Hygiene Assn. (cert.), Am. Soc. Safety Engrs. (profl.), Nat. Fire Protection Assn. Republican. Lutheran. Avocations: hunting, backpacking, snowshoeing. Home: 1568 S Elkhart St Aurora CO 80012 Office: Samsonite Corp 11200 E 45th Ave Denver CO 80239

CLAUSON, DALE WESLEY, air force officer; b. Bell, Calif., Dec. 1, 1948; s. Dale L. Clauson and Gloria R. (Tapia) Brown; m. Sherry Lou Kothmann, Feb. 28, 1980; children: Randall Thomas, Amanda Kathryn. BA in Math., San Diego State U., 1971, MS in Bus., 1975. Cert. data processor, systems profl. Commd. officer U.S. Air Force, 1971, advanced through grades to lt. col., 1986; computer programmer, Wright-Patterson AFB, Ohio, 1971-74; student Air Force Inst. Tech., San Diego, 1975; real time operating systems team chief Mil. Airlift Command, Scott AFB, Ill., 1976-79; program mgr. Air Forces Europe, W.Ger., 1979-80, command and control analyst Allied Air Forces Central Europe, W.Ger., 1980-83; chief command and control div. Pacific Air Forces, Hickam AFB, Hawaii, 1983-85; chief C3I Automated Systems, 6008 tactical air control flight, 1985-86; dir. command innovation ctr. electronic security command, Kelly AFB, Tex., 1986—. Active Boy Scouts Am., 1972, 78; big brother Montgomery County (Ohio) Schs. for Mentally Retarded, 1974; active Hawaii Heart Assn., 1985. Mem. Armed Forces Communications and Electronics Assn. (v.p. awards Hawaii chpt. 1985-86), Inst. Cert. Computer Profls., Republican. Roman Catholic.

CLAUSS, DONNA BELL, social service agency executive; b. Albuquerque, Apr. 25, 1953; d. Ueal Olen and Elise Barbara (Lowrey) Bell; m. David Otis Clauss, Dec. 31, 1974; children: Rokeya, Shannez, Joshua, Jeremy, SooJee. BA, Lone Mountain Coll. (merged into U. San Francisco), 1974; MA, U. N.Mex., 1980, postgrad. Cert. tchr., N.Mex.. Tchr. Dept. of Defense, Upper Heyford, Eng., 1975-77; counselor Hogares, Albuquerque, 1977-78; tchr. Albuquerque Indian School, 1979-80, Albuquerque Pub. Sch., 1980-85; social worker Fundacion Ascencio-Pine, Guadalajara, Mex., 1980-83; founder, exec. dir. Rainbow House, Albuquerque, 1983—; founder Pregnant Options Hotline, Albuquerque, 1985—; cons. grief and seperation counseling, Albuquerque, 1984—. Am. Field Service grantee, 1967. Mem. Am. Assn. Counseling and Devel., Joint Council Internat. Adoption. Home: 127 Square Deal Rd Belen NM 87002 Office: Rainbow House Internat 1709 Moon NE Albuquerque NM 87112

CLAVREUL, GENEVIEVE MARCELLINE, management consultant; b. Paris, May 18, 1940; d. Marcel Henri and Emilie (Cauchois) Clavreul; children—Patricia, Christina, James E., Eric P. B.A. in Psychology, Columbus (Ga.) Coll., 1976, M.Ed., 1977; M.A. in Pub. Adminstrn., Calif. State U.-Bakersfield, 1979; Ph.D. in Mgmt., Beverly Hills U., 1983. Registered nurse, Ga., Calif., S.D. Head nurse Med. Ctr. Columbus (Ga.), 1974-77; asst. dir. nursing Sioux Valley (S.D.) Hosp., 1977-78; dir. nursing San Joaquin Community Hosp., Bakersfield, 1978-79; coordinator quality assurance Cedar-Sinai Med. Ctr., Los Angeles, 1978; pres. mgmt. cons. firm Catalyst Concept Mgmt. Cons., Los Angeles, 1978—; cons., lectr. U. Calif.-Irvine, Stanford U., State N.J., Calif. State U.-Bakersfield, Phoenix U., Columbus Coll.; internat. cons. in AIDS. Recipient award for best grad. paper So. Sociol. Assn., 1975. Mem. Hosp. Council So. Calif., Calif. Hosp. Assn., Assn. Western Hosps., Am. Soc. Healthcare Edn. Tng., Hollywood C. of C., West Hollywood C. of C. Beverly Hills C. of C. Author: Keep Those Nurses, 1982; contbr. articles to profl. jours. Home and Office: 4119 Los Feliz Blvd Suite 9 Los Angeles CA 90027

CLAWSON, ARIC THOMAS, architect; b. Phoenix, Ariz., Dec. 5, 1960; s. Alan Ted and Cathrine Marie (Babrich) C. BArch., U. Ariz., 1984. Assoc. architect Grygutis & Co., Tucson, 1983-84, Anderson & Assocs., Phoenix, 1984-86; archtl. project mgr. Gosnell Devel. Corp., Phoenix, 1986-87; assoc. architect J. Barry Moffitt & Assocs., Ltd., Phoenix, 1987—. Avocations: automotive restoration, photography. Home: 2141 W Indianola Phoenix AZ 85015

CLAWSON, LEANNA LYNN, management services specialist; b. Great Falls, Wyo., May 5, 1949; d. Lester Lee Obrecht and Reta Ione (Jay) Dupree; m. Daniel Bruce Clawson, Aug. 31, 1968; 1 child, Danielle S. BA in Edn., U. Wyo., 1973. Office mgr. MSM Assocs., Rawlins, Wyo., 1978-79; legal sec. Johnson, Noecker & Noecker, Rawlins, 1979-80; mgmt. services specialist Atty. Gen., State of Wyo., Cheyenne, 1980—. Bd. dirs. Cheyenne Family YMCA, 1985—, 2d v.p., 1987. Nominated Young Career Woman Candidate Bus. and Profl. Women, Rawlins, 1976. Mem. Cheyenne Legal Secs. (sec. 1985, v.p. 1986), Nat. Assn. Atty. Gens. (mgmt. contact 1982-86). Republican. Methodist. Clubs: Cheyenne Country. Avocations: photography, painting, sewing, aerobics. Home: 4215 Hillside Cheyenne WY 82009 Office: Wyo Atty Gen 123 Capitol Bldg Cheyenne WY 82002

CLAWSON, RAYMOND WALDEN, independent oil producer; b. San Jose, Calif.; s. Benjamin B. and Mae Belle (Names) C.; LL.B., Am. U., 1936; m. Barbara M. Robbins, 1965. Ind. operator, exploration and devel. oil properties, 1936—; pub. Los Angeles Mirror, 1945-47; pres. Ariz. Securities, Phoenix, 1947-50, Transcontinental Oil Co., Los Angeles, 1947-49; geophys. cons. in offshore drilling ops. Gulf of Mexico, 1963—, North Sea, 1970—; chmn., chief exec. officer Clawco Petroleum Corp., Newport Beach, Calif., 1979—. Clubs: Balboa Bay, Acapulco Yacht. Office: PO Box 2102 Newport Beach CA 92663

CLAY, AMBROSE WHITLOCK WINSTON, telecommunication company executive; b. Marion, Ohio, Dec. 20, 1941; s. Ambrose Whitlock Winston and Ann Bernadette (Robinson) C.; m. Sharon Lee Boyd, June 25, 1966; children—Susan Rose, Allison Win. B.S.E.E., MIT, 1964; M.B.A., U. Chgo., 1972. Sr. supr. GTE Labs, Northlake, Ill., 1972-74, mgr. project plan, 1974-79, mgr. software devel., Phoenix, 1979-81; dir. systems devel. GTE Communication Systems Research and Devel., Phoenix, 1981-84, dir. tech. devel. and applications, 1985-87, corp. contact to U. Ariz., Phoenix, 1984—, v.p. research and devel. 1987— ; chmn. tech. presentation, 1979; chmn. Ariz. Math., Engring., Sci. Achievement Industry Adv. Bd., 1985—; bd. A Patentee telephone switching, 1975. Active MIT Ednl. Council, Chgo., 1972-76; mem. sch. bd. Glen Ellyn Sch. Dist. 89, 1976-79, pres. 1979; mem. computer sci. edn. com. Ariz. State U., Phoenix, 1981—. Mem. IEEE, Communication Soc. (vice-chmn. Phoenix chpt. 1982-83, chmn. 1983-84). Republican. Roman Catholic. Club: MIT (Phoenix). Home: 215 E Acapulco Ln Phoenix AZ 85022 Office: GTE Communication Systems Research & Development 2500 W Utopia Rd Phoenix AZ 85027

CLAY, CAROLYNE, metallurgist; b. Chgo., Apr. 30, 1952; d. Calvin and Leanet (May) C. B.S., Rensselaer Poly. Inst., 1974; M.S., MIT, 1976, Metall. Engr., 1978. Research asst. MIT, Cambridge, 1975-77; research metallurgist Ford Motor Co. Sci. Research Lab., Dearborn, Mich., 1977-79; sr. metallurgist Kaiser Aluminum & Chem. Co.-Trentwood Works, Spokane, Wash., 1979-85; staff metallurgist Kaiser Aluminum & Chem. Co.-Trentwood Works, 1985—; vis. com. MIT Material Sci. and Engring. Corp., 1978. Recipient Karl T. Compton award, 1977; recipient Scott MacKay award, 1974. Mem. Am. Soc. Metals, AIME, Nat. Soc. Profl. Engrs., NAACP, Sigma Xi, Delta Sigma Theta. Congregationalist. Office: Trentwood Works PO Box 15108 Spokane WA 99215 *

CLAY-PARK, BROOKE, publisher; b. N.Y.C., Mar. 18, 1944; s. Alfred George Zepp and Caroline (Warwick) Kreuttner; m. John Paul Clay, Oct. 5, 1964 (div.); children: Alexandra Neville, Scott Daniel, Bradley Warwick; m. James Thornton Park, Oct. 23, 1983. Student in Advt. Design, Pratt Inst. Co-pub. American Outlook, Altadena, Calif., 1965-77; prodn., design dir. Guest Informant, Beverly Hills, Calif., 1977-79, Talent & Booking, Los Angeles, 1979-80; prodn. dir. East/West Network, Los Angeles, 1980—. Named Calif. Businessperson of Month, Calif. C. of C., Sacramento, 1978. Mem. Publ. Prodn. Club So. Calif. (founding mem., bd. dirs.), Colonial Dames Soc., DAR. Office: East/West Network 5900 Wilshire Blvd Los Angeles CA 90020

CLAYTON, E. BERNEICE LOWE, educator, counselor, social worker; b. Clanton, Ala., Jan. 21, 1923; d. Rueben Willis Lowe and Martha Ruth (Smith) L.; M. Norman Dale Clayton, June 30, 1948; children—Alan Foster, Stephen Fremont, Douglas Lowe. B.A. magna cum laude, U. Ala., 1945; M.A., U. Chgo., 1948; postgrad. Calif. State U.-Sacramento, 1956-60, U. Pacific, 1971-72; Ed.D., U. Nova, 1975. Lic. child, family, marriage counselor, Calif. Psychiat. social worker Calif. State Mental Hygiene Clinic, 1948-49; dir. Sutterville Coop. Sch., Sacramento, Calif., 1954-58; presch. and parent educator Sacramento City Unified Sch. Dist., 1960-64, sch. social worker, 1965-68, coordinator parent and presch. edn., 1967-68; instr., dir. Early Childhood Edn., Sacramento City Coll., 1968—, chmn. family and consumer sci. dept., 1971—, chmn. early childhood edn. and family and consumer sci. dept., coordinator child devel. ctr. programs, 1985—; cons. pvt. and pub. presch. programs, children and child care ctrs; bd. dirs. Alan Short Found. Devel. Disabilities Services, Inc., sec., 1986—. Ala. Bd. dirs. Grace Day Home, 1973-85; mem. Calif. Community Coll. Home Econs. Task Force, 1984-85. active Sacramento Child Care Commn., 1973-85; mem. Calif. Community Coll. Home Econs. Task Force, 1984-85. Recipient outstanding Calif. home econs. prof. award Calif. Community Colls., 1982-83. Mem. Sacramento Valley Assn. Edn. Young Children (pres. 1976), Calif. Community Colls., Early Childhood Educators (pres. 1982-83). Author: An Administrative Design for Group Infant Care, 1975. Home: 79 Lakeshore Circle Sacramento CA 95831 Office: Sacramento City Coll 3835 Freeport Blvd RS 284 Sacramento CA 95822

CLAYWORTH, JOSEPH FRANCIS, data processing executive; b. Oakland, Calif., July 10, 1942; s. Robert Edgar and Rhoda Gene (Kenney) C.; m. Randy Charline Otto, May 21, 1962 (div. June 1975); 1 child, Elizabeth Jeanne. Student, Santa Rosa Jr. Coll., 1962-63, Portland Community Coll., 1969-71. Police officer Oakland Police Dept., 1963-67; programmer Simon Stores, Oakland, 1967-68; mgr. of programming Service Bureau Corp., Portland, Oreg., 1968-73; mgr. systems devel. Ga.-Pacific Corp., Portland, 1973-80; v.p., data processing Physicians Assn. of Clackamas County, Portland, 1980—; cons. Clackamas Health Care Consortium, Milwaukie, Oreg., 1983. Served with U.S. Army, 1959-62, Korea. Mem. Model A Ford Club (v.p. 1974-75). Republican. Episcopalian. Lodge: Elks. Avocations: antique auto restoration, photography, outdoor activities. Home: 220 Monroe St Oregon City OR 97045 Office: Physicians Assn Clackamas County 18600 SE McLoughlin Milwaukie OR 97222

CLEARY, JAMES W., university president; b. Milw., Apr. 16, 1927; married, 1950. Ph.B., Marquette U., 1950, M.A., 1951; Ph.D. (Univ. fellow 1954-55), U. Wis., 1956. Instr., dir. forensics high sch. Wis., 1949-51; instr. speech, head coach debate Marquette U., 1951-53; from instr. to prof. speech U. Wis., 1956-63, vice chancellor academic affairs, 1966-69; pres. Calif. State U., Northridge, 1969—; mem. Pres.'s Commn. NCAA. Author: books in field including Robert's Rules of Order Newly Revised, 1970, 80; editor: books in field including John Bulwer's Chirologia . . . Chironomia, 1644, 1974; co-editor: books in field including Bibliography of Rhetoric and Public Address, 1964. Served to 2d lt. AUS, 1945-47. Named one of the 100 Most Effective Coll. Pres. in the U.S., Exxon Edn. Found., 1986. Mem. Speech Assn. Am., Am. Assn. State Colls. and Univs. (chmn. 1983), NCAA (pres.' commn. 1984—, chmn. div. II com.). Address: Calif State Univ Office of the Pres 18111 Nordhoff St Northridge CA 91330

CLEAVE, STEWART W., architect; b. Morristown, N.J., Oct. 17, 1947; s. Kingdon and Catherine (Johnson) C.; m. Judith Morey, June 12, 1981; children—Shawn, Jennifer, Christopher, Richard. B.Arch., Mont. State U., 1971. Assoc. architect Sakellar & Assocs., Tucson, 1973-75, Steimer & Assocs., Downingtown, Pa., 1971-73; pres. Cleave-Lundgren, Benson, Ariz., 1975—. Mem. AIA. Office: Cleave-Lundgren & Assocs 131 E 5th St Benson AZ 85602

CLECAK, DVERA VIVIAN BOZMAN, psychotherapist; b. Denver, Jan. 15, 1944; d. Joseph Shalom and Annette Rose (Dveirin) Bozman; m. Pete Emmett Clecak, Feb. 26, 1966; children: Aimée, Lisa. BA, Stanford U., 1965; postgrad., U. Chgo., 1965; MSW, UCLA, 1969. Lic. clin. social worker, Calif., marriage, family and child counselor, Calif. Social work supr. Harbor City (Calif.) Parent Child Ctr., 1969-71; therapist Orange County Mental Health Dept., Laguna Beach, Calif., 1971-75, area coordinator, 1975-79; pvt. practice psychotherapy Mission Viejo, Calif., 1979—; founder, exec. dir. Human Options, Laguna Beach, 1981—; mem, co-chmn. domestic violence com. Orange County Commn. on Status of Women, 1979-81; mem. mental health adv. com. extension U. Calif., Irvine, 1983, counseling psychologist, 1980, lectr., 1984-85; lectr. Saddleback Community Coll., Mission Viejo, 1981-82, Chapman Coll., Orange, 1979; field instr. UCLA, 1970-71, 77-78. Mem. Nat. Assn. Social Workers, Calif. Marriage Family Child Counselors' Assn., Phi Beta Kappa. Office: 28261 Marguerite Pkwy #255 Mission Viejo CA 92692

CLEM, CASEY GALYEAN, real estate broker, accountant; b. Jacksonville, Tex., Mar. 2, 1954; s. Ross Albert and Genevieve Ruth (Keith) C. BBA, Baylor U., 1975. CPA, N.Mex. Adminstrv. asst. Major Brick Co., Henderson, Tex., 1970-75; acct. audit services Main Hurdman, Waco, Tex., 1976-78, Neff & Co., Albuquerque, 1978-79, Main Hurdman, Dallas, 1981-82; exec. ptnr. Clem Investments, Santa Fe, N.Mex., 1982—; gen. ptnr. Century House II, Santa Fe, 1982—, Clem Enterprises, Santa Fe, 1981—; chmn. Galyean Ltd., Santa Fe, 1978—; owner Casey G. Clem, CPA, Santa Fe; v.p. Houtman & Co., P.C., CPA's, 1984-86 . Mem. major gifts com. Ballet at Santa Fe, 1983. Mem. Am. Inst. CPA's, Tex. Soc. CPA's, N.Mex. Soc. CPA's. Republican. Episcopalian. Lodge: Kiwanis (Waco, Tex.). Office: 121 Sandoval St Santa Fe NM 87501

CLEMANS, BETTIE KING, college educator; b. Gibbon, Nebr., Sept. 10, 1927; d. Lewallan C. and Opal (Houtz) King; A.A., Central Ariz. Coll., 1972; B.A., Ariz. State U., 1975, M.A., 1977; Ph.D., Pacific Western U., 1985; children—Michael James, Richard Alan, Robin Ann and Dana Ellen (twins), James Roy. Office mgr. R.G. Clemans, Atty., Casa Grande, Ariz., 1957-62; adminstrv. asst. Community Action Program, Coolidge, Ariz., 1962-67; pres.'s adminstrv. asst. Pinal County Community Coll. Dist., Coolidge, 1967-78, research asst., 1978-79; dir. instl. aid program Cen. Ariz. Coll., Coolidge, 1979-85, dir. vocat. office skills Gila River Career Ctr., 1985-86, prof. bus., 1986—. Mem., past pres. Pinal County Fine Arts Council, Inc.; mem. Nat. Council on Resource Devel., Am. Assn. Community and Jr. Colls. (intern 1978), Bus. and Profl. Women (past pres. Coolidge Club, asst. dir. Ariz. dist. 3), Nat. Secs. Assn. (cert. profl. sec., founding pres. Desert Rose chpt.), Nat. Bus. Educators Assn., Ariz. Coordinating Council on Resource Devel. (pres. 1979-80), AAUW (Casa Grande br.), Pi Omega Pi, Kappa Delta Pi. Lodge: Zonta. Author: Sixty Seasons: A History of Pinal County Community College District, 1976, A Study of the Federal Role in Higher Education, 1985. Office: Central Ariz Coll Woodruff at Overfield Rd Coolidge AZ 85229

CLEMENT, KATHI DEE, physician, educator; b. Malden, Mo., Aug. 16, 1951; d. John Elton and Lois Lorraine (Moore) C. BS, SE Mo. State U., 1973; MD, U. Mo., 1979. Diplomate Am. Bd. Family Practice. Intern in family practice U. Wyo., Casper, 1979-80, resident in family practice, 1980-82, chief resident in family practice, 1981-82; practice medicine specializing in family practice Sundance, Wyo., 1982-84; asst. prof. family medicine U. Wyo./Cheyenne Family Practice Ctr., 1984—; mem. Bd. Pub. Health, Laramie County, Wyo., 1987—. Bd. dirs. YWCA, Cheyenne, 1985—, Casey Family Ctr., Cheyenne, 1986—, Cheyenne Health Fair, 1985. Fellow Am. Acad. Family Physicians; mem. Wyo. Med. Soc., Wyo. Acad. Family Physicians (alt. del. 1982-84, del. 1984—), Am. Med. Women's Assn., Laramiey County Med. Soc. Democrat. Methodist. Avocations: softball, racquetball, travelling. Home: 4108 Clark Cheyenne WY 82009 Office: U Wyo Cheyenne Family Practice Ctr 821 E 18th Cheyenne WY 82001

CLEMENT, MICHAEL SCOTT, medical services administrator, pediatrician; b. Logan, Utah., Mar. 31, 1939; s. Erwin and Leona Clement; m. Mary Y. Clement, May 15, 1971 (dec. Oct. 1978); 1 child, Dean Brian; m. Roberta Mary Edwards, May 11, 1979; children: Sarah Amanda, Carolyn Edwards. Student U. Ariz., 1956-59; M.D., U. Utah, 1963. Diplomate Am. Bd. Pediatrics. Research fellow dept. pediatrics U. Utah, Salt Lake City, 1961-64, postdoctoral research fellow, 1966-68; clin. instr., 1968-72; practice medicine specializing in pediatrics, Murray, Utah, 1968-72, Tucson, 1972-75, Sierra Vista, Ariz., 1975-78; dir. Cochise County Health Dept., Bisbee, Ariz., 1978-81; asst. dir. Ariz. Dept. Health Service, Tempe, 1981-85; dir. ambulatory services Phoenix Children's Hosp. Mem. Joint Legis. Com. on Maternal and Child Health, Phoenix, 1982, Ariz.-Mexico Commn., Phoenix, 1982. Recipient Mosby Research award U. Utah, 1960, Achievement award Nat. Assn. Counties, 1982, MCH Golden Anniversary award Ariz. Dept. Health Service, 1985. Fellow Am. Acad. Pediatrics; mem. Maricopa County Pediatric Soc., U.S.-Mexico Border Health Assn., Am. Acad. Pediatrics (Ariz. chpt.), Am. Pub. Health Assn. Mormon. Office: Phoenix Childrens Hosp Outpatient Ctr 909 E Brill St Phoenix AZ 85006

CLEMENT, PAUL WAYNE, clinical psychologist; b. Aberdeen, Wash., Mar. 6, 1939; s. Albert Wayne and Helen Marguerite (Norin) C.; m. Katherine Majovski, June 13, 1959; children: Paul, Blake, Erika. BS, U. Wash., 1960, BA, 1961; student, Pepperdine U., 1957-58, MA, 1962; PhD, U. Utah, 1965. Lic. psychologist, Calif.; diplomate Am. Bd. Profl. Psychology, 1970. From instr. to asst. prof. med. psychology in residence UCLA, 1965-67; clin. psychologist II Harbor Gen. Hosp., Torrance, Calif., 1965-67; from asst. prof. to prof. psychology, 1967—; dir. clin. tng. Grad. Sch. Psychology, Fuller Theol. Sem., Pasadena, Calif., 1967-76, dir. Psychol. Ctr., 1976—; cons. to hosps., clinics, schs., editorial bds. Co-author: Clinical Prodecures for Behavior Therapy, 1981; contbr. articles to profl. jours. Named Health Service Provider, Council Nat. Register Health Service Providers in Psychology, 1975; recipient Alumni Bd. Dirs. award Pepperdine U., 1975; named Disting. Mem. Western Assn. Christians for Psychol. Studies,

1977; Harbor Gen. Hosp. grantee, 1965-66, USPHS grantee, 1966-68, 71, 74-76. Fellow Am. Psychol. Assn.; mem. Western Psychol. Assn., Calif. Psychol. Assn. (pres. 1975, award 1977), Assn. Aviation Psychologists, Flying Psychologists, Pasadena Area Psychol. Assn. (pres. 1970), Council Univ. Dirs. Clin. Psychology Nat. Council Schs. Profl. Psychology (sec., treas. 1982-84), Sigma Xi, Phi Delta Kappa, Psi Chi. Presbyterian. Home: 221 Mariners View Ln La Canada CA 91011 Office: Fuller Theol Sem Psychol Ctr 180 N Oakland Ave Pasadena CA 91101

CLEMENT, WALTER HOUGH, railroad executive; b. Council Bluffs, Iowa, Dec. 21, 1931; s. Daniel Shell and Helen Grace (Hough) C.; A.A., San Jose (Calif.) City Coll., 1958; Ph.D., World U., 1983; m. Shirley Ann Brown, May 1, 1953; children—Steven, Robert, Richard. Designer, J.K. Konerle & Assocs., Salt Lake City, 1959-62; with U.P. R.R. Co., 1962—, class B draftsman, Salt Lake City, 1971-75, sr. right of way engr. real estate dept., 1975-80, asst. dist. real estate mgr., 1980-83, field engr., 1983—; Mem. Republican Nat. Com., Rep. Congl. Com. Served with USN, 1950-54; Korea. Lic. realtor, Utah. Mem. Am. Ry. Engring. Assn., Execs. Info. Guild (asso.), Bur. Bus. Practice. Republican. Methodist. Home: 290 West 1200 North Bountiful UT 84010 Office: 406 West 100 South Salt Lake City UT 84101

CLEMENTE, CARMINE DOMENIC, anatomist, educator; b. Penns Grove, N.J., Apr. 29, 1928; s. Ermanno and Caroline (Friozzi) C.; m. Juliette Vance, Sept. 19, 1968. A.B., U. Pa., 1948, M.S., 1950, Ph.D., 1952; postdoctoral fellow, U. London, 1953-54. Asst. instr. anatomy U. Pa., 1950-52; mem. faculty UCLA, 1952—, prof., 1963—, chmn. dept. anatomy, 1963-73, dir. brain research inst., 1976—; hon. research asso. Univ. Coll., U. London, 1953-54; cons. Sepulveda VA Hosp., NIH; mem. med. adv. panel Bank Am.-Giannini Found.; chmn. sci. adv. com., mem. bd. dirs. Nat. Paraplegia Found. Author: Aggression and Defense: Neurol Mechanisms and Social Patterns, 1967, Physiological Correlates of Dreaming, 1967, Sleep and the Maturing Nervous System, 1972, Anatomy, An Atlas of the Human Body, 1975, 3d edit., 1987; editor: Gray's Anatomy, 1973—, 30th Am. edit., 1985, also Exptl. Neurology; asso. editor: Neurol. Research; contbr. articles to sci. jours. Recipient award for merit in sci. Nat. Paraplegia Found., 1973; 23d Ann. Rehfuss Lectr. and recipient Rehfuss medal Jefferson Med. Coll., 1986. Mem. Pavlovian Soc. N.Am. (Ann. award 1968, pres. 1972), Brain Research Inst. (dir. 1976—), Am. Physiol. Soc., Am. Assn. Anatomists (v.p. 1970-72, pres. 1976-77), Am. Acad. Neurology, Am. Acad. Cerebral Palsy, Am. Neurol. Assn., Assn. Am. Med. Colls. (exec. com. 1978-81, disting. service mem. 1982), Council Acad. Socs. (adminstrv. bd. 1973-81, chmn. 1979-80), Assn. Anatomy Chairmen (pres. 1972), Biol. Stain Commn., Inst. Medicine of Nat. Acad. Scis. (sci. adv. bd.), Internat. Brain Research Orgn., AMA-Assn. Am. Med. Colls. (liaison com. on med. edn. 1981—), Med. Research Assn. Calif. (dir. 1976—), N.Y. Acad. Sci., Nat. Bd. Med. Examiners, Nat. Acad. Sci. (mem. com. neuropathology, BEAR coms.), Japan Soc. Promotion of Sci. (Research award 1978), Sigma Xi. Democrat. Home: 11737 Bellagio Rd Los Angeles CA 90049 Office: UCLA Ctr Health Scis Los Angeles CA 90024

CLEMENTS, MICHAEL REID, engineering executive; b. Los Angeles, Apr. 21, 1943; s. Reid William and Phyllis Marie (Hoopes) C.; m. Genay Shumway, Aug. 30, 1967; children—Tamara, Michelle, Reid, Sean, Scott, Tiffani. A.A., Ricks Coll., Rexburg, Idaho, 1965; B.E.S., Brigham Young U., Provo, Utah, 1968; postgrad. Stanford U., 1968-69. Engr., IBM, Menlo Park, Calif., 1968-69; sr. engr. Multi-Access Systems, Cupertino, Calif., 1969-70; system design mgr. Amdahl Corp., Sunnyvale, Calif., 1970-75, dir. computer devel., 1977-78, corp. v.p. engring., 1978-82, chief tech. officer, 1982—; mgr. electronic design and data systems EG & G Idaho Falls, Idaho, 1975-77. Mem. IEEE, Am. Mgmt. Assn., Tau Beta Pi. Republican. Mormon. Patentee in field. Home: 95 W Sunset Circle Rexburg ID 83440 Office: 143 N 2d St E Rexburg ID 83440

CLEMMENS, ALBERT JONATHAN, civil engineer, researcher; b. Norfolk, Nebr., Dec. 19, 1953; s. William Clarence and Elizabeth Ann (Magdanz) C.; m. Regina Gail Albers (div.); m. Lynn Marie Tomchak, Apr. 20, 1985. BCE, Ariz. State U., 1975, MCE, 1979, postgrad., 1982—. Engr. in tng. U.S. Soil Conservation Service, Phoenix, 1975-76; engr., hydrologist Appalachian Coal Surveys, Pitts., 1979; research hydraulic engr. U.S. Agrl. Research Service, Phoenix, 1976-79, 1980—. Author: Flow Measuring Flumes for Open Channel Systems, 1984; patentee in field. Mem. ASCE (chmn. com. Operation and Maintenance Irrigation and Drainage Systems), Am. Soc. Agrl. Engrs., Internat. Commn. Irrigation and Drainage, Inst. Indsl. Engrs., Sigma Xi (hon.), Phi Kappa Phi (hon.), Tau Beta Pi (hon.), Alpha Phi Mu (hon.). Avocations: hiking, biking, softball, soccer, chess. Office: US Water Conservation Lab 4331 E Broadway Phoenix AZ 85040

CLEMONS, J. KING, insurance executive; b. Columbus, Ohio, Jan. 21, 1936; s. Frank M. and Ethel K. Clemons; B.S. in Physics, Colorado Coll., 1958; M.S. in Stats., U. Iowa, 1966; m. Ann Douglass, June 2, 1959; children—Mike, Steve, Karl. Research physicist White Sands Missile Range, N.Mex., 1958; actuarial asst. A.S. Hansen, Inc., Lake Bluff, Ill., 1966-67, cons. in tng., Lake Bluff, 1967-69, subject cons., Milw., 1969-70, subject cons., Los Angeles, 1970-72; pres. Western Res. Life Ins. Co., Grand Junction, Colo., 1972—; elected pres. Colo. Life Conv., 1986. Pres., Grand Junction Eagles Baseball, 1976-83; active YMCA Fund Drive, Milw., 1969; chmn. Grand Junction/Mesa County Indsl. Devel. Revenue Bond Com., 1981—; mem. pres.'s adv. bd. Mesa Coll., 1980—; mem. Mesa County Revolving Loan Fund Com., 1985—. Served to capt., Ordnance Corps, U.S. Army, 1958-64. Recipient Disting. Service award YMCA, 1969; named Businessman Yr. for Colo. and USA, Phi Beta Lambda, 1986. Mem. Western Colo. Estate Planning Council, North Ave. Trade Assn. (dir. 1978-82), Grand Junction C. of C. (pres. 1980). Republican. Club: Lions. Home: 2561 I Rd Grand Junction CO 81501 Office: Western Res Life Ins Co 2755 North Ave Grand Junction CO 81501

CLERC, CHARLES, English language educator; b. Pocatello, Idaho, Mar. 16, 1926; s. Clemence Clerc; m. Virginia Willson, 1946 (div. 1949); 1 child, Kim; m. Maria Labriola, 1966 (div. 1974); children: Claudette, Caroline, Rebecca; m. Sjaan Francesca VandenBroeder Fries, 1977 (div. 1986). BA, Idaho State U., 1949, 55; MA, U. Utah, 1957; PhD, U. Iowa, 1963. Instr. English U. Iowa, Iowa City, 1962-63; asst. prof. U. Pacific, Stockton, Calif., 1963-66, assoc. prof., 1966-70, dir. NDEA Inst. Modern Critical Methods, 1967, prof. English, 1970—, acting chmn. dept. English, 1968-69, chmn. dept., 1982—; disting. vis. prof. USAF Acad., 1980-81. Author, editor: Approaches to Gravity's Rainbow, 1983; author: (play) The Pillar, 1973; author short novels, articles to profl. jours. Served to lt. U.S. Army, 1952-53, Korea. Recipient Spanos award U. Pacific, 1980; Faculty Research grantee U. Pacific, 1971, 74. Mem. MLA. Office: U of the Pacific Eng Dept Knoles Hall 206 Stockton CA 95211

CLERK, NORMAN JEFFREY, advertising agency executive; b. Oakland, Calif., Mar. 3, 1923; s. Ira and Winifred (Mastick) C.; m. Anne Linderman, Apr. 28, 1951; children: Norman G., Bradford L., Amyann M. Student Modesto Jr. Coll., 1942-43, Armstrong Coll., 1948-49, U. Calif. at Berkeley, 1949. Owner, N.J. Clerk & Asso., San Francisco, 1954-64; account exec. Kennedy, Hannaford & Dolman, Inc., Oakland, 1964-65, v.p., 1966-69; owner, pres. N.J. Clerk & Assos., Oakland, 1969—; instr. advt. Laney Jr. Coll., 1966-67. Contbr. articles to profl. jours. Club: Encinal Yatch (Alameda, Calif.). Lodge: Elks. Home: 1809 San Jose Ave Alameda CA 94501 Office: 414 Pendleton Way Oakland CA 94621 *

CLEVELAND, JESSE MARVIN, research chemist; b. Newnan, Ga., July 3, 1929; s. Jesse Marvin and Mildred (Sewell) C.; m. Janice Marie Forney, June 16, 1951; 1 child, Jane Alison. BS, Ga. Inst. Tech., 1951; MS, U. Colo., 1955, PhD, 1959. Chemist Phillips Chem. Co., Dumas, Tex., 1951-52; chemist Dow Chem. Co., Golden, Colo., 1952-57, assoc. scientist, 1963-76; sr. scientist Gen. Electric Co., Pleasanton, Calif. and Richland, Wash., 1959-61, 61-63; research project chief U.S. Geol. Survey, Denver, 1977—; mem. NRC Workshop on Transplutonium Element Research, 1983, Earth Scis. Review Com. Lawrence Berkeley (Calif.) Lab., 1985—; adj. prof. Colo. State U., Ft. Collins, 1985—. Author: The Chemistry of Plutonium, 1970; co-author: The Plutonium Handbook, 1967; contbr. articles to profl. jours.; patentee in field. Mem. Am. Chem. Soc., Sierra Club. Methodist. Avocations: photography, hiking, camping, music.

CLEVELAND, JOHN TRUMAN, graphic designer; b. Long Beach, Calif., June 3, 1939; s. Truman Weston and Verna Grace (Jones) C.; divorced; children: Tracy Allison, Christopher John. BA, Art Ctr. Coll. of Design, 1963. Design dir. J. Chris Smith Inc., Los Angeles, 1963-68; ptnr. The Co., Los Angeles, 1969-76; prin. John Cleveland Inc., Los Angeles, 1976—. Recipient Gold medal Art Dir.'s Club of N.Y., 1981. Mem. Art Dirs. Club of Los Angeles (pres. adv. com. 1979-80, Gold medal 1969, 78, Hugo Hammer medal 1969), Am. Inst. Graphic Arts, Soc. Typographic Arts, Univ. and Coll. Designers Assn. (hon.). Republican. Clubs: Riviera Tennis (Gov. 1977-79), Pacific Mariners Yacht (Los Angeles). Home: 13900 Marquesas Way Marina del Rey CA 90291

CLEWETT, RAYMOND WINFRED, mechanical design engineer; b. Upland, Calif., Nov. 7, 1917; s. Howard Jasper and Pansy Gertrude (Macy) C.; m. Hazel Royer, June 11, 1938; children: Alan Eugene, Patricia Gail, Charles Raymond, Richard Howard, Beverly Lynn. Student, Chaffey Jr. Coll., 1937. Exptl. mechanic Douglas Aircraft Co., Santa Monica, Calif., 1937-51; shop foreman, exptl. designer Lear, Inc., Los Angeles, 1945-51; design engr., shop mgr. The RAND Corp., Santa Monica, Calif., 1951-83, also design cons.; owner, mgr. HY-TECH Engring. and Devel. Lab., Malibu, Calif., 1983—; design cons. Pacific-Sierra Research Corp. works include mech. design of JOHNNIAC early model electronic computer on permanent display Los Angeles County Mus.; designer variouscomputer input/output devices, 1953-70; developer low vision reading aids for the blind, 1970-75; design and constrn. spl. equipment for sci. and research, 1983—; patentee in field. Mem. AAAS, Soc. Mfg. Engrs., Am. Soc. Metals. Republican.

CLIFFORD, HAROLD JOSEPH, retired oil and gas company executive; b. San Francisco, May 10, 1924; s. Michael Joseph and Margaret (King) C.; m. Caroline L. Roy, Aug. 1946 (div. 1973); children: Christine N., Paul C., Peter S., Marc J.; m. C. Jeanne Elliott, July 11, 1975. BS, U. Utah, 1951; postgrad., U. Calif., Berkeley, 1952. Registered geologist, Calif. Sr. geologist Shell Oil Co., Los Angeles, 1952-74; chief geologist Ageco, Benghazi, Libya, 1975-79; exploration mgr. Natural Gas Corp Calif., San Francisco, 1979-86; pvt. practice cons. geologist Vista, 1986—. Scout leader Boy Scouts Am., Bakersfield, Calif., 1960-62. Served as sgt. U.S. Army, 1943-46. Mem. AAAS, Am. Assn. Petroleum Geologists. Republican. Roman Catholic. Club: Commonwealth (San Francisco). Avocations: photography, music, reading. Home: 514 Jobe Hill Dr Vista CA 92083

CLIFFORD, RICHARD ARTHUR, engineer; b. Salt Lake City, Apr. 22, 1939; s. Arthur Harris and Ruth (Langdon) C.; m. Janet May Dunlop, Sept. 27, 1963; children: Gordon B., Jenny May, Bridget, Patrick T., Katie, Ruthanne, Rebecca. Student, U. Utah, 1958-59, Lincoln Extension Inst., 1967-72, U. Phoenix, 1986—. Sales and collection agt. Hercules, Inc., Magna, Utah, 1961, technician, 1962-69, asst. engr., 1969-80, tech. asst., 1980-82, engr., 1982—. Author: (with others) Air Launched Missile Motor Behavior 1981; contbr. articles to profl. jours. Scoutmaster Boy Scouts Am., Gt. Salt Lake Council, 1962, 74-78; del., voting dist. chmn. Rep. Party, Salt Lake City, 1970-78; bishop Ch. Jesus Christ of Latter Day Saints. Salt Lake City, 1978-83; mem. high council, Salt Lake Riverside Stake, 1985—. Recipient Silver Beaver award Boy Scouts Am., 1982, Wood Badge, 1966; named Master M Man Young Men's Mut. Improvement Assn., 1966. Mem. Utah Genealogical Assn. (chpt. pres. 1974, 81), William Carter Family Orgn. (pres. 1983-87). Club: Hercules Camera (Magna) (Historian 1982—). Avocations: photography, hunting, genealogy and family history. Office: Hercules Inc Bacchus Works PO Box 98 MS/A3 Magna UT 84044-0098

CLIFTON, CHARLES ELLIS, JR., oomputer scientist; b. San Francisco, Aug. 12, 1949; s. Charles Ellis and Dorotha Lynn (Gooch) C.; m. Joyce Ray, Sept. 29, 1973; children: Dionne, Trevor, Carmin, Monica, Tanya, Blake, Trent. B.S, in Math., Ariz. State U., 1971; M.S. in Computer Sci., Brigham Young U., 1978. Programmer analyst Honeywell, Phoenix, 1972-78; chief programmer GTE Automatic Electric, Phoenix, 1978-79; software engr. Sperry Avionics, Phoenix, 1979-82; software cons. Cactus Software, Inc., Peoria, Ariz., 1982—, pres., 1981—; software cons. CATV div. GTE, El Paso, Tex., 1982-83, Sperry Avionics, 1983-85, AT&T Bell labs., Naperville, Ill., 1985—; founder pres. Cactus Software, Inc., 1981—. Author computer program: Colography, 1983; Computer program Plotography, 1984. Served to 1st lt. USAF, 1971-72. Mormon. Home: 6727 Corrine Ave Peoria AZ 85345 Office: Cactus Software Inc PO Box 880 Peoria AZ 85345

CLIFTON, ROBERT BLAINE, educator, aviation maintenance training consultant; b. Sabina, Ohio, Dec. 1, 1937; s. Ulysis Blaine and Olive Imogene (Storer) C.; m. Regina Esposito, Aug. 26, 1961; children: Christopher Blaine, Jennifer Regina. Cert. teaching, UCLA, 1970; B in Vocat. Edn., Calif. State U., Long Beach, 1971, MA, 1973. Mechanic Los Angeles Airways, 1959-62, 63-66, ERA Helicopters, Anchorage, 1962; FAA designee, engring. flight test technician Hughes Tool Co., Culver City, Calif., 1966-69; asst. prof. aviation tech. Orange Coast Coll., Costa Mesa, Calif., 1969-74, assoc. prof., 1974-79, prof., 1979—, asst. div. chmn. tech., 1979-84; designated mech. examiner, FAA, Long Beach, 1971—; exec. com. mem. Aviation Tech. Edn. Council, 1986—. Creator (films) Aviation Tech. Tng., 1974. coach Huntington Beach (Calif.) Youth Soccer Club, 1985-86, Am.Youth Soccer Orgn., 1978-85, Westminster (Calif.) Lil' Miss Softball, 1979-83, Little League Baseball, Huntington Beach, 1972-79. Served with U.S. Army, 1956-59. Mem. Am. Vocat. Assn., Calif. Assn. Vocat. Edn., Am. Helicopter Soc., Calif. Internat. Tech. Edn. Commn., 101st Airborne Div. Assn., Orange Coast Coll. Airframe and Powerplant Club (chmn. 1976-86), Kappa Delta Pi. Republican. Roman Catholic. Avocations: sports, rebuilding antique cars. Office: Orange Coast Coll 2701 Fairview Rd Costa Mesa CA 92626

CLINARD, FRANK WELCH JR., materials scientist, researcher; b. Winston-Salem, N.C., Aug. 4, 1933; s. Frank Welch and Hazel Helen (Hauser) C.; m. Elva Adams Hyatt, Apr. 2, 1968. BSME, N.C. State U., 1955, MSMetE, 1957; PhD, Stanford U., 1965. Staff mem. Sandia Corp., Albuquerque, N.Mex., 1957-61; research asst. Stanford U., Palo Alto, Calif., 1961-64; staff mem. Los Alamos (N.Mex.) Nat. Lab., 1964-77, sect. leader, 1977—; adj. prof. materials sci. U. N.Mex., Albuquerque, 1967-70; cons. in field, Los Alamos, N.Mex., 1983—. Contbr. articles to profl. jours. Bd. dirs. County Pub. TV Orgns., Los Alamos, N.Mex., 1981-82; state chmn. Libertarian Party N.Mex., 1986—. Fellow Am. Ceramic Soc.; mem. AAAS, ACLU, Amnesty Internat., Am. Soc. Metals (chmn. local chpt. 1969-70), Am. Nuclear Soc., Materials Research Soc., Sports Car Club del Valle Rio Grande (pres. 1967), Sigma Xi, Phi Kappa Phi, Tau Beta Pi, Pi Tau Sigma. Unitarian. Avocations: fishing, hunting, hiking, sports cars. Home: 2940 Ariz Ave Los Alamos NM 87544 Office: Los Alamos Nat Lab Mail Stop E546 Los Alamos NM 87545

CLINE, CARL FRANKLIN, physicist, consultant; b. Detroit, Nov. 25, 1928; s. Carl Alexander and Edythe Nadine (Reynolds) C.; m. Karen Marie Gormley, Aug. 21, 1954; children: Cathy, Cheryl, Michael, Steven. BS in Ceramic Engring., Ga. Inst. Tech., 1953; MS in Metallurgy, Niagara U., 1958; postgrad., U. Calif., Berkeley, 1959-62. Sr. engr. Carborundum Co., Niagara Falls, N.Y., 1955-58; sect. leader Lawrence Livermore (Calif.) Nat. Lab., 1958-70, metallurgist, 1974—, with physics dept., 1983—; dept. mgr. Physics Internat. Co., San Leandro, Calif., 1970-72, Allied Corp., Morristown, N.J., 1972-74; cons. Teledyne Corp., New Caanan, Conn., 1983—, Kennametal Corp., Latrobe, Pa., 1983—; bd. dirs. Dynamic Computer Internat., Pleasanton, Calif. Contbr. articles to profl. jours; inventor and patentee in field. Served with USN, 1945-47. Recipient IR-100 award, 1976. Mem. AAAS, Am. Ceramic Soc., Am. Soc. Metals, Am. Phys. Soc., Sigma Xi. Republican. Roman Catholic. Home: 728 Liquidamber Pl Danville CA 94526 Office: Lawrence Livermore Nat Lab PO Box 808 Livermore CA 94526

CLINE, CAROLYN JOAN, plastic and reconstructive surgeon; b. Boston; d. Paul S. and Elizabeth (Flom) Cline. B.A., Wellesley Coll., 1962; M.A., U. Cin., 1966; Ph.D., Washington U., 1970; diploma Washington Sch. Psychiatry, 1972; M.D., U. Miami (Fla.) 1975. Research asst. Harvard Dental Sch., Boston, 1962-64; research asst. physiology Laser Lab., Children's Hosp. Research Found., Cin., 1964, psychology dept. U. Cin., 1964-65; intern in clin. psychology St. Elizabeth's Hosp., Washington, 1966-67; psychologist Alexandria (Va.) Community Mental Health Ctr., 1967-68; research fellow NIH, Washington, 1968-69; chief psychologist Kingsbury Ctr. for Children, Washington, 1969-73; sole practice clin. psychology, Washington, 1970-73; intern internal medicine U. Wis. Hosps., Ctr. for Health Sci., Madison, 1975-76; resident in surgery Stanford U. Med. Ctr., 1976-78; fellow microvascular surgery dept. surgery U. Calif.-San Francisco, 1978-79; resident in plastic surgery St. Francis Hosp., San Francisco, 1979-82; practice medicine, specializing in plastic and reconstructive surgery, San Francisco, 1982—; cons. VA Hosp. Stanford U., Palo Alto. Contbr. articles to profl. jours. Address: 450 Sutter St Suite 2431 San Francisco CA 94108

CLINE, DANA WORTH, software designer; b. Corpus Christi, Tex., June 1, 1957; s. Richard Worth and Allene Roberta (Phillips) C.; m. Theresa An Lindsey, July 23, 1980; 1 child, Travis Richard. Student, Tex. A&M U., 1977-80. Software designer INACOM Internat., Denver, 1983-85; mgr. software devel. US West Knowledge Engring., Denver, 1985—; cons. Tanstaafl Software, Lakewood, Colo., 1985—; instr. Vertical Adventures, Lakewood, 1987—. Named to Eagle Scouts Boy Scouts Am., Corpus Christi, 1972. Mem. Assn. for Computing Machinery (siggraph treas. Denver/Boulder chpt. 1986—). Avocations: computing, reading, rock climbing. Home: 1579 S Flower Ct Lakewood CO 80226 Office: US West Knowledge Engring 4380 S Syracuse Denver CO 80237

CLINE, ROBERT CORDÉ, governmental relations advocate; b. San Francisco, May 6, 1933; s. John Wesley and Edith Bertha (Cordé) C.; m. Betty Robison, Aug. 24, 1955 (div. 1979); children: Bruce Cordé, Caren Jamie. AB, U. Calif., Berkeley, 1955, MBA in Finance, 1961. Financial analyst Litton Ind., Inc., Beverly Hills, Calif., 1961-65; owner Robert C. Cline Co., Canoga Park, Calif., 1965-70; ptnr. Cline Holzberg, Woodland Hills, Calif., 1970-77; mem. Calif. Assembly, 1970-80; owner, pres. R.C. Cline Co., Sacramento, 1980—; lobbyist Associated Builders and Contractors Calif. Inc., Calif. Ind. Producers Assn., N.Am. Assn. Inventory Services, Boxers/Wrestlers Benefit Fund, 1984—, Butte Sink Waterfowl Assn., Sacramento, 1986—. Rep. cen. committeeman, Sacramento, 1962-80. Served with U.S. Army, 1956-58. Mem. Inst. Govtl. Advs., Associated Builders and Contractors, Calif. Waterfowl Assn. (bd. dirs. 1985—). Episcopalian. Club: Colusa Shooting (Calif.). Avocations: waterfowl hunting. Home: 1596 Newborough Dr Sacramento CA 95833 Office: 1127 11th St #822 Sacramento CA 95814

CLINE, ROBERT STANLEY, air freight company executive; b. Urbana, Ill., July 17, 1937; s. Lyle Stanley and Mary Elizabeth (Prettyman) C.; m. Judith Lee Stucker, July 7, 1979; children: Lisa Andre, Nicole Lesley, Christina Elaine, Leslie Jane. B.A., Dartmouth Coll., 1959. Asst. treas. Chase Manhattan Bank, N.Y.C., 1960-65; v.p. fin. Pacific Air Freight Co., Seattle, 1965-68; exec. v.p. fin. Airborne Freight Corp., Seattle, 1968-78; vice chmn., chief fin. officer, dir. Airborne Freight Corp., 1978-84, chmn., chief exec. officer, dir., 1984—. Trustee Seattle Repertory Theatre, 1974—, Children's Orthopedic Hosp. Found., 1983—; chmn. bd. Seattle Repertory Theatre, 1979-83. Served with U.S. Army, 1959-60. Home: 10058 SE 16th St Bellevue WA 98004 Office: 3101 Western Ave Seattle WA 98121

CLINE, WILSON ETTASON, retired judge; b. Newkirk, Okla., Aug. 26, 1914; s. William Sherman and Etta Blanche (Roach) C.; student U. Ill., 1932-33; A.B., U. Okla., 1935, B.S. in Bus. Adminstrn., 1936; J.D., U. Calif., Berkeley, 1939; LL.M., Harvard U., 1941; m. G. Barbara Verne Pentecost, Nov. 1, 1939 (div. Nov. 1960); children—William, Catherine Cline MacDonald, Thomas; m. Gina Lana Ludwig, Oct. 5, 1969; children—David Ludwig, Kenneth Ludwig. Admitted to Calif. bar, 1940; atty. Kaiser Richmond Shipyards, 1941-44; pvt. practice, Oakland, 1945-49; atty., hearing officer, asst. chief adminstrv. law judge, acting chief adminstrv. law judge Calif. Pub. Utilities Commn., San Francisco, 1949-80, ret., 1981, dir. gen. welfare Calif. State Employees Assn., 1966-67, chmn. retirement com., 1965-66, mem. benefit com., 1980-81, mem. ret. employees div. council dist. C, 1981-82. Trustee Cline Ranch Trust, various family trusts. Mem. ABA, State Bar Calif., Conf. Calif. Pub. Utility Counsel (steering com. 1967-71), Am. Judicature Soc., Boalt Hall Alumni Assn., Phi Beta Kappa (pres. No. Calif. assn. 1969-70), Beta Gamma Sigma, Delta Sigma Pi (Key award, 1936), Phi Kappa Psi, Phi Delta Phi, Pi Sigma Alpha. Republican. Mem. United Ch. Christ. Clubs: Harvard, Commonwealth (San Francisco); Sleepy Hollow Swim and Tennis (Orinda, Calif.); Masons, Sirs (Peralta chpt. 12). Home: 110 St Albans Rd Kensington CA 94708 Office: 1400 Webster St Suite 212 PO Box 526 Alameda CA 94501

CLINTON, JOHN HART, lawyer, editor; b. Quincy, Mass., Apr. 3, 1905; s. John Francis and Catherine Veronica (Hart) C.; m. Helen Alice Amphlett, Feb. 18, 1933 (dec. 1965); children: Mary Jane (Mrs. Raymond Zirkel), Mary Ann (Mrs. Christopher Gardner, Jr.), John Hart; m. Mathilda A. Schoorel van Dillen, Feb. 22, 1969. A.B., Boston Coll., 1926; J.D., Harvard U., 1929. Bar: Calif. 1930, Mass. 1930. Since practiced in San Francisco; assoc. Morrison, Foerster, Holloway, Clinton & Clark, and predecessor, 1929-41, ptnr., 1941-72; of counsel Morrison & Foerster, 1972—; Vice pres., gen. counsel Indsl. Employers and Distbrs. Assn., Emeryville, 1944-72; pres. Leamington Hotel, Oakland, Calif., 1933-47, Amphlett Printing Co., San Mateo, Calif., 1943—; pub. San Mateo Times, 1943-87, editor, 1960—. Hon. mem. exec. com. San Mateo County council Boy Scouts Am.; bd. dirs., pres. Bay Meadows Found.; regent emeritus Notre Dame Coll., Belmont, Calif. Decorated Knight Equestrian Order of Holy Sepulchre of Jerusalem. Mem. FCC, Am., San Francisco, San Mateo County bar assns., State Bar Calif. (past chmn. fair trial/free press com., past co-chmn. Calif. bench/bar media com.), Am. Judicature Soc., Nat. Lawyers Club, Am. Law Inst., San Mateo County Devel. Assn (pres. 1963-65), San Mateo County Hist. Assn. (pres. 1960-64), Calif. Press Assn. (pres. 1970, chmn. membership com.), Am. Newspaper Pubs. Assn. (govt. affairs com., press/bar relations com.; Am. Bar Assn.-Am. Newspapers Pubs. Assn. task force), Calif. Newspaper Pubs. Assn. (pres. 1969), Wine and Food Soc. San Francisco, Am. Soc. Newspaper Editors, Assn. Cath. Newsmen, Nat. Press Photographers Assn., Internat. Platform Assn., Newcomen Soc. Clubs: Commonwealth of Calif. (San Francisco) (past pres.), San Francisco Comml. (San Francisco), Bohemian (San Francisco); Bombay Bicycle Riding (Burlingame, Calif.); Sequoia (Redwood City, Calif.). Lodges: Elks; Rotary (San Mateo past pres.). Home: 131 Sycamore Ave San Mateo CA 94402 Office: 1080 S Amphlett Blvd San Mateo CA 94402

CLOUD, JAMES MERLE, university administrator; b. Winston-Salem, N.C., Feb. 16, 1947; s. Merle Vail and Jane Crawford (Moore) C.; B.A., U. N.C., 1970; Ph.D., Columbia Pacific U., 1979. Co-founder Wholistic Health and Nutrition Inst., Mill Valley, Calif., 1974, dir. edn., 1974-76, dir. health resource consultation, 1976-78; admissions dir. Columbia Pacific U., 1978-84, sec.-treas., dir., 1978-84; v.p. Calif. U. for Advanced Studies, Novato, 1984-85; dir. Wholistic Health and Nutrition Inst., 1974-85. Mem. Assn. Holistic Health (v.p. 1976). Mem. Airplane Owners and Pilots Assn., Pacific Internat. Trapshooters Assn. Author: The Healthscription, 1979; anthologies of poems: Aeolus, 1971, No One Loves With Solitude, 1970. Home: 4286 Redwood Hwy San Rafael CA 94903

CLOUD, PRESTON, geologist, author, consultant; b. West Upton, Mass., Sept. 26, 1912; s. Preston E. and Pauline L. (Wiedemann) C.; m. Janice Gibson, 1972; children by previous marriage: Karen, Lisa, Kevin. B.S., George Washington U., 1938; Ph.D., Yale U., 1940. Instr. Mo. Sch. Mines and Metallurgy, 1940-41; research fellow Yale U., 1941-42; geologist U.S. Geol. Survey, 1942-46, 48-61, 74-79, chief paleontology and stratigraphy br., 1949-59; research geologist 1959-61, 74-79; asst. prof., curator invertebrate paleontology Harvard U., 1946-48; prof. dept. geology and geophysics U. Minn., 1961-65, chmn., 1961-63; prof. geology UCLA, 1965-68; prof. biogeology and environ. studies dept. geol. scis. U. Calif., Santa Barbara, 1968-74, prof. emeritus, 1974—; vis. prof. U. Tex., 1962, 78; H.R. Luce prof. cosmology Mt. Holyoke Coll., 1979-80; Sr. Queens fellow Baas-Becking Geobiology Lab., Canberra, Australia, 1981; internat exchange scholar Nat. Sci. and Engring. Research Council Can., 1982; hon. vis. prof. U. Ottawa (Ont. Can.), 1982; Nat. Sigma Xi lectr., 1967; Emmons lectr. Colo. Sci. Soc.; Bownocker lectr. Ohio State U.; French lectr. Pomona Coll.; Dumaresq-Smith lectr. Acadia Coll., N.B., Can.; A.L. DuToit Meml. lectr. Royal Soc. and Geol. Soc. of South Africa; mem. governing bd. NRC, 1972-75; mem. Pacific Sci. Bd., 1952-56, 62-65; del. internat. sci. congresses; cons. to govt., industry, founds. and assns. Author: Terebratuloid Brachiopoda of the Silurian and Devonian, 1942; (with Virgil E. Barnes) The Ellenburger Group of Central Texas, 1948; (with others) Geology of Saipan, Mariana Islands, 1957; Environment of Calcium Carbonate Deposition West of Andros Island,

Bahamas, 1962, Cosmos, Earth and Man, 1978, Oasis in Space, 1987; editor and co-author: (with others) Resources and Man, 1969, Adventures in Earth History, 1970; Author articles. Recipient A. Cressey Morrison prize natural history, 1941, Rockefeller Pub. Service award, 1956, U.S. Dept. Interior Distinguished Service award and gold medal, 1959, Medal, Paleontol Soc. Am., 1971, Lucius W. Cross medal Yale U., 1973, Penrose medal Geol. Soc. Am., 1976, C.D. Walcott medal Nat. Acad. Scis., 1977, R.C. Moore medal Soc. Econ. Paleontologists and Mineralogists, 1986; J.S. Guggenheim fellow, 1982-83. Fellow Am. Acad. Arts and Scis. (com. on membership 1978-80, council 1980-83); mem. Am. Philos. Soc., Nat. Acad. Scis. (com. on sci. and pub. policy 1965-69, mem. council 1972-75, exec. com. 1973-75, chmn. com. on resources and man 1965-69, chmn. ad hoc com. nat. materials policy 1972, chmn. study group on uses of underground space 1972, chmn. com. mineral resources and environment 1972-73, chmn. com. geology and climate 1977, chmn. sect. geology 1976-79, mem. assembly math. and phys. scis. 1976-79), Polish Acad. Scis. (fgn. assoc.), Geol. Soc. Am. (council 1972-75), Paleontol. Soc. Am., Paleontol. Soc. India (hon.), AAAS, Geol. Soc. Belgium (hon. fgn. corr.), Phi Beta Kappa, Sigma Xi, Sigma Gamma Epsilon. Field work 6 continents and 2 oceans. Home: 400 Mountain Dr Santa Barbara CA 93103 Office: Dept Geol Scis U Calif Santa Barbara CA 93106

CLOUSE, CHARLES HERCEL, educator; b. Pasadena, Calif., Nov. 12, 1946; s. Hercel Pledger and Marion Catherine (Collins) C.; m. Jan Louise Parker, Aug. 3, 1968. BA, U. Calif., Santa Barbara, 1968, MA, 1971. Cert. secondary tchr., Calif. Instr. adult edn. Santa Barbara City Coll., 1969-74; instr. Dos Pueblos High Sch., Goleta, Calif., 1972—; free-lance journalist Santa Barbara, 1984. Contbg. editor The Weekly, 1984—; contbr. over 50 articles to various mags. Mem. U. Calif. Alumni Assn. Avocations: music, photography, theatre. Home: 1722 Prospect Ave Santa Barbara CA 93103

CLOUSE, LAWRENCE HENRY, military officer, physician, hematologist; b. Milw., June 14, 1951; s. Henry Marvin and Mildred (Walter) C.; m. Janet Lynn Underwood, May 21, 1980. AB, Harvard U., 1972; MD, U. Calif., San Diego, 1976. Diplomate Am. Bd. Internal Medicine, Hematology. Intern in medicine U. Calif. Med. Ctr., San Diego, 1976-77; resident U. Okla., Oklahoma City, 1981-83, chief med. resident, 1983-84; fellow in Hematology/Oncology Ariz. Cancer Ctr., Tucson, 1984-87; commd. 1st lt. USAF, 1977, advanced through grades to maj., 1977-81, 85—. Mem. ACP, AMA, Ariz. State Med. Soc., Assn. Mil. Surgeons of U.S., Pima County Med. Soc. Office: Ariz Cancer Ctr 1501 N Campbell Tucson AZ 85724

CLOWER, ROBERT WAYNE, economics educator, consultant; b. Pullman, Wash., Feb. 13, 1926; s. Fay Walter and Mary Valentine (Gilchrist) C.; m. Frances Hepburn, Jan. 7, 1946 (div. July 1975); children: Ailsa, Leslie, Robert, Stephanie, Valerie; m. Georgene Helen Thousendfriend, Jan. 30, 1976; children: Anastasia, Kathryn. B.A in Econs., Wash. State U., 1948, M.A. in Econs., 1949; M.Litt. in Econs., Oxford U., Eng., 1952, D.Litt., 1978. Asst. prof. econs. Wash. State U., Pullman, 1952-56; prof. econs. Northwestern U., Evanston, Ill., 1957-70; prof. econs., dean Sch. Social Studies Essex U., Wivenoe, Eng., 1968-69; prof. econs. UCLA, 1971-86; Lane prof. econs. U. S.C., 1986—; cons. editor Penguin Books, Ltd., London, 1967-85. Author: Introduction to Mathematical Economics, 1957, Microeconomic Analysis, 1972, Money and Markets, 1984; editor: Readings in Monetary Theory, 1968; mng. editor Am. Econ. Rev., 1980-85. Served with AUS, 1974. Rhodes scholar, 1949; Guggenheim fellow, 1965; hon. fellow Brasenose Coll., Oxford, Eng., 1978. Fellow Econometric Soc.; mem. Am. Econs. Assn. (exec. com. 1978-81), Royal Econ. Soc., Western Econ. Assn. Internat. (editor econ. inquiry 1973-80, pres. 1986). Office: U SC Dept Econs Columbia SC 29208

CLUTE, PETER RANDOLPH, petroleum geologist, petroleum consultant; b. Schnectady, N.Y., Sept. 16, 1949; s. Gerald P. and Janice (Campbell) C. AB, Lafayette Coll., 1971; MS, SUNY, Fredonia, 1974. Jr. geologist Western Nuclear, Inc., Casper, Wyo., 1974; geologist Anderson Oil Co., Denver, 1974-77, Interam. Petroleum Corp., Denver, 1977-78, No. Natural Gas Co., Denver, 1978-80, Eagle Exploration Co., Denver, 1980; ind. cons. geologist, Denver, 1980—; v.p. Queen City Exploration Co., Denver, 1981-83, Contbr. geologic articles to profl. jours. Mem. Am. Assn. Petroleum Geologists, Am. Inst. Profl. Geologists (cert. profl. geol. scientist), Soc. Econ. Paleontologists and Mineralogists, Wyo. Geol. Assn., Rocky Mountain Assn. Geologists. Republican. Presbyterian. Home: 2526 Albion St Denver CO 80207 Office: 909 17th St Suite 335 Denver CO 80202-2715

CLYDE, CALVIN GEARY, civil engineer, educator; b. Springville, Utah, Sept. 5, 1924; s. Edward and Hannah (Mendenhall) C.; m. Brigitta Straumer, Nov. 24, 1948; children: Rixa, Eric S., DeAnn, Carla, Andrea, Loretta, Mark E., Tania. Student, Utah State U., 1942-43, No. State Tchrs. Coll., 1943-44, Brigham Young U., 1946; BS, U. Utah, 1951; degrees in civil engring., U. Calif., Berkeley, MS, 1952, PhD, 1961. Registered engr. and land surveyor, Utah; consecrated Bishop Mormon Ch., 1976. Assoc. prof. civil engring. U. Utah, Salt Lake City, 1953-63; prof. Utah State U., Logan, 1963—, assoc. dir. Utah Water Research Lab., 1965-77, acting dir. Utah Water Research Lab., 1975-76; cons. in ground water, fluid mechanics, hydraulics, hydropower, hydrology and water resources planning, 1953—. Contbr. articles to profl. jours. Served with U.S. Army, 1943-46, ETO. Science faculty fellow NSF, Berkeley, 1959-60. Fellow ASCE (pres. Utah sect. 1969-70, Utah Civil Engr. of Yr. 1979); mem. Am. Soc. Engring. Edn. (chmn. Rocky Mountain sect. 1962-63), AIAA, Nat. Water Well Assn., Internat. Assn. Hydraulic Research. Republican. Lodge: Kiwanis. Avocations: skiing, hiking, camping, fishing. Home: 839 N 1400 E Logan UT 84321 Office: Utah State U Water Research Lab 82 Logan UT 84322

CLYDE, EDWARD WILBUR, lawyer, b. Heber City, Utah, Nov. 23, 1917; s. Lionel Dean and Adell (Buhler) C.; m. Betha Jensen, Aug. 14, 1941; children—Carolyn, Susan, Steven, Thomas. B.S., Brigham Young U., 1939; J.D., U. Utah, 1942, LL.D. (hon.), 1981. Bar: Utah. Law clk. Utah Supreme Ct., Salt Lake City, 1941-45; asst. atty. gen. State of Utah, Salt Lake City, 1945-48, Utah Land Bd., Salt Lake City, 1956-60; commr. Utah Oil and Gas Commn., 1956-60; ptnr. Clyde and Pratt, Salt Lake City, 1943—; chmn. Utah Constl. Revision Commn., 1970-74. Contbr. numerous articles to profl. jours. Mem. bd. regents U. Utah, 1964-69, chmn. bd. regents, 1966-68; chmn. Instl. Council, 1969-81. Mem. Am. Coll. Trial Attys., ABA (chmn. natural resources law sect. 1976-77), Soc. Bar and Gavel, Phi Kappa Phi. Home: 1329 Blaine Ave Salt Lake City UT 84105 Office: Clyde & Pratt Am Savs Plaza Suite 200 77 W 2d S Salt Lake City UT 84101 *

CLYMA, WAYNE, irrigation educator; b. Keota, Okla., Aug. 1, 1935; s. Joe and Rose (Strickland) C.; m. Marjorie Marie Sappington, July 9, 1960; children: Gary Wayne, Howard Earl. BS, Okla. State U., 1958, MS, 1963; PhD, U. Ariz., 1971. Registered profl. engr., Tex. Agrl. engr. Agrl. Research Service of USDA, Bushland, Tex., 1958-64; asst. prof. irrigation engring. Okla. State U., Alemaya, Ethiopia, 1964-66; asst. prof., research assoc. U. Ariz., Tucson, 1966-71; assoc. prof. Colo. State U., Ft. Collins, 1971-72, Islamabad, Pakistan, 1972-76; prof. Colo. State U., Ft. Collins, 1976—. Contbr. numerous articles to profl. jours. Recipient Superior Service award Reader's Digest, 1969, Interdisciplinary Research award Colo. State U., 1977. Mem. Am. Soc. Agrl. Engrs., Am. Geophys. Union, Internat. Commn. on Irrigation and Drainage, Sigma Xi. Republican. Baptist. Avocation: church work. Home: 1405 Skyline Dr Fort Collins CO 80521 Office: Colo State U Agrl and Chem Engring Dept Fort Collins CO 80521

COAD, PETER, chemistry educator, consultant; b. San Francisco, Oct. 17, 1926; s. John Francis and Mary Katherine (Davis) C.; m. Raylene Elizabeth Adams, June 25, 1950; children: Anne Carter, Peter Jr., Michael, Patrick, Molly Raylene. BS, U. Calif., Berkeley, 1948, MS, 1949; PhD, Oreg. State U., 1953. Cert. secondary tchr., Calif. Head div. natural sci. Chapman Coll., Orange, Calif., 1956-63; research chemist Am. Potash, Trona, Calif., 1965-70; research mgr. Kerr-McGee, Oklahoma City, 1970-74; prof. physics Harbor Coll., Wilmington, Calif., 1979—; prof. chemistry Los Angeles Trade Tech. Coll., 1974-79, Biola U., La Mirada, Calif., 1982—; dep. adminstr. Walter Reed ARI, Washington, 1963-65; cons. in field. Contbr. articles to profl. jours.; patentee in field. Grantee NSF, NIMH, Petroleum Research Corp., 1961-63; fellow DuPont, Oreg. State U., 1951, NSF, 1961-63. Mem. Am. Sci. Affiliation, Am. Chem. Soc. (organic div. Orange County sect.), Internat. Union Pure and Applied Chemistry (assoc.), Nat. Assn. Sci. Tchrs. Baptist. Avocations: choir, ch. activities. Home: 15925 F Alta Vista Dr La Mirada CA 90638 Office: Biola U 13800 Biola Ave La Mirada CA 90639

COAD, RAYLENE ELIZABETH ADAMS, chemistry educator, consultant; b. South Pasadena, Calif., Apr. 11, 1926; d. Charles Donald and Dorothy Mae (Morgan) Adams; m. Peter Coad, June 25, 1950; children: Anne Carter, Peter Jr., Michael, Patrick, Molly Raylene. BS, MS, U. Calif., Berkeley, 1947, PhD, 1950; MA, Radcliffe Coll., 1949. Research assoc. Oreg. State U., Corvallis, 1950-52; asst. prof. chemistry Chapman Coll., Orange, Calif., 1956-63; research assoc. USDA, Beltsville, Md., 1963-64; instr. chemistry Oscar Rose coll., Midwest City, Okla., 1970-74; prof. chemistry El Camino Coll., Torrance, Calif., 1974—, Biola U., La Mirada, Calif., 1982—; cons. in field. Contbr. articles to profl. jours. Chancellor's grant for Innovative Teaching, 1981. Mem. Am. Chem. Soc. (Orange County sect.), Nat. Assn. Sci. Tchrs. Baptist. Avocations: choir, church activities. Home: 15925 F Alta Vista Dr La Mirada CA 90638 Office: Biola U 13800 Biola Ave La Mirada CA 90639

COAKLEY, JAY JOSEPH, sociology educator; b. Chgo., Jan. 24, 1944; s. Jeremiah Joseph and Lois (Larkin) C.; m. Nancy Carr, Aug. 20, 1966; children: Dennis Jay, Danielle Marie. BS, Regis Coll., 1966; MA, U. Notre Dame, 1969, PhD, 1971. Instr. sociology St. Mary's Coll., Notre Dame, Ind., 1969-70; asst. prof. No. Ariz. U., Flagstaff, 1970-72; prof. U. Colo., Colorado Springs, 1972—; vis. research fellow West Sussex Inst. Higher Edn., Chichester, Eng., 1985-86. Author: Sport in Society, 1978, 2d rev. edit., 1986; editor Sociology of Sport Jour., 1983—; contbr. articles to profl. jours. Bd. dirs. Pikes Peak Area Spl. Olympics, Colorado Springs, 1973-79, Pikes Peak Hospice, Colorado Springs, 1985. Mem. N.Am. Soc. Sociology of Sport (exec. bd. 1981—), Sport Sociology Acad. AAHPERD (chmn. 1983). Democrat. Avocations: recreational and competitive sports. Home: 5101 Mira Loma Circle Colorado Springs CO 80918 Office: U Colo Dept Sociology Austin Bluffs Pkwy Colorado Springs CO 80933-7150

COAN, CAROL RUTH, biochemist; b. Salt Lake City, Dec. 20, 1943; d. Dwight and Maurine (Olsen) Hemingway; children: Alisa, Jacob. BA, Goucher Coll.; PhD, U. Ga., 1971. Asst. prof. biochemistry U. Pacific, San Francisco, 1977-84, assoc. prof., 1984—. Contbr. articles to profl. jours. Mem. Am. Chem. Soc., Biophys. Soc. Am., N.Y. Acad. Scis. Office: U Pacific Sch Dentistry 2155 Webster St San Francisco CA 94115

COATES, ROBERT CRAWFORD, municipal court judge; b. Torrance, Calif., Jan. 31, 1937. B.S. in Engring. Geology, San Diego State U., 1959; J.D., Calif. Western Sch. Law, 1970; Bar: Calif., U.S. Supreme Ct. 1974. Adminstrv. analyst city mgr.'s staff City of San Diego, 1961-63,; ptnr. firm Coates & Miller, San Diego, 1977-82; judge Mcpl Ct., County of San Diego, 1982—; adj. prof. environ. and natural resource law U. San Diego, 1981—. Nominee for Calif. legislature, 1964, 66; pres. Mental Health Assn., 1978, chmn. found. bd., 1982, chmn. bd. advisers, 1984; mem. exec. bd. San Diego County council Boy Scouts Am., 1984. Served with C.B., USNR, 1955-63. Contbr. to law revs. and other legal pubs. Author book of poetry: Ships Crossing At The Dead of Night, 1984. Recipient Lifesaving award ARC, 1967; Founder's Recognition award Crime Victims Fund, 1982; Poetry First prize San Diego Writers and Editors Guild, 1982; Community Service award San Diego Housing Commn., 1984. Mem. San Diego Trial Lawyers Assn. (dir. 1980-82), Rocky Mountain Mineral Law Found. (law tchrs. com. 1981—), San Diego Ecology Ctr. (pres. 1984), San Diego Assn. Geologists, Calif. Mining Assn., Navy League, Calif. Judges Assn., ABA, Sierra Club, Eagle Scout Alumni Assn. (dir. 1980-83, pres. 1983-85). Office: San Diego Mcpl Ct 220 W Broadway San Diego CA 92101

COATS, HUBERT S., JR., banker; b. Julesberg, Colo., Feb. 26, 1927; s. Hubert S. and Ruth (Lang) C.; pre-standard cert. Am. Inst. Banking, 1951, standard cert., 1955; grad. Pacific Coast Bankers Sch., 1970; m. Edna Mae, July 13, 1946; children—Larry Dale, Matthew Daniel. With First Security Bank, Jerome, Idaho, 1946-55, 57-59, asst. mgr. timeway credit, 1953-55, asst. mgr., 1957-59; asst. mgr. Hailey (Idaho) First Security Bank, 1955-57; v.p., cashier First Security Bank Twin Falls (Idaho), 1959-67; mgr. First Security Bank, Rupert, Idaho, 1967-69; v.p. ops. eastern div. First Security Bank, Pocatello, Idaho, 1967-72, v.p., asst. mgr., 1972-73, mgr., 1977; mgr., v.p. First Security Bank, Coeur d'Alene, Idaho, 1973-77; v.p., area mgr. Idaho Bank & Trust Co., Boise, 1977-78, sr. v.p., 1978—. Pres. PTA, Hailey, Idaho, 1955-56; treas. Pocatello Jr. Achievement, 1970-71, pres., 1969-70; chmn. bd. trustees First Methodist Ch., Coeur d'Alene; treas. Kootenai County (Idaho) YMCA, 1972-75, dir., 1972—; chmn. Idaho Housing Agy.; chmn. St. Luke's Charity Ball, 1983; bd. dirs., chmn. gen. div. United Way, Boise; vice chmn. Idaho Council on Econ. Edn.; treas. Funday. Served with USN, 1944-46. Named Businessman of Yr., Twin Falls Credit Women's Club, 1954, Man of Yr., Kootenai Family YMCA, 1975; recipient Disting. Service award Coeur d'Alene C. of C., campaign award Kootenai County United Way, 1976. Mem. Idaho Bankers Assn. (chmn. public relations com. 1979-80), Sales and Mktg. Execs. of Boise (2d v.p.). Boise C. of C. Clubs: Hillcrest Country, Arid (Boise), Boise Southwest Rotary (pres.-elect). Home: 817 Argyll Dr Boise ID 83702 Office: PO Box 2800 Boise ID 83701

COBANOGLU, ADNAN, cardiothoracic surgeon; b. Ankara, Turkey, June 21, 1951; came to U.S., 1974; s. Mahmot Nedim and Kamuran Cobanoglu. BA, ANkara Coll., 1968; MD, Ankara U., 1974. Cert. Am. Bd. Surgery, Am. Bd. Thoracic Surgery. Asst. prof. surgery Oreg. Health Scis. U., Portland, 1981-83, assoc. prof., 1984—, asst. chief cardiopulmonary surgery, 1984—, assoc. dir. heart transplant program, 1984—; asst. prof. Thomas Jefferson U., Phila., 1983-84. Contbr. articles to profl. jours.; chpts. to books. Fellow ACS, Soc. Thoracic Surgeons, Am. Coll. Cardiology, Internat. Coll. Surgeons, Am. Coll. Chest Physicians. Office: Oreg Health Scis U 3181 SW Sam Jackson Park Rd Portland OR 97201

COBB, ALONZO FLOYD, JR., marketing and finance professional, management consultant; b. N.Y.C., Jan. 12, 1947; s. Alonzo Floyd Sr. and Lorene (Brown) Cobb; m. Ernestine Mitchell (div.); children: Tarik Walden, Tammy Melissa. AS in Chemistry, Nassau Community Coll., 1976; BBA in Finance, Baruch Coll., 1979; MA in Econs. and Bus., Stanford U., 1983. Internal auditor Crocker Bank, San Francisco, 1979-80; fin. analyst Castle & Cooke, San Francisco, 1981-82; fin. planner Childers, Swan & Co., Fremont, Calif., 1983-85; mktg. analyst Pacific Bell Directory, San Francisco, 1985-87; sr. fin. analyst Pacific Bell, San Ramon, 1987—. Tutor San Francisco Sch. Vols., 1986—; com. mem. Corp. Action in Pub. Schs., 1986—. Served with U.S. Army, 1966-70. Republican. Adventist. Avocations: Japanese lang. and mgmt. studies, photography, chess, sports. Home: 607 8th Ave San Francisco CA 94118 Office: Pacific Bell 2600 Camino Ramon Room 3S250E San Ramon CA 94583

COBB, DAVID WAYNE, educational video producer, script writer; b. Parkersburg, W.Va., Dec. 6, 1950; s. William and Mary Geneva (Godbey) C.; m. Debra Jean Fisher, Nov. 16, 1974. BS, W.Va. U., 1972; MA, U. Denver, 1979. Editor Talking Books Pub., Denver, 1976-79; freelance writer Los Angeles, 1979-82; producer, writer Medcom Inc., Garden Grove, Calif., 1982—. Mem. Internat. TV Assn. (Silver Angel award 1985). Democrat. Avocations: camping, hiking, travel.

COBB, JAMES L., JR., business executive; b. Port Chester, N.Y., Feb. 28, 1948; s. James L. and Jeanne H. (Wilson) C.; m. Wanda Freeman, May 27, 1972; children—Jennifer Joy, Ciara Faith, Victoria Kristine, James L. III. A.A., Los Angeles City Coll., 1968; B.S., Calif. State U.-Long Beach, 1973; M.B.A., Washington U., St. Louis, 1977. Mfg. engr. 3M Co., St. Paul, 1973-74, coll. recruiter, 1974-75; mktg. rep. Data Processing div. IBM, St. Louis, 1977-80; 3d party mktg. specialist Hewlett-Packard Co., Cupertino, Calif., 1980-81, Canadian sales devel., 1981-82, computer systems product mgr., Roseville, Calif., 1982-86, info. systems ops. mgr., 1984—; owner, ptnr. Cobb & Co. Cons., Roseville, Calif., 1986—; dir., pres. mktg. Hurrican Industries, San Jose, Calif., 1980-81; dir. Computer Sci. & Data Processing Dept. Am. River Coll., Sacramento; instr. Calif. State U.-San Jose, 1980-81, Sacramento, 1983-86. Author: Configuration Design and Procurement, 1983. Chmn. computer acquisition com. St. Rose Catholic Sch., Roseville, Calif., 1982-83. Mem. Consortium Grad. Studies in Mgmt. for Minorities (pres. 1976-77).

COBB, JEWEL PLUMMER, college president; b. Chgo., Jan. 17, 1924; divorced; 1 child. A.B., Talladega Coll., 1944; M.S., N.Y. U., 1947, Ph.D. in Biology, 1950. Fellow Nat. Cancer Inst., 1950-52; instr. anatomy U. Ill. Coll. Medicine, 1952-54; research surgery Postgrad. Med. Coll., N.Y. U., 1955, asst. prof., 1955-60; Cancer Research Found. prof. biology Sarah Lawrence Coll., 1960-69; prof. zoology, dean Conn. Coll., 1969-76; prof. biology, dean Douglass Coll., Rutgers U., 1976-81; pres. Calif. State U.-Fullerton, 1981—; Dir. Travelers Ins. Co.; Former mem. commn. on acad. affairs Am. Council on Edn.; Bd. dirs. 21st Century Found., Nat. Center Resource Recovery, Nat. Sci. Bd., 1974-80, Nat. Inst. Medicine, CPC Internat., Inc., Allied/Signal Corp., First Interstate Bancorp. Recipient Alumnae Woman of Yr. award N.Y. U., 1979. Fellow N.Y. Acad. Scis., Tissue Culture Assn.; mem. AAUW, Sigma Xi. Spl. research on tissue culture studies human neoplasms, changes produced by promising chemotherapeutic agts., mechanisms normal and abnormal pigment cell metabolism. Office: Calif State U Fullerton CA 92634

COBB, ROY LAMPKIN, JR., professional services company executive; b. Oklahoma City, Sept. 23, 1934; s. Roy Lampkin and Alice Maxine (Ellis) C.; B.A., U. Okla., 1972; postgrad. U. Calif., Northridge, 1976-77; m. Shirley Ann Dodson, June 21, 1958; children—Kendra Leigh, Cary William, Paul Alan. Naval aviation cadet U.S. Navy, 1955, advanced through grades to comdr., 1970; ret., 1978; mktg./project staff engr. Gen. Dynamics, Pomona, Calif., 1978-80; prin. engr. Advanced Tech., Inc., Camarillo, Calif., 1980—. Decorated Navy Commendation medal, Air medal. Mem. Assn. Naval Aviators, Soc. Logistic Engrs. Republican. Methodist. Club: Las Posas Country. Home: 2481 Brookhill Dr Camarillo CA 93010 Office: Advanced Tech Inc 1000 Paseo Camarillo Camarillo CA 93010

COBB, SHIRLEY ANN, public relations specialist, journalist; b. Oklahoma City, Jan. 1, 1936; d. William Ray and Irene (Fewell) Dodson; m. Roy Lampkin Cobb, Jr., June 21, 1958; children—Kendra Leigh, Cary William, Paul Alan. B.A. in Journalism with distinction, U. Okla., 1958, postgrad., 1972; postgrad. Jacksonville U., 1962. Info. specialist Pacific Missle Test Ctr., Pt. Mugu, Calif., 1975-76; corr. Religious News Service, N.Y.C., 1979-81; splty. editor fashion and religion Thousand Oaks (Calif.) News Chronicle, 1977-81; pub. relations cons., Camarillo, Calif., 1977—; sr. mgmt. analyst pub. info City of Thousand Oaks, 1983—. Trustee Ocean View Sch. Bd., 1976-79; pres. Pt. Mugu Officers' Wives Club, 1975-76; bd. dirs. Camarillo Hospice, 1983-85. Recipient Spot News award San Fernando Valley Press Club, 1979. Mem. Sigma Delta Chi, Pub. Relations Soc. Am., Phi Beta Kappa. Republican. Club: Las Posas Country. Contbr. articles to profl. jours. Home: 2481 Brookhill Dr Camarillo CA 93010 Office: 401 W Hillcrest Dr Thousand Oaks CA 91360

COBB, STEPHEN HENRY (STEVE), state senator; b. Honolulu, Dec. 5, 1942; s. William B. and Olivine (Steffens) C.; married; 1 child; student U. Hawaii, 1961-64; BA in Journalism, Calif. State U.-Los Angeles, 1966. With mktg. and loans dept. Bank of Hawaii, 1970-72; adminstrv. asst. Pacific Resources Inc., 1976; mem. Hawaii Ho. of Reps. from 8th Dist., 1972-78, Hawaii Senate from 7th, 12th Dists., 1978—, chmn. consumer protection and commerce com., 1979—, majority floor leader, 1981—. Treas., Hawaii Little League Baseball, 1971-75. active numerous Dem. campaigns, 1960—. Served with AUS, 1966-70; Vietnam. Decorated Silver Star, Bronze Star medal, Army Commendation medal, Purple Heart, Air medal. Named Kiwanis Vet. of Yr., Hawaii, 1970. Mem. DAV, Sigma Delta Chi. Roman Catholic. Office: State Capitol Bldg Room 215 Honolulu HI 96813

COBB, STEVEN MICHAEL, individual, marriage and family therapist, counselor; b. Memphis, Nov. 8, 1945; s. James Andrews Cobb and Dorothy Kathleen (Harrell) Stevens; m. Victoria Ann Hayner, Sept. 2, 1967; children—Brian Robert, Heidi Marie, Martha Michelle. B.S. in Psychology and Sociology, Eastern N.Mex. U., 1969, Ed.S. in Counseling and Psychology, 1976; M.A. in Sociology, N.Mex. State U., 1973; Ph.D. in Edn., Counseling Psychology, U. N.Mex., 1979. Lic. profl. counselor, Tex.; cert. profl. counselor; cert. clin. mental health counselor, marriage and family therapist. Counselor and clin. dir. resource ctr. Eastern N.Mex. U., Portales, 1974-76; intern, therapist Adams Lovekin, Ph.D., Psychologist, Albuquerque, 1976-78; private practice individual, marriage and family therapy, Albuquerque, 1978-79; clin. dir. counseling Community Counseling Ctr., Roswell, N.Mex., 1979-80; clin. dir., therapist Artesia Counseling Ctr., N.Mex., 1980-81; private practice individual, marriage and family therapy, Roswell, 1981—; vocat. cons. Office of Hearings and Appeals, Social Security Adminstrn., 1981-82; pvt. cons., 1981—; cons. Stress Mgmt. div. Roswell City Fire Dept., 1985pvt. practice rep. Behavioral Health Coordination Council, State of N.Mex., 1981-84. Served with U.S. Army, 1970-73. Mem. Am. Psychol. Assn., Am. Assn. Counseling and Devel., Am. Assn. for Marriage and Family Therapy, N.M. Assn. of Marriage and Family Therapists (sec. 1979-80, v.p. 1980-81), Am. Group Psychotherapy Assn., Am. Mental Health Counselors Assn., N.Mex. Assn. for Mental Health Counselors, N.MEx. Assn. for Marital and Family Therapists, N.MEx. Assn. for Counseling and Devel. (chmn. ethics and profl. devel. 1986—). Republican. Lodge: Elks. Home: 1302 Hall Dr Roswell NM 88201 Office: Family Therapy Practice 105 W 3rd St Roswell NM 88201

COBBLE, JAMES WIKLE, educator; b. Kansas City, Mo., Mar. 15, 1926; s. Ray and Crystal Edith (Wikle) C.; m. Margaret Ann Zumwalt, June 9, 1949; children—Catherine Ann, Richard James. Student, San Diego State Coll., 1942-44; B.A., No. Ariz. U., 1946; M.S., U. So. Calif., 1949; Ph.D., U. Tenn., 1952. Chemist Oak Ridge Nat. Lab., 1949-52; postdoctoral research asso. U. Calif., Berkeley, 1952-55; instr. dept. chemistry U. Calif., 1954; asst. prof. dept. chemistry Purdue U., Lafayette, Ind., 1955-58; asso. prof. Purdue U., 1958-61, prof., 1961-73; prof., dean Grad. div. San Diego State U., 1973—; cons. in field. Contbr. articles to sci. publs. Bd. visitors USAF U., 1984—, chmn-elect, 1986—; v.p. San Diego State U. Found., 1975—. Served to lt. (j.g.) USNR, 1945-46. Recipient E.O. Lawrence award U.S. AEC, 1970; Guggenheim fellow, 1966; Robert A. Welch Found. lectr., 1971. Fellow Am. Inst. Chemists, Am. Phys. Soc.; mem. Am. Chem. Soc., Sigma Xi, Phi Kappa Phi, Alpha Chi Sigma, Phi Lambda Upsilon. Home: 1380 Park Row La Jolla CA 92037 Office: Dept Chemistry San Diego State Univ San Diego CA 92182

COBBLE, MILAN HOUSTON, mechanical engineer, educator; b. St. Paul, Mar. 13, 1922; s. Houston Ira and Lillian Betty (Strom) C.; m. Nancy Lewis Musselman, July 16, 1949; children: Steven B., Brian K., Kevin S., David M. BME, U. Mich., 1948; MME, Wayne U., 1952, PhD, 1958. Registered profl. engr., Del. Asst. prof. mech. engring. U. Del., Newark, 1956-59, acting chmn. mech. engring., 1960-61, assoc. prof., 1959-62; prof. mech. engring. N.Mex. State U., Las Cruces, 1962-65, 68—, prof. math., 1965-66, prof. computer sci., 1966-67, research assoc. Solar Energy Inst., 1980-82; vis. prof. mech. and aerospace engring. U. Tenn., Knoxville, 1976, sr. cons. EERC, 1982; disting. vis. prof. U. Mich., Dearborn, 1984—; cons. N.Mex. State U., 1979-85. Contbr. articles to profl. jours. Served with U.S. Army, 1943-46, ETO. Fellow NSF, 1959-61, Shell U., 1954-55, Engring. Research Inst. U. Mich. 1955-56; recipient Western Electric Fund award, 1967, Bromilow award Haltburton Edn. Found., 1981, Naval Research Lab. Publ. award, 1982. Fellow AAAS; mem. Internat. Assn. Sci. and Tech. Devel., Computers in Edn., Sigma Xi, Phi Kappa Phi, Pi Tau Sigma. Democrat. Presbyterian.

COBURN, GARY NELSON, investment firm executive; b. Pasadena, Calif., May 19, 1946; s. George Nelson and Frances (Colton) C.; m. Carol Lucille Schmidt, Sept. 13, 1969; children—Brian, Jeffrey. B.A. in Econs., U. Calif.-Berkeley, 1968, M.B.A. in Fin., 1969. Vice pres., gen. ptnr. Scudder, Stevens & Clark, Inc., San Francisco, 1970—, also dir., Los Angeles. Mem. Security Analyst Soc. of San Francisco, Fin. Analysts Fedn., U. Calif. Alumni Assn. Republican. Clubs: University (San Francisco), Moraga Country, San Francisco Yacht (Belvedere). Home: 192 Alice Ln Orinda CA 94563 Office: Scudder Stevens & Clark Inc 101 California St Suite 4100 San Francisco CA 94111

COBURN, HORACE HUNTER, physics educator; b. Cambridge, Mass., May 10, 1922; s. Charles A. and Viola M. (Hunter) C.; m. Hope Pleyl, Dec. 24, 1947; children: Lynn L., Carol A., James H. BS, Ohio State U., 1943; MS, U. Ill., 1947; PhD, U. Pa., 1956. Physicist Manhattan Dist., Oak Ridge, Tenn., 1944-46; assoc. prof. physics Moravian Coll., Bethlehem, Pa.,

1950-51; prof. N.Mex. State U., Las Cruces, 1954—; lectr. U.S. AID, India, 1966, 69; pres., bd. dirs. Las Alturas Devel. Corp., Las Cruces. Mem. Optical Soc. Am., Am. Assn. Physics Tchrs., Nat. Sci. Tchrs. Assn., Soc. Photo-optical and Instrumentation Engrs. Mem. Christian Ch. Avocation: bicycling. Home: Box 906 Mesilla Park NM 88047 Office: NMex State U Physics Dept Las Cruces NM 88003

COBURN, MARJORIE FOSTER, psychologist, Montessori/special educator; b. Salt Lake City, Feb. 28, 1939; d. Harlan A. and Alma (Ballinger) Polk; m. Robert Byron Coburn, July 2, 1977; children—Robert Scott Coburn, Kelly Anne Coburn, Polly Klea Foster, Matthew Ryan Foster. B.A. in Sociology, UCLA, 1960; Montessori Internat. Diploma honor grad. Washington Montessori Inst., 1968; M.A. in Psychology, U. No. Colo., 1979; Ph.D. in Counseling Psychology, U. Denver, 1983. Licensed clin. psychologist. Probation officer Alameda County (Calif.), Oakland, 1960-62, Contra Costa County (Calif.), El Cerrito, 1966, Fairfax County (Va.), Fairfax, 1967; dir. Friendship Club, Orlando, Fla., 1963-65; tchr. Va. Montessori Sch., Fairfax, 1968-70; spl. edn. tchr. Leary Sch., Falls Church, Va., 1970-72, sch. administr., 1973-76; tchr. Aseltine Sch., San Diego, 1976-77, Coburn Montessori Sch., Colorado Springs, Colo., 1977-79; psychotherapist, supervised pvt. practice, Colorado Springs, 1979-82, San Diego, 1982—; cons. spl. edn., agoraphobia, women in transition. Mem. Am. Psychol. Assn., Am. Orthopsychiat. Assn., Phobia Soc., Council Exceptional Children, El Paso Psychol. Assn., Calif. Psychol. Assn., Acad. San Diego Psychologists, AAUW, NOW, Mensa. Episcopalian. Contbr. articles to profl. jours.; author: (with R.C. Orem) Montessori: Prescription for Children with Learning Disabilities, 1977. Office: 826 Prospect Suite 201 La Jolla CA 92037

COBURN, THOMAS TYLER, chemist; b. Montebello, Calif., May 8, 1943; s. H. Tyler Coburn and Betty Simpson; m. Marie Eda Mandelbaum, Jan. 15, 1981; children: Matthew, Katherine, Anna, Margaret. BS, Harvey Mudd Coll., 1965; MS, Yale U., 1966; PhD, U. Fla., 1973. Instr., asst. prof. chemistry Mount St. Mary Coll., Newburgh, N.Y., 1967-70; research chemist Ciba-Geigy Pharms., Basel, Switzerland, 1973-75; asst. prof. Bost U., 1975-78; sr. chemist Ky. Ctr. for Energy Research Lab., Lexington, 1978-84; synfuels chemist Lawrence Livermore Nat. Lab., Livermore, Calif., 1984—. Mem. Am. Chem. Soc. Office: Lawrence Livermore Nat Lab PO Box 808 L-207 Livermore CA 94550

COBURN, TIMOTHY CRAIG, research statistician; b. Houston, May 10, 1951; s. Robert Reeves and Doris Madeline (Gardner) C. BS, BSE, Abilene Christian U., 1973; MS, Okla. State U., 1975, PhD, 1980. Cert. tchr., Tex. Grad. asst. dept. stats. Okla. State U., Stillwater, 1973-75, grad. asst., cons. statistician Statis. Lab., 1978-80; regional statistician USDA-Food and Nutrition Service, Dallas, 1975-78; cons. statistician USDA-Food and Nutrition Service, Washington, 1977; statistician Phillips Petroleum Co., Bartlesville, Okla., 1980-83; research statistician Phillips Petroleum Co., Denver, 1983-85; sr. scientist Marathon Oil Co., Littleton, Colo., 1985-87; statis. cons. Carson and Tratner Attys., Oklahoma City, Okla., 1975; cons. statistician Miss. State U. Dept. Gen. Sci., Jackson, 1981-83, Ctr. Environ., Energy and Sci. Edn., Jackson; cons. in field, Dallas, 1975; lectr. Secondary Sch. Lecture Program, Dallas, 1977. Contbg. editor: Current Index to Statistics, 1985-86; pub. referee Communications in Statistics, 1984, Jour. Official Stats. Sweden, 1986; contbr. articles to profl. jours. Mem. bd. visitors Abilene (Tex.) Christian U., 1985—, eval. team Okla. State U. Ctr. Local Govt.Tech., 1975. Grantee Research Corp., 1973, USDA Food and Nutrition Service, Washington, 1979; recipient Carl Marshall award Okla. State U., 1980. Mem. AAAS, Am. Statis. Assn. (pres. Okla. chpt. 1983-84, mem. energy stats. com., adv. group for Energy Info. Adminstrn.), Internat. Assn. Math. Geology, Internat. Biometric Soc., Am. Soc. Quality Control, Colo. Alliance Sci. (vis. scientist), Sigma Xi. Democrat. Mem. Ch. Christ. Avocations: sailing, skiing, travel, hand-made pottery. Home: 7350 S Eudora Ct Littleton CO 80122 Office: Marathon Oil Co 7400 S Broadway Littleton CO 80122

COCANOWER, DAVID LEHMAN, lawyer; b. Elkhart, Ind., Dec. 3, 1939; s. Glen Merl and Augusta Mae (Lehman) C.; m. Liana Cheryl Miller, Sept. 21, 1983; 1 child, Emily Elizabeth; children by previous marriage: Michael Whitten, Joseph Charles. BS with high distinction, Ind. U., 1967, JD magna cum laude, 1970. Bar: Ariz. 1970, U.S. Dist. Ct. Ariz. 1970, U.S. Ct. Appeals (9th cir.) 1970. Assoc., Lewis and Roca, Phoenix, 1970-73, ptnr., 1973—; chmn. sect. corp. banking and bus. law State Bar Ariz., 1978-79. Articles editor Ind. U. Law Jour., 1969-70. Bd. dirs. Ariz. Kidney Found., 1978-82, Hospice of the Valley, Phoenix, 1977-82, Neighborhood Housing Services of Phoenix, 1976-78, Phoenix Integrated Surgical Residency Program Found., Inc., 1980—. Served with USN, 1961-65. Mem. ABA (Ariz. liaison com. corp. laws 1979—), Maricopa County Bar Assn., Nat. Assn. Bond Lawyers, Indiana U. Alumni Club of Phoenix (pres. 1976-77), Order of Coif, Beta Gamma Sigma, Beta Alpha Psi, Phi Delta Phi, Delta Sigma Pi, Tau Kappa Epsilon. Republican. Presbyterian. Clubs: Ariz., Mansion. Lodge: Rotary (pres. Phoenix East 1981-82, dir. 1979-84, dist. 549 gov. 1987-88). Office: Lewis and Roca 100 W Washington St 22d Floor Phoenix AZ 85003

COCANOWER, LIANA CHERYL, lawyer; b. Salt Lake City, June 19, 1953; d. Elbert Ernest and Dorothy June (Smith) Miller; m. Michael A. Thiessen, Aug., 1973 (div. 1975); m. Michael Andrew Maher, Oct. 15, 1975 (div. Feb. 1981); m. David Lehman Cocanower, Sept. 21, 1983; children—Michael Whitten, Joseph Charles, Emily Elizabeth. B.E., Western Wash. State Coll., 1973; J.D., McGeorge Sch. Law, U. Pacific, 1979; LL.M. in Taxation, NYU, 1980. Bar: Calif. 1979, Ariz. 1980. Assoc. Lewis and Roca, Phoenix, 1980-85, ptnr., 1985-87; assoc. Storey & Ross, 1987—. Served with USAF, 1975-76. Mem. ABA (tax sect., com. small bus., coauthor ann. report on recent devels. in small bus., real property, probate and trust div., vice chmn. com on spl. problems of bus. owners), Calif. State Bar, Ariz. State Bar (cert. tax specialist, tax sect.), Phi Delta Phi. Republican. Presbyterian. Home: 202 E McLellan Blvd Phoenix AZ 85012 Office: Storey & Ross 4742 N 24th St Ct One 4th Floor Phoenix AZ 85016

COCHRAN, ANNE WESTFALL, public relations executive; b. Cairo, Ill., Sept. 16, 1954; d. Howard Thurston and Flora Isabelle (Stone) Westfall; m. Charles Eugene Cochran, June 14, 1975; 1 child. BA in Advt., So. Ill. U., 1974; MA in Communications, U. Wis., Milw., 1975. Dir. advt. Sight and Sound Systems Inc., Milw., 1975-76; nat. publicity/promotions mgr. 20th Century Fox Classics, Los Angeles, 1981-85; nat. publicity dir. Cannon Films Inc., Los Angeles, 1985-86; publicist, staff writer Warner Bros. Inc., Burbank, Calif., 1986-87; v.p. mktg. Cinetel Films, Inc., Los Angeles, 1987; dir. nat. publicity and promotion Cineplex Odeon Films, Inc., Los Angeles, 1987—; mktg. cons., Los Angeles, 1976-81; freelance publicity writer, Los Angeles, 1982-86; mem. Ind. Feature Project West, Los Angeles, 1985-86. Mem. Los Angeles Conservancy, 1986. Mem. Publicists Guild. Democrat. Mem. Ch. Religious Sci. Home: 1632 N Dillon St Los Angeles CA 90026 Office: Cinetel Films Inc 9200 Sunset Blvd Suite 1215 Los Angeles CA 90060

COCHRAN, DONALD JAMES, audio products manufacturing executive, consultant; b. Riverside, Calif., June 20, 1935; s. Burke Baihley and Joyce Irene (McWilliams) C.; m. Patricia Ann Yetter, 1965 (div. 1968); 1 child, Scott Allen. Engr. IBM Corp., Poughkeepsie, N.Y., 1954-60, Ampex Corp., Redwood City, Calif., 1960-65; staff cons. Echo Sci. Corp., Mountain View, Calif., 1965-74; chief engr. Merlin Engring., Palo Alto, Calif., 1974-77; propr. Design Cons., San Mateo, Calif., 1977-85; owner, operator Don J Cochran Inc., Palo Alto, Calif., 1985—. Patentee in field. Mem. Soc. Motion Picture and TV Engrs., Audio Engring. Soc. Avocations: astrophysics, photography. Home: 2012 King's Ln San Mateo CA 94402 Office: 1900 Embarcadero Rd Palo Alto CA 94303

COCHRAN, FRED L(LOYD), author, editor, nuclear science consultant; b. Hobart, Ind., July 24, 1936; s. Fred G. and Grace Jewel (Stark) C.; m. Joan Boertje, Dec. 19, 1959; children—Elizabeth, Danielle. Lab. chemist U.S. Steel Corp., Gary, Ind., 1954-55; research asst. materials research Collins Radio Co., Burbank, Calif., 1955-56; sr. research analyst Atomics Internat., Canoga Park, Calif., 1956-58, research engr., 1958-60; research chemist Culligan Inc., San Bernardino Calif., 1958-59; chief metallographer Gulf Gen. Atomic Inc., San Diego, 1960-72; corr. AP, 1971; editor-in-chief Mountain Messenger, v.p. Roos-Cochran Publs., Downieville, Calif., 1973—; mem. com. on metallography AEC. Served with USAFR 1954-62. Mem. Internat. Metallographic Soc. (co-founder, v.p. 1967-72), Am. Nuclear Soc., ASTM, Am. Soc. Metals, Internat. Microstructural Analysis Soc., Authors League (N.Y.C.), Authors Guild, Sigma Delta Chi. Republican. Jewish. Author: Handbook of Optical Metallography, 1968-70; 5 novels. Editor: Metallography, an Internat. Jour., 1968-73; U.S. editor Metallographie, 1968-74. Contbr. articles to sci. publs. Home: PO Box 475 Downieville CA 95936 Office: The Mountain Messenger Downieville CA 95936

COCHRAN, JAMES ALAN, mathematics educator; b. San Francisco, May 12, 1936; s. Commodore Shelton and Gwendolyn Audrey (Rosenau) C.; m. Katherine Koehler Kern, Sept. 6, 1958; children: Cynthia Royal, Sarah Lynn. BS in Physics, Stanford U., 1956, MS in Physics, 1957; PhD in Math., Stanford U., 1962. Mem. tech. staff, supr. applied math. Bell Telephone Labs.Inc., Whippany, N.J., 1962-72; prof. math. Va. Poly. Inst. and State U., Blacksburg, 1972-78; prof., chmn. dept. math. Wash. State U., Pullman, 1978—; vis. prof. math. Stanford U., 1968-69, Wash. State U., 1977, U. New South Wales, Sydney, Australia, 1985, Deakin U., Victoria, Australia, 1987; fgn. scholar math. and mechanics Nanjing (People's Republic China) Inst. Tech., 1984; vis. fellow Deakin U., Victoria, Australia, 1985. Author: Analysis of Linear Integral Equations, 1972, Applied Mathematics: Principles, Techniques, and Applications, 1982, Advanced Engineering Mathematics, 1987; also articles. Mem. nat. council Boy Scouts Am., 1973-76; chmn bd. commrs. Morris County (N.J.) Area Library System, 1971-72. Gordon vis. fellow, Deakin U., Victoria, Australia, 1985. Mem. Am. Math. Soc., Math. Assn. Am., Soc. Indsl. Applied Math., Nat. Eagle Scout Assn. (young man pres. 1957-58, adviser 1958-71, Disting. Service award 1976), Phi Beta Kappa, Sigma Xi, Golden Key, Alpha Phi Omega. Republican. Presbyterian. Home: SE 825 Derby St Pullman WA 99163 Office: Wash State U Dept Math Pullman WA 99164

COCHRAN, JOHN ROBERT, hospital administrator; b. Chgo., Apr. 27, 1945; s. John Robert and Patricia (Parker) C.; m. Kathryn Neilsen, July 22, 1972; children: John Robert IV, Colin Michael. BS, U. Oreg., 1966, MS, 1968; cert., Harvard U., 1978. Legis. dir. Los Angeles County Dept. Health, 1968-72; assoc. fin., dir. Cedars-Sinai Hosp., Los Angeles, 1972-75; fin. dir. Children's Hosp., Oakland, Calif., 1975-78; assoc. dir. U. Hosp., Columbia, Mo., 1978-82; sr. v.p. Verdugo Hills Hosp., Glendale, Calif., 1982-86; chief exec. officer La Palma (Calif.) Hosp., 1986—. Chmn. glendale United Way, 1983-84; mem. fund raising com. YMCA, La Canada, Calif., 1985—; bd. dirs. Vis. Nurse Assn., Glendale, 1984—. Served with U.S. Army 1968-74. Mem. Am. Coll. Hosp. Adminstrn., Hosp. Fin. Mgmt. Assn. (advanced), Hosp. Council (chmn. legis. com. 1984-85). Lodge: Kiwanis.

COCHRAN, MARY KATHRYN, school psychologist; b. Ft. Wayne, Ind., June 30, 1942; d. Joseph Leo and Ruth Pearl (Pelkey) Oddou; m. Farlene Obert Cochran, Aug. 9, 1965 (div. June 1973); children: Ronald, Julianne. BS in Edn., Ohio U., 1963; MS in Counseling, Calif. State U., Long Beach, 1981. Cert. tchr., Calif. Tchr. Long Beach Unified Sch. Dist., 1963-80; counselor &, 1980-85, sch. psychologist, 1986—. Mem. Assn. of Long Beach Edn. Mgrs. (sec. 1984-85), Long Beach Pupil Personnel Assn. (elem. rep. 1983-86), Calif. Sch. Counselors Assn. (area rep. S. Los Angeles County 1984-86), Delta Kappa Gamma. Republican. Roman Catholic. Avocations: tennis, travel. Home: 6351 Santa Catalina Garden Grove CA 92645 Office: Long Beach Unified Sch Dist 701 Locust Long Beach CA 90813

COCHRAN, PATRICIA LUELLA, small business owner; b. Modesto, Calif., Nov. 13, 1944; d. L.V. and Mary Pauline (Wilson) Ingram; m. Ronald Lee Campbell, May 13, 1961 (div. Apr. 1984); children: Rebecca Lyn, Ronald Lee Jr., Patrick Lawrence, Sherri Anne; m. Adrian Lester Cochran, June 20, 1984. Student, Modesto Jr. Coll., 1971-72, diploma, 1981; diploma, CLS Design Acad., 1983; student, U. Calif., Berkeley, 1983—; cert., Keye Productivity Ctr., 1984; mem. Lic. cosmetologist and instr., Calif. Foreclosure officer Cen. State Title Ins. Co., Modesto, 1974-79; bookkeeper North Adrians, Modesto, 1979-82; instr. Adrians Beauty Coll., Modesto, 1982-84, also bd. dirs. Author: Adrians Beauty College Student Handbook, 1985. Mem. Nat. Assn. Cosmetology Schs. (diploma 1985), Calif. Cosmetology Assn. Democrat. Office: 950 Oakdale Rd Suite N Modesto CA 95350

COCHRAN, PATRICK HOLMES, research soil scientist; b. Guthrie Center, Iowa, Oct. 14, 1937; s. Bert Frank Cochran and Mildred (Holmes) Dennis; m. Joan Marie Meland, June 10, 1961; children: Tamara, Lyle, Wayne. BS in Forestry, Iowa State U., 1959; MS in Soils, Oreg. State U., 1963, PhD in Soils, 1966. Asst. prof. silviculture SUNY, Syracuse, 1966-67; research soil scientist USDA Forest Service, Bend, Oreg., 1967—. Contbr. articles to profl. jours. Served as pvt. U.S. Army, 1959-60. Mem. Soc. Am. Foresters, Am. Soc. Agronomy, Oreg. Soc. Soil Scientists, Sigma Xi. Republican. Baptist. Avocations: reading, fishing. Home: 480 SE Airpark Dr Bend OR 97702 Office: USDA Silviculture Lab 1027 NE Trenton Ave Bend OR 97701

COCHRAN, RUTH ELAINE BEARDSLEY, nurse, ethicist, philosopher, instructor; b. El Paso, Tex., June 14, 1936; d. David Albert and Theona Elaine (Lambert) Beardsley; m. Thomas Crowther Cochran Jr., Sept. 17, 1958; children: Thomas David, Laura Elaine. BS in Nursing, U. Utah, 1958; MA, U. Colo., 1975, PhD, 1985. RN, Utah, Colo. Staff and asst. head nurse Bernalillo County Indian Hosp., Albuquerque, 1958-59; instr. nursing Columbus Hosp. and Sch. Nursing, Great Falls, Mont., 1960-61, St. Margaret's Hosp. and Sch. Nursing, Montgomery, Ala., 1967-68; instr. philosophy Pikes Peak Community Coll., Colorado Springs, Colo., 1980—, U. So. Colo., Pueblo, 1986—; cons. private clients and institutions, 1985—; leader discussion groups Penrose Pub. Library, Colorado Springs, 1970-75. Writer, producer ednl. film Language Distortion and Propaganda Techniques, 1983-84. Friend, participant Hastings Ctr. Grantee NEH, 1982. Mem. Pikes Peak Weavers' Guild (pres. 1983-84). Democrat. Unitarian. Avocations: weaving, spinning, skiing, distance swimming. Home: 18060 E Forest Dr Monument CO 80132 Office: Pikes Peak Community Coll 5675 S Academy Blvd Colorado Springs CO 80906

COCHRANE, PEGGY, architect, writer; b. Alhambra, Calif., July 9, 1926; d. E. Elliott and Gladys (Moran) C.; B.A., Scripps Coll., 1945; postgrad., U. So. Calif., 1951-52, Columbia U., 1954; m. Hugh Bowman, Nov. 24, 1954 (div.). Job capt. Kahn and Jacobs, N.Y.C., 1954-55; project architect Litchfield, Whiting, Panero & Severud, Teheran, Iran, 1956; archtl. designer Daniel, Mann, Johnson and Mendenhall, Los Angeles, 1956-59; individual practice architecture, Sherman Oaks, Calif., 1966—. Recipient Architecture prize Scripps Coll., 1945. Mem. Assn. Women in Architecture (life), Union Internationale des Femmes Architects. Republican. Episcopalian. Club: Dionysians (S. Pasadena). Author (musical) Mayaland, 1979; (play) I Gave at the Office, 1980; The Witch Doctor's Manual, 1984; The Witch Doctors' Cookbook, 1984; mem. editorial bd. Los Angeles Architect, 1978—; contbr. to Contemporary Architects. Office: 14755 Ventura Blvd Suite 1-626 Sherman Oaks CA 91403

COCKBURN, ROBERT MILROY, physician, surgeon; b. Walla Walla, Wash., Feb. 4, 1928; s. George Samuel and Mildred Ione (Nettleship) C.; m. Gloria Fae Douma, June 12, 1955; children: Timothy Ryan, Dan Kinman, Brigitte Andrea. BA, U. Oreg., 1950, MS in Biochemistry, MD, 1955. Diplomate Am. Bd. Family Practice. Intern Multnomah County Hosp., Portland, Oreg., 1955-56; gen. practice medicine Portland, 1958—. Contbr. articles to profl. jours. Served to capt. USAR, 1956-58. Mem. AMA, Oreg. Med. Assn., Multnomah County Med. Soc., Am. Acad. Family Physicians (edn. commn. 1978-84), Oreg. Acad. Family Physicians (pres. 1983-84), , Sigma Xi. Republican. Episcopalian. Avocations: woodworking, stained glass, collections. Home: 10776 SE Idleman Rd Portland OR 97266 Office: Mt. Scott Med Ctr 9204 SE Mitchell Portland OR 97266

COCKE, JAMES WILL, banker, former army officer; b. Clarksville, Tenn., Apr. 6, 1917; s. James Gordon and Kate (Powell) C.; m. Marjorie Warwick, Oct. 26, 1941 (dec. 1961); 1 child, Robert D.; m. Joan Waterson, Oct. 31, 1964; stepchildren: David Hopping, Spencer B. Hopping, Ann Louise Hopping, Amy Louise Hopping Horton. Student Vanderbilt U., 1938-54; BS, U. Md., 1958; postgrad., U. Ariz., 1961-63; student Indsl. Coll. Armed Forces, 1960-61. Commd. 2d. lt., U.S. Army, 1940, advanced through grades to lt. col., 1961; instr. U.S. Army Cavalry Sch., 1945-46, U.S. Army Ground Gen. Sch., 1947-49, U.S. Army Armor Sch., 1959-61; prof. mil. sci. Vanderbilt U., 1954-57; with Valley Nat. Bank, Tucson, 1963-84; asst. v.p., 1968-73, v.p. econ. div. dept., 1973-83, v.p. corp. affairs, 1983-84; prin. James W. Cocke & Assocs., devel., mktg. and pub. affairs service cons., 1984—; lectr. mktg. and pub. relations, econ. devel. to various civic and coll. groups; mem. assoc. faculty Pima Community Coll. Bus. and Mgmt. Contbr. articles to mil. jours. Bd. dirs. Tucson Festival Soc., 1963-69, Jr. Achievement Tucson, 1963-69; chmn. community growth and devel. and objectives sub-com. Pima Community Coll., 1966; pres. Tucson Child Guidance Clinic, 1968-69, Tucson Council of the Arts, 1968-70; bd. dirs. Pima County Real Estate Research Council, 1969—, chmn. 1973-74, sec. treas. emeritus 1985—; pres. Tucson Trade Bur., 1970-71, Ariz. Tng. Ctr. for The Handicapped, 1971-73; mem. Tucson Regional Planning Bd., 1972—, Ariz. Assn. for Indsl. Devel., 1973-86, water com. Pima Assn. of Govts., 1977-78, Tucson Com. on Foreign Relations, 1978-80, Citizens Water Adv. Com. City of Tucson, 1979-83, Community Adv. Bd. Stas. KUAT-TV AM-FM Pub. Radio, 1979-82, Ariz. Dist. Export Council, U.S. Dept. Commerce, 1983—; bd. dirs. Ariz. Econ. Devel. Council, 1973-84, chmn., 1978; mem. City of Tucson Overall Econ. Planning Com., CETA Adv. Com., 1978—; v.p. OEPC, 1979-82, chmn. 1982—; chmn. Trunk 'N' Tusk com. Pima County Republican Club, 1979-80; pres. Pima Coll. Found., 1983—; treas. So. Ariz. Water Resources Assn. Bd., 1982-84; v.p. Pima County Acad. Decathlon Assn., 1983—. Mem. Flecha Caida Homeowners Assn. (pres. 1970-76), Mil. Order of World Wars and Retired Officers Assn. (life), U. Md. Alumni Assn. (life), Tucson Met. C. of C. (gen. chmn. Tucson Town Hall on Community Devel. 1974, chmn. task force on comprehensive planning 1973-74, chmn. 1967-68, chmn. Internat. Trade com. 1986—, bd. dirs. 1973-74, Chmn. of Yr. 1968), Tucson Ret. Officers Assn. (pres. 1981), U.S. Army Assn. So. Ariz., Tucson Marching and Chowders Soc., U. Md. Alumni Assn., Vanderbilt U. Alumni Assn. Presbyterian. Clubs: Old Pueblo, Davis Monthan AFB Officers. Lodge: Rotary. Home and Office: 4045 La Cadena Ave Tucson AZ 85702

COCKRELL, WILLIAM JASPER, III, accountant; b. Jacksonville, Fla., July 7, 1942; s. William Jasper and Bethel Aurora (Hughes) C.; BSBA, Calif. State Coll., Los Angeles, 1968; MBT, U. So. Calif., 1974; MBA, Pepperdine U., 1978; m. Sharon Lee Gerrie, Sept. 9, 1967. Tax supr. Laventhol & Horwath, Los Angeles, 1973-74; prin. Palmer, Wiggs & Heston, Agana, Guam, 1974-75; tax supr. Laventhol & Horwath, Los Angeles, 1975-76; tax mgr. Arthur Young & Co., Beverly Hills, Calif., 1977-78, Price, Waterhouse & Co., Newport Beach, Calif., 1978-79; pvt. practice acctg., Newport Beach, 1979—; bd. dirs. MBAN V, Inc., Newport Beach, CCC Steel, Inc., Compton, Calif.; instr. Northrop U., 1976-77. Co-trustee T.F. Haller Trust, 1978—. Served with USN, 1960-61. CPA, Calif., Guam. Mem. Am. Inst. CPA's, Calif. Soc. CPA's (ethics com., taxation com.), U. So. Calif. Alumni Assn., Newport Beach-Irvine Estate Planning Council, Phi Kappa Tau. Clubs: Athletic (Los Angeles), 1000, Acctg. Circle (U. So. Calif.). Contbr. articles to profl. jours. Office: PO Box 337 Balboa Island CA 92662

COCKRUM, ELMER LENDELL, biology educator; b. Sesser, Ill.; s. Ernest Elmer and Alta May (Quillman) C.; m. Irma Pauline Schutte, Nov. 9, 1943; children: David Lendell, Ward Andrew. BEd, So. Ill. U., 1942; PhD, U. Kans., 1951. Postdoctorate research assoc. U. Kans., Lawrence, 1951-52; asst. prof. zoology U. Ariz., Tucson, 1952-55, curator of mammals, 1955-76, assoc. prof., 1959-63, prof., 1963—, dir. Desert Biology Sta., 1966-67, prof. biol. scis., 1967-76, mammalogist Agrl. Experiment Sta., 1971-76, acting head dept. ecology and evolutionary biology, 1976-77, head dept., 1977-85; desert ecologist U.S. AID/MIT Sahel Drought Project, 1973-74. Author: Mammals of the Southwest 1982; cons. editor Encyclopedia Americana, 1980—; contbr. articles to profl. jours. Served to lt. USNR, 1942-45. Research grantee Smithsonian Inst., 1972-75. Fellow AAAS, Ariz.-Nev. Acad. Sci.; mem. Am. Soc. Mammalogists (life). Presbyterian. Club: Ariz. Philatelic Rangers. Lodge: Elks. Home: 846 W Palma de Coco Tucson AZ 85704 Office: U of Ariz Ecology & Evolutionary Biology Tucson AZ 85721

COCKRUM, WILLIAM MONROE, III, investment banker, consultant, educator; b. Indpls., July 18, 1937; s. William Monroe II C. and Katherine J. (Jaqua) Moore; m. Andrea Lee Deering, Mar. 8, 1975; children: Catherine Anne, William Monroe, IV. A.B. with distinction, DePauw U., Greencastle, Ind., 1959; M.B.A. with distinction, Harvard U., 1961. With A.G. Becker Paribas Inc., 1961-84, mgr. nat. corp. fin. div., 1968-71; mgr. pvt. investments A.G. Becker Paribas Inc., Los Angeles, 1971-84; fin. and adminstrv. officer A.G. Becker Paribas Inc., 1974-80, sr. v.p., 1975-78, vice chmn., 1978-84, also dir.; mem. faculty Northwestern U., 1961-63; UCLA Grad. Sch. Mgmt., 1984—; dir. Knapp Communications Corp., Cinema Capital Mgmt., Inc. ; trustee Bruin-Trojan Superstar Classic; vis. lectr. UCLA Grad. Sch. Mgmt., 1984—. Mem. Delta Kappa Epsilon. Clubs: University (Chgo.); Monterey (Palm Desert, Calif); Deke (N.Y.C.); Alisal Golf (Soluang, Calif.).

COCKS, GEORGE GOSSON, chemical microscopy educator; b. Sioux City, Iowa, Mar. 22, 1919; s. George Green and Nellie Patricia (Gosson) C.; m. Marian L. Singer, May 11, 1942; children: Gary, Kathleen (Mrs. Thomas Sadlowski), Francis, Kenneth. B.S. in Chemistry, Iowa State U., 1941; Ph.D. in Chem. Microscopy, Cornell, 1949. Researcher Battelle Meml. Inst., Columbus, Ohio, 1949-64; prof. chem. microscopy Cornell U., 1964-81, prof. emeritus, 1981—; cons. Los Alamos Sci. Lab., 1980-81, staff mem. chem. microscopy dept., 1981—. Scoutmaster Central Ohio council Boy Scouts Am., 1956-64. Served to lt. comdr. USNR, 1942-45. NSF grantee to study crystallization inorganic materials in polymers, 1966-68, to study biomed. uses collagen, 1972—. Fellow AAAS (council 1970-75); mem. Am. Optical Soc., Am. Soc. Metals, Am. Chem. Soc., Electron Microscopy Soc. Am. (exec. sec. 1964-76), Sigma Xi, Phi Kappa Phi. Patentee in field. Home: 549 Todd Loop Los Alamos NM 87544 Office: Los Alamos Nat Lab Mail Stop J979 Los Alamos NM 87544

COE, DAVID KELLY, university management consultant, educator, philosopher, author; b. Seattle, Oct. 31, 1941; s. Foster Witham and Maxine Milton (Kelly) C.; m. Patricia Grace Smith, 1970 (div. 1973); m. Barbara Ann Wright, May 31, 1975. BA, U. Hawaii, 1969, MA, 1971, PhD, 1981. Grad. teaching asst. in philosophy U. Hawaii at Manoa, Honolulu, 1970-73; dir. human resources coordination Colo. R-9 Commn., Durango, 1975-77; dir. Colo. INVEST program Colo. State Bd for Community Colls., Denver, 1977-81; dir. adult edn. Regis Coll., Denver, 1982-83; dir. Rocky Mountain mgmt. seires U. Colo., Denver, 1983-86; dir. Assn. Bay Area Govts. Tng. Inst., 1986—; pres. Denver chpt. Am. Soc. Pub. Adminstrn., 1981-82, pres. Colo. chpt., 1976-80. Author: Angst and the Abyss, 1985; contbr. articles to profl. jours. Mem. Colo. Right-to Read Acad., 1978-80; bd. dirs. high cardinal Lifespring, Inc. Leadership program, Denver, 1985—. Mem. Am. Soc. Tng. and Devel., Denver Art Mus. Avocations: classical guitar, fiction writing, aerobic exercise, jogging, cross-country skiing. Home: 1 Embarcadero W #353 Oakland CA 94607 Office: Assn Bay Area Govts Tng Inst PO Box 2050 Oakland CA 94604

COE, JOHN EMMONS, research immunologist; b. Evanston, Ill., Sept. 1, 1931; s. Emmons S. and Lillian E. (Beckman) C.; m. Nancy Rowland, June 18, 1954; children—Kristine Wing Coe-Sutton, Anne Lindstrom, Paul Rowland. B.A., Oberlin Coll., 1953; M.D., Hahnemann Med. Coll., 1957. Intern, U. Ill. Research and Ednl. Hosp., Chgo., 1957-58; resident in medicine U. Colo. Med. Ctr., Denver, 1958-60; surgeon USPHS, NIH, Hamilton, Mont., 1960-63; fellow dept. pathology Scripps Clinic and Research Found., La Jolla, Calif., 1963-65; med. officer Nat. Inst. Allergy and Infectious Diseases, NIH Rocky Mountain Lab., Hamilton, 1965—; affiliated prof. dept microbiology U. Mont., Missoula, 1966—. Contbr. articles to sci. jours. Pres. bd. dirs. Mill Lake Irrigation Dist., 1982—. Mem. Am. Assn. Immunologists, Hamster Soc. (pres. 1983-84), Soc. to Preserve Mauser, Alpha Omega Alpha. Clubs: Lacrosse (pres. 1965—), Handball (Hamilton). Home: NW 986 Orchard Dr Hamilton MT 59840 Office: Rocky Mountain Lab NIH Hamilton MT 59840

COE, RICHARD NELSON, French educator; b. Rustington, Eng., Oct. 27, 1923; s. Frederick Augustus and Stella Mary (Caslon) C.; m. Valentina Stefanovna Jukova, Sept. 3, 1949 (div. 1963); children: Antonia, Andrew; m. Ada Biagi, Feb. 3, 1972; children: Terance, Dominic, Laura-Julia. Acad. diploma in Bulgarian, U. London, 1943; BA and MA in Modern Langs., Oxford (Eng.) U., 1949; postgrad., Sorbonne U., Paris, 1949-50; PhD in French, U. Leeds, Eng., 1954. Lectr. U. Leeds, 1950-62; sr. lectr. U. Queensland, Brisbane, Australia, 1962-63; reader U. Melbourne, Australia, 1963-

66, 69-72; prof. U. Warwick, Coventry, Eng., 1966-69, 72-79; prof. French U. Calif., Davis, 1979—. Author: Morelly, 1961, Ionesco, 1961, Beckett, 1964, Genet, 1968, When the Grass Was Taller, 1985; contbr. articles to scholarly jours.; mem. editorial bd. Stand, 1959-62, Australian Jour. French Studies, 1963—, Comparison, 1975-85, New Comparison, 1986—. Served with British Army, 1943-46. Fellow Humanities Research Council, 1976, Can. Council, 1976. Fellow Australian Acad. of the Humanities (ann. address 1976). Club: Arts Theater (London). Avocations: cookery, detective stories. Office: U Calif Dept French and Italian Sproul Hall 508 Davis CA 95616

COE, WILLIAM CHARLES, psychology educator; b. Hanford, Calif., Oct. 22, 1930; s. Bernard and Bertha (Vaughan) C.; children: Karen Ann, William Vaughan. B.S., U. Calif., Davis, 1958; postgrad., Fresno State Coll., 1960-61; Ph.D. (NSF fellow), U. Calif., Berkeley, 1964. Research helper Fresno State Coll., 1960-61; research asst. U. Calif., Berkeley, 1961-62, 63-64; NSF research fellow U. Calif., 1963-64; clin. psychology trainee VA Hosp., San Francisco, 1962-63; staff psychologist Langley Porter Neuropsychiat. Inst., San Francisco, 1964-66; pvt. practice psychology Fresno, Calif., 1965—; asst. clin. prof. med. psychology U. Calif. Sch. Medicine, San Francisco, 1965-66; instr. corr. div. U. Calif., Berkeley, 1967-76; asst. prof. psychology Fresno State Coll., 1966-68; assoc. prof. psychology Calif. State U., Fresno, 1968-72; prof. Calif. State U., 1972—, chmn. dept. psychology, 1979-84; instr. Calif. Sch. Profl. Psychology, Fresno, 1973, Northeastern U., Boston, 1974; research assoc. U. Calif., Santa Cruz, 1975; cons. Tulare and Kings County Mental Health Clinics, Kingsview Corp., 1966-68, Visalia Unified Sch. Dist., 1967-68; Head Start Program, Fresno, 1970-71, Fig Garden Hosp., Fresno, 1972-73, Concentrated Employment Program, Fresno, 1973-74, VA Hosp., Fresno, 1974. Author: (with T.R. Sarbin) The Student Psychologists Handbook: A Guide to Source, 1969, Hypnosis: A Social Psychological Analysis of Influence Communication, 1972, Challenges of Personal Adjustment, 1972, (with L. Gagnon and D. Swiercinsky) instructors Manual for Challenges of Personal Adjustment, 1972, Psychology X118: Psychological Adjustment, 1973, (with T.R. Sarbin) Mastering Psychology, 1984; Contbr.: chpts. to Behavior Modification in Rehabiliation Settings, 1975, Helping People Change, 1975, 80, Encyclopedia of Clinical Assessment, 1980; contbr. articles to profl. jours. Served with USAF, 1951-55. Decorated D.F.C., Air medal with oak leaf cluster.; NSF grantee, 1967, 71. Fellow Am. Psychol. Assn. (pres. div. 30 psychol. hypnosis 1986-87); fellow Soc. for Clin. and Exptl. Hypnosis; mem. Western Psychol Assn., Calif. Psychol Assn., San Francisco Psychol Assn. (editor San Francisco Psychologist 1966), Central Calif. Psychol. Assn. (pres. 1969, dir. 1972-73), Assn. for Advancement Behavior Therapy, Phi Beta Kappa, Sigma Xi, Phi Kappa Phi, Psi Chi. Office: Dept Psychology Calif State U Fresno CA 93740

COELHO, TONY, congressman; b. Los Banos, Calif., June 15, 1942; s. Otto and Alice (Branco) C.; m. Phyllis Butler, June 10, 1967; children: Nicole, Kristin. B.A., Loyola U., Los Angeles, 1964. Agr. asst. to Rep. B.F. Sisk, 1965-70, adminstrv. asst., 1970-78; mem. 96th-100th Congresses from 15th Calif. Dist.; majority whip-at-large 96th-100th Congresses; majority whip 100th Congress; sec.-treas. United Democrats for Congress; chmn. Dem. Congressional Campaign Com.; mem. Dem. Steering and Policy Com. Mem. nat. implementation task force Epilepsy Found. Am. Roman Catholic. Office: 403 Cannon House Office Bldg Washington DC 20515

COFFEY, MARVIN DALE, biology educator; b. Midvale, Idaho, Apr. 25, 1930; s. Raymond Stanfield and Agnes (Hutchinson) C.; m. Wanda Kirchgestner, June 6, 1952; children: Susan, Gregory, Lorilee, Mark, Todd. Student, Whitman Coll., 1948-49; AB in Zoology, Brigham Young U., 1952, MA, 1953; PhD in Entomology, Wash. State U., 1957. Instr. dept. biology So. Oreg. State Coll., Ashland, 1957-59, asst. prof., 1959-63, assoc. prof., 1963-67, prof., 1967—, chmn. dept. biology, 1965-70; asst. prof. biology Fresno (Calif.) State Coll., 1964-65; vis. prof. U. Ky., Lexington, 1976-77, Tex. A&M U., Coll. Sta., 1969-70; cons. in field. Contbr. articles to profl. jours. Mem. AAAS, Am. Inst. Biol. Scis., Entomol. Soc. Am., Wash. State Entomol. Soc., Oreg. Entomol. Soc. Mormon. Office: So Oreg State Coll Dept Biology Ashland OR 97520

COFFEY, PHILIP JOHN, civil engineer; b. Holyoke, Mass., Dec. 6, 1910; s. John and Mildred (Knappett) C.; B.S. in Civil Engring. (scholar 1930-32), MIT, 1933; M.A. in Journalism, U. Colo., 1970; m. Lydia Spomer, Aug. 15, 1942; 1 son, Cecil. With USPHS, Chgo., San Francisco, Addis Ababa, Ethiopia. Cin., Denver, 1936-42, 57-68, san. engr. dir., until 1968; san. hydraulic engr. Calif. Depts. Fin. and Water Resources, San Francisco, Sacramento, 1946-48, 51-57; engr. Inst. Inter-Am. Affairs, Asuncion, Paraguay, 1949-51; spl. exam. commr. Calif. Bd. Registration for Profl. Engrs., Sacramento, 1952; mem. tech. adv. com. Calif. Senate Com. Radiation Protection, Sacramento, 1956-57; mem. faculty Water and Sewage Plant Operators' Sch., U. Colo., 1966-67. Served to lt. col., C.E., AUS, 1942-46. Registered profl. engr., Calif., Colo. Mem. Ret. Officers Assn., DAV, Kappa Tau Alpha. Lodge: Masons. Contbr. articles to tech. publs. Address: 67 S Benton Dr Lakewood CO 80226

COFFILL, MARJORIE LOUISE (MRS. WILLIAM CHARLES COFFILL), civic leader; b. Sonora, Calif., June 11, 1917; d. Eric J. and Pearl (Needham) Segerstrom; A.B. with distinction in Social Sci., Stanford U., 1938, M.A. in Edn., 1941; m. William Charles Coffill, Jan. 25, 1948; children—William James, Eric John. Asst. mgr. Sonora Abstract & Title Co. (Calif.), 1938-39; mem. dean of women's staff Stanford, 1939-41; social dir. women's campus Pomona Coll., 1941-43, instr. psychology, 1941-43; asst. to field dir. ARC, Lee Moore AFB, Calif., 1944-46; partner Riverbank Water Co., Riverbank and Hughson, Calif., 1950-68. Mem. Tuolumne County Mental Health Adv. Com., 1963-70; mem. central advisory council Supplementary Edn. Center, Stockton, Calif., 1966-70; mem. advisory com. Columbia Jr. Coll., 1972—, pres., 1980—; pres. Columbia Found., 1972-74, bd. dirs., 1974-77; mem. Tuolumne County Bicentennial Com., 1974—; active PTA, ARC. Pres., Tuolumne County Republican Women, 1952—, asso. mem. Calif. Rep. Central Com., 1950. Trustee Sonora Union High Sch., 1969-73, Salvation Army Tuolumne County, 1973—; bd. dirs. Lung Assn. Valley Lode Counties, 1974—. Recipient Pi Lambda Theta award, 1940; Outstanding Citizen award C. of C., 1974. Mem. AAUW (charter mem. Tuolumne County br., pres. Sonora br. 1965-66). Episcopalian (mem. vestry 1968, 75). Home: 376 E Summit Ave Sonora CA 95370

COFFMAN, DAVID RICHARD, lawyer, investigator; b. Swindon, Eng., Feb. 4, 1946; came to U.S., 1946 (parents Am. citizens); s. Richard and Mary Nanette (Gregg) C.; m. Patricia Anne Kipp, Oct. 7, 1972; children—Allison, Julia. B.A. cum laude, Widener U., 1971; J.D., Del. Law Sch., 1979. Bar. D.C. 1982. Investigator Organized Crime Task Force, Phila., 1972-78; regional inspector gen. U.S. Dept. Labor, Phila., 1978-80, dir. Office of Investigation, Washington, 1980-83, spl. agent-in-charge, western regional ops. racketeering Office of Labor, Los Angeles, 1983-85; mng. atty. Law Offices of Larry Parker, Long Beach, Calif., 1985—. Editor: Prosecutor's Desk Ref., 1982. Served to capt. U.S. Army, 1967-69. Temple U. fellow, Phila., 1971. Mem. ABA, Assn. Trial Lawyers Am., Calif. Bar Assn., D.C. Bar Assn. Republican. Lutheran.

COFFMAN, RIST JAMES, sales manager; b. Emporia, Kans., Sept. 19, 1942; s. Harry Deward and Bertha Lois (Farmer) C.; m. LoRie JoAnn Loomis, June 4, 1966; 1 child, Mattson Joel. Student in Bus. Adminstrn., Emporia State U., 1960-64. Meat cutter, clk., store mgr. Coffman's Food Market, Emporia, 1952-66; sales mgr. H.J. Heinz Co., Denver, New Orleans and Mobile, Ala., 1966-74; sr. dist. mgr. Kitchens of Sara Lee, Southwestern U.S. states, Hawaii, 1974—. Deacon, landscape worker First Christian Ch. Irvine, Calif., 1983-85; fund-raiser Univ. High Sch. Football, Irvine, 1985. Mem. Frozen Food Council So. Calif. Republican. Mem. First Christian Ch. Avocations: weight-lifting, football, evangelism, travel. Office: Kitchens of Sara Lee 3360 Paseo Halcon San Clemente CA 92672

COGAN, RONALD JAMES, writer, editor and editorial services company executive; b. Cleve., Dec. 5, 1952; s. John Patrick and Alice Marie (Zollner) C.; m. Sheree K. Gardner, Nov. 20, 1982; children: Stefanie, Caitlin. Student, Calif. State Poly. U., Pomona, 1971-74. Staff writer newsletter Biomed. Safety and Standards, City of Industry, Calif., 1974; sr. staff writer Select Promotions, Irvine, Calif., 1975; sr. editor Petersen's Vans and Pickups/4 Wheel and Off-Road/Hot Rod Specialty Publs., Los Angeles, 1977-80; editor Custom Rodder mag., Anaheim, Calif., 1980; prin. R.J. Cogan and Assocs., Montclair, Calif., 1980—, Level One Prodns., Rancho Cucamonga, Calif., 1987—; co-pub. Foothills View mag., Rancho Cucamonga, 1980-83; cons. to mags. Editor: Hot Rod's Kit Car Ann. #2, 1981, Hot Rod's VW Classics Ann. #1, 1981, Petersen's Big Book of Volkswagens, 1981, Motor Trend's Road Tests, 1986, 87, Musclecar Classics, 1986, 4 Wheel and Off-Road Ann., 1986, 87, Car Craft Ann., 1987.

COGBURN, MARTIN ARTHUR, accountant, real estate broker; b. Fancy Hill, Ark.; s. Francis Marion and Mary Isabell (Beezeley) C.; student U. Calif. at Berkeley, 1932-34; B.S., Golden Gate U., 1940; grad. Realtors Inst.; m. Metta Naomi Stockdal, Feb. 18, 1956; children—Martin Arthur, Thomas Stockdal; children from previous marriage—Robert F., Nancy Ann. Instr., Golden Gate U., 1945-49; accountant, San Francisco, 1944—; prin. Cogburn Comml. Brokerage, San Francisco, 1963—, Cogburn Mortgage & Investment Co., San Francisco, 1963—. Councilman, City of Lafayette (Calif.), 1968-70; treas. Springhill Valley Assn., 1967; pres. Lafayette-Morage-Orinda Republican Assembly, 1967-68, 1970-73, congressional dist. state dir., 1971-73. C.P.A., Calif.; cert. comml. investment mem. Realtors Nat. Mktg. Inst. Mem. Calif. Soc. C.P.A.s, Calif., Nat. assns. realtors, San Francisco Bd. Realtors, Contra Costa Bd. Realtors, Sierra Club, Tower and Flame, Beta Alpha Phi. Republican. Clubs: Commonwealth, Masons, Shriners. Home: 3447 Black Hawk Rd Lafayette CA 94549 Office: 1910 Olympic Blvd Suite 314 Walnut Creek CA 94596

COGGESHALL, RANDY LYNN, composite materials research engineer; b. Garrett, Ind., Sept. 26, 1955; s. Ray Daniel Coggeshall and Carol Ann (Banta) Coggeshall Detwiler; m. Heidi Louise Anderson, Feb. 2, 1985. BSCE, Purdue U., 1977; MBA, Seattle U., 1986. Specialist engr. The Boeing Co., Seattle, 1977—; instr. The Boeing Co., Seattle, 1985—. Contbr. articles to profl. jours. Mem. AIAA, Soc. Advancement Materials and Process Engring. Republican. Avocation: bicycling. Home: 1015 N 48th Seattle WA 98103 Office: The Boeing Co PO Box 3707 MS6C-11 Seattle WA 98124

COGGIN, CHARLOTTE JOAN, cardiologist, educational administrator, educator; b. Takoma Park, Md., Aug. 6, 1928; d. Charles Benjamin and Nanette (McDonald) Coggin; B.A., Columbia Union Coll., 1948; M.D., Loma Linda U., 1952. Intern, Los Angeles County Gen. Hosp., Los Angeles, 1952-53, resident in medicine, 1953-55; fellow in cardiology Children's Hosp., Los Angeles, 1955-56, White Meml. Hosp., Los Angeles., 1955-56; research assoc. in cardiology, house physician Hammersmith Hosp., London, 1956-57; resident in pediatrics and pediatric cardiology Hosp. for Sick Children, Toronto, Ont., Can., 1965-67; cardiologist, co-dir. heart surgery team Loma Linda (Calif.) U., asst. prof. medicine , 1961-73, asso. prof., 1973—, asst. dean Sch. Medicine Internat. Programs, 1973-75, assoc. dean, 1975—, co-dir., cardiologist heart surgery team missions to Pakistan and Asia, 1963, Saigon, Vietnam, 1974, 75, to Saudi Arabia, 1976—, China, 1984, Hong Kong, 1985; mem. Pres.'s Advisory Panel on Heart Disease, 1972—. Appointed to Med. Quality Rev. Com.-Dist. 12, 1976-80. Recipient award for service to people of Pakistan City of Karachi, 1963, Medallion award Evangelismos Hosp., Athens, Greece, 1967, Gold medal of health South Vietnam Ministry of Health, 1974, Charles Elliott Weinger award for excellence, 1976; named Honored Alumnus Loma Linda U. Sch. Medicine, 1973, Outstanding Women in Gen. Conf. Seventh-day Adventists, 1975, Alumnus of Yr., Columbia Union Coll., 1984. Diplomate Am. Bd. Pediatrics. Mem. Am. Coll. Cardiology, AMA (physicians adv. com. 1969—) Calif. Med. Assn. (com. on med. schs., com. on member services), San Bernardino County Med. Assn. (chmn. communications com. 1975-77, editor bull. 1975-76), Am. Heart Assn., AAUP, Med. Research Assn. Calif., Calif. Heart Assn., AAUW, Am. Acad. Pediatrics, World Affairs Council, Internat. Platform Assn., Calif. Museum Sci. and Industry MUSES (Outstanding Woman of Year in Sci. 1969), Am. Med. Women's Assn., Loma Linda Sch. Medicine Alumni Assn. (pres. 1978), Alpha Omega Alpha. Author: Atrial Septal Defects, motion picture (Golden Eagle Cine award and 1st prize Venice Film Festival 1964); contbr. articles to med. jours. Democrat. Home: 11495 Benton St Loma Linda CA 92354 Office: Loma Linda U Med Ctr Loma Linda CA 92354

COGHLAN, PAUL, electronics executive; b. N.Y.C., June 12, 1945; s. Patrick J. and Nellie (McCormack) C.; m. Angela Sowa, Sept. 15, 1973; children: Nicole, Monica. BA, Boston Coll., 1966; MBA, Babson Coll., 1968. CPA, Mass. Mgr. Price Waterhouse, Paris, 1973-76; sr. mgr. Price Waterhouse, Boston, 1976-81; corp. controller GenRad, Inc., Waltham, Mass., 1981-83, v.p., 1984-86; v.p., gen. mgr. GenRad, Inc., Milpitas, Calif., 1985-86; v.p., chief fin. officer Linear Tech. Corp., Milipitas, Calif., 1986—. Mem. Am. Electronics Assn., Am. Inst. CPA's. Home: 686 Bicknell Rd Los Gatos CA 95030 Office: Linear Tech Corp 1630 McCarthy Blvd Milipitas CA 95035

COHEN, ALBERT DIAMOND, merchandising executive; b. Winnipeg, Man., Can., Jan. 20, 1914; s. Alexander and Rose (Diamond) C.; m. Irena Kankova, Nov. 6, 1953; children: Anthony Jan, James Edward, Anna Lisa. LLD (hon.), U. Man., Can., 1987, 1987. Pres. Gendis Inc., Winnipeg, 1953—; chmn., chief exec. officer Gendis, Inc., Winnipeg, 1987—; chmn. exec. com. Met. Stores of Can., Ltd., Winnipeg, 1961—, Greenberg Stores Ltd.; sec., treas., dir. Saan Stores Ltd.; chmn., chief exec. officer Sony of Can. Ltd., 1975—. Pres. Winnipeg Clin. Research Inst., 1975-80, Paul H.T. Thorlakson Research Found., 1978-80.; hon. chmn. St. John's Ravenscourt Sch., 1984. Served with Royal Can. Navy, 1942-45. Recipient Order of Can., 1984. Office: Gendis Inc, 1370 Sony Pl, Winnipeg, MB Canada R3C 3C3

COHEN, BARRY DANIEL, psychologist; b. Bklyn., Mar. 17, 1952; s. Monroe Howard and Annette (DeKaye) C. B.A., SUNY-Buffalo, 1973; M.A., Vanderbilt U., 1975, Ph.D., 1977. Lic. psychologist, Calif. Psychologist UCLA, 1978, Kaiser-Permanente, Los Angeles, 1978-84; dir. psychol. services Pain Mgmt. Ctr., St. John's Hosp., Santa Monica, Calif., 1984—. Co-editor: Psychological Factors in Health Care, 1980. Contbr. articles to profl. jours. Mem. Am. Psychol. Assn., Soc. Clin. and Exptl. Hypnosis, Internat. Assn. for Study of Pain, Phi Beta Kappa. Office: Pain Mgmt Ctr St Johns Hosp 1328 22d St Santa Monica CA 90404

COHEN, CLARENCE BUDD, aerospace engineer; b. Monticello, N.Y., Feb. 7, 1925; s. Isidor and Dora Cohen; m. Beatrice Sholofsky, Jan. 1, 1947; children: William David, Deborah Ann. BAE, Rensselaer Poly. Inst., 1945, MAE, 1947; MA, Princeton U., 1952, PhD, 1954. Aerospace research scientist NASA, Cleve., 1947-56; assoc. chief. spl. projects br. TRW Electronics and Def., Redondo Beach, Calif., 1957—, head hypersonics research section, 1957-61; mgr. aerodynamics dept. TRW Electronics and Defense, Redondo Beach, Calif., 1961-63, mgr. aero scis. lab., 1966-69, dir. tech. application, 1970-80, dir. technology, 1980—. Contbr. articles to profl. jours; patentee manned spacecraft with staged reentry. Served with USNR, 1943-46. Recipient Class of 1902 research prize Rensselaer Poly. Inst., 1945. Fellow AIAA; mem. Licensing Execs. Soc., Research Soc. Am. (past pres.), Indsl. Research Inst. (alt. rep.), Sigma Xi. Club: King Harbor Yacht. Home: 332 Via El Chico Redondo Beach CA 90277 Office: TRW Electronics and Defense 1 Space Park E2/10063 Redondo Beach CA 90278

COHEN, DANIEL MORRIS, museum administrator, marine biology researcher; b. Chgo., July 6, 1930; s. Leonard U. and Myrtle (Gertz) C.; m. Anne Carolyn Constant, Nov. 4, 1955; children—Carolyn A., Cynthia S. B.A., Stanford U., 1952, M.A., 1953, Ph.D., 1958. Asst. prof., curator fishes U. Fla., Gainesville, 1957-58; systematic zoologist Bur. Comml. Fisheries, Washington, 1958-60; dir. systematics Nat. Marine Fisheries Service, Washington, 1960-81; sr. scientist Nat. Marine Fisheries Service, Seattle, 1981-82; chief curator life scis. Los Angeles County Mus. of Natural History, Los Angeles, 1982—; adj. prof. biology U. So. Calif., 1982—. Contbr. numerous articles to profl. jours. Fellow AAAS; mem. Am. Soc. Ichthyologists and Herpetologists (v.p. 1969, 70, pres. 1985), Biol. Soc. Washington (pres. 1971-72), Soc. Systematic Zoology (mem. council 1976-78). Avocation: gardening. Home: 3667 Greve Dr Rancho Palos Verdes CA 90274 Office: Los Angeles Co Mus of Nat Hist 900 Exposition Blvd Los Angeles CA 90007

COHEN, DAVID EDWARD, publisher; b. Springfield, Mass., Nov. 17, 1950; s. Philip J. and Marjorie (Rednor) C.; m. Barbara Elia, Dec. 31, 1979; children: Daniel Elia, Dustin Elia. BA, Windham Coll., 1971; postgrad., Internat. Acad. Continous Edn., 1974. Advt. mgr. Valley Adv. Newspaper, Springfield, 1976-79; assoc. pub. L.A. Weekly, Los Angeles, 1979-85; pub. METRO, San Jose, Calif., 1985—. Bd. dirs. San Jose Symphony Assn., 1986—; mem. adv. bd. Rockers Against Drunk Driving, 1986—, San Jose Shelter Found., 1987. Mem. San Jose Women in Advt., Advt. Club San Jose, San Jose Jazz Soc. (bd. dirs. 1986—), San Jose Downtown Assn. (bd. dirs.). Avocations: stone sculpting, skiing. Home: 4838 Rue Bordeaux San Jose CA 95136 Office: Metro 410 S First St San Jose CA 95113

COHEN, ELINOR IRISH (MAISIE), computer management specialist, consultant; b. Pasadena, Calif., Apr. 16, 1930; d. John Marion and Elizabeth (Herrington) Irish; m. William Cohen, June 16, 1956; children—David, Cathy, Andrew, Deborah, Michael, Daniel. B.A., U. Calif.-Berkeley, 1951; M.A. summa cum laude, Stanford U., 1952. Tchr. high sch., China Lake, Calif., 1952-56, Arlington County, Va., 1956-61; info. specialist, programmer analyst Informatics, Inc., Washington, 1967-71; cons., tech. writer Culler Harrison Inc. Systems, Santa Barbara, Calif., 1976-77; tchr. English dept. Santa Barbara City Coll., 1978-79; founding prin. MicroXchange, Santa Barbara, 1979-85; founding ptnr. The Santa Barbara Group, 1985—. Author study commodity coding Dept. Transp., 1970; cons., pub. MicroXchange. Mem. Data Processing Mgrs. Assn. (chmn. edn. com. chpt. 1982, dir.-at-large 1983), Santa Barbara C. of C., Assn. Computer Users (editorial bd.), Ind. Computer Cons. Assn., Data Entry Mgmt. Assn., Internat. Info./Work Processing Assn., Phi Beta Kappa, Delta Kappa Gamma. Club: Santa Barbara Piano (founder). Office: The Santa Barbara Group 1727 State St Santa Barbara CA 93101

COHEN, GENE, food processing company executive; b. Oshkosh, Wis., June 14, 1941; s. Lawrence A. and Ethel (Borenstein) C.; m. Judith Deborah Barchas, Dec. 22, 1962; children—Kathryn, Brett, Laura. B.S., U. Wis., 1963. Pres. Tranco Industries, Inc., Spokane, Wash., 1970—, K B L Enterprises, Inc., Spokane, 1975—, Triangle Nut Co., Spokane, 1980—. Active Spokane Lilac Festival, Wampum Charities, Spokane Civic Adv. Bd., 1979—. Mem. West Plains Businessman Assn. (founder, bd. dirs.), Conv. and Visitors Bur., Spokane C. of C., Club: Spokane. Lodges: Kiwanis. Office: PO Box 88 Spokane WA 99210

COHEN, HOWARD JEROME, software engineer, consultant; b. N.Y.C., Aug. 25, 1945; s. Leon Abraham and Blanche (Farkas) C.; m. Barbara L. Joseph, July 3, 1973; children: Tanya, Kendra. BS in Physics, CCNY, 1966; MA in Physics, Brandeis U., 1968, PhD in Physics, 1974. Lectr. various Bay Area Colls., Calif., 1974-76; mem. tech. staff Computer Sci. Corp., Mountain View, Calif., 1974-76; program mgr. research and devel. Ocean Routes Co., Palo Alto, Calif., 1976-79; sr. scientist Ensco Corp., Sunnyvale, Calif., 1979-82; sr. software engr. Daisy Systems Corp., Mountain View, 1982-86; with ETAK, Menlo Park, Calif., 1986—; cons. ROLM, Santa Clara, Calif., 1979, Ocean Routes Co., Palo Alto, 1980-82, 1985-86, Integrated CMOS Systems, Santa Clara, 1986. Treas. Garfield Sch. PTA, Redwood City, Calif., 1976-79, Palo Alto Sch. for Jewish Edn., 1978-86; co-founder Arden House Group, Cambridge, Mass., 1970-71. Grantee NSF, Washington, 1970; Ettore Majorona scholar Scuola di Fisica Cosmica Erice, Italy, 1971; N.Y. State Grad. fellow N.Y. State Regents, Albany, N.Y., 1966, Predoctoral fellow Racah Inst. Physics, Jerusalem, 1971-73. Mem. AAAS, Am. Phys. Soc., IEEE, Soc. Computer Simulations. Avocations: reading, travel. Home: 3272 Cowper St Palo Alto CA 94306 Office: ETAK 1455 Adams Dr Menlo Park CA 94025

COHEN, JAMES SAMUEL, research physicist; b. Houston, July 29, 1946; s. Herman and Jimmie Ruth (Harrington) C.; m. Marion Fay Daniel, Dec. 28, 1968; children: Stephen, Christy. BA, Rice U., 1968, MA, 1970, PhD, 1972. Staff mem. Los Alamos (N.Mex.) Nat. Lab., 1972—; vis. assoc. prof. Rice U., Houston, 1979-80; vis. scientist Scheizerisches Inst. fur Nuklearforschung, Villigen, Switzerland, 1983; Centre d'Etudes Nucleaires, Saclay, France, 1984; coordinator, theory of Muon-Catalyzed Fusion Dept. Energy, Washington, 1984—. Contbr. articles to profl. jours. Grantee Div. Advanced Energy Projects Dept. Energy, 1984. Mem. Am. Phys. Soc., Phi Beta Kappa, Sigma Xi. Home: 330 Valle del Sol Los Alamos NM 87544 Office: Los Alamos Nat Lab T-12 MS-J569 Los Alamos NM 87545

COHEN, JEFFREY LEWIS, psychotherapist; b. N.Y.C., Jan. 17, 1950; s. Irving and Betty (Sussman) C. BA, L.I. U., 1972; MS, Calif. State U., Los Angeles, 1975; postgrad., Calif. Grad. Inst., 1983—. Lic. marriage, family and child counselor, Calif. Instr. Santa Monica (Calif.) Coll., 1974-83; counselor Los Angeles Pierce Coll., Woodland Hills, 1977—; pvt. practice specializing in psychotherapy Encino, Calif., 1983—. Author: Asserting Yourself in the Job Market, 1979. Mem. Calif. Assn. Marriage and Family Therapists. Democrat. Jewish. Office: Los Angeles Pierce Coll 6201 Winnetka Ave Woodland Hills CA 91371

COHEN, JEREMY, journalist, educator; b. Buffalo, N.Y., Oct. 6, 1949; s. Ernest Cohen and Ruth Loretta (Isenberg) C.; m. Catherine Jordan, July 3, 1982; children: Leah, Joshua. BA, San Francisco State U., 1973; MA, U. so. Calif., 1979; PhD, U. Wash., 1983. Asst. prof. journalism U. Oreg., Eugene, 1982-84; asst. prof. communications Stanford (Calif.) U., 1984—. Contbr. articles to profl. jours. Mem. Am. Journalism Historians Soc., Assn. for Edn. in Journalism and Mass Communication. Avocation: whitewater canoeing. Office: Stanford Univ Dept Communications McClatchy Hall Stanford CA 94305

COHEN, JOANNE E., educator; b. Rochester, N.Y., May 19, 1954; d. Harvey and Doris B. Cohen. B.S. in Edn. and English, SUNY-Cortland, 1976; M.A. in Speech Communication, U. Denver, 1980. Cert. tchr., N.Y. Tchr. English and speech Elmira (N.Y.) Free Acad., 1976-78; tchr. English, Broadway Jr. High Sch., Elmira, 1978-79; tchr. English, speech and drama Southside High Sch., Elmira, 1978-80; instr. pub. speaking Community Coll. Denver, Aurora, Colo., 1982—; tng. coordinator UNIPAC Service Corp., Aurora, 1981-84; cons. human resources ECLECON, Lakewood, Colo., 1984—; Bd. dirs., adviser Pupil Assistance in Learning Club, Big Brother/Sister Orgn., Elmira, 1977-80. Mem. Am. Soc. Tng. and Devel. (pres. Rocky Mountain chpt., 1986), Exec. Profl. Women's Council. Home: 3300 S Tamarac Dr Apt G 301 Denver CO 80231 Office: 390 Union Blvd Suite 310 Lakewood CO 80228

COHEN, JONATHAN ALLAN, research psychoanalyst; b. Troy, N.Y., Dec. 4, 1939; s. Irwin Jeremiah and Gertrude Ann (Willig) C.; m. Leslie Jordan, Apr. 28, 1973; children: Joshua, Adrienne. Student, Yale U., 1956-59; BS in Phys. Chemistry, UCLA, 1963, MD, 1967. Diplomate Am. Bd. Psychiatry and Neurology. Clin. instr. dept. psychiatry U. Colo. Med. Ctr., Denver, 1971—; pvt. practice psychoanalysis and psychiatry Denver, 1974—; assoc. dept. psychiatry Med. U. S.C., Charleston, 1972-74; research assoc. Ctr. Psychoanalytic Research, London, 1982—; cons. video archives for holocaust testimonies Yale U., New Haven, 1981—; cons. dept. psychiatry W. Va. U. Sch. Medicine, Charleston, 1985—. Contbr. articles to profl. jours. Served to lt. comdr. USN, 1972-74. Mem. AAAS, Am. Psychiatric Assn., Fedn. Am. Scientists, Internat. Psychoanalytic Studies Orgn., ACLU, Common Cause. Democrat. Jewish. Avocations: skiing, sailing, travel. Home: 2114 S Clayton St Denver CO 80210 Office: 2005 Franklin St #500 Denver CO 80205

COHEN, JORDAN LEE, pharmacy educator; b. Milw., Aug. 14, 1942; s. Irving A. and Ruth (Altman) C.; m. Jana Ellen Hong, July 1, 1972; children: Justin Lee, Jamie Ellen. BS, U. Wis., 1965, MS, 1967, PhD, 1969. Registered pharmacist, Wis. Asst. prof. U. So. Calif., Los Angeles, 1969-73, assoc. prof., 1974-84, prof. pharmacy, 1984—; assoc. prof. Med. Coll. Va., Richmond, 1973-74; cons. WHO, FTC, Washington, Allergan Pharm., Irvine, Calif., 1971-77, Searle Pharm., Skokie, Ill., 1986—, Smith Kline & French Labs., 1986. Contbr. numerous articles to sci. jours. Nat. Cancer Inst. grantee, 1971—. Mem. Am. Chem. Soc., Am. Pharm. Assn., Acad. Pharm. Scis., Am. Assn. Colls. Pharmacy. Democrat. Jewish. Avocations: running, tennis, skiing. Office: U So Calif 1985 Zonal Ave Sch of Pharm Los Angeles CA 90033

COHEN, JULIUS MILTON, retired association executive; b. Rochester, N.Y., Feb. 14, 1914; s. Abraham V. and Lillian (Pontesof) C.; B.A., Cornell

U., 1935; postgrad. Rochester Bus. Inst., 1939, Columbia, 1943, U. N.C., 1948, Stanford, 1954; m. Sophie Katz, Feb. 14, 1956. Mng. editor, columnist Jewish Ledger Publs., Rochester, 1935-43; area dir. U.S.O.-Nat. Jewish Welfare Bd., 1943-63, So. Calif. area, Los Angeles, 1952-63; community devel. dir. Gateways Hosp., Los Angeles, 1963-65; exec. dir. Western region Am. Jewish Congress Los Angeles, 1965-81, ret., 1981; investment officer Am. Savs. & Loan, Seal Beach, 1984—. Mem. Los Angeles City Atty.'s Task Force Nursing Home Reform, 1972-74; bd. dirs. Inter-racial Council Bus. Opportunity, 1966-78, Bus. Devel. Center, 1979—, North Seal Beach Sr. Citizens Ctr., 1981—; pres. council presidents Pacific S.W. region United Synagogue Am., 1984—; pres. Leisure World Congregation Sholom, 1981-84. Recipient USMC award, Los Angeles, 1960; 6th Army award, 1963; Gateways award, 1965; City of Los Angeles Bicentennial Salute, 1980; 40th Anniversary award USO, 1981, Adv. Council award for disting. service to sr. citizens of Orange County, 1983, others; Disting. Service award Leisure World Congregation Sholom, 1985. Mem. Nat. Assn. Jewish Center Workers (past pres. Western states sect.), Acad. Certified Social Workers (charter), Nat. Assn. Social Workers (charter), Nat. Assn. Inter-Group Relations Ofcls. (v.p. So. Calif.), Assn. for Study Community Orgn. (sec.). Mem. B'nai B'rith (past pres. Rochester, Distinguished Service award 1961). Columnist Seal Beach Jour., Huntington Harbour Sun, 1981-86, Orange County Register, 1987—. Home: 13200 Del Monte Dr Seal Beach CA 90740

COHEN, KENNETH BRUCE, hospital administrator; b. Springfield, Mass., Jan. 19, 1950; s. Samuel A. and Shirley F. (Austin) C.; m. Deborah F. Roberts, Aug. 3, 1975; children: Kimberly A., Lauren B., Meredith L. BS, Ithaca Coll., 1971; M in Hosp. Adminstrn., George Washington U., 1975. Budget dir. Meml. Hosp., Hollywood, Fla., 1976-77; asst. adminstr. Meml. Hosp., Hollywood, 1977-78, sr. asst. adminstr., 1978-83; chief ops. officer Hollywood (Fla.) Med. Ctr., 1983-85; adminstr. Riverside (Calif.) Gen. Hosp., 1985—. Mem. Health Planning and Devel Council, Fla., 1985, bd. Nursing Home Adminstrs., Fla., 1981-84. Mem. Health Care Fin. Mgmt. Assn., Am. Hosp. Assn., Calif. Hosp. Assn., Calif. Assn. Pub. Hosps., Nat. Assn. Pub. Hosps., Am. Coll. Health Care Execs. Avocations: golf, softball, raquetball, photography. Home: 5342 Lescoe Ct Riverside CA 92503 Office: Riverside Gen Hosp 9851 Magnolia Ave Riverside CA 92506

COHEN, LEONARD, medical equipment leasing company executive; b. 1925; married. BS, UCLA, 1948; LLB, Loyola U., 1951. Ptnr. Ervin, Cohen & Jessup, 1952-68; with Nat. Med. Enterprises, Los Angeles, 1968—, pres., chief operating officer, 1983—, now also vice-chmn., dir. Served USAR, 1948-53. Office: Nat Med Enterprises Inc 11620 Wilshire Blvd Los Angeles CA 90025 *

COHEN, MICHAEL FREDERICK, psychologist, coll. dean; b. N.Y.C., Oct. 29, 1941; s. Joseph Nathaniel and Lee (Nagler) C.; m. Sharna Delaine Eberlein, Apr. 1, 1975; children—Isa, Alexandra, Theodore. B.A. with honors, Fla. State U., Tallahassee, 1962; M.S., U. Wis. Madison, 1965, Ph.D. (USPHS fellow), 1968. Lic. psychologist, Calif. Program adminstr. Community Workers' Program, Santa Clara County Mental Health, San Jose, Calif., 1968-71; chmn. community psychology program Calif. Sch. Profl. Psychology, San Francisco, 1971-75; pres. and dir. evaluation Inst. Study Social and Health Issues, San Francisco, 1971—; dean Profl. Sch. Psychology, San Francisco, 1978—; pvt. practice clin. psychology, Rohnert Park, Calif., 1981—; orgn. and evaluation cons., 1971—. HEW grantee, 1971-77; Inst. for Study Social and Health Issues fellow, 1971. Mem. Am. Psychol. Assn., Soc. Psychol. Study Social Issues. Jewish. Author: A Systems Approach to Health Manpower Utilization: A Technical Procedures Manual, 1971; Procedures for the Development of a Career Opportunity System: A Technical Manual, 1973; also articles. Office: 1714 Lombard St San Francisco CA 94123

COHEN, NORM, chemist; b. N.Y.C., Dec. 13, 1936; s. Moshe and Yetta (Pickman) C.; m. Anne Elizabeth Billings, July 11, 1959 (div. 1986); children: Alexandra Elizabeth Rachel, Carson Benjamin; m. Verni Greenfield, Feb. 6, 1987. BA in Chemistry, Reed Coll., 1958; MA in Math., U. Calif., Berkeley, 1960, PhD in Chemistry, 1963. Mem. tech. staff Aerospace Corp., El Segundo, Calif., 1963-72, head dept. chem. kinetics, 1972-84, sr. scientist, 1984—; exec. sec. John Edwards Mem. Forum, Los Angeles, 1969—. Author: Long Steel Rail, 1981 (Chgo. Folklore prize 1982, ASCAP Deems Taylor award 1982, Am. Folklore Soc. Botkin prize 1983); editor: Ozark Folk Songs, 1982, John Edwards Meml. Forum Quarterly, 1966-83, 85-86; asst. editor Int. J. Chemical Kinetics, 1977-83; editor, producer (album) Minstrels and Tunesmiths, 1982 (grammy nomination 1982); contbr. articles and revs. to chemistry and folkmusic jours. Grantee NEA, NEH. Mem. Calif. Folklore Soc. (v.p. 1984-85), Am. Folklore Soc., Am. Chem. Soc., Sigma Xi. Democrat. Jewish. Avocations: travel, photography, music, art. Home: 633 Crestmoore Pl Venice CA 90291 Office: Aerospace Corp MS M5/747 PO Box 92957 Los Angeles CA 90009

COHEN, NORMAN ABBY, electrical engineering consultant; b. Bklyn., Dec. 4, 1925; s. Jacob Barnet and Jane Lillian (Rader) C.; m. Leatrice L. Silverstein, Aug. 24, 1947 (div. May 1970); children: Maureen, Melinda Swavely, Jane Tyndzik; m. Elsie Jean Offer, May 13, 1970. Elec. engr. So. Calif. Edison Co., Los Angeles, 1946-47; elec. engring. assoc. Dept. Water and Power, Los Angeles, 1947-52; pres. Frumhoff & Cohen, Inc., Los Angeles, 1956-72, Cohen & Kanwar, Inc., Santa Monica, Calif., 1972—. Mem. IEEE, Illuminating Engrs. Soc. (Edwin Guth award 1968), Cons. Engrs. Council, Con. Elec. Engrs. Council. Home: 1347 Stradella Rd Los Angeles CA 90077 Office: Cohen & Kanwar Inc 1753 Cloverfield Blvd Santa Monica CA 90404

COHEN, NORMAN RICHARD, lawyer; b. Phila., Feb. 21, 1937; s. Barnet Cohen and Sally Weiss; m. Diana Fredman, Mar. 14, 1970. BS in Econs., U. Pa., 1958, LLB, 1961. Bar: Pa. 1961, Calif. 1966. Assoc. Buchalter, Nemer, Fields, Chrystie & Younger, Los Angeles, 1968-73, ptnr., 1973-82; exec. v.p. The Veta Grande Cos., Inc., Los Angeles, 1982-84; pres. Hamer & Cohen Assocs., Inc., Los Angeles, 1984-87; sole practice Los Angeles, 1987—; arbitrator NASD, Inc., AAA. Served to capt. USAF, 1963-66. Mem. ABA, Calif. Bar Assn., Los Angeles Bar Assn., AMEX. Avocations: sailing, skiing. Office: 11500 W Olympic Blvd Suite 400 Los Angeles CA 90064

COHEN, RICHARD J., physician, researcher in oncology; b. Bklyn., Jan. 16, 1936; m. Sandra N.; children: Aaron, Eve. AB, Columbia U., 1957; MD, SUNY, Bklyn., 1961. Lic. physician, N.Y., Calif.; cert. hematology and oncology Am. Bd. Internal Medicine. Intern Walter Reed Gen. Hosp., Walter Reed Army Inst. Research, Washington, 1961-62, asst. chief hematology, 1967-68; resident internal medicine Letterman Gen. Hosp., San Francisco, 1962-65; instr. medicine U. Saigon, Vietnam, 1966-67; clin. instr. medicine George Washington U., Washington, 1967-69; asst. clin. prof. medicine U. Calif., San Francisco, 1969-75, assoc. clin. prof. medicine, 1975-82, clin. prof. medicine, 1982—; chief hematology Mt. Zion Hosp. and Med. Ctr., San Francisco, 1973-79; chief med. oncology hematology Children's Hosp. and Adult Med. Ctr., San Francisco, 1979—; research assoc. U. Calif. Med. Ctr. Cancer Research Inst., San Francisco, 1968; attending physician medicine, hematology, med. oncology Children's Hospital and Adult Med. Ctr., 1968—, San Francisco Gen. Hosp., 1968—, Mt. Zion Hosp. and Med. Ctr., 1970—, Marshall Hale Meml. Hosp., 1972—; cons. physician medicine, hematology, and med. oncology Presbyn. Hosp. Pacific Med. Ctr., 1968—, St. Luke's Hosp., 1968—, French Hospital, 1968—, St. Mary's Hosp., 1968—, H.C. Moffitt Hosp. U.Calif. Med. Ctr., 1968—; cons. med. oncology hemotology Surgeon Gen. U.S. Army Letterman Gen. Hosp., 1970—. Contbr. numerous articles to profl. jours.; mem. manuscript rev. bd. Western Jour. Medicine. Decorated Bronze Starm, 1967, Doctor Charles Noble award Children's Hosp. and Adult Med. Ctr., 1974, Outstanding Excellence in Teaching award U. Calif. Sch. Med., 1973; named Outstanding Teacher in Medicine, Mt. Zion Hosp. and Med. Ctr., 1970-71, 71-72. Fellow ACP; mem. AAAS, AMA (manuscript rev. bd.), Am. Soc. Hematology (edn. com. 1978-82), Am. Soc. Clin. Oncology (com. unorthodox cancer treatments 1980-82, clin. practices com. 1982-84), Am. Fedn. for Clin. Research, Calif. Acad. Medicine, San Francisco Internal Medicine (pres. 1974-75), Am. Cancer Soc. (bd. dirs. San Francisco div. 1978-84), The Leukemia Soc. Am. (bd. dirs. no. Calif. div. 1983-85). Home: 3838 California St San Francisco CA 94118

COHEN, STANLEY NORMAN, educator, geneticist; b. Perth Amboy, N.J., Feb. 17, 1935; s. Bernard and Ida (Stolz) C.; m. Joanna Lucy Wolter, June 27, 1961; children: Anne, Geoffrey. B.A., Rutgers U., 1956; M.D., U. Pa., 1960. Intern, Mt. Sinai Hosp., N.Y.C., 1960-61; resident Univ. Hosp., Ann Arbor, Mich., 1961-62; clin. asso. arthritis and rheumatism br. Nat. Inst. Arthritis and Metabolic Diseases, Bethesda, Md., 1962-64; sr. resident in medicine Duke U. Hosp., Durham, N.C., 1964-65; Am. Cancer Soc. postdoctoral research fellow Albert Einstein Coll. Medicine, Bronx, 1965-67, asst. prof. devel. biology and cancer, 1967-68; mem. faculty Stanford (Calif.) U., 1968—, prof. medicine, 1975—, prof. genetics, 1977, chmn. dept. genetics, 1978-86; mem. com. recombinant DNA molecules Nat. Acad. Sci.-NRC, 1974; mem. com. on genetic experimentation Internat. Council Sci. Unions, 1977—. Mem. editorial bd.: Jour. Bacteriology, 1973-79; asso. editor: Plasmid, 1977-86. Served with USPHS, 1962-64. Guggenheim fellow, 1975; Josiah Macy Jr. Found. faculty scholar, 1975-76; recipient Burroughs Wellcome Scholar award, 1970, V.D. Mattia award Roche Inst. Molecular Biology, 1977, Albert Lasker basic med. research award, 1980, Wolf prize, 1981, Marvin J. Johnson award, 1981, Disting. Grad. award U. Pa. Sch. Medicine, 1986, Disting. Service award Miami Winter Symposium, 1986. Mem. Nat. Acad. Sci., Am. Acad. Arts and Sci., Am. Soc. Biol. Chemists, Genetics Soc. Am., Am. Soc. Microbiology, Am. Soc. Pharmacology and Exptl. Therapeutics, Am. Soc. Clin. Investigation, Phi Beta Kappa, Sigma Xi, Alpha Omega Alpha. Office: Dept Genetics S-337 Stanford U Sch Medicine Stanford CA 94305

COHEN, STEPHEN ROBERT, optometrist, army officer; b. Bklyn., Dec. 19, 1950; s. Stanley and Ida (Wexler) C.; m. Tina Lillian Vega, Jan. 27, 1978; children: Richard Stanley, David Emanuel, Sarah Lillian. BA, Hofstra U., 1971; OD, Mass. Coll. Optometry, 1974; MEd, U. So. Calif., 1984; grad., U.S. Army Command and Gen. Staff Coll., 1984. Commd. 1st. lt. U.S. Army, 1974, advanced through grades to maj., 1985; officer in charge optometry Yongsan Health Clinic, Seoul, Republic of Korea, 1983-84; chief optometry U.S. Army Health Clinic, Hawaii, 1984-86, Tripler Army Med. Ctr., Hawaii, 1986—; mem. adj. faculty So. Calif. Coll. Optometry, Fullerton, 1984—, Pacific U., Forest Grove, Oreg., 1984—. Mem. Armed Forces Optometric Soc. (chmn. edn. com. 1985-87), Am. Optometric Assn., Assn. Mil. Surgeons U.S., Better Vision Inst. Home: 435 Baldwin Rd Wahiawa HI 96786 Office: Tripler Army Med Ctr TAMC HI 96859

COHEN, STUART HARVEY, research internist; b. Chgo., Mar. 11, 1953; s. Jerome and Norma Judith (Moss) C. BS, U. Ill., 1974; MD, U. Chgo., 1978. Diplomate Am. Bd. Internal Medicine, Am. Bd. Infectious Diseases. Resident U. N.Mex., Albuquerque, 1978-81; postdoctoral fellow U. Calif., Davis, 1981-83, instr. infectious diseases, 1983-84, adj. asst. prof., 1984-86, asst. prof., 1986—. Contbr. articles to profl. jours. Mem. ACP, AAAS, Am. Soc. Microbiology, Infectious Diseases Soc. Am., Am. Fedn. Clin. Research. Democrat. Jewish. Avocations: guitar, basketball. Home: 1132 Derick Way Sacramento CA 95822 Office: U Calif Div Infectious Diseases 4301 X St Davis CA 95817

COHEN, WILLIAM ALAN, marketing educator, author, lecturer, consultant; b. Balt., June 25, 1937; s. Sidney Oliver and Theresa (Bachman) C.; m. Janice Dawn Stults, Jan. 3, 1963 (div. Jan. 1966); 1 child, William Alan II; m. Nurit Kovnator, May 28, 1967; children—Barak, Nimrod. B.S., U.S. Mil. Acad., 1959; M.B.A., U. Chgo., 1967; M.A., Claremont Grad. Sch., 1978, Ph.D., 1979. Registered profl. engr., Israel. Project mgr. Israel Aircraft Industries, 1970-73; mgr., research and devel. Sierra Engring. Co., Sierra Madre, Calif., 1973-76; pres. Global Assocs., 1973—; mgr., advanced tech. mktg. McDonnell-Douglas Co., Huntington Beach, Calif., 1976-78; dir. research Advanced Materials Tech., Costa Mesa, Calif., 1978-79; prof. mktg. Calif. State U.-Los Angeles, 1979—, dir. Bur. Bus. and Econ. Research, 1979-83, chmn. mktg. dept., 1986—; dir. Small Bus. Inst.; cons. Fortune 500 cos. Author: The Executives Guide to Finding a Superior Job, 1978, 83, Principles of Technical Management, 1980, Successful Marketing for Small Business, 1981, How To Sell To Government, 1981, The Entrepreneur and Small Business Problem Solver, 1983, Direct Response Marketing, 1984, Building a Mail Order Business, 1982, 85, Making It Big as a Consultant, 1985, Winning on the Marketing Front, 1986, High Tech Management, 1986, Developing A Winning Marketing Plan, 1987, The Students Guide To Finding A Superior Job, 1987; contbr. numerous articles to profl. jours. Served to maj. USAF, 1959-70, lt. col. Res. Decorated D.F.C. with 3 oak leaf clusters, Air medal with 11 oak leaf clusters ; recipient Ministry Def. award State of Israel, 1976; Outstanding Service award Nat. Mgmt. Assn., 1979; Pres.'s award West Point Soc., 1982; Outstanding Prof. award Calif. State U.-Los Angeles, 1983; Chgo. Trib Gold Medal; George Washington medal Freedoms Found at Valley Forge, 1986; numerous grants. Fellow Acad. Mktg. Sci.; mem. Direct Mktg. Assn. (fellow 1980, 83) bd. World Mktg. Congress (del. N.S. 1983), Direct Mktg. Club So. Calif. (bd. dirs. 1980—, grantee 1981), Am. Mktg. Assn. (award 1982), West Point Soc. (pres., bd. dirs. 1981-82). Republican. Jewish. Office: Calif State U-Los Angeles Sch Bus and Econs Los Angeles CA 90032

COHN, DAVID D., investment holding co. exec.; b. Chgo., Dec. 30, 1937; s. Albert H. and Helen F. (Baker) C.; student (research honors) Am. U., 1958; B.A., Pomona Coll., 1959; M.A. in Social Service Adminstrn., U. Chgo., 1977; m. Elizabeth Ann Curtis, Dec. 29, 1960; children—David Curtis, Robert Curtis. Salesman, Universal Battery Co., Chgo., 1959-62, v.p., 1962-66, pres., 1966-69, pres. Universal Battery div. Whittaker Corp., Chgo., 1969-70; pres., dir. Universal Res. Corp., Tucson, 1966—; cons., lectr. employee assistance programs, orgns. and industry. Vice pres. Francis W. Parker Sch. Alumni Assn., 1969-71; bd. dirs. Albert H. Cohn Found., Tucson Symphony, 1979-84, Tucson Urban League, 1982-84, Ariz.-Sonora Desert Mus. Found., 1982—; trustee Green Fields Country Day Sch., 1979-82, exec. com., 1980-82; mem. adv. bd. Ariz.-Sonora Desert Mus., 1981-84, trustee, 1984—, pres. 1985-86. Mem. Nat. Assn. Social Workers, Council Social Work Edn. Unitarian. Clubs: Tucson Country, Skyline Country Tucson); Pres.'s (U. Ariz. Found.). Research in field; speaker profl. confs. Home: 5455 E Camino Bosque Tucson AZ 85718 Office: Universal Res Corp 6801-A E Camino Principal Tucson AZ 85715

COHN, LAWRENCE STEVEN, physician, medical educator; b. Chgo., Dec. 21, 1945; s. Jerome M. and Francis C.; B.S., U. Ill., 1967, M.D., 1971; m. Harriett G. Rubin, Sept. 1, 1968; children—Allyson and Jennifer (twins). Intern, Mt. Zion Hosp., San Francisco, 1971-72, resident, 1972-73; resident U. Chgo., 1973-74; practice medicine specializing in internal medicine, Paramount, Calif.; pres. med. staff Charter Suburban Hosp., 1981-83; mem. staff Long Beach Meml. Hosp., Harbor Gen. Hosp; clin. asst. prof. medicine UCLA. Served to maj. USAF, 1974-76. Recipient Disting. Teaching award Harbor-UCLA Med. Center, 1980; diplomate Am. Bd. Internal Medicine. Mem. A.C.P., AMA, Calif. Med. Assn., Los Angeles County Med. Assn., Am. Heart Assn., Soc. Air Force Physicians, Phi Beta Kappa, Phi Kappa Phi, Phi Lambda Upsilon, Phi Eta Sigma, Alpha Omega Alpha. Home: 6608 Via LaPaloma Rancho Palos Verdes CA 90274 Office: 16243 Colorado Ave Paramount CA 90723

COHN, LINDA DOCK, dental consultant, author; b. Indpls., June 24, 1952; d. Ben and Gertrude (Siegel) Dock; m. Michael Jay Cohn, Mar. 22, 1986. AS in Dental Hygiene, Ind. U., 1973, BS in Pub. Health Dental Hygiene, 1974, postgrad., 1979-82. Cert. dental hygienist. Dental hygienist Indpls., 1973-82; founder, pres. Oral Health Mgmt., Indpls., 1985, Scottsdale, Ariz., 1986—; cons. community dental health State of Ind., Community Hosp., Oral Health Research Inst., Indpls., 1974-82. Pub., author, creator ednl. material, 1985—; pub., pres. OHM Publ., 1986—. Named one of Outstanding Young Women Am., 1986. Mem. ADA, Ind. U. Alumni Assn., Am. Assn. Pub. Health Dentistry, Nat. Speakers Assn., Alpha Omega. Jewish. Avocations: reading, music, travel, art work. Office: OHM Pub PO Box C-6000 #164 Scottsdale AZ 85261-6000

COHN, MAJOR LLOYD, neuroscientist, physician.; b. N.Y.C., Oct. 29, 1927; s. Isidore and Pauline (Burstein) C.; m. Marthe Hoffnung, Feb. 9, 1958; children: Stephan Jacques, Remi Benjamin. MD, U. Geneva, 1956; MS, U. Minn., 1966; PhD, U. Pitts., 1969. Dir. anesthesia research U. Pitts., 1969-79, asst. prof., 1969-79, dir. respiratory therapy, 1969-76; prof. UCLA Drew Med. Sch., 1979—, dir. pain clinic, 1979—, dir. anesthesia research, 1979—. Contbr. articles to profl. jours. Served with USN, 1945-46. Fellow Sloan Kettering Inst, 1960-61, NIH, 1966-69, Am. Cancer Soc., 1963-66; recipient Henry L. Moses award Montefiore Staff & Alumni Assn., 1978, Am. Assn. Orthopaedic Medicine Outstanding Investigator of Yr. award, 1985. Fellow: Royal Soc. Medicine; mem. AAAS, Am. Soc. Pharmacology and Exptl. Therapeutics, Am. Pain Soc., Soc. Neurosci. Democrat. Jewish. Avocations: bicycling, hiking, swimming, reading, music. Home: 4015 Exultant Dr Rancho Palos Verdes CA 90274 Office: Surf Med Ctr 3655 Lomita Blvd Suite 410 Torrance CA 90505

COHN, NANCY, interior designer; b. Phila., Dec. 24, 1952; d. David and Diana (Selman) C. Student, Phila. Coll. Art, 1974-76; BA, UCLA, 1984. Designer McDonnell Douglas Corp., Huntington Beach, Calif., 1976-81, Rockwell Internat., Anaheim, Calif., 1981-84; prin. NCI, Huntington Beach, 1984—; cons. Northrop Corp., Anaheim, 1985—, Polar Products, Torrance, Calif., 1984—. Prin. works include La Barritz Restaurant, 1985, Zoom Boutique, 1985, Polar Products office renovation, 1986. Mem. Illuminating Engring. Soc., Am. Soc. Interior Designers. Avocations: art, travel, skiing, photography. Office: NCI 16414 Martin Ln Huntington Beach CA 92649

COHRSSEN, BARBARA RUTH, industrial hygienist; b. N.Y.C., Nov. 4, 1937; d. Hans and Alice (Natt) C. BS, Alfred U., 1959; MLS, Carnegie Lib. Sch., 1962; MS, U. Cin., 1977. Info. systems analyst J.L. Thompson, Washington, 1966-68; environ. engr. Kaiser Engrs., Oakland, Calif., 1968-74; project mgr. Kaiser Found. Internat., Oakland, 1974-76; environ. engr. Raymond Kaiser Engrs., Oakland, 1978-80; indsl. hygienist Stanford (Calif.) U., 1980-86, San Francisco Pub. Utilities Commn., 1986—; prin. Cohrssen Assocs., San Francisco, 1980—; tech. cons. WHO, Geneva, 1984; indsl. hygienist DOL/OSHA, Washington, 1977-78. Bd. dirs. Am. Lung Assn. of San Francisco, 1984—. Mem. AAAS, Am. Pub. Health Assn., Soc. Women Engrs., Am. Conf. of govt. Indsl. Hygienists (chmn. com. on women and occupational health), Am. Indsl. Hygiene Assn. (pres. No. Calif. sect. 1986—).

COIT, R. KEN, financial planner; b. Los Angeles, Aug. 26, 1943; s. Roger L. and Thelma D. C.; B.S., U. Ariz., 1967; M.B.A., Pepperdine U., 1981; m. Donna M. Schemanske, Oct. 8, 1977; children—Kristin M., Shannon, Darren, Lauryn. Co-founder, pres. Coit-Gemmer Fin. Inc., 1981; mem. adj. faculty Coll. Fin. Planning, Denver, 1978-79. Recipient Outstanding Alumnus award Pepperdine U. Sch. Bus. and Mgmt., 1986. Mem. Internat. Assn. Fin. Planners (chpt. pres. 1978-79), Inst. Cert. Fin. Planners, Fin. Planners Equity Corp. Clubs: East Bay Gourmet, Blackhawk Country. Office: 1655 N Main St Suite 270 Walnut Creek CA 94596

COLANGELO, JERRY JOHN, professional sports executive; b. Chicago Heights, Ill., Nov. 20, 1939; s. Larry and Sue (Drancek) C.; m. Joan E. Helmich, Jan. 20, 1961; children—Kathy, Kristen, Bryan. B.A., U. Ill., 1962. Partner House of Charles, Inc., 1962-63; assoc. D.O. Klein & Assocs., 1964-65; dir. merchandising Chgo. Bulls basketball club, 1966-68; gen. mgr. Phoenix Suns basketball club, 1968—, now also exec. v.p. Mem. Basketball Congress Am. (exec. v.p., dir.), Phi Kappa Psi. Republican. Baptist. Clubs: University, Phoenix Execs. Office: Phoenix Suns PO Box 1369 Phoenix AZ 85001 also: Phoenix Suns 2910 N Central Phoenix AZ 85012 *

COLBURN, GENE LEWIS, insurance consultant; b. Bismarck, N.D., July 12, 1932; s. Lewis William and Olga Alma (Feland) C.; Ph.D., UCLA, 1982. Pres., gen. mgr. Multiple Lines Ins. Agy., Auburn, Wash., 1953-79; ins. and risk mgmt. cons., Auburn, Wash., 1980—; pres. Feland Safe Deposit Corp.; bd. dirs. Century Service Corp. sub. Capital Savs. Bank, Olympia, Wash.; mem. exec. com. Great Republic Life Ins. Co., Portland, Oreg., 1971-75; mem. Wash. State Ins. Commrs. Test Devel. Com., 1986—. Councilperson Auburn City, 1982-85; Mayor-pro tem, City of Auburn, 1984; co-incorporator, chmn. bd. SE Community Alcohol Center, 1971-75; mem. Wash. State Disaster Assistance Council, 1981—, founding mem.; pres. Valley Cities Mental Health Center, 1980; mem. instn. rev. com. Auburn Gen. Hosp., 1978—; prin. trustee Dr. R. B. Bramble Med. Research Found.; bd. dirs. Wash. Assn. Chs. (Luth. Ch. in Am.), Columbia Luth. Home, Seattle, 1985—. Cert. ins. counselor, 1978. Recipient Disting. Alumni award Green River Community Coll., 1982. Fellow Acad. Producer Ins. Studies (charter); mem. Internat. Platform Assn. Lodge: Auburn Lions (past pres.). Office: 201 A St NW Auburn WA 98002

COLBY, BARBARA DIANE, interior designer; b. Chgo., Dec. 6, 1932; d. Raymond R. and Mertyl Shirley (Jackson) C.; 1 son, Lawrence James. Student Wright Jr. Coll., 1950, Art Inst. Chgo., UCLA. Owner, F.L.S., Los Angeles, 1971-77; ptnr. Ambiance Inc., Los Angeles, 1976-77; owner Barbara Colby, Ltd., Los Angeles, 1977-81; bus. adminstr. Internat. Soc. Interior Designers, Los Angeles, 1982—; owner Chromanetics; instr. Otis/Parsons Sch. Design, Los Angeles Fashion Inst. Design and Merchandising; also lectr. in field. Contbg. editor Giftware News. Recipient award for Best Children's Room, Chgo. Furniture Show, 1969. Mem. Am. Soc. Interior Designers, Color Mktg. Group of U.S. Contbr. to profl. jours. Office: 101 E Stocker St Glendale CA 91207

COLBY, CAROLYN ANNE, business executive; b. St. Louis; d. Leonard and Iselena Anne Savage. B.S., Edgewood Coll.-St. Mary's Coll., 1970. Head nurse U. Chgo., 1975; clin. specialist Michael Reese Hosp., Chgo., 1976; br. mgr. Kimberly Services Inc., Overland Park, Kans., 1979-80, regional dir., 1980-82, regional mgr., 1982-83, ops. cons., 1983—; exec. dir. Am. Nursing Resources, Marina del Rey, Calif., 1982—. Mem. Nat. Assn. Female Execs. Buddhist. Office: 4551 Glencoe Suites 215 and 217 Marina del Rey CA 90292

COLDIRON, LYNETTE RAE, marketing consultant; b. Olivia, Minn., Apr. 1, 1951; d. Donald Douglas and Ellen Emma (Preslicka) McIlree; m. James Richard Coldiron, June 21, 1980. Student Normandale Community Coll., 1973; B.A., Simmons Coll., 1974, M.B.A., 1975. Mktg. analyst CBS, Inc., N.Y.C., 1970-76; product mgr. Litton Microwave, Mpls., 1976-79, Totino's Pillsbury, Mpls., 1979-80, Norris Industries, Los Angeles, 1980-81; asst. v.p., sr. product mgr. Wells Fargo Bank, San Francisco, 1981-82; sr. mktg. cons. Info Processing Group, Xerox Co., Fremont, Calif., 1982—. Recipient New Product Devel. award Litton Microwave Cooking, 1978, Spl. Recognition award Xerox, 1986; Northfield High Sch. journalism scholar, 1968; CBS scholar, 1974. Republican. Lutheran. Home: 4397 Nicolet Ave Fremont CA 94536 Office: Xerox Corp Info Processing Group PO Box 5030 Dept FM 313 Fremont CA 94537

COLE, CHARLES WESLEY, management educator; b. Springfield, Oreg., Jan. 21, 1929; s. Edward Charles and Lucille Ruth (Lambert) C.; m. Colleen Kohler, Mar. 20, 1949; children—Gregory, Sara Moore. B.S., Oreg. State U., 1950; postgrad. U.S. Naval Postgrad. Sch., 1955; M.A., George Washington U., 1964; postgrad. Armed Forces Indsl. Coll., 1969-70. Commd. ensign U.S. Navy, 1950; advanced through grades to capt., 1970; various mgmt. and command positions, 1950-69; asst. chief staff ops. and chief staff Amphibious Group Eastern Pacific, Coronado, Calif., 1970-74; chief mut. def. assistance office Am. Embassy, Tokyo, 1974-77; comdr. Naval Inactive Ship Maintenance Facility, Bremerton, Wash., 1977-79; ret., 1979; dir., instr. Internat. Bus. Program Grad. Sch. Mgmt., 1982—. Chmn. Eugene-Springfield Met. Area Planning Adv. Com.; bd. dirs. Lane County MADD; mem. Dist. Export Council, exec. com. Willamette Valley World Trade Ctr. Decorated Silver Star, Legion Merit, Bronze Star (2); named Outstanding Citizen Lane Council Govts., 1982. Mem. Am. Mgmt. Assn. Rubicon Soc. Republican. Lutheran. Clubs: Ret. Officers Assn. (Eugene); Elks. Home: 1245 Inglewood Ave Eugene OR 97401 Office: U Oreg Coll Bus Adminstrn Eugene OR 97403

COLE, DAVID MACAULAY, newspaper and magazine editor, computer consultant; b. Richmond, Calif., Feb. 17, 1954; s. Frederick George and Norma Ann (Caudle) C.; Student San Francisco State U., 1972-77. Mng. editor feed/back, The Calif. Journalism Rev., San Francisco, 1974-77, exec. editor, 1977-82, editor, gen. mgr., 1982-84; editorial asst. Rolling Stone, San Francisco, 1976-77; asst. news editor San Francisco Examiner, 1977-80, systems editor, 1980-85, art dir., 1985—; guest lectr. U. Calif.-Berkeley, Stanford U., San Francisco State U. Bd. dirs. West Contra Costa ARC, 1970. Mem. Media Alliance, Sigma Delta Chi, San Francisco Press Club. Office: PO Box 7260 San Francisco CA 94120

COLE, EDGAR MARION, physicist, engineer; b. Dallas, Mar. 12, 1925; s. Robert Vernon and Erma Lee (Garrett) C.; m. Anne Elizabeth Wilson, June 24, 1950 (div. Feb. 1983); children: Gail Elizabeth, Edgar Marion Jr., Adrienne Louise, Kevin Anthony, David Theodore. BA in Physics, Fisk U., 1950; MS in Physics, Howard U., 1953. Research physicist Harry Diamond Labs., Washington, 1950-54; supr. Hughes Aircraft CO., Culver City, Calif., 1954-58; project engr. Space Technology Labs., Redondo Beach, Calif., 1958-60, Aerospace Corp., El Segundo, Calif., 1960-62, TRW Systems, Inc., Redondo Beach, Calif., 1962-66; lab. dir. Litton Data Systems, Van Nuys, Calif., 1966-73; program mgr. Xerox Corp., Rochester, N.Y., 1973-83; program mgr., asst. lab. mgr. Hughes Aircraft Co., El Segundo, 1983—; instr. math. and sci. Trade Tech. Community Coll., Los Angeles, 1971-73. Contbr. articles to profl. jours. Served as cpl. USMC, 1943-46. Recipient Disting. Alumni award Fisk U.; scholar Fisk U. Mem. NAACP (life), Nat. Urban League, Montford Point Marines Assn. (life), Howard U. Alumni Assn., Fisk U. Alumni Assn. (pres. 1983-84), Washington-Lincoln Alumni Assn. Baptist. Lodge: Masons. Avocations: amateur radio, coin collecting, poetry.

COLE, JAMES RANDOLPH, II, oral and maxillofacial surgeon; b. Albuquerque, May 19, 1941; s. James Randolph and Orrel (Brooks) C.; m. Judith Campbell, Aug. 8, 1964; (div. Jan. 1985); children—Kristin, Kimberly. B.S., U. N.Mex., 1963; D.D.S., U. Mo.-Kansas City, 1967; cert. in oral maxillofacial surgery, U. Okla., 1973. Diplomate Am. Bd. Oral and Maxillofacial Surgeons. Practice oral and maxillofacial surgery, Albuquerque, 1973—. Served to capt. USAF, 1967-73. Fellow Am. Soc. Oral Maxillofacial Surgeons; mem. Rocky Mt. Soc. Oral Surgeons (pres. 1985-86), Albuquerque Dist. Dental Soc. (pres. 1985-86), Coll. Dentists, N.Mex. Dental Assn. Republican. Episcopalian. Lodge: Rotary. Office: Oral Maxillofacial Surgery Assocs 6800 A Montgomery St NE Albuquerque NM 87109

COLE, JOHN FRANCIS, biotechnology executive; b. Burwood, Australia, Feb. 15, 1943; s. Gordon Francis and Irene Jean (Eggleton) C.; m. Kaisa Inkeri Aalto, Sept. 28, 1967; children: Peter Gordon, Jason John. BSc, U. Sydney, 1964, MSc, 1966; PhD, U. London, 1969; diploma, Imperial Coll. Sci. and Tech., London, 1969. Mgr. quality control and environ. conservation Shell Oil Co., Wood River, Ill., 1977-80; mgr. dept. chemistry Shell Devel. Co., Houston, 1980-82, mgr. chem. research applications, 1982-83; dir. research Triton Bioscis., Inc., Alameda, Calif., 1983-85, v.p. research and devel., 1985—. Mem. Southwestern Ill. Indsl. Assn. (Outstanding Mem. award 1977), Sierra Club. Republican. Avocations: fine arts, backpacking, skiing, literature. Office: Triton Bioscis Inc 1501 Harbor Bay Pkwy Alameda CA 94501

COLE, KAREN LORRAINE, operating engineer; b. Norco, Calif., Apr. 12, 1954; d. William G. Willis and Lorraine Ruth (Buratti) Willis Beisner; children: Cirdon Brion, Vanna Alia. Apprentice, Trade Tech., Los Angeles, 1980-84, Journeyman Grad., 1984. Apprentice engr. Cushman & Wakefield, Los Angeles, 1980-83, Bank of Calif., 1983-84, chief operating engr., 1984—. Active Boy Scouts Am. Mem. Nat. Assn. Female Execs., Bldg. Owners and Mgrs. Assn., Local 501 Internat. Union Operating Engrs. Avocations: design and construct stained-glass windows. Office: Cushman & Wakefield Calif Inc 515 S Flower St Suite 2200 Los Angeles CA 90071

COLE, MALVIN, physician, educator; b. N.Y.C., Mar. 21, 1933; s. Harry and Sylvia (Firman) C.; A.B. cum laude, Amherst Coll., 1953; M.D. cum laude, Georgetown U. Med. Sch., 1957; m. Susan Kugel, June 20, 1954; children—Andrew James, Douglas Gowers. Intern, Seton Hall Coll. Medicine, Jersey City Med. Ctr., 1957-58; resident Boston City Hosps., 1958-60; practice medicine specializing in neurology, Montclair and Glen Ridge, N.J., Montville, N.J., 1963-72, Casper, Wyo., 1972—; teaching fellow Harvard Med. Sch., 1958-60; Research fellow Nat. Hosp. for Nervous Diseases, St. Thomas Hosp., London, Eng., 1960-61; instr. Georgetown U. Med. Sch., 1961-63; clin. assoc. prof. neurology N.J. Coll. Medicine, Newark, 1963-72, acting dir. neurology, 1965-72; clin. assoc. prof. neurology U. Colo. Med. Sch., 1973—; mem. staff Martland Hosp., Newark, Wyo. Med. Ctr., Casper, U. Hosp., Denver. Served to capt. M.C., AUS, 1961-63. Licensed physician, Mass., N.Y., Calif., N.J., Colo., Wyo.; diplomate Am. Bd. Psychiatry and Neurology, Nat. Bd. Med. Examiners. Fellow ACP, Am. Acad. Neurology, Royal Soc. Medicine; mem. Assn. Research Nervous and Mental Disease, Acad. Aphasia, Am. Soc. Neuroimaging, Internat. Soc. Neuropsychology, Harveian Soc. London, Epilepsy Found. Am., Am. Epilepsy Soc., Am. EEG Soc., N.Y. Acad. Sci., Osler Soc. London, Alpha Omega Alpha. Contbr. articles to profl. jours. Home: Spring Valley Ranch Casper WY 82644 Office: 246 S Washington St Casper WY 82601

COLE, PETER WILLIAM, financial executive; b. Berkeley, Calif., Oct. 8, 1939; s. William Robertson and Bernadette Marie (Jordan) C.; B.S. in Engring., U. Calif., Berkeley, 1962; M.B.A., U. So. Calif., 1965; m. Sharleen Martin, June 7, 1969; children—Peter Martin, Megan McKenzie, Christian Granger (dec.), Meredith Elizabeth. Self employed investor, fin. adviser Peter Cole Co., Piedmont, Calif., 1978—; ptnr. L.H. Alton and Co., 1986—; bd. dirs. Amtec Corp.; mng. gen. ptnr. Menlo Park Assocs.; asst. to v.p. Bechtel Corp., San Francisco, 1965-70; investment officer Am. Express Investment Mgmt. Co., San Francisco, 1970-76; investment officer Bank Am. Capital Corp., San Francisco, 1976-78. Served with U.S. Army, 1962. Mem. Nat. Assn. Petroleum Investment Analysts, U. Calif. Engring. Alumni Soc. Address: 1070 Winsor Avenue Piedmont CA 94610

COLE, RICHARD, environmental consulting executive; b. N.Y.C., Apr. 16, 1924; s. Albert and Celia (Ast) C.; m. Margaret Cooney, June 2, 1947; children: Ann Irene, Carol Beatrice. BS in Chem. Engring., CCNY, 1944; MS, U. Ill., 1948, PhD, 1952. Chemist, ops. research analyst U.S. Naval Radiol. Def. Lab., San Francisco, 1952-59, head countermeasures evaluation br., 1959-64, head chem. tech. div., 1964-69; v.p. Environ. Sci. Assoc., San Francisco, 1969—; also bd. dirs. Environ. Sci. Assocs., San Francisco, 1974—. Served with USN, 1944-46, PTO. Mem. Am. Chem. Soc., Ops. Research Soc. Am., N.Y. Acad. Scis., Assn. Environ. Profls. (pres. San Francisco Bay Area Chpt., 1978, state dir. 1979-81), Air Pollution Control Assn., Sigma Xi, Phi Lambda Upsilon. Office: Environ Sci Assocs 760 Harrison St San Francisco CA 94107

COLE, RICHARD GEORGE, public administrator; b. Irvington, N.J., Mar. 11, 1948; s. Warner W. and Laurel M. (Wilson) C. AS in Computer Sci., Control Data Inst., Anaheim, Calif., 1972; BA in Sociology, Calif. State U., Los Angeles, 1974; MA in Social Ecology, U. Calif., Irvine, 1976; postgrad., So. Oreg. State Coll., 1979. Computer operator Zee Internat., Gardena, Calif., 1971; teaching asst. U. Calif., Irvine, 1974-75; planner Herman Kimmel & Assocs., Newport Beach, Calif., 1976-78; program analyst The Job Council, Medford, Oreg., 1980-81, compliance officer, 1981-82, mgr. adminstrv. services, 1982—; dir. fin. system devel. project Oreg. Joint Pub. Venture, Salem, 1986—; instr. Calif. Community Coll.; chmn. bd. trustees Job Council Pension Trust, Medford, 1982—; mem. curriculum adv. com. Rogue Community Coll., Grants Pass, Oreg., 1986; mgr. computer project State of Oreg., Salem, 1983-84; mem. Oreg. Occupational Info. Coordination Com., Salem, 1982-84. Pres. bd. trustees Vector Control Dist., Jackson County, Oreg., 1985, treas., 1986; candidate bd. dirs. Area Edn. Dist., Jackson County, 1986; treas. Job Service Employer Com., Jackson County, 1986, 87; dir.fin. system development project Oreg. Joint Public Venture. Fellow LaVerne Noyes, U. Calif., Irvine, 1974; Dr. Paul Doehring Found. scholar, Glendale, Calif., 1973; Computer Demonstration grantee State of Oreg., Salem, 1983. Mem. Am. Soc. Personnel Adminstrn., Assn. So. Oreg. Pub. Adminstrs., Oreg. Employment and Tng. Assn., Pacific N.W. Personnel Mgmt. Assn. (chpt. treas. 1985—, Appreciation award 1985). Home: 575 Morey Rd Talent OR 97540 Office: The Job Council 3069 Crater Lake Ave Medford OR 97504

COLE, RICHARD KEITH, electrical engineer; b. Colorado Springs, Colo., Apr. 11, 1959; s. Gene Paul and Mary Blanche (Cieloha) C.; m. Linda Elaine Harris, June 16, 1979; children: Stephanie Renee, Sabrina Rachelle. BSEE, U. Colo., 1983. Design draftsman Aero Engring., Colorado Springs, 1980-82; safety tech. NCR, Colorado Springs, 1982-83, process engr., 1983—. Mem. Soc. Creative Anachronism. Avocations: hunting, fishing, camping, skiing, woodworking. Home: 1200 Chippewa Trail Box 4365 Woodland Park CO 80866 Office: NCR 1635 Aeroplaza Colorado Springs CO 80916

COLE, ROBERT VIRGIL, insurance broker; b. Dallas, Aug. 8, 1937; s. Robert Eugene and Inez (Hearn) C.; m. Carol Ann Wiker, July 31, 1960; children: Richard, Michael, Patricia. BS in Polit. Sci., UCLA, 1960; postgrad., Pepperdine, 1969-71, UCLA, 1971-73. Ins. broker Tolman and Wiker Ins. Brokers, Ventura, Calif., 1961—; founder, chmn. bd. Mfg. Tech. Inc., Ventura, Venvirotek, Ventura; founder ptnr. Bread n' Honey Music, Ventura, 1977—; prin. founder, dir. Affordable Homes, Ventura, 1985—. Bd. dirs. Narramore Found., Rosemead, Calif.; elder Bible Fellowship Ch., Ventura, 1984—; lay leader United Meth. Ch., Ventura, 1978-79. Served with USCG, 1955-62. Mem. Ins. Brokers Assn., Ind. Ins. Agts. Assn. (pres. 1966-68), Jr. C. of C. (bd. dirs. 1963-67). Republican. Lodge: Lions. (pres. 1974-75). Avocations: camping, water skiing, fishing. Office: Tolman and Wiker PO Box 1388 Ventura CA 93003

COLE, ROGER DAVID, biochemist, educator; b. Berkeley, Calif., Nov. 17, 1924; s. Naylor Elmer and Frances (Slankard) C.; m. Thelma Bennett, July 11, 1944; children—David Naylor, Miriam Faith, Janice Joy. B.S., U. Calif. at Berkeley, 1948, Ph.D., 1954. Jr. research biochemist U. Calif. at Berkeley, 1954-55, faculty, 1958—, prof. biochemistry, 1965—, chmn. dept. biochemistry, 1968-73, dir. Electron Microscopy Lab., 1978-84; Nat. Found. Infantile Paralysis fellow Nat. Inst. Med. Research, London, Eng., 1955-56; research asso. Rockefeller Inst. Med. Research, N.Y.C., 1956-58; Guggenheim Meml. fellow Lab. for Molecular Biology, Cambridge, Eng., 1966-67; mem. adv. com. Am. Cancer Soc., 1972-75, 79; external examiner Chinese U., Hong Kong, 1974-77; com. mem., sect. chmn., lectr. sci. confs., 1955—, cons. numerous pubs., 1960—. Mem. editorial bd.: Archives Biochemistry and Biophysics, 1965-77, Biochimica Biophysica Acta, 1966-78, Biochemistry, 1971-76, Jour. Biol. Chemistry, 1973-79, Internat. Jour. Peptide and Protein Research, 1985—; contbr. articles to profl. jours. Hon. lectureship-Newmark Lectr., 1987. Mem. AAAS, Am. Soc. Biol. Chemists, Am. Chem. Soc. (nominating com. biol. chemistry div. 1976-77, alt. councillor 1984-86, vice chmn. 1986-88), Sigma Xi (pres. Calif. chpt. 1974-75). Home: 1147 Park Hills Rd Berkeley CA 94708 Office: U Calif Biochemistry Bldg Berkeley CA 94720

COLE, TERRY RONALD, financial consultant; b. Hancock, Mich., Sept. 18, 1945; s. Homer Theodore Cole and M. Betty (Bianchi) Cole Grohne; m. Melissa Joan Meyer, Mar. 30, 1985; 1 child, Anthony Theodore. BS in Fin., U. Ill., 1967; MBA, Mich. State U., 1969; cert. chartered fin. cons., The Am. Coll., Bryn Mawr, Pa., 1982. Prin. T.R. Cole & Assocs., Kent, Ohio, 1971-77; v.p. Fin. Planning Service Inc., Colorado Springs, Colo., 1978-81; pres. J.M.I. Fin. Group Inc., Colorado Springs, 1982—. Pres. North End Comml. Assn., Colorado Springs, 1984-86—. Mem. Internat. Assn. Fin. Planning, Registry of Fin. Planning Practitioners. Republican. Club: Plaza (Colorado Springs). Avocation: snow skiing. Home: 418 Valley Hi Circle Colorado Springs CO 80910 Office: JMI Fin Group Inc 731 N Weber St Colorado Springs CO 80903

COLE, WILLIAM MANNING, social science educator; b. Los Angeles, Apr. 11, 1930; s. Carroll Manning and Doris (Mullarky) C.; m. Sharon Burkherd, Dec. 28, 1958 (div. Aug. 1976); children: Kenneth, Michael, Julie, Victoria, Jeannine. Bachelor, U. Calif., Santa Barbara, 1954; Master, Calif. State U., Los Angeles, 1960; PhD, Tex. A&M U., 1976. Tchr., coordinator Los Angeles Unified Schs., 1954-65; prof. health and safety studies Calif. State U., Los Angeles, 1965—; mem. nat. transp. research bd. Nat. Research Council, Washington, 1984—. Editor: Jour. Traffic Safety Edn., 1985-86. Mem. Los Angeles County Com. on Affairs of the Aging, 1984-86. Served with USN, 1951-53, Korea. Mem. Calif. Assn. Safety Edn. (bd. dirs. 1977—), Am. Driver and Traffic Safety Edn. Assn. (bd. dirs. 1979-81), Phi Kappa Phi, Phi Delta Kappa. Republican. Presbyterian. Avocation: amateur radio. Office: Calif State U 5151 State University Dr Los Angeles CA 90032

COLE-BEUGLET, CATHERINE MARIE, radiology educator; b. Windsor, Ont., Can.; came to U.S., 1962; d. John McKay Cole and Mary Electa Downey; m. Charles Paul Beuglet, May 29, 1973; 1 child, Charles Cole. BS, U. Western Ont., London, 1958, MD, 1962. Diplomate Am. Bd. Radiology. Asst. prof. radiology McGill U., Montreal, Que., Can., 1970-75; asst. prof. U. Wash., Seattle, 1975-76; assoc. prof. Thomas Jefferson U., Phila., 1978-82, prof., 1982-85; prof. U. Calif. Irvine, Orange, 1985—. Mem. editorial bd. Jour. Health Care Tech.; jour. reviewer Jour. Am. Med. Assn., Jour. Clin. Ultrasound, Jour. Ultrasound in Medicine, Roentgen Ray Jour.; contbr. articles to profl. jours. Fellow Am. Coll. Radiology, Royal Coll. Physicians and Surgeons of Can., Am. Inst. Ultrasound Medicine; mem. AMA, Am. Roentgen Ray Soc., Can. Assn. Radiologists, Radiological Soc. North Am. (editorial bd. jour. 1980—), Assn. Univ. Radiologists, Breast Imaging Soc., Soc. Study of Breast Disease. Office: U Calif Irvine Med Ctr 101 City Dr S Orange CA 92668

COLE KYLE, DIANA MURIEL, dance educator; b. Danville, Pa., Oct. 2, 1943; d. Eugene A. and Aunda Ann (McCool) Cole; m. John Orme Kyle, Aug. 11, 1984. BFA in Ballet magna cum laude, U. Utah, 1966, MA in Ballet, 1971; postgrad., Colo. Coll., 1968-69; BFA in Drama and Dance, U. Mont., 1980. Cert. drama and dance educator, Mont. Instr., head of dance dept. Eastern N.Mex. U., Portales, 1967-70; dance instr. U. Iowa, Iowa City, 1971-72; pvt. practice dance instr. Kalispell, Mont., 1973-75, Terpsichore Sch., Kalispell, 1981-82; dance instr. Flathead Valley Community Coll., Kalispell, 1983-87; ethnic Spanish dance instr. Luisa Triana, Los Angeles, 1958, 59, 61 and 63; José Greco, West Baden, Ind., 1968; advanced tap instr. De Rae Dance Studio, Los Angeles, summers 1958, 59, 61 and 63; performing ballet Utah Civic Ballet Co., U. Utah, Salt Lake City, 1963-67; dance instr. U. Utah, 1966-67; performing modern dance Colo. Coll., Colorado Springs, 1968, 69; summer dance workshop instr. U. Mont., Missoula, 1982-85; with Danceworks, Missoula, summer 1986. Choreographer (modern) The Dreamer, 1968; (ballets) The Bird of Time, Eastern N.Mex. U., 1968, Transfigured Night, Eastern N.Mex. U., 1969. U. Utah Pres. grantee, 1965; Hanya Holm scholar, 1969. Mem. Mont. Dance Arts Assn., Phi Kappa Phi, Alpha Lambda Delta. Episcopalian. Avocations: photography, watercolors, piano, hiking, archery. Home: 773 5th Ave WN Kalispell MT 59901 Office: Flathead Valley Community Coll Humanities Dept Kalispell MT 59901

COLEMAN, BARBARA NASH, library executive; b. Lincolnton, Ga., d. Harvey Morgan and Daisy (Murray) Nash; m. James H. Coleman (dec.). B.A., Spelman Coll., 1956; M.S. in L.S., Atlanta U., 1962. Asst. librarian Donaldson AFB, Greenville, S.C., 1959-62, head librarian, 1962-63; head librarian Paine AFB, Everett, Wash., 1963-66, Hamilton AFB, Ignacio, Calif., 1966-73; library mgr. Peterson AFB, Colorado Springs, Colo., 1973—; cons. Calif. Pub. Library Devel. Bd., 1969-72. Creator Intercultural Festival, 1969, Future Scis. and Astronauts Program, 1983; designer Frustration Symposium, 1972. Recipient Sustained Superior Performance award Peterson AFB, 1983, 84, 85, Air Force Pub. Relations award, 1985. Mem. ALA (pres. armed forces librarians sect. 1975), LWV. Republican. Roman Catholic. Home: 5235 S Carefree Circle Colorado Springs CO 80917 Office: Base Library Stop 60 Peterson AFB CO 80914

COLEMAN, BERNARD WAYNE, airline executive; b. Ashland, Oreg., Sept. 20, 1946; s. Wayne and Violet Mae (Moore) C.; m. Judith Elaine Libby, May 10, 1966; 1 child, Michele Elaine. AS, Sacramento City Coll.; BA, Loma Linda U. Lic. comml. pilot. Dir. flight observation South Am. Conf. S.D.A. North Coast, Fortelaza, Brazil, 1975-77; exec. v.p. Memphis Aero Corp., 1977-83; gen. mgr. CSX Beckett Aviation Co., Oakland, Calif., 1983-84; pres. AAR Western Skyways, Inc., Troutdale, Oreg., 1984—. Mem. Nat. Air Transp. Assn. (cert.). Republican. Avocations: snowskiing, flying, sailing, scuba diving. Home: 14232 Meadow Grass Lake Oswego OR 97034 Office: AAR Western Skyways Portland-Troutdale Airport Troutdale OR 97060

COLEMAN, BERNICE E., psychiatrist; b. Jersey City, June 15, 1925. BA, Cleve. State U., 1955; MD, Howard U., 1968; MPH, Yale U., 1973. Diplomate Am. Bd. Psychiatry and Neurology. Lectr., instr. Yale U., New Haven, 1972-73; med. dir. Salvation Army Addiction Treatment Facility, Honolulu, 1973—; pvt. practice psychiatry Honolulu, 1973—; asst. prof. psychiatry U. Hawaii Sch. Medicine, 1974-82; chief of psychiatry Queens Med. Ctr., Honolulu, 1982—; assoc. clin. prof. psychiatry, U. Hawaii, 1982—; disability determination cons. Div. Vocat. Rehab., State of Hawaii, 1978—. Fellow Am. Psychiat. Assn.; mem. Hawaii Psychiat. Soc. (pres. 1979-82), Hawaii Med. Assn., Am. Med. Soc. on Alcoholism and Other Drug Dependencies, ACLU (Hawaii bd. dirs. 1980—). Avocations: music, theater, swimming. Home: 4182-1 Keanu St Honolulu HI 96816 Office: 3624 Waokanaka St Honolulu HI 96817

COLEMAN, DOROTHY IRENE HART, public relations executive; b. Juneau, Alaska, Nov. 9, 1924; d. Julius Harold and Dorothy (Canfield) Hart; m. Don Coryell, May 20, 1952 (div. 1957); m. 2d, Patrick Coleman, Dec. 15, 1957; children—Mary Patricia and Anne Dorothy (twins). B.A., U. Wash., 1947, postgrad., 1947-50; postgrad. UCLA, 1956-60. Asst. to dir. U. Wash. Sch. Journalism, Seattle, 1947-50; reporter Seattle Post-Intelligencer, 1945-57, 50-52; columnist Honolulu Star-Bull., 1952-53; women's editor Vancouver (B.C.) News Herald, 1953-54; pub. relations dir. U. B.C., Vancouver, 1954-55; news editor Wenatchee (Wash.) Daily World, 1955-56; feature writer Los Angeles Mirror, 1956-59, women's editor, 1959-62; asst. family sect. editor Los Angeles Times, 1962; women's editor Los Angeles Herald-Examiner, 1963-68; pub. relations dir. Hollywood Presbyn. Hosp., 1968-72; pres. Dorothy Coleman Pub. Relations, Los Angeles, 1972-73; dir. communications Braille Inst. Am., Inc., 1973-82; dir. community relations Meml. Med. Centers, Inc., 1982—. Served to lt. comdr., USNR, 1950-65. Mem. Los Angeles Press Club, San Francisco Press Club, Honolulu Press Club, Wash. State Press Club, Can. Women's Press Club, Am. Women in Radio and TV, Am. Coll. Pub. Relations Assn., Women in Communications (chpt. pres. 1964), Pub. Relations Soc. Am., Los Angeles Advt. Women, Los Angeles Publicity Club, Gifted Children's Assn., Kappa Alpha Theta. Home: 32 Cedar Tree Ln Irvine CA 92715 Office: 1111 W La Palma Ave Anaheim CA 92803

COLEMAN, ESTHER MARIE, nurse; b. Bakersfield, Calif., Jan. 13, 1940; s. Johnnie Folmer and Florence Elizabeth (Hershey) P.; m. Kenneth Neal Coleman, June 20, 1964; children: Laury, Gary, Michael. RN, Knapp Coll. Nursing, 1960; BS, U. Calif., San Francisco, 1962; MS, Calif. State U., Los Angeles, 1986. Staff nurse Kaiser Permanente, San Francisco, 1961-63; pub. health nurse Alameda County, San Rafael, Calif., 1962-64, Los Angeles County, Glendale, Calif., 1964-69; staff nurse Burbank (Calif.) Community Hosp., 1980-82; home health nurse Meml. Hosp., Glendale, 1982—; staff therapist Fuller Seminary, Pasadena, Calif., 1984—; speaker Elder Abuse Heritage House and Issues of Aging and Caregiving, Pasadena, 1984—. Leader Cub Scouts and Girl Scouts, Glendale, 1973-82; pres. PTA, Glendale, 1980; elder and tchr. Grandview Presbyn., Glendale. Mem. Calif. Nurses Assn., Los Angeles County Mental Health Assn., Christian Assn. Psychol. Services. Republican. Avocations: traveling, camping, reading, family. Home: 1924 Chilton Dr Glendale CA 91201 Office: Heritage Ho 447 N El Molino Pasadena CA 91101

COLEMAN, GLENN ELDRIC, architect, illustrator; b. Seattle, May 1, 1941; s. Charles John and Eva Marie (Mason) C.; 1 child, Jake. Student U. Calif.-Berkeley, 1959-63. Lic. architect, Calif. Archtl. intern AIA, Santa Rosa, Calif., 1977—; illustrator. Mem. AIA (editor chpt. newsletter 1977-80). Democrat. Address: 2458 Gad's Hill Std 38 Santa Rosa CA 95401

COLEMAN, JEFFREY OWEN, electrical engineer; b. Louisville, Oct. 1, 1953; s. Everett Shannon Coleman and Rose Marie Fain; m. Teresa Gae Dame, 1972 (div. 1986); 1 child, David Jason. BSEE, MIT, 1975; MSEE, Johns Hopkins U., 1979. Mem. tech. staff Watkins-Johnson Co., Gaithersburg, Md., 1975-76, Digital Communications Corp., Gaithersburg, 1976-77; sr. design engr. Penril Corp., Rockville, Md., 1977-78; electronics engr. Naval Research Lab., Washington, 1978-85; contract engr. The Boeing Co., Seattle, 1985—; elec. engring. fellow U. Wash., Seattle, 1986—. Contbr. articles to profl. publs. Mem. IEEE, Assn. Computing Machinery, Inst. Cert. Computers Profls., Sigma Xi, Tau Beta Pi, Eta Kappa Nu. Home: PO Box 95680 Seattle WA 98145-2680 Office: U Wash Dept Elec Engring FT 10 Seattle WA 98195

COLEMAN, JOHN RANDALL, anesthesiologist; b. Franklin, Tenn., Jan. 23, 1943; s. Edgar Alexander and Jane A. Wilkins) C.; m. Angela Martinez, Dec. 20, 1975. B.A., Vanderbilt U., 1965; M.D., U. Tenn., 1970. Diplomate Am. Bd. Emergency Medicine. Intern Los Angeles County-U. So. Calif. Med. Ctr., Los Angeles, 1971-72, resident physician in anesthesiology, 1983-85, chief resident, 1985; staff anesthesiologist Kaiser Found. Hosp., Panorama City, Calif., 1985—, Meml. Hosp., Glendale, Calif.; resident in obgyn Kaiser Found. Hosp., Los Angeles, 1974-75; dir. emergency dept. Meml. Hosp. of Glendale, Calif., 1977-82; emergency physician St. Joseph Med. Ctr., Burbank, Calif., 1982-83; resident physician in anesthesiology Los Angeles County-U. So. Calif. Med. Ctr., Los Angeles, 1983-85; chief resident physician, 1985—. CPR instr. Am. Heart Assn., Los Angeles, 1975-83. Named Doctor of Yr., Stanton Community Hosp., 1972. Mem. Am. Soc. Anesthesiologists, Calif. Soc. Anesthesiologists, Los Angeles County Soc. Anesthesiologists. Office: Kaiser Found Hosp 13642 Cantera St Panorama City CA 91402

COLEMAN, ROBERT TRENT, vocational rehabilitation and career counselor, consultant human relations; b. Gary, Ind., Feb. 4, 1936; s. Robert Clinton and Lucille Verna C.; m. Dorothy Agnes, Aug. 1957; children—Sean, Bryce, Daniel; m. 2d, Patricia Lou, June 13, 1976; m. 3d Polly Anderson, Sept. 15, 1984. B.A. in Speech Therapy, U. Wash., Seattle, 1962; postgrad. in speech U. Redlands, 1963-64; M.S. in Rehab. Counseling, U. Oreg., 1971. Cert. rehab. counselor, career counselor; nat. cert. counselor. Social worker, San Bernardino City Welfare Dept., 1963-64; correctional counselor Calif. Rehab. Center, Norco, 1964-67; sr. counselor Job Corps, Clearfield, Utah, 1967; assoc. dir. Ednl. Systems Corp., Washington, 1968-69; ptnr. Black Fir Jade Mines, Big Sur, Calif., 1971-76; vocat. specialist Internat. Rehab. Assn., San Diego, 1976-77; vocat. rehab. counselor Sharp Hosp., San Diego, 1977-80; clin. coordinator San Diego Pain Inst., 1981; cons. in rehab. counseling, career guidance, human relations, Carlsbad, Calif., 1981-83; propr. R.T.C. Cons. Services, Escondido and San Diego, 1983—. Commr., Handicapped Appeals Commn., San Marcos, Calif., 1981-83. Served with U.S. Army, 1955-58. Mem. Am. Assn. for Counseling and Devel. (pres.), San Diego Career Guidance Assn. (pres. 1984), Assn. Indsl. Rehab. Reps. (pres. 1983), Am. Rehab. Counseling Assn., Nat. Assn. Rehab. Profls. in Pvt. Sector (standards and ethics com. 1986—). Republican. Home: 538 Glenheather Dr San Marcos CA 92069 Office: 210 S Juniper St Suite 100 Escondido CA 92025

COLEMAN, ROGER DIXON, bacteriologist; b. Rockwell, Iowa, Jan. 18, 1915; s. Major C. and Hazel Ruth Coleman; A.B., UCLA, 1937; postgrad. Balliol Coll., Oxford (Eng.) U., 1944; M.S., U. So. Calif., 1952, Ph.D., 1957; m. Lee Aden Skov, Jan. 1, 1978. Sr. laboratorian Napa (Calif.) State Hosp., 1937-42; dir. Long Beach (Calif.) Clin. Lab., 1946—, pres., 1980—; mem. Calif. State Clin. Lab. Commn., 1953-57. Served as officer AUS, 1942-46. Diplomate Am. Bd. Bioanalysts. Mem. Am. Assn. Bioanalysts, Am. Assn. Clin. Chemists, Am. Soc. Microbiologists, Am. Chem. Soc., Am. Venereal Disease Assn., AAAS (life), Calif. Assn. Bioanalysts (past officer), Med. Research Assn. Calif., Bacteriology Club So. Calif., Sigma Xi, Phi Sigma (past chpt. pres.). Author papers in field. Home: 30041 Running Deer Ln Laguna Beach CA 92677 Office: Cen Diagnostic Lab 3500 W Lomita #104 Torrance CA 90505

COLEMAN, ROGER W., institutional food distribution company executive; b. Newark, Mar. 30, 1929; s. Bernard Simpson and Evelyn (Bornstein) C.; m. Ruth Rykoff (div. Apr. 1982); children—William, Wendy, Paul, Eric; m. Francesca Marie Wesselius, Sept. 1983. B.S., UCLA, 1950. Gen. mgmt. positions Rogay Food Supply div. S. E. Rykoff & Co., Los Angeles, 1951-58; purchasing and gen. mgmt. positions S.E. Rykoff & Co., Los Angeles, 1958-63, gen. mgr., 1963-67, pres., chief exec. officer, 1967—; pres. John Sexton, 1983-86, Rykoff-Sexton, Inc., 1983—. Bd. dirs. Los Angeles Conv. Ctr., Reiss-Dis Child Study Ctr., Los Angeles. Mem. Nat. Inst. Food Service (bd. dirs.), United Instnl. Distbrs. Inc. (pres.), N.Am. Foodservice Corp. (pres.). Clubs: Los Angeles Athletic, Hillcrest Country. Avocation: golf. Home: 515 Homewood Rd Los Angeles CA 90049 Office: Rykoff-Sexton Inc 761 Terminal St Los Angeles CA 90021

COLEN, ALLYN R., engineer; b. Cleve., Jan. 19, 1920; s. Morry M. and Ann M. (Minsky) C.; m. Joy Rosalind Colen; children: Russell, Laurel. BSME, Ohio State U., 1949; BEd, Ariz. State U., 1967, MEd, 1970.

Registered profl. engr. Ariz., Calif., Nev., N.Mex., Okla., Colo., Wash. Prin. ETC Engring., Phoenix, 1976-78; dir. engring. Enercom, Inc., Tempe, Ariz., 1978-81; engr. Airresearch, Inc., Phoenix, 1981-82; prin. A.R. Colen Engring., Phoenix, 1982-84; v.p. Johannessen & Girand Engrs., Phoenix, 1984—, Diversified Engring., Phoenix, 1985—. Chmn. Electric League, Phoenix, 1985, Energy Civic Program, Phoenix, 1982. Served to sgt. U.S. Army, 1941-45. Mem. ASHRAE, ASPE, Assn. Energy Engrs. (charter), Electric League Ariz. Jewish. Office: Diversified Engring Co 8940 N 19th Ave Phoenix AZ 85021

COLER, JOEL H., motion picture company executive; b. Bronx, N.Y., July 27, 1931; s. Irving A. and Pauline (Leader) C.; B.A. in Journalism and Sociology, Syracuse U., 1953; m. Sandra Cohen, Oct. 10, 1959; children—Karen, Linda. With NBC, N.Y.C., 1955-59, advt. asst., 1955-59; asst. account exec. Grey Advt. Inc., N.Y.C., 1959-64; dir. internat. advt. and publicity 20th Century Fox Film Corp., Los Angeles, 1964-81, v.p. advt. and publicity 20th Century Fox Internat., 1981—; lectr. internat. film. mktg. U. So. Calif., UCLA; film industry rep. Scandinavia Today Com. Mem. adv. bd. local pvt. schs.; mem. Los Angeles Olympic Adv. Com., 1982-84; trustee Scott Newman Found., 1984—. Served to capt. USAF, 1953-55. Mem. Motion Picture Acad., N.Y. Fgn. Press Assn. Home: 18744 Kenya St Northridge CA 91326 Office: 10201 W Pico Blvd Los Angeles CA 90213

COLES, BRAD, investor, realtor; b. San Francisco, Aug. 23, 1949; s. Alberto Gomez and Nadine (Reveron) C.; m. Theresa Renee Beaman, Aug. 23, 1982; children—James Alberto, Yvonne Marie. B.A., U. San Francisco, 1972. Ins. salesman Mut. of Omaha, San Francisco, 1972-76; v.p. D&D, Inc. dba Oil Can Harry's Disco, San Francisco, 1976-80; ptnr. Tess & Assocs., Honolulu, 1982—; communication exec. Hawaiian Tel GTE, Honolulu, 1986—; owner TRB Mgmt., Honolulu, 1986— . Mem. Friends of Fasi, 1978—, Hawaii Deaf Awareness Assn., 1979. Mem. Life Underwriters Assn., Honolulu Bd. Realtors, San Francisco Tavern Owners Assn. Republican. Club: Plaza (Honolulu). Home and Office: 1860 Ala Moana Blvd #1606 Honolulu HI 96815

COLETTA, GERARD CHARLES, management consultant; b. Cambridge, Mass., Dec. 9, 1944; s. Gerard Charles and Eileen Gertrude (Barrett) C.; m. Pamela S. Wight, June 30, 1984; children: Nadine, Sean. BSChemE, Tufts U., 1966; MSChemE, MIT, 1968; postgrad., U. Calif., Berkeley, 1969-71. Design engr. Standard Oil of Calif., San Francisco, 1968-71; staff cons. Arthur D. Little, Inc., Cambridge, 1971-78; corp. dir. of safety and health Nat. Semiconductor Corp., Santa Clara, Calif., 1978-81; sr. cons. Risk Planning Group, Darien, Conn., 1981-83; pres. Risk Control Services, Tiburon, Calif., 1983-86; practice mgr. Tillinghast div. TPF&C, San Francisco, 1986—. Contbr. articles to profl. jours. Mem. ASTM (chmn. com. 1980-85, bd. dirs. sub-com. 1987—, Spl. Service award 1985, Achievement award 1986), Am. Soc. Safety Engrs., Nat. Safety Mgmt. Soc., Tufts U. Chem. Engring. Alumni Council. Republican. Avocations: tennis, skiing, jogging. Office: Tillinghast div TPF&C 101 California St San Francisco CA 94111

COLEY, SORAYA MOORE, social work educator; b. Wilmington, N.C., Nov. 25, 1950; d. John H. Moore and Majoria (McWilliams) Morgan; m. Ron T. Coley, Aug. 18, 1979. BA, Lincoln U., 1972; MSW, Bryn Mawr Coll., 1974, PhD, 1981. Project dir. Nat. Urban League, N.Y.C., 1975-76, research cons., 1976—; survey mgr. Mathematica Policy Research, Princeton, N.J., 1979-81; assoc. prof. Calif. State U., Fullerton, 1981—; research cons. Planned Parenthood, Santa Ana, Calif., 1984-85; acad. panel chmn. Coalition Concerned with Adolescent Pregnancy, Santa Ana, 1986—. Mem. United Way, Garden Grove, Calif., 1984—, Orange County Health Planning Council, Tustin, Calif., 1984-85. Recipient Vol. award United Way, 1983, 84, faculty research award Calif. State U., 1983; NIMH fellow U. Mich., 1984. Mem. Nat. Assn. Social Workers, Nat. Coalition Against Domestic Violence, Black Women's Forum, Delta Sigma Theta. Club: Links (Orange County). Avocation: jogging. Office: Calif State U Human Services 800 N State College Blvd Fullerton CA 92634

COLGIN, RUSSELL WEYMOUNT, clinical psychologist, consultant screenwriter, producer; b. Ontonagon, Mich., May 10, 1925; s. Russell W. and Signe E. (Peterson) C.; divorced; children—Dennis, Russell, Marc, Kevin, Sean, Siobhan. B.S., Lake Forest Coll., 1949, M.A., 1950; Ph.D., Northwestern U., 1953. Cert. clin. psychologist, Calif. Psychologist VA Hosp., Downey, Ill., 1949; asst. prof. Lake Forest Coll. (Ill.), 1950-53; asst. prof. North Park Coll., Chgo., 1951-53; pvt. practice clin. psychology, 1953—; cons. to Big Bros. of Los Angeles 1965-78, Midtown Sch., Los Angeles, 1968-78; instr. Los Angeles State U., Northridge, 1965-66; producer, chmn. bd. Star Cinema Prodns., Hollywood, Calif., 1980—. Served with USN, 1942-45. Mem. Am. Psychol. Assn., Los Angeles County Psychol. Assn., AAUP, Los Angeles World Affairs Council, Sigma Xi. Club: Rotary of Los Angeles. Contbr. articles to profl. jours.; screenwriter Young Warriors, 1982. Office: 648 N Doheny Dr Los Angeles CA 90069

COLHOUR, DONALD BRUCE, theater, TV producer-director; b. Ellsworth, Kans., May 28, 1946; s. Bruce and Ruth (Williams) C. BS in Journalism, U. Kans., 1969. Unit prodn. mgr. ABC, Inc., Los Angeles, 1969-80; mgr. spl. projects ABC Entertainment, Los Angeles, 1980-83, dir. spl. projects, 1983—; exec. producer Los Angeles Bach Festival, Los Angeles, 1985-86; cons. Claremont Sch. Theology, 1986—. Producer theatrical concerts Dionne Warwick, 1984, Dudley Moore, 1983, John Denver, 1983, Wayne Newton, 1983, Perry Como, 1982; theatrical rev. You'll Love It, 1986. Lay minister 1st Congl. of Los Angeles; communicator on ministry Nat. Assn. Congregation Chs., Los Angeles, 1986—; producer AIDS Project, Los Angeles, 1985, Beverly Hills B'Nai B'Rith, 1985, Devereux Found., 1983, 84, 85, United Jewish Fund, 1984, Boys Club of Am., 1984, Am. Jewish Com., 1984, Nat. Conf. Christians and Jews, 1984, 86, United Cerebral Palsy Tennis Festival, 1983-87, Entertainment Industries Council Drug Abuse, 1986. Mem. Hollywood Radio and TV Soc., Acad. TV Arts and Scis. Lodge: Masons. Avocations: religion, arts, music. Office: ABC Entertainment 2020 Ave of the Stars Los Angeles CA 90067

COLLADAY, JOHN STEPHEN, banker; b. Riverside, Calif., Mar. 18, 1940; s. John Louis and Marcella (Webster); m. Paula Swaney, Oct. 23, 1965; 1 child, John Stephen Jr. BA, U. So. Calif., 1963; M in banking, U. Wash. Grad. Pacific Coast Banking Sch., 1982. First v.p. Security Pacific Bank, Riverside, 1985—. Chmn. bd. dirs. community ventures corp. Riverside Community Hosp., 1985-86; chmn. Keep Riverside Ahead, 1986—; pres. World Affairs Council, 1981-85; treas. Riverside Vis. and Conv. Bur., 1984-86; bd. dirs. Riverside Community Hosp., 1982-85, U. Calif. Riverside Found., 1981—; mem. econ. devel. com. City Riverside, 1982—, econ. devel. com. County Riverside, 1983—; named campaign chmn. United Way Western Riverside County, 1986. Recipient Leadership Achievement trophy B'nai Brith, 1986. Mem. Greater Riverside C. of C. (pres. 1984-85, bd. dirs. 1981—, pres. econ. devel. div., 1982-84), Internat. Wine and Food Soc. Republican. Episcopalian. Clubs: Victoria; Frank Miller (chmn. 1985—). Home: 2824 Rumsey Dr Riverside CA 92506 Office: Security Pacific Nat Bank 3737 Main St Riverside CA 92501

COLLER, RICHARD WALTER, sociology educator; b. St. Paul, Aug. 29, 1925; s. Walter A. and Helen E. (Kretz) C.; m. Alicia Mabuhay Peruda, Aug. 12, 1950; children—Louis, Margarite, Ann, James, Katherine, Susan, William, Mark, Claire, Ruth, Patrick. B.A., U. Minn., 1948, Ph.D., 1959; M.A., U. Hawaii, 1951. Lectr., U. of East, Manila, 1951; instr., then prof. sociology U. Philippines, Quezon City, 1952-62; tng. instr. Peace Corps, Hilo, Hawaii, 1962-66; prof. sociology Kauai Community Coll., Lihue Kauai, Hawaii, 1966-84. Served with U.S. Army, 1943-46. Mem. Community Coll. Social Sci. Assn., Soc. Applied Anthropology, Am. Sociol. Assn., Philippine Studies Assn. Roman Catholic. Club: Filipino Cath. of St. Catherine's Parish. Author: Barrio Gacao, 1962; co-author: Sociology in the Philippine Setting, 1954, Filipinos in Rural Hawaii, 1984. Home and Office: 4911 Lani Rd Kapaa HI 96746

COLLET, RICHARD JOSEPH, joint venture expert, business manager; b. Los Angeles, Mar. 14, 1949; s. Rudolph Joseph and Bernal June (Rippe) C.; m. Rebecca Romney, Apr. 21, 1979; children: Rachel Michelle, Denise Ruth, Joseph Ben. BS in Acctg., Brigham Young U., 1973; JD, U. Calif., San Francisco, 1976. Law clk. to presiding justice Nev. Superior Ct., Las Vegas, 1976; exec. v.p. Uni-Mgrs., Internat., Los Angeles, 1977-83; regional mgr. Automated Lang. Processing Systems, Santa Monica, Calif., 1983-84; dir. med. practice devel. Am. Med. Internat., Inc., Brea, Calif., 1985-86; field coordinator real estate devel. sect. Am. Med. Internat., Inc., Beverly Hills, Calif., 1986—; v.p. and bd. dirs. Italimex, Beverly Hills; chief exec. officer, gen. mgr. Spangolf Enterprises, Inc., Los Vegas, 1986—. Named Eagle Scout Boy Scouts Am., Las Vegas, 1963; Jaycees scholar, Las Vegas, 1967. Democrat. Mormon. Avocations: linguistics, guitar, history, genealogy, skiing. Home: Ruiz Zorrilla 16-2 J, 39009 Santander Spain

COLLIER, ALICE LOUISE (TSCHANEN), speech pathologist; b. Marion, Ohio, Sept. 18, 1931; d. Charles Frederick Tschanen and Luella (Gravina) Dixon; m. Charles Theodore Collier, Sept. 18, 1954; children: Catherine Anne Collier-Edmands, Michael Alan, Kevin Charles, John Harold. BS in Edn., Bowling Green State U., 1953; MS in Edn., Western N.Mex. U., 1955; postgrad., Portland State U., 1963. Speech therapist Huron County Schs., Norwalk, Ohio, 1953-54; tchr. Bagdad (Ariz.) Pub. Schs., 1961-62; speech pathologist Beaverton (Oreg.) Sch. Dist., 1962-66, 70-85; mem. spl. edn. profl. enhancemnt program Beaverton Sch. Dist. 48, 1986—. Editor Speech and Language Development, 1985. Pres. Bagdad PTA, 1961-62; v.p. Whitford Parent-Tchrs. Club, Beaverton, 1967-68, pres., 1968-69; council mem. Band Parents Assn. Beaverton High Sch., 1984-85; mem. Mary Lee Singers, Beaverton, 1971-76. Recipient 19-Yr. Employee Service Recognition award Beaverton Sch. Dist., 1986. Mem. NEA, Oreg. Edn. Assn., Beaverton Edn. Assn., Am. Speech Lang. Hearing Assn., Oreg. Speech Lang Hearing Assn. (state council 1965-68), Delta Zeta. Democrat. Episcopalian. Avocations: tennis, bicycling, sewing, singing. Home: PO Box 546 Beaverton OR 97075 Office: Beaverton Sch Dist 48 PO Box 200 Beaverton OR 97075

COLLIER, CLARENCE ROBERT, educator, physician; b. Freeport, Ill., Mar. 25, 1919; s. William Henry and Bertha (Berg) C.; m. Helen Louise Watson, Sept. 3, 1942; children: Roberta, David, Barbara (Mrs. Bob Acquistapace). B.A., Andrews U., 1940; M.D., Loma Linda U., 1949. Intern White Meml. Hosp., Los Angeles, 1948-49; resident White Meml. Hosp., 1949-52; instr. medicine Loma Linda U., 1952-56, asst. prof. medicine, 1956-57, asso. prof. physiology, 1957-64, prof., chmn. dept. physiology and biophysics, 1964-70; asso. prof. medicine U. So. Calif., Los Angeles, 1970-71; prof. medicine and physiology U. So. Calif., 1971-83, prof. emeritus, 1983—; vis. prof. physiology U. de Montemoreles, Mex., 1987—; cons. in physiology Christian Med. Coll., Vellore, India, 1972—; chmn. research screening com. Calif. Air Resources Bd., 1983—; chief med. sci. service Rancho Los Amigos Hosp., Downey, Calif., 1962-64. Editorial bd.: Am. Physiol. Soc. 1965-71. Served with AUS, 1941-44. Research fellow Nat. Found. Infantile Paralysis, 1955-56; Sr. research fellow NIH, 1959-62. Fellow ACP; mem. Am. Physiol. Soc., Western Soc. Clin. Research, AAAS, Am. Fedn. Clin. Research, Am. Thoracic Soc. Research in respiratory physiology. Office: 6930 Casa Contenta Somerset CA 95684

COLLIER, DOUGLAS WAYNE, JR., food service design and construction company executive, consultant; b. Indpls., Sept. 25, 1940; s. Douglas Wayne and Ethel Jeanne (Workman) C.; m. Judith Sue Pruyn, Nov. 27, 1963 (div.); m. 2d, Catherine Leach, Sept. 13, 1980; children: Douglas Wayne III, Adam Bryon Collier. Student Purdue U., 1962, Los Angeles Valley Coll., 1963-66, UCLA, 1970-71. Cert in real estate and site selection Nat. Restaurant Assn. Designer, Parvin Dohrmann Corp., Los Angeles, 1963-68; dir. equipment and fixtures Internat. Industries, Inc., Beverly Hills, Calif., 1968-76; v.p. Design Concept, Inc., Phoenix, 1976-80; pres. Douglas Collier & Assocs., Inc., Phoenix, 1980—; cons. food service; lectr. Purdue U., Scottsdale Community Coll., Ariz. State U.; mem. Nat. Housing Adv. Panel, 1979. Chmn., Republican Legis. Dist., Phoenix, 1980-82; pres. Scottsdale (Ariz.) Rep. Forum, 1982; program chmn. Phoenix Rep. Forum, 1982, v.p. 1984, pres. 1985, sec. 1986, 87; mem. Ariz. Rep. State Com., 1980-86, del. nat. conv. Dallas, 1984; bd. dirs. Central Ariz. Mus. History, Phoenix. Served with USMC, 1958-66. Recipient award of commendation, Ariz. State U. Coll. Architecture, 1981; Food Facilities Design award Sheraton Tucson El Conquistador Golf and Tennis Resort, 1983. Mem. Internat. Foodservice Execs. Assn., Ariz. Restaurant Assn., Ariz. Hotel/Motel Assn., Am. Polit. Collectors (pres. 1986-87), Ariz. Archeol. Soc., Ariz. Assn. Fine Woodworkers. Club: Masons (Scottsdale). Designer numerous projects including: MGM Grand Hotel fire remodel and new tower, Las Vegas, Nev., El Conquistador Resort and Conf. Ctr., Tucson, Beside the Pointe, Phoenix, The Boulders Resort, Carefree, Ariz., Hotel Westcourt in the Buttes, Phoenix, Embassy Suites Hotels, Ariz., Calif., Fla., Utah, Va. Office: 4251 E Thomas Rd Phoenix AZ 85018

COLLIER, MARLENE LUCRETIA, advertising executive; b. Fullerton, Calif., Dec. 29, 1933; d. Jay Jefferson Lilley and Alice Elizabeth (Killen) Goodman; m. Robert C. Chavez, Oct. 15, 1955 (div. May 1978); children: Loraine L., James Jay, Richard Charles; m. Robler Heigh, July 11, 1979. Grad. high sch., Fullerton, Calif. Apprentice Orange County Printing Co., Fullerton, 1940-54; typesetter, prodn. artist Covina (Calif.) Sentinental, 1954-56; typesetter, prodn. artist, bindery various locations, Calif., 1956-62; typesetter, assoc. pub. Visitor Internat. Publs., Las Vegas, 1964-79; advt. dir. Miller Mags., Ventura, Calif., 1980—; prodn., circulation cons. Image Style Mag., Panorama City, Calif., 1983—. Mem. Women in Satellite Communications. Avocations: dancing, singing, knitting, horseback riding. Home: 325 Fourth St Fillmore CA 93015 Office: Miller Mags 2660 E Main St Ventura CA 93003

COLLIER, MARSHA ANN, publishing executive; b. N.Y.C., Dec. 4, 1950; d. Samuel Schleimer and Claire (Schmelzer) Tracy; m. David Dickman, June 4, 1978, (divorced); 1 child, Susan Marie. Student, Miami Dade Jr. Coll., 1968-70, U. Miami, 1970-72. Advt. account exec. Miami (Fla.) Herald, 1977; spl. projects mgr. Daily News, Los Angeles, 1977-84; pres. Collier Advt. & Promotion inc., Northridge, Calif., 1984—; bridal show dir. Daily News, Los Angeles, 1978-83; gen. mgr. Dodger Blue, Los Angeles, 1982-83; pub. So. Calif. Autoracing Newspaper, 1985—, Score News-(official pub. of Score Internat.), 1986—. Mem. Am. Autoracing Writers and Broadcasters Assn., Advt. Club Los Angeles, So. Calif. Mktg. Dirs. Assn., Internat. Council Shopping Ctrs. Republican. Avocation: photography.

COLLIER, RICHARD BANGS, foundation executive; b. Hastings, Nebr., Aug. 12, 1918; s. Nelson Martin and Stella (Butler) C.; B.A., U. Wash., 1951. Fgn. aid officer GS14, civil aviation Am. embassy, Bangkok, Thailand, 1958-63; founder, dir. Pleneurethic Internat., Spokane, Wash., 1963—. Carnegie fellow Inst. Public Affairs, Grad. Sch., U. Wash., 1950-51. Nat. adv. bd. Am. Security Council. Served to capt. USAF, 1965-66. Mem. Assn. Supervision and Curriculum Devel., Soc. Health and Human Values, Internat. Platform Assn., Acad. of Polit. Sci., AAAS, Royal Inst. Philosophy (Eng.), Senatorial Club. Republican. Author Pleneurethic, 13 vols., 1964-81. Home: PO Box 1256 Tacoma WA 98401

COLLIER, TRACY KIM, biochemist, researcher; b. Renton, Wash., Feb. 9, 1954; s. Tracy Marvin and Eleanor Ann (Sipila) C.; m. Katherine L. Larson, June 17, 1978; children, Sarah May, Christopher Jacob. BS, U. Wash., 1976, MS, 1978, postgrad., 1984—. Technician NOAA, Nat. Marine Fisheries Service, Seattle, 1972-76, fishery biologist, 1976-78, research chemist, 1978—. Contbr. articles to sci. publs. Mem. Pacific Northwest Assn. Toxicologists (charter), Sigma Xi. Avocations: carpentry, gardening, cross country skiing. Home: 9390 Miller Rd NE Bainbridge Island WA 98110 Office: Nat Oceanic Atmospheric Assn Nat Marine Fisheries Service 2725 Montlake Blvd E Seattle WA 98112

COLLINGS, CELESTE LOUISE, marketing executive, professional artist; b. Highland Park, Ill., Dec. 9, 1948; d. Robert Zane Jr. and Laura (Vasaly) C.; m. John Austin Darden III, July 17, 1971 (div. July 1975); 1 child, Desiree Anne; m. John Cochran Barber, Dec. 13, 1984. BA, U. Ariz., 1970; postgrad., N.Mex. State U., 1975; completed mktg. mgr. seminar, U. Calif., Irvine, 1978; cert. of achievement, Wilson Learning Course, 1983. Art tchr. Devargas Jr. High Sch., Santa Fe, 1971; artist, pvt. tchr. Las Cruces, N.Mex., 1971-75; sales rep. Helpmates Temp. Services, Santa Ana, Calif., 1975-76; sales account mgr. Bristol-Myers Products, N.Y.C., 1976-82; sales mgr. Profl. Med. Products, Greenwood, S.C., 1982-85; mktg. mgr. med. products Paper-Pak Products, La Verne, Calif., 1985—; mgmt. trainee Bristol-Meyers, Kansas City, Mo., 1978; sales trainee Profl. Med. Products, Greenwood, 1983, product strategy, 1984, chmn. nat. adv. com., 1983-84; owner and pres. Accent Soji Screens, Newport Beach, Calif., 1981. Exhibited in one-woman art shows at Nancy Dunn Studio and Gallery, San Clemente, Calif., 1980, The Collectables, San Francisco, 1980, Laguna Beach (Calif.) Festival of the Arts Art-A-Fair, 1981, Ariz. Inter-Scholastic Hon. Exhibit, 1st place award, 1962-66, Glendale Fed. Savs. Art Exhibition, 1982; numerous others. Mem. Orange County Performing Arts Ctr., Corona Del Mar, Calif., 1981. Recipient 10 sales awards Bristol-Meyers, 1976-82, Western Zone Sales Rep. award Profl. Med. Products, 1984, Gainers Club award, 1984; named Nat. Sales Rep. of Yr. Profl. Med. Products, 1984. Mem. U. Ariz. Alumni Assn., Kappa Alpha Theta Alumni. Roman Catholic. Office: Paper-Pak Products Inc 1941 White Ave La Verne CA 91750

COLLINGS, CHARLES LEROY, supermarket executive; b. Wewoka, Okla., July 11, 1925; s. Roy B. and Dessie L. C.; m. Frances Jane Flake, June 28, 1947; children—Sandra Jean, Dianna Lynn. Student, So. Methodist U., 1943-44, U. Tex., 1945. Sec., controller, dir. Noble Meat Co., Madera, Calif., 1947-54; chief accountant Montgomery Ward & Co., Oakland, Calif., 1954-56; with Raleys, Sacramento, 1956—; sec. Raleys, 1958—, pres., 1970—, also dir. Bd. dirs. Pro Athlete Outreach, Youth for Christ. Served with USNR, 1943-46. Mem. Calif. Grocers Assn. (dir., officer). Republican. Baptist. Home: 6790 Arabela Way Sacramento CA 95831 Office: Raleys 500 W Capitol Ave Broderick CA 95605

COLLINS, ASHTON BUDD, JR., management consultant; b. Birmingham, Ala., Mar. 28, 1932; s. Ashton Budd and Hughie (Beatty) C.; m. Susan Elizabeth May; children: Ashton Budd III, Kimball Prince. BA, Cornell U., 1954. V.p. Reddy Communications, Inc., Greenwich, Conn., 1961-63, pres., 1963—, chief exec. officer, 1969—; bd. dirs. Pub. Service Co. N.Mex., Albuquerque, 1979—. Trustee Thomas Alva Edison Found., Nat. Found. Sudden Infant Death, 1967-72. Served to capt. USAF, 1955-57. Mem. Pub. Relations Soc. Am. (dir. utilities sect.), Issues Mgmt. Assn., Edison Electric Inst. (lectr. exec. mgmt. course). Republican. Episcopalian. Clubs: Round Hill, Albuquerque Tennis. Office: Reddy Communications Inc PO Box 3209 Albuquerque NM 87190

COLLINS, BENJAMIN IRESON, geologist in oil, gas, minerals; b. New Britian, Conn., Nov. 23, 1942; s. Laurence Walker Collins and Margery (Robinson) Morehouse; m. Phyllis Ann Parrington, Feb. 28, 1970 (div.); m. Joyce Ann Seelen, Apr. 12, 1986. BA, Windham Coll., Putney, Vt., 1969; MA, Dartmouth Coll., 1971; PhD, U. Mont., 1975. Staff geologist N. Am. Exploration, Charlottesville, Va., 1975-77; staff geologist Anaconda Minerals Co., Denver, 1977-80, dist. geologist, 1980-82; sr. geologist ARCO Exploration, Denver, 1982-85; v.p. Schreider & Collins, Denver, 1985—. Served with USN, 1962-65. Mem. Am. Assn. Petroleum Geologists, Am. Inst. Profl. Geologists, Sigma Xi (research grant 1973). Avocations: skiing, hunting, fishing. Office: Schreider & Collins 1660 Lincoln Suite 1900 Denver CO 80264

COLLINS, BRADLEY JAMES, planning consultant; b. Flint, Mich., July 22, 1948; s. Dale Edward and Ruth Estella (Shue) C.; m. Janice Anne Dean, June 14, 1969; children: Alexander, Brianna. BA, Albion Coll., 1970; M in Urban Planning, U. Wash., 1979. Environ. planner Environ. Works, Seattle, 1970-73; land use planner Wilsey & Ham, Bellevue, Wash., 1974; housing planner II King County, Seattle, 1975-77; self-employed cons./planner, Seattle, 1977; prin./planner The Phoenix Group, Seattle, 1978-81; planning dir. City of Tukwila, Wash., 1981-86; prin. Collins & Assocs., 1986—; mem. exec. bd. Seattle 2000 Commn., 1972-73, citizen task force River Basin Coordination Com., Seattle, 1972-75; instr. Grad. Sch. Urban Planning, U. Wash., 1979-81; bd. dirs. Environ. Works, Inc., Seattle, 1971-84. Mem. Capitol Hill Community Council, Seattle, 1972-73, subcom. King County Environ. Devel. Commn., Seattle, 1972-73. Exchange student Am. Field Service, Grusch, Switzerland, 1965. Mem. Am. Inst. Cert. Planners, Urban Land Inst. (assoc.), Am. Planning Assn. (pres. Puget Sound sect.), Phi Alpha Theta. Club: Capital Hill Soccer (coach 1972-82), Bainbridge Island Water Polo, Bainbridge Island Youth Soccer (coach 1985—). Office: 411 First Ave S Merrill Pl Suite 660 Seattle WA 98104

COLLINS, CHARLES THOMPSON, biology educator, ornithological consultant; b. Long Branch, N.J., Mar. 9, 1938; s. Cyril Kenneth and Frances Boyce (Thompson) C.; m. Patricia Hart Meehan, May 24, 1985. BA, Amherst Coll., 1960; MS, U. Mich., 1962; PhD, U. Fla., 1966. Asst. prof. Fairleigh Dickinson U., Madison, N.J., 1967-68; from asst. prof. to prof. biology Calif. State U., Long Beach, 1968—; Fulbright research prof., India, 1974-75. Contbr. articles to profl. jours. Chapman Research fellow Am. Mus. Natural History, 1966-67. Mem. Cooper Ornithol. Soc. (treas. 1981—), Am. Ornithologists Union. Home: 6001 Fairbrook St Long Beach CA 90815 Office: Calif State U Dept Biology Long Beach CA 90840

COLLINS, DOROTHY (MRS. AKIBA EMANUEL), advertising and public relations agency executive; b. Salt Lake City; d. Joseph L. and Dorothy (Frey) C.; A.B., U. Denver; m. Akiba Emanuel; 1 dau., Lynn Collins. Woman's page editor Rocky Mountain News, Denver; fashion editor NBC, N.Y.C.; pub. relations dir. Shwayder Bros., Denver; account exec. Ellington & Co., N.Y.C.; v.p. Infoplan, N.Y.C.; v.p., mgr. consumer group Burson-Marsteller, N.Y.C.; sr. v.p., chief exec. officer Public Relations div. Sam Lusky Assos., Inc., Denver, 1981-83; v.p., dir. consumer mktg. Burson Marsteller, Denver, 1983—. Former nat. dir. women's activities Nat. Jewish Hosp., Denver; active Girl Scouts U.S.A.; trustee Marymount Coll., 1979-80, Spalding Rehab. Hosp., 1984—. Mem. Nat. Home Fashions League (pres. N.Y. chpt. 1977-79, pres. Rocky Mountain chpt. 1985-86), Women's Forum, Exec. Women in Pub. Relations, Colo. Press Assn. Club: Denver Women's Press, Denver Press. Home: 2950 Albion St Denver CO 80207

COLLINS, EARL ROGERS, JR., mechanical engineer; b. Green Castle, Ind., Apr. 30, 1929; s. Earl Rogers and Ruby (Larkin) C.; m. Dorothy Fautley, Jan. 1, 1953; children: Michael, Jo Ann. BSME, U. So. Calif., 1960. Owner, operator Collins Mfg. Co., Los Angeles, 1957-60; mem. tech. staff Jet Propulsion Lab., Pasadena, 1960—; v.p., bd. dirs. Ennis Parking Corp., Pasadena; bd. dirs. Calif. Inst. Tech. Fed. Credit Union. Inventor mech. devices (numerous NASA awards 1965—). Home: 801 Craig Ave La Canada CA 91011 Office: Jet Propulsion Lab 4800 Oak Grove MS 171/301 Pasadena CA 91109

COLLINS, EUGENE BOYD, chemist, consultant; b. Los Angeles, May 28, 1917; s. Harold Porter and Mina Rosannah (Eversoll) C.; m. Frances Louise File, Aug. 4, 1946 (div. May 1962); children: Dana, Diane, Eric; m. Helen Lucille Schultz, Oct. 16, 1966; 1 child, Dane. BS in Chemistry, UCLA, 1951, diploma in edn., 1962; DSc (hon.), De Landas U., 1952; cert. advanced med. tech., Calif. State U., Dominguez Hills, 1977; MD, U. Cen. del Este, San Pedro, Dominican Republic, 1982. Lic. clin. lab. technologist, Calif.; cert. tchr., Calif. Assoc. dir. spectroscopy Union Oil Co. (Unocal), Wilmington, Calif., 1951-57; prof. chemistry Los Angeles Harbor Coll., Wilmington, 1957-74; cons. chemist Collins and Assocs., Carson, Calif., 1974-79, 83—; pres. Boyd Collins Co., South Gate, Calif., 1960-70; cons. Holley Carburetor Co. Research Lab., San Pedro, Calif., 1957-60. Contbr. articles to profl. jours. Commr. Boy Scouts Am., Long Beach, Calif., 1958-59. Served as sgt. U.S. Army, 1944-46, ETO. Mem. AAAS, Am. Chem. Soc., Internat. Union of Pure and Applied Chemistry (affiliate), Am. Pharm. Assn., Acad. Pharm. Scis., N.Y. Acad. Scis., Am. Assn. Clin. Chemsitry. Mormon. Lodge: Optomists (Hollywood, Calif.) (treas. 1977-78). Avocations: history, chess, internat. affairs. Home: 317 Gina Dr Carson CA 90745 Office: 3868 Carson St Suite 332 Torrance CA 90503

COLLINS, GEORGE TIMOTHY, computer software consultant; b. Connersville, Ind., Aug. 21, 1943; s. Robert Emerson and Oma (Richie) C.; m. Martha Elizabeth Holt, Apr. 30, 1966; children: Kirsten Stephanie, Eowyn Erika. BA in Math., Ind. U., 1966; MS in Computer Sci., Rensselaer Poly. Inst., 1971. Engr. program analyst Sikorsky Aircraft, Stratford, Conn., 1966-70; research mathematician Peter Eckrich, Ft. Wayne, Ind., 1970-75; sr. systems analyst Pyrotek Data Service, Ft. Walton Beach, Fla., 1975-77; sr. aerosystems engr. Gen. Dynamics, Ft. Worth, 1977-79; sr. specialist Electronic Data Systems, Las Vegas, Nev., 1979-81; sr. assoc. CACI Fed., San Diego, 1981-82; prin., gen. mgr. Structured Software Systems, Escondido, Calif., 1982—; cons. Hi-Shear Corp., Los Angeles, 1973-75. Developer (computer model and data base) Aircraft Stores Interface, 1975; (computer model) TAC Disrupter, 1981; co-developer (computer model) Tactical Air

Def. Battle Model, 1978, Tactical Air and Land Ops., 1980. Bd. dirs. Family and Children's Service, Ft. Wayne, 1974. Mem. Assn. Computing Machinery (assoc.). Unitarian. Club: North County Chess (Escondido). Avocations: chess, tennis, astronomy. Office: Structured Softwares Systems 121 W Eighth Ave Escondido CA 92025

COLLINS, JACK CARL, automotive executive; b. San Mateo, Calif., July 18, 1946; s. Jack C. and Josephine J. (Buda) C.; m. Bonnie M. Urrere, Dec. 15, 1973; children: Catherine, Jennifer. BS in Mktg., San Jose State U., 1970; MBA, UCLA, 1972. Various sales and mktg. positions Ford Motor Co., Oakland, Calif., St. Louis and Detroit, 1973-81; nat. advt. mgr., nat. bus. planning mgr. Toyota Motor Sales USA, Torrence, Calif., 1981-85; mktg. dir. Hyundai Motor Am., Garden Grove, Calif., 1985—. Served to 1st lt. arty. U.S. Army, 1965-68, Vietnam. Office: Hyundai Motor Am 7373 Hunt Ave Garden Grove CA 92642

COLLINS, JAMES ARTHUR, fast food company executive; b. Huntington Park, Calif., Dec. 20, 1926; s. Albert Preston and Lucile Marie (Riglesberger) C.; m. Carol Elizabeth Leonard, July 15, 1950; children: Cathleen E., Kelly L., Michael J., Melissa L. B.S. in Civil Engring., UCLA, 1950. Civil engr. Thiesen Constrn. Co., Pasadena, Calif., 1950-52; owner, operator Airport Village Hamburger Handout, Culver City, Calif., 1952-68; chmn., chief exec. officer Collins Foods Internat., Inc., Los Angeles, 1968—; also dir. Collins Foods Internat., Inc. Bd. dirs. YMCA Met. Los Angeles; past chmn. bd. mgrs. Westside Los Angeles YMCA; chmn., past pres. U. Calif. at Los Angeles Found.; past regent U. Calif. Served with USN, 1944-46. Named Foodservice Operator of Yr. Internat. Foodservice Mfrs. Assn., 1977; recipient Univ. Service award UCLA, 1977, Profl. Achievement award UCLA, 1981, Alumnus of Yr. award UCLA, 1982, Operator of Yr. award Multi-Unit Food Service Operators, 1986, Horatio Alger award, 1987. Mem. Nat. Restaurant Assn., Calif. Restaurant Assn. (dir., past pres.), Bay Area Restaurant Hotel Assn. (past pres.), Chief Execs. Forum, U. Calif. at Los Angeles Alumni Assn. (past pres.), Young Pres. Orgn. (past chmn. Los Angeles chpt.). Republican. Methodist. Club: Rotary (pres. 1962-63). Office: Collins Food Internat 5400 Alla Rd Los Angeles CA 90066

COLLINS, JOHN WENDLER, consumer products company executive; b. Rutherford, N.J., Nov. 7, 1930; s. Nelson Haley and Agnes Lucinda (Maier) C.; m. Martha E. Raiff, Oct. 26, 1952; children: Bruce, Nancy, Susan; m. Janet Doyle, July 17, 1975. B.A., Dartmouth Coll., 1952. V.p. Procter & Gamble Co., Cin., 1955-76; group v.p. Clorox Co., Oakland, Calif., 1976—, pres., 1986—, dir., 1983—. Trustee East Oakland Youth Devel. Ctr., Oakland, 1976—; com. mem. United Way, Bay Area, 1976—. Served to lt. USNR, 1952-55. Mem. Phi Beta Kappa. Democrat. Home: 19 Honey Hill Rd Orinda CA 94563 Office: Clorox Co 1221 Broadway Oakland CA 94612 *

COLLINS, JON DAVID, engineering consultant, company executive; b. Flint, Mich., Mar. 14, 1935; s. David and Mary Marie (Palmer) C.; m. Nancy Jean Witham, June 22, 1957; children: Mark, Stephen, Paul, Laura. BS in Aero. Engring., U. Mich., 1957; MSME, U. Colo., 1959; PhD in Engring., UCLA, 1967. Registered profl. engr. (mechan., safety, quality), Calif. Engr. The Martin Co., Denver, 1957-59; sect. head TRW Systems, Redondo Beach, Calif., 1959-69; v.p., tech. dir. J.H. Wiggins Co., Redondo Beach, Calif., 1969-81; pres. ACTA, Inc., Torrance, Calif., 1982—; cons. Fed. Electric Co., Lompoc, Calif., 1982—. Contbr. articles to profl. jours. Recipient New Tech. award NASA, 1976. Fellow AIAA (assoc.); mem. ASCE, ASME, Risk Analysis Soc., Systems Safety Soc., Ops. Research Soc. Am. Republican. Mem. Covenant Ch. Am. Avocations: sports. Home: 27817 Longhill Dr Rancho Palos Verdes CA 90274 Office: ACTA Inc 24430 Hawthorne Blvd Torrance CA 90505

COLLINS, KEITH ROGER, medical imaging company executive; b. St. Louis, Aug. 29, 1946; s. Malcolm Keith and Joan Mary (Brown) C. BS, U. Portland, 1968. Sales engr. Gen. Electric Med. Systems, Glendale, Calif., 1972-75, Rohe Sci. Corp., Santa Ana, Calif., 1975-76; systems cons. ADAC Labs., Sunnyvale, Calif., 1977-81; field sales mgr. Schiff Photo-Mechanics, Santa Ana, 1981-85; nuclear medicine mktg. mgr. Toshiba Med. Systems, Tustin, Calif., 1985—. Mem. Soc. Nuclear Medicine, Am. Inst. Ultrasound in Medicine, Am. Diabetes Assn. Republican. Home: 7890 E Spring St Number 18F Long Beach CA 90815 Office: Toshiba Med Systems 2441 Michelle Dr Tustin CA 92680

COLLINS, LORENCE GENE, geology educator; b. Vernon, Kans., Nov. 19, 1931; s. Floyd Iven and Ethyl Faye (Randall) C.; m. Barbara Jane Schenck, Feb. 26, 1955; children: Glenn, Elizabeth, Gregory, Kevin, Rachel. BS, U. Ill., 1953, MS, 1955, PhD, 1959. Instr. geology U. Ill., Champaign, 1958-59; from asst. prof. to assoc. prof. Calif. State U., Northridge, 1959-66, prof., 1966—. Served to 1st lt. USAF, 1955-57. Shell fellow Shell Oil Co., 1954, NSF fellow, 1955. Fellow Geol. Soc. Am. Republican. Methodist. Avocations: nature, photography. Home: 139 Prentiss St Thousand Oaks CA 91360 Office: Calif State U Dept Geol Scis 18111 Nordhoff St Northridge CA 91330

COLLINS, MARY BETH, association executive; b. Detroit, Jan. 3, 1925; d. James Edward and Mildred Ina (Barding) Hughes; B.A., Manhattanville Coll. Sacred Heart, 1947; M.A., Ariz. State U., 1970; m. Taber Loree Collins, Aug. 7, 1947; children—Louise Collins Alton, James, Suzanne, Mary Beth Collins Brenner, Mildred Collins Hittner, Marguerite Collins Zeller, Miriam Collins Huston, Frank, Jesse, Kathleen Collins Cheo, Martha DeVault. Community services coordinator Alcohol and Drug Abuse div. Ariz. Health Dept., Phoenix, 1967-68, acting dir., 1968-70; coordinator City of Phoenix Drug Control, 1970-73; exec. dir. Drug Action Coalition, Montgomery County, Md., 1973-74; exec. dir. Community Orgn. for Drug Abuse Control, 1974-76; adminstr. Office Substance Abuse Services, Mich. Dept. Pub. Health, Lansing, 1977-78; chmn. N.Y. State Commn. Prevention and Edn. of Alcohol and Substance Abuse, Albany, 1978-79; exec. dir. Internat. Assn. Prevention Programs, 1974—. Pres. Ariz. Family, Inc., 1970-71; bd. dirs. Community Orgn. for Drug Abuse Control, 1969-73; mem. adv. bd. Good Samaritan Hosp., Mental Health Services; mem. bd. Nat. Coordinating Council on Drug Edn., 1974-76. Mem. Internat. Council on Alcoholism and Addictions, Drugs, Alcohol and Women's Health Coalition (regional chmn.), Ariz. Alumnae of Sacred Heart (founding pres. 1963-64), Pi Lambda Theta. Home: PO Box 1825 Cave Creek AZ 85331 Office: PO Box 812 Carefree AZ 85377

COLLINS, MICHAEL J., food company executive; b. Milw., Dec. 14, 1947; s. Louis J. and Catherine (Daly) C.; m. Sharon A. Manley, Dec. 18, 1971; children: Patrick, Megan. BA, U. Notre Dame, 1969. Sales rep. Procter & Gamble, Dayton, Ohio, 1971-77; dist. sales mgr. Pepsi Cola Co., Indlps., 1977-79; area sales mgr. Pepsi Cola Co., San Francisco, 1979-81; div. v.p. Pepsi Cola Co., Chgo., 1981-84; v.p. franchise sales Taco Bell div. Pepsi Cola Co., Irvine, Calif., 1985—. Served to 1st lt. U.S. Army, 1969-71, Vietnam. Mem. Notre Dame Alumni Assn. Roman Catholic. Office: Taco Bell Corp 16808 Armstrong Irvine CA 92714

COLLINS, MICHAEL SEAN, physician; b. Yankton, S.D., Sept. 8, 1951; s. Edward Daniel and Joyce (Slatky) C.; m. Judy Furman, Sept. 20, 1975; children: Lauren, Sean, Carolyn. BS, Davidson Coll., 1973; MD, Med. U. S.C., 1977. Diplomate Am. Bd. Ob-Gyn. Chief resident in ob-gyn Med. U. S.C., Charleston, 1980-81; instr. in ob-gyn U. Oreg. Health Scis. Ctr., Portland, 1981—; chmn. dept. ob-gyn Good Samaritan Hosp., Portland, 1983-85; cons. Prepared Childbirth Assn., Portland, 1981—, Triplet Connection, Los Angeles, 1985—. Fellow Am. Coll. Ob-Gyn; mem. AMA, Oreg. Med. Assn., Oreg. Ob-Gyn Soc., Am. Fertility Soc., Porsche Club Am. Republican. Roman Catholic. Avocations: photography, rose gardening, jogging, traveling. Home: 3844 SW Jerald Way Portland OR 97221 Office: NW Women's Clinic 2222 NW Lovejoy Portland OR 97210

COLLINS, ROBERT FLOYD, optometrist; b. Cleve., Aug. 11, 1935; s. Aaron J. and Ethel M. (Zalkind) C.; m. Shari A. Ballonoff, Dec. 2, 1956; m. 2d Sheila Joan Berkley, Nov. 28, 1981; children—Robyn, Wendy, Teri, Jay, Mark, Wayne. B.S., U. So. Calif., 1961; O.D., So. Calif. Coll. Optometry, 1964. Lic. optometrist, Calif. Pvt. practice optometry, North Hollywood, Calif., 1966—; dir. Vision Safeguard Health Plan, Whittier, Calif., 1982—. Office: 6765 Lankershim Blvd North Hollywood CA 91606

COLLINS, ROBERT OAKLEY, history educator; b. Waukegan, Ill., Apr. 1, 1933; s. William George and Louise Van Horsen (Jack) C.; m. Janyce Hutchins Monroe, Oct. 6, 1974; children by previous marriage: Catharine Louise, Randolph Ware, Robert William. B.A., Dartmouth Coll., 1954; A.B. (Marshall scholar 1954-55), Balliol Coll., Oxford U., 1956, M.A., 1960; M.A. (Ford fellow), Yale U., 1958, Ph.D., 1959. Instr. history Williams Coll., Williamstown, Mass., 1959-61; lectr. U. Mass. Extension, Pittsfield, 1960-61; vis. asst. prof. history Columbia U., N.Y.C., 1962-63; asst. prof. history Williams Coll., 1963-65; mem. faculty U. Calif., Santa Barbara, 1965—; prof. history U. Calif., 1969—; dir. U. Calif. (Center for Study Developing Nations), 1967-69, acting vice chancellor for research and grad. affairs, 1970-71, dean grad. div., 1971-80; vis. sr. assoc. fellow Oxford U., Eng., 1980-81; Trevelyan fellow Durham U., 1986—. Author: The Southern Sudan, 1883-1898, 1962, King Leopold, England and the Upper Nile, 1968, Problems in African History, 1968, The Partition of Africa, 1969, Land Beyond the Rivers: The Southern Sudan, 1898-1918, 1971, Europeans in Africa, 1971, An Arabian Diary, 1969, The Southern Sudan in Historical Perspective, 1975, Shadows in the Grass: Britain in the Southern Sudan, 1983, The British in the Sudan, 1898-1956, 1984. NDEA lang. fellow, 1960-61; Social Sci. Research Council fellow, 1962-63; Rockefeller Found. scholar-in-residence Bellagio, Italy, 1979, 87; Ford Found. fellow, 1979-81; Fulbright sr. research fellow, 1982; Woodrow Wilson fellow, 1983; recipient Gold class award Order Scis. and Arts Dem. Republic of Sudan, 1980; John Ben Snow Found. prize, 1984; Trevelyan fellow Coll. Fellows Durham U., 1986, fellow Balliol Coll., Oxford U., 1986-87. Mem. Am. Hist. Assn., African Studies Assn., Western River Guides Assn., Explorers Club, Phi Beta Kappa. Home: 735 Calle De Los Amigos Santa Barbara CA 93105 Office: Dept History U Calif Santa Barbara CA 93106

COLLINS, TERRENCE LEE, human resources executive, retired army officer; b. Los Angeles, Aug. 31, 1942; s. Albert Newton and Martha Zeta (Merrill) C.; m. Cheryl Jean Brokaw, Jan. 25, 1978; children—Sean Alexander, Patrick Dean, Michael Paul, Christopher Lee. B.S. in Bus. Adminstrn., Columbia Coll., 1977; M.B.A., Pepperdine U., 1979. Cert. instr. effectiveness mgmt., U.S. Army Organizational Tng. Inst. Enlisted U.S. Army, 1959, commd. capt., 1973, advanced through grades to maj., 1977; multiple assignments primarily in human resources mgmt.; ret., 1979; profl. relations mgr. Nat. Med. Enterprises Inc., Los Angeles, 1979-81; personnel dir. HR Textron Inc., Valencia, Calif., 1981-85; v.p. employee relations VSI Aerospace Products div. Fairchild, Inc., Culver City, Calif., 1985—. Decorated Legion of Merit, 2 Bronze Stars, 4 Meritorious Service medals, Air medal, Army Commendation medal, Nat. Def. Service medal; Vietnam Cross Gallantry, Vietnam Service medal. Mem. Am. Soc. Tng. and Devel., Employment Mgmt. Assn., Am. Soc. Personnel Adminstrs., Army Assn. U.S., Nat. Mgmt. Assn. Republican. Methodist. Author textbook for sr. Army ednl. tng. course. Home: 6184 E Palomino Circle Somis CA 93066 Office: VSI Aerospace Products div Fairchild Inc 3630 Eastham Dr Culver City CA 90232

COLLINS, WILLIAM LEROY, telecommunications engineer; b. Laurel, Miss., June 17, 1942; s. Henry L. and Christene E. (Finnegan) C. Student, La Salle U., 1969; BS in Computer Sci., U. Beverly Hills, 1984. Sr. computer operator Dept. Pub. Safety, Phoenix, 1975-78, data communications specialist, 1978-79, supr. computer ops., 1981-82; mgr. network control Valley Nat. Bank, Phoenix, 1979-81; mgr. data communications Ariz. Lottery, Phoenix, 1982-85; mgr. telecommunications Calif. Lottery, Sacramento, 1985—. Served as sgt. USAF, 1964-68. Mem. Data Processing Mgmt. Assn., Am. Mgmt. Assn., Assn. Computing Machinery. Roman Catholic. Lodge: K.C. Home: 7238 W Mackenzie Dr Phoenix AZ 85033 Office: Calif State Lottery 600 N 10th St Sacramento CA 95814

COLLMAN, JAMES PADDOCK, chemistry educator; b. Beatrice, Nebr., Oct. 31, 1932; married. B.Sc., U. Nebr., 1954, M.S., 1956; Ph.D. (NSF fellow), U. Ill., 1958. Instr. chemistry U. N.C., Chapel Hill, 1958-59; asst. prof. U. N.C., 1959-62, asso. prof., 1962-67; prof. chemistry Stanford U., 1967—, George A. and Hilda M. Daubert prof. chemistry, 1980—; Frontiers in Chemistry lectr., 1964, Nebr. lectureship, 1968; Venable lectr. U. N.C., 1971; Edward Clark Lee lectr. U. Chgo., 1972; vis. Erskine fellow U. Canterbury, 1972; Plenary lectr. French Chem. Soc., 1974; Dreyfus lectr. U. Kans., 1974; distinguished inorganic lectr. U. Rochester, 1974; Reilley lectr. U. Notre Dame, 1975; William Pyle Philips lectr. Haverford Coll., 1975; Merck lectr. Rutgers U., 1976; FMC lectr. Princeton, 1977; Julius Steiglitz lectr. Chgo. sect. Am. Chem. Soc., 1977; Pres.'s Seminar Series lectr. U. Ariz., 1980; Frank C. Whitmore lectr. Pa. State U., 1980; Plenary lectr. 3d IUPAC Symposium on Organic Synthesis, 1980, 2d Internat. Kyoto Conf. on New Aspects Inorganic Chemistry, 1982, Internat. Symposium on Models of Enzyme Action, Brighton, Eng., 1983, Internat. Symposium, Italy, 1984; Brockman lectr. U. Ga., 1981; Samuel C. Lind lectr. U. Tenn., 1981, Syntex Disting. lectr. Colo. State U., 1983; disting. vis. lectr. U. Fla., 1983; vis. prof. U. Auckland, New Zealand, 1985; Nelson J. Leonard lectr. U. Ill., 1987. Recipient Disting. Teaching award Stanford U., 1981, Calif. Scientist of Year award, 1983; named George A. and Hilda M. Daubert Prof. Chemistry (endowed chair, Stanford U.), 1980; Guggenheim fellow, 1977-78, 85-86. Mem. Am. Chem. Soc. (Calif. Sect. award 1972, soc. award in inorganic chemistry 1975, Arthur C. Cope award 1986), N.Y. Acad. Sci., Chem. Soc. (London), Nat. Acad. Sci., Am. Acad. Arts and Scis., Phi Beta Kappa, Sigma Xi, Phi Lambda Upsilon, Alpha Chi Sigma. Office: Stanford U Stauffer II Stanford CA 94305

COLLMER, RUSSELL CRAVENER, data processing exec.; b. Guatemala, Jan. 2, 1924; s. G. Russell and Constance (Cravener) C.; B.S., U. N.M., 1951; postgrad. Calif. Inst. Tech., 1943-44; M.S., State U. Iowa, 1955; m. Ruth Hannah Adams, Mar. 4, 1950; 1 son, Reed Alan. Staff mem. Mass. Inst. Tech., Lincoln Lab., Lexington, 1955-57; mgr. systems modeling, computer dept. Gen. Electric, Phoenix, 1957-59; mgr. ARCAS Thompson Ramo Wooldridge, Inc., Canoga Park, Cal., 1959-62; asso. mgr. tech. dir. CCIS-70 Bunker-Ramo Corp., 1962-64; sr. asso. Planning Research Corp., Los Angeles, 1964-65; pres. R. Collmer Assos., Benson, Ariz., 1965—; pres. Benson Econ. Enterprises Corp., 1968-69. Lectr. computer scis. Pima Community Coll., Tucson, 1970—. Served with USAAC, 1942-46, to capt. USAF, 1951-53. Mem. IEEE, Am. Meteorol. Soc., Assn. for Computing Machinery, Phi Delta Theta, Kappa Mu Epsilon. Republican. Baptist. Office: PO Box 864 Benson AZ 85602

COLLOPY, GEORGE FRANCIS, printing co. exec.; b. San Francisco, Sept. 12, 1921; s. James Edward and Gertrude Frances (Wilhelm) C.; B.A., St. Mary's Coll., 1943; student Jean Turner Art Cntr., 1938-43, Calif. Sch. Fine Arts, 1946-48, Golden Gate Coll., 1946-47; m. Dorothy Rose O'Leary, Aug. 25, 1946; children—Christopher, Kevin, Michael, Jon, Liam, Siobhan. Art dir. Pan Am. World Airways, San Francisco, 1946-59; v.p. Michelson Advt., Palo Alto, Calif., 1959-64; mgr. communications Raychem Corp., Menlo Park, Calif., 1964-74; art dir. George Group Printing Cos., San Francisco, 1975-87; developer art standards for State of Calif. Apprenticeship Program. Bd. dirs. Burlingame Art Assn., 1968-69; mem. Archdiocese Commn. of Worship, Art and Music, Roman Catholic Ch., 1978-81. Served with USAAF, 1943-46. Recipient awards Nat. Cath. Press Assn., 1974-86, 3 awards Printing Industries Am., 1987, 1st award Peninsula Art Assn., 1960. Mem. Am. Inst. Graphic Arts, Soc. Western Art Dirs., San Francisco Art Dirs. Club, San Francisco Soc. Communicating Arts. Contbg. author: Modern Liturgy Handbook (John F. Mossi), 1976; illustrator: Celebrating, 1979, A Festival Day Book (Thomas Kane), 1979. Home: 1345 Cabrillo Ave Burlingame CA 94010 Office: 650 2d St San Francisco CA 94107

COLN, WILLIAM ALEXANDER, III, transportation executive; b. Los Angeles, Mar. 20, 1942; s. William Alexander and Aileen Henrietta (Shimfessel) C.; m. Lora Louise Getchel, Nov. 15, 1969 (div. July 1979); 1 child, Caryn Louise. BA in Geography, UCLA, 1966. Cert. airline transport pilot, flight engr. Commd. USN, Pensacola, Fla., 1966; pilot, officer USN, Fighter Squadron 102, 1969-71, Port Mugu, Calif., 1975-77; pilot, officer USNR, Port Mugu, Calif., 1971-75, advanced through grades to lt. comdr., 1978; ret. USNR, 1984; airline pilot Delta Airlines (formerly Western Airlines Inc.), Los Angeles, 1972—. Recipient Nat. Def. medal USN, 1966. Mem. Nat. Aero. Assn., Airline Pilots Assn., Aircraft Owners and Pilots Assn., UCLA Alumni Assn., Am. Bonanza Soc. Democrat. Club: Santa Barbara (Calif.) Athletic. Avocations: sailing, scuba diving, flying, computers, electronics. Home: 519 West Quinto St Santa Barbara CA 93105 Office: Delta Airlines Inc 6060 Avion Dr Los Angeles CA 90009

COLOMBO, LOUIS JOHN, policy analyst; b. St. Louis, Feb. 8, 1947; s. Louis John and Mary (Boffetti) C. AB, Georgetown U., 1969; MA, Howard U., 1972; PhD, U. Mich., 1981. Mem. staff U.S. Ho. Reps., Washington, 1965-69; research assoc. Inst. for Social Research, Ann Arbor, Mich., 1976; dir. applied research program Sch. Archtl. Planning U. N.Mex., Albuquerque, 1980-83; prin. S.W. Land Research Inc., Albuquerque, 1983—; adj. assoc. prof. U. N.Mex. Sch. Architecture and Planning, Albuquerque, 1981-83; cons. City of Albuquerque Dept. Human Services, 1980, State of N.Mex. Dept. Human Services, 1983, Environ. Simulations Lab. U. Mich., Ann Arbor, 1975, Albuquerque Pub. Schs., 1982. Contbr. numerous articles to profl. jours. Founder Citizens for Alternatives to Radioactive Dumping, Albuquerque, 1977-80; mem. N.Mex. Council on Crime and Delinquency, Albuquerque, 1983—. Rackham predoctoral fellow, 1976. Mem. AAAS, Am. Planning Assn., Urban Land Inst., Kappa Delta Pi. Democrat. Avocations: river running, jogging, photography, cross-country skiing. Home: 2313 Camino de los Artesanos Albuquerque NM 87107 Office: SW Land Research Inc 2400 Louisina Blvd Suite 470 Albuquerque NM 87110

COLOVIC, ALEX JOHN, florist; b. Lubeck, Germany, Aug. 14, 1947; came to U.S., 1953, naturalized, 1959; s. John Daniel and Mary Colovic; student Marquette U., 1965-67; UCLA, 1968-69, U. Calif.-Northridge, 1969-70; m. Goldi Tolliver, May 4, 1978. Asst. oral pathology dept. Marquette U., 1963; clk. Kroger Co., Milw., 1964-66; asst. Chinese chef, Milw., 1965-67; clk. Fedco Foods, Inc., Van Nuys, Calif., 1967-70; sales rep. Symmar Dist., Vernon, Calif., 1971; sales rep. Kennedy Wholesale, Glendale, Calif., 1971-73; owner, operator Plantasia, Glendale, 1973—. Served with Calif. N.G., 1970-76. Mem. Cactus and Succulent Soc., Begonia Soc., Fern Soc., Glendale C. of C., U.S. C. of C. Democrat. Eastern Orthodox. Inventor self humidifying pottery, resin clothing plant stands. Office: Plantasia 2840 N Verdugo Rd Glendale CA 91208

COLPRON, MERLYN DALLAS, insurance executive; b. Newfolden, Minn., June 25, 1933; s. Ismael Charles and Freda Olivia (Nesterud) C.; m. Patricia Rose Gilbert, May 26, 1960; children—Cynthia Jean, David Allen. A.A. in Bus. Adminstrn., Lower Columbia Jr. Coll., 1953; B.A. in Fin., U. Wash., 1955. C.P.C.U. Ins. mgr. United Grocers Inc., Portland, Oreg., 1970-75; bur. chief Idaho Bur. Risk Mgmt. Boise, 1975-76; v.p., cons. Diversified Risk Mgmt. Services Inc., Boise, 1976-80; sec. Assoc. Loggers Mgmt. Corp., Boise, 1979—; v.p. Bayly, Martin & Faye Inc., Boise, 1980-82; pres. U.S. Risk Mgmt. Services Inc., Boise, 1982-86; pres. North/South Ins. Cons., Inc., Miami/Boise, 1986—; dir. Assoc. Loggers Exchange, Boise, 1979—. Served with U.S. Army, 1955-57. Mem. Soc. C.P.C.U. Methodist. Home: 4014 Kingswood Dr Boise ID 83704

COLSON, ELIZABETH FLORENCE, anthropologist; b. Hewitt, Minn., June 15, 1917; d. Louis H. and Metta (Damon) C. B.A., U. Minn., 1938, M.A., 1940; M.A., Radcliffe Coll., 1941; Ph.D. (AAUW Traveling fellow), 1945; Ph.D. (hon.), Brown U., 1978, D.Sociology, 1979; D.Sc., U. Rochester, 1985. Asst. social sci. analyst War Relocation Authority, 1942-43; research asst. Harvard, 1944-45; research officer Rhodes-Livingstone Inst., 1946-47, dir., 1948-51; sr. lectr. Manchester U., 1951-53; assoc. prof. Goucher Coll., 1954-55; research assoc., assoc. prof. African Research Program, Boston U., 1955-59, part-time, 1959-63; prof. anthropology Brandeis U., 1959-63; prof. anthropology U. Calif.-Berkeley, 1964-84, prof. emeritus, 1984—; Lewis Henry Morgan lectr. U. Rochester, 1973. Author: The Makah, 1953, Marriage and the Family Among The Plateau Tonga, 1958, Social Organization of the Gwembe Tonga, 1960, The Plateau Tonga, 1962, The Social Consequences of Resettlement, 1971, Tradition and Contract, 1974; jr. author Secondary Education and the Formation of an Elite, 1980, Voluntary Efforts in Decentralized Management, 1983; sr. editor: Seven Tribes of British Central Africa, 1951; jr. editor People in Upheaval, 1987. Fellow Center Advanced Study Behavioral Scis., 1967-68; Fairchild fellow Calif. Inst. Tech., 1975-76. Fellow Am. Anthrop. Assn., Brit. Assn. Social Anthropologists, Royal Anthrop. Inst. (hon.); mem. Nat. Acad. Sci., Am. Acad. Arts and Scis., Phi Beta Kappa. Office: Dept Anthropology U Calif Berkeley CA 94720

COLT, JOHN ERNEST, engineer, medical center administrator; b. Yonkers, N.Y., May 8, 1943; s. John E. and Alma (Negrini) C.; m. Beth Turner, June 13, 1976 (div.); 1 dau., Rebecca. B.S. Otterbein Coll., 1963; M.S. in Engring., Delaware Valley Agronomy Engr. Coll., 1966. Fgn. service officer U.S. Dept. State Frankfurt, W.Ger., 1967-68; engr. U.S. Postal Service, Washington and Pitts., 1973-75; dir. plant service Presbyn. U. Hosp., Pitts., 1975-81; founder, pres. Unique Cuisine Inc., Pitts., 1976-81; dir. plant ops. Cedars Sinai Med. Ctr., Los Angeles, 1981; assoc. prof. evening div. U. Pitts. Served to capt. U.S. Army, 1968-73. Decorated Air Medal, Purple Heart, Bronze Star. Mem. Am. Inst. Plant Engrs., Assn. Energy Engrs., Am. Hosp. Assn., Nat. Fire Protection Assn., Calif. Soc. Hosp. Engrs. Home: 18875 Kirkcolm Ln Northridge CA 91326 Office: Cedars Sinai Med Ctr 8700 Beverley Blvd Los Angeles CA 90048

COLTON, ROY CHARLES, management consultant; b. Phila., Feb. 26, 1941; s. Nathan Hale and Ruth Janis (Baylinson) C.; B.A., Knox Coll., 1962; M.Ed., Temple U., 1963. With Sch. Dist. of Phila., 1963-64; systems analyst Wilmington Trust Co., 1967-69; exec. recruiter Atwood Consultants Inc., Phila., 1969-71; pres. Colton Bernard Inc., San Francisco, 1971—; occasional lectr. Fashion Inst. Tech., Phila. Coll. Textiles and Scis. Served with AUS, 1964-66. Mem. San Francisco Fashion Industries, San Francisco C. of C., Calif. Exec. Recruiter Assn., Nat. Assn. Exec. Recruiters, Am. Apparel Mfrs. Assn., Am. Arbitration Assn. (panel arbitrators). Office: Colton Bernard Inc 417 Spruce St San Francisco CA 94118

COLWELL, ARTHUR RALPH, JR., physician; b. Chgo., Mar. 27, 1924; s. Arthur Ralph and Jane (Haskins) C.; m. Bettie Jane Norton, Sept. 4, 1948; children: Christina Jeane, Arthur Ralph, E. David, Julia Beth. Diplomate Am. Bd. Internal Medicine. Rotating intern Abington (Pa.) Meml. Hosp., 1947-48; resident in internal medicine Evanston (Ill.) Hosp., 1950-51, 53, attending physician, 1955-79, chief div. rheumatology, 1972-78; attending physician VA Research Hosp., Chgo., 1954-55; fellow Northwestern U. Med. Sch., Evanston, 1954-65, asst. prof. medicine, 1965-71, assoc. prof., 1971-80; attending physician VA Research Hosp., Chgo., 1954-55, Boswell Meml. Hosp., Sun City, Ariz., 1979—; speaker, hon. lectr. 33d Ann. Phi Delta Epsilon mtg. U. Louisville, 1974. Author: Understanding Your Diabetes, 1978. Served as capt. U.S. Army, 1951-53. Grantee NIH, 1966-69. Fellow ACP; mem. Am. Diabetes Assn., Am. Rheumatism Assn., Am. Fedn. Clin. Research, Sigma Xi. Republican. Episcopalian. Club: Palmbrook Country (Sun City). Home: 10325 Bayside Rd Sun City AZ 85351 Office: 13260 N 94th Dr Peoria AZ 85345

COLWELL, GARY GEORGE, college administrator; b. Woodstock, N.B., Can., Feb. 21, 1944; s. Edward F. and Faye M. (Merrithew) C.; m. Sheila Ada Maxwell, June 24, 1967; children—Jason, David. B.A., U. N.B., 1967, M.A., 1970; Ph.D., U. Waterloo, 1979. Mem. field staff Inter-Varsity Christian Fellowship, Fredericton, N.B., 1970-73; vis. asst. prof. Biola U., La Mirada, Calif., 1980; Interim asst. minister Highland Baptist Ch., Kitchener, Ont., Can., 1980-81; instr. philosophy Medicine Hat Coll., Alta., Can., 1981-82, dir. liberal arts, 1982—; inter-denominational supply minister, N.B., Ont. and Alta., 1968—. Contbr. articles to theol. and philos. jours.; referee Dialogue: Can. Philos. Rev., 1983—. Mem. Can. Philos. Assn., Can. Sci. and Christian Affiliation (assoc.). Baptist. Home: 18 Buttercup Ct SE, Medicine Hat, AB Canada T1B 2G9 Office: Medicine Hat College, 299 College Dr SE, Medicine Hat, AB Canada T1A 3Y6

COMANOR, WILLIAM S., economist; b. Phila., May 11, 1937; s. Leroy and Sylvia (Bershad) C.; children: Christine, Katherine. Student, Williams Coll., 1955-57; BA, Haverford Coll., 1959; MA, PhD, Harvard U., 1963; postgrad., London Sch. Econs., 1963-64. Spl. econ. asst. to asst. atty. gen. Antitrust div. U.S. Dept. Justice, Washington, 1965-66; asst. prof. econs. Harvard U., Cambridge, Mass., 1966-68; assoc. prof. Stanford (Calif.) U., 1968-73; dir. bur. econs. FTC, Washington, 1978-80; prof. econs. U. Calif., Santa Barbara, 1975—, dept. chmn., 1984-87. Author: National Health

Insurance in Ontario, 1980, Advertising and Market Power, 1974; contbr. articles to profl. jours. Mem. Am. Econ. Assn. Home: 621 Miramonte Dr Santa Barbara CA 93109 Office: Univ of Calif Santa Barbara Dept of Economics Santa Barbara CA 93106

COMBS, DOUGLAS LEE, management consultant; b. Cin., Dec. 16, 1946; s. Francis G. and Nellie Marie (Lauterwasser) C.; married. B.S. with honors in Advt., U. Fla., 1972; M.B.A., U. Ala., 1979. Dir., Combs & Assocs., Gainesville, Fla., 1971; communications dir. Gainesville C. of C., 1972; dir. public relations Blount Bros. Corp., Montgomery, Ala., 1973-77; dir. promotions So., Living, Decorating & Craft Ideas, Progressive Farmer mags., Birmingham, 1977-82; circulation dir. Omega Group, Ltd., Boulder, Colo., 1982-84; sr. ptnr. William K. Douglas Co., Los Angeles, 1984—. Bd. dirs. United Appeal, 1975—. Served with Intelligence Corps, U.S. Army, 1964-68; Vietnam. Mem. Pub. Relations Soc. Am., Direct Mail Mktg. Assn., Soc. Profl. Journalists, Am. Soc. Personnel Adminstrs., Assn. MBA Execs., Alpha Delta Sigma. Republican. Home: 330 E Cordova St #130 Pasadena CA 91101 Office: 84 N Wilson Suite #205 Pasadena CA 91106

COMEAU, CAROL SMITH, elementary educator; b. Berkeley, Calif., Sept. 4, 1941; d. Floyd Franklin and Bessie Caroline (Campbell) Smith; m. Dennis Rene Comeau, Dec. 27, 1962; children—Christopher, Michael, Karen. B.S. in Edn., U. Oreg., 1963; M.Pub. Sch. Adminstrn., U. Alaska, 1985. Third grade tchr., Springfield, Oreg., 1963-64; elem. sch. tchr. Ocean View Elem. Sch., Anchorage, 1975-84, 6th grade tchr., 1977-84; 6th grade tchr. Spring Hill Elem. Sch., Anchorage, 1985-86; adminstrv. intern Tudor Elem. Sch., Anchorage, 1986-87; community activist ednl. issues. Named Tchr. of Yr., Anchorage Sch. Dist. PTA Council, 1976. Mem. Anchorage Edn. Assn. (Tchr. of Yr. 1986), NEA, Nat. Council Tchrs. English, Alaska Tchrs. English, Am. Soc. Curriculum and Devel., Anchorage Prins. Assn., Nat. Council Tchrs. Math., Nat. Council Social Studies, Phi Delta Kappa, Kappa Delta Pi. Democrat. Home: 13632 Jarvi Dr Anchorage AK 99515 Office: Tudor Elem Sch 1666 Cadre Dr Anchorage AK 99507

COMER, BRUCE EDWARD, business executive; b. Sanford, N.C., Oct. 2, 1948; s. Edward Lee and Percilla Martin; m. Pamela Shear Parsons, June 18, 1972; children—Catherine, Mark. B.S. in Bus. Adminstrn., East Carolina U., Greenville, N.C., 1971. Ter. mgr. Sperry & Hutchinson, Wilmington, N.C., 1971-73; spl. accounts mgr. Nobel-Syslo, Albuquerque, 1973—; pres. Data Trac Inc., Albuquerque. Creator computer programs. Republican. Methodist. Home: 3108 Camino Real Ct NE Albuquerque NM 87111

COMES, ROBERT GEORGE, sr. research scientist; b. Bangor, Pa., July 7, 1931; s. Victor Francis and Mabel Elizabeth (Mack) C.; student U. Detroit, 1957-58, Oreg. State Coll., 1959-60, U. Nev., 1960, Regis Coll., 1961-62; m. Carol Lee Turinetti, Nov. 28, 1952; children—Pamela Jo, Robert G. II, Shawni Lee, Sheryl Lynn, Michelle Ann. Tech. liaison engr. Burroughs Corp., Detroit, 1955-60, mgr. reliability and maintainability engring., Paoli, Pa., 1962-63, Colorado Springs, Colo., 1963-67; sr. engr. Martin Marietta Corp., Denver, 1960-62; program mgr., research scientist Kaman Scis. Corp., Colorado Springs, 1967-75; dir. engring. Sci. Applications, Inc., Colorado Springs, 1975-80; mgr. space def. programs Burroughs Corp., Colorado Springs, 1980-82; tech. staff Mitre Corp., Colorado Springs, 1982-85; dir. Colorado Springs opn. Beers Assoc., Inc., 1985; dir. space programs Electro Magnetic Applications, Inc., Colorado Springs, 1985-87; dir. Space Systems, Profl. Mgmt. Assocs., Inc., 1987—; chmn. Reliability and Maintainability Data Bank Improvement Program, Govt.-Industry Data Exchange Program, 1978—; cons. in field. Youth dir. Indian Guides program YMCA, 1963-64; scoutmaster Boy Scouts Am., 1972-73; chmn. bd. dirs. Pikes Peak Regional Sci. Fair, 1972-84. Served with USAF, 1951-55. Mem. AAAS, IEEE, Inst. Environ. Scis., Soc. Logistics Engrs., Am. Soc. Quality Control. Lutheran. Club: Colorado Springs Racquet. Author: Maintainability Engineering Principles and Standards, 1962. Inventor Phase Shifting aircraft power supply, 1957. Home: 4309 Tipton Ct Colorado Springs CO 80915 Office: Profl Mgmt Assocs 4309 Tipton Ct Colorado Springs CO 80915

COMINGS, DAVID EDWARD, physician; b. Beacon, N.Y., Mar. 8, 1935; s. Edward Walter and Jean (Rice) C.; m. Shirley Nelson, Aug. 9, 1958; children: Mark David, Scott Edward, Karen Jean.; m. Brenda Gursey, Mar. 20, 1982. Student, U. Ill., 1951-54; B.S., Northwestern U., 1955, M.D., 1958. Intern Cook County Hosp., Chgo., 1958-59; resident in internal medicine Cook County Hosp., 1959-62; fellow in med. genetics U. Wash., Seattle, 1964-66; dir. dept. med. genetics City of Hope Med. Center, Duarte, Calif., 1966—; mem. genetics study sect. NIH, 1974-78; mem. sci. adv. bd. Hereditary Disease Found., 1975—, Nat. Found. March of Dimes, 1978—. Editor: (with others) Molecular Human Cytogenetics, 1977, Am. Jour. Human Genetics, 1979—; editorial bd.: (with others) Cytogenetics and Cell genetics, 1979—; editor-in-chief Am. Jour. Human Genetics, 1978-88. Served with U.S. Army, 1962-64. NIH grantee, 1967—. Mem. Assn. Am. Physicians, Am. Soc. Clin. Investigation, AAAS, Am. Soc. Human Genetics (dir. 1974-78, pres. 1988), Am. Soc. Cell Biology, Am. Fedn. Clin. Research, Western Soc. Clin. Research, Council Biology Editors. Office: City of Hope Med Center 1500 E Duarte Rd Duarte CA 91010

COMMON, KENNETH DOUGLAS, optometrist; b. Jersey City, Oct. 8, 1949; s. William Kenneth and Ida May (See) C.; m. Roxie M. Shannon, Mar. 11, 1978; children—Ronni, Paula, Jennifer, Daniel. B.A., Rutgers U., 1971; O.D., Mass. Coll. Optometry, 1976. Practice medicine specializing in optometry, Redmond, Wash.; instr. So. Calif. Coll. Optometry, 1982; team optometrist Seattle Mariners, 1983—. Served to lt. USN, 1976-81, to maj. USAFR. Mem. Am. Optometric Assn. (mem. sportsvision sect. 1984—), Wash. Optometric Assn. (chmn. sportsvision com. 1985—), King County Optometric Soc., Nat. Acad. Sports Vision (charter mem.), B & L Council Sports Vision. Baptist. Club: Rutgers of Puget Sound (treas. 1985—). Lodge: Gideons (sec. 1987—). Home: 126 Bremerton Ave SE Renton WA 98056 Office: 642 228th Ave NE Redmond WA 98053

COMPEAN, RICHARD EDWARD, human resources development administrator; b. Globe, Ariz., Sept. 21, 1945; s. Albert and Carmen (Quijada) C.; A.B. with honors, U. San Francisco, 1967; M.A., U. Calif.-Davis, 1969, Ph.D., 1973. Tchr., cons. U. Calif.-Davis, 1969-73, 78-80; tng. analyst Calif. Dept. Social Services, 1973-74; tng. dir. Calif. Pub. Utilities Commn., San Francisco, 1974-76; sr. tng. analyst Western States Bankcard Assn., Crocker Nat. Bank, 1976-77; regional coordinator continuing profl. edn. Kaiser Permanente Med. Care Program, Oakland, Calif., 1977—; tchr., cons. U. San Francisco, San Francisco Community Coll. Dist., Civil Service Coll., San Francisco Community Tng. and Devel. Project; teaching assoc. U. Calif., Davis, 1969-73. Mem. Am. Soc. Tng. and Devel., Orgn. Devel. Network, Am. Soc. Health Care Edn. and Tng. Democrat. Roman Catholic. Editor Am. Soc. Tng. and Devel. Newsletter, 1976-77, 80-82. Home: 810 38th Ave San Francisco CA 94121 Office: Kaiser Permanente Med Care Program 3505 Broadway Oakland CA 94611

COMPTON, ALLEN T., justice state supreme court; b. Kansas City, Mo., Feb. 25, 1938; m. Sue Ellen Tatter; 3 children. B.A., U. Kans.; LL.B., U. Colo. Staff atty. legal services office in Colo., later entered pvt. practic; supervising atty. Alaska Legal Services, Juneau, 1970-73; sole practice Juneau, 1973-76; judge Superior Ct., Alaska, 1976-80; justice Alaska Supreme Ct., Anchorage, 1980—. Mem. 4 bar assns. including Juneau Bar Assn. (past pres.). Office: Alaska Supreme Ct 303 K St Anchorage AK 99502

COMPTON, JOHN DOUGLAS, lawyer; b. Norfolk, Va., July 1, 1951; s. Emmett Mobley and Alice Compton; m. Nina Helene Nickerson, June 19, 1982. BA, U. Va., 1973; JD, Mercer U., 1978. Bar: N.Mex. 1979, U.S. Dist. Ct. N.Mex. 1979, Ga. 1980, U.S. Dist. Ct. (mid. dist.) Ga. 1980, U.S. Ct. Appeals (10th cir.) 1979, U.S. Ct. Appeals (11th cir.) 1983. Assoc. Bivins, Weinbrenner & Regan, Las Cruces, N.Mex., 1979-81, Bovis, Kyle & Bruch, Atlanta, 1982-83, Kemp, Smith, Duncan & Hammond, Albuquerque, 1983-85, Shaffer, Butt, Thornton & Baehr, Albuquerque, 1985—; adj. prof. N.Mex. State U., Las Cruces, 1981-82; guest lectr. Ga. State U., Atlanta, 1983. Mem. ABA (litigation sect., tort sect., ins. sect., com. trial practice), Assn. Trial Lawyers Am., Albuquerque Bar Assn., N.Mex. Bar Assn. (adv. opinions com. 1984), Ga. Bar Assn., Atlanta Bar Assn., Order of Barristers, U. Va. Alumni Assn. Republican. Clubs: Albuquerque Lawyers, Petroleum, Tanoan Tennis Country. Office: Butt Thornton & Baehr 2155 Louisiana Blvd NE 7000 City Pl Albuquerque NM 87190

COMPTON, NINA HELENE, business law educator, lawyer; b. Santa Fe, Oct. 21, 1950; d. Myron Hull and Helene (Dunn) Nickerson; m. Richard D. Adamson, Dec. 30, 1974 (div. 1980); m. 2d J. Douglas Compton, June 19, 1982. B.A., U. N.Mex.-Albuquerque, 1971, M.A., 1973; J.D., Del. Law Sch., 1978. Bar: N.Mex. 1979; Cert. tchr., N.Mex. Jud. law clk. Mcpl. Ct., Wilmington, Del., 1975-78; legal drafting staff Office of Gov., Santa Fe, 1979; assoc. Martin, Martin, Lutz & Cresswell, Las Cruces, N.Mex., 1979-81; asst. prof. bus. law N.Mex. State U., Las Cruces, 1981—, advisor Pre-Law Student Assn., 1981—; adj. faculty prof. bus. law, Ga. State U., 1982-83; pres. Latin Am. Studies Forum, Las Cruces, 1984—. Author: Study Guide to accompany The Legal Environment of Business (Kolasas), 1983; author research papers. Bd. dirs. and corp. council Amigos de las Americas Charity, Las Cruces, 1983; chmn. for univ. dept. United Way, Las Cruces, 1982-83; apptd. counselor to N.Mex. Border Commn., Santa Fe, 1981-83, mem. immigration subcom., 1983. Recipient Outstanding Tchr. award Coll. Bus. Adminstrn., N.Mex. State U., 1981, named Top Ten Campus-wide Faculty Mems., 1982; recipient cert. appreciation Office of Gov. N.Mex., 1982, 83. Mem. ABA, N.Mex. Bar Assn., Dona Ana County Bar Assn. sec. 1982—), Womens Trial Lawyers Caucus of Assn. Trial Lawyers Am., Am. Bus. Law Assn., Atlanta Bar Assn., Blue Key, Phi Gamma Nu (advisor 1982). Democrat. Episcopalian. Clubs: Las Cruces Jr. Womens, Faculty Womens. Home: 1073 Hillrise Ct Las Cruces NM 88001 Office: N Mex State Univ Dept Mktg and Gen Bus PO Box 5280 Las Cruces NM 88003

COMPTON, STEPHEN PAUL, police officer; b. Whittier, Calif., Dec. 12, 1953; s. A.D. and Dorothy Faye (Yarbrough) C.; m. Terry Lynn Breckley, Apr. 7, 1979; children: Cathy, Kelly, Kenny. AA, Cerro Coso Coll., 1983; BA, U. Redlands, 1984, MA, 1986. Police officer Dept. Def., China Lake, Calif., 1975-77, 1978-79, City of Wasco, Calif., 1977-78, City of Ridgecrest, Calif., 1979—; bd. dirs. Desert Counseling Clinic, Ridgecrest. Served as sgt. USAF, 1973-75. Named Officer of Yr., Exchange Club, Ridgecrest, 1983. Mem. Peace Officers Research Assn. (bd. dirs. 1983), Cerro Coso Alumni Assn. (bd. dirs. 1985-86). Avocations: fishing, boating. Office: City of Ridgecrest Police Dept 128 E Coso Ave Ridgecrest CA 93555

COMSTOCK, NANCY MURRAY, educator, consultant; b. Phoenix, Sept. 16, 1933; d. George Harold and Mary Lois (Lambert) Crose; m. William Clarence Comstock, Feb. 24, 1951; children—William G., Jeanne Marie Comstock Weber, Cynthia Ann Comstock Jenkins. B.A., Fresno State U., 1966; M.A., Bakersfield State Coll., 1976. Cert. elem., secondary, adminstrv., reading specialist, Calif. Jr. high sch., reading tchr., Bakersfield, Calif., 1966-72; resource tchr. Lerdo Sch. Dist., Bakersfield, 1972-76; primary cons. Kern County Supt. Schs. Office, Bakersfield, 1976-79, reading cons., 1979-82, staff devel. cons., 1979-82, tchr. edn., computer ctr. dir., 1982—. Mem. Calif. Tchrs. Assn., Assn. Calif. Sch. Adminstrs., Assn. Supervision and Curriculum Devel., Internat. Reading Assn., Calif. Reading Assn., Kern Math. Council, Phi Delta Kappa. Democrat. Roman Catholic. Author publs. in field. Home: 6404 Landfair Dr Bakersfield CA 93309 Office: Kern County Supt Schools Office 5801 Sundale Bakersfield CA 93309

CONAWAY, MARY ELLEN, museum administrator, anthropologist; b. Barstow, Calif., Feb. 2, 1944; d. Ray Levern and Rosalie Joan (Frankovich) C.; m. Larry Allen Goodwin, June 18, 1983. BA, U. Calif., Riverside, 1968; MA, U. Wis., Milw., 1970; PhD, cert. in Latin Am. studies, U. Pitts., 1976. Curator of exhibits, asst. prof. U. Tex. and El Paso Centennial Mus., 1978-80; asst. dir. and curator exhibits Oreg. State U. Horner Mus., Corvallis, 1980-82; curator Roger Williams Park Mus. of Natural History, Providence, 1982-84; mus. adminstr. City of Tempe, Ariz., 1984—; vis. asst. prof. U. Okla., Norman, 1976-77, U. So. Fla., Tampa, 1977-78; adj. faculty mem. anthropology Ariz. State U., Tempe, 1984—; assoc. faculty mem. Brown U., Providence, 1982-83; cond. R.I. Coll., Providence, 1983-84, NEH/Washington Hillsborough County Mus., Tampa, 1977-78. Author: (monograph) Still Guahilpo, Still Moving, A Study of Circular Migration and Marginality in Venezuela, 1984; co-editor: Self, Sex and Gender in Cross Cultural Field Work, 1986; contbr. articles to profl. jours. Mem. Tempe Sister Cities Corp., 1984—. Orgn. Am. States grantee; Mellon predoctoral fellow, 1975. Mem. Cen. Ariz. Mus. Assn. (bd. dirs. 1986—, program chmn. 1985—, sec. 1986—), Mus. Assn. Ariz. (bd. dirs. 1986—, east-cen. rep.), Am. Assn. Mus., Am. Assn., State and Local History, Mountain Plains Mus. Assn. (parlimentarian 1979-80), Archaeol. Assn. R.I. (founder), Sigma Xi. Avocations: hiking, nature programs, fishing, sewing. Office: Tempe Hist Mus 3500 S Rural Rd Tempe AZ 85282

CONCA, ROMEO JOHN, winemaker, consultant; b. New Haven, May 11, 1926; s. Matteo Celeste and Giulietta Maria (Bossi) C.; m. Irene Elizabeth Fritz, Sept. 4, 1946 (dec. Sept. 1982); children: Stephen E., David J. BS, Yale U., 1949, PhD, 1953. Research asst. Princeton (N.J.) U., 1952-53; research chemist GD Searle and Co, Skokie, Ill., 1953-55; research chemist group leader ITT Rayonier Inc, Shelton, Wash., 1955-62, sect. leader, research supr., 1962-79, mgr. tech. support, 1979-81; owner, winemaker Lost Mountain Winery, Sequim, Wash., 1981—; cons. in field, Sequim, 1983—. Contbr. articles to profl. jours.; patentee in field. Bd. dirs. Mason County Fed. Credit Union, Shelton, 1956-65. Served with USN, 1944-46. Proctor and Gamble fellow Yale U., 1950-52. Fellow The Royal Hort. Soc.; mem. TAPPI, Am. Chem. Soc., N.W. Sci. Assn., Sigma Xi. Avocations: horticulture, fly-fishing, cooking. Home and Office: Lost Mountain Winery 730 Lost Mountain Rd Sequim WA 98382

CONDÉ, RICHARD LOUIS, psychiatrist; b. Waterloo, Iowa, Sept. 16, 1922; s. Louis and Mildred Lucille (Kunce) C.; B.S. in Medicine, U. Minn., 1946, M.D., 1949; m. Mary Lou McLear, Apr. 10, 1948; children—Thomas John, Ann Louise, Mary Elizabeth. Intern, Ancker Hosp., St. Paul, 1948-49; resident Walter Reed Army Hosp., Washington, 1952-54; clin. dir. Anoka (Minn.) State Hosp., 1956-57; practice medicine specializing in psychiatry Colorado Springs, Colo., 1957—. Served to maj. U.S. Army, 1950-56. Decorated Bronze Star. Mem. AMA, Colorado Springs Psychiat. Soc. (pres. 1975-76) Colo. Med. Soc. (chmn. council pub. health 1968-75, chmn. com. alcoholism and drug abuse 1966-75), Am. Psychiat. Assn. Clubs: Cheyenne Mountain Country, Broadmoor Golf. Home: 11 El Encanto Colorado Springs CO 80906 Office: 2131 N Tejon St Colorado Springs CO 80907

CONDIE, CAROL JOY, anthropologist, research facility administrator; b. Provo, Utah, Dec. 28, 1931; d. LeRoy and Thelma (Graff) C.; m. M. Kent Stout, June 18, 1954; children: Carla Ann, Erik Roy, Paula Jane. BA in Anthropology, U. Utah, 1953; MEd in Elem. Edn., Cornell U., 1954; PhD in Anthropology, U. N.Mex., 1973. Edn. coordinator Maxwell Mus. Anthropology, U. N.Mex., Albuquerque, 1973, interpretation dir., 1974-77; asst. prof. anthropology U. N.Mex., 1975-77; cons. Albuquerque, 1977-78; pres. Quivira Research Ctr., Albuquerque, 1978—; cons. anthropologist U.S. Congl. Office Tech. Assessment, chair Archeol. Resources Planning Adv. Com., Albuquerque, 1985-86. Author: The Nighthawk Site (LA 5685), a Pithouse Site on Sandia Pueblo Land, Bernalillo County, New Mexico, 1982, Five Sites on the Pecos River Road, 1985; co-editor: Anthropology of the Desert West, 1985; also articles. Mem. Downtown Core Area Schs. Com., Albuquerque, 1982. Ford Found. fellow, 1953-54. Fellow Am. Anthropol. Assn., mem. Soc. Am. Anthropology (chmn. Native Am. Relations com. 1983-85), N.M. Archeol. Council (pres. 1982-83), Maxwell Mus. Assn. (bd. dirs.), Las Arañas Spinners and Weavers Guild (pres. 1972). Democrat. Avocations: spinning, weaving, gardening. Home: 1809 Notre Dame NE Albuquerque NM 87106 Office: Quivira Research Ctr 3017 Commercial NE Albuquerque NM 87107

CONDIE, HELEN CROWTHER, home economics educator; b. Salt Lake City; d. Norman W. and Gwenfred (Jones) C.; m. Wilmar W. Condie, July 22, 1950; children—Gwendalyn Condie Lloyd, Steven Norman. B.S. in Home Econs. Edn., Utah State U.-Logan, 1948, M.S., 1954; Ed.D., Brigham Young U., 1983. Cert. tchr., Idaho. Tchr. home econs. Provo (Utah) High Sch., 1948-50, Preston (Idaho) High Sch., 1950-55; with dept. home econs. Idaho State U., Pocatello, 1956—, prof. consumer econs., 1970—; condr. workshops Idaho State Bd. Vocat. Edn. Recipient Idaho Vocat. Edn. Disting. Service award, 1976; Idaho Future Homemakers of Am. Award of Merit, 1982. Mem. Am. Home Econs. Assn., Idaho Home Econs. Assn. (cert. award 1981), Am. Vocat. Assn., Idaho Vocat. Assn., Home Econs. Edn. Assn., Nat. Assn. Home Econs. Tchr. Educators. Republican. Mormon. Authored curriculum guides; contbr. article to profl. jour. Office: Idaho State U Pocatello ID 83209

CONDON, ERIKA MARY, library administrator; b. Ft. Monmouth, N.J., Dec. 14, 1949; d. William Maurice and Ingeborg Ursula (Neitzke) C.; m. Darryl Laws, Jan. 1975 (div. 1978). B.A. in English, Calif. State U.-Sacramento, 1972, M.P.A., 1977; M.A. in Librarianship, U. Denver, 1973. Info. desk librarian Calif. State U.-Sacramento, 1974-75, social sci. and bus. adminstr. reference librarian, 1975-77; textbook acquisition and distbn. mgr. Long Beach Unified Sch. Dist., Calif., 1977-78; library dir. Mt. St. Mary's Coll., Los Angeles, 1978—. Calif. State scholar, 1968-72. Mem. ALA, Calif. Library Assn., So. Calif. Online Users Group, Soc. for Pub. Adminstrn. Democrat. Roman Catholic. Office: Mt St Marys Coll 12001 Chalon Rd Los Angeles CA 90049

CONDON, WILLIAM EDWARD, marketing consultant; b. Tampa, Fla., Jan. 30, 1949; s. Alwin J. and Patricia B. Condon; m. Carol J. Moskal. Student, Broward Community Coll., 1973-74. Lic. real estate broker; cert. police officer, Fla. Pres. Southwest Mktg. Assocs., Phoenix, 1981—; mktg. cons. DashMat Co., Phoenix, 1982—; v.p., bd. dirs. M.A.N., Inc., 1986—; v.p., mktg. dir., OJOP Inc. Named Man of Yr. Automotive Accessory Industry-Automotive Mdse. News mag., 1984, 1985; Mfrs. Rep. of Yr., Western Internat. Distbn., 1982; nominated Man of Yr. Sales and Mktg. Mgmt. mag., 1985. Mem. Sales and Mktg. Execs. of Greater Phoenix, Mfrs. Agts. Assn. of Am. Republican. Presbyterian. Avocation: boating. Office: Southwest Mktg Assocs PO Box 37338 Phoenix AZ 85069

CONE, RAYMOND ANDREW, media company executive; b. Glendale, Calif., Oct. 29, 1939; s. Marvin Mook and Claire (Warren) C.; m. Claire Maria Dorman, May 26, 1960; children—Mary, Jeff. Student Los Angeles Valley Coll., 1957-60. Salesman Am. Blueprint Co., North Hollywood, Calif., 1960-62; dist. sales mgr. GAF Corp., La Habra, Calif., 1962-68; nat. sales mgr. Nashua Corp., N.H., 1968-74; div. mgr. Noland Paper Co., San Jose, Calif., 1974-82; pres. Bay Repro Media, Inc., San Jose, 1982—, dir., 1984—. Bd. dirs. Joint Venture-EYOA, Pacoma, 1968; bd. dirs. Civic Action Merrimack Beacon Drive, Merimack, N.H., 1973. Served with USAF, 1960-63. Mem. Nat. Office Machine Dealers Assn. (bd. dirs.), CAP (maj. 1954-74). Republican. Presbyterian. Office: Bay Repro Media Inc 694 Kings Row San Jose CA 95112

CONE, RIC IAN, neuroendocrine scientist and educator; b. Chgo., Jan. 8, 1947; s. Gilbert George Cone and Frances M. Shapiro. BA in Biochemistry, U. Calif., 1971; PhD in Neurosci., U. Wis., 1980. Research assoc. Wis. Primate Ctr., Madison, 1975-80; research fellow Stanford (Calif.) U., 1980-83; asst. prof. So. Calif. Coll. Optometry, Fullerton, 1983; research biochemist Mt. View, Calif., 1983-85; research biochemist Zoecon Corp., Palo Alto, Calif., 1985-86, cons., 1986—; Referee Nat. Sci. Found., Washington, 1982—, Brain Research Bull., San Antonio, 1983—, Life Scis. Jour., Tucson, 1983—, Biology Reproduction, Madison, Wis., 1985—; vis. scholar Calif. Coll. Medicine, 1983, Stanford U. Med. Ctr., 1985; lectr. U. So. Calif., Los Angeles, 1983, Albany Med. Sch., 1984, El Camino Hosp. Continuing Edn., Mt. View, 1985. Contbr. articles to profl. jours. Volunteer VA Hosp., Menlo Park, Calif., 1986. Mem. Am. Assn. Advanced Sci., Soc. Neurosics., U. Calif. Alumni Assn., U. Wis. Alumni Assn., Nat. Inst. Drug Abuse (Nat. Research Service award 1980-83). Clubs: Internat. Allied Health Assn., Am. Physical Fitness. Lodge: ALS-JCC. Avocations: weightlifting, aerobics, bicycling, running, tennis.

CONFORTI, EMILE RALPH, plastics mfg. co. exec.; b. Torrington, Conn., Oct. 22, 1928; s. Emile Domenic and Catherine C.; B.A., Providence Coll., 1950; m. Kathleen Ann Zullo, Dec. 27, 1953; children—Diane, Donna, David. Mktg. mgr. Monsanto Co., St. Louis, 1956-68; pres., chief exec. officer Hollywood Plastics subs. Shell Chem., Los Angeles, 1968-73; pres., chief exec. officer, dir. Ampro Corp., Anaheim Calif., 1974, now pres., chief exec. officer; chmn. bd. Western Empire Savs. and Loan. Mem. Planning Commn. City of Placentia. Served with U.S. Army, 1951-53. Mem. Soc. Plastic Engrs., ASTM, Anaheim C. of C., Ostomy Assn. Orange County (pres.). Club: Yorba Linda Country. Office: 1340 N Jefferson St Anaheim CA 92807

CONGDON, JONATHAN BLANCHARD, chemist, physicist, biologist, educator; b. Portland, Oreg., Mar. 27, 1954; s. Roger Douglas and Gwendolyn (Britt) C.; m. Harriet Nori Reed, Nov. 28, 1956; children: David William, Daniel Scott, Michael Reed. BS, Wheaton (Ill.) Coll., 1976; grad. cert., Multnomah Sch. of the Bible, 1977; MS, Oreg. State U., 1980. Cert. secondary edn. tchr. Sci. instr. Columbia High Sch., Troutdale, Oreg., 1979—; cons. in field, 1984-85. Deacon community Bible fellowship, Portland, 1983-86. Recipient $5000.00 award for excellence in sci. teaching Oreg. Mus. Sci. and Industry in assn. with the Tectronics Found., 1984. Mem. Am. Chem. Soc. Republican. Avocations: home builder, craftsman, cello, collegiate wrestling. Home: 139 NE 160th Portland OR 97230 Office: Columbia High Sch 1698 SW Cherry Park Troutdale OR 97060

CONGDON, ROGER DOUGLASS, theology educator, minister; b. Ft. Collins, Colo., Apr. 6, 1918; s. John Solon and Ellen Avery (Kellogg) C.; m. Rhoda Gwendolyn Britt, Jan. 2, 1948; children: Rachel Congdon Lidbeck, James R., R. Steven, Jon B., Philip F., Robert N., Bradford B., Ruth A., Rebecca Congdon Skones, Rhoda J., Marianne C., Mark Alexander. BA, Wheaton Coll., 1940; postgrad, Eastern Bapt. Sem., 1940-41; ThM, Dallas Theol. Sem., 1945; ThD, Dallas Theology Sem., 1949. Ordained to ministry Bapt. Ch., 1945. Exec. sec., dean Altanta Bible Inst., 1945-49; prof. theology Carver Bible Inst., Atlanta, 1945-49; prof. Multnomah Sch. of the Bible, Portland, Oreg., 1950—; served as past dean of faculty, dean of edn., v.p., chmn. library com., chmn. achievement-award com., chmn. lectureship com., advisor grad. div. and mem. pres.'s cabinet all at Multnomah Sch. of the Bible; chmn. Chil Evang. Fellowship of Greater Portland, 1978—; founder, pres. Preaching Print Inc., Portland, 1953—. Author: the Doctrine of Conscience, 1945. Chmn. Citizen's Com. Info. on Communism, Portland, 1968-75. Recipient Outstanding Educators of Am. award, 1972, Loraine Chafer award in Systematic Theology, Dallas Theol. Sem. Mem. Am. Assn. Bible Colls. (chmn. testing com. 1953-78), N.Am. Assn. Bible Colls. (N.W. rep. 1960-63), Near East Archaeol. Soc., Evang. Theol. Soc. Republican. Home: 16539 NE Halsey St Portland OR 97230 Office: Multnomah Sch of the Bible 8435 NE Glisan St Portland OR 97220

CONGER, JOHN JANEWAY, psychologist, educator; b. New Brunswick, N.J., Feb. 27, 1921; s. John C. and Katharine (Janeway) C.; m. Mayo Trist Kline, Jan. 1, 1944; children: Steven Janeway, David Trist. B.A. magna cum laude, Amherst Coll., 1943; M.S., Yale U., 1947, Ph.D., 1949; D.Sc. (hon.), Ohio U., 1980, Amherst Coll., 1983. Asst. prof. psychology Ind. U., 1949-53; chief staff psychologist U.S. Naval Acad., 1951-52; mem. faculty U. Colo. Sch. Medicine, prof. psychology, 1957—, assoc. dean, 1961-63, v.p. for med. affairs, 1963-70, dean, 1963-68, acting chmn. dept. psychiatry, 1983-84, acting chancellor, 1985-86; fellow Center for Advanced Study in Behavioral Scis., Stanford, Cal., 1970-71; vis. scholar Inst. Human Devel., U. Calif., Berkeley, 1978; v.p., dir. health program John D. and Catherine T. MacArthur Found., 1980-83, cons., 1983—; cons. to NIH, VA, USPHS.; Vice chmn. Colo. Bd. Psychology Examiners, 1961-64; mem. Gov. Colo. Com. Mental Health, 1957; chmn. mental health adv. council Colo. Dept. Pub. Health, 1957-61; mem. tng. com. Nat. Inst. Mental Health, 1959-62; mem. Western council mental health research and tng. Western Interstate Commn. Higher Edn., 1959-66; chmn. research com. President's Com. Traffic Safety, 1960-63; vice chmn. nat. motor vehicle safety adv. council Dept. Transp., 1967-70; mem. inter-council com. constrn. univ.-affiliated facilities for mentally retarded Dept. Health, Edn. and Welfare, 1967-70, mem. sec.'s adv. com. traffic safety, 1966-69; council research and planning Am. Hosp. Assn., 1965-68; nat. adv. mental health council USPHS, 1965-69; nat. adv. com. John F. Kennedy Center for Research on Edn. and Human Devel., 1965-76, chmn., 1970-74; mem. adv. com. on undergrad med. edn. AMA, 1969-70; adv. com. on casualty ins. Dept. Transp., 1970; mem. Pres.'s Task Force on Hwy. Safety, 1970, President's Commn. on Mental Health, 1977-78; mem. com. study nat. needs for biomed. and behavioral sci. research personnel Nat. Acad. Scis., 1976-80; mem. Inst. Medicine/Nat. Acad. Scis., 1983—, bd. mental health and behavioral medicine, 1986—. Author: Child Development and Personality, 6th edit, 1984, Readings in Child Development, 1964, 3d edit., 1984, Personality, Social Class and Delinquency, 1965, Adolescence and Youth: Psychological Development in a Changing World, 3d edit., 1984, Basic and Contemporary Issues in Developmental Psychology, 1975, Contemporary Issues in Adolescent Development, 1975, Psychological Development: A Life-Span Approach, 1979, Adolescence: Generation Under Pressure, 1979, Essentials of Child Development and Personality, 1980, also articles. Served to lt. USNR, 1944-46, 51-52. Recipient Stearns Alumni medal for extraordinary service U Colo., 1970, U. Colo. medal, 1986, disting. profl. achievement award Am. Bd. Profl. Psychology, 1979. Fellow Am. Psychol. Assn. (mem. policy and planning bd. 1967-70, rec. sec., dir. 1974-79, pres. 1980-82, award for outstanding contbns. health psychology 1983), AAAS, Soc. Research in Child Devel. (program chmn. 1975); mem. Am. Psychol. Found. (pres. 1985-86), Denver Med. Soc. (hon. mem.), Colo. Psychol. Assn. (pres. 1959, disting. service award 1963, 84), Colo. Med. Soc. (disting. Service award 1970), Phi Beta Kappa, Sigma Xi, Alpha Omega Alpha (hon.). Club: Cosmos. Home: 130 S Birch St Denver CO 80222

CONKLE, GALEN EUGENE, accountant, corporate director; b. Clark, Ohio, Feb. 26, 1933; s. Maynard S. and Mary (Parks) C.; B.S. in Accounting, Sacramento State Coll., 1959; m. Lureen A. Edgar, Apr. 27, 1962; children—Galen John, Ramona Jean, Rebecca Lureen. Prin., Galen E. Conkle, C.P.A., Oceanside, Calif., 1963-66; ptnr. Conkle, Sigrist & Co., C.P.A.'s, Oceanside, Calif., from 1966; later ptnr. Reschly & Conkle, C.P.A.s, Escondido; prin. Galen E. Conkle, C.P.A. Escondido, Calif.; now corp. dir.; instr. accounting and fed. income taxes Palomar Coll., San Marcos, Cal., 1964-68, 75-79. Served with USNR, 1951-55. Mem. Calif. Soc. C.P.A.'s. Republican. Home: 16520 Green Valley Truck Trail Ramona CA 92065 Office: Conkle CPAs 420 W 5th Ave Escondido CA 92025

CONKLIN, MARIE ECKHARDT, biologist, educator; b. Derby, Conn., Sept. 30, 1908; d. Malcolm Moyer and Elizabeth Nancy (McLean) Eckhardt; m. G. Howard Conklin, June 27, 1931 (dec.); children—Elizabeth Nancy, George William. A.B., Wellesley Coll., 1929; M.S., U. Wis., 1930; Ph.D., Columbia U., 1936. Teaching asst. dept. botany Wellesley Coll., 1930-31; research Bklyn. Botanic Garden, 1935-36; research assoc. dept. genetics Carnegie Inst. of Washington at Cold Spring Harbor, 1936-41; instr. to prof. Adelphi U., 1943-72, chmn. dept. biology, 1953-67; research collaborator Brookhaven Nat. Lab., 1959-72; lectr./adj. prof. San Diego State U., 1977-85, dean, sr. v.p. Continuing Edn. Ctr., 1980—; v.p. for acad. affairs Continuing Edn. Ctr. at Rancho Bernardo; dir. Adelphi Coll., NSF, and AEC summer insts. and in-service programs for high sch. tchrs. sci., 1959-64. Author: Genetic and Biomedical Aspects of the Development of Datura, 1976, (with D.L. Hartl) Genetics Study Guide, 1977. Mem. AAAS, Sigma Xi, Sigma Delta Epsilon. Home: 12062 Caminito Cadena Rancho Bernardo San Diego CA 92128 Office: Continuing Edn Ctr 16789 Bernard Ctr Dr Suite 202 Home Fed Savs Loan San Diego CA 92128

CONLAN, MICHAEL DAVID, electronics engineer; b. San Jose, Calif., May 29, 1933; s. Paul Peter and Mary Helen (Hansen) C.; m. Patricia Ann Krell, May 19, 1962 (div. Feb. 1981); children: Michael David, Christopher John, Steven Joseph. Technician Varian Assocs., Palo Alto, Calif., 1961-68, engr., 1982—; engr. Aydin Corp., Palo Alto, 1968-77; owner, operator CC Graphics Printing Co., Mountain View, Calif., 1974-82. Served with U.S. Army, 1954-57, Korea. Club: Optimists (Palo Alto) (pres. 1977-78, lt. gov. 1978-79). Home: 1774 Bethany Ave San Jose CA 95132 Office: Varian Assocs 3200 Patrick Henry Dr Santa Clara CA 95054

CONLEY, ZEB BRISTOL, JR., art gallery director; b. Andrews, N.C., Feb. 12, 1936; s. Zeb Bristol and A. Elizabeth (Faircloth) C.; student N.C. State Coll., 1954-55, Mars Hill Coll., 1955-57, Coll. William and Mary, 1957-61; m. Betty Ann Wiswall, May 25, 1974; stepchildren—Peter Wiswall Betts, Stephen Wood Betts, Frederick Beale Betts, III. Designer, Seymour Robins, Inc., N.Y.C., 1961; with First Nat. Bank, Las Vegas (N.Mex.), 1964-65; gen. mgr. Swanson's Inc., Las Vegas, 1965-73, v.p., 1969—; dir. Jamison Galleries, Santa Fe, 1973—, guest curator Alfred Morang: A Retrospective at Mus. of S.W. Midland, Tex., 1985; sec. Marbasconi, Inc., d.b.a. Jamison Galleries, 1974-80, pres., 1980—. Bd. dirs. Las Vegas Mental Health Assn., 1963-65; office mgr. Las Vegas Opera Guild, 1971-73. Republican. Home: PO Box 2534 Santa Fe NM 87501 Office: The Jamison Galleries 111 E San Francisco St Santa Fe NM 87501

CONLON, WILLIAM MARTIN, engineer; b. N.Y.C., Nov. 2, 1953; s. William Martin and Dorothy Margaret (Figueroa) C.; m. Judith Ellen Schwartz, May 13, 1983. BS, Rensselaer Poly. Inst., 1975, MS in Engring., 1977, PhD, 1982. Registered profl. engr., Calif. Engr. Pacific Gas and Electric Co., San Francisco, 1982-84; sr. engr. Internat. Power Tech., Palo Alto, Calif., 1984-85, mgr. new product devel., 1986—. patentee in field. Mem. IEEE, AAAS, ASME, Am. Nuclear Soc., Sigma Xi. Avocations: handball, jogging, tennis, gardening. Home: 2330 Bryant St Palo Alto CA 94301 Office: Internat Power Tech 2800 W Bayshore Rd Palo Alto CA 94303

CONLY, JOHN FRANKLIN, engineering educator, researcher; b. Ridley Park, Pa., Sept. 11, 1933; s. Harlan and Mary Jane (Roberts) C.; m. Jeannine Therese McDonough, Apr. 14, 1967; children: J. Paul, Mary Ann. B.S., U. Pa., 1956, M.S., 1958; Ph.D., Columbia U., 1962. Instr. U. Pa., Phila., 1956-58; research asst. Columbia U., N.Y.C., 1959-62; asst. prof. engring. San Diego State U., 1962-65, assoc. prof., 1965-69, prof., 1969—, chmn. dept., 1971-74, 77-85, wind tunnel dir., 1978—. D. and F. Guggenheim fellow, 1958. Assoc. fellow AIAA (sect. chmn. 1970 best U.S. sect.). Republican. Episcopalian. Office: San Diego State U Dept Aerospace Engring San Diego CA 92182

CONN, MICHAEL P., social worker; b. Salt Lake City, May 18, 1956; s. Raymond A. Conn and Shirley (Lamb) Justet; m. June Solomon, Feb. 3, 1978 (div. Nov. 83); 1 child, Jeremy M.; m. Sylvia Anderson, Nov. 16, 1985. BS in Polit. Sci. and Sociology, U. Utah, 1981, MSW, 1984. Cert. social worker. Property clk. Bur. Land Mgmt., Salt Lake City, 1976-84; youth specialist Youth Services, Salt Lake City, 1982-83; sr. treatment counselor Div. Youth Corrections, Salt Lake City, 1984—. Author: Sociology Student Guide, 1981. Served withs U.S. Army, 1973-75. Recipient Spl. Achievement award Bur. Land Mgmt., Salt Lake City, 1980, Length of Service award Bur. Land Mgmt., Salt Lake City, 1984; named one of Outstanding Young Men of Am. Jaycees, Salt Lake City, 1984. Mem. Nat. Assn. Social Workers, Am. Correctional Assn., Utah Correctional Assn., Utah Pub. Employees Assn. Avocations: tennis, camping, golf, hiking, sports. Home: 329 C St Salt Lake City UT 84103 Office: Div Youth Corrections 61 W 3900 S Salt Lake City UT 84117

CONNELL, MARK THOMAS, test engineer; b. Cheyenne, Wyo., June 5, 1961; s. Paul Thomas and Grace Marie (Biehl) C. BA in Physics, U. Colo., 1983. Test engr. Colo. Mfg. Tech., Colorado Springs, 1983-85, engring. mgr., 1985-86; test engr. Rolm subs. IBM, Colorado Springs, 1986—. Judge Boulder (Colo.) County Sci. Fair, 1980—. Named Eagle Scout Boy Scouts Am., 1976. Mem. Am. Soc. Test Engrs., Soc. Mfg. Engrs. (sr. mem.), Mass. Inst. Tech. Enterprise Forum, Am. Prodn. Inventory Control Soc. Republican. Roman Catholic. Avocations: golfing, woodworking. Home: 7925 Lindsey Dr Colorado Springs CO 80918 Office: Rolm Telecommunications 4678 Alpine Meadow Ln Colorado Springs CO 80919

CONNELL, RICHARD M., civil engineer; b. Erie, Pa., Sept. 13, 1925. BS, U.S. Mil. Acad., 1949; MS in Civil Engring., MIT, 1955; grad., U.S. Army Command and Gen. Staff Coll., 1974, U. Pitts. Mgmt. Program for Execs. Registered Profl. engr., Calif., Wash., Alaska, D.C. Commd. 2d lt. C.E. U.S. Army, 1949, advanced through grades to brig. gen., ret., 1984; dist. engr. U.S. Army, Walla Walla, Wash., 1970-73; later div. engr. U.S. Army, S. Pacific; v.p. T.Y. Lin Internat., 1985—. Fellow Am. Soc. Mil. Engrs.; mem. Am. Pub. Works Assn., ASCE, The Beavers, U.S. Com. on Large Dams. Office: TY Lin Internat 315 Bay St San Francisco CA 94133 *

CONNELLEE-CLAY, BARBARA, laboratory administrator; b. Hereford, Tex., Dec. 4, 1929; d. Herman and Audrey Stella (Carroll) Galbraith; m. Edward Lee Clay, 1983; children—Alison Elaine Stephens, Rebecca Diane Connellee Crabtree, Calvin Clay, Larry Clay, Becky Inge. B.S., U. N.Mex., 1976, M.B.A., 1981. Mem. adminstrv. staff U. Calif. Los Alamos Nat. Lab., 1976—. Pres., Wesleyan Service Guild, 1958. Recipient Women at Work award region 8 Dept. Labor Council on Working Women, 1983, N.Mex. Women at Work Spl. award Council Working Women Inst. Women and Minority Affairs, 1985. Mem. Nat. Assn. Female Execs., Laser Inst. Am., Optical Soc., Women in Sci., Internat. Assn. Quality Circles (cert. facilitator). United Methodist (past dir. edn.). Office: PO Box 1663 MS E 505 Los Alamos NM 87544

CONNELLY, THEODORE SAMPLE, communications executive; b. Middletown, Conn., Oct. 15, 1925; s. Herbert Lee and Mabel Gertrude (Wells) C.; B.A., Wesleyan U., 1948, postgrad., 1951; postgrad. U. Paris, 1950. Sec., Nat. Com. on Edn., Am. Trucking Assn., Inc., Washington, 1952-54; dir. public affairs Nat. Automobile Club, San Francisco, 1955-62; pres., chmn. Connelly Corp., San Francisco, 1963—; treas. Ednl. Access Cable TV Corp.; dir. Mission Neighborhood Centers, Inc., Neighborhood Devel. Corp.; mem. adv. com. on Calif. motor vehicle legis., 1955-62, Calif. State C. of C. com. on hwys., 1958-62. Trustee, sec., v.p. Lincoln U.; sec. Lincoln U. Found., 1968-80; bd. dirs. San Francisco Program for Aging; founder Communications Library, 1963, Communications Inst., 1978; founding mem. Calif. Council for UN Univ., 1976; organizer Internat. Child Art Collection; co-founder African Research Commn., 1970; established Connelly Fund, 1981. Served with USNR, 1943-54. Recipient cert. of merit San Francisco Jaycees, 1959; award of merit USPHS, 1980, citation, 1981. Mem. AAAS, AAUP, Public Relations Round Table San Francisco, Atlanta Hist. Soc., Asian Mass Communication and Info. Centre (Singapore), NAACP, SAR, Press Club San Francisco, UN Assn. U.S.A., Nat. Sci. Tchrs. Assn. (bus.-industry sect.). Club: Dolphin Swimming and Boating (San Francisco). Author/compiler: BCTV Bibliography on Cabletelevision, 1975—; Electromagnetic Radiation, 1976; CINCOM: Courses in Communications, 1978; editor: An Analysis of Joint Ventures in China, 1982; contbr. articles to profl. jours.; producer, writer, dir. numerous TV programs.

CONNICK, ROBERT ELWELL, educator; b. Eureka, Calif., July 29, 1917; s. Arthur Elwell and Florence (Robertson) C.; m. Frances Spieth, Dec. 19, 1952; children—Mary Catherine, Elizabeth, Arthur, Megan, Sarah, William Beach. B.S., U. Calif. at Berkeley, 1939, Ph.D., 1942. Faculty U. Calif., Berkeley, 1942—; research Manhattan project U. Calif., 1943-46, asst. prof. then asso. prof. chemistry, 1945-52, prof., 1952—, chmn. dept., 1958-60; dean U. Calif. (Coll. Chemistry), 1960-65, vice chancellor acad. affairs, 1965-67, vice chancellor, 1969-71. Contbr. articles profl. jours. Guggenheim fellow, 1949, 59. Mem. Am. Chem. Soc., Nat. Acad. Scis., Phi Beta Kappa, Sigma Xi, Pi Mu Epsilon. Home: 50 Marguerita Rd Berkeley CA 94707

CONNOLLY, HUGH FRANCIS, lawyer; b. N.Y.C., Sept. 16, 1928; s. John Patrick and Helen Marie (Reid) C.; m. Paulette Marie Tobin, Feb. 9, 1952; children—Colleen Connolly Lippett, Maureen Connolly Holmes, Brian, Thomas, Christopher. A.B. in Greek, Fordham U., 1951, J.D., 1958. Admitted to Calif. bar, 1958; ptnr. firm Anderson, McMillan & Connolly, Burlingame, Calif., 1958-82; individual practice law, Burlingame, 1982—; instr. real estate law Coll. of San Mateo, 1968-74; pres. Seton Med. Office Ctr., Inc.; gen. counsel Seton Med. Ctr., St. Catherine Hosp., San Mateo-Burlingame Bd. Realtors, Redwood City-San Carlos-Belmont Bd. Realtors, North San Mateo County Bd. Realtors; dir. Diagnostic Networks Inc. Pres., Cath. Social Service San Mateo County, Cath. Social Service San Francisco Archdiocese, Serra High Sch. Bd. Edn., San Mateo County Easter Seal Soc., chmn. legal affairs com. Cath. Health Assn. U.S. Served to 1st lt., AUS, 1951-53. Recipient Vol. of Yr. award San Mateo County Easter Seal Soc., 1977. Mem. ABA, Am. Soc. Hosp. Attys., Burlingame C. of C. (pres.), Calif. Assn. Cath. Hosps. (pres.). Republican. Roman Catholic. Club: Burlingame Kiwanis (pres.). Office: 1450 Chapin Ave Burlingame CA 94010

CONNOLLY, JOHN EARLE, surgeon, educator; b. Omaha, May 21, 1923; s. Earl A. and Gertrude (Eckerman) C.; m. Virginia Hartman, Aug. 12, 1967; children: Peter Hart, John Earle, Sarah. A.B., Harvard U., 1945, M.D., 1948. Diplomate: Am. Bd. Surgery (bd. dirs. 1976-82), Am. Bd. Thoracic and Cardiovascular Surgery, Am. Bd. Vascular Surgery. Intern. in surgery Stanford U. Hosps., San Francisco, 1948-49, surg. research fellow, 1949-50, asst. resident surgeon, 1950-52, chief resident surgeon, 1953-54, surg. pathology fellow, 1954, instr. surgery, 1957-60, John and Mary Markle Scholar in med. scis., 1957-62; surg. registrar professional unit St. Bartholomew's Hosp., London, 1952-53; resident in thoracic surgery Bellevue Hosp., N.Y.C., 1955; resident in thoracic and cardiovascular surgery Columbia-Presbyn. Med. Ctr., N.Y.C., 1956; from asst. prof. to assoc. prof. surgery Stanford U., 1960-65; prof., chmn. dept. surgery U. Calif.-Irvine, 1965-78; attending surgeon Stanford Med. Ctr., Palo Alto, Calif., 1959-65; chmn. cardiovascular and thoracic surgery U. Calif.-Irvine Med. Ctr., 1968—; attending surgeon St. Joseph's Children's Hosp., Orange, Calif., 1968—; Anaheim Meml. Hosp. (Calif.), 1970—; A.H. Duncan vis. prof. U. Edinburgh, 1984; Hunterian prof. Royal Coll. Surgeons Eng., 1985-86; mem. adv. council Nat. Heart, Lung, and Blood Inst.-NIH, 1981—; cons. Long Beach VA Hosp., Calif., 1965—, Long Beach Naval Hosp., Calif. Contbr. articles to profl. jours.; editorial bd.: Jour. Cardiovascular Surgery, 1974—, chief editor, 1985—; editorial bd. Western Jour. Medicine, 1975—, Jour. Stroke, 1979—, Jour. Vascular Surgery, 1983—. Bd. dirs. Audio-Digest Found., 1974—; bd. dirs. Franklin Martin Found., 1975-80. Served with AUS, 1943-44. Recipient Cert. of Merit, Japanese Surg. Soc. Fellow ACS (gov. 1964-70, regent 1972-82, vice chmn. bd. regents 1980-82, v.p. 1984-85), Royal Coll. Surgeons Eng. (hon.), Royal Coll. Surgeons Ireland (hon.); mem. Am. Surg. Assn., Soc. Univ. Surgeons, Am. Assn. Thoracic Surgery (council 1974-78), Pacific Coast Surg. Assn. (pres. 1985-86), San Francisco Surg. Soc., Los Angeles Surg. Soc., Soc. Vascular Surgery, Western Surg. Assn., Internat. Cardiovascular Soc. (pres. 1977), Soc. Internat. Chirurgie, Soc. Thoracic Surgeons, Western Thoracic Surg. Soc. (pres. 1978), Orange County Surg. Soc. (pres. 1984-85), James IV Assn. Surgeons (councillor 1983—). Clubs: California (Los Angeles); San Francisco Golf, Pacific Union, Bohemian (San Francisco); Cypress Point (Pebble Beach, Calif.); Harvard (N.Y.C.); Big Canyon (Newport Beach). Home: 7 Deerwood Ln Newport Beach CA 92660 Office: U Calif Dept Surgery Irvine CA 92717

CONNOLLY, JOHN STEPHEN, research scientist; b. Butte, Mont., Nov. 23, 1936; s. Stephen Joseph and Helen Marguerite (Harkins) C.; m. Elaine Frances Berson, Jan. 19, 1963; children: Elizabeth, Helen, Jeffrey. AB cum laude, Carroll Coll., 1958; MS, U. Minn., 1960; postgrad., U. Calif., Berkeley, 1962-63; PhD, Brandeis U., 1969. Staff scientist C.F. Kettering Research Lab., Yellow Springs, Ohio, 1969-72; Nat. Acad. Scis./ NRC sr. research research assoc. U.S. Army Natick (Mass.) Labs., 1973-74; dir. research life sci. div. Tech. Inc., San Antonio, 1974-76; adj. assoc. prof. U. Tex. Health Sci. Ctr., San Antonio, 1975-78; sr. scientist Solar Energy Research Inst., Golden, Colo., 1977-83, prin. scientist, 1983—; vis. scientist USAF Aerospace Research Labs., Wright-Patterson AFB, Ohio, 1972-73; cons. in field, Yellow Springs, 1972-74, San Antonio, 1974-77, Golden, 1977—; bd. dirs. Photon Tech. Internat., Princeton, N.J., 1985—. Editor: Photochemical Conversion and Storage of Solar Energy, 1981; contbr. articles to profl. jours. Chmn. Antioch Sch. Assn., Yellow Springs, 1970-71; com. person Jefferson County Democrats, Lakewood, Colo., 1978-85, capt. 1980—, ho. dist. chmn. 1984-85, ho. dist. vice-chmn., 1986. Served to lt. USN, 1960-63. Mem. Am. Chem. Soc. (councilor 1981-83, 86-88), Am. Soc. Photobiology, AAAS, European Photochemistry Assn., Inter-Am. Photchem. Soc., Sigma Xi, Phi Lambda Upsilon, Delta Epsilon Sigma. Roman Catholic. Avocations: photography, computers. Home: 75 Flora Way Golden CO 80401 Office: Solar Energy Research Inst 1617 Cole Blvd Golden CO 80401

CONNOLLY, THOMAS JOSEPH, bishop; b. Tonopah, Nev., July 18, 1922; s. John and Katherine (Hammel) C. Student, St. Joseph Coll. and St. Patrick Sem., Menlo Park, Calif., 1936-47, Catholic U. Am., 1949-51; J.C.D., Lateran Pontifical U., Rome, 1952; D.H.L. (hon.), U. Portland, 1972. Ordained priest Roman Catholic Ch., 1947; asst. St. Thomas Cathedral, Reno, 1947; asst., rector St. Thomas Cathedral, 1953-55; asst. Little Flower Parish, Reno, 1947-48; sec. to bishop 1949; asst. St. Albert the Gt., Reno, 1952-53; pastor St. Albert the Gt., 1960-68, St. Joseph Ch., Elko, 1955-60, St. Theresa's Ch., Carson City, Nev., 1968-71; bishop Baker, Oreg., 1971—. Tchr. Manogue High Sch., Reno, 1948-49; chaplain Serra Club, 1948-49; officialis Diocese of Reno; chmn. bldg. com., dir. Cursillo Movement; moderator Italian Cath. Fedn.; dean, mem. personnel bd. Senate of Priests; mem. Nat. Bishops Liturgy Com., 1973-76; region XII rep. to adminstrv. bd. Nat. Conf. Cath. Bishops, 1973-76, 86-89, mem. adv. com., 1974-76; bd. dirs. Cath. Communications Northwest, from 1977. Club: K.C. (state chaplain Nev. 1970-71). Home: 3805 N Cedar St Baker OR 97814 Office: 2215 First St PO Box 826 Baker OR 97814 *

CONNOLLY-O'NEILL, BARRIE JANE, interior designer; b. San Francisco, Dec. 22, 1943; d. Harry Jr. and Jane Isabelle (Barr) Wallach; m. Peter Smith O'Neill, Nov. 27, 1983. Cert. of design, N.Y. Sch. Interior Design, 1975; BAF in Environ. Design, Calif. Coll. Arts and Crafts, 1978. Profl. model Brebner Agy., San Francisco, 1963-72; TV personality KGO TV, San Francisco, 1969-72; interior designer Barrie Connolly & Assocs., Boise, Idaho, 1978—. Best Interior Design award Mktg. and Merchandising Excellence, No. Calif., 1981, 1984, Sales and Mktg. Council, San Diego, 1985. Mem. Mannequin League of Marin. Avocations: tennis, skiing, gardening, art. Home: 2188 Bluestem Ln Boise ID 83706

CONNOR, GARY EDWARD, manufacturing company marketing executive; b. S.I., N.Y., Nov. 13, 1948; s. Everett M. and Josephine (Amato) C.; B.S. in Elec. Engring., U. Md., 1973; M.B.A., U. Santa Clara (Calif.), 1979. Quality assurance engr. Frankford Arsenal, 1973; quality assurance engr., field service engr. Lockheed Electronics Co., 1973-74; group leader memory test engring. sect. head bipolar product engring. Nat. Semicondr. Corp., 1975-79; internat. mktg. mgr. Am. Microsystems Inc., 1979-80; mktg. mgr. GenRad-STI, Santa Clara, 1980-82; prodn. mktg. exec. AMD, Sunnyvale, Calif., 1982-86; mktg. mgr. IDT, Santa Clara, Calif., 1986—. Mem. IEEE, Electronics Internat. Adv. Panel, Am. Security Council (nat. adv. bd.), Franklin Mint Collectors Soc. Republican. Home: 5121 Kozo Ct San Jose CA 95124 Office: IDT 3236 Scott Blvd PO Box 58015 Santa Clara CA 95052

CONNOR, WILLIAM ELLIOTT, physician, educator; b. Pitts., Sept. 14, 1921; s. Frank E. and Edna S. (Felt) C.; m. Sonja Lee Newcomer, Sept. 19, 1969; children: Rodney William, Catherine Susan Connor Mulford, James Elliott, Christopher French, Peter Malcolm. B.A., U. Iowa, 1942, M.D., 1950. Diplomate: Am. Bd. Internal Medicine, Am. Bd. Nutrition. Intern USPHS Hosp., San Francisco, 1950-51; resident in internal medicine San Joaquin Gen. Hosp., Stockton, Calif., 1951-52; practice medicine specializing in internal medicine Chico, Calif., 1952-54; resident in internal medicine VA Hosp., Iowa City, 1954-56; cons. 1967-75; mem. faculty U. Iowa Coll. Medicine, 1956-75, prof. internal medicine, 1967-75; acting dir., then dir. Clin. Research Center, 1967-75, dir. lipid-atherosclerosis sect., cardiovascular div., 1974-75; vis. prof. Basic Sci. Med. Inst., Karachi, Pakistan, 1961-62, Baker Med. Research Inst., Melbourne, Australia, 1982; vis. fellow clin. sci. Australian Nat. U., Canberra, 1970; prof. cardiology and metabolism-nutrition, dept. medicine, 1975-79, head sect. clin. nutrition, 1979—, acting head, head div. endocrinology, metabolism and nutrition, 1984—, dir. lipid-atherosclerosis lab., assoc. dir. Clin. Research Center, Oreg. Health Scis. U., Portland, 1975—; chmn. heart and lung program project com. Nat. Heart and Lung Inst., NIH, 1974-75, chmn. rev. com. A, 1975-76, chmn. lipid metabolism adv. com., 1971-72, mem. gen. clin. research centers com., 1976-80; mem. arteriosclerosis, lipid metabolism and hypertension com. Natl. Heart and Lung Inst., NIH, 1982-84; mem. food and nutrition bd. Nat. Acad. Scis., 1983—. Contbr. numerous articles to med. jours.; Editor: Jour. Lab. and Clin. Medicine, 1970-73; mem. editorial bds., reviewer profl. jours. Mem. Johnson County (Iowa) Central Democratic Com., 1965-69; mem. nat. council Fellowship Reconciliation; nat., North Central and Pacific Northwest bds. Am. Friends Service Com. Served with AUS, 1943-46. Research fellow Am. Heart Assn., 1956-58; A.C.P. traveling fellow Sir William Dunn Sch. Pathology, Oxford, Eng., 1960; recipient Career Devel. Research award Nat. Heart Inst., 1962-73. Mem. AAAS, A.C.P., Am. Diabetes Assn. (vice chmn. food and nutrition com. 1972-74), Am. Fedn. Clin. Research, Am. Heart Assn. (chmn. council arteriosclerosis 1975-78, exec. com. council epidemiology 1967-70, exec. com. council cerebral vascular disease 1966-68), Am. Soc. Clin. Nutrition (pres. 1978), Am. Inst. Nutrition, AMA, Am. Oil Chemists Soc., Am. Physiol. Soc., Am. Soc. Clin. Investigation, Am. Soc. Study Arteriosclerosis, Assn. Am. Physicians, Central Soc. Clin. Research, Nutrition Soc., Soc. Exptl. Biology and Medicine (council 1971-72, pres. Iowa sect. 1971-72), Western Assn. Physicians, Western Soc. Clin. Research, AAUP (pres. U. Iowa chpt. 1968-69, pres. Oreg. Health Sci. U. chpt. 1978-79), Phi Beta Kappa, Sigma Xi, Alpha Omega Alpha. Research in nutrition, lipid metabolism, blood vessel diseases. Home: 2600 SW Sherwood Pl Portland OR 97201 Office: Oreg Health Scis U Portland OR 97201

CONNORS, DENNIS MICHAEL, infosystems executive; b. Anaconda, Mont., June 13, 1943; s. Dennis Anthony and Vivian Helen (Mahaulos) C.; m. Sandra Lee Haubrich, Sept. 15, 1962; children: Brad, Kevin, Karrie, Timothy, Tricia. AA, El Camino Sch., 1966; Cert. in Tech. of Info. Mgmt., U. Calif., Long Beach, 1967; degree in bus. mgmt., U. Mont., 1963; postgrad., Stanford U. Sr. Exec. Program, 1985. Mgr. TRW Systems, Los Angeles, 1965-77; dir. Levi Strauss & Co., San Francisco, 1977-79; dir. Mervyn's, Hayward, Calif., 1979-81, v.p., 1981—; mem. info. systems adv. bd. Golden Gate U., San Francisco, 1984. Vice chmn. Bay Area Urban League, Oakland, Calif., 1983—. Mem. Data Processing Mgmt. Assn., Am. Mgmt. Assn., Nat. Retail Mchts. Assn. (bd. dirs. info. systems div. 1984—). Avocation: golf. Office: MERVYN'S 22301 Foothill Blvd Hayward CA 94541

CONNORS, STEPHEN WILFRED, lawyer; b. Monroe, Wis., Mar. 11, 1918; s. Patrick J. and Alice (Norder) C.; student U. Wis., 1937-41, U. Minn., 1951; B. Sci. Law, St. Paul Coll. Law, 1950, LL.B. cum laude, 1952; J.D., William Mitchell Coll. Law, 1969; m. Louise Pharr, Feb. 4, 1946; children—Maureen, Patricia, Constance, Mary, Michele, Kelly. Bar: Minn. 1952, Ariz. 1954, U.S. Dist. Ct., 1954, U.S. Ct. Appeals (9th cir.) 1963, U.S. Supreme Ct., 1960; practice Phoenix, 1953—; pres. Olympia Realty, Inc.; dir. Truten Investment Corp. Mem. Ariz. State Athletic Commn., 1961; founding mem. Ariz. State U. Law Sch.; mem. adv. council Am. Security Council; precinct committeeman Democratic Party, 1954-59, 61-72, 84—; mem. Dem. State Central Com., 1954-59, 61-72. Served as sr. pilot USAF, 1943-53, disch. capt. Mem. Am., Ariz., Maricopa County, Minn., Ramsey County bar assns., VFW (life), Am. Legion, Amvets, Hump Pilots Assn. (life), Mil. Flight Service (life dir., legal officer, past pres.), Air Force Assn., Fraternal Order of Police, Friendly Sons of St. Patrick, Am. Trial Lawyers Assn., Internat. Assn. Jewish Lawyers and Jurists, Internat. Acad. Law and Sci., Am. Judicature Soc., Academia Internationali Lex et Scientia. Roman Catholic. Moose. Clubs: Phoenix Execs., Prescott Mountain, Phoenix Press, Terrace, Arizona, Thunderbird Country (founding mem.), Statesman's, Westerner. Home: 8650 E Sandalwood Dr Scottsdale AZ 85253 Office: 810 Clubhouse Dr Prescott AZ 86301

CONNORS, TIMOTHY DAVID, theatre educator; b. Lynn, Mass., Feb. 26, 1951; s. Ernest Delmont and Jean Marie (Franey) C.; m. Miriam Paula Goodman, Aug. 22, 1972; 1 child, Janeice Marie. BA, Culver-Stockton Coll., 1972; MA, Cen. Mo. State U., 1973; PhD, U. Kans., 1981. Asst. instr. theatre U. Kans., Lawrence, 1974-77; instr. Midwestern State U., Wichita Falls, Tex., 1977-81; asst. prof. No. Ariz. U., Flagstaff, 1981-86, chmn. dept. theatre and dance, 1984—, assoc. prof., 1986—; vice chmn. Tex. Am. Coll. Theatre Festival, 1979-81, Ariz. Coll. Theatre Festival, 1984-86, chmn., 1986—. Dir. high sch. and coll. theatre prodns.; contbr. articles to profl. jours. Bd. dirs. Backdoor Community Theatre, Wichita Falls, 1979-81; merit badge advisor Boy Scouts Am., Wichita Falls, 1979-81; mentor Gifted Opportunity Program, 1984-85. Named one of Outstanding Young Men Am., 1985. Mem. Assn. for Theatre in Higher Edn., Ariz. Theatre Educators Assn., United Inst. for Theatre Tech. Roman Catholic. Avocations: writing, raquetball, jigsaw puzzles. Home: 6225 N Dodge Flagstaff AZ 86004 Office: No Ariz U Dept Theatre and Dance Flagstaff AZ 86011

CONOVER, JERRY NEIL, marketing educator; b. Terre Haute, Ind., Oct. 30, 1950; s. James August and Jane (Pittman) C.; m. Carey Lea Lumpkin, June 2, 1979; children: Michael David, Robert Steven. AB in Psychology, U. Mich., 1972; MA in Psychology, U. Mo., 1975; PhD in Psychology, U. MO., 1979; PhD in Bus. Adminstrn., U. Mo., 1982. Grad. instr. U. Mo., Columbia, 1979-81; asst. prof. U. Ariz., Tucson, 1981-85, No. Ariz. U., Flagstaff, 1985—; pres. Market Insight, Flagstaff, 1983—. Contbr. articles to profl. jours. Research grantee U. Ariz. and No. Ariz. U., 1982-86; doctoral consortium fellow Am. Mktg. Assn., 1980. Mem. Am. Mktg. Assn., Assn. for Consumer Research, Am. Psychol. Assn. Republican.

Home: PO Box 22189 Flagstaff AZ 86002 Office: No Ariz Univ Box 15066 Flagstaff AZ 86011

CONOVER, JOHN CARLISLE, III, electrical engineer; b. Tulsa, Apr. 17, 1943; s. John Carlisle and Evelyn Loretta (Cole) C.; m. Florence Consuelo Williams, Sept. 2, 1967. BSEE, U. N.Mex., 1973. Design engr. Tex. Instruments, Dallas, 1973-74, Motorola, Phoenix, 1973-76; staff engr. Fairchild Corp., Mountain View, Calif., 1976—81; with Siliconix, Santa Clara, Calif., 1982-83; mgr. engr. MCE, Sunnyvale, Calif., 1981-83; dir. engring. SMOS Systems, San Jose, Calif., 1983—. Contbr. articles to profl. jours. Mem. IEEE. Avocations: sports cars, racing cars.

CONOVER, ROBERT WARREN, librarian; b. Manhattan, Kans., Oct. 6, 1937; s. Robert Warren and Grace Darline (Grinstead) C.; B.A., Kans. State U., 1959; M.A., U. Denver, 1961. Librarian, supervising librarian County of Fresno, Calif., 1961-66; county librarian County of Yolo, Woodland, Calif., 1967-68; dir. City of Fullerton (Calif.) Pub. Library, 1968-73, City of Pasadena (Calif.) Pub. Library, 1973-80, City of Commerce (Calif.) Pub. Library, 1985—. Palos Verdes Library Dist., Palos Verdes Peninsula, Calif., 1980-85. Recipient Pres.'s award Fresno Jaycees, 1963. Mem. ALA, Orange County Library Assn. (pres. 1971), Spl. Libraries Assn., Calif. Library Assn. (pres. Yosemite chpt. 1965, mem. council 1981), Santiago Library System Council (pres. 1972), Pi Kappa Alpha. Republican. Episcopalian. Clubs: University (Pasadena); Los Angeles Athletic. Office: City of Commerce Pub Library 5655 Jillson St City of Commerce CA 90040

CONRAD, JUANA CAROL, court administrator; b. Callaway, Nebr., July 4, 1939; d. Norris Elwood and Madeline Gwendolyn (Stapelman) Whaley; m. James Edward Williams, Feb. 7, 1959 (div. July 1963); m. Samuel Charles Conrad, Sept. 2, 1966; children: Scott James, Jason Charles. Asst. supr. Los Angeles Mcpl. Ct., 1964-65, supr., 1965-66, ct. clk., 1966-79, dep. chief, 1979-82; ct. adminstr. East Los Angeles Mcpl. Ct., 1982—. Pres. Women for Internat. Peace and Arbitration, Glendale, Calif., 1985, founder; appointed to nat. com. on women Baha'is of U.S. Fellow Inst. Ct. Mgmt.; mem. Mcpl. Cts. Los Angeles, Assn. of Los Angeles County Mcpl. Ct. Adminstrs. (mem. jury auto. com. 1982—), Nat. Assn. Trial Ct. Adminstrs. Avocation: skiing. Office: East Los Angeles Mcpl Ct 4837 E Third St Los Angeles CA 90022

CONRAD, KENNETH ALLEN, internal medicine, pharmacology educator; b. Reading, Pa., Sept. 30, 1946; s. Roger Stapleton and Margaret (Miller) C.; m. JoAnne Ruth Castonguay, Aug. 30, 1974; children: Heather, Allison. BS, Albright Coll., 1968; MD, U. Pa., 1972. Diplomate Am. Bd. Internal Medicine. Asst. prof. Med. Coll. Pa., Phila., 1976-77; asst. prof. U. Ariz., Tucson, 1977-83, assoc. prof., 1983—. Editor: Drug Therapy for the Elderly, 1982. Fellow ACP; mem. AMA, Am. Soc. Clin. Pharmacology and Therapeutics, Am. Fedn. Clin. Research. Office: U Ariz Med Ctr 1501 N Campbell Ave Room 6335 Tucson AZ 85724

CONRAD, PAUL FRANCIS, editorial cartoonist; b. Cedar Rapids, Iowa, June 27, 1924; s. Robert H. and Florence G. (Lawler) C.; m. Barbara Kay King, Feb. 27, 1954; children: James, David, Carol, Elizabeth. B.A., U. Iowa, 1950. Editorial cartoonist Denver Post, 1950-64, Los Angeles Times, 1964—; cartoonist Los Angeles Times Syndicate, 1973—; lectr. Cooke-Daniels Lecture Tours, Denver Art Mus., 1964; Richard M. Nixon chair Whittier Coll., 1977-78. Exhibited sculpture and cartoons, Los Angeles County Mus. Art, 1979; (Recipient Editorial Cartoon award Sigma Delta Chi 1963, 69, 71, 81, 82, Pulitzer prize editorial cartooning 1964, 71, 84); Author: The King and Us, 1974, Pro and Conrad, 1979, Drawn and Quartered, 1985. Served with C.E. AUS, 1942-46, PTO. Recipient Journalism award U. So. Calif., 1972, Overseas Press Club award, 1970, 81, Robert F. Kennedy Journalism award, 1st Prize, 1985. Fellow Soc. Profl. Journalists; mem. Phi Delta Theta. Democrat. Roman Catholic. Office: Times Mirror Sq Los Angeles CA 90053

CONROY, THOMAS FRANCIS, insurance company executive; b. Chgo., Sept. 26, 1938; s. Thomas Francis and Eleanor Althea (Heatherly) C.; m. Mary Elizabeth Schaeffer, June 19, 1965; children: Alexandra, Margaret. BSc, De Paul U., 1959; MBA, U. Chgo., 1969. CPA, CDP. Mgr. Ernst & Whinney, Chgo., 1959-74; exec. v.p. fin. Security Life of Denver, 1974—. Served to capt. U.S. Army, 1960-62. Fellow Life Mgmt. Inst. Office: Security Life Ins Denver 1616 Glenarm Pl Denver CO 80202

CONROYD, MAUREEN ANN, social worker; b. Chgo., Nov. 3, 1944; d. Walter Francis and Margaret Ann (McAuliff) C.; m. Thomas M. Fitzgerald, Aug. 24, 1968 (div. Mar. 1974); 1 child, Maureen Ann. BS, Loyola U., Chgo., 1967; MSW, U. Wash., 1981. Cert. Mental Health Adminstr., Wash. Social worker Child and Family Service, Chgo., 1972-75; assoc. adminstr. Child and Family Advocated, Evanston, Ill., 1975-78; mgr. child and family program Eastside Mental Health, Bellevue, Wash., 1978-84; dir. Conroyd & Assocs., Everett, Wash., 1984—; tchr. Everett Community Coll., 1986—; cons. in field. Contbr. articles to profl. jours. Adv. bd. mem. Issaquah Youth and Family Service, 1983-84; chmn. Children's Service Coordinator's com. King County Mental Health Ctrs., Seattle, 1979-81; chmn. of adv. com. METRO Ctr. YMCA Single Parent Project, Seattle, 1978-79; health adv. com. Evanston Mental Health Consortium Child and Adolescent Task Force, 1976-78; rep. Ill. State Adv. com. Child Care, Springfield, 1972-74. Mem. U. Wash. Alumni Assn. Social Workers (sec. 1985-86, pres. elect. 1986-87), N.W. Officers Devel. Assn., Nat. Assn. Social Workers (cert.), Acad. Cert. Social Workers. Roman Catholic. Lodge: Zonta. Avocations: golfing, hiking, traveling, sailing. Home: 7002 25th Ave NW Seattle WA 98117 Office: 3325 Wetmore Everett WA 98201

CONSANI, WILLIAM PAUL, insurance company executive; b. San Francisco, Dec. 14, 1931; s. Angelo Paul and Mable (Wood) C.; m. Maria Cuenca, Feb. 24, 1951 (dec. 1954); m. 2d Delilah A. Daniels, Apr. 24, 1955 (div. Jan. 1984); children—Betty Lin, Julie Ann, William P., Cheryl Lee, Ronald Allen, Delilah Gayle; m. 3d Elaine C. Moore, Mar. 1, 1985. Student Lincoln U. Law Sch., 1971-73. Enlisted U.S. Air Force, 1948; advanced to sgt., 1970; ret., 1971; adjuster Underwriters Adjusting Co., Chico, Calif., 1971-77, br. claims mgr., 1977-82, dist. mgr., 1982-84, mgr. franchising/spl. accounts Citrus Heights, Calif., 1984-85; mgr. franchising Pacific Region, 1985—. Mem. USAF Paralegal Assn. Home: 15 Kaseberg Dr Roseville CA 95678 Office: Underwriters Adjusting Co 11031 Sun Ctr Dr Rancho Cordova CA 95670

CONSTANT, CLINTON, chemical engineer; b. Nelson, B.C., Can., Mar. 20, 1912; came to U.S., 1936, naturalized, 1942; s. Vasile and Annie (Hunt) C.; m. Margie Robbel, Dec. 5, 1965. B.Sc. with honors, U. Alta., 1935, postgrad., 1935-36; Ph.D., Western Res. U., 1939. Registered profl. engr. Devel. engr. Harshaw Chem. Co., Cleve., 1936-38, mfg. foreman, 1938-43, sr. engr. semi-works dept., 1948-50; supt. hydrofluoric acid dept. Nyotex Chems., Inc., Houston, 1943-47, chief devel. engr., 1947-48; mgr. engring. Ferro Chem. Co., Bedford, Ohio, 1950-52; tech. asst. mfg. dept. Armour Agrl. Chem. Co. (name formerly Armour Fertilizer Works), Bartow, Fla., 1952-61, mfg. research and devel. div., 1961-63, mgr. spl. projects Research div. (co. name changed to USS Agri-Chems 1968), 1963-65, project mgr., 1965-70; chem. adviser Robert & Co. Assocs., Atlanta, 1970-79; chief engr. Almon & Assocs., Inc., Atlanta, 1979-80; project mgr. Engring. Service Assocs., Atlanta, 1980-81; v.p. engring. ACI Inc., Hesperia, Calif., 1981-83; sr. v.p., chief engr. MTI (acquisition of ACI), Hesperia, 1983-86; engring. cons. San Bernardino County APCD, Victorville, Calif., 1986—. Fellow AAAS, Am. Inst. Chemists, Am. Inst. Chem. Engrs., N.Y. Acad. Scis., AIAA (assoc.); mem. Am. Chem. Soc., Am. Astron. Soc., Astron. Soc. Pacific, Royal Astron. Soc. Can., Nat. Soc. Profl. Engrs., Am. Water Works Assn., Calif. Water and Pollution Control Assn., Air Pollution Control Assn., Soc. Mfg. Engrs., NSPE, Calif. Soc. Profl. Engrs. Author tech. reports, sci. fiction; patentee in field. Office: San Bernardino County APCD 15505 Civic Dr Victorville CA 92392

CONSTANTEN, CARL PHILIP, mechanical engineer; b. Hackensack, N.J., Sept. 20, 1951; s. Frank Costos and Lillian Barbara (Stone) C.; m. Roberta Kay McDermott, Nov. 13, 1975. BS in Engring. and Applied Sci., Calif. Inst. Tech., 1972, MS in Mech. Engring., 1973; MBA, U. So. Calif., 1982. Cons. engr. Dino A. Morelli, Inc., Pasadena, Calif., 1972-73; lead engr. F-5 hydraulic systems Northrop Corp., Hawthorne, Calif., 1973-82, mgr. F-5/F-20 mech. design, 1982-86, mgr. sybsystems design and analysis, 1986—. Area chmn. Calif. Inst. Tech. Alumni Fund, 1978-84, Los Angeles regional chmn., 1984—. Howard R. Hughes scholar, 1968-69, Gen. Motors scholar, 1970-71. Mem. AIAA, Soc. Automotive Engrs., Beta Gamma Sigma. Republican. Home: 5849 Woodglen Dr Agoura Hills CA 91301 Office: Northrop Corp 1 Northrop Ave Hawthorne CA 90250

CONTI, DANIEL JOSEPH, health management executive; b. Somerville, N.J., Feb. 22, 1949; s. Daniel A. and Helen (Glab) C.; m. Carolynn E. Frush, Aug. 10, 1982. BS, St. Bonaventure U., 1970; MS, U. Ariz., 1979. Sr. physiologist Los Angeles County Occupational Health Dept., 1979-80; exec. dir. Inst. Health Mgmt., San Francisco, 1980-82; owner, pres. Health Mgmt. Cons., San Francisco, 1982-86; v.p., chief ops. officer Nat. Inst. Cardiovascular Tech., Inc., Newport Beach, Calif., 1986—, also bd. dirs.; facility design mgmt. cons. Norland Properties, Inc., San Francisco, 1985—; mgmt. cons. Physis, Inc., San Francisco, 1983-85. Editor Health Mgmt. Newsletter, 1982-84. Mem. Am. Coll. Sports Medicine, Assn. Fitness in Bus. Democrat. Avocations: fitness, computer sci. Office: Nat Inst Cardiovascular Tech 1542 Monrovia Ave Newport Beach CA 92663

CONTI, PETER SELBY, astronomy educator; b. N.Y.C., Sept. 5, 1934; s. Attilio Carlo and Marie (Selby) C.; m. Carolyn Safford, Aug. 26, 1961; children—Michael, Karen, Kathe. B.S., Rensselaer Poly. Inst., 1956; Ph.D., U. Calif-Berkeley, 1963. Research fellow Calif. Inst. Tech., Pasadena, 1963-66; asst. prof. astronomy U. Calif./Santa Cruz, 1966-71; astronomer Lick Obs., Santa Cruz, 1966-71; prof., fellow Joint Inst. Lab. Astrophysics U. Colo., Boulder, 1971—, chmn. dept. astrophys., planetary and atmospheric scis., 1980-86; Bd. dirs. Assoc. Univs. for Research in Astronomy, Inc., Tuscon, chmn. bd. dirs. 1983-86; vis. prof. U. Utrecht, The Netherlands, 1969-70. Editor: Mass Loss and Evolution of O-type Stars, 1979; contbr. articles to profl. jours. Served to lt. (j.g.) USNR, 1956-59. Recipient Gold medal U. Liege, Belgium, 1975; Fulbright fellow, 1969-70. Fellow AAAS (chmn. sect. D. in astronomy 1980); mem. Am. Astron. Soc. (councillor 1983-86), Astron. Soc. of Pacific, Internat. Astron. Union (organizing com. 1983-85, v.p. 1986—, commn. 29 stellar spectra). Democrat. Home: 516 College Ave Boulder CO 80302 Office: U Colo Joint Inst Lab Astrophysics Box 440 Boulder CO 80309

CONTI, SAMUEL, judge; b. Los Angeles, July 16, 1922; s. Fred and Katie C.; m. Dolores Crosby, July 12, 1952; children: Richard, Robert, Cynthia. B.S., U. Santa Clara, 1945; LL.B., Stanford U., 1948, LL.D. Bar: Calif. 1948. Pvt. practice San Francisco and Contra Costa County, 1948-60; city atty. Concord, Calif., 1960-69; judge Superior Ct. Contra Costa County, 1968-70, U.S. Dist. Ct., No. Dist. Calif., San Francisco, 1970—. Mem. Bd. Edn. Pittsburg Unified Sch. Dist., 1952-58; mem. Sch. Redistricting Com. for Contra Costa County, 1956-58. Served with AUS, 1940-44. Mem. Central Contra Costa Bar Assn. (pres.), Concord C. of C. (pres.), Alpha Sigma Nu. Office: US Dist Court House PO Box 36060 San Francisco CA 94102

CONTO, ARISTIDES, advertising agency executive; b. N.Y.C., Feb. 10, 1931; s. Gus Dimitrios and Osee (Kenney) C.; B.A., Champlain Coll., 1953; M.S. in Journalism, UCLA, 1958, certificate in indsl. relations, 1965; m. Phyllis Helen Wiley, June 22, 1957; 1 son, Jason Wiley. Reporter, City News Service, Los Angeles, 1958; dir. pub. relations Galaxy Advt. Co., Los Angeles, 1959-60; news media chief Los Angeles County Heart Assn., 1960-61; pub. relations asso. Prudential Ins. Co., Los Angeles, 1961-64; advt. mgr. Aerospace Controls Co., Los Angeles, 1964-65; comml. sales promotion coordinator Lockheed-Calif. Co., Burbank, 1965-73; pres. Jason Wiley Advt. Agy., Los Angeles, 1973—; dir. Tower Master, Inc., Los Angeles. Served with U.S. Army, 1955-56. Recipient advt. awards. Mem. Nat. Soc. Published Poets, Los Angeles Press Club, Bus.-Profl. Advt. Assn. Los Angeles, Public Relations Soc. . Author: The Spy Who Loved Me, 1962; The Diamond Twins, 1963; author screenplays: Lannigan, 1973; Haunted Host, 1976; Captain Noah, 1977; (screenplay) Government Surplus, 1983. Office: 1506 W 12th St Los Angeles CA 90015

CONTOS, PAUL ANTHONY, engineer, investment advisor; b. Chgo., Mar. 18, 1926; s. Anthony Dimitrios and Panagiota (Kostopoulos) C.; m. Lilian Katie Kalkines, June 19, 1955 (dec. Apr. 1985); children: Leslie, Claudia, Paula, Anthony; m. Elsa Saxton, Mar. 7, 1987. Student, Am. TV Inst., Chgo., 1946-48, U. Ill., 1956, U. So. Calif., 1956-57. Engr. J.C. Deagan Co., Inc., Chgo., 1951-53, Lockheed Missile and Space Co., Inc., Sunnyvale, Calif., 1956-62; engring. supr. Lockheed Missile and Space Co., Inc., Sunnyvale, 1962-65, staff engr., 1965—; pres. PAC Investments, Saratoga, Calif., 1984—, also adv., 1984—. Served with U.S. Army, 1944-46, ETO. Decorated Purple Heart. Mem. DAV (commdr. Chgo. unit 1948-51), Pi Sigma Phi (pres. 1951-53). Republican. Greek Orthodox. Home and Office: 13878 Malcolm Ave Saratoga CA 95070

CONVERY, FREDRICK RICHARD, orthopaedic surgeon; b. Olympia, Wash., June 12, 1932; s. Fredrick Rudolph and Francis (Lockwood) C.; m. Janet Lea Carlson, Aug. 21, 1955 (div. Dec. 1977); children: Kristine, Linda, Mark; m. Martha Minteer, Dec. 1977. BA, U. Wash., 1954, MD, 1958. Instr. U. Wash., Seattle, 1967-68, asst. prof., 1968-71, assoc. prof., 1971-72; assoc. prof. U. Calif.-San Diego, La Jolla, 1972-77, prof., 1977—. Contbr. numerous articles to profl. jours. Mem. Am. Acad. Orthopaedic Surgeons (Kappa Delta award 1973), Am. Orthopaedics Assn., Western Orthopaedics Assn. (Vernon G. Thompson award 1964), Wislon-Bost Interurban Club, Am. Rheumatology Assn., Internat. Soc. of the Knee. Served to lt. (M.C.) USNR, 1959-61. Avocations: skiing, property development. Home: 5772 La Jolla Corona Dr La Jolla CA 92037 Office: U Calif San Diego Med Ctr 225 Dickinson St H-776 San Diego CA 92103

CONWAY, JOHN GEORGE, research physicist; b. Pitts., May 16, 1922; s. John George and Irene M. (Clifford) C.; m. Florence M. Bittner, Oct. 21, 1947; children: John George III, Jane M., Michael F., Ann S., Kathleen M., Patrick K., Caroline M. BS in Physics and Engring., U. Pitts., 1944. Mem. staff Los Alamos (N.Mex.) Sci. Lab., 1944-46; research assoc. U. Pitts., 1946-47, CNRS, Orsay, France, 1973-74; with Lawrence Berkeley (Calif.) Lab., 1947—, sr. staff scientist, 1950—. Contbr. articles to profl. jours. Mem. El Cerrito (Calif.) City Council, 1958-63, mayor, 1961. Named Outstanding Man of Yr. El Cerrito Jaycees, 1959; recipient Louis A. Strait award No. Calif. Soc. Spectroscopy, 1978. Fellow Optical Soc. Am. (William F. Meggers award 1980); mem. AAAS, Am. Phys. Soc., Soc. Applied Spectroscopy. Home: 1153 King Dr El Cerrito CA 94530 Office: Lawrence Berkeley Lab 1 Cyclotron Rd Berkeley CA 94720

CONWAY, JOHN JOSEPH, technical consulting company executive; b. Cleve., Mar. 22, 1929; s. John Anthony and Mary Alice (Gallagher) C.; m. Maxine Waite, June 30, 1959 (div. 1969). Student, John Carroll U., 1947-49; A.A., Orange Coast Coll., Calif., 1977; B.A., Calif. State U.-Fullerton, 1979, M.B.A., 1981. Mgr. component engring. Litton Data Systems, Van Nuys, Calif., 1962-80; microelectronics cons. Northrop Electronics, Hawthorne, Calif., 1980-81, Magnavox Adv. Products, Torrance, Calif., 1981-82, TRW Electronics & Def., Redondo Beach, Calif., 1982—; pres. Conway Software Inc., Irvine, Calif., 1980—. Mem. Standards Engring. Soc. (chmn. Los Angeles sect. 1959-60), IEEE. Republican. Home: 8 Northcove Irvine CA 92714

CONYERS, JAMES FRANKLIN, educational adminstrator; b. Mattoon, Ill., May 24, 1945; s. Milton Elmore and Juanita Virginia (Welch) Bareither C.; m. Dolores Marie Kester, Aug. 16, 1970; children—Timothy James, Ivy Marie. B.S. in Edn., Eastern Ill. U., 1967, Ed.S., 1974; M.S. in Edn., Western Ill. U., 1970. Vol. U.S. Peace Corps, The Gambia, 1967-69; grad. asst. Western Ill. U., Macomb, 1969-70; tchr., counselor Navajo Meth. Mission, Farmington, N.Mex., 1970-74; guidance counselor Mesa Alta Jr. High Sch., Bloomfield, N.Mex., 1974-83, prin., 1983—. Mem. Assn. for Supervision and Curriculum Devel., N.Mex. Sch. Adminstrs., N.Mex. Middle Sch. Educators, Phi Delta Kappa. Methodist. Club: San Juan Rabbit Breeders (Aztec, N.Mex.) (pres.). Lodge: Kiwanis. Home: 436 S Johnson St Bloomfield NM 87413 Office: Mesa Alta Jr High Sch 329 Bergin Ln Bloomfield NM 87413

COODLEY, ALFRED EDGAR, psychiatrist, psychoanalyst; b. Los Angeles, Apr. 25, 1922; s. Oscar and Rae (Korot) C.; m. Gloria May Drexler, Feb. 9, 1947 (div. 1975); children: Roger Stuart, Mitchell Ross; m. Inga Charlotte Steinberg, Nov. 1985. Student, UCLA, 1940; BA, U. Calif., Berkeley, 1941; MD, U. Calif., San Francisco, 1943; PhD, So. Calif. Psychoanalytic Inst., 1955. Diplomate Am. Bd. Psychiatry and Neurology. Intern Los Angeles County Gen. Hosp., 1943-44; asst. chief dept. neurology, asst. chmn. dept. neuropsychology Letterman Gen. Hosp., San Francisco, 1946-47; sr. resident and fellow in psychiatry Cin. Gen. Hosp., 1947-49; clin. assoc. So. Calif. Psychoanalytic Inst., Beverly Hills, 1950-55; pvt. practice psychiatry Los Angeles, 1949—; assoc. clin. prof. psychiatry Loma Linda (Calif.) Sch. Medicine, 1954-61, UCLA Sch. Medicine, 1962—; tng. and supervising analyst So. Calif. Psychoanalytic Inst., Beverly Hills, 1972—; clin. prof. emeritus U. So. Calif. Sch. Medicine, 1977-85; psychiat. cons. USPHS, Los Angeles, 1949-68, Los Angeles County Juvenile Hall, 1949-71, Psychiat. Sect. Los Angeles County Superior Ct., 1950-57, Criminal div., 1971—, State of Calif. Parole Clinic, 1962—, Allergy Clinic UCLA Med. Ctr., 1962-82, Family Med. Dept., 1982-85, Oncology Dept., 1987—. Contbg. editor: Ann. Survey of Psychoanalysis, 1961, 63-64; assoc. editor The Psychoanalytic Forum, 1966-70; mem. editorial bd. Am. Jour. Forensic Psychiatry; contbr. 85 articles to profl. jours. Mem. Los Angeles World Affairs Council, 1960—, Los Angeles Town Hall, 1980—. Served to maj. M.C., U.S. Army, 1944-47. Fellow Am. Psychiat. Assn. (life), Am. Orthopsychiat. Assn. (life), Am. Assn. for Social Psychiatry; mem. Am. Psychoanalytic Assn. (exec. councilor 1970-78, pres. 1968-69), Am. Psychosomatic Soc. (exec. councilor 1970-78), So. Calif. Psychoanalytic Soc. (pres. 1967-68), So. Calif. Psychiat. Soc. (exec. councilor 1962-65, treas. 1965-66), So. Calif. Psychotherapy Affiliation (pres. 1977-82), Los Angeles County Med. Assn. (pres.-elect sect. psychiatry 1986—), Am. Acad. Psychiatry and Law, Acad. Psychosomatic Medicine, Phi Delta Epsilon (historian 1986—). Democrat. Jewish. Avocations: travel, art, music, theatre, football. Office: 10921 Wilshire Blvd #614 Los Angeles CA 90024

COOGAN, EDWARD RICHARD, psychotherapist; b. Archbald, Pa., Sept. 1, 1931; s. John Edward and Dora Marie (McHale) C.; m. Patricia Ann Hardwick, Dec. 19, 1955 (div. May 1975); children—Christine, Lynne, Cynthia; m. Kathryn Theresa Stevens, June 4, 1977. B.A., Chapman Coll., 1974; M.S. with distinction, Calif. State Coll.-Stanislaus, 1983. Lic. marriage, family and child counselor, Calif.; lic. hypno-analyst, Calif. Commd. 2d lt. U.S. Air Force, 1953, advanced through grades to col., 1975; ret., 1977; psychotherapist Family Service Agy., Turlock, Calif., 1978-83; pvt. practice psychotherapy, Modesto, Calif., 1983—; child custody mediator Stanislaus County, Modesto, 1983—; cons. Eastern Wash. U., Cheney, 1979—. Mem. adv. bd. Salvation Army, Turlock, 1982-84. Decorated Silver Star. Mem. Calif. Assn. Marriage, Family and Child Therapists, Phobia Soc. Am. (therapist 1984), Ret. Officers Assn. (bd. dirs. Merced, Calif. 1984), Mensa. Democrat. Roman Catholic. Home: 1150 La Rosa Ct Turlock CA 95380 Office: Coogan Counseling Services 1400 K St Suite C Modesto CA 95354

COOK, ANNE WELSH, mathematics educator; b. Hilo, Hawaii, July 9, 1948; d. Charles Edward and Charlotte Annabelle (Redfield) Welsh; m. Thomas Rollin Kramer, Sept. 12, 1970 (div. Dec. 1981); 1 child, Jeanne Elizabeth; m. Jeffrey Dean Cook, June 22, 1985; 1 child. BS in Math., Duke U., 1970, MA in Math., Computer Sci., 1971; PhD in Stats., Am. U., 1983. Programmer, researcher Duke U. Hosp., Durham, N.C., 1969-71; math. statistician Bur. Census, Suitland, Md., 1971-73; sr. programmer, mgr. EG&G Mason REsearch, Rockville, Md., 1973-74, 75-78; project mgr. Price, Williams & Assocs., Silver Spring, Md., 1974-75; instr. Am. U., Washington, 1981-82; asst. prof. math. Pacific Luth. U., Tacoma, 1983—; statis. cons. Donald Murtha, Washington, 1981-83, EPA, Washington, 1982-83; cons. Fairchild, Puyallup, Wash.; elected mem. rank and tenure com. Pacific Luth. U., 1984—. Sec. bldg. com. St. Joseph/St. John's Episcopal Ch., Tacoma, 1986. Mem. Am. Statis. Assn. Home: 7231 Interlaaken Dr SW Tacoma WA 98499 Office: Pacific Luth U Math and Computer Sci Dept Tacoma WA 98447

COOK, BLANCHE MCLANE, artist; b. Moulton, Iowa, July 1, 1901; d. Alva Randolph and Eva (Wynn) Mclane; m. Harry Christian Cook, Feb. 19, 1938 (dec. 1983); m. Rankin A. Nebinger. Honor grad., Phila. Sch. Design for Women, 1928; student, Temple U., 1929; BA, Cen. Wash. State Coll., 1959, MA, 1965. Tchr. Phila. Sch. Design and Baldwin Sch., 1927-29; free-lance comml. artist 1928—; with irrigation dept. Yakima County Treas., Wash., 1930-34, chief dep. treas., 1934-40; pvt. instr. art 1930—; art instr. Yakima Valley Jr. Coll., 1933-48, 57-58; portrait painter, 1928—; art instr., counselor Moxee Elem. Sch., Yakima, 1959-60; art instr. Wilson Jr. High Sch., Yakima, 1961-66, chmn. art dept., 1962-66. Works exhibited at Larson Gallery, Yakima, 1954-63, Seattle Art Mus., Woessner Gallery, Studio Gallery, Palace Legion of Honor, San Francisco, Spokane (Wash.) Art Gallery, others; represented in permanent collections Seattle Art Mus., Frye Mus., Yakima Valley Coll. Home: Madison House 21500 72d Ave W Edmonds WA 98020

COOK, CHERYL DIANE MORTENSEN, municipal official; b. Delta, Utah, June 7, 1948; d. Hans Ronald and Fern (Whicker) Mortensen; m. Robert David Cook, June 22, 1968. BS, U. Utah, 1976; grad., Am. Banking Assn. Nat. Sch. Bank Investments, Champagne, Ill., 1979. Asst. v.p., investment officer Comml. Security Bank, Salt Lake City, 1976-82; treas. City of Salt Lake City, 1982—; mem. Utah Money Mgmt. Council, Salt Lake City, 1983—, chmn., 1987; instr. U. Utah, 1982. Mem. Govt. Fin. Officers Assn., Mcpl. Treasurers Assn., Utah Bond Club (pres. 1983), Money Mgrs. Club. Avocations: skiing, sailing, golf, biking. Office: City and County Bldg Room 209 Salt Lake City UT 84111

COOK, DONALD E., pediatrician; b. Pitts., Mar. 24, 1928; s. Merriam E. and Bertha (Gwin) C.; B.S., Colo. Coll., 1951; M.D., U. Colo., 1955; m. Elsie Walden, Sept. 2, 1951; children—Catherine, Christopher, Brian, Jeffrey. Intern, Fresno County Gen. Hosp., Calif., 1955-56; resident in gen. practice Tulare (Calif.) County Gen. Hosp., 1956-57; resident in pediatrics U. Colo., 1957-59; practice medicine specializing in pediatrics, Aurora, Colo., 1959-64, in pediatrics, Greeley, Colo., 1964—; clin. faculty U. Colo., 19—, clin. prof., 1977—; mem. adv. bd. Nat. Center Health Edn., San Francisco, 1978-80; mem. adv. com. on maternal and child health programs Colo. State Health Dept., 1981-84, chmn., 1981-84; preceptor Sch. Nurse Practitioner Program U. Colo., 1978—. Mem. Weld County Dist. 6 Sch. Bd., 1973-83, pres., 1973-74, 76-77, chmn. dist. 6 accountability com., 1972-73; mem. adv. com. dist. 6 teen pregnancy program, 1983-85; mem. Weld County Task Force on teenaged pregnancy, 1986—, Dream Team Weld County Task Force on sch. dropouts, 1986—, Weld County Interagy. Screening Bd., Weld County Community Ctr. Found., 1984—; group leader neonatal group Colo. Action for Healthy People Colo. Dept. Pub. Health, 1985-86; co-founder Colorodoans for seatbelts on sch. buses, 1985—; co-founder, v.p. Coalition of primary care physicians, Colo., 1986; mem. adv. com. Greeley Central Drug and Alcohol Abuse, 1984-86, Rocky Mountain Ctr. for Health Promotion and Edn., 1984—. Served with USN, 1946-48. Recipient Disting. Service award Jr. C. of C., 1962, Disting. Citizenship award Elks, 1975-76, Service to Mankind award Sertoma Club, 1972; Community Service award Phi Delta Kappa, 1981, Spark Plug award U. No. Colo., 1981. Diplomate Am. Bd. Pediatrics. Mem. Colo. Soc. Sch. Health Com. (chmn. 1967-78), Am. Acad. Pediatrics (chmn. sch. health com. 1975-80, chmn. Colo. chpt. 1982—, mem. task force on new age of pediatrics 1982-85, Ross edn. and award com. 1985-86; media spokesperson Speak Up for Children 1983—), AMA (chmn. sch. and coll. health com. 1980-82), Adams Aurora Med. Soc. (pres. 1964-65), Weld County Med. Soc. (pres. 1968-69), Colo. Med. Soc. (com. on sports medicine, 1980—, com. chmn. 1986—, A.H. Robbins Community Service award 1974), Centennial Pediatric Soc. (pres. 1982-86). Republican. Methodist. Club: Rotary. Home: 1710 21st Ave Greeley CO 80631 Office: 1650 16th St Greeley CO 80631 Office: Greeley Sports Medicine Clinic 16th St and 34th Ave Greeley CO 80634

COOK, DONALD WYNNE, engineering company executive; b. Berkeley, Calif., Aug. 20, 1926; s. Harold Wynne and Caroline (Peters) C.; m. Jemik Elayan, Apr. 4, 1958; children: Jeffrey Wynne, Elizabeth Cheryl. Student, U. Calif., Berkeley, 1944; BS in Naval Tech., U. Minn., 1946; MSME, Stanford U., 1947. From trainee to asst. plant mgr. Continental Can Co., various locations, 1949-59; plant mgr. Continental Can Co., Denver, 1959-64; mgr. div. engring. Continental Can Co., Chgo., 1964-65; dir. ops. Metal div. Ball Corp., Golden, Colo., 1965-73; pres., chief exec. officer Container Tech. Corp., Wheatridge, Colo., 1974—; pres., Eagle Leasing Co., Wheatridge, 1983—, Container Support Internat., Wheatridge, 1980—, Omnitech, Wheatridge, 1980—; gen. ptnr. Rainbow Creek Ltd., Denver, 1976—. Contbr. articles to profl. jours. Mem. legis. affairs com. Colo. C. of C., Denver, 1963-64. Served to lt. (j.g.) USNR, 1952-53, Korea. Republican. Club: Rolling Hills Country. Lodge: Rotary, Masons. Avocations: tennis, skiing, fishing, reading. Home: 2419 Ward Dr Lakewood CO 80215 Office: Container Tech Corp 11465 W 48th Ave Wheatridge CO 80033

COOK, EARL KAAE, oil company executive; b. Provo, Utah, Oct. 17, 1939; s. Earl and Lera (Smith) C.; m. Yvonne Marie Ames, Nov. 24, 1959; children—Karlyn, Jenifer, Shuri, Jason, Heather, Brett. Acctg. degree Stevens Henager Bus. Coll., Salt Lake City, 1962. Rep. Frontier Refining Co., Salt Lake City, 1965-67, Northwestern Refining Co., St. Paul, 1967-68; pres. Telum, Inc., Provo, Utah, 1968—; chmn., dir. Am. Telemedia Network, Provo. Bd. dirs. Provo City Library, 1983, Provo Airport, 1983—, Provo Cultural Affairs, 1982. Recipient Free Enterprise award Sertoma Club, 1983; Disting. Alumni award Stevens Henager Bus. Coll., 1978; Second Miler Service award Utah Nat. Parks council Boy Scouts Am., 1976. Mem. Young Pres.'s Orgn. Republican. Mormon. Initiated self-serve diesel fuel concept to trucking industry in U.S., 1968. Office: Telum Inc 890 E 3650 N Provo UT 84604

COOK, HAROLD RODNEY, army medical center administrator; b. Sterling, Colo., Feb. 13, 1944; s. Harold E. Cook and Adelaide Cook; m. Shirley Carnel; children: Dawn, Danae, Kevin. BS in Bus., Psychology and Sociology, Kearney State Coll., 1973, MA in Psychology, 1974; M Hosp. Adminstrn., Baylor U., 1985. Commd. 2d lt. U.S. Army, 1974, advanced through grades to maj., 1986; med. adminstr. 130th Gen. Hosp., Nürnberg, Germany, 1975-78; comdr. 560th Ambulance Co., Korea; chief ops. med. med./surg. div. Acad. of Health Service, Ft. Sam Houston, Tex., 1980-83; with health care adminstrn. Baylor U., Waco, Tex., 1983-85; surgery administr. Fitzsimons Army Med. Ctr., Aurora, Colo., 1985—. Mem. Am. Coll. Hosp. Adminstrs., Am. Soc. Mgmt., Nat. Assn. Collegiate Vets. (exec. bd.). Clubs: Fitz Alpine (pres. 1985—), Pantera. Home: 12064 E Maple Ave Aurora CO 80012 Office: Fitzsimons Army Med Ctr PO Box 6065 Aurora CO 80045

COOK, LIA, art educator; b. Ventura, Calif., Nov. 25, 1942; d. James and Esther Miriam (Holman) Polese. BA, U. Calif., Berkeley, 1965, MA, 1973. Prof. art Calif. Coll. Arts and Crafts, Oakland, Calif., 1976—; lectr. art various univs. and orgns., U.S. One-woman shows include B.Z. Wagman Gallery, St. Louis, 1985, The Allrich Gallery, San Francisco, 1984, 82, 81, 78, No. Ill. U. Gallery 200, De Kalb, 1984, Galerie Nationale de la Tapisserie et d'Art Textile, Beauvais, France, 1983, San Jose (Calif.) Mus. Art, 1980; exhibited in group shows at Milw. Art Mus., 1986, Three Rivers Art Festival, Pitts., 1986, Albuquerque Mus. Art, History and Sci., 1985, Susan Cummins Gallery, Mill Valley, Calif., 1985, Evanston (Ill.) Art Ctr., 1984, First Street Forum, St. Louis, 1984, The Hand and the Spirit Crafts Gallery, Scottsdale, Ariz., 1984, Ill. State U., Normal-Bloomington, 1984, Kohler Arts Ctr., Sheboygan, Wis., 1984, Meadows Mus., So. Meth. U., Dallas, 1984, Schick Art Gallery, Saratoga Springs, N.Y., Southwest Tex. State U., San Marcos, 1984, Stanislaus State Coll., Turlock, Calif., 1984, Swan Gallery, Phila., 1984, The Allrich Gallery, San Francisco, 1983, Traver Sutton Gallery, Seattle, 1983, Hillwood Art Gallery, Long Island (N.Y.) U., 1983, Brunnier Gallery and Mus. Iowa State U., 1982, Mus. of Art, R.I. Sch. Design, 1982, Cooper-Hewitt Mus., N.Y.C., 1982, Nelson Gallery of Art, Akins Mus. Fine Arts, Kansas City, Mo., 1982, numerous others; represented in permanent collections Mus. Modern Art, N.Y.C., Galerie Nat. de la Tapisserie et d'Art Textile, Am. Craft Mus., N.Y.C., Univ. Tex. Art Mus., Austin, Rensselaer Poly. Inst., AT&T Co., N.Y.C., Art in Architecture Program U.S. GSA, Richmond, Calif., numerous others; contbr. articles, chpts. and revs. to books, catalogues, profl. jours. Fellow NEA, 1974, 77; Jacquard grantee NEA, 1981. Home: 2127 Bonar St Berkeley CA 94702 Office: Calif Coll Arts and Crafts Dept Crafts 5212 Broadway Oakland CA 94618

COOK, LODWRICK M., petroleum company executive; b. 1928; married. B.S., La. State U., 1950, B.S. in Petroleum Engring., 1955; M.B.A., So. Meth. U., 1965. Petroleum engr. Union Producing Co., 1955-56; with Atlantic Richfield Co., Inc., Los Angeles, 1956—, engring. trainee, 1956-61, adminstrv. asst., 1961-64, sr. personnel dept., then personnel mgr., 1964-67, labor reins. con., 1967-69, mgr. labor reins. dept., 1969-70, v.p., gen. mgr. product div. Western area, 1970-72, v.p. mktg. products div., 1972-73, v.p. corp. planning div., 1973-74, v.p. products div., 1974-75, v.p. transp. div., 1975-77, sr. v.p. transp. div., 1977-80, exec. v.p., dir., 1980-85, pres., chief exec. officer, 1985, chmn., chief exec. officer, 1986—. Bd. dirs. Nat. Jr. Achievement, Nat. Action Council for Minorities in Engring.; bd. regents Pepperdine U., La. State U. Found.; exec. bd. Edwin L. Cox Sch. Bus., So. Meth. U. Served as 1st lt. U.S. Army, 1950-53. Mem. Bus. Roundtable, Nat. Petroleum Council, Am. Petroleum Inst. (dir.), U.S. C. of C. (dir.). Office: Atlantic Richfield Co Inc 515 S Flower St Los Angeles CA 90071 *

COOK, LYLE EDWARDS, fund-raising executive, consultant; b. Astoria, Oreg., Aug. 19, 1918; s. Courtney Carson and Fanchon (Edwards) C.; m. Olive Freeman, Dec. 28, 1940; children: James Michael, Ellen Anita Cook Otto, Mary Lucinda Cook Vaage, Jane Victoria. A.B. in History, Stanford U., 1940, postgrad., 1940-41. Instr. history Yuba Jr. Coll., Marysville, Calif., 1941-42; methods analyst Lockheed Aircraft Corp., 1942-45; investment broker Quincy Cass Assocs., Los Angeles, 1945-49; mem. staff Stanford U., 1949-66, asso. dean Sch. Medicine, 1958-65; sr. staff mem. Lester Gorsline Assos., Belvedere, Calif., 1966-72, v.p., 1967-70, exec. v.p., 1970-72; v.p. univ. relations U. San Francisco, 1973-75; fund-raising and planning cons. 1975; dir. fund devel. Children's Home Soc. Calif., 1976-78; exec. dir. That Man May See, Inc., San Francisco, 1978—; trustee, chmn. bd. The Fund Raising Sch., 1967-86; spl. cons. NIH, 1960-62. Mem. Nat. Soc. Fund Raising Execs. (bd. dirs. Inst.), Stanford Assos., Theta Delta Chi. Episcopalian. Club: Belvedere Tennis. Home: 25 Greenwood Bay Dr Tiburon CA 94920 Office: That Man May See Inc 374 Parnassus Ave Suite 312 San Francisco CA 94143

COOK, M(ELVIN) GARFIELD, chemical company executive; b. Woodbury, N.J., June 17, 1940; s. Melvin Alonzo and Wanda (Garfield) C.; m. Margo Dawn Taylor, Aug. 24, 1965; children: Dawn Ann, Melvin, Katherine, JoAnn, Carol, Mary, Taylor, Stephen, Michael. B.S. in Physics, U. Utah, 1966. Research assoc. IRECO Chems., Salt Lake City, 1966-67; gen. mgr. Mesabi Blasting, Inc., Biwabik, Minn., 1967-69; v.p. ops. IRECO Chems., 1969-71, exec. v.p., 1971-72, pres., chief exec. officer, 1972—; dir. Def. Systems, Inc., Salt Lake City, Nobel Ins. Ltd.; advisor on explosives and propellants Dept. Def., Washington, 1979—; bd. govs. Inst. of Makers of Explosives, Washington, 1972—. Author: Everlasting Burnings, 1981, Ency. Modern Explosives, 1972—, (with M.A. Cook) Science and Mormonism, 1967. Vice pres. N.E. Bench Region Council, Salt Lake City, 1974; chmn. voting dist. Republican Party, 1973. Served with USAR, 1958-66. Mem. Mayflower Soc. Republican. Mormon. Lodge: Rotary. Office: IRECO Incorporated 11th Floor Crossroads Tower 50 S Main St Salt Lake City UT 84144

COOK, PAUL M., chemical manufacturing company executive; b. Ridgewood, N.J.. B.S. in Chem. Engring, M.I.T., 1947. With Stanford Research Inst., Palo Alto, Calif., 1949-53, Sequoia Process Corp., 1953-56; with Raychem Corp., Menlo Park, Calif., 1957—, former pres., now chmn., chief exec. officer, bd. dirs. Office: Raychem Corp 300 Constitution Dr Menlo Park CA 94025 *

COOK, ROBERT CROSSLAND, research chemist; b. New Haven, Conn., June 5, 1947; s. Russell C. and Tensia (Veazey) C. BS in Chemistry, Lafayette Coll., 1969; PhM in Phys. Chemistry, Yale U., 1971, PhD in Theoretical Chemistry, 1973. Mem. faculty Lafayette Coll., Easton, Pa., 1973-81; staff scientist Lawrence Livermore (Calif.) Nat. Lab., 1981—; instr. Calif. State U., Hayward, 1985-86; instr. (part-time) Chabot Coll., 1986—; vis. faculty Dartmouth Coll., Hanover, N.H., 1977, 78, 79, Colo. State U., Ft. Collins, 1980. Contbr. articles to profl. jours. Grantee in field. Mem. Am. Chem. Soc., Am. Phys. Soc., Sigma Xi. Office: Lawrence Livermore Nat Lab L-338 Livermore CA 94550

COOK, ROBERT DONALD, business executive; b. Chicago Heights, Ill., Nov. 1, 1929; s. Webster Warren and Gladys (Miner) C.; m. Maxine Jensen, Nov. 11, 1950; children: Carolyn Jean, Robert Donald II. B.S. in Bus, U. Md., 1956; grad. advanced mgmt. program, Harvard U., 1973. C.P.A., Md. Audit mgr. Arthur Andersen & Co. (CPAs), Washington, 1956-63; comptroller Peoples Drug Stores, Washington, 1963-68; v.p., controller Booz, Allen & Hamilton, Inc., Chgo., 1968-72; pres. Cookemper Rentals, Inc., Barrington, Ill., 1971-73; controller Esmark, Inc., Chgo., 1973-77; pres., chief operating officer Castle & Cooke, Inc., San Francisco, 1977-86; chmn. R.D. Cook Mgmt. Corp., 1986—. Served with USNR, 1948-52. Mem. Inst. C.P.A.s, Fin. Execs. Inst., Beta Alpha Psi. Clubs: Masons (32 deg.), Shriners. Home and Office: 75 Rolling Hills Rd Tiburon CA 94920

COOK, ROGER NOLAN, safety manager; b. Helen, W. Va., Aug. 18, 1945; s. Raleigh Newson and Erma Lois (Cook) C.; m. Saundra Dianne Cook, Aug. 17, 1971; children: John Andrew, Ian Philip. BS, Concord Coll., 1971; cert. mining, W. Va. U., 1973; cert. radiation, Colo. Sch. Mines, 1982; postgrad., Utah State U., 1984. Saftey inspector, tng. Pittston Corp., Beckley, W. Va., 1972-77; sr. safety specialist Syncrude Can., Ft. McMurry, Alta., 1977-79; advisor safety, security Getty Oil, Salt Lake City, 1979-85; mgr. safety, security Titanium Metals Corp. Am., Henderson, Nev., 1985—. Scout master Boy Scouts Am., Henderson, 1985-86; bd. dirs. Casper (Wyo.) Youth Hockey Assn., 1980-81, Spl. Olympics, W. Va., 1974-76; pres. Syncrude Softball Assn., Ft. McMurray, 1978-79. Served with USN, 1963-66. Named one of Outstanding Young Men of Am., Jaycees, Utah, 1982. Mem. Nev. Safety Council (bd. dirs. 1986—), Am. Soc. Safety Engrs. (profl., sec. 1986—, v.p. 1987), World Safety Orgn. (cert.), Am. Soc. Indsl. Security (profl., treas. 1983), Nat. Intelligence and Counter Intelligence Assn., Nat. Safety Council (com. health and hygiene 1984—). Republican. Episcopalian. Avocations: fishing, reading. Home: 2349 Red Willow Ln Henderson NV 89105 Office: Titanium Metals Corp AM PO Box 2128 Henderson NV 89015

COOK, RUDOLPH EMANUEL, psychologist; b. Chgo., May 30, 1928; m. Shirley Thrower, Aug. 3, 1973. Ph.B., Northwestern U., 1949; M.A., Loyola U., Chgo., 1956; Ph.D., U. Oreg., 1965. Lic. psychologist, Calif. Boys' counselor Cook County Juvenile Home, Chgo., 1952-56; psychologist Elgin (Ill.) State Hosp., 1956-62; teaching asst. U. Oreg., Eugene, 1962-65; poverty worker Portland (Oreg.) Urban League, 1965-66; psychol. counselor San Jose (Calif.) State U., 1966—; forensic evaluator Santa Clara County (Calif.) Superior Ct.; psychologist Calif. Disability Evaluation Div. Recipient Service award Continental Socs., 1982-83. Fellow Am. Orthopsychiat. Assn., Royal Soc. Health; mem. Nat. Register Health Service Providers in Psychology, Pathway Socs. (Service award 1977), Afro-Am. Community Ctr., Campus Christian Ctr., Kappa Alpha Psi (Service award 1975, 76). Democrat. Home: 1094 Pomeroy Ave Santa Clara CA 95051 Office: San Jose State Univ Adm 201 San Jose CA 95192

COOK, S. ALAN, lawyer, accountant; b. Bangor, Maine, Mar. 25, 1947; s. Harry George and Margaret (Black) C.; 1 child, Heather Alison. B.S., U. R.I., 1972; J.D., U. Ariz., 1978. Bar: Ariz. 1978, U.S. Dist. Ct. Ariz. 1978, U.S. Ct. Appeals (9th cir.) 1978, U.S. Supreme Ct., 1985; CPA, Ariz., R.I. Law clk. to chief judge U.S. Dist. Ct. Ariz., Phoenix, 1978-81; clk. of ct. Ariz. Supreme Ct., Phoenix, 1981-85; sole practice law Phoenix, 1985—; bd. visitors U. Ariz. Coll. Law, Tucson, 1983—. Editorial staff Appellate Ct. Adminstrn. Rev., 1982-83. Area chmn. Western region Nat. Eagle Scout Assn., 1983—. Served as chief warrant officer, U.S. Army, 1966-69, Vietnam; mem. Ariz. Army N.G. (capt. JAGC). Decorated Air medal with 29 clusters, Army Commendation medal. Mem. Nat. Conf. Appellate Ct. Clks. (chmn. various coms. 1981—), Am. Inst. C.P.A.s, U. Ariz. Law Coll. Assn. (exec. com. 1983—), Phi Kappa Phi, Beta Gamma Sigma, Beta Alpha Psi. Republican.

COOK, SHARON EVONNE, academic administrator, educator; b. Pocatello, Idaho, July 16, 1941; d. Willard Robert and Marian (Bartlett) Leisy; m. John Fred Cook, June 19, 1971 (div. Nov. 1980). BEd, No. Mont. Coll., 1970; M in Secondary Edn., U. Alaska, Juneau, 1980; postgrad. in Edn., U. San Francisco, 1980—. Cert. secondary sch. tchr., Alaska. Loan officer 1st Nat. Bank, Havre, Mont., 1964-68; adminstrv. asst. Alaska State Legis., Juneau, 1970-71; tchr. Juneau Dist. High Sch., 1971-75; instr. Juneau Dist. Community Coll., 1975-79; assoc. prof. U. Alaska, Juneau, 1979—, dean Sch. Bus. and Pub. Adminstrn.,, 1986—; editor in chief office tech. McGraw Hill Book Gregg Div., N.Y.C., 1983-84; mem. exec. bd. statewide assembly U. Region V Vocat. Assn., 1978-80, del. 1982. Treas. Alaska State Vocat. Assn., 1980-82, pres.-elect, 1986, pres., 1987; pres. U. Alaska Juneau Assembly, 1978-80, v.p., 1980-82. No. Mont. Coll. scholar, Havre, 1968-70; named Outstanding Tchr., U. Alaska, 1976. Republican. Avocations: hiking, fishing, skiing, knitting. Home: 2400 Douglas Hwy #5 Juneau AK 99801 Office: U Alaska Sch Bus & Pub Adminstrn 1108 F St Juneau AK 99801

COOK, SID FRANK, marine biologist; b. Reno, Dec. 14, 1953; s. Harold Raymond Cook and Doramae Catherine (Deal) Jakobson. BS in Vertebrate Zoology, U. Pacific, 1977; postgrad., Oreg. State U., 1978-80. Project mgr. Cook, Stolowitz and Frame, Visalia, Calif., 1978-81; cons. Argus-Mariner Cons. Scientists Inc., Corvallis, Oreg., 1981—; cons. Calif. Cedar Products Co., Stockton, 1977, UN Indsl. Devel. Orgn., 1986—; fgn. observer Nat. Marine Fisheries Service, Bering Sea, Alaska, 1979. Author: Cook's Book, 1985; contbr. articles to profl. jours.; patentee underwater storage facilities. Active Community Foodbank, Corvallis; advisor Luth. Campus Ministries, Corvallis, 1985; bd. dirs. Grace Luth Ch. Food Gleaning Project, Corvallis, 1985. Mem. Am. Elasmobranch Soc., Desert Fishes Council, Am. Soc. Photogrammetry, Am. Soc. Ichthyologists and Herpetologists. Home and Office: PO Box 393 Corvallis OR 97339-0393

COOK, STANLEY JOSEPH, linguist; b. Spicer, Minn., June 9, 1935; s. William Joseph and Lillie Esther (Feeland) C.; B.A., U. Minn., 1957; M.A., U. Utah, 1966, Ph.D. (NDEA fellow), 1969; m. Janet Lucille Terry, Oct. 9, 1964; children—John Hildon, Laurel Erin. Project specialist in English, U. Wis., Madison, 1967; instr. English, U. Utah, Salt Lake City, 1968-69; prof. English and modern langs. Calif. State Poly. U., Pomona, 1969—; cons. communications. Served with USMCR, 1958-64. NSF grantee, 1966; Calif. State U. and Colls. grantee, 1973-74. Mem. Dialect Soc., Western Photog. Soc., Phi Beta Kappa. Democrat. Roman Catholic. Editor: Language and Human Behavior, 1973, Man Unwept: Visions from the Inner Eye, 1974; author: (with others) The Scope of Grammar: A Study of Modern English, 1980. Home: 1744 N Corona Ave Ontario CA 91764 Office: Calif State Poly U 3801 W Temple Ave Pomona CA 91768

COOK, SYBILLA AVERY, librarian, educator; b. Buffalo, Aug. 20, 1930; d. Edward Carrington and Elizabeth (Boorum) Avery; m. John D. Cook, June 12, 1951; children: Harold John, Robert Sherman, Raymond Avery. BS, Northwestern U., 1951; MALS, Rosary Coll., River Forest, Ill., 1968; MA, U. Oreg., 1982. Cert. ednl. media tchr. and supr., Oreg., Ill. Tchr. Glenview (Ill.) Pub. Schs., 1951; librarian Deerfield (Ill.) Pub. Schs., 1968-69; media specialist Des Plaines (Ill.) Pub. Schs., 1969-76; librarian Dillard (Oreg.) Pub. Schs., 1976-78; library media specialist Glide (Oreg.) Pub. Schs., 1978—; instr., cons. pub. schs., Yoncalla, Oreg. and Oakland, Oreg., 1986. Author: Instructional Library Design, 1986; contbr. articles to profl. jours. Mem. Am. Assn. Sch. Librarians, Am. Library Assn., Pacific Northwest Library Assn., Oreg. Library Assn., Lane Douglas Regional Library Assn. (chmn. 1982-84), Oreg. Ednl. Media Assn. (Tchr. of Yr. 1984), Children's Book Writers Assn., Beta Phi Mu. Home: 19 N River Dr Roseburg OR 97470 Office: Glide Elem Sch 1477 Glide Loop Rd Glide OR 97443

COOK, WILLARD EUGENE, SR., automotive executive; b. Mandan, N.D., Aug. 18, 1912; s. Valentine Ralph and Myrtle Eugenia (McVey) C.; m. Anne Elizabeth Sanders, July 27, 1938; children—Willard, Stephen B., Judith Anne Cook Garber, Janet R. Grad. high sch., Great Falls. Bookkeeper, Mont. Power Co., Great Falls, 1929-34; credit desk Gen. Motors Acceptance Corp., Great Falls, 1934-36; sales Gen. Mills., Inc., Mpls., 1937-47; v.p. Scales Motor Co., Sheridan, Wyo., 1947-54; pres. Cook Ford Sales, Inc., Sheridan, 1954—. Trustee, Sch. Dist. #7, 1950-68; mem. Sheridan County Welfare Bd., 1960-65; pres., bd. dirs. Sheridan chpt. Salvation Army; bd. dirs. YMCA, 1966-78, Whitney-Benefits, Inc., 1970-86, pres., 1986-87; mem. Wyo. Gov.'s Commn. on Edn., 1963-64; deacon, trustee, elder Presbyterian Ch., 1955-75. Recipient Golden Bell award Wyo. Sch. Bd. Assn., 1968; 1st pl. Quality Dealer award Time mag., 1975; Disting. Service in Bus. award Coll. Commerce, U. Wyo., 1976. Mem. Nat. Auto Dealers Assn., Sheridan Auto Dealers Assn. (past pres.), Wyoming Auto Dealers Assn. (dir.), Ford Regional Dealers Council, Rocky Mountain Ford Dealers Advt. Assn., Future Farmers Am. (hon. life). Presbyterian. Clubs: Sheridan Country, Lions (past pres.), Executive (dir.) Sportsman, Elks, Masons, Shriners. Home: 566 W Loucks St Sheridan WY 82801 Office: 103 N Gould St PO Box 863 Sheridan WY 82801

COOK, WILLIAM HOWARD, architect; b. Evanston, Ill., Dec. 19, 1924; s. Clare Cyril and Matilda Hermine (Schuldt) C.; m. Nancy Ann Dean, Feb. 1, 1949; children—Robert, Cynthia, James. B.A., U. Cal. at Los Angeles, 1947; B.Arch., U. Mich., 1952. Chief designer Fabrica de Muebles Camacho-Roldan, Bogota, Colombia, S.Am., 1949-52; asso. architect Orus Eash, Traverse City, Mich., Ft. Wayne, Ind., 1952-60; partner Cook & Swaim (architects), Tucson, 1961-68; project specialist in urban devel. Banco Interamericano de Desarrollo, Buenos Aires, Argentina, 1968-69; pres. Cain, Nelson, Wares, Cook and Assocs., architects, Tucson, 1969-82; vis. lectr. architecture U. Ariz., 1980—, coordinator archtl. exchange with U. LaSalle, Mexico City, 1983, 85. Served to lt. (j.g.) USNR, 1943-46. Fellow AIA (pres. So. Ariz. 1967); mem. Ariz. Soc. Architects (pres. 1970), Ariz. Soc. of AIA (Architect's medal 1981). Presbyterian. Home: 7065 Mesa Grande Ct Tucson AZ 85715 Office: Studio of William H Cook 7065 Mesa Grande Ct Tucson AZ 85715

COOKE, EDNA MARIE, fire protection co. exec., restaurant owner; b. Hogansburg, N.Y., Dec. 27, 1935; d. Thomas and Agnes E. (Jock) Lazare; student Pasadena Coll., 1965, Citrus Coll., 1966-67; m. Charles Ronald Cooke, July 2, 1955 (div.); children—Leanna Jane, Ramona Gale, Craig Ronel. Various positions, 1953-65; sec.-treas., part owner Vanguard Automatic Sprinkler Co., Santa Fe Springs, Calif., 1967-74; owner LaZar House of Beauty, Glendora, Calif., 1974-83, Jacques Restaurant, Glendora, 1974—; pres., owner Eagle Fire Protection, Glendora, 1974—, Fasah, Inc., 1983—. Ways and means chairperson San Gabriel Valley Symphony Assn., 1966. Mem. Glendora C. of C., Calif. Restaurant Assn. Democrat. Roman Catholic. Club: Glendora Country. Office: 906 Cataract San Dimas CA 91773

COOKE, JACK KENT, diversified company executive; b. Hamilton, Ont., Can., Oct. 25, 1912; s. Ralph Ercil and Nancy (Jacobs) C.; m. Barbara Jean Carnegie, May 5, 1934 (div.); children: Ralph Kent, John Kent; m. Jeanne Maxwell Williams, Oct. 31, 1980 (div.). Student, Malvern Collegiate. Joined No. Broadcasting and Pub. Ltd.,, Can., 1937; ptnr. Thomson Cooke Newspapers, 1937-52; pres. Sta. CKEY, Toronto, Ont., Can., 1944-61, Liberty of Can. Ltd., 1947-61, Toronto Maple Leaf Baseball Club Ltd., 1941-64, Micro Plastics, Ltd., Acton, Ont., Can., 1955-60, Robinson Indsl. Crafts, Ltd., London, Ont., Can., 1957-63, Precision Die Casting Ltd., Toronto, Ont., Can., 1955-60, Consol. Frybook Industries, Ltd., 1952-61; chmn. bd., pres. Consol. Press Ltd., 1952-61; pres. Aubyn Investments, Ltd., 1961-68, Continental Cablevision Inc., 1965-68; chmn. Jack Kent Cooke Inc., 1964—; chmn. bd. Transamerica Microwave, Inc., 1965-69; chmn. Pro-Football Inc., Washington Redskins, NFL, 1960—; pres. Calif. Sports, Inc. (Los Angeles Lakers, NBA, Los Angeles Kings, NHL), 1965-79, The Forum of Inglewood, Inc., 1966-79; dir., chmn. exec. com. H&B Am. Corp, 1969-70; chmn., chief exec. officer Teleprompter Corp., 1974-81; chmn. Group W Cable Inc. (formerly Teleprompter Corp.), 1981-85, Cooke Properties Inc., N.Y.C., 1966—, Kent Farms, Byrnley Farms, 1979—, Cooke Media Group, Inc. (Daily News), Los Angeles, 1985—, Cooke CableVision Inc., Warner Ctr., Calif., 1986—, Ercil Pub. Inc., 1976—, Kent Plaza, Phoenix, 1983-85, Elmendorf Farm, Inc., Lexington, Ky., 1984—, Video Tape Enterprises, 1976-85. Trustee Little League Found. Mem. Nat. Athletic Inst. (bd. dirs.).

COOKE, (JAMES) PHILIP, chemical engineer; b. Rossland, B.C., Can., Nov. 29, 1909; s. James Hugh and Lois Vietta (Adams) C.; m. Faith Elinor Beamer, Sept. 5, 1931; 1 child, Elinor Joanne Perlich. BS in Chem. Engring., Oreg. State U., 1934; MSMetE, U. Idaho, 1939. Registered profl. engr., Oreg., Wash. Cons. in mining engring. Portland, Oreg., 1936-41; process engr. ammunition mfg. Remington Arms, Salt Lake City, 1941-43; constrn. engr., radiation protection engr., project engr., devel. engr. E.I. DuPont, Gen. Electric, United Nuclear Corp., Richland, Wash., 1943-69; control officer, administrator Tri County Air Pollution Control Authority, Richland, 1971—. Mem. Am. Inst. Chem. Engrs. (local sec., treas. 1950), Wash. State Air Pollution Control Assn. Republican. Congregationalist. Avocations: gardening, traveling. Home: 1824 Riverside Richland WA 99352 Office: Tri County Air Pollution Control Authority 650 George Washington Way Richland WA 99352

COOLE, WALTER ALTON, mathematics and philosophy educator; b. Dallas, July 6, 1929; s. Walter Alton and Ruth (Musgrave) C.; m. Valya Vladimirovna Vonzell, May 30, 1947 (dec. 1949); m. Marjorie Josephine Wrinch, Aug. 5, 1975; children: Barbara Ruth Richman, Walter Allen, Valya Lara; 1 stepdau., A. Elizabeth Moorthy. BA, Trinity U., 1956; MA, Tex. U., 1958. Systems analyst System Devel. Corp., Santa Monica, Calif., 1959-64; tchr. Skagit Valley Coll., Mount Vernon, Wash., 1965—; prin. Scaramouche, Mount Vernon, 1982—. Author: Bourbaki Strikes Again, 1969, Greenbook System, 1973. Mem. select commn. Non-Traditional Studies, Olympia, Wash., 1971-73. Served to 1st lt. Med. Service Corps, U.S. Army, 1952-55. Mem. AAUP, NEA, Am. Philos. Assn., Assn. Electronic Cottagers. Democrat. Avocations: mopeds, sewing, leathercrafts. Home: 1325 Shirley Pl Mount Vernon WA 98273 Office: Skagit Valley Coll 2405 E College Way Mount Vernon WA 98273

COOLEY, DONALD WAYNE, research engineer; physicist; b. Kirksville, Mo., July 28, 1952; s. Elmo Franklin and Deloris Coleen (Bowers) C.; m. Yolanda A. Florencio, Feb. 28, 1985. B.A. in Physics, U. Colo., 1974, M.S. in Physics, 1976, M.S. in Elec. Engring., 1981. Sr. research engr. SRI Internat., Menlo Park, Calif., 1981—. Contbr. articles to profl. jours. Gates Found. scholar Gates Rubber Co., 1970-74. Mem. IEEE, Am. Phys. Soc., Soc. Indsl. and Applied Math., Phi Beta Kappa, Sigma Pi Sigma. Home: 1730 Halford Ave Apt 154 Santa Clara CA 95051 Office: SRI Internat 333 Ravenswood Ave Menlo Park CA 94025

COOLEY, RICHARD PIERCE, banker; b. Dallas, Nov. 25, 1923; s. Victor E. and Helen (Pierce) C. B.S., Yale, 1944. With Wells Fargo Bank, San Francisco, 1949-82; exec. v.p. Wells Fargo Bank, 1965-66, pres., chief exec. officer, 1966-79, chmn. bd., chief exec. officer, 1979-82, also dir.; chmn., chief exec. officer, pres. Seattle-1st Nat. Bank (now Seafirst Corp.),, 1983-86; chmn., chief exec. officer 1986—; chmn. bd., chief exec. officer, dir. Wells Fargo & Co., 1968-83; dir. UAL, Inc., Howmett Turbine Components Corp., Pechiney Ugine Kuhlmann Corp. Trustee Children's Hosp., San Francisco, Rand Corp., Calif. Inst. Tech., Pasadena. Served to 1st lt. Armed Services. Decorated Air medal. Mem. Assn. Res. City Bankers, Smithsonian Instn. Nat. Assn. (bd. dirs.), Calif. C. of C. (bd. dirs.). Office: Seafirst Corp PO Box 3977 Seattle WA 98124 *

COOLIDGE, CARLTON CROMER, financial consultant; b. Cin., Apr. 5, 1943; s. James Henry and Emily (Mashburn) C.; m. Nancy Belden, Aug. 15, 1965 (div. Apr. 1974); children: Courteney Mashburn, Lindsay Vliet, K. Whitney; m. Cynthia Antoniello, Sept. 15, 1976. Student, U. Va., 1961-63; BSBA, Babson Inst., 1966. Registered rep. Smith Barney & Co., Cleve., 1966-72; pres. Daley Coolidge & Co., San Francisco, 1972-76, Coolidge & Co., San Francisco, 1976-79; v.p. Fidelity Brokerage, San Francisco, 1979-84; fin. cons. Shearson Lehman Bros., San Francisco, 1984-86; cons. New Enterprise Assocs., San Francisco, 1986—. Trustee Cleve. Zoo, 1968-72; bd. dirs. San Francisco Opera Assn. Mem. Nat. Assn. Securities Dealers. Republican. Episcopalian. Clubs: Union (Cleve.); St. Francis Yacht (San Francisco). Avocations: hunting, fishing, tennis, golf, collecting antique cars. Home: 65 Normandie Terr San Francisco CA 94115 Office: New Enterprise Assocs 235 Montgomery St #1025 San Francisco CA 94104

COOMBE, GEORGE WILLIAM, JR., lawyer, banker; b. Kearny, N.J., Oct. 1, 1925; s. George William and Laura (Montgomery) C.; A.B., Rutgers U., 1946; LL.B., Harvard, 1949; m. Marilyn V. Ross, June 4, 1949; children—Susan, Donald William, Nancy. Bar: N.Y. 1950, Mich. 1953, Calif.

1976, U.S. Supr. Ct. Practice in N.Y.C., 1949-53, Detroit, 1953-69; atty., mem. legal-staff Gen. Motors Corp., Detroit, 1953-69, asst. gen. counsel, sec., 1969-75; exec. v.p., gen. counsel Bank of Am., San Francisco, 1975—. Served to lt. USNR, 1942-46. Mem. Am., Mich., Calif., San Francisco, Los Angeles, N.Y.C. bar assns., Phi Beta Kappa, Phi Gamma Delta. Presbyterian. Home: 2190 Broadway #2E San Francisco CA 94115 Office: Bank of Am Nat Trust & Savs Assoc Bank of Am Center 555 California St San Francisco CA 94104

COOMBS, WILLIAM ELMER, accountant, lawyer; b. Keosauqua, Iowa, Jan. 17, 1911; s. Elmer Clyde and Myra Ann (Moon) C.; AB in Econs., U. Calif. at Los Angeles, 1933; JD, Loyola U., Los Angeles, 1954; m. Katheryn Rose Logan, Oct. 20, 1934 (dec. May 1984); children: Katheryn M. Coombs Kirkendoll, Rose Ann (Mrs. Luciano Siracusa); m. Elta Louise Pfister, Feb. 17, 1985. CPA, Calif.; bar: Calif. 1955, U.S. Dist. Ct. (cen. dist.) Calif. 1955, U.S. Dist. Ct. (no. dist.) Calif. 1957, U.S. Supreme Ct. 1960, U.S. Ct. Appeals (9th cir.) 1963, U.S. Dist. Ct. (so. dist.) Calif. 1980. Acct., Shell Oil Co., Los Angeles, 1933-36, So. Calif. Edison Co., Los Angeles, 1936-37; auditor State of Calif., Los Angeles, 1937-41; sr. acct. Arthur Andersen & Co., 1941-43; controller Case Constrn. Co., San Pedro, Calif., 1943-46; C.P.A., Roberts & Coombs, 1946-49, Deloitte, Plender, Griffths & Co., 1949-52; controller Ford J. Twaits Co., Los Angeles, 1952-55; overseas auditor Morrison-Knudsen Internat., San Francisco, 1955-56; asst. prof. bus. Calif. State U., Chico 1956-58; sec.-treas., dir., house counsel Matich Corp., Colton, Calif. 1958-61; practiced in Rialto, 1962—; mem. Calif. Senate, 1967-73, Calif. Adv. Council on Econ. Devel., 1984—; city atty. Rialto, 1977-81, Big Bear Lake, Calif., 1980-82. Mem. Rialto City Planning Commn., 1960-62; councilman, Rialto, 1962-67; bd. dirs. Regional Econ. Devel. Council, 1964-67, pres., 1944—. Mem. Calif. Bar Assn., ABA, Am. Inst. CPAs, Calif. Soc. CPAs, Calif., San Bernardino County Bar Assn. (pres. 1966-67) taxpayers assns. Rotarian. Author reference book: Construction Accounting and Financial Management 1968. Home and Office: 5810 Date Ave Rialto CA 92376

COONEY, ROBERT VINCENT, chemical researcher; b. Fremont, Nebr., Dec. 13, 1953; s. William Calvin and Alice Ellen (Richardson) C.; m. Kay Chiemi Nakakura, July 15, 1978. BA, Washington U., St. Louis, 1976; PhD, U. Calif., La Jolla, 1981. Research fellow UCLA Harbor Med. Ctr., Torrance, 1981-84; asst. researcher U. Hawaii, Honolulu, 1984—. Contbr. articles to profl. jours. Mem. Am. Chem. Soc. Office: Cancer Research Ctr of Hawaii 1236 Lauhala St Honolulu HI 96813

COONS, DAVID JOEL, physician, psychiatrist; b. Oakland, Calif., Mar. 16, 1947; s. Harold S. Coons and Maxine (Beard) Flowers; m. Jean Elizabeth Curtiss, Sept. 15, 1970; children: Daniel, Michael, Christine. BS, U. Utah, 1969, MD, 1973. Diplomate Am. Bd. Psychiatry and Neurology, Am. Bd. Forensic Psychiatry. Intern Good Samaritan Hosp., Phoenix, 1973-74, resident, 1977; dep. dir. psychiatry Indian Health Services, Anchorage, 1977-78; asst. supt. Alaska Psychiat. Inst., Anchorage, 1978-82; practice medicine specializing in psychiatry Anchorage, 1982—; cons. S. Cen. Counseling, Anchorage, 1982—; assoc. clin. prof. U. Wash., Seattle, 1978—. Contbr. articles to profl. jours. Den and pack officer Anchorage council Boy Scouts Am., 1985-86. Served as surgeon USPHS, 1977-78. Mem. Am. Psychiat. Assn., Alaska Psychiat. Assn. (legis. rep. 1950-83, pres.-elect 1986—), AMA. Congregationalist. Avocations: music, reading, canoeing, computers. Office: 3710 E 20th Ave Anchorage AK 99508

COONS, MARLIS JUTTA, nurse; b. Berlin, July 2, 1943; came to U.S., 1969; d. Fritz and Erika (Modrack) Unbekannt; m. Darryl Coons, Aug. 16, 1968; children: Bettina, Sylvester. Lic. vocat. nurse, Bellaire Gen Hosp. Sch. Vocat. Nursing, 1976; AA, Houston Community Coll., 1981. Office nurse Dr. Jospeh Lucci Jr. & Assocs., Houston, 1978-79; staff nurse cardiovascular div. St. Lukes Episc. Hosp., Houston, 1981-82; staff nurse intensive care unit Meml. Southwest Hosp., Houston, 1982-85, VA Hosp., Martinez, Calif., 1985—. Mem. Am. Med. Joggers Assn., Am. Assn. of Critical Care Nurses. Republican. Lutheran. Clubs: Pres. First Lady, The Landing at Seven Coves Yacht and Country (Houston). Home: 123 Panorama Dr Benicia CA 94510 Office: PO Box 6569 Concord CA 94524

COOPER, ALFRED WILLIAM MADISON, physics educator; b. Dublin, Ireland, June 12, 1932; s. Alfred John and Lilian May (Smyth) C.; m. Gail Williams Niemoeller, May 6, 1961; children: Nigel William, David Owen, Colin Roy. BA with honors, Trinity Coll., Dublin, 1955, MA, 1958; PhD, Queen's U., Belfast, No. Ireland, 1961. Asst. lectr. Queen's U., 1956-57; from asst. and assoc. prof. Naval Postgrad. Sch., Monterey, Calif., 1957-75, prof. physics, 1976—; dir. Naval Acad. Ctr. Infared Tech., 1985—; cons. Aerospace Corp., El Segundo, Calif., 1964-68, Ministry fo Defence, Singapore, 1982. Contbr. articles to profl. jours. Found. scholar Dublin U., 1954. Mem. AAUP (local chpt. pres. 1984-86), Am. Phys. Soc., Optical Soc. Am., Electronic Def. Assn., Sigma Xi (Research award 1974). Republican. Episcopalian. Avocations: music, rugby, refereeing. Home: PO Box 224 Pebble Beach CA 93953 Office: Naval Postgrad Sch Monterey CA 93943

COOPER, ANITA LUCILE, retired chamber of commerce executive; b. Rocky Ford, Colo., June 23, 1909; d. Frank Alan and Eunice Harriet (Casebeer) Crowe; m. Roy Doig Cooper, May 27, 1936; children—Alice Eunice Deatherage, Virginia Jessie Grimsley. Cert., Colo. State Tchrs. Coll., Greeley, 1929, student summer 1931. Elem. sch. tchr. rural schs. Bent and Otero counties, Colo., 1929-36; vol. community work, 1936-75; sec.-mgr. Las Animas-Bent County C. of C., 1976-84, ret., 1984. 4-H club leader, Rixey, Colo.; past officer various community orgns. Recipient Santa Fe Trail Day award as Outstanding Citizen of the Community of Las Animas, Las Animas High Sch., 1980; Citizen of the Year award for Outstanding Community Service, Las Animas-Bent County C. of C., 1981. Republican. Presbyterian. Clubs: Eastern Star, Rixey Country Club., PEO.

COOPER, ANTHONY ROGER, chemist, researcher; b. Coventry, Eng., Oct. 24, 1941; came to U.S., 1967; s. Frank and Edith May (Thomas) C.; m. Audrey Carol Stelter, Sept. 3, 1983; children from previous marriage: Richard Anthony, Julie Elizabeth. BSc., London U., Eng., 1963, PhD, 1966; postgrad., Santa Clara U., 1985—. Chartered chemist. Research chemist Chevron Research Co., Richmond, Calif., 1967-70; research fellow U. Strathclyde, Glasgow, Scotland, 1970-71; research asst. U. Conn., Storrs, 1971-73; prin. scientist Dynapol, Palo Alto, Calif., 1973-80; staff scientist Lockheed Missiles and Space Co., Palo Alto, 1981-86, sr. staff scientist, 1986—; vis. prof. San Jose State U., 1987—. Editor: Ultrafiltration Membranes and Applications, 1981, Polymeric Separation Media, 1982; contbr. over 70 articles to profl. jours. Fellow Royal Soc. Chemistry, Soc. Plastics Engrs. (sr.); mem. Am. Chem. Soc., Sierra Club, Audubon Soc., Nat. Geographic Soc., Soc. Plastics Engrs. Avocations: soccer, car restoration, travel. Home: 10620 Creston Dr Los Altos CA 94022

COOPER, AUSTIN MORRIS, chemist, chemical engineer, consultant, researcher; b. Long Beach, Calif., Feb. 1, 1959; s. Merril Morris and Charlotte Madeline (Wittmer) C. BS in Chemistry, Baylor U., 1981; BSChemE, Tex. Tech U., 1983, MSChemE, 1985. Solar energy researcher U.S. Dept. Energy, Lubbock, Tex., 1983-85; advanced mfg. and process engr., chem. and mech. cons. and researcher McDonnell-Douglas Astronautics Co., Huntington Beach, Calif., 1986—. Contbr. articles to profl. jours. Mem. Am. Inst. Chem. Engrs., Am. Chem. Soc., Sigma Xi, Omega Chi Epsilon, Kappa Mu Epsilon, Beta Beta Beta. Lutheran. Avocations: gymnastics, bee keeping.

COOPER, CAROL EILEN, social worker; b. Los Angeles, Jan. 19, 1940; d. Harry and Barbara (Prupis) C. BA, U. Calif., Berkeley, 1962; diploma, Calif. Acupuncture Sch., 1984; MSW, Calif. State U., 1972. Diplomate Nat. Commn. Cert. Acupuncturists. Psychiat. social worker II Los Angeles County Forensic Unit, 1973—; pvt. practice psychotherapy Los Angeles, 1975—. Mem. Am. Fellowship Ch. Healing Arts (minister 1979—). Office: 441 Bauchet St Los Angeles CA 90012

COOPER, DENNIS CHARLES, ophthalmologist; b. St. Louis, May 22, 1945; s. Irving and Muriel (Kolker) C.; children—Douglas, Michael. M.D., Washington U., St. Louis, 1971. Diplomate Am. Bd. Ophthalmology. Intern, Mt. Sinai Med. Ctr., Cleve., 1971-72, resident, 1972-75; ophthalmologist Affiliated Ophthalmologists, Scottsdale, Ariz., 1977—. Served as maj. U.S. Army, 1975-77. Decorated Army Commendation medal. Fellow Am. Acad. Ophthalmology; mem. Phoenix Ophthalmol. Soc. (sec.-treas. 1982-83). Office: Affiliated Ophthalmologists 1402 N Miller Rd #C-2 Scottsdale AZ 85257

COOPER, DIANE ELIZABETH, home economist; b. Chgo., Feb. 2, 1942; d. Donald Howard and Margaret (Kingsley) C.; B.S. in Home Econs., U. Ariz., 1969. Home economist, research test kitchen supr. Sunbeam Appliance Co., Oak Brook, Ill., 1970-77; product devel. research home economist Ore-Ida Foods, Inc., Ontario, Oreg., 1977—. Mem. Am. Home Econs. Assn., Home Economists in Bus., Oreg. Home Econs. Assn. (dist. dir.), Treasure Valley Home Economists. Office: 175 NE 6th Ave Ontario OR 97914

COOPER, DOUGLASS WILLIAM, architect, industrial designer; b. Pitts., July 10, 1956; s. John Coleman and Martha Jane (Douglass) C.; m. Sherry Lou McKibben, Oct. 2, 1985. BS, Pa. State U., 1978; MArch, Yale U., 1981. Designer, draftsman Pitts. History and Landmarks Found., 1978, Lucian Caste Architects, Pitts., 1978-81; project architect Jay Alpert Architect, Woodbridge, Conn., 1981; sr. designer Gruen Assocs., N.Y.C., 1982-85; designer Heller & Leake Architects, San Francisco, 1986; architect William Turnbuh Assocs Architects, San Francisco, 1987—. Designer of sports car, 1984 (Runner-up Internat. Automotive Design Competition). Mem. Omicron Delta Kappa. Avocations: furniture design, industrial design, automotive design. Home: 1395 Masonic Ave # 3 San Francisco CA 94117 Office: William Turnbuh Assoc Architects Pier 1 1/2 The Embarcadero San Francisco CA 94103

COOPER, EDWARD MARK, marketing educator, consultant, researcher; b. Bklyn., Apr. 6, 1950; s. Jack J. and Evelyn (Weinfeld) C.; m. Anita J. Ross, June 6, 1970. B.A. in Psychology and Sociology, U. Colo., 1973, M.A. in Counseling and Personnel, 1976, Ph.D. in Higher Edn. Adminstrn. and Mktg., 1979. Research assoc. Nat. Ctr. for Higher Edn. Mgmt. Systems, Boulder, Colo., 1975-77; dir. instl. research, dir. program evaluation and outcomes research Met. State Coll., Denver, 1977-79, assoc. prof. mktg., 1979—; co-founder, dir., v.p. mktg. Internat. Data Systems, Inc., Denver, 1982; founder Cooper & Marcum Advt., Denver and Boulder; pres., chmn. Mktg. and Mgmt. Services of the Rockies, Inc. Chmn. Met. State Coll. United Way Campaign, 1981-82; mem. Needs Assessment Com., Mile High United Way, internat. sci. vis. host. El Rancho Colo. Corp. grantee, 1982. Mem. So. Mktg. Assn., Southwestern Mktg. Assn., Internat. Assn. for Instl. Research (chmn. internat. forum), Am. Mktg. Assn. (exec. com. No. Colo.), Denver Advt. Fedn., Colo. Assn. Planners and Instl. Researchers (pres. 1980-81), Western Mktg. Educators. Democrat. Contbr. writings to publs. in field. Office: Met State Coll Mktg Dept Box 13 1006 11th St Denver CO 80204

COOPER, FRANK EVANS, banker; b. Seattle, Nov. 28, 1928; s. Frank Homer and Marguerite Caroline (Madison) C.; m. Erlene Rose Johnson, June 30, 1951; children—Dawn Rene, Frank Evans. B.B.A., U. Wash., 1950; M.B.A., Pacific Coast Grad. Sch. Banking, 1958-61. Br. mgr. Comml. Credit Corp., Eugene, Oreg., 1951-58; v.p. Puget Sound Nat. Bank, Tacoma, 1958-64; pres., chief exec. officer, dir. Bank of Tacoma, 1965-68; supr. banking State of Wash., Olympia, 1968-70; sr. v.p. Bank of Hawaii, Honolulu, 1970-72; pres., chief exec. officer, dir. Bank Honolulu, 1972-76; owner Frank Cooper & Assos., 1976-80; pres., chief exec. officer Equitable Savs. & Loan, Huntington Beach, Calif., 1980—; dir. Security & Gen. Bank, Ltd., Vila, New Hebrides, World Finance, Honolulu, Guardian Finance, Honolulu, Mahalo Acceptance, Honolulu, Hula Records, Ltd., Honolulu, Keehi Drydock Corp., Honolulu; internat. fin. and mgmt. cons. Chmn. Western States Commrs. Banking, 1970; dir. Nat. Assn. Bank Commrs., 1970. Mem. bd. Tacoma Community Coll., 1967-69; mem. adv. bd. Nat. Consumer Finance Assn., 1969; Del. Wash. Rep. Convs., 1958-68; precinct committeeman, Tacoma, 1950-69; del. Rep. Nat. Conv., 1964, 68; mem. Wash. Ho. of Reps., 1963-64; chmn. Hawaii Rep. Com., 1978-80; bd. dirs. Jessie Dslyn Boys' Ranch, Tacoma, Mary Bridge Children's Hosp.; trustee Annie Wright Girls' Acad., U. Wash. Grad. Sch. Banking. Mem. C. of C. Hawaii (chmn. visitor industry com.), Hawaii Bankers Assn. (exec. com.), Navy League, Sales and Mktg. Execs. Honolulu. Clubs: Oahu Country (Hawaii), Outrigger Canoe (Hawaii), Honolulu Press (Hawaii), Plaza (Hawaii), Univ. Union (Hawaii) (pres.), Pacific (Hawaii), Waikiki Yacht (Hawaii); Masons, Shriners, Jesters, Elks, Rotary, Lions. Home: 16783 Beach Blvd Huntington Beach CA 92647 Office: Equitable Savs & Loan PO Box 2700 Huntington Beach CA 92647

COOPER, HAL, television director; b. N.Y.C., Feb. 23, 1923; s. Benjamin and Adeline (Raichman) C.; m. Marta Lucille Salcido, June 26, 1971; 1 son, James Benjamin; children by previous marriage: Bethami, Pamela. B.A., U. Mich., 1946. Performer Big Bro.'s Rainbow House, Mut. Network, 1936-41, asst. dir. Dock Street Theatre, Charleston, S.C., 1946-48; writer, producer TV Babysitter, DuMont TV Network, 1948-52, The Magic Cottage, 1950-56; dir., producer various daytime TV shows including Kitty Foyle, others, 1950-57; producer stage play The Troublemakers, London, 1952; dir. TV shows including Death Valley Days, 1952-72, Dick Van Dyke Show, 1961-66, Gilligan's Island, 1964-67, I Dream of Jeannie, 1965-70, I Spy, 1965-68, That Girl, 1966-71, Courtship of Eddie's Father, 1969-72, The Odd Couple, 1970-75, Mary Tyler Moore, 1970-77, All in the Family, 1971-79; dir., exec. producer: TV shows including Maude, CBS, Hollywood, Calif., 1972-78, Phyl and Mikky, 1980, Love, Sydney, 1982-83, Gimme a Break, 1983-87. Served to lt. (j.g.) USNR, 1943-46. Mem. Writers Guild Am., ASCAP, Screen Actors Guild, AFTRA, Actors Equity, Dirs. Guild Am. (trustee 1964-75, mem. benevolent and edn. com. 1963-75, trustee pension plan 1964-75). Address: 2651 Hutton Dr Beverly Hills CA 90210

COOPER, IRVING, manufacturing company executive; b. London, July 29, 1920; came to U.S., 1946; s. Nathan and Mary (Caseman) C.; m. Wanda Mae Jackson, Apr. 14, 1955; children—Barbara Gwendolyn, Leah Ginnette. Student London U., 1938. Dist. mgr. Ajax Corp., N.Y.C., 1948-50; agt., asst. sales mgr. Beneficial Standard Life Ins., Los Angeles, 1951-54; br. mgr. Frankel Mfg. Co., Los Angeles, 1954-64, nat. sales mgr., Denver, 1964-74, v.p. sales/mktg., 1975-84, sr. v.p., 1984-87; cons. in field; adv. to Frye Copysystems div. Allied Signal Co., 1985-86. Served as lt. Royal Navy Res., 1938-45. Lodges: Elks, Kiwanis (bd. dirs. Rancho Bernardo, Calif.). Home: 15542 Vista Vicente Dr San Diego Country Estates Ramona CA 92065-4319

COOPER, JAMES ARLIN, electrical engineer; b. Pueblo, Colo., Oct. 23, 1935; s. Richard Gilbert and Effie Lorine (Cotner) C.; m. Patricia Estelle Smith, June 14, 1958 (div. June 1980); children—David Arlin, Douglas Kent, Scott Garret, Brenton Grant; m. Dana Louise Frook, May 30, 1982. B.S.E.E., U. N.Mex., 1957, M.S.E.E., 1958; Ph.D., Stanford U., 1964. Instrumentation engr. Rocketdyne div. N.Am. Aviation, Canoga Park, Calif., 1958-60, engr. in charge, 1960-61; div. supr. Sandia Labs., Albuquerque, 1963—. Author: Microprocessor Background for Managers, 1981; Computer-Security Technology, 1984. Author-editor: Electromagnetic Pulse Handbook for Missiles and Aircraft in Flight, 1972. Patentee electrical devices. Cubmaster Kit Carson council Boy Scouts Am., 1968-70, co-pres. Embudo Elem. Sch. PTA, Albuquerque, 1971-72; mem. career edn. site selection com. Albuquerque Pub. Schs., 1972. Mem. IEEE (sr.). Home: PO Box 5093 Kirtland AFB NM 87185 Office: Sandia Labs Box 5800 Kirtland AFB NM 87185

COOPER, JON HUGH, public TV executive; b. Wynnewood, Okla., Aug. 6, 1940; s. John Hughes and Sarah Edna (Ray) C.; m. L. Ilene Batty, Dec. 16, 1961 (div. Jan. 1984); children: Jon Shelton, Geoffrey Harold. BA, Okla. State U., 1962. Mgmt. positions with Evening Star Broadcasting, Washington and Lynchburg, Va., 1962-67, Sta. KUAT-AM-TV, Tucson, 1967-73; exec. dir. Rocky Mountain Network, Denver, 1973-77; exec. dir. Pacific Mountain Network, Denver, 1977-79, also bd. dirs.; gen. mgr. Sta. KNME-TV, Albuquerque, 1979—; mem. interconnection com. Pub. Broadcasting Service, Washington, 1983—, bd. dirs., 1986—; panel judge N. Mex. Moot Ct. Competition, 1986, 87; bd. dirs. Native Am. Pub. Broadcasting Consortium, Inc.; bd. dirs., mem. Japan Survey Team Pacific Mountain Network. Co-chmn. cultural deve. Sisters Cities Albuquerque; host N.Mex. Internat. Student Program; bd. dirs., v.p. Pueblo Los Cerros Homeowners Assn.; bd. dirs. Samaritan Counseling Ctr. Albuquerque, Albuquerque Council for Internat. Visitors.

COOPER, LLOYD GAYLE, education educator; b. Carrizozo, N.Mex., Apr. 22, 1935; s. Dennis Scott and Josephine Edward (Peters) C.; m. Carolynn Ann France, Apr. 14, 1956; children: Mark, Kirk, Kelt, Shaun. BS, N.Mex. State U., 1957, MA, 1960; DEd, U. Oreg., 1962. Tchr. Las Cruces (N.Mex.) Pub. Schs., 1957-60; teaching asst., instr. U. Oreg., Eugene, 1960-62; from asst. prof. to prof. edn. U. Tex., El Paso, 1962-67; from assoc. prof. to prof. N.Mex. State U., Las Cruces, 1967-80, head dept. edn. adminstrn., 1980—; state pres. N.Mex. Assn. Higher Edn., Santa Fe, 1976-78. Served to 2d lt. USAR, 1957—. Mem. Nat. Council Profs. of Edn. Adminstrn., Am. Assn. Sch. Adminstrs., Internat. Planning Assn., Phi Delta Kappa. Republican. Club: Toastmasters (Las Cruces) (pres. 1974, area gov. 1975-76). Home: 2020 Tyre Circle Las Cruces NM 88001 Office: NMex State U Box 3N Las Cruces NM 88003

COOPER, MARTIN JACOB, engineer, research and development executive; b. Detroit, June 27, 1939; s. Bernard Harold and Betty Fern (Feldman) C.; m. Sharon Fae Frank, June 10, 1965; children: Sena, Lara. BSE, U. Mich., 1961, MS in Physics, 1963; PhD in Physics, Brandeis U., 1966. Engr. various depts. U.S. Govt., Washington, 1966-79; mgr. strategic planning Occidental Petro-Research and Devel., Irvine, Calif., 1979—; prin. MJC and Assocs., Irvine, 1981—. Contbr. articles to profl. jours. Research fellow Nat. Acad. Scis. research, Washington, 1966-68, White House fellow, 1974-75. Mem. Am. Phys. Soc., Am. Chem. Soc., IEEE, Nat. Conf. for Advancement of Research (bd. dirs. 1979—). Office: 18662 MacArthur #200 Irvine CA 92715

COOPER, MARTIN MICHAEL, communications executive, author; b. Phila., Aug. 13, 1941; s. Al and Anne Rae (Katzen) C.; m. Barbara A. Roisman, Aug. 13, 1961. B.A., UCLA, 1963. Advt. and promotion mgr. Disneyland, Anaheim, Calif., 1963-69; mktg. dir. recreation div. Universal City (Calif.) Studios, 1968-70; sr. v.p. pub. relations Harshe-Rotman & Druck, Inc., Los Angeles, 1970-79; sr. v.p. corp. communications and corp. mktg. dir. Playboy Enterprises, Inc., Los Angeles, 1979-82; pres. Cooper Communications, Inc., Los Angeles, 1982—; v.p. devel. and mktg. London Trust Prodns.; instr. mag. writing UCLA Extension Div.; speaker pub. relations seminars; author: Academy Awards Oscar Annual, 1979; contbr. chpt. to book, articles to mags. Chmn. pub. relations adv. com. sta. KCET, Los Angeles. Recipient Gold Key award Pub. Relations News, 1980, 81, Pro awards, Publicity Club of Los Angeles, 1974-76, 78, So. Calif. Chpt. of Am. Mktg. Assn. award, 1980, Los Angeles Advt. Women award, 1980. Mem. Acad. Motion Pictures Arts and Scis., Pub. Relations Soc. Am. (Silver Anvil award 1974, Prisms award 1978). Am. Film Inst., Acad. TV Arts and Scis. (co-chmn. Emmy adv. council). Office: 16250 Ventura Blvd Suite 335 Encino CA 91436

COOPER, RALPH SHERMAN, physicist; b. Newark, May 25, 1931; s. Morris David and Fay Bella (Gottfried) C.; m. Sandra Lenore Kleeman, Jan. 30, 1956; children: Laurie Mara, Brett Edward. B in Chem. Engring., Cooper Union U., 1953; MS in Physics, U. Ill., 1954, PhD in Physics, 1957. Chief scientist Douglas Labs., Richland, Wash., 1965-69; assoc. div. leader Los Alamos (N.Mex.) Sci. Lab., 1957-65, 69-75; dep. dir. research and devel. Physics Internat., San Leandro, Calif., 1975-82; dir. systems INESCO, Inc., San Diego, 1982-84; pres. Apogee Research Corp., San Diego, 1984-87; Long Beach, 1987—; assoc. dean research Dept. Engring. Calif. State U., Long Beach, 1987—. Patentee in field. Recipient Young Author prize Am. Electrochemistry Soc., 1956. Mem. AIAA, Am. Assn. Artificial Intelligence, Am. Phys. Soc., Am. Nuclear Soc., Sigma Xi, Tau Beta Pi. Office: Calif State U Sch Engring Long Beach CA 90840

COOPER, ROBERT MELVIN, laboratory director; b. Angels Camp, Calif., Jan. 7, 1924; s. George Proctor and Cora Alice (Field) C.; m. Lorraine Marjorie Brown, Oct. 7, 1956. BA in Criminalistics, U. Calif., Berkeley, 1950, postgrad., 1950-52. Criminalist Oakland (Calif.) Police Dept., 1952-63; criminalist Alameda County Sheriff's Dept., Oakland, 1963-68, dir. crime lab., 1968—; cons. in field, Lafayete, Calif., 1965—. Contbr. articles to profl. Served with U.S. Army, 1943-45. Recipient Sheriff's Commendation, Alameda County Sheriff's Dept., 1983. Fellow Am. Acad. Forensic Scis.; mem. Calif. Assn. Criminalists (pres. 1964-65), Calif. Assn. Crime Lab. Dirs., Am. Soc. Crime Lab. Dirs. Republican. Office: Alameda County Sheriff's Dept 15001 Foothill Blvd San Leandro CA 94578

COOPER, RODNEY STERLING, production operations executive; b. Earl Park, Ind., Mar. 16, 1933; s. Matthew William and Gertrude Geraldine (Hitzman) C.; m. Donna Mae Damico, June 27, 1956; children: Connie Sue, Michael Sterling. BSEE, Purdue U., 1955. Subcontract quality leader Eastman Kodak Co., Rochester, N.Y., 1964-65; with TRW Systems, Redondo Beach, Calif., 1964-69; mgr. Viking program Martin Marietta Corp., Denver, 1969-76, mgr. parts tech. labs., 1976-80, mgr. mfg., 1980-83, mgr. prodn. ops., 1983—; sec., treas. Sterling Techs. Inc., Evergreen, Colo., 1985—. Recipient Pub. Service award NASA, Denver, 1976. Avocations: computer sci., photography, woodworking. Home: 29 Pinyon Pine Rd Littleton CO 80127

COOPER, SONNI (SANDRA LENORE), writer; b. N.Y.C., July 9, 1934; d. Edward Emmanuel and Mollie (Hantman) Kleeman; m. Ralph Sherman Cooper, Jan. 30, 1956; children: Laurie Mara, Brett Edward. Grad., The Cooper Union, 1954; BFA, U. Colo., 1955. Pres. Northwestern Assn. on Indian Affairs, Richland, Wash., 1968-72; exec. asst. Eight No. Indian Pueblos Council, San Juan Pueblo, N.Mex., 1973-76; v.p. Apogee Research Corp., San Diego, 1985—, chmn. bd. dirs.; pres. Creative Enterprises, San Diego, 1978—, writer, 1980—. Author: As The World Turns, 1983, Black Fire, 1984 (#3 Best Seller list), Forbidden Passions, 1985, Love Trap, 1985. Mem. Sci. Fiction Writers Am., Screen Actor's Guild (v.p. N.Mex. br. 1976-78), Screen Extra's Guild, Mensa. Jewish. Home and Office: 10323 Rue Finisterre San Diego CA 92131

COOPER, STEVEN JON, health care management consultant, educator; b. Oct. 19, 1941; B.A., U. Calif., Los Angeles, 1966; M.Ed., Loyola U., 1973; postgrad. Union Sch., 1977—; m. Sharon M. Lepack; children—Robin E., Erik S. Ednl. coordinator dept. radiology Mt. Sinai Hosp. Med. Center, Chgo., 1969-72; chmn. dept. radiol. scis. U. Health Scis., Chgo. Med. Sch., VA Hosp., North Chicago, 1972-79; v.p. C&S Inc., Denver, 1980-81; pres. Healthcare Mktg. Corp., Denver, 1981-84; corp. officer Sharon Cooper Assocs. Ltd., Englewood, Colo., 1984—; cons. HEW; lectr. in field. Served with USAF, 1960-64, USAFR, 1964-66. Mem. W.K. Kellogg Found. grantee. Mem. Am. (mem. edn., curriculum review coms., task force), Ill. (chmn. annual meeting 1976, program Midwest conf., 1977) socs. radiol. tech., Coll. Radiol. Scis., Am. Hosp. Radiology Adminstrs. (mem. edn. com., treas. Midwest region, nat. v.p.), AMA (com. on allied health edn. and accreditation), Sigma Xi. Author numerous publs. in field. Home: 8522 E Dry Creek Pl Englewood CO 80112 Office: 9085 E Mineral Circle Suite 160 Englewood CO 80112

COOPER, THOMAS ASTLEY, banker; b. Phila., July 19, 1936; m. June Danenberger; children: Aleta, Anita, Alane, Allison, Anne, Thomas. BA, Haverford (Pa.) Coll., 1957; BD, Drew U., 1960; postgrad., U. Pa.; PMD, Harvard U., 1973. Asst. br. mgr., asst. treas. Girard Bank subs. Girard Co., Bala Cynwyd, Pa., 1967-68, asst. v.p., 1968-70, v.p., 1970-73, sr. v.p., 1973-74, vice chmn. bd., 1974-80, pres., 1980-84; vice chmn. Mellon Nat. Corp., 1983-84; exec. v.p., dir. BankAm. Payment Services, 1985; pres. Bank of Am. Nat. Trust & Savs. Assn., San Francisco, 1986-87; pres., chief operating officer BankAm. Corp., San Francisco, 1986-87, former mem. mng. com., loan policy com.; bd. dirs. S.E. chpt. ARC; trustee Haverford Coll., Thomas Jefferson U., Thomas Jefferson Hosp. Club: Brant Beach Yacht (commodore 1984). Office: Bank of Am Nat Trust & Savs Assoc Bank of Am Center 555 California St San Francisco CA 94104

COOPER, VICTORIA ANN, magazine editor; b. Boston, Dec. 27, 1945; d. Thaddeus Walter and Mabel Isabel (Kittredge) Kowilcik; m. Kent Leland Groninger, Oct. 12, 1968 (div. Feb. 1980); children: Jennifer Louise, Heather Louise; m. David Lawrence Cooper, May 5, 1985. Student, Emmanuel Coll., 1964-67, Cornell U., 1968-69, U. Colo., 1980-82. Manuscript editor MIT, Cambridge, 1967-68; publs. editor Cornell U., Ithaca, N.Y., 1968-70; mng. editor Boulder (Colo.) Monthly, 1979; editor Sunday mag. Boulder Daily Camera, 1980-84, mem. writing staff, 1980-83; editor Empire mag. The Denver Post, 1985—; book editor Westview Press Co., Boulder, 1976-78.

Avocations: swimming, hiking, biking, dancing, movies. Office: The Denver Post 650 15th St Denver CO 80202

COOPER, WILLIAM CLARK, physician; b. Manila, P.I., June 22, 1912 (father Am. citizen); s. Wibb Earl and Pearl (Herron) C.; M.D., U. Va., 1934; M.P.H. magna cum laude, Harvard U., 1958; m. Ethel Katherine Sicha, May 1, 1937; children—Jane Willoughby, William Clark, David Jeremy, Robert Lawrence. Intern, asst. resident U. Hosps., Cleve., 1934-37; commd. asst. surgeon USPHS, 1940, advanced through grades to med. dir., 1952; chief occupational health Field Hqrs., Cin., 1952-57; mem. staff div. occupational health USPHS, Washington, 1957-62, chief div. occupational health, 1962-63; ret., 1963; research physician, prof. occupational health in residence Sch. Pub. Health, U. Calif.-Berkeley, 1963-72; med. cons. AEC, 1964-73; sec.-treas. Tabershaw-Cooper Asso., Inc., 1972-73, v.p., sci. dir., 1973-74; v.p. Equitable Environ. Health Inc., 1974-77; cons. occupational medicine, 1977—. Served to 1st lt. M.C., U.S. Army, 1937-40. Diplomate Am. Bd. Internal Medicine, Am. Bd. Preventive Medicine, Am. Bd. Indsl. Hygiene. Fellow AAAS, Am. Pub. Health Assn., Am. Coll. Chest Physicians, Am. Occupational Medicine Assn., Am. Acad. Occupational Medicine, Royal Soc. Medicine (London); mem. Internat. Commn. on Occupational Health, Western Occupational Med. Assn., Am. Indsl. Hygiene Assn. Club: Cosmos (Washington). Contbr. articles to profl. jours. Home: 8315 Terrace Dr El Cerrito CA 94530 Office: 3687 Mt Diablo Blvd Suite 320 Lafayette CA 94549

COOPERSMITH, SHIRLEY ANN, insurance company executive; b. Kansas City, Mo., Feb. 4, 1944; d. Louis and Yetta (Swartz) Agronin, m. Henry Joseph Coopersmith, Sept. 3, 1970 (div. 1978); children: Marc Daniel, Stacy Janine. AAS, Kans. City Jr. Coll., 1963; student, U. Alberta, 1964. Project mgr. Optigan Inc., Compton, Calif., 1971-72; cons. Tustin, Calif., 1972-78; sr. mktg. analyst Basic Four Corp., Irvine, Calif., 1978-80; regional mgr. Data Solutions Inc., Santa Ana, Calif., 1980-82; info. resources mgr. Pacific Nat. Ins. Co., Fullerton, Calif., 1982—. Bd. dirs. Tustin Village II, 1985-86. Mem. Data Processing Mgmt. Assn. (legis. com. 1985-86), Calif. State Homeopathic Med. Soc., Internat. Found. Homeopathy. Libertarian. Avocations: homeopathy, weaving, sailing, astrology. Office: Pacific Nat Ins Co 680 Langsdorf Dr Fullerton CA 92631

COORS, JOSEPH, brewery executive; b. 1917. With Adolph Coors Co., Golden, Colo., v.p., from 1947, vice chmn., 1975, pres., 1977-85, vice chmn., chief operating officer, 1982—. Office: Adolph Coors Co East of Town Golden CO 80401 *

COORS, WILLIAM K., brewery executive; b. Golden, Colo., 1916. Chmn. bd., chief exec. officer Adolph Coors Co., Golden, Colo. Office: Adolph Coors Co Golden CO 80401

COOX, ALVIN DAVID, history educator; b. Rochester, N.Y., Mar. 8, 1924; s. Irving and Ruth (Werner) C.; m. Hisako Suzuki, Apr. 7, 1954; 1 child, Roy Alan. BA, NYU, 1945; MA, Harvard U., 1946, PhD, 1951. Teaching fellow Harvard U., Cambridge, Mass., 1948-49; sr. historian Johns Hopkins U., Washington, 1949-54; lectr. U. Calif. Far East Div., Tokyo, 1954-56, U. Md. Far East Div., Tokyo, 1956-64; prof. history San Diego State U., 1964—, dir. Japanese Studies, 1985—, dir. Asian Studies, 1966-79; vis. prof. Shiga Nat. U., Hikone-Otsu, Japan, 1954-55; historian Japanese Research Div., Tokyo, 1955-57; adj. prof. U.S. Naval War Coll., San Diego, 1985—. Author: Japan: The Final Agony, 1970, Tojo, 1975, Anatomy of a Small War, 1977, Nomonhan 1939, 1985; co-editor: China and Japan, 1978; editor Orient/West Mag., 1958-65. Fellow Rockefeller Found., 1961-64, Japan Found., 1983-84, NEH, 1985; named Outstanding Prof. Calif. State U. System, 1973. Mem. Assn. Calif. State Univ. Profs., Assn. Asian Studies, Internat. House Japan, Calif. Pacific Rim Commn., Phi Beta Kappa (pres. 1973). Avocation: writing. Office: San Diego State U Dept History 5300 Campanile Dr San Diego CA 92182-0380

COPE, CONNIE LOU, accountant, educator; b. San Diego, July 22, 1944; d. Arlise Lanesome Jr. and Mary Norbourne (Gordon) Cope; m. Gearl Bennett, July 9, 1977; children—Robert Neal Bennett, Terri Ann Bennett Minney Shields, Gearl Don Bennett, Danny Lynn Bennett, Johnny Ray Bennett. A.A. in Secretarial Sci., Western N.Mex. U., 1964, B.A. in Bus. and History Edn., 1972; postgrad. Eastern N.Mex. U., 1979-81. Cert. tchr., Tex., N.Mex.; lic. gen. contractor, N.Mex. Tchr., counselor Allstate Bus. Coll., Dallas, 1973-77; tchr. Hobbs (N.Mex.) Pub. Schs., 1977-78; tchr. N.Mex. Jr. Coll., Hobbs, 1978-80; owner, mgr. Energy Coating Co., Hobbs, 1980-82; acct. Guidance Ctr. Lea County, Hobbs, 1982—. Mem. Am. Soc. Tng. and Devel., N.Mex. Farm and Livestock Bur. Presbyterian. Club: Women of Moose (Hobbs). Office: Guidance Ctr Lea County 924 E Sanger St Hobbs NM 88240

COPELAND, EUGENE LEROY, lawyer; b. Fairfield, Iowa, Mar. 5, 1939; BA, Parsons Coll., 1961; JD with distinction, U. Iowa, 1965. Admitted to Colo. bar, 1965, Iowa bar, 1965, U.S. Supreme Ct. bar, 1966; individual practice law, Denver, 1965-66; sr. v.p., gen. counsel, sec. Security Life of Denver, 1966—; gen. counsel Nationale Nederlanden U.S. Corp., 1986—; lectr., speaker at legal and industry convs., seminars, meetings; participant contemporary issue program Today show NBC, 1980. Bd. dirs. Buffalo Mountain Met. Dist., Summit County, Colo.; bd. dirs., chmn. investment com. Friends Found. of Denver Pub. Library; mem. Denver Pub. Library Commn.; bd. dirs., 1st v.p. Adult Edn. Council Met. Denver. Served with inf. U.S. Army. Fulbright scholar. Mem. Inter-Am. Bar Assn., ABA, Colo. Bar Assn., Denver Bar Assn., Iowa Bar Assn., Assn. Life Ins. Council, Am. Council Life Ins. (state v.p. 1973-83, legis. com., reins. com., policyholder tax com.), Colo. Life Conv. (legis. chmn. 1973-86), Colo. Assn. Corp. Counsel, Denver Estate Planning Council, Colo. Assn. Life Underwriters (co-author learning guide 1978), Law Club Denver, Phi Kappa Phi. Unitarian. Author: Preventive Law for Medical Directors and Underwriters, 1973; Underwriting in a New Age of Legal Accountability, 1978; Insurance Law, 1982; bd. editors Iowa Law Rev., 1965. Office: Security Life Ctr 1290 Broadway Denver CO 80203

COPELAND, PHILLIPS JEROME, former university administrator, former air force officer; b. Oxnard, Calif., Mar. 22, 1921; s. John Charles and Marion Moffatt) C.; student U. So. Calif., 1947-49; B.A., U. Denver, 1956, M.A., 1958; grad. Air Command and Staff Coll., 1959, Indsl. Coll. Armed Forces, 1964; m. Alice Janette Lusby, Apr. 26, 1942; children—Janette Ann Copeland Bosserman, Nancy Jo Copeland Briner. Commd. 2d lt. USAAF, 1943, advanced through grades to col. USAF, 1964, pilot 8th Air Force, Eng., 1944-45; various flying and staff assignments, 1945-51; chief joint tng. sect. Hdqrs. Airsouth (NATO), Italy, 1952-54; asst. dir. plans and programs USAF Acad., 1955-58; assigned to joint intelligence, Washington, 1959-61; plans officer Cincpac Joint Staff, Hawaii, 1961-63; staff officer, ops. directorate, then team chief Nat. Mil. Command Center, Joint Chiefs Staff, Washington, 1964-67; dir. plans and programs USAF Adv. Group, also adviser to Vietnamese Air Force, Vietnam, 1967-68; prof. aerospace studies U. So. Calif., Los Angeles, 1968-72, exec. asst. to pres., 1972-73, assoc. dir. office internat. programs, 1973-75, dir. adminstrv. services Coll. Continuing Edn., 1975-82, dir. employee relations, 1982—. Decorated D.F.C., Bronze Star, Air medal with 3 clusters; Medal of Honor (Vietnam). Mem. Am. Econ. Assn., Air Force Assn., Order of Daedalians. Home: 81 Cypress Way Rolling Hills Estates CA 90274

COPELAND, ROBERT MILTON, librarian; b. Lincoln, Ill., Sept. 23, 1938; s. William Duncan and Mary Evelyn (Stannard) C.; m. Julia Fillmore Wallace, 1962 (div. 1969); 1 child, Jonathan Robert; m. Nora R. Shirajian. BA, Carleton Coll., 1960; MLS, U. Minn., 1963; MA in History, Colo. State U., 1981. Reference librarian Coll. St. Thomas, St. Paul, 1963-64; head librarian Colo. Coll., Colorado Springs, 1964-68; assoc. univ. librarian Am. U. of Beirut, 1968-76; head librarian Kans. Wesleyan U., Salina, 1976-79; program adminstr. reference and local history Ft. Collins (Colo.) Pub. Library, 1983—. Author: A Sesquicentennial History of the Community Church of Beirut 1823-1973, 1974. Served to sgt. USNG, 1961-67. Mem. Colo. Library Assn., Nat. Trust for Hist. Preservation, Georgetown Hist. Soc., Colo. Hist. Soc., Ft. Collins Hist. Soc. (bd. dirs. 1985—), Phi Kappa Phi, Phi Alpha Theta. Presbyterian. Avocations: photography, historical research, gardening, hiking, camping. Home: 1313 Crestmore Pl Fort Collins CO 80521 Office: Ft Collins Pub Library 201 Peterson St Fort Collins CO 80524

COPELOF, RUTH ANN, clinical social worker; b. Culver City, Calif., July 11, 1959; d. Donald Stanton and Esther Adele (Kusnitz) C. BA, Calif. State U., Northridge, 1982; MSW, Ohio State U., 1984. Lic. clin. social worker. Social work intern Childhood League Ctr., Columbus, Ohio, 1983, Nisonger Ctr., Columbus, 1983-84; clin. social worker Maryvale, Rosemead, Calif., 1984—. Recipient Stillman Scholarship Ohio State U., 1983-84. Mem. Nat. Assn. Social Workers, Council of Exceptional Children, San Fernando Valley Child Care Consortium, Social Work Alumni, Alpha Xi Delta. Democrat. Jewish. Avocations: folk dancing, sports. Office: Maryvale 7600 E Graves Rosemead CA 91770

COPLEY, HELEN KINNEY, newspaper publisher; b. Cedar Rapids, Iowa, Nov. 28, 1922; d. Fred Everett and Margaret (Casey) Kinney; m. James S. Copley, Aug. 16, 1965 (dec.); 1 child, David Casey. Attended, Hunter Coll., N.Y.C., 1945. Assoc. The Copley Press, Inc., 1952—, chmn. exec. com., chmn. corp., dir., 1973—, chief exec. officer, sr. mgmt. bd., 1974—; chmn. bd. Copley News Service, San Diego, 1973—; chmn. editorial bd. Union-Tribune Pub. Co., 1976—; pub. The San Diego Union and The Tribune, 1973—. Chmn. bd., trustee James S. Copley Found., 1973—; mem. Friends of Internat. Center, La Jolla, La Jolla Mus. Contemporary Art, La Jolla Town Council, Inc.; life patroness Makua Aux.; San Diego Hall of Sci., life mem.; mem. San Diego Soc. Natural History; Scripps Meml. Hosp. Aux., Life mem. Star of India Aux., Zool. Soc. San Diego; mem. YWCA; hon. chmn., bd. dirs. Washington Crossing Found.; trustee, mem. audit and compensation com. Howard Hughes Med. Inst. Mem. Inter Am. Press Assn., Calif. Press Assn., Am. Soc. Newspaper Editors, Am. Press Inst., Am. Newspapers Publs. Assn., Calif. Newspaper Pubs. Assn., Greater Los Angeles, Nat., San Diego, San Francisco press clubs, Am. Newspapers Assn., Sigma Delta Chi. Republican. Roman Catholic. Clubs: Aurora (Ill.) Country; Army and Navy (D.C.); San Diego Yacht, Univ., La Jolla Beach and Tennis, La Jolla Country. Office: PO Box 1530 La Jolla CA 92038

COPMAN, LOUIS, naval officer, radiologist; b. Phila., Jan. 17, 1934; s. Jacob and Eve (Snyder) C.; m. Avera Schuster, June 8, 1958; children: Mark, Linda. BA, U. Pa., 1955, MD, 1959. Diplomate Am. Bd. Radiology; Nat. Bd. Med. Examiners. Commd. ensign Med. Corps USN, 1958; advanced through grades to capt. Naval Hosp., 1975; asst. chief radiology dept. Naval Hosp., Pensacola, Fla., 1966-69; chief radiology dept. Doctors Hosp., Phila., 1969-73; radiologist Mercer Hosp. Ctr., Trenton, N.J., 1973-75; chmn. radiology dept. Naval Hosp., Phila., 1975-84; chief. radiology dept. Naval Med. Clinic, Pearl Harbor, Hawaii, 1984—; cons. Radiology Services, Wilmington, Del., 1978-84, Yardley (Pa.) Radiology, 1979-84. Author: The Cuckold, 1974. Recipient Albert Einstein award in Medicine, U. Pa., 1959. Mem. AMA, Assn. Mil. Surgeons of the U.S., Royal Soc. Medicine, Radiol. Soc. N.Am., Am. Coll. Radiology, Photographic Soc. Am., Sherlock Holmes Soc., Phi Beta Kappa, Alpha Omega Alpha. Jewish. Avocations: photography, hang-gliding, scuba diving. Home: 1774 Akaakaawa St Kailua HI 96734 Office: Naval Med Clinic PO Box 121 Pearl Harbor HI 96860

COPPOLA, FRANCIS FORD, director, producer, film writer; b. Detroit, Apr. 7, 1939; s. Carmine C.; m. Eleanor Neil; children: Roman, Sofia, Gian-Carlo (dec.). B.A., Hofstra U., 1958; Master of Cinema, UCLA, 1968. Artistic dir., Zoetrope Studios.; Dir.: motion pictures Tonight for Sure, 1961, Dementia 13, 1964, You're a Big Boy Now, 1967, Finian's Rainbow, 1968, The Rain People, 1969, One from the Heart, 1981; writer: motion pictures This Property Is Condemned, 1966, Reflections In a Golden Eye, 1967, The Rain People, 1969, Is Paris Burning, 1966, Patton, 1970, The Great Gatsby, 1974, Peggy Sue Got Married, 1986; writer, producer and dir.: motion pictures The Godfather (Acad. awards for Best Screenplay and Best Picture, nominee for Best Dir., Film Dir.'s award Dirs. Guild Am. 1972), The Godfather, Part II, 1974 (Acad. awards for Best Screenplay, Best Dir. and Best Picture), The Conversation, 1974 (Golden Palm award Cannes Film Festival 1974), Apocalypse Now, 1979; producer: TV movie The People; co-writer, producer, dir.: motion picture The Outsiders, 1983, Rumble Fish, 1983; producer: motion pictures THX 1138, 1971; exec. producer: motion pictures Black Stallion, 1979; producer: motion picture The Black Stallion Returns, 1983; co-writer, producer, dir.: motion picture The Escape Artist, 1982; exec. producer motion picture Hammett; dir., co-screenwriter The Cotton Club, 1984; co-exec. producer Mishima, 1985; dir., co-producer Gardens of Stone, 1986; dir. play Private Lives, opera The Visit. Mem. Dirs. Guild Am. Inc. Office: Zoetrope Studios 916 Kearny St San Francisco CA 94133 *

COPPOLINO, ROBERT NUNZIO, mechanical engineer; b. N.Y.C.; s. Louis Joseph and Nancy Grace (Bonarrigo) C.; m. Catherine Gayle Stafford; children: Michael, Melissa, Kenneth, Peter. BS in Aerospace Engring., Polytech. Inst. Bklyn, 1966, MS in Applied Mechanics, 1967, PhD, 1973. Sr. engr. Grumman Aerospace Corp., Bethpage, N.Y., 1967-75; sect. mgr. The Aerospace Corp., El Segundo, 1975-83; br. mgr. MacNeal Schwendler Corp., Los Angeles, 1983—; lectr. engring. U. So. Calif., Los Angeles, 1978-83; cons. engr. in field, 1980-83. Contbr. numerous articles to profl. jours. Recipient Outstanding Accomplishment award The Aerospace Corp., 1979, Outstanding Accomplishment award NASA, 1981. Mem. AIAA (mem. structural dynamic com.), Soc. Automotive Engrs., Sigma Xi. Home: 11866 Laughton Way Northridge CA 91326 Office: The MacNeal-Schwendler Corp 815 Colorado Blvd Los Angeles CA 90041

CORBELL, BOBBY HAROLD, laboratory technical staff member, electrical engineer; b. Charleston, Ark., June 22, 1952; s. Billy Harold and Eula Ann (McMurtry) C.; m. Deborah Faye Mobley, Aug. 2, 1975; children: William Harold, Andrew Nelson, Christopher James. BSEE, U. Ark., 1978, MSEE, 1981. Research asst. U. Ark., Fayetteville, 1979-80; mem. tech. staff Sandia Nat. Labs., Albuquerque, 1981—. Asst. coach tee ball little league, Albuquerque, 1986. Served with U.S. Army, 1972-74. Mem. NSPE. Republican. Avocations: hunting, fishing, woodworking, auto mechanics. Home: 1018 Grace NE Albuquerque NM 87112 Office: Sandia Nat Labs PO Box 5800 Albuquerque NM 87185

CORBETT, GARY MACKAY, graphic designer; b. Nampa, Idaho, Dec. 24, 1942; s. Walter Colvin and Ann (MacKay) C.; m. Judith Rose Hanel, Aug. 9, 1963 (div. Jan. 1976); children: Jeffrey, Tracy, Bree; m. Kathleen Ann Hodgson, Dec. 11, 1976. Student, Art Ctr. Coll. of Design, Los Angeles, 1964-67. Staff designer Perine/Jacoby, Newport Beach, Calif., 1967-69; art dir. Westcliff Advt., Newport Beach, Calif., 1969-70; designer Huerta Design Assn., Los Angeles, 1970-71; owner Gary Corbett Design, Santa Ana, Calif., 1971-75, cons., 1976—; creative dir. The Realist, Santa Ana, Calif., 1975-76; v.p., creative dir. KNT Plusmark, Inc., Irvine, Calif., 1976-86; owner, pres. Corbett Design Assn., Newport Beach, Calif., 1986-87; co-owner Corbett & Hinds, Inc., Newport Beach, 1987—; faculty Art Ctr. Coll. of Design, Pasadena, Calif., 1984-85. Mem. Orange County Ad Fedn. (Golden Orange award 1980), Art Dirs. and Designers of Orange County (treas. 1980-81). Avocations: dog shows, horses, karate. Office: Corbett & Hinds Inc 4001 Westerly Pl Suite 110 Newport Beach CA 92660

CORBIN, JOHN STEPHEN, aquaculture development program executive; b. Secaucus, N.J., Aug. 21, 1946; s. John Patrick and Edith Pauline (Herbig) C.; m. Elizabeth Ruth Wolf, June 10, 1978; 1 child, Catherine Elizabeth. BS, U. Miami, 1968; MS, U. Hawaii, 1977. Combat photographer, correspondent U.S. Army, Socialist Republic of Vietnam, 1969-71; research asst. U. Hawaii, Honolulu, 1971-74, research assoc., 1976-77; planner dept. planning and econ. devel. State of Hawaii, Honolulu, 1975, specialist aquaculture devel. prog., 1977-78, mgr. aquaculture devel. prog., 1978—; cons. State of Hawaii, 1976-77; advisor Congl. Office Tech. Assessment, Washington, 1985—; mem. adv. bd. West Coast Aquaculture Found., Monterey, Calif., 1982-84, Internat. Aquaculture Ctr., Hagerman, Idaho, 1983—. Co-author aquaculture devel. plan for Hawaii, 1978; contbr. chpts. to books, articles to profl. jours. Mem. Pacific Asian Affairs Council, Honolulu, 1982—. Served with U.S. Army, 1969-71, Vietnam. Recipient Gov.'s Disting. State Service award State of Hawaii, 1984. Mem. AAAS, World Aquaculture Soc., Am. Fisheries Soc. (cert.), Am. Planning Assn. Democrat. Episcopalian. Avocations: photography, writing, skin diving, fishing. Home: 47-215 Iuiu St Kaneohe HI 96744 Office: State of Hawaii Aquaculture Devel 335 Merchant St Room 359 Honolulu HI 96813

CORBIN, ROBERT K., state attorney general; b. 1928; married; 3 daus. B.S., Ind. U., 1952, J.D., 1956. Bar: Ind. 1957, Ariz. 1958. County atty. Maricopa County, 1965-69; chmn. Maricopa County Bd. Suprs., 1974-77; atty. gen. State of Ariz., Phoenix, 1979—; former mem. stats. adv. bd. U.S. Bur. Justice; chmn. Ariz. Criminal Justice Commn. Served with USN, 1946-48. Mem. Ariz. State Bar Assn. (past mem. ethics com.), Ariz. County Attys. Assn., NRA (bd. dirs.), Nat. Assn. Attys. Gen. (chmn. antitrust com. 1981-83), Americans for Effective Law Enforcement (pres. 1974), Conf. Western Attys. Gen. (chmn. 1982). Republican. Club: Masons. Home: 1275 W Washington Phoenix AZ 85007 Office: Office of the Attorney General Dept of Law State Capitol 1275 W Washington Phoenix AZ 85007

CORBOY, JAMES MCNALLY, investment banker; b. Erie, Pa., Nov. 3, 1940; s. James Thomas and Dorothy Jane (Schluraff) C.; BA, Allegheny Coll., 1962; MBA, U. Colo., 1986. m. Suzanne Shaver, July 23, 1965; children: Shannon, James McNally. Sales staff Boettcher & Co., Denver, 1964-70; sales staff Blyth Eastman Dillon, Denver and Chgo., 1970-74; sales staff William Blair & Co., Chgo., 1974-77; mgr. corp. bond dept. Boettcher & Co., Denver, 1977-79; ptnr. in charge William Blair & Co., Denver, 1979-86; first v.p. Stifel, Nicolaus & Co., 1986—. Served with USMC, 1962-67. Mem. Securities Industry Assn., Republican. Presbyterian. Clubs: The Attic (Chgo.), Glenmoor Country, Metropolitan. Home: 5723 S Florence St Englewood CO 80111 Office: 5445 DTC Pkwy Suite 1025 Englewood CO 80111

CORBRIDGE, JAMES NOEL, JR., chancellor, educator; b. Mineola, N.Y., May 27, 1934; s. James Noel Sr. and Edna (Springer) C.; m. Charlotte Ivans Mixon, July 18, 1938; children: Lisa, Stuart. AB, Brown U., 1955; LLB, Yale U., 1963. Assoc. Lord, Day & Lord, N.Y.C., 1963-65; asst. prof. law U. Colo., Boulder, 1965-67, assoc. prof., 1967-73, prof., 1973—, v.p. student affairs, 1970-72, v.p. student and minority affairs, 1972-74, vice chancellor acad. affairs, 1974-77, interim vice chancellor acad. services, 1979-81, acting vice chancellor acad. affairs, 1986, chancellor, 1986—; vis. scholar Inst. for Advanced Legal Studies U. London, 1977, 85, Univ. Linkoping, Sweden, 1985. Contbr. articles to profl. jours. Served to lt. (j.g.) USNR, 1957-60. Mem. Colo. Bar Assn., Boulder County Bar Assn., Internat. Assn. Water Lawyers, Internat. Water Resources Assn. Episcopalian. Club: Boulder Country. Avocations: golf, bird carving, birding. Office: Univ of Colo Campus Box 17 Boulder CO 80309 Home: 7112 Old Post Rd Boulder CO 80301 *

CORCORAN, CHRISTOPHER MATTHEW, advertising executive; b. Los Angeles, Sept. 19, 1951; s. James George and Anne Giovana (DeLuca) C.; m. Anne Hodges, Mar. 1, 1986; 1 child from previous marriage, Christopher Matthew. Student Loyola U., Los Angeles, 1968-73; B.S.L., Irvine U. Sch. Law, 1977. Pres., Ultimate Performance Group, Anaheim, Calif., 1976—; dir. communications United Technologies Corp., Santa Ana, Calif., 1978-80; mktg. dir. Promotion Ltd., Santa Ana, 1980-81; v.p., account mgmt. supr. Dailey & Assocs., Los Angeles, 1981-83; pres. Corcoran & Assocs., 1983—; cons., lectr. in field. Bd. dirs., producer Hollywood Bowl Easter Sunrise Service, 1974-79. Mem. Pub. Relations Soc. Am. Roman Catholic. Office: 1215 Red Gum St Suite A Anaheim CA 92806

CORDER, MICHAEL PAUL, physician, educator; b. Zanesville, Ohio, Jan. 20, 1940; s. Thurman E. and Dorothy S. C.; children: Anita, Jennifer, Wendy. BS, Capital U., 1963; MD, Ohio State U., 1965. Diplomate Am. Bd. Internal Medicine, Am. Bd. Internal Oncology. Asst. chief hematology and oncology service Letterman Med. Ctr., San Francisco, 1971-75, chief oncology sect., 1972-75; from asst. prof. to assoc. prof. medicine U. Iowa, Iowa City, 1975-80; chief div. oncology and hematology Kern Med. Ctr., Bakersfield, Calif., 1983—; adj. prof. medicine UCLA, 1983—; cons. Nat. Cancer Inst., Bethesda, Md., 1978—; exec. com. San Joaquin Valley (Calif.) Regional Cancer Registry Planning Bd., 1986. Contbr. articles to profl. jours. V.p. Kern Unit Am. Cancer Soc., 1986—. Served to col. USAR. Fellow ACP (A. Blaine Brower Traveling scholar 1981), Internat. Soc. Hematology; mem. Am. Soc. Clin. Oncology (membership com. 1984—), Am. Assn. Cancer Research, Western Soc. Clin. Investigation, Calif. Acad. Medicine. Unitarian Universalist. Clubs: Petroleum, Rio Bravo Golf & Tennis (Bakersfield). Avocations: tennis, oriental rugs, cycling. Home: 12430 Cattle King Dr Bakersfield CA 93306 Office: Kern Med Ctr 1830 Flower St Bakersfield CA 93306

CORDINGLEY, JOHN STUART, biochemist, educator; b. Keighley, Yorkshire, Eng., May 22, 1953; came to U.S., 1984; s. Francis and Doreen (Hoyle) C.; m. Pamela Joyce Langer, June 1, 1985. BSc in Zoology, U. St. Andrews, Scotland, 1975; PhD in Biology, U. Essex, Eng., 1978. Scientist med. research council, Cambridge, Eng., 1978-81; research fellow dept. pathology Cambridge U., 1981-84; research fellow Harvard U. Med. Sch., Boston, 1984-85; prof. U. Wyo., Laramie, 1985—. Contbr. articles to profl. jours. Charles and Katherine Darwin research fellow Darwin Coll., Cambridge, 1980-83. Mem. AAAS. Avocations: climbing, mountaineering, folk music. Office: U Wyo Dept Biochemistry PO Box 3944 University Sta Laramie WY 82071

CORDINGLEY, WILLIAM ANDREW, JR., advertising executive; b. Mpls., July 18, 1948; s. William Andrew and Mary Jeannette (Bowles) C.; m. Pamela Cotter, Apr. 2, 1950. A.B., Harvard U., 1971; M.B.A., M.S., Columbia U., 1975. Account mgr. Ogilvy & Mather, N.Y.C., 1975-77, Foote, Cone & Belding/Honig, San Francisco, 1977-80; pres. Bill Cordingley Advt., San Anselmo, Calif., 1980-85; pres. and founder eVisages, Inc., San Anselmo, 1985—. Mem. Harvard Fund, San Francisco area Harvard Campaign com., 1982; founder, pres. San Anselmo Resident's Forum; chmn. tax initiative San Anselmo, 1982; vice-mayor City of San Anselmo, 1986-87; mem. Town Council, 1984—, mayor, 1987—. Home and Office: 10 Elkhorn Way San Anselmo CA 94960

CORDINGLEY, WILLIAM ANDREW, newspaper publisher; b. Des Moines, Aug. 24, 1917; s. William Andrew and Louise (Cookerly) C.; m. Mary Jeannette Bowles, Mar. 17, 1942; children: William Andrew, Thomas Kent, Constance Louise. Grad., Phillips Exeter Acad., 1936; B.S., Harvard U., 1940. With Mpls. Star and Tribune, 1940-65, nat. advt. mgr., 1949-65; pub., pres. Great Falls (Mont.) Tribune, 1965—; pres. South Idaho Newspapers, Inc., 1977-82, chmn., 1982—; dir. Mont. Mag., Northwestern Nat. Bank, Great Falls.; Vice chmn. Helena br. Mpls. Fed. Res. Bank, 1970, 72, chmn., 1971, 73, 74, 75. Trustee Breck Sch., Mpls., 1962-65; bd. dirs. Great Falls Symphony, 1965-70, Russell Gallery, Great Falls, 1965-76, Mpls. Curative Workshop, 1952-65; mem. council of 50, U. Mont., 1966-70; mem. U. Mont. Citizens Council, 1979-83; mem. pres.'s council Coll. Great Falls, 1971—, trustee, 1979—, vice chmn. bd. trustees, 1981-83; bd. dirs. Endowment and Research Found., Mont. State U., 1968-73; Mem. regional adv. group Mountain State Regional Med. Programs, 1967-71. Served to lt. col. AUS, 1941-46, ETO, MTO and NATOUSA. Mem. Am. Newspaper Pubs. Assn., Mpls. Sales and Mktg. Execs. (v.p. 1963-65), Great Falls C. of C. (dir. 1967-70), Sigma Delta Chi. Episcopalian. Clubs: Hazeltine Nat. (Mpls.) (bd. govs. 1962-65); Meadowlark Country (Great Falls) (bd. dirs. 1966-69); Harvard Varsity. Lodge: Rotary. Office: Great Falls Tribune Great Falls MT 59405

CORDON, FRANK JOSEPH, insurance company executive; b. Los Angeles, Oct. 11, 1925; s. Frank and Ramona (Sesma) C.; m. Lillian Davis, Apr. 19, 1953; children: Cecilia Leta, Peter Francis. BSBA, U. So. Calif., 1950. Founder Yeakel and Cordon Ins. Agy., North Hollywood, Calif., 1950-57, Cordon & Co., Los Angeles, 1957-64; co-founder Heritage Life Ins. Co., Los Angeles, 1957—; pres. bd. dirs. Heritage Ins. Group and subs.; bd. dirs. Quaker State Oil Refining Corp., Oil City, Pa., Kingsley Found., Los Angeles. Pres. North Hollywood C. of C., 1952-53. Served with USNR, WWII. Mem. Am. Legion, Phi Kappa Psi. Republican. Roman Catholic. Avocations: hunting, fishing, gardening. Office: 30851 Agoura Rd Agoura Hills CA 91301

CORDOVA, ERNEST LEROY, architect; b. Denver, Dec. 30, 1950; s. Forrest Ernest and Joy Jean (Garber) C.; m. Karen Lynne Masters, June 28, 1975; children: Rylan Andrew, Beth Evonne, Brent Avery. BA magna cum laude, U. No. Colo., 1973; MArch., Washington U., St. Louis, 1979. Registered architect, Colo. Job capt. SLP, Inc., Denver, 1978-79; project architect Pouw Outland Assoc., Inc., Denver, 1979-81; assoc. Murata Outland Assoc.,

Inc., Denver, 1981—. Prin. works inlcude Scenic artist stage set designs Endgame, 1971 (best technician award), Oliver, 1973 (best technician award). V.P. Colo. Baptist Youth Fellowship, 1969-70; council pres. Messiah Luth. Ch., Denver. Recipient Helen Langworthy award Little Theatre of the Rockies, U. No. Colo., 1973, Award of Excellence, Archtl. Woodwork Inst., 1986. Republican. Lutheran. Avocations: skiing, racquetball, snooker, volleyball, restoration. Home: 2865 S High St Denver CO 80210 Office: Murata Outland Assoc Inc 1660 17th St #200 Denver CO 80202

CORDOVA, JUAN ALBERTO, health care company executive; b. Guayaquil province, Ecuador, June 24, 1947; came to U.S., 1958; s. Servio Tulio Cordova and Violeta (Velez) Cordova Rogowski. Degree in aerospace tech., SUNY, Farmingdale, 1968; degree in aero. engring., Utah State U., 1970; M in Health Adminstrn., Duke U., 1978; postgrad., U. LaVerne, Calif. Asst. hosp. adminstr. Kaiser Found. Hosps., Los Angeles, 1978-82; asst. med. group adminstr. Permanente Med. Group, Los Angeles, 1982—. Contbr. articles to profl. jours. Served to lt. comdr. USN, 1970—, reservist. Decorated D.F.C. Mem. Am. Coll. Hosp. Adminstrs. (cert.), Navy Officer Res. Assn., Health Care Execs. Assn. Roman Catholic. Club: Los Angeles Athletic. Avocations: flying, skiing, bicycling, scuba diving, fine arts. Home: 163 N Parkwood Ave #1 Pasadena CA 91107 Office: Permanente Med Group 1505 Edgemont Ave Los Angeles CA 90027

COREY, JON MICHAEL, psychologist, educator; b. New Kensington, Pa., Nov. 23, 1946; s. Frederick and F. Sara (Elias) C.; m. Barbara Stanton, July 11, 1982; children: Jon, Michael, James, Karen, Chissy, Matthew. BA, Washington and Jefferson U., 1968; MS, U. So. Calif., 1972, PhD, 1977. Lic. psychologist. Commd. 2d lt. U.S. Army, 1968, advanced through grades to maj., combat arms officer, 1968-69, resigned, 1979; clin. dir., psychologist White House staff U.S. Govt., Washington, 1979-80; mgmt. exec. INTERACT, Inc., Frankfurt, Fed. Republic Germany, 1980-85; v.p. human resources Profl. Adv. Group, Ltd., Frankfurt, Fed. Republic Germany, 1985-86; corp. prof. mgmt. EG&G, Inc., Idaho Falls, Idaho, 1985-86; v.p. profl. services Caditz & Assocs., Seattle, 1986—; prof. psychology, mgmt. U. So. Calif., UCLA, U. Md., U. Ala., Schiller Internat. U., Heidelberg, Fed. Republic Germany, 1974-85. Author: "Classified" U.S. Government, 1977. Decorated Silver Star, Dist. Flying Cross, Bronze Star, Purple Heart; Civilian Exec. award U.S. Govt., 1979, 80. Mem. AAUP, Am. Coll. Hosp. Execs., Assn. Mil. Surgeons U.S., Inst. Behavior Health, Inst. Indsl. Engrs. Lodge: Masons. Avocations: running, reading. Home: 4317 130th Pl SW Lynnwood WA 98037 Office: The Globe Bldg Mercer Island WA 98040

COREY, JOSEPH ROBERT, advertising executive; b. Corning, N.Y., Aug. 28, 1944; s. Joseph Marshall and Margaret Elizabeth (Emhiser) C.; m. Sally Jeanne Davis, Aug. 24, 1967; children: Joseph, Matthew. BA, Taylor U., 1966; postgrad., Temple U., 1966-67. Enlisted U.S. Army, 1967, advanced through grades to capt., 1970, resigned, 1982; with sales and mktg. dept. Ford Motor Co., Detroit, 1972-82; advt. exec. Sales div. Toyota Motor Corp., Torrance, Calif., 1982-85; nat. advt. mgr. Hyundai Motor Co. Am., Garden Grove, Calif., 1985—. Republican. Avocations: swimming, gardening, sports. Home: 21942 Calderas Mission Viejo CA 92691 Office: Hyundai Motor Am 7373 Hunt Ave Garden Grove CA 92642

CORLESS, ELIZABETH ANN, interior design professional; b. Olds, Alta., Can., Oct. 18, 1959; came to U.S., 1978; d. Larry and Shirley Ann (Herdman) C. BS in Interior Design, Woodbury U., 1980. Sr. designer Judith Wilson Design, Studio City, Calif., 1980-84; design dir. Impact Images, Santa Ana, Calif., 1984-85; mgr. environ. resources Pacific Bus. Interiors, Los Angeles, 1985—; instr. Brooks Coll., Long Beach, Calif., 1986-87; lectr. Woodbury U., Los Angeles, 1985-86. Mem. Inst. Bus. Designers (treas. 1981-83, v.p. programs 1983-85, nat. trustee 1985—, recipient Appreciation award 1983, 85), Internat. facility Mgmt. Assn. Episcopalian. Office: Pacific Bus Interiors 8687 Melrose Ave M-3 Los Angeles CA 90069

CORLESS, JOHN CONDIE, accountant, educator; b. Prosser, Wash., June 30, 1943; s. John M. and Zelda (Condie) C.; m. Ronda Sims, Mar. 18, 1969; children: John S., Preston, Brady, Andrew, Justin. BS, Brigham Young U., 1967; MS, U. Minn., 1969, PhD, 1971. CPA. Asst. prof. U. Conn., Storrs, 1971-75, assoc. prof., 1976-80; assoc. prof. U. Wyo., Laramie, 1980-84; prof. accountancy Calif. State U., Sacramento, 1984—; faculty resident Arthur Andersen & Co., Hartford, Conn., 1972-73. Contbr. articles and revs. to profl. jours. Served mission to West Cen. States, 1962-64. Mem. Am. Inst. CPA's, Am. Acctg. Assn., Inst. Internal Auditors, Beta Alpha Psi, Beta Gamma Sigma. Republican. Mormon. Office: Calif State U 6000 J St Sacramento CA 95819-2694

CORLETT, DONNA JEAN, education educator; b. Seattle, Sept. 28, 1934; d. J. Earl and Margaret N. (Whitehall) Broyles; divorced; 1 child, Shannon Hayes. BA, U. Idaho, 1955; MEd, U. Oreg., 1965; EdD, U. Portland, 1969. Cert. tchr., Wash. Tchr. pub. schs. Wash. and Idaho, 1955-63; instr. Portland (Oreg.) State U., 1964-66; assoc. prof. elem. edn. U. Portland, 1968—, coordinator elem. edn., 1974—. Honored juror Jour. Adminstrn. and Supervision, 1983—; contbr. articles to profl. jours. Nat. v.p. AAUW, Washington, 1970. Mem. Internat. Reading Assn., NW Assn. Tchr. Educators (pres. 1987—), Willamette Writers Club, Phi Delta Kappa (local v.p. 1981-82), Delta Kappa Gamma. Democrat. Lodge: Zonta (local pres. 1976-78). Avocations: writing, painting, outdoors, cooking, travel. Office: U Portland 5000 N Willamette Blvd Portland OR 97203

CORLETT, EMMA JEAN, social worker; b. Knox City, Tex., Aug. 4, 1926; d. LeRoy and Luella (Burns) Massey; B.A. in Secondary Edn. cum laude, N.W. Nazarene Coll., 1965; M.S.W. with honors, U. Utah, 1972; m. John Paul Corlett, Jan. 1, 1946 (dec. 1969); children—Jeanne Marie, Thomas Lee, Jan Louise. Feature writer Statesman Newspaper, Boise, Idaho, 1960-63; caseworker Idaho Dept. Pub. Assistance, Boise, 1965-68; mental health counselor Community Inst. Human Resources, Boise, 1969-70; dir. patient and family counseling Mercy Med. Center, Nampa, Idaho, 1972-75; edn. counselor U.S. Army, Seoul, S. Korea, 1975-76; med. social worker Kern Med. Center, Bakersfield, Calif., 1976-78, dir. med. social services, 1978-79; dir. med. social services Santa Barbara (Calif.) Cottage Hosp., 1979—. Named Mrs. Idaho, 1959; licensed clin. social worker, Calif. Mem. Nat. Assn. Social Workers, Acad. Certified Social Workers, Internat. Register Clin. Social Workers, AAUW, Soc. Hosp. Social Worker Dirs., Am. Hosp. Assn., U.S. Postal Clks. Aux. (nat. v.p. 1959-63). Phi Delta Lambda. Office: Santa Barbara Cottage Hosp Pueblo at Bath St Santa Barbara CA 93105

CORLETT, THERESA NIEMEIER, science facility administrator; b. Seattle, Mar. 14, 1937; d. Edward A. and Jean (Gilbreath) Niemeier; m. Richard C. Corlett; children: John Helton, Douglas Helton, Catherine, Cynthea. BBA, U. Wash., 1957. Program mgr. U. Wash., Seattle, 1972-84; project coordinator Fred Hutchinson Cancer Ctr., Seattle, 1984-87; supr. regulatory affairs CooperVision, Bellevue, Wash., 1987—. Mem. Soc. Research Adminstrs., Nat. Council Univ. Research Adminstrs., Info. Processing Assn. Home: 909 N 35th #303 Seattle WA 98103 Office: CooperVision 3190 160th SE Bellevue WA 98008-5496

CORLEY, JOHN MICHAEL, educator; b. Reno, Nov. 22, 1929; s. Roscoe Theodore and Delta Baynard (Lagerquist) C.; m. Dagmar Christine Neick, Jan. 26, 1958 (div. July 1975); children: Christopher Shaun, Kathleen Elise; m. Sherie Prowell, Feb. 5, 1976. BA, U. Calif., Berkeley, 1956; MA, U. N.Mex., 1965. Salesman Dobeckmun Corp., Berkeley, 1956-58; instr. Herlong (Calif.) High Sch., 1958-59, Willits (Calif.) High Sch., 1959-62, Santa Cruz (Calif.) High Sch., 1962-68; instr. Merced (Calif.) Coll., 1968—, chmn. div., edn. con.; chmn. bd. dirs. Cen. Valley Opportunity Ctr., Merced. Dem. chmn. Willits and Mendocino Counties, 1960; mem. City Sch. Bd., Merced, 1970-73; pres. Merced Community Concert Assn., 1969-72; active San Joaquin Balley Boy Scouts Am., Merced. Served as sgt. USMC, 1950-52, Korea. Fellow NDEA, Albuquerque, 1964-65, NDEA, Buffalo, N.Y., Florence, Italy, 1968-69, NEH, Rutgers U., N.J., 1978. Mem. SAR (pres. Fresno chpt. 1984-86), Sons of Calif. Pioneers, Huguenot Soc. S.C., Delta Chi (alumni council 1980—). Democrat. Avocations: fly fishing, backpacking, philately, bridge, reading. Home: 3312 M St #1 Merced CA 95348 Office: Merced Coll 3600 M St Merced CA 95340

CORLISS, DOUGLAS RALPH, politician; b. Bremerton, Wash., Oct. 29, 1930; s. Verne Francis and Thora Ingrid (Hansen) C.; m. Lucille Joan Davis, Oct. 2, 1949; children—Roni, Randal, Rockford, Rene, Ragan, Robin, Roger. A.A., Olympic Coll., 1955; B.A., Central Wash. U., 1957; postgrad. U. Puget Sound, 1962. Music dir. pub. schs., Belfair, Wash. and Federal Way, Wash., 1957-72; owner, operator Corliss Trucking Co., 1972-73; mgr. constrn. Blazing Tree Ranch, Friday Harbor, Wash., 1973-77; owner, operator Harbor Rental Equipment, Friday Harbor, 1977; heavy equipment operator F.H. Gravel, Friday Harbor, 1977-80; gen. mgr. Friday Harbor Motor Inn, 1980-84; pres. North Mason Investment Group, Belfair, Wash., 1960-62; chmn. North Mason Edn. Assn., 1963. Chmn. salary com. North Mason Schs., Belfair, 1962-63; commr. San Juan County, 1985—, freeholder, 1983; bd. dirs. San Juan Island Whale Mus. Leader Community Stage Band, Friday Harbor, 1978-85; v.p. Community Youth Council, Friday Harbor, 1982; chmn. City Parks Action Com., Friday Harbor, 1983-84; rep. region 4 Tourist Assn., 1984; counsel San Juan County Ferry Adv. Com.; mem. N.W. Regional Council; spearheaded com. fund raising campaign for whale mus., Friday Harbor; mem. Blue Ribbon Com. Wash. Dept. Transp., 1985; sec., v.p. Wash. State Ferry Riders Coalition, 1985-86; ambassador State of Wash., 1986. Served with USN, 1947-51. Mem. NEA, Wash. State Edn. Assn., Music Edn. Assn., San Juan C. of C. (pres. 1984, bd. dirs. 1985), Am. Legion, Assn. Counties. Republican. Lodge: Lions (bd. dirs. 1982-84). Home: PO Box 286 Friday Harbor WA 98250

CORMIE, DONALD MERCER, investment company executive; b. Edmonton, Alta., Can., July 24, 1922; s. George Mills and Mildred (Mercer) C.; B.A., U. Alta., 1944, LL.B., 1945; LL.M., Harvard U. 1946; m. Eivor Elisabeth Ekstrom, June 8, 1946; children—John Mills, Donald Robert, Allison Barbara, James Mercer, Neil Brian, Bruce George, Eivor, Robert. Admitted to bar, 1947; Queens counsel 1964; sessional instr. faculty law U. Alta., 1947-53; sr. partner Cormie, Kennedy, Fitch & Patrick, Edmonton, 1954—; dir. Prin. Equity Fund, Inc., Prin. World Fund, Prin. Cash Mgmt. Fund, Inc., Prin. Mgmt., Inc. instr. real estate law Dept. of Extension, U. Alta., 1958-64; pres., dir. Prin. Group Ltd., Prin. Life Ins. Co. Can., Collective Securities, Ltd., Collective Mut. Fund Ltd., Cormie Ranch, Ltd., Prin. Certificate Series, Inc., Prin. Investors Corp., Prin. Venture Fund Ltd.; chmn., dir. Prin. Savs. & Trust Co. Served with Canadian Mcht. Marine, 1943-44. Recipient Judge Green Silver medal in Law. Mem. Law Soc. Alta., World Bus. Council, Chief Execs. Forum (dir. 1976-79), Canadian Bar Assn. (mem. council 1961-76, chmn. adminstrv. law com. 1963-66, chmn. taxation 1972-82, v.p. Alta. 1968-69). Home: 12436 Grandview Dr, Edmonton, AB Canada T6H 4K4 Office: 3000 Principal Plaza, Edmonton, AB Canada T5J 3NG

CORMIER, CHRISTIE ANN, computer company professional; b. Denver, Colo., Apr. 22, 1952; d. G. Robert and Marjory C. (Dibblee) Gilbert; 1 child, R. Jason. Outreach worker Community Social Services, Grand Junction, Colo., 1973-76; personnel adminstr. Pikes Peak Mental Health Ctr., Colorado Springs, Colo., 1976-81; personnel adminstr. Digital Equipment Corp., Colorado Springs, Colo., 1981-84, instructional designer, 1984—. Group coordinator The Way Internat., Colorado Springs. Mem. Am. Soc. Tng. and Devel. Republican. Avocations: camping, dancing, music, biblical research.

CORN, JO ANN PHYLLIS, hospital administrator; b. Manomen, Minn., July 17, 1937; d. Joseph Jacob and Dorothy Claire (Oleson) Matysek; m. Poe Rolland, June 8, 1958 (div.); children—Poe David, Clayton Jay, Kelly Ann. Student Colo. State U., 1955-58; B.A., Adams State Coll., 1969; M.S.W., Our Lady of the Lake Coll., San Antonio, 1971; postgrad. U. Colo., 1973-75, U. No. Colo., 1980. Patient and family counselor St. Anthony Hosp., Denver, 1971-75, adminstrv. coordinator human resources, 1975-80, dir. human resources dept., 1980; dir. St. Anthony Hosp. North, Westminster, Colo., 1980-86; cons., dir. profl. relations Humana Hosp., Mountain View, 1986—; dir. Internat. Banks, Engelwood, Denver, Wheatridge and Federal Heights, Colo.; bd. dirs. Central Colo. Health Planning Council, Denver, 1982-83; del. Denver Hosp. Liaison Com., 1982—; dir. St. Anthony's Hosp.. Mem. Adams County Econ. Devel. Council, 1982—; bd. dirs. Adams County ARC, 1983-84. Mem. Western Hosp. Assn. (del. 1982—), Colo. Hosp. Assn. (mem. task force on aging 1983—), Colo. Women's Forum for Health Care, Clear Creek Med. Soc., North Suburban Bus. and Profl. Women (bd. dirs. 1982-84, found. chmn. 1982-84), Met. Denver Hosp. Council (del. 1982—), Metro North C. of C., Broomfield C. of C., Lafayette C. of C., Louisville C. of C. Republican. Home: 2328 S Troy St Aurora CO 80014 Office: St Anthony North Hosp 2551 W 84th Ave Westminster CO 80030

CORNABY, KAY STERLING, lawyer, state senator; b. Spanish Fork, Utah, Jan. 14, 1936; s. Sterling A. and Hilda G. (Stoker) C.; m. Linda Rasmussen, July 23, 1965; children: Alyse, Derek, Tara, Heather, Brandon. AB, Brigham Young U., 1960; postgrad. law Heidelberg (W.Ger.), 1961-63; JD, Harvard U., 1966. Bar: N.Y. 1967, Utah 1969, U.S. Patent and Trademark Office 1967. Assoc. Brumbaugh, Graves, Donahue & Raymond, N.Y.C., 1966-69; ptnr. Mallinckrodt & Cornaby, Salt Lake City, 1969-72; sole practice, Salt Lake City, 1972-85; assoc. Jones, Waldo, Holbrook & McDonough, Salt Lake City, 1985—; mem. Utah State Senate, 1977—, majority leader, 1983-84. Chmn. 2d Congl. Dist., Utah Rep. Party, 1973-77; mem. council legal advisers Rep. Nat. Com., 1981—. chmn. North and East Regional Council of Neighborhoods, 1976-77; mem. Salt Lake County Commn. on Youth, 1979—; mem. Utah Health Cost Found., 1979-86, chmn., 1979-84; mem. Utah State Jud. Conduct Commn., 1983—, chmn. 1984-85; bd. dirs. Friends of KUED, 1982—, chmn. 1985-87; bd. dirs. Salt Lake Conv. and Visitors Bur., 1985—; mem. adv. council Salt Lake dist. Small Bus. Assn.; pres. Utah Opera Co., 1985-86. Mem. Utah Bar Assn., Utah Harvard Alumni Assn. (pres. 1977-79), Harvard U. Law Sch. Alumni Assn. (v.p. 1979—). Mormon. Club: Alta (Salt Lake City). Office: Jones Waldo Holbrook & McDonough 1500 First Interstate Plaza 170 S Main St Salt Lake City UT 84101

CORNELIUS, BYRON GRANT, lawyer; b. Tallahassee, Nov. 8, 1951; s. Curtis Harding and Kathryn Louise (Laury) C.; m. Hilda O. Cornelius, July 28, 1973; 1 child, Camille Renee. AA, Grossmont Coll., 1979; BSL, Western State U., 1981, JD, 1982. Bar: Calif. 1983, U.S. Dist. Ct. (eas. dist., so. dist.) Calif. 1983, U.S. Ct. Appeals (9th cir.) 1983, U.S. Supreme Ct., 1986. Assoc. Davies, Barwick & Knowlton, Lemon Grove, Calif., 1983-84, Vaughan de Kirby, A.P.C., San Diego, 1984-86; ptnr. Epsten & Cornelius, San Diego, 1986—; tchr. legal analysis Western State U., San Diego, 1983-85, profl. respon, 1985—; tutor BAR/BRI Bar Rev., San Diego, 1984-85; tchr. law. Barpassers Bar Rev., Los Angeles, 1985-86. Author, editor: Professional Responsibility, 1985; editor: Criminal Justice Jour., 1981. Minister, elder Lamar Congregation Jehovah's Witnesses, Spring Valley, Calif., 1983—. Served with USN, 1969-73. Mem. San Diego County Bar Assn., San Diego Trial Lawyers, Assn. Trial Lawyers of AM. Home: 8728 Harness St Spring Valley CA 92077 Office: Epsten & Cornelius 2150 First Ave San Diego CA 92101

CORNELL, DAVID ROGER, hospital administrator; b. Glens Falls, N.Y., Apr. 5, 1944; s. Junius R. and Isabelle R. C.; B.A., U. Vt., 1966; cert. phys. therapy Duke U., 1967; M.B.A., U. S.C., 1973; PhD Columbia Pacific U., 1986; m. Alma Files Cornell, Dec. 16, 1967; children—Kimberley Anne, Kelly Elizabeth. Dir. phys. therapy Univ. Hosp., Augusta, Ga., 1970-72, adminstrv. resident, 1972; adminstrv. asst. Drs. Hosp., Augusta, 1973-74; asst. adminstr. Cypress Community Hosp., Pompano Beach, Fla., 1974; assoc. adminstr. North Ridge Gen. Hosp., Ft. Lauderdale, Fla., 1975-77, adminstr., 1977-79; pres. Mont. Deaconess Med. Center, Great Falls, 1979—; dir. First Bank System, Great Falls. Bd. dirs. Mont. unit ARC. Served with U.S. Army, 1968-69. Fellow Am. Acad. Med. Adminstrs., Am. Coll. Health Care Adminstrs., Am. Coll. Health Execs.; mem. Am. Hosp. Assn. (del. 1984—), Mont. Hosp. Assn., Beta Gamma Sigma. Clubs: Rotary, Meadowlark Country. Office: Mont Deaconess Med Ctr 1106 26th St S Great Falls MT 59405

CORNELL, GARY WARREN, state forestry official; b. Utica, N.Y., Sept. 4, 1951; s. William Fredrick and Marie (Detraglia) C.; m. Patricia Wright, July 1, 1976 (div. Oct. 1978); m. Jean C. Reddoor, Sept. 10, 1982; (div. Oct. 1984); children—Denise, Chris. B.S. in Forest Mgmt., No. Ariz. U., 1973. Firefighter, USDA Forest Service, Camelo, Ariz., 1967-70, 71-72, forestry tech. supr., Sierra Vista, Ariz., 1973-75; asst. area forester Utah State Lands and Forestry Dept., Heber City, 1976-77, area forester, 1977-78, fire mgmt. officer, Salt Lake City, 1978—. Developer, instr. basic wildland fire course, Utah. Tech. Coll., 1980. Recipient cert. Appreciation USDA Forest Service Nat. Forest, 1981, Park City Vol. Fire Dept., 1981. Mem. Soc. Am. Foresters, Am. Forestry Assn., Utah County Chief Fire Officers Assn., Forestry Conservation Communications Assn. (agy. rep. 1978—), Intermountain Fire Council (agy. rep. 1978—), Gt. Basin Incident Mgmt. Team, Western Fire Mgrs. Office: Utah State Lands and Forestry 355 W North Temple 3 Triad Center Suite 400 Salt Lake City UT 84180

CORNETT, LAUREEN ELIZABETH, photographer; b. San Diego, Nov. 14, 1946; d. Clarence Alex and Barbara Ann (Mesku) Lane; m. Bruce Walter Cornett, Oct. 17, 1981; children: Cherie Ann, Robert Michael, John David. Student, San Diego State U., 1964-70. Exec. sec. Boyle Engring., San Diego, 1964-69, Design Cons., San Diego, 1969-71; owner Laureen's Secretarial Service, San Diego, 1979-83; exec. sec. Covi Corp., San Diego, 1979-83; owner Word Processing Co., San Diego, 1982-84; owner, photographer Panoramix, San Diego, 1984—. Photographer for brochures, newspaper ads. Mem. Communicating Arts Group San Diego, San Diego C. of C., Better Bus. Bur. Democrat. Methodist. Office: Panoramix PO Box 15323 San Diego CA 92115

CORNETTE, WILLIAM MAGNUS, scientist, research director; b. San Francisco, Apr. 17, 1945; s. William Magnus and Elisabeth Louise (Stone) C.; m. Patricia Ruth King, Mar. 24, 1968 (div. Oct. 1981); children: Christopher Scott, David Warren; m. Sylvia Annette Martin, Jan. 6, 1982; 1 child, Jennifer Nicole. BS with high honors, U. Fla., 1967; MS, U. Chgo., 1969; PhD, U. Denver, 1973. Mathematician Naval Weapons Ctr., China Lake, Calif., 1973-77; specialist engr. Boeing Co., Seattle, 1977-80; v.p., dir. Photon Research Assocs., La Jolla, Calif., 1980—; cons. Denali Software Systems, San Diego, 1983—. Contbr. articles to profl. jours. Served with USAF, 1969-73. Mem. Optical Soc. Am., Optical Soc. San Diego, Soc. Photo-Optical Instrumentation Engrs., Sierra Club, Wilderness Soc., Germany Philatelic Soc. (working group chmn. 1985—), Phi Beta Kappa, Sigma Xi. Avocations: backpacking, river running, photography. Home: 7905 Port Royale Dr San Diego CA 92126 Office: Photon Research Assocs 3377 N Torrey Pines Ct La Jolla CA 92037

CORNTHWAITE, RUTH LOUISE, marketing professional; b. Harbor City, Calif., June 26, 1958; d. William Guy and Nancy Jane (Hirl) C. BS in Communication Arts, Calif. State Poly. U., Pomona, 1984. Mktg. mgr. Jr. Achievement, Anaheim, Calif., 1984—. Mem. Pub. Relations Soc. Am. (Lindbeck Meml. scholar, 1984). Republican. Avocations: cooking, swimming, tennis. Home: 600 Central Ave #128 Riverside CA 92507 Office: Jr Achievement 730 N Euclid Suite 211 Anaheim CA 92801

CORNWELL, JAMES EDWARD, insurance sale executive; b. Covina, Calif., Aug. 25, 1947; s. Arthur Wheeler and Patricia (Purcell) C.; m. Donna Jean Watkins, Jan. 29, 1972 (div. Feb. 1979); m. Carla Dobbs, Mar. 17, 1979; children: Lester, Greg, Phillip. AA, Fresno City Coll., 1969. CLU, chartered fin. cons. Mgr. Snoking Stamp, Inc., Lynnwood, Wash., 1971-73; life ins. agt. Conn. Mut. Life Ins. Co., Fresno, Calif., 1973-82; life ins. sales mgr. Pacific Mutual Life Ins. Co., Fresno, 1982-83; life ins. mgr. Met. Life Ins. Co., Bakersfield, Calif., 1983—. Mem. Estate Planning Council, Bakersfield, 1984—. Served as cpl. USMC, 1966-68, Vietnam. Mem. Am. Soc. CLU (edn. chmn. 1985—, v.p. 1986—, pres. Bakersfield chpt. 1987-88), Nat. Assn. Life Underwriters, Fresno Life Underwriters (membership com. 1978-79), Life Underwriter Tng. Council (instr. bus. ins. 1982-83, 86-87). Republican. Club: Clovis Water Ski (Fresno) (pres. 1979-80). Lodges: Lions (pres. Fresno club 1979-80), Rotary (sec. Bakersfield chpt. 1986, bd. dirs. 1987-89). Avocations: snow skiing, slalom water skiing, flying, snorkeling, tennis. Home: 5905 Preston Ct Bakersfield CA 93309 Office: Met Ins Co 200 New Stine Rd #295 Bakersfield CA 93309

CORNYN, JOHN EUGENE, III, management consultant; b. Evanston, Ill., May 5, 1945; s. John Eugene and Virginia Ryder (Shannahan) C.; m. Alice Patricia Sellers, May 8, 1965 (div. Apr. 1974) 1 child, Kelly. B.S. in Hotel and Restaurant Adminstrn., Okla. State U., 1968. Mgr. Indian Trail Restaurant, Winnetka, Ill., 1970-71; employee services mgr. Zenith Corp., Chgo., 1971-72; mgr. Red Lion Corp., Portland, Oreg., 1973; cons. Pannell, Kerr, Forster, Chgo., 1973-75; pres., owner John Cornyn & Assocs., Portland 1976—; v.p. Seven Seas, Inc., Winnetka, Ill., 1978—, All Seas, Inc., Winneka, 1980—. Served to 1st lt. U.S. Army, 1968-70. Mem. Foodservice Cons. Soc. Internat. (chmn. mgmt. cons. com. 1983—), Inst. Mgmt. Cons. Republican. Club: Portland City. Home: 3350 NE Holladay St Portland OR 97232 Office: John Cornyn & Assocs 917 SW Oak St Suite 312 Portland OR 97205

CORONITI, FERDINAND VINCENT, physics educator, consultant; b. Boston, June 14, 1943; s. Samuel Charles and Ethel Marie (Havlik) C.; m. Patricia Ann Smith, Aug. 30, 1969; children: Evelyn Marie, Samuel Thomas. A.B., Harvard U., 1965; Ph.D., U. Calif.-Berkeley, 1969. Research physicist UCLA, 1967-70, asst. prof. physics, 1970-74, assoc. prof., 1974-78, prof. physics and astronomy, 1978—; cons. TRW Systems. Contbr. articles to sci. jours. NASA grantee, 1974; NSF grantee, 1974. Mem. Am. Geophys. Union, Am. Astron. Soc., Internat. Union Radiol. Sci., Am. Phys. Soc. Home: 10475 Almayo Ave Los Angeles CA 90064 Office: UCLA Dept Physics 401 Hilgard Ave Los Angeles CA 90024

CORRENTI, JOHN DAVID, steel company executive; b. Rochester, N.Y., Apr. 1, 1947; s. Nicholas William and Sara Rita (Annalora) C.; m. Dawn Jane Major, Nov. 22, 1980; 1 child, Nicholas John. BCE, Clarkson U., 1969. Supr. of contrn. U.S. Steel, Pitts., 1969-80; v.p., gen. mgr. Nucor Corp., Plymouth, Utah, 1980—. Mem. Gov's. Club, Salt Lake City. Mem. Iron and Steel Inst. Republican. Lodges: Rotary, Elks. Home: 901 N Main St Brigham City UT 84302 Office: Nucor Steel PO Box 488 Plymouth UT 84330

CORRIGAN, MICHAEL EDWARD, investment executive; b. Northfield, Minn., Jan. 3, 1955; s. Robert Willoughby Corrigan and Mary Kathryn Corrigan-Welsh; children: Cailen O'Neill, Daniel Thomas. BA, Evergreen State Coll., 1977; MBA, U. Wash., 1978. Account exec. Merrill Lynch, Pierce, Fenner & Smith, Inc., subs. Merrill Lynch & Co., Inc., Seattle, 1979-81, regional mgr. tax investments, 1981-82; v.p. mktg. Great Northern Insured Annuity Corp., Seattle, 1982-85; pres. Gibraltar Fin. Securities Corp., Beverly Hills, Calif., 1985—, also bd. dirs. Mem. Interfin. Assn. Democrat. Episcopalian. Clubs: Wash. Athletic, Snohomish Track (Seattle). Avocation: track and field. Home: 1803 N Courtney Ave Los Angeles CA 90046 Office: Gibraltar Fin Securities Corp 9111 Wilshire Blvd Beverly Hills CA 90210

CORRY, LAWRENCE LEE, sugar company executive; b. Portland, Oreg., Oct. 31, 1939; s. Rowland Parry and Clara Hannah (Orton) C.; m. Rhea Kathleen Reeder, May 29, 1964; children—Kamille, Todd L., Matthew D., Jill, Steffani, Melanee. A.S. in Bus. Mgmt., Weber State Coll., 1959; B.A., Brigham Young U., 1963, M.B.A., 1965. Indsl. engr. Arabian Am. Oil Co., Saudi Arabia, 1958; fin. analyst Standard Oil Co. Calif., San Francisco, Houston, 1965-68; fin. analyst, asst. to pres. Amalgamated Sugar Co., Ogden, Utah, 1968-73, dist. agrl. mgr., Nampa, Idaho, 1973-75, dir. indsl. and pub. relations, Ogden, Utah, 1975-77, v.p., 1977-84, exec. v.p., 1984—; mem. Dept. Agrl. Mktg. Allotment Task Force, 1986-74; dir. Curtis Grain Co. Mem. North Ogden City Citizens Planning Commn., 1973. Mem. Am. Soc. Sugarbeet Technologists. Clubs: Rotary (Nampa); Kiwanis (Ogden). Mormon. Home: 5547 S 100 East St Ogden UT 84405 Office: Amalgamated Sugar Co 2400 Washington Blvd Ogden UT 84401

CORSE, DEAN MCNEIL-COLONSAY, federal civil servant; b. N.Y.C., Dec. 16, 1919; s. Murray Pichot and Lilla Elizabeth Benham Pierce (Dielman) C.; m. Robyn Patrick Bell, June 13, 1972; stepchildren—Robert Huntley Bell, Steven Jeffrey Bell. Student Parsons Sch. Design, N.Y.C., 1938-41; B.S., Northeastern U., 1970; M.A., Emerson Coll., 1978. Lic. broadcaster FCC. Writer, broadcaster for French Govt., Morocco, 1953-56; broadcaster Armed Forces Network, Casablanca, Rabat, Morocco, 1952-56, Italy, 1956-60; weekly columnist On the Road to Rabat, The Moroccan

Courier, 1952-56; v.p., sec. Inc. Meliphon, parent orgn. WRNW-Radio, Mt. Kisco, N.Y, 1960-62; program dir., chief announcer The Concert Network, Boston, 1962-64; writer, editor Boston, N.Y.C., 1964-66; lectr. communications arts Emerson Coll., Boston, 1966-69; sole practitioner in restoration of Colonial houses, Boston, 1969-78; quality control mgmt. specialist U.S. Navy, Alameda, Calif., 1980—; lectr. to ROTC, San Francisco. Served with U.S. Army, 1942-46. Mem. Actor's Equity Assn., Mil. Order of Loyal Legion of U.S., English Speaking Union, Airborne Assn., Navy League, Aztec Club of 1847, Soc. Cin. (pres. Calif. Assn.), S.A.R. (past pres. San Francisco chpt.), Assn. U.S. Army, Armed Forces Broadcasters Assn., Social Register. Episcopalian.

CORSO, PHILIP DANIEL, real estate broker, developer, instructor; b. Jersey City, June 9, 1952; s. Salvatore and Ann (Bradican) C.; m. Deborah S. Mahalick, Dec. 14, 1979; children: Michael, Jeffrey. BA, Wilkes Coll., 1974; MA, Ariz. State U., 1977. Lic. real estate broker; cert. tchr., Ariz. Tchr. Washington Schs., Phoenix, 1975-77; real estate salesman, mgr. Bud Melcher Realtors, Phoenix, 1977-80; chief exec. officer, pres. PCI Assocs. Ltd., Scottsdale, Ariz., 1980—; instr. Ariz. Sch. of Real Estate, Scottsdale, 1979—; bd. dirs., organizer Scottsdale Savs. and Loan. Mem. Nat. Assn. of Office Parks, Nat. Assn. of Realtors, Scottsdale C. of C. (bd. dirs. 1986), Urban Land Inst. Republican. Avocations: skiing, sailing, traveling. Office: PCI Assocs Ltd 6991 E Camelback 0220 Scottsdale AZ 85251

CORSON, GALE CHAPMAN, engineering and management consultant; b. Los Angeles, Apr. 15, 1934; s. Asa LeRoy and Merna Louise (Chapman) C.; B.S. in Bus. Adminstrn. with honors, Aurora Coll., 1955; B.S. in Engring., UCLA, 1960, M.B.A., 1964; m. Anita Jeanne Durr, June 12, 1953; children—Don, Glen, Diana. Engr., Aeroquip Corp., Burbank, Calif., 1955-59; engr. Parker Hannifin Corp., Los Angeles, 1960-61; contracts adminstr. Hughes Aircraft Corp., Culver City, Calif., 1962-65; treas., bus. mgr. Aurora (Ill.) Coll., 1965-74; chief engr. Nissen Corp., Cedar Rapids, Iowa, 1974-76; gen. mgr., pres. Center 4 Engring., Redmond, Oreg., 1977-82; pres. Gale C. Corson Engring., Bend, Oreg., 1982—; v.p. engring. Energy Kinematics Inc., Springfield, Oreg., 1983-84; interim dir. Citizens' Utility Bd. of Oreg., 1984-86. Chmn., Central Oreg. Energy Policy Com., 1979-81. Registered profl. engr., Calif., Oreg., Iowa. Mem. Architects-Engrs. Soc. Central Oreg. (past pres.), ASME, IEEE, ASTM, ASHRAE. Methodist. Author: Hydroelectric Power Resources in the Pacific N.W., 1981; contbr. articles to profl. jours. Home: 594 SE Craven Rd Bend OR 97702

CORTÉS, CARLOS ELISEO, history educator; b. Oakland, Calif., Apr. 6, 1934; s. Carlos Federico and Florence Frieda (Hoffman) C.; m. Laurel Vermilyea, Apr. 26, 1986; 1 child, Alana Madrugada. BA in Communications and Pub. Policy, U. Calif., Berkeley, 1956; MS in Journalism, Columbia U., 1957; B in Fgn. Trade, Am. Inst. for Fgn. Trade, 1962; MA in Portuguese and Spanish, U. N.Mex., 1965, PhD in History, 1969. Lab. asst. Jensen-Salsbery Chem. Co., Kansas City, Mo., 1952; cable splicer Whitaker Cable Corp., North Kansas City, Mo., 1953-54; editor Univ. Calif. yearbook Blue and Gold, Berkeley, 1955-56; gen. asst. Boxoffice Mag., Kansas City, Mo., 1956; asst. to dir. of pub. relations Am. Shakespeare Festival, Stratford, Conn., 1957; exec. editor Phoenix Sunpapers, 1959-61; proofreader Am. Men of Sci., Tempe, Ariz., 1961; reporter AP, Phoenix, 1961; asst. to dir. area studies Am. Inst. Fgn. Trade, Phoenix, 1961-62; teaching machine programmer Learning Inc., Tempe, 1961-62; acting asst. prof. history U. Calif., Riverside, 1968-69, asst. prof. history, 1969-72, chmn. Latin Am. Studies, 1969-71, asst. to vice chancellor for acad. affairs, 1970-72, assoc. prof. history, 1972-76, 1972-76, chmn.Chicano Studies Program, 1972-79, prof. history, 1976—, chmn. dept. history, 1982-86; cons. in field to govt. agys., sch. systems, univs., mass media and pvt. bus.; lectr.in field. Author numerous books and articles to profl. jours. Served with U.S. Army, 1957-59. Kraft scholar; recipient numerous grants and fellowships, Vernon J. Scott award, Hubert Herring Meml. award, Pacific Coast Council on Latin Am. Studies, 1974, Disting. Teaching award, U. Calif.-Riverside, 1976, Eleanor Fishburn award, Washington EdPress Assn., 1977 Disting. Calif. Humanist award, Calif. Council for Humanities, 1980, Keys to the City, Kansas City, Mo. and Kansas City, Kans., 1982; named Bildner Fellow, Assn. Am. Schs. in South Am.; fellow Japan Found., 1986, Rockefeller Found., 1986-87. Mem. AAUP, Am. Hist. Assn., Assn. Supervision and Curriculum Devel., Assn. Borderlands Scholars, Assn. Calif. Intergroup Relations Educators, Calif. Council for Social Studies, Conf. on Latin Am. History, Historians Film Com., Immigration History Soc., Internat. Assn. Audio-Visual Media in Hist. Research and Edn., Internat. Communication Assn., Latin Am. Studies Assn., Nat. Assn. Chicano Studies, Nat. Council Social Studies, Pacific Coast Council on Latin Am. Studies, Social Sci. Edn. Consortium, Soc. for Study of Multi-Ethnic Lit. of the U.S., So. Calif. Social Sci. Assn., Western History Assn., Phi Beta Kappa, Phi Alpha Theta, Phi Kappa Phi. Home: 3088 Pine St Riverside CA 92501 Office: U Calif Dept History Riverside CA 92521

CORTES, MICHAEL EDUARDO, academic director; b. Berkeley, Calif., May 15, 1946; m. Susan Elaine Jankowski, Aug. 27, 1966 (div. Dec. 1982); two children. AB, U. Calif., Berkeley, 1968, M Pub. Policy, 1976, postgrad., 1982—; MSW, U. Mich., 1971. Project dir. Interstate Research Assocs., Washington and S. Tex., 1971-74; v.p. Nat. Council of La Raza, Washington, 1977-80; dir. planning, fin. and adminstrn. Levi Strauss Found., San Francisco, 1980-82; dir. pub. policy Summer Inst. U. Calif., Berkeley, 1984—; cons. in policy research and pub. mgmt. Author: Handicapped Migrant Farm Workers, 1976; contbr. articles to profl. jours. Mem. Equal Rights for Fathers, Albany, Calif., 1980—. Recipient Music Achievement award Bank of Am., 1964. Mem. Nat. Assn. Social Workers, Assn. for Pub. Policy Analysis and Mgmt., Raza Alumni Assn. Democrat. Mem. Unitarian Ch. Avocations: chamber music, computers, bicycling, hiking. Office: U Calif Grad Sch Pub Policy 2607 Hearst Ave Berkeley CA 94720

CORTESE, RICHARD ANTHONY, computer company executive; b. New London, Conn., Dec. 4, 1942; s. Anthony John and Winifred Silvia (Beebe) C.; m. Susan Louise Turner, Feb. 13, 1965 (div. 1973); m. Cindy Sue Folsom, Feb. 9, 1982; children: Cynthia Ann, Jennifer Lynn. BS, U. So. Calif., 1965, MBA, 1967. Fin. dir. Nat. Semiconductor Corp., Santa Clara, Calif., 1973-78; fin. control dir. TRW Corp., Los Angeles, 1978-79; v.p. fin. Northern Telecom Systems Corp., Minn. and Calif., 1979-80; v.p., gen. mgr. Gen. Automation Inc., Anaheim, Calif., 1980-82; pres., chief exec. officer Alpha Microsystems, Santa Ana, Calif., 1982—, also bd. dirs.; mem. adv. bd. Bus.-to-Bus., RimTech, Los Angeles, 1985—; bd. dirs. So. Calif. Tech. Network. Active Young Pres.'s Orgn., Orange County, Calif. Named All-Am. in track and field NCAA, 1964, All-Am. in track and field AAU, 1964. Mem. Computer Communication Industry Assn. (mem. exec. com. 1983—), SoCal 10 (founding mem., bd. dirs. 1983—). Club: Chancellor's. Avocations: reading.

CORTEZ, JOSE ONESIMO, college administrator, vocational educator, consultant; b. Laredo, Tex., Jan. 20, 1942; s. Onesimo and Herminia (Obregon) C.; m. Bonnie Jean Frampton, Jan. 4, 1964 (div.); children—Sonya, Mathew, Carl. B.A. cum laude, Calif. State U., Long Beach, 1976, M.A., 1980. Tool and die maker Huck Mfg. Co., Carson, Calif., 1971-76; indsl. engr. ITT Cannon Electric, Santa Ana, Calif., 1976-78; asst. prof. metals tech. Los Angeles Trade Tech. Coll., 1978-83, asst. dean, 1983—, instr. tool and die making, numerical control, 1978—; cons. in field; mem. com. on gen. edn. Community Coll. State Chancellor, Sacramento, 1982, mem. task force on acad. quality, 1983. Los Angeles Trade Tech. Coll. Pres.'s grantee, 1981. Mem. Computer Assisted Systems Assn., Soc. Mfg. Engrs., Am. Vocat. Assn., Phi Kappa Phi, Epsilon Pi Tau. Democrat. Roman Catholic. Office: Los Angeles Trade Tech Coll 400 W Washington Blvd Los Angeles CA 90015

CORTINES, RAMON, Supt. of schools city of San Francisco. Office: San Francisco Sch Dist Office of the Supt of Schools 135 Van Ness Ave San Francisco CA 94102 *

CORTNER, GARY VICTOR, criminalist; b. Sanger, Calif., Apr. 6, 1947; s. Victor Henry and Edith (Lombardi) C.; m. Sandra Lee Barros, Oct. 13, 1973; children: Alysia M., Tara E. AA, Fresno City Coll., 1967; BA in Chemistry, Calif. State U., Fresno, 1972, MS in Criminology, 1977. Criminalist I Calif. Dept. Justice, Sacramento, 1972; criminalist I, II, III Calif. Dept. Justice, Fresno, 1972-75, 75-77, 78—. Recipient Homicide Investigation award Clovis Police Dept., 1976. Mem. Calif. Assn. Criminalists, Cen. Valley Arson Investigators Assn. (pres. 1983), Am. Chem. Soc., Phi Kappa Phi. Democrat. Roman Catholic. Avocations: guitar, softball, hunting, photography. Office: Calif Dept Justice Fresno Regional Lab 6014 N Cedar Fresno CA 93710

CORTNER, JAY CURTIS, chemical executive, engineer; b. Herlong, Calif., Sept. 30, 1954; s. James Clarence and Maureen L. (McDonnel) C.; m. Jeannette Moss Trompeter, Aug. 24, 1985. BS in Chemistry, U. N.Mex., 1978, MSChemE, 1980. Chem. engr. Dow Chemical Co., Freeport, Tex., 1979; chemist Octopus System, Albuquerque, 1980-83; chem. engr. Hanna Industries, Portland, Oreg., 1983-85; prin. Chemtech Chem. Corp., Santa Ana, Calif., 1985—. Patentee in field. Mem. Am. Chem. Soc. Republican. Avocations: sports, treasure hunting. Office: Chemtech Chem Corp 2760 S Grand Ave Santa Ana CA 92705

CORWIN, JEFFREY TODD, biology educator; b. Riverhead, N.Y., Oct. 15, 1951; s. Frank Madison and Muriel Ester (Stein) C. BS, Cornell U., 1973; MS, U. Hawaii, 1975; PhD, U. Calif., San Diego, 1980. NIH postdoctoral fellow Lab. of Marine Biol Assn. U.K., Plymouth, Eng., 1980-81; asst. to assoc. prof. neurobiology and zoology U. Hawaii, Honolulu, 1981—; assoc. dir. summer program Grass Found., Woods Hole, Mass., 1984-85. Contbr. articles to profl. jours. Recipient Nat. Research Service award USPHS, 1980, NIH Research Career Devel. award USPHS, 1986; Grass fellow, 1983. Mem. Internat. Soc. Neuroethology, Soc. Neurosci., Am. Soc. Cell Biology, Am. Soc. Zoologists, Assn. Research Otolaryngology, Hawaii Neurosci. Group (pres. 1985—), Honolulu Zoo Hui. Avocations: sailing, fishing, ice hockey. Office: U Hawaii 1993 East-West Rd Honolulu HI 96822

CORWIN, VICTORIA LYNN, retail executive; b. Mpls., May 8, 1959; d. Milton Harris and Sheila Rae (Markus) Corwin. BA in Econs., Wellesley Coll., 1981. Mgr. in tng. The Gap Stores, Inc., San Jose, Calif., 1982, store mgr., 1982-83, inventory analyst, 1983-84; inventory analyst Mervyn's, Hayward, Calif., 1984; owner The Postery, Phoenix, Ariz., 1984—. Republican. Jewish. Office: The Postery 1912 E Camelback Rd Phoenix AZ 85016

CORY, JOHN THOMAS, engineer, accountant; b. Elko, Nev., Mar. 7, 1942; s. John Lloyd and Anita Paddock (McElrath) C.; m. Patricia Hinckley Ashton, Aug. 26, 1966; 1 child, Jean Trisha. BS in Engring. Sci., U. Nev., 1968, MS in Nuclear Engring., 1969, postgrad., 1969-70. Registered profl. engr., Wis. Nuclear engr. Puget Sound Naval Yard, Bremerton, Wash., 1970-72; sr. engr. Aerojet Nuclear Co., Idaho Falls, Idaho, 1972-74; start up and test engr. Babcock and Wilcox Co., Lynchburg, Va., 1974-76; mason Ashton Constn. Co., Salt Lake City, 1976-77; project engr. Fairbanks-Morse, Beloit, Wis., 1977-79; staff engr. Utah Power & Light Co., Salt Lake City, 1979—; engring. cons. UP&L Co., Salt Lake City, 1979—. Del. Salt Lake County Republican Conv., 1982, 84. Mem. Sigma Xi, Phi Kappa Phi, Sigma Tau. Republican. Mormon. Club: Toastmasters (v.p. 1984) (Salt Lake City). Avocations: home remodeling, swimming, music. Home: 2060 Evergreen Ave Salt Lake City UT 84109 Office: Utah Power and Light Co. 1407 W North Temple Salt Lake City UT 84116

COSART, WILLIAM PRIMM, engineering educator, academic administrator; b. Chgo., Jan. 17, 1936; s. Lee D. and Jacqueline (Primm) C.; m. Nanette Otness, June 1957; children: Jann M., Jill M., Kara J. BSChemE, Stanford U., 1958, MSChemE, 1960; PhD, Oreg. State U., 1973. Research assoc. Oreg. Primate Ctr., Beaverton, 1962-64; asst. prof. chem. engring. U. Ariz., Tucson, 1968-73, assoc. prof., 1973—, asst. dean mines, 1972-81, acting dean mines, 1981-84, assoc. dean engring., 1984—. Served to lt. Chem. Corps, U.S. Army, 1960-62. Recipient Outstanding Teaching award U. Ariz., 1972. Mem. Am. Inst. Chem. Engrs. (chmn. edn. program 1980—, Outstanding Student chpt. advisor 1978), Mining Club of S.W. (bd. dirs. 1982-86), Sigma Xi, Tau Beta Pi (life). Republican. Episcopalian. Avocations: hiking, music, photography. Office: U Ariz Coll Engring and Mines Tucson AZ 85721

COSGROVE, JOAN NALEZYTY, speech-language pathologist; b. Detroit, Aug. 1, 1935; d. Walter Clement and Florence (Somerfeldt) Nalezyty; children: Michael, Sean, Kelly, Christopher. BS, Wayne State U., 1957; MS, U. Miss., 1969. Dir. speech lang. pathology dept. Millard Fillmore Hosp., Buffalo, 1976-83, R.I. Nursing Home Co., Buffalo, 1983-84; speech-lang. pathologist Cen. Consolidated, Shiprock, N.Mex., 1984—; cons. SUNYAB Sch. of Nursing, Buffalo, 1975-76; presenter telephone lecture network Med. Edn. Services, Buffalo, 1975-80. Author: Assessment and Intervention in Language Disorders. Pres. PTA, Jackson, Miss., 1957, Buffalo, 1975, 77. Mem. Am. Speech-Lang. Hearing Assn. (cert.), N.Y. State Speech-Lang. Hearing Assn. (del. 1982-84), Speech Hearing Lang. Assn. of Western N.Y. (2d v.p. 1976-77, 82-83), Bd. Stroke Assn. Western N.Y. Home: PO Box 3563 Shiprock NM 87420

COSGROVE, THOMAS JOHN, academic administrator; b. Jamaica, N.Y., Mar. 18, 1940; s. James Thomas and Helen Veronica (Gilmore) C.; m. Karen Lee Kraus, Aug. 1935; children: Jennifer Ellen, Sean David James. BA in English, U. Dayton, 1961; MA in Theology, St. Louis U., 1971; MEd in Counseling, U. San Diego, 1975, EdD in Ednl. Leadership, 1984. Tchr. Chaminade High Sch., Mineoli, N.Y., 1961-64, 65-66, Colegio San Jose, San Juan, Puerto Rico, 1964-65; program coordinator The Cir. U., Reno, 1969-70; tchr. Convent of Sacred Heart, El Cajon, Calif., 1970-72; program coordinator U. San Diego, 1972-73, assoc. dean students, 1973—; dir. Univ. Ctr., 1986—. Contbr. articles to profl. jours. Bd. dirs. San Diego Crew Classic, 1982-85; v.p. bd. dirs. San Diego Rowing Council, 1985-86; bd. dirs. Friends of San Diego Rowing, 1979—. Mem. Nat. Assn. Campus Activities (nat. com. chmn. 1986—, host dir. programming west workshop 1978, 1983-85, chmn. leadership com. 1986—), Assn. Coll. Unions Internat. (host com. nat. conv. 1985), Am. Personnel and Guidance Assn., U. San Diego Sch. Edn. Alumni Assn. (bd. dirs. 1980-82). Democrat. Roman Catholic. Avocations: rowing, tennis, art, photography, music. Office: U San Diego Alcala Park San Diego CA 92110

COSSMAN, PAUL JOSEPH, lawyer; b. Maywood, Calif., July 3, 1955; s. Harry and Ann Sabina (Kohn) C.; m. Julia Elizabeth Bishop, June 14, 1980. BA, Humboldt State U., 1980; JD, U. Oreg., 1984. Bar: Oreg. 1984, U.S. Dist. Ct. Oreg., Wash. 1985, U.S. Dist. Ct. (we. dist.) Wash., Alaska, 1985; U.S. Dist Ct. Alaska. Law clk. to Judge Douglas Spences Eugene, Oreg., 1984-85; lawyer Bernard P. Kelly & Assocs., Anchorage, 1985—. Mem. Am. Trial Lawyers Assn. (pub. affairs rep. for Alaska, 1986—), Order of Coif, Nat. Panel of Consumer Arbitrators. Democrat. Office: Bernard P Kelly & Assocs 310 K St Suite 506 Anchorage AK 99501

COSTA, LUCIO GUIDO, toxicologist; b. Milan, Oct. 14, 1954; came to U.S., 1980; s. Ugo and Silvia (Trisolini) C. PhD, U. Milan, 1977. Postdoctoral fellow U. Tex., Houston, 1980-81, research scientist, 1982-83; research asst. prof. U. Wash., Seattle, 1983-87; research assoc. prof. U. Washington, Seattle, 1987—. Contbr. articles to profl. jours. Fellow N.Y. Acad. Scis.; mem. Soc. Toxicology, Soc. Neurosci., Internat. Neurotoxicology Assn. (charter). Roman Catholic. Office: U Wash Dept Environ Health SC-34 Seattle WA 98195

COSTANDI, WAHIB ASSAAD, accounting educator; b. Cairo, Jan. 16, 1939; came to U.S., 1966; s. Assad and Alice (Aristidis) C.; m. Mireille Rothstein, July 3, 1969. BSc in Chemistry, Am. U., Cairo, 1964; MBA, U. San Francisco, 1974; PhD in Fin., U. Santa Clara, 1981. Sr. fin. analyst Memorex, Santa Clara, Calif., 1970-74; mgr. cost acctg. Precision Monolithic, Santa Clara, 1974-75; mgr. ops. acctg. IVC, Sunnyvale, Calif., 1975-78; v.p. fin. 3H Industries, Sunnyvale, 1980-84; assoc. prof. bus. adminstrn. San Jose (Calif.) State U., 1984—; fin. and acctg. cons. Mem. Am. Acctg. Assn., Am. Fin. Assn., Nat. Acctg. Assn. Home: 22999 Voss Ave Cupertino CA 95014 Office: San Jose State U Dept Fin Acctg Sch Bus Adminstrn San Jose CA 95192-0066

COSTANTINO, MARSHALL UGO, credit official; b. West Palm Beach, Fla., Apr. 19, 1949; s. Ugo A. and Gloria R. C.; m. Sharon London, Sept. 22, 1974; 1 son, David Adam. B.S., U. Fla., 1972; M.S., S.D. State U., 1975. Credit research mgr. Diners Club Internat., Denver, 1976-79; credit policy mgr. Citicorp Person-to-Person Fin. Services, Inc., Aurora, Colo., 1979-83; asst. v.p. Citicorp Retail Services, Inc., Englewood, Colo., 1983—; pres. Analysis, Research & Design, Inc.; instr. Webster U., also other teaching assignments. Served to capt. USAF, 1972-76. Mem. Ops. Research Soc. Am. (chpt. treas. 1982—), Assn. Managerial Economists, Am. Statis. Assn. Author: A Handbook for Time Series Analysis and Prediction, 1981. Home: 8062 S Niagara Way Englewood CO 80112 Office: Citicorp Retail Services Inc 5889 Greenwood Plaza Blvd Englewood CO 80111

COSTELLO, DANIEL WALTER, banker; b. Mich., June 17, 1930; s. Walter William and Rose Angela (Dimond) C.; B.S. in Engring. Sci., Purdue U., 1952; children: Michael Joseph, Colleen Marie. Various sales, mktg. and real estate positions Shell Oil Co., 1955-63; dir. real estate and constrn., planning mgr. Ford Motor Co., U.S. and Can., 1963-71; dir. real estate devel. and constrn. Ford Land Devel. Corp., Dearborn, Mich., 1971-75; chmn. Am. Express Realty Mgmt. Co., N.Y.C., 1975—; corporate sr. v.p. real estate and gen. services Am. Express Co. and subs., N.Y.C., 1975-82; exec. v.p. corp. real estate div. Bank of Am., San Francisco, 1982—. Served with U.S. Army, 1952-56; Korea. Mem. Nat. Assn. Rev. Appraisers (bd. dirs.), Internat. Real Estate Inst. (bd. govs.), Nat. Assn. Corp. Real Estate Execs., San Francisco Real Estate Bd. (cert. master corp. real estate), Bldg. Owners and Mgrs. Assn. Theta Xi. Clubs: Meadows Country; San Francisco Bankers. Office: Bank of Am Nat Trust & Savs Assoc Bank of Am Ctr 555 California St San Francisco CA 94104

COSTELLO, JOHN JAMES, restaurateur; b. Fresno, Calif., July 9, 1959; s. Leo Francis and Nadine Theresa (Rocha) C. BA in Communications, Santa Clara U., 1981. Talent agy. operator Sound Ethics Talent Agy., San Jose, Calif., 1981-83; pub. relations agt. PRX Co., Cupertino, Calif., 1982-83; sales rep. ATV Systems, Inc., San Francisco, 1983-84; restaurant analyst Saga Corp., Menlo Park, Calif., 1984—; restaurant mgr. Spoons Grill & Bar, 1986—; freelance photographer Menlo Park, 1977—; disc jockey Mr. DJ, Santa Clara County, Calif., 1981-83; freelance pub. relations agt. Carter, Callahan & Assocs., San Jose, 1983; advisor Career Choice Handbook, Humanities Dept. U. Santa Clara, 1985. Republican. Roman Catholic. Avocations: photography, tennis, golf, bicycling. Home: 1230 Orange Ave Menlo Park CA 94025 Office: Saga Corp 1 Saga Ln Menlo Park CA 94025

COTSAKOS, CHRISTOS MICHAEL, postal shipping executive; b. Paterson, N.J., July 29, 1948; s. Michael John and Lillian (Scoulikas) C.; m. Hannah Batami Fogel, July 1, 1973; 1 child, Suzanne Renee. BA in Communications and Polit. Sci., William Paterson Coll., 1972; MBA, Pepperdine U., 1984. Tour guide Universal Studios, Burbank, Calif., 1973; courier Fed. Express Corp., Burbank, 1973-74; sales rep. Fed. Express Corp., Long Beach, Calif., 1974; sta. mgr. Fed. Express Corp., San Jose, Calif., 1974; we. dist. mgr. Fed. Express Corp., 1974; region engring. mgr. Fed. Express Corp., Denver, 1975; mng. dir. Fed. Express Corp., Chgo., 1975-80; v.p. Fed. Express Corp., Sacramento, Calif., 1980—; instr. Consumers River Coll., Placerville, Calif., 1985-86; bd. dirs. Airlifeline, Sacramento. Served as sgt. U.S. Army, 1967-70, Vietnam. Decorated Bronze Star, 1967, Purple Heart, 1967. Clubs: Sutter, Comstock. Office: Fed Express Corp 8950 Cal Ctr Dr Sacramento CA 95826

COTTER, JEFFREY LEE, pastor; b. Los Angeles, May 14, 1946; s. Lawrence L. and Frankie Marie (Marlow) C.; m. Patricia Allen Hodges, May 19, 1973; children: Meghan, Marlo. BA, UCLA, 1969; M of Divinity, Fuller Theol. Sem., 1973. Ordained to ministry Presbyn. Ch., 1973. Dir. drug rehab. Hollywood (Calif.) First Presbyn. Ch., 1968-71; dir. student ministries Bel Air Presbyn. Ch., Los Angeles, 1971-73; univ. pastor Fremont Presbyn. Ch., Sacramento, Calif., 1973-76, pastor and founder, dir. Logos Study Ctr.,, 1976-79; pastor Santa Ynez Valley Presbyn. Ch., Solvang, Calif., 1979—; speaker Calvin Crest Confs., Fresno, Calif., 1973-78, Young Life Campaign Sacramento Young Life, 1974-78; cons. in Youth Outreach Sacramento Area Youth Ministries, 1974-76; cons. New Ch. Devel. Presbyn. Ch., Santa Barbara; lectr. Japan Ch. Growth Inst., Tokyo, 1986; cons., speaker Nepali Pastors Conf., Nepal. Contbr. articles to profl. jours. Mem. adv. bd. Drug Rehab., Hollywood, Calif., 1968; mem. steering com. Extension Edn. Grad. Theol. Union, Berkeley, Calif., 1981, Fuller Theol. Sem. for Santa Barbara County, 1982-84; preaching pastor for President and Mrs. Ronald Reagan, Santa Ynez Valley, Calif., 1982, 86; mem. gen. council Santa Barbara Presbyetery; co-founder Cross Roads Counseling Ctr., Santa Ynez, Valley Friendship Ctr., Santa Ynez; cons., charter founder Great Commn. Tng. Ctr., Bangalore, India. Named one of Outstanding Young Men of Am., 1975. Mem. Presbyn. Panel (research and mktg. 1982, 84), Serving God Found. (adv. com. bd. dirs. 1984—). Republican. Avocations: piano, competition road bicycle racing, writing. Office: Santa Ynez Presbyn Ch 1825 Alamo Pintado Rd Solvang CA 93463

COTTER, LAWRENCE R., management consultant; b. Albany, Calif., Aug. 13, 1933; s. Malcolm Thompson Cotter and Una Elyse Raffety. AA, U. Calif., Berkeley, 1953, BA in Astronomy, 1956; MS in Bus. Adminstrn., The George Washington U., 1967; PhD in Mgmt. Theory, UCLA, 1977. Commd. USAF, 1956, advanced through grades to col., ret., 1982; orbital analyst, network controller Project Space Track USAF, Bedford, Mass., 1958-61; staff scientist Hdqs. N.Am. Air Def. Command, Colorado Springs, Colo., 1962-66, Hdqrs. USAF, Washington, 1967-70; dir. test and deployment def. support program USAF, Los Angeles, 1975-76; commdr. detachment 1 Electronic Systems Div. USAF, Tehran, Iran, 1976-78; system program dir. Electronic Systems div. USAF, Bedford, Mass., 1978-79; dep. commdr. network plans and devel. AF Satellite Control Facility USAF, Sunnyvale, Calif., 1979-82; mgmt. cons. Berkeley, 1982—; adminstrv. asst. Arnold Air Soc., Washington, 1959-72. Co-author: The Arnold Air Soc. Manual, 1956; (computer program) SPACE, 1970; editor: The Arnold Air Soc. Manual 1964-72. Recipient Departmental Citation U. Calif. Berkeley, 1955, Citation of Honor, Arnold Air Soc., 1967. Mem. AF Assn., The Royal AF Club, Beta Gamma Sigma.

COTTER, WILLIAM JOSEPH, data processing specialist; b. N.Y.C., Jan. 27, 1952; s. William Anthony and Grace Agnes (McCann) C.; m. Carol Roberta Muller, Mar. 17, 1984; 1 child, Margot Grace. BS in Electrical and Computer Engring., Clarkson U., 1973. Computer design engr. Gen. Electric, Pittsfield, Mass., 1973-75; product rep. Honeywell, Albany, N.Y., 1975-76; EDP auditor Walt Disney Prodns., Burbank, Calif., 1976-82; EDP audit mgr. Warner Brothers, Burbank, 1982-84, dir. internat. data processing, 1984—. Cr. correspondent Starlog Mag., 1978—; columnist Movie Collectors World, 1983—, Video Shopper, 1987—; contbr. over 100 articles to profl. jours. Eagle Scout Boy Scouts Am., 1970, troup leader, 1973-76; pres. Tierre Verde Homeowners Assn., Burbank, 1981-86; chmn. supervisory com. 1st Entertainment Fed. Credit Union. Mem. IEEE, EDP Auditors Assn., Confederate Air Force, Experimental Aircraft Assn., Warbirds of Am. Roman Catholic. Avocations: flying airplanes, scuba diving, photography. Office: Warner Brothers 4000 Warner Blvd Burbank CA 91522

COTTINGHAM, SUSAN MARIE, infosystems specialist; b. Denver, July 14, 1950; d. Cyril Francis and Nancy Lee (Meyer) Kipp; m. Ronald Lynn Cottingham, Apr. 26, 1973. BFA, Colo. State U., 1972; postgrad., R.I. Sch. Design, 1972-73. Programmer Larimer County Govt., Ft. Collins, Colo., 1978-81, lead analyst, 1981-84, mgr., 1984—. Mem. Am. Mgmt. Assn., Data Processing Mgmt. Assn., Inst. Cert. Computer Profls. (cert., assoc.), Career Women's Roundtable (co-founder), Am. UNIVAC Users Assn., AAU, Ft. Collins Potter's Guild (v.p. 1977-78). Democrat. Avocations: weightlifting, genealogy, gourmet cooking, gardening.

COTTON, DANIEL FRANCIS LEIGH, hospital management company executive; b. Mt. Vernon, N.Y., Jan. 16, 1931; s. Harold Heath and Dorothy Submit (Avery) C.; B.A., Pacific Union Coll., Angwin, Calif., 1952; M.A., Andrews U., Berrien Springs, Mich., 1954, B.D., 1956; m. Marilyn Dillow, Feb. 27, 1955; children—Patrice Lynn, Jennifer Leigh, Elizabeth Anne, Lori Jean. Assoc. prof. religion Columbia Union Coll., Takoma Park, Md., 1959-62; assoc. prof. religious philosophy Loma Linda (Calif.) U., 1962-69; developer, pres. Heritage Health Care Inc. Loma Linda, 1966—; developer, pres. Loma Linda Community Hosp., 1972-82; pres. Colorado Springs Community Hosp., 1974-78; chmn. bd., chief exec. officer United Med. Mgmt. Inc., 1978—. Chmn. bd. Nat. Child Health Council, 1977-82; chmn. bd., chief exec. officer The Am. Heritage Group, 1986—; pres. Loma Linda Health Care Found., 1979-82; dir., sec. Health Care Funding Corp., 1986—.

Fellow Am. Coll. Health Care Adminstrs.; mem. AAUP, Hosp. Fin. Mgmt. Assn., Loma Linda C. of C. (past dir.). Republican. Club: Rotary. Home: 1300 Propsect Dr Redlands CA 92373 Office: 25271 Barton Rd Loma Linda CA 92354

COTTON, EILEEN GIUFFRÉ, educator; b. Oakland, Calif., Apr. 23, 1947; d. Leonard and Helen Marie (Weiss) Giuffré; B.A., Calif. State U., Hayward, 1968; M.A. in Edn., Calif. State U., Sacramento, 1976; Ph.D. in Adminstrn., Supervision and Curriculum, U. Md., 1979; m. Chester C. Cotton, Apr. 3, 1971. Elem. tchr. Hayward (Calif.) Unified Sch. Dist., 1969-70, Rescue (Calif.) Union Sch. Dist., 1970-72, Chico (Calif.) Unified Sch. Dist., 1972-76; curriculum dir. Crownsville (Md.) Hosp. Center, 1976-77; vis. asst. prof. edn., Calif. State U., Chico, 1978-82, vis. assoc. prof., 1982-84, assoc. prof., 1984-85, 86—, coordinator Elem. Edn. Program, 1986—; chmn. dept. reading U. Guam, Mangilao, 1985-86. Mem. Am. Psychol. Assn., Am. Edn. Research Assn., Calif. Reading Assn., Assn. Supervision and Curriculum Devel., Internat. Reading Assn., Internat. Assn. Applied Psychology, Assn. Calif. Sch. Adminstrs., Phi Delta Kappa, Kappa Delta Pi. Author: A Guide to Community Re-entry, 1977; contbr. to ednl. jours. Office: Calif State U Dept Edn Chico CA 95929-0222

COTTON, ERNEST KUESTER, pediatric medicine educator; b. Denver, Aug. 9, 1927; s. George Kuester Cotton and Frances Ester (Wiegle) Roberts; m. Joan Elizabeth Cotton, Aug. 27, 1949 (div. July 1983); children: George, Melanie, Gerald, Theodor, Ernest, Mary; m. Margo Ann Pinney, Oct. 13, 1984. BS, U. Colo., 1951, MD, 1954. Resident pediatrics Cleve. City HOsp., 1954-58; practice medicine specializing in pediatrics Denver, 1958-61; fellow pulmonary physiology U. Calif., San Francisco, 1961-63; from asst. prof. to assoc. prof. pediatrics U. Colo., Denver, 1963-72, prof., 1972—, dir. Cystic Fibrosis ctr., 1963—, head pediatric pulmonary sect., 1964—; pulmonary cons. Fitzsimons Army Hosp., 1976—, Nat. Jewish Hosp., Denver, 1980—. Contbr. articles to profl. jours. Served with USN, 1945-46, PTO. NIH fellow, San Francisco, 1962-63; grantee NIH, 1975—, Nat. Cystic Fibrosis Found., 1965—. Mem. Am. Pediatrics Soc. (program com.), Am. Thoracic Soc. (sec. 1978-79), Western Soc. Pediatric Research. Democrat. Avocations: skiing, biking, mountain climbing, photography, gardening. Home: 1340 Jersey Denver CO 80220 Office: U Colo Health Scis Ctr 4200 E 9th Ave C220 Denver CO 80262

COUCH, GEORGE WALTER, III, beverage distributor; b. Washington, Sept. 22, 1947; s. George W. Jr. and Geraldine Catherine (Glockner) C. AB in Econs., Stanford U., 1969; MBA, Harvard U., 1971. Securities analyst Fidelity Mgmt., Boston, 1971-73; chmn., pres. Couch Distbg. Co., Watsonville, Calif., 1973—; bd. dirs. Trammell Crow Hotel, Dallas, 1984—. Chmn. governing bd. Cabrillo Community Coll., Aptos, Calif., 1985—; bd. govs. State Bar of Calif., 1982-85. Mem. Calif. Beer and Wine Wholesalers Assn. (bd. dirs. 1984—), Phi Beta Kappa. Democrat. Avocations: breeding and racing thoroughbred horses. Home: 100 Merk Rd Watsonville CA 95076 Office: Couch Distbg Co Inc 104 Lee Rd PO Box 183 Watsonville CA 95077

COUCH, JOHN C., diversified company executive. BS in Engring., U. Mich., 1964, MS in Engring.; MBA, Stanford U., 1976. Chief marine engr. Ingalls Shipbldg. div. Litton Corp., from 1967, pres., chief operating officer, 1976; with Alexander and Baldwin, Inc., exec. v.p., 1985, pres., chief operating officer, 1985—, also bd. dirs. Office: Alexander & Baldwin Inc 822 Bishop St Honolulu HI 96813 *

COUCHER, ROBERT JAMES, engineer; b. Salt Lake City, Jan. 12, 1955; s. Robert George and F. LaDene (Hawkins) C.; m. Shelley L. Zeboray, Aug. 8, 1981 (div. May 1985); m. Marilyn C. King, Nov. 30, 1985. BS in Physics, U. Utah, 1978. Engr. ADDS, Salt Lake City, 1979-81, Tektronix, Beaverton, Oreg., 1981-83; engring. mgr. Tektronix, Forest Grove, Oreg., 1983—. Home: Rt 1 Box 355 Hillsboro OR 97124

COUGHRAN, BRUCE EDWARD, software engineer, computer graphics specialist; b. Kenniwick, Wash., Aug. 29, 1955; s. Edward Henry Coughran and Virginia Marie (Phillips) Johnson; m. Shelley J. Plumb, Apr. 27, 1980; 1 child, Richard Aaron. Diploma, Dick Grove Sch. Music, 1979; BA, U. Calif., San Diego, 1983. Research asst. U. Calif., San Diego, 1981-83; mgr. devices ISSCO, San Diego, 1983-87; graphics and telecommunications specialist Computer Intelligence Corp., La Jolla, Calif., 1987—. Contbr. articles to profl. jours. Mem. IEEE (P610 computer dictionary working group), Assn. Computing Machinery, Spl. Interest Group Graphics, Am. Nat. Standards Inst. (accredited standards com. X3H3 1984—). Home: 4394 Donald Ave San Diego CA 92117 Office: Computer Intelligence Corp 3344 N Torrey Pines Ct La Jolla CA 92037

COULSON, KINSELL LEROY, meteorologist; b. Hatfield, Mo., Oct. 7, 1916; s. Charles Samuel and Nora Madge (Swank) C.; m. Vera Vivien Vainer, Mar. 23, 1947. B.S., Northwest Mo. State Tchrs. Coll., 1942; M.A., UCLA, 1952, Ph.D., 1959. Jr. meteorologist U.S. Weather Bur., Chgo., 1942; meteorologist UN, Shanghai, China, 1946-47, Naval Civil Service, China Lake, Calif., 1950-51; assoc. research meteorologist UCLA, 1951-59; meteorologist Stanford Research Inst., Menlo Park, Calif., 1959-60; mgr. geophysics Gen. Electric Space Scis. Lab., Phila., 1960-65; prof. meteorology U. Calif.-Davis, 1965-79, prof. emeritus, 1984—; dir. Mauna Loa Obs., Hilo, Hawaii, 1979-84; cons., lectr. Author: Solar and Terrestrial Radiation: Methods and Measurements, 1975, (with J.V. Dave and Z. Sekera) Tables Related to Radiation Emerging, From a Planetary Atmosphere with Rayleigh Scattering, 1960; contbr. articles to profl. jours.; patentee atmospheric density calulator. Served with USN, 1943-46. Recipient numerous research grants. Mem. Am. Meteorol. Soc., Am. Geophys. Union, Am. Solar Energy Soc., AAAS, No. Calif. Energy Assn., Planetary Soc., Mauna Kea Astron. Soc., Sigma Xi. Home: 119 Bryce Way Vacaville CA 95688

COULTER, BORDEN MCKEE, JR., management consultant; b. Casper, Wyo., Feb. 9, 1917; s. Borden McKee and Josephine Helen (Grother) C.; B.S., UCLA, 1939, M.B.A., 1947; m. Emily Sawtelle, Aug. 23, 1950; children—Borden, Terry Lynn, Leigh, Richard. Research analyst Australian Nat. R.R., 1939-40; indsl. engr. Lockheed Aircraft, 1940-47, staff indsl. engr., 1948-50; with div. indsl. engring. U.S. Steel Corp., 1947; mgr. prodn. control Bakewell Products, 1947; supr. orgn. and procedures Norris Industries, 1950-53; gen. mgr. Roed Engring. Assos., 1943—; prin., sr. v.p., dir. The Emerson Cons., Inc., mgmt. cons., N.Y.C., 1954—. Mem. Am. Inst. Indsl. Engrs. (pres. Los Angeles), Am. Mgmt. Assn. (Wall of Honor), Am. Inst. Plant Engrs., Nat. Assn. Accountants Am., Newcomen Soc., U.S. Naval Inst., Navy League U.S., Internat. Mgmt. Consultants, Nat. Petroleum Refiners Assn., Am. Arbitration Assn., Nat., Tex. socs. profl. engrs., Houston Soc. Cons. Engrs. Blue Key, Kappa Kappa Psi, Alpha Kappa Psi, Tau Kappa Alpha, Phi Gamma Delta. Club: Petroleum (Houston). Home: 12351 Escala Dr San Diego CA 92128

COULTER, C(LAUDE) ALTON, research physicist, consultant; b. Phenix City, Ala., Mar. 30, 1936; s. Leonard Alton and Winslow Lanae (Gullatt) C.; m. June Karolyn Ketchum, Feb. 6, 1960; children: Kathryn Lanae, Kimberly Lorraine. BA, Samford U., 1956; MS, U. Ala., 1959; MA, Harvard U., 1963, PhD, 1964. Asst. prof. physics U. Ala., Tuscaloosa, 1963-66, from assoc. prof. to prof., 1971-81; from asst. prof. to assoc. prof. Clark U., Worcester, Mass., 1966-71; mem. lab. staff Los Alamos (N.Mex.) Nat. Lab., 1982—; cons. Army Missile Command, Redstone Arsenal, Ala., 1963-81. Contbr. articles to profl. jours. Mem. Am. Phys. Soc., Inst. Nuclear Materials Mgmt., Sigma Xi. Office: Los Alamos Nat Lab N-4 MS E541 Los Alamos NM 87545

COULTER, DEE JOY, neuroscience educator; b. Oak Park, Aug. 20, 1939; d. Clifford Whitney and Phyllis Rose (Marks) Joy; m. John Eugene Coulter, Mar. 23, 1974; 1 child, Scott Whitney. BA in English and Psychology, U. Mich., 1961, MA in Spl. Edn., 1962; EdD in Neurol. Studies, U. No. Colo., 1981. Cert. English and Spl. Edn. tchr. Spl. edn. tchr. Monona Pub. Schs., Madison, Wis., 1963-70; tchr., dir. Outreach Ctr., Englewood, Colo., 1971-73; dir. Tchr. Enrichment Ctr., Englewood, 1973-75; adj. faculty U. No. Colo., Boulder, 1975—, Naropa Inst., Boulder, 1986—; grant writer, dir. Sheridan Pub. Schs., Englewood, 1976-80; workshops, inservices 1975—; conf. speaker, 1975—; cognitive evaluator, 1982—; co-dir. Coulter Publs., 1986—. Founding bd. dirs. Boulder Waldorf Sch. Assn., 1982-83. Grantee Innovative Edn., Dept. Edn. Colo., 1982; named Woman of Yr., Monona Jaycettes, 1968, Tchr. of Yr., Wis. and Upper Mich. Kiwanis, 1968; recipient Outstanding Speaker award, Dept. Edn. Wyo., 1979. Mem. AAAS. Avocations: skiing, tng. Icelandic horses, biodynamic gardening, writing. Home and Office: 4850 Niwot Rd Longmont CO 80501

COULTER, MARY ELISE, speech pathologist; b. Chgo., June 4, 1946; d. J. Joseph and Helen (Bair) Biery; m. Thayne Arthur Coulter II, Nov. 18, 1967 (div. May 1987); children: Sabrina Elise, Benjamin Thayne. Student, Grinnell Coll., 1964-65; BS in Edn., U. Kans., 1967; MA in Speech Pathology, Kans. State U., 1974. Lic. speech pathologist, Utah. Tchr. Ft. Devens Elem. Sch., Ayer, Mass., 1967-68; tchr. nongraded Nurnberg Am. Elem. Sch., Federal Republic of Germany, 1969-70; tchr. 1st grade Shawnee Mission (Kans.) Sch. Dist., 1969-70, Erlangen Am. Elem. Sch., Federal Republic of Germany, 1970-71; tchr. resource spl. edn. Davis County Sch. Dist., Farmington, Utah, 1975-80; speech pathologist, Head Start program Granite Sch. Dist., Salt Lake City, 1984-86, teaching resource spl. edn., 1986—; docent Hogle Zoo, Salt Lake City, 1980-85. Sunday sch. tchr. Christ United Meth. Ch., Salt Lake City, 1983—. Grinnell Coll. grantee, 1964-65. Mem. Am. Speech Lang. Hearing Assn. (cert.); PEO (chpt. W sec. 1982-84, chpt. AH organizer, pres. 1984-85). Republican. Clubs: Book (Salt Lake City). Avocations: traveling, reading, swimming, needlepoint, cross country skiing. Home: 4710 Fortuna Way Salt Lake City UT 84124

COUMIDES, ANDREAS DEMOSTHENOUS, mining company executive; b. Limassol, Cyprus, Feb. 10, 1928; came to U.S., 1947, naturalized, 1952; s. Demosthenis C. and Christalia A. (Philippou) C.; m. Amalia Aragon, Nov. 17, 1957; children—Michael A., Andreas Demosthenous, Francisco X. B.S. with high distinction in Bus. Adminstrn., U. Ariz., 1951. Various acctg. position Asarco Inc., El Paso, Tex., 1951-53, Mex., 1953-59, mgr. mining unit, Mex., 1960-63, co. treas., Mexico City, 1963-65, various managerial acctg. positions, southwestern mining dept. Tucson, 1965-79, asst. to v.p. mining, Tucson, 1979—; v.p., dir. Midetco, Ltd.; dir. United Park City Mines Co.; dir.-examiner Mex. Desarrollo Indsl. Minero and various subs. Mem. research com., bd. dirs. Ariz. Acad. Recipient award citation Jr. Achievement, 1969. Mem. AIME, Ariz. Mining Assn., Ariz. Tax Research Assn. (dir.), Inst. of Property Taxation, Alpha Kappa Psi, Beta Gamma Sigma, Phi Kappa Phi. Democrat. Roman Catholic. Club: Mexico City Bankers. Home: 3625 Calle Del Prado Tucson AZ 85716 Office: Asarco Inc 1150 N 7th Ave Tucson AZ 85705

COUNELIS, JAMES STEVE, education educator; b. Streator, Ill., June 26, 1927; s. Steve and Mary (Drivas) C.; m. Anna Catherine Marakas, Nov. 25, 1962; children: Steven George, George James. AA, Chgo. City Jr. Coll., 1948; AM, U. Chgo., 1951, PhD, 1961. Cert. high sch., jr. coll. tchr., pub. sch. principal, Ill. High sch. tchr. Chgo. Pub. Schs., 1951-55; asst. prof. history and social scis. Chgo. City Jr. Coll., Woodrow Wilson br., 1955-62, dir. evening program, 1962-64; asst. prof. edn. Chgo Tchrs. Coll., 1964-66; assoc. prof. edn. Pa. State U., University Park, 1966-67; sr. adminstrv. analyst U. Calif., Berkeley, 1968-70; prof. edn. U. San Francisco, 1970—, dir. instl. studies and mgmt. info. systems, 1971-75, Sch. Edn. Coordinator of Evaluation, 1986—. Author, editor: To Be a Phoenix: The Education Professoriate, 1969; contbr. articles, reviews and papers to profl. publs. pres., trustee Greek Orthodox Ch. of the Ascension, Oakland, Calif., 1973; pres. Hellenic Am. Profl. Soc., San Francisco, 1974, 75; trustee tenure Hellenic Coll./Holy Cross, 1951-53, trustee, 1982-86; mem. Calif. Council on Criminal Justice, 1987. Served with Signal Corps, U.S. Army, 1946-47. Recipient Archon Chartoularius (honoris causa) award Ecumenical Patriarchate of Canstantinople and New Rome, 1976, Norbert Wiener award The World Orgn. Gen. Systems and Cybernetics, 1978, Scholar U. Chgo., 1951, 52, 60-61, Pacific Sch. Religion, 1958; U. Calif., Berkeley grantee, 1962; Coolidge Research fellow Andover-Newton Theol. Sch., 1985, Wayne J. Doyle Research award, 1986. Mem. AAAS, Am. Assn. Instl. Research, Am. Ednl. Research Assn., Am. Ednl. Studies Assn., Hellenic Am. Profl. Soc. (Axion award 1982), Orthodox Theol Soc. Am., Soc. Gen. Systems Research, U. San Francisco Faculty Assn., Mensa, Gold Key, Phi Delta Kappa. Avocations: travel, photography, reading, music. Office: U San Francisco Sch Edn San Francisco CA 94117-1080

COUNT, EARL WENDEL, anthropology educator, clergyman; b. Irvington-on-Hudson, N.Y., Oct. 22, 1899; s. Elmer Ernest and Viette Ella (Thompson) C.; m. Maude Augusta Poole, July 6, 1928 (dec. July 1982); m. Alice Lawson, Sept. 28, 1984. AB, Williams Coll., 1922; BDiv, Garrett Theol. Sem., 1926; PhD, U. Calif., Berkeley, 1935. From instr. to asst. prof. biology San Jose (Calif.) State U., 1928-36; from. asst. prof. to assoc. prof. anatomy N.Y. Med. Coll., N.Y.C., 1936-46; research assoc. Wenner-Gren Found. Anthropol. Research Ctr., N.Y.C., 1946-47; prof. anthropology, dept. chmn. Hamilton Coll., Clinton, N.Y., 1947-68; vis. prof. Syracuse U., 1956, Brandeis U., Tulane U., Northwestern U., 1968, Purdue. U., 1978. Author: 4000 Years of Christmas, 1948, This is Race, 1950, Das Biogramm: Anthropologische Studien, 1970, Being and Becoming Human, 1978; co-author, co-editor: Fact and Theory in Social Science, 1964; translator: Contemporary Raciology and Racism, 1960, The Dualistic Creation of the World, 1960; contbr. articles to profl. jours. Research grantee NIH, 1960-61, travel grantee Wenner-Gren Edn. Found., 1964,66, 68, 83, 85. Fellow AAAS, Am. Anthropol. Assn.; mem. European Sociobiol. Soc., Lang. Origins Soc., Sigma Xi, Phi Beta Kappa (key reporter nat. book com. 1956—). Episcopalian. Home: 2616 Saklan Indian Dr #2 Walnut Creek CA 94595

COUNTRYMAN, RICHARD ALVA, state official, environmental horticulturist; b. Rochelle, Ill., July 28, 1926; s. Leon A. and Lola Margaret (Parker) C.; m. Betty Jeanne Branum, Feb. 5, 1950. B.S. in Agrl. Econs., U. Ariz., 1951, M.S. in Horticulture, 1958. Dist. entomologist Ariz. Commn. Agr. and Horticulture, Casa Grande, 1953-62, state seed insp., Phoenix, 1962-69, dir. div. compliance and dists., 1969-83, dir. Western region, 1983—. Author: Monthly Garden, Sun Gardener 1971—; Gardening, Mens Garden Club of Am., 1983-84. Mem. Environ. Edn. Council, 1965-77; bd. dirs. Clean Cities Systems, Phoenix, 1970—; commr. Maricopa County Fair, Phoenix, 1975—; chmn. Glendale Ariz. Com. Juvenile Concerns, 1978—, Theodore Roosevelt council Boy Scouts Am., 1963-83; exec. bd. Gov.'s Commn. on Ariz. Environ., 1974-84; vice chmn. State Vandalism Program, 1983—. Recipient Ariz. Farmer degree Future Farmers Am., Phoenix, 1976. Mem. Ariz. Native Plant Soc., Am. Assn. Seed Control Ofcls. (pres. 1982, 83), Western Assn. Seed Control Ofcls. (pres. 1969-70, 75-77, sec.-treas. 1970-75). Democrat. Methodist. Clubs: Valley of the Sun (Phoenix) (pres. 1970-85); Mens Garden Club Am. (Des Moines) (Johnny Appleseed award 1984). Home: Glendale AZ 85301 Office: Ariz Commn Agr and Horticulture 1688 W Adams St Phoenix AZ 85007

COUPE, RODGER, JR., civil engineer; b. Montclair, N.J., Sept. 25, 1947; s. Rodger Sr. and Harriet Louise (Stults) C.; m. Evelyn Lorraine Meneken, Feb. 1, 1971; children: Brandon Tyler, Alyssa Jill. BSCE, The Citadel, Charleston, S.C., 1969. Registered profl. engr. Calif., Wash., Nev., Oreg. Civil engr. Lawrence Livermore (Calif.) Lab., 1974-77; project engr. Creegan & D'Angelo, Dublin, Calif., 1977-78; civil engr. Creegan & D'Angelo, Pleasanton, Calif., 1980—; project mgr. Wilsey & Ham, Bellevue, Wash., 1978-79, Plummer & Assocs., Concord, Calif., 1979-80. Contbr. articles to mags. Chmn. Dublin Sign Com., 1984. Served to 1st lt. U.S. Army 1969-71, Vietnam. Recipient Project Mgmt. for Small Design Firm award Civil Engring. Expo'86. Mem. Livermore C. of C. (growth com. 1984), Dublin C. of C. Presbyterian. Home: 2154 6th St Livermore CA 94550 Office: Creegan & D'Angelo 6150 Stoneridge Mall Rd Suite 100 Pleasonton CA 94566

COURNOYER, MICHELE LOUISE, social worker; b. Sacramento, Sept. 19, 1960; d. Leo Franklin and Lorraine Rita (Roy) C. B in Sociology, Calif. State U., Fresno, 1982, MSW, 1984. Claim mgr., sec. Am. Investors, San Jose, Calif., 1979-81; hosp. hotline counselor Rape Counseling Service, Fresno, 1980-81; cash controller IBM Corp., San Jose, 1982; advocacy worker, counselor Young Women's Christian Assn., Fresno, 1983-84; social service practitioner Child Protective Service, Bakersfield, Calif., 1984—. Coauthor: (pamphlet) Everything You Wanted to Know About Rape But Were Afraid to Know. Vol. earthquake disaster ARC, Fresno, 1983—. Mem. Nat. Assn. Social Workers. Avocations: stitchery, belly dancing, horseback riding, racketball. Office: Child Protective Service 1800 19th St Bakersfield CA 93309

COURSON, THOMAS KLINGLER, banker; b. Sept. 9, 1947; married, 1971; 2 children. BS, U. Colo., 1969; Masters in Banking, U. Wis., 1979. Office mgr., credit analyst First Comml. Corp., Denver, 1969-71, asst. v.p., comml. loan officer, 1973-74; asst. sec., comml. loan officer Union Investment Co., Detroit, 1971-73; asst. v.p. United Bank Denver Nat. Assn., 1974-78; exec. v.p. United Bank Lakewood (Colo.) Nat. Assn., 1978—; bd. dirs. United Bank Arvada (Colo.) Nat. Assn. Treas., bd. dirs. Jefferson Found.; treas., bd. dirs. Lakewood Civic Found. Inc.; gen. chmn. Leadership Lakewood Program; bd. dirs. Lakewood Polit. Action Com.; bd. mgrs. S.W. Family YMCA; elder session bd. First Presbyn. Ch. Littleton, Colo. Mem. Lakewood/South Jefferson County C. of C. (vice chmn. bd. dirs.), Colo. Bankers Assn., Roberts Morris Assocs., U. Colo. Alumni Assn., Buff Club. Home: 9963 W Laurel Pl Littleton CO 80127

COURT, ALLEN HENRY, banker; b. Bklyn., June 15, 1942; s. Henry John and Ellen (Jack) C. B.S. in Bus. Adminstrn., Norwich U., 1964; M.B.A., Pepperdine U., 1980. Sr. credit analyst Mfrs. Hanover Trust Co., N.Y.C., 1966-71; loan officer Union Bank, Los Angeles, 1971-74; v.p., mgr. Toronto Dominion Bank, Irvine, Calif., 1974-80; sr. v.p., mgr. regional office Mitsui Mfrs. Bank, Newport Beach, Calif., 1980-86; sr. v.p., divisional mgr. Calif. div. Mitsui Mfrs. Bank Corp. Hdqrs., Los Angeles, 1986—. Mem. Friends of Sherman Library and Gardens, Corona Del Mar, Calif., 1980—; mem. benefactors com. South Coast Repertory, Costa Mesa, Calif., 1980-84. Served to 1st lt. U.S. Army, 1964-66. Mem. Robert Morris Assocs. Republican. Episcopalian. Clubs: Big Canyon Country, Jonathan, Balboa Bay, Pacific. also: Mitsui Mfrs Bank 1 Newport Pl 1301 Dove St Newport Beach CA 92660 Home: 163 Tangelo Irvine CA 92714

COURT, ARNOLD, climatologist; b. Seattle, June 20, 1914; s. Nathan Altshiller and Sophie (Ravitch) C.; m. Corinne H. Feibelman, May 27, 1941 (dec. Feb. 1984); children: David, Lois, Ellen. BA, U. Okla., 1934; postgrad., U. Wash., 1938, MS, 1949; PhD, U. Calif., Berkeley, 1956. Reporter and city editor Duncan (Okla.) Banner, 1935-38; observer, meteorologist U.S. Weather Bur., Albuquerque, Washington, Little Am., Los Angeles, 1938-43; chief meteorologist U.S. Antarctic Service, 1939-41; climatologist office Q.M. Gen. U.S. Army, Washington, 1946-51; research meteorologist U. Calif., Berkeley, 1951-56; meteorologist U.S. Forest Service, Berkeley, 1956-60; chief applied climatology, Cambridge Research Labs. USAF, Bedford, Mass., 1960-62; sr. scientist Lockheed-Calif. Co., Burbank, 1962-65; prof. climatology San Fernando Valley State Coll. (now Calif. State U.), Northridge, 1962-85, chmn. dept. geography, 1970-72, prof. emeritus, 1985—; part-time prof. Calif. State U., Northridge, 1985—, UCLA, 1987—. Editor: Eclectic Climatology, 1968; assoc. editor Jour. Climate and Applied Meteorology, 1978—; chmn. editorial bd. Jour. Weather Modification, 1978-86; contbr. articles and revs. to profl. jours. Served to 1st lt. USAAF, 1943-46. Recipient Spl. Congl. medal, 1944. Fellow AAAS, Am. Meteorol. Soc., Royal Meteorol. Soc.; mem. Am. Geophys. Union, Am. Statis. Assn., Assn. Am. Geographers, Assn. Pacific Coast Geographers (pres. 1978-79), Bernouilli Soc. for Math. Stats. and Probability, Calif. Geog. Soc., Weather Modification Assn. (trustee 1973-76), Western Snow Conf., Sigma Xi, Phi Beta Kappa. Home: 17168 Septo St Northridge CA 91325 Office: Calif State U Dept Geography Northridge CA 91330

COUSER, WILLIAM GRIFFITH, medical educator, academic administrator, nephrologist; b. Lebanon, N.H., July 11, 1939; s. Thomas Clifford and Winifred Priscilla (Ham) C. B.A., Harvard U., 1961, M.D., 1965; B.M.S., Dartmouth Coll. Med. Sch., 1963. Diplomate Am. Bd. Internal Medicine. Intern Moffitt Hosp./U. Calif. Med. Ctr., San Francisco, 1965-66, 66-67; resident Boston City Hosp., 1969-70; asst. prof. medicine U. Chgo., 1972-73; asst. prof. Boston U., 1972-77, assoc. prof., 1977-82; prof. U. Wash., Seattle, 1982—, head div. nephrology, 1982—; head div. nephrology U. Wash., 1982—; mem. sci. adv. bd. Kidney Found. Mass., Boston, 1974-82; mem. research grant com. Nat. Kidney Found., N.Y.C., 1981-86; mem. rev. bd. for nephrology VA, Washington, 1981-84; mem. exec. com. Council on Kidney in Cardiovascular Disease, Am. Heart Assn., Dallas, 1982-85; mem. pathology A study sect. NIH, subspecialty bd. in nephrology Am. Bd. Internal Medicine. Contbr. numerous articles, chpts., abstracts to profl. publs. Mem. editorial bd. Kidney Internat., 1982, Am. Jour. Kidney Diseases, Contemporary Nephrology, Clin. Updates in Nephrology, Seminars in Nephrology, Contemporary Nephrology. Served to capt. U.S. Army, 1967-69, Vietnam. Recipient Research Career Devel. award NIH, 1975-80; Nat. Kidney Found. fellow, 1971; NIH fellow, 1973, grantee, 1974—. Fellow ACP; mem. Am. Soc. Clin. Investigation, Am. Assn. Physicians, Am. Soc. Nephrology, Internat. Soc. Nephrology, Am. Assn. Pathologists, Am. Assn. Immunologists, Western Assn. Physicians. Avocation: boating. Office: U Wash Nephrology div 1959 NE Pacific Ave Rm 11 Seattle WA 98195

COUSINEAU, PIERRE, health administrator; b. Montreal, Que., Dec. 30, 1948; s. Emile and Madeleine (Labrèche) C.; m. Mary Putnam, May 4, 1974; children: Michael, Jacqueline. BS in Bus., Northeastern U., 1971; M in Health Adminstrn., Duke U., 1974. Asst. adminstr. ambulatory care U.S. Army Hosp., Wuerzburg, Fed. Republic Germany, 1974-77; comdr. Med. Clearing Co., Ft. Ord, Calif., 1977-78; exec. officer 8th Combat Support Hosp., Ft. Ord, 1978-79; asst. adminstr. Natividad Med. Ctr., Salinas, Calif., 1979—. Served to capt. U.S. Army, 1974-79. Mem. Am. Coll. Healthcare Execs. Presbyterian. Club: Toastmasters Internat. (Salinas). Avocations: jogging, camping, swimming. Home: 1072 University Ave Salinas CA 93901 Office: Natividad Med Ctr PO Box 81611 Salinas CA 93912

COUVELIER, MELVILLE BERTRAM, minister of finance and corporate relations; b. Vancouver, B.C., Can., Jan. 20, 1931; s. Melville George and Hilda Kate Couvelier; m. Mildred Anne Couvelier, Sept. 22, 1949; children: Richard, Rodney, Melissa. Acct. Crown Zellerbach Can. Ltd., 1950-58; retail and food wholesaler 1959-72; minister of fin. and corp. relations Victoria, B.C. Roman Catholic. Office: Ministry Fin and Corp Relations, Parliament Bldgs, Victoria Can V8T 1X4

COUZENS, STANLEY ANTHONY II, entrepreneur; b. Detroit, May 21, 1940; s. Stanley Anthony I and Caroline Marie (Andrus) C.; m. Marilyn Reed, June 14, 1980 (div. 1985); children: Cammille Ann, Stanley Anthony III, Corey Jean. Student, Ariz. State U. Art dir. McCutcheon Advt., Phoenix, 1960-61; asst. art dir., asst. prodn. mgr. John Bond Corp., Phoenix, 1961-64; staff artist Automated Bus. Forms, Goleta, Calif., 1964-67; art dir. Designed Systems, Santa Barbara, Calif., 1970—; owner, founder SAC-Art Bus. Forms, Santa Barbara, Calif., 1970—; forms cons. County Savs. Bank, Santa Barbara, 1985—; printing cons., Santa Barbara, 1970—. Author: Culinary Survival Guide, 1986, (booklet) Date Rater, 1986; devel. File-a-Disc, 1987, File-a-Film, 1987. Recipient Service Appreciation award Tres Condados Girl Scout Council, 1983. Mem. Data Processing Mgmt. Assn. (pres. 1978-79), Purchasing Mgmt. Assn., Tri County Assn. of Small Systems Users, Santa Barbara Jaycees (Outstanding Service award, 1971-75, Spark of Yr., 1971). Republican. Roman Catholic. Club: Ski Club (Santa Barbara) (pres. 1978-79). Lodges: Elks. Avocations: skiing, camping, fishing, photography, marksman. Office: SAC ART Bus Forms and Printing 375 Pine Ave Goleta CA 93117

COVAN, JAMES PARKER, safety engineer, industrial hygienist; b. Urbana, Ill., Aug. 23, 1940; s. Jack Phillip and Thelma Elizabeth (Parker) CoV.; m. Brenda Sample, June 14, 1964; children: Cynthia Faith, Candace Hope, Heather Alisa. Student, U.S. Naval Acad., 1958-59; BS in Chemistry, Tex. A&M U., 1962, ME in Indsl. Engring., 1974. Pilot USN, Barbers Point, Hawaii, 1962-67, 70-72; shift supr. Procter & Gamble, Dallas, 1967-70; safety analyst Phillips Petroleum Co., Pasadena, Tex., 1974-76; staff indsl. hygenist Tenneco Inc., Houston, 1976-84; safety and health cons. Tech. Serving People, Inc., Houston, 1984-85; system safety mgr. Aerospace Ops. div. Boeing Co., Moffett Field, Calif., 1985—; lectr. U. Houston, Clear Lake City, Tex., 1983-85. Mem. Am. Indsl. Hygiene Assn. (chpt. sec. 1982-83), Am. Soc. Safety Engrs. (profl.), Am. Chem. Soc., System Safety Soc. (chpt. pres. 1983-85). Republican. Baptist. Avocations: clarinet, swimming. Home: 847 Canada Dr Milpitas CA 95035 Office: Boeing Aerospace Ops Ames 244-2A Moffett Field CA 94035

COVELL, RUTH MARIE, medical educator, medical school administrator; b. San Francisco, Aug. 12, 1936; d. John Joseph and Mary Carolyn (Coles) Collins; m. James Wachob Covell, 1963 (div. 1972); 1 child, Stephen; m. Harold Joachim Simon, Jan. 4, 1973; 1 child, David. Student, U. Vienna, Austria, 1955-56; BA, Stanford U., 1958; MD, U. Chgo., 1962. Clin. prof. and assoc. dean sch. medicine U. Calif. San Diego, La Jolla, 1969—; gov. bd. Health Systems Agy. San Diego and Imperial Counties; bd. dirs. Beverly Found., Pasadena; cons. Nat. Ctr. for Health Services Research and Technology Assessment; med. adv. bd. Alzheimers Family Ctr., San Diego, San Diego Epilepsy Soc. Contbr. articles on health planning and quality of med. care to profl. jours. Mem. AMA, Am. Health Scis. Research, Assn. Tchrs. Preventive Medicine, Am. Pub. Health Assn., Assn. Am. Med. Colls. Group on Instl. Planning (chair 1973-74, sec. 1983-84), Phi Beta Kappa, Alpha Omega Alpha. Home: 1604 El Camino de Teatro La Jolla CA 92037 Office: U Calif San Diego Sch Medicine M-002 La Jolla CA 92093

COVIN, DAVID L., political science educator; b. Chgo., Oct. 3, 1940; s. Odell Jerry and Lela Jane (Clements) Johnson; m. Judy Bentinck Smith, May 7, 1965; children: Wendy, Holly. BA, U. Ill., 1962; MA, Colo. U., 1966; PhD, Wash. State U., 1970. Asst. prof. govt. and Pan African studies Calif. State U., Sacramento, 1970-72, assoc. dean gen. studies, 1972-74, assoc. prof. govt. and Pan African studies, 1975-79, acting dir. Pan African studies, 1979-81, prof. govt. and Pan African studies, 1979—, dir. Pan African studies, 1986—; adj. prof. Union Grad. Sch., 1979-82; commr. Edn. Mgmt. and Evaluation Commn., 1977-81; bd. trustees Congl. Black Caucus, Washington, 1977—; mem. Criminal Justice Brain Trust. Contbr. articles to profl. jours. Active Com. for the Fair Adminstrn. of Justice, Sacramento, 1985—; edn. co-chmn. Sacramento Black Community Activist Com., 1985—; co-chmn. Nat. Black Ind. Polit. Party, Sacramento, 1981-85; active Sacramento Black Area Caucus, 1972—. Recipient Community Service award Omega Psi Phi, 1982, Community Service award All African People's Revolutionary Party, 1986, Community Service award Sacramento Area Black Caucus, 1976. Mem. Nat. Council Black Studies, Nat. Conf. Black Polit. Scientists. Avocations: fishing, skiing, reading. Home: 4131 44th St Sacramento CA 95820 Office: Calif State U 6000 J St Sacramento CA 95819

COVINO, JOSEPHINE, research chemist; b. Sturno, Avellino, Italy, June 24, 1957; came to U.S., 1966; d. Generoso and Stella (Todisco) C.; m. Mark Hrbacek, Dec. 29, 1984. BS in Chemistry magna cum laude, Adelphi U., 1979; PhD in Inorganic Chemistry, Brown U., 1982. Research asst. Brown U., Providence, 1979-82, Exxon Research, Lindon, N.J., 1980; research chemist Naval Weapons Ctr., China Lake, Calif., 1982—. Contbr. numerous articles to sci. jours.; patentee in field. Recipient Hon. award Am. Inst. Chemists, 1979. Mem. Am. Chem. Soc., Am. Ceramic Soc., Sigma Xi. Republican. Roman Catholic. Home: 608 Alice Ridgecrest CA 93555 Office: Naval Weapons Ctr Code 3891 China Lake CA 93555

COVITZ, CARL D., real estate and investment executive; b. Boston, Mar. 31, 1939; s. Edward E. and Barbara (Matthews) C.; m. Aviva Habert, May 15, 1970; children—Philip, Marc. B.S., Wharton Sch., U. Pa., 1960; M.B.A., Columbia U., 1962. Product mgr. Bristol-Myers Co., N.Y.C., 1962-66; dir. mktg. Rheingold Breweries, N.Y.C., 1966-68; nat. mktg. mgr. Can. Dry Corp., N.Y.C., 1968-70; v.p. mktg., dir. corp. devel. ITT/Levitt & Sons, Lake Success, N.Y., 1970-73; owner, pres. Landmark Communities, Inc., Beverly Hills, Calif., 1973—. Exec. com. Presl. Commn. Cost Control and Efficiency (Grace Commn.); co-chmn. Dept. Def. Task Force; past chmn. ops. com. Mus. Contemporary Art Los Angeles; chmn. Los Angeles County Delinquency and Crime Commn.; dir. Columbia U. Grad. Bus. Sch. Alumni Assn. Mem. Young Pres. Orgn. Home: 818 Malcolm Ave Los Angeles CA 90024 Office: Landmark Communities Inc 9595 Wilshire Blvd Beverly Hills CA 90212

COWAN, GEORGE ARTHUR, chemist, bank executive, director; b. Worcester, Mass., Feb. 15, 1920; s. Louis Abraham and Anna (Listic) C.; m. Helen Dunham, Sept. 9, 1946. BS, Worcester Poly. Inst.; DSc, Carnegie-Mellon U. Research asst. Princeton U., 1941-42, U. Chgo., 1942-45; mem. staff Columbia U., N.Y.C., 1945; mem. staff Los Alamos (N.Mex.) Sci. Lab., 1945-46, sr. fellow, 1949—; teaching fellow Carnegie Mellon U., Pitts., 1946-49; chmn. bd. dirs. Los Alamos Nat. Bank, Trinity Capital Corp., Los Alamos; pres. Santa Fe Inst., 1984—; mem. White House Sci. Council, Washington, 1982-85, cons., 1985—, AFTAC, 1952—. Contbr. sci. articles to profl. jours. Bd. dirs. Santa Fe Opera, 1964-79; treas. N.Mex. Opera Found., Santa Fe, 1970-79; regent N.Mex. Inst. Tech., Socorro, 1972-75. Recipient E.O. Lawrence award, 1965, Disting. Scientist award N.Mex. Acad. Sci. 1975, Robert H. Goddard award Worcester Poly. Inst., 1984. Fellow AAAS, Am. Physics Soc.; mem. Am. Chem. Soc., N.Mex. Acad. Sci. Club: Cosmos (Washington). Avocation: skiing. Home: 721 42nd St Los Alamos NM 87544 Office: Los Alamos Nat Lab PO Box 1663 MS A114 Los Alamos NM 87545

COWAN, STUART MARSHALL, lawyer; b. Irvington, N.J., Mar. 20, 1932; s. Bernard Howard and Blanche (Hertz) C.; m. Marilyn R.C. Toepfer, Apr., 1961 (div. 1969); m. Jane Alison Averill, Feb. 24, 1974; children—Catherine R.L., Erika R.L., Bronwen P. B.S. in Econ., U. Pa., 1952; LL.B., Rutgers U., 1955. Bar: N.J. 1957, Hawaii 1962, U.S. Supreme Ct., 1966. Atty., Greenstein & Cowan, Honolulu, 1961-70, Cowan & Frey, Honolulu, 1970—; arbitration Fed. Mediation & Conciliation Service, Honolulu, 1972—, Am. Arbitation Assn., Honolulu, 1978—, Hawaii Pub. Employees. Relation Bd., 1972—. Served to lt. USN, 1956-61. Mem. Hawaii Bar Assn., ABA, Am. Judicature Soc., Trial Lawyers Assn. of Am. (state committeeman for Hawaii 1965-69, bd. govs. 1972-75), Hawaii Trial Lawyers Assn. (v.p. 1972-78), Japan-Hawaii Lawyers Assn. Jewish. Clubs: Waikiki Yacht (Honolulu), San Francisco Comml., Hawaii Scottish Assn. (chieftain 1983-85), Caledonian Soc. (vice chieftain 1983-85), St. Francis Yacht, Honolulu Club, Honolulu Pipes and Drums (sec.-treas. 1985-87). Lodges: Masons, Pearl Harbor (master 1971), Composite. Home: 47-339 Mapumapu Rd Kaneohe HI 96744 Office: Cowan & Frey 1600 Grosvenor Ctr Towers 733 733 Bishop St Honolulu HI 96813

COWART, BILLY FRANK, academic administrator; b. San Benito, Tex., Aug. 5, 1932; m. Janet Marie Dube, Aug. 6, 1954; 1 child, Richard. BS, Tex. A&I U., 1954; MA, Stephen F. Austin State Coll., 1959; PhD, U. Tex., 1963. Asst. mgr. Brownie Butane, Inc., McAllen, Tex., 1956-57; office mgr. Cowart Cattle co., Henderson, Tex., 1957-59; tchr. Tivy Jr. High Sch., Kerrville, Tex., 1963-66; dir. secondary student teaching Tex. A&I U., Kingsville, 1963-66, dir. project Upward Bound, 1966-69; pres. Laredo (Tex.) State U., 1969-84; provost Western Oreg. State Coll., Monmouth, 1984—. Contbr. articles to profl. jours. Pres. United Fund of Laredo, 1980; chmn. Laredo Council for the Arts, 198-84, Borderfest steering com., Laredo, 1980-83. Served to 1st lt. U.S. Army, 1954-56. Named Man of Yr., Laredo Times, 1979, Exec. of Yr., Colegio de Licenciados in Administracion de Nuevo, 1981. Mem. SW Philosophy Edn. Soc. (pres. 1970-71). Home: 322 Marr Ct Monmouth OR 97361 Office: Western Oreg State Coll Office of the Provost 345 N Monmouth Ave Monmouth OR 97361

COWDEN, CHESTER LYLE, accountant; b. Cedar Rapids, Iowa, Oct. 6, 1917; s. James Fenimore and Beulah Hayes (Gilchrist) C.; m. Kathryn Roseanna Phillips, Mar. 21, 1943; children—James Franklin, Patricia Kathryn Cowden Seifert. B.S., U. Iowa, 1942, M.A., 1948. C.P.A., Iowa, Calif. Acting head cost dept., head br. factory ledger acct. Cherry-Burrell Corp., Cedar Rapids, Iowa, 1942-48; semi-sr. acct. Allen & Co., C.P.A.s, Des Moines, 1948-50; stores auditor, trainee fgn. asst. controllership Firestone Tire & Rubber Co., Des Moines, 1950-52; internal auditor Contra Costa County, Martinez, Calif., 1952-57; staff acct. Heruth-Thyken & Smith, 1954-55, Cowden and Koskinen, C.P.A.s, 1958-64, Cowden, Koskinen & Westenrider, C.P.A.s, 1964-65; pvt. practice acctg., Concord, Calif., 1965—. Mem. Am. Inst. C.P.A.s, Am. Acctg. Assn., Nat. Assn. Accts. (sec., dir. Oakland-East Bay chpt., Most Valuable mem. 1961-62, 63-64), Calif. Soc. C.P.A.s, Estate Planning Council Diablo Valley, Concord C. of C. (dir. 1962-65). Republican. Presbyterian. Clubs: Masons, Elks, Kiwanis (dir., treas., v.p.) (Concord, Calif.). Home: 4649 Benbow Ct Concord CA 94521 Office: 1875 Willow Pass Rd Suite 306 Concord CA 94520

COWELL, ERNEST SAUL, lighting designer, consultant; b. Hollywood, Calif., Jan. 27, 1927; s. Ernest S. and Bernice Michael (Waterman) C.; m. Beverly Sue Bloom, Apr. 15, 1950 (div. May 1960); children: Steven Richard, Craig Wesley, Marilyn Tobiann. BA, UCLA, 1950; student, Moorpark Coll., 1971, Cerritos Jr. Coll., 1979. Regional mgr. Prentice Hall Inc., San Francisco, 1954-59; pvt. practice indsl. and govtl. sales Los Angeles, 1959-70; area mgr. Philips Lighting, Los Angeles, 1970-79; v.p. Conns & Cowell Lighting Unltd., Thousand Oaks, Calif., 1979-83; pres. Lighting Designs, Thousand Oaks, 1983—; cons. City of Thousand Oaks, 1970—. Mem. Rep. Presdl. Task Force, 1978—; founder, pres. Sunset Hills Homewoners Assn., Thousand Oaks, 1968; pres. Conejo Valley Homeowners Assns., Thousand Oaks, 1970; chmn. City of Thousand Oaks Housing Mix Com., 1973; mem. gen. plan com. City of Thousand Oaks, 1967, gen. plan rev. com. City of Thousand Oaks, 1984, 86. Served as sgt. U.S. Army, 1943-46, PTO, with Res. 1950-58, 70—. Recipient Edison award Excellence in Lighting, Gen. Electric Corp., 1985. Fellow Inst Advancement Engring.; mem. Illuminating Engring. Soc. (bd. dirs. So. Calif. sect. 1977-85, nat. chmn. schs and colls. lighting standards com. 1984—, residential lighting standards com. 1985—, Internat. Illumination Design award 1983, 84, 85), Internat. Assn. Lighting Designers, U.S. Nat. Com. to Internat. Commn. Illumination, Internat. Soc. Interior Designers (design assoc.), Am. Soc. Interior Designers (design affilate), Inst. Bus. Designers (allied), Navy League,. Lodge: Kiwanis (pres. Westlake Village club 1977-79). Avocations: sailing, photography, travel. Office: Lighting Designs PO Box 2061 Thousand Oaks CA 91360

COWEN, DONALD EUGENE, physician; b. Ft. Morgan, Colo., Oct. 8, 1918; adopted s. Franklin and Mary Edith (Dalton) C.; B.A., U. Denver, 1940; M.D., U. Colo., 1943; m. Hulda Marie Helling, Dec. 24, 1942; children—David L., Marilyn Marie Cowen Dean, Theresa Kathleen Cowen Cunningham, Margaret Ann. Intern, U.S. Naval Hosp., Oakland, Calif., 1944; gen. practice medicine, Ft. Morgan, 1947-52; resident internal medicine U. Colo. Med. Center, Denver, 1952-54; practice medicine specializing in allergy, Denver, 1954—; mem. staff Presbyn. Med. Center, Denver, Porter, Swedish hosps., Englewood, Colo.; clin. asst. prof. medicine U. Colo. Med. Center, 1964—; postgrad. faculty U. Tenn. Coll. Medicine, Memphis, 1962—; cons. Queen of Thailand, 1973, 75, 77. Pres. Community Arts Symphony Found., 1980-82. Served to lt. M.C., USN, 1943-47. Fellow ACP, Am. Coll. Chest Physicians (vice chmn. com. on allergy 1968-72, 75-87, sec.-treas. Colo. chpt. 1971-77, pres. 1978-80), Am. Coll. Allergists, Am. Assn. Clin. Immunology and Allergy, Soc. Clin. Ecology (charter mem.), Acad. Internat. Medicine, West Coast Allergy Soc., Southwest Allergy Forum, Am. Acad. Otolaryngic Allergy; mem. Am., Colo. socs. internal medicine, Am. Thoracic Soc., Colo. Allergy Soc. (past pres.), Ill. Soc. Opthalmology and Otolaryngology (hon.), Denver Med. Soc. (chmn. library and bldg. com. 1963-73). Presbyterian (ruling elder 1956—). Club: Lions. Contbr. numerous articles to profl. jours. Home: 1501 E Quincy Ave Cherry Hills Village Englewood CO 80110 Office: 3510 S Marion St Englewood CO 80110

COWIE, BRUCE EDGAR, communications executive; b. Prince Albert, Sask., Can., Mar. 6, 1938; s. Louis Leroy and Janet Louise (Anderson) C.; m. Marlene Lehman, July 28, 1958; children—Cameron, Robert, Caron-Dawn. Student pub. schs., Prince Albert. Announcer Sta. CKOM, Saskatoon, Sask., 1956-59; with Sta. CKCK-TV (and subsidiaries), Regina, Sask., 1959—; gen. mgr. sta. Sta. CKCK-TV (and subsidiaries), 1972-77, v.p., gen. mgr., 1978-81; v.p., dir. Harvard Devels. Ltd., 1981—; pres. Braeloch Cons. Ltd. (communications cons.), Braeside Holdings; dir. Western Surety Co., Can. TV Network; mem. program com. CTVTV Network; founding chmn. Canpro, 1974; vice-chmn. TV Bur. Can. Alderman, City of Regina, 1963-67; pres. Sask. Roughrider Football Club, 1976, Western Football Conf., 1980; bd. dirs. Can. Football League Exec. Com. Served to 2d lt. Regina Rifle Regiment Res., 1965. Mem. Western Assn. Broadcasters (pres. 1976-77, Broadcaster of Yr., 1981), Canadian Assn. Broadcasters (dir.), Nat. Assn. TV Program Execs., Broadcast Promotion Assn., Regina C. of C., United Services Inst. Clubs: Assinabdia, Wascana Golf and Country. Home: 113 Tibbitts Rd, Regina, SK Canada Office: PO Box 2000, Regina, SK Canada S4P 3E5

COWLES, JEANNINE BOUCHARD, personal services co. exec.; b. Memphis, Oct. 14, 1928; d. Horace Louis and Melissa Oldham (Boyd) Bouchard; student Phila. Acad. Vocal Arts, 1948-51, Hartt Coll. Music, 1963-65; 1 dau. by previous marriage, Ann. Singer, actress, Broadway, summer stock, opera, 1951-67; mem. Am. Opera Co., Phila., then Hartt Opera Theatre, Hartford; pres., chief exec. officer Weight Watchers of Oreg., Inc., Portland, 1969—. Mem. Portland Met. Performing Arts Theatre Task Force, 1976-77, City of Portland Downtown Housing Adv. Com., 1978-79; bd. dirs. Portland Opera Assn., 1973-79, chmn. personnel com., 1977-78; mem. adv. council for Sch. of Fine and Performing Arts Portland State U., 1987—; bd. dirs. The Musical Co., 1987—. Mem. Portland C. of C. (chmn. cultural resources com. 1976-77, dir. 1977-80), Women's Advt. Club (dir. 1977-78), Internat. Platform Assn. Episcopalian. Club: Multnomah Athletic. Home: 2221 SW 1st Ave Portland OR 97201 Office: 9200 Barnes Rd SW Portland OR 97225

COWLES, WILLIAM HUTCHINSON, 3RD, newspaper publisher; b. Spokane, Wash., Mar. 4, 1932; s. William Hutchinson and Margaret (Paine) C.; m. Allison Stacey, Mar. 28, 1959; children: William Stacey, Elizabeth Allison. B.A., Yale U., 1953; J.D., Harvard U., 1959. Bar: Wash. 1959. Pres., pub. Cowles Pub. Co. (pubs. The Spokesman-Rev., Spokane Chronicle), N.W. Farmer-Stockman, Inc. (pubs. Wash. Farmer-Stockman, Oreg. Farmer-Stockman, Idaho Farmer-Stockman, Utah Farmer-Stockman), Spokane, 1970—, Mont. Farmer-Stockman, Inc. (pubs. Mont. Farmer-Stockman), Billings, 1970—; v.p., dir. Inland Empire Paper Co., Millwood, Wash., 1964—; dir. Allied Daily Newspapers, 1970-71, pres., 1972-74; dir. AP, 1974-83, 1st vice-chmn., 1982-83. Bd. dirs. Inland Empire council Boy Scouts Am., 1960—, Spokane Symphony Soc., 1961-78; bd. dirs. United Crusade Spokane County, 1963-74, pres., 1970; bd. overseers Whitman Coll., 1966—. Served to lt. USNR, 1953-56. Mem. Am. Soc. Newspaper Editors, Am. Newspaper Pubs. Assn. (dir. 1980—), Newspaper Advt. Bur. (dir. 1968—, chmn. 1978-80), Beta Theta Pi, Sigma Delta Chi. Club: Spokane. Office: The Spokesman-Review and Spokane Chronicle W 999 Riverside Ave Spokane WA 99201

COWLEY, JOHN MAXWELL, educator; b. Peterborough, South Australia, Feb. 18, 1923; came to U.S., 1970; s. Alfred Ernest and Doris (Milway) C.; m. Roberta Joan Beckett, Dec. 15, 1951; children—Deborah Suzanne, Jillian Patricia. B.Sc., U. Adelaide, Australia, 1942, M.Sc., 1945, D.Sc., 1957; Ph.D., Mass. Inst. Tech., 1949. Research officer Commonwealth Sci. and Indsl. Research Orgn., Melbourne, Australia, 1945-62; chief research officer, head crystallography sect. Commonwealth Sci. and Indsl. Research Orgn., 1960-62; prof. physics U. Melbourne, Australia, 1962-70; Galvin prof. physics Ariz. State U., Tempe, 1970—; Mem. U.S. Nat. Com. for Crystallography, 1973-78, 84-86. Author: Diffraction Physics, 1975; Editor: (with others) Acta Crystallographica, 1971-80; Contbr. (with others) articles to profl. jours. Fellow Australian Acad. Sci., Inst. Physics (London), Australian Inst. Physics, Royal Soc. (London), Am. Phys. Soc.; mem. Internat. Union Crystallography (mem. exec. com. 1963-69), Am. Inst. Physics, Am. Crystallographic Assn., Electron Microscope Soc. Am. (dir. 1971-75). Home: 2625 E Southern Ave C-90 Tempe AZ 85282

COWPER, STEVE CAMBRELENG, governor, lawyer; b. Petersburg, Va., Aug. 21, 1938; s. Stephanie Smith; m. Michael Margaret Stewart; children: Katherine, Grace, Wade. B, U. N.C., 1960, JD, 1963. Sole practice Norfolk, Va.; asst. dist. atty. State of Alaska, Fairbanks, 1968-70; ptnr. Cowper & Madson, Fairbanks, 1971-84; mem. legislature Alaska Ho. of Reps., Fairbanks and Juneau, 1974-78; gov. State of Alaska, Juneau, 1986—. Columnist Alaska newspapers, 1979-80, 85. Mem. Alaska Native Brotherhood Klawock Camp, Eielson Area Grange, Fairbanks. Served with U.S. Army, 1960. Democrat. Episcopalian. Club: Sundawgs Rugby. Avocations: banjo, rugby, scuba diving, reading. Office: Office of the Gov State Capitol PO Box A Juneau AK 99811

COX, BENJAMIN VINCENT, electrical engineer; b. Chgo., Jan. 25, 1934; s. Benjamin and Lorretta Deloris (Jozwiak) C.; B.S. in Elec. Engring., U. Utah, 1963, M.S., 1969, Ph.D., 1979; m. Mary Patricia Mitchell, Apr. 18, 1959; children—Linda Marie, Stephen Martin. With Sperry Univac Co. (now UNISYS), 1963-73, 74—, staff engr., 1974-78, engring. mgr., advanced research and devel., dir. advanced tech., Salt Lake City, 1978—; engring. dir. Naval Civil Engring. Lab., Port Hueneme, Calif., 1973-74; adj. prof. U. Utah. Served with U.S. Army, 1954-57. Mem. AIAA (council Utah chpt. 1980-81), IEEE, Am. Def. Preparedness Assn., Air Force Assn., Assn. Old Crows. Author papers, reports in field. Home: 2760 E Blue Spruce Dr Salt Lake City UT 84117 Office: 640 N Sperry Way Salt Lake City UT 84116-2988

COX, CARLMAN, architect; b. Aug. 19, 1937; s. Otis Printiss and Mabel Molly (Price) C.; m. Grethe Germansen, July 21, 1966; children—Kevin Jens, Rikke Ann. A.A., San Bernardino Valley Coll., 1960; student Ariz. State U., 1962, U. Calif.-Riverside, 1964. Registered architect, Calif., Ariz. Pvt. practice architecture, Indio, Calif., 1973—. Chmn. Indio Bldg. and Housing Bd. Appeals, Econ. Devel. Com. Recipient honor award Masonry Inst., 1982. Mem. AIA, Constrn. Specifications Inst. Republican. Club: Exchange (past pres.). Lodges: Masons, Elks. Office: Carl Cox AIA Architect Profl Plaza 47-159 Youngs Ln Indio CA 92201

COX, CATHLEEN RUTH, zoologist, educator; b. Vallejo, Calif., Oct. 20, 1948; d. Charles W. and Betty A. (Born) Cox; B.A., U. Calif.-San Diego, 1970, Ph.D., Stanford U., 1976; m. William S. Bain, Dec. 14, 1985. Postdoctoral fellow Am. Mus. Natural History, N.Y.C., 1976-78; research assoc. Barnard Coll., N.Y.C., 1978-79; research zoologist UCLA, 1979-82; asst. prof. Calif. State U.-Northridge, 1980—; dir. research Los Angeles Zoo, 1981—. Recipient W.C. Allee award Animal Behavior Soc., 1976; NSF research grantee, 1978. Mem. Assn. Women in Sci. (exec. bd. Los Angeles chpt.), Am. Assn. Zool. Parks and Aquaria, Am. Ornithol. Union, Animal Behavior Soc., Am. Primatol. Soc. Contbr. articles to profl. jours. Office: 5333 Zoo Dr Los Angeles CA 90027

COX, CLARK BURGESS, dentist; b. St. George, Utah, Feb. 23, 1929; s. Emerald Lane and Elsie (Burgess) C.; Asso. Sci., Dixie Jr. Coll., 1949; D.D.S., U. So. Calif., 1953; m. Donna Anderson, July 15, 1949; children—David C., Craig E., Suzanne, Dianne, Gary L., Cynthia. Practice dentistry, Delta, Utah, 1955—; v.p. Habb Corp., Delta, 1962—, Cox Trucking Inc., Delta, 1976—; farmer, livestock rancher, 1960—; dir. Del-Tex Corp., Oasis Seed Corp.; partner Fransworth-Cox Real Estate; vice chmn. W. Millard Soil Conservation Service, 1970-76. City councilman, Delta, 1968-76, mem. bd. adjustment, 1978—. Served with Dental Corps, AUS, 1953-55. Mem. Acad. Gen. Dentistry, Am., Utah, Provo Dist. dental assns., Brigham Young U. Acad. Dentists (charter), Alpha Tau Epsilon, Psi Omega. Mem. Ch. Jesus Christ of Latter-day Saints (Delta 2d ward bishopric 1962-65, high councilor Delta West stake). Home: RFD Delta PO Box 695 Delta UT 84624 Office: Hobb Bldg Main St Delta UT 84624

COX, DENNIS WILLIAM, medical social worker; b. Pomona, Calif., Aug. 19, 1955; s. Arthur Harold and Yvonne (Coreen) C.; m. Cheryl Elaine Groves, Aug. 20, 1983; 1 child, Erin Nicole. BA magna cum laude, U. Calif., Santa Barbara, 1977; MSW, U. Calif., Berkeley, 1981. Lic. clin. social worker. Med. social worker Kentfield (Calif.) Med. Hosp., 1981-83; social work cons, discharge planner Community Vis. Nurses, Sacramento, Calif., 1983-84; med. social worker Home Health and Counseling, Auburn, 1983-84; bereavement group facilitator Auburn (Calif.) Faith Hospice, 1983-85; med. social worker Vis. Nurse Assn., Auburn, 1983-87; pvt. practice psychotherapy Auburn, 1986—; supr. community services program supr. U. Calif. Davis Multi Sr. Services Project, 1987—; Coordinator Alzheimer's Disease Training Program Home Health and Counseling, Auburn, 1984-85; bereavement com. chmn., Auburn Faith Hospice, 1985-87; cons. Foothill Oaks Convalescent Hosp., Auburn, 1986-87, Auburn Gardens Convalescent Hosp., 1987. Mem. Nat. Assn. Social Workers, Am. Soc. Aging. Democrat. Avocations: skiing, softball, motorcycle riding. Home: 1740 Sierra View Dr Meadow Vista CA 95722 Office: U Calif Multi Sr Services Program 2000 Stockton Blvd Suite 200 Sacramento CA 95017

COX, DOROTHY MARIE, public administrator; b. Wellpinit, Wash., Jan. 21, 1931; d. John West Potter and Ethel (Wynecoop) Davis; m. Milton Richard Cox, Aug. 13, 1951; 1 child, Steven Milton. AA, Lower Columbia Coll., Longview, Wash., 1971; BS, City U., Seattle, 1980; cert. in personnel adminstrn., Portland State U., 1985. Personnel coordinator City of Longview, Wash., 1977-82, mgmt. asst., personnel adminstr., 1982—. Com. mem. Pvt. Industry Council-Planning, Cowlitz County, Wash., 1985—, Lower Columbia Mental Health Task Force, Cowlitz County, 1984—; sec.-examiner Longview Civil Service Commn., 1980—; com. mem. and bd. dirs. Lower Columbia Community Action Council, Cowlitz County, 1983—; mem. job service employers com., 1984—, chmn., 1986-87. Recipient Meritorious scholarship City U., 1980. Mem. Pacific Northwest Personnel Mgrs. Lower Columbia chpt. (treas. 1983-84, vice chmn. 1985-86); Altrusa (community services chmn. 1982). Lutheran. Avocations: antique glass collecting, reading, piano. Office: City of Longview 1575 Broadway PO Box 128 Longview WA 98632

COX, ENID ELAINE, home economist; b. Eugene, Oreg., Feb. 28, 1935; d. James Artie and Bessie Agnes (Foster) Tanner; student Central Oreg. Coll., 1956; B.S., Oreg. State U., 1958, M.S., 1964; m. Manuel Ernest Cox, Jan. 7, 1950; children—Kathryn A., Carol A. Tchr. vocat. homemaking, chmn. dept. Scappoose (Oreg.) High Sch., 1958-67; instr. home econs. Marylhurst (Oreg.) Coll., 1967-68; coop. ext. agt. Wash. State U., Pullman, 1968; ext. agt. 4-H youth Clark County, Wash., 1968-75, home economist, 1975-82; coop. extension agt., home economist Walla Walla County (Wash.), 1982-86, chmn. Klickitat County, 1986—. Mem. Nat. Elec. Women's Round Table (bd. dirs., chmn. Oreg. chpt. 1978-79), Nat. Extension Home Economists Assn., Blue Mountain Home Econs. Assn. (pres. 1982-83), Am. Home Econs. Assn. (western regional coordinator 1986-87, pres. unit leadership adv. com. 1987, resolution adv. com. 1987—), Wash. Home Econs. Assn. (sec. 1983-85, pres. 1986—). Lutheran. Clubs: Daughters of Pioneers of Wash., Scappoose Woman's (past pres.). Office: 228 W Main St Room 210 Goldendale WA 98620

COX, GARY ROBERT, engineer; b. Chgo., Jan. 20, 1953; s. Henry Hale and Ethel Margaret (Lindemann) Cox; m. Nancy Mary Lange, Feb. 3, 1973 (div. June 1980); m. Susan Margaret McLean, Nov. 27, 1983. AS, William Rainey Harper Coll., 1974; BS, So. Ill. U., 1976; MS, Wash. State U., 1980; hazardous waste specialist, U. Mo., 1983. Research asst. Wash. State U., Pullman, 1976-78; research technologist Northrup-King Seed Co., Mpls., 1978-79; sr. engr. Rockwell Internat. Hanford, Richland, Wash., 1979-85, UNC Nuclear Industries, Richland, 1985—. Contbr. articles to profl. jours. Bd. dirs. Yakima (Wash.) Area Arboretum, 1983—. So. Ill. U. Found. scholar, Carbondale, 1974-76. Mem. Agronomy Soc. Am. (cert.), Western Crop Soc., Spill Control Prevention Soc. Am. (cert.), Nat. Environ. Tng. Assn. (cert.), Soc. Range Mgmt., Enological Soc. (bd. dirs. 1986—), Sigma Xi. Democrat. Lutheran. Club: Yakima Cougar (pres. 1982—). Avocations: flyfishing, backpacking, mountaineering, canoeing, winemaking. Home: 2510 McCullough Rd Yakima WA 98903 Office: UNC Nuclear Industries PO Box 490 Richland WA 99352

COX, GREGORY RICHARDSON, mayor; b. San Diego, July 2, 1948; s. Gordon Barter and Doris Margaret (Richardson) C.; m. Cheryl Sue Willett, Dec. 20, 1975; children: Elizabeth Karin, Emily Anne. BA, San Diego State U., 1970, MA, 1977. Tchr. Bonita Vista High Sch., Chula Vista, 1971-72, dean of activities, 1972-82; city councilman City of Chula Vista, Calif., 1976-81, mayor, 1981—. V.p. League of Calif. Cities, Sacramento, 1986-87, bd. dirs. 1984—, pres. San Diego div., 1985-86; chmn. Chula Vista Parks and Recreation Commn., 1974; pres. Chula Vista Rep. Club, 1972, Chula Vista Jaycees, 1974-75; mem. San Diego Bay Cities Bd. Realtors, 1981—; bd. dirs. ARC, San Diego, 1984—, United Way, San Diego, 1983—. Named one of Five Outstanding Californians, Calif. Jaycees, 1982, Man of Yr., Chula Vista Star-News, 1983; recipient Outstanding Citizen award Chula Vista C. of C., 1985, Disting. Service award Chula Vista Jaycees, 1973, 82. Mem. San Diego Assn. Govts. (bd. dirs. 1981—), Theta Chi Alumni Assn. (Disting. Service award 1982). Congregationalist. Lodges: Optimists, Elks, Rotary, Kiwanis. Avocations: golf, coin collecting. Home: 647 Windsor Circle Chula Vista CA 92010 Office: Office of the Mayor 276 4th Ave Chula Vista CA 92010

COX, J. WILLIAM, health educator; b. St. Louis, Aug. 31, 1928; s. William E. and Evelyn (Schenck) C.; m. Anne Maczewsk, June 11, 1949; 1 child, William E. Student, Washington U., St. Louis; MD, St. Louis U., 1952, PhD, 1953. Diplomate Am. Bd. Internal Medicine. Chief research labs. VA Hosps., St. Louis, 1953-54; commd. med. officer USN, 1954, advanced through grades to Vice Adm., ret., 1983; chief medicine, dir. clinics Naval Hosp., Subic Bay, Philippines, 1961-63; chief medicine, dir. research Naval Hosp., Phila., 1965-69; dir. edn., tng. USN Med. Dept., Washington, 1971-77; comdg. officer Naval Regional Med. Ctr., San Diego, 1978-80; Surgeon Gen. USN, Washington, 1980-83; assoc. dir. Grad. Sch. Pub. Health San Diego State U., 1983-87; dir. dept. health services County of San Diego, 1987—; cons. in pub. health, profl. relations AMA, Chgo., 1983—. Contbr. numerous tech. reports, articles to profl. jours. Mem. House of Dels. AMA, 1970-83, 1986—; chmn. tech. adv. group San Diego County Bd. Suprs., 1986—; chmn. spl. services div. San Diego County Council Boy Scouts Am., 1986—. Recipient Borden award for Med. Research Borden Corp., St. Louis U., 1951, Disting. Alumni Merit award St. Louis U., 1981, Spl. award for Meritorious Service AMA, 1983, Disting. Service award Uniformed Services Univ. Health Scis., Bethesda, Md., 1983. Fellow Am. Coll. Physicians, Am. Coll. Chest Physicians, Phila. Coll. Physicians, Am. Coll. Cardiology; mem. AMA (Ho. of Dels. 1970-83, 86—). Republican. Lodge: Rotary. Avocations: swimming, music. Office: Dept Health Services San Diego County 1700 Pacific Hwy San Diego CA 92101

COX, JACQUELINE ROSALIE, telecommunications company executive; b. San Francisco, Mar. 29, 1942; d. Jack Domenic Pera and Rose Catherine (Koziel) Frazier; m. Eugene Clyde Batson, Nov. 22, 1975 (dec. Mar. 1981); children: Gerald, James, Joelle, Jennifer, Eugene Jr.; m. Nicholas Jay Cox, June 3, 1983; 1 stepchild, Adryan. Grad. high sch., Calif. Pub. Schs. Night mgr. Paul Bunyon Restaurant, Sacramento, Calif., 1961-65; floor mgr. Calif. Almond Growers, Sacramento, 1965-67; office mgr. Strasburg (Colo.) Telephone Co., 1976—. Contbr. articles to newspaper. Mem. Hist. Soc. Strasburg. Democrat. Roman Catholic. Club: Watkins (Colo.) Gun. Avocations: trap shooting, hunting for Indian arrowheads, reading, boating, fishing. Home: Rt 1 Box 140 1816 Aspen St Strasburg CO 80136 Office: Strasburg Telephone Co PO Box 535 1450 Arapahoe Strasburg CO 80136

COX, JIM DALE, general contracting company executive; b. Harris, Mo., Nov. 24, 1931; s. John Clarence and Helen LuVerna (Holiday) C.; A.A. in Indsl. Mgmt., Independence (Kans.) Jr. Coll., 1951; B.S. in Real Estate and Constrn., U. Denver, 1956, M.B.A. in Fin., 1970; m. Joan Gregerson Green, Mar. 14, 1980; children—Susan J., John H., Charles Green, Andrea Green. Gen. mgr. Hopkins Mfg. Co., 1951-53, Shepard Constrn. Co., 1957-60; pres. Cox Constrn. Co., Colorado Springs, Colo., 1960-70, Village Contractors, Inc., Colorado Springs, 1980—; ptnr. SCS Co., constrn. mgmt., Colorado Springs, 1970—, Village Cos., Colorado Springs, 1972—; dir. First Bank Colorado Springs, Colo. Western Properties, Denver; lectr. U. Denver, 1965—. Mem. El Paso County Courthouse Com., 1969-72, Colo. Small Bus. Council; vice chmn. Colorado Springs Contractors Bd., 1964-65; chmn. Colorado Springs Fire Bd., 1979-86; chmn. adv. bd. Regional Bldg. Dept., 1987—; vice chmn. Regional Bldg. Dept., 1984-87. Mem. Home Builders Assn. Met. Colorado Springs (pres. 1963-64), Colorado Springs C. of C. Republican. Episcopalian. Clubs: El Paso, Garden of Gods, Country of Colo., Jaguar Clubs N. Am., U. Denver Pikes Peak Alumni (pres.). Home: 52 Polo Dr Colorado Springs CO 80906 Office: 104 S Nevada Ave Suite 107 Colorado Springs CO 80903

COX, JOHN HENRY, religious organization administrator, aeronautical engineer; b. Dorking, Surrey, Eng., May 17, 1941; s. William Edward and Ethel May (Bailey) C.; m. Elizabeth Mary Iris O'Brien, June 26, 1965; children: Jared Selvoy, Rachel Sonia. Diploma, Southall Coll. Technology, Eng., 1965. Lic. airline engr.; chartered engr. Asst. chief engr. British Airways, Eng., 1965-72, chief engr., 1972-77; national dir. Latter-day Saints Ch., Eng., 1977-83; internat. dir. Latter-day Saints Ch., Salt Lake City, 1983-85, welfare dir., 1985—. Mem. Inst. Mech. Engrs., Royal Aero. Soc., Brit. Inst. Mgmt. Avocation: photography.

COX, LARRY GLEN, engineering and construction company executive; b. Pampa, Tex., Jan. 16, 1938; s. Odis and Dorothy Izela (Woods) C.; B.S., U.S. Naval Acad., 1960; children—Terri, David. Commd. ensign, U.S. Navy, 1960, advanced through grades to lt. comdr.; with Polaris Nuclear Submarine Service, 1960-69; engr., mgr. prodn. ops. Exxon Gas System, King Ranch Gas Plant, Gulf Coast, Tex., 1969-76; mem. mgmt. staff Prudhoe Bay Prodn. Facilities Project, Pasadena, Calif., div. supervising engr., 1976-79; v.p. ops. Williams Instrument Co., Inc. and partner U.S.A. Industries, Inc., Valencia, Calif., 1979-81; prin. project mgr. The Ralph M. Parsons Co., Pasadena, Calif., 1981-82; dep. program dir. Sohio Endicott Arctic Ocean Prodn. Facilities, Beaufort Sea, Alaska, 1983; offshore programs bus. devel. advisor, Parsons Co., 1984—; project dir. Amerada Hess North Star Arctic Project, 1985; proposal mgr. office of civilian radioactive waste salt repository project Dept. Energy, 1986—; pres. Precision Systems Internat., Valencia, Calif., 1987—. Active Boy Scouts Am.; elder 1st Presbyterian Ch., Newhall, Calif. Served to capt. USNR. Registered profl. engr., Tex. Mem. ASME (chmn. Arctic ops. com.), Calif. Export Mgrs. Assn., Soc. Petroleum Engrs., Pacific Energy Assn., Pacific Coast Gas Assn. Club: Rotary. Office: 23528 San Fernando Rd #5 Newhall CA 91321-3121

COX, LYLE ASHTON, physicist; b. Atchison, Kans., Nov. 16, 1921; s. George King and Jessie Viola (Prather) C.; m. Jane Leecraft, Mar. 1, 1947; 1 son, Lyle A. B.S., U.S. Naval Acad., 1944; M.S. in Physics, MIT, 1953. Commd. ensign U.S. Navy, 1944, advanced through grades to comdr., 1960; served on U.S.S. Enterprise, 1944-45; student aviator, Corpus Christi, Tex., Pensacola, Fla., 1946-47; naval aviator, naval ordnance engr., Norfolk, Va., and other bases, 1947-64; physicist and dep. assoc. dir. Lawrence Livermore Nat. Lab., U. Calif., 1964—. Mem. AIAA, Sigma Xi. Republican. Club: Commonwealth of Calif. Home: 569 Escondido Circle Livermore CA 94550 Office: Lawrence Livermore Nat Lab U Calif Livermore CA 94550

COX, MARCUS BUD, educational administrator; b. Miami, Ariz., Aug. 5, 1944; s. Bud and Mildred (Bell) C.; m. June Arlene Milne, June 26, 1971; children—John David, Arlene Rebecca. B.A. in Elem. and Spl. Edn., U. Ariz., 1969, M.Ed. in Counseling and Guidance, 1977, M.Ed. in Ednl. Adminstrn., 1979. Tchr. Savannah Sch. Dist., Anaheim, Calif., 1969-71, Coolidge (Ariz.) Unified Schs., 1971-78, supr. counselor, dir. Indian edn., 1978-79, asst. prin., 1979-82; elem. sch. prin. Casa Grande (Ariz.) Elem. Dist. 4, 1982—. Scoutmaster Boy Scouts Am., 1974-75; coach Little League, 1982—. Mem. Ariz. Sch. Administrs., Nat. Assn. Elem. Sch. Prins. Republican. Roman Catholic. Lodges: Optimists, Lions Internat. Co-author physical edn. handbook, special edn. plan. Home: 1213 Avenida Grande Casa Grande AZ 85222 Office: 501 S Florence St Casa Grande AZ 85222

COX, MARK STANLEY, public relations professional; b. Uvalde, Tex., May 9, 1953; s. George Washington and Ora Faye (Wilson) C.; m. Jennifer Holinsworth Tidwell, Jan. 10, 1972 (div. Feb. 1977); 1 child, Amy Melissa; m. June Lynn Long; children: George Michael, Stephen William. BA, U. Okla., 1980; MS in Mass Communications, San Diego State U., 1983. Asst. editor Communicator Mag., San Diego, 1982-83; pub. info. coordinator City of Chula Vista, Calif., 1983—. Served with USAF, 1972-76. Named one of Outstanding Young Men of Am., 1984, 86. Mem. Pub. Relations Soc. Am., Chula Vista C. of C., San Diego Quarterdeck Club (chmn. 1986-87). Democrat. Roman Catholic. Club: San Diego. Avocations: fiction writing, guitar, ship modeling. Home: 790 Oaklawn Ave #B Chula Vista CA 92010 Office: City of Chula Vista 276 4th Ave Chula Vista CA 92101

COX, MILO LAWSON, retired agriculture educator; b. Denison, Tex., Aug. 27, 1916; s. Milo Rockwell and Effie Maude (Price) C.; m. Thelma Ann Thomson, Nov. 24, 1942; children: Karen Ann, Kelly Brent. Student, U. Tex., 1935-37; BS, Tex. A&M U., 1941; MS, U. Nebr., 1955, PhD, 1957; postgrad., Johns Hopkins U., 1962; PhD (hon.), U. Nebr., 1976. Ecologist Tex. State Govt., 1940-41, 46-48, Tex. Research Found., Renner, Tex., 1949-51; aquatic biologist Lake Improvement Co., Austin, Tex., 1948-49; asst. prof. U. Nebr., Lincoln, 1954-57; agrl. devel. specialist AID, Asia, Africa, South Am., 1957-75; prof. Renewable Nat. Resources, U. Ariz., Tucson, 1975-86; cons. NASA, Brooking Instn., NSF, Nat. Acad. Sci., Dept. of State, Rockefeller Found., 1975-86. Contbr. articles to sci. jours. Served with USN, 1941-46. Recipient Sr. FAculty award Fgn. Service Instn., Dept. of State, 1973. Mem. Soc. Range Mgmt., Soc. Agronomy, Sigma Xi. Home: 3356 E 5th Tucson AZ 85716

COX, PAUL ALAN, biologist, educator; b. Salt Lake City, Oct. 10, 1953; s. Leo A. and Rae (Gabbitas) C.; m. Barbara Ann Wilson, May 21, 1975; children: Emily Ann, Paul Matthew, Mary Elisabeth, Hillary Christine. BS, Brigham Young U., 1976; MSc, U. Wales, 1978; AM, Harvard U., 1978, PhD, 1981. Teaching fellow Harvard U., Cambridge, Mass., 1977-81; Miller research fellow Miller Inst. Basic Research in Sci., Berkeley, Calif., 1981-83; asst. prof. Brigham Young U., Provo, Utah, 1983-86, assoc. prof., 1986—; ecologist Utah Environ. Council, Salt Lake City, 1976; staff ecologist Utah MX Coordination Office, Salt Lake City, 1981. Mem. editorial bd. Pacific Studies. Recipient Bowdoin prize; Danforth Found. fellow, 1976-81, Fulbright fellow, 1976-77, NSF fellow, 1977-81, Melbourne Univ. fellow, 1985-86; named Presdl. Young Investigator, 1985—. Mem. Brit. Ecol. Soc., N.Y. Acad. Scis., Am. Soc. Naturalists, Assn. for Tropical Biology, AAAS, New Eng. Bot. Club. Mormon. Office: Brigham Young U Dept Botany Provo UT 84602

COX, RAYMOND WHITTEN, III, political science educator, academic director; b. Cambridge, Mass., Aug. 21, 1949; s. Raymond Whitten Cox Jr. and Louise Carolyn Holmes; m. Charlene Marie Sharp, Oct. 9, 1975 (div. Jan. 1981); 1 child, Geoffrey; m. Susan Jane Buck, Feb. 5, 1982; children: Joshua, Bethany. BA, Northeastern U., 1972; M in Pub. Adminstrn., Suffolk U., 1975; PhD, Va. Poly. Inst., 1983. Asst. dir. research Mass. Ho. of Reps., Boston, 1970-77; program dir. NSF, Washington, 1977-82; instr. Va. Poly. Inst., Blacksburg, 1982-83; asst. prof. Bemidji (Minn.) State U., 1983-85; dir. pub. adminstrn. programs No. Ariz. U., Flagstaff, 1985—; cons. Beltrami County Welfare Office, Bemidji, 1984-85, Yuma (Ariz.) Econ. Devel. Corp., 1986. Contbr. articles to profl. jours. Mem. exec. com. Beltrami County Dem. Farmer Labor Party, Bemidji, 1984-85; mem. Dem. precinct com. Coconino County, Flagstaff, 1985—, vice chmn. Coconino County Dems., 1987—; mem. fund-raising com. No. Ariz. U. Campus Christian Ctr., Flagstaff 1986—. Recipient Outstanding Performance award Dept. of Def., Hartford, Conn., 1969; named one of Outstanding Young Men of Am., Jaycees, 1981. Mem. Am. Polit. Sci., Acad. Polit. Sci., Wester Polit. Sci. Assn. (membership com. 1986—), Am. Soc. Pub. Adminstrn. (nat. council 1986—). Democrat. Episcopal. Avocations: tennis, reading. Home: 1807 Deer Crossing Rd Flagstaff AZ 86001 Office: No Ariz U Dept Polit Sci Box 15036 Flagstaff AZ 86011

COX, RICHARD HORTON, civil engineering executive; b. Paia, Hawaii, Oct. 10, 1920; s. Joel B. and Helen Cliford (Horton) C.; m. Hester Virginia Smith, Dec. 12, 1942; children: Millicent, Janet, Lydia, Evelyn, David, Samuel. BS, Calif. Inst. Tech., 1942, MS, 1946. Registered profl. engr., surveyor, Hawaii. Supr. rocket range Calif. Inst. Tech., Pasadena, 1942-46; civil engr. McBryde Sugar Co., Eleele, Hawaii, 1946-56; land mgr. Alexander & Baldwin, Honolulu, 1956-71, v.p., 1971-86; engring. cons. Honolulu, 1986—. Fellow ASCE; mem. AAAS, NSPE, Am. Geophys. Union, Hawaiian Sugar Technologists. Mem. Soc. of Friends. Home: 1951 Kakela Dr Honolulu HI 96822

COX, SANDERS BROWNLOW, process engineer, solid state physicist; b. Dallas, Aug. 31, 1945; s. Sanders Brownlow and Clara Sue (Haywood) C.; m. Linda Sue Dupree, June 4, 1967 (div. 1984); children: Meredith, Brandon; m. Phyllis Cecile Pei, June 14, 1986. BS, So. Meth. U., 1967; MA, U. Tex., Arlington, 1973. Program mgr., sr. processor Tex. Instruments, Dallas, 1973-84; mgr. semiconductor engring. Signetics Corp., Albuquerque, 1984—, cons. on radiation effects, 1973—; lectr. physics U. Tex., Arlington, 1975-80; project officer underground nuclear testing USAF, 1971-73; researcher on semiconductor devices, quantum theory of solids, energy band theory, 1967—. Contbr. articles to profl. jours. Served to capt. USAF, 1967-71. Mem. IEEE, ASTME, Electrochem. Soc., Am. Phys. Soc., Sigma Pi Sigma. Home: 5713 Papaya Pl Albuquerque NM 87111 Office: Signetics Corp 9201 Pan Am Freeway Albuquerque NM 87184

COX, WENDELL, transportation consultant; b. Los Angeles, Dec. 14, 1944; s. Raymond and Shirley (Miller) C.; student U. So. Calif., 1963-65; B.A. in Polit. Sci., Calif. State U.-Los Angeles, 1968; M.B.A., Pepperdine U., Los Angeles, 1981; divorced; children: Deanna, Jeffrey, Gregory. Credit mgr. Marshall Imports Co., Los Angeles, 1967-68; asst. credit mgr. Bishop Industries, Union, N.J., 1969; mem. credit dept. United Factors (named changed to Crocker Comml. Services, 1977), Los Angeles, 1969-73, mgmt. cons., 1973-76, asst. mgr. credit services dept., 1977-78, mgr., 1978-79, mgr. client services, 1979-82; mktg. mgr. Crocker Nat. Bank, Los Angeles, 1983-85; urban transp. cons., 1985—. Bd. dirs. Rice Ctr. Joint Ctr. for Urban Motality Research, Houston; chmn. Mayor's San Fernando Valley Adv. Com. on Transp., 1975-76; mem. Calif. Dept. Transp., I-405 Diamond Ln. Adv. Com., 1976, mem. transit performance measures project rev. com., 1981—; mem. Los Angeles County Transp. Commn., 1977-85, chmn. service coordination com., 1978-85, mem. fin. rev. com., 1978-85, chmn. energy task force, 1979, mem. ad hoc rapid transit com. 1981-85 ; chmn. Nat. Conf. on Energy Contingency Planning in Urban Areas, Houston, 1983; mem. Urban Mass Transit Adminstrn. Bus Line Costing Procedures Rev. Panel, U.S. Dept. Transp., 1981-83; adj. prof. transp. Calif. State U., Long Beach, 1985—; Subsidy Allocation Rev. Panel, 1982-84 ; bd. govs. Tng. Rev. Panel, 1982-84 ; mem. Pvt. Sector Operation of Pub. Transit Rev. Panel, 1982-85 ; mem. pvt. sector/public sector commuter bus study com. So. Calif. Assn. Govts., 1981-83; vice chmn. Crocker People Care Charitable Contbn. Campaign, 1983-84. Mem. Transp. Research Bd. (chmn. energy contingency planning com. 1982-84, mem. com. on pub. cooperation in providing pub. transit service 1982—), Am. Pub. Transit Assn. (mem. performance indicators com. and governing bds. com., chmn. policy and planning com. 1982-84), Am. Bus. Assn. (bd. dirs. mass transit programs 1985—). Contbr. articles to profl. publs. Home and Office: PO Box 8083 Belleville IL 62222

COX, WILLIAM HAROLD, writer, photographer; b. Atlanta, June 23, 1940; s. Harold A. Cox and Mary L. (Lewis) Midlam; m. Patricia Anne Sullivan, Aug 20, 1965 (div. 1984). Student, U. Alaska, 1958-60, U. N.Mex., 1960-61, 63-65. Tech. writer McDonnell Douglas, Long Beach, Calif., 1966-74; editor Plane and Pilot Mag., Encino, Calif., 1975-78, Keep Flying Mag., Ft. Atkinson, Wis., 1978-80; freelance writer, photographer Long Beach, 1980—; assoc. producer/writer ABC Wide World of Flying, Los Angeles, 1985—. Mem. Aviation Space Writers Assn. Home and Office: 4556 Faculty Ave Long Beach CA 90808

COY, TIMOTHY KIRK, advertising executive; b. Chgo., Mar. 4, 1958; s. Shirley Delbert and Bette Kathleen (Havens) C.; m. Elizabeth Ann Martin, Sept. 27, 1980. BJ, U. Colo., 1980. Advt. acct. exec. Rocky Mountain News, Denver, 1981—. Republican. Episcopalian. Avocations: skiing, computer programming. Home: 365 Pheasant Run Louisville CO 80027 Office: Rocky Mountain News 400 W Colfax Ave Denver CO 80204

COYLE, DOUGLAS JEFFERSON, state official; b. Lebanon, Oreg., Mar. 14, 1943; s. Alton Jefferson and Doris Marie (Cutts) C.; m. Karen Denise Edwards, Aug. 16, 1981; children by previous marriage—Alan Jefferson, Jeanette Marie. B.S., Oreg. State U., 1965. Forester Linn Fire Patrol, Foster, Oreg., 1963-67; forest insp. Oreg. Forestry Dept., Grants Pass, 1967-68, forest fire protection analyst, Salem, 1968-70, unit forester, Wallowa County, 1971-72, head forestry mapping, 1972-74, area mgr., 1977—, dist. forester, LaGrande, 1974-77; fire boss state-wide fire team State of Oreg., 1976-78; fire investigator specialist, 1973—. Mem. Union County Planning Com., LaGrande, 1975-77, Econ. Devel. Dist., 1976-77; advisor Eastern Oreg. State Coll. Curriculum, 1977; mem. Marion County Econ. Devel. Com., 1983. Mem. Soc. Am. Foresters (chmn. 1975-76, 80-81). Republican. Lutheran. Lodges: Elks, Eagles. Home: 2532 Gray Oak Ln Salem OR 97302 Office: Oreg Forestry Dept 2600 State St Salem OR 97310

COYLE, ROBERT EVERETT, federal judge; b. Fresno, Calif., May 6, 1930; s. Everett LaJoya and Virginia Chandler C.; m. Faye Turnbaugh, June 11, 1953; children—Robert Allen, Richard Lee, Barbara Jean. B.A., Fresno State Coll., 1953; J.D., U. Calif., 1956. Bar: Calif. Ptnr. McCormick, Barstow, Sheppard, Coyle & Wayte, 1958-82; judge U.S. Dist. Ct. (ea. dist.) Calif., 1982—. Mem. Fresno County Bar Assn. Office: 5116 U S Courthouse Fresno CA 93721 •

COYNE, BRIAN JOSEPH, lawyer; b. Yonkers, N.Y., Apr. 8, 1940; s. John Henry and Della (O'Brien) C.; m. Fumiko Hoshida; Mar. 26, 1965; children: Cheryl Lee, Moira Julliette. BA, Cornell U., 1963; PhD, U. Chgo., 1968; JD, Boston U., 1976. Bar: Wash. 1976, U.S. Patent Office 1980. Asst. atty. gen. State of Wash., Olympia, 1976-81; assoc. J. Leggett, Tacoma, 1981-83; sole practice Olympia, 1983-85; ptnr. Miles, Way, Coyne & Humphrey, Olympia, 1985—. Sec., treas. Capital Area Community TV Assn., Olympia, 1985—. Mem. Wash. State Bar Assn. Home: 2918 S Orange St Olympia WA 98501 Office: Miles Way & Coyne Heritage Fed Savs Bldg Olympia WA 98501

COYOLI, EDMUND CHARLES, advertising account manager, consultant; b. Kansas City, Mo.; s. Edmundo S. and Edna Jane (Taylor) C.; m. Kathleen Michelle Haddow, June 10, 1972; children—Christopher Edmund, Suzanne Michelle. B.A. in Liberal Studies, Calif. State U.-Northridge, 1977; postgrad. UCLA, 1981—. Gen. mgr. Stanley Holden Dence Center, West Los Angeles, Calif., 1971-74; account exec. classified, Los Angeles Times, 1974-77, advt. account exec. display, 1977-80; sr. advt. account exec. Bernard Hodes Advt., Inc. div. Doyle Dane Bernbach, Encino, Calif., 1980—; free lance advt. cons. Club: Advt. Los Angeles. Office: Bernard Hodes Advt Inc 16027 Ventura Bldg Suite 300 Encino CA 91436

COYTE, CAROLINE R., contracts administrator, writer; b. Panama C.Z., June 9, 1951; d. Hugh Wayne and Gloria (Scott) Randel; student Am. U., 1969-71, George Washington U., 1972-73; B.A. in Polit. Sci., U. Ariz., 1973; grad. Western State U. Coll. Law, 1984; m. Michael Alan Coyte, June 26, 1978; 1 child, Alistair Jeremy. Profl. staff/writer U.S. Senate Republican Policy Com., Washington, 1973-77; legis. asst./speechwriter U.S. Senator Cliff Hansen, Washington, 1977-78; dir. legislation Nat. Asphalt Pavement Assn., Washington, 1979-80; with Wickes Cos., San Diego, 1981-82, corp. govt. affairs analyst, 1982; with ICA Mortgage Corp., La Jolla, Calif., 1984-86; with Mgmt. Analysis Co., Del Mar, Calif., 1986—. Mem. Nat. Assn. Female Execs. Presbyterian.

COZART, MARJORIE LEE, computer software executive, consultant; b. Kensington, Kans., Dec. 19, 1930; d. Ervin Wayne and Clementine Elizabeth (Zrubec) Oliva; m. Jack Dean Conway, Dec. 25, 1947; m. Cornelius Garrett Cozart, July 12, 1975; children: Judith Conway Hawkins, Douglas Jack Conway. Student, Parks Bus. Coll., Denver, 1963-64. Lic. real estate salesman. Property mgr., acct. Van Schaack & Co., Denver, 1958-63; office mgr. Computer Listing Services, Denver, 1961-65, Pennant Petroleum Co., Denver, 1965-66; v.p. Petroleum Data Systems, Denver, 1967-71; pres., owner, founder Oil-Tronix Ltd., Denver, 1972—, computerized oil and gas accting. software and timesharing services, land mgmt. acctg., application software designer. Mem. Denver Assn. Petroleum Landmen, Am. Assn. Petroleum Landmen, Bus. and Profl. Women's Orgn., Denver C. of C. Democrat. Club: Denver Country. Lodges: Zonta, Order Eastern Star. Contbr. articles to profl. pubs. Home: 1299 Gilpin St Park Towers 5W Denver CO 80218 Office: Oil-Tronix Ltd 1580 Lincoln Suite 1240 Denver CO 80203

CRABBS, ROGER ALAN, consultant, publisher, small business owner; b. Cedar Rapids, Iowa, May 9, 1928; s. Winfred Wesley and Faye (Woodard) C.; m. Marilyn Lee Westcott, June 30, 1951; children—William Douglas, Janet Lee, Ann Lee. B.A. in Sci., State U. Iowa, 1954; M.B.A., George Washington U., 1965, D.B.A., 1973; M.Christian Leadership, Western Conservative Bapt. Sem., 1978. Commd. 2d lt. USAF, 1950, advanced through grades to lt. col., 1968; Ret. U.S. Air Force, 1972; asst. prof. mgmt. U. Portland, Oreg., 1972-74; assoc. prof. U. Portland, 1974-79; prof. bus. George Fox Coll., Newberg, Oreg., 1979-83; pres. Judson Bapt. Coll., The Dalles, Oreg., 1983-85; corp. cons. Harmon & Assocs., Inc., Stanwood, Wash., 1985—; pres., assoc. pub. Host Pubs. Inc. doing bus. as Travel Host of Portland, 1985; pres. Crabbs, Braden & Pamplin, Inc., 1974-77, Walt Morgan Travel and Tours, Inc., 1976-77, Plain & Fancy Fencing, Inc., 1979-80; chmn. bd. Micro-Tech., Inc., 1979-86; treas., dir. Blascmb B Corp.; chmn. bd. UOA of Embarcadero, Inc., Climax Mfg., Inc., Yaquina Rental Agy., Inc.; cons. to various orgns., corps. and agys. Author: The Storybook Primer on Managing, 1976; The Infallible Foundation for Management-The Bible, 1978; The Secret of Success in Small Business Management-Is in the Short Range, 1983. Pres. bd. dirs. Living Rehab. Ctr., Inc., 1975-79; v.p. bd. dir. Young Audiences of Oreg., Inc., 1975-78; bd. dirs. George Fox. Coll. Found., Inc., 1979-83; chmn. bd. dirs. Western's Mt. Tabor Ednl. Services Found.; trustee Western Conservative Bapt. Sem., 1980-86; deacon, mem. long-range planning com. N. Am. Bapt. Conf.; mem. Small Bus. Adv. Council, Oreg. dist. SBA, 1983—. Decorated Air Force Commendation medal with oak leaf cluster, Meritorious Service medal Dept. Def.; rated Command Air Force Missileman; recipient regional, dist. and nat. awards SBA; U. Portland grantee, 1976-78. Mem. Acad. Mgmt., Am. Soc. Personnal Adminstrn., Small Bus. Inst. Dirs. Assn., Am. Arbitration Assn., Service Corps. Ret. Execs./Active Corps of Execs., Air Force Assn., Alpha Kappa Psi, Delta Epsilon Sigma. Republican. Club: Portland Officers. Lodges: Rotary, Masons. Office: Harmon and Assocs Inc 13563 NW Cornell Rd Suite 173 Portland OR 97229-5892

CRABTREE, SAMUEL EPSTEIN, sailing educator, charter skipper, delivery captain; b. Los Angeles, Mar. 1, 1935; s. Edward Crabtree and Pauline Epstein; m. Linda Arleen Friedland, Sept. 2, 1957 (div. 1975); children: David Owen, Robbin Dale, Michele Elise. AA, Los Angeles City Coll., 1955; student, U. Calif., Davis, Los Angeles, Berkeley, 1955-58, U. So. Calif., 1959; BSCE, Sacramento State Coll., 1960. Jr. civil engr. City of Woodland, Calif., 1960; asst hwy. engr. State of Calif. div. Hwys., Bishop, 1961-63; assoc. civil engr. City of Walnut Creek, Calif., 1964; pvt. practice civil engring. Antioch, Calif., 1965—; instr. sailing Crabtree Maritime Services, Antioch, 1983—. Mem. Waterfront Com., Antioch, 1977. Mem. ASCE, NSPE, Calif. Soc. Profl. Engrs., Calif. Land Surveyors Assn., U.S. Yacht Racing Union, Diablo Sailing Club (commodore 1985), SYRA of San Francisco Bay (chmn. protest com. 1975-85), Catalina 22 Nat. Sailing Assn. (nat. commodore 1974-75), Oceanic Soc. San Francisco (instr. 1984—), Richmond Yacht Club, Ocean Cruising Club. Office: Crabtree Maritime Services PO Box 529D Pittsburg CA 94565

CRAFT, C. DOUGLAS, research chemist; b. Pensacola, Fla., Oct. 4, 1953; s. Manuel Charles and Betty Odell (Boyd) C.; m. Audrey Jeanne Daniels, Nov. 15, 1981. BS in Chemistry, U. W. Fla., 1975, BS in Scis. Interdisciplinary, 1975. Research chemist U.S. Bur. Reclamation, Denver, 1976—. Contbr. articles to profl. jours. Mem. citizens adv. council Colo. Craniosynostosis Project. Mem. Am. Chem. Soc., Soc. Environ. Toxicology and Chemistry, Chemometrics Soc. Avocations: music, writing, visual arts, philosphy. Home: 13642 W 65th Pl Arvada CO 80004 Office: US Bur Reclamation PO Box 25007-D-1523A Denver CO 80225-0007

CRAIB, KENNETH BRYDEN, resource development executive, physicist, economist; b. Milford, Mass., Oct. 13, 1938; s. William Pirie and Virginia Louise (Bryden) C.; m. Gloria Faye Lisano, June 25, 1960; children—Kenneth Jr., Judith Diane, Lori Elaine, Melissa Suzanne. B.S. in Physics, U. Houston, 1967; M.A. in Econs., Calif. State U., 1982. Aerospace technologist NASA, Houston, 1962-68; staff physicist Mark Systems, Inc., Cupertino, Calif., 1968-69; v.p. World Resources Corp., Cupertino, 1969-71; dir. resources devel. div. Aero Service Corp., Phila., 1971-72; dir. ops. Resources Devel. Assocs., Los Altos, Calif., 1972-80, pres., chief exec. officer, Diamond Springs, Calif., 1980-85; owner Sand Ridge Arabians, 1980—; chmn., dir. Resources Devel. Assocs., Inc., 1982—, Devel. Support Internat. Inc., Placerville, Calif., 1981—; pres., chmn., dir. RDA Internat., Inc., 1986—; dir. Sierra Gen. Investments, 1985—. Contbr. articles to profl. jours. Served with USAF, 1957-61. Recipient Sustained Superior Performance award NASA, 1966. NASA grantee, 1968. Mem. Am. Soc. Photogrammetry, Soc. Internat. Devel., Agrl. Research Inst., Calif. Select Com. Remote Sensing, Internat. Assn. Natural Resources Pilots, Remote Sensing Soc. (council), Am. Soc. Oceanography (charter), Aircraft Owners and Pilots Assn., Gulf and Caribbean Fisheries Inst., Placerville C. of C. Republican. Universalist. Home: 6431 Mary Ann Ln Placerville CA 95667 Office: RDA Internat Inc 801 Morey Dr Placerville CA 95667

CRAIG, ARNOLD CHARLES, chemistry professor; b. Johnstown, N.Y., Sept. 5, 1933; s. Arnold Henry Craig and Burdella Louisa (Fonda) Stone; m. Rhoda Evelyn Richardson, May 30, 1959; children: Heather S.R., Lindsay A.R., Colin R.F. BA, Utica Coll., 1954; PhD in Chemistry, Cornell U., 1959. Sr. research chemist Eastman Kodak Co., Rochester, N.Y., 1959-65; asst. prof. Mont. State U., Bozeman, 1965-68, assoc. prof., 1968-74, prof. chemistry, 1974—. contbr. articles to profl. jours. Mem. Am. Chem. Soc. (chmn. local sect. 1986-87), Inter-Am. Photochem. Soc., Mont. Acad. Scis.

Home: 1216 S Grand Bozeman MT 59715 Office: Mont State U Chemistry Dept Bozeman MT 59717

CRAIG, JOHN CYMERMAN, chemistry educator; b. Berlin, Jan. 23, 1920; came to U.S., 1960; m. Elaine Cuyler Roddy, Aug. 24, 1967; 1 child, Elizabeth Anne. BS with 1st class honors, Assoc. Royal Coll. Sci., Imperial Coll. U. London, 1942, diploma, 1945; PhD, U. London, 1945; DSc, Sydney (Australia) U., 1961. Research chemist Boots Pure Drug Co., Eng., 1945-47; from lectr. to sr. lectr. U. Sydney, 1948-60; prof. chemistry U. Calif., San Francisco, 1960—, from vice chmn. to dept. chmn., 1963-70, assoc. dean, 1980—; lectr. U. London, 1947-48; mem. preclin. psychopharmacology research rev. com. NIMH, Washington, 1963-79; mem. and chmn. panel vapor-phase pollutants Nat. Acad. Scis., Washington, 1970-75. Contbr. numerous articles to profl. jours. Nuffield Found. fellow Oxford (Eng.) U., 1955-57; faculty research lectrship. U. Calif., San Francisco, 1974-75; recipient Research Achievement award Am. Pharm. Assn. Research Found., 1967. Fellow Royal Soc. Chemistry; mem. Am. Chem. Soc., Am. Coll. Neuropsychopharmacology. Home: 103 Mendosa Ave San Francisco CA 94116 Office: U Calif Room 926-S San Francisco CA 94143

CRAIG, LARRY EDWIN, congressman; b. Council, Idaho, July 20, 1945; s. Elvin and Dorothy C. B.A., U. Idaho; postgrad, George Washington U. Farmer, rancher Midvale area, Idaho; mem. Idaho Senate, 1974-80, 97th-100th Congresses from 1st Dist. Idaho; mem. com. on govt. ops., com. on standards of official conduct, com. on interior and insular affairs.; Chmn. Idaho Republican State Senate Races, 1976-78. Pres. Young Rep. League Idaho, 1976-77; mem. Idaho Rep. Exec. Com., 1976-78; chmn. Rep. Central Com. Washington County, 1971-72; advisor vocat. edn. in public schs. HEW, 1971-73; mem. Idaho Farm Bur., 1965-79. Served with U.S. Army N.G., 1970-74. Mem. NRA (bd. dirs. 1983-87), Future Farmers of Am. (v.p. 1965). Methodist. Office: 1034 Longworth House Office Bldg Washington DC 20515

CRAIG, LEXIE FERRELL, career vocational guidance counselor; b. Halls, Tenn., Dec. 12, 1921; d. Monroe Stancil and Hester May (Martin) Ferrell; m. Philip L. Craig, May 19, 1951; children—Douglas H., Laurie K., Barbara J. B.S. magna cum laude, George Peabody Coll., Vanderbilt U., 1944; M.A. with honors, Denver U., 1965; postgrad. Colo. U., 1972—, Colo. State U., 1964—, U. No. Colo., 1964—. Cert. local vocat. adminstr., vocat. guidance specialist, vocat. bus. specialist, vocat. home econs. specialist, reading specialist, nat. recreation dir. specialist. Danforth grad. fellow Mich. State U., East Lansing, 1944-46; nat. student counselor, field dir. student counseling dept. higher edn. Am. Bapt. Conv., summer service career projects dir. U.S. and Europe, 1946-51; coordinator religious and career activities counselor, Colo. U., 1951-52; tchr. home econs., phys. edn., counseling, dist. 96, Riverside, Ill., 1952-54; substitute tchr., psychometrist, reading specialist part time, Deerfield, Ill., 1956-59; substitute tchr. Littleton (Colo.) Dist. VI, 1961-63, guidance and career counselor Littleton Pub. Schs., 1963-67, 68—, now career vocat. counselor specialist, guidance counselor, Littleton High Sch., Dist. VI, 1985—, also mem. vocat. needs and assessment com., career curriculum task force; dir., counselor YWCA Extension Program, Job Corps, Denver, 1967-68; tchr. adult edn. home econs. evenings, 1963-66; mem. Colo. State Career Task Force, 1973-77, Lay conf. rep. Meth. Ch. Pastor/Parish Commn.; bd. dirs. Powell Careers Post Council Boy Scouts Am., also mem. Colo. Career Awareness Council; bd. dirs. So. Suburban Recreation, Littleton Community Arts Ctr.; adv. council Powell PTO; adv. com. SEMBCS area vocat. schs.; mem. local caucus com. Republican Party; mem. Dist. Environ. Sci. Council. Didcott scholar, 1942; Danforth home econs. and leadership scholar, 1943; Am. Leadership Camp Found. scholar, Shelby, Mich., 1942-45; Hildegarde Sweet Scholar, 1983; recipient Sullivan award and grant, named outstanding grad., 1944; named Littleton Mother of Year, 1977, Colo. Vocat. Counselor of Yr., 1978, Colo. Vocat. Guidance Assoc. Counselor of Yr., 1984; recipient plaque for recruiting and career guidance Navy and Air Force, 1980, Clifford G. Houston award, 1985. Mem. NEA, AAUW, Colo. Edn. Assn., Littleton Edn. Assn., Am. Vocat. Assn., Colo. Vocat. Assn., Am. Assn. Counseling and Devel., Colo. Assn. for Counseling and Devel. (exec. bd.), Nat. Career Devel. Assn. (membership chmn.), Colo. Career Devel. Assn. (past pres., membership chmn.), Nat. Vocat. Guidance Assn. (Colo. rep.), Colo. Sch. Counselors Assn., Am. Field Service (pres. Littleton chpt.), Lit. Book Club Littleton Arts Ctr., Home Economists in Homemaking (Littleton and Bega, Australia clubs), Phi Delta Kappa, Delta Kappa Gamma Alpha Delta (chpt. pres.), Delta Pi Epsilon (past pres.), Pi Omega Pi (past pres.), Pi Gamma Mu (past pres.), Kappa Delta Pi (past pres.). Clubs: Order Eastern Star, Country Western Dance, Editor, pub. Join in a Song, 1949; editor The Church Follows Its Youth, 1950, curriculum units in consumer edn., home econs., careers, parenting classes.

CRAIG, MAYADELLE DELL, counselor, organizational development consultant; b. Wildrose, N.D., June 14, 1937; d. Willie O. and Olive May (Holland) Evenson; m. John Takas, 1979 (dec.); children: Cynthia, Joni. BA, U. Nev., Las Vegas, 1978; MA, Whitworth Coll., 1982; postgrad. Saybrook Inst. Cert. alcoholism counselor Wash. State Profl. Staff Soc., 1982. Counselor, group therapist Ct. Referral Services, Las Vegas, 1977-79; counselor, employee assistance program facilitator Southwest Community Alcohol Ctr., Seattle, 1979-81; pres. Dell Craig Therapists Inc., Des Moines, Wash., 1981—; developer, cons. employee assistance programs; franchiser catalyst plans on alcoholism recovery, organizational enhancement. Mem. Wash. State Council on Alcoholism, Am. Personnel and Guidance Assn., Psi Chi. Club: Toastmasters (Buren, Wash.). Office: Dell Craig Therapists Inc 22030 7th Ave S Suite 204 Seattle WA 98188

CRAIG, ROBERT WALLACE, educational administrator; b. Long Beach, Calif., Sept. 16, 1924; s. Harold Fleming and Ellen Amelia (Stagg) C.; m. Carol Williams Gallun, Nov. 5, 1957; children: Kathleen Elizabeth, Jennifer Courtney, Michael Brian. BS, BA cum laude, U. Wash., 1949; MA, Columbia U., 1951. V.p., exec. dir. Aspen (Colo.) Inst. for Humanistic Studies, 1954-64; v.p. Unimark Interior Design Inc., Aspen and Chgo., 1965-71; prin. Robert Craig & Assocs., 1965-73; ptnr. Genesis Inc., 1971-73, Rieben & Craig, Denver, 1973-75; pres. The Keystone (Colo.) Ctr., 1975—; mountain and cold weather tng. cons. U.S. Army, 1951-54; hon. trustee, co-founder Aspen Ctr. for Physics. Author (with others): K-2, The Savage Mountain, 1954, rev. ed., 1979, Storm and Sorrow, 1978. Bd. dirs. Summit Ski Edn. Found., Keystone, 1985—, Snake River Health Clinic, Keystone, Colo. Outward Bound, 1985—. Served to lt. (j.g.) USN, 1943-46, PTO. Democrat. Episcopalian. Clubs: Am. Alpine (pres. 1983-86), Century (N.Y.C.); Cactus (Denver); Bohemian (San Francisco). Leader Am.-Tibetan expedition, Mt. Everest, 1983; co-leader Am. expedition, Pamirs, USSR, 1974. Home: 624 Montezuma Rd Keystone CO 80435 Office: The Keystone Ctr PO Box 606 Keystone CO 80435

CRAIG, ROGER LEE, professional baseball manager; b. Durham, N.C., Feb. 17, 1930; m. Carolyn Anderson, Dec. 22, 1951; children: Sherri, Roger Jr., Teresa, Vicki. Student, N.C. State U. Pitcher various minor league teams, 1950-55, 58, 59; with Bklyn. (later Los Angeles) Dodgers, 1956-58, 59-61, N.Y. Mets., 1962-63, St. Louis Cardinals, 1964, Cin. Reds, 1965, Phila. Phillies, 1966; mgr. Albuquerque, Tex. League, 1968; coach San Diego Padres, Nat. League, 1969-72; pitching coach Houston Astros, 1974-75, San Diego Padres, 1978-79, Detroit Tigers, Am. League, 1980-84; mgr. San Francisco Giants, Nat. League, 1985—; pitcher World Series, 1955, 56, 59, 64. Office: care San Francisco Giants Candlestick Park San Francisco CA 94124 *

CRAIG, STEPHEN WRIGHT, business consultant; b. N.Y.C., Aug. 28, 1932; s. Herbert Stanley and Dorothy (Simmons) C.; m. Margaret M. Baker, June 10, 1958 (div. 1984); children: Amelia Audrey, Janet Elizabeth, Peter Baker; m. Bette Piller, 1984. A.B., Harvard U., 1954, J.D., 1959. Reporter Daily Kennebec Jour., Augusta, Maine, 1956; engaged in pub. relations with Am. Savoyards, 1957; atty. IRS, San Francisco, 1959-61; atty.-adviser U.S. Tax Ct., 1961-63; ptnr. Snell & Wilmer, Phoenix, 1963-78, Winston & Strawn (formerly Craig, Greenfield & Irwin), Phoenix, 1978-87, Myers, Craig & Co., Phoenix, 1987—; guest lectr. Amos Tuck Sch. Bus., Dartmouth, 1962; lectr. Ariz. and N.Mex. Tax Insts., 1966-67; guest lectr. Ariz. State U. Sch. Law, 1984, adj. prof. law, 1985-87. Chmn. Jane Wayland Child Guidance Center, 1968-70; mem. Maricopa County Health Planning Council, chmn. mental health task force.; mem. Ariz. Republican Com., 1967-72; bd. dirs. Combined Met. Phoenix Arts, 1968, adv. bd., 1968-69; adv. bd. Ariz. State U. Tax Insts., 1968-70; bd. dirs. Phoenix Community Council, 1970-73, Ariz. Acad. Served with AUS, 1954-56. Mem. state bars Ariz., Calif., Maine, Hasty Pudding Inst., Sigma Alpha Epsilon. Office: Myers Craig and Co 3636 N Central Ave Suite 680 Phoenix AZ 85012

CRAIGMILE, THOMAS KAY, neurological surgeon; b. Muncie, Ind., Dec. 28, 1924; s. William Wallace and Hallie (Metzker) C.; B.S., Northwestern U., 1946, M.B., 1948, M.D., 1949; m. Doris Wolfe, Apr. 15, 1950; children—Suzanne, Christine, Elizabeth, Marianne, Kathleen. Intern, Chgo. Wesley Meml. Hosp., 1949; resident neurol. surgery Northwestern U., 1952-54; asst. resident neurology Presbyn. Hosp., N.Y.C., 1956-57; chief resident neurol. surgery U. Colo. Med. Center, Denver, 1957-58, clin. instr. neurosurgery, 1959-61, asst. clin. prof. neurosurgery, 1961-69, assoc. clin. prof. neurol. surgery, 1969-84, clin. prof. neurol. surgery, 1984—. Served to capt., M.C., USAF, 1954-56. Diplomate Am. Bd. Neurol. Surgery. Fellow ACS; mem. Am. Assn. Neurol. Surgeons, Congress Neurol. Surgeons, Rocky Mountain Neurosurg. Soc. (sec. 1966-69, pres. 1970-71), Western Neurosurg. Soc. (v.p. 1974-75, pres. 1983-84), Colo. Neurosurg. Soc. (pres. 1978-79). Home: 4431 E 6th Ave Denver CO 80220 Office: U Colo Med Ctr 2005 Franklin St Suite 440 Midtown II Med Bldg Denver CO 80205

CRAIK, CHARLES SCOTT, biochemistry educator, researcher; b. Midland, Pa., June 5, 1954; s. Donald H. and Betty J. (Blair) C. BS, Allegheny Coll., 1976; MA, Columbia U., 1977, MPhil, 1980, PhD, 1981. Adj. asst. prof. biochemistry U. Calif., San Francisco, 1983-85, asst. prof., 1985—, asst. prof. pharm. chemistry, 1985—, co-dir. Biomolecular Research Ctr., 1985—. Contbr. articles to profl. jours. Doane Disting. scholar, Richard Lee scholar Allegheny Coll., Meadville, Pa., 1975; named one of Top 100 Innovators Sci. Digest, 1986; Am. Cancer Soc. fellow, U. Calif., San Francisco, 1981-83. Mem. AAAS, Am. Chem. Soc., Am. Soc. Biol. Chemists, Am. Assn. Pharm. Scientists, Sigma Xi, Phi Beta Kappa. Avocation: writing. Office: Univ Calif Dept Pharm Chemistry and Biochemistry/Biophysics San Francisco CA 94143-0448

CRAIN, BRIAN J(OHN), optometrist; b. Winnipeg, Man., Can., Dec. 6, 1942; came to U.S., 1948, naturalized, 1956; s. Irvin J. and Phyllis M. (Howick) C.; m. Joyce Carol Knudsen, Sept. 24, 1966; children—Sean Brian, Aaron John. B.A. in Journalism, U. Wash., 1966; postgrad. Pacific Luth. U., 1973; O.D., Pacific U., 1978. Advt. mgr., asst. Assoc. Grocers, Seattle, 1968-73; practice optometry, Auburn, Wash., 1978—; instr. optometric technician program Tacoma Community Coll., 1979-80; instr. continuing edn. for optometric technicians. Bd. dirs. Auburn Parks and Recreation Dept., 1982—; deacon bd. N.Am. Bapt. Ch., 1979-86; mem. White River Presbyn. Ch., 1986—. Mem. Am. Optometric Assn., Wash. Optometric Assn., Optometric Editors Assn., Beta Sigma Kappa. Club: Rotary (pres. Auburn 1985-86). Editor Wash. Optometry Today, 1979-84. Home: 1235 25th St SE Auburn WA 98002 Office: 921 Suite A Harvey Rd Auburn WA 98002

CRAIN, CHARLES ANTHONY, telephone company executive; b. Decatur, Ill., 1931. Grad., U. Ill., 1955. Pres. Hawaiian Telephone Co., Honolulu; exec. v.p. Gen. Telephone Co. of Calif., Thousand Oaks, also bd. dirs. Office: Hawaiian Telephone Co PO Box 2200 Honolulu HI 96841 *

CRAMER, DOUGLAS SCHOOLFIELD, broadcasting executive; b. Louisville, Aug. 22; s. Douglas Schoolfield and Pauline (Compton) C.; m. Joyce Haber, Sept. 25, 1966 (div. 1973); children: Douglas Schoolfield, III, Courtney Sanford. Student, Northwestern U., 1949-50, Sorbonne, Paris, 1951; B.A., U. Cin., 1953; M.F.A., Columbia U., 1954. Prodn. asst. Radio City Music Hall, N.Y.C., 1950-51; with script dept. Metro-Goldwyn-Mayer, 1952; mng. dir. Cin. Playhouse, 1953-54; instr. Carnegie Inst. Tech., 1955-56; TV supr. Procter & Gamble, 1956-59; broadcast supr. Ogilvy, Benson & Mather, 1959-62; v.p. program devel. ABC, 1962-66, 20th Century-Fox-TV, Los Angeles, 1966-68; exec. v.p. in charge prodn. Paramount TV, 1968-71; ind. producer, pres. Douglas S. Cramer Co., 1971—; exec. v.p. Aaron Spelling Prodns., 1976—. Exec. producer: Bridget Loves Bernie, CBS-TV, 1972-73, QB VII, 1973-74, Dawn: Portrait of a Teenage Runaway, NBC-TV, 1976; co-exec. producer: Love Boat, ABC, 1977-86, Vegas, ABC, 1978-81, Wonder Woman, ABC, 1975-77, CBS, 1977-78; co-exec. producer: Dynasty, 1981-87, Matt Huston, 1982-84, Hotel, 1983-86, Colbys, 1985-87, Crossings, 1986; co-exec. producer, ABC, 1981; author: plays Call of Duty, 1953, Love Is A Smoke, 1957, Whose Baby Are You, 1963. Bd. dirs., v.p. Ctr. Theatre Group, Los Angeles Music Ctr.; v.p. trustee, mem. exec. com. Mus. Contemporary Art, Los Angeles; bd. dirs. Am. Ballet Theatre. Served with U.S. Army, 1954. Mem. Beta Theta Pi. Club: Univ. (N.Y.C.). Office: Warner Hollywood Studios 1041 N Formosa Los Angeles CA 90046

CRAMER, EDWARD A(LFRED), JR., real estate broker; b. Cin., May 12, 1932; s. E. Alfred and Ruth Joann (O'Donnell) C.; m. Connie Faye Hanks, Jan. 25, 1958 (div. Mar. 1985); children: Carla Michelle, Caryn Denise, Christina Lynn. BA in Internat. Relations, UCLA, 1956; postgrad., Mich. State U., 1968-71; MS, Pepperdine U., 1974; postgrad., Nat. U., 1982-83. Enlisted USMC, 1950; commd. ensign USN, 1956, advanced through grades to comdr., 1970, ret., 1975; br. mgr. Floyd & Boltz Century 21, Chula Vista, Calif., 1975-76; mgr. San Diego dist. Grubb & Ellis Real Estate Brokerage Inc., Oakland, Calif., 1977-78; regional dir. Realty Register of U.S., Los Angeles, 1979-80; prin., owner Circle Investment Realty Co., San Diego, 1980—; instr. real estate U. Calif., San Diego, 1981-86. Author: Introduction to Real Estate Sales, 1979, Real Estate Management, 1980. Mem. San Diego County Flood Control Commn., 1978-82, Assessment Appeals Bd., San Diego, 1984-87, Calif. Dept. Fair Housing and Employment, Sacramento, 1984-85; chmn. Sweetwater Community Planning Group, San Diego County, 1974-80. Mem. Nat. Assn. Realtors (bd. dirs. 1982-88), Calif. Assn. Realtors (regional v.p. 1985), San Diego Bd. Realtors (v.p. 1983, pres. 1984), Realtors Nat. Mktg. Inst. (residential brokerage council), Am. Arbitration Assn. (panelist 1980-87). Republican. Avocations: photography, tennis, golf, travel. Home: 5648 Menorca Dr San Diego CA 92124 Office: Circle Realty and Investment Co 4973 A Clairemont Dr San Diego CA 92117

CRAMER, HARRISON EMERY, environmental scientist; b. Johnstown, Pa., May 27, 1919; s. Frank Wilson and Ella Field (Emery) C.; m. Virginia Myrtle Viets, Dec. 22, 1942; children: Anne Cramer Tupker, Dorothy Cramer Kitchen, Nancy Cramer Donoghue, William H. AB, Amherst Coll., 1941; SM, MIT, 1943, ScD, 1948. Lab. instr. MIT, Cambridge, 1942-44, research assoc., 1946-49, research meteorologist, 1949-65; dir. environ. scis. lab. tech. div. GCA Corp., Bedford, Mass., 1965-72; pres. H.E. Cramer Co., Inc., Salt Lake City, 1972-85, cons. Salt Lake City, 1986—; mem. shuttle environ. effects team NASA, 1981. Contbr. articles to profl. jours. Served as ensign USNR, 1944-46, PTO. Amherst (Coll.) Meml. fellow, 1941-42. Fellow AAAS, Am. Meterol. Soc., Royal Meterol. Soc.; mem. Air Pollution Control Assn., Am. Geophys. Union, Phi Beta Kappa, Sigma Xi. Home: 1581 Millbrook Rd Salt Lake City UT 84106

CRAMER, ROGER EARL, chemistry educator; b. Findlay, Ohio, Sept. 14, 1943; s. Wallace and Laura Mae (Kring) C.; m. Katherine Fusae Kawasaki, June 11, 1967; children: Christine, Jennifer. BS, Bowling Green State U., 1965; MS, U. Ill., 1967, PhD, 1969. Asst. prof. chemistry U. Hawaii, Honolulu, 1969-73, assoc. prof., 1973-80, prof., 1980—, assoc. chmn. dept. chemistry, 1980-84, chmn. dept., 1986—; vis. prof. Northwestern U., Evanston, Ill., 1978. Contbr. articles to profl. jours.; patentee in field. Recipient Nat. Research Service award NIH, 1978. Mem. Am. Chem. Soc. (sec. Hawaii sect. 1975, chmn. 1977, councilor 1978—, mem. com. chem. edn. 1979-80, com. divisional activities 1983—). Republican. Methodist. Home: 896 Hao Honolulu HI 96821 Office: U Hawaii Dept Chemistry Honolulu HI 96822

CRAMOND, RICHARD, JR., structural engineer, diversified electronics company executive; b. Mpls., June 30, 1945; s. Richard Sr. and Emelia Hilma (Lundstrom) C.; m. Helen A McNalis, Feb. 28, 1987. AS, Long Beach (Calif.) City Coll., 1966; BSE cum laude, Calif. State U., Long Beach, 1968; MSCE, U. N.Mex., 1970; PhD in Structural Engring., U. Ill., 1974. Registered profl. civil engr., Calif. Naval architect Long Beach Naval Shipyard, 1968; research asst. E.H. Wang Civil Engring. Research Facility, Albuquerque, 1968-70, A. H-S Ang, Cons. Engr., Urbana, Ill., 1972-73; mem. tech. staff TRW Corp., 1973-75, engring. analysis sect. head, 1975-78, sr. project engr., 1978-80, facilities dept. mgr., 1980-84; silo hardening tech. dept. mgr. TRW Corp., San Bernardino, Calif., 1984-86; hml mgr. TRW Corp., San Bernardino, 1987—. Treas. Country Village Homeowners Assn., Yucaipa, Calif., 1980—. Mem. Soc. Exptl. Stress Analysis (sec.-treas. 1969), ASCE, AIAA, Tau Beta Pi, Chi Epsilon, Phi Kappa Phi. Democrat. Presbyterian. Avocations: hiking, fishing. Home: 36226 Ginger Tree Trail Yucaipa CA 92399 Office: TRW PO Box 1310 San Bernardino CA 92402

CRANDALL, GARY JOSEPH, real estate developer, consultant, investor; b. Pratt, Kans., June 4, 1947; s. Joseph Walter and Arlene Kay C.; B.B.A. (Wall St. Jour. Achievement award), U. N.Mex., 1969, M.B.A. (Sam Angel Meml. scholar), 1973; m. Jane Ellen Russell, Sept. 2, 1966; children—Melanie Anne, Martin Leslie, Maurice Spencer, Michelle Marie. Prin., corp. treas. Energy Conversion Systems, Inc., Albuquerque, 1969-70; mgr. acctg. Computer Micro Image Systems, Inc., Los Angeles, 1970-71; trainee Bank of N.Mex., Albuquerque, 1971-72, asst. cashier, mgr. credit dept., 1972-74, v.p., comml. loan officer, 1974-77; exec. v.p., prin. Bruce J. Pierce & Assos., Inc., Albuquerque, 1977—; v.p., dir. Colorview Services Inc., 1981—; instr. Am. Inst. Banking, 1973-77. Loaned exec. United Fund, Albuquerque, 1974; mem. Gov.'s Devel. Credit Corp. Adv. Com., 1976; bd. dirs. Urban Enhancement Trust Fund. Mem. Albuquerque Assn. Credit Mgmt. (past pres., dir.), Albuquerque Conservation Assn. (past bd. dirs., mem. exec. com.), Albuquerque C. of C. (local govt. affairs com.), Pi Kappa Alpha Alumni Assn. Republican. Clubs: Petroleum, U. N.Mex. Lobo. Home: 13301 Manitoba Dr NE Albuquerque NM 87111 Office: Bruce J Pierce & Assoc Inc 320 Central Ave SW Suite 30 Albuquerque NM 87102

CRANDALL, IRA CARLTON, consulting electrical engineer; b. South Amboy, N.J., Oct. 30, 1931; s. Carlton Francis and Claire Elizabeth (Harned) C.; m. Jane Leigh Ford, Jan. 29, 1954; children—Elizabeth Anne, Amy Leigh, Matthew Garrett. BS in Radio Engring., Ind. Inst. Tech., 1954, BS in Elec. Engring., 1958; BS in Electronics Engring., U.S. Naval Postgrad. Sch., 1962; PhD, U. Sussex, 1964; MA, Piedmont U., 1967, DSc (hon.), 1968; LLB, Blackstone Sch. Law, 1970; DLitt, St. Matthew U., 1970; EdD, Mt. Sinai U., 1972; Assoc. Bus., LaSalle U., 1975, B in Computer Sci., 1986. Tchr. Madison Twp. Pub. Schs., N.J., 1954-55; commd. ensign U.S. Navy, 1955, advanced through grades to lt. comdr., 1965, released to inactive duty, 1972; engring. cons. Concord, Calif., 1972—; pres. 7C's Enterprises, Concord, 1972—; v.p. Dickinson Enterprises, Concord, 1973-77, Williamson Engring., Inc., Walnut Creek, Calif., 1974-82; pres., chmn. bd. I.C. Crandall and Assocs., Inc., Concord and Westminster, Calif., Tigard, Oreg., 1976-82; pres. Internat. Research Assocs., Concord, 1982—; chief elec. engr. Gayner Engring. Inc., San Francisco, 1982—. Vice pres. PTA, Concord, 1969; tribal organizer Mt. Diablo YMCA Indian Guide Program, 1971-74; pres. Mt. Diablo Unified Schs. Interested Citizens. Decorated Vietnamese Cross of Valor. Fellow Am. Coll. Engrs.; mem. U.S. Naval Inst. Am. Naval Assn., Assn. Elec. Engrs., IEEE, Am. Inst. Tech. Mgmt. (sr.), Soc. Am. Mil. Engrs., Nat. Model Ry. Assn., Assn. Old Crows, Concord Homeowners Assn., Concord Chamber Singers, Concord Blue Devils, SAR, Pi Upsilon Eta, Gamma Chi Epsilon, Alpha Gamma Upsilon. Republican. Methodist (adminstrv. bd. ch. 1971-76). Clubs: Navy League, Century. Lodge: Optimists (pres.). Home: 5754 Pepperridge Pl Concord CA 94521 Office: PO Box 3268 Walnut Creek CA 94598

CRANDALL, JERRY CECIL, artist, historian; b. LaJunta, Colo., Apr. 1, 1935; s. Cecil and Nancy (Murray) C. m. Judith Ann Neulreich, July 4, 1976. Student Woodbury Coll. Los Angeles, 1960-62. Comml. artist JWC Publs., Van Nuys, Calif., 1966-69, M. Douglass Corp., Long Beach, Calif., 1969-73; free-lance artist, historian, Sedona, Ariz., 1973—; tech. adv., historian Columbia Pictures, Hollywood, Calif., 1979, Universal Pictures, 1978; speaker on profl. motivation in the arts U. Calif.-Riverside, 1980-81. Prin. works include Little House on the Prairie, 1974, Wild Bill Hickock, 1975, Robert Conrad as Pasquinelle, 1978, Custer's Last Stand, 1980, The Gulf of Sidra Incident, 1987; commissions The 49ers, 1986, James Bowie, 1987; represented in permanent collections Favell Mus. Western Art, Klamath Falls, Oreg., Koshare Mus., la Junta, Colo. Served with U.S. Army, 1955-57. Recipient hon. mention Death Valley 49ers Ann. Art Show, 1975; silver medal Western Artists Am., 1981, gold medal, 1981. Mem. Little Big Horn Assocs., Am. Fighter Aces Assn. (assoc.), 91st Bomb Group (assoc.), Golden Eagle Soc., Am. Soc. Aviation Artists, Am. Mt. Men, Internat. Plastics Modelers Soc. Home: PO Box 2606 Sedona AZ 86336 Office: Eagle Editions Ltd PO Box 1830 Sedona AZ 86336

CRANDALL, RICHARD EUGENE, research physics educator; b. Ann Arbor, Mich., Dec. 29, 1947; s. Harold E. and Janice A. (Brandt) C. BA, Reed Coll., 1969; PhD, MIT, 1973. Chief engr. Electronics Research Group, Arlington, Mass., 1973-75; dir. environ. tech. Nat. Kinney Corp., N.Y.C., 1975-77; chmn. Innovations Group Electro-Sci. Industries, Portland, Oreg., 1977-78; pres. Metaresearch, Inc., Portland, 1979—, chmn. bd. dirs., 1981—; asst. prof. physics Reed Coll., Portland, 1978-83, assoc. prof., 1983—, chmn. dept. physics, 1978-85. Contbr. articles to sci. jours.; patentee in field. Fellow Ednl. Tech. Ctr. of Next, Inc. Home: 6106 SE 44th Portland OR 97206 Office: Reed Coll Dept Physics 3203 SE Woodstock Portland OR 97202

CRANDALL, VERN JAY, computer science educator, consultant; b. Logan, Utah, Mar. 18, 1939; s. Bliss Hansen and Mildred (Johnson) C.; m. Linda Rae Storms, Jan. 28, 1972; children: Lance Vernon, Shane Lewis, Scott David. BA, Brigham Young U., 1963; MS, Kans. State U., 1966; PhD, U. Wash., 1972. Machine operator, systems programmer DHI Computing Service, Provo, Utah, 1954-63, statistician, 1963-65, v.p. research and devel., 1965-79; asst. prof. computer sci. and stats. Brigham Young U., Provo, 1968-72, assoc. prof., 1972-79, prof., 1979—; pres., chmn. Vern J. Crandall & Assocs. Inc., Provo, 1982—; bd. dirs., treas. Innovation Enterprises, Inc., 1972-79; cons. Inst. Logopedics Wichita (Kans.) State U., 1963-65, IBM, Sperry Corp., IOMEGA Corp., Pacific Telesis, Novell Corp., others 1978—. Author: Problem Solving and Writing Commercial Grade Programs Using Pascal, 1986; also articles to profl. jours. Grantee NIH Kans. State U., 1963-65, U. Wash., Seattle, 1965-68, 72, NSF, 1971-72, others. 1982—. Mem. IEEE, Assn. Computing Machinery. Republican. Mormon. Lodge: Lions (officer Provo club 1968-74). Avocations: classical music, oil painting, playing brass instruments, reading and writing murder mysteries, hiking. Home: 1224 E 700 South Provo UT 84601 Office: Brigham Young U 236 TMCB Provo UT 84602

CRANE, JULIAN COBURN, retired educator, agriculturist; b. Morgantown, W.Va., Mar. 7, 1918; s. Harley Lucious and Fern (Coburn) C.; m. Elizabeth Dorsey, Sept. 18, 1942; 1 child, Diana Carolyn (dec.). BS in Horticulture, U. Md., 1939, PhD in Horticulture, 1942. Horticulturist USDA, Washington, 1942, agronomist, 1943-45; asst. prof. pomology U. Calif., Davis, 1946-52, assoc. prof., 1952-58, prof., 1958-85. Contbr. articles to profl. jours. Recipient Merit award Calif. Fig Inst., 1954; Fellow NSF, 1957. Fellow Am. Soc. Hort. Sci.; mem. AAAS, Am. Soc. Plant Physiology, Sigma Xi, Alpha Zeta. Republican. Presbyterian. Home: 3508 Lakeview Dr El Macero CA 95618 Office: U Calif Dept Pomolgy Davis CA 95616

CRANE, PETER MARSTON, research psychologist; b. Rochester, N.Y., Apr. 9, 1950; s. Edward M. and Sarah (Perry) C.; m. June Minns, Dec. 16, 1972; children: Nathan J., Eleanor S. BA, Wittenberg U., 1972; MA, Miami U., Oxford, Ohio, 1974, PhD, 1977. Asst. prof. psychology Miami U., Oxford, 1977-79, U. Pitts., 1979-84; research psychologist U. Dayton Research Inst., Higley, Ariz., 1984-86, Air Force Human Resources Lab., Williams AFB, Ariz., 1986—. Contbr. articles to profl. jours. Mem. Human Factors Soc., Soc. Info. Display. Office: Air Force Human Resources Lab AFHRL/OTE Williams AFB AZ 85240

CRANE, TERESE ANN, educator, researcher; b. Van Nuys, Calif., Oct. 3, 1947; d. Walter James and Leontine Emma (Karle) Riendeau; m. Bruce Allen Crane, Dec. 21, 1968; children: Matthew, Adam, Ambrose, Alexis. AA, Los Angeles Valley Coll., 1967; BA, Mt. St. Mary's Coll., 1969; MA, Calif. State U., Los Angeles, 1978; EdD, UCLA, 1984. Cert. tchr., Calif. Elem. tchr. Los Angeles Archdiocese, 1969-74, 76-79; instr. Mt. St. Mary's Coll., Los Angeles, 1982; tchr. St. Genevieve Sch., Panorama City, Calif., 1982-83; tchr., asst. prin. Our Lady of Peace Sch., Sepulveda, Calif., 1983-85; elem. tchr. Los Angeles Unified Schs., 1985—. Contbr. articles to profl. mags. Mem. Am. Edn. Research Assn., Assn. Supervision Curriculum Devel., Phi Delta Kappa, Pi Lambda Theta. Democrat. Roman Catholic. Avocations: reading, writing, family. Home: 17906 Wellhaven St Canyon

Country CA 91351 Office: Plainview Elem Sch 10819 Plainview Ave Tujunga CA 91042

CRANMER, DAVID CHARLES, ceramics engineer; b. Lakewood, N.J., Jan. 13, 1954; s. Joseph Edgar and Marjorie (Richardson) C.; m. Joan Hockridge, May 28, 1977; 1 child, Alexana. BS in Ceramic Scis., Pa. State U., 1976; SM in Ceramics, MIT, 1978, PhD in Ceramics, 1981. Mem. tech. staff Advanced Tech. Ctr. Bendix Corp., Columbia, Md., 1981-83; mem. tech. staff Materials Scis. Lab. Aerospace Corp., El Segundo, Calif., 1984-86; ceramic engr. U.S. Nat. Bur. Standards, Gaithersburg, Md., 1986—. Contbr. articles to profl. jours. Mem. Am. Ceramic Soc. (program chmn. so. Calif. sect. 1985-86), Materials Research Soc., Soc. Glass Tech., Soc. Advancement of Materials and Process Engring., Keramos (v.p. 1974-75, pres. 1975-76), Sigma Xi. Avocations: running, skiing, softball, soccer.

CRANS, DEBBIE CATHARINA, chemistry educator; b. Copenhagen, Aug. 13, 1955; came to U.S., 1980; d. Flemming Holten Nielsen and Sytje Gerritje Crans. BS, Copenhagen U., 1890; PhD, Harvard U., 1984. Research asst. Copenhagen U., 1978-80; teaching asst. Harvard U., Cambridge, Mass., 1980-81, tutor, 1981-84, research asst., 1982-84; research asst. MIT, Cambridge, 1981-82; postdoctoral fellow UCLA, 1984-86, instr., 1986; asst. prof. Colo. State U., Ft. Collins, 1986—. Scholarstipendium Copenhagen U., 1979-80; recipient Egmond H. Petersen Fund stipend, Erlangen, Fed. Republic Germany, 1980; Am. Heart fellow, Los Angeles, 1986. Mem. AAAS, Am. Chem. Soc., Magisterforeningen (Danish). address: Colo State U Dept Chemistry Fort Collins CO 80523

CRANSTON, ALAN, U.S. senator; b. Palo Alto, Calif., June 19, 1914; s. William MacGregor and Carol (Dixon) C.; m. Norma Weintraub, May 19, 1978; children: Robin MacGregor (dec.), Kim MacGregor. Student, Pomona Coll., 1932-33, U. Mexico, 1933; A.B., Stanford, 1936. Fgn. corr. Internat. News Service, Eng., Italy, Ethiopia, Germany, 1936-38; Washington rep. Common Council Am. Unity, Washington, 1940-41; chief fgn. lang. div. O.W.I., Washington, 1942-44; exec. sec. Council for Am.-Italian Affairs, Inc., Washington, 1945-46; partner bldg. and real estate firm Ames-Cranston Co., Palo Alto, Calif., 1947-58; controller State of Calif., 1959-67; pres. Homes for a Better America Inc., 1967-68; v.p. Carlsberg Financial Corp., Los Angeles, 1968; mem. U.S. Senate from Calif., 1969—; Democratic whip U.S. Senate, 1977—; mem. com. on banking, housing and urban affairs, chmn. subcom. housing and urban affair, mem. com. on fgn. relations, chmn. subcom. East Asia affairs, chmn. com. on vets. affairs, mem. Dem. steering com., Dem. policy com. and Select com. on Intelligence. Author: The Big Story, 1940, The Killing of the Peace, 1945. Mem. exec. com. Calif. Democratic Central Com., 1954-60; pres. Calif. Dem. Council, 1953-57. Served with AUS, 1944-45. Mem. United World Federalists (nat. pres. 1949-52). Club: Overseas Press Am. Office: 112 Hart Senate Bldg Washington DC 20510

CRANSTON, HOWARD STEPHEN, lawyer; b. Hartford, Conn., Oct. 20, 1937; s. Howard Samuel and Agnes (Corvo) C.; m. Karen Youngman, June 16, 1962; children: Margaret, Susan. BA cum laude, Pomona Coll., 1959; LLB, Harvard U., 1962. Bar: Calif. 1963, U.S. Dist. Ct. (cen. dist.) Calif. 1966, U.S. Dist. Ct. (no. dist.) Calif. 1973, U.S. Dist. Ct. (so. dist.) Calif. 1976, U.S. Supreme Ct. 1980. Assoc. MacDonald & Halsted, Los Angeles, 1964-68; ptnr. MacDonald, Halsted & Laybourne, Los Angeles, 1968-82, of counsel, 1982-86; pres. Knapp Communications, Los Angeles, 1982-87; pres. S.C. Cons. Corp., 1987—; mem. Conf. Bd. Legal Trust Services Commn., 1985-86. Served to 1st lt. U.S. Army, 1962-64. Republican. Episcopalian. Club: Harvard (N.Y.C.). Office: Knapp Communications Corp 5900 Wilshire Blvd Los Angeles CA 90036

CRAPO, LAWRENCE MARTIN, physician; b. Portland, Oreg., Sept. 12, 1938; s. Philip Madison and Audrey Vivienne (Petterson) C.; m. Kathleen Alice Ranney; children: Larisa, Bryan. BS, U. Calif., Berkeley, 1960; PhD, Harvard U., 1964; MD, Stanford U., 1973. Cert. Bd. Internal Medicine, Bd. Endocrinology and Metabolism. Asst. prof. medicine Stanford (Calif.) U., 1978-84, assoc. prof., 1984—. Author: Vitality and Aging, 1981, Hormones: The Messengers of Life, 1985. Mem. ACP, Am. Fedn. Clin. Research, Endocrine Soc. Avocations: jazz, tennis. Home: 690 Salvatierra St Stanford CA 94305 Office: Santa Clara Valley Med Ctr 751 S Bascom Ave San Jose CA 95128

CRAPO, MICHAEL DEAN, laywer; b. Idaho Falls, Idaho, May 20, 1951; s. George LaVelle and Melba (Olsen) C.; m. Susan Diane Hasleton, June 22, 1974; children: Michelle, Brian, Stephanie, Lara, Paul. BA, Brigham Young U., 1973; JD, Harvard U., 1977. Bar: Calif. 1977, Idaho 1979. Law clk. to judge U.S. Ct. Appeals, San Diego, 1977-78; atty. Gibson, Dunn & Crutcher, Los Angeles, 1978-79; ptnr. Holden, Kidwell, Hahn & Crapo, Idaho Falls, 1979—. Senator Idaho State Legis., Boise, 1985—; leader Boy Scouts Am., Calif, Idaho, 1977—. Named one of Outstanding Young Men of Am., 1985. Mem. ABA, Idaho State Bar. Republican. Mormon. Lodge: Rotary. Avocations: sports, backpacking. Office: Holden Kidwell Hahn Crapo PO Box 129 Idaho Falls ID 83402

CRARY, JAMES HERBERT, data processing executive; b. Denver, Sept. 4, 1928; s. John Howard and Lucile Teresa (Jaeger) C.; m. Beth Jackson, Sept. 6. 1949; children: Susan, Nancy, Anne. BSEE, U. Denver, 1950; MSEE, Stanford U., 1951, PhDEE, 1961. Research engr. Stanford (Calif.) U., 1953-61; electronic engr. Dept. of Commerce, Boulder, Colo., 1961-73; cons. Boulder, 1973-74; electronic engr. The Pentagon, Washington, 1974-75; computer programmer, analyst Jefferson County, Golden, Colo., 1975—; cons. Boulder, 1973—. Contbr. articles to profl. jours. Mem. Internat. Sci. Radio Union, Sigma Xi. Avocations: radio electronics, photography, computers, volleyball. Home: 947 Crestmoor Dr Boulder CO 80303 Office: Jefferson County Mgmt Info Systems 1700 Arapahoe Golden CO 80419

CRASWELL, ELLEN, state senator; b. Seattle, May 25, 1932; m. Bruce A. Craswell, 1953; children—Richard Bruce, James Arthur, Patricia Louise Craswell Johnson, Jill Ellen Craswell Solano. Student U. Wash. Mem. Wash. State Senate, pres. task force to sec. edn. Am. Legis. Exchange Council; dir. Gt. N.W. Fed. Savs. and Loan. Bd. dirs. Seattle Hearing and Speech Clinic. Republican. Methodist. Club: Altrusa. -1 Office: Senate of Wash State Capitol Olympia WA 98504 *

CRAVEN, EDWARD PATRICK, JR., accountant; b. Memphis, Dec. 22, 1952; s. Edward Patrick Sr. and Mary Ellen (Heuertz) C. BBA in Accountancy, U. Miss., 1974. CPA Tex., Nev. From staff auditor to sr. auditor Arthur Andersen & Co., Houston, 1974-78; controller Lansky Bros. Mens Stores, Memphis, 1978; sr. internal auditor, supr. internal auditing Holiday Corp., Memphis, 1979-81, mgr. consol. reporting and corp. acctg., 1981-84; dir. internal auditing Harrah's, Reno, 1984—. Mem. Nev. Soc. CPA's, Am. Inst. CPA's, Tex. Soc. CPA's, Inst. Internal Auditors (bd. govs. Nev. chpt. 1984—). Republican. Roman Catholic. Avocations: golf, fishing. Home: 4520 Gorc Way Reno NV 89502 Office: Harrah's PO Box 10 Reno NV 89520

CRAVEN, HOMER HENRY, JR., pilot, aviation consultant; b. Seattle, Jan. 31, 1925; s. Homer Henry and Juanita Normah (Briscoe) C.; student S.W. Tex. State Coll.; m. Mary Kathleen Weaver, May 3, 1945; children—James Michael, Scott Marshall, Anne Elizabeth Craven McDonald. With Boeing Airplane Co., Seattle, 1946-48, Smith Aviation, Renton, Wash., 1948-52; pilot Northwest Orient Airlines, Seattle, 1952-85, B-747 capt., 1976-85; aviation cons. 19—. Served with USAAF, 1943-45; PTO. Decorated Air medal. Mem. Am. Soc. Aerospace Edn., Nat. Aero. Assn., Exptl. Aircraft Assn., Aircraft Owners and Pilots Assn., 14th Air Force Assn., Northwest Captain's Club, Confederate Air Force. Episcopalian. Author research papers on fuel conservation. Home: 1060 89th St NE Bellevue WA 98004 Office: Northwest Airlines Sea-Tac Airport Seattle WA 98001

CRAVENS, DANIEL LESTER, engineering geologist, hydrogeologist; b. Albuquerque, Nov. 26, 1957; s. Phillip William and Elizabeth Ann (Olmstead) C. B.S. in Phys. Sci., Colo. State U.-Ft. Collins, 1980; M.S. in Geology N.Mex. State U., 1983. Research geophysicist N.Mex. State U., Las Cruces, 1980-83; engring. geologist, hydrogeologist Leedshill-Herkenhoff Engring., Albuquerque, 1983—; cons. geohydrologist, Albuquerque, 1983—; pres. Rocky Mountain Geotech, 1987. Fellow Am. Assn. Petroleum Geologists, Assn. Engring. Geologists; mem. Nat. Waterworks Assn., N.Mex. Geol. Soc. Republican. Clubs: Internat. Health (Albuquerque); Christian Cowboys (Las Cruces). Home: PO Box 398 Tijeras NM 87059 Office: Leedshill-Herkenhoff PO Box 1217 Albuquerque NM 87059

CRAVENS, JAMES ELLIOT, hospital supply company executive; b. Los Angeles, June 2, 1949; s. James Elliott and Hazel Nelle (Harvey) C.; m. Janice Mary Dziekan, Nov. 29, 1974; children: Mary Nelle, James John. BS, UCLA, 1973. Med. specialist Burroughs-Wellcome Research, Triangle Park, Calif., 1974-77; parenteral specialist Travenol Labs., Deerfield, Ill., 1977-79; chmn. Dealex Hosp. Supply, Brea, Calif., 1979—; founder, pres. Packaging Techologies, Brea, 1982-84; founder, v.p. Pathfinder Group, Horsham, Pa., 1984—. Bd. dirs. Diamond Bar (Calif.) Community Schs., 1985-86. Mem. Nat. Intravenous Therapy Assn. Democrat. Roman Catholic. Avocations: music, guitar, photography. Office: Dealex Hosp Supply 266 Viking Ave Brea CA 92621

CRAVER, JOHN STONE, management consultant; b. Honesdale, Pa., Nov. 2, 1928; s. Myron Beach and Elizabeth (Stone) C.; m. Joan Marion Rau, Aug. 25, 1950 (div. 1971); children: John Stone, Diane Stone, Kenneth Stone, Sarah Elizabeth; m. Gay Griswold, July 10, 1971 (div. 1975); 1 child, Linda Griswold; m. Jacqueline Rose, Aug. 5, 1976. BS, Lehigh U., 1950; MBA, U. Pa. Wharton Sch Fin., 1955. Securities broker H.M. Byllesby & Co., Phila., 1950-51; systems designer RCA, Camden, N.J., 1951; systems engr. Piasecki Helicopter Corp., Morton, Pa., 1951-52; systems analyst Bethlehem (Pa.) Steel Co., 1953-59; mgr. product planning UNIVAC, Los Angeles, Phila. and Norwalk, Conn., 1959-61; mgr. engring. Philco Computer div., Phila., 1961-62; designer computer complex NASA man spacecraft control ctr. Philco Computer div., Houston, 1962-63; cons. Informatics Inc., Sherman Oaks, Calif., 1963-64, Hobbs Assoc., Corona Del Mar, Calif., 1964-66; dir. mktg. Dartex div. Tally Corp., Tustin, Calif., 1966-68; v.p. mktg. Tri Data Corp., Mountain View, Calif., 1968-71; program mgr. Newell Industries, Sunnyvale, Calif., 1971-72; v.p. Omron Research and Devel., Mountain View, 1972-75; exec. v.p. H.P. Books, Tucson, 1976-80; cons. Cypress, Calif., 1980—; bd. dirs. Citrivine Corp., SRB Devel. corp., Fisher Found., Omron Research and Devel., Omron Systems, Am. Vidconetics, Inc., Internat. Liquid Crystal Corp., Data Disk, Inc.; lectr. computer design UCLA, 1969-72; chmn. Santa Clara County Mental Health Adv. Bd., San Jose, Calif., 1973-75; cons. Office of Naval Research, Washington, 1963-65. Author: Graph Paper from your Copier, 1979, Visicals for Apple II, II , IIE, 1983; inventor elastomeric connector for micro circuits.

CRAWFORD, ARTHUR WALLACE, investment broker; b. Chgo., Mar. 24, 1921; s. Arthur Wallace and Elizabeth (Merrill) C.; A.B. cum laude, Harvard, 1941; m. Genevieve Byers Johnston, July 16, 1941 (div. 1976); children—Priscilla, Marie Crawford Saale, Carol, Susan Crawford Marsh; m. 2d, Norma Silvas Myers, May 21, 1976 (dec. Aug. 1986). Market research analyst L. E. McGivena & Co., N.Y.C., 1941; exec. asst. N.Am. Aviation, Inc., Los Angeles, 1941-44, 1946-57; investment broker J. Barth & Co., Los Angeles, 1957-65, Dominick & Dominick, Inc., Los Angeles, 1965-67, White, Weld & Co., Los Angeles, 1967-73, Shields & Co., Los Angeles, 1973-75; investment broker Smith, Barney Harris Upham & Co., Inc., Los Angeles, 1975—, v.p.-sales div. Served as lt. (j.g.) USNR, 1944-46; in U.S.S. Fred T. Berry. Republican. Clubs: Athletic. Lectr. on investments. Author: Practical Portfolio Management, 1971. Home: 9160 Florence Ave #303 Downey CA 90240 Office: Smith Barney Harris Upham and Co 800 W 6th St 11th Floor Los Angeles CA 90017

CRAWFORD, CAROL A., marketing executive; b. San Francisco, Jan. 17, 1945; d. Kenneth H. and Marcella (Schloesser) C. B.A., San Jose State U., 1967; M.B.A. in Mktg., Golden Gate U., 1985. Food publicist J. Walter Thompson, San Francisco 1967-70; asst. mktg and sales promotion dir. Eastridge Shopping Ctr., San Jose, Calif., 1970-72; consumer info. specialist Carl Byoir & Assocs., San Francisco, 1972-78; account supr. Ketchum Pub. Relations, San Francisco, 1978-80; v.p., dir. pub. relations Grey Advt., San Francisco, 1980-82; dir. corp. communications S&O Cons., San Francisco, 1982-84; mgr. mktg. and pub. relations GTE Sprint, 1984-86; dir. pub. relations U.S. Sprint, 1986; instr. pub. relations Golden Gate U., 1987; cons., lectr. in field, 1987—. Bd. mgrs. YMCA, Embarcadero, 1980-82. Mem. Pub. Relations Soc. Am. (past chpt. pres.), Am. Women in Radio and TV (past chpt. membership chmn.), Home Economists in Bus. (past chpt. chmn., past chmn. nat. pub. relations). Home and Office: 1350 California St #307 San Francisco CA 94109

CRAWFORD, DON LEE, bacteriologist, educator; b. Santa Anna, Tex., Sept. 28, 1947; s. Lester Crawford and Doris D. (Smith) Norman; m. Melinda S. Blanchard, July 30, 1970; 1 child, Sarah. BA in Biology, Okla. City U., 1970; MS in Bacteriology, U. Wis., 1972, PhD in Bacteriology, 1973. Asst. prof. biology George Mason U., Fairfax, Va., 1973-76; asst. prof. bacteriology U. Idaho, Moscow, 1976-80, assoc. prof., 1980-82, prof., 1982—; bd. dirs. Idaho Research Found., Inc., Moscow; pres. Crawford Norman, Inc., Moscow, 1982—; cons. in biotech., 1980—. Contbr. articles to profl. jours.; patentee in field. Mem. Am. Soc. Microbiology, Gamma Sigma Delta (Outstanding Researcher U. Idaho Coll. Agr. 1985). Avocation: photography. Office: U Idaho Dept Bacteriology Biochemistry Moscow ID 83843

CRAWFORD, JOYCE CATHERINE HOLMES, psychologist; b. Kansas City, Mo., May 30, 1918; d. Morton Henry and Lillian Catharine (Burton) Holmes; student Kansas City Jr. Coll., 1934-36; B.S. in Edn., U. Mo., 1938; M.A. in Guidance and Counseling, No. Ariz. U., 1957; Ph.D. in Ednl. Psychology, Ariz. State U., 1976; m. Merle Eugene Crawford, Dec. 18, 1938; children—Hal Wayne, Kent Holmes. Tchr., Sedona, Ariz., 1948-49, Verde Valley Sch., 1949-51, Cottonwood, Ariz., 1952-69; sch. psychologist, child study cons., Phoenix, 1971-75, Riverside Sch. Dist., 1972-74, Avondale Sch. Dist., 1971-83. Ranger-naturalist Tuzigoot Nat. Monument, U.S. Park Service, summers 1959-66; mem. Ariz. Gov.'s Adv. Com. on Mental Health, 1964-65, Ariz. Hosp. Survey and Constrn. Adv. Council, 1965-68; head start chmn. Cottonwood Neighborhood Council, 1967-69; sec. Yavapai County Head Start Policy Adv. Com., 1968-71; bd. dirs. Yavapai County Econ. Opportunity Council, 1967-70, sec., 1968-69; bd. dirs. Ariz. Assn. Mental Health, 1955-67, sec., 1961-64, founder Verde Valley chpt., 1956, pres., 1959-61; incorporating com. Verde Valley Community Guidance Clinic, 1965, bd. dirs., 1965-70; bd. dirs. No. Ariz. Comprehensive Guidance Center, 1967-69; bd. dirs., recreation chmn. Ariz. Congress Parents and Tchrs., 1954-55; bd. dirs. Westside Mental Health Services, 1980-87, pres., 1980, v.p., 1980-81; chmn. profl. referral com. Westside Children's Mental Health Service, 1983-87; bd. dirs. Southwest Community Network, 1985—. Cert. Ariz. Bd. Psychologist Examiners. Mem. Nat. Assn. Sch. Psychologists, Ariz. Assn. Sch. Psychologists (chmn. profl. standards com. 1980-81, pres. 1982-83, awards chmn. 1983-84), Am. Psychol. Assn., Ariz. Psychol. Assn., Ariz. Assn. Children with Learning Disabilities, Psychologists for Social Responsibility, Planned Parenthood, Common Cause, ACLU, Delta Kappa Gamma. Democrat. Home: 1606 N 161st Ave Goodyear AZ 85338

CRAWFORD, NATALIE WILSON, applied mathematician; b. Evansville, Ind., June 24, 1939; d. John Moore and Edna Dorothea (Huthsteiner) Wilson; B.A. in Math., U. Calif., Los Angeles, 1961, postgrad., 1964-67; m. Robert Charles Crawford, Mar. 1, 1969. Programmer analyst N.Am. Aviation Corp., El Segundo, Calif., 1961-64; mem. tech. staff Rand Corp., Santa Monica, Calif., 1964—, project leader, engring. tech., theater conflict and force employment programs, 1975—; cons., joint tech. coordinating group munition effectiveness. Named YWCA Woman of Yr., 1983. Mem. Am. Def. Preparedness Assn., USAF Assn., IEEE. Republican. Home: 20940 Big Rock Dr Malibu CA 90265

CRAWFORD, NEIL STANLEY, Canadian provincial official; b. Prince Albert, Sask., Can., May 26, 1931; d. William Francis and Hannah (Hoehn) C.; m. Catherine May Hughes, Sept. 3, 1951; children: Scot, Teresa, Ian, Elaine, Sandra, Robert. Bar: Alta. 1955. Created Queen's Counsel, 1972; practice law Alta., 1955-61, 63-71; exec. asst. to Prime Minister of Can. 1961-63; mem. Alta. Legis. Assembly, 1971—; apptd. Provincial Cabinet as Minister of Health and Social Devel., 1971, apptd. Minister of Labor, 1975, apptd. Atty. Gen. and Govt. House Leader, 1979—; apptd. Minister of Mcpl. Affairs 1986—. Alderman City of Edmonton, 1966-71. Served to lt/ Can. Arty., 1950-51. Mem. Can. Bar Assn., Law Soc. Alta. Progressive Conservative. Office: 227 Legislature Bldg, Edmonton, AB Canada T5K 2B6

CRAWFORD, PHILIP STANLEY, bank executive; b. Wichita, Kans., Nov. 30, 1944; s. Carson Eugene and Elizabeth Ellen (Childs) C. BA, Sterling Coll., 1967; MBA, Baruch Coll., 1973. Programmer, analyst City of N.Y., 1968-72; planning analyst Fed. Reserve Bank, Boston, 1972-74; cons. Index Systems, Cambridge, Mass., 1974-79; sr. cons. Ernst & Whinney, Los Angeles, 1979; v.p. Union Bank, Los Angeles, 1979—. Mem. Mgmt. Info. Continuing Seminar (pres. 1985), Assn. Computing Machinery, Ops. Research Soc. Am., Inst. Mgmt. Sci. Republican. Avocations: photography, genealogy. Office: Union Bank 445 S Figueroa Los Angeles CA 90071 Home: 173 Santa Ana Long Beach CA 90803

CRAWFORD, RICHARD WHITTIER, analytical chemist; b. Modesto, Calif., Aug. 18, 1936; s. Charles Dewey and Mary Christine (Gruening) C.; m. Patricia Cogswell, Apr. 3, 1960; children: Alicia C., Maria B. BS in Chemistry, San Jose State U., 1958. Chemist, group leader for mass spectrometry Lawrence Livermore Nat. Labs., Livermore, Calif., 1958—. Contbr. articles to profl. jours. Mem. Am. Chem. Soc., Am. Soc. of Mass Spectrometry, Bay Area Mass Spectrometry. Methodist. Avocations: bike riding, hiking. Office: Lawrence Livermore Nat Labs PO Box 808 L-310 Livermore CA 94550

CRAWFORD, TERRY NORMAN, marketing professional; b. Los Angeles, Apr. 24, 1945; s. Norman Oscar and Harriet (Hedelund) C.; m. Margaret Ann Kliks, Feb. 7, 1970; children: Ian Ross, Jennifer Ann. BA, U. Oreg., 1967; MBA, Portland State U., 1979. Salesman Mead Johnson Labs., Walnut Creek, Calif., 1972-73, Belton Dickson, Walnut Creek, 1973-76; sales mgr. Fiber Optics Engring., Hayward, Calif., 1976-77; customer mktg. mgr. Intel Corp., Hillsboro, Oreg., 1980-83, product mgr., 1983-86, program mgr., 1986—; research asst. Grubb Stern Mktg. Research, Portland, Oreg., 1978-79. Served to lt. USN, 1967-72. Mem. Am. Mktg. Assn. (v.p. local chpt. affairs 1982-83, pres. elect 1983-84, pres. 1984-85, com. chmn), Concord Jaycees (pres. 1975). Republican. Episcopalian. Avocations: running, gardening. Home: 7100 SW Ventura Dr Portland OR 97223 Office: Intel Corp 5200 NE Elam Young Pkwy Hillsboro OR 97124

CRAWFORD, TIMOTHY ROY, cleaning company executive; b. Medford, Oreg., Nov. 27, 1940; s. George J. and Doris E. (Macfarland) C.; student Portland State U., 1962; m. Carole L. Bothwell, June 23, 1959; children—Timothy Roy, Carrie, Chriss, Todd, Teauge. Laundry mgr. Troy Laundry Co., Portland, Oreg., 1957-67; gen. mgr. Alaska Cleaners, Anchorage, 1967—; gen. mgr. Alaska Cleaners, Alaska Textiles, Far North Equipment and Supply, Harris & Martens Enterprises. Mem. Textile Rental Services Am., Internat. Fabricare Inst., Nat. Muzzle Loading Rifle Assn. (life), Mckinley Mountainmen (past pres.), Nat. Rifle Assn. (life), Izaak Walton League (past trustee). Contbr. articles to Linen Supply News. Home: 10034 Goodnews Circle Anchorage AK 99515 Office: Alaska Cleaners 715 W Fireweed Ln Anchorage AK 99503

CRAWFORD, WILLIAM RICHARD, psychologist; b. Plant City, Fla., Feb. 5, 1936; s. W.R. and Thelma Lorene (Brown) C. B.S., Fla. State U., 1958, M.S., 1960, Ed.D., 1966. Lic. psychologist, Calif.; diplomate Am. Acad. Behavioral Medicine; registrant Nat. Register Health Service Providers in Psychology. Asst. prof. psychology San Francisco State U., 1967-69; asst. prof. Coll. Medicine U. Ill., Chgo., 1969-72; project coordinator UCLA, 1972-76; postdoctoral fellow Wright Inst., Los Angeles, 1976-78, clin. supr., 1978—; pvt. practice psychology Los Angeles, 1978—; vis. lectr. UCLA, 1980-86; adj. assoc. prof. U. So. Calif., 1984—; mem. psychology examining com. Calif. Bd. Med. Quality, 1981-86, 86—, chmn., 1984-86, vice-chmn. 1987; exec. com. Am. Assn. State Psychology Bds., 1984-86; cons. African Regional Office WHO, 1978. Author: The Psychology of Learning and Instruction: Educational Psychology, 2d edit., 1974; Thai Home Cooking from Kamolmal's Kitchen, 1985. Contbr. articles to profl. jours. Served to 1st lt. USAR, 1959-63. Recipient Disting. and Dedicated Service award Los Angeles Soc. Clin. Psychologists, 1979. Mem. Am. Psychol. Assn., Calif. State Psychol. Assn. (treas. 1981), Los Angeles County Psychol. Assn., Am. Ednl. Research Assn. Home: 12310 Hesby St North Hollywood CA 91607 Office: 1430 Howe Ave Sacramento CA 95825

CRAWSHAW, RALPH, psychiatrist; b. N.Y.C., July 3, 1921. A.B., Middlebury (Vt.) Coll., 1943; M.D., N.Y. U., 1947. Diplomate: Nat. Bd. Med. Examiners, Am. Bd. Psychiatry and Neurology. Intern Lenox Hill Hosp., N.Y.C., 1947-48; resident Menninger Sch. Psychiatry, Topeka, 1948-50, Oreg. State Hosp., Salem, 1950-51; practice medicine specializing in psychiatry Washington, 1954; staff psychiatrist C.F. Menninger Meml. Hosp., Topeka, 1954-57; asst. chief VA Mental Hygiene Clinic, Topeka, 1957-60; staff psychiatrist Community Child Guidance Clinic, Portland, Oreg., 1960-63; founder, clinic dir. Tualatin Valley Guidance Clinic, Beaverton, Oreg., 1961-67; pvt. practice medicine, specializing in psychiatry Portland, 1960—; mem. staff Holladay Park Hosp., 1961—; lectr. dept. child psychiatry U. Oreg. Med. Sch., 1961-63, clin. prof. dept. psychiatry, 1976; lectr. Sch. Social Work, Portland State U., 1964-67; founder Benjamin Rush Found., 1968, pres., 1968—; founder Friends of Medicine, 1969, Ct. of Man, 1970, Club of Kos, 1974. Contbr. editor: AMA Jour. of Socio-Econs, 1972-75; Columnist: Prism mag, 1972-76, The Pharos, 1972—, Portland Physician, 1975; Contbr. articles to med. jours. Cons. Bur. Hearings and Appeals, HEW, 1964—; cons. Albina Child Devel. Center, Portland, 1965-75, HEW Region 8 Health Planning, 1979; mem. Inst. Medicine, Nat. Acad. Sci., 1978, Oreg. Health Coordinating Council, 1979; Mem. Gov.'s Adv. Com. on Mental Health, 1966-72; ad hoc com. Nat. Leadership Conf. on Am. Health Policy, 1976, Gov.'s Adv. Com. on Med. Care to Indigent, 1976—; trustee Millicent Found., 1964-67, Multnomah Found. for Med. Care, 1977; vis. scholar Center for Study Democratic Instns., 1969, Jack Murdock Charitable Trust, 1977, U.S.-USSR exchange scholar, 1973. Served with AUS, 1943-46; to lt., M.C. USN, 1951-54. Named Oreg. Dr./Citizen of Yr., 1978; U.S.-USSR exchange scholar, 1973, 79. Fellow Am. Psychiat. Assn.; mem. AMA, Nat. Med. Assn., Oreg. Med. Assn. (trustee 1972—), Multnomah County Med. Soc. (pres. 1975), Royal Soc. Medicine, Inst. of Medicine of Nat. Acad. Sci., Am. Psychol. Assn., N.Pacific Soc. Neurology and Psychiatry, Soc. for Psychol. Study Social Issues, Western European Assn. Aviation Psychology, Am. Med. Writers Assn., AAAS, Portland Psychiatrists in Pvt. Practice (pres. 1971), Alpha Omega. Address: 2525 NW Lovejoy St Suite 404 Portland OR 97210

CREAGER, CLIFFORD RAYMOND, editor; b. N.Y.C., Oct. 8, 1937; s. Clifford Henry and Catherine (Raymond) C.; m. Dorothy Ann Carlson, Dec. 18, 1965; children: Christopher, Curtis. AB, U. Mich., 1960. Reporter, wire editor, photographer Grand Haven (Mich.) Daily Tribune, 1960-61; reporter, photographer, city editor, editor Covina (Calif.) Sentinel, weekly, 1963-72; mng. editor Car Craft mag., Los Angeles, 1972-75, Motor Trend mag., Los Angeles, 1975-81; free-lance writer, editor 1981-85; program dir. Safety Edn. Ctr., 1986—; editor, co-founder Profl. Counselor mag., 1986—; v.p. A/D Communications Corp., 1986—. Served with AUS, 1961-63. Mem. U. Mich. Alumni Assn., Calif. Assn. Alcoholism And Drug Abuse Counselors.

CREAGER, JOE SCOTT, geology and oceanography educator; b. Vernon, Tex., Aug. 30, 1929; s. Earl Litton and Irene Eugenia (Keller) C.; m. Barbara Clark, Aug. 30, 1951; children: Kenneth Clark, Vanessa Irene. B.S., Colo. Coll., 1951; postgrad., Columbia, 1952-53; M.S., Tex. A. and M. U., 1953, Ph.D., 1958. Asst. prof. dept. oceanography U. Wash., Seattle, 1958-61; assoc. prof. U. Wash., 1962-66, prof. oceanography, 1966—, asst. chmn. dept. oceanography, 1964-65, prof. geol. scis., 1981—, assoc. dean arts and scis. for earth and planetary scis., also assoc. dean for research, 1966—; program dir. for oceanography NSF, 1965-66; chief scientist numerous oceanographic expdns. to Arctic and Sub-arctic including Leg XIX of Deep Sea Drilling project, 1959—; vis. geol. scientist Am. Geol. Inst., 1962, 63, 65; U.S. Nat. coordinator Internat. Indian Ocean Expedition, 1965-66; vis. scientist program lectr. Am. Geophys. Union, 1965-72; Battelle cons., advanced waste mgmt., 1974; cons. to U.S. Army C.E., 1976, U.S. Depts. Interior and Commerce, 1975; exec. sec., exec. com., chmn. planning com. Joint Oceanographic Insts. Deep Earth Sampling, 1970-72, 76-78. Editorial bd.: Internat. Jour. Marine Geology, 1964—; assoc. editor: Jour. Sedimentary Petrology, 1963-76; asst. editor: Quaternary Research, 1970-79;

contbr. articles to profl. jours. Skipper Sea Scout Ship, Boy Scouts Am., Bryan, Tex., 1957; coach Little League Baseball, Seattle, 1964-71, sec., 1971; cons. sci. curriculum Northshore Sch. Dist., 1970; mem. Seattle Citizens Shoreline Com., 1973-74, King County Shoreline Com., 1980. Served with U.S. Army, 1953-55. Colo. Coll. scholar, 1949-51; NSF grantee, 1962-82; ERDA grantee, 1962-64; U.S. Army C.E. grantee, 1975-82; Office of Naval Research grantee; U.S. Dept. Commerce grantee; U.S. Geol. Survey grantee. Fellow Geol. Soc. Am., AAAS; mem. Internat. Assn. Quaternary Research, Am. Geophys. Union, Internat. Assn. Sedimentology, Internat. Assn. Math. Geologists, Soc. Econ. Paleontologists and Mineralists, Marine Tech. Soc. (sec.-treas. 1972-75), Sigma Xi, Beta Theta Pi, Delta Epsilon. Club: Explorers. Home: 6320 NE 157th St Bothell WA 98011 Office: U Wash Dept Oceanography WB-10 Seattle WA 98195

CREAGER, WILLIAM BRONSON, consulting engineer; b. Los Angeles, Dec. 1, 1948; s. William Boyd and P. Rowena (D'Albini) C.; m. Linda Anne Dahlke, Feb. 5, 1972; children: William Ray, Brent Russell, Heath David. BS in Civil Engring., U. Ariz., 1971, MS in Civil Engring., 1972. Structural design engr. Bechtel Power Corp., Los Angeles, 1972-77; field resident engr. Bechtel Power Corp., Buckeye, Ariz., 1977-78; project engr. Benson & Gerdin Inc., Phoenix, 1978-85, ptnr., v.p., 1985—. Coach Am. Youth Soccer Orgn., Glendale, Ariz., 1984—. Mem. Structural Engrs. Assn. Office: Benson & Gerdin Inc 3150 N 7th St Phoenix AZ 85014

CREAN, JOHN C., housing and recreational vehicles manufacturing company executive; b. Bowden, N.D., 1925; married. Founder Fleetwood Enterprises, Inc., Riverside, Calif., 1951, now chmn., chief exec. officer, also dir. Served with USN, 1942; with U.S. Mcht. Marines, 1944-45. Office: Fleetwood Enterprises Inc 3125 Myers St Riverside CA 92523 *

CREBER, WILLIAM JOHN, motion picture production designer and art director; b. Los Angeles, July 26, 1931; s. Lewis H. and Annie Valentine (Williamson) C. Art dir. film Greatest Story Ever Told, George Stevens Prodns., 1963, Planet of the Apes, 20th Century Fox Film Corp., 1967; prodn. designer films Poseidon Adventure, 20th Century Fox Film Corp., 1972, Towering Inferno, 20th Century Fox film Corp., 1974, Islands in the Stream, Paramount, 1975, Yes, Giorgio, MGM, 1981, Twice in a Lifetime, Yorkin Co., 1984. Mem. Soc. Motion Picture and TV Art Dirs., Acad. Motion Picture Arts and Scis.

CREESE, IAN NIGEL RICHARD, neuroscience educator; b. Bristol, Eng., Apr. 4, 1949; came to U.S., 1978; s. Douglas James and Marjorie Florence (Hennell) C.; m. Paula Anne Tallal, July 21, 1972. BA, U. Cambridge, Eng., 1970, MA, PhD, 1973. Postdoctoral fellow John Hopkins U., Balt., 1973-76, asst. research prof., 1976-78; asst. prof. neurosci. U. Calif. at San Diego, La Jolla, 1978-80, assoc. prof., 1980-84, prof., 1984—, dir. neurosci. grad. program, 1985—; study sect. reviewer NIMH, Washington, 1974-84;. Research grantee NIMH, Nat. Inst. Aging, Nat. Inst. Neurol. and Communicative Disorders, 1979—. Mem. Am. Coll. Neuropsychopharmacology, Soc. Neurosci., Am. Soc. Pharmacology and Exptl. Therapeutics, Am. Soc. Neurochemistry, European Soc. Neurosci. Office: U Calif San Diego M-008 Dept Neurosci La Jolla CA 92093

CREIGHTON, DAVID EDWARD, JR., civil engr.; b. Los Angeles, Aug. 27, 1923; s. David Edward and Ethel (Collier) C.; B.S., U. Ariz., 1948; student Washington U., 1943-44; m. Judith Matlock, June 3, 1947; children—James Matlock, Nancy Jean, Hannah Pauline, Robert David. Civil engr., dams sect. U.S. Bur. Reclamation, Sacramento, 1948-50, materials engr. Cachuma project, Goleta, 1950, constrn. engr. Cachuma Day, 1951, constrn. mgmt. engr. Cachuma Dam, 1952; plans and estimate engr. U.S. Bur. Reclamation, Goleta and Santa Barbara, 1953-57; planning engr. Consumnes River div. Central Valley Project, Sacramento, 1957-61, planning coordinator Central Ariz. Project and Pacific S.W. Water Plan, Phoenix, 1961-65, chief planning and reports div. Phoenix Devel. Office, 1965-72, chief environ. reports br. Ariz. Projects Office, 1972-73, projects environ. officer, 1973-77, environ. engr. Regional Office of Environment, 1977; environ. coordinator Western Area Power Adminstrn., Dept. Energy, 1977-78; civil engr. Ariz. Water Commn., Ariz. Groundwater Study Commn., 1978-79; civil engr. phase I Nat. Dam Safety Program, Dept. Water Resources, 1979-81; cons. engr., 1981-83, 84-86; civil engr. Div. Dam Safety, Ariz. Dept. Water Resources, 1983-84, water resources engr. flood control planning, 1986—. Mem. nominating com. Presbyn. of Phoenix, United Presbyn. Ch., 1965-67, mem. rev. Presbytery records com. Synod of Ariz., 1968-72, Synod of S.W., 1973-75, Ganado Commn., 1979; mem. ch. support com. Presbytery of Grand Canyon, 1984-86; leader environ. impact workshop U. Wis., 1974, chmn. com. T-201, 1968-77, instrl. rep., 1978-83 ; adv. chmn. Boy Scouts Am., Explorer Scouts 1964-69, chmn. Scottsdale Dist. bd. rev., 1966-72. Served with U.S. Army, 1943-45. Decorated Purple Heart, Bronze Star; recipient certificate of superior performance U.S. Dept. Interior, 1963, certificate of meritorious service, 1966, performance award, 1973; registered profl. engr., Ariz. Calif. Fellow ASCE; mem. U.S. Com. on Large Dams, Nat. Rifle Assn (life), Theta Tau. Club: Santa Ynez Valley Rifle and Pistol (v.p. 1955) (Solvang, Calif.). Home: 7308 E Fillmore St Scottsdale AZ 85257 Office: Ariz Dept Water Resources div Flood Control Planning 99 E Virginia Phoenix AZ 85004

CREPS, PHILIP LLOYD, chemist; b. Bowling Green, Ohio, Dec. 16, 1951; s. Wayne LeRoy and Elsie Marie (Frank) C.; m. Barbara Dawn Keller, Dec. 11, 1976; children: Jesse Jean, Sarah Marie. BS, Bowling Green (Ohio) State U., 1973; BA, U. Toledo, 1980, MS, 1987; AS, Aurora (Colo.) Community Coll., 1986. Research project dir. Mich. State U., East Lansing, 1984-85; instr. Lansing Community Coll., 1984-85; environ. scientist Ohio EPA, Bowling Green, 1985; research chemist Fitzsimmons Med. Ctr., Aurora, 1985—. Youth dir. Assembly of God Ch., Fostoria, Ohio, 1969-71; music dir. 1st Assembly of God Ch., Toledo, 1977-79; sec. Citizen's Council #3, Lansing, 1980-83. Served with USN, 1980-83. Recipient Alfred award South Counties Council, Newport, R.I., 1981, Mayor's Commendation City of Toledo, 1980. Mem. Am. Chem. Soc., Alpha Epsilon Delta, Psi Chi, Beta Beta Beta. Libertarian. Avocatins: dairy farming, gardening, swimming, jogging, singing.

CRESS, JEAN ELIZABETH, television executive; b. Sacramento, Nov. 10, 1951; d. Earl Sylvester and Nancy Louise (Cress) Gimblin. Student, Sacramento City Coll., 1969-70, Calif. State U., Sacramento, 1974-75. Dir. pub. affairs Sta. KRTH, Los Angeles, 1978-79; promotion and advt. dir. Roaring Camp R.R., Felton, Calif., 1981; news dir. Sta. KMFO, Aptos, Calif., 1981-82, program dir., 1982-84, gen. mgr., 1984-85; sales and mktg. mgr. Group W Cable, Santa Cruz, Calif., 1985-86; promotion dir. Sta. KCBA-TV, Salinas, Calif., 1986—. TV hostess Cinema Classics, Sta. KRUZ-TV, 1985-86, Focus-35, 1986—. Bd. dirs. Film Commn., Santa Cruz, 1985—. Recipient Sam Seagull award Monterey Ad Club, 1985. Democrat. Episcopal. Office: Sta KCBA TV PO Box 3560 Salinas CA 95012

CRESWELL, DONALD CRESTON, management consultant, marketing specialist; b. Balt., Mar. 28, 1932; s. Carroll Creston and Verna Moore (Taylor) C.; student Johns Hopkins U., 1951-52; M.B.A., U. Dayton, 1966; postgrad. bus. Stanford U., 1975; m. Terri Sue Tidwell, Dec. 28, 1958; 1 son, Creston Lee. Cons. engr. A.D. Ring & Assocs., Washington, 1956-58; sales and mktg. mgr. Ampex Corp., Redwood City, Calif., 1959-68; dir. mktg., magnetic products div. RCA Corp., N.Y.C., 1968-71; staff v.p. sales and advt. Pan Am. World Airways, N.Y.C., 1971-74; mktg. v.p. Rocor Internat., Palo Alto, Calif., 1975; v.p., chief operating officer, gen. mgr., Am. AmBuCar Services, Inc., San Francisco, 1976; prin. mgmt. cons., dir. mktg. services Stanford Research Inst., Menlo Park, Calif., 1977-86 ; v.p. mktg. mgmt. cons. SDG Decisions Systems, 1987—; dir. Rogerson Aircraft Controls, 1981-85 ; lectr. planning and mktg. mgmt. Am. Mgmt. Assn., 1968-69; program chmn. Grad. Bus. Assn., 1965; rep. to Electronics Industries Assn., 1968-71, to Internat. Air Transport Assn., 1971-74. Bd. dirs. Peninsula Youth Soccer Club, 1981-82; nat. dir. referee assessment, mem. referee com. U.S. Soccer Fedn., 1986—; regional chief referee San Carlos Am. Youth Soccer Orgn., 1981-85; State dir. assessment Calif. Soccer Assn., 1982-85 ; mem. Los Angeles Olympics Organizing Com., 1983-84; ofcl. N. Am. Soccer League, 1983-84. Mem. Am. Theatre Organ Assn. (bd. dirs. 1978-79), Nat. Intercollegiate Soccer Ofcls. Assn., U.S. Soccer Fedn. (cert. soccer referee). Republican. Club: Wings. Home: 3328 Brittan Ave San Carlos CA 94070 Office: SDG Decision Systems 3000 Sand Hill Rd Park CA 94025

CRESWICK, WESLEY GOODHALL, commodities broker; b. Providence, Mar. 24, 1948; s. Franklin Goodhall and Olivia Ryder (Wood) C.; m. Theresa Ruth Koepke, June 12, 1969 (div. Jan. 1976); children: Elizabeth Margarite, Scott Owen, Laura Noel; m. Melissa Moss Murchison, Sept. 15, 1978. Student, Shimer Coll., 1967, St. Claires Hall, Oxford, Eng., 1968; BA, U. Pacific, 1969. Lic. commodity broker, Calif. Ranch acct. South Lake Farms Inc., Corcoran, Calif., 1970-73; mgr. imperial div. Balfour-Guthrie & Co. Ltd., Fresno, Calif., 1973-77; mgr. No. Calif. ops. Koppel Inc., Long Beach, 1977-79; asst. mgr. M. Rinus Boer Co., Fresno, 1979-82; mng. gen. ptnr. Cen. Calif. Commodity Co., Clovis, 1982—; Founder, chmn. bd. dirs. Calif. Dairy Feeds Inc., Visalia. Mem. Calif. Feed and Grain Assn. (chmn. transp. com. 1985-86, bd. dirs. 1986—), No. Calif. Grain Exchange, Nat. Cottonseed Products Assn., Calif. Cotton Producers Assn., Oreg. Feed Dealers Assn., Austin/Healey Owners Assn., U. Calif. Fresno Bulldog Found., Calif. Dressage Soc. (pres. Fresno chpt. 1981—). Democrat. Episcopalian. Avocations: sailboat racing, antique sports car restoration. Home: 5351 E Nees Ave Clovis CA 93612 Office: Cen Calif Commodity Co 1715 Minnewawa Suite 106 Clovis CA 93612

CRETARA, DOMENIC ANTHONY, artist, educator; b. Chelsea, Mass., Mar. 29, 1946; s. Anthony Mario and Carmella (Addivinola) C.; B.F.A. magna cum laude, Boston U., 1968, M.F.A., 1970; m. Elizabeth Tarquinio, June 20, 1970; children—Jeanette, Anthony. One-man shows: Art Inst. Boston, 1976, Boston U., 1977, Camargo Found., Cassis, France, 1979, Helen Bumpus Gallery, Duxbury, Mass., 1980, Coll. William and Mary, 1980, U. Mass., 1980, Duxbury Art Complex Mus., 1982, First St. Gallery, N.Y.C., 1983, Segal Gallery, N.Y.C., 1985; group shows: Fitchburg (Mass.) Art Mus., 1973, Am. Embassy, Rome, 1975, Inst. Internat. Edn., N.Y.C., 1978, Boston Cyclorama, 1980, Drawing Center, N.Y.C., 1983, Weatherspoon Art Gallery, Greensboro, N.C., 1983, others; represented in permanent collections: Boston U., Art Inst. Boston, Met. Mus.; represented by Segal Gallery, N.Y.C., Koplin Gallery, Los Angeles; instr. painting DeCordova Mus. Sch., Lincoln, Mass., 1971-73, Fitchburg Art Mus., 1970-74; chmn. fine arts dept. Art Inst. Boston, 1975-78, instr. painting and drawing, 1970-83, assoc. prof. painting, 1983-86; assoc. prof. art Calif. State U.-Long Beach, 1986—. Fulbright-Hays grantee, Italy, 1974-75; resident painter Camargo Found., Cassis, France, 1978-79; Boston-Padua Sister Cities grantee, 1984. Mem. Boston Visual Artists Union. Drawings and paintings reproduced in: Figure Drawing, 1976; The Art of Responsive Drawing, 1977; Painting: Visual and Technical Fundamentals, 1979. Office: Calif State U Art Dept 1250 Bellflower Blvd Long Beach CA 90840

CREUTZ, EDWARD CHESTER, physicist, museum consultant; b. Beaver Dam, Wis., Jan. 23, 1913; s. Lester Raymond and Grace (Smith) C.; m. Lela Rollefson, Sept. 13, 1937 (dec. Feb. 1972); children: Michael John, Carl Eugene, Ann Jo Carmel Creutz Cosgrove; M. 2d. Elisabeth B. Cordle, Oct. 5, 1974. B.S., U. Wis., 1936, Ph.D., 1939. Research assoc. Princeton U., 1939-40, instr. physics, 1940-41; physicist NDRC, 1941-42, Metall. Lab., U. Chgo., 1942-44, Manhattan Project, Los Alamos, 1944-46; assoc. prof. Carnegie Inst. Tech., Pitts., 1946-49, prof., head dept. physics, dir. Nuclear Research Ctr., 1948-55; dir. John Jay Hopkins Lab. for Pure and Applied Sci., 1955-59; dir. research Gen. Atomic Div. Gen. Dynamics Corp., San Diego, 1955-59; v.p. research and devel. Gen. Atomic div. Gen. Dynamics Corp., San Diego, 1959-67; v.p. research and devel Gulf Gen. Atomic, San Diego, 1967-70; asst. dir. NSF, Washington, 1970-77, acting dep. dir., 1976-77; dir. Bernice Pauahi Bishop Mus., Honolulu, 1977-84; cons. Bernice Pauahi Bishop Mus., 1984—; mem. adv. council Water Resources Ctr., U. Calif.-Berkeley, 1958-65; mem. sea water conversion com. Water resources Ctr., U. Calif.-Berkeley, 1958-68; adv. com. office Sci. Personnel NRC, 1960-63; mem. exec. council Argonne Nat. Lab. (1946-51); cons. NSF, 1950-68; scientist-at-large Project Sherwood div. research AEC, 1955-56; mem. com. sr. reviewers Dept. Energy, 1972-79, fusion power coordinating com., 1971-79; cons. Oak Ridge Nat. Lab., 1946-58; adv. panel gen. scis. Dept. Def., 1959-63; research adv. com. electrophysics NASA, 1964-71, tech. adv. com., 1971-77; adj. prof. physics and astronomy U. Hawaii, 1977—. Co-editor: Handbuch der Physik, vols. 14, 15; mem. editorial bd. Ann. Rev. Nuclear Sci., 1961-66, 72-75, Handbook of Chemistry and Physics, 1961-71; mem. editorial bd.: Interdisciplinary Science Reviews, London, 1976—; editorial adv. com.: Nuclear Sci. and Engring., 1959-72. Bd. dirs. San Diego Hall Sci. and Planetarium, v.p., 1956-70; v.p. San Diego Industry-Edn. Council, 1956-65; mem. adv. council Dept. Edn. San Diego County. Fellow Am. Phys. Soc. (NRC rep. 1956-57), Am. Nuclear Soc., AAAS, Explorers Club; mem. Nat. Acad. Scis., Social Sci. Assn. Honolulu, Am. Assn. Physics Tchrs., Internat. Platform Assn., ASCAP, Phys. Soc. Pitts. (pres. 1949), Am. Soc. Engring. Edn., ASME, AAUP, IEEE, Am. Inst. Physics (dir.-at-large bd. govs. 1965-68). Home: 3964-D Old Pali Rd Honolulu HI 96817

CREVELT, DWIGHT EUGENE, computer company executive; b. Kansas City, Mo., Jan. 16, 1957; s. James Robert and Louise Gwendolynn (Wolchek) C.; m. Jean Anne Cassens, Aug. 11, 1979; children: William Michael, Michelle Anne. Student U. Las Vegas, 1973-74, U.S. Naval Acad., 1975-77; BS in Computer Engring., Iowa State U., 1979. Computer engr., cons., Las Vegas, Nev., 1972-73; software engr. Gamex Industries, Las Vegas, 1973-74, United Audio Visual, Las Vegas, 1977; computer engr. Sircoma, Las Vegas, 1979-80; dir. research Mills-Jennings, Las Vegas, 1981; pres., chmn. Crevelt Computer, Las Vegas, 1977—. Author: (computer programs) CDC160/NCR310 Disassembler, 1971; Computer Networking, 1983; Telephone Access Control, 1984; Fiber Optic Network, 1984. Mem. Nat. Eagle Scout Assn., U.S. Congl. Adv. Bd. Mem. Soc. Naval Engrs., Sales Mktg. Execs. Assn., Am. Philatic Soc., U.S. Naval Acad. Alumni Assn. (sec.), USN League, U.S. Naval Inst. Republican. Office: Crevelt Computer System Inc 3111 S Valley View E-103 Las Vegas NV 89102

CREWDSON, JOHN MARK, journalist, author; b. San Francisco, Dec. 15, 1945; s. Mark Guy and Eva Rebecca (Doane) C.; m. Prudence Gray Tillotson, Sept. 11, 1969; children: Anders Gray, Oliver McDuff. A.B. with great distinction in Econs., U. Calif., Berkeley, 1970; postgrad. studies in politics, Oxford U., Eng., 1971-72. Reporter N.Y. Times, Washington, 1973-77; nat. corr N.Y. Times, Houston, 1977-82; nat. news editor Chgo. Tribune, 1982-83, met. news editor, 1983-84; west coast corr. Chgo. Tribune, Los Angeles, 1984—. Author: The Tarnished Door, 1983, By Silence Betrayed, 1987. Recipient Bronze medallion Sigma Delta Chi, 1974; Goldberg award N.Y. Deadline Club, 1977; Page One award N.Y. Newspaper Guild, 1977; Pulitzer prize, 1981.

CREWS, RICHARD LAWRENCE, university president, psychiatrist; b. N.Y.C., July 11, 1937. B.A. magna cum laude, Williams Coll., 1959; M.D., Harvard U., Boston, 1963. Intern, San Francisco Gen. Hosp., 1963-64; resident in psychiatry Letterman Gen. Hosp., Presidio of San Francisco, 1965-68; practice medicine specializing in psychiatry, Mill Valley, Calif., 1971—; clin. practice homeopathy and nutritional counselling, Mill Valley, 1977-80; co-founder, pres. Columbia Pacific U., 1978—; mem. staff Marin Gen. Hosp., Ross Gen. Hosp., Marin County, Calif.; co-founder Brookwood Gen. Hosp., Santa Rosa, Calif., 1971, mem. staff, 1973-79; cons. Calif. Disability Evaluation Bd., 1974—; lectr. U.S. Army Edn. Ctr., Ft. Bragg, N.C., 1969-70, U. N.C. Grad. Sch. Social Work, 1970-71, Coll. Marin, 1971-72; lectr. and cons. in psychology Dominican Coll., 1972-75; exec. and clin. dir. Creative Living Ctrs. of Marin County, 1972-75; pres. Brookwood Hosp. Corp., 1975-80; exec. and clin. dir. Wholistic Health and Nutrition Inst., Mill Valley, 1977-79, bd. dirs., 1977—; co-founder N.Am. Coll. Natural Health Scis., Mill Valley and San Rafael, Calif., 1978, designer, adminstr., educator nutrition curriculum, 1978-80. Served to maj. M.C., U.S. Army, 1964-71. Decorated Legion of Merit. Mem. MENSA. Author: Introductory Workbook in Homeopathy, 1978. Office: Columbia Pacific U 1415 3d St San Rafael CA 94901

CREWS, STEPHEN THOMAS, molecular biologist; b. High Point, N.C., Aug. 11, 1953; s. Roy Elmer and Wilma (Carmichael) C.; m. Rose Agnes Kovarik, Feb. 3, 1978. BA in Zoology with highest honors, U. Tex., 1975; PhD in Biochemistry, Calif. Inst. Tech., 1982. Research fellow Calif. Inst. Tech., Pasadena, 1982-83, U. Toulouse, France, 1983, Stanford (Calif.) U., 1983—. Contbr. articles to profl. jours. Mem. Sigma Xi, Phi Beta Kappa, Phi Kappa Phi. Office: Stanford U Dept Biol Scis Stanford CA 94305

CRIBBS, ROBERT W., electronics company executive; b. Leechburg, Pa., Apr. 10, 1938; s. Robert W. and Isabell T. (Shaner) C.; m. Donna Lee Witzel, June 6, 1957; children: Robert, Mark, Sherry. Student, Pa. State U., 1957-58; BS in Physics, Carnegie-Mellon U., 1960; MS in Applied Math., Calif. State U., Sacramento, 1965; postgrad., U. Calif., Davis, 1961-62, 65-67. Project engr. Aerojet Gen., Nimbus, Calif., 1960-67; dir. engring. Electra-Physics, Folsom, Calif., 1967-75, pres., 1975-79; cons. Placerville, Calif., 1979-82; dir. research Folsom Research, 1982—, also bd. dirs.; cattle rancher Placerville, 1970—; adj. prof. Calif. State U., Sacramento, 1970—; cons. Gen Electric, Rancho Cordova, Calif., 1979-82, Electric Power Research Inst., Palo Alto, Calif., 1980-82, Sound Imaging, Folsom, 1982-84. Contbr. numerous articles to profl. jours.; patentee in field. Mem. various adv. coms., El Dorado County, Calif., 1982—, adv. bd. Calif. State U., Sacramento, 1983—. Fellow Am. Soc. Nondestructive Testing (chmn. Sacramento sect. 1984-85). Avocations: Egyptian archaeology, airplane piloting, scuba diving. Home: 4001 Lakeview Dr Placerville CA 95667 Office: Folsom Research 526 E Bidwell St Folsom CA 95630

CRICK, FRANCIS HARRY COMPTON, biologist, educator; b. June 8, 1916; s. Harry and Annie Elizabeth (Wilkins) C.; m. Ruth Doreen Dodd, 1940 (div. 1947); 1 son; m. Odile Speed, 1949; 2 daus. B.Sc., Univ. Coll., London; Ph.D, Cambridge U., Eng. Scientist Brit. Admiralty, 1940-47, Strangeways Lab., Cambridge, Eng., 1947-49; biologist Med. Research Council Lab. of Molecular Biology, Cambridge, 1949-77; Kieckhefer Disting. prof. Salk Inst. for Biol. Studies, San Diego, 1977—, non-resident fellow, 1962-73; adj. prof. psychology and chemistry, U. Calif.-San Diego; vis. lectr. Rockefeller Inst., N.Y.C., 1959; vis. prof. chemistry dept. Harvard U., 1959, vis. prof. biophysics, 1962; fellow Churchill Coll., Cambridge, 1960-61, UCLA, 1962; Warren Triennial prize lectr. (with J.D. Watson), Boston, 1959; Korkes Meml. lectr. Duke U., 1960; Henry Sedgewick Meml. lectr. Cambridge U., 1963; Graham Young lectr., Glasgow, 1963; Robert Boyle lectr. Oxford U., 1963; Vanuxem lectr. Princeton U., 1964; William T. Sedgwick Meml. lectr. MIT, 1965; Cherwell-Simon Meml. lectr. Oxford U., 1966; Shell lectr. Stanford U., 1969; Paul Lund lectr. Northwestern U., 1977; Dupont lectr. Harvard U., 1979, numerous other invited, meml. lectrs. Author: Of Molecules and Men, 1966, Life Itself, 1981; contbr. papers and articles on molecular and cell biology to sci. jours. Recipient Prix Charles Leopold Mayer French Academies des Sciences, 1961; recipient (with J.D. Watson) Research Corp. award, 1961, Nobel Prize for medicine, 1962, Gairdner Found. award, 1962, Royal Medal Royal Soc., 1972, Copley Medal, 1976, Michelson-Morley award, 1981. Fellow AAAS, Royal Soc.; mem. Am. Acad. Arts and Scis. (fgn hon.), Am. Soc. Biol. Chemistry (hon.), U.S. Nat. Acad. Scis. (fgn. assoc.), German Acad. Sci., Am. Philos. Soc. (fgn. mem.), French Acad. Scis. (assoc. fgn. mem.). Office: Salk Inst for Biol Studies PO Box 85800 San Diego CA 92138

CRIDER, HOYT, health care executive; b. Arley, Ala., June 5, 1924; s. Lindsey C. and Bessie P. C.; student Ga. Sch. Tech., 1942-43; B.S. in Naval Sci. and Tactics, U. S.C., 1946; M.A. in Polit. Sci., U. Ala., 1949; D.Pub. Adminstrn., U. So. Calif., 1954; m. Judie Watkins, Nov. 2, 1951; children—Kim, Marc. Vis. asst. prof., dir. research U. So. Calif. team, Iran, 1954-56; adminstrv. analyst Chief Adminstrv. Offices Los Angeles County, 1956-59; v.p. Watkins & Watkins Constrn. Co., Hanford and Morro Bay, Calif., 1959-64; co-owner, adminstr. Kings Convalescent Hosp., Hanford, Calif., 1964-66; adminstr. Villa Capistrano Convalescent Hosp., Capistrano Beach, Calif., 1966-68; partner Hunt and Crider, San Diego Convalescent Hosp., 1968-70; pres., chief exec. officer Health Care Enterprises, Inc., San Clemente, Calif., 1970—; mem. Regional Health Planning Commn. Kings County, 1963-64. Served with USNR, 1941-46. Fellow Am. Coll. Nursing Home Adminstrs. (pres. 1976-77), Am. Coll. Health Care Adminstrs.; mem. Calif. Assn. Health Facilities (past v.p. local chpt. 1964), Gerontol. Soc., AAAS. Club: San Clemente Kiwanis (Kiwanian of Yr. 1970, pres. 1970-71). Home: 214 Calle Cortez San Clemente CA 92672 Office: 407 N El Camino Real Suite C San Clemente CA 92672 Office: 1209 W Hemlock Way Santa Ana CA 92707

CRILL, J(ERRY) PAT, plant pathologist, breeder; b. Blaine, Colo., June 29, 1939; s. Jack and Inez (Hickey) C.; m. Paulene Brite, Jan. 29, 1961; children: Jack Paul, James Perry. BS, Panhandle State U., 1961; MS, Okla. State U., 1963; PhD, U. Wis., 1968. Asst. prof. U. Fla., Gainesville, 1968-72, assoc. prof., 1972-74; sr. plant breeder Petoseed Co., Inc., Woodland, Calif., 1974-78; prof. U. Philippines, Los Banos, 1978-81; head plant pathology dept. Internat. Rice Research Inst., Manila, 1978-81; pres. JOPOCO Agrl. Research and Prodn., Campo, Colo., 1981—. Contbr. research articles to profl. jours.; devel. 19 named varieties of tomato, 6 named varieties of cantaloupe; co-devel. 15 named varieties of tomato and cantaloupe. Recipient Bronze medal for Floramerica tomato, All-Am. Selections Bd. Govs., 1977, research award for excellence Fla. Fruit and Vegetable Assn., 1978; Council Meml. Research award Fla. State Hort. Soc., 1976. Mem. Am. Phytopath. Soc., Am. Genetic Assn., Am. Soc. Hort. Sci., Philippine Phytopath. Soc. (life), Am. Soc. Agronomy, Crop Sci. Soc. Am. Avocations: fresh and salt water fishing, breeding registered Hereford cattle. Home: PO Box 501 Walsh CO 81090 Office: JOPOCO Agrl Research and Prodn 43400 Rd C Campo CO 81029

CRILLY, EUGENE RICHARD, engineering specialist; b. Phila., Oct. 30, 1923; s. Eugene John and Mary Virginia (Harvey) C.; m. Alice Royal Roth, Feb. 16, 1952; M.E., Stevens Inst. Tech., 1944, M.S., 1949; M.S., U. Pa., 1951; postgrad. UCLA, 1955-58. Sr. research engr. N.Am. Aviation, Los Angeles, 1954-57; sr. research engr., Canoga Park and Downey, Calif., 1962-66; process engr. Northrop Aircraft Corp., Hawthorne, Calif., 1957-59; project engr., quality assurance mgr. HITCO, Gardena, Calif., 1959-62; sr. research specialist Lockheed-Calif. Co., Burbank, 1966-74; engring. specialist N.Am. aircraft ops. Rockwell Internat., El Segundo, Calif., 1974—. Author tech. papers. Served with USNR, 1943-46; comdr. Res. ret. Mem. Soc. for Advancement Material and Process Engring. (chmn. Los Angeles chpt. 1978-79, gen. chmn. 1981 symposium exhbn., dir. 1979-86, treas. 1982-85), Soc. Mfg. Engrs. (sr.), Naval Inst., Naval Res. Assn., VFW, Mil. Order World Wars (adjutant San Fernando Valley chpt. 1985, 2d vice comdr. 1986, commdr. 1987—), Former Intelligence Officers Assn., Naval Intelligence Profls. Assn., Sigma Xi, Sigma Nu. Republican. Roman Catholic. Home: 18646 Ludlow St Northridge CA 91326 Office: Rockwell Internat N Am Aircraft Ops PO Box 92098 Los Angeles CA 90009

CRIMINALE, WILLIAM OLIVER, JR., applied mathematics educator; b. Mobile, Ala., Nov. 29, 1933; s. William Oliver and Vivian Gertrude (Sketoe) C.; m. Ulrike Irmgard Wegner, June 7, 1962; children: Martin Oliver, Lucca. B.S., U. Ala., 1955; Ph.D., Johns Hopkins U., 1960. Asst. prof. Princeton (N.J.) U., 1962-68; asso. prof. U. Wash., Seattle, 1968-73; prof. oceanography, geophysics, applied math. U. Wash., 1973—, chmn. dept. applied math., 1976-84; cons. Aerospace Corp., 1962-65, Boeing Corp., 1968-72, AGARD, 1967-68, Lennox Hill Hosp., 1967-68; guest prof., Can., 1965, France, 1967-68, Germany, 1973-74, Sweden, 1973-74, Scotland, 1985, Nat. Acad. exchange scientist, USSR, 1969, 72, Scotland, 1985. Author: Stability of Parallel Flows, 1967; Contbr. articles to profl. jours. Served with U.S. Army, 1961-62. Boris A. Bakmeteff Meml. fellow, 1957-58; NATO Postdoctoral fellow, 1960-61; Alexander von Humboldt Sr. fellow, 1973-74. Mem. AAAS, Am. Phys. Soc., Am. Geophys. Union, Fedn. Am. Scientists, Soc. Indsl. and Applied Math. Home: 1635 Peach Court E Seattle WA 98112 Office: U Wash Applied Math FS-20 Seattle WA 98195

CRIMMINS, PHILIP PATRICK, metallurgical engineer, lawyer; b. Poughkeepsie, N.Y., Aug. 1, 1930; s. Philip Patrick and Eva (Booth) C.; m. Janet E. Ballou, Feb. 14, 1953; children: Lisa Jane, Philip Patrick, Michael Mathew. B.S., MIT, 1952; M.S., Wayne State U., 1959; J.D., U. Pacific, 1972. Registered profl. metall. engr. Metall. engr. Ford Motor Co., Livonia, Mich., 1954-58; dir. engring. Aerojet Tactical Systems Co., Sacramento, 1958—. Served with AUS, 1952-54. Recipient William Sparagen award Am. Welding Soc., 1968. Calif. Fellow Am. Inst. Chemists; mem. Am. Soc. Metals, Fed., Am., Calif. bar assns. Home: 9113 Rosewood Dr Sacramento CA 95826 Office: PO Box 13400 Sacramento CA 95813

CRINELLA, FRANCIS MICHAEL, neuropsychologist, science foundation director; b. Petaluma, Calif., Dec. 22, 1936; s. Marino Peter and Marian (Eleanor) C.; m. Terrie Kay Lynd, Sept. 19, 1959; children: Ramona, Gina, Peter, Andrew, Christina. BA, U. Notre Dame, 1958; MS, San Francisco

State U., 1962; PhD, La. State U., 1969. Lic. clin. and exptl. psychologist, Calif. Staff psychologist USAF Hosp., Travis AFB, 1962-66; staff psychologist Sonoma State Hosp., Eldridge, Calif., 1969-72, sr. psychologist, 1972-77; research psychologist Brain Behavior Research Ctr., Eldridge, 1969-77; dir. Fairview State Hosp., Costa Mesa, Calif., 1977-85; assoc. clin. prof. psychiatry U. Calif., Irvine, 1977—, assoc. clin. prof. physical medicine, 1981—; dir. Devel. Research Insts., Costa Mesa, 1985—; pres. Rehab. Ctr. for Brain Dysfunction, Irvine, 1982—. Contbr. articles on neuropsychiatry to profl. jours. Bd. dirs. United Way Orange County, Calif., Orange County Epilepsy Soc., also pres., 1978—. Served to capt. USAF, 1958-66. Recipient Career Scientist award Rehab. Ctr. Brain Dysfunction Inc., 1983; grantee Nat. Inst. Child Health and Human Devel., 1972, Nat. Inst. Neurol. Diseases and Sci., 1973, Nat. Inst. Aging, 1985. Mem. AAAS, Am. Psychol. Assn., Nat. Acad. Neuropsychologists, Western Psychol. Assn. Republican. Roman Catholic. Club: Mesa Verde Country (Costa Mesa). Avocations: golf, hunting, fishing, amateur theatre. Office: State Devel Research Insts 2501 Harbor Blvd Costa Mesa CA 92626

CRISCUOLO, WENDY LAURA, lawyer, interior design consultant; b. N.Y.C., Dec. 17, 1949; d. Joseph Andrew and Betty Jane (Jackson) C.; m. John Howard Price, Jr., Sept. 5, 1970 (div. Apr. 1981). AB with honors in Design, U. Calif., Berkeley, 1973; JD, U. San Francisco, 1982. Space planner GSA, San Francisco, 1973-79; sr. interior designer E. Lew & Assocs., San Francisco, 1979-80; design dir. Beier & Gunderson, Inc., Oakland, Calif., 1980-81; sr. interior designer Environ. Planning and Research, San Francisco, 1981-82; interior design cons., Mill Valley, 1982—; law clk. to Judge Spencer Williams, U.S. Dist. Ct., San Francisco, 1983-84; atty. Ciros Investments, Mill Valley, 1985—. Co-author: Guide to the Laws of Charitable Giving, 3d rev. edit., 1983; mem. U. San Francisco Law Rev., 1983. Bd. dirs. Marin Citizens for Energy Planning. Mem. ABA, State Bar Calif., Queen's Bench (San Francisco), Calif. Women Lawyers. Republican. Episcopalian. Club: Commonwealth (San Francisco). Avocation: creative writing.

CRISMAN, MARY FRANCES BORDEN, librarian; b. Tacoma, Nov. 23, 1919; d. Lindon A. and Mary Cecelia (Donnelly) Borden; m. Fredric Lee Crisman, Apr. 12, 1975 (dec. Dec. 1975). BA in History, U. Wash., 1943, BA in Librarianship, 1944. Asst. br. librarian in charge work with children Mottet br. Tacoma Pub. Library, 1944-45, br. librarian, 1945-49, br. librarian Moore br., 1950-55, asst. dir., 1955-70, dir., 1970-74, dir. emeritus, 1975—; librarian Frank Russell Co., 1985—; chmn. Wash. Community Library Council, 1970-72. Hostess program Your Library and You, Sta. KTPS-TV, 1969-71. Mem. Highland Homeowners League, Tacoma, 1980—, incorporating dir. 1980, sec. and registered agt., 1980-82. Mem. ALA (chmn. mem. com. Wash. 1957-60, mem. nat. library week com. 1965, chmn. library adminstrn. div. nominating com. 1971, mem. ins. for libraries com. 1970-74, vice chmn. library adminstrn. div. personnel adminstrn. sect. 1972-73, chmn. 1973-74, mem. com. policy implementation 1973-74, mem. library orgn. and mgmt. sect. budgeting acctg. and costs com. 1974-75), Am. Library Trustee Assn. (legis. com. 1975-78, conf. program com. 1978-80, action devel. com. 1978-80), Pacific N.W. (trustee div. nominating com 1976-77), Wash. (exec. bd. 1957-59, state exec., dir. Nat. Library Week 1965, treas., exec. bd. 1969-71, 71-73), library assns., Urban Libraries Council (editorial sec. Newsletter 1972-73, exec. com. 1974-75), AAUW (2d v.p., mem. chmn. Tacoma 1958-59), Ladies Aux. to United Transp. Union (past pres. Tacoma), Friends Tacoma Pub. Library (registered agt. 1975-83, sec. 1975-78, pres. 1978-80, bd. dirs. 1980-83), Smithsonian Assocs., Nat. Railway Hist. Soc. Roman Catholic. Club: Quota (sec. 1957-58, 1st v.p. 1960-61, pres. 1961-62, treas. 1975-76, pres. 1979-80) (Tacoma). Home: 6501 Burning Tree Ln Tacoma WA 98406 Address: Frank Russell Co 1201 Pacific Ave Tacoma WA 98402

CRISMOND, LINDA FRY, county librarian; b. Burbank, Calif., Mar. 1, 1943; d. Billy Chapin and Lois (Harding) Fry; m. Donald Burleigh Crismond, 1965 (div. Sept. 1980). B.S., U. Calif.-Santa Barbara, 1964; M.L.S., U. Calif.-Berkeley, 1965. Cert. county librarian, Calif. Reference librarian, EDP coordinator San Francisco Pub. Library, 1965-72, head acquisition, 1972-74; asst. univ. librarian U. So. Calif., Los Angeles, 1974-80; chief dep. county librarian Los Angeles County Pub. Library, Los Angeles, 1980-81; county librarian Los Angeles County Pub. Library, Downey, 1981—; Western rep. quality control council Ohio Coll.l Library Ctr., Columbus, 1977-80; mem. Am. Nat. Standards Inst., N.Y.C., 1978-80; bd. councillors U. So. Calif. Sch. Library and Info. Mgmt., 1980-83; adv. bd. mem. UCLA Library Sch., 1981—; chmn. bd. dirs. Los Angeles Pub. Library Found., 1982—. Author: Directory of San Francisco Bay Area, 1968. Named Staff Mem. of Year San Francisco Pub. Library, 1968. Mem. ALA (chmn. Percy Jury 1976-78, chmn. Gale Jury 1982-84, exec. com. resources and tech. services div. resources sect. 1980-82), Calif. Library assn. (council 1980-82), Calif. County Librarians Assn. (v.p., pres.-elect. 1984—). Home: 15985 Alcima Ave Pacific Palisades CA 90272 Office: Los Angeles County Pub Library 7400 E Imperial Hwy Downey CA 90241

CRISP, ANN CATHERINE, college administrator; b. Anderson, Ind., Nov. 27, 1946; d. Edward Vernon and Virginia Ruth (Hersberger) Dillie; m. Houston Wynnlee Crisp, Aug. 17, 1968 (div. 1980). B.S. in Edn., Ball State U., 1969; postgrad. U. Alaska, 1971-73; M.Home Econs., Oreg. State U., 1975, postgrad., 1982—. Youth nutrition specialist U. Alaska, Fairbanks, 1970-73, extension mgmt. info. coordinator, 1972-73; specialist nutrition edn. Oreg. State U., Corvallis, 1975; parent edn., home econs. coordinator Linn-Benton Community Coll., Albany, Oreg., 1975-77; Albany Ctr. dir., 1977-79, Benton Ctr. dir. 1979-85, community edn. div. dir., 1985—, spl. asst. to v.p. bus. affairs, 1987; research assoc. Western Oreg. State Coll., Monmouth, 1983; chmn., task force Community Edn. Dirs., Oreg., 1983; mem. UN Forum 85, Nairobi, Kenya. Author: Annotated Bibliography Nutrition Education Resources, 1975; Program Planning Activities Nutrition for Elderly, 1975; co-producer movie Alaskan Food Choices, 1973; author bulls. for B-4 Nutrition Program, 1971. Sec. Benton County United Way, 1984-87. Named Leader of the 80s League for Innovation in Community Colls., 1982. Mem. N.W. Adult Edn. Assn. (pres. 1984-85, Adult Educator of Yr. 1987), Am. Assn. Adult and Continuing Edn., Oreg. Home Econs. Assn. (sec. 1979-81, disting. leader 1984), Am. Home Econs. Assn., Oreg. Community Edn., Corvallis Women's Network, Phi Kappa Phi, Sigma Zeta. Democrat. Mem. Christian Ch. (Disciples of Christ). Lodge: Zonta (pres. Corvallis club 1982-83, internat. del. 1982, alt. 1984, African study tour 1985). Office: Linn-Benton Community Coll 6500 SW Pacific Blvd Albany OR 97321

CRISP, TERRY ARTHUR, professional hockey coach; b. Parry Sound, ON, Canada, May 28, 1943. Player, Nat. Hockey League 1965-77, with Boston , 1965-66 season, St. Louis, 1967-72, New York, 1972-73, Philadelphia, 1973-77; formerly coach Soo Greyhounds, Ont. Hockey League; coach Calgary Flames farm club, Moncton, 1985-87, Calgary Flames, Nat. Hockey League, Calgary, Alta., 1987—. Office: Calgary Flames, PO Box 1540, Station M, Calgary, AB Canada T2P 3B9 *

CRISPO, RICHARD CHARLES, artist, ethnologist, minister; b. Bklyn., Jan. 13, 1945; s. Frank C. and Irene M. (Lamont) C. M.F.A., Trinity Hall Coll., 1975; Ph.D., Collegii Romanii, Rome, 1976, Th.D., 1977. Instr. art Monterey Peninsula Coll., 1968-69, instr. ethnic studies, 1976; instr. art history Hartwell Coll.; now coordinator Arts in Corrections, Art Project, Soledad Prison; instr. pub. sch. art, Monterey, Calif., 1967-72; counselor Intrim, Inc., Monterey, 1976; founder Mus. on Wheels, 1973-74; founder World Folk Art Collection, Monterey, 1972; 53 murals and 63 one-man shows; executed half-mile-long mural at Soledad Prison; priest N. Am. Old Roman Catholic Ch. Recipient numerous awards including 1st prize Calif. State Fair, 1964; UNESCO award, 1971-73; Calif. Arts Council grantee. Mem. Artist Equity, Found. for the Community of Artists, Carmel Art Assn., Pacific Grove Art Center. Contbr. articles to art jours.

CRISSEY, JOHN THORNE, physician, educator; b. Tonawanda, N.Y., July 19, 1924; s. Earl Guy and Sadie Kay (Harris) C.; m. Alice Jessamine Hogue, Jul. 30, 1949; children: Jennifer, Kaye, John Jr. MD, U. Buffalo, 1946. Diplomate Am. Bd. Dermatology and Syphilology. Assoc. prof. medicine U. Buffalo, 1952-64; clin. prof. medicine U. So. Calif. Sch. Medicine, Los Angeles, 1964—. Author: Classics in Clinical Dermatology, 1952 (Garrison-Morton Classic award 1952), The Dermatology and Syphilology of the 19th Century, 1981, Syphilis, 1984. Served to capt. U.S. Army, 1943-49. Recipient Gougerot prize for med. history Société de Dermatologie Gougerot, 1985. Fellow Am. Acad. Dermatology. Republican. Presbyterian. Avocations: musical composition, photography. Home: 608 Sierra Madre Blvd San Marino CA 91108 Office: U So Calif Sch Medicine 960 E Green St Pasadena CA 91106

CRISSEY, KAYE PRISCILLA, speech-language educator; b. Tonawanda, N.Y., Feb. 3, 1953; d. John Thorne and Alice J. (Hogue) C.; m. Henry H.Y. Chang, Dec. 18, 1976 (div. Dec. 1983). BA, Calif. State U., Fullerton, 1979; MA, Whittier Coll., 1981. Cert. clin. competence, Calif. Instr., chmn. dept. speech Western High Sch., Anaheim, Calif., 1979-85; instr. speech Polaris High Sch., Anaheim, 1985—; instr. Northrop Corp., Anaheim, 1986—. Mem. Am. Speech-Lang. and Hearing Assn., Calif. Tchrs. Assn. Republican. Presbyterian. Club: Diving, Altrusa (Anaheim). Avocations: bowling, needle point, square dancing.

CRISSMAN, HARRY ALLEN, research cell biologist; b. Lock Haven, Pa., Aug. 16, 1935; s. Allen Russell and Rose Mary (Severino) C.; m. Faith Ann Sweitzer, Jan. 17, 1965 (div. Mar. 1981); 1 child, Angela Rose. BS in Biology cum laude, Lock Haven U., 1962; MS in Zoology, Pa. State U., 1968, PhD in Zoology, 1971. Tchr. biology Ovid (N.Y.) Cen. Sch., 1965-67; instr. biology Pa. State U., University Park, 1968; postdoctoral fellow Los Alamos (N.Mex.) Nat. Lab., 1971-73, mem. staff, 1973—; cons. Becton Dickenson, Mountainview, Calif and Rsearch Triangle Park, N.Y., 1980. Contbr. articles to profl. jours., chpts. to books. Mem. choir Los Alamos Choral, 1976-80, Cath. Ch. choir, Los Alamos, 1976—. Served with U.S. Army, 1958-60. Fulbright scholar, 1979-80; Nat. Def. Edn. Act IV predoctoral fellow, 1968-71. Mem. Histochem. Soc., Cell Kinetics Soc. (councillor), Am. Soc. Cell biology, Soc. Analytical Cytology. Lodge: Elks (officer Lockhaven club 1963-65). Avocations: skiing, music, singing. Office: Los Alamos Nat Lab Life Scis Div LS-4 MS M888 Los Alamos NM 87545

CRISTIANO, MARILYN JEAN, speech communication educator; b. New Haven, Jan. 10, 1954; s. Michael William Mary Rose (Porto) C. BA, Marquette U., 1975, MA, 1977; postgrad., Ariz. State U., 1977—. Speech communication instr. Phoenix Coll., 1977-87, Paradise Valley Community Coll., Phoenix, 1987—; cons. IBM, various locations, Scottsdale (Ariz.) Pub. Schs., Mayo Clinic, Scottsdale, Ariz. Pub. Service, Phoenix. Mem. Women in Higher Edn. in Ariz. (v.p.), Am. Soc. Tng. and Devel., Speech Communication Assn., Western Speech Communication Assn., Ariz. Communication Assn. Avocation: golf, breeding Lhasa Apso dogs. Office: Paradise Valley Community Coll 18401 N 32d St Phoenix AZ 85032

CRISTOL, STANLEY JEROME, chemistry educator; b. Chgo., June 14, 1916; s. Myer J. and Lillian (Young) C.; m. Barbara Wright Swingle, June 1957; children: Marjorie Jo, Jeffrey Tod. B.S., Northwestern U., 1937; M.A., UCLA, 1939, Ph.D., 1943. Research chemist Standard Oil Co., Calif., 1938-41; research fellow U. Ill., 1943-44; research chemist U.S. Dept. Agr., 1944-46; asst. prof., then asso. prof. U. Colo., 1946-55, prof., 1955—, Joseph Sewall disting. prof., 1979—, chmn. dept. chemistry, 1960-62, grad. dean, 1980-81; vis. prof. Stanford U., summer 1961, U. Geneva, 1975, U. Lausanne, Switzerland, 1981; with OSRD, 1944-46; adv. panels NSF, 1957-63, 69-73, NIH, 1969-72. Author: (with L.O. Smith, Jr.) Organic Chemistry, 1966; editorial bd., Chem. Revs., 1957-59, Jour. Organic Chemistry, 1964-68; contbr. research articles to sci. jours. Guggenheim fellow, 1955-56, 81, 82; recipient James Flack Norris award in phys.-organic chemistry, 1972. Fellow AAAS (councilor 1986—), Chem. Soc. London; mem. Am. Chem. Soc. (chmn. organic chemistry div. 1961-62, adv. bd. petroleum research fund 1963-66, council policy com. 1968-73), AAUP, Colo.-Wyo. Acad. Sci., Nat. Acad. Scis., Phi Beta Kappa, Sigma Xi, Phi Lambda Upsilon. Home: 2918 3d St Boulder CO 80302 Office: U Colo Dept Chemistry CB 215 Boulder CO 80309

CRISWELL, KIMBERLY ANN, computer company executive, dancer; b. Los Angeles, Dec. 6, 1957; d. Robert Burton and Carolyn Joyce (Semko) C. B.A. with honors, U. Calif.-Santa Cruz, 1980. Instr., English Lang. Services, Oakland, Calif., 1980-81; freelance writer Gambit mag., New Orleans, 1981; instr. Tulane U., New Orleans, 1981; instr., editor Haitian-English Lang. Program, New Orleans, 1981-82; instr. Delgado Coll., New Orleans, 1982-83; instr., program coordinator Vietnamese Youth Ctr., San Francisco, 1984; dancer Khadra Internat. Folk Ballet, San Francisco, 1984—; dir. mktg. communications Centram Systems West, Inc., Berkeley, Calif., 1984—; communications coordinator Safeway Stores, Inc., Oakland, 1985. Writer speeches articles, press releases, brochures, users manuals. Vol. coordinator Friends of Haitians, 1981, editor, writer newsletter, 1981; dancer Komenka Ethnic Dance Ensemble, New Orleans, 1983; mem. Contemp. Art Ctr.'s Krewe of Clones, New Orleans, 1983, Californians for Nonsmokers Rights, Berkeley, 1985. Mem. Nat. Assn. Female Execs., Dance Action, Bay Area Dance Coalition. Democrat. Avocations: visual arts, travel, creative writing. Office: Centram Systems West Inc 2560 Ninth St Berkeley CA 94710

CRISWELL, MARVIN EUGENE, civil engineering educator, consultant; b. Chappell, Nebr., Oct. 31, 1942; s. Wilbur Arthur and Evelyn Lucille (Jeffries) C.; m. Lela Louise Kennedy, Sept. 5, 1965; children: Karin Lee, Glenn Alan, Dianne Marie, Melanie Anne. BSCE, U. Nebr., 1965; MSCE, U. Ill., 1966, PhD in Civil Engring., 1970. Registered profl. engr., Colo. Structural engr. Clark & Enerson, Olson, Burroughs & Thompson, Lincoln, Nebr., 1965; research structural engr. U.S. Army Corps Engrs. Waterways Experiment Station, Vicksburg, Miss., 1967-69; asst. prof. civil engring. Colo. State U., Ft. Collins, 1970-75, assoc. prof., 1975-84, prof., 1984—; bd. dirs., sec. Engring. Data Mgmt., Inc., Ft. Collins, 1983-85. Co-author: Properties and Tests of Engineering Materials, 1978. Recipient Abel Faculty Teaching award Colo. State U., 1984. Mem. ASCE, Am. Soc. Engring. Edn. (chmn. civil engring. div. 1981-82, chmn.-elect Rocky Mountain sect. 1986-87, Dow Outstanding Young Faculty award 1978), ASTM, Am. Concrete Inst., Accreditation Bd. Engring. and Tech. Methodist. Avocations: photography, hiking, travel. Home: 1536 Freedom Ln Fort Collins CO 80526 Office: Colo State U Dept Civil Engring Fort Collins CO 80523

CRITCHFIELD, HOWARD JOHN, geographer; b. Vernon, Colo., Sept. 24, 1920; s. Owen Isaac and Mable Luella (McCutchan) C.; m. Rose Doreen Caygill, Feb. 17, 1950 (dec. July 1969); children: David, Anne Louise. Student, Lewiston State Normal, 1940, U. N.C., 1943; BA, U. Wash., 1946, MA, 1947, PhD, 1952. Elem. tchr. Sch. Dist. 2, Boundary County, Idaho, 1940-42; instr. Wash. State U., Pullman, 1947-48; vis. lectr. U. Canterbury, Christchurch, New Zealand, 1948-50; prof. geography Western Wash. U., Bellingham, 1951—, state climatologist, 1976—. Author: General Climatology, 1983; contbr. articles to profl. jours. Mem. Bellingham City Planning Commn., 1957-62. Served to staff sgt. USAF, 1942-46. Grantee Carnegie Corp. 1948, Nat. Acad. Sci., 1979; Fulbright scholar Inst. Internat. Edn., 1950. Fellow Am. Geog. Soc. (life); mem. Assn. Am. Geographers (life), Nat. Council for Geog. Edn. (life), AAAS (life), Am. Assn. State Climatologists (pres. 1979-80 council mem.). Club: Bellingham Yacht. Home: 156 Forest Ln Bellingham WA 98225 Office: Western Wash U Bellingham WA 98225

CRITCHLOW, B. VAUGHN, primate research administrator; b. Hotchkiss, Colo., Mar. 5, 1927; s. Arthur Burtis and Nancy Gertrude (Lynch) C.; children: Christopher, Eric, Jan, Carey. B.A., Occidental Coll., 1951; Ph.D., UCLA, 1957. Instr. to prof. anatomy Coll. Medicine Baylor U., Houston, 1957-72; prof., chmn. anatomy Oreg. Health Scis. U., Portland, 1972-82; dir. Oreg. Regional Primate Research Ctr., Beaverton, Oreg., 1982—. Served with USN, 1945-46. NIH research career devel. awardee, 1959-69; NIH research grantee, 1958-87. Mem. Am. Assn. Anatomists, Endocrine Soc., Am. Physiol. Soc., Soc. for Neurosci., Internat. Soc. Neuroendocrinology, Internat. Brain Research Orgn., Am. Soc. Primatologists. Office: Oregon Regional Primate Research Center 505 NW 185th Ave Beaverton OR 97006

CRITTENDON, ROBERT RUSSELL, advertising executive; b. Brookhaven, Miss., Sept. 30, 1930; s. Atha Floyd and Birdie Louise (Canady) C.; m. Kelly Ruth Welch, Apr. 17, 1959; children—Kelli Jaye, Tracy Lynn. B.S., Okla. Bapt. U., 1953. Cert. bus. communicator. Account exec. Roger T. Case Assocs., Long Beach, Calif., 1957-59; advt. specialist Beckman Elec. Components, Fullerton, Calif., 1960-63; advt. mgr., 1963-67, advt. mgr. sci. instruments, 1967-69; corp. mgr. Mktg. Communications, 1969-85, dir. communications, 1986—; trustee Center for Mktg. Communications, 1975-78; dir. Media Comparability Council, 1982-83, Bus. Pub. Audit, 1982-86. Nat. bd. dirs. Leukemia Soc. Am., 1982-83. Served to capt. USMC, 1952-55. Recipient Crain Found. award, 1978. Mem. Bus./Profl. Advt. Assn. (internat. pres. 1974-75), Assn. Nat. Advertisers, Advt. Research Found. Republican. Club: El Niguel Country. Contbr. to book. Office: Mktg Communications 2500 Harbor Blvd Fullerton CA 92634

CRNIC, LINDA SMITH, psychobiologist, educator; b. Ft. Wayne, Ind., Mar. 29, 1948; d. Herman Edward and Patricia Ellen (Leeth) Smith; m. David Michael Crnic, June 21, 1969 (div. June 1976); m. Stanley Loyd Wilks, May 3, 1986. AB, U. Chgo., 1970; MA, U. Ill., Chgo., 1972, PhD, 1975. Postdoctoral fellow U. Colo. Sc. Medicine, Denver, 1975-77, instr. psychobiology, 1977-78, asst. prof. psychobiology, 1979-85, assoc. prof. psychobiology, 1985—. Contbr. articles to profl. jours. NIH grantee, 1975—. Mem. Internat. Soc. Devel. Psychobiology (sec./treas. 1983-86), Internat. Soc. Devel. Neurosci., Soc. Neurosci.(chmn. Rocky Mountain region group 1983-86), Western Soc. Pediatric Research, Animal Behavior Soc. Home: 1811 S Quebec Way #187 Denver CO 80231 Office: U. Colo Sch Medicine 4200 E 9th Ave C233 Denver CO 80262

CROCK, DOLORES LAVERNE, business educator; b. Marquette, Mich., Oct. 17, 1937; d. Henry LaVern and Ann (Dybing) Zweifel; m. Glenn Dale Crock, Mar. 1, 1973. BSBA, Wayne State U., 1964, MA in Teaching, 1967. Cert. tchr.; life vocat. edn. tchr., Mo. Sec. No. Mich. U., Marquette, 1956-60, Moses & Cline Forest Products, Dallas, 1964-66; instr. Cen. Mo. State U., Warrensburg, 1968-73, Laramie County Community Coll., Cheyenne, Wyo., 1974—. Mem. Wyo. Bus. Edn. Assn., Nat. Bus. Edn. Assn., Mountain Plains Bus. Edn. Assn., Wyo. Vocat. Assn., Am. Bus. Women's Assn., Assn. Info. Systems Profls. Republican. Presbyterian. Lodge: Order Eastern Star. Home: 3422 Warren Ave Cheyenne WY 82001 Office: Laramie County Community Coll 1400 E College Dr Cheyenne WY 82007

CROCKER, RICHARD EBEN, petroleum company executive; b. Detroit, Mar. 11, 1932; s. Clinch Nathaniel and Doris Lee (Campbell) C.; m. Mary Joanne Kendrick, Aug. 15, 1954; children: Nancy Joanne, James Richard, Steven Clinch. BS, U. Redlands, 1953; PhD, Mich. State U., 1959. Dir. research and tech. service Witfield Chem. Co., Long Beach, Calif., 1964-66; research assoc. ARCO Chem. Co., Anaheim, Calif., 1966-69; sr. research chemist Chevron Research Co., Richmond, Calif., 1969-73, sr. research assoc., 1973-79, mgr. lubricants div., 1979—. Patentee in field. Recipient Author's award Nat. Lubricating Grease Inst., 1976, Fellow's award Nat. Lubricating Grease Inst., 1978. Mem. Am. Chem. Soc. Office: Chevron Research Co 576 Standard Richmond CA 94802

CROCKER, THOMAS DUNSTAN, economics educator; b. Bangor, Maine, July 22, 1936; s. Floyd M. and Gloria F. (Thomas) C.; m. Sylvia Fleming, Dec. 31, 1961 (div. Sept. 1986); children: Sarah Lydia, Trena Elizabeth. AB, Bowdoin Coll., 1959; PhD, U. Mo., 1967. Asst. prof. econs. U. Wis., Milw., 1963-70; assoc. prof. U. Calif., Riverside, 1970-75; prof. U. Wyo., Laramie, 1975—. Co-author: Environmental Economics, 1971; author, editor: Economic Perspectives on Acid Deposition Control, 1984; contbr. articles to profl. jours. Grantee NSF, 1968, 73, 81, EPA, 1971—. Mem. Am. Econ. Assn., Assn. Environ. Resource Econs., Air Pollution Control Assn. Republican. Home: 2225 Skyview Ln Laramie WY 82070 Office: Univ Wyo Dept Econs Laramie WY 82071

CROCKETT, DONALD LEE, small business owner; b. Oxnard, Calif., Sept. 11, 1942; s. Burney Byron and Josephine (Genova) C.; m. Norma Lee Crabtree, Nov. 9, 1968; children: Carrie Ann, Anthony Joseph. Student, Allan Hancock Coll., 1962-63. Asst. mgr. Beneficial Fin. Co., Santa Maria, Calif., 1965-68, 70; installment loan officer Wells Fargo Bank, Santa Maria, 1971-77, asst. v.p. and mgr., 1978-82; owner, chief exec. officer The Paint Works, Inc., Santa Maria, 1982—. Bd. dirs., region chmn. March of Dimes, 1979-82. Served to sgt. U.S. Army, 1968-69. Democrat. Roman Catholic. Club: Exchange (Santa Maria) (Ventura) (charter pres. 1974, treas. 1980). Lodge: Elks. Avocations: bird hunting, boating, water skiing, gardening. Home: 4630 Lydia Ln Santa Maria CA 93455 Office: The Paint Works Inc 721 S Miller St Santa Maria CA 93454

CROCKETT, JAMES GROVER, III, publisher, musician; b. San Francisco, Feb. 13, 1937; s. James Grover and Virginia (Adams) C.; married; children: Chenoa Denelle, Doya Laurenne, Cordell Miller, Kessel Robinson. B.A. in Communications, Coll. of Pacific, 1958; M.A. in Communications, U. of Pacific, 1960. Various positions radio and TV stas. Stockton, Calif., Sacramento, Grants Pass, Oreg., Spokane, Wash., 1952-62; instr. radio-TV dept. U. Idaho, Moscow, 1961-63; concert producer, freelance writer 1963-70; owner, mgr. Books Universal, Livermore, Calif., 1963-70; arts editor, columnist, writer Livermore Ind., 1968-70; asst. editor Guitar Player mag., Los Gatos, Calif., 1970-71; editor Guitar Player mag., 1971, pub., editor, 1971—; v.p. GPI Corp., 1971-82, pres., 1982—; also pub. Keyboard mag., Frets mag.; speaker various trade confs. Free-lance musician, writer, 1955—; Pub. 1st non-objective coloring book for children, guitar repair manual. Active Music Educators' Nat. Conf., Music Industry Council. Mem. Fretted Instrument Guild Am., Nat. Assn. Music Mchts., Nat. Assn. Rec. Arts and Scis., Alpha Epsilon Rho, Phi Mu Alpha. Office: Guitar Player Dalton Communications 20085 Stevens Creek Cupertino CA 95014

CROFFORD, HELEN LOIS, accountant; b. Mesa, Ariz., Sept. 1, 1932; d. Elmer Earl and Lillian Irene (Williams) C.; grad. Lamson Bus. Coll., Phoenix, 1952. Acct., Bob Fisher Enterprises, Inc., Holbrook, Ariz., 1964-78; office mgr. for physician, Holbrook, 1978-79; office mgr. Trans Western Services, Inc., Holbrook, 1979; acct., Northland Pioneer Coll., Holbrook, 1980—. Squadron comdr. CAP, 1965-67, mission coordinator, 1970-79, group comdr., 1972-77, mem. regional staff, 1977-79, wing. historian, 1984—; mem. Navajo Fair Commn., 1966-75; mem. Navajo County Natural Resource Conservation Dist., 1970—, sec.-treas., 1971-81, chairperson, 1981-85; chmn. Navajo County Emergency Service Council, 1984-85. Mem. Ariz. Assn. Conservation Dists. (exec. bd. 1977-78, sec., 1979-80, v.p. 1981-82, pres. 1983-84, past pres. 1985), Nat. Assn. Conservation Dists., Nat. Assn. Female Execs., D.A.R. Democrat. Home: Box 36 Woodruff AZ 85942 Office: 1200 E Hermosa Dr Holbrook AZ 86025

CROFT, HUGO WILLIAM, engineering executive; b. Tacoma, Jan. 30, 1945; s. Bliss Henry and Nellie Blanche (Bost) C.; m. Carolynn Betty Akagi, June 15, 1968; children: Jennifer, Alexis. Student, Worcester Poly. Inst., 1963-64; BS, U.S. Mil. Acad., 1968; MSCE, Stanford U., 1974, MSME, 1974; MBA, Santa Clara U., 1982. Registered profl. engr., Va. Commd. 2d lt. U.S. Army, 1968, advanced through grades to capt., 1978—; product engr. Ford Motor Co., Dearborn, Mich., 1978-79; sr. design engr. ordnance div. FMC Corp., San Jose, Calif., 1979-82, system engr., 1982-84, project engr., 1984-85, mgr. survivability, 1985—; asst. prof. U.S. Mil. Acad., West Point, N.Y., 1974-77; adj. lectr. U. Mich., Dearborn, 1979. Decorated Bronze Star with 2 oak leaf clusters. Mem. Am. Assn. Artificial Intelligence, Soc. Automotive Engrs., Beta Gamma Sigma. Lutheran. Avocations: gardening, computers, running, swimming, family. Office: FMC Corp Ordnance div 1105 Coleman Ave San Jose CA 95108

CROKER, ROBERT ERNEST, vocational education educator; b. East Chicago, Ind., Feb. 10, 1946; s. David Robert and Donna Lorraine (Williams) C.; m. Susan Joan Relinski, Sept. 3, 1966; children: Amy, Allison, Amanda, Adam. BS, Purdue U., 1979; MS, Ind. State U., 1980; EdD, Wash. State U., 1986. Tchr. Tech. Vocat. High Sch., Hammond, Ind., 1976-79, Edison High Sch., Lake Station, Ind., 1979-81; grad. teaching asst. Wash. State U., Pullman, 1981-83; asst. prof. vocat. indsl. edn. Brigham Young U., Laie, Hawaii, 1983—. Served with USN, 1963-67. Mem. Nat. Assn. Indsl. Tech., Am. Vocat. Assn., Hawaii Indsl. Arts Assn., Internat. Tech. Edn. Assn., Inds. Tech. Students Assn. (advisor 1982), Phi Delta Kappa. Mormon. Avocations: camoeing, camping. Home: 55-474 Moana St Laie HI 96762 Office: Brigham Young U PO Box 1730 SS-220 Kulanui Laie HI 96762

CROMAR, MICHAEL EARL, transportation company executive; b. Salt Lake City, July 2, 1947; s. Earl B. and Mary L. (Peterson) C.; m. Nancy E. Maher, Feb. 5, 1973 (div. Oct. 1984); children: Matthew M., Martha E.; m.

Robin Ann McMullen, May 11, 1985. BS in Bus., U. Utah, 1972. CPA, Calif. Asst. controller Natomas Co., San Francisco, 1980-82; controller Am. Pres. Lines, Oakland, Calif., 1982-84; v.p., controller Computerland Corp., Oakland, 1984; v.p. Royal Viking Lines, San Francisco, 1984-85; controller Am. Pres. Cos., Oakland, 1985—. Served to capt. inf. U.S. Army, 1966-69, Vietnam. Mem. Am. Inst. CPA's, Calif. Soc. CPA's. Republican. Club: San Francisco Yacht (Belvedere, Calif.). Avocations: small yacht racing, skiing, woodworking. Office: American Pres Cos 1800 Harrison St Oakland CA 94612

CROMWELL, DERMONT GLOVER, chemist; b. Chatham, Ont., Can., Oct. 12, 1913; came to U.S., 1950; s. William G. and Alice H. (Shreve) C.; m. Nancye Trumbo, Apr. 10, 1939 (div. June 1941); m. Etta Mae Curtis, Dec. 16, 1942; children—Alice V., Beverly L., Sherry L. B.S., Wilberforce U., 1939. Lab. technician Chrysler Corp., Detroit, 1939-40; salesman N.C. Mut. Ins. Co., Nashville, 1940-42; chemist Monsanto Chem. Corp., Vancouver, B.C., Can., 1943-50; chemist Sinclair Paint Co., Los Angeles, 1951-81, tech. dir., 1981—. Mem. Los Angeles Soc. Coatings Tech. (dir. 1967-74, sec./treas. 1967-68, v.p. 1969, pres. 1970; Outstanding Service award 1981). Republican. Christian Scientist. Home: 9407 S LaSalle Ave Los Angeles CA 90047 Office: Sinclair Paint Co 6100 S Garfield Blvd Los Angeles CA 90040

CRONE, RICHARD ALLAN, cardiological physician, clinical instructor; b. Tacoma, Nov. 26, 1947; s. Richard Irving and Alla Marguerite (Ernst) C.; m. Rita Louzetta Mitchell, June 9, 1972 (div. Oct. 1981); m. Mika Jane Hinkle, Feb. 12, 1983. BA in Chemistry, U. Wash., 1969, MD, 1973. Intern Madigan Army Med. Ctr., Tacoma, 1973-74, resident in medicine, 1974-76, fellow in cardiology, 1977-79; commd. med. officer U.S. Army, Tacoma, Denver, San Francisco, 1972; advanced through grades to lt. col. U.S. Army, 1981; dir. coronary care unit Fitzsimons Army Med. Ctr., Denver, 1979-81; practice medicine specializing in cardiology Stevens Health Clinic, Edmonds, Wash., 1981—, also dir. coronary care unit, 1982—; clin. instr. U. Wash. Sch. Medicine, Seattle, 1983—. Nat. Merit scholar, 1965. Fellow Am. Coll. Angiology; mem. AMA, Am. Coll. Cardiology, Am. Heart Assn., Seattle Acad. Internal Medicine, Wash. State Soc. Internal Medicine, Wash. State Med. Assn., BMW Am. Republican. Roman Catholic. Avocations: skiing, wood carving, fishing, nature walks. Home: 10325 66th Pl W Everett WA 98204 Office: Stevens Health Clinic 21700 76th Ave W #100 Edmonds WA 98020

CRONIN, GEORGE THOMAS, lawyer; b. San Francisco, May 18, 1913; s. Daniel W. and Florence (Brenzel) C.; m. Terese A. Mango, Feb. 6, 1943; children—Susan Cronin Laird, Thomas Michael, Terese A., Kevin Charles. B.S., U. San Francisco, 1936, J.D., 1939. Bar: Calif. 1939. Atty., City and County of San Francisco, 1940-42; assoc. Brobeck, Phleger & Harrison, San Francisco, 1942-52, ptnr., 1952—; of counsel, 1986—. Mem. adv. bd. St. Mary's Hosp. and Med. Ctr., San Francisco, 1970—; mem., chmn. St. Mary's Found.; v.p., bd. dirs. Harney Found.; v.p., bd. dirs. Atholl McBean Found.; regent U. San Francisco; mem. adv. bd. Marianist Province of the Pacific. Fellow Am. Coll. Probate Counsel; mem. Internat. Acad. Estate and Trust Law (academician), Am. Acad. Hosp. Attys., Calif. State Bar (mem. com. bar examiners 1956-61, chmn., 1960-61), ABA, Am. Judicature Soc., Nat. Conf. Bar Examiners (sec. 1961-62), Internat. Bar Assn. Clubs: Pacific-Union, San Francisco Golf, Olympic, Commonwealth. Home: 35 Santa Clara Ave San Francisco CA 94127 Office: 2700 Spear St Tower One Market Plaza San Francisco CA 94105

CRONIN, GILBERT FRANCIS, insurance company executive; b. Rosetown, Sask., Can., Feb. 16, 1923; came to U.S., 1925, naturalized, 1943; s. Michael E. and Mary A. (Dawson) C.; m. Dorothy M. Fahey, Feb. 5, 1949; children: Michael, Timothy, Patricia, Vincent. A.B., Loyola U., Los Angeles, 1947. With Sears Roebuck and Co., Los Angeles, 1947-48, Prudential Ins. Co. Am., 1948-53, Scott-Hindenach Cons., Los Angeles, 1953-54; with Occidental Life Ins. Co. of Calif., Los Angeles, 1954—, exec. v.p.; chmn. bd. dirs. Transam. Life Ins. and Annuity Co., Los Angeles, 1977—; pres., chief exec. officer Transam. Ins. Securities Sales Corp., Los Angeles; bd. dirs. Transam-Occidental Life Ins. Co., Transam Life Ins. & Annuity Co., Transam Ins. Security Sales Corp., Transam. Assurance, Trans. Fin. Resources, First Transam. Life Ins. Co. of N.Y., Transam. Life Assurance Co. Bd. dirs. Los Angeles chpt. ARC, ins. council City of Hope, Los Angeles Mchts. & Mfrs. Assn. Served with parachute inf. U.S. Army, 1943-46, 1950-52, Korea. Decorated Silver Star, Bronze Star, Combat Inf. badge with star. Mem. Western Pension Conf. (past pres. Los Angeles chpt.), Am. Council Life Ins., Nat. Assn. Securities Dealers (prin. officer), Internat. Found. of Health, Welfare and Pension Plans, Assn. Pvt. Pension and Welfare Plans, Los Angeles Merchants and Mfg. Assn., Employee Benefit Research Inst. Republican. Roman Catholic. Office: Transamerica Life Ins and Annuity Co 1150 S Olive St Los Angeles CA 90015

CRONIN, JOHN READ, chemistry educator; b. Marietta, Ohio, Mar. 5, 1937; s. Lester A. and Mary (Read) C.; m. Muriel McLaughry Hill, Mar. 30, 1963; children: Paul R., Martha S., Sarah M. BA, Coll. Wooster, 1959; PhD, U. Colo., 1964. NIH postdoctoral fellow Yale U., New Haven, 1963-66; asst. prof. chemistry Ariz. State U., Tempe, 1966-72, assoc. prof., 1972-78, prof., 1978—. Contbr. articles to profl. jours. Mem., chmn. research adv. com. Am. Heart Assn., Phoenix, 1977-83. Faculty fellow Am. Soc. Engring. Edn., Stanford U., 1974-75; research grantee NIH, NASA, NSF, Am. Heart Assn., 1966—. Mem. Am. Soc. Biol. Chemistry, Am. Chem. Soc., Meteoritical Soc., AAAS, Internat. Soc. Study Origin of Life, Sigma Xi. Home: 409 E Laguna Dr Tempe AZ 85282 Office: Ariz State U Dept Chemistry Tempe AZ 85287

CRONK, MILDRED (MILI) SCHIEFELBEIN, special education consultant; b. Waverly, Iowa, May 29, 1909; d. Emil August and Nettie Marie (Berger) Schiefelbein; m. Dale Cronk, July 20, 1930; children: Barbara Cronk Burress, Bruce, Margaret, Michael. Student, Wartburg Coll., Waverly, 1927, Tampa (Fla.) U., 1944-45, Los Angeles City Coll., 1957; BA in Psychology, Calif. State U., 1960, MA in Spl. Edn. Supervision, 1971. Aircraft communicator, weather observer CAA, Fla. and Calif., 1942-49; dir. Parkview Nursery Sch., Los Angeles, 1956-57; tchr. trainable mentally retarded Hacienda-LaPuente United Sch. Dist., LaPuente, Calif., 1961-74; cons. spl. edn. La Mirada, Calif., 1975—; in-service trainer for tchrs; mem. spl. Olympics Southeast Los Angeles County com., 1977; treas. Very Spl. Arts Festival com., Orange County, 1977—, Internat. Very Spl. Arts Festival com., 1981; bd. dirs. Very Spl. Arts Calif., 1986—; active Common Cause. Author: Create With Clay, 1976, Vocational Skills Taught Through Creative Arts, 1978, Career Education for Trainable Mentally Retarded Students--It's For Life!, 1982, others. Mem. Am. Assn. on Mental Deficiency (bd. dirs. region II, editor Newsette, 1975-77, chmn. publicity com., 1977-79, presenter ann. confs.), Council for Exceptional Children (bd. dirs. Calif., editor Calif. State Fedn./Council for Exceptional Children Jour., 1977-80, past pres. San Gabriel Valley chpt. 538, mem.-at-large South Calif. div. Mental Retardation, 1976-79, pres. Calif. div. Mental Retardation, 1980-81, chmn. com. on officers' handbook, nat. council, div. Mental Retardation, 1977-78, spl. recognition awards, 1976, 77, 78, 79), Nat. Assn. for Retarded Citizens (rec. sec. 1980-81), Nat. Soc. Autistic Children (nat., state, local orgns.), Nat. Ret. Tchrs. Assn. (nat., state, local orgns.), Am. Ceramic Soc. (design div.), Smithsonian Instn., Wilderness Soc., Psi Chi. Democrat. Home and Office: 13116 Clearwood Ave La Mirada CA 90638

CRONKLETON, THOMAS EUGENE, physician; b. Donahue, Iowa, July 22, 1928; s. Harry L. and Ursula Alice (Halligan) C.; B.A. in Biology, St. Ambrose Coll., 1954; M.D., Iowa Coll. Medicine, 1958; m. Wilma Agnes Potter, June 6, 1953; children—Thomas Eugene, Kevin P., Margaret A., Catherine A., Richard A., Robert A., Susan A., Phillip A. Rotating intern St. Benedict's Hosp., Ogden, Utah, 1958-59; Donahue, Iowa, 1959-61, practice family medicine, Davenport, Iowa, 1961-66, Laramie, Wyo., 1966—; asso. The Davenport Clinic, 1961-63, partner, 1963-66; active staff St. Luke's Hosp., Mercy Hosp., Davenport; staff physician U. Wyo. Student Health Service, 1966-69, 70-71, 74-75; staff physician outpatient dept. VA Hosp., Iowa City, 1969-70; staff physician outpatient dept. VA Hosp., Cheyenne, Wyo., 1971-74, chief outpatient dept., 1973-74; dir. Student Health Service Utah State U., Logan, 1975-76; physician (part-time) dept. medicine VA Hosp., Cheyenne, 1976-81; staff physician U. Wyo. Student Health Service, Laramie, 1976—. Active Long's Peak council Boy Scouts Am., 1970—, scout chaplain Diocese of Cheyenne, 1980—, mem. Diocesan Pastoral Council, 1982-85. Served with USMC, World War II, Korea. Recipient Dist. Scouter award Boy Scouts Am., 1974, St. George Emblem, Nat. Cath. Scouter award, 1981. Recipient 5-, 10-, and 15-yr. service pins Boy Scouts Am. Diplomate Am. Bd. Family Practice. Fellow Am. Acad. Family Practice; mem. Wyo. State Med. Soc., Albany County (Wyo.) Med. Soc., Iowa Med. Soc., Johnson County (Iowa) Med. Soc. Democrat. Roman Catholic. Club: K.C. (4 deg.). Home: 2444 Overland Dr Laramie WY 82070 Office: Univ of Wyo Student Health Service Laramie WY 82071

CRONN, DAGMAR RAIS, atmospheric chemistry educator; b. Vicksburg, Miss., Nov. 9, 1946; d. Wesley Edward and Sarah Margaret (Courtney) Rais; m. Robert Stuart Cronn, June 22, 1968. BS, U. Wash., 1969, MS, 1972, PhD, 1975. Teaching asst. U. Wash., Seattle, 1969-71, research asst., 1971-75; asst. research chemist Wash. State U., Pullman, 1975-79, asst. prof., 1977-79, assoc. prof., 1979-86, prof. atmospheric chemistry, 1986—, asst. program dir., 1985-86, chair environ. sci. and regional planning program, 1986-88; cons. Am. Plywood Assn., Tacoma, 1977, EPA, Research Triangle Park, N.C., 1979-81, Meteorology Research Inc., Santa Rosa, Calif., 1981, Environ. Research and Tech., Inc., Westlake Village, Calif., 1981, W.K. Kellogg Found., Battle Creek, Mich., 1985, NSF, Washington, 1986. Contbr. numerous articles to profl. jours. Kellogg Found. fellow, 1981-84; Welsh Fund scholar, 1965-69. Air Pollution Control Assn. (chair regional meeting 1982), Soc. Women Engrs. (nat. keynote speaker 1983), Antarctican Soc. (speaker 1986), Sigma Xi. Home: Rt 2 Box 596 Pullman WA 99163 Office: Wash State U Pullman WA 99164

CRONQUIST, BRIAN EDWARD, process engineer; b. Roanoke, Va., Aug. 22, 1957; s. William Edward and Roberta Ann (Huston) C.; m. Jaymelynn Green, June 6, 1979; children: Lucannus Edward, Paul Michael. BS in Chemistry, U. Santa Clara, 1979. Process devel. engr. Synertek, Inc., Santa Clara, Calif., 1979-83; staff process research and devel. engr. Am. Microsystems Inc., Santa Clara, 1983-84; sr. process engr. Sierra Semicondr., San Jose, Calif., 1984—. Contbr. articles to profl. jours. Mem. Am. Chem. Soc., IEEE, Electrochem. Soc. Republican. Baptist. Avocations: chess, personal computers. Office: Sierra Semicondr 2075 N Capitol Ave San Jose CA 95132

CRONSHAW, JAMES, biology educator; b. Lancashire, Eng., Mar. 11, 1933; came to U.S., 1962; s. William and Edith (Wilkinson) C.; m. Patricia Birwhistle, Sept. 1, 1956; 1 child, Caroline Anne. BS in Botany, U. Leeds, Eng., 1954, PhD, 1957, DSc, 1973. Demonstrator dept. botany U. Leeds, 1955-57; research officer, div. forest products Commonwealth Sci. and Indsl. Research Orgn., Melbourne, Australia, 1957-62; demonstrator dept. botany U. Melbourne, 1957-62; asst. prof. biology Yale U., New Haven, 1962-65, assoc. prof. biol. scis. U. Calif., Santa Barbara, 1965-71, prof., 1971—. Contbr. articles to profl. jours. Grantee NSF, 1962-64, 65-66, 67-69, 69-72, 75-78, 80-86, NIH, 1962-67, Santa Barbara Med. Found. Clinic, 1974-76, Dickson Blanchard Pathology Group, 1978, U.S. Dept. Interior, 1976-80, USDA, 1985, U.S. Dept. Energy, 1985. Fellow AAAS, Royal Microscopical Soc.; mem. Am. Soc. Cell Biology, Bot. Soc. Am., Electron Microscopy Soc. Am., So. Calif. Soc. for Electron Microscopy, Soc. Exptl. Biology, Sigma Xi. Office: U Calif Dept Biol Scis Santa Barbara CA 93106

CROOK, SEAN PAUL, aerospace systems engineer; b. Pawtucket, R.I., July 6, 1953; s. Ralph Frederick and Rosemary Rita (Dolan) C.; m. Mary Wickman, June 10, 1978; children: Kimberly Anne, Kelly Dolan, Erin Webster, Mary Katherine. BSME, U.S. Naval Acad., 1975. Commd. ensign USN, 1975, advanced through grades to lt., 1979, resigned, 1981; sr. systems engr. space div. Gen. Electric Co., Springfield, Va., 1982-84; sr. aerospace systems engr. Martin Marietta Aero Def. Systems, Long Beach, Calif., 1984—, now sr. aerospace system engring. mgr. Served to lt. commdr. USNR, 1981-84. Mem. Am. Mgmt. Assn. Avocation: fin. planning. Home: 19281 Weymouth Ln Huntington Beach CA 92646 Office: Martin Marietta Aerospace 1501 Hughes Way Suite 300 Long Beach CA 92646

CROSBY, JOHN O'HEA, conductor, opera manager; b. N.Y.C., July 12, 1926; s. Laurence Alden and Aileen Mary (O'Hea) C. Grad., Hotchkiss Sch., 1944; B.A., Yale U., 1950; Litt.D. (hon.), U. N.Mex., 1967; Mus. D. (hon.), Coll. of Santa Fe, 1968; Mus.D. (hon.), Cleve. Inst. Music, 1974; L.H.D. (hon.), U. Denver, 1977. pres. Manhattan Sch. Music, 1976-86. Accompanist, opera coach, condr., N.Y.C., 1951-56, gen. dir., mem. conducting staff, Santa Fe Opera, 1957—; guest condr. various opera cos. in U.S. and Can., 1967—; condr.: U.S. stage premiere Daphne, 1964; world premiere Wuthering Heights, 1958. Served with inf. AUS, 1945-46, ETO. Roman Catholic. Clubs: Metropolitan Opera (N.Y.C.), Century Assn. (N.Y.C.), University (N.Y.C.). Office: PO Box 2408 Santa Fe NM 87501

CROSS, DEL S., school superintendent. Supt. Tacoma Pub. Sch. System, Wash. Office: Tacoma Sch Dist 10 Administrv Offices Box 1357 Tacoma WA 98401 *

CROSS, GLENN LABAN, engineering company administrator; b. Mt. Vernon, Ill., Dec. 28, 1941; s. Kenneth Edward and Mildred Irene (Glenn) C; m. Kim Lien Duong, Aug. 30, 1968 (div. Oct. 1975); m. 2d Tran Tu Thach, Dec. 26, 1975; children—Cindy Sue, Cristy Luu; B.A., Calif. Western U., 1981, M.B.A., 1982. Hosp. adminstr. pub. health div. AID, Dept. State, Washington, 1966-68; personnel mgr. Pacific Architects and Engrs., Inc., Los Angeles, 1968-70, contract adminstr., 1970-73, mr. mgmt. services, 1973-75; contracts adminstr. Internat. Services div., AVCO, Cin., 1975-77; sr. contract adminstr. Bechtel Group, Inc., San Francisco, 1977-80, Arabian Bechtel Co. Ltd.; contract adminstrv. supr. Jubail Industrial City, Saudi Arabia, 1980-85; cons. Bechtel Western Power Corp., Jakarta, Indonesia, 1985—. Author: Living With a Matrix: A Conceptual Guide to Organizational Variation, 1983. Served as sgt. 1st spl. forces group, airborne, AUS, 1962-65; Okinawa, Vietnam. Decorated Combat Infantryman's Badge. Mem. Internat. Personnel Mgmt. Assn., Assn. Human Resource Systems Profls., Human Resource Planning Soc., Assn. MBA Execs., Am. Mgmt. Assn., Am. Arbitration Assn., Internat. Records Mgmt. Council, Adminstrv. Mgmt. Soc. Home: 2841 Cottingham St Oceanside CA 92054 Office: Bechtel Group Inc 50 Beale St San Francisco CA 94119

CROSS, JOHN WILLIAM, biochemist; b. Memphis, Feb. 9, 1947; m. Susan Jean McLarty, Dec. 29, 1973; 2 children. BA, Vanderbilt U., 1969; PhD, Calif. Inst. Tech., 1976. Sr. research scientist Pfizar Cen. Research, Groton, Conn., 1978-85; sr. research biochemist Sogetal, Inc., Hayward, Calif., 1985—. Contbr. articles to profl. jours. Design project moderator Holy Cross Episc. Ch., Castro Valley, Calif., 1986. Carnegie Inst. fellow, 1976-78. Mem. AAAS, Am. Chem. Soc., Am. Soc. Plant Pathologists, Phi Beta Kappa. Research on plant growth substances, plant molecular biology and plant tissue culture. Office: Sogetal Inc 3872 Bay Center Pl Hayward CA 94545

CROSS, LINDA MARIE, state corrections official; b. Pasco, Wash., Feb. 14, 1950; d. Roosevelt and Vivian (Miles) Duncan; m. Lilton Cross Jr., June 22, 1972 (div. 1975); 1 child, Shawn L. AA in Sociology, San Bernardino Valley Jr. Coll., 1969; BA in Sociology, Los Angeles U., 1972; student, UCLA, 1980—. Cert. parole agt., Calif. Correctional counselor State Calif. Dept Corrections, Norco, 1980-82; women's program coordinator, equal employment analyst State Calif. Dept Corrections, Sacramento, 1982-83; parole agt. State Calif. Dept Corrections, Orange County, Calif., 1983—. Mem. Citizen's for Alternative Sentencing; adminstrv. v.p. Coalition for Women in State Service, Sacramento, 1982; com. mem. Affirmative Action, Sacramento, Calif., 1983; team mother Little League, Rialto, Calif. Recipient Dedication of Service award Chicano Pintos Inc., 1984, Dedication of Tutorer award Oak Glen Rehab. Camp, 1969-70. Mem. Friends Outside (vice chairperson 1984), Correctional Counselor Assn., Calif. Correctional Peace Officers Assn., Women's Liaison Council (head of resources 1985—), Orange County Calif. Chpt. NOW, Workers Employment Resource Council, Orange County Task Force, Women's Programs Corrections. Democrat. Baptist. Club: Toastmasters (vice chairperson 1980-82). Avocations: decorating, sewing, reading, swimming, aerobics. Home: 19413 Anaconda St Rialto CA 92376 Office: Calif State Dept Corrections 9500 Norwalk Rd Sante Fe Springs CA 90670

CROSS, ROBERT CLINTON, director of training, consultant; b. Paducah, Ky., Mar. 22, 1944; s. Robert C. and Barbara Nell (Stigall) C.; m. Judith Ellen Johnson, Jan. 28, 1967; children: Micheil, Shaun, Erin, Meghan. BA, Ky. Wesleyan Coll., 1967; MDiv, Vanderbilt U., 1970; EdM, Union Coll., 1975. Ordained Episcopal priest, 1971, renounced, 1986; instr. Sch. Nursing, Harlan, Ky., 1976-79; asst. St. Michael's Cathedral, Boise, Idaho, 1979-81; interim rector St. David's Ch., Caldwell, Idaho, 1981-82; cons. Boise, 1982-86; dir. tng. Laser Magic, Boise, 1986—; coordinator Diocese of Idaho, Boise, 1984-86; founder Sch. for Faith and Ministry, Boise, 1985. Author: (study guide) Promises, Promises, 1981. Mem. Am. Soc. Tng. and Devel., Episcopal Educators of N.W. Democrat. Home: 3112 Good St Boise ID 83703 Office: Laser Magic 816 W Bannock Suite 400 Boise ID 83702

CROSSLAND, HARRIET KENT, portrait painter; b. Cleve., Sept. 8, 1902; d. Carl and Harriet Emily (Bacon) Dueringer; pupil of Margaret McDonald Phillips; m. Paul Marion Crossland, Sept. 20, 1959. Portrait painter, 1952—; freelance editor med. papers, 1953-70; represented in permanent collection John F. Kennedy Library, Boston. Fund raiser Am. Cancer Soc.; mem. fund raising com. Vol. Action Bur.; mem. Santa Rosa Symphony League; mem. art mus. com. Luther Burbank Center for the Arts, Santa Rosa, 1982—. Recipient award of merit Am. Cancer Soc., 1979, 84. Mem. Artists Round Table, Sonoma County Med. Assn. Aux., Am. Med. Women's Assn. (friend), Am. Cancer Soc., DAR, Stanford U. Alumni Assn. Clubs: Ret. Officers Wives, Sonoma County Press, Sat. Afternoon. Editor, illustrator: X-Rays and Radium in Treatment of Diseases of the Skin, 1967. Prin. donor Crossland Lab. for Audiovisual Learning in Dermatology, Stanford U. Sch. Medicine. Address: 2247 Sunrise Dr Santa Rosa CA 95405

CROSSLAND, WILLIAM EDWARD, safety engineer; b. Detroit, July 13, 1932; s. Ernest Edward and Clara Gertrude (Davis) C.; m. Helen Charlene Thompson, July 23, 1976. B.S. in Safety Engring., U. Ala., 1960; postgrad. U. So. Calif., 1975. Registered profl. engr., Calif.; cert. safety profl., Ill.; lic. pvt. pilot; cert. police officer. Founder, chmn. bd. Internat. Safety Cons., Inc., 1969-81; dir. safety Handy Andy Corp., San Antonio, 1972-73; safety engr. Royal Globe Ins. Co., 1973-74; dir. safety U.S. Air Force, Oklahoma City, 1974-77; safety and health mgr. Dept. Labor, Kansas City, Mo., 1977-84; safety and health mgr. U.S. Air Force, Hawaii, 1984—; tchr. safety engring. Okla. State U.; cons. AF Community Coll.; mem. energy com. Fed. Exec. Bd., 1979-84. Composer: Never, 1958; Is It the Same, 1978. Contbr. articles to profl. jours. Vol. Kansas City chpt. ARC. Served with USAF, 1951-72. Decorated Commendation Medal with 3 oak leaf clusters, Meritorious Service Medal with 2 oak leaf clusters; named Top Civilian Safety Dir. in USAF, 1974. Mem. Assn. Fed. Safety and Health Profls. (past pres.), Am. Soc. Safety Engrs., Vets. Safety Internat. (pres.), Nat. Safety Mgmt. Soc., System Safety Soc., Am. Legion. Baptist. Office: 15ABW/SEG Hickham AFB HI 96853

CROSSLEY, FRANK ALPHONSO, metallurgical engineer; b. Chgo., Feb. 19, 1925; s. Joseph Buddie and Rosa Lee (Brefford) C.; m. Elaine J. Sherman, Nov. 23, 1950; 1 child, Desne Adrienne. B.S. in Chem. Engring, Ill. Inst. Tech., 1945, M.S. in Metall. Engring, 1947, Ph.D. in Metall. Engring, 1950. Instr. Ill. Inst. Tech., Chgo., 1948-49; sr. scientist Ill. Inst. Tech. Research Inst., 1952-66; prof. foundry engring., head dept. foundry engring. Tenn. Agrl. and Indsl. State U., 1950-52; sr. mem. research lab. Lockheed Missiles & Space Co., Palo Alto, Calif., 1966-74; mgr. dept. producibility and standards Lockheed Missiles & Space Co., 1974-78, mgr. dept. missile body mech. engring., 1978-79, cons. engr. missile systems div., 1979-86; dir. research propulsion materials Aerojet Propulsion Research Inst., 1986-87; cons. engr. Aerojet TechSystems Co., Sacramento, Calif., 1987—. Contbr. articles to metall. jours. and symposia, 1952-86. Served to ensign USNR, 1944-46, PTO. Fellow Am. Soc. for Metals; mem. Metall. Soc. of AIME, AIAA, SAMPE, Sigma Xi. Congregationlist. Patentee Transage titanium alloys. Home: 7575 Woodborough Dr Roseville CA 95661 Office: Aerojet Propulsion Research Inst PO Box 13502 Sacramento CA 95853-4502

CROSSMAN, HARLAN JAY, lawyer; b. Bklyn., July 27, 1941; s. Sydney Russell and Mary Lee (Cohen) C.; m. Gayla Glascock, July 1, 1964; children—Monica Ann, Avery Naomi. Student Menlo Coll., 1958-60; B.A., U. N.Mex., 1962, J.D., 1965. Bar: Ariz. 1968. Clk. to presiding judge N.Mex. Ct. Appeals, Santa Fe, 1966-67; atty. Navajo Legal Services Program, Window Rock, Ariz., 1967-69; atty. state compensation fund, Phoenix, 1969-72; pres. Harlan J. Crossman, P.C., 1972—; adj. prof. law Ariz. State U., 1985. Pres., Temple Solel, 1974-76; mem. Ariz. Gov.'s Com. on Workmen's Compensation, 1980-81; vice chmn. YMCA, 1980-84, chmn. youth com., 1981—, mem. nominating com., 1982. Mem. Maricopa County Bar Assn., State Bar Ariz. (sec. workmen's compensation sect. 1979—), ABA, Ariz. Trial Lawyers Assn. Democrat. Jewish. Club: Temple Solel Men's. Contbr. articles to profl. jours. Office: Suite 520 11 W Jefferson St Phoenix AZ 85003

CROTEAU, BRIAN ROLAND, personnel managment; b. Burlington, Vt., Dec. 8, 1956; s. Roland Francis and Kathryn Stella (Dubie) C. BS in Secondary Edn., U. Vt., 1978; postgrad., Chapman Coll., 1984—. Tng. specialist Aerosci. Corp., Anaheim, Calif., 1983-84, supr. personnel, 1984-85, mgr. adminstrn., 1985-86; supr. employee relations Amoco Foam Products, La Mirada, Calif., 1986—. Served to 1st lt. U.S. Army, 1978-83, capt. comdr . Res. 1986—. Methodist. Lodge: Masons. Avoctions: camping, backpacking, reading, ch. choir. Home: 4821 Keywood Ln Santa Ana CA 92703

CROUCH, BARBARA LEE, human resources management consultant; b. Sebring, Fla., Oct. 8, 1936; d. Elmer Nichols and Emily (Dreiss) Butler; m. Ralph Dean Crouch, Dec. 4, 1931; children: Ralph Dean, Barbara Lee, Clair Christopher, Kelly Andrew. Student, Long Beach City Coll., 1975, Cerritos (Calif.) Coll., 1976; cert. personnel mgmt., UCLA, 1978. Asst. to cons. Merchants and Mfrs. Assn., Los Angeles, 1975-78, library mgr., 1978-80; personnel mgr. TAD Avanti, Inc., Compton, Calif., 1980-82, Ole's Home Ctrs., Pasadena, Calif., 1982-84; staff cons. Merchants and Mfrs. Assn., Tustin, Calif., 1984-85; mgr. inland empire Merchants and Mfrs. Assn., Ontario, Calif., 1986—; coordinator Inland Empire Legis. Task Force, San Bernardino, Riverside Counties, Calif., 1986; mem. adv. bd. Employer Adv. Council, Ontario and Riverside, 1985—, Dept. Fair Employment Housing Commn. Regional Round Table, San Bernardino, Riverside Counties, 1985—. Contbr. articles to newsletters and profl. jours. Mem. Inland Empire Liaison Group Inc., San Bernardino, Riverside counties, 1985—. Mem. Indsl. Relations Research Assn. (conf. coordinator 1986, mem. planning bd. 1986, bd. dirs. 1986—), Personnel Indsl. Relations Assn. (treas. 1981, program chair 1981, 82), Assn. Labor-Mgmt. Adminstrs. and Cons. on Alcoholism, Pomona Valley Personnel Adminstrn. Democrat. Baptist. Winner Gold medal Amateur Roller Skating Assn. Am., 1971, 72, 73. Avocations: sewing, swimming, reading, cooking and gardening. Home: 436 Peach Tree Dr Mira Loma CA 91752 Office: Merchants and Mfrs Assn 337 N Vineyard Ave Suite 400 Ontario CA 91764

CROUT, ELEANOR MUECKE, civic worker; d. Berthold Muecke, Jr. and Eleanor B. Thalmann; B.A., Mt. Holyoke Coll.; M.A., Columbia; children—Alexandra Lynn, Stephen Andrew, Charles Merrill. Mem. Jr. Welfare Assn., Santa Fe, program chmn., treas., pres., then pub. relations chmn.; chmn. Community Christmas Store, Santa Fe; co-chmn. ticket sales Heart Fund Benefit; active March of Dimes drive, Heart Fund, Am. Cancer Soc. Drive, United Way; mem. St. Vincent Hosp. Aux.,, chmn. com., benefit; mem. Santa Fe Council Internat. Relations; chmn. Girl Scout Expn. Bd. dirs. Jr. Welfare Assn., Girl's Club, Shelter Care for Youth; bd. dirs., chmn. personnel services Sangre de Cristo council Girl Scouts U.S.A.; bd. dirs. St. Michael's High Sch., Santa Fe; coordinator City Elementary Sch. Competitive Swimming Program. Mem. Mt. Holyoke Alumnae Assn., Delta Kappa Pi, Phi Lambda Theta. Club: Santa Fe Garden (co-chmn. house and garden tours, sec., dir., publicity chmn. 1974-76). Episcopalian. Address: 32 Old Arroya Chamisa Rd Santa Fe NM 87505

CROWE, DANIEL WALSTON, lawyer; b. Visalia, Calif., July 1, 1940; s. J. Thomas and Wanda (Walston) C.; m. Nancy V. Berard, May 10, 1969; children—Daniel W., Karyn Louise, Thomas Dwight. B.A., U. Santa Clara, 1962; J.D., U. Calif. Hastings Coll. Law, 1965. Bar: Calif. 1966, U.S. Dist. Ct. (ea. dist.) Calif. 1969, U.S. Dist. Ct. (cen. dist.) Calif. 1973, U.S. Ct. Appeals (9th cir.) 1973, U.S. Supreme Ct. 1973. Assoc. Crowe, Mitchell & Crowe, and predecessors, Visalia, Calif., 1968-74, ptnr., 1974-83; ptnr. Crowe & Williams, 1983—; sec., treas., dir. The Exeter Devel. Co.; dir., treas.

Willson Ranch Co., 1983—. Founding mem., dir. Visalia Balloon Assn., Inc. Served to capt. U.S. Army, 1965-68. Decorated Bronze Star, Air medal, Purple Heart, Nat. Def. Service medal. Mem. ABA, Calif. Bar Assn., Tulare County Bar Assn. Republican. Roman Catholic. Clubs: Visalia Rotary, Elks, Moose, Am. Radio Relay League, DAV. Address: PO Box 1110 Visalia CA 93279

CROWE, DEVON GEORGE, physicist, engineering consultant; b. Portland, Oreg., Mar. 11, 1948; s. Frank Irving and Jeannie Campbell (Scott) C. B.S. in Astronomy and Math., U. Ariz., 1971, M.B.A. in Ops. Mgmt., 1977, M.S. in Optical Scis., 1980. Sr. research asst. Kitt Peak Nat. Obs., 1975-76; chief systems devel. and ops. Bell Tech. Ops. Corp., Tucson, 1978-80; mgr. tech. analysis div., sr. scientist Sci. Applications, Inc., Tucson, 1980—; pres. Desert Cat Software, Ltd., 1984—; cons. in field. Served to lt. USAF, 1971-74. Fellow Brit. Interplanetary Soc.; mem. IEEE, AAAS, Optical Soc. Am. (past pres. Tucson sect.), Photo-Optical Instrumentation Engrs., Am. Astron. Soc. Co-author: Optical Radiation Detectors, 1984; contbr. articles in field to profl. jours. Home: PO Box 11755 Tucson AZ 85734 Office: 5151 E Broadway St Suite 1100 Tucson AZ 85711

CROWE, DOUGLAS MARTIN, wildlife management administrator, biologist; b. Arkansas City, Kans., Nov. 7, 1939; s. Richard Martin and Shirley Rose (McCumber) C.; m. Timothea Barrett, Feb. 25, 1961; children—Ardith Jeanette, Martin Gregory, Marcella Ann. B.S., U. Wyo., 1970, Ph.D., 1974. Sales mgr. Wyo. Wholesalers, Casper, 1960-68; planner Wyo. Game and Fish Dept., Cheyenne, 1974-75, planning supr., 1975-85, asst. dir., 1985—; mem. Internat. Conv. Adv. Commn., Washington, 1982-83; cons. State Wildlife Agys. (Oreg., Alaska, Ohio, Wis., Mont., others) 1980—. Author: Comprehensive Planning for Wildlife Resources, 1984, Furbearers of Wyoming, 1986. Contbr. articles to Jour. Wildlife Mgmt., Jour. Mammalogy. Mem. Govs.' Task Force on Policy and Instl. Arrangements, Cheyenne, 1977. Served with U.S. Army, 1958-60. Named Outstanding Conservationist Wyo. Wildlife Fedn., 1981; NSF research grantee, 1972. Mem. Orgn. Wildlife Planners (pres. 1980), Wildlife Soc. (bd. dirs. Wyo. chpt. 1979), Am. Soc. Mammalogists, Phi Beta Kappa, Phi Kappa Phi, Wyo. Wildlife Fedn. Office: Wyo Game and Fish Dept 5400 Bishop Blvd Cheyenne WY 82002

CROWE, JOHN T., lawyer; b. Cabin Cove, Calif., Aug. 14, 1938; s. J. Thomas and Wanda (Walston) C.; m. Marina Protopapa, Dec. 28, 1968; 1 dau., Erin Aleka. B.A., U. Santa Clara, 1960, J.D., 1962. Bar: Calif. 1962, U.S. Dist. Ct. (no. dist.) Calif. 1964, U.S. Dist. Ct. (ea. dist.) Calif. 1967. Practiced in Visalia, Calif., 1964—; ptnr. firm Crowe, Mitchell & Crowe, 1971-85; referee State Bar Ct., 1976-82; gen. counsel Sierra Wine, 1986—. Bd. dirs. Mt. Whitney Area council Boy Scouts Am., 1966—, pres., 1971, 72; bd. dirs. Visalia Associated In-Group Donors (AID), 1973-81, pres., 1978-79; mem. Visalia Airport Commn., 1982—. Served to 1st lt. U.S. Army, 1962-64; col. Res. Decorated Meritorious Service Medal, Army Commendation Medal; named Young Man of Yr., Visalia, 1973; Senator, Jr. Chamber Internat., 1970; recipient Silver Beaver award Boy Scouts Am., 1983. Mem. ABA, Tulare County Bar Assn., Nat. Assn. R.R. Trial Counsel, State Bar Calif., Visalia C. of C. (pres. 1979-80). Republican. Roman Catholic. Clubs: Rotary (pres. 1980-81 ; Downtown (Fresno, Calif.). Home: 3939 W School St Visalia CA 93291

CROWE, TODD WILLIAM, architect; b. Bloomington, Ill., Jan. 19, 1956; s. John Stanley and Nancy Lee (Breen) C.; m. Faye Ellen Johnson, Sept. 22, 1979. BArch magna cum laude, Ariz. State U., 1979. Intern design Jack Peterson & Assocs., Phoenix, 1979-80; architect Backen, Arrigoni & Ross Inc., San Francisco, 1980-81; prin., pres. Dokken Crowe Architects, Frisco, Colo., 1981—; bd. dirs. Summit County Builders Assn., 1984-85. Furniture designs represented at Denver Regional Art Exhibit, 1986, Hibberd/McGrath Gallery, 1986. Chmn. Frisco Parks and Recreation Adv. Com., 1984—. Recipient Reynold Aluminum Design award 1979, Design award WOOD Inc., 1984, 86. Mem. AIA (cert., Colo. Design award 1984, Western Regional award 1984), Colo. Soc. Architects, Internat. Conf. Bldg. Officials, Summit County C. of C. Office: PO Box 569 Frisco CO 80443

CROWLE, ALFRED JOHN, immunology educator; b. Mexico City, Apr. 15, 1930; s. Alfred C. and Hazel Araminta (Mason) C.; m. Clarice Marjorie Futrelle, Oct. 22, 1954; children—Nelson Frederick, Cynthia Nanette. A.B., San Jose State Coll., 1951; Ph.D., Stanford U., 1954. Instr. immunology U. Colo. Sch. Medicine, Denver, 1956-59, asst. prof., 1959-65, assoc. prof., 1965-75, prof., 1974—; research microbiologist Webb-Waring Lung Inst., Denver, 1956-59, head div. immunology, 1965—; cons. U.S. Army, NSF, others. Author: Delayed Hypersensitivity in Health and Disease, 1962, Immunodiffusion, 2d edit., 1973; contbr. articles to profl. jours. Active Boy Scouts Am., 1966-71. Nat. Tb Assn. fellow, 1953-55, Nat. Acad. Scis.-NSF postdoctoral fellow, 1955; James Alexander Miller fellow N.Y. Tb and Health Assn., 1960-61; grantee NIH, NSF, others. Mem. Reticuloendotheial Soc., Am. Assn. Immunologists, AAAS, AAUP, Am. Soc. Microbiology, Soc. Exptl. Biology and Medicine. Clubs: Cherry Creek Gun (pres. 1967-70, 85), Colorado Mountain (head Rock Climbing Sch. Denver group 1977-82, dir.). Office: B-122 E 9th Ave Denver CO 80262

CROWLEY, JOHN CRANE, real estate developer; b. Detroit, June 29, 1919; s. Edward John and Lean Helen (Crane) C.; m. Barbara Wenzel Gilfillan, Jan. 12, 1945; children: F. Alexander, Leonard, Philip, Eliot, Louise, Sylvia. BA, Swarthmore Coll., 1941; MS, U. Denver, 1943. Mem. staff Pub. Adminstrn. Service, Chgo., 1942-46; asst. dir. Mcpl. Finance Officers Assn., Chgo., 1946-48; So. Calif. mgr. League Calif. Cities, Los Angeles, 1948-53; mgr. City of Monterey Park, Calif., 1953-56; v.p. Community Facilities Corp., Los Angeles, 1956-59, DSI Corp., Beverly Hills, Calif., 1961—; founder, exec. v.p. Nat. Med. Enterprises, Los Angeles, 1968; pres. Ventura Towne House (Calif.), 1963—; mem. faculty U. So. Calif. Sch. Pub. Adminstrn., 1950-53. Contbr. articles to profl. jours. Mem. State Adv. Council on Retirement Housing, 1965-68, Los Angeles County Com. on Affairs of Aging, 1966—; Mayor City of Pasadena, 1986—; city dir. Pasadena, 1979—; bd. dirs. Nat. Mcpl. League, 1986—, Pacificulture Found. and Asia Mus., 1971-76, pres., 1972-74; bd. dirs. Pasadena Area Liberal Arts Ctr., 1962-72, pres., 1965-68; trustee Pacific Oaks Friends Sch. and Coll., Pasadena, 1954-57; chmn. Pasadena Cultural Heritage Commn., 1975-78; pres. Pasadena Civic Improvement Corp., 1985—; bd. mgrs. Swarthmore Coll., 1986—. Recipient Disting. Citizen award Nat. Mcpl. League, 1984; Sloan Found. fellow, 1941-43. Mem. Internat. City Mgmt. Assn., Nat. Mcpl. League (nat. bd. 1980—), Phi Delta Theta. Democrat. Unitarian. Home: 615 Linda Vista Ave Pasadena CA 91105 Office: PO Box 93223 Pasadena CA 91109

CROWLEY, JOSEPH NEIL, univ. pres.; b. Oelwein, Iowa, July 9, 1933; s. James Bernard and Nina Mary (Neil) C.; m. Johanna Lois Reitz, Sept. 9, 1961; children—Theresa, Neil, Margaret, Timothy. B.A., U. Iowa, 1959; M.A., Calif. State U., Fresno, 1963; Ph.D. (Univ. fellow), U. Wash., 1967. Reporter Fresno Bee, 1961-62; asst. prof. polit. sci. U. Nev., Reno, 1966-71; asso. prof. U. Nev., 1971-79, prof., 1979—, chmn. dept. polit. sci., 1976-78, pres., 1978—; bd. dirs. Citibank Nev., Channel 5 Pub. TV; policy formulation officer EPA, Washington, 1973-74; dir. instl. studies Nat. Commn. on Water Quality, Washington, 1974-75; cons. in field. Author: Democrats, Delegates and Politics in Nevada: A Grassroots Chronicle of 1972, 1976; editor: (with Robert Roelofs and Donald Hardesty) Environment and Society, 1973. Mem. Commn. on Colls., 1980—, adv. commn. on mining and minerals research U.S. Dept. Interior, 1985—; bd. dirs., campaign chmn. No. Nev. United Way, 1985—. Recipient Thornton Peace prize U. Nev., 1971; Nat. Assn. Schs. Public Affairs and Adminstrn. fellow, 1973-74. Mem. Am. Polit. Sci. Assn., Western Polit. Sci. Assn., No. Calif. Polit. Sci. Assn. Roman Catholic. Club: Rotary. Home: 1265 Muir Dr Reno NV 89503 Office: Pres's Office U Nev Reno NV 89557

CROWLEY, ROBERT TINKHAM, physician; b. Galion, Ohio, Dec. 10, 1913; s. Forrest Glen and Frances Mae (Tinkham) C.; grad. Mercersburg Acad., 1930; M.D., Syracuse U., 1937; M.S. in Surgery, Wayne State U., 1946; M.Sc.Med., N.Y. Med. Coll., 1947; m. Cecilia Rita Smith, Dec. 23, 1956. Intern N.Y. Med. Coll., N.Y.C., 1937-38, resident in pathology and medicine, 1938-39; resident surgery Detroit Receiving Hosp., 1939-43, 45-46; adj. attending surgeon Lenox Hill Hosp., N.Y.C., 1947-54, chief women's div. Cancer Detection Clinic, 1950-54; chief surgery Meml. Med. Center, Williamson, W.Va., 1956-62; partner Kinsman (Ohio) Clinic, 1962-67; asst. prof. clin. surgery N.Y. U. Postgrad. Med. Sch., 1948-54; assoc. prof. surgery Wayne State U. Coll. Medicine, 1954-56; practice medicine specializing in thoracic surgery, Lancaster and Palm Dale, Calif.; chief surg. service Palm Dale Gen. Hosp., 1968-74; surg. cons. Los Angeles County Mira Loma Hosp., 1980—; cons. surgeon Lancaster Community Hosp.; med. cons. U.S. Dept. Justice, 1979—. Commr. Calif. Bd. Med. Quality Assurance, 1985. Served from capt. to maj., M.C., AUS, 1943-45; ETO. Named Disting. Citizen of Golden State, 1974. Diplomate Am. Bd. Surgery, Am. Bd. Thoracic Surgery, Nat. Bd. Med. Examiners. Fellow ACS, Am. Assn. Surgery Trauma, Royal Soc. Health (London), N.Y. Acad. Medicine; mem. Internationale Societe de Chirurgie, N.Y. Surg. Soc., N.Y. County Med. Soc., Western, Central surg. assns., Am. Coll. Geriatrics, Am. Coll. Angiology, Lyman Brewer II Internat. Surgery Soc., Internat. Platform Assn., Am. Platform Soc., Am. Authors League, Authors Guild, Sigma Xi. Episcopalian. Author: (novels) The Coffer of Saturno, 1961; Some with Steel, 1965; Not Soldiers All, 1967; Contract Surgeon, 1969; (poetry) Haste to The Red Brides Wedding, 1971; Lessons from Fright School, 1976; Robert T. Crowley research collection at Mugar Inst. Creative Writing, Boston U.; contbr. articles to med. jours. Office: PO Box 1058 Palmdale CA 93550

CROWLEY, THOMAS B., marine transportation company executive; b. 1914; married. With Crowley Maritime Corp., San Francisco, 1935—, now chmn., pres., dir. Office: Crowley Maritime Corp 101 California St San Francisco CA 94117 *

CROWLEY, WARD RAYMOND, real estate broker, investor; b. Des Moines, Jan. 14, 1927; s. Orville Wilfred and Hazel Aileen (Stevens) C.; m. Charlotte Klemenz, Aug. 19, 1958 (div. Jan. 1965); m. Gay Armistine Zohon, June 26, 1970. B.A., U. Iowa, 1950. Account exec. sta. KGHL, Billings, Mont., 1951-53, sta. KVTV, Sioux City, Iowa, 1953-55, sta. KLZ Denver, 1955-71; owner, operator Holiday Motor Lodge, Estes Park, Colo., 1971-76; sales assoc. Sovereign Motels Ltd., Denver, 1976-79; broker assoc. Morrison & Morrison, Denver, 1979-83; mgr. mem. services Printing Industries Assn. Mountain States, Denver, 1983-85. Precinct committeeman Denver Dem. Com., 1968. Served with USN, 1945-46. Recipient Salesman of Yr. award Sales and Mktg. Execs., 1961. Mem. Estes Park C. of C. (pres. 1974), Estes Park Accomodations Assn. (bd. dirs. 1973-75), Colo. Motel Assn. (v.p., 1974-75), Phi Beta Kappa, Alpha Delta Sigma. Lutheran. Lodge: Lions (bd. dirs. Denver 1963-65, pres. Estes Park 1975-76). Home and Office: 712 Allison St Lakewood CO 80215

CROWN, KATHLEEN JORDAN, speech/language pathologist; b. Washington, Oct. 30, 1959; d. Edward Daniel and Margaret Ann (Moran) Jordan; m. Ross Lee Crown, Jr., June 16, 1984. BA summa cum laude, Cath. U. Am., 1981; MS, U. Mich., Ann Arbor, 1983. Cert. clin. speech/lang. pathologist. Speech/lang. pathologist Albuquerque Hearing and Speech Ctr., 1983—, acting dir., 1985—. Named One of Outstanding Young Women Am., 1985; recipient Nat. Ambuc scholarship for Therapists, 1982, Kappa Kappa Gamma Rehab. scholarship, 1982, U. Mich. Alumni Council scholarship, 1982. Mem. Am. Speech Lang. and Hearing Assn. (cert.), N.Mex. Speech Lang. and Hearing Assn., Albuquerque Speech and Hearing Profls. (v.p. 1986), Blue Key, Phi Beta Kappa, Phi Eta Sigma, Sigma Epsilon Phi, Kappa Gamma Pi. Republican. Roman Catholic. Club: Exec. Sports (Albuquerque). Avocation: weightlifting. Home: 4408 Kellia Ln NE Albuquerque NM 87111 Office: Albuquerque Hearing and Speech Ctr 1011 Buena Vista Dr SE Albuquerque NM 87106

CROWSON, DAN MICHAEL, electrical engineer; b. Tulsa, Aug. 1, 1953; s. Bobby Earl and Virginia Marie (Stoops) C.; m. Brenna Leigh Gentry, Oct. 16, 1982; 1 child, Bobby Christopher. AS in Elec. Engring. Tech., Okla. State U., 1975, BS in Engring. Tech., 1976. Engr. Xerox Corp., Oklahoma City, 1977-81, Phillips Petroleum, Dallas, 1981-82, H.P. Smith Paper Co., Chgo., 1982-83; engr., designer Stearns-Catalytic World Corp., Denver, 1984-87; electrical engr. Master Palletizer Systems, Inc., Denver, 1987—; computer cons., Denver, 1985—. Office: Master Palletizer Systems Inc 1401 W Stanford Ave Englewood CO 80110

CROWTHER, RICHARD LAYTON, architect, consultant, researcher, author, lecturer; b. Newark, Dec. 16, 1910; s. William George and Grace (Layton) C.; m. Emma Jane Hubbard, 1935 (div. 1949); children: Bethe Crowther Allison, Warren Winfield, Vivian Crowther Tuggle; m. 2d Pearl Marie Tesch, Sept. 16, 1950. Student, Newark Sch. Fine and Indsl. Arts, 1928-31, San Diego State Coll., 1932, U. Colo., 1956. Registered architect, Colo. Prin. Crowther & Marshall, San Diego, 1946-50, Richard L. Crowther, Denver, 1951-66, Crowther, Kruse, Landin, Denver, 1966-70, Crowther, Kruse, McWilliams, Denver, 1970-75, Crowther Solar Group, Denver, 1975-82, Richard L. Crowther FAIA, Denver, 1982—; lectr. U. Wis., Madison, 1974, U. Ky., Shakertown, 1977, Smithsonian Inst., Washington, 1977, U. Nebr., Lincoln, 1981; judge solar archtl. competition State of Ill., Chgo., 1977. Author: Sun/Earth, 1975 (Progressive Architecture award 1975), rev. edit., 1983, Affordable Passive Solar Homes, 1983, Paradox of Smoking, 1983, Women/Nature/Destiny: Female/Male Equity for Global Survival, 1987, (monographs) Context in Art and Design, 1985, Existence, Design and Risk, 1986, Indoor Air: Risks and Remedies, 1986, Migration in Solar Homes for Seasonal Comfort and Energy Conservation, 1986. NSF grantee, 1974-75. Fellow AIA (commr. research, edn. and environ. Colo. Central chpt. 1972-75, bd. dirs. chpt. 1973-74 AIA Research Corp. Solar Monitoring Program contract award).

CROWTHER, TED JOSEPH, electrical engineer, researcher; b. Alamosa, Colo., Jan. 29, 1937; s. Horace C. and Almorine (Cunningham) C.; m. Suzanne Nixon, June 3, 1957; children: Mark J., Sharon, David T., Robyn, Autumn, Randolph. BS, Brigham Young U., 1960; MS, Stanford U., 1963. Sr. scientist Lockheed Research Labs., Palo Alto, Calif., 1960-65; sr. elec. project Ultek div. Perkin Elmer, Palo Alto, 1965-71; engr. mgr. Syntex, Cupertino, Calif., 1973-78; chief engr. Triax Co., Alpine, Utah, 1979-83, Eyring Research Inst., Provo, Utah, 1978-79, 83—; instr. Brigham Young U., Provo, 1985—. Patentee in field; contbr. articles to tech. jours. Mem. IEEE. Mormon. Avocations: gardening, photography, backpacking, model building. Office: Eyring Research Inst 1455 W 820 N Provo UT 84601

CRUIKSHANK, SUSAN FRANK, entrepreneur; b. Indpls., May 2, 1945; d. Frank Tupper Greenwald and Geraldine Phyllis (Frank) Greenwald; m. Lanric Hyland, July 4, 1968 (div. Jan. 1975); m. Dale Paul, Oct. 4, 1975; 1 child, Jeffrey. BA in Psychology, San Francisco State U., 1968; MEd, U. Hawaii, 1980. Sec. dept. geology San Francisco State U., 1969-72; adminstrv. asst. trauma ctr. San Francisco Gen. Hosp., 1972-74; personnel officer Inst. for Astronomy, U. Hawaii, Honolulu, 1974-79; personnel mgmt. specialist City and County of Honolulu, 1979-82; owner children's store The Rubber Ducky, Honolulu, 1982—; owner women' store Just Ducky, Honolulu, 1986—. Mem. Nat. Fedn. Ind. Bus., Mchts. Assn. (bd. dirs. 1982—). Avocation: oil painting. Office: The Rubber Ducky Koko Marina Shopping Ctr Honolulu HI 96825

CRULL, TIMM F., food company executive; b. 1931; married. BA, Mich. State U., 1955. Chief operating officer Norton Simon Inc., 1977-79; with Carnation Co., Los Angeles, 1955-77, 80—, exec. v.p., 1980-83, pres., 1983—, chief exec. officer, 1985—, also bd. dirs. Office: Carnation Co 5045 Wilshire Blvd Los Angeles CA 90036

CRUMBAKER, MARY KATHRYN (MRS. WILLIAM GOODMAN WILLIAMSON), business educator; b. Gt. Falls, Mont.; d. Calvin and Kathryn Elizabeth (Harbaugh) Crumbaker; student U. Mont., 1939, Southwestern U. at Memphis, 1942-43, Whitman Coll., 1939-41; B.S., U. Oreg., 1946; postgrad. Hochschule for Music, Vienna, Austria, 1947-48; M.Ed., Oreg. State U., 1966; Ph.D., Nat. Christian U. Dallas, 1974; m. William Goodman Williamson, Dec. 17, 1941 (dec. Oct. 1970); children—James Calvin, Albert Jerome, Kathryn Erilda. Sec., exec. sec. Granada (Miss.) Elem. Sch., also U.S. C.E., 1941-44; substitute sec. U. Oreg., 1944-46; head comml. studies Internat. Trade Coll., Chgo., 1948-51; tchr. Mich. Dept. Rehab., Am. Legion Tb Hosp., Battle Creek, 1952-53; tchr. U.S. Army, Kokura, Japan, 1954-56; tchr. Clark Bus. Coll., Topeka, 1956-58; charm sch. dir., dir. tng. Eugene (Oreg.) Bus. Coll. 1959-70, mgr., corp. sec.-treas., 1970—, pres., 1974-85, prof. emeritus, 1986—; prof. bus. Eugene Coll. Bus. and Tech., 1985—; lectr., Am. econ. system and music Austro-Am. Soc., Vienna, 1946-48. Mem. exec. bd. S.W. Oreg. Mus. Sci. and Industry, 1972-75; den mother Oreg. Trail council Boy Scouts Am., 1959-69; chmn. West Univ. Neighborhood, 1981, 82; mem. Neighborhood Leaders Council, 1981; treas. Eugene WCTU, 1980-82; precinct committeeman Republican party, 1960—; pres. Central Lane Rep. Women, 1970; chmn. constn. and bylaws Lane County Council Orgns., 1985—; pres. Lane County WCTU, 1985—. Named Troop Mother of Yr. Boy Scouts Am., 1971. Mem. Nat. Fedn. Bus. and Profl. Women's Clubs, Oreg. Fedn. Bus. and Profl. Women (found. chmn. 1986—), Am. Bus. Women, Am. Inst. Profl. Cons., Rubicon Soc., Eugene Bus. and Profl. Women's Club (pres. 1966, 79), DAR, Daus. of Nile, Am. Forestry Assn., Nat. Rifle Assn., PEO (treas. chpt. H, 1986-87), AAUW, Beta Gamma Sigma, Mu Phi Epsilon. Clubs: Eugene City (life mem.), Zonta (pub. Newsletter 1984—), Dial (pres. Eugene 1973-74). Lodges: Order Eastern Star (musician), White Shrine of Jerusalem (musician), Order of Amaranth (musician; condr. 1982-83, royal matron 1984-85). Kiwanis (hon.). Author: Typing with Less Than 2 Hands, 1962. Home: 1031 Mill St Eugene OR 97401 Office: 383 E 11th St Eugene OR 97401

CRUMP, GERALD FRANKLIN, lawyer; b. Sacramento, Feb. 16, 1935; s. John Laurin and Ida May (Banta) C.; m. Glenda Roberts Glass, Nov. 21, 1959; children—Sara Elizabeth, Juliane Kathryn, Joseph Stephen. A.B., U. Calif.-Berkeley 1956, J.D., 1959; M.A., Baylor U., 1966. Bar: Calif. 1960. Dep. county counsel Los Angeles County, 1963—, legis. rep., 1970-73; chief pub. works div. Los Angeles County Counsel, 1973-84, sr. asst. county counsel, 1984-85, chief asst. county counsel, 1985—; lectr. Pepperdine U., 1978, U. Calif., 1982. Served to capt. USAF, 1960-63; to col. USAFR, 1963—. Mem. ABA, State Bar of Calif. (del.), Los Angeles County Bar Assn. (chmn. govtl. law sect. 1983-84), Am. Judicature Soc., Am. Acad. Polit. and Social Sci., Res. Officers Assn., Air Force Assn., Phi Alpha Delta, Delta Sigma Phi. Home: 4020 Camino de la Cumbre Sherman Oaks CA 91423 Office: 648 Hall of Administration Los Angeles CA 90012

CRUMP, MICHAEL JOHN, Computerized tax services company executive; b. Los Angeles, Oct. 11, 1946; s. Eugene L. and Elizabeth M. (Finn) C.; m. Susan Jane Pendergast, Apr. 5, 1975; 1 dau., Catherine. B.A., U. San Francisco, 1968; J.D., U. San Diego, 1972. Research asst. U.S. Dist. Ct., San Diego, 1974-75; tax analyst Marshall Acctg., Long Beach, Calif., 1975; tax analyst Tymshare Unitax, Anaheim, Calif., 1975-78, tax mgr., 1978—; mem. IRS Task Force, 1982-86; apptd. v.p. Unitax-McDonnell Douglas Corp., 1986; lectr. in field. Mem. Nat. Soc. Pub. Accts., Nat. Assn. Computerized Tax Processors (treas. 1978-81, v.p. 1981-82, pres., 1982-84), Xplor (v.p. 1980-81). Democrat. Roman Catholic. Author manuals in field. Deceased Sept. 1986.

CRUMPTON, EVELYN, psychologist, educator; b. Ashland, Ala., Dec. 23, 1924; d. Alpheus Leland and Bernice (Fordham) Crumpton. A.B., Birmingham So. Coll., 1948; M.A., UCLA, 1953, Ph.D. in Psychology, 1955. Lic. psychologist, Calif. Research psychologist VA Hosp., Brentwood, Los Angeles, 1955-77; asst. chief, psychology service, coordinator clin. training VA Adminstrn. Med. Ctr., West Los Angeles, 1977-85; sr. assoc. chief, dir. intern training, Psychology Service VA Adminstrn. Med. Ctr., West Los Angeles, 1985-87; clin. prof. dept. psychology UCLA, assoc. research psychologist dept. psychiatry, UCLA Sch. Med., 1957—; cons. chief of staff 2d psychology services, Brentwood div., VA Adminstrn. Med. Ctr., West Los Angeles, Calif. Recipient Profl. Service award, Assn. Chief Psychologists VA, 1979. Fellow Soc. Personality Assessment; mem. Am. Psychol. Assn., Western Psychol. Assn., Sigma Xi. Contbr. numerous articles to profl. jours.

CRUSE, ALLAN BAIRD, mathematician, computer scientist, educator; b. Birmingham, Ala., Aug. 28, 1941; s. J. Clyde and Irma R. Cruse. A.B., Emory U., 1959-62, Ph.D., 1974; postgrad. (Woodrow Wilson fellow) U. Calif.-Berkeley, 1962-63, M.A., 1966; teaching fellow Dartmouth Coll., 1963-64. Instr., U. San Francisco, 1966-73, asst. prof. math., 1973-76, assoc. prof., 1976-79, prof., 1979—; vis. instr. Stillman Coll., summer 1967; vis. assoc. prof. Emory U., spring 1978; prof. computer sci. Sonoma State U., 1983-85; cons. math edn. NSF fellow, 1972-73. Mem. Am. Math. Soc., Math. Assn. Am., Calif. Math. Council, Computer Soc. of IEEE, Assn. Computing Machinery, Am. Mgmt. Assn., U. San Francisco Faculty Assn., Sigma Xi (Dissertation award 1974). Author: (with Millianne Granberg) Lectures on Freshman Calculus, 1971; research, publs. in field. Office: Harney Sci Center U San Francisco San Francisco CA 94117

CRUTCHFIELD, SUSAN RAMSEY, neurophysiologist; b. Pasadena, Calif., Oct. 7, 1941; d. Henry Colwell Ramsey and Rowena Ruth (Lockett) Banning; m. Ralph L. Crutchfield, Sept. 26, 1964 (div. Sept. 1973); children: Pamela Montague, Ashley Noland. AA, Pine Manor Coll., 1961; student, Sorbonne U., Paris, 1961-62; BA, George Washington U., 1964; MA, U. Calif., San Diego, 1978; PhD, Aston U., Birmingham, Eng., 1986. Research assoc. U. Calif. Med. Ctr., San Diego, 1978-80, researcher, 1986—; researcher Birmingham U., 1980-86. Mem. San Diego Jr. League. Mem. AAAS, N.Y. Acad. Scis., European Neurosci. Soc., Royal EEG Soc. Club: Warwick (Eng.) Boat, La Jolla Beach and Tennis Club. Avocations: camping, horseback riding, hiking, photography, gardening. Home: 1624 Ludington Ln La Jolla CA 92037 Office: U Calif Med Ctr San Diego CA 92115

CRUZ, BENJAMIN JOSEPH FRANQUEZ, judge; b. Agana, Guam, Mar. 3, 1951; s. Juan Quenga Cruz and Antonia (Franquez) Guerrero. BA, Claremont Men's Coll., 1972; JD, U. Santa Clara, 1975. Asst. consumer counsel Office Atty. Gen., Agana, 1975; gov.'s legal counsel Gov. of Guam, Agana, 1975-79; sole practice law Agana, 1979-82; minority legal counsel Guam Legis., Agana, 1979-82; dir. Guam/Wash. Liaison Office, Washington, 1983-84; judge Superior Ct. Guam, Agana, 1984—. Pres. Am. Cancer Soc., 1978-80; committeeman Dem. Nat. Com., Washington, 1984; TV co-host Muscular Dystrophy Assn. Telethon, Agana, 1977-78; exec. dir. Dem. Party Guam, Agana, 1979-83. Mem. Nat. Judges Assn., Nat. Assn. Juvenile and Family Ct. Judges. Avocations: aerobics, weightlifting. Home: PO Box 3326 Agana GU 96910 Office: Superior Ct of Guam 110 W O'Brien Dr Agana GU 96910

CRYER, RODGER EARL, educational administrator; b. Detroit, Apr. 2, 1940. A.B. in Fine Arts, San Diego State U., 1965; M.A. in Edn. Adminstrn., Stanford U., 1972; PhD in Psychol. Services Counseling, Columbia-Pacific U., 1985. Cert. tchr., N.J., Calif.; cert. gen. adminstrn., Calif. Spl. asst. to commissioner N.J. State Dept. Edn., Trenton, 1967-68; cons. N.J. Urban Sch. Devel., Trenton, 1969-70; mgmt. cons. Rodger E. Cryer, Co., Pinole, Calif., 1970-73; adminstrv. asst. Franklin McKinley Sch. Dist., San Jose, Calif., pres. Chief Exec. Tng. Corp., San Jose, 1981-82; prin. McKinley Sch., 1986—. Mem. Nat. Sch. Pub. Relations Assn. (sec. 1975—), Calif. Sch. Pub. Relations Assn. (pres.). Contbr. articles to profl. jours. Home: PO Box 21917 San Jose CA 95151 Office: McKinley Sch 651 Macredes Ave San Jose CA 95116

CSENDES, ERNEST, chemist, corporate and financial executive; b. Satu-Mare, Romania, Mar. 2, 1926; s. Edward O. and Sidonia (Littman) C.; came to U.S., 1951, naturalized, 1955; m. Catharine Vera Tolnai, Feb. 7, 1953; children: Audrey Carol, Robert Alexander Edward. BA, Protestant Coll., Hungary, 1944; BS, U. Heidelberg (Ger.), 1948, MS, PhD, 1951. Research assoc. biochemistry Tulane U., New Orleans, 1952; fellow Harvard U., 1953; research chemist organic chems. dept. E. I. Du Pont de Nemours and Co., Wilmington, Del., 1953-56, elastomer chems. dept., 1956-61; dir. research and devel. agrl. chems. div. Armour & Co., Atlanta, 1961-63; v.p. corp. devel. Occidental Petroleum Corp., 1963-64, exec. v.p. research, engring. and devel., 1964-68, also mem. exec. com.; exec. v.p. Occidental Research and Engring. Corp., 1963-68; pres., chief exec. officer Tex. Republic Industries, Inc., 1968—; gen. ptnr. Tex. Republic Investors, Ltd., 1971-72; pres., chief exec. officer TRI Ltd., Bermuda, 1971—; chmn. TRI Internat., Ltd., Bermuda, 1971—; mng. dir. TRI Capital N.V. (Netherlands), 1971—; chmn., chief exec. officer Micronic Techs., Inc., 1981-85. Contbr. articles to profl. jours.; patentee in field. Recipient Pro Mundi Beneficio medal Brazilian Acad. Humanities. Fellow AAAS, Am. Inst. Chemists; mem. Am. Chem. Soc., German Chem. Soc., N.Y. Acad. Sci., Royal Soc. Chemistry (London), Acad. Polit. Sci., Am. Acad. Polit. and Social Sci., Global Action Econ. Inst., Am. Mgmt. Assn., AIM, AIAA, Am. Def. Preparedness Assn., Sigma Xi. Research in area of elastomers, rubber chemicals, dyes and intermediates, organometallics, organic and biochemistry, high polymers, phosphates, plant nutrients, pesticides, process engring. and design of fertilizer plants, ammonia, urea, sulfur, iron, potash and phosphate ore mining and metallurgy; also acquisitions, mergers, internat. fin. related to leasing, banking, trusts and ins.; regional devel. related to agr. and energy resources. Home: 514 Marquette St Pacific Palisades CA 90272

CSICSERY, SIGMUND MARIA, chemist, consultant; b. Budapest, Hungary, Feb. 3, 1929; s. Sigmund and Pálma (Tahy) C.; m. Gabrielle Maria Szemere, Dec. 1, 1956. BSChemE, Tech. U., Budapest, Hungary, 1950, MSChemE, 1951; PhD in Organic Chemistry, Northwestern U., Evanston, Ill., 1961. Research chemist Monsanto Chem. Co., Dayton, Ohio, 1957-59, Chevron Research Co., Richmond, Calif., 1961-66; sr. research chemist Chevron Research Co., Richmond, 1966-70, sr. research assoc., 1970-86; instr. U. Calif., Berkeley, 1965-66. Contbr. articles to profl. jours.; patentee in field. Mem. Am. Chem. Soc., Calif. Catalysis Soc. (pres. 1973-74), Catalysis Soc. N. Am. (bd. dirs. 1976-80). Avocations: mountain climbing, skiing, windsurfing, hiking, scuba. Home: PO Box 843 Lafayette CA 94549

CUARÓN, ALICIA VALLADOLID, educator, community activist, business owner; b. Oxnard, Calif., Mar. 1, 1939; d. Rosendo Alfaro and Guadalupe Valladolid (Perez) V.; 1 dau., Alexis Maritza. B.A. in Edn., U. Tex.-El Paso, 1961, M.A. in Adminstrn., 1972; Ed.D. in Curriculum and Instrn., U. No. Colo., Greeley, 1975. Cert. tchr., supr., Tex. Tchr., Pub. Schs. El Paso, 1961-72; asst. prof. edn. Met. State Coll., Denver, 1974-80; social sci. program specialist U.S. Dept. Labor Women's Bur., Denver, 1979; exec. dir. Colo. Econ. Devel. Assn., Denver, 1980; nat. adminstr. Nat. Assn. Constrn. Enterprises, Denver, 1981-82; dir. Hispanic Access to Services Project, Community Coll. Denver, Auraria Campus, 1982; pres. Cuarón & Silvas & Assocs., 1983-85, Cuarón & Gomez, 1985-87; bilingual/bicultural presch. coordinator Denver Headstart, 1972; project dir. Bilingual/Multicultural Edn. project, 1975; cons. Hispanic Displaced Homemakers project, 1981. Founder, Nat. Adelante Mujer Hispana Conf., 1980, Nat. Network Hispanic Women, 1981, Colo. Network Hispanas, 1981; chair Colo. Ctr. Women and Work, 1980-84; mem. Colo. State Fair Commn., Colo. Supreme Ct. Nominating Commn. Recipient award Colo. Big Sisters, 1983. Mem. Nat. Assn. Hispanas in Econ. Devel. and Enterpreneurship (founder), Colo. Women's Forum, League United Latin Am. Citizens, Denver Hispanic C. of C. (sec.), Phi Delta Kappa. Democrat. Roman Catholic. Author: Hispana Displaced Homemakers Training Model, 1982; producer/host TV and radio programs, 1981-83. Home: 1000 S Monaco St #30 Denver CO 80224 Office: Cuarón & Gomez Inc 1391 N Speer Blvd Suite 460 Denver CO 80218

CUCHNA, MICHAEL JOHN, chemistry, physics, computer science educator; b. Chgo., Oct. 11, 1946; s. Gerald Frank and June Loretta (Lynge) C.; m. Judith Lynn Belon, Sept. 3, 1969; children: Laura Lynn, Karen Michelle. BA in Chemistry, Chico State U., 1968, MA in Phys. Sci., 1969; MEd, Chapman Coll., 1978; postgrad., U. Pacific, 1978—. Cert. secondary and community coll. tchr., Calif. Tchr. Merced (Calif.) Union High Sch. Dist., 1971-82; instr. U. Calif., Davis, 1981—, Merced Coll., 1983—, U. Golden Gate, San Francisco, 1985—; bd. dirs. Cen. Calif. Sci. Project, Modesto, 1983—; mem. Curriculum Devel. and Supplemental Materials Commn., Sacramento, 1983—; cons. Merced Coll., 1982-83. Mem. policy bd. Region VII Tchr. Edn. and Computer Ctr., Modesto, 1985—; bd. dirs. Merced Sch. Employees Credit Union, 1986—, Merced Coll. Found., 1985—. Served to sgt. U.S. Army, 1969-71. Named Merced County Tchr. of Yr., Merced County Dept. Edn., 1978. Mem. Nat. Sci. Tchrs. Assn., Computer Using Educators (Modesto chpt.), Phi Delta Kappa. Democrat. Roman Catholic. Avocations: photography, skiing, sailing, computer programming. Home: 2942 El Camino Real Merced CA 95340 Office: Merced Coll 3600 M St Merced CA 95340

CUCINOTTA, JOSEPH ROGER, transportation company executive; b. Mount Holly, N.J., Oct. 6, 1940; s. Anthony Roger and Edith (Serchia) C.; m. Nancy Jernee Ellis, Oct. 19, 1968; children: J. Matthew, Paul David. A. Acad. Traffic, 1964. Sales coordinator Sea-Land Service, Phila., 1966-67; ops. supr. Sea-Land Service, Trenton, N.J., 1967-69; documentation supr. Sea-Land Service, Elizabeth, N.J., 1969-71; documentation mgr. Sea-Land Service, Seattle, 1971-78; adminstrn. mgr. Sea-Land Service, Oakland, Calif., 1978-80, Tacoma, 1980—. Served with USMC, 1959. Mem. Puget Sound Steamship Operators. Republican. Roman Catholic. Clubs: Oak Harbor (Wash.) Yacht; U.S. Power Squad (Bellevue, Wash.). Avocations: yachting, gourmet cooking. Home: 14003 Bear Creek Rd NE Woodinville WA 98072 Office: Sea-Land Service Inc 3600 Port of Tacoma Rd Tacoma WA 98424

CULL, CHRIS ALAN, operations executive; b. Las Cruces, N.Mex., Jan. 3, 1947; s. William Roy Cull and Doris Jean (Compton) Morgan; m. DuAnne Elizabeth Diers King, July 26, 1967 (div. 1979); children: Joey Lynn, Jamie Ayn, Brandon Alan. BS, N.Mex. State U., 1976. Bus. mgr. Lloyd McKee Chrysler-Plymouth Inc., Albuquerque, 1972; lab./field technician N.Mex. State U., Las Cruces, 1973-76; research soil scientist Mont. State U., Bozeman, 1976-77; reclamation supr. Western Energy Co., Colstrip, Mont., 1977-80; mgr. ops. permitting Western Energy Co., Billings, Mont., 1980-85; asst. project mgr. En Tech Inc., Butte, Mont., 1985-86; mgr. ops. Spl. Resource Mgmt. Inc., Billings, 1986—. Contbr. articles to profl. jours. Mem. Assn. Environ. Scientists and Adminstrs. (charter), Nat. Resource Conservation Soc. (pres. 1975-76), Nat. Assn. Environ. Profls., Soil Conservation Soc. Am. (chmn. surface mine reclamation com. 1978-80, mem. univ. and coll. relations com. 1977-78, spl. task force surface mine reclamation div. 1977-79, pres. Mont. chpt. 1980-82), Mont. Coal Council (co-chmn. environ./tech. com. 1983-85), Mining and Reclamation Council Am. (tech. com. 1983-85), Am. Council on Sci. and Health. Avocations: hunting, fishing, camping, gardening, leatherwork. Home: 4237 Palisades Park Dr Billings MT 59106 Office: Spl Resource Mgmt Inc 3333 2d Ave N Suite 250 Billings MT 59101

CULLEY, JOHN HENRY, legal history educator; b. Buna Vista, Tex., Aug. 14, 1947; s. John Henry and Venla Myrtle (Reynolds) C. BA in History cum laude, U. Colo., 1969, JD, 1971; MA, U. Calif., Santa Barbara, 1979, PhD, 1986. Bar: Colo. 1972, U.S. Dist. Ct. 1972, U.S. Ct. Military Appeals 1973, U.S. Supreme Ct. 1975, U.S. Ct. Appeals (10th cir.) 1982. Judge advocate USAF, Chanute AFB, Ill., Taipei, Taiwan, and March AFB, Calif., 1972-76; judge advocate reserve USAFR, Lowry AFB, Colo., 1976—; teaching asst. U. Calif., Santa Barbara, 1979-81; staff atty. Hyatt Legal Services, Northglenn, Colo., 1984. Contbr. book reviews and pubs., articles to profl. jours. (Ellison prize 1978). Served to capt. USAF, 1972-76. Mem. ABA, Am. Judicature Soc., Am. Legion. Republican. Mem. United Ch. Christ. Avocations: tennis, skiing, ice skating, war games. Home and Office: 811 Tucson St Aurora CO 80011

CULLINAN, VINCENT, lawyer; b. San Francisco, Jan. 22, 1911; s. Eustace and Katherine (Lawler) C.; m. Elizabeth Erlin, Oct. 16, 1937; children—Terrence, Kathleen Cullinan Merchant, Sheila Cullinan Wheeler. A.B. magna cum laude, U. Santa Clara, 1933; LL.D., Stanford U., 1936. Bar: Calif. bar, U.S. Supreme Ct. bar, Fed. Ct. bars of Calif. Partner firm Cushing, Cullinan, Duniway & Gorrill, San Francisco, 1936-41, Cullinan, Hancock, Rothert and Burns, 1946-71, Cullinan Brown and Helmer, San Francisco, 1971-77, Cullinan and Lyons, San Francisco, 1978—; dir. Schlage Lock Co. Served with M.I., USN, 1941-45. Mem. ABA, San Francisco Bar Assn. (pres. 1968), Am. Law Inst., State Bar Calif. (v.p. 1969). Republican. Roman Catholic. Club:, Bohemian. Office: 100 Bush St Suite 1100 San Francisco CA 94104

CULMER, COLEEN ANN, special education administrator; b. Salt Lake City, Mar. 16, 1956; s. Fred Lawrence and Beverly Marie Bahr; m. John Russell Culmer, June 6, 1945; children: Chris, Aaron, Brian, Kayla. BA summa cum laude, Wash. State U., 1978, MA, 1979, postgrad., 1984. Communication disorders specialist Kennewick (Wash.) Sch. Dist., 1979-86, program mgr. spl. edn. dept., 1986—; pvt. practice communication disorders specialist, Kennewick, 1979-84. Mem. Am. Speech and Hearing Assn. (cert. clin. competence), Wash. Speech and Hearing Assn. Home: 8517 W Entiat Pl Kennewick WA 99336 Office: Spl Services 200 S Dayton Kennewick WA 99336

CULP, GERARD HUBBARD, assets protection executive; b. Reno, Nev., Jan. 16, 1930; s. W. Ray and Ruth Lee (Hubbard) C.; m. Audrey Elizabeth Crompton, May 26, 1955 (div. Sept. 1977); children—Stephen Gerard, Heather Janeane; m. Sandra Lee Jaksina, Dec. 23, 1977. B.A., U. Redlands, 1958; postgrad. U. Maine, 1966. Cert. protection profl. Enlisted U.S. Air Force, 1951, advanced through grades to col., 1973; served in U.S., Can., Eng., Pakistan; dir. personnel investigations ctr. Dept. Def., Balt., 1975-76, ret., 1976; dir. corp. security Pa. Power & Light Co., Allentown, 1977-80; mgr. nuclear security Portland Gen. Electric Co., Oreg., 1980—. Contbr. articles to profl. jours. Decorated Air Force Commendation medal with one oak leaf cluster, Meritorious Service medal, Joint Service Commendation medal, Legion of Merit. Mem. Am. Soc. Indsl. Security (chpt. chmn.), Geneal. Forum Oreg., Am. Assn. Individual Investors, Am. Mgmt. Assn., Phi Kappa Phi.

CULP, MILDRED L., business owner; b. Ft. Monroe, Va., Jan. 13, 1949; d. William W. and Winifred (Stilwell) C. BA in English, Knox Coll., 1971; AM Divinity Sch., U. Chgo., 1974, PhD, 1976. Coll. faculty, adminstr. 1976-81; dir. Exec. Resumés, Seattle, 1981—; pres. Exec. Directions Internat., Inc., Seattle, 1985—. Columnist Seattle Daily Jour. Commerce, 1981—; radio commentator, Seattle; contbr. articles and book revs. to profl. jours. Admissions advisor U. Chgo., 1981—. Mem. Network Exec. Women (bd. dirs. 1981-82), Am. Soc. Personnel Adminstrn., Pacific NW Personnel Mgmt. Assn., Nat. Alliance for Mentally Ill, Nat. Sibling Network (adv. bd. 1987), WAMI, SOS/CAMI. Club: U. Chgo. Alumni (bd. dirs. 1982-86). Office: Seattle Tower 1218 3d Ave Suite 2404 Seattle WA 98101

CULP, ROBERT DUDLEY, engineering educator; b. McAlester, Okla., Feb. 28, 1938; s. Chesley Key and Irma Lucille (Combs) C.; m. Elizabeth Lovelace Poor, Dec. 2, 1960; children: Robert Dielman, Thomas Dudley. BS, U. Okla., 1960; MS, U. Colo., 1963, PhD, 1966. With ops. research dept. Convair-Gen. Dynamics, Ft. Worth, 1958, with internal aerodynamics dept., 1959; with applied research dept. Martin Co., Denver, 1960-62; prof. engring. U. Colo., Boulder, 1966—. Author: Hypersonic and Planetary Entry, 1980; contbr. articles and short stories tp profl. publs. Fellow Am. Astronautical Soc. (v.p. 1982-84), AIAA; mem. Am. Soc. Engring. Educators, Sigma Xi, Boulder Tennis Assn. (pres. 1972). Democrat. Methodist. Club: The Ranch (Westminster, Colo.). Home: 10536 Lipan St Northglenn CO 80234 Office: U Colo Campus Box 429 Boulder CO 80309

CULPEPPER, WILLIAM WARREN, bank executive; b. Denver, May 20, 1928; s. William Augustus and Constance Lenore (Haldeman) C.; m. Mary Louise Brown, Dec. 28, 1964 (div. July 1984); children: William Warren Jr., Carolyn Louise, Kathryn Marie. BS in Bus. Adminstrn., U. Colo., 1949; cert., Am. Sch. Banking, 1967; grad., Stonier Grad. Sch. Banking, 1975. Credit mgr. H.W. Moore Equipment Co., Denver; asst. sec., treas. Colo. Builders Supply Co., Denver; v.p. Cen. Bank of Denver, 1962-82; sr. v.p. Dominion Nat. Bank, Denver, 1982-83, sr. v.p., sr. loan and credit officer, 1983—, exec. v.p., 1984—; bd. dirs. U.S. Welding Inc., Robert Morris & Assocs.; advisor Kellogg Corp., Denver, 1975-83; pres. Colo. Motor Carrier Allied Conf., Denver, 1960's. Candidate for legis. in Rep. Primary, Denver, 1970; committeeman Legis. Dists. 14 and 10, Denver, 1970-84; mem. adv. bd. Sch. of Bus. U. Colo., Boulder; bd. dirs. Rocky Mountain Assn. Credit Mgmt. Mem. Denver Area Alumni Assn. (pres. 1968), Deta Alpha Psi. Methodist. Club: Buff (Boulder) (pres. 1976). Lodge: Masons, Shriners, Consistory. Home: 1020 15th St Apt 10A Denver CO 80202 Office: Dominion Nat Bank 600 17th St Denver CO 80202

CULVERWELL, HOWARD GLENDON, rancher; b. Concordia, Kans., May 18, 1911; s. Albert Sutcliff and Mabel Amelia (Middaugh) C.; student public schs.; m. Erma Frances Martin, Dec. 31, 1939; children—Gerald, Norman, Jon, Carolyn, Melvin, Melodie. Engaged in sheep, cattle, wheat and hay ranching, Craig, Colo., 1946—; past pres. Moffat County Farm Bur. Mem. Dist. 13 Sch. bd., also pres., 9 yrs., then mem. County Wide Bd., 16 yrs.; bd. dirs. Colo. Assn. Sch. Bds., 1965-71. Mem. Profl. Farmers Am., Farmers Union, Nat. Farmers Orgn. Republican.

CULWELL, CHARLES LOUIS, manufacturing company executive; b. Putnam, Tex., Apr. 26, 1927; s. Willie and Ila Alberta (Crosby) C.; m. Virginia Green, June 10, 1949; children—Andrew Scott, Perry Neal, Curtis Austin, Travis Lee. B.S. in Elec. Engring, U.S. Naval Acad., 1949; M.S. in Mgmt, U.S. Naval Postgrad. Sch., 1969. Commd. ensign U.S. Navy, 1949, advanced through grades to capt., 1969; service in Korea and Vietnam; comdg. officer Naval Supply Center, Oakland, Calif., 1975-76; ret. 1976; asst. to pres., then v.p. Purex Corp., 1976-79; group v.p., gen. mgr. indsl., instl. and comml. products Purex Industries, Inc., Lakewood, Calif., 1979-84; v.p., asst. to chief exec. officer Purex Industries Inc., Carson, Calif., 1984-86; v.p., asst. to chief exec. officer Purex Industries Liquidation, Carson, Calif., 1986-87, retired, 1987. Decorated Legion of Merit, Bronze Star with combat V, Meritorious Service medal. Mem. U.S. Naval Acad. Alumni Assn. Republican. Presbyterian. Office: 24600 S Main St Carson CA 90749-4408

CUMBOW, ROBERT CHARLES, corporate communications executive; b. Columbus, Ohio, Oct. 22, 1946; s. Robert M. and Margaret Joan (O'Connor) C.; m. Grace Blond, Sept. 6, 1975; children: Rachel Elizabeth, Irena Alexis. BA in English, Seattle U., 1967, MA in English, 1969. Info. mgr. Northwest Indian Fisheries Commn., Olympia, Wash., 1978-81; writer, lectr. Seattle, 1981—; info. specialist Seattle City Light, 1983-84; leader exec. seminars Seattle U., 1985—; news media rep. Puget Sound Power and Light, Bellevue, Wash., 1984-86, corp. communications coordinator, 1986—. Author: Pardon Me, Roy, 1983, ONCE UPON A TIME: The Films of Sergio Leone, 1987; contbr. articles on film to profl. jours. Juror, New City Theatre Dirs. Festival, 1985, Seattle Arts Commn., 1986. Served with U.S. Army, 1969-71. recipient Copy Desk awards Dept. Def., 1970-71, Army Commendation medal Dept. Def., 1971. Mem. Pub. Relations Soc. Am., Am. Film Inst. Republican. Roman Catholic. Avocations: film, music, games, puzzles. Office: Puget Sound Power & Light Co Puget Power Bldg Bellevue WA 98009

CUMMING, FREDERICK LITTLEFIELD, III, safety engineer; b. N.Y.C., Nov. 20, 1943; s. Frederick L. Jr. and Corinne Marie (Kast) C.; m. Lavera Elaine Yakel, Oct. 18, 1969; children: Sean, Kirk. BA, Holy Cross Coll., 1965; MA, Calif. State U., Los Angeles, 1975. Registered profl. safety engr., Calif. Safety dir. City of San Diego, 1969-87; loss control mgr. San Diego Office of Edn., 1987—. Editor: Readings in Stress Management, 1985; contbr. articles to profl. jours. Active Madeleine Sch. Bd., San Diego, 1984; bd. dirs. San Diego Safety Council, 1970-80; adv. bd. San Diego Community Coll., 1970—. Served to 1st lt. inf. Army, 1965-68, Vietnam. Mem. Am. Soc. Safety Engrs. (pres. 1978), Nat. Safety Mgmt. Assn. (v.p. 1978-80), City Safety Mgmt. Assn. (founder 1971). Roman Catholic. Avocations: running, reading, cooking. Home: 4031 Mt Barnard Ave San Diego CA 92111 Office: San Diego Office of Edn 6401 Linda Vista Rd #705 San Diego CA 92111

CUMMINGS, GARTH ELLIS, nuclear safety engineer; b. Oakland, Calif., Jan. 31, 1934; s. Ellis N. and Dorothy M. (Boyd) C.; m. Shirley E. Wolfe, Nov. 10, 1956; children: Gregg A., Jill L. BSME, U. Calif., Berkeley, 1956, MS in Nuclear Engring., 1959; PhDME, U. Calif., Davis, 1978. Registered profl. engr., Calif. Chief research reactor Lawrence Livermore (Calif.) Nat. Lab., 1964-67, mem. staff space power reactor, 1967-68, AEC reactor safety study, 1972-73, AEC reactor regulation, 1973-74, leader engring. mechincal section, 1979-82, leader nuclear systems safety program, 1984—; mem. SP-100 Safety Adv. Com., 1983—. Chmn. com. Boy Scouts Am., Danville, Calif., 1976-78; mem. adv. com. De Molay, Walnut Creek, Calif., 1979-80. Mem. AAAS, Am. Nuclear Soc. (chmn. No. Calif. sect. 1971-72). Home: 1551 Harlan Dr Danville CA 94526 Office: Lawrence Livermore Nat Lab PO Box 808 L-198 Livermore CA 94550

CUMMINGS, JOHN PATRICK, optometrist; b. Sheridan, Wyo., Dec. 17, 1952; s. John Francis and Ivy Lee (Borksdale) C.; m. Pamela Gwen Miller, Aug. 30, 1981. A.S., Sheridan Coll., 1973; B.S., Pacific U., 1975, O.D., 1977. Gen. practice optometry, Sheridan, Wyo., 1977—; pres. Wyo. Vision Service, 1984-86; cons. optometrist Sheridan VA Med. Ctr. Mem. Nat. Ski Patrol, asst. patrol leader, 1980, jr. adv., 1980-83, regional first aid adv., 1982-83, div. first aid advisor, 1982-84, nat. 1st aid com. mem. Story-Banner Vol. Emergency Service; bd. dirs. Wyo. Youth Found., Crime Stoppers. Recipient Sheridan Community Disting. Service award, 1982; Jaycee of Yr. award, 1979-80. Mem. Assn. VA Optometrists, Am. Optometric Assn. (charter mem. contact lens sect.), Sheridan County C. of C. (ambassador), Sheridan County Pilots Assn. (bd. dirs.). Lodge: Lions. Contbr. articles to profl. jours. Office: 116 S Main St Sheridan WY 82801

CUMMINGS, JOHN PATRICK, lawyer; b. Westfield, Mass., June 28, 1933; s. Daniel Thoams and Nora (Brick) C.; m. Dorothy June D'Ingianni, Dec. 27, 1957 (div. May 1978); children: John Patrick, Mary Catherine, Michael Brick, Kevin Andrew, Colleen Elise, Erin Christine, Christopher Gerald; m. Marilyn Ann Welch, May 23, 1980. BS, St. Michael's Coll., 1955; PhD, U. Tex., 1969; JD, U. Toledo, 1973, MCE, 1977. Bar: Ohio 1973, U.S. Mil. Appeals 1974, U.S. Dist. Ct. (no. dist.) Ohio 1979. Instr. U. Tex., Austin, 1962-68; scientist Owens Ill., Toledo, Ohio, 1968-75, atty., 1976-83; legal counsel Ecotherm Ltd., Sacramento, 1982—; pres. Hansa World, Toledo, 1983—; cons. EPA, Washington, 1970-74, Owens Corning Fiberglass, Toledo, 1978-79; bd. dirs., v.p. World Wide Tramsport, Toledo; bd. dirs. Interport Systems, Houston; adj. prof. U. Toledo, 1978-82. Contbr. articles to profl jours.; patentee in field. Mem. Bay Area Pub. Affairs Council, San Francisco. Served to col. USAFR, 1955-85. USPHS fellow, 1963-66. Fellow The Chem. Soc.; mem. ABA, Am. Chem. Soc., ASTM (chmn. 1979), Am. Ceramic Soc. (chmn. 1973), Res. Officers Assn. (legis. chmn. 1979—), Am. Legion. Roman Catholic. Club: Toledo Press. Lodge: KC. Avocations: reading, traveling, coin and stamp collecting. Home: 843 Barcelona Dr Fremont CA 94536 Office: Hansa World 1507 21st St Suite 340 Sacramento CA 95814

CUMMINGS, LARRY CARL, analytical chemist; b. San Jose, Calif., Apr. 6, 1951; s. Elmer Carl and Julia Ann (Hagan) C.; m. Rachel Jean Bronder, June 21, 1980. BA in Biology, U. Calif., Santa Cruz, 1974. Chem. quality control technician Churchill Chem. Corp., Los Angeles, 1974; research chemist Los Angeles County/U. So. Calif. Med. Ctr., 1974-77; quality assurance officer Alpha Omega Services, Paramount, Calif., 1977; research asst. Calif. Inst. Tech., Pasadena, 1977-80; quality assurance mgr. Compositek Engring. Corp., Buena Park, Calif., 1980-84, cons., 1984-85; research chemist Restech Industries, Inc., Eugene, Oreg., 1985; ops. chemist Laurence David Inc., Eugene, 1986—; cons. Goldsworthy Engring. Inc., Torrance, Calif., 1984. Contbr. articles to profl. jours. Mem. ASTM, Am. Chem. Soc., Am. Inst. Chemists (cert.), Soc. Advancement Materials and Process Engring., N.Am. Thermal Analysis Soc. Democrat. Unitarian. Avocations: scuba diving, photography, computer software devel., hiking, backpacking. Office: Laurence David Inc PO Box 2484 Eugene OR 97402

CUMMINGS, MARY EISELE, clinical psychologist; b. Chgo., Oct. 3, 1939; d. Charles Wesley and Blanche Mae (Kennell) Eisele; m. David Peter Adam, 1961 (div.); m. 2d, Ronald Beavers, 1969 (div.); 1 child, John Miller Adam; m. 3d, F.L. Patrick Cummings, 1986. B.A. in History cum laude, Radcliffe Coll., 1962; M.A., U. Ariz., 1970, Ph.D. in Psychology, 1973. Cert. psychologist, Ariz. Clin. psychologist Student Counseling Service, U. Ariz., Tucson, 1972-76, asst. dir., 1976-84, acting dir., 1980, assoc. dir., 1985—, tng. dir., 1985—, dir. univ.-wide honors program, 1980-85, lectr. dept. psychology, 1973-75; Ariz. coordinator Catalyst Network for Nat. Women's Info. Co-founder Tucson Gilbert & Sullivan Theatre, 1966, bd. dirs., 1966-71; mem. Ariz. Opera Co. Chorus, 1975—; mem. adminstrv. bd. St. Francis in the Foothills Meth. Ch., 1978-81. Recipient faculty achievement award U. Ariz. Alumni Assn., 1983; NIMH fellow, 1968-69. Mem. Am. Psychol. Assn., Ariz. Psychol. Assn., So. Ariz. Psychol. Assn., Ariz. Group Psychotherapy Soc., Internat. Transactional Analysis Assn., Nat. Collegiate Honors Council. Democrat. Contbr. articles to profl. jours. Office: Student Counseling Service Old Main 200 W U Ariz Tucson AZ 85721

CUMMINGS, NICHOLAS ANDREW, psychologist; b. Salinas, Calif., July 25, 1924; s. Andrew and Urania (Sims) C.; m. Dorothy Mills, Feb. 5, 1948; children—Janet Lynn, Andrew Mark. A.B., U. Calif.-Berkeley, 1948; M.A., Claremont Grad. Sch., 1954; Ph.D., Adelphi U., 1958. Chief psychologist Kaiser Permanente No. Calif., San Francisco, 1959-76; clin. dir. Biodyne Inst., San Francisco, 1976—; pres. Am. Biodyne Ctrs. Inc., San Francisco, 1985—; co-dir. Golden Gate Mental Health Center, San Francisco, 1959-75; pres. Calif. Sch. Profl. Psychology, Los Angeles, San Francisco, San Diego, Fresno campuses, 1969-76; chmn. bd. Calif. Community Mental Health Centers, Inc., Los Angeles, San Diego, San Francisco, 1975-77; pres. Blue Psi, Inc., San Francisco, 1972-80, Inst. for Psychosocial Interaction, 1980-84; mem. mental health adv. bd. City and County San Francisco, 1968-75; bd. dirs. San Francisco Assn. Mental Health, 1965-75; pres., chmn. bd. Psycho-Social Inst., 1972-80; dir. Mental Research Inst., Palo Alto, Calif., 1979-80; pres. Nat. Acads. of Practice, 1981—. Served with U.S. Army, 1944-46. Fellow Am. Psychol. Assn. (dir. 1975-81, pres. 1979); mem. Calif. Psychol. Assn. (pres. 1968). Pioneer prepaid mental health plans, profl. schs. psychology. Office: Biodyne 400 Oyster Point Blvd South San Francisco CA 94080

CUMMINGS, RITA, advertising agency executive; b. Dundee, Scotland, May 11, 1950; came to U.S., 1972; d. Harold Stuart and Mary Winifred (Reid) C. MA with Honors, U. St. Andrews, Scotland, 1972; MA in English Lit., U. Calif., 1974. Assoc. prof. U. Calif., Santa Barbara, 1974-76; sr. mktg. mgr. Banks of Am., San Francisco, 1976-83; pres. Cummings & Assoc., San Francisco, 1983—; pub. relations cons. Nat. Assn. Bank Women, San Francisco, 1985. Co-author: Collected Book of Poetry, 1981. Pres. Camp Fire Girls, San Francisco, 1979-83, Older Women's League, San Francisco, 1983-85; bd. dirs. Women's Found., San Francisco, 1983-84.

CUMMINGS, RULON CAINE, financial counselor; b. Salt Lake City, Nov. 4, 1925; s. James R. and Gwendelyn M. (Caine) C.; B.S., Northwestern Coll. Allied Sci., 1980; Assoc. in Bus., LaSalle Extension U., 1960; m. Jeannine Mae Astler, Aug. 14, 1947; children—Craig S., Rulon K., Douglas W., Celia M., Cynthia I., Anna Lisa. Chief adminstrn. sect. Utah Army Depot, Ogden, 1950-53, adminstrv. asst. engr. supply sect., 1953-59; mgmt, analyst Def. Depot Ogden, 1959-66, asst. chief methods and standards br., 1966-70, safety and health dir., 1970-82, dir. installation services, 1982-86; instr. Nat. Safety Council, 1970-86; safety and health cons., 1970-86; chmn. exec. com. Fed. Safety Council, 1979-80; mem. Clearfield City Council, 1982—. Pres., Wasatch Little League Football, 1959-60; coach Little League Football, 1958-62; coach community softball, volleyball and basketball teams, Clearfield, Utah, 1964-86. Served with U.S. Army, 1944-46. Recipient Supply Agy. Meritorious Civilian Service award, 1973, Superior Performance award Defense Depot, 1968-80, Cert. Appreciation, Asst. Sec. Labor, 1980, Exceptional Civilian Service award Def. Logistics Agy., 1986.. Mem. Am. Soc. Safety Engrs., Armed Forces Mgmt. Assn., Quartermaster Assn., Soc. Am. Mil. Engrs., Methods Time Measurement Assn. for Standards and Research. Republican. Mem. Ch. Jesus Christ of Latter-day Saints (counselor in stake presidency, high councilor, bishop, clk., pres.). Club: Kiwanis. Home: 749 E 300 South Clearfield UT 84015 Office: 420 E South Temple 5th Floor Salt Lake City UT 84111

CUMMINGS, WILLIAM BARTON, educational administrator; b. Richmond, Va., Apr. 26, 1929; s. Frank Letelle and Dallas (Burrows) C.; m. Beatrice Martin, Feb. 18, 1950 (div. Jan. 1971); children—William Barton, Thomas, Judith, Scott; m. Lois Anderson, Jan. 7, 1972. B.A., Moravian Coll., 1953; M.A., Temple U., 1968; Ed.D., U. San Francisco, 1979. Cert. tchr., adminstr., Calif. Tchr., adminstr. Centennial Joint Schs., Warminster, Pa., 1954-67; supr. gifted program Pa. Dept. Edn., 1967-68, San Francisco Unified Sch. Dist., 1968-77; dir. curriculum, area supr. Fall River Joint Unified Sch. Dist., Cassel, Calif., 1981-87, asst. supt., 1987—; cons. gifted child edn.; instr. U. Ill., U. San Francisco, San Francisco State U., Dominican Coll. Served with USN, 1946-48. Mem. Assn. for Gifted, Calif. Assn. Gifted (past pres.), Council Exceptional Children, Assn. Calif. Sch. Adminstrs., Assn. Supervision and Curriculum Devel. Home: PO Box 66 Cassel CA 96016 Office: PO Box 89 Cassel CA 96016

CUMMINGS, WILLIAM (BILL) STEWART, advertising executive; b. Glendive, Mont., Jan. 4, 1959; s. Donald Stewart and Helen Jean (Richard) C.; m. Karen Lynn Crivello, Aug. 27, 1983. Student, Dawson Coll., 1976-77; AA in Bus., Fresno (Calif.) City Coll., 1977-78. With display advt. dept. E. Gottschalks Co., Fresno, 1977-78; media mgr. Sun Stereo Inc., Fresno, 1978-79; with pub. relations dept. Northwest Sch., Fresno, 1979-82; owner, creative dir. Madison Ave. Group, Fresno, 1982—. Creative dir. advt. campaign No on Proposition 41, Cent., Calif., 1984 (Golden Oak award 1985), multimedia campaign Pediatrics Plus Ctr., 1985 (Golden Oak award 1986). Pres. Sunrise Meadows Assn., Fresno, 1979—; bd. dirs. Northwest

Sch. System, Fresno, 1979—. Mem. Am. Inst. Graphic Arts, Fresno Advt. Club. Avocations: sailing, boating, swimming, touring. Office: The Madison Ave Group 1500 W Shaw Suite 303 Fresno CA 93711

CUMMINS, JOHN STEPHEN, bishop; b. Oakland, Calif., Mar. 3, 1928; s. Michael and Mary (Connolly) C. A.B., St. Patrick's Coll., 1949. Ordained priest Roman Catholic Ch., 1953; asst. pastor Mission Dolores Ch., San Francisco, 1953-57; mem. faculty Bishop O'Dowd High Sch., Oakland, 1957-62; chancellor Diocese of Oakland, 1962-71; rev. monsignor 1962, domestic prelate, 1967; exec. dir. Calif. Cath. Conf., Sacramento, 1971-77; consecrated bishop 1974; aux. bishop of Sacramento, 1974-77; bishop of Oakland, 1977—; Campus minister San Francisco State Coll., 1953-57, Mills Coll., Oakland, 1957-71; Trustee St. Mary's Coll., 1968-79. Home: 634 21st St Oakland CA 94612 Office: Oakland Diocese 2900 Lake Shore Ave Oakland CA 94610 *

CUMMINS, KEVIN, chemist; b. Durango, Colo., Mar. 24, 1948; s. Mark A. and Mary L. (Wethington) C.; m. Mary Virginia O'Brien, Jan. 3, 1976; children: Patrick Kevin, Joseph Michael, Brendan Thomas. BS in Chemistry, Colo. State U., 1970; MS in Chemistry, U. Calif., San Diego, 1972; MPH in Indsl. Hygiene, U. Utah, 1986. Mgr. Holiday Motel, Canon City, Colo., 1974-76; chemist Occupational Health and Safety Adminstrn., U.S. Dept. Labor, Salt Lake City, 1976—. Mem. Am. Indsl. Hygiene Assn. (sec. Utah sect. 1984). Democrat. Avocations: gardening, politics. Home: 10110 S 3345 W South Jordan UT 84065 Office: US Dept Labor Occupational Health Safety Adminstrn 1781 S 300 W Salt Lake City UT 84115

CUMMINS, NEIL JOSEPH, JR., land surveyor; b. Oxnard, Calif., Sept. 14, 1945; s. Neil Joseph and Helen Louise (Porter) C.; student Claremont Men's Coll., 1962-64, Calif. State Poly. Coll., 1965-67; JD, Mid Valley Coll. Law, 1978; Bar: Calif. 1978. m. Lynn D. Mealer, Sept. 16, 1967. Designer, Ludwig Engring., San Bernardino, Calif., 1967-69; field supr. Sikand Engring., Van Nuys, Calif., 1969-77; land surveyor, Reseda, Calif., 1977—; lectr. civil engring. Calif. Poly. Coll., Pomona, 1979-80; admitted to Calif. bar, 1978. Registered profl. engr., Ariz., Calif., Nev.; registered land surveyor, Calif., Nev., Ariz. Fellow ASCE; mem. Am. Congress Surveying and Mapping (chmn. So. Calif. sect. 1984), Am. Water Works Assn., ABA, Los Angeles County Bar Assn., Calif. Land Surveyors Assn. Office: 7122 Reseda Blvd Reseda CA 91335-4210

CUNDALL, DONALD ROGER, rancher, state senator; b. Glendo, Wyo., May 30, 1925; s. Edwin Paul and Ruth Frances (Troupe) C.; m. Doris Moran, May 18, 1946; children—Jerry, Ronald, Tyler, Michael. Student, Mont. Sch. Mines, Colo. Coll. Ranche; mem. Wyo. Senate, 1972—, chmn. health, edn. and welfare com., 1976-87, pres., 1981—. Served with U.S. Navy, 1944-48. Republican. Office: Wendover Rt Guernsey WY 82214

CUNDIFF, MEL (MILFORD) FIELDS, natural science educator, editorial consultant; b. Baker, Oreg., Dec. 7, 1936; s. Carmon William Cundiff and Margaret Jane (Crockett) Davis; m. Tildie Elmore, June 6, 1963 (div. July 1973); children: Scott G., Kimberly A.; m. Sharon Little, May 25, 1981. Student, U. Oreg., 1955-56; BS Sci. Edn., U. Colo., 1960, PhD, 1966; postgrad., U. Wash., Friday Harbor, summer 1962, La. State U., summers 1966, 67, 68. Teaching asst. U. Colo., Boulder, 1958-61, teaching assoc., 1961-62; from instr. to assoc. prof. Austin Coll., Sherman, Tex., 1964-70; assoc. prof. U. Colo., Boulder, 1970—; editorial cons. various pub. cos., 1970—. Contbr. articles to profl. jours. Pres. Parents Without Ptnrs., Boulder and 4-state region, 1975-78, Parent, Tchr. Orgns., Boulder, 1979-81. Grantee NSF/AEC 1966-68; NDEA fellow, U. Colo., 1962-64. Fellow Tex. Acad. Sci.; mem. Am. Inst. Biol. Scis., Colo.-Wyo. Acad. Sci., Southwestern Assn. Naturalists, Sigma Xi. Democrat. Avocations: bridge, wilderness backpacking, horsepacking, scuba diving. Home: 5014 Gallatin Pl Boulder CO 80303 Office: U Colo Nat Sci Program Boulder CO 80309

CUNNEEN, WALLACE VINCENT, JR., marketing consultant; b. York, Pa., Sept. 18, 1922; ed. U.S. Naval Acad., 1941-44, U. Pa., 1947, Naval Aviator 1945-47; m. Joan Eleanor Frederick, Jan. 8, 1955; children—Wallace, Mary, James. Sales rep. Diebold, Inc., Canton, Ohio, 1947-49; v.p. The Cunneen Co., Phila., 1949-57, Welton Becket & Asso., Los Angeles, 1957-64; v.p., dir. John Carl Warnecke Asso., San Francisco, 1964-69; v.p. programs devel. Daniel, Mann, Johnson & Mendenhall, Los Angeles, 1969-71; programs devel. Hoover Assos., Palo Alto, 1972-74; owner mktg.-cons. practice, Los Altos Hills, 1974—; bd. dirs. Winkler Tawa McManus Advt. Author Essential Element; founder San Jose Nat. Bank, 1982; mem. adv. com. AIA Research Corp. Chmn. Santa Clara County, United Fund Los Altos, 1958-62; exec. bd. Stanford Area council Boy Scouts Am., 1977-78; pres. Los Altos PTA, 1961; council pres. & nat. bd. dirs. Navy League, 1979-81; chmn. Navy Moffett Field 50th Anniversary Celebration Hangar I Dinner. Republican. Roman Catholic. Clubs: Fremont Hills (Los Altos Hills); Commonwealth (San Francisco); St. Claire (San Jose, Calif.). Home and Office: 26666 Laurel Ln Los Altos Hills CA 94022

CUNNIFF, GREGORY NIXON, manufacturers representative; b. Great Falls, Mont., Jan. 26, 1947; s. Gordon N. and Helen I. (Roquet) C.; m. Candy K. Parchen, Aug. 16, 1969; children: Lori L., Staci A. BSME, Mont. State U., 1969, MSME, 1970. Registered profl. engr., Mont. Mech. engr. Drapes Engring. Inc., Great Falls, Mont., 1970-81; prin. Vemco, Inc., Great Falls, 1981—; mem. adv. com. Energy and Man's Environment, Dillon, Mont., 1978-82; mem. Consulting Engrs. Council Mont., Great Falls, 1978-81. Chmn. Alumni Assn. Leadership Great Falls, 1986—; bd. dirs. Voluntary Action Ctr., Great Falls, 1981. Mem. ASHRAE (state research com. chmn. 1983), ASME, Mont. Ambassadors, Mont. State U. Alumni Assn. (chmn. alumni scholarship com. 1982). Club: Meadowlark Country (Great Falls). Lodge: Optimists (pres. Great Falls club 1981, Disting. Pres. award 1981). Avocations: golf, running, woodworking. Home: 742 33 B Ave NE Great Falls MT 59404 Office: Vemco Inc 300 7th Ave S Box 2027 Great Falls MT 59403

CUNNINGHAM, DENNIS, electrical engineer; b. N.Y.C., Sept. 24, 1929; s. Joseph Patrick and Alice Rose C.; A.A., Harbor Coll., 1957; B.S.E.E., Calif. State U., Long Beach, 1970; m. Dorothy Jane Laughton, Dec. 7, 1963; 1 son, Kevin Laughton. Field engr. TRW Inc., Redondo Beach, Calif., 1957-62, sr. system engr., 1962-70; mem. tech. staff Hughes Aircraft Co., El Segundo, Calif., 1971, sect. head, 1971; staff engr. ESL Inc., Sunnyvale, Calif., 1971-79; research specialist Lockheed Missiles and Space Co., Sunnyvale, Calif., 1979-84, staff engr., 1984-86, sr. staff engr., 1986—. Served with USN, 1948-54. Mem. Tau Beta Pi, Eta Kappa Nu. Home: 20269 Northwest Square Cupertino CA 95014 Office: Lockheed Missiles and Space Co 1111 Lockheed Way Sunnyvale CA 94086

CUNNINGHAM, DENNIS DEAN, microbiology, molecular genetics educator; b. Des Moines, Iowa, Aug. 16, 1939; s. Melvin B. and Laura (Jones) C. BA, U. Iowa, 1961; PhD, U. Chgo., 1967. Postdoctoral fellow Princeton (N.J.) U., 1968-70; asst. prof. U. Calif., Irvine, 1970-74, assoc. prof., 1974-78, prof. microbiology and molecular genetics, 1978—; bd. dirs. Irvine Med. Ctr., 1985—; mem. study sect. NIH, Bethesda, Md., 1975-80, Am. Cancer Soc., 1982-86. Editor: Control of Cellular Division and Development, 1980, Proteases in Biological Control and Biotechnology, 1986; assoc. editor Jour. Cellular Physiology, 1978—; mem. editorial bd. Jour. Cellular Biochemistry, 1979—; contbr. articles to sci. jours. Recipient Research Career Devel. award NIH, 1975-80; research grantee NIH, 19706. Mem. Am. Soc. Biol. Chemists, Am. Soc. Cell Biology. Home: 1215 Brangwyn Way Laguna Beach CA 92651 Office: U Calif Dept Microbiology and Molecular Genetics Irvine CA 92717

CUNNINGHAM, DOROTHY FAY, early childhood development educator; b. Briton, S.D., Aug. 28, 1933; d. Elmer H. and Emma O. (Pearson) Alberts; m. David R. Cunningham, Aug. 18, 1956; children: Cynthia D., Belinda K., Kenneth D. BA, Cen. Wash. U., 1956; postgrad., Seattle Pacific U., 1963; MEd, U. Wyo., 1969. Cert. tchr., Wyo. Tchr. Yakima (Wash.) Pub. Schs., 1956-58, Broomfield (Colo.) Consol. Sch., 1958-59, Edmonds (Wash.) Sch. Dist., 1964-65, Federal Way (Wash.) Sch. Dist., 1965-66; asst. prof. Univ. Sch., Laramie, Wyo., 1966—; cons. Child Devel. Assn., Wyo., Colo., Nebr., S.D., N.D., Mont., Tex., S.C., 1974—. Editor: Preschool Curriculum, 1978; contbr. articles to profl. jours. Mem. Internat. Reading Assn. (state rep. 1978—), Nat. Council Tchrs. English, Nat. Assn. Childhood Educators, Nat. Assn. Edn. Young Children, Nat. Accreditation Tchrs. Educators, Assn. Tchrs. Educators (sec.-treas. 1978), Kappa Delta Pi, Delta Kappa Gamma (chmn. membership com. 1980). Avocations: yoga, tennis, walking, cooking, travel. Home: 1407 Kearney Laramie WY 82070 Office: U Wyo Univ Sch Coll Edn Laramie WY 82071

CUNNINGHAM, GARY LEROI, historian, criminologist, educator, writer; b. Los Angeles, July 18, 1947; s. Earle Maxwell and Gladys Seward (Belding) C.; m. Gerry Sue Gibson, Sept. 1, 1974; children: Jacob Arthur, Joshua Edward. Student UCLA, 1965-66, Calif. State Coll.-Dominguez Hills, 1969; AA, Harbor Coll., 1969; BA, U. Calif., Santa Barbara, 1970, M.A., 1972, PhD, 1980. Life secondary teaching credential, life community coll. supr. credential, Calif. Short entry writer ABC-Clio Press, Santa Barbara, 1979-80; research historian U. Calif.-Santa Barbara, 1980—; instr. history Santa Barbara City Coll., 1981-83, Oxnard Coll., Calif., 1981—, Ventura Coll., Calif., 1982—; coll. coordinator, instr. Calif. Youth Authority Ventura Sch., Camarillo, 1983—; speaker various pub., civic, profl. groups, 1978—. Author: Moral Corruption in the American West (Prostitution and Gambling), 1980. Contbr. chpt., articles to profl. publs.; contbr. book revs. to Los Angeles Times, 1981—. Counselor juvenile offenders Calif. Youth Authority, Camarillo, 1983—; cons. deviant juvenile behavior. U. Calif.-Santa Barbara instructional devel. grantee, 1977, 78. Mem. Am. Hist. Assn., Orgn. Am. Historians, Western History Assn., Alcohol History Group, Correctional Edn. Assn., Internat. Platform Assn. (Am. Lyceum), Kans. State Hist. Soc. Jewish. Office: Calif Youth Authority/Ventura Sch 3100 Wright Rd Camarillo CA 93010

CUNNINGHAM, GARY WATSON, publishing executive; b. Denver, Jan. 15, 1943; s. Benjamin W. and Virginia M. (Lewark) C.; m. Behnaz Ghorbani-Nik, Aug. 26, 1980; children—Erin, Cameron, Kelan. B.A., U. Pacific, 1965; M.S., Eastern Wash. U., 1971. Cert. speech pathologist. Peace Corps cons. for Ministry of Ednl. TV., Medellin, Colombia, 1966-68; cons. to Ministry Spl. Edn., San Jose, Costa Rica, 1973; speech pathologist North Clakamas Sch. Dist., Milwaukie, Oreg., 1973-76; pres. C.C. Publs., Inc., Tualatin, Oreg., 1976—; dir. Oracle Computing Systems, Inc., Tualatin; cons. in field. Recipient cert. of appreciation Lyndon B. Johnson, 1968; Ednl. grantee Eastern Mont. U., 1961, Eastern Wash. U., 1969, 70, 71. Mem. Am. Speech and Hearing Assn., Oreg. Speech and Hearing Assn. Republican. Episcopalian. Club: Partners of Ams. Contbr. articles to profl. jours. Home: 2 Cellini Ct Lake Oswego OR 97034 Office: C C Publs Inc 19576 SW 90th Ct Tualatin OR 97062

CUNNINGHAM, JOHN FRANCIS, mechanical/electrical consulting company executive; b. Denver, Apr. 24, 1941; s. John Francis and Virginia Thora (Brown) C.; m. Bonnie K. Franson, Apr. 22, 1965 (dec. Oct. 1983); children: Christopher, Shon, Virginia; m. Mary Elizabeth Richards, May 18, 1985. Student, Colo. Sch. Mines, 1963. Registered profl. engr., Colo., Calif., Ariz. Designer Paul B. Crews Engrs., Anchorage, 1962-63, Behrent Engrs., Denver, 1965-66; pvt. practice engr. Grand Junction, Colo., 1966-86; pres. Burke Assocs. Inc., Grand Junction, 1986—. Served with U.S. Army, 1963-64. Mem. ASHRAE, NSPE, Cons. Engrs. Council. Club: Civitan (Grand Junction) (sec. 1972-74). Home: 306 32 1/2 Rd Palisade CO 81526 Office: Burke Assocs Inc 145 Grand Ave Suite A Grand Junction CO 81501

CUNNINGHAM, KIRKWOOD MASON, chemist; b. Tampa, Fla., Aug. 23, 1944; s. Kirkwood Bracher and Martha Nell (Shaffer) C. BS in Chemistry, Westminster Coll, 1966; PhD in Phys. Chemistry, Yale U., 1971. Post-doctoral fellow Nat. Research Council, Ottawa, Can., 1971-73, Wayne State U., Detroit, 1973-74, U. Denver, 1974-75; conservation scientist Smithsonian Inst., Washington, 1975-77; research chemist U.S. Geol. Survey, Denver, 1977—. Contbr. articles to profl. jours. Mem. Am. Chem. Soc., Sierra Club (Colo. chpt. conservation chmn. 1979—), Sigma Xi. Democrat. Avocations: hiking, camping, environ. advocacy.

CUNNINGHAM, LOREN DUANE, religious organization administrator; b. Taft, Calif., June 30, 1935; s. Thomas Cecil and Jewell Etta (Nicholson) C.; m. Darlene Joy Scratch; children: Karen Joy, David Loren. BA in Bible Studies, BA in Religious Edn., Cen. Bible Inst. and Sem., 1957; BA in Religion, MA in Adminstrn. of Edn., U. So. Calif., 1958; DD (hon.), Latin Am. Bible Coll., 1982. Founder, pres. Youth With A Mission, Kailua-Kona, Hawaii, 1960—; chmn. nat. exec. bd. Yr. of the Bible, Hawaii, 1983—; mem. exec. bd. Freedom Council Nat. Am. for Jesus, Virginia Beach, Va.; mem. internat. council Second Internat. Conf. on World Evangelization; pres. Pacific and Asia Christian U., Kailua-Kona; mem. exec. com. Wash. for Jesus, 1988—; mem. adv. com. Open Doors with Bro. Andrew, Assn. Internat. Missions Services. Author: Is That Really You God?, 1984. Mem. Women's Aglow (internat. adv. bd.), Christian Broadcasting Assn. (exec. bd.), Active Am. Coalition (exec. bd.), Full Gospel Chaplains Assn. (exec. bd.). Home: Kuakini Hwy Kailua-Kona HI 96740 Office: Youth With A Mission 75-5851 Kaukini Hwy Kailua-Kona HI 96740

CUNNINGHAM, MARY ELIZABETH, physician; b. Newark, Apr. 21, 1931; d. William Rutherford and Mary Agnes (Harvey) C. AB, Mt. Holyoke Coll., 1953; MS, U. Ill., 1955; PhD, U. Oreg., 1964; MD, U. Conn., 1982. Grad. asst. dept. physics U. Oreg., Eugene, 1957-64; sr. physicist Lawrence Livermore (Calif.) Nat. Lab., 1964-78, cons. Earth Scis. div., 1978-80; resident Mich. State. U. Affiliated Hosps., Lansing, 1982-85; physician Permanente Med. Group, Sacramento, 1985—. Contbr. articles to profl. jours. Mem. AMA, Am. Coll. Emergency Physicians, Am. Phys. Soc., N.Y. Acad. Scis., Sigma Xi (research grantee 1963-64), Phi Beta Kappa. Roman Catholic. Avocation: photography. Office: The Permanente Med Group 2025 Morse Ave Sacramento CA 95825

CUNNINGHAM, PAUL BERNARD, strategic planner, researcher; b. San Fancisco, Jan. 10, 1943; s. Forrest Eugene and Lois Berdeen (Caster) C.; m. Patricia Lynn Jewett, Oct. 21, 1971; children: Erin, Dara. BS, Humbolt State U., 1970; MS, Calif. State U., Arcata, 1979. Research biologist Alaska Dept. Fish and Game, King Salmon, 1971-73; arctic area biologist Alaska Dept. Fish and Game, Nome, 1973-76; dep. dir. Alaska Dept. Fish and Game, Juneau, 1979-81; mgmt. biologist Quinault Indian Nation, Taholah, Wash., 1978; planner, demographer Alaska Dept. Community and Regional Affairs, Juneau, 1981—. Chmn. Luth. Ch. council, Juneau, 1983-86, mem. adv. com. City of Nome, 1974-76; mem. Iditarod Trail Race Com., Nome, 1973-76. Served with U.S. Army, 1961-64, Korea. Mem. AAAS, Alaska Assn. for Advancement of Sci. and Engring., Am. Planning Assn., Am. Fisheries Soc., Appraisers and Measures Soc. (charter). Lutheran. Avocations: Nordic skiing, flying, fly-casting, scuba diving, gardening. Office: Community and Regional Affairs Box BH Juneau AK 99802

CUNNINGHAM, PAUL THOMAS, research chemist; b. Newton, Iowa, Oct. 16, 1936; s. Lynn D. and Margaret (Henderson) C.; m. Mary Jane McCullough, Oct. 28, 1961; children: David H., Robert P., Alan C. BS, U. Idaho, 1958; MS, San Diego State Coll., 1965; PhD, U. Calif., Berkeley, 1968. Mem. staff Argonne (Ill.) Nat. Lab., 1968-75, group leader, 1975-76, sect. head chem. engring., 1976-82; group leader chemistry div. Los Alamos (N.Mex.) Nat. Lab., 1982-86, program dir. nuclear materials, 1986—. Contbr. articles to profl. jours.; patentee in field. Served to lt. USNR, 1958-61. Fellow AAAS; mem. Am. Chem. Soc., Optical Soc. Am. Avocations: wood working, reading. Home: 1127 San Ildefonso Los Alamos NM 87544

CUNNINGHAM, RAY EARL, municipal court commissioner; b. Highland Park, Mich., Oct. 4, 1948; s. Raymond and Jane Elizabeth (Rathbun) C.; m. Karen Irene Zaninovich, July 4, 1975 (div. Aug. 1982); 1 child, Raymond Jeremy; m. Linda Jean Zuccolotto, Oct. 2, 1982; children: Jason Adam, Suzanne Elizabeth. BA in Govt., U. San Francisco, 1970, JD, 1973. Bar: Calif. 1973, Idaho 1983. Sole practice Palo Alto, Calif., 1973-76; dep. dist. atty. Santa Clara County, San Jose, Calif., 1976-82, 1983-84, mcpl. ct. commr., 1984—; dep. prosecuting atty. Kootenai County, Coeur d'Alene, Idaho, 1982-83; chmn. Santa Clara County Mcpl. Ct. Traffic Com., San Jose, 1985—. Mem. Santa Clara County Bar Assn. (bench-bar-media police com. 1983—), Idaho State Bar (assoc.), Calif. State Bar. Republican. Congregationalist. Home: 5270 Rio Grande Dr San Jose CA 95136 Office: Santa Clara County Mcpl Ct 200 W Hedding San Jose CA 95110

CUPP, MARY KATHERINE HYER, social worker; b. Clay, W.Va., Jan. 17, 1932; d. Oral Otis and Icie Arlene (McCracken) Hyer; divorced. BA, W.Va. State Coll. (now W.Va. Coll. Grad. Studies), 1967; MSW, W.Va. U., 1970. Lic. clin. social worker, Calif.; cert. jr. coll. tchr., Calif. Statistician W.Va. Dept. Welfare, Charleston, 1967-70; social worker Calif. Dept. Mental Hygiene, South Gate, 1970-73; adoptions worker Los Angeles County (Calif.) Dept. Adoptions, West Covina, 1973; social worker Camarillo (Calif.) State Hosp., 1973-86; parole agt. Calif. Dept. Corrections, North Hollywood, 1986—; cons. Psychiat. Residency Program, Camarillo, 1982-86. Pres. Save our Streetlights, Camarillo, 1979-81. Recipient award State Calif., 1983. Mem. Nat. Assn. Social Workers, Camarillo Bridge Club. Democrat. Methodist. Home: 1091 Dara St Camarillo CA 93010 Office: Calif Dept Corrections Parole and Community Services div 6736 Laurel Canyon Blvd Suite 207 North Hollywood CA 91606

CURELARU, IRINA MARIANA, materials scientist, engineer, educator; b. Iasi, Romania, Sept. 29, 1935; came to U.S., 1981.; children: Maria, John. BS, Bucharest (Romania) U., 1957; MS, Inst. Atomic Physics, Bucharest, 1957; CPS, Joint Inst. Nuclear Physics, Dubna, USSR, 1964; PhD, Chalmers U. Tech., Gothenburg, Sweden, 1980. Research assoc. Inst. Atomic Physics, 1957-62, 64-72, Joint Inst. Nuclear Physics, 1962-64, Inst. Nuclear Tech., Bucharest, 1972-74; research assoc., teaching asst. Chalmers U. Tech., 1974-80, research assoc., asst. prof., 1980-81; assoc. prof. U. Utah, Salt Lake City, 1981—; research collaborator Nat. Synchrotron Light Source, Brookhaven Nat. Lab., Upton, N.Y., 1984—; vis. prof. Fritz-Haber Institut der Max-Planck Gesellschaft, Berlin, 1986. Contbr. articles to profl. jours. Fellow Internat. Atomic Energy Agy.; mem. Am. Phys. Soc., Am. Vacuum Soc., Am. Ceramic Soc., European Phys. Soc., N.Y. Acad. Scis., AAAS. Home: 6249 S 440 E Murray UT 84107 Office: U Utah Dept Materials Sci and Engring Salt Lake City UT 84112

CURIEL, RAMON, international public relations educator; b. Guadalajara, Mexico, Nov. 18, 1945; came to U.S., 1956; s. Santos and Consuelo (Sanchez) C.; m. Leticia Perez, Feb. 28, 1970; children—Yvette, Leticia Marie, Vanessa. B.A. in Psychology, St. John's Coll., 1967; M.A. in Romance Langs., U. So. Calif.-Los Angeles, 1969, M.P.A., 1974. Research analyst County of Los Angeles, 1967-69; manpower programs coordinator 1969-70; manpower programs coordinator County of Orange, Santa Ana, Calif., 1970-72, affirmative action officer, 1972-74; affirmative action officer U. Calif.-Irvine, 1974-77, asst. chancellor, 1977—, assoc. vice chancellor govt. and community affairs, 1984-86; pres., dir. So. Calif. Health Resources Ctr., Tustin, 1983—; owner, pres. Curiel Internat., 1986—; cons. State of Calif. Dept. Edn., Sacramento, 1976-82; founding pres. Orange County Affirmative Action Officers Assn., Santa Ana, 1974; founding mem. Am. Assn. for Affirmative Action, Austin, Tex., 1976. Author: Contemporary Issues in Government, 1983; contbr. articles to profl. jours. Bd. dirs. Orange County ARC, Santa Ana, 1978—, Orange County Health Planning Council, Santa Ana, 1979—, Big Bros. of Orange County, Santa Ana, 1981, Amigos de Ser, Santa Ana, 1976-82; cabinet mem. United Way campaign, Orange County, 1984, bd. dirs., 1986—; founding mem. Orange County Protocol Com., 1984. U. Calif.-Irvine fellow, 1976, 75; v.p. Hist. and Cultural Found. of Orange County, 1986—. Mem. Nat. Chicano Council on Higher Edn. (council), Raza Adminstrs. and Counselors in Higher Edn., Nat. Council of Higher Edn. Mgmt. Systems, Personnel Mgmt. Assn. Aztlan. Democrat. Roman Catholic. Lodge: Irvine Lions (v.p. 1984—). Home: 13842 Loretta Dr Santa Ana CA 92705 Office: 1905 E 17th St Santa Ana CA 92701

CURL, JAMES CRAIG, mathematician, educator; b. Jefferson, Iowa, May 27, 1941; s. Dale Frank and Irene René (Edwards) C.; A.A., Modesto Jr. Coll., 1961; B.A., San Francisco State U., 1963; M.S., U. Santa Clara, 1968; Ed.D., U. No. Colo., 1976; m. Evelyn Ruth Ewen, July 4, 1963 (div. 1982); children—Brian Mitchell, Darren Matthew, Heather Michele. Tchr. math. high sch., San Mateo, Calif., 1964-66, Tracy (Calif.) Joint Union High Sch., 1966-68; instr. math. Modesto (Calif.) Jr. Coll., 1968—; teaching asst. in math. U. No. Colo., 1974-75. Mem. Calif. Math. Council Community Colls. (past pres., founding dir.), Calif. Math. Council, Nat. Council Tchrs. Math., Math. Assn. Am. Author: Developmental Arithmetic-An Individualized Approach, 1973; Developmental Arithmetic-A Computational Review, 1978, 3d edit., 1985; contbr. articles to profl. jours. Office: Modesto Jr Coll College Ave Modesto CA 95350

CUROTTO, RICKY JOSEPH, lawyer, corporate executive; b. Lomita Park, Calif., Dec. 22, 1931; s. Enrico and Nora M. (Giusso) C.; m. Lynne Therese Ingram, Dec. 31, 1983; children—Dina L., John F., Alexis J. B.S. cum laude, U. San Francisco, 1953, J.D., 1958. Bar: Calif. 1959. Assoc. Peart, Baraty & Hassard, San Francisco, 1958-60; sr. counsel, asst. sec. Utah Internat. Inc., San Francisco, 1960—; of counsel Curotto Law Offices, San Francisco and Sacramento, Calif., 1984—; counsel, sec. Ross Valley Homes, Inc., Greenbrae, Calif.; dir. First Security Realty Services Corp., Simco Indsl. Mortgage Co., Garden Hotels Investment Co. Trustee, U. San Francisco. Served to 1st lt. U.S. Army, 1954-56. Named to U. San Francisco Athletic Hall of Fame, 1985; recipient Bur. Nat. Affairs award, 1958, Disting. Service award U. San Francisco, 1981. Mem. State Bar Calif., San Francisco Bar Assn., ABA, Am. Arbitration Assn. (nat. panel arbitrators), Am. Corp. Counsel Assn. Republican. Roman Catholic. Club: Commonwealth of Calif. (San Francisco). Contbr. articles to law revs. Office: Utah Internat Inc 550 California St Suite 700 San Francisco CA 94104

CURRAN, CAROL ANNE, commercial real estate company official; b. San Francisco, Nov. 2, 1943; d. Andrew Joseph and Verna Maude (Woodman) Geiser; A.A. in Bus., City Coll. San Francisco; A.A. in Bus. Adminstrn., Foothill Coll.; B.S. in Bus. Adminstrn., San Jose State U., M.B.A., 1978; teaching credential Calif. Community Coll. System, 1980. Employee recruiter, employment rep., asst. mgr. Pacific Telephone Co., San Francisco, 1962-65; with Stanford U., 1965-68; with mktg. dept. Varian Assocs., Palo Alto, Calif., 1968-71; with Michael C. Fields, Menlo Park, Calif., 1971-72; adminstrv. asst., editor co. newsletter Time/Data Corp., Palo Alto, Calif., 1972-74; ind. cons. Olson Labs., Anaheim, Calif., 1977-78; office bldg. specialist, sr. sales cons. Coldwell Banker Comml. Real Estate Services, San Jose, Calif., 1978—. Trustee Music and Arts Found. Santa Clara County 1984-85; mem. City of San Jose Mayor's Econ. Devel./Image Bd., 1986. Named Office Bldg. Broker of Yr., San Jose C. of C., 1982; named to Comml. Real Estate Hall of Fame, City of San Jose, 1986. Mem. Assn. South Bay Brokers (dir. 1981). Office: Coldwell Banker Comml Real Estate 226 Airport Pkwy Suite 150 San Jose CA 95110

CURRENT, JERRY HALL, oil company research associate; b. Anderson, Ind., Mar. 2, 1935; s. James Abraham and Frances (Hall) C.; m. Diane Evalice Miller, June 23, 1961; children: Karen Eileen, Pamela Sue, James Robert Miller. BS in Chemistry, U. Ind., 1957; PhD in Chemistry, U. Wash., 1961. Instr. U. Calif., Berkeley, 1963-64; asst. prof. U. Mich., Ann Arbor, 1964-70; research chemist Gulf Oil Corp., Pitts., 1970-74, sr. research chemist, 1974-79, sect. dir., 1979-83; mgr. research support services Gulf Oil Corp., Houston, 1983, sr. research assoc., sect. dir., 1983-85; sr. research assoc. Chevron Research Co., Richmond, Calif., 1985—. Contbr. articles to profl. jours. Served as 2d lt. U.S. Army, 1957. NSF fellow, Berkeley, 1961-62. Mem. Am. Chem. Soc. (sect. sec., pres. 1968-69), Instrument Soc. Am., Soc. Petroleum Engrs., Union Concerned Scientists, Alpha Chi Sigma, Sigma Alpha Epsilon. Republican. Presbyterian. Avocations: gardening, walking, reading. Home: 1040 Lea Dr San Rafael CA 94903 Office: Chevron Research Co 576 Standard Ave Richmond CA 94802

CURRIE, JAMES WILLIAM, economist, engineer; b. Old Town, Maine, Aug. 8, 1942; s. James Wallace and Edith Mabel (Sage) C.; m. Andrea Jean Miskoski, Aug. 29, 1964; children—Dana Lorelle, James Brandon. B.S. in Mech. Engring., U. Maine, 1964, M.S. in Resource Geography, Oreg. State U., 1971, Ph.D. in Resource Econs., Civil Engring., 1975. Engr., Smithsonian Astrophys. Obs., Maui, Hawaii, 1964-67; engr. Ga. Pacific Corp., Bellingham, Wash., 1968; sr. researcher, research and devel. mgr. Battelle Pacific N.W. Labs., Richland, Wash., 1974—; mgr. bus. planning Office Tech. Planning and Analysis. Mem. Am. Econ. Assn., Am. Agrl. Econ. Assn., Am. Geophys. Union, Western Econ. Assn., Western Agrl. Econ. Assn., Internat. Assn. Energy Economists, World Future Soc., Soc. Risk Analysis. Club: Masons. Author publs. on project feasibility analysis, investment analysis, energy economics. Office: PO Box 999 Richland WA 99352

CURRIE, MADELINE ASHBURN, business administration educator; b. Rankin, Tex., Sept. 28; d. Herman and Ivan G. Vinson; BS, Tex. Woman's U., 1962; MA, Calif. State U., 1967; EdD, UCLA, 1974; m. Gail G. Currie; children: Robb Ashburn, Mark Ashburn, Michael Ashburn. Tchr., Edgewood High Sch., West Covina, Calif., 1962-69 ; instr. Rio Hondo Coll., Whittier, Calif., 1968-69; prof., dir. grad. programs Sch. Bus. Adminstrn., Calif. State Poly. U., Pomona, 1969—. Recipient award Alpha Lambda Delta; Exceptional Merit award Calif. State Poly. U., 1984. Mem. Grad. Sch. Edn., UCLA. Mem. Calif. Bus. Edn. Assn. (Recognition award), Tex. Woman's U. Alumnae Assn., Delta Pi Epsilon, Pi Lambda Theta, Delta Kappa Gamma, Delta Mu Gamma. Office: Calif State Poly U Sch Bus Adminstrn Pomona CA 91768

CURRIE, MALCOLM RODERICK, scientist, aerospace and automotive executive; b. Spokane, Wash., Mar. 13, 1927; s. Erwin Casper and Genevieve (Hauenstein) C.; m. Sunya Lofsky, June 24, 1951; children—Deborah, David, Diana; m. Barbara L. Dyer, Mar. 5, 1977. A.B., U. Calif. at Berkeley, 1949, M.S., 1951, Ph.D., 1954. Research engr. Microwave Lab., U. Calif. at Berkeley, 1949-52, elec. engring. faculty, 1953-54; lectr. U. Calif. at Los Angeles, 1955-57; research engr. Hughes Aircraft Co., 1954-57, v.p., 1965-66; head electron dynamics dept. Hughes Research Labs., Culver City, Calif., 1957-60; dir. physics lab. Hughes Research Labs., Malibu, Calif., 1960-61; asso. dir. Hughes Research Labs., 1961-63, v.p., dir. research labs., 1963-65, v.p., mgr. research and devel. div., 1965-69; v.p. research and devel. Beckman Instruments, Inc., 1969-73; dir. def. research and engring. Office Sec. Def., Washington, 1973-77; pres. missile systems group Hughes Aircraft Co., Canoga Park, Calif., 1977-83; exec. v.p. Hughes Aircraft Co., 1983—; pres., chief exec. officer Delco Electronics Corp., also bd. dirs.; dir. Hughes Aircraft, GM Hughes Electronics Co. mem. Def. Sci. Bd. Author articles. Mem. adv. bd. U. Calif., Berkeley, UCLA, U. Tex. Served with USNR, 1944-47. Decorated comdr. Legion of Honor France; named nation's outstanding young elec. engr. Eta Kappa Nu, 1958, one of 5 outstanding young men of Calif. Calif. Jr. C. of C., 1960. Fellow IEEE, AIAA; mem. Nat. Acad. Engring., Am. Phys. Soc., Phi Beta Kappa, Sigma Xi, Lambda Chi Alpha. Club: Cosmos. Patentee in field. Home: 28780 Wagon Rd Agoura CA 91301 Office: Hughes Aircraft Co 7200 Hughes Terr Los Angeles CA 90045

CURRIER, RICHARD PAUL, software consulting company executive, educator; b. Orange, Calif., Oct. 1, 1952; s. Myrl L. and Dolores A. (Ervin) C.; M. Karen Lorraine Mair, Aug. 11, 1973; 1 son, Brett. B.A. in Mgmt. Info. Systems, Calif. State U.-Fullerton, 1979. Cert. data processing Inst. Cert. Computer Profls. Systems. Programmer/analyst Rio Hondo Coll., Whittier, Calif., 1979-81; sr. programmer Bourns, Inc., Riverside, Calif., 1981-82; systems analyst Carter Hawley Hale Stores, Inc., Anaheim, Calif., 1982-84; pres. Currier Software Cons. Services, Inc.; instr. computer ops., devel. new curriculum Rio Hondo Coll. Served with USN, 1971-75. Mem. Assn. Systems Mgmt. Home: 11584 Kiwi Ct Sunnymead CA 92388

CURRY, BO UNDERWOOD, chemist; b. Augusta, Ga., May 10, 1951; s. Thomas Fortson and Mary Ann (Kemper) C.; m. Clelia Maria Krietsch, July 12, 1971 (div. Jan. 1977); children: Soren Christopher, Arwen Lee, Maya Ruth; m. Ilona Anna Palings. BS in Chemistry, Ga. Inst. Tech., 1973; PhD in Chemistry, U. Calif., Berkeley, 1983. Staff chemist Environ. Analysis Labs., Richmond, Calif., 1974-77; mem. tech. staff Hewlett-Packard Labs., Palo Alto, Calif., 1983—. Contbr. articles to profl. jours. Mem. Am. Chem. Soc., AAAS, ACLU, Sierra Club, Sigma Xi. Democrat. Avocations: hiking, reading, childraising. Home: 26417 Mockingbird Ln Hayward CA 94544 Office: Hewlett-Packard Labs 1651 Page Mill Rd Palo Alto CA 94304

CURRY, FRANCIS JOHN, physician; b. San Francisco, July 19, 1911; s. William Martin and Madonna (Burke) C.; m. Beryl Marguerite Swannel, Apr. 10, 1948; children: Francis John, Joan F., Elizabeth Anne, Patrick F., Thomas F., Robert, William, James. B.S., U. San Francisco, 1936, Sc.D. (hon.), 1984; M.D., Stanford U., 1946; M.P.H., U. Calif., 1964. Diplomate Am. Bd. Preventive Medicine. Teaching asst., research asst. Stanford U., 1942-43; intern San Francisco Gen. Hosp., 1945-46; resident Fresno (Calif.) Gen. Hosp., 1946-47; resident, asst. dir. Ahwahnee Tri-county Hosp., Madera, Calif., 1947-50; resident Santa Clara County (Calif.) Hosp., 1951-53; practice medicine specializing in pulmonary diseases and internal medicine San Francisco, 1956—; chief Tb div. San Francisco Health Dept., 1960-74, dir. health, hosps. and mental health, 1970-76; prof., spl. lectr. U. Calif., Berkeley, 1966—; prof. health care adminstr. Golden Gate U., 1973—; mem. staff San Francisco Gen. Hosp., 1956—, dir. chest clinic, 1956-74; mem. staff U. Calif. Hosp.; asst. clin. prof. medicine Stanford U., 1957-70, clin. prof., 1970—; asst. clin. prof. U. Calif., San Francisco, 1958-68, asso. clin. prof., 1968-70, clin. prof., 1970—; clin. prof. community dentistry U. Pacific, 1970—; project dir. Tb Control Project for San Francisco, USPHS, 1962-76; vice chmn. med. advisory com. San Francisco Hosp. Service Study Project, 1962—; mem. U. Calif. at San Francisco Gen. Hosp. Planning Com., 1963-78; mem. adv. council Tb Control Surgeon Gen. USPHS, 1965-78; cons., lectr. in field. Contbr. articles to profl. jours. Served as capt. AUS, 1953-55. Fellow ACP, Am. Coll. Preventive Medicine, Am. Coll. Chest Physicians (pres. Calif. chpt. 1962-63, regent 1971-78), Am. Pub. Health Assn.; mem. AMA, Calif. Med. Assn., Sci. Research Soc. Am., Am. Thoracic Soc., Royal Soc. Health, Acad. Preventive Medicine, Internat. Coll. Chest Physicians (dir. 1972-78), Am. Legion, Sigma Xi. Home: 217 Kensington Way San Francisco CA 94127 Office: U Calif Med Ctr Div Ambulatory & Com Medicine 3d & Parnassus Ave San Francisco CA 94143

CURRY, JANE HELEN, school principal; b. Stockton, Calif., Jan. 2, 1936; d. James Arthur and Mary Jane (Wakefield) C. BA, U. Pacific, 1957; MEd, U. So. Calif., 1965, EdD, 1975. Social worker County of San Joaquin, Stockton, Calif., 1957-58; supr. Occidental Life, Los Angeles, 1958-60; tchr. Valle Lindo Sch. Dist., El Monte, Calif., 1960-64; tchr. reading Rosemead (Calif.) Sch. Dist., 1964-70; cons. Hayward (Calif.) Unified Sch. Dist., 1970-78, prin., 1978—; mem. adv. panel Subject Matter Preparation of Elem. Tchrs. Mem. Hayward Area Festival of Arts, Lawrence Hall Sci., Berkeley. Named Woman of Yr., AAUW, Hayward, 1977. Mem. Women in Mgmt. (pres. 1983-85), Internat. Reading Assn., Elem. Sch. Sci. Assn., Internat. Vis. Ctr., Calif. Math Council, Assn. Calif. Sch. Adminstrs. (treas. 1976), Calif. Reading Assn. (bd. dirs. 1978-81), San Francisco Zoo, Delta Kappa Gamma (pres. 1979-80). Avocations: traveling, reading, theatre. Home: 3827 Mabel Ave Castro Valley CA 94546 Office: Hayward Unified Sch PO Box 5000 Hayward CA 94540-5000

CURRY, LINDA WILSON, business development consultant; b. Long Branch, N.J., Mar. 17, 1945; d. Sidney Meadow and Josephine Barbara (Dremel) Meadow Oswald; B.S. in Math., Bucknell U., 1966; M.S. in Numerical Sci., Johns Hopkins U., 1970; Ph.D. candidate in bus. adminstrn. Pacific Western U.; m. James Prescott Curry, Aug. 22, 1980. Various positions as mathematician, 1966-69; ops. research analyst Dept. Transp., 1970-73; mgr. Planning Research Corp., 1973-75; exec. v.p. Automated Scis. Group, Inc., 1975-77; pres. Excel Corp., 1978; mgr. info. systems Commonwealth Research Corp., 1978; pres., chmn. bd. Wilson Hill Assocs., Inc., 1978-81; pres. South Bay Introductions, Inc., Manhattan Beach, Calif., 1981-82; v.p. bus. devel. Automated Scis. Group, Manhattan Beach, 1982-84; pres. Curry Assocs. Inc., 1984-86; pres. INMAR Corp., 1986—; instr. Calif. State U.-Dominguez Hills, Harbor Coll. Mem. IEEE, Am. Def. Preparedness Assn., Air Force Assn., Navy League, Tech. Mktg. Soc. Am., Army Assn., Armed Forces Communications and Electronics Assn., Am. Mgmt. Assn., Am. Entrepreneurs Assn., Phi Beta Kappa. Jewish. Home: 154 Anacapa Dr Camarillo CA 93010 Office: NMAR Corp 350 N Lantana St Suite 157 Camarillo CA 93010

CURRY, MICHAEL ARTHUR, telecommunications company executive; b. Bklyn., Nov. 9, 1949; s. Arthur and Charlotte (Farrell) C.; m. Phyllis Wymer, Aug. 21, 1971; children: Michele, Christopher. BA in Econs., Rutgers U., 1976; postgrad., Pepperdine U., 1985—. Analyst Lionel Liesure, Phila., 1979-82; sr. tech. Anacorp, Cherry Hill, N.J., 1982-83; v.p. Security Pacific Data Transmission Corp., Glendale, Calif., 1983—; bd. dirs. Granda Park Inc.; tech. cons. Price Waterhouse, Los Angeles, Eckerd Drugs, Fla., Kinney Shoes, Pa. Youth leader YMCA, Yorba Linda, Calif., 1983—. Mem. Internat. Tanden Users Group. Republican. Roman Catholic. Avocation: sailing. Home: 424 New Jersey Ln Placentia CA 92670 Office: Security Pacific Data Transmission 330 N Brand Glendale CA 91203

CURRY, SEAN, research engineer; b. Ottawa, Ont., Can., June 23, 1953; s. Francis Darby and Mary Nancy (McTaggart) C.; m. Mary Ann Pfister, Sept. 9, 1984. B in Tech., Ryerson Poly. Inst., Ont., Can., 1979; MSc, U. Calif., Berkeley, 1981, PhD, 1985. Photogrammetrist J.D. Barnes, Toronto, Ont., 1981; research engr. U. Calif., San Francisco, 1981-85, Vexcel, Boulder, Colo., 1985—; cons. Shriners Hosp., San Francisco, 1985, Found. for Glaucoma Research, San Francisco, 1985. Contbr. articles to profl. jours.; inventor mandibular motion analysis system, 1986. Recipient Ryerson Gold Medal Ryerson Poly. Inst., 1978, Wild Heerbrugg Photogrammetric award Wild Heerbrugg, 1981. Mem. Am. Soc. Photogrammetry, British Photogrammetric Soc., Can. Inst. Surveying, Soc. Photo-Optical Instrumentation Engrs. Office: Vexcel Corp 2905 Wilderness Pl Boulder CO 80301

CURRY, STEPHEN MARTINDALE, physicist, laser engineer; b. Dallas; s. Duncan Ford and Frances Janella (Martindale) C. BS, So. Meth. U., 1967; MS, Stanford U., 1969, PhD, 1972. Asst. prof. U. Tex., Dallas, 1973-78; research scientist Vought Corp., Dallas, 1978-79, cons., 1979-81; sr. laser engr. Cooper LaserSonics, Santa Clara, Calif., 1981-85; pres. Sound Decisions, Cupertino, 1985—; research assoc. Stanford (Calif.) U., 1972-73. Fellow NSF, 1967-71, Sloan Found., 1977-78. Mem. Optical Soc. Am., Am. Phys. Soc., Phi Beta Kappa, Phi Eta Sigma. Democrat. Home: 520 Fern Ridge Ct Sunnyvale CA 94087-3261 Office: Sound Decisions 19925 Stevens Creek Blvd Cupertino CA 95014

CURTIN, SUSAN, employee assistance program administrator; b. Burbank, Calif., June 8, 1953; s. John Daniel and Patricia (Humphrey) C.; m. Damon Schamu, Sept. 7, 1985. BS, San Diego State U., 1975, MS, 1977. Rehab. counselor San Diego Mesa Coll., 1977-84; market rep. Orgn. Stress Testing, San Diego, 1983-84; employee assistance program adminstr. City of San Diego, 1984—. Bd. dirs. Rancho Mission Villas, San Diego, 1979-80, Peninsula YWCA Soccer League, San Diego, 1981-82; adv. mem. San Diego State Vocat. Grant, 1982-83. Mem. Nat. Rehab. Assn. (local pres. 1981-82), Calif. Rehab. Assn. (treas. 1982-83), Assn. Labor Mgmt. and Cons. on Alcoholism (sec. 1984-86, pres. San Diego chpt. 1986—). Avocations: soccer skiing, softball, areobics, jogging. Office: City San Diego Dept Employee Assistance 1010 2d Ave #300C San Diego CA 92101

CURTIN, THOMAS LEE, ophthalmologist; b. Columbus, Ohio, Sept. 9, 1932; s. Leo Anthony and Mary Elizabeth (Burns) C.; B.S., Loyola U., Los Angeles, 1954; M.D., U. So. Calif., 1957; children—Michael, Gregory, Thomas, Christopher. Intern, Ohio State U. Hosp., 1957-58; resident in ophthalmology U.S. Naval Hosp., San Diego, 1961-64; practice medicine specializing in ophthalmology, Oceanside, Calif., 1967—; mem. staff Tri City, Palomar Meml., Scripps Meml. Mercy hosps.; sci. adv. bd. So. Calif. Soc. Prevention Blindness, 1973-76; cons. in field. Trustee, Carlsbad (Calif.) Unified Sch. Dist., 1975-83, pres., 1979, 82, 83. Served as officer M.C., USN, 1958-67. Diplomate Am. Bd. Ophthalmology. Mem. Am., Calif. med. assns., San Diego County Med. Soc., Am. Acad. Ophthalmology, Am. Assn. Ophthalmology, Soc. Cryobiology, Aerospace Med. Assn., Pacific Coast Ophthalmology and Otolaryngology Assn., San Diego Acad. Ophthalmology (pres. 1979), Calif. Assn. Ophthalmology (dir.), San Diego Surg. Soc. Republican. Roman Catholic. Clubs: Carlsbad Rotary, El Camino Country. Home: 2014 Ave of Trees Carlsbad CA 92008 Office: 3231 Waring Ct Suite S Oceanside CA 92056

CURTIS, DWAYNE HERBERT, human physiologist; b. Caldwell, Idaho, May 9, 1930; s. Jesse Benjamin Curtis and Edith May (Pottenger) Allen; m. Ardys Arlene Atchley, June 10, 1954; children: Jess Alan, Jeanine Ann, Craig Shelby, Connie Sue. AA, Boise Jr. Coll., 1951; BS, Idaho State Coll., 1953; MA, U. Utah, 1960, PhD, 1963. Prof. biol. scis. Calif. State U., Chico, 1963—; pulmonary function technician N.T. Enloe Meml. Hosp., Chico, Calif., 1969-70; instr. Butte Coll., Durham, Calif., 1970-71; adv. com. mem. respiratory therapy program Butte Coll., 1971—. Author: Human Physiology Laboratory Manual, 1974, rev. edits. 1977, 81, 84; contbr article to profl. jours. Ranger, naturalist Crater Lake Nat. Park, Oreg., 1965-69; edn. bd. dirs. Chico Christian Sch.; chmn. bd. dirs. 1976-77; bd. dirs. Lung Assn. Superior Calif., 1963-80, pres. 1968-69, 71-72; del. Lung Assn. State of Calif., 1970-73. Served with U.S. Army, 1954-56. Grantee Chico State Coll. Found., 1969, 70, 71, 72, NSF, 1970,. Republican. Mem. Evangelical Christian Ch. Avocation: geneology of family history. Office: Calif State U Dept Biol Scis Chico CA 95929

CURTIS, JESSE WILLIAM, JR., U.S. district judge; b. San Bernardino, Calif., Dec. 26, 1905; s. Jesse William and Ida L. (Seymour) C.; m. Mildred F. Mort, Aug. 24, 1930; children: Suzanne, Jesse W., Clyde Hamilton, Christopher Cowles. A.B., U. Redlands, 1928, LL.D., 1973; J.D., Harvard U., 1931. Bar: Calif. 1931. Pvt. practice 1931-35; mem. firms Guthrie & Curtis, San Bernardino, 1935-40, Curtis & Curtis, 1946-50, Curtis, Knauf, Henry & Farrell, 1950-53; judge Superior Ct. of Calif., 1953-62; U.S. judge Central Dist. of Calif., 1962—; Rep. dist. ct. on Jud. Council U.S., 1972-74. Chmn. San Bernardino Sch. Bd., 1942-46, mem., 1946-49; mem. Del Rosa Bd. Edn., 1950-53; Chmn. San Bernardino County Heart Fund; dir., past pres. YMCA; dir. Good Will Industries, Crippled Children's Soc., Arrowhead United Fund; adv. bd. Community Hosp. Mem. Am., Los Angeles County bar assns., Calif. State Bar, Am. Judicature Soc., Am. Law Inst., Los Angeles World Affairs Council, Town Hall, Phi Delta Phi. Democrat. Conglist. Club: Newport Harbor Yacht. Home: 305 Evening Star Ln Newport Beach CA 92660 Office: US Court House Los Angeles CA 90012

CURTIS, KERRY PARK, banking and marketing executive; b. Blackfoot, Idaho, Jan. 1, 1942; s. Joseph Wesley and Marjorie (Park) C.; m. Lynn Walton, June 21, 1969; children: Rebecca, Elisabeth, Christopher. AB, U. Calif., Berkeley, 1963, MBA, 1965; PhD, U. Pa., 1969. With Bank of Am., San Francisco, 1969-74, head of locations planning, 1974-76, head mktg. research, 1976-77, asst. to chief exec. officer, 1978-80; head ops. mgmt. Bank of Am., London, 1980-82; head info. mgmt. Bank of Am., San Francisco, 1982-84, head mktg. info., 1984—. Bd. dirs. San Francisco Planning and Urban Research, 1983—, Friends of Langley Porter Psychiat. Inst., 1977—. Office: Bank of Am PO Box 37000 Dept 3672 San Francisco CA 94137

CURTIS, MACHELLE MCKINLEY, telemarketing executive; b. Racine, Wis., Mar. 22, 1948; d. Wilbert Leon and Alma Jean (Baird) McKinley; m. William Childs Curtis, Aug. 23, 1980. Student, U. Wis., La Crosse, 1966-68; BS, No. Ill. U., 1971; MS, Emerson Coll., 1974. Speech and lang. pathologist Lincoln (Mass.) Bd. Edn., 1974-79; v.p. Mitterling Method, Boston, 1980-82; pres. Tele-Connections, Aurora, Colo., 1983—; lectr., pub. speaker various orgns. Co-author: Winning Words: A New Approach to Developing Effective Speaking Skills, 1980. Grantee Racine Environment Com., 1968, 69; fellow Emerson Coll., Boston, 1972. Mem. Am. Soc. Tng. and Devel., Rocky Mountain Telemktg. Assn. (sec. 1985-86, exec. v.p. 1986—, bd. dirs.). Office: Tele-Connections PO Box 440025 Aurora CO 80044

CURTIS, MARY PACIFICO, advertising agency executive; b. Chgo., Feb. 22, 1953; d. Louis Enrico Pacifico and Margaret (Geneva) Peterson; m. Douglas Reid Curtis, Jan. 2, 1982. B.S., Northwestern U., 1973. Assoc. producer Panorama Prodns., Santa Clara, Calif., 1975-76; copy chief Moorhead Mktg., San Francisco, 1976-77; pres. Pacifico & Assocs. Inc., San Jose, Calif., 1977—; founder Silicon Valley Bank, San Jose, 1984—. Bd. dirs. Childrens Counseling Ctr., Santa Clara, 1980—, pres.; bd. dirs. San Jose Symphony Assn., 1984-85. Recipient San Francisco Cable Car award San Francisco Ad Club, 1978; Best in the West awards of merit, 1979, 80; Maggie award, 1980; Addy award, 1984; Joey award, 1984; Murphy award, 1984, 85, 86. Mem. San Jose Ad Club, Peninsula Women in Advt., San Jose Women in Advt., Western States Ad Agys. Assn., Am. Mktg. Assn. Roman Catholic. Avocations: photography; tennis; skiing. Office: Pacifico & Assocs Inc 2145 The Alameda San Jose CA 95126

CURTIS, ORLIE LINDSEY, JR., lawyer; b. Hutchinson, Kans., Feb. 27, 1934; s. Orlie Lindsey and Lillian Esther (Barnes) C.; m. Idella Mae Krueger, June 5, 1955; children: Elizabeth, Victoria. B.A. with high distinction, Union Coll., Lincoln, Nebr., 1954; M.S., Purdue U., 1956; Ph.D., U. Tenn., 1961; J.D., U. So. Calif., 1977. Bar: Calif. 1977. Group chief Oak Ridge Nat. Lab., 1956-63; lab. dir., sci. fellow Northrop Corp., Hawthorne, Calif., 1963-77; since practiced in Stockton; ptnr. firm Kroloff, Belcher, Smart, Perry & Christopherson, 1980—; vis. lectr. physics U. Calif., Berkeley, 1970-71; adv. bd. physics dept. U. Ky., 1970-73; lectr. Nat. Symposia Products Liability and Ins. Law. Author: Point Defects in Solids, 1975; contbr. articles to profl. jours. Bd. dirs. So. Calif. conf. Seventh-day Adventists, 1970-74, Newbury Acad. Park Acad., 1970-74, Lodi Acad., 1979-84, No. Calif. conf. Seventh-day Adventists, 1980-86, Dameron Hosp. Found., 1985—. Fellow Am. Phys. Soc., IEEE (chmn. radiation effects com. 1970-73); mem. Am. Bar Assn., Def. Research Inst., State Bar Calif., San Joaquin County Bar Assn., Adventist Attys. Assn. (pres. 1983-84), Order of Coif. Patentee in field. Home: 9794 N Fernwood Rd Stockton CA 95212 Office: Kroloff Belcher Smart et al 1044 N El Dorado St Stockton CA 95201

CURTIS, STANLEY BARTLETT, radiation biophysicist; b. Evanston, Ill., Feb. 16, 1932; s. Harold Bartlett and Margaret (Furrey) C.; children: Kathryn, Elizabeth, Charles; m. Mary Catherine Pirruccello, Nov. 20, 1982. BA, Carleton Coll., 1954; PhD, U. Wash., 1962. Physicist Lockheed Calif. Co., Belair, 1962-64; biophysicist Boeing Co., Seattle, 1964-65; biophysicist Lawrence Berkeley (Calif.) Lab., 1965-78, sr. biophysicist, 1978—, also dep. group leader, 1985—. Contbr. research and rev. articles to profl. jours. Eleanor Roosevelt Internat. Cancer fellow Am. Cancer Soc., 1970-71; Fogarty Internat. Sr. fellow NIH, 1981-82. Mem. AAAS, Am. Phys. Soc., Radiation Research Soc. (council mem. 1972-75), Nat. Council Radiation Protection. Home: 800 Spruce St Berkeley CA 94707 Office: Lawrence Berkeley Lab Bldg 74 Rm 159B Berkeley CA 94720

CURTIS, VERN O., restaurant chain executive; b. 1934; married. B.S. in Acctg., U. Utah, 1959. Acct. Arhur Young & Co, 1960-66; controller Data Dynamics, Inc., 1966-68; with Denny's Inc., La Mirada, Calif., 1968—, successively treas, treas. and asst. sec., v.p. fin. and treas., exec. v.p. and treas., now pres., chief exec. officer, dir. Served to capt. U.S. Army, 1959-60. Office: Dennys Inc 16700 Valley View Ave La Mirada CA 90638 *

CURTIS, WILLIAM HENRY, real estate developer, broker; b. Kansas City, Mo., Aug. 6, 1936; s. William Edward and Helen (Neuer) C.; m. Margaretha Reidenboch, May 8, 1965; children: Michelle, Kathleen, Stephanie, David. BA, U. Mo., 1958; MBA, U. Pa., 1964. Lic. real estate broker. Analyst Fairchild Semi, Mountain View, Calif., 1966-71; broker Grubb & Ellis Co., San Jose, Calif., 1971-75; prin. William Curtis Assocs., San Jose, 1975-77; ptnr. McMillan Moore & Buchanan, San Jose, 1977-79; owner CRI Properties, San Jose, 1979—; bd. dirs. San Jose Nat. Bank, Children's Discovery Mus., San Jose, YMCA, San Jose, O'Connors Hosp., San Jose. Served with USN, 1959-79, Vietnam. Mem. Assn. South Bay Brokers (tours chmn. 1977-78), San Jose C. of C. Republican. Episcopalian. Lodge: Rotary (program chmn. San Jose club 1984-85). Avocations: skiing, sailing, swimming, golf. Home: 15981 Grandview Monte Sereno CA 95030 Office: CRI Properties 2021 The Alameda #19 San Jose CA 95126

CURTISS, ELDEN F., bishop; b. Baker, Oreg., June 16, 1932; s. Elden F. and Mary (Neiger) C. B.A., St. Edward Sem., Seattle, M.Div., 1958; M.A. in Ednl. Adminstrn, U. Portland, 1965; postgrad., Fordham U., U. Notre Dame. Ordained priest Roman Catholic Ch., 1958; campus chaplain 1959-64, 65-68; supt. schs. Diocese of Baker (Oreg.), 1962-70; pastor 1968-70; pres./rector Mt. Angel Sem., Benedict, Oreg., 1972-76; bishop of Helena (Mont.), 1976—; mem. priests senate Archdiocese of Portland, 1974-76; mem. ecumenical ministries State of Oreg., 1972; mem. pastoral services com. Oreg. State Hosp., Salem, 1975-76; Mem. adminstrv. bd. Nat. Conf. Cath. Bishops, 1976-80, mem. pro-life com., from 1977; bd. dirs. Cath. Mut. Relief Soc., from 1977, Mont. Cath. Conf., from 1976; mem. N.W. Assn. Bishops and Major Religious Superiors, 1976—, Mont. Assn. Chs., 1976—. Mem. Nat. Cath. Ednl. Assn. (Outstanding Educator 1973). Address: 515 N Ewing PO Box 1729 Helena MT 59624

CUSHING, COLBERT ELLIS, aquatic ecologist, researcher; b. Ft. Collins, Colo., Jan. 9, 1931; s. Colbert Ellis and Mabel May (Skalla) C.; m. Jacqueline Agnes Roddy, Sept. 9, 1959; children: Robert, Thomas, Laurie. BS in Fisheries Mgmt., Colo. State U., 1952, MS in Zoology, 1956; PhD in Biology, U. Saskatchewan, Saskatoon, Can., 1961. Fisheries technician Colo. Game and Fish Dept., Grand Lake, 1956-57; fisheries research biologist Mont. Fish and Game Dept., Kalispell, 1958; sr. research scientist Battelle Meml. Inst., Richland, Wash., 1961—; cons. Nat. Acad. Scis., 1980; mem. adv. com. Ill. Natural History Survey, 1983-86. Editor: Radioecology and Energy Resources 1976; contbr. articles to profl. jours. Pres. bd. trustees YMCA, Richland, 1974-78, v.p., sec. treas.; coach Wash. Spl. Olympics, Richland, 1985—. Served to 1st. lt. U.S. Army, 1954-56. Grantee Colo. State U. Research Found., 1956, NSF, 1961, 75, 80. Mem. Ecol. Soc. Am. (bulletin editor 1983—), Am. Soc. Limnology and Oceanography (mem. at large 1976-79), N.Am. Benthological Soc. (bd. dirs. 1984-86), Am. Fisheries Soc., Internat. Soc. Limnology, Freshwater Biol. Assn. Republican. Club: Columbia Basin Flycasters (Richland). Avocations: hunting, fishing, collecting and selling Western Art. Home: 1610 Woodbury Richland WA 99352 Office: Battelle Menly Inst Pacific Northwest Lab PO Box 999 Richland WA 99352

CUSHING, JIM MICHAEL, research mathematics educator; b. North Platte, Nebr., Mar. 20, 1942; s. Harry Joseph and Lorraine Francis (Rohr) C.; m. Dagmar Maria Ostendorf, July 30, 1971; children: Alina Stephanie, Lara Jennifer. BA magna cum laude, U. Colo., 1964; PhD, U. Md., 1968. Asst. prof. math. U. Ariz., Tucson, 1968-72, assoc. prof., 1973-82, prof., 1983—. Author: Integrodifferential Equations, 1979; editor Rocky Mountain Jour. Math., 1985—; contbr. articles to profl. jours. Fellow IBM, Yorktown Heights, N.Y., 1971-72, Humboldt Found., West German Govt., Tübingen, 1977-78; NSF grantee, 1980-87. Mem. Am. Math. Soc., Soc. Indsl. and Applied Math. Avocations: chamber music, long distance running, hiking. Office: U Ariz Dept Math Bldg 89 Tucson AZ 85721

CUSUMANO, JAMES ANTHONY, chemical company executive; b. Elizabeth, N.J., Apr. 14, 1942; s. Charles Anthony and Carmella Madelow (Catalano) C.; m. Jane LaVerne Melvin, june 15, 1985; children: Doreen Ann, Polly Jean. BA, Rutgers U., 1964, PhD, 1968. Mgr. catalyst research Exxon Research and Engring. Co., Linden, N.J., 1967-74; pres. Catalytica Assocs., Mountain View, Calif., 1974-85, chmn., 1985—, also bd. dirs. Author: Catalysis in Coal Conversion, 1978; also articles to profl. jours.; patentee in field. Recipient Surface Chemistry award Continental Oil Co., 1964. Mem. Am. Chem. Soc., Am. Inst. Chem. Engrs., Am. Phys. Soc., N.Y. Acad. Sci., Sigma Psi. Republican. Roman Catholic. Avocations: skiing, hiking, sailing, swimming, travelling. Home: 1611 Morton Ave Los Altos CA 94022 Office: Catalytica Assocs Inc 430 Ferguson Dr Bldg 3 Mountain View CA 94022

CUTLER, ANDREW HALL, research chemist; b. Gary, Ind., Nov. 29, 1956; s. Robert Cutler and Estelle (Gorbatoff) C. BS in Physics, U. Calif., Riverside, 1978; PhD in Chemistry, Princeton U., 1985. Lab. asst. U. Calif. Physics Dept., Riverside, 1976-78; teaching, research and library asst. Chemistry Dept. Princeton (N.J.) U., 1978-82; programming cons. Princeton U. Computer Ctr., 1981; research assoc. Hawaii Nat. Energy Inst., Manoa, 1982-83; postgrad. research chemist Calif. Space Inst., San Diego, 1983-86; prin. scientist Energy Sci. Labs., San Diego, 1986—; cons. Energy Sci. Labs., 1984—, Earth Space Ops. and Large Scale Projects Inst., Austin, Tex., 1984—; presenter research papers at various profl. confs., 1983—. Mem. AAAS, AIAA, Am. Astron. Assn., Am. Chem. Soc., L-5 Soc. (pres. Honolulu chpt. 1982-83, program chmn. San Diego chpt. 1986—). Avocations: contra dancing, cooking, history and sociology of sci., sci. fiction. Home: 3030 Suncrest #214 San Diego CA 92116

CUTLER, HELEN ELMQUIST, historian, writer, lawyer; b. Iowa City, Iowa, Aug. 31, 1938; d. Homer S. and Mercedes (Shaw) Elmquist; m. Allan Harris Cutler, Dec. 8, 1961. BA, U. So. Calif., 1960; JD, UCLA, 1981. Bar: Calif. 1981, U.S. Dist. Ct. (so.and ea. dists.) Calif. 1982, U.S Ct. Appeals (9th cir.) 1981. Assoc. Manatt, Phelps et al, Los Angeles, 1981-82; sole practice Los Angeles, 1982—. Author: Jew as Ally of Muslim, 1986. Avocations: fgn. travel, hiking, biking, music, ballet. Home and Office: 1016 S Alfred St Los Angeles CA 90035

CUTLER, KENNETH ROSS, pension funds investment counsel; b. Tacoma, Mar. 5, 1920; s. Clarence William and Matilda Roxanne (Ross) C.; m. Pat Virginia Reinecke, Aug. 6, 1943; children—Geoffrey William, Craig Lee, Brooke Roxanne. Student U. Chgo., 1941-42, UCLA, 1945. Broker,

William R. Staats & Co., 1945-47, Dempsey-Tegeler & Co., Los Angeles, 1950-53; pres. Calif. Fund, Los Angeles, 1953-62; investment counsel, Van Nuys, Calif., 1962-66; broker Dean Witter & Co., Century City, Calif., 1966-72; mgr. spl. accounts dept. Paine Webber, Los Angeles, 1972-77; chmn. Cutler & Co., Inc., Medford, Oreg., 1977—. Mem. Phi Delta Theta. Republican. Presbyterian. Clubs: Balboa Bay, Pacific (Newport Beach); Rogue Valley Country; Commonwealth (San Francisco). Home: 4300 Livingston Rd PO Box 1411 Jacksonville OR 97530 Office: Cutler & Co Inc 132 W Main St Suite 204 Medford OR 97501

CUTLER, LORRAINE MASTERS, interior designer; b. Indpls., Oct. 19, 1943; d. James Mark and Dorothy Aileen (DeLawter) Masters; m. Albert B. Cutler III, June 3, 1965 (div.); children: Valina Dawn, Anthony Bret. BFA, Ariz. State U., 1973, BA, 1974. Intern Walsh Bros., Phoenix, 1973, jr. designer, 1973-74, staff designer, 1978-80; dir. interior design Dick, Fritsche and Assocs., Phoenix, 1980-84; dir. interior design and space planning HNC Inc., Phoenix, 1984—. Participant Interior Designer Efforts for Ariz. Legis., Phoenix, 1986-87. Mem. Inst. Bus. Designers (profl., pres. 1985-87, v.p. programs 1983-85, sec. 1981-83, Cert. Appreciation, 1981), Am. Soc. Interior Designers (profl., bd. dirs. 1984-85, Presdl. Citation, 1984). Avocations: glider pilot, tennis, ice skating, antique refinishing. Home: 2548 N 29th St Phoenix AZ 85008 Office: HNC Inc 7330 N 16 St #110 Phoenix AZ 85020

CUTLER, MARTHA MARIE EMERY, publishing executive; b. Lodi, Calif., Sept. 15, 1939; d. Wallace Haile and Elizabeth Dorothy Emery; m. David H. Cutler, Dec. 6, 1959; children—Geoffrey Horton, Gregory Abbott. B.A. in Elem. Edn., Calif. State U.-Los Angeles, 1965. Corp. v.p. Merchant Mag., Inc., Newport Beach, Calif., 1965—, also dir.; corp. v.p. Cutler Pub., Inc., Newport Beach, 1981—, also dir. Mem. Jr. League Newport Harbor, Talents, South Coast Orgn. of Planned Parenthood, Orange County Philharm. Soc., Spyglass Philharmonic. Recipient award for vol. hours given to Huntington Meml. Hosp., Huntington Meml. Clinic Aux., Pasadena, Calif., 1972. Republican. Episcopalian. Clubs: Newport Beach & Tennis, Seaview Swim and Tennis. Home: 2011 Yacht Vindex Newport Beach CA 92660 Office: 4500 Campus Dr Suite 480 Newport Beach CA 92660

CUTLER, RUTH ELLEN LEMON, publisher; b. York, Nebr., Feb. 26, 1928; d. Harry Oliver and Ruby Elizabeth (Hartgrave) Lemon; student Latter-day Saints Bus. Coll., 1946; m. Harold Max Cutler, Nov. 17, 1944 (div. 1971); children—Sheryl, Harold Max, Pamela. Sec., photostat operator IRS, Salt Lake City, 1951-54; sec. Purdue U. Sch. Civil Engring., West Lafayette, Ind. and engring. firms, 1954-60; exec. sec. Rico Argentine Mining Co., Salt Lake City and Rico, Colo., 1960-63; exec., legal sec. Manpower, Inc., Salt Lake City, 1959-71; owner, operator Mountain View Motel and Country Club Motel, Salt Lake City, 1963-64; exec. sec., adminstrv. asst. to clin. psychologist in pvt. practice, Salt Lake City, 1964-70; legal sec., head office staff Watkins & Faber, attys., Salt Lake City, 1971-73; adminstrv. sec. F-15 Radar div. Hughes Aircraft Co., El Segundo, Calif., 1973—; dir., v.p., sec. Cutler Enterprises, Inc., Salt Lake City, 1963-71; founder, pres., pub. Gallant House Inc., Heber City, Utah, 1983—. State del. Utah Republican party, 1967-69; active various community drives. Mem. League Utah Writers. Home: 8628 S 300 E Sandy UT 84070

CUTLER SHAW, JOYCE, artist, educator; b. Detroit, June 25, 1932; d. Joseph and Lola (Wienstien) C.; m. Jerome Shaw, Aug. 10, 1954; children: Michael, Steven, Rachel. BA, N.Y.U., 1953; MFA, U. Calif., San Diego, 1972; postgrad., Columbia U., 1954. Mem. faculty art dept. Palomar Coll., San Marcos, Calif., 1974-78; dir. Art and Artists Audio/Video Archive, San Diego, Calif., 1974—; vis. faculty art dept. San Diego State U., 1978-80; vis. faculty visual arts U. Calif., Irvine, 1979-80; founding dir., sec. Landmark Art Projects Inc., 1979-85; pres. Landmark Art Projects Inc. 1985-87. One-person shows include La Mamelle Gallery, San Francisco, 1977, Occidental Coll., Los Angeles, 1978, U. Mo., 1978, Apropos Gallery, Luzern, Switzerland, 1979, San Jose Inst. Contemporary Art, 1983, Mus. Natural History, San Diego, 1984-85, Herbert F. Johnson Mus. Art, Cornell U., Ithaca, N.Y., 1986, Nat. Acad. Scis., Washington, 1986, Performance Am. Mus. Natural History, N.Y.C., 1986; exhibited in group shows at Museo Carrillo Gil, Mex. City, 1980, Museu de Arte Contemporanea, Universidade de Sao Paulo, Brazil, 1980, Muestra Internacional de Arte Grafico, Bilbao, Spain, 1982, Pacific Design Ctr., Los Angeles, 1985, Clocktower, N.Y.C., 1986; prin. works include Unesco Patronage Survival Evolution Project, U.N., 1982. Founding mem. Pub. Art Adv. Council, San Diego County, 1976, chmn. 1978. Mem. Art Advt. Commn., Coll. Art Assn., Woman's Caucus for the Arts. Studio: 7969 Engineer Rd #211 San Diego CA 92111

CUTRELL, WAYNE ALLEN, government official; b. Greencastle, Ind., July 27, 1943; s. Myron Keneth and Florence (Wardlow) C.; m. Kathy Goldstein, May 16, 1978; children: Wayne Allen, William Andrew. Student, U. Ga., 1961-65; BBA cum laude, Southland U., 1985. Contract specialist EPA, Durham, N.C., 1969-75, HUD, Washington, 1975-77; mgr. contracts Dept. of Energy, New Orleans, 1977-84; dir. contracts GSA, Auburn, Wash., 1984—; mem. U.S. del. on contract mgmt. to People's Republic China, 1986. Served with USAF, 1966-69. Mem. Nat. Contract Mgmt. Assn. Home: PO Box 2004 Auburn WA 98071 Office: US GSA GAS CTR Auburn WA 98001

CUTRULES, ALEXANDER JAMES, history educator, writer, bibliophile; b. Sanford, Maine, Apr. 25, 1933; s. James Nicholas and Marika (Kalbouros) C. B.S., Boston U., 1959; M.A. in History, U. Ariz., 1960; postgrad. Columbia U. Tchr's Coll., U. London, Makerere U. Coll., 1961, U. Hawaii, 1968, Summer Inst. East Asian History and Current Affairs. Tchr. Govt. Secondary Sch., Mpwapwa, Tanganyika, 1961-64; research aide dept. history U. Ariz., Tucson, 1964-65; tchr. history and humanities Kofa High Sch., Yuma, Ariz., 1965—. Author: Alexander of Macedon, 1958. Contbr. hist. and archeol. letters and articles to profl. jours., Yuma Daily Sun, other newspapers, Mankind, Newsweek, Argosy, Greek Accent, Saturday Rev., Nat. Observer and other mags.; columnist Yuma Daily Sun, 1985—. Traveled to archeol. and hist. sites in more than 50 nations. Recipient Travel Essay prize Ellinismos Amerikis, 1957, Appreciation award Greek Embassy, Washington, 1985. Fellow Columbia U. Tchrs. Coll., 1961; U. Hawaii grantee, 1968. Mem. Soc. for Preservation of Greek Heritage, Archeol. Inst. Am., Bibl. Archeology Soc., L.S.B. Leakey Found., Ariz. Educ. Assn., NEA, Phi Delta Kappa. Hiked Hadrian's Wall, 1969, explored Nile from Lake Victoria to Cairo, 1964. Office: Kofa High School 3100 Ave A Yuma AZ 85664

CYR, ROB ROY, engineer; b. Parlier, Calif., Jan. 15, 1921; s. William Albion and Jean Lucille (Little) C.; m. Verna Florence Demichelli, Nov. 27, 1942; children: Rodney William, Stephen Michael. BSME, U. Calif., Berkeley, 1943. Registered profl. mech. engr., Calif. Pres., chief engr. Mirra-Cote Co., Inc., El Segundo, Calif., 1950-57; sales and applications engr. King Knight Co., San Francisco, 1957-61; v.p. engring. and quality control Kinney Vacuum Co., Boston, 1961-72; dir. engring. Scott Aviation, Lancaster, N.Y., 1972-81; chief scientist Scott Aviation, Monrovia, Calif., 1981-86; pvt. practice cons. Laguna Hills, Calif., 1986—. Contbr. articles to profl. jours. Cubmaster Torrance, Calif. council Boy Scouts Am., 1955-58, asst. scoutmaster Mill Valley, Calif. council, 1959-61. Mem. AAAS, Am. Vacuum Soc., Inst. Environ. Scis. Am. Indsl. Hygiene Assn., Internat. Soc. Respiratory Protection. Republican. Clubs: Via Verde Country (San Dimas, Calif.), Lancaster (N.Y.) Country. Avocations: golf, photography, woodwork. Home and Office: 2148C Ronda Granada Laguna Hills CA 92653

CZANDERNA, ALVIN WARREN, surface scientist; b. LaPorte, Ind., May 27, 1930; s. Walter Stanley and Alvina Wilhelmina (Koch) C.; m. Lucile Jean Delp, Feb. 14, 1953; children: Kathy K. Porak, Karel C. Shirkey, Kani L. BS with distinction in Metall. Engring., Purdue U., 1951, PhD, 1957. Jr. research metallurgist USAF, Dayton, Ohio, 1951-53; sr. research physicist Union Carbide, Parma, Ohio, 1957-63; research scientist Union Carbide, South Charleston, W.Va., 1963-65; cons. Union Carbide, South Charleston, 1969, 77; prof. physics Clarkson Coll., Potsdam, N.Y., 1965-78; research fellow Solar Energy Research Inst., Golden, Colo., 1978—; cons. Owens-Ill., Toledo, 1969, Los Alamos (N.Mex.) Sci. Lab., 1968-76, Lawrence Livermore (Calif.) Lab., 1977, Exxon, Baton Rouge, 1981, W.R. Grace, Columbia, Md., 1982-84; vis. scientist Fritz Haber Inst., West Berlin, Republic of Germany. Editor; patentee in field; contbr. articles to profl. jours. Mem. Lutheran Ch. Bd. for Higher Edn. Services, St. Louis, 1973-86, vice chmn., 1979-81, chmn., 1981-83. Served as staff sgt. USAF, 1951-53. Recipient Indsl. Research IR-100 award, 1977. Fellow Am. Phys. Soc., N.Y. Acad. Scis.; mem. Am. Chem. Soc. (exec. com 1975-77), Am. Vacuum Soc. (chmn. edn. com. 1979-81, bd. dirs. vacuum tech. div. 1980-81), Materials Research Soc., Catalysis Soc., Sigma Xi. Republican. Office: Solar Energy Research Inst 1617 Cole Blvd Golden CO 80401

CZUHA, MICHAEL, JR., instrument company executive, researcher; b. Peninsula, Ohio, July 20, 1922; s. Michael and Theresa (Sipos) C.; m. Dorothy Haburt, May 12, 1951. BS in Chemistry magna cum laude, Kent State U., 1944. Research chemist U. Akron, Ohio, 1946-53, A.O. Beckman Inc., South Pasadena, Calif., 1953-56, Consolidated Electronics, Pasadena, 1956-64; sr. research chemist Bell & Howell, Pasadena, 1959-64; prin. engr. Bell & Howell, Monrovia, Calif., 1964-70; sr. engr. E.I. Du Pont de Nemours & Co., Monrovia, 1970-80; prin. Bubble-O-Meter, La Verne, Calif., 1980—. Contbr. articles to profl. jours.; patentee in field. Mem. Am. Chem. Soc., Instrument Soc. Am. Mem. Eastern Orthodox Ch. Avocation: golf. Home: 6510 Wheeler Ave La Verne CA 91750 Office: Bubble-O-Meter PO Box 297 La Verne CA 91750

CZYZEWSKI, HARRY, metallurgical and mechanical engineer, consultant; b. Chgo., Feb. 13, 1918; s. Leon and Irene (Mierczynska) C.; m. Wilma E. Hood, Nov. 27, 1943; children: Sharon, Bettina, Marie. MSMetE, U. Ill., 1949. Registered profl. engr. Oreg., Alaska, Calif., Wash. Instr. war tng. program Bradley U., 1942-45; research metallurgist Caterpillar Tractor Co., 1941-46; asst. prof. phys. metallurgy research U. Ill., Urbana, 1947-51; pres. Metall. Engrs., Inc., Portland, Oreg., 1946-69, MEI-Charlton, Inc., Portland, 1969-83, Oreg. Tech. Services Ctr., Inc., Portland, 1965—; chmn. indsl. devel. com. Assoc. Oreg. Industries, 1965. Contbr. numerous articles to profl. jours.; patentee in field. Mem. Oreg. Gov.'s Manpower Coord. Com., 1968-71. Recipient Pres.'s Citation for extraordinary service Cons. Engrs. Council Oreg., 1979, 82, Alumni Honor award/Gallo medal U. Ill., 1979. Fellow Am. Inst. Chemists; mem. Am. Council Ind. Labs. (nat. pres. 1978-80, Outstanding Service award 1985), Am. Cons. Engrs. Council (pres. Oreg. chpt. 1960, Honor and award Engring. Excellence awards competition 1977), Am. Foundrymen's Soc. (pres. Oreg. chpt. 1955), Profl. Engrs. Oreg. (pres. 1959, Oreg. Engr. of Yr., 1972). Home: 1966 NW Ramsey Crest Portland OR 97229 Office: Oreg Tech Services Ctr Inc 2245 SW Canyon Rd Portland OR 97201

DAAMS, FREDERIC LUCAS, electronics engineer; b. N.Y.C., June 19, 1953; m. Rosa Luz Iraheta, Dec. 20, 1980. BS, Iowa State U., 1976. Sr. engr. Litton Industries, Van Nuys, Calif., 1977-80, prin. engr., 1981-82; sr. engr. Litton Industries, Woodland Hills, Calif., 1984-86; sr. mem. tech. staff Plantronics Systems Corp., Sepulveda, Calif., 1980; engr. Pay-Fone Systems Inc., West Los Angeles, 1982; sr. engr. Ocean Tech. Inc., Burbank, Calif., 1982-83; cons. Teledyne Systems Co., Northridge, Calif., 1986—. Fellow Inst. for Advancement Engring.; mem. IEEE (chmn. San Fernando Valley sect. 1980-81, Centennial medal 1985). Avocations: electronics, camping. Home: PO Box 4716 Panorama City CA 91412 Office: Teledyne Systems Co 19601 Nordhoff St Northridge CA 91324

DABBERDT, WALTER F., meteorologist; b. N.Y.C., Oct. 12, 1942; s. Richard J. and Marie Dabberdt; m. Meredith Mueller, Aug. 25, 1967; children: Jennifer, Geoffrey. BS, SUNY, Bronx, 1964; MS, U. Wis., 1966, PhD, 1969. Nat. Research Council fellow U.S. Army Labs., Natick, Mass., 1969-70; dir. meteorology program SRI Internat., Menlo Park, Calif., 1970-85; dir. boundary layer sensing group Nat. Ctr. for Atmospheric Research, Boulder, Colo., 1985—; instr. Foothill Coll., Los Altos, Calif., 1974-77; cons. EPA Adv. Bd., 1980—; mem. tech. adv. council Bay Area Air Quality Mgmt. Dist., 1980-85; mem. com. transp. and air quality Transp. Reseach Bd., Washington, 1974—. Author: Whole Air Weather Guide, 1976; Weather for Outdoorsmen, 1981; sci. editor: Weather in the West, 1975; editor: Atmospheric Dispersion of Hazardous/Toxic Materials for Transport Accidents, 1984; pub. Solstice Publs., Los Altos, 1976—; contbr. articles to profl. jours. Fellow Alexander von Humboldt Found., 1977-78. Mem. Am. Meteorol. Soc., Air Pollution Control Assn., Transp. Research Bd., Sigma Xi. Office: Nat Ctr for Atmospheric Research PO Box 3000 Boulder CO 80307

DABELL, RICHARD W., psychologist; b. Idaho Falls, Idaho, Nov. 11, 1951; s. Burdette and Dorothy (Williams) D.; m. Hoda Mahmoudi, June 21, 1975; 1 son, Bijan. B.S., U. Utah, 1974, M.S., 1978, Ph.D., 1979. Lic. psychologist, Utah, Calif. Psychologist, Salt Lake County Div. Mental Health, Salt Lake County, 1979-84, psychologist Utah div. rehab., 1981-84, Los Angeles County Dept. Mental Health, 1985—. Recipient Carnegie Hero Fund ednl. award, 1972. Mem. Am. Psychol. Assn., Utah Psychol. Assn., AAAS. Baha'i. Contbr. articles to profl. jours. Home: 960 19th St Apt C Santa Monica CA 90403

DABUL, BARBARA LOHMAN, speech pathologist; b. Evergreen Park, Ill., Oct. 5, 1942; d. Wilfred Goetzinger Lohman and Barbara (Murray) Seagreaves; 1 child, Amy. Student, Occidental Coll., 1960-61; BA, U. So. Calif., 1965, MA, 1967, PhD, 1970. Lic. speech pathologist, Calif. Asst. prof. speech pathology Calif. State U., Northridge, 1969-70; speech pathologist VA Outpatient Clinic, Los Angeles, 1970-76; assoc. prof. La Verne (Calif.) Coll., 1977-78; asst. dir. Am. Speech Lang. Hearing Assn. Clinic and Hosp. Programs, Rockville, Md., 1978-79; assoc. prof. Calif. State U., Los Angeles, 1979-80; chief speech sect. Sepulveda (Calif.) VA Hosp., 1980-83; speech pathologist Los Angeles County-U. So. Calif. Med. Ctr., 1983-85; dir. speech sect. San Gabriel Valley (Calif.) Med. Ctr., 1985—. Mem. bilingual adv. com. Fremont Sch., 1979-80, Dir.'s Council So. Calif. Mem. AAUW (v.p. program com. 1980), Am. Speech Lang. Hearing Assn. (cert., quality assurance com.), Calif. Speech Lang. Hearing Assn. (sec. 1982-84, commr. research, pubs. and documents 1986—), Calif. Assn. Bilingual Lang. Speech Specialist (treas. 1986), Mensa. Democrat. Congregationalist. Home: 315 E Broadway Apt 209 San Gabriel CA 91776 Office: San Gabriel Valley Med Ctr 218 S Santa Anita St San Gabriel CA 91776

DACH, JOHN RICHARD, food company executive, farmer; b. Long Beach, Calif., Dec. 18, 1945; s. Richard John and Lilas Elizabeth (Retzlaff) D.; 1 child, Elise Christine. AA, Long Beach City Coll., 1966; BS in Mktg., Long Beach State Coll., 1972. Tour dir. and office mgr. Novitiate Winery, Los Gatos, Calif., 1970-72; ptnr., corp. vineyard mgr. Dach Vineyards, Philo, Calif., 1972-83; ptnr., operator Bearcreek Winery, Los Gatos, 1971-74; mgr. Dach Ranch, Philo, 1976—; corp. officer Anderson Valley Beverage Corp./Grapple, Philo, 1985—; cons. Philo, 1978—; ptnr. Anderson Valley Agrl. Services, Philo, 1974-78. Served with USCG, 1967-73. Recipient Quartermaster award Explorer Scout div. Boy Scouts Am. Mem. Calif. Farm Bur., Calif. Cert. Organic Farmers (statewide rep. and cons. 1978—). Republican. Lodge: Lions. Avocations: diving, fishing, boating, swimming, handball.

DADESHO, SARGON OSHANA, physiologist; b. Habbanya, Bet-Nanrain, Iraq, Sept. 18, 1948; came to U.S., 1965; s. Oshana Shimon and Ester (Nimrod) D.; A.A., Modesto Jr. Coll., 1968; B.A., Calif. State U., 1970; M.S., U. Calif.-Davis, 1972; Ph.D. U. Calif.-Davis and Pacific Western U., 1978. Scientist, writer life Research Ctr., Modesto, Calif., 1976—; gen. mgr. Bio-Med. Electronics, Turlock, Calif., 1981—; pres. Assyrian Christian Coll., Ceres, Calif., 1980-81. Editor Bet-Nahrain, 1974—. Author: The Assyrian Nat. Question, 1984. Contbr. articles to profl. jours. Mass media dir. Radio Sta. KBES-TV, Bet Nahrain, Inc., 1974—; chmn. Assyrian Nat. Congress, Modesto, 1983. Modesto Jr. Coll. Internat. scholar, 1967; Bet-Nahrain Inc. Award of Merit, 1977. Mem. Christian Ch. Address: 3704 N Veneman Ave Modesto CA 95356

DADISMAN, LYNN ELLEN, financial services marketing executive, writer; b. Los Angeles, Mar. 1, 1946; d. Orlan Sidney and Erna Lou (Harris) Friedman; m. Kent Dadisman, May 1973 (div. 1974). Student UCLA, 1963-65, 71-72, Willis Bus. Coll., 1965-66, Fin. Schs. Am., 1982, Viewpoints Inst., 1970-71. Office mgr. Harleigh Sandler Co., Los Angeles, 1965-67; customer service Investors Diversified Services, West Los Angeles, Calif., 1968-76; exec. sec. McCulloch Oil Corp., West Los Angeles, 1976; mgr. publs. Security 1st Group, Century City, Calif., 1976-80; office mgr. Morehead & Co., Century City, 1980-81; dir. mktg., mgr. customer service Ins. Mktg. Services, Santa Monica, Calif., 1981-82; v.p. Decatur Petroleum Corp., Santa Monica, 1982-83; asst. v.p., broker services dir. Angeles Corp., Los Angeles, 1984—. Mem. Nat. Assn. Securities Dealers, Internat. Assn. Fin. Planning, Nat. Assn. Female Execs. Club: Migi Car Am. (pres., sec., newsletter editor) (Canoga Park, Calif.). Fin. and ins. writer; contbr. poetry to UCLA Literary Mag., 1964. Home: 3442 Centinela Ave Apt 15 Los Angeles CA 90066

DAE, DONNA, speech pathologist; b. Fresno, Calif., Sept. 8, 1943; s. Clarence Netzler and Myrl LaVern (Martin) Johnson; m. Gary Orr, Aug. 29, 1964 (div. Dec. 1980). BA, Calif. State U., Fresno, 1965; MA, San Francisco State U., 1973. Speech, lang. pathologist Santa Clara County (Calif.) Office Edn., San Jose, 1977-79, 80-82; compliance coordinator Santa Clara County (Calif.) Office Edn., 1979-80; research assoc. U. Santa Clara, San Jose, 1980-82; pvt. practice speech pathology Sacramento, 1982—; exec. dir. DAE Assn., Sacramento, 1984—. Chmn. Nat. Women's Polit. Caucus, Sacramento, 1984—; coordinator Cranston Re-election campaing, Sacramento, 1986; mem. Dem. State Cen. Com., 1984—. Mem. Am. Speech Lang. Hearing Assn. (cert.), Calif. Speech Lang. Hearing Assn., Council for Exceptional Children. Club: Truman (woman's campaign fund). Avocation: needlepoint. Home and Office: 7982 Cavalli Way Fair Oaks CA 95628

DAELEY, JON MICHAEL, airforce officer, electrical engineer; b. Seattle, June 30, 1961; s. Vernon LeRoy and Mary Lee (Moffitt) D.; m. Maurine Diane Gunn, Aug. 21, 1982; 1 child, Jenna Leigh. Student, U. Wash., 1980-81; BS in Chemistry, Western Wash. U., 1983; BSEE, U. N.Mex., 1986. Commd. 2d lt. USAF, Albuquerque, 1984—; advanced through grades to 1st lt. USAF, Loma Linda, Calif., 1986. Mem. Tau Beta Pi, Eta Kappa Nu. Republican. Avocations: golf, photography, hiking. Home: 25633 Coulston St Loma Linda CA 92354

DAGGETT, ROBERT SHERMAN, lawyer; b. La Crosse, Wis., Sept. 16, 1930; s. Willard Manning and Vida Naomi (Sherman) D.; m. Lee Sullivan Burton, Sept. 16, 1960; children: Ann Sherman, John Sullivan; m. Helen Ackerman, July 20, 1976. A.B. with honors in Polit. Sci. and Journalism, U. Calif.-Berkeley, 1952, J.D., 1955. Bar: Calif. 1955, U.S. Supreme Ct. 1967. Assoc. firm Brobec, Phleger & Harrison, San Francisco, 1958-66, ptnr., 1966—; counsel Calif. Senate Reapportionment Com., 1972-73; adj. prof. evidence and advocacy Hastings Coll. Law, 1982—; demonstrator-instr. Nat. Inst. for Trial Advocacy, 1981—, Hastings Ctr. for Trial and Appellate Advocacy, 1981—, mem. adv. bd., 1983—; vol. pro tem small claims judge San Francisco Mcpl. Ct., 1981—. Bd. editors: Calif. Law Rev., 1953-55; contbr. articles to profl. jours. Rep. Pacific Assn. AAU, 1973; bd. dirs. San Francisco Legal Aid Soc.; bd. visitors Coll. V U. Calif.-Santa Cruz. Served to 1st lt. JAGC U.S. Army, 1958-62. Walter Perry Johnson scholar, 1953. Mem. ABA, State Bar Calif. (chmn. local adminstrv. com. 1964-65), San Francisco Bar Assn. (past dir.), Am. Judicature Soc., Order of Golden Bear, Phi Delta Phi, Theta Xi. Republican. Club: Bohemian, Commonwealth, Commercial (San Francisco). Office: Brobeck Phleger & Harrison Spear St Tower One Market Plaza San Francisco CA 94105

DAGGETT, WILLIAM PATRICK, accountant; b. Carthage, Mo., June 19, 1943; s. Sherwood Homer and Roberta Louise (Prunty) D.; m. Susan Helene Burke, Sept. 4, 1965; children—Christine Nicole, Patrick Tomas. B.S., Ariz. State U., 1972; A.A., Glendale Community Coll., 1971. C.P.A., Ariz. Acct., Seely Mullins & Assocs., Glendale, Ariz., 1970-82; pvt. practice acctg., Sun City, Ariz., 1982—; pres. Ariz. C.P.A. Found. for Edn. and Research, Tempe, 1981-82, bd. dirs., 1981—. Instr. project bus. Jr. Achievement, Phoenix, 1983; instr. CPR, ARC Sun City, 1982-84; mem. coop. edn. com. Deer Valley High Sch., Glendale, 1983-84. Served with USAF, 1962-70. Mem. Am. Inst. C.P.A.s, Ariz. Soc. C.P.A.s (Outstanding com. chmn. 1980-81). Democrat. Roman Catholic. Lodge: Sun City del Sol Rotary (pres. 1979-80). Home: 7602 W Villa Rita Peoria AZ 85345

DAGLE, GERALD EUGENE, veterinary pathologist; b. Seattle, July 12, 1939; s. Tillman T. and Ruby (Smoke) D.;m. Margaret Kathleen Ellingson, Sept. 16, 1961; children: Laura, Jeffery, Robert. DVM, Wash. State U., 1963; PhD, Colo. State U., 1973. Research fellow Merck, West Point, Pa., 1965-69; staff pathologist Battelle, Richland, Wash., 1973—; scientist Nat. Cancer Inst., 1973-76, Dept. Energy, 1975—; lectr. Joint Ctr. Grad. Study, Richland, 1973—, Whitman Coll., Walla Walla, Wash., 1980-84. Served to capt. USAR, 1963-65. Mem. AVMA, Am. Coll. Vet. Pathologists (diplomate), Internat. Acad. Pathology, AAAS, Sigma Xi. Republican. Lutheran. Home: 2426 Harris Ave Richland WA 99352

DAHL, GARDAR GODFREY, JR., geologist, coal company executive; b. Hood River, Oreg., May 27, 1946; s. Gardar Godfrey Sr. and Margaret Jean (North) D.; m. Eva Lorraine Skolmen, Nov. 10, 1973. BS in Geol. Engring., Mont. Coll. Mineral Sci. and Tech., 1969, MS in Geol. Engring., 1971. Registered profl. geologist. Asst. geologist Burlington No., St. Paul, 1971-72; mining geologist Burlington No., Seattle, Wash. and Billings, Mont., 1972-75; mgr. coal exploration and devel. Burlington No., Billings, 1975-79; dir. resource devel. Peabody Coal Co., Flagstaff, Ariz., 1979-81; chief geologist Cyprus Coal Co., Englewood, Colo., 1981-85, mgr. geology, 1985—. Mem. AIME, Internat. Assn. Math. Geology, AAAS, Rocky Mountain Coal Inst., Am. Assn. Profl. Geologists. Lutheran. Home: 6432 E Mineral Pl Englewood CO 80112 Office: Cypress Coal Co 7200 S Alton Way Englewood CO 80112

DAHL, LOREN SILVESTER, judge; b. East Fairview, N.D., Mar. 1, 1921; s. William T. and Maude (Silvester) D.; m. Luana Siler, Apr. 5, 1942 (dec.); children: Candy Dahl Hanson, Walter Ray.; m. Mary Anne Bristow, Jan. 20, 1979. AA, Coll. of Pacific, 1940; LLB, JD, U. Calif., San Francisco, 1949. Bar: Calif., 1950, U.S. Supreme Ct., 1957; lic. instrument pilot and aerial navigator. Sole practice Sacramento, 1950; sr. ptnr. Dahl, Hefner, Stark & Marois, Sacramento, 1950-80; judge U.S. Bankruptcy Ct. (ea. dist.) Calif., Sacramento, 1980—. Pres. Golden Empire Council Boy Scouts Am., Sacramento, 1955-56, chmn. bd. trustees, 1956, exec. com. region 12, 1958, regional chmn. 1968-70, nat. exec. bd. 1968-70; Sacramento County Juvenile Justice Commn.; bd. dirs. Salvation Army, Sacramento, 1954-57; Sacramento Symphony Assn., 1958-59, Sacramento Safety Council. Served with USAAF, 1942-46. Recipient Disting. Service award Jaycees, 1957, Silver Beaver award, Boy Scouts Am., 1957, Silver Antelope award, Boy Scouts Am., 1963, Disting. Eagle Scout award, Boy Scouts Am. Mem. Univ. of Pacific Alumni Assn. (pres., bd. regents, Disting. Alumnus award 1963), ABA, Calif. Bar Assn. (lectr. bankruptcy, continuing edn.), Am. Judicature Soc., Phi Delta Phi. Club: Del Paso Country. Lodge: Masons, Shriners, Lions (dir. Sacramento club 1952-53). Home: 842 Lake Oak Ct Sacramento CA 95864 Office: US Bankruptcy Ct 650 Capitol Mall Sacramento CA 95814

DAHL, RANDY LYNN, engineer, consultant; b. Devils Lake, N.D., Aug. 30, 1957; s. Duane Edward and Louise Mary (Cash) D. BS, N.D. State U., 1981, MS, 1983. Systems engr. Motorola, Scottsdale, Ariz., 1981—; project engr. Am. Crystal Sugar Research Ctr., Moorhead, Minn., 1982-83; cons. Scottsdale, 1984—. Patentee in field. Mem. IEEE, Soc. Photo-optical Instrumentation Engrs. Avocations: skiing, hunting, fishing, hiking, competition shooting. Office: Motorola GEG 8220 E Roosevelt Scottsdale AZ 85222

DAHL, VICTOR CHARLES, history educator; b. Dickinson, N.D., Dec. 11, 1928; s. Charles Hans and Nora E. (Joubert) D.; m. Beryl Alice Brechbill, Feb. 20, 1954; children: Victor Charles Jr., Camilla Bernice, Antonia Elizabeth, Marcella Rosalia. BA in History, U. Mont., 1950, MA in Polit. Sci., 1951; PhD in History, U. Calif., Berkeley, 1959. Clk. No. Pacific Ry., Missoula, Mont., 1951-52, 54-55; mem. faculty Portland (Oreg.) State U., 1959—, prof. history, 1974—, asst. dean grad. studies, 1980—, dir. internat. programs, 1985—. Contbr. articles to profl. jours. Served to lt. USAF, 1952-54. Am. Council Edn. fellow, 1967-68; recipient sr. lectureship Fulbright Commn., 1982-83. Mem. Pacific Coast Council Latin Am. Studies (pres. 1982-83), Western Slavic Assn., Portland Com. Fgn. Relations. Democrat. Roman Catholic. Avocation: antique automobile restoration. Home: 15136 SW Glen Eagles Ct Lake Oswego OR 97034 Office: Portland State U PO Box 751 Portland OR 97207

DAHLE, JOHN LEE, consulting engineer; b. Titusville, Pa., Dec. 30, 1949; s. Wayne John and June Rose (Penick) D.; m. Helyn Margeret Horne, Aug.

27, 1970; children: Jeneane, David. BS in Aerospace Engring., U. Pitts., 1971, postgrad in Mech. Engring., 1971-75. Mech. engr. U.S. Bur. of Mines, Pitts., 1971-75, supr. mech. engr., 1975-78; dir. Mining Equipment Safety Lab., Triadelphia, W.Va., 1978-80; sr. program mgr. Woodward Assocs., Inc., San Diego, 1980-82, v.p., 1982-86; pres. JDA Sci. Enterprises, San Diego, 1986—; cons. Can. Standards Org., Montreal, Queb., 1981-86. Contbr. numerous articles to profl. jours.; patentee in field. Recipient Outstanding Achievement award U.S. Dept. Interiors, 1972, 1974, U.S. Dept. Labor, 1976. Mem. Soc. Automotive Engrs., Human Factors Soc., Nat. Forensic Ctr. Club: Southwestern Yacht. Avocations: racing sailboats, windsurfing. Home: 13779 Via Tres Vistas San Diego CA 92129 Office: JDA Sci Enterprises 16496 Bernardo Ctr Dr San Diego CA 92128

DAHLEN, ALICE LOUISE, hospital administrator; b. Kenmare, N.D., Nov. 22, 1934; d. Gudmund Bernhard and Alice Marie (Gissel) Rundstrom; student Augsburg Coll., 1952-53; diploma in nursing Emanuel Hosp. Sch. Nursing, 1956; B.S. in Nursing, U. Oreg. Health Scis. Center, 1969, M.S. in Nursing Edn., 1971; Ph.D. in Health Services Adminstrn., Columbia Pacific U.; m. Charles Raymond Dahlen, Mar. 16, 1957; children—Kirsten Ann, Lisa Elaine. Sch. nurse Hillcrest Sch. for Girls, 1957-58; nursing home adminstr. Salem (Oreg.) Methodist Home, 1963-64, Willamette Lutheran Home, Salem, 1966-67; asst. dir. nursing service Emanuel Hosp., Portland, 1970-73; dir. nursing service, asst. adminstr. Meridian Park Hosp., Tualatin, Oreg., 1973-84; v.p. patient services St. Joseph's Hosp. and Health Ctr., Tucson, 1984—; mem. clin. faculty U. Oreg. Health Scis. Center, 1974-84; clin. prof. U. Ariz. Coll. Nursing, 1986—. Mem. Oreg. League Nursing (pres. 1980-82), Nat. League Nursing (bd. dirs., exec. com. 1983—), Am., Oreg. (past pres. dist. 1) nurses assns., Am. Soc. for Hosp. Nursing Service Adminstrs. (bd. dirs. 1979-81, bd. rev. 1983-84), Portland Council Dirs. Nursing Service and Edn. (chmn. 1976), Oreg. Soc. Nursing Adminstrs. (chmn. 1977, pres. 1978), Am. Coll. Healthcare Execs., Sigma Theta Tau. Republican. Lutheran. Home: 4269 N Vereda Rosada Tucson AZ 85746 Office: 350 N Wilmot Rd Tucson AZ 85711

DAHLQUIST, JOHN PAUL, economics educator; b. Oakland, Calif., Jan. 1, 1939; s. Paul Theodore and Margaret Ann (Ekroot) D. BS in Bus., San Jose State U., 1965, MA in Econs., 1974. Systems analyst Gen. Electric, San Jose, 1965-69; instr. econs. Peralta Community Coll. Dist., Oakland and Alameda, Calif., 1971—. Author, narrator: (films) A Demand Schedule for Wumpets, 1980, A Supply Schedule for Wumpets, 1981. Bd. dirs. San Jose Community Concerts Assn., 1967-70. Mem. Balalaika and Domra Assn. Am. (contbr. revs. to newsletter 1979-82), Joaquin Miller Heights Homeowners Assn. (bd. dirs. 1985-86). Democrat. Avocations: music, hiking, catamaran sailing, wine collecting. Office: Coll Alameda 555 Atlantic Ave Alameda CA 94501

DAHLSTEN, DONALD LEE, enviromental biology, forest entomology educator; b. Clay Center, Nebr., Dec. 8, 1933; s. Leonard Harold and Shirley B. (Courtright) D.; m. Reva D. Wilson, Sept. 19, 1959 (div.); children: Dia Lee, Andrea; m. Janet Clair Winner, Aug. 7, 1965; stepchildren: Karen Rae, Michael Allen. BS, U. Calif., Davis, 1956, MS, U. Calif., Berkeley, 1960, PhD, 1963. Asst. prof. Los Angeles State Coll., 1962-63; asst. entomologist U. Calif., Berkeley, 1963-65, lectr., 1965-68, asst. prof., 1968-69, assoc. prof., 1969-74, prof. entomology, 1969—, also chmn. div. Biol. Control, 1980—; vis. prof. Yale Sch. Forestry and Environ. Studies, 1980-81, Integrated Pest Mgmt. Team People's Republic China, 1980. Mem. AAAS, Am. Inst. Biol. Scis. (vis. prof., lectr. 1970-71), Entomol. Soc. Am., Entomol. Soc. Can., Soc. Am. Foresters. Office: U Calif Div Biol. Control Berkeley CA 94720

DAHLSTROM, DONALD ALBERT, chemical and metallurgical engineering educator, former equipment manufacturing company executive; b. Mpls., Jan. 16, 1920; s. Raymond Estin and Dora Adina (Bloomgren) D.; m. Betty Cordelia Robertson, Dec. 4, 1942; children: Mary Elizabeth, Donald Raymond, Christine Dora, Stephanie Lou, Michael Jeffrey. Student, Macalester Coll., 1937-39; B.S. in Chem. Engring, U. Minn., 1942; Ph.D., Northwestern U., 1949. Petroleum engr. Internat. Petroleum Co., Ltd., Negritos, Peru, 1942-45; from instr. to asso. prof. chem. engring. Northwestern U., 1946-56; with Eimco Corp., Palatine, Ill., 1952-69; v.p., dir. research and devel. Eimco Corp., 1960-80, also dir.; v.p. research and devel. Envirotech Corp., Salt Lake City, 1969-84; v.p., dir. Erco-Environtech, 1974-84; sr. v.p. research and devel. Eimco Process Equipment Co., 1981-84; research prof. chem., metall. and fuels engring. U. Utah, Salt Lake City, 1984—; dir. Process Engrs., Inc.; Am. mem. internat. sci. com. 6th Internat. Mineral Processing Congress, 1963; mem. adv. council on engring. NSF. Contbr. to handbooks. Mem. State Air Conservation Com. State Utah, 1971-78, vice chmn., 1977-78, Mem. sch. bd. dist. 110, Deerfield, Ill., 1959-61; pres. Riverwoods Residents Assn., 1962-63; chmn. bd. Northwestern YMCA, 1950-52; trustee Village of Riverwoods, 1966-69. Served with USNR, 1945-46. Recipient Merit award Northwestern U., 1965. Mem. Am. Inst. Chem. Engrs. (dir. 1960-62, v.p. 1963, pres. 1964-65, chmn. environ. div. 1971, Founders award 1972, Environ. award 1977, One of 30 Emminent Chem. Engrs at 75th anniversary), AIME (disting. mem., hon. mem., chmn. minerals benefication div. 1963-64, bd. dirs. soc. mining engrs. 1965-67, pres. soc. mining engrs. 1974-75, dir. 1973-76, Rossiter W. Raymond award 1952, Richards award 1976, Krumb lectr. 1980, Taggart award 1983), Am. Chem. Soc. (hon.), Nat. Acad. Engring., The Filtration Soc. (London), Mining and Metall. Soc. Am. (dir. Engrs. Council Profl. Devel.), Am. Soc. Engring. Edn., Nat. Acad. Engrs., Sigma Xi (Holgate award Northwestern U. chpt. 1949), Phi Lambda Upsilon, Tau Beta Pi (nat. pres. 1958-62). Presbyterian. Home: 5340 Cottonwood Ln Salt Lake City UT 84117 Office: Chem Engineering Dept Univ of Utah Salt Lake City UT 84112

DAHLSTROM, JOHN ALEXANDER, banker, lawyer; b. Ogden, Utah, Dec. 11, 1934; s. Nephi Harold and Marjorie (Brewer) D.; m. Marylin Hatch; children—Elizabeth Anne Dahlstrom Cook, John Alexander Jr., Kathryn Alison Wadsworth, James Derek, Amy Alexandra. B.S. in Acctg., U. Utah, 1956; J.D., George Washington U., 1960. Bar: Utah, 1960, U.S. Tax Ct. 1961, U.S. Ct. Claims 1961, U.S. Ct. Customs and Patent Appeals 1960, U.S. Supreme Ct. 1968. Tax lawyer IRS, Washington, 1958-61; auditor GAO, Washington, 1956-58; assoc. Ray Quinney & Nebeker, Salt Lake City, 1961-65; ptnr. Parsons Behle & Latimer, Salt Lake City, 1965-85; chmn. bd., dir. Tracy-Collins Bank and Trust Co., Salt Lake City, Tracy Bancorp, Salt Lake City; bd. dirs. Utah Hotel Co.; Salt Lake br. Fed. Res. Bank San Francisco. Chmn. Fed. Jud. Selection Com., 1978; chmn. instl. council U. Utah, Salt Lake City, 1979—; Bd. dirs. Eyring Research Inst., Served to capt. JAGC, U.S. Army, 1956-66. Mem. ABA (tax sect. 1961—), Utah State Bar Assn. (chmn. tax sect. 1966), Salt Lake County Bar Assn., Salt Lake Area C. of C. (chmn., bd. govs. 1984-85). Mormon. Clubs: Salt Lake Country, Alta, Pacific (Honolulu), Bear River.

DAHY, EDWARD JOHN, education specialist; b. Los Angeles, June 21, 1930; s. Edward John Jr. and June Claudia (Thompson) D.; m. Nancy Ann Pall, Sept. 24, 1952; children: Edward John, James Patrick, Mary Elizabeth, Paul Christopher. AB, Gonzaga U., 1952; MA, Mont. State U., Missoula, 1957; EdD, Mont. State U., Bozeman, 1977. Tchr., Absarokee, Belt, Mont., 1955-57; Served with USMC, 1952-54, 57-71; advanced through grades to lt. col., 1970; supr. student tchrs. Coll. Gt. Falls, Mont., 1971-72; prin., Centerville, Mont., 1973-77; Navy edn. specialist State of Mont., Butte, 1977—. Decorated Bronze Star with V, others; recipient Edn. Specialist of Yr. award, 1982, 83, cert. of commendation, 1983, 84, 85, 86. Mem. NEA, Am. Assn. for Counseling and Devel., Am. Vocat. Assn., Mil. Educators and Counselors Assn., Marine Corps Assn., Phi Delta Kappa. Roman Catholic. Home: 104 Star Ln Butte MT 59701 Office: NRPS Butte Finlen Complex 100 E Broadway Butte MT 59701

DAIGNAULT, DAVID WILLIAM, insurance company executive; b. Spencerport, N.Y., Oct. 25, 1939; s. Louis Joseph and Marian Agnes (VanGeison) D.; m. Lynn Grace Crossan, Nov. 11, 1961; children: Chari Lynn, Melanie Danielle, Jacqulyn, Leigha Rene. BA, Alfred U., 1961; MS in System Mgmt., U. So. Calif., 1976. Commd. 2d lt. U.S. Army, 1961, advanced through grades to lt. col., 1978, ret., 1983; mng. dir. ERA Magnum Properties, Aiea, Hawaii, 1983-84; ops. mgr. T.I. of Hawaii Inc., Honolulu, 1984-86, exec. v.p., 1986; pres. Communicative Pubs., Inc., 1986—; bd. dirs. ERA Beacan, Pearl City, Hawaii, 1985—; pres. bd. dirs. Hawaii Philharm., Honolulu, 1985—; market mgmt. coll. instr. Mem. Kaneohe (Hawaii) Neighborhood Bd., 1985—, chmn. 1986-87; mem. Small Bus. Hawaii Polit. Action Com., Honolulu, 1985-86. Decorated Bronze Star, Legion of Merit. Mem. Yacht Club Terrace Owner's Assn. (pres. 1984-87). Republican. Lodge: Rotary. Avocations: golf, jogging, aerobics. Office: TI of Hawaii Inc 1001 Bishop Suite 700 Honolulu HI 96813

DAILEDA, DAVID ALLEN, architect; b. Phoenix, Jan. 19, 1949; s. Dominic Jacob and Mary Julia (Pavidus) D.; m. Cynthia Ann Strembel, Aug. 23, 1972 (div.); children—Ryan, Christopher. B. Arch., U. Ariz., 1971; postgrad., Ariz. State U., 1976-77. Registered architect, Nev., Ariz., Calif., Tex., Utah, Colo., Mont., Wyo. Draftsman Haver, Nunn & Nelson, Phoenix, 1971-72; design draftsman Stimmel-VonFange Architects, Phoenix, 1972-77, Devenney & Stahm Architects, Phoenix, 1977-78; designer Zick & Sharp Architects, Las Vegas, Nev., 1978-81; assoc. architect Harris Sharp Assocs., Las Vegas, 1981-83, pres., 1983-86; v.p. CHD Architects, Denver, Cody, Wyo.; ptnr. Design Group, Cody, Wyo., 1984, CHD Architects Cody and Denver, 1986-87; v.p. mktg. Mariani & Assoc., Washington, 1986—. Chmn. combined bd. bldg. appeals Clark County, Nev., 1982-86; mem. residential design exam. rev. jury Nev. State Bd. Architects, 1981-83; big bro. Valley Big Bros., Phoenix, 1972-78. Max C. Fleishmann Found. scholar, 1966-67. Mem. AIA (pres. Las Vegas chpt. 1981, sec. West Mountain region 1982-83, nat. bd. dirs. 1985-87), Nev. Soc. Architects (pres. 1984). Lodge: Rotary.

DAILEY, DAVID ARTHUR, risk control specialist; b. South Bend, Ind., Dec. 12, 1953; s. Arthur W. Dailey and Margaret (Bruggner) Carberry; m. Deborah S. Baker, Sept. 1, 1979; 1 child, Anessa Virginia. AB, Ind. U., 1976, MS, 1978; cert., Ins. Sch. Chgo., 1979. Cert. Safety Profl. Am. Bd. Safety Profls. Shift mgr. Am. Diversifies Foods Co., Bloomington, Ind., 1974-78; risk improvememt rep. Arthur J. Gallagher & Co., Rolling Meadows, Ill., 1979-80; loss prevention cons. Gallagher-Bassett Services, Sacramento, 1980-84; safety cons. Beaver Ins. Co., San Francisco, 1984; loss control cons. SWS, Inc., Bremerton, Wash., 1984-85; hazard control engr. Lockheed Missiles and Space Co., Sunnyvale, Calif., 1985—. Contbr. articles to profl. jours. Counselor San Francisco Suicide Prevention Program, 1981-82. Mem. Nat. Mgmt. Assn., Nat. Safety Mgmt. Soc. (state dir. pub. affairs 1983-85, dir. edn., 1981-83, sec. Golden Gate chpt. 1982), Am. Soc. Safety Engrs. (assembly del., chmn. pub. relations com. 1985-87, treas. 1987-88, editor region I newsletter). Mem. Ch. Nichiren Soka Gakkai of Am. Club: Toastmasters (Sunnyvale) (sgt. at arms 1986—). Avocations: sports, travel, music, culinary arts, yoga. Office: Lockheed Missiles & Space Co 0/47-20 B/102 1111 Lockheed Way Sunnyvale CA 94088-3504

DAILEY, FRED WILLIAM, hotel exec.; b. Aurora, Ill., Feb. 3, 1908; s. Louis A. and Frances (McCoy) D.; m. Elizabeth Murphy, Apr. 22, 1946; children—Michael K., Pam Sue Hinman. Builder, operator tourist resorts, 1933-42; builder, So. Calif., 1946-52; pres. Mokuleia Assos., Mokuleia Polo Farms, Inc., Waikiki Corp., A.D. Corp. Adv. bd. Hawaii, Army; past mem. Honolulu Bd. Water Supply. Served as maj. AUS, World War II. Decorated Purple Heart. Mem. U.S. Air Force Assn., C. of C., Am. Hotel Assn. (past dir.), Hawaii Hotel Assn. (past pres.), Hawaii Horse Show Assn. (past pres.), Hawaii Polo and Racing Assn. (pres.), U.S. Polo Assn. (gov.). Clubs: Los Angeles Athletic; Hawaii Polo (Honolulu); Santa Barbara Polo; Big Bend Ranch (pres.) (Korbel). Author: Blood, Sweat and Jeers; One Man's Meat, Polo Is A Four Letter Word. Address: Waikikian Hotel Honolulu HI 96815 Address: Mokuleia Polo Farm Inc Gahu HI 96815

DAILEY, JACOB EDWARD, school superintendent; b. Danville, Pa., July 23, 1927; s. Jacob Lawrence and Minnie Mildred (Young) D.; m. Rose Katharine McKean, Aug. 16, 1947; children—Suzanne Marie, Jacob Edward. B.S., Bloomsburg State Coll., 1952; M.Ed., Temple U., 1956, Ed.D., 1968. Tchr. Central Bucks High Sch., Doylestown, Pa., 1952-53; prin., tchr. Doylestown Twp. Schs., 1953-56; prin., supr. Exeter Twp. Schs., Reading, Pa., 1956-61; supt. schs. Pottsgrove Schs., Pa., 1961-72, Bristol Twp., Levittown, Pa., 1972-76, No. Syracuse, N.Y., 1976-79, Natrona County Sch. Dist., Casper, Wyo., 1979—. Served with USNR, 1945-46. Pres. Daniel Boone Nat. Found., 1970-74, mem. Phila. Suburban Study Council, 1969. Mem. Am. Assn. Sch. Adminstrs., Phi Delta Kappa. Home: 2460 Allyson Pl Casper WY 82604 Office: Natrona County Sch Dist Office of Sch Supt 970 N Glenn Rd Casper WY 82601 *

DAILY, JAMES WALLACE, engineering educator, consultant; b. Columbia, Mo., Mar. 19, 1913; s. Wallace Edgar and Marjory Isabel (McGrath) D.; m. Sarah Vanderlip Atwood, Sept. 10, 1938; children: John Wallace, Sarah Anne Vanderlip (Mrs. Charles Rosenberg). A.B., Stanford U., 1935; M.S., Calif. Inst. Tech., 1937, Ph.D., 1945. Registered profl. engr. Test engr. Byron Jackson Co., Berkeley, Calif., 1935; research asst. hydraulics Calif. Inst. Tech., 1936-37, research fellow, mgr. hydraulic machinery lab., 1937-40, instr. mech. engring., 1940-46; hydraulic engr. OSRD, Navy Research Projects, 1941-46; asst. prof. hydraulics M.I.T., 1946-49, asso. prof., 1949-55, prof., 1955-64; prof. engring. mechanics, chmn. dept. U. Mich., 1964-72, prof. fluid mechanics and hydraulic engring., 1972-81, prof. emeritus, 1981—; vis. prof. Tech. U. of Delft, Netherlands, 1971; vis. scientist Electricite de France Centre de Recherches et d'Essais, Paris, 1971; mem. U.S. del. water resources specialists to, People's Republic of China, 1974; vis. prof. East China Coll. Hydraulic Engring., Nanking, 1979; domestic and internat. cons. various firms. Author: (with D.R.F. Harleman) Fluid Dynamics, (with R.T. Knapp and F.G. Hammitt) Cavitation; Contbr. tech. articles Am., fgn. jours. Mem. sch. com. Town of Arlington, Mass., 1959-65. Recipient Naval Ordnance Devel. award, 1945. Mem. Nat. Acad. Engring., Internat. Assn. Hydraulic Research (hon. mem., pres. 1967-71, mem. Council 1963-65, 71-77), ASCE (Rouse lectr. 1985), ASME (hon.), Japan Soc. C.E. (hon.), Sigma Xi, Tau Beta Pi, Chi Epsilon. Congregationalist. Clubs: Athenaeum (Pasadena), Cosmos (Washington). Home: 2968 San Pasqual St Pasadena CA 91107

DAILY, PAUL JAMES, retired air force officer, laser electro-optics educator; b. Winchester, Idaho, Aug. 16, 1928; s. Garland Gale and Anna Bell (Graham) D.; m. Jean Elton Dammarell, Aug. 28, 1949; children—Mark Elton, Michael James. B.S. in Edn., U. Idaho, 1950, M.S., 1952; postgrad. U. Utah, 1961-63; grad. Air War Coll., 1974. Commd. 2d lt. U.S. Air Force, 1950, advanced through grades to col., 1973; teaching fellow in physics U. Idaho, Moscow, 1950-52; pilot SAC, Biggs AFB, Tex., 1953-57; computer analyst, Kirtland AFB, N.Mex., 1957-61, project scientist, 1963-66; research and devel. dir., Air Force Office Sci. Research, Air Force Rocket Propulsion Lab, Air Force Weapons Lab., 1967-78; ret., 1978; instr. laser optics Albuquerque Tech. Vocat. Inst., 1981—; mem PEN-X com. Def. Advanced Research Projects Agy., Washington, 1964-65. Vice pres. Springfield Art Guild, Va., 1972-73. Decorated Air Force Commendation medal, Meritorious Service medal with oak leaf cluster, Legion of Merit. Mem. Arnold Air soc., Planetary Soc., Sigma Pi Sigma, Tau Kappa Epsilon. Home: 12904 Hugh Graham Rd NE Albuquerque NM 87111

DAILY, WILLIAM DEAN, research physicist; b. Dallas, Oct. 5, 1943; s. William Dean and Dollie Virginia (Hudson) D.; m. Kathleen Bosworth, Aug. 21, 1967; children: William, Daxton, Jared, Devany, Drue, Jesse. BS, Brigham Young U., 1967, PhD, 1971. Research assoc. NSF, Moffett Field, Calif., 1971-72; research asst. Eyring Research Inst., Provo, Utah, 1972-80; physicist Lawrence Livermore (Calif.) Lab., 1980—; cons. Geotomographics, Alamo, Calif., 1983—. Contbr. articles to profl. jours.; patentee in field. Cubmaster Boy Scouts Am., Sunnyvale, Calif., 1977-80, scoutmaster, Livermore, 1981—. Mem. Am. Geophys. Union. Avocation: mountaineering. Home: 2671 Waverly Way Livermore CA 94550 Office: Lawrence Livermore Nat Lab Livermore CA 94550

DAJANI, JARIR SUBHI, civil engineer; b. Jerusalem, Apr. 5, 1940; s. Subhi T. and Lisa (Stori) D.; came to U.S., 1965, naturalized, 1974; B. Engring., Am. U. of Beirut, 1961; M.S., Stanford U., 1966; Ph.D. in Urban Systems Engring., Northwestern U., 1971; m. Rihab Dajani, Aug. 23, 1965; children—Jumana, Subhi, Dina. Asst. resident engr. Riyadh and Al-Khobar, Asso. Cons. Engrs., Saudi Arabia, 1961-62, resident engr., 1962-63, mgr. br. office, Amman, Jordan, 1963-65; estimator Bechtel Corp., San Francisco, 1966; project engr. Asso. Cons. Engring., Beirut, Lebanon, 1966-67; instr. Construction Engring. Center, Jerusalem, 1967-68; constrn. mgmt. and bldg. constrn. Vocat. Tng. Center, Jerusalem, 1967-68; research asst. Northwestern U., Evanston, Ill., 1968-71; part-time asso. transp. and community planning, DeLeuw, Cather & Co., Chgo., 1968-71; asst. prof. civil engring. Duke U., Durham, N.C., 1971-75, asst. prof. civil engring. and policy scis., 1974-75, asso. prof. civil engring. and policy scis., 1975-76; asso. prof. civil engring., chmn. urban studies com. Stanford (Calif.) U., 1976-82; sr. tech. adv. Abu Dhabi Fund for Econ. Devel., 1982—; cons. to AID, 1978—, EPA, 1978—, FAA, 1976-77, IBRD (World Bank), 1979—; v.p. Public Systems Assos., Inc., Durham, 1974-78; mem. Transp. System Planning Group, Transp. Research Bd., NRC, 1971-76. Mem. ASCE, Am. Soc. Pub. Adminstrn., Ops. Research Soc. Am., Regional Sci. Assn., Am. Planning Assn., Sigma Xi. Author: (with Dennis Warner) Water and Sewer Development in Rural America, 1975; contbr. articles on urban systems engring. and planning to profl. jours.; asso. editor Jour. of High Speed Ground Transportation, 1977—; editorial bd. Policy Analysis and Information Systems, 1977—. Home: 1565 Klamath Dr Sunnyvale CA 94087 Office: PO Box 814, Abu Dhabi United Arab Emirates

DALE, DAVID C., medical educator, physician; b. Knoxville, Tenn., Sept. 19, 1940; s. John Irvin and Cecil (Chandler) D.; m. Rose Marie Wilson, June 22, 1963. B.S. magna cum laude, Carson-Newman Coll., 1962; M.D. cum laude, Harvard U., 1966. Intern and resident Mass. Gen. Hosp., 1966-68; resident U. Wash. Hosp., Seattle, 1971-72; clin. assoc. NIH, 1968-71; prof., assoc. chmn. dept. medicine U. Wash., Seattle, 1976-82, dean Sch. of Medicine, 1982-86. Contbr. numerous articles to profl. jours. Served to comdr. USPHS, 1968-70, 72-74. Mem. Am. Soc. Hemetology, Assn. Am. Physicians, Am. Soc. for Clin. Investigation, ACP. Avocations: woodworking; gardening; backpacking; sports. Office: U Wash Sch of Medicine RG-22 Seattle WA 98195

DALE, DENVER THOMAS, III, retired marine officer, educator; b. Santa Barbara, Calif., July 30, 1931; s. Denver Thomas Jr. and Ethel Helen (Squire) D.; m. Elizabeth Ann Donleavy, Nov. 17, 1956 (div. Oct. 1978); children: Denver Thomas IV, Matthew J., Jeffrey N.; m. Peggy Frances Altice, Nov. 19, 1982. Student Va. Mil. Inst., 1948-52; BA, San Francisco State U., 1959; MS, Cen. Conn. State U., 1969. Cert. secondary educator, Calif. Enlisted USMC, 1952, advanced through grades to lt. col., 1975; comdg. officer Co. K., 3d Bn., 4th Marine Regt., Kaneohe Bay, Hawaii, 1961-64; manpower mgmt. officer 1st Marine Aircraft Wing, Iwakuni, Japan and Danang, Vietnam, 1964-65; exec. officer, comdg. officer 3d Bn., 5th Marine Regt., An Hoa, Vietnam, 1969-70; head officer force mgmt. unit Hdqrs. U.S. Marine Corps, Washington, 1970-73; exec. officer, comdg. officer, assoc. prof. naval sci. NROTC Unit, Rice U., Houston, 1973-75; ret., 1975; project mgr. Telemedia, Inc., Teheran, 1978; sr. marine instr. Marine Corps jr. ROTC unit, Portage High Sch., Ind., 1979-81, North High Sch., Bakersfield, Calif., 1981—, chmn. dept. mil. sci., 1981—, high sch. varsity boys tennis coach, 1983-86; chmn. USMC. Grad. Edn. Com., Washington, 1970-73; prin. speaker at numerous civic, frat., vets., high sch. and coll. groups, 1965—. Chmn. Navy Relief Charity Drive, Camp San Onofre, Calif., 1966; asst. scoutmaster Boy Scouts Am., 1970-73; regional bd. dirs.-at large Navy Mut. Aid Assn., Houston, 1973-75. Decorated Bronze Star medal with v device, Comdt. U.S. Marines commendation; Vietnamese Cross of Gallantry. Mem. Marine Corps Assn., VFW, Am. Legion, Republican. Lodge: Masons. Home: 5604 Logan St Bakersfield CA 93308 Office: USMC JROTC Unit North High Sch 300 Galaxy Ave Bakersfield CA 93308

DALE, FRANCIS LYKINS, sports executive, performing arts officer; b. Urbana, Ill., July 13, 1921; s. Charles Sherman and Sarah (Lykins) D.; m. Kathleen Hamlin Watkins, Mar. 20, 1947; children: Mitchell Watkins, Myron Lykins, Kathleen Hamlin, Holly Moore. A.B., Duke U., 1943; LL.B., U. Va., 1948; LL.D. (hon.), Eastern Ky. U., U. Cin., Ohio Wesleyan U., Salmon P. Chase Coll. of Law, Bloomfield Coll., Pepperdine Sch. of Bus. Bar: Ohio 1948. Assoc. Frost & Jacobs, Cin., 1948-53; partner Frost & Jacobs, 1953-65; Asst. sec. Cin. Enquirer, Inc., 1952-65, pres., pub., 1965-73; pres. The Cin. Reds, Inc., 1967-73, vice-chmn., 1973-80; pub. Los Angeles Herald Examiner, 1977-85; commr. Major Indoor Soccer League, Los Angeles, 1985-85; pres. The Music Ctr. of Los Angeles County, 1986—; Chmn. Nat. Council Crime and Delinquency, 1973-74, vice chmn., 1975—; chmn. Commn. White House fellows, 1973-74; U.S. ambassador and rep. to European Office of UN and other internat. orgns., Geneva, Switzerland, 1974-76; spl. asst. to asst. sec. state, 1976; spl. adviser U.S. del. 31st Gen. Assembly; bd. dirs. United Meth. Pub. House Inc., Viratek Inc., Lear-Sigler Inc., Beneficial Standard Life Ins. Co. Active United Appeal, Cin.; bd. dirs. Goodwill Industries, Cin., v.p., 1968; bd. dirs., mem. exec. com. Cin. area chpt. ARC; bd. dirs. Boys Clubs' Am., Bethesda Hosp., Boys' Club Cin., Taft Inst., Natural History Museum, also symphony, opera, ballet cos.; trustee Am. U., Occidental Coll., Claremont Sch. Theology; chmn. bd. councilors U. So. Calif. Coll. Continuing Edn.; bd. councilors Sch. Internat. Relations and Sch. Bus.; bd. dirs. Los Angeles chpt. ARC, Central City Assn., 1978-84, Meth. Hosp. So. Calif., 1980-85, Huntington Meml. Research Inst., 1985—, Operating Co.-Music Center, Los Angeles World Affairs Council, Los Angeles chpt. NCCJ, Town Hall Calif., Greater Los Angeles Visitors and Conv. Bur.; bd. dirs., pres. Los Angeles County council Boy Scouts Am., 1983-84, mem. nat. adv. bd., 1984—. Served with USNR, World War II. Named Outstanding Young Man of Year Cin., 1951; recipient Gov.'s award for adding prestige Ohio, 1968; Superior Honor award State Dept., 1976; Freedoms Found. award, 1976; Silver Beaver award Boy Scouts Am., 1969. Fellow Am. Bar Assn.; mem. Ohio Bar Assn. (pres. 1966-67), Cin. Bar Assn. (pres. 1961-62), Los Angeles C. of C. (v.p., dir.), Council Chs. Greater Cin. (pres. 1959-61), Frat. of Friends (v.p.), Order of Coif, Omicron Delta Kappa, Phi Kappa Psi, Sigma Nu Phi. Methodist (dist. lay leader 1958-64; mem. bd. publs. 1977-82). Clubs: Lincoln, Rotary; Comml. (Cin.); Annandale Golf (Los Angeles), Los Angeles Athletic (Los Angeles), Calif. (Los Angeles); Bohemian (San Francisco); Valley Hunt (Pasadena). Office: The Music Ctr 135 N Grand Ave Los Angeles CA 90012

DALE, JOHN MCCLELLAN, educational administrator; b. Fayetteville, Ark., June 24, 1934; s. Gilbert R. and Arna (Pursell) D.; m. Frances A. Bruner, Aug. 18, 1958; children—Elizabeth, John E., Sara. BA, U. Colo., 1956, MA, 1987; MA, Colo. Coll., 1962; student Denver U. Profl. Ctr., 1968-70. Tchr., Pueblo, Colo., 1956-62, Barcelona Sch., Albuquerque, 1962-63; tchr., Aurora, Colo., 1963-66, prin., 1971—; instr. Met. State Coll., Denver, 1982—. Bd. dirs. Denver Catholic Community Services; mem. Hoffman Heights Neighborhood Assn. Mem. Nat. Assn. Elem. Sch. Prins., Assn. Supervision and Curriculum Devel., Colo. Assn. Sch. Execs., Sixth Ave. Sch. PTA, Sch. Execs. Aurora, Phi Delta Kappa, Phi Alpha Theta. Democrat. Contbr. articles to profl. jours. Home: 1179 Salem St Aurora CO 80011 Office: 560 Vaughn St Aurora CO 80011

DALE, PAUL ROSS, operations manager; b. Los Angeles, June 27, 1915; s. William Lester and Rose (Roth) D.; m. Martha Goodman, Oct. 14, 1973; children by previous marriage; Patricia Rose, Nadine Ann. Student San Francisco Tech. Coll., 1935-36. Asst. supt. communications Aramco, Saudi Arabia, 1938-41, 46-52; chief communications engr. Mil. Adv. Group, TDC, Taipei, Taiwan, 1953-57; regional mgr. Henningsen & Co. Ltd., Seoul, Korea, 1957-58; v.p. ITT-Far East Ltd., Hong Kong, 1959-68; dir. Laboratoire Electronique et D'Automatione Dauphinois, Grenoble, France, 1968-79; ops. mgr. Sanag div. Sanitek Products, Los Angeles, 1980—; mgr. Corp. Mgmt. Services, Los Angeles, 1973-79. Contbr. articles to profl. jours. Served with USN, 1941-46; PTO. Mem. IEEE. Republican. Lodge: Masons (past master), Shriners.

DALE, THERESA MARIE, marketing communications executive; b. Loma Linda, Calif., July 2, 1957; d. C.F. and Ruth Elizabeth (Bretsch) D. BA, U. Redlands, 1979. Cert. Bus. Communicator. Advt. specialist Beckman Instruments, Fullerton, Calif., 1980-84; acct. mgr. Intel Corp., Chandler, Ariz., 1984, GenRad, Inc., Phoenix, 1984-85; mktg. communications mgr. Magnavox, Torrance, Calif., 1986—; mktg. communications cons. Calif., 1984—. Mem. Bus. Profl. Advt. Assn. Republican. Roman Catholic. Office: Magnavox Advanced Products and Systems Co 2829 Maricopa St Torrance CA 90503

DALENBERG, ROBERT VAN RAALTE, lawyer, utility company executive; b. Chgo., Nov. 1, 1929; s. John R. and Helene (Van Raalte) D.; m. Diane Curtis, June 19, 1954; children: Douglas, Donald, Betsy. Student, Morgan Park Jr. Coll., 1947-49; J.D., U. Chgo., 1953. Bar: Ill. 1956, Calif. 1973. Assoc. firm Essington, McKibben, Beebe & Pratt, Chgo., 1955-58; assoc. firm Schuyler, Stough & Morris, Chgo., 1958-64, ptnr., 1965-67; gen. atty. Ill. Bell Telephone Co., Chgo., 1967-72; assoc. gen. counsel Pacific Tel. & Tel. Co., San Francisco, 1972-76, v.p., gen. counsel, 1976-82; exec. v.p., gen. counsel, sec. Pacific Telesis Group and Pacific Bell, 1983—. Served to lt. USCGR, 1953-55. Mem. Am., Ill., Chgo., Calif. bar assns., Am. Judicature Soc., Phi Kappa Psi, Legal Club Chgo., Law Club Chgo. Office: Pacific Telesis and Pacific Bell 140 New Montgomery St San Francisco CA 94105

DALEY, LAURENCE STEPHEN, plant physiologist, biochemist; b. Liverpool, Eng., Sept. 21, 1936; came to U.S., 1962; s. Leonard and Leonela (García-Iñiguez) D.; m. Natalie Sue Cohen, June 12, 1967; children: Kara Hope, Ethan Leonard Henry, Jillian Bena. BSA, U. Fla., 1964, MSA, 1965; PhD, U. Calif., Davis, 1975. Assoc. prof. plant biochemistry dept. horticulture Oreg. State U., Corvallis, 1983—. Contbr. articles to profl. jours. Mem. Am. Soc. Plant Physiologists, Bot. Soc. Am., Am. Soc. Hort. Sci. Office: Natural Clonal Germplasm Repository 33447 Peoria Rd Corvallis OR 97333

DALEY, PAUL FREEMAN, environmental scientist; b. Glendale, Calif., Aug. 7, 1952; s. Marcus Freeman and Wanda Victoria (Pietrusewicz) D. BS, U. Calif., Davis, 1974, MS, 1977; PhD in Entomol. Sci., U. Calif., Berkeley, 1981. Postdoctoral fellow U. Laval, Quebec, Can., 1981-84, Lawrence Livermore (Calif.) Nat. Lab., 1984—. Contbr. articles to profl. jours. Mem. AAAS, Am. Soc. Plant Physiologists, Entomol. Soc. Am., Apple 32 Users, Berkeley Macintosh Users Group. Avocations: skiing, photography, microcomputer graphic design. Office: U Calif Lawrence Livermore Nat Lab PO Box 5507 Livermore CA 94550

DALEY, RODGER CLEVELAND, lawyer; b. Waukegan, Ill., Sept. 27, 1952; s. Arthur Charles and Margie Francis (Simmons) D.; m. Linda Mongiovi, Oct. 7, 1978. BS in Biology, Upsala Coll., 1974; M in Pub. Adminstrn., U. Colo., 1979; JD, U. Denver, 1982. Bar: Colo. 1982, U.S. Dist. Ct. Colo. 1983, U.S. Ct. Appeals (10th cir.) 1983. Assoc. Canges & Volpe, Denver, 1983-86, E.L. Volpe, P.C., Denver, 1986—. Mem. ABA, Colo. Bar Assn., Denver Bar Assn., Order of St. Ives. Roman Catholic. Avocations: snow skiing, softball, fishing. Home: 3026 D W Prentice Ave Littleton CO 80123 Office: E L Volpe PC 303 E 17th Ave Suite 850 Denver CO 80203

DALEY, VIRGINIA BROWN, retired educator, reading consultant; b. Chico, Calif., Nov. 7, 1918; d. Walter W. and Alice A. (Kinner) B.; B.A., San Francisco State Coll., 1953; M.A., U. LaVerne (Calif.), 1971; m. John W. Daley, Nov. 10, 1939; children—Virginia, Pamela. Elem. sch. tchr., then reading specialist schs. in Calif., 1949-70; reading specialist Lehigh Elem. Sch., Montclair, Calif., 1971-81; reading cons. West End Child Devel. Ctrs. Inc., 1981—; extension instr. U. Calif., Riverside, 1973, summer sch. lead tchr., 1974; cons., speaker in field. Mem. Internat. Reading Assn., NEA, Calif. Reading Assn., Reading Specialists Calif., Native Daus. Golden West (past chpt. pres.), Friends of Mus. (charter mem., pres.), Delta Kappa Gamma (past chpt. pres.). Republican. Episcopalian. Clubs: Order Eastern Star, Pomona Valley Lady Anglers.

DALIS, IRENE, mezzo-soprano, opera administrator; b. San Jose, Calif., Oct. 8, 1925; d. Peter N. and Mamie (Boitano) D.; m. George Loinaz, July 16, 1957; 1 child, Alida Mercedes. A.B., San Jose State U., 1946; M.Mus. (hon.), San Jose State Coll., 1957, M.S. (hon.), 1957; M.A., Columbia U. Tchrs. Coll., 1947; studied voice with, Edyth Walker, N.Y.C., 1947-50, Paul Althouse, 1950-51, Dr. Otto Mueller, Milano, Italy, 1952-72. Prof. music San Jose State U., Calif., 1976—; gen. dir. Opera San Jose, 1979—. Operatic debut as dramatic mezzo-soprano Oldenburgisches Staatstheater, 1953, Berlin Staedtische Opera, 1955; debut Met. Opera, N.Y.C., 1957, leading mezzo-soprano, to 1976, 1st Am.-born singer, Kundry Bayreuth Festival, 1961, opened, Bayreuth Festival in, Parsifal, 1963; commemorative: Wagner 150th Birth Anniversary; opened: 1963 Met. Opera Season in, Aida; premiered: Dello Joio's Blood Moon, 1961, Henderson's Medea, 1972; rec. artist, Philips Records. Recipient Fulbright award for study in Italy, 1951; Tower award San Jose State U., 1974; Disting. Service award Tchrs. Coll., Columbia U., 1961; Woman of Achievement award Commn. on Status of Women, 1983; Disting. Alumna award San Jose State U., 1983; President's award Nat. Italian Am. Found., 1985; award of merit People of San Francisco, 1985; inducted into Calif. Pub. Edn. Hall of Fame, 1985, also other awards. Office: Opera San Jose 12 S 1st St Suite 900 San Jose CA 95113

DALLARA, JON GEORGE, systems engineer; b. Mt. View, Calif., Oct. 23, 1958; s. George Peter and Nadine M. (Vill) D.; m. Toni Marie Laureano, Aug. 11, 1985; children: Ralph Michael Hale, Melissa Enos. Student, U. Santa Clara, 1976-82. Technician Hewlett-Packard, Palo Alto, Calif., 1978-83; systems engr. Hewlett-Packard, San Jose, Calif., 1983—; software cons., Santa Clara, Calif., 1984—. Mem. San Jose Search and Rescue Team, 1983-86. Avocations: skiing, computers, radio controlled models, woodworking. Home: 4904 Calle De Escuela Santa Clara CA 95054 Office: Hewlett Packard 350 W Trimble Rd San Jose CA 95131-1096

DAL PRA, CHRISTOPHER JOSEPH, mental health therapist; b. Rockford, Ill., Nov. 26, 1953; s. Virginio Peter and Mary Jane (Conus) Dal P.; m. Rhea White, May 31, 1975; children: Christopher Joseph, Tiffany Diane. B.S., Rockford Coll., 1975; M. Counseling, Ariz. State U., 1980. Asst. mgr. Mid-West Punch & Die Co., Rockford, Ill., 1975; psychiat. asst. Camelback Hosp., Phoenix, 1976; youth counselor St. Lukes Med. Ctr., Phoenix, 1977-80; mental health counselor Maricopa County Atty.'s Office, Phoenix, 1980; dir. Youth Service Bur., Chandler, Ariz., 1980—; cons. and youth counselor. Mem. Am. Personnel and Guidance Assn., Am. Mental Health Counselors Assn. Office: 250 E Commonwealth St Chandler AZ 85224

DALRYMPLE, STEPHEN HARRIS, computer scientist, consultant; b. Austin, Tex., Dec. 2, 1932; s. Dewey Culberson and Marian Francis (Harris) D.; m. Sonia Beatrice Curd, Nov. 28, 1952; children—Sheri Lynn, Cindy Marie, Stephen Harris, Terrance Christopher. B.A., U. Tex., 1954, M.A., 1959. Staff mem. Los Alamos Sci. Lab., N.Mex., 1954-60; unit chief, sr. advisor Autonetics, Anaheim, Calif., 1960-65, 67-69; sr. specialist Planning Research Corp., Westwood, Calif., 1965-67; dir. ops. Central Computer Corp., Anaheim, Calif., 1969-70; br. chief McDonnell Douglas Astronautics, Huntington Beach, Calif., 1970-81; sr. specialist Sci. Applications Internat. Corp., La Jolla, Calif., 1981—. Pres. Tustin High PTO, Calif., 1974; scoutmaster Orange County council Boy Scouts Am., 1971. AEC grad. fellow, Los Alamos, N.Mex., 1958. Mem. Assn. Computing Machinery, IEEE, Acacia. Republican. Clubs: Soc. Am. Magicians, Internat. Brotherhood of Magicians. Home: 1332 Arloura Way Tustin CA 92680 Office: Sci Applications Internat Corp 1332 Arloura Way Tustin CA 92680

DALTON, DOUGLAS, lawyer; b. Astoria, Oreg., Sept. 1, 1929; s. Mervyn Edgar and Julia Margaret (Hitchcock) D.; m. Shirley Kirkpatrick, Aug. 29, 1953; children—Julia M., Douglas C., John D., Matthew J., Bartholomew P. B.A., UCLA, 1951; J.D., U. So. Calif., 1956. Bar: Calif. bar 1956. City prosecutor Long Beach, Calif., 1956-60; partner Ball, Hunt, Hart, Brown & Baerwitz, Los Angeles, 1960-77; prin. Dalton & Godfrey, Inc., Los Angeles, 1977—; adj. prof. law Pepperdine U. Sch. Law, Los Angeles, 1978-80. Counsel Pres. Nixon's Commn. on Campus Unrest, 1970. Served with USN, 1951-53. Fellow Am. Coll. Trial Lawyers; mem. ABA, State Bar Calif. (bd. govs. 1985—), County Bar Los Angeles. Republican. Office: Dalton & Godfrey Inc 4525 Wilshire Blvd 3d Floor Los Angeles CA 90010

DALTON, JAMES EDWARD, business executive, retired air force officer; b. N.Y.C., Oct. 17, 1930; s. Edward A. and Marion (Conway) D.; m. Betty Jane Irwin, Nov. 29, 1958; children: Christopher, Stephanie, Todd. B.S., U.S. Mil. Acad., 1954; M.S.E. in Instrumentation Engring, U. Mich., 1960, M.S.E. in Aero./Astronautical Engring, 1960; grad. with distinction, Air Command and Staff Coll., 1965, Indsl. Coll. Armed Forces, 1970. Commd. 2d lt. U.S. Air Force, 1954, advanced through grades to gen., 1983; served in numerous operational and research assignments 1954-73; comdr. 39th Aerospace Rescue and Recovery Wing, Eglin AFB, Fla., 1973-75, Air Res. Personnel Center, Denver, 1975-76; dep. dir. concepts Hdqrs. USAF, Washington, 1976-77; dep. dir. Force Devel. and Strategic Plans, Plans and Policy Directorate, Office Joint Chiefs of Staff, Washington, 1977-78; vice dir. Joint Staff, 1978-80; commandant Indsl. Coll. of Armed Forces, Washington, 1980-81; dir. Joint Staff, 1981-83; chief of staff SHAPE, 1983-85; pres. R & D Assocs.; corp. v.p. Logicon. Decorated Def. Disting. Service medal with two oak leaf clusters, Legion of Merit with 1 oak leaf cluster, D.F.C., Bronze Star, Air medal with 5 oak leaf clusters, Meritorious Service medal with 2 oak leaf clusters, Air Force Commendation medal. Mem. Air Force Assn., Assn. Grads. U.S. Mil. Acad., Council Fgn. Relations. Roman Catholic. Home: 61 Misty Acres Rd Rolling Hills Estates CA 90274

DALTON, PATRICK DALY, JR., biology educator; b. Salt Lake City, Oct. 11, 1922; s. Patrick Daly and Ora (Johnson) D.; m. Lela Jesperson, Dec. 20, 1948; children: Tanya, Erin Colleen, Mark Edward. BS, Ariz. State U., 1949; MS, Utah State U., 1951; PhD, U. Ariz., 1961. Reporter, printer Mesa (Ariz.) Jour. Tribune, 1939-42, Los Angeles Times, 1942, Sta.'s Corp., Los Angeles, 1942; lab. and teaching asst. Ariz. State U., Tempe, 1945-49; research and teaching asst. Utah State U., Logan, 1949-51; range mgr., adminstrn., research and instrn. Soil Conservation Service USDA, Tooele, Utah, 1951-52; range mgr., adminstrn. and instrn. Bur. Land Mgmt. U.S. Dept. Interior, Price, Utah, 1952; instr. math., phys. and biol. scis., agrl. and indsl. arts, supt. bldgs. and grounds, assoc. plantation mgr. Tongan Mission Liamhoma High Sch., Nuku'alofa, Tonga, 1953-55; pres. Tongan Mission, Nuku'alofa, Tonga, 1963-66; asst. prof., dir. farm ops. Depts. Agrl. and Phys. Sci. Ch. Coll. Hawaii, Laie, 1955-58, assoc. prof. biol. scis., 1966-70; prof. biol. scis. Ch. Coll. Hawaiinow Brigham Young U. Hawaii, Laie, 1970—; research and teaching assoc. Dept. Plant Sci. U. Ariz., Tucson, 1958-61; asst. prof. range mgmt. U. Nevada, Reno, 1961-62; dir. forest and range research and rehab. UNESCO, Soeul, Rep. of Korea, 1962-63. Contbr. articles to profl. jours. Active Windward council Boy Scouts Am. dist. commr. 1980—, Laie Elem. Sch. PTA, Kahuku (Hawaii) High Sch. PTA., Jesus Christ Latter Day Saints. NSF fellow 1959-60; Named Eagle Scout with Bronze, Gold and Silver palms, Silver Beaver award, Gold Service medal Boy Scouts Am., Scouter's award Boy Scouts Am., Order of Merit award Boy Scouts Am., Order of Arrow award Boy Scouts Am. Mem. AAAS, Am. Inst. Biol. Sci., Ecol. Soc. Am., Am. Soc. Range Mgmt., Nat. Geographic Soc., Hawaiian Acad. Sci., Hawaiian Bot. Soc., Blue Key, Sigma Xi, Alpha Gamma Rho, Alpha Phi Omega, Lambda Delta Sigma, Alpha Zeta, Beta Beta Beta, Xi Sigma Pi, Delta Sigma Pi. Office: Brigham Young U-HC Box 1846 Laie HI 96762

DALY, CHRISTOPHER JOSEPH, lawyer; b. Butte, Mont., May 25, 1951; s. Gene William and Mona Elizabeth (Boyle) D. BA, U. Mont., 1973; MA, U. Alta., Can., 1975; PhD, U. Mich., 1979; JD, U. Mont., 1984. Bar: Mont. 1984, U.S. Dist. Ct. Mont. 1984. Sole practice Missoula, Mont., 1984—. Mem. ABA, State Bar Mont., Am. Trial Lawyers Assn. Office: 101 E Broadway Suite 200 Missoula MT 59802

DALY, PAUL SYLVESTER, university chancellor; b. Belmont, Mass., Jan. 8, 1934; s. Matthew Joseph and Alice Mary (Hall) D.; m. Maureen Teresa Kenny, May 25, 1957; children: Judith Mary, Paul S. Jr., Susan Marie, John Joseph, Maureen H. BS in Engring. Sci., Naval Postgrad. Sch., 1968; MBA, U. W. Fla., 1971. Coll. dean Embry-Riddle Aero. U., Daytona Beach, Fla., 1979-81; chancellor Embry-Riddle Aero. U., 1981—; lectr. seminars, 1977-85; cons. British Aerospace, 1979-84, McDonnell Douglas, 1979-84, IBM, 1983-84; sr. faculty U. Phoenix, 1983-86. Bd. dirs. Yavapai Regional Med. Ctr., Prescott, Ariz., 1983-86, Ariz. Hosp. Fedn., Prescott C. of C., 1982-84; chmn. Ariz. State Bd. of Pvt. Postsecondary Edn., Phoenix, 1985, Interactive Health Corp.; pres. Ind. Coll. and Univs. of Ariz., Phoenix, 1982-86. Served to capt. USN, 1953-79. Decorated Legion of Merit. Mem. Ariz. Airport Assn., Retired Officers Assn., Ariz. Town Hall, USAF Assn. Republican. Roman Catholic. Avocation: sports. Office: Embry-Riddle Aero U 3200 N Willow Creek Rd Prescott AZ 86301

DALY, ROBERT ANTHONY, motion picture company executive; b. Bklyn., Dec. 8, 1936; s. James and Eleanor D.; m. Nancy MacNeil, Oct. 7, 1961; children: Linda, Bobby, Brian. Student, Bklyn. Coll. From dir. bus. affairs to v.p. bus. affairs, to exec. v.p. CBS TV Network, 1955-77; pres. CBS Entertainment Co., 1977—; co-chmn. and co-chief exec. officer Warner Bros., Inc., Burbank, Calif., from 1980, now chmn., chief exec. officer; Bd. dirs. Am. Film Inst. Mem. Acad. Motion Picture Arts and Scis., Nat. Acad. TV Arts and Scis., Hollywood Radio and TV Soc., Motion Picture Pioneers. Roman Catholic. Club: Bel Air Country. Office: Warner Bros Inc 4000 Warner Blvd Burbank CA 91522

D'AMBROSIO, BLANCHE FADA GRAWE, hotel executive; b. Baton Rouge, Mar. 18, 1926; d. Walter Theodore and Blanche Laura (Causey) Bozant; m. Arthur Nolan Grawe, June 5, 1949; children—Cary Nolan, Geoffrey Allan; m. 2d, Anthony Francis D'Ambrosio, Feb. 18, 1978. Student La. State U., 1943-45, U. So. Calif., 1945-47. Society editor Herald Am. newspaper, Compton, Calif., 1957-61; asst. editor Host mag., Oreg. Restaurant and Beverage Assn., Portland, 1962-66; agt. Oreg. Liquor Control Commn., Portland, 1966-69; dir. sales and catering Cosmopolitan El Mirador, Sacramento, Calif., 1969-71; mgr. Umpqua Hotel, Roseburg, Oreg., 1971-74; gen. mgr. Inn at Spanish Head, Lincoln City, Oreg., 1974—. Mem. Lincoln City Advt. Com.; mem. job service employers com. Dept. Human Resources of Lincoln County. Mem. Nat. Restaurant Assn., Oreg. Hotel and Motel Assn. (past pres., chmn. bd.), Am. Hotel and Motel Assn., Oreg. Motor Hotel Assn. (dir.), Restaurants of Oreg. Assn., Lincoln City Motel Assn. (dir.), Women's Assn. of Allied Beverage Industry (past pres. Portland chpt), Oreg. Lodging Assn. (sec., treas.). Club: Norwalk (Calif.) Jr. Women's (life mem., past pres.). Office: Inn at Spanish Head 4009 S Hwy 101 Lincoln City OR 97367

DAMERON-LICHTENBERG, CLARICE ELAINE, speech/language pathologist; b. Granite City, Ill., Sept. 9, 1934; d. Leo Alonzo and Cora Frances (Carriger) Dameron; m. Larry Ray Lichtenberg, Dec. 23, 1961; 1 child, Isabel Dameron. B.S. in Speech Communications, N.E. Mo. State U., 1961; postgrad. Ill. Normal U., 1963, Ariz. State U., 1968-76. Third grade tchr. Harris Sch., Madison, Ill., 1957-59; asst. mgr. Dameron Sheltered Care Home, Roodhouse, Ill., 1959-60; speech-lang. pathologist Washington Elem. Schs., Phoenix, 1969—; dir. learning disabilities program Sweetwater Ch., Glendale, Ariz., 1978-79; supr. Adult Homebound Ministry, The Valley Cathedral, Phoenix, 1979-80; spl. edn. cons. Christian schs., Maricopa County, Ariz.; coordinator nat. patriotism week Washington Elem. Sch. Dist., 1981; pub. relations co-chmn. Ariz. Speech/Hearing Assn. Mktg. analyst Intel, Phoenix, 1983; computer programming trainer, summer 1984. Pub. relations dir. Federated Women's Club, Bloomington, Ill.; pres. Nat. Asthmatic Club, Bloomington; bicentennial dir. Evangelical Ch. Pageant, Maricopa County; met with U.S. Pres. Ronald Reagan at White House for Nat. Patriotism Week, 1981, mem. Ariz. Gov.'s Statue of Liberty Centennial Commn., 1986-87, Ariz. Commn. on Bicentennial of U.S., 1986—. Recipient Am. Educator medal Valley Forge Freedoms Found., 1981, State of Ariz. Gov.'s. Proclamations for Speech and Hearing Month, 1969-73. Mem. Am. Soc. Tng. and Devel., NEA, Ariz. Edn. Assn., Nat. Christian Edn. Assn., DAR. Author: Arizona's Heritage Blessed by God Pageant Souvenir Coloring Book, 1975; numerous brochures and newsletters.

DAMEROW, RICHARD AASEN, physicist, division supervisor; b. Thief River Falls, Minn., Sept. 4, 1936; s. Albert M. and Patricia P. (Aasen) D.; m. Yvonne D. Armbruster, Oct. 12, 1957; children: Cynthia K., Michelle R. BS in Physics, U. Minn., 1958, MS in Physics, 1960, PhD in Physics, 1963. Mem. tech. staff Sandia Nat. Labs., Albuquerque, 1963-71, div. supr., 1971-78, 1979—; sci. adv. U.S. Dept. Energy, Washington, 1978-79. Contbr. articles to profl. jours. Recipient award of Excellence U.S. Dept. Energy, 1982. Mem. Am. Phys. Soc., Am. Assn. Physics Tchrs. Avocations: piloting, fishing, reading. Home: 2924 Espanola NE Albuquerque NM 87110

D'AMICO, MICHAEL, architect, urban planner; b. Bklyn., Sept. 11, 1936; s. Michael and Rosalie (Vinciguerra) D.; B.Arch., U. Okla., 1961; postgrad. So. Meth. U. Sch. Law, 1962-63; m. Joan Hand, Nov. 26, 1955; children—Michael III, Dion Charles. Supr. advanced planning sect. Dallas Dept. City Planning, 1961-63; designer, planner in charge Leo A. Daly Co., San Francisco, 1963-66; project planner Whisler, Patri Assos., San Francisco, 1966-67; architect, urban planner D'Amico & Assocs., San Francisco, N.Y., Guam, 1967-73, pres. D'Amico & Assocs., Inc., Mill Valley, Calif., and Guam, 1973—; pres. Jericho Alpha Inc., 1979-82; cons. architect, planner City of Seaside (Calif.), 1967-72, 79-81; cons. urban redevel. Eureka (Calif.), 1967-82; cons. planner, Lakewood, Calif.; redevel. cons. to Daly City (Calif.), 1975-77; redevel. adviser to Tamalpais Valley Bus. Assn., 1975-77; archtl. and hist. analyst to Calif. Dept. Transp., 1975-77; agt. for Eureka, Calif. Coastal Commn., 1977-79. Mem. steering com. San Francisco Joint Com. Urban Design, 1967-72. Recipient Community Design award AIA, 1970; First prize award Port Aransas (Tex.) Master Plan Competition, 1964. Mem. AIA, Am. Planning Assn., Calif. Assn. Planning Cons. (sec., treas. 1970-72), Am. Soc. Cons. Planners, World Future Soc., Solar Energy Soc. Am. Office: 525 Midvale Way Mill Valley CA 94941 Office: Agana Guam

DAMISCH, PETER WHITON, diversified technical company engineering manager; b. Chgo., Feb. 27, 1953; s. John W. and Harriet D. (Darley) D.; m. Kathleen R. Reilly, May 14, 1977. BS in Aerospace Engring., U.S. Naval Acad., 1975; MS in Nuclear Engring., NPS/NPTU, 1976; M in Mgmt. and MBA with distinction, Northwestern U., 1982. Cert. nuclear chief engr. USN. Commd. ensign USN, 1975, advanced through grades to lt., resigned, 1980, congressionl aide, 1975, elec. div. officer USS Nimitz, 1977-79, combat info. ctr. officer USS Texas, 1979-80; program mgr. No. Ordnance div. FMC, 1982-83; mgr. strategic planning and bus. devel. Def. Systems Group FMC, San Jose, Calif., 1983-84; dir. bus. devel. Def. Systems Internat. div. FMC, Santa Clara, Calif., 1985-86; mgr. system engring. Ordnance div. FMC, San Jose, 1986—; bd. dirs. Ideamatics, Inc., Washington; pres., v.p. Am. Inst. Aeronautics and Astronautics, USNR, 1973-75; student tchr. computer sci. U.S. Naval Acad., 1974-75. V.p. Almaden Hills Estates Homeowner's Assn., San Jose, 1984—; campaign worker Sam Young Congressional campaign, Skokie, Ill., 1970. Mem. U.S. Naval Inst. (life), U.S. Navy League (life), U.S. Naval Acad. Alumni Assn. (life), Northwestrn Univ. Alumni Assn. (life), San Jose Astron. Assn. Avocations: swimming, squash, bicycling, microcomputing, telescopic astronomy. Home: 1045 Mazzone Dr San Jose CA 95120 Office: FMC Corp Ordnance div 1115 Coleman Ave PO Box 1201 M/D 690 San Jose CA 95108

DAMOOSE, GEORGE LYNN, lawyer; b. Grand Rapids, Mich., Feb. 2, 1938; s. George G. and Geneva J. (Joseph) D.; m. Carol Sweeney, Dec. 7, 1968; children: Alison Dana, George Christopher. AB cum laude, Harvard U., 1959; JD, Harvard Law Sch., 1965. Bar: Calif. 1965. Assoc. O'Melveny and Myers, Los Angeles, 1965-72; shareholder, prin. Jennings, Engstrand, Henrikson, P.C., San Diego, 1972-76; ptnr. Procopio, Cory, Hargreaves, and Savitch, San Diego, 1976—. Bd. dirs. San Diego Civic Light Opera Assn., 1984—; trustee The Bishops Sch, La Jolla. Served to lt (j.g.) USN, 1959-62). Mem. Am. Bar Found, San Diego County Bar Assn. (chmn. tax sect. 1974-75, 86-87), Calif. Bar Assn. (ind. inquiry and rev. panel, program for certifying legal specialists 1986-87). Republican. Episcopalian. Club: La Jolla Beach and Tennis. Avocations: tennis, bicycling. Home: 208 Avenida Cortex La Jolla CA 92037 Office: Procopio Cory Gargreaves Savitch 530 B St Suite 1900 San Diego CA 92101

DAMRON, CARINA KAY CASTAGNETO, educator; b. Longview, Wash., Dec. 26, 1942; d. William James and Beverly Jean (Marshall) Castagneto; B.S.Ed. in Child Devel., Brigham Young U., 1965; postgrad. U. Utah, 1965-76; m. William E. Damron, June 11, 1973. Tchr., Salt Lake City Bd. Edn., 1965-76, Centennial Sch. Dist., Portland, Oreg., 1976—. Active March of Dimes, United Fund, Am. Cancer Soc.; vol. Primary Children's Med. Center, Salt Lake City, 1966-68; active Big Sisters Program, 1967-68; mem. Com. for Defeat of Oreg. Initiative to Limit Property Taxes, 1980. Named Tchr. of Yr., Golden Gleanner Outstanding Woman award Ch. Jesus Christ of Latter-day Saints, 1972. Mem. Salt Lake Tchrs. Assn., Utah Tchrs. Assn., Centennial Edn. Assn., NEA, Oreg. Edn. Assn., Assn. of Early Childhood Educators, Assn. Early Childhood Edn. Republican. Mem. Ch. Jesus Christ of Latter-day Saints. Club: Women's Century. Home: 14427 NE Alton Ct Portland OR 97230 Office: Centennial Sch Dist 1546 SE 169th Pl Portland OR 97233

DAMSBO, ANN MARIE, psychologist; b. Cortland, N.Y., July 7, 1931; d. Jorgen Einer and Agatha Irene (Schenck) D. B.S., San Diego State Coll., 1952; M.A., U.S. Internat. U., 1974, Ph.D., 1975. Commd. 2d lt. U.S. Army, 1952, advanced through grades to capt., 1957; staff therapist Letterman Army Hosp., San Francisco, 1953-54, 56-58, 61-62, Ft. Devers, Mass., 1955-56, Walter Reed Army Hosp., Washington, 1958-59, Tripler Army Hosp., Hawaii, 1959-61, Ft. Benning, Ga., 1962-64; chief therapist U.S. Army Hosp., Ft. McPherson, Ga., 1964-67; ret. U.S. Army, 1967; med. missionary So. Presbyterian Ch., Taiwan, 1968-70; psychology intern Naval Regional Med. Ctr., San Diego, 1975, pre-doctoral intern, 1975-76, postdoctoral intern, 1975-76, chief, founder pain clinic, 1977-86; lectr., U.S., Can., Eng., France, Australia, cons. forensic hypnosis to law enforcement agys. Contbr. articles to profl. publs., chpt. to book. Tchr. Sunday sch. Methodist Ch., 1945—. Fellow Am. Soc. Clin. Hypnosis; mem. San Diego Soc. Clin. Hypnosis (pres. 1980), Am. Phys. Therapy Assn.; Mem.; mem. Calif. Soc. Clin. and Hypnosis (bd. govs.), Internat. Soc. Clin. and Exptl. Hypnosis, Internat. Platform Assn. Republican. Club: Toastmasters (local pres.). Lodges: Job's Daus., Zonta. Home and Office: 1062 W 5th Ave Escondido CA 92025

DANA, DEANE, county government official; b. N.Y.C., July 9, 1926; s. Deane and Dorothy Bartlett (Lawson) D.; m. Doris Weiler, July 14, 1951; children: Deane III, Marguerite, Diane and Dorothy (twins). BSME, Stevens Inst., 1951; LLD(hon.), Pepperdine U., 1985. Registered profl. engr., Calif. Engring. exec. Pacific Telephone, Los Angeles, 1953-80; fourth dist. supr. Los Angeles County Bd. Suprs., 1980—. Past pres. Coliseum Commn.; mem. Regional Airport Authority, Town Hall Calif.; chmn. Los Angeles County Transp. Commn., 1986; bd. dirs. Calif. Shore and Beach Preservation, Los Angeles Area council Boy Scouts Am. Served to 1st lt. USAF, 1945-47, 51-53. Recipient Torch of Liberty award Anti-Defamation League of B'nai Brith, 1986; named Most Caring Pub. Ofcl., Calif. Ctr. Family Survivors of Homicide, 1985. Mem. Calif. Assn. Compensatory Edn., Navy League U.S., Am. Legion, Calif. Motion Picture Council, Californians for a Strong Am. Republican. Episcopalian. Lodges: Elks, Rotary. Avocations: golf, tennis, water skiing. Office: Los Angeles County Bd Suprs 500 W Temple #822 Los Angeles CA 90012

DANCE, FRANCIS ESBURN XAVIER, communication educator; b. Bklyn., Nov. 9, 1929; s. Clifton Louis and Catherine (Tester) D.; m. Nora Alice Rush, May 1, 1954 (div. 1974); children: Clifton Louis III, Charles Daniel, Alison Catherine, Andrea Frances, Frances Sue, Brendan Rush; m. Carol Camille Zak, July 4, 1974; children: Zachary Esburn, Gabriel Joseph, Caleb Michael, Catherine Emily. B.S., Fordham U., 1951; M.A., Northwestern U., 1953, Ph.D., 1959. Instr. speech Bklyn. Adult Labor Schs., 1951; instr. humanities, coordinator radio and TV U. Ill. at Chgo., 1953-54; instr. Univ. Coll., U. Chgo., 1958; asst. prof. St. Joseph's (Ind.) Coll., 1958-60; asst. prof., then assoc. prof. U. Kans., 1960-63; mem. faculty U. Wis.-Milw., 1963-71, prof. communication, 1965-71; dir. Speech Communication Center U. Wis-Milw., 1963-70; mem. faculty U. Denver, 1971—; partner Helix Press, Shorewood, Wis., 1970-71; cons. in field. Author: The Citizen Speaks, 1962, (with Harold P. Zelko) Business and Professional Speech Communication, 1965, 2d edit., 1978, Human Communication Theory, 1967, (with Carl E. Larson) Perspectives on Communication, 1970, Speech Communication: Concepts and Behavior, 1972, The Functions of Speech Communication: A Theoretical Approach, 1976, Human Communication Theory, 1982, (with Carol C. Zak-Dance) Public Speaking, 1986; editor: Jour. Communication, 1962-64, Speech Tchr, 1970-72; adv. bd.: Jour. Black Studies; editorial bd.: Jour. Psycholinguistic Research; Contbr. articles to profl. jours. Bd. dirs. Milw. Mental Health Assn., 1966-67. Served to 2d lt. AUS, 1954-56. Knapp Univ. scholar in communication, 1967-68; recipient Outstanding Prof. award Standard Oil Found., 1967; Master Tchr. award U. Denver, 1985, University Lectr. award U. Denver, 1986. Fellow Internat. Communication Assn. (pres. 1967); mem. Speech Communication Assn. (pres. 1982), Psi Upsilon. Office: U Denver Dept Speech Communication Denver CO 80208

DANDOY, SUZANNE EGGLESTON, physician, educator; b. Los Angeles, Jan. 2, 1935; d. Leonard Lester and Catherine (Wheelwright) Eggleston; m. Jeremiah Richard Dandoy, June 14, 1958; children: Kevin, Bret, Jolyn. BA, U. Calif., Los Angeles, 1956; MD, UCLA, 1960, MPH, 1963. Diplomate: Am. Bd. Preventive Medicine. Intern, Los Angeles Harbor Gen. Hosp., Torrance, Calif., 1960-61; resident Los Angeles Health Dept., 1961-62, 63-64; epidemiologist San Diego Dept. Pub. Health, 1967-68; chief Ariz. Dept. Health Service, Phoenix, 1970-73; asst. commr. Ariz. Dept. Health Service,

1973-74, asst. dir., 1974-75, dir., 1975-80; prof. health adminstrn. Ariz. State U., Tempe, 1981-85; exec. dir. Utah Dept. Health, Salt Lake City, 1985—; adj. assoc. prof. U. Utah. Contbr. articles to profl. jours. Bd. dirs. Child Crisis Ctr., Tempe St. Lukes Hosp.; adv. com. on immunization practices HEW; pres. Utah Women's Forum. Recipient award Ariz. Dietetic Assn., 1976; award Maricopa County Med. Soc., 1980. Fellow Am. Pub. Health Assn., Am. Coll. Preventive Medicine; mem. AMA, Utah Med. Assn., Utah Pub. Health Assn., Ariz. Med. Assn., Phi Beta Kappa, Delta Omega. Democrat. Mormon. Home: 990 S Oak Hills Way Salt Lake City UT 84108 Office: Utah Dept Health PO Box 16700 Salt Lake City UT 84116-0700

DANFORTH, HOLLY ELIZABETH, clinical social worker; b. Lancaster, Pa., Dec. 22, 1957; d. Theodore Scofield and Susan Francis (Kessler) D.; m. Robert Luther Grossman, Nov. 22, 1980 (div. Mar. 1986). Student, U. Pitts., 1975-76; BA in Psychology summa cum laude, Millersville U., 1978; MSW, UCLA, 1985; postgrad., U. Calif., Berkeley, 1987—. Crisis intervention counselor York (Pa.) Mental Health, 1979-80; case mgr. N. Cen. Mental Health, Columbus, Ohio, 1980-82; geriatric social worker Whittier (Calif.) Care Ctr., 1982-83; research asst. dept. social work UCLA, 1984—; psychiat. social worker Los Angeles County Hosp. U. So. Calif., 1985-86; clin. social worker Neuropsychiat. Inst. UCLA, 1986—. Co-author: Support Groups in Social Work, 1986. Intake interviewer, emergency counselor Planned Parenthood, Lancaster, 1978-79, vol. 1977-79. Senatorial and gymnastics scholar U. Pitts., 1975-76. Mem. Nat. Assn. Social Workers, Soc. Clin. Social Work, Beyond War, Sierra Club. Democrat. Avocations: ballet and jazz dancing, swimming, naturalist interests. Home: 1243 12th St #8 Santa Monica CA 90401 Office: UCLA Neuropsychiat Inst 760 Westwood Plaza #A7-361 Los Angeles CA 90024

DANGELO, J. CARLOS, electrical engineer; b. Lins, Brazil, May 19, 1946; came to U.S., 1976; s. Bonifacio and Rosa Dangelo; m. Catherine Cappetta, Jan. 8, 1983. BSEE, Escola Eng. Maua, Sao Paulo, Brazil, 1971; MSEE, Carnegie Mellon U., 1977, PhDEE, 1981. Research assoc. Carnegie Mellon U., Pitts., 1976-81; staff engr. Nat. Semicondr., Santa Clara, Calif., 1981-83; sr. staff Fairchild Semicondr., Milpitas, Calif., 1983-84; design automation mgr. Fairchild SemiCond., Milpitas, CA, 1984—; sr. cons. UN, N.Y.C., 1984. Author: Energy Conversion, 1975 (Best Text award 1977); contbr. articles to profl. jours. Recipient Best text award SP Industry Fedn. Mem. IEEE. Republican. Jewish. Avocations: piano, A-I programming, Italian art. Home: 3522 McCoppin Ct San Jose CA 95124 Office: Fairchild Semicond Gate Array 1801 McCarthy Blvd Milpitas CA 95035

DANHOF, CYNTHIA CAMPBELL, executive search consultant; b. Cleve., Sept. 26, 1952; d. Clifford Blaine and Jeanne (Maher) C. BSBA, Menlo Coll., 1976. Advt. mgr. Seagull Inc., Palo Alto, Calif., 1976-79; research assoc. The Advisory Group, Portola Valley, Calif., 1979-80; gen. mgr. PLB Co., Menlo Park, Calif., 1980-81; assoc. Bradsbury Co., Cupertino, Calif., 1981-83, Boyden Internat. Inc., Menlo Park, 1983-86, Apple Computer, Cupertino, Calif., 1986—. Mem. Assn. Exec. Search Cons., Calif. Exec. Recruiters Assn., Nat. Assn. Female Execs., Phi Chi Theta (nat. counselor 1975-76). Republican. Episcopalian. Club: Decathalon (Santa Clara). Home: 4043 Olga Dr San Jose CA 95117 Office: Apple Computer 20525 Mariani Ave MS 9-C Cupertino CA 95014

DANIEK, MAUREEN LOUISE, social worker; b. Brewster, Wash., June 6, 1949. BA in Sociology, Wash. State U., 1971; MSW, U. Wash., 1975. Cert. social worker. Mem. psychiat. team Harborview Hosp., Seattle, 1974-75; therapist U. Wash. Dept. Psychiatry, Seattle, 1976-83; pvt. practice specializing in phobias Seattle, 1983—. Mem. membership com. Womens Network, Seattle, 1984. Mem. Nat. Assn. Social Workers, Am. Assn. Behavior Therapy, Phobia Soc. Am., Phi Beta Kappa. Home and Office: 19040 3d NE Seattle WA 98155

DANIEL, JAMES ALLEN, mechanical engineer; b. Alamogordo, N.M., Nov. 15, 1953; s. Quinton Edward and Kathryn May (Skelley) D.; m. Peggy Ann Gaddy, June 30, 1984. BSME, N.M. State U., 1975; MSME, N.Mex. State U., 1987. Registered profl. engr. N.M., Tex. Sr. design engr. Gen. Dynamics, Ft. Worth, 1975-81; v.p. engring. Daniel Engring. Co., Alamogordo, 1981-83; mech. engr. Radar Backscatter div. Dynalectron Corp., Alamogordo, 1983—; instr. N.M. State U., Alamogordo, 1983-84. Mem. ASME, NSPE. Democrat. Methodist. Avocations: aviation, astronomy, photography, jogging. Home: 2905 Comanche Ct Alamogordo NM 88310 Office: Dynalectron Corp Radar Backscatter Div PO Drawer O Holloman AFB NM 88330

DANIELS, DIANE, computer software engineering and development executive; b. Valdosta, Ga., Dec. 4, 1945; d. Harry A. and Mary M. (Curry) Davidson. B.A. with honors, Mich. State U., 1966. With IBM Corp., 1966-73, computer programmer on Apollo 11, also Pentagon Intelligence, Washington, Saigon, Vietnam, 1968-70; mgmt. info. systems cons. to Govt. of Iran, Louis Berger Internat., 1973-75, staff, 1978; system engr. automated medicaid and welfare systems, EDS Corp., San Francisco, 1976-77; founder, pres. Info. Orgn. Corp., San Francisco, 1979—. Pres. bd. dirs. Pacific Heights Place Owners Assn., 1980-82, Fairspace Dancing Theatre, 1976-78; chmn. Com. for Ann. Fundraiser for San Francisco Moving Co., Modern Dance, Inc., 1982; Mem. Assn. Records Mgrs. and Adminstrs. (dir. 1980-81, cert. of recognition 1981), Assn. Systems Mgrs. (cert. of recognition 1982), Women Entrepreneurs, Profl. and Tech. Cons. Assn., Profl. Women's Network (bd. dirs. 1986), Profl. Women's Bus. Exchange. Inventor, copyright holder in field. Office: Info Orgn Corp 30 Grant Ave San Francisco CA 94108

DANIELS, DIANNE COMBS, social services administrator; b. Kingston, N.Y., Dec. 21, 1958; d. Alan Combs and Judy Chong Nim (Sin) Lee; m. Michael Kevin Daniels, Aug. 11, 1985. Student, U. Ariz., 1975-77; BA, Western Mich. U., 1979, MSW, 1981. pvt. practice social worker, Albuquerque, 1985—. Contractor Dianne Combs Drapes, Kalamazoo, 1977-81; social worker N.Mex. Dept. Human Services, Albuquerque, 1981-83; adoption social worker Chaparral Adoptions, Albuquerque, 1983-84, maternity supr., 1984-85; dir. Meth. Home, Albuquerque, 1985—; bd. dirs., sec., vol. publicity com. Bright Horizons, 1986—. Bd. dirs. adv. bd. Families for Children Adoption Agy., 1987—. Mem. Albuquerque Metro. Adoption Group, Nat. Assn. Social Workers (bd. dirs. N.Mex. chpt.), Individuals Making Positive Action for Children Today, N.Mex. Youth Work Alliance, N.Mex. Assn. Community Edn. Devel., Ultimate Players Assn. Democrat. Roman Catholic. Avocations: graphic design, ultimate frisbee, basketball. Home: 2603 Harvard Dr SE Rio Rancho NM 87124 Office: Methodist Home 8100 Mountain Rd NE Suite 112 Albuquerque NM 87110

DANIELS, EDWARD BAY, health care executive; b. Chgo., Nov. 4, 1950; s. Edward William and Harriet (Zimmerman) D.; m. Merle Joy Daniels, Apr. 21, 1973; children: Scott, Alan, Leslie. BA in Psychology, So. Ill. U., 1972; MA in Indsl. Engring., SUNY, 1976. Ops. analyst Henry Ford Hosp., Detroit, 1976-77, mgr. systems devel., 1977-79, dir. systems and programming, 1979-81, dir. ops. analysis, 1981-82; dir. healthcare systems Arthur Young and Co., Detroit, 1982-85; v.p. GeriMed of Am., Denver, 1985—. Mem. Healthcare Mgmt. Systems Soc. (v.p. Mich. chpt. 1982), Healthcare Fin. Mgmt. Assn. (chmn. systems com. 1984), Nat. Space Inst., NRA, L-5 Soc. Avocations: martial arts, outdoor activities, swimming. Home: 165 Pine Rd Golden CO 80401 Office: GeriMed of Am Inc 1400 1 Denver Pl Denver CO 80202

DANIELS, ETHEL MARY, reading specialist; b. Phoenix, Feb. 26, 1942; d. Eddie Ernest and Alberta (Evans) D. BA in Edn., Ariz. State U., 1964; MA in Reading, U.S. Internat. U., 1976. Elem. tchr., Phoenix, 1964-67, San Diego, Calif., 1967—; demonstration tchr. reading and math., 1974-75; reading specialist San Diego City Schs., Robert E. Lee Elem. Sch., 1979—. Participant San Diego writing project, 1985. Recipient Service award PTA, 1981. Mem. San Diego Tchrs. Assn., Calif. Tchrs. Assn., NEA, Assn. Supervision and Curriculum Devel., Reading Specialists Calif., Greater San Diego Reading Assn., Calif. Reading Assn., Computers and Writing Summer Inst. (mentor tchr. 1985—). Democrat. Baptist. Clubs: Mountain View Tennis (Service award 1976, 82), Balboa Tennis, Helix South Tennis. Home: 3041 Picasso Dr Bonita CA 92002 Office: Robert E Lee Elem Sch 6196 Childs Ave San Diego CA 92139

DANIELS, JEFFREY IRWIN, environmental scientist; b. San Mateo, Calif., Dec. 26, 1951; s. Henry Marcus and Ruth (Fox) D.; m. Danita Jenny Carter, Jan. 17, 1982; 1 child, Sarah Ilse. BA in Biology, UCLA, 1974, D in Environ. Sci. and Engring., 1981; MS in Microbiology, Calif. State U., Northridge, 1976. Adminstrv. asst. UCLA Hosp. and Clinics, 1972-79; environ. scientist Environ. Sci. div. Lawrence Livermore Nat. Lab., Livermore, Calif., 1979—. Contbr. articles to profl. jours. Mem. AAAS, Soc. Risk Analysis (charter), No. Calif. Chpt. Health Phys. Soc., Environ. Sci. and Engring. Soc. (charter). Democrat. Jewish. Lodge: Masons. Home: 328 Camaritas Way Danville CA 94526 Office: Lawrence Livermore Nat Lab Environ Sci Div L-453 PO Box 5507 Livermore CA 94526

DANIELS, LESLIE BETH, city ofcl.; b. Kansas City, Mo., July 14, 1951; d. Charles Lee and Helen Atanasoff D.; B.A., U. Ariz., 1972; M.A., U. Phoenix, 1981; postgrad. U. Okla. Econ. Devel. Inst., 1983. Copywriter public relations, Tucson, 1972-74, graphic artist/electronic typesetter, 1974-75, polit. campaign mgr., 1972-77; adminstrv. asst. City Mgrs. Office, City of Tucson, 1978-85; transit coordinator City of Tucson Transp. Dept., 1985—; bd. dirs. Tucson Clean and Beautiful Com. Editor, State Republican Com. newspaper, 1975-76; chmn. Pima County Young Rep. League, 1973-74; dist. 9 chmn. Pima County Rep. Central Com., 1974. Mem. Kappa Tau Alpha, Delta Sigma Pi. Republican. Methodist. Club: Pima County Trunk 'n Tusk (publicity chmn. 1974-77). Home: 7369 E 20th St Tucson AZ 85710 Office: PO Box 27210 Tucson AZ 85726

DANIELS, LYDIA M., medical records administrator; b. Louisville, Dec. 21, 1932; d. Effort and Gladys T. (Turner) Williams; student Calif. State U., Hayward, 1967, 69, 70, 71, 72, Golden Gate U., 1979, 86; cert. Samuel Merritt Hosp. Sch. Med. Record Adminstrs., 1959; student Central State Coll., Ohio, 1950-52; children by previous marriage—Danny Winston, Jeffrey Bruce, Anthony Wayne. Sec. chemistry dept. Central State Coll., Wilberforce, Ohio, 1950-52; co-dir. Indian Workcamp, Pala Indian Reservation, Pala, Calif., 1956-58; clk.-typist Camarillo (Calif.) State Hosp., 1956-58; student med. record adminstr. Samuel Merritt Hosp., Oakland, Calif., 1958-59, asst. med. record adminstr., 1962-63, asst. chief med. record adminstr., 1965, chief med. record adminstr., 1965-72; med. record adminstr. Albany (Calif.) Hosp., 1964-65; asst. med. record adminstr. Children's Hosp., San Francisco, 1960; co-dir. interns in community service Am. Friends Service Com., San Francisco, 1960-61; med. record adminstr. Pacific Hosp., Oakland, Calif., 1963-64; med. record cons. Tahoe Forest Hosp., Truckee, Calif., 1969-73; chief med. record adminstr. Highland Gen. Hosp., Oakland, 1972-74; dir. med. record services U. Calif. San Francisco Hosps. and Clinics, 1975-82; mgr. patient appointments, reception and registration Kaiser-Permanente Med. Ctr., 1982—; adj. prof. mgmt., office automation Golden Gate U., 1978—. Girl scout leader Oakland area council, 1960-62; Sunday sch. tchr. Soc. of Friends, Berkeley, Calif., 1961-63, mem. edn. com., 1965-68; mem. policy and adv. bd. Far West Lab. Demonstration Sch., Oakland, 1973—. Recipient Mgmt. Fellowship award U. Calif., San Francisco, 1979-80. Mem. Am. Med. Record Assn., Calif. Med. Record Assn. (editorial bd. 1976-77, pres. 1974-75), East Bay Med. Record Assn. (chmn. edn. com. 1971-72, pres. 1969-70), Assn. Systems Mgmt., Am. Mgmt. Assn., San Francisco Med. Records Assn. (pres.-elect 1982-83, pres. 1983-84). Author: Health Record Documentation: A Look at Cost, 1981; Inservice Training as a Tool in Managing the Changing Environment in the Medical Record Department, 1983; the Budget as a Management Tool, 1983. Issues editor Topics in Health Record Management, Parts I and II, 1983. Home: 545 Pierce St #1105 Albany CA 94706 Office: Kaiser-Permanente Med Ctr 280 W MacArthur Blvd Oakland CA 94611

DANIELS, MICHAEL CLAUDE, geologist; b. Grand Junction, Colo., Dec. 28, 1955; s. Harold Eugene and Claudell (Jackson) D. BS in Geology, Ft. Lewis Coll., 1978; MS in Geology, W.Va. U., 1982. Geologist Cliffs Minerals inc., Morgantown, W.Va., 1978-82, Chevron USA, New Orleans, 1982-85; devel. geologist Chevron USA, Ventura, Calif., 1985-86, sr. devel. geologist, 1987—. Contbr. geol. reports to profl. publ. Mem. Am. Assn. Petroleum Geologists, Coast Geol. Soc. Republican. Congregationalist. Avocations: raquetball, bicycling, target shooting. Home: 323 S Lomita Ojai CA 93023 Office: Chevron USA 1000 Hill Rd Ventura CA 93006

DANIELS, RICHARD MARTIN, marketing communications company executive; b. Delano, Calif., Feb. 24, 1942; s. Edward Martin and Philida Rose (Peterson) D.; m. Kathryn Ellen Knight, Feb. 28, 1976; children: Robert Martin, Michael Edward. A.A., Foothill Coll., 1965; B.A., San Jose State U., 1967; M.A., U. Mo., 1971. News reporter Imperial Valley Press, El Centro, Calif., summers 1963-66, San Diego (Calif.) Evening Tribune, 1967-68, Columbia Daily Tribune (Mo.), 1969-70; nat. news copy editor Los Angeles Times, 1966-67; staff writer San Diego Union, 1971-74, real estate editor, 1974-77; v.p. pub. relations Hubbert Advt. & Pub. Relations, Costa Mesa, Calif., 1977-78; ptnr. Berkman & Daniels Mktg. Communications, San Diego, 1979—; lectr. various bus. groups and colls. Chmn. bd. dirs. March of Dimes San Diego County, mem. Nat. Council Vols.; bd. dirs. San Diego-Imperial Counties Devel. Services, Inc., Com. of 100. Served with USN, 1959-62. Recipient Excellence award Communicating Arts Group San Diego, 1981. Mem. Pub. Relations Soc. Am., Building Industry Assn. San Diego County, Nat. Assn. Real Estate Editors (best home sect. in U.S. award 1976, best real estate analysis, consumer oriented story, real estate features awards 1977), Sigma Delta Chi. Republican. Home: 1717 Kettner Blvd San Diego CA 92101 Office: Berkman & Daniels Mktg Communications 1717 Kettner Blvd Suite 100 San Diego CA 92101

DANIELS, WILLIAM ANTHONY, writer; b. San Francisco, Aug. 29, 1956; s. William Edward and Violetta (Remedios) D.; m. Cheryl Ann Cureton, June 21, 1986. BA in Radio/TV, San Francisco State U., 1981. Air personality Sta. KREM-FM, Spokane, Wash., 1977-78; writer, producer Video D. Prodns., Mountain View, Calif., 1979-84; reporter, critic Daily Variety, Hollywood, Calif., 1984-87. Author: The Adventures of Osmond Otter, 1986, The Bad Bears of Barrier Boulevard, 1987; dir. (art video) I Love A Parade, 1980; producer, writer (documentary) Earth Power, 1981. Roman Catholic. Avocations: scuba diving, computers, collecting hats.

DANIELSON, MICHAEL JON, minister; b. Moscow, Idaho, May 30, 1960; s. Jon Jay and Marilyn Ann (Stewart) D. BS in Archtl. Studies, Wash. State U., 1982, BArch cum laude, 1983; M in Ministry, Seattle U., 1987. Youth minister St. John Vianney Ch., Spokane, Wash., 1983-84, St. Mary's Ch., Spokane, 1983—; mem., dir. Cath. Youth Ministries of Spokane, 1983-85; mem. Channel Lay Ministers Program, Spokane, 1983-85; founder, dir. Christian Rock Music workshops and seminars, 1983-85. Roman Catholic. Avocations: tennis, snow and water skiing, juggling, drama, dancing. Home: E 1908 35th Spokane WA 99203 Office: St Mary's Religious Edn S 304 Adams Spokane WA 99216

DANIELSON, WALTER GEORGE, lawyer; b. Anaconda, Mont., July 3, 1903; s. John and Tekla Christina (Jonsson) D.; m. Beryl Marie Pearce, Aug. 17, 1935; children—Karin Lynn Godfrey, John Howard. LL.B., U. Mont., 1929, J.D. (hon.), 1970; diploma of honor Pepperdine U., 1980. Bar: Calif. 1929, ptnr. firm Danielson & St. Clair, Los Angeles; vice consul for Sweden, Los Angeles, 1937-55, consul, 1955-69, consul gen., 1969-76, emeritus, 1976; sec. Los Angeles Consular Corps, 1976—. Trustee Luth. Hosp. Soc. So. Calif., Los Angeles; bd. dirs. Calif. Hosp. Decorated Knight Royal Order Vasa, comdr. Royal Order Vasa, comdr. Royal Order North Star (Sweden); officers cross (Hungary); Knight Royal Order St. Olav (Norway); Knight's cross 1st class Royal Order Dannebrog (Denmark). Mem. Calif. State Bar, Los Angeles Bar Assn. Clubs: California, Vasa Order Am., Swedish (Los Angeles). Home: 68 Fremont Pl Los Angeles CA 90005 Office: Danielson & St Clair 643 S Olive St Suite 600 Los Angeles CA 90014

DANIELSON, WALTER RUSSELL, JR., engineering company executive; b. Wharton, N.J., Dec. 30, 1927; s. Walter Russell and Annie May (Lawrence) D.; m. Paulette Sazerat, Oct. 30, 1957; children: David Walter, Veronique France, Marc Patrick. ME with honors, Stevens Inst. Tech., 1951; MSAE, Air Force Inst. Tech., 1954; MBA with honors, U. Chgo., 1962, Air War Coll., 1974. System mgmt. and acquisition specialist USAF, advanced through grades to lt. col.; served in Ethiopia, France, Ger., Belgium, Portugal and Guam; ret., 1979; project head DSM system engring. group System Devel. Corp., Sunnyvale, Calif., 1979-83; support engr. specialist Lockheed Missiles & Space Co., Sunnyvale, 1983; sr. staff engr. Ultrasystems Def. and Space Inc., 1983—; faculty mgmt. sci. Boston Coll. MSBA program, Brussels, 1978-79. Trustee St. Andrews Meth. Ch., Cherry Hill, N.J., 1964-65; bd. dirs., treas. Am. Community Sch., Addis Ababa, Ethiopia, 1967-68. Served with USMC, 1946-48. Decorated Meritorious Service medal with two oak leaf clusters, Air Force Commendation medal, Joint Services Commendation medal, USAF Outstanding Unit award with 2 oak leaf clusters. Mem. AAAS, Air Force Assn., Mil. Order World Wars, Ret. Officers Assn., Am. Security Council, Armed Forces Communications Electronics Assn. (chpt. dir. 1982-83), L-5 Soc., Ingenieurs et Scientifics de France, Alliance Francaise, Tau Beta Pi, Beta Theta Pi, Beta Gamma Sigma. Republican. Club: L'Ile de France. Lodge: Masons. Home: 2578 Ohlone Dr San Jose CA 95132 Office: Ultrasystems Def and Space Inc 1327 Orleans Dr Sunnyvale CA 94089

DANIHER, JOHN M., engineer; b. LaJunta, Colo., Aug. 2, 1926; s. Gerald and Mary Isabelle (Manly) D.; A.B., Western State Coll., Gunnison, Colo., 1948; postgrad. Idaho State U., 1957-74, U. Idaho, 1974-76; m. Edna Erle Hoshall, Sept. 4, 1948; children—Lyn Mari, Suzanne Laurie, Patricia Gail, Jerome Matthew, Michael Kevin. High sch. tchr., Grand Junction, Colo., 1948-52; salesman Century Metalcraft, Denver, 1952-53; chem. plant supr. U.S. Chem. Corps., Denver, 1953-56; sr. engr. instrument and controls Phillips Petroleum Co., Idaho Falls, 1956-76; project engr. E G & G Idaho, Idaho Falls, 1976—, engring. specialist, 1985—; adv. Eastern Idaho Vocat. Tech. Sch., 1975-80. Cubmaster, Boy Scouts Am., 1970-75, asst. scoutmaster, 1975-80. Recipient Cub Man of Yr., Boy Scouts Am., 1973. Mem. Am. Nuclear Soc. Roman Catholic. Club: K.C. (state dep. 1979-81, Supreme council 1981-84) Home: 250 12th St Idaho Falls ID 83401

DANKE, VIRGINIA, educator, travel consultant; b. Spokane, Wash., Mar. 9, 1925; d. William Ernest and Daisy May (Norton) D. B.S., Wash. State U., 1947; M.Ed., Whitworth Coll., 1950; postgrad. LaSalle U., 1973. Cert. tchr., Wash. Tchr., counselor Clarkston, Sch. Dist. (Wash.), 1947-48; head phys. edn. dept. Spokane Sch. Dist., 1948-77; travel cons. Viking Travel, Spokane, Empire Tours, Spokane, 1982—. Co-author, editor: Marching Together, 1955. Treas. Fedn. Western outdoor Clubs, 1980—; com. mem. Future Spokane, 1981—; bd. dirs. Pacific Crest Trail Conf., Santa Ana, Calif., 1984. Recipient Scroll of Honor-Hall of Fame, Spokane C. of C., 1983; award Greater Spokane Sports Assn., 1973. Mem. Spokane Edn. Assn. (com. chmn. 1960-70), Spokane Ret. Tchrs. Assn. (pres. 1981-82), Wash. Edn. Assn., Nat. Ret. Tchrs. Assn., Wash. State Officials Assn. Clubs: Hobnailers, Hangman Golf (Spokane). Lodge: Soroptimist (pres. 1970). Home: E 1103 14th Spokane WA 99202

DANNA, KATHLEEN JANET, virologist, educator; b. Beaumont, Tex., Aug. 21, 1945; d. William Eugene and Elsie Pearl (Fisher) D.; m. Richard Lloyd Kautz, Nov. 27, 1976; 1 child, Timothy D. B.S., N.Mex. Inst. Mining and Tech., 1967; Ph.D., Johns Hopkins Sch. Medicine, 1972. Postdoctoral fellow in molecular biology Rijksuniversiteit-Gent, Ghent, Belgium, 1972-73, MIT, Cambridge, 1973-75; asst. prof. U. Colo., Boulder, 1975-83, assoc. prof., 1983—. Author chpts. in books, research articles. NIH, NSF grantee, 1975—; recipient Wilson S. Stone Meml. award for basic biomed. research M.D. Anderson Hosp., U. Tex.-Houston, 1973. Mem. Am. Soc. Microbiology, Am. Soc. Virology, Am. Women in Sci., Johns Hopkins Surg. and Med. Soc., Am. Rock Garden Soc. Office: U Colo Campus Box 347 Boulder CO 80309

DANNA, ROBERT, consulting engineer; b. N.Y.C., June 28, 1951; s. Albert Ralph and Anna (Damiano) D.; m. Janice Sarah Agnello, Aug. 31, 1974 (div. July 1984); m. Janis Lee Wind, Dec. 23, 1984; 1 child, Elizabeth Michelle. BA in Physics, CUNY, 1973, MA in Physics, 1975; MS in Engring., U. Cen. Fla., 1979. Registered profl. engr. Research asst. Research Found., N.Y.C., 1974; lectr. Hunter Coll., N.Y.C., 1973-76; dir. physics div. Naval Nuclear Power Sch., Orlando, Fla., 1976-80; instr., dir. engring. services Gen. Physics Corp., Columbia, Md. and San Diego, 1980—. Contbr. articles to profl. jours. Served to lt. comdr. USNR, 1976—. Mem. ASME, Am. Soc. Metals, Am. Soc. Quality Control, San Diego C. of C., Sigma Pi Sigma. Republican. Club: Physics (CUNY) (pres. 1974-76). Office: Gen Physics Corp 2251 San Diego Ave B110 San Diego CA 92110

DANNEMEYER, WILLIAM EDWIN, congressman; b. South Gate, Calif., Sept. 22, 1929; s. Henry William and Charlotte Ernestine (Knapp) D.; m. Evelyn Hoemann, Aug. 27, 1955; children—Bruce, Kim, Susan. B.A., Valparaiso U., 1950; J.D., U. Calif., 1952. Bar: Calif. bar, U.S. Supreme Ct. bar. Individual practice law Fullerton, Calif., 1957-79; asst. city atty. City of Fullerton, 1959-62; mem. Calif. Assembly, 1963-66, 77-78; judge pro tem Mcpl. Ct., 1966-76, Superior Ct., 1966-76; mem. 96th Congress from 39th Calif. Dist. Bd. dirs. Orange County Luth. High Sch., 1972-78; bd. dirs. Luth. Ch.-Mo. Synod, So. Calif. Dist.; spl. gifts chmn. Capital Fund drive Boy Scouts Am. Served with U.S. Army, 1950-52. Mem. Orange County Bar Assn. (dir.), Orange County Criminal Justice Council. Republican. Office: 1214 Longworth House Off Bldg Washington DC 20515 *

DANNER, DARRELL KENNETH, health science facility research administrator; b. Carthage, Mo., Oct. 31, 1942; s. Harold Kenneth Danner and Virginia Lee (Hoel) Kropp; m. Joyce Lee Long, Mar. 26, 1961 (div. Oct. 1976); children: Darrell Christopher, Timothy Harold; m. Barbara Dianne Herring, July 31, 1982. BS, N.Mex. State U., 1970, BA, 1971, M Urban and Regional Planning, 1972; postgrad., U. Kans., 1981. City planner City of Las Cruces, N.Mex., 1968-72; dir. regional planning Mid Mo. Council Govts., 1972-74; asst. prof. U. Mo., Columbia, 1974-79; research assoc. U. Kans., Lawrence, 1979-80; chief research and evaluation Ariz. State Hosp., Phoenix, 1980—; cons. in field; pres. Good Homes, Inc., Phoenix, 1984—. Contbr. articles to profl. jours. Mem. AAUP, Am. Planning Assn., Assn. Am. Geographers. Republican. Episcopalian. Office: Ariz State Hosp 2500 E Van Buren Phoenix AZ 85008

DANSKIN, WESLEY ROBERT, hydrogeologist; b. Berwyn, Ill., Nov. 22, 1952; s. Robert Eugene and Alice Josephine (Hintz) D.; m. Rita E. Hoffmann, July 4, 1983. BA, Carleton Coll., 1978; MS, Stanford U., 1986. Hydrologist U.S. Geol. Survey, San Diego, 1978—. Served with USN, 1973-75. Mem. Am. Geophys. Union, Nat. Water Well Assn., Sigma Xi.

DANSON, EDWARD BRIDGE, anthropologist; b. Glendale, Ohio, Mar. 22, 1916; s. Edward Bridge and Ann (Allen) D.; m. Jessica Harriet MacMaster, Nov. 7, 1942; children: Jessica Ann, Edward Bridge III. B.A., U. Ariz., 1940; M.A., Harvard, 1948, Ph.D., 1953. Asst. prof. anthropology U. Colo., 1948-50, U. Ariz., 1950-56; asst. dir. Mus. No. Ariz., 1956-58, dir., 1959-75; pres. Mus. of No. Ariz., 1975-79, bd. dirs., 1979-84; adj. prof. anthropology No. Ariz. U., 1973-75. mem. adv. bd. Nat. Park Service, 1958-64, mem. adv. council, 1964-85; mem. Ariz. Hist. Adv. Com., 1966-84; chmn. Colo. Plateau Environmental Adv. Council, 1970-74; mem. Ariz. Council Humanities and Pub. Policy, 1973-75; Mem. adv. bd. Southwestern Parks and Monuments Assn., 1958-85; trustee Folklife Center, Library of Congress, 1976-85, chmn., 1979; bd. dirs. Flagstaff Symphony Assn., 1962-71, chmn., 1967-69; bd. dirs. Fred Harvey Fine Arts Found., 1970-77, Ariz. Hist. Soc., 1975-84, Robert T. Wilson Found., 1971-74, v.p., 1972-74. Served to lt. comdr. USNR, 1942-45. Recipient Dept. Interior Conservation Service award, 1986. Fellow Am. Anthrop. Assn., AAAS, Ariz. Acad. Sci. (pres. 1958-59); mem. Soc. Am. Archaeology, Am. Anthrop. Soc., Am. Assn. Museums, Sigma Xi. Episcopalian. Home: PO Box 379 Sedona AZ 86336

DANZBERGER, ALEXANDER HARRIS, chemical engineer, consultant; b. N.Y.C., Mar. 23, 1932; s. George Harris and Ruth P. (Alexander) D.; m. Jacqueline P. Pilcher, Mar. 12, 1954; children—Alison, Alexander, Diana, Robert; m. Anne Griggs Pierson, Apr. 23, 1977; stepchildren—Jennifer Pierson, Priscilla Pierson, Stephanie Pierson. BSChemE, MIT, 1953. Registered profl. engr., Mass., Colo. Mem. staff Arthur D. Little Inc., Cambridge, Mass., 1953-60; engring. mgr. Linde div. Union Carbide Corp., Tonawanda, N.Y., N.Y.C., 1961-70; chief engr. Booz, Allen & Hamilton, Florham Park, N.J., 1971-72, Marcom Cons., N.Y.C., 1973-75; v.p. Hydrotechnic Corp., N.Y.C., 1976-81; mgr. pollution control group Dames & Moore, Golden, Colo., 1982-83; founder, prin. Danzberger and Assocs. Cons. Engrs., Golden, Colo., 1983—. Served to 1st lt. U.S. Army, 1956-68. Recipient Kenneth B. Allen award N.Y. Water Pollution Control Assn., 1983. Fellow Am. Inst. Chem. Engrs. (chmn. environ. div.); mem. Am. Acad. Environ. Engrs. (diplomate), Water Pollution Control Fedn., Am. Water Works Assn.,

ASME, AIME, AAAS. Republican. Presbyterian. Club: N.Y. Yacht. Lodges: Corinthians, Masons. Home and Office: 13245 Willow Ln Golden CO 80401

DANZIG, LARRY ARIEL, orthopaedic surgeon; b. Manchester, N.H., Jan. 18, 1944; s. Martin E. and May (Berg) D.; m. Valerie Goodwin, Jan. 2, 1982; children: Elizabeth Sarah, Matthew Isaac. BA cum laude, Rutgers U., 1965; MD, SUNY, Syracuse, 1969. Diplomate Nat. Bd. Med. Examiners., Am. Bd. Orthopaedic Surgery. Surgical intern Univ. Hosp. of San Diego County, 1969-70, surgical resident, 1970-71; resident in orthopaedic surgery U. Calif. at San Diego Med. Sch., 1971-75; chief reconstructive surgery and rehabilatative medicine March AFB Regional Hosp., USAF, Riverside, Calif., 1975-77; orthopaedic surgeon Orthopaedic Group, Santa Ana, Calif., 1977—; clin. assoc. prof. orthopaedic surgery and radiology U. Calif. San Diego Med. Sch., 1981—; cons. orthopaedic surgery San Diego VA Adminstrn. Med. Ctr., 1978—. Assoc. editor Jour. Orthopaedics, 1980—; contbr. numerous articles, papers and book chpts. to med. publs. Recipient cert. of appreciation Roentgen Ray Soc., 1984. Fellow: Am. Acad. Orthopaedic Surgeons, Am. Coll. Surgeons, Orthopaedic Research Soc., Western Orthopaedic Assn.; mem. AMA, Am. Orthopaedic Soc. for Sports Medicine, Arthroscopy Assn. North Am., Internat. Arthroscopy Assn., Calif. Med. Assn., Orange County Med. Assn., Soc. Mil. Orthopaedic Surgeons, Am. Coll. Sports Medicine, North Am. Spine Soc., Phi Beta Kappa. Avocations: skiing, jogging. Office: Orthopaedic Group Orange County 1200 N Tustin Ave 250 Santa Ana CA 93705

DAPELO, MARIE CLAIRE, credit company financial representative; b. San Francisco, May 11, 1961; d. Louis George and Claire Virginia (Morris) D.; 1 child, Daniel Louis. BS, Calif. State U., Hayward, 1985. Restaurant mgr. Foodmaker Inc., Hayward, 1978-85; account exec. Transworld Systems, Sacramento, 1985-86; fin. rep. Credithrift Fin., Sacramento, 1986—. Mem. NOW, Nat. Assn. Female Execs., Sierra Club. Democrat. Roman Catholic. Home: 8508 Cherry Crest Ct Elk Grove CA 95624 Office: Credithrift and Loan Inc 1418 K St Sacramento CA 95814

DARBY, ROBERT LOUIS, interior designer; b. Detroit, Oct. 30, 1921; s. Leo William and Mary Elizabeth (Gilligan) D.; 1 dau., Mariel Elizabeth. BS, Wayne State U. 1952; MFA, U. Rome, 1954. Prin. Robert L. Darby Assocs., Woodside, Calif.; guest lectr. Can. Coll., Redwood City, Calif., tchr. in field. Recipient 1st prize Ohline Corp.'s Design Competition, 1980. Mem. Internat. Soc. Interior Designers (past internat. v.p., pres. No. Calif. chpt.), Interior Designers Co., Nat. Home Fashion League, Alpha Delta Sigma, Sigma Nu. Contbr. articles to profl. mags., newspapers. Office: 2995 Woodside Rd Suite 400-401 Woodside CA 94062

DARBY, WESLEY ANDREW, clergyman, educator; b. Glendale, Ariz., Sept. 19, 1928; s. Albert Leslie and Beulah E. (Lamb) D.; student Bible Inst. Los Angeles, 1946, No. Ariz. U., 1946-47, Rockmont Coll., Denver, 1948-50, Ariz. State U., 1965, St. Anne's Coll., Oxford (Eng.) U., 1978; m. Donna Maye Bice, May 29, 1947; children—Carolyn Darby Eymann, Lorna Dale, Elizabeth Darby Bass, Andrea Darby Perdue. Ordained minister Baptist Ch., 1950; pastor Sunnyside Bapt. Ch., Flagstaff, Ariz., 1947-48, First Bapt. Ch. of Clifton, Ariz., 1950-55, West High Bapt. Ch., Phoenix, 1955—; dep. assessor Greenlee County, 1951-55; instr. English lit. and pastoral subjects Southwestern Conservative Bapt. Bible Coll., Phoenix, 1961—. Chmn. bd. Conservative Bapt. Found. Ariz., 1974-83, Gospel Wings, 1960—; v.p. Ariz. Bapt. Conf., 1976-83; pres. Ariz. Alcohol-Narcotic Edn. Assn., 1968—. Recipient God, Family and Country award Freeman Inst., 1981. Mem. Evang. Philos. Soc., Greater Phoenix Assn. Evangelicals (pres. 1960-63). Republican. Club: Ariz. Breakfast (chaplain 1969—). Contbr. articles to profl. jours. Home: 5628 N 11th Dr Phoenix AZ 85013 Office: 3301 N 19th Ave Phoenix AZ 85015

D'ARCY-CLARKE, EDMUND THOMAS, personnel manager, educator; b. Englewood, N.J., Dec. 21, 1921; s. John Peter and Mary Agnes (Costello) D'Arcy-C.; m. Vera Annaliese Addix, Jan. 12, 1952; children—Peggy Ann, Evelyn Jeanne, Edmund, Charles John. A.A., Riverside City Coll., 1966; B.S. in Bus., Calif. State U.-Fresno, 1973, M.S. in Bus., 1977. Cert. community coll. instr., personnel mgr. Entered U.S. Army, 1942, advanced through grades to master sgt., 1953; ret., 1964; adminstrv. asst. Angeles Nat. Forest, Pasadena, Calif., 1964-65; resource adminstrv. asst. San Bernardino (Calif.) Nat. Forest, 1965-66; personnel mgmt. specialist Sierra Nat. Forest, Fresno, Calif., 1966-69, personnel officer, 1969-76; pre-retirement planning instr. Centers div. San Francisco Community Coll. Dist., 1978-84; facilitator retirement planning programs various fed. and state agys., 1976—. Mem. curriculum adv. com. Reedley Coll., 1969-74; former mem. Fresno Commn. on Aging., 1979-80. Decorated Bronze Star, Army Commendation medal. Mem. Am. Soc. Personnel Adminstrn., Am. Assn. Ret. Persons, Nat. Assn. Ret. Fed. Employees, Internat. Platform Assn. Roman Catholic. Home: 1243 E Escalon Ave Fresno CA 93710

DARDEN, JEROME WINN, financial analyst; b. PortArthur, Tex., Apr. 11, 1956; s. Jerome Kirby and Martha Dell (Winn) D. BS in Chemistry cum laude, U. Tex., 1980, MBA, 1986. Lab. technician Neville Chem. Co., Pitts., 1975-76, Gulf Oil Chems., Houston, 1976-78; chemist Texaco Chem. Co., Austin, Tex., 1980-83, cons. chemist, 1983—; sr. financial analyst Exxon Corp., Thousand Oaks, Calif., 1986—. Patentee in field. Advisor Jr. Achievement, Austin, 1981-82; participant The Washington Campus, 1984. Mem. AAAS, Am. Chem. Soc., Phi Kappa Phi, Beta Gamma Sigma. Avocations: running, basketball. Home: 1374 E Hillcrest Dr #330 Thousand Oaks CA 91362 Office: Exxon Corp Western Prodn 225 W Hillcrest Dr Thousand Oaks CA 91359

DARGER, STANFORD PARLEY, banker; b. Salt Lake City, Oct. 15, 1920; s. Perry Stanford and Eva (Williams) D.; m. Arlene Barlow, June 17, 1946; children—Stanford Parley, Janet, Ann Darger Hatch, Jane Darger Thomas, John Barlow. B.S., U. Utah, 1944. Pres. Darger Co., Salt Lake City, 1947-53, Darger Ford, Magna, Utah, 1953-55; exec. v.p. Retail Mchts. Assn., Salt Lake City, also div. mgr. Salt Lake City Area C. of C., 1955-73; sr. v.p., mktg. mgr. Valley Bank and Trust Co., Salt Lake City, 1973—; dir., mem. exec. com. Utah Resources Internat.; pres., chmn. Sport Pix, Inc., Salt Lake City, 1984—. Fin. sec., bus. mgr. Mormon Tabernacle Choir, 1958-75; mem. Utah Ho. of Reps., 1962-72, chmn. appropriations com., 1967, majority whip, 1968; del. Utah State Republican Conv., 1962, 64, 68; mem. exec. com., treas. Salt Lake City Conv. and Visitors Bur. Named Exec. of Yr., Nat. Retail Assn., 1970. Mem. Am. Inst. Banking, Bank Mktg. Assn. (pres.-elect western chpt.). Utah C. of C. (pres. 1971). Club: Fort Douglas Country. Office: 185 State St Salt Lake City UT 84111

DARKO, DENIS FRANK, physician; b. Indpls., July 13, 1947; s. Charles O. and Agnes Mary (Lauck) D.; m. Ann Marie Barker, Oct. 15, 1983; 1 child, Emily Marie. BS in Physics, U. Notre Dame, 1969; MD, Ind. U., 1975. Diplomate Am. Bd. Psychiatry and Neurology. Research technician biols. div. Eli Lilly Co., Indpls., 1970, U. Colo. Sch. Medicine, 1971; resident physician family practice Scotsdale (Ariz.) Meml. Hosp., 1975-76; resident physician psychiatry Good Samaritan Med. Ctr., Phoenix, 1977-80, chief resident in psychiatry, 1979-80; pvt. practice psychiatry, Scottsdale, Ariz., 1980-83; cons. psychiatrist Phoenix Indian Med. Center, 1980-81; supr. psychiatry residency program Maricopa Med. Center, 1980-83; instr. premed. program Ariz. State U., 1980-83; instr. family practice residency program, 1980-83; fellow in consultation/liaison psychiatry U. Calif.-San Diego Med. Ctr., 1983-84, fellow in psychopharmacology and psychobiology Clin. Research Center, 1984-85; asst. prof. psychiatry U. Calif., San Diego Sch. Medicine, 1985—, attending physician Univ. Hosp., 1985—; ward chief and staff psychiatrist, San Diego VA Med. Ctr., 1985—. Recipient review article award Am. Coll. Allergists; USPHS fellow, 1972. Mem. Am. Phys. Soc., Am. Chem. Soc., Am. Math. Soc., AAAS, ACP, Am. Psychiat. Assn., Central Neuropsychiat. Assn., Am. Psychosomatic Soc., Calif. Psychiat. Assn., San Diego Psychiat. Soc. Office: U Calif San Diego Sch Medicine Dept Psychiatry M-003 La Jolla CA 92093

DARLING, RICHARD LEO, real estate developer; b. Brainard, Minn., Aug. 24, 1938; s. Delbert E. and Trudy (Etzler) D.; m. Arlene Herbert, 1958 (div.); children: Richard L. Jr., Robert L. (dec.); m. Victoria Killough, 1974 (div. 1974). BS, U. So. Calif., 1961. Lic. contractor and real estate broker. Pres. Tandam Builders Inc., Santa Monica, Calif., 1985—; bd. dirs., founder City Savings and Loan Assn., Westlake Village, Calif. Author: Handbook of Real Estate Investment Formulas, 1970. Mem. Urban Land Inst., Los Angeles Conservancy. Clubs: Bel Air Country, North Ranch Country, Johnathan. Avocations: skiing, tennis, sailing. Office: Tandam Builders Inc 1631 16th St Santa Monica CA 90401

DARLING-ROSENFELD, SANDRA KAYE, educator; b. Portland, Oreg., Aug. 6, 1953; d. Howard Wayne and Ruth Eileen (Russell) Darling; m. Stephen Barry Rosenfeld, June 25, 1983; 1 child, Austin Harrison. BS in Edn., Portland State U., 1975, MS in Edn., 1983. Ticket agt. Meml. Coliseum, Portland, 1971—, Civic Stadium, Portland, 1975—; early childhood educator Portland pub. schs., 1975—. Adminstrv. asst., sisterhood membership chmn. Congregation Neveh Shalom. Mem. Portland Assn. Tchrs. (mem. contract maintenance com., sec. exec. bd.), Theatrical Employees Union Local B-20 (pres.). Home: 6837 SW 11th Dr Portland OR 97219 Office: 4906 NE 6th Ave Portland OR 97211

DARNALL, DENNIS WAYNE, biochemistry educator, university administrator, research facility administrator; b. Glenwood Springs, Colo., Dec. 14, 1941; s. Harvey Glen and Lois Marie (Coleman) D.; m. Judy Marcell Thornton, May 31, 1963; children: Nichol Michelle, Beth Denise. BS in Chemistry, N.Mex. Inst. Mining and Tech., 1963; PhD in Biochemistry, Tex. Tech U., 1966. Asst. prof. biochemistry N.Mex. State U., Las Cruces, 1968-72, assoc. prof., 1972-74, prof., 1974—, assoc. dean, 1983—, dir. research ctr., 1983—; Pres. Bio-Clean, Inc., Las Cruces, 1985—. Editor: Methods for Determining Metal Ion Environments in Proteins, 1979; contbr. articles to profl. jours.; inventor chem. method mineral recovery. NIH fellow Northwestern U., Evanston, Ill., 1966-68. Fellow AAAS; mem. Am. Chem. Soc., Am. Soc. Biol. Chemists, Soc. Research Adminstrs., Nat. Council of Univ. Research Adminstrs. Lodge: Rotary (bd. dirs. Las Cruces chpt.). Avocations: hunting, fishing, backpacking, traveling. Home: PO Box 502 Mesilla NM 88046 Office: NMex State U PO Box RC Las Cruces NM 88003

DARNALL, ROBERTA MORROW, university official; b. Kemmerer, Wyo., May 18, 1949; d. C. Dale and Eugenia Stayner (Christmas) Morrow; B.S., U. Wyo., Laramie, 1972; m. Leslie A. Darnall, Sept. 3, 1977; children: Kimberly Gene, Leslie Nicole. Tariff sec., ins. adminstr. Wyo. Trucking Assn., Casper, 1973-75; asst. clerical supr. Wyo. Legislature, Cheyenne, 1972-77; congl. campaign press aide, 1974; pub. relations dir. in Casper, Wyo. Republican Central Com., 1976-77; asst. dir. alumni relations U. Wyo., 1977-81, dir. of alumni, 1981—; exec. com. Higher Edn. Assn. Rockies. Mem. Council Advancement and Support Edn. (membership com.), Higher Edn. Assn. Rockies, Am. Soc. Assn. Execs., Laramie C. of C. (pizzazz and acad. instns. com.), PEO (courtesy com.), Sigma Delta Chi. Republican. Episcopalian. Home: 1172 Frontera Dr Laramie WY 82070 Office: Box 3137 Univ Station Laramie WY 82071

DARNELL, DANIEL ROE, academic administrator; b. Wyandott, Mich., Dec. 22, 1945; s. Willard Carver and Mavis Geraldine D.; m. Donna Lynn Baker, July 12, 1980; children—Raymond, Scott, Christine, Jeffery. B.A., Okla. Christian Coll., 1967; M.A., Pepperdine U., 1970; postgrad. U. So. Calif.-Los Angeles, 1972-76. Asst. registrar Pepperdine U., Los Angeles, 1967-71, asst. prof., 1972-77, asst. provost, dir., 1972-77; asst. dean Eastern Ill. U., Charleston, 1971-72; dir. instructional service Cerro Coso Community Coll., Ridgecrest, Calif., 1977-79, assoc. dean instruction, 1979-83, acad. dean, 1983—. Chmn. budget adv. com. Sierra Sands Unified Sch. Dist., Ridgecrest, 1983-84; sec. Council on Alcohol Awareness, Ridgecrest, 1979-84; founding mem. Community Youth Ctr. Orgn., Ridgecrest, 1984; founding bd. dirs. Pepperdine Employee Fed. Credit Union, Los Angeles, 1974; youth coordinator Sunset chpt. Calif. Credit Union Assn., Santa Monica, 1975; active Kern County Rep. Cen. Com.; treas. Rep. League. Mem. Assn. Community Coll. Adminstrs., Nat. Council on Resource Devel., World Future Soc., Nat. Council of Staff, Program and Organizational Devel., Phi Alpha Theta (v.p. Eta Zeta chpt. 1970-71). Home: 700 Randall St Ridgecrest CA 93555 Office: Cerro Coso Community Coll 3000 College Heights Blvd Ridgecrest CA 93555

DARNELL, LEONARD ROBERT, information technology consultant; b. Beirut, Lebanon, Dec. 12, 1957 (parents Am. citizens); s. Robert Carter and Mary Lucy (Tunison) D.; m. Denise Michelle Cates, July 15, 1979. B.S. in Math., Loma Linda U., 1978. Programmer, analyst Loma Linda Med. Ctr., Calif., 1979-81; sr. programmer, analyst TRW, Orange, Calif., 1981-82; sr. mgr. Price Waterhouse, Los Angeles, 1983—; chmn. bus. trade show Bus. Net '85; speaker on info. tech. Contbr. articles to profl. jours. Mem. Assn. for Cert. Computer Profls., Los Angeles Jr. C. of C. (chmn. bus. affairs 1985-86, bd. dirs. 1986-87, v.p., treas. 1987—). Republican. Seventh-Day Adventist. Office: Price Waterhouse 400 S Hope St Los Angeles CA 90071

DARRAH, JAMES GORE, physicist, financial executive, real estate developer; b. Milford, Mich., Nov. 28, 1928; s. Carl Williard and Marie (Rathburn) D.; m. Maud Gray, June 27, 1953; children Kimberley D., Sandra Gray Capalongan. BS in Metall. Engring., Rensselaer Poly. Inst., 1952, MS in Metall. Engring., 1953; PhD, Lehigh U., 1955. Project engr. Gen. Motors Corp., Warren, Mich., 1956-58; mgr. nuclear research and devel. United Aircraft Corp., East Hartford, Conn., 1958-64; div. mgr. Eimac-Varian, San Carlos, Calif., 1964-65; gen. mgr. Teledyne-Monolith, Mountain View, Calif., 1965-68; pres. Stratamet Corp., Sunnyvale, Calif., 1968-84; also chmn. bd. dirs. Stratamet Corp., Fremont, Calif.; pres. Darrah Capital Corp., Menlo Park, Calif., 1984—; chmn. bd. dirs. Ceramic Products Corp., Fremont, Calif., 1975—, Gold Mind of N.Y., Buffalo, 1985—, Darco Leasing Co., Menlo Park, 1984—. Patentee in field. Served as cpl. U.S. Army, 1946-47. Mem. Sigma Xi, Tau Beta Pi. Republican. Presbyterian. Avocations: tennis, traveling, amateur playwrighting, musician. Home and Office: 927 Continental Dr Menlo Park CA 94025

DAS, SANJOY KUMAR, ceramic engineer; b. Calcutta, India, Oct. 12, 1953; came to U.S., 1979; s. Sudhangshu Kumar and Mira (Nandy) Das; m. Gopa Roy, July 13, 1984. B of Tech. in Ceramic Engring., Inst. Tech., Banaras Hindu U., Varanasi, India, 1977; MS in Cermaic Engring., Ga. Inst. Tech., 1983. Ceramic engr. Perfect Refractories, Bharatpur, India, 1977-78; sr. ceramist Bombay Potteries, 1978-80; research and devel. engr., materials mgr. R&W Products, Inc., Auburn, Calif., 1983—. Mem. Am. Ceramic Soc., Nat. Inst. Ceramic Engrs. Hindu. Avocations: photgraphy, pottery, hiking, long distance cycling. Home: 11365 #52 Quartz Dr Auburn CA 95603 Office: R&W Products Inc 13079 Earhart Ave Auburn CA 95603

DASH, ALAN, computer software company executive, consultant; b. N.Y.C., May 18, 1934; s. John and Grace (Apfel) D.; m. Kay Kyoko Yokoyama, Jan. 25, 1968; 1 child, June. B.A. in Psychology, UCLA, 1955; M.S. in Computer Sci., West Coast U., 1976. Computer programmer Info. Systems Co., Los Angeles, 1965-68; systems analyst UNIVAC (now UNISYS Corp.), Pasadena, Calif., 1968-70; mgr. systems support Computer Scis. Corp. (INFONET), El Segundo, Calif., 1970-81; dir. internat. mktg., sr. v.p. Fuyo Info. Systems, Gardena, Calif., 1981—. Mem. Assn. Data Processing Service Orgns., Japan Bus. Assn. So. Calif., Japan Am. Soc., Japan C. of C. Home: 14772 Bodger Ave Hawthorne CA 90250 Office: Fuyo Info Systems 1875 Redondo Beach Blvd Gardena CA 90247

DASHIELL, FREDERICK KNOWLES, JR., mathematician; b. Asheville, N.C., June 12, 1941; s. Frederick KNowles and Mfary V. (Grisette) D.; m. Paula R. Rochford, Sept. 11, 1971; children: Emily, Stephanie. BS in Physics, U. N.C., 1963, MA in Math., 1966; PhD in Math., U. Calif., Berkeley, 1973. Adj. asst. prof. UCLA, 1973-75; Bateman research instr. Calif. Inst. Tech., Pasadena, 1975-77; sr. research scientist R and D Assocs., Marina Del Rey, Calif., 1977-81; prin. mem. tech. staff Transaction Tech., Inc., Santa Monica, Calif., 1981-84; staff scientist Inference Corp., Los Angeles, 1984—; lectr. Creative Initiative, 1979-84. Mem. AAAS, IEEE, Am. Math. Soc., Assn. Computing Machinery, Math. Assn. Am., Sierra Club. Democrat. Office: Inference Corp 5300 W Century Blvd Los Angeles CA 90045

DAUB, CLARENCE THEODORE, JR., astronomer, educator; b. Hagerstown, Md., Nov. 27, 1936; s. Clarence Theodore Sr. and Sarah Ellen (Myers) D.; m. Barbara Ruth Lien, June 22, 1963 (div. Dec. 1982); children: Jonathan Andrew, Douglas Matthew. BA, Carleton Coll., 1958; PhD, U. Wis., 1962. Asst. prof. physics Iowa State U., Ames, 1962-67; assoc. prof. astronomy San Diego State U., 1967-73, prof. astronomy, 1973—, chmn. astronomy dept., 1984—. Contbr. articles to sci. jours. Mem. Am. Astron. Soc., Astron. Soc. of Pacific. Office: San Diego State U Astronomy Dept San Diego CA 92182

DAUBEN, WILLIAM GARFIELD, chemist, educator; b. Columbus, Ohio, Nov. 6, 1919; s. Hyp J. and Leilah (Stump) D.; m. Carol Hyatt, Aug. 8, 1947; children—Barbara, Ann. A.B., Ohio State U., 1941; A.M., Harvard U., 1942; Ph.D., 1944; PhD. hon. degree, U. Bordeaux, France, 1980. Edward Austin fellow Harvard U., 1941-42, teaching fellow, 1942-43, research asst., 1943-45; instr. U. Calif. at Berkeley, 1945-47, asst. prof. chemistry, 1947-52, assoc. prof., 1952-57, prof., 1957—; lectr. Am.-Swiss Found., 1962; pres. Organic Reactions, Inc., 1967-84; mem. med. chem. study sect. USPHS, 1959-64; mem. chemistry panel NSF, 1964-67; mem. Am.-Sino Sci. Cooperation Com., 1973-76; mem. assembly math. and phys. scis. NRC, 1977-80. Mem. bd. editors: Jour. of Organic Chemistry, 1957-62; bd. editors: Organic Syntheses, 1959-67; bd. dirs., 1971—; editor-in-chief: Organic Reactions, 1967-83, bd. dirs. 1967—; contbr. articles profl. jours. Recipient award Calif. sect. Am. Chem. Soc., 1959; Guggenheim fellow, 1951, 66; sr. fellow NSF, 1957-58; Alexander von Humboldt Found. Fellow, 1980. Fellow London Chem. Soc., Swiss Chem. Soc.; mem. Am. Chem. Soc. (chmn. div. organic chemistry 1962-63, councilor organic div. 1964-70, mem. council publ. com. 1965-70, mem. adv. com. Petroleum Research Fund 1974-77, Ernest Guenther award 1973), Nat. Acad. Scis. (chmn. chemistry sect. 1977-80), Am. Acad. Arts and Scis., Pharm. Soc. Japan (hon.), Phi Beta Kappa, Sigma Xi, Phi Lambda Upsilon, Phi Eta Sigma, Sigma Chi. Club: Bohemian. Home: 20 Eagle Hill Berkeley CA 94707

DAUGHERTY, LYNN BAYLISS, psychologist; b. Durham, N.C., Aug. 24, 1947; d. Welden Cushman and Vivian Lynn (Burroughs) Bayliss; m. Charles Hines Daugherty, June 11, 1968 (div. 1979); m. Lawrence Gabriel Michelsohn, Sept. 29, 1984; 1 child, Moses James Michelsohn. Student Middlebury Coll., 1965-68; B.A., U. Tulsa, 1970; Ph.D., U. Mont., 1977. Lic. psychologist, Mont.; cert. psychologist, N.Mex. Psychologist Warm Springs State Hosp., Mont., 1975-80; dir. N.Mex. Forensic Evaluation Team, Roswell, 1980-81; psychologist Community Counseling Ctr., Roswell, 1981-83; pvt. practice psychology, Roswell, 1981—; cons. psychologist Tabosa Tng. and Devel. Ctr., Roswell, 1983-84, bd. dirs., 1984—; cons. psychologist Roswell Girls Club, 1984—, Roswell Ind. Sch. Dist., 1984-86; cons. psychologist Roswell Refuge Battered Adults, 1983—, bd. dirs., 1984-86, cons. psychologist Roswell Job Corps Ctr., 1986—. Author: Why Me? Help for Victims of Child Sexual Abuse, 1984. Contbr. articles to profl. jours. Chmn. area selection com. Am. Field Service, Missoula, Mont., 1974-76; pres. adv. bd. Chaves County Widowed Person's Service, Roswell, 1984—. Am. Field Service scholar, Italy, 1964-65; NSF fellow, 1970-74. Mem. Am. Psychol. Assn., N.Mex. Psychol. Assn., Nat. Acad. Neuropsychologists, Am. Psychology-Law Soc., Nat. Audubon Soc., Sigma Xi. Club: Altrusa Internat. Office: 200 W 1st St Suite 842 Roswell NM 88201

DAUGHTERS, ROBERT ALDEAN, artist; b. Trenton, Mo., Feb. 17, 1929; s. Donald Rupert and Ona Gladys (Warner) D.; m. Sandra L. McWhorter, Aug. 29, 1953; children—Ward Tyler, Lynn Renee, Nancy Lee. Grad. Kansas City Art Inst. and Sch. of Design, Mo., 1953. Curator part-time St. Joseph Mus. of Natural History, Mo., 1950-53; fashion artist Harzfeld's, Kans. City, Mo., 1953-54; advt. artist Hallmark Cards, Kansas City, 1954; ptnr., art dir. Moyer Crandall, Inc., Kansas City, 1954-70; artist, painter, Taos, N.Mex., 1970—. Contbr. articles to profl. jours. Served to corp. U.S. Army, 1946-49; Europe. Recipient Best of Show and Merit awards Kansas City Artists Guild, Mo., 1954-70; Best of Show and Gov. Purchase award N.Mex. State Fair, Albuquerque, 1972. Mem. Nat. Soc. Art Dirs. Republican. Baptist.

DAUGHTON, CHRISTIAN GAAEI, environmental toxicologist, consultant; b. Balt., June 14, 1948. BA, U. Calif. San Diego, La Jolla, 1971; PhD, U. Calif. Davis, 1976. Postdoctoral assoc. Cornell U., Ithaca, N.Y., 1976-77, NIH postdoctoral fellow, 1978-79; asst. research toxicologist U. Calif. Berkeley, Richmond, 1979-87; staff scientist research dir. synfuels project Lawrence Berkeley Nat. Lab., 1987—; research dir. oil shale project Lawrence Berkeley (Calif.) Nat. Lab., 1980-86; oil industry cons., 1985—. Patentee contaminated water purification, chromatographic mixer; contbr. articles to profl. jours. NIH fellow, 1972-76, 78. Mem. Am. Chem. Soc., Am. Soc. Microbiology. Avocation: nordic ski racing. Office: U Calif Berkeley SEEHRL 112 RFS 1301 S 46th St Richmond CA 94804

DAUPHINE, RICHARD TIERNEY, orthopedic surgeon; b. San Francisco, Dec. 16, 1942; m. Susan Miller, June 15, 1968; children: Marc, Nicole, Carl, David. BS, Yale U., 1964; MD, Georgetown U., 1968. Intern Boston City Hosp., 1968-69; resident in orthopedics Mayo Clinic, Rochester, Minn., 1969-70, 72-75; practice medicine specializing in orthopedic surgery Monterey, Calif., 1975—; med. dir. Sports Medicine Ctr., Monterey, 1983—. Served to lt. comdr. USNR, 1970-72. Fellow ACS, Am. Acad. Orthopedic Surgeons; mem. AMA, Arthrosurgery Assn. N.Am., Calif. Med. Assn. Club: Yale (Monterey) (bd. dirs. 1985—). Office: 980 Cass St Monterey CA 93940

DAUT, KENNETH RICHARD, industrial engineer, production supervisor; b. Santa Monica, Calif., Aug. 3, 1952; s. Kenneth C. and Betty (Coggins) D.; m. Pamela Jaye Braxton, Feb. 12, 1983; children—Matthew Christopher, Peter Nicholas, Kelly Erin. B.A., UCLA, 1975; cert. in engring. mgmt. Calif. Inst. Tech., 1984. Account exec. Metropolitan Life Ins. Co., Torrance, Calif., 1976-77; bus. devel. officer Community Bank, Huntington Park, Calif., 1977-78; mfg. fin. analyst Northrop Corp., Hawthorne, Calif., 1978-80, indsl. engr. comml. aircraft div., 1980-82, mil. fabrication center, 1982-83, facilities engr., 1983-84, prodn. supr., 1984-85, sr. industrial engr. and indsl. supr. comml. fabrication, 1985—; mem. Northrop Mgmt. Club. Mem. Youth Motivation Task Force, Los Angeles County, 1979-80. Recipient Metropolitan Life Career Booster award, 1976, Northrop Performance award, 1979, Boeing 747 efficiency awards (3), 1982. Mem. Am. Inst. Indsl. Engrs., Nat. Assn. Accts., Hawthorne Jr. C. of C. (sec. 1983, Outstanding Jaycee of Yr. 1984), Torrance Jr. C. of C. Republican. Roman Catholic. Home: 1069 Ridgewood Long Beach CA 90807 Office: Northrop Corp Dept Comml Fabrication One Northrop Ave Hawthorne CA 90250

DAVENPORT, DAVID, university president, lawyer; b. Sheboygan, Wis., Oct. 24, 1950; s. E. Guy and Beverly J. (Snoddy) D.; m. Sally Nelson, Aug. 13, 1977; children—Katherine, Charles. B.A., Stanford U., 1972; J.D., U. Kans., Lawrence, 1977. Bar: Calif., 1977, U.S. Dist. Ct. (so. dist.) Calif.; ordained to ministry Ch. of Christ. Assoc. Gray, Cary, Ames & Frye, San Diego, 1977-78; minister Ch. of Christ, San Diego, 1979; law prof. Pepperdine U., Malibu, Calif., 1980—, gen. counsel, 1981-83, exec. v.p., 1983-85, pres., 1985—; bd. dirs. Colls. of So. Calif., Los Angeles, 1985—; legal cons. Calif. Christian Schs., San Fernando, 1982-83, World Outreach Found., Inc., Malibu, 1982-83. Contbr. articles to profl. jours.; contbr. to Fed. Antitrust Law, 1985. Mem. Adminstrv. Conf. of U.S., Washington, 1984-86; bd. dirs. Mchts. and Mfrs. Assn., Los Angeles, 1985—. Mem. ABA, State Bar Calif., Am. Council on Edn., Nat. Assn. Colls. and Univ. Attys., Am. Assn. Pres. of Ind. Colls. and Univs. (bd. dirs. 1985—, treas.), Order of Coif. Republican. Home: 24255 Pacific Coast Hwy Malibu CA 90265 *

DAVENPORT, JOHN SCOTT, corporate executive, researcher; b. Decatur, Ill., Aug. 12, 1925; s. Omer Earl and Mary Margaret (Baldis) D.; m. Dorothy Matilda Milliken, Feb. 8, 1948; children: Douglas M., Alice J. McCarthy, Margaret E. Hirsch, Geneva L. BS, U. Ill., 1946, MS, 1947; PhD, U. Iowa, 1952; student, U. Redlands and Va. Mil. Inst. Cert. profl. genealogist. Editor, pub. Bur. Valley Chief, Princeton, Ill., 1952-55; dir. research Albert B. Cord Co., Cin., 1955-58; exec. asst. to chmn. of bd. E.W. Scripps Co., Cin., 1958-72, dir. corp. research, 1960-72, corp. research cons., 1972-73; dir. research Foutz Family Found., Honolulu, 1978-85; dir. Davenport Found., Long Beach, Calif., 1985—; lectr. media mgmt. Washington & Lee U., Lexington, Va., 1978; assoc. prof. communication Brigham Young U., Provo, Utah, 1978-79, prof., 1979-80; pub. Daily Universe Brigham Young U., Provo, 1979-80; cons. Phila. Inquirer, 1963-66, Bur. of Census, Washington, 1966-68, City of Cin., 1973-75; dean Kent (Ohio) State U., 1980-81; pres., chief exec. officer Ma-RT Services, Inc., Farmington, N.Mex. and Salt Lake City, 1981-85; v.p. research and analysis, corp. budget officer Bonneville Internat. Corp., Salt Lake City, 1985—. Author: Newspaper Circulation, 1949; contbr. articles on journalism and genealogy to mags. Asst. dir. Labor State of Ill., Springfield, 1954; commnr. of Parks, Green Twp., Ohio, 1972-75. Served with USMC, 1943-45, ATO. Scholar U. Chgo., 1943; fellow Inter. Circulation Mgrs., 1946; named Marine of Yr. Marine Corps League, 1973. Mem. Am. Inst. Indsl. Engrs. (sr.), Am. Mktg. Assn. (Outstanding Contbrn. award 1961), Newspaper Bur. Advt. Research Adv. Council (past chmn.), Nat. Assn. Broadcasters (sr., task force on radio audience measurement 1985—), The Planning Forum (v.p. Salt Lake City chpt. 1986), Sigma Delta Chi, Alpha Delta Sigma, Kappa Tau Alpha, Phi Kappa Phi. Republican. Mormon. Lodges: Elks, Kiwanis, Masons, Shriners, K.T. Avocations: genealogy, fishing, travel. Home: 1101N Am Towers 48 W 300 S Salt Lake City UT 84101 Office: Bonneville Internat Corp Broadcast House Salt Lake City UT 84180-1160

DAVEY, SCOTT ARTHUR, stockbroker; b. Erie, Pa., Apr. 3, 1955; s. Donald Arthur and Gladys Wilma (Paul) D. BA, Allegheny Coll., 1977; JD, U. Houston, 1981; M in Internat. Bus., U. Stockholm, 1982. Bar: Tex. 1982. Salesman Dictaphone Corp., Houston, 1978-80; stockbroker Merrill Lynch, San Francisco, 1983-85, E.F. Hutton & Co., Inc., San Francisco, 1985—. Grad. fellow Rotary Internat., Stockholm, 1981. Mem. ABA, Nat. Assn. Security Dealers, Calif. Ins. Bd. Republican. Lodge: Rotary (San Francisco). Avocations: sailing, cross-country skiing, mountain climbing. Office: EF Hutton & Co Inc 580 California St San Francisco CA 94104

DAVIAU, DONALD GEORGE, German educator; b. Medway, Mass., Nov. 30, 1927; s. George and Jenny (Burbank) D.; m. Patricia Edith Mara, Aug. 20, 1950; children: Katherine, Robert, Thomas, Julie. BA, Clark U., 1950; MA, U. Calif., Berkeley, 1952, PhD, 1955. From asst. prof. to prof. U. Calif., Riverside, 1955-. Author; editor Modern Austrian Lit., 1974; contbr. articles to profl. jours. Mem. MLA, Am. Assn. Tchrs. of German, German Studies Assn., Philo. Assn. Pacific Coast, Am. Council Study Austrian Lit. (pres. 1980-), Internat. Arthur Schnitzler Research Assn. (pres. 1974-). Avocations: tennis, motorcycle riding, stamp collecting. Home: 184 Nisbet Way Riverside CA 92507 Office: U Calif Dept Lit and Langs Riverside CA 92521

DAVID, FLORENCE NIGHTINGALE, statistician; b. Leominster, Eng., Aug. 23, 1909; d. William Richard and Florence Maude (James) D. BSc, U. London, 1931, PhD, 1938, DSc, 1951. Asst. lectr. U. London, 1935-39, lectr./reader/prof., 1945-67; statistician Eng. Ministry Home Security, London, 1939-45; prof., chmn. dept. stats. U. Calif., Riverside, 1967-77; research biostatistician U. Calif., Berkeley, 1977—; statis. cons. Pacific State Hosp., Pomona, Calif., 1965-77, U.S. Forest Service, Berkeley, 1964—. Author: Games, Gods and Gambling, others; contbr. articles to profl. jours. Fellow AAAS, Royal Statis Soc., Am. Statis Assn., Inst. Math. Stats.; mem. Internat. Statis. Inst., Biometric Soc. Home: 156 Highland Blvd Berkeley CA 94708 Office: U Calif Dept Stats Berkeley CA 94720

DAVID, LEON THOMAS, judge, educator, former army officer; b. San Francisco, Aug. 25, 1901; s. Leon Kline and Ella Nancy (Thomas) D.; A.B., Stanford, 1924, J.D., 1926; M.S. in Pub. Adminstrn., U. So. Calif., 1935, Dr. Pub. Adminstrn., 1957; m. Henrietta Louise Mellin, May 22, 1927; children—Carolyn L. Eskra, Leon Colby. City editor Vallejo (Calif.) Times, 1920-21; free-lance journalist, 1921-26; admitted to Calif. bar, 1926, U.S. Supreme Ct., 1932; pvt. practice law; mem. Malcolm & David, Palo Alto, Calif., 1926-31; dep. and acting city atty. Palo Alto, 1926-31; mem. faculty Sch. Law, U. So. Calif., 1931-34, Sch. Pub. Adminstrn., 1934-41, 1947-67; sr. asst. city atty. Los Angeles, 1934-41, 46-50; spl. counsel Los Angeles Harbor Commn., 1939-41; judge Municipal Ct., Los Angeles Jud. Dist., 1950-53; judge Superior Court, 1953-67, appellate dept., 1958-60, ret., 1967; asso. justice pro tem Calif. Ct. Appeal, 1969-73. Mem. Calif. Gov.'s Adv. Com. Law Enforcement, 1959-67. Chmn. legal aid com. State Bar Calif. intermittently to 1950, chmn. state bar com. history of law, 1975-78; bd. dirs., past pres. Los Angeles Legal Aid Found. Served from 2d lt. to maj. F.A.-O.R.C., 1924-42; from lt. col. to col. arty. AUS, 1942-46; comdt. U.S. Army Sch. for Spl. Services, 1942-43, chief Spl. Services, N. Africa and Mediterranean theaters of operation, 1943-45; col. AUS (ret.). Decorated Legion of Merit (U.S.), Hon. Officer Order Brit. Empire, Medaille d'Honneur d'Or (France), Medalha do Guerra (Brazil), Comdr. Crown of Italy; recipient Reginald Heber Smith medal for distinguished legal aid service to indigent, 1962. Mem. Los Angeles Bar Assn., Contra Costa County Bar Assn., Am. Legion (past comdr.), Calif. Judges Assn. (life), Stanford, U. Calif., U. So. Calif. Alumni assns., Calif. Hist. Soc., Mt. Diablo Amateur Radio Club, Soc. Mayflower Descendants, Phi Alpha Delta, Phi Kappa Phi, Pi Sigma Alpha, Blue Key, Order of Coif. Mason (K.T., 32d degree, Shriner), DeMolay Legion of Honor (life). Presbyn. (elder, mem. laws and regulations com., social edn. and action com. Los Angeles Presbytery, 1965-69). Clubs: Commonwealth, Kiwanis (pres. Palo Alto 1931, Los Angeles 1962, lt. gov. Div. 1 Calif.-Nev.-Hawaii dist. 1967). Author: Municipal Liability for Tortious Acts and Omissions, 1936; Administration of Public Tort Liability in Los Angeles, 1939; Tort Liability of Public Officers, 1940; Law and Lawyers, 1950; Role of the Lawyer in Public Administration, 1957; Law of Local Government, 1966; Old 89, My Horse, and Other Tales, Essays and Verse, 1974; History of State Bar of California, 1979; also articles in field of municipal law, ct. procedure and practice, legal history, legal aid, pub. adminstrn. Home: 240 Kuss Rd PO Box 656 Danville CA 94526

DAVIDGE, MARY ANGELA, interior design executive; b. Corning, Calif., Nov. 10, 1952; d. Leland Anson and Alma Jean (Tolan) Williams; m. Barney Norwood Davidge, June 3, 1978; 1 child, John Gordon. BS in Interior Design, San Jose State U., 1977. Designer Pacific Design Gruop, San Jose, Calif., 1977-78; designer Western Design Assocs. Inc., San Jose, 1978-80, project mgr., 1980-83, design dir., 1983-84, v.p., mng. prin., 1984—. Mem. Inst. Bus. Designers (chmn. Western regional conf. 1985-86). Democrat. Roman Catholic. Avocations: skiing, scuba diving, backpacking. Office: Western Design Assocs Inc 175 Stockton Ave San Jose CA 95030

DAVIDOV, HARRY LOUIS, infosystems specialist; b. Camden, N.J., Sept. 17, 1948; s. Martin Abraham and Dorothy (Schwartz) D. BA, Rutgers U., 1973. With Navy Ships Parts Control Ctr., Mechanicsburg, Pa., 1973-86; sr. info. specialist Western Instrument Corp., Ventura, Calif., 1986—. Author of pub. poems. Meritorious Civilian Service award USN, 1981. Mem. Small Press Writers and Artists Orgn., Sci. Fiction Poetry Assn. Republican. Jewish. Club: Los Angeles Sci. Fantasy Soc. Avocations: sports, chess, reading.

DAVIDS, FRANCINE ELISSA, speech pathologist; b. N.Y.C., May 3, 1953; d. William Ernest and Marie (Lipira) Piazza; m. Noah Seth Davids, Aug. 16, 1981; 1 child, Joseph. BA, Adelphi U., 1975; MS, Ariz. State, 1983. Speech pathologist Ariz. Tng. Program, Tucson, 1977-78, Mesa (Ariz.) Pub. Sch., 1978, New Way Sch., Scottsdale, Ariz., 1978-79, Washington #6, Phoenix, 1979—. Author: The Coarticulated /s/, 1986. Mem. Am. Speech Hearing and Lang. Assn. Democrat. Roman Catholic. Avocations: aerobic excercise, computers, writing.

DAVIDSON, BYRON WILLIS, insurance executive; b. Lincoln, Nebr., Sept. 2, 1934; s. Dean S. and Jeanette P. Davidson; m. Janet L., June 10, 1956 (div. Apr. 1959); m. Sandra Gail Chiate, Oct. 4, 1960; children—Keith J., Gary D. BS, U. Ariz., 1956. CPCU. Assoc. in risk mgmt. Ins. agt. Dean S. Davidson Ins. Agy., Inc., Phoenix, 1956—, pres., 1979—; bd. dirs. Insgroup Ins. Co., Denver. Bd. dirs. Valley Big Bros., Phoenix, 1969—, Community Orgn. for Drug Control, Phoenix, 1973; pres. Youth Etc., Phoenix, 1982. Served with U.S. Army, 1957-58. Mem. Assurex Internat. (com. chmn. 1987), Profl. Ind. Mass Mktg. Assn. (nat. pres. 1984-86), Assn. State Ins. Adminstrs. (pres. 1984-85), Maricopa County Agts. Assn. (pres. 1966-67), Soc. C.P.C.U.s (chpt. pres. 1967-68), Ariz. Agts. Assn. (dir. 1972-73), Nat. Casualty and Surety Assn. (coms. 1982-84, bd. dirs. 1986—). Lodges: Masons, Shriners. Home: 302 E State St Phoenix AZ 85016 Office: Dean S Davidson Ins Agy 4620 N 16th St Phoenix AZ 85016

DAVIDSON, CHARLES FREDERICK, metallurgical engineer, chemist; b. Ogden, Utah, Feb. 15, 1951; s. Sherman Aruthur and Donna (Newman) D.; m. Kristen Carter, Jan. 21, 1972; children: Audrey, Erica, Hilary, Lydia, Clarice, Alex Charles, Ashley, Quinn Alvin. BS in Chemistry, Weber State Coll., 1973, BS in Geology, 1973; MS in Metallurgy, U. Utah, 1975, PhD in Metallurgy, 1977. Technician GSL Chems. and Minerals, Ogden, 1973; metallurgist Fansteel, North Chicago, Ill., 1973-77; research metallurgist Gen. Electric, Detroit, 1977-78, U.S. Bur. Mines, Salt Lake City, 1978—; cons. in field, Salt Lake City. Patentee in field; contbr. articles to profl. jours. Recipient Sustained Performance award U.S. Govt. Dept. Interior, 1986. Republican. Mormon. Avocations: hiking, skiing, woodworking, gardening. Home: 2830 N 725 W Layton UT 84041 Office: US Bur Mines 729 Arapeen Dr Salt Lake City UT 84108

DAVIDSON, DARWIN E., brewing company official; b. Rockford, Ill., May 5, 1943; s. Arthur T. and Jane (Kindell) D.; m. Claire M. Janse, Nov. 23, 1965; children: Elizabeth A., Michael J. BS, Oreg. State U., 1965; MS, U. Wyo., 1967; PhD, Duke U., 1971. Research assoc. U. Wyo., Laramie, 1972-74; research assoc. Adolph Coors Co., Golden, Colo., 1974-76, brewing research supr., 1976-80, research mgr., 1980—; pres. HOP Research Council, 1982—. Contbr. articles to profl. jours. Mem. AAAS, Am. Soc. Brewing Chemists. Avocations: running, basketball, reading. Home: 500 21st St Golden CO 80401

DAVIDSON, GEORGE WINFIELD RAYMOND, III, chemical engineer, researcher; b. Macon, Ga., Oct. 16, 1956; s. George Winfield Raymond Jr. and Dolores (English) D.; m. Katherine Lynn Williamson, Dec. 30, 1978; 3 children. BChemE, Ga. Inst. Tech., 1978; MSChemE, Purdue U., 1982, PhD in Chem. Engring., 1985. Staff researcher Syntex Research, Palo Alto, Calif., 1985—. Mem. Am. Inst. Chem. Engrs., Am. Chem. Soc., Am. Assn. Pharm. Scientists, N.Y. Acad. Scis., Sigma Xi. Avocations: microcomputers, ballet. Office: Syntex RI-266 3401 Hillview Ave Palo Alto CA 94303

DAVIDSON, GORDON, theatrical producer, director; b. Bklyn., May 7, 1933; s. Joseph H. and Alice (Gordon) D.; m. Judith Swiller, Sept. 21, 1958; children: Adam, Rachel. B.A., Cornell U.; M.A., Case Western Res. U.; L.H.D. (hon.), Bklyn. Coll.; D. Performing Arts (hon.), Calif. Inst. Arts; D.F.A. (hon.), Claremont U. Ctr. Stage mgr. Phoenix Theatre Co., 1958-60, Am. Shakespeare Festival Theatre, 1958-60, Dallas Civic Opera, 1960-61, Martha Graham Dance Co., 1962; mng. dir. Theatre Group at UCLA, 1965-67; artistic dir. Center Theatre Group Mark Taper Forum, 1967—; co-founder New Theatre For Now, Mark Taper Forum, 1970; Past mem. theatre panel Nat. Endowment for Arts; past pres. Theatre Communications Group; mem. adv. council Internat. Theatre Inst.; mem. adv. com. Cornell Ctr. for Performing Arts; cons. Denver Center for the Performing Arts. Prod., dir.: numerous theatrical prodns. including The Deputy, 1965, Candide, 1966, The Devils, 1967, Who's Happy Now, 1967, In the Matter of J. Robert Oppenheimer, 1968, Murderous Angels, 1970, Rosebloom, 1970, The Trial of the Catonsville Nine, 1971, Henry IV, Part I, 1972, Mass, 1973, Hamlet, 1974, Savages, 1974, Too Much Johnson, 1975, The Shadow Box, 1975, And Where She Stops Nobody Knows, 1976, Getting Out, 1977, Black Angel, 1978, Terra Nova, 1979, Children of a Lesser God, 1979, The Lady and the Clarinet, 1980, Chekhov in Yalta, 1981, Tales from Hollywood, 1982, The American Clock, 1984, The Hands of Its Enemy, 1984, Traveler in the Dark, 1985, The Real Thing, 1986, Ghetto, 1986; prod.: numerous prodns. including Robert Frost: Promises To Keep, 1965, Yeats and Company, 1965, Oh What a Lovely War, 1965-66, Next Time I'll Sing to You, 1966, The Birthday Party, 1966, Poor Bitos, 1966, The Sorrows of Frederick, 1967, The Marriage of Mr. Mississippi, 1967, The Miser, 1968, Camino Real, 1968, The Golden Fleece, 1968, Muzeeka, 1968, The Adventures of the Black Girl in Her Search for God, 1969, Chemin de Fer, 1969, Uncle Vanya, 1969, Crystal and Fox, 1970, Story Theatre, 1970, Dream on Monkey Mountain, 1970, Rosebloom, 1970, Metamorphoses, 1971, Othello, 1971, Major Barbara, 1971, Godspell, 1971, Here Are the Ladies, Volpone, 1972, Old Times, 1972, Don't Bother Me I Can't Cope, 1972, Mass, 1973, The Mind with the Dirty Man, 1973, Forget-Me-Not Lane, 1973, The Hot'l Baltimore, 1973, The Mahogany Songplay, 1973, The Measures Taken, 1973, Hamlet, 1974, The Charlatan, 1974, Juno and the Paycock, 1974, The Dybbuk, 1974, Me and Bessie, 1975, Sizwe Banzi Is Dead, 1975, Once in a Lifetime, 1975, Ashes, 1975, Cross Country, 1975, Three Sisters, 1975, Ice, 1976, Travesties, 1976, The Importance of Being Earnest, 1976, A History of the American Film, 1976, Angel City, 1976, Bugs/Guns, 1976, Leander Stillwell, 1976, For Colored Girls Who Have Considered Suicide/When the Rainbow Is Enuf, 1977, Comedians, 1977, Zoot Suit, 1978, Dusa, Fish, Stas & Vi, 1978, The Tempest, 1978, Talley's Folly, 1979, 5th of July, 1979, I Ought To Be in Pictures, 1979, Says I, Says He, 1979, Division Street, 1979, Billy Bishop Goes to War, 1980, Hoagy, Bix and Wolfgang Beethoven Bunkhaus, 1980, Tintypes, 1980, Twelfth Night, 1980, A Lesson from Aloes, 1981, A Tale Told, 1981, Number Our Days, 1981, A Flea in Her Ear, 1981, The Misanthrope, 1981, A Soldier's Play, 1982, Metamosphosis, 1982, Accidental Death of an Anarchist, 1982, Grownups, 1982, A Month in the Country, 1982, Richard III, 1982, Cat on a Hot Tin Roof, 1982, An American Comedy, 1983, Quilters, 1984, The Genius, 1984, Wild Oats: A Romance of the Old West, 1984, Moby Dick-Rehearsed, 1984, Viva, Vittorio!, 1984, Passion Play, 1984, In the Belly of the Beast, 1985, Undiscovered Country, 1985, Measure for Measure, 1985, Beautiful Lady, 1985, Romance Language, 1986, 'night Mother, 1986, Green Card, 1986, Hedda Gabler, 1986, The Immigrant, 1986, Burn This, 1987, The Traveler, 1987, Roza, 1987; dir.: operas including Cosi Fan Tutte, Otello, Beatrice and Benedick, Carmen, La Boheme, Il Trovatore, Harriet, A Woman Called Moses; TV film The Trial of the Catonsville Nine, 1971; exec. producer Zoot Suit, 1981; prod.: for TV Its the Willingness, PBS Visions Series, 1979, Who's Happy Now?, NET Theatre in Am. Series. Trustee Ctr. for Music, Drama and Art; past pres. League Resident Theatres; past v.p. Am. Nat. Theatre Acad; advisor Fund for New Am. Plays. Recipient N.Y. Drama Desk award for direction, 1969; recipient Los Angeles Drama Critics Circle awards for direction, 1971, 74, 75, Margo Jones award New Theatre for Now, 1970, 76, Obie award, 1971, 77, Outer Critics Circle award, 1977, Tony award for direction, 1977, award John Harvard, award Nat. Acad. TV Arts and Scis., award Nosotros Golden Eagle, award N.Y. League for Hard of Hearing, award N.Y. Speech and Hearing Assn., award Am. Theatre Assn., award Los Angeles Human Relations Commn.; Guggenheim fellow, 1983. Mem. League Resident Theatres (past pres.), ANTA (v.p. 1975). Office: Center Theatre Group 135 N Grand Ave Los Angeles CA 90012

DAVIDSON, HERMAN LAMONT, aerospace co. exec.; b. Denver, May 26, 1930; s. William Franklin and Hazel Arnetta (Lenhard) D.; Asso. Sci., Allan Hancock Coll., 1976; m. Virginia Jane Taylor, Oct. 1, 1949; children—Pamela, William, Virginia, David. Mechanic, Leeman Auto Co., Denver, 1948-51; insp. Martin Marietta Co., Denver, 1957-58, engr./supr., 1958-59, quality project chief, 1959-61, chief inspection missile site, Vandenberg, Calif., 1961-68, chief quality assurance, 1968-76, mgr. quality, 1977—, central quality mgr. programs, 1978-82, dir. mission assurance Space Transp. System, Ground Support System, mgr. quality and safety Vandenberg ops., 1982—, mgr. product assurance and safety, 1987. Served with USN, 1951-57; Korea. Registered profl. engr., Calif. Mem. Am. Soc. for Quality Control (sr.), Nat. Mgmt. Assn. (Gold Knight of Mgmt. 1983), Calif. Soc. Profl. Engrs. Air Force Assn., Am. Inst. Aeros. and Astronautics. Home: 937 Empress Circle Santa Maria CA 93454 Office: Martin Marietta Corp Vandenberg Ops PO Box 1681 Vandenberg AFB CA 93437

DAVIDSON, JAMES WALTER, aerospace chemist; b. Santa Barbara, Calif.; s. Claurice Walter and Jessie Mary (Matthams) D.; m. Rhea Fae Newman, July 18, 1978 (div. Apr. 1979). BS, U. Calif.-Santa Barbara, Goleta, 1959; postgrad., N.Mex. Highlands U., 1959-60. Chemist Gen. Motors Corp., Goleta, 1961, U. Calif.-Santa Barbara, Goleta, 1961-62, Energy Mgmt. Lab., Vandenberg AFB, Calif., 1962—; vol. cons. VITA, Arlington, Va., 1961—. Bd. dirs. Santa Barbara Easter Seal Soc., 1983-84, UN Assn. of Santa Barbara, 1963-65; pres. Mental Health Assn. (pres. 1983), Lompoc, Calif., 1980—. Mem. AIAA, Am. Chem. Soc., Am. Scandinavian Found. (treas. 1962-85), Finlandia Found., Fedn. Am. Scientists, AIC Santa Barbara Peace Resource Ctr., ACLU Nuclear Age Peace Found., Peacekeepers, ISCOS. Democrat. Mem. Vedanta Ch. Home: 3319 Via Arnez Lompoc CA 93436 Office: Energy Mgmt Lab Bldg 7422 SFTLE Vandenberg AFB CA 93437

DAVIDSON, JOEL, sales executive; b. Phila., Nov. 26, 1943; s. Sutherland Packart and Mae (Sandos) D.; m. Francine Beatrice Orner, 1984. AA with honors, Los Angeles City Coll., 1968; AS, Laney Coll., 1972. Sales mgr. William Lamb Corp., North Hollywood, Calif., 1982—. Author: Solar Electric Home, 1983; pub./editor Living in the Ozarks, 1973; (newsletter) PV Network News, 1982-85. Served with U.S. Army, 1962-65. Named Solar Man of Yr., 1984; recipient World's Fastest Solar Vehicle award Guinness Book World Records, 1986. Avocations: solar design, computer, art. Office: William Lamb Corp 10615 Chandler Blvd North Hollywood CA 91601

DAVIDSON, KENNETH WALTER, federal official; b. July 28, 1937. BA, U. B.C., Can., 1962. Mem. Vancouver City Police Force, B.C., 1958-65; mgr. Western Can. McNeil Labs. Ltd. subs. Johnson and Johnson; gen. mgr. Western Optical, Vancouver; dir. pub. library commn., mem. planning commn. City of Vancouver, 1972-75; exec. asst. Parliament of Burnaby-Richmond-Delta, B.C.; mem. Legis. Assembly, Delta, 1975, 79; dep. speaker Legis. Assembly, B.C., 1980, speaker, 1982, 83. Office: Parliament Bldg, Office of Speaker, Victoria Can V8V 1X4

DAVIDSON, ROBERT WILLIAM, printing company executive; b. Colfax, WA, Sept. 18, 1949; s. William Martin and Lena (Soli) D.; m. Molly Evoy, Apr. 16, 1977; children: Ford Patrick, Matthew Harpur, Marshall Andrew. AB, Harvard U., 1971. Exec. dir. Sabre Found., Cambridge, Mass., 1971-72; adminstrv. asst. Congressman Joel Pritchard, Washington, 1973-79; asst. sec. state State of Wash., Olympia, 1979-80; pres. Frayn Fin. Printing, Seattle, 1982—, Frayn Printing Co., Seattle, 1985—; mem. adv. com. Wash. State Software Ind. Devel. Bd., 1984—. Chmn. pub. funding com. Mayor's Zoo Commn., Seattle, 1984-85; pres. Seattle Zool. Soc., 1986—. Republican. Roman Catholic. Clubs: Rainier, Wash. Athletic (Seattle); Harvard (N.Y.C.); Overlake Golf and Country (Bellevue, Wash.). Avocation: tennis. Office: Frayn Printing Co 2518 Western Ave Seattle WA 98121

DAVIDSON, SANDRA LEE DRESMAN, sales engineer; b. Long Beach, Calif., Feb. 16, 1947; d. George Anton and Sophia Genevive (Buczynski) Jecmen; m. Robert Davidson, Oct. 7, 1971 (div. Feb. 1973); m. Craig S. Dresman, June 24, 1978. BSM in Mgmt., Pepperdine U., 1981. Mgr. west region sales Precision Dynamics, Burbank, Calif., 1976-78; dir. profl. relations Westminster (Calif.) Hosp., 1978-80; sales rep. Foregger, Hayward, Calif., 1981-83, Kontron, Hayward, Calif., 1983-84; sales engr. Philips T&M, Garden Grove, Calif., 1984—; mktg. cons. Vortran, Los Angeles, 1983-84, ADA, 1980-85; instr. CPR, Orange County, Calif., 1980-85. Lay minister Crystal Cathedral, Garden Grove, 1985—. Home: 6279 E Woodsboro Ave Anaheim CA 92807 Office: Philips T&M 12882 Valley View Garden Grove CA 92683

DAVIDSON, SHELDON JEROME, medical facility director; b. N.Y.C., Oct. 21, 1939; s. Leo and Lee (Levy) D.; m. Golda Feldman, Sept. 16, 1962; children: Larry, Debra, Sara. BA summa cum laude, NYU, 1960; MD, Albert Einstein U., 1964. Diplomate Am. Bd. Internal Medicine, Am. Bd. Hematology. Intern Maimonides Med. Ctr., Bklyn., 1964-65; fellow in hematology Mt. Sinai Med. Ctr., N.Y.C., 1967-68, resident internal medicine, 1965-67; fellow in hematology, oncology U. So. Calif. Med. Ctr., Los Angeles, 1971-72; with So. Calif. Hematol-Oncology Med. Group, Los Angeles, 1972-77, Valley Hematol-Oncology Med. Group, Los Angeles, 1977—; bd. dirs. oncology Holy Cross Hosp., Mission Hills, Calif., 1978—; assoc. clin. prof. dept. medicine UCLA Sch. Medicine, 1976—; chief dept. of medicine Holy Cross Hosp., Mission Hills, 1985—, Valley Presbyn. Hosp., Van Nuys, Calif., 1986-87. Served to maj. U.S. Army, 1968-71. Cert. of Appreciation dept. medicine UCLA, 1984.4. Mem. ACP, Am. Legion, Am. Soc. Hematology, Am. Soc. Clin. Oncology, Alpha Omega Alpha. Democrat. Jewish. Home: 14960 Dickens St Sherman Oaks CA 91403 Office: Valley Hematol-Oncology Med Group 6850 Sepulveda Van Nuys CA 91405

DAVIDSON, THOMAS J, JR., soil chemistry educator, researcher; b. Los Angeles, Dec. 1, 1935; s. Thomas J. and Thelma Jean Davidson; m. Anna Louise Dawson, July 15, 1961; children: Thomas, Todd, Nancy, Gail, Rosa. BS with honors, Calif. Poly. State U., San Luis Obispo, 1958; MSc., Ohio State U., 1961, PhD, 1963. Asst. instr. Ohio State U., Columbus, 1958-63; asst. soil chemist U. Fla., Quincy, 1963-65; sr. scientist Castle & Cooke, Honolulu, Oreg. and Honduras, 1965-82; prof. soil sci. U. Hawaii, Honolulu, 1984—; with U. South Pacific, Apia, Western Samoa, 1984—. Bd. dirs. Wahiawa (Hawaii) Community Garden, 1977-79. Mem. Am. Soc. Agronomy (cert.), Soil Sci. Soc. Am. (cert.), Crop Sci. Soc. Am., Soil Conservation Soc. Am., Council of Agrl. Scientists and Technologists, Soil and Crop Sci. Soc. of Fla., Sigma Xi, Gamma Pi Delta. Republican. Presbyterian. Home: U S Pacific/Alafua Campus, Pvt Bag, Apia Western Samoa Office: U Hawaii 115 Gilmore Hall 3050 Maile Way SPRAD Honolulu HI 96822

DAVIE, EUGENE NEWTON, international language center executive; b. Oakland, Calif., Apr. 3, 1942; s. Eugene Newton and Marjorie Inez (Sifford) D.; m. Mary Jane Whitelam, May 19, 1967 (div. Feb. 1968). B.A., San Francisco State U., 1965; postgrad. Syracuse U., 1968-69, U. Calif. and U. Hawaii, 1961-63. With Burman-Johnson & Assocs., 1965-66; tchr. spl. children San Raphael Mil. Acad., 1966-67; head English dept. St. Hilda's and Hughes Sch., 1969-69; with LanFranco Corp., San Francisco, 1972—, pres., 1976—, chmn. bd., 1979—; guest lectr. Soviet Consulate. Mem. San Francisco Tb and Lung Assn.; bd. dirs. San Francisco Spring Opera, also mem. exec. and planning coms.; mem. San Francisco Opera Fair., English Speaking Union of San Francisco. Tenn. squire, 1973. Mem. Theta Alpha Phi. Episcopalian.

DAVIES, DARLENE GOULD, communicologist; educator; b. Los Angeles, Apr. 28, 1939; d. Allen Charles and Loretta Catherine (Geary) Geer; B.A. with honors, San Diego State U., 1962, M.A., 1965; postgrad. Purdue U., 1965-66; m. Lowell Davies (dec.); 1 son, David Gould. Instr. speech and drama Bishop's Sch., La Jolla, Calif., 1961; speech pathologist, supr. chmn. speech pathology dept. Children's Health Ctr., San Diego, 1967-71; dir. speech and hearing clinic Naval Regional Med. Ctr., Balboa Naval Hosp., 1971-76; clinic coordinator, asst. prof. communicative disorders San Diego State U., 1976—; mem. prof. adv. bd. San Diego Speech and Hearing Neurosensory Ctr., 1971-74; faculty Point Loma Coll. Grad. Sch. Edn.; cons. several San Diego county sch. dists., 1977-81; community producer of arts features Sta. KPBS-FM Radio, 1985-86; interviewer, narrator (TV films) Learning Resource Ctr., San Diego State U., 1983-86. Mem. San Diego City Adv. Bd. on Women, 1981; bd. visitors Bishop's Sch., La Jolla, 1983; founder Old Globe Theatre, bd. dirs. 1986—. Lic. in speech pathology Calif. Bd. Med. Quality Assurance. Mem. Am. Speech Lang. and Hearing Assn. (cert. clin. competence in speech pathology; asst. book rev. editor), Alexander Graham Bell Assn. for Deaf, Univ. Women San Diego, Mortar Bd. Alumni Assn. Contbr. articles to profl. and gen. interest publs.; asst. book rev. editor Am. Speech-Lang-Hearing Assn., 1981-84. Office: San Diego State U Dept Speech Pathology San Diego CA 92182

DAVIES, DAVID HUW, manufacturing company executive; b. Tredegar, Monmouth, U.K., Oct. 29, 1942, came to U.S., 1967, naturalized, 1972; s. Vivian Jones and Maynance (Richards) D.; m. Josephine Lockwood, July 22, 1966; children—Susan, Sarah. B.S., Univ. Coll., London, 1964, Ph.D., 1967; M.B.A., U. Pitts., 1972. Sr. scientist Westinghouse Electric Co., Pitts., 1967-72, mgr. thin film div., 1972-77; v.p. tech. Kylex Inc. affiliate Exxon Enterprises, Mountain View, Calif., 1977-81; mgr. optical recording div. 3M Co., Mountain View, 1981—: Contbr. articles to profl. jours.; patentee in field. Mem. IEEE (sr.; vice chmn. chpt., 1977-79), Optical Soc. Am., Electrochem. Soc., Soc. Info. Display, Beta Gamma Sigma. Home: 10157 Myer Place Cupertino CA 95014 Office: 3M Co 420 Bernardo Ave Mountain View CA 94043

DAVIES, EDWARD DAVID, architect, educator; b. Madison, Wis., Sept. 4, 1911; s. Howell D. and Julia Hosford (Merrell) D.; m. Marjorie Scheflow, Jan. 30, 1936; 1 child, Robert Huntington. Student, Ill. Inst. Tech. (formerly Armour Inst.), 1930-31, Cranbrook Acad. Art., 1933-34, U. Ill., 1934. Registered architect, Calif., Ariz., Nev. Archtl. designer J. Robert F. Swanson, Detroit, 1935; automobile designer Fisher div. Gen. Motors Corp., Detroit, 1937; plant layout engr. Bigelow-Liptak Corp., Detroit, 1937-38, Marblehead Lime Co., Chgo., 1939-40; designer new stores, warehouses Montgomery Ward & Co., Chgo., 1940—; chief coordinator Army and Navy project Convair Aircraft Corp., San Diego and Ft. Worth, 1941-45; architect Richard J. Neutra, 1945-46, Wiseman & Goldsmith, Los Angeles, 1946-47; theatre architect S. Charles Lee, 1947-50; cons. architect Hayden-Lee Devel. Corp., 1950-52; pvt. practice architecture Pasadena, Calif., 1953—; v.p., founder-dir. Pacific Architects Collaborative, Pasadena. Prin. works include layout and design Los Angeles Airport Indsl. Tract, 1950-53, Hayden-Lee Corp., 1952; designer Los Angeles County Ctrs., Compton, Calif., 1950; architect 25 Luth. chs. including Torrance, Calif., 1954, San Clemente, Calif., 1956, Reno, 1957, Phoenix, 1959, Pasadena, 1961. Pres. Pasadena Beautiful Found., 1961-62; vice-chmn. Citizens Urban Renewal Adv. Com., Pasadena, 1961-62; pres. Pasadena Citizens Council Planning, 1963-64; mem. Mayor's Fgn. Cities Affiliation Com.; mem. exec. com. Forward Pasadena Assn., 1961-62. Recipient Silver Cup, Pasadena Beautiful Found., 1982. Mem. AIA (pres. Pasadena chpt. 1959, mem. nat. nominating com. 1959-61), Calif. Council Architects (bd. dirs. 1958-60, sec. 1960), Planning and Conservation

League (founder, v.p. 1965—), Pasadena C. of C. (bd. dirs. 1961-63), Pasadena Art Mus., Los Angeles Mus., Scarab, Mask and Bauble, 20 Club U. So. Calif. Republican. Avocations: fgn. travel, archtl. research, gardening, photography. Home and Office: 45100 Brest Rd PO Box 1081 Mendocino CA 95460

DAVIES, HUGH MARLAIS, museum director; b. Grahamstown, South Africa, Feb. 12, 1948; came to U.S., 1956; s. Horton Marlais and Brenda M. (Deakin) D.; m. Sally E. Yard, Dec. 21, 1981. A.B. summa cum laude, Princeton U., 1970, M.F.A., 1972, Ph.D., 1976. Dir., Univ. Gallery, U. Mass., Amherst, 1975-83, La Jolla Mus. Contemporary Art, Calif., 1983—; vis. prof. fine arts Amherst Coll., 1980-83; mem. mus. com. Rose Art Mus., Brandeis U., 1981-83. Author: Francis Bacon: The Early and Middle Years: 1928-58; co-author: Sacred Art in a Secular Century: 20th Century Religious Art, 1978, Francis Bacon (Abbeville), 1986. Nat. Endowment Arts fellow, 1982. Mem. Am. Assn. Mus., Coll. Art Assn. Office: La Jolla Mus of Contemporary Art 700 Prospect St La Jolla CA 92037

DAVIES, INGEBURG CHRISTEL, educator; b. Halle, Germany, Nov. 26, 1937; d. Hans Werner and Ursula Anna Helene (Mücke) Kreimann; m. Charles Raymond Davies, Apr. 2, 1963; children—Evelyn Christel, Roxanne Natascha, Charles Ryan. Diplôme de Langue, Alliance Française, Paris, 1956; B.A., U. Utah, 1976, M.A., 1980. Cert. secondary tchr. Utah. Sec., translator West German State Dept., Bonn, 1958-59, Dept. Army, Frankfurt, 1967-71; tchr. Jordan Sch. Dist., Salt Lake City, 1980—; fgn. lang. specialist. Former sec.-treas. Res. Officers' Assn. Ladies. Mem. NEA, Jordan Educators Assn., Utah Educators Assn., Phi Beta Kappa. Lutheran. Author fgn. lang. instrn. text, elem. level. Home: 688 Terrace Hills Dr Salt Lake City UT 84103 Office: Jordan Sch Dist 7350 S 900 E Midvale UT 84047

DAVIES, JAMES SCOTT, architect; b. Fond du Lac, Wis., Apr. 14, 1958; s. Richard C. and Lois (Nett) D.; m. Pamela Jean Acheson, June 30, 1984. AS, U. Wis., Fond du Lac, 1978; BArch with honors, U. Wis., Milw., 1980; MArch in Solar and Appropriate Techs., U. N.Mex., 1986. Designer, draftsman Bridgers & Paxton, Albuquerque, 1981-82, Lohse & Assocs., Albuquerque, 1981-85; job capt. The Burns, Peters, Long, Waters Group, Albuquerque, 1985—. Mem. AIA, ASHRAE, CSI. Republican. Roman Catholic. Avocations: hunting, fishing, softball, weight lifting, windsurfing. Home: 772 Metro Ln NE Albuquerque NM 87123

DAVIES, KENNETH, research physicist; b. Merthyr Tydfil, Wales, Jan. 28, 1928; came to U.S., 1955; s. William Rees and Hannah Elizabeth (Broad) D.; m. Joyce Alice Demerchant, Feb. 20, 1958; children: Russell, Elizabeth, Kenneth. BSc, U. Wales, 1949, PhD, 1953. Physicist Defence Research Bd., Ottawa, Can., 1952-55; asst. prof. Brown U., Providence, 1956-58; physicist Dept. Commerce, Boulder, Colo., 1958-85, sr. scientist, 1985—. Author: Ionospheric Radio Propagation, 1965, Ionospheric Radio Waves, 1969, Phase and Frequency Instabilities, 1970; contbr. over 120 articles to profl. jours. Chmn. Plan Boulder County; pres. Boulder Council for Internat. Visitors. Webster fellow U. Queensland, Brisbane, Australia, 1975-76. Fellow AAAS, IEEE. Avocation: antiques. Office: SEL/ERL/NOAA 325 Broadway Boulder CO 80303

DAVIES, MERTON EDWARD, planetary scientist; b. St. Paul, Sept. 13, 1917; s. Albert Daniel and Lucile (McCabe) D.; A.B., Stanford, 1938, post-grad., 1938-39; m. Margaret Louise Darling, Feb. 10, 1946; children—Deidra Louise (Mrs. Chris Stauff), Albert Karl, Merton Randel. Instr. math. U. Nev., 1939-40; group leader Math. Lofting, Douglas Aircraft Co., El Segundo, Calif., 1940-48; sr. staff Rand Corp., Santa Monica, Calif., 1948-59, 62—, liaison USAF, Washington, 1959-62. U.S. observer inspected stas. under terms Antarctic Treaty, 1967; TV co-investigator Mariner Mars, 1969, 71, Mariner Venus/Mercury 1973 Mission, Voyager Mission, Galileo Mission, Magellan Mission. Asso. fellow AIAA; mem. Am. Soc. Photogrammetry, AAAS. Author: (with Bruce Murray) The View from Space, 1971; (with others) Atlas of Mercury, 1978. Patentee in field. Home: 1414 San Remo Dr Pacific Palisades CA 90272 Office: Rand Corp 1700 Main St Santa Monica CA 90406

DAVIES, PAUL LEWIS, JR., lawyer; b. San Jose, Calif., July 21, 1930; s. Paul Lewis and Faith (Crummey) D.; m. Barbara Bechtel, Dec. 22, 1955; children: Laura (Mrs. Segundo Mateo), Paul Lewis III. A.B., Stanford U., 1952; J.D., Harvard U., 1957. Bar: Calif. 1957. Assoc. Pillsbury, Madison & Sutro, San Francisco, 1957-63; ptnr. Pillsbury, Madison & Sutro, 1963—; also gen. counsel Chevron Corp., 1984—; dir. FMC Corp., Indsl. Indemnity Co., So. Pacific Transp. Co. Hon. trustee Calif. Acad. Scis., trustee, 1970-83, chmn., 1973-80; pres. Herbert Hoover Found.; bd. overseers Hoover Instn., chmn., 1976-82; bd. regents U. of Pacific; bd. dirs. Merritt Peralta Med. Ctr. Served to 1st lt. U.S. Army, 1952-54. Mem. State Bar Calif., ABA, San Francisco Bar Assn., Phi Beta Kappa, Pi Sigma Alpha. Republican. Clubs: Bankers, Bohemian, Pacific-Union, Stock Exchange, Villa Taverna, World Trade (San Francisco); Claremont Country, Lakeview (Oakland, Calif.); Cypress Point (Pebble Beach, Calif.); Sainte Claire (San Jose, Calif.), Collectors, Explorers, Links (N.Y.C.); Metropolitan, 1925 F St. (Washington); Chicago, Mid-America (Chgo.). Office: Pillsbury Madison and Sutro 225 Bush St San Francisco CA 94104

DAVIES, THOMAS MOCKETT, JR., history educator; b. Lincoln, Nebr., May 25, 1940; s. Thomas Mockett and Faith Elizabeth (Arnold) D.; m. Eloisa Carmela Monzón Ábate, June 10, 1968; 1 dau., Jennifer Elena. B.A., U. Nebr., 1962, M.A., 1964; student, Universidad Nacional Autónoma de México, 1961; Ph.D., U. N.Mex., 1970; postdoctoral fellow, U. Tex., Austin, 1969-70. Lectr. U. N.Mex. Peace Corps Tng. Center, 1964-66; asst. prof. Latin Am. history San Diego State U., 1968-72, asso. prof., 1972-75, prof., 1975—; dir. Center Latin Am. Studies, Henry L. and Grace Doherty Charitable Found. fellow, 1966-68. Author: Indian Integration in Peru: A Half Century of Experience, 1900-1948, 1974 (co-winner Hubert Herring Meml. award Pacific Coast Council on Latin Am. Studies 1973), (with Victor Villaneuva) 300 Documentos Para la Historia del APRA; Conspiraciones Apristas de 1935 a 1939, 1979, Secretos Electorales del APRA: Correspondencia y Documentos de 1939, 1982; (with Brian Loveman) The Politics of Anti-Politics: The Military in Latin America, 1978, Che Guevara: Guerrilla Warfare, 1985 (Hubert Herring Meml. award 1985); mem. editorial bd. Hispanic Am. Hist. Rev., 1985—; Contbr. (with Brian Loveman) articles to profl. jours. Grantee Dept. Edn. for Nat. Resource Ctr. for Latin Am. Studies, 1979—; summer research grants San Diego State U. Found., 1971-73, 75, 76, 79, 80; recipient Outstanding Faculty award San Diego State U. Alumni and Assos., 1981—, Exceptional Merit Service award San Diego State U., 1984, Meritorious Performance and Profl. Promise award San Diego State U., 1985. Mem. Latin Am. Studies Assn., Conf. Latin Am. History (exec. sec. 1979-84), Pacific Coast Council Latin Am., Rocky Mountain Council on Latin American Studies (exec. com. 1980—). Home: 4617 Edenvale Ave LaMesa CA 92041 Office: San Diego State U Dept History San Diego CA 92182

DAVIESS, STEVEN NORMAN, geology consultant; b. Cedar Rapids, Iowa, Jan. 25, 1918; s. Harry Marston and Mary Alice (Davidson) D.; m. Frances Ober, May 16, 1944; children: Norman Frederick, Frank Arthur. BA in Geology, UCLA, 1940, MA in Geology, 1942. Registered profl. geologist, Calif.; cert. petroleum geologist. Geologist U.S. Geol. Survey, U.S. and Cuba, 1942-46, Gulf Oil Corp., Cuba, Mozambique, other countries., 1946-59; mgr. Gulf Oil Co. of Spain subs. Gulf Oil Corp., 1959-67; mgr. explorations Gulf Mineral Resources Co. subs. Gulf Oil Corp., Denver, 1967-78; cons. geologist Englewood, Colo., 1978—. Contbr. articles to profl. jours. Fellow Standard Oil Co. Calif., 1971-72. Fellow Geol. Soc. Am., Geol. Soc. Republic S. Africa, Geol. Soc. London, Sigma Xi; m. Am. Assn. Petroleum Geologists. Club: Valley Country (Denver).

DAVIS, ALEXANDER SCHENCK, architect; b. San Francisco, Jan. 3, 1930; s. William Schenck and Amelia (Francisco) D.; B.A. with honors in Architecture, U. Calif.-Berkeley, 1953, M.A. in Architecture (D. Zelinsky & Sons Found. Grad. scholar), 1957; m. Nancy Leah Barry, Oct. 21, 1953; children—Arthur Barry, Laurel Davis Bowden, Pamela Davis Bennett. With Hammarberg & Herman, Architects, El Cerrito, Calif., 1956-62; project architect Bonelli, Young & Wong, Architects and Engrs., San Francisco, 1962-67; chief architect Earl & Wright, Cons. Engrs., San Francisco, 1967-73; constrn. mgr. Fisher Devel., Inc., San Francisco, 1973-74; project architect Keller & Gannon, Cons. Engrs., San Francisco, 1974-77; individual practice architecture, Albany, Calif., 1977-81. Served with USCGR, 1951-56, active duty 1953-55. Registered architect, Calif., Alaska, U.K.; cert. Nat. Council Archtl. Registration Bds. Fellow Soc. Am. Registered Architects, mem. AIA, Royal Inst. Brit. Architects, Soc. Am. Mil. Engrs., Constrn. Specifications Inst. Home: 928 Contra Costa Dr El Cerrito CA 94530

DAVIS, ALLEN, professional football team executive; b. Brockton, Mass., July 4, 1929; s. Louis and Rose (Kirschenbaum) D.; m. Carol Segall, July 11, 1954; 1 son, Mark. Student, Wittenberg Coll., 1947; A.B., Syracuse U., 1950. Asst. football coach Adelphi Coll., 1950-51; head football coach Ft. Belvoir, Va., 1952-53; player-personnel scout Baltimore Colts, 1954; line coach The Citadel, 1955-56, U. So. Calif., 1957-59; asst. coach San Diego Chargers, 1960-62; gen. mgr., head coach Oakland Raiders (now Los Angeles Raiders), 1963-66, owner, mng. gen. ptnr., 1966—; former mem. mgmt. council and competition com. Nat. Football League. Served with AUS, 1952-53. Named Profl. Coach of Year A.P., Profl. Coach of Year U.P.I., Profl. Coach of Year Sporting News, Profl. Coach of Year Pro-Football Illustrated, 1963; Young Man of Yr. Oakland, 1963. Mem. Am. Football Coaches Assn. Only individual in history of profl. football to be an asst. coach, head coach, gen. mgr., league commr. and owner. Office: Los Angeles Raiders 332 Center St El Segundo CA 90245 *

DAVIS, BETTY JEAN BOURBONIA, real estate investment executive; b. Ft. Bayard, N.Mex., Mar. 12, 1931; d. John Alexander and Ora M. (Caudill) Bourbonia; B.S. in Elem. Edn., U. N.Mex., 1954; children—Janice Ann Cox Plagge, Elizabeth Ora Cox. Gen. partner BJD Realty Co., Albuquerque, 1977—. Bd. dirs. Albuquerque Opera Guild, 1977-79, 81-83, 85-86, membership co-chmn., 1977-79; mem. Friends of Art, 1978-85, Friends of Little Theatre, 1973-85, Mus. N.Mex. Found. Recipient Matrix award for journalism Jr. League. Mem. Albuquerque Mus. Assn., N.M. Hist. Soc., N.Mex. Symphony Guild, Jr. League Albuquerque, Alumni Assn. U. N.Mex. (dir. 1973-76), Mus. N.Mex. Found., Alpha Chi Omega. Republican. Methodist. Clubs: Tanoan Country, Internat., Century (U. N.Mex.), Order Eastern Star, Order Rainbow for Girls (past grand worthy adv. N.Mex., past mother adv. Friendship Assembly 50), Alpha Chi Omega (mem. Beta Gamma Beta chpt., chpt. adv. 1958 building corp. 1962-77). Home: 9505 Augusta NE Albuquerque NM 87111

DAVIS, BRENT LEE, software development company executive; b. Haskell, Tex., May 22, 1947; s. Don Wimberly and Frances Wynell (Norman) D. BA in Biology, Tex. Technol. Coll., 1969; MS in Biology, Tex. Tech U., 1975, postgrad., 1975-78. V.p. ops. Bus. Solutions, Inc., Lubbock, Tex., 1978-81; internal systems cons. Delta Engring. Co., Houston, 1981-82; tech. sales support staff Software Mgmt. Systems, Houston, 1981-82; mgr. software engring. Software Mgmt. Systems, Denver, 1982-84; cons. Williams and Burrows, Inc., Belmont, Calif., 1983-84; v.p. Project Mgmt. Techs., Inc., Belmont, 1983—; cons. CRS/Sirrene, Houston, Associated Supply and Equipment Co., Lubbock. Contbr. articles to profl. jours. Grantee NSF, 1970-71, 1975, Smithsonian Instn., 1974-75; recipient Eagle Scout award Boy Scouts Am., 1961. Mem. Project Mgmt. Inst. Democrat. Avocations: photography, art, book collecting, reading. Home: 33 Scott St Apt 2 San Francisco CA 94117 Office: Project Mgmt Techs Inc 1601 El Camino Real Suite 201 Belmont CA 94002

DAVIS, BRUCE WELDON, chemistry researcher; b. Glendale, Calif., July 19, 1937; s. M.W. and Betty (Preston) D.; m. Nancy Lee Borst, June 27, 1964; children: Alice, Kelly, Laureen, Wendelyn. BS, U. So. Calif., 1960, MS, 1962; PhD, U. Calif., Riverside, 1964. Post-doctoral fellow U. N.C., Chapel Hill, 1964-66; asst. prof. Ga. Inst. Tech., Atlanta, 1966-72; sr. research chemist Chevron Oil Field Research Co., LaHabra, Calif., 1973-80, sr. research assoc., 1980—; vis. asst. prof. Cornell U., Ithaca, N.Y., 1972-73. Mem. Am. Chem Soc. (councilor local sect.), Soc. Petroleum Engrs., Assn. U. So. Calif. Chemists (pres. 1985-86), Sigma Xi, Phi Lambda Upsilon. Office: Chevron Oil Field Research Co PO Box 446 La Habra CA 90631

DAVIS, CAROLYN LEIGH, psychotherapist; b. Houston, Mar. 18, 1936; d. William Harvey Speight and Veral Audra (Nunn) Speight Poole; m. John C. Rogers, June 22, 1957 (div. Nov. 1970); children: Elizabeth Leigh Porterfield, Rena Kathleen, John; m. L.B. Davis, Jr. Oct. 14, 1972. Diploma in nursing, U. Houston, 1956; MSW, U. Denver, 1981. RN, Tex., Colo.; lic. social worker II, Colo.; cert. alcohol, drug counselor, Colo. Therapist Bethesda Mental Health Ctr., Denver, 1972-73; supr. emergency alcoholism services Denver Gen. Hosp., 1973-74; dir. alcoholism services Jefferson County Health Dept., Lakewood, Colo., 1974-78; pvt. practice psychotherapy Lakewood and Littleton, Colo., 1981—; adj. prof. Grad. Sch. Social Work, U. Denver, 1982—; cons. employee assistance program FAA, Longmont, Colo., 1984—; mem. adv. bd. Nurses of Colo., Denver, 1984—. Author: The Most Important Months of Your Child's Life: Fetal Alcohol Syndrome, 1976. Mem. Nat. Assn. Social Workers, Assn. Labor and Mgmt. Administrs. and Cons. on Alcoholism. Republican. Episcopalian. Avocations: bridge, music. Office: 6909 S Holly Circle Suite 260 Englewood CO 80112 other: 720 Kipling Lakewood CO 80215

DAVIS, CHARLES JOSEPH, security specialist; b. Portland, Oreg., July 8, 1948; s. Melvin E. and Eloise (Pashak) D.; m. Scottie Lynn Nix, July 31, 1970 (div. 1978); children—Jeffrey S., Amy L.; m. Sheryl Marie Dwyer, Sept. 2, 1980. B.A., Western Wash. U., postgrad. U. So. Calif., 1983, Northwestern U., 1985, S.D. State U., 1986—. Enlisted in U.S. Air Force, 1971; security specialist, Korea, 1971-73, Spokane, Wash., 1973-74, Thailand, 1975, W.Ger., 1977-80, Marysville, Calif., 1981-85, Ellsworth AFB, S.D., 1985—. Tchr., asst. preacher Ch. of Christ, Rapid City, S.D., 1984. Decorated Meritorious Service medals, others. Mem. Air Force Assn., Wilderness Soc., Bibl. Archaeology Soc., Nat. Wildlife Assn. Home: 9708 A Madison Ellsworth AFB SD 57706

DAVIS, CHARLES TRUMAN, ophthalmologist, clergyman; b. El Dorado, Ark., Aug. 16, 1920; s. Jesse Gilbert and Dixie Ethel (Britt) D.; student So. State Coll., Magnolia, Ark., 1939-40, U. Mich., 1945-46, U. Tenn., Knoxville, 1946, M.D., Memphis, 1950; M.S. in Ophthalmology, U. Minn., Rochester, 1955; D.Sc. (hon.), Grove City Coll., 1970; m. Jean Elizabeth Lowe, Aug. 23, 1943; children—Elizabeth Jean (Mrs. Poynter), Nancy Lynn (Mrs. Burritt), Charles Truman. Intern, Gorgas Hosp., Panama Canal Zone, 1950-51; resident Kennedy Hosp., Memphis, 1951-52; fellow in ophthalmology Mayo Clinic, Rochester, 1952-55; staff ophthalmologist Scott & White Clinic, Temple, Tex., 1955-58; pvt. practice medicine specializing in ophthalmology, Mesa, Ariz., 1958—; asst. prof. ophthalmology U. Tex., 1955-58; ordained priest Old Catholic Ch., 1974; consecrated bishop Anglican Chs. Am., 1983; pastor Trinity Ch., Anglican, Ind., Mesa, 1973—; mem. staffs Mesa Luth., Doctors, Desert Samaritan hosps. Trustee Grove City Coll., 1969—; pres. Trinity Found., Mesa, 1970—; dir. Trinity Christian Sch., Mesa, 1970—. Served to 1st lt. U.S. Army, 1940-45. Diplomate Am. Bd. Ophthalmology. Fellow Am. Acad. Ophthalmology; mem. Maricopa County (Ariz.) Med. Soc., Ariz., Am. med. assns., Am. Assn. Ophthalmologists (1st v.p. 1973-74), Ariz. Ophthalmol. Soc. (pres. 1964-65), Contact Lens Soc. Ophthalmologists, Alpha Omega Alpha. Republican. Patentee in field. Office: 1150 N Country Club Dr Mesa AZ 85201

DAVIS, CLYDE EDWARD, chemistry educator; b. Glenns Ferry, Idaho, June 24, 1937; s. Clyde Edward and Beulah Norris (Defur) D.; m. Phyllis Margaret Neef, Aug. 23, 1959; children: Sydney Noel, Scott Edward. BS, Coll. of Idaho, 1959; MS, Oreg. State U., 1962; PhD, Colo. State U., 1968. Chemistry tchr. Casper (Wyo.) Coll., 1961-64, Calif. State Poly. Coll., San Luis, 1967-69, Humboldt State U., Arcata, Calif., 1969—. Mem. Am. Chem. Soc. Republican. Avocations: camping, gardening, rock collecting. Home: 171 Anderson Ln Trinidad CA 95570 Office: Humboldt State U Chemistry Dept Arcata CA 95521

DAVIS, COLEEN COCKERILL, educator; b. Pampa, Tex., Sept. 20, 1930; d. Charles Clifford and Myrtle Edith (Harris) Cockerill; m. Richard Harding Davis, June 22, 1952 (div. Dec. 1984); children: David Christopher, Denis Benjamin (dec. 1979). B.S., U. Okla., 1951; M.S., UCLA, 1952; postgrad. U.So. Calif., Whittier Coll., UCLA. Cert. tchr., Calif. Chmn, dept. home econs., tchr. Whittier Union High Sch. Dist., Calif., 1952-85; substitute tchr., 1985—; home tchr., 1985—, cons. 1986—; co-host America's Bed & Breakfast, Whittier, 1983—, also founder, pres., exec. dir. Contbr. articles to newspapers. Founder Children of Murdered Parents, Whittier, 1984, Coalition of Orgns. and People, Whittier, 1984, Whistle, Ltd., Whittier, 1984; chpt. leader Parents of Murdered Children, Whittier. Mem. Calif. Tchrs. Assn., NEA, Whittier C. of C. (ambassador). Republican. Episcopalian. Avocation: volunteer worker. Office: PO Box 9302 Whittier CA 90608

DAVIS, CRAIG CARLTON, aerospace co. exec.; b. Gulfport, Miss., Dec. 14, 1919; s. Craig Carlton and Helen Lizette (Houppert) D.; B.S., Ga. Inst. Tech., 1941; J.D., Harvard U., 1949; children—Kimberly Patricia, Craig Carlton. Instr. aeros. Escola Tecnica de Aviacao, Sao Paulo, Brazil, 1946; contract adminstr. Convair, Fort Worth, 1949-51; mgr. contracts and pricing, atomics internat. and autonetics divs. N.Am. Aviation, Anaheim, Calif., 1954-62, asst. corp. dir. contracts and proposals, El Segundo, Calif., 1963-70; dir. contracts Aerojet Electro Systems Co., Azusa, Calif., 1971-81, v.p., 1982—. Served with AUS, 1941-45; USAF, 1951-53, to col. res., 1953-66. Mem. ABA, Fed. Bar Assn., D.C. Bar Assn., Res. Officers Assn., Harvard U. Alumni Assn., Ga. Tech. Alumni Assn. Republican. Episcopalian. Club: Harvard. Home: 10501 Wilshire Blvd Apt 1208 Los Angeles CA 90024 Office: Aerojet Electro Systems Co 1100 W Hollyvale St Azusa CA 91702

DAVIS, DANIEL EDWARD, museum director; b. Creston, Iowa, July 3, 1922; s. Fred M. and Myrtle A. D.; m. Mary Joan Kelly, July 15, 1947; children: Daniel B., Nancy, Terry, Barbara, Michelle. Student, U. Iowa, Nat. U. Mex., U. N.Mex., U. Mont. With Nat. Park Service, 1948-77; asso. regional dir. Nat. Park Service, Omaha, 1973-77; dir. Ariz.-Sonora Desert Mus., Tucson, 1977—; adv. bd. Sch. Renewable Natural Resources, U. Ariz., 1980-81; adv. Arab Center Studies Arid Zones, Kouf Nat. Park, Libya.; cons. Egyptian Wildlife Service, Nat. Parks, Netherlands West Indies, Saudi Arabia Nat. Park Service, Thumamah Nat. Park, Kuwait Inst. Sci. Research. Author: Hikers Guide to Grand Canyon, 1956, Boatman's Guide to the Colorado River, 1957, The Little Colorado, 1958, Backcountry Travel, Sequoia National Park, 1961. Served with AUS, 1943-46. Recipient Meritorious Service award Dept. Interior, 1956, Environ. Leadership medal UN, 1982. Mem. Sierra Club, Nature Conservancy. Office: Route 9 Box 900 Tucson AZ 85743

DAVIS, DORIS A., former mayor, business executive; B.Ed., U. Chgo.; M. Adminstrn., Northwestern U.; postgrad. U. Chgo., U. Cal. at Los Angeles; Ph.D., Lawrence U.; 2 children. Tchr. elementary sch., Chgo.; tchr., adminstr. Los Angeles City Schs.; city clk. City of Compton, Calif., 1965-73, mayor, 1973-77. Owner, pres. Heritage Unltd., Inc.; pres. Davis, Edgerton Assocs.; lobbyist State of Calif.; owner Heritage Bus. Products; Pres. Daisy, civic orgn. Mem. Nat. Democratic Policy Council; del., speaker Dem. Nat. Conv., 1972; founder Heritage Polit. Forum. Recipient meritorious award Internat. Inst. Municipal Clks., recognition for community service State of Calif. Legislature. Mem. U.S. Conf. of Mayors, So. Calif. City Clks. Assn. (dir.), LWV, Nat. League of Cities, Calif. Tchrs. Assn., NAACP (dir.), Nat. Urban League, Conf. Negro Elected Ofcls., Nat. Council Negro Women, Links Internat., Phi Beta Kappa, Iota Lambda Phi (Woman of Year), Alpha Kappa Alpha. Address: 4206 E Rosecrans Compton CA 90221

DAVIS, DWIGHT M., superintendent schools, retired; b. Lynnville, Iowa, Mar. 12, 1920; s. Orland G. and Gertrude (McClung) D.; m. Alice Fredrickson, Aug. 20, 1941; children: Gilbert Kenneth, Trevor Dwight; m. Arleen M. Schultze, Nov. 2, 1980. B.A., Iowa State Tchrs. Coll., 1941; M.A., State U. Iowa, 1947, Ph.D., 1953. Tchr. math Williamsburg, Iowa, 1941-42, Iowa Falls, Iowa, 1942-43; prin. high sch., dean jr. coll. Bloomfield, Iowa, 1947-48; prin. high sch. Hampton, Ia., 1948-50, U. High Sch. of State U. Iowa, Iowa City, 1950-53; dean Moline (Ill.) Community Coll., 1953-55; supt. schs. Moline, 1955-65, Des Moines, 1965-80, Colorado Springs, Colo., 1980-85. Pres. Girls-Home Sch.; active Community Chest, Boy Scouts Am.; mem. Gov.'s Task Force on Edn.; life mem. P.T.A.; Trustee Joint Council Econ. Edn.; bd. dirs. Mid-Am. Arts Alliance. Served with C.E. AUS, 1943-46. Mem. NEA, Am. Assn. Sch. Adminstrs. (exec. com., pres. 1985-86), Phi Delta Kappa, Phi Mu Epsilon. Lodges: Kiwanis, Rotary. Home: 2927 Highland Dr Colorado Springs CO 80909

DAVIS, EDWARD MICHAEL, state senator; b. Los Angeles, Nov. 15, 1916; s. James Leonard and Lillian (Fox) D.; m. Aileen Bobbie Nash, Jan. 7, 1984; children: Michael, Christine Hart, Mary Ellen Burde. BS in Pub. Adminstrn. cum laude, U. So. Calif., 1961; LLD (hon.), Western Sierra Law Sch., 1972. Chief of police Los Angeles Police Dept., 1969-78; senator State of Calif., Los Angeles, 1980—; adj. prof. U. So. Calif., Los Angeles, 1967-68. Author: Staff One, 1978. Served with USN, 1942-45. Recipient George Washington Honor medal Freedom Found., Flame of Truth award Fund for Higher Edn., 1976; named Man of Yr., B'nai Brith, 1974, Outstanding Am., Los Angeles Philanthropic Found., 1977. Mem. Am. Legion (post 381 commdr. 1968-69), Internat. Assn. Chiefs of Police (pres. 1976-77). Republican. Episcopalian. Office: Calif Dist Senate Office 11145 Tampa Ave 21B Room 2048 State Capitol Northridge CA 91326

DAVIS, GARY DUANNE, insurance executive; b. Youngstown, Ohio, Apr. 25, 1945; s. Foster and Ruth Jane (Tate) D.; m. Susan Nancy O'Connor, Apr. 29, 1979; 1 child, Steven Michael. AA, Chaffey Coll., 1965; BA, U. Calif., Riverside, 1967, postgrad. Field rep. Calif. Casualty Ins. Co., Riverside, 1970-72; product developer Calif. Casualty Ins. Co., San Mateo, 1977-79; underwriter, sales mgr. mass mktg. INA Corp. subs. Cigna Corp., Phila., 1972-77; dir. mass mktg. Wausau Ins. Co., St. Louis, 1979-81; v.p. personal lines, mass mktg. Marsh & McLennan, Los Angeles, 1981-85; v.p. sales and mktg. Ins. Office of Am., Inc., El Toro, Calif., 1985—. Republican. Presbyterian. Avocations: travel, running, sports. Home: 24621 Cresta Ct Laguna Hills CA 92653 Office: Ins Office of Am Inc 22481 Aspan St El Toro CA 92630

DAVIS, GARY THAYNE, county official; b. Topeka, July 22, 1938; s. Kenneth Doud and Ruth Nylene (Grabow) D.; B.S., George Washington U., 1972; M.Sc., Naval Postgrad. Sch., 1974; children—Gary Thayne, Alisa Diane, Sheila Rene Hamilton. Enlisted in U.S. Navy, 1955, commd. ensign M.S.C., 1967, advanced through grades to lt. comdr., 1977, ret., 1981; comptroller Naval Regional Med. Clinics, Pearl Harbor, Hawaii, 1981-82; adminstrv. officer Jefferson County Health Dept., Lakewood, Colo., 1982—; acctg. instr. U. Guam, 1976. Mem. Gov.'s Com. for Armed Forces Day, 1976; committeeman Littleton Republican Com.; co-chmn. South Jefferson County Pride, 1985; officer South Jefferson County Rep. Com., 1985. Decorated Navy Commendation medal (U.S.), Cross of Gallantry (Vietnam). Mem. Assn. Govt. Accts. (cert. of merit, pres. Guam 1976-77), Assn. Mil. Comptrollers, Advanced Hosp. Fin. Mgmt. Assn., Am. Hosp. Assn., Colo. Pub. Health Assn., Colo. Health and Environ. Council (chmn. bd. dirs. 1986-87). Clubs: Nat. Sojourners (pres. Hawaii 1980-81), Hero of '76, Dragoman (pres. 1986—). Lodges: Jesters, Masons, Shriners. Home: 10147 W Fremont Pl Littleton CO 80127

DAVIS, GAY RUTH, psychotherapist, social welfare educator, consultant; b. Bellingham, Wash., Sept. 19, 1935; d. Lee Laverne Wickersham and Altha Pearl (Lund) Wickersham Knight; m. Paul Cushing Davis, Dec. 20, 1956; children: Jeffrey Richards, Jennifer Lynn. Student, Brigham Young U., 1953-55; BA summa cum laude, Western Wash. U., 1976; MSW, U. Wash., 1978, PhD, 1985. Dir. social services dept. Sound Health Assn., Tacoma, 1977-78; social work profl. Harborview Med. Ctr., Seattle, 1979-81; lectr. social work U. Wash., Seattle, 1984-85; pvt. practice cons. social work and psychotherapy Seattle, 1985—; cons. Virginia Mason Hosp. Separation and Loss Inst., Seattle, 1985—. Contbr. articles to profl. jours. Grantee Wash. Dept. Health and Human Services, 1981-82. Mem. Nat. Assn. Social Workers, Wash. Assn. Social Workers, Council on Social Work Edn., Gerontol. Soc. Am. Democrat. Mormon. Avocations: geneology, writing.

DAVIS, GERI TURNER, educator; b. Eden, N.C., Mar. 23; d. William Rosamond and Mary Thelma (Barnes) Turner; m. Bruce Reynolds DAvis, Nov. 28, 1957 (div. 1974). AA, Lees-McRae Coll., 1954; BA, U. N.C., 1957; MA, U. So. Calif., 1962; PhD, U.S. Internat. U., 1981. Tchr. Forsyth County (N.C.) Pub. Schs., Winston-Salem, 1957; tchr. San Diego City Schs., 1957-62, 63-86, mentor tchr., 1984-86; researcher, writer CBS TV, Los Angeles, 1962-63; tchr. U. Calif., San Diego, 1985—; dir., coach theater arts Mission Bay HIgh Sch., San Diego, 1957-62, 64-75; coach speech arts Point Loma High Sch., San Diego, 1975-86. Author (play) A Cat Called Jesus,

1965, (5 awards 1965); contbr. articles to mags. Named Outstanding Young Woman of Am.; grantee Humanities Inst. U. Calif., San Diego, 1984; recipient Excellence in Edn. award Rotary Internat.. Mem. Nat. Forensic League, Nat. Tchrs. Assn.; Calif. Tchrs. Assn., San Diego Tcrs. Assn., ACLU, Alpha Delta Kappa. Avocations: dancing, reading, talking, theater, arts. Home: 5251 Pacifica Dr San Diego CA 92109 Office: Point Loma High Sch 2335 Chatsworth Blvd San Diego CA 91106

DAVIS, GLENN ALFRED, management analyst, army intelligence specialist; b. Gastonia, N.C., July 28, 1938; s. Glenn Howard Davis and Virginia (Self) Barnes; m. Patsy Jean George, Aug. 9, 1958; children: William Eugene, Douglas Glenn. AS in Indsl. Mgmt., El Paso (Tex.) Community Coll., 1974. Enlisted U.S. Army, advanced through grades to command sgt. major, 1977; command sgt. major U.S. Army Field Sta., Pyongtaek, Republic of Korea, 1978-79, U.S. Army Intelligence Sch., Ft. Huachuca, Ariz., 1979-81; ret. U.S. Army, 1981; asst. tech. dir. Mantech Internat., Sierra Vista, Ariz., 1981-83; dep. dir. dept. human intelligence U.S. Army Intelligence Ctr., Ft. Huachuca, 1983-85; mgmt. analyst, team leader U.S. Army Info. Systems Command, Ft. Huachuca, 1985—. Mem. Am. Soc. Mil. Comptrollers, Assn. Old Crows. Democrat. Baptist. Lodge: Masons. Avocation: home computing. Home: 19 Danser Dr NE Sierra Vista AZ 85635 Office: US Army Info Systems Command Mgmt Engring Activity Fort Huachuca AZ 85613-5000

DAVIS, GLENN WILLIAM, personnel executive; b. Springfield, Ill., Mar. 11, 1943; s. Loren Garland and Ida Louise (Carraro) D.; m. Pamela Louise Broyles, Mar. 1, 1964; children: Kersten, Krista. BA, Eastern Ill. U., 1965; MEd, U. Ill., 1969, Cert. Advanced Studies, 1976; postgrad., Ariz. State U. Tchr. Springfield Pub. Schs., 1965-69, prin., 1970-78; prin. Cave Creek (Ariz.) Schs., 1979-81; prin. Kyrene Schs., Tempe, Ariz., 1982-84, dir. personnel, 1985—. Home: 3357 W Sandra Terr Phoenix AZ 85023

DAVIS, GUILLETT GERVAISE, III, lawyer; b. Marshalltown, Iowa, Nov. 18, 1932; s. Guillett Gervaise and Alice V. (Denison) D.; m. Kathleen Anderson,June 22, 1955; children: Virginia, Cynthia, Susan, Shauna. BS, Georgetown U., 1954, JD, 1958. Law clk. to presiding justice U.S. Ct. Appeals, Los Angeles, 1958-59; assoc. Lillick, Geary, Wheat, Adams & Charles, San Francisco, 1959-60; ptnr. Walker, Schroeder, Davis & Brehmer, Monterey, Calif., 1960-78; sr. ptnr. Schroeder, Davis & Orliss, Inc., Monterey, 1978—; v.p. legal, dir. Am. Recreation Ctrs., Sacramento, 1959—; sec., dir. Digital Research Corp., Monterey, 1977-85; v.p., sec., bd. dirs. Lifetree Software, Monterey, 1983—. Author: Software Protection: Practical and Legal Steps to Protect and Market Computer Programs, 1985 (Hon. Mention Assn. Am. Pubs. 1985). Served as sgt. U.S. Army, 1954-56. Home: 1150 Alta Mesa Rd Monterey CA 93940 Office: Schroeder Davis & Orliss Inc 215 W Franklin St Monterey CA 93940

DAVIS, HELEN NANCY MATSON (MRS. CHAUNCEY D. DAVIS), real estate broker, civic worker; b. Zanesville, Ohio, Nov. 18, 1905; d. Austin F. and Georgianna (Hale) Matson; grad. high sch.; m. Chauncey D. Davis, May 1, 1924; children—James Harvey, Robert Lee. Real estate broker, South Bend, Wash., 1964—. Exec. sec. Pacific County Tb League, 1936-62; chmn. Park Bd., South Bend, 1955—; ofcl. Pacific County Bicentennial Pageant; trustee Pacific County Hist. Soc. Named Woman of Yr. Pacific County C. of C., 1949, 61. Mem. Nat. League Am. Pen Women, Dramatists Guild Inc., Propaelaeum Study Club, Chinook Indian Tribe (hon.), Delta Kappa Gamma. Republican. Methodist. Rebekah. Club: Garden (South Bend). Composer: Washington, My Home (ofcl. state song Wash.), 1959; Eliza and the Lumberjack (mus. play). Home: 606 W 2d St South Bend WA 98586 Office: 705 Robert Bush Dr South Bend WA 98586

DAVIS, HELENA LANG, human relations consultant, writer; b. Richmond, Va., Sept. 21, 1942; d. Harold and Regina (Lang) Pfeffer; m. Richard Earl Davis, Dec. 18, 1966; 1 dau., Rebekah Caroline Beatty Davis. B.A., U. Md., 1965; secondary teaching credential San Francisco State U., 1972, postgrad. in Am. Indian edn., 1973-75; postgrad. in curriculum design, U. San Francisco, 1978-80; Instr. Native Am. studies U. San Francisco, 1971-72; Emergency Sch. Aid Act reading coordinator San Francisco Unified Sch. Dist., 1973-75, chmn. native Am. sub-com., 1974; tchr. English and lang. arts Ramah Navajo High Sch., N.Mex., 1976; coordinator acad. support services U. San Francisco, 1979-80; fgn. expert East China Normal U., Shanghai, People's Republic China, 1980-81; dir. School Initiatives program Community Bd. Ctr. for Policy and Tng., San Francisco, 1982-85, assoc. dir., 1985-86; founder, exec. dir. Connections, 1986—; cons. Human Rights Commn., San Francisco, 1973-74, Filipino Edn. Ctr., San Francisco, 1974-75, Title IV Am. Indian Edn. Project, San Francisco, 1974-75, J. Gary Mitchell Film Productions, 1984—, Paul Rupert Assocs., 1986—, Camp Thoreau-in-Vermont, 1985-86; British Columbia Justice Inst., 1985-86; curriculum cons. Chinese-Am. People's Friendship Assn., San Francisco, 1975-76; program cons. UN U. for Peace, Costa Rica, 1984; mem. Consortium on Peace Research, Edn. and Devel., 1984; adv. bd. Meadowlark Camp for Peace; program organizer Third Nat. Conf. on Peacemaking and Conflict Resolution, Denver, 1986; co-founder World Mediation Congress, 1985.Author: Conflict Resolution for Youth: An Experiential Approach, 1982; China Year, 1981; Indians in America's Past, 1971; author, editor: Conflict Manager Program Implementation and Training Manual, 1983; The Teacher as Trainer in Conflict Management Programs, 1984. Contbr. articles to Profl. jours. Mem. Parents Coalition, 1984, M.H. deYoung Mus., 1978-84. Mem. Calif. Acad. Sci., Am. Soc. for Tng. and Devel., Nat. Assn. Mediators in Edn. (steering com. 1984), Pi Lambda Theta (rec. sec. 1973-74, nat. conf. del. 1975), Phi Delta Kappa. Office: Connections 40 Delano Ave San Francisco CA 94112

DAVIS, HOWARD MURRAY, electrical engineer, technical management consultant; b. Greenfield, Mass., Feb. 28, 1920; s. Murray E. and Mildred I. (Leonard) D.; m. Mary Eileen Cowan, Apr. 10, 1943; children—James Howard, John Leonard. B.E.E., Rensselaer Poly. Inst., 1950. Chief electronic counter measures project coordinator Army Air Force Proving Ground, Eglin Field, Fla., 1943-46; various engring. mgmt. positions Sperry Co., Great Neck, N.Y., 1950-83; pvt. engring. cons., San Diego and Washington, 1983—. Contbr. articles on project mgmt. to profl. jours. Served to capt. USAF, 1943-46. Mem. IEEE (sr.), Am. Def. Preparedness Assn. (steering com. combat system), Tau Beta Pi, Eta Kappa Nu. Home and Office: 12504 Avenida Tineo San Diego CA 92128

DAVIS, JAMES FRANKLIN, III, public relations executive; b. Marshall, Tex., Feb. 1, 1943; s. James Franklin Jr. and Jimmie (Johnston) D.; m. Ann Gaither, June 20, 1970; 1 child, April Elaine. BS in Radio, TV and Film, U. Tex., 1970; MEd, Chapman Coll., 1983; postgrad., U. S.C., 1983. Program dir. Sta. KHFI-TV, Austin, Tex., 1972-87; commd. 2d lt. U.S. Army, 1970, advanced through grades to capt., 1976, ret., 1983; pub. affairs officer Dept. of Army, Ft. Ord, Calif., 1983—. Mem. Pub. Relations Soc. Am., DAV (2d Jr. vice comdr. 1986—), Monterey C. of C. (mil. affairs com. 1985-86), Salinas C. of C. (mil. affairs com. 1985-86). Republican. Methodist. Avocations: music, performance cars. Home: 9956 Cockle Bur Ct Salinas CA 93907 Office: Pub Affairs Office Fort Ord CA 93941

DAVIS, JEAN MARGARET, career counselor, educator; b. Antioch, Calif., Dec. 31, 1945; d. Clyde W. and Elizabeth Jean (Heaton) D.; m. Robert F. King, 1967; 1 child, Jody Lynn; m. Charles J. Harris, Dec. 17, 1979. BA in Sociology summa cum laude, with honors, Dickinson Coll., 1967; MS in Edn. Sci., SUNY, Albany, 1976. Social worker Susquehanna Valley Home, Binghamton, N.Y., 1967-69; asst. dir. career counseling Trinity Coll., Hartford, Conn., 1976-78; coordinator career planning Keystone Jr. Coll., La Plume, Pa., 1978-79; counselor, instr. Santa Rosa (Calif.) Jr. Coll., 1981—. Editor Pacific Woodworker mag., 1982-84, contbr. articles, 1984-85. Mem. Sonoma County Women's Soccer League (bd. dirs. 1984-85), Phi Beta Kappa. Avocations: soccer, softball, gardening, playing trumpet and french horn. Office: Santa Rosa Jr Coll 1501 Mendocino Ave Santa Rosa CA 95401

DAVIS, JEREMY MATTHEW, chemist; b. Bakersfield, Calif., Aug. 5, 1953; s. Joseph Hyman and Mary (Pavetto) D.; m. Bernadette Sobkiewicz, Aug. 28, 1976; 1 child, Andrew Jeremy. BS, U. Calif., 1974; M in Pub. Adminstrn., Calif. State U., Long Beach, 1983. Salesman Camera World, San Diego, 1974-75, Gailey Photo Supply, Escondido, Calif., 1975-76; lab.

technician Crosby Labs., Orange, Calif., 1976-77; chemist I, II, Orange County Water Dist., Fountain Valley, Calif., 1977-84, supervising chemist, 1984—. Named Lab. Person of Yr., Calif. Water Pollution Control Assn., Santa Ana River Basin, 1984. Mem. Am. Chem. Soc. (chem. health and safety sect.), Am. Water Works Assn., Am. Soc. Pub. Adminstrn., Water Pollution Control Fedn., Calif. Water Pollution Control Assn. (bd. dirs. Santa Ana River Basin chpt., Lab. Person of Yr., 1984). Office: Orange County Water Dist PO Box 8300 Fountain Valley CA 92728-8300

DAVIS, JOEL ANTHONY, freelance writer; b. Ventura, Calif., Oct. 11, 1948; s. Gerald Herbert and Antonia (Farkas) D.; m. Marie Ann Celestre, Aug. 30, 1975. BA in English, Calif. Luth. U., 1970; MLS, U. Oreg., 1976. Registered profl. librarian, Wash. Librarian Spokane County Library System, Wash., 1977-78; reporter Spokane Community Press, 1978-79; freelance writer Spokane and Olympia, Wash., 1979—. Author: Endorphins: New Waves in Brain Chemistry, 1984, Flyby: The Interplanetary Odyssey of Voyager 2, 1987; contbr. numerous articles to publs. Recipient 1st place sci. writing award Soc. Profl. Journalists, 1985. Mem. AAAS, Am. Soc. Journalists and Authors, Nat. Assn. Sci. Writers, Sci. Fiction Writers Am. Democrat. Roman Catholic. Avocations: weightlifting, racquetball, bicycling, science fiction. Home: 902 N Quince St Olympia WA 98506 Office: care Scott Meredith Lit Agy Inc 845 Third Ave New York NY 10022

DAVIS, JOHN CHARLES, IV, food service company executive; b. Denver, Nov. 16, 1944; s. John Charles III and Margaret Regene (Stenseth) D.; m. Carol Ann Rymer, May 9, 1969; children: Heather Mead, Marne Anne. Student, U. Vt., 1963-65. V.p., gen. mgr. Davis Bros., Inc., Albuquerque, 1974-78; pres. Balloonport of Albuquerque, 1976—; pres., gen. mgr. Restaurant Industries, Inc., Albuquerque, 1984—. Mem., past. chmn. Bernalillo County Planning Commn., Albuquerque, 1972-84; mem. Albuquerque Environ. Planning Commn., 1985—; bd. dirs. Albuquerque Internat. Balloon Fiesta, past. pres., past chmn. bd. dirs. Named Accident Prevention Counselor of Yr., FAA, 1984. Mem. Balloon Fedn. Am. (Pres.'s award 1977). Republican. Episcopalian. Clubs: Albuquerque Country; Colo. Arlberg. Avocations: hot air ballooning, skiing, bicycling, computers. Home: 1312 Los Arboles Ave NW Albuquerque NM 87107

DAVIS, JOHN ROWLAND, university adminstrator; b. Mpls., Dec. 19, 1927; s. Roland Owen and Dorothy (Norman) D.; m. Lois Marie Falk, Sept. 4, 1947; children—Joel C., Jacque L., Michele M., Robin E. B.S., U. Minn., 1949, M.S. 1951; postgrad., Purdue U., 1955-57; Ph.D., Mich. State U. 1959. Registered profl. engr., Calif., Oreg. Hydraulic engr. U.S. Geol. Survey, Lincoln, Nebr., 1950-51; instr. Mich. State U., 1951-55; asst. prof. Purdue U., 1955-57; lectr. U. Calif. at Davis, 1957-62; hydraulic engr. Stanford Research Inst., South Pasadena, Calif., 1962-64; prof. U. Nebr., Lincoln, 1964-65; dean U. Nebr. Coll. (Engring. and Architecture), 1965-71; prof., head dept. agrl. engring. Oreg. State U., Corvallis, 1971-75; instl. athletic rep. Oreg. State U., 1972—; dir. Agrl. Expt. Sta., asso. dean Sch. Agr., Oreg. State U., 1975-85, dir. spl. programs Office of Academic Affairs, assoc. dir. athletics, 1987—; mem. governing bd. Water Resources Research Inst., 1975-85; dir. Western Rural Devel. Center, 1975-85, Agrl. Research Found., Jackman Inst.; cons. Stanford Research Inst., Dept. Agr., Consortium for Internat. Devel.; dir. Engrs. Council Profl. Devel., 1966-72; pres. Pacific-10 Conf., 1978-79. Contbr. articles to profl. jours. Served with USNR, 1945-46. Fellow Am. Soc. Agrl. Engrs. (dir. 1971-73, agrl. engr. of year award Pacific N.W. region 1974), Nat. Coll. Athletic Assn. (v.p. 1979-83, sec.-treas. 1983-85, pres. 1985-87). Home: 2940 NW Aspen St Corvallis OR 97330 Office: Oreg State U Gill Coliseum Corvallis OR 97331

DAVIS, KAREN ROSEMARY, educational administrator; b. San Bernardino, Calif., Sept. 4, 1947; d. Lewis William and Florence Mary (Gramlich) Little; m. Richard Ross Davis, Jan. 17, 1970. BA, MA, Calif. State Poly. U., Pomona, 1970. Cert. elem. tchr., Calif., reading tchr., Calif. Tchr. Hacienda-LaPuente (Calif.) Unified Sch. Dist., 1970-73, reading specialist, 1973-76, curriculum specialist, 1976-80; staff devel. program Riverside (Calif.)-San Bernadino County Supt. of Schs., 1980-83, mgr. region 13 tchr. edn. and computer ctr., 1983-85; asst. supt., instr. tchr. edn. and computer ctr. Hesperia (Calif.) Sch. Dist., 1985—. Mem. Assn. Calif. Sch. Adminstrs., Assn. Supervision and Curriculum Devel., Computer Users in Edn., Calif. Reading Assn., Internat. Reading Assn., Calif. State Commn. for Tchr. Credentialing (mem. profl. growth com. 1985), Phi Delta Kappa (v.p. of programs, Service Key award 1985). Avocation: oil painting. Home: 2463 N San Fernando Ct Claremont CA 91711 Office: Hesperia Sch Dist 9144 Third Ave Hesperia CA 92345

DAVIS, KATHLEEN EDDINS, interior designer; b. Lewistown, Pa., Mar. 15, 1948; d. Arthur Henry and Elizabeth (Weldgen) Eddins; m. John Thomas Malloy, Jr., Apr. 20, 1968; children: John Thomas III, Michele Ann; m. Charles Joseph Davis, Dec. 27, 1980. BS, San Jose State U., 1975; AA, San Jose City Coll., 1971. Asst. interior designer B. Terry Interiors, Campbell, Calif., 1973; asst. interior designer Charles Falls & Assocs., Los Altos, Calif., 1973-75; interior designer W & J Sloane Inc., San Jose, Calif., 1975-79; interior designer, owner Kathleen Malloy ASID, Palo Alto, Calif., 1979-83; ptnr. Davis/Rudd Design Assocs., Menlo Park, Calif., 1983-86; Davis/Wilson Design Assocs., Menlo Park, 1986—. Chmn. Gamble House Project, City Palo Alto, 1982, Los Angeles Sch. dist. Coordinating Council, 1984-85; pres. La Entrada PTA, 1983-84, Menlo-Atherton (Calif.) High Sch, 1986-87; chmn. coordinating council Los Lomitas (Calif.) Sch. Dist., 1984-85; mem. Menlo-Atherton High Sch. PTA, 1986—; Mem. Menlo Park C. of C., San Mateo County Better Bus. Bur. (arbitrator), AAUW, Am. Soc. Interior Designers (pres. Peninsula chpt. 1981-82, recipient presdl. citation 1977, 79, 80). Republican. Office: Davis/Wilson Design Assocs 883 Oak Grove Ave Menlo Park CA 94025

DAVIS, LARRY ERNEST, neurologist, educator; b. N.Y.C., Aug. 16, 1940; s. Lloyd E. and Ruth (Leopard) D.; m. Geraldine Temples, Apr. 26, 1968 (dec. 1983); children: Meredith, Colin. BA, Stanford U., 1963, MD, 1966. Instr. Johns Hopkins U., Balt., 1973-75; asst. prof. U. N.Mex., Albuquerque, 1975-79, assoc. prof., 1979-83, prof. neurology and microbiology, 1983—, vice chmn. dept. neurology, 1980—; chief neurology service VA Med. Ctr., Albuquerque, 1976—; neurobiology specialist, advisor VA, Washington, 1983-86. Contbr. chpts. to books and articles to profl. jours. Recipient Moore award Am. Assn. Neuropathologists, 1979, Wiel award Am. Assn. Neuropathologists, 1984. Fellow Am. Acad. Neurology; mem. Am. Neurol. Assn., Am. Neuropathology Assn., Am. Coll. Medicine. Democrat. Home: 1115 Tijeras NW Albuquerque NM 87102 Office: U NMex Dept Neurology Albuquerque NM 87131

DAVIS, LINDA CLAIRE, public relations consultant; b. San Bernardino, Calif., Aug. 25, 1942; d. Rudolph Lafayette (Curttright) and Dorothy Kaufman; m. John P. Duden, Jan. 15, 1963 (div. Feb. 1966); 1 child, John L.; m. Tigi Mataalii, Nov. 8, 1968 (div. Feb. 1971); 1 child, Siniva V.; m. Charles H. Davis, Nov. 3, 1984. Grad. high sch., Venice, Calif. Dir. sales promotion Gannett Outdoor, Los Angeles, 1976-78; dir. pub. relations Sta. KIIS AM/FM, Hollywood, Calif., 1978-79; v.p. Liljenwall Group Advt./ Pub. Relations, Long Beach, Calif., 1980-85; owner, chief exec. officer Media Concepts Pub. Relations, Hollywood, 1985—, Celebrity Concepts, Hollywood, 1986—; cons. Red de Publicidad Exterior, Spain, 1975-76. Editor: Long Beach Bus. mag., 1985—. Bd. dirs. Long Beach Area C. of C., 1985—, chmn. Olympic Opportunity Com., 1984; active Am. Heart Assn., Long Beach, 1985-86, Civic Light Opera Women's Guild, Long Beach, 1985—. Served with USAF, 1962-63. Mem. Pub. Relations Soc. Am., Publicity Club of Los Angeles, Sales and Mktg. Execs. Internat. Democrat. Jewish. Avocations: writing, equestrians, tennis. Office: Media Concepts 1024 Bennett Ave Suite 201 Long Beach CA 90804

DAVIS, L(LOYD) WAYNE, research company executive; b. Medicine Lodge, Kans., July 16, 1929; s. Lloyd and David Elda (Furnas) D.; B.S. in Engring. Physics (Summerfield scholar), U. Kans., 1952; M.S. in Elec. Engring. (fellow), U. N.Mex., 1959; m. Betty Louise Pyke, Sept. 7, 1963; 1 son, William W.; children by previous marriage—Robert L., Cheryl S. Staff mem. systems analysis dept. Sandia Corp., Albuquerque, 1952-56, cons. 1956-57; research physicist Dikewood Corp., Albuquerque, 1957-60, sr. research physicist 1960-64, head weapons effects div., 1964-67, dep. tech. dir., 1967-69, asst. v.p. 1969-72, sec., 1970-80, dir., 1971-82, v.p., 1972-77, sr. v.p. 1977-80, pres., chmn. bd., 1980-82; v.p. Kaman Scis. Corp., gen. mgr.

Dikewood Div., Albuquerque, 1982-83; sci. cons., 1983—. Mem. IEEE (sr.), Am. Phys. Soc. (S.E. sect.), Sigma Xi, Phi Kappa Phi, Tau Beta Pi, Sigma Tau, Sigma Pi Sigma, Kappa Mu Epsilon, Beta Gamma Sigma, Delta Sigma Pi, Sigma Chi. Republican. Mem. Christian Ch. (trustee 1970-73). Research on nuclear weapons effects and phenomenology effects on personnel and complex mil. systems; developed urban nuclear-casualty prediction model for high-yield nuclear bursts from Japanese data base over many years; presented paper in Eng. on Japanese Blast Casualty Experience at Brit. Home Office (Govt.) request, 1984. Home: 4411 Altura Ave NE Albuquerque NM 87110

DAVIS, LOUIS ELKIN, management educator, consultant; b. N.Y.C., Sept. 10, 1918; s. David George and Anna (Elkin) D.; m. Edith Kaufmann, Mar. 26, 1944 (dec. Sept. 1986); children: Jonathan F., Carol Davis Berezin. BSME, Ga. Inst. Tech., 1940; MS, U. Iowa, 1942. Registered engr., Calif. Prof. mgmt. U. Calif., Berkeley, 1947-66, UCLA, 1966—; pres. The Davis Group Inc., Beverly Hills, Calif., 1975—; sr. cons. OECD, Paris, 1957-58; LUCAS prof. U. Birmingham, Eng., 1962-63; sr. research fellow Tavistock Inst., London, 1965-66, Work Research Inst., Oslo, 1965-66. Author: Quality of Working Life, 1975, Design of Jobs, 1979; contbr. articles to profl. jours. Commr. Calif. Man Power Commn., Sacramento, 1963-68. Grantee Research Ctr., 1970—; recipient Hayhow medal Coll. Hosp. Adminstrs., 1971. Mem. Nat. Acad. Sci. (maritime research bd. 1968-74). Home: 1149 Calle Vista Dr Beverly Hills CA 90210 Office: UCLA 450 Hilgard Ave Los Angeles CA 90024

DAVIS, LOWELL LIVINGSTON, thoracic and cardiovascular surgeon; b. Urbanna, Va., Dec. 14, 1922; s. Jordan and Mary Emma (Wright) D.; B.S., Morehouse Coll., 1949; M.S., Atlanta U., 1950; M.D., Howard U., 1955; postgrad. U. Pa. Grad. Sch. Medicine, 1959-60. Rotating intern Jersey City Med. Center, 1955-56; resident in obstetrics Margaret Hague Maternity Hosp., Jersey City, 1956-57; asst. resident in obstetrics and gynecology Elmhurst (N.Y.) Gen. Hosp., 1957-58, chief resident, 1958-59; resident in gen. surgery VA Hosp., Tuskegee, Ala., 1960-61; resident in gen. surgery Meadowbrook Gen. Hosp., Hempstead, N.Y., 1961-63, chief resident, 1963-64; resident and chief resident in cardiothoracic surgery Cook County Hosp., Chgo., 1967-69; fellow in cardiopulmonary surgery U. Oreg. Med. Sch., Portland, 1972; fellow in cardiovascular surgery St. Vincent Hosp., Portland, 1972; fellow in coronary revascularization surgery Med. Coll. Wis., Milw., 1973; fellow in cardiovascular surgery Insts. Med. Scis., Pacific Med. Center, San Francisco, 1974; instr. Meharry Med. Coll., Nashville, 1950-51; instr. surgery U. Ill., 1969; vis. surgeon Hosp. for Sick Children, London, 1977; clin. asst. prof. dir. thoracic surgery U. So. Calif., 1981—; fellow cardiac surgery, quest lectr. Hadassah Med. Sch., Jerusalem, 1987. Served with USNR, 1943-46; to capt., M.C., USNR, 1971. Diplomate Am. Bd. Surgery, Am. Bd. Thoracic Surgery. Fellow A.C.S., Internat. Coll. Surgeons, Am. Coll. Angiology, Internat. Coll. Angiology, Am. Coll. Chest Physicians, Am. Coll. Cardiology, N.Y. Acad. Medicine; mem. Soc. Thoracic Surgeons, Am. Assn. Thoracic Surgeons, Albert Starr Cardiac Surgery Soc. (founding), Assn. Mil. Surgeons U.S., Lyman Brewer III Internat. Surg. Soc., Royal Soc. Medicine (affiliate), Los Angeles Surgical Soc., Denton Cooley Cardiovascular Soc., Western Thoracic Surgery Soc., Sampson Thoracic Surgery Soc., Chi Delta Mu. Home: 4316 Marina City Dr G-308 Marina Del Rey CA 90291

DAVIS, MICHAEL JOHN, aerospace engineer, administrator, researcher; b. Escanaba, Mich., May 25, 1954; s. Edward Mackin and Mildred Olive (Groos) D.; m. Sharon Ann Vest, Sept. 6, 1981; children: Keith Mackin, Nathan Edward. BS in Aerospace Engring., U. Mich., 1976; M in Aeronautics, George Washington U., 1977; MBA, Mich. State U., 1979; postgrad., Def. Systems Mgmt. Coll., 1981. Chief, engring. econ. analysis Martin Marietta Corp., Denver, 1979-85; advance tech. program mgr. Martin Marietta Aerospace, Denver, 1985-87, account exec. commercial launch vehicles, 1987—. NASA-Langley research scholar, 1976-77. Mem. Am. Def. Preparedness Assn. Home: 5224 S Jellison St Littleton CO 80123

DAVIS, MICHAEL WILLIAM, research biologist; b. Chgo., Oct. 5, 1949; s. Roger E. and Diane D. Davis. BS, Marlboro Coll., 1973; MS, U. Vermont, 1975; PhD, Oreg. State U., 1981. Postdoctoral fellow Harbor Br. Found., Ft. Pierce, Fla., 1982-83; research biologist Oreg. State U., Corvallis, 1983-84; fishery biologist Nat. Marine Fisheries Service, Newport, Oreg., 1984—. Contbr. articles to profl. jours. Mem. AAAS, Phycol. Soc. Am., Estuarine Fedn. Am., Sigma Xi. Home: PO Box 174 South Beach OR 97366 Office: Hatfield Marine Sci Ctr Newport OR 97365

DAVIS, NICHOLAS HOMANS CLARK, finance company executive; b. N.Y.C., Dec. 1, 1938; s. Feltz Cleveland and Loraine Vanderpool (Homans) D.; children from previous marriage: Loraine, Helen, Alexandra, Christopher, Katherine, Eleanor, John; m. Brenda Jean Molen, Dec. 18, 1982. BA in Geology with honors, Princeton U., 1961; MBA in Fin., Stanford U., 1963. Chartered fin. analyst; cert. NYSE supervisory analyst. Research analyst Fahnestock & Co., N.Y.C., 1963-67; mgr. research Andresen & Co., N.Y.C., 1967-71; dir. research Boettcher & Co., Denver, 1971-75; v.p. corp. fin. White Weld & Co., Denver, 1975-78; v.p. asset mgmt. Paine Webber Co., Denver, 1978—; Trustee, investment officer Thenen Found., Montclair, N.J., 1966—. Founder Denver Internat. Film Festival, 1977-80; founder, treas. Greenwich Vill. (N.Y.) Montessori Sch., 1965-71; Bishop's Sch. Lay Ministry, Denver, 1984—; bd. dir. Colo. Mus. Festival, Boulder, 1980-82. Mem. Venture Capital Assn. Colo. (founder, bd. dirs., treas. 1982—), Denver Soc. Security Analysts (chmn., pres. 1972-76). Republican. Episcopalian. Clubs: Racquet & Tennis, (N.Y.C.), N.Y. Yacht; Denver Country, Mile High (Denver). Avocations: skiing, flyfishing, deepwater voyaging, writing, backpacking. Home: 9823 W 83d Ave Arvada CO 80005 Office: Paine Webber Co 1600 Broadway #2200 Denver CO 80202

DAVIS, NISSEN AVROY, communications executive; b. Windhoek, Namibia, Nov. 21, 1933; came to U.S. 1961; s. Sam and Sera (Levin) D.; m. Pamela Warder, Apr. 16, 1954 (div. 1970); children: Janine, Glenn; m. Susan Taylor, Jan. 16, 1978; 1 child, Scott. Dir. pub. relations J. Walter Thompson, Los Angeles, 1967-72; dir. pub. affairs ACTION, Washington, 1972-74; v.p. pub. relations and advt. Flying Tiger Line, Los Angeles, 1974-83; sr. v.p. pub. relations Welton Becket Assocs., Santa Monica, Calif., 1983-84; dir. communications Douglas Aircraft Co., Long Beach, Calif., 1984—; pres. Aero Club So. Calif., Los Angeles, 1981, Aero Exhibits Corp., Los Angeles, 1981—. Mem. Pub. Relations Soc. Am. (accredited), Aviation Space Writers Assn. Club: Publicity (Los Angeles). Office: Douglas Aircraft Co 3855 Lakewood Blvd Long Beach CA 90846

DAVIS, PHILIP ARTHUR, JR., research geologist; b. Toledo, Aug. 3, 1950; s. Philip Arthur and Nancy (Michoff) D.; m. Laura Smith, Sept. 18, 1982; 1 child, Philip Charles. BS, Bowling Green State U., 1972; MS, Miami U., Oxford, Ohio, 1974; PhD, U. Ky., 1977. Postdoctoral research chemist U. Calif. San Diego, La Jolla, 1977-79; sr. research scientist Jet Propulsion Lab, Pasadena, Calif., 1979-80; research geologist U.S. Geol. Survey, Flagstaff, Ariz., 1979—. Contbr. articles to profl. jours. Fellow Alfred P. Sloan Found., 1977, George W. Pirtle, 1977. Mem. Am. Geophys. Union, Geol. Soc. Am., Am. Soc. Photogrammetry, Geochem. Soc., Sigma Xi. Office: US Geol Survey Astrogeology Br 2255 N Gemini Dr Flagstaff AZ 86001

DAVIS, R. W., chemical company executive; b. 1924; married. M.S., MIT, 1950; M.B.A., Northwestern U., 1966. With Chevron Chem. Co., 1951—; pres., chief exec. officer, 1982—, also dir. Office: Chevron Chemical Co 575 Market St San Francisco CA 94105 *

DAVIS, RICHARD ADDISON, state official; b. Berkeley, Calif., Nov. 25, 1935; s. Richard E. and Ruby C. (Silva) D.; m. Nancy Orr, Feb. 17, 1957; children: Kathleen, Patricia. BS in Mktg., U. Oreg., 1960. Dir. human resources State of Oreg., Salem, 1976-79; various mktg. positions with Pacific N.W. Bell Telephone, Portland, Oreg., 1960-76; mgr. mktg. div. Pacific N.W. Bell Telephone, Seattle, 1979-80, asst. v.p. sales, 1980-82, asst. v.p. mktg., 1982-85; dir. labor and industry State of Wash., Olympia, 1985—; bd. dirs. Am. Bioclin., Portland, 1985—; mem. State Wash. Investment Bd. Roman Catholic. Club: Cen. Park Tennis. Lodge: Rotary. Office: Dept Labor Industry Gen Adminstrv Bldg Olympia WA 98504

DAVIS, RICHARD ERNEST, engineer; b. San Francisco, Nov. 20, 1936; 1 child, Richard Jr.; m. Sharon L. Buss, Aug. 26, 1961; children: Dawn, Michelle. BS in Engring., Calif. State Poly. U., San Luis Obispo, 1967. Facilities engr. Naval Weapons Ctr., China Lake, Calif., 1967-77; program coordinator U.S. Dept. Energy, Oakland, Calif., 1977-78; program mgr. Solar Energy Research Inst., Golden, Colo., 1978-80; engring. specialist Holmes & Narver, Mercury, Nev., 1980—. Contbr. articles to profl. jours. Served with USAF, 1954-62. Mem. Assn. Energy Engrs. (sr.). Avocations: mountain rescue, hiking, camping. Home: SR 15 Box 495 Amargosa Valley NV 89020 Office: Holmes & Narver Inc PO Box I Mercury NV 89023

DAVIS, RICHARD MALONE, emeritus economics educator; b. Hamilton, N.Y., June 2, 1918; s. Malone Crowell and Grace Edith (McQuade) D. AB, Colgate U., 1939; MA, Cornell U., 1941, PhD, 1949. From instr. to assoc. prof. econs. Lehigh U., Bethlehem, Pa., 1941-54; assoc. prof. econs. U. Oreg., Eugene, 1954-62, prof., 1962-83; prof. emeritus U. Oreg., 1983—. Contbr. articles to profl. jours. Served with U.S. Army, 1942-45, CBI. Mem. Am. Econ. Assn., Phi Beta Kappa. Republican. Home: 1040 Ferry St Apt 503 Eugene OR 97401 Office: Univ Oreg Dept Econs Eugene OR 97403

DAVIS, ROBERT DEE, utility company executive; b. Whitney, Idaho, July 25, 1932; s. James Edward and Olive Belle (Willes) D.; m. Marian Linford, Nov. 13, 1953; children—Dee, Bruce, Roberta, Kimberly, Parley, Stephanie. B.S. in Civil Engring., Utah State U., 1957. Design and constrn. engr. Riverside County Flood Control & Water Conservation Dist., Calif., 1957-68; hydrologist Soil Conservation Service, Salt Lake City, 1968-69; solar ponds engr. N.L. Industries, Salt Lake City, 1970-72; project supr. coal-fired and geothermal power plants Utah Power & Light Co., Salt Lake City, 1973—, project mgr. coal-fired power plants, project mgr. spl. research and devel. geothermal projects, planning engr; ptnr. D&D Mining, Bountiful, Utah, 1983—. Served with U.S. Army, 1954-55. Democrat. Mormon. Home: 446 E 1700 South Bountiful UT 84010 Office: Utah Power & Light Co 1407 W North Temple Salt Lake City UT 84116

DAVIS, ROBERT DENNIS, advertising executive; b. Salt Lake City, Aug. 14, 1945; s. James Zimmiri and Blossom (Traver) D.; m. Jeannette Lynn Cader, Oct. 1, 1982. BS, U. Utah, 1967, postgrad., 1967. Creative dir. J. Walter Thompson, San Francisco, 1981-83; v.p., creative dir. Grey Advt., San Francisco, 1983-84; prin. Robert Davis Advt., Inc., Santa Rosa, Calif., 1984—. Contbr. articles to profl. jours. Active Big Brothers of San Francisco; v.p. North Va. Spl. Olympics, Fairfax City, Va., 1974-75. Recipient 4 Best in the West awards Am. Adv. Fedn., 1984. Mem. Ad Club San Francisco, Direct Mktg. Creative Guild, Am. Assn. Fundraising Execs, Miline Club San Francisco, Sonoma County Ad Club. Republican. Episcopalian. Avocations: tennis, reading, fishing, golf, writing children's stories. Home: 2359 Morningside Circle Santa Rosa CA 95405 Office: Robert Davis Advt Inc 4415 Sonoma Hwy C Santa Rosa CA 95405

DAVIS, ROBERT HEATER, chemical engineering educator; b. Paris, Mar. 26, 1957; came to U.S., 1957; s. Richard Malcolm and Helen (Heater) D.; m. Shirley Lynn Giles, Dec. 28, 1982. BS, U. Calif., Davis, 1978; MS, StanfordU., 1979, PhD, 1983. Postdoctoral fellow Cambridge (Eng.) U., 1982-83; asst. prof. chem. engring. U. Colo., Boulder, 1983—. Contbr. articles to profl. jours. Bd. dirs. univ. program First. Presbyn. Ch., Boulder, 1985—. NSF fellow, 1982; recipient Univ. Gold medal U. Calif., Davis, 1978, Presdl. Young Investigator award NSF, 1985. Mem. Am. Inst. Chem. Engrs., Am. Phys. Soc., Sigma Xi, Phi Kappa Phi, Tau Beta Pi. Republican. Avocations: hiking, bicycling. Office: U Colo Dept Chem Engring Campus Box 424 Boulder CO 80309-0424

DAVIS, ROBERT WAYNE, broadcasting executive; b. Snohomish, Wash., May 9, 1947; s. Hugh Edward and Lorraine Mae (Tronsrud) D.; m. Joan Carol Miller, June 21, 1969; children—Emily Lyn, Alison Kay. B.B.A., U. Wash., 1969. Sales rep. Sta. KNDO-TV, Yakima, Wash., 1969-70, ops. mgr., program mgr., 1971-73, v.p., gen. mgr., 1977; acct. exec., Simpson/Reilly & Assoc., Seattle, 1974-76, Sta. KOMO-TV, Seattle, 1978-81; pres., gen. mgr. Sta. KMTR-TV, Eugene, Oreg., 1982—. Mem. Oreg. Assn. of Broadcasters, Nat. Assn. Broadcasters. Lodge: Rotary. *

DAVIS, RONALD FRANKLIN, mechanical engineer, real estate broker; b. Asheville, N.C., June 17, 1943; s. Edgar Franklin and Geneva Snow (Kuykendall) D.; m. Karen Starleaf, Aug. 2, 1980. B.S. in Aerospace Engring., N.C. State U., 1968; postgrad. in aerospace engring. U. Tenn. Space Inst., Tullahoma, 1968-70; M.B.A., U. So. Calif., 1985. Engring. scientist/specialist McDonnell Douglas Astronautics Co., Huntington Beach, Calif., 1970-80; sr. engr. Interstate Electronics Corp., Anaheim, Calif., 1980-81; engring. specialist Ford Aerospace & Communications Co., Newport Beach, Calif., 1981-85; dep. program mgr. JWP Communication Mfg. Co., Long Beach, Calif., 1985— . Author: (with K. Starleaf) Microkey, 1982. Served with USAF, 1961-65. Mem. AIAA, Am. Mgmt. Assn. Office: JWP Communication Mfg Co 3300 E Spring St Long Beach CA 90801

DAVIS, RUSSELL LEONARD, librarian; b. Blackfoot, Ida., Oct. 25, 1924; s. John Leonard and Mary Verna (Robertson) D.; m. Emma Lou Barnes, June 10, 1949; childrenDan, Kathleen, Kirk, Susan, Eileen, Alan, Julie, Grant. Student, Weber Jr. Coll., 1948-50; B.S., Utah State U., 1952; A.M. in L.S, U. Mich., 1952-53. Teaching asst. U. Mich. Lib. Sch., 1952-53; engring. librarian Utah State U., 1953-54, circulation librarian, 1954-57, instr. library sci., 1953-57, extension librarian, 1955-57; dir. Utah State Library Commn., 1957—. Mem. A.L.A., Utah Library Assn. (pres. 1960-61), Mountain Plains Library Assn. (pres. 1964-65). Mem. Ch. of Jesus Christ of Latter-day Saints (bishop). Office: Utah State Library Commn 2150 S 3d W Salt Lake City UT 84115

DAVIS, STANFORD MELVIN, engineering executive, publishing consultant; b. Camden, N.J., June 12, 1941; s. Winford and Rose Marie (Rich) D.; m. Pamela Davis, Nov. 25, 1967 (div. 1980); children: Peter, Shawna; m. Laura A. Rudolph, Feb. 21, 1987. AB, BSEE, Rutgers U., 1964; postgrad., UCLA, 1967; MBA, U. Portland, 1984. Elec. engr. RCA, Van Nuys, Calif., 1966-68; project engr. Tek, Wilsonville, Oreg., 1968-79; S/W mgr. Tektronix, Wilsonville, 1979-81, mgr. mktg., 1981-83; v.p. engring. Concept Technologies, Portland, 1983-86; mgr. engring. program INTEL, Hillsboro, Oreg., 1986—. Patentee in field. Served to capt. U.S. Army, 1964-66. Recipient Outstanding Product award Datapro, Delran, N.J., 1985. Mem. Assn. of Computing Machinery, IEEE. Avocations: skiing, gardening, camping, tennis, fishing. Home: 7320 SW 103d Ave Beaverton OR 97005

DAVIS, STEPHEN EDWARD, consulting engineer; b. Dayton, Ohio, Oct. 28, 1946; s. Melvin Wellington and Frieda (Plummer) D.; m. Marvel Elizabeth Fegursky, Aug. 14, 1971; children: Derek Andrew, Alison Elizabeth. BS, U. Ariz., 1968, MS, 1971;Registered profl. engr., Ariz., registered land surveyor, Ariz. Civil engr./planner Marum & Marum, Tucson, 1971-72; water planning adminstr. Tucson Water, City of Tucson, 1974-84, John Carollo Engrs., 1984-86, Malcolm Pirnie, Inc., Phoenix, 1986—; mem. adv. council Gov.'s Commn. on Ariz. Environ. Served to capt. USAF, 1972-74. NSF fellow, 1968-71. Mem. ASCE, Am. Water Resources Assn., Am. Water Works Assn., Ariz. Water and Pollution Control Assn., Ariz. Hydrological Soc., Internat. Platform Assn., U. Ariz. Alumni Band, Tau Beta Pi, Phi Eta Sigma, Phi Mu Alpha Symphonia. Democrat. Presbyterian (elder, deacon). Clubs: Tucson Sailing, Ariz. Yacht; Phoenix City. Contbr. articles to profl. jours. Home: 2444 S El Dorado Mesa AZ 85202 Office: Malcolm Pirnie Inc 2650 S 46th St Suite 102 Phoenix AZ 85034-7416

DAVIS, STEPHEN PARKES, lawyer, administrator; b. Denver, May 2, 1951; s. Robert Charles and Bonna Ann (Blankenship) D.; m. Sheila Ann Higgins, Apr. 2, 1976. AA, CCD West, 1972; BA, U. Colo., 1976; JD, U. Denver, 1979. Bar: Colo. 1980, U.S. Dist. Ct. Colo. 1980, Nebr. 1983, U.S. Dist. Ct. Nebr. 1983. Legis. aide to Rep. Gerald Kopel, Denver, 1978-80; assoc. Lobato Bleidt & Bleidt, Lakewood, Colo., 1980-81; assoc. Gerald Kopel, Denver, 1981-83; assoc. dir. Colo. Bar Refresher, Inc., Denver, 1981-85, dir. 1985—; sole practice, Denver, 1983—. Committeeman Jefferson County, Colo. Democratic Com., 1972; committeeman Denver Dem. Com., 1978, co-capt., 1980; campaign mgr. Com. to Re-elect Kopel, Denver, 1982, treas. 1984-86. Mem. ABA, Colo. Bar Assn., Denver Bar Assn. (exec. council, gen. practice sect. 1985—), Colo. Trial Lawyers Assn. (exec. council, gen. practice sect. 1985—), Assn. Trial Lawyers Am. Democrat. Club: DU-ATLA (pres. 1979-80). Lodge: Masons (officer Aurora chpt. 1986—). Home: 3635 S Roslyn Way Denver CO 80237 Office: 1616 Glenarm Pl Suite 1718 Denver CO 80202

DAVIS, THOMAS CASEY, marketing professional; b. Phoenix, Oct. 4, 1961; s. Eugene Phillip and Beverly Jean (Melander) D.; m. Charlene Anne Manilla, Apr. 13, 1985. Student, Ariz. State U. Graphic designer Tempe, Ariz., 1980—; mktg. dir. KOOL Radio, Phoenix, 1984—. Organizer Phoenix Children's Hosp., 1985-86; com. mem. Muscular Distrophy Assn., 1985-86, Cystic Fibrosis, 1985-86. Mem. Broadcast Promotion and Mktg. Execs., (voting mem. 1985—), Phi Gamma Delta (pres. 1985). Republican. Lutheran. Avocations: golf, art, music. Home: 4137 E Alan Ln Phoenix AZ 85023 Office: KOOL Broadcasting Co 2196 E Camelback Phoenix AZ 85016

DAVIS, TIM DOUGLAS, plant scientist, educator; b. Sonoma, Calif., Jan. 27, 1956; s. Lewis Douglas and Josephine Gloria (Mazzoni) D.; m. Patricia Frances Clifford, May 7, 1977; children: Lance, Trevor. BS, Brigham Young U., 1978; MS, Oreg. State U., 1980, PhD, 1983. Research asst. Oreg. State U., 1978-82; asst. prof. Brigham Young U., Provo, Utah, 1982—. Contbr. articles to sci. and trade jours. Internat. Soc. Arboriculture Research grantee, 1986. Mem. Am. Soc. Hort. Sci., Am. Soc. Plant Physiologist, Plant Growth Regulator Soc. Am., Internat. Plant Propagator's Soc., Japanese Soc. Plant. Physiologists, Sigma Xi Sci. Research Soc. Avocations: athletics, gardening. Home: 237 W 255 S Orem UT 84058 Office: Dept Agronomy and Hort 271 WIDB BYU Provo UT 84602

DAVIS, WANDA ROSE, lawyer; b. Lampasas, Tex., Oct. 4, 1937; d. Ellis DeWitt and Julia Doris (Rose) Cockrell; m. Richard Andrew Fulcher, May 9, 1959 (div. 1969); 1 son, Greg Ellis; m. Edwin Leon Davis, Jan. 14, 1973 (div. 1985). B.B.A., U. Tex., 1959, J.D., 1971. Bar: Tex. 1971, Colo. 1981, U.S. Dist. Ct. (no. dist.) Tex. 1972, U.S. Dist. Ct. Colo. 1981, U.S. Ct. Appeals (10th cir. 1981, U.S. Supreme Ct. 1976. Atty. Atlantic Richfield Co., Dallas, 1971; assoc. firm Crocker & Murphy, Dallas, 1971-72; prin. Wanda Davis, Atty. at Law, Dallas, 1972-73; ptnr. firm Davis & Davis Inc., Dallas, 1973-75; atty. adviser HUD, Dallas, 1974-75, Air Force Acctg. and Fin. Ctr., Denver, 1976—; co-chmn. regional Profl. Devel. Inst., Am. Soc. Mil. Comptrollers, Colorado Springs, Colo., 1982; chmn. Lowry AFB Noontime Edn. Program, Exercise Program, Denver, 1977-83; mem. speakers bur. Colo. Women's Bar, 1982-83, Lowry AFB, 1981-83; mem. fed. ct. liaison com. U.S. Dist. Ct. Colo., 1983; mem. Leaders of the Fed. Bar Assn. People to People Del. to China, USSR and Finland, 1986. Contbr. numerous articles to profl. jours. Bd. dirs. Pres.'s Council Met. Denver, 1981-83; mem. Lowry AFB Alcohol Abuse Exec. Com., 1981-84. Recipient Spl. Achievement award USAF, 1978; Upward Mobility award Fed. Profl. and Adminstrv. Women, Denver, 1979. Mem. Fed. Bar Assn. (pres. Colo. 1982-83, mem. nat. council 1984—, Earl W. Kintner Disting. Service award 1983, 1st v.p. 10th cir. 1986—), Colo. Trial Lawyers Assn., Bus. and Profl. Women's Club (dist. IV East dir. 1983-84, dist. dir. 1983-84, Colo. 1st v.p. 1986—), Am. Soc. Mil. Comptrollers (pres. 1984-85), Denver South Met. Bus. and Profl. Women's Club (pres. 1982-83), Denver Silver Spruce Am. Bus. Women's Assn. (pres. 1981-82; Woman of Yr. award 1982), Colo. Jud. Inst., Colo. Concerned Lawyers, Profl. Mgrs. Assn., Fed. Women's Program (v.p. Denver 1980), Dallas Bar Assn., Tex. Bar Assn., Denver Bar Assn., Altrusa, Zonta, Denver Nancy Langhorn Federally Employed Women. (pres. 1979-80). Christian. Office: Air Force Acctg and Fin Ctr AFAFC/JAL Denver CO 80279

DAVIS, WILLIAM EUGENE, university administrator; b. Wamego, Kans., Feb. 15, 1929; s. Eugene Kenneth and Willa (Dickinson) D.; m. Pollyanne Peterson, Mar. 17, 1951; children: Deborah, Rebecca, Douglas, Brooke, Bonnie. B.S., U. Colo., 1951; M.A., U. No. Colo., 1958; Ed.D., U. Colo., 1963. Asst. to dean men U. Colo., 1951; tchr. English, coach Loveland, Colo., High Sch., 1954-55, Rapid City (S.D.) High Sch., 1955-59, Greeley (Colo.) High Sch., 1959-60; alumni dir., head football coach, dean men U. Colo., 1960-63; exec. asst. to pres. U. Wyo., 1963-65; pres. Idaho State U., Pocatello, 1965-75; commr. Western Interstate Commn. Higher Edn., Idaho, 1965-75, N.Mex., 1978-82, Oreg., 1983—; pres. U. N.Mex., Albuquerque, 1975-82; chancellor Oreg. System Higher Edn., Eugene, 1983—; Idaho commr. Western Interstate Commn. for Higher Edn., 1965-75, vice chmn., 1973-74, chmn., 1974-75; N.Mex. commr. Western Interstate Commn. Higher Edn., 1978-82; mem. N.Mex. Selection Com. for Rhodes scholars, 1976-82, Pres.'s Council Western Athletic Conf., 1975-82, chmn., 1978-79; mem. N.Mex. Gov.'s Com. on Tech. Excellence, 1975-82, Nat. Collegiate Athletic Assn. Theodore Roosevelt Award Jury, 1974-79; chmn. Idaho Rhodes Scholarship Selection Com., 1971-75; mem. Gov.'s Corp. Voluntarism Com., 1982—, Am. Council Edn., 1982—, AFL-CIO Labor/Higher Edn Council, 1982—. Author: Glory Colorado-A History of the University of Colorado, 1965, Nobody Calls Me Doctor, 1972. Served to capt. USMCR, 1951-54. Mem. Western Coll. Assn. (exec. com. 1981—), Assn. Western Univs. (bd. dirs. 1975-82), Oreg. Hist. Soc. (bd. dirs. 1982—), Am. Assn. State Colls. and Univs. (com. governance 1985—), Alpha Tau Omega, Phi Delta Kappa, Omicron Delta Kappa. Methodist. Clubs: Elk, Rotarian. Office: Oreg State System Higher Edn PO Box 3175 Eugene OR 97403

DAVIS, WILLIAM EVANS, psychology consultant; b. Denver, Apr. 16, 1929; s. Roblin Henry and Margaret (Evans) D.; m. Nancy Caroline Yaw, Aug. 8, 1962; children: Caroline Josephine, William Scott, Roblin Gray. AB magna cum laude, Princeton U., 1951; PhD, U. Denver, 1959. Instr. psychology U. Denver, 1959-60; dir. admissions Alaska Meth. U., Anchorage, 1961-64, asst. prof. psychology, edn., 1961-65, assoc. prof., 1965-70, prof., 1973-75; sr. policy analyst Office Tech. Assessment U.S. Congress, Washington, 1976-82; project dir. Cultural Dynamics Ltd., Anchorage, 1982—; mem. adv. council Alaska Title III ESEA, 1969-76, Alaska Rescue Group, 1962-68. Contbr. articles to profl. jours. Mem. Anchorage Com. on Alcoholism, 1963-67; chmn. Rep. Precinct Com., Anchorage, 1965-67; pres. local PTA, 1977-79; mem. community task force Prince George's County Pub. Schs., 1978-79, Citizens Adv. Edn. Concerns Com. 1983—. Recipient Armsey Excellence in Teaching award Alaska Meth. U., 1966; NSF fellow U. Wash., Seattle, 1967-68. Mem. AAAS, Cross-Cultural Edn. Consortium, Am. Psychol. Assn., Western Psychol. Assn., Sigma Xi. Episcopalian. Clubs: Am. Alpine (Alaska sect.); Colo. Mountain; Alpine Can. Home: 1634 Hidden Ln Anchorage AK 99501-4918

DAVIS, WILLIAM LANDON, JR., chemical engineer; b. Chatham, Va., Oct. 2, 1923; s. William Landon and Vera Estelle (Turner) D.; m. Catharine Antonette Skrak, Dec. 16, 1950; children: Catharine Vera, William Landon III, MIchael Thomas. BSChemE, U. Va., 1950; MSChemE, Ill. Inst. Tech., 1958. Registered profl. engr., Pa. Research cons. U.S. Steel Corp., Pitts., 1952-73; mgr. Kennecott Corp., Salt Lake City, 1974-77; pres. Hicap Engring. Corp., Salt Lake City, 1977-78; mgr. Occidental Petroleum Corp., Bakersfield, Calif., 1978-82; supr. Unocal Corp., Grand Junction, Colo., 1982—. Contbr. 35 articles to profl. jours.; patentee in field. Served to 1st lt. Chem. Corps U.S. Army, 1943-46, PTO. Mem. Am. Inst. Chem. Engrs., Am. Chem. Soc. Republican. Episcopalian. Lodge: Masons. Avocation: golf. Home: 3336 Northridge Dr Grand Junction CO 81506 Office: Unocal Energy Mining div PO Box 76 Parachute CO 81635

DAVIS, WILLIE, data processing executive; b. Tuskegee, Ala., June 18, 1949; s. Willie and Catherine (Coley) D.; m. M.C. Van Deventer-Zutphen, June 18, 1983. BA, St. Louis U., 1971, MS, 1974. Program support rep. IBM, San Francisco, 1979—. Mem. Soc. for Psychol. Study of Social Issues. Democrat. Methodist. Avocation: filmmaking. Office: IBM B/O 388 425 Market St San Francisco CA 94105

DAVISON, NED J., Spanish educator, researcher; b. Salt Lake City, Oct. 3, 1926; s. Ralph Henry and Mabel (Kauffman) D.; m. Donna Jean Hansen, Aug. 2, 1948 (dec. Sept. 1970); children: Ronald H., Alan R., Christopher N.; m. Ruth Esther Mercado-Sherman, June 5, 1972. BA, U. Utah, 1949; MA, UCLA, 1952, PhD in Hispanic langs. and lit., 1957. Instr. French Coll. of Idaho, Caldwell, 1954; from instr. to asst. prof. Spanish U. Oreg., Eugene, 1954-63; assoc. prof. Spanish U. N.Mex., Albuquerque, 1963-67, prof. Spanish, 1967-70; prof. Spanish U. Utah, Salt Lake City, 1970—. Author: Sobre Eduardo Barrios y Otros: Estudios y Crónicas, 1966, The Concept of Modernism in Hispanic Criticism, 1966, Eduardo Barrios, 1970, El Concepto de Modernismo en la Crítica Hispánica, 1971, Particles: Poems 1960-70, 1971, Sound Patterns in a Poem of José Martí: Phonemic Patterning and Poetic Musicality, 1975; co-author Prosas y Poesías de Espana e Hispanoamérica, 1968; rev. editor Modern Lang. Jour., 1970-76; adv. editor Studies in 20th Century Literature, 1977—; assoc. editor Am. Assn. Tchrs. of Spanish and Portugese, 1984—; columnist Las Últimas Noticias, 1960-68; articles on Spanish lit. to profl. jours. Served with U.S. Army, 1945-46. Recipient Research award Am. Philos. Soc., 1961, 65, Research award Lit. Am. Studies dept. U. N.Mex., 1968, Research award Fulbright-Hays Commn., 1968, 69. Mem. Am. Assn. Tchrs. of Spanish and Portugese. Democrat. Avocations: tennis, fishing, photography, drawing, computer programming. Home: 1373 Butler Ave Salt Lake City UT 84102 Office: U Utah Dept Lang and Lit Salt Lake City UT 84112

DAWES, WILLIAM LINTON, sales executive; b. San Francisco, July 27, 1956; s. Lyell Clark Dawes and Patricia (Clinton) Williams. BA in History, Denison U., 1980. Dir. pub. relations Dwight-Englewood Sch., Englewood, N.J., 1980-81; sr. account exec. Dun & Bradstreet Corp., San Francisco, 1981-84, regional sales mgr., 1984—. Mem. Am. Mktg. Assn., San Francisco C. of C., San Francisco Soc. Prevention Cruelty to Animals. Club: San Francisco Press, Bayview Yacht (vice commodore 1985-86). Avocations: skiing, sailboat racing. Home: 504 Wisconsin St San Francisco CA 94107 Office: The Dun & Bradstreet Corp 400 Oyster Point Blvd San Francisco CA 94080

DAWSON, DONALD ROY, business executive; b. Hamilton, Ont., Can., Aug. 7, 1921; s. Roy Elgin and Margaret Hannah (O'Connor) D.; B.A., McMaster U., 1949; M.B.A., U. Toronto, 1951; m. Beatrice K. Kanahele, June 2, 1956; children—Victoria Lani, Kathryn Malia, Donne Leinani, Christopher Burwood. Pres., Dawson Assocs., Honolulu, 1960-63, Dawson Corp., Honolulu, 1963-70; dir. export programs U.S. Dept. Commerce, Honolulu, 1970-80; pres. Dawson Internat. Inc. and Hawaii Prepaid Legal Plan, Honolulu, 1980—. Chmn. Hawaii-Pacific Export Expansion Council, Gov.'s Commn. on Hawaii's Econ. Future. Served with Can. Army, 1939-45. Named Small Businessman of Year, SBA, 1967. Mem. Hawaii World Trade Assn., C. of C. Hawaii. Republican. Episcopalian. Clubs: Pacific, Plaza, Oahu Country. Lodge: Rotary (Oahu) (past pres.). Home: 3966 Nuuanu Pali Dr Honolulu HI 96817

DAWSON, JUDITH M. SHEEHAN, educational administrator; b. Honolulu, Nov. 3, 1939; d. Wade Edmund and Barbara Montague (Guard) Sheehan; m. Donald D. Dawson, Apr. 4, 1964 (div. Aug. 1979); children—Mark Lynn, Starr Montague. Student Wellesley Coll., 1957-59; B.A., U. Calif.-Berkeley, 1962; M.A., U. Hawaii, 1977. Exec. sec. Halekulani Hotel, Honolulu, 1962-64; reservations mgr. Waikiki Grand Hotel, Honolulu, 1964-65; community relations officer East-West Ctr., Honolulu, 1965-66; dir. devel. Punahou Sch., Honolulu, 1978—. Bd. dirs. Boys Club Am., Honolulu, 1982—; trustee, v.p. Atherton Family Found., Honolulu, 1980—; trustee Hawaiian Mission Childrens Soc., 1982—, pres., 1986—. Mem. Hawaii Soc. Fund-Raising Execs. (trustee, bd. dirs. 1983—), Oriental Art Soc. (bd. dirs. 1979—). Republican. Episcopalian. Club: Oahu Country (Honolulu). Home: 3155 Kaohinani Dr Honolulu HI 96817 Office: Punahou Sch 1601 Punahou St Honolulu HI 96822

DAWSON, MARK H., university administrator. Chancellor U. Nev. system, 1987—. Office: Univ of Nevada System Office of Chancellor Reno NV 89509 *

DAWSON, MICHAEL EDWARD, psychologist, educator; b. Chgo., Mar. 31, 1940; s. Peter F. and Clara (Stephens) D.; m. Lavina Thersa Caparella, June 16, 1962; children: Michael, Christopher. BS, Ariz. State U., 1963; PhD, U. So. Calif., 1967. Lic. psychologist, Calif. Asst. prof. Calif. State Coll., Los Angeles, 1967-69; research psychologist Gateways Hosp., Los Angeles, 1969-79; adj. assoc. prof. UCLA, 1979-84; assoc. prof. U. So. Calif., Los Angeles, 1984—. Co-author: Emotions and Bodily Response, 1978; assoc. editor jour. Psychology, 1980-83; contbr. articles to profl. jours. NIMH grantee, 1969—. Mem. AAAS, Am. Psychol. Assn., Soc. Psycholphys. Research (bd. dirs. 1981-84). Office: U So Calif Dept Psychology SGM 501 Los Angeles CA 90089-1061

DAWSON, WILLIAM JAMES, JR., orthodontist; b. San Francisco, May 16, 1930; s. William James and Augusta (Rude) D.; A.B., U. Calif. at Berkeley, 1948-52; D.D.S., U. Calif. Med. Center, San Francisco, 1958; m. Judith Elizabeth Riede, Aug. 11, 1962; children—William James, Wendy, Nancy Garms, Sarah Rankin, Evelyn Elizabeth. Pvt. practice orthodontics, San Rafael, Calif., 1958—; clin. instr. oral histology, U. Calif. Med. Center, San Francisco, 1958-61; clin. instr. orofacial anomolies, 1964-75, asst. research dentist, 1968-75; mem. Calif. Bd. Dental Examiners, 1985—. Mem. bd. adminstrn. Calif. Pub. Employees Retirement System, 1969-76. Mem. adv. com. Marin council Boy Scouts Am., 1965—; chmn. citizen's adv. com. Dominican Coll. San Rafael, 1974-76; mem. city council, Ross, Calif., 1967-69; assoc. mem. Calif. Rep. Cen. Com., 1967-68, 85—, regular mem., 1971-73; pres. Marin County Property Owners Assn., 1980-82; bd. dirs. Marin County Coalition, 1980-86, chmn., 1983-84; mem. adv. bd. Terwilliger Nature Ctr.; trustee Marin Gen. Hosp. Found., 1985—. Served with USAF, 1951-54. Diplomate Am. Bd. Orthodontics (charter mem. Coll. of Diplomates). Fellow Royal Soc. Health, Internat. Coll. Dentists, Acad. Dentistry Internat.; mem. ADA, Am. Assn. Orthodontists, Fedn. Dentaire Internationale, Marin County C. of C. (dir. 1976—, pres. 1986—), Am. Rifle Assn. (life), Sierra Club (life), Trout Unltd. (life), Omicron Kappa Upsilon, Chi Phi, Xi Psi Phi. Republican. Episcopalian. Rotarian (dir. San Rafael 1971-73, pres. 1978-79, Paul Harris fellow). Clubs: Lagunitas Country (pres. 1973-75), Bohemian; Lincoln of No. Calif., Meadow. Contbr. articles to profl. jours. Home: PO Box 977 Ross CA 94957 Office: 11 Greenfield Ave San Rafael CA 94901

DAY, ANTHONY, newspaper editor; b. Miami, Fla., May 12, 1933; s. Price and Alice (Alexander) D.; m. Lynn Ward, June 25, 1960; children—John, Julia. A.B. cum laude, Harvard U., 1955, postgrad. (Nieman fellow), 1966-67; L.H.D. (hon.), Pepperdine U., 1974. Reporter Phila. Bull., 1957-60, Washington, 1960-69; chief Washington bur. Phila. Bull., 1969. Chief editorial writer: Los Angeles Times, 1969-71; editor editorial pages, 1971—. Served with AUS, 1955-57. Mem. Am. Soc. Newspaper Editors, Signet Soc. Harvard, Asia Soc., Inter Am. Press Assn. Office: Los Angeles Times Times Mirror Sq Los Angeles CA 90053 *

DAY, BEVERLY JEAN, state insurance examiner; b. Tacoma, Wash., July 29, 1942; d. Therial Etheon and Georgia Ykema (Fisher) Wright; A.A., Riverside City Coll., 1962; B.A., U. Md., 1969; M.B.A., U. Utah, 1975; m. Dallas Glenn Day, June 13, 1964; 1 child, Linda Gayle. Cert. fin. examiner and accredited record technician. Acct., Toledo Scale Corp., Riverside, Calif., 1962-64, Dikeou Bros., Denver, 1964-65, Redlands (Calif.) Community Hosp., 1965-66, Titan Constrn. Co., Denver, 1969-72; med. record technician U.S. Air Force Hosp., RAF Lakenheath, England, 1973-76; insurance examiner State of Colo. Ins. Div., Denver, 1977—, sr. ins. examiner. Recipient scholarship Am. Soc. Women Accountants, 1961. Mem. Soc. Fin. Examiners (state chmn., mem. ins. examination rev. com.), Am. Mgmt. Assn., Assn. M.B.A. Execs., Nat. Assn. Female Execs., Inc., Am. Med. Record Assn., AAUW. Republican. Methodist. Home: 10330 W Burgundy Ave Littleton CO 80127 Office: Div Ins State of Colo First Western Plaza Bldg 303 W Colfax Ave Suite 500 Denver CO 80204

DAY, CARMEL MARTI, educator; b. Long Beach, Calif.; children: Alexander Jered, Michele Louise. MS in Biol., Calif. State Polytech. U., 1974; MA, Cen. Mich. U., 1976; MAM, Claremont Grad. Sch., 1979, PhD in exec. mgmt., 1981. Cert. clin. lab. dir. Med. tech. program dir. City of Hope, Duarte, Calif., 1974-78, adminstrv. technologist, 1978-79; asst. lab. mgr. Brotman Med. Ctr., Culver City, Calif., 1979-80; prof., dir. health mgmt. U. LaVerne, Calif., 1980—; co-dir. Health Mgmt. Analysts, West Covina, Calif., 1978—; exec. dir. Mgmt. Diagnostics, West Covina, 1982—; bd. dirs. Community Health Projects, West Covina, 1976—. Contbr. articles to profl. jours. Active West Covina Republican Club. Recipient Disting. Alumna award, Calif. Polytech. U., 1980. Mem. AAUW, Am. Soc. Med. Tech. (profl. achievement award 1980), Assn. Western Hosps., Women in Health Adminstrn., Arabian Horse Assn., West Covina C. of C. (chmn. health services 1986), Beta Beta Beta, Omicron Sigma (outstanding service award). Avocations: showing and breeding Arabian horses, skiing, raquetball. Office: U La Verne 1950 Third St La Verne CA 91750

DAY, HAROLD EDWARD, hospital adminstrator; b. Norristown, Pa., June 30, 1948; s. Harold Elsworth and Irene (Whonovitch) D.; m. Melinda S. Dewey, Apr. 3, 1971 (div.); m. Loretta H. Gaines, Aug. 29, 1981. Student U.S. Internat. U., 1970. Pres. RDQ Inc., Dana Point, Calif., 1970—, Capistrano Hosp. Corp., Dana Point, 1970—; chief exec. officer Capistrano by the Sea Hosp., Dana Point, 1968—. Mem. Assn. Mental Health Adminstrs., U.S. C. of C. Office: PO Box 398 Dana Point CA 92629

DAY, JOSEPH DENNIS, librarian; b. Dayton, Ohio, Sept. 23, 1942; s. John Albert and Ruth (Pearson) D.; m. Mary Louise Herbert, Oct. 10, 1964; children: Cindy, Jeff, Chris, Steve, Tom. B.A., U. Dayton, 1966; M.L.S., Western Mich. U., 1967. Community librarian Dayton-Montgomery Pub. Library, 1967-70; dir. Troy-Miami County Pub. Library, Troy, Ohio, 1970-76, Salt Lake City Pub. Library, 1976—; chmn. Miami Valley Library Orgn., 1971-73; pres. Ohio Library Assn., 1975-76; project dir. planning and constrn. first solar powered library in world, 1973-76. Pres. Troy Area Arts Council, 1973-74; v.p. SLC Salvation Army Bd., 1986—. Recipient Disting. Community Service award Troy C. of C., 1974; John Cotton Dana award, 1975, 77, 83-85; AIA-ALA architecture award, 1977. Mem. ALA (chmn. intellectual freedom com. 1981-84, exec. bd. 1987-88), Utah Library Assn. (pres. 1979-80, Disting. Service award 1985), Am. Soc. Pub. Adminstrn., Freedom To Read Found. (pres. 1986-87). Club: Kiwanis (pres. Troy 1975-76, Disting. Service award Troy 1973, pres. Salt Lake-Foothill 1979-80). Address: 209 East 5th South Salt Lake City UT 84111

DAY, LUCILLE ELIZABETH, educator, author; b. Oakland, Calif., Dec. 5, 1947; d. Richard Allen and Evelyn Marietta (Hazard) Lang; A.B., U. Calif., Berkeley, 1971, M.A., 1973, Ph.D., 1979; m. Frank Lawrence Day, Nov. 6, 1965; 1 dau., Liana Sherrine; m. 2d, Theodore Herman Fleischman, June 23, 1974; 1 dau., Tamarind Channah. Teaching asst. U. Calif., Berkeley, 1971-72, 75-76, research asst., 1975, 77-78; tchr. sci. Magic Mountain Sch., Berkeley, 1977; specialist math. and sci. Novato (Calif.) Unified Sch. Dist., 1979-81; instr. sci. Project Bridge, Laney Coll., Oakland, Calif., 1984-86; sci. writer and dir. of precoll. edn. programs, Lawrence Berkeley (Calif.) Lab., 1986—; author numerous poems, articles and book reviews; author: (with Joan Skolnick and Carol Langbort) How to Encourage Girls in Math and Science: Strategies for Parents and Educators, 1982; Self-Portrait with Hand Microscope (poetry collection), 1982. NSF Grad. fellow, 1972-75; recipient Joseph Henry Jackson award in lit. San Francisco Found., 1982. Mem. No. Calif. Sci. Writers Assn., Phi Beta Kappa, Iota Sigma Pi. Home: 109 Monte Vista Ave Oakland CA 94611

DAY, RICHARD ELLEDGE, newspaper editor; b. Denver, June 27, 1939; s. Bartle Henry and Clara Violet (Smith) D.; student Mesa Jr. Coll., 1958-60; B.A., Western State Coll. Colo., 1962. Reporter, Rock Springs (Wyo.) Daily Rocket and Sunday Miner, 1962-64, Casper (Wyo.) Star-Tribune, 1964-66; reporter Montrose (Colo.) Daily Press., 1967-68, mng. editor, 1968—. Mem. accountability adv. com. Montrose County Sch. Dist., 1979—. Republican precinct committeeman, Montrose, 1968—; mem. exec. com. Montrose County Rep. party; bd. dirs. Montrose County United Fund, 1972, Western Slope Tb and Respiratory Disease Assn., 1968-73; trustee Colo. Western Coll., 1971-72. Mem. Nat. Press Photographers Assn., Denver Press Club, AP Mng. Editors Assn., Montrose County C. of C. (dir., chmn. hwy. com. 1973—), Sigma Delta Chi. Mem. Christian Ch. Clubs: Masons, Elks, Kiwanis. Home: PO Box 957 844 N 5th St Montrose CO 81401 Office: PO Box 850 535 S 1st St Montrose CO 81401

DAY, RICHARD SOMERS, author, editorial consultant; b. Chgo., June 14, 1928; s. Milo Frank and Ethel Mae (Somers) D.; m. Lois Patricia Beggs, July 8, 1950; children—Russell Frank, Douglas Matthew, Gail Leslie. Student, Ill. Inst. Tech., 1946, U. Miami, 1947. Promotion writer, editor Portland Cement Assn., Chgo., 1958-62, promotion writer, 1963-66; editor Am. Inst. Laundering, Joliet, Ill., 1962-63; freelance writer, Monee, Ill., 1966-69, Palomar Mountain, Calif., 1969—; cons. editor home and shop Popular Sci. mag., N.Y.C., 1966—. Author numerous home repair books including: Patios and Decks, 1976; Plumb-It-Yourself the Easy Way with Genova, 1977; Automechanics, 1982; Do Your Own Plumbing, 1987. Editor: (newspaper) Powderlines, 1958; (mag.) Concrete Hwys. and Pub. Improvements, 1958-62; (mag.) Soil-Cement News, 1960-62; (mag.) Fabric Care, 1962-63. Contbr. chpts. to books. Bd. dirs. Land Use Council, San Diego, 1977, Palomar Mountain Planning Orgn., 1984—. Mem. Nat. Assn. Home and Workshop Writers (mng. editor newsletter 1982—, bd. dirs., pres. 1984-85). Home: Palomar Mountain CA 92060

DAY, ROBERT JAMES, industrial safety manager; b. Phoenix, Nov. 21, 1937; s. James Robert and Marion Virginia (Cook) D.; m. Margaret Elizabeth Eccles, June 28, 1957 (div. June 1979); children: Robert J. Jr., Steven C., Dennis S.; m. Arnita Joyce Zinn, Oct. 11, 1981. AA, Phoenix Coll., 1976. cert. health and safety technologist. Lineman apprentice Ariz. Pub. Service, Phoenix, 1959-64, lineman journeyman, 1964-72, safety specialist, 1972-80, 83-85, sr. safety specialist, 1985—; plant safety analyst Ariz. Pub. Service, Joseph City, 1980-83; sec., treas., bd. dirs. DLD Safety cons., Phoenix, 1985—. Past coach, mgr., v.p., pres. Westwood Little League; past coach West Cen. Assn. Pop Warner Tootball; past pres. Seabee Vets. Am. Island, Phoenix; past elder Campbell Ave. Christian Ch., choir dir., vice chmn. bd. dirs., trustee; mem. Westwood Sch. PTA; vol. Cub Scouts; mem. adv. council Westwood Community Sch.; mem. com. Alhambra (Calif.) Elem. Sch. Dist. Declining Enrollment. Served with USNR, 1955—. Mem. Am. Soc. Safety Engrs. (sec. 1985-86), Ariz. Safety Engrs. Assn., Soc. Fire Protection Engrs., World Safety Orgn. Republican. Home: 2214 W Myrtle Ave Phoenix AZ 85021 Office: Ariz Pub Service Co 2121 W Cheryl Phoenix AZ 85021

DAY, ROBERT WINSOR, research administrator; b. Framingham, Mass., Oct. 22, 1930; s. Raymond Albert and Mildred (Doty) D.; m. Jane Alice Boynton, Sept. 6, 1957 (div. Sept. 1977); m. Cynthia Taylor, Dec. 16, 1977; children: Christopher, Nathalia. Student, Harvard U., 1949-51; MD, U. Chgo., 1956; MPH, U. Calif., Berkeley, 1958, PhD, 1962. Intern USPHS, Balt., 1956-57; resident U. Calif., Berkeley, 1958-60; research specialist Calif. Dept. Mental Hygiene, 1960-64; asst. prof. sch. medicine UCLA, 1962-64; dep. dir. Calif. Dept. Pub. Health, Berkeley, 1965-67; prof., chmn. dept. health services Sch. Pub. Health and Community Medicine, U. Wash., Seattle, 1968-72, dean, 1972-82; dir. Fred Hutchinson Cancer Research Ctr., Seattle, 1981—; cons. in field. Pres. Seattle Planned Parenthood Ctr., 1970-72. Served with USPHS, 1956-57. Fellow Am. Pub. Health Assn., Am. Coll. Preventive Medicine; mem. Soc. Pediatric Research, Assn. Schs. Pub. Health (pres. 1981-82), Am. Assn. Cancer Insts. (bd. dirs. 1983—, v.p. 1984-85, pres. 1985-86, chmn. bd. dirs., 1986—). Office: Fred Hutchison Cancer Research Ctr 1124 Columbia St Seattle WA 98104

DAY, THOMAS BRENNOCK, university president; b. N.Y.C., Mar. 7, 1932; s. Frederick and Alice (Brennock) D.; m. Anne Kohlbrenner, Sept. 5, 1953; children: Erica, Monica, Mark, Kevin, Sara, Timothy, Jonathan, Patrick, Adam. B.S., U Notre Dame, 1953; Ph.D., Cornell U., 1957. Prof. U. Md., College Park, 1964-78, vice chancellor for acad. planning and policy, 1970-77, spl. asst. to pres., 1977-78, vice chancellor for acad. affairs Baltimore County, 1977-78; pres. San Diego State U., 1978—; cons. Bendix Corp., IBM Corp., Digital Equipment Corp.; vis. physicist Brookhaven Nat. Lab., 1963; cons. Argonne Nat. Lab., Ill., 1967. Contbr. articles to profl. jours. Mem. Nat. Sci. Bd., Am. Phys. Soc., Sigma Xi, Phi Kappa Phi. Republican. Roman Catholic. Lodge: Rotary. Office: San Diego State U Office of Pres San Diego CA 92182

DAY, WILLIAM H., chemistry educator; b. Trawick, Tex., July 6, 1921; s. Benjamin R. and Minnie M. (Hill) D.; m. Dorothy M. Burrell, June 22, 1948; children: Sharon Johnson, Winston H., Janis B. Parker, Keith. BS, Tex. Coll., 1947; MS, Tex. So. U., 1954, Okla. State U., 1960. Cert. chemist, tchr. Tchr. San Augustine (Tex.) High Sch., 1948-54, LaMarque (Tex.) High Sch., 1954-60, Fresno (Calif.) High Sch., 1960-64; mem. faculty Fresno City Coll., 1964—; med. technologist Hosp., Fresno, 1961-65; advisor Chemistry Dept. Fresno City Coll., 1964—; mem. Acad. Standards Com. (chmn. 1983-85), Chancellors Task Force (co-chmn. 1985). Served to capt. USAAF, 1943-46. Shell Merit fellow, 1958, NFS fellow, 1948, 60-61, 68, 72. Mem. Calif. Assn. Chem. Tchrs. (pres. 1976-76), Alpha Phi Alpha (pres. Fresno 1985-86). Democrat. Avocations: golfing, gardening, walking, reading. Home: 866 E Fir Fresno CA 93710 Office: Fresno City Coll Div MS & E Dept Chemistry 1101 University Ave Fresno CA 93741

DAYAN, RON, interior designer; b. Eng., Oct. 21, 1956; m. Barbara Jean Felise, Sept. 13, 1981. BA, Polytech. No. London, 1978; BS, Woodbury U., 1981. Owner, dir. interior design Piccadilly Designs, Los Angeles, 1983—. Designer Marina City Club Penthouses. Mem. Brit. Inst. Interior Design, Beverly Hills C. of C. Office: Piccadilly Designs 2617 Harlesden Ct Los Angeles CA 90046

DAY-GOWDER, PATRICIA JOAN, association executive, consultant; b. Lansing, Mich., Apr. 9, 1936; d. Louis A. and Johanna (Feringha) Whipple; m. Duane Lee Day, Jan. 7, 1961 (div.); children—Kevin Duane, Patricia Kimberely; m. William A. Gowder, Nov. 30, 1986. B.A., Mich. State U., 1958; M.A., Lindenwood (Mo.) Coll., 1979; postgrad. U. So. Calif., 1982-83. Cert. secondary tchr., Calif. Health edn. asst. YWCA, Rochester, N.Y., 1958-59; tchr. jr. high schs., Flint, Mich., 1959-61; tchr. Brookside Acad., Montclair, N.J., 1963-68; adult program dir. YMCA, Long Beach, Calif., 1968-73; community edn. dir. Paramount (Calif) Unified Sch. Dist., 1973-78; exec. dir. counseling ctr., Arcadia, Calif., 1978-80; sr. citizens program dir. City of Burbank (Calif.), 1981-83; div. dir. Am. Heart Assn., Los Angeles, 1983-87 ; exec. dir. Campfire Orgn., Psadena, 1987—; cons. community edn. State Dept. Edn., Fed. Office Community Edn., Los Angeles County Office Edn. Bd. dirs., v.p. Children's Creative Ctr., Long Beach, Calif., 1969-73, Travelor's Aid Soc., 1969-72; vice-chmn. Cerritos YMCA, 1968-73. Mott Found. fellow, 1977-78. Mem. Western Gerontology Assn., Calif. Community Edn. Assn. (sec.-treas., 1974-77), LWV. Democrat. Congregationalist. Club: Soroptimist, AAUW. Home: 837 Silver Maple Dr Azusa CA 91702 Office: Campfire Orgn 391 S Madison Pasadena CA 91724

DAYS, SHEILA TRUNZO, distributing company executive, consultant; b. Charlottesville, Va., Apr. 10, 1946; d. Louis and Beirne Wiley (Moon) Trunzo. B.S., Radford Coll., 1968; student UCLA-TESOL Inst., 1980, mktg. program, 1981, 82, 83. Cert. secondary sch. tchr., Va. Tchr. French and English, Va. Pub. Schs., 1968-74; writer, researcher Sta. WBRA-TV (PBS affiliate), Roanoke, Va., 1974-75; mgr. Libreria Britanica (English lang. bookstore), Mexico City, 1976-79; promotion mgr. ELS Publs., Los Angeles, 1979-81; rep. Regents Publ. Co., Inc., Los Angeles, 1982; owner, pres. The Lang. Works (publs. distbr.), Los Angeles, 1983—; cons. English as 2d lang. Mem. Nat. Assn. Female Execs., TESOL, Calif. TESOL, Calif. Council Adult Edn., Calif. Assn. Bilingual Educators, Am. Soc. Tng. Dirs. Creator Sta. WBRA-TV (PBS affiliate) show Cast Your Own Shadow, 1975.

DEA, MOON SUEY, telecommunications executive; b. Hong Kong, June 21, 1950; came to U.S., 1954; d. William and Jean Dea. BA, U. So. Calif., 1972, MLS, 1973; MBA, UCLA, 1982. Cert. tchr., Calif. Sr. librarian Los Angeles Pub. Library, 1977-80; tech. cons. AT&T Info. Systems, Los Angeles, 1983-85; product specialist Lexar div. United Techs. Communications Co., Westlake Village, Calif., 1985-86; product mgr. Security Pacific Network Services Co., Los Angeles, 1986-87, dir. planning and analysis, 1987—. Mem. adv. bd. Friends of Chinatown Library, Los Angeles, 1986—, bd. dirs. 1984-85, pres., 1983-84. Calif. State scholar, 1968-72; Calif. PTA LIbrary scholar, 1972; fellow Gen. Telephone and Electronics, 1981. Mem. Asian Bus. League, Chinese Hist. Soc., Phi Beta Kappa. Home: 339 W Wilson Ave #303 Glendale CA 91203 Office: Security Pacific Network Services Co 330 N Brand Blvd Suite 300 Glendale CA 91203

DEA, PHOEBE KIN-KIN, chemistry educator; b. Canton, Kwong-Tung, Peoples Republic of China, June 17, 1946; came to U.S., 1964; d. Kwok-Hung and Hon-Kuan (Lau) Wong; m. Frank J. Dea, Dec. 23, 1967; children: Denise, Melvin. BS, UCLA, 1967; PhD, Calif. Inst. Tech., 1972. Research fellow ICN Nucleic Acid Research Inst., Irvine, Calif., 1972-74; head dept. ICN Pharm., Irvine, 1974-76; asst. prof. Calif. State U., Los Angeles, 1976-79, assoc. prof., 1979-84, prof. chemistry, 1984—. Author: Practical Introductory Quantitative Analysis, 1983; contbr. articles to profl. jours. Grantee NSF, NIH, Am. Chem. Soc. Petroleum Research Fund. Mem. So. Calif. Thermal Analysis Group (treas. 1985—), Phi Kappa Phi (bd. dirs. 1985—). Home: 1155 Sherwood Rd San Marino CA 91108 Office: Calif State U 5151 State University Dr Los Angeles CA 90032

DEACETIS, SHIRLEY MARGARET, social worker; b. Modesto, Calif., Feb. 18, 1941; d. Walter Henry and Martha A. (Quinley) Zimmerman; m. William DeAcetis, June 8, 1963. BA, U. Calif., Berkeley, 1963; BA in Gerontology, Iona Coll., 1981; MSW, Fordham U., 1984. Social worker YM, YWHA, Scarsdale, N.Y., 1983, Westchester Jewish Community Services, New Rochelle, N.Y., 1984; project dir. West-Care Adult Day Health Care Ctr., Modesto, 1986—. Mem. Nat. Assn. Social Workers (cert.), Scarsdale Audubon Soc. (bd. dirs. 1980-84), Delta Epsilon Sigma. Democrat. Avocations: gardening, hiking, tide-pooling. Home: 807 High St Modesto CA 95354 Office: West-Care 918 Sierra Dr Modesto CA 95351

DEAL, PATRICIA LOU EISENBISE, educational administrator; b. Reading, Pa., Mar. 25, 1932; d. Jasper Paul and Mae (Rozycki) Eisenbise; B.S., Albright Coll., 1954; M.A., Pacific Lutheran U., 1978; m. Robert Lee Deal, May 31, 1955; children—Robert Lee Jr., David Alan, James Edward. Tchr. aide instr.-coordinator Clover Park Vocat.-Tech. Inst., Tacoma, Wash., 1970-78, asst. to program supr. of secondary vocat. edn., 1979, career edn. asst., fed. and spl. projects asst., 1979-81, asst. dir. Elective High Sch., 1981-82, dir., 1982-84, 85, dir. Elective High Sch. and Adult Edn., 1985-86; dir. Singletree Estates, Yelm, Wash., 1981-84, 85; trustee Lakes Dist. Library, 1986—. Recipient Community Service award United Way, 1980; honoree Clover Park Found., 1984, 85, 86. Mem. Wash. Vocat. Assn. (pres. Clover Park local unit 1981-82, legis. chmn. 1980-81, exec. bd. local chpt. 1985-86), Wash. Assn. Career Edn. (mem. exec. bd. 1980-81), Am. Vocat. Assn., C. of C., Pierce County Adminstrv. Women in Edn., South Sound Women's Network, Nat. Council Local Adminstrs., Wash. Assn. Vocat. Adminstrs. (bd. dirs. 1986—). Home: 8401 Woodlawn Ave SW Tacoma WA 98499 Office: 4500 Steilacoom Blvd SW Tacoma WA 98499

DEAN, BURTON VICTOR, educator; b. Chgo., June 3, 1924; s. Samuel and Dorothy (Eisner) D.; m. Barbara Louise Arnoff, Nov. 26, 1958; children: Howard David, Paul Evan, Heather Diana, Theodore Samuel. B.S., Northwestern U., 1947; M.S., Columbia U., 1948; Ph.D., U. Ill., 1952. Instr. math. Columbia U., 1947-49, Hunter Coll., 1949-50; research fellow math. U. Ill., 1950-52; mathematician Nat. Security Agy., 1952-55; research mathematician Ops. Research, Inc., 1955-57; assoc. prof. operations research Case Western Res. U., Cleve., 1957-65; prof. ops. research, chmn. dept. Case Western Res. U., 1965-76, 79-85, prof. ops. research, 1965-85; prof. ops. mgmt., chmn. dept. orgn. and mgmt. San Jose State U., 1985—; on leave as vis. prof. indsl. and mgmt. engring. Technion-Israel Inst. Tech., 1962-63; assoc. Inst. Public Adminstrn., Washington, 1972-76, 79-82, Booz, Allen & Hamilton, 1980-82; cons. U.S. industry and govt., 1957—, TAHAL Water Planning for Israel, 1962-64; vis. prof. U. Louvain, Belgium, Ben Gurion U., U. Tel Aviv, 1978, Zero-Base Budgeting Seminars, Belgium, Egypt, Israel, Greece, Spain, 1978, Greece, Spain, Japan, 1979, Greece, Spain, 1980; lectr. U.S. CSC, 1977-80; adv. dir. Sourcenet Inc.; vis. prof. indsl. engring., mgmt. engring. Stanford U., 1985. Author: Operations Research in Research and Development, 1963, reprinted, 1978, (with Sasieni and Gupta) Mathematics of Modern Management, 1963, reprinted 1978, Evaluation, Selection and Control of R & D Projects, 1968, (with Reisman, Salvador and Oral) Industrial Inventory Control, 1974, (with Goldhar) Management of Research and Innovation, 1980, Project Management, 1985; also articles and chpts. in profl. jours, books Ency. Profl. Mgmt; editor Mgmt. Sci, 1962—; assoc. editor OPSEARCH, 1968-74; editor: IEEE Trans. on Engring Mgmt, 1968—, North Holland Studies in Management Science and Systems, 1974—, Jour. Bus. Venturing, 1985—. Recipient Centennial medal IEEE Engring. Mgmt. Soc., 1984; Centennial Scholar medal Case Inst. Tech., 1981. Fellow AAAS (chmn. indsl. sci. sect. 1976); mem. IEEE (vice chmn. seminars Santa Clara Valley chpt., founding chmn. Cleve. chpt. 1984-85), Am. Prodn. and Inventory Control Soc. (academic liaison Santa Clara Valley chpt., 1986—, instr. mfg. strategies program, 1987), Acad. Mgmt. (prodn./ops. mgmt. div. program reviewer 1987), Ops. Research Soc. (council 1973-76, chmn. ORSA/AAAS com. 1976-82), Inst. Mgmt. Scis. (chmn. coll. research and devel. 1969-73, council 1966-67, past chmn. No. Ohio chpt., council coll. engring. mgmt. 1978-85, founding chmn. Coll. Innovation Mgmt. and Entrepreneurship 1986—), Am. Math. Soc., Omega Rho (founding mem. 1977, pres. 1980-82, exec. council 1984-86). Home: 161 Gabarda Way Portola Valley CA 94025

DEAN, JEFFREY STEWART, dendrochronologist, archaeologist; b. Lewiston, Idaho, Feb. 10, 1939; s. Kenneth Franklyn and Margaret Mary (Mitchell) D; children: Alison Elizabeth, Carrie Margaret. Student, U. Idaho, 1957-58; BA, U. Ariz., 1961, PhD, 1967. Instr. U. Ariz., Tucson, 1966-67, asst. prof., 1967-72, assoc. prof., 1972-77, prof., 1977—; sr. scientist So. Ill. U., Carbondale, 1985-86; cooperating scientist Black Mesa Archeol. Project, Carbondale, 1979—; peer reviewer Ariz. State Museum, Tucson, 1981—; cons. in field. Author: Chronological Analysis of Tsegi Phase Sites in Northeastern Arizona, 1969; (with others) SW Dendroclimate, 680-1970, 1977, Arroyo Hondo Paleoclimate, 1981; also numerous articles. Grantee U.S. Nat. Park Service, 1967-77, NSF, 1985—. Fellow Am. Anthrop. Assn.; mem. AAAS, Soc. Am. Archaeology (treas. 1977-80), Tree-Ring Soc. (sec. 1974—), Sigma Xi. Office: U Ariz Lab of Tree-Ring Research Tucson AZ 85721

DEAN, KENNESON GENE, geologist, researcher; b. Miami, Fla., Nov. 9, 1948; s. Gene Wendell and Ann Sofia (Wasekanes) D.; m. Deborah Ann Lipke, Sept. 6, 1975; children: Kristin, Holly. Student, U. Md., 1967-69; AA in Engring., Anne Arundel Community Coll., 1970; BS, No. Ariz. U., 1972; MS, U. Alaska, 1979. Engr. Greiner Co., Balt., 1972-74; geologist Shannon & Wilson Geotech. Cons., Fairbanks, Alaska, 1975, R&M Cons. Inc., Fairbanks, 1975-76; engr. geologist Bechtel Corp., Fairbanks, 1976-77; remote sensing geologist Geophys. Inst. U. Alaska, Fairbanks, 1977—; tchr. U. Alaska, 1983-85; prin. investigator NASA-U. Alaska, 1979—. Contbr. articles to profl. jours. Mem. AAAS, Geol. Soc. Am., Am. Soc. Photogrammetry and Remote Sensing, Alaska Geol. Soc. Republican. Roman Catholic. Avocations: fishing, camping. Office: U Alaska Geophys Inst Fairbanks AK 99775-0800

DEAN, KENNETH, design executive, educator; b. Chgo., May 10, 1939; s. Wayne Edwin and Genevieve Julia (Kyll) Smith; m. Linda Elizabeth Benitez, Sept. 27, 1980. B.A. in Design, Los Angeles Coll., 1959. Cer. profl. interior designer, Calif. pres. Dean Interior Design, Studio City, Calif., 1971—; dean Los Angeles Sch. Design, 1980—. Debater, lectr. People for the Am. Way. Served to lt. Army N.G., 1955-63. Recipient Award of Merit for Outstanding Design, Los Angeles County Fair, 1979; Best Actor awards, 1962, 1963, 1965. Mem. Am. Soc. Interior Designers, Internat. Soc. Interior Designers (Designer of the Yr. award 1986), Constrn. Specifications Inst. Democrat. Roman Catholic. Club: Optimist. Contbr. articles to profl. design mags. Office: Dean Interior Design 13045 Ventura Blvd Studio City CA 91604 Office: Dean Interior Designs 16507 Soledad Canyon Canyon Country CA 91351

DEAN, RAY BARTLETT, former educator; b. Portland, Oreg., Apr. 17, 1901; s. Murray and Hazel (Bartlett) D.; B.S., Whitman Coll., 1925; M.A., U. Wash., 1928; Ed.D., Stanford, 1943; m. Grace V. Burgett, Sept. 2, 1924; children—James, Norma, Robert. Instr., coach high sch., Dayton, Wash., 1925-26; instr., coach, Longview, Wash., 1926-29; playground dir., Longview, 1929; prin. elementary sch., Longview, 1929-30; vice prin. elementary and jr. high sch., Sacramento, 1930-33, prin. elementary sch., 1933-44; instr. Chico State Coll., summers 1936-41, Stanford, summer 1945, U. So. Calif., summer 1948-49; asst. supt. schs., Sacramento, 1945-63; mem. faculty Calif. State U. at Sacramento, 1964-76; dir. men's personnel Bercut-Richards Packing Co., Sacramento. Mem. Calif. State Curriculum Commn., 1944-46. Mem. Sacramento Prins. Assn., Calif. Elementary Prins. Assn., Phi Delta Theta, Phi Delta Kappa. Author numerous tech. articles in profl. jours. Home: 2923 25 St Sacramento CA 95818

DEAN, WILLIAM EVANS, aerospace, environmental, electronics systems company executive; b. Greenville, Miss., July 6, 1930; s. George Thomas Dean and Martha Myrtle (Evans) Carlton; m. Dorothy Sue Hamilton, Oct. 14, 1953; children—Janet Lea, Jody Anne, Justin H. B. Aero. Engring., Ga. Inst. Tech., 1952; M.B.A., Pepperdine U., 1970. Cert. flight instr. Commd. officer U.S. Air Force, 1952, advanced through grades to maj.; div. mgr., dir. Rockwell Internat. Corp., Los Angeles, 1962-67, v.p., div. gen. mgr., 1967-80; exec. v.p. Acurex Corp., Mountain View, Calif., 1981-82, pres., chief operating officer, 1982-83, pres., chief exec. officer, 1983—, dir., 1981—; dir. Aerotherm Corp., Mountain View, Calif., 1982—; bd. dirs. Acurex Export Sales, Ltd., Bridgtown, Barbados, 1985—, Cryopro, Inc., Huntsville, Ala., Anacom. Assn., Los Angeles, 1986—. Contbr. articles on gen. mgmt. and aero. engring. to profl. jours. Bd. dirs. NCCJ, San Jose, Calif., 1984—, Santa Clara County Mfg. Group, San Jose, 1984—, Saddleback Community Coll., Mission Viejo, Calif., 1976-77, United Fund, Orange County, Calif., 1971 ; United Way, Santa Clara County, San Jose, 1985—. Served to maj. USAF, 1952-62. Assoc. fellow AIAA (bd. dirs. 1979-86, space shuttle award 1984); fellow Am. Astron. Soc.; mem. Am. Electronics Assn. (edn. found. 1982—), Nat. Mgmt. Assn. (Silver Knight award 1978), Aircraft Owners and Pilots Assn., Air Force Assn., ARmed Forces Communications and Electronics Assn. Republican. Baptist. Avocations: aviation, breeding and showing horses. Office: Acurex Corp 555 Clyde Ave Mountain View CA 94039

DEANGELO, MARLENE ANN, social services administrator; b. Orland, Calif., Aug. 14, 1937; d. Elmar Laurence and Gloria Arnel (Warren) Zimmerman; m. Ernest Lewis DeAngelo; children: Kippi Lynn, Scott. AA, Sierra Coll., 1973; BA, Calif. State U., Sacramento, 1979, MA, 1980. Tchr. Roseville (Calif.) Adult Ctr., 1978-81; counselor supr. Aquarian Effort Inc., Sacramento, 1981-85; program dir. Assn. Retarded Ctr. Placer County Auburn (Calif.) Activity Ctr., 1985—. Mem. AAUW, Auburn C. of C., Assn. Retarded Ctr. Democrat. Club: Toastmasters. Avocations: gardening, painting. Home: 5000 9th Ave Sacramento CA 95820 Office: ARC-PC Auburn Activity Ctr 11517 F Ave Auburn CA 95603

DE ARAGON, RAGENA CHERI, history educator; b. Boulder, Colo., May 29, 1952; d. Raymond John and M. ErvaGene (Alden) DeA. BA in History, U. Santa Clara, 1974; MA in History, U. Calif., Santa Barbara, 1977, PhD in History, 1982. Vis. asst. prof. history Wichita (Kans.) State U., 1981-83; asst. prof. Gonzaga U., Spokane, 1983—. Editor: Kings, Saints and Parliaments, 1979; contbr. articles to profl. jours. Grantee NEH, 1978, 85. Mem. Am. Hist. Assn., Conf. Brit. Studies, Haskins Soc. Anglo-Saxon, Viking, Anglo-Norman and Angevin History. Democrat. Roman Catholic. Avocations: photography, wine-tasting. Office: Gonzaga U Dept History E 502 Boone Spokane WA 99258

DE ARMENT, SAMUEL W., publishing executive; b. Lewistown, Pa., Feb. 1, 1945; s. William S. and Edna P. (Earnest) De A.; m. E. Jeanne Singleton, Feb. 17, 1969; children: Stacey, Bradley Alan. Product mgr. Norden Labs., Lincoln, Nebr., 1970-83; nat. sales mgr. Ft. Dodge (Iowa) Labs., 1983-85; owner, pub. Vet. Practice Pub. Co., Santa Barbara, Calif., 1985—; owner, mgr. Ties and Accessories, Lincoln, 1982-83, Fashion Station, Ft. Dodge, 1984-85. Patentee double syringe for livestock enclosures, 1984. Served as capt. U.S. Army, 1964-69, Vietnam. Decorated Bronze Star, Purple Heart; recipient numerous sales awards. Mem. Am. Vets. Exhibition Assn. (bd. dirs. 1986), Western Pub. assn., Young Reps. assn. Lodges: Elks, Toastmasters. Avocations: sailing, golf, chess, walking. Home: 2559 Calle Galicia Santa Barbara CA 93109 Office: Vet Practice Pub Co PO Box 4457 Santa Barbara CA 93103

DEASY, WILLIAM JOHN, corporate executive; b. N.Y.C., June 22, 1937; s. Jeremiah and Margaret (Quinn) D.; m. Carol Ellyn Lemmons, Feb. 1, 1963; children: Cameron, Kimberly. B.S. in Civil Engring, Cooper Union, 1958; LL.B., U. Wash., 1963. With Morrison Knudsen, Boise, Idaho, 1970—, v.p. N.W. region, 1972-75, v.p. mining, 1975-78, group v.p. mining, 1978-83, exec. v.p. mining, shipbuilding and mfg., 1983-84, pres., chief operating officer, 1984-85, chmn., pres., chief exec. officer, from 1985, also bd. dirs.; bd. dirs. MK-Engrs., MK-Ferguson, Emkay Devel., Moore Fin. Group, Boise; mem. eximbank adv. com. Export-Import Bank U.S., Washington, 1986-87. Bd. dirs. St. Luke's Regional Med. Ctr., 1984—. Mem. Soc. Mining Engrs., Soc. Mil. Engrs., Beavers, Moles. Home: 4611 Hillcrest

Dr Boise ID 83705 Office: Morrison Knudsen Corp PO Box 7808 Boise ID 83729

DEATS, WAYNE LAWTON, JR., oil company executive; b. Houston, Feb. 21, 1941; s. Wayne Lawton and Margaret (Brown) D.; m. Judy Linda Gill, Jan. 4, 1963; 1 son, Wayne Lawton III. B.A. in Acctg., U. St. Thomas, Houston, 1974. Data processing and payroll mgr. Ethyl Corp., Houston, 1974-77; cash control mgr. Amerada Hess Oil Co., V.I., 1977-80; corp. sec., controller Berry Holding Co., Taft, Calif., 1980-85, v.p., 1983-85; prin. Taft Bus. Services, 1985—; v.p., bd. dirs. Liquid Waste Mgmt. Corp., 1982-84; bd. dirs. Ind. Oil Producers Agy. Chmn. Taft Planning Commn.; sr. warden St. Andrew's Episcopal Ch., 1983-84; elected mayor City of Taft, 1986—; active Taft City Personnel Rev. Commn. Served with USN, 1963-67. Mem. Nat. Assn. Accts., Petroleum Accts. Soc., Calif. Ind. Accts. Assn., Nat. Soc. Pub. Accts., Taft C. of C. (bd. dirs. 1982-84). Club: Rotary (bd. dirs.) (Taft). Home: 309 Church St Taft CA 93268 Office: Taft Bus Services 330 North St Taft CA 93268

DE BARTOLO, EDWARD J., JR., owner pro football team; b. Youngstown, Ohio, Nov. 6, 1946; s. Edward J. and Marie Patricia (Montani) DeB.; m. Cynthia Ruth Papalia, Nov. 27, 1968; children: Lisa Marie, Tiffanie Lynne, Nicole Anne. Student, U. Notre Dame, 1964-68. With Edward J. DeBartolo Corp., Youngstown, Ohio, 1960—; v.p. Edward J. DeBartolo Corp., 1972-75, exec. v.p., 1975—; pres., chief adminstrv. officer EJD Corp., 1979; owner, mng. partner San Francisco 49ers, 1977—. Trustee Youngstown State U., 1974-77; mem. nat. adv. council St. Jude Children's Research Hosp., 1978—, local chmn., 1979-80; local chmn. fund drive Am. Cancer Soc., 1975—, City of Hope, 1977; mem. Nat. Cambodia Crisis Com., 1980—; chmn. 19th Ann. Victor awards City of Hope, 1985. Served with U.S. Army, 1969. Recipient Man of Yr. award St. Jude Children's Hosp., 1979, Boys' Town of Italy in San Francisco, 1985; Salvation Army Citation of Merit, 1982. Mem. Internat. Council of Shopping Centers. Roman Catholic. Clubs: Tippecanoe Country, Fonderlac Country, Dapper Dan (dir. 1980—). Office: Edward J DeBartolo Corp 7620 Market St Youngstown OH 44512 and: care San Francisco 49ers 711 Nevada St Redwood City CA 94061

DE BERGE, EARL VINCENT, market research executive; b. Phoenix, June 7, 1941; s. Ray Henry de B. and Lorraine (May) Sharp; M. Suzanne Martha Sonderegger, June 26, 1965. BA, Antioch Coll., 1964; MA, U. Ariz., 1965. Research dir. Behavior Research Ctr., Phoenix, 1965—, also bd. dirs. Contbr. articles to profl. jours.; editor Rocky Mountain Poll, 1970—. Chmn. Maricopa County Planning Commn., Phoenix, 1975—, Ariz. Land Appeals Bd., Phoenix, 1982-86; mem. Ariz. Planning Commn.; mem. exec. com. Phoenix Econ. Growth Corp. 1985—; bd. dirs. Phoenix Symphony 1986—. Named one of Young Men of Yr., Phoenix Jaycees, 1975. Avocation: metal sculpture. Office: Behavior Research Ctr 1117 N 3rd St Phoenix AZ 85004

DEBLASE, ANTHONY FRANK, publishing company executive, biology educator, consultant; b. South Bend, Ind., Apr. 3, 1942; s. Stephan and Ida (Macri) D.; m. Alyce Mae Myers, Aug. 19, 1969 (dec. Mar. 1976). A.B., Earlham Coll., 1964; Ph.D. in Zoology, Okla. State U., 1971. Asst. dir. museums Earlham Coll., dir. Conner Prairie Mus. (now Conner Prairie Pioneer Settlement), Noblesville, Ind., 1964-66; chief of security and visitor services Field Mus. of Natural History, Chgo., 1970-78; assoc. prof. biology Roosevelt U., Chgo., 1969-78; pres., pub. Desmodus Publs., Inc., Chgo., 197886; v.p. pub. Desmodus, Inc, San Francisco, 1986—. Named expdn. co-mammalogist W.S. & J.K. Street Expdn. to Iran, Field Mus. Natural History, 1968. Mem. Am. Soc. of Mammalogists (life). Club: CHC (Chgo.). Author (with Robert E. Martin) A Manual of Mammalogy (2d edit.), 1981; author tech. publs., short stories; contbr. articles to profl. jours. Office: Desmodus Inc PO Box 11314 San Francisco CA 94101

DEBOER, CATHY PATRICE, electronics company executive; b. Kokomo, Ind., Nov. 14, 1949; d. Lowell Jay and Juanita Monelle (Gasaway) Somsel; m. Robert Lee DeBoer, Feb. 15, 1970; children: Julienne Rae, Christa Michelle. AA, Pikes Peak Community Coll., 1981. Automated data processing systems mgr. DOD MERB, Colorado Springs, Colo., 1976-77; functional A.D. mgr. Air Force Acad., Colorado Springs, 1977-79; automated data processing systems mgr. AFPRO TRW, Redondo Beach, Calif., 1981—; chmn. Computer Resources Bd., Redondo Beach. Named Technician of Yr. Air Force Acad., Colorado Springs, 1979, Outstanding Technician Fed. Exec. Bd., 1983. Mem. AFTRA, S.B. Local IBM Personal Computer User's Group. Avocation: acting. Home: 2841 Gramercy Ave Torrance CA 90501 Office: AFPRO TRW Redondo Beach CA 90278-1078

DEBON, GEORGE A., security services company executive. Chmn. Loomis Corp., Seattle. Office: Loomis Corp 720 Olive Way Seattle WA 98101 Other Office Address: Loomis Armored Inc 10 Corporated Pl S Piscataway NJ 08854 *

DEBRETTEVILLE, SHEILA LEVRANT, educator, artist; b. Bklyn., Nov. 4, 1940. Student Barnard Coll.; B.A. in Art History, Columbia U.; M.F.A., Yale U. Group shows include Am. Inst. Graphics Art, 1972, 5e Biennale des Arts Graphiques, Brno Czech, 1972, Whitney Mus., 1974; represented in permanent collections N.Y., Mus. Modern Art, N.Y.C., Community Gallery, Los Angeles; commns. include Archtl. League, N.Y., 1965, Yale Art Gallery, 1966, book design Canavese, Olivetti, Milan, Italy, 1968, poster design Calif. Inst. Arts, Valencia, 1970, spl. issue design Art Soc. Wis., 1970; typographer Yale U. Press, 1969-74; co-founder, pres. Woman's Bldg. Community Gallery, 1973—; dir. graphic design dept. Calif. Inst. Arts, 1970-74; co-founder, editor, designer Chrysalis Mag., 1977; design dir. Los Angeles Times, 1978-81; chmn. dept. communication, design and illustration Otis Art Inst., Parsons Sch. Design, Los Angeles, 1981—; judge Nat. Endowment Arts-Civil Service Commn., 1975; lectr. various colls. and univs. Recipient Grand Excellence award Soc. Pub. Designers, 1971, Communication Graphics awards Am. Inst. Graphic Arts, 1972. Mem. Am. Inst. Graphic Arts. Office: Otis Art Institute Parsons Sch Design 2401 Wilshire Blvd Los Angeles CA 90057

DEBREU, GERARD, educator, economist; b. Calais, France, July 4, 1921; came to U.S., 1950, naturalized, 1975; s. Camille and Fernande (Decharne) D.; m. Françoise Bled, June 14, 1945; children: Chantal, Florence. Student, Ecole Normale Supérieure, Paris, 1941-44, Agrégé de l'Université, 1946; D. Scis., U. Paris, 1956; Dr. Rerum Politicarum honoris causa, U. Bonn, 1977; D. Scis. Economiques honoris causa, U. Lausanne, 1980; D. Sci.h.c., Northwestern U., 1981; D.h.c. U. des Sciences Sociales de Toulouse, 1983. Research assoc. Centre Nat. De La Recherche Sci., Paris, 1946-48; Rockefeller fellow U.S., Sweden and Norway, 1948-50; research assoc. Cowles Commn., U. Chgo., 1950-55; assoc. prof. econs. Cowles Found., Yale, 1955-61; fellow Center Advanced Study Behavioral Scis., 1960-61; vis. prof. econs. Yale U., fall 1961; prof. econs. U. Calif. at Berkeley, 1962—, prof. math., 1975—, Univ. prof., 1985—; Guggenheim fellow, vis. prof. Center Ops. Research and Econometrics, U. Louvain, 1968-69, vis. prof., fall 1971, winter, 1972; Erskine fellow U. Canterbury, Christchurch, New Zealand, 1969, vis. prof., 1973; Overseas fellow Churchill Coll., Cambridge, Eng., spring 1972; vis. prof. Cowles Found. for Research in Econs., Yale U., fall 1976; sr. U.S. scientist awardee Alexander von Humboldt Found.; vis. prof. U. Bonn, 1977; research asso. CEPREMAP, Paris, fall 1980. Author: Theory of Value, 1959, Mathematical Economics: Twenty Papers of Gerard Debreu, 1983; Asso. editor: Internat. Econ. Rev, 1959-69; mem. editorial bd.: Jour. Econ. theory, 1972—; mem. adv. bd.: Jour. Math. Econs, 1974—. Served with French Army, 1944-45. Decorated chevalier Légion d'Honneur; recipient Nobel Prize in Econ. Scis., 1983, Commandeur de l'Ordre du Merite, 1984. Fellow Am. Acad. Arts and Scis., AAAS, Econometric Soc. (pres. 1971); Disting. fellow Am. Econ. Assn.; mem. Am. Philos. Soc., Nat. Acad. Scis., French Acad. Scis. (fgn. assoc.). Office: Dept of Economics Univ of Calif at Berkeley Berkeley CA 94720

DE BRUIN, HENDRIK CORNELIS, academic administrator; b. Passaic, N.J., Jan. 3, 1929; s. William and Jane (Van Hoek) deB.; m. Marie Annicharico, July 5, 1952 (div. Aug. 1974); children: Mari, Derik; m. Jo Ann Buck, Nov. 29, 1974. BA, Montclair State U., 1951; MEd, U. Ariz., 1953, PhD, 1962. From sci. tchr. to supt. of schs. various high schs., 1951-61; asst. prof. edn. Mont. State U., Bozeman, 1962-64; dir. grad. program Butler U., Indpls., 1964-68; dean Coll. of Edn. Eastern N.Mex. U., Portales, 1968-76; chmn. div. of edn. Ind. U., South Bend, 1976-79; head dept. edn. The Citadel, Charleston, S.C., 1979-82; dir. instrn. U. N.Mex., Gallup, 1982—. Contbr. articles to profl. jours. Deacon Sunnyside Presbyn. Ch., South Bend, 1979-82, Westminister Presbyn. Ch., Gallup, 1983-85. Served as cpl. U.S. Army, 1946-48. Named one of Community Leaders of the World, 1985, Man of Achievement, 1973, 77, 84, one of 2000 Men of Achievement, 1971; Westinghouse Sci. fellow Carnegie Inst. Tech., 1952, Montclair State Coll. scholar, 1948-51. Mem. Nat. Orgn. Legal Problems of Edn. (state dir. 1969-76, 79-85, bd. dirs. 1972-74), Tchr. Edn. Council State Colls. and Univs. (accreditation com. 1981), Am. Assn. Coll. Tchr. Edn. (chief instl. rep. 1968-82), Assn. Tchr. Educators (nat. com. 1980), Ind. Assn. Colls. Tchr. Edn. (pres 1979, v.p., pres. elect 1978), Nat. Assn. Trade and Tech. Schs. (evaluation team), N.Mex. Assn. Colls. Tchr. Edn. (pres. 1972-74), Am. Arbitration Assn. (mem. ednl. panel 1970-83), Apache County Adminstr. Assn. (pres. 1961), Yavapai County Tchrs. Assn. (pres. 1959), Am. Assn. Community Jr. Colls. Democrat. Lodges: Shriners, Elks, Masons. Avocations: golf, photography, writing. Home: 505 Mountain View Circle Gallup NM 87301

DEBUS, BEMI (ELIZABETH BEMIS), naturalist, lecturer, writer, consultant; b. Littleton, Colo., Aug. 5, 1916; d. Edwin Arnold and Katherine (Prescott) Bemis; m. Louis Kissam DeBus, Sept. 22, 1941; children—David Waring, Edwin Bemis, Maya Ruffner. B.A., U. Colo., 1937; student U. Paris Med. Sch., 1937-38. Spl. teaching credential, Calif. First U.S. woman radio news analyst Sta. KLZ, Denver, 1939-40; news analyst Sta. WLW, Cin., 1940-42, Sta. CBS-TC, N.Y.C., 1942-43; news writer/analyst Office of War Info., N.Y.C., 1943-45; with pub. relations and publicity dept. So. Calif. Horticulture Inst., Los Angeles, 1963-69; lectr., resource person, Santa Monica, 1970—; aquatic life tour guide to Hawaiian Islands, China, Baja, Calif., Channel Islands; resource person for European Inst. Edn.; lectr. on whales, dolphins to various schs.; TV lectr. for Nova-Oceanus series, 1980; mem. U.S.-Japan Whaling Problems Com., Tokyo, 1970; counselor Marine Tech. Soc., Los Angeles, 1965-72. Author, editor monthly newsletters, Whalewatcher, 1968-77, You-Are-Invited, 1970—, Roundhouse Reporter, 1983. Patentee sewing gadget, 1956. Co-pres., bd. dirs. Stevens House, UCLA 1960—; bd. dirs. Support Group, UCLA Neuropsychiat. Hosp., 1981—; judge, clk. Santa Monica Election Bd., 1982—; active library service Shut-Ins, Santa Monica Pub. Library, 1983—; tour guide Visitors Center UCLA, 1983—. Recipient Community Services award City of Los Angeles, 1982; Magnet Sch. award Los Angeles County Schs., 1983-84. Mem. Western Soc. Naturalists, Oceanic Soc., Am. Cetacean Soc. (co-founder 1967, editor 1968-74, bd. dirs., award 1982, ambassador-at-large 1984), Soc. for Marine Mammology, Oceanographic Teaching Stations (bd. dirs. 1980—), Assoc. Ethnic Arts (pres. 1986). Democrat. Unitarian. Clubs: Westwood Coop Folkdance (Los Angeles), Southern Calif. Folk Dance Fedn. (Van Nuys). Home and Office: 901 25th St Santa Monica CA 90403

DEBUS, ELEANOR VIOLA, business management company executive; b. Buffalo, May 19, 1920; d. Arthur Adam and Viola Charlotte (Pohl) D.; student Chown Bus. Sch., 1939. Sec., Buffalo Wire Works, 1939-45; home talent producer Empire Producing Co., Kansas City, Mo., sec. Owens Corning Fiberglass, Buffalo; public relations and publicity Niagara Falls Theatre, Ont., Can.; pub. relations dir. Woman's Internat. Bowling Congress, Columbus, Ohio, 1957-59; publicist, sec. Ice Capades, Hollywood, Calif., 1961-63; sec. to controller Rexall Drug Co., Los Angeles, 1963-67; bus. mgmt. acct. Samuel Berke & Co., Beverly Hills, Calif., 1967-75; Gadbois Mgmt. Co., Beverly Hills, 1975-76; sec., treas. Sasha Corp., Los Angeles, 1976—; bus. mgr. Dean Martin, Shirley MacLaine, Debbie Reynolds; pres. Tempo Co., Los Angeles, 1976—. Mem. Nat. Assn. Female Execs., Nat. Notary Assn., Nat. Film Soc., Am. Film Inst. Republican. Lodge: Order Eastern Star. Contbr. articles to various mags. Office: Tempo Co 1900 Ave of Stars #1230 Los Angeles CA 90067

DE BUTTS, EDWARD H(ERBERT), JR., diversified chemical company executive; b. Front Royal, Va., Dec. 23, 1922; s. Edward H(erbert) and Inez Love (Anderson) de B.; m. Jacqueline Eleanor Alderton, Dec. 28, 1946; children: Harold, Rebecca, Richard. BS, George Washington U., 1943; PhD, U. Ill., 1948. Instr. Harvard U., Cambridge, Mass., 1948-51; research chemist Hercules Inc., Wilmington, Del., 1951-62; research mgr. Hercules ABL, Cumberland, Md., 1962-71; tech. mgr. Hercules/Bacchus, Magna, Utah, 1971-82; dir. tech. devel. Hercules Aerospace, Salt Lake City, 1982-86; cons. U.S. Govt., Washington, 1965—. Contbr. articles to profl. jours.; patentee in field. Mem. AIAA (sec. chmn. 1982-83), Am. Chem. Soc. (sec. chmn. 1969-70), Am. Def. Preparedness Assn., Sigma Xi, Phi Lambda Upsilon. Democrat. Episcopalian. Clubs: Willow Creek Country (Sandy, Utah); Briarwood Country (Sun City West, Ariz.). Avocations: golfing, fishing, history. Home and Office: 13913 Pennystone Dr Sun City West AZ 85375

DECAUSEMAKER, RONALD JAMES, computer systems consultant; b. San Francisco, June 23, 1949; s. Richard Edward and Violet Betty DeC.; B.S., E.E.C.S., U. Calif.-Berkeley, 1971; postgrad. Stanford U., 1974; m. Nada Nenadovic; 1 dau., Heidi Hope. Devel. engr. GTE Sylvania, 1972-76; dir. spl. projects Planning Research Corp., Info. Scis. Co., San Jose, 1976-77; mem. tech. staff Intercon Systems, Santa Monica, Calif., 1977-78; owner Yosemite System Services, Fresno, Calif., 1978—; dir. ops. Sun Stereo, Fresno, 1980-81; prof. Am. Leadership Coll., Oseola, Iowa, 1980—; bus. mgr. Nenadovic Chiropractic Life Ctr., 1981—; computer cons. Ernst & Whinney, 1982. Lic. spiritual cons., Peace Community Ch. Cert. computer programmer, cert. data processor. Mem. Assn. for Computing Machinery, Data Processing Mgmt. Assn. Libertarian.

DECHERT, PETER, photographer, writer, foundation administrator; b. Phila., Dec. 17, 1924; s. Robert and Helen Hope (Wilson) D.; m. Phoebe Jane Booth; children—Sandra, Robin Booth, Caroline. B.A., U. Pa., 1948, M.A., 1950, Ph.D., 1955. Owner, Peter Dechert Assocs., Bryn Mawr, Pa., 1956-68; asst. dir. Sch. of Am. Research, Santa Fe, 1968-71; pres. Indian Arts Fund, Santa Fe, 1971-72; pres. Southwest Found. for Audio-Visual Resources, Santa Fe, 1973-77; self-employed photographer, Santa Fe; tchr., cons. photog. communications, 1964—; pres. St. Vincent Hosp. Found., 1981-83, v.p., 1983-84. Author: Canon Rangefinder Cameras, 1933-68; contbg. editor Shutterbug mag., other photographic periodicals; contbr. articles on early Canon cameras, research on history and design of miniature cameras and other photog. topics to profl. publs. Bd. dirs. St. Vincent Hosp. Found. (pres. 1981-83, v.p. 1983-84). Served with AUS, 1943-46. Mem. N.Mex. Poetry Soc. (pres. 1969-74), Am. Studies Assn., Am. Soc. Mag. Photographers, SAR, Southwest Assn. Indian Affairs. Club: New Mexico Jazz Workshop. Research on history of early Canon, other miniature cameras. Address: PO Box 636 Santa Fe NM 87504

DE CIUTIIS, ALFRED CHARLES MARIA, medical oncologist, TV producer; b. N.Y.C., Oct. 16, 1945; s. Alfred Ralph and Theresa Elizabeth (Manko) de C. B.S. summa cum laude, Fordham U., 1967; M.D., Columbia U., 1971. Diplomate Am. Bd. Internal Medicine, Am. Bd. Med. Oncology. Intern N.Y. Hosp.-Cornell Med. Ctr., N.Y.C., 1971-72, resident, 1972-74; fellow in clin. immunology Meml. Hosp.-Sloan Kettering Cancer Ctr., N.Y.C., 1974-75, fellow in clin. oncology, 1975-76, spl. fellow in immunology, 1974-76; guest investigator, asst. physician exptl. hematology Rockefeller U., N.Y.C., 1975-76; practice medicine, specializing in med. oncology Los Angeles, 1977—; host cable TV shows, 1981—; med. editor Cable Health Network, 1983—, Lifetime Network, 1984—; mem. med. adv. com. 1984 Olympics; active staff South Bay Hosp., Little Co. of Mary Hosp., Torrance Meml. Hosp., Bay Harbor Hosp.; co-founder Meditrina Med. Ctr., free out-patient surg. ctr., Torrance, Calif. Producer numerous med. TV shows; contbr. articles to profl. jours. Founder Italian-Am. Med. Assn., 1982; co-founder Italian-Am. Med.-Legal Alliance, Los Angeles, 1982—; mem. Italian-Am. Civic Com., Los Angeles, 1983. Served to capt. M.C., U.S. Army, 1972-74. Leukemia Soc. Am. fellow, 1974-76; N.Y. State Regents scholar, 1963-67, 67-71; recipient Physicians Recognition award AMA, 1978-80, 82-85; proclamation Senate Rules Com., State of Calif., 1982. Fellow ACP; mem. AMA, Am. Union Physicians and Dentists, Am. Soc. Clin. Oncology, N.Y. Acad. Sci. (life), Calif. Med. Assn., Los Angeles County Med. Assn., Internat. Health Soc., Am. Pub. Health Assn., AAAS, Am. Geriatrics Soc., Drug Info. Assn., Am. Soc. Hematology, Nat. Geog. Soc., Mensa, Phi Beta Kappa, Alpha Omega Alpha, Sigma Xi. Republican. Roman Catholic. Avocations: collecting; reading; hunting; fishing; astronomy. Office: c/o Dr Gene Leone 4305 Torrence Blvd Suite 101 Torrance CA 90503

DE CIUTIIS, VINCENT LOUIS, hospital administrator, anesthesiology educator; b. N.Y.C., Oct. 11, 1924; s. Alfredo Vincent and Chiara Mary (Giannone) de C.; m. Claire Adele Ostuni, June 28, 1947 (div. 1976); children—Vilia, Nadine, Vincent, Mario, Elena, Michael, Elisa, Carl; m. Patricia Therese Paulson, June 3, 1976; children—James, Marianna, Michelle, Donald. B.A., Columbia U., 1945; M.D., N.Y. Med. Coll., 1948; grad. Walter Reed Army Med. Ctr., 1954; M.B.A., Pepperdine U., 1976; grad. U.S. Army Command and Gen. Staff Coll., 1986. Diplomate Am. Bd. Anesthesia. Intern Met. Hosp., N.Y.C., 1948-49, resident in anesthesia, 1949-51; resident Fitzsimons Army Hosp., Denver, 1952-53; chief anesthesiology U.S. Army Hosp., Ft. Dix, N.J., 1951-52, Misericordia Hosp., Bronx, 1958-62, Torrance Meml. Hosp., Calif., 1971-79; chief anesthesiology, assoc. prof. Met. Hosp. N.Y. Med. Coll., N.Y.C., 1956-58; asst. prof. UCLA Med. Sch., Los Angeles, 1958-86, assoc. prof., 1986—; prof. surgery, anesthesiology Coll. Osteo. Medicine U. of the Pacific, Stockton, Calif., 1985; adminstr. Riviera Community Hosp., Torrance, 1963-64; adminstr., med. dir. Surg. Ctr. S. Bay, Torrance, 1979—; cons. U.S. Army Hosp., Ft. MacArthur, Calif., 1965-71; dir. med. edn. Torrance Meml. Hosp., 1972-76. Producer/dir. med. documentary with KNBC, 1972; inventor intravenous catheter laryngoscope, 1973; contbr. articles to profl. jours. Served to lt. col. U.S. Army. Decorated World War II Victory medal, Korean Service medal, Commendation ribbon. Fellow Am. Coll. Anesthesiologists; mem. AMA, Los Angeles County Med. Assn., Calif. Med. Assn., Disabled Am. Vets., Assn. Mil. Surgeons U.S. Republican. Roman Catholic. Home: 254 Via Linda Vista Redondo Beach CA 90277 Office: Alternacare Corp Surg Ctr of S Bay 23500 Madison St Torrance CA 90505

DECKARD, GARY DENNISON, moving and storage company executive; b. Newark, Ohio, Nov. 8, 1942; s. Raymond Vance and Mary Helen (Young) D.; m. Victoria Deckard; children: Jason Paul, Meredith Cole. BA in Communications, Ohio State U., 1971. Mgr. So-Fro Fabrics, Columbus, Ohio, 1971-73; sales rep. Xerox Corp., Anchorage, 1973-75; mgr. Sourdough Express, Fairbanks, Alaska, 1975-80; v.p. World Wide Movers, Anchorage, 1980-83; pres. Cole Deckard Inc., Colorado Springs, Colo., 1983—. Committeeman Dem. Party Cen. Com., Fairbanks, 1976. Mem. Nat. Def. Transp. Assn. (bd. dirs. 1986—), Armed Forces Communications and Electronics Assn. Avocations: hunting, computer programming. Home: 7825 Prism Ct Colorado Springs CO 80918 Office: Cole Deckard Inc 615 Valley St Colorado Springs CO 80915

DECKARD, LAWRENCE ARTHUR, educator; b. Chgo., Nov. 25, 1936; s. Lawrence Alexander and Evelyn (Larson) D.; m. Shirley Adelaide Slight, July 3, 1958; children—Deborah, Daniel, Dawn. B.A., Calif. State U.-Sacramento, 1961, M.A., 1975; Ed.D., U. So. Calif., 1982. Gen. elem. credential; adminstrv. service credential, Calif. tchr. elem. schs. Rio Linda Union Sch. Dist., North Highlands, Calif., 1961—; track coach Grant Unified Sch. Dist., North Highlands, 1979; phys. edn. resource person Oakdale Sch., North Highlands, 1974-77, mem. comprehensive arts com., 1980-81; mem. curriculum support com., 1980-82. Hon. life mem. PTA. Mem. Assn. Calif. Sch. Adminstrs., Assn. Supervision and Curriculum Devel., NEA, Rio Linda Edn. Assn., Calif. Tchrs. Assn., Phi Delta Kappa (pres. Sacramento chpt. 1985-86). Democrat. Baptist. Contbr. articles to profl. jours. Home: 7979 Gilardi Rd Newcastle CA 95658

DECKER, DONALD WESLEY, aerospace engineer; b. Fruitland, Wash., Apr. 6, 1935; s. Alfie LeRoy and Lois Elizabeth (Murbach) D.; m. Lanora Jeanette Carson, June 8, 1956; 1 child, Penny Ann. BSE, Wash. State U., 1956; MSE, Seattle U., 1961. Flight test engr. Lockheed Aircraft, Palmdale, Calif., 1956-57; flight control staff engr. Boeing Airplane Co., Seattle, 1957-63; sr. engr. Northrup Space Labs., Huntsville, Ala., 1963-64; staff engr. Boeing, Huntsville, 1964-66; sr. engr. dept. head Sperry Corp., Phoenix, 1966-83; sr. staff engr. Sperry Corp., Albuquerque, 1983—. Mem. IEEE, Phoenix Bowling Assn., Ariz. State Bowling Assn. (named to Hall of Fame 1985). Republican. Avocations: computer programming, camping, hunting. Home: 13117 Bear Dancer Trail NE Albuquerque NM 87112 Office: Sperry Aerospace & Marine Group PO Box 9200 Albuquerque NM 87119

DECKER, FRED WILLIAM, meteorologist; b. Portland, Oreg., July 5, 1917; s. John William and Emma Sophia (Schlickaiser) D.; m. Charlotte Eleanor Menker, Oct. 3, 1942; children: Charlotte Jane, William Allen, Lorraine Anne Takalo. Assoc. in Engring., Multnomah Coll., 1937; BS, Oreg. State U., 1940, PhD, 1952; MS, NYU, 1943. Meteorologist U.S. Weather Bur., various locations, 1937-41; instr. meteorology NYU, University Heights, 1941-44; weather officer USAAF, 1942-46; from instr. to assoc. prof. Oreg. State U., Corvallis, 1946-81; prin. dep. asst. sec. U.S. Dept. Edn., Washington, 1981-85; meteorol. expert Corvallis, 1985—. Author: (with John A. Day) Rudiments of Weather, 1958; The Weather Workbook, 1958, last edition 1981, Weather Map Study, 1958, last edition 1981, Science Travel Guide, 1971. Mem. edn. com. C. of C., Corvallis, 1970-82; pres. Citizens for Corvallis, 1975-81, Mount Hood Soc., Portland, 1982—; Rep. committeeman, Corvallis, 1956—. Served to lt. col. USAFR, 1937-67. Recipient Excellence award Am. Security Council, 1967. Fellow AAAS, Royal Meteorol. Soc.; mem. Am. Meteorol. Soc., Am. Phys. Soc., Am. Assn. Physics Tchrs., Mont Pelerin Soc., U. Profs. Acad. Order (pres. 1974, bd. dirs. 1970—), Phila. Soc. Lutheran. Club: Toastmasters (Corvallis) (gov., Evaluation Champion award 1978). Lodge: Masons. Home and Office: 827 NW 31st St Corvallis OR 97330

DECKER, JAMES THOMAS, psychotherapist; b. Dayton, Ky., Jan. 16, 1944; s. Frank and Edith (Mountain) D.; m. Jane Campbell Fisher, May 6, 1972; children: Peter Campbell, James Mountain, Christina Campbell. AA, Los Angeles Pierce Coll., 1970; BA, Calif. State U., Northridge, 1972; MSW, SUNY, Stony Brook, 1974; PhD, U. Minn., 1976. Research asst. U. Minn., Mpls., 1974-76; asst. prof. San Diego State U., 1976-78; dir., assoc. prof. U. Tex., El Paso, 1978-80; dir. cons. Kern View Hosp., Bakersfield, Calif., 1980-82; exec. dir. J.T. Decker Profl. Group, Bakersfield, Calif., 1982—; adj. prof. Calif. State Coll., Bakersfield, 1981—; sch. psychotherapist Friends Sch., Bakersfield, 1983—; nursing mgmt. cons. Meml. Hosp., Bakersfield, 1983—; out placement cons. Tosco Inc., Bakersfield, 1983—; employee asst. coordinator various orgns., Bakersfield, 1982—. Contbr. articles to profl. jours. Bd. dirs. Consumer Credit Counselors, Bakersfield, 1982—; chmn. Human Resources Com., Bakersfield, 1980-85; bd. dirs. Health Care Mgmt. Adv. Council, Bakersfield, 1982—; bd. dirs. United Way., San Diego and El Paso, Tex., 1977-80. Served with U.S. Army, 1960-64. Recipient Outstanding Alumni award Sch. Social Work, SUNY. Mem. Assn. Labor Mgmt. Administrs. and Cons. on Alcoholism, Nat. Assn. Social Workers (cert.). Avocation: golf. Home: 231 Oleander St Bakersfield CA 93304 Office: JT Decker Profl Group 2109 19th St Bakersfield CA 93301

DECKER, JANICE LYON, consulting firm executive, protective services official; b. Troy, N.Y., May 12, 1942; d. Everett Francis and Rita Theresa (Kelly) Lyon; 1 child, Barton Shields Decker. BA, Coll. New Rochelle, N.Y., 1964. Dir. employee relations SUNY system, Albany, 1971-77; dir. personnel services U. Mont., Missoula, 1977-78; dir. employee relations Calif. State Univ. system, Long Beach, 1979-80, Oakland (Calif.) Housing Authority, 1980-85; pres. Solutions, Oakland, 1986—, Decker Litigation Services, Oakland, 1986—; cons. various firms, Calif. and N.Y., 1971-85; guest lectr. St. Mary's Coll., Moraga, Calif., 1984-85. Mem. Bay Area Profl. Women's Network. Democrat. Avocation: ballet. Home and Office: Solutions 3871 Piedmont Ave Oakland CA 94611

DECKER, RICHARD KELSEY, equipment distribution company executive; b. Monrovia, Calif., Dec. 31, 1927; s. Raymond Grant and Dorothy Irene (Heady) D.; m. Barbara Carolyn Carlson, 1956; children—Richard Brian, Carolyn Ann Decker Johnson. B.S., U. So. Calif., 1952. Cost. acct. S.W. Products Co., Monrovia, 1953-55; controller Scotsman Refrigeration Inc., Monterey Park, Calif., 1955-64; with Scotsman Distbrs. of Los Angeles, Inc., La Verne, Calif., 1964—, pres., chief exec. officer, 1976—. Served with USN, 1945-47. Mem. Alpha Kappa Psi (pres.), Beta Gamma Sigma. Office: Scotsman Distributors of Los Angeles Inc 1480 Arrow Hwy La Verne CA 91750

DECKERT, HARLAN KENNEDY, JR., manufacturing company official; b. Evanston, Ill., May 22, 1923; s. Harlan Kennedy and Lady Otey (Hutton) D.; B.S., U. Calif., Berkeley, 1949; M.B.A., U. So. Calif., 1962; m. Mary Emma Eldredge, Nov. 27, 1971; children—Mary Adrienne, Christine Ann, Daniel Gregory, Deborah Alice. Systems analyst Northrop Corp., Hawthorne, Calif., 1949-53, supr. engring. adminstrv. services, 1953-57, adminstrv. systems engr., 1957-59; with AiResearch Indsl. div. Garrett Corp., Torrance, Calif., 1959—, systems service adminstr., 1962-72, mgr. adminstrv. services, 1972-75, adminstr. internat. ops., 1975-80, sr. staff advisor Garrett Automotive Group Allied-Signal, Inc., 1980-87, retired. Patron, Los Angeles County Mus. Art; zoo docent Greater Los Angeles Zoo Assn.; mem. UCLA Art Council. Mem. Los Angeles County Mus. Natural History, San Diego Zool. Soc., Palm Springs Living Desert Res., World Wildlife Found. Served with USAAF, 1943-46; CBI. Home: 2509 20th St Santa Monica CA 90405

DE CONCINI, DENNIS, U.S. Senator, lawyer; b. Tucson, May 8, 1937; s. Evo and Ora (Webster) DeC.; m. Susan Margaret Hurley, June 6, 1959; children: Denise, Christina, Patrick Evo. B.A., U. Ariz., 1959, LL.B., 1963. Bar: Ariz. bar 1963. Mem. firm Evo DeConcini, Tucson, 1963-65; partner firm DeConcini & McDonald, 1968-73; dep. Pima County atty. Sch. Dist. 1, 1971-72, county atty., 1973-76; mem. U.S. Senate from Ariz., 1977—, U.S. Senate from Ariz. (Appropriations com.), U.S. Senate from Ariz. (Judiciary com.), U.S. Senate from Ariz. (subcom. on Treasury, Postal Service and gen. govt.), U.S. Senate from Ariz. (subcom. on fgn. ops.), U.S. Senate from Ariz. (subcom. on Interior), U.S. Senate from Ariz. (subcom. on State, Justice, Commerce and Judiciary), U.S. Senate from Ariz. (subcom. on Constn.), U.S. Senate from Ariz. (subcom. on immigration), U.S. Senate from Ariz. (select com. on Indian Affairs), U.S. Senate from Ariz. (select com. on vets. affairs); formerly pres., now dir. Shopping Centers, Inc. Chmn. legis. com. Tucson Community Council, 1966-67; mem. major gifts com., devel. fund drive St. Joseph's Hosp., 1970, mem. devel. council, 1971-73; mem. major gifts com. Tucson Mus. and Art Center Bldg. Fund, 1971; adminstr. Ariz. Drug Control Dist., 1975-76; precinct committeeman Ariz. Democratic Party, 1958—; mem. Pima County Dem. Central Com., 1958-67, Dem. State Exec. Com., 1958-68; state vice chmn. Ariz. Dem. Com., 1964-66, 70-72; vice chmn. Pima County Dem. Com., 1970-73. Served to 2d lt. JAG U.S. Army, 1959-60. Named Outstanding Ariz. County Atty., 1975. Mem. Am., Ariz., Pima County bar assns., Nat. Dist. Attys. Assn., Ariz. Sheriffs and County Attys. Assn., Am. Judicature Soc., Ariz. Pioneer Hist. Soc., NAACP, U. Ariz. Alumni Assn., Tucson Fraternal Order Police, Phi Delta Theta, Delta Sigma Rho, Phi Alpha Delta. Roman Catholic. Clubs: Nucleus (Tucson), Old Pueblo (Tucson), Pres.'s U. Ariz. (Tucson), Latin Am. (Tucson), Latin Am. Social (Tucson). Office: 328 Hart Senate Bldg Washington DC 20510

DECORE, LAURENCE G., mayor; b. Vegreville, Alta., Can., June 28, 1940. BA, U. Alta., 1961, LLB, 1964. Alderman City of Edmonton, 1974-77, former chmn. econ. affairs com., budget com., pub. affairs com., mayor, 1983—; ptnr. Decore and Co.; co-founder QCTV, Ltd. Chmn. Nat. Can. Conservative Council on Multiculturalism, 1980-83, mem. various coms.; mem. Edmonton Multiculturalism com., Ukrainian Community com. on multiculturalism, St. John's Ukrainian Greek Orthodox Parish, Edmonton; former vice-chmn. devel. appeal bd.; bd. dirs. local Bd. Health, 1974-77, Royal Alexander Hosp., 1975-77. Served to lt. JAG Dept., Royal Can. Navy. Recipient Province of Alta. Community Service Achievement award, 1982; named to Order of Can., 1983. Mem. Elizabeth Fry Soc. (bd. dirs., fin. chmn.), Alta. Law Soc., Can. Bar Assn., Edmonton and Dist. Soccer Assn., (past adminstrv. sec.), Alta. Soccer Assn. (past adminstrv. sec.), Ukrainian Profl. and Bus. Fedn. of Can., Ukrainian Can. Com. (past sec.), Can. Found. of Ukrainian Studies (past bd. dirs.), Greater Edmonton Found., Alta. Heritage Council (past 1st chmn.). Club: Ukrainian Profl. and Businessmen's (Alta.) (past pres.). Office: City Hall, Office of Mayor, 1 Sir Winston Churchill Sq, Edmonton, AB Canada T5J 2R7

DEEDWANIA, PRAKASH CHANDRA, cardiologist; b. Ajmer, India, Aug. 28, 1948; came to U.S., 1971; s. Gokul C. and Paras (Garg) D.; m. Catherine E. Deewania; 1 child, Anne. BS, U. Rajasthan, Jaipur, India, 1963, MD, 1969. Diplomate Am. Bd. Internal Medicine, Am. Bd. Cardiology, Am. Bd. Pulmonary Medicine. Rotating intern J.L.N. Med. Coll. Hosp. Ctr., Ajmer, 1970, postgrad. resident, 1970-71; intern in medicine Coney Island Hosp. Maimonides Med. Ctr., Bklyn., 1971-72; resident in medicine VA Med. Ctr. Bronx, Mt. Sinai Sch. Medicine, N.Y.C., 1972-73, chief resident in medicine and pulmonary sect., 1973-75; cardiology fellow dept. medicine UL. Ill. Abraham Lincoln Sch. Medicine, Chgo., 1975-76, sr. research fellow in cardiology, 1976-77; chief cardiology VA Med. Ctr. U. Va., Salem, 1977-78; dir. non-invasive lab. VA. Med. Ctr. U. Ill., Chgo., 1978-80; chief cardiology VA Med. Ctr. U. Calif. San Francisco Sch. Medicine, Fresno, 1980—; dir. electrophysiology VA Med. Ctr. U. Ill., Chgo., 1978-80, co-dir. critical care unit, 1978-80; dir. critical care unit VA Med. Ctr. U. C. San Francisco, Fresno, 1980—; hosp. appointments include supervising attending physician St. Joseph's Hosp., N.Y.C., 1973-75, supervising physician Weiss Meml. Hosp., Chgo., 1975-77, cons. in cardiology and pulmonary Bd. Health, Chgo., 1976-77; teaching appointments include instr. medicine Abraham Lincoln Sch. Medicine U. Ill., Chgo., 1975-76, assoc. in medicine 1976-77, asst. prof. 1978-80; asst. prof. medicine U. Va., Charlottesville, 1977-78; assoc. clin. prof. U. Calif. San Francisco Sch. Medicine, Fresno, 1980—. Contbr. numerous articles to profl. jours. Grantee Hoffman La Roche, 1976, Pfizer, 1981, 1984, Ciba-Geigy, 1981, Merck Sharp and Dohme, 1982, Miles Labs., 1982, 83, New England Nuclear, 1983, McNeil Labs., 1984, 1985, Am. Critical Care, 1984, Squibb Pharms., 1984, 1985, Bristol-Meyers, 1985, Merrell Dow Research Inst., 1985. Fellow Royal Coll. Physicians and Surgeons (Can.), Am. Coll. Chest Physicians, ACP, Am. Coll. Cardiology, Am. Heart Assn. (clin. council cardiology); mem. N.Y. Acad. Scis., Am. Thoracic Soc., N.Y. Trudeau Soc., Am. Fedn. Clin. Research. Avocations: study of cultures, photography, travel, penfriendship, reading. Office: VA Med Ctr 111 2615 E Clinton Ave Fresno CA 93703

DEESE, E(THEL) HELEN, English educator; b. San Diego, Sept. 15, 1925; d. Clyde Thomas and Ethel (Findlay) Smith; m. Rupert Julian Deese, Mar. 4, 1951; children: Rupert Thomas, Mary Ann, Franklin William, Richard Samuel. BA, U. Calif., Riverside, 1968, MA, 1970, PhD, 1977. Lectr. U. Calif., Riverside, 1977-79, 81-83, Calif. State Poly. U., Pomona, 1979-81; assoc. prof. English Mt. St. Mary's Coll., Los Angeles, 1983—. Critic So. Calif. drama, Shakespeare Bull., N.Y.C. 1985—; editor: Robert Lowell: A Reference Guide, 1982, Robert Lowell: New Essays on the Poetry, 1986, Critical Essays on Wallace Stevens; also articles. Mem. MLA, Internat. Shakespeare Assn., Shakespeare Assn. Am., Nat. Council Tchrs. English. Democrat. Unitarian. Home: 601 E Baseline Rd Claremont CA 91711 Office: Mt St Mary's Coll Dept English 2901 Chalon Rd Los Angeles CA 91711

DEFAZIO, LYNETTE STEVENS, dancer, choreographer, educator, chiropractor; b. Berkeley, Calif., Sept. 29; d. Honore and Mabel J. (Estavan) Stevens; student U. Calif., Berkeley, 1950-55, San Francisco State Coll., 1950-51; D. Chiropractic, Life-West Chiropractic Coll., San Lorenzo, Calif., 1983, BA in Humanities, New Coll. Calif., 1986; children—Joey H. Panganiban, Joanna Pang. Contract child dancer Monogram Movie Studio, Hollywood, Calif., 1938-40; dance instr. San Francisco Ballet, 1953-64; performer San Francisco Opera Ring, 1960-67; performer, choreographer Oakland (Calif.) Civic Light Opera, 1963-70; fgn. exchange dance dir. Academie de Danses-Salle Pleyel, Paris, France, 1966; dir. Ballet Arts Studio, Oakland, 1960—; teaching specialist Oakland Unified Sch. Dist.-Childrens Centers, 1968—; instr. Peralta Community Coll. Dist., Oakland, 1971—, chmn. dance dept., 1985—; cons., instr. extension courses UCLA, Dirs. and Suprs. Assn., Pittsburg Unified Sch. Dist., Tulare (Calif.) Sch. Dist., 1971-73; researcher Ednl. Testing Services, HEW, Berkeley, 1974; resident choreographer San Francisco Childrens Opera, 1970—, Oakland Civic Theater; ballet mistress Dimensions Dance Theater, Oakland, 1977-79; cons. Gianchetta Sch. Dance, San Francisco, Robicheau Boston Ballet, television series Patchwork Family, CBS, N.Y.C.; choreographer Ravel's Valses Nobles et Sentimentales, 1976. Author: The Opera Ballets; A Choreographic Manual, Vols. I-V, 1986. Recipient Foremost Women of 20th Century, 1985, Merit award San Francisco Children's Opera, 1985. Mem. Profl. Dance Tchrs. Assn. Am. Author: Basic Music Outlines for Dance Classes, 1960, rev., 1968; Teaching Techniques and Choreography for Advanced Dancers, 1965; Basic Music Outlines for Dance Classes, 1965; Goals and Objectives in Improving Physical Capabilities, 1970; A Teacher's Guide for Ballet Techniques, 1970; Principle Procedures in Basic Curriculum, 1974; Objectives and Standards of Performance for Physical Development, 1975. Asso. music arranger Le Ballet du Cirque, 1964, Techniques of a Ballet School, 1970, rev., 1974; asso. composer, lyricist The Ballet of Mother Goose, 1968; choreographer: Walses Nobles Et Sentimentales (Ravel); Cannon in D for Strings and Continuo (Pachelbel), 1979. Home and office: 4923 Harbord Dr Oakland CA 94618

DEFAZIO, PETER A., congressman; b. Needham, Mass., May 27, 1947; m. Myrnie Daut. BA in Econs. and Polit. Sci., Tufts U., 1969; postgrad., U. Oreg., 1969-71, MS in Pub. Adminstrn./Gerontology, 1977. Aide to U.S. rep. Jim Weaver, 1977-82, sr. issues specialist, caseworker, dist. field office, 1977-78, legis. asst. Washington office, 1978-80, dir. constituent services, 1980-82; mem. commn. representing Springfield Lane County (Oreg.) Commn., 1982-86; mem. U.S. Ho. Reps. from 4th Oreg. dist., 1987—, mem. interior and insular affairs com., pub. works and transp. com., com. on small bus., mem. subcoms. on water and power, nat. parks and pub. lands, aviation, water resources, regulation and bus. opportunities, mem. Dem. study group, environ. and energy study conf., mem. arts caucus, populist caucus, arms control and fgn. policy caucus, travel and tourism caucus, human rights caucus, co-chmn. freshman task force on trade. Mem. Lane County Econ. Devel. com., Ingergovtl. Relations com.; bd. dirs. Eugene/Springfield Met. Partnership; Lane County Dem. precinct person, 1982—. Served with USAF. Mem. Assn. of Oreg. Counties (legis. com.), Nat. Assn. of Counties (tax and fin. com.). Office: US House of Reps Office of House Mems 1729 Longworth House Office Bldg Washington DC 20510

DEFFNER, JOHN FREDERICK, research chemist; b. Pitts., Aug. 7, 1932; s. Joseph J. and Mary M. (Snyder) D.; m. Mary T. Bonner, June 28, 1958; children: Mary P. Patterson, Cecile M., Margaret M. Mullen, Joseph J. BS in Chemistry, Duquesne U., 1954, MS in Organic Chemistry, 1956. Chemist E.I. DuPont de Nemours, Wilmington, Del., 1956-57; research chemist Gulf Oil, Pitts., 1957-75, sr. research chemist, 1975-80, research assoc., 1980-85; sr. research chemist Chevron Research Co., Richmond, Calif., 1985—. Patentee in field. Pres. Parent Tchrs. Guild, Vincentian High Sch., Pitts., 1979-80; treas. St. Bonaventure Sch., Pitts., 1973-74. Mem. Am. Petroleum Inst. (chmn. task force 1980-85), Soc. Automotive Engrs. (sect. chmn. Pitts. 1984-85, Outstanding Sect. award 1985), Am. Chem. Soc., Pitts Chem. Club. Lodge: Elks. Avocations: jogging, gardening. Office: Chevron Research Co PO Box 1627 Richmond CA 94802

DE FILIPPO, RITA MARCELLA, budget analyst; b. N.Y.C.; d. Sal and Margaret (Jaeger) DeF.; student Los Angeles City Coll., 1957, City Coll. San Francisco, 1975, U. San Francisco, 1976; cert. acctg. LaSalle U., 1968. Asst. advt. dir. Gump's, Inc., San Francisco, 1959; research statistician Honig-Cooper & Harrington, San Francisco, 1960-61; salesperson Landau Realty, San Francisco, 1962-63; mgmt. analyst Oakland Army Base (Calif.), 1978-80; budget analyst Dept. Army, San Francisco, 1980—. Recipient Outstanding Performance award Fed. Govt., 1979. Mem. Am. Bus. Women's Assn. (treas. 1978-79), Am. Soc. Mil. Comptrollers, Assn. Women in Sci., Assn. U.S. Army, Nat. Fedn. Fed. Employees (trustee 1972), World Affairs Council, Sierra Club. Home: 1348 C Scott St San Francisco CA 94115

DE FOREST, EDGAR LESTER, actor, poet, educator; b. Hull, Mass.; s. Edgar Leonard and Ellen Marian (Huntington) De F.; m. Beulah Mary Ingalls, Nov. 21, 1940; children: Peter, Stephen, David, Richard. Diploma, Leland Powers Sch. of Theatre, Boston, 1937; BS, Boston U., 1940; MA, U. So. Calif., 1941; EdD, Columbia U., 1954. Cert. elem. tchr., Calif. (life); cert. secondary tchr., Calif. (life); cert. sch. adminstr., Calif. (life). Dir. reading Mich. State U. (formerly Mich. State Coll.), East Lansing, 1945-48, asst. dir. summer program, 1954-57; dir. students Suffolk U., Boston, 1948-52; assoc. survey research Columbia U., N.Y.C., 1952-53; acting dean instruction Ventura (Calif.) Coll., 1957-60; prof. Coll. Desert, Palm Desert, Calif., 1962-78, prof. emeritus continuing edn., 1979—; dean of ship U. Seven Seas, Whittier, Calif., 1964-65. Author poems. Mem. Mayor's cultural planning 2000 com., Palm Desert, 1985-86; pres. Friends of the Library Coll. of the Desert, Palm Desert, 1983-85. Named Ideal Citizen of the Age of Enlightenment, World Govt. for the Age of Enlightenment, 1971. Mem. Mich. Reading Assn. (founder, pres. 1954-55). Democrat. Avocations: hiking, cats. Home: 220 Pinyon Crest Mountain Center CA 92361 Office: Coll Desert 43 500 Monterey Ave Palm Desert CA 92260

DEFRAIN, DENNIS ALLEN, education director, retired army officer; b. Fairbury, Nebr., Mar. 3, 1943; s. Howard Willis and Anna Pauline (Eisenhauer) De F.; m. Carol Jean Daugherty, Nov. 21, 1964; 1 child, Darren Craig. B.Sc., U. Nebr., 1965; M.Sc., U. So. Calif., 1972; Ed.D., Catholic U. Am., 1983. Commd. 2d lt. U.S. Army, 1965, advanced through grades to lt. col., 1982; adminstrv. officer 2d Bn., 1st Arty., Fort Wainwright, Alaska, 1965-66, unit comdr., 1966-67; adminstrv. officer Adv. Team 55, Rach Gia, Vietnam, 1968-69; unit comdr. 2d Bn., 59th Arty., El Paso, Tex., and Schwabach, W.Ger., 1970-71, personnel mgr., Schwabach, 1971-73; asst. prof. U. Wis.-Oshkosh, 1973-76; personnel mgr. U.S. Army Personnel Ctr., Alexandria, Va., 1976-78; faculty devel. adminstr., instructional technologist Command and Gen. Staff Coll., Fort Leavenworth, Kans., 1979-82; prof. mil. sci. Weber State Coll., Ogden, Utah, 1982-85 , dir. distance edn., 1985—. Dir. youth bowling Ft. Leavenworth Youth Activities, 1979-80, dir. rifle marksmanship, 1981-82. Decorated Bronze Star medal, Army Commendation medal, Meritorious Service medal with two oak leaf clusters. Mem. Mil. Testing Assn., Nat. Univ. Continuing Edn. Assn., Am. Assn. for Adult and Continuing Edn., Layton C. of C.(bd. dirs.), Alliance for Distance Learning, Alpha Gamma Rho. Home: 2762 E Brinton Way Layton UT 84041 Office: Weber State Coll Ogden UT 84408

DEFREES, DOUGLAS JOHN, research scientist; b. Oneida, N.Y., July 4, 1952; s. Herbert Lansing and Bernice Martha (Berger) D.; m. Diane Rae Yates, Sept. 4, 1976; 1 child, Caleb John. BS, Clarkson U., 1974; PhD, U. Calif., Irvine, 1978. Postdoctoral research assoc. Carnegie-Mellon U., Pitts., 1978-80; research scientist Molecular Research Inst., Palo Alto, Calif., 1980—, also bd. dirs., v.p., chief fin. officer, sec. Co-author: (book) Carnegie-Mellon Quantun Chemistry Archive, 1981, (computer program) Gaussian 82, 1983; co-editor: Exobiology in Earth Orbit, 1987; contbr. articles to profl. jours. Grantee NASA, 1984—; Regents Intern fellow U. Calif., Irvine, 1974-78. Mem. Am. Chem. Soc., Astron. Soc. Pacific, Phi Kappa Phi, Gamma Sigma Epsilon. Avocations: backpacking, bicycling, camping, reading. Home: 477 Sieber Ct San Jose CA 95111 Office: Molecular Research Inst 701 Welch Rd Suite 213 Palo Alto CA 94304

DEGENER, ISA IRMGARD MARGARETE ELISABETH HANSEN, botanist, botanical writer; b. Berlin, Apr. 27, 1924; came to U.S. 1953; d. Walter Hansen and Elisabeth (Raasch) Hansen Kuhle; m. Otto Degener, Jan. 10, 1953. Student U. Freiburg, Breisgau, Germany, 1944; Dr. natural Scis. magna cum laude U. Berlin, 1949. Bot. asst. Bot. Mus., Berlin-Dahlem, Germany, 1945-46; lab. asst., 1946-52, botanist, 1949-52; collaborator Hawaiian Botany resident in Hawaiian Islands, N.Y. Bot. Garden, 1953. Contbr. articles to profl. jours. Extensive field work and plant collecting in Hawaiian Islands and Fiji Islands, Canton Atoll, Central Am., Tasmania, N.Z., Australia, Canary Islands, Madeira, Azores and other tropical and subtropical areas. Mem. Internat. Bot. Congress, Montreal, 1959, Edinburgh, 1964, Leningrad, 1975, Sydney, 1981. Author: (with O. Degener) Flora Hawaiiensis or New Illustrated Flora of the Hawaiian Islands, Book 5, 1956-57, Book 6, 1957-63, Book 7, 1963-86. Active plant and animal conservationist, Hawaii, 1953—. Home and Office: PO Box 154 Volcano HI 96785

DE GOES, LOUIS, resort development executive; b. Maui, Hawaii, June 23, 1914; s. John and Mary De G.; m. Allison Virginia Hammond, June 3, 1944; children: Michael Louis, John Macline, Ginger Allison. Cert. geol. engr., Colo. Sch. of Mines, 1941; MS in Geology, Stanford U., 1950. Registered engring. geologist, Calif. Commd. USAF, 1941, advanced through grades to col., retired, 1966; exec. sec. polar bd. Nat. Acad. Scis., Washington, 1967-81; v.p. Kino Devel. of Am. Inc., Irvine, Calif., 1982-84; pvt. cons., Bellevue, Wash., 1982-84. Recipient Silver Anniversary All-Am. award Sports Illustrated, N.Y.C., 1964. Fellow Geol. Soc. Am., Arctic Inst. N.Am.; mem. AAAS, ASCE, Soc. Am. Mil. Engrs., Theta Tau, Alpha Tau Omega. Episcopalian. Club: Explorer's (N.Y.C.). Avocations: reading, writing, fishing, boating, travel. Office: Kino Devel Am Inc 10900 NE 8th St Suite 900 Bellevue WA 98004

DEGRACIE, JAMES SULLIVAN, school district official, educational consultant; b. Marshfield, Wis., Aug. 30, 1939; s. Harold William and Julia Helen DeG.; m. Marlene Louise McDonald, Feb. 5, 1939; children—Debra, Daniel, Donald, Darren. B.S. in Math., Calif. State Poly. Coll., San Luis Obispo, 1962, M.A. in Edn., 1963; M.S. in Stats., Kans. State U.-Manhattan, 1965; Ph.D. in Stats., Iowa State U., 1968. Instr., Iowa State U., 1964-68; sr. statistician Control Data Corp., Dugway, Utah, 1968-70; project mgr. Litton Sci. Support Lab., Ft. Ord, Calif., 1970-71; sr. scientist Human Resources Research Orgn., Monterey, Calif., 1971-72; functioning chief statistician Nat. Ctr. for Edn. Stats., Washington, 1981-82; dir. dept. research adn evaluation Mesa (Ariz.) Pub. Schs., 1972—; vis. prof. No. Ariz. U., Flagstaff, 1979—; exec. dir. Info. Analysis Assocs., Mesa, 1973—. Bd. dirs. Community Orgn. for Drug Abuse Systems, 1975-76; mem. adv. bd. Cen. Ariz. Health Systems, 1976-77; mem City of mesa Planning and Zoning Bd., 1985—. Inst. Ednl. Leadership Edn. Policy fellow, 1981-82. Mem. Am. Ednl. Research Assn. (sec. Div. H, 1982-84, program chmn. 1979, 81), Am. Statis. Assn., Mesa Sch. Adminstrs. Assn. (pres. 1976-77), Sigma Xi, Kappa Mu Epsilon, Phi Kappa Phi. Republican. Roman Catholic. Mem. bd. editorial advisors Education Research Service, 1982; contbr. articles to profl. jours. Home: 2104 E Encanto St Mesa AZ 85203 Office: 549 N Stapley Dr Mesa AZ 85203

DEGRASSE, ROBERT WOODMAN, information services executive; b. Yakima, Wash., July 4, 1929; s. M.A. and Pearl L. (Pape) DeG.; m. Marilyn Lucille Haglund, Aug. 16, 1952; children: Robert W. Jr., Lori E., Cheryl L., Donald H. BSEE, Calif. Inst. Tech., 1951; MSEE, Stanford U., 1954, PhDEE, 1958. Mem. tech. staff Bell Telephone Lab., Murray Hill, N.J., 1957-63; mgr. research and devel. Microwave Elec. Corp., Palo Alto, Calif., 1960-63; group v.p. Quantum Sci. Corp., Palo Alto, 1963-69; v.p., dir., founder Quantor Corp. (acquired by NCR), Mountain View, Calif., 1969-78; dir. research and devel. Micrographics Systems div. NCR, Mountain View, 1978-82; sr. v.p., dir. Quantum Sci. Corp., Los Altos, Calif., 1982—; also bd. dirs. Quantum Sci. Corp., N.Y.C., 1978—. Patentee in field. Mem. IEEE, Sigma Xi. Republican. Presbyterian. Office: Quantum Sci Corp 4966 El Camino Real Suite 101 Los Altos CA 94022

DEGRASSI, LEONARD RENÈ, art historian, educator; b. East Orange, N.J., Mar. 2, 1928; s. Romulus-William and Anna Sophia (Sannicolo) DeG.; m. Dolores Marie Welgoss, June 24, 1961; children: Maria Christina, Paul. BA, U. So. Calif., 1950, BFA, 1951, MA, 1956; postgrad., Harvard U., 1953, U. Rome, 1959-60, UCLA, 1970-73. Tchr. art Redlands (Calif.) Jr. High Sch., 1951-53, Toll Jr. High Sch., Glendale, Calif., 1953-61, Wilson Jr. High Sch., Glendale, 1961; mem. faculty Glendale Coll., 1962—, prof. art history, 1974—, chmn. dept., 1972. Prin. works include: (paintings) high altar at Ch. St. Mary, Cook, Minn., altar screen at Ch. St. Andrew, El Segundo, Calif., 1965-71, altar screen at Ch. of the Descent of the Holy Spirit, Glendale, 14 Stas. of the Cross at Ch. of St. Benedict, Duluth, Minn; also research, artwork and dramatic work for Spaceship Earth exhbn. at Disney World, Orlando, Fla., 1980. Decorated knight Order of Merit of Republic of Italy, 1972; knight comdr. Holy Sepulchre (Papal); knight St. John of Jerusalem, 1974; Cross of Merit, 1984. Mem. Art Educators Assn., Glendale Art Assn., Egypt Exploration Soc. London, Am. Research Ctr. Egypt, Tau Kappa Alpha, Kappa Pi, Delta Sigma Rho. Office: 1500 N Verdugo Rd Glendale CA 91206

DE GUZMAN, RENÉ VIÑAS, chemist; b. Lipa City, Philippines, Nov. 29, 1956; came to U.S., 1980; s. Rufino Lapeña and Cristeta (Viñas) De G. BSChemE, Adamson U., Manila; MBA, De LaSalle U., Manila; MS in Nuclear Engring., U. Philippines, Manila; postgrad., Calif. State U., Northridge. Registered profl. engr., Philippines. Cadet engr. Filsyn, Laguno, Philippines, 1977, process engr., 1978, plant safety engr., 1978-79; nuclear health physicist PNPP, Quezon City, Philippines, 1979-80; computer programmer Transam. Corp., Los Angeles, 1981-85; chemist E.I. Du Pont de Nemours, Sun Valley, Calif., 1985—. Mem. Am. Chem. Soc., Soc. Applied Spectroscopy, Am. Soc. Metals, Am. Ceramic Soc. Democrat. Roman Catholic. Avocations: swimming, bowling, outdoor activities. Office: E I Du Pont de Nemours 11078 Fleetwood St Sun Valley CA 91352

DE HAAS, MARLIN JACKIE, consulting engineer; b. North Powder, Oreg., June 12, 1933; s. Charles and Lola (Brothers) De H.; m. Marie B. Wagner, Sept. 29, 1961; children: Linda, Sharon, Julie, Brian. BS, Oreg. State U., 1955. Cert. profl. engr., Oreg., Wash.; cert. profl. land surveyor, Oreg. Project engr. Worthington and Assocs., Corvallis, Oreg., 1962-66; asst. city engr. City of Corvallis, 1966-68; city engr. City of Forest Grove, Oreg., 1968-70; dir. pub. works City of Lake Oswego, Oreg., 1970-76; pres. DeHaas and Assocs., Inc., Wilsonville, Oreg., 1976—. Served to 1st lt. U.S. Army, 1956-58. Mem. Am. Pub. Works Assn. (pres. Oreg. chpt. 1976), Nat. Soc. Profl. Engrs., Am. Cons. Engrs. Council. Republican. Methodist. Lodge: Rotary. Avocations: tennis, elk and deer hunting, fishing. Home: 1425 Cherry Crest Dr Lake Oswego OR 97034 Office: De Haas and Assocs Inc 9450 Commerce Circle Wilsonville OR 97070

DE HALAS, DON RICHARD, metals company executive; b. San Francisco, Mar. 16, 1930; s. Andrew and Delorys (Thatcher) De H.; m. Roberta B. Zulauf, Mar. 30, 1956; children: Jeff, Jay, Molly, Mitz. BS, U. Calif., Berkeley, 1952; MS in Chemistry, U. Idaho, 1955; PhD in Chemistry, Oreg. State U., 1960. Registered profl. engr., Colo., Va. Mgr. bus. devel. Exxon Nuclear Corp., Seattle, 1970-71; gen. mgr. nuclear fuel Babcock & Wilcox, Lynchburg, Va., 1972-73; cons. Lynchburg, 1974-77; pres. Colo. Nuclear Corp., Monument, 1978-82; pres. Am. Strategic Metals, Monument, 1983—, also bd. dirs.; bd. dirs. Colo. Nuclear Corp. Republican. Avocations: computer programming, mountain climbing. Office: Am Strategic Metals PO Box 1010 1200 Synthes Monument CO 80132

DEHAVEN, KENNETH LE MOYNE, physician; b. The Dalles, Oreg., Mar. 28, 1913; s. Luther John and Dora (Beeks) DeH.; B.S., North Pacific Coll. Oreg., 1935; M.D., U. Mich., 1946; m. Ledith Mary Ewing, Jan. 11, 1937; children—Marya LeMoyne DeHaven Keeth, Lisa Marguerite DeHaven Jordan, Camille Suzanne DeHaven Ludlow. Intern USPHS Hosp., St. Louis, 1947; intern Franklin Hosp., San Francisco, 1947-48, resident, 1949; clinician Dept. Pub. Health, City San Francisco, Dept. V.D., 1949-51; practice gen. medicine, Sunnyvale, Calif., 1955—; mem. staff El Camino Hosp., Mt. View, Calif., San Jose Hosp. (Calif.). Pres. Los Altos Hills Assn. Served to capt., USAF, 1952-55. Fellow Am. Acad. Family Practice; mem. Calif. Med. Assn., Santa Clara County Med. Soc., The Royal Astron. Soc. Can., Brit. Astron. Assn., Astron. Soc. Pacific, Sunnyvale C. of C. (dir. 1955-56), AAAS, Alpha Kappa Kappa. Republican. Mason. Clubs: Press and Union League, Commonwealth, Book (San Francisco). Home: 9348 E Casitas Del Rio Dr Scottsdale AZ 85255 Office: 665 Knickerbocker Dr Sunnyvale CA 94087

DEHMER, CARLOS, computer engr.; b. Rosario Tala, Argentina, Aug. 30, 1949; came to U.S., 1961; s. Arturo Jorge and Irma Elena (Kloss) D.; m. Elena Margarita Abalo, July 25, 1971; 1 child, Lizette Elaine. BS in Engring., Calif. State U., Los Angeles, 1977; MBA, Pepperdine U., 1980. Engr. So. Calif. Gas Co., Los Angeles, 1977-85, sr. systems analyst, 1985—; prin. Tower Engring. Co., Pasadena Calif., 1982-84, Color Graphics, Arcadia, Calif., 1980-82; owner, cons. Carlos Dehmer Cons., Arcadia, 1985—. Mem. Soc. Hispanic Profl. Engrs., Berkeley Macintosh Users Club, Tau Beta Pi. Republican.

DEIHL, RICHARD HARRY, savings and loan association executive; b. Whittier, Calif., Sept. 9, 1928; s. Victor Francis and Wilma Aileen (Thomas) D.; m. Billie Dantz Beane, Mar. 24, 1952; children: Catherine Kent, Michael, Victoria, Christine. A.B., Whittier Coll., 1949; postgrad., UCLA, 1949, U. Calif.-Berkeley, 1949-50. With Nat. Cash Register Co., Pomona, Calif., 1955-59; trainee Rio Hondo Savs. & Loan, Calif., 1959-60; loan cons. Home Savs. & Loan Assn. (now Home Savs. Am., A Fed. Savs. & Loan Assn.), Los Angeles, 1960-63; loan agt., supr., v.p. Home Savs. & Loan Assn. (now Home Savs. Am., A Fed. Savs. & Loan Assn.), 1964, loan service supr., 1964, v.p. ops., v.p. loans, 1965, exec. v.p., 1966, pres., 1967-84, chief exec. officer, 1967-84, chmn., 1984—, also dir.; chief exec. officer, dir. H.F. Ahmanson Co., 1984—; bd. dirs. Fed. Home Loan Bank, Fed. Asset Disposition Assn., Atlantic Richfield Good Samaritan Hosp. Contbr. articles to profl. jours. Served to 1st lt. USAF, 1951-55. Decorated D.F.C., Air medal with three clusters. Republican. Club: Fairbanks Ranch Country (Rancho

Santa Fe). Office: H F Ahmanson & Co 3731 Wilshire Blvd Los Angeles CA 90010 *

DEINES, HARRY J., agr. and livestock co. exec.; b. Loveland, Colo., Nov. 5, 1909; s. John and Mary (Maseka) D.; B.M.E., U. Colo.; grad. Advanced Mgmt. Program, Harvard; m. Eleanor Vrooman, 1932; children—Gretchen Deines Langston, Mark, Katrina, Stephen. Advt. mgr. Gen. Electric Co., 1930-45; v.p. Fuller & Smith & Ross, 1945-49; gen. advt. mgr. Westinghouse Electric Corp., 1949-53; v.p. J. Walter Thompson, N.Y.C., 1953-56, Fuller & Smith & Ross, N.Y.C., 1956-59; exec. v.p., dir. Campbell, Mithun, Inc., Mpls., 1959-71; mng. partner Deines Agr. & Livestock Co., Ft. Collins, Colo., 1971—; pres. Collectors' Books Ltd. Home and office: 1707 Country Club Rd Fort Collins CO 80524

DEINES, LOIS ANN, b. Los Angeles, Jan. 17, 1923; d. Richard Hart and Ellen Alira (Brownell) Wellington; m. Robert Louis Deines, June 6, 1944; children—Robert Dale, Dean Allen, Dwight Kenneth. B.S., U. So. Calif., 1944, M.L.S., 1967. Catalog and reference librarian San Marino (Calif.) Pub. Library, 1966-69, asst. city librarian, 1970-75, city librarian, 1976—. Mem. ALA, Calif. Library Assn., Women's Archtl. League, San Marino Hist. Soc., Friends of the Old Mill, LWV, Beta Phi Mu, Phi Beta Kappa, Phi Kappa Phi. Home: 2956 Lombardy Rd Pasadena CA 91107 Office: 1890 Huntington Dr San Marino CA 91108

DEINHARDT, CAROL LUCY, counselor, musician; b. Huntington, N.Y., Nov. 8, 1946; d. John and Florence (Hoag) D. Student, Douglass Coll., Rutgers U., 1964-66; B.A. in Anthropology with honors, Stanford U., 1969; M.A., Harvard U., 1973; Ph.D. in Psychology, Calif. Western U., 1982; BTh L.I.F.E. Bible Coll., 1987. Vol. VISTA, 1966; research asst. Johns Hopkins U., Balt., 1967; teaching fellow Harvard U., Cambridge, Mass., 1970-73; psychologist Salem Hosp., Mass., 1972-73; dir., psychologist Child Devel. Ctr., S.E. La. Hosp., Mandeville, 1973-75; asst. prof. City Coll., Loyola U., New Orleans, 1975-80; dir. Women's Ctr. for Greater New Orleans, 1975-80; research assoc., psychology bd. U. Calif., Santa Cruz, 1982-84; counselor Alpha Counseling Ctr., Los Angeles, 1985—; asst. pastor Thousand Oaks (Calif.) Foursquare Ch.; cons. in field. Author: Personality Assessment and Psychological Interpretation, 1983; contbr. articles to profl. jours. Recipient YWCA Bicentennial Achievement award, 1976; Ford Found. Research grantee, 1968; NSF fellow, 1969-71; NIMH fellow, 1972. Mem. Am. Assn. Counseling and Devel., Am. Psychol. Assn., Am. Mental Health Counselors Assn., Nat. Vocat. Guidance Assn. Club: Harvard (N.Y.C.). Address: 32142 Lakemeadow Ln Westlake Village CA 91361

DEININGER, JAMES PAUL, research electrochemist, engineer; b. Ft. Collins, Colo., May 15, 1950; s. James Paul and Rose Marie (Glancy) D.; m. Susan Marie Sontag, Dec. 28, 1976; children: Keith David, Kevin Paul. BS, N.Mex. Tech., 1972; MSChemE, N.Mex. State U., 1976. Research engr. Diamond Shamrock, Painesville, Ohio, 1976-80; assoc. devel. engr. Olin Chem., Charleston, Tenn., 1980-85; staff mem., electrochemist Los Alamos (N.Mex.) Nat. Lab., 1985—. Patentee in field. Mem. Am. Inst. Chem. Engrs., Electrochem. Soc., Am. Chem. Soc. Republican. Presbyterian. Avocation: music. Home: 44 La Paloma Los Alamos NM 87544 Office: Los Alamos Nat Lab Mailstop E517 Los Alamos NM 87545

DEININGER, RICHARD CRAIG, aerospace physicist; b. Poughkeepsie, N.Y., Nov. 4, 1955; s. Charles Richard and Rita (Essig) D. BS in Atmospheric Sci., SUNY, Albany, 1978; PhD in Meteorology, MIT, 1983. Assoc. research scientist Lockheed Missiles and Space Co., Sunnyvale, Calif., 1983-85, research specialist, 1985-87; tech. prin. Deskin Research Group, Inc., San Jose, 1987—. Contbr. articles to sci. jours. Fellow Univ. Corp. for Atmospheric Research, 1978-79, Woods Hole Oceanographic Instn., 1980. Mem. AAAS, AIAA, Am. Meteorol. Soc. (Howard H. Hanks scholar 1978), U.S. Ski Assn., Wine Investigation for Novices and Enophiles, U.S. Ski Coaches Assn., U.S. Recreational Ski Assn., Les Amis du Vin. Republican. Club: Eastern. Avocations: bicycling, running, enology. Home: 10635 Cordova Rd Cupertino CA 95014 Office: Deskin Research Group Inc 2880 Zanker Rd Suite 204 San Jose CA 95134

DEININGER, WILLIAM DWIGHT, physicist; b. Nov. 2, 1956; s. Charles Richard and Rita Hellen (Essig) D.; m. Kelly Marie Ward, June 28, 1980; 1 child, Christopher Ward. BS, SUNY, Cortland, 1979; MS, Colo. State U., 1982; student, U. So. Calif., 1984—. Student aide, research asst. Argonne (Ill.) Nat. Lab., 1978-79; mem. tech. staff Jet Propulsion Lab., Pasadena, Calif., 1982—. Contbr. articles to profl. jours. Mem. AIAA, Am. Assn. Physics Tchrs., Materials Research Soc. Club: JPL Ski Club (v.p. 1985). Home: 802 East Mountain Pasadena CA 91104 Office: Jet Propulsion Lab 125-224 4800 Oak Grove Dr Pasadena CA 91109

DEIOTTE, CHARLES EDWARD, computer software company executive; b. Gary, Ind., Jan. 31, 1946; s. Raymond Louis and Dorothy Jane (Paulson) D.; A.A., Skagit Valley Jr. Coll., 1966; student Wash. State U., 1970; m. Margaret Williams Tukey, Sept. 11, 1971; children—Raymond, Karl, Ronald. Programmer, Wash. State U., Pullman, 1969-70; project dir. AGT Mgmt. Systems, Renton, Wash., IEEE, AAAS, sr. tech. cons., sect. mgr. McDonnell-Douglas Automation, Bellevue, Wash., 1972-73; sr. engr. Boeing Computer Services, Seattle, 1973-75, computer based instrn. specialist, Tng. div., 1975-79; mgr. microprocessor design support center Boeing Aerospace Co., Kent, Wash., 1979-80; mgr. concept research Federal Express Corp., Colorado Springs, Colo., 1980-81, mgr. microprocessor support group, 1981-82; pres. Deitron Systems, Inc., Auburn, Wash., 1976-81; pres., chmn. bd. Logical Systems Inc., Colorado Springs, 1981—; chmn. bd. Summit Med. Systems, Inc., 1985-86 . Neighborhood commr. Chief Seattle council Boy Scouts Am., 1971-72; v.p. REACT alert, Seattle, 1974; advisor Jr. Achievement, Colorado Springs, 1980. Recipient Boeing Aerospace Co. Cert. of Achievement, 1979. Mem. Assn. Computing Machinery, IEEE, AAAS, Data Processing Mgmt. Assn., Am. Mgmt. Assn., Gamma Sigma Epsilon. Home: 2973 Fascination Circle Colorado Springs CO 80917 Office: 6295 Lehman Dr Suite B-101 Colorado Springs CO 80918

DEISENROTH, CLINTON WILBUR, electrical engineer; b. Louisville, Aug. 9, 1941; s. Clifton Earl and Nell (Pierce) D.; B.E.E., Ga. Inst. Tech., 1965; m. Lisbeth D. Isaacs, May 10, 1974; 1 dau., Susan Michelle. With Raytheon Co., 1966—, div. mgr. Addington Labs., Inc., solid state products div., Santa Clara, Calif., 1975-77, program mgr. electromagnetic systems div., Goleta, Calif., 1977-79, dir. surface navy electronic warfare systems, 1979-81; sr. v.p. systems div. Teledyne-MEC, 1981-84; pres. Teledyne CME, 1984—. Mem. IEEE, Am. Mgmt. Assn., Am. Def. Preparedness Assn., Navy League, Assn. Old Crows. Home: 1274 Pitman Ave Palo Alto CA 94301 Office: PO Box 58133 Santa Clara CA 95052

DEITCH, ARLINE DOUGLIS, research scientist; b. N.Y.C., Mar. 12, 1922. BA cum laude, CUNY, 1944; MA in Zoology, Columbia U., 1946, PhD in Zoology, 1954. Postdoctoral fellow Neurology and Blindness div. NIH, 1955-56; research assoc. Columbia U., N.Y.C., 1956-62, asst. prof. microbiology, 1962-68, asst. prof. pathology, 1968-73, assoc. prof. clin. pathology, 1973-81, assoc. prof. clin. pathology and urology in anatomy, 1981-84; adj. prof. urology U. Calif. Davis Sch. Medicine, Sacramento, 1984—; researcher various projects NIH, 1967-77, 83—, Nat. Cancer Inst. 1985—; dir. NIH cancer research grant, 1977-81; local chmn. Third Internat. Congress Histochemistry and Cytochemistry, N.Y.C., 1968. Contbr. articles to profl. jours. Mem. Soc. for Analytical Cytology, Am. Soc. Cell Biology, Histochem. Soc. (program chmn. 1964-68, council mem. 1964-68, 1973-77), Tissue Culture Assn. (organizer symposium on flow cytometry Meml. Sloan-Kettering Cancer Ctr. 1982), Sigma Xi. Office: U Calif Davis Med Sch Dept Urology 4301 X St Profl Bldg Suite 2220 Sacramento CA 95817

DEITRICH, ROBERT FRANKLIN, health care administrator; b. Pitman, Pa., May 24, 1933; s. Thomas Jefferson and Blanche Irene (Wetzel) D.; m. Lillie Esther, Apr. 9, 1955; children—Linda Esther, Lois Elaine. B.A., U. Md., 1966; M.S., U. No. Colo., 1977. Enlisted in USAF, 1951, advanced through grades to capt., 1970; ret., 1977; dir. central services, mgmt. analyst Univ. Hosp., U. Colo. Health Sci. Ctr., Denver, 1980—; faculty mil. sci. U.S. Air Force Sch. Aerospace Medicine, Brooks AFB, Tex., 1960-63. Deocrated Air Force Meritorious Service award with oak leaf cluster, Air Force Commendation medal; named Outstanding Registrar, Med. Service Sch., 1967. Mem. Nat. Rifle Assn., Health Care Material Mgmt. Soc. Am. Hosp. Assn. Republican. Mem. Evangelical Ch. Clubs: American Sportsman, Internat. Arabian Horse Assn., Am. Arabian Horse Assn. Home: 14804 E Iliff Pl Aurora CO 80014 Office: 4200 E 9th Ave Denver CO 80262

DEITZ, ROBERT JOSEPH, allergist; b. Garfield, N.J., May 15, 1932; s. Joseph and Ellen (Billy) D.; m. Sonya Makarewich, Mar. 21, 1959; children: Robert J. II, Jeffrey B., Lydia A., Darcy L. AA, Trenton Jr. Coll., 1956; BS, U. Utah, 1957, MS, 1958; PhD, Rutgers U., 1961; MD, Temple U., 1965. Intern USPHS Hosp., San Francisco, 1965-66, resident in internal medicine, 1966-67, 69-70, chief allergy and rheumatology, 1970-71, cons. in allergy and rheumatology, 1971-79; clin. fellow in allergy, immunology and rheumatology Scripps Clinic and Research Found., La Jolla, Calif., 1968-69; acting. med. dir. Dept. Labor, San Francisco, 1971; practice medicine specializing in allergy and rheumatology San Francisco, 1971—; asst. clin. prof. medicine U. Calif., San Francisco, 1972—; chief allergy clinic Pacific Presbyn. Med. Clinic, San Francisco, 1977—; hosp. appointments include U. Calif. Med. Ctr., San Francisco, 1971—, St. Mary's Hosp. and Med. Ctr., San Francisco, 1971—, St. Francis Meml. Hosp., San Francisco, 1972—, Children's Hosp., San Francisco, 1975—, Pacific Presbyn. Med. Ctr., San Francisco, 1974—, Seton Med. Ctr., Daly City, Calif., 1985—, Ross (Calif.) Gen. Hosp., 1975—. Served with USN, 1950-54, Korea; comdr. USPHS, 1965-71, col. Res. NSF fellow, 1959-60; recipient Robert Wood Johnson Found. award, 1961-65; named Outstanding Internal Medicine Resident, USPHS Hosp., 1967-68. Mem. AMA, ACP, Am. Coll. Allergists, Am. Acad. Allergy and Clin. Immunology, Am. Assn. Clin. Immunology and Allergy, Am. Rheumatism Assn., Am. Soc. Internat. Medicine, Calif. Med. Assn., San Francisco Med. Assn., Western Soc. Allergy and Immunology, Calif. Soc. Allergy and Clin. Immunology, Assn. Mil. Surgeons of U.S., Ducks Unltd., Nat. Rifle Assn., Calif. Rifle and Pistol Assn., Calif. Waterfowl Assn., Quail Unltd. Republican. Lutheran. Clubs: Pacific Rod and Gun, Sausalito Yacht. Avocations: hunting, fishing, traveling the back roads of Calif. Home: 127 Kinross Dr San Rafael CA 94901 Office: 2001 Union St Suite 625 San Francisco CA 94123

DEJARNATT, ARLIE URBAN, senator; b. Glezen, Ind., Nov. 13, 1923; s. Clyde Oscar and Clara Etta (Weeks) DeJ.; m. Donna Lee Stoffel, Sept. 4, 1946; children: Judith Ann, John Douglas, Steven Herrick, Susan Lee, Lise Jeanne. AB, Cornell Coll., 1948; MA, U. No. Colo., 1951. Cert. tchr., Colo., Wash. Social sci. tchr. Sterling (Colo.) High Sch., 1948-53, Longview (Wash.) Schs., 1953-76; fed. program analyst, supt. pub. instrn. Olympia, Wash., 1976-78; dist. asst. Congressman Don Bonker, Longview, 1980-85; state senator Olympia, 1985—. Chmn. Logan County Dem. com., Colo., 1952-53; pres. Cowlitz County Young Dems., Wash., 1956-57; state committeeman Cowlitz Dem. Cen. Com., Wash., 1976. Served as cpl. U.S. Marine Corps, 1943-46. Mem. Phi Delta Kappa. Mem. Unitarian Ch. Lodge: Rotary. Avocations: reading, gardening, fishing. Home: 7401 Willow Grove Rd Longview WA 98632 Office: 401 B Legislative Bldg Olympia WA 98504

DE JARNETTE, JAMES EDWARD, psychoanalyst, psychotherapist; b. Atlanta, Mar. 22, 1948; s. Charles Nathan and Sarah Holmes (Phillips) deJ. B.A., Shorter Coll., 1970; M.A., W. Ga. Coll., 1971; Ph.D., Sussex Coll., 1973. Exec. dir. Middle Ga. Counseling Center, Macon, 1972-80; exec. dir. Power Ferry Psychotherapy Clinic, 1976-80, deJarnette and Assocs., Beverly Hills, Calif., 1979—; chmn. bd. Leonidas Ltd., Inc.; dir. Alpha-Omega Enterprises, Inc.; chmn. bd. trustees Center for Meditative Living, Inc. Bd. dirs. Ga. Mental Health Assn., 1975, Macon/Bibb County Mental Health Assn., 1975. Fellow Am. Orthopsychiat. Assn., Am. Acad. Behavioral Sci.; mem. Am. Mental Health Couselors Assn., Nat. Psychiat. Assn., Internat. Soc. Adlerian Psychology, Mensa, Tripple Nine Soc. Pi Gamma Mu. Republican. Episcopalian. Contbr. articles to profl. jours. Home: 8535 W Knoll Dr Apt 215 Los Angeles CA 90069

DEKA, NIREN, molecular biologist, biochemist; b. Gauhati, India, June 29, 1955; came to U.S., 1979; s. Tarini Charan and Binapani Deka. BSc, Cotton Coll., Gauhati, India, 1975; MSc, Jawaharlal Nehru U., New Delhi, 1978; PhD, U. Mo., Kansas City, 1984. Postdoctoral fellow U. Calif., Davis, 1984—. Contbr. articles to profl. jours. Mem. AAAS, Sigma Xi. Hindu. Home: 609 E 7th St #3 Davis CA 95616 Office: U Calif Dept Chemistry Davis CA 95616

DEKORTE, JOHN MARTIN, chemistry educator, textbook consultant; b. Grand Rapids, Mich., Sept. 20, 1940; s. Simon and Jeannette (Mieras) DeK.; m. Carolyn Marie Meindertsma, Aug. 10, 1963; children: Bradley John, Carrie Joy. AS, Grand Rapids Junior Coll., 1960; BA, Hope Coll., 1962; PhD, Purdue U., 1969. Asst. prof. chemistry No. Ariz. U., Flagstaff, 1966-72, assoc. prof., 1972-81, prof., 1981—; summer research assoc. Dow Chem. Co., Midland, Mich., 1962; cons. and devel. reviewer gen. chemistry textbooks, 1966—. Author: Student Solutions Manual to Accompany General Chemistry, 2d edit., and Gen. Chemistry with Qualitative Analysis, 2d edit., 1984, Student Solutions Manual to Accompany Principles of Chemistry, 1984. Recipient Burlington No. Found. Teaching award No. Ariz. U., 1986. Mem. Am. Chem. Soc. Republican. Avocations: backpacking, hiking. Home: 1645 Linda Vista Flagstaff AZ 86004 Office: No Ariz U Chemistry Dept Box 5698 Flagstaff AZ 86011

DEKRUIF, ROBERT M., financial services company executive. Vice chmn. bd. H.F. Ahmanson & Co., Los Angeles. Office: HF Ahmanson & Co 3731 Wilshire Blvd Los Angeles CA 90010

DE LAFUENTE, JOSÉ RAMÓN, speech and language pathologist; b. Amherst, Tex., Nov. 23, 1951; s. Leon Garciá and Juana Rios (Rivera) De LaF.; m. Sylvia Antonia Abalos, June 8, 1974; children: José Alejandro, Maria Elena. BA (2), U. No. Colo., 1974, MA, 1976. Cert. speech-lang. pathologist, Colo. Speech-lang. pathologist, pub. schs. Weld County Sch. Dist. 6, Greeley, Colo., 1975—. Mem. Am. Speech-Lang. and Hearing Assn. (cert., co-trainer bilingual lang. systems 1983-84). Avocation: Korean karate instr. Home: 208 Todd Ave La Salle CO 80645

DELAND, DIANE O. AMMONS, business executive; b. Redding, Calif., Jan. 3, 1940; d. Mark T. and Lucille I. (Wissert) Ammons; m. Maurice Graham DeLand, Feb. 19, 1966 (div. 1974); 1 child, Charles Maurice DeLand. B.A., U. Calif.-Berkeley, 1961; Cert., Goethe Inst., Berlin, 1961; postgrad. Am. U., 1969-71. Economist, AID, U.S. Dept. State, Washington, 1962-70; sr. economist U.S. EPA, Washington, 1970-73, PBGC, Washington, 1974-76; rep. U.S. Govt. Inter-Agy. Task Force, Washington, 1978; dir. tech. programs Pension Benefit Guaranty, Washington, 1976-79; pres. Pension Corp., Los Angeles, 1979—; cons. and lectr. in field. Co-author: (tech. booklet) Guidelines on Plan Termination, 1977; Syllabus on Pension Plans, 1981. Headmaster council Indian Mountain Sch., Conn., 1984—. Named Life mem. Calif. Scholastic Soc., 1957, U.S. Pres.'s Govt. exchange scholar, 1978-79. Mem. Women in Bus., Nat. Assn. Female Execs., Am. Soc. Pension Actuaries (assoc.), Jr. League. Avocations: Painting; reading; skiing; tennis; travel. Office: Pension Corp 429 Santa Monica Blvd Suite 320 Santa Monica CA 90401

DELANEY, MARION PATRICIA, advertising agency executive; b. Hartford, Conn., May 20, 1952; d. William Pride Delaney and Marian Patricia (Utley) Murphy. BA, Union Coll., Schenectady, N.Y., 1973. Adminstrv. asst. N.Y. State Assembly, Albany, 1973-74; account exec. Foote, Cone & Belding, N.Y.C., 1974-78; sr. account exec. Dailey & Assocs., Los Angeles, 1978-81; pub. relations cons. NOW, Washington, 1981-83; account supr. BBDO/West, Los Angeles, 1983-85; v.p. Grey Advt., Los Angeles, 1985—. Del. Dem. Nat. Conv., San Francisco, 1984; v.p. NOW, Los Angeles, 1980-83, pres. 1984, advisor 1985—. Mem. Bus. and Profl. Women Assn., Los Angeles Advt. Club. Congregationalist. Home: 3682 Fillmore St San Francisco CA 94123 Office: Grey Advt 50 California St San Francisco CA 94111

DELANEY, MATTHEW SYLVESTER, educator, coll. adminstr.; b. Ireland, Nov. 26, 1927; s. Joseph C. and Elizabeth M. (Berrigan) D.; came to U.S., 1947, naturalized, 1952; student St. John's Coll., 1947-51; B.A., Immaculate Heart Coll., Los Angeles, 1958; M.S., Notre Dame U., 1960; Ph.D., Ohio State U., 1971. Ordained priest, Roman Catholic Ch., 1951; assoc. pastor Los Angeles Cath. Diocese, 1951-55; instr. math., physics Pius X High Sch., Downey, Calif., 1955-58, vice prin., 1960-62; instr. math. Immaculate Heart Coll., Los Angeles, 1962-65, asst. prof., 1965-72, assoc. prof., 1972-76, prof., 1976—; asst. acad. dean, 1973-78; dean acad. devel. Mt. St. Mary's Coll., Los Angeles, 1978-82, acad. dean, 1982—. NSF grantee, 1959-60, 61. Mem. Am. Math. Soc., Math. Assn. Am., Am. Conf. Acad. Deans. Democrat. Contbr. articles to math. publs. Home: 922 S Detroit St Los Angeles CA 90036 Office: Mt St Mary's Coll 12001 Chalon Rd Los Angeles CA 90049

DELANEY, RICHARD JAMES, investment banking executive; b. Pottsville, Pa., Jan. 4, 1946; s. James F. and Ann M. (Giacoia) D.; B.S. in Indsl. Engring., Lehigh U., 1968; M.B.A., U. Pa., 1970; m. Mary D. McGuire, Aug. 16, 1969; children—Jennifer, Kelly. With Carrier Air Conditioning Co., N.Y.C., 1968-69; with Dean Witter & Co., San Francisco, 1970; v.p., instl. rep. White, Weld & Co., San Francisco, 1971-78; v.p. Shearson, Hayden-Stone, 1978-79; sr. v.p. Donaldson, Lufkin & Jenrette, 1979—; pres., dir. U.S. Global Trading Corp.; dir. Pacific Mellon Corp. Pres. No. Calif. Cystic Fibrosis Found., 1974-75, trustee, 1973-76. Mem. Am. Assn. Indsl. Engrs., Lehigh Alumni of No. Calif. (pres.). Democrat. Roman Catholic. Clubs: San Francisco Bond, Calif. Golf, Wharton Bus. Sch., Lehigh Alumni (pres. 1978—). Lodge: Elks. Home: 7 Highlands Ct Belmont CA 94002 Office: Donaldson Lufkin and Jenrette 1 Montgomery St Suite 1210 San Francisco CA 94104

DELANEY, THOMAS ALTON, musician, educator; b. Yonkers, N.Y., Dec. 24, 1944; s. Joseph and Julia (Romanchick) D.; m. Marianne Elizabeth Krolicki, Mar. 26, 1966; children—Tim, Judy. Diploma in Arranging/Composition, Berklee Coll. Music, Boston, 1969; B.A. in Music, Sierra Nevada Coll., 1983. Freelance musician jazz and popular music, 1958—; condr., contractor, arranger, N.Y., 1958-62, N.Y., Boston, 1963-70, Reno, Tahoe, Nev., 1970—; tchr. music theory, composition and music history, band dir. Sierra Nevada Coll., Incline Village, Nev., 1972—, chmn. music dept., 1980—. Composer: Khroma, string Quartet, 1983; numerous jazz compositions, 1980—, also arrangements for jazz bands. Mem. Reno Musicians Union. Home: PO Box 4584 Incline Village NV 89450 Office: Sierra Nevada Coll PO Box 4269 Incline Village NV 89450

DE LANGE, HANS, travel agency executive. Pres. Ask Mr. Foster West, Van Nuys, Calif. Office: Ask Mr Foster West 7833 Haskell Ave Van Nuys CA 91406 *

DE LA PEÑA, RAMON SERRANO, agronomist; b. San Jacinto, Pangasinan, Philippines, Oct. 2, 1936; s. Marcelino Reyes and Maria Serrano de la P.; B.S., U. Philippines, 1958; M.S., U. Hawaii, 1964, Ph.D., 1967; m. Harriet Enriqueta Viloria, Jan. 26, 1963; children—Marjorie Joy Leilani, Ramon, Raynard Don, Ryan Mel. Research asst. U. Philippines, 1958-60; asst. in plant physiology U. Hawaii, 1960-65, jr. soil scientist, 1965-67, asst. agronomist, 1967-76, rice tng. officer, 1968-72, assoc. specialist in agronomy Kauai br. sta., Kapaa, 1976-81, supt. sta., 1978-81; assoc. agronomist, assoc. prof. dept. agronomy and soil sci., 1981-83, agronomist, prof. agronomy, 1983—; dir. econ. devel. County of Kauai, 1973-74; cons. tropical agr. AID, World Bank, Universe Tankships; panel mem. Nat. Acad. Sci. Mem. Kauai County Employment and Tng. Planning Council; mem. Office of Elderly Affairs Policy Bd., County of Kauai. Grantee U.S. Dept. Agr., State of Hawaii, County of Kauai. Mem. Am. Soc. Agronomy, Asian-Pacific Weed Sci. Soc., Hawaiian Acad. Sci., Internat. Soc. Tropical Root Crops, Internat. Soc. Soil Sci., Soil Sci. Soc. Am., Weed Sci. Soc. Am., Weed Sci. Soc. Philippines, Sigma Xi, Gamma Sigma Delta. Roman Catholic. Editor Internat. Soc. Tropical Root Crops Newsletter, 1980—; contbr. articles to profl. jours. Home: 6155 Kala Kea Pl Kapaa HI 96746 Office: 7370-A Kuamoo Rd Kapaa HI 96746

DELAPLANE, STANTON HILL, newspaper columnist; b. Chgo., Oct. 12, 1907; s. Frank Hugh and Marion (Hill) D.; m. Miriam Moore, Dec. 6, 1940 (div. 1958); children: Kristin Moore, Thomas; m. Susan Aven, Feb. 2, 1961 (div. May 1973); children: Andrea Aven, John Berry Hill; m. Laddie Marshack, Oct. 19, 1979. Student, Hyde Park, Chgo., Santa Barbara, Cal., Monterey high schs., 1922-26. Editor Aperitif Mag. (pub. by Baroness Emily Von Romberg), 1933-36; reporter San Francisco Chronicle, 1936—, editor women's dept., 1937; now columnist; also columnist Chronicle Features, San Francisco; Organizer Calif. Young Democrats; and editor The Young Democrat, 1933-34; U.S. war corr. San Francisco Chronicle, 1944-45. Author: Pacific Pathways; Contbr. to: etc. Served to lt. comdr. USMC, Maritime Commn., 1942-44, Washington. accredited corr. U.N. Conf., 1945; Recipient Pulitzer prize for regional reporting of movement of Calif.-Oreg. border counties to secede and form the 49th state, 1941, Nat. Headlines journalism award for feature series titles, Ding Dong Daddy of the D Car Line, 1946; Nat. Headlines award, 1959; 1st Ann. Writers award for best N. Am. article on sea travel Transpacific Passenger Conf. Club: San Francisco Press (pres. 1970-71, dir). Home: 1730 Kearny Apt A-1 San Francisco CA 94133 Office: San Francisco Chronicle San Francisco CA 94103

DELAQUIS, NOEL, bishop; b. Notre-Dame de Lourdes, Man., Can., Dec. 25, 1934; s. Louis and Therese (Hebert) D. B.A., U. Man., 1954; B.Th., U. Laval, 1958; J.C.L., Latran, Rome, 1962. Ordained priest Roman Catholic Ch., 1958; asst. priest Christ the King Parish, St. Vital, Man., 1958-60; prof. canon law St. Boniface Sem., Man., 1962-68; chancellor Archdiocese of St. Boniface, Man., 1965-73; bishop of Gravelbourg, Sask., Can., 1974—. Address: CP 690, Gravelbourg, SK Canada S0H 1X0

DELASHMUTT, WILLIAM ALLEN, electrical engineer; b. La Grande, Oreg., May 30, 1949; s. William Robert and Etta Lucinda (McCabe) DeL.; m. Charle Marie Rankin, June 10, 1972; 1 child, Darcie Kay. BAEE, Oreg. State U., 1972. Registered profl. engr., Oreg. Asst. dist. engr. CP Nat. Corp., La Grande, 1972-77, dist. engr., 1977—; resource instr. Ea. Oreg. State Coll., La Grande, 1982-84. Asst. Ea. Oreg. State Coll. Triathlon, 1985; laborer antenna tower Island City (Oreg.) Fire Dept., 1982; engring. lighting poles Ea. Oreg. State Coll., 1981. Mem. IEEE (sr.). N.W. Electric Light and Power Assn. (underground com. 1980—). Republican. Methodist. Lodges: Elks (com. mem. 1972—). Avocations: dancing, amateur radio, running, hunting, hiking. Office: CP Nat Corp 107 Elm St La Grande OR 97850

DE LASSEN, JAN FOLMER, university administrator; b. Copenhagen, Jan. 25, 1934; came to U.S., 1980; s. Ivar Christian and Edith (Christiansen) De L.; m. Magali Florelia Cumare, Sept. 23, 1972; children—Magalita, Jan Folmer Jr., Michelle. B.S. in Math. (Gulf Oil Co. scholar), Tex. A&M U., 1959. Computer programmer Mobil Oil Co., Caracas, Venezuela, 1959-60; systems analysis, procedure supr. Gen. Electric of Venezuela, 1961-72; computer ops. mgr. Savoy Group, 1973-75; computer ops. mgr. ACO Group, Caracas, 1976-79; gen. mgr. Boulton Group, Caracas, 1980; dir. computer application services Brigham Young U., Provo, Utah, 1981—; owner JDL and Assocs.; cons. in field. Mem. Assn. System Mgmt. (past pres. Venezuela), Am. Assn. Artificial Intelligence, Office Systems Research Assn., Utah Council on Computers for Edn., Tex. Aggie Former Students Assn. Mormon. Office: Brigham Young University 193 TCMB Provo UT 84602

DE LA TORRE, JOLYNN KAE HINGER, public relations professional; b. Riverside, Calif., Sept. 17, 1960; d. Larry Leland Hinger and Joyce Marlene (Runck) Bates; m. Eduardo de la Torre, Aug. 30, 1981. Student, Union Coll., 1978-79; BA, Loma Linda U., 1982. Communications asst. County Supt. Schs., San Bernardino, Calif., 1982-84; asst. dir. pub. relations Loma Linda U., Riverside, 1984—; asst. dir. TV prodn. Univ. Ch., Loma Linda, Calif., 1984—. Mng. editor La Sierra Today mag., 1984—. Council for Advancement and Support of Edn. dist. scholar, 1985. Mem. Pub. Relations Soc. Am. (sec. 1986). Avocations: video prodn., comml. art, calligraphy, photography. Office: Loma Linda U Riverside CA 92515

DE LAURENTIIS, DINO, motion picture producer; b. Torre Annunziata, Italy, Aug. 8, 1919; s. Rosario Aurelio and Giuseppina (Salvatore) De L.; m. Silvana Magnano, July 17, 1949; children: Veronica, Rafaella, Francesca. Ed. high sch. and comml. sch., Centro Sperimentale di Cinematografia, Rome. Prin. De Laurentiis Entertainment Group Studios, Wilmington, DE, 1984—; prin. De Laurentiis Entertainment Group, Inc., 1985—, now chmn. bd. dirs.; purchased Embassy Pictures, 1985; formed De Laurentiis Entertainment Ltd. (Australia), 1986. Mem. actor's sch., Expt. Film Center,

Rome, 1937-39, organized first film prodn. co., 1941; productions include Bitter Rice, 1952, Ulysses, 1955, War and Peace, 1956, La Strada, 1956 (Acad. award), Nights of Cabiria, 1957 (Acad. award), This Angry Age, 1958, The Tempest, 1959, Under Ten Flags, 1960, The Best of Enemies, 1962, Barabbas, 1962, Three Faces of a Woman (Soraya), 1964, The Bible, 1966, Barbarella, 1967, Anzio, 1967, Waterloo, 1970, Valachi Papers, 1972, The Stone Killer, 1973, (moved to N.Y. 1973), Serpico, 1974, Death Wish, 1974, Mandingo, 1975, Three Days of the Condor, 1975, (moved to Los Angeles 1975), Lipstick, 1976, Face to Face, 1976, Buffalo Bill and the Indians, 1976, The Shootist, 1976, King Kong, 1976, Orca, 1977, The Serpent's Egg, 1977, King of the Gypsies, 1978, The Great Train Robbery, 1978, The Brink's Job, 1979, Hurricane, 1979, Flash Gordon, 1980, Ragtime, 1981, Striking Back, 1982, Conan The Barbarian, 1982, The Dead Zone, 1983, Firestarter, 1984, The Bounty, 1984, Conan The Destroyer, 1984, Dune, 1984, Cat's Eye, 1985, Red Sonja, 1985, Year of the Dragon, 1985, Marie, 1985, Silver Bullet, 1985, Raw Deal, 1986, Maximum Overdrive, 1986, Tai-Pan, 1986, Blue Velvet, 1986, 1986, King Kong Lives, 1986, Manhunter, 1986, Trick or Treat, 1986, Crimes of the Heart, 1986, Date With an Angel, 1987, The Bedroom Window, 1987, From the Hip, 1987, Million Dollar Mystery, 1987, Traxx, 1987, Weeds, 1987, Rampage, 1987, Collision Course, 1987, Dracula's Widow, 1987, Pumpkinhead, 1987. Office: De Laurentiis Entertainment Group 8670 Wilshire Blvd Beverly Hills CA 90211 *

DE LAY, BABETTE WALES, consultant, real estate agent, radio broadcaster; b. Buffalo, Sept. 5, 1954; d. Lee R. De Lay and Virginia W. Schive. BS in English and Behavioral Scis., Westminster Coll., 1976, BS in Bus. Communications, 1979. Social worker County Jail, Salt Lake City, 1975-78; exec. editor Rocky Mountain Woman Mag., Salt Lake City, 1976-79; mktg. coordinator Westminster Coll., Salt Lake City, 1979; dir. communications Great Salt Lake area United Way, 1980-82; radio broadcaster Sta. KRCL-FM 91, Salt Lake City, 1981—; pub. relations cons., Salt Lake City, 1979-84; real estate agt. Carli & Co. Realtors, 1984—. Coordinator Utah Arts Festival, 1983—; coordinator U.S. Film Festival, 1987. Editor Salt Lake Realtor Mag., 1987. Recipient poster of the year award United Way Am., 1982. Mem. Utah Advt. Fedn. (Gold award 1982, Silver award 1981), Internat. Assn. Bus. Communicators (Best Poster award 1981, Merit in Photography award 1981), Pub. Relations Soc. Am. Office: 2196 S 700 E Salt Lake City UT 84106

DELAY, EUGENE RAYMOND, psychologist, educator, researcher; b. Coeur d'Alene, Idaho, Dec. 24, 1948; s. Raymond Joseph and Fairy Louise (Fisher) D.; m. Rona Jane Moore, Sept. 12, 1971; 1 child, Shawn Patrick. BS in Psychology, U. Idaho, 1972; MS in Biopsychology, U. Ga., 1977, PhD in Biopsychology, 1979. Asst. prof. Regis Coll., Denver, 1979-84, assoc. prof., 1984—; provisional clin. cons. Denver VA Hosp., 1981—; research cons. Brenau Coll., Gainesville, Ga., 1978. Contbr. articles to profl. jours. Served with U.S. Army, 1973-75. Mem. Am. Psychol. Assn., Southeastern Psychol. Assn., N.Y. Acad. Sci., Rocky Mountain Neurosci. Group, Rocky Mountain Psychol. Assn. Avocations: fishing, woodworking, racquetball. Home: 2819 Dundee Ct Fort Collins CO 80525 Office: Regis Coll Dept Psychology W 50th & Lowell Blvd Denver CO 80221

DE LEON, DOROTEO, JR., aerospace engineer; b. Pueblo, Colo., Jan. 5, 1929; s. Doroteo and Guadalupe (Lugo) DeL.; m. Ann Garner Lewis; children: Doroteo III, Damian, Dawn Marie. AS in Engring., U. So. Colo., 1949; BSEE, Colo. State U., 1951. Sr. design engr. Martin Marietta Corp., Denver, 1959-76, group engr., 1977—; sr. design engr. EG&G, Idaho Falls, Idaho, 1976-77. Contbr. articles to profl. jours. State bd. dirs. League United Latin Am. Citizens, Denver, 1972-73. Served to lt. USN, 1951-58. Republican. Mormon. Home: 1056 E Costilla Way Littleton CO 80122 Office: Martin Marietta Aerospace Corp PO Box 179 Denver CO 80201

DELEWSKI, CATHIE HANES, social worker; b. Salt Lake City, Dec. 5, 1955; d. Angelo and Helen Ludlow (Cope) Hanes; m. Richard Edwin Delewski, Aug. 5, 1983; 1 child, Megan Rachel. BS in Psychology, U. Utah, 1976, MSW, 1979, DSW, 1986. Dir. social services Lakeview Hosp., Bountiful, Utah, 1979-81; sr. social worker U. Utah Med. Ctr., Salt Lake City, 1981-83; research analyst U. Utah, 1983-85; crisis specialist Salt Lake City Mental Health, 1983-85, U. Utah Health Scis. Ctr., 1985—; co-chmn. Nat. Family Sex Edn. Week, Salt Lake City, 1985. Contbr. articles to profl. jours. Mem. Nat. Assn. Social Workers, Nat. Register Clin. Social Workers. Democrat. Mormon. Avocations: cross country skiing, backpacking, biking, swimming, handicrafts. Home: 729 E Roosevelt Ave Salt Lake City UT 84105 Office: U Utah Health Services Ctr 50 N Medical Dr Salt Lake City UT 84132

DELFINO, MICHELANGELO, scientist; b. Bronx, N.Y., June 19, 1950; s. Cosimo A. Delfino and Mary Nicolosi; m. Joan Marie Tolomer, Dec. 26, 1971; children: Michel John, Janine Marie, Robert Jon. BS, St. John's U., Jamaica, N.Y., 1972; MS, Fordham U., 1977, PhD, 1979. Assoc. profl. Philips Labs., Briarcliff Manor, N.Y., 1973-78; sr. staff mem. Signetics div. Philips Labs., Sunnyvale, Calif., 1983—; assoc. profl. Exxon Enterprises, Elmsford, N.Y., 1978-79; sr. staff mem. research and devel. div. Fairchild Corp., Palo Alto, Calif., 1979-83. Contbr. 50 articles to profl. jours.; 8 patents in field. Mem. IEEE, Materials Research Soc., Electrochem. Soc. Avocations: mountaineering, numismatics, wine tasting. Home: 2141 Deodara Rd Los Altos CA 94022 Office: Philips Labs div Signetics 811 E Arques Ave Sunnyvale CA 94088

DELIS, NICHOLAS PETER, JR., producer dealer, real estate mortgage loan broker; b. San Francisco, Nov. 25, 1949; s. Nick Peter and Pearl S. (Pallios) D.; m. Stephanie A. Morf, Aug. 27, 1972; children—Nicholas III, Katina. B.A. in Mktg., San Francisco State U., 1972. Mktg. and sales dir. Nick Delis Co., Inc., Millbrae, Calif., 1967-75, pres., 1975—, chief exec. officer, 1983—; chief exec. officer Nicholas Peter Delis Investments, 1976—. Mem. Rep. Nat. Com. (sustaining) San Mateo County, Calif. Mem. Save the Redwood League (life), Nat. Rifle Assn. (life), Save San Francisco Bay Assn. Greek Orthodox. Club: Pan Cretan Assn. Am. (San Francisco). Office: 1001 Broadway Suite 2-C Millbrae CA 94030

DELISLE, HAROLD FREDERICK, biology educator; b. Los Angeles, Feb. 18, 1933; s. Frederick James and Kathleen M. (O'Brien) DeL. BA, St. John's Coll., Camarillo, Calif., 1955; BS, Loyola U., Los Angeles, 1968; MS, U. Puerto Rico, 1970; PhD, UCLA, 1980. Tchr. high schs. 1955-76; asst. prof. biology U. Pasadena, Calif., 1980—; cons. BLM, Riverside, Calif., 1978-79. Author: Wildlife of Southern California Mountains, 1975. Mem. AAAS, So. Calif. Acad. Sci., Southwest Herpetology Soc. (pres. 1983-84), Soc. for Study of Amphibians and Reptiles, Nat. Assn. Biology Tchrs. Home: PO Box 292 North Hollywood CA 91603 Office: U Pasadena 1505 N Marengo Pasadena CA 91103

DELLAS, ROBERT D., investment banker; b. Detroit, July 4, 1944; s. Eugene D. and Maxine (Rudell) D.; m. Shila L. Clement, Mar. 27, 1976; children—Emily Allison, Lindsay Michelle. B.A. in Econs., U. Mich., Ann Arbor, 1966; M.B.A., Harvard U., Cambridge, 1970. Analyst Burroughs Corp., Detroit, 1966-67, Pasadena, Calif., 1967-68; mgr. U.S. Leasing, San Francisco, 1970-76; pres., dir. Energetics Mktg. & Mgmt. Assn., San Francisco, 1978-80; sr. v.p. E.F. Hutton & Co., San Francisco, 1981-85; prin. founder Captial Exchange Internat., San Francisco, 1976—; gen. ptnr. Kanland Assocs., Tex., 1982, Claremont Assocs., Calif., 1983, Lakeland Assocs., Ga., 1983, Americal Assocs., Calif., 1983, Chatsworth Assocs., Calif., 1983, Walnut Grove Assocs., Calif., 1983, Somerset Assocs., N.J., 1983, One San Diego Assocs., Calif., 1984. Mem. U.S. Trotting Assn., Calif. Harness Horse Breeders Assn. (Breeders award for Filly of Yr. 1986). Home: 1911 Sacramento St San Francisco CA 94109 Office: E F Hutton & Co Inc 580 California St San Francisco CA 94104

DELLINGER, EVAN PATCHEN, surgery educator; b. Newark, Jan. 2, 1944; s. David and Elizabeth (Peterson) D.; m. Lissa D'Orlando, July 1, 1967; children: Kira Lauren, Seth Berton. BA in Math., Swarthmore Coll., 1966; MD, Harvard U., 1970. Diplomate Am. Bd. Surgery. Resident in surgery Beth Israel Hosp., Boston, 1970-73, 1975-77; research fellow Tufts U.-New Eng. Med. Ctr., Boston, 1973-75; asst. prof. surgery U. Wash., Seattle, 1977-82, assoc. prof., 1982—. Contbr. articles to profl. jours., chpts. to books. Fellow ACS; mem. Soc. Univ. Surgeons, Surg. Infection Soc. (sci. studies com. 1983-86, treas. 1986—), Am. Soc. Microbiology, Infectious Diseases Soc. Am. Avocations: skiing, sailing, tennis. Office: Harborview Med Ctr Dept Surgery ZA-16 325 9th Ave Seattle WA 98104

DELLUMS, RONALD VERNIE, congressman; b. Oakland, Calif., Nov. 24, 1935; m. Leola Roscoe Higgs; 3 children. A.A., Oakland City Coll., 1958; B.A., San Francisco State Coll., 1960; M.S.W., U. Calif., 1962. Psychiat. social worker Calif. Dept. Mental Hygiene, 1962-64; program dir. Bayview Community Center, San Francisco, 1964-65; from assoc. dir. to dir. Hunters Point Youth Opportunity Center, 1965-66; planning cons. Bay Area Social Planning Council, 1966-67; dir. concentrated employment program San Francisco Econ. Opportunity Council, 1967-68; sr. cons. Social Dynamics, Inc., 1968-70; mem. 92d-100th Congresses from 8th Calif. Dist.; chmn. house com. D.C. 1979—, chmn. house armed services subcom. on mil. installations and facilities, 1983—; Lectr. San Francisco State Coll., U. Calif. at Berkeley; mem. U.S. del. North Atlantic Assembly. Author: Defense Sense: The Search For A Rational Military Policy, 1983. Mem. Berkeley City Council, 1967-71. Served with USMCR, 1954-56. Democrat. Home: Washington DC Office: 2136 Rayburn House Office Bldg Washington DC 20515

DELMAR, EVELYN EMAN, public relations agency executive; b. N.Y.C., Dec. 31, 1949; d. John and Gay (Simon) Eman; m. Larry Edward Delmar, Nov. 26, 1982. Student NYU, 1975-76, Baruch Coll., 1981-82. Asst. mgr. Vanderbilt Athletic Club, N.Y.C., 1967-68; pub. relations mgr. DEC Enterprises, Inc., N.Y.C., 1968-73; exec. interviewer Dun & Bradstreet, Inc., N.Y.C., 1974; pub. relations rep. Parsons & Whittemore, Inc., N.Y.C., 1974-77; corp. mgr. pub. relations NEC Am., Inc., Melville, N.Y., 1977-82; pres. Perception Plus, Colorado Springs, Colo., 1982—. Recipient Merit cert. Publicity Club of N.Y., 1976-77, Silver Quill award, IABC, 1986, Women of Achievement award Women in Communications, 1986. Mem. Colorado Springs Conv. and Visitors Bur., Internat. Assn. Bus. Communicators (v.p. programming 1984-85, pres. 1985-86, Gold Nuggets award 1984, 85, 86), The Promoters (pres. 1984), Pub. Relations Soc. Am., Colorado Springs Press Assn. (Gridiron award 1986), Pikes Peak Advt. Fedn. (Addy awards 1986), Colo. Springs C. of C. Contbg. editor: PR Essay, 1976-77; editor Women's Exchange Network Newsletter, 1983; contbr. articles to profl. jours.; composer popular songs. Office: Perception Plus PO Box 38880 Colorado Springs CO 80937

DELMAR-MCCLURE, NELLIE, psychologist, educator; b. San Antonio, Tex., Sept. 25, 1940; d. Eduardo and Maria (Lopez-Bravo) Delmar; m. Robert E. McClure, June 30, 1962; children—David Robert, Michael Robert. B.A., Pepperdine U., 1962, M.A., 1966; Ph.D., U.S. Internat. U., San Diego, 1974. Lic. psychologist, Calif. Instr. psychology Pepperdine U., Los Angeles, 1966-69, Rio Hondo Coll., Whittier, Calif., 1968-72; prof. psychology U. Autonoma de Guadalajara, Mex., 1974-75; asst. clin. prof. dept. pediatrics U. Calif.-Irvine, 1982-84; asst. prof. Fuller Grad. Sch. Psychology, Pasadena, 1983—; psychologist Los Angeles Psychol. Ctr., 1966-67, Rancho Los Amigos Hosp., Downey, Calif., 1966-67, pvt. practice, 1974—; lectr. on parent-child issues, 1966-72. Spina bifida grantee Nat. Found., 1980; recipient Pollygramatic award for psychology, 1961, Zeta Kappa award for psychology, 1961, Phi Beta award, 1961. Mem. Am. Psychol. Assn., Calif. Psychol. Assn., Psi Chi. Democrat. Presbyterian.

DEL MORAL, ROGER, botany educator, ecological consultant; b. Detroit, Sept. 13, 1943; children: Sara, Andrea. BA, U. Calif., Santa Barbara, 1965, MA, 1966, PhD, 1968. Cert. sr. ecologist. Asst. prof. U. Wash., Seattle, 1968-74, assoc. prof., 1974-83, prof., 1983—; prin. del Moral & Assocs., Seattle, 1984—; Contbr. articles to profl. jours. NFS research grantee, 1971, 75, 79, 81, 82, 84. Mem. Ecol. Soc. Am., Bot. Soc. Am. (sec. 1983-86), Brit. Ecol. Soc., Internat. Union Vegetation Scientists, Northwest Sci. Assn. (bd. dirs. 1984-85). Avocations: photography, hiking. Office: U Wash Dept Botany KB 15 Seattle WA 98195

DELOACH, ROBERT EDGAR, business executive; b. Daytona Beach, Fla., Jan. 6, 1939; s. Ollie Newman and Sally Gertrude (Schrowder) DeL. Student U. Alaska-Anchorage, 1967-69, Alaska Meth. U., 1970, Pacific Luth. U., 1972. Lic. elec. engr. and adminstr., Alaska, 1979; lic. pvt. pilot; lic. real estate agt. Former chmn. bd. Alaska Stagecraft, Inc., Anchorage; pres. BG Systems Co., BG Tax & Acctg., Inc., The Electric Doctor, Inc.; former pres. Coastal Electronics, Inc.; former owner-mgr. Bargain Towne, Anchorage. Active Anchorage Community Theatre, Anchorage Theater Guild. Mem. Assn. Ind. Accts., Internat. Assn. Theatrical Stage Employees and Moving Picture Machine Operators U.S. (pres. local 770), Ind. Elec. Contractors Assn., Internat. Assn. Elec. Insps. Home: 1207 W 47th Ave Anchorage AK 99503 Office: 7910 King St Anchorage AK 99502

DELONG, WILLIAM JAMES, state senator, retired business executive; b. Albany, N.Y., Mar. 27, 1930; s. Harry and Pearl Smith (Sickles) DeL.; m. Loretta Strzelecki, 1977; children—Peter, Linda DeLong, William R., James R., Lee, Robin. Student U. Md., two years. Vice pres. Merodias Constrn. Co., Tucson, 1978, Automated Printing & Mailing, Inc., Tucson, 1979-81; gen. mgr. Complete Personnel Service, Tucson, 1978-79, Today's Bus. Mag., Tucson, 1979-81; owner Complete Trophy Ctr., Tucson, 1979-82; mem. Ariz. Ho. of Reps., from 1981; now Ariz. State Senate. Chief dep. county treas. Pima County, Ariz., 1969-70; city clk. Tucson, 1971-72, manpower dir., 1972-73, asst. city mgr., 1973. Served to maj., AGC, U.S. Army, 1947-68; Korea, Vietnam. Decorated Legion of Merit, 6 Army Commendation Medals. Mem. Big Bros. (dir.), Council State Govts., Edn. Commn. of the States. Republican. Clubs: Catalina Midtown Optimist (pres. 1976), Tanque Verde Optimists. Home: 551 S Brighton Ln Tucson AZ 85711 Office: Arizona State Senate Phoenix AZ 85007

DE LOS SANTOS, HECTOR C(RESCIND, physician, consultant; b. Bulacan, Philippines, Sept. 20, 1924; came to U.S., 1948; s. Benigno and Sofia (Crescini) de los S.; m. Melencia B. Syta, Nov. 14, 1948 (div. 1982); children: Victoria, Carlos, Divina, Hector, Sophia, Ramon, George; m. Pacita B. Manalo, Aug. 5, 1982. AA, U. Santo Tomas, Manila, 1942, MD summa cum laude, 1948. Rotating intern U. Santo Tomas Hosp., 1947-48, resident in medicine, 1948-49; fellow in surgery Hosp. Provincial de Madrid, 1949-51; resident in surgery Boston City Hosp., 1951-52; sec. Coll. Medicine, U. Santo Tomas, 1952-62, chmn. dept. gen. practice, 1962-66, chmn. dept. anatomy, 1966-68, dir. clin. programs, 1968-71, prof. surgery, 1952-80; dir. med. edn. Trinity Gen. Hosp., Manila, 1971-76; dean Med. Sch., v.p. med. affairs Perpetual Help System, Laguna, Philippines, 1979-80, dean emeritus, 1984—; practice medicine specializing in family practice, Reno, 1983—; v.p. acad. affairs Internat. Med. Mgmt. Assocs., Ltd., Berrien Springs, Mich., 1982—; med. dir. Rodoza, Inc., Manila, 1977-80, Perpetual Help Med. Ctr. of Rizal, Philippines, 1977-79; prof. sch. Nursing, La Concordia Coll., Manila, 1970-71, Perpetual Help Coll. Medicine, Laguna, 1977-80, U. Nev., Reno, 1983-84; mem. staff St. Mary's Hosp., Reno; mem. cons. staff Nev. Health Assn. Inc., Hawthorne, Nev. Health Consortium, Babitt, 1984; mem. staff Mount Grant Gen. Hosp., Hawthorne; med. dir. U.S. Army Health Clinic HWAAP, Hawthorne; v.p. U. Santo Tomas Med. Missions Inc., 1960-64, now mem. Author: Integrated Anatomy and Physiology, 1958; Homo Sapiens, 1974; co-author: Health, Preservation and Maintenance, 1961. Pres. Tenpin Bowlers' Assn. Makati, Manila, 1973-74, 77, 79; v.p. Philippine Bowling Congress, Manila, 1979. Med. scholar Institutio Cultura Hispanica, Madrid, 1949, Metro Drug Co., Manila, 1949. Fellow Philippine Coll. Surgeons, Philippine Coll. Gastroenterology, Sociedad de Gastroenterologia y de la Nutricion (Spain), Philippine Hosp. Assn. (pres. Laguna chpt. 1979-80), AMA, Nev. Med. Assn., Washoe County Med. Assn., Assn. Philippine Med. Colls., Philippine Med. Assn., Manila Med. Soc. (bd. dirs. 1955-57), Philippine Heart Assn., Fedn. Pvt. Med. Practitioners (Philippines), Colegio Medico-Farmaceutico de Filipinas, Cath. Physicians Guild of Philippines, U. Santo Tomas Med. Assn. Roman Catholic. Clubs: Altadena Golf (Birmingham); Walker Lake Golf (Hawthorne). Home: 3455 San Mateo Ave Reno NV 89509 Office: US Army Health Clinic HWAAP Hawthorne NV 89415

DEL PAPA, FRANKIE SUE, state official; b. 1949. BA, U. Nev.; JD, George Washington U. Bar: Nev. 1974. Sec. of state Nev., 1987—. Democrat. Office: Office of Secretary of State Capitol Complex Carson City NV 89710 *

DEL SANTO, LAWRENCE A., retail merchandising company executive; b. 1934; married. B.S., U. San Francisco, 1955. With Household Merchandising Inc., Des Plaines, Ill., from 1957, with advt. dept. subs. Vons Grocery Co., 1957-58, asst. advt. mgr., 1958-61, advt. mgr., 1961-68, mgr. sales and mdse., 1968-71, sr. v.p., 1971-73, pres., chief exec. officer, 1973-75, corp. sr. v.p., 1975-79, exec. v.p., from 1979, also bd. dirs.; exec. v.p. Lucky Stores Inc., Dublin, Calif., to 1986, pres., 1986—. Served with U.S. Army, 1955-57. Office: Lucky Stores Inc 6300 Clark Ave Dublin CA 94568

DELUCA, MARLENE ANDEREGG, biochemist, educator; b. LaCrosse, Wis., Nov. 10, 1936; s. Ruben H. and Yerda T. (Harris) Anderegg; m. William D. McElroy, Aug. 28, 1967; 1 child, Eric Gene. BS, Hamline U., 1958; PhD, U. Minn., 1962. Postdoctoral fellow Johns Hopkins U., Balt., 1962-64, asst. prof., 1965-69; asst. prof. biochemistry Georgetown U., Washington, 1969-72; assoc. prof. U. Calif. San Diego, La Jolla, 1972-78, prof., 1978—. Editor: Methods in Enzymology, 1978, Methods in Enzymology Bioluminescence and Chemiluminescence Part B, 1986, Basic Chemical and Analytical Applications, 1981; contbr. articles to profl. jours. Recipient Career Devel. awards NIH, 1967-69, 72-73; named one of Outstanding Young Women in Am. Mem. Am. Chem. Soc., Am. Soc. Biol. Chemistry, Am. Soc. for Photobiology, Sigma Xi. Democrat. Congregationalist. Home: 9651 Blackgold Rd La Jolla CA 92037 Office: U Calif San Diego Chemistry Dept M-001 La Jolla CA 92093

DELUCIA, ELIZABETH DIANE, public relations executive; b. Harbor City, Calif., Nov. 4, 1957; d. Joe A. and Margarita Dominguez; m. Donald Francis DeLucia, June 7, 1980. AA, Los Angeles Harbor Coll., 1979; BA in Pub. Relations, Calif. State U., Long Beach, 1985. Creative sec. Dancer Fitzgerald Sample, Torrance, Calif., 1980-83; jr. acct. exec. in pub. relations Cox and Burch Advt. Co., Newport Beach, Calif., 1983-84; mgr. merchandising and pub. relations Pentel of Am., Ltd., Torrance, Calif., 1984—. Mem. Nat. Speleological Soc. (pub. relations cons. 1982), So. Calif. Grotto. Democrat. Roman Catholic. Office: Pentel Am Ltd 2805 Columbia St Torrance CA 90503

DE LUTIS, DONALD CONSE, investment manager, consultant; b. Rome, N.Y., Apr. 25, 1934; s. Conse R. and Mary (Fasani) D.; m. Ruth L. Schlosser, Sept. 7, 1974; 1 child, Dante. B.S. in Econs., Niagara U., 1956; M.B.A., Boston Coll., 1962. Vice pres. John Nuveen & Co., Inc., San Francisco, 1968-74; acct. exec. Dean Witter & Co., London, 1975-77; sr. investment officer Buffalo Savs. Bank, N.Y., 1978-80; exec. v.p. Robert Brown & Co., Inc., San Francisco, 1980—; exec. v.p., dir. Pacific Securities, Inc., San Francisco, 1980—. Commr. San Francisco Bay Conservation and Devel. Commn., 1983—, State of Calif. Commn. Housing and Community Devel., 1974-77. Served with USAF, 1957-58. Mem. Nat. Assn. Bus. Economists, Nat. Economist Club, Bus. Economists Council, San Francisco Bond Club. Republican. Roman Catholic. Club: San Francisco Press. Office: Robert Brown & Co Inc 655 Montgomery St San Francisco CA 94111

DELWICHE, CONSTANT COLLIN, geobiologist, educator; b. Green Bay, Wis., Nov. 26, 1917; s. Edmund J. and Alice (Collin) D.; m. Alice Kerr, June 21, 1943; children: Norman, Mark, Joseph, James, Richard, Charles. BS, U. Wis., 1940; PhD, U. Calif., Berkeley, 1950. From asst. to assoc. profl. plant biochemistry M. Theodore Kearney Found., U. Calif., Berkeley, 1950-63; prof. geobiology, biochemist Experiment Sta. dept. Land Air and Water Resources U. Calif., Davis, 1963—, dept. chmn., 1965-69. Editor: Nitrification, Denitrification and Atmospheric Nitrous Oxide, 1981; contbr. articles to profl. jours. Served to capt. U.S. Army, 1940-46, ETO, maj. gen. Res. Fellow AAAS; mem. Am. Soc. Microbiology, Soil Sci. Soc. Am. Home: Rt 2 Box 2275 Davis CA 95616 Office: U Calif LAWR Davis CA 95616

DEMARCHI, ERNEST NICHOLAS, aerospace engineering administrator; b. Lafferty, Ohio, May 31, 1939; s. Ernest Costante and Lena Marie (Cireddu) D.; B.M.E., Ohio State U., 1962; M.S. in Engring., UCLA, 1969; m. Carolyn Marie Tracz, Sept. 17, 1960; children—Daniel Ernest, John David, Deborah Marie. With Space div. Rockwell Internat., Downey, Calif., 1962—, engring. mgr., mem. Apollo, Skylab and Apollo-Soyuz missions design team in electronic and elec. systems, mem. mission support team for all Apollo and Skylab manned missions, 1962-74, mem. Space Shuttle design team charge elec. systems equipment, 1974-77, in charge Orbiter Data Processing System, 1977-81, in charge Orbiter Ku Band Communication and Radar System, 1981-85, in charge orbitor elec. power distbr., displays, controls, data processing, 1984-87, in charge space based kinteic energy weapon system, 1987—. Active, YMCA Indian Guide program, 1969-74, bd. dirs., 1971-74; vol. instr. community program of tech. tng. for high-sch. students, 1970-78; youth athletics coach, 1975-76; pres. Little League, 1976-78; bd. dirs. high sch. athletic boosters club, 1980-84. Recipient Apollo Achievement award NASA, 1969, Apollo 13 Sustained Excellent Performance award, 1970, Astronaut Personal Achievement Snoopy award, 1971; Exceptional Service award Rockwell Internat., 1972, Outstanding Contbn. award, 1976; NASA ALT award, 1979; Shuttle Astronaut Snoopy award, 1982; Pub. Service Group Achievement award NASA, 1982; Rockwell Pres.'s award, 1983; registered profl. engr., Ohio. Mem. ASME, Varsity O Alumni Assn. Home: 25311 Maximus St Mission Viejo CA 92691 Office: 12214 Lakewood Blvd Downey CA 90241

DEMARCO, RALPH JOHN, real estate developer; b. N.Y.C., Mar. 22, 1924; s. Frank and Mary (Castriota) DeM.; B.A., Claremont Men's Coll., 1956; m. Arlene Gilbert, July 1, 1945; children—Sheryl DeMarco Grahn, Stephen, Laura DeMarco Wilson. Assoc. John B. Kilroy Co., Riverside, Calif., 1960-64, also mgr. operations Riverside, San Bernardino counties, 1960-64; v.p. Marcus W. Meairs Co., 1964-67; pres. Diversified Properties, Inc., Riverside, 1967-72; v.p. Downey Savs. & Loan Assn. (Calif.), 1972-75; exec. v.p. DSL Service Co., 1972-75; pres. Interstate Shopping Ctrs., Inc., Santa Ana, Calif., 1975—. Mem. City of Riverside Planning Commn., 1955-59, Airport Commn., 1960-70; mem. Urban Land Inst. Served to 1st lt. USAF, 1942-45. Mem. Internat. Council Shopping Ctrs. Home: 23022 Java Sea Dr South Laguna CA 92677 Office: 735 Ohms Way Costa Mesa CA 92627

DEMAREE, BETTY, artist, educator; b. Denver, Oct. 19, 1918; d. Nathaniel and Margaret Elizabeth (Sanderson) Wolfson; m. Dean Clay DeMaree, Jan. 15, 1962; 1 stepchild. Student Cooper Union Sch. Art, 1938-41. Textile designer Am. Textile Co., N.Y.C., 1940-43; self-employed greeting card designer, Los Angeles, 1945-48; self-employed designer, Bolivia, 1948-53; self-employed custom ceramics designer, Denver, 1954-65; self-employed painter, tchr., Denver, 1967—; condr. numerous workshops; judge various art shows; bd. dirs. Rocky Mountain Nat. Watermedia Soc. ann. exhbn. Exhibited in group shows at Southwestern Watercolor Soc., Dallas, 1968-84, Am. Watercolor Soc., N.Y.C., 1976-80, San Diego Watercolor Soc. 1983, Ky. Watercolor Soc., 1984-86, Allied Artists Am., N.Y.C., 1977-78; Rocky Mountain Nat. Watermedia Exhbn., 1975-85, Gallery A, Taos, N.Mex., Cason Gallery, Helena, Mont., La Porta Gallery, Englewood, Colo., Art of Denver Gallery, Parker-Blake Galleries; represented in permanent collections Los Alamos Nat. Lab., United Bank of Denver, Mason, Reuler and Peake, Denver, Central Bank and Trust, Denver, Colo. State U., Fort Collins, Rocky Mountain Energy Corp., Broomfield, Colo., Dwight Energy Data, Natkin & Co., Englewood, Denver, James Inc. Co., Denver, Sheraton Hotel, Ft. Lauderdale, Fla., Combs-Gates Airport, Denver, Harris Bank and Trust, Scottsdale, Ariz., Utah State U., Logan, others. Mem. Southwestern Watercolor Soc. (named Best of Show 1969, selected for travelling show 1969), Am. Watercolor Soc. (Emily Lowe Meml. award 1976), Allied Artists Am. (John Young-Hunter award 1977, Winsor Newton award for watercolor 1978), Audubon Artists Am., Rocky Mountain Nat. Watermedia Soc., Colo. Watercolor Soc. Denver Artists Guild, Colo. Artist Assn. (award 1981, Best of Show award 1986), San Diego Watercolor Soc. Republican. Christian Scientist. Home and Office: Betty DeMaree Studio 4725 W Quincy Ave Denver CO 80236

DEMARTINI, JAMES CHARLES, college professor, veterinarian; b. Los Angeles, Apr. 29, 1942; s. James Paul and Thelma (Lidtka) DeM.; m. Ruth Trayer; children: Mary, Sarah, Amy, Laura. BS, U. Calif., 1964, DVM, 1966, PhD, 1972. Diplomate Am. Coll. Veterinary Pathologists. Veterinary pathologist Intermountain Labs., Salt Lake City, 1972-73; clin. asst. prof. U. Utah, Salt Lake City, 1973-74; asst. prof. Colo. State U., Ft. Collins, Colo., 1974-78, assoc. prof., 1979-85, prof., 1985—. Contbr. articles to profl. jours. Mem. Am. Assn. Advancement Sci., Am. Coll. Veterinary Pathologists, Wildlife Disease Assn., Am. Assn. Pathologists, Sigma Xi. Club: Sierra (San

Francisco). Avocations: backpacking, hiking, photography. Home: 947 Lochness Ct Fort Collins CO 80524 Office: Colo State U Dept Pathology Fort Collins CO 80523

DE MASSA, JESSIE G., librarian. BJ, Temple U.; MLS, San Jose State U., 1967; postgrad., U. Okla., U. So. Calif. Tchr. Palo Alto (Calif.) Unified Sch. Dist., 1966; librarian Antelope Valley Joint Union High Sch. Dist., Lancaster, Calif., 1966-68, ABC Unified Sch. Dist., Artesia, Calif., 1968-72; dist. librarian Tehachapi (Calif.) Unified Sch. Dist., 1972-81; also media specialist, free lance writer, 1981—. Contbr. articles to profl. jours. Fellow Internat. Biog. Assn.; mem. Calif. Media and Library Educators Assn., Calif. Assn. Sch. Librarians (exec. council), AAUW (bull. editor, assoc. editor state bull., chmn. publicity 1955-68), Hon. Fellows John F. Kennedy Library (founding mem.). Home: 9951 Garrett Circle Huntington Beach CA 92646

DEMBE, ALLARD EOMER, safety and standards engineer, insurance executive; b. Cleve., Aug. 11, 1952; s. Harold N. and Shirley E. (Roseman) D.; m. Susan I. Permut, Aug. 15, 1982. BA summa cum laude, Vanderbilt U., 1974; MA, Cornell U., 1977. Lic. profl. engr., Calif.; cert. safety profl., Calif. Instr. Grinnell (Iowa) Coll., 1977-78; loss prevention rep. Liberty Mutual Ins. Co., Bala Cynwyd, Pa., 1978-79, sr. loss prevention rep., 1979-81; indsl. tech. cons. Liberty Mutual Ins. Co., San Francisco, 1981-83, tech. div. dir., 1983, dist. loss prevention mgr., 1983—; mem. adv. com. Calif. Occupational Safety and Health Adminstrn., Sacramento, 1981—. AEC fellow, 1973; Danforth fellow, 1974-77; Alfred P. Sloan fellow, 1974. Fellow Soc. Values in Higher Edn.; mem. Am. Soc. Safety Engrs. (profl.), Soc. Mfg. Engrs. (sr.), Human Factors Soc., Phi Beta Kappa. Jewish. Avocations: religious activities, tennis, volleyball, hiking, camping. Home: 718 W 27th Ave San Mateo CA 94403 Office: Liberty Mutual Ins Co 216 Pine St San Francisco CA 94104

DEMELLO, JOHN LOUIS, psychotherapist, writer; b. São Miguel, Portugal, Nov. 16, 1945; came to U.S., 1948; s. Humberto Medeiros and Deolinda (Gallego) DeM.; m. Gloria Narvaez, Dec. 20, 1978 (div. Apr. 1981); 1 child, Vannessa. BA, Southeast Mass. U., 1969; MSW, U. Wash., 1972; PhD, Columbia Pacific U., 1982. Lic. clin. social worker, Calif. Postgrad. fellow Mt. Zion Hosp., San Francisco, 1972-74; program dir. Marin Found., San Rafael, Calif., 1974-75; clin. social worker U. Calif., San Francisco, 1976-81; counselor Hawaii Job Corps, Hilo, 1982-83; child protective worker Dept. of Social Services, Hilo, 1983-84; psychiat. social worker Hilo Counseling Ctr., 1985—; v.p. U. Calif. Hosp. Worker's Local 1650, San Francisco, 1979, 80. Author: Niagara Curtain, 1984, Cave Roads, 1985, Return of Sebastian's Army, 1986. Dem. state del., Honolulu, 1984, Hilo, 1986, 1st dist. Dem. vice chmn., Hilo, 1986, co-chmn. Sunshine coalition Hawaii Dems., mem. state cen. com. on legislation; treas. Big Island Com. for Peace in Cen. Am., 1986. Mem. Nat. Assn. Social Workers (cert.). Democrat. Club: Chiefie Mehau Tennis (Hilo). Home: 1911 Kalanianaole #407 Hilo HI 96720 Office: Hilo Counseling Ctr 37 Kekaulike Hilo HI 96720

DEMERSMAN, JAMES RICHARD, museum administrator; b. Rochester, N.Y., July 31, 1957; s. Richard Oscar and Carolyn Ruth (Morse) DeM.; m. Pricilla Ann McClellan, Nov. 29, 1980. B.A. in History and Bus., Houghton Coll., 1980. Asst. dir. edn. Genesee Country Village, Rochester, 1980; dir. edn. Hist. Speedwell Village, Morristown, N.J., 1980-83; dir. edn. Rosemount Victorian House Mus., Pueblo, Colo., 1983—, exec. dir.; media judge Nat. History Day, Newark, 1982, 83. Author: (exhibit catalog) Going to the Ball, 1981, Life of a Soldier, 1981; research assoc.: At Speedwell, 1982. Mem. Pueblo Visitor & Conv. Bur., 1983-87. Discover Pueblo Com., 1983-87; treas. Pueblo Arts Council, 1987; mem. bd., pres. Friends of Library, Pueblo, 1986, 87. Mem. Am. Assn. State and Local History (mem. seminars 1981, 83), Am. Assn. for Mus., Mountain-Plains Mus. Assn., Colo.-Wyo. Assn. Museums, Alliance of SW Mus. Educators. Democrat. Presbyterian. Home: 2500 Mountainview Ave Pueblo CO 81008 Office: Rosemount Victorian House Mus 419 W 14th St Pueblo CO 81003

DEMETRESCU, MIHAI CONSTANTIN, computer company executive, scientist; b. Bucharest, Romania, May 23, 1929; s. Dan and Alina (Dragosescu) D.; M.E.E., Poly. Inst. of U. Bucharest, 1954; Ph.D., Romanian Acad. Sci., 1957; m. Agnes Halas, May 25, 1969; 1 child, Stefan. Came to U.S., 1966. Prin. investigator Research Inst. Endocrinology Romanian Acad. Sci., Bucharest, 1958-66; research fellow dept. anatomy UCLA, 1966-67; faculty U. Calif.-Irvine, 1967—, asst. prof. dept. physiology, 1971-78, assoc. researcher, 1978-79, assoc. clin. prof., 1979-83; v.p. Resonance Motors, Inc., Monrovia, Calif., 1972—; pres. Neurometrics, Inc., Irvine, Calif., 1978-82; pres. Lasergraphics Inc., Irvine, 1982-84, chmn., chief exec. officer, 1984—. Mem. com. on hon. degrees U. Calif.-Irvine, 1970-72. Postdoctoral fellow UCLA, 1966. Mem. Internat. Platform Assn., Am. Physiol. Soc., IEEE (sr.). Republican. Contbr. articles to profl. jours. Patentee in field. Home: 20 Palmento Way Irvine CA 92715 Office: 17671 Cowan Ave Irvine CA 92714

DEMETRION-BOATRIGHT, HELEN KATHLEEN, speech pathologist; b. Pomona, Calif., June 6, 1957; d. Nicholas and Starling (Grueser) Demetrion; m. Donald W. Boatright, Dec. 27, 1979. BA, U. LaVerne, 1978; MS, U. Redland, 1982. Lic. speech pathologist, Calif. Speech-lang. specialist Chaffey High Sch., Ontario, Calif., 1979—, Speech-Lang. Devel. Ctr., Buena Park, Calif., 1980; pvt. practice San Bernardino, Calif., 1985—; chmn. Better Hearing and Speech Month, Chaffey High Sch., 1980—, mem. Work Study Project, 1980, chmn. Project Succeed, 1981, mem. Video Tape Mainstream, 1983; advisor Keywanettes, 1984—, SET Club, 1985—. Recipient Tchr. Recognition award Chaffey High Sch., Ontario, 1983; named Outstanding Club Advisor, Kiwanis, 1985. Mem. Calif. Speech Hearing Assn., 1979—, Am. Speech-Lang.-Hearing Assn. (cert.). Democrat. Greek Orthodox.

DE MICHELE, O. MARK, utility company executive; b. Syracuse, N.Y., Mar. 23, 1934; s. Aldo and Dora (Carno) De M.; m. Faye Ann Venturin, Nov. 8, 1957; children: Mark A., Christopher C., Michele M., Julianne; m. Barbara Joan Stanley, May 22, 1982. B.S., Syracuse U., 1955. Mgr. Seal Right Co., Inc., Fulton, N.Y., 1955-58; v.p., gen. mgr. L.M. Harvey Co. Inc., Syracuse, 1958-62; v.p. Niagara Mohawk Power, Syracuse, 1962-78; v.p. Ariz. Pub. Service, Phoenix, 1978-81, exec. v.p., 1981-82, pres., 1982—, dir.; dir. Am. West Airlines. Pres. Jr. Achievement, Syracuse, 1974-75, pres., Phoenix, 1982-83; pres. United Way of Central N.Y., Syracuse, 1978, Ariz. Opera Co., Phoenix, 1981-83, Phoenix Symphony, 1984-86; chmn. bd. Valley of Sun United Way, 1984-86; pres. United Way, Phoenix, 1985-86. Named Outstanding Young Man of Yr. Syracuse Jaycees, 1968. Mem. Phoenix C. of C. (chmn. bd. 1986-87). Republican. Clubs: Phoenix Country, Ariz. (Phoenix). Home: 77 E Missouri Ave Phoenix AZ 85012 Office: Ariz Pub Service Co 411 N Central Ave Phoenix AZ 85036

DEMING, MARY BEARD, environmental specialist, consultant; b. Washington, Sept. 30, 1946; d. Raimon Lewis and Francis Janes (Clark) B.; m. Richard Lynn Deming, June 21, 1969; children: Ann Elizabeth, Laura Janes. BA, Carleton Coll., 1968; MA, U. Chgo., 1971, PhD, 1975. Asst. prof. sociology U. Vt., Burlington, 1974-77; research asst. prof. Social Sci. Research Inst. U. So. Calif., Los Angeles, 1977-81, research assoc. social policy lab. Andrus Gerontology Ctr., 1979-81; sr. market analyst So. Calif. Edison Co., Rosemead, 1981-84, environ. specialist, 1985—; adj. prof. U. Mass., 1984; cons. Burlington Bd. Sch. Commrs., 1976. Contbr. articles to profl. jours. Elder Morningside Presbyn. Ch., Fullerton, Calif., 1986—. NDEA fellow, 1969-72; grantee Vt. Council on Humanities and Pub. Issues, 1976, NIMH, 1979. Mem. Population Assn. Am., Am. Sociol. Assn., Pacific Sociol. Assn., Sociologists for Women in Soc., Sigma Xi. Presbyterian. Avocations: music, crafts, gardening. Home: 705 N Wilson Ave Fullerton CA 92631 Office: So Calif Edison Co PO Box 800 2244 Walnut Grove Ave Rosemead CA 91770

DEMLING, JOSEPH ANTHONY, technical publications supervisor, writing and editing consultant; b. Denver, Mar. 30, 1936; s. Francis Charles Demling and Mary Frances (Kempter) Moss; m. Janice Louise Laub, Aug. 15, 1965 (div. Mar. 12, 1987); children: Joseph Adam, Jennifer Annette, James Andrew. AEE, Colo. Tech. Inst., 1960. Electronics technician Hathaway Instruments, Denver, 1960-61; sr. tech. writer Cushing and Nevell, Denver, 1961-62; tech. publs. engr. Martin Marietta Corp., Denver, 1962-66; writing dept. supr. Tech. Graphics Inc., Denver, 1966-68; sr. writer, editor Honeywell Inc., Littleton, Colo., 1968-79, supr. tech. publs., 1979—; writing cons. Tech. Documentation Assocs., Denver, 1975-78. Writer and editor numerous tech. articles. Served as cpl. USMC, 1954-57. Mem. Mensa (columnist Matrix Mag. of Denver chpt.), Intertel. (contbr. articles to jour.). Avocations: chess, four-wheeling, running, weight training, reading. Home: 10021 W Exposition Dr Lakewood CO 80226 Office: Honeywell Inc Test Instruments Div 4800 E Dry Creek Rd Littleton CO 80122

DE MONSABERT, WINSTON RUSSELL, JR., environmental planning engineer; b. New Orleans, Apr. 22, 1957; s. Winston Russell and Eleanor (Ranson) de M.; m. Sharon Kay Mishler, July 11, 1981; 1 child, W. Russel. BS in Chemistry, U. Md., 1979; MS in Environ. Engring., Purdue U., 1982. Environ. engr. Naval Civil Engring. Lab., Port Hueneme, Calif., 1982-85, environ. program mgr., 1985—. Mem. ASCE, Am. Chem. Soc., Soc. Am. Mil. Engrs., Alpha Chi Sigma. Home: 3240 Landen St Camarillo CA 93010 Office: Naval Civil Engring Lab Port Hueneme CA 93043

DE MONTE-CAMPBELL, ALPHA, writer; b. Munich; came to U.S, 1969; d. Philippe and Vicky (von May-Menzinger) de Monte; m. Robert James Campbell, Dec. 24, 1968. Student, U. Munich, 1957. Author: (novels) It Began in Cannes, 1956, O'Hara, 1963, She Followed Him to Ireland, 1965, In Return for..., 1983; (novelette) The Doll and the Old Man, 1985. Roman Catholic.

DEMOSS, ARLENE ANNAN, speech-language pathologist; b. Boston, Mar. 12, 1937; d. David Paul and Rachael (Epstein) Annan; m. Donald J. Sherman, Apr. 20, 1958 (div. July 1970); children: Lee Sidney, Lori Marcia Raineri; m. Richard Allen DeMoss, Aug. 1, 1982. AA, Colby-Sawyer Coll.; BA, San Jose State U., MA, 1980. Speech-lang. pathologist Evergreen Sch. Dist., San Jose, Calif., 1974—; cons., adv. com. Speech Pathology Dept. San Jose State U., 1981—; interview team for commn. on teaching credentialing, San Jose State U., 1986—. Author: (with others, grant handbook) Parent as Partners: A Guide to Pre-School Language Development, 1984, (legis. handbook) How to Be Pro-Active in a Reactive World, 1986; contbr. articles to infant and teens mags. Mem. Calif. Speech-Lang. Hearing Assn. (adv. com. 1984—, num. com. 1982-84, dir. elect. 1986-88, cert.), Calif. Tchrs. Assn. (pub. relations com. Santa Clara County chpt. 1985—), Evergreen Tchrs. Assn. (membership chairperson Santa Clara Valley chpt. 1974—), Brandeis U. Women's Com. (founding pres. Western region 1966-70, nominating com. 1971). Club: Aprés Ski Club (Mountain View, Calif.) (assoc. editor newsletter 1980-81, Outstanding Service award 1981). Office: Evergreen Sch Dist 3188 Quimby Rd San Jose CA 95148

DEMPSEY, BEVERLY JUNE, university academic administrator, English educator; b. Detroit, Sept. 24, 1932; d. Edgar Rae and Betty Pearl (DeGonia) Luke; m. Cedric Warren Dempsey, Aug. 22, 1953; children: Linda Sue, David Earl, Marcia Kay. AB, Albion Coll., 1954; EdM, U. Ariz., 1967; EdD, U. Houston, 1985. Cert. elem. and secondary tchr., reading specialist, Ariz., Calif., Mich. Tchr. pub. schs. Albion, Mich., 1954-56, 61, Tucson, 1966-67, Stockton, Calif., 1967-69; instr. English and div. chmn. Joaquin Delta Coll., Stockton, 1969-79; assoc. prof. U. Houston, 1979-82; dir. extended univ. and summer seesion U. Ariz., Tucson, 1983—; cons. Maui (Hawaii) Community Coll. Dist., 1977, Tex. Jr. Coll. Assn., 1978. Contbr. chpts. to books, articles to profl. jours. Sec. bd. dirs., exec. com. Palo Verde Hosp., Tucson, 1985-86; exec. com. Palo Verde Mental Health Services, Tucson, 1985-86, also fin. com. Detroit Free Press scholar, 1952, Meth. scholar, 1950-54. Mem. Internat. Reading Assn., Western Coll. Reading and Learning Assn. (pres. 1974-75, v.p., bd. dirs., Disting. Speaker award 1978), Nat. Assn. Devel. Edn. (pres.-elect 1980-81, bd. dirs., cert. merit 1981), Palo Verde Mental Health Assn. , Pi Lambda Theta, Delta Kappa Gamma. Republican. Presbyterian. Avocations: tennis, golf, travel, writing. Office: U Ariz Adminstrn 509 Tucson AZ 85721

DEMPSEY, JULIAN NED, civil engineer; b. Wichita, Kans., Dec. 6, 1942; s. Clevelon and Edna Dempsey; m. Charlene Zeigler, Sept. 1, 1984; children: Karen, Chris. BCE, San Jose State U., 1970, MS in Sanitary Engring., 1971. Pres. Century West Engring. Corp., Bend, Oreg., 1973—; Registered profl. engr., Oreg., Wash., Calif., Nev., Idaho. Vice chmn. Oreg. Commn. on Futures, Salem, 1984—; adv. Cen. Oreg. Econ. Council, Bend., 1984—. Named Small Bus. Entrepreneur Oreg. Bus. mag., 1984; recipient Top 10 Growth award Portland mag., 1985. Mem. Pacific NW Waterworks Assn., Am. Waterworks Assn., NSPE, ASCE, Pacific NW Pollution Control Assn. Republican. Club: City (Portland). Lodge: Rotary. Avocations: travel, skiing, boating. Office: Century West Engring Corp 2121 SW Broadway Suite 300 Portland OR 97201

DEMPSTER, ANTHONY JOHN, display company executive, exhibit designer; b. Los Angeles, Feb. 15, 1942; s. Albert Taylor and Catherine Cajori (Hull) D.; m. Joyce Lynne Kipper, Apr. 20, 1974; children—Adam, Matthew. Student Calif. State U.-Northridge, 1960-62, Art Center Coll. Design, 1962-64, Calif. Inst. Arts, 1965-66. Film designer Tom McGowan Prodns., Los Angeles, 1966; film designer, prodn. illustrator Walt Disney Prodns., 1966-70, Warner Bros. Studios, 1970; art dir., exhibit designer Internat. Displays Inc., Los Angeles, 1970-73; owner, designer Dempster Assocs., Los Angeles, 1973; co-owner, mgr. Carsten Dempster Displays Inc., Los Angeles, 1974—. Active Rep. Nat. Com., Apartment Assn. San Fernando Valley. Mem. Notre Dame Alumni Club, Art Ctr. Alumni Club, Brit. Am. C. of C., Smithsonian Instn., So. Calif. Furniture Mfrs. Assn. Office: Carsten Dempster Displays Inc 11164 Bradley Ave Pacoima CA 91311

DEMPSTER, WILLIAM FRED, computer systems analyst, engineer; b. Berkeley, Calif., Dec. 10, 1940; s. John Ross and Anna Julia (Ramsperger) D.; m. Sue Wight (div. 1966); children: David Allen, Carolyn Sue. BA, U. Calif., Berkeley. Computer programmer Lawrence Berkeley (Calif.) Lab., 1964-66, systems analyst, 1966-69; ranch foreman Synergia Ranch, Santa Fe, 1969-73; dir. Inst. of Ecotechnics, Santa Fe, 1973-85, pres., 1984—; systems engr. Space Biospheres Ventures, Oracle, Ariz., 1985—; expedition chief Amazon River expedition Inst. Ecotechnics, London, and Santa Fe, 1980-81; bd. dirs. Sarbid, Ltd., London. Mem. AAAS, Soc. Mfg. Engrs., The Planetary Soc., Pronatura. Avocation: Japanese bd. game Go.

DEMUTH, ALAN CORNELIUS, lawyer; b. Boulder, Colo., Apr. 29, 1935; s. Laurence Wheeler and Eugenia Augusta (Roach) DeM.; m. Susan McDermott; children—Scott Lewis, Evan Dale, Joel Millard. B.A. magna cum laude, U. Colo., 1958, LL.B., 1961. Bar: Colo. 1961, U.S. Dist. Ct. Colo. 1961, U.S. Ct. Appeals (10th cir.) 1962. Assoc. Akolt, Turnquist, Shepherd & Dick, Denver, 1961-68; ptnr. Akolt, Dick, Rovira, DeMuth & Eiberger, 1968-73, Rovira, DeMuth & Eiberger, 1973-76, DeMuth, Eiberger, Kemp & Backus, 1976-79, DeMuth, Kemp & Backus, 1979-82, DeMuth & Kemp, 1982—. Conf. atty. Rocky Mountain Conf. United Ch. of Christ, 1970—; bd. dirs. Friends of U. Colo. Library, 1978-86; bd. dirs., sponsor Denver Boys Inc. Mem. ABA, Colo. Bar Assn., Denver Bar Assn., Phi Beta Kappa, Sigma Alpha Epsilon, Phi Delta Phi. Republican. Mem. United Ch. of Christ. Club: Denver Athletic. Lodge: Rotary. Office: DeMuth & Kemp 718 17th St Suite 1600 Denver CO 80202

DENARO, ROBERT PETER, aerospace engineer; b. Glen Rock, N.J., Jan. 28, 1949; s. Angelo and Helene Marie (Warschauer) D.; m. Carolyn Rae McSemek, June 28, 1975; children—Brian , Tracy, Andrew. B.S. in Engring. Scis., U.S. Air Force Acad., 1971; M.S. with distinction in Elec. Engring., Air Force Inst. of Tech., Dayton, Ohio, 1973; M.S. in Systems Mgmt., U. So. Calif., 1978. Commd. 2d lt. U.S. Air Force, 1971, advanced through grades to capt., 1975, resigned, 1979; sr. engr. Systems Control Inc., Palo Alto, Calif., 1979-81; founder dir., TAU Corp., Los Gatos, Calif., v.p., mgr. Nav. Systems div. 1981—. Decorated Air Force Commendation medal, Air Force Meritorious Service medal. Mem. IEEE, AIAA, Inst. Nav., Eta Kappa Nu. Republican. Clubs: Kona Kai Swim and Racquet, Los Gatos Athletic. Contbr. numerous articles to tech. jours. Office: 485 Alberto Way Los Gatos CA 95030

DE NEUFVILLE, JUDITH INNES, planning educator; b. Boston, Jan. 18, 1942; d. Charles John and Vera Fern (Jensen) Innes; m. Richard de Neufville, May 23, 1964 (div. 1979); 1 child, Robert Eustace. AB, Radcliffe Coll., 1963; PhD, MIT, 1973. Legis. asst. U.S. Congress, Washington, 1965-66; asst. prof. Harvard U., Cambridge, Mass., 1974; asst. prof., assoc. program dir. Tufts U., Medford, Mass., 1975; assoc. prof. city and regional planning U. Calif., Berkeley, 1976—, chmn. faculty Coll. Environ. Design, 1982-83. Author: Social Indicators and Public Policy, 1975; editor/author: The Land Use Policy Debate in the U.S., 1981; assoc. editor Jour. Planning Edn. and Research., 1983—. Mem. Albany (Calif.) Waterfront Com., 1984—. Mem. Assn. Collegiate Schs. Planning (exec. bd. 1984—, planning accreditation bd. 1987—). Avocations: skiing, sailing, hiking.

DENKE, CONRAD WILLIAM, motion picture producer and dir.; b. Cottonwood, Ariz., July 23, 1947; s. Lee Ernest and Barbara Ann (Russell) D.; B.A. in Radio-TV Communications and Psychology, U. Wash., 1969; m. Laura Lee Nielson, Aug. 22, 1975; 1 son, Alexander Lee. Dir., Sta. KCTS-TV, Seattle, 1967-69; dir. prodn. Cinema Assos., Seattle, 1973-78; pres. Am. Motion Picture Co., Seattle, Am. Video Lab., Studio One, Am. Tape Duplicating Co., 1978—; owner Studio One, motion picture sound stage. Subcom. chmn. cultural arts com. Seattle C. of C., 1979—; bd. dirs. Seattle Children's Ballet, 1980—. Served with USAF, 1969-73. Recipient Cine Golden Eagle award Council on Internat. Nontheatrical Events, 1977, 79, Silver Cindy award Info. Film Producers Am., 1977, Gold Camera award U.S. Indsl. Film Festival, 1978. Mem. Internat. TV Assn. (dir. Seattle chpt. 1980—, chpt. pres. 1982-83), Wash. Film and Video Assn. (bd. dirs.), Associated Latter Day Media Artists (pres. Seattle chpt.), AICP (v.p. N.W. chpt. 1986—). Republican. Mormon. Dir. and editor documentary: More Than Bows and Arrows, 1978 (various awards including Western Heritage Arts award for dir. best Western documentary 1978); producer TV series Adventures on Sinclair Island; co-inventor process to transfer slide programs to film. Office: Am Motion Picture Co 7023 15th NW Seattle WA 98117

DENKE, PAUL HERMAN, aircraft engineer; b. San Francisco, Feb. 7, 1916; s. Edmund Herman and Ella Hermine (Riehl) D.; m. Beryl Ann Lincoln, Feb. 10, 1940; children—Karen Denke Mottaz, Claudia Denke Tesche, Marilyn Denke Kunert. B.C.E., U. Calif.-Berkeley, 1937, M.C.E., 1939. Registered profl. engr., Calif. Stress engr. Douglas Aircraft Co., Santa Monica, Calif., 1940-62, mgr. structural mechanics Long Beach, Calif., 1962-65, chief sci. computing, 1965-71, chief structures engr. methods and devel., 1972-78, chief scientist structural mechanics, 1979-84, staff mgr. MDC fellow, 1985—; mem. faculty dept. engring. UCLA, 1941-50. Assoc. fellow AIAA; mem. Soc. Automotive Engrs. (Arch T. Colwell Merit award 1966, IAE Outstanding Engr. Merit award 1985), Sigma Xi, Tau Beta, Chi Epsilon. Democrat. Pioneered and developed finite element method of structural analysis; author numerous technical papers. Home: 32646 Coastsite Dr Rancho Palos Verdes CA 90274

DENMARK, LAWRENCE M., psychologist; b. Bklyn., Jan. 10, 1946; s. Bernard and Claire P. (Katz) D.; m. Raina M. Moskowitz, Oct. 20, 1968; children—Abrahan, Miriam, Daniel. B.S., NYU, 1968, M.A., 1969; Ed.D., U. No. Colo., 1978. Lic. psychologist, Colo. Psychologist, The Point, Ft. Collins, Colo., 1973-75, Help Ctr., Somerset, Pa., 1975-77, Larimer County Mental Health, Ft. Collins, 1977-83, Poudre Valley Hosp., 1983—; pvt. practice psychology, Ft. Collins, 1978—; cons. organizational devel., Colo., 1978—; clin. dir. Larico Ctr. Youth Addictions; instr. Colo. State U., 1977—. Bd. dirs. Larimer County Council on Alcholism, 1978—, Island Grove Ctr., Greeley, Colo., 1978—; mem. program devel. com. Larico Youth Homes. 1977—. Mem. Am. Psychol. Assn. Democrat. Jewish. Lodge: Lions. Office: 141 S College Ave Fort Collins CO 80524

DENMON, PEARLEN BURNETT STRAWTHER, educator; b. Whaton County, Tex., Jan. 1; d. James and Almer Lee (Brown) Strawther; m. J.C. Denmon, Mar. 30, 1950; 1 child, Phillis Pearl. B.A., Tillotson-Huston Coll., 1947; postgrad. Tex. So. U., summers, 1950-54, San Diego State U., 1962-66, Long Beach U., 1974-75. Cert. gen. secondary tchr., spl. secondary tchr in Home Econs., Calif., Tex. Tchr., Woodsboro Ind. Sch. Dist., 1947-51, San Diego United Sch. Dist., 1968—; Bell Jr. High Sch., 1985-86. Recipient Cert. of Appreciation, United Negro Coll. Fund, 1980. Mem. Am. Home Econs. Assn., Calif. Home Econs. Assn. (state chmn. clothing and textile 1969-71, state chmn. health and welfare 1972-74), San Diego Tchrs. Assn., Calif. Tchrs. Assn., Alpha Kappa Alpha (grad. advisor Epsilon Xi Omega chpt. 1981-83). Baptist. Office: San Diego High Sch San Diego CA 92117

DENNEY, AL B., JR., motion picture producer; b. Waco, Tex., Mar. 15, 1935; s. Albert B. and Mary E. (Fason) D.; m. Christine Denney; 1 son, Rick L. Student San Antonio Jr. Coll., 1953, 57-58, Tex. Chiropractic Coll., 1953, 57-58. Screen writer, newsreel cameraman; dir., cinematographer Ind. Artists Prodns., Winnetka, Calif., 1965—, owner, producer, distbr., 1970—; owner/broker DenReal Co., 1961—; owner/designer The Dennehy Touch, 1972—. Served with USMC, 1953-56. Mem. Internat. Photographers, Internat. Alliance Theatrical Stage Employees, Dirs. Guild Am. (dir. 1978—), Am. Film Inst., Am. TV Arts and Scis., Am. Soc. Lighting Dirs., Underwater Photog. Soc., Internat. Platform Assn., VFW, Am. Legion. Republican. Club: Elks. Office: 20360 Haynes St Winnetka CA 91306

DENNEY, GARY EVANS, association executive; b. Farmersburg, Ind., Apr. 17, 1934; s. Richard Elias and Helen Marie (Hopewell) D.; m. Joann Farley, Dec. 4, 1954; children: Teresa, Kimberly, Richard, Kristine, Robert. Student, Ind. State U., 1954-56, Butler U., 1957-58, Inst. Organizational Mgmt., 1970-75. Asst. advt. staff mem. Citizen Gas, Indpls., 1954-56; asst. advt. mgr. The Flintkote Co., Los Angeles, 1956-64; assoc. dir. So. Calif. Dental Assn., Los Angeles, 1964-73, San Diego Med. Soc., 1973—. Mng. editor Jour. So. Calif. Dental Assn., 1964-73, San Diego Physician Mag., 1973—. Bd. dirs. San Diego Blood Bank, San Diego, 1975-81. Served with USMCR, 1952-59. Mem. Profl. Conv. Mgmt. Assn., Am. Assn. Med. Soc. Exec., San Diego Soc. Assn. Execs. (pres. 1974-76), Western Conf. Assn. Execs. (chmn. 1977). Republican. Clubs: San Diego Yacht, Santa Monica Yacht. Avocations: yachting, traveling. Home: 874 Loma Valley Pl San Diego CA 92106 Office: San Diego County Med Soc PO Box 23581 San Diego CA 92123

DENNEY, TALBERT L., real estate investment broker, antique and classic automobile dealer; b. Leedey, Okla., Apr. 23, 1928; s. James Harden and Myrtle Mae (Eaton) D.; student pub. schs., Stockton, Calif.; m. Barbara Pilcher, Feb. 17, 1951; children: Melanie Ann, Monica Susan. Owner cleaning co., Portland, Oreg. and Santa Barbara, Calif., 1959-67; co-founder, pres. Servpro Industries, Inc., Rancho Cordova, Calif., 1967-78, chmn. bd. 1978-84; condr. seminars on principles of success. Served with U.S. Army, 1950-52. Mem. Am. Mgmt. Assn., Internat. Franchise Assn, Airplane Owners and Pilots Assn., Am. Bonanza Soc. Office: PO Box 1648 Gardnerville NV 89410

DENNING, GREGORY JOHN, real estate investment executive; b. Coos Bay, Oreg., Jan. 2, 1946; s. Jack and Evelyn T. (Tretter) D.; m. Cheryl L. Topham (div.). B.A. in Psychology and Sociology, Northeastern Ill. U., Chgo., 1973. With Sta. KWRO, Inc., Coquille, Oreg., 1962-64; sales rep. Mead Papers, Chgo., 1965-67; asst. sales/mktg. mgr. Arvey Corp., Chgo., 1968-72; regional sales mgr. Emerson Electric Co., Chgo. and Seattle, 1973-75; nat. sales mgr. Manoir Internat., Chgo., 1976-78; regional mgr. Becton-Dickinson Co., 1978-80; investment counselor Baird and Warner, Chgo., 1981-82; ptnr., v.p., Equest Real Estate and Fin. Corp., Chgo., 1982-84; v.p. Oak Brook Capital Corp., Ill., 1985-86; mgr. Property Mgmt. Services, Inc., Vancouver, Wash., 1986—. Recipient numerous top sales producer awards. Mem. Chgo. Symphony Soc. Clubs: Gold Coast Ski, Chgo. (v.p. 1976-79). Home: 15214 NE 76th St Vancouver WA 98682 Office: Property Mgmt Services Inc 1104 Main Vancouver WA 98660

DENNING, MICHAEL MARION, computer company executive; b. Durant, Okla., Dec. 22, 1943; s. Samuel M. and Lula Mae (Waitman) D.; m. Suzette Karin Wallance, Aug. 10, 1968 (div. 1979); children—Lila Monique, Tanya Kerstin, Charlton Derek; m. Donna Jean Hamel, Sept. 28, 1985; 1 child, Caitlin Shannon. Student USAF Acad., 1963; B.S., U. Tex., 1966; B.S., Fairleigh Dickinson U., 1971; M.S., Columbia U., 1973. Mgr. systems IBM, White Plains, N.Y., 1978-79, mgr. service and mktg., San Jose, Calif., 1979-81; nat. market support mgr. Memorex Corp., Santa Clara, Calif., 1981, v.p. mktg., 1981-82; v.p. mktg. and sales Icot Corp., Mountain View, Calif., 1982-83; exec. v.p. Phase Info. Machines Corp., Scottsdale, Ariz., 1983-84; exec. v.p. Tricom Automotive Dealer Systems Inc., Hayward, Calif., 1985—; pres. ADS Computer Services, Inc., Toronto, Ont., Can., 1985—. Served with USAF, 1962-66; Vietnam. Mem. Phi Beta Kappa, Lambda Chi Alpha (pres. 1965-66). Republican. Methodist. Home: 959 Shoreline Dr San Mateo CA 94404 Office: 3400 Arden Rd Hayward CA 94545

DENNING, MITCHELL EDWARD, educational administrator, teacher; b. Los Angeles, Sept. 8, 1941; s. Ralph Edward and Pearl Genevieve (Mitchell) D.; m. Mary Catherine McGee, Aug. 22, 1964; children: Elizabeth, Lisa, Robert. BA, Westmont Coll., 1963; MA, San Francisco State Coll., 1971; postgrad., Gonzaga U. Cert. elem. and secondary tchr. Tchr. pub. schs. Torrance, Calif., 1964-65, Mt. Diablo Sch. Dist., Concord, Calif., 1965-74; asst. prin. Clatskanie (Oreg.) High Sch., 1974-77, West Valley High Sch., Spokane, Wash., 1977-79; dir. inst. programs Ednl. Service Dist. 101, Spokane, 1979—; prin. Juvenile Detention Sch., Spokane, 1986—. Elder Northview Bible Ch., Spokane, 1983-85, 87—. Mem. Wash. State Assn. Supervision and Cirriculum Devel. (conf. chmn. 1984-86), Wash. Assn. Sch. Adminstrs. (chmn. profl. devel. com. 1983-84). Republican. Avocations: fishing, camping, tennis. Office: Ednl Service Dist 101 W 1025 Indiana Spokane WA 99205

DENNIS, BRIAN CHRISTOPHER, statistician; b. Des Moines, Oct. 8, 1952; s. Lawrence Edward and Lorraine May (Bradt) D.; m. Barbara Ann Bajusz, Feb. 25, 1978 (div. Dec. 1981); m. Virginia Lee Vanderschaaf, June 9, 1984; 1 child, Christopher John. BA, Roger Williams Coll., 1973; MA, Pa. State U., 1981, PhD, 1982. Research asst. Pa. State U., University Park, 1976-81, grad. fellow, 1977-78; asst. prof. forestry, stats. U. Idaho, Moscow, 1981—, mem. staff stats. cons. ctr., 1982—. Contbr. articles to profl. jours. Nat. Wildlife Fedn. fellow 1976; recipient Outstanding Research award Coll. Forestry U. Idaho, 1986. Mem. AAAS, Am. Statis. Assn., Resource Modeling Assn., Sierra Club, Friends of the Earth, Pa. State U. Outing Club, Sigma Xi (U. Idaho Faculty Research Paper award 1985), Phi Kappa Phi. Democrat. Avocations: mountaineering, backpacking, classical piano. Home: 985 Colt Rd Moscow ID 83843 Office: U Idaho Dept Forest Resources Moscow ID 83843

DENNIS, DOUGLAS ALAN, orthopedic surgeon; b. Toledo, Apr. 20, 1954; s. Ronald I. and Donna M. (Canning) D.; m. Debra L. Russell, June 18, 1976; children: Kendall N., Travis R. BS, Bowling Green State U., 1976; MD, Med. Coll. of Ohio, 1979. Lic. physician, Ohio, Colo.; Diplomate Nat. Bd. Med. Examiners. Resident in orthopedic surgery Ohio State U., Columbus, 1979-84; fellow in orthopedic surgery St. Joseph Hosp., Denver, 1984-85; orthopedic surgeon Joint Implant Surgeons, Columbus, 1985-86, Denver Orthopedic Clinic, 1986—; clin. instr. div. orthopedic surgery Ohio State U., Columbus, 1980—. Contbr. articles to profl. jours. Mem. AMA, Ohio Orthopedic Soc., Columbus Orthopedic Soc., Denver Med. Soc., Ohio State Med. Assn. Republican. Presbyterian. Avocations: tennis, running, gardening, piano. Home: 865 Aster Way Golden CO 80401 Office: Denver Orthopedic Clinic 2005 Franklin St #550 Denver CO 80205

DENNIS, EDWARD ALAN, chemistry educator; b. Chgo., Aug. 10, 1941; s. Sol E. and Ruth (Marks) D.; m. Martha S. Greenberg; Mar. 30, 1969; children: Jennifer, Evan, Andrew. BA, Yale U., 1963; MA, Harvard U., 1965, PhD, 1968. Research fellow Harvard Med. Sch., Boston, 1967-69, vis. prof., 1983-84; asst. prof. chemistry U. Calif.-San Diego, La Jolla, 1970-75, assoc. prof., 1975-81, prof., 1981—, vice chmn. dept. chemistry, 1984—; mem. NSF adv. panels, 1981-85. Editor: Methods in Enzymology Cumulative Indexes, 1975—; contbr. over 100 articles to profl. jours. Guggenheim fellow, 1983-84; grantee NSF, 1970—, NIH, 1970—. Fellow AAAS; mem. Biophys. Soc. (chmn. biopolymers subgroup 1981-82), Am. Chem. Soc., Am. Soc. Biol. Chemists (mem. com. 1979-81), N.Y. Acad. Sci., Sigma Xi, Alpha Chi Sigma Chem. Home: 2731 Glenwick Pl La Jolla CA 92037 Office: U Calif-San Diego Dept Chemistry M-001 La Jolla CA 92093

DENNISON, RONALD WALTON, consulting engineer; b. San Francisco, Oct. 23, 1944; s. S. Mason and Elizabeth Louise (Hatcher) D.; m. Sandra Lee Johnson; children—Ronald, Frederick. B.S. in Physics and Math., San Jose State U., 1970, M.S. in Physics, 1972. Physicist, Memorex, Santa Clara, Calif., 1970-71; sr. engr. AVCO, San Jose, Calif., 1972-73; advanced devel. engr. Perkin Elmer, Palo Alto, Calif., 1973-75; staff engr. Hewlett-Packard, Santa Rosa, Calif., 1975-79; program gen. mgr. Burroughs, Westlake Village, Calif., 1979-82; dir. engring., founder EIKON, Simi Valley, Calif., 1982-85. Author tech. publs. Served to sgt. USAF, 1963-67. Mem. IEEE, Am. Vacuum Soc., Internat. Soc. Hybrid Microelectronics, Am. Nat. Standards Inst. (com. rigid disks), Semiconductor Equipment and Materials Inst. Republican. Methodist. Mem. Aircraft Owners and Pilots Assn., Internat. Comanche Soc., Ventura County Aviators Assn. Home: 2764 Granvia Place Thousand Oaks CA 91360

DENNISON, TERRY ALAN, consultant; b. Milw., Jan. 8, 1947; s. Willard Lawrence and Delphia Marie (Willis) D.; m. Lynn Celeste Kovacic, Mar. 30, 1974. B.A., U. Wis., 1969, M.B.A., 1972. C.P.A., Ill. Vice pres. systems devel. Ins. Computing Corp., Madison, Wis., 1971-72; v.p., mgr. investment tech. and investment analytical services divs. Continental Ill. Nat. Bank & Trust Co., Chgo., 1972-84; v.p., mgr. data processing div. Wilshire Assocs., Santa Monica, Calif., 1984—. Mem. Am. Inst. CPA's, Ill. Soc. CPA's. Office: Wilshire Assocs 1299 Ocean Ave Suite 700 Santa Monica CA 90401

DENNY, BREWSTER CASTBERG, educator, university dean; b. Seattle, Sept. 5, 1924; s. Merle Wilson and Margaraith (Castberg) D.; m. Patricia Virginia Sollitt, June 14, 1950; 1 child, Maria Janet. A.B., U. Wash., 1945; M.A., Fletcher Sch. Law and Diplomacy, 1948, Ph.D., 1959. Instr. Mass. Inst. Tech., 1948-52; with Office of Sec. of Def., 1952-60; profl. staff mem. Sub-Com. on Nat. Policy Machinery, U.S. Senate, 1960-61; asso. prof. pub. affairs U. Wash., 1961-64, prof. pub. affairs, 1964—, 1st dir. Grad. Sch. Pub. Affairs, 1962-68, 1st dean, 1968-80, dean emeritus, 1980—, chmn. marine affairs bd., 1972-79; U.S. rep. to 23d gen. assembly UN, 1968; cons. to RAND Corp., 1961-68; mem. vis. com. dept. govt. Harvard, 1967-72; mem. Presdl. Adv. Council on Intergovtl. Personnel Policy, 1971-74; chmn. Gov.'s Task Force on Exec. Orgn., 1968-72; presdl. mem. U.S.-P.R. Commn. on Status of P.R., 1964-66; mem. bd. sci. and tech. in devel. Nat. Acad. Scis., 1976-81, co-chmn. Korean com. on sci. and tech., 1977-82. Author: Seeing American Policy Whole, 1985; contbr. to Am. Polit. Sci. Rev., Sci., Pub. Adminstrn. Rev.; author, co-author, editor articles, books, chpts., and reports. Trustee 20th Century Fund, 1975—, vice chmn., 1982-86, chmn., 1986—. Served to ensign USNR, 1943-46; to lt. 1952-54. Mem. UN Assn. U.S.A. (mem. nat. policy panel on UN capabilities in the 1970's 1970-71), Nat. Acad. Pub. Adminstrn., Am. Soc. for Pub. Adminstrn., Am. Polit. Sci. Assn., Council Fgn. Relations, AAAS (com. on new directions 1975-78, charter mem. com. on sci. and pub. policy 1968-72, com. on arms control 1980—), Nat. Assn. Schs. Pub. Affairs and Adminstrn. (pres. 1968-69). Home: 2021 1st Ave Seattle WA 98121 Office: U Wash Grad Sch Pub Affairs DP-30 Seattle WA 98195

DENOVA, DOLORES THERESA, business educator; b. Baton Rouge, La., Jan. 1, 1931; d. Theodore Florencio and Alvina Loretta (Cassagne) Crespo; m. Charles C. Denova, Jan. 27, 1951; children: Charlene Clare, Bruce Philip, Keith Louis. AA, San Diego City Coll., 1958; BS, Calif. State U., Long Beach, 1968; MA, Calif. State U., Los Angeles, 1970. Cert. community coll. instr., Calif. Instr. bus. Cerritos (Calif.) Coll., 1971, Long Beach City Coll., 1971-77, El Camino Coll., Torrance, Calif., 1971-87, Los Angeles Trade Tech. Coll., 1975-76, Cypress (Calif.) Coll., 1979-80, Calif. State U., Los Angeles, 1980-81, Santa Monica (Calif.) Coll., 1975-87, Los Angeles Harbor Coll., Wilmington, Calif., 1975—; dir. programs for unemployed Office Automation/Word Processing Program, State of Calif., Los Angeles, 1986—; cons. curriculum Los Angeles Harbor Coll., 1978-79, Long Beach City Coll., 1980; presenter workshops on mainstreaming physically handicapped student. Editor Bus. Tchrs.'s Newsletter, 1984-86. Mem. Assn. Info. Systems Profls., Internat. Bus. Edn. Assn., Nat. Bus. Edn. Assn., Western Bus. Edn. Assn., Calif. Bus. Edn. Assn., Phi Kappa Phi, Delta Pi Epsilon, Theta Alpha Delta (v.p. 1979-80, pres. 1981-83, 87—). Home: 729 N Paulina Ave Redondo Beach CA 90277 Office: Los Angeles Harbor Coll 1111 Figueroa Pl Wilmington CA 90744

DENT, CHARLES ALLAN, radio communications executive; b. Edmonton, Alta., Can., July 20, 1951; s. Ivor Graham and Aileen (Anderson) D.; m. Eileen Della Siega, Aug. 29, 1981. BA, U. Alta., 1976. Exec. asst. City of Yellowknife, N.W.T., Can., 1976-79; pres., gen. mgr. Sta. CJCD, Yellowknife, 1979—. Alderman City of Yellowknife, 1984-85; pres. N.W.T. Assn. Municipalities, 1984-85.

DENT, ERNEST DUBOSE, JR., physician; b. Columbia, S.C., May 3, 1927; s. E. Dubose and Grace (Lee) D.; student Presbyn. Coll., 1944-45; M.D., Med. Coll. S.C., 1949; m. Dorothy McCalman, June 16, 1949; children—Christopher, Pamela; m. 2d, Karin Frehse, Sept. 6, 1970. Intern U.S. Naval Hosp., Phila., 1949-50; resident pathology USPHS Hosp., Balt., 1950-54; chief pathology USPHS Hosp., Norfolk, Va., 1954-56; asso. pathology Columbia (S.C.) Hosp., 1956-59; pathologist Columbia Hosp., S.C. Baptist Hosp., also dir. labs., 1958-69; with Straus Clin. Labs., Los Angeles, 1969-72; staff pathologist St. Joseph Hosp., Burbank, Calif., Hollywood (Calif.) Community Hosp., 1969-72; dir. labs. Meml. Hosp. of Glendale, 1972—. Diplomate clin. pathology and pathology anatomy Am. Bd. Pathology. Mem. Am. Cancer Soc., AMA, Los Angeles County Med. Assn. (pres. Glendale dist. 1980-81), Calif. Med. Assn. (councillor 1984—), Am. Soc. Clin. Pathology, Coll. Am. Pathologists (assemblyman S.C. 1965-67; mem. publs. com. bull. 1968-70), Los Angeles Soc. Pathologists (trustee 1984—), Los Angeles Acad. Medicine, S.C. Soc. Pathologists (pres. 1967-69). Lutheran. Author papers nat. med. jours. Home: 1526 Blue Jay Way Los Angeles CA 90069 Office: 1420 S Central Ave Glendale CA 91204

DENTON, KAREN, sociologist, consultant; b. Stamford, N.Y., Feb. 15, 1949; d. Hiram McKenzie and Mary Lousia (Baldwin) D. BA, SUNY, Oswego, 1971; MSW, Syracuse U., 1974; PhD, U. Utah, 1984. Cert. social worker, Utah. Social worker Jewish Family Service Bur., Syracuse, N.Y., 1974-77; asst. prof. U. Utah, Salt Lake City, 1977-78; program mgr. Salt Lake City Aging Ctr. Health Screening Ctr. U. Utah, 1983-86; adminstr. Sr. Day Ctr., Salt Lake City, 1978-79; cons. sociology Salt Lake City, 1986—; bd. dirs. Multi Ethnic Housing Corp., Salt Lake City; co-founder Older Women's League of Salt Lake City, 1984—; cons. St. Joseph's Villa, Salt Lake City, 1985—, State Div. on Alcohol and Drugs, 1980-82; co-chmn. Gynecology Teaching Assn., 1980—; adj. asst. prof. sociology U. Utah, 1984—. Editor with Wadsworth Pub. Co., Belmont, Calif., 1980—. Campaign worker Frances Farley polit. campaigns, Salt Lake City, 1984, 86, Palmer DePaulis for mayor, 1986; active nuclear disarmament efforts, Salt Lake City, 1986—. Nominated for Superior Teaching award U. Utah, 1986; grantee Marrines S. Eccles Found., 1984—, Bamberger Found., 1985-86. Mem. Internat. Network for Social Network Analysis, Nat. Assn. Social Workers, Am. Sociol. Assn., Am. Soc. Aging, Rural Am. Women, Sociologists for Women in Soc., Utah Sierra Club (registered lobbyist). Democrat. Avocations: weaving, tennis, skiing, hiking, biking. Home and Office: 161 F St Salt Lake City UT 84103

DENTON, MARK, ballet company executive; b. Boston, July 19, 1949; s. Clarence and Elizabeth Jane (Silver) D. AB, Kenyon Coll., 1972; MBA, UCLA, 1976. Gen. mgr. Oakland Ballet Co., Calif.; Asst. editor G.P. Putnam and Sons, N.Y.C., 1972-74; asst. dir. San Francisco Art Commn., Neighborhood Arts Program, 1976-77, dir., 1977-80; gen. mgr. Oakland (Calif.) Ballet Co., 1980—. Mem., site visitor Calif. Arts Council Dance Panel; mem. festivals and spl. events panel Oakland Arts Council; mem., then pres. Bay Area Dance Coalition.; advisor Mgmt. Ctr. Office: Oakland Ballet Co 2700 MacArthur Blvd Oakland CA 94602

DENTON, SHELA IVA, health science association executive; b. Aug. 27, 1934. Student, Moravian Coll., 1952-53, Ithaca Coll., 1953-55, Bklyn. Coll., 1956-58. Cert. in AAMA, CAE. V.p. Fulton Gold Copr., N.Y.C.; asst. editor/elected sec. Nat. Assn. Phys. Therapists, Inc., West Covina, Calif., 1978-80, exec. dir., 1978—. Recipient Louis M. London Adminstrv. award, 1980. Address: Nat Assn of Physical Therapists PO Box 367 West Covina CA 91793

DENVER, DANIEL JOSEPH, utilities executive, nuclear engineer; b. N.Y.C., Dec. 21, 1944; s. Daniel Joseph and Katherine Ann (Boland) D.; m. Maureen Diane Conroy, June 11, 1966; children: Daniel Thomas, Molly Kathryn, Tammy Maureen, Katherine Eileen. Registered profl. engr., Va. Scientist Westinghouse Bettis Atomic Power Lab., West Mifflin, Pa., 1967-71; assoc. engr. Pub. Service Electric and Gas Co., Newark, 1971-73; sr. reactor physicist Yankee Atomic Electric Co., Westboro, Mass., 1973-77; v.p. ops. Energy, Inc., Idaho Falls, 1977. Mem. fin. com. Town of Holliston, Mass., 1975-76. Fellow Atomic Energy Commn. MIT, 1966-67. Mem. Am. Nuclear Soc., ASME. Roman Catholic. Avocation: photography. Home: 2907 Laguna Dr Idaho Falls ID 83401 Office: Energy Inc One Energy Way Idaho Falls ID 83401

DE ORTO, BARBARA ROSE, correctional educator; b. San Diego, Mar. 5, 1927; d. Kenneth Ries Reichert and Charlotte Bernice (Muckler) Rosegrant, m. Russell Clarence De Orto, Dec. 13, 1947; children: Allen Ries (dec.), Kenneth Charles, David Allen, Joanne Michelle. BA, U. Calif., Riverside, 1976. Cert. Ryan multisubject life teaching credential; ordained to ministry Ch. of Gospel of Truth, 1986. Substitute tchr. Corona (Calif.) Norco Unified Sch. Dist., 1973-76, adult edn. ESL, 1976-78; correctional educator Calif. Inst. For Men, Chino, Calif., 1976—; cons. curriculum Calif. Dept. Corrections, Corrections Adv. Commn. on Edn., 1984-86. Avocations: miniatures, needlework.

DEPAOLIS, POTITO UMBERTO, food co. exec.; b. Mignano, Italy, Aug. 28, 1925; s. Giuseppe A. and Filomena (Macchiaverna) deP.; Vet. Dr., U. Naples, 1948; Libera Docenza, Ministero Pubblica Istruzione (Rome, Italy), 1955; m. Marie A. Caronna, Apr. 10, 1965. Came to U.S., 1966, naturalized, 1970. Prof. food service Vet. Sch., U. Naples, Italy, 1948-66; retired, 1966; asst. prof. A titre Benevole Ecole Veterinaire Alfort, Paris, France, 1956; vet. inspector U.S. Dept. Agr., Omaha, 1966-67; sr. research chemist Grain Processing Corp., Muscatine, Iowa, 1967-68; v.p., dir. product devel. Reddi Wip, Inc., Los Angeles, 1968-72; with Kubro Foods, Los Angeles, 1972-73, Shade Foods, Inc., 1975—; pres. Vegetable Protein Co., Riverside, Calif., 1973—, Tima Brand Food Co., 1975—, Dr. Tima Natural Foods, 1977—. Fulbright scholar Cornell U., Ithaca, N.Y., 1954; British Council scholar, U. Reading, Eng., 1959-60; postdoctoral research fellow NIH, Cornell U., 1963-64. Mem. Inst. Food Technologists, Italian Assn. Advancement Sci., AAAS, Vet. Med. Assn., Biol. Sci. Assn. Italy, Italian Press Assn., Greater Los Angeles Press Club. Contbr. articles in field to prol. jours. Patentee in field. Home: 131 Groverton Pl Bel Air Los Angeles CA 90077 Office: 8570 Wilshire Blvd Beverly Hills CA 90211 also: 6878 Beck Ave North Hollywood CA 91605

DEPAOLO, DONALD JAMES, earth science educator; b. Buffalo, N.Y., Apr. 12, 1951; s. Dominic James and Lorraine Marie (Nassiff) DeP.; m. Geraldine Sue Adler, Apr. 14, 1973 (div. Oct. 1984); 1 child, Tara Michelle; m. Bonnye Lynn Ingram, Aug. 24, 1985. BS in Geology, SUNY, Binghamton, 1973; PhD in Geology, Calif. Inst. Tech., 1978. Asst. prof. UCLA, 1978-81, assoc. prof., 1981-83, prof., 1983—; mem. various research coms. NRC, 1983—; mem. sci. adv. com. DOSECC, 1985-87. Contbr. articles to profl. jours. Fellow Am. Geophys. Union (chmn. award coms., Macelwane award 1983); mem. AAAS, Geol. Soc. Am. (Clarke medal 1978), Geochem. Soc. (chmn. award coms.). Avocations: guitar, skiing, tennis. Office: UCLA Dept Earth & Space Scis 405 Hilgard Ave Los Angeles CA 90024

DEPAULIS, PALMER ANTHONY, city mayor; b. Oakland, Calif., Jan. 17, 1945; s. Hugo Benjamin and Genevieve Amalia (Fontana) D.; m. Jeanne Marie Laufenberg, June 26, 1970; children—Patrick, Margaret. B.A. in English, Sacred Heart Sem., Detroit; M.A., Wayne State U., Detroit. Tchr. St. Mary's of the Wasatch, Salt Lake City, 1969-70, St. Mary of Redford, Detroit, 1970-72, Judge High Sch., Salt Lake City, 1972-74; dist. mgr. All-state Ins. Co., Salt Lake City, 1974-83; pub. works dir. Salt Lake City Corp, 1983-85; mayor Salt Lake City, 1985—. Democrat. Roman Catholic. Home: 834 S 600 E Salt Lake City UT 84102 Office: 300 City-County Bldg Salt Lake City UT 84111

DE PETRIS, CARLA NICOLE CAPIRONE, fine arts cons.; b. Torino, Italy; came to U.S., 1956, naturalized, 1961; d. Giovanni Giuseppe and Albina Luigia (Ferraris) Capirone di Montanaro; ed. Italian and Calif. schs.; cert. in arts mgmt. U. Calif.; m. Wilmer Anthony DePetris, Dec. 4, 19S5; 1 son, Walther Gian Carlo. Internat. cons. fine arts, interior design and hist. preservation, Sonoma, Calif., 1969—; co-owner Fine Arts Research Assos.; tchr. art and art appreciation Sonoma Cath. Elem. Sch.; Arabian horse breeder, Am. Saddlebred breeder. Bd. dirs. Cath. Social Service, 1967-69, treas., 1968; active Pacific Mus. Soc., San Francisco, 1968-69; pres. Sonoma League Hist. Preservation, 1979; sec.-treas. Sonoma Land Trust, 1977-78; founder St. Francis the Ch. Mouse; diocese interior decorator and appraiser; archtl. rev. commr. City of Sonoma; adv. com. Sonoma Parks and Recreation; bd. dirs. Sonoma County Art Council; chmn. spl. events Pres.'s Assos., Sonoma State U. Recipient award Sonoma Parks and Recreation, 1975; Calif. State Office Preservation grantee, 1978. Mem. Associated Photographers Internat. Republican. Research on archtl. style and social devel. from 1840-1940 in So. Sonoma County.

DE PIETRO, MARY RITA ANN, personnel service executive; b. Youngstown, Ohio, May 22, 1933; d. Stephen J. and Mary E. (Kuntz) Montella; m. Orlando J. DePietro, Feb. 16, 1953; children: Larry, Michael. Student, Youngstown Coll., 1950-51. Owner Arcadia (Calif.) Pub. Steno, 1961-85, Arcadia Data Services, 1984—. Active Arcadia Rep. Women's Club. Roman Catholic. Lodge: Sons of Italy in Am. (local sec. 1967-75). Avocations: thoroughbred horses, reading, computers, fiction writing. Home: 1501 Hyland Ave Arcadia CA 91006 Office: Arcadia Data Service 37 E Huntington Dr Arcadia CA 91006

DEPNER, ROBERT KURT, architect, planning cons., builder, developer, property mgmt. exec.; b. Calgary, Alta., Can., Sept. 1, 1944; s. Kurt Rudolf and Dagny Kristine (Beim) D.; student U. B.C. (Can.), 1967-69; B.Arch. with distinction, Wash. State U., 1972; children—Kendall Ann, Ashley Elizabeth, Cooper Mitchell. Draftsman, designer Calgary (Can.) Regional Planning Commn., 1966-67; designer Expo '74' (Spokane) Architects & Planners, 1972-74; designer Higgins, McClarty and Johnson, 1974-77; v.p. McClarty, Johnson, Depner & Milbrandt, Inc., Bellevue, Wash., 1977-80; pres. Depner Assn., 1980—; owner Depner Properties, 1980—; pres. Depner Architects & Planners, Inc.; instr. design Wash. State U., 1975-76. Lic. architect, Wash., Oreg., Idaho, Colo., Utah; cert. Nat. Council Archtl. Registration Bds. Mem. AIA, Nat. Assn. Am. Home Builders, Wash. State Assn. Home Builders (dir.), Wash. State U. Alumni Assn. Home and Office: 4205 148th St NE Suite 100 Bellevue WA 98007

DEPNER, THOMAS ARNOLD, nephrology educator; b. Medford, Oreg., Apr. 8, 1943; s. Arnold Martin and Helen Lois (Swan) D.; m. Celeste Marie White, June 29, 1968; children: Charles, Kristine, Ivy. BS, U. Portland, 1965; MD, Johns Hopkins U., 1969. Intern Case Western Res. U. Hosps., Cleve., 1969-70, resident in medicine, 1970-72, fellow in nephrology, 1972-74; asst. prof. nephrology U. Calif., Davis, 1974-81, assoc. prof., 1981—; dir. renal dialysis unit U. Calif.-Davis Med. Ctr., 1980—. Mem. Internat. Soc. Nephrology, Am. Soc. Nephrology, Internat. Soc. Artifical Organs, Am. Kidney Found. Democrat. Roman Catholic. Office: U Calif 4301 X St Davis CA 95817

DEPOORTER, GERALD LEROY, ceramic engineer, chemist; b. Everett, Wash., Mar. 4, 1940. BS in Ceramic Engring., U. Wash., 1961; MS in Engring., U. Calif., Berkeley, 1963; PhD in Engring., U. Calif., 1965. Mem. staff Los Alamos (N.Mex.) Nat. Lab., 1965-83, project mgr., 1983—. Contbr. articles to profl. jours, chpts. to books. Mem. Am. Chem. Soc., Am. Ceramic Soc., Keramos, Sigma Xi, Tau Beta Bi, Zeta Mu Tau. Republican. Lutheran. Avocations: flying, hiking, camping, fishing, model railroading. Home: 505 Oppenheimer Dr #413 Los Alamos NM 87544 Office: Los Alamos Nat Lab MS-F619 Los Alamos NM 87545

DE PRIESTER, CORAL LEE, oil company executive, technology development consultant; b. Jackson, Mich., Apr. 24, 1922; s. Harold Lee De Priester and Blanche Elsie Trafford; m. M. Margaret Stebbins; children: Susan A. Freeman, Bruce L. BSChemE, U. Mich., 1947, MSChemE, 1948. Research engr. Chevron Oil Field Research, La Habra, Calif., 1948-57, sr. research engr., 1957-58, research assoc., 1962-68; chief reservoir engr. Chevron Venezuela, Maracaibo, 1958-60, chief engr., 1960-62; licensing exec. Chevron Research Co., San Francisco, 1968-82; pres. CORAMAR, Inc., Moraga, Calif., 1982—; cons. Creative Engring., Bakersfield, Calif., 1983—, Petroleum Testing Service, Santa Fe Springs, Calif., 1983—, Phoenix Filtration, Larkspur, Calif., 1984—; pres. Robstrig Corp., Bakersfield, 1982-85. Author video tape and text Sand Control, 1969; patentee in field. Pres. Elem Sch. Bd., Fullerton, Calif., 1965-68, Planned Parenthood Shusta-Diablo, Walnut Creek, Calif., 1984-85; lay leader St. Mark's United Meth. Ch., Orinda, Calif., 1986—. Decorated Bronze Star. Mem. Am. Inst. Chem. Engrs., Soc. Petroleum Engrs. (chmn. San Francisco chpt. 1983-84), AAAS. Republican. Avocations: fishing, hiking, nature study, cultural history. Home and Office: CORAMAR Inc 142 Selborne Way Moraga CA 94556

DER, CHANNING JOSEPH, molecular biologist, researcher; b. San Francisco, Mar. 9, 1953; s. Albert Joseph and May (Lai) D.; m. Kathleen Kimiko Yasui, Aug. 8, 1981. BA, UCLA, 1975; PhD, U. Calif., Irvine, 1981. Research fellow Harvard Med. Sch. and Dana-Farber Cancer Inst., Boston, 1981-85; staff scientist La Jolla (Calif.) Cancer Research Found., 1985—. Contbr. articles to profl. jours. NIH predoctoral fellow 1976-81, NIH postdoctoral fellow 83-85, NIH grantee 1986—; Damon-Runyon/Walter Winchell postdoctoral fellow, 1982-83. Mem. AAAS, Union Concerned Scientists. Democrat. Avocations: running, tennis, basketball, racquetball, photography. Home: 1638 Gitano St Encinitas CA 92024 Office: La Jolla Cancer Research Found 10901 N Torrey Pines Rd La Jolla CA 92037

DER-BALIAN, GEORGES PUZANT, immunologist; b. Montmorency, France, June 22, 1943; s. Hagop and Azniv (Andelian) Der B. M in Physics, Sorbonne U., Paris, 1965, M in Biochemistry, 1969; M in Immunology, U. Calif., Berkeley, 1971, PhD in Immunology, 1976. Dir. immunology Axonics, Mountain View, Calif., 1982; v.p. research Hemogenetics, San Mateo, Calif., 1983-85; head infectious disease section SCLAVO, San Jose, Sunnyvale, Calif., 1985—. Inventor in field; contbr. articles to profl. jours. Mem. Am. Soc. Microbiology, N.Y. Acad. Scis., Am. Chem. Soc. Home: 505 Cypress Point Dr #8 Mountain View CA 94043

DERBES, DANIEL WILLIAM, manufacturing company executive; b. Cin., Mar. 30, 1930; s. Earl Milton and Ruth Irene (Grauten) D.; m. Patricia Maloney, June 4, 1952; children: Donna Ann, Nancy Lynn (dec.), Stephen Paul. B.S., U.S. Mil. Acad., 1952; M.B.A., Xavier U., Cin., 1963. Devel. engr. AiResearch Mfg. Co., Phoenix, 1956-58; with Garrett Corp., 1958-80; v.p., gen. mgr., then exec. v.p. Garrett Corp., Los Angeles, 1975-80; dir. Garrett Corp., 1976—; pres. Advanced Tech. Group, Signal Cos., Inc., La Jolla, Calif., 1980-85; pres. Allied-Signal Internat. Inc., 1985—; exec. v.p. Allied-Signal, Inc., Morristown, N.J., 1985—; bd. dirs. Allied- Signal Can., Inc., San Diego Gas & Electric Co., WD-40 Co. Bd. dirs. Ind. Colls. So. Calif., 1980—, United Way, San Diego, 1981—; v.p. nat. council Boy Scouts Am., 1981—; trustee U. San Diego, 1981—; mem. adv. bd. U. S.C., 1986—. Served with AUS, 1952-56. Republican. Roman Catholic. Office: 11255 N Torrey Pines Rd La Jolla CA 92037

DERBY, CHARLES WALLACE, bank executive; b. Scottsbluff, Nebr., Sept. 16, 1939; s. George Brinton and Agnes Viola (Marshall) D.; m. Francine Fort, June 21, 1963; children: Richard George, Jennifer Paige, Brett William. AA, Scottsbluff Coll., 1959; BBA, U. Denver, 1961. Ops. officer United Bank Denver, 1959-72; exec. v.p. Bank Woodmoor, Monument, Colo., 1972-75; v.p., cashier Cherry Creek Nat. Bank, Denver, 1975-77, Wyo. Nat. Bank, Casper, 1977-83; v.p. Affiliated Bank Corp., Casper, 1983-85; pres. Norwest Bank Kemmerer (Wyo.), 1985—, also bd. dirs. Pres. Casper Civic Chorace, 1983. Mem. Bank Adminstrn. Inst. (pres. Wyo. chpt. 1983). Republican. Lodges: Rotary, Lions (local bd. dirs. 1985), Kiwanis (v.p. Monument chpt. 1974), Elks. Avocations: golf, bridge, skiing, reading. Home: 8701 E Roundtree Ave Englewood CO 80111 Office: Norwest Bank Kemmerer 716 Sage Ave Kemmerer WY 83101

DERDENGER, PATRICK, lawyer; b. Los Angeles, June 29, 1946; s. Charles Patrick and Drucilla Marguerite (Lange) D.; m. Jo Lynn Dickins, Aug. 24, 1968; children—Kristin Lynn, Bryan Patrick, Timothy Patrick. B.A., Loyola U., Los Angeles, 1968; M.B.A., U. So. Calif., 1971, J.D., 1974; LL.M. in Taxation, George Washington U., 1977. Bar: Calif. 1974, U.S. Ct.

Claims 1975, Ariz. 1979, U.S. Ct. Appeals (9th cir.) 1979, U.S. Dist. Ct. Ariz. 1979, U.S. Tax Ct. 1979, U.S. Supreme Ct. 1979. Trial atty. honors program Dept. Justice, Washington, 1974-78; ptnr. Lewis and Roca, Phoenix, 1978—; adj. prof. taxation Golden Gate U., Phoenix, 1983—. Author: Arizona State and Local Taxation, Cases and Materials, 1983, Arizona Sales and Use Tax Guide, 1986; Served to capt. USAF, 1968-71. Recipient U.S. Law Week award Bur. Nat. Affairs, 1974. Mem. ABA (taxation sect., various coms.), Ariz. Bar Assn. (taxation sect., various coms., chmn. dept. revenue com.), Maricopa County Bar Assn., Nat. Assn. Bond Lawyers, Inst. Property Taxation, Phoenix Met. C. of C., Ariz. C. of C. (sales tax com.), Phi Delta Phi. Home: 9501 N 49th Pl Paradise Valley AZ 85253 Office: Lewis and Roca 2200 1st Interstate Bank Plaza 100 W Washington St Phoenix AZ 85003

DEREGT, JOHN STEWART, real estate development executive; b. San Francisco; s. Christian Anthony and Mary Margaret (Stewart) deR.; B.C.E., U. Santa Clara, 1950; m. Mal Padgett, Mar. 21, 1981; children—Kenneth, Thomas, James, Lauren, Mary, Jordan, Keith, Stewart. Pres. Carl Holvick Co., Palo Alto, Calif., 1957-75; v.p. Holvick deRegt Koering, Sunnyvale, Calif., 1960-75, pres., owner 1975-86; indsl. and office park counsel Urban Land Inst., 1978—; pres., owner Golden Devel. Co., Inc., 1987—. Contbr. feature articles to Corporate Times, Santa Clara, Calif. Mem. bd. regents Bellarmine High Sch., San Jose, 1977—; bd. dirs. Food Bank, San Jose, Calif., 1980—, San Mateo County Devel. Assn., San Mateo, Calif., 1975—; YMCA, 1984—; adv. bd. Santa Clara U. Sch. Bus., 1984— ; mem. Exec. Com., 1980—. Served with U.S. Army, 1951-53. Mem. Nat. Assn. Indsl. Office Parks. Club: Sharon Heights Country (Menlo Park, Calif.). Home: 97 Elena Ave Atherton CA 94025 Office: 1230 Oakmead Pkwy 212 Sunnyvale CA 94088

DE RIOS, MARLENE DOBKIN, medical anthropologist, educator; b. N.Y.C., Apr. 12, 1939; d. Bernard and Anne Dobkin; m. Yando Rios, Nov. 9, 1969; 1 child, Gabriela. BA in Psychology, Queens Coll., 1959; MA in Anthropology, NYU, 1963; PhD, U. Calif., Riverside, 1972. Prof. anthropology Calif. State U., Fullerton, 1969—; research anthropologist U. Calif., Irvine, 1974-75; health sci. adminstr. Nat. Inst. Mental Health, Rockville, Md., 1980-81. Author: Hallucinogens-Cross Cult Perspective, 1984, Visionary Vine, 1984. Fellow Am. Anthrop. Assn.; mem. Internat. Soc. Clin. and Exptl. Hypnosis. Office: Calif State U Dept Anthropology 800 N State Coll Dr Fullerton CA 92634

DERLACKI, WALTER RICHARD, forest products company executive, consultant; b. Chgo., Nov. 13, 1923; s. Walter and Jadwiga Derlacki; m. Joyce Bratton, Apr. 24, 1948; children: David, Donald, Douglas. BSME, Northwestern U., 1945; MSME, MIT, 1947. Registered profl. engr., Ohio, Calif. Project mgr. Procter & Gamble, Cin., 1947-59; gen. mgr. engring. Luria div. Ogden Corp., Cleve., 1959-69; v.p. ops. M.A. Nishkian & Co., Long Beach, Calif., 1969-71; v.p. engring. Benham-Kite & Co., Los Angeles, 1971-72; v.p. design services Fruin-Colnon Corp., St. Louis, 1972-74; mgr. cons. services Weyerhaeuser Co., Tacoma, 1974-86. Bd. dirs. Seattle Philharm. Orch., 1981, Friends of Phila., String Quartet, Seattle, 1981, Belle Arte Concerts, Bellevue, Wash., 1985. Mem. NSPE, TAPPI, Project Mgmt. Inst., Am. Engring. Model Soc. Republican. Avocations: violin music, golfing.

DERLIN, JANE CAROL, clinical psychologist; b. Sheboygan, Wis., June 19, 1926; d. Edgar Carl and Jennie Rose (Knocke) Derlein; 1 child, Roberta Lee. BS, U. Wis., La Crosse, 1948; MA, U. Mich., 1961. Lic. psychologist; cert. sch. psychologist. Tchr. phys. edn. Oconto Falls (Wis.) Sch. Dist., 1950-53; tchr. phys. edn. Sheboygan (Wis.) Sch. Dist., 1953-61, all city supr. phys. edn., 1960-61, sch. psychologist, 1961-68; sch. psychologist Plymouth, Wis., 1969-75, dir. Title I Activities, 1974-75; sch. psychologist Racine (Wis.) Unified Sch. Dist., 1975-85; dir. Psychol. Services, Racine, 1973—; pvt. practict clin. psychology 1961—; cons. psychologist New Concepts Found. Northeastern Wis., 1968-75, Southeastern Wis. Med. and Social Services, Inc., 1985—. Mem. Am. Psychol. Assn., Wis. Psychol. Assn., Wis. Sch. Psychologists Assn., Wis. Women Entrepreneurs (mem. mentor com. 1984—), Wis. Hunter and Jumper Assn., Ill. Hunter and Jumper Assn. Avocations: equestrian activities.

DERMODY, JOHN, oceanographer; b. Needham, Mass., Mar. 28, 1924; s. Frank J. and Frances (Frawley) D.; m. Tommy Anne Black, Mar. 5, 1950; children—Grant M., Robin Anne, Todd F. B.S., Holy Cross Coll., 1945; postgrad. U. Wash., 1957-58; MIT, 1959. With U.S. Coast and Geodetic Survey, 1948-56; oceanographer U. Wash., Seattle, 1957-75; mgr. programs U. Alaska, Fairbanks, 1976-79; lab. dir. Ocean Inst. of Wash., Seattle, 1979-81; tech. mgr. Raven Systems & Research, Seattle, 1981—. Contbr. articles to profl. jours. Served with USN, 1942-46. Adult leader Boy Scouts Am., Seattle, 1968-74; exec. sec. Pres.'s Commn. on Marine Sci., Engring. and Resources, 1967-68; mem. Gov.'s Tech. Com., Alaska, 1976-79. Recipient award of yr. U.S. Dept. Commerce, 1956. Mem. Soc. Naval Architects and Marine Engrs., Inst. of Navigation, The Hydrographic Soc., Marine Tech. Soc. Republican. Roman Catholic.

DERONDE, JOHN ALLEN, JR., lawyer, author; b. Albany, N.Y., July 22, 1947; s. John Allen and Kathleen (Doran) DeR.; m. Marianne E. Karlsson, Mar. 19, 1983. B.A., U. Calif.-Davis, 1969; J.D., U. Pacific, 1972. Bar: Calif. 1974, U.S. Dist. Ct. (ea. and no. dists.) Calif. 1978, U.S. Supreme Ct. 1981, U.S. Tax Ct. 1984. Law clerk DeRonde & Brewer, Vacaville, Calif., 1972-73; dep. trial counsel State Dept. Motor Vehicles, Sacramento, 1973-74; ptnr. DeRonde & Geandrot, Fairfield, Calif., 1974-76, sole practice, Fairfield, 1976-78; ptnr. DeRonde & DeRonde, Fairfield and Pleasant Hill, Calif., 1978—; dir. Calif.-Hawaii Corp., 1979—, Pietro's Pizza Parlors, Inc., 1975—. Contbr. numerous articles to profl. jours. Active Vacaville, Fairfield and Concord, Calif. chambers of commerce. Recipient Highest Score award Jessup Internat. Moot Ct. Competition, Seattle, 1972. Mem. Calif. State Bar Assn. (legal econs. and family law sect.), ABA, Calif. Trial Lawyers Assn., Assn. Trial Lawyers Am., Am. Judicature Soc., Barristers Club No. Calif., No. Calif. Soc. Cert. Family Law Specialists, Calif. Assn. Realtors, Notaries Pub. Assn. Calif., Am. Overseas Employees Assn., Nat. Fedn. Ind. Bus., U.S. Justice Found., Pacific Legal Found., Bay Area Auto Dismantlers Assn., Nat. Restaurant Assn. Republican. Roman Catholic. Lodge: Lions Internat. Home: 47 Portsmouth Circle Pleasant Hill CA 94523 Office: 627 Delaware St Fairfield CA 94533 also: 101 Gregory Ln Suite 30 Pleasant Hill CA 94523

DE ROO, REMI JOSEPH, bishop; b. Swan Lake, Man., Can., Feb. 24, 1924; s. Raymond and Josephine (De Pape) De R. Student, St. Boniface (Man.) Coll.; S.T.D., Angelicum U., Rome, Italy. Ordained priest Roman Catholic Ch., 1950; curate Holy Cross Parish, St. Boniface, 1952-53; sec. to archbishop of St. Boniface 1954-56; diocesan dir. Cath. action Archdiocese St. Boniface, 1953-54; exec. sec. Man. Cath. Con., 1958; pastor Holy Cross Parish, 1960-62; bishop of Victoria, B.C., Can., 1962—; Canadian episcopal rep. Internat. Secretariat Apostleship See, 1964-78; chairperson Human Rights Commn. B.C., 1974-77; mem. social affairs commn. Can. Conf. Cath. Bishops, 1973—, chmn., 1980-85; pres. Western Cath. Conf. Bishops, 1980—. Address: 230-1555 McKenzie Ave, Victoria, BC Canada V8N 1A4 *

DE ROPP, JEFFREY SYLVESTER, biophysicist, spectroscopist; b. Nyack, N.Y., Nov. 17, 1955; s. Robert Sylvester and Kathleen Elizabeth (Knowlman) DeR. BS, Sonoma Coll., 1976; PhD, U. Calif., Davis, 1981. Post-doctoral researcher U. Calif., Davis, 1981-84, research spectroscopist, 1985—. Giannini fellow, 1983, 84. Mem. Am. Chem. Soc. Republican. Avocations: bicycling.

DERR, JOHN FREDERICK, health care products company executive; b. Chgo., Aug. 23, 1936; s. Harry Louis and Annette Bollow D.; student Purdue U., 1954-58, Ind. U., 1970-71, Columbia U., 1972; m. Polly Laughlin Pease, Sept. 7, 1963; children: Deborah L., Jennifer. B. Projects mgr., hosp. group product mgr., dir. hosp. market planning, dir. products and systems devel. E.R. Squibb & Sons, Princeton, N.J., 1966-74; v.p. mktg. Searle Diagnostics, Des Plaines, Ill., 1974-76, v.p. imaging mktg. products group, gen. mgr. sales/service div. 1977-80; v.p., div. mgr. Nuclear and Ultrasound div. Siemens Med. Systems, Iselin, N.J., 1980; sr. v.p. mktg. internat., pres. Internat. Equipment div. Nat. Med. Enterprises, Santa Monica, Calif., 1981-82; exec. v.p., chief operating officer, dir. Internat. Remote Imaging Systems, Chatsworth, Calif., 1982-85; pres., chief exec. officer The Westlake Group, Westlake Village, Calif., 1986—; pres., bd. dirs. Beck Analytical Services, Bloomington, Ind.; bd. dirs. Sports Optiks, Westlake Village, Med. Imaging Systems, Riverside, Calif.; mem. Ind. Grad. Sch. Bus. Exec. Adv. Bd., 1970—. Dir. planning Naval Res. Region 19, San Diego, 1986—; mem. pres.'s council Purdue U. Served to capt. USN, 1959-63, USNR, 1964—. Mem. Am. Mktg. Assn., Res. Officers Assn., Naval Res. Assn., Chief Exec. Officers Club, U.S. Arab C. of C., Soc. Nuclear Medicine, Sigma Phi Epsilon (pres. alumni bd. dirs. UCLA chpt.; bd. govs. edn. found.), Purdue U. Pres. Council. Republican. Presbyterian. Clubs: Big Ten Los Angeles. Home: 1659 Larkfield Westlake Village CA 91362 Office: 2659 Townsgate Rd Suite 214 Westlake Village CA 91361

DERR, JOHN SEBRING, geophysicist, seismologist; b. Boston, Nov. 12, 1941; s. Thomas Sieger and Mary Ferguson (Sebring) D.; m. Patricia Louise Barker, July 14, 1985; children: Alex, Mary, Nathan. BA, Amherst Coll., 1963; MA, U. Calif., Berkeley, 1965, PhD, 1968. Geophysicist Pan Am. Petroleum Corp., Midland, Tex., 1964; research assoc. MIT, Cambridge, 1968-70; research scientist Martin-Marietta Aerospace Corp., Denver, 1970-74; chief ops. Nat. Earthquake Info. Service U.S. Geol. Survey, Golden, Colo., 1974-79, chief spl. seismol. analysis project, 1983—; chief tech. reports U.S. Geol. Survey, Menlo Park, Calif., 1980-83. Contbr. articles to profl. jours. Mem. AAAS, Am. Geophys. Union, AIAA, Royal Astron. Soc., Seismol. Soc. Am., Soc. Sci. Exploration (councilor 1986—), Sigma Xi. Avocations: aircraft constrn., choral singing, bicycling. Office: US Geol Survey Fed Ctr MS967 Box 25046 Denver CO 80225

DERR, KENNETH T., oil company executive. m. Donna Mettler, Sept. 12, 1959; 3 children. B.A., M.B.A., Cornell U. With Chevron Corp. (formerly Standard Oil Co. of Calif.), 1960—, v.p., 1972-85; pres. Chevron U.S.A., Inc. subs. Chevron Corp., 1978-84; head merger program Chevron Corp. and Gulf Oil Corp., 1984-85; vice-chmn. Chevron Corp., 1985—. Trustee Alta Bates Corp., Cornell U. Mem. Am. Petroleum Inst. (dir.). Clubs: Orinda Country (Calif.); Pacific Union, Stock Exchange (San Francisco). Office: Chevron Corp 225 Bush St San Francisco CA 94104 *

DERR, ROGER DARRELL, retail executive; b. Red Cloud, Nebr., Feb. 12, 1936; s. Darrell L. and Winifred I. (Hall) D.; m. Charlene Nixon, Oct., 1955 (div. Apr. 1968); children: Rick Lee, Scott Roger; m. Patricia Houlihan, Mar. 6, 1970; 1 child, Sean Patrick. Store mgr. Cannon Shoe Co., Oklahoma City and Kansas City, 1955-59; from buyer to store mgr. Joslins Dept. Store, Denver, 1959-85; pres. Hennesy's, delendrecie's and Glass Block Dept. Stores, Mont., N.D., Minn., 1985—.

DERTIEN, DONALD CHARLES, prosthodontist, air force officer; b. Kearney, Neb., Sept. 9, 1936; s. Charles John and Florence Hilda (Voetberg) D.; m. Helen Dolores Henson, Apr. 5, 1963; children—Craig Charles, Evan Carleton, Sarah Angela, Cheyenne Anita. D.D.S., U. Nebr., 1960; M.S. U. Tex.-Houston, 1969. Diplomate Am. Bd. Prosthodontics. Commd. 1st lt. U.S. Air Force, 1960, advanced through grades to lt. col., 1978; dental intern U.S. Army, Ft. Benning, Ga., 1960-61; gen. dentist, RAF Croughton, Eng. and Myrtle Beach AFB, S.C., 1961-66, prosthodontist, Wright-Patterson AFB, Ohio, USAF Acad., Colo., Yokota Air Base, Japan, 1969-79; chief prosthodontics, Edwards AFB, Calif., 1979-85; pvt. practice prosthodontics Colorado Springs, Colo., 1985—. Active Boy Scouts Am., 1975-85. Fellow Am. Coll. Prosthodontists; mem. ADA, Internat. Acad. Gnathology. Republican. Home: 1314 Shrider Rd Colorado Springs CO 80918 Office: Chapel Hills Dental Bldg 7970 N Academy Blvd Colorado Springs CO 80918

DE SANTIS, NUNZIO PASQUALE, nuclear pharmacy executive; b. Cansano, Italy, Mar. 24, 1951; s. Luciano and Velia (Di Giacomo) De S.; B.S. in Pharmacy, U. N.Mex., 1974; m. Sherolyn Kay Smith, Aug. 12, 1973; children—Louie, Rhonda, Paul. Pres., Radiopharmacy Assocs., Inc., El Paso, 1974-75; dir. Nuclear Pharmacy, Inc., 1975-83, mgr. Eastern dist., Phila., 1979, v.p. ops., Albuquerque, 1980, sr. v.p. ops., 1980-81, exec. v.p., 1981-83, chief operating officer, 1982-83, sec.-treas., 1982-83; founder, pres., chief exec. officer Diagnostek, Inc., 1983. Mem. Am. Pharm. Assn., Soc. Nuclear Medicine. Republican. Home: 807 Alhambra NW Albuquerque NM 87103 Office: 5651 Kircher NE Albuquerque NM 87109

DESCAMP, JOHN BAYARD, JR., lawyer; b. Shelton, Wash., July 24, 1943; s. John Bayard and Jean Marienne (Lemieux) D.; m. Julie Powers, Sept. 21, 1974; children—Margaret, Amy, John, Daniel, Melinda, Robin. A.A. magna cum laude, Northwest Mich. Coll., 1963; B.A. magna cum laude, Seattle U., 1965; J.D. cum laude, Lewis and Clark Law Sch., Portland, Oreg., 1974. Bar: Oreg. 1974, U.S. Dist. Ct. Oreg. 1974, U.S. Ct. Appeals (9th cir.) 1975. Analyst U.S. Nat. Bank, Portland, 1965-66; mktg. rep., cons. IBM Corp., Portland, 1967-74; assoc. Rives Bonyhadi Drummond, Portland, 1974-78, Dahl, Zalutsky, Portland, 1978-79; ptnr. Weiss, DesCamp and Botteri, Portland, 1979—; dir. Block Bus. Forms, Portland, 1981—, Oreg. Sch. Design, 1985—. Contbr. articles to profl. jours. Active Republican Party, other civic orgns; bd. trustees Doernbecher Hosp. Guild, 1986—. Mem. ABA, Nat. Tax Inst., Computer Law Assn., Oreg. State Bar. Republican. Episcopalian. Clubs: Arlington, University, Multnomah Athletic (Portland). Home: 2550 SW Ravensview Dr Portland OR 97201 Office: Weiss DesCamp & Botteri 111 SW Fifth Ave Portland OR 97204

DE SERIO, JOSEPHINE, electronic office equipment company executive, consultant; b. Matewan, W.Va., Feb. 6, 1942; d. Arthur and Ruth (Justus) Charles; m. George Raymond DeSerio, June 15, 1963; 1 child, Sheila Ann. Gen. office clk. Twentieth Century, Norfolk, Va., summer 1959; invoice clk. J.C. Penney Co., Norfolk, 1963-65, catalog mgr., Charleston, W.Va., 1968-72; corp. sec. APD, Inc., Stanton, Calif., 1973-75; pres. DSJ Bus. Systems, Fountain Valley, Calif., 1975—. Mem. Nat. Office Machine Dealer Assn., Fountain Valley C. of C. Office: DSJ Bus Systems 11577 C Slater Ave Fountain Valley CA 92708

DES GRANGES, MAINO, engineering company executive, retired naval officer; b. Fullerton, Calif., Aug. 2, 1918; s. Paul Ray and Julia Teresa (Maino) des G.; m. Dorothy Elizabeth Beckley, Sept. 19, 1942; children—Paul Scott, Jeanne Marie (Mrs. James Vivoli), Anne Michelle (Mrs. Ned Chambers). B.E.E., U.S. Naval Acad., 1941. Lic. contractor, Calif. Commd. ensign U.S. Navy, 1941, advanced through grades to capt.; officer in charge Exptl. Diving Unit, Washington, 1955-57; comdr. Submarine div., 1957-59; naval attaché U.S. Embassy, New Delhi, 1962-64; commdg. officer 6 submarines and surface ships, 1943-66; gen. ptnr. Des Granges Land, Ltd., San Diego, 1968—; pres. Superior CATV Constrn., El Cajon, Calif., 1972—, also dir.; established NATO missions Office Chief Naval Ops., 1948-50. Editor manual on U.S. Navy diving; originator tables on U.S. Navy repetitive diving, 1957; patentee diving decompression calculator. Mem. El Cajon C. of C., Huntington Beach C. of C., Von Mises Inst., San Diego Associated Builders and Contractors, Am. Soc. Concrete Constrn. Republican. Clubs: San Diego Yacht; Parkway Tennis and Swim (El Cajon). Home: 1474 Liggett Way San Diego CA 92106 Office: Superior CATV Constrn Inc 843 Gable Way El Cajon CA 92022

DESHAIES, KENNETH JOSEPH, lobbyist, private investigator; b. Lawrence, Mass., Oct. 2, 1946; s. Joseph Oscar and Lucille Eva (Fawcett) D.; m. Sandra Freund, Apr. 19, 1981 (div. May 1982); 1 child, Heather Marie; m. Kathleen Anne Aguirre, Aug. 4, 1985. Grad. high sch., Colorado Springs, Colo. Ptnr. Do-More Constrn. Co., Colorado Springs, 1972-73; owner Walton Creek Mgmt. Co., Steamboat Springs, Colo., 1973-74; prin. Deshaies & Assocs., Denver, 1976—; pres. Win/Win Bus. Forum, Inc., Denver, 1985-86. Contbr. articles to pubs. Founder and pres. Colo. Health Research Coalition, Denver, 1977—. Served with USN, 1966-70, Vietnam. Mem. Profl. Pvt. Investigators Assn. Colo. (pres.), World Assn. Detectives, Inst. Internat. Edn., Am. Soc. Indsl. Security. Avocations: Nordic skiing, backpacking, tennis. Office: Deshaies & Assocs 56 Steele St Denver CO 80206

DESHPANDE, NILENDRA GANESH, physics educator; b. Karachi, Pakistan, Apr. 18, 1938; came to U.S., 1961; s. Ganesh V. and Myna G. (Junnarkar) D.; m. Kanchan S. Karnik, May 15, 1960; children: Pranay N., Rahul N. BS with honors, U. Madras, India, 1959, MA in Physics, 1960, MS in Physics, 1961; PhD, U. Pa., 1965. Asst. prof. physics Northwestern U., Evanston, Ill., 1967-73; assoc. prof U. Tex., Austin, 1973-75; assoc. prof U. Oreg., Eugene, 1975-83, prof., 1983—. Contbr. articles to profl. jours. Named Outstanding Jr. Investigator, U.S. Dept. Energy, 1981-86; prin. investigator High Energy Physics Grant, U.S. Dept. Energy, 1981—. Mem. Am. Phys. Soc. (organizer annual meeting div. particles and fields 1985), Sigma Xi. Home: 90 E 47th St Eugene OR 97405 Office: Inst Theoretical Sci U Oreg Eugene OR 97403

DES MARAIS, DAVID J., research biogeochemist; b. Richmond, Va., Jan. 12, 1948; s. Stanley Ferdinand and Irma (Fredricks) DesM.; m. Shirley Lee, Aug. 15, 1970; children: David Lee, Andrea Catherine. BS in Chemistry, Purdue U., 1969; MS in Geology, Ind. U., 1972, PhD in Geochemistry, 1974. Postdoctoral research assoc. Ind. U., Bloomington, 1974-75; research fellow UCLA, 1975-78; research chemist Ames Research Ctr. NASA, Moffett Field, Calif., 1976—; prin. investigator lunar samples NASA, 1977-79. Assoc. editor Lunar and Planetary Sci. Conf., 1979; mem. editorial bd. Biogeochemistry Jour., 1983—; contbr. chpts. to books, articles to profl. jours; patentee in field. Sec. Willows Assn. Homeowners group, Menlo Park, Calif., 1982-83. Fellow Ind. U., 1972, 74, NASA Ames Research Ctr., 1983. Fellow Nat. Speleological Soc. (nat. conv. chmn. 1973); mem. Cave Research Found. (bd. dirs. 1972-76, joint venturer), Geochem. Soc., Am. Geophys. Union, Internat. Symposia on Environ. Biogeochemistry (mem. Internat. com. 1984—), Sigma Xi. Avocations: speleology, photography. Home: 1015 Woodland Ave Menlo Park CA 94025 Office: NASA Ames Research Ctr Mail Stop 239-4 Moffett Field CA 94035

DE SOLA, RALPH, author, editor, educator; b. N.Y.C., July 26, 1908; s. Solomon and Grace (von Geist) DeS.; m. Dorothy Clair, Dec. 24, 1944. Student, Columbia U., 1927, 29, 31, Swarthmore Coll., 1928. Collector N.Y. Zool. Soc., N.Y.C., 1928-29, 30-33, Am. Mus. Natural History, N.Y.C., 1930, Tropical Biology Soc., Miami, Fla., 1933-34; zool. editor Fed. Writers Project, N.Y.C., 1935-39; tech. dir. U.S. Microfilm Corp., N.Y.C., 1939-49; hist. dir. Travel U.S. 90 and Mex. Border Trails Assn., Del Rio, Tex., 1951-54; publs. editor Convair div. Gen. Dynamics Corp., San Diego, 1955-68; instr. tech. English San Diego Unified Colls., 1962—. Author: (with Fredrica De Sola) Strange Animals and Their Ways, 1933, Microstat Technicians Handbook, 1943, Microfilming, 1944, Worldwide What and Where, 1975; compiler Abbreviations Dictionary, 1958, 7th rev. edit., 1984, Crime Dictionary, 1982, (booklet) Great Americans Discuss Religion, 1963, (booklet) Quotations from A to Z for freethinkers and other skeptics, 1985, (with Dorothy De Sola) A Dictionary of Cooking, 1969; Great Americans Examine Religion, 1983; editor: International Conversion Tables, 1961; compiler-editor Whitman books, specializing in zool. juveniles, 1937-41; translator: Beethoven-by-Berlioz, 1975; cons. on microfilming to USN, on abbreviations to Dept. Def.; contbr. articles to Copeia, 1928-32, revs. to classical records and concerts to Freeman, Del Rio News-Herald, San Diego Engr., Downtown. Home: 1819 Puterbaugh St San Diego CA 92103

DE SOLLAR, DANIEL CHARLES, aircraft company executive; b. Cin., Sept. 21, 1955; s. James Clamor and Eileen Mary (Norris) DeS.; m. Kathy L. Cork, Dec. 16, 1984; children: Marcus, James. B.S. in Indsl. Engring., Purdue U., 1978; M.S. in Mgmt., West Coast U., 1981; M.B.A., 1982; M.S. in Indsl. and Systems Engring., U. So. Calif., 1984. Mfg. engr. Cin. Milacron, 1977-78; indsl. engr. Hughes Aircraft Co., Fullerton, Calif., 1978-80, project mgr., 1980—. Hughes Aircraft Co. fellow, 1982. Mem. Am. Inst. Indsl. Engrs., Theta Xi, Alpha Pi Mu. Republican. Roman Catholic. Home: 7524 E Woodsboro Ave Anaheim Hills CA 92807 Office: Hughes Aircraft Co 7000 Village Dr Buena Park CA 90620

DESPOL, JOHN ANTON, state deputy labor commissioner; b. San Francisco, July 22, 1913; s. Anton and Bertha (Balzer) D.; m. Jeri Kaye Steep, Dec. 7, 1937; children—Christopher Paul, Anthony John. Student, U. So. Calif., 1931, Los Angeles Jr. Coll., 1929-30. Sec.-treas., council Calif. CIO, Los Angeles, 1950-58, gen. v.p. Calif. Labor Fedn. AFL-CIO, San Francisco, 1958-60; internat. rep. United Steelworkers Am., Los Angeles, 1937-68; with Dempsey-Tegeler & Co., Inc., 1968-70; rep. Bache & Co., 1970-71; commr. Fed. Mediation and Conciliation Services, Los Angeles, 1972-73; indsl. relations cons., 1971-76; dep. labor commr. State of Calif., 1976—; mem. Nat. Steel Panel Nat. War Labor Bd., 1944-45; chmn. bd. trustees Union Mgmt. Ins. Trust Fund, Los Angeles, 1948-68. Mem. Calif. Def. Council, 1939-41, 10th Regional War Manpower Commn., 1942-46; bd. dirs. So. Calif. region NCCJ, 1960-68; bd. dirs. Los Angeles Community Chest, Los Angeles World Affairs Council, 1951-80, Braille Inst. of Am., 1961—; del. Nat. Democratic Conv., 1948, 52, 56, 60; mem. Los Angeles County Dem. Com., 1942-44; mem. exec. com. Calif. Dem. Com., 1952-56; chmn. Calif. Congl. dist., 1954-56; mem. Calif. Legislative Adv. Commn. to State Legislature, 1956-59; del. Nat. Republican Conv., 1968; bd. dirs. Los Angeles World Affairs Council, 1953-81, Braille Inst. Am., 1961—; bd. govs. Town Hall, Los Angeles, 1941-44, 67-70, chmn. econ. sect., 1964-65; mem. Los Angeles Com. Fgn. Relations, 1946—; mem. Calif. Job Tng. and Placement Council, 1967-68. Mem. Indsl. Relations Research Assn., Inst. Indsl. Relations, Assn. Calif. State Attys. and Adminstrv. Law Judges. Home: 4717 Willis Ave Apt 7 Sherman Oaks CA 91402 Office: 6150 Van Nuys Blvd Suite 200 Van Nuys CA 91401

DETELS, ROGER, epidemiologist, physician, former university dean; b. Bklyn., Oct. 14, 1936; s. Martin P. and Mary J. (Crookr) D.; m. Mary M. Doud, Sept. 14, 1963; children: Martin, Edward. B.A., Harvard U., 1958; M.D., NYU, 1962; M.S. in Preventive Medicine, U. Wash., 1966. Am. Bd. Preventive Medicine. Intern U. Calif. Gen. Hosp., San Francisco, 1962-63; resident U. Wash., Seattle, 1963-66, practice medicine specializing in preventive medicine, 1966—; med. officer, epidemiologist Nat. Neurol. Diseases, Bethesda, Md., 1969-71; assoc. prof. epidemiology Sch. Pub. Health, UCLA, 1971-73, prof., 1973—; dean 1980-85; head div. epidemiology Sch. Pub. Health, UCLA, 1972-80; guest lectr. various univs., profl. confs. and med. orgns., 1969—; research physician Wadsworth Hosp. Center, Los Angeles, 1972; mem. sci. adv. com. Am. Found. AIDS Research. Contbr. articles to profl. jours. Served as lt. comdr. M.C. USN, 1966-69. Grantee in field. Fellow Am. Coll. Preventive Medicine; mem. Am. Epidemiological Soc., Soc. Epidemiologic Research (pres. 1977-78), Assn. Tchrs. Preventive Medicine, Calif. Acad. Preventive Medicine (chmn. essay com. 1971), Am. Public Health Assn., Am. Assn. Cancer Edn. (membership com. 1979-80), Am. Thoracic Soc., Internat. Epidemiological Assn. (treas. 1984—), AAAS, Associated Schs. Pub. Health (sec.-treas. 1984-85), Sigma Xi, Delta Omega. Office: UCLA Sch Public Health Los Angeles CA 90024

DETHLEFS, WILLIAM WALTER, social worker; b. Spokane, Wash., July 24, 1954; s. Theodore Alvin and Luella Louise (Peterson) D. BS, U. Oreg., 1977; MSW, U. Wash., 1981. Intern-program dir. Community Council, Portland, Oreg., 1979-80; adminstrv. intern State of Wash., Tukwila, 1980-81; loaned exec. United Way of King County, Seattle, 1981; dir. employee assistance Employment Enterprises, Bellevue, Wash., 1981-82; regional mgr. Employee Support Systems Co., Seattle, 1982-85; adminstr. employee relations Gen. Telephone Co., Everett, Wash., 1985—. Co-author: Social Services and Work, 1983, Initiating Social Work Services, 1985. Chmn. panel United Way of King County, Seattle, 1984-85; bus. rep. Corp. Involvement in Child Care, Seattle, 1983-86; mem. adv. com. King County Red Cross, Seattle, 1985. Mem. Nat. Assn. Social Workers (pres. Wash. State chpt. 1985-87), Employee Assistance Soc. N.Am., Assn. Labor Mgmt. Adminstrs. and Cons. on Alcoholism, The Work Inst. (bd. dirs. 1983—), Acad. Cert. Social Workers. Office: Gen Telephone Co Northwest PO Box 1003 5-ER Everett WA 98206

DETTERMAN, ROBERT LAWRENCE, geologist; b. Green Springs, Ohio, Apr. 20, 1919; s. Wade Hampton and Ruth Elizabeth (Stigamire) D.; m. Janis Morlie Scott, May 1, 1954; children: Mark Eugene, Lynda Jean. BA, Miami U., Oxford, Ohio, 1941. Registered geologist, Calif. Geologist U.S. Geol. Survey, Menlo Park, Calif., 1947—. Contbr. articles to profl. jours. Served to sgt. USAAF, 1942-45, PTO. Fellow AAAS; mem. Am. Assn. Petroleum Geologists, Soc. Econ. Paleontologists and Mineralogists, No. Calif. Geol. Soc., Geol. Soc. of Wash. Democrat. Avocations: backpacking, hiking, antique clock repair. Home: 1725 Chitamook Ct Sunnyvale CA 94087 Office: U S Geol Survey 345 Middlefield Rd Menlo Park CA 94025

DETTERMAN, ROBERT LINWOOD, energy company executive; b. Norfolk, Va., May 1, 1931; s. George William and Jeanneille (Watson) D.; m. Virginia Armstrong; children: Janine, Patricia, William Arthur. B.S. in Engring., Va. Poly. Inst., 1953; Ph.D. in Nuclear Engring., Oak Ridge Sch. Reactor Tech., 1954; postgrad. Engring. test dir. Foster Wheeler Co., N.Y.C., sr. research engr. Atomics Internat. Co., Canoga Park, Calif., 1959-62; chief project engr. Rockwell Internat. Co., Canoga Park, 1962-68, dir. bus. devel., 1968—, fin. planner, 1983—; dir. Bo-Gin, Inc.; dir. Arabian Horse Fed. Credit Union, 1974-82. Trustee, mem. exec. com. Morris Animal Found.; treas., trustee Arabian Horse Trust; chmn. Cal Bred Futurity; Mem. Soc. for the Preservation of Variety Arts, Am. Nuclear Soc., Inst. Cert. Fin. Planners, Atomic Indsl. Forum, Acad. Magical Arts, Am. Horse Shows Assn., Am. Horse Council, Tau Beta Phi, Eta Kappa Nu, Phi Kappa Phi. Republican.

DETTWEILER, JACK H(ENRY), JR., real estate broker, developer; b. Washington, Nov. 21, 1945; s. John Henry Dettweiler and Mary Camila (Calnan) Sterner. Student, St. Louis U., 1963-64; grad., U. N.Mex., 1964-68. Stockbroker Doherty & Co., Albuquerque, 1968-70; pvt. practice real estate broker Albuquerque, 1971—; broker Berger-Briggs Real Estate, Albuquerque, 1978-84; pres. Equity Securities Inc., 1982—; faculty Am. Savs. and Loan Inst., Albuquerque, 1973-76; founder Real Estate Exchangors, Albuquerque, 1981—; bd. dirs. Energy Concepts Internat. Bd. dirs. Nat. Football League Sports Charities, 1986—; v.p., bd. dirs. NFL Sports Charities, 1986—. Named one of 50 Most Eligble Bachelors, Drs. King & Nichols, N.Mex., 1983. Mem. Albuquerque Bd. Realtors (bd. dirs. 1983-84, Exchangors award 1982-83), Realtors Assn. N.Mex., Nat. Assn. Realtors, U. N.Mex. Top 100 Club (bd. dirs. 1983—), Sigma Chi (alumni chpt. pres. 1973-75). Democrat. Roman Catholic. Avocations: golf, handball, fishing. Home: PO Box 8341 Albuquerque NM 87110 Office: 3636 Menaul NE #321 Albuquerque NM 87110

DETZ, CLIFFORD MICHAEL, chemical research and development executive; b. N.Y.C., Dec. 16, 1942; s. Arthur and Sylvia (Diskin) D.; m. Roberta Kleinsinger, Oct. 2, 1966; children: Joanna, Alissa. AB, Brown U., 1964; MS, U. Chgo., 1966, PhD, 1970. Research chemist Union Carbide Corp., Tarrytown, N.Y., 1970-75, group leader, 1975-78; mgr. mineral processing research Chevron Research Co., Richmond, Calif., 1978-82, mgr. process devel., 1982—. Contbr. articles to profl. jours.; patentee in field. Mem. Am. Chem. Soc., Am. Inst. Chem. Engrs. Avocations: skiing, swimming, reading. Office: Chevron Research Co 576 Standard Ave Richmond CA 94903

DEUKMEJIAN, GEORGE, governor California; b. Albany, N.Y., June 6, 1928; s. C. George and Alice (Gairdan) D.; m. Gloria M. Saatjian, 1957; children—Leslie Ann, George Krikor, Andrea Diane. B.A., Siena Coll., 1949; J.D., St. John's U., 1952. Bar: N.Y. 1952, Calif. 1956, U.S. Supreme Ct. 1970. Partner firm Riedman, Dalessi, Deukmejian & Woods, Long Beach, Calif., to 1979; mem. Calif. Assembly, 1963-67; mem. Calif. Senate, 1967-79, minority leader; atty. gen. State of Calif., 1979-82, gov., 1983—; former dep. county counsel Los Angeles County. Mem. exec. bd. Long Beach council Boy Scouts Am. Served with U.S. Army, 1953-55. Mem. Long Beach Bar Assn., Am. Bar Assn., State Bar Calif., Long Beach C. of C. (past dir.), Navy League, YMCA. Republican. Episcopalian. Clubs: Lions, Elks. Office: Office of Gov State Capitol Sacramento CA 95814 *

DEUPREE, ROBERT MARSHALL, physician, retired government official; b. Elizabeth, Colo., Dec. 26, 1912; s. Elmer Burton and Mary Ayer (Griffin) DeuP.; student Santa Ana Coll., 1930-33, Los Angeles City Coll., 1937-38; D.O., Coll. Osteo. Physicians and Surgeons, 1942; M.D., Met. U., 1948; postgrad. UCLA, 1952-53; A.B., Calif. State U., Fullerton, 1962; M.A., Calif. State U., Long Beach, 1963; postgrad. (Nat. Inst. Dental Health fellow) Purdue U., 1963-64; m. Harriett Ann Janetos, Oct. 11, 1963; children—Carol J., R. Scott. Intern, Wilshire Hosp., Los Angeles, 1942-43, resident in neurology, 1943-44; practice medicine, Los Angeles, 1944-57, El Monte, Calif., 1957-58, Newport Beach, Calif., 1958-59; dir. Rush-Merced Clinic, 1957-58; asso. med. dir. Aerojet Gen. Corp., Azusa, Calif., 1967-69, Am. Airlines, Los Angeles, 1969; ships surgeon U. Calif. Scripps Inst. Oceanography, 1969; area med. officer Div. Fed. Employee Health, USPHS, Los Angeles, 1970—; head dept. internal medicine and radiology Hiss Orthopedic Clinic, Los Angeles, 1953-57; instr. differential diagnosis Coll. Osteo. Physicians and Surgeons, Los Angeles, 1945-49; instr. med. terminology N. Orange Community Coll. Dist., 1966-78; pres., Deustar Internat. Corp.; research fellow VA Hosp., Long Beach State Coll., UCLA Inst. Laryngol. Research, 1962-63. Diplomate in aerospace medicine and occupational medicine. Fellow Royal Soc. Health, N.Y. Acad. Scis., Am. Occupational Med. Assn., Am. Aerospace Med. Assn. (assoc.); mem. Royal Soc. Medicine, Aviation Hall of Fame (charter), Asclepiad. Author, editor: DeuPree International Emergency Medical Translations, 1972; co-author: Travis' Handbook of Speech Pathology and Audiology, 1972; editor Jour. Pro-Re-Nata, 1947-50. Home: 2625 W Huckleberry Rd Santa Ana CA 92706

DEUTSCH, BARRY JOSEPH, management development company executive; b. Gary, Ind., Aug. 10, 1941; s. Jack Elias and Helen Louise (La Rue) D.; B.S., U. So. Calif., 1969, M.B.A. magna cum laude, 1970; m. Gina Krispinsky, Feb. 20, 1972. Lectr. mgmt. U. So. Calif., Los Angeles, 1967-70; pres., founder The Deutsch Group, Inc., mgmt. cons. co. tng. upper and middle mgmt., Los Angeles, 1970—, chmn. bd., 1975—; dir. Red Carpet Corp. Am., 1975-77, United Fin. Planners, 1984-86. Chmn. bd. govs. Am. Hist. Center, 1980—. Served with M.I., U.S. Army, 1964-66. Mem. Am. Mgmt. Assn., Am. Soc. Bus. and Mgmt. Cons.'s, Am. Soc. Tng. and Devel., Internat. Mgmt. by Objectives Inst. Author: Leadership Techniques, 1969; Recruiting Techniques, 1970; The Art of Selling, 1973; Professional Real Estate Management, 1975; Strategic Planning, 1976; Employer/Employee: Making the Transition, 1978; Managing by Objectives, 1980; Conducting Effective Performance Appraisal, 1982; Advanced Supervisory Development, 1984. Home: 4848 Fir Ave Seal Beach CA 90740

DEUTSCH, FRANCINE, developmental psychology educator; b. Reading, Pa., Aug. 9, 1948; d. Arthur and Dorace Gertrude (Asher) D. A.B., Albright Coll., 1969; M.S., Pa. State U., 1970, Ph.D., 1972. Instr. child and adolescent devel. Pa. State U., 1969-72, dep. head Pa. Day Care Project, 1972, research assoc. child and family relationships, 1972-73, asst. prof. human devel., 1973-77, asst. prof. child devel., child services, prof.-in-charge child devel. and child services lab., 1977-81; prof. child devel., family relationships San Diego State U., 1981—, dir. Family Life Edn. Project, 1981-83. NSF trainee, 1971-72; Danforth fellow, 1979—. Mem. AAAS, Am. Ednl. Research Assn., Am. Psychol. Assn., Am. Home Econs. Assn., Nat. Assn. Early Childhood Tchr. Educators, Nat. Council Family Relations, Orthopsychiat. Assn., Soc. Research in Child Devel. Democrat. Jewish. Author: Life-Span Individual and Family Development, 1977; Adult Development and Aging: A Life-Span Perspective, 1981; Child Services: On Behalf of Children, 1983. Contbr. articles to profl. jours.

DEUTSCH, VICTOR HENRY, financial executive; b. Chgo., Dec. 3, 1923; s. Lester Lesserman and Sylvia (Friedman) D.; m. Ailsa Lange, Jan. 8, 1950; children: Judith Sharon, Lynne Karen. PhB, U. Chgo., 1943, MBA, 1947. Asst. controller Western Tire Auto Stores, Chgo., 1950-58; asst. to treas. Allied Radio Corp., Chgo., 1958-63; controller Globe Class Mfg. Co., Chgo., 1963-64, Fuller Paint Co., Los Angeles, 1964-65; dir. fin. Jewish Fedn. Council, Los Angeles, 1965-75; v.p. fin. Fishking Processors Inc., Los Angeles, 1975—. Served to capt. USCG Aux., 1980-81. Mem. Fin. Exec. Inst. (vice chmn. info. mgmt. com. 1986—, chmn. mgmt. info. systems com. Los Angeles chpt. 1984-86), Los Angeles Area C. of C. (exec. edn. com. 1984—), Nat. Fedn. Temple Brotherhoods (asst. sec. 1985-86). Jewish. Avocations: tennis, sailing. Home: 750 S Spaulding Ave #233 Los Angeles CA 90036 Office: Fishking Processors Inc 1324 E 15th St Los Angeles CA 90021

DEV, VASU, chemistry educator; b. Lahore, India, Mar. 18, 1933; s. Bhim Dev and Satyavati (Pandey) Shastri; m. Barbara C. Zimmerman, Dec. 19, 1963; children—Rajan, Nisha. B.S., Punjab (India) U., 1951, B.S. with honors, 1953, M.S., 1954; Ph.D., U. Calif., Davis, 1962. Chemist Regional Drug Research Lab., Jammu, India, 1955-56; chemist Med. Coll., Patiala, India, 1956-59; research asso. U. Chgo., 1963-64; asst. prof. dept. pharm. medicinal chemistry U. Tenn., Memphis, 1964-65; prof. chemistry Calif. State Poly. U., Pomona, 1965—; chmn. dept. Calif. State Poly. U., 1971-78; U.S. India exchange scientist, 1982. Contbr. articles to profl. jours. NSF research grantee, 1966-67; Calif. Poly. U. creative activity leave grantee, 1970. Mem. Am. Chem. Soc., Chem. Soc. London, Am. Soc. Pharmacognosy, Calif. Assn. Chemistry Tchrs., Sigma Xi. Home: 1210 Cambridge Ave Claremont CA 91711 Office: Dept Chemistry Calif Poly U Pomona CA 91768

DEVANEY, JOSEPH JAMES, physicist, educator; b. Boston, Mass., Apr. 29, 1924; s. Joseph Patrick and Madeline Elinor (Darragh) D.; m. Marjorie Ann Jones, Sept. 9, 1954; 1 child, Kathleen. Student, Tex. Tech U., 1943-44, USCG Acad., 1944-45; SB, MIT, 1947, PhD, 1950. Research asst. MIT, Cambridge, 1942, 46-48; staff physicist Los Alamos (N.Mex.) Nat. Lab., 1950—; adj. prof. math. U. N.Mex., Los Alamos, 1956-59, adj. prof. physics, 1959-79. Contbr. articles to profl. jours. Adv. Gov.'s policy bd. on pollution, State of N.Mex., 1969-70; mem. County and State Cen. Com., Los Alamos and Santa Fe, 1953-71; co-founder Anti-Smog Fedn. N.Mex., 1967, patrolman Nat. Ski Patrol, 1953-82, water safety and first aid instr. ARC, Los Alamos, 1952-79. Served with AUS, 1942-44; served with USCG, 1944-45. MIT scholar, 1941, 42, 45, 46, 47; AEC fellow, 1947-50. Mem. Am. Phys. Soc., Am. Nuclear Soc., Los Alamos Ski Club (ski patrol leader 1962-63), Sigma Xi. Home: 4792 Sandia Dr Los Alamos NM 87544 Office: Los Alamos Nat Lab X-6 MS B226 PO Box 1663 Los Alamos NM 87545

DEVENPORT, RICHARD LINDSEY, management consultant; b. Burbank, Calif., June 18, 1954; s. Richard Ligon and Nancy Crump (Lindsey) D.; m. Myra Ann Baudoin, Aug. 1974 (div. Apr. 1979); m. Jeanne Angela Humphreys, Dec. 12, 1981. AA in Bus. Adminstrn., Diablo Valley Coll., 1975; BA in Bus. Econs., Golden Gate U., 1979. Payroll acct. Western Pacific, San Francisco, 1974-76; lead acctg. asst. Chevron, USA, Concord, Calif., 1977-79; analyst Gulf Oil Exploration and Prodn. Co., New Orleans, 1977-82; coordinator new systems Petro-Lewis, Denver, 1982-84; mgr. Price Waterhouse Cons., Denver, 1985—. Mem. Ind. Petroleum Assn. Mountain States, Council Petroleum Accts. Soc., Smoky Hill Owners Assn. (bd. dirs. 1985). Republican. Episcopalian. Avocations: snow skiing, fishing, camping. Home: 18278 E Belleview Pl Aurora CO 80015 Office: Price Waterhouse Cons 950 17th St Suite 2600 Denver CO 80202

DE VENUTA, ANTHONY CHARLES, management consultant; b. Newark, July 11, 1946; s. Anthony Joseph and Mary (Kahanec) DeV.; student Fairleigh Dickinson U., 1964-67; AA, Monterey Peninsula Coll., 1970; BA, No. Mich. U., 1971; postgrad. U. So. Calif., 1977-79; m. Francine Mary Ranuio, Oct. 10, 1976; children: Gina Marie, Anthony Joseph, Dominic D., Maretta Lubov, Joseph Michael. Jr. acct. Fidelity Union Trust Co., Newark, 1965-67; mgmt. intern, indsl. mgmt. analyst Naval Air Rework Facility, Alameda, Calif., 1975-78, supervising indsl. mgmt. analyst, 1979, project mgr., 1979, supervising prodn. controller, project mgr., 1980; pvt. practice indsl. mgmt., systems, office automation cons., Lafayette, Calif.; dir. info. systems devel. Mil. Sealift Command, Oakland, Calif., 1982-83; dir. info. systems, 1983—. Chmn. ADP adv. com. Laney Coll., Oakland, Calif., 1984. Served with U.S. Army, 1967-69. Mem. Assn. Systems Mgrs., Naval Employees Assn. (past dir.), Alameda Def. Mgmt. Assn. (past dir.). Roman Catholic. Home: 3283 Walnut Ln Lafayette CA 94549 Office: Bldg 310-5 P-8 Oakland CA 94625

DE VERE, JULIA ANNE, educator; b. Onaga, Kans., Nov. 2, 1925; d. Goodlet Clarence and Anna (Fairbanks) Bonjour; m. Robert E. DeVere; 1 child, David E. Student Emporia State U., U. Kans., Kans. State Coll.; B.A. in Edn. and Psychology, U. Denver, 1957, M.A., 1961; postgrad. in edn. psychology and social work, U. Md., Sacramento State Coll., U. Calif., Santa Cruz, U. Denver, U. Pacific, San Jose State U. Cert. tchr. mentally retarded, elem. tchr.; specialist in edn., counseling. Elem. tchr. Buckeye-Jackson County, Kans., 1943-45, Bancroft (Kans.) Grade Sch., 1945-46, Belvue (Kans.) Grade Sch., 1946-53, Westmoreland Elem. Grade Sch., Kans., 1953-56; tchr. spl. edn. Stockton United Sch. Dist., Calif., 1957-64; tchr. spl. edn. Cupertino United Sch. Dist., Calif., 1964—, now specialist tchr. for learning disabilities Meyerholz Sch. Contbr. articles to profl. jours. Mem. Nat. Assn. for Retarded Citizens, Santa Clara Chpt. Assn. Retarded Citizens, NEA, Cupertino Edn. Assn., Calif. Tchrs. Assn., Assn. Retirement Credit for Out of State Service, Council Exceptional Children, Delta Kappa Gamma.

DEVEREAUX, J. PETER, architect; b. Allentown, Pa., Apr. 9, 1956. BS, Pa. State U., 1978; MArch, Yale U., 1982. Designer Moore Grover Harper P.C., Essex, Conn., 1979-82, Cesar Pelli & Assocs., New Haven, 1982-85; prin. in charge of design Fields & Silverman, Los Angeles, 1985—. Curator exhbn. An Ideology for Making Architecture, 1981; editor Yale Architecture Jour., Perspecta 20, 1983. Charles Matchum scholar Yale U., 1982. Home: 1037 3d St Santa Monica CA 90403 Office: Fields & Silverman 116 N Robertson Blvd Suite 802 Los Angeles CA 90048

DEVINCENZI, STEVEN LEE, business equipment company executive; b. Santa Monica, Calif., Oct. 29, 1943; s. Peter Louis and Jeanne Louise (Simms) DeV.; student El Camino Coll., 1963-65; B.S., Calif. State U.-Long Beach, 1967; m. Norma Mary Ashby, June 17, 1984; children—D'Arcy Ann, Anthony David, Dana Ann. Sales mgr. A. B. Dick Co., Los Angeles, 1971-73, br. sales mgr., 1973-74, market planning mgr., Chgo., 1974-75; Western regional mgr. Apeco Corp., Los Angeles, 1975-77; Western region mgr. Royal Bus. Machines, Los Angeles, 1977-79; pres. Pacific Photocopy of Calif., North Hollywood, Calif., 1979-85; v.p. sales and mktg. Bus. World Techs., North Hollywood, 1985—; cons. sales tng. Tratec; PMC Corp.; A.B. Dick Distbrs. Served with USNR, 1961-63. Mem. North Hollywood C. of C., Sun Valley C. of C., Los Angeles C. of C., Nat. Office Machine Dealers Assn., Western Office Machines Dealers Assn., Am. Mktg. Assn. Republican. Home: 3693 Dixie Canyon Sherman Oaks CA 91423 Office: 11905 Vose St North Hollywood CA 91605

DEVINE, GRANT, Canadian premier; b. Regina, Sask., Can., 1944; m. Chantal Guillaume, July 1966; children: Michelle, Monique, David, John William, Camille. B.S.A., U. Sask., 1967; M.Sc. in Agr. Econs., U. Alta., 1969, M.B.A., 1970; Ph.D., Ohio State U., 1976. Assoc. prof. agr. U. Sask., 1975-79; mktg. specialist Fed. Govt. Ottawa Agr. Commodity Legislature, 1970-72; leader Progressive Conservative Party of Sask., 1979; premier Province of Sask., 1982—; adv. to Food Prices Rev. Bd. and Province Govts. Contbr. articles to profl. jours. Mem. Am. Econ. Assn., Am. Mktg. Assn., Am. Assn. Consumer Research, Canadian Agr. Econ. Soc. (recipient Cert. of Merit, Vanier award 1983), Consumers Assn. Can. Office: 148 Legislative Bldg, Regina, SK Canada S4S 0B3

DEVOE, VIOLET ANN, systems analyst; b. Chgo., Sept. 27, 1940; d. Lambert Fred and Jean Mary (O'Hagan) Craemer; B.A. in Math., Mt. St. Mary's Coll., 1962; postgrad. in bus. adminstrn. San Diego State U.; cert. in data processing; m. Daniel Franklin Devoe, Dec. 29, 1962; children—Debra Jean, Alan Daniel, Lambert Theodore. Research asst. RAND Corp., Santa Monica, Calif., 1962-63; sci. programmer Litton Industries, Canoga Park, Calif., 1964; programmer analyst Lockheed-Calif. Co., Burbank, Calif., 1965-66, 69-72; sr. systems analyst County of San Diego (Calif.), 1972-80; sr. systems analyst Acctg. Corp. Am., San Diego, 1980-84, ICA Services Corp., San Diego, 1984-85, Presidio Components Inc., San Diego, 1985—. Mem. Data Processing Mgmt. Assn., Coronado Schs. Found., Am. Mensa Ltd. Republican. Roman Catholic. Club: Soroptimists (Coronado, Calif.). Home: 610 First St Coronado CA 92118 Office: PO Box 81576 San Diego CA 92138

DEVON, MICHAEL F., personnel service company executive; b. Vancouver, Wash., Sept. 3, 1949; s. Frank Paul and Marlene Marie Feist; BS, Portland State U., 1975; Salesman Riback and Navaroo Interiors, Vancouver, Wash., 1967-69, Vancouver Furniture Co., 1969-74; sales rep. Paper Cybernetics, Culver City, Calif., 1974-75; pres., owner Devonshire Personnel Service, Inc., Garden Grove, Calif., 1976-84; owner Devon & Devon Personnel Service Inc., Orange, Calif., 1984—. Mem. Am. Employment Assn. Republican. Home: 10717 Wilshire Blvd Penthouse 2 Los Angeles CA 90024 Office: One City Blvd W Suite 1710 Orange CA 92668 Office: 4200 Campus Drive Suite 100 Newport Beach CA 92660

DE VORE, ZETH BLEVENS, educator; b. Oakland, Calif., 1931; B.A. in Edn., San Francisco State U., 1951, M.A. in Spl. Edn., 1964; married; 3 children. Tchr. trainable mentally retarded Kailua (Hawaii) schs., 1966-69; tchr. educationally handicapped Rich-Mar Sch. Dist., San Marcos, Calif., 1969—, now dist. spl. edn. adminstr. Mem. NEA, Council Exceptional Children (pres. N. County chpt. 1980-81), Am. Assn. Mental Deficiency, Calif., Rich-Mar (pres. 1974-76) tchrs. assns., Assn. Calif. Sch. Adminstrs. Office: 270 San Marcos Blvd San Marcos CA 92069

DE VOTO, TERENCE ALAN, radio station executive; b. San Francisco, Aug. 2, 1946; s. Albert Anthony and Virginia Louise (Kohnke) De V.; m. Christine McKannay, Jan. 24, 1976; children: Tommy, Mark, Julie, Carolyn. BBA in Mktg., Gonzaga U., 1968. V.p. trading Birr, Wilson & Co., San Francisco, 1968-74; account exec. Sta. KFOG Radio, San Francisco, 1974-78, Sta. KSFO Radio, San Francisco, 1978-81; nat. sales mgr. Sta. KYUU Radio, San Francisco, 1981-83, gen. sales mgr., 1983-84, gen. mgr., 1984—. Mem. No. Calif. Broadcasters Assn. (bd. dirs. 1985—). Republican. Roman Catholic. Clubs: The Olympic, Merchandising Execs. (San Francisco). Avocations: sports, music. Home: 50 Wolfe Canyon Rd Kentfield CA 94904 Office: NBC/KYUU Radio 530 Bush St San Francisco CA 94108

DEVOUASSOUX, JEAN SAMUEL (JOHN), infosystems specialist; b. Lyon, France, Mar. 23, 1940; came to U.S., 1983; s. Gaston and Rose Olympe (Gallice) D.; m. Line Sachot, Aug. 27, 1967; children: Hans, Yann. Engr., I.N.S.A., France, 1964; PMD, Harvard U., 1976. Tech. advisor Govt., Algiers, Algeria, 1965-66; data processing staff Ferodo Group, Paris, 1967-69; data processing cons. Diebold Group, Paris, 1969-70; mgr. mgmt. infosystems Le Nickel Group, Paris, 1970-75; data processing mgmt. cons. Dev. Enterprise, Los Angeles, 1977-84, pres.; mgr. mgmt. infosystems Bridgestone, Los Angeles, 1985—; cons. in field, San Diego, 1984—. Chief of Cabinet Counseil de Gouvernement, Noumea, New Caledonia, 1981; in charge of fin. and economy Services Economique, New Caledonia, 1983. Mem. Data Processing Mgmt. Assn. Avocation: ocean sailing. Home: PO Box 7808 Laguna Niguel CA 92677 Office: Bridgestone 2000 W 190 St Torrance CA 90509

DE VRIES, KENNETH LAWRENCE, mechanical engineer, educator; b. Ogden, Utah, Oct. 27, 1933; s. Sam and Fern (Slater) DeV.; m. Kay M. DeVries, Mar. 1, 1959; children—Kenneth, Susan. A.B., Weber State Coll., 1953; B.S., U. Utah, 1959, Ph.D., 1962. With Convair, Fort Worth, 1957; mem. faculty U. Utah, Salt Lake City, 1961—; prof. mech. engring. U. Utah, 1969-76, prof. dept. mech. and indsl. engring., 1976—, chmn. dept., 1970-81, assoc. dean research Coll. Engring., 1983—; head polymer program NSF, 1975-76; mem. Utah Council Sci. and Tech., 1973-77. Author: Analysis and Testing of Adhesive Bonds, 1977; contbr. articles on polymers, dental materials, rock mechanics, adhesive design to profl. jours. Mem. ASME, Am. Phys. Soc., Internat. Soc. Dental Research, Am. Chem. Soc., ASTM, Material Soc. Mormon. Home: 1466 Penrose St Salt Lake City UT 84103 Office: U Utah 3008 Mech Engring Bldg Salt Lake City UT 84112

DEWALL, KAREN MARIE, advertising executive; b. Phoenix, May 31, 1943; d. Merle C. and Agnes M. (Larson) Feller; m. Charles E. DeWall, Sept. 3, 1963; 1 child, Leslie Karen. A.A., Phoenix Coll., 1969. Media buyer Wade Advt., Sacramento, 1964-66; media dir., Harwood Advt., Phoenix, 1967-71; co-owner, account exec. DeWall & Assocs. Advt. Co., 1971—; bd. dirs. Phoenix Festivals, Inc., N. Cen. Phoenix Homeowners Assn.; sustaining mem. Jr. League of Phoenix. Named Ad-2 Advt. Person of Yr., Phoenix, 1984. Mem. Am. Women in Radio and TV (achievement award 1986). Republican. Club: Phoenix Country. Home: 32 West Marlette St Phoenix AZ 85013 Office: DeWall and Assocs Advt 737 West McDowell St Phoenix AZ 85007

DEWAN, SAT PAUL, nutritionist, consultant; b. Lahore, Punjab, Pakistan, Jan. 5, 1937; came to U.S., 1964; . Vidya Sagar and Kaushalya Devi (Chaudhry) D.; m. Raj K. Dhaliwal, Apr. 4, 1967; children: Asheesh, Puneet. BS in Pharmacy, Birla Inst. Sci., Pilani, India, 1960; MS in Pharmacy, Punjab U., Chandigarh, India, 1964; PhD in Nutrition, U. Nebr., 1969. Research scientist Tech. Inc., Houston, 1970-75; research dir. Plus Products, Irvine, Calif., 1976; dir. quality control U.S. Labs., Orange, Calif., 1977-78; tech. dir. D&F Industries, Orange, 1979—; cons. Herbalife Internat., Los Angeles, 1982—; mem. staff Apollo and Skylab nutrition programs, NASA, 1970-75. Author: (with others) Nutrition, 1980. Mem. Am. Chem. Soc., Am. Assn. Nutritional Cons. Republican. Avocations: wood working, photography, badminton, table tennis. Home: 15 Rainstar Irvine CA 92714 Office: D&F Industries 1800 E Pacifico St Anaheim CA 92805

DEWAR, JACQUELINE MICHELE, mathematics educator. d. James Martin and Dorothy Elizabeth Deveny; m. James A. Dewar; children: Jeremy, Margot. B, St. Louis U., 1968; M, U. So. Calif., 1970, PhD, 1973. Prof. math. Loyola Marymount U., Los Angeles, 1973—, chairperson dept. math, 1982-86. Co-author: Basic Mathematics for Calculus, 2d rev. edit., 1983; contbr. articles to profl. jours. Mem. Math. Sci. Interchange (co-founder), Assn. Women in Math. (council mem.), Math. Assn. Am., Nat. Council Tchrs. Math., Phi Beta Kappa. Office: Loyola Marymount U Dept Math Los Angeles CA 90045

DEWEESE, MALCOLM LESLIE, JR., social sciences educator, consultant; b. Moultrie, Ga., Nov. 11, 1935; s. Malcolm Leslie DeWeese Sr. and Mary Katherine (Harryman) Harper; m. Catherine Marie McGuern, Jan. 28, 1963 (div. 1984); 1 child, Abraham. AA, Valley Coll., 1957; BA cum laude, U. Ariz., 1965; PhD, U. Wash., 1973, MBA, 1979. Sr. research investigator Wash. State Hosp. Commn., Olympia, 1979-81; sci. systems programmer U. Wash., Seattle, 1981—; prin. investigator Prospective Reimbursement Program, Health and Human Services, Washington, 1979-81; cons. Geriatric Studies, Seattle, 1981—, Inst. on Aging, U. Hosp., Seattle, 1981-84; vis. faculty The Evergreen State Coll., Olympia, 1986—. Author: (software program) Electragrade, 1986; contbr. articles to profl. jours. Served with U.S. Army, 1958-60. Grantee U. Wash., 1970; Ford Found. fellow, 1965. Fellow Am. Math. Assn.; mem. Am. Econ. Assn., Nat. Assn. Bus. Economists, Nat. Econometric Assn., Medieval Acad. Am. Democrat. Roman Catholic. Avocation: microcomputer software creation. Home: 13739 1st Ave NW Seattle WA 98177 Office: U Wash Speech Communication Dept MS DL-15 Seattle WA 98105

DEWELL, WENDY ANDERSON WESTOVER, indsl. engr.; b. Denver, Jan. 23, 1950; d. Alden DeLancey and Faye Anderson (Smillie) Westover; BA in Math. magna cum laude, UCLA, 1972; MS in Ops. Research, Stanford U., 1973; m. David Kent Dewell, Feb. 19, 1978; 1 child, Elizabeth Anderson; stepchildren: David Todd, Ginger Anne, Thomas Steven. Asso. indsl. engr. IBM, San Jose, Calif., 1973-76, sr. assoc. indsl. engr. Gen. Products Div., 1976-77, project engr. indsl. engring., 1977-79, new products program adminstr., 1979-81, project mgr., 1981-84, mfg. staff, 1984-87, adv. engr., 1987—. Mem. Soc. Women Engrs. (sec. San Francisco Bay Area sect. 1977-78), Phi Beta Kappa, Alpha Xi Delta (treas. Santa Clara Valley chpt. 1977-79, v.p. 1979-80, pres. 1980-81, regional alumnae dir. 1981-83, pres. Alpha Xi chpt. 1971-72. Republican. Presbyterian. Home: 57B Mount Hamilton Rd San Jose CA 95114 Office: 5600 Cottle Rd San Jose CA 95193

DE WETTER, HERMAN PETER, health care corp. exec.; b. New Rochelle, N.Y., Jan. 28, 1920; s. Herman and Louise (Hurlbutt) de W.; student public, pvt. schs.; m. Margaret Belding, Aug. 7, 1943; children—Charles, David, Robert. Trainee, R.H. Macy, N.Y.C., 1938-39; prodn. mgr. Napier Co., Meriden, Conn., 1940-42; buyer White House Dept. Store, El Paso, Tex., 1945-48; mdse. mgr. Guberman's Dept. Store, Colorado Springs, Colo., 1949-51; partner OK Van & Storage, El Paso, 1951-61; chmn. bd. OK Van & Storage Co., Las Cruces, N. Mex., 1961-71; pres., chief exec. officer Bekins Co., Los Angeles, 1971-79; exec. v.p. Nat. Med. Enterprises, Inc., Los Angeles, 1979—, also dir.; dir. Thomas J. Lipton, Inc., Englewood Cliffs, N.J., BSC Ptrns.,Los Angeles. Mem. nat. adv. council Goodwill Industries Am.; bd. dirs. So. Calif. Bd. of NCCJ, Music Center Operating Co., Los Angeles, YMCA Metro Los Angeles; trustee City of Hope; mayor, City of El Paso, 1969-70. Served to maj. U.S. Army, 1942-45. Decorated Bronze Star. Recipient Thanks Badge, Girl Scouts U.S.A., 1965, Leadership award West Tex. C. of C., 1969, Outstanding Community Service award City of El Paso (Tex.), 1970, Humanitarian award NCCJ, 1981. Mem. Mchts. and Mfrs.' Assn. (dir.), Am. Heart Assn., Newcomen Soc., SR. Clubs: Calif.,

Lincoln, 100, Valley Hunt, Twilight; Rotary (Los Angeles). Office: 11620 Wilshire Blvd Los Angeles CA 90025 *

DEWEY, CHRISTOPHER GERARD, protective services official; b. Janesville, Wis., June 8, 1956; s. Floyd James and Eleanor Alice (Kauffman) D. BA in Philosophy and Chemistry, Cornell Coll., 1978; MS in Inorganic Chemistry, U. Minn., 1983. Chemist Rock Paint and Chem. Co., Ft. Atkinson, Wis., 1978-79; instr. Blackhawk Tech. Inst., Beloit, Wis., 1978-80; chem. specialist Dana Corp., Edgerton, Wis., 1979-80; research asst. chemistry dept. Cornell Coll., Mt. Vernon, Iowa, 1980; tech. Wis. Lab. of Hygiene, Madison, 1984; hazardous materials inspector Bellevue (Wash.) Fire Dept., 1984—, Kirkland (Wash.) Fire Dept., 1986—; cons. chemist Kent (Wash.) Fire Dept., 1985—. Mem. solid waste adv. com. Puget Sound Council Govt., Seattle, 1985—, Tukwila (Wash.) Fire Dept., 1986—. Mem. Am. Chem. Soc. (Jr. Analytical Chem. award 1977), Internat. Union Pure and Applied Chemistry, Wash. State Assn. Fire Chiefs (fire prevention officers sect.), Am. Inst. Chemists. Office: Bellevue Fire Prevention Bur 666 Bellevue Way SE Bellevue WA 98004

DEWEY, JAMES WILLIAM, seismologist; b. Glen Ridge, N.J., Jan. 21, 1943; s. Horace William and Margaret Ann (Avery) D.; m. Anne Katherine Redo, Mar. 18, 1967; children: Nicholas John, Elizabeth Anne. AB, U. Calif., Berkeley, 1965, MA, 1967, PhD, 1971. Research geophysicist Nat. Oceanic Atmosphere Adminstrn., Boulder, Colo., 1971-73, U.S. Geol. Survey, Denver, 1973—. Editor: Geophys. Jour., 1977-81; assoc. editor: Jour. Geophys. Research, 1984—. Fellow Royal Astron. Soc.; mem. Seismol. Soc. Am., Am. Geophys. Union, AAAS. Home: 2840 Dover Dr Boulder CO 80303 Office: US Geol Survey Stop 967 Fed Ctr Denver CO 80225

DEWEY, MICHAEL LEE, wood technologist; b. Spokane, Wash., Nov. 9, 1944; s. Leland Sullivan and Lorraine Margaret (Kofmehl) D.; m. Beverly Jean Thompson, Dec. 30, 1967; children—Cheryl, Michelle, Marci, Monica. B.S. in Wood Tech., U. Idaho, 1968, B.S. in Chemistry, 1969; A.A. in Acctg., Mendocino Community Coll., 1980, A.A. in Bus. Adminstrn., 1980. Chemist, U.S. Plywood, Lebanon, Oreg., 1969-70; wood chemist Koppers Co., Orrville, Ohio, 1971-76; process engr. Masonite Co., Ukiah, Calif., 1976-79, sr. process engr., 1979-82, cost acct., fin. analyst, 1982-83, acctg. mgr., 1983—. Served with USNR, 1966-70. Mem. Am. Chem. Soc., Am. Mgmt. Assn., Forest Products Research Soc., Soc. Wood Sci. and Tech., Am. Legion, Alpha Phi Omega. Republican. Lodges: Elks, Lions (Ukiah treas. 1986—). Home: 650 Chablis Ct Ukiah CA 95482 Office: Masonite Co 300 Ford Rd Ukiah CA 95482

DEWEY, RICHARD WILLIAM, automotive company public affairs manager; b. Detroit, June 30, 1930; s. Richard Sydney and Viola Katherine (Rau) D.; m. Dora Belle Byerly, Dec. 27, 1952; children—Steven Richard, Cheryl Katherine Dewey Hartman. B.A., U. Mich., 1955. Reporter, bus. writer Owosso (Mich.) Argus-Press, 1955-56; with pub. relations staff Chrysler Corp., 1956-57, Burroughs Corp., 1957; account exec., pub. relations McCann Erickson, 1958-60, Kenneth Drake Assocs., 1960-61; with Ford Motor Co., 1961—, overseas pub. info. mgr. Ford Tractor Ops., 1965-70, corp. info. mgr. internat. ops., 1970-71, corp. internat. plans mgr., 1971-74, asst. pub. relations mgr. Ford Tractor Ops., 1974-76, asst. mgr. pub. relations Western Region, 1976-83, regional mgr. pub. affairs staff, San Jose, Calif., 1983—. Nat. adv. bd. Northwood Inst., Midland, Mich., bd. dirs. Blue Lake Fine Arts Camp, Twin Lake, Mich., 1972—; adv. com. Crittendon Hosp., Rochester, Mich. Served to lt. U.S. Army, 1953-55. Mem. Pub. Relations Soc. Am. (accredited). Clubs: San Francisco Press, Commonwealth.

DEWHURST, WILLIAM GEORGE, psychiatrist, educator, administrator, researcher; b. Frosterley, Durham, Eng., Nov. 21, 1926; came to Can., 1969; s. William and Elspeth Leslie (Begg) D.; m. Margaret Dransfield, Sept. 17, 1960; children—Timothy Andrew, Susan Jane. B.A., Oxford U., Eng., 1947, B.M., B.Ch., 1950; MA, Oxford U., 1961; D.P.M. with distinction, London U., 1961. House physician, surgeon London Hosp., 1950-52, jr. registrar, registrar, 1954-56; registrar, sr. registrar Maudsley Hosp., London, 1957-62, cons. physician, 1965-69; lectr. Inst. Psychiatry, London, 1962-64, sr. lectr., 1965-69; assoc. prof. psychiatry U. Alta., Edmonton, Can., 1969-72, prof., 1972—, chmn. dept. psychiatry, 1975—, co-dir. Neurochem. Research Unit, 1979—, hon. prof. pharmacy and pharm. scis., 1979—, hon. prof. oncology, 1983—; cons. psychiatrist Royal Alexandra Hosp., Edmonton, Edmonton Gen. Hosp.; chmn. med. council Can. Test Com., 1977-79, Royal Coll. Test Com. in Psychiatry, 1971-80, examiner, 1975—. Neurobiology of Trace Amines, 1984, Co-editor: Pharmacotherapy of Affective Disorders, 1985; also conf. procs. Referee Nature, Can. Psychiat. Assn. Jour., Brit. Jour. Psychiatry; mem. editorial bd. Neuropsychobiology, Psychiat. Jour. U. Ottawa. Contbr. articles to profl. jours. Mem., chmn. Edmonton Psychiat. Services Steering Com., 1977—; mem. Provincial Mental Health Adv. Council, 1973-79, Mental Health Research Com., 1973—, Edmonton Bd. Health, 1974-76, Can. Psychiat. Research Found., 1985—; bd. dirs. Friends of Schizophrenics, Ctr. Gerontology, Alta., Can. Psychiat. Research Found.; grant referee Health & Welfare Can., Med. Research Council Can., Ont. Mental Health Found., Man. Health Research Council, B.C. Health Research Found. Served to capt. Royal Army M.C., 1952-54, Hong Kong. Fellow Can. Coll. Neuropsychopharmacology (pres. 1982-84), Am. Coll. Psychiatrists, Am. Psychiat. Assn., Royal Coll. Psychiatrists, Royal Coll. Physicians and Surgeons Can. (nucleus speciality com. 1987—); mem. Alta. Psychiat. Assn. (pres. 1973-74), Can. Psychiat. Assn. (pres. 1983-84), Royal Coll. Physicians, Alta. Coll. Physicians and Surgeons, Alta. Med. Assn., AAAS, Am. Assn. Chmn. Depts. Psychiatry, Assn. for Acad. Psychiatry, Brit. Med. Assn., Can. Assn. Anglican. Club: Faculty (Alta.). Avocations: music; hockey; football; chess; athletics. Office: U Alberta, Dept Psychiatry, 1E7 44 Mackenzie Centre, 8440-112 St, Edmonton, AB Canada T6G 2B7

DEWITT, ELIZABETH KATHLEEN, social worker; b. Kansas City, Mo., Feb. 20, 1947; d. George Anderson Flud and Lenora Margaret (Brown) Robinson; m. Ronald Lee DeWitt, May 7, 1966 (div. Jan. 1983); children: Brian, Tonia. B in Social Work, N.Mex. State U., 1979, MA in Counseling and Edn. Psychology, 1981. Exec. sec., asst sales mgr. United Med. Labs., Portland, Oreg., 1968-72; stas. mgr. Gulf Oil Co., Portland, 1972-74; social work aide S.W. Mental Health Ctr., Las Cruces, N.Mex., 1978-79; Child Protective Services social worker N.Mex. Dept. Human Services, Las Cruces, 1980-85; social work supr. N.Mex. Dept. Human Services, Albuquerque, 1985—; cons. Crisis Rap Ctr., Las Cruces, 1978-80; vol. Battered Women's Shelter, Las Cruces, 1980-83; dir. S.W. regional conf. Nat. Fedn. Social Workers, Las Cruces, 1979-80. Author: Megavitamin Therapy for Hyperactive Children, 1981. Named one of Outstanding Young Women of Am., 1979-80; Harry S. Truman scholar N.Mex. State U., 1977. Mem. Nat. Assn. Social Workers (sec., treas. N.Mex. chpt. 1982-84), Nat. Assn. Christians in Social Work (bd. dirs. 1979-81, pres. N.Mex. chpt. 1978—), Nat. Assn. Prevention Child Abuse, Phi Kappa Phi. Democrat. Adventist. Avocations: bowling, swimming, softball, sewing, cooking. Home: 4723 Glendale Rd NW Albuquerque NM 87105 Office: NMex Dept Human Services PO Box 669 Albuquerque NM 87103

DEWITT-RUIZ, VALERI JEAN (VAL), corporate communications director; b. San Bernardino, Calif., Jan. 17, 1950; d. Howard William and Beverly Jean (Williamson) DeWitt; m. Edward John Ruiz, May 21, 1983; 1 child, Cameron. B, San Diego State U., 1974, postgrad. in bus., 1985-87; postgrad. in orgn. devel., U. San Francisco, 1986—. Staff Sentinal Newspapers, San Diego, 1974-76, Press-Courier Pub. Co., San Diego, 1976-78; communications coordinator Home Fed. Savs. and Loan, San Diego, 1978-80; dir. pub. relations Cox Cable, San Diego, 1980-82; corp. communications mgr. IVAC Corp., San Diego, 1982-85; corp. communications counsel Solar Turbines, Inc., San Diego, 1985—; cons. in field, San Diego, 1980—. Contbr. writing, photography, design to various publs. (numerous awards). Chmn. Tribute to Women and Industry, San Diego YWCA, 1980-84. Mem. Internat. Assn. Bus. Communicators (bd. dirs. 1978-80, v.p. 1980-82, pres. 1982-84, Communicator of Yr. 1980), Women in Communications (v.p. 1980-81, pres. 1982, Woman of Achievement 1981), Pub. Relations Soc. Am., Soc. Profl. Journalists. Club: San Diego Press. Avocations: photography, writing, camping. Office: Solar Turbines Inc 2200 Pacific Hwy San Diego CA 92138

DEWOLF, ROBERT BORDON, II, chemical engineer; b. Birmingham, Ala., May 2, 1945; s. Robert Borden and Betty Joan (Wright) DeW.; m. Eva Jane Brockman, June 21, 1969. BA in Gen. Sci., Bridgewater Coll., 1968; BS in Chem. Engring., U. Md., 1974. Chemist Patuxent Research, Laurel, Md., 1971-73; chem. engr. Davison Chem., Curtis Bay, Md., 1975-78, Nuclear Fuel Service, Erwin, Tenn., 1978-83; sr. process engr. Rockwell Hanford, Richland, Wash., 1983—. Patentee in field. Served to sgt. U.S. Army, 1968-70, Vietnam. Mem. Am. Chem. Soc., Am. Inst. Chem. Engrs. Republican. Methodist. Club: Richland Rod and Gun. Avocations: bridge, sci. fiction, hunting, fishing.

DE WOODY, CHARLES, lawyer; b. Chgo., Oct. 18, 1914; s. Charles and Oneta (Ownby); student U. Fla., 1931-33, U. Mich., 1933-35, Columbia U., 1935-36, Western Res. U., 1936-38; m. Nancy Tremaine, June 15, 1940; children—Charles, Nancy. Office atty. Oglebay, Norton & Co., Cleve., 1939-43; ptnr. Arter, Hadden, Wykoff & Van Duzer, 1943-61; sole practice, 1961—; dir. Nat. Extruded Metal Products Co., Ferry Cap and Set Screw Co., Meteor Crater Enterprises, Inc.; gen. partner Bar-T-Bar Ranch, Mem. Am., Ohio, Cleve. bar assns., Cleve. Law Library Assn. Clubs: Rancho Santa Fe Tennis; Chagrin Valley Hunt (Gates Mills, Ohio). Home: El Mirador Box 1169 Rancho Santa Fe CA 92067

DEXHEIMER, HENRY PHILLIP, II, ins. agy. exec.; b. Dayton, Ohio, Sept. 16, 1925; s. Henry Phillip and Helene Francis (Veach) D.; B.S. in Commerce, U. So. Calif., 1952; children—James Phillip, Jana Helene. Sales account exec. with various cos. and newspapers, 1946-51; broadcasting sales exec. Sta. KBIG, KTLA-TV, Los Angeles, 1952-58; broadcasting sales exec. Sta. KFXM, San Bernardino, Calif., 1956-57, pres., 1956-57; founder, owner, pres. Dexheimer Co., Los Angeles, 1958—. Served with inf. and adj. gen.'s dept. U.S. Army, 1943-46; PTO. Recipient Sammy award Los Angeles Sales Execs. Club, 1955; Silver Sales trophy Radio Advt. Bur. N.Y., 1955; named Agt. of Year, Los Angeles office Travelers Ins. Cos., 1978, 83, 84, 85; Hal Parsons award, 1983. C.L.U. Mem. Am. Soc. C.L.U.s (nat. dir. Travelers chpt. 1972-73, 80-81), Am. Coll. Life Underwriters, Advt. Assn. West, Radio and TV Soc. Hollywood, Life Ins. and Trust Council Los Angeles, Los Angeles Life Underwriters Assn. (dir. 1963-65, v.p. 1967-69), Million Dollar Round Table (life, honor roll), World Affairs Council Los Angeles, Internat. Assn. Fin. Planners, U. So. Calif. Acctg. Circle, Am. Art Council, Decorative Art Council of Los Angeles County Art Mus., Alpha Delta Sigma, Phi Kappa Tau. Republican. Presbyterian. Clubs: Town Hall (Los Angeles); Beverly Hills Men's (Calif.); Masons (32 degree), Shriners, Legion of Honor. Office: Dexheimer Co Marina Bus Ctr 13160 Mindanao Way Suite 222 Marina del Rey CA 90292 *

DEXTER, THOMAS RAY, radio station executive; b. Denver, July 22, 1938; s. Ernest Ray and Lelia (Blevins) D.; m. Sharon Estelle Madison, Sept. 1, 1962 (div. Nov. 1976); children: Paul Thomas, John Thomas; m. Purificacion A. Mendoza, July 4, 1986. AA, Valley Coll., Van Nuys, Calif., 1959; student, Calif. State U., Northridge, 1959-60, Don Martins, 1960-61, Bakersfield Coll., 1976-79; CPA, Becker CPA Review, 1984-85. CPA; lic. gen. operator's, FCC. Disc jockey, news reporter Sta. KZIP, Amarillo, Tex., 1966, Sta. KVOD, Albuquerque, 1966-67; various positions Wagenvoold Broadcasting Co., New Orleans, 1967-69; with news, prodn. depts. Sta. WTAN, Clearwater, Fla., 1969-71; disc jockey Sta. KVBM, Lancaster, Calif., 1971; dir. programming Sta. KCHJ, Delano, Calif., 1971—; tax preparer Benificial Fin., Delano, 1980; cons. Bloom & Co., Studio City, Calif., 1986, Melvin Crosby, Hollywood, Calif., 1987, James Lyles, Bakersfield, Calif., 1987. Contbr. articles Contemporary Comedy mag., 1975. Dir. Delano Wine and Harvest Festival, 1975. Mem. Filipino-Am. Soc. Tulare County (pres. 1984), Acad. Magical Arts. Lodge: Eagles. Avocations: music, magic. Home: PO Box 562 Delano CA 93216 Office: Sta KCHJ 16th and 122d Aves Delano CA 93216

DEXTER, TOMME SCOTT, developmental engineer, consultant; b. Glendale, Calif., Feb. 1, 1950; s. Dennie Dary and Martha Verne (Fullmer) D.; m. Lorraine Ruth Ritter, Feb. 14, 1976; children: Michelle Lisa, Cameron Paul, Kimberley Maie, Gregory Dean. BS in Engring., Calif. State U., Northridge, 1975. With Alpha Loc, St. George, Utah, 1975; quality assurance supr. Inspiron, Upland, Calif., 1975-77; production supr. Hosp. Med. Corp., Santa Ana, Calif., 1977; sr. project engr. Am. Pharmaseal, Irwindale, Calif., 1977-84; devel. engr. Cilco, Inc., Pomona, Calif., 1984—; cons. in field. Inventor. Mem. ASME, Am. Nat. Standards Inst., Am. Standard Test Methods, Soc. Mfg. Engrs. Clubs: West End Gun (Ontario, Calif.) (pres. 1983-85); Prado Tiro (Chino, Calif.). Avocations: photography, hunting, fishing, hiking, racquetball. Home: 13203 E Highland Ave Etiwanda CA 91739 Office: CILCO Inc 2865 Pomona Blvd Pomona CA 91769

DE YARMIN, RAYMOND WESLEY, museum curator, naval historian, author, lectr.; b. Dinuba, Calif., May 25, 1924; s. William Franklin and Helen Augusta (Johnson) de Y.; B.G.S., Chaminade U., 1981; M.P.S., Central Mich. U., 1983; m. Dorothy Jean Mills, Mar. 11, 1949; children—Richard Michael, Karen Sue, Daniel Raymond, Thomas Grady; m. 2d Constance Marie Fedor, July 16, 1966. Curator, Pacific Submarine Mus., Naval. Submarine Base, Pearl Harbor, Hawaii, 1979—. Served with USN, 1942-77; World War II, Korea, Vietnam. Mem. Hawaiian Mus. Assn., Submarine Vets., Naval Submarine League, Fleet Res. Assn., Internat. Submarine Assn. (Brit. sect.), VFW (life), Naval Inst. (assoc.), Maritime Hist. Soc. (assoc.), Sigma Iota Epsilon. Democrat. Episcopalian. Lodge: Elks. Author: Japanese Midget Submarine Attack on Pearl Harbor, 1981; History of Submarine Base, Pearl Harbor, 1984, Saga of the I-25, 1985. Office: Pacific Submarine Mus Naval Submarine Base Pearl Harbor HI 96860

DEZEMBER, RAYBURN STUART, banker; b. Evansville, Ind., Jan. 24, 1931; s. Larry O. and Dalpha Fay (Haley) D.; m. Joan Erreca, Sept. 11, 1954; children: Rebecca, Brent, Cherilee, Kathleen. B.A. in Sociology, Whittier Coll., 1953. Chmn., pres. Am. Nat. Bank, Bakersfield, Calif., 1967-83, chmn., 1983—; chmn. Bakersfield Ready Mix Inc., 1967—; owner Service Transport Inc., Bakersfield, 1966—; chmn., pres., chief exec. officer Central Pacific Corp., Bakersfield, 1981—; dir. Bakersfield Californian Newspaper, Fed. Res. Bank San Francisco Los Angeles br., 1972-77, Fed. Res. Bank San Francisco, 1984—; mem. Stanford Ado Group, Palo Alto, Calif., 1975-77. Bd. dirs. Pacific Coast Banking Sch. U. Wash.-Seattle, 1972-78; bd. trustees Whittier Coll., (Calif.), 1970—, Kern High Sch. Dist., Bakersfield, 1968-80. Mem. Bank Adminstrn. Inst. (bd. dirs., exec. com., chmn. 1983—), Am. Bankers Assn. (leadership council 1982-83), Calif. Bankers Assn. (pres. 1980-81, bd. dirs 1983—). Republican. Congregationalist. Clubs: Jonathan (Los Angeles); Stockdale County (Bakersfield). Lodge: Elks. Office: Central Pacific Corp PO Box 5500 5016 California Ave Bakersfield CA 93309 *

DHALL, PREM KUMAR, research chemist; b. Churkhana, Punjab, India, Dec. 4, 1938; came to U.S., 1970; s. Boota Ram and Mohan Devi (Sabarwal) D.; m. Bimla Kandhari, Sept. 15, 1966; children: Anjna, Leena, Neeta. BS, Lucknow U., India, 1957, MS, 1959; MS, U. Wyo., 1972. Lectr. Boys Anglo Bengali Coll., Lucknow, 1959-61; sci. officer Atomic Energy Establishment, Bombay, 1961-70; sr. analyst Phelps Dodge Corp., Playas, N.Mex., 1975-78; research chemist Stauffer Chem. Co., Green River, Wyo., 1978—. Home: 1430 Moran Dr Green River WY 82935 Office: Stauffer Chem Co PO Box 513 Green River WY 82935

DHARANIPRAGADA, RAMALINGA MURTY, organic chemist; b. Vijayawada, India, Nov. 9, 1956; came to U.S., 1978; s. Late Viswanadha Sarma and Sesha Yamma Dharanipragada. BS, Andhra Loyola Coll., Vijayawada, 1975; MS, Indian Inst. Tech., Bombay, 1977; PhD in Organic Chemistry, W.Va. U., 1985. Teaching asst. W.Va. U., Morgantown, 1978-85, research assoc., 1985; postdoctoral chemist UCLA, 1985—. Contbr. chpts. to books. Mem. Am. Chem. Soc. Home: 1923 Camden Ave Los Angeles CA 90025 Office: UCLA Dept Chemistry and Biochemistry Los Angeles CA 90024

DHAWAN, GULSHAN KUMAR, chemical engineer; b. Rawalpindi, India, Oct. 30, 1944; came to Can., 1966; s. Ram Saran and Krishna (Khanna) D.; m. Rajni Kalra, Dec. 18, 1973; children: Anjli, Manisha, Sonali. BTech in Chem. Engring., India Inst. Tech., Delhi, 1966; MASc., Waterloo U., Ont., Can., 1968, PhD in Chem. Engring., 1972. Registered profl. engr. Research and devel. engr. Electrohome, Kitchener, Ont., Can., 1972-74, mgr. reverse osmosis, 1974-77; mgr. environ. systems Electrohome, Kitchener, Ont., Can, 1977-80; mktg. mgr. UOP Fluid Systems, San Diego, 1980-82, market devel. mgr., 1982-83; pres. Applied Membranes, Inc., San Diego, 1983—; cons. Nitto Denko, Santa Clara, Calif., 1984-85, Eastman Kodak, Rochester, N.Y., 1985—, Hydromation, Detroit, Mich., 1986—. Contbr. articles to profl. jours. Grantee Nat. Research Council, 1966, 68; postdoctoral fellow Nat. Research Council, 1972. Mem. Am. Inst. Chem. Engrs., Am. Chem. Soc., Water Quality Assn. Avocations: hiking, tennis. Home: 13343 Bavarian Dr San Diego CA 92129 Office: Applied Membranes inc 635 N Twin Oak Valley Rd San Marcos CA 92069

DHAWAN, JAGJIT RAJ KUMAR, marketing executive; b. Nowshera, India, Apr. 14, 1944; came to U.S., 1969, naturalized, 1973; s. Badrinath and Savitri Devi (Bhola) D.; B.S. with honors, St. Xavier's Coll., 1967; cert. in exec. program in mgmt., UCLA, 1978, Exec. M.B.A., 1984; m. Georgene Rose Cain, Aug. 27, 1969. Quality control technician Mobil Chem. Co., Vernon, Calif., 1970-73; math. analyst Jet Propulsion Lab., Pasadena, Calif., 1974; supr. quality control and product control Champion Internat., Monrovia, Calif., 1975-76; tech. dir. Ferro Corp., Culver City, Calif., 1977-80, mktg. dir., 1980-87, gen. mgr. composites div., 1987—; bd. dirs., trustee Pan Pacific Ctrs., Pacific Palisades, Calif., 1974-78; bd. dirs. Alsthom-Ferro Composites; chmn. mktg. com. Suppliers of Advanced Composites Materials. Recipient awards of merit Internat. Vegetarian Congress, 1961, Bombay Humanitarian League, 1962, St. Xavier's Coll., 1967. Mem. Am. Chem. Soc., Am. Mgmt. Assn., Soc. for Applied Material and Process Engring., Internat. Student Assn., Suppliers Advanced Composites Materials Assn. (chmn. mktg. com. 1986). Mem. Evangelical Free Ch. Contbr. articles to profl. jours. Office: Ferro Corp 5915 Rodeo Rd Los Angeles CA 90016

DHRUV, HARISH RATILAL, textile chemist/colorist; b. Ahmedabad, India, Mar. 14, 1946; came to U.S., 1970, naturalized, 1978; s. Ratilal Chhaganial and Shantaben Hariprasad (Dave) D.; m. Kaumudini Vasudev Vyas, June 21, 1971; 1 child, Nirav H. BS in Chemistry, St. Xavier's Coll., Gujarat U., India, 1966; diploma in textile chemistry, M.S. U., Baroda, India, 1967; BS in Textile Chemistry, Phila. Coll. Textiles and Sci., 1972. Trainee supr. Mafatlal Fine Mills, Ahmedabad, 1967-68; supr. Calico Mills, Ahmedabad, 1969-70; quality control and processing mgr. fashion prints U.S. Industries Co., Allentown, Pa., 1972-77; print supt., v.p. mfg. Pacific Fabric Printers, Vernon, Calif., 1977-80; owner textiles importing, converting and printing bus. South Pasadena, Calif., 1980—. Pres. India Assn. of Lehigh Valley, 1974, 75, 76. Recipient Bicentennial medal for pub. service to community City of Allentown, 1977. Mem. Am. Assn. Textile Chemists and Colorists, Am. Chem. Soc., Assn. Western Furniture Suppliers (sec.), West Coast Furniture Fabric Club (sec. 1984, treas. 1985, v.p. 1986, pres. 1987—), Bharatiya Cultural Soc. (pres. 1976). Democrat. Hindu. Home: 269 Saint Albans Ave South Pasadena CA 91030

DIAL, OLIVER EUGENE, political scientist, educator; b. Woodriver, Ill., Nov. 10, 1922; s. Oliver Lee and Julia Lavina (Botkin) D.; m. Bette Jeanne Wynkoop, Dec. 28, 1944; 1 child, Oliver Eugene. LL.B., Blackstone Coll. Law, 1954; B.A., San Diego State Coll., 1959, M.S. in Pub. Adminstrn, 1962; Ph.D. in Polit. Sci. (Sch. fellow), Claremont Grad. Sch., 1965. Time motion study engr. Owens Ill. Glass Co., Alton, 1940-42; commd. 2d lt. U.S. Marine Corps., 1942, advanced through grades to maj., 1953; ret. 1963; lectr. govt. San Diego State Coll., 1963-64; asst. prof. govt. Calif. Poly. U., San Luis Obispo, 1964-65; chmn. dept. govt. Idaho State U., 1965-68; vis. prof. polit. sci., mem. staff Urban Systems Lab., Mass. Inst. Tech., 1968-69; mem. faculty Joint Center Urban Studies, Harvard U., 1968-69; chmn. dept. polit. sci., supr. grad. program pub. adminstrn. Baruch Coll. CUNY, 1969-70; prof. urban affairs U. Colo. Grad. Sch. Pub. Affairs, 1973-81; prof. elec. and computer engring. U. Colo., 1981-85, ret., 1985; cons. fed. intergovtl. agys. com. urban regional info. systems, Washington, 1968-80. Author: Programming and Statistics for Basic Research, 1969, Bibliography on Urban Affairs, 1970, (with Kraemer, Mitchell, Weiner) Municipal Information Systems: The State of the Art in 1970, 1971, Integrated Municipal Information Systems: The USAC Approach, 1972, Integrated Municipal Information Systems: The Use of the Computer in Local Government, 1973, (with Goldberg) Privacy, Security, Computers and the City: Guidelines for Municipal Information Systems, 1974; Editor: policy forum info. systems dedication Bureaucrat, 1972; editor: policy forum info. systems dedication Urban Geocoding, 1975; Contbr. numerous articles to profl. publs. and popular computer mags. Mem. Am. Bar Found. (adv. com. land records improvement 1973-85), Urban Regional Info. Systems Assn. (pres. 1979-80), Am. Polit. Sci. Assn., AAUP, Am. Soc. Pub. Adminstrn., AAAS.

DIAMOND, BERNARD LEE, educator, psychiatrist; b. San Francisco, Dec. 8, 1912; s. Leon Isaac and Rose (Cohen) D.; m. Ann Landy, Feb. 10, 1946; children: Joan, Lynn (Mrs. Alan Feiger), Larry, Lisa, Judy, Jan. A.B., U. Calif-Berkeley, 1935; M.D., U. Calif. at Berkeley and San Francisco, 1939. Intern, resident psychiatry U. Mich. Neuropsychiat. Inst., 1938-40, 41-42; grad. San Francisco Psychoanalytic Inst., 1952; pvt. practice psychiatry and psychoanalysis San Francisco, 1945-64; faculty U. Calif. at Berkeley, 1963—, prof. law, 1964-80, emeritus, 1980—, clin. prof. psychiatry, 1968—, acting dean Sch. Criminology, 1969-70, 74-76; dir. Dr. of Mental Health program U. Calif.-San Francisco, 1980-86; mem. adv. com. criminal justice mental health standards project ABA dir. Am. Bd. Forensic Psychiatry, 1978-82. Contbr. articles to profl. jours. Bd. advisers Atascadero State Hosp., 1974-76. Served to lt. col. M.C. AUS, 1940-41, 42-45. Recipient J. Elliot Royer award U. Calif., 1964; Gold medal award Mt. Airy Found., 1972. Fellow AAAS, Am. Psychiat. Assn. (Isaac Ray award 1968), Am. Orthopsychiat. Assn. (bd. dirs. 1968-71); mem. AMA (diagnostic and therapeutic tech. assessment panel), Am. Sociol. Assn., Am., Internat. psychoanalytic assns., Am. Acad. Psychiatry and Law (Golden Apple award 1975), No. Calif. Psychiat. Soc. (past pres.). Home and Office: PO Box 999 Ross CA 94957

DIAMOND, DIANA LOUISE, editor; b. Floral Park, N.Y., Feb. 4, 1937; d. Louis Bartholomew and Helen Stephanie (Strzelecki) Chmielewski; student Middlebury Coll., 1954-56; B.A. in English, U. Mich., 1958; m. Horace Williams Diamond, Jr., June 29, 1958 (div. 1975); children—Bruce Williams, Scott Kenneth, Kent Christopher, Mark Patrick. Editorial asst. dept. higher edn. NEA, Washington, 1958-59; pvt. tchr. art, Sunnyvale, Calif., 1964-68; reporter Pioneer Press, Highland Park, Ill., 1969-70; reporter Lerner Newspapers, Highland Park, 1970-72, mng. editor, 1972-78, suburban coordinator, 1974-78; corr. (part-time) The N.Y. Times, 1975-78; profl. journalism fellow Stanford U., 78-79, sr. writer, editor, spl. asst. to pres., 1983—; asst. dir. univ. relations Stanford U., 1985—; editorial writer, mem. editorial bd. San Jose (Calif.) Mercury News, 1979-80, editor Sunday Opinion sect., spl. projects editor, 1980; editor-in-chief Calif. Lawyer, 1981-83; moderator, co-producer League Women Voters TV show Left, Right and Center, 1968; sr. writer Stanford U., 1983-85. Pres. Deerfield (Ill.) Area Human Relations Com., 1968-70; mem. Deerfield Human Relations Commn., 1969-70; bd. dirs. YWCA, Highland Park, 1977-78, New Forum, 1985—, Palo Alto Civic League, 1986—; Chgo. Philharmonic Soc., 1977-78; bd. dirs. Midpeninsula Citizens for Fair Housing, pres., 1983-86; mem. Calif. Freedom on Info. Com., 1983—; mem. Calif. Freedom of Info. Com., 1984—. Recipient Nat. Blue Ribbon Newspaper award, 1976, 77, 78; 3d pl. Ill. Editor of Year contest, 1974; 1st pl. for Best Feature Story, Ill. Press Assn., 1976, Suburban Newspapers Am., 1977; 2d pl. for Best Column, Nat. Newspaper Assn., 1977; Maggie award Western Pubs. Assn. Mem. LWV (dir. Deerfield 1968-70), Sigma Delta Chi. Home: 4146 Thain Way Palo Alto CA 94306

DIAMOND, JAMES MORRIS, physician; b. N.Y.C., Jan. 6, 1938; s. Solomon and Florence Diamond.; m. Michiyo Ishii, Nov. 9, 1960; children: Naomi, Emily. AB, Stanford U., 1959; MD, U. Calif., San Francisco, 1975. Diplomate Am. Bd. Pediatrics. Intern Kaiser Found. Hosp., San Francisco, 1975-76, resident, 1976-78; from physician to sr. physician The Permanente Med. Group, South San Francisco, 1978—. Fellow Am. Acad. Pediatrics; mem. Physicians for Social Responsibility. Avocations: photography, bicycling, canoeing, writing. Office: The Pemanente Med Group 1200 El Camino Real South San Francisco CA 94080

DIAMOND, JONI LYNN, psychotherapist; b. Cin., Apr. 1, 1956; d. Sidney David and Elaine Shirley (Gindy) D. BSW, Ohio State U., 1977; MSW,

Atlanta U., 1980. Lic. clin. social worker, Calif.; diplomate in clin. social work. Evaluation cons., trainer S.E. Regional Support Ctr., A.L. Nellum and Assocs., Atlanta, 1979-80; social worker Coosa Valley (Ga.) Community Mental Health Ctr., Cartersville, 1980-81; program dir. Vols. of Am., Los Angeles, 1981-83, Gateways Hosp. and Mental Health Ctr., Los Angeles, 1983-86; psychotherapist Balog Med. Group, Pasadena, Calif., 1984—; program mgr. Drug/Alcohol Recovery Team, Pasadena, 1986-87; psychotherapist Balog Med. Ctr. Group, Pasadena, 1987—; pvt. practice psychotherapy North Hollywood, Calif., 1987—; cons. to various agys. and orgns. San Fernando Valley, Calif., Beverly Hills, Calif., 1986—; mem. adv. bd. Nursing Services Internat., Beverly Hills, 1986—. Mem. Nat. Assn. Social Workers (cert., bd. dirs. 1987—), Bus. and Profl. Women (exec. bd. dirs., 1st v.p. 1986-87, pres. 1987—), So. Calif. Jewish Communal Workers, Jewish Prisoners (mem. adv. bd.), Escalon Group (hon., bd. dirs. 1981—, program chmn. 1984-85). Avocations: traveling, reading, cooking, camping, racquetball. Home: 12352-2 Runnymede St North Hollywood CA 91605 Office: Balog Med Group 33 S Catalina #202 Pasadena CA 91106

DIAMOND, MARIA SOPHIA, lawyer; b. Portland, Oreg., Aug. 29, 1958; d. Harry and Nitsa (Fotiou) D. BA in Eng., U. Wash., 1980; JD, U. Puget Sound, 1983. Bar: Wash. 1983, U.S. Dist. Ct. (we. dist.) Wash. 1983, U.S. Ct. Appeals (9th cir.) 1985. Assoc. Levinson, Friedman, Vhugen, Duggan, Bland & Horowitz, Seattle, 1983—. Named to Nat. Order of the Barristers U. Puget Sound, 1983. Mem. ABA, Wash. State Trial Lawyers Assn., Wash. Women Lawyers, Seattle-King County Bar Assn. (young lawyers sect., mem. com. legal problems disadvantaged 1984-86, legis. com. 1986—), Women's Fisheries Network, U. Wash. Alumni Assn., Alpha Gamma Delta Alumni Assn. Avocations: fgn. langs. (Greek and French), travel, golf, swimming. Office: Levinson Friedman Vhugen et al 1500 One Union Sq Seattle WA 98101

DIAZ, FERNANDO J(ERONIMO), interior designer; b. Veguitas, Cuba, Nov. 14, 1952; came to U.S., 1966; s. Jose Amador and Mercedes H. (Jimenez) D. BA, Ottawa (Kans.) U., 1968-73; cert. in Interior Design, UCLA. Corp. mgr. and designer Budget Furniture Rentals, Santa Monica, Calif., 1974—; designer Fernando Interior Design, Santa Monica, Calif., 1980—. Mem. Am. Soc. Interior Designers (assoc.), Alpha Psi Omega. Baptist. Home: 2638-28th St #10 Santa Monica CA 90405

DIAZ, LUIS F., environmental executive, consultant; b. Lima, Peru, Apr. 20, 1946; came to U.S., 1962; s. Julio G. and Luisa C. (Campodonico) D.; m. Sharon L. Clark, Oct. 19, 1968; children: Daniel, David. BSME, San Jose State U., 1972; MME, U. Calif., Berkeley, 1973, PhD in ME, 1976. Research engr. U. Calif., Berkeley, 1976-77, instr., 1977; instr. San Francisco State U., 1980-81; pres. Cal Recovery System, Richmond, 1975—; cons. World Bank, WHO, U.S. Aid, UN Indsl. Devel. Orgn. Author: Organic Wastes for Fuel and Fertilizer in Developing Countries, 1980, Resource Recovery from Municipal Solid Wastes, 1982; contbr. articles to publs. Served with USAR, 1971-76. Recipient Engring. Award of Distinction, San Jose State U., 1982. Mem. ASME, Am. Soc. Agrl. Engring., Soil Conservation Soc. Am., Sigma Xi. Office: 160 Broadway Suite 200 Richmond CA 94804

DIAZ, RAMON VALERO, judge; b. Manila, Oct. 13, 1918; came to Guam, 1951; s. Vicente and Bibiana (Valero) D.; m. Josefina Dela Concepcion, July 3, 1945; children: Carlos, Marilu, Mariles, Maribel, Marilen, Maryann, Anthony, Vincent, Ramon, Maricar. PhB, U. St. Tomas, Manila, 1940, LLB, 1941; grad. U.S. Army J.A.G. Sch., 1945; Diploma Jud. Skills, Am. Acad. Jud. Edn., 1984. Bar: Philippines 1941, Guam 1956, U.S. Ct. Appeals (9th cir.) 1966, High Ct. of Trust Territories 1977, No. Marianas 1985. Assoc. Diokno Law Office, Manila, 1943-44; sole practice, Guam, 1960-80; judge Superior Ct. of Guam, Agana, 1980—; mem. U.S. Selective Service Bd. Appeals, Guam, 1950-62. Permanent deacon Roman Catholic ch. Served with PhilippineArmy, j.g., 1941-45. Mem. Am. Judges Assn., Nat. Council Juvenile and Family Ct. Judges, VFW. Survivor Bataan Death March, 1942. Home: 41 San Antonio St Dededo GU 96912 Home: PO Box AR Agana GU 96910 Office: Superior Ct of Guam Route 4 O'Brien St Agana GU 96910

DIAZ-JIMENO, FELIPE, foreign language/ area studies educator, consultant; b. Madrid, Aug. 9, 1937; came to U.S., 1958; s. Felipe Díaz and Emilia Jimeno; m. Stephanie Ferrara, Aug. 26, 1967; children: Celeste, Felipe R. BA in Latin Am. Area Studies, U. Kans., 1968; MA in Spanish, U. Tex., 1973, PhD in Spanish, 1978; PhD, U. Madrid, 1988. Internat. exec., coordinator European and Latin Am. div. Sybron Corp., 1968-71; vis. lectr. U. Ill., Chgo., 1976-77; paleographer and translator Béxar Archive of Tex., Austin, 1977-78; instr. Spanish U. Tex., Austin, 1978-79; vis. prof. Spanish Pa. State U., Univsity Park, 1979-80; asst. prof. Spanish U. Ga., Carrollton, 1980-83; assoc. prof. Spanish U. Colo., Denver, 1983—; cons. U.S. govt., 1977-81, Westinghouse Corp., Spain, AT&T, Spain, Gen. Motors, Spain and Portugal, 1984-86, others; advisor U.S.-Spain Commn. for Cultural Exchange, 1975-80; participant U.S. Nat. Fgn. Policy Conf., Dept. State, 1982. Author: Fate & Fortune in XVI Century Spain, 1987; contbr. articles to profl. jours. Served with U.S. Army, 1962-65. Grantee Spanish Ministry Fgn. Affairs, 1974-75, Spanish U. Found., 1975-78, Fulbright, 1974-75. Mem. Am. Assn. Tchrs. Spanish (higher edn. rep., chmn. study abroad com. Colo. chpt. 1986—), MLA, Rocky Mountain MLA, European Assn. Profs. Spanish, South Eastern Latin Am. Area Studies Assn., Philol. Assn. the Carolinas, Phi Sigma Iota. Democrat. Roman Catholic. Avocations: drawing, painting, sculture, mountain climbing, soccer. Home: 2840 Colby Dr Boulder CO 80303 Office: U Colo Denver Box 178 1100 14th St Denver CO 80202

DIBATTISTA, JOHN, JR., sales manager; b. McKeesport, Pa., Sept. 22, 1949; s. John Sr. and Jean (Sposato) DiB.; m. Caryl Lee King, Aug. 26, 1967; children: Christine Ann, John III. AS, Community Coll. Alleghany, 1972; BS, SUNY, Albany, 1976; MBA, Pepperdine U., 1985. Mgr. retail store Fox Grocery Store, Belle Vernon, Pa., 1975-76; area sales rep. S.C. Johnson & Son, Inc., Pitts., 1976-77, dist. sales mgr., 1977-78; regional sales mgr. S.C. Johnson & Son, Inc., Cleve., 1978-82, Los Angeles, 1982-86; v.p. retail ops. Normark & Assocs. Food Brokers, Los Angeles, 1986—. Served to maj. USMCR, 1972—. Republican. Methodist. Home: 24902 Avenida Libre El Toro CA 92630 Office: Normark & Assocs 3200 W Temple St Los Angeles CA 90026

DIBBLE, ROSAMOND, educator; b. Sprague, Wash., Nov. 28, 1932; d. James Tilden and Keithe Stella (Robertson) Swannack; m. Neil Lawrence Dibble, Apr. 5, 1955; children: Susan Lynn, Craig Evan, Lisa Anne, Dawn Marie. BA, Wash. State U., 1953, MA, 1957. Tchr. bus. edn. Pateros (Wash.) Pub. Schs., 1954-56, Omak (Wash.) Pub. Schs., 1960—; adj. instr. bus. edn. Cen. Wash. U., 1985—. Active disaster res. ARC, Burlingame, Calif., 1973—. Named Tchr. of Yr. Omak Sch. Dist., 1978. Mem. Wash. State Bus. Edn. Assn., Wash. Vocat. Assn., Cen. Wash. Bus. Edn. Assn. (treas. 1976-77, pres. 1978-79), Wash. Women's Bowling Assn. (treas. 1984-86, bd. dirs. 1975-84). Avocations: bowling, playing piano and organ, reading, hunting, fishing. Home: Rt 3 PO Box 450 Omak WA 98841 Office: Omak High Sch PO Box 833 Omak WA 98841

DICHTL, RUDOLPH JOHN, aerospace company executive; b. Chgo., May 16, 1939; s. Max and Anna (Eibl) D.; m. Joan Lottie Smith, June 11, 1960; children: Angela S., Kristopher R., Mary K., John R. BSEE, Ill. Inst. Tech., 1961; MS in Physics, Air Force Inst. Tech., 1966. Commd. 2d lt. USAF, 1961, advanced through grades to lt. col., ret., 1981; asst. prof. U. Colo., Boulder, 1978-81; proposal mgr. Ball Aerospace Systems Div., Boulder, 1981-82, mgr. new tech., 1982-85, program mgr., 1985—; bd. dirs Shroud of Turin Research Project, Inc., Amston, Conn. 1978—. Exchange scientist Fed. Republic Germany, 1972; recipient Community Service award Ball Corp., 1985. Mem. Am. Def. Preparedness Assn., Am. Astronautical Soc. Republican. Roman Catholic. Lodge: Kiwanis (pres. Foothills club, named disting. sec. Rocky Mountain Dist. 1983, disting. pres. 1985). Avocations: stamp and coin collecting, construction of scientific prototypes. Home: 41 Pineview Ln Boulder CO 80302-9414 Office: Ball Aerospace Systems Div PO Box 1062 Boulder CO 80306

DICK, BERTRAM GALE, JR., physics educator; b. Portland, Oreg., June 12, 1926; s. Bertram Gale and Helen (Meengs) D.; m. Ann Bradford Volkmann, June 23, 1956; children—Timothy Howe, Robin Louise, Stephen Gale. B.A., Reed Coll., 1950; B.A. (Rhodes scholar), Wadham Coll., Oxford (Eng.) U., 1953, M.A., 1958; Ph.D., Cornell U., 1958. Research assoc. U. Ill., 1957-59; mem. faculty U. Utah, 1959—, prof. physics, 1965—, Univ. prof., 1979-80, chmn. dept., 1964-67, dean grad. sch., 1987—; cons. Minn. Mining and Mfg. Co., 1960-67; vis. prof. Technische Hochschule, Munich, 1967-68; vis. scientist Max Planck Institut Für Festkörperforschung, Stuttgart, Fed. Republic Ger., 1976-77; faculty Semester at Sea, fall 1983, 86. Mem. Alta Planning and Zoning Commn., 1972-76; pres. Chamber Music Salt Lake City, 1974-76. Served with USNR, 1944-46. Fellow Am. Phys. Soc.; mem. AAAS, Am. Alpine Club, Sierra Club, Phi Beta Kappa, Sigma Xi. Research in theory solid state. Home: 1377 Butler Ave Salt Lake City UT 84102 Office: U Utah Dept Physics Salt Lake City UT 84112

DICK, JUSTIN, performance hall administrator, entrepeneur, film producer; b. Colorado Springs, Colo., July 27, 1957; s. Howard Millhouse and Nancy Elizabeth (Kilzer) D. BS in Biochemistry, Evergreen State Coll., 1979. Freelance film producer N.Y.C., 1979-81; geophysicist Western Geophys. Co. subs. Litton Industries, Denver, 1981-82; dir. adminstrn. rec. and research ctr. Denver Ctr. Performing Arts, 1982—; pres. Transp. Designs, Denver, 1983—. Produced over 250 film and videotape pieces including Spellbound (Festival of the Am.'s award Houston Internat. Film Festival), Renew (Alfie award), The Winning Edge (Silver award Internat. Film and TV Festival of N.Y. 1984), Magic Box (Bronze award Internat. Film and TV Festival of N.Y. 1985, Festival of the Am.'s award 1986), Center Stage Breakin' (Ace award 1985, Nat. Hometown USA award 1985, Frannie award 1985). Active campaigns Nancy Dick for State Rep., 1976, Nancy Dick for Lt. Gov., 1978, 82, Nancy Dick for U.S. Senate, 1984. Mem. Colo. Film and Video Assn. Home: 1421 Gilpin #7 Denver CO 80218 Office: Denver Ctr Performing Arts 1245 Champa Denver CO 80204

DICK, NANCY E., former state lieutenant governor; b. Detroit, July 22, 1930; m. Stephen Barnett; children: Margot, Timber, Justin. B.A. in Resort Mgmt., Mich. State U. Worked in resort mgmt., conv. dir., interior design, bookkeeping; mem. Colo. Gen. Assembly, 1974-79, vice chmn. transp. and energy com.; lt. gov. State of Colo., 1979-86; fin. chmn. Fedn. Rocky Mountain States; mem. adv. panel U.S. Oil Shale Environ. Com., 1974-78; del. Nat. Democratic Party Convention, 1980; mem. Fordham Planning Commn., U.S. Health Care Cost Containment, 1981; Rocky Mt. bd. dirs. Inst. Internat. Edn., 1980-87; exec. bd. Gov's. Interstate Indian Council, 1981-83; chmn. regional selection White House Fellows, 1981, panelist, 1979-80; chmn. Colorado-Human Indsl. Conf. Planning Com.; del. Women's Leadership Conf. on Nat. Security. Trustee Denver Symphony Assn.; hon. chmn. Friends of the Urban League; mem. rural health com. Colo. Med. Soc., 1975-76; exec. bd. U.S. Army War Coll., 1981. Recipient Disting. Alumni award Mich. State U., 1980; recipient Florence Sabin award Colo. Pub. Health Care Assn., 1980, Outstanding Alumnus award Coll. Bus., Mich. State U., 1981, Outstanding Citizen Nat. Rural Primary Care Assn., 1981, Found. scholarship Nat. Ctr. Creative Leadership, 1981. Democrat. Office: Office of Lt Gov State Capitol Bldg Room 144 Denver CO 80203 *

DICKENS, A. TERRANCE, real estate developer; b. Torrance, Calif., Nov. 20, 1944; s. Alvin Tennyson and June (Hansen) D.; m. Vicky Lee Knight, June 11, 1966; children: Geoffrey, Michelle, Brandon, Ryan. BA, Calif. State U., Fullerton, 1967. Property mgr. Bryan Indsl. Properties, Anaheim, Calif., 1962-64; ind. real estate appraiser La Habra, Calif., 1964-68; area analyst br. locations Bank of Am., Los Angeles, 1968-70; dir. real estate Alpha Beta Co., La Habra, 1970-78; sr. v.p., dir. real estate Downey Savs. and Loan, Costa Mesa, Calif., 1978-82; real estate developer, gen. ptnr. Terrawin Group Ltd., Fullerton, 1982-86; gen. ptnr., real estate devel. DP Properties, Inc., Fullerton, 1986—; instr. Calif. State U., Fullerton, 1982—. Scout leader Boy Scouts Am., Fullerton, 1978—; pres. conf. Calif. State U., Fullerton Alumni Exec. Council, 1984-85. Mem. Internat. Council Shopping Ctrs. (state dir. 1976-79), Calif. Bus. Properties Assn. (pres. 1980-81, chmn. bd. dirs. 1981-82). Republican. Mormon. Office: DP Properties 680 Langsdorf Dr Suite 203 Fullerton CA 92631

DICKENSON, DONALD DWIGHT, sugar company executive, researcher; b. Paris, Ill., Jan. 15, 1925; s. John Herbert and Eloise Elma (Muncie) D.; m. Virginia Mae Adams, June 16, 1946; children: Susan Gay, Ann Elizabeth, Robin Lee, Donald Curtis. BS, U. Ill., 1949, MS, 1950; PhD, U. Minn., 1953. Plant breeder Holly Sugar Corp., Sheridan, Wyo., 1953-54; plant breeder Holly Sugar Corp., Tracy, Calif., 1954-62, asst. dir. agrl. research, 1962-66, dir. agrl. research, 1966-71; dir. agrl. research Holly Sugar Corp., Colorado Springs, Colo., 1971-86. Contbr. articles to jours. Mem. city planning commn. Tracy, 1964-71. Recipient Meritorious Service award Beet Sugar Devel. Found., 1974. Mem. Am. Soc. Sugar Beet Technologists, Cropsci. Soc. Am., Am. Soc. Agronomy, Soil Sci. Soc. Am., Am. Phytopath Sci. Avocations: photography. Office: Holly Sugar Corp PO Box 1052 Colorado Springs CO 80909

DICKER, DORN SUE, corporate relations executive; b. Wichita, Kans., June 27, 1946; d. James Frederick, Jr., and Joan C. (Callais) Barlow; BA, U. Kans., 1968; MBA, U. So. Calif., 1970. V-p. for security Pacific Nat. Bank, Los Angeles, 1969-73; dir. adminstrn. Pacific Resources, Inc., Honolulu, 1975-76; owner, dir. Island Internat., Honolulu, 1976-79; v.p., dir. corp. relations Parsons Corp., Pasadena, Calif., 1979—; leader seminars and workshops, panelist, speaker. Trustee, past pres. Dispute Resolution Ctr., Pasadena; trustee Pasadena Polit. Action Com.; mem. adv. council Girls' Club Pasadena. Commerce Assns.fellow, 1968-70; recipient Outstanding Leadership award Am. Cancer Soc., 1983, 84. Mem. Nat. Investor Relations Inst., Pub. Relations Soc. Am., Women in Bus., Beta Gamma Sigma.

DICKERSON, ERIC DEMETRIC, football player; b. Sealy, Tex., Sept. 2, 1960; s. Helen Dickerson. Student, So. Meth. U. Running back Los Angeles Rams, 1983—. Named NFL Player of Yr., 1983, Pro Football Writers Rookie of Yr., 1983. Player Pro Bowl, 1984, 85; holds single season rushing yardage record, 1984; lead NFL in rushing 1983, 84, 86. Office: Los Angeles Rams 2327 W Lincoln Ave Anaheim CA 92801 *

DICKERSON, MORGAN WILLIAM FISHER, III, social worker, county/city ofcl.; b. Pueblo, Colo., Apr. 10, 1941; s. Morgan William Fisher and Ellen Morehead (Weddington) B.; B.S., McPherson (Kans.) Coll., 1966; M.S W., Portland State U., 1972, M.P.A., 1978; m. Patricia A. Pitts, June 16, 1968; children—Laura Noelle, Scott Irving. Asst. rehab. coordinator Goodwill Industries of Oreg., 1968-70; asst. dir. Ret. Sr. Vol. Program, City of Portland/County of Multnomah, Oreg., 1973-74, dir. 1975-76, planner Commn. on Aging, 1974-75, assoc. dir., from 1976, planner Area Agy. on Aging, 1975; geriatric specialist North/N.E. Community Mental Health Center Inc., 1982-83; adult therapist Ctr. for Community Mental Health, 1983-85, Portland Pub. Schs., 1985—. Contbr. articles to profl. jours. Served with U.S. Army, 1966-68; with res. Mem. Nat. Council on Aging, Nat. Assn. Social Workers, Nat. Assn. Black Social Workers (pres. 1986-87). Club: Lions (pres. 1983-84). Office: 531 SE 14th St Portland OR 97211

DICKERSON, WILLIAM ROY, lawyer; b. Uniontown, Ky., Feb. 15, 1928; s. Banjamin Franklin and Honor Mae (Staples) D. B.A. in Acctg., Calif. State U.; J.D., UCLA, 1948. Bar: Calif. 1959. Dep. atty., ex-officio city prosecutor City of Glendale, Calif., 1959-62; assoc. James Brewer, Los Angeles, 1962-68, LaFollette, Johnson, Schroeter & DeHaas, Los Angeles, 1968-73; sole practice, Los Angeles, 1973—; lectr. and speaker in field. Bd. dirs. LosFeliz Improvement Assn., Zoning Commn.; co-chmn. Streets and Hwys. Commn. Mem. ABA, Calif. Bar Assn., Los Angeles County Bar Assn., Soc. Calif. Accts., Assn. Trial Lawyers Am., Century City Bar Assn., Fed. Bar Assn., Nat. Soc. Pub. Accts., Assn. So. Calif. Def. Counsel, Am. Film Inst., Internat. Platform Assn. Home and Office: 813 N Doheny Dr Beverly Hills CA 90210

DICKEY, RITA M., tourism and corporate research training, education consultant; b. Hartford, Conn., Oct. 16, 1925; d. Joseph and Edwina Curtis (Partridge) Durkee; m. Franklin Miller Dickey, Apr. 19, 1947 (div.); 1 dau., Sarah Coulter Lazarus. Student U. Calif.-Berkeley, 1943, 47. Writer, editor, Teaching Machines, Inc., Albuquerque, 1961-64, EVCO, Inc. Behavioral Research & Devel., Albuquerque, 1966-70; editorial dir. Individual Learning Systems, Inc., San Rafael, Calif., 1970-71, mktg. dir., 1972-74; dir. tourism devel. No. Pueblo Enterprises, Santa Fe, 1971-72; v.p. Sipapu Inst., San Francisco, 1976-80, pres., 1980-82; part-time faculty Coll. Bus. Adminstrn., U. San Francisco, 1981; pvt. practice communications cons., San Francisco, 1976-85, Honolulu, 1985—. Docent Haas-Lillienthal House, 1982-83; dir. tng. and devel. Travel Industry; mem. Internat. Visitors Ctr., San Francisco; vol. Com. to Save Cable Cars. Democrat. Club: Commonwealth (San Francisco). Home: 11707 W Darlington #9 Los Angeles CA 90049 Office: Dr Martha D D Brumbaugh & Assocs 1234 Franklin Suite A Santa Monica CA 90404

DICKINSON, ELEANOR CREEKMORE, artist, educator; b. Knoxville, Tenn., Feb. 7, 1931; d. Robert Elmond and Evelyn Louise (Van Gilder) C.; m. Ben Wade Oakes, June 12, 1952; children: Mark Wade, Katherine Van Gilder, Peter Somers. B.A., U. Tenn., 1952; postgrad., San Francisco Art Inst., 1961-63, Académie Grande Chaumiere, Paris, 1971; M.F.A., Calif. Coll. Arts and Crafts, 1982. Escrow officer Security Nat. Bank, Santa Monica, Calif., 1953-54; mem. faculty Calif. Coll. Arts and Crafts, Oakland, Calif., 1971—; assoc. prof. art Calif. Coll. Arts and Crafts, 1974-84, prof., 1984—, dir. galleries, 1976-86. Author: Revival, 1974, That Old Time Religion, 1975, The Complete Fruit Cookbook, 1972; also museum catalogs; illustrator Human Sexuality: A Search for Understanding, 1984; one person exhbns. include Corcoran Gallery Art, Washington, 1970, 74, San Francisco Mus. Modern Art, 1965, 68, Fine Arts Mus. San Francisco, 1969, 75, touring exhbn., Smithsonian Inst., 1975-81, Oakland Mus., 1979, Tenn. State Mus., 1981-82, Galeria de Arte y Libros, Monterrey, Mexico, 1978, Hatley Martin Gallery, San Francisco, 1986; represented in permanent collections Nat. Collection Fine Arts, Corcoran Gallery Art, Library of Congress, Smithsonian Instn., San Francisco Mus. Modern Art, Butler Inst. Art, Oakland Mus., Santa Barbara Mus. Bd. dirs. Calif. Confederation of the Arts, 1983—, Bay Area Lawyers for the Arts, 1976-78, 86—; mem. council bd. San Francisco Art Inst., trustee, 1964-67; sec., bd. dirs. YWCA, 1955-62; treas., bd. Westminster Center, 1955-59; bd. dirs. Children's Theater Assn., 1958-60, Internat. Child Art Center, 1958-68, Calif. Confedn. for the Arts, 1983—; trustee Art Inst., 1964-67, mem. council, 1966—. Mem. Coalition of Women's Art Orgns. (dir., v.p. 1978-80), Coll. Art Assn., AAUP, San Francisco Art Assn. (sec., dir. 1964-67), NOW, Artists Equity Assn. (nat. v.p., dir. 1978-84), Arts Advocates, Women's Caucus for Art (nat. Affirmative Action officer 1978-80). Democrat. Episcopalian. Office: 5212 Broadway Oakland CA 94618

DICKINSON, JACOB JOHN LOUIS, mechanical engineer; b. Honolulu, Dec. 17, 1957; s. Jacob Alan and Ruth (Curd) D.; m. Janis Miyeko Kibe, Feb. 25, 1983; 1 child, Jacob Carl Toshiro. Student, Deep Springs Coll., 1976-78, Washburn U., 1979; BSME, U. Wash., 1982; student, UCLA, 1985—. Sr. engr. Douglas Aircraft, Long Beach, Calif., 1983—. Chmn. decade fundraising Deep Springs Coll. Mem. ASME, AAAS, Am. Assn. for Artificial Intelligence. Avocations: bicycling, cooking, reading history, writing.

DICKINSON, ROBERT EARL, atmospheric scientist, administrator; b. Millersburg, Ohio, Mar. 26, 1940; s. Leonard Earl and Carmen L. (Ostby) D.; m. Nancy Mary Mielinis, Jan. 5, 1974. AB in Chemistry and Physics, Harvard U., 1961; MS in Meteorology, MIT, 1962, PhD in Meteorology, 1966. Research assoc. MIT, Cambridge, 1966-68; scientist Nat. Ctr. Atmospheric Research, Boulder, Colo., 1968-73, sr. scientist, 1973—, head climate sect., 1975-81, dep. dir. A.A.P. div., 1981-86, acting dir., 1986—; mem. climate research com. NRC, Washington, 1985—, com. earth scis., 1985—, UNU steering com. Climatic, Biotic and Human Interactions in Humid Tropics, 1984—, steering com. Internat. Satellite Land Surface Climatology project, 1984—. Editor: The Geophysiology of Amazonia, 1986; contbr. articles to profl. jours. Fellow AAAS, Am. Meteorol. Soc. (Meisinger award 1973, Editors award 1976); mem. Am. Geophys. Union, Assn. Meteorol. and Atmospheric Physics (sec. climate commn. 1983—). Democrat. Home: 2835 Iliff St Boulder CO 80303 Office: Nat Ctr Atmospheric Research PO Box 3000 Boulder CO 80307

DICKINSON, ROBERT VANCE, computer company executive; b. Susanville, Calif., Nov. 16, 1941; s. Fred Eugene and Doris Elida (Vance) D.; m. Janet Lucy Mayfield, July 17, 1965 (div. Apr. 1975); m. Sylvia Olivia Avenente, May 17, 1975; 1 child Lauren Elissa. AB in Physics, U. Calif., Berkeley, 1963; MS in Physics, U. Wash., 1964. Dir. engring. Singer Co., San Leandro, Calif., 1964-75; dir. product mgmt. TRW Inc., Los Angeles, 1976-78; v.p. engring. Systems Devel. Corp., Los Angeles, 1978-80; v.p., gen. mgr. Burroughs Corp., Danbury, Conn., 1981-83, Zilog Inc., Campbell, Calif., 1983; pres., chief exec. officer Mouse Systems Corp., Santa Clara, Calif., 1984-86, Verticom Inc., Sunnyvale, Calif., 1987—; bd. dirs. First Systems Corp. Contbr. articles to profl. jours.; inventor in field. Sloan Found. fellow Stanford (Calif.) U. Sch. Bus., 1972-73. Mem. IEEE, AAAS, Stanford Bus. Sch. Alumni Assn. Republican. Club: Ladera Oaks Country, Ladera Oaks Swim and Tennis. Avocations: running, skiing, reading, wine. Office: Verticom Inc 545 Weddel Dr Sunnyvale CA 94089

DICKINSON, WADE, physicist, research and development company executive; b. Sharon, Pa., Oct. 29, 1926; s. Ben Wade Orr and Gladys Grace (Oakes) D.; m. Eleanor Creekmore, June 12, 1952; children: Mark, Katherine, Peter. Student, Carnegie Inst. Tech., 1944-45; BS, U.S. Mil. Acad., 1949; postgrad., Oak Ridge Sch. Reactor Tech., 1950-51. Commd. 2d lt. USAF, 1949, advanced through grades to capt., 1954, resigned, 1954; cons. physicist Rand Corp., Santa Monica, Calif., 1952-54; engring. cons. Bechtel Group, Inc., San Francisco, 1954—; tech. advisor U.S. Congress, Washington, 1957-58; pres. Agrophysics, Inc., San Francisco, 1968—; ptnr. Petrolphysics Ltd., San Francisco, 1975—, Radialphysics Ltd., San Francisco, 1980—, Robotphysics Ltd., San Francisco, 1983—; vis. prof. engring. U. Calif., Berkeley, 1984—; cardiology cons. Mt. Zion Hosp., San Francisco; chmn. bd. Calif. Med. Clin. Psychotherapy. Contbr. articles to profl. jours; patentee in field. Trustee World Affair Council, 1958-62; mem. San Francisco Com. Fgn. Relations; pres. Young Republicans, Calif. Mem. Am. Physicists Soc., Am. Soc. Petroleum Engrs. Episcopalian. Club: Bohemian (San Francisco). Lodges: Masons, Guardsmen. Home: 2125 Broderick St San Francisco CA 94115 Office: Petrolphysics Ltd 2101 Third St San Francisco CA 94107

DICKMAN, SHERMAN RUSSELL, educator; b. Buffalo, Jan. 15, 1915; s. Albert Aaron and Anna (Singer) D.; m. Marion Jeannette Lund, June 11, 1941; children: Susan, William, Thomas. BS, Pa. State Coll., 1936; MS, U. Ill., Urbana, 1937, PhD, 1940. Asst. prof. biochemistry U. Utah, Salt Lake City, 1947-50, assoc. resident prof. biochemistry, 1951-52, assoc. prof. biochemistry, 1952-67, prof. biochemistry, 1967—. Pres. Chamber Music Soc. of Salt Lake City, 1966-69, Planned Parenthood of Utah, Salt Lake City, 1970-73. Mem. AAAS, Am. Chem. Soc. (pres. 1956-57), Fedn. Am. Soc. Exptl. Biologists, Am. Soc. Biol. Chemists, Sigma Xi (pres. 1970-73). Avocations: photography, hiking, skiing, tennis. Home: 1560 Indian Hills Dr Salt Lake City UT 84108 Office: U Utah Dept Biochemistry 410 Chipeta Way Salt Lake City UT 84108

DICKS, NORMAN DE VALOIS, congressman; b. Bremerton, Wash., Dec. 16, 1940; s. Horace D. and Eileen Cora D.; m. Suzanne Callison, Aug. 25, 1967; children: David, Ryan. B.A., U. Wash., 1963, J.D., 1968. Bar: Wash. 1968. Salesman, Boise Cascade Corp., Seattle, 1963; labor negotiator Kaiser Aluminum Co., Seattle, 1964; legis. asst. to Senator Warren Magnuson of Wash., 1968-73, adminstrv. asst., 1973-76; mem. 95th-100th Congresses from 6th Wash. Dist., mem. appropriations com., interior, mil. constrn., def. subcoms. Mem. U. Wash. Alumni Assn., Sigma Nu. Democrat. Lutheran. Office: 2429 Rayburn House Office Bldg Washington DC 20515 *

DICKSON, LYNDA FAYE, sociology educator; b. Akron, Ohio, Jan. 3, 1948; d. George L. and Katherine (Poland) D.; 1 child, Melissa. BA, We. Ky. U., 1970, MA, 1972; PhD, U. Colo., 1982. Instr. Auburn (Ala.) U., 1972-74, U. Colo., Boulder, 1975-82; asst. prof. sociology Bradley U., Peoria, Ill., 1982-84, U. Colo., Colorado Springs, 1984—; equal employment opportunity specialist NOAA Environ. Research Lab., Boulder, 1975-76; retention analyst U. Colo., Boulder, 1981-82; research cons. Tng. and Research Assistance Corp., Denver, 1978, Reseach Triangle Inst., Research Triangle Park, N.C., 1980; speaker and lectr. for various civic orgns. Grantee U. Colo., Colorado Springs, 1985. Mem. Am. Sociol. Assn., We. Social Sci. Assn. (cofacilitator sociology 1986—), Colo. Womens Studies Assn, NAACP. Democrat. Home: 705 Bridger Dr Colorado Springs CO 80909-7156 Office: U Colo at Colorado Springs Austin Bluffs Pkwy Colorado Springs CO 80933

DICKSON, PAUL WESLEY, JR., physicist; b. Sharon, Pa., Sept. 14, 1931; s. Paul Wesley and Elizabeth Ella (Trevethan) D.; m. Eleanor Ann Dunning, Nov. 17, 1952; children—Gretchen Ann, Heather Elizabeth, Paul Wesley. B.S. in Metall. Engring., U. Ariz., 1954, M.S., 1954; Ph.D. in Physics, N.C. State U., 1962. With Westinghouse Electric Corp., Large, Pa., 1963-84, mgr. weapon systems, 1965-68, mgr. advanced projects, 1969-72, mgr. reactor analysis and core design, Madison, Pa., 1972-79, tech. dir., Oak Ridge, 1979-84; with EG & G Idaho, Idaho Falls, 1984—, mgr. new tech. devel., 1984—; mem. adv. com. on advanced propulsion systems NASA, Washington, 1970-72; mem. adv. com. reactor physics AEC/Dept. Energy, 1974-79; mem. rev. com. applied physics Argonne (Ill.) Nat. Lab., 1978-83, chmn., 1980; mem. rev. com. engring. physics Oak Ridge Nat. Lab., 1982-86, chmn. 1986; mem. sci. and tech. adv. com. Argonne Nat. Lab., 1985—. Contbr. numerous sci. articles to profl. publs. Served to capt. USAF, 1955-63. Phelps Dodge fellow, 1953-54. Mem. Am. Nuclear Soc., Am. Phys. Soc., N.Y. Acad. Scis., AIME (pres. student chpt. 1953-54), AAAS. Republican. Methodist. Subspecialties: Nuclear fission; Nuclear engineering. Current work: Nuclear reactor development. Office: EG&G Idaho Inc PO Box 1625 Idaho Falls ID 83415 Home: 4850 Loma Circle Idaho Falls ID 83401

DICKSTEIN, IRWIN LLOYD, government official; b. Chgo., Apr. 19, 1929; s. Morris and Dorothy (Levin) D.; m. Ina Ruth Pivitz, Sept. 23, 1951; children—Steven, William, Sheila, Margary. B.S., U. Ill., 1951; M.A., Ind. U., 1956, M.B.A., 1957; LL.B., La Salle Law Sch., 1974. Chief chemist Bloomington (Ind.) Dept. Utilities, 1954-64; chief chemistry unit Ohio River Basin Project, Fed. Water Pollution Control Adminstrn., Eumsville, Ind., 1965-67, chief lab. service, 1967-68, chief pollution surveillance, Cin., 1968-69; dir. Office Regulatory Programs, EPA, Cin., 1969-71, dir. enforcement div. R-8, Denver, 1971-78, dir. environ. services div. R-8, 1978-85, dir, air and toxics div., 1985—. Served to 1st lt. USAF, 1951-54; lt. col. Res. (ret.). Recipient numerous govt. awards, including Outstanding Service award EPA, 1973, 76, 77, 81, 82, Fed. Womens Program award, 1977. Mem. Am. Chem. Soc., Am. Water works Assn., Water Pollution Control Fedn., Sigma Xi, Sigma Iota Epsilon, Omega Beta Pi. Jewish. Clubs: Optimists, Toastmasters. Home: 6739 S Willow Englewood CO 80112 Office: 1860 Lincoln St Denver CO 80203

DIDOMIZIO, VINCENT JAMES, fin. and strategic planner; b. Waterbury, Conn., Mar. 5, 1939; s. James V. and Carmella M. (Cipriano) DiD.; B.S., Post Coll., 1961; LL.B., LaSalle U., 1965; M.B.A., Calif. Western U., 1974; m. Alexandria Ramanauskas, Oct. 27, 1962; children—Kim, Vincent, Robert. Group controller Timex Corp., 1976-78, dir. planning and control, 1980; dir. planning and control Timex Clock Co., 1978-80; dir. govt. fin. Talley Industries, Mesa, Ariz., 1980-82; pres. VJ Assocs., 1983—; v.p. fin. Dynamic Science, Inc.; chief fin. officer Stencel Aero. Engring. Corp., 1985—; dir. Lasting Impressions, Inc. Budget com. United Fund, recipient award. Served with AUS, 1957, 61-62. Recipient Outstanding Fin. Achievement award Timex Corp., 1978. Mem. Nat. Assn. Accts., Nat. Contract Mgmt. Assn., Nat. Indsl. Security Assn. Republican. Roman Catholic. Clubs: KC, Civitan (award). Contbr. articles on acctg., govt. contracting and strategic planning to profl. jours. Home: 11093 E Mercer Ln Scottsdale AZ 85259 Office: PO Box 1140 Phoenix AZ 85029

DIECKHOFF, MARK ANTHONY, data processing manager; b. Los Angeles, Apr. 24, 1962; s. Donald Orman and Myrna Alta (Taylor) D.; m. Susan Marie Crawford, Nov. 14, 1981; children: Joshua Patrick Allen, Lindsay Leigh Ann. A in Engring., Oreg. Inst. Tech., 1982, BS, 1983. Data processing mgr. Calif. Maritime Acad., Vallejo, 1983—; cons. CMA Found., Vallejo, 1985—, D&M Auto Repair, Eugene, Oreg., 1986—. Avocations: sports, sports officiating. Home: 4 Selfridge Vallejo CA 94590 Office: Calif Maritime Acad PO Box 1392 Vallejo CA 94590

DIEDRICK, GERALDINE ROSE, nurse; b. Chgo.; d. Milton Edward and Rose Agnes (Michalski) Goodman; R.N., Mt. San Antonio Coll., Walnut, Calif., 1963; B.S., Calif. State U., Los Angeles, 1966; M.S., UCLA, 1968; divorced; 1 son, Scott Wesley. Nurse, State of Calif., 1960-83, dir. nursing Met. State Hosp., Norwalk, 1977-83; cons. in mental health, devel. disabilities. Recipient Letter of Commendation, State of Calif., 1974-77. Mem. Am. Nurses Assn., Nat. League Nursing, Am. Assn. Devel. Disabilities, Calif. Nurses Assn. (service awards), Am. Hosp. Assn., World Future Soc., Town Hall Calif. Democrat. Lutheran. Contbr. to profl. jours.

DIEHL, CAROL SUSAN, counselor, educator; b. Uniontown, Pa., Dec. 6, 1949; d. Robert Francis and Charlotte Marilyn (Newcomer) D. BA, Juniata Coll., 1971; MA, W.Va. U., 1976, EdD, 1981. Counselor Search Group Home, Betterway, Inc., Elyria, Ohio, 1971-72; counselor I Youth Devel. Ctr., Waynesburg, Pa., 1972-73, counselor II, cottage supr., 1973-75, crisis intervention supr., 1977-78; staff counselor Student Counseling Service W.Va. U., Morgantown, 1979-82; staff counselor Ctr. Health and Counseling, asst. prof. counseling Behavioral Scis. and Human Services, U. Alaska, Fairbanks, 1982—, acad. cons. dept. athletics, 1983—. Vol. Spl. Olympics, Fairbanks; active Alaska Women's Lobby, Fairbanks, 1984—. Mem. Am. Assn. Counseling and Devel., Assn. Multicultural Counseling and Devel., Assn. Counselor Edn. and Supervision, Fairbanks Golf Assn. (sec. 1986-87). Democrat. Mem. Ch. Brethren. Avocations: travel, art history, crafts, photography, sports. Home: 1089 Chena Ridge Rd Fairbanks AK 99709 Office: U Alaska Ctr Health Counseling Fairbanks AK 99775-0440

DIEHL, DIGBY ROBERT, journalist; b. Boonton, N.J., Nov. 14, 1940; s. Edwin Samuel and Mary Jane Shirley (Ellsworth) D.; m. Kay Beyer, June 6, 1981; 1 dau., Dylan Elizabeth. A.B. in Am. Studies (Henry Rutgers scholar), Rutgers U., 1962; M.A. in Theatre Arts, UCLA, 1966, postgrad., 1969—. Editor Learning Center, Inc., Princeton, N.J., 1962-64; dir. research Creative Playthings, Los Angeles, 1964-66; editor Coast mag., Los Angeles, 1966-68, Show mag., Los Angeles, 1968-69; book editor Los Angeles Times, 1969-78; v.p., editor-in-chief Harry N. Abrams, Inc., N.Y.C., 1978-79; book editor Los Angeles Herald Examiner, 1980-86; movie critic, entertainment editor Sta. KCBS TV, Los Angeles, 1986—; instr. journalism UCLA, 1969-78; jurist Nat. Book Awards, 1972; mem. nominating com. Nat. Medal for Lit., 1972-75; v.p. Nat. Book Critics Circle, 1975-78, bd. dirs., 1981—; jurist Am. Book Awards, 1981-85, v.p. programming, 1984-86. Author: Supertalk: Extraordinary Conversations, 1974, Front Page, 1981. Trustee KPFK-Pacifica Found. Recipient; Irita Van Doren award, 1977. Mem. Am. Soc. Journalists and Authors, AAUP, Phi Beta Kappa, Phi Sigma Delta. Home: 788 S Lake Ave Pasadena CA 91106 Office: Los Angeles Herald Examiner 1111 S Broadway Los Angeles CA 90015

DIEL, LEOPOLD, lawyer; b. Fresno, Calif., Nov. 1, 1923; s. Frederick and Mary D.; m. Brunhilda Wallach, Sept. 20, 1947; children—Garrance Stark, Gregory, Mark, Martel. B.A., Princeton U., 1947; J.D., San Francisco Law Sch., 1952. Bar: Calif. 1952. Asst. city atty. City of San Jose (Calif.), 1952-54; ptnr. Bean, Bergna, & Diel, San Jose, 1954-57; sole practice, San Jose, 1957—; arbitrator Superior Ct. of Santa Clara County, 1981—; judge pro tem San Jose Mcpl. Ct., intermittently 1981—. Served to 1st lt. U.S. Army, 1943-45. Presbyterian. Club: Rotary (Saratoga, Calif.).

DIENER, ROYCE, health care services company executive; b. Balt., Mar. 27, 1918; s. Louis and Lillian (Goodman) D.; m. Jennifer S. Flinton; children: Robert, Joan, Michael. BA, Harvard U.; LLD, Pepperdine U. Comml. lending officer, investment banker various locations to 1972; pres. Am. Med. Internat., Inc., Beverly Hills, Calif., 1972-75, pres., chief exec. officer, 1975-78, chmn., chief exec. officer, 1978-85, chmn. bd., chmn. exec. com., 1986—; dir. Calif. Econ. Devel. Corp.; mem. bd. Applied Circuit Tech., Acuson, Advanced Tech. Venture Funds. Author: Financing a Growing Business, 1966, 3d edit., 1978. Bd. dirs. Los Angeles Philharm. Assn., Los Angeles Red Cross, Heritage Sq. Mus., Santa Monica; mem. vis. com. Harvard Med. Sch. and Sch. Dental Medicine, Harvard U.; bd. visitors Grad. Sch. Mgmt., UCLA; trustee Andrus Gerontol. Inst., U. So. Calif.; mem. adv. bd. Fishman-Davidson Inst. Served to capt. USAF, 1942-46, PTO. Decorated D.F.C. with oak leaf cluster. Mem. Los Angeles C. of C. (bd. dirs.), Calif. C. of C. (bd. dirs.), Calif. Bus. Round Table (bd. dirs.). Clubs: Harvard, Regency, California Yacht, Riviera Country (Los Angeles); Marks (London). Office: Am Med Internat Inc 414 N Camden Dr Beverly Hills CA 90210

DIERAUF, LESLIE ANN, veterinarian, consultant; b. Boston, Feb. 7, 1948; d. Curtis John and Adeline M. (Kirk) D. BS in Microbiology, English cum laude, U. Mass., 1970; DVM, U. Pa., 1974; postdoctoral, U. Calif., Davis, 1974-77. Lic. vet. Calif., Wash., Oreg., Nev., N.Y., Vt.; cert. community coll. tchr., Calif. Instr. physiology U. Calif., Davis, 1976-77; staff vet. Elk Grove (Calif.) Vet. Clinic, 1977, Midtown Animal Hosp., Sacramento, 1978-79, Marin County Vet. Emergency Clinic, San Rafael, Calif., 1979—; staff vet. Calif. Marine Mammal Ctr., Ft. Cronkhite, 1979-82, dir. vet. services, 1982-84, bd. sci. advisors, 1984—; instr. animal health tech. Western Sch. Allied Health Professions, Sacramento, 1977-79; cons. Marine Mammal Cons. Services, Novato, Calif., 1985—; cons. Naval Ocean Systems Ctr., 1984—, Calif. Marine Mammal Ctr., 1984—, Pribilof Island Fur Seal Program, 1981-84, San Francisco Zoo, 1979-84, Calif. State U., Hayward, 1979-84, ; bd. sci. advisors West Quoddy Marine Research Sta., Lubec, Maine, 1979—; bd. examiners Calif. Dept. Consumer Affairs, 1978-85. Mem. editorial bd. Diseases of Aquatic Organisms, 1985—; contbr. articles to profl. jours. Mem. com. to Save Squaw Valley Meadow; dir. Calif. Marine Mammal Ctr. Run for Seals; mem. Wildlife Care Assn., Sacramento, Sacramento Jr. Sci. Mus., Sacramento Community Orch., Sacramento Intramural Softball and Volleyball; vol. Belchertown State Hosp. Recipient Erickson Ednl. Found. award 1982-83; Thouron scholar U. Pa., 1974, U. Pa. scholar 1970-73; U. Calif., Davis grantee 1974-76; U. Calif. fellow, 1974-75, Teaching fellow U. Calif., 1975-77. Mem. AVMA (editorial asst. 1986), Internat. Assn. Aquatic Animal Medicine (pres. 1986-87), Soc. Marine Mammalogy, Am. Assn. Wildlife Vets., Am. Animal Hosp. Assn., Am. Assn. Avian Vets., Women's Vet. Med. Assn., Marin County Vet. Med. Assn., Wildflife Disease Assn., Calif. Vet. Med. Assn., Am. Assn. Vet. Immunology, Calif. Acad. Scis., Calif. Marine Mammal Ctr., Friends of Sea Otter. Democrat. Episcopalian. Avocations: skiing, bicycling, climbing, writing, running. Home: 33 Martin Dr Novato CA 94947 Office: Marin County Vet Emergency Clinic 4240 Redwood Hwy San Rafael CA 94903

DIERINGER, HELMUT OTTO, health care industry executive; b. Selb, Germany, May 14, 1942; came to U.S., 1982; s. Franz-Xaver and Elise Emma (Krauss) D.; m. Asuncion Rodriguez, Oct. 31, 1968; 1 child, Javier-Helmut. BBA, German Chamber of Industry and Commerce, 1962; corr. in English and French and Spanish, Auslandskorrespondentenschule, Fed. Republic Germany, 1964; MBA, Internat. Bus. Sch., Spain, 1975; PhD, Pacific Western U., 1984. Tech. sales mgr. Gebrueder-Netzsch, Selb, Fed. Republic Germany and Barcelona, Spain, 1960-67; mktg. mgr. Squibb & Sons, Barcelona, 1967-69; dir. mktg. Abbott Labs., Madrid, 1969-77, Schering-Plough, Madrid, 1977-78; mng. dir. Boehringer Pharm., Brussels, 1978-79; gen. mgr. Pharmacodex, Fed. Republic Germany, 1979-81; v.p., chief exec. officer Compretox Labs., Inc., Inglewood, Calif., 1982—; pres., chief exec. officer Quit for Good, Inglewood, 1984—. Home: 10404 Summer Holly Circle Bel Air CA 90077

DIERS, CAROL JEAN, psychology educator; b. Bellingham, Wash., July 16, 1933; d. William Donald and Alice H. (West) D.; m. Herbert C. Taylor Jr., Aug. 17, 1973. BA, BEd, Western Wash. State Coll., 1956; MA, U. B.C., Vancouver, Can., 1958; PhD, U. Wash., 1961. Tchr. Bellevue (Wash.) Pub. Schs., 1956-57, 58-59; instr. Olympic Community Coll., Bremerton, Wash., 1961-63; asst. prof. psychology Western Wash. U., Bellingham, 1963-65, assoc. prof., 1965-74, prof., 1974—, dir. honors program, 1970-74. Contbr. articles to profl. jours. Mem. AAAS, AAUP, Animal Behavior Soc., Sigma Xi, Psi Chi. Avocations: golf, photography, travel. Home: 3004 Cherrywood Ave Bellingham WA 98225 Office: Western Wash U Dept Psychology Bellingham WA 98225

DIES, GREGORY BAIRD, distribuitng company official; b. Seattle, Dec. 7, 1948; s. Roy Miller, Jr. and Mary Louise (Baird) D.; m. Mary Joyce Coffee, June 10, 1971; children—Andrew Jennings, Elizabeth Baird. B.S., U.S. Naval Acad., 1971. Commd. ensign USN, 1971, advanced through grades to lt. comdr., 1980; resigned, 1981, comdr., Res.; sr. analyst Analysis & Tech., Inc., Arlington, Va., 1981-82; central region mgr. Mfr.'s Packaging Co. (name changed to Dyn Logistics Services Co. subs. Dynalectron Corp. 1984), Alexandria, Va., 1982-83, asst. to pres., San Diego, 1983, v.p. ops., 1984, v.p., western region mgr., National City, Calif., 1984-85; pres. Sticklen and Dies, Inc., Escondido, Calif., 1986—. Republican. Presbyterian. Home: 17110 Pacato Ct San Diego CA 92128 Office: Sticklen and Dies Inc 600 S Andreasen Suite I Escondido CA 92025

DIESTELKAMP, DAWN LEA, laboratory data processing specialist; b. Fresno, Calif., Apr. 23, 1954; d. Don and Joy LaVaughn (Davis) Diestelkamp. B.S. in Microbiology, Calif. State U.-Fresno, 1976, M.S. in Pub. Adminstrn., 1983. Lic. clin. lab. technologist, Calif.; cert. clin. lab. dir. Clin. lab. technologist Valley Med. Ctr., Fresno, Calif., 1977-82, quality control coordinator, 1983-84; cons., instr. in field. Mem. Nat. Assn. Female Execs. Democrat. Office: 445 S Cedar Ave Fresno CA 93702

DIETER, ALICE HUNT, journalist; b. Denver, Apr. 16, 1928; d. Thomas Addison and Alice (McCullough) Hunt; B.A. cum laude in English Lang., U. Colo., 1949; m. Leslie Louis Dieter, Sept. 10, 1948; children—Alice Dieter Crowley, Philip Leslie, Paul Wesley. Columnist, reporter, feature writer Intermountain Observer, Boise, Idaho, 1962-72, asst. editor, 1965-72, also TV news reporter Sta. KBOI, and news librarian, 1966-73; stringer Newsweek mag., 1970-73; editorial assoc. corp. communications Boise Cascade Corp., 1973-83; ret., 1983; weekly editorial columnist Idaho Daily Statesman, 1977-85. Chair, Idaho Assn. Humanities, 1972-78; bd. dirs. Idaho Farm Workers Services, Inc., 1963-69, pres., 1965-69; mem. Boise Com. Fgn. Relations, 1975—; mem. Idaho Gov.'s Commn. on Excellence in Edn., 1983; mem. Idaho Selection Com. for Rhodes Scholars, 1983-84; pres. Boise LWV, 1957-59; Idaho rep. UNICEF, 1963-65; mem. Boise Valley World Affairs Assn., 1956-65; mem. Boise City Park Bd., 1964-79; co-chair Idaho Johnson for Pres., 1964, Citizens for Andrus for Gov., 1966; del. Women's Conf., Houston, 1978; active YWCA, St. Michael's Episcopal Parish, Boise Philharm., Friends of Boise Library, Idaho Hist. Soc. Recipient Idaho Press awards for feature writing and news photography, 1967, for gen. interest column, 1983. Mem. Idaho Press Club (bd. dirs.), Phi Beta Kappa. Home: 1147 Santa Maria Dr Boise ID 83712

DIETLE, CARROLL EUGENE, II, real estate developer exec., lawyer; b. Toledo, Jan. 4, 1940; s. Carroll Eugene and Martha (Haley) D.; children—Aimee Marie, Brandon Carroll, Chad Justin. B.A., U. Mich., 1961; J.D., U. Ariz., 1964. Bar: Ariz. 1964. With Anchor Nat. Life Ins. Co., Phoenix, 1968-83, gen. counsel, 1968-83, asst. sec., 1968-71, sec., 1971, v.p., 1970-78, sr. v.p., 1978-82, exec. v.p., 1982-83, dir. 1978-83; exec. v.p. Patrick Properties, Inc., Phoenix, 1984—. Mem. ABA, Ariz. Bar Assn., Maricopa Bar Assn. Club: Arizona. Home: 4302 E Fanfol Dr Phoenix AZ 85028 Office: 4250 E Camelback Rd Phoenix AZ 85018

DIETRICH, ROBERT EHRLICH, real estate appraiser; b. Salinas, Calif., July 15, 1947; s. Robert Erlich and Mary Louise (Zimbleman) D.; m. Linda Ann Saunders, Dec. 22, 1970; children—Robert E., Lauren Marie. B.S. in Fin. and Real Estate, U. Ariz., 1969. Research assoc. Burke, Hansen, Homan & Klafter, Tucson, 1974, mgr., 1974-77, ptnr., mgr., 1978-80, treas., mgr. Tucson office, 1980—; dir. Burke, Hansen & Homan, Inc., Mining & Constrn. Suppliers, Inc. Mem. exec. council Catalina Council, Tucson, 1983—. Served to 1st. lt. U.S. Army, 1969-73. Mem. Am. Inst. Real Estate Appraisers, Am. Soc. Farm Mgrs. and Rural Appraisers. Democrat. Lutheran. Lodge: Rotary (pres. 1983-84, bd. dirs.). Home: 4640 N Avenida del Cazador Tucson AZ 85718 Office: Burke Hansen Homan & Klafter 335 N Wilmot Suite 500 Tucson AZ 85711

DIETZ, DOROTHY BRILL, artist, designer; b. San Bernardino, Calif.; d. Henry Edward and Anna Mae (Parfitt) Brill. Student, San Bernardino Jr. Coll., U. So. Calif., Oreg. State U., Mills Coll., Coll. of Desert, Rudolph Schaefer's Sch. Design, Academie Julian, France, 1959, Art Acad., Honolulu, L'Ecole du Cordon Bleu, France; grad., Japanses Art Ctr., San Francisco, 1957, Wash. Sch. Art, 1964, Unity Sch. Christianity, 1969; U.S. student, Instituio San Miguel de Allende, Mex., 1960, Sorbonne, France, 1959. Ct. reporter San Bernardino Justice Ct., San Bernardino Superior Cts., six yrs.; practice as interior designer 1947—. One-woman shows include Dietz Galleria, 1959-69, Bank of Am., Palm Desert, Calif., 1962, Ferrall's Playhouse, Palm Springs, 1961, The Villages, San Jose, Calif., Del Mesa Carmel, Calif., 1980; one-woman and group shows in Calif., Mex., Honolulu. Mem. Honolulu Acad. Arts, Honolulu Symphony Soc. Recipient Taka Mizu Dietz award Japanese Govt., 3 1st Place awards, 1 5th Place award nat. art contests. Mem. Assn. of Unity Chs., North Shore Animal League, Alpha Chi Omega. Republican. Club: President's (Oreg. State U.). Home: Royal Iolani 581 Kamoku St #408 Honolulu HI 96826

DIETZ, WILLIAM ANTHONY, product designer; b. New Ulm, Minn., Jan. 14, 1927; s. William Lawrence and Mabel Irene (Simmet) D.; m. Isabel Hamer Smith, Apr. 29, 1978. B.A., St. John's U., 1950. Draftsman Honeywell, Inc., Mpls., Los Angeles, 1951-58; design draftsman Litton Industries, Beverly Hills, Calif., 1958-61; chief design dept. Schurz Corp., Los Angeles, 1966-80; product designer, R G Sloane Mfg. Co., Sun Valley, Calif., 1980—. Served with USAAF, 1945-47. Winner 8th Bachner Award Competition, 1976; San Francisco br. award for unique indsl. plastic product Soc. Plastics Engrs., 1982. Patentee water conditioning control valve, drain valve and fluid coupling. Home: 1564 Talmadge St Los Angeles CA 90027 Office: 7660 N Clybourn Ave Sunvalley CA 91352

DIGHT, MARJORIE LEE, state official; b. McAlister, Okla., Jan. 21, 1926; d. Lee Andrew and Ora Etta (Ryles) Jones; m. William Russell Dight, Oct. 14, 1944; 1 child, Reardon Russell. Student Phoenix Coll., 1967-68. Claims specialist Indsl. Commn. of Ariz., Phoenix, 1947-69, asst. claims mgr., 1969-70, claims mgr., 1970—; lectr. on workers compensation. Author/editor ednl. pamphlets on worker's compensation claim reporting. Mem. Internat. Assn. of Indsl. Accident Boards and Commns. (exec. bd.). Democrat. Methodist. Club: Toastmasters.

DIGIORGIO, JOSEPH BRUN, chemistry educator; b. San Francisco, Aug. 4, 1932; s. Salvatore A. and Helen Marie (Brun) DiG.; m. Velta Erdmanis, June 15, 1957 (div. 1984); children: Joseph B. Jr., Ann, Edward V., Kathleen, Carol, James S.; m. Carol Diane Usher, Jan. 24, 1985. BE, Johns Hopkins U., 1954, MA, 1957, PhD, 1960. Asst. prof. chemistry Calif. State U., Sacramento, 1964-67, assoc. prof., 1967-70, prof., 1970—; owner Analytical Assocs. Inc., Sacramento, 1977—. Fellow Chem. Soc. London; mem. AAAS, Am. Chem. Soc. Avocations: photography, stamp collecting, model bldg. Office: Calif State U Chem Dept 6000 J St Sacramento CA 95819

DIGIORGIO, ROBERT, retired consumer products executive; b. N.Y.C., Dec. 2, 1911; s. Salvatore and Marie (Meyer) Di G.; m. Eleanor Vollmann, Jan. 20, 1940 (div.); children: Ann, Barbara, Christine, Dorothy; m. Patricia Kuhrts Sharman, Aug. 7, 1964. A.B., Yale, 1933; B.L., Fordham U., 1936. Bar: N.Y. 1937. With Di Giorgio Corp., San Francisco, 1937-85, pres., 1962-71, chmn. bd., chief exec. officer, 1971-82, chmn. bd., 1982-86, chmn. exec. com., 1986—. Clubs: Metropolitan (N.Y.C.); California (Los Angeles); Pacific-Union (San Francisco), Commonwealth (San Francisco), Bohemian (San Francisco). Office: One Maritime Plaza San Francisco CA 94111

DIGNAM, ROBERT JOSEPH, physician; b. Manchester, N.H., July 8, 1925; s. Walter Joseph and Margaret Veronica (Lowe) D.; m. Evelyn Pettitt, Aug. 4, 1961; children—Stephen Mark, Lyn Shore, Margaret Gale. B.S., Bates Coll., 1945; M.D., Tufts U., 1949. Intern Boston City Hosp., 1949-50, resident in orthopedic surgery, 1954-57; resident in orthopedic surgery Lahey Clinic, Boston, 1953-54; practice medicine specializing in orthopedic surgery Santa Monica, Calif., 1960—; mem. staff St. Johns Hosp. UCLA Med. Center; clin. prof. orthopedic surgery UCLA. Served to lt., M.C. USN, 1951-54. Fellow A.C.S.; mem. AMA, Mass. Med. Soc., Calif. Med. Assn., Am. Acad. Orthopedic Surgeons. Club: Jonathan. Home: 821 Alma Real Pacific Palisades CA 92072 Office: 2021 Santa Monica Blvd Santa Monica CA 90404

DIGNAM, WILLIAM JOSEPH, obstetrician, gynecologist, educator; b. Manchester, N.H., Aug. 11, 1920; s. Walter Joseph and Margaret Veronica (Lowe) D.; m. Winifred Kennedy, June 7, 1947; children—Mary Brett, Kevan Jean, Erin Margaret, Meighan Ann. A.B., Dartmouth Coll., 1941; M.D., Harvard U., 1943. Intern Boston City Hosp., 1944; resident in ob-gyn U. Kans. Med. Ctr., Kansas City, 1947-50; From asst. prof. to prof. ob-gyn UCLA, 1951—; affiliated with UCLA Med. Ctr., St. John's Hosp., Los Angeles, Cedars Sinai Med. Ctr., Los Angeles, Harbor UCLA Med. Ctr. Roman Catholic. Home: 820 Alma Real Dr Pacific Palisades CA 90272 Office: UCLA Sch Medicine Dept Ob-Gyn 10833 LeConte Los Angeles CA 90024

DIGRAZIA, PETER MICHAEL, dentist; b. Battle Mountain, Nev., Aug. 30, 1939; s. Eugene John and Julia Marie (Nannini) DiG.; m. Susan Lee Cavitt, June 21, 1965; children—Michaelle, Jill, John, Susan. B.A., U. Nev., 1964; D.M.D., U. Oreg., 1966. Gen. practice dentistry, Reno, 1968—; mem. Nev. State Bd. Dental Examiners, 1973-81, pres., 1980-81; mem. joint commn. Nat. Dental Examinations, 1986—; chmn. Nev. State Bd. health, 1985—, ann. meeting Nev. State Dental Conv., 1971-72; vice chmn. Nev. State Bd. Health, Reno, 1981—. Served to capt. U.S. Army, 1966-68. Fellow Acad. Gen. Dentistry, Acad. Dentistry Internat.; mem. Western Conf. Dentists and Dental Examiners (pres. 1978-79), Am. Assn. Dental Examiners (pres. 1984), ADA (nat. hygiene com. 1983, nat. fragmentation com. 1985-86), Acad. Children's Dentistry. Democrat. Roman Catholic. Clubs: Italian Benevolent Soc. (sec. 1986—), Reno Aquatics (bd. dirs. 1984). Lodges: Mt. Rose Lions (pres. 1983-84), Sunrise Exchange, (Reno); KC (Battle Mountain). Office: Peter DiGrazia DMD Ltd Lakeside Dr Reno NV 89509

DI GRAZIA, RICHARD EDWARD, finance executive; b. Oakland, Calif., Aug. 24, 1938; s. Guido William and Vera Margherita (Fenzi) Di G.; m. Helen Doris Munch, Sept. 1, 1984; 1 child, Molly Alexandra Munch. BA, U. Calif., Berkeley, 1966; MA, San Francisco State U., 1973. Acct. Community TV, Oakland, 1975-77, Calif. Acad. Scis., San Francisco, 1977-78; asst. dir. fin. Roman Cath. Archdiocese San Francisco, 1978—. Served with USN, 1956-59. Democrat. Avocation: writing, swimming, bicycling. Home: 920 Carmel Ave Albany CA 94706 Office: Roman Cath Archdiocese 445 Church St San Francisco CA 94114

DIJULIO, RALPH (CHIP), commercial decorator; b. Seattle, Dec. 6, 1944; s. Guy and Norma DiJulio; m. Sigrid DiJulio, June 24, 1979; children—Loyd McBroom, Simone McBroom, Nick Roberts. B.A., Gonzaga U., 1966; postgrad. U. Wash., 1970. Mgr. Jonas Bros., Seattle, 1969-70; entertainer, 1970-74; personnel mgr. Weyerhauser Co., Everett, Wash., 1974-76, St. Regis Paper Co., Seattle, 1976-78; sales rep. Male, Pierre Cardin,, 1978-81; territory mgr. Valley Decorating, Fresno, Calif., 1981—; career cons. and instr. State Prison, Monroe, Wash., 1974-76. Served to capt. U.S. Army, 1966-69. Roman Catholic. Home and Office: 24028 Brier Way Brier WA 98036

DIKELSKY, BURTON E., performing arts producer; b. Chgo., Feb. 18, 1945; s. Samuel and Helen (Berman) D.; m. Sandra Dikelsky, June 16, 1966 (div. June 1980); 1 child, Michael; m. Mayo S. Dikelsky, Mar. 26, 1983; 1 child, Sheryl. BS, So. Ill. U., 1967; MA, Northeastern Ill. U., 1975. Cert. secondary edn. tchr., Ill. Tchr. Naperville (Ill.) Pub. Schs., 1965-80; pub. relations dir. Albuquerque Little Theater, 1979-80; sales mgr. Barn Dinner Theatre, Albuquerque, 1981-83; exec. dir. Albuquerque Civic Light Opera, 1983—; mem. tourism com. Albuquerque Conv. and Visitors Bur., 1982-86; mem. fin. com. S.W. Theatre Conf., Albuquerque, 1983-86. Mem. Nat. Alliance of Mus. Theatre Producers, S.W. Theatre Conf. Democrat. Jewish. Office: Albuquerque Civic Light Opera 4201 Ellison NE Albuquerque NM 87109

DILGER, PAUL HERMAN, agricultural engineering educator, computer consultant; b. Cin., Jan. 12, 1939; s. Paul George and Dorothy Mae (Moser) D.; m. Dixie Lee York, Aug. 25, 1966; 1 son, Bryce Edward. A.A. in Chemistry, Los Angeles Valley Coll., 1964; B.S. in Soil Chemistry, U. Calif.-Davis, 1967; M.S. in Agrl. Engring., Calif. Poly. U., 1974. Elec. and telemetry technician Atomics Internat., Chatsworth, Calif., 1961-62; research technician space div. N.Am. Aviation, Canoga Park, Calif., 1962-64, Kearney Found., U. Calif.-Davis, 1964-68; vocat. agr. instr. Cuyama Valley (Calif.) High Sch., 1968-71; assoc. prof. agr. and computers Coll. of Desert, Palm Desert, Calif., 1971-84; assoc. prof. agrl. engring. Calif. State Poly. U., San Luis Obispo, 1984—; cons. computers in agr. and bus. Cubmaster and scoutmaster Boy Scouts Am., 1979-83; mem. adv. com. Hemet Future Farmers Am., 1981—. Served with U.S. Army, 1957-59. Mem. Am. Soc. Agrl. Engrs., Calif. Agr. Tchrs. Assn., Am. Vocat. Assn., Am. Farm Assn., Farm Bur., Fluid Power Soc., Faculty Assn. Calif. Community Colls.

Republican. Presbyterian. Clubs: Cuyama Exchange, Anza Valley Lions. Designed particulate control and evaluation for liquid rocket engine fuels; discovered biochemical cause of grass tetany in range land cattle. Home: PO Box 908 Santa Margarita CA 93453 Office: Calif Poly State U Agrl Engring Dept San Luis Obispo CA 93407

DILL, RICHARD EVERETT, software company marketing executive; b. Landstuhl, Fed. Republic of Germany, Mar. 12, 1952; came to U.S., 1956; s. Harlon Jewel and Marilyn Francis (Ritchie) D.; m. Nancy Ann McFarland, Jan. 10, 1981; 1 child, Megan Elizabeth Dill-McFarland. BS in Computer Sci., Wash. State U., 1974. Resource mgr. Boeing Computer Services, Seattle, 1977-79; project lead Allied Stores Corp., Seattle, 1979-80; systems engr. Data Gen. Corp., Bellevue, Wash., 1980-82; systems engring. mgr. Data Gen. Corp., Denver, 1982-83; Original Equipment Mfr. support mgr. Microsoft Corp., Redmond, Wash., 1983-85, product mktg. group mgr., 1985-86, program mgr. OS/2 Windows, 1986—. Editor: Windows Developers Seminar Notes, 1986. Mem. Delta Tau Delta (treas. 1973-74). Republican. Avocations: sailing, skiing, woodworking. Office: Microsoft Corp 16011 NE 36th Way Redmond WA 98073-9717

DILL, ROBERT FLOYD, marine geologist; b. Denver, May 25, 1927; s. Robert Kirby and Eldora A. (Fisk) D.; m. Sonia B. Daswick, Dec. 27, 1963; children: Robert F. II, Kathryn Baslee, Marc C., James M. BS in Geology, U. So. Calif., 1950, MS in Geology, 1952; PhD in Marine Geology, U. Calif.-San Diego, La Jolla, 1964. Cert. petroleum geologist. Geologist, oceanographer USN Elec. Lab., San Diego, 1951-72; geologist NOAA, Rockville, Md., 1972-75, 1981-83; geologist U.S. Geol. Survey, Washington, 1975; dir., prof. geology West Indies Lab. Fairleigh Dickenson U., St. Croix, U.S. Virgin Islands, 1975-81, Dept. Interior, Los Angeles and San Diego, 1983-86; cons. Geomarex, San Diego, 1986-87; owner, dir. Dill Geomarine Cons., San Diego, 1987—; commr. Virgin Island Water Resources Commn., St. Croix, 1979-81. Author: (with others) Submarine Canyons, 1966; producer motion picture Submarine Canyons, 1967, Deeply Submerged Terraces, 1968 (Nat. Ind. Picture Assn. 1969); contbr. 75 articles to profl. jours. Served with USN, 1945-47. Recipient Golden Bear award Calif. Resources Agy., 1964. Fellow Geol. Soc. Am.; mem. Am. Assn. Petroleum Geologists, Soc. Econ. Paleontologists and Minerologists, Marine Tech. Soc., St. Croix C. of C. Republican. Avocations: underwater photography, scuba diving. Home: 610 Tarento Dr San Diego CA 92106

DILL, THOMAS DOUGLAS, JR., chemist, consultant; b. Los Angeles, May 22, 1954; s. Thomas Douglas Sr. and Dorothy Mae (West) D.; m. Marla La Rae Newell, Oct. 20, 1984; children: Le Conte Jeanine, Kristina Dionne. BS in Chemistry, Calif. State U., Dominguez Hills, 1979. Analytical chemist Purex Corp., Carson, Calif., 1980-85; supr. Allergan Pharm., Irvine, Calif., 1985—; cons. Helene Curtis Inc., Industry, Calif., 1984-85. Mem. Am. Chem. Soc., Nat. Orgn. Profl. Advancement Black Chemists and Chem. Engrs. (v.p. 1983—). Democrat. Baptist. Home: 11860 Overland Dr Fontana CA 92335

DILLARD, JOHN MARTIN, lawyer, pilot; b. Long Beach, Calif., Dec. 25, 1945; s. John Warren and Clara Leora (Livermore) D.; student U. Calif., Berkeley, 1963-67; B.A., UCLA, 1968; J.D., Pepperdine U., 1976; m. Patricia Anne Yeager, Aug. 10, 1968; 1 son, Jason Robert. Instr. pilot Norton AFB, Calif., 1973-77; admitted to Calif. bar, 1976; asso. firm Magana, Cathcart & McCarthy, Los Angeles, 1977-80, Lord, Bissell & Brook, Los Angeles, 1980-85, Finley, Kumble, Wagner, 1985—. Served to capt. USAF, 1968-73; Vietnam. Mem. Am. Trial Lawyers Assn. (aviation litigation com.), Am. Bar Assn. (aviation com.), Fed. Bar Assn., Los Angeles County Bar Assn. (aviation com.), Century City Bar Assn., Internat. Platform Assn., Res. Officers Assn., Sigma Nu. Aircraft comdr. 1st Mil. Airlift Command relief mission for Turkish earthquake, 1976. Home: 19621 Verona Ln Yorba Linda CA 92686 Office: 4400 MacArthur Blvd Suite 300 Newport Beach CA 92660

DILLER, BARRY, entertainment company executive; b. San Francisco, Feb. 2, 1942; s. Michael and Reva (Addison) D. Vice pres. feature films and movies of week ABC, 1971-73, ABC (prime time TV), 1973-74; chmn. bd. Paramount Pictures Corp., 1974-84; pres. Gulf & Western Leisure Time Group, 1983-84; chmn., chief exec. officer Twentieth Century Fox Film Corp., Los Angeles, 1984—, Fox, Inc., 1985—; jr. ptnr. TCF Holdings, Inc., from 1984. Mem. Am. Film Inst., Variety Clubs Internat., Hollywood Radio and TV Soc., Acad. Motion Picture Arts and Scis., ACLU, NCCJ. Office: Twentieth Century-Fox Film Corp 10201 W Pico Blvd Los Angeles CA 90035 *

DILLER, PERRY, small business owner; b. Alameda, Calif., Feb. 3, 1950; s. Sherwood Anderson and Phyllis Ada (Driver) D.; m. Julie Sirchuk, Oct. 7, 1978; children: Christopher Driver, Cory Anderson. Student, U.S. Internat. U., 1969-71, UCLA, 1971-72. V.p. and part-owner The Escrow Shoppe, Encino, Calif.; v.p. Equity Title, Santa Monica, Calif.; pres. and chief exec. officer Diller Escrow, Woodland Hills, Calif., Computer Data Control, Calabasas, Calif.; founder 1st Charter Bank Los Angeles, also bd. dirs. Mem. Rep. Nat. Task Force, Washington, 1984-86, Mayor's Fund for Homeless. Named to Hon. Order Ky. Cols., 1986. Mem. Calif. Escrow Assn., Bd. Realtors So. Calif., Internat. Soc. Financiers (cert.), Am. Mgmt. Assn., Am. Escrow Assn., Orange County Escrow Assn., Escrow Inst. Calif., Calif. C. of C., Sales and Mktg. Council of Los Angeles. Office: Computer Data Control 24007 Ventura Blvd #130 Calabasas CA 91302

DILLINGHAM, LOWELL SMITH, diversified company executive, state legislator; b. Honolulu, June 17, 1911; s. Walter Francis and Louise Olga (Gaylord) D.; m. Harriet Barbour, June 12, 1936; children—Gail Louise Dillingham Williams, Heather Barbour Dillingham Suhr. Grad., Harvard U., 1930-34. With Dillingham Corp. and subs., Honolulu, 1934—; pres. Dillingham Corp. and subs., 1955-70, pres., chief exec. officer, 1969-70, chmn. bd., chief exec. officer, 1971-77, chmn. bd., from 1977, now vice chmn.; also dir. and dir. subs.; former mem. Hawaii Ho. of Reps., Honolulu; dir. Hawaiian Western Steel Ltd., Nat. Properties, Inc., Econ. Devel. Corp. Honolulu; mem. internat. adv. bd. Pan Am. World Airways, 1984—. Trustee Punahou Sch., Hawaii, 1963-86; trustee emeritus Pacific Tropical Bot. Garden, N.Y. and Hawaii; mem. sr. adv. council Japan-Am. Soc. Honolulu, 1976—. Recipient award for outstanding achievement in constrn. The Moles, 1969. Republican. Clubs: Oahu Country, Outrigger Canoe and Pacific, Pacific Union. Avocation: quarter horse breeding. Office: Dillingham Corp 1441 Kapiolani Blvd Honolulu HI 96801

DILLON, FRANCIS PATRICK, human resources executive, management consultant; b. Long Beach, Calif., Mar. 15, 1937; s. Wallace Myron and Mary Elizabeth (Land) D.; B.A., U. Va., 1959; M.S., Def. Fgn. Affairs Sch., 1962; M.B.A., Pepperdine U., 1975; m. Vicki Lee Dillon, Oct. 1980; children—Cary Randolph, Francis Patrick Jr., Randee, Rick. Traffic mgr., mgr. personnel services Pacific Telephone Co., Sacramento and Lakeport, Calif., 1966-69; asst. mgr. manpower planning and devel. Pan-Am. World Airways, N.Y.C., 1969-71; mgr. personnel and orgn. devel. Continental Airlines, Los Angeles, 1971-74; dir. personnel Farwest Services, Inc., Irvine, Calif., 1974; dir. human resources Bourns, Inc., Riverside, Calif., 1974-80; dir. employee and community relations MSI Data Corp., 1980-83; pres. Pavi Enterprises, 1983—; mgmt. cons., 1983—; pres., chief exec. officer Personnel Products & Services Inc., 1984—; pres. Meditrans Inc. Bd. dirs. Health Services Maintenance Orgn., Inc., Youth Services Center, Inc.; vol. precinct worker. Served to lt. comdr. USN, 1959-66; asst. naval attaché, Brazil, 1963-65. Recipient Disting. Service award Jaycees, 1969; Jack Cates Meml. Vol. of Year award Youth Service Center, 1977. Mem. Assn. Internat Mgmt. Cons.'s, Am. Soc. Personnel Adminstrn., Personnel Indsl. Relations Assn., Am. Soc. Tng. and Devel. Republican. Episcopalian. Clubs: Mission Viejo Sailing, YMCA Bike, Mission Viejo Ski, Caving, Toastmasters (pres. 1966-67), Have Dirt Will Travel. Home: 3700 S Susan Suite 100 Mission Viejo CA 92692 Office: Personnel Products and Services Inc 3700 S Susan Suite 100 Santa Ana CA 92704

DILLON, GREGORY RUSSELL, hotel executive; b. Chgo., Aug. 26, 1922; s. Gregory Thomas and Margaret Moore (Russell) D.; m. Nancy Jane Huntsberger, Nov. 8, 1969; children: Michael Gregory, Patricia Jean, Margaret Esther, Richard Thomas, Daniel Russell. Student, Elmhurst Coll., Ill., 1941-43, 45-46; JD, DePaul U., Chgo., 1948. Bar: Ill. Sole practice Chgo.; ptnr. Friedman Mulligan Dillon & Urist, Chgo., 1950-63; asst. to pres. Hilton Hotels Corp., Beverly Hills, Calif., 1963-65, v.p., asst. sec., 1965-71, sr. v.p., asst. sec., 1971-80, exec. v.p., also bd. dirs., 1980—; pres. Conrad Internat. Hotels, 1986—, also bd. dirs.; trustee Wells Fargo Mortgage & Equity Trust, San Francisco, 1975—; bd. dirs. Jupiters Mgmt. Ltd., Surfers Paradise, Queensland, Australia. Served to 1st lt. USAAF, 1943-46, ETO. Mem. Urban Land Inst. (trustee 1980—, trustee found. 1981—), ABA, Ill. Bar Assn., Chgo. Bar Assn., Nat. Realty Com. (chmn. exec. com. 1979), Am. Hotel and Motel Assn. Republican. Roman Catholic. Clubs: Chicago Athletic (Chgo.); Bel-Air Country (Los Angeles); Marco Polo (N.Y.C.). Office: Hilton Hotels Corp 9336 Civic Ctr Dr Beverly Hills CA 90210

DILLON, JOHN THOMAS, geologist, educator; b. Tarrant County, Tex., Dec. 17, 1947; s. Stephen Patrick and Carol C. (Lychak) D.; m. Mary A. Moorman, Dec. 26, 1976; children: Stephen P. Noah Dillon, Panika Marie C., Abraham Francis M. BS, Calif. State U., Los Angeles, 1970; PhD, U. Calif., Santa Barbara, 1975. Exploration geologist Falcon Bridge Nickle Mines, Vancouver, B.C., Can., 1970; lectr. U. Calif., 1974; marine geologist U.S. Bur. Land Mgmt., Pacific Outer Continental Shelf, Los Angeles, 1975-77, asst. chief geologic mapping, 1982-84; geologist IV Alaska Geol. Survey, Fairbanks, 1977—; asst. prof. U. Alaska, Fairbanks, 1978—. Contbr. geologic maps. and reports to profl. pub. NSF fellow, 1970-72, NDEA Fellow, 1972-74. Mem. Am. Assn. Petroleum Geologists, Geol. Soc. Am., Am. Geol. Inst., So. Economic Paleontologists and Mineraloists, Fed. Am. Scis. Avocations: surfing, aircraft pilot. Home: PO Box 81123 Fairbanks AK 99708 Office: Alaska Geol Survey 794 University Ave Fairbanks AK 99701

DILLON, MARGARET HAFER, educational administrator; b. Chgo., June 25, 1920; d. Lawrence Grover and Beatrice Stella (McGrath) Hafer; m. George Gustave Dillon, Dec. 19, 1942; children—David Lee, Michael George. Telegrapher, Western Union Co., Chgo., 1939-43; disbursing agt. Naval Air Sta., Whidbey Island, Wash. and Seattle, 1943-45; stock control supr. Ship Store Ashore, Atsugi, Japan, 1953-54; dir. purchasing and stores Grossmont Union High Sch. Dist., La Mesa, Calif., 1957-83. Bd. dirs. Aztec Athletic Found. San Diego State U., 1982—. Mem. Calif. Assn. Sch. Bus. Ofcls. (chmn. purchasing com.), Calif. Assn. Pub. Purchasing Officers (pres. San Diego chpt.), San Diego Council Adminstrv. Women, Ednl. Heartland Sch. Adminstrs. Assn., Grossmont Hosp. Aux. Republican.

DILLON, PAUL LEE, electrical engineer, consultant, real estate manager; b. Walla Walla, Wash., Aug. 21, 1914; s. William Louis and Dema Ellen (Thomas) D.; m. Esther Melissa Pickett, June 4, 1939; children: Paul Lee Jr., Ferman Lewis, Wilson Kent, Eileen Ruth, Warren Michael. BSEE, Wash. State U., 1937. Engr. Gen. Electric Co., Schenectady, N.Y., San Francisco, Los Angeles, Portland, Oreg., 1937-49; owner, operator farm, Spokane, Wash., 1949-56; elec. engr. Indsl. Electric Co., Roseburg, Oreg. and Everett, Wash., 1956-64; sr. elec. engr. Hughes Helicopters, Culver City, Calif., 1968-74, Hallanger Engrs., Bellingham, Wash., 1974-81; elec. engr. cons. Profl. Engr. and Cons. Service, Bellingham, Wash., 1981—. Mem. Am. Inst. Plant Engrs. (cert., pres. Los Angeles chpt. 1973-74). Republican. Methodist. Avocations: boating, fishing, traveling. Home: 1322 Lowe Ave Bellingham WA 98226

DI LORETO, CHRIS MICHAEL, architect, interior designer; b. Portland, Oreg., Apr. 27, 1955; s. Eugene Peter and Florence Marie (Polster) DiL.; m. Ann Lenore Talbott, Sept. 10, 1977; children: Matthew, David, Bryan. BArch, U. Oreg., 1978. Registered architect, Oreg. Design architect Balhizer, Longwood, Smith et al., Eugene, Oreg., 1978-79, Broome, Orngdulph, O'Toole and Rudolph, Portland, 1979-84; prin. Chris Michael DiLoreto, Architects, Portland, 1984—; guest critic Oreg. Sch. Design, 1986—. Bd. dirs. North/Northeast Bus. Boosters Tourism Council, Portland, Hist. Preservation League of Oreg. Recipient Portland Women's Archtl. League award, 1977. Mem. AIA, Nat. Trust Hist. Preservation, Chi Psi Alumni Corp. Democrat. Roman Catholic. Office: 911 N Skidmore Studio #1 Portland OR 97217-3156

DILTS, MELVIN RUSSELL, national customer service organization executive; b. Salem, Mass., Oct. 31, 1946; s. Harry Leslie and Marjorie Elizabeth (Townsend) D.; m. Donna Murphy, div. 1977; m. Jonilynn Andresen, Apr. 16, 1983. A.S.E.T. in Electronics, Wentworth Inst., Boston, 1972; B.S.E.T. in Electronics, Wentworth Coll., Boston, 1974. Maintenance foreman Lyncor Plastics, Lynn, Mass., 1971-73; mgr. Hamilton Test Systems, Tucson, 1974—; speaker U. Phoenix, Tucson, 1983-84, Pima Community Coll., Tucson, 1983-84. Author of various computer bus. programs. Served with U.S. Army, 1966-69, Vietnam. Mem. Internat. Customer Service Orgn. Clubs: Tucson Rod and Gun, Sabbar Gun (pres. 1986—), Tucson Pistol League (bd. dirs., 1986). Lodges: Shriners (pres. motorized unit 1984, road capt., 1982—), Masons, Elks. Home: 11421 E Limberlost Rd Tucson AZ 85749 Office: Hamilton Test Systems Inc 2301 N Forbes Blvd Tucson AZ 85745

DIMAIO, VIRGINIA SUE, gallery owner; b. Houston, July 6, 1921; d. Jesse Lee and Gabriella Sue (Norris) Chambers; AB, U. Redlands, 1943; student U. So. Calif., 1943-45, Scripps Coll., 1943, Pomona Coll., 1945; m. James V. DiMaio, 1955 (div. 1968); children: Victoria, James V. Owner, Capistrano Trading Post, San Juan Capistrano, Calif., 1946—; owner, dir. Galeria Capistrano, San Juan Capistrano and Santa Fe, N.Mex., 1979—; cons., appraiser Southwestern and Am. Indian Handcrafts; lectr. Calif. State U., Long Beach; established ann. Helen Hardin Meml. scholarship for woman artist grad. Inst. Am. Indian Art, Santa Fe, also ann. Helen Hardin award for outstanding woman artist at Indian Market, S.W. Assn. on Indian Affairs, Santa Fe. Mem. Indian Arts and Crafts Assn., S.W. Assn. Indian Affairs, Heard Mus., San Juan Capistano C. of C. Republican. Roman Catholic. Office: 31681 Camino Capistrano San Juan Capistrano CA 92675 also: 409 Canyon Rd Santa Fe NM 87501

DIMENT, WILLIAM HORACE, research geophysicist, consultant; b. Oswego, N.Y., Oct. 15, 1927; s. James Smith and Priscilla Rose (Faatz) D.; m. Evelyn Virginia East, Nov. 12, 1958; children: Evelyn Patricia Diment Chamberlain, James Howell, William David. AB, Williams Coll., 1949; AM, Harvard U., 1951, PhD, 1954. Registered geophysicist, Calif. Geophysicist Standard Oil Co., New Orleans, 1953-56; geophysicist, br. chief U. S. Geol. Survey, Washington, Menlo Park, Calif., Denver, 1956-65; research geophysicist U.S. Geol. Survey, Washington, Menlo Park, Calif., Denver, 1973-83, Golden, Colo., 1981—; prof. geology U. Rochester, N.Y., 1965-73; cons. on reactor siting U.S. AEC, Washington, 1965-69, on radioactive waste disposal, 1965-69, 71; mem. various panels, NSF, NRC. Served with USNR, 1945-46; served to 1st lt. USAFR, 1949-58. Sr. postdoctoral fellow NSF, Yale U., 1964-65; prin. investigator NSF grants, 1966-73. Fellow AAAS (council 1961-62), Geol. Soc. Am.; mem. Soc. Exploration Geophysicists (rep. AAAS council 1961-62). Republican. Congregationalist. Home: 1822 Arapahoe St Golden CO 80401 Office: US Geol Survey 1711 Illinois St Golden CO 80401

DIMICK, WALTER STEVEN, motion picture director, producer; b. Portland, Oreg., Mar. 3, 1950; s. Norman Caples and Winifred I. (Rayner) D.; m. Patricia Ann Weeks, Nov. 13, 1971 (div. June 1983); m. Barbara Janet Andersen, Apr. 14, 1984; children: Jeffrey Steven, Brian Jens. Student, Portland State U. V.p. Dimick Motion Picture Service Inc., Portland, 1971-85, pres., 1985—; mem. film and video adv. bd. Oreg. Dept. Econ. Devel., Salem, 1983—. Director TV commls. (Best in the West award Am. Advt. Fedn. 1982, 86). Mem. Oreg. Media Prodn. Assn. (bd. dirs. 1982-87, pres. 1983-85, Disting. Service award 1985). Democrat. Avocation: tennis. Office: Dimick Motion Picture Service 5253 NE Sandy Portland OR 97213

DIMMICK, CAROLYN REABER, federal judge; b. Seattle, Oct. 24, 1929; d. Maurice C. and Margaret T. (Taylor) Reaber; m. Cyrus Allen Dimmick, Sept. 10, 1955; children: Taylor, Dana. B.A., U. Wash., 1951, J.D., 1963; LL.D., Gonzaga U., 1982. Bar: Wash. Asst. atty. gen. Wash., 1953-55; judge Dist. Ct., 1965-75, Superior Ct., 1976-80; justice Wash. Supreme Ct., 1981-85; judge U.S. Dist. Ct. (we. dist.) Wash., 1985—; pros. atty. King County, Wash., 1955-59, 60-62; sole practice law, 1959-60, 62-65. Recipient Matrix Table award, 1981, World Plan Execs. Council award, 1981, others. Mem. Am. Judges Assn. (gov.), Nat. Assn. Women Judges, World Assn. Judges, Am., Wash. bar assns., Am. Judicature Soc. Clubs: Wash. Athletic, Wingpoint Golf and Country, Harbor. Office: U.S. District Court 816 US Courthouse 1010 Fifth Ave Seattle WA 98104

DIMON, MICHAEL PRATT, metals company executive; b. Atlantic City, Sept. 8, 1949; s. Bruce Pratt and Ruth (Burns) D. B.A., Dickinson Coll., 1971; postgrad. Pace U., 1971-73; M.B.A., Harvard U., 1976. C.P.A., N.Y. Staff acct. Price Waterhouse & Co., N.Y.C., 1971-73; sr. acct. Price Waterhouse & Co., N.Y.C., 1973-74, 76-78; sr. bus. analyst Cabot Corp., Boston, 1978-81; project mgr. High Tech. Materials div. Cabot Corp., Kokomo, Ind., 1981-82, mktg. mgr., 1982-83, mgr. bus. planning and communications Cabot Wrought Products div., 1983-84, mgr. bus. devel. Cabot Stellite div., 1984-86; corp. dir. mktg. Stoody Deloro Stellite, Inc., 1986—; dir. Shanghai Stellite Co. Ltd. Mem. Am. Mktg. Assn., Am. Soc. Metals, Am. Inst. C.P.A.s. Methodist. Club: Cuyamaca (San Diego). Office: 610 W Ash St Suite 1510 San Diego CA 92101-3348

DIMOND, JEFFREY JOHN, information services executive; b. St. Paul, Jan. 26, 1952; s. John R. and Joyce A. (Crooks) D.; m. SarahA. Fail, July 31, 1982. BJ, U. Ala., 1974; MBA in Sports Adminstrn., U. Ariz., 1982. Field rep. Am. Cancer Soc., Huntsville, Ala., 1975-76; aquatic dir. City of Huntsville, 1976-80; sports info. asst. U. Ariz., Tucson, 1980-82; dir. sports info. Calif. State U., Bakersfield, 1982-83; dir. info. U.S. Swimming, Colorado Springs, Colo., 1983—; media staff U.S. Olympic Com., Los Angeles, 1984, Caracas, Venezuela, 1983, Colorado Springs, 1983, Baton Rouge, 1985; press chief U.S. Aquatic Sports, Madrid, 1986. Contbr. articles on swimming to various pubs. Mem. Pub. Relations Council Ala., Coll. Sports Info. Dirs. Am. Methodist. Avocation: jogging. Home: 4955 Old Farm Cir W Colorado Springs CO 80917 Office: US Swimming 1750 E Boulder Colorado Springs CO 80909

DIMSDALE, JOEL EDWARD, psychiatry educator; b. Sioux City, Iowa, Apr. 16, 1947; s. Lewis J. and Phyllis (Green) D.; m. Nancy Kleinman, Sept. 17, 1978; 1 child, Jonathan Jared. BA in Biology, Carleton Coll., 1968; MA in Sociology, Stanford U., 1970, MD, 1973. Diplomate Am. Bd. Psychiatry. Resident in psychiatry Mass. Gen. Hosp., Boston, 1973-76; instr. psychiatry Harvard U. Sch. Medicine, Boston, 1976-80, asst. prof., 1980-84, assoc. prof., 1984-85; assoc. prof. U. Calif., San Diego, 1985—; cons. to Pres.'s Commn. on Mental Health, Washington, 1977-78, NIH, Washington, 1980—. Editor: Survivors, Victims and Perpetrators, 1980; contbr articles to profl. jours. Fellow Am. Psychopathol. Assn.; mem. Am. Psychiat. Assn., Am. Psychosomatic Soc. (council 1982-85), Sigma Xi. Home: 1684 Lugano Ln Del Mar CA 92014 Office: U Calif Med Ctr 225 Dickinson St San Diego CA 92037

DINARDO, LUELLA KAY, bookkeeper, special events coordinator; b. Montrose, Colo., May 3, 1948; d. William Edgar and Evelyn Ruth (Carlson) Bray; m. Monte Talbot, Aug. 22, 1970 (div. May 1972); m. John Nicholas Di Nardo, Sept. 25, 1976; 1 child, Nicholas John. B.S., Colo. State U., 1970. With accounts payable and receivable dept. Beaver Mesa Exploration, Denver, 1976-79; pres. Independant Bookkeeping Services, Denver, 1986—; pres. Planned Occasions Unltd., Inc., Denver, 1986—. Charter mem. Republican Presdl. Task Force, 1981—; mem. Nat. Fedn. Rep. Women, 1983—. Served to 2d lt. USAF, 1973-75. Mem. Nat. Assn. Female Execs., Women Bus. Owners Assn., Denver C. of C., Centennial C. of C., Beta Epsilon. Congregationalist. Avocations: reading, aerobic dance. Home and Office: 3921 S Narcissus Way Denver CO 80237

DINEGAR, ROBERT HUDSON, research chemist; b. N.Y.C., Dec. 18, 1921; m. Ann Elizabeth Knolle, July 11, 1942 (dec. June 1980); children: Janice Ann Boyd, Barbara Hudson Menicucci, Robert William Leonard; m. Athalie N. Moore, Apr. 26, 1986. AB in Chemistry, Cornell U., 1942; cert. in meteorology, NYU, 1943; AM in Chemistry, Columbia U., 1947, PhD in Phys. Chemistry, 1951; AB in Theology, Coll. Santa Fe, 1976. Ordained priest Episcopal Ch., 1962. Asst. in chemistry Columbia U., N.Y.C., 1945-50; mem. research staff Los Alamos (N.Mex.) Nat. Lab., 1950—; adj. instr. chemistry U. N.Mex., Los Alamos, 1970—; chmn. chemistry dept. USN enlisted sci. edn. program, San Diego, 1971-74; owner, cons. SYCON, Los Alamos, 1984—; bd. dirs. Shroud of Turin Research Project, Amston, Conn., 1977—. Co-inventor low voltage explosive detonator, 1982, high temperature explosive detonator, 1987. Priest The Episcopal Ch., Diocese of Rio Grande, 1959—. Served to comdr. USNR, 1942-75, PTO. Fellow Am. Inst. Chemists (cert.); mem. Am. Chem. Soc., Am. Meteorol. Soc., Sigma Xi, Phi Lambda Upsilon. Republican. Clubs: Baker St. Irregulars (N.Y.C.); Bros. Three Moriarty (Santa Fe). Home: 15 Tesuque Los Alamos NM 87544 Office: Los Alamos Nat Lab PO Box 1663 MS P950 Los Alamos NM 87545

DINGES, RICHARD ALLEN, entrepreneur; b. Englewood, N.J., June 17, 1945; m. Kathie A. Headley; children: Kelly, Courtney. Grad., Jersey City State Coll., 1967; MEd, U. Hawaii, 1972; postgrad., William Peterson Coll., 1974-79. Cert. sch. adminstr.; cert. sch. spl. services dir., N.J., Ariz., Hawaii. Pres. Resumes Plus, Sierra Vista, Ariz., 1979—, Fed. Career Cons., Sierra Vista, Ariz., 1985; dir. Nat. Scholarship Locators, Sierra Vista, 1985—. Editor: Guide to U.S. Defense Contractors, 1985, 87, 10 Step Guide to College Selection, Salary Negotiations for Military, How to Survive the Job Interview. Mem. Ariz. Better Bus. Bur., Cochise County Merit Commn., Sierra Vista C. of C., The Career Network. Home and Office: 2713 Pawnee Dr Sierra Vista AZ 85635

DINGMAN, JAMES DANIEL, public health sanitarian; b. Longmont, Colo., Feb. 1, 1954; Leo Willis and Helen Pearl (Fishburn) D.; m. Cheryl Elizabeth Maronde, Jan. 8, 1983; 1 child, Andrew James Daniel. BS, Colo. State U., 1976; MS, U. Denver, 1980. Instr. biol. scis. U. Denver, 1980-81; researcher Denver Mus. Natural History, 1981-82; sanitarian Tri-County Health Dept., Englewood, Colo., 1982—. Contbr. articles to profl. jours. Mem. City of Longmont (Colo.) Smoking Task Force, 1986. Denver Audubon Soc. grantee 1979. Mem. Colo. Pub. Health Assn. (bd. dirs., treas. 1983—), Colo. Environ. Health Assn. (v.p. 1985, pres. 1986-87, bd. dirs. 1983—, editor newsletter 1984-85), Nat. Environ. Health Assn., Sigma Xi. Democrat. Lodge: Elks (lectring. knight 1984-85, loyal knight 1985-86, leading knight 1986-87). Avocations: photography, hunting. Home: 1516 Mayfield Ln Longmont CO 80501 Office: Tri County Health Dept 2200 E 104th Ave Suite 115 Thornton CO 80233

DINGMAN, MICHAEL DAVID, industrial company executive; b. New Haven, Sept. 29, 1931; s. James Everett and Amelia (Williamson) D.; m. Jean Hazlewood, May 16, 1953 (div.); children: Michael David, Linda Channing (Mrs. Michael S. Cady), James Clifford; m. Elizabeth G. Tharp, Apr. 13, 1984; children: James Tharp, David Ross. Student, U. Md. Various mgmt. positions Sigma Instruments, Inc., Braintree, Mass., 1954-64; gen. and ltd. ptnr. Drexel Burnham Lambert, Inc. (formerly Burnham & Co.), N.Y.C., 1964-70; pres., chief exec. officer, bd. dirs. Wheelabrator-Frye, Inc., Hampton, N.H., 1970-83; chmn. bd. Wheelabrator-Frye Inc., Hampton, N.H., 1977-83; pres., bd. dirs. The Signal Cos., Inc., La Jolla, Calif., 1983-85, Allied-Signal Inc., Morristown, N.J., 1985-86; chmn. bd., chief exec. officer The Henley Group, Inc., La Jolla, 1986—; bd. dirs. Ford Motor Co., Time Inc.; mem. adv. bd. Mellon Bank Corp. Trustee John A. Hartford Found. Mem. IEEE (mem. adv. bd.). Clubs: Links, Bd. Room, N.Y. Yacht (N.Y.C.); Union (Boston); Cruising of Am. (Conn.); Bohemian (San Francisco), Fairbanks Ranch Country; Lyford Cay (Nassau); La Jolla Country, San Diego Yacht. Office: Henley Group Inc 375 Park Ave New York NY 10152 also: Signal Cos Inc 11255 North Torrey Pines La Jolla CA 92037

DINGMAN, ROGER VINCENT, history educator; b. Los Angeles, Oct. 19, 1938; s. Alvin Boyd and Rose Irene (Brennan) D.; m. Linda Susan Story, Aug. 21, 1965; children: Charles Edward, Margaret Rose, Zachary John, Andrew Patrick. BA, Stanford U., 1960; MA, Harvard U., 1963, PhD, 1969. History instr. Harvard U., Cambridge, Mass., 1969-71; asst. prof. U. So. Calif., Los Angeles, 1971-75, assoc. prof., 1976—; prof. strategy U.S. Naval War Coll., Newport, R.I., 1977-78; vis. prof. Griffith U., Brisbane, Australia, 1985; disting. lectr. Assn. Asian Studies, Western U.S., 1983. Author: Power in the Pacific, 1976 (Best Book award Soc. Historians Am. Fgn. Relations 1977); editor: Japan and The Outside World, 1974; contbr. articles to profl. jours. Tng. chmn. Los Angeles council Boy Scouts of Am., 1986, activities chmn., 1984-85; chmn. Speakers Bur. Citizens for Carter/Mondale, 32d Congl. Dist., 1976. Served to lt. (j.g.) USN, 1960-62. Fellow Am. Council Learned Socs., 1983, 86, NEH Australian Nat. U., Yoshida Found. Tokyo, 1982, Naval War Coll., 1980, Am. Philos. Soc., 1976, Hoover

Instn., 1973, Asia Found. (Japan), 1973, Social Scis. Research Council, 1973. Fellow Am. Council Learned Socs.; mem. Soc. Historians Am. Fgn. Relations (program chmn. 1985), Am. Hist. Assn. (Pacific coast br. nomination chmn. 1985), Japan Soc. for Occupation Hist. Democrat. Roman Catholic. Club: Internat. House of Japan (Tokyo). Avocations: swimming, photography. Home: 1532 W 238th St Harbor City CA 90710 Office: U So Calif Dept History Los Angeles CA 90089-0034

DINKELSPIEL, PAUL GAINES, investment banking and public financial consultant; b. San Francisco, Feb. 12, 1935; s. Edward Gaines and Pauline (Watson) D.; A.B., U. Calif.-Berkeley, 1959. Gen. ptnr. Stone & Youngberg, San Francisco, 1961-71; 1st v.p. Shearson/Lehman and predecessor firms, San Francisco, 1971-79; pres., chmn. bd. dirs. Dinkelspiel, Belmont & Co., Inc., investment banking and pub. fin. cons., San Francisco, 1979—. Served with AUS, 1959-60. Mem. Mcpl. Fin. Officers Assn., Am. Water Works Assn., San Francisco Mcpl. Forum, Pub. Securities Assn. (public fin. com.), Sigma Chi. Clubs: San Francisco Comml., Commonwealth of Calif., Mcpl. Bond. Home: PO Box 727 Stinson Beach CA 94970 Office: One California St San Francisco CA 94111

DINSMORE, PHILIP WADE, architect; b. Gilroy, Calif., Nov. 4, 1942; s. Wilbur Allen and Elizabeth Eleanor (Hill) D.; m. Mary Kathryn Mead; children—Robert Allen, Kerry Philip. B.Arch., U. Ariz., 1965. Registered architect, Ariz., Calif., Nev. Designer, William L. Pereira & Assocs., Los Angeles, 1965-67; assoc. CNWC Architects, Tucson, 1967-69; prin., ptnr. Architecture One Ltd., Tucson, 1970—. Mem., chmn. Archtl. Approval Bd., City of Tucson, 1974-75, 77. Fellow AIA (nat. bd. dirs. 1981-84, nat. sec. 1984—, Ariz. Architects Medal 1985, Western Mountain Region Citation award 1973, 76, 78, Award of Honor 1983); mem. Constrn. Specifications Inst., Ariz Soc. Architects Citation award 1977-80), Bldg. Stone Inst. (Tucker award 1986). Republican. Presbyterian. Office: Architecture One Ltd 6303 E Tanque Verde Rd Suite S200 Tucson AZ 85715

DINWIDDIE, DOUGLAS M., museum director; b. July 18, 1951; s. Ralph Alonzo and Vernie (Brown) D.; m. Rebecca Louise Smith, Aug. 21, 1971; children: Aaron, Amber. BA, Western N.Mex. U., 1973, MA, 1975; postgrad., No. Ariz. U., 1983-86. Curator Western N.Mex. U. Mus., Silver City, 1974-77, dir., 1977—; history instr. Western N.Mex. U., 1980—. Mem. Am. Assn. Mus., Am. Assn. State and Local History, Westerners Internat. (program chmn. Silver City chpt. 1976—). Democrat. Presbyterian. Avocations: team sports, Western Am. history. Home: 2311 Paul Pl Silver City NM 88061 Office: Western NMex U Mus Coll Arts and Letters Silver City NM 88062

DIRENFELD, LORNE KENNETH, neurologist; b. Toronto, Ont., Can., July 18, 1949; s. Edel and Bess (Olenick) D.; m. Marianna Knottenbelt, Sept. 3, 1976. BS, U. Toronto, 1971, MD, 1975. Diplomate Am. Bd. Psychiatry and Neurology. Intern Royal Columbian Hosp., New Westminster, B.C., Can., 1975-76; resident in internal medicine St. Michael's Hosp., Toronto, 1977-78; resident in neurology Boston U. Sch. Medicine, 1978-81, instr. neurology, neurobehavior fellow, 1981-83; practice medicine specializing in neurology Maui Neurol. Assoc. Inc., Kahului, Hawaii, 1983—. Contbr. articles to sci. jours. Recipient Clin. Investigator award NIH, Inst. on Aging, 1981-83. Fellow Royal Coll. Physicians of Can.; mem. Am. Acad. Neurology, Behavioral Neurology Soc., AMA. Home: PO Box 6070 Kahului HI 96732 Office: Maui Neurol Assn Inc 53 Puunene Ave Kahului HI 96732

DIRICCO, LEO, chemical engineer; b. Raymond, Wash., Sept. 16, 1922; s. Ferdinand and Eugenia (delFrate) diR.; B.S., Wash. State U., 1949, M.S., 1950; Ph.D., U. Colo., 1955; m. Cecilia DiFalco, Sept. 22, 1947. Staff engr. IBM, 1960-65; mgr. chem. devel. Singer Bus. Machines, 1965-68; mgr. magnetic media devel. Honeywell Info. Systems, 1968-70; prin. engr. Ampex Corp., 1970-72; cons. Ball Bros. Research, Boulder, 1972-74; mgr. materials and processes devel. Applied Magnetics, Goleta, Calif., 1974-78; mgr. chem. devel. rigid media and components div. Memorex Corp., San Jose, Calif., 1978-83, sr. v.p. research and devel. Kearney Magnetics, San Jose, 1983—. Served with USAF, 1943-47; CBI, ETO. Socony-Vacuum fellow, 1953-54. Mem. Am. Chem. Soc., Sigma Xi, Tau Beta Pi, Phi Lambda Upsilon, Sigma Tau. Republican. Roman Catholic. Patentee in field.

DIRKS, LESLIE CHANT, communications, electronics company executive; b. New Ulm, Minn., Mar. 7, 1936; s. Emerald Francis and Eva Gay (Fabianke) D.; m. Eleanor Gertrude McPeake, Feb. 10, 1959; children: Anthony, Jason, Elizabeth. BS in Physics, MIT, 1958; BS, Oxford (Eng.) U., 1960. Registered electrical engr. Instr. physics Philips Acad., Andover, Mass., 1960-61; with office directorate of Sci. & Tech. U.S. Govt., Washington, 1961-71, dir. Office of Spl. Projects., 1971-76, dep. dir. Sci. and Tech., 1976-82; corp. v.p. of research and devel. Raytheon Corp., Lexington, Mass., 1982-84; v.p. Space and Communications group Hughes Aircraft Co., El Segundo, Calif., 1984—. Recipient Nat. Security Metal Pres. U.S., 1978. Mem. Nat. Acad. Engring., Nat. Research Council (mem. Army-Space com. 1986—). Unitarian. Avocations: hiking, bicycling. Office: Hughes Aircraft Co Space & Communications Group PO Box 92919 Los Angeles CA 90009

DIRKS, LOLITA ANN, interior designer; b. Washington, Feb. 14, 1944; d. America Matthew and Lucille Francis (Neznanski) Borzello; m. Algimantas J. Rutelionis, May 6, 1967 (div.); 1 child, Ari A.; m. Joseph Edward Dirks, Nov. 7, 1981. BS, U. Md., 1966. Interior display designer Hecht Co., Washington, 1966-69, May D&F, Denver, 1969-70; mgr. C.J. Welch Co., Denver, 1970-72; owner, operator Wall Art, Denver, 1972-74; v.p., owner Possibilities for Design, Inc., Denver, 1974—; tchr. retailing and merchandising Barbazon Schs., Englewood, Colo., 1976-80; lectr. bldg. industry, 1985—. Illustrator (book) Historic Costume, 1977; contbr. articles to profl. jours. Chmn. com. Colo. Folk Life Festival, Denver, 1972, 73. Mem. Nat. Assn. Home Builders, Home Builders Assn. Colorado Springs, Inst. Residential Mktg., Nat. Sales and Mktg. Council (Mame award 1985, 86), Colo. Assn. of Home Builders, Home Builders Assn. Denver, Lithuanian Orgn. Colo. (officer 1970-71). Roman Catholic. Avocation: skiing. Office: Possibilities for Design Inc 600 Elati Denver CO 80204

DIRKSEN, CHARLES JOSEPH, dean emeritus, consultant; b. Springfield, Ill., Aug. 27, 1912; s. Frank T. Dirksen and Mary A. Cloney; m. Rita C. Seneker, Aug. 16, 1941; children: Charles Jr., Frank, Victor, Mary Lula (dec.), Mary Rita (dec.), J. Anthony. BS, St. Louis U., 1935, MS, 1938; LLD, U. Santa Clara, 1965. CPA, Calif. Coach, tchr. Cathedral High Sch., Springfield, 1936-37; dean and prof. U. Santa Clara, Calif., 1938-79; vis. prof. mktg. Harvard U., Cambridge, Mass., 1953, U. So. Calif., Los Angeles, 1954-55, Stanford U., Palo Alto, Calif, 1972-73; founder, bd. dirs. Bank of Santa Clara, 1972; mem. First Western Bank, World Airways, Newcomb Hotel, Vasconi & Assocs., Western G Car Corp., World Am. Investment Inc. Author books on mktg. and advt. Chmn. Calif. Student Aid Commn., Sacramento, 1968-78; bd. dirs. Santa Clara C. of C., 1947-51; chmn. San Jose (Calif.) Ind. Study, 1981-82. Recipient St. Louis U. Alumni Merit award, 1965, Western Assn. Coll. Schs. of Bus. Disting. Educator award, 1979; named to St. Louis U. Sports Hall of Fame, 1976. Mem. Am. Mktg. Assn., Am. Assn. Collegiate Schs. of Bus. (pres. 1965-66, Dow Jones award 1977). Lodge: Rotary (pres. Santa Clara club 1947-48). Home and Office: 1465 Calaveras Ave San Jose CA 95126

DIRUSCIO, LAWRENCE WILLIAM, business executive; b. Buffalo, Jan. 2, 1941; s. Guido Carmen and Mabel Ella (Bach) DiR.; m. Gloria J. Edney, Aug. 19, 1972; children—Lawrence M., Lorie P., Darryl C., Teresa M., Jack D. With various broadcast stas. and instr., adminstr. Bill Wade Sch. Radio and TV, San Diego, San Francisco, Los Angeles, 1961-69; account exec. Sta. KGB Radio, San Diego, 1969, gen. sales mgr., 1970-72; pres. Free Apple Advt., San Diego, 1972—, Fin. Mgmt. Assocs., Inc., San Diego, 1979-84, Self-Pub. Ptnrs., San Diego, 1981—, Media Mix Assocs. Enterprises, Inc., 1984-86; pres. Press-Courier Pub. Co., Inc., 1985-86; pres. Media Mix Advt. and Pub. Relations, 1985—; lectr., writer on problems of small bus. survival. Served with USN, 1958-60. Mem. Nat. Acad. TV Arts and Scis. Democrat. Roman Catholic. Office: 3926 Iowa St San Diego CA 92104

DISHMAN, C. MICHAEL, computer industry executive; b. Missoula, Mont., Dec. 11, 1940; s. Charles Francis and Margaret Zoe (Ross) D.; m. Nuria Rosa Maureso, July 15, 1968. B.A. in Pre Law, U. Mont., 1963; B.B.A., U. Md.-College Park, 1968; M.B.A., U. So. Calif., 1969. Sales mgr. RCA Computer Div., Century City, Calif., 1968-71; mktg. mgr. Xerox Data Systems, El Segundo, Calif., 1971-76; v.p. mktg. Computer Scis. Corp., El Segundo, 1976-81; prin., v.p. Input, Mountain, Calif., 1981-82; founder, v.p. OEMTEK San Jose, Calif., 1982-84; prin. Input, Mountain View, Calif., 1984—. Author: (research) Decision Support Systems, 1982; Fourth Generation Languages, 1984; Annual Report on the Computer Services Industry, 1985. Contbr. articles to profl. jours. Served to capt. USAF, 1964-68. Mem. Data Processing Mgmt. Assn., Nat. Corp. Planners Am., Soc. Magical Arts. Republican. Methodist. Lodge: DeMolay (state master counselor 1957-58). Office: Input 1943 Landings Dr Mountain View CA 94043

DISHNO, DUANE ALLAN, educational administrator; b. Missoula, Mont., Oct. 26, 1941; s. Thomas Charles and Nellie Montana (Managhan) D.; m. Pauline Amelia Schwandt, Aug. 17, 1968; children—Joel Thomas, Chris Edward. Student, Wash. State U., 1959-60; B.A., Eastern Wash. U., 1963; M.A., Calif. State U.-Long Beach, 1972; student U. Calif.-Riverside, 1975-76; Ed.D., U. La Verne, 1984. Cert. pre-sch.-adult adminstr., tchr. Classroom tchr., reading specialist, learning analyst Westminster (Calif.) Sch. Dist., 1963-73; lectr. Calif. State U.-Los Angeles, 1973-74; coordinator compensatory edn. Westminster Sch. Dist., 1973-75; prin. Huntington Beach (Calif.) City Sch. Dist., 1975-77, dir. spl. services, 1977-82, asst. supt. ednl. services, 1982-84; supt. El Monte City Sch. Dist., Calif., 1984—; pres. El Monte/South El Monte Coordinating Council; cons. Calif. State Dept. Edn.; mem. adv. com. bilingual tchr. preparation Calif. State U., 1980-81, mem. adv. com. ethnic heritage studies, 1981-83; adv. com. instructional aide program Goldenwest Community Coll., 1975. Dist. rep. United Crusade, 1975-77; sustaining mem. Calif. Republican Com., 1981—; bd. dirs. San Gabriel Valley Boys' Club; mem. El Monte C. of C. Mem. Assn. Calif. Sch. Adminstrs., Calif. Soc. Ednl. Program Auditors and Evaluators, Orange County Reading Assn., Calif. Assn. Compensatory Edn., Orange County Adminstrs. Spl. Edn., Educare, Assn. Supervision and Curriculum Devel., West Orange County Tchrs. Center (mem. policy bd., v.p.). Republican. Roman Catholic. Lodge: Kiwanis. Home: 7652 Concordia Pl Westminster CA 92683 Office: 3540 N Lexington Ave El Monte CA 91731

DISTEFANO, PETER ANDREW, insurance executive; b. N.Y.C., Nov. 26, 1939; s. Peter Julian and Marie Antoinette (Onorato) D.; student City Coll. San Francisco, 1965, Costa Mesa (Calif.)-Orange Coast Coll., 1975; cert. enrolled employee benefits, Wharton Sch., U. Pa., 1980; children: Diane, Daniel, Donald. Agt., Mut. N.Y., San Francisco, 1971-73; regional mgr. Hartford Ins. Group, Santa Ana, Calif., 1972-77; v.p. Lachman & Assos., Inc., ins., Lafayette, Calif., 1977-80; pres., owner Distefano Ins. Services, Benicia, Calif., 1980—; lectr., cons. risk mgmt., employee benefits. Pres. Contra Costa/Solano County Easter Seal Soc. Served with USNR, 1957-62. Recipient various ins. sales awards; registered profl. disability and health ins. underwriter. Fellow Acad. Producer Ins. Studies; mem. Nat. Assn. Health Underwriters, Nat. Assn. Life Underwriters, Soc. Registered Profl. Health Underwriters, Nat. Assn. Security Dealers, Internat. Found. Employee Benefit Plans, Profl. Ins. Agts. Calif./Nev., Oakland/East Bay Assn. Life Underwriters. Greek Orthodox. Home: 845 First St PO Box 696 Benicia CA 94510 Office: Distefano Ins Services Inc 845 First St PO Box 696 Benicia CA 94510

DITHRIDGE, BETTY, civic worker; b. Los Angeles, Sept. 11, 1920; d. Thomas Edward and Louise (Miles) Mitchell; m. Andrew Morrison Dithridge, May 11, 1940; 1 child, Andrew Morrison Jr. Student, UCLA, 1937-39. Boy scout and cub scout leader Los Angeles Orphan's Home Soc., 1952-69, sec. extension com., 1959-61, chmn., 1966-68; vol. worker USO; mem. Los Angeles Jr. Philharmonic Com., 1949—; active Symphonies for Youth Concerts, 1958-59; founder, chmn. San Marino Protection Com., 1971-72; sec. Los Angeles County Grand Jury, 1974-75; bd. dirs. Pasadena chpt. ARC, 1961-62, Vol. Service Bur. Pasadena; bd. dirs., treas. Wilshire Community Police Council, 1979-81; mem. citizens adv. com. Los Angeles Olympics Organizing Com., 1982-84. Recipient awards for work with local youth groups. Mem. Wilshire C. of C. (chmn. women's bur. 1957-59), Los Angeles C. of C. Assocs. Los Angeles City Coll., Orange County Marine Inst., Friends of Huntington Library, D.A.R., Friends of San Juan Capistrano Library, Los Angeles Grand Jurors Assn., Alpha Phi, Sigma Alpha Iota. Clubs: Los Angeles Tennis, Wilshire Country. Home: 35411 Beach Rd Capistrano Beach CA 92624

DITMORE, MICHAEL CONRAD, medical company executive; b. Mpls., May 14, 1943; s. Conrad William and June Carol (VanNest) D.; student U.S. Air Force Acad., 1961-64; B.A., U. Wash., 1966; M.B.A., Stanford U., 1970; m. Rebecca Patterson Ditmore; children—Brooke, Nathan, Nicholas. With IBM, Portland, Oreg., 1966-68; dir. European ops. Canberra Industries GmbH, Wiesbaden, Germany, 1970-72; regional sales mgr. Rolm Corp., Santa Barbara, Calif., 1972-73; cons. to NASA-Gen. Research Corp., Santa Barbara, 1973-74; divisional mgr. Gyrex Corp., Santa Barbara, 1974-75; v.p. mktg. and fin. Browne Corp., Santa Barbara, 1975-78; pres. Endotek Corp., Santa Barbara, 1978-84; chmn., chief exec. officer Group Techs. Corp., Santa Barbara, 1984—. Mem. Montecito Sch. Bd., 1975-79; mem. Santa Barbara alumni bd. Stanford U., 1976-78, 86—; Santa Barbara Symphony bd., 1986—. Served with USAF, 1961-64. Mem. IEEE, Fgn. Relations Com. EpiscopaBlian. Clubs: Birnam Wood Golf, Channel City. Home: 211 Rametto Rd Santa Barbara CA 93108 Office: 4 E Yanonali St Santa Barbara CA 93101

DITO, WILLIAM ROBERT, pathology educator; b. Alameda, Calif., Aug. 8, 1929; s. Salvatore Mario and Mary Josephine (Silvestri) D.; m. Bridget Claire O'Rourke, Sept. 25, 1954; children: Robert W., David M., Matthew T., Mark A., William K. BS, U. San Francisco, 1950; MD, Loyola U., Chgo., 1954. Diplomate Am. Bd. Pathology; Clin. and Anatomical Pathology Radioisotopic Pathology. Commd. capt. U.S. Army, 1955, advanced through grades to major, 1961; chief lab. service U.S. Army Hosp., Nuremberg, Fed. Republic Germany, 1961-64; resigned U.S. Army, 1965; chief clin. lab. Letterman Gen. Hosp., San Francisco, 1964-65; dir. labs., dir. Sch. Med. Tech. Pontiac (Mich.) Gen. Hosp., 1965-73; assoc. prof. pathology U. Ariz., Tucson, 1973-76; med. dir. Sch. Med. Tech. Ariz. Med. Ctr., Tucson, 1974-76; head div. lab. medicine Scripps Clinic and Research Found., La Jolla, Calif., 1976—; adj. instr. Wayne State U., Detroit, 1970-73; adj. assoc. prof. pathology, U. Calif.-San Diego, La Jolla, 1977-86, assoc. clin. prof., 1986—; chief of labs. VA Hosp., Tucson, 1973-74. Co-editor: (with Nakamura and Tucker) Immunologic Analysis—Recent Progress in Diagnostic Laboratory Immunology, 1982; (jour.) Informatics in Pathology, 1985—; mem. editorial bd. Lab. Medicine, 1978-85; also numerous articles and monographs in field. Fellow. Coll. Am. Pathologists, Am. Soc. Clin. Pathologists (mem. editorial bd. 1979-82, Disting. Service award 1980), Internat. Acad. Pathology. Republican. Roman Catholic. Club: La Jolla Profl. Mens. Avocations: golf, photography, computers. Office: Scripps Clinic and Research Found 10666 N Torrey Pines Rd La Jolla CA 92037

DITTMAN, DEBORAH RUTH, real estate broker; b. Sacramento, Apr. 15, 1932; s. Charles Harwood and Ruth Boice (Potter) Kinsley; m. John Alvin Cardoza, Sept. 1950 (div. 1964); children: Harold, Nancy Cardoza Tolbert, John Allan, Gregory, Janice, Cardoza Boswell; m. Edgar Marshall Dittman, Jan. 22, 1967 (dec. Jan. 1982); 5 stepchildren. Student Humprey's Coll., Stockton, Calif., 1966, San Joaquin Delta Coll., 1977; grad. real estate sales Anthony Schs., 1974. Real estate broker, Calif. Sec., Calif. Dept. Water Resources, Patterson and Tracy, 1966-72; hostess Welcome Wagon, Tracy, 1973-74; assoc. realtor Reeve Assocs., Tracy, 1975-80; broker Allied Brokers, Tracy, 1980-83; ptnr. real estate Putt, Fallavena, Willbanks & Dittman, Tracy, 1983—. Mem. Tracy Bd. Realtors (pres. 1981, 85, dir. 1976, 77, 80-83, 85-86), Calif. Assn. Realtors (dir. 1980-81, 85), Tracy C. of C. Presbyterian. Home: 12134 Midway Dr Tracy CA 95376 Office: 1300 W 11th St Tracy CA 95376

DITZ, JOHN ADAMS, construction company executive; b. Stockton, Calif., Mar. 4, 1921; s. George Armand and Janet (Adams) D.; m. Elizabeth Ann Goodwin, June 14, 1947; children: Susan, Elizabeth, Nancy, Janet. A.B., Stanford U., 1942. V.p. Ditz Bros., San Jose, Calif., 1948-60; v.p. Ditz-Crane, Santa Clara, Calif., 1954-82, pres., 1982-85, also bd. dirs.; v.p. McKesson Corp., San Francisco, 1975-85; pres. McKesson Property Co., San Francisco, 1975-85; pres. Foremost Homes Hawaii, Honolulu, 1975-80, McKesson Property Co., San Francisco, 1975-85. Chmn. Santa Clara Heart Assn., San Jose, 1951; trustee Stanford U., Palo Alto, Calif., 1982—, Palo Alto Med. Found., 1982—. Served to lt. USN, 1942-46, PTO. Republican. Episcopalian. Clubs: Bohemian (San Francisco), Pacific Union (San Francisco). Office: 1 Post St Suite 2225 San Francisco CA 94104

DIVINE, THEODORE EMRY, electrical engineer; b. Hailey, Idaho, May 27, 1943; s. Theodore Clyde and Muriel Juanita (Kirtley) D.; BEE, U. Wash., Seattle, 1966, MBA, 1970; m. Roberta Louise Erickson, Mar. 19, 1966; children: Timothy Shannon, Brianna Kristine, Rachel Melissa. Engr., Gen. Telephone Co. of N.W., 1968-69; mem. tech. saff NW ops. Computer Scis. Corp., 1970-72; research engr. Battelle Pacific N.W. Labs., Richland, Wash., 1973—, research sect. mgr., 1978, staff engr. def. programs, 1980—. Pres., Mid-Columbia Sci. Fair Assn., 1975-76; ruling elder First Presbyn. Ch., Prosser, Wash., 1982-84. Served as officer Signal Corps, USAR, 1966-84; Vietnam, 1967. Decorated Bronze Star. Mem. IEEE, Am. Def. Preparedness Assn., Assn. of U.S. Army, Am. Soc. Agrl. Engrs. (com. chmn. 1977-78, 82-83, chmn. nat. conf. on electronics in agr. 1983), Beta Gamma Sigma. Mem. editorial adv. bd. Internat. Jours. Computers & Electronics in Agr., Elsevier, The Netherlands, 1983—.

DIVITA, FRANK GEORGE, artist; b. Genoa, Italy, Apr. 30, 1949; came to U.S. 1960; s. Salvatore A. and Anna (Mazzoca) DiV.; m. Marsha Kay Buzzard, Mar. 2, 1974; 1 child, Suzanne. B.F.A., U. Mont., 1972. Illustrator, U.S. Forest Service, Missoula, Mont., 1973; tchr. art Flathead High Sch., Kalispell, Mont., 1974-80; one man shows include Ctr. Gallery, U. Mont., 1974-75; exhibited in group shows at Peking Exhibition Ctr., Peking, Peoples Rep. of China, 1980, C.M. Russell Mus., Great Falls, Mont., 1978-82, Mus. of Native Am. Culture, Spokane, Wash., 1974-80, Trailside Galleries, 1980-84, Driscol Gallery, Denver, 1980, Connally and Altermann Galleries, Dallas; represented in permanent collections at the White House, Washington, NBC Bldg., N.Y., Peking Exhibition Ctr., U. Mont., Missoula, State Capital, Helena, Mont., Neuman Ctr., Missoula, Beatrice Foods Co., Calif., Wrigley Bldg., Chgo., Am. Container Corp., Sweden, Dubai Natural Gas Corp., United Arab Emerates. Contbr. articles to profl. jours. Recipient Best of Show, Charles M. Russell Art Show, 1978. Home: 461 S Many Lake Dr Kalispell MT 59901 Office: PO Box 1437 Kalispell MT 59901

DIX, CHRISTOPHER SCOVELL, newspaper publisher; b. Lockport, N.Y., Feb. 17, 1948; s. Elliott Tillinghast and Margaret Elizabeth (Scovell) D.; children: Alissa Jane, Rachel Elizabeth. BA, U. Rochester, 1970; JD, SUNY, Buffalo, 1973. Bar: Hawaii 1976. Confidential clk. N.Y. Supreme Ct., Buffalo, 1973-75; legal counsel Johnson & Higgins, Honolulu, 1975-76; gen. counsel Hawaii Newspaper Agy., Honolulu, 1976-82; pub., pres. The Bellingham (Wash.) Herald, 1982-84, The Stockton (Calif.) Record, 1984—. Home: 3347 Cove Circle Stockton CA 95204 Office: The Stockton Record 530 E Market St Stockton CA 95202

DIXON, FRANK JAMES, medical scientist, educator; b. St. Paul, Mar. 9, 1920; s. Frank James and Rose Augusta (Kuhfeld) D.; m. Marion Edwards, Mar. 14, 1946; children: Janet Wynne, Frank, Michael. B.S., U. Minn., 1941, M.B., 1943, M.D., 1944. Diplomate: Am. Bd. Pathology. Intern U.S. Naval Hosp., Great Lakes, Ill., 1943-44; research asst. dept. pathology Harvard, 1946-48; instr. dept. pathology Washington U., 1948-50, asst. prof., 1950-51; prof., chmn. dept. pathology U. Pitts. Med. Sch., 1951-60; chmn. dept. exptl. pathology Scripps Clinic and Research Found., La Jolla, Calif., 1961-74; chmn. biomed. research depts. Scripps Clinic and Research Found., 1970-74, dir. research inst., 1974-86, dir. emeritus, 1986—; research assoc. dept. biology U. Calif. at San Diego, 1961-64, prof. in residence in dept. biology, 1965-68, adj. prof. dept. pathology, 1968—; sci. adviser NIH, Nat. Found., Helen Hay Whitney Found., St. Jude's Med. Center, Christ Hosp. Inst., Cin.; mem. expert adv. panel on immunology WHO; sci. adv. bd. Nat. Kidney Found.; Pahlavi lectr. Ministry of Sci. and Higher Tech., Iran, 1976. Co-editor: Advances in Immunology; Editorial bd.: Excerpta Medica, Jour. Exptl. Medicine, Am. Jour. Pathology, Cellular Immunology, Kidney Hosp. Practice, Perspectives in Biology and Medicine; Contbr. articles to profl. jours. Served with M.C. USNR, 1943-46. Recipient Theobald Smith award, 1952; Parke-Davis award in exptl. pathology, 1957; Disting. Achievement award Modern Medicine, 1961; Martin E. Rehfuss award in internal medicine, 1966; Von Pirquet medal Ann. Forum on Allergy, 1967; Bunim medal Am. Rheumatism Assn., 1968; Internat. award Gairdner Found., 1969; Mayo Soley award Western Soc. Clin. Research, 1969; Albert Lasker Basic Med. Research award, 1975; Dickson prize U. Pitts., 1975; Homer Smith award N.Y. Heart Assn., 1976; Rous-Whipple award Am. Assn. Pathologists, 1979, Gold-Headed Cane award, 1987; Regents award U. Minn., 1985; H.P. Smith award Am. Soc. Clin. Pathologists, 1985; Distinguished Service award Lupus Found. Am., 1987. Mem. Nat. Acad. Scis., N.Y. Acad. Scis. Western Assn. Physicians, Western Soc. Clin. Research, Soc. Exptl. Biology and Medicine, Transplantation Soc., AAAS, Am. Soc. Clin. Investigation, Am. Acad. Allergists, Interurban Path. Soc., Harvey Soc. (lectr. 1962), Am. Soc. Exptl. Pathology (pres. 1966), Am. Assn. Immunologists (pres. 1972), Am. Assn. for Cancer Research, Assn. Am. Physicians, Am. Acad. Arts and Scis., Sigma Xi, Nu Sigma Nu, Alpha Omega Alpha. Office: Scripps Clinic and Research Found 10666 N Torrey Pines Rd La Jolla CA 92037

DIXON, JOHN ELVIN, agricultural engineering educator; b. Roseburg, Oreg., Mar. 23, 1927; s. Ned Elvin and Marjorie May (Whipple) D.; m. Winifred Augusta Powers, June 18, 1948; children: Jeffery Alan, Pauline Ellen Dixon Scheurman. BS in Agrl. Engring., BS in Agrl. Mech., Oreg. State U., 1951; MS in Agrl. Engring., U. Idaho, 1957; PhD in Agrl. Engring., Mich. State U., 1979. Registered profl. engr., Idaho, Calif. Instr. agrl. engring. Colo. State U., Ft. Collins, 1951-54; instr. agrl. engring. U. Idaho, Moscow, 1954-57, asst. prof., 1957-64, assoc. prof., 1964-79, dir. profl. advisory service, 1970-72, prof., 1979—; agrl. engring. advisor A.P. Agrl. U., Hyderabad, India, 1967-69; agrl. engring. cons. Pragma Corp., Falls Church, Va., Cairo, 1984. Author: Environmental Control for Agriculture Buildings, 1986; also articles to profl. jours. Served with USN, 1945-46. Mem. Am. Soc. Agrl. Engrs. (bd. dirs. 1983-85), Am. Soc. Engring. Engrs., NSPE, Idaho Soc. Profl. Engrs., Sigma Xi, Alpha Zeta. Lodge: Lions (pres. Moscow Paradise club 1983-84), Elks. Avocations: gardening, swimming, travelling. Home: 1350 Walenta Dr Moscow ID 83843 Office: U Idaho Agrl Engring Dept Moscow ID 83843

DIXON, JULIAN CAREY, congressman; b. Washington, Aug. 8, 1934; m. Betty Lee; 1 son, Cary Gordon. B.S., Calif. State U., Los Angeles, 1962; LL.B., Southwestern U., Los Angeles, 1967. Mem. Calif. State Assembly, 1972-78; mem. 96th-100th Congresses from Calif. 28th Dist., mem. House Appropriations Com., chmn. Com. on Stanards Ofcl. Conduct, mem. Black Caucus; pres., bd. dirs. CBC Found., Inc. Served with U.S. Army, 1957-60. Mem. NAACP, Urban League, Calif. Arts Commn. Democrat. Office: 2400 Rayburn Bldg Washington DC 20515

DIXON, MARK G., computer systems engineer, analyst; b. Gooding, Idaho, Mar. 29, 1953; s. Ken and Dixie (Gardner) D.; m. Claudia Lee Dent, Aug. 6, 1976; children: Heidi Ann, David Mark, Angela Michelle. BSEE, Brigham Young U., 1978. Engr. Eyring Research, Provo, Utah, 1977-82, dir. mktg., 1982-83; program dir. Eyring Computer Systems, Provo, 1982-86, exec. v.p., 1986—. Advisor Boy Scouts Am., Am. Fork, Utah., 1985-86. Mem. IEEE, Tau Beta Pi, Eta Kappa Nu, Phi Kappa Phi. Mormon. Photography. Office: Eyring Computer Systems 1450 W 820 N Provo UT 84601

DIXON, RICHARD DEAN, lawyer, educator; b. Columbus, Ohio, Nov. 6, 1944; s. Dean A. and Katherine L. (Currier) D.; m. Kathleen A. Manfrass, June 17, 1967; children—Jennifer, Lindsay. B.S. in Elec. Engring., Ohio State U., 1967, M.S. in Elec. Engring., 1968; M.B.A., Fla. State U., 1972, J.D., 1974. Bar: Fla. 1975, U.S. Dist. Ct. (mid. dist.) Fla. 1975, U.S. Patent and Trademark Office, 1975, Colo. 1985, U.S. Dist. Ct. Colo. 1985. Telemetry systems engr. Pan Am. World Airways, Patrick AFB, Fla., 1968-72; sole practice, Melbourne and Orlando, Fla., 1975-80; sr. counsel Harris Corp., Melbourne, 1980-85; corp. counsel Ford Microelectronics, Inc., Colorado Springs, Colo., 1985—; adj. prof. bus. law U. Central Fla., Cocoa, 1977, Fla. Inst. Tech., Melbourne, 1980-84. Cooper Industries Engring. scholar Ohio State U., 1964-67. Mem. Licensing Execs. Soc., Am. Intellectual Property Law Assn., Am. Corp. Counsel Assn., ABA, Sigma Iota Epsilon, Eta Kappa Nu, Phi Eta Sigma. Home: 225 Woodmoor Dr Monument CO 80132 Office: Ford Microelectronics Inc 10340 State Hwy 83 Colorado Springs CO 80908

DIXON, ROBERT CLYDE, communication systems engineer, consultant; b. Greensboro, N.C., Jan. 8, 1932; s. Earnest Patrick and Alma Leona (Moore) D.; m. Nancy Tom Zurborg, July 9, 1955; children—David Thomas, Theresa Anne, Robert Weldon. B.S. in Elec. Engring., Pacific States U., 1961; M.S. in Systems Engring., West Coast U., 1968; cert. bus. for tech. personnel, UCLA, 1971, profl. designation in bus., 1972. Registered profl. engr., Calif. Sr. engr. Magnavox Research Labs., Torrance, Calif., 1959-68; staff engr. TRW, Redondo Beach, Calif., 1968-71; sr. research engr. Northrop Corp., Palos Verdes, Calif., 1971-74; sr. tech. staff asst. Hughes Aircraft Co., Fullerton, Calif., 1974-75; chief scientist, Irvine, Calif., 1982-84; pres. Spectrack Systems Inc., Cypress, Calif., 1975-82; cons. R.C. Dixon & Assocs., Cypress, 1975—; chief scientist Spread Spectrum Scis., Palmer Lake, Colo., 1981—; lectr. UCLA, Westwood, 1975—, George Washington U., 1976—. Author: Spread Spectrum Systems, 1976, 84; editor: Spread Spectrum Techniques, 1976; contbr. articles to tech. jours. Elder's pres. Ch. of Jesus Christ of Latter Day Saints, Cypress, 1975, mem. High Council, 1977-83. Served with USN, 1951-55. Mem. IEEE (sr. mem., co-editor spl. issue communications transactions 1978, mem. prceedings editorial bd.), Armed Forces Communications and Electronic Assn. Mormon. Home: 14717 Perry Park Rd Palmer Lake CO 80133 Office: Spread Spectrum Scis PO Box 100 Palmer Lake CO 80133

DIXON, ROBERT GENE, educator, mechanical company executive; b. Clatskanie, Oreg., Feb. 15, 1934; s. Hobart Jay and Doris Marie D.; m. Janice Lee Taylor, Sept. 19, 1954; children—Linda Dixon Johnson, Jeffrey, David. A.S. in Indsl. Tech., Chemeketa Community Coll., 1978, various special courses, 1978-80. Journeyman machinist, cert. welder, Oreg., cert. mfg. engr. Machine apprentice to asst. mgr. A.B. McLauchlan Co., Inc., 1956-69; supt. engring. and prodn. Stevens Equipment Co., 1969-70; co-owner, operator Pioneer Machinery, 1970-72; supt. constrn. and repair Stayton Canning Co., 1972-73; mgr. Machinery div. Power Transmission, 1973-75; owner, operator Dixon Mech., Salem, Oreg., 1975—; instr., program coordinator mfg. engring. tech. Chemeketa Community Coll., 1975—; cons. Served with U.S. Navy, 1952-56. Named Tchr. of Yr., Chemeketa Deaf Program, 1978, Outstanding Instr. of Yr., Am. Tech. Edn. Assn., 1983. Mem. Am. Vocat. Assn. (Outstanding Tchr. award 1981), Oreg. Vocat. Assn. (Instr. of Yr. 1980; pres. 1984), Oreg. Vocat. Trade Tech. Assn. (Instr. of Yr. 1979; pres. 1981; Pres.'s Plaque 1982), Soc. Mfg. Engrs. (sr., chmn. Oreg. sect. 1987—), Am. Welding Soc., Am. Soc. Metals, Chemeketa Edn. Assn. (pres. 1979), Am Soc. Quality Control, Computer Automated Systems Assn. Author: Benchwork, 1980; Procedure Manual for Team Approach for Vocational Education Special Needs Students, 1980; designer, patentee fruit and berry stem remover. Home: 4242 Indigo St NE Salem OR 97305 Office: PO Box 14007 Salem OR 97309

DIXON, ROBERT MORTON, soil scientist; b. Leon, Kans., May 30, 1929; s. William Gilld and Vivian (Marshall)D.; B.S., Kans. State U., 1959, M.S., 1960; Ph.D., U. Wis., 1966; children—James, Curtis, Donna, Gregory. Instr., Kans. State U., Manhattan, 1959-60; irrigation specialist Ford Found., Cairo, 1967; research soil scientist U.S. Dept. Agr., 1960-85, Tucson, 1973-85; water infiltration control specialist AID, Port-au-Prince, Haiti, 1977; agrl. cons. U.S. Agy. Internat. Devel., Haiti, 1978; People-to-People Irrigation del. People's Republic of China, 1982. Served with U.S. Army, 1954-56. Mem. Internat. Soc. Soil Sci., Am. Soc. Agronomy, Am. Geophys. Union, Am. Soc. Agrl. Engrs., Soil Sci. Soc. Am., Soil Conservation Soc. Am., Internat. Platform Assn., Soc. Range Mgmt., Ariz.-Nev. Acad. Sci., Land Imprinting Found. (organizer 1986, chmn. 1986—). Democrat. Unitarian. Contbr. articles to profl. jours. Patentee land imprinter. Home and Office: 1231 E Big Rock Rd Tucson AZ 85718

DIXON, STEVEN BEDFORD, lawyer; b. San Bernardino, Calif., Dec. 25, 1945; s. Harold James Dixon and Jane Anna (Bedford) Kennedy; m. Lucy Pearson; children—Melanie Anne, Zachary David; stepchildren: Michael, Katherine. B.A., U. Hawaii-Hilo, 1975; J.D., Calif. Western Sch. Law, 1978; postgrad. Chaminade U. of Hawaii, Hawaii Tax Inst., 1978-82. Bar: Hawaii, U.S. Dist Ct. Hawaii, U.S. Tax Ct. Law clk. firm Linley, McDougal, Meloche & Murphy, El Cajon, Calif., 1976, D. Stephen Boner, San Diego, 1977, Tyson & Churchill, San Diego, 1977; law intern Legal Aid Soc. of Hawaii, 1978; law clk., investigator Stephen Christensen, Hawaii, 1978; gen. ptnr. Altman, Dicker & Dixon, tax attys., Hilo, 1978-79, Altman Dixon & Assocs., tax attys., Hilo, 1979-81; sole practice as tax atty., Hilo, 1981-82; gen. ptnr. Dixon & Okura, Hilo, 1982—; speaker, news columnist in field; writer; instr. bus. law U. Hawaii-Hilo, 1979-80, Vitousek Real Estate Sch. (cert.); bd. dirs. Elec. Co-operative Hawaii Inc. Columnist Money, Real Estate and You; radio show 50 Minutes with Steve Dixon. Past v.p. Hawaii Concert Soc.; counsel discharge Vets. Outreach, San Diego, 1976; bd. dirs. Big Island Substance Abuse Council, Elec. Coop. of Hawaii, Inc; active community services. Served to 1st lt. 1967-70, Vietnam. Decorated Bronze Star. U. Hawaii-Hilo scholar, 1973. Mem. Hawaii County Bar Assn. Lodge: Rotary. Office: 155 Wailuku Dr Hilo HI 96720 also: Kailua Kona HI 96740

DJERASSI, CARL, chemist, educator, writer; b. Vienna, Austria, Oct. 29, 1923; s. Samuel and Alice (Friedmann) D.; m. Norma Lundholm (div. 1976); children: Dale, Pamela (dec.); m. Diane W. Middlebrook, 1985. A.B. summa cum laude, Kenyon Coll., 1942, D.Sc. (hon.), 1958; Ph.D., U. Wis., 1945; D.Sc. (hon.), Nat. U. Mex., 1953, Fed. U., Rio de Janeiro, 1969, Worcester Poly. Inst., 1972, Wayne State U., 1974, Columbia, 1975, Uppsala U., 1977, Coe Coll., 1978, U. Geneva, 1978, U. Ghent, 1985, U. Man., 1985. Research chemist Ciba Pharm. Products, Inc., Summit, N.J., 1942-43, 45-49; asso. dir. research Syntex, Mexico City, 1949-52; research v.p. Syntex, 1957-60; v.p. Syntex Labs., Palo Alto, Calif., 1960-62; v.p. Syntex Research, 1962-68, pres., 1968-72; pres. of Zoecon Corp., 1968-83, chmn. bd., 1968-86; prof. chemistry Wayne State U., 1952-59, Stanford, 1959—; dir. Cetus Corp., Teknowledge, Inc., Sandoz Crop Protection Corp.; chmn. bd. trustees Djerassi Found. Resident Artists Program; lectr. various univs. and orgns. Mem. editorial bd. Jour. Organic Chemistry, 1955-59, Tetrahedron, 1958—, Steroids, 1963—, Proc. of Nat. Acad. Scis, 1964-70, Jour. Am. Chem. Soc, 1966-75, Organic Mass Spectrometry, 1968—, Chemica Scripta, 1985—; author 7 books.; Contbr. numerous articles to profl. jours., poems and short stories to lit. publs. Recipient Intrasci. Research Found. award, 1969; Freedman Patent award Am. Inst. Chemists, 1970; Chem. Pioneer award, 1973; Nat. Medal Sci., 1973; Perkin medal, 1975; Wolf prize in chemistry, 1978; John and Samuel Bard award in Sci. and Medicine, 1983; named to Nat. Inventors Hall of Fame, 1978. Mem. Nat. Acad. Scis., Am. Chem. Soc. (award pure chemistry 1958, Baekeland medal 1959, Fritzsche award 1960, award for creative invention 1973, award in chemistry of contemporary tech. problems 1983), Swiss Chem. Soc., Royal Soc. Chemistry (hon. fellow, Centenary lectr. 1964), Am. Acad. Arts and Scis., German Acad. (Leopoldina), Royal Swedish Acad. Scis. (fgn.), Royal Swedish Acad. Engring. Scis. (fgn.), Am. Acad. Pharm. Scis. (hon.), Brazilian Acad. Scis. (fgn.), Mexican Acad. Sci. Investigation, Bulgarian Acad. Scis. (fgn.), Phi Beta Kappa, Sigma Xi, Phi Lambda Upsilon (hon.). Office: Stanford U Dept Chemistry Stanford CA 94305

DLUGATCH, IRVING, industrial engineer, consultant; b. N.Y.C., Jan. 20, 1910; s. Louis and Lena (Segal) D.; m. Helen Rosenberg, Dec. 22, 1935; children: Harvey E., Norman J. BSEE, West Coast U., 1964, MS in Systems Engring., 1965; PhD in Math., Los Angeles U., 1976. Pres. IDL Industries, Los Angeles, 1972-79; program mgr. Hughes Aircraft Co., Culver City, Calif., 1969-75; mgmt. cons. Eric Blum & Assocs., Chgo., 1976-79; dean engring. sch. Calif. Western U., Santa Ana, 1977-81; indsl. engr. Rockwell Internat., Anaheim, Calif., 1982-86. Author: Dynamic Cost Reduction, 1979; contbr. and author Engineering and Industrial Graphics Handbook, 1982. Fellow AIAA (assoc.); mem. Inst. Indsl. Engrs. (sr.), Computer and Advanced Systems Assocs. (sr.), Sigma Xi. Avocations: painting, guitar, writing, bridge. Home: 2302-D Via Puerta Laguna Hills CA 92653

DMYTRYK, JOHN WILLIAM, controller; b. Tampa, Fla., Jan. 15, 1943; s. William Dmytryk and Margaret Rush; m. Geraldine Scandariato, Apr. 25, 1970; children: Bernadette, Brian. BS, L.I. U., 1965. Fin. controller Citibank, United Arab Emirates, 1976-81; v.p. Citibank, Puerto Rico, 1981-83; v.p. fin. Citicorp Retail Services, Denver, 1983—. Home: 7936 S Corona Ct Littleton CO 80122 Office: PO Box 1558 Englewood CO 80111

DMYTRYSHYN, BASIL, historian, educator; b. Poland, Jan. 14, 1925; came to U.S., 1947, naturalized, 1951; s. Frank and Euphrosinia (Senchak) Dmytryshyn; m. Virginia Roehl, July 16, 1949; children: Sonia, Tania. B.A., U. Ark., 1950; M.A., U. Ark, 1951; Ph.D., U. Calif.-Berkeley, 1955. Asst. prof. history Portland State U., Oreg., 1956-59; assoc. prof. Portland State U., 1959-64, prof., 1964—, assoc. dir. Internat. Trade and Commerce Inst., 1984—; vis. prof. U. Ill., 1964-65, Harvard U., 1971, U. Hawaii, 1976, Hokkaido U., Sapporo, Japan, 1978-79. Author books including: Moscow and the Ukraine, 1918-1953, 1956, Medieval Russia, 900-1700, 2d edit., 1973, Imperial Russia, 1700-1917, 2d edit., 1974, Modernization of Russia Under Peter I and Catherine II, 1974, Colonial Russian America 1817-1832, 1976, A History of Russia, 1977, U.S.S.R.: A Concise History, 4th edit., 1984, The End of Russian America, 1979, Civil and Savage Encounters, 1983, Russian Statecraft, 1985, Russian Conquest of Siberia 1558-1700, 1985, Russian Penetration of the North Pacific Archipelago, 1700-1799, 1987, The Soviet Union and the Middle East, 1917-1985, 1987; contbr. articles to profl. jours., U.S., Can., Yugoslavia, Italy, South Korea, Fed. Republic Germany, France. State bd. dirs. PTA, Oreg., 1963-64; mem. World Affairs Council, 1965—. Fulbright-Hays fellow W. Germany, 1967-68; fellow Kennan Inst. Advanced Russian Studies, Washington, 1978; recipient John Mosser award Oreg. State Bd. Higher Edn., 1966, 67; Branford P. Millar award for faculty excellence Portland State U., 1985. Mem. Am. Assn. Advancement Slavic Studies (dir. 1972-75), Am. Hist. Assn., Western Slavic Assn., Can. Assn. Slavists, Oreg. Hist. Soc., Nat. Geog. Soc., Conf. Slavic and East European History (nat. sec. 1972-75). Office: Portland State U Dept History Portland OR 97207

DO AMARAL, LUIZ HENRIQUE DE FILIPPIS DE STEFANO REZENDE, architect, interior designer, construction company executive; b. Rio De Janeiro, Oct. 18, 1952; came to U.S., 1964; s. Jefferson R. and Erminia D. Do Amaral. BArch, U. Calif., Berkeley, 1975. Lic. gen. contractor. Sr. ptnr. Do Amaral, Brower & Stewart, Santa Clara, Calif., 1976-77, Do Amaral & Stewart, Santa Clara, 1977-78; prin. Do Amaral Assocs., Santa Clara, 1978-80, Do Amaral Assocs. Definitive Environments & Arch-West Constrn. Co., Los Gatos, Calif., 1980-82; pres., chief exec. officer Amalgamated Devel. Enterprises, Inc., Los Gatos, 1982—. Charles M. Marshall Found. scholar, 1972. Mem. Am. Inst. Bldg. Design (cert. bldg. designer, bd. dirs. 1978-79, chpt. v.p. 1979-80), Internat. Conf. Bldg. Officials, Constrn. Specifications Inst., Pi Lambda Phi, Alpha Mu Gamma. Roman Catholic. Office: Amalgamated Devel Enterprises 61 E Main St Suite C Los Gatos CA 95030

DOBBIN, MURIEL ISABELLA, newspaper reporter, writer; b. Ayrshire, Scotland; d. George and Isabella Lightbody (Laird) Hunter. Ed. Scottish Acad. Reporter, Ayrshire Post, 1953-56, Rochester (N.Y.) Democrat and Chronicle, 1956-56; reporter Balt. Sun, 1959-62; reporter Washington Bur., 1959-77, West Coast Bur. chief, San Francisco, 1977-85; west coast corr. U.S. News and World Report, San Francisco, 1985—. Clubs: Gridiron, Washington Press (Washington). Author novels: A Taste for Power, 1980; Joe's World, 1983.

DOBBINS, GEORGE C., horticulture educator; b. Courtland, Calif., July 30, 1916; B.A. in Zoology-Botany, U. Calif.-Berkeley, 1946; children—Barbara, Dan (dec.). Dist. nursery insp. Nursery Service, Calif. Dept. Agr., Sacramento, 1953-56; hort. instr. Am. River Coll., Sacramento, 1966-84; hort. cons. Rusch Bot. Garden, Citrus Heights, Calif., 1978—. Bd. dirs. Sacramento Tree Found., Inc. Served to 1st lt. U.S. Army, World War II. Mem. Am. Hort. Soc., Calif. Assn. Nurserymen (Bert Kallman award 1967, Edn. award 1971), Calif. Native Plant Soc., Sierra Club. Author: Sacramento: City of Trees, 1980. Home and Office: 2813 Elvyra Way #128 Sacramento CA 95821

DOBBS, ANDREW JAMES, engineer; b. Huntington, N.Y., Sept. 9, 1960; s. Alex and Gladys (O'Mera) D.; m. Sue Lynn Sherwood, Sept. 7, 1982; children: Michael, Christopher. BS ChemE, U. Mass., 1982. Process engr. Hughes Aircraft, El Segundo, Calif., 1982-84; mfg. engr. Motorola Corp., Scottsdale, Ariz., 1984—. Recipient Cost Improvement award Hughes Corp., 1983, Process Improvement Spl. Achievement award Motorola, 1985. Mem. Am. Inst. Chem. Engrs. Roman Catholic. Avocations: photography, reading, sports. Office: Motorola Corp 8201 E McDowell Scottsdale AZ 85252

DOBBS, LINDA LEE, state official; b. San Francisco, Oct. 7, 1948. B.A. in Sociology, Calif. State U.-Los Angeles, 1973; M.S.Ed. (fellow), U. So. Calif., 1980. Cert. community coll. student personnel worker, instr. psychology, counselor, basic pupil personnel services, Calif. Various positions Calif. State U.-Los Angeles, 1972-75; counselor asst. Los Angeles Unified Sch. Dist., 1978; employment and claims asst. State of Calif., Van Nuys, 1976-77, employment devel. officer, El Monte, 1978-80, employment counselor, San Fernando, 1980—; counselor Immaculate Conception Home for Girls, Los Angeles, 1972, McKinley Jr. High Sch., Pasadena, Calif., 1973, Found. for Jr. Blind, Los Angeles, 1978; intern Occidental Coll., Los Angeles and Los Angeles Community Coll. Dist., 1979; family counselor Ctr. for Study of Drug Abuse, Tarzana Psychiat. Hosp., 1979; TV guest Jobs and the Jobless, Sta. KCLS, 1985; program counselor Nat. Issues Forum, Washington, San Fernando, 1980—; appointed mem. Calif. State Spl. Projects Team, 1985; chmn. community adv. council N. Valley Occupational Ctr., 1983—. Mem. civil service div. Calif. State Employees Assn. Recipient Lit. award St. Vincent High Sch., 1966, Commendation for Job Opportunity Fair, USAF, 1984. Mem. Nat. Soc. Internships and Experiential Edn., Am. Personnel and Guidance Assn., Los Angeles County Personnel and Guidance Assn., Calif. Personnel and Guidance Assn., LWV. Office: 1520 San Fernando Rd San Fernando CA 91340

DOBBS, WARREN CRAIG, community organization executive; b. Atlanta, Apr. 15, 1928; s. Samuel C. and Marjorie D. (Frampton) D.; student Yale U., 1945-47, various mil. schs., 1950-53, San Francisco State Coll., 1956-57, Coll. Notre Dame, 1966, Wash. State U., 1976; grad. United Community Funds and Councils Inst., 1969; m. Mary Anne Karish, Sept. 27, 1950; children—Marjorie Stanish, Catherine Candler, Warren Craig. Ind. sales contractor, San Francisco, 1957-62; exec. dir. United Cerebral Palsy, Oakland, Calif., 1962-65; area dir. United Crusade, San Francisco, 1965-69, asso. exec. dir., Sacramento, 1969-72; exec. dir. United Way of Benton and Franklin Counties, Kennewick, Wash., 1972-82, United Way Spokane County, 1982—; community orgn. cons. Office Community Devel., State of Wash., 1977-79. Bd. dirs. Benton Franklin Opportunities Industrialization Center, 1978-79; trustee Mid-Columbia Symphony Soc., 1977-79; pres. Mid-Columbia Arts Council, 1975-76; regional adv. com. Wash. State Dept. Social and Health Services, 1982—; mem. Spokane Human Services Adv. Bd., 1983—; mem. SSS Bd., 1984—. Served with Transp. Corps, U.S. Army, 1950-56; Korea. Republican. Presbyterian. Club: Rotary (pres. Pasco-Kennewick 1981-82). Contbr. articles to profl. jours.; founder of Counterpart, an interracial orgn. Home: W 403 21st Ave Spokane WA 99203 Office: PO Box 326 Spokane WA 99210

DOBELIS, GEORGE, manufacturing company executive; b. July 31, 1940; s. John and Dorothy (Arins) D.; m. Dolores Ann Nagle, Dec. 2, 1972; children: Sally Ann Berg, Christian Eric Berg, Kurt Conrad Berg. AA in Engring., Santa Monica Coll., 1963; student, Control Data Inst., 1970. Engring. Masterite Ind., Torrance, Calif., 1969-70; engring. mgr. Elco Corp., El Segundo, Calif., 1964-76, mgr. new products, 1976-77; pres. Connector Tech. Inc., Anaheim, Calif., 1977—; V.p. Guide Services, Calif., 1982—. Patentee in field; contbr. articles to profl. jours. Served as sgt. N.G., 1963-69. Mem. IEEE. Republican. Lutheran. Club: Palm Valley. Avocations: golf, skiing, camping, hiking.

DOBLER, NORMA (MRS. CLIFFORD DOBLER), state legislator, civic worker; b. Haines, Oreg., May 2, 1917; d. Lester and Bessie (Bircket) Woodhouse; student U. Cin., 1935-37; B.S. in Bus., U. Idaho, 1939; m. Clifford Dobler, June 14, 1941; children—Sharon Louise Dobler Vega, Carol Marie Dobler Harris, Terry Lee. Sec. to registrar U. Idaho, 1939-41; sec. to judge, Caldwell, Idaho, 1945; sec. Am. Express Co., Seattle, 1943; lab. technician U. Idaho Coll. Forestry, Moscow, 1963-69; mem. Idaho Ho. of Reps., 1973-77, Idaho Senate, 1977-87 ; mem. health and human services com. Nat. Conf. State Legislators; mem. Idaho Job Tng. Coordinating Council; mem. Idaho Developmental Disabilities Adv. Council, 1977-81; chairperson Gov.'s Task Force Independence, alternative nursing homes; mem. Commn. on Nursing and Nursing Edn.; mem. State Edn. Equity Com., 1986—, State Adv. Council on Aging, 1986—. Mem. LWV, 1951—, bd. dirs. Moscow, 1953-68, pres. Idaho, 1968-71; county adv. bd. trustee Moscow Sch. Dist., 1963-69, vice chmn., 1966-69; bd. dirs. Idaho Sch. Trustees Assn., 1969; leader 4-H Club, 1951-64; pres. Moscow PTA, 1958-59, life mem. Recipient Service award Idaho Home Economists, 1979; Conservation Legislator of Yr. award Idaho Wildlife Fedn., 1984; named Citizen of Yr. Nat. Assn. Social Workers, Idaho chpt., 1980; Outstanding Alumna award dept. home econs. U. Idaho, 1984; Conservation Legislator of Yr. award Idaho Wildlife Fedn., 1984. Mem. AAUW (hon.), Delta Kappa Gamma (hon.). Methodist (pres. Woman's Soc. Christian Service 1972, supt. ch. sch. 1953-65, mem. ofcl. bd. 1953-67, 72). Home: 1401 Alpowa St Moscow ID 83843

DOBROWOLSKI, JAMES PHILLIP, range and watershed science educator; b. Los Angeles, June 2, 1955; s. Joseph Adolph and Lois Ann (Hibbs) D.; m. Janet Ann Brown, Mar. 10, 1984; children: Jessica, Jonathan. BS, U. Calif., Davis, 1977; MS, Wash. State U., 1979; PhD, Tex. A&M U., 1985. Systems analyst The Norac Co., Inc., Azusa, Calif., 1980-81; W.G. Mills fellow in hydrology Tex. Water Resources Inst., College Station, 1981-83; Tom Slick fellow in Agr. Tex. A&M U., College Station, 1983-84; research asst. prof. Utah State U., Logan, 1984-85, asst. prof., 1985—; cons. Dern & Polk Cons., Belton, Tex., 1981; co-dir. Inst. Land Rehab., Logan, 1985—. Contbr. articles to profl. jours. Jr. warden St. John's Episcopalian Ch., Logan, 1986. Mem. Soc. Range Mgmt. Am. Water Resources Assn., Am. Soc. Agrl. Engrs. (affiliate), N.Y. Acad. Scis., Sigma Xi, Phi Kappa Phi. Avocations: cross-country skiing, fishing, camping. Office: Utah State U Dept Range Sci Logan UT 84322-5230

DOCHTERMAN, CLIFFORD LEE, university administrator; b. Cridersville, Ohio, Dec. 13, 1925; s. Earl R. and Audrey G. (Yantis) D.; m. Dorothy Jane Coset, July 4, 1954; children—Claudia Jane, Clifford Lee II. A.B., Ohio Wesleyan U., 1947; M.A., U. Calif.-Berkeley, 1950; LL.D., Coll. of Idaho, 1980. Field dir. Calif. Alumni Assn., 1950-58; asst. to pres. U. Calif.-Berkeley, 1958-70; dir. pub. relations Edn. Commn. of States, Colo., 1970-72; v.p. Univ. of the Pacific, Stockton, Calif., 1972—; lectr. Golden Gate U., 1962-70; dir. Nat. Space Sci. and Urban Life Conf., Oakland, Calif., 1962-63. Author: Understanding Education's Financial Dilemma, 1972; co-author: Directions to Better Education, 1970; Directions to Excellence in Education, 1970; Future Directions to State Financing of Education, 1972. Bd. dirs. Calif. Council Humanities, San Francisco, 1975-80. Recipient Silver Antelope award Boy Scouts Am., 1981, Silver Beaver, 1977; Honor medal Freedoms Found., 1975; Disting. Achievement award Ohio Wesleyan U., 1987. Mem. Stockton C. of C. (pres. 1977-78), Council Advancement & Support Edn., Am. Assn. Sch. Adminstrs., Am. Coll. Pub. Relations Assn. Republican. Methodist. Lodge: Rotary (v.p. 1984-85, dir. 1983-85). (Disting. Service award 1983). Home: 9027 Frankford Ln Stockton CA 95212 Office: Univ of the Pacific Stockton CA 95211

DOCKRY, NANCY SUE, producer; b. Niagara Falls, N.Y., Mar. 24; d. Walter Edward Cazen and Adolpha (Jacek) Dezik; m. John Dockry, Aug. 19, 1961 (div. Aug. 1968). BS, Syracuse U., 1958; PhD, Columbia U., 1961. Freelance writer 1956-60; with corp. tng. program ABC, 1960-62; with Dancer, Fitzgerald and Sample, 1962-70; v.p. advt. Am. Home Products, 1970-75; office sr. agt. William Morris Agy., N.Y.C., 1975-76; office sr. agt., v.p. William Morris Agy., Los Angeles, 1975-78; sr. v.p. Nephi Prodns., 1978-79; v.p. TV MCA-Universal, 1979-80; v.p. Time-Life TV Inc., 1980-81; v.p. TV Columbia Pictures Inc., 1981-82; sr. v.p. Jay Bernstein Prodns., 1983-85; ind. producer Dockry Prodns., 1985—; bd. dirs. Entertainment Industries Council, Los Angeles and Washington; cons. Tree Music Pub., Nashville, 1980—. Producer Maneaters, Cheapshow, The Plant Family, Gauguin, Masada, Galactica, Minnesota Strip, Nobody's Perfect, Semi-Tough, The Bunker, The Wall, Mom the Wolfman and Me, Dial M for Murder, Baker's Dozen, Night Heat, The Blue and the Gray, Shadow Riders, Be-At-Rice, Ripley's Believe It or Not, Money on the Side, Ain't Misbehavin', Malibu, Mickey Spillane's Mike Hammer, Susan Hayward, Suddenly A Stranger, Two By Two, Houston Knights, Johnny Aladdin, The Great Diamond Robbery, Clash of Eagles, The America's Cup, Last Cheaters, Stiff, Harry, Stranger Dangers. Panel mem. Pres. Commn. on Whitehouse Fellows, Los Angeles, N.Y.C., Washington, 1979—. Mem. TV Acad., Motion Picture Acad. Republican. Avocations: tennis, swimming, skiing, reading, travel. Home: 2528 Hutton Dr Beverly Hills CA 90210

DOCKSON, ROBERT RAY, savings and loan executive; b. Quincy, Ill., Oct. 6, 1917; s. Marshall Ray and Letah (Edmondson) D.; m. Katheryn Virginia Allison, Mar. 4, 1944; 1 child, Kathy Kimberlee. A.B., Springfield Jr. Coll., 1937; B.S., U. Ill., 1939; M.S. in Fgn. Service, U. So. Calif., 1940, Ph.D., 1946. Lectr. U. So. Calif., 1940-41, 45-46, prof., head dept. mktg., 1953-59; dean U. So. Calif. (Sch. Bus. Adminstrn.); and prof. bus. econs. 1959-69; vice chmn. bd. Calif. Fed. Savs. & Loan Assn., Los Angeles, 1969-70; pres. Calif. Fed. Savs. & Loan Assn., 1970-77, chmn., 1977—, chief exec. officer, 1973-83; chmn. CalFed Inc., 1984—, chief exec. officer, 1984-85, also dir.; instr. Rutgers U., 1946-47, asst. prof., 1947-48; dir. Bur. Bus. and Econ. Research, 1947-48; economist Western home office Prudential Ins. Co., 1948-52, Bank of Am., San Francisco, 1952-53; econ. cons., 1953-57; dir. McKesson Corp., IT Corp., Pacific Lighting Corp., Transam. Capital Fund, Inc., Transam. Income Shares, Inc., Internat. Lease Fin. Corp., Computer Scis. Corp., Fed. Res. Bank of San Francisco. Am. specialist for U.S. Dept. State; mem. Town Hall, 1954—, bd. govs., 1963-65, hon. bd. govs., 1965—, pres., 1961-62; Trustee John Randolph Haynes and Dora Haynes Found., Rose Hills Meml. Park Assn., Com. for Econ. Devel., Calif. Council for Econ. Edn.; trustee, pres. Orthopedic Hosp.; bd. councilors Grad. Sch. Bus. Adminstrn., U. So. Calif.; bd. regents, chmn. univ. bd. Pepperdine U.; chmn. housing task force Calif. Roundtable. Served from ensign to lt. USNR, 1942-44. Decorated Star of Solidarity Govt. of Italy.; Recipient Asa V. Call Achievement award; Disting. Community Service award Brandeis U.; Whitney M. Young Jr. award Urban League, 1981, Albert Schweitzer Leadership award; Man of Yr. award Nat. Housing Conf., 1981; Industrialist of Yr. award Calif. Mus. Sci. and Industry, 1984. Mem. Calif. C. of C. (pres. 1980, dir. 1981—), Los Angeles C. of C. (dir.), Am. Arbitration Assn., Newcomen Soc. North Am., Hugh O'Brian Youth Found., Phi Kappa Phi (Diploma of Honor award 1984), Beta Gamma Sigma. Clubs: (, Bohemian, California, Los Angeles Country, One Hundred, Silver Dollar, Birnam Wood Golf, Thunderbird Country. Office: 5670 Wilshire Blvd Los Angeles CA 90036

DOCKSTADER, JACK LEE, materiel executive; b. Los Angeles, Dec. 14, 1936; s. George Earl and Grace Orine (Travers) D.; student UCLA, 1960-70. Rate analyst Rate Bur., So. Pacific Co., Los Angeles, 1954-57; traffic analyst traffic dept. Hughes Aircraft Co., Fullerton, Calif., 1957-58, Culver City, Calif., 1958-59, traffic mgr. Hughes Research Labs., Malibu, Calif., 1959-70, materiel mgr., 1970-75; materiel mgr. Hughes Aircraft Co., Culver City, 1975-80, prodn. materiel mgr. Electro-Optical and Data Systems Group, El Segundo, Calif., 1980-84, mgr. materiel total quality 1984-85, mgr. cen. materiel ops. 1986—. Mem. adv. council transp. mgmt. profl. designation program UCLA, 1966-80, mem. Design for Sharing Com., 1977-82; adv. com. transp. program Los Angeles Trade Tech. Coll., 1970-80. Served with USNR, 1954-76. Mem. UCLA Alumni Assn., Nat. Contracts Mgmt. Assn., Naval Enlisted Res. Assn., Hughes Aircraft Co. Mgmt. Club, Delta Nu Alpha (pres. San Fernando Valley chpt. 1965-66, v.p. Pacific S.W. region 1969-71, region man of year 1971). Republican. Presbyn. Home: 2701 Armacost Ave Los Angeles CA 90064 Office: PO Box 902 El Segundo CA 90245

DOCTORS, SAMUEL I., management educator; b. Phila., July 1, 1936; s. Abraham and Celia (Lakoff) D.; divorced, 1973; children: Eric, Rachel; m. Judith Blackfield Cohen, Feb. 1, 1982; 1 child: Rebecca. BS, U. Miami, 1956; JD, Harvard U., 1967, DBA, 1969. Bar: Mass. 1967. Assoc. engr. Westinghouse Electric Corp., Balt., 1956-58; sr. math. analyst AC Sparkplug div. Gen. Motors, El Segundo, Calif., 1958-59; sr. devel. engr., work dir. aero. div. Honeywell, St. Petersburg, Fla., 1961-64; cons. tech., mgmt., econs. various orgns., 1968-81; project mgr. N. Lawndale Econ. Devel. Corp. & NUGSM, 1971-73; assoc. prof. Northwestern U., Evanston, Ill., 1969-73; faculty advisor, dir. Mgmt. Asst. Clinic, Northwestern U., Chgo., 1969-73; prof. U. Pitts., 1974-84, co-prin. investigator, project monitor, 1977-79;

project mgr. Allegheny County Energy Study, 1977; prin. investigator Urban Tech. System Evaluation, NSF, 1978-81, Small Bus. Adminstrn. and Dept. Energy, Washington, 1979-80; prof., adminstrn. Calif. State U., Hayward, 1982—; lctr. Harvard Bus. Sch., 1968-69; chmn. research and devel. workshop, U.S. Office edn. Task Force Minority Bus. Edn. and Tng., 1972-73; bus. advisor David Community Devel. Corp., Ky., 1973-76; bd. dirs. Energy Policy Inst., U. Pitts., 1979-81; vis. prof. U. Calif. Sch. Bus., Berkeley, 1980-82; tech. advisor Western Gerontol. Soc., 1984—; owner, mgr. vineyard and tasting room, Mendocino County, Calif., 1985—. Author books (9) and over 40 articles on management. V.p., bd. dirs. Sr. Citizens Service Corp., Pitts.; chairperson Energy Outlook '78, Allegheny County Air Pollution Control Bd. Sponsoring Agy. Mem. ABA, Am. Polit. Sci. Assn., Am. Econ. Assn., Nat. Assn. Community Devel., AAAS, Nat. Council Small Bus. Devel., Nat. Acad. Mgmt. (sounding bd. manpower div.), Pitts. C. of C. Home: PO Box 50 Yorkville CA 95494 Office: Calif State U Hayward Mgmt Scis Dept Hayward CA 94542

DODD, JOE DAVID, safety engineer, consultant, administrator; b. Walnut Grove, Mo., Jan. 22, 1920; s. Marshall Hill and Pearl (Combs) D.; m. Nona Bell Junkins, Sept. 17, 1939; 1 dau. Linda Kay Dodd Helmick. Student SW Mo. State U., 1937-39, Wash. U., 1947-55. Cert. profl. safety engr. Calif. Office asst. retail credit co., Kansas City, Mo., 1939-42; bus driver City of Springfield (Mo.), 1945-47; ops., engring., and personnel positions Shell Oil Co., Wood River (Ill.) Refinery, 1947-66; health and safety dept. mgr. Martinez Mfg. Complex, Calif., 1966-83, retired 1983; exec. dir. Fire Protection Tng. Acad., U. Nev.-Reno; rep. Shell Oil Co., Western Oil and Gas Assn., 1970-81. Mem. Republican Presdl. Task Force. Served with USMC, 1942-45. Decorated Presdl. Citation. Mem. Western Oil and Gas Assn. (Hose Handler award 1972-81, Outstanding mem. award), Am. Soc. Safety Engrs., Veterans Safety, State and County Fire Chiefs Assn., Peace Officers Assn., Nat. Fire Protection Assn. Presbyterian (elder). Established Fire Protection Tng. Acad., U. Nev.-Reno, Stead Campus.

DODD, WILLIAM FRANCIS GILL, consultant; b. Henderson, N.C., June 30, 1936; s. Claude Swanson and Rebekah (Young) D.; m. Joy Taber, Aug. 16, 1958; children—William Isaac, Marie Celeste. A.B. in Bus. Adminstrn., Duke U., 1958; EDP cert. IBM, 1960, NCR, 1960. Sales mgr. Kendall Co., Boston, 1964-74, Colgate Palmolive, N.Y.C., 1974-76; v.p. sales-mktg. NIDCO of Colo., Denver, 1976-78; owner, pres. NASMARC, Inc., Englewood, Colo., 1979—; cons. to U.S. mgrs. and importers in the devel. of sales and mktg. programs of consumer products, Australian Depts. of Commerce and Trade, U.S. Dept. Trade. Republican. Methodist. Home: 10428 E Dorado Pl Englewood CO 80111 Office: Nasmarc Inc 5150 S Syracuse Circle Suite 206 Suite 206 Englewood CO 80110

DODGE, EUGENE EDWARD, optometrist; b. Denver, Feb. 21, 1947; s. George Harcourt and Helen Margaret (Moore) D.; m. Lynda Kay Thomsen, June 7, 1969; children—Christian Edward, Casey Lynn, Carrie LeAnne. B.A., U. No. Colo., 1969; O.D., Pacific U., 1974. Lic. optometrist, Colo. Biology tchr. Littleton, Colo., 1969-70; chief optometry sect. 15th Med. Bn., 1st Cav. Div., Ft. Hood, Tex., 1974-77; pvt. practice optometry Aurora, Colo., 1977—. Served to maj. USAR. Mem. Am. Optometric Assn., Colo. Optometric Assn., Assn. Mil. Surgeons, Res. Officers Assn., Council Sports Vision, Aurora C. of C. Republican. Baptist. Clubs: Kiwanis (Aurora); Masons, Shriners. Home: 5376 S Salida Ct Aurora CO 80015 Office: 999 18th St Suite 146 Denver CO 80202

DODGE, JAMES EDWARD, lawyer; b. Salina, Kans., Feb. 8, 1953; s. James Ernest and Donna Jane (Downey) D.; m. Constance Winther; children: Anna, Christopher, David. BA with honors, U. Oreg., 1977, JD, 1982. Bar: Oreg. 1983, U.S. Dist. Ct. Oreg. 1984, U.S. Ct. Appeals (9th cir.) 1985. Assoc. MB McLord, Bend, Oreg., 1982-84, Hall & Hall, P.C., Eugene, 1984—. Mem. Assn. Trial Lawyers Am., Oreg. Trial Lawyers Assn., Oreg. Workers Compensation Clamaint's Attys. Assn. Home: 3910 Hilyard Eugene OR 97405 Office: PO Box 10287 899 Pearl Eugene OR 97440-2287

DODGE, THEODORE AYRAULT, geological mining consultant, drilling company executive; b. Chgo., Jan. 17, 1911; s. Robert Elkin Neil and Katherine Eleanor (Staley) D.; m. Isabelle Stebbins, June 15, 1935; children—Eleanor Dodge Gray, Janet, Richard Neil, Thomas Marshall. A.B. in Geology, Harvard Coll., 1932; A.M. in Geology, Harvard U., 1935, Ph.D. in Geology, 1936; M.A. in Geology, U. Wis., 1933. Registered geologist, Ariz. Geologist, sr. geologist Cerro de Pasco Copper Corp., Morococha, Peru, 1935-38; geologist, petroleum engr. various cos., 1939-41; geologist Anaconda Copper Mining Co., Las Cruces, N.Mex., 1941-42; geologist, acting chief geologist Cananea Consol. Copper Co., Cananea, Mexico, 1942-45; cons. geologist various companies, Ariz. and Mex. 1946-70; mgr. Christmas div. Inspiration Consol. Copper Co., Christmas, Ariz., 1971-75; pres. Hoagland & Dodge Drilling Co., Inc., Tucson, 1976—; instr. geology U. So. Calif., Los Angeles, 1940. Contbr. articles to profl. jours. Fellow Geol. Soc. Am., Mineral. Soc. Am.; mem. Ariz. Geol. Soc. (pres. 1955), Soc. Econ. Geologists, Am. Inst. Mining Engrs., Phi Beta Kappa, Sigma Xi. Baha'i. Club: Mining of the Southwest (Tucson). Home and Office: 3 Potter Place Tucson AZ 85719

DODGEN, HAROLD WARREN, educator; b. Blue Eye, Mo., Aug. 31, 1921; s. James Monroe and Lora (Myers) D.; m. Harriet Keddie Ralston, Jan. 20, 1945; children—Cynthia Jeanne, Gilbert Keddie, Stephen LaRele. Student, Long Beach Jr. Coll., 1939-41; B.S., U. Calif. at Berkeley, 1943, Ph.D., 1946. Research asst. Manhattan Dist. Project, U. Calif. at Berkeley, 1943-46; post-doctorate fellow Inst. Nuclear Studies, U. Chgo., 1946-48; asst. prof. chemistry Wash. State U., 1948-52, asso. prof., 1952-59, prof. chemistry, 1959-63, prof. chemistry and physics, 1963—; dir. Wash. State U. (Nuclear Reactor Project), 1954-68, chmn. chem. physics program, 1968-77. Fellow Am. Inst. Chemists, AAAS; mem. Am. Chem. Soc., Am. Phys. Soc., Am. Nuclear Soc., AAUP, Phi Beta Kappa, Sigma Xi, Alpha Chi Sigma. Home: NW 905 Fisk St Pullman WA 99163

DODSON, ARLEEN CECILIA, language educator; b. Alhambra, Calif., Mar. 18, 1953; d. Moses and Olivia Beatrice (Potts) Baca; m. Walter Anthony Dodson, June 24, 1979; children: Robert, Elizabeth. AA, East Los Angeles Coll., 1973; BA in Spanish, Calif. State U., Los Angeles, 1978. Cert. life tchr., Calif. Bilingual aide Alhambra High Sch., 1977-78; tchr. 4th grade St. Anthony's, San Gabriel, Calif., 1982-84; bilingual tchr. 1st and 2d grades Garvey Sch. Dist., Rosemead, Calif., 1984-86; bilingual tchr. 4th grade Hacienda La Puente Unified Sch. Dist., 1986—; Spanish interpreter Fed. Bldg. Immigration Ct., Los Angeles, 1977,. Mem. adult choir St. John Vianney. Recipient Outstanding Service award Garvey Sch. Dist., 1986. Mem. NEA, Calif. Tchrs. Assn., Assn. Curriculum Devel. Democrat. Roman Catholic. Avocations: teaching music. Home: 15320 Pintura Dr Hacienda Heights CA 91745 Office: Hacienda La Puente Unified Sch Dist 15959 Gale Ave La Puente CA 91774

DODSON, FRANK ROBERT, hotelier, real estate investor; b. Albuquerque, Dec. 15, 1946; s. Conrad C. and Martha (Ellen) D. Student, UCLA, 1965-66, San Diego State U., 1966-68, U. N.Mex., 1970-71. Bus. cons. Dodson & Assocs., Albuquerque, 1970-84, real estate developer, 1980—; hotelier, owner Royal Inn of Albuquerque, 1971—; pres., founder Albuquerque Innkeepers Assn., 1972-73, Albuquerque Conv. & Visitors Bur., 1981-82, Cen. Ave. Assn. Albuquerque, 1982-84. Mgr. Econ. Adv. Council to Mayor, Albuquerque, 1977-83. Served with USN, 1968-69. Named Educator of Yr. award Am. Hotel-Motel Assn.,1976 1st person cert. as Hotel Adminstr. in N.Mex., 1977; recipient Cen. Ave. Assn. Beautification Program City Honor, 1984. Republican. Roman Catholic. Lodge: Rotary. Home: 1017 Madison NE Albuquerque NM 87110 Office: 4119 Central Ave NE Albuquerque NM 87108

DODSON, JEROME L., financial executive; b. Oak Park, Ill., May 14, 1943; s. Leo D. and Grace Edith (Shoup) D.; m. Thao Nguyen, Apr. 20, 1975; children: Stephen Jerome, Katrina Kim. AB, U. Calif., Berkeley, 1965; MBA, Harvard U., Cambridge, Mass., 1971. Fgn. service officer Dept. State, Washington, 1966-69; fin. analyst San Francisco Local Devel. Corp., 1971-73; mgmt. cons., San Francisco, 1973-75; founder, pres. Continental Savs. & Loan, San Francisco, 1976-82, Working Assets Money Fund, San Francisco, 1982-84; pres. The Parnassus Fund, 1984—; mem. Gov.'s Pub. Investment Task Force Calif., 1981-82. Mem. Found. for San Francisco's Archtl. Heritage, World Affairs Council No. Calif. Mem. Harvard Bus. Sch. Assn. of No. Calif. Clubs: Commonwealth, Harvard (San Francisco). Office: The Parnassus Fund 244 California St San Francisco CA 94111

DODSON-EDGARS, JEANNIE ELIZABETH, public relations executive; b. El Paso, Tex., July 12, 1950; d. Minot Boyd and Florence Elizabeth (Smith) Dodson; m. Darryl Eugene Edgars, Sept. 18, 1973; 1 child, Ginja Rachel. BS, UCLA, 1972. Radio program producer NEH, Portland, Oreg., 1978-79; cons., audio-visual producer Pub.'s Paper Co., Oregon City, Oreg., 1982, Southwest Wash. Hosps., Vancouver, Wash., 1982; founder, prin. Chandler Pub. Relations, Portland, 1984—; prin. GWT, Inc., 1986—. Bd. dirs. Meet the Leaders, 1986-87; steering com. Women in the Yr. 2000, Portland, 1985-86. Mem. Women in Communications (v.p. fin. adminstrn. 1987—), Nat. Assn. Female Execs., Network of Bus and Profl. Women. Club: The City Club of Portland. Avocations: gardening, hiking, reading, fishing.

DOEH, GIYORA, real estate broker; b. Tiberias, Israel, Aug. 12, 1934; came to U.S., 1936, parents Am. citizens; s. Benjamin Benzion and Pearl (Kerner) D.; m. Wendy Ann Standridge, Oct. 13, 1961 (div. Jan. 1977); children: Cole Adam, Tamara Lark Shannan, Thomas David. BSME, The Cooper Union, 1956; MS, MIT, 1958. Registered profl. engr., Calif. Adminstrv. asst. Lockheed Aircraft Co., Ontario and Burbank, Calif., 1958-60; mem. tech. staff Hughes Aircraft Co., Los Angeles, 1960-66; sr. indsl. engr. N.Am. Aviation, Los Angeles, 1966-67; sr. staff engr., material systems advisor TRW Systems Group, Redondo Beach, Calif., 1967-78; cons. Coca-Cola Bottling Co., Redondo Beach, 1978; pres. Century 21 W. Los Angeles Realty, 1979—. Active Los Angeles United Way, 1969-75; pres. bd. dirs. S. Bay Childrens Health Ctr., Redondo Beach, 1971-74. Mem. ASME, Inst. Mgmt. Sci., Los Angeles Bd. Realtors (bd. dirs. 1983-86). Avocations: sailing, philosophy, hiking. Home: 3432 Colonial Ave Los Angeles CA 90066 Office: Century 21 W Los Angeles Realty 10511 W Pico Blvd Los Angeles CA 90064

DOERFLING, HANK, aerospace engr.; b. San Pedro, Calif., Nov. 3, 1936; s. Laurence Howard and Julia Margret (Rusbarsky) D.; B.S. in Physics, Oreg. State U., 1958, M.S., 1963; M.Pub. Adminstrn., Pepperdine U., 1975; m. Elaine Carole; children—Howard, Carrie, Cassie, Tony, Evon. Analyst, No. Am. Aviation Co., Downey, Calif., 1963-64; mem. tech. staff TRW Systems Redondo Beach, Calif., 1964-66, adminstrv. and project mgr. Logicon, San Pedro, Calif., 1966-77; mgr. data processing mgmt. info. div., space and communications group Hughes Aircraft Co., El Segundo, Calif., 1977—. Mem. Hermosa Beach Improvement Commn., 1970-72, chmn., 1971-72; mem. City of Hermosa Beach City Council, 1972-80, mayor, 1973-74, 79-80; pres. South Bay Cities Assn., 1975-76; commr. South Coast (Calif.) Regional Coastal Commn., 1977-80, Calif. Coastal Commn., 1978-80. Served with USN, 1958-61. Mem. Hermosa Beach C. of C. (bd. dirs. 1970-71), League Calif. Cities, Sigma Pi Sigma. Home: 1011 2d St Hermosa Beach CA 90254 Office: Hughes Aircraft Co 650 N Sepulveda Blvd El Segundo CA 90245

DOERING, RICHARD, educator; b. Cleve., May 17, 1939; s. Roy A. and Gertrude (Koubek) D.; m. Clara Mae Weber, Aug. 1, 1969; children: Bart Lee, Karl Curtis, Marlena Rae, Mark Richard. BA, Ohio Wesleyan U., 1960; MA, Columbia U., 1962; BSEd, Kent State U., 1967; MA, U. Calif., Riverside, 1974, PhD, 1975. Instr. Cen. Wyo. Coll., Riverton, 1968-70; research sociologist U. Calif., Riverside, 1972-74; instr. Orange Coast Coll., Costa Mesa, Calif., 1975-76, Golden West Coll., Huntington Beach, Calif., 1975-76; asst. prof. sociology and statistics Calif. State U., Los Angeles, 1977—; evening instr. Chaffey Coll., Alta Loma, Calif., 1976—. Contbr. articles to profl. jours. Recipient Leland Publs. award, 1960. Mem. Am. Sociol. Assn., Am. Psychol. Assn., Calif. Assn. for Gifted, Mensa, Psi Chi, Kappa Delta Pi, Tau Kappa Epsilon. Home: 7286 Nixon Dr Riverside CA 92504 Office: Calif State U Dept Sociology and Social Work Los Angeles CA 90032

DOERR, MARK ERWIN, radio broadcasting educator; b. San Francisco, June 9, 1945; s. Luke Erwin Doerr and Eleanor Alberta (Mark) Kidd; m. M. Catherine Haupt, Aug. 9, 1975; children: Elizabeth Ann, Emily Christine. BA, Eastern Wash. U., 1967, MA, 1979. News dir. Sta. KSMK, Kennewick, Wash., 1971-74; writer, advt. dir. The Outdoor Press, Spokane, Wash., 1974-76; owner, dir. Mark Doerr ABH Advt. and Promotion, Spokane, Wash., 1976-81; educator Spokane Falls Community Coll., Spokane, Wash., 1981—. Served to sgt. USAF, 1967-71. Democrat. Office: Spokane Falls Community Coll W 3410 Ft George Wright Dr Spokane WA 99204

DOERR, ROBERT DOUGLAS, psychologist, educator, poet; b. Burlington, Vt., Apr. 9, 1944; s. Robert Joseph and Betty Jane Catlin (Whitney) D. BA, Rollins Coll., 1966; MA, San Francisco State U., 1969; PhD, Saybrook Inst., San Francisco, 1978. Cert. biofeedback technician; cert. tchr., Calif. From instr. to prof. Columbia Coll., Alameda, Calif., 1970—; dir. Alameda Biofeedback and Peak Performance Ctr., 1980—; ednl. cons., 1981—. Peace Corps vol., Nepal, 1966-68. Recipient Order of Oseola award Rollins Coll., 1966. Fellow Am. Psychol. Assn.; mem. Biofeedback Soc. Am., Assn. for Humanistic Psychology, Am. Fedn. Tchrs., AAAS. Taoist. Author: Good Better Best; contbr. articles to profl. jours.; editor Saybrook Rev., 1979—. Office: 1810 Eagle Ave Alameda CA 94501

DOGGETT, WILLIAM HOWARD, chiropractic physician; b. Chgo., July 27, 1951; s. William Howard and Ila Darlene (Edwards) D.; m. Diane Hilary Polasky, Oct. 24, 1976; 1 child: Leryn Rose. Student, George Mason U., 1978-79, No. Va. U., 1978-79, No. Ill. U., 1969-71; D Chiropractic, Los Angeles Chiropractic Coll. ASB pres. Los Angeles Community Coll., 1982-83; dir. CareMore Chiropractic Ctrs., Albuquerque, 1983—. C. Gonstead Found. grantee, 1982. Mem. Bernalillo County Chiorpractic Assn., (pres. 1984-86), N.Mex. Chiropractice Assn. (bd. dirs. 1985-86), Am. Chiropractic Assn. Democrat. Jewish. Avocations: herbology, gardening, camping. Office: CareMore Chiropractic Ctrs 1664 Bridge SW Albuquerque NM 87105

DOHERTY, GEORGE WILLIAM, research psychologist, counselor; b. N.Y.C., Oct. 18, 1941; s. William George and Catherine Marguerite (Nierenhausen) D.; B.S., Pa. State U., 1964; M.S., Miss. State U., 1977; postgrad. Baylor U., 1972, North Texas State U., 1979. Cert. Nat. Acad. Cert. Clin. Mental Health Counselors. Program coordinator, dir. youth devel. program Econ. Opportunities Advancement Corp., Waco, Texas, 1968-71; psychol. counselor, parent tng. Counseling or Referral Assistance Services, Phila., 1973-75; psychologist III, Rural Clinics Community Counseling Ctr., Ely, Nev., 1980-85; counselor, researcher, Ely, 1985—; mem. faculty No. Nev. Community Coll., Ely, 1980-85; cons., research, counseling, 1985—. Served to capt. U.S. Air Force, 1964-68. Fellow Am. Biog. Inst. (life, commemorative medal of honor); mem. Am. Psychol. Assn. (assoc.), Western Psychol. Assn., Tex. Psychol. Assn., Nev. Psychol. Assn., Psychol. Study of Social Issues, Inter-Am. Soc. Psychology, Internat. Assn. Applied Psychology, Assn. Behavior Analysis, Am. Assn. Counseling and Devel., Biofeedback Soc. Am., Assn. Counselor Edn. and Supervision, Western Assn. Counselor Edn. and Supervision, Assn. Measurement Edn. and Guidance, Am. Mental Health Counselors Assn., Air Force Assn., World Future Soc., AAAS, Pa. State Alumni Assn., Smithsonian Assoc., Irish-Am. Cultural Inst., O'Dochartaigh Family Research Assn., Am. Legion, Wilderness Soc., Nat. Audubon Soc. Democrat. Home and Office: Box 607 Ely NV 89301

DOHERTY, RICHARD MICHAEL, law firm adminstr.; b. San Francisco, Mar. 29, 1943; s. George Daniel and Alice Elizabeth (Kehl) D.; B.S. in Biochemistry, U. Santa Clara, 1965, M.B.A., 1968; m. Karen Lynn Kinney, Aug. 18, 1980; children—Shannon Elizabeth, Matthew John. Mgr. data processing Pacific Telephone Co., San Jose, Calif., 1966-69; mgr. internat. fin. Memorex Corp., Santa Clara, Calif., 1969-73; group controller Rohr Industries, San Diego, 1973-76; v.p. fin. and adminstrn. Photosonics, Inc., Los Angeles, 1976-79; v.p. fin. and adminstrn. Korn/Ferry Internat., Los Angeles, 1979-81; mng. dir., partner firm Cox, Castle, Nicholson, Los Angeles, 1981—; vis. prof. UCLA, U. Calif., Berkeley. Served to lt. U.S. Army, 1965-66. Mem. Nat. Assn. Accts., Am. Inst. Corp. Controllers. Republican. Clubs: Century West, Beverly Hills Gun.

DOI, LOIS KIKUMI, psychiatric social worker; b. Honolulu, Oct. 24, 1951; d. James Masato and Thelma Kimiko Miyamoto; m. Brian Kenji Doi, May 26, 1972; children: Michael Leslie, Lorian Naomi. BS, U. Hawaii, 1974, MSW, 1978. Lic. clin. social worker, Calif. Psychiat. social worker, child specialist Desert Community Mental Health Ctr., Indio, Calif., 1979—, coordinator children's day treatment program, 1982—; pvt. practice psychiat. social worker Indio, 1983—; counselor Los Angeles Urban League, 1975-76. Vol. advisor Community Recreation Ctr. Youth Group, Hawaii, 1967-69; vol. interviewer ARC Food Stamp Program, Hawaii, 1973; vol. asst. YWCA Programs Young Mothers and Teens, Hawaii, 1973; vol. group leader YWCA Juvenile Delinquent Program, Hawaii, 1973; placement counselor Vols. In Service to Am., Los Angeles, 1975. Mem. Nat. Assn. Social Workers. Avocations: needlework, reading. Office: Desert Community Mental Health Ctr 82-485 Miles Ave Indio CA 92201

DOI, MARY ELLEN, research chemist, laboratory administrator; b. Memphis, Mo., Jan. 15, 1933; d. Earl Edward and Beulah Mae (Leach) Tucker; m. Minoru Doi, June 16, 1962; 1 child, Paul Edward. BS, Northeast Mo. State U., 1953. Cert. med. technologist, 1957. Tchr. chemisty, biology Princeton (Mo.) High Sch., 1953-54; tchr. sci. Evans Jr. High Sch., Ottumwa, Iowa, 1954-56; lab. technician Shelby County Hosp., Shelbyville, Ill., 1957-58; med. chemist Barnes Hosp., St. Louis, 1958-60; research chemist Monsanto Chem. Co., St. Louis, 1960-63; chief chemist, dir. lab. E.S. Erwin and Assocs., Tolleson, Ariz., 1963—. Active Rep. campaign, 1976. Mem. Am. Chem. Soc., Assn. Official Analytical Chemists, Ariz. Assn. Cert. Labs. Republican. Methodist. Club: Bus. and Profl. Women (Maryvale, Glendale, Ariz.) (past sec.-treas., v.p., pres., Woman of Yr. 1974, 79). Avocations: investments, coins, stamps, traveling, reading. Home: 5963 W Hazelwood Phoenix AZ 85033 Office: Nutrition-Lab Services PO Box 237 Tolleson AZ 85353

DOI, MAY YOKO, city official; b. Los Angeles, May 30, 1926; d. Paul Mitsugu and Hideko (Nakatani) Horiuchi; m. Carl Kaoru Doi, Aug. 28, 1949; children—Ronald M., Kevin K., Conrad T.; B.S., U. So. Calif., 1971, M.S. cum laude, 1972; A.A. (Kiwanis scholar), Los Angeles Harbor Coll., 1969; student U. Calif., Santa Cruz, Pepperdine U., Occidental Coll. Cert. city clk. Sec. Internat. Inst., Detroit, 1946; YMCA, Detroit, 1947-48; Warehousing Service, Los Angeles, 1948-51; Douglas Aircraft, 1952-54; tchr. Los Angeles Unified Sch. Dist., 1971-80; sec. TRW Systems, Redondo Beach, Calif., part-time summers 1974-81; city clk. City of Gardena (Calif.), 1980—. Vice chmn. Gardena Citizens Adv. Com., 1978, Gardena Planning Commn., 1979; pres. Gardena Valley Japanese Am. Citizens League, 1983; chmn. bd. Gardena Valley YMCA, 1984—; bd. dirs. ARC; pres. Gardena council PTA, 1966; pres. Amestoy PTA, 1962, hon. life mem.; den mother Los Angeles council Boy Scouts Am., 1960-67; mem. chmn., mem. allocations and planning coms. United Way, 1983-86. Recipient Resolution of Commendation, City of Gardena, 1980; recognition award Japanese Am. Citizens League, 1981, plaque, 1982; named Outstanding Woman in Govt., Soroptimists, 1985. Mem. So. Calif. City Clks. Assn., Calif. City Clks. Assn., Records Mgmt. Assn., Nat. Micrographics Assn., Soc. So. Calif. Archivists, Internat. Inst. Mcpl. Clks., Calif. Hist. Soc., Gardena Valley C. of C. (govt. affairs com.), Alpha Gamma Sigma. Baptist (sec. Dorcas Circle 1966). Club: South Bay (fin. dir., bd. dirs.). Lodge: Zonta. Office: 1700 W 162d St Gardena CA 90247-6803

DOI, ROY HIROSHI, biochemist, educator; b. Sacramento, Mar. 26, 1933; s. Thomas Toshiteru and Ima (Sato) D.; m. Joyce Takahashi, Aug. 30, 1958; children: Kathryn E., Douglas A. AB in Physiology, U. Calif., Berkeley, 1953, AB in Bacteriology, 1957; MS in Bacteriology, U. Wis., 1958, PhD in Bacteriology, 1960. NIH postdoctoral fellow U. Ill., Urbana, 1960-63; asst. prof. Syracuse (N.Y.) U., 1963-65; asst. prof. U. Calif., Davis, 1965-66, assoc. prof., 1966-69, prof. biochemistry, 1969—; cons. NIH, Bethesda, Md., 1975-79, 82-84, Syntro Corp., San Diego, 1983—; treas. Internat. Spores Conf., Boston, 1980—. Served with U.S. Army, 1953-55. Fellow NSF, 1971-72; recipient Sr. Scientist award, von Humboldt Found, Munich, 1978-79, vis. scholar award Naito Found, Tokyo. Mem. AAAS, AAUP, Am. Soc. Biol. Chemists, Am. Soc. Microbiology, Sigma Xi. Democrat. Unitarian. Avocations: photography, sports. Office: U Calif Dept Biochemistry and Biophysics Davis CA 95616

DOIG, DALE E., mayor, educator; b. Los Angeles, July 24, 1935; s. Frank Finnamore and Pauline (Turner) D.; m. Sally Fletcher, Aug. 30, 1958; children—Lisa Carrera, Ken Doig. A.B., Fresno State Coll., M.A. Cert. tchr., Calif. Tchr. Fresno Unified Sch. Dist., Calif.; mayor City of Fresno, Calif., 1985—; Elected to Fresno City Council, 1973, 77, 81. Pres. Fresno County Young Democrats, 1966; mem. Fresno County Dem. Central Com., 1966-68. Served with N.G., U.S. Army, 1957-60. Recipient Fresno's Outstanding Young Educator award, Jaycees, 1969; Fresno's Outstanding Young Citizen award Jaycees, 1970. Mem. Fresno Tchrs. Assn., Calif. Tchrs. Assn., NEA. Lodge: Elks. Avocations: stamp collecting; jogging; fishing. Office: City of Fresno 2326 Fresno St Fresno CA 93721

DOLBEAR, GEOFFREY EMERSON, industrial research scientist, writer; b. Richmond, Calif., June 1, 1941; s. William C. and Verda L. (Sharp) D.; m. Catherine Alice Croker, Aug. 26, 1961; children: Cynthia Ann, Douglas Emerson. BS, U. Calif., Berkeley, 1962; PhD, Stanford U., 1965. Research chemist E.I. DuPont de Nemours, Wilmington, Del., 1965-68, W.R. Grace & Co., Columbia, Md., 1968-75; research mgr. Occidental Petroleum, Irvine, Calif., 1975-82; research assoc. Unocal Sci. Tech., Brea, Calif., 1982—. Editor: Chemtech mag., 1984—; contbr. articles to profl. publs.; patentee in field. Pres. Occidental Employees Fed. Credit Union, Irvine, 1980-81. NSF fellow, 1963, Allied Chem. Corp., 1964. Mem. AAAS, Am. Chem. Soc., N.Am. Catalysis Soc., Orange County Fly Fishers. Home: 23050 Aspen Knoll Dr Diamond Bar CA 91765 Office: Unocal Sci & Tech 376 S Valencia Brea CA 92621

DOLE, MALCOLM, JR., economist; b. Evanston, Ill., Apr. 24, 1935; s. Malcolm and Frances Hibbard (Page) D.; m. Margaret Hoffman Dole, June 30, 1962; children—Malcolm, Heather McAdie. B.A., Northwestern U., 1957; Ph.D., UCLA, 1974. Cert. community coll. instr., Calif. Research asst. UCLA, 1961-64, teaching asst., 1964-67; prof. Calif. State U., 1967-72; sr. economist Calif. State Air Resources Bd., Sacramento, 1973-76, research mgr., 1976—. Recipient award of Appreciation, United Way, 1979. Mem. Am. Econ. Assn., Western Regional Sci. Assn. Clubs: Commonwealth; Sheridan Shore Yacht (Wilmette, Ill.). Home: G25-1 Woodside Sierra Ln Sacramento CA 95825 Office: PO Box 2815 Sacramento CA 95812

DOLENC, MAX RUDOLPH, geologist, researcher; b. Rock Springs, Wyo., Jan. 15, 1943; s. Max Jack and Elsie Rose (Yardas) D.; m. Jeanne Marie Greenhalgh, June 22, 1963 (div. Aug. 1973); children—Patrick Vincent, Paige Marie; m. 2d, Louise Edna Peterson, Nov. 8, 1980; stepchildren—Theresa Satoyo Togo, Tami Kyoko Togo. B.S. in Chemistry, U. Wyo.-Laramie, 1966, B.S. in Bus. Adminstrn., 1969; postgrad. in geology, U. Idaho-Moscow, 1982—. Radiation specialist Wyo. Health Dept., Cheyenne, 1967-69; field mgr. ATCOR, Inc., Denver, 1969-70; research physicist El Paso Natural Gas, 1970-76; environ. geosci. mgr. EG&G Idaho, Inc., Idaho Falls, 1976-78, sr. geosci. engr., 1978-83, sr. project engr., 1983—. Contbr. articles in field. Mem. Am. Assn. Petroleum Geologists, Assn. Petroleum Goechem. Explorations, Soc. Petroleum Engrs., Phi Epsilon Phi. Roman Catholic. Home: 2272 Enell St Idaho Falls ID 83402 Office: EG&G Idaho Inc PO Box 1625 Idaho Falls ID 83415

DOLEZAL, HENRY, retired research chemist; b. San Francisco, June 20, 1925; s. Frank Charles and Teresa (Garcia) D.; m. Lucille Ethel Gregersen, Nov. 29, 1958; children: Carolyn Ann Padgett, Linda Sue Mulcock, Thomas Albert Harrison. AA, City Coll. San Francisco, 1949; BA, U. Calif., Berkeley, 1952. Research chemist U.S. Bur. Mines, Boulder City, Nev., 1952-62, Salt Lake City, 1962-83. Contbr. articles to profl. jours.; patentee in field. Served to 1st lt. U.S. Army, 1943-46. Mem. Am. Legion (treas. Boulder City chpt. 1961—). Democrat. Roman Catholic. Lodge: Elks. Avocations: photography, cooking. Home: 3900 Autumn St Las Vegas NV 89120

DOLGOW, ALLAN BENTLEY, management consultant; b. N.Y.C.; BIE, NYU, 1959, MBA, 1972; m. Nina Kim; children—Nicole, Marc, Ginger, Kimbie. with, Republic Aviation Corp., Farmingdale, N.Y., 1959-60; mgr.

Internat. Paper Co., N.Y.C., 1960-73; project mgr. J.C. Penney Co. Inc., N.Y.C., 1973-75; dir. mfg. and planning Morse Electro Products, N.Y.C., 1975-77, exec. mgr. Morse Electrophonic Hong Kong Ltd., 1976-77; internat. project mgr. Revlon Inc., Edison, N.J., 1977-79: mgmt. cons. SRI Internat., Menlo Park, Calif., 1979—. Served with U.S. Army; Germany. Office: 333 Ravenswood Ave Menlo Park CA 94025

DOLICH, ANDREW BRUCE, professional baseball team administrator; b. Bklyn., Feb. 18, 1947; s. Mac and Yetta (Weiselter) D.; m. Ellen Andrea Fass, June 11, 1972; children: Lindsey, Caryn, Cory. B.A., Am. U., 1969; M.Ed., Ohio U., 1971. Adminstrv. asst. to gen. mgr. Phila. 76ers, NBA, 1971-74; v.p. Md. Arrows Lacrosse, Landover, 1974-76; mkg. dir. Washington Capitals, NHL, Landover, 1976-78; exec. v.p., gen. mgr. Washington Diplomats Soccer, 1978-80; v.p. bus. ops. Oakland A's Baseball, Calif., 1980—; dir. Sports Adminstrs. Program Ohio U., Athens, 1978-82, U. Mass., Athens, 1979—; dir. Maj. League Baseball Promo Corp. Bd. dirs. Bay Area Sports Hall of Fame, 1982—, Carden Sch., Oakland Conv. and Visitors Bur. Recipient Alumni of Yr. award Ohio U. Sports Adminstrs. Program, Athens, 1982; recipient Clio award Am. Advt. Fedn., 1982. Democrat. Office: Oakland A's Baseball Oakland Coliseum Oakland CA 94621

DOLIM, DENNIS WILLET, distribution company executive; b. Honolulu, Apr. 5, 1947; s. Lorrin Willet and Evelyn (Holmberg) D.; m. Andrea Leinaala Wilson, July 4, 1974; children: Traciann Lei, Douglas Pekelo. BS, St. Mary's Coll., Moraga, Calif., 1969. Sales mgr. Holsum/Oroweat, Honolulu, 1969-80; owner D.D. Brokerage, Honolulu, 1980—; pres. T.A.P. Dists., Honolulu, 1980—. Bd. dirs. United Cerebral Palsy Assn. Hawaii, Honolulu, 1985—. Mem. Hawaii Food Industry Assn., Food Industry Assn. (bd. dirs.). Democrat. Roman Catholic. Club: Oahu Country (Honolulu). Home: PO Box 29447 Honolulu HI 96820 Office: T A P Distributors Inc 3207 N Nimitz Hwy Honolulu HI 96819

DOLINAY, THOMAS V., bishop; b. Uniontown, Pa., July 24, 1923. Student, St. Procopius Coll., Ill. Ordained priest Roman Catholic Ch., 1948. Ordained titular bishop Tiatira and aux. bishop Byzantine rite Diocese of Passaic, 1976-81; aux. bishop Byzantine rite Diocese of Van Nuys Calif., 1981; installed 1982—. Editor: Eastern Cath. Life, 1966-82. Office: Chancery Office 5335 Sepulveda Blvd Van Nuys CA 91411 *

DOLL, LINDA A., artist, teacher; b. Bklyn., May 5, 1942; d. William James Harrington and Ann B. (Casey) Cook; m. William John Doll, Feb. 4, 1962; children: Patricia, William Jr. AA, Palomar Coll., 1974; BA, San Diego State U., 1976. chairperson Arts Adv. Com. to Congressman Jim Bates, 1983-84; U.S. Coast Guard Artist, 1985. Exhibited in group shows with Am. Watercolor Soc. (selected for one yr. nat. travel show) N.Y.C., 1986, Canton, Ohio, 1985, Nat. Watercolor Soc., Brea, Calif., 1984-85, Watercolor West Annual, Riverside, Calif., 1982, 84-86 (E. Gene Crain Purchase Selection award 1985, Second Place Jurors award 1982), Rocky Mountain Nat., Golden, Colo., 1984-85, Midwest Annual, Davenport, Iowa, 1983, 85, Nat. Watercolor Soc., Riverside, 1985 (Selected for one yr. nat. travel show), Watercolor Internat., San Diego, 1978-79, 82-84 (Selected for one yr. nat. travel show, 1983-84), Watercolor Okla., 1982-84 (Harry Hulett Jr. award 1984), Pa. Soc. Watercolor Painters, Harrisburg, 1982 (hon. mention); represented in permanent collections including E. Gene Crain Collection, Scripps Hosp., La Jolla, Calif., Redlands Community Hosp., Riverside, Campbell River Community Art Council, Can., Simpact Assocs. Inc., San Diego. Mem. San Diego Watercolor Soc. (past pres.), Nat. Watercolor Soc., Watercolor West, Knickerbocker Artists, Am. Watercolor Soc. (chmn. of assocs. 1985), Midwest Watercolor Soc. (assoc. mem., annual show chmn. 1985). Office: 17490 Matinal Dr Rancho Bernardo CA 92127-1238

DOLL, WILLIAM ELDER, JR., educator; b. Detroit, Jan. 29, 1931; s. William Elder and Anne (Moran) D.; B.A. in Philosophy, Cornell U., 1953; M.A., Boston U., 1960; Ph.D. in Edn., Johns Hopkins U., 1972; m. Mary Elizabeth Aswell, June 25, 1966; 1 son, William Campbell. Tchr., Mass., Colo. and N.Y. State, 1954-64; headmaster Valley Sch., Owings Mills, Md., 1964-67; mem. faculty SUNY Coll.-Oswego, 1971-85. Assoc. prof. edn., 1975-85, chmn. dept. elem. edn., 1980-82, coordinator, 1983-85; dir. tchr. preparation programs U. Redlands, Calif., 1985—. Mem. Fulton Bd. Edn., 1983-85. Grantee SUNY, 1979, 80. Mem. Am. Ednl. Research Assn., Am. Ednl. Studies Assn., Assn. Supervision and Curriculum Devel., John Dewey Soc., Philosophy of Edn. Soc., Soc. Profs. Curriculum, Soc. Profs. Edn. Democrat. Roman Catholic. Author papers in field. Home: 1565 E Highland Ave Redlands CA 92374 Office: U Redlands Larsen Hall Redlands CA 92373-0999

DOLLARHIDE, COLETTE THERESA, college administrator, consultant; b. Lancaster, Calif., Nov. 12, 1956; d. Charles Wesley and Kathleen Colette (Scherr) Reding; m. Jerry Glen Dollarhide, Mar. 24, 1975; 1 child, Shiloh Colette. BA in Polit. Sci., Calif. State U., 1980; postgrad. U. Nevada-Reno, 1980—; adminstrv. asst. City of Norwalk, Calif., 1979-80; GED proctor/audiovisual technician Washoe County Sch. Dist., Reno, 1980-82; evening coll. dir. Reno Bus. Coll., 1982—, dean edn., 1985—, cons., 1983-84. Author: The Better Sentence, 1984. Dep. registrar of voters Washoe County Registry of Voters, Reno, 1982; bd. dirs. Reno Bus. Coll. Found., 1984. Mem. Am. Assn. Counseling and Devel., Am. Coll. Personnel Assn., Nat. Employment Counselors Assn., Nat. Devel. Assn., No. Nev. Assn. Tchrs. English. Roman Catholic. Office: Reno Bus Coll 140 Washington St Reno NV 89503

DOLLINGER, ARMAND LEON, pathologist; b. Los Angeles, June 16, 1931; s. G. Glenn and Alethea D. (Morrison) D.; B.A. in Chemistry, La Sierra Coll., 1952; M.D., Loma Linda (Calif.) U., 1956; m. Martha Alice Dobias, June 13, 1975; children by previous marriage—Barbara, John, Robert, Elizabeth, Mary, Rebecca, Andrew, Matthew, Bradley, Kelly. Intern, White Meml. Hosp., Los Angeles, 1956-57; resident in pathology Loma Linda U. Hosp., 1957-63; assoc. pathologist Riverside County Coroner, Riverside, Calif., 1963-73; pathologist, co-dir. Biolabs., Colton, Calif., 1963-73; pathologist, owner, dir. Dollinger Pathology Med. Group, Inc., Hanford, Calif., 1973—; forensic pathologist Kings County Coroner, Hanford, 1973; pathologist, lab. dir., past pres. med. staff Hanford Community Hosp.; guest lectr. forensic pathology Loma Linda U. Med. Center, 1972; chief forensic pathologist, Kern County Coroner's Office, Bakersfield, 1984; pathology cons., lab. dir. U.S. Naval Hosp., Lemoore, Calif.; adv. bd. Kings County Drug Adv. Bd., chmn. 1985, 86; cons. in field, pathologist to coroners' offices. Served with M.C., USNR, 1958-60, now capt. Res. Diplomate Am. Bd. Pathology. Fellow Am. Soc. Clin. Pathologists, Coll. Am. Pathologists; mem. Am. Acad. Forensic Scis., Naval Res. Assn., Nat. Rifle Assn. (endowment), Calif. Rifle and Pistol Assoc. (life), Kings County Med. Soc. (bd. govs. 1975—, pres. 1984), Nat. Assn. Med. Examiners, Kings County Peace Officers Assn., Calif. Res. Peace Officers Assn., Calif. Rifle and Pistol Assn. (life), Loma Linda U. Alumni Assn. (life). Republican. Seventh-day Adventist. Author papers in field. Office: 1222 West Lacey Blvd PO Box 1308 Hanford CA 93230

DOLLIVER, JAMES MORGAN, state supreme court justice; b. Ft. Dodge, Iowa, Oct. 13, 1924; s. James Isaac and Margaret Elizabeth (Morgan) D.; m. Barbara Babcock, Dec. 18, 1948; children: Elizabeth, James, Peter, Keith, Jennifer, Nancy. BA in Polit. Sci. with high honors, Swarthmore Coll., 1949; LLB, U. Wash., 1952; D in Liberal Arts (hon.), U. Puget Sound, 1981. Bar: Wash. 1952. Clk. to presiding justice Wash. Supreme Ct., 1952-53; sole practice Port Angeles, Wash., 1953-54, Everett, Wash., 1961-64; adminstrv. asst. to Congressman Jack Westland, 1955-61, Gov. Daniel J. Evans, 1965-76; justice Supreme Ct. State of Wash., 1976—, chief justice, 1985-86; 2d v.p. conf. Chief Justices, 1985-86. Chmn. United Way Campaign Thurston County, 1975, pres., 1976, mem. exec. bd., 1977—; chmn. Wash. chpt. Nature Conservancy, 1981—; pres. exec. bd. Tumwater Area council Boy Scouts Am., 1972-73, Wash. chpt. The Nature Conservancy, 1981-83, mem. 1979—, Wash. State Capital Hist. Assn., 1976-80, 85—, also trustee, 1983-84; trustee Deaconess Children's Home, Everett, 1963-65, U. Puget Sound, 1970—, Wash. 4-H Found., 1977-84, also v.p., 1983—, Claremont (Calif.) Theol. Sem., assoc. mem., Community Mental Health Ctr., 1977-84; bd. mgrs. Swarthmore Coll., 1980-84; bd. dirs. Thurston Mason Community Health Ctr., 1977-84, Thurston Youth Services Soc., 1969-84, also pres., 1983, mem. exec. com., 1970-84, Safety Tng. and Research Assn. Wash., 1979—, Wash. Women's Employment and Edn., 1982-84; mem. jud. council United Meth. Ch., 1984—, gen. conf., 1970-72, 80—, gen. bd. ch. and society, 1976-84; adv. council Retired Senior Vol. program, 1979-83; mem. bd. visitors Cen. Wash. U. Coll. of Letters, Arts and Scis., 1983—. Served as ensign USCG, 1945-46. Recipient award Nat. Council Japanese Am. Citizens League, 1976; Silver Beaver award, 1971; Silver Antelope award, 1976. Mem. Am., Wash. bar assns., Am. Judges Assn., Am. Judicature Soc., Pub. Broadcast Found. (bd. dirs. 1982—), Am. Acad. Youth Exchange (adv. council 1983—). Clubs: Masons, Rotary. Office: Wash Supreme Ct Temple of Justice Olympia WA 98504

DOLLY, JOHN PATRICK, university dean, educational psychologist; b. N.Y.C., May 16, 1942; s. Thomas Joseph and Anna Maria (Baron) D.; m. Carol Ann Dolly, Oct. 23, 1966; children—Sheila, Erin. B.S., Manhattan Coll., 1964; M.S., SUNY, 1966; Ed.D., U. Ga., 1973. Area dir. Founds. of Edn. U. S.C., Columbia, 1975-78, asst. dean acad. affairs Coll. Edn., 1978-79, acting dean, 1979-80, asst. dean research and devel., 1980; dean Coll. Edn. U. Wyo., Laramie, 1981-86, U. Hawaii, Manoa, 1986—; cons., lectr. in field. Co-author: Learning to Teach: A Decision Making System. Contbr. articles to profl. jours. Served to capt. USAF, 1966-70. Vocat. Rehab. Adminstrn. trainee, 1964-66. Mem. Am. Psychol. Assn., Am. Ednl. Research Assn., Phi Delta Kappa, Phi Kappa Phi, Kappa Delta Pi. Office: Coll Edn U Hawaii 1776 University Ave Manoa HI 96822

DOLNICK, DAVID BENJAMIN, occupational safety, health consultant; b. Chgo., Dec. 4, 1950; s. Norman I. and June Blythe (Fogelstrom) D.; m. Marjorie Isabelle Wagus, May 7, 1969 (div. 1979); children: Sonja Lynn, Rachel Elizabeth; m. Janice Lee Cimbalo, Nov. 1, 1980; 1 child, Michael Anthony. BA, Ripon Coll., 1972. Cert. Occupational Hearing Conservationist, Comml. Pesticide Applicator, Calif. Engrng. aide Ralph M. Parsons Co., Pasadena, Calif., 1975-77; sales rep. Mut. of N.Y., Los Angeles, 1977; payroll auditor State Compensation Ins. Fund, Los Angeles, 1978-79; safety cons. State Compensation Ins. Fund, Los Angeles, San Diego, 1979-83; supr. loss control Fremont Indemnity Co., San Diego, 1983-86; with policy holder services Citation Ins. Co., San Diego, 1986-87; mgr. San Diego Terr. Citation Ins. Co., 1987—; dir. risk mgmt. and safety Univ. Industries, San Diego, 1987—; Chmn. 8th, 9th Ann. Pacific Southwest Safety and Health Seminars, San Diego, 1985,86, Nat. Safety in Workplace Week, San Diego, 1984, 86; cons. BackTalk/Work Hardening Program, San Diego, 1981, 83—, Back Pain Clinic, Escondido, Calif., 1984-86, Profl. Seminars, Inc., San Diego, 1981-82. Bd. dirs. San Diego County Safety Council, 1984—. Mem. Am. Soc. Safety Engrs. (pres. local chpt. 1985-86), Nat. Safety Mgmt. Soc., San Diego Fire Protection Engrs. Democrat. Avocations: deep sea fishing, photography, painting, writing poetry. Office: Citation Ins Co 3111 Camino del Rio N San Diego CA 92108

DOLOWITZ, DAVID AUGUSTUS, otolaryngologist, educator; b. N.Y.C., Nov. 3, 1913; s. Alexander and Florence Reda (Levine) D.; A.B., Johns Hopkins U., 1933; M.D., Yale U., 1937; M.A., U. Utah, 1951, Sc.D. (hon.), 1978; m. Frances Marie Fleisher, May 6, 1937 (dec. 1967); children—David S., Julia Louise, Wilma Florence, Susan Reda, Fridolyn Gimble; m. 2nd Emma Ruth Halvorsen, June 11, 1968. Intern, Morristown (N.J.) Meml. Hosp., 1937-38, Albany (N.Y.) Hosp., 1938-39; resident Johns Hopkins Hosp., Balt., 1939-43; practice medicine, specializing in otolaryngology, Salt Lake City, 1946-78; asst. otolaryngology Johns Hopkins U., Balt., 1938-39, instr., 1942-43; instr. U. Utah, Salt Lake City, 1943-48, assoc. clin. prof., 1948-58, assoc. prof., chief otolaryngology, 1958-67, clin. prof. otolaryngology, 1967—; instr. biology Dixie Coll., St. George, Utah, 1987—; staff Holy Cross Hosp., VA Hosp., Salt Lake City, U. Utah Med. Hosp., Primary Children's Hosp., Salt Lake City, all 1946-78; councilman, treas. Town of Toquerville (Utah), 1982—. Chmn. bd. Pioneer Craft House, Salt Lake City, 1965-84; mem. gov.'s com. study exceptional children, Utah, 1967; mem. otolaryngologic del. to China, People to People, 1986. Served with M.C., U.S. Army, 1943-46. NIH fellow, U. Lund, Sweden, 1959-60. Fellow ACS; mem. AMA, Utah Med. Assn., Am. Bd. Otolaryngology, Am. Acad. Otolaryngology, Am. Bd. Clin. Allergy, Am. Otol. Soc., Deafness Research Found., Soc. Univ. Otolaryngologists (adv. com. pulmonary-allergy drugs 1973-78), Am. Laryngology, Rhinology and Otolaryngology Soc., Barany Soc., C. of C. Democrat. Jewish. Author: Basic Otolaryngology, 1964; editor: Allergy in Otolaryngologic Practice: The Otolaryngologic Clinics of North America, 1971; Transactions of Am. Soc. Ophthalmologic and Otolaryngologic Allergy, 1973-78; contbr. articles to profl. jours. Home: PO Box 189 Toquerville UT 84774

DOLOWY, WILLIAM CLARENCE, veterinarian; b. Chicago Heights, Ill., Jan. 13, 1927; s. William and Sophia (Bombrys) D.; m. Joan Elizabeth Hallstead, June 24, 1955; children: Elizabeth, Cynthia. BS in Chemistry, U. Ill., 1948, MS in Zoology, 1949, BS in Veterinary Medicine, 1951, DVM, 1953. Diplomate Am. Coll. Lab. Animal Medicine. Adminstr. med. research lab. U. Ill. Med. Ctr., Chgo., 1954-67; prof. and chmn dept. exptl. animal medicine U. Wash., Seattle, 1967-73; prof. microbiology Chgo. Med. Sch., 1974-75, Loyola U., Maywood, 1975-76; practice medicine specializing in lab. animals, Animal Care Hosp. of Mercer Island, Wash., 1976—; cons. numerous VA and private hosps., 1955-73. Contbr. articles to profl. jours. Served with USN, 1945-46. Grantee Diagnostic Lab. in Exptl. Animal Medicine, 1968-74, NIH, 1968-76. Mem. AVMA, Wash. State Vet. Med. Assn., King County-Seattle Vet. Med. Assn., AAAS, Am. Soc. Microbiology, Am. Coll. Lab. Animal Medicine, Am. Assn. Cancer Research, Am. Soc. Lab. Animal Practitioners, Conf. Research Workers in Animal Diseases, Soc. Exptl. Biology and Medicine. Avocation: paleozoology. Office: Animal Care Hosp Mercer Island 2705 76th SE Mercer Island WA 98040

DOLSEN, DAVID HORTON, mortician; b. Durango, Colo., Feb. 27, 1940; s. Donald B. and Florence I. (Maxey) D.; B.A., Southwestern Coll., 1962; Mortuary Sci. Degree, Dallas-Jones Coll. Mortuary Sci., 1963; m. Jo Patricia Johnson, Dec. 23, 1962; children—Wendy, Douglas. Apprentice, Davis Mortuary, Pueblo, Colo., 1963-64; bus. mgr. George F. McCarty Funeral Home, Pueblo, 1964-65; owner Dolsen Mortuary, Lamar, Colo., 1965-72; v.p., gen. mgr., dir. Almont, Inc., Lamar, 1972—; sec. Dolsen, Inc., 1967—; treas. Wilson Funeral Dirs. Inc., Itoh-Wilson Funeral Dirs., Inc.; gen. ptnr. Let's Talk Travel, Ltd. Mem. Lamar City Council, 1969-73; mayor City of Lamar, 1971-73. Bd. dirs. Lamar Community Coll., 1967-73, Prowers County Hist. Soc., 1966—, San De Cristo Arts and Conf. Center, 1979-85; bd. dirs., sec. Pueblo Met. Mus. Assn., 1975-79; chmn. council on fin. and adminstrn. Rocky Mountain Conf. United Meth. Ch., 1976—, del. Gen. Conf., 1979—; mem. Pres.'s Council Nat. Meth. Found., 1978—, Iliff Sch. Theology, 1986—; trustee, mem. exec. com. Southwestern Coll., Winfield, Kans., 1979—; dist. chmn. Boy Scouts Am., 1981—; treas., mem. exec. com. Girl Scouts U.S.A., 1981—; mem. council on fin. and adminstrn. Western Jurisdiction, United Meth. Ch., 1980—; trustee, gen. council on fin. and adminstrn. United Meth. Ch., 1980—; trustee Meth. Corp., 1980—, United Meth. Ch. Ins. Trust, 1982—; mem. World Service Commn., Meth. Episcopal Ch., 1980—; mem. gen. council on adminstrn., bd. adminstrn. Ch. of United Brethren in Christ, 1980—; trustee Sunny Acres Retirement Community, 1986, bd. dirs. Mem. Nat. Funeral Dirs. Assn., Nat. Selected Morticians, Cremation Assn. Am., Monument Builders N.Am., Colo. Funeral Dirs. Assn. Pi Sigma Eta, Pi Kappa Delta, Pi Gamma Mu. Methodist (cert. lay speaker). Clubs: Masons, Shriners, Elks, Rotary (Paul Harris fellow). Home: 3503 Morris Ave Pueblo CO 81008 Office: 401 Broadway Pueblo CO 81004

DOMBECK, MICHAEL PAUL, fisheries biologist; b. Stevens Point, Wis., Sept. 21, 1948; s. Leonard Barney and Estelle Evelyn (Gross) D.; m. Patricia Ann Rider, July 25, 1975; 1 child, Mary Rider. BS, U. Wis., Stevens Point, 1971, MS, 1974; MS, U. Minn., 1977; PhD, Iowa State U., 1984. Fishing guide Hayward, Wis., 1963-77; instr. zoology U. Wis., Stevens Point, 1971-74; research specialist Bell Mus., Mpls., 1975-77; staff columnist Visitor Mag., Hayward, 1975—; fisheries biologist Forest Service, Milw., 1978-84; regional fisheries program mgr. Forest Service, San Francisco, 1985—; cons. Freshwater Fishing Hall of Fame, Hayward, 1984—, bd. govs. (life); program chmn. Internat. Muskellunge Symposium, 1984. Contbr. articles to profl. jours.; inventor oxygen stratification (nat. award 1985). T. Roosevelt fellow Am. Mus. Natural History, 1975; recipient "Ding" J.N. Darling Conservation Writers award, 1981, 82, 83, Outdoor Writer's Assn. Am. scholarship, 1983. Mem. Am. Fisheries Soc. (cert., sec./treas. Wis. chpt. 1983-85), Am. Inst. Fisheries Research Biologists, Sigma Xi, Gamma Sigma Delta. Avocations: fishing, camping, hiking, oil painting, music. Office: Forest Service Fish and Wildlife Mgmt 630 Sansome St San Francisco CA 94111

DOMBECK, THOMAS WALTER, physicist, researcher; b. Ellwood City, Pa., Feb. 7, 1945; s. Walter John and Cecelia Mary (Topolski) D.; m. Bonnie Marcia Rosen, Dec. 21, 1968; children: Heidi Jayne, Daniel Andrew. BA, Columbia U., 1967; PhD, Northwestern U., 1972. Research assoc. Imperial Coll., London, 1972-75, Argonne (Ill.) Nat. Lab., 1975-78; asst. prof. U. Md., College Park, 1978-81; staff mem. Los Alamos (N.Mex.) Nat. Lab., 1981—; referee Dept. of Energy, Gathersburg, Md., 19786; cons. Argonne Nat. Lab., 1980; mem. gen. research bd. U. Md., 1980. Contbr. articles to sci. jours.; inventor computer storage device. Mem. AAAS, Am. Phys. Soc. Democrat. Avocations: sailing, skiing, hiking, racquetball. Home: 550 Canyon Rd Los Alamos NM 87544 Office: Los Alamos Nat Lab Box 1663 MS D449 Los Alamos NM 87545

DOMBROWSKI, JOANNE MORGAN, science educator; b. Charlotte, Mich., July 1, 1946; d. Charles Andrew and Marian Hazel (Dickinson) Morgan; m. Stanley Alfred Dombrowski, Aug. 27, 1966; children: Christopher Charles, Arick Duncan. BS, No. Ariz. U., 1967, MA, 1968, EdD, 1983. Adj. instr. Ariz. State U., Tempe, 1976-77; adj. prof. No. Ariz. U., Flagstaff, 1985—; tchr. sci. Kofa High Sch., Yuma, Ariz., 1968—, sci. dept. chmn., 1976—; co-dir. safety seminar Ariz. Dept. Edn., Phoenix, 1983, cons. 1984-85, Scottsdale Pub. Sch., 1984; co-dir. research survey Lab. Safety, State of Ariz., 1985. Co-producer lab. safety notes posters, 1984; writer lab safety filmstrips, 1985; contbr. articles to profl. jours. Mem. Somerton Sch. Bd. Dist., 1987—. Recipient Pres. award NSF, Excellence in Sci. and Math award, 1985. Mem. Nat. Sci. Tchrs. Assn. (bd. dirs. The Sci. Tchr. 1985—), Nat. Assn. Biology Tchrs., Ariz. Sci. Tchrs. Assn. (bd. dirs. 1985—), NEA, Ariz.-Nev. Acad. Sci. (chmn. awards 1986, Sci. Tchr. of Yr. award 1984-85), Phi Delta Kappa (sec. 1986—), Alpha Delta Kappa (sec. 1975-76). State semi-finalist Ariz. Tchr. in Space, 1985. Home: PO Box 503 Somerton AZ 85350 Office: Kofa High Sch 3100 Ave A Yuma AZ 85364

DOMENICI, PETE (VICHI DOMENICI), U.S. senator; b. Albuquerque, May 7, 1932; s. Cherubino and Alda (Vichi) D.; m. Nancy Burk, Jan. 15, 1958; children: Lisa, Peter, Nella, Clare, David, Nanette, Helen, Paula. Student, U. Albuquerque, 1950-52; B.S., U. N.Mex., 1954, LL.D. (hon.); LL.B., Denver U., 1958; LL.D. (hon.), Georgetown U. Sch. Medicine; H.H.D. (hon.), N.Mex. State U. Bar: N.Mex. 1958. Tchr. math. pub. schs. Albuquerque, 1954-55; ptnr. firm Domenici & Bonham, Albuquerque, 1958-72; mem. U.S. Senate from N.Mex. 1972—; mem. energy and natural resources com., chmn. subcom. on energy research and devel.; mem. com. on environ. and public works; chmn. budget com.; mem. spl. com. on aging; mem. Presdl. Adv. Com. on Federalism. Mem. Gov.'s Policy Bd. for Law Enforcement, 1967-68; chmn. Model Cities Joint Adv. Com., 1967-68; mem. Albuquerque City Commn., 1966-68, chmn. and ex-officio mayor, 1967. Mem. Nat. League Cities, Middle Rio Grande Council Govts. Home: 11110 Stephalee Ln Rockville MD 20852 Office: 434 Dirksen Senate Office Bldg Washington DC 20510 *

DOMINO, GEORGE, psychology educator; b. Turin, Italy, June 13, 1938; came to U.S., 1949; s. Tommaso and Maria (Oglietti) D.; m. Valerie Gerencser, Aug. 14, 1965; children: Brian, Marisa, Marla. BS, Loyola U., Los Angeles, 1960; PhD, U. Calif., Berkeley, 1967. Registered psychologist. Instr. U. San Francisco, 1962-65; asst. prof. psychology Calif. State U., Fresno, 1965-66; prof., dir. counselling Fordham U., N.Y.C., 1966-75; prof. U. Ariz., Tucson, 1975—. Contbr. articles to profl. jours. Mem. Am. Psychol. Assn., Western Psychol. Assn., Rocky Mountain Psychol. Assn. Roman Catholic. Office: U Ariz Dept Psychology Tucson AZ 85721

DOMONDON, OSCAR, dentist; b. Cebu City, Philippines, July 4, 1924; s. Antero B. and Ursula (Maglasang) D.; D.M.D., Philippine Dental Coll., 1951; D.D.S., Loma Linda U., 1964; m. Vicky Domondon. children—Reinelda, Carolyn, Catherine, Oscar. Came to U.S., 1954, naturalized, 1956. Dentist, Manila. (Philippines) Sanitarium and Hosp., 1952, U.S. embassy, Manila, 1952-54; pvt. practice dentistry, Long Beach, Calif., 1964—. Dentist, Children's Dental Health Center, Long Beach, part-time, 1964-68; past mem. Calif. State Bd. Dental Examiners. Past pres., Filipino Community Action Services, Inc. Served with AUS, 1946-49, 54-60. Fellow Acad. Dentistry International, Acad. Gen. Dentistry, Internat. Inst. Community Service, Acad. Internat. Dental Studies, Internat. Coll. Dentists, Am. Coll. Dentists; mem. Am. Soc. Dentistry Children, ADA, Am. Acad. Oral Radiology (award 1964), Internat. Acad. Orthodontists, Am. Soc. Clin. Hypnosis, Am. Endodontic Soc., Western Conf. Dental Examiners and Dental Sch. Deans, Fedn. of Assns. of Health Regulatory Bds., Calif. Assn. Fgn. Dental Grads. (past pres.), Filipino Dental Soc. (past pres.), Philippine Tech. and Profl. Soc. (v.p.), Am. Acad. Dentistry for Handicapped, Am. Assn. Dental Examiners, Nat. Assn. Filipino Practicing Dentists in Am. (pres.), Pierre Fauchard Acad., Acad. Continuing Edn. Republican. Lodges: Lions (past pres.), Elks (past chmn. rangers), Masons. Home: 3570 Aster St Seal Beach CA 90740 Office: 3714 Atlantic Ave Long Beach CA 90807

DONAHOO, STANLEY ELLSWORTH, orthopaedic surgeon; b. St. Joseph, Mo., Dec. 3, 1933; s. Charles Ellsworth and Opal (Cole) D.; m. Cheryl R. Donahoo; children—Shan Maureen, Brian Patrick, Mary Kathleen, Jane Eileen; stepchildren: Trina Person, Kevin Person. MD, U. Wash., 1963. Resident, Duke U., Durham, N.C., 1967-68, U.S. Naval Hosp., Oakland, Calif., 1963-67; commd. lt., U.S. Navy, 1963 advanced through grades to lt. comdr. (orthopaedic surgeon), 1971, ret. 1971; practice medicine, specializing in orthopaedic surgery, Roseburg, Oreg., 1971—; chief surgery Mercy Hosp., Roseburg, 1973-74; chief surgery Douglas Community Hosp., Roseburg, 1973, chief of staff, 1974—; cons. Guam Meml. Hosp., co-dir. rehab. unit, 1970-71; cons. orthopaedic surgery VA Hosp., Roseburg, 1971—; chmn. Douglas County (Oreg.) Emergency Med. Services Com., 1973-74. Trustee Douglas Community Hosp., 1975. Served with AUS, 1952-55. Diplomate Am. Bd. Orthopaedic Surgery. Fellow Am. Acad. Orthopaedic Surgeons (admissions com. region 14), North Pacific Orthopaedic Assn. (v.p. 1984-85); mem. Piedmont Orthopaedic Soc., AMA, Oreg. Med. Assn. (mem. sports medicine com., ins. and fee rev. com. 1981), Guam Med. Soc. (pres. 1970), Am. Trauma Soc. (founding mem.), Roseburg C. of C. (bd. govs. 1978—). Home: 205 Wildfern Dr Winchester OR 97495 Office: 1813 W Harvard St Suite 201 Roseburg OR 97470

DONALD, IAN, wood products company executive. Formerly pres. Crown Forest Industries Ltd, Vancouver, B.C., Can.; pres. Brit. Col. Forest Products Ltd, Vancouver, B.C., Can., 1987—. Office: Brit Col Forest Products Ltd, Office of Pres, 1050 W Pender St, Vancouver, BC Canada V6E 2X3 *

DONALDSON, CHARLES RUSSELL, state justice; b. Helena, Mont., Feb. 2, 1919; s. Charles Mortimer and Mabel (King) D.; children: Karen, Holly, Jean, Laurel, Sarah, Charles. Student, Willamette U., 1937-38; B.A., U. Idaho, 1941, LL.B., 1948; postgrad., George Washington Law Sch., 1943-44. Bar: Idaho 1948. Practice law Boise, 1948-64; dist. judge 1964-68; justice Idaho Supreme Ct., Boise, 1969—, chief justice, 1973, 79-80, 83-86; mem. Idaho Ho. of Reps., 1955-57; justice of peace, 1960-64. Mem. governing com. Idaho chpt. Arthritis and Rheumatism Found. Served with Signal Corps, AUS, World War II. Mem. Conf. Chief Justices (dep. chmn. 1980—). Methodist. Lodges: Kiwanis (past pres.), Masons, Shriners. Office: Supreme Ct Bldg Boise ID 83720

DONALDSON, EDWARD ENSLOW, physicist, educator; b. Wenatchee, Wash., Mar. 7, 1923; s. George Howard and Milbra Frances (Enslow) D.; m. (Helen) Virginia Voss, Apr. 28, 1946; 1 child, Dinah Lee. AA, Wenatchee Jr. Coll., 1946; BS in Physics, Wash. State Coll., 1948, PhD in Physics, 1953. Radiol. physicist Gen. Electric, Hanford, Wash., 1953-57; asst. prof. Wash. State U., Pullman, 1957-64, prof. physics, 1967, dept. chmn., 1967-74, 81-85; program chmn. Surface Physics Symposia, Wash. State U., Pullman, 1963-67, 69, 71. Contbr. articles to profl. jours. Served as cpl. U.S. Army, 1943-46. Mem. Am. Phys. Soc., Am. Vacuum Soc. (sr., bd. dirs. 1966, program com. 1965, chmn. 1966), Am. Inst. Physics, Am. Assn. Physics Tchrs. Republican. Presbyterian. Avocations: bagpiping, organ, skiing. Home: SE 500 Water St Pullman WA 99163 Office: Wash State U Dept Physics Pullman WA 99164

DONALDSON, GEORGE BURNEY, chemical company executive; b. Oakland, Calif., Mar. 16, 1945; s. George T. and L.M. (Burney) D.; m. Jennifer L. Bishop, Feb. 16, 1974; children: Dawn Marie, Paul Matthew. AS in Criminology, Porterville Coll., 1972. Police officer City of Lindsay (Calif.), 1966-67; distbn. mgr. Ortho div. Chevron Chem. Co., Lindsay, 1967-73; safety specialist Wilbur-Ellis Co. Fresno, Calif., 1973-77, safety dir., 1977-79, dir. regulatory affairs, 1979—; industry rep. to White House Inter-Govtl. Sci. Engring., and Tech. Adv. Panel, Task Force on Transp. of Non-Nuclear Hazardous Materials, 1980; industry rep. Transp. Research Bd.'s Nat. Strategies Conf. on Transp. of Hazardous Materials and Wastes in the 1980's, Nat. Acad. Scis., 1981, Hazardous Materials Transp. Conf., Nat. Conf. of State Legislatures, 1982; hazardous materials adviser, motor carrier rating com. Calif. Hwy. Patrol, 1978-79. Served with U.S. Army, 1962-65. Mem. Western Agrl. Chems. Assn. (chmn. transp., distbn. and safety com., outstanding mem. of year 1981, govtl. affairs com.), Nat. Agrl. Chems. Assn. (chmn. transp. and distbn. com., occupational safety and health com., environ. mgmt. com.), Am. Soc. Safety Engrs., Calif. Fertilizer Assn. (transp. and distbn. com., environ. com.), Fresno City and County C. of C. (agrl. steering com., govt. affairs com.), Calif. C. of C. (environ. policy com.). Republican. Lodge: Elks. Office: 191 W Shaw Ave Suite 107 Fresno CA 93704

DONATHAN, ANN G., food products executive; b. San Francisco, Feb. 18, 1937; d. Ralph Vincent and Bridgie M. (Mullen) D.; student U. San Francisco, 1955-61, Munson's Sch. Bus., 1957-58, D'Youville Coll., 1965, DeAnza Jr. Coll., 1967-68. Clk. typist to buyer F.W. Woolworth Co., San Francisco, 1955-58; asst. law librarian, sec. City Atty.'s Office, San Francisco, 1958-59; sec., girl friday P.J. Rhodes and Co., San Francisco, 1959-61; sec. to Western sales mgr. Firestone Tire and Rubber Co., San Francisco, 1961-64; sec. to pres. Beal's McCarthy & Rodgers, Inc., Buffalo, 1964-67, Pacific Abrasive/Carborundum Co., Santa Clara, Calif., 1967-69; adminstrv. sec. to pres., chmn. bd. Kanda Corp., San Jose, Calif., 1969-73; sec. to v.p. Western div. Am./Dixie Sales, Am. Can Co., Hayward, Calif., 1973-76, sales analyst, 1976-78, sales devel. analyst, 1978; mgr. sales planning Calif. Canners and Growers, San Francisco, 1978-79, mgr. sales planning and control, 1979-80, mgr. sales and mktg. services, 1980-84; brand product mgr. Tri/Valley Growers, San Francisco, 1984-87; sales adminstrn. mgr. Brands, 1987—. Mem. Am. Mgmt. Assn., Montalvo Assn. Arts. Democrat. Roman Catholic. Club: Commonwealth (San Francisco). Home: 100 Kinross Dr Apt 17 Walnut Creek CA 94598 Office: Tri/Valley Growers 1255 Battery St PO Box 7114 San Francisco CA 94120

DONEGAN, JUDITH HIGGINS, physician, anesthesiology educator; b. Peoria, Ill., Aug. 14, 1939; d. John Franklin and Jane (Walker) Higgins; m. William Laurence Donegan, Dec. 21, 1963; children: William David, Elizabeth. MD, Washington U., St. Louis, 1964; PhD, Med. Coll. Wis., 1983. Diplomate Am. Bd. Anesthesiology. Resident in anesthesiology U. Mo. Sch. Medicine, Columbia, 1965-67, asst. prof. anesthesia, 1968-74; staff anesthesiologist Boone County (Mo.) Hosp., Columbia, 1967-68; asst. prof. Med. Coll. Wis., Milw., 1975-80, assoc. prof., 1980-84; prof. U. Calif., San Francisco, 1984—. Author, editor: Cardiopulmonary Resuscitation, 1982; contbr. articles to profl. jours., chpts. to books. Fellow Am. Coll. Anesthesiologists (bd. govs.); mem. Internat. Anesthesia Research Soc. (trustee 1981—), Soc. Neurosurg. Anesthesia, Am. Soc. Anesthesiologists, Calif. Soc Anesthesiologists. Avocations: horseback riding, skiing. Office: U Calif Dept Anesthesia C-455 San Francisco CA 94143

DONGES, SAMUEL ARNOLD, process control engineer; b. Ashland, Ohio, Oct. 9, 1938; s. George H. and Cathlean (Vanosdall) D. Student, Metro State Coll., 1970-74. Ore inspector Martin Co., Denver, 1961-62; water commr. City of Frisco, Colo., 1962-65; contract adminstr. Man. Services Inc., Huntsville, Ala., 1966-68; prodn. supr. Honeywell Inc., Denver, 1969-70; process CTL engr. Armco Autometrics, Boulder, 1970—. Vol. Fire Dept., Boulder, 1970—. Served with USN, 1956-60. Mem. Instrument Soc. Am. Lodges: Elks, Masons (32 degree). Avocations: photography, electronics, computers. Home: PO Box 1384 Boulder CO 80301 Office: Armco Autometries 7077 Winchester Circle Boulder CO 80301

DONISTHORPE, CHRISTINE ANN, state senator; b. Christina, Mont., May 31, 1932; d. Lambert A. and Ludmilla (Hruska) Benes; m. Oscar Lloyd Donisthorpe, 1951; children—Paul, Karen, Bruce, Brian. Student U. Mont., 1951-53, San Juan Coll., N.Mex. Real Estate Sch., 1958-70. Pres. Bd. of Edn., Bloomfield, N.Mex., 1975-81; mem. N.Mex. State Senate, 1979—, mem. edn. com., 1979, fin. com., 1980, edn. study com., 1981; mem. Bd. Realtors San Juan County, 1978-81. Adv. bd. Salvation Army, 1970-75; active C. of C. Recipient U.S. Soil and Water Conservation award, 1967; Hon. State Future Farmers Adv. award, 1975. Mem. N.Mex. Hay Growers Assn. Republican. Methodist. Address: PO Box 746 Bloomfield NM 87413

DONLEY, RUSSELL LEE, III, engineer, former state representative; b. Salt Lake City, Feb. 3, 1939; s. R. Lee and Leona (Sherwood) D.; m. Karen Kocherhans, June 4, 1960; children: Tammera Sue, Tonya Kay, Christina Lynn. B.S. in Civil Engring. with honors, U. Wyo., 1961; M.S. in Engring., U. Fla., 1962. Registered profl. engr., Wyo., Mont., Colo., N.Y. land surveyor, Wyo. Mem. Wyo. Ho. of Reps., 1969-84, chmn. appropriations com., 1975-78, mem. rules com., 1973-84; chmn. rules com. Wyo. Ho. Reps., 1983-84; majority floor leader Wyo. Ho. of Reps., 1979-80, speaker pro tem, 1981-82, chmn. legis. mgmt. council, 1983-84, speaker of house, 1983-84; chmn. bd. Nat. Ctr. Constl. Studies, Wyo. region 1983—. Chmn. Western Region Council State Govts., 1982-83; Republican candidate for gov. Wyo., 1986; precinct committeeman Rep. Party, 1967; chmn. Wyo. Young. Reps., 1968; fin. chmn. Natrona County Rep. Party, 1970; pres. bd. dirs. YMCA, Casper, 1976-77. Recipient award for engring. excellence Am. Cons. Engrs. Council; recipient Legislator of Yr. award Nat. Republican Legislators Assn., 1981; named Wyo. Outstanding Young Engr. Sigma Tau, 1974, Disting. Wyo. Engr. Tau Beta Pi., 1976. Former mem. Am. Water Works Assn., Nat. Soc. Profl. Engrs., Wyo. Soc. Profl. Engrs., Wyo. Engring. Soc., Wyo. Assn. Cons. Engrs. and Surveyors. Mormon. Home: 1140 Ivy Ln Casper WY 82609 Office: 240 S Wolcott St Casper WY 82601

DONNELLY, GARY DENNIS, public relations representative; b. Newport, Oreg., May 11, 1944; s. Wallace J. and Dorothy Mildred (VanHine) D.; m. Betty Jo Glessner, Sept. 7, 1963 (div. 1974); children: Matthew Scott, Robert Christian. Student, Oreg. Coll. Edn. With prodn. dept. KEZI-TV, Eugene, Oreg., 1964-68; reporter, photographer KVAL-TV, Eugene, 1968-74; div. news rep. Pacific Power, Casper, Wyo., 1974-78, sr. pub. info./ pub. relations rep., 1978—; pres. Wyo. Advt. Fedn., Casper, 1976-77; chmn. pub. relations com. Rocky Mt. Elec. League, Denver, 1976-78. Mem. One Cent Sales Tax Subcom., Casper, 1977; bd. dirs. Jackson County March of Dimes, Medford, Oreg., 1981, So. Oreg. Air Show, Medford, 1982-83; coordinator Amateur Radio Emergency Services, Medford, 1983-85. Charter mem. Oreg. Broadcast Pioneers; mem. Oreg. Assn. Broadcasters, Casper C. of C. Republican. Episcopalian. Lodges: Lions, Elks, De Molay. Avocations: amateur radio, athletics. Home: 1005 Wabash PO Box 613 Medford OR 97501 Office: Pacific Power PO Box 459 Medford OR 97501

DONNELLY, GARY MICHAEL, marketing educator; b. Wendell, Idaho, Feb. 22, 1950; s. Paul E. Donnelly and Marjorie (Brown) Ehresman; m. Julie Halseth, June 30, 1978; children: Stephanie Lynn, Katie Lynn, Gary Michael Jr. AA, Coll. So. Idaho, 1970; BS in Bus. Edn., U. Idaho, 1974, MEd, 1978. Tchr. bus. Globe (Ariz.) High Sch., 1974-76; salesman Hudsons Shoes, Twin Falls, Idaho, 1976-79; tchr. bus. Boise (Idaho) High Sch., 1979-80, Emmett (Idaho) High Sch., 1980-81; instr. mktg. and retail Casper (Wyo.) Coll., 1981—; mktg. cons. Donnelly & Assocs., Casper, 1981—; counselor Small Bus. Adminstrn., Casper, 1982—. Mem. vertical bus. curriculum com., Casper, 1985—; mem. subcom. Wyo. Bus. Devel. Ctr., 1985—. Named to Distributive Edn. Hall of Fame, Mktg. and Distributive Edn. div. Am. Vocat. Assn., 1975. Mem. Western Mktg. Educators Assn. Avocation: traveling. Home: 5221 S Oak Casper WY 82601

DONNELLY, JOHN JAMES, munition researcher; b. Chgo., Aug. 21, 1946; s. Walter John and Arleen (Gilman) D.; m. Ann M. Miller, June 1966 (div. 1975); children: Jill Marie, Jason John; m. Judy Ann, July, 1985. Student, Mass. Coll. Pharmacy, 1964-65, Boston Coll., 1966. Owner NAI/Ballistek, Lake Havasu City, Ariz., 1970—; planner Gates Learjet, Tucson, 1978-79; sr. mfg. engr. Mc Culloch Corp., Lake Havasu City, 1979-82; handloading editor Communication Group, Ft. Lauderdale, Fla., 1982—; editor Am. Firearms Industry mag., 1982—; indsl. engr. Crpft Metals, 1986—. Author: Handloader's Guide to Cartridge Conversions, 1986; contbr. articles to profl. jours. Mem. Soc. Mining Engrs., Soc. Mfg. Engrs., Nat. Rifle Assn. (life). Republican. Avocations: reading, writing, computer tech., mfg. tech. Home: 2387 Clarke Dr Lake Havasu City AZ 86403 Office: Northwest Ariz Industries Ballistek PO Box 535 Lake Havasu City AZ 86403

DONNELLY, KURT DENNIS, architectural designer; b. Roseburg, Oreg., Mar. 24, 1959; s. William Leslie and Jacqueline Nell (Kennedy) D.; m. Maria Katsoulis, Nov. 3, 1984; 1 child, Jacqueline Demetra. BArch, U. Oreg., 1982. Draftsman S. Harriman and Assocs., Walnut Creek, Calif., 1982-83; sr. designer Dahlin Group, Inc., San Ramon, Calif., 1983—. Official umpire Amateur Softball Assn., Oreg., 1978-82. Greek Orthodox. Lodges: Masons (Master Mason), Order of Demolay. Avocations: collecting baseball cards, theater, sports. Home: 1743 Carmel Dr #33 Walnut Creek CA 94596

DONOVAN, DENNIS FRANCIS, banker, lawyer; b. Duluth, Minn., Jan. 29, 1925; s. Dennis Francis and Gertrude (Flaherty) D.; m. Lila Lindeman Munyon, Aug. 12, 1950; children: Kathleen Donovan Walsh, Theresa Donovan Brown, Dorothy Donovan; m. Marie Kendrick, Oct. 9, 1983. B.A., U. Minn., 1948, 1952, J.D., 1952. Bar: Minn. 1952, Calif. 1962. Ptnr. McCabe, VanEvera, et al, Duluth, 1952-61; assoc. U.S. atty. U.S. Dept. Justice, Los Angeles, 1961-64; assoc. Gendel, Raskoff, et al, Los Angeles, 1964-67; ptnr. Donovan & Somers, Los Angeles, 1967-82; v.p., sr. counsel Union Bank, Los Angeles, 1982; v.p., asst. gen. counsel Mitsui Mfrs. Bank, Los Angeles, 1983—; ptnr. Esters & Donovan, 1986—; judge pro-tem Los Angeles Mcpl. Court, 1972-84; mem. exec. com. trial lawyer's sect. Los Angeles County Bar, 1977-80; dir. Legal Aid Soc., Duluth, 1957-59. Editor, contbr. to legal jours. Bd. dirs. Duluth Jr. C. of C., 1958, Duluth Playhouse, 1958; chmn. Duluth Port Authority Com., 1959. Served with USN, 1944-46, PTO. Mem. ABA, Los Angeles County Bar Assn. (exec. com. 1977-80), State Bar of Calif. (conf. of dels. 1977-78), U. Minn. Alumni Assn. (chmn. Los Angeles chpt. 1970). Club: Los Angeles Athletic. Home: 105 Crest Verde Dr Rolling Hills Estates CA 90276 Office: Mitsui Mfrs Bank 135 E 9th St Los Angeles CA 90055

DONOVAN, JESSICA ELLEN, geologist; b. Phila., Dec. 17, 1949; d. Neil Benjamin and Dorothy Ellen (Olszewski) D.; m. Jonathan F. Stebbins. B.A., Rutgers U., 1975, M.A., Harvard U., 1977. Registered geologist, Calif., 1983. Sr. geologist, project geologist, staff geologist Dames & Moore, Honolulu, 1977-79, San Francisco, 1979—; speaker Options in Engring. and Sci., Expanding Your Horizons career confs. Mem. Assn. Women Geoscientists (nat. pres. 1981-82, disting. service award 1986), Geol. Soc. Am., Mineral. Soc. Am., AAAS. Club: Commonwealth (San Francisco). Author conf. abstracts. Office: 221 Main St Suite 600 San Francisco CA 94105

DONZE, JERRY LYNN, electrical engineer; b. Wauneta, Nebr., June 12, 1943; s. John Henry and Virgina May (Francis) D.; m. Marilyn Grace Bascue, Feb. 22, 1964 (div. May. 1980); children: Scott. L., Michele A.; m. Sandra Kay Morris, July 25, 1981. Cert. technician, Denver Inst. Tech., 1964; BSEE, U. Colo., 1972; postgrad., Advanced Metaphysics Inst. Religios Sci., 1986. Electronic technician A.B.M. Co., Lakewood, Colo., 1964-71; computer programmer Nat. Bur. Standards, Boulder, Colo., 1971-72; electronic engr. Autometrics Co., Boulder, Colo., 1972-76, Gates Research and Devel., Denver, 1976-77; devel. engr. Emerson Electric Co., Lakewood, 1977; engring. mgr. Storage Tech., Louisville, Colo., 1977—; cons. Sun Co., Arvada, Colo., 1974-75. Patentee in field. Mem. IEEE Student Soc. (treas. 1971-72), Eta Kappa Nu. Religious Scientist. Avocation: giving workshops and presentations. Home: 6658 Alkire Ct Arvada CO 80004 Office: Storage Tech 2270 S 88th Tape Power M/S 3R Louisville CO 80004

DOOLEY, GEORGE JOSEPH, III, metallurgist; b. Greenwich, Conn., Aug. 8, 1941; s. George Joseph and Susan Marilyn (Robustelli) D.; m. Betty Louise Roach, Sept. 7, 1963 (div.); children: Deborah Susan, Jennifer Ann, Daniel Paul; m. Mary Khrys Von Tellrop, Oct. 27, 1984; children: Samantha Joel, Charles Douglas, Anastacia Halley, James Huston, Cynthia Maureen, Sandra Robin. BS, U. Notre Dame, 1963; MS, Iowa State U., 1966; PhD, Oreg. State U., 1969. Research asst. Ames (Iowa) Lab. AEC, 1963-66; research metallurgist U.S. Bur. Mines, Albany, Oreg., 1966-68, dir. Albany Research Ctr., 1984—; research scientist Aerospace Research Labs. USAF, Wright Patterson AFB, Ohio, 1968-72; dir. research and devel. Oreg. Metall. Corp., Albany, 1974-83, dir. metall. and quality assurance, 1983-84; mem. metallurgy adv. bd. Linn Benton Community Coll., Albany, 1976—. Contbr. articles to profl. jours. Served to capt. USAF, 1968-72. Mem. Am. Soc. Metals, AIME, Am. Vacuum Soc., Am. Phys. Soc., Sigma Xi, Alpha Sigma Mu, Phi Lambda Upsilon. Democrat. Roman Catholic. Home: 8804 NW Arboretum Rd Corvallis OR 97330 Office: US Bur Mines Albany Research Ctr 1450 Queen Ave SW PO Box 70 Albany OR 97321

DOOLEY, GERALD FRANCIS, univ. adminstr., former marine corps officer; b. Lowell, Mass., Apr. 26, 1935; s. William Edmund and Gertrude Frances (Killeen) D.; m. Eleanor Josephine Bernat, Oct. 31, 1955; children: Deborah Jean, Stephen Patrick, David Gerald. Diploma, U.S. Armed Forces Inst., 1954, U.S. Air Force Sch. Applied Aerospace Scis., 1976; degree in polit. sci. Saddleback Coll., 1979. Enlisted in U.S. Marine Corps, 1953, advanced through grades to lt. col., 1974; presdl. helicopter pilot, 1967-70; ret., 1978; dir. facilities Saddleback Coll. Dist., Mission Viejo, Calif., 1980-85; dir. facilities Trammell Crow Co., Irvine, Calif., 1985—; aviation cons. Coach, Metro. Collegiate Baseball League, 1972-79, personnel dir., 1979—; chmn. Workman Med./Rehab. Fund, 1975—; mem. Nat. Rep. Congl. Com., 1982, presdl. task force. Decorated D.F.C. (2), Air medal (32), Purple Heart; recipient Presdl. Medal of Merit, 1983. Mem. Assn. Profl. Energy Engrs., DAV, Mil. Order of Purple Heart, Marine Corps Assn., Ret. Officers' Assn. Roman Catholic. Contbr. articles to profl. jours. Home: 26372 Via Conchita Mission Viejo CA 92691 Office: 3333 Michelson Dr Irvine CA 92715

DOOLEY, HELEN BERTHA, artist, art gallery owner; b. San Jose, Calif., July 27, 1907; s. George W. and Frances (Arwine) Macrae D. AB, San Jose State Coll., 1928; MA, Claremont Grad. Sch., 1939; postgrad. Douglas Donaldson Sch. of Design, Hollywood, 1933, Calif. Sch. Fine Arts, 1933-34, Chouinard Art Inst., Los Angeles, 1935, U. Calif., Berkeley, 1937-39, Columbia U., 1948. Tchr. Scripps Coll., 1937-39, San Jose State Coll., 1940-55, 56; art supr. Kern County Schs., 1939-48; prof. U. Pacific Stockton, 1948-68; owner Dooley Gallery, Carmel, Calif., 1965—. One man shows include U. of the Pacific, 1961, 63, 68, San Jose Art League Gallery, 1962, Artists' Guild, Carmel, 1962, Haggin Mus. and Art Gallery, Stockton, 1962, Seven Arts Gallery, Bakersfield, 1963, Lord and Taylor Galleries, N.Y.C., 1969, Carmel Art Assn. Galleries, 1965, 71, 73, 77, 79, Art Works Gallery, Fair Oaks, Calif., 1978, 80, Stary-Sheets Gallery, Gualala, Calif., 1983, Farnsworth Gallery, San Francisco, 1986; exhibited in group shows at Am. Watercolor Soc., Nat. Acad. Galleries, N.Y.C., Pa. Acad. Fine Arts, Oakland Art Mus., Laguna Beach Art Festival, Los Angeles County Art Exhbn., Mission Galleries, Taos, N.Mex., West Coast Watercolor Soc., San Francisco traveling shows, Royal Watercolor Soc., London, Gronbeck Gallery, Morro Bay, Watercolor Gallery, Berkeley, Noroton Gallery, Darien, Conn.; represented in permanent collections: Shimizu Art Mus., Japan, U. Pacific, Stockton, Monterey Peninsula Mus. Art, Irving Coleman Library, U. of the Pacific, Stockton; also pvt. collections. Recipient First and Third awards Soc. Western Artists, DeYoung Mus., San Francisco, 1951, 54, Stockton Art League, Haggin Mus., 1956, 1st and 2d awards Monterey County Fair, 1955, Grumbacher award Crocker Gallery, Sacramento, 1954, Mother Lode Art Assn., Sonora, 1971, 1st Prize watercolor Lodi Art Assn., Top award 6th Ann. Exhibit Contemporary Religious Art, Carmel, 1967, award in contemporary oil painting Calif. State Fair, 1965, award Monterey Peninsula Mus. Art, 1967. Mem. Carmel Art Assn., West Coast Water Color Soc. Republican. Methodist. Office: Dooley Gallery Box 5577 Carmel CA 93921

DOOLITTLE, WILLIAM HOTCHKISS, internist; b. Cheshire, Conn., June 20, 1929; s. Joseph Delos and Geraldine (Lincoln) D.; B.S., U. Vt., 1956, M.D., 1960; m. Marla M. Rescott; 1 son, William Lawrence. Commd. lt. M.C., U.S. Army, 1959, advanced through grades to lt. col., 1971; intern U.S. Army Hosp., Fort Bragg, N.C., 1959-60; resident in internal medicine Walter Reed Gen. Hosp., Washington, 1961-64, ret., 1973; practice medicine specializing in internal medicine, Fairbanks, Alaska, 1973—; dir. Arctic Med. Research Lab. Alaska, Ft. Wainwright; pres. Fairbanks Internal Medicine and Diagnostic Center; staff Fairbanks Meml. Hosp., chief of staff, 1974-76. Bd. dirs. Fairbanks Meml. Hosp. Found. Served with USAF, 1947-53. Decorated Army Commendation medal, Legion of Merit. Diplomate Am. Bd. Internal Medicine. Fellow A.C.P.; mem. AAAS, AMA, Alaska Med. Assn., Fairbanks Med. Soc., Assn. Mil. Surgeons, Alpha Omega Alpha. Republican. Episcopalian. Club: Rotary. Contbr. articles in field to profl. jours. Home: 666 11th Ave Apt 207 Fairbanks AK 99701 Office: 1919 Lathrop St Fairbanks AK 99701

DOOR, JO EVELYN, social work administrator; b. Tulsa, Aug. 1, 1945; d. Robert Joseph and Evelyn (Emerson) Harlan; m. Raymond Ivan Kelley, July 21, 1964 (div. Oct. 1984); children: Mary Evelyn Kelley Armstead, Christina; m. Jo James Michael Door. Student, Connor State Coll., 1963-64; BA in Social Studies, Northeastern State U., Tahlequah, Okla., 1966; MA in Guidance Counseling, U. Mo., 1972. Social studies tchr. Hartshorne (Okla.) Pub. Schs., 1966-67; elem., secondary sch. tchr. Sullivan (Mo.) Pub. Schs., 1967-72; regional sales rep. Photo Corp. of Am. of Kans., Lenexa Bus. Ctr., 1973; caseworker I State of Mo. Div. Family Services, St. Louis, 1975, social service worker, 1975-76, socila service supr. I, 1976-77, social supr. II, 1977-78, staff devel. specialist I, 1978-79; program, policy devel. specialist State of Mo. Div. Family Services, Jefferson City, 1979; social service supr. V-Eastern region grants and contract mgr. State of Mo. Div. Aging, St. Louis, 1979-81; social service supr. V-statewide assessment coordinator, service dept. mgr., acting dept. dir. State of Mo. Div. Aging, Jefferson City, 1981; agy. adminstr. Medigroup Mgmt. Corp. Coodinated Health Services, St. Louis, 1981-82; adminstr. I Beverly Enterprises Sullivan Nursing Ctr., Sullivan, Mo., 1982-84, sr. adminstr. I, 1984-85, regional mgr. Colo. and N.Mex., 1985—. Named Bus. Person on Month, Sullivan C. of C., 1983. Mem. Bus. and Profl. Women's Club (program chmn. 1982-86), Pi Gamma Mu, Alpha Chi. Roman Catholic. Home: 741 Lone Pine Dr PO Box 3934 Estes Park CO 80517 Office: Beverly Enterprises 2121 Mesa Dr Boulder CO 80302

DOPP, ALICE FLORENCE, librarian; b. Detroit, Oct. 28, 1931; d. Kenneth Wilton and Florence Caroline (Gabriel) Marsh; m. James Wellington Dopp, Jr., Aug. 1, 1969; m. Harold Lewis Allen, Aug. 1, 1953 (div. July 1960); 1 child, Laurie Jeanne. B.A., Wayne State U., 1965; M.L.S., U. Mich., 1967. Reference librarian Detroit Pub. Library, 1967-69; cataloger San Luis Obispo (Calif.) City Library, 1970-73; head tech. services San Luis Obispo City/County Library, 1973-78; head tech. services Las Vegas-Clark County Library Dist., 1981—; cons. San Luis Obispo Friends of Library, 1975-78; organizer, cons. Second Edit. Book Store, Las Vegas, 1982-83. Art tchr. local 500, United Auto Workers, Detroit, 1964; bd. mem. Detroit Pub. Library Staff Credit Union, Detroit, 1968; chmn. Internat. Inst. Supper Club, Detroit, 1967. Mem. ALA, Mich. Library Assn., Calif. Library Assn., Nev. Library Assn. (chmn. S.O.U.P. 1983-84), Black Gold Tech. Services Com. (chmn. 1977-78), AAUW. Democrat. Lutheran. Club: Silver Queens Investment (acctg. ptnr. 1981-83) (Las Vegas). Office: Las Vegas-Clark County Library Dist 1401 E Flamingo Rd Las Vegas NV 89119

DOPP, WILLIAM FLOYD, publishing executive; b. Watertown, Wis., Apr. 30, 1942; s. William M. and June K. (White) D.; m. Janet M. Bochnowski, Sept. 8, 1962; children—William J., Douglas F. B.S. in Bus. and Journalism, Ind. U., 1969. With Wall St. Jour., N.Y.C., 1965-68, Chgo. Tribune, 1969-71; v.p., sales mgr. Chicagoland Broadcasters, Inc., 1971-76; pres. TDM Advt., Arlington Heights, Ill., 1976-79; pres., owner Great Western Advt., San Diego, 1979-84; editor, pub. Exec. News bus. mag., Escondido, Calif., 1984—; seminar leader San Diego State U., Palomar, Calif. Author: Copywriter's Idea Book, 1982. Founder, treas. Rancho Bernardo Hist. Soc., San Diego. Mem. Advt. Writers League Calif., Rancho Bernardo C. of C., Escondido (Calif.) C. of C., Ind. U. Alumni Assn. (San Diego), Sigma Chi, Sigma Chi Alumni Assn. of San Diego (pres.). Episcopalian. Lodge: Elks. Home: 2141 N Nutmeg St Escondido CA 92026 Office: Exec News Mag 1523 E Valley Pkwy Escondido CA 92027

DORAN, DOROTHY FITZ, business educator; b. Nekoosa, Wis., Feb. 27, 1934; d. Edwin E. and Ruby E. (Burch) Larson; m. John David Doran; children—Jean Marie Fitz Harkey, Kenneth Lee Fitz, Cynthia Ann Fitz Whitney. B.S. with high distinction in Bus. and English, No. Ariz. U., 1969; M.A. in English, 1971; Ed.D. in Bus., Ariz. State U., 1980. Tchr. English, Cottonwood (Ariz.) Oak Creek Elem. Sch., 1969-70; tchr. bus. and English, Mingus Union High Sch., Cottonwood, 1970-79, dir. vocat. edn., 1976-79; mem. faculty dept. office adminstrn. Yavapai Coll., 1979—, chairperson Bus. div., 1981—; cons. Ariz. Dept. Edn. Mem. Ariz. Bus. Edn. Assn. (pres. 1980-81), Nat. Bus. Edn. Assn., Am. Vocat. Assn., Ariz. Edn. Assn., NEA, Internat. Word/Info. Processing Assn., Pi Omega Pi, Delta Pi Epsilon, Phi Kappa Phi, Alpha Delta Kappa, Phi Delta Kappa. Republican. Club: Soroptimists Internat. Editor Ariz. Bus. Edn. Newsletter, 1972-74. Home: 1195 Solar Heights Dr Prescott AZ 86301 Office: 1100 E Sheldon Prescott AZ 86301

DORAN, MARTHA SUTTON, corporation executive, accountant; b. Escondido, Calif., Mar. 7, 1952; d. Carl Leon and Jean (Godard) Sutton; m. Gary Wayne Doran, Dec. 27, 1975. B.A., Stephens Coll., 1973; postgrad. Ariz. State U., 1979-80, postgrad. studies, Portland (Ore.) State U., 1984—. C.P.A., Calif. Acct. Acosta, Cordova & Pittman C.P.A.s, Phoenix, 1978-80, Apodaca, Finocchiaro & Co. C.P.A.s, Pasadena, Calif., 1980-81; controller Bill Palmer Assocs., El Monte, Calif., 1981-84; supervising sr. tax dept. KMG Main Hurdman, Portland, Ore., 1984-85; mgr. comml. acctg. Acosta, Cordova and Pittman, Phoenix, 1985—. Mem. Am. Inst. CPA's, Ariz. Soc. CPA's, Stephens Coll. Alumnae Assn. (pres. San Gabriel Valley). Republican. Christian Scientist.

DORAN, VINCENT JAMES, steel fabricating company consultant; b. Ephrata, Wash., June 13, 1917; s. Samuel Vincent and Sarah Anastasia (Fitzpatrick) D.; B. Phil., Gonzaga U., Spokane, 1946; m. Jean Arlene Birrer, Jan. 15, 1949; children—Vincent James, Mollie Jean, Michele Lee, Patrick Michael. Mgr., Flying Service, Coulee Dam, Wash., 1947-58; mgr. constrn. Morrison-Knudsen Co., Wash. and Alaska, 1959-60; co-owner C.R. Foss Inc., constrn., Anchorage, 1961-64; mgr. Steel Fabricators, Anchorage, 1965-86. Active Boy Scouts Am.; co-founder, pres. Chugach Rehab. Assn., 1962; mem. Alaska Gov.'s Rehab. Adv. Bd., 1962-63; mem. CAP. Served with USAAF, 1943-45, USAF, 1949-50. Decorated Air medal with 4 clusters. Mem. Anchorage C. of C., Welding Inst. Alaska (co-organizer, dir. 1977-78). Roman Catholic. Club: Toastmasters. Compiler, pub. home owners' and builders' guide to sun's positions in N.Am. during solstices and equinoxes, designer packaged water, sewage treatment plants and water collection systems Arctic communities. Home: 3811 Knik Ave Anchorage AK 99517 Office: Steel Fabricators 2131 Railroad Ave Anchorage AK 99501

DORAY, ANDREA WESLEY, marketing consultant, account services executive, writer; b. Monte Vista, Colo., Oct. 4, 1956; d. Dant Bell and Rosemary Ann (Kassap) D.; m. Paul Dean Doray, Nov. 25, 1978. BA, U. No. Colo., 1977. Cert. post secondary tchr. Asst. advt. mgr. San Luis Valley Publ. Co., Monte Vista, 1977-78; mktg. dir. Stuart Scott & Assocs. (formerly Philip Winn & Assocs.), Colorado Springs, 1978-80; sr. v.p. Heisley Design and Advt., Colorado Springs, 1980-85; pres., creative dir. Doray Doray, Monument, Colo., 1985—; account services dir. Praco Ltd., Advt., Colorado Springs, 1987—; pt. time instr. Pikes Peak Community Coll., Colorado Springs, 1983-86;project bus. cons. Jr. Achievement, Colorado Springs, 1985-86; mem. mktg. adv. council Pikes Peak Community Coll., Colorado Springs, 1985—; spkr. Colorado Springs C. of C. Small Bus. Council, 1985, Pikes Peak Advt. Fedn., Colorado Springs, 1986—; guest lectr. Colo. Mountain Coll., 1982-84, U. So. Colo., 1983, Pikes Peak Community Coll, 1983—. Author: The Other Fish, 1976, Oil Painting Lessons, 1986, Coming to Terms, 1986, Roger Douglas, 1987; contbg. editor Colorado Springs Bus. Mag., 1984—; creative writer World Cycling Fedn. Championships, Colorado Springs, 1986. Mem. mktg. adv. council Pikes Peak Community Coll., Colorado Springs, 1985-86; chmn. Colorado Springs Local Advt. Review Program, 1985; chmn., advt. pub. relations task force exec. com. U.S. Olympic Hall of Fame, 1986; mem. State Legis. Alert and Action Coalition, 1985—. Named one of Colorado Springs Leading Women, Colorado Springs Gazette Telegraph, 1984, Outstanding Young Woman of Yr., State of Colo., 1986. Mem. Pikes Peak Advt. Fedn. (pres. 1984-86, Advt. Person of Yr. award), Am. Advt. Fedn. (chmn. dist. 12 legis. com. 1985—, pub. relations com. 1986, Silver medal award 1986). Avocations: sports, reading, writing, skiing, cycling. Office: Praco Ltd PO Box 387 Colorado Springs CO 80901

DORE, BONNY ELLEN, film and TV production company executive; b. Cleve., Aug. 16, 1947; s. Reber Hutson and Ellen Elizabeth (McNamara) Barnes; m. James Llewellyn Metz, Feb. 20, 1977 (div. Aug. 1986); m. Sanford Astor, May 22, 1987. BA, U. Mich., 1969, MA, 1975. Cert. tchr., Mich. Dir., tchr. Plymouth (Mich.) Community Schs., 1969-72; gen. mgr. Sta. WSDP-FM, Plymouth, 1970-72; prodn. supr. pub. TV N.Y. State Dept. Edn., 1972-74; producer TV series Hot Fudge Sta. WXYZ-TV, Detroit, 1974-75; mgr. children's programs ABC TV Network, Los Angeles, 1975, dir. children's programs, 1975-76, dir. prime time variety programs, 1976-77; dir. devel. Hanna-Barbera, Los Angeles, 1977; v.p. devel. and prodn. Krofft Entertainment, Los Angeles, 1977-81, Centerpoint Prodn., Los Angeles, 1981-82; pres., owner The Greif-Dore Co. in assn. with Orion TV, Los Angeles, 1983—. Producer (TV series) The Krofft Superstar Hour, 1978 (2 Emmy awards 1979), (mini-series) Sins, 1986, numerous others. Named Outstanding Young Tchr. of Yr., Cen. States Speech Assn., 1973; Cert. of Appreciation, Gov. of Mich., 1985, City of Beverly Hills, Calif., 1985. Mem. Women in Film (v.p. 1978-81, pres. 1980-81), Women in Film Found. (trustee 1981—), Acad. TV Arts and Scis., Beverly Hills C. of C. (cons. 1985). Home: 15150 Dickens Condo 307 Sherman Oaks CA 91403 Office: Orion TV Studios 11500 W Olympic Blvd Suite 300 West Los Angeles CA 90064

DORE, FRED HUDSON, state supreme ct. justice; b. Seattle, July 31, 1925; s. Fred Hudson and Ruby T. (Kelly) D.; B.S.F.S., Georgetown Fgn. Service Sch., 1946; J.D., Georgetown U., 1949; m. Mary S. Shuham, Nov. 26, 1956; children: Margaret, Fred Hudson, Teresa, Tim, Jane. Bar: Wash. 1949. Practiced in Seattle, 1949-77; mem. Wash. Ho. of Reps., 1953-59, Wash. State Senate, 1959-74; judge Wash. State Ct. Appeals, 1977-80; justice Wash. State Supreme Ct., Olympia, 1981—. Office: State Supreme Ct Temple Justice Olympia WA 98504

DORF, MILTON IRVING, law office administrator; b. Newport News, Va., June 4, 1921; s. Samuel Leonard and Mary Madeline (Moore) D.; A.B. magna cum laude, Washington Coll., Chestertown, Md., 1942; m. Barbara Elaine Levine, Oct. 19, 1949; children—Lauren, Steven. Buyer gen. mdse. Penn Fruit Co., Phila., 1955-60, dir. gen. mdse., 1960-69, also dir. Quaker Drug store chain div., 1967-69; dir. gen. mdse. Bohack Corp., N.Y.C., 1969-71, also v.p. Bohack Super Drugs stores, 1970-71; pres. Drug Pride Corp. div. Food Fair Stores, Inc., Phila., 1971-78; mem. exec. com. J. M. Fields Dept. Store, Phila., 1975—; pres. Argold Press, Inc., 1978—; mem. gen. mdse. com. Supermarket Inst., also Topco Assocs.; owner The Magic Lens.; office mgr. Law Offices of Steven B. Dorf, Los Angeles, 1984—. Pres., Laverock Civic Assn., Wyncote, Pa., 1956-69. Served to lt. USCG, 1942-45. Mem. Nat. Assn. Chain Drug Stores. Jewish. Club: Rotary. Home: 8455 Fountain Ave Apt 722 Los Angeles CA 90069

DORFMAN, HERBERT, chemist, staff scientist; b. N.Y.C., Jan. 6, 1919; s. William Dorfman and Gussie (Weiss) Singer; m. Frances Teresa Allen, Feb. 15, 1975. BS, U. Wis., 1950; postgrad., Bklyn. Coll. of CUNY, U. Calif., Berkeley, De Anza Coll., Foothill Coll. Ordnance chemist Picatinny Arsenal, Dover, N.J., 1951-53; ordnance engr. Temco, Inc., Nashville, 1953-56; research chemist Atlantic Research, Saugus, Calif., 1956-58; sr. staff scientist Lockheed Missiles and Space Co., Sunnyvale, Calif., 1958—; lectr. Ctr. Profl. Advancement, San Mateo, Calif. and East Brunswick, N.J., also various socs. and symposiums. Contbr. elec. and tech. articles to profl. jours. Served with U.S. Army, 1941-45. Named Employee of Month, Lockheed Missiles and Space Co., Sept. 1983; recipient Material Command award USN, 1983. Mem. Calif. Circuits Assn. (Lockheed Missiles and Space co. rep.), Inst. for Interconnecting and Packaging Elec. Circuits (mem. process effects, multilayer and Environ. protection coms.), Internat. Electronics Packaging Soc., Am. Electroplaters Soc. Lodges: Elks, Masons. Avocations: sailing.

DORFMAN, STEVEN DAVID, space and communications company executive; b. Bklyn., Sept. 26, 1935; s. Murray Dorfman and Eleanor Judith (Blitzer) Pisani; m. Georgina Breckenridge (divorced): 1 child, Jennifer; m. Beverly Joan Pain, Dec. 28, 1965; children: Lorraine, Gene, Lynn. BSEE, U. Fla., 1957; MSEE, U. So. Calif., 1959. Mgr. adv. programs Hughes Aircraft Co., El Segundo, Calif., 1967-72, mgr. Pioneer Venus, 1972-78, assoc. mgr. NASA Systems Div., 1978-82, mgr. NASA Systems Div., 1982-83, exec. v.p. Hughes Communications Div., 1983-86; pres., chief exec. officer Hughes Communications Div. Hughes Aircraft Co., Los Angeles, 1983-86, corp. v.p., 1986—; cons. NASA, Space Systems Technology Adv. Com., Washington, 1982—; mem. U.S. Info. Agy. TV/Telecom Adv. Council, Washington, 1985—. Contbr. articles to profl. jours.; patentee in field. State (Fla.) Senate scholar, 1955-56; recipient Disting. Pub. Service Medal, NASA, 1980. Home: 517 Veteran Ave Los Angeles CA 90024 Office: Hughes Aircraft Co Space & Communications Group PO Box 92919 S41/B345 Los Angeles CA 90009

DORFMONT, LINDA BERNICE, industrial engineer, consultant; b. Los Angeles, Feb. 9, 1947; d. Elmer and Bernice Alberta (Bechestobill) D. BA, Calif. State U., Long Beach, 1968; MBA, U. So. Calif., 1975. Cert. mfg. engr. With Hughes Aircraft Co., Los Angeles, 1969—; prin. Linda Dorfmont E.A., Lawndale, Calif., 1983—; cons. Calif. State U., Fullerton and Northridge, 1984—. Contbr. articles to profl. jours. Mem. Inst. Indsl. Engrs. (sr., v.p. 1977-78, pres. 1979-80, chmn. annual conf. 1985, bd. dirs.), Calif. Soc. Enrolled Agts. (bd. dirs.), Productivity Ctr. S.W. (bd. dirs. 1977-83). Libertarian. Byzantine Catholic. Club: Toastmasters. Avocations: archtl. history, bicycling, Oriental rugs, cartography. Home: 11638 Truro Hawthorne CA 90250 Office: Hughes Aircraft Co PO Box 92426 R1O/10066 Los Angeles CA 90009

DORLAND, FRANK NORTON, art conservator; b. Peru, Nebr., Oct. 11, 1914; s. Frank Norton and Marion Hope (Abbot) D.; student Calif. Christian Coll., 1931-33; San Diego State Coll., 1933-38; m. Mabel Vyvyan Jolliffe, July 29, 1938. Artist preliminary design engring. Convair Co., San Diego, Calif., 1938-49; pvt. practice as art conservator, La Jolla, Calif., 1949-59, San Francisco, 1959-63, Mill Valley, Calif., 1963-73, Santa Barbara, Calif., 1973-85; engaged in authentication and classification art objects; cons. for art assns. galleries, museums, collectors, churches. Mem. Internat. Inst. for Conservation, Internat. Council Museums, Am. Mus. Assn. Pioneer in use of spl. waxes in painting; inventor oil and water mix wax mediums; engaged in research and devel. waxes and resins and properties and usage of electronic quartz crystals, also pioneer biocrystallographer, researcher on crystals and the human mind. Address: PO Box 6233 Los Osos CA 93412-6233

DORMAN, SCOTT JEFFREY, marketing professional; b. St. Louis, Aug. 21, 1957; s. David Alan and Evelyn Ruth (Schwartz) D. B in Journalism, U. Mo., 1980. Promotion mgr. Playboy Enterprises, N.Y.C., 1980-82; nat. sales dir. Nat. Field Mktg., N.Y.C., 1982-85; nat. promotions dir. Diener-Hauser-Bates, Los Angeles, 1985—. Jewish. Club: Young Variety (Los Angeles) (bd. dirs.). Avocations: writing, skiing, tennis.

DORN, DOLORES, actress; b. Chgo., Mar. 3; d. Edward Dorn Heft and Alice Ellen Eagmin; m. Frachot Tone, May 14, 1956 (dec. 1968); m. Ben Piazza, Aug. 6, 1969 (div.). BFA, Goodman Theater; studied with, Uta Hagen, N.Y.C., 1954-56, Lee Strasberg, N.Y.C., 1957-58. Tchr. Am. Film Inst., Los Angeles, 1977—, Lee Strasberg Theater Inst., Los Angeles, 1983—; pvt. coach to stars Los Angeles, 1974—; coach Star Search 1984, Los Angeles, 1984; mem. The Actor's Studio, N.Y.C., here continued work with Lee Strasberg, 1958-82. Appeared in TV shows Simon and Simon, Night Cries, Intimate Strangers, Charlie's Angels, Jigsaw John, Tenafly, Girls of Huntington House, Run for Your Life, Strawberry Blonde, Capitol; appeared in motion pictures Tell Me A Riddle, The Stronger, The Candy Snatchers, Thirteen West Street, Underworld U.S.A., The Bounty Hunter, Uncle Vanya, Murders of the Rue Morgue; appeared in Broadway plays The Midnight Sun, Starward Ark, Hide and Seek; appeared in off-Broadway plays The Pinter Plays, To Damascus, Plays for Bleeker Street, Lime Green Khaki Blue, Between Two Thieves, Uncle Vanya, A Mighty Man Is He. Recipient Best Actress award San Francisco Internat. Film Festival, 1957. Mem. Women in Flim, Actor's Studio, Am. Film Inst. (hon.). Office: care Am Film Inst 2021 N Western Ave Los Angeles CA 90027

DORN, MARIAN MARGARET, educator, sports management administrator; b. North Chicago, Ill., Sept. 25, 1931; d. John and Marian (Petkovsek) Jelovsek; m. Eugene G. Dorn, Aug. 2, 1952 (div. 1975); 1 child, Bradford Jay. B.S., U. Ill., 1953; M.S., U. So. Calif., 1961. Tchr., North Chicago Community High Sch., 1954-56; tchr., advisor activities, high sch., Pico-Rivera, Calif., 1956-62; tchr., coach Calif. High Sch., Whittier, 1962-65; prof. phys. edn., chmn. dept., coach, asst. chmn. div. women's athletic dir. Cypress (Calif.) Coll., 1966—; mgr. Billie Jean King Tennis Ctr., Long Beach, Calif., 1982-86; founder King-Dorn Golf Schs., Long Beach, 1984; pres. So. Calif. Athletic Conf., 1981. Recipient cert. of merit Cypress Elem. Sch. Dist., 1976; Outstanding Service award Cypress Coll., 1986. Mem. Calif. (v.p. So. dist.), San Gabriel Valley (pres.) assns. health, phys. edn. and recreation, So. Calif. Community Coll. Athletic Council (sec., dir. pub. relations), NEA, Calif. Tchrs. Assn., AAHPERD, Ladies Profl. Golf Assn. Republican. Conglist. Author: Bowling Manual, 1974. Home: 21303 Norwalk #121 Lakewood CA 90716 Office: 9200 Valley View Cypress CA 90630

DORN, MICHAEL RAYMOND, city planner; b. Oakland, Calif., Nov. 19, 1948; s. John E. and Virginia (Henneman) D.; B.A., U. Calif.-Berkeley, 1971; M.Urban Planning, San Jose State U., 1976. Archtl. designer Carl Swenson Co., San Jose, Calif., 1971-73; cons. Bini & Assocs. Engrs., Santa Clara, Calif., 1972-75; planning intern City of Menlo Park, 1975-76; planning aide City of Roseville (Calif.), 1977; assoc. planner City of Gilroy (Calif.), 1977-78, dir. planning, 1978—; teaching asst. San Jose State U., 1975-76; guest instr. U. Calif.-Berkeley, 1982; guest lectr. San Jose State U., 1979—. Editor: Historic Building Study, vols. I and II, 1981-82. Pres. bd. dirs. Gilroy Community Theatre, 1984; v.p. bd. dirs. Gilroy Hist. Soc., 1983-84. Mem. Am. Inst. Cert. Planners, Am. Planning Assn., Santa Clara County Assn. Planning Officers, Am. Soc. Pub. Adminstrs. Office: City of Gilroy 7351 Rosanna St Gilroy CA 95020

DORN, ROSE MARIE, advertising executive, computer consultant; b. Milw., Jan. 23, 1946; d. John Paul and Irene Mary (Korenak) D. B.A., U. Wis.-Milw., 1968. Buyer, McCann-Erickson, Milw., 1968-74; sr. media planner and buyer Eisaman Johns & Laws Advt., Los Angeles, 1974-77; sr. media supr. Chiat/Day Advt., Los Angeles, 1977-79; asst. media dir. Dailey & Assocs., Los Angeles, 1979-85; advt., media and computer cons., 1986—; guest lectr. mktg. U. So. Calif. Active McGovern presdl. campaign, 1972, Advt. Industry Emergency Fund, Equal Rights Amendment ratification. Democrat. Roman Catholic. Home and Office: 1522 S Centinela Ave #202 Los Angeles CA 90025

DORNAN, ROBERT KENNETH, congressman; b. N.Y.C., Apr. 3, 1933; s. Harry Joseph and Gertrude Consuelo (McFadden) D.; m. Sallie Hansen, Apr. 16, 1955; children—Robin Marie, Robert Kenneth II, Theresa Ann, Mark Douglas, Kathleen Regina. Student, Loyola U., Westchester, Calif., 1950-53. Nat. spokesman Citizens for Decency Through Law, 1973-76; mem. 95th-97th Congresses from 27th Calif. Dist., 1977-83, 99th-100th Congresses from 38th Calif. Dist., 1985—. Host TV polit. talk shows in Los Angeles, 1965-73; host, producer: Robert K. Dornan Show, Los Angeles, 1970-73; combat photographer/broadcast journalist assigned 8 times to Laos-Cambodia-Vietnam, 1965-74; originator POW/MIA bracelet. Served to capt. as fighter pilot USAF, 1953-58, as fighter pilot and amphibian rescue pilot USAFR, 1958-75. Decorated Commendation awards. Mem. Am. Legion, Navy League, Air Force Assn., Assn. Former Intelligence Officers, AFTRA. Republican. Roman Catholic. Lodge: K.C. Office: Room 301 Cannon House Office Bldg Washington DC 20515 *

DORNEMAN, ROBERT WAYNE, manufacturing engineer; b. Oaklawn, Ill., Nov. 13, 1949; s. Robert John and Julia (Vorchenia) D.; M. Katrina Holland, July 30, 1977; children: Tamara, Tiana. BA in Biol. Sci., Calif. State U., Fullerton, 1974. Mfg. engr. Gen. Telephone Co., Anaheim, Calif., 1974-77, Xerox/Century Data, Anaheim, 1977-80; advance mfg. engr. MSI Data, Costa Mesa, Calif., 1980-83; sr. mfg. engr. Parker Hannifin, Irvine, Calif., 1983-86; sr. advanced mfr. engr. Western Digital, Irvine, 1986—; specialist automated assembly of circuits; cons. Base 2, Fullerton, 1980. Contbr. articles in 3M-Alert to profl. jours. Mem. Nat. Assn. Realtors (broker), N. Orange County Bd. Realtors (broker), Calif. Assn. Realtors, Internat. Soc. Hybrid Mfg., Phillips Ranch Assn., Tau Kappa Epsilon. Republican. Avocations: real estate, auto restorations, landscape architecture, billiards, bridge. Home: 56 Meadow View Dr Phillips Ranch Pomona CA 91766 Office: Western Digital 2801 Main St Irvine CA 92714

DORPAT, THEODORE LORENZ, psychoanalyst; b. Miles City, Mont., Mar. 25, 1925; s. Theodore Ertman and Eda (Christiansen) D.; m. Damaris Elisabeth Suttle, Aug. 11, 1972; 1 dau., Joanne Katherine. B.S., Whitworth Coll., 1948; M.D., U. Wash., 1952; grad., Seattle Psychoanalytic Inst., 1964. Resident in psychiatry Seattle VA Hosp., 1953-55, Cin. Gen. Hosp., 1955-56; instr. in psychiatry U. Wash., 1956-58, asst. prof. psychiatry, 1958-59, assoc. prof., 1969-75, prof., 1976—; practice medicine specializing in psychiatry Seattle, 1958-64; practice psychoanalysis 1964; instr. Seattle Psychoanalytic Inst., 1966-71, tng. psychoanalyt, 1971—, dir., 1984; chmn. Wash. Gov.'s Task Force for Commitment Law Reform; trustee Seattle Community Psychiat. Clinic; pres., trustee Seattle Psychoanalytic Inst. Contbr. numerous articles, revs. to profl. books and jours. Served to ensign USNR, 1943-46. Fellow Am. Psychiat. Assn.; mem. Am. Psychoanalytic Assn., AMA, Seattle Psychoanalytic Soc. (sec.-treas. 1965-67, pres. 1972-73), AAAS, Alpha Omega Alpha, Sigma Xi. Home: 3815 46th Ave NE Seattle WA 98105 Office: 2271 NE 51st St Seattle WA 98105

DORR, AIMEE, educator; b. Los Angeles, Sept. 20, 1942; d. Thomas Osborn and Mary Alice (Perkey) D.; m. Larry John Leifer, Dec. 19, 1962; 1 child, Simeon Kel Leifer; m. Donald Warren Bremme, Aug. 6, 1977; 1 child, John Thomas Dorr-Bremme. B.S., Stanford U., 1964, M.A., 1966, Ph.D. in Psychology, 1970. Acting asst. prof. communication Stanford U., 1967-70, research assoc. in psychiatry and communication, 1970-71, research assoc. in psychiatry, acting asst. prof. communication, childcare policy analyst in Pres.'s Office, 1971-72; asst. prof. edn. Harvard U., Cambridge, Mass., 1972-76, assoc. prof., 1976-78; assoc. prof. communications Annenberg Sch. Communication U. So. Calif., Los Angeles, 1978-81; prof. Annenberg Sch. Communication U. So. Calif., Los Angeles, 1981; prof. edn. UCLA, 1981—; cons. Children's TV Workshop, NBC, KCET, Joyce Hakansson Assoc., Children's Advt. Rev. Unit, NIMH, Action for Children's TV, others. Author: Television and Children: A Special Medium for a Special Audience, 1986; editor: (with Edward L. Palmer) Children and the Faces of Television-Teaching, Violence, Selling, 1980, 2d edit., 1981; contbr. articles to profl. jours. Fellow Am. Psychol. Assn., Am. Ednl. Research Assn., Soc. Research in Child Devel., Internat. Communication Assn., Amnesty Internat., Friends Com. on Nat. Legis. Democrat. Office: UCLA Moore Hall Los Angeles CA 90024

DORR, ROBERT CHARLES, lawyer; b. Denver, Jan. 7, 1946; s. Owen and Rose Esther (Tudek) D.; m. Sandra Leah Gehlsen, Feb. 25, 1971; children—Bryan, Aric. B.S.E.E., Milw. Sch. Engring., 1968; M.S.E.E., Northwestern U., 1970; J.D., U. Denver, 1975. Bar: Colo. 1975, U.S. Dist. Ct. Colo. 1975, U.S. Patent Office 1975. Mem. tech. staff Bell Labs., Naperville, Ill., 1968-72, patent staff, Denver, 1975-76; ptnr. Burton & Dorr, Denver, 1976-86; sr. ptnr. Dorr, Carson, Sloan & Peterson, Denver, 1986—; ptnr. Internat. Practicum Inst., Denver, 1979—; owner The Lawyers Edge, Inc., 1985—; seminar speaker various profl. orgns. Contbr. articles to profl. jours. Active Citizens Com. for Retention of Judges, Denver, 1984. Milw. Sch. Engring. scholar, 1964-68; named Outstanding Young Man Am., 1976. Mem. Douglas-Elbert County Bar Assn. (pres. 1983—), IEEE, AAAS, ABA, Colo. Trial Lawyers Assn., Sigma XI. Republican. Roman Catholic. Home: 519 Willowlake Dr PO Box 116 Franktown CO 80116 Office: Dorr Carson Sloan Peterson 3010 E 6th Ave Denver CO 80222

DORRANCE, STURGES DICK, III, broadcasting executive; b. N.Y.C., Jan. 1, 1942; s. Sturges Dick and Marjorie Colt (Wooster) D; m. Pamela Winters, Sept. 21, 1963; children—Elizabeth, Sarah, Meredith, Jennifer. B.A. in English, Dartmouth Coll., 1963. With King Broadcasting, Seattle, 1966—, gen. sales mgr., 1976-82, v.p., gen. mgr. King-TV, 1982—. Past pres. Northwest Chamber Orch., trustee United Way, Pacific Med. Ctr., TV Acad. Arts and Scis., Wash. State Broadcasters, Seattle Chamber Festival. Served to 1st lt. U.S. Army, 1964-66. Com. Anglican. Club: Wash. Athletic. Office: King-TV 333 Dexter N Seattle WA 98109

DORRENCE, SAMUEL MICHAEL, research administrator; b. Rock Springs, Wyo., May 21, 1939; s. Samuel William and Ila Ozella (Coulston) D.; m. Marilyn Ann Toth, Dec. 30, 1960; children: Julie, Michael, Maria. BA, U. Utah, 1961, PhD in Organic Chemistry, 1964. Research chemist Celanese Chem. Co., Clarkwood, Tex., 1964-67, group leader, 1967; research assoc. Laramie Energy Tech. Ctr., Laramie, Wyo., 1967-80, div. mgr., 1980-83; office dir. Western Research Inst., Laramie, 1983-87, v.p. phys. scis., 1987—; adj. prof. fuels engring. U. Utah, 1975—; adv. bd. Enhanced Oil Recovery Inst. U. Wyo., Laramie, 1984—. Mem. editorial bd. Fuel Sci. and Tech. Internat., 1983—; contbr. articles to profl. jours. Mem. budget com. United Way Albany County, Wyo., 1973-75. Mem. Am. Chem. Soc. (fuel and petroleum divs.), Laramie Area C. of C., Sigma Xi. Democrat. Roman Catholic. Avocations: fishing, bird hunting, boating, reading, backpacking. Office: Western Research Inst PO Box 3395 University Sta Laramie WY 82071

DORSEY, HELEN DANNER, writer, author, educator; b. Tarentum, Pa., Jan. 18, 1928; d. Frederick William and Harriet (Wiggins) Danner; m. Thomas Brookshier Dorsey, June 30, 1951; children: Diana, F. Blinn. BA, U. Iowa, 1949; postgrad., U. Wis., 1950. Food columnist Herald Tribune News Service, N.Y.C., 1956-58; remedial education educator U.S. Army, Hoechst, Federal Republic of Germany, 1954-56; food editor Am. Weekend, Frankfurt, Federal Republic of Germany, 1954-56; with elec. drafting dept. Newport News (Va.) Shipbuilding and Dry Dock Co., 1952-54; tchr. George Wythe Jr. High Sch., Hampton, Va., 1951-52; home econs. tchr. Keokuk (Iowa) High Sch., 1949-51; tchr. Thomas Jefferson Jr. High Sch., Arlington, Va., 1956-57; tchr. home econs. Sr. High Sch., Massapequa, N.Y., 1958-59; contbg. editor Forecast Mag., N.Y.C., 1958-59, 50 Mag., N.Y.C., 1958-60; asst. food editor LOOK mag., N.Y.C., 1962-64; celebrity cookbook columnist Newsday Spls. (syndicated), Garden City, N.Y.C., 1964-69, Chgo. Tribune-N.Y. News Syndicate, N.Y.C., 1969-75, Los Angeles Times Syndicate, 1975-87; celebrity foodstyles producer, writer Family Circle mag., N.Y.C., 1985—; contbg. correspondent USA Today & USA Weekend, Arlington, Va., 1985—; contbg. editor The Phila. Inquirer Mag., 1985—; celebrity cookbook columnist Celebrity Foodstyle Syndicate, Los Angeles, 1987—; columnist Editors Press Service, Inc., N.Y.C., Miller Services, Ltd., Can., 1987—; cons. in field. Author of 25 cookbooks, 1974—; contbr. articles to mags. and newspapers. Avocations: swimming, reading, tennis. Home and Office: 9239 Doheny Rd Los Angeles CA 90069

DOSS, ROBERT PAUL, plant physiologist; b. Madera, Calif., May 25, 1945; s. Jesse Paul and Rhea March (Trethewey) D.; m. Elke Felizitas Mittmann, June 7, 1968; children: Lynn E., Christopher P. BA, Calif. State U., Fullerton, 1968; PhD, U. Calif., Davis, 1974. Plant physiologist USDA, Corvallis, 1976—. Editorial adv. bd. mem. Internat. Soc. Hort. Sci., 1982—; contbr. articles to profl. jours. Served with U.S. Army, 1969-71. Mem. AAAS, Am. Soc. Plant Physiologists, Internat. Soc. Chem. Ecology. Republican. Lutheran. Avocations: hunting, fishing, hiking, gardening. Home: 3209 NW Charmyr Vista Dr Corvallis OR 97330 Office: USDA-ARS 3420 NW Orchard Ave Corvallis OR 97330

DOSSETT, LAWRENCE SHERMAN, professional services company official; b. Santa Ana, Calif., May 11, 1936; s. Wheeler Sherman and Eunice Elizabeth (Bright) D.; student U. Ariz., 1957-58, U. Calif., Irvine, 1973-75, Loyola Marymount Coll., 1974; m. Joanne Kallisch; children—Todd Sherman, Garrick Robert (dec.), Dana Shelene, Ryan William. Engring. draftsman Hughes Aircraft Co., Tucson, 1955-57, John J. Foster Mfg. Co., Costa Mesa, Calif., 1958, Standard Elec. Products, Costa Mesa, 1959; engring. mgr. Electronic Engring. Co., Santa Ana, 1959-79; product quality mgr. Farwest Data Systems, Irvine, Calif., 1979-82; dist. mgr. profl. services, nat. cons. mgr. Comserv/MSA, 1982—, Western Electronic Mfrs. Assn., Am. Prodn. and Inventory Control Soc., 1976-82, Computer Mfrs. Conf., 1980. Cert. in mgmt. Am. Mgmt. Assn., 1968. Mem. Am. Prodn. and Inventory Control Soc. Co-author patent reel spindle, 1972.

DOTO, IRENE LOUISE, statistician; b. Wilmington, Del., May 7, 1922; d. Antonio and Teresa (Tabasso) D. B.A., U. Pa., 1943; M.A., Temple U., 1948, Columbia U., 1954. Engring. asst. RCA-Victor, 1943-44; research asst. U. Pa., 1944; actuarial clk. Penn Mut. Life Ins. Co., 1944-46; instr. math. Temple U., 1946-53; commd. sr. asst. health services officer USPHS, 1954, advanced through grades to dir., 1963; statistician Communicable Disease Ctr., Atlanta, 1954-55, Kansas City, Kans., 1955-67; chief statis. and publ. services, ecol. investigations program Ctr. for Disease Control, Kansas City, 1967-73, chief statis. services, div. hepatitis and viral enteritis, Phoenix, 1973-83; statis. cons., 1984—; mem. adj. faculty Phoenix Ctr., Ottawa U., 1982—. Mem. Am. Statis. Assn., Biometrics Soc., Am. Pub. Health Assn., Ariz. Pub. Health Assn., Ariz. Council Engring. and Sci. Assn. (treas. 1982-83, 84-86, sec. 1986-87), Primate Found. Ariz. (mem. animal care and use com. 1986—), Bus. and Profl. Women's Club Phoenix, Sigma Xi, Pi Mu Epsilon. Office: PO Box 22197 Phoenix AZ 85028

DOTSON, ROSE DOLORES, civil servant; b. Santa Fe, Aug. 30; d. Matias and Irene (Martinez) Gonzales; m. Gerald Richard Dotson; children: Roberta Ann Dotson Dettman, Deborah Irene, Matthew Charles. AA, Loretto Acad. Community Coll., 1978. With 1st Nat. Bank, Santa Fe, 1955-60, Santa Fe Nat. Bank, 1960-62; with sch. tax div. State of N.Mex., Santa Fe, 1962-64; with Social Security Adminstrn., Santa Fe, 1964-79; loan servicing specialist HUD, Denver, 1979—. Treas. Nat. Fedn. Fed. Employees local #1900, Denver, 1983—. Roman Catholic. Lodges: Elks (local sec. 1978-79), KC (pres. ladies aux. 1979-80). Avocations: bowling, knitting, crocheting, sewing. Home: 8469 Otis Dr Arvada CO 80003

DOTTS, DONALD VERN, education educator; b. Covina, Calif., Nov. 7, 1935; s. John Ward and Lela Mae (Folsom) D.; m. F. Annis Jones, June 7, 1958; children: Deborah Ann, John David. BA, Ariz. State U., 1958. Asst. exec. dir., editor Ariz. State U. Alumni Assn., Tempe, 1958-67, exec. dir., 1967—. Active Maricopa County Air Pollution Hearing Bd., Phoenix, 1968-74; chmn. bd. dirs. YMCA, Tempe, 1984-86. Served to capt. USAR, 1958-66. Mem. Am. Alumni Council (mem. nat. bd. 1968-70), Council for Advancement and Support of Edn. (mem. nat. bd. 1980-83, dist. chmn. 1980-83, Dist. VII Tribute award 1986), Phi Sigma Kappa (editor 1974-79, dist. gov. 1958—). Democrat. Methodist. Avocations: traveling, skiing. Home: 1206 E Harbor View Dr Tempe AZ 85283 Office: Ariz State U Alumni Ctr Tempe AZ 85287

DOTY, CLAUDIA REGINA, vocal educator, performer; b. St. George, Utah, Mar. 21, 1954; d. Claudius Delbert and Maria Magdalena (Stock) D. BA, U. Nev., Las Vegas, 1977; MusM, Brigham Young U., 1982. Pvt. vocal instr. Las Vegas, Nev. and Provo, Utah, 1976-86; music tchr. Yamaha Music Sch. for Children, Las Vegas, 1977-78; vocal instr. Brigham Young U., Provo, 1979-82, Nev. Sch. of the Arts, Las Vegas, 1983—, U. Nev., Las Vegas, 1983—; opera singer Las Vegas Opera Co., 1983—, Nev. Opera Theater, 1986—. Young women's camp dir. Ch. of Jesus Christ of Latter-Day Saints, Kolob, Utah, 1985—, youth choir dir., Las Vegas, 1984—; 1st festival adjudicator Clark County Sch. Dist., Las Vegas, 1985. Recipient 1st Place in competition N.Y. Met. Opera Auditions Nev., 1976, 2d Place in competition N.Y. Met. Opera Auditions, Nev., 1984. Mem. Nat. Assn. of Tchrs. of Singing (Las Vegas chpt. recruitment chmn. 1986—, pres. 1987—, recipient 1st place in competition, Utah, 1982, 3d place in competition, Calif., 1982). Republican. Avocations: artwork, sewing, aerobics, jogging. Home: 1455 E Katie #D23 Las Vegas NV 89119 Office: U Nev Las Vegas Music Dept 4505 Maryland Pkwy Las Vegas NV 89154

DOTY, HORACE (JAY), JR., theater administrator, arts consultant; b. St. Petersburg, Fla., May 25, 1924; s. Horace Herndon and Mabel (Bruce) D.; student Sherwood Music Sch., Chgo., 1942-43; BA in Music, Pomona Coll., 1950; cert. La Verne Coll., 1969; MA in Edn., Claremont Grad. Sch., 1972; cert. in Bus. Adminstrn., 1984; m. Wanda L. Flory, Dec. 27, 1947; 1 child, Janet. Propr. Jay Doty's Inc., Claremont, 1960-68; concert mgr. Claremont Colls., 1968-73, supr. Garrison Theater, U. Ctr. Box Office, dir. Auditorium, theater events, coordinator programs, 1973-79, 81—; exec. dir. Flint Ctr. for Performing Arts, Cupertino, Calif., 1979-81. Mem. blue ribbon com. Fox Theater Restoration, Pomona, Calif., 1982; mem. Claremont Bicentennial

Com. for Performing Arts, 1975—; mem. touring adv. panel Calif. Arts Council; mem. exec. bd., Calif. Presenters. Served with inf. AUS, 1943-46. NEA fellow, 1986. Mem. Assn. Coll. and Univ. Concert Mgrs. (dir. 1983—), Western Alliance Arts Adminstrs. (pres. 1975-77), Auditorium Mgrs., Claremont C. of C. (pres. 1965-66). Home: 4145 Oak Hollow Rd Claremont CA 91711 Office: Claremont Colls Center Performing Arts Bridges Auditorium Claremont CA 91711

DOUGHERTY, CELIA BERNIECE, educator; b. Toronto, Ohio, Aug. 7, 1935; d. Ernest Merle and Dorothy Grace (Erwin) Putnam; student (scholar) Ohio U., 1953-54; B.A., Calif. State U., Fullerton, 1971, M.S., 1974; doctoral candidate U. So. Calif.; m. William Vincent Dougherty, May 14, 1955; children—Marie Collette, Michael Charles. Reading specialist Anaheim (Calif.) Union High Sch. Dist., 1972-78, asst. prin. jr. high, 1978-80; asst. prin. jr. high Orange (Calif.) Unified Sch. Dist., 1980—; trustee Anaheim City Sch. Dist., 1986—. Leader, Girl Scouts, 1968-71; mem. alumni council Calif. State U., Fullerton. Mem. Orange County Reading Assn. (dir. 1978-83, pres. 1982-83), Calif. Reading Assn., Internat. Reading Assn., Assn. Calif. Sch. Adminstrs., Calif. Sch. Bd. Assn., Assn. Supervision and Curriculum Devel., Educare. Phi Kappa Phi, AAUW, Phi Alpha Theta, Phi Delta Gamma. Democrat. Home: 860 S Cardiff St Anaheim CA 92806 Office: 370 N Glassell St Orange CA 92666

DOUGHERTY, DENNIS A., chemistry educator; b. Harrisburg, Pa., Dec. 4, 1952; s. John E. and Colleen (Canning) D.; m. Ellen M. Donnelly, June 3, 1973; children: Meghan, Kayla. BS, MS, Bucknell U., 1974; PhD, Princeton U., 1978. Postdoctoral fellow Yale U., New Haven, 1978-79; asst. prof. Calif. Inst. Tech., Pasadena, 1979-85, assoc. prof. chemistry, 1985—. Contbr. articles to sci. jours. Fellow Alfred P. Sloan Found., 1983; Camille and Henry Dreyfus Tchr. scholar, 1984. Mem. Am. Chem. Soc., Phi Beta Kappa. Office: Calif Inst Tech Div Chemistry and Chem Engring Pasadena CA 91125

DOUGHERTY, FREDERICK EARL, county ofcl.; b. Oconomowoc, Wis. June 16, 1929; s. Bert F. and Eleonore L. Dougherty; A.A., Pasadena City Coll., 1949; B.A., Occidental Coll., 1952; M.S., Calif. State U., 1963; postgrad. U. So. Calif., 1963-64; m. Viola M. Takaro, Apr. 21, 1956; children—Frederick Earl, Devon D. Real estate appraiser Los Angeles County, 1957-60, sr. appraiser, 1961-64, prin. appraiser, 1964-69, chief appraiser, 1971-80; ops. mgr. Govt. Ctr., 1968-71, chief spl. services div., 1980-82; chief real estate div. Los Angeles County Assessor, 1982—; tchr. Los Angeles Community Coll. Dist., 1963-68. Active local council Boy Scouts Am.; pres. S. Pasadena Band Parents, 1971-73; mem. exec. com. Pasadena Tournament of Roses, 1976—. Served with U.S. Army, 1953-55. Recipient medal of Merit, Silver Beaver award, Order of Arrow, Boy Scouts Am. Cert. rev. appraiser. Mem. Internat. Assn. Assessors, Nat. Assn. Rev. Appraisers, Soc. Real Estate Appraisers, Assn. Govt. Appraisers, Western Govtl. Research Assn., Sigma Zeta Psi, Pi Sigma Alpha. Methodist. Contbr. articles to profl. jours. Office: 500 W Temple St Los Angeles CA 90012

DOUGHERTY, HOWARD WILLIAM, oil and gas producer; b. Kansas City, Mo., Jan. 5, 1915; s. Frank C. and Elsie (Braecklein) D.; m. Violeta van Rozelen, Aug. 3, 1940; children—William, Robert, Patrick, Michael, Mary, Peter. B.S. in Earth Sci., Stanford U., 1938. Oil and gas producer, Pasadena, Calif., 1947—; dir. Santa Anita Consol., Inc.; pres. Pioneer Kettleman Co., Book Cliffs Oil & Gas Co. Mem. Conservation Com. Calif.; trustee Neuro Scis. Inst. Mem. Ind. Petroleum Assn. Am., Beta Theta Pi. Clubs: Los Angeles Country, California, Bohemian; Valley Hunt (Pasadena); Birnham Wood Golf (Santa Barbara); Mil. Order of St. Lazarus (comdr.). Office: 2234 E Colorado Blvd 2d Floor Pasadena CA 91107-3608

DOUGHERTY, (MARY) PATRICIA, history educator; b. Monterey, Calif., Dec. 7, 1944; d. John Francis Dougherty and Clotilde (Quarelli) Hoefle. BA, Dominican Coll., 1967; MA, Georgetown U., 1979, PhD, 1984. Tchr. St. Michael's, Livermore, Calif., 1968-72; tchr., vice-prin. St. Cyril's Sch., Oakland, Calif., 1972-77; teaching asst. dept. history Georgetown U., Washington, 1978-81, 82-83; chmn. dept. history Dominican Coll., San Rafael, Calif., 1984—. Fulbright fellow, Paris, 1981-82, Georgetown U. fellow, Washington, 1978-81, 82-83. Mem. Am. Hist. Assn., Am. Cath. Hist. Assn., Soc. French Hist. Studies. Office: Dominican Coll 1520 Grand Ave San Rafael CA 94901

DOUGHERTY, RALEIGH GORDON, manufacturer's representative; b. Saginaw, Mich., Aug. 19, 1928; s. Raleigh Gordon and Helen Jean (McCrum) D.; 1 dau., Karen Kealani. Salesman, H.D. Hudson Mfg. Co., Chgo., 1946-48; field sales rep. Jensen Mfg. Co., Chgo., 1948-50; field sales mgr. Regency Idea, Indpls., 1950-54; mgr. Brenna & Browne, Honolulu, 1954-56; owner, pres. Dougherty Enterprises, Honolulu, 1956—. Served with U.S. Army, 1950-52. Mem. Hawaii Hotel Assn., Internat. Home Furnishings Reps. Assn., Air Force Assn., D.A.V. (life), Am. Soc. Interior Designers (industry found.), Navy League U.S., Am. Legion, Hawaii Restaurant Assn., Nat. Fedn. Ind. Bus., Korean Vet. Small Bus. of Hawaii, Hawaii Visitors Bur. Republican. Methodist. Lodge: Elks. (past trustee Hawaii). Home: 7 Poipu Dr Honolulu HI 96825 Office: PO Box 25400 Honolulu HI 96825

DOUGHERTY, RICHARD L., accountant, educator; b. Redlands, Calif., May 14, 1934; s. Robert L. and Esther L. D.; m. Mary Mann, Sept. 19, 1959; children—Michael, William. B.A. in Econs., U. Redlands, 1956; M.S. in Taxation, Golden Gate U., 1982. C.P.A., Calif. Staff acct. Arthur Andersen & Co., Los Angeles, 1956-60; ptnr. Harris & Corp., C.P.A.s, Los Angeles, 1960-75, Fox & Co., C.P.A.s, Los Angeles, 1975-80; prin. R. L. Dougherty & Co., C.P.A.s, Los Angeles, 1980-83, mng. ptnr. Dougherty & Co., C.P.A.s, 1983—; instr. in banking and fin. Golden Gate U.; commnr. ins. and corps. Calif. State Senate. Served with U.S. Army, 1957-59. Mem. Am. Inst. C.P.A.s, Calif. Soc. C.P.A.s. Office: 606 S Olive St Suite 1500 Los Angeles CA 90014

DOUGHERTY, THOMAS ANTHONY, aerospace manager; b. Wichita, Kans., Dec. 31, 1937; s. Ralph C. and Minnie (Daly) D.; m. Joyce Allegro, June 15, 1963; children—Jennifer, Gregory, Mitchell, Kevin. B.S. in Chemistry, Wichita State U., 1960, M.S. in Chemistry, 1962; Ph.D. in Phys. Chemistry, Iowa State U., 1966. Research engr. Boeing Co., Wichita, 1966-69, sr. research specialist, Seattle, 1969-72; sr. staff scientist Ford Aerospace, Palo Alto, Calif., 1972-78, spacecraft mktg. mgr., 1978-80, spacecraft engring. mgr., 1980-82, dep. program mgr., 1982-84, program mgr., 1984—. Mem. AIAA, Am. Mgmt. Assn., Phi Lambda Upsilon. Republican. Roman Catholic. Clubs: WDL Golf (Palo Alto), KC. Contbr. articles profl. jours. Patentee in field. Home: 1804 Frobisher Way San Jose CA 95124 Office: 3939 Fabian Way Palo Alto CA 94303

DOUGLAS, JOHN EDWARD, academic administrator, chemistry educator; b. Normal, Ill., June 29, 1926; s. Johnathan Park and Frances (Green) D.; m. Gertrude A. Horn, Aug. 25, 1951 (div. Dec. 1982); children: James, Carl, Elizabeth; m. Eileen Marie Starr, June 4, 1983. Student, Ill. State U., 1943-44; BS, U. Chgo., 1947, MS, 1949; PhD, U. Wash., 1952. Mem. chemistry faculty U. Wyo., Laramie, 1952-56; chemist Stanford Research Inst., Menlo Park, Calif., 1956-60; mem. chemistry faculty Eastern Wash. U., Cheney, 1960-79, vice provost, graduate program, 1979—; vis. research prof. Canterbury U., Christchurch, New Zealand, 1968-69, U. Calif., San Francisco, 1978-79. Contbr. articles to profl. jours. Mem. AAAS, Nat. Council Univ. Research Adminstrs. Avocations: backpacking, cross-country skiing. Home: S 4711 Magnolia Spokane WA 99223 Office: Eastern Wash U Academic Affairs Cheney WA 99004

DOUGLAS, JOY ANNE MARGARET, social worker, consultant; b. Spokane, May 20, 1935; d. Walter Franklin and Ella Mildred (James) Jones; m. Mark Newel Douglas, July 19, 1954; children: Sheryll Diane (dec.), Carl Herbert, Eric Stuart, Ward Austin, Kevin Alexander. BA in Edn. and Psychology cum laude, San Jose State U., 1958; MSW, U. Calif., Berkeley, 1972; cert. in legal assistanceship, U. Calif., Santa Cruz, 1981, cert. in advanced gerontology, 1982. Cert. adult educator (life), Calif. Tchr. elem. sch. Santa Clara (Calif.) County and Princess Anne (Md.) County Pub. Schs., and Agana, Guam, 1954-62; social worker children's protective services various county agys., Prince George County, Md. and Santa Cruz County, Ca., 1965-71; dir. med. social services Community Hosp. of Santa Cruz, Calif., 1972-74; dir. long term care ombudsman program Santa Cruz and San Benito (Calif.) Counties, 1976-81; health facilities evaluator Calif. Dept. Health Licensing and Cert., 1982-85; licensing program analyst Calif. Dept. Social Services, 1985—; chmn. Santa Cruz County Nursing Home Adv. Com., 1982; mem. long term care needs assessment task force Mid-Coast Health Systems Agy., Salinas, Calif. 1979-80; officer Santa Cruz County Long Term Care Commr., 1983-85; mem. long term care Planning Group, Sacramento, 1981. Contbr. articles to profl. jours. Bd. dirs. Community Council Santa Cruz, 1973-77; pres. Tri County R.S.V.P. Santa Cruz and Monterey (Calif.), 1975-79, bd. dirs.; bd. dirs. Behind the Times Theatre, Santa Cruz, 1986—. Mem. Am. Soc. Aging, Nat. Council Aging, Nat. Assn. Social Workers, Calif. Assn. Long Term Care Ombudsman (pres. 1978-81, hon. life mem.). Avocations: hiking, sewing. Home: 2905 Pine Flat Rd Santa Cruz CA 95060

DOUGLAS, MARION JOAN, labor negotiator; b. Jersey City, May 29, 1940; d. Walter Stanley and Sophie Frances (Zysk) Binaski; children: Jane Dee, Alex Jay. BA, Mich. State U., 1962; MSW, Sacramento State Coll., 1971; MPA, Calif. State U.-Sacramento, 1981. Owner, mgr. Linkletter-Totten Dance Studios, Sacramento, 1962-68, Young World of Discovery, Sacramento, 1965-68; welfare worker Sacramento County, 1964-67, welfare supr., 1968-72, child welfare supr., 1972-75, sr. personnel analyst, 1976-78, personnel program mgr., 1978-81, labor relations rep., 1981—; cons. State Dept. Health, Sacramento, 1975-76; cons. in field. Author/editor: (newsletter) Thursday's Child, 1972-74. Presiding officer Community Resource Orgn., Fair Oaks, Calif., 1970-72; exec. bd. Foster Parent's Assn., Sacramento, 1972-75; organizer Foster Care Sch. Dist. liaison programs, 1973-75; active Am. Lung Assn., 1983-87; rep. Calif. Welfare Dirs. Assn., 1975-76; county staff advisor Joint Powers Authority, Sacramento, 1978-81; mem. Mgmt. Devel. Com., Sacramento, 1979-80; vol., auctioneer KVIE Pub. TV, Sacramento, 1970-84; adv. bd. Job and Info. Resource Ctr., 1976-77; spl. adv. task force coordinator Sacramento Employment and Tng. Adv. Council, 1980-81; vol. leader Am. Lung Assn., Sacramento, 1983-86 Calif. Dept. Social Welfare ednl. stipend, 1967-68, County of Sacramento ednl. stipend, 1969-70. Recipient Achievement award Nat. Assn. Counties, 1981. Mem. Mgmt. Women's Forum, Indsl. Relations Assn. No. Calif., Indsl. Relations Research Assn., Nat. Assn. Female Execs., Mensa. Republican. Avocations: real estate, nutrition. Home: 7812 Palmyra Dr Fair Oaks CA 95628 Office: County of Sacramento Dept Personnel Mgmt 700 H St Sacramento CA 95814

DOUGLAS, PAUL JAMES, aerospace engineer; b. Sioux Falls, S.D., Sept. 13, 1930; s. James Paul and Smaragda D. B.S. in Aero. Engring., U. Ill., 1956; m. Marianne P. West, Nov. 14, 1953; children—Pamela, Paula, Patricia, James. With Lockheed Missiles and Space Co., Sunnyvale, Calif., 1956—, group engr., 1983-85, staff engr., 1985—. Served with USAF, 1951-52. Mem. AIAA. Office: PO Box 3504 Sunnyvale CA 94088-3504

DOUGLASS, CRAIG BRUCE, computer graphics executive; b. Santa Monica, Calif., July 3, 1956; s. W. Bruce and Frances A. (Ellingwood) D. AB, Dartmouth Coll., 1978; MBA, U. Chgo., 1980. Sr. bus. devel. analyst Bell & Howell Co., Chgo., 1980-82, product mgr., 1982-83, sr. product mgr., 1983, mgr. product and market devel., 1983-86; v.p. product and market devel. Bell & Howell Co., Torrance, Calif., 1986—. Inventor digital film recording. Mem. Nat. Computer Graphics Assn. (pres. Ill. chpt. 1985-86, v.p. Los Angeles Orange County chpt. 1986—, nat. com. 1986—). Republican. Mem. Christian Ch. Club: Dartmouth (Chgo.) (v.p. 1984-85), Los Angeles (bd. dirs. 1986—). Avocations: yacht racing, skiing, scuba diving. Home: 506 N Helberta #1 Redondo Beach CA 90277 Office: Bell & Howell Co 411 Amapola Ave Torrance CA 90501

DOUGLASS, DONALD ROBERT, banker; b. Evanston, Ill., Oct. 7, 1934; s. Robert William and Dorothy (Gibson) D.; B.B.A., U. N.Mex., 1959, M.B.A., 1966; m. Susan Douglass. With Security Pacific Nat. Bank, Los Angeles, 1961—, mgmt. trainee, 1962-63, asst. mgr. Vernon (Calif.) br., 1963-64, asst. mgr. Whittier (Calif.), 1964, asst. v.p., 1965, asst. v.p., credit officer regional adminstrn., Los Angeles, 1966-69, v.p., San Francisco, 1969-74, mgr. corp. accounts credit adminstrn. No. Calif. Corp. Banking, 1974-77; group v.p. Annco Properties, Burlingame, Calif., 1977-79; v.p., sr. loan officer Borel Bank and Trust Co., San Mateo, Calif., 1979-83, sr. v.p., 1983-84, exec. v.p. mortgage banking div. comml. property sales, Los Altos, 1984-87; ptnr. Key Equiteis, Inc., San Mateo, 1987—; instr. Am. Inst. Banking, 1963, Coll. San Mateo, 1982—. Served with AUS, 1954-56. Mem. U. N.Mex. Alumni Assn., Sigma Alpha Epsilon, Delta Sigma Phi. Republican. Presbyn. Home: 745 Celestial Lane Foster City CA 94404

DOUGLASS, ENID HART, educational director; b. Los Angeles, Oct. 23, 1926; d. Frank Roland and Enid Yandell (Lewis) Hart; m. Malcolm P. Douglass, Aug. 28, 1948; children: Malcolm Paul Jr., John Aubrey, Susan Enid. BA, Pomona Coll., 1948; MA, Claremont (Calif.) Grad. Sch., 1959. Research asst. World Book Ency., Palo Alto, Calif., 1953-54; exec. sec., asst. dir. oral history program Claremont Grad. Sch., 1963-71, dir. oral history program, 1971—, history lectr., 1977—; mem. Calif. Heritage Preservation Commn., 1977-85, chmn. 1983-85. Contbr. articles to hist. jours. Mayor pro tem City of Claremont, 1980-82, Mayor, 1982-86; mem. planning and research adv. council State of Calif., mem. city council, Claremont, 1978-86; bd. dirs., founder Claremont Heritage, Inc., 1977-80. Mem. Oral History Assn. (pres. 1979-80), Southwest Oral History Assn. (founding steering com. 1981, J.V. Mink award 1984), Nat. Council Pub. History, LWV (bd. dirs. 1957-59). Democrat. Avocation: tennis. Home: 1195 Berkeley Ave Claremont CA 91711 Office: Claremont Grad Sch Oral History Program 900 N College Ave Claremont CA 91711

DOUGLASS, JOHN MICHAEL, physician; b. Takoma Park, Md., Apr. 13, 1939; s. Jones All and Helen Louise D.; BA, Columbia Union Coll., Takoma Park, 1959; MD (Salerni Collegium scholar), U. So. Calif., 1964; DPh Pacific West U., 1986; PhD Clayton U., 1987. m. Sue Nan Peters, May 15, 1962; children: Dina Lynn, Lisa Michele. Rotating intern Los Angeles County, U. So. Calif. Med. Ctr., 1964-65, resident internal medicine, 1965-67, home care physician, 1965-68; practice medicine specializing in internal medicine, Cin., 1968-70, Los Angeles, 1970—; physician Pasadena Emergency Center, 1965-68, Deaconess Hosp., 1968-70; postdoctoral fellow automobile safety and trauma research U. Calif., Los Angeles, 1967-68, med. cons. Emergency Med. Services Project, 1970-71; commd. med. officer USPHS, 1968-70; asst. sci. adviser, injury control program ECA, USPHS, Cin., 1968-69, med. specialities cons. Office Product Safety, FDA, USPHS, 1969-70; internal medicine cons. East End Neighborhood Community Health Center, Cin., 1968-70; lt. comdr.-04, USPHS Res. officer, 1970-82; internal medicine cons. Hollywood Sunset Free Clinic, 1971-72; sr. med. cons. multidisciplinary hwy. accident investigation unit U. So. Calif., 1971-73; staff internist, coordinator health improvement service Kaiser Found. Hosp., Los Angeles, 1970—; instr. biomedical engring. course U. Calif., Los Angeles, 1968, instr. internal medicine, 1971-74; instr. internal medicine U. Cin. Sch. Medicine, 1968-70; instr. kinesthesiology, traumatic anatomy and head injury U. So. Calif., 1971-74, instr. foodstyle and lifestyle, 1977—; mem. med. adv. bd. Dominican Sisters of Sick Poor, 1969; traffic safety cons. Countywide Conf. on Emergency Med. Services, 1972; mem. nutrition council Las Virgenes Sch. Dist., 1977. Active mgmt. devel. program Boy Scouts Am. Execs., 1966; bd. dirs. Calif. Assn. Pvt. Schs. and Colls., 1967, Coronary Club (adult jogging program), 1967-68; co-organizer Oriental rug exhibit Pacificulture Mus., Pasadena, Calif., 1973; v.p. Los Angeles Med. Milk Commn. Diplomate Nat. Bd. Med. Examiners, Am. Bd. Internal Medicine. Comdr. USPHS Officers Res. Corps. Fellow ACP; mem. AMA, Calif. Med. Assn., Los Angeles County Med. Assn., Am., Calif., Los Angeles socs. internal medicine, Am. Assn. Automotive Medicine (exec. com. Western chpt. 1977-82), Nutrition Today Soc., Internat. Hajji Baba Soc., Decorative Arts Council, Los Angeles Mus. Art, Sierra Club, Phi Delta Epsilon, Alpha Omega Alpha, Phi Kappa Phi. Author: The Lost Language; contbr. articles to profl. jours. Home: 29154 S Lakeshore Dr Agoura CA 91301 Office: 1510 N Edgemont St Los Angeles CA 90027

DOUGLASS, ROBERT JOSEPH, JR., computer scientist; b. Moline, Ill., June 8, 1951; s. Robert Joseph and Hattie Jane (Holmes) D.; m. Barbara Walker Mahan, June 3, 1973 (div. Aug. 1981). BEE magna cum laude, Princeton U., 1973; MS in Computer Scis., U. Wis., 1974, PhD in Computer Scis., 1978. Postdoctoral researcher dept. physics and astronomy U. London, 1978; asst. prof. computer sci. U. Va., Charlottesville, 1978-81; assoc. group leader for research Los Alamos (N.Mex.) Nat. Lab., 1981-85, collaborating scientist, 1985—; machine ingelligence unit head Martin Marietta, Denver, 1985, dep. program mgr. Autonomous Land Vehicle, 1985—; Mem. panel Computer Architecture Pres.'s Sci. adv. Nat. Acad. Sci., Washington, 1984. Editor: Parallel Programs and Algorithms, 1986; assoc. editor Jour. Parallel and Distributed Processing, 1984—; contbr. articles to profl. jours. Mem. IEEE, Assn. Computing Machinery, Assn. Computational Linguistics, AAAS. Avocations: paleoanthropology, alpine skiing, boxing, karate, soccer. Office: Martin Marietta Mail Stop TO427 PO Box 179 Denver CO 80201

DOUTHART, RICHARD JAMES, physical chemist; b. Chgo., June 11, 1935; s. Richard Charles and Anna Marie (Baur) D.; m. Irene Rosalind McKelvey, June 5, 1961; children: William Richard, Julia Celleste. BS in Chemistry, U. Ark., 1962; PhD in Phys. Chemistry, U. Ill., 1968. Sr. biophysicist Lilly Research Labs., Indpls., 1968-72, research scientist, 1972-81; mgr. biotech. devel. Battelle Northwest Labs., Richland, Wash., 1981—; adj. faculty mem. Wash. State U., Pullman, 1983—; lectr. biotech., computer systems for various civic orgns. Contbr. articles to profl. jours.; patentee anti tumor therapy, genetic engring. Served with USAF, 1953-57. Recipient Top 100 Innovator award Sci. Digest, 1985, IR 100 award 1986. Mem. AAAS, Am. Chem. Soc., Sigma Psi. Avocation: astronomy. Home: 209 Enterprise Dr Richland WA 99352 Office: Battelle Pacific NW Lab Battelle Blvd Richland WA 99352

DOUTT, JEFFREY (THOMAS), marketing and management specialist, university dean; b. Oakland, Calif., Mar. 30, 1947; s. Richard L. and Lucinda M. (Killian) D.; B.S., U. Calif.-Berkeley, 1968, M.S., 1970, Ph.D., 1976. Assoc. in bus. adminstrn. U. Calif.-Berkeley, 1974; asst. prof. mgmt. Sonoma (Calif.) State U., 1974-78, assoc. prof., 1978-83, prof., 1983—, chmn. dept. mgmt. studies, 1976-80, dean Sch. Social Scis., 1980-86, dean Sch. Bus. and Econs., 1986—; prin. assoc. Mgmt. Devel. Internat.; cons. mktg. and mgmt. Recipient Internat. Exchange award Rotary Found., 1979; Giannini Found. fellow, 1968-70. Mem. Am. Mktg. Assn., Am. Agrl. Econs. Assn., Am. Econ. Assn., Am. Inst. Decision Scis., Acad. Mktg. Sci., Acad. Internat. Bus., Am. Soc. Tng. and Devel., Internat. Communication Assn., Soc. Intercultural Edn. Tng. and Research, Am. Bus. Communication Assn., Western Mktg. Educators Assn., Phi Beta Kappa. Democrat. Club: Rotary. Contbr. articles to profl. jours. Home: 5130 Gilchrist Rd Sebastopol CA 95472 Office: 1801 E Cotati Ave Rohnert Park CA 94928

DOVE, DONALD AUGUSTINE, city planner, consultant, lecturer; b. Waco, Tex., Aug. 7, 1930; s. Sebert Constantine and Amy Delmena (Stern) D.; m. Cecelia Mae White, Feb. 9, 1957; children—Angela Dove Gaddy, Donald, Monica, Celine, Austin, Cathlyn, Dianna, Jennifer. B.A., Calif. State U.-Los Angeles, 1951; M.A. in Pub. Adminstrn., U. So. Calif., 1966. Planning and devel. cons. D. Dove Assocs., Los Angeles, 1959-60; supr. demographic research Calif. Dept. Pub. Works, Los Angeles, 1960-66, environ. coordinator, Sacramento, 1971-75; dir. transp. employment project State of Calif., Los Angeles, 1966-71, chief Los Angeles Region transp. study, 1975-84; chief environ. planning Calif. Dept. Transp., Los Angeles, 1972-75; dir. U. So. Calif. Praetors, Los Angeles, 1984-87; panelist, advisor Pres. Conf. on Aging, Washington, 1970—, Internat. Conf. on Energy Use Mgmt., 1981; guest lectr. univs. western U.S., 1969—. Author: Preserving Urban Environment, 1976; Small Area Population Forecasts, 1966. Chmn. Lynwood City Planning Commn., Calif., 1982—; pres. Area Pastoral Council, Los Angeles, 1982-83; mem., del. Archdiocesan Pastoral Council, Los Angeles, 1979—, Compton Community Devel. Bd., Calif., 1967-71. Served to cpl. U.S. Army, 1952-54. Mem. Am. Planning Assn., Am. Inst. Planners (transp. chmn. 1972-73), Am. Inst. Cert. Planners, Assn. Environ. Profls. (co-founder 1973). Democrat. Roman Catholic. Lodges: Optimists (sec. 1978-79), K.C., Knights of Peter Claver (fin. sec. 1984—). Home: 11356 Ernestine Ave Lynwood CA 90262 Office: Calif Dept Transp 120 S Spring St Los Angeles CA 90012

DOVER, HAROLD LEON, state senator, building contractor; b. Lewistown, Mont., Oct. 1, 1933; s. John Wesley and Martha Elizabeth (Johnson) D.; B.A., Westmont Coll., Santa Barbara, Calif., 1951-55; m. Marian Leona Prentice, Sept. 1, 1956; children—Stephen Harold, Timothy Prentice, Bryan Hayden. Tchr. elem. sch., Calif. and Mont., 1955-58; gen. bldg. contractor, Lewistown, 1969-83; pres. Dover Constrn. Co., Inc.; ordained to ministry Ind. Bible Chs., 1962; pastor, 1958-76; mem. Mont. Senate, 1976-84; exec. dir. Nat. Gasahol Commn., 1978-81. Served with USAF, 1956-57. Mem. Lewistown C. of C. (pres. 1975-76). Republican. Club: Rotary (sec. 1978-79).

DOW, MARY ALEXIS, accountant; b. South Amboy, N.J., Feb. 19, 1949; d. Alexander and Elizabeth Anne (Reilly) Pawlowski; m. Russell Alfred Dow, June 19, 1971. B.S. with honors, U. R.I., 1971. C.P.A., Oreg. Staff acct. Deloitte, Haskins & Sells, Boston, 1971-74; sr. acct. Price Waterhouse, Portland, Oreg., 1974-77, mgr., 1977-81, sr. mgr., 1981-84; chief fin. officer Copeland Lumber Yards Inc., Portland, 1984-86; ind. cons. in field, 1984—. Mem. fin. com. Oreg. Mus. Sci. and Industry; bd. dirs. Oreg. Trails chpt. ARC; mem. budget rev. com. Multnomah County. Mem. Am. Inst. CPAs, Oreg. Soc. CPAs, Fin. Execs. Inst. Roman Catholic. Clubs: City (bd. govs.), University (Portland), Multnomah Athletic. Contbr. articles to profl. publs.

DOWD, DONALD G., communications executive; b. Milw., June 18, 1933; s. Grover Daniel and Katheryn Wilhelmina (Kauppila) D. Grad. high sch., Royal Oak, Mich. Dir. Sperry Univac, N.Y.C., 1959-80; v.p. A B Dick Corp., Chgo., 1980-83; pres. Don Dowd Communications Inc., Belmont, Calif., 1983—; bd. dirs. Peninsula Mktg. Assn. Mem. San Francisco Host Com., San Francisco C. of C., Am. Assn. for Artificial Intelligence, Bus. Profl. Advt. Assn., Assn. Computing Machinery, Asian Am. Mfrs. Assn., Asian Bus. League. Club: San Francisco Press. Home and Office: Don Dowd Communications Inc 300 Davey Glen Rd Suite 3623 Belmont CA 94002

DOWD, MICHAEL BURKE, architect; b. Alexandria, Va., Dec. 1, 1958; s. Thomas John and Catherine Jean (Burke) D.; m. Hilary Mackenzie, Aug. 16, 1986. BA, U. Wash., 1980, MArch, 1983. Registered architect, Wash., Oreg. Designer Charles Bergmann, Architect, Seattle, 1983, Ibsen Nelsen & Assocs., Seattle, 1983-84, GBGBD Architects, Portland, Oreg., 1984—. Contbr. and Portland correspondent to ARCADE Jour., 1983—; archtl. drawings published in various mags. and jours. Recipient Blue Ribbon ARCADE Jour., 1985, 1st prize Arts N.W., 1982, Portland Landmarks Commn. award, 1986. Avocation: classic autos, distance running. Home: 2024 NW Overton St Portland OR 97209 Office: GBGBD Architects 920 SW 3d Ave Portland OR 97204

DOWDY, WILLIAM LOUIS, management consultant, director; b. San Antonio, Dec. 3, 1937; s. Eugene Joseph and Estelle Helen (Schmid) D.; m. Frances Anne Tyson, May 31, 1962 (div. Sept. 1981); children: Mark Allen, John Joseph, Daniel Patrick. BS in Physics, St. Mary's U., San Antonio, 1959; M in Nuclear Engring., Tex. A&M U., 1964. Registered profl. engr., Calif. Mgr. advanced programs Rockwell Internat., N. Am., Downey, Calif., 1964-73; gen. mgr. Air Monitoring Ctr., Rockwell Internat., Newbury Park, Calif., 1973-77; mgr. program devel. Electric Power Research Inst., Palo Alto, Calif., 1977-78; dir. new product devel. BSP div. Envirotech Corp., Belmont, Calif., 1978-80; dir. feasibility evaluation Lurgi Corp., Belmont, 1980-83; dir. tech. and innovation mgmt. SRI Internat., Menlo Park, Calif., 1983—; pvt. cons., Thousand Oaks, Calif., 1976-77. Contbr. numerous articles on tech. and mgmt. to profl. jours. Bd. dirs. March of Dimes, San Mateo, Calif., 1980-83. Recipient Tech. Utilization award NASA, 1968, Apollo Achievement award NASA, 1969. Mem. Am. Mgmt. Assn., World Future Soc. Club: Commonwealth (San Francisco). Home: 27 Old Spanish Trail Portola Valley CA 94025 Office: SRI Internat 333 Ravenswood Ave Menlo Park CA 94025

DOWELL, FLONNIE, theoretical physicist; b. Marietta, Ga., Feb. 7, 1947. BA, U. So. Fla., 1969; MS, Tex. Woman's U., 1974; PhD, Georgetown U., 1977. Tchr. various pub. schs., Fla. and Tex., 1970-71; research, teaching asst. Tex. Woman's U., Denton, 1971-73, Georgetown U., Washington, 1973-77; research scientist Nat. Bur. Standards, Washington, 1977-79, Oak Ridge (Tenn.) Nat. Lab., 1979-81, Los Alamos (N.Mex.) Nat.

Lab., 1981—. Contbr. articles to profl. jours. Recipient Travel award NSF-NATO, 1977; postdoctoral research associateship Nat. Research Council, 1977-79. Mem. Am. Phys. Soc., N.Y. Acad. Scis., AAAS, (assoc.) Royal Soc. Chemistry, Sigma Xi. Office: Los Alamos Nat Lab Theoretical Div MS-B221 Los Alamos NM 87545

DOWELL, FRANK HERBERT, research entomologist; b. Birmingham, Ala., Aug. 27, 1926; s. Arthur Maultsby and Alma (Papot) D; m. Marian Craig Moore, Aug. 29, 1951; children: Craig, Karen, Mark. AB, Birmingham-So. U., 1948; MS, U. Tenn., 1949, PhD, 1964; diploma, Air Command and Staff Coll., 1953. Instr. U. of South, Sewannee, Tenn., 1950; commd. USAF, 1951, advanced through grades to maj., entomologist, parasitologist, 1951-66, resigned, 1966; mgr. biol. research Olin Corp., New Haven, 1966-67, Dow Chem. Co., Midland, Mich. and Walnut Creek, Calif., 1968-74; cons. Concord, Calif., 1975-76; ops. analyst Concord Police, 1977—; adj. assoc. prof. So. Conn. State U., New Haven, 1966-67; cons., instr. Calif. Dept. Justice, Sacramento, 1985—, Search, Inc., Sacramento, 1986—; cons. various Police Depts., Calif., 1983—, WHO, Washington, 1967. Contbr. articles to profl. jours. Vice-chmn. Armed Forces Pest Control Bd., Washington, 1962. Served with U.S. Army, 1944-46, ETO. Recipient Outstanding Performance award Dow Chem. Co., 1968-74, Exceptional Achievement award City of Concord, 1986. Mem. AAAS. Republican. Episcopalian. Avocations: painting, computers. Home: 4824 Eagle Way Concord CA 94521 Office: Concord Police Dept Planning and Research Dept Willow Pass Rd and Parkside Dr Concord CA 94519

DOWELL, JAMES CALVIN, civil engineer, consultant; b. Berwyn, Ill., Mar. 31, 1950; s. James Calvin and Marilyn (Parkhurst) D.; m. Elisabeth Totok, Oct. 4, 1975; 1 child, Michael J. BS in Engring., Stanford U., 1972. Design engr. Wilson & Co., Salina, Kans., 1972-80, dept. head., 1980-85; office mgr. Wilson & Co., Phoenix, 1985—. Mem. Ariz. Water and Pollution Control Assn., Ariz. Assn. County Engrs. Republican. Episcopalian. Avocations: golf, fishing, hunting. Home: 2132 W Isthmus Loop Mesa AZ 85202 Office: Wilson & Co 4100 E Broadway #130 Phoenix AZ 85040

DOWELL, MARIAN MOORE DOWELL, registered nurse; b. Seneca, S.C., Apr. 1, 1929; s. Clarence Craig and Leontine (Werner) Moore; m. Frank Herbert Dowell, Aug. 29, 1951; children: Craig M., Karen G., Mark C. BA, Winthrop Coll.; MEd, Clemson U., S.C.; BSN, U. Calif., San Francisco; MSN, U. Calif. Registered nurse. Tchr. Liberty (S.C.) High Sch., 1965-66, Wilbur Cross High Sch., New Haven, 1966-68, NE Intermed. Sch., Midland, Mich., 1968-71; staff nurse, ins. instr. Contra Costa County Hosp., Martinez, Calif., 1974-80; staff nurse coronary care unit Kaiser Hosp., Walnut Creek, Calif., 1980—. Mem. Am. Nurses Assn., Sigma Theta Tau. Republican. Episcopalian. Home: 1425 S Main St Walnut Creek CA 94596

DOWELL, ROBERT VERNON, entomologist, state agency offical; b. San Francisco, Sept. 13, 1947; s. Robert Leroy and Clair Adele (Smith) D.; m. Linda Kay Wange, Mar. 15, 1973. BS, U. Calif., Irvine, 1969; MS, Calif. State U., Hayward, 1973; PhD, Ohio State U., 1976. Asst. research scientist U. Fla., Ft. Lauderdale, 1977-80; pest mgmt. specialist Calif. Dept. Food and Agriculture, Sacramento, 1980-82, econ. entomologist, 1982-85, primary state entomologist, 1985—; tchr. integrated post mgmt. Consumnes River Coll., Sacramento, 1981-84, exotic insect pests and Calif. agriculture U. Calif., Davis, 1984—; lectr., Sierra Coll., 1984—. Contbr. chpts. to books, articles to profl. jours. Recipient Superior Achievement award Calif. Dept. Food and Agriculture, 1984. Mem. AAAS, Ecol. Soc. Am., Entomol. Soc. Am., Entomol. Soc. Can., Internat. Orgn. Biol. Control, Soc. Population Biology, Xerces Soc. Office: Calif Dept Food and Agriculture 1220 N St Sacramento CA 95814

DOWLER, WARREN LEROY, chemical engineer; b. Denver, Feb. 24, 1930; s. Leroy Charles and Ruth C. (Dubbs) D.; m. Louise Bishop, Sept. 20, 1952; children: Randy, Danny, Candy. BS in Chem. Engring., U. Colo., 1952; MS in Chem. Engring., S.D. Sch. Mines and Tech., 1956. Chem. engr. Union Carbide Chems. Co., South Charleston, W. Va., 1952, Gen. Mills Inc., Kankakee, Ill., 1954-55; research engr. Jet Propulsion Lab., Pasadena, Calif., 1956-59; mgr. engring. and test sects. Stanford Research Inst., Menlo Park, Calif., 1959-63; research engring. specialist Aerojet-Gen. Corp., Sacramento, 1963-65; supr. advanced tech. group in solid propellant engring. sect. Stanford Research Inst., Menlo Park, Calif., 1965-75, mem. tech. staff, 1975-78, acting group supr., 1978-82; mem. tech. staff, prin. investigator Jet Propulsion Lab., Pasadena, Calif., 1982—. Author with L. Dowler Lake Powell Boat and Tour Guide, 1973, 4th rev. edit., 1983, Lake Powell and Rainbow Bridge, 1982; contbr. articles to profl. jours.; patentee in field. Served to 1st lt. U.S. Army, 1952, maj. Res. ret. Fellow AIAA (chmn. solid rockets tech. com. 1971-72, 1981); mem. Am. Chem. Soc. (treas. so. Calif. sect.), Am. Inst. Chem. Engrs., AAAS, Flying Samaritans, Kankakee Jaycees, Pershing Rifles, NSPE, The Combustion Inst., Am. Def. Preparedness Assn., New Pictorialist Soc. (bd. dirs., treas.), Planetary Soc., Sigma Xi, Alpha Chi Sigma. Republican. Presbyterian. Home: 526 Camillo St Sierra Madre CA 91024 Office: Calif Inst Tech Jet Propulsion Lab 4800 Oak Grove Dr Pasadena CA 91109

DOWLIN, KENNETH EVERETT, librarian; b. Wray, Colo., Mar. 11, 1941; s. Ross Everett and Fern Mae (Peterson) D.; m. Janice Marie Simmons, Mar. 11, 1961; children: Kevin Everett, Kristopher Everett. B.A., U. Colo., 1963, M.P.A., 1981; M.A., U. Denver, 1966. Bookmobile librarian, library asst. Adams County Public Library, Westminster, Colo., 1961-63; library asst. II Denver Public Library, 1962-64; head librarian Arvada Public Library, Colo., 1964-68; adminstrv. asst. Jefferson County Public Library, Colo., 1969; dir. Natrona County Public Library, Casper, Wyo., 1969-75, Pikes Peak Regional Library Dist., Colorado Springs, Colo., 1975—; instr. Casper Coll., 1971-73; chmn. Colo. Libraries in Coop., 1975-76, Colo. Ad-hoc Com. Networking, 1976; mem. Western Interstate Commn. Higher Edn. Library Network Task Force; past trustee Wyo. Dept. Library, Archives and History; mem. Library of Congress Commn. on Book of Future; bd. dirs. Satellite Library Info. Network; vis. instr. U. Denver, 1980, 81; cons. in cable TV. Editorial bd. Microcomputers for Info. Mgmt., Library Hi Tech. Mem. adv. bd. for series on tech. WNET, N.Y.C., 1981—; bd. dirs. Citizens Goals for Colorado Springs, 1981—; bd. govs. Colo. Tech. Coll., 1982-85. Served with USMCR, 1959-65. Recipient Disting. Alumni award U. Denver Grad. Sch. for Library and Info. Mgmt. Mem. ALA (council 1985—, commn. on equality and freedom access to info. 1984-85, chmn. awards com. 1985-86, Hammond Inc. Library Award Jury 1968), ALA Library and Info. Tech. Assn. (long range planning com. 1981-82, pres. 1983-84), Mountain Plains Library Assn., Colo. Library Assn. (pres. 1968-69), Denver Council Govts. (chmn. librarians com. 1966), Colo. Mcpl. League (chmn. librarians sect. 1967), Bibliog. Ctr. Rocky Mountains (pres. 1972-74), Pikes Peak Area C. of C. (chmn. cultural affairs com. 1976-77). Home: 2477 N Circle Dr Colorado Springs CO 80909 Office: PO Box 1579 Colorado Springs CO 80901

DOWNARD, BOB HANSON, composer, librettist; b. Orange, Calif., Sept. 11, 1946; s. Marshall Clem and Dorothy Mae (Hanson) D.; m. Teresa Lee Morgan, May 31, 1984. BA summa cum laude, Calif. State U., Hayward, 1968; MusM summa cum laude, U. So. Calif., 1970. Mus. dir. Artist's Repertory Theatre, Los Angeles, 1976-79; accompanist Los Angeles City Coll., 1980-83; faculty mem. Loretto Heights Coll., Denver, 1983—; mus. dir., accompanist, Hayward, Los Angeles, Denver, 1960—; organist, asst. conductor Panorama Presbyn. Ch., Panorama City, Calif., 1976-83; critic Opera Guide, Los Angeles, 1981-83. Composer, lyricist, librettist: Roundheads, 1976 (Bicentennial Commendation), Evening Shadows, 1977 (Dramalogue Critics award 1978), Celebration of the Angels, 1980, Martin Avdeich: A Christmas Miracle, 1985 (Pulitzer Prize nomination 1986). Mem. Dramatists' Guild, Nat. Writers' Club. Republican. Avocations: travel, reading, singing. Home: 231 S Bryant St Denver CO 80219 Office: Loretto Heights Coll 3001 S Federal Blvd Denver CO 80236-2798

DOWNES, DAVID ANTHONY, English educator; b. Victor, Colo., Aug. 17, 1927; s. David Michael and Julia (Zitnik) D.; m. Audrey Romaine Ernst, Sept. 7, 1949; children: Mary Kathryn, Jane Frances, Daniel Ross, Michelle Marie. BA cum laude, Regis Coll., 1949; MA, Marquette U., 1950; PhD, U. Wash., 1956. Instr. English Gonzaga U., Spokane, Wash., 1950-53; asst. prof., then prof., chmn. dept. Seattle U., 1953-68; prof. English, dean humanities and fine arts Calif. State U., Chico, 1968—, dir. ednl. devel. projects, 1972—, chmn. English dept., 1978—. Author: Gerard Manley Hopkins: A Study of His Ignatian Spirit, 1959, Victorian Portraits: Hopkins and Pater, 1965, Pater, Kingsley and Newman, 1972, Ruskin's Landscape of Beatitude, 2d edit. 1984, The Great Sacrifice: Studies in Hopkins, 1983, Hopkins: Sanctifying Imagination, 1985, other studies on Hopkins; editor Univ. Journal, 1974-78; contbr. articles to Thought, Victorian Poetry, other jours. Grantee Western Gear Found., 1960, Seattle U., 1961, 62, 67, Andrew Mellon Found., Stanford U., 1982, Pres. Merit award, 1984, Profl. Achievement award, 1984. Office: Calif State U Dept English Chico CA 95926

DOWNEY, TED L., management consultant; b. Tiskilwa, Ill., Dec. 3, 1949; s. Harold L. and Mary L. (Hasselman) D. BA, Sangamon State U., Springfield, Ill., 1970, MA, 1971. Analyst Ill. Office of Gov., Springfield, 1972-74; sr. mgr. Price Waterhouse, Sacramento, 1974-86, Peat Marwick, Los Angeles, 1986—; advisor Nat. Govs. Assn., Washington, 1978-82. Contbg. Author: Papers in Public Finance, 1975; contbr. guest articles to numerous newspapers. Participant Grace Commn., Washington, 1983-84. White House Conf. on Productivity, Washington, 1984, Gov.'s Efficiency Teams, Sacramento, 1983; co-found. Nat. Student Lobby, Washington, 1970-72. Mem. Inst. Mgmt. Consulting (chpt. bd. dirs. 1985-86), Am. Arbitration Assn. Home: 8190 W Hidden Lakes Dr Roseville CA 95661

DOWNING, CHRISTINE ROSENBLATT, theology educator; b. Leipzig, Germany, Mar. 21, 1931; came to U.S., 1935; d. Edgar Fritz and Herta (Fischer) Rosenblatt; m. George Downing, June 9, 1951, (div. Jan. 1978); children: Peter, Eric, Scott, Christopher, Sandra; m. River Malcolm, Sept. 2, 1984. BA, Swarthmore Coll., 1948; PhD, Drew U., 1966; MA, U.S. Internat. U., 1982. From instr. to assoc. prof. religion and psychology Rutgers U., New Brunswick, N.J., 1963-75; prof., chmn. dept. religious studies San Diego State U., 1974—; mem. core faculty Calif. Sch. Profl. Psychology, Pomona, 1974—. Author: The Goddess, 1981; co-author: Face to Face to Face, 1975; contbr. articles to profl. jours. Fellow NEH, 1982-83. Fellow Soc. Values in Higher Edn. (bd. dirs. 1966-81); mem. AAUP, Am. Acad. Religion (pres. 1973-74). Office: San Diego State U Dept Religious Studies San Diego CA 92182

DOWNS, GEORGE, politicial science educator; b. Darby, Pa., Aug. 6, 1946; s. George W. Sr. and Ruth (McFarland) D. BA, Shimer Coll., 1967; PhD, U. Mich., 1976. From asst. prof. to prof. polit. sci. U. Calif., Davis, 1976—. Author: Bureaucracy, Innovation and Public Policy, 1976, The Search for Government Efficiency, 1986; contbr. articles to profl. jours. Served to capt. USAF, 1967-71. Recipient Youden Prize Am. Soc. Quality Control, 1982. Mem. AAAS, Am. Polit. Sci. Assn. Home: 2801 Bodega Bay Pl Davis CA 95616 Office: U Calif Polit Sci Dept Davis CA 95616

DOWNS, MARION PFAENDER, audiologist, researcher; b. New Ulm, Minn., Jan. 26, 1914; d. Albert and Marie Therese (Neumann) Pfaender; m. George R. Downs, Sept. 22, 1934 (dec. 1984); children: Josephine, George R. Jr., Sara. BA, U. Minn., 1935; MA, U. Denver, 1951; D. Human Services(hon.), U. No. Colo., 1979. Asst. prof. U. Denver, 1951-59; prof. audiology U. Colo. Med. Sch., Denver, 1959-82, prof. emerita, 1982—. Author: (with others) Auditory Disorders in School Children, 1983, Hearing in Children, 1984. Home hearing test grantee NIH, 1986; Marion Downs Children's Hearing Ctr. Fund named in her honor U. Colo. Health Scis. Ctr., 1986. Fellow Am. Speech Lang. Hearing Assn. (cert.), Soc. Ear Nose Throat Advances in Children; hon. mem. Colo. State Speech Hearing Assn. (pres. 1955, 78). Avocations: tennis, skiing, mountain climbing. Home: 735 Grape St Denver CO 80220 Office: U Colo Health Scis Ctr 4200 E 9th Ave Denver CO 80262

DOYLE, DEBORAH, marketing executive; b. Phila., Oct. 15, 1959; d. William David and Carole Ann (McIntire) D. BA in English, Pa. State U., 1980. Dir. community relations Tempe (Ariz.) Daily News, 1983-84; dir. promotional publicity Barclay Communications, Phoenix, 1985-86; regional. mktg. mgr. Arby's Inc., Scottsdale, Ariz., 1986—. Sec., treas. Tempe All-City Assn., 1985. Mem. Ad2 Phoenix (sec., treas. 1984-85, pres. 1985-86), Phoenix Advt. Club. Democrat. Roman Catholic. Office: Arbys Inc Regional Office 4412 N Miller Rd Scottsdale AZ 85251

DOYLE, EDWARD JOHN, III, banking executive; b. Evanston, Ill., Nov. 3, 1944; s. Edward John and Doris (Lane) D.; m. Eileen Ryan, Nov. 25, 1967; children: Kara, John. BS, Marquette U., 1967, MBA, 1975. Comml. loan officer Marshall & Isley Bank, Milw., 1967-85; sr. v.p. Crocker Bank, Los Angeles, 1985—, Calif. Fed. Savs. and Loan, Los Angeles, 1985—; pres., bd. dirs. Cal Fed Investment Services, Los Angeles. Active YMCA, Los Angeles. Mem. Consumer Bankers Assn., Calif. League Savs. Instns. (comml. coms. 1985—). Roman Catholic. Club: Riviera Tennis (Pacific Palisades, Calif.). Lodge: Rotary. Home: 16407 Akron St Pacific Palisades CA 90272 Office: Calif Fed Savs & Loan 5670 Wilshire Blvd #1990 Los Angeles CA 90036

DOYLE, THERESA LIPARI, real estate executive, public relations specialist; b. Long Beach, Calif., Aug. 27, 1957; d. Joseph and Joyce Lorraine (Wagle) Lipari; m. Timothy Xavier Doyle, June 26, 1982. BA, Calif. State U., Fullerton, 1980. Fundraising asst. Am. Heart Assn., Santa Ana, Calif., 1980; account exec. Kerr & Assocs. Pub. Relations, Huntington Beach, Calif., 1980-83; dir. mktg. Covington Homes, Fullerton, Calif., 1983-86; dir. sales and mktg., Covington Homes, Orange County, Calif., 1986, v.p. sales and mktg., 1986—; pub. relations cons. Am. Heart Assn., 1980-84, Family Crisis Ctr., Orange County, 1980-83. Recipient Outstanding Pub. Relations award Publicity Club Los Angeles, 1980, 3 Mem. Inst. Residential Mktg. awards Nat. Assn. Home Builders, 1986. Mem. Women in Communications, Inc. (Outstanding Mag. Article award 1980, Outstanding Pub. Relations award 1980), Bldg. Industry Assn. (dir. sales and mktg. 1984-86, 5 Major Achievment in Merchandising Excellence awards, 1984-85), Nat. Assn. Female Execs., Southern Calif. Women in Advertising, Calif. State U., Fullerton Alumni Assn. Republican. Roman Catholic. Office: Covington Homes 1748 W Katella Ave Suite 106 Orange CA 92667

DOYLE, WILFRED EMMETT, bishop; b. Calgary, Alta., Can., Feb. 18, 1913; s. John Joseph and Mary (O'Neill) D. B.A., U. Alta, 1935; D.C.L., U. Ottawa, Ont., Can., 1949. Ordained priest Roman Cath. Ch., 1938; chancellor Archdiocese Edmonton, Alta., Can., 1949-58; bishop Nelson, B.C., Can., 1958—; Chmn. bd. govs. Notre Dame U., Nelson, 1963-74. Address: 813 Ward St, Nelson, BC Canada V1L 1T4

DRABEK, THOMAS EDWARD, sociology educator; b. Chgo., Feb. 29, 1940; s. Thomas Francis and Glenna Marie (Martin) D.; m. Ruth Ann Obduskey, June 10, 1960; children—Deborah Kaye, Russell Ray. B.A., U. Denver, 1961; M.A., Ohio State U., 1963, Ph.D., 1965. Asst. prof. U. Denver, 1965-69, assoc. prof., 1969-74, prof., 1974—. Author: Disaster in Aisle 13, 1968; (with G.M. Sykes) Law and the Lawless, 1969; Laboratory Simulation of a Police Communication System Under Stress, 1969; Complex Organizations: A Sociological Perspective, 1973; (with J.E. Haas) Understanding Complex Organizations, 1974; (with D. Mileti and J. E. Haas) Human Behavior in Extreme Environments, 1975; (with D. Q. Brodie, J. Edgerton and P. Munson) The Flood Breakers: Citizens Band Radio Use During the 1978 Flood in the Grand Forks Region, 1979; (with H. Tamminga, T. Kilijanek and C. Adams) Managing Multiorganizational Emergency Responses: Emergent SAR Networks in Natural Disaster and Remote Area Settings, 1981; (with A. Mushkatel and T. Kilijanek) Earthquake Mitigation Policy: The Experience of Two States, 1983; (with W. H. Key) Conquering Disaster: Family Recovery and Long-Term Consequences, 1984, Emergency Management: The Human Factor, 1985, Human System Responses to Disaster, 1986. Recipient Disting. Teaching award U. Denver, 1969. Mem. Am. Sociol. Assn., Midwestern Sociol. Soc., Pacific Sociol. Soc., Western Social Sci. Assn. (pres. 1971-72). Home: 7643 E Navarro Pl Denver CO 80237 Office: Dept Sociology U Denver Denver CO 80208

DRACH, GEORGE WISSE, urology educator; b. Trenton, N.J., Aug. 24, 1935; s. John D. and Johanna (Opthof) D.; m. Paula Thomas, June 15, 1957; children: Diane David, Cora. BA, U. Ariz., 1957; MD, Case Western Res. U., 1961. Diplomate Am. Bd. Urology (trustee 1986—). Intern in surgery U. Hosps., Cleve., 1961-62, resident in surgery, 1962-63; research fellow in urology Bowman-Gray Sch. Medicine Wake Forest U. and N.C. Bapt. Hosp., Winston-Salem, 1965-66, asst. resident in urology, 1965-68, chief resident in urology, 1968-69; fellow in immunology U. N.Mex. Sch. Medicine, 1969-70; instr. surgery U. N.Mex., Albuquerque, 1969-70; asst. prof., chief urology U. Ariz., Tucson, 1970-74, assoc. prof., chief urology, 1974-77, acting assoc. dean acad. affairs, 1977-79, prof., chief urology, 1977—; cons. urology VA Hosp., Tucson, 1970—; mem. NIH site visit teams, 1979-82; trustee Am. Bd. Urology, 1985—; mem. research and grants com. Nat. Kidney Found., 1982—; chmn. com. of 9 U. Ariz. Coll. Medicine, 1972-74, mem. curriculum com., 1974-80; sci. coordinator FDA Clin. Study Extracorporeal Shock Wave Lithotripsy, 1982—. Asst. editor Jour. Urology, 1972-78, ad hoc reviewer, 1972—; mem. editorial bd. Investigative Urology, 1972-78, ad hoc reviewer, 1972—; ad hoc reviewer Sci.; ad hoc reviewer Urol. Research; contbr. numerous articles to profl. jours.; numerous chpts. to books. Served to lt. comdr. USNR, 1963-65. Fogarty Sr. Internat. Research fellow Gen. Infirmary, Leeds, Eng., 1980; recipient Resident Essay award Cleve. Surgical Soc., 1963; Am. Geriatrics Soc. Resident Research fellow, 1966-68; Nat. Inst. Arthritis and Metabolic Disease spl. fellow, 1969-70. Fellow ACS (pres. Ariz. chpt. 1981); mem. AMA, Am. Urol. Assn. (research com. 1978-81, pubs. com. 1981—, chmn. pubs. com. 1985-86, 1st award sci. exhibit S.E. sect. 1968, 2d award sci. exhibit Nat. Conv., 1975, Hugh Hampton Young award 1986), Clin. Soc. Genitourinary Surgeons, Am. Assn. Genitourinary Surgeons, Soc. Univ. Surgeons, Ariz. Med. Assn., Western Urol. Forum, Ariz. Urol. Soc. (pres. 1980-81), Tucson Urol. Soc. (pres. 1982-83), Am. Assn. Med. Colls., Soc. Univ. Urologists, Internat. Soc. Nephrology, Soc. Internat. de Urologie, Sigma Xi, Phi Beta Kappa, Phi Kappa Phi. Avocation: ethnobotany. Home: 2681 E Calle Los Altos Tucson AZ 85718-2060 Office: U Ariz Health Scis Ctr 1501 N Campbell Ave Tucson AZ 85724

DRAGON, ELIZABETH ALICE, research molecularbiologist; b. Mineola, N.Y., June 12, 1948; d. Harry L. and Alice L. (Clayton) Oosterom; m. Frank X. Dragon, Aug. 24, 1972; 1 child, Michael. BS, U. N.H., 1970; PhD, Yeshiva U., 1980. Postdoctoral fellow Brookhaven Nat. Lab., Upton, N.Y., 1980-82; research scientist CODON, Brisbane, Calif., 1982—. Research grantee NIH, 1983—. Mem. AAAS, Am. Soc. Microbiology, Am. Soc. Parasitologists. Avocations: reading, bowling, roses. Home: 42 Park Lane Dr Orinda CA 94563 Office: CODON 430 Valley Dr Brisbane CA 94005

DRAINE, ROBERT WILCO, real estate executive; b. Los Angeles, Jan. 31, 1925; s. George Neiland and Ruth (Jewett) D.; m. Patricia Lee Hayes, Feb. 1, 1952; children—Janet, Cameron, Steven. Student Occidental Coll., 1943, Ind. U., 1943-44, UCLA, 1944-49. Cert., Soc. Indsl. Realtors. Mgr. Minn. Mining & Mfg., 1952-57; exec. v.p. Coldwell Banker Group, 1957-83; chmn. Robert Draine Group, Pacific Palisades, Calif., 1978—, ptnr. Draine/Poulson Group, Los Angeles, 1983—. bd. dirs. Watson Land, Los Angeles, CalFed Ptnrs., Los Angeles. Chmn. Los Angeles County Econ. Devel. Commn., 1980-81, Calif. Land Use Council, 1977-78, Los Angeles Econ. and Job Devel. Council, 1981-82; trustee UCLA Found.; bd. dirs. Orthopedia Hosp. Served with U.S. Army,, 1943-44. Mem. Soc. Indsl. Realtors (past pres.), Los Angeles C. of C. (past dir., So. Calif. Industrialist of Year, 1971). Presbyterian. Clubs: California , Los Angeles Country. Home: 1495 Capri Dr Pacific Palisades CA 90272 Office: Draine/Poulson Group 12217 W Pico Blvd Los Angeles CA 90064

DRAKE, DORIS CLAIRE, clinical social worker, biofeedback therapist; b. Santa Monica, Calif., Nov. 3, 1955; d. Edward Plumere and Doris Claire (Bentley) D. BSW, Calif. State U., Chico, 1977; MSW, UCLA, 1981. Lic. clin. social worker, Calif. Social worker Children's Home Soc., Los Angeles, 1981-83; mental health clinician Calif. Dept. Mental Health, Ukiah, Calif., 1983—; pvt. practice biofeedback therapy Ukiah, 1985—; adj. instr. Mendocino Community Coll., Ukiah, 1983-85; cons. Child Sexual Abuse Treatment Program, Ukiah, 1985—. Founder Community Social Work Library, Ukiah, 1984. Mem. Nat. Assn. Social Workers (unit chair 1983—), Biofeedback Soc. Am. (cert.), Biofeedback Soc. Calif., Children's Home Soc. Calif. (assoc.). Democrat. Methodist. Avocations: windsurfing, skiing, backpacking, music, geneaology. Home: PO Box 1204 Ukiah CA 95482 Office: Calif Mental Health Dept 564 S Dora St Ukiah CA 95482

DRAKE, HARRINGTON, business services and communications executive; b. Kansas City, Mo., Sept. 2, 1919; s. Embree and Orpha (Anderson) D.; m. Shirley Grant, Feb. 18, 1942; children: Ted G., Jeffrey, Anderson. B.A., Colgate U., 1941, LL.D. (hon.), 1985. With Reuben H. Donnelley Corp., N.Y.C., 1947-72; pres., prin. exec. officer Reuben H. Donnelley Corp., 1968-72; exec. v.p. Dun & Bradstreet, Inc., 1971-72; pres., chief operating officer The Dun & Bradstreet Corp., 1972-75, chief exec. officer, 1975-84, also bd. dirs.; bd. dirs. Rockwell Internat. Corp., Baxter Travenol Labs.; adv. dir. Irving Bank Corp., Irving Trust Co. Chmn. emeritus bd. trustees Colgate U. Clubs: Valley of Montecito (Calif.) Golf; Birnam Wood Golf (Santa Barbara, Calif.); Cypress Point Golf (Pebble Beach, Calif.); Links (N.Y.C.); Los Angeles Country-Golf, The Calif. (Los Angeles); Los Caballeros Golf (Wickenburg, Ariz.).

DRAKE, (LEROY) KENNETH, aerospace engineer; b. Cheyenne, Okla., Dec. 9, 1933; s. Elton Mnu and Verna M. (Rupp) D.; m. Donna Mae Good, Mar. 15, 1964 (div. Jan. 1977); children: Melanie, Vonita, Pamela Sue, Derek Kenneth; m. Carmen Proulx Belisle, May 28, 1977; children: Alain, Marc. Student, Long Beach Coll., 1957-61, Citrus Coll., 1961-63. Sr. cost analyst HITCO, Gardena, Calif., 1976-79, operation planning mgr., 1979-80, engring. service mgr., 1980-83, program mgmt., 1983-85, bus. mgr., 1985-86, mem. tech. staff mfg. engring. office, 1986—. Served with USN, 1951-54. Mem. Soc. Mfg. Engrs., Soc. Advancement Material and Process Engring., Nat. Contract Mgmt. Assn. Republican. Club: Am. Contract Bridge League. Office: Aerospace Corp 2350 E El Segundo Blvd El Segundo CA 90245

DRAKE, LUCIUS C., JR., school administrator; b. Tacloban, Philippines, June 29, 1946; s. Lucius Charles and Victoria (Badiles) D. BA, Fisk U., 1968; EdM, Temple U., 1970. Cert. sch. adminstr.; cert. guidance counselor. Math. tchr. Sch. Dist. of Phila., 1968-70, Gary (Ind.) City Schs., 1970-72, Dept. Defense Dependents Sch., Fed. Republic Germany and Okinawa, 1972-77; elemtary tchr. Dept. Defense Dependents Sch., Philippines, 1977-79; guidance counselor Dept. Defense Dependents Sch., Japan and Korea, 1979-83; asst. prin. Dept. Defense Dependents Sch., Seoul and Taegu, Korea, 1983—; chmn. math dept. Sayre Jr. High Sch., Phila., 1969-70; math. curriculum rev. com., Dept. Defense Dependents Schs., Karlsruhe, Fed. Republic Germany, 1972-73; dir. Far East Basketball Tourney, Taegu, Korea, 1984-86; mem. regional mgmt. council, Dept. Defense Dependents Schs., Okinawa, 1985-86. Recipient Disting. Educator award IDEA Acad. Fellows, Denver, 1985. Fellow Am. Bd. Master Educators (disting.); mem. Nat. Assn. Secondary Sch. Prins., Nat. Assn. Elem. Sch. Prins., Internat. Educator's Inst., Phi Delta Kappa, Alpha Phi Alpha (edn. sec. Seoul chp. 1984-85). Democrat. Baptist. Avocations: weight tng., travel, chess, basketball, karate. Home: 2143 Westbourn Dr Loveland CO 80537 Office: Seoul Am Elementary Sch US Army Installation Seoul, Korea APO San Francisco CA 96301-0005

DRAKE, RONALD DOUGLAS, consulting engineer, real estate developer; b. Denver, Sept. 22, 1951; s. Donald Neil and Betty Lee (Estes) D.; m. Louise Margaret Bauer, Oct. 26, 1979; children: J.B., Lee. BS in Mining Engring., Colo. Sch. Mines, 1973. Registered profl. engr., Colo. President Drake Engring. and Constrn. Co., Winter Park, Colo., 1979-86; pres., chmn. bd. Berthoud Tunnel Bldg. Authority, Winter Park, 1986—; pres. Winter Park Corp., 1982-86. Mem. Winter Park Town Council, 1986—; bd. dirs. Winter Park Devel. Authority, 1985-86, Grand County Water & San Distr., 1986. Served to capt. C.E., U.S. Army, 1974-78. Decorated Army Commendation medal with oak leaf cluster. Mem. NSPE, Profl. Engrs. of Colo. Republican. Presbyterian. Avocations: skiing, golf, outdoor activities. Home: 320 Vasquez Rd Winter Park CO 80482 Office: Berthoud Tunnel Bldg Authority PO Box 3096 Winter Park CO 80482

DRAKE, STEVE JOEL, mining executive; b. Iron River, Mich., May 14, 1948; s. Thomas Watts and Ermaline Rita (Parrotta) D.; m. Jo Ann Steele, Aug. 30, 1966 (div. Oct. 1976); children: Julie Ann, Stephanie Ann; m. Leslie Ellen Sims, Apr. 6, 1985. Attended high sch., Globe, Ariz. Mine gen. foreman Ranchers Exploration, Miami, Ariz., 1975-79, mine supt., 1979-81; gen. mgr. Ranchers/Territorial Corp., Slate Creek, Alaska, 1981-84; mine ops. supt. Homestake McLaughlin Mine, Lower Lake, Calif., 1984—. Avocations: hunting, fishing, snow and water skiing, golf. Home: 9303 Yaquima Dr Kelseyville CA 95451 Office: McLaughlin Mine Homestake Mining Co PO Box 1010 Lower Lake CA 95457

DRAKE, SUSAN FREIMER, telecommunications consultant; b. Bklyn., May 23, 1946; d. Leo and Beatrice (Samuels) Freimer; m. Stanley Rosenzweig, July 16, 1967; m. 2d, Richard P. Drake, Nov. 15, 1981. B.A., CUNY, 1967. Communications cons. N.Y. Telephone, N.Y.C., 1970-75; communications analyst Nat. Telephone Planning Corp., Yonkers, N.Y., 1975-78; cons. Peat, Marwick Mitchell & Co., N.Y.C., 1978-79; dir. Los Angeles ops. Contel Info. Systems, Great Neck, N.Y., 1979-82; owner, mgr. Suritel Assocs., Los Angeles, 1982—. Contbr. articles to profl. jours. Bd. dirs., residential chmn. Am. Cancer Soc., Yonkers, 1977-78. Mem. Internat. Orgn. Women in Telecommunications, Valley Interchange of Entrepreneurial Women (founding dir., pres. 1982-86), Nat. Assn. Female Execs. Home and Office: 17246 Braxton St Granada Hills CA 91344

DRAPER, JAMES EDWARD, research physics educator; b. Kansas City, Mo., Sept. 14, 1924; s. Raymond Edward and Doris Isabelle (Aiken) D.; m. Helen Caryl Andrews, June 12, 1948; children: Lorna, Jeffrey, John, Anna. BA, Williams Coll., 1945; PhD, Cornell U., 1952. Assoc. physicist Brookhaven Nat. Lab., Upton, N.Y., 1952-56; from asst. to assoc. prof. Yale U., New Haven, 1956-63; prof. physics U. Calif., Davis, 1964—, chmn. dept. physics, 1966-71; cons. Lawrence Berkeley (Calif.) Lab., 1980—; research assoc. nuclear physics div. Atomic Energy Research Establishment, Harwell, Eng., 1971, 79. Contbr. numerous articles to profl. jours. Fellow AAAS, Am. Phys. Soc. Home: 22 Almond Ln Davis CA 95616 Office: U Calif Physics Dept Davis CA 95616

DRATLER, JAY, JR., lawyer, educator; b. Los Angeles, June 11, 1945; s. Jay Dratler and Berenice (Tolins) Eunson. AB in Physics, U. Calif., Berkeley, 1966; MS in Physics, U. Calif. San Diego, 1968, PhD in Physics, 1971; JD, Harvard U., 1978. Bar: Calif. 1978, U.S. Dist. Ct. (no. dist.) Calif. 1978, Hawaii 1987. Physicist Diax Corp., La Jolla, 1972-73; research scientist U. Calif., Berkeley, 1973-75; geophysicist U.S. Geol. Survey, Menlo Park, Calif., 1975; assoc. Morrison & Foerster, San Francisco, 1978-81, Fenwick, Davis & West, Palo Alto, Calif., 1981-86; assoc. prof. law U. Hawaii, Honolulu, 1986—; cons. York U., Downsview, Ont., Can., 1974, Geonomics, Inc., Berkeley, 1975, Fenwick, Davis & West, Palo Alto, Calif., 1986—. Articles editor Harvard U. Law Rev., 1976-78. Fellow NSF, 1966-70, NATO, 1971-72. Mem. AAAS, ABA (chmn. subcom. 1985—), Computer Law Assn., Sierra Club, Mensa, Phi Beta Kappa. Democrat. Jewish. Avocations: jogging, guitar, symphony, hiking, opera.

DRAUT, JOHN EDWARD PAUL, electrical engineering consultant; b. N.Y.C., Aug. 12, 1950; s. William John and Rona (Roberts) D.; m. Dianne Kathleen Paar, June 30, 1979. BEE with honors, Pratt Inst., 1973; MSEE, Stanford U., 1977. Design engr. Intersil, Inc., Sunnyvale, Calif., 1976-80; prin. engr. Genrad Semiconductor Test Co., Milpitas, Calif., 1980-81; sr. logic engr. Magnuson Devel. Co., San Jose, Calif., 1981-82; mgr. engring. Davong Systems, Inc., Sunnyvale, 1982-85; founder, prin. J. Draut Cons., Menlo Park, Calif., 1985—. Mem. Tau Beta Pi, Eta Kappa Nu. Avocations: tropical fish, downhill skiing. Home and Office: 207 Robin Way Menlo Park CA 94025

DRECHSLER-PARKS, DEBORAH MARIE, research physiologist; b. Lakewood, Ohio, Apr. 27, 1952; d. Albert Carl and Dorothea Marie (Angersbach) Drechsler; m. Edward Parks, Oct. 29, 1983. AB, Westmont Coll., 1974; MA, U. Calif., Santa Barbara, 1976; PhD, Pa. State U., 1981. Postdoctoral fellow U. Calif., Santa Barbara, 1981-85, asst. research physiologist, 1985—. Contbr. articles to publs. Health Effects Inst. grantee, 1983-85, EPA grantee, 1986-89. Mem. AAAS, N.Y. Acad. Scis. Orthodox Presbyterian. Avocations: jogging, dogs, raising African violets, classical music and lit. Office: U Calif Inst Environ Stress Santa Barbara CA 93106

DREICER, HARRY, physicist; b. Bad Lausick, Fed. Republic of Germany, Oct. 6, 1927; came to U.S., 1939; s. Alfred and Jean Dreicer; m. Roberta J. Waldman, July 30, 1950; children: Emily, Victor, Jared. BS in Physics, MIT, 1951, PhD in Physics, 1954. Mem. staff Los Alamos (N.Mex.) Nat. Lab., 1954-66, group leader, 1966-75, asst. div. leader, 1975-76, div. leader, 1977—; prof. physics U. Colo., Boulder, 1977-78. Fellow MIT, Cambridge, 1952-53. Fellow AAAS, Am. Phys. Soc. (chmn. div. plasma physics 1984-85, vice-chmn. 1983-84). Office: Los Alamos Nat Lab Controlled Thermonuclear Research MS F640 Los Alamos NM 87545

DREIER, DAVID TIMOTHY, U.S. congressman; b. Kansas City, Mo., July 5, 1952; s. H. Edward and Joyce (Yeomans) D. BA cum laude, Claremont McKenna Coll., 1975; MA in Am. Govt., Claremont Grad. Sch., 1976. Dir. corp. relations Claremont McKenna Coll., 1975-78; dir. mktg. and govt. relations Indsl. Hydrocarbons, San Dimas, Calif., 1978-81; mem. 97th Congress from 35th Calif. Dist., 98th-100th Congresses from 33d Calif. Dist.; mem. banking com., small bus. com.; vice-chmn. Energy and Agr. subcom.; active Calif. Reps., POW/MIA Task Force, Afghanistan Task Force; mem. Calif. Rep. Party vice chmn. Energy and Agriculture subcommittee; POW/MIA Task Force, Afghanistan Task Force. Office: 410 Cannon House Office Bldg Washington DC 20515

DREISBACH, JOHN GUSTAVE, investment banker; b. Paterson, N.J., Apr. 24, 1939; s. Gustave John and Rose Catherine (Koehler) D.; AB, N.Y.U., 1963; m. Janice Lynn Petitjean. With Shields & Co., Inc., 1965-68, Model, Roland & Co., Inc., N.Y.C., 1968-72, F. Eberstadt & Co., Inc., N.Y.C., 1972-74; v.p. Bessemer Trust Co., 1974-78; pres. Community Housing Capital, Inc., 1978-80; chmn., pres. John G. Dreisbach, Inc., Santa Fe, N.Mex., 1980—; JGD Housing Corp., 1982—; bd. dirs., pres. The Santa Fe Investment Conf., 1986— Served with USAFR, 1964. Mem. Mensa, Santa Fe C. of C. Republican. Episcopalian. Clubs: St. Bartholomew's Community, Essex, Hartford, Amigos del Alcalde. Office: 1 Sunflower Circle Santa Fe NM 87501-8503

DRENNAN, MICHAEL ELDON, bank executive; b. Yakima, Wash., June 24, 1946; s. George Eldon and Jane (Nilsson) D.; m. Alice Marie Seabolt, May 13, 1972; children: Brian, David. BS in Fin., U. Oreg., 1968. Ops. officer First State Bank, Aloha, Oreg., 1972-73; ops., loan officer First State Bank, Portland, Oreg., 1973-74; asst. mgr. First State Bank, Milwaukie, Oreg., 1974-76; asst. v.p. Citizens Bank, Corvallis, Oreg., 1976-80, v.p., 1980-81; pres., chief exec. officer Bank of Corvallis, 1981—. Bd. dirs. Cascades W. Fin. Services, Inc., 1983—, United Way Benton County, 1984—; trustee Good Samaritan Hosp. Found., 1984—; bd. dirs. Jr. Achievement of Benton County, 1983-85, treas. 1984-85, mem. exec. bd., 1984-85; bd. dirs. Benton County Family YMCA, 1978-80, sec. 1979, mem. fin. com., 1978-80, mem. personnel com. 1979, active sustaining membership dr.; bd. dirs. Community Club, 1978-83, pres., 1978, treas. 1979-80; active Corvallis Ambassadors, 1976—; mem. mgmt. com. Corvallis Conv. and Vis. Bur., 1982-85; fund. raising chmn. Com. City Improvemnt Levy, 1980; mem. exec. com. Pack 17 Boy Scouts Am., 1984—, treas. 1984—. Served to lt. USN, 1968-71. Mem. Corvallis C. of C. (v.p. fin. 1980-83, pres. 1985-86, chmn. bd. dirs. 1986-87, Econ. Devel. award 1978, Chmn. of Bd. award, 1979, George award 1980-81, Devel. award 1983), Am. Inst. Banking (cert.), Chi Phi, Alpha Kappa Psi, Beta Gamma Sigma. Home: 4060 NE Pin Oak Corvallis OR 97330 Office: Bank of Corvallis 2600 NW Ninth St Corvallis OR 97330

DRENNON, BARRY JAMES, life sciences technician; b. Morristown, N.J., Dec. 12, 1944; s. Winfield Kinsley and Rose Marie (Morris) D.; m. Barbara Jo Benavente, Oct. 29, 1962; m. 2d, Marsha Kay Long, Dec. 13, 1969; children—Scott Patrick, Felicia Anne, Jeffrey Todd, Deborah Michele, Laura Nicole. Customer service rep. IBM, Phila., Atlanta, 1966-70; lab. technician Devro Inc., Somerville, N.J., 1970-74; chem. technician Controls for Environ. Pollution, Santa Fe, 1974-76; life scis. technician III U. Calif. Los Alamos Nat. Lab., 1976—. Vestryman, sr. warden, mem. Acolyte Guild, Episcopalian Church. Served with USN, 1963-66. Mem. Am. Soc. Agronomy, Soil Sci. Soc. Am., Calumet Photographic Soc., Western History Assn., N. Mex. Barbed Wire Collectors Assn. Democrat. Contbr. numerous articles to profl. publs. Home: 1780 Fort Union Dr Santa Fe NM 87501 Office: PO Box 1663 Los Alamos Nat Lab Los Alamos NM 87545

DRESANG, RICHARD WAYNE, social services director; b. Kimberly, Wis., May 11, 1947; s. Norbert E. and Margie (Tracy) D.; m. Barbara Ann Rooyakkers, Sept. 7, 1967 (div. Feb. 1979); children: Jill Renee, Vicki Ann; m. JoEllen Jorgensen, Mar. 7, 1980; children: Christopher Richard, Nicklaus Norbert. BSSW, U. Wis., Oshkosh, 1971; student, U. Wis., Madison, 1971-73, U. Wyo., 1981—. Co-dir. La Rasa, Fond du Lac, Wis., 1970-71; social worker Brown County Dept. Social Services, Green Bay, Wis., 1971-74; adminstr. Green Bay Free Clinic, 1974-80; asst. mgr. Homax Oil Co., Glenrock, Wyo., 1980-82; dir. Youth Crisis Ctr., Casper, Wyo., 1982—; cons. Wyo. Dept. Health and Social Services, Cheyenne, 1984—, Converse County Group Home, Douglas, Wyo., 1985—; pres. Wyo. Youth Services Assn., 1985—; pres. elect. Wyo. Human Resource Conf., 1986—. Community organizer Brown County Youth Resource Council, Green Bay, 1972, Oneida Tribe Youth Resource Council, Green Bay, 1972, Green Bay Street Worker Program, 1972, Women, Infants, and Children's Program, Casper, Wyo., 1981. Recipient President's award Wis. Med. Assn., 1979. Mem. Nat. Assn. Social Workers, Am. Pub. Welfare Assn., Natrona County Child Protection Team. Democrat. Roman Catholic. Avocations: camping, food preparation, fishing, carpentry. Home: 6658 Sharrock Rd NBU 9 Casper WY 82604 Office: Youth Crisis Ctr Inc 242 S Jefferson Casper WY 82601

DRESBACH, LINDA ELAINE, accountant; b. San Jose, Calif., Nov. 27, 1955; d. George Robert and Frances May (Dickie) D. BS, San Jose State U., 1977, teaching cert., 1978. Acctg. supr., systems analyst Zeta Lab. Inc., Santa Clara, Calif., 1978—. Mem. Am. Mgmt. Assn. Republican. Presbyterian. Avocations: tennis, snow skiing, outrigger canoe paddling.

DRESSER, JESSE DALE, investor, real state officer; b. San Diego, May 5, 1906; s. Charlwood Fessenden and Ora (Evans) D.; m. Mary A. Goldsworthy, June 9, 1934; children—Dennis T., Brian D., Linda A. Ed. pub. schs. Trainee Union Title Ins. Co., San Diego, 1926; sr. title examiner, chief title officer, v.p. So. Title & Trust Co., San Diego, 1927-51; v.p., chief title officer Security Title Ins. Co., San Diego, 1951-54; asst. to pres. San Diego Fed. Savs. & Loan Assn., 1954-55, v.p., sec., 1955-56, exec. v.p., dir., 1956-70; v.p., dir. Calif. Gen. Mortgage Service, Inc., 1967-70, San Diego Federated Ins. Agy., Inc., 1967-70; real estate investments La Mesa, Calif., 1970—. Home: 3833 Acacia St Bonita CA 92002 Mailing Address: PO Box 418 Bonita CA 92002

DRESSER, MILES JOEL, physicist, educator; b. Spokane, Wash., Dec. 19, 1935; s. Lloyd Joel and Stella Christine (Nelson) D.; m. Muriel Louise Hunt, June 7, 1959; children: Don Joel, Marilyn Louise, Laura Jill. BA, Linfield Coll., 1957; PhD, Iowa State U., 1964. Research asst. Ames (Iowa) Lab. AEC, 1959-64; asst. prof. Wash. State U., Pullman, 1964-70, assoc. prof. physics, 1970—; vis. physicist Nat. Bur. Standards, Washington, 1972; vis. prof. physics U. Pitts., 1984-88—; mem. exec. council Wash. State U. Resident Instrs. Staff, 1983—; prof. short course Wash. State U., 1981-84. Contbr. articles to profl. jours. Bd. dirs. Pullman United Way, 1972-75, Common Ministry, Wash. State U., 1980-84. Mem. Am. Phys. Soc., Am. Assn. Physics Tchrs., Am. Vacuum Soc., Sigma Xi. Baptist.

DRESSLER, FREDERIC MICHAEL, cable TV executive; b. N.Y.C., Sept. 23, 1941; s. Martin and Anne (Kaufman) D.; children—Kevin, Douglas. B.S., Syracuse U., N.Y., 1963; postgrad. U. Denver, 1979, Negotiation Inst., 1981. News reporter, editorial dir. sta. KBTV, Denver 1967-74; exec. news producer Sta. KMGH-TV, Denver, 1974-76; system mgr. Fresno, Calif., 1977; div. mgr. Am. TV and Communications Corp., Englewood, Colo., 1977-80, v.p. Denver, 1980-87, v.p. programming 1987—; pres., bd. dirs. Mile Hi Cablevision Inc., Denver, 1982-86, also chief exec. officer; lectr. U. Colo., 1971-74. V.p., bd. dirs. Colo. Easter Seal Soc., 1980; adv. bd. Mexican-Am. Legal Def. and Edn. Fund. Served with USNG, 1963-69. Recipient Award for Disting. Service in Journalism, 1971, Commendation for Investigative Reporting, 1973, Service Recognition Award, Nat. Broadcast Editorial Assn., 1975. Mem. Nat. Cable TV Assn., Nat. Broadcast Editorial Assn. (founding dir., officer 1972, pres. 1975, Radio-TV Editorial Jour. adv. bd. 1974-76), Colo. Cable TV Assn. (polit. action com. 1983—), Alpha Epsilon Rho. Lodge: Denver Rotary. Home: 13302 E Jewell Ave #203 Aurora CO 80012

DRESSLER, MARGARET DAWN, physics educator; b. Portland, Oreg., July 11, 1927; d. Marcus Driver and Mary Elsie (Everett) O'Day; m. Robert Lyle Dressler, July 31, 1948; children: Elizabeth Meyer, Katherine Shea, Mary Dressler. AB, Wellesley Coll., 1948. Research asst. Cruft Lab., Boston, 1948-49; electrical engr. Bonneville Power Adminstrn., Portland, 1949-50; instr. Portland State U., 1962-69, sr. instr., 1969-79, asst. prof., 1979-86, assoc. prof., 1986—. Chair Energy Facility Siting Council State Oreg., 1977-78; pres. Oreg. Psychoanalytic Found. Bd., Portland, 1986—; moderator 1st Congl. Ch., Portland, 1981. Mem. AAUW (hon. Portland br. 1981, pres. 1986—), AAAS (chmn. steering com. Women's caucus 1975-77), Am. Assn. Physics Tchrs., AAAS (pres. Oreg. sect. 1982-83). Republican. Mem. United Ch. Christ. Club: Zonta (Portland) (pres. 1983-84). Avocations: camping, canoeing, cooking. Home: 2340 Bellaire Portland OR 97233 Office: Portland State U SW 6th and Harrison Box 751 Portland OR 97207

DRESTI, MAURO GIUSEPPE, design engineer; b. Detroit, Oct. 5, 1959; s. Luigi and Francesca (Savini) D. BSEE, Oakland U., Rochester, Mich., 1982. Elec. engr. USN, Pomona, Calif., 1983-84; design engr. Transducer Techs., Inc., Pasadena, Calif., 1984-86; metrologist So. Calif. Edison, Westminster, Calif., 1986—. Republican. Roman Catholic. Avocation: rebuilding old cars. Home: 917 S Easthills Dr West Covina CA 91792

DREVDAHL-ORCHARD, JEAN MARIE, safety supervisor, industrial hygienist, nurse; b. Tucson, Feb. 16, 1961; d. Elmer R. and Joan B. (Levine) D.; m. Mark S. Orchard. AD, Clark Coll., Vancouver, Wash., 1981; BS, Oreg. State U., 1983; MS, Portland State U., 1986. RN, Assoc. Safety Profl., Emergency Med. Technician. RN, intravenous therapist S.W. Wash. Hosps., Vancouver, 1981-83; occupational health nurse Crown Zellerback Corp., West Linn, Oreg., 1983-85; safety supr. N.W. Natural Gas, Portland, Oreg., 1985—; instr. Clark Coll., 1986—. Mem. Am. Indsl. Hygiene Assn. (Indsl. Hygiene scholar Pacific Sect. 1981), Am. Soc. Safety Engrs. (sec. Portland chpt. 1986—). Avocations: sailing, bike riding, sewing. Home: 396 SE 39th Ave Hillsboro OR 97123 Office: NW Natural Gas 220 NW 2d Ave Portland OR 97209

DREW, CHARLES MILTON, chemist; b. McKinney, Tex., Feb. 13, 1921; s. Andrew Everett and Lutie Lella (Weger) D.; divorced; children: Darrell Everett, Donna Lee, Lynn Milton, Carl Allen. BS, U. N. Tex., 1943. Supr. chemist Columbia Southern, Corpus Christi, Tex., 1943-47; research scientist Naval Weapons Ctr., China Lake, Calif., 1947-70; cons. U. Ariz., Tucson, 1980—. Author: Principles of Gas Chromatography, 1959; contbr. articles to profl. jours.; patentee in field. Mem. Research Soc. Am., Sigma Xi. Clubs: Glider Club (China Lake, Colo.) (pres. 1967-70), Rockhounds Club (pres. 1949-50). Avocations: soaring, hot air balloons, nature, creative glass working. Home: 0614 Bobcat Ln Redstone/Carbondale CO 81623 Office: Glass by Charles PO Box 336 Carbondale CO 81623-0336

DREW, CLIFFORD JAMES, educator; b. Eugene, Oreg., Mar. 9, 1943; s. Albert C. and Violet M. (Caskey) D. B.S. magna cum laude, Eastern Oreg. Coll., 1965; M.Ed., U.Ill., 1966; Ph.D. with honors, U. Oreg., 1968. Asst. prof. edn. Kent (Ohio) State U., 1968-69; asst. prof. dir. research and spl. edn. U. Tex., Austin, 1969-71; assoc. prof. spl. edn. U. Utah, Salt Lake City, 1971-76; prof. U. Utah, 1977—; asst. dean Grad. Sch. Edn., 1974-77, assoc. dean, 1977-79, prof. spl. edn. and ednl. psychology, 1979—; cons. HEW, 1969—; Bd. dirs. Far West Lab. Ednl. Research and Devel., San Francisco, 1974-80; mem. exec. bd. Salt Lake County Assn. Retarded Children, 1971-72; mem. adv. com. Mental Retardation Counseling Service, Tex. Dept. Mental Health Mental Retardation, 1969-70. Author: (with P. Chinn and D. Logan) Mental Retardation: A Life Cycle Approach, 2d edit, 1979, Introduction to Designing Research and Evaluation, 2d edit. 1980, (with M. Hardman and H. Bluhm) Mental Retardation: Social and Educational Perspectives, 1977, (with D. Gelfand and W. Jenson) Understanding Children's Behavior Disorders, 1982, 2d edit. 1988, (with D. Logan and M. Hardman) Mental Retardation: A Life Cycle Approach, 4th edit, 1988, Designing and Conducting Behavioral Research, 1985, (with M. Hardman and W. Egan) Human Exceptionality: Society, School, and Family, 1984, 2d edit. 1987; numerous articles in field. NDEA fellow, 1965-66; U.S. Office Edn. fellow, 1966-68. Fellow Am. Assn. Mental Deficiency; mem. Am. Psychol. Assn., Am. Ednl. Research Assn., Council Exceptional Children. Office: Grad Sch Edn MBH 221 Univ of Utah Salt Lake City UT 84112

DREW, RICHARD BRIAN, sales representative; b. N.Y.C., Dec. 10, 1952; s. Louis and Kay (Friedman) D.; m. Barbara Goldenberg, July 16, 1978; children: Matthew, Justin. BS, SUNY, Fredonia, 1974. Sales rep. VWR Sci. Inc., N.Y.C., 1975-80; dist. sales mgr. VWR Sci. Inc., Batavia, Ill., 1980-83; nat. furniture mgr. VWR Sci. Inc., Plano and Irvine, Tex., 1983-85; dist. mgr. VWR Sci. Inc., Denver, 1985—. Lake Erie Environ. Studies grantee, 1973. Avocations: racquetball, tennis. Office: VWR Sci Inc 3700 Havana St Denver CO 80239

DREXLER, KENNETH, lawyer; b. San Francisco, Aug. 2, 1941; s. Fred and Martha Jane (Cunningham) D.; BA, Stanford U., 1963; JD, UCLA, 1969. Bar: Calif. 1970. Assoc., David S. Smith, Beverly Hills, Calif., 1970, McCutchen, Doyle, Brown and Enersen, San Francisco, 1970-77; assoc. Chickering & Gregory, San Francisco, 1977-80, ptnr., 1980-82; ptnr. Drexler & Leach, San Rafael, Calif., 1982—. Served with AUS, 1964-66. Mem. ABA, Calif. State Bar (resolutions com. conf. of dels. 1979-83, chmn. 1982-83, adminstrn. justice com. 1983—), Marin County Bar Assn. (bd. dirs. 1985—), Bar Assn. San Francisco (dir. 1980-81), San Francisco Barristers Club (pres. 1976, dir. 1975-76), Marin Conservation League (bd. dirs. 1985—). Office: 1330 Lincoln Ave Suite 300 San Rafael CA 94901

DREXLER, KIM ERIC, author, researcher; b. Oakland, Calif., Apr. 25, 1955; s. Allan Barry and Hazel Edna (Gassmann) D.; m. Christine Louise Peterson, June 18, 1981. BS in Interdisciplinary Sci., MIT, 1977, MS in Engring., 1979. Freelance author, researcher, lectr., inventor Cambridge, Mass., 1980-85, Palo Alto, Calif., 1985—; research affiliate MIT Space Systems Lab., Cambridge, 1980-86, MIT Artificial Intelligence Lab., 1986—; vis. scholar Stanford (Calif.) U. Computer Sci. Dept., 1986—; bd. dirs., pres. The Foresight Inst., Palo Alto, 1986. Author: Engines of Creation, 1986; also articles to profl. jours.; inventor high performance solar sail, method for processing and fabricating metals in space. sec. bd. dirs. L5 Soc., Tucson, 1981, bd. dirs. 1979—, advisor, 1979—, co-editor jour., 1983-84. Fellow NSF, MIT, 1977. Mem. AAAS, Am. Assn. Artificial Intelligence, Authors Guild. Office: The Foresight Inst PO Box 61058 Palo Alto CA 94306

DRIGGS, GARY HARMON, financial executive; b. Phoenix, July 13, 1934; s. Douglas H. and Effie (Killian) D.; m. Kay Taylor, June 9, 1959; children: Rebecca Driggs-Campbell, Kimberly, Taylor, Benjamin. Student, Stanford U., 1952-54; BA, Brigham Young U., 1959; MBA, Ind. U., 1960, DBA, 1962. Economist Western Savs. and Loan Assn., Phoenix, 1962—, v.p., 1969-73, pres., chief exec. officer, 1973—; faculty lectr. real estate dept. Ind. U. Grad. Sch. Bus., 1960-62, vis. lectr. urban econs., 1962-76; lectr. econs. Ariz. State U., 1963-67; pres. Ariz. Tomorrow, Inc., chmn. Visions of Future; div. dir. Nat. Council Savs. Instns.; mem. dean's adv. council Ind. U. Sch. Bus.; bd. dirs. Thousand Trails, Inc., Newell Cos., Weidner Communications Inc.; v.p. Valley Leadership; mem. corp. adv. bd. Karl Eller Ctr.; chmn. nat. task force Gov.'s Com. Nat. and Internat. Commerce; fin. chmn. Gov.'s Transportation Task Force; mem. Maricopa Cts. Commn. Author: How to Reduce Risk in Apartment Lending, 1966. Mem. exec. bd. Phoenix Community Alliance; bd. dirs. Phoenix Together; adv. bd. Morrison Inst. Pub. Policy, Ariz. Rep. Caucus; mem. Ariz. State U. Centennial Bus. Support Com., dean's council of 100 Ariz. State U. Coll. Bus.; bd. advisors, exec. com. U. Ariz.; chmn. Phoenix Streets Adv. Com., Gov.'s State Urban Lands Task Force; bd. dirs. Silent Witness Program; served ch. mission Mormon Ch., Finland. Named Outstanding Young Man of Yr., Ariz. Jr. C. of C., 1968, named Outstanding Young Man of Yr., Phoenix Jr. C. of C., 1968-69; recipient Disting. Citizen award U. Ariz. Alumni Assn., 1982, Disting. Citizen award Ind. U. Sch. Bus. Acad. Alumni Fellows, 1983. Mem. Nat. Assn. State Savs. and Loan Supvrs. (future planning com.), Internat. Union Bldg. Socs. and Savs. Assns., U.S. League (legis. policy com., spl. task force on deficit reduction, com. econ. affairs, com. capital stock and holding cos., mem. home ownership task force), Savs. and Loan League Ariz. (past pres.), Phoenix 40, Assn. for Corp. Growth, Chief Execs. Orgn., World Bus. Council, Inc. (chief exec. officer), U.S. C. of C. (banking, monetary and fiscal affairs com.). Republican. Lodge: Rotary. Avocations: tennis, mountain climbing, skiing. Office: Western Savs and Loan Assn Fin Ctr 3443 N Central Ave Phoenix AZ 85012

DRIGGS, JOHN D., bank executive; b. 1929. Grad., Stanford U., 1953. Chmn. Western Savs. and Loan Assn., Phoenix. Office: Western Savs & Loan Assn 6001 N 24th St Phoenix AZ 85014

DRINKER, KIMBERLY, psychotherapist, mediator, educator; b. Anchorage, Jan. 22, 1955; d. Henry Russell and Marion Lee (Wilson) D. Student, U. Colo., 1973-74; BA in Psychology, U. Calif., Santa Cruz, 1977; MSW, U. Calif., Berkeley, 1980. Family therapist Community Human Services Project, Monterey, Calif., 1980-84; instr. Chapman Coll., Monterey, 1982—; child custody mediator Superior Ct. of Monterey County, Salinas, Calif., 1984—; pvt. practice psychotherapy Pacific Grove and Salinas, Calif., 1983—; bd. dirs. Beacon House; therapist Confidential Recovery, Fresno, Calif., 1985—; trainer Domestic Violence Council of Monterey, 1984—. Mem. Nat. Assn. Social Workers (lic.). Avocations: reading, skiing, aerobics, running, swimming. Office: 667 Lighthouse Ave Pacific Grove CA 93950 also: 154 Central Ave Salinas CA 93902

DRISCOLL, NEIL JOSEPH, III, lawyer; b. Chgo., Nov. 14, 1948; s. Neil Joseph and Regina Frances (Golden) D.; m. Linda Rae Fallon, June 30, 1973; children—Amelia Tara, Ethan Hancock. B.S., Portland State U., 1974; J.D., Lewis & Clark Law Sch., 1977. Bar: Oreg. 1978, U.S. Dist. Ct. Oreg. 1978, U.S. Tax Ct. 1982. Sole practice, Portland, Oreg., 1980—. Served with U.S. Army, 1971-72. Decorated Air medal, Purple Heart, U.S. Army Commendation medal, Armed Forces Honor medal (Vietnam). Mem. Oreg. Bar Assn., Multnomah Bar Assn. Republican. Club: Willamette Athletic (Portland). Home: 63 Aquinas Lake Oswego OR 97035 Office: 3405 SW Barbur Blvd Portland OR 97201

DRISS, MARILYN GENSMAN, social worker; b. Ajo, Ariz., July 5, 1953; d. Owen A. and Mary C. (Kormayer) Gensman; m. Leon A. Driss, May 6, 1984; 1 child, Daniel A. BA in Social Welfare, Ariz. State U., 1974, MSW, 1978. Lic. clin. social worker, Calif. Social worker Maricopa Med. Ctr., Phoenix, 1980-83; social worker Glendale (Calif.) Meml. Hosp., 1983-84, dir. social services, 1984-86; dir. clin. social services Los Robles Regional Med. Ctr., Thousand Oaks, Calif., 1986—. Bd. dirs. Jewish Family Services, Ventura, Calif. Mem. Nat. Assn. Social Workers (cert.), Soc. Hosp. Social Work Dirs. Jewish. Home: 7018 Sonora Ct Ventura CA 93003 Office: Los Robles Regional Med Ctr 215 W Janss Rd Thousand Oaks CA 91360

DROLET, CYNTHIA JUNE, communication aids company executive; b. Hammond, Ind., July 21, 1945; d. Gerald and Darline (Larason) Kackley; m. Kenneth James Drolet, July 27, 1970. BS, Purdue U., 1967; MA, Calif. State U., Los Angeles, 1975. Speech, lang. pathologist Balt. County Schs., 1967-70, Los Angeles County Schs., 1970-81; owner, operator Imaginart Communication Products, Los Angeles and Idyllwild, Calif., 1981—. Author: Unipix: Universal Language of Pictures, 1982; author ednl. material Touch'n Talk Communication Stickers, 1983, Touch'n Talk Micros, 1985, Pick 'n Stick Color Packs, Pocket Picture Holder; producer communication aid Eye-Com Board, 1985. Mem. Am. Speech-Lang. Hearing Assn., So. Calif. Communication Group, Internat. Soc. for Augmentative and Alternative Communication, Idyllwild C. of C. (brochure chmn. 1985, beautification com. 1985, essence of Idyllwild com. 1985-86), Phi Kappa Phi. Lodge: Soroptimists (sec. Idyllwild club 1985-86, pub. relations com. 1986-87). Avocations: traveling, reading, dancing. Home: PO Box 1868 Idyllwild CA 92349 Office: Imaginart Communication Products 25680 Oakwood St Idyllwild CA 92349

DROPESKY, BRUCE J., nuclear chemist; b. Phila., Apr. 29, 1924; m. Beatrice M. Stehling, June 20, 1948; children: Bruce Phillip, Elaine Suzanne. BS in Chemistry, Rensselaer Poly. Inst., 1949; PhD, U. Rochester, 1953. Staff mem. Los Alamos (N.Mex) Sci. Lab., 1953-70; assoc. group leader Los Alamos Nat. Lab., 1970-85, mem. staff, 1985—; vis. prof. Kyoto U., 1985; lectr. People's Republic China, 1985. Contbr. articles to profl. jours. Served with USAF, 1942-45, ETO. Mem. Am. Chem. Soc. (chmn.-elect 1977, chmn. nuclear chemistry and tech. div. 1978), Am. Phys. Soc., N.Mex. Acad. Sci., Sigma Xi. Home: 213 Los Pueblos Los Alamos NM 87544 Office: Los Alamos Nat Lab INC DO MS J519 Los Alamos NM 87545

DROSDICK, JOHN G., oil company executive; b. Hazelton, Pa., Aug. 9, 1943; m. Gloria J. Shenosky, May 10, 1944; children: Scott E., Candice M., Courtney J., Brooke K. BSChemE, Villanova U., 1965; MSChemE, U. Mass., 1968. Crude oil coordinator Exxon USA, Houston, 1973-74, marine planning mgr., 1974-76, corp. analysis mgr., 1978-81; facilities devel. dept. head Exxon USA, Baton Rouge, 1976-78, refinery ops mgr., 1981-83; v.p. refining Tosco Corp., Santa Monica, Calif., 1983-85, sr. v.p. refining, 1985-86, exec. v.p., 1986-87, pres., chief ops. officer, 1987—, also bd. dirs. Mem. Nat. Petroleum Refiners Assn. (bd. dirs. 1985—), Am. Petroleum Refiners Assn. (bd. dirs. 1985—). Roman Catholic. Club: Jonathan. Avocations: running, skiing, tennis, golfing. Office: Tosco Corp 2401 Colorado Ave Box 2401 Santa Monica CA 90406

DROST, KATHLEEN ANDERSON, speech pathologist, small business owner; b. Jamestown, N.Y., Apr. 8, 1957; d. Robert James and Joyce Mary (Palm) Anderson; m. Russell Charles Drost, June 29, 1985; 1 child, Russell Charles Jr. AA, Orange Coast Community Coll., 1978; BA, Calif. State U., Long Beach, 1980; MA, Calif. State U., Fullerton, 1983. Lic. speech patholigst, Calif.; cert. clin. rehab. services and competency, Calif., nursery sch. edn., Calif. Speech, lang. pathologist La Habra (Calif.) City Schs., 1983, Jurupa Unified Sch. Dist., Riverside, Calif., 1983—. Mem. Am. Speech Lang. Hearing Assn., Calif. Speech Lang. Hearing Assn., Nat. Tchrs. Assn., Calif. Tchrs. Assn., Yorba Linda C. of C., Phi Kappa Phi. Democrat. Roman Catholic. Home: 21850 Feather Ave Yorba Linda CA 92686 Office: Jurupa Unified Sch Dist 3924 Riverview Dr Riverside CA 92509

DROW, DORIS LARSEN, microbiologist, researcher; b. Highland Park, Ill.; d. Harold Otis and Alice Irene (Evans) Larsen; m. Wilbert Russell Erickson, Jan. 27, 1956 (div.); m. Gregg Stanley Drow, Nov. 10, 1970. AB, U. Ill., Urbana, 1947; MS, Northwestern U., 1949; PhD, U. Wis., 1978. Lab. dir. The Duluth (Minn.) Clinic, 1965-69; microbiology supr. Madison (Wis.) Gen. Hosp., 1969-79; asst. prof. Tex. Tech Med. Sch., El Paso, 1979-84; research prof. U. Tex., El Paso, 1984—; faculty El Paso Community Coll., 1986—. Contbr. articles to profl. jours. Founder Pet-a-Pet, El Paso, 1982; bd. dirs. El Paso Council on Aging, El Paso, 1981—, El Paso Literacy Council, 1986. Mem. Am. Acad. Microbiology (cert.), Am. Soc. for Microbiology, Sigma Xi, Beta Beta Beta. Presbyterian. Avocations: horseback riding, skiing, stained glass. Home: 141 Sundance Ct PO Box 532 Santa Teresa NM 88008

DROWN, EUGENE ARDENT, govt. ofcl.; b. Ellenburg, N.Y., Apr. 25, 1915; s. Frank Arthur and Jessie Kate D.; B.S., Utah State U., 1938; postgrad. Mont. State U., 1939-40; Ph.D. in Public Adminstrn., U. Beverly Hills, 1979; m. Florence Marian Munroe, Mar. 5, 1938; children—Linda Harriett Oneto, Margaret Ruth Lunn. Park ranger Nat. Park Service, Yosemite Nat. Park, 1940-47; forest ranger U.S. Forest Service, Calif. Region, 1948-56; forest mgr. and devel. specialist U.S. Bur. Land Mgmt., Calif., 1956—; forest engring. cons., 1970—; research and devel. coordinator U.S. Army at U. Calif., Davis., 1961-65. Mem. adv. bd. Sierra Coll., Rocklin, Calif., 1962—; active Boy Scouts Am.; instr. ARC, 1954—. Served with AUS, 1941-45. Decorated Bronze Star, Silver Star; registered profl. engr., profl. land surveyor, profl. forester, Calif. Recipient Nat. Service medal ARC, 1964. Mem. Nat. Soc. Profl. Engrs., Soc. Am. Foresters, Am. Inst. Biol. Scientists, Ecol. Soc. Am., Res. Officers Assn. U.S., Nat. Rifle Assn., Internat. Rescue and First Aid Assn., Internat. Platform Assn., Bulldog Sentinels of Superior Calif. Methodist. Clubs: Masons, Shriners. Home: 5624 Bonniemae Way Sacramento CA 95824

DROZD, ANDREW PETER, brewery executive; b. Bklyn., May 20, 1947; s. Adam Andrew and Helen Ann (Golebwski) D.; m. Barbara Jean Coughlin, Mar. 15, 1969 (div. June 1978); m. Kathleen Kelly, June 23, 1984; 1 child, Allyson Patricia. BBA, Marist Coll., 1968. Prin. Caboose Tavern, Poughkeepsie, N.Y., 1972-78; supr. River Distbg., Poughkeepsie, 1978-82, gen. mgr., 1982-83; gen. sales mgr. Miller Brands, Ft. Myers, Fla., 1983-84; gen. mgr. Miller Brands, Portland, Oreg., 1984—. Bd. dirs. United Cerebral Palsey, Portland, 1985—, Boys and Girls Clubs, Portland, 1985—, Alcohol Safety Action Program, Portland, 1985—, Pete Ward Baseball Clinic, Portland, 1985—. Served as sgt. U.S. Army, 1968-70, Vietnam. Decorated Bronze Star. Mem. Marist Alumni Assn. (class agt. 1972—), Grocery Sales Mgrs. Club, Inspirators Club. Roman Catholic. Avocations: golf, skiing, softball, travelling. Office: Miller Brands 5825 NE Skyport Way Portland OR 97218

DROZD, LEON FRANK, JR., lawyer, energy and mining company executive; b. Victoria, Tex., Sept. 11, 1948; s. Leon Frank and Dorothy Lucille (Smith) D.; BBA, Tex. A&M U., 1971; J.D., U. Denver, 1979. Bar: Colo., U.S. Dist. Ct. Colo. U.S. Ct. Appeals (10th cir.). Legis. asst. U.S. Ho. of Reps., also Dem. Caucus, Washington, 1971-74, chief clk. com. on sci. and tech., 1974-75; asst. to dean for devel. Coll. Law, U. Denver, 1975-79; v.p. Braddock Publs., Inc., Washington, 1975-79; land and legal counsel Chevron Shale Oil Co., Chevron Resources Co., 1980—, Chevron Overseas petroleum and White Nile Petroleum Co. Ltd. (Sudan), 1983. Colo. elector Anderson/Lucey Nat. Unity Campaign, 1980. Mem. ABA, Fed. Bar Assn., Colo. Bar Assn., Colo. Trial Lawyers Assn., Denver Bar Assn., Denver C. of C. (steering com. 1981-82). Club: Nat. Lawyers (Washington). Home: 1856 Pacific Ave Apt 3 San Francisco CA 94109 Office: Chevron Resources Co PO Box 7147 San Francisco CA 94120-7147

DRUCKER, PETER FERDINAND, writer, consultant, educator; b. Vienna, Austria, Nov. 19, 1909; came to U.S., 1937, naturalized, 1943; s. Adolph Bertram and Caroline D.; m. Doris Schmitz, Jan. 16, 1937; children: Kathleen Romola, J. Vincent, Cecily Anne, Joan Agatha. Grad., Gymnasium, Vienna, 1927; LL.D., U. Frankfurt, 1931; 16 hon. doctorates, U.S. and fgn. univs. Economist London Banking House, 1933-37; Am. adviser for Brit. banks, Am. corr. Brit. newspapers 1937-42; cons. maj. bus. corps. U.S., 1940—; prof. philosophy, politics Bennington Coll., 1942-49; prof. mgmt. NYU, 1950-72, chmn. mgmt. area, 1957-62, disting. univ. lectr., 1972—; Clarke prof. social sci. Claremont Grad. Sch. (Calif.), 1971—; prof. dept art Pomona Coll., Calif., 1979-85. Author: The End of Economic Man, 1939, The Future of Industrial Man, 1941, Concept of the Corporation, 1946, The New Society, 1950, Practice of Management, 1954, America's Next Twenty Years, 1957, The Landmarks of Tomorrow, 1959, Managing for Results, 1964, The Effective Executive, 1966, The Age of Discontinuity, 1969, Technology; Management and Society, 1970, Men, Ideas and Politics, 1971, Management: Tasks, Responsibilities, Practices, 1974, The Unseen Revolution: How Pension Fund Socialism Came to America, 1976, People and Performance, 1977, Management, An Overview, 1978, Adventures of a Bystander, 1979, Managing in Turbulent Times, 1980, Toward the Next Economics and Other Essays, 1981, The Changing World of the Executive, 1982, Innovation and Entrepreneurship, 1985; The Frontiers of Management, 1986; (fiction) The Last of All Possible Worlds, 1982, The Temptation to Do Good, 1984; producer: movie series The Effective Executive, 1969, Managing Discontinuity, 1971, The Manager and the Organization, 1977, Managing for Tomorrow, 1981. Recipient gold medal Internat. U. Social Studies, Rome, 1957; Wallace Clark Internat. Mgmt. medal, 1963; Taylor Key Soc. for Advancement Mgmt., 1967; Presdl. citation NYU, 1969; CIOS Internat. Mgmt. gold medal, 1972; Chancellor's medal Internat. Acad. Mgmt., 1987. Fellow AAAS (council), Internat., Am. acads. mgmt., Brit. Inst. Mgmt. (hon.), Am. Acad. Arts and Scis.; mem. Soc. for History Tech. (pres. 1965-66), Nat. Acad. Pub. Adminstrn. (hon.).

DRUM, WILLIAM ORTON, educator; b. Circleville, Ohio, July 27, 1937; s. Orwin D. and Wilhelmina B. (Strehle) D.; B.A. with distinction, U. Ariz., 1959, M.Ed., 1964; m. Peggy Jo Hoover, Aug. 12, 1962; children—David Michael, Douglas Allen. Tchr., Ohio, 1959-62; chmn. dept. bus. edn. Rincon High Sch., Tucson, 1962-84; pres. Drum Research Assn. Inc.; mem. assoc. faculty Pima Community Coll., U. Ariz.; edn. industry asst. IBM. Mem. NEA, Computer Users in Edn., Ariz. Edn. Assn., Ariz. Bus. Edn. Assn., Tucson Edn. Assn., Tucson Bus. Educators Assn., Phi Kappa Phi, Pi Omega Pi. Republican. Co-author: Structured Basic Programming, 1982, Database Applications, 1986. Home: 801 N Sahuara Ave Tucson AZ 85711 Office: 7454 E Broadway Tucson AZ 85710

DRUMHELLER, GEORGE JESSE, motel chain executive; b. Walla Walla, Wash., Jan. 30, 1933; s. Allen and Ila Margaret (Croxdale) D.; student Wash. State U., 1951-52, Whittier Coll., 1955-58; m. Carla Rene Cunha, May 4, 1965 (div. 1984). Asst. mgr. Olympic Hotel, Seattle, 1959; jr. exec. Westin Hotels, Seattle, 1959-63; founder, pres. George Drumheller Properties, Inc., motel holding co., Pendleton, Oreg., 1963—; founder, chmn. bd. Dalles Tapadera, Inc., motel and hotel holding co., The Dalles, Oreg., 1964-77; founder, pres. Lewiston Tapadera, Inc. (Idaho), motel holding co., 1970-77; founder, pres. Yakima Tapadera, Inc. (Wash.), 1971-77; founding partner Drumheller & Titcomb (Tapadera Motor Inn), Ontario, Oreg., 1972-84; merger with Tapadera motel holding cos. and George Drumheller Properties, Inc., 1978—, founder Tapadera Budget Inns, Kennewick and Walla Walla, Wash., 1981-85, also merged with George Drumheller Properties, Inc., 1986; engaged in farming, eastern Wash., 1958-80. Served with USCG, 1952-55. Mem. Am. Hotel and Motel Assn. (nat. dir. 1980-84, pres.'s exec. com. 1983-84), Oreg. Hotel Motel Assn. (dir. 1974-78), Wash. State Lodging Assn. (dir., v.p. 1976-84). Clubs: Spokane, Walla Walla Country, Washington Athletic, Rancho Santa Fe, LaJolla Beach and Tennis, San Diego. Home: 244 Marcus St PO Box 1106 Walla Walla WA 99362 Office: George Drumheller Properties Inc PO Box 1234 Walla Walla WA 99362

DRUMMER, DONALD RAYMOND, banking executive; b. Binghamton, N.Y., Oct. 10, 1941; s. Donald Joseph and Louise Frances (Campbell) D.; A. Sci., Broome Community Coll., 1962; B.S., U. Colo., 1972; M.B.A., Regis Coll., 1981; m. Rita Kovac, May 22, 1965; children—Shelley Rita, Adam Donn. With, Lincoln First Bank, Binghamton, N.Y., 1962-69; asst. comptroller Adams & Horne, Denver, 1969; with Colo. State Bank, Denver, 1969—, v.p., 1972-81, comptroller, 1972—, sr. v.p., 1981—; treas., trustee Colorado State Bank Found.; adj. faculty Regis Coll., mem. grad. edn. task force, 1986—. Mem. fin. com. Holy Family Grade Sch. Mem. Nat. Assn. Accts. (dir. 1975-79, v.p. 1977-79), Am. Acctg. Assn., Am. Taxation Assn. Clubs: Denver Sertoma (past pres.), City (v.p., dir. 1979-83), Denver Athletic. Editor: Chronicle, 1980-81. Office: Colorado State Bank 1600 Broadway Denver CO 80202

DRUMMOND, GERARD KASPER, resource development company executive, lawyer; b. N.Y.C., Oct. 9, 1937; s. John Landells and Margaret Louise (Kasper) D.; m. Donna J. Mason, Sept. 14, 1957 (div. 1976); children: Alexander, Jane, Edmund; m. Sandra Hamilton, Aug. 31, 1985. B.S., Cornell U., 1959, LL.B. with distinction, 1963. Bar: Oreg. 1963. Assoc. Davies, Biggs, Strayer, Stoel & Boley, Portland, Oreg., 1963-64; assoc., ptnr. Rives, Bonyhadi, Drummond & Smith, Portland, 1964-77; pres. Nerco, Inc., Portland, 1977—; mem. corp. policy group PacifiCorp, Inc. 1979—. Pres. Tri-County Met. Transit Dist., Portland, 1974-86, bd. dirs., 1974-86; mem. Oreg.-Korea Econ. Coop. Com., Portland, 1981-85, Oreg. Investment Council, 1987—; trustee Reed Coll., 1982—; bd. dirs. Oreg. Contemporary Theatre, 1983-85; community bd. dirs. Providence Hosp., 1986—. Served to 1st lt. USAR, 1959-67. Mem. ABA, Oreg. Bar Assn., Am. Mining Congress (bd. dirs. 1986—), Oreg. Investment Council. Club: Arlington. Home: 28815 S Needy Rd Canby OR 97013 Office: Nerco Inc 111 SW Columbia St Portland OR 97201

DRUMMOND, OLIVER LEE, city official; b. Van Nuys, Calif., Oct. 7, 1947; s. Joseph Lester and Ollie Lee (Rodabaugh) D.; m. Deborah Louise Clark, Oct. 14, 1970; 1 dau., Deborah Lee. B.S. in Criminology, Calif. State U.-Long Beach, 1974; advanced grad. cert. in exec. mgmt. Pacific Christian Coll., 1979; postgrad. in human behavior Newport U., 1979—; L.H.D. (hon.) Newport Internat. U., 1979; LL.D. (hon.) Van Norman U., 1980. Community coll. lifetime tchr. credential, Calif.; basic, intermediate, advanced and mgmt. certs., exec. cert. Calif. Dept. Justice. Police officer Santa Ana (Calif.) Police Dept., 1970-75, sgt., 1975-78, lt., 1978-82; chief of police Hanford (Calif.) Police Dept., 1982—; instr. Advanced Investigators Acad., Saddleback Coll., 1981-83. Mem. sch. site council Kings River-Hardwick Sch., 1982—, mem. sch. attendance rev. bd., 1982—; bd. dirs. Kings County Vol. Bur., 1982—, chmn., 1985. Served with Army N.G., 1969-75; served to lt., Mil. Police Corps, USAR, 1972-76. Recipient Profl. Service award Santa Ana Police Dept., 1982; Meritorious Service/Valor award Santa Ana Police Benevolent Assn., 1973; named Chief of Yr., Calif. Law Enforcement Mgmt. Ctr., 1982. Mem. Internat. Assn. Chiefs of Police, Internat. Police Assn., ABA (criminal justice sect.), Calif. Peace Officers Assn. (law and legis. com.), Calif. Chiefs Assn., Calif. Police Chiefs Assn. (standards and ethics com., tng. com.), Calif. Assn. Police Tng. Officers, Calif. Assn. Adminstrn. of Justice Educators, Calif. Robbery Investigators Assn., Kings County Peace Officers Assn., League of Calif. Cities (2d v.p. police chiefs sect.), Hanford C. of C. (dir. 1983, pres. 1985, mem. ambassador corps, City Employee of Yr. award 1982, President's award 1984), SAR (Law Enforcement Commendation medal), Lodge: Rotary (sgt.-at-arms 1983-84). Office: 425 N Irwin St Hanford CA 93230

DRURY, GERALD IRWIN, periodontist, educator; b. Chgo., July 23, 1944; s. Daniel and Dorothy (Chait) D.; m. Tineke Willy Ten Hagen, Dec. 25, 1970; children: Charles, Justin. BA, U. Ill., 1966; BSD, U. Ill., Chgo., 1970, DDS, 1972; MS, Med. Coll. Va., 1968; cert. in periodontics La. State U., 1979. Diplomate Am. Bd. Periodontology. Intern N.E. Fla. State Hosp., MacClenny, 1972-73; resident in anesthesiology VA Hosp., New Orleans, 1978; resident in medicine Charity Hosp., New Orleans, 1978, vis. resident periodontist, 1978-79; instr. La. State U. Sch. Dentistry, New Orleans, 1977-79; clin. asst. prof. dept. surg. scis. periodontics sect. U. So. Calif. Sch. Dentistry, Los Angeles, 1979, asst. prof. dept. surg. scis., 1979-81, clin. asst. prof. grad. div., 1981-85, clin. assoc. prof., 1985—; dir. predoctoral periodontal surgery clinic, 1980-81, course dir. current lit. rev. grad. periodontics, 1982-86; mem. adv. com. Bryman Sch. Dental Assts., 1983; pvt. practice dentistry, Fort Myers Beach, Fla., 1973-77, specializing in periodontics, Irvine, Calif., 1981, Hermosa Beach, Calif., 1981—; provisional med. staff Little Company of Mary Hosp., Torrance, Calif., 1986. Recipient cert. of appreciation U. So. Calif., 1981. Mem. Am. Acad. Periodontology (local arrangements com., fgn. relations com.), Am. Assn. Dental Research, Internat. Assn. Dental Research (research award of excellence New Orleans chpt.), ADA, Western Soc. Periodontology (co-chmn. periodontal publs. com. 1977), Western Dental Soc. (membership com. 1981—), Calif. Soc. Periodontists. Home: 1100 Pacific Coast Hwy Apt F Hermosa Beach CA 90254 Office: U So Calif Sch Dentistry PO Box 77951 Los Angeles CA 90007

DRUXMAN, MICHAEL BARNETT, public relations executive; b. Seattle, Feb. 23, 1941; s. Harry Irving and Florence Evelyn (Barnett) D.; m. Terry M. Lundy, Mar. 18, 1966 (div. 1979); 1 son, David Michael; m. Laurie Patricia Singer, July 3, 1983 (div. 1984); 1 stepdau., Wendy Lynn Russ. B.A. in Sociology, U. Wash., 1963. Real estate salesman Pope & Talbot, Inc., Seattle, 1963; investigator Retail Credit Co., Los Angeles, 1964-65; owner Michael B. Druxman & Assocs., Los Angeles, 1965—; tchr. pub. relations UCLA, 1980. Author: Paul Muni, 1974; Basil Rathbone, 1975; Make It Again, Sam, 1975; Merv, 1976; Charlton Heston, 1976; One Good Film Deserves Another, 1977; The Musical, 1980; (plays) Gable, 1984, Tracy, 1984; monthly columnist Coronet Mag., 1973-74. Address: PO Box 8086 Calabasas CA 91302

DRYDEN, ROBERT EUGENE, lawyer; b. Chanute, Kans., Aug. 20, 1927; s. Calvin William and Mary Alfreda (Foley) D.; m. Jetta Rae Burger, Dec. 19, 1953; children: Lynn Marie, Thomas Calvin. A.A., City Coll., San Francisco, 1947; B.S., U. San Francisco, 1951, J.D., 1954. Bar: Calif. 1955; diplomate: Am. Bd. Trial Advs. Assoc. Barfield, Barfield, Dryden & Ruane (and predecessor firm), San Francisco, 1954—; jr. partner Barfield, Barfield, Dryden & Ruane (and predecessor firm), 1960-65, gen. partner, 1965—; lectr. continuing edn. of the bar, 1971-77. Served with USMCR, 1945-46. Fellow Am. Coll. Trial Lawyers, Am. Bar Found; mem. ABA, San Francisco Bar Assn., State Bar Calif., Am. Judicature Soc., Assn. Def. Counsel (dir. 1968-71), Def. Research Inst., Internat. Assn. Ins. Counsel, Fedn. Ins. Counsel, Am. Arbitration Assn., U. San Francisco Law Soc. (mem. exec. com. 1970-72), U. San Francisco Alumni Assn. (bd. govs. 1977), Phi Alpha Delta. Home: 1320 Lasuen Dr Millbrae CA 94030 Office: Suite 3125 1 California St San Francisco CA 94111

D'SA, DEREK, financial executive; b. Mangalore, India, Sept. 20, 1942; came to U.S., 1969; s. Apollinaris M. and Eunice (Pinto) D'Sa. BSEE, U. Mysore, India, 1965; MBA, San Jose State U., 1974. Prodn. supt. AMERON Inc., Honolulu, 1974-78; cash mgr. Hydril Co., Los Angeles, 1979-84; v.p., treas. Angeles Corp., Los Angeles, 1985—. Mem. Cash Mgmt. Assn. of So. Calif. (treas. 1983, pres. 1984). Home: 1711 Dixon St Redondo Beach CA 90278 Office: Angeles Corp 10301 W Pico Blvd Los Angeles CA 90064

DUAL, PETER A(LFRED), school administrator, management consultant; b. Alexandria, Va., Jan. 27, 1946; s. Peter Lloyd and Averlee Lucritia (Coco) D.; m. Toni Irene Nixon, Aug. 24, 1968; children—Nikki Averlee, Peter Aaron, Tony Ahmaad, Alfred Michael. A.A., Lake Mich. Coll., 1966; B.S., Western Mich. U., 1969, M.A., 1971; Ph.D., Mich. State U., 1973; M.P.H., U. Tex.-Houston, 1975. Counselor Neighborhood Youth Corps, Benton Harbor, Mich., 1967-69; tchr., Benton Harbor, 1968-69, Battle Creek, Mich., 1969-70; adminstrv. asst. to dir. sch. community relations Kalamazoo pub. schs., assoc. corm dir. Western Mich. U., Kalamazoo, 1970-71; counselor multi-ethnic counseling ctr., Mich. State U., East Lansing, 1971-72, asst. to ombudsman, 1971-73; asst. chmn. African and Afro-Am. Studies and Research Ctr., U. Texas, Austin, 1973-74, asst. prof. cultural founds. and ethnic studies, 1973-75; assoc. dir. continuing edn., asst. prof. health behavior and health edn. U. Mich., Ann Arbor, 1975-78, dir., asst. to dean Grad. Sch. Pub. Health, 1978-80; acad. dean, prof. health services adminstrn., Eastern Mich. U., Ypsilanti, 1980-83; acad. dean Coll. Health and Human Services, prof. pub. health San Diego State U., 1983—. Active Greater Detroit Area Hosp. Council, 1982, Nat. Health Council, 1979. Mem. Am. Council Edn., Am. Pub. Health Assn., Am. Assn. Higher Edn., Nat. Assn. Supervision and Curriculum Devel., Am. Soc. Allied Health Professions, NEA, Adult Edn. Assn., Mich. Pub. Health Assn. Club: Rotary. Contbr. articles to profl. jours.

DUARTE, BONITA KATHLEEN BOWMAN, temporary help company executive; b. Hagerstown, Md., Jan. 26, 1947; d. John Edward and Ruth Kathleen (Harrison) Boward; m. Wiliam Patrick FitzGerald Duarte, June 30, 1979. Student, U. Nebr., 1969-70, U. Md., 1972, 74. Dep. planner Lincoln Action Program, Lincoln, Nebr., 1968-70; asst. adminstr. Howrey & Simon, Washington, 1970-76; adminstr. Bergson, Borkland et al, Washington, 1977-78; asst. adminstr. Steptoe & Johnson, Washington, 1978-79; adminstr. Pendleton & Sabian, Denver, 1979-80; v.p., chief fin. officer Temporary Profls. Inc., Denver, 1983-86; v.p., fin. officer Duarte & Duarte Inc., Denver, 1987—. Dir. Five Thanks Found. Inc., Denver, 1983-86. Mem. Mensa. Avocation: tailor. Office: Duarte & Duarte Inc PO Box 8621 Denver CO 80201-8621

DUARTE, RAMON GONZALEZ, nurse; b. San Fernando, Calif., Jan. 5, 1948; s. Salvador Revelez and Juanita (Gonzalez) D.; m. Sophia Constant Garabedian, Apr. 17, 1983; children: David Ramon, John Robert. AA in Nursing, Los Angeles Valley Coll., 1972; student, Calif. State U., Los Angeles, 1972-76. RN; Cert. Bd. Nephrology Examiners. Staff nurse hemodialysis unit U. So. Calif. Med. Ctr., Los Angeles, 1971-75; charge nurse self care hemodialysis unit Kaiser Found. Hosp., Los Angeles, 1976, Culver City (Calif.) Dialysis Services, Inc., 1981-82; adminstrv. head nurse hemodialysis unit Valley Prebyn. Hosp., Van Nuys, Calif., 1976-78; adminstrv. head nurse Kidney Dialysis Care Units, Lynwood, Calif., 1980-81; ind. nursing contractor Nursing Services in Nephrology, Van Nuys, 1982—, clin. instr., researcher, 1980—; coordinator clin. research Valley Dialysis Assocs., Inc., Van Nuys, 1978-80; mem. research com. Valley Presbyn. Hosp. Research. Mem. editorial bd. Dialysis and Transplantation mag.; contbr. articles to med. publs. Founder Mus. Hope, Van Nuys. Recipient Dedicated Service award Hemodialysis Found., 1976; named Allied Health Profl. of Yr. Nat. Kidney Found. So. Calif., 1986; scholar Am. G.I. Forum, 1966, Am. Legion Forty and Eight Coll., Los Angeles Valley Coll. Associated Students. Mem. Am. Assn. Artificial Internal Organs, Am. Assn. Nephrology Nurses and Technicians, Kidney Found. So. Calif., Am. Assn. Critical Care Nurses, Ind. Nurses' Assn., Nat. Assn. Patients on Hemodialysis and Transplantation Inc., Am. Soc. Nephrology. Democrat. Roman Catholic. Home and Office: 6849 Oak Park Ave Van Nuys CA 91406

DUBBERKE, KATHARINE MARY, architectural design executive; b. Milw., May 4, 1960; d. Edwin Henry and Joan Alene (Zimmerlee) D. BA in Communication, Wartburg Coll., 1982. Office mgr. The Movie Channel, Waterloo, Iowa, 1983-84; asst. dir. spl. projects Scottsdale (Ariz.) Conf. Ctr., 1984; v.p. techniques Techniques, Tempe, Ariz., 1985—. Aid Assn. for Lutherans scholar, 1978-82. Avocations: reading, piano. Home: 4527 N 40 St #2 Phoenix AZ 85018 Office: Techniques Illustration & Design 1403 W 10 Pl Suite B114 Tempe AZ 85281

DUBBERLY, RONALD ALVAH, library director; b. Jacksonville, Fla., Oct. 25, 1942; s. Chester Alvah and Mary Margaret (Jessup) D.; m. Bonnie Rose Bazemore, June 15, 1963; children: Pamela Rose, Kenneth Alvah. BA in History, Jacksonville U., 1964; MA in LS, Fla. State U., 1965. Reader's adviser asst. Jacksonville Pub. Library, 1961-64; reference librarian, br. librarian Baltimore County (Md.) Pub. Library, 1965-67, adminstrv. asst. to dir., 1967-69; dir. Sioux City (Iowa) Pub. Library, 1969-75, Seattle Pub. Library, 1975-87, Atlanta-Fulton Pub. Library, 1987—; exec. bd. Md. Library Assn., 1969; cons. Iowa State Library, 1970-72; exec. bd. Iowa Library Assn., 1971-73, 75, chmn. legis. com., 1973-75; mem. Wash. Adv. Council Libraries, 1975-77; chair planning and devel. com. Wash. State Library, 1984—; mem. exec. bd. Urban Libraries Council, 1981-87, chmn. long range planning com., 1984; pres. Wash. Literacy, 1985-86; adminstrv. agt. Pub. Library Devel. Program Project, 1985-87; auxilliary faculty U. Washington, 1985-86. Mem. editorial bd. Jour. Library Adminstrn., 1979-85. Recipient Spl. Service award Iowa Library Assn., 1975. Mem. ALA (v.p., pres.-elect pub. library assn. 1976-78, pres. 1978-80, standardscom. 1983-87), new standards task force com. 1984-86), Am. Library Trustee Assn. (bd. dirs. 1980-81), Wash. Library Assn. (legis. com. 1981-87), Pub. Library Assn. (chmn. pub. libraries principles task force 1980-82, goals, guidelines and standards com. 1982-86, mem. new standards task force 1984-86). Office: One Margaret Mitchell Square NW Atlanta GA 30303

DUBBS, SCOTT ARTHUR, educator; b. Gt. Falls, Mont., Feb. 13, 1957; s. Arthur LeRoy and Colleen (Bennett) D.; m. Vickie Lynn Smail, Sept. 5, 1976; children: Kyle David, Letha René. BS in Phys. Edn., Sci., Mont. State U., 1980. Tchr., coach Harlowton (Mont.) High Sch., 1980—. Named Coach of Yr. SC Athletic Conf., 1984-85, 85-86, Coach of Yr. So. Div., 1985. Mem. NEA, Mont. Edn. Assn., Nat. Sci. Tchrs. Assn., Mont. Sci. Tchrs. Assn., Mont. Coaches Assn. Methodist. Home: PO Box 1 Harlowton MT 59036 Office: Harlowton High Sch PO Box 288 Harlowton MT 59036

DUBIN, MARK WILLIAM, neuroscientist, educator; b. N.Y.C., Aug. 30, 1942; s. Sidney Stanley and Dorothy (Cirinsky) D.; m. Alma Hermine Heller, June 27, 1964; children—Lila Rachel, Miriam Rebecca. AB in Biophysics, Amherst Coll., 1964; PhD in Biophysics, Johns Hopkins U., 1969. Research fellow Australian Nat. U., Canberra, 1969-71; asst. prof. dept. molecular, cellular and devel. biology U. Colo., Boulder, 1971-77, assoc. prof., 1977-82, prof., 1982—, chmn. dept., 1983—; sci. cons. Wills Found., 1981—; cons., mem. bd. sci. advisors Columbine Venture Fund, Denver, 1984—. Contbr. articles to profl. jours. Bd. dirs. Congregation Har Ha-Shem, Boulder, 1976-80, pres., 1978, 79. Grantee NIH-Nat. Eye Inst., 1972—, NSF, 1976-83, March of Dimes Found., 1982-83; Fight for Sight fellow Australian Nat. U., 1969-71. Mem. Assn. Research in Vision and Ophthalmology (sect. chmn. 1981), AAAS, Soc. Neurosci., Internat. Soc. Devel. Neurosci., Sigma Xi. Democrat. Jewish. Avocation: reading. Home: 1868 Del Rosa Ct Boulder CO 80302 Office: Univ Colo Dept Molecular Cellular and Devel Biology PO Box 347 Boulder CO 80309

DUBOFF, LEONARD DAVID, legal educator; b. Bklyn., Oct. 3, 1941; s. Rubin Robert and Millicent Barbara (Pollach) DuB.; m. Mary Ann Crawford, June 4, 1967; children—Colleen Rose, Robert Courtney, Sabrina Ashley. J.D. summa cum laude, Bklyn. Law Sch., 1971. Bars: N.Y. 1974, U.S. Dist. Cts. (so. and ea. dists.) N.Y. 1974, U.S. Ct. Appeals (2d cir.) 1974, U.S. Customs Ct. 1975, U.S. Supreme Ct. 1977, Oreg. 1977. Teaching fellow Stanford (Calif.) U. Law Sch., 1971-72; mem. faculty Lewis & Clark Coll. Northwestern Sch. Law, Portland, Oreg., 1972—, prof. law, 1977—; instr. Hastings Coll. Law Coll. Civil Advocacy, San Francisco, summers 1978, 79.

Founder, past pres. Oreg. Vol. Lawyers for Arts; mem. lawyers' com. ACLU, 1973-78, bd. dirs. Oreg., 1974-76; mem. Mayor's Adv. Com. Security and Privacy, 1974; bd. dirs. Portland Art Mus. Asian Art Council, 1976-77, Internat. Assn. Art Security, N.Y.C., 1976-80; Gov. Oreg. Com. Employment of Handicapped, 1978-81; cons., panelist spl. projects Nat. Endowment for Arts, 1978-79; mem. Mayor's Adv. Com. on Handicapped, 1979-81; mem. Wash. State Atty. Gen.'s Com. to Reorganize Maryhill Mus.; Oreg. Commn. for Blind; Oreg. Com. for Humanities, 1981-87. Recipient Bklyn. Law Sch. Stuart Hirschman Property, Jerome Prince Evidence, Donald W. Matheson Meml. awards, 1st scholarship prize; Hofstra U. Lighthouse scholar 1965-71; recipient Hauser award, 1967, Howard Brown Pickard award, 1967-69. Mem. Am. Soc. Internat. Law, Assn. Alumni and Attenders of Hague Acad. Internat. Law, Assn. Am. Law Schs. (chmn. sect. law and arts 1974-80, standing com. sect. activities 1975), ABA, N.Y. State Bar Assn., Oreg. Bar Assn., Delta Kappa Phi, Sigma Pi Sigma, Sigma Alpha. Spl. columnist on craft law, The Crafts Report; editor, contbr. materials to legal and art textbooks; author textbooks and articles for legal and art jours. Office: Lewis & Clark Law Sch 10015 SW Terwilliger Portland OR 97219

DUBOFSKY, JEAN EBERHART, justice Colorado Supreme Court; b. 1942; B.A., Stanford U., 1964; LL.B., Harvard U., 1967; m. Frank N. Dubofsky; children: Joshua, Matthew. Admitted to Colo. bar, 1967; legis. asst. to U.S. Senator Walter F. Mondale, 1967-69; atty. Colo. Rural Legal Services, Boulder, 1969-72, Legal Aid Soc. Met. Denver, 1972-73; ptnr. Kelly, Dubofsky, Haglund & Garnsey, Denver, 1973-75; dep. atty. gen. Colo., 1975-77; counsel Kelly, Haglund, Garnsey & Kahn, 1977-79; justice Colo. Supreme Ct., Denver, 1979—. Office: 465 State Judicial Bldg 2 E 14th Ave Denver CO 80203

DUBOIS, DONALD FRANK, physicist; b. Little Falls, N.Y., Jan. 4, 1932; s. Harold J. and Gertrude A. (Hebrank) DuB.; m. Rosemary Peters, July 16, 1955; children: Donn, David, Andrew. AB, Cornell U., 1954; PhD, Calif. Inst. Tech., 1959. Research physicist Rand Corp., Santa Monica, Calif., 1959-62; sr. scientist Hughes Research Labs., Malibu, Calif., 1962-72; group leader Los Alamos (N.Mex.) Nat. Lab., 1973-83, fellow, 1983—; cons. Rand Corp., 1962-72; cons., adj. prof. U. Colo., Boulder, 1970—, vis. prof., 1972-73. Contbr. articles to profl. jours. J.S. Guggenheim fellow, 1981. Fellow Am. Phys. Soc.; mem. AAAS. Office: Los Alamos Nat Lab MS B262 Group T-Dot Los Alamos NM 87545

DUBOIS, MARSHA, interior designer; b. Elyria, Ohio, May 21, 1949; d. Sanford and Ann Louise (DuBois) Burnstein. AA in Bus., East Los Angeles City Coll., 1972; BA in Psychology, Calif. State U., Long Beach, 1975; diploma, Interior Designers Inst., 1986. Med. sales rep. Mallinckrodt Inc., St. Louis, 1976-77, Mead Johnson Labs, Evansville, Ind., 1977-79; account rep. 3M Co., St. Paul, 1979-80; territory mgr. Minnetonka Inc., Chaska, Minn., 1981-82, Bates Mfg. Co., Hackettstown, N.J., 1983-84; interior designer W. Lee & Assocs., Laguna Beach, Calif., 1985-87; co-owner DuBois et Cie, Interior Design, Laguna Beach, 1987—. Office: DuBois et Cie PO Box 4967 Laguna Beach CA 92652

DUBOIS, PHILIP LEON, political science educator; b. Oakland, Calif., Oct. 17, 1950; s. Fernand Edmond and Germaine (Goodrich) D.; m. Lisa Lewis, Aug. 28, 1976. A.B. with highest honors in Polit. Sci., U. Calif.-Davis, 1972; M.A. in Polit. Sci. (Ford Found. fellow), U. Wis.-Madison, 1974, Ph.D. in Polit. Sci. (scholar), 1978. Asst. prof. polit. sci. U. Calif.-Davis, 1976-82, assoc. prof., faculty asst to vice chancellors, 1982-83, asst. vice chancellor acad. programs, 1983—; cons. profl. jours., comml. book pubs. Jud. fellow U.S. Supreme Ct., 1979-80. Mem. Am. Polit. Sci. Assn. (Edward S. Corwin award, 1978), Am. Judicature Soc., Phi Beta Kappa, Pi Sigma Alpha. Democrat. Author: From Ballot to Bench: Judicial Elections and the Quest for Accountability, 1980; editor: The Analysis of Judicial Reform (Philip L. Dubois), 1982; The Politics of Judicial Reform (Philip L. Dubois), 1982; contbr. numerous articles, book revs. to law revs. and jours., other profl. publs. Home: 6301 Holstein Way Sacramento CA 95831 Office: U Calif Dept Polit Sci Davis CA 95616

DUBOSE, FRANCIS MARQUIS, clergyman; b. Elba, Ala., Feb. 27, 1922; s. Hansford Arthur and Mayde Frances (Owen) DuB.; BA cum laude, Baylor U., 1947; MA, U. Houston, 1958; BD, Southwestern Bapt. Sem., 1957, ThD, 1961; postgrad. Oxford (Eng.) U., 1972; m. Dorothy Anne Sessums, Aug. 28, 1940; children: Elizabeth Anne Parnell, Frances Jeannine Stevens, Jonathan Michael, Celia Danielle Carmichael. Pastor, Bapt. chs., Tex., Ark., 1939-61; supt. missions. So. Bapt. Conv., Detroit, 1961-66; prof. missions Golden Gate Bapt. Sem., 1966—, dir. World Mission Ctr., 1979—; lectr., cons. in 115 cities outside U.S., 1969-82; v.p. Conf. City Mission Supts., So. Bapt. Conv., 1964-66; trustee Mich. Bapt. Inst., 1963-66; mem. exec. bd. San Francisco Conf. Religion, Race and Social Concern. Mem. Internat. Assn. Mission Study, Am. Soc. Missiology, Assn. Mission Profs. Co-editor: The Mission of the Church in the Racially Changing Community, 1969; author: How Churches Grow in an Urban World, 1978, Classics of Christian Missions, 1979, God Who Sends: A Fresh Quest for Biblical Mission, 1983, Home Cell Groups and House Churches, 1987; contbr. to Toward Creative Urban Strategy; Vol. III Ency. of So. Baptists, also articles to profl. jours. Home: 21 Platt Ct Mill Valley CA 94941 Office: Golden Gate Bapt Sem Mill Valley CA 94941

DUBOVOY, WYNNE SEGAL, social worker; b. Richmond, Va., Jan. 7, 1959; d. Harry William Segal and Marie Anne (Cardani) White; m. Mark Dubovoy, Aug. 4, 1985. BA in Anthropology and Sociology, St. Andrews Coll., 1980; MSW, Va. Commonwealth U., 1982. Lic. social worker I, Colo. Intern The Daily Planet, Richmond, Va., 1980-81, Med. Coll. Va., Richmond, 1981-82; outpatient therapist Arapahoe House, Littleton, Colo., 1982-84; dir. social work Humana Hosp. Mountain View, Thornton, Colo., 1984—; field instr. U. Denver Grad. Sch. Social Work, 1985—, Colo. State U. Sch. Social Work, Ft. Collins, 1984—. Author numerous poems (runner-up free verse Va. Poetry Soc. contest, 1976). Chair planning com. young profls. div. Allied Jewish Fedn., Denver, 1983-84. Flora McDonald Scholar St. Andrews's Coll., 1976-80. Mem. Nat. Assn. Social Workers (cert.), Rocky Mountain chpt. of Hosp. Social Workers Soc., Adams County Social Service Multidisciplinary Rev. Team. Avocations: creative writing, cooking, outdoor activities, travelling. Office: Humana Hosp Mountain View 9191 Grant St Thornton CO 80229

DUBOVSKY, STEVEN LEW, physician, educator, researcher; b. Pueblo, Colo., July 12, 1944; s. Mortimer Herbert and Gladys (Levy) D.; m. Anne Lois Gallupe, May 27, 1972; children: Amelia, Elizabeth. BA, NYU, 1965, MD, 1969. Diplomate Am. Bd. Psychiatry and Neurology. Intern, Vancouver Gen. Hosp., B.C., Can., 1969-70; resident in psychiatry Colo. Psychiat. Hosp., Denver, 1970-73; mem. faculty Med. Sch. U. Colo., Denver, assoc. prof. psychiatry, 1979-83, assoc. dean acad. and faculty affairs, 1983—, assoc. prof. psychiatry and medicine, 1983—; assoc. dir. Colo. Psychiat. Hosp.; cons. psychiatry Fitzsimmons Army Hosp., Denver, 1978—; external examiner King Saud U., Riyadh, 1982; vis. prof. U. Oreg., U. Man., U. Tex. examiner Am. Bd. Psychiatry and Neurology, 1978—; v.p. med. bd. U. Hosp. Author: Clinical Psychiatry in Primary Care, 3rd edit., 1985, Psychotherapeutics in Primary Care, 1981; editor: Psychiatric Decision Making, 1984; numerous contbr. articles to profl. jours. Grantee NIMH, 1978-80, Bur. Health Manpower, 1979-81. Fellow Am. Psychiat. Assn.; mem. Group Advancement Psychiatry, Colo. Psychiat. Soc., Phi Beta Kappa. Office: U Colo Med Sch 4200 E 9th Ave Box C260 Denver CO 80262

DUBUC, GERARD PIERRE, JR., beverage industry exec.; b. Versailles, France, Jan. 18, 1941; came to U.S., 1962; s. Gerard P. and Claire E. (Dobes) D.; Baccalaureat, Academie Nationale Française, 1960, B.S. in Bus. Adminstrn., 1962; LL.B., LaSalle U., 1969. Mgr. data processing Young's Market Co., Los Angeles, 1966-72; v.p. ops., dir. Joseph J. Battle Corp., Oakland, Calif., 1973-74; dir. ops. Automatic Data Processing Co., San Francisco, 1974-75; dir. systems, gen. office mgr. Nat. Distbg. Co., Los Angeles, 1975-81; adminstr. Anaheim Eye Med. Group, Inc., and mng. dir. Anaheim Profl. Services, Inc., 1981-83; v.p., dir. M.I.S. Nat. Distbg. Co., Atlanta, 1983-84; v.p., dir. ops. Nat. Distbg. Co., Los Angeles, 1984-87; exec. v.p., dir. ops., Intra-State Marketers, Inc., San Francisco and North Hollywood, Calif., 1987—. Served with JAGC, U.S. Army, 1964-66. Mem. Data Processing Mgmt. Assn. (dir. 1969-72), Am. Mgmt. Assn., Townhall of Calif., Med. Group Mgmt. Assn., Am. Group Practice Assn. Republican. Home: 2415 E Ocean Blvd Suite 1 Long Beach CA 90803 Office: 11428 Sherman Way North Hollywood CA 91605 also: 427 Valley Dr Brisbane CA 94005

DUCKWORTH, GUY, musician, educator; b. Los Angeles, Dec. 19, 1924; s. Glenn M. and Laura (Lysle) D.; m. Ballerina Maria Farra, May 23, 1948. B.A., UCLA, 1951; M.A., Columbia U., 1953, Ph.D., 1969. Piano soloist Metro Goldwyn Mayer Studios, 1936-41; piano soloist Warner Bros. Studios, 1936-41, sta. KFI, Los Angeles, 1938, sta. KNX, Los Angeles, 1939, sta. KHJ, Los Angeles, 1940; asst. prof. music. U. Minn., Mpls., 1955-60; assoc. prof. U. Minn., 1960-62; prof. piano Northwestern U., Evanston, Ill., 1962-70; chmn. dept. preparatory piano Northwestern U., 1962-70; prof. music U. Colo., Boulder, 1970—; originator, coordinator masters and doctoral programs in mus. arts U. Colo.; piano concert tours in U.S., Can., Mexico, 1947-49; condr. various music festivals, U.S., 1956—; dir. Walker Art Children's Concerts, Mpls., 1957-62; nat. piano chmn. Music Educators Nat. Conf., 1965-71; vis. lectr., scholar 75 univs., colls. and conservatories, U.S. and Can., 1964—; cons. to Ill. State Dept. Program Devel. for Gifted Children, 1968-69. Author: Keyboard Explorer, 1963, Keyboard Discoverer, 1963, Keyboard Builder, 1964, Keyboard Musician, 1964, Keyboard Performer, 1966, Keyboard Musicianship, 1970, Guy Duckworth Piano Library, 1974, Guy Duckworth Musicianship Series, 1975; contbr. articles on pedagogy of music to various jours.; producer, performer video tapes on piano teaching; producer, writer (film) The Person First: A Different Kind of Teaching, 1984. Served with U.S. Army, 1943-46. Recipient All-Univ. Teaching award for excellence, U. Colo., 1981. Mem. Music Tchrs. Nat. Assn., Colo. State Music Tchrs. Assn., Coll. Music Soc., Music Educators Nat. Conf., Phi Mu Alpha, Pi Kappa Lambda. Home: 1020 15th St Denver CO 80202 Office: U Colo Boulder CO 80302

DUCLOS, RUSSELL LEO, banker; b. Berkeley, Calif., Apr. 7, 1939; s. Roger Joseph and Gladys Augustine (Lavorni) D.; m. Ruth Ann Crowell, Jan. 14, 1967; children—Rachel Marie, Russell Philip. A.A., Am. River Coll., 1971. With Crocker Bank, Sacramento, 1961-69, asst. v.p., 1969-72, asst. v.p., Redding, Calif., 1972-79, v.p., mgr., Sacramento, 1979-82; v.p., sr. loan officer Redding Bank of Commerce, 1982-84, sr. v.p., sr. loan officer, 1984-85; exec. v.p., 1985—. Served with U.S. Army, 1961-67. Mem. Redding C. of C. (bd. dirs. 1986—), Private Industry Council (bd. dirs. 1986). Republican. Roman Catholic. Club: Riverview Golf and Country. Lodges: Exchange (v.p. 1976), Rotary (sec.-treas. 1980).

DUDICS, SUSAN ELAINE, interior designer; b. Perth Amboy, N.J., Oct. 22, 1950; d. Theodore W. and Joyce M. (Ryals) D. B.S. in Sociology, W.Va. U., 1972; postgrad. Rutgers U., 1975-78, U. Calif.-Irvine, 1979-81, Can. Coll., 1981—. Programmer Prudential Life, Newark, 1972-73; sr. systems analyst Johnson & Johnson, New Brunswick, N.J., 1973-78, Sperry Univac, Irvine, Calif., 1978-80; sr. systems analyst, project leader Robert A. McNeil, San Mateo, Calif., 1981-83; design dir. TransDesigns, Woodstock, Ga., 1982—. High sch. mentor Directions, San Francisco, 1985-86. Named one of Outstanding Young Women in Am., 1985. Mem. Women Entreprenuers (membership com., treas. 1983—), Central N.J. Alumni Assn. (assoc. sec., founder, pres.), Delta Gamma. Recipient awards TransDesigns, Woodstock, Ga., 1984, 85, 86; named one of Outstanding Women Am., 1985. Club: Leads. Avocations: skiing; sewing; scuba diving; ballet; hand crafts.

DUENSING, CAROL JANET, corporate professional; b. Bellflower, Mo., Apr. 14, 1937; d. Charles Donald and Mary Lois (Drewer) Buermann; m. George Herman Duensing, Aug. 26, 1967; children: Mary Theresa, Julie Ann. Student, Suburba Sch. Music. Office mgr. Dempsey Tegeler, Corpus Christi, Tex., 1960-62; sec. Goldman Sachs Investment Co., Los Angeles, 1962-63; sec., treas. Music Systems Enterprises Inc., Orange, Calif., 1966—. Recipient Community Service award Tustin (Calif.) Schs., 1976. Mem. Pacific Coast Buckskin Horse Assn. (sec. 1980-86). Republican. Home: 18901 Valley Dr Villa Park CA 92667 Office: Music Systems Enterprises Inc PO Box 1744 935 N Main Orange CA 92668

DUERDEN, GREGORY CLAUDE, editor, writer, heraldry and genealogy researcher and consultant; b. Salt Lake City, May 4, 1949; s. Claude Bronson Duerden and Claudia (Young) Breinholt; m. Katherine Jo Rasmussen, Aug. 21, 1971; children: Doris, Holly, Michelle, Rachel, Garrett, Mackenzie. Student Brigham Young U., 1967-68, 70-71, St. Leo's Coll., 1976; Historian Cert., Air U., Birmingham, Ala., 1977. Cert. research herald, pursuviant herald. Div. mgr. Heraldry Div. Associated Investigations, Nev., Utah, Ohio, Va., 1970-80; gen. mgr. Zavadu Features Syndicate, Roosevelt, Utah, 1982-87; chief exec. officer, regent Am. Coll. of Arms, Roosevelt, 1984; syndicated newspaper columnist, 1977-80. Columnist The Coat Tree, 1974—; developer, producer, writer radio/TV segment Coat Tree, visual or audio, 1984; author corr. courses on genealogy and heraldry Am. Coll. Arms, 1983; editor Uintah Basin Standard, 1984-87; editor Rifle Telegram, 1987—; contbr. articles to publs. Chmn. pub. awareness com. Citizens for Drug-Free Youth, Roosevelt, 1983-87; publicity chmn. Unitah Basin Indsl. Conv., 1982, 83; candidate for City Council, Roosevelt, 1983; chmn. Duchesne County Preservation Commn., 1985—. Served with USAF, 1973-78, U.S. Vietnam. Fellow Am. Coll. Arms; mem. Duchesne County Hist. Soc. (founder 1985—), Roosevelt C. of C. (charter mem. ambassadorial group Rough Riders 1980-87), VFW, Am. Legion. Mormon. Lodge: Lions. Office: Uintah Basin Standard PO Box 370 Roosevelt UT 84066 Address: Am Coll Arms Box 89-11 Roosevelt UT 84066

DUERR-LEVINE, DIANE, marketing executive; b. Tulsa, Mar. 8, 1938; d. Arthur and Reta (Reeves) Duerr; B.A. in Math., U. Mich., 1960; M.B.A., Columbia U., 1963; m. Matthew A. Levine, June 9, 1963; children: Arielle, Sarsh. Systems engr. Xerox Corp., N.Y.C., 1963-64; products mgr. Lever Bros. Corp., N.Y.C., 1964-68; sr. br. mgr. Am. Home Products Corp., N.Y.C., 1968-71; account supr. Honig-Cooper Herrington (now Foote Cone/Honig), San Francisco, 1971-72; v.p. advt. and sales promotion Continental Airlines, Los Angeles, 1973-76; dir. mktg. and communications San Francisco Bay Area Transit Dist., 1976-78; pres., founder Inst. Health Mgmt., San Francisco, 1978-85; prof. San Francisco State U., 1982-85. Bd. dirs. Greybridge, Palo Alto, Calif., Pacific Select Corp., San Francisco; chmn. membership com. Bus. Adv. Bd., San Francisco State U., chmn. membership com.; cons. Solar Energy Research Inst., No. Calif. Coalition for ERA. Mem. Columbia U. Grad. Sch. Bus. Alumni Assn., Kappa Kappa Gamma, Beta Gamma Sigma. Recipient numerous mktg. and advt. awards. Democrat. Mem. Soc. of Friends. Author: Executive Edge, 1981; Vital Living after Fifty, 1982.

DUFFER, DON RAY, airline pilot; b. Quinlan, Tex., Aug. 3, 1942; s. Emmett L. and Loyce M. (Mack) D.; student U. Tex., Arlington, 1960-62, Saddleback Coll., 1974-76; m. Linda Jo A. Cooley, Mar. 18, 1967; children—Don, Mark. Capt. Continental Airlines, Los Angeles, 1967—; owner, mgr. Domar Properties, Dana Point, Calif., 1973—; pres. Domar European Imports, Dana Point, 1979—; v.p. M & M Patchworks, Inc. Asst. scoutmaster Boy Scouts Am., 1979—. Served with USMC, 1962-67, to col. USMCR, 1967—. Decorated Air medal. Mem. Marine Corps Res. Officers Assn. Marine Corps Aviation Assn. Republican. Club: Dana Point Yacht. Home: 33452 Cockleshell Laguna Niguel CA 92677 Office: 7300 World Way W Los Angeles CA 90009

DUFFY, JAMES WILLIAM, national guard officer; b. Mullan, Idaho, Feb. 17, 1930; s. Bernard Bevan and Mary Teresa (Hrella) D.; student Carroll Coll., 1948-50; grad. Command and Gen. Staff Coll., 1975, CD Mgmt. Sch., 1980; m. Barbara Joan Mergenthaler, Aug. 28, 1954; children—Jeanne, Joan, William, Jeffrey, Daniel. Operator farm, Helena Valley, Helena, Mont., 1950-55; commd. 2d lt., Med. Service Corps, Mont. Army N.G., 1956, promoted to maj. gen., 1981; detachment comdr. Separate Detachment 1049th Engr. Co., 1960-63, detachment comdr. Hdqrs. Detachment, 1963, asst. G-1, 1970, reassigned as asst. G-4, 1972, Mil. Support to Civil Authorities Sect., 1973, dir. State Area Command, 1980, adj. gen., State of Mont., Helena, 1981—. Decorated Army Commendation medal, Meritorious Service medal, Legion of Merit. Mem. N.G. Assn. of U.S., Mont. N.G. Assn., Helena C. of C., Great Falls C. of C. Democrat. Roman Catholic. Club: Lions. Home: PO Box 961 Montana City Route Clancy MT 59634 Office: PO Box 4789 1100 N Main St Helena MT 59604

DUFRESNE, ARMAND FREDERICK, management and engineering consultant; b. Manila, Aug. 10, 1917; s. Ernest Faustine and Maude (McClellan) DuF.; m. Theo Rutledge Schaefer, Aug. 24, 1940 (dec. Oct. 1986); children: Lorna DuFresne Turnier, Peter, m. Lois Burrell Klosterman, Feb. 21, 1987. BS, Calif. Inst. Tech., 1938. Dir. quality control, chief product engr. Consolidated Electrodynamics Corp., Pasadena, Calif., 1945-61; pres., dir. DUPACO, Inc., Arcadia, Calif., 1961-68; v.p., dir. ORMCO Corp., Glendora, Calif., 1966-68; mgmt., engring. cons., Duarte and Cambria, Calif., 1968—; dir., v.p., sec. Tavis Corp., Mariposa, Calif., 1968-79; dir. Denram Corp., Monrovia, Calif., 1968-70, interim pres., 1970; dir., chmn. bd. RCV Corp., El Monte, Calif., 1968-70; owner DUFCO, Cambria, 1971-82; pres. DUFCO Electronics, Inc., Cambria, Calif., 1982—, chmn. bd. 1982-86; pres. Freedom Designs, Inc., Northridge, Calif., 1982-86, also chmn. bd. dirs. Patentee in field. Bd. dirs. Arcadia Bus. Assn., 1965-69; bd. dirs. Cambria Community Services Dist., 1976, pres., 1977-80; mem., chmn. San Luis Obispo County Airport Land Use Commn., 1972-75. Served to capt. Signal Corps, AUS, 1942-45. Decorated Bronze Star medal. Mem. Instrument Soc. Am. (life), Arcadia (dir. 1965-69), Cambria (dir. 1974-75) C. of C., Tau Beta Pi. Home: 901 Iva Ct Cambria CA 93428

DUGAN, LINDA JOAN, school social worker; b. Urbana, Ill., Oct. 12, 1940; d. Lyndan Marshall and Joan Helen (Tempel) Merriman; m. Frank John Dugan (dec. Oct. 1974); children: G. Christopher Stinson, Kimberlee Sutherland, Craig L. Stinson. BSW, Colo. State U., 1977; MSW, U. Denver, 1978. Sch. social worker St. Vrain Valley Sch., Longmont, Colo., 1978-79, Laramie County Sch. Dist. #1, Cheyenne, Wyo., 1979—; dist. coordinator parental edn. Laramie County Sch. Dist. #1, 1985—; diagnostic team mem. Youth Alternatives, Cheyenne, 1985—. Bd. dirs. Spl. Friends of Cheyenne, YMCA. Mem. Nat. Assn. Social Workers (1st v.p. Wyo. chpt. 1985-86, pres. 1986—), Zonta Internat. Democrat. Avocations: weaving, spinning, Southwestern arts, crafts, and culture.

DUGDALE, RICHARD COOPER, biological oceanographer, educator; b. Madison, Wis., Feb. 6, 1928; s. Bryan R. and Esther D.; m. Vera Alexander; children—Graham, Elizabeth; m. Jane Joiner MacIsaac, Aug. 25, 1966 (dec. Oct. 1982); 1 child, Alexis; m. Frances Plevna Wilkerson, Nov. 15, 1986. B.S. in Elec. Engring., U. Wis., 1950, M.S. in Zoology and Botany, 1951, Ph.D. in Zoology, 1955. Postdoctoral fellow Marine Inst., U. Ga., 1956; instr. in zoology U. Ky., 1957; instr. in zoology U. Pitts., 1958-60, asst. prof. zoology, 1960-62; assoc. prof. marine sci. U. Alaska, 1965-67; research prof. oceanograph U. Wash., Seattle, 1967-75; research scientist Bigelow Lab. Ocean Sci., West Boothbay Harbor, Maine, 1975-79; assoc. dir. marine sci. Inst. Marine and Coastal Studies, U. So. Calif., Los Angeles, 1979-83; prof. biol. scis. U. So. Calif., Los Angeles, 1979—; dir. Allan Hancock Found., U. So. Calif., Los Angeles, 1981-86; vis. scientist CNRS, France, 1987—. Served to 2d lt. Signal Corps, U.S. Army, 1952. Fulbright research fellow, Athens, Greece, 1972-73; NSF grantee. Fellow AAAS, Calif. Acad. Scis.; mem. Am. Soc. Limnology and Oceanography (pres. 1976), Phycological Soc. Am., Am. Geophys. Union, Internat. Assn. Ecology, Sigma Xi. Greek Orthodox. Avocations: sailing; camping; skiing. Office: U So Calif Allan Hancock Found University Park 0371 Los Angeles CA 90089

DUGGAN, CATHERINE MARIE, investment advisory services company executive; b. St. Louis, June 15, 1949; d. William Joseph and Fern Beatrice (Dodson) D.; 1 child, Christina Jennifer. Lic. real estate assoc., Calif.; registered mortgage underwriter. Salesperson, Schauer Realty, Los Angeles, 1975-76; sales mgr. Property Store, Los Angeles, 1976-77; cons. Expert Realtor, Los Angeles, 1977-79; ptnr. Duggan, Ruggieri & Co., Los Angeles, 1979-82; v.p. Am Cal Co., Los Angeles, 1982—. Mem. Apt. Owners Assn., Nat. Assn. Female Execs., Calif. Mortgage Bankers Assn., Young Mortgage Bankers, Nat. Assn. Rev. Appraisers and Mortgage Underwriters. Roman Catholic. Avocation: Tang Soo Do karate. Office: Am Cal Co 4730 Woodman St Suite 220 Sherman Oaks CA 91423

DUGGAR, GEORGE STROWAN, sculptor; b. St. Louis, Aug. 20, 1915; s. Benjamin M. and Marie Livingston (Robertson) D.; m. Margaret Pelton, Aug. 27, 1938; children: Eleanor Pfeiffer, John Robertson, Margaret Louise. BA, U. Wis., 1936, MA, 1937; AM, Harvard U., 1943, PhD, 1956; MA in Art, San Francisco State U., 1981. Housing and planning assoc. U.S. Govt., Washington, N.Y., and Los Angeles, 1940-48; sr. planner City of San Francisco, 1948-52; research assoc. U. Calif., Berkeley, 1952-61; prof., chmn. urban affairs dept. U. Pitts., 1961-70; cons., dir. UN Ctr. for Regional Devel., Nagoya, Japan, 1970-72; sculptor Belmont, Calif., 1978—; vis. prof. U. Calif., Irvine and UCLA, 1974-76, San Diego State U., 1976-77; prof. Coll. Europe, Bruges, Belgium, 1958-59; cons. Balt. Urban Renewal Study Bd., 1956, Nat. Planning Bd. Pakistan, 1969-70, Korea Inst. Sci. and Tech., 1974, William Spangle and Assocs., Menlo Park, Calif., 1975-77, U. Calif. Pub. Policy Research Orgn., Irvine, 1974. Prin. works include Sierra Stalemate, 1983 (San Francisco Art Commn. Merit award 1985), Errant Comma, 1984 (San Francisco Art Festival award 1984); author: Industrial Worker Housing in Karachi, 1968, Urban Renewal Objectives and Practices of Local Government, 1965; editor: The New Renewal, 1962. Sec., chmn., bd. dirs. Arts Council of San Mateo County, 1980-86; vice chmn., bd. dirs. Hillbarn Theatre, Inc., San Mateo County, 1982-86; bd. dirs. Belmont Planning Commn., 1955, Bd. of Design, 1981. Served with U.S. Army, 1945-46. Fulbright fellow, 1958, 74, Sr. fellow East-West Ctr., 1973-75, Ford Found. fellow, 1964. Mem. Am. Inst. Cert. Planners (charter), Peninsula Sculptors Guild (founder). Democrat. Mem. Unitarian Ch. Home: 551 South Rd Belmont CA 94002 Office: 1870 Gallery and Studios 1870 Ralston Ave Belmont CA 94002

DUKA, LONNIE DANIEL, photographer; b. Queens, N.Y., July 14, 1951; s. Daniel Louis and Sophie (Pashun) D.; m. Melanie Schwartz, Aug. 18, 1952; children: Daniel, Roxane. Student, Clark U., 1969-73, NYU, 1969-73. Camera operator Cinecom Inc., Boston, 1972-73; dir. Francis Selfo Films Inc., Cambridge, Mass., 1973-75; freelance cinematographer, editor northeastern U.S., 1976-81; lead photographer Fluor Corp., Irvine, Calif., 1981-85; freelance photographer Laguna Beach, Calif., 1986—. Editor: (indsl. film) An Extrodinary Enterprise, 1981 (Indy 1981 award); photographer (appointment book) Insight, 1981 (Belding award 1981), The World's Wonders, 1983 (Golden Orange award 1983), The Yr. of the Athlete, 1984 (Clio cert. of merit 1985). Recipient Cert. of Excellence, Am. Inst. Graphic Arts, 1981, Kodak Preis award, 1985, Award of Excellence, Communication Arts mag., 1985, Merit award Art Dir.'s Club., 1985. Mem. Am. Soc. Mag. Photographers, Art Direction and Design in Orange County, Orange County Advt. Fedn. Home and Office: 919 Oriole Dr Laguna Beach CA 92651

DUKE, CLESSON MARSH, JR., computer software company executive; management consultant; b. Manchester, N.H., Mar. 30, 1940; s. Clesson Marsh Sr. and Gertrude (Siddall) D.; m. Lauren Ann Sowles, Dec. 20, 1985; children—Brett David, Darryl Paul, Christopher John, Deanna Lynne, Dhana Lauren, Lewis William. BSEE, Ariz. State U., 1962. Regional mgr. Victor Bus. Systems, Bellevue, Wash., 1965-72; gen. mgr. (div.) Western Marine Electronics Co., Seattle, 1972-74; v.p. Integrated Circuits Inc., Bellevue, 1974-78; dep. dir. Wash. State Dept. of Energy, Olympia, 1978-79; pres. Revere NW, Redmond, Wash., 1979—; mem. Wash. State Energy Building Code Com., Olympia, 1978, Gov.'s Energy Task Force, Olympia, 1978, Gov.'s Econ. Devel. Task Force, Olympia, 1978; cons., Bellevue, 1979—. Mem. Am. Electronics Assn. Republican. Episcopalian. Office: Revere NW 15127 NE 24th St Suite 310 Redmond WA 98052

DUKE, DONALD NORMAN, publisher; b. Los Angeles, Apr. 1, 1929; s. Roger V. and Mabel (Weineger) D. B.A. in Ednl. Psychology, Colo. Coll., 1951. Comml. photographer Colorado Springs, Colo., 1951-53; pub. relations Gen. Petroleum, Los Angeles, 1954-55; agt. Gen. S.S. Corp., Ltd., 1956-57; asst. mgr. retail advt., sales promotion Mobil Oil Co., 1958-63; pub. Golden West Books, Alhambra, Calif., 1964—; dir. Pacific R.R. Publs., Inc., Athletic Press.; Pub. relations cons. Santa Fe Ry., 1960-70. Author: The Pacific Electric—A History of Southern California Railroading, 1958, Southern Pacific Steam Locomotives, 1962, Santa Fe... Steel Rails to California, 1963, Night Train, 1961, American Narrow Gauge, 1978; editor: Water Trails West, 1977. Recipient Spur award for Trails of the Iron Horse Western Writers Am., 1975. Mem. Ry. and Locomotive Hist. Soc. (dir. 1944—), Western History Assn., Newcomen Soc., Lexington Group of Western Historians, Western Writers Am., P.E.N. Internat. (v.p. 1975-77),

Authors Guild Am., Book Pubs. Assn. So. Calif. (dir. 1968-77), Cal. Writers Guild (dir. 1976-77), Calif. Book Pubs. Assn. (dir. 1976-77), Westerners Internat. (editor Branding Iron 1971-80), Hist. Soc. So. Calif. (dir. 1972-75), Kappa Sigma (lit. editor Caduceus 1968-80). Home: PO Box 80250 San Marino CA 91108 Office: 525 N Electric St Alhambra CA 91801

DUKE, HAROLD BENJAMIN, JR., business executive; b. Washington, Iowa, Jan. 11, 1922; s. Harold Benjamin and Norlica (Wells) D.; m. Maud Barnard Banks, June 11, 1949; children: James Lenox, Harold Benjamin III, Peter Wells, Lester Perrin, Charles Banks. B.A., Williams Coll., 1943. With Gates Corp., Denver, 1946—; mem. exec. com. Gates Corp., 1959—, v.p., 1960-73, exec. v.p., 1973-83, pres., 1983-87, vice-chmn., 1987—, also dir.; bd. dirs. subs. cos. Gates Corp., A-Bar-A Ranches, Gates Energy Products, Gates Land Co., Gates Learjet. Mem. Denver Com. on Fgn. Relations, 1967-85; Bd. dirs. Boys Clubs of Denver, 1960—; pres., trustee Denver Country Day Sch., Englewood, Colo., 1958-71; trustee Social Sci. Found., U. Denver, 1967-75, pres., 1972-75; trustee Denver Pub. Library Found., 1974—, pres., 1976-79; nat. dir. Jr. Achievement, 1986—. Served with U.S. Army, 1943-45. Decorated Bronze Star medal, Purple Heart. Mem. Nat. Assn. Mfrs. (nat. dir. 1986—). Republican. Clubs: University, Mile High, Denver Country, Country of Colo, Castle Pines. Office: PO Box 5887 Denver CO 80217

DUKE, LELAH KAY (LEE), nursing educator; b. Brigham, Utah, Sept. 23, 1937; d. Jack Earl and Eunice (Isaacs) Wright; m. Harold Clyde Duke, Jan. 10, 1957; children: Rebecca, Roberta, Michael, Linda, Jeffery. AS, Weber; BSN, U. Utah, 1975, MS, 1980; postgrad., Brigham young U. RN. Asst. prof. nursing Weber State Coll., Salt Lake City, 1975—, program coordinator, 1983—; critical care staff nurse St. Mark's Hosp., Salt Lake City, 1981—. Mem. Am. Nurses Assn. (membership com.), Utah Nurses Assn. (recording sec. 1984-86), Am. Assn. Critical Care Nurses, Nat. League for Nursing, Western Inst. Higher Edn. in Nursing, Greater Salt Lake City Chpt. Am. Assn. Critical Care Nurses (pres.-elect 1985-86, pres. 1986-87), N.Am. Nursing Diagnosis Assn., Sigma Theta Tau, Phi Kappa Phi. Avocation: running. Home: 868 E 725 S Centerville UT 84014 Office: PO Box 30808 Salt Lake City UT 84130

DUKE, ROY BURT, research organic chemist; b. Houston, Sept. 20, 1932; s. Roy B. and Helen (Sabayrac) D.; m. Theadus Ann Schrader, Mar., 1951; children: Larry, Paul, Dwight. BS, U. Houston, 1956, MS, 1960; PhD, Ga. Inst. Tech., 1966. Chemist Amoco Oil Co., Texas City, Tex., 1956-60; research chemist Eastman Kodak Co., Longview, Tex., 1960-62; instr. Ga. Inst. Tech., Atlanta, 1962-66; research chemist Marathon Oil Co., Littleton, Colo., 1966—. Mem. Am. Chem. Soc., Soc. Petroleum Engrs. Office: Marathon Oil Co Box 269 Littleton CO 80160

DUKE, WILLIAM EDWARD, petroleum company executive; b. Bklyn., July 18, 1932; s. William Robert and Amy Margaret (Devlin) D.; B.S., Fordham U., 1954; m. Leilani Kamp Lattin, May 7, 1977; children by previous marriage, William Edward, Jeffrey W., Michael R. City editor Middletown (N.Y.) Record, 1956-60; asst. state editor Washington Star, 1961-63; exec. asst. to U.S. Senator from N.Y. State, Jacob K. Javits, Washington, 1963-69; dir. pub. affairs Corp. Pub. Broadcasting, Washington, 1969-72; dir. fed. govt. relations Atlantic Richfield Co., Washington, 1973-78, mgr. pub. affairs, Los Angeles, 1978—; cons. in field. Community trustee Greater Washington Ednl. Telecommunications Assn., WETA-TV-FM, chmn. radio com., exec. com., 1976-78; assoc. Georgetown U. Center Strategic and Internat. Studies, 1975—. Mem. Pub. Relations Soc. Am. (accredited, bd. dirs. pub. affairs sec., Los Angeles chpt.), Am. Petroleum Inst. Clubs: Nat. Press, Internat., Capitol Hill, Los Angeles Athletic. Office: Atlantic Richfield Co 515 S Flower St Los Angeles CA 90071

DUKES, PETER PAUL, biochemist, educator; b. Vienna, Austria, June 27, 1930; came to U.S., 1954; s. Paul Stephan Dukes and Vera P. (Przibram) Teleki; m. Lois Jean Pinta, May 5, 1961 (dec. 1982); children: Leslie Ann, Ian Paul. Student, Karl Franz U., Graz, Austria, 1953; PhD, U. Chgo., 1958. Research asst. biochemistry U. Chgo., 1954-55, from instr. to asst. prof., 1958-67; biochemist div. hematology, oncology Children's Hosp. Los Angeles, 1967—; asst. prof. biochemistry and pediatrics U. So. Calif. Sch. Medicine, Los Angeles, 1967-71, assoc. prof. biochemistry and pediatrics, 1971-82, prof. biochemistry and pediatrics, 1982—; acting dir. research Children's Hosp., Los Angeles, 1986—. Contbr. articles to profl. jours. USPHS fellow, 1964-65. Mem. AAAS, Am. Soc. Biol. Chemists, Am. Soc. Hematology (chmn. sub-com. on Erythropoietin 1974), Internat. Soc. Exptl. Hematology (chmn. mem. com. 1981-87), Gesellschaft für Biologische Chemie. Office: Childrens Hosp Los Angeles 4650 Sunset Blvd PO Box 54700 Los Angeles CA 90054

DULBECCO, RENATO, biologist, educator; b. Catanzaro, Italy, Feb. 22, 1914; came to U.S., 1947, naturalized, 1953; s. Leonardo and Maria (Virdia) D.; m. Gulseppina Salvo, June 1, 1940 (div. 1963); children: Peter Leonard (dec.), Maria Vittoria; m. Maureen Muir; 1 dau., Fiona Linsey. M.D., U. Torino, Italy, 1936; D.Sc. (hon.), Yale U., 1968, Vrije Universiteit, Brussels, 1978; LL.D., U. Glasgow, Scotland, 1970. Asst. U. Torino, 1940-47; research asso. Ind. U., 1947-49; sr. research fellow Calif. Inst. Tech., 1949-52, asso. prof., then prof. biology, 1952-63; sr. fellow Salk Inst. Biol. Studies, San Diego, 1963-71; asst. dir. research Imperial Cancer Research Fund, London, 1971-74; dep. dir. research Imperial Cancer Research Fund, 1974-77; disting. research prof. Salk Inst., La Jolla, Calif., 1977—; prof. pathology and medicine U. Calif. at San Diego Med. Sch., La Jolla, 1977-81, mem. Cancer Ctr.; vis. prof. Royal Soc. Great Britain, 1963-64, Leeuwenhoek lectr., 1974; Clowes Meml. lectr., Atlantic City, 1961; Harvey lectr. Harvey Soc., 1967; Dunham lectr. Harvard U., 1972; 11th Marjory Stephenson Meml. lectr., London, 1973, Harden lectr., Wye, Eng., 1973, Am. Soc. for Microbiology lectr., Los Angeles, 1979; Mem. Calif. Cancer Adv. Council, 1963-67; adv. bd. Roche Inst., N.J., 1968-71, Inst. Immunology, Basel, Switzerland, 1969-84; chmn. sr. council Internat. Assn. Breast Cancer Research, 1980-84; pres., trustee Am.-Italian Found. for Cancer Research. Trustee LaJolla Country Day Sch. Recipient John Scott award City Phila., 1958; Kimball award Conf. Pub. Health Lab. Dirs., 1959; Albert and Mary Lasker Basic Med. Research award, 1964; Howard Taylor Ricketts award, 1965; Paul Ehrlich-Ludwig Darmstaedter prize, 1967; Horwitz prize Columbia U., 1973; with David Baltimore and Howard Martin Temin Nobel prize in medicine, 1975; Targa d'oro Villa San Giovanni, 1978; Mandel Gold medal Czechoslovak Acad. Scis., 1982; named Man of Yr. London, 1975; Italian Am. of Yr. San Diego County, Calif., 1978; hon. citizen City of Imperia (Italy), 1983; Guggenheim and Fulbright fellow, 1957-58; decorated grand ufficiale Italian Republic, 1981; hon. founder Hebrew U., 1981. Mem. Nat. Acad. Scis. (Selman A. Waksman award 1974), Am. Acad. Arts and Scis., Am. Assn. Cancer Research, Internat. Physicians for Prevention Nuclear War, Accademia Nazionale dei Lincei (fgn.), Accademia Ligure di Scienze e Lettre (hon.), Royal Soc. (fgn. mem.). Club: Athenaeum. (London). Home: 7525 Hillside Dr La Jolla CA 92037 Office: Salk Inst PO Box 1809 San Diego CA 92112

DULEY, CHARLOTTE DUDLEY, vocational counselor; b. Lincoln, Nebr., Oct. 2, 1920; d. Millard Eugene and Inez Kathryn (Miller) Dudley; student U. Nebr., 1938-41; M.A. in Guidance Counseling, U. Idaho, 1977; B.S., Lewis and Clark State Coll., 1973; m. Phillip D. Duley, Mar. 28, 1942; (dec. Sept. 1984) children—Michael Dudley, Patricia Kaye. Tchr., Nebr. schs., 1951-56; with Dept. of Employment, Lewiston, Idaho, 1958-81, local office counselor handling fed. tng. programs, 1958-81; ind. job cons.; counselor. Pres. bd. dirs. Civic Arts, Inc., 1972-81; mem. women's service league Wash.-Idaho Symphony Orch., 1972—; bd. dirs. YWCA, 1980—, treas., 1981—; dir. artist series Lewis and Clark State Coll., 1984—. Mem. Am., Idaho personnel guidance assns., Idaho State Employees Assn., Internat. Assn. Employees in Employment Security, Am. Assn. of Counsleing and Devel., Idaho State Employment Counselors Assn. (pres. 1979-80), Stateline Guidance and Counseling Assn. (sec.-treas. 1964, 76-77), Lewiston Community Concert Assn. (bd. dirs., pres. 1980—), Greater Lewiston C. of C. (chmn. conv. and tourism com. 1984—). Presbyterian. Club: Altrusa (bd. dirs.). Lodge: Elks (pres. 1986-87, exec. bd. 1985—, election bd. chmn. 1986—). Home: 1819 Ridgeway Dr Lewiston ID 83501

DULMAGE, DONALD WRIGHT, audio-visual producer; b. San Francisco, July 31, 1936; s. Claude Samuel and Archylene Bernice (Wright) D.; m. Bonnie Lillian Goodrich, Nov. 24, 1957; children—Debora Dawn Dulmage Moore, Christopher Wright. B.A., Stanford U., 1958. Dir. photography Sta. KNTV, San Jose, Calif., 1962-69; free lance audio-visual producer, 1964-69; founder Panorama Prodns., Santa Clara, Calif., 1969, pres., owner, 1972—; advisor De Anza Coll., Foothill Coll. Ford Found. fellow, 1957-58; recipient IFPA Cindy awards, SJAC Murphy awards, SFAC awards, AMI awards, others. Mem. Profl. Photographers Am., Info. Film Producers Am., San Jose Ad Club, San Francisco Ad Club, Profl. Photographers Greater Bay Area, Profl. Photographers Calif., others. Republican. Methodist. Club: Decathlon. Home: PO Box 38 New Almaden CA 95042 Office: 2353 De La Cruz Blvd Santa Clara CA 95050

DUMAINE, R. PIERRE, bishop; b. Paducah, Ky., Aug. 2, 1931; student St. Joseph Coll., Mountain View, Calif., 1945-51, St. Patrick Sem., Menlo Park, Calif., 1951-57; Ph.D., Cath. U. Am., 1962. Ordained priest Roman Cath. Ch., 1957; asst. pastor Immaculate Heart Ch., Belmont, Calif., 1957-58; mem. faculty dept. edn. Cath. U. Am., 1961-63; tchr. Serra High Sch., San Mateo, Calif., 1963-65; asst. supt. Cath. schs., Archdiocese of San Francisco, 1965-74, supt., 1974-78; ordained bishop, 1978, bishop of San Jose, Calif., 1981—; dir. Archdiocesan Ednl. TV Ctr., Menlo Park, Calif., 1968-81. Mem. Pres.'s Nat. Adv. Council on Edn. of Disadvantaged Children, 1970-72; bd. dirs. Cath. TV Network, 1968-81, pres., 1975-77; bd. dirs. Pub. Service Satellite Consortium, 1975-81. Mem. Nat. Cath. Edn. Assn., Assn. Cath. Broadcasters and Allied Communicators, Internat. Inst. Communications, Assn. Calif. Sch. Adminstrs. Office: St Patrick Cathedral 389 E Santa Clara St San Jose CA 95113 *

DUMAS, HERBERT SCOTT, engineer, educator; b. Albuquerque, Aug. 14, 1957; s. Herbert Monroe and Patricia Ann (Johnson) D. B.A. in French and Physics, Rice U., 1979; M.A. in Math., U. Colo., 1981; Ph.D. candidate in Applied Math., U. N.Mex., 1985. Teaching asst. U. Colo., Boulder, 1979-81; engr. Jet Propulsion Lab., Pasadena, Calif., 1982; research asst. Naval Research Lab., Washington, 1984, 85. Fulbright fellow, Paris, 1986-87; recipient DAAD award, 1986. Mem. Soc. Indsl. and Applied Math., Am. Math. Soc., Pi Delta Phi, Phi Kappa Phi. Home: 1304 Florida St NE Albuquerque NM 87110 Office: U N Mex Albuquerque NM 87131

DUMAS, KATHERINE ANN, research physicist; b. Boston, Oct. 13, 1950; d. Anthony Peter and Ann (Katilus) D.; m. Randall Thomas Swimm, June 21, 1975. BS, Lowell Tech. Inst., 1972; MS, Coll. William and Mary, 1974, PhD, 1978. Mem. tech. staff Jet Propulsion Lab., Pasadena, Calif., 1979—. Editor: High-Speed Crystal Growth, 1984, Growth of High-Efficiency Material, 1985; contbr. articles to profl. jours. Recipient Cert. Recognition, NASA, 1983, Exceptional Pub. Service award Dept. of Energy, 1986. Mem. IEEE, Materials Research Soc. Roman Catholic. Avocations: backpacking, cross country skiing, traveling, reading, gardening. Office: Jet Propulsion Lab 4800 Oak Grove Dr MS 238-343 Pasadena CA 91109

DUMBACHER, JOSEPH DALE, marketing professional; b. Indpls., Oct. 14, 1960; s. John Louis and Rita Mae (Schoborg) D. BS, U. Ala., Huntsville, 1982; MBA, U. So. Calif., 1984. Dir. mktg. Southwest Data Systems Co., Burbank, Calif., 1984—. Mem. Am. Mktg. Assn. Club: Toastmasters (treas. 1983). Home: 1419-D Monterey Rd South Pasadena CA 91030 Office: Southwest Systems Data Mktg 3017 San Fernando Blvd Burbank CA 91504

DUMESNIL, CARLA DAVIS, interior design educator; b. Plainfield, N.J., Oct. 15, 1946; d. Carlton Carlise and Jenny (Katz) Davis; m. Randolph Dumesnil, July 5, 1971 (div. 1979); 1 child, Bretta. BS, U. Conn., 1968, MA, 1971. Lectr. Ga. So. Coll., Statesboro, 1969-71; instr. Westmoreland Community Coll., Greensburg, Pa., 1977; assoc. instr. U. Utah, Salt Lake City, 1977-80, asst. prof. interior design, 1980—; cons. IDEAS-Interior Design, Salt Lake city, 1982—, Interior Design Cons., Salt Lake City, 1975-83. Author: An Invitation to Design, 1982, Study Guide of Interior Design, 1979; house assembly designer Harbin Homes, 1974. Recipient Contbn. to Y-teen Home award YWCA, Salt Lake City, 1982; David P. Gardner Research grantee U. Utah, 1982. Mem. AIA (assoc.), Am. Soc. Interior Design, Environ. Design Research Assn., Am. Home Econs. Assn. (Expressions in Visual Arts award 1977), Internat. Facility Mgmt. Assn. Avocations: weaving, photography.

DUMKE, GLENN S., university and college chancellor emeritus; b. Green Bay, Wis., May 5, 1917; s. William F. and Marjorie S. (Schroeder) D.; m. Dorothy Deane Robison, Feb. 3, 1945. A.B., Occidental Coll., 1938, M.A., 1939, LL.D., 1960; Ph.D., U. Calif., 1942; H.L.D., U. Redlands, 1962, Hebrew Union Coll., 1968, Windham Coll., 1969; LL.D., U. Bridgeport, 1963, Transylvania Coll., 1968, Pepperdine Coll., 1969, Our Lady of the Lake U., 1977, Dickinson State Coll., 1978, Calif. State U., 1982. Teaching asst. U. Calif. at Los Angeles, 1940-41; instr. history Occidental Coll., 1940-43, asst. prof., 1943-46, assoc. prof., 1947-50, prof. history, 1950, Norman Bridge prof. Hispanic Am. history, 1954, dean faculty, 1950-57; pres. San Francisco State Coll., 1957-61; vice chancellor acad. affairs Calif. State Colls., 1961-62; chancellor Calif. State Univ. and Colls., 1962-82; pres. Inst. for Contemporary Studies, 1982-86, Found. 21st Century, 1986—; bd. dirs. Farmers Ins. Group, Trust Services Am., Forest Lawn Co., Barclays Bank of Calif.; 1st chmn. Calif. Council Econ. Edn., 1968; past mem. exec. com., chmn. Western Interstate Commn. for Higher Edn.; Mem. founding bd. Civilian/Mil. Inst., USAF Acad. Found.; former chmn. bd. Econ. Lit. Council Calif.; former mem. exec. com., chmn. fin. com. Council on Post-secondary Accreditation; former trustee Community TV So. Calif.-KCET; past mem. exec. com. Calif. Council for Humanities in Pub. Policy, 1974-77; chmn. Calif. Selection Com. for Rhodes Scholarships, 1966; former mem. com. on state relations Am. Assn. State Colls. and Univs.; bd. visitors USAF Air U.; past mem. bd. visitors USAF Acad.; bd. commrs. Nat. Commn. on Accrediting, 1959-65, 70-74; bd. dirs. Am. Council Edn., 1967-68; trustee Calif. Industry-Edn. Council. Author: The Boom of the Eighties in Southern California, 1944, Mexican Gold Trail, 1945, (with Dr. Osgood Hardy) A History of the Pacific Area in Modern Times, 1949, (under name Glenn Pierce) The Tyrant of Bagdad, 1955, King's Ransom, 1986, (under name Jordan Allen) Cavern of Silver, 1982; Co-author, editor: From Wilderness to Empire: A History of California, 1959; Contbr. articles to profl. and popular pubs. Alt. del. Republican nat. conv., 13th dist. Calif., 1948, 24th dist. Calif., 1952; trustee emeritus U. Redlands. Research fellow Huntington Library, 1943-45; Haynes Found. grantee, 1943. Mem. Los Angeles World Affairs Council (dir.), Calif. Hist. Soc., Joint Council Econ. Edn. (dir. 1969—), Western Coll. Assn. (past chmn. membership and standards com.), Am. Mgmt. Assn. (dir. 1970-73, 74-77, 79-82), Inst. Internat. Edn. (West Coast adv. bd. 1972—), Calif. C. of C. (dir.), Phi Beta Kappa. Methodist. Clubs: California, Bohemian, Town Hall, Commonwealth, Regency. Home: 16332 Meadow Ridge Rd Encino CA 91436 Office: 2650 Camino del Rio North San Diego CA 92108

DUMMETT, CLIFTON ORRIN, dentist, educator; b. Georgetown, British Guiana, May 20, 1919; came to U.S., 1936; s. Alexander Adolphus and Eglantine Annabella (Johnson) D.; m. Lois Maxine Doyle, Mar. 6, 1943; 1 son, Clifton Orrin. B.Sc. in Psychology, Roosevelt U., Chgo., 1941; D.D.S., Northwestern U., 1941, M.Sc.D., 1942, D.Sc. (hon.), 1976; M.P.H., U. Mich., 1947; Sc.D. (hon.), U. Pa., 1978. Diplomate Am. Bd. Periodontology, Am. Bd. Oral Medicine. Dean, and prof. periodontology Meharry Med. Coll., Nashville, 1945-49; chief dental service VA Hosp., Tuskegee, Ala., 1949-65, assoc. chief staff for research and edn., 1958-65; chief dental service VA Hosp., Chgo., 1965-66; dental dir., dir. ctr. Watts Health Ctr., Los Angeles, 1966-69; assoc. dean, prof., chmn. dept. community dentistry U. So. Calif. Sch. Dentistry, Los Angeles, 1969-75, prof. dentistry, 1975—; vis. prof. cons. Sch. Vet. Medicine, Tuskegee Inst., 1962-65; trustee Am. Fund Dental Health, Chgo., 1968-78; chmn. devel. component rev. panel Calif. Regional Med. Programs, Los Angeles, 1975-77; mem. President's Com. on Nat. Health Ins., 1977. Author: Community Dentistry, 1974, Charles Edwin Bentley, 1982; (editorial) Nor Yet the Last, 1962 (W.J. Gies award 1963), The Hillenbrnd Era, 1986; editor: Nat. Dental Assn., 1953-75; contbr. over 250 papers and articles to profl. jours., chpts. to books. Chmn. adv. bd. Econ. and Youth Opportunity Agy. Project Head Start, Tuskegee, Ala, 1964-65; mem. spl. health adv. com. Calif. Bd. Edn., Los Angeles, 1972-74; mem. Los Angeles regional hearing planning council, President's Com. on Health Edn., Los Angeles, 1973-74. Served to lt. col. USAF, 1955-58. Recipient Fones Gold medal Conn., Dental Assn., 1976; Pierre Fauchard Gold medal Pierre Fauchard Acad., 1980; Alumni award of Merit, Northwestern U., 1971. Fellow Internat. Coll. Dentists, Am. Coll Dentists, Am. Pub. Health Assn., AAAS (chmn. dental sect. 1975-76, 87—), Am. Acad. History of Dentistry (pres. 1982-83); mem. ADA (hon. mem.), Internat. Assn. Dental Research (pres. 1969-70), Assn. Mil. Surgeons U.S., (life), Am. Assn. Dental Editors (editor 1963-72, pres. 1974-75, Disting. Service medal 1976), Sigma Xi, Sigma Pi Phi, Alpha Phi Alpha, Omicron Kappa Upsilon (pres. Nashville chpt. 1947-49), Delta Omega. Democrat. Episcopalian. Avocations: music; politics; track. Home: 5344 Highlight Pl Los Angeles CA 90016 Office: U So Calif Sch of Dentistry PO Box 77006 Los Angeles CA 90007

DUNBAR, PATRICIA LYNN, new product development consultant; b. St. Louis, Feb. 11, 1953; d. William R. and Beryl Ione Noland (Ferrand) Dunbar; m. Michael R. Jeffrey, Oct. 2, 1950. BS, Northwestern U., 1973, MFA, 1975. With NBC-TV, Chgo., 1975-79; regional sales/mktg. mgr. Home Box Office, Chgo., 1979-81; sr. product mgr. Bank of Am., San Francisco, 1981-82, v.p., 1982-84; interactive communications services cons., 1984—. Mem. Women in Cable (1st pres. Chgo. chpt. 1981), Jr. League Seattle. Episcopalian. Patentee on child's chair, 1973. Office: 9640 SE 61st Pl Mercer Island WA 98040

DUNBAR, ROBERT GEORGE, historian, educator; b. LaGrange, Wis., Apr. 30, 1907; s. Charles Sales and Johannah (Van de Vrede) D.; B.A., Milton Coll., 1929; M.A., U. Wis., 1933, Ph.D., 1935; m. Mary Snell Albertson, June 19, 1937; children—Ann Marie, George Roger. High sch. tchr., Colby, Wis., 1929-31; asst. prof. history U. S.D., 1935-37; faculty Colo. State U., 1937-47, asso. prof., 1943-47; faculty Mont. State U., Bozeman, 1947—, prof. history, 1950-72, emeritus prof., 1972—, dir. Center for Intercultural Programs, 1966-72. Served with USNR, 1944-45. Mem. Orgn. Am. Historians, Agrl. History Soc. (pres. 1966-67), Western History Assn. (award of honor 1978), Phi Kappa Phi, Phi Alpha Theta. Author: Farmer and the American Way, 1952; Forging New Rights in Western Waters, 1983; editorial bd. Agrl. History, 1943-77. Home: 715 S Grand Ave Bozeman MT 59715

DUNCAN, ANSLEY MC KINLEY, aerospace co. mgr.; b. Homer City, Pa., Jan. 25, 1932; s. William McKinley and Marion Melissa (Davis) D.; student U. Denver, 1955-57, Pa. State U., 1957-59. Engring. adminstr. RCA, Van Nuys, Calif., 1959-61; program evaluation coordinator N.Am. Aviation, Anaheim, Calif., 1961-66; mfg. supr., Rockwell Internat., Anaheim Calif., 1966-70, program adminstr., 1970-76, program controls mgr., 1976-81, plans/schedule advisor, 1981—. Served with USN, 1951-55. Home: 12600 Willowood Ave Garden Grove CA 92640 Office: 3370 Miraloma Ave Anaheim CA 92803

DUNCAN, JAMES ALAN, chemistry educator; b. Osage, Iowa, Aug. 14, 1945; s. Wendell Alden and Karen Marie (Johnson) D. BA cum laude, Luther Coll., 1967; student, U. Ill., 1967-68; PhD, U. Oreg., 1971. Substitute asst. prof. chemistry Morgan State Coll., Balt., 1971-72; asst. prof. chemistry U. Notre Dame, Ind., 1972-74, Boston U., 1974-75; vis. asst. prof. chem. Reed Coll., Portland, Oreg., 1975-77; vis. scientist MIT, Cambridge, 1983-84; assoc. prof. chemistry Lewis and Clark Coll., Portland, 1977—. Contbr. articles to profl. jours. Grantee Research Corp. 1982-83, 85—, NSF, 1983, Petroleum Research Fund, 1983-85. Mem. Am. Chem. Soc. Home: 6813 SE Flavel St Portland OR 97206 Office: Lewis and Clark Coll 615 SW Palatine Hill Rd Portland OR 97219

DUNCAN, JERRY RAY, data processing executive; b. Portland, Oreg., Mar. 29, 1944; s. Robert Ray and Louise Elizabeth (Henderson) D.; m. Marilyn Mae Dietz, Mar. 20, 1965 (div. Jan. 1984); children: Julie Ann, Laurie Mae; m. Irene Patricia Garvey, June 16, 1984. Tech. support mgr. First Nat. Bank of Oreg., Portland, 1975-80; tech. support mgr. Farwest Fed. Bank, Portland, 1976-80, systems and programming mgr., 1980-84, mgr. data div., 1984—. Mem. Data Processing Mgmt. Assn., Soc. Info. Mgrs., Fin. Mgrs., Assn. Info. Mgrs. Republican. Clubs: Mountain Park Racquet (Lake Oswego, Oreg.); Oreg. Motorcycle Owners Assn. (Portland). Avocations: running, motorcycle racing, antique car restoration, tennis. Home: 17520 SE Paradise Dr Milwaukie OR 97267 Office: Farwest Fed Bank 44 SW 5th Ave Portland OR 97204

DUNCAN, JOHNNY LEE, electrical engineer; b. Adair, Okla., Feb. 2, 1939; s. Lloyd Talbot Duncan and Ruby Adelia Jeans; m. Kerin Dale Boston, June 17, 1961; children: Glenn Keith, David Lloyd (dec.), Melinda Elizabeth. A.A., Northeastern Okla. A&M U., 1959; B.S. in Elec. Engring., Okla. State U., 1962; M.S. in Elec. Engring., U. N.Mex., 1964. Mem. staff Sandia Labs., Albuquerque, 1962—, div. supr., 1969—, test mgr. cruise missile warhead, 1978-82, test and evaluation mgr. Trident II fuze, 1982—; mem. Trident II Blue Ribbon Com., 1986—. Served with U.S. Army, 1957. Mem. IEEE (sr.). Democrat. Baptist. Home: 10820 Nelle St Albuquerque NM 87111 Office: Kirtland AFB Sandia Labs Albuquerque NM 87185

DUNCAN, LINDA HELEN, elementary school teacher; b. Fitchburg, Mass., Sept. 10, 1947; d. Arvo Theodore and Helen (Kukkula) Heikkila; m. William David Duncan, Dec. 22, 1971; stepchildren: Joye Brady, Glen Scot, Jill Becksted, Jana Brinkman. AA, Palm Beach Jr. Coll., 1967; BA, Fla. Atlantic U., 1970; MEd, Utah State U., 1978. Cert. tchr., Wyo. Elem. sch. tchr. Rock Springs (Wyo.) Sch. Dist. 1, 1970-72; elem. sch. tchr. Green River (Wyo.) Sch. Dist. 2, 1972—, local young author program coordinator, 1981—. Recipient State K-3 1st Place award Wyo. Ednl. Media Assn., 1984, 2d Place, 1985. Mem. NEA, Green River Edn. Assn., Wyoming Edn. Assn., Beta Sigma Phi. Democrat. Congregationalist. Avocations: painting, writing. Office: Wilson Elem Sch 351 Monroe Ave Green River WY 82934

DUNCAN, RAYDEAN MARY, printing company executive; b. Ponca City, Okla., Aug. 26, 1936; d. Ray Edward and Nadine Catherine (Ivers) Cox; m. Dale Keith Duncan, Nov. 22, 1953 (div. 1982); children: Brian Keith, Lisa Renee. Grad. high sch., Owasso, Okla. Typesetter Douglas Aircraft Co., Tulsa, 1954-58, Tulsa Composition Co., 1959-63; typesetting mgr. Litho Negative Service, Tulsa, 1963-66; composition mgr. Bus. Controls, Tulsa, 1966-69; typesetter Duraset Composition, Los Angeles, 1969-71; pres. Forms Design & Typesetting Inc., Los Angeles, 1972—. Author: Forms Design Specifications, 1981. Named Woman of Yr., Graphic Arts Tech. Found., Washington, 1985. Mem. Bus. Forms Mgmt. Assn. (employment chmn. 1976—), Nat. Composition Assn. (numerous offices and awards 1973—), Los Angeles Composition Assn. (pres., bd. dirs. 1973-83), Printing Industries Calif. (bd. dirs. 1982-84), Printing Industries of So. Calif., Los Angeles Typographers Assn. (founding pres. 1984-85). Roman Catholic. Avocations: skiing, traveling, painting, entertaining. Office: Forms Design & Typesetting Inc 3016 E Olympic Blvd Los Angeles CA 90023

DUNCAN, RICHARD LEE, JR., educational psychologist; b. Lincoln, Nebr., June 1, 1940; s. Richard L. Duncan; m. Charlotte Fish; children: Dana, Dwight, Derick, Denise, Darlene. BA in Edn., Ariz. State U., 1963, MA in Counseling and Ednl. Psychology, 1965; EdD in Psychology, Western Colo. U., 1975. Cert. elem. and secondary tchr., counselor, psychologist, adminstr. Psychologist Mesa (Ariz.) Pub. Schs., 1969-71, guidance cons., 1971-74, dir. Title III, 1973-74, head psychologist, 1974-76, dir. psychol. services, 1976—, pres. clin. communications systems, 1978—; cons. nat. tng. on Stanford Binet Intelligence Test, edit. IV, 1986—; adj. prof. Ariz. State U., 1982—; vis. faculty Mesa Community Coll., 1969—. Editor: Creative Action Counseling Techniques and Useful Strategies, 1976. Bd. dirs. Maricopa County Youth Services Bur., Tri-City Community Behavioral Health Ctr., 1983—, pres., 1986-87; active Boy Scouts Am., YMCA (mem. LYFE found. bd. dirs.), Right to Life Assn. Recipient Merit award Boy Scouts Am., 1986. Mem. Nat. Assn. Sch. Psychologists, Ariz. Assn. Sch. Psychologists (pres. 1970-71), Am. Personnel and Guidance Assn., Ariz. Personnel and Guidance Assn. (pres. 1975-76), Am. Sch. Counselors Assn., Ariz. Sch. Counselors Assn., Kappa Delta Pi, Phi Delta Kappa. Mormon. Home: 1530 Alameda Dr Tempe AZ 85282 Office: 549 N Stapley Dr Mesa AZ 85203

DUNGEY, JOAN MARIE, educational consultant; b. Seattle, Nov. 24, 1944; d. Richard Allan and Bonita Florence (Slane) Osterholt; m. Ronald Eugene Dungey; children: Keenan, Philip. BA in Zoology, U. Wash.,

Seattle, 1966; MEd in Reading, Seattle Pacific U., 1983. Cert. reading resource specialist, profl. edn. cert., Wash.; cert. tchr., Tex. Sci. tchr. Meridian High Sch., Bellingham, Wash., 1967-69, Seoul Am. High Sch., Republic of Korea, 1969-70; english, reading tchr. Estacado Jr. High Sch., Plainview, Tex., 1979-81; dist. ESL evaluator Northshore Pub. schs., Bothell, Wash., 1982-84; tech. writer Computer Fin. Services, Bellevue, Wash., 1982—; cons. Baptist Young Women, N.W. Baptist Conv., 1975-77, Seattle Area Literacy Tutors, 1982-84; cons. ESL research, Addison-Wesley Pub. Co., Reading Mass., 1983; assoc. literacy missions, Home Mission Bd., Atlanta, 1984—. Author: Bible Studies for New English Speakers, 1982, Teaching the Bible to New English Speakers (video), 1986; contbr. articles to edn. jours. bd. dirs. ESL Sunday Sch. First Bapt. Ch., Bothell, Washington, 1982-84. Mem. Tch. of English to Speakers of Other Langs., Internat. Reading Assn., Nat. Council Tchrs. English, Popular Culture Assn., Laubach Literacy Action, Literacy Missions Assn. (Home Mission bd. 1984). Baptist. Avocations: swimming, photography.

DUNIGAN, PAUL FRANCIS XAVIER, JR., federal agency administrator; b. Richland, Wash., June 22, 1948; s. Paul Frances Xavier Sr. and Eva Lucille (Reckley) D.; m. Elizabeth Anne Henricks, Apr. 8, 1978; children: Katherine Anne, Theresa Anne. BS in Biology, Gonzaga U., 1970; MS in Environ. Sci., Washington State U., 1973. Tech. program mgr. ERDA, AEC, Richland, 1972-75; environ. biologist U.S. Dept. Energy, ERDA, Richland, 1975-81; waste mgmt. engr. U.S. Dept. Energy Waste Mgmt., Richland, 1981-84; civilian program mgr. Surplus Facilities Mgmt. Program U.S. Dept. Energy, Richland, 1984—. Contbr. articles to profl. jours. Named Eagle Scout Boy Scouts Am., 1962. Mem. AAAS, Water Pollution Control Fedn., Pacific Northwest Pollution Control Fedn. Roman Catholic. Home: 1612 Judson Richland WA 99352 Office: US Dept Energy PO Box 550 Richland WA 99352

DUNIKOSKI, FREDERICK, transportation executive; b. N.Y.C., Aug. 1, 1925; s. Helen (Czajkowski) D.; m. Rita A. McQuade, Oct. 11, 1947; children—Susan, Fred, Donna, Robert. Student, U. Ill. With Greyhound Lines, Inc., 1942—, dir. transp., 1969-70, v.p. transp., 1970-78, exec. v.p. ops., 1978-79; pres., chief operating officer Greyhound Lines, Inc., Phoenix, 1979—; also dir. subs. Greyhound Lines, Inc.; pres. Greyhound de Mexico, Greyhound World Tours. Bd. dirs. Travelers Aid Soc., Cleve., 1961-69, Devereux Ctr. Learning Disabled, Phoenix; bd. dirs., chmn. elect Phoenix Conv. and Visitors Bur.; treas. Community Orgn. for Drug Abuse Control, 1973-75. Served with USMC, 1943-45. Mem. Am. Bus. Assn. (bd. dirs.), United Bus. Owners Am. Democrat. Roman Catholic. Office: Greyhound Lines Inc Greyhound Tower Phoenix AZ 85077 *

DUNIN-WASOWICZ, EDWARD, advertising company executive; b. Rio de Janiero, Aug. 21, 1951; came to U.S., 1953; s. Walenty Dunin-Wasowicz and Victoria Bueno-Brandao; m. Karen Louise McGarrity, Aug. 27, 1977; children: Damien, Jeremy. BA, So. Ill. U., 1973. Dir. creative services Chgo. Sun-Times, 1974-76; writer, researcher So. Ill. U., Carbondale, 1976-78; copywriter, creative dir. Owens & Assocs. Advt., Tucson, 1978-86, cons., 1986—; owner, creative dir. Creative Accomplice, Tucson, 1986—. Recipient 1985 Addy Best of Show award Tucson Ad Club, 1985, Creative Excellence awards Tucson Ad Club, 1979-86. Home: 4159 W Sugarcane Tucson AZ 85741 Office: Creative Accomplice 1200 A N El Dorado Pl Suite 150 Tucson AZ 85715

DUNIPACE, IAN DOUGLAS, lawyer; b. Tucson, Dec. 18, 1939; s. William Smith and Esther Morvyth (McGeorge) D.; B.A. magna cum laude, U. Ariz., 1961; J.D. cum laude, 1966; m. Janet Mae Dailey, June 9, 1963; children: Kenneth Mark, Leslie Amanda. Reporter, critic Long Branch (N.J.) Daily Record, 1963; admitted to Ariz. bar, 1966, U.S. Supreme Ct. bar, 1972; assoc. firm Jennings, Strouss, Salmon & Trask, Phoenix, 1966-69, Jennings, Strouss & Salmon, 1969-70, ptnr., 1971—. Reporter, Phoenix Forward Edn. Com., 1969-70; bd. mgmt. Downtown Phoenix YMCA, 1973-80, chmn., 1977-78; bd. dirs. Phoenix Met. YMCA, 1976—, chmn., 1984-85; bd. mgmt. Paradise Valley YMCA, 1979-82, chmn., 1980-81; bd. mgmt. Scottsdale/Paradise Valley YMCA, 1983, mem. legal affairs com. Pacific Region YMCA, 1978-81; bd. dirs. Beaver Valley Improvement Assn., 1977-79, Pi Kappa Alpha Holding Corp., 1968-72; trustee Paradise Valley Unified Sch. Dist. Employee Benefit Trust, 1980—, chmn., 1987—; trustee First Meth. Found. of Phoenix, 1984—; mem. Greater Paradise Valley Community Council, 1985—. Served to capt. AUS, 1961-63. Mem. State Bar Ariz. (securities regulation sect. 1970—, sect. council 1983—, mem. sect. unauthorized practice of law 1972-84, chmn. 1975-83, mem. corp. law sect. 1981—, chmn., 1984-85), Am., Fed. (sec. Ariz. chpt. 1978-79, pres. 1980-81), Maricopa County bar assns., Ariz. Zool. Soc., U. Ariz. Law Coll. Assn. (bd. dirs. 1983—, pres. 1985-86), Heard Mus. Assn., Smithsonian Assn., U. Ariz. Alumni Assn. (bd. dirs. 1985-86), Phi Beta Kappa, Phi Kappa Phi, Phi Delta Phi, Phi Alpha Theta, Sigma Delta Pi, Phi Eta Sigma, Pi Kappa Alpha (nat. counsel 1968-72). Democrat. Methodist (mem. met. Phoenix commn. 1968-71, lay leader 1975-78, trustee 1979-81, pres. 1981; mem. Pacific S.W. ann. conf. 1969-79, lawyer commn. 1980-85, chancellor Desert S.W. ann. conf. 1985—). Clubs: Mansion, Renaissance. Lodges: Masons, Kiwanis (pres. Phoenix 1984-85, lt. gov. 1986-87). Comments editor Ariz. Law Rev., 1965-66. Home: 3601 E Mountain View Phoenix AZ 85028 Office: Jennings Strouss & Salmon 2 N Central 1 Renaissance Square Phoenix AZ 85003

DUNLAP, JOHN CRANDALL, mathematician, financial consultant; b. Casper, Wyo., Nov. 12, 1957; s. John Udell and Virginia Kathleen (Eddy) D. SB in Math., SB in Physics, MIT, 1979; postgrad., U. Calif., Berkeley, 1980-84. Teaching asst. U. Calif., Berkeley, 1980-84; fin. cons. BARRA, Berkeley, 1984—. Recording sec. San Francisco Lesbian/Gay Freedom Day Com., 1986, co-chmn. safety com., 1985, bd. dirs., 1986-87. Fulbright Commn. scholar, Fed. Republic of Germany, 1979-80. Mem. Am. Math. Soc., Assn. Symbolic Logic, Sigma Xi, Phi Beta Kappa. Democrat. Avocations: dancing, roller skating. Home: 602 Castro St San Francisco CA 94114 Office: BARRA 2001 Addison St Berkeley CA 94704

DUNLAP, KATHLEEN JANE, public relations executive, communications consultant; b. Roanoke, Va., Jan. 1, 1946; d. James Grantham and Kathleen Meredith (Haggerty) D. A.B. in English, Greensboro Coll., N.C., 1967; grad. publishing procedures Radcliffe Coll., 1970; M.A. in Mass Communication Research/Journalism, U. N.C., 1971. Tchr., Dept. Edn., Va., 1968-70; asst. dir. devel. Washington and Lee U., Lexington, Va., 1970-73; dir. devel., instr. So. Sem. Jr. Coll., Buena Vista, Va., 1973-74; admissions rep. Art Inst. of Ft. Lauderdale, 1974-78; pres. Dunlap Assocs., Seattle, 1979—; communications cons. Kramer, Chin & Mayo, Inc., Seattle, 1979-80; communications cons. Washington Environ. Tng. Research Inst., Auburn, Wash., 1981—; publs. cons. U. Wash., 1980-83, Puget Sound Power & Light, Bellevue, Wash., 1982—, Weyerhauser Co., 1984—; communications cons. Am. Plywood Assn., Tacoma, 1983—. Writer video script, 1983 (Bronze medal Internat. Film & TV festival of N.Y. 1984). Editor: Outlet, 1982-84 (Pacesetter awards Internat. Assn. Bus. Communicators 1982, 83, 84); Live Wires, 1984—. Mem. pub. relations com. Seattle Women's Commn., 1984—. Mem. Pub. Relations Soc. Am., Internat. Assn. Bus. Communicators, Women in Communications, Wash. Sch. Pub. Relations Assn., Am. Med. Writers Assn., Greater Seattle C. of C. Presbyterian. Club: Sound of the Baskervilles (pub. relations officer 1984—) (Seattle). Lodges: DAR (editor Silver Anniversary Yearbook Francis Broward chpt. 1976), Virginia Soc. Colonial Dames of 17th Century. Office: Dunlap Assocs 140 A S 108th St Seattle WA 98168

DUNLAP, STEVEN EUGENE, military officer, chemistry educator; b. Mobile, Ala., Jan. 6, 1951; s. Rudolf Benz and Agnes Leon (Powell) D.; m. Linda Sue mosley, Dec. 31, 1971 (div. Nov. 1975); children: Kathryn, Autumn; m. Patricia Lamar Pearson, Apr. 14, 1979; children: Melissa Michelle. BS in Chemistry cum laude, U. So. Ala., 1973; MA in Mgmt., Webster Coll., 1981; MS in Chemistry, Stanford U., 1985, postgrad., 1985—. Commd. USAF, 1973, advanced through grades to maj., 1973—, fighter pilot, 1973—; instr. chemistry USAF Acad., Colorado Springs, Colo., 1985—. Named Eagle Scout, Boy Scouts Am., 1965. Mem. Officer's Christian Fellowship, Am. Chem. Soc., Tau Kappa Epsilon. Presbyterian. Avocation: golfing. Home: Quarters 4511 I USAF Acad Colorado Springs CO 80840 Office: DFC USAF Acad Colorado Springs CO 80840

DUNLEVIE, ERNIE G., Realtor; b. N.Y.C., Aug. 3, 1917; s. George B. and Adelaide (Thompson) D.; children—Jon Taylor, Scott George, Michael Raymond, Geoffrey Kyle Dunlevie; m. 2d, Joy R. Nicholson, Nov. 8, 1982. Ptnr., Desert Bermuda Devel. Co., Bermuda Dunes, Calif., 1957—; pres. Dunray Land Co., Inc., 1957—, Ernie Dunlevie Assos., Palm Springs, Calif., 1946—. Past pres. Bob Hope Desert Classic. Served with USAAF, 1942-45. Decorated Air medal with 3 oak leaf clusters, D.F.C. Mem. Palm Springs C. of C. (dir. 1958), Calif. Real Estate Assn. (v.p. 1959, dir.), Palm Springs Bd. Realtors (past pres.). Clubs: Bermuda Dunes Country, Bermuda Dunes Racquet; Balboa Bay (Newport Beach); Mt. Kenya Safari (Africa); Catalina Island Yacht. Home: 79-050 Ave 42 Bermuda Dunes CA 92201

DUNLOP, RICHARD GALBRAITH, retail company executive; b. Phila., Nov. 24, 1942; s. Robert Galbraith and Emma (Brownback) D.; m. Kathleen Sittig, Aug. 11, 1967; children: Robert Galbraith II, Allison Suzanne. B.A. in Econs., Trinity Coll., 1965; M.B.A. in Fin., U. Pa., 1968. Asst. controller Acme Markets Inc., Phila., 1974-75, controller, 1975-80; v.p., asst. to chmn. Am. Stores Co., Salt Lake City, 1980-81; v.p., sec. Am. Stores Co., Salt Lake Co., 1981-82; exec. v.p., sec. Am. Stores Co., Salt Lake City, 1982-83, vice chmn. bd., treas., chmn. exec. com., 1983-85; vice chmn. bd., treas., chmn. exec. com. Am. Stores Co., 1985—; dir. First Interstate Bank of Utah N.A. Republican. Presbyterian. Club: Ft. Douglas (Salt Lake City). Home: 609 N Perrys Hollow Rd Salt Lake City UT 84103 Office: American Stores Co 709 E South Temple Salt Lake City UT 84102

DUNN, A. DALE, livestock and agricultural products company executive; b. Montpelier, Idaho, 1923; married. MSChemE, U. Idaho, 1949. With J.R. Simplot Co., Boise, Idaho, 1953—, pres. minerals and chems. div., 1970-78, pres., chief exec. officer, 1978—, also bd. dirs. Office: J R Simplot Co PO Box 27 Boise ID 83707 *

DUNN, BRUCE CLEVELAND, construction executive; b. Lawrenceburg, Ind., May 9, 1943; s. Fenmore Emerson and Hattie (Ballard) D.; m. Sue Ann Jeosephson, Nov. 8, 1975. BSME, U. Colo, 1965; BSBA, U. Colo., 1969. Product engr. Dow Chem. Co., Golden, Colo., 1966-73; engr., mgr. Stearns-Roger div. United Engrs. and Constructors, Denver, 1973—. Bible tchr. Trinity United Presbyn. Ch., Arvada, Colo. Mem. ASME, Am. Soc. Cost Engrs., Project Mgmt. Inst., Pi Tau Sigma, Sigma Tau. Republican. Office: Stearns-Roger Box 5888 Denver CO 80217

DUNN, CAL, artist, motion picture producer and director; b. Georgetown, Ohio, Aug. 31, 1915; s. Forester Eugene and Mary Achsa (Calvin) D.; m. Eleanor Frances Little, Sept. 4, 1937; 1 son, Michael Hamilton. Student Cin. Art Acad., 1927, Central Acad. Comml. Art, 1932-34. Engaged in layout and illustration studios and advt. agys., Cin., Detroit, Iowa, 1935-43; freelance cartoonist, 1943; founder Cal Dunn Studios, Inc., Chgo., 1947-79; artist, Santa Fe, 1980—; one-man shows include: A.B. Closson Gallery, Cin., 1941, Etc. Gallery, Chgo., 1952, Tavern Club, Chgo., 1962-81; numerous group shows including: Cin. Art Mus., 1941, Davenport (Iowa) Municipal Art Gallery, 1941, Art Inst. Chgo., 1946, 50, Artists Guild Chgo., 1946, 48, 49, 50-55, 58-63, 65, Santa Fe Festival Arts, 1978, 80; represented in permanent collections Albuquerque Mus., N.Mex. Mus. Fine Art, Santa Fe. Recipient numerous awards including Artists Guild Chgo., 1946, 48, 49-51, 55, Disting. Achievement award The Seasoned Eye, 1986, Emmy award Acad. TV Arts and Scis., 1959, Best Dir. award Chgo. Audiovisual Producers Assn., 1977. Mem. Am. Watercolor Soc. (Bronze medal 1956), N.Mex. Watercolor Soc. (hon. life mem.), Artist Guild Chgo. (past pres.), Dirs. Guild Am. Address: Route 9 Box 86L Sunlit Hills Santa Fe NM 87505

DUNN, DAVIS DEAN, JR., corporate executive; b. Mare Island, Calif., May 20, 1945; s. Davis Dean and Carol Lucille Dunn; m. Candida Louise Conklin, Dec. 31, 1982. B.S., Utah State U., 1967; postgrad. Syracuse U., 1974. Mgr. Quality control and tech. services Corning Glassworks, N.Y., 1973-76; dir. tech. services Texana Industries, Austin, 1976-77; dir. mountain services Vail Assocs. Inc., Colo., 1977-81; v.p. Pleasant Mountain Recreation Corp., Bridgton, Maine, 1981-82; gen. ptnr. Western Racing Equipment and Engring., Grand Junction, Colo., 1982-84, pres. D.D. Dunn & Co., Avon, Colo.; cons. microbiology; mem. Standards Com. Blood Collection Systems, Tissue Culture Products. Active various civic fund-raising programs. Served with M.C., USN, 1967-71. Decorated Navy Commendation medal. Mem. Am. Soc. Microbiology. Home: PO Box 27 Avon CO 81620

DUNN, IMA CHARLENE, special education administrator; b. Pueblo, Colo., Jan. 29, 1941. A.A., U. So. Colo., 1960; B.A., U. No. Colo., 1962, Ed.D. in Spl. Edn., 1973; postgrad. U. N.Mex.; M.A. in Spl. Edn., Central State U., Edmond, Okla., 1966; postgrad. Western State Coll., Gunnison, Colo., 1975; postgrad Ft. Hays State U., 1981. Tchr. pub. schs., Albuquerque, 1962-65; tchr. developmental reading and reading methods U. So. Colo., Pueblo, 1966-68; coordinator secondary reading Pueblo Dist. #70, 1968-71, 73-74, dir. spl. services, 1974—; specialist in field experiences U. No. Colo., 1971-73; lectr. and cons. in field. Contbr. articles to profl. jours. Recipient Masonic Educators award. Mem. NEA (life), Central State U. Alumni Assn. (life), Assn. Sch. Curriculum Devel. (sec.-treas. Pueblo chpt. 1974-75), Colo. Assn. Sch. Execs., Council Exceptional Children (pres. Pueblo chpt. 1975-76, pres. Colo. Fedn. 1976-78), Council Adminstrs. in Spl. Edn., Kappa Delta Pi, Phi Delta Kappa, Pi Lambda Theta. Office: Pueblo Sch Dist 70 24951 E Hwy 50 Pueblo CO 81006

DUNN, JACK HIBBARD, neurological surgeon; b. Clayton, N.Y., Apr. 5, 1944; s. Jack K. and Helen (Hibbard) D.; m. Rosemary Moroney, May 1, 1980; children: Erica Rose, Allison Marie. BA, Yale U., 1967; MD, Wayne State U., 1971. Diplomate Am. Bd. Med. Examiners, Am. Bd. Neurol. Surgery. Clin. instr. surgery NYU, N.Y.C., 1971-72, clin. instr. neurosurgery, 1974-79; asst. chief physiol. neurosurgery West Chester County Med. Ctr., N.Y.C., 1980; asst. prof. surgery, neurosurgery U. Ariz., Tucson, 1980-82; v.p. Western Neurosurgery, Tucson, 1982—. Served to lt. M.C., USN, 1972-74. Home and Office: 5182 E Farness Dr Tucson AZ 85712

DUNN, JAMES MICHAEL, physician, pharm. co. exec.; b. Long Beach, Calif., May 8, 1937; s. Joseph Shelby and Mary Juanita (Fowler) D.; B.S., U. Oreg., 1958; M.D., U. Calif., Irvine, 1962; m. Carolyn Kay Olson, Oct. 23, 1971; children—Shannon, Lisa, Christopher, Kevin. Intern, Sacred Heart Gen. Hosp., Eugene, Oreg., 1962-63; resident in ob-gyn Kaiser Found. Hosp., Oakland, Calif., 1965-67; practice medicine specializing in ob-gyn, Fairfield, Calif., 1967-74, Oreg. McLean Clinic, Oregon City, 1974-75; asst. dir. clin. pharmacology Abbott Labs., 1975-76; asso. dir. clin. pharmacology, then dir. clin. research Wallace Labs., 1976-79; v.p. med. affairs Boots Pharms., Inc., 1979-80; pres. Verex Labs., Inc., Englewood, Colo., 1980-82, pres., chief exec. officer, chmn., 1982—; asst. prof. family medicine and pharmacology La. State U. Med. Sch., 1979-81. Served as officer M.C., USAF, 1963-65. Fellow Am. Coll. Clin. Pharmacology, Am. Soc. Abdominal Surgeons, Royal Soc. Medicine, Internat. Coll. Physicians and Surgeons; mem. Am. Soc. Clin. Pharmacology and Therapeutics, AMA, N.Y. Acad. Sci., Am. Fertility Soc., AAAS, Western Soc. Ob-Gyn (a founder), Drug Info. Assn., Sigma Xi. Roman Catholic. Author articles in field, also poems, short stories. Address: 8925 E Nichols Ave PO Box 3817 Englewood CO 80112

DUNN, JESSIE JOYCE, psychotherapist, consultant; b. Pineville, Mo., July 16, 1930; d. Silas and Lucretia (Packwood) Clark; m. Robert E. Dunn, Dec. 13, 1958 (div. 1970); 1 child, Jonathan. BA in Soc. and Justice magna cum laude, U. Wash., 1974, MSW, 1977. Counselor Salvation Army, Seattle, 1977-78; therapist Divorce Lifeline, Seattle, 1977-84; pvt. practice specializing in psychotherapy Seattle, 1980—; practicum instr. U. Wash. Sch. Social Work, 1980-81. Screen clients Mcpl. Probations and Parole, Seattle, 1974; bd. dirs. Seattle Counseling, 1973-74, v.p.; coordinator of adult single programs Univ. Unitarian Ch., Seattle, 1979-83. Mem. Nat. Assn. Social Workers, Phi Beta Kappa. Democrat. Avocations: walking, dancing, football, gardening, movies.

DUNN, JOHN MAXIMILLIAN, physical education educator; b. Du Quoin, Ill., Oct. 3, 1945; s. Francis George and Arah Mae (Bush) Dunne; m. Linda Dell Turner, Aug. 28, 1971; children: Matthew Michael, Michael Turner, Kerry Frances. BS, No. Ill. U., 1967, MS, 1969; EdD, Brigham Young U., 1972; postdoctorate, Temple U., 1973. Grad. teaching asst. Brigham Young U., Provo, Utah, 1970-72; asst. prof. phys. edn. U. Conn., Storrs, 1972-75; asst. prof. phys. edn. Oreg. State U., Corvallis, 1975-77, assoc. prof., 1977-83, chmn. dept. phys. edn., 1981—, prof., 1983—; program dir. Camp Coventry, Mansfield, Conn., 1974-75; cons. in field. Author: Adaptive Physical Education, 1979; co-author: Physical Education for the Severely Handicapped, 1986, Special Physical Education, 1984, Physical Education for the Handicapped, 1979; contbr. articles to profl. jours. Mem. State Adv. Council for the Handicapped; bd. dirs. Corvallis 509J Sch. Dist. Sch. Bd., Corvallis, 1980—. Grantee Dept. Edn., 1986—, 83-86, 80-83, Bur. of Edn. for Handicapped, 1979-80, 77-80, 76, State Dept. Edn., 1978, 78-85. Mem. Am. Diabetes Assn., U.S. Assn. for Blind Athletes, Assn. for Severely Handicapped, Oreg. Assn. Retarded Citizens, Nat. Assn. Retarded Citizens, AAHPERD (life, fellow research consortium, ARAPCS Honor award 1982), Nat. Assn. for Phys. Edn. in Higher Edn., Nat. Consortium on Phys. Edn. and Recreation for Handicapped (charter, Disting. Service award 1985). Democrat. Roman Catholic. Avocations: running, gardening, reading, traveling. Office: Oreg State U Dept Phys Edn Langton 214 Corvallis OR 97331

DUNN, MICHAEL AUSTIN, writer, producer; b. Tucson, Mar. 5, 1958; s. James Richard and Patricia (Sargeant) D.; m. Linda Poulson, May 1, 1980; children: Jeffrey P., Braden T. BS, U. Utah, 1981. Reporter, producer KUTV TV, Salt Lake City, 1982-83; pub. relations exec. Fotheringham & Assocs., Salt Lake City, 1983—. Contbr. articles to newspapers and mags. Recipient Telly award, 1983, 85; named Best in Dist., Coll. Sports Info. Dirs. of Am., 1982. Mem. Pub. Relations Soc. Am., Utah Advt. Fedn. Mormon. Avocations: biking, skiing. Home: 3711 Ceres Dr Salt Lake City UT 84124 Office: Fotheringham & Assocs 215 S State St #300 Salt Lake City UT 84111

DUNN, STEPHEN PORTER, research anthropologist; b. Boston, Mar. 24, 1928; s. Leslie Clarence and Louise (Porter) D.; m. Ethel Deikman, Oct. 6, 1956. BA, Columbia Coll., 1950, PhD, 1959. Researcher Inst. Contemporary Russian Studies Fordham U., Bronx, N.Y., 1959-63; researcher Ctr. Slavic and East European Studies U. Calif, Berkeley, 1964-68; dir. research Highgate Rd. Social Sci. Research Sta., Berkeley, 1969—. Author: The Fall and Rise of the Asiatic Mode of Production, 1982; co-author: The Peasants of Central Russia, 1967; translator Alexander Yanov, The Russian New Right, 1978; editor Soviet Anthropology and Archaeology, Soviet Sociology, ME Sharpe, Inc.; contbg. editor: The Station Relay. Fellow Am. Anthrop. Assn. Avocations: poetry, polit. commentary. Home and Office: Highgate Rd Social Sci Research 32 Highgate Rd Berkeley CA 94707

DUNN, THOMAS GUY, biology educator, university administrator; b. Livingston, Mont., Jan. 31, 1935; s. Thomas L. and E. Gretchen (Gibson) D.; m. Nancy Jane Murphy, Aug. 6, 1960; children: T. James, Michael M. BS, Mont. State Coll., 1962; MS, U. Nebr., 1965; PhD, Colo. State U., 1969. Asst. prof. animal sci. Purdue U., West Lafayette, Ind., 1968-70; asst. prof. animal physiology U. Wyo., Laramie, 1970-73, assoc. prof., 1973-77, prof., 1977—, dean Grad. Sch., 1984—; acting dean Coll. Agr. U. Wyo., Laramie, 1983-84; vis. prof. Colo. State U., Ft. Collins, 1979; sr. trustee Consortium Internat. Devel., Tuscon, 1983—. Refereed sci. jours.; contbr. articles to profl. jours., chpts. to books. Trustee Mus. of Rockies, Bozeman, Mont., 1986—. Served with U.S. Army, 1956-58. Grantee NIH, FDA, USDA, Human Growth Found., Nat. Assn. Animal Breeders. Mem. AAAS, Am. Soc. Animal Sci., Soc. Study of Reprodn., Am. Fertility Soc. Republican. Avocations: team roping, hunting, fishing, flying, skiing. Home: PO Box 4268 Univ Sta Laramie WY 82071 Office: U Wyo Grad Sch PO Box 3108 Univ Sta Laramie WY 82071

DUNNE, THOMAS, geology educator; b. Prestbury, U.K., Apr. 21, 1943; came to U.S., 1964; s. Thomas and Monica Mary (Whitter) D. BA with honors, Cambridge (Eng.) U., 1964; PhD, The Johns Hopkins U., 1969. Research assoc. USDA-Agrl. Research Service, Danville, Vt., 1966-68; research hydrologist U.S. Geol. Survey, Washington, 1969; asst. prof. McGill U., Montreal, Que., Can., 1969-73; from asst. prof. to prof. U. Wash., Seattle, 1973—; vis. prof. U. Nairobi, Kenya, 1969-71; cons. in field, 1970—. Author (with L.B. Leopold) Water in Environmental Planning. Grantee NSF, NASA, Rockefeller Found., 1969—. Mem. AAAS, Am. Geophys. Union, Geol. Soc. Am., Brit. Geomorphol. Research Group, Sigma Xi. Office: U Wash Dept Geol Scis AJ-20 Seattle WA 98195

DUNNELL, ROBERT CHESTER, archaeologist, educator; b. Wheeling, W.Va., Dec. 4, 1942; s. Arthur and Kathryn (McCarter) D.; m. Mary Jewett Davidson, June 4, 1966. B.A., U. Ky., 1964; Ph.D. (Woodrow Wilson fellow, Univ. fellow), Yale U., 1967. Asst. prof. anthropology U. Wash., Seattle, 1967-71; asso. prof. U. Wash., 1971-74, prof., 1974—, chmn. dept. anthropology, 1973-85; prin. investigator Nat. Park Service contracts, U.S. Army Corps Engrs. contracts; adj. curator N.Am. archaeology Burke Meml. Wash. State Mus., 1971—; mem. sci. com. Wash. Archaeol. Research Center, 1975-79; adj. prof. Quaternary Research Center, 1976—; council from Anthropology to Quaternary Research Center Adv. Council, 1976-79; curatorial affiliate in anthropology Peabody Mus. Natural History, Yale U., 1985-90. Mem. editorial bd.: Advances in Archaeological Theory and Method, 1977—. Fellow AAAS, Am. Anthrop. Assn., N.Y. Acad. Sci.; mem. Classification Soc., Soc. for Am. Archaeology, Assn. Field Archaeology (pres. 1985-87), Am. Soc. for Conservation Archaeology. Office: Dept Anthropology U Wash Seattle WA 98195

DUNNER, DAVID LOUIS, medicine educator; b. Bklyn., May 27, 1940; s. Edward and Reichel (Connor) D.; m. Peggy Jane Zolbert, Dec. 27, 1964; children: Laura Louise, Jonathan Michael. AA, George Washington U., 1960; MD, Washington U., St. Louis, 1965. Diplomate Am. Bd. Psychiatry and Neurology. Intern Phila. Gen. Hosp., 1965-66; resident in psychiatry Barnes Renard Hosp. of Washington U., St. Louis, 1966-69; research psychiatrist N.Y. State Psychiat. Inst., N.Y.C., 1971-79; from asst. prof. to assoc. prof. clin. psychiatry Columbia U., N.Y.C., 1972-79; chief psychiatry Harborview Med. Ctr., Seattle, 1979—; prof. psychiatry and behavioral scis. U. Wash., Seattle, 1979—; cons. Found. for Depression and Manic Depression, N.Y.C., 1974—. Contbr. articles to profl. jours. Served to lt. comdr. USPHS, 1969-71. Fellow Am. Psychiat. Assn., Am. Psychopathol. Assn. (pres. 1986), Am. Coll. Neuropsychopharmacology, West Coast Coll. Biol. Psychiatry (charter, pres. 1987); mem. Psychiat. Research Soc. (pres. 1984). Office: Harborview Med Ctr 325 9th Ave ZA-15 Seattle WA 98104

DUNNETT, DENNIS GEORGE, state official; b. Auburn, Calif., Aug. 5, 1939; s. George DeHaven and Elizabeth Grace (Sullivan) D. AA in Elec. Engring., Sierra Coll., 1959; AB in Econs., Sacramento State Coll., 1966. Engring. technician State of Calif., Marysville, 1961-62; data processing technician State of Calif., Sacramento, 1962-67, EDP programmer and analyst, 1967-74, staff services mgr. and contract adminstr., 1974-76, hardware acquisition mgr., 1976-86, support services br. mgr., information security officer, 1986—; instr. Am. River Coll., 1972; cons. to state personnel bd. on data processing testing, 1983. Mem. Data Processing Mgmt. Assn. (certs.), Calif. State U. Sacramento Alumni Assn. (life), Assn. Computing Machinery, IEEE Computer Soc., Assn. Inst Cert. of Computer Profls., Intergovtl. Council on Tech. of Info. Processing, The Mus. Soc., San Francisco Opera Guild. Home: 729 Blackmer Circle Sacramento CA 95825-4704 Office: Box 13436 Sacramento CA 95813-4436

DUNNIGAN, MARY ANN, former educational administrator; b. St. Maries, Idaho, Sept. 7, 1915; d. William Henry and Mary Ellen (Kelly) D.; B.A., Holy Names Coll., Spokane, 1942; M.A., Gonzaga U., Spokane, 1957; postgrad. U. Idaho, UCLA. Tchr. rural schs. Bonner County, 1936-41, elem. schs., 1941, 45-59, high sch., 1942, 45, coordinator elem. edn., 1959-78; prin. kindergarten Sch. Dist. 271, Coeur d'Alene, Idaho, 1978-81; tchr. extension classes U. Idaho; curriculum chmn. Gov.'s Conf. on Edn.; adv. council Head Start. Adv. council Council for Aging; mem. N. Idaho Mus., Community Council, Community Concerts, Community Theater, N. Idaho Booster Club, Mayor's Com. on Handicapped; mem. task force and diocesan bd. Catholic Edn. of Idaho, 1969-74. Bd. dirs. Coeur d'Alene Tchrs. Credit Union, 1958—, pres., treas., 1976—; hist. chmn. Coeur d'Alenecentennial, 1986—. Named Citizen of Yr., N. Idaho Coll., 1974, Idaho Cath. Dau. of Year, 1968. Mem. Idaho Edn. Assn., NEA, Kootenai County Ret. Tchrs. Assn. (pres. 1983-87), Delta Kappa Gamma. Club: Cath. Daus. Am. (state regent 1956-62). Home: 720 9th St Coeur d'Alene ID 83814

DUNNING, KENNETH LAVERNE, research physicist; b. Yale, Iowa, Sept. 24, 1914; s. Howard Grant and Gertrude Estelle (Dygert) D.; m. Ruth Ellen Pyle, Sept. 2, 1941; children: David M., Jane B., John K., Marion Leigh. BEE, U. Minn., 1938; MS in Physics, U. Md., 1950; PhD in Physics, Cath. U. Am., 1968. Engr. Western Union, N.Y.C., 1938-41; physicist U.S. Naval Research Lab., Washington, 1945-80; cons. Port Ludlow, Wash., 1981—. Contbr. articles to profl. jours. Pres. Highland Greens Condominium Assn., Port Ludlow, 1983-84, v.p. 1984-85. Served to maj. U.S. Army, 1941-45. Recipient Research Pub. award Naval Research Lab., 1971. Mem. IEEE, Am. Phys. Soc., Coll. Club Seattle, Sigma Xi, Tau Beta Pi, Eta Kappa Nu. Home and Office: 101-6 Highland Greens Port Ludlow WA 98365

DUNNING, LAWRENCE MORTON, editor, writer, creative writing educator; b. Kansas City, Mo., Aug. 8, 1931; s. Lawrence M. and Virginia Elizabeth (Morisey) D.; m. Barbara Lee Adams, Apr. 11, 1958; children: Melissa Ann, Tracey Lee, Jennifer Kay. Student, Rice Inst., 1948-49; BJ, So. Meth. U., 1952. Freelance writer Denver, 1960—; sr. editor Air Force Acctg. and Fin. Ctr., Denver, 1962-84, pubs. mgr., 1984—; tchr. creative writing U. Colo., Denver, 1983-85, U. Denver, 1980-83. Author: Neutron Two is Critical, 1977, Keller's Bomb, 1978, Taking Liberty, 1981. Served with USAF, 1952-56. Short story listed in Best Am. Short Stories, 1971. Mem. The Author's Guild, Inc., Colo. Authors League (Top Hand award 1979), Mensa. Home: 1211 S Quebec Way #4-101 Denver CO 80231 Office: USAF Acctg & Fin Ctr/DAP Denver CO 80279-5000

DUNNING, ROBERT LEWIS, chemistry consultant; b. Portland, Oreg., Jan. 18, 1931; s. Owen Chase and Alice Eudora (Mowes) D.; m. Anne Mae Kitts, Feb. 7, 1952; children: Michael, Patti Baird, Jan Johnson, Teresa Henderson. BS in Chemistry, Lewis and Clark Coll., 1954; MS in Chemistry, Oreg. State U., 1956. Research chemist Shell Chem. Co., Torrance, Calif., 1956-62; mgr. research and devel. Douglas Oil Co., Paramount, Calif., 1963-72; chemist, sec./treas. La Belle Cons., Santa Ana, Calif., 1972-74; pres. Petroleum Scis., Inc., Anaheim, Calif., 1974-76, Spokane, Wash., 1976—. Contbr. articles to profl. jours. Served with USAF, 1951-52. Mem. Am. Chem. Soc., Soc. Rheology, Math. Assn. Am., Spokane C. of C., Sigma Xi. Republican. Lodge: Kiwanis (pres. 1986—). Avocations: skiing, fishing. Office: Petroleum Scis Inc N 4817 Freya #3 Spokane WA 99207

DUNOYER, PHILIPPE, petroleum industry executive; b. Paris, May 3, 1930; s. Bernard and Suzanne (De Mones) D.; m. Cynthia Troxell, Apr. 4, 1956; children: Cecilia, Louis, François, Jean. Grad. Engr., École Polytechnique, Paris, 1951; Certificate of Geology, U. Montpellier, France, 1952; postgrad. in geophysics, Colo. Sch. Mines, 1952-53, U. Calif., Los Angeles, 1953-54; postgrad. exec. program, Stanford U., 1970. With Total Compagnie Française des Petroles and Affiliates, 1954—; chmn. bd., pres., chief exec. officer Total Petroleum (N.Am.) Ltd. Trustee Alma Coll., 1976, Denver Symphony, 1982. Served with French Army, 1953-54. Mem. Am. Petroleum Inst. (dir.), French Assn. Oil Industry Profls. (chmn. econ. com. 1968-71). Roman Catholic. Club: Denver (pres. 1986). Home: 2000 E 12th Ave Box 22 Denver CO 80206 *

DUNST, LAWRENCE WILLIAM, electronics company executive; b. Bellfonte, Pa., Aug. 19, 1947; s. Joseph William and Elaine Louise (Zwicker) D.; m. Carol Carter Davenport, Dec. 10, 1977; children: William, Catherine. BS in Engring. Sci., Pa. State U., 1969, MS in Physics, 1971; postgrad., Johns Hopkins U., 1974, Westinghouse Sch. Applied Engring. Sci., 1973-78, Ariz. State U., 1980, UCLA, 1981. Research asst. Martin Marietta Labs., Balt., 1972-73; simulation and computer analyst Westinghouse Electric Co., Balt., 1973-80, sr. radar engr., 1973-80; prin. staff engr. Motorola, Inc., Tempe, Ariz., 1980, group leader systems software, 1980-81, task leader aerospace payload section, 1982-82; software cons. Gen. Electric Corp., Utica, N.Y., 1982-83; group leader F-16 Displays Sperry Flight Systems, Phoenix, 1982-84, systems and Software cons. avionics div., 1984—; lead engr. Neurologics, Inc., Nashville, 1984-85; pres. Laurence Resources, Inc., 1982—. Contbr. articles to profl. jours. Supporter Jr. League of Phoenix, 1980-86; active YMCA, Scottsdale. Named Eagle Scout Boy Scouts Am., 1964. Mem. Tau Beta Pi, Sigma Tau, Pi Mu Epsilon. Republican. Presbyterian. Club: Village Tennis (Scottsdale). Avocations: tennis, boating, camping, hiking, swimming. Home and Office: 5825 E Lewis Ave Scottsdale AZ 85257

DUNSTAN, LARRY KENNETH, insurance company executive; b. Payson, Utah, May 26, 1948; s. Kenneth Leroy Dunstan and Verna Matilda (Carter) Taylor; m. Betty K. Limb, Sept. 23, 1966 (div. June 1975); children: Tamara, Thane; m. Jacqueline Lee Darron, Oct. 7, 1975; children: Tessa, Matthew, Bennett, Spencer, Adam. Mgr. Diamond Bar Inn Ranch, Jackson, Mont., 1972-73; agt. Prudential Ins. Co., Missoula, Mont., 1973-77; devel. mgr. Prudential Ins. Co., Billings, Mont., 1977-78; div. mgr. Prudential Ins. Co., Gt. Falls, Mont., 1978-83; pres. Multi-Tech Ins. Services, Inc., Oswego, Oreg., 1983—; agy. mgr. Beneficial Life Ins. Co., Portland, Oreg., 1983—; CLU; CPCU; chartered fin. cons. Mem. planning commn. City of West Linn, Oreg., 1986; mem. bishopric Ch. Jesus Christ of Latter Day Sts., West Linn, 1984-86; scouting coordinator Boy Scouts Am., West Linn, 1984-86, scoutmaster various troops. Named Eagle Scout Boy Scouts Am., 1965, recipient Heroism award 1965. Mem. Gen. Agts. and Mgrs. Assn. (bd. dirs. 1981-82), Life Underwriter Tng. Council (bd. dirs. 1980-81), Am. Soc. CLU (pres. 1982-83). Republican. Avocations: sports, stamp collecting, oil painting, gardening, photography. Home: 19443 Wilderness Dr West Linn OR 97068 Office: Multi-Tech Ins Services Inc 1 Centerpointe Dr #330 Lake Oswego OR 97034

DUPLER, MARGE L(OU)., bank executive; b. Madison County, Tex., July 30, 1950; d. W. Robert and Laura Lavinia (Mosley) Brown; m. T.L. Dupler, Oct. 17, 1970. BBA in Fin., Sam Houston State U., 1978; MBA in Fin., Tex. A&M U., 1980. Credit analyst Republic Bank Houston, 1980-81, energy banking officer, 1981-84; asst. v.p. Bank of Montreal, Houston, 1984-85, Los Angeles, 1985—. Precinct chmn. Rep. Party Harris County, Houston, 1984-85; chmn. Gallery Aides Craft and Folk Art Mus., Los Angeles, 1986—. Mem. Houston Women Profl. Group (asst. sec. 1984—). Lutheran. Avocations: scuba diving, skiing, photography. Home: 507 N Highland Ave Los Angeles CA 90036

DUPONT, CHARLES J., retired safety engineer, consultant; b. Garyville, La., Apr. 25, 1923; s. Watson Stanhope and Leona (Schroeder) DuP.; m. Genevieve Joan Wojnas, June 25, 1949 (div. 1972); children: Sara Ann Leach, Barbara Jean Eppenger; m. Carol Francis Eckhardt, Aug. 4, 1978. BS, No. Ariz. U., 1974; MS, U. So. Calif., 1975. Commd. USAF, 1941, advanced through grades to maj., 1962; aviation mgr. Clarke Spraying Co., LaGrange, Ill., 1966-69; chief pilot Grand Canyon (Ariz.) Helicopters, 1969-70; owner, mgr. Multi Service Enterprises, Flagstaff, Ariz., 1971-73; research assoc. U. So. Calif., Los Angeles, 1975-78; system safety engr. Hughes Aircraft Co., Long Beach, Calif., 1978-84; prin. Spec. Safety Services, Camp Nelson, Calif., 1975—. Co-author: Multidisciplinary References for Aircraft Accident Investigation, 1975. Decorated DFC 1951; recipient Air medal 1951. Mem. System Safety Soc. Republican. Lodge: Elks. Avocations: hunting, fishing, hiking, gardening. Address: 315 View Dr PO Box 64 Camp Nelson CA 93208-0064

DUPONT, FRANCES MARGUERITE, plant physiologist; b. Duluth, Minn., May 23, 1944; d. John Francis and Florence Marguerite (Anderson) Milne. BA, U. Calif., Berkeley, 1965; MA, UCLA, 1971; PhD, U. Calif., Riverside, 1979. Research assoc. Cornell U., Ithaca, N.Y., 1979-81, ARCO Plant Cell Research Inst., Dublin, Calif., 1981-83; plant physiologist USDA, Albany, Calif., 1983—. Contbr. articles to profl. jours. USDA grantee, 1985. Mem. AAAS, Am. Soc. Plant Physiologists. Office: USDA ARS/WRRC 800 Buchanan St Albany CA 94804

DUPONT, JOHN, TV producer, director, writer; b. Troy, N.Y., June 5, 1948; s. William and Marian Theresa (Northrup) D. A.A.S. in Media Tech., Pima Community Coll., Tucson, 1982. Organist, 1959-71; Organ sales mgr. Muller Music Ctr., Tucson, 1973-74; printed circuit bd. digitizer Compuroute, Inc. Dallas, 1974-77; computer operator for various firms, Tucson, 1977-79; TV producer/dir. Tucson Med. Ctr., 1979—; music instr. Baldwin Music Ctr., Tucson, 1982-85. Composer numerous songs. Served with U.S. Army, 1971-73. Republican. Roman Catholic. Office: Tucson Med Ctr 5301 E Grant Rd Tucson AZ 85733

DUPPER, FRANK FLOYD, health care facility executive; b. La Salle, Colo., Jan. 20, 1933; s. Henry and Caroline (Beierle) D.; m. Norma Jean Eder, June 24, 1956; children: Debbie, Brent. BA, Union Coll., 1954. Treas. Newbury Park (Calif.) Acad., 1959-64; controller Glendale (Calif.) Sanitarium, 1964-68; asst. adminstr. Glendale Adventist Hosp., 1968-72; v.p. fin. Glendale Adventist Med. Ctr., 1972-74; v.p. Adventist Health Service, Glendale, 1974-79; pres. Adventist Health System/West, Roseville, Calif., 1980—; cons. Loma Linda (Calif.) U., 1981-82. Bd. dirs. United Way, Glendale, 1986. Recipient William G. Follmer award Fin. Mgmt. Assn., 1975, Robert H. Reeves award Fin. Mgmt. Assn., 1979. Fellow Hosp. Fin. Mgmt. Assn. (Fredrich Muncie award 1985); mem. Am Acad. Med. Adminstrs., Am. Coll. Hosp. Execs., Am. Hosp. Assn., Am. Protestant Hosp. Assn., Ariz. Assn. Homes for Aging, Assn. Western Hosps., Calif. Hosp. Assn., Hosp. Council So. Calif. (Outstanding Service to Hosps. award 1979), Pres.' Assn.,. Home: 6305 Oakhill Dr Roseville CA 95661 Office: Adventist Health System West 2100 Douglas Blvd Roseville CA 95678

DUPREE, MAHLON GRIFFIS, JR., programmer analyst; b. Memphis, Jan. 9, 1947; s. Mahlon Griffis and Thelma Beatris (Higgins) D.; children: Cherrish Ann, Charles John Griffis. BA, Rhodes Coll., 1969; AS, State Tech. U., 1982. EDP liaison Tenn. Dept. Human Services, Memphis, 1976-83; programmer Am. Lebanese Syrian Associated Charities-St. Jude, Memphis, 1983-85; programmer, analyst Hughes Aircraft Corp., Los Angeles, 1985—. Served with USN, 1969-75. Rhodes Coll. grantee, 1969. Democrat. Avocations: photography, restoring old railroad cars. Home: 13600 Doty Ave Apt 29 Hawthorne CA 90250 Office: Hughes Aircraft co 200 N Sepulveda Blvd El Segundo CA 90245

DUPUY, HOWARD MOORE, JR., lawyer; b. Portland, Oreg., Mar. 15, 1929; s. Howard Moore and Lola (Dunham) D.; m. Anne Irene Hanna, Aug. 26, 1950; children—Loanne Kay, Brent Moore. B.A., U. Portland, 1951; postgrad., Willamette U., Salem, Oreg., 1951; LL.B., Lewis and Clark Coll., 1956. Bar: Oreg. bar 1956. Since practiced in Portland; assoc. Green, Richardson, Green & Griswold, 1956; ptnr. Morton & Dupuy, 1957-67, Black & Dupuy (and predecessor firm), 1968—. Mem. fin. com. Oreg. Rep. Cen. Com., 1962. Served with AUS, 1946-47. Mem. Am., Oreg., Multnomah County Bar Assns., Am. Arbitration Assn. (nat. panel arbitrators), World Trade Club, Oregon Trial Lawyers Assn., Judicature Soc. Club: World Trade (Portland). Home: 16116 NE Stanton St Portland OR 97230 Office: 400 SW 6th Ave Suite 800 First Farwest Bldg Portland OR 97204

DURAN, JUNE CLARK, legal research company executive; b. Los Angeles, June 10, 1919; d. Willis W. and Ethel M. (King) Clark; m. Frank M. Duran, Apr. 26, 1940; children—Timothy Clark, Patricia Ellen. Student Santa Monica Jr. Coll., 1936-37, UCLA, 1937-38; B.A., U. So. Calif., 1949; postgrad. U. Calif.-Berkeley, 1951-53; LL.B., LaSalle U. Personnel mgr., dir. ops. Calif. Test Bur., Los Angeles, 1950-65, asst. to gen. mgr., Monterey, Calif., 1965-66, asst. v.p., managing editor, 1966-68; asst. v.p. CTB/McGraw-Hill, Monterey, 1968-84; pres. Legal Research and Services Ctr., Monterey, 1985—; dir. First Nat. Bank Monterey County. Pres. Clark Found.; trustee Community Hosp. Monterey Peninsula; bd. dirs. Alliance on Aging, 1971-82; mem. Monterey County Republican Central Com., 1963-78; mem. governing bd. Monterey Peninsula Coll. Mem. Copyright Soc. U.S.A., Monterey Peninsula C. of C. (dir. 1973-75), Calif. Elected Women's Assn. for Evaluation and Research. Office: 810 Airport Rd Monterey CA 93940

DUREIN, JOSEPH FLUHR, bookbinding company executive; b. Alameda, Calif., Apr. 19, 1912; s. Louis John and Alice Elizabeth (Fluhr) D.; m. Alice Catherine Gibson, Oct. 10, 1935; children: Douglas, Alice. Student, San Francisco State U. Prin. Durein & Fluhr, San Francisco, 1937-47; with Am. Binder Co., San Francisco, 1947-71, Am. Durein Co., San Francisco, 1971—. Bd. dirs. Alameda (Calif.) Pub. Library, 1959-76, Alameda Pub. Utility, 1976-85. Lodges: Elks (exalted ruler 1952), Masons, Native Sons (pres. 1985-86). Home: 3110 Thompson Ave Alameda CA 94501

DURHAM, BARBARA, state justice; b. 1942. B.S.B.A., Georgetown U.; law degree, Stanford U. Bar: Wash. 1968. Formerly judge Wash. Superior Ct., King County; then judge Wash. Ct. Appeals; assoc. justice Wash. Supreme Ct., 1985—. Office: Temple of Justice Olympia WA 98504 *

DURHAM, KATHLEEN ERICKSON, communication disorders specialist; b. Mojave, Calif., June 3, 1944; d. John Stahlberg and Evelyn Lyle (Shriver) Erickson; m. Dennis Irvin Smith (div. Mar. 1968); m. John King Durham (div. Dec. 1976). BA cum laude, U. Utah, 1968, MA, 1969. Lic. speech pathologist, Utah. Resource tchr. Salt Lake City Schs., 1971-76, communication disorders specialist, 1969-70, 76—, tchr. spl. edn., 1985—; communication disorders specialist Orange (Calif.) Unified Schs., 1970-71; aux. faculty U. Utah Dept. Communication Disorders, Salt Lake City, 1976—; chmn. com. for practical examination speech pathology licensure Utah Dept. Bus. Regulations, Salt Lake City, 1984, 86. Project chmn., recording sec. Salt Lake Jr. League, 1973-85; chmn. Youth Services Adv. Bd., 1976-78; treas., trustee Parent Support Inc., 1976—; coms. chmn. Salt Lake Jr. Achievement, 1974-78, bd. dirs. Named Vital Vol., Salt Lake County Commn., 1986. Mem. NEA, Salt Lake Tchrs. Assn., Utah Tchrs. Assn., Am. Speech Lang. Hearing Assn. (cert.), Utah Speech Lang. Hearing Assn., AAUW, Pi Beta Phi Alumnae Club (sec. 1971-72, chmn. 1972-73, philanthropy chmn. 1973-75, pledges advisor 1978-80, house advisor 1985-86, adv. com. chmn. 1986—), Phi Kappa Phi. Democrat. Mem. Christian Scientist Ch. Avocations: skiing, golfing. Home: 5219 S Gravenstein Park Murray UT 84123 Office: Salt Lake Bd Edn Communication Disorders Dept 440 E 1st S Salt Lake City UT 84111

DURKEE, RICHARD CURTIS, organizational consultant; b. Nyack, N.Y., Jan. 22, 1930; s. Paul Curtis and Elizabeth (Ganung) D.; B.S., U. Rochester, 1951; m. Carmeleta Mary Reichl, May 22, 1952; children—Robert Curtis, Barbara Suzanne. With Transam. Occidental Life Ins. Co. 1951-85, dir. tng. and manpower devel., 1971-73, asst. v.p., 1973-75, 2d v.p. personnel and organizational devel., 1975-80, 2d v.p. orgnl. devel., 1980-85. Trustee group ins. trust Am. Heart Assn., Dallas, 1979-84, bd. dirs., 1979-84; chmn. bd. Am. Heart Assn., Los Angeles, 1980-81; adv. Gov.'s Office for Citizen Initiative and Voluntary Action, 1978-82; chmn. Kellogg-United Way Tng. Ctr., 1983—; bd. dirs. United Way Los Angeles, 1983—. Recipient Vol. of Yr. award City of Los Angeles, 1977; Heart of Gold award Am. Heart Assn., 1983. Fellow Life Mgmt. Inst. Home: 133 E Arthur Ave Arcadia CA 91006 Office: PO Box 3685 Arcadia CA 91006 Office: Involvement Corps 15515 Sunset Blvd Suite 108 Pacific Palisades CA 90272

DURKIN, TERRY EDWARD, locomotive engineer, small business owner; b. Oakland, Calif., Dec. 8, 1942; s. Bernard Joseph and Twila Fern (Roe) D. BA, U. San Diego, 1966; MA, U. Calif., San Diego, 1967; PhD, Royal Coll., Dublin, Ireland, 1968. Locomotive engr. Santa Fe Ry., San Diego, 1963—; pres. Pacific Southwest Ry. Mus., San Diego, 1961-72. Mem. United Transp. Union (local chmn. 1972—), Pacific Southwest Ry. Mus. (pres. 1961-72, chmn. 1983—, named founding father 1982), San Diego Hist. Soc., Nat. Soc. Hist. Preservation, Smithsonian Inst., Rolls Royce Owners Club (vice chmn. 1980, recipient appreciation awards, 1970—). Democrat. Roman Catholic. Avocation: antique preservation. Home: 3754 Pringle St San Diego CA 92103

DURLAND, STEVEN RICHARD, magazine editor; b. Long Beach, Calif., Jan. 18, 1951; s. Richard Floyd and Sheila Virginia (Hayes) D.; m. Diane Sipprelle, Aug. 18, 1974. BFA, U. S.D., 1974; MFA, U. Mass., Amherst, 1979. Freelance artist N.Y.C., 1979-82; gen. mgr. Astro Artz, Los Angeles, 1983-85; mng. editor High Performance mag., Los Angeles, 1983-85, editor, 1986—; artist in residence S.D. Arts Council, Sioux Falls, 1974-76; cons. arts and mktg., El Salvador, 1978. Contbr. articles to profl. jours. Office: High Performance 240 S Broadway 5th floor Los Angeles CA 90012

DUROST-FISH, REBECCA BERNICE, editor; b. Lewiston, Maine, Nov. 29, 1958; d. Richard Edward and Sarah Louise (Marstaller) D. BA, The King's Coll., 1980. Asst. to the editor Christian Herald, Chappaqua, N.Y., 1980-81, asst. editor, 1981-82, assoc. editor, 1982-84; mng. editor Virtue mag., Sisters, Oreg., 1984-85; editor Virtue Mag., Sisters, Oreg., 1985—. Mem. Evang. Press Assn. (sec. 1986—). Office: Virtue Mag 548 Sisters Parkway PO Box 850 Sisters OR 97759

DURRANT, BARBARA SUSAN, reproductive physiologist; b. Lansing, Mich., Aug. 22, 1949; d. Charles William and Ruth Elizabeth (DePuyt) D. BS, N.C. State U., 1972, MS, 1975, PhD, 1979; postgrad., U. Ga., 1975-76. Post doctoral fellow Zool. Soc. San Diego, 1979-81, reproductive physiologist, 1981—; cons. San Diego City Schs., 1982—, Women's Career Devel., San Diego, 1982—; advisor Scimitar-Horned Oryx Species Survival Plan, Springfield, Mo., 1985—. Contbr. articles to profl. jours. Judge Greater San Diego Sci. Fair, 1984—. Mem. Internat. Embryo Transfer Soc., Am. Assn. Zool. Parks and Aquariums, Am. Soc. Andrology, Sigma Xi. Avocations: classical lit., sci. fiction, showing dogs, travel. Office: Zool Soc San Diego PO Box 551 San Diego CA 92112

DURRANT, DEAN OBORN, podiatrist; b. Tooele, Utah, Dec. 1, 1929; s. Rendell Porter and Emily (Oborn) D.; B.A., City Coll. San Francisco, 1955; B.S., Calif. Coll. Podiatric Medicine, 1956-57; D.Podiatric Medicine, 1960; m. Dian Overson, Apr. 10, 1953; children—Kathrine, Calleen, Russell Dean, Joyce, Suzanne, Ronda, LaDean. Gen. practice podiatry, Vallejo, Calif., 1960—; chief podiatry staff Broadway Hosp., Vallejo, 1978-81. Mem., sec. Solano County Comprehensive Health Planning Council, 1974-75; trustee Calif. Coll. Podiatric Medicine, 1974-75; councilor Boy Scouts Am., 1963-64; bd. dirs. Vallejo Symphony Assn., 1968-72. Served with USN, 1953-55. Mem. Calif. Podiatric Assn. (pres. 1974-75), Am. Podiatry Assn. (commr. Region 12 1970-79), Redwood Empire Soc., Sons Utah Pioneers. Democrat. Mem. Ch. Jesus Christ Latter-day Saints. Club: Toastmasters. Lodges: Masons, Shriners, Elks. Home: 1325 Hestia Way Napa CA 94558 Office: 609 Georgia St Vallejo CA 94590

DURRETT, JOHN CHARLES, aerospace corporation executive; b. Fort Worth, Feb. 5, 1939; s. John H. and H. Beatrice (Burkhart) D.; B.S., U. Kans., 1962; M.S., Air Force Inst. Tech., 1963; Ph.D., U. Colo., 1970; m. Leilani Mary Gresham, July 31, 1976; children by previous marriage: Michelle Rene, John Edward. Commd. 2d lt. USAF, 1962, advanced through grades to lt. col., 1978; flight test engr. Edwards AFB, Calif., 1963-67; supervising engr. Air Force Flight Dynamics Lab., Wright-Paterson AFB, Ohio, 1970-73; assoc. prof. astronautics USAF Acad., Colo., 1973-77; space test program spacecraft program mgr. Space and Missile Systems Orgn., Los Angeles, 1977-79, dep. dir. space test program office, space div., Los Angeles, 1979-80, dir. space sensor test directorate, space div., 1980-82, ret., 1982; dep. program mgr. Def. Systems, Martin Marietta Aerospace Corp., Denver, 1983, program mgr. def. systems, 1984-85, spacecraft design mgr., 1985—. Decorated Meritorious Service medal with oak leaf cluster, Air Force Commendation medal with 2 oak leaf clusters. NASA summer faculty fellow Stanford U., 1975. Mem. AIAA, Am. Astron. Soc. Club: Toastmasters (Calif. area gov. 1966-67). Office: Martin Marietta Aerospace Mail Stop 8030 PO Box 179 Denver CO 80201

DUSENBURY, DAVID ALLAN, police officer; b. Alhambra, Calif., Mar. 20, 1940; s. Jack Hamlin and Mildred Leigh (Galloway) D.; A.A., Compton Coll., 1967; BS, Calif. State U., Los Angeles, 1970, MS, 1976; m. Nancy Nugent Dusenbury, July 16, 1966; children—Debra Ann, David Alan. With Lynwood (Calif.) Police Dept., 1961-68; with Long Beach (Calif.) Police Dept., 1968—, police sgt., 1976, police lt., 1981, police comdr., 1985, dep. chief police, 1986—; instr. Long Beach City Coll. Served with U.S. Army, 1963-65. Mem. Am. Soc. Pub. Adminstrn., Mensa. Republican. Office: 400 W Broadway Long Beach CA 90802

DUTTLE, PATRICIA GOULD, social worker; b. N.Y.C., Apr. 7, 1928; d. Bertram Cheever and Lucy (Vigus) Gould; m. George J. Duttle, Apr. 23, 1946 (div. Oct. 1980). BA, N.Mex. State U., 1975. Social worker I, II N.Mex. Human Services Dept., Las Cruces, 1976-81, social worker II, III, 1983-84; social work supr. N.Mex. Human Services Dept., Truth or Consequences, N.Mex., 1984-85; nephrology social worker Las Cruces Dialysis Ctr., 1981-83; social worker Puerta de Carino, Las Cruces, 1985-87; mem. staff N.Mex. Child Protective Services Tng., Santa Fe, 1983-85; mem. field faculty and field faculty rev. team N.Mex. State U., 1986-87. Mem. Citizens Adv., Las Cruces, 1972-74. Honored for Efforts, Human Services Consortium of Doña Ana County, 1984. Mem. Nat. Assn. Social Workers (sec. N.Mex. chpt. 1983-84, mem. at large 1984-86 named social worker of yr. Doña Ana Program Unit, dist. rep. 1986-87). Democrat. Roman Catholic. Home: PO Box 747 Mesilla Park NM 88047

DUTTON, DENNIS LEE, computer consultant; b. Independence, Mo., Sept. 20, 1950; s. Clifford and Ruby Flora (Paylor) D.; 1 dau., Fonda Marie. B.S. in Math., S.E. Mo. U., 1974, A.S. in Computer Sci., 1974. System analyst, computer programmer Quik Serv Systems, Kansas City, Mo., 1974-76, Recordata West, Inc., Los Angeles, 1976-77, Eastern Wash. U., Cheney, 1977-78, Stephens Nelsen Computer Ctr., Spokane, Wash., 1978-83; cons., 1983—. Assoc. adv. Explorers Post 135, Boy Scouts Am. Served with USN, 1970-72. Mem. Associated Systems Mgrs., Alpha Iota Delta. Mormon. Home: 717 W 15th St Apt D Spokane WA 99203

DUTTON, JOHN EDGAR, librarian; b. Lethbridge, Alta., Can., Aug. 30, 1924; s. Edgar Evans and Hannah Eleanor (Turner) D.; m. Helen Irene, Nov. 28, 1945; children: Corinne Eleanor, Carolyn Ann, Dianne Lillian. B.A. with honors in History, U. Alta., Can., 1950; B.L.Sc., U. Toronto, Ont., Can., 1951. Librarian U. Alta. Library, Edmonton, Can., 1951-53; chief librarian Lethbridge Pub. Library, Alta., 1953-63, North York Pub. Library, Toronto, Ont., Can., 1963-77; city librarian Winnipeg Pub. Library, Man., Can., 1977-79; dir., sec.-treas. Calgary Pub. Library, Can., 1979—. Contbr. articles to profl. jours. and encys. Served with RCAF, 1943-46. Mem. Library Assn. Alta. (pres. 1962), Can. Library Assn. (2d v.p.), Ont. Library Assn. (pres. 1969-70), Nat. Library Adv. Bd. Progressive Conservative. Mem. United Ch. of Canada. Office: Calgary Pub Library, 616 MacLeod Terr SE, Calgary, AB Canada T2G 2M2

DUTTON, PAULINE MAE, fine arts librarian; b. Detroit, July 15; d. Thoralf Andreas and Esther Ruth (Clyde) Tandberg; B.A. in Art, Calif. State U., Fullerton, 1967; M.S. in Library Sci., U. So. Calif., 1971; m. Richard Hawkins Dutton, June 21, 1969. Elem. tchr., Anaheim, Calif., 1967-68, Corona, Calif., 1968-69; fine arts librarian Pasadena (Calif.) Public Library, 1971-80; art cons., researcher, 1981—. Mem. Pasadena Librarians Assn. (sec. 1978, treas. 1979-80), Calif. Library Assn., Calif. Soc. Librarians, Art Librarians N.Am., Nat. Assn. Female Execs., Am. Film Inst., Am. Entrepreneurs Assn., Gilbert and Sullivan Soc., Alpha Sigma Phi. Club: Toastmistress (local pres. 1974).

DUVALL, BETTY JEAN, educator; b. Ft. Benton, Mont., Jan. 31, 1932; d. Ernest Charles and Thelma Louise (Brown) Schultz; m. Richard W. Duvall, Dec. 17, 1955; children—Debbie Ripsom, Denise Wolff, Carla, Tracee. B.S., Eastern Mont. Coll., 1968; M.S., No. Mont. Coll., 1975; Ed.D., Mont. State U., 1984. Cert. elem. tchr., Mont. Tchr., Great Falls, Mont., 1964-83, curriculum coordinator, 1983-85; adj. prof. Western Mont. Coll., Seattle Pacific U., U. Mont.; cons. to sch. dists. Mem. NEA, Mont. Ednl. Assn., Assn. Suprs. and Curriculum Dirs., Internat. Reading Assn., Soc. Scribes, Soc. Italic Handwriting. Author: Can Do, 1976; Duvall Method of Handwriting, 1981; Learn to Write Italic Style, 1981; The Formal Italic Hand, 1981; Handwriting Abecedarian, 1983; Writing Right, 1986. Home: 3303 E Fairway Coeur d'Alene ID 83814 Office: 422 W Appleway Coeur d'Alene ID 83814

DUVALL, DAVID JOHN, zoology and physiology educator; b. Los Angeles, Mar. 14, 1948; s. David Eugene and Virginia Lee (Maupin) D.; m. Jeanne Marie Trupiano, Aug. 3, 1979. AB in Psychology, U. Calif., Berkeley, 1973; MA in Psychology, San Jose State U., 1976; PhD in Biology, U. Colo., 1980. Lab. asst. comparative endocrinology dept. zoology U. Calif., Berkeley, 1970-71, curatorial asst. in herpetology Mus. Vertebrate Zoology, 1971-73; research asst. comparative endocrinology dept. EPO biology U. Colo., Boulder, 1976-77, research asst. reptilian behavioral ecology dept. psychology, 1978, research asst. comparative reproduction dept. EPO biology, 1977-79, research asst. mammalian behavioral ecology dept. environ., population and organismic biology, 1979-80; gen. biology coordinator, asst. prof. zoology and physiology U. Wyo., Laramie, 1980-84, asst. prof., 1984-85, assoc. prof., 1985—; lectr. and instr. in field; mem. Zoology Dept. Ecology and Wildlife Curriculum Com., 1981—, Zoology Dept. Physiology Curriculum Com., 1981—, Arts and Scis. Coll. Honors Program Com., 1983-84, Univ. Scholars Program Com., 1983-85, Gen. Biology Organizing Com., 1984-85, v.p. Acad. Affairs Search Com., 1985-86; chmn. Gen. Biology Organizing Com., 1980-84, Gen. Biology Lab. Coordinator Search Com., 1982-83, Arts and Scis. Coll. Honors Com., 1984-86, Univ. Scholars Program Com., 1985-86; faculty sponsor Univ. Honors/Scholars Student Orgn., 1985; dir. U. Wyo. Hons. program, 1987—; co-organizer, co-host U. Wyo./Wyo. Community Colls. Biology Articulation Conf., N.W. Community Coll., Powell, 1982; co-organizer U. Wyo./Wyo. Community Colls. Biology Articulation Conf., Casper (Wyo.) Coll., 1983; chmn. Internat. Organizing Com. Chem. Signals in Vertebrates Conf. Series, 1984-86; host. 4th Internat. Conf. Chem. Signals in Vertebrates U. Wyo., 1985. Author (with S.M. Feldkamp) Gen. Biology 301 Lab. Manual, 1983; editor: (with others) The Evolution and Ecology of Animal Behavior, 1983, Chemical Signals in Vertebrates 4, 1986; mem. editorial bd. Am. Biology Tchr., 1982-85; contbr. numerous articles and abstracts to profl. jours. Recipient John P. Ellbogen Meritorius Classroom Teaching award U. Wyo., 1984; Dudley Moorehead Grad. scholar San Jose State U., 1974; grantee U. Wyo., 1980, U. Wyo., 1981, U. Wyo., 1983, Nat. Park Service, 1984, Union Carbide Corp., 1984, NSF, 1984, U. Wyo., 1984, Wyo. Game and Fish Dept., 1985, NSF, 1986, 1987—. Mem. AAAS, Soc. Study Amphibians and Reptiles (Kennedy award 1983), Am. Soc. Naturalists, Am. Soc. Zoologists, Animal Behavior Soc., Colo.-Wyo. Acad. Scis. Herpetologist's League, Internat. Soc. Chem. Ecology, Nat. Assn. Biology Tchrs., Nat. Geographic Soc., Nat. Wildlife Fedn., Sigma Xi. Democrat. Avocations: music, skiing, hiking, travelling, reading. Home: 1918 Thornburgh Dr Laramie WY 82070 Office: U Wyo Dept Zoology and Physiology Laramie WY 82071

DUVALL, FERN PARK, II, ethnologist, consultant; b. Detroit, Dec. 19, 1953; s. Fern Park and Bernice Therese (Mintus) D.; m. Eva-Maria Renate Gassmann, Oct. 6, 1981; children: Anna Therese, Kai Allen. BSBA in Germanic Language with honors, U. Mich., 1976; Dr. Rerum Naturum, Die Freie U. Berlin, 1983. Teaching Fellow, lectr. Die Freie U. Berlin, West Berlin, 1978-81; lectr. U. Md., Berlin, 1981; cons. 'Alala Project, Dept. Land and Natural Resources, State of Hawaii, Hilo, 1984-. Contbr. articles to profl. jours. Mem. AAAS, Nat. Audobon Soc., Nature Conservancy, World Wildlife Fund, Animal Behavior Soc., Ethologische Gesellschaft, Deutsche Zoologische Gesellschaft, Am. Ornithol. Union, Cooper Ornithol: Soc. Avocations: painting, hiking, flying. Office: Hawaii Div Forestry and Wildlife Endangered Species Facility 535 Olinda Maui Rd Makawao HI 96768

DUVAUL, THOMAS HINES, clinical social worker; b. Columbus, Georgia, Sept. 23, 1934; s. Charles Wesley and Ganelle (Black) DuV.; m. Joy Dean Smedley, June 27, 1957; children: Michael Sean, Denise Toni. BA in Instrumental Music, W.Va. State Coll., 1956; cert. social welfare, U. Calif., Berkeley, 1965; MSW, Calif. State U., Sacramento, 1970; cert. human effect tng., Calif. State Health Ctr., Berkeley, 1976; cert. behavior mgmt., Med. Coll. Wis., San Francisco, 1981; cert. Child Sexual Abuse Treatment Tng., Inst. for Community as Extended Care, San Jose, Calif., 1986; cert. Decision Making in Child Welfare Practice, San Jose State U., 1986. Lic. clin. social worker, Calif. Social worker Solano County Welfare Dept., Vallejo, Calif., 1964-65; social worker II Santa Clara County Social Services, San Jose, Calif., 1965-68, social worker children's services, 1970-74, social worker child protective services, 1974-85, social worker sexual abuse, 1986—; pvt. practice social work San Jose, 1983—; cons., social worker Berryessa Sch. Dist., San Jose, 1977-84; field instr. San Jose State U., 1976-84, U. Calif., Berkeley, 1980-81, San Francisco State U., 1982-83. mem. adv. bd. East Valley Youth Service Bur., San Jose, 1974-76, Slonaker Community Sch. Alum Rock Dist., San Jose, 1974-76; mem. sch. attendance review bd. Berryessa Sch. Dist., San Jose, 1984-85; bd. dirs. Afro-Am. Community Service Agy., San Jose, 1985—. Recipient Certificate of Recognition, Senator Mervyn M. Dymally, 1970, Certificate of Award, United Christian Ctrs., 1970, Disting. Service and Leadership award Boy Scouts Am., 1975-76. Mem. Calif. Chpt. of Nat. Assn. Social Workers, Nat. Assn. Black Social Workers, (v.p. San Jose 1978-79; pres. San Jose 1979-80), NAACP, Urban League, Omega Psi Phi (past v.p., past treas.). Democrat. Avocations: classical and jazz music, bike riding, walking. Home: 4721 Corrales Dr San Jose CA 95136 Office: Santa Clara County Social Services Children's Protective Services 55 W Younger Ave San Jose CA 95110

DUVE, JOHN LARRY, university administrator, transportation systems consultant; b. Pullman, Wash., Sept. 14, 1949; s. John Eugene and Ada (Popkema) D.; m. Paulette Ann Cunningham, May 3, 1987. B.S., U. Nebr., 1972. With prodn. dept. M & M/Mars Co., Chgo., 1969-70; staff Zenith Radio Corp., Chgo., 1970; shift comdr. Univ. Police Dept., U. Nebr., Lincoln, 1971-74, asst. to dir., 1974-78, parking adminstr. bus. and fin., 1978-80; dir. parking and transp. systems U. Calif., Irvine and Med. Center, 1980—; village/venue transp. mgr. Los Angeles Olympic Organizing Com., 1983, asst. dir. adminstrn. U. So. Calif. Olympic Village, 1984; mem. chancellor's adv. com. on status of handicapped persons and disabled vets. U. Calif., 1980—, also exec. dir. parking and transp. adv. com.; pvt. cons. parking and transp. systems mgmt., 1976—. Mem. City of Lincoln Carpool Resource Com., 1976-80; exec. sec. U. Nebr.-Lincoln Parking Adv. Com., 1974-80; mem. Irvine Transp. Corridor Adv. Bd., 1981—; mem. Orange County Transp. Commn., 1982-83; bd. advisors Instl. and Mcpl. Parking Congress. Mem. Instl. and Mcpl. Parking Congress, Am. Mgmt. Assn., Nat. Assn. Vanpool Operations, Triangle Fraternity. Congregationalist. Home: 43 Esplanade Irvine CA 92715 Office: U Calif Parking and Transp Services Irvine CA 92717

DUXBURY, ALISON BEATRIX SAUNDERS, oceanography educator; b. San Francisco, Nov. 6, 1932; s. John B. de C.M. and Alison Jean (Ramsay) Saunders; m. Alyn Crandall Duxbury, Dec. 20, 1956; children: Andrew Saunders, Alison Jean, Alec Ramsay. BA, U. Calif., Berkeley, 1954, MA, 1956. Research technician Tex. A&M U., College Station, 1958-60, Yale U., New Haven, 1960-62; instr. oceanography and biology Seattle Cen. Community Coll., 1973—. Author: The World's Oceans, 1984. Trustee Seattle Acad. Arts and Scis., 1983-87. Mem. Phi Beta Kappa. Congregationalist. Home: 3823 44th Ave NE Seattle WA 98105 Office: Seattle Cen Community Coll 1701 Broadway Seattle WA 98122

DUZETT, ANNETTE, junior high school principal; b. Emery, Utah, Feb. 5, 1952; d. Robert Courtney and Dawn (Lewis) D. B.A., U. Utah, 1973, M.A., 1976; Ph.D., Brigham Young U., 1979. Cert. secondary tchr., adminstr., Utah. Tchr., chmn. dept. fgn. lang. West Lake Jr. High Sch., Granite Sch. Dist., Utah, 1974-80, acting asst. prin., 1980; chmn. internat. edn. West Valley Area, Granite Sch. Dist., 1980-81; acting prin. Oquirrh Hills Elem. Sch., Granite Sch. Dist., 1980, acting asst. prin. Kennedy Jr. High Sch., Granite Sch. Dist., 1981, asst. prin., 1981-83; prin. Kearns Jr. High Sch., 1983—; adv. bd. Granite Sch. Dist., 1984—; pres.-elect, sec. Jr. High Asst. Prins., Granite Sch. Dist., 1981-82, pres., 1982-83. Mem. NEA, Nat. Carl Schultz Assn., Smithsonian Instn., Utah Edn. Assn., Granite Edn. Assn., Granite Assn. Sch. Adminstrs. (officer 1984-85), Am. Assn. Tchrs. of German, Nat. Assn. Secondary Sch. Prins., Phi Delta Kappa, Phi Kappa Phi. Office: Kearns Jr High Sch 4040 W 5305 S Kearns UT 84118

DWINELL, LORIE LADEAN, psychotherapist; b. Albuquerque, Oct. 23, 1939; d. John Willis Richard Engholm and Betty Lou (Jones) Archer. BA, U. N.Mex., 1969; MSW, U. Wash., 1971. Caseworker N.Mex. Dept. Pub. Welfare, Albuquerque, 1962-67; health educator Alcohol Research Tng., Albuquerque, 1967-69; psychiat. social worker Winslow (Ariz.) Navajo County Guidance Ctr., 1971-72; health educator Project Escape, Kent, Wash., 1972-73; instr. social work U. Wash., Seattle, 1973-77; pvt. practice psychotherapy Elliott Bay Therapy Assocs., Seattle, 1977—; trainer State Wash. Bur. Alcohol Substance Abuse, Olympia, 1973—; faculty mem. alcohol studies program Seattle U., 1975-84, children fo alcoholics confs. U.S. Jour. Drugs and Alcohol, Pompano Beach, Fla., 1983—, Inst. Integral Devel., Colorado Springs, Colo., 1984—. Co-author: After the Tears: Reclaiming the Personal Losses of Childhood, 1986. Mem. Nat. Assn. Social Workers (cert.). Avocations: travelling, collecting S.W. art, collecting antiques. Office: Elliott Bay Therapy Assocs Merrill Pl Suite 530 411 1st Ave S Seattle WA 98104

DWORSKY, DANIEL LEONARD, architect; b. Mpls., Oct. 4, 1927; s. Lewis and Ida (Fineberg) D.; m. Sylvia Ann Taylor, Aug. 10, 1957; children: Douglas, Laurie, Nancy. B.Arch., U. Mich., 1950. Practice architecture as Dworsky Assocs., Los Angeles, 1953—; design critic, lectr. arch. UCLA, 1983-84. (Recipient Design citation Progressive Arch. mag. 1967, Gov. Calif. award 1966, 3 Los Angeles Grand Prix awards So. Calif. AIA and City of Los Angeles 1967); Prin. works include Angelus Plaza Elderly Housing, Los Angeles, 1981, Ontario (Calif.) City Hall, 1980, CBS Exec. Office Bldg, North Hollywood, Calif., 1970, U. Calif. at Los Angeles Stadium, 1969, Fed. Res. Bank Bldg., Los Angeles, 1987—; U. Mich. Crisler Arena at Ann Arbor, 1968, Dominguez Hills State U. Theatre, 1977, Ventura County Govt. Center, 1979, Lloyds Bank Ops. Ctr., Los Angeles, 1980, The Park Office Bldgs., Los Angeles, 1980, Skyline Condominiums, Los Angeles, 1982, Northrop Electronics Hdqrs., Los Angeles, 1983, Hewlett-Packard Region Office, North Hollywood, 1984, Los Angeles County Mcpl. Cts. Bldg., 1985. Fellow AIA (20 awards So. Calif. chpt., including 11 honor awards; Nat. honor award 1974, 1968-69, merit award Calif. chpt. 1985, Firm award Calif. chpt. 1985). Home: 9225 Nightingale Dr Los Angeles CA 90069 Office: 2029 Century Park E Suite 350 Los Angeles CA 90067

DWYER, JAMES RICHARD, librarian, consultant; b. Seattle, July 21, 1949; s. William Carroll and Ellen Dagmar (Carlson) D. BA in English, U. Wash., 1971, MLS, 1973. Cataloger SUNY, Albany, 1973-76, U. Oreg., Eugene, 1976-82; cataloging coordinator No. Ariz. U., Flagstaff, 1982-86; head bibliographic services Calif. State U., Chico, 1986—; vis. asst. prof. U. Wash., Seattle, 1978; library cons. Maricopa County Library, Phoenix, 1985—. Contbg. editor (jour.) Technicalities, 1980—, cons. editor Library Hi Tech, 1986—; contbr. articles to profl. jours. Canvassing coordinator Friends of Flagstaff Pub. Library, 1985; mem. Earth First, Flagstaff, 1985—, Bus. and Profl. People for Sane Energy, Eugene, 1980-82. Named Poet Laureate, Olde Dexter (Oreg.) Theatre, 1978. Mem. ALA (councilor 1981-85, Disting. Service award 1985, Shirley Olofson Novia award 1974), Library Info. Tech. Assn., Ariz. State Library Assn. (chmn. IFC 1985-86), Serials Online Ariz. (steering com. 1984-86), Social Responsibilities Round Table (action council 1979-81). Democrat. Avocations: backpacking, wilderness preservation, reading, art, music. Home: 1286 Filbert Ave Chico CA 95926 Office: Calif State U Meriam Library Chico CA 95929-0295

DWYER, JAMES ROBERT, social work administrator; b. N.Y.C., Nov. 10, 1947; s. Francis James and Elizabeth Rita (McCabe) D.; m. Susan Steblay O'Hara, June 21, 1986. BA in English, U. Wis., 1973; MSW, U. Tenn., 1980. Lic. clin. social worker. Co-dir. Hoyt Counseling Ctr., N.Y.C., 1973-74; supr. Nat. Save-A-Life League, N.Y.C., 1975-76; recruiter Peace Corps (Action Agy.), Rochester, N.Y., 1976-78; social worker VA Med. Ctr., Los Angeles, 1978-83; dir. Vietnam Vets. Liaison Unit, Los Angeles, 1983—; vol. VISTA-Operation Vet. Reach, Wichita, Kans., 1974-75; media cons. regarding Vets. various TV/Motion Picture Orgns., Los Angeles. Author: PTSD-What to Look For, 1986; contbr. book revs. Dist. capt. John Lindsay for Mayor, N.Y.C., 1965. Served with U.S. Army, 1967-69. Mem. Nat. Assn. Social Workers (cert.), Soc. Traumatic Stress Studies, Phi Kappa Phi. Avocations: camping, hiking, baseball, literature. Home: 5068 Lemona Ave Sherman Oaks CA 91403 Office: Vietnam Vets Liaison Unit Wilshire and Sawtelle Blvds Los Angeles CA 90073

DWYER, ROBERT FRANKLIN, II, arts administrator; b. Lake City, Fla., Dec. 7, 1943; s. Robert Franklin and Maxine Delores (Stenberg) D.; children—Erin Adair, Robert Franklin III. A.B., U. Calif.-Berkeley, 1967; M.T.S., Harvard U. Div. Sch., 1969; cert in arts mgmt., U. Chgo., 1981. Pub. affairs dir. Sta. KYDO-TV 3, Salem, Oreg., 1969-74; dir. mktg. Specialists Internat., Reno, Nev., 1974-77; dir. devel. Sierra Arts Found., Reno, 1977—; bd. dirs. Nev. Alliance for Arts, 1979—, v.p., 1980; cons. in field. Named Arts Adminstr. of Yr., Arts Mgmt. mag., 1982. Mem. Am. Council on Arts, Assn. Coll., Univ. and Community Arts Adminstrs., Nat. Assembly Community Arts Agys. Editor: Snow Peach, 1980; producer, writer TV documentary: Art Works, 1981.

DWYER, TERRY TAYLOR, editor; b. Alexander, N.D., Apr. 4, 1922; s. James William and Grace Isabel (Taylor) D.; m. Marie Gustafson, May 17, 1941; children—VerNel Carver, Colleen Lulf, Maureen Downey, Kelly, Sean. Reporter, Ind.-Record, Helena, Mont., 1946-53; reporter Tribune, Great Falls, Mont., 1953-65, city editor, 1965-74, mng. editor, 1974—, corp. v.p., mng. editor, 1984—. Recipient Disting. Reporting of Pub. Affairs award Am. Polit. Sci. Assn., 1962. Mem. Sigma Delta Chi. Office: Great Falls Tribune 205 River Dr S PO Box 5468 Great Falls MT 59403

DYAN, ANN, paralegal; b. Decatur, Ill., Sept. 26, 1942; d. Arthur Woodrow and Margaret Ruth (Rutherford) Lawler; m. Richard Marks, May 29, 1964 (div. 1975); children: Kelby, Marla; m. Robert Michael Dyan, May 26, 1984. BS in Edn., Emporia State U., 1964. Cert. paralegal, Colo. Paralegal Church's Fried Chicken Inc., San Antonio, 1978-79, La Quinta Motor Inns Inc., San Antonio, 1979-80; loan adminstr. Wells Fargo Realty Advisors, Los Angeles, 1980-81; paralegal Ashkenazy Enterprises, Los Angeles, 1981-83, Cox, Castle & Nicholson, Los Angeles, 1983-86; asst. v.p. Metmor Financial, Inc., 1986—; ptnr., panelist Dynamic Info. Seminars, Los Angeles, 1983—; instr. San Antonio Coll., 1980. Mem. Los Angeles Paralegal Assn., Los Angeles Arts Council, Women in Comml. Real Estate. Jewish. Avocations: photography, reading. Office: Metmor Fin Inc Income Property Loan Closing Dept 8074 4525 Wilshire Blvd Suite 150 Los Angeles CA 90010

DYCUS, SUSAN JOHNSON, laywer, registered nurse; b. Galveston, Tex., Dec. 10, 1953; d. John Edward and Mary Shirley (Jimmerson) Johnson; m. Dale Wyatt Dycus, Mar. 8, 1976 (dec. July 1985). AAS in Nursing cum laude, Tarrant County Jr. Coll., 1975; BA in Polit. Sci. summa cum laude, U. Tex., 1980; student, So. Meth. U., 1980-82; JD, U. Denver, 1983. Bar: Colo. 1984, U.S. Dist. Ct. Colo. 1984. R.N. various hosps., Colo. and Tex., 1975-82; law clk. to U.S. Atty. Dist. of Colo., Denver, 1982-83; law clk. to referee U.S. Dist. Ct. Colo., Colorado Springs, 1983; sole practice Denver, 1984—; cons. Kripke, Esptein, Lawrence, P.C., Denver, 1983; instr. Continuing Nursing Edn., 1986. Amelia Lundull scholar, 1974. Mem. Am. Assn. Crit. Care Nurses, Colo. Bar. Assn., Am. Trial Lawyers Assn., Denver and Arapahoe County Bar Assns., Delta Theta Phi (baliff 1982-83). Avocations: ham radio, fire buff, scuba diving. Office: 155 S Madison #308 Denver CO 80209

DYER, ALAN GORDON, educator, educational administrator, consultant; b. San Diego, Mar. 30, 1941; s. Robert Beakley and Velma Ann (Griffin) D.; m. Beverly Anne Stipe, May 27, 1961; children—Dale Alan, Donna Diane. B.A. in Sociology, Calif. State U.-San Bernardino, 1968; M.A. in Edn., Pepperdine U., 1975. Adult edn. and community coll. life teaching and adminstrv. credentials, Calif. Child social worker Good Samaritan Boys' Home, Corona, Calif., 1968-69; tchr. manpower devel. tng. program San Hidalgo Inst., San Bernardino, 1971-74; adult edn. instr. San Bernardino Adult Sch., 1974—; high sch. equivalency instr., lead tchr. supr. Rialto (Calif.) Adult Sch., 1974—; instr. in English, Upward Bound Program, Calif. State Coll.-San Bernardino, 1978—; instr. extended edn. Calif. State U., San Bernardino, 1986—; cons. adult edn. community services; dir. ednl. services Merrill Community Services, Fontana, Calif. Sec./treas. Corona Jaycees, 1973-74; elder Ch. of Jesus Christ of Latter-day Saints, Rialto, Calif.. Served with USNR, 1959-68; staff sgt. Air N.G. Decorated Meritorious Service medal. Recipient Ednl. Excellence award Program Dir. and Students of Upward Bound Program, Calif. State Coll.-San Bernardino, 1981. Mem. Assn. Calif. Sch. Adminstrs., Calif. Council Adult Edn., Am. Social. Assn., Alumni Calif. State Coll.-San Bernardino (life), Phi Delta Kappa. Democrat. Home: 19256 Arbeth St Rialto CA 92376 Office: Merrill Community Services 16846 Merrill Ave Suite 202 Fontana CA 92335

DYER, ANDREW ROY, manufacturing executive; b. Nashville, Apr. 30, 1951; s. Andrew Johnson and Gladys Marie (Kelly) D. B.S., U. Tenn., 1973; B.E., Vanderbilt U., 1974; M.B.A., U. Tenn., 1975. Prin. systems analyst Teledyne Brown Engring., Huntsville, Ala., 1976-78; ops. auditor Data Design Labs., Cucamonga, Calif., 1978-80; sr. acctg. systems analyst Calif. Federal, Los Angeles, 1980-81; sr. mem. tech. staff Teledyne Systems Co., Northridge, Calif., 1981—. Sustaining mem. Mount Wilson Obs. Assn., Pasadena, 1983—. Named Best Econ. Forecaster of the Year, So. Calif. Corp. Planning Assn., 1980; Sturges Meml. scholar, U. Tenn., 1976. Fellow Brit. Interplanetary Soc.; mem. AIAA, IEEE, Planning Execs. Inst., World Future Soc. Los Angeles (pres. 1979-80), Orgn. for Advancement of Space Industrialization and Settlement, Los Angeles Astron. Soc., Orange County Astronomers. Home: 22446 Burbank Blvd Woodland Hills CA 91367 Office: Teledyne Systems Co 19601 Nordhoff St Northridge CA 91324

DYER, ANN, oil painting artist; b. Marion, Ind., Sept. 19, 1938; d. Clarence William and Charlottee (Woodmansee) Middlesworth; m. Otto Earl Dyer, May 20, 1967. Studies with Sebastian Capella, La Jolla, Calif., 1982-85. One-woman shows include Exeter Gallery, Rancho Bernardo, Calif., 1985—; completed commissioned works for private parties in several states, 1966-86; freelance illustrator Warner Press Publs., Anderson, Ind., 1967-70. Prin. works include oil paintings "The Courtyard," 1976 (1st prize 1976), "Basket of Eggs," 1984 (4th prize 1984), Cottage at the Beach. Recipient Hon. Mention award So. Calif. Exposition, Del Mar, 1984; nominated for Art Achievement awards Artists' Soc. Internat., 1987. Mem. San Dieguito Art Guild (bd. dirs. 1977-78, 1st prizes for hanging works 1976-78), San Diego Art Inst. Avocations: hiking, traveling, Bible studies, lay counseling. Home and Studio: 231 Via Sarasan Encinitas CA 92024

DYER, DAVID LINDSEY, advertising executive; b. Gardiner, Maine, May 21, 1955; s. Milton Earl and Doris Liz (Decker) D. AA, U. Maine, 1976; student, Art Inst., Atlanta, 1978. Mktg. dir. William Hobbs Ltd., Atlanta, 1978-80; art dir. Visual Continuum, San Diego, 1981-83; dir. advt. Marcel Schurman Co., Oakland, Calif., 1982—, creative dir., 1986—; corp. image cons. R.T.S. Prodns., San Francisco, 1984—. Mem. San Francisco Mus. Modern Art, San Diego Mus. Photography. Mem. San Francisco Ad Club, Direct Mktg. Creative Guild. Avocations: video presentations and documentaries. Home: 2855 Union St San Francisco CA 94123 Office: Marcel Schurman Co Inc 954 60th St Oakland CA 94608

DYER, GREGORY CLARK, lawyer; b. Stanford, Calif., May 29, 1947; s. Allen Clayton and Mary Louise (Sutter) D.; m. Karyne Lee Clough, June 28, 1980; children: Ashley, Chelsea. AB, Stanford U., 1970, JD, 1971. Bar: Calif. 1972, U.S. Ct. Appeals (9th cir.) 1972. Sole practice Mill Valley, Calif., 1972—. Judge pro tem Marin County (Calif.) Mcpl. Ct., 1981—; bd. dirs. Legal Aid Soc. Marin, 1979-81. Mem. Marin County Bar Assn. (bd. dirs. 1980-82, treas. 1985, pres.-elect 1986, pres. 1987), Am. Arbitration Assn. Republican. Lodge: Rotary (pres. 1984-85, area rep. 1986-87, fgn. exchange team leader 1981, 87). Avocations: travel, tennis, reading, gardening, hiking. Office: 16 Buena Vista Ave Mill Valley CA 94941

DYER, JAMES HARRISON, lawyer; b. Phoenix, Oct. 25, 1952; s. Harvey L. and Nonavie (Harman) D. BA, U. Ariz., 1975, JD, 1978. Bar: Ariz. 1978, U.S. Dist. Ct. Ariz. 1980. Assoc., Healy & Beal, P.C., Tucson, 1978-86; sole practice, Tucson, 1986—; instr. Ariz. State Bar, 1984-85; arbitrator Am. Arbitration Assn., 1980—. Chmn. for So. Ariz., Republican Commitment '80 campaign; mem. Ariz. Town Hall, 1981; pres. Tucson Sport Fishing Festival, 1983-85; surrogate speaker Reagan/Bush Campaign, 1984. Mem. ABA, Ariz. Bar Assn., Pima County Bar Assn., Assn. Trial Lawyers Am., Ariz. Trial Lawyers Assn., Blue Key, Phi Gamma Delta. Club: U. Ariz. Pres.'s, 20/30 Internat. Tucson (charter, bd. dirs. 1986-87, chmn. polo tournament 1986-87). Home: 2125 E Hampton Tucson AZ 85719 Office: 239 N Church Tucson AZ 85701

DYER, JOHN NORVELL, physics educator; b. Norfolk, Va., July 19, 1930; s. Leslie Roland and Elizabeth (Jennings) D.; m. Raye Allan Smith, May 21, 1975. BS in Physics, U. Calif., Berkeley, 1956, PhD in Physics, 1960. Prof. physics Naval Postgrad. Sch., Monterey, Calif., 1961—, chmn. dept. physics, 1979-83, dean sci. and engring., 1983-87. Served to 1st lt. U.S. Army, 1951-53. Home: 270 Mar Vista Dr Monterey CA 93943 Office: Naval Postgrad Sch Monterey CA 93943

DYER, RICHARD AVERY, utility company executive; b. Salt Lake City, Apr. 6, 1951; s. Richard A. and Raquel (Peterson) D.; m. Laurie Teuscher, June 12, 1974; children: Rachel, Richard, Jonathan, Rebecca, Scott. BA, U. Portland, Oreg., 1977. CPA, Wash., Oreg. Acct. Touche Ross, Portland, 1976-77; account rep. NCR Corp., Portland, 1977-79; audit supr. Moss Adams, Portland, 1979-83; dir. fin. Clark Pub. Utility Dist., Vancouver, Wash., 1983—. Bd. dirs. Cascade Pk., Vancouver. Lodge: Rotary. Home: 15007 SE Graham Rd Vancouver WA 98694 Office: Clark Pub Utility Dist 1200 Fort Vancouver Way Vancouver WA 98668

DYER, ROBERT EUGENE, SR., academic administrator; b. Everett, Wash., Sept. 7, 1936; s. Peter Reubin and Georgia Ann (Duncan) D.; m. Juanita M. Hanford, Sept. 30, 1956 (div. Sept. 1972); children: Robert E. Jr., Loretta Kaye; m. Noreen Faye Harris, Oct. 7, 1972; children: Vikki LaRee, Stephen Peter. BS in Bus. Edn., Cen. Wash. U., 1982. Cert. tchr., Wash., Alaska. Appliance mgr. Pay Less Drug, Wenatchee, Wash., 1966-67; ops. officer Rainier Bank, Seattle, 1967-76; chief acct. Pybus Steel Co., Wenatchee, 1976-80; instr. U. Alaska, Juneau, 1982-84; instr., coordinator Alaska Vocat. Inst., Juneau, 1984—. Designed Alaska Vocat. Inst. Ednl. Ctr., 1985. Served with USN, 1956-64. Mem. Alaska Vocat. Assn., Nat. Bus. Edn. Assoc. Home: 4949 Hummingbird Ln Juneau AK 99801

DYGERT, HAROLD PAUL, JR., physician; b. Rochester, N.Y., June 21, 1919; s. Harold Paul and Elsie Viola (Howe) D.; m. Helen Adelaine Nelson, Apr. 22, 1944; children: Harold Paul III, William Nelson, Peter Howe. BA, U. Rochester, 1941; postgrad., Alfred U., 1942-43; MD, Syracuse U., 1950. Diplomate Am. Bd. Internal Medicine. Intern Receiving Hosp., Detroit, 1950-51, resident internal medicine, 1951-53, chief resident, 1953-54; instr. medicine Wayne State U., Detroit, 1954-55; mem. staff VA Hosp., Vancouver, Wash., 1955-59; practice medicine specializing in cardiology and internal medicine Vancouver, 1959—; chmn. Health Care Consortium, 1974—. Pres. Wash. State Med., Ednl. and Research Found., 1971-73; bd. dirs. Wash.-Alaska Regional Med. Program, 1966-72; participant Manhattan Project, 1943-46. Served with AUS, 1943. Fellow ACP, Am. Coll. Cardiology; mem. AMA (del. 1976-77), Am. Fedn. Clin. Research, Wash. State Med. Assn. (pres. 1973-74), Portland Heart Club (pres. 1975-77), Wash. State Soc. Internal Medicine (trustee 1976-80). Home: 8407 SE Evergreen Hwy Vancouver WA 98664 Office: 2101 E McLoughlin Blvd Vancouver WA 98661

DYKSTRA, DAVID CHARLES, accountant, management consultant, author, educator; b. Des Moines, July 10, 1941; s. Orville Linden and Ermina (Dunn) D.; B.S.Ch.E., U. Calif., Berkeley, 1963; M.B.A., Harvard U., 1966; m. Ello Paimre, Nov. 20, 1971; children—Suzanne, Karin, David S. Corp. controller Recreation Environments, Newport Beach, Calif., 1970-71, Hydro Conduit Corp., Newport Beach., 1971-78; v.p. fin. and adminstrn. Tree-Sweet Products, Santa Ana, Calif., 1978-80; pres., owner Dykstra Cons., Irvine, Calif., 1980—; pres. Easy Data Corp., 1981—; pub. Easy Data Computer Comparisons, 1982—; prof. mgmt. info. systems Nat. U.-Irvine, Calif., 1984—. Chmn. 40th Congressional Dist. Tax Reform Immediately, 1977-80; mem. nat. com. Republican Party; vice-chmn. Orange County Calif. Rep. Assembly, 1979-80; v.p., dir. Corona Del Mar Rep. Assembly, 1980—. CPA, Calif. Mem. Am. Inst. CPAs, Am. Mgmt. Assn., Calif. Soc. CPAs, Data Processing Mgmt. Assn., Ind. Computer Consultants Assn., Internat. Platform Assn., Data Processing Mgmt. Assn., Orange County C. of C., Newport Beach C. of C., Harvard Bus. Sch. Assn. Orange County (dir. 1984—, v.p 1984-86, pres. 1986-87), Harvard Bus. Sch. Assn. So. Calif. (dir. 1986-87), Town Hall, Harvard Bus. Sch. Assn. So. Calif. (bd. dirs. 1986-87). Clubs: Rotary Internat. (dir. 1984-86), John Wayne Tennis, Lido Sailing. Author: Manager's Guide to Business Computer Terms, 1981; Computers for Profit, 1983; contbr. articles to profl. jours. Home: 1724 Port Ashley Pl Newport Beach CA 92660 Office: 2192 Dupont Dr Irvine CA 92715

DYMALLY, MERVYN MALCOLM, congressman; b. Trinidad, W.I., May 12, 1926; s. Hamid A. and Andreid S. (Richardson) D.; m. Alice M. Gueno; children: Mark, Lynn. B.A., Calif. State U., Los Angeles, 1954; M.A., Calif. State U., Sacramento, 1970; LL.D. (hon.), U. West Los Angeles, 1970; Ph.D. in Human Behavior, U.S. Internat. U., 1978; J.D. (hon.), Lincoln U., Sacramento, 1975; Ph.D. (hon.), Shaw U., N.C., 1981. Lectr. Whittier and Claremont Colls.; mem. Calif. Assembly, 1962-66, Calif. Senate, 1967-74; lt. gov. Calif., 1975-79; mem. 97th-100th Congresses from 31st Calif. Dist., 1981—; chmn. bd., pres. Caribbean Am. Research Inst.; founder Congl.

Inst. for Space, Sci. and Tech. Author: Black Politician-His Struggle for Power. Chmn. Congl. Caucus on Sci. and Technology; chmn. bd. Caribbean Action Lobby; trustee Shaw U.; bd. govs. Joint Ctr. Polit. Studies. Mem. AAUP, Am. Acad. Polit. Sci., Am. Polit. Acad., Phi Kappa Phi Honor Soc. Address: 1717 Longworth House Office Bldg Washington DC 20515

DYRUD, RICHARD ERIC, real estate syndicator, sales and property manager; b. Prairie du Chien, Wis., Dec. 27, 1944; s. Martinus Jacob and Blanche (Paris) D.; m. Jackie Ann McCallister, Aug. 2, 1975; children: Adam Paris, Erica Robin. BA, Lawrence U., 1967; postgrad., U. Utah, 1971-72. Commd. USAF, 1967, advanced through grades to capt., 1970; owner Alaska Tax Service, Anchorage, 1975-77; salesman Hanson-Ohrt, Anchorage, 1977-79; owner, syndicator Associated Brokers, Anchorage, 1979—. Decorated D.S.M. with bronze oak leaf cluster. Mem. Anchorage Bd. Realtors, Alaska Assn. Realtors (chmn. edn. com. 1985-86), Real Estate Security and Syndication Inst. (nat. mem. com. 1986—, pres. Alaska chpt. 1984—). Republican. Episcopalian. Avocations: fishing, skiing. Office: Associated Brokers 640 W 36th Ave Suite 1 Anchorage AK 99503

DYSON, RICHARD SAMUEL, public school administrator; b. Anderson, Ind., Feb. 12, 1947; s. Robert Bonner and Naomi Ruth (Cade) D.; B.A. in Polit.Sci., Ind. U., 1969; postgrad. Harvard U., 1973; M.S. in Bus. Org. and Mgmt., U. LaVerne, 1984; m. Kristen Keith, Aug. 21, 1976; children—Jeffrey Brantford Keith, Jonathan Richard Blackledge. Adminstr. employee services RCA Alascom, Inc., 1975-77; mktg. account exec. Totem Ocean Trailer Express, Inc., 1978-79; mgr. compensation Anchorage Sch. Dist., 1979—. Chmn. public edn. com. Anchorage unit Am. Cancer Soc., 1976, bd. dirs. for Alaska, 1978—; chmn. pacesetter fundraising drive United Way Alascom, 1976; chmn. Bike-O-Thon for Anchorage, Am. Diabetes Assn., 1979, 80, bd. dirs. for Alaska, 1979—; bd. dirs. Community Council, 1986. Served with USAR, 1969-72. Recipient award Alaska Press Club, 1977; Merit award Am. Cancer Soc., 1978; Outstanding Service award Am. Diabetes Assn., 1979, 80. Mem. Am. Soc. Personnel Adminstrs., Pacific N.W. Personnel Mgmt. Assn., Alaska Assn. Sch. Bus. Ofcls., Anchorage Personnel Assn. (treas. 1980-81), Ind. U. Alumni Assn., Sigma Phi Epsilon. Episcopalian. Club: Rotary (treas. Anchorage 1978, chmn. public relations 1980). Home: 4900 Hartman Circle Anchorage AK 99507 Office: Anchorage Sch Dist PO Box 196614 Anchorage AK 99519

EACHO, ROSA LEE, business executive; b. Elk River, Idaho, Dec. 27, 1931; d. Quinto and Lily Esther (Harlan) Paolini; m. Richard Gerald Eacho, Oct. 20, 1950 (div.); children—Rex, Roxanne Paolini, Rochelle Carroll, Rebecca. Sec., Salewoman Farmers Ins., Wenatchee, Wash.; owner Boatique Ltd., Seattle, Danish Waffle Sundae. Republican. Presbyterian Office: 7001 Seaview Ave NW Seattle WA 98117

EACKER, RICHARD MYRON, electrical engineer; b. Weiser, Idaho, May 3, 1948; s. Ray Alfred and Mina Marie (Hudson) E.; m. Sandra Lynn Porter, Mar. 22, 1969; children: Stephen Matthew, Michael Shawn. BA in Biology, Portland State U., 1970, BSEE, 1977. Registered prof. elec. engr., Alaska, Wash., Oreg., Idaho. Journeyman electrician Portland (Oreg.) State U., 1974-77; estimator, constrn. scheduler Pacific Power and Lights Co., Portland, 1977-79; elec. engr. Elcon Assocs. Inc., Beaverton, Oreg., 1979-81, Ace Electric Co., Portland, 1981-82, Winzler & Kelly, Portland, 1982-83; sr. elec. engr. Coffman Engrs. Inc., Anchorage, 1983—; mem. subcom. Anchorage Bldg. Bd., 1985—. Scout coordinator Boy Scouts Am., Anchorage, 1985-86. Served as sgt. U.S. Army, 1971-74. Mem. IEEE (editor newsletter 1985—), Internat. Assn. Elec. Inspectors. Lutheran. Avocations: weight lifting, tennis, swimming. Home: 6832 Cape Lisburne Loop Anchorage AK 99504 Office: Coffman Engrs Inc 550 W 7th Ave #700 Anchorage AK 99501

EADES, LUIS ERIC, artist; b. Madrid, June 25, 1923; came to U.S., 1949, naturalized, 1967; s. Alwyn Turley and Luisa (Olmedo) E.; m. Ursula Jean Lambert, Dec. 27, 1957; children—Peter Luis, Helen Elisabeth. Student, Bath (Eng.) Sch. Art, 1940-42, London U. Slade Sch., 1947-48, Nat. Poly. Inst. Mex., 1948-49; B.A. summa cum laude, U. Ky., 1952. Instr., then asst. prof. U. Tex., 1954-61; faculty fine arts dept. U. Colo., Boulder, 1961—; prof. U. Colo., 1970—. Exhibited one-man shows, Carlin Galleries, Fort Worth, Tex., 1968, 71, 74, 77, 80, Janet Nessler Gallery, N.Y.C., 1960, 64, Carson/Sapiro Gallery, Denver, 1979, group shows include, Mus Modern Art, N.Y.C., 1962, A.F.A., N.Y.C., 1970; represented in permanent collections, Whitney Mus. Am. Art, N.Y.C., Dallas Mus. Fine Arts. Served with Brit. Intelligence Corps, 1943-45. U. Tex. research grantee, 1960; U. Colo. grantee, 1966, 72, 78. Mem. Phi Beta Kappa. Roman Catholic. Home: 1627 5th St Boulder CO 80302 Office: Fine Arts Dept U Colo Boulder CO 80309

EADS, RICHARD CHARLES, broadcast manager; b. Bryan, Tex., Mar. 26, 1947; s. Richard Bailey and Florence (Richey) E. B. in Bus. Adminstrn., Tex. A&M U., 1969. Sales rep. Otis Elevator Co., Los Angeles, 1971-76; account exec. KGRL/KXIQ Radio, Bend, Oreg., 1976-78; sales mgr. KGAL Radio, Albany, Oreg., 1978, gen. mgr., 1979-80; owner, v.p., gen. mgr. KGAL Radio and Eads Broadcasting Corp., Albany, 1981—. Mem. bd. dirs. Red Cross, Linn County, Oreg., 1980—, United Way, 1982—; chmn. Conv. and Vistors Commn., Albany, 1983-86; pres. Albany Concert Band. Mem. Oreg. Assn. of Broadcasters, Nat. Assn. of Broadcasters, Radio Advertising Bur. Republican. Presbyterian. Lodge: Rotary (Greater Albany) (treas. 1984-85). Office: Station KGAL Box 749 Albany OR 97321

EAGLES, STUART ERNEST, business executive; b. Saint John, N.B., Can., July 29, 1929; s. Ernest Lyle and Evelyn Gertrude (Feltmate) E.; m. Margaret Anne Gulliver, Sept. 20, 1952; children: James Stuart, Patricia Anne, Mark Edward. B.Sc., Acadia U., 1949. With statis. dept. Can. Pacific Ltd., 1949-62, asst. to v.p., 1962-64; asst. to pres. Can. Pacific Investments, 1964-65; asst. gen. mgr. Marathon Realty, Montreal, 1965-69, v.p. Eastern region, 1969-70; pres. Marathon Realty, Toronto and Calgary, Alta., Can., 1970-77; chmn., pres., chief exec. officer Marathon Realty, Toronto, 1977-83; pres. Can. Pacific Enterprises, Calgary, 1983-86; v.p. corp. Can. Pacific Ltd., Montreal, 1986—; chmn., mem. exec. com. Marathon Realty; chmn. Can. Pacific Cons. Services; bd. dirs. The Algoma Steel Corp. Ltd., Can. Pacific Enterprises Ltd., Can. Pacific Securities, Can. Pacific (U.S.) Inc., Maple Leaf Mills Ltd., PanCan. Petroleum, Maritime Life Assurance Co. Bd. dirs. Resources Can. Fund, Jr. Achievement Can.; bd. govs. Acad Univ. Mem. Can. C. of C., Ont. C. of C. Clubs: National (past pres.), Canadian, Empire. Home: 24 Garfield Ave, Toronto, ON Canada M4T 1E7 Office: Can Pacific Ltd, 123 Front St W, Suite 800, Toronto, ON Canada M5J 2M8 *

EAKS, IRVING LESLIE, plant physiologist; b. Saivtelle, Calif., May 24, 1923; s. Elvis Agustus and Irene Clara (Springer) E.; m. Catherine Delp, Aug. 10, 1948; children: Joanne, Gerald Edward, Jeanette. BS, Colo. A&M U., 1948; MS, U. Calif., Davis, 1950, PhD, 1952. Plant physiologist U. Calif., Riverside, 1952—. Bd. dirs. Riverside Symphony Soc., 1956-70, 78-83, house mgr., 1965-70. Served with U.S. Army, 1943-46. Mem. Am. Soc. Hort. Sci. (Vaughn award 1958), Am. Soc. Plant Physiologists, AIBS, Sigma Xi, Alpha Zeta. Avocation: wood working. Home: 5865 Shaker Dr Riverside CA 92506 Office: U Calif Dept Biochemistry Riverside CA 92521

EAMER, RICHARD KEITH, health care company executive, lawyer; b. Long Beach, Calif., Feb. 13, 1928; s. George Pierce and Lillian (Newell) E.; m. Eileen Laughlin, Sept. 1, 1951; children: Brian Keith, Erin Maureen. B.S. in Acctg., U. So. Calif., 1955, LL.B., 1959. Bar: Calif. 1960; C.P.A., Calif. Acct. L. H. Penney & Co. (C.P.A.s), 1956-59; assoc. firm Ervin, Cohen & Jessup, Beverly Hills, Calif., 1959-63; partner firm Eamer, Bell and Bedrosian, Beverly Hills, 1963-69; chmn. bd., chief exec. officer Nat. Medical Enterprises, Inc., Los Angeles, 1969—; also dir. Nat. Med. Enterprises, Inc.; dir. Union Oil Co. Calif., Imperial Bank. Mem. Am. Bar Assn., Am. Inst. C.P.A.s, Calif. Bar Assn., Los Angeles County Bar Assn. Republican. Clubs: Bel Air Country, Bel Air Bay; California. Office: Nat Med Enterprises Inc 11620 Wilshire Blvd Los Angeles CA 90025 *

EARDLEY, JOHN KENNETH, JR., civil engineering consultant; b. Chgo., Feb. 24, 1923; s. John Kenneth and Janet Inez (Gallagher) E.; m. Betty Jane Berger, Feb. 23, 1943; children: Sharon Eileen Melton, Kenneth Michael, Melanie Christine. BSCE, U. Ariz., 1950; postgrad., U. So. Calif., 1956-57. Registered profl. civil engr., Calif., Ariz., Nev.; registered safety engr., Calif. Mem. engring. staff City of Tucson, 1946-50, mem. dept. bldg., 1950-52; mem. engring. staff U.S. Bur. Reclamation, Yuma, Ariz., 1950, S.B. Barnes and Assocs. Cons., Los Angeles, 1952-53, 59-60; mem. plant devel. staff Harvey Aluminum, Inc., Torrance, Calif., 1953-56; mem. staff Albert C. Martin and Assocs. Architects and Engrs., Los Angeles, 1956-57; mem. refinery staff Richfield Oil Corp., Wilmington, Calif., 1957-58; mem. cons. staff Ralph M. Parsons Co., Los Angeles and Fairbanks (Alaska), 1958-59, Stacy and Skinner, Los Angeles, 1960-61; prin. John K. Eardley & Assocs., Torrance, 1961—; participant numerous residential and comml. bldg. projects, investigative reports and expert witness to back up. Mem. Torrance, Culver City and Carson Sister City Assns.; bd. dirs. So. Calif. Council Japan/Am. Sister Cities, 1973-76, past vice-chmn.; merit badge counselor Boy Scouts Am., mem. dist. com.; past mem. Torrance City Planning Commn.; mem. adv. bds. So. Calif. Regional Occupational Ctr., Los Angeles Harbor Community Coll., S.O.C.S. Internat. Inst. English, Glendale, Calif.; very active student exchange programs, U.S. and Japan. Recipient Service award, City of Torrance, 1964, Cert. Appreciation Lomita (Calif.) C. of C., 1967, Cert. Appreciation City of Lomita, 1971, Cert. Appreciation Torrance Area C. of C., 1975. Mem. NSPE (bd. dirs. 1965-67, 72-76, pres. local chpt. 1964-65, bd. dirs. 1960-77, 80-81), Structural Engrs. Assn. So. Calif., Cons. Structural Engrs. Soc. of Los Angeles (bd. dirs. 1970-71), Am. Arbitration Assn. (panelist), Japanese Am. Citizens League (chmn. scholarship com., bd. dirs., v.p.), Calif. Taido Assn., Amerika Ueki Trimming Assn. (mem. adv. bd.). Republican. Mem. Ch. Christian Sci. Lodge: Lions. (past holder numerous offices). Avocations: photography, poetry, bonsai culture, lapidary. Office: 1629 Crenshaw Blvd Torrance CA 90501

EARL, BOYD L., chemistry educator; b. Burley, Idaho, Aug. 17, 1944; s. Boyd Wilde and Alismae (Melton) E.; m. Judy Mathewson, June 1, 1980; stepchildren: Christina, Frances, Charles. BS, U. Idaho, 1966; MS, PhD, U. Calif., Berkeley, 1973. Adj. asst. prof. chemistry CUNY, Bklyn., 1973-75; asst. prof. U. Nev., Las Vegas, 1976-82, assoc. prof., 1982—, chmn. dept. chemistry, 1982-86. Contbr. articles to profl. jours. NSF fellow, 1966-68. Mem. AAAS, Am. Chem. Soc., Sigma Xi. Office: U Nev Dept Chemistry Las Vegas NV 89154

EARL, WILLIAM JOHN, software engineer; b. East Stroudsburg, Pa., July 5, 1950; s. Lawrence William and Helen Olga (Gaisler) E.; m. Marion Helen Kaufman, Feb. 11, 1977; children: John William, Lesley Ann. BS, Calif. Inst. Tech., 1972; postgrad., U. Calif., Irvine, 1972-77. Sr. programmer Varian Data Machines, Irvine, 1976-77; supervising programmer Sperry Univac, Irvine, 1977-80; software designer Tandem Computers, Cupertino, Calif., 1980-84; software engr. Daisy Systems, Mountain View, Calif., 1984-86; mgr. operating systems group Am. Info. Tech., Cupertino, 1986—. Mem. Assn. Computing Machinery. Republican. Presbyterian. Avocations: hiking, skiing, sailing. Office: Am Info Tech 10201 Torre Ave Suite 250 Cupertino CA 95014

EARLE, DEBRA, manufacturing company executive; b. Newark, July 9, 1954. Software engr. Digital Equipment Corp., Maynard, Mass., 1978-79; mfg. engr. Digital Equipment Corp., Burlington, Vermont, 1979-80; robotics corp. cons. Gen. Electric Co., Schenectady, N.Y., 1980-82; mgr. robotics engring. Tektronix, Inc., Beaverton, Oreg., 1983-86; chief mfg. systems, robotics Rohr Industries, Inc., Riverside, Calif., 1986—; cons. in field, Tualatin, Oreg., 1982—; advisor, panelist Mt. Hood Community Coll. of Gresham, Oreg., 1983; panelist Consumer Network, Phila., 1983—. Advisor, panelist Mt. Hood C. of C., Gresham, Oreg., 1983; panelist Consumer Network, Phila., 1983—. Mem. Soc. Mech. Engrs. (mem. adv. com. Robots West Conf., 1984), Robotics Internat. of Soc. Mfg. Engrs. (Cert. of Appreciation, 1982, 84), Robot Industries Assn. of Soc. Mech. Engrs. (Tektronics Corp. rep. 1982-85), Women in Mgmt. Taoist. Avocations: profl. musician, gourmet cooking, photography, hist. restoration. Office: Rohr Industries Inc 8200 Arlington Ave Bldg 5 Riverside CA 92503-1499

EARLE, SYLVIA ALICE, biologist, oceanographer; b. Gibbstown, N.J., Aug. 30, 1935; d. Lewis Reade and Alice Freas (Richie) E. B.S., Fla. State U., 1955; M.A., Duke U., 1956, Ph.D., 1966. Resident dir. Cape Haze Marine Lab., Sarasota, Fla., 1966-67; research scholar Radcliffe Inst., 1967-69; research fellow Farlow Herbarium, Harvard U., 1967-75, researcher, 1975—; research assoc. in botany Natural History Mus. Los Angeles County, 1970-75; research biologist, curator Calif. Acad. Scis., San Francisco, 1976—; research assoc. U. Calif.-Berkeley, 1969-75; founder, v.p., sec.-treas., dir. Deep Ocean Tech., Inc., Oakland, Calif., Deep Ocean Engring., Oakland, 1981—. Author: Exploring the Deep Frontier, 1980. Editor: Scientific Results of the Tektite II Project, 1972-75. Contbr. 60 articles to profl. jours. Trustee World Wildlife Fund U.S., 1976-82, council mem., 1984—; trustee World Wildlife Fund Internat., 1979-81, council mem., 1981—; trustee Charles A. Lindbergh Fund., Ocean Trust Found.; council mem. Internat. Union Conservation Nature, 1979-81; corp. mem. Woods Hole Oceanographic Inst.; mem. Nat. Adv. Com. Oceans and Atmosphere, 1980-84. Recipient Conservation Service award U.S. Dept. Interior, 1970, Boston Sea Rovers award, 1972, 79, Nogi award Underwater Soc. Am., 1976, Conservation service award Calif. Acad. Sci., 1979, Lowell Thomas award Explorer's Club, 1980, Order of Golden Ark Prince Netherlands, 1980; named Woman of Yr. Los Angeles Times, 1970, Scientist of Yr., Calif. Mus. Sci. and Industry, 1981. Fellow AAAS, Marine Tech. Soc., Calif. Acad. Scis., Explorers Club, Calif. Acad. Sci.; mem. Internat. Phycological Soc. (sec. 1974-80), Phycological Soc. Am., Am. Soc. Ichthyologists and Herpetologists, Am. Inst. Biol. Scis., Brit. Phycological Soc., Ecol. Soc. Am., Internat. Soc. Plant Taxonomists. Club: Explorers (fellow). Home: 12812 Skyline Blvd Oakland CA 94619 Office: Calif Acad Scis Golden Gate Park San Francisco CA 94118

EARLE, TED CHARLES, publisher, editor; b. Palo Alto, Calif., Aug. 31, 1946; s. Ellis P. and Ida Mae (Parker) E.; m. Gloria E. Alvillar, Aug. 11, 1984; children: Christopher R., Erik L., Dominique L. BSChemE, U. Tex., 1969, MBA, 1974. Research engr. Universal Oil Products div. Signal Co., Des Plaines, Ill., 1969-70; field engr. Universal Oil Products div. Signal Co., Turkey, Italy and Japan, 1971-73; planner, budgeter, forecaster ARAMCO, Dhahran, Saudi Arabia, 1974-76; publisher, editor Market Timing Report, Tucson, 1979—; forecasting cons. Port of Jeddah, Saudi Arabia, 1976-77. Mem. Market Technicians Assn., Tau Beta Pi, Phi Eta Sigma. Libertarian. Avocations: country swing dancing, hiking, bicycling, jogging. Home: 1422 E Mabel Tucson AZ 85719 Office: Market Timing Report 2755-C W Ankam Rd Tucson AZ 85745

EARLEY, PAUL CHRISTOPHER, psychology educator, organizational consultant; b. Pitts., Aug. 21, 1959; s. James William and Shirley Irene Earley; m. Claudia Carstens Smith, Jan. 10, 1981. BA, Knox Coll., 1980; MA, PhD, U. Ill., 1984. Indsl. researcher Dunlop Tyre Co., Birmingham, Eng., 1978; mgmt. trainee Deere and Co., Waterloo, Iowa, 1979; orgnl. cons. U. Ill., Champaign, 1981, instr. psychology, 1980-84; asst. prof. Claremont (Calif.) McKenna Coll., 1984-86, U. Ariz., Tucson, 1986—; asst. dir. student research InterFuture, N.Y.C., 1982—. Author: Industrial Psychology, 1983; contbr. research articles to profl. jours. Grantee U. Ill., 1983-84, InterFuture, 1979. Mem. Acad. Mgmt., Am. Psychol. Assn., Champaign Computer Club. Office: Univ Ariz Dept Mgmt and Policy Tucson AZ 85721

EARLY, JAMES MICHAEL, research consultant; b. Syracuse, N.Y., July 25, 1922; s. Frank J. and Rhoda Gray E.; m. Mary Agnes Valentine, Dec. 28, 1948; children—Mary, Kathleen, Joan Early Farrell, Rhoda Early Alexander, Maureen Early Mathews, Rosemary, James, Margaret Mary. B.S., N.Y. Coll. Forestry, Syracuse, N.Y., 1943; M.S., Ohio State U., 1948, Ph.D., 1951. Instr., research assoc. Ohio State U., Columbus, 1946-51; dir. lab. Bell Telephone Labs., Murray Hill, N.J., 1951-64, Allentown, Pa., 1964-69; research and devel. dir. Fairchild Semicondr. Corp., Palo Alto, Calif., 1969-83, sci. advisor, 1983-86; research cons. 1986—. Served with U.S. Army, 1943-45. Fellow IEEE (recipient J.J. Ebers award IEEE Electron Device Soc. 1979); mem. AAAS, Am. Phys. Soc., Electrochem. Soc., Internat. Platform Assn. Roman Catholic. Club: Palo Alto (Calif.) Yacht. Home: 740 Center Dr Palo Alto CA 94301 Office: Fairchild Semiconductor Corp 4001 Miranda Ave Palo Alto CA 94304

EARP, KENNETH ROLAND, psychology educator; b. Denver, Oct. 30, 1929; s. John Rosslyn and Kathleen May (Goodliffe) E.; m. Sherrie McGillivray, Oct. 1, 1961 (div. 1983); children: Dwight David Vandegrift, Valerie Victoria, Susan Marie, Timothy A.; m. Dorothy Louise Palmer, Nov. 26, 1983. BS, U. N.Mex., 1956, MS, 1959. Cert. secondary tchr., Calif.(life). Research assoc. U. N.Mex., Albuquerque, 1958-59; ednl. psychologist Human Resources Inst., Albuquerque, 1959-62; tchr. high sch. dist. El Cantro, Calif., 1960-63, Salinas, Calif., 1983-86; coordinator testing, high sch. dist. Salinas, 1984—. Pres. Unitarian Universalist Fellowship Salinas, 1976-86. Served as cpl. U.S. Army, 1947-51. Mem. Am. Psychol. Assn. (assoc.), Calif. Tchrs. Assn. (v.p., pres. local chpt.), Sigma Xi, Phi Delta Kappa. Democrat. Unitarian. Avocations: music, gardening, bowling. Home: 644 University Ave Salinas CA 93901 Office: Salinas Union High Sch Dist 431 W Alisal St Salinas CA 93901

EASH, DIANNE MARY, charitable financial planning executive; b. Long Branch, N.J., Apr. 8, 1944; d. George Henry and Hazel Mary (Ball) E. B.A., UCLA, 1966; M.A., Calif. State Coll., Bakersfield, 1973; grad. gemologist Gemological Inst. Am., 1979. Instr. English and math. Kern High Sch. Dist. (Calif.), 1967-80, coordinator communications, 1975-78; instr. Bakersfield Adult Sch., 1973-80, Calif. State Coll., Bakersfield, 1976-77; engaged in research and devel. Gemological Inst. Am., Santa Monica, Calif., 1980, adminstrv. coordinator research, 1981-82, spl. projects coordinator, 1981-82, asst. exec. dir. Gemological Inst. Am. Alumni Assn., 1982; spl. cons. E/H Graphic Communications, 1982—; pres. Nat. Assn. Philanthropic Planners, Long Beach, Calif., 1983—; dir. adminstrn./sales PhilanthroTec, Inc., Los Angeles, 1983-85; pres. Wealth Devel. Resources, Long Beach, 1985—. Editor: Internat. Gemological Symposium Procs., 1982; (with others) Diamonds: From Birth to Eternity, 1982. Mem. NEA, Calif. Tchrs. Assn. Office: Wealth Devel Resources 1001 Oberlin Ct Bakersfield CA 93305

EASLEY, DAVID THOMAS, orthopaedic surgeon; b. Detroit, Oct. 29, 1941; s. Maynard Millington and Alicia Nelletta (Vines) E.; m. Suzanne Whitney Martin, Aug. 24, 1963 (div. Feb. 1982); children: Kirsten Braidwood, Kevin Thomas; m. Terri Janene Pelton, Aug. 11, 1984; 1 child, Ryan Taylor. BS, Wayne State U., 1965; MD, U. Mich., 1971. Diplomate Nat. Bd. Med. Examiners, Am. Bd. Orthopaedic Surgeons. Intern U. Wis. Hosps., Madison, 1971-72; resident Blodgett Meml. Hosp., East Grand Rapids, Mich., 1972-75; chief resident Blodgett-Butterworth Hosps., East Grand Rapids, Mich., 1974-75; pratice medicine specializing in orthopaedic surgery La Mesa, Calif., 1975—; mem. med. staff U. Calif. San Diego Hosp., 1975—; vice chmn. orthopaedic dept. Grossmont Hosp., La Mesa, 1982-83, chmn., 1982-83; lectr. in arthroscopy; bd. dirs. Holiday Bowl; mem. adv. bd. First La Mesa Bank. Bd. dirs. Girls Club El Cajon, Calif., 1978-80, Boys Club East County, El Cajon, 1979—; mem. Inner Circle Rep. Senatorial Com., 1984. Fellow ACS, Am. Acad. Orthopaedic Surgeons; mem. AMA, Calif. Med. Assn., San Diego County Med. Soc., Western Orthopaedic Assn. Methodist. Avocations: skiing, sailing, flying. Office: Coast Pointe Orthopaedic Med Group 8530 La Mesa Blvd Suite 201 La Mesa CA 92041

EASLEY, GEORGE WASHINGTON, construction executive; b. Williamson, W.Va., Mar. 14, 1933; s. George Washington and Isabel Ritchie (Saville) E.; student U. Richmond, 1952-56; children—Bridget Bland, Kathy Clark, Saville Woodson, Marie Alexis, Isabell Roxanne, George Washington, Laura Dean. Hwy. engr. Va. Dept. Hwys., Richmond, 1956-62; dep. city mgr. City of Anchorage, 1962-68; prin. assoc. Wilbur Smith & Assos., Los Angeles, 1969-70; commr. pub. works State of Alaska, Juneau, 1971-74; exec. v.p. Burgess Internat. Constrn. Co., Anchorage, 1974, pres., 1975; pres., chmn. bd. George W. Easley Co., Anchorage, 1976-83 ; pres. Alaska Aggregate Corp., Fairbanks Sand & Gravel Co., 1986—; chmn. bd. Central Services, Inc. DBA Yellow Cab of Anchorage, 1982—; dir. Totem Ocean Trailer Express, Inc., Life Ins. Co. Alaska. Mem. New Capital Site Planning Commn. State of Alaska, 1981—; bd. dirs. Anchorage YMCA. Recipient commendations City of Anchorage, 1966, Greater Anchorage, Inc., 1969, Ketchikan C. of C., 1973, Alaska State Legis., 1974, Gov. of Alaska, 1974; named one of Outstanding Young Men, Anchorage Jaycees, 1964. Registered profl. engr., Calif. Mem. U.S. C. of C. (nat. com. on small bus.), Alaska C. of C. (dir. 1978—, chmn. 1982-83), Anchorage C. of C. (sec.-treas. 1976, v.p. 1977, pres.-elect 1978, pres. 1979-80, dir. 1982-85, Gold Pan award 1969, 77), Hwy. Users Fedn. Alaska (dir. 1972—, treas. 1974—), Orgn. Mgmt. of Alaska's Resources (past dir.), Am. Pub. Works Assn., Anchorage Transp. Commn. (past chmn.), Associated Gen. Contractors (dir. Alaska chpt. 1978—, chpt. treas. 1980-81, sec. 1981, pres. 1984, nat. com. labor relations), Am. Mil. Engrs. (v.p. Alaska chpt. 1978), Inst. Mcpl. Engrs., Inst. Traffic Engrs., Internat. Orgn. Masters, Mates and Pilots (hon.), Common Sense for Alaska (past pres.), Commonwealth North (charter). Democrat. Presbyterian. Club: Tower. Lodge: Rotary. Home: 333 M St #210 Anchorage AK 99501 Office: 7800 Lake Otis Blvd Anchorage AK 99507

EASON, BARBARA BENNETT, health care and community services administrator; b. Pontiac, Ill., Aug. 14, 1945; d. Charles William and Bess Margaret (Anderson) Bennett; m. Kenneth Michael Blumenthal, May 4, 1964 (div. Aug. 1969); 1 child, Fawn Phaedra; m. Charles Warren Strait III, Dec. 20, 1969 (dec. May 1974); m. David Lynn Eason, Nov. 23, 1975. BS in Radio-TV, So. Ill. U., 1976; MS in Urban Affairs, U. Wis., Milw., 1979. Pub. relations specialist Children's Service Soc., Milw., 1979; instr., coordinator U. Wis., Milw., 1979-81; asst. program dir. Viacom Cablevision, Milw., 1981-83; research cons. KUED-TV sta., Salt Lake City, 1984; mgr. mem. services FHP, Salt Lake City, 1984-86; dir. Intermountain Women's Ctr. LDS Hosp., Salt Lake City, 1986—. Mem. Community Devel. Adv. Bd., Salt Lake City, 1984—; fund-raising com. Utah Issues, Salt Lake City, 1986. Mem. Pub. Relations Soc. Am. Home: 1164 Herbert Ave Salt Lake City UT 84105 Office: LDS Hosp Intermountain Women's Ctr 8th Ave and C St Salt Lake City UT 84103

EASON, ERNEST DAY, consulting mechanical engineer; b. Denver, Apr. 10, 1949; s. Maurice Verne and Elma Iris Eason; m. Laurie Parker, Aug. 23, 1969. B.S. with spl. honors in Engring. Design and Econ. Evaluation, U. Colo., 1971; M.Eng. in Mech. Engring., U. Toronto (Can.), 1972; Ph.D. in Mech. Engring., U. Calif.-Berkeley, 1975. Registered profl. engr., Calif. Mem. tech. staff Sandia Labs., Livermore, Calif., 1976-79; mgr. mech. engring., mgr. engring. computer ctr. and prin. Failure Analysis Assocs., Palo Alto, Calif., 1979—. Prin. trombonist Ohlone Community Band, 1979—. Recipient Pres.'s award as outstanding mem. jr. class U. Colo., 1970; Nat. Honor Soc. scholar, 1967; Nat. Merit scholar, 1967-71, Adolf Coors Co. scholar, 1967-71; NSF grad. fellow, 1971-74. Mem. ASME, Mathematical Programming Soc., NACE, Tau Beta Pi (past chpt. v.p.), Sigma Xi. Contbr. articles to profl. jours. and books. Office: Failure Analysis Assocs 2225 E Bayshore Rd Palo Alto CA 94303

EASTERLY, JEAN LUCEY, education educator; b. Chgo., May 29, 1939; d. Lawrence Y. and Elizabeth (Fischer) Lucey; m. Charles H. Easterly, June 4, 1960; children: Kevin, Lawrence, Elizabeth. BS, Bradley U., 1961; MA, U. Ariz., 1967, EdD, 1972. Cert. elem. tchr., Ariz., Ill. Tchr. elem. schs. Peoria, Ill., 1960-64, Tucson, 1967-69; supr. Ariz. State U., Tempe, 1972; from asst. prof. to assoc. prof. edn. Oakland U., Rochester, Mich., 1972-84; chmn. dept. tchr. edn. Calif. State U., Hayward, 1984—. Contbr. articles to prof. jours. Mem. Assn. Tchr. Edn. (bd. dirs. 1986—, pres. Calif. chpt. 1986—), Am. Ednl. Research Assn., Am. Assn. Colls. for Tchr. Edn. Office: Calif State U Dept Tchr Edn Hayward CA 94542

EASTIN, JAMES THOMAS, actor, educator; b. San Francisco, Sept. 23, 1938; s. Thomas Drake and Muriel Margaret (Arnold) E. BA, U. Denver, 1962; MA, San Francisco State U., 1966. Prof., track coach San Francisco State U., 1962-64; tchr. Canyon High Sch., Castro Valley, Calif., 1964-65; prof., track coach, basketball coach Coll. San Mateo (Calif.), 1965-68; mgr. Beverly Hills Health Club, Hollywood, Calif., 1969-71; actor Don Schwartz Agy., Hollywood, 1970—; cons. Frontier Adjusters, Phelan, Calif., 1982—. Bd. dirs. New County Steering Com., Victorville, Calif., 1986. Named Man of Yr., U. Denver, 1962, All-Am., Amatuer Athletic Union, 1963-64, Track Coach of Yr., Alameda County Coaches Assn., 1965. Mem. Scren Actors Guild, AFTRA, Am. Film Soc., Sons and Daughters of the Golden West, Phi Kappa Sigma. Democrat. Clubs: Olympic (San Francisco); Los Angeles Athletic. Avocations: sports, traveling, photography. Home: PO Box 79 Phelan CA 92371 Office: Don Schwartz and Assocs 8721 Sunset Blvd Hollywood CA 90069

EASTLAKE, CARLETON CHESMORE, screenwriter, producer, lawyer; b. N.Y.C., Dec. 23, 1947; s. Alfred Chesmore and Marion Hilda Eastlake; m. Loraine Depsres, Nov. 24, 1985; 1 stepson, David Mulholland. Student Columbia U., 1965-66; AB, UCLA, 1969; JD, Harvard U., 1972. Bar: Calif. 1973, U.S. Dist. Ct. (cen. dist.) Calif. 1982. Atty. FTC, Washington, 1972-74, atty., advisor Office of Comm. Nye, 1974-76; atty. Los Angeles Regional Office FTC, 1977-79, acting regional dir., asst. dir., 1979-83; assoc. Lawler, Felix & Hall, Los Angeles, 1976-77; screenwriter, pres. The Eastlake-Despres Co., Los Angeles, 1983—; producer Warner Bros. TV. Writer (TV movies, series) Murder She Wrote, The Equalizer, Airwolf, V, Crime Story. Mem. Writers Guild Am., Calif. Bar Assn., ABA, Zuma Beach Protective Assn. Democrat. Avocations: computer tech., horsemanship. Home and Office: 6403 Seastar Dr Malibu CA 90265

EASTMAN, ELKE-ROSEMARIE GRIMM, public relations professional; b. Swinemuende, Pomerania, Germany, June 8, 1941; came to U.S., 1964, naturalized, 1969; d. Heinz Willi and Elli Johanna (Morgenstern) Grimm; m. Richard Phillip Eastman, Mar. 4, 1967 (div. 1977); children: Stephen Peter, Jay Stuart. AA, Santa Ana Coll., 1975; BA in Communications, Calif. State U., Fullerton, 1980. Purser, Pan. Am. World Airways, San Francisco, 1965-67, sr. purser, Los Angeles, 1967-68; assoc. pub. relations rep. Beckman Instruments, Inc., Fullerton, Calif., 1978-79, staff writer, 1979-83, sr. staff writer, 1983-86, sr. press relations rep., 1986—. Mem. Pub. Relations Soc. Am. (officer Orange County chpt. 1984-85, bd. dirs., Protos awards 1978, 79, 84, 85, Excellence awards 1980, 83, 84). Office: Beckman Instruments Inc 2500 Harbor Blvd Fullerton CA 92634

EASTMAN, GLEN PRESTON, engineer; b. St. Louis, Oct. 14, 1948; s. Warren Harding and Willma Jane (Prator) E.; m. Gloria Jean Temple, June 5, 1971; children: Jonathan Warren, Erin Rebekah. BS in Indsl. Tech., Southeast Mo. State U., 1975. Mfg. engr. II Emerson Electronics, St. Louis, 1975-79; sr. engr. Digital Equipment Corp., Colorado Springs, Colo., 1979—. Patentee in field. Served with USN, 1969-73, Vietnam. Mem. Soc. Mfg. Engrs. (cert.), Mfg. Tech. Robotics Internat. (cert.). Republican. Methodist. Avocations: sports cars, motorcycles. Home: 1065 Allegheny Dr Colorado Springs CO 80919 Office: Digital Equipment Corp 301 Rockrimmon Blvd S Colorado Springs CO 80919-2398

EASTMAN, JANET L(OUISE), magazine editor; b. Memphis, Feb. 25, 1957; d. Paul T. and Nancy J. (McGrath) Kuras; m. Kenneth J. Eastman, Sept. 7, 1979; one child, Eric J. BS, Calif. State U., Fullerton, 1979. Editor Orange Coast mag., Costa Mesa, Calif., 1979—. Mem. Calif. Soc. Press. Assn. (com. chmn., instr. 1979—). Avocations: traveling, reading, tennis. Office: Orange Coast Mag 245-D Fischer Costa Mesa CA 92626

EASTON, JAMES PATRICK, public administrator; b. Bloomington, Ind., Mar. 18, 1949; s. Fred Charles and Elizabeth Maxine (Blackmore) E.; m. Rhonda Susan Johnson, June 26, 1971; children: Aimee Reid, Benjamin James. BA, Ind. U., 1971; MPA, U. Colo., 1978. Security officer Miesau Army Depot, W.Ger., 1971-74; dir. security U.S. Army, Ft. Carson, Colo., 1974-76; program mgr. Ridefinders Transp. Info. Ctr., Colorado Springs, Colo., 1978-80, Air Quality Control El Paso County Health Dept., Colorado Springs, 1980—; chmn. air quality tech. com. Pikes Peak Area Council Govts., Colorado Springs, 1982-85. Co-developer computer software online rideshare matching system, 1979. Council mem. Am. Lung Assn., Colorado Springs, 1980—; bd. dirs. Energy Resource Ctr., 1981—; mem. Comprehensive Plan Com., 1982-83. Recipient Blue Sky award Am. Lung Assn., 1983, Zoya Miller award, 1984. Mem. Am. Soc. Pub. Adminstrn. (pres. 1982-83), Colo. Pub. Health Assn. (chmn. clean air task force 1983-85), U. Colo. Alumni Assn. (pres.-elect 1986-87), Citizens Goals of Colorado Springs, Pi Alpha Alpha. Roman Catholic. Office: El Paso County Health Dept Air Quality Control 501 N Foote Ave Colorado Springs CO 80909

EASTON, LOIS EVELYN, writing specialist, educator; b. Detroit, Nov. 6, 1946; d. John Wallace and Christine (Chambers) Brown; m. Martin Edward Easton, Nov. 12, 1966 (div. Mar. 1987); 1 son, Michael David Brown. Student MacMurray Coll., Jacksonville, Ill., 1964-65; B.A. in Humanities and English Edn., Colo. State U., 1970; M.A. in Secondary Edn., U. Ariz., 1983. Cert. tchr., Ariz. Tchr., Poudre Sch. Dist., Ft. Collins, Colo., 1970-75, Colo. Mountain Coll., Glenwood Springs, 1975-77; author-in-residence The Economy Co., Ednl. Publishers, Oklahoma City, 1977-80; tchr. lang. arts Catalina Foothills Sch. Dist., Tucson, 1980-85; writing specialist Sch. Improvement Unit Ariz. Dept. Edn., 1985—; cons. in field. Authored ednl. materials; editor: (jour.) Ariz. Reading, 1982-83. Mem. Colo. Lang. Arts Soc., Ariz. English Tchrs. Assn. (pres. 1986-87, Ariz. Jr. High English Tchr. of Yr. 1984), Nat. Council Tchrs. English (steering com. secondary edn. sect. 1987), Internat. Reading Assn., Ariz. State Reading Assn., Assn. Supervision and Curriculum Devel., Phi Kappa Phi, Phi Delta Kappa. Democrat. Unitarian. Home: 1521 W Pierson #3 Phoenix AZ 85015 Office: Ariz Dept Edn 1535 W Jefferson Phoenix AZ 85007

EASTON, ROBERT (OLNEY), author, environmentalist; b. July 4, 1915; s. Robert Eastman and Ethel (Olney) E.; m. Jane Faust, Sept. 24, 1940; children: Joan Easton Lentz, Katherine Easton Renga (dec.), Ellen Easton Brumfiel, Jane. Student, Stanford U., 1933-34, postgrad., 1938-39; B.S., Harvard U., 1938; M.A., U. Calif.-Santa Barbara, 1960. Ranch hand, day laborer, mag. editor 1939-42; co-pub., editor Lampasas Dispatch, Tex., 1946-50; instr. English Santa Barbara City Coll., 1959-65; writing and pub. cons. U.S. Naval Civil Engring. Lab., Port Hueneme, Calif., 1961-69. Author: The Happy Man, 1943, (with Mackenzie Brown) Lord of Beasts, 1961, (with Jay Monaghan and others) The Book of the American West, 1963, The Hearing, 1964, (with Dick Smith) California Condor: Vanishing American, 1964, Max Brand: The Big Westerner, 1970, Black Tide: The Santa Barbara Oil Spill and Its Consequences, 1972, Guns, Gold and Caravans, 1978, China Caravans: An American Adventurer in Old China, 1982, This Promised Land, 1982; editor: Max Brand's Best Stories, 1967; co-editor: Bullying the Moqui (Charles F. Lummis), 1968; contbr. stories and articles to mags., including Atlantic and N.Y. Times mag., also anthologies, including Great Tales of the American West. Co-chmn. Com. for Santa Barbara; trustee Santa Barbara Mus. Natural History. Served to 1st lt., F.A., Tank Destroyer Command, inf. U.S. Army, 1942-46. Co-founder Sisquoc Sanctuary for Calif. condor, 1937, also first wilderness area established under Nat. Wilderness Act, Los Padres Nat. Forest, Calif., 1968. Home: 2222 Las Canoas Rd Santa Barbara CA 93105

EATER, LLOYD EUGENE, chemical engineer; b. Mt. Vernon, Ill., May 16, 1927; s. Truman W. and Jessie A. (Yearwood) E.; m. Terrie F. Frank, Aug. 13, 1977; children: Daniel, Rebecca. BSChemE, Washington U., 1949. Works mgr. Trane Co., La Crosse, Wis., 1952-74; v.p. Sentry Equipment Corp., Oconomowoc, Wis., 1974-83; sr. engr. RCT Inc., San Jose, Calif., 1983-86; v.p. Ultrapure, Inc., San Jose, 1987—. Mem. ASTM, ASME. Home: 165 Arroyo Way San Jose CA 95112 Office: Ultrapure Inc 90 Great Oaks Blvd #206 San Jose CA 95119

EATON, ANTHONY RONALD, television producer; b. London, May 31, 1949; came to U.S., 1957; s. Ronald Jack and Doris Lillian (Neville) E.; m. Reneá Eve Sulick, Dec. 15, 1981 (div. June 1986); 1 child, Alexandra Margaux. BA, U. Calif., Berkeley, 1970. Producer Tall Pony Prodns., Los Angeles, 1977—; lectr. UCLA extension, 1983—. Producer (TV programs) George Jones, 1981 (Bronze medal Chgo. Film Festival 1981, Silver medal N.Y. Film Festival, 1981), David Bowie, 1984 (Award for Cable Excellence 1984), Huey Lewis, 1985 (Grammy award Nat. Acad. Recording Arts Scis. 1985). Episcopalian. Avocations: travel, hiking, archeol. explorations. Office: Tall Pony Prodns 9000 Sunset Blvd # 612 Los Angeles CA 90069

EATON, GARETH RICHARD, chemistry educator, dean; b. Lockport, N.Y., Nov. 3, 1940; s. Mark Dutcher and Ruth Emma (Ruston) E.; m. Sandra Shaw, Mar. 29, 1969. BA, Harvard U., 1962; PhD, MIT, 1972. Asst. prof. chemistry U. Denver, 1972-76, assoc. prof., 1976-80, prof., 1980—, dean natural scis., 1984—. Contbr. articles to profl. jours. Served to lt. USN, 1962-67. Mem. AAAS, Am. Chem. Soc., Royal Soc. Chemistry (London), Internat. Soc. Mag. Resonance, Soc. Applied Spectroscopy, Am. Physical Soc. Office: U Denver Dean Natural Scis Denver CO 80208

EATON, PAULINE, artist; b. Neptune, N.J., Mar. 20, 1935; d. Paul A. and Florence Elizabeth (Rogers) Friedrich; m. Charles Adams Eaton, June 15, 1957; children—Gregory, Eric, Paul, Joy. B.A., Dickinson Coll., 1957; M.A., Northwestern U., 1958. Lic. instr., Calif. Instr., Mira Costa Coll., Oceanside, Calif., 1980-82, Idyllwild Sch. Music and Arts, Calif., 1983—; juror, demonstrator numerous art socs. Recipient award Haywood (Calif.) Area Forum for the Arts, 1986. Exhibited one-woman shows Nat. Arts Club, N.Y.C., 1977, Designs Recycled Gallery, Fullerton, Calif., 1978, 80, 84, San Diego Art Inst., 1980, Spectrum Gallery, San Diego, 1981, San Diego Jung Ctr., 1983, Marin Civic Ctr. Gallery, 1984; group shows include Am. Watercolor Soc., 1975, 77, Butler Inst. Am. Art, Youngstown, Ohio, 1977, 78, 79, 81, NAD, 1978; represented in permanent collections including Butler Inst. Am. Art, St. Mary's Coll., Md., Mercy Hosp., San Diego, Sharp Hosp., San Diego, Redlands Hosp., Riverside, 1986; work featured in books: Watercolor, The Creative Experience, 1978, Creative Seascape Painting, 1980, Painting the Spirit in Nature, 1984. Trustee San Diego Art Inst., 1977-78, San Diego Mus. Art, 1982-83. Mem. Nat. Watercolor Soc. (exhibited traveling shows 1978, 79, 83, 85), Rocky Mountain Watermedia Soc. (Golden award 1979, Mustard Seed award 1983), Nat. Soc. Painters in Acrylic and Casein (hon.), Watercolor West (Strathmore award 1979, Purchase award 1986), Marin Arts Guild (instr. 1984—), San Diego Watercolor Soc. (pres. 1976-77, workshop dir. 1977-80), Artists Equity (v.p. San Diego 1979-81), San Diego Artists Guild (pres. 1982-83), Western Fedn. Watercolor Socs. (chmn. 1983, 3d prize 1982, Grumbacher Gold medal 1983), West Coast Watercolor Soc. (exhbns. chmn. 1983—). Democrat. Presbyterian. Home: 10 Alta Mira Ave Kentfield CA 94904

EATON, ROBERT CHARLES, biologist, educator; b. Los Angeles, Aug. 14, 1946; s. Charles Hardman Eaton and Ruth Irene (Cook) Christopher; 1 child, Christopher Charles Eaton. BA with honors, U. Calif., Riverside, 1968; MS, U. Oreg., 1970; PhD, U. Calif., Riverside, 1974. Asst. research neuroscientist U. Calif., San Diego, 1974-78; asst. prof. U. Colo., Boulder, 1978-83, assoc. prof., 1983—. Editor: Neural Mechanisms of Startle Behavior, 1984. Recipient Nat. Research Service award Nat. Inst. Health, 1974; research fellow INSERM, CHU Pitie-Saltpetriere, Paris, 1976. Mem. Soc. for Neurosci., AAAS, Internat. Soc. for Neuroethology. Office: U Colo Dept Biology EPO Box 334 Boulder CO 80309

EATON, SANDRA SHAW, chemistry educator; b. Boston, Jan. 23, 1946; d. James Headon and Vera (Chapman) S.; m. Gareth Richard Eaton, Mar. 29, 1969. BA, Wellesley Coll., 1968; PhD, MIT, 1972. Asst. prof. U. Colo., Denver, 1973-80, assoc. prof. chemistry, 1980-86, prof., 1986—. Contbr. articles to profl. jours. Predoctoral fellow NSF, 1969-71. Mem. Am. Chem. Soc., Phi Beta Kappa, Sigma Xi. Office: U Colo Dept Chemistry 1100 14th St Denver CO 80202

EATOUGH, DELBERT JAY, chemistry educator; b. Provo, Utah, Sept. 15, 1940; s. Richard George and Thelma Elizabeth (Burr) E.; m. Judith Mae Pursley, Mar. 5, 1964; children: Michael, Michele, David, Rebecca, Melinda, Jennifer, Elizabeth. BS, Brigham Young U., 1964, PhD, 1967. Chemist Shell Devel. Co., Emeryville, Calif., 1967-70; dir. Thermochem. Inst. Brigham Young U., Provo, 1979-85, prof. chemistry, 1985—. Author: Heats of Metal Ligand Interactions, 1978; editor, author: Titration Calorimetry, 1977, 3d rev. edit. 1985; contbr. numerous articles to sci. jours. Scoutmaster Boy Scouts Am., Provo, 1975-86. mem. Calorimetry Conf. (sec., treas. 1976-85, chmn. 1985—), Am. Chem. Soc., Am. Pollution Control Assn., Am. Assn. Aerosol Research. Mormon. Home: 1252 N Uinta Dr Provo UT 84604 Office: Brigham Young U 276 FB Provo UT 84602

EATOUGH, NORMAN LEROY, chemistry educator; b. Bingham Canyon, Utah, Oct. 18, 1833; s. Richard G. and Thelma (Burr) E.; m. Marilyn Buckner, Sept. 13, 1956; children: LaRae, Craig, Steven, Jerry, Jason. BS, BES, MS, Brigham Young U., 1959, PhD, 1968; MSChemE, U. Wash., 1960. Sr. devel. engr. Hercules Inc., Salt Lake City, 1960-64, cons., 1965-66; instr. chemistry Dixie Coll., St. George, Utah, 1964-65; instr. chem. engring. Brigham Young U., Provo, Utah, 1965-67, research prof., 1985—; prof. chemistry Calif. Poly. State U., San Luis Obispo, 1968—. Author: Study Guide for Chemistry, 1983. Served with U.S. Army, 1953-55, Korea. Recipient Disting. Tchr. award Calif. Poly. State U., 1983. Mem. Am. Chem. Soc., Air Pollution Control Soc., Sigma Xi. Home: 1508 Gulf St San Luis Obispo CA 93401 Office: Calif Poly State U Chemistry Dept San Luis Obispo CA 93407

EBBEN, THOMAS HARVEY, optical engineer; b. Menominee, Wis., Nov. 12, 1957; s. Ronald Joseph and Joanna Myrtle (Badzinski) E.; m. Mary Francis Moretti, June 16, 1984; 1 child, Christina Marie. AS in Laser Tech., and Electronics Tech., N. Cen. Tech. Inst., 1980; student, U. Colo., 1984—. Technician Storage Tech. Corp., Louisville, Colo., 1980-85; designer Ball Aerospace Corp., Boulder, Colo., 1985—. Mem. Internat. Soc. Optical Engrs., Sigma Alpha Lambda. Avocations: photography, golf. Home: 1413 Centaur Circle Lafayette CO 80026 Office: Ball Aerospace Corp PO Box 1062 High Tech Products MS BE-5 Boulder CO 80306

EBERHARD, CHRISTINE LUCILLE, public relations executive; b. Fremont, Ohio, Jan. 12, 1951; d. Richard Lesley and Elva Lucille (Ransom) E. Student U. Am., Cholula, Mex. 1972-73; B.A. in Internat. Studies, Ohio State U. 1973. Account exec. News-Times Pub. Co., Anaheim, Calif. 1975-77; asst. dir. pub. relations and devel. Hawthorne Community Hosp. 1977-80; dir. pub. relations Presbyterian Intercommunity Hosp., Whittier, Calif. 1980-82; pres. CommuniQuest, Manhattan Beach, Calif., 1982—. Bd. dirs. Los Angeles South Bay-Harbor Industry Edn. Council 1978-81. Serving with USAR 1973—. Mem. Res. Officers Assn. (Outstanding Jr. Officer 1983), So. Calif. Soc. Hosp. Pub. Relations, Profl. Helicopter Pilots Assn. (bd. dirs.), Publicity Club Los Angeles, Internat. Assn. Bus. Communicators, Helicopter Assn. Internat. (mem. heliport and airway com.), Aero Club. So. Calif., Nat. Def. Transp. Assn. (bd. dirs.), Manhattan Beach C. of C., Los Angeles Internat. Airport C. of C. (bd. dirs.), Los Angeles Area C. of C. Home: 115 1/2 31st St Hermosa Beach CA 90254 Office: CommuniQuest 1020 Manhattan Beach Blvd #109 Manhattan Beach CA 90266

EBERHARDT, CLIFFORD ERIE, education specialist; b. Portland, Oreg., May 28, 1932; s. Ernest and Dorothy (Jackson) E.; m. Dorothy Mae Engel, Aug. 10, 1958; children—Ellen, Paul. B.S., Western Oreg. State Coll., 1953; M. Ed., U. Oreg., 1957; postgrad. Stanford U., 1962-63; D.Ed., Oreg. State U., 1972. Tchr. elem. schs., Oakridge and Portland, 1955-62; sch. adminstr. Lewis and Clark Sch., Astoria, Oreg., 1966-69; specialist for low achieving students Oreg. Dept. Edn., Salem, 1971—. Served with U.S. Army. Mem. Assn. for Supervision and Curriculum Devel., Am. Assn. Sch. Adminstrs., Am. Ednl. Research Assn., Phi Delta Kappa. Presbyterian. Home: 4585 Graber NE Salem OR 97305 Office: Oreg Dept Edn 700 Pringle Pkwy SE Salem OR 97310

EBERHARDT, LESTER LEE, quantitative ecologist; b. Valley City, N.D., Oct. 15, 1923; s. Lester W. and Gladys M. (Bonine) E.; m. Shirley L. Sage, Jan. 4, 1943; children: Laurie L., Lester E., Lynn R. BS, N.D. State U., 1947; PhD, Mich. State U., 1961; postgrad., U. Calif., Berkeley, 1961-62. Biometrician Mich. Dept. Conservation, Lansing, 1953-61; scientist Gen. Electric Co., Richland, Wash., 1962-65; sr. staff scientist Battelle Meml. Inst., Richland, 1965—. Contbr. numerous sci. articles to profl. jours. Fellow AAAS; mem. Am. Statis. Assn., Biometrics Soc., Ecol. Soc., Wildlife Soc., Sigma Xi. Home: 2528 W Klamath Kennewick WA 99336

EBERHART, HELEN ANN, psychotherapist; b. Follansbee, W.Va., Nov. 13, 1936; d. Sante and Piacenza America (Borghese) Trequatrini; m. James Gettins Eberhart, Aug. 16, 1958; children: Karen Ann, Brian James. Cert. dental hygiene, Ohio State U., 1956, BS in Edn., 1958; MSW, George Williams Coll., 1979. Lic. clin. social worker. Social worker Community Unit Sch. Dist. 200, Wheaton, Ill., 1979-81; psychotherapist Wholistic Health Ctr., Woodridge, Ill., 1980-82; med. social worker Meml. Hosp., Colorado Springs, Colo., 1982-84; pvt. practice as psychotherapist Colorado Springs, 1982—. Mem. Nat. Assn. Social Workers, Acad. Cert. Social Workers, Am. Assn. Marriage and Family Therapy, Colo. Soc. Clin. Social Work, El Paso County Psychol. Soc. Democrat. Roman Catholic. Avocations: tennis, hiking, swimming. Home: 6720 Northrim Ln Colorago Springs CO 80919 Office: Univ Office Park 1843 Austin Bluffs Pkwy Colorado Springs CO 80907

EBERL, DENNIS DONALD, research geologist; b. Buffalo, Sept. 1, 1943; s. Donald L. and Erma E. (Griswold) E.; m. Patricia Jo Buschman, Mar. 7, 1970; children: Karuna, Lucas. BA, Dartmouth Coll., 1965; PhD, Case Western Res. U., 1971. Asst. prof. No. Ill. U., DeKalb, 1974-75; from asst. prof. to assoc. prof. geology U. Ill., Urbana, 1975-81; project chief U.S. Geol. Survey, Denver, 1981—. Assoc. editor Clays and Clay Minerals, Jour. Sedimentary Petrology, Applied Clay Sci.; contbr. articles to profl. jours.; inventor slow release fertilizer. NSF grantee, 1975-80. Mem. Am. Chem. Soc., Clay Minerals Soc., Assn. Internat. pour l'Etude des Argiles. Club: Am. Alpine (N.Y.C.). Participant first ascent direct south face Mt. McKinley, 1967, first Am. ascent north face Matterhorn, 1968. Home: 6451 Kilimanjaro Dr Evergreen CO 80439 Office: US Geol Survey Federal Center MS404 Denver CO 80225

EBERLE, DONALD CRAMER, lawyer, governmental relations consultant; b. Balt., Dec. 29, 1948; s. William Cramer and Margaret Elizabeth (Mullaney) E.; m. Dr. Patricia Ann Poisson, Aug. 14, 1971. B.A., U. Colo., 1970, J.D., 1974; advanced studies Harvard, 1984. Bar: Colo., 1974. Asst. dean students U. Colo., Denver, 1970-72; dep. dist. atty., Denver, 1974-77; chief counsel Met. Econ. Crime Office, Denver, 1977-79; sr. appellate atty. Office of Denver Dist. Atty., 1979-80; state rep. Color. House of Reps., 1980-82; dir. legis. affairs gov. Colo., 1982-84; dir. external affairs MCI-West, Denver, 1984—; lectr. Colo. District Attys. Assn., 1978-80; vice chmn. State Bd. Equalization, 1985—; bd. dirs. Capitol Complex Commn., 1983-85, Denver Civic Ventures, 1985—, Colo. Dance Festival, 1986—. Mem. DRCOG Clean Air Task Force, Colo., 1980-82; mem. adv. com. on Crime Reclassification, Colo., 1981-83; bd. dirs. Capitol Hill Community Ctr., Denver, 1981-82. Harvard scholar Gates Found., 1984. Mem. ABA, Colo. Bar Assn., Nat. Dist. Attys. Assn., Colo. Dist. Attys. Assn. Democrat. Home: 379 Dahlia Denver CO 80220 Office: MCI West ARCO Towers Denver CO 80202

EBERT, JAMES IAN, consulting archaeologist; b. Washington, June 30, 1948; s. Ian Oleria and Doris Elizabeth (Fuller) E.; m. Eileen Lois Camilli, June 28, 1980. BA in Anthropology, Mich. State U., 1971; MA in Anthropology, U. N.Mex., 1977, PhD in Anthropology, 1986. Archaeologist Nat. Park Service, Dept. Interior, Albuquerque, 1972-82; pres. Ebert & Assocs., Albuquerque, 1983—; cons. forensics, devel. anthropology, remote sensing and archaeology, 1972—; spl. cons. N.Y. State Police Forensic Unit, 1985—; research assoc. Wash. State U., Pullman, 1983—, Tech. Applicatoins Ctr. NASA/U. N.Mex., Albuquerque. Contbr. numerous articles to profl. jours. Mem. Am. Anthropol. Assn., Am. Acad. Forensic Scis., Am. Soc. Photogrammetry and Remote Sensing (cert.), Soc. Am. Archaeology, Kalahari Peoples Fund. (pres. 1982—). Home and Office: 3100 9th St NW Albuquerque NM 87107

EBERT, ROBERT BALDWIN, video production company executive; b. Milw., Oct. 22, 1912; s. Walter R. and Elsie A. (Koepsel) E.; m. Charlotte King, Dec. 24, 1960; children: Anthony, Nancy, Michael, Timothy, Judith, Elisabeth. B in Engring., U. Wis., 1936. Registered profl. engr., Calif. Pres. Pacific Prodns., Honolulu, 1946—. Contbr. articles to profl. jours. Sec. bd. mgmt. Armed Forces YMCA, Honolulu, 1980—. Served with U.S. Army, 1944-46. Republican. Lutheran. Address: 700 Richards St #2710 Honolulu HI 96813

EBERWEIN, BARTON DOUGLAS, wood products company executive, consultant; b. Balt., Aug. 19, 1951; s. Bruce George and Thelma Joyce (Cox) E. BS, U. Oreg., 1974. Sales mgr. Teleprompter of Oreg., Eugene, 1974-75; pres., owner Oreg. Images, Eugene, 1975-80; mktg. mgr. Clearwater Productions, Eugene, 1980-82; sales mgr. Western Wood Structures, Portland, Oreg., 1982-84, mktg. coordinator, 1984-85, mktg. dir., 1985—; chmn. Forest Products Com., Portland, 1984—, Am. Inst. Timber Constrn., Denver, 1985—; cons. Dept. Econ. Devel., Oregon City, 1984—, Oreg. Forest Industry, Salem, 1985—. Editor: (jour.) Why Wood, 1984; prod. video Vault of Man, 1984. Bd. Dirs. N.W. Youth Corps, Eugene, 1984—; vol. Portland Marathon Com., 1984—, Portland Festival Arts, 1986—; vol. Clackamas County (Oreg.) Econ. Devel., 1985—. Recipient Johnny Horizen award U.S. Dept. Interior Bur. Land Mgmt., 1978; named Mktg. Firm of Yr., Portland C. of C., 1984. Mem. Soc. Mktg. Profl. Services, Am. Mktg. Assn., Constrn. Specifications Inst., Nat. League Cities, Internat. Assn. Bus. Communication. Democrat. Methodist. Clubs: Oreg. Road Runners, Trails End (Portland). Avocations: rare books, photography, outdoor recreation, architectural preservation. Home: PO Box 1014 Tualatin OR 97062 Office: Western Wood Structures 20675 SW 105th St Tualatin OR 97062

EBERWEIN, KENNETH MARTIN, infosystem executive; b. Topeka, Kans., Aug. 24, 1946; s. Leonard Rex and Pauline Claire (Vogel) E.; 1 child, Jason Neil. BS in Math., Washburn U., 1968. Mathematician Fleet Analysis Ctr. USN, Corona, Calif., 1968-72, lead, sr. programmer, 1972-75, staff engr., 1975-80, supr., 1980-85, project mgr., 1985—. Designer software system D.I.A.L., 1971, OA network D.I.S., 1984. Home: 2765 Wildcat Ln Riverside CA 92503 Office: USN Fleet Analysis Ctr Corona CA 91720-5000

EBINER, ROBERT MAURICE, lawyer; b. Los Angeles, Sept. 2, 1927; s. Maurice and Virginia (Grand) E.; m. Paula H. Van Sluyters, June 16, 1951; children—John, Lawrence, Marie, Michael, Christopher, Joseph, Francis, Matthew, Therese, Kathleen, Eileen, Brian, Patricia, Elizabeth, Ann. J.D., Loyola U., Los Angeles, 1953. Bar: Calif. 1954, U.S. dist. ct. (cen. dist.) Calif. 1954. Solo practice, West Covina, Calif., 1954—; judge pro tem Los Angeles Superior Ct., 1964-66, arbitrator, 1979—; judge pro tem Citrus Mcpl. Ct., 1966-70; instr. law Alhambra Evening High Sch., 1955-58; mem. disciplinary hearing panel Calif. State Bar, 1968-75. Bd. dirs. West Covina United Fund, 1958-61, chmn. budget com. 1960-61; organizer Joint United Funds East San Gabriel Valley, 1961, bd. dirs. 1961-68; bd. dirs. San Gabriel Valley Cath. Social Services, 1969—, pres., 1969-72; bd. dirs. Region II Cath. Social Service, 1970—, pres. 1970-74; trustee Los Angeles Cath. Welfare Bur. (now Cath. Charities), 1978—; charter bd. dirs. East San Gabriel Valley Hot Line, 1969-74, sec., 1969-72; charter bd. dirs. N.E. Los Angeles County unit Am. Cancer Soc., 1973-78, chmn. by-laws com. 1973-78; bd. dirs. Queen of the Valley Hosp. Found., 1983—, West Covina Hist. Soc., 1982—; active Calif. State Democratic Central Com., 1963-68. Served with AUS, 1945-47. Recipient Los Angeles County Human Relations Commn. Disting. Service award, 1978; named West Covina Citizen of Yr., 1986. Mem. ABA, Calif. Bar Assn., Los Angeles County Bar Assn., Fed. Ct. So. Dist. Calif. Assn., Los Angeles Trial Lawyers Assn., Eastern Bar Assn. Los Angeles County (pres. Pomona Valley 1965-66), West Covina C. of C. (pres. 1960), Am. Arbitration Assn. Clubs: K.C., Bishop Amat High Sch. Booster (bd. dirs. 1973—, pres. 1978-80), Kiwanis (charter West Covina, pres. 1976-77, lt. gov. div. 35 1980-81, Kiwanian of Yr. 1978, 82, Disting. Lt. Gov. 1980-81, bd.dirs. Calif., Nev. and Hawaii Internat. Found. 1986—). Office: 1502 W Covina Pkwy West Covina CA 91790

EBY, FRANK SHILLING, research scientist; b. Kansas City, Mo., Apr. 6, 1924; s. Frank Shilling and Irene (Trissler) E.; m. Nancy Rea Vinsonhaler, Sept. 2, 1958; children: Elizabeth, Susan, Carl. BS, U. Ill., 1948, MS, 1949, PhD, 1954. Group leader fusion research Lawrence Livermore (Calif.) Nat. Lab., 1954-58, group leader, 1958-66, div. head, 1967-72, sr. scientist, 1973—. Inventor classified mil. weaponry. Served to 1st lt. USAAF, 1942-46, PTO. Mem. AAAS. Avocations: hiking, camping, gardening, music. Home: 27 Castlewood Dr Pleasanton CA 94566 Office: Lawrence Livermore Nat Lab Dept Spl Projects Livermore CA 94550

ECCLES, SPENCER FOX, banker; b. Ogden, Utah, Aug. 24, 1934; s. Spencer Stoddard and Hope (Fox) E.; m. Cleone Emily Peterson, July 21, 1958; children: Clista Hope, Lisa Ellen, Katherine Ann, Spencer Peterson. B.S., U. Utah, 1956; M.A., Columbia U., 1959. Trainee First Nat. City Bank, N.Y.C., 1959-60; with First Security Bank of Utah, Salt Lake City, 1960-61, First Security Bank of Idaho, Boise, 1961-70; exec. v.p. First Security Corp. Salt Lake City, 1970-75, pres., 1975—, chief operating officer, 1980-82, chmn. bd., chief exec. officer, 1982—, also dir.; dir. Union Pacific Corp., Amalgamated Sugar Co., Anderson Lumber Co., Zions Corp., Merc. Instn., Aubrey G. Lanston & Co., Inc.; mem. adv. council U. Utah Bus. Coll. Served to 1st lt. U.S. Army. Mem. Am. Bankers Assn., Assn. Bank Holding Cos., Assn. Res. City Bankers, Young Pres. Orgn. Clubs: Salt Lake Country, Alta, Arid. Office: First Security Corp 79 S Main St PO Box 30006 Salt Lake City UT 84125 •

ECHOLS, THOMAS JOHN, geologist; b. Washington, Aug. 1, 1958; s. William Edward and Rosemary Anne (Gilleeny) E. B.S., Tulane U., 1980. Geol. field asst. U.S. Geol. Survey, Menlo Park, Calif., 1981-82; geologist Calif. Energy Co., Santa Rosa, Calif., 1982—. Mem. Geol. Soc. Am., Am. Geophys. Union, Geothermal Resources Council, Sigma Gamma Epsilon. Home: 1106 Linden St Apt 204 Riverside CA 92507 Office: Calif Energy Co 3333 Mendocino Ave Santa Rosa CA 95401

ECK, CHARLES PAUL, chemist, educator; b. Morristown, N.J., July 15, 1956; s. John Clifford and Helen A. (Behrendt) E.; m. Alice Anne Whittaker, Jan. 2, 1982. BA, Johns Hopkins U., 1978; MS, U. Ariz., 1983, postgrad., 1983—. Pilot plant technician McCormick & Co., Inc., Balt., 1978-80; assoc. faculty mem. Pima Community Coll., Tucson, 1985—. Mem. AAAS, Am. Chem. Soc., Am. Inst. Chemists, N.Y. Acad. Scis. Republican. Evangelical. Avocations: choral and vocal performance, lapidary, photography, skiing. Office: U Ariz Dept Chemistry Tucson AZ 85721

ECK, DOROTHY FRITZ, state senator; b. Sequim, Wash., Jan. 23, 1924; d. Ira Edward and Ida (Hokanson) Fritz; B.S. in Secondary Edn., Mont. State U., 1961, M.S. in Applied Sci., 1966; m. Hugo Eck, Dec. 16, 1942; children—Lauvrence, Diana. Co-mgr. archtl. and property mgmt. bus., 1955—; conf. coordinator Am. Agrl. Econs. Assn., 1967-68; state-local coordinator Office of Gov. Mont., Helena, 1972-77; mem. Mont. State Senate, 1981—; mem. Mont. Environ. Quality Council, 1981—. Bd. dirs. Methodist Youth Fellowship, 1960-64, Mont. Council for Effective Legislature, 1977-78, Rocky Mountain Environ. Council, 1982—; del., Western v.p. Mont. Constl. Conv., 1971-72; chmn. Gov.'s Task Force on Citizen Participation, 1976-77; mem. adv. com. No. Rockies Resource and Tng. Center (now No. Lights Inst.), 1979-81. Recipient Outstanding Alumna award Mont. State U., 1981. Mem. LWV (state pres. 1967-70), Common Cause, Nat. Women's Polit. Caucus. Democrat. Office: Mont Senate Helena MT 59620 *

ECKARD, CECIL ORAIN, statistician, consultant; b. Middletown, Md., Nov. 5, 1927; s. Amidee Edward and Olive Elizabeth (Guyton) E.; m. Marilyn Faye Williams, Mar. 31, 1951; children: Donald Alan, Bruce Michael. BA, Bridgewater Coll., 1948; MEA, U. Utah, 1973. Phys. chemist Dept. of the Army, Frederick, Md., 1948-52, research mathematician, 1952-62; math. statistician Dept. of the Army, Ft. Douglas, Utah, 1962-69; phys. scientist Dept. of the Army, Dugway, Utah, 1969-84; sr. scientist Andrulis Research Corp., Salt Lake City, 1984—. Mem. advancement com. Boy Scouts Am., Md. and Utah. Mem. Am. Statistical Assn., Sigma Xi. Home: 1136 Wales Pl Cardiff by the Sea CA 92007 Office: Andrulis Research Corp 35 Hempstead Way Salt Lake City UT 84113

ECKARDT, ROBERT E(DWARD), toxicologist, consultant; b. Fanwood, N.J., May 1, 1916; s. Emil and Florence (Archer) E.; m. Mary Lenore Harvey, July 1, 1950 (dec. July 1965); children: Robert E. Jr., Nancy Jean; m. Elvira Berry, Aug. 30, 1965; children: Carol Donahue. BS, Antioch Coll., 1937; MS, Case Western Res. U., 1939, PhD, 1940, MD, 1943. Diplomate Am. Bd. Internal Medicine, Am. Bd. Preventive Medicine. Intern Cornell U. Hosp., N.Y.C., 1943-44, resident, 1947-48; spl. research physician Standard Oil Co. of N.J., N.Y.C., 1948-51; dir. med. research div. Exxon Research and Engring. Co., Linden, N.J., 1951-74; dir. research and environ. health div., assoc. med. dir. Exxon Corp., Linden, 1974-78; practice medicine specializing in toxicology Scottsdale, Ariz., 1981—; assoc. clin. prof. medicine Cornell U., 1943-78; clin. assoc. prof. environ. health NYU, 1948-78. Author: Industrial Carcinogens, 1959; editor Jour. Occupational Medicine, 1978. Served to maj. AUS, 1944-47. Named Disting. Fellow Toxicology Forum, 1986; recipient Knudsen award Am. Occupational Medicine Assn., 1965, Robert A. Kehoe award Am. Acad. Occupational Medicine, 1978. Home and Office: 6720 E Kelton Ln Scottsdale AZ 85254

ECKER, DONALD NESS, accountant; b. Gettysburg, Pa.. Mng. ptnr. Ernst & Whinney, Riverside, Calif., 1978-82, dir. physician services, 1982—. Mem. Estate Planning Council, Riverside County; chmn. edn. com. Inland Empire Young Pres.'s Orgn., pres., 1987; pres. Riverside Area United Way, 1984-85; co-founder Riverside County 2% and 5% Club, chmn. bd. dirs. 1985-86; original organizer Keep Riverside Ahead, gen. campaign chmn.; mem. World Affairs Council, Monday Morning Group. Recipient United Way Vol. of Yr. award, 1985, Chamber Vol. of Yr. award, 1985. Mem. Am. Inst. CPA's, Calif. Soc. CPA's (state bd. dirs.), Citrus Belt Chpt. CPA's (pres. 1985), Med. Group Mgmt. Assn., Am. Group Practice Assn, Greater Riverside C. of C. (pres.-elect 1985, pres. 1986), Los Angeles C. of C. (bd. dirs.). Office: Ernst & Whinney 3750 University Ave Suite 600 PO Box 1270 Riverside CA 92502-1270

ECKERSLEY, NORMAN CHADWICK, banker; b. Glasgow, Scotland, June 18, 1924; s. James Norman and Beatrice (Chadwick) E.; m. Rosemary J. Peters, May 23, 1986, 1 child, Anne. With Chartered Bank, London and Manchester, 1947-48; acct., Bombay, 1948-52, Singapore, 1952-54, Sarawak, 1954-56, Pakistan, 1956-58, Calcutta, 1958-59, Hong Kong, 1959-60, asst. mgr. Hamburg, 1960-62, mgr. Calcutta, 1962-67, Thailand, 1967-69; pres. Chartered Bank London, San Francisco, 1964-74, chmn., chief exec., 1974-79; chmn. Standard Chartered Bancorp, San Francisco, 1978-81; dep. chmn. Union Bank, Los Angeles, 1979-82; chmn., chief exec. officer The Pacific Bank, San Francisco, 1982—. Served with RAF, 1940-46. Decorated D.F.C.; comdr. Order Brit. Empire. Mem. Overseas Banks Assn. Calif. (chmn. 1972-74), Calif. Council Internat. Trade, San Francisco C. of C., World Trade Assn., World Trade Club. Mem. Ch. of Scotland. Clubs: Royal and Ancient, Royal Troon Golf (Scotland); San Francisco Golf, Pacific Union (San Francisco). Home: 401 El Cerrito Hillsborough CA 94010 Office: Pacific Bank 351 California St San Francisco CA 94104

ECKHARDT, JOHN ROBERT, water resources engineer, civil engineer; b. Greeley, Colo., Sept. 21, 1948; s. Robert Arthur and Elsie Pearl (Miller) E.; m. Trudy Christine Pritchard, June 21, 1969; children—Heidi Lynn, Heather Johnn. B.S. in Civil Engring. with high distinction, Colo. State U., 1970, M.S. in Civil Engring., 1976, postgrad. Colo. State U. Registered profl. engr., Colo. Design engr. Standard Oil Co. Calif., San Francisco, 1970-71; design, resident, project engr. NHPQ, Greeley, 1971-74; water resources engr. Engrs. Office, State of Colo., Denver, 1976; with No. Colo. Water Conservancy Dist., Loveland, 1976—, div. head engring. and computer services, 1980-85, dept. head, ops., scheduling and forecasting, 1985—; guest lectr. in field; life mem. U.S. Com. on Irrigation, Drainage and Flood Control. Contbr. articles to profl. jours. Edward B. House scholar Colo. State U., 1969. Mem. ASCE (vice chmn . conveyance and distbn. com. Irrigation and Drainage div.), Am. Water Works Assn., Kappa Mu Epsilon, Chi Epsilon, Sigma Tau, Phi Kappa Phi. Lutheran. Club: Loveland Swim. Home: 1637 Pinyon Ct Loveland CO 80538 Office: No Colo Water Conservancy Dist PO Box 679 Loveland CO 80537

ECKHARDT, WILLIAM BOYDEN, credit union executive; b. Bellefonte, Pa., Aug. 31, 1949; s. Boyden and Maxine Alice (Young) E.; BBA, Oreg. State U., 1971. Adminstrv. officer Alaska U.S.A. Fed. Credit Union, Anchorage, 1971-72, ops. mgr., 1972-74, asst. gen. mgr., 1974-79, pres., 1979—; chmn. bd. Alaska USA Ins., Inc., 1986—; chmn. Alaska Option Services Corp.; dir. Alaska League Services Corp. Mem. Credit Union Execs. Soc. (pres. Alaska council 1975—), Alaska Credit Union League (pres. Anchorage chpt. 1979-81), Credit Union Nat. Assn. (dir.). Club: Elks. Home: 12850 Ben Ct Anchorage AK 99515 Office: Mail Pouch 6613 4000 Credit Union Dr Anchorage AK 99502

EDDE, HOWARD JASPER, engineering executive; b. Page City, Kans., Dec. 14, 1937; s. Gilbert Herman and Jennie (Foulke) E.; m. Marilyn Ann Scheleen, Sept. 5, 1961; children: Michael, Heather, Sonja. BS, Kans. State U., 1959; MS, U. Kans., 1961; PhD, U. Tex., 1967. Registered profl. engr., Wash., Tex., N.C., Va., Md., Pa., Alaska, B.C.; diplomate Am. Acad. Environ. Engrs. Project engr. State of Kans. Dept. Highways, Topeka, 1959-60, Nat. Council Paper Industry for Air and Steam Improvement, Baton Rouge, La., 1961-64; regional engr. Nat. Council Paper Industry for Air and Steam Improvement, Balt., 1967-70; project engr. Roy F. Weston Co., West Chester, Pa., 1966-67; v.p. EKONO OY, Helsinki, Finland, 1970-74; pres. Howard Edde, Inc., Redmond, Wash., 1974—; affiliate prof. U. Wash., Seattle, 1972—; lectr. Johns Hopkins U., Balt., 1967-70, numerous other speaking engagements. Author: Environmental Control for Pulp and Paper Mills, 1984; contbr. over 50 articles on energy conservation and environ. control to profl. jours. Fellow ASCE (various coms.); mem. TAPPI (chmn. wastewater treatment com. 1978-81, process energy use subcom. 1984), Water Pollution Control Fedn. (program chmn. 1981-84, session mgr. 1984). Republican. Lutheran. Club: Neptune Sailing (Kirkland, Wash.) (pres. 1979-80). Avocations: skiing, sailing. Home: 3001 164th Pl NE Bellevue WA 98008 Office: 15436 NE Bell-Red Rd Redmond WA 98052

EDDY, FRANK WARREN, anthropology educator; b. Roanoke, Va., May 7, 1930; s. Frank D. and Mamie Dunn (Mosher) E.; m. Edna Lobato, Apr. 1963 (div. Aug. 1974); 1 child, Frank. BA, U. N.Mex., 1952; MA, U. Ariz., 1958; PhD, U. Colo., 1968. Curator Mus. N.Mex., Santa Fe, 1958-65; research asst. U. Colo. Mus., Boulder, 1965-68; assoc. dir. Tex. Archaeol. Salvage Project U. Tex., Austin, 1968-69; asst. prof. anthropology U. Colo., Boulder, 1970-74, assoc. prof., 1974—. Author: Archaeology: A cultural-evolutionary approach, 1984; contbr. articles, monographs, abstracts to profl. publs. Served as cpl. U.S. Army, 1952-54. Grantee Comins Fund, U. Ariz., 1958, Council on Research and Creative Work, 1972, NEH, 1985. Mem. Soc. Am. Archaeology (com. pub. archaeology 1973-76, state coordinator Colo. 1978-79), Am. Quaternary Assn., Colo. Archaeol. Soc. (exec. sec. 1971-74, adv. com. Office State Archaeologist 1973-74, 80-82), Colo. Council Profl. Archaeologists (v.p. 1979, pres. 1980, exec. com. 1981). Democrat. Episcopalian. Avocations: hiking, swimming, cross country skiing. Home: 3443 Cripple Creek Sq Boulder CO 80303 Office: U Colo Dept Anthropology Boulder CO 80309

EDDY, LOWELL PERRY, retired research chemistry educator; b. Portland, Oreg., Nov. 25, 1920; s. Delmar and Anna Belle (Weisenborn) E.; m. M. Caroline Wall, Jan. 13, 1946; children: Candice M., Kati J., Lowell Stacy. BS, Oreg. State U., 1942, MS, 1947; PhD, Purdue U., 1952. Instr. chemistry U. Wyo., Laramie, 1950-51; research assoc. Reed Coll., Portland, 1951, instr., 1951-53; research chemist Puget Sound Pulp and Timber Co., Bellingham, Wash., 1953-57; from instr. to assoc. prof. chemistry Western Wash. U., Bellingham, 1957-85, ret., 1986; vis. assoc. prof. U. New South Wales, Sydney, Austrialia, 1975; hon. research asst. U. Coll. London, 1964. Contbr. articles to profl. jours. Served to 1st lt. inf. U.S. Army, 1942-46. Mem. Am. Chem. Soc., Sigma Xi. Republican. Mem. Christian Ch. Lodge: Kiwanis (pres. Bellingham club 1980-81). Home: 206 N Garden St Bellingham WA 98225 Office: We Wash U Chemistry Dept Bellingham WA 98225

EDELMAN, LORI ANN, programmer/analyst; b. Ventura, Calif., Feb. 16, 1959; d. Hy and Bernice (Eisenstein) Canter; m. Michael James Edelman, May 1, 1983; 1 child, Brandon Jacob. BS, Calif. Poly. State U., 1982. Asst. programmer Fed. Systems div. IBM Corp., Westlake village, Calif., 1982-83; software engr. Tektronix, Inc., Beaverton, Oreg., 1983-86, programmer/analyst, 1986—. Recipient Acad. Excellence award Atlantic Richfield Co., 1981, Gold Seal Calif. Scholarship Fedn., 1977; scholar J.W. Van Dyke Meml. Atlantic Richfield Co., 1980, 81, Clyde P. Fischer Calif. Poly. State U., 1979. Mem. Math. Assn. Am., Calif. Poly. State U. Alumni Assn., Phi Kappa Phi, Kappa Mu Epsilon. Home: 14035 SW Maverick Ct Beaverton OR 97005 Office: Tektronix Inc PO Box 500 Beaverton OR 97077

EDELSON, ANDREW CHARLES, aerospace program executive; b. Chgo., Apr. 23, 1946; s. Mark and Ricalin (Waller) Edelson; m. Joyce Francine Simpson, Dec. 18, 1977. BSEE, UCLA, 1968. Pres. Acetronics, Los Angeles, 1969-77; sr. staff engr. Lear Sieglar, Santa Monica, Calif., 1977-80; program mgr. Teledyne Controls, Los Angeles, 1981—; cons. Air Force Logistics Ctr., San Antonio, 1985—. Inventor, patentee in field. Mem. Am. Def. Preparedness Assn. (Mgmt. award Gavel 1984-85), Teledyne Mgmt. Club (pres., 1984-85, v.p. 1986), Teleco Club (pres. 1986). Democrat. Jewish. Avocations: exotic cars, organist, dancing, theater, competitive target shooting. Home: 5035 Overland Ave Culver City CA 90230 Office: Teledyne Controls 12333 W Olympic Blvd Los Angeles CA 90230

EDELSTEIN, ROSE MARIE, nurse educator, consultant; b. Drake, N.D., Mar. 3, 1935; d. Francis Jerome and Myrtle Josephine (Merbach) Hublou; m. Harry George Edelstein, June 22, 1957; children—Julie, Lori, Lynn, Toni Anne. B.S. in Nursing, St. Teresa's Coll., 1956; M.A. in Edn., Holy Names Coll., 1977; Ed.D., U. San Francisco, 1982; postgrad. U. Ariz., 1985—; cert. public health nurse U. Calif., Berkeley, 1972. Dir., clin. supr. San Francisco Sch. for Health Professions, 1971-74, Rancho Arroyo Sch. of Vocat. Nursing, Sacramento, 1974-75; intensive care nurse Kaiser-Permanente Hosp., San Rafael, Calif., 1976-77; dir. inservice edn. Ross Hosp., Calif., 1977-78; assoc. dir. nursing, nursing edn. St. Francis Meml. Hosp., San Francisco, 1978—; med.-legal cons.; instr. CPR. Served to lt. col. USAR Med. Res. Mem. Calif. Nurses Assn., Am. Heart Assn., Sigma Theta Tau. Roman Catholic. Author: (with Jane F. Lee) Acupuncture Atlas, 1974; The Influence of Motivator and Hygiene Factors in Job Changes by Graduate Registered Nurses, 1977; Effects of Two Educational Methods Upon Retention of Knowledge in Pharmacology, 1981. Home: PO Box 696 Ross CA 94957

EDELSTEIN, STEPHANIE CORINNE, academic administrator; b. Wilmington, Del., Sept. 13, 1945; d. William Boyd Bush and Joy Ruth (Coleman) Dwyer; m. Garland Lloyd Caughran, Apr. 16, 1966 (dec. Apr. 1970); 1 child, Sean Garland; m. Mark Gerson Edelstein, Jan. 29, 1982. RN, St. Joseph's Hosp. Sch. Nursing, Phoenix, 1966; AA, San Diego City Coll., 1984; cert. emergency nurse, U. Calif., San Diego, 1978; student, St. Joseph's Coll., Windham, Maine. RN St. Joseph's Hosp., Phoenix, 1966, Palomar Hosp., Escondido, Calif., 1966-67, Rees-Stealy Med. Clinic, San Diego, 1967-69, Bernalillo County Med. Ctr., Albuquerque, 1971-72, R. Hecker DDS, La Jolla, Calif., 1975-77, Scripps Meml. Hosp., Encinitas, Calif., 1977-83; owner, dir. North County Med. Edn., San Diego, 1982—; cons. Grossmont Hosp., San Diego, 1986. Mem. Emergency Nurses Assn., Com. Quality in Edn. Democrat. Avocations: reading, skiing, gardening, cooking, entertaining. Office: North County Med Edn 1117 Santa Luisa Solana Beach CA 92075

EDEN, RAYMOND LER, assn. exec.; b. Lee, Ill., July 19, 1925; s. S. Bennie and Hannah (Edwards) E.; B.S., No. Ill. U., 1950 with high honors; postgrad. Northwestern U., 1950, N.Y. U., 1955, U. Chgo., 1961, U. So. Calif., 1973; m. Ellen M. Mercer, Aug. 17, 1945; 1 son, Steven M. Exec. sec. Crippled Children's Center, Peoria, Ill., 1953-59; exec. dir. Crippled Children's Service, Milw., 1959-62, Ill. Heart Assn., Springfield, 1962-66, Calif. Heart Assn., San Francisco, 1966-69; adminstr. San Mateo (Calif.) Med. Clinic, 1969-70; exec. v.p. Am. Heart Assn., Los Angeles, 1970-86; assoc. dean adminstrn. UCLA Sch. Medicine, 1986—. Chmn. objectives com. Calif. Regional Med. Program, 1968-73; v.p. Comprehensive Health Planning Agy., 1973-75; bd. dirs. UCLA Unicamp, 1974-76, Comprehensive Health Planning Council of Los Angeles County, 1975-77; mem. adv. com. UCLA Profl. Designation program for Voluntary Agy. Execs., 1972-74; faculty Center for Non-Profit Mgmt., 1978-82; pres. Council on Vol. Health Agys., Los Angeles, 1976-79, Los Angeles CPR Consortium, 1979-81; mem. Cardiac Care com. State of Calif., 1980-83; treas., chmn. fin. com. Little Co. of Mary Hosp., Torrance, 1977-81; chmn. South Bay (Los Angeles) Com. for Pres. Ford, 1976; mem. Atty. Gen.'s Task Force on Solicitations, 1977; chmn. Younger for Gov. Com., South Bay, 1978; chmn. bd. trustees Neighborhood Ch., Palos Verdes Estates, Calif., 1975; mem. Claremont Grad. Sch. Exec. Program adv. council, 1979-82; mem. clean air com., Los Angeles Area C. of C., 1980-82. Served with U.S. Army, 1944-46. Decorated Purple Heart, Bronze Star. Soc. Heart Assn. Profl. Staff fellow, 1980-81, 82-83; Alpha Gamma Delta Fellow award, 1955. Mem. Soc. Heart Assn. Profl. Staff (pres. 1981-82), Nat. Assn. Social Workers, Acad. Cert. Social Workers, So. Calif. Assn. Execs., Los Angeles Area C. of C., Sigma Alpha Eta. Republican. Clubs: Rotary, California, Masons, Shriners. Home: 9961 Durant Dr Beverly Hills CA 90212 Office: UCLA Sch Medicine 12-138 CHS Los Angeles CA 90024

EDENS, GARY DENTON, broadcast company executive; b. Asheville, N.C., Jan. 6, 1942; s. James Edwin and Pauline Amanda (New) E.; m. Hannah Suellen Walter, Aug. 21, 1965; children—Ashley Elizabeth, Emily Blair. B.S., U. N.C., 1964. Account exec. PAMS Prodns., Dallas, 1965-67; account exec. Sta. WKIX, Raleigh, N.C., 1967-69; gen. mgr. Sta. KOY, Phoenix, 1970-81; sr. v.p. Harte-Hanks Radio, Inc., Phoenix, 1978-81, pres., chief exec. officer, 1981-86; chmn., pres. Edens Broadcasting, Inc.; dir. Gt. Western Bank & Trust Ariz., 1975-86, Citibank Ariz., 1986—. Bd. dirs. Valley Big Bros., 1972-80, Ariz. State U. Found., 1979—, COMPAS, 1979—, Men's Arts Council, 1975-78. Named One of Three Outstanding Young Men, Phoenix Jaycees, 1973. Mem. Phoenix Execs. Club (pres. 1976), Nat. Radio Broadcasters Assn. (dir. 1981—), Radio Advt. Bur. (dir. 1981—), Young Pres.'s Orgn. Republican. Methodist. Clubs: Phoenix Country, Univ. Phoenix. Office: 840 N Central Ave Phoenix AZ 85004

EDGAR, BRUCE CHARLES, aerospace engineer; b. Bartlesville, Okla., July 25, 1942; s. Maurice Russell and Natalie (Flynn) E.; m. Nancy Gale Raymond, Aug. 24, 1968; children: Timothy, William. BSEE, Okla. State U., 1964, MSEE, 1965; PhDEE, Stanford U., 1972. Research asst. Stanford (Calif.) Electronic Labs., 1965-72; postdoctoral research assoc. U. Fla., Gainesville, 1972-74; mem. tech. staff Aerospace Corp., El Segundo, Calif., 1974—. Contbg. editor Speaker Builder mag., 1980—; contbr. articles to profl. jours. Active local Boy Scouts Am. Mem. Am. Geophys. Union, Audio Engring. Soc. Democrat. Presbyterian. Avocation: cycling. Office: Aerospace Corp PO Box 92957 Los Angeles CA 90009

EDGAR, BRYAN CYRUS, dentist; b. Kamloops, B.C., Can., Apr. 19, 1950; came to U.S., 1957, naturalized, 1968; s. Arthur Osmund and Laura Belle (Lapsley) E.; m. Linda Carol Johansen, June 23, 1973; 1 child, David. BS with distinction in Zoology, U. Wash., 1972, DDS, 1976. Gen. practice resident Irwin Army Hosp., Ft. Riley, Kans., 1976-77; dentist Madigan Army Med. Ctr., 1977-80; pvt. practice dentistry, Federal Way, Wash., 1979-81; pres. Bryan C. Edgar, D.D.S., P.S., Federal Way, 1981—; bus. and entrepreneurship cons.; owner Profl. Devel. Systems. Served with Dental Corps, U.S. Army, 1976-80, USAR, 1980—. Mem. ADA, Bible Study Fellowship, Acad. Gen. Dentistry (fellow 1984), Seattle-King County Dental Soc., Wash. State Dental Assn. Office: 32114 1st Ave S Suite 200 Federal Way WA 98003

EDGAR, JAMES MACMILLAN, JR., management consultant; b. N.Y.C., Nov. 7, 1936; s. James Macmillan Edgar and Lilyan (McCann) E.; B. Chem. Engring., Cornell U., 1959, M.B.A. with distinction, 1960; m. Judith Frances Storey, June 28, 1958; children—Suzanne Lynn, James Macmillan, Gordon Stuart. New product rep. E.I. duPont Nemours, Wilmington, Del., 1960-63, mktg. services rep., 1963-64; with Touche Ross & Co., 1964-78, mgr., Detroit, 1966-68, partner, 1968-71, partner in charge, mgmt. services ops. for No. Calif. and Hawaii, San Francisco, 1971-78, partner Western regional mgmt. services, 1978; prin. Edgar, Dunn & Conover, Inc., San Francisco, 1978—; mem. San Francisco Mayor's Fin. Adv. Com., 1976—, mem. exec. com., 1978—, Blue Ribbon com. for Bus., 1987—; mem. Alumnae Resources adv. bd., 1986—, mem. San Francisco Planning and Urban Research Bd., 1986—; mem. alumni exec. council Johnson Grad. Sch. Mgmt. Cornell U., 1985—, Cornell Council. Recipient Award of Merit for outstanding pub. service City and County of San Francisco, 1978; Honor award for outstanding contbns. to profl. mgmt. Johnson Grad. Sch. Mgmt., Cornell U., 1978. CPA, cert. mgmt. cons. Mem. Assn. Corp. Growth (v.p. membership San Francisco chpt. 1979-81, v.p. programs 1981-82, pres. 1982-83, nat. bd. dirs. 1983-86), Am. Inst. C.P.A.s, Calif. Soc. C.P.A.s, Am. Mktg. Assn., Inst. Mgmt. Cons. (regional v.p. 1973-80, dir. 1975-77, bd. v.p. 1977-80), Tau Beta Pi. Clubs: Univ., Commonwealth of San Francisco, Marin Rod and Gun. Patentee nonwoven fabrics. Home: 10 Buckeye Way Kentfield CA 94904 Office: Edgar Dunn & Conover Inc 847 Sansome St San Francisco CA 94111

EDGERTON, ROBERT B., construction company executive; b. Silverton, Oreg., Oct. 23, 1953; s. Robert R. and Marylou A. (Billings) E.; m. Janene Edgerton, June 18, 1977; children: Lisa Marie, Andrea Lee. BS, Oreg. State U., 1976. Mgr. quality control Riverbend Sand and Gravel Co., Salem, Oreg., 1976-80; mgr. constrn. CH2M Hill, Bellevue, Wash., 1980-86; cost and schedule mgr.Capital Products Office Edmonds Sch. Dist. #15, Lynnwood, Wash., 1986—. Mem. Am. Assn. Cost Engrs. (pres. Oreg. chpt. 1983-84, v.p. Seattle chpt. 1986—, nat. subcom. chmn. telecommunications 1986—), Project Mgmt. Inst., Am. Inst. Constructors (assoc.). Republican. Methodist. Office: Edmonds Sch Dist #15 3800 196th St SW Lynnwood WA 98039-5789

EDGETT, STEVEN DENNIS, transportation consultant; b. Indpls., June 3, 1948; s. Robert Neil and Elizabeth Catherine (Hatch) E.; m. Catherine Ann Bartel, June 19, 1971; children: Jeffrey Steven, Christopher Steven. Student, N.Mex. State U., 1965-68, U. Cin., 1968-69, Grossmont Coll., 1972-74, San Diego State U., 1974-75. Lead designer U.S. Elevator Corp., Spring Valley, Calif., 1970-76; safety engr. State of Calif., San Diego, 1976-78; assoc. Skidmore, Owings & Merrill, San Francisco, 1978-86; pres. Edgett Williams Cons. Group Inc., Mill Valley, Calif., 1986—. Mem. Constrn. Specifications Inst. Home: 541 Shasta Way Mill Valley CA 94941 Office: Edgett Williams Cons Group Inc 100 Shoreline Hwy Mill Valley CA 94941

EDISON TAK-BUN, LIU, physician, molecular biologist; b. Hong Kong, Feb. 9, 1952; s. Shih Chiu and Grace (Tam) L.; married; 1 child, Ashton. BS, Stanford U., 1973, MD, 1978. Cert. Am. Bd. Internal Medicine. Fellow Damon Runyon Cancer Fund, 1983-85; instr. Cancer Research Inst., San Francisco, 1985—, Hooper Found., San Francisco, 1985—. Recipient Clin. Investigator award Nat. Cancer Inst., 1985. Mem. Am. Fedn. Clin. Research. Avocation: music. Office: U Calif San Francisco M 1282 Cancer Research Inst Parnassus Ave San Francisco CA 94143

EDLIN, RAY LAWAYNE, real estate consultant and instructor; b. Nara Visa, N.Mex., Apr. 16, 1930; s. George William and Dorothy Evelyn (Gragg) E.; m. Barbara Ann Dalcero, Mar. 17, 1953 (dec. June 1957); m. Jean Ewing Duff, Aug. 4, 1959; children: Jane, Peter, Suzanne, Guy. BSc, Calif. Poly State U., San Luis Obispo, 1951; MSc, Rutgers U., 1961, PhD, 1962. Research fellow Rutgers U., New Brunswick, N.J., 1958-62; sr. chemist Kelco Co., San Diego, Calif., 1962-68; tech. dir., mgr. ops. Gentry Internat., Gilroy, Calif., 1968-70; dir. quality control Foodmaker Corp., San Diego, 1970; instr. Rutgers U. and U. Calif. San Diego, 1959—; prin. Edlin Realty, San Diego, 1970—; bd. dirs. Calif. Bd. Realtors; instr. San Diego Bd. Realtors, 1978—; cons. Contbr. articles to profl. jours; patentee in field. Rep. precinct worker, Poway, Calif., 1966-68; mem. sch. bd. Poway Sch. Dist., 1966-68; vol. La Jolla (Calif.) Cancer Soc., 1984-86, sr. citizens orgns., San Diego, 1978—. Served as sgt. U.S. Army, 1954-57. Mem. Nat. Assn. Realtors, Calif. Assn. Realtors, Nat. Council Exchangors (bd. dirs. 1978-79, cert.), Certified Exchangors (bd. dirs. 1983—, v.p. 1985—, plaque 1985-86), San Diego Problem Solvers (pres. 1978-79, plaque 1978-79). Club: Toastmasters (pres. Escondido chpt. 1966-68). Lodges: Kiwanis (v.p. local chpt. 1967), Elks. Avocations: reading, traveling, swimming, woodworking, walking. Office: Edlin Realty PO Box 99938 San Diego CA 92109

EDLUND, MELVIN COLLINS, retired chemist; b. Renovo, Pa., Mar. 9, 1919; s. Ivar and Louise (Holtz) E.; m. Barbara Jean Coiteux, Apr. 27, 1956; children: Thomas Ivar, David John. BS, U. Calif., Berkeley, 1952; postgrad., Oak Ridge Inst. Nuclear Studies, 1967. Research chemist Fibrebd. Research Div., Antioch, Calif., 1952-57; chemist Continental Chem. Co., Sacramento, 1957-59; chemist, supr. pub. health lab. State Calif., Berkeley, 1959-67; pub. health physicist charge radiol. environ. surveillance State Kans., Topeka, 1967-68; air pollution chemist Humboldt Co., Eureka, Calif., 1969-70; agrl. chemist State Calif., Sacramento, 1970-79; pesticide registration chemist Calif. Dept. Food and Agrl., Sacramento, 1979-81. Contbr. articles to profl. jours.; patentee in field. Mem. North Coast Region of State of Calif. Regional Water Quality Control Bd., 1983—; com. chmn. instl. rep., treas. Golden Empire council Boy Scouts Am., 1971—. Served with M.C., AUS, 1944-45, ETO. Decorated Bronze Star. Fellow Am. Inst. Chemists; mem. Am. Chem. Soc. (ret. status). Lutheran (past deacon). Lodges: Vasa Order Am. (vice chmn. Balder club 1986—), Odd Fellows. Home: PO Box 6606 5845 Walnut Dr Eureka CA 95502 Office: Calif Regional Water Quality Control Bd North Coast Region 1440 Guerneville Rd Santa Rosa CA 95401

EDMISTON, JOSEPH TASKER, state ofcl.; b. Monterey Park, Calif., Oct. 27, 1948; s. Tasker Lee and Beula Viola (Bates) E.; m. Pepper Salter Abrams, 1985; 1 child, William Tasker. A.A., East Los Angeles Coll., 1968; A.B., U. So. Calif., 1970. Mgr. of ct. process Roy Rottner & Associates, Hollywood, Calif., 1970-73; So. Calif. Coastal coordinator Sierra Club, Los Angeles, 1973-76, energy coordinator, Sacramento, Calif., 1976-77; dir. State of Calif. Santa Monica Mountains Land Acquisition Program, 1979-80; exec. dir. Santa Monica Mountains Comprehensive Planning Commn., Los Angeles,

1977-79; exec. dir. Santa Monica Mountains Conservancy, State of Calif., 1980—. Pres. Associated Students, East Los Angeles Coll., 1968. Recipient Weldon Heald Conservation award Sierra Club, 1970; Hollywood Heritage, Inc. (bd. dirs.). Mem. Marine Tech. Soc. (dir. Los Angeles region sect. 1975-77), Coastal Soc., Phi Rho Pi, Delta Sigma Rho, Tau Kappa Alpha. Democrat. Office: 107 S Broadway Los Angeles CA 90012

EDMONDS, CHARLES HENRY, publisher; b. Lakewood, Ohio, Sept. 4, 1919; s. Howard H. and Mary Frances (Galena) E.; student Woodbury Bus. Coll., 1939-40; m. Ruth Audrey Windfelder, Nov. 4, 1938; children—Joan Dickey, Charles Henry, Carolyn Anne, Dianne Marie. Owner, Shoreline Transp. Co., Los Angeles, 1946-58; mgr. transp. Purity Food Stores, Burlingame, Calif., 1958-61; supr. Calif. Motor Express, San Jose, 1961-64; account exec. Don Wright Assos., Oakland, Calif., 1964-65; sales mgr. Western U.S., Shippers Guide Co., Chgo., 1965-70; pub. No. Calif. Retailer, San Jose, 1970-83; v.p. Kasmar Publs., 1983—. Recipient journalism awards various orgns. Republican. Roman Catholic. Contbr. articles to profl. jours. Home: 1442 Sierra Creek Way San Jose CA 95132

EDMONDS, IVY GORDON, author; b. Frost, Tex., Feb. 15, 1917; s. Ivy Gordon and Delia Louella (Shumate) E.; student pub. schs.; m. Reiko Mimura, July 12, 1956; 1 dau., Annette. Freelance writer; author books including: Ooka the Wise, 1961; The Bounty's Boy, 1963; Joel of the Hanging Gardens, 1966; Trickster Tales, 1966; Taiwan—the Other China, 1971; The Magic Man, 1972; Mao's Long March, 1973; Motorcycling for Beginners, 1973; Micronesia, 1974; Pakistan, Land of Mystery, Tragedy and Courage, 1974; Automotive Tuneups for Beginners, 1974; Ethiopia, 1975; The Magic Makers, 1976; The Shah of Iran, 1976; Allah's Oil: Mid-East Petroleum, 1976; Second Sight, 1977; Motorcycle Racing for Beginners, 1977; Islam, 1977; Buddhism, 1978; The Mysteries of Troy, 1977; Big U Universal in the Silent Days, 1977; D.D. Home, 1978; Bicycle Motocross, 1979; Girls Who Talked to Ghosts, 1979; The Magic Brothers, 1979; (with William H. Gebhardt) Broadcasting for Beginners, 1980; (with Reiko Mimura) The Oscar Directors, 1980; The Mysteries of Homer's Greeks, 1981; The Kings of Black Magic, 1981; Funny Car Racing for Beginners, 1982; The Magic Dog, 1982; author textbooks: (with Ronald Gonzales) Understanding Your Car, 1975, Introduction to Welding, 1975; pub. relations mgr. Northrop Corp., Anaheim, Calif., 1968-79, indsl. editor, Hawthorne, Calif., 1979-86. Served with USAAF, 1940-45, USAF, 1946-63. Decorated D.F.C., Air medals, Bronze Star. Mem. Authors' Guild, Authors' League Am. Home: 5801 Shirl St Cypress CA 90630

EDMUND, RUDOLPH WILLIAM, coll. adminstr.; b. Lockridge, Iowa, Mar. 9, 1910; s. Amos Daniel and Minnie Elizabeth (Odean) E.; A.B., Augustana Coll., 1934; M.S., State U. Iowa, 1938, Ph.D., 1940; D.Sc. (hon.), Calif. Luth. Coll., 1980; m. Doris Irene Swanson, June 8, 1939; children—Diane (Mrs. Jack Griffin), Janice (Mrs. Steven Smith), Linda (Mrs. David Kuntzman). Instr. Coe Coll., 1939-40; geologist Shell Oil Co., Tulsa, 1940-45, Globe Oil & Refining Co., Oklahoma City, 1945-48, 51-53; prof. Augustana Coll., 1948-51, 61-69; v.p. Sohio Petroleum Co., Oklahoma City, 1953-60; v.p. acad. affairs Calif. Luth. Coll., Thousand Oaks, 1969-74, dir. life long learning, prof. geology, 1974-80, emeritus, 1980—; partner Harris & Edmund Geol. Cons., Oklahoma City, 1945-46. Active in restructuring grad. record exam. in geology Ednl. Testing Service, 1968-72. Bd. dirs. Augustana Research Found., 1962-69; mem. adv. bd. Sch. Engring., Okla. State U., 1954-60; bd. dirs. Davenport Pub. Mus., 1964-69, vice chmn., 1968; bd. regents Calif. Luth. Coll., 1982—. Recipient outstanding service award Augustana Coll., 1960. Fellow Geol. Soc. Am., Am. Assn. Petroleum Geologists, AAAS; mem. Nat. Assn. Geology Tchrs. (pres. Central sect. 1967), Soc. Exploration Geophysicists, Phi Beta Kappa, Sigma Xi, Omicron Delta Kappa. Lutheran. Author: Structural Geology and Physiography of the Northern End of the Teton Range, Wyoming, 1951; (with E. Goebel) Subsurface Waste Disposal Potential in Salina Basin of Kansas, 1968; Sharing God's Gifts, 1978. Contbr. articles profl. jours. Home: La Serena Retirement Village 3575 N Moorpark Rd Thousand Oaks CA 91360

EDUALINO, EMILIO QUIAL, educator; b. Agutaya, Palawan, Philippines, May 13, 1917; s. Telesforo Saldivia and Agapita (Quial) E.; came to U.S., 1979; Elem. tchr. cert. Philippine Normal Coll., Manila, 1935; B.S. in Edn., Far Eastern U., Manila, 1948; M.A., U. Mich., 1956, Ph.D., 1958. Tchr. then elem. sch. adminstr. various schs., Philippines, 1935-46; curriculum writer Dept. Edn., Manila, 1946-48; instr. edn. Philippine Normal Coll., Manila, 1948-48, master tchr., 1949-53, supr. student tching., 1953-55, dir. field units, prof. edn., 1957-64; primary edn. expert UNESCO, Guyana, S.Am., 1964-66, tchr. edn. expert Afghanistan, 1969-74, chief tech. adviser, Sierra Leone, 1974-79; prof. edn., chmn. dept. elem. edn. U. of the East, Manila,, 1966-69; tchr. St. Mary's Elem. Sch., Los Angeles, 1979—; cons.; mem. U.S. Edn. Found. selection com., Manila. Philippine Govt. travel fellow, 1948-49; U.S. Edn. Found. grantee, 1955-57. Mem. Childhood Edn. Internat., NEA, Nat. Soc. Study of Edn., Assn. Supervision and Curriculum Devel., Phi Delta Kappa. Roman Catholic. Lodge: Lions Internat. Clubs: Michigan (San Gabriel, Calif.); Michigan Alumni (Ann Arbor). Author: (with others) Integration as Practiced in the Philippine Normal College, 1952; also children's songs and reading materials; contbr. articles to profl. jours. Home: 2950 Manhattan Ave Glendale CA 91214 Office: 406 Saint Louis St Los Angeles CA 90033

EDWARDS, BRUCE JACK, designer, consultant; b. Salt Lake City, May 6, 1951; s. Jack Grant and Mary Voyn (Griffeth) E.; m. Joyce Lohner, April 3, 1974; children—Rochelle, Nicholas, Christel. B.F.A., Brigham Young U, 1977. Cert., Nat. Council Interior Design Qualification. Design intern Level Two Design Co., Salt Lake City, 1976; design cons. Greenhouse Design Studio, Salt Lake City, 1977-79; pres., owner B.J. Edwards Environments, Salt Lake City, 1977—; mgr. interior design and space planning Ch. of Jesus Christ of Latter Day Saints; design cons. Boy Scouts Am.; educator, lectr.; stage set designer Murray City Theatre, Osmond Studios, 1976. Council commr. Boy Scouts Am.; acad. adv. bd. Ricks Coll. Recipient AIA honor award for interior design, 1982. Mem. Am. Soc. Interior Designers (pres. Utah chpt. 1982-83, chmn. nat. ednl. found. com.), Tech. Assistance Network, Nat. Ctr. Barrier Free Environment. Republican. Contbr. articles in field to publs. Office: LDS Ch Hdqrs Salt Lake City UT 84150

EDWARDS, BRUCE LYNN, mechanical engineer; b. Decatur, Ill., Oct. 10, 1948; s. Roy W. and Lila L. (Severe) E.; m. Lynn V. Cooley, May 16, 1982. BSME, Bradley U., 1970; MBA, U. Denver, 1977. Registered profl. engr., Wash., Colo., Ariz. Nuclear reactor test engr. Newport News (Va.) Shipbuilding, 1970-73; power engr. Stone & Webster, Denver, 1974-77; supervising engr. R.W. Beck, Seattle, 1977-80; project mgr. HDR, Seattle, 1981—. Mem. ASME, Am. Pub. Works Assn. Club: Wash. Athletic (Seattle). Avocations: basketball, golfing, sailing. Office: HDR 1100 Eastlake Ave E Seattle WA 98109

EDWARDS, CARL VAUGHN, consulting engineer; b. Boise, Idaho, May 1, 1938; s. Lafell Hamblin and Marjorie Katherine (Justesen) E.; m. Diane Claudine Schraft, Sept. 11, 1961 (div. Apr. 1982); children: Carla Dalice, Sandrea Dee, Hunter James, Melinda Mae; m. Ruth Ann Barlow, Mar. 24, 1983; children: David Glyn, Dian Belle, Dana Lorrie, Daniel John, Joshua Lafell. BSCE, U. Idaho, 1964. Area engr. U.S. Forest Service, Yreka, Calif., 1956-63, Morrison Knudsen Co., Boise, 1964-72; prin. Edwards, Howard & Martens, Inc., Twin Falls, Grangeville, Idaho, 1972—. Mem. Soc. Profl. Engrs., Cons. Engr. Council, Nat. Soc. Cons. Engrs. Mormon. Avocations: fishing, hunting, rafting, outdoor sports. Home: Cove Rd Grangeville ID 83530 Office: Edwards Howard & Martens Inc 238 E South St Grangeville ID 83530

EDWARDS, CHARLES RICHARD, printing equipment and supplies co. exec.; b. S. Bend, Ind., July 16, 1931; s. Bernard Stuart and Mary Irene (Chamberlaine) E.; student pub. schs.; m. Joanne Wood, Dec. 15, 1950; children—Timothy Stuart, Terry Lynne, David Bryan. Pressman, Toastmasters Internat., Santa Ana, Calif., 1954-60; with 3M Co., 1960-69, Salesman, Western U.S. tech. service and nat. market mgr., St. Paul, 1966-69; chief exec. officer, sec., chief fin. officer, co-owner Graphic Arts Supplies, Inc., Orange, Calif., 1969-86; bus. and trade cons., 1986—; instr., cons. in field. Bd. dirs., treas. #1 Network, Inc., Chgo., 1982-86. Served with USAF, 1950-54; Korea. Mem. Nat. Assn. Lithographic Clubs (chpt. co-founder, officer, dir.), Nat. Assn. Printing House Craftsmen (past chpt. pres., regional officer). Republican. Club: Toastmasters. Home: 7221 Judson Ave Westminster CA 92683

EDWARDS, CLIFFORD MURRAY, oil company executive; b. Ft. Worth, Sept. 23, 1952; s. Charles E. and Mary Ann (Ramsey) E. BS in Geophysics summa cum laude, Tex. A&M U., 1973, MS in Geophysics magna cum laude, 1975; MS in Bus. Adminstrv. Sci., U. Tex., Dallas, 1979. Geophysicist exploration Mobil, Dallas, 1975-79; supr. exploration Mobil, New Orleans, 1979-82; supt. exploration Mobil, The Hague, The Netherlands, 1982-84, Houston, 1984-85; mgr. geophysics Mobil, Denver, 1985-87; sr. planning cons. Mobil, N.Y.C., 1987—. Mem. Am. Assn. Petroleum Geologists, Soc. Exploration Geophysics. Republican. Presbyterian.

EDWARDS, DAN C., labor union administrator; b. Denver, July 16, 1939; s. Carlyle M. and Dorothy R. (Perry) E.; m. Bonnie M. McClure, 1956 (div. 1975); children: Cynthia Lynn Edwards Vaughn, Sharyn Lee Edwards Smith, Chris Ann Edwards Bass; m. Carylon JoAnn Copeland, Mar. 13, 1976. Grad. high sch., Commerce City, Colo. Refinery worker Conoco Inc., Commerce City, 1957-71; local officer Oil Chemical and Atomic Workers Internat. Union affiliate AFL-CIO, Commerce City, 1959-71; internat. rep. Oil Chemical and Atomic Workers Internat. Union affiliate AFL-CIO, Corpus Christi (Tex.) and Houston, 1971-81; health and safety rep. Oil Chemical and Atomic Workers Internat. Union affiliate AFL-CIO, Denver, 1981-82, health and safety dir., 1982—; adv. mem. Hazardous Liquids Pipeline Safety Standards Com., U.S. Dept. Transp., 1984—. Vol. South Adams County (Colo.) Fire Dept., 1960-71, also command officer. Mem. Am. Pub. Health Assn., Colo. Pub. Health Assn. Office: Oil Chem & Atomic Workers Internat Union Denver CO 80201

EDWARDS, DANIEL WILLIAM, psychologist, educator; b. Torrance, Calif., Jan. 18, 1943; s. Eugene M. and Jean (Alderson) E.; divorced; 1 child, Tiffany. BA, Calif. State U., Fullerton, 1967; PhD, U. Mich., 1971, MPH, 1972. Lic. psychologist, Calif. Asst. dir. research Thomas Jefferson U., Phila., 1972-74; asst. prof. U. Calif., Davis, 1974-79, assoc. prof., 1979-80, assoc. clin. prof., 1980—; pvt. practice psychology Sacramento Phobia Clinic, 1980—; lectr. U. So. Calif., 1980, Thomas Jefferson U., 1972-74; assoc. prof. psychology Calif. State U., Sacramento, 1982-83; cons. Ypsilanti (Mich.) State Hosp., 1971-72, E. Carolina U., 1972-74. Co-author: Planning: The Design of Mental Health Programs, 1980, Monitoring: The Evaluation of Mental Health Programs, 1981; contbr. numerous articles to jours. Mem. AAAS, Am. Pub. Health Assn., Am. Psychol. Assn., Western Psychol. Assn., Soc. Psychotherapy Research, Evaluation Research Soc., Sacramento Soc. Profl. Psychologists, Sacramento Valley Psychol. Assn., Calif. State Psychol. Assn., Evaluation Network, Am. Mgmt. Assn. Home: 142 Cedro Circle Sacramento CA 95833 Office: Sacramento Phobia Clinic 5900 Coyle Ave Suite D Carmichael CA 95608

EDWARDS, DIANNE CAROL, educator; b. San Jose, Calif., July 20, 1945; d. Wallace Robinson and Ethel Louise (Egling) Murray; m. Jack Lee Edwards, Dec. 14, 1968; 1 child, Jennifer Lynn. BA, San Jose State U., 1966; MA, U. San Francisco, 1976. Cert. secondary tchr., Calif. (life). Secondary tchr. Santa Clara (Calif.) Unified Sch. Dist., 1967—, mem. dist. com. on communication skills, 1978-80, mem. dist. com. on reading, 1980-85. Author: (with M.L. Luchetti) Wear Comfortable Shoes and Bring a Sack Lunch, 1976. Active San Jose Civic Light Opera. Named Tchr. of Yr., Wilcox High Sch., 1977. Mem. Nat. Council Tchrs. English, Santa Clara County Reading Council, Calif. Tchrs. Assn., Nat. Tchrs. Assn., Sons of the Desert, Smithsonian Inst., Automatic Musical Instruments Collectors Assn. (founding chpt.), Delta Kappa Gamma (1st v.p. Delta Rho chpt.). Republican. Lutheran. Avocations: automatic musical instruments. Home: 1681 Mount Vernon Dr San Jose CA 95125 Office: Wilcox Sr High Sch 3250 Monroe St Santa Clara CA 95051

EDWARDS, DON, congressman; b. San Jose, Calif., Jan. 6, 1915; s. Leonard P. and Clara (Donlon) E.; children—Leonard P., Samuel D., Bruce H., Thomas C., William D.; m. Edith Wilkes. A.B., Stanford, 1936; student, Law Sch., 1936-38. Agt. FBI, 1940-41; mem. 88th-93d congresses from 9th Calif. Dist., 94th-100th congresses from 10th Calif. Dist.; Nat. chmn. Americans for Democratic Action, from 1965. Served to lt. USNR, 1941-45. Democrat. Unitarian. Office: 2307 Rayburn House Office Bldg Washington DC 20515 *

EDWARDS, GLENN THOMAS, history educator; b. Portland, Oreg., June 14, 1931; s. Glenn Thomas E. and Marie Ann (Cheska) McMullen; m. Nannette Wilhelmina McAndie, June 15, 1957; children: Randall Thomas, Stephanie Lynn. B.A., Willamette U., 1953; M.A., U. Oreg., 1960, Ph.D., 1963. Asst. prof. San Jose State U., 1962-64; asst. prof. Whitman Coll., Walla Walla, Wash., 1964-68, assoc. prof., 1968-75, prof., 1976—; cons. TV documentary Yakima Valley Mus. on William O. Douglas, Yakima, Wash., 1981-82; trustee Wash. Commn. of Humanities, Olympia, 1980-86. Co-editor: Experiences in a Promised Land: Essays on Pacific Northwest History, 1986; contbr. articles to profl. jours. Mem. pub. edn. adv. com. State Supt. of Pub. Instrn., Olympia, 1975-78; mem. bd. curators Wash. State Hist. Soc., 1983—. Served with U.S. Army, 1954-56. Grantee Am Philos. Soc., 1971. Mem. Orgn. Am. Historians, So. Hist. Assn., Oreg. Hist. Soc., Washington Hist. Soc. (photography cons. 1980). Congregationalist. Office: Whitman Coll Dept History Walla Walla WA 99362

EDWARDS, JACK A., state agency professional; b. Riverside, Calif., Nov. 17, 1948; s. Douglas Eugene and Billie Sue (Pruitt) E.; m. Donna Lee Klahr, Dec. 20, 1968 (div. Mar. 1973); m. Carolyn Ann Strause, May 7, 1983. Student, Riverside City Coll.; BS in Zoology, U. Calif., Davis, 1975; postgrad., Calif. State U., Sacramento. Horseshoer Riverside, Calif., 1972-75; park ranger asst. Sacramento Parks and Recreation, 1975-77; game warden Calif. Dept. Fish and Game, Half Moon Bay, Calif., 1977-81; game warden Calif. Dept. Fish and Game, Sacramento, 1981-86, patrol capt., statewide hunter edn. coordinator, 1986—. Co-author, editor: Defense Tactics and Arrest Techniques, 1985; author: Wildlife Protection Computer Database for California Fish and Game. Mem. South Sacramento Planning Com., 1985-86. Served to staff sgt. USAF, 1968-72. Mem. Calif. Fish and Game Warden's Protective Assn. (treas. 1981-86, pres. 1986—), N.Am. Wildlife Officers Assn. Republican. Home: 7288 Gardner Ave Sacramento CA 95828

EDWARDS, JACK GRANT, state agency administrator; b. Kenilworth, Utah, Mar. 8, 1928; s. D. Grant and Norma (Umber) E.; m. Mary Voyn Griffeth, June 28, 1949; children: Bruce Jack, Eileen Edwards Loveless, Leslie Vance. AS, Coll. Eastern Utah, 1949; student, U. Utah, 1958-59. Agy. sales mgr. Mut. of Omaha Ins., Salt Lake City, 1950-59; dep. commr. ins. dept. State of Utah, Salt Lake City, 1959-80, dir. adminstrv. services, 1980—; pres., owner Jack-O-Lite Co., Salt Lake City, 1960—. Bd. dirs. Utah State Pub. Employees Assn., Salt Lake City, 1965-68. Mem. Utah Assn. Wang Users (pres. 1983). Republican. Mormon. Avocations: squash, racquetball, tennis. Home: 1218 W 4800 S Salt Lake City UT 84123 Office: State Utah Ins Dept 160 E 300 S PO Box 5803 Salt Lake City UT 84410

EDWARDS, JAMES RICHARD, lawyer; b. Long Beach, Calif., Apr. 14, 1951; s. Nelson James and Dorothy June (Harris) E. B.S., Colo. State U., 1973; J.D., U. San Diego, 1977. Bar: Calif. 1977. Atty., Downtown Sr. Ctr., San Diego, 1977-78, Getty Oil Co., Los Angeles, 1978-80; atty. Logicon, Inc., Torrance, Calif., 1980-85, sec., 1982-85, gen. counsel, 1981-85; ptnr. Mirassou, Nyznyk & Edwards, 1985-87; gen. counsel, sec. GA Techs., Inc., San Diego, 1987—. Recipient championship medals U.S. Parachute Assn., 1977, 79, 80. Mem. ABA, State Bar Calif., Los Angeles County Bar Assn. Office: GA Techs Inc 10955 John Joy Hopkins Dr San Diego CA 92121

EDWARDS, JAUNA CARPENTER, public accountant, city treasurer, educator; b. Childress, Tex., Mar. 16, 1935; d. Carl and Mildred (O'Daniel) C Carpenter; m. Carl M. Hall, Feb. 10, 1952; 1 son, Hal; m. 2d, John M. Edwards, Feb. 14, 1963; children—Nelta M., Bryant T. A.A., Tanana Valley Community Coll., 1982; student U. Alaska, 1977-83. Sec. to logistics mgr. RCA Service Co. at BMEWS, Clear, Alaska, 1961-62, sec. to sta. mgr. NASA Sta., Fairbanks, Alaska, 1962-64; pub. acct., Clear, 1966-83; city treas., Anderson, Alaska, 1968-83; treas. Tri-Valley Investment Corp., 1977-83. Chmn., Anderson Community Sch. Com. Mem. Nat. Soc. Pub. Accts., Alaska Soc. Ind. Accts., Clear Bus. and Profl. Women's Club. Democrat. Episcopalian. Home: Family Ranchette PO Box 3129 Palmer AK 99645

EDWARDS, KATHRYN INEZ, instructional media consultant; b. Los Angeles, Aug. 26, 1947; d. Lloyd and Geraldine E. (Smith) Price; m. Gregor Quentin Edwards, June 7, 1969; 1 child, Bryan. BA in English, Calif. State U.-Los Angeles, 1969, supervision credential, 1974, adminstrn. credential, 1975; MEd in Curriculum, UCLA, 1971; PhD, Claremont Grad. Sch., 1979. Tchr., Los Angles Pub. Schs., 1969-78, adv. specially funded programs, 1978-80, advisor libraries and learning-resource program, 1980-81, instructional specialist, 1981-84; cons. instructional media Los Angeles County Office of Edn., Downey, Calif., 1984—; cons. Walt Disney Prodns., Alfred Higgins Prodns., others. Author guides and curriculm kits. Mabel Wilson Richards scholar, 1968; Calif. Congress Parents and Tchrs. scholar, 1968; UCLA fellow, 1968; others. Mem. Nat. Assn. Minority Polit. Women, Alpha Kappa Alpha, Los Angeles Reading Assn. (v.p.), Calif. Assn. Tchrs. of English (conf. del. 1982), Assn. Supervision and Curriculum Devel., Calif. Media and Library Educators Assn., Nat. Assn. Media Women. Democrat. Roman Catholic. Avocations: reading; gardening; sewing. Home: 6005 Wooster Ave Los Angeles CA 90056 Office: Los Angeles County Office Edn 9300 E Imperial Hwy Downey CA 90242

EDWARDS, (FLOYD) KENNETH, journalist, educator, mgmt. cons., marketing executive; b. Salina, Kans., Sept. 29, 1917; s. Floyd Altamus and Grace Frances (Miller) E.; A.B., Fort Hays State U., 1940; M.S., 1970; m. Virginia Marie Lewark, Sept. 10, 1970; children—Elaine Patricia, Diana, Kenneth, John Michael, Melody, Daniel J. Ins. sales exec., Denver, 1947-50; reporter Sterling (Colo.) Daily Jour., 1950, editor, 1950-52; editor Waverly (Iowa) Newspapers, 1953-55; editor, pub. Edina (Minn.) Courier Newspapers, 1955-56; v.p., editor Mpls. Suburban Newspapers, Hopkins, Minn., 1956-65; editor, gen. mgr. Valley of the Sun Newspapers, Tempe, Ariz., 1968; instr. Mankato (Minn.) State U., 1970-72, asst. prof., 1972-73; assoc. prof. U. Ala., 1973-80, prof., 1980; vis. prof. communications U. Portland (Oreg.), 1981-83; mktg. and sales dir. C.C. Publs., Tualatin, Oreg., 1983-86; cons. on newspaper mgmt.,mktg., videotex ops. Pres. Calhoun-Harriet Home Owners Assn., Mpls., 1958-60; bd. dirs. Hennepin County Assn. for Mental Health, 1959-60, S.W. Activities Council, 1960-61, S.W. High Sch. PTA, Mpls., 1960-61. Served with USN, World War II. Grantee Ford Found., 1976, U. Ala., 1977. Recipient awards for community service and editorial writing. Mem. Inst. Newspaper Controllers and Fin. Officers, Am. Mgmt. Assn., Nat. Conf. of Editorial Writers. Republican. Contbr. articles to profl. jours., chpts. to books; author newspaper profit planning and management manual. Home: 8 Sudden Valley Bellingham WA 98226

EDWARDS, LYDIA JUSTICE, state official; b. Carter County, Ky., July 9, 1937; d. Chead and Velva (Kinney) Justice; m. Frank B. Edwards, 1968; children: Mark, Alexandra, Margot. Student, San Francisco State U. Began career as acct, then Idaho state rep., 1982-86; treas. State of Idaho, 1987—; legis. asst. to Gov. Hickel, Alaska, 1967; conf. planner Rep. Gov.'s Assn., 1970-73; mem. Rep. Nat. Commn., 1972, del. to nat. conv., 1980. Mem. Rep. Womens Fedn. Congregationalist. Office: State Treasurer's Office State Capitol Bldg Rm 102 Boise ID 83720 *

EDWARDS, MARIE BABARE, psychologist; b. Tacoma; d. Nick and Mary (Mardesich) Babare; B.A., Stanford, 1948, M.A., 1949; m. Tilden Hampton Edwards (div.); 1 son, Tilden Hampton Edwards III. Counselor guidance center U. So. Calif., Los Angeles, 1950-52; project coordinator So. Calif. Soc. Mental Hygiene, 1952-54; pub. speaker Welfare Fedn. Los Angeles, 1953-57; field rep. Los Angeles County Assn. Mental Health, 1957-58; intern psychologist UCLA, 1958-60; pvt. practice, human relations tng., counselor tng. Mem. Calif., Am., Western, Los Angeles psychol. assns., AAAS, Nat. Acad. Religion and Mental Health, Soc. Advancement Mgmt., So. Calif. Soc. Clin. Hypnosis, Internat. Platform Assn. Author: (with Eleanor Hoover) The Challenge of Being Single, 1974, paperback edit., 1975. Office: 6100 Buckingham Pkwy Culver City CA 90230

EDWARDS, MICHAEL RUSS, sales consultant; b. Duncan, Okla., July 24, 1935; s. Marshall James Edwards and Emma Elizabeth Persson; A.A., Casper Coll. (Wyo.), 1969; B.S., U. Wyo., 1974, postgrad., 1984. With Mid-Continent Supply Co., Ft. Worth, 1974-82, expeditor, Ft. Worth 1974-77, mktg. systems analyst, Ft. Worth and Houston, 1977-79, pricing and inventory control specialist, Farmington, N.Mex., 1979-82; mktg. mgmt. analyst, 1983-85; ind. sales cons., Casper, 1985—. Casper, Wyo. Served with USAF, 1957-60. Mem. Am. Mktg. Assn., Am. Mgmt. Assn., U. Wyo. Alumni Assn. Democrat. Presbyterian. Address: 1724 N Grass Creek Rd Casper WY 82604

EDWARDS, RALPH M., librarian; b. Shelley, Idaho, Apr. 17, 1933; s. Edward William and Maude Estella (Munsee) E.; m. Winifred Wylie, Dec. 25, 1969; children: Dylan, Nathan, Stephen. B.A., U. Wash., 1957, M.Library, 1960; D.L.S., U. Calif.-Berkeley, 1971. Librarian N.Y. Pub. Library, N.Y.C., 1960-61; catalog librarian U. Ill. Library, Urbana, 1961-62; br. librarian Multnomah County Library, Portland, Oreg., 1964-67; asst. prof. Western Mich. U., Kalamazoo, 1970-74; chief of the Central Library Dallas Pub. Library, 1975-81; city librarian Phoenix Pub. Library, 1981—; accrediting team site visitor for library schs. ALA Com. on Accreditation, 1975. Author: Role of the Beginning Librarian in University Libraries, 1975. U. Calif. doctoral fellow, 1967-70; library mgmt. internship Council on Library Resources, 1974-75. Mem. ALA, Ariz. Library Assn., Pub. Library Assn. Democrat. Home: 4839 E Mulberry Dr Phoenix AZ 85018 Office: Phoenix Pub Library 12 E McDowell Rd Phoenix AZ 85004

EDWARDS, RICHARD HARVEY, corporate investment banking executive; b. Buffalo, Aug. 11, 1951; s. Leonard Harden and Carolyn (Drumheller) E.; m. Deborah Louise McCarthy, Jan. 27, 1954; 1 child, Scott Thornton. BSBA, Bucknell U., 1973; MBA, Cornell U., 1977. Asst. dir. admissions Bucknell U., Lewisburg, Pa., 1973-75; intern Citibank, N.Y.C., 1976; fin. assoc., sales rep., nat. sales mgr. Continental Group, Inc., Stamford, Conn., 1977-81; nat. sales mgr. Crocker Bank, San Francisco, 1981-85, v.p. West coast utilities and telecommunications group, 1985-86; v.p., group exec. West coast utilities and telecommunications Mfrs. Hanover Trust Co., San Francisco, 1986—; treas. Oakland (Calif.) Bd. Mgrs., 1982—. Youth advisor Lafayette Presbyn. Ch., 1981-83, fund chmn.; bd. dirs. Alameda County (Calif.) YMCA; chmn. alumni assn. Bay Area Bucknell U., 1983—; food chmn. San Francisco Boy Scouts Am., 1984; chmn. Oakland YMCA Fund, 1985; treas. bd. mgrs. Oakland YMCA; soccer coach Walnut Creek (Calif.) Youth Soccer League, 1987. Republican. Avocations: soccer, church, skiing, hiking, cooking. Home: 255 Dover Dr Walnut Creek CA 94598 Office: Mfrs Hanover Trust Co 50 California St 26th Floor San Francisco CA 94111

EDWARDS, ROGER YORKE, biologist, forester, museologist, consultant, writer; b. Toronto, Ont., Can., Nov. 22, 1924; s. John Macham and Agnes Cornelia (York) E.; m. Joan Claudia Thicke, Dec. 1, 1951; children—Claudia Anne, Jane Yorke. B.Sc.F., U. Toronto, 1948; M.A., U. B.C., Vancouver, Can., 1950. Research officer B.C. Forest Service, Victoria, Can., 1951-58; research supr B.C. Forest Service, 1958-59; park officer B.C. Parks Br., Victoria, 1959-67; interpretation specialist Can. Wildlife Service, Ottawa, Ont., 1967-72; asst. dir. B.C. Provincial Mus., Victoria, 1972-74; dir. B.C. Provincial Mus., 1974-84, curator emeritus, 1984—; cons., writer Victoria, 1984—. Author: The Mountain Barrier, 1970; The Land Speaks, 1979; also sci. papers and numerous popular, tech. articles, 1945—. Recipient award of achievement Interpretation Can., 1979. Fellow Can. Mus. Assn. (accredited), Royal Can. Geog. Soc.; mem. Wilson Ornithol. Club, Ottawa Naturalists Club (hon.), B.C. Mus. Assn. (hon.). Avocations: ornithology; writing; natural history; museums. Home and Office: 663 Radcliffe Ln, Victoria, BC Canada V8S 5B8

EDWARDS, SAMUEL ROGER, physician; b. Santa Barbara, Calif., Aug. 11 1937; s. Harold S. and Margaret (Spaulding) E.; m. Marcia Elizabeth Dutton, June 17, 1961; children—Harold S. II, Charles Dutton. B.A., Harvard U., 1960; M.D., U. So. Calif., 1964. Intern, Presbyn. Hosp., Phila., 1964-65; resident in internal medicine Presbyn. Med. Ctr., San Francisco, 1965-66, U. Calif. Hosps., San Francisco, 1968-70; fellow in cardiology Pacific Presbyn. Med. Ctr., San Francisco, 1970; pvt. practice specializing in internal medicine, Santa Paula, Calif., 1971—; med. dir. Santa Paula Convalescent, Twin Pines Convalescent Hosps.; pres. med. staff Ventura County Med. Ctr., Calif., 1979-80, med. dir., 1983—; clin. faculty UCLA Sch. Medicine, Westwood; dir. utilization and past rev. activities all Santa Paula acute and convalescent hosps.; dir. Citizens State Bank of Santa Paula, Limoneira Assocs.; chief dept. medicine Ventura County Gen. Hosp., 1975; chief med. staff Santa Paula Meml. Hosp., 1977. Served to lt. comdr. USNR, 1966-68. Recipient Disting. Service award Ventura County Heart Assn., 1974. Fellow ACP, Royal Soc. Medicine; mem. AMA, Calif., Ventura County Med. Assn., Calif. Med. Assn., Am. Coll. Cardiology, Am. Soc. Internal Medicine, Calif. Soc. Internal Medicine. Episcopalian. Home: 19789 E Telegraph Rd Santa Paula CA 93060 Office: 243 March St Santa Paula CA 93060

EFRON, BRADLEY, mathematics educator; b. St. Paul, May 24, 1938; s. Miles Jack and Esther (Kaufman) E.; m. Gael Guerin, July 1969 (div.); 1 son, Miles James; m. Nancy Troup, June 1986. B.S. in Math., Calif. Inst. Tech., 1960; Ph.D., Stanford U., 1964. Asst. and assoc. prof. stats. Stanford U., Calif., 1965-72, chmn. dept. stats., 1976-79, chmn. math. scis., 1981—, prof. stats., 1974—; statis. cons. Alza Corp., 1971—, Rand Corp., 1962—, Aprex Corp., 1986. Author: Bootstrap Methods, 1979, Biostatistics Casebook, 1980. MacArthur Found. fellow, 1983; named Outstanding Statistician of the Yr. Chgo. Statis. Assn., 1981; Wald and Rietz Lectr. Inst. Math. Stats., 1977, 81. Fellow Inst. Math. Stats. (pres.-elect 1986), Am. Statis. Assn.; mem. Internat. Statis. Assn., Nat. Acad. Scis. Democrat. Office: Stanford U Dept Statistics Sequoia Hall Stanford CA 94305

EGAN, JOHN TINNERMAN, rancher; b. Cleve., May 18, 1948; s. Robert Brooks and Elisabeth Neubauer (Tinnerman) E.; m. Carolyn Jane Clinton, Nov. 23, 1973 (div. Apr. 1979); children: Joseph Clinton, Elisabeth Lindsay Jane; m. Deborah Anne Montoya, Oct. 12, 1986. BA, Loretto Heights Coll., 1973; BA (hon.), Coll. Santa Fe, 1982. Gen. mgr. Rancho Encantado, Santa Fe, 1968-83, owner, mgr., 1983—; chmn. Encantado Mgmt., Santa Fe, 1985—. Author: The Present, 1973. Bd. dirs. Symphony Santa Fe, 1986—; pres. N.Mex. North, Santa Fe, 1982; mem. Council Dist. 2, 375th Anniversary Comm. City Santa Fe, 1986—. Named one of Outstanding Young Men Am., U.S. Jaycees, 1984. Mem. Santa Fe Lodgers Assn. (pres. 1981), N.Mex. Amigos, Santa Fe C. of C. (pres. 1986—, Dir. Yr. award 1982). Republican. Methodist. Club: Santa Fe Country. Lodge: Eagles. Office: Rancho Encantado Inc Rt 4 Box 57-C Santa Fe NM 87501

EGAN, RAYMOND DAVIS, electronics engineer; b. Honolulu, Aug. 22, 1931; s. Raymond Davis and Florence (Carter) E.; m. Christine Hunt, Sept. 17, 1955; children: Kathleen, Karen, Carol, Brian. BSEE, Stanford U., 1955, MSEE, 1956, PhD, 1960. Research assoc. Stanford (Calif.) U., 1956-60; project engr. Granger Assoc., Palo Alto, Calif., 1961-65; v.p. research Granger Assoc., Palo Alto, 1966-70; v.p. engring. Granger Assoc., Santa Clara, Calif., 1971-78, v.p. corp. devel., 1979-81; v.p. engring. Lynch Communications Systems, Reno, 1985—. Contbr. articles to profl. jours. Served to sgt. USAF, 1951-54. Mem. IEEE (chmn. no. Nev. sect. 1986—), Assn. Computing Machinery, Sigma Xi. Home: 8355 Lakeside Dr Reno NV 89511 Office: Lynch Communications Systems 204 Edison Way Reno NV 89520

EGAN, WILLIAM EUGENE, labor union leader; b. Hawthorne, Calif., Aug. 23, 1936; s. Eugene and Charlotte (Baldwin) E.; m. Marlene R. McEwen, Sept. 30, 1956; children: Edward, Richard, James, Pamela. Student pub. schs., Butte, Mont. Lic. electrician, various states. With Anaconda Co., Butte, 1952-54, Victor Chem., Butte, 1955-56, Tierney Bros., Butte, 1957-60; operating engr. F & S Constrn., Butte, 1960-62; electrician Elec. Industries, various locations, 1962-76; bus. mgr. fin. sec. Internat. Brotherhood Elec. Workers, Local #122, Great Falls, Mont., 1976—; v.p. Mont. State Bldg. and Constrn. Trades, Helena, 1976—; pres. Mont. Conf. Elec. Workers, Cascade County Trades and Labor Assembly; mem. exec. bd. Mont. Elec. Constrn. Labor and Mgmt. Coop. Com.; bd. dirs. Mont. Elec. Joint Apprenticeship Tng., Helena, 1976—; mem. adv. bd. No. Mont. Coll., 1985—; trustee Mont. Elec. Health and Accident Trust, 1976—; advisor trustee 8th Dist. Elec. Pension Trust, Denver, 1976—. Bd. dirs. Western Environ. Trade Assn., Helena, 1977—, Great Falls Econ. Growth Council, 1981-83; adv. bd. Pacific N.W. Power Planning Council, 1980—; advisor Butte VoTech Ednl. Ctr., 1974—. Mem. Mont. Mining Assn. (pres. 1968-71), Internat. Found. of Employment Benefit Plans. Democrat. Methodist. Home: 2920 7th Ave S Great Falls MT 59405 Office: Elec Workers IBEW 1112 7th St S Great Falls MT 59405

EGBERT, ROBERT L., consulting geologist; b. Union, Utah, Apr. 11, 1928; s. John W. and Hazel I. (Wardle) E.; m. Lolita Knighton, Aug. 1, 1952; children: Mark David, Matthew Robert, Karl Lee. BS, U. Utah, 1950, MS, 1955. Geologist Sun Oil Co., Salt Lake City, 1953; geologist Phillips Petroleum Co., Salt Lake City, 1954-56, project geologist, Billings, Mont., 1957-60, Rocky Mountain exploration geologist, Denver, 1960-67, project geologist, Santa Barbara, Calif., 1967, area geologist, Denver, 1968-77, tech. services mgr., Denver, 1978-85; cons. geologist, Golden, Colo., 1985—. Editor: Geologic Guidebook, 1960. Served with AUS, 1950-52, Korea. Mem. Am. Assn. Petroleum Geologists (del. 1976-79), Rocky Mountain Assn. Geologists (assoc. editor Rocky Mountain Geologic Atlas 1978), Computer Oriented Geol. Soc. Republican. Mormon. Home and Office: 2251 Braun Dr Golden CO 80401

EGELUND, KATHLEEN CHRISTINE, social worker; b. Logan, Utah, Jan. 27, 1951; d. Leonard Milton and Kathryn (Campbell) E. BSW, U. Denver, 1975; MSW, U. Utah, 1983. Art therapist Porter Meml. Hosp., Denver, 1974-75, social worker, 1975; program dir. Utah Tech. Coll. Skills Ctr. div., Salt Lake City, 1979-81; social worker U. Utah Med. Ctr., Salt Lake City, 1981, VA Med. Ctr., Salt Lake City, 1982, Utah State Prison, Draper, 1984—; women's correctional facility rep., camp social worker Half Way House Transition com. Dept. State Corrections, Utah, 1985—. Art dir. Fred Harris for Pres., Iowa, 1976; dem. campaign organizer state reps. Francis Farley, Olene Walker, Palmer DePaulis, Salt Lake City, 1976. Grantee CETA/FIPS Fund for the Improvement of Post Secondary Edn., Wash., 1979-81. Mormon. Avocations: art-painting, tennis, snow skiing, golf, European travel. Home: 185 Virginia St Salt Lake City UT 84103 Office: Utah State Prison 14400 Frontage Rd Draper UT 84309

EGERMAN, HOWARD DOUGLAS, federal agency administrator; b. San Francisco, Aug. 2, 1946; s. Alvin Prinz and Enid June (Yampol) E.; m. Diane Lynne Shapiro, Sept. 6, 1981. BA in Polit. Sci., U. Calif., Davis, 1968; MA in Polit. Sci., U. Calif., Riverside, 1969. Service rep. Social Security, Oakland, Calif., 1973-76, claims rep., 1976-84, field rep., 1984—; v.p. Am. Fedn. Govt. Employees, No. and Cen. Calif., 1984—, health and safety rep. Am. Fedn. Govt. Employees, Calif., Nev., Ariz., Hawaii, 1984—. Chmn, Calif. Aggie Alumni Scholarship Com., Alameda County, 1985—; vol. Home for Jewish Parents Outreach, Oakland, 1983—. Served with USN, 1969-73. Mem. Silver Chimes Internat. Tng. in Communication Club (ednl. chmn. 1984—). Jewish. Avocations: reading, writing. Home: 3216 Davis St Oakland CA 94601 Office: Social Security Adminstrn 10700 MacArthur Blvd Oakland CA 94605

EGGERDING, FAYE ADELE, medical educator, researcher; b. St. Louis, Nov. 7, 1944; d. Victor Charles and Helen Rose (Bowler) E. BA, U. Calif., Berkeley, 1966; MD, St. Louis U., 1971; PhD, Washington U., St. Louis, 1978. Resident in pathology Wash. U. Sch. Medicine, St. Louis, 1971-78, research fellow, 1973-78; asst. prof. pathology UCLA Sch. Medicine, 1978-86; research biologist UCLA Neuropsychiatric Inst., 1986—. Contbr. articles to profl jours. Mem. AAAS, Am. Soc. Microbiology. Office: UCLA Sch Medicine Dept Neurosurgery Room 17-382 NPI Los Angeles CA 90024

EGGERS, ALFRED J., JR., research corporation executive; b. Omaha, June 24, 1922; s. Alfred John and Golden May (Meyers) E.; m. Elizabeth Ann Hills, Sept. 9, 1950; children—Alfred John III, Philip Norman. B.A., U. Nebr.-Omaha, 1945; M.S., Stanford U., 1951, Ph.D., 1957. Aerospace scientist NASA Ames Research Ctr., Mountain View, Calif., 1944-64; dep. assoc. adminstr. NASA, Washington, 1964-68; Hunsaker prof. MIT, Cambridge, 1969-71; asst. dir. NSF, Washington, 1971-77; dir. Lockheed Research Lab., Palo Alto, Calif., 1977-79; pres., chief exec. officer RANN Inc., Palo Alto, Calif., 1979—, dir., 1981—; mem. sci. adv. bd. U.S. Air Force, Washington, 1958-72, Nat. Acad. Engring., 1973—, Aerospace Engring. Bd., Washington, 1973-77; mem. adv. bd. Solar Energy Research Inst., Golden, Colo., 1985—; chmn. A.J. Eggers & Co., Atherton, Calif., 1981—. Author: Hypersonic Flow, 1962; contbr. articles to profl. jours.; patentee in field. Vice chmn. Sch. Community Devel. Com., Los Altos Hills, Calif., 1963-64; mem., chmn. troop com. Boy Scouts Am., Arlington, Va., 1968-75; mem. safety com. ARC, Arlington, 1975-77. Served to lt. (j.g.) USN, 1943-46. Recipient Exceptional Service medal NASA, 1971; Disting. Service medal NSF, 1975; Disting. Service medal Pres. of U.S., 1977; commendation Nat. Sci. Bd., 1977. Fellow AIAA (Sylvanus Albert Reed award 1961), Am. Astron. Soc., AAAS; mem. Nat. Acad. Engring. long range planning and devel. com. 1983-85). Republican. Club: Washington Golf and Country (Arlington). Avocations: swimming; golf; skiing. Home: 23 Fair Oaks Ln Atherton CA 94025 Office: RANN Inc 260 Sheridan Ave Suite 414 Palo Alto CA 94306

EGGERS, LARRY ALAN, tax and financial planning company executive; b. Maryville, Tenn., Oct. 15, 1941; s. Robert Carroll and Pearl Etta Glen (Jenkins) E.; A.S. in Edn. (High Scholastic scholar), Ricks Coll., 1965; B.S. in Bus. Adminstrn., U. Redlands, 1979; m. Ruth Ann Pearson, Apr. 4, 1963; children—Laurie Ann, Mark, David, Robert, Amber, April, Jason, Michelle. With toll transmission dept. Am. Telephone Co., Long Lines, Pocatello, Idaho, 1965-66; operations engr. Lockheed Co., Sunnyvale, Calif., 1966-72; owner, gen. mgr. Eggers Tax Service, San Jose, Calif., 1968-78, editor The ETS Taxpayer, 1972-78; v.p. Mighty-Mite Computer Systems, Inc., San Jose, 1975—, chmn. bd., 1975—; gen. partner E.T.S. Real Estate Partnership, San Jose, 1978—; pres. E.T.S. & Assocs., Inc., San Jose, 1978—; tax and fin. cons. Active Better Bus. Bur. Lic. real estate broker, life and disability agt., securities agt. Mem. Nat. Assn. Tax Cons., Calif. Assn. Realtors, Nat. Assn. Realtors, Internat. Assn. Fin. Planners, San Jose Real Estate Bd. Mormon. Author: Basic Federal Income Tax Training Course, 1971, 72, 73; Copyrighted Tax Questionaire Booklet, 1974, 80, 82, 83, 84; programming cons. income tax software for mini-computers, acctg. software for minicomputers. Home: 700 Dartmouth Pl Gilroy CA 95020 Office: 7174 Santa Teresa Blvd Suite A-2 San Jose CA 95139

EGGERT, PAUL RICHARD, computer researcher, consultant; b. Lincoln, Nebr., Dec. 4, 1954; s. Richard Herman and Elizabeth June (Bredthauer) E. BA, Rice U., 1975; MS, UCLA, 1978, PhD, 1980. Asst. prof. U. Calif., Santa Barbara, 1980-83; chief scientist Silogic Inc., Los Angeles, 1983-86; sr. advisor to mgmt. Unisys Corp., Santa Monica, Calif., 1986—. Co-author: (computer programs) Knowledge Work Bench Core, 1985. Bd. dirs. Tigertail Assocs., Los Angeles, 1983—. Mem. Assn. for Computing Machinery, Computing Soc. of IEEE. Home: 3495 Stoner Ave Los Angeles CA 90066 Office: Unisys Corp 2525 Colorado Blvd Santa Monica CA 90406

EGGERTSEN, FRANK THOMAS, research chemist; b. Provo, Utah, Mar. 26, 1913; s. Burton Simon and Anne (Thomas) E.; m. Beth Marie Krueger, Dec. 29, 1939; children: Karl F., Thomas K., Grace Ann. BA, U. Utah, 1934; PhD, U. Minn., 1939. Research chemist Sherwin-Williams Co., Chgo., 1939-43, Shell Devel. Co., Emeryville, Calif., 1943-72; prin. research scientist Calif. Ink Co. div. Flint Ink Corp., Berkeley, Calif., 1973—. Contbr. articles to profl. jours.; patentee in field. Shevlin fellow U. Minn., 1938-39. Mem. Am. Chem. Soc., Sigma Xi, Phi Lambda Upsilon, Phi Kappa Phi. Democrat. Mormon. Avocations: tennis, violin, bridge. Home: 21 Daryl Dr Orinda CA 94563 Office: Calif Ink Co div Flint Ink Corp 711 Camelia St Berkeley CA 94710

EGGLESTON, KATHLEEN A., manufacturer, marketing consultant; b. Chgo., Feb. 6, 1947; d. Kirkland James and Johnnie Viola Rand; m. Ed Arnold, Nov. 24, 1968 (div. 1972); m. Michael William Eggleston, Dec. 25, 1982. Student, San Francisco State U. Investigator, research cons. Ill. Supreme Ct., Chgo., 1970; account exec. ETA Pub. Relations, Chgo., 1970-72; pub. relations and promotion dir. Sta. WTVS TV, Detroit, 1972; pub. affairs dir. Sta. WJLB Radio, Detroit, 1972-74; pvt. practice bus. resource and research cons. K.H. Arnold, San Francisco, 1974-80; spl. projects coordinator The Hdqrs. Co. subs. United Techs., San Francisco, 1980-81; adminstrn. mgr. Nat. Alliance of Bus.-Region IX, San Francisco, 1981-83; pres. Michael St. Michael/Corp. Leather and Leather Goods Mfr., Menlo Park, Calif., 1983—. Mem. Acad. Ind. Scholars, Soc. for Study of Women in Legal History, Inst. for Hist. Study, NOW, Women's Inst. for Freedom, Am. Women in Radio and TV Inc., Vallejo C. of C. (com. mem. 1985—), San Francisco C. of C. (com. mem. 1984—), World Trade Assn., Bay Area Purchasing Council (com. mem. 1986—), Urban Coalition West, (bd. dirs. Phoenix chpt. 1986—). Home: 181 Santa Margarita Ave Menlo Park CA 94025

EGLEY, THOMAS ARTHUR, computer services executive, accountant; b. Aberdeen, S.D., June 23, 1945; s. Ralph Joseph and Cora Ellen (Wade) E.; m. Cecelia K. Kuskie, Feb. 22, 1984. BBA, U. Mont., 1967, postgrad., 1973-75. CPA, Mont. Programmer, analyst Comml. Data, Missoula, Mont., 1973-77; data processing mgr. John R. Daily, Inc., Missoula, 1977-78; ptnr. Egley & White CPA's, Missoula, 1978-84; ptnr. Egley & White Computer Services, Missoula, 1978-85, pres., 1982—; pres. Able Fin., Inc., Missoula, 1984—; lectr., Missoula, 1973—. Bd. dirs. Missoula Children's Theater, 1975-82. Served to sgt. U.S. Army, 1968-71. Mem. Am. Inst. CPA's, Mont. Soc. CPA's, Nat. Assn. Accts., EDP Auditors Assn., Mont. Data Processing Assn., Phi Sigma Kappa Alumni Club (pres. 1973—). Republican. Lutheran. Lodge: Elks. Avocations: fishing, photography, travel. Home and Office: E&W Computer Services Inc PO Drawer 2729 Missoula MT 59806-2729

EGNEW, THOMAS ROMINE, family medicine educator, counselor; b. Billings, Mont., Dec. 4, 1947; s. Charles Leaman and Dorothy Elizabeth (Hawk) E.; m. Kathleen Louise Cucciardi, July 25, 1968 (div. Feb. 1978); children: Danielle Marie, Aaron Thomas. BA, Rocky Mountain Coll., 1970; MA, U. Chgo., 1972. Social work officer Madigan Army Med. Ctr., Tacoma, 1972-75, behavioral scientist, 1975-77; clin. dir. Tacoma Girls' Club Children's Indsl. Home, 1978-79; behavioral scientist Tacoma Family Medicine, 1979—; adj. faculty Pacific Luth. U., Tacoma, 1975-82; pvt. counseling practice Tacoma, 1978—; clin. assoc. U. Wash. Dept. Family Medicine, 1980—. Served to capt. U.S. Army, 1972-77. Mem. Nat. Assn. Social Workers (cert.), Am. Assn. Marital and Family Therapy, Soc. Tchrs. of Family Medicine. Episcopalian. Avocations: reading, cooking, guitar, vocal music. Office: Tacoma Family Medicine 419 South L St Tacoma WA 98405

EGUCHI, YASU, artist; b. Japan, Nov. 30, 1938; came to U.S., 1967; s. Chihaku and Kiku (Koga) E.; m. Anita Phillips, Feb. 24, 1968. Student, Horie Art Acad., Japan, 1958-65. Exhibited exhbns., Tokyo Mus. Art, 1963, 66, Santa Barbara Mus. Art, Calif., 1972, 73, 74, 85, Everson Mus. Art, Syracuse, N.Y., 1980, Nat. Acad. Design, N.Y.C., 1980-87, one-man shows, Austin Gallery, Scottsdale, Ariz., 1968-87, Greystone Galleries, Cambria, Calif., 1969, 70, 72, Copenhagen Galleries, Calif., 1970-78, Charles and Emma Frye Art Mus., Seattle, 1974, 84, Hammer Galleries, N.Y.C., 1977, 79, 81, City of Heidenheim, W. Ger., 1980, Artique Ltd., Anchorage, 1981-86; pub. and pvt. collections, Voith Gmbh, W. Ger., City of Giengen and City of Heidenheim, W. Ger., represented, Deer Valley, Utah, Hunter Resources, Santa Barbara, Am. Embassy, Paris, Charles and Emma Frye Art Mus., Seattle, Nat. Acad. Design, N.Y.C.; author: Der Brenz Entlang, 1980; contbr. to jours in field. Active Guide Dogs for the Blind, San Raphael, Calif., 1976; active City of Santa Barbara Arts Council, 1979, The Eye Bank for Sight Restoration, N.Y., 1981, Anchorage Arts Council, 1981. Recipient Selective artist award Yokohama Citizen Gallery, 1965; recipient Artist of Yr. award Santa Barbara Arts Council, 1979, Hon. Citizen award City of Heidenheim, 1980, The Adolph and Clara Obrig prize Nat. Acad. Design, 1983. Home: PO Box 30206 Santa Barbara CA 93130

EHERENMAN, DARVIN GENE, salesman, food service consultant; b. Warsaw, Ind., Jan. 27, 1933; s. Harry Oakley Eherenman and Blanche Fay (Rickel) Bair; m. Helen Louise Bean, Dec. 27, 1955; children: Kimberly Ann, Kurt Steven, Kevin Forrest, Kent Charles. BA, Wabash Coll., 1956. Salesman John Sexton, Las Vegas; v.p., gen. mgr. Henny Penny Foods, Las Vegas; dir. purchasing Caesars Tahoe Hotel, Stateline, Nev.; sales rep. Atlas Horn Food Service, Las Vegas. Mem. Internat. Food Execs. Assn. (sec.). Republican. Roman Catholic. Lodge: Elks. Avocations: music, boating, camping. Home: 3100 W Avalon Las Vegas NV 89107 Office: Atlas-Horn Food Service 6255 Sunset Blvd Hollywood CA

EHLERS, ELEANOR MAY COLLIER (MRS. FREDERICK BURTON EHLERS), civic worker; b. Klamath Falls, Oreg., Apr. 23, 1920; d. Alfred Douglas and Ethel (Foster) Collier; B.A., U. Oreg., 1941; secondary tchrs. credentials Stanford, 1942; m. Frederick Burton Ehlers, June 26, 1943; children—Frederick Douglas, Charles Collier. Tchr., Salinas Union High Sch., 1942-43; piano tchr. pvt. lessons, Klamath Falls, 1958—. Mem. Child Guidance Adv. Council, 1956-60; mem. adv. com. Boys and Girls Aid Soc., 1965—; mem. Gov.'s Adv. Com. Arts and Humanities, 1966-67; bd. mem. Friends of Mus. U. Oreg., 1966-69, Arts in Oreg., 1966-68, Klamath County Colls. for Oreg.'s Future, 1968—; co-chmn. Friends of Collier Park, Collier Park Logging Mus., 1986—; chpt. pres. Am. Field Service, 1962-63; mem. Gov.'s Com. Governance of Community Colls., 1967; bd. dirs. Favell Mus. Western Art and Artifacts, 1971—, Community Concert Assn., 1950—, pres., 1966-74; established Women's Guild at Presbyn. Intercommunity Hosp., 1965, trustee hosp. sec. bd. trustees, 1962-65, 76—, mem. bldg. com. 1962-67, mem. planning com., chmn. edn. and research com. hosp. bd., 1967—. Named Woman of Month, Klamath Herald News, 1965; named grant to Oreg. Endowed Fellowship Fund, AAUW, 1971; recipient greatest Service award Oreg. Tech. Inst., 1970-71, Internat. Woman of Achievement award Quota Club, 1981, U. Oreg. Pioneer award, 1981. Mem. AAUW (local pres. 1955-56), Oreg. Music Tchrs. Assn. (pres. Klamath Basin dist. 1979—), P.E.O. (Oreg. dir. 1968-75, state pres. 1974-75, trustee internat. Continuing Edn. Fund 1977-83, chmn. 1981-83), Pi Beta Phi, Mu Phi Epsilon, Pi Lambda Theta. Presbyterian. Address: 1338 Pacific Terr Klamath Falls OR 97601

EHLERS, FREDERICK DOUGLAS, real estate developer; b. San Francisco, Aug. 18, 1945; s. Frederick Burton and Eleanor (Collier) E.; BBA, U. Oreg., 1967; children: Claire Collier, Janet Victoria. V.p. Swan Lake Moulding Co., Klamath Falls, Oreg., 1971—; real estate developer, 1978—; mng. ptnr. Jefferson Sq. Mall, Klamath Falls, 1979—; owner, operator North Fork Hydro, Klamath Falls, 1979—; developer of North Fork Hydro Plant, 1981—. Prin. oboe, bd. dirs. Plum Ridge Symphony; mem. Klamath County Rep. Cen. Com.; bd. dirs. Klamath Falls YMCA. Served with AUS, 1967-71. Decorated Bronze Star, Air medal with five oak leaf clusters. Mem. Internat. Council Shopping Ctrs., Klamath County Econ. Devel. Assn., Nat. Retail Hardware Assn., Nat. Bldg. Materials Assn., Western Bldg. Materials Assn. Presbyterian. Club: Klamath Yacht (past commodore). Lodge: Rotary. Home: Box 7148 Klamath Falls OR 97602 Office: Box 5148 Klamath Falls OR 97601

EHNINGER, STEPHEN MARTIN, architect; b. Salt Lake City, May 17, 1948; s. Martin Carlye and Winona (Dahlquist) E.; m. Sandra Collison, June 30, 1966; children: Amy, Andrew. BFA, U. Utah, 1966, MArch, 1974. Graphic designer Young Electric Sign Co., Salt Lake City, Gardiner Advt., Salt Lake City; architect Scott, Louie & Browning, Salt Lake City, 1979—; mem. architects registration bd., Salt Lake City, 1985—. Author: Administration Master Plan Study, 1985. Served to staff sgt. USAF, 1969-72. Mem. AIA, Am. Inst. Graphic Arts. Episcopal.

EHRENTHAL, FRANK FREDERIC, architect, planner, educator; b. Budapest, Hungary, Jan. 22, 1910; s. Alexander S. and Eugenie (Deutch) E.; came to U.S., 1939, naturalized, 1944; student U. Padua, Italy, 1928-29, Brunn Inst. Tech., Czechoslovakia, 1929-32; D.Arch., U. Firenze, Italy, 1935; L.H.D. (hon.), Starr King Sch. for Ministry, Berkeley, 1966; m. Julie Ann Deutch, 1941; children—Robert, Ann, Sylvia. Asso. various archtl. firms, Czechoslovakia, Italy, U.S., 1931—; pvt. practice architecture, San Francisco, 1946-63; vis. lectr. various colls., 1948-63; prof. architecture and urban design Pa. State U., 1963-66, Okla. State U., 1966-68; prof., chmn. grad. urban design program Center for Urban and Regional Studies, Coll. Architecture, Va. Poly. Inst. and State U., Blacksburg, 1968-69, prof., chmn. grad. urban and regional planning and urban design programs Environ. and Urban Systems div. Coll. Architecture and Urban Studies, 1969-70, prof. urban and regional studies, chmn. grad. urban design program, 1970-80, prof. emeritus, 1980—. Recipient 1st and Grand prize Archtl. Forum, NAMP Internat. Competition, 1952, honorable mention Franklin Delano Roosevelt Meml. Competition, Washington, 1960, Spl. honorable mention Centro Direzionale Fontivegge Bellocchio Internat. Competition, Perugia, Italy, 1971, hon. mention Rainbow Center Plaza Competition, Niagara Falls, 1972. Past chmn. com. on extension San Francisco Council Chs.; past mem. com. on extension Calif.-Nev. Council Chs.; past mem. Mayor's San Francisco Forward Com. Task Force, Fedn. Am. Scientists; founder Centre Citizens Planning Assn. (Pa.). Mem. AIA, Va. Citizens Planning Assn. (past dir.), Environ. Designers and Planners for Social Responsibility (founder), Architects/Designers/Plannersfor Social Responsibility (founding dir. nat. bd.). Contbr. articles to profl. jours.; work featured in various profl. publs. Home: 140 Agnes Ct Vallejo CA 94589

EHRHORN, RICHARD WILLIAM, electronics company executive; b. Marshalltown, Iowa, Jan. 21, 1934; s. Theodore Raymond and Zelda Elizabeth (Axtell) E.; B.S.E.E., U. Minn., 1955; M.S.E.E., Calif. Inst. Tech., 1958; m. Marilyn Patrick, Aug. 1, 1959; children: Scott Patrick, Kimberlee Dawn. Sr. engr. Gen. Dynamics Corp., Pomona, Calif., 1956-60; sr. research engr. Calif. Inst. Tech. Jet Propulsion Lab., Pasadena, 1960-63; mgr. advanced devel. lab. Electronic Communications Inc., St. Petersburg, Fla., 1963-68; gen. mgr. Signal/One div., 1968-70; pres. Ehrhorn Tech. Ops., Inc., Canon City, Colo., 1970—. Bd. dirs. Fremont County (Colo.) Econ. Devel. Council, 1978-84; trustee, bd. dirs. St. Thomas More Hosp., Canon City, 1981—; trustee First United Meth. Ch., Canon City, 1980-85; mem. Fremont Re-1 Dist. Bd. Edn., 1983—, pres., 1985—. Mem. IEEE (sr.; chmn. sect. 1967-68), Mfrs. Roundtable, Armed Forces Communications and Electronics Assn., Am. Radio Relay League, Radio Club Am., Quar. Century Wireless Assn. Author: (with others) Principles of Electronic Warfare, 1959; patentee in field. Office: PO Box 888 Canon City CO 81212

EHRLICH, EUGENE, communications executive; b. N.Y.C., Jan. 10, 1930; s. Max Ehrlich and Rose Krauthamer; children: Karen, Jeffrey. BS, NYU, 1951. Program mgr. NASA, Washington, 1962-79; communications engr. Aerospace Corp., El Segundo, Calif., 1979-81, Spacecom, Gaithersburg, Md., 1981-82; sr. communications engr. TRW Inc., Redondo Beach, Calif., 1982—. Avocations: tennis, hiking. Home: 8180 Manitoba St #227 Playa del Rey CA 90293 Office: TRW Inc 1 Space Park Communications Div M/S 87/1519 Redondo Beach CA 90278

EHRLICH, PAUL RALPH, biology educator; b. Phila., May 29, 1932; s. William and Ruth (Rosenberg) E.; m. Anne Fitzhugh Howland, Dec. 18, 1954; 1 dau., Lisa Marie. A.B., U. Pa., 1953; A.M., U. Kans., 1955, Ph.D., 1957. Research assoc. U. Kans., Lawrence, 1958-59; asst. prof. biol. scis. Stanford, 1959-62, asso. prof., 1962-66, prof., 1966—, Bing prof. population studies, 1976—, dir. grad. study dept. biol. scis., 1966-69, 1974-76; cons. Behavioral Research Labs., 1963-67. Author: How to Know the Butterflies, 1961, Process of Evolution, 1963, Principles of Modern Biology, 1968, Population Bomb, 1968, 2d edit., 1971, Population, Resources, Environment: Issues In Human Ecology, 1970, 2d edit., 1972, How to Be a Survivor, 1971, Global Ecology: Readings Toward a Rational Strategy for Man, 1971, Man and the Ecosphere, 1971, Introductory Biology, 1973, Human Ecology: Problems and Solutions, 1973, Ark II: Social Response to Environmental Imperatives, 1974, The End of Affluence: A Blueprint for the Future, 1974, Biology and Society, 1976, Race Bomb, 1977, Ecoscience: Population, Resources, Environment, 1977, Insect Biology, 1978, The Golden Door: International Migration, Mexico, and the U.S, 1979, Extinction: The Causes and Consequences of the Disappearance of Species, 1981, The Machinery of Nature, 1986, Earth, 1987, The Science of Ecology, 1987; contbr. articles to profl. jours. Fellow Calif. Acad. Scis., Am. Acad. Arts and Scis.; mem. Nat. Acad. Scis., Soc. for Study Evolution, Soc. Systematic Zoology, Am. Soc. Naturalists, Lepidopterists Soc., Am. Mus. Natural History (hon. life mem.). Address: Stanford U Biological Scis Stanford CA 94305

EHRLICH, STEVEN DAVID, architect; b. N.Y.C., June 12, 1946; s. Samuel J. and Betty Ehrlich; m. Marlo Lani, Jan. 3, 1981; children: Vanessa, Sarah. BS, Rensselaer Poly. Inst., 1968, BArch., 1969. Registered architect, Calif. Architect, Peace Corps, Morocco, 1969-71; tchr. Ahmadu Bello U., Nigeria, 1974-77; pvt. practice architecture, Venice, Calif., 1978—; tchr. U. So. Calif., Los Angeles, 1982-83, Sci.-Arch, Santa Monica, Calif., 1983, UCLA, 1985. Recipient Builders Choice Grand award, 1983, 85. Mem. AIA

(Design awards Los Angeles chpt. 1981, 82, 83, Calif. chpt. 1983-84, Sunset chpt. 1983). Office: Ehrlich Architects 76 Market St Venice CA 90291

EHRMANTRAUT, HARRY CHARLES, medical consultant, researcher; b. Washington, Nov. 25, 1921; s. Edward Joseph and Elizabeth (Kaufmann) E.; m. Shirley Lee Anderson, Mar. 26, 1948; children: Lisa, Lynn. BA in Botany, George Washington U., 1947; MS in Chemistry, Georgetown U., 1948; PhD in Biophysics, U. Ill., 1950. Pres. Mechrolab, Inc., Mountain View, Calif., 1959-65, Videonetics, Inc., Sunnyvale, Calif., 1966-68, Gymnas corp., Los Altos, Calif., 1968-71, AVM Assocs., Inc., Los Osos, Calif., 1977-81; dir. mktg. Alpha Thermistor, Inc., San Diego, 1986-87; pres. Alchem Assocs., San Diego, 1987—; ptnr. Bus. Analysis Assocs., San Carlos, Calif., 1972-76; bd. dirs. I.I.M., Inc., San Diego, IDS, Inc. Author: Headaches, 1980, 2d ed., 1987; co-author, editor 4 books on instrumentation, 1954-65; patentee in field. Served to cpl. USAAF, 1942-46. Mem. IEEE, Biophys. Soc. (founding), Am. Chem. Soc., N.Y. Acad. Scis., Sigma Xi. Home: 10631 Porto Ct San Diego CA 92124 Office: Alchem Assocs 10615 Tierrasanta Blvd Suite 168 San Diego CA 92124

EICHINGER, BRUCE EDWARD, chemistry educator; b. Canby, Minn., Oct. 25, 1941; s. Howard and Gladys C. (Dahl) E.; m. Mary Kathryn Gabriel, Sept 1, 1962; children: Gregory, Gretchen, Jason. B in Chemistry, U. Minn., 1963; PhD, Stanford U., 1967. Postdoctoral fellow Yale U., New Haven, 1967-68; from asst. prof. to prof. U. Wash., Seattle, 1968—, acting chmn. chemistry dept., 1985—; cons. in field. Mem. Am. Chem. Soc., Tau Beta Pi. Avocations: skiing, woodworking. Home: 1111 38th Ave Seattle WA 98122 Office: U Wash Dept Chemistry Seattle WA 98195

EICKHOFF, DENNIS RAYMOND, financial services company executive; b. Indpls., Aug. 13, 1944; s. Raymond Alvin and Wilma Irma (Franke) E.; m. Janice Kay Ryder, Aug. 27, 1966; children: Christopher David, Stephen Dennis. BS in Math., Purdue U., 1966, MS in Indsl. Adminstrn., 1967. Market analyst Esso Internat., Inc., N.Y.C., 1967-69; mgmt. cons. Touche Ross & Co., N.Y.C., 1969-74; exec. v.p. Citicorp Person to Person, Inc., St. Louis and San Diego, 1974-82; chief operating officer Citicorp Savs., Oakland, Calif., 1982-83; pres., chief exec. officer Gibraltar Moneycenter, Inc., San Diego, 1983—; bd. dirs. Gibraltar Life Ins. Co., Phoenix, 1984—, Am. Fin. Services Assn., Washington, 1986—. Republican. Lutheran. Club: University. Avocations: racquetball, gardening, automobiles. Office: Gibraltar Moneycenter Inc 9696 Business Park Ave San Diego CA 92131

EICKHOFF, THEODORE CARL, physician; b. Cleve., Sept. 13, 1931; s. Theodore Henry and Clara (Strassen) E.; m. Margaret Heinecke, Aug. 24, 1952; children: Stephen, Mark, Philip. B.A., Valparaiso U., 1953; M.D., Case Western Res. U., 1957. Diplomate: Am. Bd. Internal Medicine. Intern, then resident Harvard Med. Services, Boston City Hosp., 1957-59; fellow in medicine Harvard Med. Sch.-Boston City Hosp., 1961-64; epidemiologist Center for Disease Control, 1964-67; prof. medicine U. Colo. Med. Ctr., 1975—, head div. infectious disease, 1967-80; vice chmn. dept. medicine U. Colo. Med. Center, 1976-81; dir. internal medicine Presbyn./St. Luke's Med. Ctr.; dir. medicine Denver Gen. Hosp., 1978-81; cons. FDA, Centers for Disease Control, Am. Hosp. Assn. Contbr. articles to med. jours. Served with USPHS, 1959-67. Mem. Am. Fedn. Clin. Research, ACP, Am. Soc. Clin. Investigation, Assn. Am. Physicians, Infectious Diseases Soc. Am. (sec. 1978-82, pres. 1983-84), Am. Epidemiol. Soc. (pres. 1985-86). Home: 15 S Franklin Circle Littleton CO 80121 Office: St Lukes Hosp 601 E 19th Ave Denver CO 80201

EIDE, CRAIG DONALD, accountant; b. Mpls., May 13, 1949; s. Lloyd Norman and Donna Mae (Mickelson) E.; m. Linda Ann Briggs, Dec. 17, 1971; 1 child, Eric. BS, USCG Acad., 1971; MBA, U. Chgo., 1976. CPA, Wash. Commd. ensign USCG, various, 1971; advanced through grades to lt. USCG, various locations, 1974; staff acct. Coopers & Lybrand, Portland, Maine, 1977-79; sr. acct. Baumgartner, Kueckelhan, Seattle, 1979-81; controller Northwest Steel Rolling Mills, Seattle, 1981-84, Trade Products Inc., Lynnwood, Wash., 1984—. Mem. Wash. Soc. CPA's. Democrat. Lutheran. Office: Trade Products Inc 2807 Lincoln Way Lynnwood WA 98046

EIDSON, ROBERT LEE, computer company executive; b. Portland, Oreg., Aug. 1, 1940; s. Bernard F. and Mary I. (Eldred) E.; m. Barbara Anne Demerath, Dec. 23, 1967; children: Jennifer, Scott. BS, U. Oreg., 1963; MBA, U. Santa Clara, 1973. Computer programmer Wells Fargo, San Francisco, 1963-67; systems programmer ESL Corp., Sunnyvale, Calif., 1967-73; systems analyst Stanford (Calif.) U., 1973-77; project mgr. FWFS Corp., Portland, 1977-80; capacity mgr. Tektronix, Inc., Vancouver, Wash., 1980—; cons. Springbrook Systems, Lake Oswego, Oreg., 1983—; adj. prof. Oreg. Inst. Tech., Portland. Mem. IEEE, Computer Soc. of IEEE (bd. dirs. 1983—). Republican. Roman Catholic. Home: 14825 SW Rainbow Dr Lake Oswego OR 97035 Office: Tektronix Box 3500 Vancouver WA 98668

EIFLER, CARL FREDERICK, ret. psychologist; b. Los Angeles, June 27, 1906; s. Carl Frederick and Pauline (Engelbert) E.; Ph.D., Ill. Inst. Tech., 1962; B.D., Jackson Coll.; m. Margaret Christine Aaberg, June 30, 1963; 1 son, Carl Henry; 1 adopted son, Byron Hisey. Insp., U.S. Bur. Customs, 1928-35, chief insp., 1936-37, dep. collector, 1937-56; bus. mgr. Jackson Coll., Honolulu, 1954-56, instr., 1955-56; grad. asst. instr., research asst. Ill. Inst. Tech., Chgo., 1959-62; psychologist Monterey County Mental Health Services, Salinas, Calif., 1964-73; ret., 1973. Served with U.S. Army, 1922-23, 40-47; col. ret. Decorated Combat Infantryman's Badge, Legion of Merit with 2 oak leaf clusters, Bronze Star medal, Air medal, Purple Heart. Mem. Am., Western States, Calif., Monterey County psychol. assns., AAUP, Res. Officers Assn. (Hawaii pres. 1947), Assn. Former Intelligence Officers (bd. govs., Western coordinator), Pearl Harbor Survivors, 101 Assn., Assn. U.S. Army, Vets. of OSS (western v.p.), Am. Law Enforcement Officers Assn., Nat. Intelligence Study Center, Security and Intelligence Fund, Ret. Officers Assn., Psi Chi. Clubs: Masons, KT, Shriners, Elks, Nat. Sojourners. Contbg. author Psychon. Sci., vol. 20, 1970; co-author: The Deadliest Colonel; author: Jesus Said. Home: 22700 Picador Dr Salinas CA 93908

EIKENBERRY, KENNETH OTTO, state attorney general; b. Wenatchee, Wash., June 29, 1932; s. Otto Kenneth and Florence Estelle E.; m. Beverly Jane Hall, Dec. 21, 1963. B.A. in Polit. Sci., Wash. State U., 1954; LL.B., U. Wash., 1959. Bar: Wash. 1959. Spl. agt. FBI, 1960-62; dep. pros. atty. King County (Wash.), Seattle, 1962-67; with firm Richey & Eikenberry, 1967-68, Clinton, Andersen, Fleck & Glein, Seattle, 1968-73; legal counsel King County Council, 1974-76; chmn. Wash. Republican party, 1977-80; atty. gen. State of Wash., 1981—; judge pro tem Seattle Mcpl. Ct., 1979-80; mem. Pres.'s Task Force on Victims of Crime, Pres.'s Child Safety Partnership, 1986—, state Criminal Justice Training Commn. 1980—, state Corrections Standards Bd. 1980—. Chmn., King County Rep. Conv., 1974, 78; mem. Wash. Ho. of Reps., 1970-74. Served with AUS, 1954-56. Named Legislator of Year, Young Americans for Freedom/Wash. Conservative Union, 1974, Rep. Man of Year, Young Men's Rep. Club King County, 1979. Mem. Wash. Bar Assn., Western Conf. Attys.-Gen. (chmn. 1983-84), Soc. Former Spl. Agts. FBI, Nat. Assn. Attys.-Gen. (chmn. energy com. 1983-84, sub-com. on RICO issues, 1984—), Internat. Footprint Assn., Delta Theta Phi, Alpha Tau Omega. Clubs: Kiwanis, Rainrunners. Office: Temple of Justice Office Atty Gen Olympia WA 98504

EIKREM, LYNWOOD OLAF, business executive; b. Lansing. Mich., June 11, 1919; s. Arthur Rudolph and Gatha (Zupp) E.; m. Margaret Rosemarie McDonough, July 13, 1946; children: Margaret, John, Marie, Jeanne. BS, Mich. State U., 1941; MS, MIT, 1948. Assoc. prof. chemistry La. Poly. Inst., 1946; tech. dir. Jarrell-Ash Co., Newtonville, Mass., 1949-53; project engr. Baird-Atomic, Cambridge, Mass., 1953-59; staff engr. Geophysics Corp. Am., Bedford, Mass., 1959-60; mgr. product devel. dept. David W. Mann Co. div. Geophysics Corp. Am., Lincoln, Mass., 1960-63, dir. mktg., Burlington, Mass., 1963-65; v.p. mktg. Applied Research Labs. subs. Bausch & Lomb Inc., Sunland, Calif., 1965-72; dir. mktg. Darling & Alsobrook, Los Angeles, 1972-75; prin. Darling, Paterson & Salzer, 1975-79; pres. Paterson & Co., 1979-81; chmn. Strategic Directions Internat., 1981—. Fellow Am. Inst. Chemists; mem. Optical Soc. Am., ASTM, N.Y. Acad. Scis., Sales and Mktg. Execs. Assn., VFW. Lodge: K.C. Home: 605 N Louise St #201 Glendale CA 92106 Office: Strategic Directions Internat 6242 Westchester Pkwy Suite 100 Los Angeles CA 90045

EILS, RICHARD GEORGE, retail company executive; b. Milw., 1937; married. Grad., U. Wis., 1960. With Thrifty Corp., Los Angeles, 1956-65; treas. Thrifty Corp., 1972-74, v.p., 1974-76, sr. v.p., 1976-77, exec. v.p., 1977-79, pres., 1979—, also chief operating officer, chief fin. officer, dir.; pres., dir. Thrifty Realty Co.; bd. dirs. United Merchandising Corp., Newman Importing Co. Inc., FTM Sports, Thrifty Jr. Inc., Thrifty Wilshire Inc., MC Sporting Goods, Gart Bros. Sporting Goods. Office: Thrifty Corp 3424 Wilshire Blvd Los Angeles CA 90010 *

EINSTEIN, CLIFFORD JAY, advertising executive; b. Los Angeles, May 4, 1939; s. Harry and Thelma (Bernstein) E.; m. Madeline Mandel, Jan. 28, 1962; children: Harold Jay, Karen Holly. A.B. in English, UCLA, 1961. Writer Norman, Craig & Kummel, N.Y.C., 1961-62, Foote, Cone & Belding, Los Angeles, 1962-64; partner Silverman & Einstein, Los Angeles, 1965-67; pres., creative dir. Dailey & Assos., Los Angeles, 1968—; also dir. Dailey & Assos.; dir. Campaign '80, advt. agy. Reagan for Pres., 1980; lectr. various colls.; dir. El Segundo First Nat. Bank. Producer: play Whatever Happened to Georgie Tapps, Los Angeles and San Francisco, 1980. Bd. dirs. Rape Treatment Ctr., Santa Monica Med. Ctr. Served with U.S. Army, 1957. Recipient Am. Advt. award as Best in West, 1968, 73, 79, Clio award for best radio comml., Internat. Broadcast pub. service award, 1970, Sweepstakes award Los Angeles Advt. Club, 1974, 78, Nat. Addy award for best campaign, 1979, Gov.'s award for victim services, 1987; named Creative Dir. of the West Adweek Poll, 1982, named Exec. of West, 1986. Mem. AFTRA, ASCAP, Screen Actors Guild., Dirs. Guild Am. Home: 11940 Brentwood Grove Los Angeles CA 90049 Office: Dailey & Assocs 3055 Wilshire Blvd Los Angeles CA 90010

EISELE, MILTON DOUGLAS, viticulturist; b. N.Y.C., Apr. 2, 1910; s. Charles Francis and Helen Agnes (Dolan) E.; B.A., U. Calif.-Berkeley, 1933; grad. San Francisco Stock Exchange Inst., 1938; m. Barbara Lois Morgan, July 26, 1941; children—Helen Frances Eisele Osthimer, Barbara Glennis, William Douglas. Investment cashier Wells Fargo Bank, San Francisco, 1934-39; coordinator cement sales Permanente Corp., 1940-41, constrn. supt., 1941-43; mgr. refractory div. Kaiser Aluminum, 1943-47, mgr. regional sales, Chgo., 1947-50, mgr. foil div., 1950-55, mgr. prodn., 1955-60, mgr. market and prodn. devel., 1960-65, mgr. investments, 1966-71; ret., 1971; owner, operator Eisele Vineyards, Napa Valley, Calif., 1969—. Dir., former pres. Napa Valley Found., 1981—; bd. dirs., past chmn. Vintage Hall, Inc., 1973—; bd. dirs., past pres. Napa Valley Heritage Fund, 1973—; past pres., bd. dirs. Upper Napa Valley Assocs., 1976-80; mem. adv. council Napa County Land Trust, 1976-79. Mem. Am. Soc. Enologists, Napa Valley Grape Growers Assn. (dir.), Calif. Assn. Wine Grape Growers (dir., former sec., chmn. 1986—), Wine & Food Soc. of San Francisco, Calif. Vintage Wine Soc., Agri. Council of Napa County, Wine and Winegrape Mktg. Order State of Calif. (dir. 1984), Napa Valley Vinter/Grower (chmn. bd. dirs.), Kappa Alpha Order. Republican. Episcopalian (vestryman, sr. warden 1966-69). Club: Commonwealth (San Francisco). Home and Office: 2155 Pickett Rd Calistoga CA 94515

EISELIN, ROLF, architect, artist; b. Zurich, Switzerland, Nov. 6, 1925; s. Adolph and Louise (Bäuerlein) Eiselin; divorced; children: Frances, Philip. Architecture diploma, Swiss Fed. Ins. Tech., Zurich. Registered architect, Ill., Switzerland. Architect Skidmore, Owings & Merrill, Chgo.; adminstr., organizer Prints USA Exhibition. One-man shows include San Francisco Mus. Modern Art; exhibited in group shows at Univ. Calif., Davis., U.S. Nat. Mus., Washington, Royal Ontario Mus., Nat. Mus., Singapore, Japan Print Assn. Annual, Seattle Art Mus.; represented in permanent collections San Francisco Mus. Modern Art, Achenbach Found. Legion of Honor., Oakland Art Mus., Cabo Frio CIPB collection, Brazil, Graphische Sammlung ETH, Zurich. Served to capt. Swiss Army. Recipient Medal of Honor, Nat. Exhibition, Jersey City Mus. Mem. Swiss Architects and Engrs. Assn., Swiss Painters, Sculptors and Architects Soc., Calif. Soc. Printmakers (past pres.). Home and Office: 1868 Mountain View Dr Tiburon CA 94920 Other: Rés La Côte 60, 1110 Morges Switzerland

EISENBERG, ALLAN JEROME, advertising executive; b. Bklyn., May 24, 1935; s. Jules J. and Rose d(Chenkin) E.; divorced; 1 child, Evan. BFA, Ithaca Coll., 1961. V.p., gen. mgr. Sta KUDL AM-FM, Kansas City, Mo., 1971-73; gen. mgr. Sta. WNCN-FM, N.Y.C., 1973-74; v.p. NBC Radio Network, N.Y.C., 1974-75; v.p., gen. mgr. Sta. KKSS-FM, St. Louis, 1975-79; gen. sales mgr. Sta. WRTH Radio, St. Louis, 1979-80, Sta. KSD, KCFM, St. Louis, 1980-81; dir. advt. sales Am. TV and Communications Corp., Englewood, Colo., 1981—. Served with U.S. Army. Mem. Denver Ad Fedn., Cable Ad Bur., St. Louis Media Club, Women in Cable, Speakers Bur., Cable Advt. Bur., St. Louis Advt. Club, Sales Mktg. and Mgmt. Club. Avocations: tennis, politics, music, reading. Home: 669 Washington Denver CO 80203 Office: ATC-Corp 160 Inverness Dr W Englewood CO 80112

EISENBERG, LAWRENCE, university research foundation executive, corporate planning consultant; b. N.Y.C., Aug. 5, 1939; s. Morris and Sophie (Shebutsky) E.; m. Gretchen Gary, Aug. 24, 1969; children: Jonathan Gary, David Mills. BA in History, Queens Coll. CUNY, 1960; MBA, JD, Columbia U., 1964. Program coordinator The Asia Found., San Francisco, 1964-65; asst. dir. Frederic Burk Found., San Francisco, 1965-67; exec. dir. San Francisco State U. Found. Inc., 1967—; pres. Research, Tng., Edn. Services Inc., Millbrae, Calif., 1970-76; v.p. Sensory Aids Found., Palo Alto, Calif., 1974—; sec. treas. Am. Found. Chinese Studies, 1979-83. Recipient Research Mgmt. Improvement grant NSF, U. Okla., 1974. Mem. San Francisco Bay Area Devel. Execs. Roundtable (pres. 1986—), Nat. Council of U. Research Adminstrs., Soc. Research Adminstrs. Club: Press Club of San Francisco. Home: 15 El Bonito Way Millbrae CA 94030

EISENHARDT, (EMIL) ROY, professional baseball team executive; b. 1939; m. Auban Slay, 1965 (div. 1976); m. Elizabeth Haas, 1978; children: Sarah, Jesse. BA, Dartmouth Coll., 1960; LLB, U. Calif., Berkeley, 1965. Bar: Calif. 1966. Formerly with firm Farella, Braun and Martel, San Francisco; tchr. U. Calif. Boalt Hall Sch. Law, Berkeley, 1974—; Pres. Oakland A's, Am. League, Calif., 1980—; former coach U. Calif. rowing crew. Served with USMC, 1960-62. Avocations: tennis, woodworking. Address: Oakland A's Oakland-Alameda County Coliseum Oakland CA 94621 *

EISENHEIM/HENSLER, DIANE L., speech pathologist; b. Chgo., Aug. 11, 1954; d. Alfred and Marilyn (Swenty) E. BS, Western Ill. U., 1976; MS, U. Wyo., 1978. Speech and lang. pathologist Rock Springs (Wyo.) Pub. Schs., 1976-77, Albany County Pub. Schs., Laramie, Wyo., 1977-78, Wilson Sch. Dist., Phoenix, 1978-82, Tempe (Ariz.) Union High Sch. Dist. 213, 1982—; faculty advisor Comparative Cultures Project Overseas, Tempe, 1982-85; adminstr. adult overseas tour Unique Discoveries Inc., Los Angeles, 1985—. Student coordinator Spl. Olympics, Tempe, 1979-82. Mem. Am. Speech and Hearing Assn. (cert.). Republican. Avocations: skiing, sailing, photography, music, writing. Office: Tempe Union High Sch Dist 213 500 W Guadalupe Rd Tempe AZ 85283

EISENMAN, STEPHEN ALAN, restaurant design consultant; b. Boston, Apr. 26, 1947; s. Gerald and Miriam Edna (Housman) E.; m. Kathryn Anne Soho, June 19, 1970 (div. Dec. 1974); m. Helen-Marie Kendrick, Dec. 28, 1974; children: Russell John, Karen Marie. BA, UCLA, 1970. Sales coordinator Supreme Metal Fabrication, Pico Rivera, Calif., 1970-80; pres. Beckham/Eisenman, Irvine, Calif., 1980—. Democrat. Jewish. Avocations: skiing, boating, coaching youth sports. Office: Beckham/Eisenman 16811 Milliken Ave Irvine CA 92714

EISENSHTAT, SIDNEY HERBERT, architect; b. New Haven, June 6, 1914; s. Morris and Ella (Sobole) E.; m. Alice D. Brenner, Dec. 19, 1937; children: Carole Oken, Abby Robyn. BArch, U. So. Calif., 1935. Registered architect, Calif. Prin. Sidney Eisenshtat & Assocs., Beverly Hills, Calif., 1941—; cons. Hechal Shlomo, Israel; mem. architects panel Union Am. Hebrew Congregations; bd. dirs. Internat. Tech. Coop. Ctr., Tel Aviv; pres., chmn. bd. dirs. Beth Jacob Congregation. Prin. works include House of the Book, Brandeis, Calif., 1970 (Landmark award 1979), Sinai Temple, Los Angeles, 1959 (25 yr. Landmark award 1984), Knox Presbyn. Ch., 1965 (Los Angeles Beauty award 1975), Wells Fargo Bldg., 1975 (Beverly Hills award 1978), Union Bank Bldg., 1960, Beverly Hills Exec. Life Bldg., 1966, Beverly Hills Hughes Aircraft Satellite Testing and Computer Ctr., El Segundo, Calif., Friars Club, Los Angeles, 1961, Marlton Sch. for Deaf, Los Angeles, 1968, Univ. Judaism Master Plan & Bldgs., Los Angeles, 1977, B'nai Zion Temple, El Paso, Tex., 1983, Temple Mt. Sinai, El Paso, 1962; works represented in permanent collection at Skirball Mus., Los Angeles. Recipient Nat. Sch. Adminstrs. award 1966. Fellow AIA (Honor award 1960, 66); mem. Bur. Jewish Edn. (vice-chmn. 1971-77, 86), Jewish Fedn. Council (vice-chmn. planning dept. 1971-72 chmn. emigré resettlement). Home: 2736 Motor Ave Los Angeles CA 90064 Office: 144 S Beverly Dr Beverly Hills CA 90212

EISENZIMMER, BETTY WENNER, insurance agent, executive; b. Twisp, Wash., July 25, 1939; d. Bren William and Julia Emogene (Salmon) Wenner; m. Erwin LeRoy Cook, June 19, 1955 (div. 1960); 1 child, Richard Jeffrey; m. Jerome Anthony Eisenzimmer, Feb. 18, 1966. Cert. in gen. ins. Ins. Inst. Am., 1981. Clk. typist MR Ins., Seattle, 1957-59; records clk. Assigned Risk Plan, Seattle, 1959-61; acct. asst. Robinson Jenner, Inc., Seattle, 1961-66; sec., acct. asst. Falkenberg & Co., Seattle, 1966-75, adminstrv. asst., 1975-77; ins. agt., corp. officer Service Ins. Inc., Seattle, 1975—; mem. adv. bd. Sch. Ins., Wash. State U. Coll. Bus., 1981—. Asst. editor Today's Ins. Woman, 1980-81. Exec. bd. Wash. chpt. Cystic Fibrosis Found., 1978-86, pres., 1983-85; mem. Wash. State Centennial Speakers' Bur., 1987—; mem. long range planning com. Cedar Cross United Meth. Ch., 1986—. Recipient Disting. Service award Cystic Fibrosis Found., 1984; named Vol. of Yr., Wash. chpt. Cystic Fibrosis Found., 1980. Mem. Seattle C. of C., Ins. Women Puget Sound (pres. 1970-72, Ins. Woman of Yr. 1978, 81, Industry award 1984), Ins. Women's Assn. Seattle (Ins. Woman of Yr. 1981), Nat. Assn. Ins. Women (nat. sec. 1976-77, regional dir. 1981-82, mem. exec. bd. 1976-77, 81-82, You Make the Difference award 1977, Regional IX Lace Speakoff award 1983). Ind. Ins. Agts. and Brokers Wash. (edn. com. 1982-83), Ind. Ins. Agts. and Brokers King County (chmn. bylaws 1984-85), Profl. Ins. Agts. Wash. (edn. com. 1982-86, chmn. 1983-86), Wash. Ins. Council (mem. speakers bur. 1980—), Women's Bus. Exchange, Women's Profl. and Managerial Women's Network, Nat. Assn. Life Underwriters Womens' Conf., Women Life Underwriters Conf., Acad. Producer Ins. Studies (fellow of acad.), Ins. Women of Lower Yakima Valley, Network of Exec. Women, Seattle Assn. Life Underwriters, Nat. Assn. Female Execs. Club: Toastmasters (pres. Wallingford chpt. 1986-87, ednl. v.p. 1987-88). Home: 8932 240th St SW Edmonds WA 98020 Office: Service Ins Inc 332 Securities Bldg Seattle WA 98101

EISLER, ANN OLMSTED, social worker; b. Whittier, Calif., Jan. 17, 1954; d. Alvin Herman and Joane Winette (Free) Olmsted; m. Gerald Richard Eisler, Sept. 11, 1976; 1 child, Brandon Richard. BJ, Iowa State U., 1976; MSSW, U. Tex., Austin, 1985. Cert. social worker. Copy editor and feature writer The Albuquerque Tribune, 1976-79; home visitor and social worker Ctr. Devel. Non-formal Edn., Austin, 1983-84; social worker neonatal ICU dept. Darnall Army Hosp., Ft. Hood, Tex., 1985; investigator sexual abuse Tex. Dept. Human Services, Austin, 1985-86; therapist Albuquerque Rape Crisis Ctr., U. N.Mex., 1986—. Pres. Temple Albert Sisterhood, Albuquerque, 1982-83; bd. trustees Temple Albert, 1978-83; active Albuquerque chpt. Operation Identity. Mem. Nat. Assn. Social Workers, LWV (bd. dirs. 1978-79), Phi Beta Kappa, Phi Kappa Phi. Democrat. Jewish. Avocations: bridge, reading. Home: 9713 Admiral Emerson NE Albuquerque NM 87112

EISLER, RIANE TENNENHAUS, lawyer; b. Vienna, Austria, July 22, 1931; d. David and Lisa (Greif) Tennenhaus; children: Andrea Suzanne, Loren Claire. BA, UCLA, 1952, JD, 1965. Assoc. Zagon, Schiff, Hirsch and Levine, Beverly Hills, Calif., 1966-68; sole practice Los Angeles, 1968-78; c0-dir. Inst. Futures Forecasting, Carmel, Calif., 1978—; founding dir. Los Angeles Women's Ctr. Legal Program, 1969-71; lectr. dept. anthropology UCLA, 1972, social sci. Immaculate Heart Coll., Los Angeles, 1972. Author: The Equal Rights Handbook, 1978, Dissolution, 1977, Paean to Women: A Call to Unity, 1985, The Chalice and The Blade: Out History, Our Future, 1987; contbr. articles to profl. jours. Bd. dirs. YWCA, Los Angeles, 1971, Monterey (Calif.), 1984-85, Women's Clinic, Los Angeles, 1975-78, ACLU, Monterey; mem. adv. bd. Women's Rights Reporter, 1971; NOW rep. Monterey Peninsula Women's Orgns. Network, 1981-83; mem. Nat. Women's Polit. Caucus. Mem. NOW, State Bar Calif., Gen. Evolution Research Group, Western Assn. Women Historians, Nat. Women's Conf. Com. (ERA task force 1985-86), Acad. Peace Development (research adv. bd.), Internat. Soc. Gen. Systems Research, Phi Beta Kappa, Pi Gamma Mu.

EISNER, ALAN MURRAY, social service administrator; b. Steubenville, Ohio, Mar. 30, 1938; s. Arthur and Teressa (Weis) E.; m. Rhonda Arlene Koff, July 4, 1976; children: Rachel Beth, Vickie Renee. BS, Ohio U., 1960; MSW, U. Pitts., 1970. Psychiat. social worker Met. State Hosp., Norwalk, Calif., 1970-73, Community Care Services, Los Angeles, 1973-77; licensing program analyst Community Care Licensing, Los Angeles, 1977-80, licensing program supr., 1980-85; ombudsman Child Care Ombudsman Program, Los Angeles, 1985—; mem. Los Angeles Mayor's Adv. Child Care Com., 1985—. Served with USAR, 1960-62. Mem. Licensed Clin. Social Workers, Nat. Assn. Social Workers (cert.). Home: 7238 Leescott Van Nuys CA 91406 Office: Child Care Ombudsman Program 107 S Broadway Suite 8034 Los Angeles CA 90012

EISNER, MICHAEL DAMMAN, motion picture company executive; b. N.Y.C., 1942; married. B.A., Denison U. Began career in programming dept. CBS; asst. to nat. programming dir. ABC, 1966-68, mgr. spls. and talent, dir. program devel.-East Coast, 1968-71, v.p. daytime programming, 1971-75, v.p. program planning and devel., 1975-76, sr. v.p. prime time prodn. and devel., 1976; pres., chief operating officer Paramount Pictures, 1976-84; chmn., chief exec. officer Walt Disney Prodns., Burbank, Calif., 1984—. Office: Walt Disney Productions 500 S Buena Vista St Burbank CA 91521 *

EISSMANN, WALTER JAMES, weight loss franchise owner; b. Newark, N.J., Apr. 20, 1939; s. Walter Curt Eissmann and Alice Delice (Irving) Clark; m. Dorothea Ann Donaldson, June 1, 1963; children—Patricia Helene, Walter William. B.S. in Indsl. Engring., Rutgers U., 1962. Account mgr. Gen. Electric, Englewood Cliffs, N.J., 1962-67; regional sales mgr. Tymshare, Englewood Cliffs, 1968-71, Buffalo, N.Y., 1971-73, Washington, 1973-74, v.p. mktg. service div., Cupertino, Calif., 1974-79, div. v.p., Cupertino, 1980-84; sr. v.p. McDonnell Douglas Corp., Cupertino, 1984-86; gen. ptnr. Archer Assocs., 1985—; dir. Softyme, Inc., 1984. Bd. dirs. Saratoga Little League, Calif., 1976-81, Saratoga Boosters, 1981-84; active Vienna Theatre Players, Va., 1973, mem. Church Men's Choir, Saratoga, 1980-82. Named to President's Club Tymshare, Golden Circle. Mem. Pi Tau Sigma. Republican. Office: Archer Assocs 1510 Arden Way Suite 300 Sacramento CA 95815

EITNER, LORENZ EDWIN ALFRED, art historian, educator; b. Brunn, Czechoslovakia, Aug. 27, 1919; came to U.S., 1935, naturalized, 1943; s. Wilhelm and Katherina (Thonet) E.; m. Trudi von Kathrein, Oct. 26, 1946; children: Christy, Kathy, Claudia. A.B., Duke U., 1940; M.F.A., Princeton U., 1948, Ph.D., 1952. Research unit head Nuremberg War Crimes Trial, 1946-47; from instr. to prof. art U. Minn., Mpls., 1949-63; chmn. dept. art, dir. mus. Stanford U., Calif., 1963—; organizer exhbn. works of Gericault for museums of Los Angeles, Detroit and Phila., 1971-72. Author: The Flabellum of Tournus, 1944, Gericault Sketchbooks in the Chicago Art Institute, 1960, Introduction to Art, 1951, Neo-Classicism and Romanticism, 1969, Gericault's Raft of the Medusa, 1972, Gericault, His Life and Work, 1983 (Mitchell prize 1984, C.R. Morey award 1985), An Outline of 19th Century European Painting from David through Cezanne, 1987; (with others) The Arts in Higher Education; contbr. articles to profl. jours. Mem. Regional Arts Council San Francisco Bay Area. Served as officer OSS, AUS, 1943-46. Fulbright grantee, Belgium, 1952-53; Guggenheim fellow, Munich, Federal Republic Germany, 1956-57. Mem. Coll. Art Assn. Am. (bd. dirs., past v.p.), Phi Beta Kappa. Home: 684 Mirada St Stanford CA 94305 Office: Stanford Univ Dept Art Stanford CA 94305

EKDALE, ALLAN ANTON, geology educator, paleontology researcher; b. Burlington, Iowa, Aug. 30, 1946; s. Warren E. and Marian L. (Nielsen) E.; m. Susan Faust Rostberg, July 5, 1969; children: Joan Diane, Eric Gregory. BA, Augustana Coll., Rock Island, Ill., 1968; MA, Rice U., 1973, PhD, 1974. Prof. geology U. Utah, Salt Lake City, 1974—. Fellow AAAS; mem. Geol. soc. Am., Internat. Assn. Sedimentologists, Nat. Assn. Geology

Tchrs., Paleontol. Soc., Soc. Econ. Paleontologists and Mineralogists. Office: U Utah Dept Geology and Geophysics Salt Lake City UT 84112

EKROM, ROY H., electronic equipment company executive; b. 1924. A.B., U. Wash., 1951. With Boeing Airplane Co., Seattle, 1952-58; with Aireach Mfg. Co. Ariz., Phoenix, 1959-81; v.p., mgr. Pneumatic Systems div. Garrett Corp., 1981-83; pres., chief exec. officer, dir. Ampex Corp., Redwood City, Calif., 1983-86; pres., chief exec. officer Garrett Corp., Los Angeles, 1986—. Office: Garrett Corp 9851 Sepulveda Blvd Los Angeles CA 90009 *

ELAM, ROBERT JAMES, instructional technologist, management consultant; b. Decatur, Ill., Oct. 10, 1947; s. Robert Eugene and Emma Constance (Holthaus) E.; m. Linda Rae, July 6, 1973 (div. Aug. 1983); 1 child, Shelby Jeane; m. Vicki Lynn Wells, June 16, 1984; 1 child, Gregory Joseph. BA, Quincy Coll., 1969; MA, Ariz. State U., 1971, PhD, 1974. Cert. elem. tchr., Calif.; cert. community coll. supr., Calif. Mgr. Elam's Silverfross Drive-in, Decatur, 1966-72; grad. asst. ednl. tech. dept. Ariz. State U., Tempe, 1971-73; mem. profl. staff SWRL Ednl. Research and Devel., Los Alamitos, Calif., 1973-79; mgr. human resources devel. dept. So. Calif. Edison, Rosemead, 1979-86; prin. cons. Robert J. Elam & Assocs., Calif., 1986—; Mem. adv. group U. So. Calif., Los Angeles, 1982—; various adv. cons. UCLA, 1986—; mem. Mgmt. Inst. Coastline Community Coll., Fountain Valley, 1983—; cons. Toyota Motor Sales, Torrance, Calif., 1982, Disneyland, Anaheim, Calif., 1981; disting. vis. practitioner U. So. Calif., 1982; ext. univ. instr. UCLA, 1983. Named one of Outstanding Young Men Am. U.S. Jaycees, 1980; recipient Lew Byrd Meml. award Orange County Am. Soc. Tng. and Devel., 1981. Mem. Orange (Calif.) C. of C. (cons. 1985), Am. Soc. Tng. and Devel. (pres. 1979), Los Angeles chpt. Am. Soc. Tng. and Devel. (cons. to bd. dirs.,1980). Democrat. Home: PO Box 477 Rainier WA 98576

ELAND, NANCY CAROL, infosystems specialist; b. Bremerton, Wash., Sept. 14, 1951; d. Gene Dayton and Margaret Francis (Wiley) E. BA, Oral Roberts U., 1973; MS, Cornell U., 1976, PhD, 1978; MBA, U. Hawaii, 1985. Mem. tech. staff MITRE Corp., Colorado Springs, Colo., 1978-80; mem. tech. staff MITRE Corp., Honolulu, 1980-83, mem. dept. staff, 1983-86, lead engr., 1986—. Co-chmn. Youth Edn. com. Women's Assn. of Honolulu Symphony, 1983—. Doctoral fellow AAUW, 1978. Mem. Assn. Computing Machinery, IEEE. Avocations: photography, racquetball, snow skiing. Office: MITRE Corp PO Box 29 Camp Smith HI 96861

EL-BAYOUMY, LOTFI E., manager of engineering analysis; b. Fayoum, Arab Republic of Egypt, Jan. 18, 1942; came to U.S., 1966; s. El-Sayed Ibrahim and Nageyya F. (El-Zainy) El-B.; m. Shahira A. El-Masry, Aug. 17, 1973; children: Sharif, Khalid, Dena. BS with honors, Cairo U., 1964, MS, 1966; PhD with honors, NYU, 1970. Asst. prof. NYU, 1969-70; prin. engr. Dathar Corp., Ramsey, N.J., 1970-72; advanced vibrations analyst Pratt & Whitney, East Hartford, Conn., 1972-74; group engr. Sundstrand Corp., Rockford, Ill., 1975-80; mgr. engring. analysis Western Gear Corp., Industry, Calif., 1980—; engring. cons. NASA Lewis, Cleve., 1981—; assoc. prof. mech. engring. Calif. State U., Long Beach, 1981—, No. Ill. U., Dekalb, 1979-80. Contbr. articles to profl. jours. Mem. Am. Acad. Mechanics (founding), AIAA, ASME (Power Transmision and Gearing com. 1983—), Assn. Egyptian-Am. Scholars, Nat. Mgmt. Assn., Soc. Automotive Engrs. (G-5 com. 1984—). Home: 6041 Peridot Ave Alta Loma CA 91701 Office: Western Gear Corp 14724 E Proctor Industry CA 91749

ELBEL, ROBERT EDWIN, entomologist, medical zoologist; b. Hannibal, Mo., July 8, 1925; s. Edwin R. and Nora L. (McHenry) E.; m. Lyda Louise Harris, Apr. 4, 1960; children: Ruth, Russell, Karl. BA in Entomology and Engring., U. Kans., 1948, MA in Entomology and Botany, 1950; PhD in Zoology and Plant Scis., U. Okla., 1964. Technician USPHS, Thomasville, Ga., 1950-51; plague and malaria advisor U.S. Ops. Mission, Thailand, 1951-55, 61-63; grad. asst. in zoology U. Okla., Norman, 1956-59; med. zoologist, entomologist Ecology and Epidemiology Br. U.S. Army, Dugway, Utah, 1963-75; from research assoc. to research prof. U. Utah, Salt Lake City, 1974—; research assoc. entomology Bishop Mus., Honolulu, 1982—; cons. Brigham Young U. studies on fleas of N.Am., Provo, Utah, 1976, U.S. Army Studies Br. vector-born diseases, Dugway, 1979-80, U.S. Army Environ. Ecology Br. mosquito-virus studies, Dugway, 1983-85. Contbr. articles to profl. jours. Explorer advisor Boy Scouts Am. and Christ United Meth. Ch., Salt Lake City, 1968-83, cubmaster, 1975-82, cub roundtable staff, 1976-82, cub leadership tng. staff, 1980-82. Served to lt. comdr. USNR, USPHS, 1943-45, 51-55. Named Hon. Officer Thai Dept. Pub. Health, Bangkok, 1955; 25 species of birds and parasites named in his honor. Mem. Am. Mosquito Control Assn., Biol. Soc. Washington, Kans. Entomol. Soc., Am. Assn. Zool. Nomenclature, Soc. Systematic Zoologists, Southwestern Assn. Naturalists, Internat. Council Bird Preservation Hornbill Specialist group, Phi Sigma, Sigma Xi. Home: 1518 Evergreen Ln Salt Lake City UT 84106 Office: U Utah Dept Biology Salt Lake City UT 84112

ELDREDGE, EDDA ROGERS, securities transfer company executive; b. Deseret, Utah, Feb. 15, 1915; d. James Noah and Alice (Critchley) Rogers; student Henager Bus. Coll., 1930-31, U. Utah, 1932-35; m. Frank Aubrey Eldredge, Sept. 5, 1936; children—Frank A., Noah R., Alice Lou, Julie, Joseph U. With Gen. Petroleum Corp., 1945-55; mgr. land dept. Utah So. Oil Co., 1955-62, asst. sec., 1956-62; pres., dir. Edda R. Eldredge & Co., Inc., Salt Lake City, 1967—; pres., dir. Bonneville Petroleum Corp., 1974—. Republican. Mormon. Office: 315 Newhouse Bldg 10 Exchange Pl Salt Lake City UT 84111

ELDREDGE, FRANK AUBREY, II, geneticist; b. Salt Lake City, Jan. 8, 1940; s. Frank Aubrey and Esther Edda (Rogers) E.; m. Birgitta Veronica Osterberg, Dec. 19, 1963; children: John William, Jennifer, Christine, Emilie Birgitta. Student, U. Utah, 1958-60, BA, 1965, MS, 1969, PhD, 1972. Teaching assoc. U. Utah, Salt Lake City, 1971; assoc. prof. biology Cen. Mich. U., Mt. Pleasant, 1972—. Contbr. research articles on plant cytogenetics and evolution to profl. jours. Active troop com. Lake Huron council Boy Scouts Am., 1973—. NIH genetics tng. fellow, 1967-72; faculty research and creative endeavors grantee, 1973-75, 77-79. Mem. AAAS, Am. Genetic Assn., Bot. Soc. Am., Smithsonian Assn., Amateur Radio Club, Sigma Xi, Beta Beta Beta, Phi Sigma, Phi Eta Sigma. Republican. Mormon. Office: Eldredge Resources Inc 6124 Stratler St Salt Lake City UT 84107

ELECCION, MARCELINO, computer corporate executive, lecturer, artist; b. N.Y.C., Aug. 22, 1936; s. Marcelino G. and Margaret J. (Krcha) E.; B.A., NYU, 1961; postgrad. Courant Inst. Math. Scis., 1962-64; m. Naomi E. Kor, Jan. 5, 1978; children—Mark Eaton, Jordan Kai. Electromech. draftsman Coll. Engring., NYU, Bronx, 1954-57, chief designer dept. elec. engring., 1957-60, tech. editor lab. for electrosci. research, 1960-62, editor publs. Sch. Engring. and Scis., 1962-67; asst. editor IEEE Spectrum, N.Y.C., 1967-69, assoc. editor, 1969-70, staff writer, 1970-76, contbg. editor, 1976—; dir. adminstrn. Internat. Bur. Protection and Investigation, Ltd., N.Y.C., 1976-78; account exec. Paul Purdom & Co., pub. relations, San Francisco, 1978-81, creative dir., 1981-83; dir. mktg. communications Am. Info. Systems, Palo Alto, 1983—; cons. tech. artist, 1953—; music orchestration cons., 1956-70; cons. Ency. Britannica, 1969-70, Time-Life Books, 1973; spl. guest lectr. Napa Coll., 1979—. Recipient Mayor's commendation award N.Y.C., 1971. Mem. IEEE (sr.), N.Y. Acad. Scis., Am. Math. Soc., AAAS, Optical Soc. Am., Smithsonian Assocs., Am. Numis. Assn., Nat. Geog. Soc., U.S. Judo Fedn., Athletic Congress, AAU. Fedn. Home: PO Box 486 Millbrae CA 94030

ELGAL, GALOUST MARGAR, chemical engineer; b. Armenia, Oct. 16, 1930; came to U.S., 1946; s. Margar Galoustiantz and Louise (Apcar) E.; 1 child, Vahé Mark. BS, U. Calif., Berkeley, 1953; postgrad., UCLA, 1959-60. Engr., scientist Douglas Missiles Co., Huntington Beach, Calif., 1958-67; programmer analyst Philips Industries, Sydney, Australia, 1971-74; chem. engr. Thermatech., Houston, 1974-75; research chem. engr. USDA, New Orleans, 1976-84; engr. USAF, Sunnyvale, Calif., 1984—. Contbr. articles to profl. jours.; patentee in field. Vol. emergency unit East Jefferson Hosp., Metairie, La., 1980-84. Mem. AIAA, Am. Chem. Soc., Am. Inst. Chem. Engrs., Sigma Xi. Democrat. Roman Catholic. Avocations: volleyball, dance, competition target shooting. Home: 499 N Fairoaks Ave #3 Sunnyvale CA 94086 Office: USAF/STC Sunnyvale CA 94088

ELGEE, NEIL JOHNSON, physician; b. Oxford, N.S., Can., Apr. 3, 1926; came to U.S., 1946, naturalized, 1955; s. William Harris and Lucile (Nevers) E.; m. Leona Victoria Karlsson, Aug. 18, 1951; children—Joan, Susan, Laurie, Steve, Karen. B.Sc., U. N.B., Can., 1946; M.D., U. Rochester, 1950. Intern Peter Bent Brigham Hosp., Boston, 1950-51; resident Strong Meml. Hosp., Rochester, N.Y., 1951-52; fellow in endocrinology U. Wash., 1952-54, clin. prof. medicine, 1968—; resident in medicine Harborview Med. Center, Seattle, 1954-55; practice medicine specializing in endocrinology Seattle, 1957—; mem. staff Swedish Med. Center, Harborview Med. Center, Seattle. Served as capt. USAF, 1955-57. Master ACP (gov. for Wash. and Alaska 1965-71, regent 1974-78); mem. Endocrine Soc., Inst. Medicine. Home: 3621 72d Ave SE Mercer Island WA 98040 Office: 1229 Madison St Seattle WA 98104

ELGIN-BÖDY, GITA, psychologist; b. Santiago, Chile; came to U.S., 1968, naturalized 1987; d. Serafin and Regina (Urízar) Elguin; B.S. summa cum laude, in Biology, U. Chile, Santiago, Psy.D., 1964; Ph.D. in Counseling Psychology (Chancellor's fellow, NIMH fellow), U. Calif., Berkeley, 1976; m. Bart Bödy, Oct. 23, 1971; 1 adopted child, Dio Christopher Elgin-Bödy. Clin. psychologist Barros Luco-Trudeau Gen. Hosp., Santiago, 1964-65; co-founder, co-dir. Lab. for Parapsychol. Research, Psychiat. Clinic, U. Chile, Santiago, 1965-68; research fellow Found. Research on Nature of Man, Durham, N.C., 1968; researcher psychol. correlates of EEG-Alpha waves U. Calif., Berkeley, 1972-76; originator holistic method of psychotherapy Psychotherapy for a Crowd of One, 1978; co-founder, clin. dir. Holistic Health Assos., Oakland, Calif., 1979—; lectr. holistic health Piedmont (Calif.) Adult Sch., 1979-80; hostess Holistic Perspective, Sta. KALW-FM, Nat. Public Radio, 1980. Lic. psychologist, Chile, Calif. Mem. Am. Psychol. Assn., Calif. Psychol. Assn., Alameda County Psychol. Assn., Assn. Advancement Psychology, Assn. for Holistic Health, AAAS, Montclair Health Profls. Assn. (co-founder, pres. 1983-85), Sierra Club, U. Calif. Alumni Assn. Contbr. articles in clin. psychology and holistic health to profl. jours. and local periodicals. Presenter Whole Life Expo, 1986. Office: Montclair Profl Bldg 2080 Mountain Blvd Suite 203 Oakland CA 94611

ELHAUGE, EDWARD, electronics consultant, software engineer; b. Buenos Aires, Nov. 28, 1956; s. Einer Edward and Mario Innes (Robatto) E. BS in Physics and Math., Carnegie-Mellon U., 1978. Engr. Micromation, San Francisco, 1980-81; software engr. Phase-One Systems, Oakland, Calif., 1981-82; cons. First Strike DSP and Control, San Francisco, 1982—; software engring. cons. RAMTEK, Santa Clara, Calif., 1982-83; devel. engring. cons. TAK Automation, Burlingame, Calif., 1983-84, Applied Materials, Santa Clara, 1984-86. Author: RT-Forth, 1986, Silicon Wafer Robot Handling, 1986, Crane Position Control, 1983. Mem. IEEE, Assn. Computing Machinery. Avocations: music, ecology, politics. Office: First Strike DSP and Control 1100 Tennesse St San Francisco CA 94107

ELIAS, THEODORE JOSEPH, retired chemical engineer; b. Des Moines, June 13, 1914; s. Mitchell S. and Cecelia M. (Korey) E.; B.S., Iowa State U., 1942; m. Ann Marie Kouri, Nov. 26, 1946; children—Amy Louise, Donna Marie, Theodore J., Woodrow Mark. Registered chemical engr., Calif.; safety engr., Calif.; cert. indsl. hygiene engr.; safety professional; environ. engr. Engr., Chem. Equipment Co., Los Angeles, 1945-48, Technicolor Inc., Hollywood, Calif., 1948-57, Los Angeles County, 1957-63, State of Calif., Los Angeles, 1963-68; chem. engr. Los Angeles County, Los Angeles, 1968-77, ret., 1977; div. chief occupational health and safety Los Angeles County, 1970-77; cons. Nat. Insts. Occupational Safety and Health. Served with U.S. Army, 1942-46. Decorated Purple Heart, Silver Star, Bronze Star medal; diplomate Environ. Engrs. Mem. Am. Conf. Govtl. Indsl. Hygienists (chpt. pres. 1975-76), Am. Indsl. Hygiene Assn. (chpt. pres. 1977-78), Am. Legion, VFW, Calif. Profl. Engrs. Republican. Roman Catholic. Club: Elks. Inventor in field. Home: 4943 Densmore St Encino CA 91436

ELIAS-BAKER, BARBARA ANN, research chemist; b. Oakland, Calif., June 28, 1946; d. Albert and Helen (Elias) Baker; m. Armando Peraza, Jan. 15, 1970 (div. Mar. 1978). BA in Biology, San Francisco State U., 1971; postgrad., U. Calif., Berkeley, 1971-75, cert. alcohol counseling, 1982. Outpatient clin. mgr. U. Calif., Berkeley, 1974-77; alcohol counselor Centerpoint, San Rafael, Calif., 1984—; research chemist U. Calif., San Francisco, 1977—; cons. alcohol abuse, San Francisco, 1984—. Mem. AAAS, Calif. Acad. Sci., Am. Chem. Soc., Am. Inst. Chemists. Avocations: camping, canoeing, bicycling, playing piano and bass, composing music. Office: U Calif Langley Porter Inst 401 Parnassus San Francisco CA 94143

ELION, GARY DOUGLAS, lawyer; b. N.Y.C., Mar. 3, 1947; s. Herbert A. and Sheila (Thall) E.; m. Sally Lloyd, June 30, 1968 (div. Oct. 1979); m. Kathy Dees, Nov. 20, 1979; 1 child, Leslie. BA, Williams Coll., 1969; MBA, Harvard U., 1974; JD, U. San Francisco, 1982. Bar: Calif., U.S. Dist. Ct. (no. dist.) Calif., U.S. Ct. Appeals (9th cir., 3d cir., 5th cir.). Assoc. dir. WNAC-TV, Boston, 1969-70; producer, dir. Westinghouse Broadcasting, Boston, 1970-74; exec. producer WJZ-TV, Balt., 1974-77; news dir. KPIX-TV, San Francisco, 1977-79; assoc. Alioto & Aliotoion, San Francisco, 1982-85, Bianco, Brandi & Jones, San Francisco, 1985-86; ptnr. Sturdevant & Elion, San Francisco, 1986—; cons. Program Devel., San Francisco, 1979-82; gen. counsel Inter Optical Telecommunications, Hyannis, Mass., 1985; dir. Inter Communications and Energy, 1985—. Recipient Emmy award 1979. Mem. Am. Trial Lawyers Assn., Calif. Bar Assn., San Francisco Bar Assn., Barristers Club. Home: 594 48th Ave San Francisco CA 94121 Office: Sturdevant & Elion 120 Montgomery Suite 1800 San Francisco CA 94104

ELIZONDO, ANN MOCK, advertising executive; b. Pitts., Apr. 6, 1957; d. Lawrence Edward and Mary Ann (McCoy) Mock; m. Michael Lee Elizondo, Aug. 23, 1981. BBA, Emory U., 1979; MBA, Ga. State U., 1981. Brand mgr. H.P. Hood, Boston, 1981-83; mktg. mgr. Coca-Cola Co., Atlanta, 1983-86; v.p. McCann-Erickson, Los Angeles, 1986—; mgmt. cons. intern Booz-Allen & Hamilton, Atlanta, 1979-80. Avocations: windsurfing, racquetball. Office: McCann-Erickson 6420 Wilshire Blvd Beverly Hills CA 90048

ELKIND, MORTIMER MURRAY, biophysicist, educator; b. Bklyn., Oct. 25, 1922; s. Samuel and Yetta (Lubarsky) E.; m. Karla Annikki Holst, Jan. 27, 1960; children—Sean Thomas, Samuel Scott, Jonathan Harald. B.M.E., Cooper Union, 1943; M.M.E., Poly. Inst. Bklyn., 1949; M.S. in Elec. Engring., Mass. Inst. Tech., 1951, Ph.D. in Physics, 1953. Asst. project engr. Wyssmont Co., N.Y.C., 1943; project engr. Safe Flight Instrument Corp., White Plains, N.Y., 1946-47; head instrumentation sect. Sloan Kettering Inst. Cancer Research, 1947-49; physicist Nat. Cancer Inst. on assignment to Mass. Inst. Tech., 1949-53; on assignment to Donner Lab., U. Calif. at Berkeley, 1953-54; physicist Lab. Physiology, Nat. Cancer Inst., Bethesda, Md., 1954-67; sr. research physicist Lab. Physiology, Nat. Cancer Inst., 1967-69; sr. biophysicist biology dept. Brookhaven Nat. Lab., Upton, L.I., N.Y., 1969-73; guest scientist MRC exptl. radiopathology unit Hammersmith Hosp., London, 1971-73; sr. biophysicist, div. biol. and med. research Argonne (Ill.) Nat. Lab., 1973—, asst. dir., 1976-78, head mammalian cell biology group, 1978-81; prof. radiology U. Chgo., 1973-81; prof., chmn. dept. radiology and radiation biology Colo. State U., 1981—; Mem. radiation study sect. NIH, 1962-66, molecular biology study sect., 1970-71; mem. developmental therapeutics com. Nat. Cancer Inst., 1975—. Author monograph. Served with USNR, 1944-46. Recipient E.O. Lawrence award AEC, 1967; Superior Service award HEW, 1969; L.H. Gray medal Internat. Com. Radiation Units and Measurements, 1977; E.W. Bertner award M.D. Anderson Hosp. and Tumor Inst., 1979; A.W. Erskine award Radiol. Soc. N. Am., 1980; Albert Soiland Meml. award Albert Soiland Cancer Found., 1984; 1st Henry S. Kaplan Disting. Scientist award Internat. Assn. Radiation Research, 1987; Univ. Disting. Prof. Colo. State U., 1986; Nat. Cancer Inst. Spl. fellow, 1972-74. Fellow Am. Coll. Radiology (hon.); mem. AAAS, Biophys. Soc., Radiation Research Soc. (council 1965-66, assoc. editor jour. 1965-68, pres.-elect 1980—, G. Failla Meml. award 1984), Tissue Culture Assn., Am. Assn. Cancer Research (assoc. editor jour. 1980—), Am. Soc. Therapeutic Radiology and Oncology (gold medalist 1983), Sigma Xi, Tau Beta Pi. Office: Colo State U Dept Radiology and Radiation Biology Fort Collins CO 80523

ELKINS, FRANCIS CLARK, history educator, university official; b. Scranton, Ark., Feb. 24, 1923; s. Frank and Auby (Moore) E.; m. Norma Trice, Aug. 18, 1946; 1 dau., Annette. BA, State Coll. Ark., 1943; MA, U. Ark., 1947; PhD, Syracuse U., 1953; postdoctoral, U. Minn., 1956. From instr. to prof., chmn. div. social sci. Henderson State Coll., Arkadelphia, Ark., 1946-61; pres. Chadron (Nebr.) State Coll., 1961-67, N.E. Mo. State Coll., Kirksville, 1967-69; coordinator Univ. Coll., Ark State U., 1969-70, v.p. instrn., 1970-78, v.p. univ. relations, 1979-80; v.p. univ. relations and devel. No. Ariz. U., Flagstaff, 1980-83, prof. history, 1980—, president's coordinator univ. relations, 1983—; mem. exec. com. Rocky Mountain Edn. Lab., 1965-67; examiner North Cen. Assn. Colls. and Schs.; examiner, cons. Nat. Council Accreditation Tchr. Edn., chmn. visitation and appraisal com., 1963-68; mem. Nebr. Ednl. TV Council Higher Edn., 1966-67, Ark. Council Econ. Edn., 1970-81. Mem. adv. council Mo. 4-H Found., 1968-69; mem. Ark. Adv. Council on Career Edn.; bd. dirs. United Way, 1980—. Served with USAAF, 1943-45. Decorated D.F.C., Air medal with four oak leaf clusters. Mem. Am. Assn. Colls. Tchr. Edn. (dir. 1968-71, state liaison rep. 1974-77), Asso. Orgns. Tchr. Edn. (adv. council), NEA (life), Ark. Edn. Assn. (life), Flagstaff C. of C. (dir. 1980—), Phi Delta Kappa, Kappa Delta Pi, Phi Alpha Theta, Alpha Chi, Phi Kappa Phi, Sigma Tau Gamma, Sigma Nu. Methodist. Lodges: Elks, Rotary. Home: 800 W University Heights Dr S Flagstaff AZ 86001 Office: No Ariz U Box 4094 Flagstaff AZ 86011

ELKINS, ROBERT, aerospace engineer; b. N.Y.C., Feb. 26, 1929; s. Jacob and Bertha (Biener) E.; m. Frances H. Greenwald, June 26, 1957 (div. Jan. 1973); m. Barbara Harriet London Galper, Oct. 5, 1980; children: Pamela D., Cynthia. BEE, CCNY, 1952. Mgr. small satellite project TRW Corp., Redondo Beach, Calif., 1969-72, asst mgr. communication satellites project, 1972-77, mgr. advanced systems manned satellite systems div., 1977-78, mgr. proposals missions and space div., 1978-80, asst. project mgr. def. support program, 1980-83, project mgr. laser communications subsystem, 1983—; cons. in field. 1969—. Recipient Group Achievement award, NASA Lunar Sci., 1972. Republican. Avocations: tennis, auto restoration, competitive pistol. Home: 18828 Paseo Nuevo Dr Tarzana CA 91356 Office: TRW Mil Space Systems 1 Space Park Redondo Beach CA 90278

ELKINS, ROLAND LUCIEN, printing company executive; b. Coral Gables, Fla., Aug. 8, 1945; s. George Meyer and Leona (Wolfson) E.; m. Ruth Binder, Apr. 1, 1967; children: Eric Seth, Sarah Lynn, Karen Rachel. BA, Am. U., 1967. Prodn. mgr. Am. Aviation Pub., Washington, 1968-69, Govt. Exec. Mag., Washington, 1969-72; advt. scheduling mgr. Army Times Pub. Co., Washington, 1972-75; prodn. mgr. Colo. Mag., Denver, 1975-80; gen. mgr. Guest Informant, Beverly Hills, Calif., 1980-82; exec. v.p. Williams Printing Inc., Colorado Springs, Colo., 1983—; cons. Western Pub. Assn., Los Angeles, 1980-82. Recipient First Place awards Colorado Springs Classic, 1983, Valley Rally, 1983, Gleneagle (Colo.) Baloon Regatta, 1984. Mem. Nat. Assn. Printers and Lithographers (top mgmt. award 1984). Jewish. Club: Ballooning Soc. of Pike's Peak (Colorado Springs) (pres. 1986—). Avocation: commercial balloon pilot. Office: Williams Printing Inc Centennial Blvd Colorado Springs CO 80919

ELLARD, HOWARD RAY, oil company executive; b. Mortlach, Sask., Can., Nov. 24, 1925; s. Howard Hugh and Mary Helen (Lockhart) E.; m. Margaret Marie Forsgren, May 12, 1950; children—John Howard, Ronald Ray, Marcus Patrick, Norman Hugh. Student U. Sask., 1943-45; B.Sc. in Geol. Engring., U. B.C., 1948. Registered profl. engr., Alta. Geophysicist Imperial Oil Ltd., Calgary, Alta., 1948-65; div. geophysicist Imperial Oil Enterprises, Edmonton, Alta., 1965-68, contracts negotiator, Calgary, 1969-74, sr. contracts negotiator, 1974-76; chief Landman Esso Resources, Calgary, 1976-80; ret., 1980; pres. L.K. Oil & Gas Ltd., Calgary, 1981-83, Triweb Resources Ltd., Calgary, 1984—. Bd. dirs. Calgary Zool. Soc., 1970-78; mem. senate of Calgary, 1978-84. Mem. Assn. Profl. Engrs., Geologists and Geophysicists Alta., Can. Soc. Exploration Geophysicists, Can. Assn. Petroleum Landmen, Calgary Petroleum Club, Zeta Psi, Progressive Conservative. Anglican. Club: Polo Social (Calgary). Home: Rural Route 8, Calgary, AB Canada T2J 2T9 Office: Triweb Resources Ltd, 1650 Monenco Pl, 801 6th Ave SW, Calgary, AB Canada T2P 3W2

ELLARD, TIMOTHY DANIEL, marketing research executive; b. Salem, Mass., Dec. 20, 1934; s. Daniel J. and Anna M. (Byrne) E.; m. Mary Patricia Amend, July 11, 1959; children—Marcia Ann, Daniel Joseph, Michael Patrick. A.B., Harvard U., 1956; M.B.A., U. Pa., 1958. In brand mgmt. Procter & Gamble Co., Cin., 1961-64; with Opinion Research Corp., Princeton, N.J., 1964-82, San Francisco, 1982—, sr. v.p., 1969—. Served to 1st lt. USAR, 1958-61. Mem. Am. Mktg. Assn., Am. Assn. Pub. Opinion Research, Travel and Tourism Research Assn. Home: 139 Wildwood Ave Piedmont CA 94610 Office: Opinion Research Corp 4 Embarcadero Ctr San Francisco CA 94111

ELLER, KARL, holding company executive; b. 1928; married. Student U. Ariz. Founder Eller Outdoor Advt., 1968; founder, pres., chief exec. officer Combined Communication Corp., 1968-79; pres. Columbia Pictures Communications, 1980-83; chmn., chief exec. officer, Circle K Corp., Phoenix, 1983—, dir.; chmn. Swensen's, Inc., Phoenix. Office: Circle K Corp 7th St & McDowell Box 52084 Phoenix AZ 85072 *

ELLER, PHILLIP GARY, research chemist; b. New Martinsville, W.Va., Aug. 18, 1947; s. Thaddeus and Virginia (Frohnapfel) E.; m. Terese M. Devine, May 28, 1978; children: Audrey Elizabeth, Rachel Eileen. BS in Chemistry, W.Va. U., 1967; PhD in Chemistry, Ohio State U., 1971. Postdoctoral research Ga. Inst. Tech., Atlanta, 1971-73; postdoctoral research Los Alamos (N.Mex.) Nat. Lab., 1974-75, staff mem., 1976-84, assoc. group leader, 1985—. Contbr. numerous articles to profl. jours.; patentee in field. Served to capt. USAR, 1969-79. Recipient Disting. Performance award Los Alamos Nat. Lab., 1984. Mem. Am. Chem. Soc. Office: Los Alamos Nat Lab MSC 346 INC4 Los Alamos NM 87544

ELLERSICK, STEVEN DONALD, electromagnetic effects engineer, scientist; b. Pullman, Wash., Apr. 20, 1961; s. Donald Kay and Sandra Lee (Dyke) E. Student, Pacific Luth. U., 1979-81; BSEE, Wash. State U., 1983; postgrad., U. Wash., 1984—. Elec. engr. Boeing Co., Seattle, 1983—, change engr., 1983-84, electromagnetic compatability engr., 1984-86, infra-red scientist, engr., 1986—. Vol. Mus. History and Industry, Seattle, 1986—, Seattle Nat. Archives, 1986—. Recipient Eagle Scout award Boy Scouts Am., 1976. Mem. Bioelectromagnetic Soc., IEEE, Electromagnetic Compatibility Soc.of IEEE, Quantum Electronics Soc. of IEEE, Aerospace and Electronics Systems Soc. of IEEE, Mgmt. Soc. of IEEE, Medicine and Biology Soc. of IEEE, Soc. Photo-optical Inst. Engrs. Lutheran. Avocations: basketball, racquetball, hiking, snow and water skiing, history. Home: 7333 47th Ave SW #1 Seattle WA 98136

ELLEVEN, RAYMOND A., loss control engineer; b. El Paso, Tex., Nov. 28, 1951; s. Charles Jr. and Josephine (Gilbert) E.; m. Helen I. Hudson, Apr. 16, 1975. AS, Community Coll. of USAF, 1982; BSBA, Chapman Coll., 1985. Enlisted USAF, 1971, advanced through grades to staff sgt., 1979, resigned, 1982; loss control rep. Alaska Pacific Ins. Co./Ins. Co. of N. Am. subs. CIGNA Corp., 1983-85; loss control engr. Alaska Nat. Ins. Co., 1985—. Named Safety Profl. of Yr. Am. Soc. Safety Engrs. (Alaska chpt.), 1984. Mem. Am. Soc. Safety Engrs. (treas. Alaska chpt. 1980-81, sec. 1981-82, v.p. 1982-83, pres. 1983-84, assembly del. 1984—, chmn. membership com.), Vets. of Safety (chmn. membership com.), Alaska Gov.'s Safety Conf. (mem. pub. relations com.), ARC (mem. damage assessment team), World Safety Orgn. (affiliate, cert.). Republican. Episcopal. Club: Toastmasters (sec./treas. local chpt.). Avocations: old cars, camping, fishing. Home: 1516 Ermine Anchorage AK 99504 Office: Alaska Nat Ins Co 7001 Jewel Lake Rd Anchorage AK 99502

ELLINGSEN, MARY ELIZABETH, speech-language pathologist; b. Balt., Mar. 17, 1950; d. Charles Allen and June E. (Ellingsen) Strait; m. Donald Gardner Foulke, Aug. 13, 1981; 1 child, Myra Leigh. BA magna cum laude, Temple U., 1972; MA, U. Ariz., 1974. Lic. speech pathologist, Ariz. Instr. Pima Coll., Tucson, 1975-79; speech-lang. pathologist Davis Bilingual Learning Ctr. Tucson Unified Sch. Dist., 1977—; prin., speech-lang. pathologist Ellingsen and Assocs., Inc., Tucson, Am. and Hispanic Speech-Lang. Pathology Cons. Services, Tucson; Eng. teaching fellow Centro Cultural, San José, Costa Rica, 1974; cons. Ariz. Affiliated Tribes, Phoenix, 1979—, Ariz. Dept. Edn., Phoenix, 1982, Colo. River Indian Tribes, Parker, Ariz., 1979—, Ariz. Migrant Head Start program, Phoenix, 1986, Shannon County Schs., Pine Ridge, S.D., 1985, others. NIH grantee, U. Ariz., Tucson, 1978-79. Mem. Am. Speech, Lang. and Hearing Assn. Democrat.

Avocations: gardening, cooking, travel. Home and Office: 2411 W Nebraska St Tucson AZ 85746

ELLINGTON, JESSE THOMPSON, film services executive; b. Phila., Sept. 21, 1931; s. Jesse Thompson and Elizabeth Young (Turner) E.; m. Nancy Cabell Meredith, July 19, 1959; children: Cabell, Jesse III, Meredith. BA, U. Va., 1953. Exec. producer Ellington Advt., N.Y.C., 1953-63; v.p. Young & Rubicam, N.Y.C., 1963-68; sr. v.p. Young & Rubicam, Los Angeles, 1968-70; sr. asst. postmaster gen. U.S. Postal Service, Washington, 1971-77; pres. Consol. Film, Los Angeles, 1977—. Fellow Soc. Motion Picture Engrs.; mem. Acad. Motion Picture Arts and Scis., Acad. TV Arts and Scis., Am. Soc. Cinematographers., Hollywood Radio and TV Soc. Home: 1480 Charlton Rd San Marino CA 91108 Office: Consol Film Inds 959 N Seward St Hollywood CA 90038

ELLINGTON, JOHN STEPHEN, psychotherapist; b. Moses Lake, Wash., July 7, 1950; s. John Wiley and Lydia Maria (Antognini) E.; m. Pauletta Inez Myers, June 2, 1979 (div. Aug. 1980). Student, Merced Coll., 1968-70; BA in Biology, U. Calif., Santa Barbara, 1973; MSW, Calif. State U., Fresno, 1978. Lic. clin. social worker. Psychiat. social worker Terapeutic Day Sch., Merced (Calif.) County Mental Health, 1974-76, Family-Adolescent Intervention, Merced County Mental Health, 1978-80, Turlock (Calif.) Inpatient Ctr., Stan County Mental Health, 1980-81; clinician mental health Turlock Counseling Ctr., 1981-83; prog. dir. Psychiat. Health Facility, Modesto, Calif., 1983-85; clinician mental health Adolescent Day Treatment program, Stanislaus County Mental Health, Hughson, Calif., 1985—; program dir. Pain Mgmt. Systems, Modesto, 1985—; part-time social worker Modesto Psychiat. Ctr., 1987—. Actor Loose Assn., 1982-83; bd. dirs. Friends of the Sunshine Place, Modesto. Mem. Nat. Assn. Social Workers. Home: 537 Castle Modesto CA 95350 Office: Stanislaus County Mental Health Adolescent Day Treatment program 7419 E Whitmore Hughson CA

ELLINGTON, LYNDA VENERABLE, transportation executive; b. Los Angeles, Feb. 16, 1944; s. Grant Delbert and Thelma Lorraine (Scott) Venerable; m. Owen Bernardo Ellington, June 27, 1971; children: Owen Jr., Bryan G.; Michelle L. Student, Los Angeles City Coll., 1961-63, 66-67, U. Calif., Berkeley, 1963-64; BS, Calif. State U., 1967-69; postgrad. in bus. adminstrn., Pa. State U., 1972-73; postgrad., John Robert Powers Sch. Modeling, 1983. Buyer trainee Bullock's Wilshire, Los Angeles, 1966-67; supr. operations Security Pacific Nat. Bank, Los Angeles, 1970-71; internal auditor electronic data processing Commonwealth Nat. Bank., Harrisburg, Pa., 1971-74; office mgr. Med. Office, Oakland, Calif., 1979-84; customer service rep. Wells Fargo Bank, Torrance, Calif., 1985; reservation sales agent N.W. Orient Airlines, Los Angeles, 1986—; cons., med. mgr. Henderson and Assoc., Oakland, 1980-84. Author: There's a Monster in the Closet, 1984. Treas. Com. to Elect Sch. Bd. Mem., Palos Verdes, Calif., 1985; exec. v.p. and treas. CAN-7 Cancer Screening Clinic, Oakland, 1981-84; pres. PTA 1983-84; coordinator Boy Scouts Am., 1984—. Named Champion Wheel of Fortune TV game show, Los Angeles, 1977; recipient Vol. Recognition award Palos Verdes Sch. Dist., Rancho Vista Sch., 1984, 85, Founders Day award PTA, 1984, Vol's. Recognition award Oakland Pub. Schs., 1981-82, 83-84. Mem. Alameda County-Contra Costa Med. Auxiliary, No. Calif. Med. Auxiliary, Foreign Lang. League (chmn. Oakland chpt. 1980-84). Home: 4139 Pascal Pl Palos Verdes Peninsula CA 90274

ELLION, M. EDMUND, aerospace executive; b. Boston, Jan. 20, 1923; s. Michael N. and Beatrice Elizabeth (Patterson) E.; m. Dolores Diana Rolph, July 3, 1954; children: Laurie Ann, Thomas Michael. BS, Northeastern U., 1943, Tufts U., 1944; MS, Harvard U., 1947; PhD in Engring. Physics, Calif. Inst. Tech., 1953. Exec. dir. Nat. Engring. Sci. Corp., Pasadena, Calif., 1955-60; pres. Dynamic Sci. Corp., Pasadena, 1960-64; mgr. tech. devel. GM Hughes Electronics, Los Angeles, 1964—. Patentee in field; contbr. articles to profl. jours. Served to lt. USNR, 1943-46, PTO. Fellow Am. Inst. Aeros. (assoc.), IEEE (assoc.). Republican. Avocations: organ, saxophone, playing tennis. Home: 2152 Highland Oaks Arcadia CA 91006 Office: Hughes Aircraft Co PO Box 92919 Space Communications MS/S12/V348 Los Angeles CA 90009

ELLIOT, CHARLES LOTHROP, geophysical engineer; b. Northampton, Mass., Nov. 15, 1928; s. William Samuel and Eleanore Eunice (Lothrop) E.; m. Helen McMahon, Sept. 17, 1954; children: James D., Denise E., Colin D. BS in Mining Engring. with honors, Mich. Tech. U., 1954, MS in Geophysics, 1955. Registered profl. engr., Ariz. Geophys. engr. Newmont Exploration Ltd., Jerome, Ariz., Danbury, Conn., 1955-64; research geophysicist Kennecott Exploration Services, Denver and Salt Lake City, 1964-66; owner, operator Elliot Geophys. Co., Inc., Tucson, 1966-82, pres., 1982—; cons. in field. Patentee electromagnetic instrument for geophys. exploration. Served with USN, 1946-49. Mem. Soc. Exploration Geophysicists, European Assoc. Exploration Geophysicists, AIME. Office: Elliot Geophys Co Inc 4653 E Pima St Tucson AZ 85712

ELLIOTT, GORDON RAY, non profit organization executive; b. Winnipeg, Man., Can., July 31, 1916; s. Frank George and Ethel Maud (Johnson) E.; m. Shirley Anderson, Nov. 2, 1950; 1 dau. Student U. So. Calif., Southwestern U.; grad. Am. Inst. Banking, 1936; LL.B., Pacific Coast Sch. Law, 1940. With Security First Nat. Bank (now Security Pacific Bank), Los Angeles, 1934-41; budget analyst VA, San Francisco, 1946-47, asst. to dir., Los Angeles, 1947-56, dir., Albuquerque, 1957-58, Phila., 1958-62, dir. VA for Europe, Am. embassy, Rome, 1962-65, dir. regional office, attache vets. affairs, Am. embassy, Manila, 1965-67, dir. No. Calif. Regional Office, San Francisco, 1967-70, So. Calif. Regional Office, Los Angeles, 1970-73, spl. asst. to adminstr. vets. affairs, Washington, 1974-75; gen. mgr. DAV Charities of Greater Los Angeles, Inc., 1981—; bd. chmn. Vets. on Job, Inc.; dir., past pres. Purple Heart Vets. Rehab. Services, Inc.; pres. Valley Hunt Investors, Inc.; mem. adv. com. Calif. Dept. Rehab., Calif. Vets. Employment Com., Pres. Commn. on Employment of Handicapped; mem. exec. adv. council Congl. Medal of Honor Soc., 1976. Co-chmn. Calif. Vets. for Reagan and Bush Com. for 1980 nat. election; mem. Pres.-elect Reagan Transition Team, 1980. Served with AUS, 1942-45. Recipient Civil Servant of Yr. Silver Helmet award Am. Vets. of World War II, Korea, Vietnam, 1972; Nat. Disting. Service award Mil. Order of Purple Heart, 1974; Mem. Fed. Bar Assn., Res. Officers Assn., DAV, Am. Legion, VFW, Amvets. Lutheran. Clubs: Masons, Shriners, Rotary, Town Hall, Overseas Press. Office: 13550 E Ramona Blvd Baldwin Park CA 91706

ELLIOTT, JAMES HEYER, museum dir.; b. Medford, Oreg., Feb. 19, 1924; s. Bert R. and Marguerite E. (Heyer) E.; m. Judith Ann Algar, Apr. 23, 1966 (div.); children—Arabel Joan, Jakob Maxwell. B.A., Willamette U., Salem, Oreg., 1947, D.F.A. (hon.), 1978; A.M., Harvard U., 1949. James Rogers Rich fellow Harvard U., 1949-50; Fulbright grantee Paris, 1951-52; art critic European edit. N.Y. Herald-Tribune, 1952-53; curator, acting dir. Walker Art Center, Mpls., 1953-56; asst. chief curator, curator modern art Los Angeles County Mus. Art, 1956-63, chief curator, 1964-66; dir. Wadsworth Atheneum, Hartford, Conn., 1966-76, Univ. Art Mus., Berkeley, Calif., 1976—; adj. prof. Hunter Coll., N.Y.C., 1968, U. Calif., Berkeley, 1976—; commr. Conn. Commn. Arts, 1970-76; fellow Trumbull Coll., Yale U., 1971-75; mem. museum arts panel Nat. Endowment Arts, 1974-77; bd. dirs. San Francisco Art Inst., 1980—. Author: Bonnard and His Environment, 1964. Served with USNR, 1943-46. Mem. Internat. Council Museums, Am. Assn. Museums, Coll. Art Assn., Assn. Art Mus. Dirs. (sec., trustee 1980—), Artists Space N.Y. (dir. 1980-84). Club: Arts (Berkeley). Home: PO Box 4848 Berkeley CA 94704 Office: Univ Art Mus 2626 Bancroft Way Berkeley CA 94720

ELLIOTT, JOHN ED, economics educator; b. Los Angeles, Oct. 22, 1931; s. James Edgar and Jessie Fisher (Metcalf) E.; m. Elda Rose Wilson, Dec. 22, 1975; children: John David, Richard Lee, Elizabeth Ann, James Hall. BA in Econs., Occidental Coll., 1952; MA in Polit. Sci., Harvard U., 1956, PhD in Econs., 1956. Instr. U. So. Calif., Los Angeles, 1956-59, asst. prof. econs., 1959-61, assoc. prof., 1961-66, prof., 1966—; dir. faculty seminar NEH, 1980, 82, 84, 86. Author: Comparative Economic Systems, 1985, Marx and Engels Economics Politics Society, 1981, Competing Philosophies American Political Economics, 1975; contbr. articles to profl. jours. Mem. AAUP (nat. council 1985—, pres. Calif. conf. 1985—), Assn. Social Econs. (exec. council. 1985—), Am. Econ. Assn., Western Econ. Assn., Assn. for Evolutionary Econ., Atlantic Econ. Soc., History Econs. Soc., Union Radical Polit. Econs. Democrat. Avocations: classical jazz, swimming, music. Office: U So Calif Dept Econs University Park Los Angeles CA 90041

ELLIOTT, KATHLEEN MARIE, nurse, administrator; b. San Diego, Aug. 1, 1945; d. Howard O'Dell and Mary Elizabeth (Steging) Carr; m. Richard Wayne Elliott, Apr. 16, 1966; children: Aaron Louis, Brian Scott. Grad. Knapp Coll. Nursing, 1966; BS with departmental honor in Health Sci., Chapman Coll., 1982. RN; cert. tchr. designated subjects, Calif. Nurse Atascadero (Calif.) State Hosp., 1966-76; nurse III, hosp. supr. El Paso de Robles Sch., Calif. Dept. Youth Authority, 1976-78; mgr. Planned Parenthood Clinic, Fresno, Calif., 1978-79; staff nurse Fresno (Calif.) Community Hosp., 1979-80; rehab. nurse, dir. staff devel. Sierra Meadows Convalescent Hosp., Oakhurst, Calif., 1980-82, dir. nursing services, asst. to adminstr. Med. Services, 1983-85; health service specialist infection control Napa (Calif.) State Hosp., 1985—; instr. Yosemite High Sch. nurses aide program. Mem. Calif. Soc. Nursing Service Adminstrs., Calif. Assn. Health Care Educators. Democrat. Home: 39313 John West Rd Oakhurst CA 93644 Office: Napa State Hosp 1600 Trower Ave Napa CA 94558

ELLIOTT, NORMA HOUCHIN, speech pathologist, consultant; b. Spencer County, Ky., May 27, 1938; d. Chester Dove Houchin and Louise H. (Hammand) Thompson; divorced; children: Susan Joy, Steven Michael, Melinda Caye. BS, Eastern Ky. U., 1972; MS, Vanderbilt U., 1973. Cert. clin. competence in speech lang. pathology. Infant therapist Wilkerson Hearing and Speech Ctr., Nashville, 1974-76; speech pathologist, dir. Oakwood Ctr., Somerset, Ky., 1976-79; dir. State Wide Agy., Richmond, Ky., 1979-82; speech pathologist Gompers Rehab. Ctr., Phoenix, 1983-84; pvt. practice specializing in speech pathology Phoenix, 1985—; cons. Dept. Human Resources, Frankfort, Ky., 1979-81, Tech. Assistance Delivery Systems, Chapel Hill, N.C., 1975-77; participant Ky. Com. for Autism, Frankfort, 1979-80, Ariz. Week of the Child, Phoenix, 1984. Mem. Am. Speech and Hearing Assn. Episcopalian. Avocations: drawing, painting, riding. Home: 8377 E Via de Ventura #M220 Scottsdale AZ 85258

ELLIOTT, PATRICK HAROLD, precious metal manufacturing company executive; b. El Paso, Tex., Feb. 21, 1940; s. Harold Egan and Patricia Betty (Gonzalez) E.; m. Karolyn Kay Spangler, Apr. 19, 1961; children: Jon Patrick, Roy Spangler. AA, Cypress City Coll., 1972; BA, Calif. State U., Fullerton, 1975. Sr. radar technician ITT Fed. Electric, Vandenburg AFB, Calif., 1965-68, Kentron Hawaii Ltd., Honolulu, 1968-70; plant mgr. Fusion Inc., Santa Fe Springs, Calif., 1974-82; western regional mgr. Krohn Industries Inc., Carlstadt, N.J., 1982—; cons. in field. Served with USAF, 1957-60. Mem. Nat. Rifle Assn. (benefactor). Republican. Jewish. Avocations: internat. big game hunting, photography, collecting fine art. Office: Krohn Industries Inc 448 S Hill St #704 Los Angeles CA 90013

ELLIOTT, WARD EDWARD YANDELL, political science educator; b. Cambridge, Mass., Aug. 6, 1937; s. William Yandell and Mary Louise Ward; m. Myrna Joy Victoria Krahn; children: William Yandell, Christopher David. AB, Harvard U., 1959, AM, PhD, 1968; LLB, Va. Law Sch., 1964. Bar: D.C. 1964, Va. 1964; ordained to ministry Universal Life Ch., 1969. Assoc. Covington & Burling, Washington, 1964; prof. polit. sci. Claremont (Calif.) McKenna Coll., 1968—. Author: The Rise of Guardian Democracy, 1975. V.p. Coalition for Clean Air. Served to 1st lt. U.S. Army, 1959-61. Fellow NIH, 1975, Earhart, 1975, 83, NEH, 1985; grantee NEH; recipient Roy C. Crocker prize Claremont McKenna Coll., 1984. Mem. AAAS. Republican. Clubs: Claremont McKenna Coll. East Coast (faculty sponsor), Pumpkin Papers Irregulars. Avocations: hiking, boating. Home: 875 N College Ave Claremont CA 91711 Office: Claremont McKenna Coll Pitzer Hall Claremont CA 91711

ELLIS, ALBERT TROMLY, applied mechanics educator; b. Atwater, Calif., Apr. 22, 1917; s. Walter Harwood and Mabel (Tromly) E.; m. Helen Margaret Hyder; children: Kathryn, James. BEE, Calif. Inst. Tech., 1943, MS in Physics, 1947, PhD in Mech. Engring., 1953. Lic. profl. elec. engr., Calif. Research engr. Columbia U., N.Y.C., 1944-46; research engr. Calif. Inst. Tech., Pasadena, 1947-49, sr. research fellow, 1950-54, assoc. prof., 1954-66; prof. U. Calif., San Diego, 1967—; sr. visitor Cambridge U., Eng., 1964-65, 1974; vis. fellow Oxford U., Eng., 1984, 86. Contbr. articles to profl. jours. Served with Signal Corps, U.S. Army, 1943-44. Recipient numerous grants NSF, Office of Naval Research. Republican. Presbyterian. Home: 9459 La Jolla Farms Rd La Jolla CA 92037 Office: U Calif 6120 Urey Hall Gilman and La Jolla Scenic Dr La Jolla CA 92093

ELLIS, ARTHUR LEON, social work educator; b. N.Y.C., Mar. 6, 1935; s. Arthur Leon Sr. and Pearl (Heylinger) E.; m. Yvonne Anita Davis, Aug. 3, 1957; children: Laurel, Tamara, Daryl. Dir. youth program Harlem Youth Opportunities Unltd., N.Y.C., 1967-69; exec. dir. Hudson Valley Opportunities Industrialization Ctr., Poughkeepsie, N.Y., 1969-71; internat. dir. Opportunities Industrialization Ctr., Addis Ababa, Ethiopia, 1971-72; assoc. prof. social work, dir. undergrad. social work Skidmore Coll., Saratoga Springs, N.Y., 1972-78; prof., dir. social welfare San Diego State U., 1978—. Home: 1204 Sutter St San Diego CA 92103 Office: San Diego State U College Ave San Diego CA 92158

ELLIS, DONALD GRIFFITH, bioengineer; b. Colorado Springs, Colo., Aug. 10, 1940; s. William Eugene and Lucile (Mathews) E.; m. Merle Elisabeth Landberg, May 21, 1977. BS, U. Colo., 1962; postgrad., U. Denver, 1962-63; MS, U. Mich., 1964, PhD, 1970. Postdoctoral fellow Webb-Waring Inst., Denver, 1970-72; research assoc. U. Mich., Ann Arbor, 1972-75, U. Colo., Boulder, 1975-78, U. Colo. Health Scis. Ctr., Denver, 1978-87; designer Spiderwort Design, Boulder, 1976—. Contbr. articles to profl. jours.; inventor inflatable insulating apparatus, pill dispenser, probe swivel. Mem. AAAS, ASME, Assn. Humanistic Psychology, Nat. Assn. Neuro-Linguistic Programming, ACLU. Avocations: mountaineering, skiing, painting. Home: Geneva Park Boulder CO 80302 Office: Spiderwort Design Geneva Park Boulder CO 80302

ELLIS, ELDON EUGENE, physician; b. Washington, Ind., July 2, 1922; s. Osman Polson and Ina Lucretia (Cochran) E.; B.A., U. Rochester, 1946, M.D., 1949; m. Irene Clay, June 26, 1948 (dec. 1968); m. 2d, Priscilla Dean Strong, Sept. 20, 1969; children—Paul Addison, Kathe Lynn, Jonathan Clay, Sharon Anne, Eldon Eugene, Rebecca Deborah. Intern in surgery Stanford U. Hosp., San Francisco, 1949-50, resident and fellow in surgery, 1950-52, 55; Schilling fellow in pathology San Francisco Gen. Hosp., 1955; partner Redwood Med. Clinic, Redwood City, Calif., 1955—, med. dir., 1984—; dir. Sequoia Hosp., Redwood City, 1974-82; asst. clin. prof. surgery Stanford U., 1970-80. Pres. Sequoia Hosp. Found., 1983—. Served with USNR, 1942-46, 50-52. Named Outstanding Citizen of Yr., Redwood City, 1987. Mem. San Mateo County (pres. 1961-63), Calif. (pres. 1965-66), Am. (v.p. 1974-75) heart assns., San Mateo Med. Soc. (pres. 1969-70), San Mateo County Comprehensive Health Planning Council (v.p. 1969-70), Calif., Am. med. assns., San Mateo, Stanford surg. socs., Am. Coll. Chest Physicians, Calif. Thoracic Soc., Cardiovascular Council. Republican. Mem. Peninsula Covenant Ch. Club: Commonwealth. Home: 3621 Farm Hill Blvd Redwood City CA 94061 Office: Redwood Med Clinic 2900 Whipple Ave Redwood City CA 94062

ELLIS, GEORGE EDWIN, JR., chem. engr.; b. Beaumont, Tex., Apr. 14, 1921; s. George Edwin and Julia (Ryan) E.; B.S. in Chem. Engring., U. Tex., 1948; M.S., U. So. Calif., 1958, M.B.A., 1965, M.S. in Mech. Engring., 1968, M.S. in Mgmt. Sci., 1971, Engr. in Indsl. and Systems Engring., 1979. Research chem. engr. Tex. Co., Port Arthur, Tex., 1948-51, Long Beach, Calif., Houston, 1952-53, Space and Information div. N.Am. Aviation Co., Downey, Calif., 1959-61, Magna Corp., Anaheim, Calif., 1961-62; chem. process engr. AiResearch Mfg. Co., Los Angeles, 1953-57, 57-59; chem. engr. Petroleum Combustion & Engring. Co., Santa Monica, Calif., 1957, Jacobs Engring. Co., Pasadena, Calif., 1957, Sesler & Assos., Los Angeles, 1959; research specialist Marquardt Corp., Van Nuys, Calif., 1962-67; sr. project engr. Conductron Corp., Northridge, 1967-68; information systems asst. Los Angeles Dept. Water and Power, 1969—. Instr. thermodynamics U. So. Calif., Los Angeles, 1957. Served with USAAF, 1943-45. Mem. Am. Chem. Soc., Am. Soc. for Metals, Am. Inst. Chem. Engrs., ASME, Am. Electroplaters Soc., Am. Inst. Indsl. Engrs., Am. Mktg. Assn., Ops. Research Soc. Am., Am. Prodn. and Inventory Control Soc., Am. Assn. Cost Engrs., Nat. Assn. Accts., Soc. Mfg. Engrs., Pi Tau Sigma, Phi Lambda Upsilon, Alpha Pi Mu. Home: 1344 W 20th St San Pedro CA 90731 Office: Dept Water and Power Los Angeles CA 90012

ELLIS, GEORGE RICHARD, museum adminstrator; b. Birmingham, Ala., Dec. 9, 1937; s. Richard Paul and Dorsie (Gibbs) E.; m. Sherroll Edward, June 20, 1961 (dec. 1973); m. Nancy Enderson, Aug. 27, 1975; 1 son, Joshua. B.A., U. Chgo., 1959, M.F.A., 1961; postgrad., UCLA, 1971. Art supr. Jefferson County Schs., Birmingham, 1962-64; asst. dir. Birmingham Mus. Art, 1964-66; asst. dir. UCLA Mus. Cultural History, 1971-81, assoc. dir., 1981-82; dir. Honolulu Acad. Arts, 1981—. Author various works on non-western art, 1971—. Recipient Ralph Altman award UCLA, 1968; recipient Outstanding Achievement award UCLA, 1980; fellow Kress Found., 1971. Mem. Pacific Arts Assn. (v.p. 1985—), Hawaii Mus. Assn. (v.p. 1986—), Assn. Art Mus. Dirs., Am. Assn. Mus., Los Angeles Ethnic Arts Council (hon.). Club: Pacific (Honolulu). Office: Honolulu Academy of Arts 900 S Beretania St Honolulu HI 96822

ELLIS, HENRY CARLTON, psychologist, educator; b. Bern New, N.C., Oct. 23, 1927; s. Henry Alford and Frances Lee (Mays) E.; m. Florence Pettyjohn, Aug. 24, 1957; children: Joan, Diane Elizabeth, John Weldon. B.S., Coll. William and Mary, 1951; M.A., Emory U., 1952; Ph.D. (Van Blarcom fellow), Washington U., 1958. Asst. prof. psychology U. N.Mex., Albuquerque, 1957-62, assoc. prof., 1962-67, prof. psychology, 1967—, chmn. dept., 1975-84; v.p. Gen. Programmed Teaching Corp., 1960-62; mem. vis. faculty Washington U., St. Louis, 1963-67; vis. prof. psychology U. Calif.-Berkeley, 1971, U. Hawaii, 1977; disting. vis. prof. U.S. Air Force Med. Ctr., Lackland AFB, Tex., 1978; chmn. Nat. Council Grad. Depts. Psychology, 1977-79, bd. dirs., 1976-81; vis. scholar Learning Research and Devel. Ctr., U. Pitts., 1985; cons. Fla. State Bd. Regents, U. Fla. System. Author: The Transfer of Learning, 1965, Fundamentals of Human Learning and Cognition, 1972, Fundamentals of Human Learning, Memory and Cognition, 1978, (with Bennett, Daniels and Rickert) Psychology of Learning and Memory, 1979, (with Hunt) Fundamentals of Human Memory and Cognition, 1983; editorial bd. Jour. Exptl. Psychology, 1967-74, Jour. Exptl Psychology: Human Learning and Memory, 1974-76, Perception and Psychophysics, 1971-78; co-editor Cognition and Emotion, 1986—; cons. Motivation and Emotion, 1986—; contbr. articles to profl. jours. Served with USAAF, 1946-47. Fellow Am. Psychol. Assn. (council reps. 1980-81, 83—, edn. and tng. bd. 1981-84, chmn. 1984, bd. dirs. 1986—, pres. div. exptl. psychology 1983-86, G. Stanley Hall lectr. 1986, SWIM Disting. lectr. 1987); mem. Psychonomic Soc., AAAS, Sigma Xi, Phi Kappa Phi. Methodist. Clubs: Albuquerque Tennis, Twenty-One; Cosmos (Washington). Home: 1905 Amherst Dr Albuquerque NM 87106 Office: U New Mexico Dept Psychology Albuquerque NM 87131

ELLIS, JAMES DAVID, science educator, curriculum developer; b. Coffeyville, Kans., Dec. 18, 1948; s. Stephen Stuart and Mabel Marie (Nelson) E.; m. Marsha Gail Beaty, Dec. 20, 1980. BA, U. Kans., 1970, MA, 1974, PhD, 1979. Cert. sci. tchr. Sci. tchr. Abe Hubert Jr. High Sch., Garden City, Kans., 1974-77; asst. prof. U. Tex., Austin, 1979-82; staff assoc. Biol. Scis. Curriculum Study, Colorado Springs, Colo., 1982—; project dir. Summer Inst. Dept. Edn., Austin, 1981-82, NSF project, Colorado Springs, 1985—, Health Edn. Project, Colorado Springs, 1983—; lectr. med. meetings. Author, editor sci. edn. textbooks; contbr. articles to profl. jours. Mem. Am. Ednl. Research Assn., Nat. Assn. Research in Sci. Teaching, Nat. Sci. Tchrs. Assn., Nat. Assn. Biology Tchrs., AAAS. Democrat. Avocation: personal fitness. Home: 6715 War Eagle Ln Colorado Springs CO 80919 Office: Biol Sci Curriculum Study 1115 N Cascade Ave Colorado Springs CO 80903

ELLIS, JAMES LEONARD, state senator, businessman; b. Tulsa, Oct. 28, 1928; s. Gaylord Harold and Faye (Proper) E.; m. Barbara Ella Gilligan, 1955; children—Gay Anne, Jon Thomas, Merrilee, James Clayton. Student Colo. State U., 1946-48, Western State Coll., 1948-49; B.A. in Polit. Sci., U.S. Naval Postgrad. Sch., 1965. Propr. Pacific Car Leasing, pres. Pacific Car Rental, San Diego, Calif., 1970—; mem. Calif. State Assembly, 1976-80, Calif. State Senate, 1981—. Mem. San Diego City Council, 1973-76. Served to comdr. U.S. Navy, 1949-70. Decorated D.F.C. with star, Air Medal with 10 stars, Navy Commendation medal with 2 stars, Bronze Star. Mem. El Cajon C. of C., VFW, Am. Legion, Mil. Order World Wars. Republican. Baptist. Club: Rotary. Home: 2755 Navajo Rd El Cajon CA 92020 Office: California State Senate Sacramento CA 95814 *

ELLIS, JOHN W., utility co. exec.; b. Seattle, Sept. 14, 1928; s. Floyd E. and Hazel (Reed) R.; m. Doris Stearns, Sept. 1, 1953; children: Thomas R., John, Barbara, Jim. B.S., U. Wash., 1952, J.D., 1953. Bar: Wash. State bar 1953. With firm Perkins, Coie, Stone, Olsen & Williams, Seattle, 1953-70; with Puget Sound Power & Light Co., Bellevue, Wash., 1970—; exec. v.p. Puget Sound Power & Light Co., 1973-76, pres., chief exec. officer, 1976, also dir.; chmn. Seattle br. Fed. Res. Bank of San Francisco, 1981; mem. Wash. Gov.'s Spl. Com. Energy Curtailment, 1973-74; chmn. Pacific N.W. Utilities Coordinating Com., 1976-82; bd. dirs. Wash. Mut. Savs. Bank, Seattle, SAFECO Corp., Electric Power Research Inst., 1984-89, Nat. Energy Found., 1985—. Pres. Bellevue Boys' Club, 1969-71, Seattle/King County Econ. Devel. Council, 1984—; mem. exec. dirs. Seattle/King County Boys' Club, 1972-75; bd. dirs. Overlake Hosp., Bellevue, 1974—, United Way King County, 1977—, Seattle Sci. Found., 1977—, Seattle Sailing Found., Evergreen Safety Council, 1981, Assn. Wash. Bus., 1980-81, Wash. State Bus. Round Table, 1983, Govs. Adv. Council on Econ. Devel., 1984—, Grad. Sch. Bus. Adminstrn. U. Wash., 1982—, Wash. State Econ. Ptnrship., 1984—; chmn. Seattle Regional Panel White Ho. Fellows, 1985—; trustee Seattle U., 1986—. Mem. Am., Wash., King County (Wash.) bar assns., Nat. Assn. Elec. Cos. (dir. 1977-79), Edison Electric Inst. (dir. 1978-80, exec. com. 1982), Assn. Edison Illuminating Cos. (exec. com. 1979-81), Seattle C. of C. (dir. 1980—), Phi Gamma Delta, Phi Delta Phi. Clubs: Rainier (Seattle) (sec. 1972, v.p. 1984, pres. 1985), Seattle Yacht (Seattle), Corinthian Yacht (Seattle); Meydenbauer Bay Yacht (Bellevue), Bellevue Athletic. Lodge: Rotary (Seattle). Home: 901 SE Shoreland Dr Bellevue WA 98004 Office: Puget Sound Power & Light Co PO Box 97034 OBC-15 Bellevue WA 98009-9734

ELLIS, JOHN WILLIAM, compensation specialist, industrial engineer; b. Buffalo, Apr. 2, 1935; s. Nelson Ray and Ena Mae (Hammond) E.; m. Lee Myao Lee, May 7, 1962; children: Linda Ellis Cummings, Jean, Christina. BS in Indsl. Engring., Rutgers U., 1957. With Manville Sales Corp., 1966—; chief corp. indsl. engr. Manville Sales Corp., Denver, 1969-73, prodn. engring. mgr., 1973-77, mgmt. tng. mgr., 1977-82, compensation adminstrn. mgr., 1982—. Active St. James Presbyn. Ch., Littleton, Colo., choir dir., 1973-82, treas. 1984—. Served with U.S. Army, 1958-61. Mem. Am. Compensation Assn., Am. Soc. Personnel Adminstrs., Denver Figure Skating Club (bd. dirs. 1980-83), Lambda Chi Alpha (chpt. bd. pres. 1962-72). Republican. Avocations: piano, choir, quartet singing, photography. Home: 5460 S Perry St Littleton CO 80123 Office: Manville Sales Corp PO Box 5108 Denver CO 80217

ELLIS, LARRY EDWARD, transportation executive; b. Globe, Ariz., June 25, 1945; s. James William Ellis and Margaret Helen (Habich) Vuletich; m. Karen Ann Rogers, Oct. 22, 1977; children: Christopher Ray, Heather Marie, Scotty Leonard. AA, Phoenix Coll., 1972; BS, Ariz. State U., 1976, postgrad., 1976-80. Adminstrv. asst. Motor Vehicle div Dept. Transp., Phoenix, 1972-79, mgmt. analyst, 1980, group mgr., 1980-85, project leader, 1985—; cons. Orgnl. Dynamics III, 1985. vol. Big Bros. of Am., Phoenix, 1978-81; cubmaster Boy Scouts Am., Phoenix, 1981—, asst. dist. commr., 1986. Recipient Rural Service award VISTA Office of Econ. Opportunity, 1968. Mem. Acad. Cert. Adminstrv. Mgrs., Adminstrv. Mgmt. Soc. (cert. mgr.). Lutheran. Avocations: chess, scouting, reading, backpacking. Office: Dept Transp Motor Vehicle Div 1801 W Jefferson Phoenix AZ 85001

ELLIS, LEE, newspaper/magazine publishing company executive; b. Medford, Mass., Mar. 12, 1924; s. Lewis Leeds and Charlotte Frances (Brough) E.; m. Sharon Kay Barnhouse, Aug. 19, 1972. Child actor, dancer, stage, radio, movies, Keith-Albee Circuit, Eastern U.S., 1927-37; announcer, producer, writer, various radio stas. and CBS, Boston and Miami, Fla., 1946-50; TV dir. ABC; mem. TV faculty Sch. Journalism U. Mo., Columbia, 1950-55; mgr. Sta. KFSD/KFSD-TV, San Diego, 1955-60, GM Imperial Broadcasting System, 1960-62; v.p., dir. advt., Media-Agencies-Clients, Los

Angeles, 1962-66; v.p., dir. newspaper relations Family Weekly (name now USA Weekend), N.Y.C., 1966—; lectr. gen. semantics and communications Idaho State U., Utah State U., San Diego State U. Served with USN, 1941-44; PTO. Mem. San Diego Press Club. Republican. Methodist. Home: 47-800 Madison St #53 Indio CA 92201

ELLIS, LEGRANDE CLARK, physiology educator; b. Farmington, Utah, June 20, 1932; s. Owen William and Mary Lucile (Clark) E.; m. Marilyn Peterson, Sept. 18, 1952; children: Brent P., LuAnn, Janet, L. Clark, Julie, Scott P., Jason P. BS, Utah State U., 1954, MS, 1956; PhD, Okla. State U., 1961. From instr. to asst. prof. physiology Okla. State U., Stillwater, 1957-60; research fellow U. Utah, Salt Lake City, 1962-64; asst. prof. Utah State U., Logan, 1964-66, assoc. prof., 1966-71, prof. physiology, 1971—. Contbr. articles to profl. jours. Explorer leader Boy Scouts Am., Logan, 1974-77, dist. chmn. explorer, 1981-86. Recipient Dist. Merit award Boy Scouts Am., 1983. Mem. Am. Physiol. Soc., Endocrine Soc., Soc. Exptl. Biology and Medicine, Soc. for Study of Reproduction, Am. Soc. Andrology, Am. Soc. Animal Sci., Utah Acad. Arts and Letters, Sigma Xi. Mormon. Avocations: gardening, restoration of old cars. Home: 1160 N 600 E Logan UT 84321 Office: Utah State U Dept Biology Logan UT 84322

ELLIS, MARCIA B., marketing director; b. Nashua, N.H., Oct. 21, 1942; d. Robert M. Polhemus and Lorraine (Bond) Delano; m. David Winston Ellis, Dec. 1, 1961; children: Jocelyn, Jim, Erik. BA in Theater, Ariz. State U., 1980. Artistic dir. CAS/West Masquemakers, Phoenix, 1965-81, Phoenix Little Theatre, 1983-84; freelance writer, theater critic Westsider, Phoenix, 1979-81; assoc. Buchen, Snell & Co., Phoenix, 1981-84; dir. mktg. Fountainhead Corp. Park, Tempe, Ariz., 1984—. Dir. plays Two for the Seesaw, 1983, Everything in the Garden, 1984. V.p. bd. dirs. Phoenix Little Theatre; bd. dirs. Tempe Leadership, Inc., 1985—, Valley Leadership, 1981-84, Culture Arts Soc. West, 1978-81, Tempe United Way, 1986; mem. Task Force for Hosp. Bed Needs Assessment, 1982, Rep. caucus; active Rep. Town Hall, 1984-85. Mem. Pub. Relations Soc. Am., Avondale-Goodyear-Litchfield Park C. of C. (bd. dirs. East Valley ptnrship.). Club: Goodyear Golf and Country (Litchfield Park, Ariz.). Avocations: tennis, backpacking. Office: Fountainhead Corp Park 1620 W Fountainhead Pkwy Suite 200 Tempe AZ 85282

ELLIS, MARGARET (KIT), instructional computer specialist; b. Long Branch, N.J.. BS in Chemistry, U. Wash., 1967, MS in Chemistry, 1969. Supr. chemistry lab. Seattle Cen. Community, Seattle, 1969-70, instr. chemistry, 1971-85, computer-based instrn. coordinator, 1978-85; instr. computing coordinator Wash. Community Coll. Computing Consortium, Redmond, 1985—. Mem. Am. Chem. Soc. (treas. Puget Sound sect. 1985—), Assn. Women in Computing (v.p. programs Puget Sound chpt. 1986—), Iota Sigm Pi (nat. dir. 1975-81, nat. sec. 1981-84). Avocations: swimming, crosscountry skiing. Office: Wash Community Coll Computing Consortium 4002 148th Ave NE Redmond WA 98052

ELLIS, ROBERT ELLSWORTH, electronics executive; b. White Plains, N.Y., Jan. 15, 1947. BA, Miami U., 1969; postgrad., U. Oreg., 1972-75. Pres. Bio-Dynamics Corp., Eugene, Oreg., 1980—. Mem. Am. Def. Preparedness Assn., U.S. Naval Inst., Marine Corps. Assn.

ELLIS, ROBERT HARRY, TV executive; b. Cleve., Mar. 2, 1928; s. John George and Grace Bernice (Lewis) E.; m. Frankie Jo Lanter, Aug. 7, 1954; children: Robert H. Jr., Kimberley Kay Murphy, Shana Lee. BA, Ariz. State U., 1953; MA, Case Western Res. U., 1962. Newswriter, announcer Sta. KOY Radio, Phoenix, 1953-60; dir., radio ops. Ariz. State U., Tempe, 1960-61, gen. mgr. Sta. KAET-TV, 1961—, assoc. prof., 1961—, assoc. v.p. univ. relations, 1986; exec. com. bd. dirs. Pub. Broadcasting Service, Washington, 1983—; founder Pacific Mountain Network, Denver, 1972, pres. 1973-75; mem. ednl. telecommunications com. Nat. Assn. State Univs. and Land Grant, Washington, 1982-86. Mem. Sister City, Tempe, 1986; bd. dirs. Ariz. Zool. Soc., 1986, sec., mem. exec. com. Mem. Nat. Assn. TV Arts and Scis. (life, v.p. bd. trustees 1969-70, bd. dirs. Phoenix chpt. 1986), Ariz. Broadcasters, Phoenix Met. Broadcasters, Tempe C. of C. (diplomate, bd. dirs.). Methodist. Avocations: tennis, racquetball, bridge. Home: 24 E Bishop Tempe AZ 85281 Office: Ariz State U Sta KAET-TV Tempe AZ 85287

ELLIS, RONALD JAMES, systems development manager, educator; b. Los Angeles, Mar. 13, 1952; s. Don R. and Cades A. (LeVay) E. B.A., Calif. State U.-Fullerton, 1974; M.B.A., U. So. Calif., 1978. Life cert. community coll. instr. Adminstr. Bechtel Power Corp., Norwalk, Calif., 1974-77; data engr. Ralph M. Parsons, Pasadena, Calif., 1977-79; sr. account rep. Comshare, Inc., Los Angeles, 1979, client service mgr., 1979-81; systems evaluation cons. ARCO Marine, Inc., Los Angeles, 1971-82; mgr. systems devel. ARCO Transp. Co., Long Beach, Calif., 1982-86, mgr. info. services ARCO Internat. Oil & Gas Co., Los Angeles, 1986—; instr. Coastline Community Coll., Westminister, Calif., 1982; pvt. practice cons., Brea, Calif., 1978—; lectr. in field. Developer, presenter over 20 tng. courses on computers and computer systems; frequent speaker computer confs. Various adult positions Orange County council and Los Amigos dist. Boy Scouts Am., scoutmaster, 1973—, council com. chmn., life mem., exec. bd. Orange County chpt. Nat. Eagle Scout Assn., mem. Order of Arrow, Vigil life mem.; mem. ARCO Speakers Bur.; former advisor Jr. Achievement; pres. So. Calif. Lutheran Assn. Scouters, 1986—. Recipient Scoutmasters key Boy Scouts Am., 1976, award of merit, 1977, Commr.'s key, 1977, Silver Beaver award, 1983. Mem. Planning Forum (v.p. programs 1982-83, v.p. communications 1983-84, v.p. spl. events 1984-85, pres. 1985-86), Data Processing Mgmt. Assn., Assn. M.B.A. Execs., World Future Soc. (life), U. So. Calif. Alumni Assn., Calif. State U. Fullerton Alumni Assn., Beta Gamma Sigma. Club: Toastmasters (Able Toastmaster award, past pres.). Home: 1668 W Norwood Ct Brea CA 92621 Office: ARCO Internat Oil & Gas Co 444 S Flower St Los Angeles CA 90017

ELLIS, SY, mortgage banker; b. N.Y.C., Feb. 5, 1943; s. Alan Louis and Irene (Stillman) E.; m. Marilyn Diane Sherman, Aug. 9, 1969; children—Amy, Kimberly. A.A. in Architecture, Mt. San Antonio Coll., 1963; B.S. in Fin. and Real Estate, U. So. Calif., 1965; Postgrad. UCLA. Real estate broker and notary pub., Calif. Vice pres., div. mgr. Allstate Savs. & Loan, Glendale, Calif., 1978-80; exec. v.p. Bank of Beverly Hills, Calif., 1980-84, pres., chmn. bd. subs. BBH Mortgage Co., Beverly Hills, 1984—; guest speaker on real estate fin. at numerous colls. and profl. orgns. Bd. dirs., exec. com. La Puente Valley Mental Health Dept., San Gabriel Valley, Calif. 1983—; real estate cabinet United Jewish Fund, Los Angeles, 1982—. Served to 1st lt. U.S. Army, 1965-68. Mem. So. Calif. Mortgage Bankers Assn. (bd. dirs. 1986-87), U. So. Calif. Alumni Assn.(life mem.), Real Estate Research Council So. Calif.(exec. com. 1977—), Theta Chi (vice chmn. alumni bd. dirs.). Club: Los Angeles Athletic. Office: BBH Mortgage Co 9766 Wilshire Blvd Beverly Hills CA 90212

ELLIS, THEODORE DALE, sales executive; b. Boise, Idaho, May 14, 1957; s. Jack Dale Ellis and Joy (Howell) Smith; m. Valerie Gwyn Frederickson, Aug. 1, 1975; children: Jeremiah, Shad, Christopher. Student, Boise State U. Mgr. Energy Seal, Boise, 1975-77; product mgr. Chandler Corp., Boise, 1977-83; nat. sales mgr. Canfor U.S.A. Corp., Boise, 1983—. Republican. Home: 12038 W Ramrod Boise ID 83704 Office: Canfor USA Corp 1301 N Orchard Boise ID 83701

ELLIS, WALTON PAUL, chemist, researcher; b. Mammoth Spring, Ark., Aug. 25, 1931; s. Joe Dan and Alpha Louetta (White) E.; m. Martha Lou Grove, Nov. 4, 1956; children: Elly, Carolyn. BS, U. Calif., 1953; PhD, U. Chgo., 1957. Mem. research staff Los Alamos (N.Mex.) Nat. Lab., 1957—. Contbr. articles to profl. jours. Mem. Am. Chem. Soc., Am. Vacuum Soc. Methodist. Avocations: swimming, woodworking. Home: 156 El Viento Los Alamos NM 87544 Office: Los Alamos Nat Lab Chem 2 MS G738 Los Alamos NM 87545

ELLIS, WAYNE ELMO, building materials company executive; b. Puxico, Mo., Apr. 13, 1915; s. Roscoe Clinton and Carrie Elizabeth (Palmer) E.; A.A., Bakersfield Jr. Coll., 1935; B.A., San Jose State U., 1938; m. Helen Flora Rice, Aug. 2, 1940; children—Helen Kuulei, Wayne Richard, Michael Lewis. Tchr., Dept. Pub. Instruction, Lihue, Kauai, Hawaii, 1938-42; owner, operator Lihue Hotel, 1942-46; mgr. Hale Kauai, Ltd., Lihue, 1945-50, pres., 1950-85, chmn., 1985—; dir. InterIsland Resorts; pres. Puhi Enterprises, Inc.; commr. Dept. Pub. Instrn. Ter. Hawaii, 1945-53; statehood commr. Ter. Hawaii, 1953-59; mem. adv. council for 7 western states SBA, 1955-56; mem. U.S. Army Adv. Council, 1965-78. Clubs: Rotary, Yacht, Masons, Shriners (Kauai). Home: PO Box 1749 Lihue HI 96766

ELLIS, WILLIAM, ophthalmologist, educator; b. N.Y.C., Dec. 28, 1942; s. Benson and Pauline Ellis; m. Lucy Wiltshire Bugg, July 7, 1969 (div.); children: William Benson, Charles Edward. B.S. In Elec. Engring., U. Calif.-Berkeley, 1964; M.D., Washington U., St. Louis, 1968. Diplomate Am. Bd. Ophthalmology. Intern Duke U. Med. Ctr., Durham, N.C., 1968-69; fellow in Nat. Heart and Lung Inst., NIH, Bethesda, Md., 1969-71; resident in ophthalmology Stanford U. Med. Ctr., Calif., 1971-74, lectr. postgrad. ophthalmology meetings, 1972-74; practice medicine specializing in ophthalmology, Richmond, Calif., 1975-83, Pinole, Calif., 1974—, El Cerrito, Calif., 1983—; lectr. U. Calif. Ophthalmology Conf., Letterman Hosp., 1973-74; clin. asst. prof. ophthalmology U. Calif.-San Francisco, 1981— ; asst. prof. U. Calif.-Berkeley Sch. Optometry; numerous TV and radio appearances on ophthalmology, 1983—; lectr. on retractive surgery, various internat. groups. Author: A Textbook of Radial Keratotomy and Astigmatism Surgery. Served with USPHS, 1969- 71. Fellow Am. Acad. Ophthalmology, ACS; mem. AMA, Calif. Med. Assn., Alameda-Contra Costa Med. Assn., Keratorefractive Soc., Am. Intraocular Implant Soc., Pacific Coast Oto-Ophthalmol. Soc., Tau Beta Pi, Epsilon Kappa Nu, Nu Sigma Nu. Office: 6500 Fairmount Ave El Cerrito CA 94530

ELLISMAN, ROLAND AVERY, psychotherapist, consultant, educator; b. Ventura, Calif., Apr. 10, 1951; s. Carl and Bertha (Dressler) E. BA in Philosophy, U. Calif., Santa Barbara, 1973; MSW, San Diego State U., 1979. Clin. supr. Escondido Youth Encounter, 1979; also bd. dirs. 1984—; counselor Family Service Assn., Escondido, Calif., 1979; owner, dir. Hidden Valley Family Counseling, Escondido, 1983—. Chmn. North County Assn. Divorce Mediators, Encinitas, Calif., 1984—, co-founder; active Felicita Found. for the Arts, Escondido, 1985—; supporter Ctr. Study Dem. Instns., Santa Barbara, Calif., 1984—. Fellow Soc. Clin. Social Work (elected to state bd. dirs.); mem. ACLU, Nat. Assn. Social Workers (cert.), Assn. Family and Conciliation Cts., Acad. Family Mediators (assoc.), Nat. Fedn. Socs. Clin. Social Work (com. profl. standards 1985—). Jewish. Avocations: violin, fishing, surfing. Office: Hidden Valley Family Counseling 333 S Juniper Suite 100 Escondido CA 92025

ELLISON, DIANE MARIE, timber company executive; b. Aberdeen, Wash., June 18, 1941; d. Russell M. and Syster (Edlund) E.; m. Thomas C. Rowe, Apr. 12, 1963 (div. 1969); children: Dawn M., Robert Ellison. BA in Sociology cum laude, U. Wash., 1963; teaching credential in social scis., U. Calif., Irvine, 1970; MS in Human Resource Mgmt. and Devel., Chapman Coll., 1984. Prin. Ellison Truffles Corp., Aberdeen, 1986—; speaker Chapman Coll. Enterprise Inst., 1986-87; mem. steering com. Wash. State Folklife Council. Co-author: Reach for the Sky, 1986. Counselor Seattle Detention Ctr. for Juveniles, 1963, Oakland (Calif.) YWCA, 1964; developer lesson plans St. Andrews Ch., Newport Beach, Calif., 1971-75; coach Tustin (Calif.) Hills Racquet Club and Fountain Valley Racquet Club, 1977-78. Mem. N.Am. Truffling Soc., Pacific N.W. Writers Conf., Internat. Log Rolling Orgn., Women in Timber, Aberdeen C. of C. (bd. dirs. 1986), U. Wash. Alumni Assn., Alumni Assn. Chapman Coll., Polson Mus., Mus. Aberdeen, Alpha Chi Omega. Lodge: Zonta. Guest on ABC Wide World of Sports, 1966, 68, 69, 84, and Woman to Woman. Home and Office: Rt 1 Box 142 Aberdeen WA 98520

ELLISON, KATHERINE ESTHER, journalist; b. Mpls., Aug. 19, 1957; d. Ellis and Bernice June (Bender) E. BA in Internat. Relations, Stanford U., 1979. Intern reporter Washington Post, 1979, Newsweek, London, 1979-80; reporter San Jose (Calif.) Mercury, 1980—; bd. dirs. Media Alliance, San Francisco, 1986—. Co-author articles including Hidden Billions: The Draining of the Philippines, 1985 (Pulitzer prize 1986, George Polk Meml. award 1986, Investigative Reporters and Editors award 1986). Office: care San Jose Mercury News 750 Ridder Park Dr San Jose CA 95190

ELLISOR, WILBURN LEE, real estate executive; b. Independence, Kans., Aug. 26, 1932; s. William Payne and Mary (Baty) E.; m. Ann L. Chester, Jan. 2, 1953; children—Conni L., Kristen A., William C., Susan K., Carol B. B.A., U. Wichita, 1955; grad. U.S. Army Command and Gen. Staff Coll., 1976. Program dir. Eastside br. YMCA, Wichita, Kans., 1953-56; exec. dir. Westside YMCA, Wichita, 1956-57; program dir. San Angelo (Tex.) YMCA, 1958-59, Abilene (Tex.) YMCA, 1960-64; exec. dir. Jefferson County YMCA, Lakewood, Colo., 1964-70; v.p. ops. YMCA Met. Denver, 1970—. Serving with F.A., USAR, 1955—. Recipient Disting. Service award Jaycees, Denver, 1969. Mem. Assn. Profl. Dirs. YMCA USA, N.G. Assn., Denver C. of C., Am. Camping Assn., ARC, Boy Scouts Am., Acad. Cert. Profl. Dirs., Sigma Tau Gamma, Alpha Phi Omega. Democrat. Mem. Evangelical Covenant Ch. Clubs: Kiwanis (program chmn. Denver); Optimists (pres. 1959, life). Office: YMCA Met Denver 25 E 16th Ave Denver CO 80202

ELLIS-VANT, KAREN ELLA, special education teacher; b. La Grande, Oreg., May 10, 1950; d. Ellis Eddington and Gladys Vera (Smith) McGee; m. Lynn F. Ellis, June 14, 1975 (div. Sept. 1983); children—Megan Marie, Matthew David; m. Jack Scott Vant, Sept. 6, 1986. BA in Elem. Edn., Boise State U., 1972, MA in Spl. Edn., 1979; postgrad. studies in curriculum and instruction, U. Minn., 1985—. Tchr. learning disabilities resource room New Plymouth Joint Sch. Dist., 1972-73; tchr. learning disabilities resource room Payette Joint Sch. Dist., 1973, diagnostician project SELECT, 1974-75; cons. tchr. in spl. edn. Boise Sch. Dist., 1975—; com. profl. Standards Commn., 1983-86. Active Hotline, Inc.; mem. Idaho Coop. Manpower Commn., 1984-85. Recipient Disting. Young Woman of Yr. award Boise Jaycettes, 1982, Idaho Jaycettes, 1983; Coffman Alumni scholar U. Minn., 1985-86. Mem. NEA (mem. civil rights com. 1983-85, state contact for peace caucus 1981-85, del. assembly rep., 1981-85), Idaho Edn. Assn. (bd. dirs. region VII 1981-85, pres. region VII 1981-82), Boise Edn. Assn. (v.p. 1981-82, 84-85, pres. 1982-83), Nat. Council Urban Edn. Assn., World Future Soc., Council for Exceptional Children (pres. chpt. 1978-79), Assn. Supervision and Curriculum Devel., Minn. Council for Social Studies, Calif. Assn. for Gifted, Assn. for Grad. Edn. Students. Unitarian. Contbr. articles to profl. jours.; editor, author ednl. texts and communiques; conductor of workshops. Office: Lincoln Annex Pupil Personnel 1207 Fort St Boise ID 83702

ELLSWORTH, FRANK L., college president; b. Wooster, Ohio, May 20, 1943; s. Clayton Sumner and Frances (Fuller) E.; 1 child, Kirstin Lynne. B.A., Western Res. Coll., 1965; M.Ed., Pa. State U., 1967; M.A., Columbia U., 1969; Ph.D., U. Chgo., 1976. Asst. dir. devel. Columbia Law Sch., 1968-70; dir. spl. projects, prof. lit. Sarah Lawrence Coll., N.Y., 1971; asst. dean Law Sch., U. Chgo., 1971-79, instr. social sci. collegiate div., 1975-79; pres. Pitzer Coll., Claremont, Calif., 1979—; also prof. polit. sci. Pitzer Coll., 1979—. Author: Law on the Midway, 1977, Student Activism in American Higher Education; mem. editorial bd. Calif. Lawyer; contbr. articles to profl. jours. Mem. vis. coms. Western Res. Coll.; vice chmn. bd. trustees Southwestern U.; bd. dirs., pres. Ind. Colls. So. Calif.; bd. fellows Claremont Univ. Center; trustee Brentwood Sch. Recipient Disting. Young Alumnus award Case Western Res. U., 1981. Mem. Assn. Ind. Colls. and Univs. (bd. dirs.), History Edn. Soc., Council for Advancement of Secondary Edn., Young Pres.'s Orgn. Clubs: University (Los Angeles); Zamorano (Los Angeles). Office: Pitzer Coll 1050 Mills Ave Claremont CA 91711

ELLSWORTH, RICHARD GERMAN, psychologist; b. Provo, Utah, June 23, 1950; s. Richard Grant and Betty Lola (Midgley) E.; BS, Brigham Young U., 1974, M.A., 1975; Ph.D., U. Rochester (N.Y.), 1979; postgrad. UCLA, 1980-84; Ph.D., Internat. Coll., 1983; m. Carol Emily Osborne, May 23, 1970; children—Rebecca Ruth, Spencer German, Rachel Priscilla, Melanie Star. Instr. U. Rochester, 1976-77; research assoc. Nat. Tech. Inst. for Deaf, Rochester, 1977; instr. West Valley Coll., Saratoga, Calif., 1979-80, San Jose (Calif.) City Coll., 1980; psycholinguist UCLA, 1980-81; research assoc. UCLA, 1981-85; psychologist Daniel Freeman Meml. Hosp., Inglewood, Calif., 1981-84, Broderick, Langlois & Assocs., San Gabriel, Calif., 1982—, Beck Psychiat. Med. Group, Lancaster, Calif., 1984—, Angeles Counseling Ctr., Arcadia, Calif., 1986— ; cons. LDS Social Services Calif. Agy., 1981—, Antelope Valley Hosp. Med. Ctr., 1984—, Palmdale Hosp. Med. Ctr., 1984—, Treatment Ctrs. of Am. Psychiat. Hosps., 1985—. Scoutmaster, Boy Scouts Am., 1976-79. UCLA Med. Sch. fellow in psychiatry, 1980-81. Mem. Am. Psychol. Assn., Am. Assn. Sex Educators, Counselors and Therapists, Assn. Mormon Counselors and Psychotherapists, Am. Soc. Clin. Hypnosis, Psi Chi. Contbr. articles to profl. jours. Office: 1650 W Ave J Lancaster CA 93534

ELMENDORF, WILLIAM WELCOME, anthropology educator; b. Victoria, B.C., Can., Sept. 10, 1912; s. William Judson and Mary (Johnson) E.; m. Eleanor Gerlough, Oct. 12, 1940; children: William John, Anthony Daniel. B.A., U. Wash., 1934, M.A., 1935; Ph.D., U. Calif. at Berkeley, 1949. Teaching asst. U. Calif. at Berkeley, 1940-42; instr., then asst. prof. anthropology U. Wash., 1946-57; teaching asso. Northwestern U., 1950-51; lectr., then asso. prof. Wash. State U., 1957-65; mem. faculty U. Wis., 1963—, prof. anthropology, 1964-81, prof. emeritus, 1981—; vis. prof. anthropology U. Calif.-Davis, 1982-84, research assoc., 1984—; profl. cons. Skokomish Indian Claims Case, 1956. Author: The Structure of Twana Culture, 1960, Skokomish and Other Coast Salish Tales, 1961, Lexical and Cultural Change in Yukian, 1968. Served to capt. AUS, 1942-46, 51-52. Fellow Am. Anthrop. Assn., Am. Ethnol. Soc.; mem. Linguistic Soc. Am., Central States Anthrop. Soc., Northwest Anthrop. Conf. (pres. 1958), Sigma Xi. Home: 1119 Bucknell Drive Davis CA 95616 Office: U Calif Dept Anthropology Davis CA 95616

ELMER, JEAN RADLEY, psychotherapist; b. Clifton Springs, N.Y., Aug. 6, 1946; d. Vaughn Ferris and Sara (Sutman) Radley; 1 child, William VII. BA, U. Maine, 1968; MSW, Boston U., 1971; postgrad., U. Wash., 1977-79. Caseworker Rensselaer County Dept. Social Services, Troy, N.Y., 1968-69, State of Hawaii, Honolulu, 1971-72, Seattle Children's Home, 1973-74; psychotherapist Divorce Lifeline, Olympia, Wash., 1977; outpatient therapist Mental Health N., Seattle, 1974-76, 78-82; pvt. practice psychotherapy Seattle, 1982—; pub. speaker KIRO-Radio sta., Seattle, 1984, Nat. Assn. Women in Constrn., Everett, Wash., 1986, Bothell (Wash.) C. of C., 1986, Civitan, Bellevue, Wash., 1985, Rotary Club, Seattle, 1985, Women Bus. Owners, Seattle, 1986. Contbr. articles to profl. pubs. Arbitrator Floating Homes Assn., Seattle, 1981. Mem. Am. Group Psychotherapy Assn., N.W. Group Psychotherapy Assn. (sec. 1983-85), Nat. Assn. Social Workers, Wash. State Soc. Clin. Social Workers, Assn. Women in Psychology, Women's Bus. Exchange, Women Bus. Owners. Democrat. Presbyterian. Club: Toastmasters. Avocations: single sculls rowing, 4 and 8-person shells, skiing, stained glass crafting. Home: 2349 Fairview Ave E Seattle WA 98102 Office: 1424 4th Ave Suite 903 Seattle WA 98101

ELMORE, KATHLEEN ANN MARIE, food company executive; b. Indpls., Sept. 9, 1952; s. Martin Alfred and Florence Cecilia (Miara) E. BS, Purdue U., 1974; MBA in Mktg., Central State U., Okla., 1978. Regional merchandiser Castle & Cooke Foods, Inc., Indpls., 1975, divisional merchandiser, New Orleans, 1975-76, asst. dist. sales mgr., Dallas, 1976, dist. sales mgr., Oklahoma City, 1976-77; mgr. field mktg. projects Pizza Hut div. PepsiCo, Inc., Wichita, Kans., mgr. market research, 1978; mgr. sales planning Stokely-Van Camp Inc., Indpls., 1981-83; asst. product mgr. Star-Kist Foods Inc. div. H. J. Heinz Inc., Long Beach, Calif., 1983-84, product mgr. dog snacks, 1984—. Ind. State scholar, 1970-74; Am. Bus. Women's Assn. scholar, 1971-73; Purdue U. Centennial grantee, 1974. Mem. Assn. MBA Execs. Office: H J Heinz Inc 180 E Ocean Blvd Long Beach CA 90802

ELMSTROM, GEORGE P., optometrist, writer; b. Salem, Mass., Dec. 11, 1925; s. George and Emily Irene (Wedgwood) E.; grad. So. Calif. Coll. Optometry, 1951; m. Nancy DePaul, Apr. 29, 1973; children—Pamela, Beverly, Robert. Pvt. practice optometry, El Segundo, Calif., 1951—; mem. staff So. Calif. Coll. Optometry, 1951—; book cons. Med. Econs. Books, 1970—; instrument and forensic editor Jour. Am. Optical Assn.; comml. airplane and balloon pilot, 1968—. Served with U.S. Army, World War II. Decorated Bronze Star; named Writer of Year, Calif. Optometric Assn., 1957, Man of Year, El Segundo, 1956; recipient spl. citation Nat. Eye Found., 1955. Fellow Am. Acad. Optometry, AAAS, Southwest Contact Lens Soc., Disting. Service Found. of Optometry, Internat. Acad. Preventive Medicine; mem. Am. Optometric Assn., Assn. for Research in Vision, Am. Soc. Ultrasonography, Am. Pub. Health Assn., Optometric Editors Assn., Assn. Research in Vision, Internat. Soc. Ophthalmic Ultrasound, Profl. Airshow Pilots Assn., Flying Optometrists Assn. Am., Beta Sigma Kappa, So. Calif. Coll. Optometry Alumni (pres. 1955-56). Author: Optometric Practice Management, 1963; Legal Aspects of Contact Lens Practice, 1966; Advanced Management for Optometrists, 1974; Modernized Management, 1981; mgmt. editor Optometric Monthly, 1973. Home: 15 63d Ave Playa Del Rey CA 90291 Office: 502 Main El Segundo CA 90245

ELSAYED, KHALIL MOHAMAD, aerospace engineer; b. Zahleh, Lebanon, July 9, 1950; came to U.S., 1976; s. Mohamad Hassan and Hadia Yusef (Ali Ahmed) E.; m. Wilma Beatriz Ramirez, Oct.11, 1976; children: Mohamad Omar, Marie Joumana. BS in Engring. Tech., Northrop U., 1983; BSBA, U. Phoenix, 1983, MBA, 1986; BT2, Arts and Crafts Coll., Beirut, 1972. Aircraft mechanic Middle East Airlines, Beirut, 1972-76, Steward Davis Inc., Longbeach, Calif., 1976-77; airframe and powerplant mechanics Aircraft Tank Service, Burbank, Calif., 1977-78; leadman, devel. mechanic Northrop Corp., Hawthorne, Calif., 1978-81, mfg. engr., 1981-83, sr. mfg. engr., 1983—; cons. PACTEC, Cerritos, Calif., 1983; aircraft structural designer ANOROC, Compton, Calif., 1984. Author: Arabic As Spoken in Lebanon. Active Los Angeles County Youth Motivation Task Force, 1986. Mem. soc. Mfg. Engrs., Robotics Internat., Aircraft Owners and Pilots Assn., AIAA, Young Astronauts Program (chpt. establisher, advisor 1986). Republican. Muslim. Avocations: flying, reading, camping, biking, ping pong. Home: 12533 Broadleaf Ln Moreno Valley CA 92388 Office: Northrop Corp Aircraft Div One Northrop Ave 4813/52 Hawthorne CA 90250

ELSE, CAROLYN JOAN, library system administrator; b. Mpls., Jan. 31, 1934; d. Elmer Oscar and Irma Carolyn (Seibert) Wahlberg; m. Floyd Warren Else, 1962 (div. 1968); children—Stephen Alexander, Catherine Elizabeth. B.S. Stanford U., 1956; M.L.S., U. Wash., 1957. Cert. profl. librarian, Wash. Librarian Queens Borough Pub. Library, N.Y.C., 1957-59, U.S. Army Special Services, France, Germany, 1959-62; info. librarian Bennett Martin Library, Lincoln, Neb., 1962-63; br. librarian Pierce County Library, Tacoma, Wash., 1963-65, dir., 1965—. Bd. dirs. Campfire, Tacoma, 1984. Mem. South Sound Women's Network (bd. dirs.), Wash. Library Assn. (v.p. 1969-71), Pacific Northwest Library Assn. (sec. 1969-71), ALA. Club: City (Tacoma). Office: Pierce County Rural Library Dist 2356 Tacoma Ave S Tacoma WA 98402

ELSNER, ROBERT HOLMES, medical association administrator; b. Orange, Calif., June 2, 1933; s. Ernest Edgar Elsner and Geneva Florence (Holmes) Van Zant; m. Nancy Lee Robison, June 14, 1958; 1 child, Alison. AB in Journalism, U. So. Calif., 1955. Staff Daily News Tribune, Fullerton, Calif., 1955-56; northwest mgr. Allen's Press Clipping Bureau, San Francisco and Portland (Oreg.), 1957-60; pub. relations account exec. Pacific Nat. Advt. Agy., Portland, 1960-61; pub. relations dir. Assoc. Oreg. Industries, Portland, 1961-63; exec. dir. Multhomah County Med. Soc., Portland, 1963-77; exec. v.p., chief exec. officer Los Angeles County Med. Assn., 1977-85; chief exec. officer Calif. Med. Assn., San Francisco, 1985—; pres. Northwest Oreg. Health systems, 1976-77; mem. Nat. Council on Health Planning and Resource Devel., Washington, 1976-77. Bd. dirs. Calif. Med. Polit. Action Com., San Francisco, 1979-85; pres. Oregon Rep. Club, 1964, sustaining mem. Rep. Nat. Com., 1975—. Served with USN, 1956-57. Mem. AMA (adv. com. to exec. v.p. 1974-82), Am. Assn. Med. Soc. Execs. (pres. 1975-76), Calif. Med. Execs. Conf. (chmn. 1983-84), Nat. Council Against Health Fraud, Los Angeles County Med. Assn. (hon.), Multhomah County Med. Soc. (hon.), Am. Soc. Assn. Execs. (bd. dirs. 1986—), Profl. Conv. Mgmt. Assn. (bd. dirs. 1986—), Soc. Profl. Journalists, Portland C. of C. (forum chmn. 1972-73), Delta Tau Delta. Clubs: Portland Pub. Relations Roundtable (pres. 1968), Cardinal and Gold. Home: 105 Golden Gate Ave Belvedere CA 94920 Office: Calif Med Assn 44 Gough St San Francisco CA 94103

ELSON, BRIAN BRUCE, microbiologist; b. Pueblo, Colo., Sept. 10, 1952; s. Samuel Bruce and Mary Margaret (Black) E.; m. Shari Renee VanPelt, July 7, 1984. BS in Microbiology, Colo. State U., 1976; postgrad., U. So. Colo., 1986—. Lab. tech. Pueblo Bd. Water Works, 1976-79, lab. dir., 1979-

82, water quality control supr., 1982—; inst. Operator Sch. Boulder, 1979; cons. Pueblo County Stream Standards Com., 1977, U.S. Geol. Survey Water Quality Study of Pueblo Reservoir, 1986—, Hazardous Materials Response Unit, Pueblo Fire Dept., 1986—. Chmn. Environ. Policy Adv. Com., Pueblo, 1986—. Mem. Am. Soc. Microbiologists, Am. Water Works Assn. (affiliate mem.). Democrat. Mem. Ch. of Christ. Office: Pueblo Bd Water Works 319 W 4th St Pueblo CO 81005

ELSTNER, RICHARD CHESNEY, structural engineer; b. Pitts., Jan. 23, 1924; s. Richard Alfred and Marguerite (Chesney) E.; m. Elizabeth Ann Smith, Sept. 19, 1947; children—Richard Graham, Dwight Smith, Charles William. B.S. in Civil Engring., Rose Poly. Inst., 1947; M.S. in Theoretical and Applied Mechanics, U. Ill., 1953. Registered profl. engr., Ill., Iowa, Ind., Miss., Calif., Hawaii, Wash. Instr. Rose Poly., Terre Haute, Ind., 1947-48, U. Hawaii, Honolulu, 1948-50; research assoc. U. Ill., Urbana, 1950-53; devel. engr. Portland Cement Assn., Skokie, Ill., 1953-59; prin. Wiss, Janney, Elstner, Northbrook, Ill., 1960-78, br. mgr., Honolulu, 1979—, Bd. dirs. Insulating Glass Certification Council, Chgo., 1975—. Served with U.S. Army, 1943-46; PTO. Fellow Am. Concrete Inst. (bd. dirs., Wason medal 1955); mem. ASCE (sect. pres. 1983), Cons. Engrs. Council Hawaii, Structural Engrs. Assn. Hawaii, Structural Engrs. Assn. Ill. (life). Office: Wiss Janney Elstner Assocs 1210 Auahi St Suite 108 Honolulu HI 96814

ELSTON, WOLFGANG EUGENE, geology educator, researcher; b. Berlin, Germany, Aug. 13, 1928; came to U.S., 1945; s. Frederick Gustave and Anny (Halpert) E.; m. Lorraine Hind, Dec. 26, 1952; children: Stephen, Richard. BS, CCNY, 1949; MA, PhD, Columbia U., 1953. Cert. profl. geol. scientist. Geologist N.Mex. Bur. Mines, Socorro, summers 1950-64; asst. prof. Tex. Technol. Coll., Lubbock, 1955-57; asst. prof. U. N.Mex., Albuquerque, 1957-63, assoc. prof., 1963-67, prof. geology, 1967—, acting chmn. dept. geology, 1982; lectr. Columbia U., N.Y.C., 1951-52; cons. Govt. Agys. Industry, Albuquerque, 1957—; prin. investigator NASA, 1964—, NSF, 1978—; Univ. Found. visitor U. Auckland, New Zealand, 1985-86; exchange scientist NSF, 1979, 85-86. Author, editor: Volcanism in Southwest New Mexico, 1976, Cauldrons and Ore Deposits, 1978; co-editor: Ash-Flow Tuffs, 1979; contbr. articles to profl. jours. Served with U.S. Army, 1953-55. Research fellow Royal Soc., Eng., 1986; Research grantee NASA, U.S. Geol. Survey, N.Mex. Energy Inst., 1964—. Fellow Geol. Soc. Am., AAAS; mem. Nat. Assn. Geology Tchrs. (pres. S.W. sect. 1975-76), Am. Inst. Profl. Geologists (cert., pres. N.Mex. sect. 1982), Internat. Assn. Volcanology and Chemistry of Earth's Interior (sec. working group on explosive volcanism 1983-86). Avocations: travel, hiking, sailing. Home: 1023 Columbia Dr NE Albuquerque NM 87106 Office: U NMex Dept Geology Albuquerque NM 87131

ELTON, ALBERT MAX, beverage company executive; retired air force officer; b. Yellville, Ark., Mar. 17, 1917; s. Albert M. and Maude (Lay) E.; m. Smilja Mamula, May 16, 1942 (div. Oct. 1982); children—Albert M., Kenneth, Thomas, Ann, Marian, Pat, Therese, Mary Lata; m. Patricia Ann Elton, Oct. 9, 1982; 1 child, Sean C. B.A., U. Ga., 1939; B.A., George Washington U., 1964; grad. Air War Coll., Maxwell AFB, Ala., 1964. Commd. 2d lt. U.S. Air Force, 1940, advanced through grades to lt. col., command pilot, 1964; B-52 wing comdr. SAC, 1951-63; dept. chmn. UCLA, 1964-67; ret. 1967; chmn. bd., chief exec. officer High Sierra Springs, Inc., Granada Hills, Calif., 1978—; pres. bd. dirs. Home Visitation Ctr., Inc., Pacoima, Calif., 1982—; exec. dir. Casa Loma Coll., Lakeview Terrace, Calif., 1967—. Decorated D.F.C., Air medal with 2 oakleaf clusters, Purple Heart with 1 oakleaf cluster. Mem. VFW (past comdr.), Am. Legion (past comdr.). Democrat. Roman Catholic. Home: 11916 Woodley Ave Granada Hills CA 91344 Office: Casa Loma Coll 11620 Eldridge Ave Lakeview Terrace CA 91342

ELVERUM, GERARD WILLIAM, JR., electronic and diversified company executive; b. Mpls., Sept. 29, 1927; m. Mary Jean Proverbs, Dec. 28, 1948. Student, U. Nebr., 1945, S.D. State U., 1945; B in Physics, U. Minn., 1949. Engr. Jet Propulsion Lab., Pasadena, Calif., 1949-59; sect. head, mgr. dept. Space Tech. Lab., El Segundo, Calif., 1959-62; dir. lab. Systems Group TRW, Redondo Beach, Calif., 1963-66, mgr. ops. Def. and Space Systems Group, 1969-81, v.p., gen. mgr. Applied Tech. Div./Space and Tech. Group, 1981—; mem. adv. panel NASA/Aerospace Safety Bd., Washington, 1982—. Contbr. articles to profl. jours.; patentee in field. Served with USAF, 1944-46. Recipient Spl. Achievement award ASME, 1971; named Outstanding Engr. Inst. Advancement Engring., 1972. Fellow AIAA (James H. Wyld Propulsion award 1973); mem. Am. Def. Preparedness Assn. Office: TRW ATD/STG Bldg E1 Space Park Redondo Beach CA 90278

ELWAY, JOHN ALBERT, professional football player; b. Port Angeles, Wash., June 28, 1960; s. Jack Elway; m. Janet Elway; 1 child, Jessica Gwen. BA in Econs., Stanford U., 1983. Quarterback Denver Broncos, 1983—. Mem. Mayor's Council on Phys. Fitness, City of Denver; chmn. Rocky Mountain region Nat. Kidney Found. Played in NFL Pro Bowl, 1987. Office: Denver Broncos 5700 Logan St Denver CO 80216 *

ELY, JOHN THOMAS ANDERSON, research physicist; b. San Francisco, June 24, 1923; s. John Thomas Anderson and Ruth (Mallery) E.; B.A., Eastern Wash. State U., 1952; M.S., U. Wash., 1959, Ph.D., 1969. Commd. 2d lt. USAF, 1944, advanced through grades to col., 1965, ret., 1968, pilot conventional and jet aircraft, 1947-67; cosmic ray physicist, research faculty U. Wash., Seattle, 1969—. Lectr. physics Northeastern U., 1963-65, U. Wash., 1970—; sci. cons., 1969—. Mem. Am. Phys. Soc., Sigma Xi. Club: Swedish. Contbr. articles to profl. publs. Designed experiments flown on 5 satellites; research in physics of viruses; mutagenic burden of sea-level cosmic radiation as a factor in aging and cancer; immune response in viral and neoplastic diseases; explained tumor tolerance, other immune suppression of hyperglycemia. Office: U Wash Physics Dept Seattle WA 98195

ELY, MARICA MCCANN, interior designer; b. Pachuca, Mex., May 2, 1907 (parents Am. citizens); d. Warner and Mary Evans (Cook) McCann; m. Northcutt Ely, Dec. 2, 1931; children—Michael and Craig (twins), Parry Haines. B.A., U. Calif.-Berkeley, 1929; diploma Pratt Inst. of Art, N.Y.C., 1931. Free-lance interior designer, Washington and Redlands, Calif., 1931—; lectr. on flower arranging and fgn. travel, 1931—; prof. Sogetsu Ikebana Sch., Tokyo, 1972. Art editor (calendar) Nat. Capital Garden Club League, 1957-58. Pres. Kenwood Garden Club, Md.; bd. dirs. Nat. Library Blind, Washington; v.p. bd. dirs. Washington Hearing and Speech Soc., 1969; cofounder Delta Gamma Found. Pre-Sch. Blind Children, Washington. Finalist Nat. Silver Bowl Competition, Jackson-Perkins Co., 1966; garden shown on nat. tour Am. Hort. Soc., 1985. Mem. Calif. Arboretum Found., Redlands Hort. and Improvement Soc. (bd. dirs. 1982—), Town and Country African Violet Soc., Hemerocallis Soc., Delta Gamma. Clubs: Redlands Country (Calif.); Washington, Chevy Chase (Washington); Berkeley Tennis (Calif.).

EMAN, EVELYN (EVELYN EMAN DELMAR), communications executive; b. N.Y.C., Dec. 31, 1949; d. John and Gay (Simon) Eman; m. Lawrence E. Delmar. Student NYU, 1975-76, Baruch Coll., 1981-82. Asst. mgr. Vanderbilt Athletic Club, N.Y.C., 1967-68; pub. relations mgr. DEC Enterprises, Inc., N.Y.C., 1968-73; exec. interviewer Dun & Bradstreet, Inc., N.Y.C., 1974; pub. relations rep. Parsons & Whittemore, Inc., N.Y.C., 1974-77; corp. mgr. pub. relations NEC Am., Inc., Melville, N.Y., 1977-82; pres. Perception Plus, Colorado Springs, Colo., 1982—; chmn. media relations communications adv. council World Cycling Championships, 1986. Recipient cert. of merit Publicity Club N.Y., 1976-77. Mem. Colorado Springs Conv. and Visitors Bur., Colo. Springs Press Assn. (Gridiron award 1986), Internat. Assn. Bus. Communicators (pres. So. Colo. 1985-86, Gold Nuggets awards 1984-86, Silver Quill 1986), The Promoters (dir. 1983-84, pres. 1984-85, chmn. 1985-86), Colorado Springs C. of C., Pikes Peak Advt. Fedn. (Addy awards 1986), Pub. Relations Soc. Am., Women in Communications (Women of Achievement award 1986). Composer: Face Another Day, 1973; Songbird, 1973; There's the Man, 1973; Hey Mister, 1974; In the Morning, 1974: It's Never Been Like This, 1974; contbr. editor PR Essay, 1976-77; editor: Women's Exchange Network Newsletter, 1983; contbr. articles to mags. Office: Perception Plus PO Box 38880 Colorado Springs CO 80937

EMBRY, MICHAEL HEARD, construction company executive; b. Shreveport, La., Jan. 28, 1951; s. Woodrow Wilson and Annie Dell (Heard) E.; m. Kathy Ann Hill, July 28, 1984. BS in Bldg. Constrn., NE La. U., 1976. Cost analyst, scheduler Ford Bacon and Davis, Inc., Monroe, La., 1976-77; mgr. cost control scheduling Ford Bacon and Davis, Inc., Salt Lake City, 1978—. Mem. Am. Assn. Cost Engrs. Democrat. Baptist. Avocations: skiing, model railroading. Home: 640 Parkview Dr Park City UT 84060 Office: Ford Bacon and Davis Inc 375 Chipeta Way Salt Lake City UT 84108

EMERSON, ALTON CALVIN, physical therapist; b. Webster, N.Y., Sept. 29, 1934; s. Homer Douglas and Pluma (Babcock) E.; m. Nancy Ann Poarch, Dec. 20, 1955 (div. 1972); children: Marcia Ann, Mark Alton; m. Barbara Irene Stewart, Oct. 6, 1972. BS in Vertibrate Zoology, U. Utah, 1957; cert. phys. therapy, U. So. Calif., 1959. Staff phys. therapist Los Angeles County Crippled Children's Services, 1958-65; pvt. practice phys. therapy Los Angeles, 1966—; cons. City of Hope, Duarte, Calif., 1962-72; trustee Wolcott Found. Inc., St. Louis, 1972-86, chmn. bd. trustees, 1980-85. Recipient Cert. of Achievement, George Washington U., Washington, 1986. Mem. Temple City High Twelve Club (pres. 1971), Calif. Assn. High Twelve Clubs (pres. 1986), Aston Martin Owners Club. Lodges: Masons (master Camellia club 1973), Royal Order Scotland. Home and Office: 287 W Ave de Las Flores Thousand Oaks CA 91360

EMERSON, DAVID WINTHROP, college dean; b. Littleton, Mass., Mar. 13, 1928; s. Leon Ware and Alice Sophia (Howe) E.; m. Margaret Shirley Armstrong, Sept. 4, 1954; children—Richard R., Eric H., Ellen N. A.B., Dartmouth Coll., 1952; M.S. in Chemistry, U. Mich., 1954, Ph.D., 1958. Research chemist Shell Oil Co., Houston and N.Y.C., 1957-63; mem. faculty U. Mich., Dearborn, 1963-81; prof. chemistry U. Mich., 1969-81; dean U. Mich. (Coll. Arts, Scis. and Letters), 1979-81, Coll. Sci., Math. and Engring., U. Nev., Las Vegas, 1981—. Served with AUS, 1946-47, 50-51. Mem. Am. Chem. Soc., Royal Soc. Chemistry, AAAS, AAUP, Sigma Xi, Phi Kappa Phi. Home: 4240 Woodcrest Rd Las Vegas NV 89121 Office: U Nev 4505 S Maryland Pkwy Las Vegas NV 89154

EMERSON, THOMAS OLIVER, savings and loan executive; b. Albert Lea, Minn., July 15, 1920; s. Ralph Waldo and Letha F. (Johnson) E.; m. Alma Irene Schuetz, Sept. 2, 1942; children—James Alexander, Jack Thomas, Thomas Hall. Student U. Wash., 1939-41; grad. diploma Inst. Fin. Edn., Chgo., 1965. Real estate broker, Idaho. Messenger-teller, Coffman-Dobson Bank, Chehalis, Wash., 1936-39; bookkeeper-teller Peoples Nat. Bank, Seattle, 1939-42; flying instr. U.S. Army AC, 1943-45; owner/mgr. Emerson Flying Service, Coeur d'Alene, Idaho, 1946-49; chief exec. officer First Fed. Savs. & Loan, Coeur d'Alene, 1949-82, chmn. bd., 1983—. Author: Seaplanes from Coeur d'Alene, 1973; Hangar Flying, 1984. Mem. Coeur d'Alene City Council, 1956-60; trustee N. Idaho Coll., 1978-81. Served to capt. AC, U.S. Army, 1943-46. Named Outstanding Citizen of Coeur d'Alene, 1980. Mem. U.S. League Savs. Assns. (dir. 1971-72, nat. legis. com. 1976-81), Idaho League Ins. Savs. and Loans (past pres.), Am. Inst. Real Estate Appraisers, Appraisers Inst., Coeur d'Alene C. of C. (dir. 1964-65). Republican. Clubs: Viking Booster (pres. 1966-67), Hayden Lake Country. Lodges: Rotary (pres. 1976-77), Elks, Eagles (Coeur d'Alene). Home: 1111 Mountain Ave Coeur d'Alene ID 83814 Office: First Fed Savs & Loan PO Box 400 Coeur d'Alene ID 83814

EMERY, BETTY JO, cosmetology executive, fund-raiser; b. Culver City, Calif., Oct. 27, 1947; s. Phil Sheridan and Thelma Ione (Bennett) Emery; m. Bülent Peksanli, Jan. 7, 1986. Student Bartmore Beauty Coll., Mesa Coll., U.Calif.-Irvine, 1979-81. Owner, operator Gene's of LaJolla (Calif.), 1968-70, The Hair Garden, LaJolla, 1974-78, Hairs to Ya! Dana Point, Calif., 1979—; treas., dir. fins., fund-raiser Pacific Ocean Found., Dana Point. Recipient Resolution of Commendation Orange County (Calif.) Suprs., 1982. Mem. Assn. Female Execs. Republican. Episcopalian. Office: Hairs to Ya 34213 Coast Hwy Suite C & D Dana Point CA 92629

EMERY, EARL EUGENE, steel company executive; b. Youngstown, Ohio, Apr. 1, 1931; s. Earl Eugene and Florence (Machin) E.; m. Mary Therese Orton, June 4, 1955; children—Maria, Catherine, Erin, Kevin, Martin, Sheila, Noreen, Terrence, Earl Eugene III, Mary. Met.E., Youngstown State U. Cert. purchasing mgr. Buyer, Youngstown Sheet & Tube Co., Ohio, 1959-71, mgr. purchasing, 1971-75, gen. mgr. purchasing, 1975-78; dir. purchases CF&I Steel Corp., Pueblo, Colo., 1978-83, dir. purchases and traffic, 1983—. Mem. exec. com. Mahoning County Republican Com., Youngstown, 1973-76; bd. dirs. John Neuman Catholic Sch., Pueblo, 1981-85, Goodwill Industries, Pueblo, 1982—; v.p. United Way of Pueblo, 1982-86 . Purchasing Mgmt. Assn. So. Colo. (pres. 1982-83, dir. nat. affairs 1983-84), Assn. Iron and Steel Engrs. (chpt. chmn. 1983-84, nat. bd. dirs. 1985-86), Am. Iron and Steel Inst. Lodges: Elks, K.C. Home: 7 Kingsbridge Pueblo CO 81001 Office: CF&I Steel Corp 225 Canal St PO Box 316 Pueblo CO 81002

EMERY, MICHAEL ROBERT, manufacturing company executive; b. Des Moines, Nov. 6, 1945; s. James William and Helen Loies (Lewis) E.; m. Betty Jean Beagles, Dec. 24, 1964 (div. July 1976); 1 child, Michael Robert Jr.; m. Yeasook Yi, July 1, 1977; 1 child, Chris Lee. Student, Grandview Coll., 1963-64. Field engr. Raytheon Service Co., U.S., Fed. Republic of Germany, Republic of Korea, 1967-75; engring. coordinator Raytheon Service Co., Republic of Korea, 1975-77, facilities mgr., 1977-82; ops. mgr. Raytheon Service Co., Kuwait (Kuwait) City, 1982-85, Laguna Industries Inc., Albuquerque, 1985—. Served with U.S. Army, 1963-66. Republican. Roman Catholic. Avocation: golf. Home: 10324 Karen Ave NE Albuquerque NM 87111

EMERY, MYRON DELEUW, lawyer; b. Chgo., Aug. 12, 1927; s. Charles Eugene and Dora (Guttel) E.; m. Robin Ann Wein, Oct. 22, 1954 (div. Feb. 1976); children: Meg Erin, Jason DeLeuw. AB, Stanford U., 1952; JD, U. Denver, 1956. Bar: Calif., D.C., U.S. Ct. Internat. Trade. Assoc. prof. Calif. State U., Northridge; mem. faculty U. Calif., Santa Barbara, Riverside, Irvine; sole practice Los Angeles; ptnr. Emery and Stambul, Los Angeles; gen. counsel Pub. Relations Soc. Am., Los Angeles, So. Calif. Broadcasters Assn., The Advt. Club Los Angeles, Western States Advt. Agys. Assn. Inc., Advt. Rev. Bd. So. Calif. (founder); guest lectr. U. So. Calif. Sch. Bus. Adminstrn., Los Angeles, Advt. Age Creative Workshop, Chgo.; mem. faculty UCLA., Art Ctr. Coll. Design; adj. assoc. prof. law S.W. U.; bd. govs. Internat. Community Coll.; adv. bd. govs. U. Tel Aviv Film and Communications Sch.; conducted seminars at Northwestern U., Evanston, Ill., Motorola Corp., TRW Inc., Calif. Cosmetic Assn. Inc., Sales and Exec. Advt. Club of St. Joseph City, Ind., Savs. Insts. Mktg. Soc. of Am., Security Pacific Nat. Bank, United Calif. bank, Am. Mgmt. Assn., U. Calif. Santa Barbara, Stanford (Calif.) U.; counsel to Calif. State Lottery. Contbr. numerous articles to profl. jours., chpts. to books. Commr. Olympic Citizens Adv. Commn. 1984 Olympics, Consumer Affairs for Los Angeles County; mem. exec. com. Los Angeles Police Crime Prevention Adv. Counsel. Served with USN, 1945-46. Mem. Am. Arbitration Assn. (nat. panel of arbitrators), Am. Advt. Fedn. (nat. com. govt. affairs, gen. counsel),. Office: Emery and Stambul 2049 Century Park E Suite 2400 Los Angeles CA 90067

EMERY, PHILIP ANTHONY, geologist; b. Neodesha, Kans., Oct. 20, 1934; s. Vincent A. and Whilomena B. (Kempker) E.; m. Janet L. Emery, Apr. 13, 1960; 1 child, David A. BS in Geology, Kans. U., 1960, MS in Geology, 1962. Project chief U.S. Geol. Survey, Alamosa, Colo., 1966-70; subdist. chief U.S. Geol. Survey, Pueblo, Colo., 1970-72; project chief U.S. Geol. Survey, Lincoln, Nebr., 1972-74; ground water specialist U.S. Geol. Survey, Menlo Park, Calif., 1974-75; dist. chief U.S. Geol. Survey, Louisville, Colo., 1975-81; dist. chief U.S. Geol. Survey, Anchorage, 1981—, Alaska dir.'s rep., 1985—. Contbr. articles to profl. jours. Served as sgt. U.S. Army, 1954-57. Recipient Superior Performance award Dept. Interior, 1984. Fellow Geol. Soc. Am.; mem. Am. Inst. Hydrology, Am. Inst. Profl. Geologists. Home: 18243 McCrary Rd Eagle River AK 99577 Office: US Geol Survey WRD 4230 University Dr Anchorage AK 99508

EMMANOUILIDES, GEORGE CHRISTOS, physician, educator; b. Drama, Greece, Dec. 17, 1926; came to U.S., 1955; s. Christos Nicholas and Vassiliki (Jordanopoulos) E.; married; children: Nicholas, Elizabeth, Christopher, Martha, Sophia. MD, Aristotelion U., 1951; MS in Physiology, UCLA, 1963. Diplomate Am. Bd. Pediatrics (pediatric cardiology and neonatal-perinatal medicine). Asst. prof. UCLA, 1963-69, assoc. prof., 1969-73, prof., 1973—; chief div. pediatric cardiology Harbor UCLA Med. Ctr., Torrance, Calif., 1963—; chief div. neonatology, 1963-69. Co-author: Practical Pediatric Electrocardiography, 1973; co-editor (2nd ed.) Heart Disease in Infants, Children and Adolescents, 1977, (3rd ed.) Moss' Heart Disease in Infants, Children and Adolescents, 1983; contbr. more than 70 articles in field to profl. jours. Served as 2d lt. M.C., Greek Army, 1953-55. Recipient Sherman Mellincoff award UCLA Sch. Medicine, 1982; several research awards Am. Heart Assn., 1965-83. Fellow Am. Acad. Pediatrics (cardiology section, chmn. 1978-80), Am. Coll. Cardiology; mem. Am. Pediatric Soc., Soc. for Pediatric Research, Hellenic-Am. Med. Soc. (pres.). Democrat. Greek Orthodox. Clubs: Hellenic Univ. (Los Angeles) (bd. dirs.). Avocation: gardening. Home: 4619 Brown Deer Ln Rolling Hills Estates CA 90274 Office: Harbor-UCLA Med Ctr 1000 W Carson St Torrance CA 90509

EMMELUTH, BRUCE PALMER, investment banker; venture capitalist; b. Los Angeles, Nov. 30, 1940; s. William J. and Elizabeth L. (Palmer) E.; children: William J. II (dec.), Bruce Palmer Jr., Carrie E.; m. Canda E. Samuels, Mar. 29, 1987. Sr. investment analyst corp. fin. dept. Prudential Ins. Co. Am., Los Angeles, 1965-70; with Seidler, Amdec Securities, Inc., Los Angeles, 1970—, sr. v.p., mgr. corp. fin. dept., 1976—, bd. dirs., 1974—; pres., bd. dirs. SAS Captial Corp., Venture capital subs. Seidler Amdec Securities; bd. dirs. Denar Corp., Motherhood Maternity Shops, Inc.; allied mem. N.Y. Stock Exchange, Inc. Past. bd. dirs. UCLA Grad. Sch. Mgmt. Served with Army NG, 1965-71. Mem. Assn. for Corp. Growth (pres. Los Angeles chpt. 1979-80), Beta Gamma Sigma. Republican. Presbyterian. Club: Jonathan. Home: 17146 Palisades Circle Pacific Palisades CA 90272 Office: Seidler Amdec Securities Inc 515 S Figueroa St Los Angeles CA 90071

EMMET, THOMAS ADDIS, JR., college administrator, consultant; b. Detroit, July 26, 1930; s. Thomas Addis and Leona Margaret (Schneider) E.; m. Anne Marie Baker, Mar. 3, 1972; children—Lynn, Anthony, William Novitsky. Ph.B., U. Detroit, 1952, M.Ed.. 1954; Ed.S., Ed.D., U. Mich., 1963. Asst. dean U. Detroit, 1953-57, dean men, 1957-64, dean evening coll. arts and scis., 1964-66, asst. prof. higher edn., 1964-67; asst. exec. v.p. Marquette U., 1966-67, adj. prof. higher edn. Wayne State U., Detroit, 1968-70; spl. asst. to pres., prof. edn. Regis Coll., Denver, 1972—; pres. higher edn. exec. assocs., 1967-72, 84-86; chmn. bd. Higher Edn. Group, 1986—; pres. Thomas A. Emmet & Assos., 1972-84. Cons. collective negotiations in higher edn. Edn. Commn. of States, 1971—; cons. higher edn. Opinion Research Corp.; dir. leadership seminars, sr. adviser Am. Council on Edn., 1979-85. Staff dir. Mich. State Senate Student Unrest Com., 1968-69; exec. sec. Conf. Jesuit Student Personnel Adminstrs., 1956-64; sec. Council Student Personnel Assns. in Higher Edn., 1966-69. Recipient Bernard Webster Reed award, 1963, John P. McNichols award U. Detroit, 1986. Mem. Adult Student Personnel Assn. (v.p. 1961-64), Nat. Assn. Student Personnel Adminstrs. (editor Jour. 1962-63), Phi Kappa Phi, Alpha Sigma Nu, Alpha Sigma Lambda, Phi Delta Kappa, Phi Eta Sigma. Editor: The Academic Department and Division Chairman, 1972; Collective Bargaining in Post-secondary Institutions: The Impact on the Campus and the State, 1974; asso. editor Coll. and Univ. Bus., 1969-71. Home: 3941 E Orchard Rd Littleton CO 80121 Office: Regis Coll Dept Edn 50th St and Lowell Blvd Denver CO 80221

EMMONS, ROBERT JOHN, corporate executive; b. Trenton, N.J., Sept. 18, 1934; s. Charles John and Ruth Marie (Heilhecker) E.; m. Christine Young Bebb, July 13, 1980; children: Bradley Thomas, Cathy Lynne, Christopher Robert. A.B. in Econs, U. Mich., 1956, M.B.A., 1960, J.D., 1964. Vice-pres. Baskin-Robbins Co., Burbank, Calif., 1964-68; pres. United Rent-All, Los Angeles, 1968-69, Master Host Internat., Los Angeles, 1969-71; prof. Grad. Sch. Bus., U. So. Calif., 1971-82; pres. LTI Corp., Monterey, Calif., 1982-84; pres., chief exec. officer, dir. Casino USA/SFI Corp., 1984—. Author: The American Franchise Revolution, 1970; poetry Other Places, Other Times, 1974, Love and Other Minor Tragedies, 1980. Mem. Am. Mktg. Assn., European Mktg. Assn., Am. Econ. Assn., AAUP, Beta Gamma Sigma, Pi Kappa Alpha. Clubs: Calif. Yacht (Los Angeles); Hawaii Yacht (Honolulu); Montecito Country (Santa Barbara, Calif.). Office: Casino USA SFI Corp 5933 W Century Blvd Suite 900 Los Angeles CA 90045

EMPEY, GENE F., real estate exec.; b. Hood River, Oreg., July 13, 1923; B.S. in Animal Husbandry, Oreg. State U., 1949; masters degree in tech. journalism Iowa State U., 1950; m. Janet Halladay, Dec. 27, 1950; children—Stephen Bruce, Michael Guy. Publs. dir. U. Nev., Reno, 1950-55; mgr. Zephyr Cove Lodge Hotel, Lake Tahoe, Nev., 1955-65; owner Empey Co., real estate agy., Carson City and Tahoe, Nev., 1964—; land developer, owner investment and brokerage firm. Mem. Nev. Planning Bd., 1959-72, chmn., 1961-66; mem. Nev. Tax Commn., 1982—. Served to capt., inf. U.S. Army, 1943-47; PTO. G.R.I. (grad. Realtors Inst.). Mem. Nat. Assn. Realtors, (cert. comml. investment mem.; pres. Nev. chpt. 3 times), Tahoe Douglas C. of C. (pres. 1962, dir.), Carson City C. of C., Carson-Tahoe-Douglas Bd. Realtors. Republican. Clubs: Capital City, Rotary, Heavenly Valley Ski (pres. 1968). Home: PO Box 707 Zephyr Cove NV 89448 Office: 512 S Curry St Carson City NV 89701

EMPIE, HART HALLER, artist, sculptor; b. Safford, Ariz., Mar. 26, 1909; s. Hart Dewitt and Allie Annie (Haller) E.; m. Louise O. Reinhardt, Feb. 20, 1929; children—Halene Louise, Joel Stratton, Ruth Ann. Student Capital Coll. Pharmacy, Denver, 1929, U. Ariz., 1931; student of Frederic Taubes, 1950-53; D.Pharm. (hon.), Ariz. Pharmacy Assn., 1982. Registered pharmacist, Ariz. Owner and pharmacist Duncan Drug/Art Gallery Drug, Duncan, Ariz., 1929-80; cartoonist Empie Kartoon Kards, Duncan, 1930-63; artist/tchr. Hal Empie Studio, Duncan, 1929—; judge Traditional Artists Guild; lectr. schs. and univs., Ariz. One-man shows include: El Presidio Gallery, Tucson, Valley Nat. Bank, Phoenix, 1982—, El Conquistador Mezzanine Gallery, Tucson, 1982, 83, Eastern Ariz. Coll., 1983; group shows include Traditional Artists Guild, Paramount, Calif., 1981, Phippin Meml., 1983, N.Mex. So. State Fair Invitational, 1984, Mus. Modern Art, N.Y.C., U. Ariz., Tucson. represented in permanent collections Carnegie Library, Syracuse U., Graham County C. of C., Ariz., Duncan Unified Sch. Dist., Eastern Ariz. Jr. Coll., Thatcher, 1st Meth. Ch., Duncan, Tucson Mus. Art, Phippin Meml. Mus., Prescott, Ariz. Mem. art com. 5th Congl. Dist. Ariz., 1983—. Named Man of Yr., Duncan Booster Club, 1939. Mem. Ariz. Pharmacy Assn. (hon. pres. 1983). Republican. Methodist. Lodge: Rotary (charter) (Duncan). Home: Box K Duncan AZ 85534

EMR, SCOTT DAVID, biology educator, consultant; b. Jersey City, Feb. 8, 1954; s. John Frank and Evelyn Grace (Metzger) E.; m. Michelle Christine Therrien, July 16, 1977; 1 child, Bryanna Michelle. BS, U. R.I., 1976; PhD, Harvard U., 1981. Vis. scholar NCI Frederick (Md.) Cancer Research Facility, 1979-81; traveling scholar Pasteur Inst., Paris, 1978; research fellow U. Calif., Berkeley, 1981-83; asst. prof. Calif. Inst. Tech., Pasadena, 1983—. Contbr. articles to jours. Named Presdl. Young Investigator NSF, 1985—; Searle Scholars Program grantee, 1984; Miller Research Inst. fellow, U. Calif., 1981-83. Mem. AAAS, Am. Soc. Microbiology, Phi Kappa Phi. Office: Calif Inst Tech Div Biology 147-75 Pasadena CA 91125

ENDERS, ALLEN COFFIN, anatomy educator; b. Wooster, Ohio, Aug. 5, 1928; s. Robert Kendal and Abbie Gertrude (Crandell) E.; m. Alice Hay, June 15, 1950 (div. Dec. 1975); children: Robert H., George C., Richard S., Gregory H.; m. Sandra Jean Schlafke, Aug. 5, 1976. AB, Swarthmore Coll., 1950; AM, Harvard U., 1952, PhD, 1955. From asst. prof. to assoc. prof Rice Inst., Houston, 1954-63; from assoc. prof. to prof. Washington U., St. Louis, 1963-75; prof., chmn. dept. human anatomy U. Calif., Davis, 1976-86; cons. NIH, Bethesda, Md., 1964-68, 70-73, 76-80, 83—. Author: (with others) Bailey's Microscopic Anatomy, 1984; editor: Delayed Implantation, 1964; contbr. numerous articles on anatomy and reproduction to profl. jours. Nat. pres. Perinatal Research Soc., 1981. Grantee NIH, 1959—. Fellow AAAS; mem. Am. Assn. Anatomists (v.p. 1980-82, pres. 1983-84), Soc. Study Reprodn., Am. Soc. Cell Biology. Home: Route 1 Box 1916A Davis CA 95616 Office: Univ of Calif Davis Sch of Medicine Dept of Human Anatomy Davis CA 95616

ENDERS, RICHARD JOSEPH, plastics company executive; b. Aurora, Ill., Sept. 8, 1940; s. William Jacob and Rose (Janaes) E.; m. Margaret Kile, Sept. 7, 1968; children: Sarah Margaret, Rebecca Lynne. BS in Engring., U. Ill., 1967; MBA, UCLA, 1970. With Shell Chem. Co., Houston, 1970-72, A.

Schulman, Los Angeles, 1972-78; v.p. mfg. products A. Schulman, Akron, Ohio, 1978-85; v.p. Pacific region A. Schulman, Los Angeles, 1985—. Co-author: Thermoplastic Elastomers: Rubber Technology. Mem. Soc. Plastics Engrs., Soc. Plastics Industry (rep.). Republican. Roman Catholic. Avocation: tennis. Home: 13-18th St Hermosa Beach CA 90254 Office: A Schulman Inc 101 Continental Blvd El Segundo CA 90245

ENDERUD, WILBUR DONALD, JR., data processing cons.; b. Pueblo, Colo., Nov. 4, 1945; s. Wilbur Donald and Loretta Faye (Jackson) E.; B.A. in Math., San Diego State U., 1967; M.B.A., Calif. State U., Long Beach, 1972; children—Cynthia. From programmer to project leader Mattel, Inc., Hawthorne, Calif., 1967-72; dir. mgmt. info. systems Audio-Magnetics Corp., Gardena, Calif., 1972-75; founder, 1975, since owner, prin. cons. Don Enderud & Assocs. (now Mgmt. Info. Solutions, Inc.), Diamond Bar, Calif.; founding ptnr. New Century Leasing, Diamond Bar, 1978—. Served with USAR, 1968-69; Vietnam. Decorated Army Commendation medal. Mem. Assn. Computing Machinery, Aircraft Owners and Pilots Assn. Republican. Lutheran. Office: PO Box 4237 Diamond Bar CA 91765

ENDRIZZI, JOHN EDWIN, retired plant genetics educator; b. Wilburton, Okla., July 28, 1923; s. Lui and Maria Christina (Carigano) E.; m. Yvonne B. Barbot, June 6, 1955; children: Colette, George, Regina, Carisa, Karena. BS, Tex. A&M U., 1949, MS, 1951; postgrad., U. Va., 1951-52, PhD, 1955. Asst. prof. Tex. A&M U., College Station, 1955-63; prof. plant genetics, dept. head U. Ariz., Tucson, 1963-71, prof., 1971-86; cons. cytogenetics Tex. A&M U., 1976, cons. genetics U. Ceara, Fortleza, Brazil, 1971. Assoc. editor: Jour. Heredity, 1986—; contbr. articles to sci. jours., chpts. to books. Served to sgt. U.S. Army, 1943-46, PTO. Recipient Cotton Genetics award Nat. Cotton Council, 1969. Fellow Ariz.-Nev. Acad. Sci.; mem. Genetics So. Am., Am. Genetics Assn., Genetics Soc. Can., AAAS, Am. Inst. Biol. Scis., Sigma Xi. Democrat. Roman Catholic. Avocations: fishing, hiking. Home: 2335 E 9th St Tucson AZ 85719

ENG, FREDERICK PAK-CHING, polymer organic chemist; b. Canton, Peoples Republic of China, May 29, 1951; s. Ching Foo and Lai Sau (Wong) E.; m. Yvonne The Hua, July 18, 1981; 1 child, Davina Ting. BS in Chemistry, U. Calif., Berkeley, 1974; MS in Organic Chemistry, U. Nev., 1977; PhD in Polymer Sci., Case Western Res. U., 1985. Staff chemist IBM, San Jose, Calif., 1979—. Author: Fourier Transform Infrared Studies on New Corrosion Inhibitors, 1985, Circular Dichroism Studies of Methyl and Methoxy Cholestanones; contbr. articles to profl. jours. IBM Resident Study Program grantee, 1983-85. Mem. Am. Chem. Soc., Applied Spectroscopy Soc. Avocations: singing, basketball, football, classical music. Office: IBM 5600 Cottle Rd San Jose CA 95193

ENG, HENRY, city planner; b. N.Y.C., Apr. 14, 1941; s. Foo and May Siu Moy (Mah) E.; m. Loxley Robin Len, Aug. 5, 1967; children—Robert Michael, Lisanne Aimee. Student Columbia Coll., 1958-60; B.Arch., Pratt Inst., Bklyn., 1966, M.S. in Planning, 1966. Lic. real estate salesman, Hawaii. Assoc. planner Office of Planning Coordination, N.Y.C., 1967-68; sr. planner Bechtel Assocs., N.Y.C., 1968-69; planner/architect City and County Dept. Planning, Honolulu, 1969-73; br. chief City and County Dept. Land Utilization, 1973-79, asst. dir. zoning, 1979-84; planning analyst Honolulu City Council, 1984—. Photographer: (Book) Long Island Landmarks, 1969. Troop chmn. Aloha council Boy Scouts Am., Kailua, 1979-87 . Mem. Am. Planning Assn. (Hawaii chpt. treas. 1981-82, v.p. 1982-83, pres. 1983-84), Am. Inst. Cert. Planners. Home: 1537 Akake Pl Kailua HI 96734 Office: Office of Council Services 530 S King St Honolulu HI 96813

ENGEBRECHT, RICHARD E., diversified distribution company executive. Formerly pres., chief operating officer Univar Corp., Seattle; pres., chief exec. officer VWR Corp., Seattle, 1986—. Office: VWR Corp 1600 Norton Bldg Seattle WA 98104 *

ENGEL, BERNARD EDWARD, physician; b. Birmingham, Eng., June 14, 1938; came to U.S., 1947; s. Max and Bella (Frankenheimer) E.; m. Norma Lee Scavo, June 13, 1963; children: Edward Randall, Jacqueline Yvette, Leslie Erin. BA, U. Colo., 1960, MD, 1964. Diplomate Am. Bd. Family Practice. Intern Los Angeles County Gen. Hosp., 1964-65; gen. practice medicine Thornton and Westminster, Colo., 1965—; police surgeon Fed. Heights Colo., 1975—. Water commr. Westlake Water and Sanitation Dist., Adams County, Colo., 1984—; team physician Thornton High Sch., 1985—; disaster coordinator Adams County Office Emergency Preparedness, 1974—. Mem. Am. Coll. Sports Medicine. Avocations: skiing, photography. Office: 5130 W 80th Ave Suite 100 Westminster CO 80030

ENGEL, JAN MARCIN, research physicist; b. Gdansk, Poland, May 1, 1924; came to U.S., 1946, naturalized 1951; s. Adam and Jola Rosa (Frenkel) E.; m. Janet Zelda Greenky, June 11, 1955 (dec. Sept. 1962); children: Karen Y., Stephen A. BSc, U. London, 1946; student, U. Pa., 1946-48, Temple U., 1949-50, UCLA, 1956-57. Diamond polisher Owen & Kuropatwa Ltd., London, 1941-43; engr. E. Shipton & Co. Ltd., Northwood Hills, Eng., 1943-46; research physicist Socony-Vacuum Oil Co., Paulsboro, N.J., 1950-51, Gen. Electric Co., Syracuse, N.Y., 1951-53; sr. project engr. Motorola Inc., Phoenix, 1953-54; research physicist Pacific Semicondrs. Inc., Culver City, Calif., 1954-57; adv. physicist IBM Corp., San Jose, Calif. and Poughkeepsie, N.Y., 1958-84; pres. Geneal. Data Systems, San Jose, Calif., 1980—; cons. Electro-Optical Systems, Inc., Pasadena, Calif., 1957-58; lectr. liberal arts U. Calif., Los Angeles and Berkeley, 1956-60. Contbr. articles to profl. jours. co-founder Santa Clara Valley Assn. Widows and Widowers, 1964-65, chmn. Fellow Inst. Physics London; mem. IEEE (sr. mem., founder, 1st editor IEEE Electron Devices newsletter 1966-70), Am. Phys. Soc., Am. Inst. Physics, Soc. Info. Display, Sigma Xi (founder, 1st pres. Poughkeepsie br. 1961-63). Lodge: B'nai Brith (co-founder, treas. Thomas Jefferson Lodge, Syracuse N.Y. 1952-53). Home: 2980 Cambridge Dr San Jose CA 95125

ENGEL, TIBOR, obstetrics and gynecology educator; b. Kosice, Czechoslovakia, Mar. 8, 1938; came to Mex., 1940, came to U.S., 1948, naturalized, 1954; married; 2 children. BA, U. Tex., El Paso, 1957; MD, U. Tex., Galveston, 1961. Diplomate Am. Bd. Ob-Gyn. Intern Phila. Gen. Hosp., 1961-62; resident N.Y. Hosp. Cornell U. Med. Ctr., N.Y.C., 1962-65; clin. prof. ob-gyn Health Scis. Ctr. U. Colo., Denver; asst. dir. ob-gyn Denver Gen. Hosp., 1969-74, dir. gynecologic endocrinology service, past pres. med. staff; cons. in family planning Westinghouse Learning Corp., 1970-71; med. dir. Rocky Mountain Planned Parenthood, 1973-77; editorial cons. Medcom Famous Teaching in Modern Medicine. Served to capt. M.C., U.S. Army, 1965-67. Columbia U. Med. Ctr. fellow, 1967-69. Fellow Am. Coll. Obstetricians and Gynecologists, Am. Fertility Soc.; mem. AMA, Colo. Gynecol. and Obstetrical Soc., Denver Med. Soc., Colo. Med. Soc., Am. Assn. Gynecol. Laparascopists (nat. adv. com), Endocrine Soc. Home: 220 S Eudora Denver CO 80222 Office: 4545 E 9th Ave Denver CO 80220

ENGEL, VICTOR BOYNTON, construction industry company executive; b. Keokuk, Iowa, Jan. 29, 1914; s. Martin T. and Gertrude (Boynton) E.; A.A, Calif. Concordia Coll., 1935; various bus. and mil. schs.; B.A., U. Calif. at Berkeley, 1949; certificate Acad. Internat. Law, Hague, Netherlands, 1951; M.A., Grad. Inst. Internat. Studies and U. Geneva, Switzerland, 1952; m. Dorothea Ann Messner, Mar. 18, 1944. Prof. constl. law, U.S. history U. Geneva, 1950-52; exec. mgr. Assn. Plumbing and Heating Contractors of Contra Costa County, Richmond, Calif., 1952-54; exec. dir. Contra Costa Builders Exchange, Concord, Calif., 1954—; pres. Constrn. Mgmt. Services, Inc., Metro-Mgmt. Services, Inc. Pres., Internat. Builders Exchange Execs., U.S., Can., 1962-63; chmn. Builders Exchange Council, 1971-72; pres. Builders Exchanges Constrn. Industry Conf., 1969-70. Mem. Contra Costa County Devel. Assn., Contra Costa Taxpayers Assn., Bay Area Coalition for Transp. Served with AUS, 1941-46. Recipient Dan Patrick award of merit Internat. Builders Exchange Execs., 1983. Mem. World Affairs Council No. Calif., Calif. Alumni Assn., Am. Soc. Assn. Execs., No. Calif. Soc. Assn. Execs., Assn. des Anciens l'Inst. Geneva. Rotarian. Clubs: Commonwealth (San Francisco); Concord Century, Toastmasters (Concord). Author: Significant Developments in American Society, 1952. Editor: Constrn. Weekly, 1954—. Home: 10 Gran Via Alamo CA 94507 Office: 115 Aspen Dr Pacheco CA 94553

ENGEL, WILLIAM KING, neurologist, educator; b. St. Louis, Nov. 19, 1930; s. William Ernst and Opal (King) E.; m. Valerie Askanas; children: W. Keith, Peter J., Bradford C., Eve M. B.A., Johns Hopkins U., 1951; M.D., C.M., McGill U., 1955. Diplomate: Am. Bd. Neurology and Psychiatry, Pan. Am. Med. Assn. (hon. life mem.). Intern U. Mich. Hosp., 1955-56; clin. assoc. Nat. Inst. Neurol. Diseases and Blindness, 1956-59; clin. clk. Nat. Hosp., London, 1959-60; with Nat. Inst. Neurol. Diseases and Stroke, 1960-81, chief med. neurology, 1963-78, chief neuromuscular diseases, 1978-81; clin. prof. neurology George Washington U., 1969-81; prof. neurology and pathology, chief div. neuromuscular diseases, dept. neurology U. So. Calif. Sch. Medicine, Los Angeles, 1981—; mem. med. bd. NIH, 1968-69;; founding dir. U. So. Calif. Neuromuscular Center, Hosp. of Good Samaritan, 1981—; Mem. med. adv. bd. St. Jude's Children's Research Hosp., Memphis, 1970-76, Myasthenia Gravis Found., 1970—, Amyotrophic Lateral Sclerosis Nat. Found., 1971-85, Los Angeles chpt. Muscular Dystrophy Assn., 1981—, Amyotrophic Lateral Sclerosis Soc. Am., 1980-82, (sci. adv. bd. 1982-85); vis. prof., invited lectr., advisor internat. congresses in, Europe, S.Am., Can., Far East; cons. Nat. Naval Med. Center. Former Mem. editorial bd.: Archives of Neurology; contbr. numerous papers to profl. lit., poems to mags. Past pres. Citizens Assn., Bethesda, Md., Longhouse chief YMCA Indian Guides, 1965-66; past chmn. troop com. Boy Scouts Am.; mem. edn. adv. bd. Phronesis, Spain; nat. corp. mem. Muscular Dystrophy Assn., 1985—, med. adv. bd. Los Angeles chpt., 1981—, bd. dirs. 1985—. Recipient Meritorious Service medal USPHS, 1971, various awards from Italian med. socs. Fellow Am. Acad. Neurology (S. Weir Mitchell award 1962; pres. VI Internat. Congress Neuromuscular Diseases, 1986); mem. AMA, Histochem Soc., Am. Soc. Cell Biology, Am. Assn. Neuropathologists, World Commn. Neuromuscular Disease (exec. com.), Am. Neurol. Assn., Los Angeles County Med. Assn., Société Belge d'Electromyographie (assoc.), Asociación de Distrofia Muscular de la República Argentina (hon. pres.), Soc. for Neurosci., Société Francaise de Neurologie (hon.). Office: U So Calif Neuromuscular Ctr Hosp Good S 637 S Lucas Ave Los Angeles CA 90017

ENGELKING, HENRY MARK, virology researcher; b. Burbank, Calif., May 3, 1949; s. Henry Christian and LorraineKatherine (Miehl) E.; m. Judy Ann Hagner, Sept. 15, 1979; one child, Erin Ruth. BA, U. Calif., San Diego, 1971; MS, Oreg. State U., 1974. Research asst. in biochemistry and biophysics Oreg. State U., Corvallis, 1974-78, sr. research asst. in microbiology, 1978—; cons. in field. Contbr. articles to profl. jours. Mem. AAAS, Am. Soc. Microbiology, Phi Kappa Phi. Home: 234 NW 29th Corvallis OR 97330 Office: Oreg State U Dept Microbiology Corvallis OR 97331

ENGELMEIER, ROBERT LEO, prosthodontist, military officer; b. Pitts., June 19, 1944; s. Leo Julius and Ruth Margaret (Milton) E.; m. Nancy Beth Hope, June 25, 1972; children: Tanya Hope, Lee Stephen, Robert Leo II. BS, U. Pitts., 1966, DMD, 1970; MS, U. Tex., 1978. Diplomate Am. Bd. Prosthodontics; cer. maxillofacial prosthodontist. Commd. USAF, 1970, advanced through grades to col., 1985; gen. dentist 483d div. USAF Hosp., Cam Rahn bay, Vietnam, 1970-71; gen. dentist USAF Hosp., Otis AFB, Mass., 1971-72; gen. practice dentistry Provincetown, Mass., 1972-74; resident in prosthodontics USAF, San Antonio and Houston, 1974-80; maxillofacial prosthodontist USAF Regional Hosp., Elgin AFB, Fla., 1980-84, USAF Med. Ctr., Travis AFB, Calif., 1984—; spl. cons. to Surgeon Gen., USAF, 1984—; instr. USAF hosps., San Antonio, Elgin AFB and Travis AFB, 1978—; lectr. various nat. and state profl. meetings. Contbr. numerous articles to profl. jours. Active Boy Scouts Am., Tex. and Fla., 1978-80; mem. sch. adv. bd. Elgin AFB, 1983-84. Decorated over 13 medals, USAF, 1970-84; recipient Eagle Scout award Boy Scouts Am. Fellow Am. Coll. Prosthodontics, Acad. Gen. Dentistry; mem. ADA, Fedn. Prosthodontic Orgns., Assn. Military Surgeons of U.S., Phi Gamma Delta Frat. Alumni Assn., No. Calif. Kyudo Assn., M.D. Anderson Hosp. Assocs., Smithsonian Soc., Nat. Rifle Assn. Roman Catholic. Club: Buick Am., Yolo Sportsman's. Office: PSC#4 Box 9418 Travis AFB CA 94535

ENGEN, IRVIN GRANT, podiatrist; b. Crookston, Minn., Dec. 1, 1947; s. Walter Louis and Hazel (Johnson) E.; m. Mary McDunn (div. June 1972); m. Eva M. Cornett, Dec. 7, 1974; children: Michelle C., Gina L. Sherriff, Lori R. Sherriff. D of Podiatric Medicine, Ill. Coll. Podiatric Medicine, 1974. Practice medicine specializing in podiatry Spokane, 1976—. Served with U.S. Army, 1968-69, Vietnam. Mem. Am. Podiatric Med. Assn., Wash. Podiatric Med. Assn. (treas. eastern div. 1984—). Lutheran. Lodge: Eagles. Avocations: racquetball, skiing, scuba diving, golf, do it yourselfer. Home: N 11612 Monroe Ct Spokane WA 99218 Office: N 4601 Monroe #204 Spokane WA 99205

ENGLAND, TALMADGE RAY, physicist, researcher; b. Bonham, Tex., Dec. 22, 1929; s. Bascom Curtis and Dora Mae (Hobbs) E.; m. Carol Elizabeth Odell, Mar. 26, 1949; children: Cheryl, Ana, Rebecca, Rhonda. BS, Lincoln Meml. U., 1956; MS, U. Pitts., 1962; PhD, U. Wis., 1969. Chief engr. Sta. WJMA-Radio, Orange, Va., 1949-51, Sta. WMIK-Radio, Middlesboro, Ky., 1951-56; jr. scientist Bettis Atomic Power Lab., Pitts., 1956-57, scientist, 1957-60, sr. scientist, 1960-72; mem. staff Los Alamos (N.Mex.) Lab., 1972—; chmn. fission yields data U.S. Data Files, Brookhaven Nat. Lab., Upton, N.Y., 1975—; chmn. yields standard Am. Nuclear Soc., 1975—, sec. decay power standard, 1973—. Contbr. 112 tech. articles on nuclear data. Served with USN, 1945-46. Mem. IEEE, AAAS, Am. Nuclear Soc. Democrat. Unitarian. Avocation: tennis. Home: 613 Meadow Ln Los Alamos NM 87544 Office: Los Alamos Nat Lab PO Box 1663 Los Alamos NM 87545

ENGLE, KENNETH WILLIAM, information management executive; b. Hazleton, Pa., Feb. 1, 1937; s. Ishmael Charles and Margaret Elizabeth (Bond) E.; m. Jeanne Mae Davis, June 3, 1961; children: Kenneth Richard, Jonathan Edward. BA, George Washington U., 1964; MA, Am. U., 1970; MS, Colo. State U., 1984—. Intelligence officer USAF, 1955-59, 64-82; research analyst Sci. Applications Internat., Denver, 1982-85, cons., 1985—; dir. mgmt. infosystems Hosp. Service, Inc., Ft. Collins, Colo., 1985—. Contbr. articles to profl. jours. Named Outstanding Colo. State U. Mgmt. Infosystems Grad., Denver Bus. Mag., 1984-85. Mem. Retired Officers Assn. (2d v.p. 1986—), World Future Soc. Republican. Presbyterian. Avocations: golf, tennis. Home: 2018 Rollingwood Dr Fort Collins CO 80525 Office: Hosp Service Inc PO Box 2367 200 S Coll Ave Fort Collins CO 80522

ENGLER, GEORGE NICHOLS, educator, financial consultant; b. Los Angeles, Sept. 27, 1944; s. James George and Esther (Nichols) E.; m. Suzanne J. Knudson, June 11, 1967; 1 child, Cristina Noel. B.S. in Bus., U. So. Calif., 1965; M.B.A., UCLA, 1966, Ph.D. in Bus., 1969. Asst. prof. fin. Calif. State U.-Long Beach, 1968-69; asst. prof. fin. U. So. Calif., Los Angeles, 1969-75; pres. Century Fin. Mgmt., Inc., 1973-75; prof. fin., chmn. dept. fin. and bus. law Calif. State U.-Los Angeles, 1977—; cons. Keplar, Galen & Assocs., Inc., N.J., 1977-79; dir. grad. programs Sch. Bus. and Econs. Calif. State U.-Los Angeles, 1980-83, assoc. dean grad. programs Sch. Bus. and Econs., 1983-87. Author: Business Financial Management, rev. edit., 1978; Managerial Finance: Cases and Readings, 1973; (with John Boquist) Cases in Managerial Finance, 1982. Contbr. articles to profl. bus. jours. Mem. Am. Fin. Assn., Western Fin. Assn., Fin. Mgmt. Assn., Los Angeles Area C. of C. Democrat. Christian Scientist. Lodge: Rotary. Office: Calif State U Dept Fin Sch Bus 5151 State University Dr Los Angeles CA 90032

ENGLISH, ALEXANDER, professional basketball player; b. Columbia, S.C., Jan. 5, 1954; M. Vanessa E.; 3 children. Ed., U. So. Carolina. Forward Milw. Bucks, NBA, 1976-78, Indiana Pacers, NBA, 1978-80, Denver Nuggets, NBA, 1980—; player NBA All-Star Game, 1982-86; Leader NBA scorer, 1985-86 season. Author poetry. Address: care Denver Nuggets PO Box 4658 Denver CO 80204 *

ENGLISH, CAROLYN SUE, project officer; b. Rockford, Ill., July 1, 1953; d. Willis B. and M. Sue (Holder) English. Student Okla. Christian Coll., 1973, U. N.Mex., 1982. Lic. real estate, N.Mex. Staff sec., office mgr. NASA Tech. Application Ctr., Albuquerque, 1977-79, div. mgr. 1979-83; mgr. tech. transfer, dir. Global Resources & Assocs., Inc., Albuquerque, 1983-84; project officer engring. Rogers Constrn., Inc., Albuquerque, 1984-85, CRSS/ Western Empire Constructors, Inc., Albuquerque, 1985; project mgr. Page & Wirte Constrn. Co., 1986-87; mgr. Realty World-Sterling & Co., Albuquerque, 1987—. Mem. NM Multi Housing Authority. Mem. Profl. Secs. Internat., Profl. Library Assn., NM C. of C., NM Bd. Realtors.

ENGLISH, DARREL STARR, geneticist, educator; b. Newton, Kans., Sept. 6, 1936; s. David Leslie and Velma Jean (Starr) E.; m. Yvonne Marie Osgood, June 12, 1960; children: Darrin Wayne, Melanie Lynn, Todd Gregory. BA, SW. Coll., Winfield, Kans., 1959; MS, La. State U., 1962; PhD, Iowa State U., 1968. Instr. biology Millsaps Coll., Jackson, Miss., 1961-64; instr. genetics Iowa State U., 1965-67; asst. prof. genetics No. Ariz. U., 1967-71, assoc. prof. genetics, 1971-85, prof. genetics, 1985—; vis. prof. biology M.D. Anderson Hosp. and Tumor Inst., Houston, 1978, clin. histologist William Gore and Assocs., Flagstaff, Ariz., 1979-81. Editor: Genetic and Reproductive Engineering, 1974; contbr. articles and papers to profl. jours and books. Capt. CAP., Flagstaff, 1980—. NIH Biomed. Research grantee, 1982-86. Mem. Am. Soc. Mammalogists, Am. Genetics Assn., Sigma Xi. Republican. Methodist. Office: No Ariz U Box 5640 Flagstaff AZ 86011

ENGLISH, DONALD MARVIN, insurance inspector; b. Raleigh, N.C., July 31, 1951; s. Marvin Lee and Lois (Woodard) E.; m. Rebecca Pritchard, Sept. 3, 1970 (div. 1977). Student, Miami U., Oxford, Ohio, 1969-70, 73-74, U. Cin., 1977-78, Calif. State U., Fresno, 1980—. Ins. inspector Comml. Services, Cin., 1974-78, Ohio Casualty Ins. Co., Fresno, 1978—. Served with U.S. Army, 1970-73. Mem. Am. Soc. Safety Engrs. Club: E. Fresno Exchange (pres. 1984-85). Avocation: internat. traveling. Home: 4417 N Teilman Fresno CA 93705-1053 Office: The Ohio Casualty Ins Co 4420 N First St Suite 106 Fresno CA 93755

ENGLISH, JOHN DOUGLAS, manufacturing company executive, marketing consultant; b. Columbus, Ohio, Oct. 2, 1947; s. Donald Wellsley and Frances Elizabeth (Arant) E. BA, Hobart Coll., 1970; postgrad., U. Colo., 1982. Pres. EEI, Boulder, Colo., 1979-84, The Protector Corp., Boulder, 1984—; cons. Boulder County Justice Ctr., 1983. Author: How to Care for Your Personal Computer, 1984; contbr. articles to profl. jours. Mem. Boulder County NWEC, 1982-85; bd. dirs. MANA, Boulder, 1982-85, pres. 1986. Mem. Nat. Office Products Assn. (cons.), Assn. Computer Retailers (assoc.). Club: Colo. Mountan (Denver). Office: The Protector Corp 6681 Arapahoe Boulder CO 80303

ENGLISH, JOHN MORLEY, engineering educator; b. Vancouver, B.C., Can., Oct. 17, 1915; s. John Molineaux and Maude (Treleavan) E.; m. Marva Elizabeth Connolly, Oct. 12, 1938; children: Wayne, Marshall. BS, U. British Columbia, Can., 1938; MS, U. So. Calif., 1949; PhD, UCLA, 1952. With Boeing Co., Vancouver, B.C., 1938-40; resident tech. officer British Air Commn., Los Angeles, 1940-43; mgmt. staff Lockheed Corp., Burbank, Calif., 1943-44; research staff Calif. Inst. Tech., Pasadena, Calif., 1945; lectr. U. So. Calif., Los Angeles, 1946-49; prof. UCLA, 1949—; cons. Harvey Aluminum, Torrance, Calif., 1952-60, TRW, Redondo Beach, Calif., 1960-65; cons. reasearch on CIAP Dept. of Transport, 1971-75; pres. Econergy Inc., 1975-79. Author: Project Evaluation, 1984, also articles. Mem. ASCE, AIAA, Am. Soc. Engring. Edn. (v.p. 1975-77). Home: 37202 Village 37 Camarillo CA 93010 Office: UCLA 406 Hilgard Ave Los Angeles CA 90024

ENGLISH, RAYMOND HERMAN, architect; b. Grants Pass, Oreg., May 31, 1940; s. William Herman and Sarah May (Heald) E. BA in Environ. Design, U. Wash., 1971, MArch, 1986. Archtl. apprentice Balt., 1971-78; archtl. cons., owner, pres. Pavilion, Inc., Seattle, 1978—; mem. archtl. commn. U. Wash., 1981-82. Discovered new polyhedron, U. Wash., 1971. Served as cpl. USMC, 1959-63. Home and office: 4411 SW 100th St Seattle WA 98146

ENGLUND, ALAN LLOYD, fiscal services manager; b. Portland, Oreg., Jan. 3, 1943; s. George Englund and Joyce J. (Bisbey) Wirfs; m. Patricia A. Miller, July 9, 1969; children: Gregory, Emily. BS, Marylhurst Coll., 1983; postgrad., Oreg. State U., 1985—. Asst. bus. mgr. Multnomah Coll., Portland, 1968-69; bus. mgr. Riverdale Sch. Dist., Portland, 1969-72; controller Oreg. Grad. Ctr., Beaverton, 1972-81; dir. acctg. Tigard (Oreg.) Sch. Dist., 1981-83; mgr. fiscal services Corvallis (Oreg.) Sch. Dist., 1983—; adv. com. mem. Oreg. Ednl. Coordination Commn., 1981. Recipient Cert. Achievement Tigard Sch. Dist. Sch. Bd., 1983. Mem. Assn. Sch. Bus. Officials (editorial excellence panel, pubs. research com.), Oreg. Assn. Sch. Bus. Officials (registered sch. bus. official 1985, vice-chmn. profl. devel. com.), Govt. Fin. Officers Assn. Avocations: gardening, tennis. Home: 3769 NW Tyler Pl Corvallis OR 97330 Office: Corvallis Sch Dist 1555 SW 35th Corvallis OR 97333

ENGST, EDWARD D., orthodontist; b. Seattle, July 18, 1947. Student, U. Wash., 1965-68, DDS, 1972, MS in Dentistry, 1977. Resident in gen. dentistry Davis-Monthan Hosp., Tucson, 1976; mem. faculty U. Wash. Dept. Orthodontics, Seattle, 1977-80; practice dentistry specializing in orthodontics Bellingham, Wash.; cons. orthodontics to health profls., Bellingham; research investigator serial extraction therapy, 1977, orofacial manifestations of achondroplasia, 1985. Served to capt. USAF, 1972-75. Mem. ADA, Am. Assn. Orthodontists, Pacific Coast Soc. Orthodontists, Puget Sound Orthodontic Study Group (pres. 1986), Phi Beta Kappa, Omicron Kappa Upsilon. Avocations: skiing, sailing. Office: PO Box 5145 Bellingham WA 98227-5145

ENGSTROM, DONALD ELTON, psychiatrist; b. Seattle, Oct. 26, 1934; s. Elton Elbert Elliot and Ragna Marie (Hoidal) E.; m. Arliss Verlaine Ocker, Mar. 18, 1961; children: Verlaine Elise, Alison Elizabeth, Stephen Edward. BS, U. Wash., 1956, MD, 1959. Diplomat Am. Bd. Psychiatry and Neurology. Rotating intern Phila. Gen. Hosp., 1959-60; resident in psychiatry U. Wash. Affiliated Hosps., Seattle, 1960-63; psychiatrist USAF Hosp., Elmendorf AFB, Alaska, 1963-64, chief of psychiatry, 1964-66; clin. asst. prof. psychiatry U. Wash., Seattle, 1966-75; practice medicine specializing in psychiatry Island Psychiat. Group, Mercer Island, Wash., 1966-75; chief psychiatrist Great Falls (Mont.) Clinic, 1975—; pres. med. staff Mont. Deaconess Med. Ctr., Great Falls, 1984, chief of psychiatry, 1985—. Served to capt. USAF, 1963-66. Fellow Am. Psychiat. Assn. (mem. assembly 1981-86), Mont. Psychiat. Assn. (pres. 1981, mem. exec. com. 1979-86), N. Pacific Soc. Psychiatry and Neurology; mem. Mont. Med. Assn. (mem. exec. com. 1986—), AMA, Phi Beta Kappa. Republican. Lutheran. Club: Meadow Lark Country. Avocations: history, photography, railroads. Home: 1919 Elm Ct Great Falls MT 59404 Office: Great Falls Clinic PO Box 5012 Great Falls MT 59403

ENGSTROM, ERIC GUSTAF, interior/ graphic designer; b. Plymouth, Mass., July 9, 1942; s. Walder Julius and Victoria Sarah (Brewer) E.; m. Jacqueline Suzanne Del Savio, Apr. 19, 1969; children: Lars-Eric, Kate Pratumtip. B.F.A., Rhode Island Sch. of Design, 1964; postgrad. Southeastern Mass. U., 1967-69. Cert. interior designer. Exhibits designer Plimoth Plantation Mus., Plymouth, Mass., 1964-69; designer Johnson-Hotvedt & Assocs., Boston, 1969-71, Boston Children's Mus., 1971-73; assoc., dir. Interior and Graphic Design Architects Hawaii Ltd., Honolulu, 1973-78; designer Wudtke, Watson & Davis, San Francisco, 1978-81; prin. Wudtke, Watson, Davis & Engstrom, 1981-84; pres. Interior Design Collaborative, San Francisco, 1985-87; pres., design dir. Eric Engstrom Design, Tiburon, Calif., 1987—; guest lectr. Hotel Sch. Cornell U., Ithaca, N.Y., 1981; lectr. U. Hawaii, 1977-78. Mem. Town of Fairfax Design Rev. Bd., 1982; mem. Planning Commn. Town of Fairfax, 1981-84. Recipient 1st place Design award, Chain Restaurants, 1981; 1st place Design award Fast-Food Restaurants, 1981; design awards Restaurant Hospitality mag. Mem. Am. Soc. Interior Designers (project design award 1980), Inst. Bus. Designers (sec. No. Calif. chpt. 1985—). Club: Outrigger Canoe (Honolulu). Projects published in profl. mags. Office: 33 Main St Tiburon CA 94920

ENIS, BEN MELVIN, marketing educator; b. Baton Rouge, La., Jan. 5, 1942; s. Ben Melvin Sr. and Marjorie Bowman (Wood), E.; m. Sharon Lee Coleman, Jan. 8, 1977; 1 child, Ben Melvin III. BS in Acctg., La. State U., 1963, MBA in Mgmt., 1965, PhD in Mktg. and Econs., 1967. Supr. sales So. Bell Telephone Co., 1964; from asst. prof. to prof. mktg. U. Houston, 1967-78; Bailey K. Howard World Book Prof. Mktg. U. Mo., Columbia,

1978-82; vis. prof. U. Queensland, Brisbane, Australia, 1982; prof. mktg. U. So. Calif., Los Angeles, 1982—; cons. in field; bd. dirs. Countrywide Credit Industries; expert witness to several U.S. Fed. Cts. Author: (textbooks) (with Keith K. Cox) The Marketing Research Process, 1972, Marketing Principles, 1974, 3d. edit. 1980, (with L.B. Chonko) Personal Selling: Foundations, Process, and Management, 1979, (with P.E. Murphy) Marketing, 1985; co-editor various anthologies; mem. various editorial review bds.; contbr. numerous articles to profl. jours. Humble Oil fellow, 1965-66; Ford Found. fellow, 1966-67. Mem. Am. Mktg. Assn. (nat. v.p. edn. div. 1979, bd. dirs. 1978-79, pres. Houston, 1977, various other coms.), Consumer Psychology div. of Am. Psychol. Assn., Am. Inst. Decision Scis., MENSA, Beta Gamma Sigma, Phi Kappa Phi, Phi Eta Sigma. Libertarian. Avocations: reading, science fiction, swimming, skiing. Home: 3053 Hillside Dr West Covina CA 91791 Office: U So Calif Dept Mktg Los Angeles CA 90089-1421

ENNIS, CALVIN BRADY, guidebook editor; b. Alton, Ill., Mar. 19, 1954; s. Calvin Franklin and Virginia Jo (moody) E. BA in Journalism, Tex. Christian U., 1978. Copywriter Concordia Pub. House, St. Louis, 1978; display ad rep. Ft. Worth Star-Telegram, 1979; proofreader LeWay Composing, Ft. Worth, 1979-80, Deloitte Haskins & Sells, San Francisco, 1980-83; assoc. editor ASU Travel Guide, San Francisco, 1983-86, mng. editor, 1986—; writer, cons. pub. relations Different Spokes Bicycling Club of San Francisco, 1982-83. Mem. San Francisco Advt. Club. Office: ASU Travel Guide 1325 Columbus Ave San Francisco CA 94133

ENOCH, JAY MARTIN, visual scientist, educator; b. N.Y.C., Apr. 20, 1929; s. Jerome Dee and Stella Sarah (Nathan) E.; m. Rebekah Ann Feiss, June 24, 1951; children—Harold Owen, Barbara Diane, Ann Allison. B.S. in Optics and Optometry, Columbia U., 1950; postgrad., Inst. Optics U. Rochester, 1953; Ph.D. in Physiol. Optics, Ohio State U., 1956. Asst. prof. physiol. optics Ohio State U., Columbus, 1956-58; assoc. supr. of Ohio State U. (Mapping and Charting Research Lab.), 1957-58; fellow Nat. Phys. Lab., Teddington, Eng., 1959-60; research instr. dept. ophthalmology Washington U. Sch. Medicine, St. Louis, 1958-59, research asst. prof., 1959-64, research assoc. prof., 1965-70, research prof., 1970-74; fellow Barnes Hosp., St. Louis, 1960-64, cons. ophthalmology, 1964-74; research prof. dept. psychology Washington U., St. Louis, 1970-74; grad. research prof. ophthalmology and psychology Coll. Medicine U. Fla., Gainesville, 1974-80, grad. research prof. physics, 1979-80; dir. Center for Sensory Studies, 1976-80; dean Sch. Optometry, prof. physiol. optics and optometry, chmn. Grad. Group in Physiol. Optics U. Calif., Berkeley, 1980—; prof. physiol. optics in ophthalmology U. Calif., San Francisco, 1980—; chmn. subcom. contact lens Standards Am. Nat. Standards Inst., 1970-77; mem. nat. advisory eye council Nat. Eye Inst., NIH, 1975-77, 80-84; exec. com., com. on vision NAS-NRC, 1973-76; mem. U.S. Nat. Com. Internat. Commn. Optics, 1976-79. Contbr. numerous chpts. and articles on visual sci., receptor optics, perimetry, contact lenses and infant vision to sci. jours.; contbr. chpts. in field to med. books; mem. editorial bd.: Vision Research, 1974-80, Internat. Ophthalmology, 1977—; assoc. editor: Investigative Ophthalmology, 1965-75, 80—, Sight-Saving Rev, 1974-84, Sensory Processes, 1974-80; mem. editorial bd. Binocular Vision, 1984—, optical scis.: Springer-Verlag, Heidelberg, 1978—. Mem. nat. sci. advisory bd. Retinitis Pigmentosa Found., 1977—; U.S. rep. Internat. Perimetric Soc., 1974—; also exec. com., chmn. Research Group Standards.; Bd. dirs. Friends of Eye Research, 1977—; trustee Illuminating Engring. Research Inst., 1977-81. Served to 2d lt. U.S. Army, 1951-52. Recipient Career Devel. award NIH, 1963-73. Fellow AAAS, Am. Acad. Optometry (Glenn A. Fry award 1972, Charles F. Prentice medal award 1974), Optical Soc. Am. (chmn. vision tech. sect. 1974-76), Am. Acad. Ophthalmology (assoc., honor award 1985); mem. Assn. for Research in Vision and Ophthalmology (trustee 1967-73, pres. 1972-73, Francis I. Proctor medal 1977), Internat. Strabismological Assn., Internat. Soc. for Clin. Electro-retinography, Psychonomic Soc., AAUP, Am. Psychol. Assn. (sect. 3), Concilium Ophthalmologicum Universale (chmn. visual functions com. 1982-86), Sigma Xi. Home: 54 Shuey Dr Moraga CA 94556 Office: U Calif Sch Optometry Berkeley CA 94720

ENRIGHT, THOMAS JONES, mathematics educator; b. Concord, N.H., Aug. 15, 1947; s. Cecil Thomas and Monterey (Jones) E.; m. Gwyn Stern, Aug. 20, 1973 (div. June 1978); m. Elizabeth Enos, Sept. 16, 1979; 1 child, James Thomas. BA, Harvard U., 1969; PhD, U. Wash., 1973. Asst. prof. math. UCLA, 1973-75; mem. Inst. Advanced Study, Princeton, N.J., 1975-76; prof. math. U. Calif. San Diego, La Jolla, 1976—. Contbr. articles to profl. jours. Alfred P. Sloan fellow, 1979-80. Mem. AAAS, Am. Math. Soc.

ENSIGN, JACQUELINE, social worker; b. Oakland, Calif., Sept. 14, 1931; d. John A. and Helen A. (Symons) London; m. Ernest F. Ensign, Nov. 28, 1957; children: Jane Ann, Susan Amy. BA, U. Calif., Berkeley, 1953, MSW, 1956. Social worker Jewish Family and Children's Service, Phoenix, 1963-70, St. Luke's Hosp., Phoenix, 1970-72; coordinator social services Boswell Hosp., Sun City, Ariz., 1976-84; case mgr. Sun City Area Agy. on Aging, 1985-86; pvt. practice social work Tempe, 1986—. Chmn. social work sub-com. Am. Cancer Soc., Phoenix, 1984-86. Mem. Nat. Assn. Social Workers, Acad. Cert. Social Workers, Am. Assn. Aging, Ariz. Hosp. Social Work Dirs. (chmn. edn. com. 1976-84). Democrat. Avocations: swimming, biking, gardening, tennis. Home and Office: 625 W 17th Pl Tempe AZ 85281

ENSMINGER, MICHAEL PAUL, biology researcher; b. Indpls., Dec. 31, 1952; s. Paul Warner and Lorraine (Croessant) E.; m. Kathryn Lynn Raab, Oct. 16, 1982; children: Leah, Adam, Cassandra. BA, Ind. U.; MS, Purdue U., PhD. Assoc. research biologist Stauffer Chem. Co., Mountain View, CA, 1984-86, research biologist, 1986—. Contbr. articles to profl jours. Mem. Weed Sci. Soc. Am. (mem. research subcom. 1986), Am. Soc. Plant Physiology. Home: 4840 Poston Dr San Jose CA 95136 Office: Stauffer Chem Co PO Box 760 Mountain View CA 94042

ENSTROM, JAMES EUGENE, cancer epidemiologist; b. Alhambra, Calif., June 20, 1943; s. Elmer Melvin, Jr. and Klea Elizabeth (Bissell) E.; B.S., Harvey Mudd Coll., Claremont, Calif., 1965; M.S., Stanford U., 1967, Ph.D. in Physics, 1970; M.P.H., UCLA, 1976; m. Marta Eugenia Villanea, Sept. 3, 1978. Research asso. Stanford Linear Accelerator Center, 1970-71; research physicist, cons. Lawrence Berkeley Lab., U. Calif., 1971-75; Celeste Durand Rogers cancer research fellow Sch. Pub. Health, UCLA, 1973-75, Nat. Cancer Inst. postdoctoral trainee, 1975-76, cancer epidemiology researcher, 1976-81, assoc. research prof., 1981—; program dir. for cancer control epidemiology Jonsson Comprehensive Cancer Center, 1978—, sci. dir. tumor registry, 1984—, mem. dean's council, 1976—; cons. epidemiologist Linus Pauling Inst. Sci. and Medicine, 1976—; cons. physicist Rand Corp., 1969-73, R&D Assos., 1971-75; mem. sci. bd. Am. Council on Sci. and Health, 1984—. NSF predoctoral trainee, 1965-66; grantee Am. Cancer Soc., 1973—, Nat. Cancer Inst., 1979—; Preventive Oncology Acad. award, 1981-87. Fellow Am. Coll. Epidemiology; mem. Soc. Epidemiologic Research, Am. Heart Assn., Am. Pub. Health Assn., Am. Phys. Soc., AAAS, N.Y. Acad. Scis., Galileo Soc. Author papers in field. Office: U Calif Sch Pub Health Los Angeles CA 90024

ENTREMONT, PHILIPPE, conductor, pianist; b. Rheims, France, June 7, 1934; s. Jean and Renée (Monchamps) E.; m. Andree Ragot, Dec. 21, 1955; children: Félicia, Alexandre. Student, Conservatoire National Superieur de Musique, Paris, Jean Doyen. Profl. debut at 17, in Barcelona, Spain, Am. debut at 19, at Nat. Gallery, Washington, 1953, performs throughout world; pianist-condr. debut at, Mostly Mozart Festival, Lincoln Center, N.Y.C., 1971; rec. artist, Epic, Concert Hall and Columbia records, guest condr., Royal Philharmonic, Orch. Nat. de France, Montreal Symphony, San Francisco Symphony, Vienna Chamber Orch., numerous others, music dir., prin. condr., New Orleans Philharmonic Symphony Orch., 1981—; prin. condr. Denver Symphony, 1986—. Decorated Chevalier de l'Ordre National du Merite.; A finalist Queen Elizabeth of Belgium Internat. Concours, 1952; Grand Prix Marguerite Long-Jacques Thibaud Competition, 1953; Harriet Cohen Piano medal, 1953; 1st prize Jeunesses Musicales; Grand Prix du Disque, 1967, 68, 69, 70; Edison award, 1968; Nominee Grammy award, 1972. Former mem. Academie Internationale de Musique Maurice Ravel (pres. 1975-80). Office: Denver Symphony Orch 910 15th St Suite 330 Denver CO 80202 Address: Amara-Chantaco, F-64500 Saint-Jean-de-Lux France *

ENTRIKEN, ROBERT KERSEY, management educator; b. McPherson, Kans., Jan. 15, 1913; s. Frederick Kersey and Opal (Birch) E.; m. Elizabeth Freeman, May 26, 1940 (div. Nov. 1951); children—Robert Kersey, Jr., Edward Livingston Freeman, Richard Davis; m. Jean Finch, June 5, 1954; 1 child, Birch Nelson. B.A., U. Kans. 1934; M.B.A., Golden Gate U., 1961; postgrad. City Univ. Grad. Bus. Sch., London, 1971-73. C.P.C.U. Ins. broker, Houston, Tex. and McPherson, Kans., 1935-39; asst. mgr. Cravens, Dargan & Co., Houston, 1939-42; br. mgr. Nat. Surety Corp., Memphis and San Francisco, 1942-54; v.p. Fireman's Fund Ins. Co., San Francisco. 1954-73; adj. prof. Golden Gate U., San Francisco, 1953-73, prof. mgmt., 1974—; underwriting mem. Lloyd's of London, 1985—. Contbr. articles to trade and profl. jours. Bd. dirs., sec., treas. Northstar Property Owners Assn., Calif., 1982-86. Served to capt. USNR, 1944-73, ret., 1973. Mem. Ins. Forum San Francisco (pres. 1965, trustee 1975-78, 84—), Surety Underwriters Assn. No. Calif. (pres. 1956), CPCU Soc. (pres. No. Calif. chpt. 1957, named Ins. Profl. of Yr., San Francisco chpt. 1981), Chartered Ins. Inst., Ins. Inst. London, Musicians' Union Local Ilife), Acad. Polit. Sci., U.S. Naval Inst., Phi Delta Theta. Republican. Episcopalian. Clubs: University, Marines' Meml. (San Francisco); Commonwealth. Lodge: Naval Order U.S. Office: Golden Gate U 536 Mission St San Francisco CA 94105

EPEL, DAVID, biologist; b. Detroit, Mar. 26, 1937; s. Jacob A. and Anna K. (Karse) E.; m. Lois S. Ambush, Dec. 18, 1960; children: Andrea, Sharon, Elissa. A.B., Wayne State U., 1958; Ph.D., U. Calif.-Berkeley, 1963. Postdoctoral fellow Johnson Research Found., U. Pa., 1963-65; asst. prof. Hopkins Marine Sta., 1965-70; assoc. prof., then prof. Scripps Instn. Oceanography, 1970-77; prof. biol. scis. Hopkins Marine Sta., Stanford U., Pacific Grove, Calif., 1977—; acting dir. Stanford U., Pacific Grove, 1984—; co-dir. embryology course Marine Biol. Lab., Woods Hole; mem. adv. panel on devel. and cell biology NSF. Mem. editorial bd. Expert Cell Research, Cell Differentiation, Exptl. Cell Research, Gamete Research. Guggenheim fellow, 1976-77; Overseas fellow Churchill; Coll., Cambridge, Eng., 1976-77. Fellow AAAS (mem.-at-large, sect. G 1979-84); mem. Am. Soc. Cell Biology (mem. council 1978-80), Soc. Devel. Biology, Internat. Soc. Devel. Biology, Soc. Gen. Physiologist, Am. Soc. Zoologists. Home: 25847 Carmel Knolls Dr Carmel CA 93923 Office: Hopkins Marine Station Pacific Grove CA 93950

EPLER, VENETIA, painter, muralist, sculptor; b. Linwood, W.Va., Mar. 7; d. Franklin and Anne (Farrer) E. Student of painting Slades Sch. Art, London, Ecole de Louvre, Paris, London Sch. Arts and Crafts. Motion picture illustrator, layout and background artist M.G.M., Hannah-Barbera, Wexler Documentary Films, Filmation, Cathedral Films, 1963-78; muralist Forest Lawn, Glendale, Calif., 1965-70, (with D. Huntington) paints original oil on canvas murals, recreated in tesserie as world's largest religious mosaic at Christian Heritage Mausoleum, West Covina, Calif., also Life of Christ Mural, Woodlawn Memorium, Orlando, Fla., 1987; designed 12 stained glass windows Science of Mind Ch., Beverly Hills, Calif.; painted altar mural and (with D. Huntington) designed alter windows St. Augustine Ch., East Los Angeles, 1985; painted portraits of Pres. Dwight D. Eisenhower at White House, His Excellency Peter J. Velez for Embassy of Malta to Guatemala, 1971; represented in permanent collections; San Bernardino County Mus., Redlands, Calif., De Saisset Gallery of Santa Clara (Calif.) Mus., Phiffer Hall, Claremont (Calif.) Coll., Occidental Coll., Los Angeles, Am. embassy, London, others; contbr. poems to Secrets of the Poetic Vision, 1986. Recipient Nat. First award Smithsonian Ins Instn., 1967; Gold medal Council Traditional Artists Socs., 1969; numerous others. Fellow Am. Inst. Fine Arts (Gold medal 1969), Am. Artists Profl. League; mem. San Gabriel Fine Arts Assn. (Gold medal 1971, 72), Accademia Italia delle Arti e de Lavoro (Gold medal 1979), Artists of S.W. (Lillian Prest Ferguson award 1982, Duncan Gleason Meml. award, 1986). Address: 1835 Outpost Dr Hollywood CA 90068

EPP, JEFFREY ROBERT, lawyer; b. Bethlehem, Pa., Aug. 18, 1959; s. Gari R. and Judy A. (Kline) E. BA, U. Wyo., 1981, JD, 1984. Bar: Wyo. 1984, Calif. 1986. Asst. city atty. City of Cheyenne, Wyo., 1984-85; dep. city atty. City of Escondido, Calif., 1985—. Mem. ABA (litigation sect.), Wyo. Trial Lawyers Assn. Republican. Lutheran. Avocations: racquetball, fishing, reading. Home: PO Box 58 Escondido CA 92025 Office: City of Escondido 100 Valley Blvd Escondido CA 92025

EPPERSON, DENNIS HARLEY, patent lawyer; b. Quincy, Ill., Aug. 30, 1948; s. Harley and Elma (Brickman) E.; m. Bonnie Jean Epperson, Jan. 17, 1970. BA, Park Coll., 1969; PhD, Duke U., 1978; JD, U. San Diego, 1984. Bar: Calif. 1985, Ill. 1986. Postdoctoral fellow Duke U., Durham, N.C., 1978; sr. scientist Sci. Applications Inc., San Diego, 1978-85; patent atty. Knobbe, Martens, Olson and Bear, Newport Beach, Calif., 1986—. Home: 230 W Avenida Gaviota San Clemente CA 92672 Office: Knobbe Martens Olson & Bear 610 Newport Center Dr Newport Beach CA 92660

EPPERSON, ERIC ROBERT, international tax consultant; b. Oregon City, Oreg., Dec. 10, 1949; s. Robert Max and Margaret Joan (Crawford) E.; B.S., Brigham Young U., 1973, M.Acctg., 1974; M.B.A., Golden Gate U., 1977, J.D., 1981; m. Lyla Gene Harris, Aug. 21, 1969; 1 dau., Marcie. Instr. acctg. Brigham Young U., Provo, Utah, 1973-74; supr. domestic taxation Bechtel Corp., San Francisco, 1974-78; supr. internat. taxation Bechtel Power Corp., San Francisco, 1978-80; mgr. internat. tax planning Del Monte Corp., San Francisco, 1980-82, mgr. internat. taxes, 1982-85; internat. tax specialist Touche Ross & Co., San Francisco, 1985, 87; dir. internat. tax Coopers & Lybrand, Portland, 1987—. Eagle Scout, 1965; scoutmaster, Boy Scouts Am., Provo, 1971-73, troop committeeman, 1973-74, 83—; mem. IRS Vol. Income Tax Assistance Program, 1972-75; pres. Mut. Improvement Assn., Ch. Jesus Christ of Latter-day Saints, 1972-74, pres. Sunday sch., 1977-79, tchr., 1974-80, ward clk., 1980-83, bishopric, 1983-87 . Mem. Am. Acctg. Assn., Tax Assn. Am., World Affairs Council, Japan/Am. Soc., Internat. Tax Planning Assn., Internat. Fiscal Assn., Beta Alpha Psi. Republican. Clubs: Commonwealth, Masters of Accountancy Brigham Young U. Author: (with T. Gilbert) Interfacing of the Securities and Exchange Commission with the Accounting Profession: 1968 to 1973, 1974. Office: Coopers & Lybrand 2700 First Interstate Tower Portland OR 97201 Address: 2700 First Interstate Tower Portland Ave San Francisco CA 97201

EPPERSON, VAUGHN ELMO, civil engineer; b. Provo, Utah, July 20, 1917; s. Lawrence Theophilus and Mary Loretta (Pritchett) E.; m. Margaret Ann Stewart Hewlett, Mar. 4, 1946; children: Margaret Ann (Mrs. Eric V.K. Hill), Vaughn Hewlett, David Hewlett, Katherine (Mrs. Franz S. Amussen), Lawrence Stewart. BS, U. Utah, 1953. With Pritchett Bros. Constrn. Co., Provo, 1949-50; road design engr. Utah State Road Commn., Salt Lake City, 1951-53, bridge design engr., 1953-54; design engr. Kennecott Copper Corp., Salt Lake City, 1954-60, office engr., 1960-62, sr. engr., 1962, assigned concentrator plant engr., 1969-73, assigned concentrator project engr., 1973-78; cons. engr. Vaughn Epperson Engring. Service, Salt Lake City, 1978—; project engr. Newbery-State Inc., Salt Lake City, 1980, geneal. extraction and research programs, 1983—. Scoutmaster Troop 190, Salt Lake City, 1949-51. Served to capt. AUS, 1941-45; maj. N.G., 1951; col. Utah State Guard, 1952-70. Decorated Army Commendation medal; recipient Service award Boy Scouts Am., 1949, Community Service award United Fund, 1961, Service award VA Hosp., Salt Lake City, 1977. Mem. ASCE, Am. Soc. Mil. Engrs., Sons of Utah Pioneers. Republican. Mormon. Home: 1537 Laird Ave Salt Lake City UT 84105 Office: PO Box 8769 Salt Lake City UT 84108

EPPINETTE, SHIRLEY LYNN, educator, journalist; b. New Orleans; d. Woodie Trevillion and Thelma Elizabeth (Axline) E.; A.A. (Journalism Alumni Assn. scholar), East Los Angeles, Coll., 1967; B.A. (Arthur J. Baum journalism scholar), Calif. State U., Los Angeles, 1969, postgrad., 1969-70; postgrad. U. Santa Clara, 1981, U. So. Calif., 1982, Chapman Coll., 1983, Loyola Marymount U., Los Angeles, 1986. Elem. tchr. Covina-Valley Unified Sch. Dist., 1970-74, San Gabriel (Calif.) Sch. Dist., 1974-75, Alhambra (Calif.) City Sch. Dist., 1976-78, Los Angeles City Unified Sch. Dist., 1978—; rewrite editor, staff writer San Gabriel Valley Newspaper Publs., 1975-76; mem. membership adv. group Automobile Club So. Calif. Contbr. articles to newspapers and publs. Recipient TAP award Alhambra-San Gabriel dist. Soroptimist Club, 1975; Calif. State PTA scholar, 1981. Mem. NEA, Calif. Tchrs. Assn., Los Angeles City Tchrs. Math. Assn., United Tchrs. Los Angeles, Women in Communications, Nat. Press Women, AAUW (com. internat. relations 1977-78, chmn. ednl. com. 1978-79), Humane Soc. U.S., Nat. Rifle Assn., Sigma Delta Chi. Club: Pacific Coast Press. Home: 7318 W 91st St Los Angeles CA 90045

EPPS, HARLAND WARREN, astronomy educator, optical design consultant; b. Hawthorne, Calif., July 29, 1936; s. Harland Garner and Nydia Dolly (Gall) E.; m. Susan Lou Markowitz, Oct. 10, 1976 (div. Feb. 1983); children: Melody Amanda, Brenden Putty. Student, U. Vienna, Austria, 1956-57; BA, Pomona Coll., 1959; MS, U. Wis., 1961, PhD, 1964. Asst. prof. astronomy San Diego State U., 1964-65; asst. prof. astronomy UCLA, 1965-70, assoc. prof., 1970-76, prof., 1976—; systemwide astronomer Lick Obs., Santa Cruz, Calif., 1984—; cons. Stewars Obs., Tucson, 1972—, Lick Obs., 1970—, Smithsonian Astrophys. Obs., Cambridge, Mass., 1984—, Los Alamos (N.Mex.) Nat. Lab., 1984—. Contbr. articles to profl. jours. Grantee NSF, Air Force Cambridge Research, U. Calif. Regents Opportunity Fund. Mem. Am. Astron. Soc., Internat. Astron. Union, Soc. Photooptical Instrumentation Engrs., Sigma Xi. Avocation: classical guitar. Office: UCLA Dept Astronomy 2405 N Hilgard Ave Los Angeles CA 90024

EPPSTEIN, DEBORAH ANNE, biomedical department head, researcher, pharmaceutical executive; b. Kalamazoo, Oct. 16, 1948; d. Samuel Hillel and Dorothy Jean (Dodd) E. BA, Grinnell Coll., 1970; PhD in Biochemistry, U. Ark., 1985. Research assoc. U. Calif., Santa Barbara, 1976-78; staff researcher Syntex Corp., Palo Alto, Calif., 1978-81, research sect. leader, 1982-84, head biochemistry dept., 1984—. Mem. edit. bd. Jour. Interferon Research, 1983—; patentee in field. Recipient Outstanding Teaching award, U. Ark., 1972-73; NSF fellow, 1969, Nat. Def. Edn. Act IV fellow, 1970-73, NIH fellow, 1976-78. Mem. AAAS, Am. Soc. Virology, Internat. Soc. Interferon Research. Office: Syntex 3401 Hillview Ave Palo Alto CA 94304

EPSTEIN, CHARLES JOSEPH, physician, medical geneticist, pediatrics and biochemistry educator; b. Phila., Sept. 3, 1933; s. Jacob C. and Frieda (Savransky) E.; m. Lois Barth, June 10, 1956; children: David Alexander, Jonathan Akiba, Paul Michael, Joanna Marguerite. A.B., Harvard U., 1955, M.D., 1959. Diplomate: Am. Bd. Medical Genetics. Intern in medicine Peter Bent Brigham Hosp., Boston, 1959-60; asst. resident in medicine Peter Bent Brigham Hosp., 1960-61; research assoc., med. officer and sect. chief Nat. Heart Inst. and Nat. Inst. Arthritis and Metabolic Diseases, NIH, Bethesda, Md., 1961-67; research fellow in med. genetics U. Wash., 1963-64; assoc. prof. pediatrics and biochemistry U. Calif., San Francisco, 1967-72; prof. U. Calif., 1972—, chief div. med. genetics. dept. pediatrics, 1967—; investigator Howard Hughes Med. Inst., 1976-81; mem. human embryology and devel. study sect. NIH, 1971-75; mem. mental retardation research com. Nat. Inst. Child Health and Devel., 1979-83, chmn., 1981-83; mem. com. for study inborn errors of metabolism NRC, 1972-75; mem. sci. adv. bd. Nat. Down Syndrome Soc., 1981—, chmn., 1984—; mem. recombinant DNA adv. com. NIH, 1985—; Stanley Wright Meml. lectr. Western Soc. Pediatric Research, 1986; William Potter Lectr. Thomas Jefferson U., 1987. Author: The Consequences of Chromosome Imbalance: Principles, Mechanisms and Models, 1986; editor: Human Genetics, 1985—, The Neurobiology of Down Syndrome, 1986, Am. Jour. Human Genetics, 1987—; assoc. editor: Rudolph's Textbook of Pediatrics, 18th edit., 1986; mem. editorial bd. Biology of Reproduction, 1974-78, Cytogenetics and Cell Genetics, 1975-80, Am. Jour. Med. Genetics, 1977—, Devel. Genetics, 1983-85, Jour. Embryology and Exptl. Morphology, 1983-85, Progress in Med. Genetics, 1985—, Human Genetics, 1981—; editor, 1984—. Served with USPHS, 1961-63. Recipient Henry A. Christian award Harvard Med. Sch., 1959, Research Career Devel. award NIH, 1967-72; John S. Guggenheim Meml. Found. fellow, 1973-74; Ctr. Advanced Studies in Behavioral Scis. fellow, 1983-84. Fellow AAAS; mem. Am. Fedn. Clin. Research, Am. Soc. Human Genetics (dir. 1972-75, 87), Am. Soc. Biol. Chemists, Soc. Pediatric Research (council 1972-75), Western Soc. Pediatric Research, Western Soc. Clin. Investigation, Am. Soc. Clin. Investigation, Am. Soc. Cell Biology, Soc. Devel. Biology, Am. Pediatric Soc., Western Assn. Physicians, Assn. Am. Physicians, Soc. Inherited Metabolic Disorders, Calif. Acad. Medicine, Phi Beta Kappa, Alpha Omega Alpha. Jewish. Research, numerous publs. on human and med. genetics, devel. genetics and biochemistry. Home: 19 Noche Vista Ln Tiburon CA 94920 Office: U Calif Dept Pediatrics San Francisco CA 94143-0106

EPSTEIN, EMANUEL, plant physiologist; b. Duisburg, Germany, Nov. 5, 1916; came to U.S., 1938, naturalized, 1946; s. Harry and Bertha (Lowe) E.; m. Hazel M. Leask, Nov. 26, 1943; children: Jared H. (dec.), Jonathan H. B.S., U. Calif.-Davis, 1940, M.S., 1941; Ph.D., U. Calif.-Berkeley, 1950. Plant physiologist Dept. Agr., Beltsville, Md., 1950-58; lectr., assoc. plant physiologist U. Calif.-Davis, 1958-65, prof. plant nutrition, plant physiologist, 1965—, prof. botany, 1974—; cons. to govt. and pvt. agys. Author: Mineral Nutrition of Plants: Principles and Perspectives, 1972; editorial bd.: Plant Physiology, 1962-71, 76—, CRC Handbook Series in Nutrition and Food, 1975—, The Biosaline Concept: An Approach to the Utilization of Underexploited Resources, 1978, Plant Sci., 1981—, Advances in Plant Nutrition, 1981—. Served with U.S. Army, 1943-46. Recipient Gold medal Pisa (Italy) U., 1962; Guggenheim fellow, 1958; Fulbright sr. research scholar, 1965-66, 74-75. Fellow AAAS; mem. Nat. Acad. Scis., Am. Soc. Plant Physiologists (Charles Reid Barnes Hon. Life Membership award, 1986), Scandinavian Soc. Plant Physiology, Australian Soc. Plant Physiologists, Am. Inst. Biol. Scis., Crop Sci. Soc. Am., Am. Soc. Agronomy, Common Cause, Save-the-Redwoods League, Sierra Club, Nature Conservancy, Sigma Xi. Club: U. Calif. at Davis Faculty. Research, publs. on ion transport in plants, mineral nutrition and salt relations of plants, salt tolerant crops. Office: U Calif Land Air and Water Resources Davis CA 95616

EPSTEIN, JOHN HOWARD, dermatologist; b. San Francisco, Dec. 29, 1926; s. Norman Neman and Gertrude (Hirsch) E.; m. Alice Thompson, Nov. 1953; children: Norman H., Janice A., Beverly A. B.A., U. Calif., Berkeley, 1949, M.D., 1952; M.S., U. Minn., 1956. Diplomate Am. Bd. Dermatology (dir. 1974-84, pres. 1981-82). Intern Stanford U. Med. Center, 1952-53; resident in dermatology Mayo Clinic, Rochester, Minn., 1953-56; practice medicine specializing in dermatology San Francisco, 1956—; chief dermatology Mt. Zion Hosp., 1970-80; clin. prof. U. Calif. Med. Sch., San Francisco, 1972—; cons. Letterman Army Med. Center, U.S. Naval Hosp., San Diego. Author articles in field.; Chief editor: Archives of Dermatology, 1973-78; asst. editor: Jour. Am. Acad. Dermatology, 1978—. Served with USNR, 1944-46. Fellow A.C.P.; mem. Am. Acad. Dermatology (pres. 1981-82, Silver award for exhibit 1962, Gold award 1969), Soc. Investigative Dermatology (v.p. 1979-80), Am. Dermatol. Assn. (bd. dirs. 1983—), N.Am. Dermatology Soc., Pacific Dermatol. Assn. (pres. 1985-86), San Francisco Dermatol. Soc. (pres. 1963-64), Am. Soc. Photobiology (councilor 1983-86), Academia Mexicana and Dermatologia (hon.). Office: 450 Sutter St Suite 1306 San Francisco CA 94108

EPSTEIN, JOSEPH I., steel company executive; b. Oakland, Calif., Sept. 25, 1938; s. Samual and Rebecca (Berman) E.; m. Judith Ann Rubens, Oct. 4, 1964; children: Mark Douglas, Laura Ann. BA, U. Calif., Berkeley, 1960. Mgr. Marysville (Calif.) Steel Co., 1960-70; pres. and chief exec. officer Sierra Pacific Steel Corp., Hayward, Calif., 1970—. Clubs: Berkeley Tennis, Commonwealth (San Francisco). Avocations: tennis, skiing. Office: Sierra Pacific Steel Corp 3200 Depot Rd Hayward CA 94545

EPSTEIN, L(UDWIG) IVAN, physicist; b. Duisburg, Fed. Republic Germany, Nov. 25, 1918; came to U.S., 1936; s. Fritz David and Irma (Magnus) E.; m. Thelma Ruth Vaughn, July 30, 1955. BS, Calif. Inst. Tech., 1940, MS, 1941; PhD, Ohio State U., 1967. Optical engr. Bausch & Lomb, Rochester, N.Y., 1947-54; asst. prof. physics Lowell (Mass.) Tech. Inst., 1958-63; assoc. prof. Marietta (Ohio) Coll., 1963-64, Med. Coll. of Va., Richmond, 1967-82; visiting scholar Optical Scis. Ctr. U. Ariz., Tucson, 1982—. Author: Nomography, 1958; (with B.A. Kuzava) Basic Physics in Anesthesiology, 1976. Grantee NIH, Bethesda, Md., 1975, 79. Mem. Optical Soc. Am., Assn. for Research Vision and Ophthalmology, AAUP. Club: Alliance Francaise (Tucson). Avocation: hist. of music.

EPSTEIN, ROBERT MICHAEL, advertising and public relations company executive; b. Albuquerque, Feb. 22, 1944; s. Sam and Sayde (Kitzes) E.; children: Barry, Stacey. BBA, U. N.Mex., MBA. Data processing rep. IBM Corp., Albuquerque; v.p. S.W. Coll., Albuquerque; exec. dir. U. N.Mex. Lobo Club, Albuquerque; pres. Epstein Enterprises Inc., Albuquerque,

1974—. Bd. dirs. Albuquerque C. of C., Albuquerque Little Theatre. Mem. Am. Assn. Advt. Agys., Nat. Advt. Agy. Network, Am. Advt. Fedn., Am. Diabetes Assn. (bd. dirs.). Office: Epstein Enterprises Inc 6301 Indian School Rd NE Albuquerque NM 87110

EPSTEIN, WILLIAM LOUIS, educator, physician; b. Cleve., Sept. 6, 1925; s. Norman N. and Gertrude (Hirsch) E.; m. Joan Goldman, Jan. 29, 1954; children—Wendy, Steven. A.B., U. Calif., Berkeley, 1949, M.D., 1952. Mem. faculty U. Calif., San Francisco, 1957—; asso. prof. div. dermatology U. Calif., 1963-69, dir. dermatol. research, 1957-70, acting chmn. div. dermatology, 1966-69, chmn. dept. dermatology, 1970-85; cons. dermatology Outpatient Dept.; cons. various hosps. Calif. Dept. Public Health; cons. Food and Drug Adminstrn., Washington, 1972—; dir. div. research Nat. Program Dermatology, 1970-73; Dohi lectr., Tokyo, 1982. Mem. AAAS, AMA, Am. Acad. Dermatology and Syphilology (nominating com. 1984), Pacific Dermatologic Assn., Am. Fedn. Clin. Research, Soc. Investigative Dermatology (bd. dirs., pres. 1985), Am. Dermatol. Assn., Assn. Profs. Dermatology (sec. 1983-85), Dermatology Found. (pres. 1986-87), Phi Beta Kappa, Sigma Xi. Home: 498 Sea Cliff San Francisco CA 94121

ERBACHER, KATHRYN ANNE, writer, editor; b. Kansas City, Mo., Dec. 11, 1947; d. Philip Joseph and Thelma Lillian (Hines) E. BS in Edn., U. Kans., 1970; BA magna cum laude in Art, Metro State Coll., Denver, 1983. Reporter, Kansas City Star (Mo.), 1970-71; newswriter Washington U., St. Louis, 1972-76; copy editor Kansas City Star-Times (Mo.), 1976-79; editor Petro-Lewis Corp., Denver, 1979-82; assoc. editor Artours, Inc., Denver, 1983-84; assoc. editor arts and travel editor Denver Mag., 1984-86; freelance writer, editor, 1986—. Creative dir. TV shorts for contemporary art collection Denver Art Mus., 1983. Recipient award for arts writing Denver Partnership, 1986. Mem. Women in Communications (jobs chmn. Denver 1981-82). Home: 1539 Platte St Denver CO 80202

ERBES, RUSSELL EDWARD, utility company executive, atmospheric scientist; b. Ft. Collins, Colo., July 21, 1947; s. Edward and Elizabeth Catherine (Hankel) E.; m. Peggy JoAnn Demos, Jan. 27, 1969; children: Anissa, Chris, Sara, Kelly, Robert, Cathy, Thomas. BS, N.Mex. Inst. Mining and Tech., 1969; MS, Colo. State U., 1978. Research asst. Colo. State U., Ft. Collins, 1974-75; tchr. sci. Farmington (N.Mex.) High Sch., 1975-77; atmospheric scientist Pub. Service Co. N.Mex., Albuquerque, 1977-79, supr. air/water quality, 1979-85, dir. environ. programs, 1985—; chmn. air task force WEST Assocs., 1984-85, chmn. program com. Electric Power Research Inst., 1985. Nat. bd. dirs. Cath. Engaged Encounter; mem. family life com. Archdiocese of Santa Fe, Albuquerque, 1980-85. Served to lt. USNR, 1969-74. Mem. AAAS, Nat. Water Well Assn., Air Pollution Control Assn., Am. Meteorol. Soc. Republican. Avocations: woodworking, backpacking. Home: 8105 Pickard Ave NE Albuquerque NM 87110 Office: Pub Service Co NMex Alvarado Sq Albuquerque NM 87158

ERBURU, ROBERT F., newspaper publishing company executive; b. Ventura, Calif., 1930. BA, U. So. Calif., 1952; LLB, Harvard U. Law Sch., 1955. Chmn. bd., chief exec. officer Times-Mirror Co., Los Angeles, also bd. dirs.; bd. dirs. Tejon Ranch Co.; bd. dirs., dep. chmn. Fed. Res. Bank of San Francisco. Trustee Huntington Library, Art Gallery and Bot. Gardens, 1981—, Flora and William Hewlett Found., 1980—, Brookings Instn., 1983—, Tomas Rivera Ctr., 1985—, Carrie Estelle Doheny Found., Fletcher Jones Found., 1982—, Pfaffinger Found., 1974—; mem. exec. panel on future of welfare state Ford. Found., 1985—; bd. dirs., v.p. Times Mirror Found., 1962—; bd. dirs. Los Angeles Festival, 1985—, Ralph M. Parsons Found., 1985—; mem. Nat. Gallery of Art Trustees Council. Mem. Am. Newspaper Pubs. Assn. (bd. dirs. 1980—), Council on Fgn. Relations (bd. dirs.), Bus. Roundtable, Bus. Council. Home: 1518 Blue Jay Way Los Angeles CA 90069 Office: Times Mirror Co Times Mirror Sq Los Angeles CA 90053

ERDMAN, BARRY RICHARD, clinical social worker, psychotherapist; b. Bklyn., Mar. 1, 1952; s. Herman and Shirley (Goldblatt) E. BA in Psychology, Bklyn. Coll., 1974; MSW, U. Denver, 1983. Lic. clin. social worker, Colo. Corrections counselor Weld County Sherrif's Dept., Greeley, Colo., 1979; circulation mgr. Assn. for Transpersonal Psychology, Stanford, Calif., 1980-81; social worker Boulder Valley (Colo.) Schs., 1981-82; intake caseworker III Boulder County (Colo.) Dept. Social Services, 1983; outpatient therapist Boulder (Colo.) Mental Health Ctr., 1983—; pvt. practice psychotherapy Boulder, 1983—. Mem. Nat. Assn. Social Workers (bd. dirs. and rep. Boulder County chpt., 1985—), Am. Assn. Marriage and Family Therapists (assoc.), Assn. Past Life Therapy and Research (profl., editorial bd. Regression Jour., 1985—), Assn. Transpersonal Psychology (hon.), Acad. Cert. Social Workers (cert.). Avocations: percussion music performance, Eastern religion and culture studies. Office: Boulder Mental Health Ctr 1722 14th St Suite 130 Boulder CO 80302

ERDMAN, JOHN GORDON, geoscientist, retired; b. Balt., Apr. 12, 1919; s. John Matthew and Margaret Adele (Hollmann) E.; m. Arline Juanita Calhoun, Apr. 12, 1948. BA, Johns Hopkins U., 1940, PhD, 1943. Research chemist Nat. Def. Research Com., Balt., 1943-45; petroleum fellow Mellon Inst., Pitts., 1945-56, sr. fellow, 1956-65; mgr. geochem. br. Phillips Petroleum Co., Bartlesville, Okla., 1965-74, sr. scientist, 1974-84. Contbr. numerous articles to profl. jours.; patentee in field. Fellow AAAS (com. for Interciencia), Am. Inst. for Chemists (emeritus, pres. Pitts. chpt. 1962-64), The Geol. Soc. Am., Sigma Xi; mem. Am. Petroleum Inst. (chmn. project adv. com.), Nat Acad. Sci. (Am. Petroleum Council adv. panel Organic Geochemistry), Am. Assn. Petroleum Geologists, Geochem. Soc. (chmn. Organic Geochemistry div. 1964-65, chmn. 1965-66, counselor 1969-72), Am. Chem. Soc. (div. petroleum chemistry, wood and fibre chemistry), Am. Geophys. Union (corp. rept.), Woods Hole Oceanographic Instn. (corp. rep.), Lamont -Doherty Geol. Obs. (corp. rep.), Scripps Instn. Oceanography (corp. rep.), Marine Sci. Inst. U. Tex. (corp. rep.), Tulsa Geol. Soc., European Assn. Organic Chemists, Johns Hopkins Alumni Assn. (v.p. Pitts. chpt. 1960-61, Pres. Pitts. chpt. 1961-62), Phi Beta Kappa. Republican. Presbyterian. Avocations: horticulture, photography, travel. Home: 6045 Olohena Rd Kapaa-Kauai HI 96746

ERDMANN, JOACHIM CHRISTIAN, physicist; b. Danzig, June 5, 1928; s. Franz Werner and Maria Magdalena (Schreiber) E.; doctorate Tech. U. Braunschweig (Germany), 1958; m. Ursula Maria Wedemeyer, Aug. 24, 1957; children—Michael Andreas, Thomas Christian, Maria Martha Dorothea. Physicist, Osram Labs., Augsburg, Germany, 1954-60; sr. research scientist Boeing Sci. Research Labs., Seattle, 1960-72; sr. research scientist Boeing Aerospace Co., Seattle, 1972-73; prin. engr. Boeing Comml. Airplane Co., Seattle, 1973-81, sr. prin. engr., 1981-84; sr. prin. engr. Boeing Aerospace Co., Seattle, 1984—; vis. prof. Max Planck Inst. for Metals Research, Stuttgart, Germany, 1968-69; lectr. Tech. U. Stuttgart, 1968-69; pres. Optologics Inc., Seattle, 1973—. Mem. Am. Phys. Soc., Optical Soc. Am., Soc. Photo Optical Instrumentation Engrs. Author: Heat Conduction in Crystals, 1969. Contbr. articles to profl. jours. Research in cryogenics, statis. physics and opto electronics. Home: 11245 12th Ave S Seattle WA 98168 Office: Boeing Aerospace Co PO Box 3999 Seattle WA 98124

ERICKSEN, DONALD ELROY, marriage and family counselor; b. Fresno, Calif., Nov. 8, 1922; s. Laurence A. and Mary A. (May) E.; m. Jo Ann Joy, Apr. 7, 1963; 1 dau., Patricia; stepchildren—Richard, Judith. M.A., Loma Linda U., 1965; M.A., Chapman Coll., 1981. Cert. life elem. and secondary tchr., Calif. Food processor Loma Linda (Calif.) Foods, 1943-48; self-employed salesman, 1948-52; precision honer Ace Bushings, Riverside, Calif., 1955-56; tchr. Newport-Mesa (Calif.) Unified Sch. Dist., 1958-83; marriage, family and child counselor, Orange County, Calif., 1983—; ednl. cons. Newport Mesa Unified Sch. Dist., Family Services Assn., 1986— Vol. community service orgns. Recipient Valley Forge Tchrs. Freedom Found. award, 1972; Newport Mesa Educators Assn. Educators award, 1973-74; named Alumnus of Yr., La Sierra Alumni Assn., Loma Linda U. Sch. Edn., 1984. Mem. Calif. Assn. Marriage and Family Therapists, Newport Mesa PTA (hon. life), Nat. Fedn. of Blind. Republican. Seventh-day Adventist.

ERICKSEN, JACQUELINE HOPE, communications executive; b. Buffalo, July 12, 1942; d. Patrick Harmon and Jane Elizabeth (Dietter) Hill; m. Ronald C. Ericksen, June 8, 1964; 1 child, Christin. BS, U. N.Mex., 1963, MS, 1964, PhD, 1969. Lic. Federal Communications Com. 1st class. V.p. All-Comm Inc., Albuquerque, 1972—. Contbr. articles to profl. jours. Mem. Radio Club of Am. Avocation: writing. Home: Box 666 Placitas NM 87043 Office: All-Comm Inc 301 Wyoming NE Albuquerque NM 87123

ERICKSON, ARTHUR CHARLES, architect; b. Vancouver, B.C., Can., June 14, 1924; s. Oscar and Myrtle (Chatterson) E. Student, U. B.C., Vancouver, 1942-44; B.Arch., McGill U., Montreal, Que., Can., 1950; LL.D. (hon.), Simon Fraser U., Vancouver, 1973, U. Man., Winnipeg, Can., 1978, Lethbridge U., 1981; D.Eng., Novia Scotia Tech. Coll., McGill U., 1971; Litt.D., U. B.C., 1985. Asst. prof. U. Oreg., Eugene, 1955-56; assoc. prof. U. B.C., 1956-63; ptnr. Erickson-Massey Architects, Vancouver, 1963-72; prin. Arthur Erickson Architects, Vancouver and Toronto, 1972—, Los Angeles, 1981—; dir. Campus Planning Assocs., Toronto. Prin. works include Can. Pavilion at Expo '70, Osaka (recipient first prize in nat. competition, Archtl. Inst. of Japan award for best pavilion), Robson Square/The Law Courts (honer award), Mus. of Anthropology (honor award), Eppich Residence (honor award), Habitat Pavilion (honor award), Sikh Temple (award of merit), Champlain Heights Community Sch. (award of merit); contbr. articles to profl. publs. Mem. com. on urban devel. Council of Can., 1971; bd. dirs. Can. Conf. of Arts, 1972; mem. design adv. council Portland Devel. Commn., Can. Council Urban Research; trustee Inst. Research on Pub. Policy. Served to capt. Can. Intelligence Corps, 1945-46. Recipient Molson prize Can. Council for Arts, 1967, Triangle award Nat. Soc. Interior Design, Royal Bank of Can. award, 1971, Gold medal Tau Sigma Delta, 1973, residential design award Can. Housing Council, 1975, August Perret award Internat. Union of Architects' Congress, 1975, Chgo. Architecture award, 1984, Gold medal French Acad. Architecture, 1984, Pres.' award Excellence, Am. Soc. Landscape Architects, 1979; named Officer, Order of Can., 1973, Companion, Order of Can., 1981; McLennan Travelling scholar; Can. Council fellow, 1961. Fellow AIA (hon., Pan Pacific citation Hawaiian chpt. 1963, Gold medal 1986), Royal Archtl. Inst. Can. (recipient award 1980, Gold medal 1984); mem. Archtl. Inst. B.C., Ont. Assn. Architects, Royal Can. Acad. Arts (academician), Am. Soc. Interior Designers, Ordre des Architectes du Quebec, Am. Soc. Planning Officials, Community Planning Assn. Can., Heritage Can., Planning Inst. B.C., Urban Land Inst. Clubs: Vancouver, U. B.C. Faculty, Univ. Several books and articles including Time Mag. cover article and New Yorker Mag. profile written about him. Office: Arthur Erickson Architects Inc, 80 Bloor St W, 16th Floor, Toronto, ON Canada M5S 2V1 Office: 2412 Laurel St, Vancouver, BC Canada V5Z 3T2 Office: 125 N Robertson Los Angeles CA 90048

ERICKSON, CAROL ANN, psychotherapist; b. Worcester, Mass., Dec. 26, 1933; d. Milton Hyland and Helen (Hutton) E.; m. Jean LaRue Barnes, Mar. 20, 1952 (div. Sept. 1962); children: Stephanie Free, Suzanne Hackett, Paul, Sandra Smith, Larry, Cynthia Baker. BS, Ariz. State U., 1964; MSW, Calif. State U., Fresno, 1977. Social worker Los Angeles County, 1964-83; pvt. practice psychotherapy Berkeley, Calif., 1977—; exec. dir. Erickson Inst., Berkeley, 1981—; adj. faculty U. Calif., Berkeley; adj. faculty Vermont Coll. San Francisco, 1986—. Co-writer, composer Deep Self Appreciation, 1983, Self-Hypnosis, A Relaxing Time Out, 1984, Natural Self Confidence, 1985. Bd. dirs. YWCA, Torrance, Calif., 1981-83. Mem. Internat. Soc. Hypnosis, No. Calif. Soc. Clin. Hypnosis, So. Calif. Soc. Clin. Hypnosis, Calif. Assn. Marriage and Family Therapists (cert.), Soc. Clin. and Exptl. Hypnosis, Soc. Clin. Social Workers, Nat. Assn. Social Workers (cert.), AAUW, NOW. Democrat. Avocations: writing, music, reading, camping. Office: Erickson Inst PO Box 739 Berkeley CA 94701

ERICKSON, DON, mayor Cheyenne (Wyoming); b. Chgo., Jan. 15, 1937; s. Lyden L. and Irene E. (Reich) E.; B.S., U. Ill., 1960, M.Ed., 1969; M.P.H., U. N.C., 1965; m. Jacqueline S. Jones; children—Cori Kerstin, Carie Lynn, Darryl Scott, Darren Thomas, Caryn Marie. Dir. health edn. and community services Wyo. Dept. Public Health, Cheyenne, until 1967; dir. ednl. devel. Mountain States Regional Med. Program, Cheyenne, 1967-73, Wyo. dir., 1973-76; mayor City of Cheyenne, 1977—; chmn. subcom. for arts U.S. Conf. Mayors; mem. human resources steering com., mem. fin. and goals com. Nat. League Cities; chmn. Cheyenne Area Devel. Com., 1979—; chmn. policy com. Cheyenne Area Transp. Planning Process. Former mem. Model Cities Bd., Wyo. Gov.'s Hwy. Safety Council, Spl. Sch. Dist. Adv. Com. on Policy Revisions; past pres. Wyo. Heart Assn. Mem. Wyo. Assn. Municipalities. Roman Catholic. Office: 2101 O'Neil Ave Cheyenne WY 82001

ERICKSON, ERICK KENNETH, academic administrator; b. Eureka, Calif., Feb. 26, 1923; s. Erick Werner and Hilda Carolina (Sandberg) E.; m. Charlotte Mae Helmick, Feb. 20, 1949; children: Erick Jr., Craig, Mary, Jan, Kim, Nancy. BS, U. Calif., Berkeley, 1947, MBA, 1949. Asst. acctg. officer U. Calif., Berkeley, 1947-62; acctg. officer U. Calif., San Francisco, 1962-63, asst. to chancellor, 1963-66, vice-chancellor bus. and fin. services, 1966—. Served with U.S. Army, 1942-46, ETO; lt. col. res. 1946-67. Mem. Western Assn. Coll. and Univ. Bus. Officers, Nat. Assn. Coll. and Univ. Bus. Officers. Democrat. Lutheran. Home: 1054 Hacienda Dr Walnut Creek CA 94598 Office: U Calif 145 Irving St San Francisco CA 94143

ERICKSON, JAMES DELOY, mechanical design engineer; b. Ogden, Utah, Jan. 6, 1951; s. Edward Clyde and Ruby (Bate) E.; m. Deborah Carol Dixon, Mar. 16, 1973; children: Summer, Charity, James, Russell, Isaac, Blake, Daniel. BS in Applied Physics, Weber State Coll., 1976; ME, U. Utah, 1976-78. Structural design engr. John Deere Harvester Works, Moline, Ill., 1978-83; assoc. scientist composite structures Morton Thiokol, Inc., Brigham City, Utah, 1983-86, supr. strategic composite structures, 1986—. Mem. Soc. Automotive Engrs. (mem. chmn. gov. bd. 1982-83). Mormon. Clubs: Toastmasters (Moline), John Deere (pres. 1981-82). Avocations: model rocketry, hunting, fishing. Home: 3050 N 175W Ogden UT 84404 Office: Morton Thiokol Inc PO Box 524 Brigham City UT 84302

ERICKSON, LENNART GODTFRID, industrial biochemical engineer, energy producing company executive; b. San Francisco, Mar. 8, 1914; s. Oscar Leonard and Naeoni Dorothea (Andersen) E.; m. Charlotte Rudolph, Apr. 24, 1937; 1 child, William Scott. Student U. Calif. Extension, 1932-35. Co-founder, pres., chmn. Lenkurt Electric Co., San Carlos, Calif., 1944-60; founder, pres. Willen Corp., San Mateo, Calif., 1955—; co-founder, pres. Waste=Energy Corp., San Mateo, 1982—. Patentee in communications electronics, irrigation, water mgmt. and conversion of wastes to energy. Trustee Cogswell Poly. Coll., San Francisco, 1975—, Med. Research Inst. San Francisco, 1978—. Mem. IEEE (life), Water Pollution Control Fedn. Republican. Office: Waste=Energy Corp 100 S Ellsworth Ave Suite 807 San Mateo CA 94401

ERICKSON, MICHAEL SIDNEY, controller; b. Walla Walla, Wash., Aug. 11, 1943; s. Dale Glen and Veryl LaVerne (Tucker) E.; m. Lidwina Myong Cha, Dec. 26, 1966; children: Sidney Warren, Tonya Myong. MS in Taxation, Gonzaga U., 1982. CPA, cert. fin. planner. Acct. Arick and Elliott CPA's, Spokane, Wash., 1968-70; controller Brent Homes West Inc., Spokane, 1970-72, E Z Loader Boat Trailer, Spokane, 1972—; trustee E Z Loader Profit Sharing, 1976—; bd. dirs. Spokane Fed. Credit Union, 1986—. Served with U.S. Army, 1964-67. Mem. Am. Inst. CPA's, Wash. State Inst. CPA's. Lodge: Kiwanis (Spokane chpt. pres. 1978). Office: E Z Loader Boat Trailer Inc PO Box 3263 TA Spokane WA 99220-3263

ERICKSON, ROY DENMAN, artist, interior designer, corp. exec.; b. Lincoln, Nebr., Dec. 24, 1922; s. Edwin Emmanual and Hildur (Helstrom) E.; student U. Nebr., 1940-41, Pomona Coll., 1941-42, Art Center Sch., 1942, Chouinard Art Inst., 1945-47; m. Sammye Jean Williams, Nov. 1, 1946; children—Eric Edwin, Bradford Alan. Prof. art U. Wis., 1947-49; art educator Chouinard Art Inst., Los Angeles, 1949-57; prin. Eric Hand Prints, El Segundo, Calif., 1947-60; dir. contract sales and design Sagar Assos., Los Angeles, 1960-63; pres. Erickson Assos. Inc., Alhambra, Calif., 1963—; cons. on design projects. active Luth. Ch. Served as pilot USNR, 1942-46. Decorated Air medal with four oak leaf clusters, D.F.C. with oak leaf cluster; recipient Gold Nugget award for best office, 1979. Mem. Am. Soc. Interior Designers (award 1976), Soc. Calligraphers, Am. Inst. Designers. Club: Chess. Works include Mary Kay Cosmetics office tower, Dallas, 1977, Chiat/Day Offices, San Francisco, N.Y.C., 1986, Bozell, Jacobs, Kenyon and Echardt, Westwood, Calif., 1986; major hotels, Guatemala, 1976, P.R., 1979, N.Y.C., 1976, Boca Raton, Fla., 1980, Inn on the Beach, Long Boat Key, Fla., Tampa (Fla.) Airport Hilton, Grand Butte Hotel, Crested Butte, Colo., 1986; contbr. articles to profl. publs. Home: 328 Bellefontaine Pasadena CA 91105 Office: 1112 S Garfield Alhambra CA 91801

ERICKSON, VIRGINIA BEMMELS, chemical engineer; b. Sleepy Eye, Minn., June 19, 1948; d. Gordon Boothe and Marion Mae (Rieke) Bemmels; m. Larry Douglas Erickson, Sept. 6, 1969; children: Kirsten Danielle, Dean Michael. Diploma in Nursing, Swedish Hosp. Sch. Nursing, 1969; BSChemE, U. Wash., 1983, MChemE, 1985. RN. Asst. head nurse N. Meml. Hosp., Mpls., 1970-73; intensive care RN Swedish Med. Ctr., Seattle, 1973-83; research asst. U. Wash., Seattle, 1983-85; instrumentation and control chem. engr. CH2M Hill, Bellevue, Wash., 1985—; cons. instrumentation and control engr. Leader Girl Scouts U.S., Seattle, 1985; supt. Seattle Ch. Sch., 1983; rep. United Way, 1986—. Recipient Cert. Achievement, Soc. Women Engrs., 1983. Mem. Am. Inst. Chem. Engrs., Instrument Soc. Am., Tau Beta Pi. Democrat. Mem. United Methodist Ch. Avocations: running, soccer, music, cooking. Home: 6026 24th NE Seattle WA 98115 Office: CH2M Hill 777 108th Ave NE PO Box 91500 Bellevue WA 98009-2050

ERICKSON, WILLIAM HURT, judge; b. Denver, May 11, 1924; s. Arthur Xavier and Virginia (Hurt) E.; m. Doris Rogers, Dec. 24, 1953; children: Barbara Ann, Virginia Lee, Stephen Arthur, William Taylor. Petroleum Engr., Colo. Sch. Mines., 1947; postgrad., U. Mich., 1949; LL.B., U. Va., 1950. Bar: Colo. 1951. Practiced law Denver; justice Colo. Supreme Ct., 1971—, chief justice, 1983-85; faculty NYU Appellate Judges Sch., 1972-85; mem. exec. com. Commn. on Accreditation of Law Enforcement Agys., 1980-83. Served with USAAF, 1943. Recipient award of merit Colo. Com. Continuing Legal Edn., 1968. Fellow Internat. Acad. Trial Lawyers (former sec.), Am. Coll. Trial Lawyers, Am. Bar Found. (chmn. 1985), Internat. Soc. Barristers (past pres.); mem. Am. Law Inst. (council), Practising Law Inst. (nat. adv. council, bd. govs. Colo. chpt.), Denver Bar Assn. (past pres., trustee), ABA (bd. govs. 1975-79, former chmn. com. on standards criminal justice, former chmn. council criminal law sect., former chmn. com. to implement standards criminal justice, mem. long-range planning com., action com. to reduce ct. costs and delay), Am. Bar Found. (chmn. 1985-86), Freedoms Found. at Valley Forge (nat. council trustees, 1986—), Order of Coif, Scribes (pres. 1978). Home: 10 Martin Ln Englewood CO 80110 Office: State Judicial Bldg 2 E 14th Ave Denver CO 80203

ERIKSON, GLENN ROBERT, real estate developer, architect; b. Indpls., Feb. 12, 1951; s. Erik Gunnar and Mabel Elizabeth (Anderson) E.; m. Lorie Lloyd, Aug. 30, 1977; 1 child, Annika, Sören. BArch, U. Ariz., 1974, MS in Fin., 1981. Registered architect, Calif.; cert. real estate broker, Calif., community coll. tchr., Calif. Prin. Erikson Design Group, Tucson, San Diego, Los Angeles, 1975-85; project designer, mgr. Deems/Lewis & Ptnr.s, San Diego, 1977-80; v.p. devel. Subbiondo & Assocs., Fountain Valley, Calif., 1981-82; v.p. Ctr. Fin. Group, Century City, Calif., 1982-85; gen. ptnr., exec. v.p. Los Angeles Land Co., 1985—; gen. ptnr. and exec. v.p. Los Angeles Land Co., 1985—; seminar tchr. UCLA, U. Calif., San Diego, Santa Barbara, 1982-85. Prin. works include NCR Office Bldg., San Diego, 1978, Orangegate Plaza, Westminster, Calif., 1980-85, Morton Park Apts., Los Angeles, 1985, Exposition Plaza, Los Angeles, 1985, Sherman Plaza, Los Angeles, 1986, Tustin Ctr. Plaza, Orange, Calif., 1986, 10401 Bldg., Los Angeles, 1986, New York Lake Plaza, Los Angeles, 1986, Marina Fashion Plaza, Long Beach, Calif., 1987, Magnolia Plaza, Westminster, Calif., 1987, Chaparrel Lanes, San Dimas, Calif., 1987. Young Mens Pres. Ch. Jesus Christ of Latter-day Sts., San Diego, 1978, elders quorum pres., La Jolla, Calif., 1979-80; scoutmaster Boy Scouts Am., Van Nuys, Calif., 1986. Mem. AIA, Urban Land Inst., Internat. Council Shopping Ctrs. Republican. Office: Los Angeles Land Co 1554 S Sepulveda Suite 208 Los Angeles CA 90025

ERIQAT, VICTORIA ALDERMAN, small business owner; b. Los Angeles, Mar. 20, 1940; d. James William and Ann (Sieg) Alderman; m. Albert Kareem Eriqat, Apr. 18, 1959; children: David Alan, Cheryl Anne, Joseph Michael, Suzanne Michelle. AA, Mesa Coll., 1977; BS, San Diego State U., 1979, MS, 1983. Corp. sec./treas. AKE Profl. Engrs., San Diego, 1971, also bd. dirs.; owner, operator Eriqat Enterprises, San Diego, 1971—. Bd. dirs., area chmn. San Diego council Girl Scouts U.S., 1970—; vol. cons. Small Bus. Adminstrn. San Diego, 1978-79. Merit scholar U. San Diego Sch. Law, 1984. Mem. ABA, Inst. Cert. Fin. Planners, San Diego Bd. Realtors, Phi Kappa Phi, Beta Gamma Sigma. Avocations: piano, accordion, windsurfing, skating, bodybuilding. Home: 8264 Caminito Maritimo La Jolla CA 92037 Office: AKE Profl Engrs 4443 30th St San Diego CA 92116

ERLANDSEN, KNUT ERIK, hotel executive; b. Oslo, Jan. 22, 1939; came to U.S., 1966; s. Kaare and Magnhild (Handsen) E.; m. Aasta Steen-Nielsen, Aug. 10, 1964; children: Espen, An-Margrith. BA in Bus., Wang Bus. Sch., Oslo, 1962; BA, Katedral Skolen, Oslo, 1961; cert. hotel mgmt., Lausanne (Switzerland) Hotel Sch., 1965. Mgr. Tides Inn Hotel, Petersburg, Alaska, 1966; dir. catering The Olympic Hotel, Seattle, 1967-74; dir. food and beverages The Westin Crown Ctr., Kansas City, Mo., 1974-77; asst. dir. food and beverages Westin Hotels & Resorts, Seattle, 1977-82, mgr. food and beverage devel., 1982—. Served to lt. Med. Corps Norwegian Army, 1958-59. Recipient The Golden Ivy, Instn. Mag., 1977, Most Valuable Promotion, Pepsi Cola Co., 1977. Mem. Food Service Cons. Internat., Nat. Restaurant Assn., Ancien Eleve de L'Ecole Hotel. Avocations: skiing, sailing, chinese calligraphy. Office: Westin Hotels & Resorts 2001 Sixth Ave Seattle WA 98121

ERNST, RICHARD DALE, chemistry educator; b. Long Beach, Calif., Oct. 23, 1951; s. Erwin Harry and Martha Miriam (Jircik) E.; m. Chariya Asawaroengchai, Aug. 11, 1973; children: Kenneth, Christopher, Anjulee. BS, U. Calif., Berkeley, 1973; PhD, Northwestern U., 1977. Asst. prof. chemistry U. Utah, Salt Lake City, 1977-84, assoc. prof., 1984-87, prof., 1987—; cons. Phillips Petroleum Co., Bartlesville, Okla., 1979—. Mem. AAAS, Am. Chem. Soc. Roman Catholic. Home: 3238 Oakcliff Dr Salt Lake City UT 84124 Office: U Utah Dept Chemistry Salt Lake City UT 84112

EROKAN, DENNIS WILLIAM, magazine publisher; b. Istanbul, Turkey, Aug. 20, 1950; came to U.S., 1955; s. Don H. and Athena (Caragianis) E.; m. Lori Engelfried, Dec. 18, 1976; children: Lane Katharine, Darcy Beth, William Bruce. Grad. high sch., San Jose, Calif., 1968. Bassist Green Catherine band, San Francisco and N.Y.C., 1968-74; mgr. Peter's Plum Restaurant, Boston, 1974-75; nat. sales mgr. Dean Markley Strings, Santa Clara, Calif., 1975; chief exec. officer Bam Publs., Oakland and Los Angeles, Calif., 1976—; Exec. producer, founder Bay Area Music awards, San Francisco, 1978-; pres., founder Bay Area Music Archives, San Francisco, 1979—; concert producer, Hollywood, 1983, San Francisco, 1978-83. Editor, publisher (mag.) The Mix, 1977-78, BAM, 1976— (Maggie award 1984, 86), MicroTimes, 1984—; exec. producer (TV show) The 1981 Bammies, 1981, A San Fransisco Celebration, 1986; contbr. articles to mags. Auctioneer KQED Fundraiser, San Francisco, 1978—. Mem. Nat. Acad. Songwriters (bd. dirs. 1983—), Freedom Found. (bd. dirs. 1980-83). Episcopalian. Avocations: musician, archivist, public speaking. Office: BAM Mag/BAM Rock & Video The BAM Network 5941 Canning St Oakland CA 94609

ERSKINE, JANICE MARIE, psychologist, educator; b. San Antonio, Feb. 11, 1935; d. John Elmer and Elizabeth Florence (Lanier) E.; m. Andrew James Karoly, Aug. 22, 1966 (div.). B.A., Baylor U., 1956, M.A., 1957; Ph.D., U. Mich., 1963. Research scientist Am. Inst. Research, Pitts., 1962-65; asst. prof. Humboldt State U., Arcata, Calif., 1965-71, assoc. prof. psychology, 1971-76, prof., 1976—, chmn. div. of interdisciplinary studies and spl. programs, 1976-80; assoc. acad. planning div. edn. programs and resources. Office of Chancellor, Calif. State U., 1981—, mem. acad. senate, 1975-80; cons. Environ. Cons., Arcata, 1972-76; Trustee Mattole Ctr. for Sci. and Edn. 1980-82; mem. Citizens Adv. Comm. for Humboldt Bay Harbor and Recreation Dist., 1975-77; mem. state planning com. Nat. Identification Program, Am. Council Edn., 1980—. USPHS trainee U. Mich., 1958-60; NSF fellow, 1970, 71-72; administrv. fellow Calif. State U. and Colls., 1980-81. Mem. Am. Psychol. Assn., Western Psychol. Assn., Congress of Faculty Assns. (state del. 1974-76), Am. Primatological Soc., Internat. Primatological Soc. Democrat. Home: 7842 Northlake Apt 123 Huntington Beach CA 92647 Office: Ednl Programs and Resources 400 Golden Shore Long Beach CA 90802

ERVIN, PATRICK FRANKLIN, nuclear engineer; b. Kansas City, Kans., Aug. 4, 1946; s. James Franklin and Irma Lee (Arnett) E.; m. Rita Jeanne Kimsey, Aug. 12, 1967; children: James, Kevin, Amber. BS in Nuclear

Engring., Kans. State U., 1969, MS in Nuclear Engring., 1971. Registered profl. engr., Ill., Colo. Reactor health physicist Kans. State U. Dept. Nuclear Engring., Manhattan, 1968-69, research asst., 1969-72, sr. reactor operator, temp. facility dir., 1970-72; system test engr. Commonwealth Edison Co., Zion, Ill., 1972-73, 73-74, shift foreman, 1973, shift foreman with sr. reactor operator lic., 1974-76, prin. engr., 1976-77, acting operating engr., 1977; tech. staff supr. Commonwealth Edison Co., Byron, Ill., 1977-81; lead test engr. Stone & Webster Engring. Corp., Denver, 1982-83, project mgr., 1982—, ops. services supr., 1982-86, asst. engring. mgr., 1986—. Contbr. articles to profl. jours. Served with U.S. Army N.G., 1971-77. Mem. Am. Nuclear Soc. (Nat. and Colo. chpts.), Am. Nat. Standards Inst. (working group on containment leakage testing). Republican. Roman Catholic. Avocations: hunting, fishing, camping, coin and stamp collecting, woodworking. Home: 2978 S Bahama St Aurora CO 80013 Office: Stone & Webster Engring Corp PO Box 5406 Denver CO 80217

ERWIN, JENNY LIND, education specialist, consultant; b. Maryville, Tenn., Sept. 10, 1946; d. Roland Edward and Virginia Verle (Vassey) Jett; m. William Shafer Erwin, Jr., May 25, 1968 (div.); 1 son: Douglas Roland; m. Robert V. Atkinson, Dec. 29, 1983. B.S. in Edn., Maryville Coll., 1968; M.A. with honors in Counseling, No. Ariz. U., 1977. Cert. elem. tchr., counselor and adminstr., Ariz. Tchr., Prestonia Elem. Sch., Louisville, 1968-70, Green Valley Sch., New Albany, Ind., 1970-72; owner, mgr. Flagstaff Newcomer Service (Ariz.), 1972-74; career co-ordinator Flagstaff Pub. Schs., 1972-80; project supr. Coconino County Ednl. Services, Flagstaff, 1980-81; specialist Ariz. Ctr. Vocat. Edn., Dept. Edn., Phoenix, 1981—; cons. in field. Co-dir. Camp Viola, La Grange, Ga., summer 1968; bd. dirs. Flagstaff Library, 1976-78, Big Sisters No. Ariz., 1978-81; bd. advs. Women's Shelter, 1980-81. Ariz. Dept. Edn. grantee, 1979-80. Mem. Ariz. Career Devel. Assn., Ariz. Women's Town Hall, Ariz. Guidance Assn. (pres. 1979-80), Ariz. Vocat. Assn., Am. Vocat. Assn., Vocat. Edn. Equity Council. Democrat. Methodist. Club: Toastmasters Internat. Capitol (membership award, service award 1982). Lodge: Soroptimists. Editor, publisher Connections, 1981—; author ednl. handbooks and slide tapes. Office: Ariz Ctr Vocat Edn Ariz Dept Edn 1535 W Jefferson Ave Phoenix AZ 85007

ERWTEMAN, LION SAMUEL, minister; b. Eindhoven, Noordbrabant, The Netherlands, June 30, 1949; came to U.S., 1980; s. Jacob and Esther (Segal) E.; m. Elze Elisabeth Anneke Ooms, Dec. 28, 1972; children: Rachel Mirjam, Abel David, Lydia Marta. BA in Biology, U. Amsterdam, The Netherlands, 1973, MS, 1978; MDiv., Fuller Theol. Sem., 1984. Ordained to ministry Conservative Congl. Christian Conf., 1985. Tchr. biology and gen. scis. 1977-80; sem. intern Pasadena (Calif.) Alliance Ch., 1981-82; staff missionary Jews for Jesus, Studio City, Calif., 1983; chaplain Union Rescue Mission, Los Angeles, 1983—, guest ministry supr., 1985-86; program dir. Overcomers Drug and Alcohol program, Pasadena, 1986—, Social Model Detoxification program, Pasadena, 1986—. Grantee Fuller Theol. Sem., 1981-83. Avocations: playing viola, piano and guitar. Home: 2196 E Villa St Pasadena CA 91107 Office: Union Rescue Mission 226 S Main St Los Angeles CA 90012

ERXLEBEN, WILLIAM CHARLES, lawyer; b. Chgo., Dec. 18, 1942; s. Walter Oscar and Sarah Louise (Githens) E.; m. Gayle Amelia Reichmuth, Aug. 28, 1965; children: David William, Jennifer Renée. BS in Bus., Miami U., Oxford, Ohio, 1963; JD, Stanford U., 1966. Bar: Wash. 1969. Asst. state atty. gen. Wash. State Atty. Gen.'s Office, Olympia, 1968-70; asst. U.S. atty. Dept. Justice, Seattle, 1970-72; regional dir. FTC, Seattle, 1972-79; lectr. Grad. Sch. Bus., U. Wash., Seattle, 1979-85; ptnr. Foster, Pepper & Riviera, Bellevue, Wash., 1985—; chmn., dir. Advanced Digital Tech., Bellevue, Wash., 1983-85; dir. Data I/O Corp., Redmond, Wash., 1979—; cons. bus., law, 1979-84. Contbr. articles to law revs. Mem. resource exec. com. Wash. Assn. for Children and Adults with Learning Disabilities, Seattle, 1982-86; chmn. Portwatch, Seattle, 1985; mem. advt. rev. com. Better Bus. Bur., Seattle, 1982-85; bd. dirs. Wash. Citizens for Recycling, Seattle, 1980-84. Served with USAF, 1966-68. Recipient Excellence in Supervision award FTC, 1975, Disting. Service award, 1979; Sloan exec. fellow Stanford U. Grad. Sch. Bus., 1975-76. Mem. Wash. State Bar Assn. (sec.-treas. antitrust subcom. 1981-83), Acad. Mgmt. Democrat. Home: 4531 143d Ave SE Bellevue WA 98006 Office: Foster Pepper & Riviera 777 108th Ave NE 15 Floor Rainier Bank Plaza Bellevue WA 98004

ESCALANTE, ROEL, material management executive; b. Los Angeles, July 16, 1937; s. Angel and Maria (Arellanos) E.; m. Myrna L. Walterscheid, May 3, 1985; 1 son, Anthony Miles. AA, Valley Jr. Coll., 1959. Asst. purchasing agt. Colony Paint & Chem. Co., Los Angeles, 1964-67; buyer Traid Corp., Los Angeles, 1967-69; asst. purchasing mgr. Walt Disney Prodns., Burbank, Calif., 1969-76; dir. purchasing MCA, Inc., Universal City, Calif., 1976-79, corp. dir. material, div. v.p., 1979—. Mem. Los Aneles Purchasing Mgmt. Assn., Am. Mgmt. Assn., Nat. Assn. Purchasing Mgmt. (cert.), So. Calif. Regional Purchasing Council (bd. dirs.). Republican. Roman Catholic. Home: PO Box 8836 Universal City CA 91608 Office: MCA Inc 100 Universal City Plaza Universal City CA 91608

ESCOFFIER, JEFFREY PAUL, editor, educator; b. Balt., Oct. 9, 1942; s. George Escoffier and Dorothy Iris (Miller) Wendel. BA, St. John's Coll., Annapolis, Md., 1964; M in Internat. Affairs, Columbia U., 1966; postgrad., U. Pa., 1986—. Research assoc. N.Y. Med. Coll., N.Y.C., 1967-72; research librarian Population Studies Ctr., Pa., 1972-77; instr. San. Francisco State U., 1978-80; vis. lectr. U. Calif., Berkeley, 1983-84, 86; exec. editor Socialist Rev., Berkeley, 1980—; founder, editor Gay Alternative Mag., Phila., 1972-75. Contbr. articles to profl. jours. Pres. Gay Activists Alliance Phila., 1971-72; co-founder, mem. San Francisco Lesbian and Gay History Project, 1978—. Office: Socialist Review 3202 Adeline St Berkeley CA 94703

ESGUERRA, LARRY SABARILLO, IV, banker; b. Manila, Phillippines, May 7, 1949, came to U.S., 1979; s. Hilario Gonzales Esguerra and Josefina (Soriano) Sabarillo. B.S. in Bus. Adminstrn., U. Philippines, Quezon, City, 1969. C.P.A., Philippines. Sr. auditor J.L. Maranan & Assocs., Manila, 1969-71; resident auditor CitiBank, N.A., 1971-75; pvt. practice acctg., Manila, 1970-79; fin. officer JRK Devel. Corp., Metro Manila, 1975-84; asst. v.p. Associated Citizens Bank Manila, 1976-79; v.p., cashier, comptroller Pacific Union Bank & Trust Co., Menlo Park, Calif., 1979-84; v.p. fin. Golden Bay Fed. Credit Union, Moffett Field, Calif., 1984—; bd. dirs. Corp. Resource Cons., Manila, 1977-79; lectr. Ateneo Grad. Sch. Bus., Makati, Philippines, 1978. Co-author: Commercial Banking Operations in the Philippines, 1979. Mem. Inst. Internal Auditors, Nat. Assn. Accts., Am. Mgmt. Assns., Philippine Inst. C.P.A.s, Asian Tax Assn. Roman Catholic. Office: Golden Bay Credit Union PO Box 127 NAS Moffett Field CA 94035

ESHAGIAN, JOSEPH, ophthalmologist; b. Iran, Mar. 15, 1951; s. Ebrahim and Touran (Monasebian) E.; B.S. with honors, U. Mich., 1971; M.D., SUNY, Syracuse, 1975. Intern, U. Mich. Hosp., Ann Arbor, 1975-76; resident in ophthalmology U. Iowa Hosp., Iowa City, 1976-79, assoc. dept. ophthalmology, 1979; practice medicine specializing in ophthalmology, Los Angeles, 1980—. Diplomate Am. Bd. Ophthalmology and Otolaryngology. Mem. Am. Acad. Neurology, Assn. Research in Vision and Ophthalmology, Nat. Assn. Residents and Interns, Iowa Med. Soc., Am. Assn. Ophthalmology, Contact Lens Assn. Ophthalmologists, Med. Eye Services Calif., Am. Acad. Ophthalmology, AMA, Calif. Med. Assn., Los Angeles County Med. Assn., Am. Soc. Contemporary Ophthalmology, Internat. Glaucoma Congress. Contbr. articles to med. jours. Office: 1200 N Vermont Ave Los Angeles CA 90029

ESPE, DWIGHT EARLE, marketing consultant; b. Los Angeles, Oct. 22, 1944; s. Robert Ervin and Lenore Mae (Klawiter) E.; m. Gayle Elizabeth Hunter Aug. 20, 1967 (div. 1976); m. Dorothy Juanita Burleigh, Oct. 12, 1980; children: Matthew Burleigh, Melanie Autumn, Jonathan Michael. AA, Pasadena City Coll., 1964; student, U. Colo, 1966, U. So. Calif., 1967, UCLA, 1968. Pres. Dwight Espe and Assocs., Los Angeles, 1968-71; v.p. Mktg. Assn. Services, Los Angeles, 1971-74; account exec. N.W. Ayer, Los Angeles, 1975-76; v.p. Group X, Rolling Hills Estates, Calif., 1977-80; pres. Espe & Assocs., Breckenridge, Colo., 1981—; founder Tipsy Taxi, Inc., 1987. Contbr. articles on mktg., advertising, resource conservation to profl. jours. 1st v.p. campaign Summit County United Way, Breckenridge, 1984—; treas. Summit County Alcohol and Drug Task Force, Breckenridge, 1982-85, co-founder 1982; bd. dirs. Breckenridge Music Inst., 1984—. Named one of Top 25 Mktg. Strategists, Advt. Age mag., Chgo., 1976; recipient Award of Excellence, Photography West, Los Angeles, 1969. Republican. Roman Catholic. Lodges: Rotary, Kiwanis, KC. Avocations: photography, skiing, tennis, sailing, camping. Office: Espe & Assocs PO Box 8118 Breckenridge CO 80424

ESPINOSA, SAMUEL, occupational safety health professional; b. Matanzas, Cuba, Dec. 5, 1930; came to U.S., 1953; s. Antonio and Blanca (Arencibia) E.; m. Eva Esther Hernandez, Sept. 4, 1953; children: Victor Samuel, David Samuel. BA, Columbia Union Coll., Takoma Park, Md., 1961; MA, Loma Linda U., 1966; MS, U. Tenn., 1974, EdD, 1978. Registered profl. safety engr., Calif. Dir. safety dept. Loma Linda U., Riverside, Calif., 1968-76; safety engr. Teledyne, Redlands, Calif., 1979-80, Kwikset, Anaheim, Calif., 1980-81; safety, security mgr. Western Wheel Corp., La Mirada, Calif., 1981—. Author: (manual) Occupational Safety Health Manual, 1974, (handbook) Supervisors Safety Handbook, 1983, 86, Emergency Handbook, 1985. Instr. Rehab. Ctr. for Drug Addicts, Norco, Calif. 1972-73; coach La Sierra Little League and Pony League, Riverside, 1978-82; instr. ARC, Riverside, 1979—; vice chmn. Environ. Protections Com., Riverside, 1980-84. Recipient Cert. Merit NSC, 1973, Merit award NSC, 1974, Honor award NSC, 1975. Mem. Acad. Accreditation Team Teachers, San. Diego Zool. Soc., Campus Safety Assn., Am. Soc. Safety Engrs. Avocations: tennis, photography. Home: 11262 Gramercy Pl Riverside CA 92503 Office: Western Wheel Corp 14500 Firestone Blvd La Mirada CA 90638

ESPINOZA, ARMIDA MARIE, human resources executive; b. Los Angeles, Feb. 27; d. Francisco and Francisca (Robles) E. AA, East Los Angeles Coll., 1965; BA, Calif. State U., Los Angeles, 1971. Asst. dist. customer service mgr. Montgomery Ward Stores, Rosemead, Calif., 1963-71; tng. coordinator Singer Co., Parmount, Calif., 1971-73; personnel mgr. Carter Hawley Hale Stores, Los Angeles, 1973-79; personnel dir. May Dept. Stores, Los Angeles, 1979-80; regional dir. human resources Westinghouse Broadcasting Co., Encino, Calif., 1980-84, Dorotronics, San Gabriel, Calif., 1984—; cons. Career Recruitment in Telecommunications Industries Inc., 1980-86; hon. lectr. Calif. Assn. Latinos in Broadcasting, 1980-83. Mem. West San Gabriel Valley Mayor's Com. for Employment of Handicapped, 1980-83, budget com. Los Angeles Bd. Edn. Bus., United Way, Congl. Hispanic Caucus, mem. panel on edn. Nat. Council of La Raza, 1980-84. Mem. Acad. Mgmt., Am. Compensation Assn., Am. Soc. Personnel Administrn., Am. Soc. Tng. and Devel., Personnel Indsl. Relations Assn., Personnel Women Am., Am. Women in Radio and TV, Am. Film Inst. (assoc.), Found. Community Service Cable TV, Minorities in Telecommunications, Hispanic Women's Council, Latin Small Bus. Assn., Nat. Hispanic Council for High Tech Careers. Avocations: tennis, oil painting, creative writing, music. Home: 9913 Candia Cr Whittier CA 90603 Office: Dorotronic Data Systems and Equipment Inc 260 W Ralph St San Gabriel CA 91776

ESPLIN, FREDERICK CHARLES, public TV manager; b. Cedar City, Utah, Apr. 16, 1947; s. Charles Cutler and Leah (Crofts) E.; m. Martha Dickey, Nov. 29, 1972; children: Eric, Jason, Grant, Erin. BA, So. Utah State Coll., 1971; MA, U. Utah, 1974. Writer Pub. Broadcasting Service, Washington, 1973-75; dir. devel. and pub. relations Pa. Pub. TV Network, Hershey, 1975-78; dir. devel. and planning Sta. WITF-TV FM, Hershey, 1978-79; dir. mktg. Sta. KUED-TV, Salt Lake City, 1979-81, gen. mgr., 1981—; bd. dirs. Pacific Mountain Network, Denver, 1981—; cons. Carnegie Com. on The Future of Pub. Broadcasting, 1978. Editor: Forum, 1985—; mem. editorial bd. Pub. Telecommunications Rev., 1974-80. Mem. Utah Hist. Soc., Sigma Delta Chi. Lodge: Kiwanis. Home: 2839 Glenmare St Salt Lake City UT 84106 Office: Sta KUED U Utah 101 Gardner Hall Salt Lake City UT 84112

ESPOSITO, LARRY WAYNE, planetary astronomer; b. Schenectady, N.Y., Apr. 15, 1951; s. Albert and Beverly Jane (DeLaMater) E.; m. Diane Marie McKnight, July 24, 1975; children: Rhea, Ariel. BS in Math., MIT, 1973; PhD in Astronomy, U. Mass., 1977. Research assoc. Lab. Atmospheric and Space Physics U. Colo., Boulder, 1977—, lectr., 1979-84, assoc. prof. dept. astrophys., planetary and atmospheric scis., 1984—; investigator Pioneer Venus, Pioneer Saturn, Voyager, Galileo, Mars Observer, USSR Phobos spacecraft missions, 1977—; mem. NASA Planetary Atmospheres Mgmt. Ops. Working Group, 1981-84, Nat. Acad. Scis. Space Sci. Bd. com. on planetary and lunar exploration, 1982-86; dep. chmn. Nat. Acad. Scis. Space Sci. Bd. task group on planetary exploration, 1984-86. Contbr. articles to sci. publs. Recipient Exceptional Sci. Achievement medal NASA, 1986. Mem. Am. Astron. Soc. (div. planetary scis. com. 1983-86, H.C. Urey prize 1985), Internat. Astron. Union, Am. Geophys. Union, Internat. Council Sci. Unions (exec. mem. com. space research). Methodist. Club: Boulder Go. Office: U Colo Lab Atmosphere Space Physics Boulder CO 80309-0392

ESSA, LISA BETH, educator; b. Modesto, Calif., Nov. 19, 1955; d. Mark Newyia and Elizabeth (Warda) Essa. B.A., U. Pacific-Stockton, 1977, M.A. in Curriculum and Instrn. Reading, 1980. Cert. tchr. elem., multiple subject and reading specialist, Calif. Tchr. primary grades Delhi (Calif.) Elem. Sch. Dist., 1978-80; reading clinic tutor San Joaquin Delta Community Coll., Stockton, Calif., 1980; tchr. primary grades Hayward (Calif.) Unified Sch. Dist., Supr., San Francisco host com. Dem. Nat. Conv., 1984. Femmes Club scholar, 1973; U. Calif. Optometry Alumni Assn. scholar, 1973; Jobs Daughters scholar, 1974. Mem. Internat. Reading Assn., Calif. Tchrs. Assn., Hayward Unified Tchrs. Assn., San Francisco Jr. C. of C. Democrat. Episcopalian. Home: 1960 Clay Apt 109 San Francisco CA 94109

ESSEX, HARRY, writer; b. N.Y.C., Nov. 29, 1915; s. Wolfe Wilhelm and Sarah (Bratter) E.; m. Lee Berman, June 22, 1945; children—David, Sarah Madlene. B.B.A., St. Johns U., 1936. Writer Columbia Studio, 1945-48, RKO, 1949-51, Universal, 1951-56, MGM, 1960-62, United Artists, 1962-68; script writer, story editor Warner Bros. Writer, NBC Movie of Week, 1974—, including Hostage Flight, 1987; scenarist: films The Lonely Man, 1956, Man and Boy, 1973, The Amigos, 1974, Sons of Katie Elder, 1964, He Walked by Night, 1948, It Came from Outer Space, 1953; playwright: Broadway prodns. Something For Nothing, 1954, Neighborhood Affair, 1960, One for the Dame, 1961, Twilight, 1980; play prodns. Dark Passion, 1970, Fatty, 1985; owner, head writer: Target the Corruptors, 1961-62; author: novels I Put My Right Foot In, 1954, Man and Boy, 1971, Marina, 1981; writer: series TV Untouchables, Playhouse 90. Served with AUS, 1942-44. Recipient Theatre Guild award for playwriting, 1940; recipient Venice Festival award for motion picture He Walked by Night, 1949. Mem. Dramatists League, Writers Guild Am., West Acad. Motion Picture Arts and Scis. Home: 9303 Readcrest Dr Beverly Hills CA 90210

ESSIG, RICHARD NORMAN, manufacturing company executive; b. Sanborn, Minn., May 28, 1933; s. Joseph J. and Marie D. (Pabst) E.; m. Corinne J. Skjervold, Dec. 27, 1951 (div. Dec. 1979); children: Linda J., Michael R.; m. Mary D. Morell, Jan. 5, 1980. Student, Ariz. State U., 1960-64, U. Mass., 1972-74. Maintenance journeyman Interstate Power Co., 1952-60, Ariz. Pub. Service Co., 1960-67; sales engr. MIF Industries, Inc., Branford, Conn., 1967-69; mgr. sales, mktg., engring. Synthetic Products Mfg. Corp., Leominster, Mass., 1969-74; tech. mgr., Can. sales mgr. Reliable Electric Co., Franklin Park, Ill., 1974-78; v.p. Plastigage Corp., Jackson, Mich., 1978-84, Tranpol Internat., Santa Ana, Calif., 1984-85; pres. Globe Research Assocs., San Clemente, Calif., 1985—; mgmt. cons., Calif., 1967—. Patentee insulators, elec. accessories. Recipient Gov.'s award State of Mich., 1983. Mem. IEEE, ASTM, Vt. Elec. Assn., Electric Council New Eng., Nat. Inst., Am. Soc. Mfg. Engrs., Soc. Plastics Engrs., Sales and Mktg. Execs. (pres. 1983-84), Mich. Soc. Profl. Engrs., Am. Nat. Standards Inst., Am. Mgmt. Assn., Am. Mktg. Assn., Nat. Elec. Mfrs. Assn. Office: Globe Research Assocs PO Box 4743 San Clemente CA 92672

ESSINGTON, EDWARD HERBERT, soil scientist, chemist, environmental scientist; b. Santa Barbara, Calif., Feb. 19, 1937; s. Benner Heber and Joanina Catherina (Vercelino) E.; m. Betty Joan Dacus, Sept. 15, 1957; children: Michael Edward, Laura Diane. BS in Soil Sci., Calif. State Poly. U., San Luis Obispo, 1958; MS in Plant Sci., UCLA, 1964. Soil chemist Teledyne Isotopes, Palo Alto, Calif., 1964-72, Los Alamos (N.Mex.) Nat. Lab., 1973—. Contbr. articles to profl. jours. Chmn. supervis. com. Los Alamos Credit Union, 1980. Named Most Valuable Employee, Teledyne Isotopes, 1972. Mem. AAAS, Soil Sci. Soc., Health Physics Soc. Republican. Club: Tennis (Los Alamos) (v.p. 1983-84, pres. 1985). Avocations: auto repair, tennis. Home: 118 Balboa Dr Los Alamos NM 87544 Office: Los Alamos Nat Lab PO Box 1663 MS K495 Los Alamos NM 87544

ESTES, CLARISSA PINKOLA, psychologist, analyst; b. South Bend, Ind., Jan. 27, 1949; d. Josef and Mary (Hornyak) Pinkola; m. Buffalo Kaplinski, May 1, 1967 (div. 1974); 1 child, Tiaja; m. M.R. Estes, Nov. 1, 1975. BA in Psychodymamics with distinction, Loretto Heights Coll., 1976; PhD in Ethno-Clin. Psychology, Union Grad. Sch., Cin., 1981; postdoctoral diploma, Charter of Zurich, 1984. Pvt. practice psychology specializing in therapy and Jungian Analysis Denver, 1974—; prof. lecture series women's depth psychology, 1979, methods of dream analysis, 1979-86, the wild woman of heart, 1983—, archetypes of the underworld, 1986—; co-dir. Women in Transition Safe House program, Denver, 1973-75; exec dir. Beyond Divorce, Denver, 1976-77; dir. tng., exec. dir. C.G. Jung Inst. for Edn. and Research, Denver, 1986—; professional cons. to colls. and univs., nationwide, 1980—. Mem. Inter Regional Soc. Jungian Analysts (diplomate, analyst mem.), Internat. Assn. Analytic Psychology (analyst), Jung Soc. of Denver. Club: Penrose Exec. (Denver).

ESTRIN, FRED MARSHALL, manufacturing company executive; b. Los Angeles, Oct. 7, 1940; s. Joseph and Pauline (Fromsky) E.; m. Mildred W. Estrin, Dec. 15, 1963; children: Paula Rae, David Joseph, Matthew Franklin. Student, Calif. State U., Northridge, 1964. Mem. sales staff NCR Corp., Los Angeles, 1965-70; v.p. sales Pharmacy Computer Billing Inc., Encino, Calif., 1971-72; pres. Am. Indsl. Stationers, Canoga Park, Calif., 1972-76; gen. mgr. NBS Systems Inc., Edwardsville, Ill., 1976-84, Bus. Forms div. Stationers Graphics, Los Angeles, 1984-85; sales mgr. Postal Graphics, Los Angeles, 1985-86; v.p. mktg. services Bank Printing Co., Los Angeles, 1986—. Author: Time and Territory Management, 1980. Mem. Econ. Devel. Commn., 1983, Cable TV Commn., 1983 (both Glen Carbon, Ill.). Mem. Nat. Bus. Forms Assn., Printing Industries. Democrat. Jewish. Home: 22214-1 James Alan Circle Chatsworth CA 91311 Office: Bank Printing Co Inc 1901 Santee St Los Angeles CA 90011

ESTRIN, THELMA AUSTERN, electrical engineer; b. N.Y.C., Feb. 21, 1924; d. I. Billy and Mary (Ginsburg) Austern; m. Gerald Estrin, Dec. 21, 1941; children: Margo, Judith, Deborah. BSEE, U. Wis., Madison, 1947, MSEE, 1948, PhD, 1951. Cert. clin. engr. Research engr. UCLA Brain Research Inst., 1960-70, dir. data processing, 1970-80; prof. UCLA Sch. Engring. and Applied Sci., 1980—; dir. div. electronics, computer and systems engring. NSF, Washington, 1982-84; dir. dept. engring. and sci., asst. dean Sch. of Engring. and Applied Sci. UCLA, 1984; trustee Aerospace Corp., 1979-82; mem. biomed. tech. resources com. NIH, 1981-86; mem. U.S. Army Sci. Bd., 1982-83; mem. energy engring. bd. NRC, 1985—. Contbr. articles to tech. jours. Mem. Los Angeles Women in Bus. Recipient Disting. Contbn. to Engring. Edn. award NSPE, 1985, Achievement award Soc. Women Engrs. 1981, Disting. Service citation U. Wis., 1976. Fellow IEEE (bd. dirs. 1979-80, exec. v.p. 1982, recipient Centennial medal 1984), AAAS; mem. Engring. in Medicine and Biology Soc. Jewish. Home: 500 Warner Ave Los Angeles CA 90024 Office: UCLA Sch Engring and Applied Sci Boelter Hall Room 6722 Los Angeles CA 90024

ESTWICK, LLOYD ANTHONY, oil company executive; b. Berbice, Guyana, July 22, 1935; s. Albert Estwick and Gertrude E. (Crawford) Heyliger; m. Margaret A. Glasgow, Aug. 24, 1963; children: Brian, Mark, David. BS, Calif. State U., Los Angeles, 1966; MBA, CUNY, 1973; MBT, U. So. Calif., 1978. Acct. Kalb and Kalb, CPA's, Los Angeles, 1964-66; fgn. tax analyst Atlantic Richfield Co., N.Y.C., 1971-72; internat. acct. Atlantic Richfield Co., Los Angeles, 1966-71, sr. tax. acct., 1972-78, tax analyst, 1978-86, sr. tax analyst, 1986—. Treas. Loyola High Sch. Booster Club, Los Angeles, 1984—. Mem. Am. Acctg. Assn., Am. Taxation Assn., Nat. Assn. Black Accts. (founding mem.), Pasadena City Coll. Frat. (founding mem.). Roman Catholic. Club: Pasadena Athletic. Lodge: Ionic, Ancient Order of Foresters. Home: 5401 Rock Castle Dr La Canada CA 91011

ETTER, CAROL LOUISE, energy analyst, engineer, consultant; b. Boulder, Colo., July 18, 1957; d. Alan H. and Kathryn E. (Maloney) Shapley; m. John Karl Etter, Aug. 31, 1980; 1 child, Darryl William. BS, Swarthmore Coll., 1979; MBA, U. Colo., 1987. Registered profl. engr., Colo. Research asst. Resource Planning Assn., Washington, 1979-80; cons. engr. Solar Energy Research Inst., Golden, Colo., 1980-81; research assoc. Colo. Energy Research Inst., Golden, 1981-83; engr. Energy and Resource Cons., Inc., Boulder, 1983—; cons. City of Longmont (Colo.) Electric Utility Co., 1983; pres. Colo. Council Local Energy Officials, Denver, 1983-85. Co-chmn. Energy Com. 1st Congregation Ch., Boulder, 1981-82. Mem. Internat. Assoc. Energy Economists, Am. Solar Energy Soc., Assn. Energy Engrs., Sigma Xi. Democrat. Mem. United Ch. of Christ. Avocations: music, hiking, backpacking, skiing. Office: Energy and Resource Cons Inc PO Box O Boulder CO 80306

ETTER, RICHARD FREDERICK, engineer, infosystems specialist; b. Indpls., Nov. 22, 1936; s. Richard W. and Delpha K. (Roell) E.; m. M. Eloise Whitney; 1 child, John K. BA in Math., Reed Coll., 1958. Assoc. engr. The Boeing Co., Seattle, 1958-61, sr. prin. engr., 1965—; engr. Lockheed M & S, Sunnyvale, Calif., 1961; sr. systems analyst Mellonics S-D, Sunnyvale, 1961-65. Mem. AIAA, Ops. Research Soc. Am., Space Studies Inst. Home: 2225 Evergreen Point Rd Bellevue WA 98004 Office: The Boeing Co PO Box 3707 Seattle WA 98124

ETTLICH, WILLIAM F., electrical engineer; b. Spokane, Wash., Jan. 7, 1936; s. Fred Ernest Ettlich and Dorothy Sue (Olney) Nicholls; m. Alice Dianne Lawton, Aug. 24, 1958; children: Pamela, Daniel. BS, Oreg. State U.; PMD-25, Harvard U. Registered profl. engr., Oreg., Calif., Nev., Colo., Mich., Ohio., S.D. Project engr. CH2M-Hill Corp., Corvallis, Oreg., 1959-65; pres. Neptune Microfloc, Corvallis, 1965-74; v.p. Culp Wesner Culp, Cameron Park, Calif., 1974-86, CWC-HDR, Inc., Cameron Park, 1986—; pres. Cameron Estates CSD, Cameron Park, 1977-80. Contbr. tech. articles to jours.; patentee in field. Trustee Marshall Hosp. Found. Sr. mem. IEEE, Instrument Soc. Am. Republican. Presbyterian. Lodge: Rotary (local bd. dirs. 1979, pres.-elect 1986). Avocations: skiing, woodworking. Home: 4317 Strolling Hills Rd Cameron Park CA 95682 Office: CWC-HDR Inc 3461 Robin Lane Cameron Park CA 95682

EU, MARCH KONG FONG, state official; b. Oakdale, Calif., Mar. 29, 1922; d. Yuen and Shiu (Shee) Kong; children by previous marriage—Matthew Kipling Fong, Marchesa Suyin Fong You; m. Henry Eu, July 30, 1973; stepchildren—Henry, Adeline, Yvonne, Conroy, Alaric. Student, Salinas Jr. Coll.; B.S., U. Calif.-Berkeley; M.Ed., Mills Coll., 1951; Ed.D., Stanford U., 1956; postgrad., Columbia U., Calif. State Coll.-Hayward; LL.D., Lincoln U., 1984. Chmn. div. dental hygiene U. Calif. Med. Center, San Francisco; dental hygienist Oakland (Calif.) Pub. Schs.; supr. dental health edn. Alameda County (Calif.) Schs.; lectr. health edn. Mills Coll., Oakland; mem. Calif. Legislature, 1966-74, chmn. select com. on agr., foods and nutrition, 1973-74; mem. com. natural resources and conservation, com. commerce and pub. utilities, select com. med. malpractice; sec. state State of Calif., 1975—, chief of protocol, 1975-83; chmn. Calif. State World Trade Commn., 1982-87; spl. cons. Bur. Intergroup Relations, Calif. Dept. Edn.; ednl., legis. cons. Sausalito (Calif.) Pub. Schs., Santa Clara County Office Edn., Jefferson Elementary Union Sch. Dist., Santa Clara High Sch. Dist., Santa Clara Elementary Sch. Dist., Live Oak Union High Sch. Dist.; mem. Alameda County Bd. Edn., 1956-66, pres., 1961-62, legis. adv., 1963. Mem. budget panel Bay Area United Fund Crusade; mem. Oakland Econ. Devel. Council; mem. tourism devel. com. Calif. Econ. Devel. Commn.; mem. citizens com. on housing Council Social Planning; mem. Calif. Interagy. Council Family Planning; edn. chmn., mem. council social planning, dir. Oakland Area Baymont Dist. Community Council; charter pres., hon. life mem. Howard Elementary Sch. PTA; charter pres. Chinese Young Ladies Soc., Oakland; mem., vice chmn. adv. com. Youth Study Centers and Ford Found. Interagy. Project, 1962-63; chmn. Alameda County Mothers' March, 1971-72; bd. councillors U. So. Calif. Sch. Dentistry, 1976; mem. exec. com. Calif. Democratic Central Com., mem. central com., 1963-70, asst. sec.; del. Dem. Nat. Conv., 1968; dir. 8th Congl. Dist. Dem. Council, 1963; v.p. Dems. of 8th Congl. Dist., 1963; dir. Key Women for Kennedy, 1963; women's vice chmn. No. Calif. Johnson for Pres., 1964; bd. dirs. Oakland

YWCA, 1965. Recipient ann. award for outstanding achievement Eastbay Intercultural Fellowship, 1959; Phoebe Apperson Hearst Disting. Bay Area Woman of Yr. award; Woman of Yr. award Calif. Retail Liquor Dealers Inst., 1969; Merit citation Calif. Assn. Adult Edn. Adminstrs., 1970; Art Edn. award; Outstanding Woman award Nat. Women's Polit. Caucus, 1980; Person of Yr. award Miracle Mile Lions Club, 1980; Humanitarian award Milton Strong Hall of Fame, 1981; Outstanding Leadership award Ventura Young Dems., 1983; Woman of Achievement award Los Angeles Hadassah, 1983. Mem. Am. Dental Hygienists Assn. (pres. 1956-57), No. Calif. Dental Hygienists Assn., Oakland LWV, AAUW (area rep. in edn. Oakland br.), Calif. Tchrs. Assn., Calif. Sch. Bd. Assn., Alameda County Sch. Bd. Assn. (pres. 1965), Alameda County Mental Health Assn., So. Calif. Dental Assn. (hon.), Bus. and Profl. Women's Club, Chinese Retail Food Markets Assn. (hon.), Delta Kappa Gamma. Office: State of Calif 1230 J St Sacramento CA 95814

EUBANKS, TOMMY L., accountant; b. Manchester, Ga., Oct. 12, 1948; s. Alvin Richard and Doris Fay (Cox) E.; m. Susan Louise Peterson, June 21, 1968; children: Amanda, Victoria, Rebecca, Jonathan. BA in Acctg., U. No. Colo., 1973. Acct. Chevron USA, Denver, 1973-77; mgr. revenue acctg. Ladd Petroleum Corp., Denver, 1977—; instr. Profl. Devel. Inst. N. Tex. State U., Denton, 1981—. Chmn. Boulder (Colo.) County Dems., 1978-80, treas., 1976-78. Mem. Petroleum Accts. Soc. Colo. (pres. 1983-84), Council Petroleum Accts. Socs. (v.p. 1984-85, sec. 1985—). Democrat. Lutheran. Office: Ladd Petroleum Corp 370 17th St Suite 1700 Denver CO 80501

EULENBERG, JULIA NIEBUHR, history and archives educator, consultant; b. San Angelo, Tex., Aug. 18, 1942; d. Ralph Waldo Niebuhr and Joy Niebuhr (Coatney) Holliday; m. George Edward Schairer, March 24, 1963 (div. 1975); children: Benjamin, Sarah Niebuhr; m. Michael Eulenberg, Feb. 24, 1980. BA in Polit. Sci., U. Wash., 1965, MA in History and Archives Mgmt., 1984, postgrad, 1984—. Freelance editor 1970—; editor Battelle Seattle Research Ctr., Seattle, 1974-76; records and archives specialist Battelle Seattle Research Ctrs., 1981-84; mgr. info. publs. services Battelle Human Affairs Research Ctrs., Seattle, 1976-81; archivist Wash. State Jewish Hist. Soc., Seattle, 1983-84; cons. archives and records mgmt. 1984—; vis. lectr. U Wash Sch. of Library and Info. Sci., Seattle. Author: Handbook for the Recovery of Water Damaged Business Records, 1986; contbr. articles to profl. jours. Active synagogue activities. Mem. Am. Assn. for State and Local History, Assn. of Records Mgrs. and Adminstrs., Immigration History Soc., Internat. Council of Archivists and Records Mgrs. (corresponding mem. council integrative com. 1981—), N.W. Archivists' Assn. (mem. publs. com., editor newsletter 1981-85), Pacific N.W. Historians' Guild (exec. bd. 1984-86), Soc. of Am. Archivists, Assn. Profl. Writers and Editors (v.p. program devel. 1977-78), Phi Alpha Theta. Democrat. Avocation: writing.

EVANS, CEANNE LESLIE, audiologist; b. Rochester, N.Y., Dec. 30, 1951; d. Harold Warren and Jacqueline (Ranck) E. BS, N.D. State U., 1975; MS in Audiology, U. Wyo., 1978. Audiologist Spokane (Wash.) Ear, Nose, Throat Clinic, 1978-86. Mem. Am. Speech-Lang.-Hearing Assn. (cert.), Am. Auditory Soc. Office: Spokane ENT Clinic W 104 5th Ave Spokane WA 99204

EVANS, CHRIS P., computer company executive; b. Worcester Park, Eng., Sept. 13, 1943; came to U.S., 1984; s. Evan A. and Muriel (Kitson) E.; m. Kristien Tanner, Jan. 2, 1971; children: Jeremy, Diana. BSc in Chemistry, Bristol (Eng.) U., 1965. Tchr. chemistry Karachi (Pakistan) Grammar Sch., 1965-66; sales rep. Internat. Computers Ltd., London, 1966-69, mid-east sales mgr., 1970-80; devel. specialist Axel Springer Verlag, Hamburg, Fed. Republic of Germany, 1969-70; OEM sales mgr. Siemens AG, Munich, 1980-84; sales dir. Siemens Info. Systems Inc., Anaheim, Calif., 1984—. Author: Printing World-The Decision to Computerize, 1970. Mem. Brit. Computer Soc. Club: Old King's (Wimbledon, Eng.). Avocations: travel, foreign langs., coin collecting, amateur dramatics. Office: Siemens Info Systems Inc 240 E Palais Rd Anaheim CA 92805

EVANS, (MARY) CLAIRE, painter, educator; b. Augusta, Ga., June 8, 1929; d. John Franklin Patrick and Mary Viola Dowling; m. Charles Lane Evans, Oct. 18, 1951; children—Joel Lane, Ellen Claire. B.A., Converse Coll., 1951; Tchr., lectr. Rocky Mountain Sch. Art, Denver, 1979—. One-woman shows: Foothills Art Ctr., Golden, Colo., 1978, UMC Gallery, U. Colo., Boulder, 1979; group shows include: West '82 Art and the Law, St. Paul, 1982, Joslyn Biennial, Omaha, 1984, Foothills Art Ctr., Golden, 1984, Colorado Springs Biennial, 1985; represented in corp. collections including United Bank, Amoco Prodns., Petrolewis Corp., ARCO. Studio: 2810 Wilderness Pl Suite E Boulder CO 80301 Office: 828 Pearl St Boulder CO 80302

EVANS, DANIEL JACKSON, U.S. senator; b. Seattle, Oct. 16, 1925; s. Daniel Lester and Irma (Ide) E.; m. Nancy Ann Bell, June 6, 1959; children: Daniel Jackson, Mark L., Bruce M. B.S. in Civil Engring, U. Wash., 1948, M.S., 1949. Registered profl. engr., Wash. With Assn. Gen. Contractors, Seattle, 1953-59; cons. civil engr. Seattle, 1949-51; partner Gray & Evans, structural and civil engrs., Seattle, 1959-65; mem. Wash. Ho. of Reps. from, King County, 1956-65; Republican floor leader Wash. Ho. of Reps. from, 1961-65; gov. State of Wash., 1964-77; pres. Evergreen State Coll., Olympia, 1977-83; mem. U.S. Senate from Wash. State 1983—; mem. Adv. Council on Intergovernmental Relations, 1972-77, Fed. Adv. Commn. Project Independence, 1974, Nat. Commn. on Productivity and Work Quality, 1975, President's Vietnamese Refugee Adv. Com., 1975; chmn. Pacific NW Electric Power and Conservation Planning Council, 1981-83. Keynote speaker Rep. Nat. Conv., 1968; mem. Nat. Gov.'s Conf., chmn., 1973-74; chmn. Western Gov.'s Conf., 1968-69; trustee Carnegie Found. for Advancement of Teaching, Nature Conservancy, 20th Century Fund. Served to lt. USNR, 1943-46, 51-53. Recipient Human Rights award Pacific N.W. chpt. Nat. Assn. Intergroup Relations Ofcls., 1967; Service to the Profession award Cons. Engrs. Council, 1969; Scales of Justice award Nat. Council Crime and Delinquency, 1968; Pub. Ofcl. of Year award Wash. Environmental Council, 1970; Distinguished Eagle, Silver Beaver, Silver Antelope awards Boy Scouts Am.; Distinguished Citizen award Nat. Municipal League, 1977. Congregationalist. Address: US Senate 702 Hart Senate Bldg Washington DC 20510

EVANS, DAVID LEE, retail pet supplies executive; b. St. Joseph, Mo., Oct. 9, 1951; s. Joseph Francis and Helen Marie (McCall) E.; m. Louise Guy Greco, Sept. 14, 1976 (div. Mar. 1977); m. Sandi Elizabeth Canales, Aug. 20, 1977; children: Joshua Andrew, Aaron Joseph, Megan Marie, Zachary Bryce. AA, Nat. U., 1979, student, 1979—. Retail clk. Petco Animal Supplies, La Mesa, Calif., 1974-81; v.p. Petco Animal Supplies, San Diego, 1981—. Councilor to Bishop of Ch. Jesus Christ Latter Day Saints, San Diego, 1986—, sem. instr., Sunday sch. tchr., 1977—. Served with USN, 1970-74. Avocations: water and snow skiing. Home: 9979 Riverhead Dr San Diego CA 92129 Office: Petco Animal Supplies 9151 Rehco Rd San Diego CA 92121

EVANS, DONALD BEERS, metallurgist; b. Cleve., Oct. 11, 1933; s. Frederick James and Margaret Jane (Beers) E.; m. Jo Ann Werden, May 19, 1984. BSE, MIT, 1955; MSE, U. Mich., 1959, PhD, 1963. Devel. engr. Mallinckrodt Chem. Works, St. Louis, 1958; engring. specialist Martin Marietta Corp., Balt., 1963-68; mem. tech. staff TRW Corp., Redondo Beach, 1969—. Contbr. articles to profl. jours; patentee in field. Served to 1st lt. C.E., U.S. Army, 1955-57. Mem. Am. Soc. Metals, Am. Welding Soc. Republican. Avocations: skiing, squash, golf. Home: 708 Camino Real Redondo Beach CA 90277 Office: TRW Inc One Space Park 102/1819 Redondo Beach CA 90278

EVANS, ELLIS DALE, educator, psychologist; b. Topeka, Nov. 6, 1934; s. Ellis Meredith and Ruth Alice (Burchinal) E.; m. Cynthia Ann McClure, Dec. 23, 1961; children—Jennifer Ann, Alicia Ruth. B.Music Edn., U. Kans., 1956; M.S. in Edn, Ind. U., 1962, Ed.D., 1964. Tchr. Shawnee Mission, Kans., 1957; field rep. Delta Upsilon, 1960-61; research asst., teaching asso. Ind. U., 1961-64; mem. faculty U. Wash., 1964—, prof. ednl. psychology, 1971—, chmn. ednl. psychology, 1986—; spl. instr. Shoreline Community Coll., Seattle, 1973-75; adv. Pacific Marine Research Inst.; cons. Lakeview Travel and Cruise. Author: Development and Classroom Learning, 1973, Children and Youth; Psychosocial Development, 1973, rev. edit., 1978, Contemporary Influences in Early Childhood Education, 1975, The Transition to Teaching, 1976; cons. editor: Charles E. Merrill Pubs.; Author also articles. Active local music orgns. Shoreline Schs. Served to capt. USAF, 1957-60. Fellow U.S. Office Edn., 1970-71.; Mem. Am. Ednl. Research Assn., Nat. Assn. Edn. Young Children, Soc. for Research in Adolescence, Soc. for Research in Child Devel., Am. Fedn. Musicians, Phi Delta Kappa, Omicron Delta Kappa, Delta Upsilon. Home: 19045 46th St NE Seattle WA 98155

EVANS, HANNAH IMOGENE, psychologist; b. Richmond, Va., Nov. 6, 1945; d. Charles and Ruth (Powell) E.; BA, U. Vt., 1967; MS, Pa. State U., 1970, PhD, 1972; MPA, U. Colo., Denver, 1981; m. Robert F. McKenzie, July 12, 1975. Clin. psychology intern, psychol. cons. II, Denver Dept. Health and Hosps., 1972-77; adj. faculty U. Colo., Denver, summer 1978; resource counselor Regional Transp. Dist., 1978-79; pvt. practice psychotherapy, Denver, 1976—. Mem. community adv. bd. Sch. Profl. Psychology, U. Denver; mem. grievance com. Colo. Supreme Ct., 1982—; staff affiliate Bethesda Hosp., 1979—; clin. assoc. sch. profl. Psychology, U. Denver. Mem. Gov.'s Front Range Task Force, 1980-81; bd. dirs. Denver Sexual Assault Council, 1974-80; founding bd. Colo. Center Women and Work, 1979-81; mem. Women's Forum of Colo., 1979—, selection com., 1980—; mem. Victims and Witness Assistance and Law Enforcement Bd. 2d Jud. Dist. USPHS fellow, 1968-70; named one of Faces of Colo., Colo. mag., 1976. Mem. Am. Psychol. Assn., Rocky Mountain Road Runners. Club: Phiddipides Track. Contbr. articles to profl. jours. and popular mags.

EVANS, HILTON BERNARD, geophysics consultant; b. Moab, Utah, Jan. 7, 1929; s. Hilton Byrd and Flora (Peterson) E.; m. Johan Bowen, Jan. 21, 1948 (div. June 1979); children: Teri Ann, Jama Lyn Hashbarger, Kelle Le. BA in Physics, U. Utah, 1954, PhD in Geophysics, 1959; postgrad., U. Colo., 1960-69. Registered geophysicist, Calif. Nuclear physicist U.S. Geol. Survey, Salt Lake City, 1953-59; sr. research scientist Marathon Oil Co., Littleton, Colo., 1959-73; dir. formation evaluation Gearhart Industries, Ft. Worth, 1973-76; dir. advanced tech. div. Bendix Field Engring. Corp., Grand Junction, Colo., 1976-79; mgr. integrated seismic well log services Seismograph Service Corp., Tulsa, 1979-80; cons. Applied Petro-Physics Assocs., Colo., Ariz., Tex., Utah, Calif. and Europe, 1980—; mem. logging adv. com. Deep Sea Drilling Project, La Jolla, Calif., 1968-73; cons. borehole measurements Marine Minerals Tech. Ctr., Tiburon, Calif., 1960-69; speaker Career Day Speakers, Golden, Colo., Denver, Casper, Wyo., 1968-69. Author: (3 vol. series) Formation Evaluation, 1963, (2 vol. series) Formation Evaluation Using Programmable Hand Calculators, 1981; contbr. articles to profl. jours.; patentee in field. Mem. Littleton (Colo.) Budget Com., 1965-66, Little Water Com., 1963-64. Mem. Soc. Profl. Well Log Analysts (co-chmn. arrangements symposium 1966-67, publications com. 1969-70, 77-81, tech. com. 1965-68, 74-75, 78-81, membership com. 1977-81; speaker 1965, 66, 67, 78, 79, 80, editor The Log Analyst 1980-81; First Disting. Service award 1980), Computer Oriented Geol. Soc., Soc. Petroleum Engrs. (speaker 1969), Am. Geophys. Union, Soc. Exploration Geophysicists (speaker 1968), European Assn. Exploration Geophysicists, COre Analysis Soc., Minerals and Geotechnical Logging Soc., Sigma Xi. Avocations: theater, art, opera, symphony, literature. Office: PO Box 214676 Sacramento CA 95821

EVANS, HIRAM KRAIG, forensic chemist; b. Chula Vista, Calif., July 8, 1953. BA in Chemistry, Cen. Coll., Pella, Iowa, 1975; AS in Criminal Justice, Southwestern Coll., Chula Vista, 1976; MS in Criminalistics, Calif. State U., Los Angeles, 1982. Tech. asst. Harris & Harris, Los Angeles, 1977; criminalist I Ventura County (Calif.) Sheriff's Dept., 1978-79; criminalist II San Diego County Sheriff's Dept., 1979-81; criminalist II, dep. sheriff San Bernardino County (Calif.) Sheriff's Dept. Forensic Sci. Lab., 1982—; adj. prof. forensic sci. Nat. U., San Diego, 1980-83; instr. Regional Criminal Justice Tng. Ctr., San Bernardino, 1983—. Contbr. articles to profl. jours, chpt. to book. Bd. dirs. Safety Employees Benefit Assn., San Bernardino. Fellow Am. Acad. Forensic Scis. (criminalistics sect.); mem. Am. Chem. Soc., Calif. Assn. Criminalists (nominating Com.), Am. Acad. Forensic Scis., Calif. Assn. Criminalists (sec. 1986-88), Cen. Coll. Alumni Assn. (steering com.), Pacific S.W. Ry. Mus. Assn. Republican. Lodge: Masons. Avocations: horticulture, railway history. Home: PO Box 782 Highland CA 92346-0782 Office: Regional Forensic Sci Lab PO Box 1557 San Bernardino CA 92402

EVANS, JOHN THORNLEY, lawyer; b. Salt Lake City, Mar. 14, 1938; s. Richard L. and Alice (Thornley) E. J.D., U. Utah, 1965. Bar: Utah 1965. Law clk. to chief justice Utah Supreme Ct., 1964-65; dep. atty. Salt Lake County, 1965-66; asst. atty. gen. State of Utah, Salt Lake City, 1968-73; ptnr. Clyde & Pratt, Salt Lake City, 1968-80; sole practice, Salt Lake City, 1980-86; of counsel Dart, Adamson & Parken, Salt Lake City, 1986—; speaker, lectr. numerous seminars, convs. law enforcement, legal groups. Active Greater Salt Lake council Boy Scouts Am., 1967-83, Explorer post adv., 1967-69, neighborhood commr., 1969-71, chmn. fund drive, 1982, 83. Republican conv. del. Salt Lake County, 1968, 74, State of Utah, 1978. Served as staff sgt. M.C., U.S. Army, 1961-62. Mem. ABA, Utah State Bar (exec. com. Young Lawyers sect. 1965-67, chmn. condemnation sect. 1973-74), Nat. Assn. Securities Dealers, Salt Lake County Bar Assn., Phi Delta Phi. Office: 310 S Main St Suite 1330 Salt Lake City UT 84101

EVANS, JOSEPH WILLIAM, lawyer; b. Louisville, Ky., July 1, 1948; s. William Hale and Margaret (Hollyfield) E.; m. Frances Dennis, July 26, 1969; children: Mary Elizabeth, Margaret Hollyfield. BA, U. Ky., 1973; JD, Duke U., 1976. Bar: Alaska 1976, D.C. 1984, U.S. Ct. Appeals (9th cir.) 1977, U.S. Supreme Ct. 1984. Assoc. Law Offices of Murphy L. Clark, Anchorage, 1976-77, Birch, Horton & Bittner Inc., Anchorage, 1977—. Assemblyman Anchorage Mcpl. Assembly, 1985—; bd. dirs., steering com. Alaska Mcpl. League, Juneau, 1985—; mem. Alaska Coastal Policy Council, transp. and communications com. Nat. League of Cities, Washington, 1985—; del. PTA Nat. Conv., Washington, 1985; v.p. Abbott-O-Rabbit Little League, Anchorage, 1984-85; legal chair United Way Campaign, Anchorage, 1985. Served to sgt. USMC, 1967-70, Vietnam. Mem. Assn. Trial Lawyers Am., Nat. Coll. Criminal Def. Lawyers, Alaska Bar Assn., D.C. Bar Assn., Phi Beta Kappa. Lodge: Rotary. Home: 4741 Southpark Bluff Dr Anchorage AK 99516 Office: Birch Horton & Bittner Inc 1127 W 7th Ave Anchorage AK 99501

EVANS, JUNIUS ANTHONY, physician; b. Festus, Mo., Aug. 13, 1911; s. George James and Daisy (Keiser) E.; A.B. in Chemistry, U. Tex., 1937, B.S. in Pharmacy, 1939, M.D., 1943; m. Josephine Van Zandt, Nov. 28, 1936; children—Martha Ellen (Mrs. Metarelis), Mary Daisy (Mrs. Everhart), Junius Anthony Jr. Intern U.S. Marine Hosp., New Orleans, 1943-44; resident No. Mich. Tb San., Gaylord, Mich., USPHS, Washington, 1945-46, U. Ark., VA Hosps. Little Rock and North Little Rock, 1960-62; career officer USPHS, 1943-47; pvt. practice medicine, Las Vegas, N.Mex., 1947-60; specializing in dermatology, Roswell, N.Mex., 1962—; formerly chief of staff Las Vegas, St. Anthony hosps. (both Las Vegas); staff mem. St. Mary's Hosp.; chief of staff Eastern N.Mex. Med. Center, Roswell, 1968-69; clin. assoc. dermatology U. N.Mex., 1974—. Served from ensign to lt. USCG, 1943-46; capt. Res. Recipient A.H. Robins award for Outstanding Pub. Service, 1985. Mem. Chaves County, N.Mex. (councillor 1956-59, mem. pub. relations com. 1963-73, chmn. pub. relations com. 1963-64, ho. of dels. 1969-—, mem. liaison com. to allied professions 1972-74) med. socs., Am., N.Mex. (pres. 1958) thoracic socs., Am. Acad. Dermatology, N.Mex. Tb Assn. (dir. 1950-62), Am. Acad. Tb Physicians, Am. Cancer Soc. (v.p. 1970, chmn. service com. N.Mex. div. 1965-70), Chaves County Cancer Soc. (dir. 1965-79), Am. Council Med. Staffs (regional dir. S.W. area 1972—, pres. N.Mex. council 1972-74), Assn. Am. Physicians and Surgeons, N.Mex. (dir.), Chaves County (pres. 1970-71) heart assns., S.W. Dermatol Soc. (pres. 1966-67), N.Mex. Dermatol. Soc., Rho Chi, Theta Kappa Psi. Mason (Shriner), Rotarian. Home: 2200 Palomar Dr Roswell NM 88201 Office: 207 N Union St PO Box 1226 Roswell NM 88201

EVANS, LATIMER RICHARD, chemistry educator; b. Washington, Nov. 4, 1918; s. Clifford V. and Ruth L. (Latimer) E.; m. Eloise Swick, Aug. 24, 1942; children: Carol, Beth, Marget, Scott. BS, Am. U., 1941; PhD, Purdue U., 1945. Research chemist DuPont Co., Wilmington, Del., 1946-50; prof. chemistry N.Mex. State U., Las Cruces, 1950—. Author: Lab. Manual for Organic Chemistry, 1979. Treas. Las Alturas Devel. Corp., Las Cruces, 1967—, bd. dirs. Named Outstanding Tchr. N.Mex. State U., 1986. Mem. Am. Chem. Soc., Sigma Xi. Democrat. Unitarian. Avocations: gardening, athletics, bridge. Home: 4155 Tellbrook Las Cruces NM 88001 Office: NMex State U Box 3-C Las Cruces NM 88003

EVANS, LAWRENCE JACK, JR., lawyer; b. Oakland, Calif., Apr. 4, 1921; s. Lawrence Jack and Eva May (Dickinson) E.; m. Marjorie Hisken, Dec. 23, 1944; children—Daryl S. Kleweno, Richard L., Shirley J. Coursey, Donald B. Diplomate Near East Sch. Theology, Beirut, 1951; M.A., Am. U. Beirut, 1951; Ph.D., Brantridge Forest Sch., Sussex, Eng., 1968; J.D., Ariz. State U., 1971; grad. Nat. Jud. Coll., 1974. Bar: Ariz. 1971, U.S. Dist. Ct. Ariz. 1971, U.S. Ct. Claims 1972, U.S. Customs Ct., 1972, U.S. Tax Ct. 1972, U.S. Ct. Customs and Patent Appeals 1972, U.S. Ct. Appeals (9th cir.) 1972, U.S. Supreme Ct. 1975. Served as enlisted man U.S. Navy, 1938-41; enlisted man U.S. Army, 1942-44, commd. 2d lt., 1944, advanced through ranks to lt. col., 1962; chief, field ops. and tactics div., U.S. Army Spl. Forces, 1963, chief spl. techniques div., 1964, unconventional warfare monitor, 1964-65; assigned to Command and Gen. Staff Coll., 1960; ops. staff officer J-3 USEUCOM, 1965-68; mem. Airborne Command Post Study Group, Joint Chiefs of Staff, 1967; ret., 1968; sole practice law, cons. on Near and Middle Eastern affairs, Tempe, Ariz., 1971-72, 76—; v.p., dir. Trojan Investment & Devel. Co., Inc., 1972-75; active Ariz. Tax Conf., 1971-75; mem. adminstrv. law com., labor mgmt. relations com., unauthorized practice of law com. Ariz. State Bar. Author: Legal Aspects of Land Tenure in the Republic of Lebanon, 1951; (with Helen Miller Davis) International Constitutional Law, Electoral Laws and Treaties of the Near and Middle East, 1951. Contbr. articles to mags., chpts. to books. Chmn. legal and legis. com. Phoenix Mayor's Com. To Employ Handicapped, 1971-75; active Tempe Leadership Conf., 1971-75; chmn. Citizens Against Corruption in Govt.; mem. Princeton Council on Fgn. and Internat. Studies. Decorated Silver Star, Legion of Merit, Bronze Star, Purple Heart; named Outstanding Adminstrv. Law Judge for State Service for U.S., 1974; named to U.S. Army Ranger Hall of Fame, 1981. Mem. Ranger Bns. Assn. World War II (life), Tempe Rep. Mens Club (v.p., bd. dirs. 1971-72, U.S. Army Airborne Ranger Assn. (life), Mil. Order Purple Heart (life), Nat. Rifle Assn. (life), Phi Delta Phi, Delta Theta Phi. Episcopalian. Lodges: Masons, KT (past master, past thrice illustrious master, past comdr.). Home: 539 E Erie Dr Tempe AZ 85282 Office: Tempe AZ 85282

EVANS, LOUISE, psychologist; b. San Antonio; d. Henry Daniel and Adela (Pariser) E.; B.S., Northwestern U., 1949; M.S. in Psychology, Purdue U., 1952, Ph.D. in Clin. Psychology, 1955; m. Thomas Ross Gambrell, Feb. 23, 1960. Intern clin. psychology Menninger Found., Topeka (Kans.) State Hosp., 1952-53, USPHS-Menninger Found. fellow clin. child psychology, 1955-56; staff psychologist Kankakee (Ill.) State Hosp., 1954; head staff psychologist child guidance clinic Kings County Hosp., Bklyn., 1957-58; dir. psychology clinic, instr. med. psychology Washington U. Sch. Medicine, 1959; clin. research cons. Episcopal City Mission, St. Louis, 1959; pvt. practice clin. psychology, 1960—; psychol. cons. Fullerton (Calif.) Community Hosp., 1961-81; staff cons. clin. psychology Martin Luther Hosp., Anaheim, Calif., 1963-70; lectr. clin. psychology schs. and profl. groups, 1950—; participant psychol. symposiums, 1956—; guest speaker clin. psychology civic and community orgns., 1950—. Elected to Hall of Fame, Central High Sch., Ind., 1966; recipient Service award Yuma County Head Start Program, 1972; named Miss Heritage, Heritage Publs., 1965; lic. psychologist N.Y., Calif.; diplomate Clin. Psychology. Fellow Am. Psychol. Assn., Royal Soc. Health of England, Internat. Council of Psychologists (dir. 1977-79, sec. 1962-64, 73-76), AAAS, Am. Orthopsychiat. Assn., World Wide Acad. of Scholars of N.Z.; mem. AAUP, Los Angeles Soc. Clin. Psychologists (exec. bd. 1966-67), Calif. State Psychol. Assn., Los Angeles County Psychol. Assn., Orange County Psychol. Assn. (exec. bd. 1961-62), Orange County Soc. Clin. Psychologists (exec. bd. 1963-65, pres. 1964-65), Am. Public Health Assn., Rehab. Internat., Internat. Platform Assn., Am. Acad. Polit. and Social Scis., N.Y. Acad. Scis., Purdue U. Alumni Assn. (Citizenship award 1975), Am. Judicature Soc., Center for Study of Presidency, Alumni Assn. Menninger Sch. Psychiatry, Sigma Xi, Pi Sigma Pi. Contbr. articles on clin. psychology to profl. publs. Office: 905-907 W Wilshire Ave Fullerton CA 92632

EVANS, LYNETTE EILEEN, newspaper editor; b. Everett, Wash., Apr. 26, 1941; d. Delmer H. and Georgia Mary (Johnson) Buse; B.A., U. Wash., 1963; postgrad. U. Nev., Las Vegas, 1967-68; m. John Basil Evans, Nov. 10, 1962. Sch. tchr., Everett, Wash., 1963-64; police officer, Everett, Wash., 1964-65, teaching asst. U. Nev., Las Vegas, 1967-68; reporter, women's news editor Everett (Wash.) Herald, 1969-74; dir. Learning Center Tulalip Indian Tribes, 1974-75; Sunday mag. editor Las Vegas (Nev.) Sun, 1976; news dir. Foster's Daily Democrat, Dover, N.H., 1977-79; pub. Lake Tahoe News, South Lake Tahoe, Calif., 1979-83; mng. editor San Francisco Progress, 1983—; v.p. Buse Media, Inc., Everett, Wash. Bd. dirs. San Francisco Boys and Girls Club, 1986—. Recipient State Writing awards Wash. Press Women, 1972. Mem. Calif. Soc. Newspaper Editors, Soc. Newspaper Design. Author: (with George Burley) Roche Harbor: A Saga in the San Juans, 1972. Home: 243 Byxbee San Francisco CA 94132 Office: San Francisco Progress 851 Howard San Francisco CA 94103

EVANS, MORGAN J., service, management company executive. Pres., chief exec. officer 1st Security Service Co., Salt Lake City. Office: 1st Security Service Co PO Box 30006 Salt Lake City UT 84130 *

EVANS, NORMAN ALLEN, scientist; b. Spearfish, S.D., Dec. 3, 1922; s. Allen C. and Claire (Doscher) E.; m. Jean Cole, Dec. 26, 1943; children—Douglas Robert, Elizabeth Ann, Garth William, Mathew. B.S., S.D. State U., 1944; M.S., Utah State U., 1947; Ph.D., Colo. State U., 1963. Registered profl. engr., Colo. Asst. prof. N.D. State U., 1947-51; from asst. prof. to prof. civil engring. Colo. State U., Fort Collins, 1951-59; prof., head dept. agrl. engring. Colo. State U., 1956-69; dir. Environ. Resources Ctr., 1966-78; assoc. dir. U. Expt. Sta., 1970-71; dir. Office Gen. U. Research, 1970-72; dir. Water Resources Research Inst., 1966—; cons. in field; dir. Engrs. Council for Profl. Devel., 1970-76; mem. Colo. Water Pollution Control Commn., 1966-80, vice chmn., 1970-72; mem. Fort Collins City Water Bd., 1963—, chmn., 1966-68, 81—, vice chmn., 1963-66, 68-81. Served to 1st lt. AUS, 1944-46. Fellow AAAS, Am. Soc. Agrl. Engrs. (v.p. 1968-70); mem. ASCE, Sigma Xi, Phi Kappa Phi, Chi Epsilon, Alpha Epsilon, Gamma Sigma Delta. Home: 1847 Michael Ln Fort Collins CO 80521

EVANS, RICHARD JESSE, lumber company executive; b. East St. Louis, Ill., Aug. 17, 1913; s. Elmer D. and Elizabeth (Rogers) E.; m. Lucille H. Tiefenauer, May 21, 1939; children: Joyce Carol, Sharon Gail. Student, Wash. U. Constrn. and engring. supr. S.W. Bell Telephone Co., St. Louis, 1938-64; pres., chief exec. officer United Lumber Co., Inc., Anchorage, 1964—. Republican. Baptist. Home: 2239 Susitna Dr Anchorage AK 99503 Office: United Lumber Co Box 6809 5011 Jeel Lake Rd Anchorage AK 99503

EVANS, THOMAS EDGAR, JR., title insurance agency executive; b. Toronto, Ohio, Apr. 17, 1940; s. Thomas Edgar and Sarah Ellen (Bauer) E.; B.A., Mt. Union Coll., 1963; m. Cynthia Lee Johnson, Feb. 23; children—Thomas Edgar, Douglas, Melinda, Jennifer. Tchr. Lodi, Ohio, 1963-64; salesman Simpson-Evans Realty, Steubenville, Ohio, 1964-65, Shadron Realty, Tucson, 1965-67; real estate broker, co-owner Double E Realty, Tucson, 1967-69; escrow officer, br. mgr., asst. county mgr., v.p. Ariz. Title Ins., Tucson, 1969-80; pres. Commonwealth Land Title Agy., Tucson, 1980-82, also dir.; pres. Fidelity Nat. Title Agy., 1982—; v.p. Fidelity Nat. Corp.; bd. dirs. Fidelity Nat. Fin. Inc., Fidelity Nat. Title Ins. Co., Fidelity Nat. Title Agy. Pinal, The Griffin Co.; dir., chmn. bd. Cochise Title Agy., TIPCO; v.p., dir. A.P.C. Corp. Named Boss of Year, El Chaparral chpt. Am. Bus. Women's Assn., 1977. Mem. So. Ariz. Escrow Assn., So. Ariz. Mortgage Bankers Assn. (bd. dirs. 1982-85), Ariz. Mktg. Bankers Assn., Old Pueblo Businessmen's Assn. Tucson, Tucson Bd. Realtors, Ariz. Assn. Real Estate Exchangors (bd. dirs. 1968-69), Land Title Assn. Ariz. (pres. 1984), So. Ariz. Homebuilders Assn., Blue Key, Sigma Nu. Republican. Methodist. Clubs: Old Pueblo Courthouse, La Paloma, Ventana Country, Centre Court, Elks, Pima Jaycees (dir. 1966), Sertoma (charter pres., chmn. bd. Midtown sect. 1968-70); Tucson Real Estate Exchangors (pres. 1968); Sunrise Rotary; Old Pueblo. Home: 5142 E Camino Faja Tucson AZ 85718 Office: 4903 E Broadway Suite 100 Tucson AZ 85711

EVANS, TODD EDWIN, research physicist; b. Jackson, Mich., June 3, 1947; s. Harold M. and Jane Nanette (Mounteer) E.; m. Michele Simone Deroulez, Aug. 20, 1981; children: Cassandra Nanette, Annabelle Ashley. BS with honors in Physics, Wright State U., 1978, BSE in Engring., 1978; MS in Physics, U. Tex., Dallas, 1979, PhD in Physics and E.E., U. Tex., Austin, 1984. Research scientist Fusion Research Ctr., U. Tex., Austin, 1978-84, research engr. Electronics Research Ctr., 1978-83; instr. physics Austin (Tex.) Community Coll., 1979-80; research physicist Wright Patterson AFB, Dayton, Ohio, 1978; project engr. ITT, Springfield, Ohio, 1972-75; research scientist Fusion research Ctr. and Fusion Engring. Ctr. U. Tex., Austin, 1984-85; sr. scientist fusion energy research tokamak confinement physics GA Techs. Inc., San Diego, 1985—; lectr. in physics U. Tex., Austin, 1984-85; cons. U. Tex., Austin, various high tech. firms, Austin, Nagoya (Japan) U. Mem. World Future Soc. Recipient Profl. Devel. award, U. Tex., 1982, H.L. Book Scholarship, 1979-81. Mem. IEEE, Math. Assn. Am., Am. Phys. Soc., N.Y. Acad. Scis., Sigma Xi, Sigma Pi Sigma, Phi Kappa Phi. Contbr. sci. articles to various publs. Office: GA Techs Inc PO Box 85608 MS 02-516 San Diego CA 92138

EVANS, TOMMY NICHOLAS, physician, educator; b. Batesville, Ark., Apr. 12, 1922; s. James Rufus and Carrye Mae (Goatcher) E.; m. Jessica Ray Osment, June 12, 1945; 1 child, Laura Kathreen. A.A., Mars Hill Jr. Coll., 1940; student, Duke U., 1940-41; A.B., Baylor U., 1942; M.D., Vanderbilt U., 1945. Intern U. Mich. Hosp., Ann Arbor, 1945-46; asst. resident ob-gyn U. Mich. Hosp., 1948, resident, 1948-49, jr. clin. instr., 1949-50, sr. clin. instr., 1950-51, instr., 1951-54, asst. prof., 1954-56, assoc. prof., 1956-60, prof., 1960-65; prof. ob-gyn Wayne State U., Detroit, 1965-83; dean Sch. Medicine Wayne State U., 1970-72, dir. C.S. Mott Ctr. Human Growth and Devel., 1973-83; sr. attending physician Hutzel Hosp., 1966-83, chief ob-gyn, 1966-82, vice chief of staff, 1967-70, chief of staff, 1970-74, trustee, 1975-78; mem. teaching, surgeon Harper-Grace Hosps., 1965-83, chief gynecology Harper div., 1970-83, chief ob-gyn, 1975-83; chief gynecology, sr. attending physician Detroit Receiving Hosp., 1965-83; chief gynecology U. Colo., Denver, 1983—; vice chmn. ob-gyn U. Colo., 1983—; cons. pediatric surgery Children's Hosp.; cons. Sinai Hosp. William Beaumont Hosp., Wayne County Gen. Hosp.; past mem. med. adv. com. Detroit Med. Ctr. Corp. Bd. dirs. Alan Guttmacher Inst. Fellow Am. Assn. Ob-Gyn.; mem. Am. Coll. Obstetricians and Gynecologists (past exec. bd., past pres.), ACS (adv. council ob-gyn credentials com. 1983-86, bd. govs. 1982-86), Am. Fedn. Clin. Research, Am. Fertility Soc., Am. Gynecol. Club (past pres.), Am. Gynecol. Soc. (past pres.), Am. Gynecol. and Obstetrical Soc. (council), AMA, Am. Med. Soc. Vienna, Am. Pub. Health Assn., Am. Soc. Andrology (exec. council), Am. Soc. Study Sterility, Anthony Wayne Soc., Assn. Profs. Ob-Gyn (past chmn. nominating com.), Central Assn. Ob-Gyn (past pres.), Charlie Flowers Ob-Gyn Soc., Chgo. Gynecol. Soc., Continental Gynecol. Soc., Detroit Acad. Medicine, Detroit Cancer Club (past mem. program com.), Engring. Soc. Detroit, Greater Detroit Area Hosp. Council Inc., Internat. Fedn. Ob-Gyn (exec. bd.), Internat. Soc. Advancement Humanistic Studies in Gynecology, Miami Obstet. and Gynecol. Soc., Mich. Assn. Retarded Children, Mich. Cancer Found. (trustee), Mich. Council Study of Abortion, Mich. Soc. Ob-Gyn (past pres.), Mich. State Med. Soc. (past exec. council), Mich. United Cerebral Palsy Assn., Norman Miller Gynecol. Soc., Ob-Gyn Soc. N.Y., Planned Parenthood League, Pan Am. Med. Assn., Royal Soc. Medicine, Soc. Study of Reprodn., Soc. Ob-Gyn of Can., S. Atlantic Assn. Ob-Gyn, numerous others. Republican. Presbyterian. Clubs: Country of Detroit, Detroit Athletic. Office: Health Sci Ctr 4200 E 9th Ave Denver CO 80262

EVANS, TRICIA WARD, advertising account executive; b. Franklin Lakes, N.J., Nov. 20, 1947; d. Lloyd William and Avis Louise (Nagle) Ward; m. Vic Warren; children—Eric Ward, Pamela Ward. B.A. in Pub. Adminstrn., U. La Verne (Calif.), 1979; M.A. in Vocat. Edn., Calif. State U.-Long Beach, 1985. Cert. vocat. educator, Calif. Sales mgr., tech. rep. Ford Motor Co. and Gen. Motors Corp., Manila, Philippines, 1968-75; with personnel dept. Orange County (Calif.), 1975-76; adminstr. Los Angeles County Regional Occupational Program, 1976-86; ptnr WBA Advt., Mktg. and Communications, Seattle, 1986—; instr. Cerritos Community Coll. Chmn. employer adv. group Calif. Employment Devel. Dept.; chmn. adv. group Regional Adult Vocat. Edn. Council; mem. bus. edn. adv. bd. Cerritos Coll.; mem. accreditation team Western Assn. Schs. and Colls. Recipient Pub. Service award State of Calif., 1979, 80, Legislature resolution, 1979, Internat. Women Achievement award Soroptomists, 1984. Mem. ACLU, Calif. Assn. Regional Occupational Programs, NOW, Nat. Assn. Female Execs., Assn. Calif. Sch. Adminstrs. Democrat. Unitarian. Office: WBA 1101 N Northlake Way Seattle WA 98103

EVANS, WAYNE CANNON, advertising and public relations executive; b. Salt Lake City, Aug. 26, 1931; s. David Woolley and Beatrice (Cannon) E.; m. Vella Sydne Neil, Aug. 30, 1956; children: Laurel Evans Galli, Nancy Evans Peterson, Patricia Evans Thomas, Wayne Neil. BA, U. Utah, 1957, MS in Journalism, 1959. Corp. sec., sr. v.p., dir., account exec. Evans Communications and Evans-Salt Lake, Salt Lake City, 1965—; dir. Liberty Fin. Corp. Mem. Salt Lake City Sch. Bd., 1973-84, pres., 1979-80, 83, 84; mem. Salt Lake County Parks and Recreation Bd., 1973-84, pres., 1974, 78, 82, 83; mem. Salt Lake County Arts adv. Bd., 1982; bd. dirs. Family Counseling Ctr., 1982—, pres. 1985-87 Served with U.S. Army, 1954-55. Mem. Pub. Relations Soc. Am. (accredited). Republican. Mormon. Lodge: Rotary. Home: 1246 Gilmer Dr Salt Lake City UT 84105 Office: Evans Communications and Evans Salt Lake 110 Social Hall Ave Salt Lake City UT 84111

EVANS, WAYNE HENRY, educational organization administrator; b. Browning, Mont., May 3, 1937; s. Henry and Annie Irene (Fast Buffalo Horse) E.; m. Sandy Ryan, Sept. 22, 1959 (div.); 1 child, Jordon; m. Ethel Ann Calf Boss Ribs, Feb. 15, 1972; children: Henry, Frances, Hiram, Jaunita. AA, Haskell Coll., 1958; BA, Cleve. State U., 1971. Counselor Cleve. Out Reach, 1971-72; edn. coordinator Blackfeet Native Am. Program, Browning, 1972-78; dir. Tribal Work Experience Program, Browning, 1978-81, Community Devel. Ctr., Heart Butte, Mont., 1981—. Mem. Mont. Edn. Assn., Mont. Rifleman's Assn. Democrat. Roman Catholic. Avocations: hunting, skiing, hiking, rodeoing. Office: Heart Butte Community Devel Ctr PO Box 134 Heart Butte MT 59448

EVANS, WILLIAM THOMAS, physician; b. Denver, Aug. 21, 1941; s. Alfred Lincoln and Marian Audrey (Biggs) E.; student Whitman Coll., 1959-60, U. Vienna (Austria), 1961-62; A.B., U. Colo., 1963; M.D., Baylor U., 1967; grad. Chinese Coll. U.K.; Licentiate Acupuncture, Oxford, Eng., 1976; m. Lucy Fales. Intern, Mary Fletcher Hosp., Burlington, Vt.; physician Villages of Kodiak Island and Lake Iliamna, 1968-70; founder, dir. emergency dept. St. Elizabeth Hosp., Yakima, Wash., 1970-75; practice medicine specializing in health care, practice traditional acupunture, Denver; founder, dir. Colo. Back Sch., Denver, 1979—; Friends of Earth del. Limits to Medicine Congress, 1975. Organizer, Protest Poison in Our Presence run, Colo., 1977; initiated Colo. Sun Day, 1978. Served to lt. comdr. Indian Health Service, USPHS, 1968-70. Mem. Rocky Mountain Traumatological Soc. (program chmn.), Denver County Med. Soc., Colo. Med. Soc., Am. Occupational Medicine Assn., Colo. Acad. Occupational Medicine (v.p.), AMA, Am. Coll. Sports Medicine, Traditional Acupuncture Soc. Office: 1720 S Bellaire Suite 1200 Denver CO 80222

EVANS, WINIFRED DOYLE, physicist; b. Logansport, La., Sept. 10, 1934; s. Willie Cheatune and Annie Laurie (Hawthorne) E.; m. Carolyn Trudell Hawkins, May 26, 1956; children: Julia Lynne, Randall Brian. BS in Physics, La. Tech. U., 1956; MS in Physics, UCLA, 1958; PhD in Physics, U. N.Mex., 1965. Asst. prof. physics La. Tech. U., Ruston, 1958-60; staff mem. Hughes Aircraft Co., Los Angeles, 1956-58, NASA Langley, Newport News, Va., 1960-61; with Los Alamos (N.Mex.) Nat. Lab., 1961—. Mem. Am. Astron. Soc. (exec. com. high energy astrophysics div. 1983—). Home: 390 El Conejé Los Alamos NM 87544 Office: Los Alamos Nat Lab PO Box 1663 MS D446 Los Alamos NM 87545

EVANS, WINTHROP SHATTUCK, airline captain, lawyer; b. Santa Monica, Calif., June 21, 1939; s. Clifford E. and Luella (Wyble) E.; m. Carlene D. Buschena, June 26, 1965; children—Theresa, Shalene, Shanna, Michelle. A.A., Fullerton Coll., 1969; B.A., Calif. State U.-Fullerton, 1973; J.D., Western State U., Fullerton, 1980. Bar: Calif. 1980. Enlisted in U.S. Navy, 1957, commd. ensign, 1961, advanced through grades to lt. comdr., 1969; served with U.S. Naval Reserve, 1965-76, ret. lt. comdr., 1976; airline capt. Am. Airlines, Los Angeles, 1965—; sole practice law, Placentia, Calif., 1980—; substitute tchr. Western State U. Mem. Calif. Bar Assn., Orange County Bar Assn., Aircraft Owners and Pilots Assn. Republican. Roman Catholic. Office: PO Box 532 Placentia CA 92670

EVARTS, HAL GEORGE, JR., author; b. Hutchinson, Kans., Feb. 8, 1915; s. Hal George and Sylvia (Abraham) E.; B.A., Stanford U., 1936; m. Dorothea Van Dusen Abbott, June 28, 1942; children—Virginia Leland, William Abbott, John Van Dusen. Reporter, Evening Tribune, San Diego, 1935, Call Bull., San Francisco, 1939; reporter, writer Occidental Pub. Co., San Francisco, 1938; writer N.Y. Herald Tribune, European edit., Paris, 1939-40; author novels, including: Treasure River, 1964; The Talking Mountain, 1966; Smugglers' Road, 1968; Mission to Tibet, 1970; The Pegleg Mystery, 1972; Bigfoot, 1973; author biographies: Jedediah Smith, 1958; Jim Clyman, 1959; author anthology: Fugitive's Canyon, 1955; contbr. numerous short stories to nat. mags., including Saturday Evening Post, Esquire, Collier's, Am., This Week; tchr. creative writing at workshops. Served with inf. U.S. Army, 1943-45. Recipient Charlie May Simon award for children's lit. Ark. State Sch. Council, 1976, Spl. award Mystery Writers Am., 1964, 68. Mem. Western Writers Am. (v.p. 1959-60, Spl. award 1973), Zeta Psi. Home and Office: 6625 Muirlands Dr La Jolla CA 92037

EVENHUIS, NEAL LUIT, entomologist; b. Upland, Calif., Apr. 16, 1952; s. Kornelus and Harmina (Vermeer) E. BS, Calif. State Poly. U., Pomona, 1974, MS, 1977. Sci. illustrator Bishop Mus., Honolulu, 1976-78, entomologist, 1978—; mem. internat. editorial adv. bd. USDA Catalog of Flies of the World, 1983—. Author: Bibliography of Bombyliidae, 1983 (Oberly award 1985); assoc. editor Pacific Insects, a publ. of Bishop Mus., 1980-85, sr. editor Internat. Jour. Entomology, 1985; contbr. articles to profl. jours. Fellow Smithsonian Instn., 1985; grantee Nat. Geographic Soc., 1984-85. Fellow Royal Entomol. Soc. London; mem. AAAS, Entomol. Soc. Am., Hawaiian Entomol. Soc. (sec. 1983, Disting. Service award 1984), Soc. Systematic Zoology, Sigma Xi. Tibetan Buddist. Avocations: reading, guitar playing, coin collecting, flying disc sports. Home: 2737 Pacific Heights Rd Honolulu HI 96813 Office: Bishop Mus Dept Entomology 1525 Bernice St Honolulu HI 96817-0916

EVENS, ROBLEY DUNGLISON, retired army officer, former county official; b. Pasco, Wash., July 16, 1909; s. Silas Monroe and Emma (Pays) E.; B.A. in Bus. Adminstrn., Wash. State U., 1932; postgrad Sch. Social Work, U. Calif., 1963-64; m. Edythe Mae Greene, June 7, 1931 (dec. Sept. 1979); children—Marian Louise Evens Oppenlander, Roberta Diane Evens Crownover; m. 2d, Ruth Hamilton Airey, June 1980. With Pacific Power & Light Co., Yakima County, Wash., 1933-41; apptd. 2d lt. Inf., U.S. Army Res., 1932, advanced through grades to capt., entered active duty, 1941, advanced through grades to col., 1957; comdg. officer various facilities, Ft. Buchanan, San Juan, P.R., 1944-46, U.S. Army Forces, Aruba-Curacao, 1946; service in Dutch Guiana, 1946-47, Istanbul, Turkey, 1952-53; prof. mil. sci. and tactics U. Oreg., Eugene, 1953-56; asst. chief of staff G-I, Hdqrs. U.S. Army, Pacific, 1959-61, ret., 1961; supr. social services County of Sonoma, Calif., 1961-71. Bd. dirs. Sonoma County Taxpayers Assn., 1971-80. Decorated Army Commendation medal. Mem. Ret. Officers Assn., Nat. Assn. Uniformed Services. Club: Masons. Home: 6445 Mesa Oaks Circle Santa Rosa CA 95405

EVENSON, WILLIAM EDWIN, university administrator; b. Martinez, Calif., Oct. 12, 1941; s. Raymond Fox and Berta (Woolley) E.; m. Nancy Ann Woffinden, Dec. 21, 1964; children: Brian, Elizabeth, Joann, Andrew, Bengte. BS, Brigham Young U., 1965; PhD, Iowa State U., 1968. Research assoc. U. Pa., Phila., 1968-70; asst. prof. physics Brigham Young U., Provo, Utah, 1970-73, assoc. prof., 1973-79, assoc. dir., dean gen. edn., 1980-84, prof. physics, 1979—, assoc. acad. v.p., 1985—. Contbr. articles to profl. jours. Missionary Ch. Jesus Christ Latter-Day Saints, Paris, 1961-63, mem. high council, Provo, 1970-71, 74-75, bishop, Provo, 1971-74; active Dem. Cen. Com. Utah State, Provo, 1979-81; vice chmn. Dem. Utah County, Provo, 1981-82. Fellow Woodrow Wilson Found., 1965-66, Coop. Grad. NSF, 1965-66, Danforth Found., 1965-68; named Prof. of Month Brigham Young U., 1979. Mem. Am. Assn. Physics Tchrs., Hawaiian Bot. Soc., Nat. Audubon Soc., Hawaiian Audubon Soc., Sigma Xi. Home: 629 E 2875 N Provo UT 84602 Office: Brigham Young U 1206 SFLC Provo UT 84602

EVERETT, HOWARD CHESTON, civil engineer; b. Pelahatchee, Miss., Feb. 12, 1909; s. Looney Newton and Loretta Adela (Moore) E.; m. Maude Evelyn Rockefeller, May 29, 1929; 1 son, Howard Cheston (dec.). B.Sc. in Civil Engring., U. Houston, 1950, postgrad., 1950-52; postgrad. U. Calif.-San Francisco, 1960-61, Coll. San Mateo, 1959-60. Registered profl. engr. Tex., Calif., Colo. Numerous engring. positions with United Gas and other companies in petroleum industry Tex., La., 1928-45; asst. prof., civil engring. U. Houston, 1950-51; pres. Everett-Heinen Corp., Houston, 1948-50; pres. Fairfield Park Corp., Houston, 1951-52; chief draftsman, structural engr. Holly Sugar Corp., San Mateo, Calif. and Colorado Springs, Colo., 1955-74; chief engr. Schloss & Shubart, Denver, 1974-80; instr. engring. Menlo (Calif.) Coll., 1960-63; cons. and lectr. in field. Mem. Colo. Soc. Profl. Engrs., Tau Beta Pi, Phi Kappa Phi. Lodges: Masons, Shriners. Engring. research and devel. of new machinery for waste water and sewage treatment, 1979-80.

EVERETT, NICHOLAS PAUL, biochemist, researcher; b. Rugby, Eng., Feb. 27, 1953; came to U.S., 1981; s. Norman Dennis and Elsie Henrietta (Williams) E. BSc in Applied Chemistry, Kingston Poly., Kingston-on-Thames, England, 1975; PhD in Plant Physiology, Leicester (Eng.) U., 1978. Postdoctoral research assoc. Leicester U., 1978-79; sr. research asst. Liverpool (Eng.) U., 1979-81; research biochemist Stauffer Chem. Co., Richmond, Calif., 1981-85, research group supr., 1985—. Contbr. articles to profl. jours. Mem. AAAS, Internat. Assn. Plant Tissue Culture. Avocations: hiking, camping, racquetball. Office: Stauffer Chem Co 1200 S 47th St Richmond CA 94804

EVERSLEY, FREDERICK JOHN, sculptor, engineer; b. Bklyn., Aug. 28, 1941; s. Frederick William and Beatrice Agnes (Syphax) E. B.S.E.E., Carnegie-Mellon U., 1963. Aerospace engring. exec. Wyle Labs., El Segundo, Calif., 1963-67. One man shows include Whitney Mus. Am. Art, N.Y.C., 1970, Nat. Acad. Sci., Washington, 1976, 81, Los Angeles Inst. Contemporary Art, 1976, Santa Barbara Mus., 1976, Newport Harbor Art Mus., 1976, Oakland Mus. Art, 1977, Palm Springs Desert Mus., 1978, AIA, 1981, Va. Mus., 1981, Bacardi Art Gallery, Miami, Laband Art Gallery, Loyola Marymount U., Los Angeles; represented in permanent collections Smithsonian Instn., Washington, Calif. State Coll. at Los Angeles, Oakland (Calif.) Art Mus., Milw. Art Center, Whitney Mus. Am. Art, N.Y.C., John Marin Meml. Collection, N.Y.C., U., Kans. Art Gallery, Lawrence, Long Beach (Calif.) Mus. Art, Currier Gallery Art, Manchester, N.H., Taft Mus. Art, Cin., Cranbrook Art Gallery, Bloomfield Hills, Mich., Nat. Acad. Sci., Washington, Nat. Collection Fine Arts, Washington, M.I.T., Cambridge, Neuberger Mus. Art, Purchase, N.Y., Newport Harbor Art Mus., Newport Beach, Calif., Guggenheim Mus., N.Y.C., Smith Coll. Mus. Art, Northhampton, Mass., Nat. Air and Space Mus., Mus. Contemporary Art, Los Angeles; artist in residence Nat. Air and Space Mus., Washington, 1977-80. Nat. Endowment Arts grantee, 1972. Mem. Los Angeles Inst. Contemporary Art, Artworkers Coalition. Address: 1110 W Washington Blvd Venice CA 90291 also: 29 Mercer St New York NY 10013

EVERSON, DALE OSCAR, statistician educator; b. Geneva Lake, Wis., Feb. 1, 1930; s. Oscar Martenus and Edith May (Kingery) E.; m. Darlene Marie Wamstad, Aug. 15, 1954; children: Vicki M. Keller, Sharon Kay. BS in Dairy Sci., U. Idaho, 1952, MS in Dairy Sci., 1956; PhD in Animal Breeding, Iowa State U., 1960. With biometrical services Agrl. Research Service, USDA, Beltsville, Md., 1960-62; assoc. prof. stats. U. Idaho, Moscow, 1962-66, prof. stats., 1966—. Contbr. articles to profl. jours. chmn. Sch. Bd. Moscow Sch. Dist. 281, 1985-86. Served to sgt. Q.M.C., 1952-54. Named Outstanding Tchr., Coll. Agriculture, U. Idaho, 1972, 87. Mem. Sigma Xi (pres. 1972-73), Phi Kappa Phi (pres. 1974-75), Alpha Zeta (advisor 1978-81), Gamma Sigma Delta (1982-83). Lodge: Lions (pres. 1966-67, outstanding Lion award, 1966). Avocations: fishing, waterskiing, boating. Home: 1241 Ponderosa Dr Moscow ID 83843 Office: Dept Math and Applied Stats U Idaho Moscow ID 83843

EVERTON, LOUISE MATHEWS, publishing executive; b. Providence, Utah, Oct. 22, 1934; d. Alma Erickson Mathews and Elva (Poulter) Allen; m. George Baugh Everton, Jr., Sept. 10, 1952; children: Stephen George, Carrie Louisa, Elizabeth Ann (dec.), Marion Birget, Alma Lee, Peter Mathew (dec.), Andrew Harold. Grad., Logan (Utah) Latter Day Saints Sem., 1951; B in Ornamental Horticulture, Utah State U., 1974. Book rev. editor Everton Publs., Logan, 1978—; lectr. in geneology various locations, 1960; cons. in geneology. bd. dirs. Freedom Found. Valley Forge, Salt Lake City, 1983—; sec. Cache County Rep. Women, Logan, 1974—; 2d v.p. Utah Fedn. Rep. Women, 1982—. Avocations: gardening, oil painting. Home: 825 S 4th E Providence UT 84332 Office: Everton Publs Box 306 Logan UT 84321

EVERTON, THOMAS, chemistry educator; b. Logan, Utah, Jan. 21, 1937; s. Marion Knowles and Hattie Lois (Hale) E.; m. Susan Patricia Henderson, June 3, 1963; children: Ted, Amy, John. BS, Brigham Young U., 1963; MS, U. Utah, 1968, PhD, 1972. Instr. chemistry Idaho Falls (Idaho) High Sch., 1963-64; instr. chemistry and gen. sci. Dugway (Utah) High Sch., 1964-67; teaching fellow U. Utah, Salt Lake City, 1968-71; instr. chemistry Ventura (Calif.) Coll., 1971-77, head dept. chemistry, 1977—. Served as lance cpl. USMC, 1960-66. Recipient Golden Apple award Alpha Gamma Sigma, 1978. Mem. Calif. Assn. Chemistry Tchrs., Sigma Xi. Avocations: bicycling, computer programming. Office: Ventura Coll 4667 Telegraph Rd Ventura CA 93003

EVERTS, CONNOR, artist; b. Bellingham, Wash., Jan. 24, 1926; s. William Edward and Sophia (Mehan) E.; m. Chizuko Sugita, Mar. 15, 1953; children—Anon Connor, Meigan Mariko, Geoffrey, Tamura. A.A., El Camino Coll., 1950; B.A., U. Wash., 1952. Mem. faculty dept. art Calif. State U., Northridge, 1960-62, Calif. Inst. Arts, 1962-65, Calif. State U., Long Beach, 1965, San Francisco Art Inst., 1966, U. So. Calif., 1967-69, U. Calif.-Riverside, 1972-76; graphics chmn. Cranbrook Acad. Art, Bloomfield Hills, Mich., 1976-81; exchange prof. Prahran Coll. Advanced Studies, Melbourne, Australia; artist in residence Calif. Inst. Tech., 1970-71. One man exhbns. include, Pasadena Art Mus., 1960, Michael Walls Gallery, San Francisco, 1967-69, Los Angeles Mcpl. Gallery, 1971, Meckler Gallery, Los Angeles, 1979, World Print Council, 1982, retrospective exhibit, Los Angeles Mus., 1983, Orange County Ctr. for Contemporary Art, 1986; group exhbns. include Tokyo Biann. Painting Exhbn, 1967, Homage to Lithography, Mus. Modern Art, N.Y.C., 1969, Printmaking, Oskokunst Forening, Oslo, Norway, 1974; represented in permanent collections, Chgo. Art Inst., Long Beach Mus. Art, Los Angeles County Mus. Art, Milw. Art Mus., Mus. Modern Art, N.Y.C., Pasadena Art Mus., San Francisco Mus. Modern Art, Washington Gallery Modern Art, others. Pres. adv. bd. Los Angeles Mcpl. Gallery, 1968. Served with USCG, 1946. Mem. AAUP, Los Angeles Printmaking Soc., Mich. Assn. Printmakers, Artists Equity. Studio: 2351 Sonoma St Torrance CA 90501

EWAN, JOHN ROBERT, energy company executive; b. Paso Robles, Calif., Mar. 10, 1950; s. Henry Lewis and Lydia Imogene (Teegarden) E.; m. Stephanie Ann Frediani, Mar. 27, 1982; 1 child, Renée Ann. BA, Calif. Poly. State U., San Luis Obispo, 1973, postgrad., 1973. Lic. gen. contractor, Calif. Group leader Vols. in Service to Am., Columbus, Ind., 1974-75; prin. John Ewan Builder, San Luis Obispo, 1975-80; pres. Pacific Energy Co., San Luis Obispo, 1980—. Founder The Sun Group, San Luis Obispo, 1978. Mem. Exec. Assn. San Luis Obispo (bd. dirs. 1985—), Calif. Seia Coastal Chpt. (bd. dirs. 1986—). Avocations: swimming, golf. Office: Pacific Energy Co 2121 Santa Barbara St San Luis Obispo CA 93401

EWAN, MARION, optometrist; b. Hong Kong, Apr. 19, 1952; came to U.S., 1959, naturalized, 1962; d. Nelson and Lucy (Wu) E. B.A. in Psychobiology, UCLA, 1973; O.D., So. Calif. Coll. Optometry, 1977. Lic. optometrist, Calif. Optometrist Joseph Mulach Eye Ctr., Long Beach, Calif., 1977-81, cons. contact lenses, 1981—; pvt. practice optometry specializing in contact lenses, Los Angeles, 1982—. Mem. Am. Optometric Assn., Calif. Optometric Assn., South Bay Optometric Soc. (pres. 1980-81), Japanese-Am. Optometric Assn. Clin. study on extended-wear soft contact lenses, 1981. Office: 8737 Beverly Blvd Suite 401 Los Angeles CA 90048

EWELL, A(USTIN) B(ERT), JR., lawyer; b. Elyria, Ohio, Sept. 10, 1941; s. Austin Bert and Mary Rebecca (Thompson) E.; m. Kristine Lynn Ballantyne, Feb. 14, 1976; children—Austin Bert III, Brice Ballantyne. B.A., Miami U., Oxford, Ohio, 1963; J.D., Hasting Coll. Law, U. Calif.-San Francisco, 1966. Bar: Calif. 1966, U.S. Dist. Ct. (ea. dist.) Calif. 1967, U.S. Supreme Ct. 1982, U.S. Ct. Appeals (9th cir.) 1967. Pres. A. B. Ewell, Jr., A. Profl. Corp., Fresno, 1984—; gen. counsel Kings River Water Assn., 1979—, Dudley Ridge Water Dist., 1980—, MidValley Water Dist., 1984—, Friant Water Users Authority, 1985—; pres. Western Water Recharge Corp., 1985—; chmn. San Joaquin River Flood Control Assn., 1984—; mem. task force on prosecution, cts. and law reform Calif. Council Criminal Justice, 1971-74; mem. Fresno Bulldog Found., Calif. State U. Mem. affiliated San Joaquin Valley Agrl. Water Com. 1979—; co-chmn. nat. adv. council SBA, 1981, 82, mem. 1981—; bd. dirs. Fresno East Community Ctr., 1971-73; mem. Fresno County Water Adv. Com., Fresno Community Council, 1972-73; chmn. various polit. campaigns and orgns., including Reagan/Bush, 1984, Deukmejian for Gov., 1986; mem. adv. com. St. Agnes Med. Ctr. Found., 1983—; trustee Fresno Met. Mus. Art, History and Sci. Mem. ABA (water resources com. of natural resources sect., real property probate and trust law sect.), Internat. Platform Assn., Phi Alpha Delta, Assn. Calif. Water Agys. (affiliate), U.S. Supreme Ct. Hist. Soc., Sigma Nu. Clubs: Downtown, Racquet (Fresno), Commonwealth (San Francisco), President's. Congregationalist. Office: 83 E Shaw Ave Suite 203 Fresno CA 93710

EWING, CLAIR EUGENE, geophysics educator, engineering consultant; b. Blue Rapids, Kans., Sept. 20, 1915; s. Grant and Margaret Leona (Fincham) E.; m. Evelyn Dorothea Anderson, June 19, 1942; children: Mike, Kathy, Karen, Patty, Kevin. BSCE, Kans. State U., 1941; MSCE, U. Colo., 1950; PhD in Geodetic Sci., Ohio State U., 1955; diploma, Air Command and Staff Coll., Montgomery, Ala., 1950, Indsl. Coll. of Armed Forces, Washington, 1959. Commd. 2d lt. USAF, 1941, advanced through grades to col., 1954; chief scientist ITT, Vandenberg AFB, Calif., 1969-72; cons. Lompoc, Calif., 1972—; adj. prof. Golden Gate U., San Francisco, 1976—. Named Engr. of Yr. IEEE, Vandenberg, 1970. Mem. Am. Geophys. Union (pres. Geodesy sect. 1972-74), Sigma Xi (v.p. Ventura chpt. 1963-64). Methodist. Home: 4344 Sirius Ave Lompoc CA 93436 Office: PO Box 5297 Vandenbrg AFB CA 93437

EWING, COLEMAN CLAY, architect; b. San Antonio, Oct. 11, 1944; s. William Thomas and Ina Fay (Talley) E.; student San Antonio Jr. Coll., 1963-65; B.S., U. Houston, 1970; m. Marjorie Glennda Sewell, Aug. 28, 1965; children—Christopher Coleman, Michelle InaMarie. Customer engr. IBM Co, Houston, Tex., 1965-67; draftsman Morton Levy, Houston, 1967-71, Roland Johnson, Denver, 1971-72, DMJM Phillips, Denver, 1972-73, Wheeler/Lewis, Denver, 1973-75, Frank Lundquist, Denver, 1975-76, Oliver, Hellegren, Denver, 1976-77; prin. Coleman C. Ewing Architect & Assocs., Denver, 1977-80, 86—; pres. Ewing Gorman Archtl. Group, Denver, 1980-81, also dir.; pres. Ewing Archtl. Group, P.C., 1981-86; CAD/CAM specialist archtl. dept. Martin Marietta Co., Denver, 1981-86. Republican. Mem. Ch. of Christ. Office: Ewing Architect and Assocs 6634 S Clarkson St Littleton CO 80221

EWING, GALEN WOOD, retired chemistry educator, consultant; b. Boston, Mar. 14, 1914; s. William Clinton and Florence (Wood) E.; m. Alice C. Sipple, Nov. 26, 1942; children: Martin Sipple, William Galen, Thomas Edward. BS, Coll. William & Mary, 1936; PhD, U. Chgo., 1939. Phys. chemist Winthrop Chemical Co., Rensselaer, N.Y., 1942-46; from asst. prof. to assoc. prof. chemistry Union Coll., Schenectady, N.Y., 1946-57; prof. N.Mex. Highlands U., Las Vegas, N.Mex., 1957-64, Seton Hall U., South Orange, N.J., 1964-79; retired 1979—; vis. prof. Carleton Coll., Northfield, Minn., 1983-84. Author: Instrumental Methods of Chemical Analysis, 1954, 5th rev. edit., 1985. Recipient John Dustin Clark award Am. Chem. Soc., Cen. N.Mex. sect., 1986. Fellow AAAS; mem. Am. Chem. Soc. (emeritus), Soc. Applied Spectroscopy, Sigma Xi, Phi Beta Kappa. Mem. Orthodox Baha'i Ch. Lodge: Kiwanis. Home: 707 Myrtle Ave Las Vegas NM 87701

EWING, JAMES J., laser scientist; b. Morristown, N.J., Dec. 15, 1942; s. Clyde Frederick and Katherine Augusta (Joyce) E.; m. Jane Carole Davis; children: Jennifer Barbara, Daniel Jonathon. BA, U. Calif., Riverside, 1964; PhD, U. Chgo., 1969. Faculty mem. U. Ill., Urbana, 1969-71; staff mem. AVCO Everett (Mass.) Research Lab., 1972-76; program mgr. advanced excimer fusion laser tech. Lawrence Livermore Nat. Lab., Livermore, Calif., 1976-79; v.p. laser programs Spectra Tech., Inc., Bellevue, Wash., 1979—. Contbr. chpts. to books and articles to profl. jours. Mem. Am. Phys. Soc., Sigma Xi. Home: 15305 SE 46th Bellevue WA 98006 Office: Spectra Tech Inc 2755 Northup Way Bellevue WA 98004

EWING, MARTIN SIPPLE, astronomer, electrical engr.; b. Albany, N.Y., May 4, 1945; s. Galen Wood and Alice (Sipple) E.; m. Eva Reissner, June 11, 1966; children: Margaret, Robert, Eric. BA, Swarthmore Coll., 1966; PhD, MIT, 1971. Mem. prof. staff Calif. Inst. Tech., Pasadena, 1971—; vis. assoc. CSIRO Div. Radiophysics, Sydney, Australia, 1985—. Author: Forth Manuel D'Application, 1984; contbr. articles to profl. jours. Mem. IEEE, AAAS, Internat. Astronomical Union, Assn. Computing Machinery. Episcopalian. Avocations: writing, amateur radio. Office: Calif Inst Tech Mail Stop 102-24 Pasadena CA 91125

EWING, RICHARD EVERT, orchard company executive, retired chemist; b. Webster City, Iowa, Dec. 28, 1919; s. Lee Roy and Ruth Elizabeth (Amundson) E.; m. Mildred Ann Ludt, Jan 30, 1943; children: Richard E. Jr., Ronald F., Timothy J. BS, Iowa State U., 1948; MS, U. Idaho, 1952; PhD, Wash. State U., 1958. Sr. scientist Gen. Electric Co., Richland, Wash., 1950-60, Clevite Semiconductor, Palo Alto, Calif., 1960-62; group ldr. Hewlett-Packard Co., Palo Alto, 1962-72; sr. scientist Xerox Corp., Palo Alto, 1972-75; entrepreneur Manson, Wash., 1975-84; pres. Bountiful Orchards, Inc., Manson, 1984—. Sect. Editor Jour. Chem. Abstracts, also contbr. articles to profl. jours; patentee in field. Served with U.S. Army, 1941-45, PTO. Mem. Am. Chem. Soc., Phi Lambda Upsilon. Republican. Mormon. Avocations: woodworking, fly fishing. Home and Office: Bountiful Orchards Inc 2143 Lakeshore Dr Manson WA 98831

EWING, ROBERT CRAIG, lawyer; b. Glen Ridge, N.J., May 9, 1953; s. Donald Graham and Barbara (Hansen) E.; m. Mary Arnold Hengy, Aug. 30, 1981; 1 child, Kyle Ross. B.A., Middlebury Coll., 1976; J.D., Denver U., 1980. Bar: Colo. 1980, Mass. 1981, U.S. Dist. Ct. Colo. 1980, U.S. Ct. Appeals (10th cir.) 1984. Assoc. Hall & Evans, Denver, 1981-84; part-time prof. Metro. State Coll., Denver, 1983—; assoc. Holme, Roberts & Owen, Denver, 1984—; bd. dirs. State Adv. Council on Emergency Med. Services, Denver, 1981-83; emergency med technician Am. Coll. Surgeons, Colo. Dept. Health, Denver, 1979—; bd. dirs. McArthur Ranch Homeowners Assn., 1981-85; mem. Am. Trakehner Assn., Columbus, Ohio, 1983—. Author: Emergency Medical Personnel and the Law, 1982; editor Legal Information Rev., 1983; Trends in Law Report newsletter, 1983-84. Named Charles A. Dana Scholar Middlebury Coll., Vt., 1975. Mem. ABA, Colo. Bar Assn., Denver Bar Assn., Am. Trial Lawyers Assn., Colo. Trial Lawyers Assn., Colo. Def. Lawyers Assn. Republican. Presbyterian. Clubs: Internat. Athletic, Araphaoe Hunt (Littleton). Home: 816 W Quarry Rd Littleton CO 80124

EWING, RUSSELL CHARLES, II, physician; b. Tucson, Aug. 16, 1941; s. Russell Charles and Sue M. (Sawyer) E.; B.S., U. Ariz., 1963; M.D., George Washington U., 1967; m. Louise Anne Wendt, Jan. 29, 1977; children—John Charles, Susan Lenore. Intern, Los Angeles County-U. So. Calif. Med. Center, Los Angeles, 1967-68; gen practice medicine and surgery, Yorba Linda, Calif. and Placentia, Calif., 1970—; mem. staff St. Judes Hosp., Fullerton, Calif., 1970—; mem. staff Placentia Linda Community Hosp., 1972—, vice chief staff, 1977-78, chief staff, 1978-80; sec., dir. Yorba Linda (Calif.) Med. Group, Inc., 1974—; dir. Western Empire Savs. & Loan Assn. (Calif.). Bd. dirs. Yorba Linda YMCA, 1973—, pres., 1973-74, 81; bd. dirs. Placentia Linda Community Hosp., 1974-81. Served with USN, 1968-70. Diplomate Am. Bd. Family Practice. Fellow Am. Acad. Family Practice; mem. AMA, Calif. Med. Assn. (house of del. 1978—), Orange County Med. Assn. (dir. 1983—, sec., treas. 1986-87). Republican. Episcopalian. Home: 9212 Smoketree Lane Villa Park CA 92667 Office: 4900 Prospect Yorba Linda CA 92686

EWING, VERNON RICHARD, electrical engineer; b. St. Paul, Jan. 19, 1948; s. Ivan Leon and Muriel Juliette (Skaalrude) E.; m. Carrie Frances Burkholder, Oct. 26, 1974; 1 child, Aren Matthew. BS, Colo. State U., 1970; postgrad., Colo. Sch. Mines, 1973-75. Registered profl. engr., Calif. Engr. Alumet, Golden, Colo., 1973-77, Combustion Power, Palo Alto, Calif., 1978-79, Lurgi, San Mateo, Calif., 1979-81; sr. engr. Bechtel, San Francisco, 1981—; cons. Petroleum Pipeline Co., Cairo, Egypt, 1984-86; cons. Chevron, GEO; pres. Applied Tech. Engring., 1987. Patentee in field. Served with USN, 1970-73. Mem. Instrument Soc. Am., Cairo Divers (sci. officer). Avocations: scuba diving, sailing, playing classical guitar. Home: Rural Rt #1 Box 415 Halfmoon Bay CA 94019 Office: Bechtel 50 Beale San Francisco CA 94119

EZZARD, MARTHA MCELVEEN, state senator, lawyer; b. Atlanta, Nov. 8, 1938; d. George Davant and Gladys Caroline (Lewis) McElveen; A.B. in Journalism, U. Ga., 1960; M.A., U. Mo., 1968; J.D., U. Denver, 1982; m. John A. Ezzard, Dec. 27, 1960; children—Shelly Lynne, Lisa Annette, John A. With Atlanta Jour., 1959-60, Sta. WSB-TV, Atlanta, 1960; tchr. Littleton (Colo.) High Sch., 1961-62; with Sta. KOMU-TV, Columbia, Mo., 1965-68; gov.'s press aide, 1973-75; polit. columnist Rocky Mountain Jour., Denver, 1976-77; mem. Colo. Ho. of Reps. from 37th Dist., 1978-80, Colo. Senate from 26th Dist., 1980—; assoc. Davis, Graham & Stubbs, Denver; lectr. environ. law Denver U.; bd. dirs. United Bank Littleton. Bd. dirs. Women's Found.; candidate Rep. nomination U.S. Senate, 1986. Named Outstanding Rep. Legislator, 1986, Best Legis., Westword Newspaper, 1986, Englewood Bus. and Profl. Woman of Yr., 1986; recipient Rocky Mountain Womens Inst. award, 1987. Mem. ABA (continuing legal edn. lectr.), Colo. Bar Assn., Denver Bar Assn., Women's Forum. Episcopalian. Clubs: Oxford. Office: Colo Senate State Capitol Denver CO 80203 Other: 370 17th St Denver CO 80201

FAAS, LARRY ANDREW, educator; b. Iowa City, Sept. 25, 1936; s. Merlin Andrew and Verla Lavonne (Cheney) F.; m. Patricia Middleton, Dec. 18, 1962; children—Anna Rachel, Eric Andrew, Audra Beth. B.S., Iowa State U., 1959; M.A., U. No. Colo., 1961; Ed.D., Utah State U., 1967. Instr. vocat. agr. English Valley Community Schs., North English, Iowa, 1959-60; sch. psychologist Tri-County Spl. Edn., Decorah, Iowa, 1961-63; dir. spl. edn. Tri-County Spl. Edn., 1963-65; asst. prof., dir. spl. edn. U. Nev., 1966-67; asst. prof. edn. Ariz. State U., Tempe, 1967-70; asso. prof. Ariz. State U., 1970-75, prof. edn., 1975—. Author: The Emotionally Disturbed Child, 1970, Learning Disabilities, 1972, Learning Disabilities: A Competency Based Approach, 1976, 2d edit., 198l, Children with Learning Problems: A Handbook for Teachers, 1980. Mem. Council Exceptional Children, Phi Delta Kappa. Home: 519 E Del Rio Dr Tempe AZ 85282

FABER, EDWARD E., computer retail executive; b. Buffalo, Mar. 19, 1933. BS in Indsl. and Labor Relations, Cornell U., 1955. Data processing salesman IBM Corp., Miami, Fla., 1957-62; instr. Customer Exec. Sch. IBM Corp., Endicott, N.Y., 1963; instr. European Edn. Ctr. IBM Corp., Blaricum, The Netherlands, 1964; program adminstr. New Bus. Mktg. Dept. IBM Corp., White Plains, N.Y., 1965-66; mgr. devel. info mktg. IBM Corp., San Jose, Calif., 1967-68; v.p., dir. mktg. services Memorex Sales and Services Corp., 1969-72; dir. mktg. services Four-Phase Systems Inc., 1972-75; mgr. nat. sales Omron Corp. Am., 1975, Im Sai Mfg., 1975-76; pres. Computerland Corp., Hayward, Calif., 1976-83, vice chmn., 1983-85, pres., chief exec. officer, 1985-86, chmn., chief exec. officer, 1986—. Served to capt. USMC, 1955-57. Office: Computerland Corp 30985 Santana Hayward CA 94544 *

FACCINI, ERNEST CARLO, mechanical engineer; b. Livo, Trento, Italy, May 28, 1949; s. Carlo and Elena Agnes (Pancheri) F.; parents Am. citizens; A.A., Western Wyo. Community Coll., 1969; B.S., U. Wyo., 1972, M.S., 1976. Engring. technician Laramie (Wyo.) Energy Research Center, 1968-71; field engr. Mountain Fuel Supply Co., Rock Springs, Wyo., 1972; research engr. Aberdeen (Md.) Proving Grounds, 1972-73; research asst. mech. engring. U. Wyo., Laramie, 1973-76; engring. asst. Bridger Coal Co., Rock Springs, Wyo., 1973; mech. engr. Naval Explosive Ordnance Disposal Facility, Indian Head, Md., 1976-85; sr. scientist TERA/NMIMT, Socorro, N. Mex., 1986—. Registered profl. engr., Wyo., Md. Mem. ASME (chmn. student sect. 1971-72), Am. Phys. Soc., AAAS, Am. Soc. Metals. Roman Catholic. Contbr. articles to profl. jours.; patentee in field. Researcher rapid explosive excavation techniques, underwater non-explosive excavation, surface/subsurface ordnance clearance vehicle design, remote fuse disassembly, aluminum burn bar investigation, multi-fuel combuster investigation, internal ballistics, blast effects. Home: 1211 Hilton Pl Socorro NM 87801 Office: TERA/NMIMT Socorro NM 87801

FACKLER, MARTIN L(UTHER), surgeon, researcher; b. York, Pa., Apr. 8, 1933; s. Martin Luther and Naomi Dorcas (Gibbs) F.; m. Nancy Aleen Gray, Sept. 29, 1964. AB magna cum laude, Gettysburg Coll., 1955; MD, Yale U., 1959. Diplomate Am. Bd. Surgery. Intern U. Oreg. Med. Sch. Hosp., 1959-60; enlisted USN, 1960; resident in gen. surgery U.S. Naval Hosp., Boston, 1961-65; resident in plastic surgery U.S. Naval Hosp., Bethesda, Md., 1966-67; advanced through grades to col. USN; staff surgeon NSA Hosp., DaNang, Socialist Republic of Vietnam, 1967-68, USN Hosp., Yokosuka, Japan, 1969-71; chief dept. surgery USN Hosp., Memphis, 1972-74; interservice transfer, U.S. Army, chief dept. surgery 2d Gen. Hosp., Landstuhl, Republic of Germany, 1975-80; chief dept. surgery U.S. Army Hosp., Ft. Carson, Colo., 1980-81; dir. wound ballistics lab. Presidio, San Francisco, 1981—; tech. adv. Assn. Firearm and Toolmark Examiners, 1984—; adv. forensic sci. grad. sch. U. Calif., Berkeley, 1985—; speaker on war surgery, wound ballistics, weapons effects; expert witness, cons. to various state, city and nat. law enforcement agys. and criminalistics labs.; appointed steering com. on devel. less-than-lethal weapons for law enforcement use Nat. Inst. Justice, 1986—. Contbr. articles to profl. jours.; patentee in field. Recipient Commendation 2d Gen. Hosp., Landstuhl, 1981. Fellow ACS (com. on trauma); mem. Phi Beta Kappa, Nat. Rifle Assn. (life). Club: Commonwealth (San Francisco); Franco-Am. (Berkeley, Calif.). Avocations: study of German and French, gunsmithing, welding, designing surgical instruments, tennis. Home: 1809 Wyman Ave Presidio San Francisco CA 94129 Office: Letterman Army Inst Research Presidio San Francisco CA 94129

FACTOR, MAX, III, lawyer, investment advisor; b. Los Angeles, Sept. 25, 1945; s. Sidney B. and Dorothy (Levinson) F.; m. Susan Barg, June 19, 1966; 1 child, Jennifer Lee. B.A. in Econs. magna cum laude, Harvard Coll., 1966; J.D., Yale U., 1969. Bar: Calif. 1970, U.S. Ct. Appeals (6th cir.) 1971, U.S. Dist. Ct. (cen. dist.) Calif. 1971. Law clk. U.S. Ct. Appeals (6th cir.), 1969-71; exec. dir. Calif. Law Ctr., Los Angeles, 1973-74; dir. Consumer Protection Sect., Los Angeles City Atty., 1974-77; pres. MF Capital Ltd., Beverly Hills, Calif., 1978-86; ptnr. Cooper, Epstein & Hurewitz, Beverly Hills, Calif., 1986—; expert witness numerous state and fed. bds., 1974-78; guest lectr. UCLA, U. So. Calif., Los Angeles County Bar Assn., Calif. Dept. Consumer Affairs, 1974-76; hearing examiner City of Los Angeles, 1975. Contbr. articles to profl. jours. Bd. dirs. Western Law Ctr. for the Handicapped, Los Angeles, 1977-79, Beverly Hills Unified Sch. Dist., 1979-83; pres. Beverly Hills Bd. Edn., 1983; bd. councilors U. So. Calif. Law Ctr., Los Angeles, 1983—. Recipient scholarship award Harvard Coll., 1965; Max Factor III Day proclaimed in his honor Beverly Hills City Council, 1979; recipient Disting. Service to Pub. Edn. award Beverly Hills Bd. Edn., 1979. Mem. Los Angeles County Bar Assn. (chmn. various coms. 1976-78), Beverly Hills C. of C. (pres.-elect 1986—), Beverly Hills Edn. Found. (pres. 1977-79). Democrat. Jewish. Office: Cooper Epstein & Hurewitz 9465 Wilshire Blvd Suite 800 Beverly Hills CA 90212

FADDICK, ROBERT RAYMOND, civil engineering educator; b. Sudbury, Ont., Can., May 18, 1938. BSCE, Queen's U., 1961, MSCE, 1963; PhD, Mont. State U., 1970. Hydraulic engr. Alden Research Lab. Worcester (Mass.) Polytech Inst., 1963-66; research asst. Mont. State U., Bozeman, 1966-69; prof. Colo. Sch. Mines, Golden, 1969—; pres. Slurry Pipeline Corp., Golden, 1970—. Contbr. articles to profl. jours. Mem. Assn. Profl. Engrs. Ont., ASCE, Slurry Transport Assn., Slurry Tech. Assn., soc. Rheology, Brit. Hydromechanics Research Assn. (hon. mem.). Home: 2373 Coors Dr Golden CO 80401 Office: Colo Sch Mines Engring Dept Golden CO 80401

FADEN, ALAN IRA, neurology educator; b. Phila., Jan. 11, 1945. BA in Physics, U. Pa., 1966; postgrad., Ind. U., 1966-67; MD, U. Chgo., 1971. Resident in neurology U. Calif., San Francisco, 1972-75; research neurologist Walter Reed Army Inst. Research, Washington, 1975-80; assoc. prof. neurology and medicine Uniformed Services U. of Health Scis., Bethesda, Md., 1978-84, prof. neurology and physiology, 1981-84; dir., vice chmn. neurological research Uniformed Serviced U. of Health Scis., Bethesda, Md., 1980-82, chief neurobiol. research unit, 1982-84; prof. neurology, vice chmn. dept. U. Calif., San Francisco, 1984—; chief neurology VA Med. Ctr., San Francisco, 1984—; dir. Ctr. for Neural Injury, San Francisco, 1984—; sci. dir. Nat. Research Inst. for Neural Injury, Washington, 1983—. Contbr. articles to profl. jours.; patentee in field. Named one of 100 Top Leaders of Washington, Washington mag., 1982. Fellow ACP, Am. Acad. Neurology; mem. Am. Soc. Pharmacology and Exptl. Therapeutics, Am. Soc. Clin. Investigation, Am. Physiol. Soc., Am. Neurol. Assn. Avocations: jogging, history, art collecting. Office: VA Med Ctr Neurology Service 127 4150 Clement St San Francisco CA 94121

FAGAN, WILLIAM LAWRENCE, plant engineer, hospital official; b. Middletown, Conn., Feb. 15, 1927; s. William Robert and Margaret Gonsega (Drennan) F.; m. Catherine Victoria Graham, Feb. 14, 1949; children—William R., Deborah, Jennifer, Jeffrey; m. 2d, Dorothy May Fluke, Jan. 10, 1974. Cert. in air conditioning and refrigeration Conn. State Tech. Inst., Hartford, 1948. Adminstrv. engr. Bay State Med. Ctr., Springfield, Mass., 1967-74, St. Luke's Episcopal Hosp., Houston, 1974-75; asst. adminstr. Alexandria (Va.) Hosp., 1975-77; dir. plant engring. Cedars-Sinai Med. Center, Los Angeles, 1977-81; dir. facilities devel. and constrn. Hoag Meml. Hosp., Newport Beach, Calif., 1981—. Served to chief warrant officer U.S. Army, 1945-67. Mem. Am. Soc. Hosp. Engrs., Am. Inst. Plant Engrs. (cert. plant engr., sr. mem.; Plant Engr. of Yr. award 1973), Orange County Chpt, Hosp. Engrs. (pres.) Calif. Hosp. Engrs. Soc. (bd. dir.) Am. Legion, Nat. Rifle Assn. Roman Catholic. Club: Costa Mesa (Calif.) Golf. Contbr. chpt. to Handbook for Hospital Engineers, 1974. Home: 300 Cagney Ln Apt PH 1 Newport Beach CA 92663 Office: Hoag Meml Hosp 301 Newport Blvd Box Y Newport Beach CA 92663

FAGEN, RICHARD REES, educator, author; b. Chgo., Mar. 1, 1933; s. Abel E. and Mildred (Rees) F.; children: Sharon, Ruth, Elizabeth, Michael. B.A. in English, Yale U., 1954; M.A. in Journalism, Stanford U., 1959, Ph.D. in Polit. Sci., 1962. Asst. prof. Stanford U., 1962-66, assoc. prof., 1966-70, prof. polit. sci., 1970—, Gildred prof. Latin Am. studies, 1981—; cons. Ford Found., Santiago, Chile, 1972-73; prof. Latin Am. Sch. Social Sci., Santiago, 1972-73; cons. Rockefeller Found., 1977-80; chmn.com. on Latin Am. studies Social Sci. Research Council, N.Y.C., 1981-83. Author Politics and Communication, 1966; co-author: (with David Finley and Ole Holsti) Enemies in Politics, 1967; co-author: (with Richard Brody and Thomas O'Leary) Cubans in Exile: Disaffection and the Revolution, 1968; author: The Transformation of Political Culture in Cuba, 1969; co-author: (with William Tuohy) Politics and Privilege in a Mexican City, 1972, (with Albert Fishlow, Carlos Diaz Alejandro. Roger Hansen) Rich and Poor Nations in the World Economy, 1978; author: The Nicaraguan Revolution, 1981, Choosing Peace: A New U.S. Policy Toward Cen. Am., 1987; editor, translator: Cuba: The Political Content of Adult Education, 1964; editor. author: (with Wayne Cornelius) Political Power in Latin America, 1969; editor, author: (with Julio Cotler) Latin America and The United States, 1974; editor, author: Capitalism and the State in U.S.-Latin American Relations, 1979, (with Olga Pellicer) The Future of Central America: Policy Choices for the U.S. and Mexico, 1983; co-author: Changing Course: Blueprint for Peace in Central America and The Caribbean, 1984; co-editor, author: (with Carmen Diana Deere and Jose Luis Coraggio) Transition and Development: Problems of Third World Socialism, 1986.. Mem. internat. adv. bd. Amnesty Internat., 1976—. Served with U.S. Army, 1954-56. Fellow Social Sci. Research Council, 1960-61; fellow Social Sci. Research Council, 1964, Am. Council Learned Socs., 1964, Ford Found., 1965-67, Fgn. Area Fellowship Program, 1965-67; grantee Ford Found., 1969, 79-80, 81; fellow NSF, 1970-71, 82-84, Rockefeller Found., 1977; grantee Rockefeller Found., 1978-80, Com. on Scholarly Exchange with the People's Republic of China, 1983; Guggenheim fellow, 1986. Office: Stanford U Dept Polit Sci Stanford CA 94305

FAGIN, KATHERINE DIANE, research scientist; b. N.Y.C., Oct. 25, 1954; d. Arthur E. and May (Seplow) F. AB in Bio. Sci. magna cum laude, Cornell U., 1976; PhD in Physiology, Emory U., 1980. Research asst. Emory U., Atlanta, 1976-79, U. Ala., Birmingham, 1979-80; postdoctoral fellow interdisciplinary program psychiatry/physiology U. Calif., San Francisco, 1980-82, postdoctoral fellow neuroendocrine program, 1982-83, research assoc., 1983-84; research scientist Amgen Co., Thousand Oaks, Calif., 1984—. Contbr. articles to profl. jours. Mem. AAAS, Endocrine Soc., N.Y. Acad. Scis., Internat. Soc. Neuroendocrinology. Office: Amgen Co 1900 Oak Terrace Ln Thousand Oaks CA 91320

FAGIN, RONALD, computer research manager; b. Oklahoma City, May 1, 1945; s. George J. and Maxine (Appleman) F.; m. Susan Mary Malsin, Mar. 30, 1985; children: Joshua Bejosa, Timothy Aaron. BA, Dartmouth Coll., 1967; PhD in Math., U. Calif., Berkeley, 1973. Mem. research staff Watson Research Ctr., IBM Corp., Yorktown Heights, N.Y., 1973-75, Almaden Research Ctr., IBM Corp., San Jose, Calif., 1975—; mgr. computer sci. founds. Almaden Research Ctr., IBM Corp., San Jose, 1979—. Assoc. editor Jour. Computer and System Sci., 1984—; mem. editorial bd. Theoretical Computing, 1984—. Recipient 2 Outstanding Innovation awards IBM Corp., 1981, MIT Press Pub's. Prize for Best Paper, Internat. Joint Conf. on Artificial Intelligence, 1985. Jewish. Democrat. Home: 321 Escobar Ave Los Gatos CA 95030 Office: IBM Almaden Research Ctr Dept K53/802 650 Harry Rd San Jose CA 95120

FAHNESTOCK, MARGARET, biochemist, molecular biologist; b. Pasadena, Calif., Jan. 5, 1952; d. Warren Louis and Phyllis (Rogers) Kern; m. Douglas Wade Fahnestock, Aug. 18, 1974. BS, Stanford U., 1974; PhD, U. Calif., Berkeley, 1979. Postdoctoral fellow Baylor Coll. of Medicine, Houston, 1979-81, Stanford (Calif.) U., 1981-85; biochemist SRI Internat., Menlo Park, Calif., 1984-86, sr. biochemist, molecular biologist, 1986—. Contbr. articles to profl. jours. Fellow Am. Cancer Soc., 1979, Dysautonomia Found., 1982. Mem. AAAS, Phi Beta Kappa. Avocations: horseback riding, skiing, traveling, butterfly collecting. Office: SRI Internat 333 Ravenswood Ave Menlo Park CA 94025

FAIKS, JAN OGOZALEK, state senator, real estate developer; b. Hempstead, N.Y., Nov. 17, 1945; d. Edmund Frank and Anna Marie (Chupella) Ogozalek. B.A., Florida State U., 1967. Tchr. Anchorage Sch. Dist., 1968-76, counselor, 1976-78; owner, mgr. Green Connection, Anchorage, 1978-81; mem. Alaska State Senate, Juneau, 1982—. Author: Llama Training-Who's In Charge, 1981. Editor course devel. in career math., 1976. Bd. dirs. Common Sense for Alaska, 1980—, research chmn., v.p., 1980-82; bd. dirs. Anchorage Symphony, 1984; Recipient First Lady vol. award Gov. of Alaska, 1981; President's award Common Sense for Alaska, 1981; named Outstanding Secondary Tchr., Anchorage Sch. Dist., 1977. Mem. Nat. Council State Legislators, Anchorage C. of C. (bd. dirs. 1981-86, legis. chmn. 1980-82), Gen. Fedn. Women's Club (legis chmn. 1979-82), Anchorage Symphony Women's League (pres. 1980-81), Phi Beta Phi (pres. 1974-76). Republican. Presbyterian.

FAILI, FIROOZ NASSER, research chemical engineer; b. Tehran, Iran, Nov. 24, 1953; came to U.S., 1977; s. Ali Nasser and Nayer (Nayeri) F. BSChemE, Abadan (Iran) Inst. Tech., 1977; MSChemE, San Jose State U., 1980. Sr. research assoc. IIT Cons., Loves Park, Ill., 1980-84; instrumentation specialist Syva Co., Mountain View, Calif., 1984-85; process engr. GCA Corp., Sunnyvale, Calif., 1985; research and devel. engr. Zylin div. Varian Assocs., Fremont, Calif., 1985—. Contbr. articles to profl. jours. Mem. Am. Inst. Chem. Engrs. (assoc.), Am. Chem. Soc., Electrochem. Soc. Avocations: sculpting, reading. Office: Varian Assocs Zylin Div 48501 Milmont Dr Fremont CA 94538

FAILING, WILLIAM LATIMER, JR., broadcasting company executive; b. Portland, Oreg., July 29, 1940; s. William Latimer and Ellen (Johnson) F.; m. Patricia Stipe, Feb. 11, 1966 (div. Aug. 1978); m. Michele Mary Bowler, Mar. 18, 1984; children: Edward Arthur, Josiah John. A.A., Menlo Coll., 1960; student Colgate U., 1960-61; B.A., U. Calif.-Berkeley, 1964. With sales dept. China Dry Goods, San Francisco, 1964-66, Crown Zellerbach, San Francisco, 1966-69, Sta. KYA, San Francisco, 1969; sales mgr. Sta. KISN, Portland, 1969-76, Sta. KXL, Portland, 1977-79; owner, gen. mgr. Sta. KKSN, Portland, 1979—, KKLI-FM Radio, 1985—; Classical Music Syndication, Inc., 1986—; mem. exec. com. Portland Area Radio Council, 1983—. Chmn. Vista Bridge Restoration Com., Portland, 1984; bd. dirs. French-Am. Sch., Portland, Oreg. Sch. Design, Portland, 1984, Old Ch. Soc., Portland, 1984, Artquake, 1987. Served with USCG, 1964-70. Clubs: University (Portland); Multnomah Athletic. Office: KKSN/KKLI Radio 510 SW 3d St Portland OR 97204

FAILS, THOMAS GLENN, geologist; b. Unity Twp., Ohio, Feb. 28, 1928; s. T. Glenn and Mary C. (Adams) F.; m. Mary Ivy Schmid, Mar. 1, 1959; children—Glenn Michael, Nora Anne. Geol. Engr., Colo. Sch. Mines, 1954; M.A. in Geology, Columbia U., 1955. Cert. petroleum geologist; cert. profl. geol. scientist. Geologist, Shell Oil Co., New Orleans, 1956-66; dist. geologist Trend Exploration Ltd., New Orleans, 1967-69, v.p., London, 1970-75; geologist, producer, Denver, 1975—; gen. ptnr. Glennora Holdings, Ltd., Denver, 1982—; pres. Raven Exploration, Denver, 1977—. Citizen ambassador to Peoples Republic of China, People to People Internat., 1983. Served with USMC, 1946-48, 50-51. Fellow Geol. Soc. London; mem. Am. Assn. Petroleum Geologists, Petroleum Exploration Soc. Gt. Britain (bd. dirs. 1974-75), Rocky Mountain Assn. Geologists. Republican. Lutheran. Home: 965 S Monroe St Denver CO 80209 Office: 1777 Larimer St Suite 1203 Denver CO 80202

FAIN, GORDON LEE, physiology educator; b. Washington, Nov. 24, 1946; s. Robert Forbes and Margaret (Smith) F.; m. Margery Jones, June 22, 1968; children: Timothy P., Nicholas H. Student, U. Chgo., 1964-65; BA in Biology, Stanford U., 1968; PhD in Biophysics, Johns Hopkins U., 1973. NIH predoctoral fellow Johns Hopkins U., Balt., 1968-73; NIH postdoctoral fellow biol. labs. Harvard U., Cambridge, Mass., 1973-74; Grass fellow Marine Biol. Labs., Woods Hole, Mass., 1974; exchange fellow Harvard U. Med. Sch. and Inst. Nat. de la Sante et de la Recherche Med., Lab. de Neurobiologie, Paris, 1974-75; asst. prof. ophthalmology UCLA Sch. Medicine, Jules Stein Eye Inst., 1975-78, assoc. prof., 1978-82, prof. ophthalmology, 1982—; assoc. dir. Jules Stein Eye Inst., Los Angeles, 1985—; speaker in field. Contbr. numerous articles to profl. jours. NIH grantee, 1980-85, 84-88, 85-90; NSF travel grantee, 1985-87. Mem. Assn. for Research in Vision and Ophthalmology, Biophys. Soc., Soc. Neurosci., Phi Beta Kappa. Office: UCLA Jules Stein Eye Inst Los Angeles CA 90024

FAIRBAIRN, ROBERT HENDERSON, psychiatrist; b. Calgary, Alta., Can., Oct. 28, 1934; came to U.S., 1964, naturalized, 1969; s. Robert Henderson and Vibeke Mary (Madsen) F.; m. Anne Begbie Drysdale, June 8, 1963 (div. Mar. 1984); children—John, Daniel, James. M.D., U. B.C., 1959. Rotating intern Montreal Gen. Hosp., Que., Can., 1959-60; ship's surgeon on freighter Brit. Mcht. Marine, 1961; resident in psychiatry U. B.C., Vancouver, Can., 1961-64; chief resident psychiat. service Shaughnessy Hosp., Vancouver, 1963-64; fellow dept. psychiatry U. Colo. Med. Ctr., Denver, 1964-65, instr., ward chief inpatient gen. psychiat. wards, 1956-67; asst. clin. prof., 1970—; psychiatrist II, Ft. Logan Mental Health Ctr., Colo., 1967-69; practice medicine specializing in psychiatry with spl. interest in forensic psychiatry, Denver, 1969—; seminar leader summer work program Western Interstate Council for Higher Edn., 1966, 67; psychiat. cons. asthma service Nat. Jewish Hosp., Denver, 1970-73; advisor Beta Theta Pi, U. Denver, 1973—; presenter forensic seminar dept. psychiatry Fitzsimons Army Med. Ctr., 1978, 84; mem. staff Colo. Psychiat. Hosp., Mt. Airy Psychiat. Ctr., Mercy Med. Ctr. Contbr. articles to med. jours. Mem. Am. Psychiat. Assn., Colo. Psychiat. Soc., Colo. Soc. for Study Multiple Personality Disorder. Republican. Office: 3535 Cherry Creek North Dr Denver CO 80209

FAIRBANK, JANE DAVENPORT (MRS. WILLIAM MARTIN FAIRBANK), editor, civic worker; b. Seattle, Aug. 21, 1918; d. Harold

Edwin and Mildred (Foster) Davenport; A.B. magna cum laude, Whitman Coll., 1939; postgrad. U. Wash., 1940-42; m. William Martin Fairbank, Aug. 16, 1941; children—William Martin, Robert Harold, Richard Dana. Teaching asst. U. Wash., Seattle, 1940-42; sci. staff mem. Radiation Lab., Mass. Inst. Tech., Cambridge, 1942-45. Chmn. Second Careers for Women, Stanford, Calif., 1970—; co-organizer Whitman Coll. Sr. Alumni Coll., 1985—; founding mem. Bay Area Consortium on Ednl. Needs of Women. 1971; mem. Canada Coll. Citizens Advisory Com. for Community Edn., 1968—; mem. organizing com. for conf. on frontiers of physics Stanford U., 1982. Fellow U. Wash., 1940-42. Mem. Whitman Coll. Alumni Assn. (bd. dirs. 1986—), Calif. Congress Parents and Tchrs. (hon. life), Mortar Bd., Phi Beta Kappa. Alpha Chi Omega. Mem. United Ch. of Christ. Club: Stanford Faculty Women's (pres. 1975-76). Editor: Radar Maintenance Manual (2 vols.), 1945; co-editor Near Zero: New Frontiers of Physics, 1987; Second Careers for Women: A View from the San Francisco Peninsula, 1971; Second Careers for Women, vol. II: A View of Seven Fields from the San Francisco Bay Area, 1975. Contbr. articles to sci. jours. Office: Second Careers for Women 141 E Floresta Way Menlo Park CA 94025

FAIRBANK, WILLIAM MARTIN, JR., physicist; b. New Haven, Jan. 7, 1946; s. William Martin and Jane (Davenport) F.; m. Donna Lorraine Witter, Aug. 30, 1975; children: William Henry, Mary Helen, David Martin. BA, Pomona Coll., 1968; MS, Stanford U., 1969, PhD, 1974. Research assoc. U. Ariz., Tucson, 1974-75; asst. prof. Colo. State U., Ft. Collins., 1975-78, assoc. prof., 1978-83, prof., 1983—; cons. Atom Scis., Inc., Oak Ridge, Tenn., 1984—. Fellow NSF, 1968, Alfred P. Sloan Found, 1976. Mem. Am. Phys. Soc., Optical Soc. Am., Sigma Xi.

FAIRCHILD, ARVID PERSHING, travel agency executive; b. Turlock, Calif., Jan. 6, 1925; s. Clarence Frank and Maybelle (Dunagan) F.; B.S. in Civil Engring., U. Miami (Fla.), 1955; m. Grace M. Stewart, June 20, 1943; children—Jack W., Jean A. Fairchild Gartner. Dir. ops. Interocean Airways, Luxembourg, 1961-63; flight instr. United Airlines, 1963-64; check pilot Japan Air Lines, 1964-74; pres., chmn. bd. Island Air Tours, Kilohana World Travel (formerly Scenic Island Travel), Honolulu, 1974-85; v.p. Horizon Airlines/Trans Nat. Airlines; v.p. Pacific Air Express, 1982—; dir. ops. UN airlift for Congo, 1962; capt. Seaboard Western Airlines, 1955-62. Served with USN, 1940-53. Decorated Air medal (3), Purple Heart, Army Disting. Service medal with oak leaf clusters. Mem. Nat. Assn. Businessmen. Republican. Presbyterian. Clubs: Masons, Shriners, Order Eastern Star. Author: Instrument Flight Technique; also articles in aviation publs. Home: 927 Prospect St Apt 804 Honolulu HI 96822 Office: PO Box 30622 Honolulu HI 96820

FAIRCHILD, THOMAS NEWMAN, psychologist, educator; b. Burley, Idaho, Nov. 21, 1947; s. Loyal Bryant and Bernyce Elizabeth (Rudolph) F.; m. Carolyn Ardria Yoder, Oct. 1, 1966 (div.); children—David Brian, Brandi Michelle, Nicole Kathryn; m. 2d, Ellen Lorett; children—Joshua Thomas, Megan Lorett. B.S. in Psychology, U. Idaho, 1969, M.Ed. in Guidance and Counseling, 1971, Specialist D. in Sch. Psychology, 1972; Ph.D. in Sch. Psychology, U. Iowa, 1974. Cert. sch. counselor, psychologist, Idaho; lic. profl. counselor, Idaho. Counselor, sch. psychologist Walla Walla Community Sch. Dist. (Wash.), 1971; sch. psychologist Cedar Rapids Community Schs. (Iowa), 1971-74; counselor educator, sch. psychologist trainer Coll. Edn., U. Idaho, Moscow, 1974—, chmn. dept. counseling and human services, 1978-86, coordinator sch. psychology tng. program, 1974—; cons. Kendrick, Genesee, Craigmont, Lapwai Culdesac Sch. Dists., Idaho. Mem. Rocky Mountain Assn. for Counselor Edn. Supervision (sec. treas. 1981-82), Nat. Assn. Sch. Psychologists (state del. 1984-86, Cert. Appreciation 1985, 86), Am. Assn. Counseling and Devel., Am. Psychology Assn., Council Exceptional Children, Assn. for Counselor Edn. and Supervision (resources and research com. 1982—), Idaho Assn. for Counselor Edn. and Supervision, Idaho Assn. Counseling and Devel., Idaho Sch. Psychologists Assn. (pres. 1976, 86-87, historian 1984-87, chmn. awards com. 1983-85, licensure com. 1975-82, Disting. Service award 1985), Idaho Stateline Guidance Assn., Phi Delta Kappa. Co-author: (with A. Lee Parks) How to Survive Educator Burnout, 1981, (with D. Fairchild, E. Woolums, D. Starr) Everything You Always Wanted to Know About Drinking Problems and a Few Things You Didn't Want to Know, 1978, (with A. Iriarte, M. Yutzy) The Kindergarten Primer: A Guide for Professionals and Parents, 1975; editor: Accountability for School Psychologists: Selected Readings, 1977, Crisis Intervention Strategies for School-Based Helpers, 1985; editor, author: Mainstreaming Series, 1975-77; mem. editorial bd. Psychology in the Schools, 1976-83, Sch. Psychology Rev., 1978-81; contbr. to profl. jours. and filmstrips. Home: 2201 Westview Dr Moscow ID 83843 Office: U Idaho Coll Education Moscow ID 83843

FAIRCLOTH, RICHARD WILLIAM, information management specialist; b. St. Louis, July 16, 1935; s. Paul Henry and Isabel Lewis (Smith) F.; m. Sharon Kay Lien, June 2, 1956; children: Kimberly Ann, Michele Rae. BA, Harris Tchrs. Coll., 1965; EdM, U. Mo., St. Louis, 1975. Cert. elem. and secondary tchr., Mo. (life). Computer specialist U.S. Army, St. Louis, 1969-76; supr. computer specialists U.S. Army, Delta Junction, Alaska, 1976—. Office: US Army Cold Regions Test Ctr Office of Commdr STECR-AD-I APO Seattle WA 98733-7850

FAIRWEATHER, EDWIN ARTHUR, electronics company executive; b. London, July 21, 1916; came to U.S., 1967; s. Arthur Henry and Elizabeth (Dawson) F.; m. Joan Barbara Branson, Sept. 14, 1946; children: David Martin, Janet Elizabeth Fairweather Nelson. BSME, London Poly., 1940. Quality engr. Lucas-Rotex, Toronto (Ont., Can.) and Birmingham (Eng.), 1951-58; mfg. engr. Flight Refuelling Co., Dorset, Eng., 1958-62, Spar Aerospace, Toronto, 1962-67, Sperry Flight Systems, Phoenix, 1967-71; engr. research and devel. Ford Aerospace Co., Palo Alto, Calif., 1971-85; founder, pres., chief engr. Fairweather & Co., Sunnyvale, Calif., 1980—. Patentee in field. Served with RAF, 1940-46. Avocations: sailing, golf. Home and Office: 1442 Wolfe Rd Sunnyvale CA 94087

FAISON, DELORES, government accountant; b. Atlanta, Aug. 28, 1945; d. Harry and Ella Maud (Hunter) Campbell; 1 child, Harold Ernest Campbell. Student CUNY, Helene Fuld Sch. Nursing, N.Y.C., U. Ariz.; grad. with high honors, Pima Coll., 1984. In various positions U.S. Govt., N.Y.C., 1965-74; health unit coordinator Polyclinic Med. Ctr., Harrisburg, Pa., 1978-81, St. Joseph's Hosp., Tucson, 1981-86; acctg. technician Agrl. Research Service, Dept. Agr., Tucson, 1984—; v.p. Tucson Employees Benefit Assn., 1984-85. Recipient Woman On The Move award YWCA, Tucson, 1985. Mem. Nat. Assn. Health Unit Coordinators, Nat. Assn. Female Execs., Federally Employed Women, Fed. Women's Program (alt. rep.), Phi Theta Kappa. Democrat. Baptist. Club: Federally Employed Women (com. chairperson 1985—) (Tucson). Avocations: reading; writing; singing; public speaking.

FAISON, EDMUND WINSTON JORDAN, business educator; b. Rocky Mount, N.C., Oct. 13, 1926; s. Nathan Marcus and Margery Lucille (Jordan) F.; m. Lois Harger Parker; children: Charles, Dorothy Anne, Barbara Jeane, Edmund Jr., Diane, Carol. A.B. in Psychology, George Washington U., 1948, M.A., 1950, Ph.D., 1956. Research asst. NRC, Washington, 1948-49; mgr. exptl. lab. Needham, Louis and Brorby, Chgo., 1955-56; account exec. Leo Burnett Co., 1957-58; v.p. Market Facts, Inc., Chgo., 1959; pres. Visual Research Internat., Zurich, Switzerland, 1960-61; adviser AID, Dept. State. Latin Am., 1963-68; prof. bus. adminstrn. U. Hawaii, Honolulu, 1968—; chmn. mktg. dept. U. Hawaii, 1975—; chmn. bd. Scandata Hawaii, Inc., East-West Research and Design, Inc.; vis. prof. London Grad. Sch. Bus. Studies, 1974-75. Author: Advertising: A Behavioral Approach for Managers, 1980; editorial bd.: Jour. of Mktg, 1958-63; contbr. articles to profl. jours. Served with USN, 1944-46; Served with USAF, 1950-54. Mem. Am. Psychol. Assn., Soc. Consumer Behavior, Am. Mktg. Assn. (pres. Honolulu chpt. 1973-74), Acad. Mktg. Sci., Acad. Mgmt., Am. Acad. Advt., Am. Assn. Public Opinion, Sales and Mktg. Execs. Internat., Advt. Research Found., Japan-Am. Soc., Honolulu Advt. Fedn., Market Research Soc. (U.K.), C. of C. of Hawaii, Japanese C. of C., Hawaii Visitors Bur., Small Bus. Assn. Hawaii, Honolulu Acad. Arts, All-Industry Packaging Assn. (chmn. 1961), European Packaging Fedn. (U.S. rep. 1961), World Packaging Orgn., Sigma Xi, Pi Sigma Epsilon. Clubs: Pacific, Oahu Country, Kaneohe Yacht, Rotary. Home: 619 Paopua Loop Kailua HI 96734 Office: East West Research Inst 735 Bishop St Suite 235 Honolulu HI 96813 Office: U Hawaii Honolulu HI 96822

FAITH, CHARLES ALBERT, III, insurance company executive; b. Rahway, N.J., Jan. 31, 1952; s. Charles Albert and Jessiemay (Aycock) F.; m. Barbara Ann Schertler. B.A., U.S. Internat. U., 1974. Counselor, Model Ex-Offenders, San Diego, 1974-75; loss control rep. Continental Ins. Co., San Francisco, 1976-77; Fireman's Fund Ins. Co., San Diego, 1977-80; comml. ins. broker Bromac, San Diego, 1980-84, Nationwide Ins., San Diego, 1984—. Mem. Nationwide Ins. Pres. Club. Club: Bay View Yacht. Home: 2610 Cowley Way San Diego CA 92110 Office: Nationwide Ins 8555 Aero Dr San Diego CA 92123

FALCO, CHARLES MAURICE, physicist, educator; b. Fort Dodge, Iowa, Aug. 17, 1948; s. Joe and Mavis Margaret (Mickelson) F.; m. Dale Wendy Miller, May 5, 1973; children: Lia Denise, Amelia Claire. BA, U. Calif., Irvine, 1970, MA, 1971, PhD, 1974. Asst. physicist Argonne (Ill.) Nat. Lab., 1974-76, physicist, group leader, 1976-82; prof. physics and optical scis., research prof. U. Ariz., Tucson, 1982-86, dir. lab. x-ray optics, 1986—; cons., 1976—; vis. prof. U. Paris, 1979, 86; Conf. organizing com. mem. 1978-81, 86-87; lectr. 1974—. Editor: Future Trends in Superconductive Electronics, 1978; contbr. articles to profl. jours.; patentee in field. Trainee NSF, 1970-74. Mem. IEEE, Am. Phys. Soc., Am. Vacuum Soc., Materials Research Soc. Home: 6301 N Caravan Ln Tucson AZ 85704 Office: U Ariz PAS Bldg 81 Tucson AZ 85721

FALCON, KAREN GAY, bedspread manufacturer; b. N.Y.C., Jan. 31, 1949; d. Joseph Albert Falcon and Olcay Kent. AA, Pierce Coll., 1970; BA, Calif. State U., Los Angeles, 1972. Sales mgr. Animan Designs, Los Angeles, 1972-76; pres. Kare-Free, Los Angeles, 1976-79; founder, chief exec. officer Hollywood Nights, Inc., Los Angeles, 1979—; pres. Hollywood Nights of Jamaica Ltd., 1985—; cons. European mktg. Magma Heimtex, Friesenheim, Fed. Republic Germany, 1985—; seminar speaker SBA, Los Angeles, 1982—. Sponsor Soc. for Prevention Cruelty to Animals, Los Angeles, since 1980—. Mem. Nat. Bath, Bed and Linen Assn., Waterbed Mfrs. Assn. (speaker 1977—, best trade show exhibit awards 1981, 83, 84, 85), Nichiren Shoshu Am. Democrat. Avocations: travel, music. Office: Hollywood Nights Inc 1930 E 15th St Los Angeles CA 90021

FALCONE, ALFONSO BENJAMIN, physician; b. Bryn Mawr, Pa., July 24, 1923; s. B. and Elvira (Galluzzo) F.; m. Patricia J. Lalim, Oct. 22, 1955; children: Christopher L., Steven B. AB in Chemistry with distinction, Temple U., 1944, MD with honors, 1947; PhD in Biochemistry, U. Minn., 1954. Diplomate Am. Bd. Internal Medicine subspecialty bd. endocrinology and metabolism. Intern Phila. Gen. Hosp., 1947-48, resident in internal medicine, 1948-49; teaching fellow internal medicine U. Hosps., U. Minn., 1949-51; asst. clin. prof. medicine U. Wis., Madison, 1956-59, assoc. clin. prof., 1959-63, asst. prof. Inst. Enzyme Research, 1963-66, vis. prof., 1966-67; practice medicine specializing in endocrine and metabolic diseases Fresno, Calif., 1968—; mem. staff Fresno Community Hosp., chmn. dept. medicine, 1973; mem. staff St. Agnes Hosp., Fresno, Valley Med. Ctr., Fresno; sr. corr. Ettor Majorana Ctr. for Sci. Culture, Erice, Italy. Contbr. articles to profl. jours. Served with AUS, 1944-46; served to lt. comdr. M.C., USNR, 1954-56. NIH postdoctoral fellow, 1951-53; NIH research grantee, 1958-68. Fellow ACP; mem. AMA, Am. Soc. Biol. Chemists, Cen. Soc. Clin. Research, Am. Fedn. Clin. Research, Am. Chem. Soc., Am. Soc. Internal Medicine, Am. Assn. for Study Liver Disease, Calif. Acad. Medicine, Sigma Xi, Phi Lambda Upsilon. Office: 2240 E Illinois Ave Fresno CA 93701

FALK, EUGENE L, newspaper executive; b. Smith Center, Kans., May 10, 1943; s. Lester and Esther (Hatfield) F.; m. Joanne Krys, Jan. 26, 1968; children—Laura Rae, Shannon Lynn. B.S., U. Colo., Boulder, 1967; M.B.A., Rochester Inst. Tech., N.Y., 1971. Asst. dir. prodn. Gannett Rochester Newspapers, Rochester, N.Y., 1969-71; dir. engring. Harte-Hanks Newspapers, San Antonio, 1971-73; asst. prodn. dir. Ridder Publications, Denver, 1973-75; dir. prodn. Wichita Eagle-Beacon, Kans., 1975-77; prodn. dir. San Jose Mercury News, Calif., 1977-81, dir. ops., 1981-83, v.p. ops., 1983-87; sr. v.p. Phila. Newspapers, Inc., 1987—; chmn. Western Newsprint Tech. Commn., Vancouver, B.C., 1981-86; dir. Portage Newspaper Supply Co., Akron, 1981-85;. Vice chmn. Hope Rehab. Services, San Jose, 1983-86, chmn., 1986—; trustee Hope Found., San Jose, 1984—. L.C. Paddock Meml. scholar U. Colo., 1965-67. Mem. Am. Newspapers Publishers Assn. (newsprint tech. com., vice chmn. 1986), Nat. Systems Group. Republican. Roman Catholic. Clubs: San Jose Athletic, LaRinconada Country (Los Gatos, Calif.), Courtside Tennis (Los Gatos). Lodge: Kiwanis. Home: 212 Brooke Acres Dr Los Gatos CA 95030 Office: San Jose Mercury News 750 Ridder Park Dr San Jose CA 95190

FALK, GATHIE, artist; b. Alexander, Manitoba, Can., Jan. 31, 1928; d. Cornelius and Agatha (Penner) F.; m. Dwight Allen Swanson, Nov. 11, 1974 (div. 1978). Student, U. Brit. Columbia, 1956-65. One-man shows include Canvas Shack, 1965, Odalesque Gallery, 1967, Douglas Gallery, Vancouver, 1968, Can. Cultural Ctr., Paris, 1974, Bau-Xi Gallery, Vancouver, 1976, Nat. Gallery Tour, 1976-77, Forest City Gallery, London, Ont., 1977, Edmonton Art Gallery, 1978, Artcore, Vancouver, 1978, UBC Art Gallery 1980, U. So. Alberta, Lethbridge, 1980, Glenbow Mus., Calgary, 1980, Equinox Art Gallery, Vancouver, 1981, 82, 83, 85, 87, Isaacs Gallery, Toronto, 1982, 84, 87, Painting Retrospective Art Gallery of Greater Victoria, 1985, 24 Yr. Retrospective Vancouver Art Gallery, 1985, 49th Parallel, N.Y.C., 1987; exhibited in group shows at Burnaby Art Gallery, 1964, 69, 73, 75, 80, Montreal Mus. Fine Arts, 1967, 70, 74, Art Gallery of Ont., Toronto, Can., 1970, 73, 74, Nat. Gallery of Can., 1975, 84, Art Gallery of Greater Victoria, 1973, 74, 79, Douglas Art Gallery, 1968, 69, Agnes Etherington Art Centre, Kingston, 1972-78, Edmonton U. Art Gallery, Alta. Coll. Art, Calgary, 1981, Musee d'art de Saint-Laurent, Que., 1981, Norman Mackenzie Art Gallery, Regina, Nickle Art Mus., 1982, The Art Gallery at Harbour Front, Toronto, 1977, 85, VAG, 1983, Nat. Art Gallery, O Hawa, 1975, 84, Centre Internat. d'Art Contemporaia d'Montreal, 1985; represented in permanent collections Indusman Collection, Ringhouse, Can. Comml. and Indsl. Bank, Art Gallery of Ont., Nat. Gallery, Art Bank, Vancouver Art Gallery. Grantee Can. Council, 1967, 80, Can. Council Arts Bursary, 1968, 69, 71. Recipient Sun award, 1968. Home and Office: 2861 West 3, Vancouver, BC Canada V6K 1M8

FALK, THEODORE CARSWELL, lawyer; b. Washington, Dec. 13, 1946; s. Leslie Alan And Joy (Hume) F.; m. Leila Birnbaum, July 27, 1973; children: Abram, Ariana, Phillip. Student, MIT, 1964-66; BA, Reed Coll., 1971; JD, Yale U., 1982; PhD, U. Pitts., 1985. Bar: Oreg. 1982. Psychiat. aide Haverford (Pa.) State Hosp., 1966-68; dir. library devel. Kaiser Research Ctr., Portland, Oreg., 1972-74; lectr. philosophy U. Calif., Santa Barbara, 1978-79; law clk. to presiding justice Oreg. Supreme Ct., Portland, 1982-83; assoc. Stoel, Rives et al, Portland, 1983-85, Spears, Lubersky et al, Portland, 1985—; research Psychiat. Security Rev. Bd., sponsor Yale U. Law Sch., Portland, 1981; legal asst. Mental Health Div., Portland, 1981. Contbr. articles to profl. jours. Chmn. legal subcomm. Oreg. HIV/AIDS Policy Com., Portland, 1986; campaign worker Com. to Re-elect Justice Linde, Portland, 1984. Fellow Danforth Found., St. Louis, 1971, Mellon, U. Pitts., 1971-76. Mem. ABA (health law forum), Oreg. Soc. Hosp. Atty.'s, Am. Acad. Hosp. Atty.'s, Multnomah County Bar Assn., Western Pension Conf., ACLU. Club: City Club of Portland (mem. human resources 1986—). Home: 6824 SE 34th Ave Portland OR 97202 Office: Spears Lubersky et al 520 SW Yamhill Suite 800 Portland OR 97204-1383

FALKENBERG, WILLIAM STEVENS, architect, contractor; b. Kansas City, Mo., July 21, 1927; s. John Joseph and Maraba Elizabeth (Stevens) F.; m. Janis Patton Hubner, Apr. 13, 1951; children: Ruth Elizabeth, Christopher Joseph, Charles Stevens. BS in Archtl. Engring., U. Colo., 1949. Pres. Falkenberg Constrn. Co., Denver, 1951-71, 74-84, devel. cons., 1984—; broker Hogan & Stevenson Realty, Denver, 1971-74. Chmn. constrn. Archdiocesan Housing Com., Inc.; chmn. restoration 9th St. Hist. Park; chmn. bldg. com. Four Mile House Hist. Park; chmn. Housing Trust Council, Denver, 1986-87; chmn. Rocky Mountain Better Bus. Bur., 1965-67; pres. Denver Friends of Folk Music, 1966. Served to lt. (j.g.) USNR, 1945-51. Mem. AIA (bd. dirs. Denver chpt. 1978-81, treas. 1981), Home Builder Assn. Met. Denver, Serra Internat. (pres. 1971, dist. gov. 1973), Delta Tau Delta. Clubs: Denver Athletic, Cactus, Equestrian Order of Holy Sepulchre. Home and Office: 430 Marion St Denver CO 80218

FALKENRATH, REX ELMER, automotive aftermarket executive, real estate developer; b. Salf Lake City, Feb. 11, 1954; s. Eugene Sherman and E. Maxine (England) F.; m. Corina E. Van Kwawegen, May 24, 1974 (div. Mar. 1983); children—Annika, Jennifer, Christina. Student in bus. U. Utah, 1972-73, Utah Tech. Coll., 1979-81; cert. in bus. law Nat. Inst. Credit, Salt Lake City, 1980, Assoc. Credit Mgmt., 1981. Salesman, caterer La Cetadelle, Salt Lake City, 1970-71; asst. mgr. United Rent-All, Salt Lake City, 1971-73; pres. Number 1 Performance, Salt Lake City, 1973—, Glday & Assocs., Salt Lake City, 1981—; mng. ptnr. Falkenrath Properties, Salt Lake City, 1977—; trustee Employees Profit Sharing Trust, Salt Lake City, 1975—; dir. Number 1 Tire Ctr., Inc., Salt Lake City. Republican dist. chmn., Salt Lake City, 1976; counselor Birthright, Salt Lake City, 1980-81. Mem. Nat. Assn. Credit Mgmt. (legis. chmn., Robert Morris Assocs. chmn. 1980-83), Automotive Booster Clubs B-49 (pres. 1979), Automotive Booster Club, Internat. (hon. life) (bd. dirs. 1974-82), Nat. Assn. Credit Mgmt. Intermountain (diesal products supplies chmn. 1982-83), Automotive Service Industry Assn. Presbyterian. Club: Boy Scouts Am. (Eagle). Office: Number 1 Performance 847 W 1700 S Salt Lake City UT 84121

FALLCREEK, STEPHANIE JEAN, university administrator; b. Springfield, Mo., May 6, 1950; d. Martha Jean (Barton) Wertz; m. Jerry R. Tillman, 1987; 1 child, Christopher. AB in History, U. Okla., 1972; MSW in Social Welfare, U. Calif., Berkeley, 1974, DSW in Social Welfare, 1984. Dir. Inst. for Geron. Research and Edn., N.Mex. State U., Las Cruces, 1983-87, N.Mex. State Agy. on Aging, 1987—; pres. Fallcreek & Assocs., Las Cruces, N.Mex., 1982—; sr. assoc. Age Wave Inc., Emeryville, Calif., 1985-87; cons. various hosps. and health care orgns.; speaker confs. and trade shows; guest radio and TV programs on aging. Author: (with others) A Healthy Old Age: A Sourcebook for Health Promotion with Older Adults, Health Promotion and Aging: Strategies for Action, Health Promotion and Aging: A National Resource of Selected Programs; also articles and book chpts. Danforth fellow, 1972-78. Mem. Geron. Soc. Am., Am. Soc. on Aging, Nat. Council on the Aging, Soc. for Values in Higher Edn., Nat. Assn. Social Workers, AAUW (corp. rep.). Home: 2525 Hagarty Rd Las Cruces NM 88001

FALLON, MARY PATRICIA, psychologist; b. Kansas City, Mo., Sept. 15, 1953; d. Joseph John and Ethel Mary (Schwartz) Fallon; m. Daniel Louis Coleman, July 26, 1975; B.A. in Psychology and Human Devel., U. Kans.-Lawrence, 1974; M.A. in Counseling, W. Va. U., 1976; Ph.D. in Ednl. Psychology, U. Wash., 1983. Play therapist U. Kans. Med. Ctr., Lawrence, 1971-75; fellow in genetics counseling W. Va. U. Med. Ctr., Morgantown, 1976; elem. sch. counselor, Winston-Salem, N.C., 1977-80, supr. for new counselors, 1978-80; counselor U. Wash. Counseling Ctr., Seattle, 1980-83; psychologist in pvt. practice 1983—; dir. Bulimia Treatment Program, 1982-86; cons. family styles project UCLA, 1982. Mem. Am. Psychol. Assn., Am. Assn. for Counseling and Devel., Assn. for Counselor Educators and Suprs., Assn. for Women in Psychology, Phi Beta Kappa, Pi Lambda Theta. Author: Bulimia: A Systems Approach to Treatment; contbr. numerous articles to profl. jours. Office: 1728 E Madison St Seattle WA 98122

FANCHER, MICHAEL REILLY, newspaper editor; b. Long Beach, Calif., July 13, 1946; s. Eugene Arthur and Ruth Leone (Dickson) F.; m. Nancy Helen Edens, Nov. 3, 1967 (div. 1982); children: Jason Michael, Patrick Reilly; m. 2d Carolyn Elaine Bowers, Mar. 25, 1983. B.A., U. Oreg., 1968; M.S., Kans. State U., 1971; M.B.A., U. Wash., 1986. Reporter, asst. city editor Kansas City Star, Mo., 1970-76, city editor, 1976-78; reporter Seattle Times, 1978-79, night city editor, 1979-80, asst. mng. editor, 1980-81, mng. editor, 1981-86, exec. editor, 1986—. Ruhl fellow U. Oreg., 1983. Mem. Am. Soc. Newspaper Editors, Associated Press Mng. Editors (bd. dirs. 1985—), Soc. Profl. Journalists, Nat. Press Photographers Assn. (Editor of Yr. 1986). Office: Seattle Times PO Box 70 Seattle WA 98111

FANELLI, IRENE SUSAN, health and safety professional; b. Watertown, N.Y., July 17, 1956; d. Maryagnes (Travis) Neforos. Student, Rockhurst Coll.; BS in Indsl. Hygiene, Quinnipiac Coll., 1979; MS in Occupational Safety and Health, U. So. Calif., 1984; postgrad., Southwestern U., Los Angeles, 1984-86, U. San Francisco Law Sch., 1986—. Corp. indsl. hygiene engr. Am. Can Co., Union, N.J., 1979-81; indsl. hygiene and safety adminstr. Essex Group United Techs. Corp., Ft. Wayne, Ind., 1981-82; cons. Los Angeles, 1983-85; supr. indsl. hygiene and safety Orange County (Calif.) Transit Dist., Garden Grove, 1984-85; with dept. corp. health and safety Canonie Environ. Services, San Mateo, Calif., 1985—; mem. faculty U. So. Calif., Los Angeles, 1984; guest lectr. U. Calif., Irvine, 1986; cons. occupational health abd safety So. Calif., 1983-85. Advisor Ft. Wayne Jr. Achievement, 1982. Nat. Inst. Occupational Safety and Health, 1983-84. Mem. Am. Soc. Safety Engrs., Am. Indsl. Hygiene Assn., Beta Beta Beta. Republican. Roman Catholic. Avocations: swimming, music. Home: 1210 Bellevue Ave #205 Burlingame CA 94010 Office: Canonie Environ Services 1825 S Grant St Suite 260 San Mateo CA 94402

FANNI, TAHSIN ALI, chemistry researcher; b. Jafa, Palestine, Feb. 15, 1948; came to U.S., 1979; s. Ali Hassan and Badriyeh Abdelmajid (Bawab) F.; m. Fatina Fawzi Alnabulsi, Dec. 27, 1985. PhD in Chemistry, U. Ill., 1984. Chemistry tchr. Ministry of Edn., Amman, Jordan, 1970-79; teaching and research asst. U. Ill., Chgo., 1979-84; researcher U. Calif., San Diego, 1985-87, Santa Cruz, 1987—. Author: Problems and Answers in High School Chemistry, 1977, also lab. manual, 1976; contbr. articles to profl. jours. Mem. Jordan Chem. Soc. (pres. 1975-77), Am. Chem. Soc. Avocations: sports, music, traveling. Home: 138 Palo Verde Dr Santa Cruz CA 95060 Office: U Calif Thimann Labs Santa Cruz CA 95064

FANNIN, DANIEL PAUL CLARK, information systems executive, military officer; b. Tallahassee, Dec. 17, 1942; s. Harvey Fayette and Kathryn Alice Fannin; m. Kerry Kathleen Barbour, July 14, 1980; children: Daniel Paul Clark, Kourtney Kathleen, Katie Rose. BS in Psychology, Loyola U., Los Angeles, 1965; MBA in Mgmt. with honors, U. N.D., 1974; MS in Computer Sci. with honors, N. Tex. State U., 1976. Commd. USAF, 1967, advanced through grades to lt. col., 1983; mgr. computer ctr. Strategic Air Command, Minot, N.D., 1970-74, Beale, Calif., 1970-74; program mgr. Dept. of Def. Computer Inst., Washington, 1976-79; mgr. edn. with industry Boeing Aerospace Co., Seattle, 1979-80; dir. software and data base mgmt. USAF Data Systems Evaluation Ctr., Montgomery, Ala., 1980-83; dir. info. systems 25th air div. USAF, Tacoma, 1983-87; retired USAF, 1987; chief info. systems Wash. Dept. Social and Health Services, Olympia, 98504; tech. advisor Space Transp. System, El Segundo, Calif., 1980-83; cons. Computer Security Program Office, Montgomery, 1980-83, Brit. Parliament, England, 1978, N.Y. Police Dept., N.Y.C., 1978, Maritime Adminstrn., Washington, 1978, Comptroller of the Currency, Washington, 1978, FBI, Washington, 1977-79; mem. staff Pres. Carter's Nat. Com. on Electronic Fund, Washington, 1976-79. Editor: Nat. Bur. of Standards Inst. for Computer Sci. and Tech., 1980; contbr. articles to profl. jours. Bd. dirs. Fed. Credit Union, Minot, 1973-74, Washington, 1977-79; coach Little League, Washington, 1978-79. Mem. Office of Mgmt. Budget (assoc. 1978—), Air Force Communication and Electronics Assn. (bd. dirs. 1984—), Steilacoom (Wash.) Hist. Soc. Republican. Roman Catholic. Avocations: tennis, golf, philately. Home: 48 Hewitt Dr Steilacoom WA 98388 Office: Office Infosystems Wash Dept Social/Health Services Olympia WA 98504

FANNON, JOHN J., paper company executive; b. 1934. With Champion Internat., 1960-73; with Simpson Paper Co., 1973—, v.p. mktg., 1977-79, pres., 1979—, also bd. dirs. Office: Simpson Paper Co 1 Post St San Francisco CA 94104 *

FARAH, TAWFIC ELIAS, polit. scientist; b. Nazareth, Palestine, Aug. 12, 1946; came to U.S., 1965, naturalized, 1975; s. Elias Tawfic and Itaf Fahim F.; B.A., Calif. State U., Fresno, 1970, M.A. summa cum laude, 1971; Ph.D., U. Nebr., 1975; m. Linda Maxwell, Apr. 24, 1969; children—Omar Lee, Aliya Jane. Market researcher Xerox Corp., Lincoln, Nebr., 1974-75; asst. prof. polit. sci. Kuwait U., 1975-79; pres. Calif. Ednl. Services, 1979—; vis. asso. prof. UCLA, summers 1978-83, fellow Center for Internat. and Strategic Affairs, 1980-81, Ctr. for Near Eastern Studies, 1986; Fulbright scholar, 1983. Toyota Found. grantee, 1985. Mem. Am. Polit. Sci. Assn.,

Middle East Studies Assn. Greek Orthodox. Co-author: Research Methods in the Social Sciences, 1977; A Dictionary of Social Analysis, 1980; author: Aspects of Modernization and Consociationalism: Lebanon as an Exploratory Test Case, 1975, 77; co-editor: Palestinians Without Palestine: Socialization of Palestinian Children, 1979; Learning to Become Palestinians, 1985; editor Political Behavior in the Arab States, 1983; Pan Arabism and Arab Nationalism: The Continuing Debate, 1986, Political Socialization in the Arab States, 1987, Survey Research in the Arab World, 1987; editor Jour. Arab Affairs, 1981—, Merg Analytica. Home: 4379 N 7th St Fresno CA 93726 Office: 2611 N Fresno St Fresno CA 93703

FARAONE, FRANK RAYMOND, public relations consultant; b. San Francisco, Oct. 19, 1927; s. Frank and Josephine (Lauritano) F. BBA, U. Santa Clara, 1951. With Gen. Motors Corp., 1951-81; regional mgr. Gen. Motors Corp., Dallas, 1956-58; mgr. N.Y.C. office Gen. Motors Corp., 1959-70; media relations mgr. Gen. Motors Corp., Detroit, 1970-72; dir. Washington office Gen. Motors Corp., 1973-81; pub. relations cons. San Francisco, 1982—. Served with U.S. Army, 1946-48. Address: 93 Eucalyptus Knoll Mill Valley CA 94941

FARDY, MARCIA SHIOMI, electrical engineer; b. Honolulu, Apr. 24, 1952; d. Noriyoshi and Lynn Tsuyako (Kato) Murakami; m. Douglas Alton Fardy, May 12, 1971; 1 child, Jessica. BSEE, U. Calif., Berkeley, 1978. Electronics design engr. Martin Marietta, Denver, 1978-84; gate array design engr. GTE-SSPD, Aurora, Colo., 1984; applications engr. Mentor Graphics Corp., Englewood, Colo., 1984-85; mem. tech. staff Hughes Aircraft Co., Englewood, 1985—. Served with USN, 1970-73. Mem. IEEE. Avocations: aerobics, travelling, reading, skiing. Office: Hughes Aircraft Co 8000 E Maplewood Ave MS 200 Englewood CO 80111

FARER, TOM JOEL, legal educator, writer; b. N.Y.C., July 28, 1935; s. Louis and Lola (Garfinkel) F.; m. Mika V. Ignatieff, Dec. 26, 1964; children: Paola E., Thomas V. AB magna cum laude, Princeton U., 1957; LLB, Harvard U., 1961. Bar: N.Y. Program officer AID, Washington, 1962; spl. asst. Dept. Def., Washington, 1962-63; advisor Somaili Police Force, Mogadishu, Somalia, 1963-64; assoc. Davis, Polk & Wardwell, N.Y.C., 1965-66; asst. prof., then assoc. prof. Columbia U., N.Y., 1966-71; disting. prof. law Rutgers U., Camden, N.J., 1971-85; pres. U. N.Mex., Albuquerque, 1985-86, prof. of law, 1986—; lectr. Hague Acad. Internat. Law, 1974, U. Munich, 1978-82; vis. prof. Princeton U., 1982-83, Johns Hopkins Sch. Advanced Internat. Studies, 1984. Author: Warclouds on the Horn of Africa, 1975; author, editor: Toward A Humanitarian Diplomacy, 1980, Future of Inter-American System, 1979, The Grand Strategy of the U.S. in the Western Hemisphere, 1987; note editor Harvard Law Rev., 1961. Mem. Inter-Am. Commn. Human Rights, 1976-83, pres., 1980-82; spl. asst. Dept. State, 1975. Recipient Presdl. Disting. Pub. Service award Rutgers U., 1984; sr. fellow Carnegie Endowment, 1974; sr. research fellow Council Fgn. Relations, 1975, Woodrow Wilson fellow, 1983; Fulbright scholar Glasgow U., Eng., 1957-58. Mem. Am. Soc. Internat. Law. Clubs: Cosmos (Washington); Princeton (N.Y.C.); Tennis (Albuquerque). Avocations: running, tennis, skiing. Office: U NMex Law Sch Albuquerque NM 87131

FARINHA, MARCELLA A., union official; b. Osceola, Iowa, Aug. 29, 1929; d. Raymond E. and Iva (True) Brown; m. Phil Farinha, July 22, 1950; children—Michael (dec.), Jan. Student U. Calif.-Berkeley, 1948, 49, Chabot Jr. Coll., 1976. Sec. to sr. union rep. Local 29, Office and Profl. Employees Union, AFL-CIO, 1959-73, sec.-treas., 1979-86; sec. Local 104, Sheet Metal Workers Union, 1986—. Health welfare trustee, mem. com. on polit. edn; del. Alameda County Central Labor Council; cons. labor mgmt. to grad. students. Active Workers Compensation; mem. Voice of Electorate, Democratic Party. Recipient Salute to Women of Labor award Calif. Senate, 1983. Mem. Internat. Found. Employee Benefit Plans. Office: Sheet Metal Workers Union Local 104 Emeryville CA 94608

FARISS, BRUCE LINDSAY, endocrinologist; b. Allisonia, Va., July 22, 1934; s. Alven Pierce and Hetty Jo (Lindsay) F.; B.S., Roanoke Coll., 1957; M.D., U. Va., 1961; m. Cheryl Louise Tomasie, Jan. 18, 1975; children—Bruce Lindsay, Melissa, Margaret, Susan, Henry, Sarah Jane, Caroline, Adam. Intern in medicine U. Va. Hosp., 1961-62; commd. capt. M.C. U.S. Army, 1962, advanced through grades to col., 1976; gen. med. officer, Ft. Monroe, Va., 1962-63; resident in internal medicine Brooke Gen. Hosp., Ft. Sam Houston, Tex., 1963-66; fellow in endocrinology U. Calif.-San Francisco, 1966-68; chief, endocrine service Madigan Gen. Hosp., Tacoma, Wash., 1968-71, chief clin. research service, 1968-76, asst. chief dept. medicine, 1972-73, dir. endocrine fellowship program, 1971-76, chief dept. clin. investigation, 1979-85, dir. endocrine-metabolism fellowship tng. program, 1979-85; cons. internal medicine MEDCOM Europe, 1976-79; cons. endocrinology to surgeon gen. U.S. Army, 1979-85. Diplomate Am. Bd. Internal Medicine, Am. Bd. Endocrinology; decorated Legion of Merit; with oak leaf cluster. Recipient Meritorious Service award Office of Surgeon Gen. Army, 1977. Fellow ACP; mem. Am. Fedn. Clin. Research, Endocrine Soc. (ednl. com. 1980-83), Am. Diabetes Assn. (trustee 1986—), Alpha Omega Alpha. Contbr. articles to med. jours.

FARLEY, HALE RALPH, electronic manufacturing company sales executive; b. Lick Creek, W.Va., Aug. 11, 1935; s. Wilbur Burnice and Annie May (Brown) F.; m. Imogene Croy, June 1, 1956; children—Beverly Farley McCann, Cynthia Kay Farley Kerr, Chris. A.S. in Electronic Tech., Central Tech. Inst., 1963; B.S., U. N.Mex., 1976, C.S.E.E., 1975; B.A. in Mgmt., St. Mary's Coll., 1982. Instrumentation engr. Sandia Lab., Albuquerque, 1963-73; mktg. mgr. Tektronix, Beaverton, Oreg., 1973-75, master salesman, Santa Clara, Calif., 1976-82; sales rep. Lecroy Research Systems Inc., Livermore, Calif., 1982-84; sales engr. Tektronix, Santa Clara, Calif., 1984-86; sr. sales engr. Data I/O, San Jose, 1987—; condr. in-plant seminars; presenter paper 3d Internat. Electro-Optic Conf., Tokyo, 1980; guest lectr. Stanford U., 1982. Served with USAF, 1954-57. Mem. Nat. Manpower Council. Republican. Methodist. Home: 909 Roxanne St Livermore CA 94550 Office: 1701 Fox Dr San Jose CA 95131

FARLEY, JOHN MICHAEL, steel company executive; b. Bklyn., July 10, 1930; s. John F. and Lucile J. Farley; m. Dorothy O. Stacy, Nov. 29, 1959; children: Anne L., Jean E., John O. B.C.E. magna cum laude, Syracuse U., 1952; M.S., U. Ill., 1954. Registered prof. engr., Ohio, Pa. Project mgr. Cleve. works Jones & Laughlin Steel Corp., 1957-64; mem. engring. staff Jones & Laughlin Steel Corp., Pitts., 1964-72, v.p. research and engring., 1972-75, v.p. raw materials, 1975-77; pres. raw materials div. Jones & Laughlin Steel Corp., 1977-82, v.p. raw materials, purchasing, traffic, 1982-85; v.p. research, engring. and traffic LTV Steel Co., 1985—. Served with USN, 1954-57. Mem. Am. Iron and Steel Inst., AIME, Iron and Steel Soc., Assn. Iron and Steel Engrs., Sigma Xi, Tau Beta Pi. Clubs: Duquesne (Pitts.); Union (Cleve.).

FARLEY, ROGER DEAN, university educator, neurophysiologist; b. Jefferson, Iowa; s. Reno Elsworth and Edith May (Rogers) F. BA, No. Iowa U., 1958; MS, Iowa U., 1962; PhD, U. Calif., Santa Barbara, 1967. Assoc. prof. biology U. Calif., Riverside, 1968—. Contbr. numerous research articles on the neurophysiology of desert arthropods to profl. jours. Mem. Soc. Neurosci., Soc. Neuroethology, Am. Soc. Zoologists.

FARMER, GERALD IRVINE, electronics company executive; b. Manhattan, Kans., Mar. 1, 1934; s. William Ramsdell and Margaret Helen (Burke) F.; m. Susan Jane Perry, Sept. 7, 1960; children: Gerald, Thomas, Samuel. BS in Chemistry, Law, U. Wyo., 1956; postgrad., U. Heidelberg, Fed. Republic Germany, 1962, Pa. State U., 1963; MS in Physics, Math., U. Wis., 1964, PhD in Physics, Math., 1967. Chemist Aerojet-Gen. Corp., Sacramento, 1956-58; engr. Chrysler Corp., various locations, 1958-61; various positions with IBM Corp., various locations, 1967-79; div. mgr. Xerox Corp., Pasadena, Calif., 1979-83; pres. SAI Tech., San Diego, 1983-86; sr. v.p. research and devel. Gould Image and Graphics, Fremont, Calif., 1986-87; exec. v.p. Hecht-Nielsen Neurocomputer Corp., San Diego, 1987—; mem. engring. devel. council U. Colo., Boulder, 1979—. Contbr. articles to profl. jours. Served to capt. U.S. Army, 1967. Mem. AAAS, IEEE (sr.). Home: 13502 Caminito Carmel Del Mar CA 92014 Office: Hecht-Nielsen Neurocomputer Corp 5893 Oberlin Dr San Diego CA 92121

FARMER, JAMES LEE, genetics and zoology educator; b. South Gate, Calif., Aug. 8, 1938; s. James Ira and Ellen Eliza (Sheeks) F.; m. Gladys Clark, Jan. 27, 1967; children: Sarah, Clark, Rachel, Jared, Deborah. BS in Chemistry, Calif. Inst. Tech., 1960; PhD in Biology, Brown U., 1966. Instr. biophysics U. Colo. Med. Ctr., Denver, 1966-68; from asst. prof. to prof. zoology Brigham Young U., Provo, Utah, 1969—. Contbr. articles to profl. jours. Mem. AAAS, Genetics Soc. Am., Fedn. Am. Scientists. Democrat. Mormon. Home: 222 E 4200 N Provo UT 84604 Office: Brigham Young U 591 WIDB Provo UT 84602

FARMER, JANENE ELIZABETH, artist, educator; b. Albuquerque, Oct. 16, 1946; d. Charles John Watt and Regina M. (Brown) Kruger; m. Michael Hugh Bolton, Apr. 1965 (div.); m. Frank Urban Farmer, May, 1972 (div.). B.A. in Art, San Diego State U., 1969. Owner, operator Iron Walrus Pottery, 1972-79; designer ceramic and fabric murals, Coronado, Calif., 1979-82; executed commns. for clients in U.S.A., Can., Japan and Mex.; pvt. tchr. pottery; mem. faculty U. Calif.-San Diego; substitute tchr. Calif. community colls.; designer fabric murals and bldg. interiors, Coronado and La Jolla, Calif., 1982—; tchr. Blessed Sacrament Sch., San Diego, 1982-85, San Diego Unified Sch. Dist., 1985—. Mem. Coronado Arts and Humanities Council; resident artist U. Calif.-San Diego. Recipient grant Calif. Arts Council, 1980-81; U. San Diego grad. fellow dept. edn., 1984. Mem. Am. Soc. Interior Designers (affiliate). Roman Catholic. Home: 4435 Nobel Dr #35 San Diego CA 92122

FARMER, JOHN DAVID, museum administrator; b. Washington, Ga., Jan. 25, 1939; s. John Lloyd and Frances Heard (Woolley) F.; m. Patricia Phelps Dow, Aug. 21, 1965; children: Emily Dow, Rachel Aldrich. B.A., Columbia U., 1960; M.A., U. N.C., 1963; M.F.A., Princeton U., 1965, Ph.D., 1981. Curatorial asst. Worcester (Mass.) Art Mus., 1967-69; curator Busch-Reisinger Mus. Germanic Art, Harvard, 1969-72; curator earlier painting Art Inst. Chgo., 1972-75; dir. Birmingham (Ala.) Mus. Art, 1975-78; lectr. fine arts Clark U., Worcester, 1968-69; lectr. art Harvard U., 1970; lectr. U. Ala., Birmingham, 1976-78; exec. dir. Commn. for Ednl. Exchange between U.S.A., Belgium and Luxembourg, Brussels, 1979-80; dir. U. Calif.-Santa Barbara Art Mus., 1981—; adj. prof. art history U. Calif.-Santa Barbara, 1981—. Author: The Virtuoso Craftsman: Northern European Design in the 16th Century, 1969, Concepts of the Bauhaus, 1971, German Master Drawings of the 19th Century, 1972, James Ensor, 1976, Rubens and Humanism, 1978, Rowing/Olympics, 1984, also articles. Bd. dirs. Boston Musica Viva, 1971-72. Albert M. Friend fellow, 1963-64, 65-66; Fulbright-Hayes fellow Belgium, 1966-67. Mem. Coll. Art Assn., Assn. Am. Museums, Assn. Art Mus. Dirs., U.S. Rowing Assn. Club: Odd Volumes (Boston). Office: Art Museum U Calif Santa Barbara CA 93106

FARMER, JOSEPH RILEY, protective services official; b. Rehobeth, N.Mex., Jan. 12, 1937; s. Charles Bennett Farmer and Alice Mercedes (Eppele) Herr; m. Vivian Petra Cohen, Aug. 17, 1973 (div. Feb. 1985); children: Terri Noreen, Christopher Brian. AA, Glendale Community Coll.; BA, No. Ariz. U.; postgrad., Ariz. State U. Patrol div. adminstr., homicide investigator, field detective, patrol and adminstrv. sgt. Phoenix Police Dept., advanced tng. lt., 1981-84, communications bur. comdr., 1984—; lectr., tchr. Ariz. Law Enforcement Officer Adv. Council. Contbr. articles to profl. publs. V.p. St. Edwards Parish Council, Phoenix, 1982-84. Served with USAF, 1955-59. Democrat. Roman Catholic. Club: Ariz. Athletic (Tempe). Avocations: motorcycling, reading, travel, flying, crafts. Home: 12622 S 38th Pl Phoenix AZ 85044 Office: Phoenix Police Dept 620 W Washington St Phoenix AZ 85003

FARMER, LEE R., insurance executive; b. Alliance, Nebr., Feb. 23, 1924; s. Lee R. and Berenice (Ellis) F.; student U. Nebr., 1941-43, 46-47, U. Minn., 1948; m. Constance Audrey Lang, Sept. 18, 1954; children—Diana Lee, Lee R. III, Stuart Lang. Spl. rep. Minn. Hosp. Service Assn., St. Paul, 1948-50, dist. mgr., Duluth, 1950-55; regional mgr. Continental Casualty Co., Chgo., 1955-56, supt. group div., 1956-59, asst. v.p., 1959-61, v.p., chief operating officer of gen. group div. and ind. plans div., 1961-65; exec. v.p. Nat. Ben Franklin Life Ins. Corp. and Nat. Ben Franklin Ins. Co. affiliates of Continental Ins. Co., Chgo., 1965-68; pres. Lee R. Farmer & Assos., Inc., Hinsdale, Ill. 1969-70; exec v.p. Continental Life & Accident Co., 1971-74; pres. Profl. Adminstrs., Inc., 1974—. Served to lt. (j.g.) USNR, 1943-45. Mem. Sigma Nu. Methodist. Clubs: Masons (32 deg.), Hillcrest Country. Home: 209 E Curling Dr Boise ID 83702 Office: Box 1722 Boise ID 83701

FARMER, WILLIAM MICHAEL, electronics research and development company executive; b. Nashville, May 10, 1944; s. John Campbell and Hattie Mann (Phillips) F.; m. Jan Miller, Sept. 4, 1966; children: Michael Ryan, Amanda Ford. BS in Engring. Physics, U. Tenn., 1967; MS in Phsyics, U. Tenn. Space Inst., 1968; PhD in Phsyics, U. Tenn. Sci. Inst., 1973. Engr. Arnold Research Orgn., Tullahoma, Tenn., 1967-73; staff scientist Sci. Applications Inc., Tullahoma, Tenn., 1973-75; sr. scientist Spectron Devel. Labs., Tullahoma, Tenn., 1975-77; prof. physics U. Tenn. Sci. Inst., Tullahoma, Tenn., 1977-84; v.p. research and devel. Sci. and Tech. Corp., Las Cruces, N.Mex., 1984—; cons. Solar Turbines, San Diego, Calif., 1975-77, U.S. Army/NATO, Brussels, 1980-84, 85—, U.S. Army, Edgewood, Md., 1983. Contbr. articles to profl. jours. Mem. Optical Soc. Am., Soc. Photographic Instrumentation Engrs., Sigma Xi. Methodist. Avocations: photography, reading, cycling. Home: 4309 Mission Bell Las Cruces NM 88001 Office: Sci and Tech Corp FNB Suite 940 Las Cruces NM 88005

FARNAM, HELEN MAHONEY, accounting executive, educator; b. Phoenix, Dec. 13, 1945; d. John Conroy and Clare Frances (James) Mahoney; m. Frederick W. Farnam, Feb. 14, 1971; children: Scott Alan, Shannon Frances, Michelle Rene. BA, Calif. State U., San Bernardino, 1983, MBA, 1985. Cert. lifetime teaching credential community coll. dist., Calif. Adminstr. Riverside (Calif.) County Med. Assn., 1970-72; bus. mgr. Farnam and Assocs., Redlands, Calif., 1972-75, World Life Research Inst., Grand Terrace, Calif., 1977-80; prof. bus. Crafton Hills Coll., Yucaipa, Calif., 1981-86; owner EXCALIBRE Mgmt., Redlands, 1986—; cons. Moreno Valley (Calif.) C. of C., 1986—; adv. bd. mem. Montessori Sch., San Bernardino, 1985—. Calif. State U. Sch. Bus., San Bernardino, 1985—; bd. dirs. World Life Research, Grand Terrace, Calif., Saturn Oil & Gas Co., Cheyenne, Wyo.,1966-67. Dir. Super Stars Dance Drill Team, Redlands, 1981-83; active Rep. Women's Assn., Redlands. Recipient cert. appreciation Bus. Improvement Dist., Redlands, 1979. Mem. Fin. Mgrs. Assn. (hon. soc. 1984-85), Redlands C. of C., AAUW. Lodge: Soroptimists. Avocations: interior design, furniture refinishing, water skiing, boating, camping. Office: EXCALIBRE Mgmt 236 Cajon St Suite B Redlands CA 92373

FARNER, DONALD SANKEY, biologist; b. Waumandee, Wis., May 2, 1915; s. John and Lillian O. (Sankey) F.; m. Dorothy S. Copps, Dec. 21, 1940; children: Carla M., Donald C. B.S., Hamline U., 1937, D.Sc. (hon.), 1962; M.A., U. Wis., 1939, Ph.D., 1941. Instr. zoology U. Wis., 1941-43; asst. prof. zoology U. Kans., 1946-47; faculty Wash. State U., 1947-65, prof. zoophysiology, 1952-65; dean Wash. State U. (Grad. Sch.), 1960-64; prof. zoophysiology U. Wash., Seattle, 1965-85; chmn. dept. zoology U. Wash., 1966-81, prof. emeritus, 1985—; Fulbright research scholar, hon. lectr. zoology U. Otago, N.Z., 1953-54; Guggenheim fellow U. Western Australia, 1958-59; chmn. div. biology and agr. Nat. Acad. Sci.-NRC, 1969-73; sr. U.S. scientist Alexander von Humboldt Stiftung, 1978, 85; pres. XVII Internat. Ornithol. Congress, 1978. Served to lt. USNR, 1943-46; capt. Res. ret. Fellow AAAS (council 1964-80), Am. Ornithologists Union (Brewster award 1960, pres. 1973-75); mem. Am. Physiol. Soc., Am. Soc. Zoologists (pres. 1984), Am. Inst. Biol. Scis., Internat. Union Biol. Scis. (pres. 1967-73, chmn. div. zoology 1973-82), Soc. Systematic Zoology, Cooper Ornithol. Soc. (hon. mem.; bd. govs. 1965-71), Deutsche Ornithologen-Gesell. (hon.), Ornitologiska Foreningen: Finland (hon.), Soc. for Endocrinology, Soc. for Study Reproduction, Phi Beta Kappa, Sigma Xi, Phi Kappa Phi, Phi Sigma (hon. pres. 1973-80), Gamma Alpha, Omicron Delta Kappa. Methodist. Club: Cosmos (Washington). Research and publs. in avian biology and physiology. Home: 930 E West Camano Dr Camano Island WA 98292

FARNHAM, CHARLES PETER, illumination engineer; b. Cleve., Dec. 30, 1934; s. Ralph Everett and Helena Catherine (Otto) F.; m. Shirley Jo Tinsley, Mar. 17, 1977; children—David Everett, Jeannette Elizabeth, Patricia Helena. B.A., Ohio Wesleyan U., 1954; M.F., Oreg. State U., 1956. Sales engr. Gen. Elec. Lamp div., Fresno, Calif., 1958-63, lamp engr., Seattle, 1963-72, supr. sales, 1963-72, lighting systems engr. Apparatus div., Seattle, 1972-76; pres. Lighting Tech. Inc., Bellevue, Wash., 1976—. Author: Lighting Controls Overview, 1983. Patentee retroflector. Pres., Norwood Village Corp., Bellevue, 1968; chmn. City of Bellevue Planning Bd., 1972-75, City of Medina Park Bd., 1980—. Mem. Illuminating Engring. Soc. (pres. 1969-70), Assn. Energy Engrs. (past pres.), Wash. Soc. Profl. Engrs. (past. pres. Seattle chpt.). Home: 8629 NE 6th St Bellevue WA 98004 Office: Lighting Tech Inc Box 3532 Bellevue WA 98009

FARNSWORTH, JAMES VIRGEL, accountant, corporate officer; b. El Paso, Tex., Dec. 19, 1951; s. Virgel Rayo and Abbie Fern (Keeler) F.; m. Phyllis Redd, Sept. 23, 1979; children: Yvette, Nicole, Krystle. BS in Acctg., Brigham Young U., 1974, M Acctg., 1976. CPA, Ariz. Sr. acct. Price Waterhouse & Co., Phoenix, 1976-78; controller MicroAge Computer Stores, Phoenix, 1978-80, Shamrock Foods Co., Phoenix, 1980-82; treas. Citizen Auto Stage Co., Nogales, Ariz., 1982-83, exec. v.p., 1983—. Mem. Am. Inst. CPA's, Ariz. Soc. CPA's. Home: 1575 Calle Kino Rio Rico AZ 85621 Office: Citizen Auto Stage Co 424 Grand Ave Nogales AZ 85621

FARNSWORTH, PAUL, archaeologist; b. Stockport, Cheshire, Eng., Apr. 23, 1958; came to U.S., 1980; s. Edward Ronald and Ruth (Harrison) F. BS, Leeds U., West Yorkshire, Eng., 1980; MA, UCLA, 1982, PhD, 1987. Researcher history dept. UCLA, 1981, lab. asst. dept. earth and space scis., 1981-83, computer programmer dept. earth and space scis., 1982, researcher/bibliographer archaeology program, 1983, field crew supr. Inst. Archaeology, 1983-84, instr., field dir. summer sessions, 1984—; field instr. Inst. Jamaica, Kingston, 1983; curator archaeology UCLA Mus. Cultural History, 1985—; cons. in field. Contbr. articles to profl. jours. Friends of Archaeology fellow UCLA, 1982, 84. Mem. Soc. Promotion Roman Studies, Soc. Hist. Archaeology, Soc. Post-Medieval Archaeology, Soc. Calif. Archaeology, Calif. Mission Studies Assn., Archaeol. Soc. UCLA, Archaeol. Inst. Am., Soc. for Am. Archaeology, Am. Anthrop. Assn. Home: 1338 S Carmelina Ave #3 Los Angeles CA 90025 Office: UCLA Mus Cultural History 405 Hilgard Ave Los Angeles CA 90024

FARON, JOHN FRANK, engineering executive; b Chgo., Aug. 27, 1933; s. John Theodore and Mary Rose (Szczecina) F.; m. Martha Darling, Nov. 2, 1957; children—Kathleen, Susan, Sandra, Edward. Student Ohio State U., 1951-53, U. So. Calif., 1962, Fresno State U., 1967-69; A.B., U.S. Naval Postgrad. Sch., 1971; postgrad. George Washington U., 1972; M.A., Calif. State U.-Dominguez Hills, 1982. Commd. ensign U.S. Navy, 1955; advanced through grades to comdr., 1968; pilot, 1953-78; intelligence officer, 1955-59; flight instr., 1959-61; combat pilot, Vietnam, 1962-64; aviation maintenance officer USS Hancock, 1964-66; dept. head tech. tng. Attack Squadron 125, 1966-69; exec. sec. to chief naval ops. sub-com. command, control and communication, 1971-73; chmn. ops. sub-group R-2508 enhancement program, mgr. USN portion 56M radar enhancement program, test pilot, 1973-78; ret., 1978. sr. engring. tech. writer, Comarco Engring. Inc., Ridgecrest, Calif., 1978-80; head systems effectiveness engring. group, sr. staff cons. PRC Ridgecrest Engring. Co., 1980-83; staff engr. Vitro Corp., Oxnard, Calif., 1984—. Decorated Navy Commendation medal, 1973. Mem. AIAA (chmn. China Lake sect. 1986-87), Nat. Air Racing Group, U.S. Air Racing Assn. (hon.), Assn. Naval Aviation, Tailhook Assn., Assn. Old Crows, Soc. Flight Test Engrs. (pres. China Lake chpt. 1986-87), Delta Chi. Republican. Roman Catholic. Clubs: China Lake Men's Golf, So. Calif. Golf Assn., Calif. Golf Assn. Home: 618 Scott St Ridgecrest CA 93555 Office: 2345 Statham Blvd Oxnard CA 93033

FARONE, WILLIAM ANTHONY, research director, chemist; b. Cortland, N.Y., Feb. 1, 1940; s. Anthony George and Rose (Speach) F.; m. Barbara Schroeder, Dec. 27, 1962 (div. 1981); children: Elizabeth, Stacey; m. Cynthia H. O'Donohue, Jan. 1, 1983; 1 stepchild, Diane L. BS in Chemistry with honors, Clarkson U., 1961, MS in Chemistry, 1963, PhD in Chemistry, 1965. Assoc. prof. chemistry Va. State U., Petersburg, 1965-67; sci. research dir. Lever Bros. Co., Edgewater, N.J., 1967-75; applied research dir. Philip Morris, Inc., Richmond, Va., 1976-84; sr. v.p. Bio-Solar, Inc., Elk Grove, Calif., 1984-86; research dir. X2Y2 Corp., Culver City, Calif., 1986—; bd. dirs. Advanced Sci. Applications, Inc., Richmond. Contbr. articles to profl. jours.; patentee in field. Mem. com. Bergen County (N.J.) Supervisory Bd., 1968-70. Recipient Hamlin Math. award Clarkson U., Potsdam, N.J., 1961. Mem. AAAS, Am. Chem. Soc., Am. Inst. Physics, Optical Soc. of Am., Sigma Xi. Avocations: game theory, electronics, sailing, tennis. Home: 13900 Panay Way S316 Marina Del Rey CA 90292 Office: X2Y2 Corp 5765 Uplander Way Culver City CA 90230

FAROOQUI, MUSTAHSAN RASHEED, chemist; b. Jaunpur, India, Apr. 17, 1942; came to U.S., 1969, naturalized, 1978; s. Mohammad Anas and Atiyah (Sultanah) F; m. Marilyn Laural Poling, Jan. 18, 1975; children: Summereen, Rafi. B.Sc. in Chemistry with honors, U. Karachi, Pakistan, 1963, M.Sc. in Phys. Chemistry, 1965; BS in Gen. Engring., Oreg. State U., 1974. Tech. asst. Pakistan Council of Sci. and Indsl. Research, Karachi, 1963-68; research asst. dept. chemistry Oreg. State U., Corvallis, 1969-72; chemist Evans Products, Corvallis, 1972-80, sr. chemist Evanite Battery Separators div., 1980—. Mem. AAAS, Am. Chem. Soc., Am. Contract Bridge League (life master, life mem.).

FARR, DONALD EUGENE, engineer; b. Clinton, Iowa, July 1, 1933; s. Kenneth Elroy and Nellie Irene (Bailey) F.; m. Sally Joyce Brauer, Mar. 8, 1954; children: Erika Lyn Leventis, Jolene Karyn. BA in Engring. Psychology, San Diego State U., 1961; M in Indsl. Tech. with distinction, Nat. U., 1974; postgrad., Calif. Pacific U., 1976. Human factors specialist Bunker Ramo Corp., Canoga Park (Calif.) and Fed. Republic Germany, 1964-69; design specialist Gen. Dynamics, San Diego, 1969-76; tech. staff Sandia Nat. Labs., Albuquerque, 1977-80; supr. and sr. tech. advisor Babcock & Wilcox Co., Lynchburg, Va., 1980-82; dir. human factors systems Sci. Applications, Inc., Lynchburg, 1982-83; human engring. staff scientist Lockheed Calif. Co., Burbank, 1983—; on-call energy systems cons. Dept. Energy and Nuclear Contractors, Washington, other locations, 1977—. Contbr. articles to profl. jours. Rep. precinct capt., Conejo Valley, Calif., 1964, 68. Served with USN, 1952-53. Mem. Human Factors Soc. (pres. Los Angeles chpt. 1986-87), San Diego Internat. Numismatic Soc. (pres. 1973-75). Republican. Lutheran. Avocations: bridge, stained glass, numismatics, gourmet cooking. Home: 13770 Linfield Ave Sylmar CA 91342 Office: Lockheed Calif Co Dept 69-06 Bldg 80-2 A-1 Burbank CA 91520

FARR, DONALD HAINES, hardware store executive; b. Sunnyside, Wash., Apr. 26, 1914; s. Chester Carroll and Iva Della (Haines) F.; m. Emma Frances Mulkey, Mar. 17, 1940; children—David D., Paul F., Mary F. Farr Brice, Patricia L. Farr Sisson. BS, U. Oreg., 1936; MBA, Northwestern U., 1938. Owner, ptnr. Farr's True Value Hardware Store, Coquille and Coos Bay, Oreg., 1937-75; pres. Farr's Hardware, Inc., Coquille, 1975—; instr. bus. adminstrn. Southwestern Oreg. Community Coll., Coos Bay, 1937-81; mem. Gov.'s Employment and Tng. Council, 1979-81. Trustee Emmanuel Sch. Religion, Johnson City, Tenn., 1973—; mayor City of Coquille, 1950-54; committeeman Rep. Party, 1948-64; bd. dirs. Oreg. Retail Council, Salem, 1950-83, Oregonians for Responsible State Govt., 1975-83, Assoc. Oreg. Industries Found., Salem, 1975—; elder, trustee, tchr. Bible sch. Christian Ch. Recipient Disting. Service award U. Oreg., 1960. Mem. Pacific N.W. Hardware and Implement Assn. (past pres.), North Coast Retail Hardware Assn. (past pres.), Oreg. Grange, Beta Gamma Sigma. Lodges: Rotary, Masons, Gideons. Home: HC 83 Box 681 Coquille OR 97423 Office: Farrs Hardware Inc 222 N Central Blve Coquille OR 97423

FARR, LEE EDWARD, physician; b. Albuquerque, Oct. 13, 1907; s. Edward and Mabel (Heyn) F.; B.S., Yale U., 1929, M.D., 1933; m. Anne Ritter, Dec. 28, 1936 (dec.); children—Charles E., Susan A., Frances A.; m. Miriam Kirk, Jan. 22, 1985. Asst. pediatrics Sch. Medicine, Yale U., 1933-34; asst. medicine Hosp. of Rockefeller Inst. Med. Research, 1934-37, assoc. medicine, 1937-40; dir. research Alfred I. duPont Inst. of Nemours Found., Wilmington, Del., 1940-49; vis. assoc. prof. pediatrics Sch. Medicine, U. Pa., 1940-49; med. dir. Brookhaven Nat. Lab., 1948-62; prof. nuclear medicine U. Tex. Postgrad. Med. Sch., 1962-64, prof. nuclear and environ. medicine Grad. Sch. Bio-Med. Scis., U. Tex. at Houston, 1965-68; chief sect. nuclear medicine U. Tex.-M.D. Anderson Hosp. and Tumor Inst., 1962-67, prof. environ. health U. Tex. Sch. Pub. Health, Houston, 1967-68; head disaster health services Calif. Dept. Health, 1968, chief emergency health services unit, 1968-70, 1st chief bur. emergency med. services, 1970-73; Lippitt lectr. Marquette U., 1941; Sommers Meml. lectr. U. Oreg. Sch. Med., Portland, 1960; Gordon Wilson lectr. Am. Clin. and Climatol. Assn., 1956; Sigma Xi nat. lectr., 1952-53. Mem. adv. com. on naval med. research to sec. naval and chief naval ops. NRC, 1953-68, adv. com. on atomic bomb, 1953-78, chmn. 1954-76, adv. com. on medicine and surgery, 1955-56, exec. com., 1962-65; Naval Research Mission to Formosa, 1953; tech. adviser U.S. delegation to Geneva Internat. Conf. for Peaceful Uses Atomic Energy, 1955; mem. N.Y. Adv. Com. Atomic Energy, 1956-59; mem. AMA Com. Nuclear Medicine, 1963-66; mem. com. med. isotopes NASA Manned Spacecraft Ctr., 1966-68; mem. expert adv. panel radiation WHO, 1957-79; mem. Calif. Gov.'s Ad Hoc Com. Emergency Health Service, 1968-69; mem. sci. adv. bd. Gorgas Meml. Inst., 1967-72; mem. Naval Res. Adv. Com., 1970-78, numerous other sci. adv. bds., panels; cons. TRW Systems, Inc., 1966-70, Consol. Petroleum Co., Beverly Hills, Calif., 1946-70. Mem. alumni bd. Yale, 1962-65, mem. alumni fund, 1966-76. Served as lt. comdr. M.C., USNR, 1942-46; capt. (M.C.) USNR, ret. Recipient Mead Johnson award for pediatric research, 1940; decorated Gold Cross Order of Phoenix, Greece; Order of Merit, West Germany; named community leader in Am., 1969. Diplomate Nat. Bd. Med. Examiners, Am. Bd. Pediatrics. Fellow AAAS, Royal Soc. Arts, Am. Acad. Pediatrics, N.Y. Acad. Scis., Royal Soc. Health, Am. Coll. Nuclear Medicine (disting. fellow); mem. Soc. Pediatric Research, Soc. Exptl. Biology and Medicine (chmn. adv. com. atom bomb casualties 1954-76, naval research adv. com. 1970-78), Harvey Soc., Am. Pediatric Soc., Soc. Exptl. Pathology, Am. Soc. Clin. Investigation, Radiation Research Soc., A.M.A. (mem. council on sci. assembly 1960-70, chmn. 1968-70), Houston C. of C. (chmn. subcom. on quality in living 1966-68), Med. Soc. Athens (Greece) (hon.), Alameda County Med. Assn., Sigma Xi, Alpha Omega Alpha, Phi Sigma Kappa, Nu Sigma Nu, Alpha Chi Sigma. Club: Commonwealth (San Francisco). Author articles on nuclear medicine, protein metabolism, emergency med. services, radioactive and chem. environ. contaminants, environ. noise. Home: 2502 Saklan Indian Dr Apt 2 Walnut Creek CA 94595

FARR, MELVIN MILLER, personnel director; b. Ogden, Utah, May 22, 1928; s. Lionel Ballantine and Eleanor (Miller) F.; m. Joan Bennett, Feb. 2, 1953; children: Melvin, James, David, Carol Ann, John, Daniel. BA, U. Md., 1953; JD, Georgetown U., 1960, LLM, 1964. Bar: Md. 1960, D.C. 1961, U.S. Supreme Ct. Acctg. mgr. C&P Telephone Co., Washington, 1953-64; mgr. systems analysis and programming Ch. of Jesus Christ of Latter-day Saints, Salt Lake City, 1964-69, dir. internat. personnel, 1979—; v.p. mktg. Mgmt. Systems Corp., Salt Lake City, 1969-74, v.p. prodn., 1974-79. Pres. Utah State Soc., Washington, 1955-56; asst. dir. Eisenhower Inaugural Com., Washington, 1956; chmn. Utah Systems Planning Steering Bd., 1977-79. Served to capt. USAF, 1954-58. Mem. Sigma Alpha Epsilon, Delta Theta Phi. Republican. Avocations: fishing, racquetball. Home: 3344 Oakcliff Dr Salt Lake City UT 84124 Office: Latter-day Sts Personnel 50 E North Temple Salt Lake City UT 84150

FARR, WILLIAM JOHN, industrial engineer; b. Chgo., Oct. 27, 1947; s. William Walter and Bettie May (Felkamp) F.; m. Patsy Ann Weir, Oct. 14, 1972 (div. Sept. 1980); one child, Christopher Lee; m. Kathryn Regina August, May 30, 1984. AA, Purdue U., 1974, BS, 1977; postgrad., De Paul U. Gen. foreman Internat. Harvester Co. (now called Navistar), Chgo., 1970-77; mfg. supt. Cobe Labs. Inc., Lakewood, Colo., 1977-79, mfg. engr., 1979-81; program adminstr. Storage Tech. Corp., Louisville, Colo., 1981-83, value improvement program mgr., 1983-84, indsl. engr., quality engr., 1985—; pres. Vintage Video, Lakewood, 1983—; ptnr. Video Visions and Pine Junction Video, Northglenn, Colo., 1986—. Rep. precinct capt., Chgo., 1972; emergency med. technician Luth. Hosp. and Cobe Labs., 1979. Served with USN, 1966-68. Mem. Am. Soc. Indsl. Supervision (cert.), Am. Soc. Value Engrs. (chpt. pres. 1984-85), Purdue U. Alumni Assn. Republican. Lutheran. Avocations: photography, white water rafting, skiing. Home: 30573 King's Valley Dr Conifer CO 80433 Office: Storage Technology Corp 2270 S 88th St Louisville CO 80028

FARRACE, MICHAEL ANGELO, editor, publisher; b. Berkeley, Calif., June 29, 1951; s. Raphael Alessio and Letitia Mae (Howell) F.; m. Maria Salomone, May 2, 1981; 1 child, Patrick Michael. Student, Calif. Poly. State U., San Luis Obispo, 1969-70, Calif. State U., 1970-73, 73-75, 77. Music columnist Sacramento Union, 1974-79; founder, editor, art dir. Rock-n-Roll News, Sacramento, 1975-77; record buyer Tower Records, Sacramento, 1977-80, regional advt. dir., 1980-83; editor, pub. Tower Records' Pulse, Sacramento, 1983—. Mem. Nat. Assn. Record Merchandisers, Calif. State U. Alumni Assn. Democratic. Roman Catholic. Avocations: record collecting, oil and watercolor painting. Office: Tower Record's Pulse! 2500 Del Monte St Bldg C Sacramento CA 95691

FARRAR, DONALD EUGENE, mutual fund executive; b. Seattle, Dec. 15, 1931; s. Joseph Lester and Ruth Emily (Close) F.; m. Joan Fowler Drew, July 29, 1974; children: Donald E., John M., Peter H., Cordelia G.; stepchildren: Terri J., Walter M., Jason J.W. A.B. magna cum laude, Harvard U., 1954, M.A. in Econs., 1961, Ph.D., 1961. Instr. econs. U. Wis.-Madison, 1959-61, asst. prof., 1961-62; economist Inst. Naval Studies, Cambridge, Mass., 1962-63; asst. prof. fin. MIT, 1963-66, assoc. prof., 1966-68; assoc. prof. fin. Columbia U., 1968; dir. Instn. Investor Study, SEC, Washington, 1969-71; sr. fellow U. Pa. Law Sch., Phila., 1971; sr. research assoc. Nat. Bur. Econ. Research, Cambridge, 1972; prof. fin. UCLA, 1973-76; prof. fin. U. Utah, Salt Lake City, 1976-81; exec. v.p. Benham Mgmt. Corp., Palo Alto, Calif., 1981—; bd. dirs. Mattel, Inc., 1974-83, Mattel Found., 1976-83, Capital Preservation Fund, 1975-81, Benham Mgmt. Corp., 1981—, Capital Preservation Fund II, Capital Preservation Treasury Note Trust, 1980—, Benham Nat. Tax Free Trust, 1984—, Benham Target Maturities Trust, 1985—, Benham Govt. Income Trust, 1985—, Capital Preservation Fund Internat., S.A., Luxembourg, 1983-86, Vascular Internat., Inc.; cons. in field. Served to lt. U.S. Army, 1955-56. IBM fellow, 1955; Ford Found. fellow, 1967. Mem. Western Fin. Assn. (dir. 1978-81, pres. 1980). Clubs: Harvard of San Francisco (bd. dirs. 1984—); Commonwealth of Calif, 1981-84. Author: The Investment Decision Under Uncertainty, 1962; (with others) Managerial Economics, 1970, Institutional Investor Study Report of the Securities & Exchange Commission, 8 vols., 1971; editor: Explorations in Economic Research, 1974-75; (with others) Readings in Investments, 1980. Home: 14575 DeBell Rd Los Altos Hills CA 94022 Office: Benham Mgmt Corp 755 Page Mill Rd Palo Alto CA 94304

FARRAR, ELAINE WILLARDSON, artist; b. Los Angeles, Feb. 27, 1929; d. Eldon and Gladys Elsie (Larsen) Willardson; B.A., Ariz. State U., 1967, M.A., 1969, now doctoral candidate; children—Steve, Mark, Gregory, Leslie Jean, Monty, Susan. Tchr., Camelback Desert Sch., Paradise Valley, Ariz., 1966-69; mem. faculty Yavapai Coll., Prescott, Ariz., 1970—, chmn. dept. art, 1973-78, instr. art in watercolor and oil and acrylic painting and intaglio, 1971—; one-man shows include: R.P. Moffat's, Scottsdale, Ariz., 1969, Art Center, Battle Creek, Mich., 1969, The Woodpeddler, Costa Mesa, Calif., 1979; group show Prescott (Ariz.) Fine Arts Assn., 1982, 84, 86, N.Y. Nat. Am. Watercolorists, 1982; Ariz. State U. Women Images Now, 1986, 87; works rep. local and state exhibits; supt. fine arts dept. County Fair; com. mem., hanging chmn. Scholastic Art Awards. Mem. Mountain Artists Guild (past pres.), Nat. League Am. Pen Women (Prescott br.), NEA, Ariz. Edn. Assn., Nat. Art Edn. Assn., Ariz. Coll. and Univ. Faculty Assn., AAUW, Verde Valley Art Assn., Ariz. Women's Caucus for Art, Kappa Delta Pi, Phi Delta Kappa. Republican. Mormon. Home: 635 Copper Basin Rd Prescott AZ 86303 Office: Yavapai College Art Dept 1100 E Sheldon Rd Prescott AZ 86301

FARRELL, CYNTHIA FANGMAN, speech pathologist; b. Seneca, Kans., May 18, 1958; d. Carlton Morton and Barbara Ellen (Ayers) Fangman; m. Michael Thomas Farrell, Feb. 2, 1985. BS, Kans. State U., 1980; M in Natural Sci., Ariz. State U., 1983. Cert. speech and lang. pathologist. Speech/lang. pathologist Maricopa County Headstart Program, Phoenix, 1981-83, Sweetwater Developmentally Delayed Presch., Glendale, Ariz., 1983—; pvt. practice speech and lang. pathology Phoenix, 1983—. Author: Choosing a Phonetic Context, 1986. Mem. Am. Speech Lang. Hearing Assn., Ariz. Speech Lang. Hearing Assn. Home: 4243 E Edgemont Ave Phoenix AZ 85008

FARRELL, JAMES PATRICK, hospital executive; b. San Diego, Feb. 12, 1948; s. George W. and Doris M. (Dixon) F.; children—Shelley, Karissa. B.S., U. Utah, 1972, M.S. in Bus. Adminstrn. Indsl. Relations, 1974. Coordinator job evaluation Salt Lake City Sch. Dist., 1973-74; research fellow, teaching asst. Coll. Bus., U. Utah, Salt Lake City, 1974; dir. personnel Meth. Hosp., Madison, Wis., 1975-77; v.p. personnel services Meth. Med. Ctr. of Ill., Peoria, 1977-80; v.p. human resources Sutter Community Hosp., Sacramento, 1980—. Pres. Sacramento Personnel Assn.; chmn., bd. dirs. Sacramento Urban League; bd. dirs. Sutter Solano Med. Ctr.; mem. task force Nat. Council Community Hosps., Washington. Served with USN, 1967-68. Recipient award Central Ill. Hosp. Personnel Mgmt. Assn., 1978. Mem. Am. Soc. Personnel Adminstrn., Am. Compensation Assn., Calif. Hosp. Assn. (human resources task force), Sacramento C. of C.

FARRELL, LARRY DON, microbiology educator; b. Woodward, Okla., Nov. 5, 1942; s. Donal Mervin and Frieda Marie (Rector) F.; m. Julia Ann Robinson, Aug. 8, 1965; children: Denise Eileen, Meghan Kathleen. BS, U. Okla., 1964, MS, 1965; PhD, UCLA, 1970. Postdoctoral and instr. Coll. Medicine U. Ill., Chgo., 1970-72; asst. prof. microbiology Idaho State U., Pocatello, 1972-78, chmn. microbiology dept., 1977-84, assoc. prof., 1978—. Contbr. articles to profl. jours. Mem. AAAS, Am. Soc. Microbiology, Idaho Acad. Scis., Idaho Com. Correspondence Liaison (pres. 1982—), Sigma Xi. Democrat. Avocations: bicycling, fly fishing, reading. Home: 843 N 10th St Pocatello ID 83201 Office: Idaho State U Dept Biol Scis Pocatello ID 83209

FARRELL, ROBERT SCOTT, real estate investor and developer, oil and gas executive; b. Chgo., Mar. 17, 1954; s. Robert E. and Jennifer C. (Novelli) F.; m. Catherine Ann Shell, Dec. 6, 1985. BS, Ind. U., 1976. Pres. Farrell Investment Co., Phoenix, 1979—, Parallax Energy Corp., Phoenix, 1981—, Dax Real Estate, Phoenix, 1985—. Patentee in field. Co-chmn. fundraising Phoenix chpt. Am. Cancer Soc., 1986. Mem. Beta Gamma Sigma. Republican. Club: Vega 10-1.

FARRELL, THOMAS JOSEPH, insurance company executive; b. Butte, Mont., June 10, 1926; s. Bartholomew J. and Lavina H. (Collins) F.; m. Evelyn Irene Southam, July 29, 1951; children: Brien J., Susan M., Leslie A., Jerome T. Student U. San Francisco, 1949. CLU. Ptnr. Affiliated-Gen. Ins. Adjusters, Santa Rosa, Calif., 1949-54; agt. Lincoln Nat. Life Ins. Co., Santa Rosa, 1954-57, supr., 1957-59, gen. agt., 1959-74; pres. Thomas J. Farrell & Assos., 1974-76, 7 Flags Ins. Mktg. Corp., 1976-81, Farrell-Dranginis & Assocs., 1981—; pres., bd. dirs. Lincoln Nat. Bank, Santa Rosa, San Rafael. Pres. Redwood Empire Estate Planning Council, 1981-82, Sonoma County Council for Retarded Children, 1956—, City Santa Rosa Traffic and Parking Commn., 1963; del. Calif. State Conf. Small Bus., 1980; mem. Santa Rosa City Schs. Compensatory Edn. Adv. Bd.; bd. dirs. Santa Rosa City Schs. Consumer Edn. Adv. Bd.; pres., nat. dir. United Cerebral Palsy Assn., 1954-55; nat. coordinator C. of C.-Rotary Symposia on Employment of People with Disabilities, 1985—; v.p. Vigil Light, Inc.; chmn. bd. dirs. Nat. Barrier Awareness for People with Disabilities Found.;ound., Inc.; mem. Pres.'s Com. on Mental Retardation, 1982-86; chmn. Santa Rosa Community Relations Com., 1973-76; pres. Sonoma County Young Reps., 1953; past bd. dirs. Sonoma County Fair and Expn., Inc.; bd. dirs. Sonoma County Family Service Agy., Eldridge Found., North Bay Regional Ctr. for Developmentally Disabled; trustee Sonoma State Hosp. for Mentally Retarded. Recipient cert. Nat. Assn. Retarded Children, 1962, Region 9 U.S. HHS Community Service award, 1985, Sonoma County Vendor's Human Service award, 1986, Individual Achievement award Community Affirmative Action Forum of Sonoma County, 1986. Mem. Nat. Assn. Life Underwriters, Redwood Empire Assn. CLU's (pres. 1974—), Japanese-Am. Citizens League, Jaycees (Outstanding Young Man of Year 1961, v.p. 1955), Santa Rosa C. of C. (bd. dirs. 1974-75), Calif. PTA (hon. life). Lodge: Rotary. Home: 963 Wyoming Dr Santa Rosa CA 95405 Office: 1160 N Dutton Ave Suite 160 Santa Rosa CA 95401

FARRELL, WILLIAM EDGAR, sales executive, infosystems specialist; b. Jeanette, Pa., Mar. 13, 1937; s. Arthur Richard and Lelia (Ryder) F.; m. Sara Lynnette Swing, Aug. 20, 1960; children: Wendy J., Tracy L., Rebecca J. BS in Edn., Pa. State U., 1959. Location mgr. IBM Corp., Dover, Del., 1969-72; corp. lobbyist IBM Corp., Washington, 1972-74, planning cons., 1974-78, nat. mktg. mgr., 1978-80, exec. asst., 1980-81; account exec. IBM Corp., Denver, 1981—. Founding mem. River Falls Community Assn., Potomac, Md., 1975; first reader First Ch. of Christ Scientist Chevy Chase, Md., 1976-80. Recipient Outstanding Contbn. award IBM Corp., 1968. Republican. Avocations: flying instrument and comml. airplanes. Home: 6063 S Beeler St Englewood CO 80111 Office: IBM Corp 4700 S Syracuse Pkwy Denver CO 80237

FARRER, JOHN, orchestra conductor; b. Detroit, July 1, 1941; s. John Arnold and Beulah (Finley) F.; m. Bonnie Bogle, June 3, 1967; children—Matthew, Joanna. B.Mus., U. Mich., 1964, M.Mus., 1966; diploma Mozarteum, Salzburg, Austria, 1969. Music dir. Roswell Symphony Orch., N.Mex., 1972—, Bakersfield Symphony Orch., Calif., 1975—. Mem. Am. Symphony Orch. League (mem. standing com. on artistic affairs 1981—), Condrs. Guild, Assn. Calif. Symphony Orchs. (bd. dirs. 1977-83). Lodge: Rotary. Office: Bakersfield Symphony Orch 400 Truxtun St Suite 104 Bakersfield CA 93301

FARRIMOND, GEORGE FRANCIS, JR., business educator; b. Peerless, Utah, Sept. 23, 1932; s. George Francis Sr. and Ruth (Howard) F.; m. Remor Lamon Curtis, June 3, 1952; children: George Kenneth, Ronald Kay, Carrie Frances, Holly Jean. BS, U. Utah, 1955; MBA, U. Mo., 1968; postgrad., Portland State U., 1979—. Cert. profl. contracts mgr. Enlisted USAF, 1955, advanced through grades to lt. col., 1971; master navigator USAF, various locations, 1955-71; flight commdr. 360th tactical elec. war squadron USAF, Saigon, Socialist Republic of Vietnam, 1971-72; chief procurement ops. USAF, Wright-Patterson AFB, Ohio, 1972-73, chief pricing ops. div., 1973-76; retired USAF, 1976; asst. prof. bus. So. Oreg. State Coll., Ashland, 1976-82, assoc. prof., 1982—; cons. small bus., Jackson County, Oreg., 1976-86; cons. Japanese mgmt., Jackson County, 1981-86. Author: (computer program) Spanish Verb Conjugation, 1980, (workbook) Pricing Techniques, 1983. Chmn. Wright-Patterson AFB div United Fund, 1973-76; little league coach various teams, Ark. and Mo., 1963-71; Sunday Sch. tchr. Ch. of Latter-day Saints, various states. Decorated Disting. Flying Cross, 5 Air medals; Minuteman Ednl. scholar Air Force Inst. Tech., 1964, Education with Industry scholar Air Force Inst. Tech., 1970. Mem. Am. Prodn. and Inventory Control Soc. (v.p. edn. com. 1982-84), DPMA, Air Force Soc., Beta Gamma Sigma. Republican. Avocations: oil painting, grandfather clocks, personal computers. Home: 3404 Hwy 99 S Ashland OR 97520 Office: So Oreg State Coll Sch Bus 1250 Siskiyou Blvd Ashland OR 97520

FARRINGTON, NANCY, extended care nurse, geriatric care consultant; b. Orange, N.J., Feb. 11, 1944; d. Edward Walker and Nancy (Weyers) Wilkins; m. Albert Garry Luini, Aug. 12, 1967; m. Clyde Jesse Farrington, July 26, 1973; 1 child, Ian Walker, BS in Nursing, SUNY, 1966; MS in Nursing, U. Alaska, Anchorage, 1986. RN, Alaska 1971. Nurse, tchr., Buffalo, New Haven, Calgary, Alta., Puyallup, Wash., and Anchorage, 1966-75; rehab. cons., Anchorage, 1975; regional dir. Alaska Homemaker-Home Health Aide Program, Anchorage. 1975-76, program dir., dir. ops., 1979-82; supr. of nurses Hope Cottages, Inc., Anchorage, 1977; dir. Alaska Nurses Registry, Anchorage, 1977-79; ptnr. Health and Rehab. Services of Alaska, Anchorage, 1982-85; spl. projects nurse Our Lady of Compassion Care Ctr., Anchorage, 1985—, mgr. nurses, 1986—. Past chmn. Alaska Chpt., Nat. Multiple Sclerosis Soc. Recipient service award Multiple Sclerosis Soc. Mem. Nat. Rehab. Nurses Assn. (cert. rehab. nurse 1985). Home: 13341 Alpine Dr Anchorage AK 99516 Office: Our Lady of Compassion Care Ctr 4895 Cordova Anchorage AK 99503

FARRINGTON, WILLIAM BENFORD, investment analyst; b. N.Y.C., Mar. 10, 1921; s. Harold Phillips and Edith C. (Aitken) F.; B.C.E., Cornell U., 1947, M.S., 1949; Ph.D., Mass. Inst. Tech., 1953; m. Frances A. Garratt, 1949 (div. 1955); children: William Benford, Phyllis Ashley, Timothy Colfax; m. Gertrude E. Eby, Jan. 3, 1979. Radio engr. Naval Research Labs., 1942-43; dir. Read Standard Corp., 1948-55; plant engr. Hope's Windows, Inc., 1950-51; instr. geology, geophysics U. Mass., 1953-54; research geophysicist Humble Oil & Refining Co., 1954-56; lectr. U. Houston, 1955-56; sr. investment analyst Continental Research Corp., N.Y.C., 1956-61; pres., dir. Farrington Engrng. Corp., 1958-67; partner Farrington & Light Assos., Laguna Beach, Calif., 1967-82, Farrington Assocs., 1982—; v.p. Empire Resources Corp., 1961-62; asst. v.p. Empire Trust Co., 1962-64; dir. Commonwealth Gas Corp., N.Y.C.; sci. dir. Select Com. on Govt. Research, U.S. Ho. of Reps., 1964-65; lectr. U. Calif. at Los Angeles, 1968-72; sr. cons. Trident Engrng. Assos., Annapolis, Md., 1965—; corporate assoc. Technology Assos. So. Calif., 1971—. Chmn. crusade Am. Cancer Soc., Jamestown, N.Y., 1951. Chartered fin. analyst; registered geologist, Calif. Fellow AAAS, Fin. Analysts Fedn.; mem. Am. Assn. Petroleum Geologists, AIME, Am. Petroleum Inst., Am. Inst. Aeros. and Aeronautics, Geol. Soc. Am., Los Angeles Soc. Fin. Analysts, Sigma Xi. Episcolalian. Author articles in field. Home: 1565 Skyline Dr Laguna Beach CA 92651

FARRIS, MARTIN THEODORE, economist, educator; b. Spokane, Wash., Nov. 5, 1925; s. Jacob B. and Edith S. (Gunderson) F.; m. Rhoda H. Harrington, Aug. 20, 1948; children—Christine A. Farris Zenobi, Diana Lynn, Elizabeth Farris-Fisher, M. Theodore II. B.A., U. Mont., 1949, M.A., 1950; Ph.D., Ohio State U., 1957. Grad. asst. U. Mont., 1949-50; asst. in econs. Ohio State U., Columbus, 1950-51, asst. instr., 1953-55, instr., 1955-57; asst. prof. Ariz. State U., Tempe, 1957-59, assoc. prof., 1959-62, chmn. dept. econs., 1967-69, prof. transp. and pub. utility econs., 1962—; vis. prof. U. Hawaii, 1969-70, vis. scholar, 1979. Author: (with Roy Sampson and David Shrock) Domestic Transportation: Practice, Theory and Policy, 1985; (with Roy Sampson) Public Utilities: Regulation, Management and Ownership, 1973; (with Paul McElhiney) Modern Transportation, 1973; (with Grant Davis and Jack Holder) Management of Transportation Carriers, 1975; (with Forrest Harding) Passenger Transportation, 1976; (with Dave Bess) U.S. Maritime: History and Prospects, 1981, (with Stephen Happel) Modern Managerial Economics, 1987; contbr. articles to profl. jours. Served with U.S. Army, 1944-46. Decorated Philippine Liberation medal; recipient Transp. Man of the Yr. award, 1972, Outstanding Faculty Achievement award Ariz. State U. Alumni Assn., 1978, Outstanding Faculty Researcher award Coll. Bus., Ariz. State U., 1982. Mem. Am. Econ. Assn. (Outstanding Contbn. to Scholarship in Transp. and Pub. Utilities award 1984), Western Econ. Assn. (bd. dirs. 1966-67), ICC Practitioners, Transp. Research Forum, Am. Soc. Transp. and Logistics (chief examiner 1961-73), Council of Logistics Mgmt., Traffic Clubs Internat., Phi Kappa Phi, Omicron Delta Epsilon, Sigma Phi Epsilon, Delta Nu Alpha, Beta Gamma Sigma. Episcopalian. Club: Traffic (Phoenix) (pres. 1960). Home: 6108 E Vernon Scottsdale AZ 85257 Office: Ariz State U Coll Bus Adminstrn Tempe AZ 85287

FARROW, BERNARD EDWARD, psychologist, professional trainer, educator; b. Monticello, N.Y., July 6, 1936; s. Saul and Ruth (Finkelstein) F.; B.S., SUNY-Oswego, 1961; M.A., No. Ariz. U., Flagstaff, 1971; m. Arlene Mendelson, May 30, 1960; children—Scott Andrew, Randy Mark. Tchr., Brentwood (N.Y.) Pub. Schs., 1961-62, Roslyn (N.Y.) Pub. Schs., 1962-66, Half Hollow Hills Pub. Schs., Huntington, N.Y., 1966-67; tchr. Clark County Schs., Las Vegas, Nev., 1968-72, counselor, 1978-79; adj. prof. Nova U., Fort Lauderdale, Fla., 1978—; instr. Park Coll., Nellis AFB, Las Vegas, Nev., 1979—; prof. Embry Riddle Aero. U., Nellis AFB, Las Vegas, 1978—; pvt. practice psychology, Las Vegas, 1979—; prof. Nat. U., Las Vegas; psychologist State Nev., Nev. Indsl. Commn., State Indsl. Ins. System, 1979-84; sr. tng. rep. Reynolds Elec. & Engrng. Co., Inc., employee assistance program counselor; spl. investigator child custody div. 8th Jud. Dist. Ct., 1979-80. Mem. Town Bd., Mount Charleston, Nev., 1980—, chmn., 1981—; team couple World Wide Marriage Encounter, 1982—; precinct chmn. Nev. Democratic Party, 1982; mem. Nev. Speakers Bur., 1983—. Served with USN, 1954-57. Cert. clin. neuropsychologist; cert. counselor. Mem. Assn. Humanistic Edn. and Devel. (pub. INFOCHANGE), Am. Personnel and Guidance Assn., Am. Fedn. Tchrs., Rehab. Counselors Assn., Am. Psychol. Assn., Soc. Behavioral Medicine, Nev. Adlerian Soc., Nev. State Counselors Assn., Nev. Mental Health Counselors Assn. (county rep.), Nev. Psychol. Assn., Am. Soc. Quality Control, Am. Soc. Tng. and Devel., Nat. Property Mgmt. Assn.

FARWELL, HARLEIGH ELLIS, construction consultant executive; b. Palisades, Wash., Sept. 23, 1921; s. Harley Elmer and Cecil Nan (Johnston) F.; student public schs., m. Suzanne Edwina Boehm, Jan. 8, 1966; children by previous marriage—Er. Kay Farwell Gilbertson, Sharon A. Farwell Scriba, Marilyn Z. Farwell Gala, Ellis D., Donovan W., Daniel A. Constrn. supt., gen. supt. Bank Bldg. Corp., St. Louis, 1952-60; constrn. supt., project mgr. Howard S. Wright Constrn. Co., Seattle, 1960-73, v.p., Seattle, 1973-80, sr. v.p., 1980-83; pres. Farwell Constrn. Services, Inc., Redmond, Wash., 1983—; guest lectr. Mem. accessibility design adv. com. Easter Seal Soc. Wash., 1978—. Served with AUS, 1944-45. Decorated Purple Heart. Mem. Am. Soc. Mil. Engrs., Am. Concrete Inst., Am. Arbitration Assn. Research on cost improvement methods, devel. and upgrading of unit price data. Home: 15715 NE 66th Pl Redmond WA 98052 Office: 15715 NE 66th Pl Redmond WA 98052

FARWELL, HERMON WALDO, JR., educator, speech communicator; b. Englewood, N.J., Oct. 24, 1918; s. Hermon Waldo and Elizabeth (Whitcomb) F.; A.B., Columbia, 1940; M.A., Pa. State U., 1964; m. Martha Carey Matthews, Jan. 3, 1942; children—Gardner Whitcomb, Linda Margaret (Mrs. Richard Hammer). Mil. service, 1940-66, advanced through grades to maj. U.S. Air Force; ret., 1966; instr. aerial photography Escola Tecnica de Aviação, Brazil, 1946-48; faculty U. So. Colo., Pueblo, 1966-84, prof. emeritus speech communication; cons., tchr. parliamentary procedure. Mem. Am. Inst. Parliamentarians (nat. dir. 1977-87), Commn. on Am. Parliamentary Practice (chmn. 1976), Ret. Officers Assn., Nat. Assn. Parliamentarians, Am. Legion. Author: The Majority Rules-A Manual of Procedure for Most Groups; Parliamentary Motions; Majority Motions; editor: The Parliamentary Jour. Home: 65 MacAlester Rd Pueblo CO 81001

FARWELL, LYNDON JAMES, clergyman, administrator; b. Los Gatos, Calif., Oct. 29, 1940; s. Lyndon James and Louise Catherine (Bacigalupi) F. B.A., Gonzaga U., 1964; M.A. in History, UCLA, 1968; S.T.M. in Theology, Jesuit Sch. of Theology, Berkeley, 1972; Ph.D. in Religion, Claremont Grad. Sch., 1976. Joined Soc. of Jesus, 1958; ordained priest 1971; instr. Loyola High Sch., Los Angeles, 1965-68; parish asst. Our Lady of Assumption Ch., Claremont, Calif., 1971-73; asst. prof. theology U. San Francisco, 1976-78; exec. asst. to provincial Calif. Province of Soc. of Jesus, Los Gatos, 1978-81; pres. Jesuit Sch. of Theology, Berkeley, Calif., 1981-86; asst. to provincial Calif. Province, S.J., Los Gatos, 1986—. Mem. editorial bd. Company, 1981—. Trustee U. Santa Clara, 1977-84; bd. dirs. Cath. Charities, Diocese of San Francisco, 1979-81; trustee U. San Francisco, 1981—, Grad. Theol. Union, 1981-86, mem. edn. com. Oakland Diocesan Pastoral Council, Calif., 1985-86. Mem. Am. Acad. Religion, Am. Hist. Assn., Internat. Assn. History of Religions, N.Am. Acad. Liturgy, Soc. Calif. Pioneers. Democrat. Roman Catholic. Home and Office: 300 College Ave PO Box 519 Los Gatos CA 95031

FARZAROLI, PATRICK JAMES, pension services company executive; b. Orlando, Fla., Mar. 7, 1947; s. Sam Joseph and Ann Loretta (McClernan) F.; m. Mary Elizabeth McMahon, May 17, 1969; children—Samantha Ann, Lynn Elizabeth. B.S. in Indsl. Mgmt., Rochester Inst. Tech., 1973. C.L.U.; chartered fin. cons. Tchr. The Am. Sch., Rochester, N.Y., 1970-73; agt. Conn. Mut. Life Ins. Co., Rochester, 1973-74, dir. pensions, 1974-78; sr. cons. on pensions Hicks Pension Services, Fresno, Calif., 1978-79, exec. v.p. pensions, 1979-81; pres. Farzaroli & Davey Pension Services Corp., Fresno, 1981—. Contbr. articles to profl. publs. Served with USAF, 1968-71. Mem. Am. Soc. Pension Actuaries, Internat. Assn. Fin. Planning (v.p. edn. Fresno 1981-83), Am. Soc. C.L.U.s (bd. dirs., pres. 1986-87, sec. Fresno chpt. 1983-86, pres. 1985-86). Republican. Roman Catholic. Lodge: Rotary (editor Fresno 1982-83). Home: 7308 N Hazel Ave Fresno CA 93711 Office: Farzaroli & Davey Pension Services Corp 3443 W Shaw Ave Fresno CA 93711

FASI, FRANK F., mayor of Honolulu; b. Hartford, Conn., Aug. 27, 1920. B.S., Trinity Coll., Hartford, 1942. Mem. Hawaii Senate, from 1958; Dem. mayor City and County of Honolulu, 1969-81, Rep. mayor, 1985—. Mem. Dem. Nat. Com. for Hawaii, 1952-56; del. 2d Constl. Conv., 1968; mem.-at-large Honolulu City Council, from 1965. Served to capt. USMCR. Mem. VFW (former comdr. Hawaii dept.), AFTRA (past v.p.). Office: City Hall 530 S King Honolulu HI 96813

FASS, BARBARA, city official. Mayor, Stockton, Calif., 1985—. Address: Office of Mayor 425 N El Dorado St Stockton CA 95202 *

FASSERO, DONN ANTHONY, orthopedic surgeon; b. Ellensburg, Wash., Jan. 15, 1942; s. Peter and Mary Katherine (Giolitti) F.; m. Melodee Ann Olson, June 11, 1977; children—Mia Anne, Donn Anthony. B.S., U. Wash., 1966; M.D., Georgetown U., 1974. Diplomate Am. Bd. Orthopedic Surgery. Orthopedic resident, Mayo Clinic, Rochester, Minn., 1974-79; chief orthopedic surgery Gould Med. Found., Modesto, Calif., 1979—. Served to capt. U.S. Army, 1966-69. Fellow ACS, Am. Acad. Orthopaedic Surgeons, Western Orthopaedic Assn.; mem. Alpha Omega Alpha. Republican. Roman Catholic. Home: 820 Carolyn Ave Modesto CA 95354 Office: Gould Med Found 600 Coffee Rd Modesto CA 95355

FASSIO, VIRGIL, newspaper publishing company executive; b. Pitts., Aug. 10, 1927; s. Domenico and Carolina (Pia) F.; m. Shirley DeVirgilis; children—Richard, David, Michael. B.A. with honors, U. Pitts., 1949. Founder, editor, pub. Beechview News, Pitts., 1947-51; reporter Valley Daily News, Tarentum, Pa., 1950, circulation mgr., 1951-58; circulation dir. Morning News and Evening Jour., Wilmington, Del., 1958-65; circulation dir. Detroit Free Press, 1965-71, v.p., bus. mgr., 1971; v.p., circulation dir. Chgo. Tribune, 1972-76; v.p., gen. mgr. Seattle Post-Intelligencer, 1976, pub., 1978—; lectr. Am. Press Inst.; cons., lectr. in field. Contbr. articles to profl. jours. Del. White House Conf. on Children, 1960, 70; bd. dirs. Pacific Mus. Flight, Pacific Sci. Ctr. Found., Corp. Council of Arts; bd. regents Seattle U., Washington Council on Internat. Trade; pres. Seattle-King County Conv. and Visitors Bur., 1982-84; bd. dirs. Seattle Goodwill Industries, Medic I Emergency Med. Services Found., Boys and Girls Clubs of King County, Wash. Council of Internat. Trade. Served with USNR, 1945-46, comdr. USNR (ret.). Recipient Frank Thayer award U. Wis., 1972; Varsity Letterman of Distinction award U. Pitts. 1974. Mem. Internat. Circulation Mgrs. Assn. (Man of Yr. award 1964), Inter-State Circulation Mgrs. Assn. (sec.-treas. 1954-65, Outstanding Achievement award 1967), Seattle C. of C. (bd. dirs.), Downtown Seattle Devel. Assn. (treas.), Allied Daily Pubs. Assn., Am. Newspaper Pubs. Assn. (vice chmn. industry affairs com. 1982-86), Hist. Soc. Seattle and King County (bd. dirs.), Medic One Found. (bd. dirs.). Clubs: Rainier, Wash. Athletic (bd. dirs.). Lodge: Rotary (bd. dirs.). Office: Seattle Post-Intelligencer 101 Elliott Ave West Seattle WA 98111

FASTRING, RICHARD ARTHUR, engineering executive, consultant; b. New Orleans, Oct. 25, 1938; s. Wernex Theodore and Evelyn Lucille (Bondurant) F.; m. Glenda Marie Hintz, July 13, 1960; children: Rhonda, Gregg, Roger. BSEE, Tulane U., 1959; postgrad., U. Pa., 1960-61. Engr. RCA, Camden, N.J., 1959-65; engring. mgr. Sci. Mgmt. Assocs., Haddonfield, N.J., 1965-71, Semcor Inc., Moorestown, N.J., 1971-85, Synetics Corp., San Diego, 1985—; rep. Indsl. Adv. Group, NATO,. 1975-80; mem. local area network standards com., USN, 1985—, A2K com. mem. Soc. Automotive Engrs., 1971-73. Adult Bapt. Sunday sch. tchr., San Diego, 1983—. Mem. Am. Soc. Naval Engrs. (Speakers award 1986). Republican. Office: Synetics Corp 312 Highland Ave Suite I El Cajon CA 92020

FATHAUER, THEODORE FREDERICK, meteorologist, manager; b. Oak Park, Ill., June 5, 1946; s. Arthur Theodore and Helen Ann (Mashek) F.; m. Mary Ann Neesan, Aug. 8, 1981. B.A., U. Chgo., 1968. Cert. cons. meteorologist. Research aide USDA No. Dev. Labs., Peoria, Ill., 1966, Cloud Physics Lab., Chgo., 1967; meteorologist Sta. WLW radio/TV, Cin., 1967-68, Nat. Meteorol. Ctr., Washington, 1968-70, Nat. Weather Service, Anchorage, 1970-80; meteorologist-in-charge Nat. Weather Service, Fairbanks, Alaska, 1980—; instr. U. Alaska, Fairbanks, 1975-76, USCG aux., Fairbanks and Anchorage, 1974—. Contbr. articles to weather mags. Recipient Outstanding Performance award Nat. Weather Service, 1972, 76, 83, 85, 86, Fed. Employee of Yr. award, Fed. Exec. Assn., Anchorage, 1978. Mem. Am. Meteorol. Soc. (TV seal of approval), Am. Geophys. Union, AAAS, Royal Meteorol. Soc., Western Snow Conf. Republican. Lutheran. Avocations: reading, music, skiing, canoeing. Home: 1738 Chena Ridge Rd Fairbanks AK 99701 Office: Nat Weather Service Forecast Office 101 12th Ave Box 21 Fairbanks AK 99701

FATT, IRVING, optometry and bioengineering educator; b. Chgo., Sept. 16, 1920; s. David and Annie Lily (Arkin) F.; married; 1 child, Lois Fatt White. B.S. in Chemistry, UCLA, 1947, M.S., 1948; Ph.D., U. So. Calif., 1955. Sr. research chemist Standard Oil Co., La Habra, Calif., 1948-52, group supr., 1952-57; mem. faculty U. Calif.-Berkeley, 1957—, prof. physiol. optics and engring. sci., 1962-63, Miller Research prof. engring., 1962-67, asst. dean, 1964-69, acting dean, 1975-78; cons. Berkeley, 1983—. Patentee in field. Served to 1st lt. USAAF, 1942-46. Petroleum Fund Research Career grantee, 1957. Mem. Biomed. Engring. Soc., Am. Acad. Optometry, U.K. Biol. Engring. Soc. Clubs: Berkeley Faculty, Berkeley Yacht. Home: 406 Boynton Ave Berkeley CA 94707 Office: U Calif Minor Hall Berkeley CA 94720

FAULCONER, KAY ANNE, cons. exec.; b. Shelbyville, Ind., Aug. 19, 1945; d. Clark Jacks and Charlotte (Tindall) Keenan; B.A. in English, Calif. State U., Northridge, 1968; M.B.A., Pepperdine U., 1975, M.A. in Communications, 1976; m. James Faulconer; children—Kevin Lee, Melissa Lynne. Pres., Kay Faulconer & Assos., Oxnard, Calif., 1977—; instr. Oxnard Coll., U. LaVerne. Dir. bus. adminstrn of justice programs, Ventura (Calif.) Coll.; former pres., founder Oxnard Friends of Library; former exec. bd. Ventura County March of Dimes; mem. PTA; officer, bd. dirs. Oxnard Girls Club. Named Businesswoman of Yr., Ventura Bus. and Profl. Women's Club, 1976; Woman of Achievement, Oxnard Bus. and Profl. Women's Club, 1973, recipient Career Woman award, 1974; Mark Hopkins award for excellence in teaching Oxnard Coll., 1982. Mem. Am. Soc. Tng. and Devel., Am. Assn. Women in Community and Jr. Colls. (Leaders for 80's program), Ventura County Profl. Women's Network. Club: Oxnard Jr. Monday (past pres., hon. life). Home and Office: 601 Janetwood Dr Oxnard CA 93030

FAULKNER, DEXTER HAROLD, magazine publishing executive editor; b. Grand Island, Nebr., Sept. 10, 1937; s. Jack L. and Wanetta May (Howland) F.; student U. Calif.-Fresno, 1956-58, Ambassador Coll., 1958-60; m. Shirley Ann Hume, Jan. 11, 1959; children—Nathan Timothy, Matthew Benjamin. Exec. editor Plain Truth Mag; mng. editor Good News mag., Youth/87 mag. and Worldwide News-Tabloid internat. div. Ambassador Coll., Sydney, Australia, 1960-66, news research asst. dir. Ambassador Coll. Editorial, Pasadena, Calif., 1966-71, regional editor Plain Truth mag., Washington, 1971-75, asst. mng. editor, Pasadena, 1975-78, mng. editor, 1980-82, exec. editor, 1982—, mng. editor Good News mag., Worldwide News-Tabloid, 1978-85, editor, 1986—; mng. editor Youth/87 mag., 1980-85, editor, 1986—; instr. mass communications Ambassador Coll., 1980—; columnist Just One More Thing . . ., By the Way. Mem. Inst. Journalists (London), Profl. Photographers Am. Inc., Bur. Freelance Photographers (London), Nat. Press Club, World Affairs Council (Los Angeles), Internat. Assn. Bus. Communicators, Nat. Press Photographers Assn., Am. Mgmt. Assn., Sigma Delta Chi. Mem. Worldwide Ch. God. Contbr. articles, photos on internat. relations, social issues to Plain Truth mag., Good News mag., Worldwide News Publs. Club: Commonwealth of Calif. Home: 7859 Wentworth St Sunland CA 91040 Office: 300 W Green St Pasadena CA 91129

FAULKNER, JOHN MICHAEL, marketing consultant; b. Van Nuys, Calif., Apr. 30, 1952; s. James Norman and Nadine (Harper) F.; m. Marguerite Ann Otis, July 13, 1974; children: Morgan Emmery, Drew Elizabeth. AA in Social Sci., West Valley Coll., 1972; BA in History, Humboldt State U., 1974. Mktg. mgr. BAM Publs., Inc., Oakland, Calif., 1976-81; advt. dir. Western Empire Pub., Inc., San Clemente, Calif., 1981-84; advt. exec. sales promotion Cunningham & Walsh, Advt., Fountain Valley, Calif., 1984-86; mktg. cons. Drew Morgan & Assocs., Dana Point, Calif., 1986—. Office: Drew Morgan & Assocs 24312 Cortes Dr Dana Point CA 92629

FAULKNER, MAURICE ERVIN, educator, musician; b. Fort Scott, Kans., Feb. 2, 1912; s. Ervin Philetus and Minnie Mae (Munday) F.; B.S. in Music, Fort Hays State Coll., 1932; postgrad. Interlochen, U. Mich., summer 1933; M.A., Columbia, 1936; Ph.D., Stanford, 1956; m. Ellen Marie Stradal, May 24, 1934 (div. 1951); children—Katherine Sydney, Barbara Ellen; m. 2d, Suzanne Sommerville, Oct. 18, 1958. Instr. music, pub. schs., Quinter, Kans., 1932-36; instr. instrumental music pub. schs., Clay Center, Kans., 1936-37; asst. in music Columbia U., summers 1934-40; asst. prof. San Jose State Coll., 1937-40; asst. prof., assoc. prof. U. Calif., Goleta, 1940-60, prof. music, 1960— chmn. dept., 1950-54; vis. prof. U. Tex., summer 1947; music critic Santa Barbara Star, 1951-56; research musicologist Inst. for Environ. Stress, U. Calif., Santa Barbara, 1968—, prof. emeritus, 1979—; condr. Santa Barbara Symphony Orch., 1941-44, All-Calif. High Sch. Symphony Orch., 1941-73; guest condr. Korean Symphony, 1945-46; condr., mus. dir. Santa Barbara Fiesta Bowl Mus. Show, 1951-53; condr., Kern Co. Honor Band of Calif., music cons., adjudicator Calif., Nev. festivals; free lance music, drama, art critic for Mus. Courier, Sat. Rev., Christian Sci. Monitor; research asso. Inst. for Environ. Stress, 1968—. Chmn., Santa Barbara Mayor's Adv. Com. on Arts, 1966-69. Served from lt. (j.g.) to lt. USNR, 1944-46. Recipient Max Reinhardt Meml. medal for Outstanding Service to Salzburg Festival on 50th Anniversary, Salzburg Golden Service medal, 1981. Fellow Internat. Inst. Arts and Letters (life); mem. Music Acad. West (pres., dir. 1949-82, pres. emeritus, 1954-84), So. Calif. Sch. Band and Orch. Assn. (hon. life, v.p. 1955), Musicians Union (hon. life), Nat. Music Educators Conf., Internat. Congress Traditional Music (lectr. Stockholm 1984), Phi Mu Alpha, Phi Delta Kappa. Presbyn. Mason. Brass clinic editor Instrumentalist, 1964-86. Contbr. articles to profl. jours. Ann. tours European music festivals, as adviser, critic. Home: Box 572 Goleta CA 93116

FAULKNER, SEWELL FORD, realtor; b. Keene, N.H., Sept. 25, 1924; s. John Charles and Hazel Helen (Ford) F.; A.B., Harvard, 1949; M.B.A., 1951; m. June Dayton Finn, Jan. 10, 1951 (div.); children—Patricia Anne, Bradford William, Sandra Ford, Jonathan Dayton, Winthrop Sewell; m. 2d, Constance Mae Durvin, Mar. 15, 1969 (div.); children—Sarah Elizabeth, Elizabeth Jane. Product mgr. Congoleum Nairn, Inc., Kearny, N.J., 1951-55; salesman, broker, chmn., pres. Jack White Co. real estate, Anchorage, 1956——; dir. Life Ins. Co. Alaska. Mem. Anchorage City Council, 1962-65, Greater Anchorage Area Borough Assembly, 1964-65, Anchorage Area Charter Commn., 1969-70. Pres., Alaska World Affairs Council, 1967-68; treas. Alyeska Property Owners, Inc., 1973-75, pres., 1977-78; pres. Downtown Anchorage Assn., 1974-75; mem. Girdwood Bd. Suprs. Served with USAAF, 1943-45. Mem. Anchorage Area C. of C. (dir. 1973-74), Urban Land Inst., Bldg. Owners and Mgrs. Assn., Nat. Inst. Real Estate Brokers. Clubs: Alaska Notch, Anchorage Petroleum. Home: Mt Alyeska Girdwood AK 99587 Office: Jack White Co 3201 C St Anchorage AK 99503

FAUSCH, KURT DANIEL, fishery biology educator; b. Crookston, Minn., Jan. 17, 1955; s. Homer David and Guinevere Jean (Smythe) F.; m. Deborah Anne Eisenhauer, Dec. 20, 1975; children: Emily Rebecca, Benjamin Thomas. BS, U. Minn., Duluth, 1976; MS, Mich. State U., 1978, PhD, 1981. Postdoctoral fellow U. Ill., Champaign, 1981-82; asst. prof. fisheries biology Colo. State U., Ft. Collins, 1982—. Contbr. articles to profl. jours. Mem. Am. Fisheries Soc. (Albert S. Hazzard award 1982), Ecol. Soc. Am., Sigma Xi. Office: Colo State U Dept Fishery and Wildlife Biology Fort Collins CO 80523

FAUST, MARGARET SILER, psychology educator; b. Tientsin, China, Feb. 22, 1926; came to U.S., 1928; d. Charles Arthur and Marion Louise (Pierce) Siler; m. William Langdon Faust, Aug. 26, 1950; children—Katherine, Ann, Marion. B.A., Pomona Coll., 1948; M.A., Stanford U., 1951, Ph.D., 1957. Lic. psychologist, Calif. From asst. prof. to prof. Scripps Coll., Claremont, Calif., 1960-70, prof. psychology, 1970—. Author: Somatic Development of Adolescent Girls, 1977; contbr. articles to profl. jours. Bur. for Edn. of Handicapped Postdoctoral fellow UCLA, 1980; Grant Found. grantee, 1970-72. Mem. Am. Psychol. Assn., Soc. for Research in Child Devel., Sigma Xi. Office: Psychology Dept Scripps Coll Claremont CA 91711 *

FAUTSKO, TIMOTHY FRANK, state agency administrator; b. Canton, Ohio, Dec. 27, 1945; s. Frank F. and Helen E. (Gozdan) F.; m. Carol Jean Kraig, Nov. 9, 1974; children: T. Matthew, David F. BA in English, BBA, Walsh Coll., 1967; MA in Human Services Adminstrn., U. Colo., 1972. Dir. tng. Vista Programs, Washington, 1967-70, Nat. Info. Ctr., Boulder, Colo., 1972-76; ct. adminstr. State of Colo., Boulder, 1976-80; jud. adminstr. State of Colo., Aspen, 1980—; instr. Colo. Mountain Coll., Glenwood Springs, Aspen, Colo., 1980—; co-dir. T/SDA & Assocs., Denver, 1975—. Co-author: Volunteer Programs in Prevention/Diversion, 1973, 2d rev. edit., 1975, Solving Problems in Meetings, 1980, QUID-How You Can Make the Best Decisions of Your Life, 1978, Como Tomar las Mejores Deciones de Su Vida, 1985; contbr. articles to profl. jours. Mem. Centennial Com., Glenwood Springs, 1983-85; mem. Mayor's com., Denver, 1977-78. HEW scholar, U. Colo., Boulder, 1971-72; recipient Cert. Appreciation Office of Mayor, Denver, 1978, Colo. Mountain Coll., Glenwood Springs, 1985-86. Mem. Nat. Assn. Trial Ct. Adminstrs., Nat. Orgn. Victims Assistance. Avocations: writing, teaching. Home: 1009 Walz Ave Glenwood Springs CO 81601 Office: State Colo Jud Dept PO Box 1486 Aspen CO 81612

FAW, TERRY TOD, psychologist, educator, consultant; b. San Diego, Apr. 24, 1943; s. Volney E. and Maurine H. (Haman) F.; B.S., Lewis and Clark Coll., 1965; M.A., Vanderbilt U., 1967, Ph.D., 1969; m. Karen D. Kullberg, Sept. 22, 1973; children—Justin Booth, Robert Tod. Asst. prof. UCLA, 1969-73; assoc. prof. psychology Lewis and Clark Coll., Portland, Oreg., 1973-81, Lewis and Clark prof., 1981-83, chmn. dept., 1973-83; pvt. practice psychology, 1974—; mem. and chmn. Oreg. State Bd. Psychologists Examiners. Mem. Am. Psychol. Assn., Western Psychol. Assn., Oreg. Psychol. Assn. (bd. dirs.), Theta Chi. Methodist. Author: Child Psychology, 1980. Office: 6950 SW Hampton St Tigard OR 97223

FAWCETT, WILLIAM FREDERICK, video production company executive; b. Salem, Mass., May 29, 1937; s. Frederick Stewart and Margaret (Carney) F.; m. Carol Ann Chase; children: William, Suzanne, Sandi. BA with honors, Boston Coll., 1959; MBA, Loyola U., New Orleans, 1963, LLB, 1965. Pres. Fawcett Prodns., Santa Ana, Calif., 1971-78, 81—; gen. mgr. creative dir. Bozell & Jacobs, Newport Beach, Calif., 1979-81; bd. dirs. Recognition Express, San Juan Capistrano, Women's Internat. Sucess System, Newport Beach. Author stage seminar Breaking Free, 1981; dir. TV series Athletes in Action, 1982 (Golden Angel award 1983). Recipient MAME awards, Bldg. Industry Assn., 1978, 79, 82, 83, 85, MIRM award, 1986. Republican. Roman Catholic. Clubs: Mission Hills (Ranch Mirage, Calif.); Balboa Bay (Newport Beach). Avocations: tennis, golf, art and film making. Office: Fawcett Prodns 87 Brookhollow Dr Santa Ana CA 92705

FAY, ABBOTT EASTMAN, history educator; b. Scottsbluff, Nebr., July 19, 1926; s. Abbott Eastman and Ethel (Lambert) F.; m. Joan D. Richardson, Nov. 26, 1953; children: Rand, Diana, Collin. BA, Colo. State Coll., 1949, MA, 1953; postgrad., U. Denver, 1961-63, Western State U., 1963. Tchr. Leadville (Colo.) Pub. Schs., 1950-52, elem. prin., 1952-54; prin. Leadville Jr. High Sch., 1954-55; pub. info. dir., instr. history Mesa Coll., Grand Junction, Colo., 1955-64; asst. prof. history Western State Coll. of Colo., Gunnison, 1964-76, assoc. prof. history, 1976-82, assoc. prof. emeritus, 1982—; propr. Mountaintop Books, Paonia, Colo.; bd. dirs Colo. Assoc. Univ. Press; profl. speaker in field; dir. hist. tours. Author: Mountain Academia, 1968, Writing Good History Research Papers, 1980, Ski Tracks in the Rockies, 1984; playwright: Thunder Mountain Lives Tonight!; contbr. articles to profl. jours.; freelance writer popular mags. Founder, coordinator Nat. Energy Conservation Challenge; project reviewer NEH, Colo. Hist. Soc. Served with AUS, 1944-46. Named Top Prof. Western State Coll., 1969, 70, 71; fellow Hamline U. Inst. Asian Studies, 1975, 79. Mem. Western Writers Am., Rocky Mountain Social Sci. Assn. (sec. 1961-63), Am. Hist. Assn., Assn. Asian Studies, Western History Assn., Western State Coll. Alumni Assn. (pres. 1971-73), Internat. Platform Assn., Am. Legion (Outstanding Historian award 1981), Phi Alpha Theta, Phi Kappa Delta, Delta Kappa Pi. Home: 1750 Hwy 133 Paonia CO 81428

FAY, MICHAEL JAMES, orthopedic surgeon, military officer; b. Denver, Nov. 12, 1946; s. John William and Gladys Vivian (Kassel) F.; m. Samar Sandra Margaret Freemon, June 14, 1970; children: Jason Andrew, Britten Hunter. BS, U.S. Mil. Acad., 1968; MD, Georgetown U., 1977. Commd. 2d lt. U.S. Army, 1968, advanced through grades to lt. col., 1983; orthopedic surgeon 130th Sta. Hosp., Heidelberg, Baden-Wüttemberg, Fed. Republic Germany, 1981-82, chief of orthopedic service, 1982, chief dept. surgery, 1982-84; div. surgeon, bn. comdr. 7th med. bn., Ft. Ord, Calif., 1985-87; staff orthopedic service Tripler Army Med. Ctr., Honolulu, 1987—. Fellow Am. Acad. Orthopedic Surgeons; mem. Soc. Mil. Orthopedic Surgeons, Nat. Wildlife Assn., Assn. Mil. Surgeons of U.S., Order Mil. Med. Merit, Sierra Club. Episcopalian. Avocations: horseback riding, military history. Home: 203 Saint Lo Rd Fort Ord CA 93941 Office: Hdqrs 7th Med Battalion L Fort Ord CA 93941

FAY, RICHARD JAMES, mechanical engineer, executive, educator; b. St. Joseph, Mo., Apr. 26, 1935; s. Frank James and Marie Jewell (Senger) F.; m. Marilyn Louis Kelsey, Dec. 22, 1962; B.S.M.E., U. Denver, 1959, M.S.M.E., 1970; Registered profl. engr., Colo., Nebr. Design engr. Denver Fire Clay Co., 1957-60; design, project engr. Silver Engring. Works, 1960-63; research engr., lectr. mech. engring. U. Denver, 1963-74, asst. prof. Colo. Sch. of Mines, 1974-75, founder, pres. Fay Engring. Corp., 1971—. Served with Colo. N.G., 1962. Mem. Soc. Automotive Engrs. (past chmn. Colo. sect.), ASME (past chmn. Colo. sect., regional v.p. elec., coll. relations chmn. region). Contbr. articles to profl. jours.; patentee in field. Office: 5201 E 48th Ave Denver CO 80216

FAZIO, JOHN PETER, statistician; b. Portland, Oreg., Feb. 22, 1952; s. Jack Frank and Maria Nativita (Rebagliati) F. BS in Math., Oreg. State U., 1974, MS in Stats., 1975. Statistician Texaco Research Labs., Port Arthur, Tex., 1975-77; sr. process control engr. Corning Glass Works, N.Y., 1977-78; ops. research analyst U.S. Army C.E., Portland, Oreg., 1979-82; statistician Bonneville Power Adminstrn., Portland, 1982—; cons. in field. Chpt. leader Apostolate for Family Consecration, Kenosha, Wis., 1986—. Named one of Outstanding Young Men of Am., 1983. Mem. Am. Soc. Quality Control, Am. Statis. Assn., Jaycees. Roman Catholic. Clubs: Toastmasters Internat. (Essayons ednl. v.p. 1980), KC (Portland). Developer statis. and problem-solving methods; contbr. to model to assist in planning for Northwest's energy future.

FAZIO, VIC, congressman; b. Winchester, Mass., Oct. 11, 1942; m. Judy Kern; children: Dana, Anne. BA, Union Coll., Schenectady, 1965; postgrad., Calif. State U., Sacramento. Congl. and legis. cons. 1966-75; mem. Calif. State Assembly, 1975-78; mem. 96th-100th Congresses from Calif. 4th Dist., 1979—, mem. appropriations, budget and standards of ofcl. conduct coms., chmn. legis. br. appropriations com., majority whip-at-large, mem. exec. com. Democratic Study Group, also co-chmn. Fed. Govt. Services Task Force, mem. appropriations subcom. energy and water, appropriations subcom. milt. constrn., mem. Select Com. on Hunger; Former mem. Sacramento County Charter and Planning Commns. Founder: Calif. Jour. Coro Found. fellow.; Named Environmentalist of Yr., Calif. Planning and Conservation League. Mem. Air Force Assn., Navy League, UNICO. Democrat. Office: Rayburn House Office Bldg Room 2433 Washington DC 20515 *

FECHNER, GILBERT HENRY, forestry educator; b. Northbrook, Ill., Dec. 20, 1922; s. Walter George and Minnie Anna (Fickenscher) F.; m. Maxine Mildred Nitz, July 17, 1948; children: Dudley Forrest, Jennifer Sue, Cheryl Lynne. BS, Colo. State U., 1947, MS, 1955; PhD, U. Minn., 1964. Wood technologist Hallack & Howard, Denver, 1947-49; staff forester TVA, Norris, 1949-53; prof. forestry Colo. State U., Ft. Collins, 1954—; mem. Natural Resources Adv. Bd., Ft. Collins, 1985—; cons. U.S. Peace Corps, Peru, 1974, Booz-Allen & Hamilton, Chile, 1976, FAO, Rome, 1985. Fellow Soc. Am. Foresters; mem. Xi Sigma Pi (nat. sec. 1958-60), Gamma Sigma Delta (internat. sec. 1982-86, Merit award 1980). Home: 601 W Prospect Fort Collins CO 80526 Office: Colo State U 101 Natural Resource Research Lab Fort Collins CO 80523

FECHTEL, EDWARD RAY, lawyer, educator; b. Pocatello, Idaho, Apr. 20, 1926; s. Edward Joseph and Frances Lucille (Myers) F.; m. Jewell Reagan, Apr. 7, 1950 (div.); children—Scot Gerald, Mark Edward, Kim; m. 2d Mary K. Milligan, Dec. 1983. B.A. in Bus., Idaho State U., 1949; J.D., U. Oreg., 1967; M.B.A. in Fin., 1968. Bar: Oreg. 1967, U.S. Dist. Ct. Oreg. 1967, U.S. Ct. Appeals (9th cir.) 1968. Sales rep. Genesco, 1950-59; gen. mdse. mgr. Fargo Wilson Wells Co., Pocatello, 1960-64; ptnr. Husband, Johnson & Fechtel, Eugene, Oreg., 1967-83, Ray Fechtel, P.C., 1984—; prof. bus. law U. Oreg.; lectr. Oreg. State Bar. Bd. dirs. Legal Aid Soc., Lane County, Oreg., Oreg. Citizens for Fair Land Planning. Served with USN, 1944-46. Mem. ABA, Oreg. State Bar Assn., Phi Alpha Delta. Republican. Home: 2858 Greentree Way Eugene OR 97405 Office: 975 Oak St Suite 990 Eugene OR 97401

FEDER, HOWARD MITCHELL, marine biology educator; b. N.Y.C., June 8, 1922; s. Samuel and Anna Helen (Tally) F.; m. Rosalind Limbaugh, Aug. 30, 1950 (div. 1969); children: Lyn, Jill, Susan Annette, Conrad Timothy; m. Tina Goldman, Sept. 2, 1984. BA, UCLA, 1948, MS, 1951; PhD, Stanford U., 1957. Cert. tchr. jr. coll., Calif. (life). Research asst. Calif. Inst. Tech., Point Barrow, Alaska, 1949-50; tchr. Hartnell Coll., Salinas, Calif., 1957-69; prof. marine sci. U. Alaska, Fairbanks, 1970—; research assoc. Marine Biol. Lab., Elsinore, Denmark, 1964-66; vis. scientist Dunstaffnage Marine Research Lab., Oban, Scotland, 1980-81, 83, 84. Contbr. articles to profl. jours. Mem. AAAS, Crustacean Soc., Phi Beta Kappa. Democrat. Office: U Alaska Inst Marine Sci Fairbanks AK 99775-1080

FEDERICO, PAT-ANTHONY, research psychologist; b. Newark, Mar. 4, 1942; s. Pasquale and Vincenza (Caramanna) F.; m. Suzanne Marie Boudreaux, Nov. 24, 1967. B.A. cum laude in Math. and Philosophy, U. St. Thomas, Houston, 1965; M.S. in Gen. Exptl. Psychology, Tulane U., 1967, Ph.D. in Gen. Exptl. Psychology, 1969. Research psychologist, U.S. Air Force Human Resources Lab., Denver, 1969-72; sr. research psychologist U.S. Navy Personnel Research and Devel. Center, San Diego, 1972—; honorarium faculty U. Colo., Denver, 1969-71; lectr. dept. psychology San Diego State U., 1972, 77. Served to capt. USAF, 1969-72. NDEA fellow, 1966-69; NSF presdl. intern in sci. and engring., 1972-73. Mem. Human Factors Soc. (exec. dir., pres., sec.-treas. San Diego chpt.), Cognitive Sci. Soc., Psychonomic Soc., Am. Ednl. Research Assn. Sr. author: Management Information Systems and Organizational Behavior, 1980. Co-editor Aptitude, Learning and Instruction: Vol. 1, Cognitive Process Analyses of Aptitude, Vol. 2, Cognitive Process Analyses of Learning and Problem Solving, 1980. Contbr. articles to profl. jours. Home: 4493 Pescadero Ave San Diego CA 92107 Office: Navy Personnel Research and Devel Ctr San Diego CA 92152

FEDEROW, HAROLD LOUIS, physicist, lawyer; b. Springfield, Mo., Sept. 5, 1949; s. Harry and Annette Toby (Richman) F.; m. Norine Claire Bernard, July 24, 1982; children: Ariel, Mariah. BS in Humanities and Sci., Physics, MIT, 1971; JD, U. Md., 1975; MS in Physics, U. Wash., 1986. Bar: Mo. 1975, D.C. 1976. Research assoc. Inst. Energy Analysis, Oak Ridge, Tenn., 1976-79, Nat. Conf. State Legislatures, Denver, 1980; research instr. social mgmt. tech. U. Wash., Seattle, 1980-82; dir. adminstrn. Energy Scis. Corp., Bellevue, Wash., 1982-85; v.p. Am. Heritage Fin. Corp., Bellevue, 1985-86; applied theoretical physicist Boeing Commercial Airplane Co., Seattle, 1986—. Contbr. articles to profl. jours. Chmn. Conf. on Law, War and Nuclear Policy, Seattle, 1985; chief issues vol. Evans for Congress, Seattle, 1984; issues vol. Adams for Senate, Seattle, 1986; bd. dirs. 5 County Mental Health, Oak Ridge, 1978-79. Mem. Mo. Bar Assn., D.C. Bar Assn., Fedn. Am. Scientists, World Affairs Council, Sigma Pi Sigma. Democrat. Jewish. Avocations: reading, theater, movies. Home: Boeing Commercial Airplane Co PO Box 3707/MS 47-31 Seattle WA 98124 Office: Am Heritage Fin Corp 10655 NE 4th #810 Bellevue WA 98004

FEENEY, CHARLES STONEHAM, baseball executive; b. Orange, N.J., Aug. 31, 1921; s. Thaddeus and Mary Alice (Stoneham) F.; m. Margaret Ann Hoppock, July 10, 1948; children: Katharine Willard, Charles Stoneham, John Hoppock, William McDonald, Mary Patrick. B.A., Dartmouth Coll., 1943; LL.B., Fordham U., 1949. Vice pres. San Francisco Giants, 1946-69; pres. Nat. League Profl. Baseball Clubs, San Francisco, 1970-77, N.Y.C., 1977-87, San Diego Padres, 1987—. Served to lt. USNR, 1943-46. Mem. Casque and Gauntlet, Phi Kappa Psi. Clubs: Pacific Union, Burlingame (Calif.) Country. Home: 405 E 63d St New York NY 10022 Office: San Diego Padres 9449 Friars Rd San Diego CA 92108 *

FEENEY, ROBERT EARL, research biochemist; b. Oak Park, Ill., Aug. 30, 1913; s. Bernard Cyril and Loreda (McKee) F.; m. Mary Alice Waller, Dec. 3, 1954; children: Jane, Elizabeth. Student, Rochester (Minn.) Jr. Coll.,

1932-33; BS in Chemistry, Northwestern U., 1938; MS in Biochemistry, U. Wis., 1939, PhD in Biochemistry, 1942. Diplomate Am. Bd. Nutrition. Research assoc. Harvard U. Med. Sch., Boston, 1942-43; research biochemist USDA Lab., Albany, Calif., 1946-53; prof. chemistry U. Nebr., Lincoln, 1953-60; prof. dept. food sci. and tech. U. Calif., Davis, 1960-84, prof. emeritus, research biochemist, 1984—; bd. dirs. Creative Chemistry Cons., Davis. Author: (with Richard Allison) Evolutionary Biochemistry of Proteins, 1969, (with Gary Means) Chemical Modification of Proteins, 1971, Professor On the Ice, 1974; editor: (with John Whitaker) Protein Tailoring for Food and Medical Uses, 1986. Served to capt. wound research team U.S. M.C., Army, 1943-46. Recipient Superior Service award USDA, 1953, ; Feeney Peak, Antarctica named in his honor U.S. Bd. on Geog. Names, 1968. Mem. Am. Chem. Soc. (chmn. div. agrl. and food chemistry, 1978-79, award for disting. service in agrl. and food chemistry, 1978), Am. Soc. Biol. Chemists, Inst. of Food Technologists. Democrat. Club: Explorers. Avocations: polar sci., polar exploration lit. Home: 780 Elmwood Dr Davis CA 95616 Office: U of Calif Dept of Food Sci and Technology 1480 Chemistry Annex Davis CA 95616

FEES, NANCY FARDELIUS, special education educator; b. Santa Monica, Calif., Mar. 25, 1950; d. Carl August and Dodi Emma (Hedenschau) Fardelius; m. Paul Rodger Fees, June 4, 1971; 1 child, Evelyn Wyoming. BS, Mills Coll., 1971; MA in Edn., Idaho State U., 1975. Cert. tchr., Calif., Idaho, Wyo., R.I. Specialist curriculum mgmt. Barrington (R.I.) High Sch., 1975-81; coordinator learning skills ctr. Northwest Community Coll., Powell, Wyo., 1982-84, instr., 1985—; pres. Children's Resource Ctr., 1985—, bd. dirs., 1983—. Editor (with others) The Great Entertainer, 1984. Vol. Buffalo Bill Hist. Ctr., Cody, Wyo., 1981—; mem. Centennial Com., Cody, 1983. Mem. Council Exceptional Children, Assn. Children with Learning Disabilities, Council Adminstrs. of Spl. Edn. Democrat. Episcopalian. Home: 1201 Sunset Blvd Cody WY 82414

FEHLAU, PAUL EDWARD, physicist; b. Cleve., Mar. 9, 1935; s. Carl and Elda Augusta (Scheifelbein) F.; m. Alice Esther O'Connor, June 14, 1965; children: Paul Alan, Jenny Ann. BS in Physics summa cum laude, Ohio State U., 1961, MS in Physics, 1966. Staff physicist Los Alamos (N.Mex.) Nat. Lab., 1966—. Contbr. articles to profl. jours.; inventor fuel plate scanner. Served with U.S. Army, 1953-56. Mem. AAAS, Inst. Nuclear Materials Mgmt. (sr.), Health Physics Soc. Democrat. Avocation: backpacking. Office: Los Alamos Nat Lab MS J-562 Los Alamos NM 87545

FEHR, J. WILL, newspaper editor; b. Long Beach, Calif., Mar. 8, 1926; s. John and Evelyn (James) F.; m. Cynthia Moore, Sept. 4, 1951; children—Michael John, Martha Ann. B.A. in English, U. Utah, 1951. City editor Salt Lake City Tribune, 1964-80, mng. editor, 1980-81, editor, 1981—. Served to 1st lt. USAF, 1951-53. Mem. Am. Soc. Newspaper Editors, Sigma Chi. Clubs: Hidden Valley, Fort Douglas (Salt Lake City). Home: 468 13th Ave Salt Lake City UT 84103 Office: Salt Lake City Tribune 143 S Main St Salt Lake City UT 84110

FEHRMAN, KENNETH RAY, educator, interior designer, author, researcher; b. San Antonio, Oct. 24, 1941; s. Oscar Fehrman and Ruth (Peabody) McVey; m. Cherie Christina Allen, Apr. 7, 1967. AA, Solano Coll., 1961; BA, San Francisco State U., 1963, MA, 1969; Ed D, U. San Francisco, 1986. Lic. secondary tchr., Calif. Chair art dept. The Hamlin Sch., San Francisco, 1970-77; pres. Fehrman Interior Design Ltd., San Francisco, 1976—; environ. design instr. Rudolph Schaeffer Sch., San Francisco, 1978-80; dir. edn. Western Design Inst., San Francisco, 1979-81; asst. prof.interior design San Francisco State U., 1980—. Co-author: Postwar Interior Design: 1945-1960, 1986; contbr. articles on design and decorative arts to mags.; exhibitor textile work and design projects at galleries, including San Francisco Mus. Modern Art, 1969-82. Mem. Internat. Soc. Interior Designers (founding pres., No. Calif. chpt., 1980-82), Am. Soc. Interior Designers (edn.), Inst. Bus. Designers (edn.), Nat. Home Fashions League (edn.), Am. Home Econs. Assn. (profl.), Calif. Home Econs. Assn. (profl.). Office: San Francisco State U Consumer and Family Studies Dept 1600 Holloway Ave San Francisco CA 94132

FEIDELSON, MARC, advertising executive; b. N.Y.C., Aug. 20, 1939; s. Robert and Ceil (Robbins) F.; m. Linda Sarnoff, June 11, 1964; children—Lee, Pamela. B.S. in Bus. Adminstrn., Boston U., 1961; M.A. in Psychology, CUNY, 1966. Media research analyst CBS-TV, N.Y.C., 1964-65; sr. media research analyst Ted Bates Advt., N.Y.C., 1966-67; media research dir. Benton & Bowles Advt., N.Y.C., 1967-70; media mgr. RCA Corp., N.Y.C., 1970-72; dir. advt. services Hunt-Wesson Foods, Fullerton, Calif., 1973-79; sr. v.p., media dir. Dailey & Assocs. Advt., Los Angeles, 1979—; guest lectr. UCLA. Mem. Hollywood Radio and TV Soc., Los Angeles Media Dirs. Council (pres. 1981-82). Jewish. Guest editor Media Decisions mag., Apr. 1983. Office: Dailey & Associates 3055 Wilshire Blvd Los Angeles CA 90010

FEIGE, LOUIS EDWARD, chemist; b. Newcastle-on-Tyne, Eng., Feb. 24, 1944; came to U.S., 1948; s. Rudolf and Liselotte (Altbaier) F. BA in Chemistry, U. Cin., 1966. Chemist U.S. Army C.E., Cin., 1966-67, Nat. Ctr. Air Pollution Control, Cin., 1967-70; chemist EPA, Research Triangle Park, N.C., 1970-81, Las Vegas, 1981—. Mem. Am. Chem. Soc., Am. Soc. Mass Spectrometry. Democrat. Jewish. Avocations: stamp collecting, chess, sports. Home: 1851 Teak Ct Henderson NV 89015 Office: EPA 944 E Harmon Las Vegas NV 89109

FEIGELSON, ROBERT, material scientist, educator; b. N.Y.C., Dec. 3, 1935; m. Vicki Zall, June 15, 1957; children: Gregg, Derek, Roger. BS in Ceramic Engring., Ga. Inst. Tech., 1957; MS in Ceramics Engring., MIT, 1961; PhD in Material Sci. and Engring., Stanford U., 1974. Mem. tech. staff Gen. Dynamics Corp., 1957-58, Watertown Arsenal, 1958-61, Sperry Rand Research Ctr., 1961-63; prof. research Stanford U., 1963—. Assoc. editor: Jour. Crystal Growth; contbr. articles to profl. jours. Mem. Am. Assn. Crystal Growth (past. treas., pres., editor newsletter, advisor western sect.), No. Calif. Crystal Growers Assn. Office: Stanford U Ctr for Materials Research Stanford CA 94305

FEIGIN, DAVID SIMON, radiology educator; b. N.Y.C.. AB, Cornell U., 1966; MD, NYU, 1970. Intern Bell Ctr., 1970-71; resident Johns Hopkins Med. Inst., 1971-74; fellow nuclear medincine Johns Hopkins Med. Inst., Balt., 1974; chief diagnostic radiology Armed Forces Inst. Pathology, 1975-78; instr. 1974-75; asst. prof. Johns Hopkins U., Balt., 1975-78; asst. prof. U. Calif.-San Diego, La Jolla, 1978-81, assoc. prof. radiology, 1981—. Home: 8256 Caminito Lacayo CA 92037 Office: U Calif San Diego Dept Radiology V-114 San Diego CA 92093

FEIL, LINDA MAE, tax preparer; b. Dallas, Oreg., Apr. 9, 1948; d. Fred Henry and Ruth Irene (Hoffman) F. A.A., West Valley Community Coll., 1975; student Golden Gate U. Ctr. for Tax Studies, 1975, Menlo Coll. Sch. Bus. Adminstrn., 1978. Enrolled agt. IRS. Income tax preparer, office mgr. H & R Block, Inc., Santa Clara, Calif., 1972-74, asst. area mgr., 1974-76; propr. L.M. Feil Tax Service, Santa Clara, 1976-80; ptnr. Tennyson Tax Service, Santa Clara, 1980-81; owner McKeany-Feil Tax Service, San Jose, Calif., 1981-83, Feil Tax Service, San Jose, 1983—. Tchr. Mem. Nat. Assn. Enrolled Agts. (chpt. sec. 1981-83, chpt. v.p. 1983-84), Mission Soc. Enrolled Agts. (pres. 1984-85), Calif. Soc. Enrolled Agts. (bd. dirs. 1985-86). Republican. Christian. Home: 3046 Ryan Ave Santa Clara CA 95051 Office: Feil Tax Service 4300 Stevens Creek Blvd Suite 129 San Jose CA 95129

FEIN, WILLIAM, ophthalmologist; b. N.Y.C., Nov. 27, 1933; s. Samuel and Beatrice (Lipschitz) F.; B.S., CCNY, 1954; M.D., U. Calif., Irvine, 1962; m. Bonnie Fern Aaronson, Dec. 15, 1963; children—Stephanie Paula, Adam Irving, Gregory Andrew. Intern, Los Angeles County Gen. Hosp., 1962-63, resident in ophthalmology, 1963-66; instr. U. Calif. Med. Sch., Irvine, 1966-69; mem. faculty U. So. Calif. Med. Sch., 1969—, asso. prof. ophthalmology, 1979—; attending physician Cedars-Sinai Med. Center, Los Angeles, 1966—, chief ophthalmology clinic service, 1979—, chmn. div. ophthalmology, 1981—; attending physician Los Angeles County-U. So. Calif. Med. Center, 1969—; chmn. dept. ophthalmology Midway Hosp., 1975-78; dir. Ellis Eye Ctr., Los Angeles, 1984—. Diplomate Am. Bd. Ophthalmology. Mem. Am. Acad. Ophthalmology, Am. Soc. Ophthalmic Plastic and Reconstructive Surgery, AMA, Calif. Med. Assn., Los Angeles Med. Soc. Contbr. articles to med. publs. Address: 415 N Crescent Dr Beverly Hills CA 90210

FEINAUER, LYMAN RICHARD, JR., neonatologist; b. Salt Lake City, Mar. 4, 1943; s. Lyman Richard Sr. and Lorraine (Barrett) F.; m. Karen L. Barnett, Sept. 9, 1972; children: Jonathan Richard, Christian Frederick, Richard Benjamin, Joshua James. BSChemE, U. Utah, 1965, MS in Fin., 1967, MSChemE, 1969, MD, 1971. Diplomate Am. Bd. Pediatrics, Am. Bd. Med. Examiners. Cons. Jet Propulsion Lab., Pasadena, Calif., 1965-70; intern U. So. Calif. Med. Ctr., Los Angeles, 1971-72, resident in pediatrics, 1972-73, fellow neonatology, 1974; ptnr. Salt Lake (City) Clinic, 1975-81, also ptnr. Pension Fund and Investment Council, 1975—; assoc. clin. prof. pediatrics U. Utah, 1974—; clin. investigator Eli Lilly & Co., 1979—; pres. JCRJ Investments; dir. newborn intensive care Latter Day Sts. Hosp.; bd. dirs. Deseret Health Care. Contbr. articles to med. and sci. jours. Served with USAR, 1960-68. NASA fellow, 1965-67. Fellow Am. Acad. Pediatrics, Chem. Soc. (London), Am. Chem. Soc., Am. Fedn. Clin. Research, Am. Soc. Microbiology, Sigma Xi; mem. AMA, Utah Med. Soc., Intermountain Pediatric Soc., Los Angeles Pediatric Soc., Utah Acad. Arts Scis. and Letters. Office: 857 E 200 S Suite 203 Salt Lake City UT 84102

FEINBERG, DAVID ALLEN, data processing executive; b. Seattle, Feb. 17, 1947; s. Herman Stanford and Zelda (Hindin) F.; m. Lynne Brechner, Jan. 21, 1978; stepchildren: Kerri Jeanne, Todd Breck, Jamie Leigh, Megan Dawn, Eric Anthony. BS, Stanford U., 1968; MS in Adminstrn., George Washington U., 1972. Cert. data processor. Systems programmer Stanford (Calif.) Computer Ctr., 1966-68, NCR Corp., Los Angeles, 1968-69; systems analyst System Devel. Corp., Washington, 1971-75; mgr. Boeing Co., Seattle, 1975-87; tech. dir. Spacelabs, Inc., Redmond, 1987—; lectr. various orgs., Seattle, 1983—; founder, mng. prin. M.T. Writings Co., Seattle, 1983—. Contbr. articles to profl. jours. Pres. Rainier Beach High Sch. PTSA, Seattle, 1981; advisor Seattle Recreation Dept., 1983—; official Seattle Metro League, 1980—; founder, treas. Montgomery Savoyards, Rockville, Md., 1973-75. Served to 1st. lt. Signal Corps, U.S. Army, 1969-71. Mem. Computer Soc. IEEE (affiliate), Data Processing Mgmt. Assn., Assn. Computing Machinery. Avocations: volleyball, Gilbert & Sullivan operettas, other light operas. Home: 3662 SW Othello St Seattle WA 98126 Office: Spacelabs Inc 4200 150th Ave NE PO Box 97013 Redmond WA 98073-9713

FEINBERG, JOHN DAVID, architect, educator; b. Boston, Oct. 18, 1947; s. Archibald Israel and Wilhelmina Bernice (Greenspan) F.; m. Allyn Sutherland Hansson, Sept. 6, 1969; children: Natalie Sutherland, Danielle Alleyne. BA in Environ. Design, Antioch Coll., 1970; M in Landscape Architecture in Land Planning, U. Mass., 1972. Pres. Community Services Collaborative, Boulder, Colo., 1974—; mng. ptnr. Territorial Adobe, Boulder, 1983—; vis. lectr. environ. design, U. Colo., Boulder, 1974—. Pres. Central City Bus. Assn., 1983-85; chmn. University Hill Gen. Improvement Dist., Boulder, 1980-85; exec. dir. Assn. Hist. Hotels of the Rocky Mountain West. Mem. Am. Inst. Cert. Planners, Am. Planning, Assn., Soc. Archtl. Historians, Assn. Preservation Tech., Colo. Chpt. Assn. Preservation Tech., Am. Assn. State and Local History, Assn. Hist. Hotels (exec. dir. 1984—). Office: Community Services Collaborative 1315 Broadway Boulder CO 80302

FEINBERG, RICHARD ALAN, clinical psychologist; b. Oakland, Calif., Aug. 12, 1947; s. Jack and Raechel Sacks (Hoff) F. B.A., Calif. State U.-Hayward, 1969; M.A. in Clin. Psychology, Mich. State U., 1972, Ph.D., 1979; Nat. Register of Health Service Providers in Psychology, 1980. Instr., Merritt Coll., Oakland, 1975-76; clin. psychologist Highland Gen. Hosp., Oakland, 1976-79; asso. Lafayette Center Counseling and Edn., 1978-79; clin. psychologist Tri-City Mental Health Center, Fremont, Calif., 1979-81, dir., 1981—; pvt. practice clin. psychology, 1976—; participant profl. conf. USPHS fellow, 1969-71. Mem. Am. Psychol. Assn., Calif. Psychol. Assn. Jewish. Office: 38930 Blacow Rd Suite F Fremont CA 94536

FEINMAN, JEROME, chemical engineer, consultant; b. Bklyn., Mar. 18, 1928; s. Harry D. and Gertrude (Gruschen) F.; m.Leah Joanne Schafer, Feb. 27, 1954; children: Karen Sue, Mindy Ann, Gail Ruth. BS in Chem. Engring., Poly. Inst. Bklyn., 1949; MS in Chem. Engring., Ill. Inst. Tech., 1956; PhD, U. Pitts., 1964. Registered profl. engr., Pa., Colo. Research cons. U.S. Steel Corp., Monroeville, Pa., 1952-80; dir. tech. devel. Occidental Oil Shale, Inc., Grand Junction, Colo., 1980-82; pres. J. Feinman and Assocs., Inc., Grand Junction, 1982—; bd. dirs., tech. adv. com. Particulate Solids Research Inc., N.Y.C., 1977-80. Editor: Plasma Technology in Metallurgical Processing, 1987; contbr. articles to profl. jours; patentee in field. Served as cpl. U.S. Army, 1950-52. N.Y. State Regents scholar, 1945-49. Mem. Am. Inst. Chem. Engrs., Iron and Steel Soc. of AIME, Am. Chem. Soc. Democrat. Jewish. Avocations: tennis, squash, racquetball, skiing, traveling. Home and Office: 2654 Sperber Ln Grand Junction CO 81506

FEINSTEIN, DIANNE, mayor San Francisco; b. San Francisco, June 22, 1933; d. Leon and Betty (Rosenburg) Goldman; m. Bertram Feinstein, Nov. 11, 1962 (div.); 1 child, Katherine Anne; m. Richard C. Blum, Jan. 20, 1980. B.S., Stanford U., 1955; LLB (hon.), Golden Gate U., 1977; D Pub. Adminstrn. (hon.), U. Manila, 1981; D Pub. Service (hon.), U. Santa Clara, 1981; JD (hon.), Antioch U., 1983, Mills Coll., 1985. Intern in pub. affairs Coro Found., San Francisco, 1955-56; asst. to Calif. Indsl. Welfare Commn., Los Angeles, also San Francisco, 1956-57; mem., vice-chmn. Calif. Women's Bd. Terms and Parole, Los Angeles, also San Francisco, 1962-66; chmn. San Francisco City and County Adv. Com. for Adult Detention, San Francisco, 1967-69; supr. City and County of San Francisco, 1970-78; mayor of San Francisco 1978—; pres. San Francisco City and County Bd. Suprs., 1970-72, 74-76, 78; mem. Mayor's Com. on Crime, 1967-69; chmn. Environ. Mgmt. Task Force, Assn. Bay Govts., 1976-78, exec. com., del. gen. assembly, 1970—; bd. govs. Bay Area Council, 1972—; mem. Bay Conservation and Devel. Commn., 1973-78. Chmn. bd. regents Lone Mountain Coll., 1972-75. Recipient Women of Achievement award Bus. and Profl. Women's Clubs of San Francisco, 1970, Disting. Woman award San Francisco Examiner, 1970, CORO Found. award, 1979, Brotherhood/Sisterhood award Nat. Conf. of Christians and Jews, 1986, Comdr.'s award U.S. Army, 1986, French Legion of Honor award Pres. Mitterand, 1984. Mem. Multi-Culture Inst. (dir.), Calif. Tomorrow, Bay Area Urban League, Planning and Conservation League, Friends of Earth, Chinese Culture Found., N. Central Coast Regional Commn. Clubs: Sierra, Propeller, Commonwealth. Office: Office of the Mayor City Hall San Francisco CA 94102

FELABOM, LOREN WAYNE, SR., college administrator, consultant; b. Mishawaka, Ind., July 9, 1933; s. Alden Merrit and Ida May (Airgood) F.; m. Kathleen Jeanette Anderson, Sept. 7, 1952; children—Loren, Kathleen, Pamela, Julie. B.S. in Bus. Adminstrn., Ind. U.-South Bend, 1968; M.B.A., Mich. State U., 1973; certs. in data processing and computers, IBM, Dept. Def. Cert. vocat. tchr., Ind. Instr., programmer South Bend Comml. Sch., 1963-67; supr. adminstrv. services Bendix Corp., South Bend, 1967-74, 52-60; bus. mgr. Miami Christian Coll., Fla., 1974-78; controller Mercy Coll., Detroit, 1978-79; assoc. dean bus. affairs Prince George's Community Coll., Largo, Md., 1979-82; v.p. for adminstr. Cochise Coll., Douglas, Ariz., 1983—. Deacon, First Baptist Ch., Mishawaka, Ind., 1968-72; cons. Capitol Bapt. Ch., Largo, 1982; chmn., deacon First Bapt. Ch., Bisbee, Ariz., 1984—. Served with USNR, 1951-59. Mem. Nat. Assn. Colls. and Univ. Bus. Officers (sec. 1984-85), Ariz. Assn. Coll., Bus. Ofcls. (v.p. 1985-86, pres. 1986-87, treas. 1986-88), Ariz. Assn. Community Coll. Adminstrn. (treas. 1986-87). Republican. Home: 105 Navajo Dr Bisbee AZ 85603 Office: Cochise Coll Route 1 PO Box 100 Douglas AZ 85607

FELDMAN, ARTHUR, engineer; b. St. Louis, Apr. 6, 1931; s. Sam and Sadie (Hirschfield) F.; m. Lee Gallup, Dec. 20, 1953; children: Amy Nina. BCE, Wash. U., St. Louis, 1952; MCE, U. Ill., 1954, PhD, 1960. Registered profl. engr., Mo., Ill., Colo. Research asst. U. Ill., Urbana, 1952-54, research assoc., 1954-59, asst. prof., 1959-61; assoc. prof. U. Denver, Colo., 1961-63; dept. staff engr. Martin Marietta, Denver, 1963—; Qualified Fallout Instr. Office CD, Denver, 1963—. Contbr. articles to profl. jours. Mem. and player Community Arts Symphony, Englewood, Colo., 1963—. Fellow ASCE; mem. Am. Concrete Inst., Soc. Exptl. Mechanics, Am. Acad. Mechanics. Avocation: violin playing. Home: 2045 S Filmore Denver CO 80210

FELDMAN, BURTON LEON, insurance company executive; b. Bklyn., Sept. 9, 1946; s. Samuel and Dorothy F.; m. Noanna Loyce Dix, Nov. 8, 1969; 1 dau., Andrea Eden. B.A. in Psychology, Bklyn. Coll., 1966. Rehab. adminstr. Occidental Life Ins. Co., Los Angeles, 1969-78; asst. sec., dir. rehab. Mission Ins. Co., Los Angeles, 1978—; asst. v.p., dir. rehab. services Mission Am. Ins. Co., Los Angeles, 1978-86; program dir. workers compensation case mgmt. Cost Care Inc., Huntington Beach, 1986—; cons. Neurol. Learning Ctr., South Pasadena, Calif.; tng. programs in ins. rehab. Casa Colina Hosp., Pomona, Calif., Craig Rehab. Hosp., Englewood, Colo. Mem. Mayor's Com. for Employment of the Handicapped, Los Angeles, 1976-80; mem. blue ribbon ins. com. Nat. Head Injury Found., 1981—. Mem. Nat. Rehab. Assn. (pres. Pacific region and a So. Calif. chpt. 1979-80), Nat. Rehab. Counselors Assn., Calif. Assn. Rehab. Profls., Nat. Assn. Rehab. Profls. in the Pvt. Sector, Nat. Rehab. Adminstrs. Assn., Ins. Rehab. Study Group. Clubs: Indian Palms Country (Indio, Calif.); Channel Island Shores Marina (Oxnard, Calif.). Office: 17011 Beach Blvd Huntington Beach CA 92647

FELDMAN, GLORIA A., art consulatant; b. N.Y.C., Dec. 10, 1932; d. Sol and Edith (Bogen) Cohen; m. Saul Feldman, Aug. 26, 1952; children: Mitchell Dean, Eric Adam. AAS in Dental Hygiene, NYU, 1952; BA in Psychology, Art Therapy, Am. U., 1972. Asst. v.p. Auto Train Corp., Washington, 1972-80; pvt. practice art cons. San Francisco, 1981—; cons. HealthAm., Nashville, 1982—. Club: Univ. Women's (London). Avocations: art, reading, hiking, music.

FELDMAN, HARVEY WOLF, sociologist, ethnographer, educator, social worker; b. Pitts., July 1, 1929; s. Charles and Fannie (Enoch) F. BA, U. Pitts., 1953; MSW, Columbia U., 1957; PhD, Brandeis U., 1970. Research assoc. Brandeis U., Waltham, Mass., 1967-72; fellow Drug Abuse Council, Washington, 1972-73; assoc. prof. social services St. Louis U., 1974-76; sr. research assoc. URSA Inst., San Francisco; exec. dir., pres. Youth Environ. Study, 1981—. Sr. editor: Angel Dust: An Ethnographic Study of PCP Users, 1979. Prin. investigator, NIDA-founder demonstration grant "Methods to Stop AIDS Among Intravenous Drug Users.", 1986. Served with U.S. Army, 1953-55, ETO. NIMH grantee, 1964-66. Mem. Am. Sociol. Assn., Soc. for Study Social Problems, Nat. Assn. Social Workers, Nat. Assn. Ethnography and Social Policy (sec., treas.), Western Mastiff Fanciers. Club: Mastiff Club of Am. Office: 1779 Haight St San Francisco CA 94117

FELDMAN, IRA S., accountant; b. N.Y.C., June 18, 1943; s. Meyer and Esther F.; m. Susan Haber, May 31, 1965; children—Lisa, Jason, Amy. B.S. in Bus. Adminstrn., U. Ariz., 1965; M.B.A., Ariz. State U., 1970. C.P.A., Calif., Ariz. Acct., Peat, Marwick, Mitchell & Co., Los Angeles and Phoenix, 1965-70; ptnr. Laventhol & Horwath, Phoenix, 1970-76; mng. dir. Toback & Co., P.C., Phoenix, 1976—. Bd. dirs. DeGrazia Art and Cultural Found., Small Bus. Council Am., Acctg. Firms Associated, Inc., Ariz. Small Bus. United. Del. White House Conf. on Small Bus. Mem. Am. Inst. C.P.A.s, Ariz. Inst. C.P.A.s, Phoenix Tax Workshop (dir.). Mem. editorial bd. Taxation for Accts. Contbr. articles to profl. jours. Office: 3200 N Central Ave #700 Phoenix AZ 85012

FELDMAN, IRMA S., psychiatric social worker; b. Bklyn., May 31, 1930; d. Abraham and Rose (Grand) Skraly; m. Albert Edward Feldman, June 14, 1953; children: Barry Lee, Steven Bruce. BA, Bklyn. Coll., 1952; MSW, Boston U., 1954. Social worker Mass. Eye and Ear Infirmary, Boston, 1954-55; psychiat. social worker Rehab. Programs, Inc., Poughkeepsie, N.Y., 1965-75; dir. devel. disabilities Dutchess County Dept. Mental Hygiene, Poughkeepsie, N.Y., 1975-81; psychiat. social worker Mesa (Ariz.) Lutheran Hosp., 1981-87, Apollo Behavioral Health Clinic, Mesa, 1986—; ednl. presenter Mesa Community Coll., 1983—, Scottsdale (Ariz.) Community Coll., 1984. Active adv. com. for lifelong learning Mesa Community Coll. 1981—; Mesa Community Council Com. on Aging, 1982—. Mem. Ariz. Adult Edn. Assn., Am. Soc. Aging. Lodge: B'nai B'rith. Avocations: walking, swimming, sightseeing, reading, socializing. Home: 1051 S Dobson Rd #9 Mesa AZ 85202 Office: Apollo Behavioral Health Clinic 941 S Dobson Rd Suite 220 Mesa AZ 85202

FELDMAN, JENAT LEVISON, preschool administrator, business owner; b. Nashville, Aug. 12, 1951; d. Leo and Davine Loveman (Marlow) Levison; m. Howard Dale Feldman, Aug. 28, 1977; children: Leigh Jason, Jessica Levison. BA, Am. U., 1973; MSW, Tulane U., 1975. Cert. social worker. Dir. adult services Jewish Community Ctr., Atlanta, 1976-81, supr. Zaban br., 1980-82; owner Nothing But Names, Louisville, Colo., 1983—; administr. Boulder Preschool, Denver Jewish Community Ctr., Boulder, 1985—. Recipient Lou Kraft award Jewish Welfare Bd., 1978; Boulder Arts Commn. grantee, 1986; named Vol. of Yr., Denver Jaycees, 1985. Mem. Assn. Jewish Ctr. Workers (v.p. so. chpt. 1980-82), Nat. Assn. Social Workers, Assn. Cert. Social Workers, Nat. Assn. Edn. Young Children. Democrat. Club: Hadassah (sec. Boulder chpt. 1983-84). Avocations: aerobics, cooking. Home: 1135 Hancock Dr Boulder CO 80303 Office: Jewish Community Ctr Preschool 3950 Baseline Rd Boulder CO 80303

FELDMAN, LESLIE ARTHUR, materials research scientist; b. N.Y.C., Feb. 17, 1955; s. Seymour Charles and Evelyn Aileen (Cantor) F. BS, MIT, 1976; PhD, Cornell U., 1982. Staff engr. Lawrence Berkeley (Calif.) Lab., 1978-80; mem. tech. staff The Aerospace Corp., Los Angeles, 1980—. Inventor deformable carbon-carbon composite, 1984. Recipient Inventor's Award Aerospace Corp., 1986. Mem. Am. Phys. Soc., Am. Ceramic Soc., Am. Carbon Soc., Sierra Club, Mensa, Sigma Xi. Avocations: clarinet, piano, recorder, sports. Home: 136 Concord St Apt B El Segundo CA 90245 Office: The Aerospace Corp Materials Scis Lab PO Box 92957 MS M2/248 Los Angeles CA 90009

FELDMAN, NATHANIEL E., aerospace company executive; b. New London, Conn., Oct. 7, 1925; s. Morris and Frieda (Pelenberg) F.; m. Clara Klein, Oct. 20, 1946; children: Ellis Steven, Phillip Matthew, David Daniel, Pamela Caren. BS, U. Calif., Berkeley, 1949, MS, 1951. Asst. elec. engr. U. Calif., Berkeley, 1949-50; engr. Lawrence Radiation Lab., 1951-54; instr. fire control radar Hughes Aircraft Co., Culver City, Calif., 1955; leader adv. develop def. electronic prod. div. Radio Corp. Am., 1956-60; project leader, systems analyst Rand Corp., Santa Monica, Calif., 1960-78; chief scientist Systems Research Operations Sci. Application Inc., Los Angeles, 1978-81; systems dir. advanced space communications Aerospace Corp., El Segundo, Calif., 1981-84, sr. engring. specialist, 1984—. Editor: Communication Satellites for the '70's: vol.1 Technology, vol. 2 Systems, 1971; contbr. numerous articles to profl. jours. Fellow AIAA (assoc.); mem. IEEE (sr., milcom. conf. bd. 1986-88), Sigma Xi, Tau Beta Pi, Eta Kappa Nu. Jewish. Home: 10294 Cresta Dr Los Angeles CA 90064 Office: Aerospace Corp PO Box 92957 Los Angeles CA 90009

FELDMAN, SAUL, healthcare executive; b. Bklyn., Mar. 13, 1930; s. Louis and Betty (Frankel) F.; m. Gloria Cohen, Aug. 26, 1952; children: Mitchell, Eric. BS in Acctg., Long Island U., 1951; postgrad., Bklyn. Law Sch., 1951-52, MS in Psychology, 1961; D in Pub. Adminstrn., NYU, 1967. Registered pub. acct., N.Y. Dir. staff coll. NIMH, 1973-81; exec. dir. HealthAm. Corp. Calif., Albany, 1981-83, chief exec. officer, 1983-86; pres. Bay Area Found., Berkeley, Calif., 1983—, Gen. Parametrics, Berkeley, 1986—; lectr. health and med. scis. program U. Calif., Berkeley, 1982-83, health services adminstrn. John F. Kennedy U., 1982-84; adj. prof. U. So. Calif. Grad. Sch. Pub. Adminstrn, 1978—, dept. psychiatry, Uniformed Services U. of Health Scis., 1978—, Union Grad. Sch. Antioch Coll., 1974-77; faculty assoc. Johns Hopkins U. Sch. Hygiene and Pub. Health, 1974—; vis. fellow dept. social adminstrn. U. York, Eng., 1980; cons. State Mich. Dept. Mental Health, 1979, Kellogg Commn. on Edn., 1973, New Hope Guild Ctr., 1967-73; advisor Pan Am. Health Orgn., Carácas, Venezuela, 1975-83. Cons. editor Policy and Adminstrn. in the Health and Human Services, 1981-83, Consultation mag., 1980—; mem. editorial adv. bd. NIMH monographs and reports, 1979—; editor-in-chief Administration in Mental Health, 1972—; contbr. articles to profl. jours. Mem. governing body Alameda-Contra Costa Health Systems Agy., 1984-85. Served to capt. USAF, 1952-53. Mem. AAAS, Am. Coll. Mental Health Adminstrn. (pres. 1981-82), Internat. Symposium on Future of Mentally Ill in Soc. (steering com. 1983), Am. Soc. Pub. Adminstrn., Am. Psychol. Assn., Am. Polit. Sci. Assn., Am. Pub.

Health Assn.. A. Home: 901 Powell St San Francisco CA 94108 Office: Gen Parametrics Corp 1250 9th St Berkeley CA 94710

FELDMAN, STANLEY GEORGE, judge; b. N.Y.C., Mar. 9, 1933; s. Meyer and Esther Betty (Golden) F.; m. Norma Arambula; 1 dau., Elizabeth L. Student, U. Calif., Los Angeles, 1950-51; LL.B., U. Ariz., 1956. Bar: Ariz. 1956. Practiced in Tucson, 1956—; partner firm Miller, Pitt & Feldman, 1968—; justice Ariz. Supreme Ct., 1982—; lectr. Coll. Law, U. Ariz., 1965-76, adj. prof., 1976—. Bd. dirs. Tucson Jewish Community Council. Mem. Am. Bd. Trial Advocates (past pres. So. Ariz. chpt.), ABA, Ariz. Bar Assn. (pres. 1974-75, bd. govs. 1967-76), Pima County Bar Assn. (past pres.), Am. Trial Lawyers Assn. (dir. chpt. 1967-76). Democrat. Jewish. Home: 3490 Via Guadalupe Tucson AZ 85716 Office: Supreme Ct State of Ariz State Capitol Bldg Phoenix AZ 85007

FELICITA, JAMES THOMAS, aerospace company executive; b. Syracuse, N.Y., May 21, 1947; s. Anthony Nicholas and Ada (Beech) F.; A.B., Cornell U., 1969; postgrad. Harvard U., 1969, U. So. Calif., 1970, UCLA, 1975-77. Contracting officer U.S. Naval Regional Contracting Office, Long Beach, Calif., 1974-80; sr. contract negotiator space and communications group Hughes Aircraft Co., El Segundo, Calif., 1980-81, head NASA contracts, 1981-84, mgr. maj. program contracts, 1984—. Recipient cost savs. commendation Pres. Gerald R. Ford, 1976. Mem. Nat. Contract Mgmt. Assn., Cornell Alumni Assn. So. Calif., Planetary Soc. Republican. Club: Nat. Space, Hughes Mgmt. Home: 8541 Kelso Dr Huntington Beach CA 92646 Office: 909 N Sepulveda Blvd Los Angeles CA 90245

FELIX, JOHN HENRY, investments executive; b. Honolulu, June 14, 1930; s. Henry and Melinda (Pacheco) F.; student Chaminade Coll., 1947, San Mateo Coll., 1950; grad. Advanced Mgmt. Program, Stanford, 1967, Harvard 1971; Ph.D., Walden U., 1975; m. Patricia Berry; children—Laura Marie, Melinda Susan, John Morgan, Jayne Sherry, Annette Sherry. Asst. to pres. AFL-CIO Unity House, 1955-57; exec. v.p. Hotel Operating Co. of Hawaii, 1957-60; v.p. Music Polynesia, Inc.; asst. to Gov. of Hawaii, 1960-62; pres. LaRonde Restaurants, Inc., 1962—, Hotel Assocs., Inc.; dir., mem. exec. com., chmn. personnel com. Hawaii Nat. Bank; pres., chmn. exec. com. Hawaiian Meml. Park. Chmn. ARC, 1961-63, 72; del. League Red Cross Socs.; chmn. Gov.'s Jobs for Vets. Task Force, 1971-76, Honolulu Redevel. Agy., 1971, 72, Honolulu City and County Planning Com., 1959; chmn. Bd. Water Supply, 1973-75; chmn. Honolulu City County Bd. Parks Recreation; mem. City and County Honolulu Police Commn., 1979, chmn., 1984; pres. bd. Hawaii Public Radio, 1979; bd. govs. ARC, also chmn. Pacific div.; nat. trustee March of Dimes Birth Defects Found.; mem. internat. com. Boy Scouts Am, council Commr. Pacific area; chmn. Rep. Nat. Hispanic Assembly, Hawaii, 1987; chmn. redevel. com. Castle Meml. Ctr.; U.S. del. South Pacific Commn., 1985; spl. asst. to pres. League of ARC, Red Crescent Soc., 1985 . Served with AUS, 1952-54. Named Young Man of Year, Hawaii Jr. C. of C., 1959, Distinguished Service award Sales and Marketing Execs. Hawaii, 1968, Harriman award distinguished vol. service A.R.C., 1975, Silver Beaver award Aloha Council Boy Scouts Am., 1983, Disting. Eagle award, 1983; named Salesman of Yr., Sales and Mktg. Execs. of Honolulu, 1981, others. Mem. Young Pres.'s Orgn., Hawaii Restaurant Assn. (pres. 1967), Air Force Assn. (pres. Hawaii), C. of C. of Hawaii (life), Nat. Eagle Scout Assn. (life, vice chmn. Hawaii chpt.), CAP-U.S. Air Force Aux. (comdr. Hawaii Wing 1980). Club: Waikiki Rotary (Honolulu). Home: 4731 Kahala Ave Honolulu HI 96816 Office: 700 Bishop St Suite 1012 Honolulu HI 96813

FELIX, RICHARD JAMES, engineering executive, consultant; b. Sacramento, Apr. 21, 1944; s. Joseph James and Faye Lola (Thornburg) F.; m. Nancy Tucker Thompson, 1970 (div. 1972). Cert., Electronics Tech. A Sch., Treasure Island, Calif., 1963; student, Am. River Coll., 1968-72, Calif. State U., 1972-74. Ptnr. ADRA, Sacramento, 1971-73, Doggie Domes, Sacramento, 1971-72, Fong and Co., Sacramento, 1976-79; project dir. Dynascan Project, Sacramento, 1976—; ptnr. Am. Omnigraph, Sacramento, 1985—; instr. Calif. State U., Sacramento, 1973-74; cons. KDM Design, 1985—. Creator documentary film American River College Rat Decathlon, 1974; editor publicity manual, 1978; inventor omnigraph, 1967. Vol. Leukemia Soc., Sacramento, 1984; artist Camellia City Ctr., Sacramento, 1983. Served with USN, 1962-66. Mem. Sacramento chpt. Mental Health Assn. (bd. dirs. 1980, Clifford Beers award 1983). Republican. Episcopalian. Club: New Horizons (Sacramento) (editor 1977-79). Avocations: photography, poetry, graphic design, design. Office: Dynascan Project 428 J St Suite 110 Sacramento CA 95814

FELIX, WALTER DALE, marketing executive; b. Sheridan, Wyo., May 25, 1936; s. Walter John and Alberta (Conrad) F.; m. Carolyn Fernley, Apr.15, 1958; children: Wesley, Bradley, Tara, Tania, Lishaun. Student, Weber State U., 1954-55; BS in Chemistry, U. Utah, 1958, PhD in Phys. Chemistry, 1962. Research scientist Gen. Electric Co., Richland, Wash., 1962-65; sr. research scientist Battelle-Northwest, Richland, 1965-75, sect. mgr., 1975-83, assoc. dept. mgr., 1983-85; v.p. mktg. Lee Scientific Co., Salt Lake City, 1985—; post doctoral appointment Ohio State U., Columbus, 1966. Editor: Advanced Techniques in Synthetic Fuels Analysis, 1983, Coal Conversion and the Environment, 1981. Chmn bd. Mid-Columbia Regional Ballet, Richland, 1978-86. Mem. Am. Chem. Soc. (sect. chmn. 1972-73). Home: 3097 E High Danish Rd Salt Lake City UT 84092 Office: Lee Scientific 4426 S Century Dr Salt Lake City UT 84123

FELL, BARRY (HOWARD BARRACLOUGH), educator; b. Lewes, Sussex, Eng., June 6, 1917; came to U.S., 1964; s. Howard Towne and Elsie Martha (Johnston) F.; m. Renee Clarkson, Oct. 10, 1942; children—Roger Barraclough, Francis Julian, Veronica Irene. B.Sc. New Zealand Coll., 1938, M.Sc., 1939; Ph.D., Edinburgh U.-Scotland, 1941, D.Sc., 1955; A.M. (hon.), Harvard U., 1965. Sr. lectr. zoology Victoria U., Wellington, N.Z., 1946-56, assoc. prof., 1956-64; curator Mus. Comp. Zoology, Harvard U., Cambridge, Mass., 1964-77; prof. biology Harvard U., Cambridge, 1965-77; prof. emeritus, 1977—; vis. prof. U. Tripoli, Libya, 1978; cons., author Geol. Soc. Am., Lawrence, Kans., 1963-70; cons. AAAS Com. on Panama Seaway, Washington, 1968; cons., author Woods Hole Oceanographic Inst., 1967. Author: America B.C., 1976; Saga America, 1980; Bronze Age America, 1982. Contbr. articles to profl. jours. Served to maj., Brit. Army, 1941-46. Fellow Royal Soc. N.Z. (Hector medal 1959, Hutton medal 1962), Am. Acad. Arts and Scis. (fellow emeritus); Mem. N.Z. Assn. Scientists (pres. 1948-49), Epigraphic Soc. (pres.), Sociedad Portuguesa de Antropologia e Etnologia (hon. fellow), Société d'Etude des anciens peuples (membre honoris causae). Home: 6625 Bamburgh Dr San Diego CA 92117 Office: Musuem of Comparative Zoology Harvard U Cambridge MA 02138

FELLIN, OCTAVIA ANTOINETTE, librarian; b. Santa Monica, Calif.; d. Otto P. and Librada (Montoya) F.; student U. N.Mex., 1937-39; B.A., U. Denver, 1941; B.A. in L.S., Rosary Coll., 1942. Asst. librarian, instr. library sci. St. Mary-of-Woods Coll., Terre Haute, Ind., 1942-44; librarian U.S. Army, Bruns Gen. Hosp., Santa Fe, 1944-46, Gallup (N.Mex.) Public Library, 1947—; post librarian Camp McQuaide, Calif., 1947; free lance writer mags., newspapers, 1950—; library cons.; N.Mex. del. White House Pre-Conf. on Libraries and Info. Services, 1978; dir. Nat. Library Week for N.Mex., 1959. Vice-pres., publicity dir. Gallup Community Concerts Assn., 1957-78, 85—; organizer Gt. Decision Discussion groups, 1963-85; mem. Gallup St. Naming Com., 1958-59, Aging Com., 1964-68; chmn. Gallup Mus. Indian Arts and Crafts, 1964-78; mem. publicity com. Gallup Inter-Tribal Indian Ceremonial Assn., 1966-68; mem. Gov's Com. 100 on Aging, 1967-70; N.Mex. Humanities Council, 1979; mem. U. N.Mex.-Gallup Campus Community Edn. Adv. Council, 1981-82; N.Mex. organizing chmn. McKinley Hosp. Aux., pres., 1983; mem. N.Mex. Library Adv. Council, 1971-75, vice chmn., 1974-75; chmn. adv. com. Gallup Sr. Citizens, 1971-73; mem. steering com. Gallup Diocese Bicentennial, 1975-78, chmn. hist. com., 1975; chmn. Trick or Treat for UNICEF, Gallup, 1972-77; chmn. pledge campaign Rancho del Nino San Huberto, Empalme, Mexico; bd. dirs. Gallup Opera Guild, 1970-74; bd. dirs., sec., organizer Gallup Area Arts Council, 1970-78; mem. N.Mex. Humanities Council, 1979, Gallup Centennial Com., 1980-81; mem. Cathedral Parish Council, 1980-83, v.p., 1981. Recipient Dorothy Canfield Fisher $1,000 Library award, 1961; Outstanding Community Service award for mus. service Gallup C. of C., 1969, 70, Outstanding Citizen award, 1974, Benemerenti medal Pope Paul VI, 1977, Celebrate Literary award Gallup Internat. Reading Assn., 1983-84. Mem. ALA, N.Mex. Library Assn. (v.p., sec., chmn. hist. materials com. 1964-66, salary and tenure com., nat. coordinator N.Mex. legislative com., chmn. com. to extend library services 1969-73, Librarian of Yr. award 1975, chmn. local and regional history roundtable 1978, Community Achievement award 1983), AAUW (v.p., co-organizer Gallup br., N.Mex. nominating com. 1967-—, chmn. fellowships and centennial fund Gallup br., chmn. com. on women), Plateau Scis. Soc., N.Mex. Folklore Soc. (v.p. 1964-65, pres. 1965-66), N.Mex. Hist. Soc. (dir. 1979—), Gallup Hist. Soc., Gallup Film Soc. (co-organizer, v.p. 1950-58), LWV (v.p. 1953-56), NAACP, Gallup C. of C. (organizing chmn. women's div. 1972, v.p. 1972-73), N.Mex. Women's Polit. Caucus, N.Mex. Mcpl. League (pres. librarian's div. 1979—), Dictionary Soc. N. Am., Alpha Delta Kappa (hon.). Roman Catholic (Cathedral Guild, Confraternity Christian Doctrine Bd. 1962-64, Cursillo in Christianity Movement, mem. of U.S. Cath. Bishop's Adv. Council 1969-74; corr. sec. Latin Am. Mission Program 1972-75, sec. Diocese of Gallup Pastoral Council 1972-73, corr. sec. liturgical commn. Diocese of Gallup 1977);chmn. Artists Coop., 1985—; mem. N.Mex. Diamond Jubilee/U.S. Constitution Bicentennial Gallup Com., 1986—. Author: Yahweh the Voice that Beautifies the Land. Home: 513 E Mesa Ave Gallup NM 87301 Office: 115 W Hill St Gallup NM 87301

FELLOWS, RUSHIA GLEN, architect, educator; b. Little Rock, Nov. 17, 1925; s. Winslow Fellows and Althea Mae (Sampson) King; m. Alice Nello Tease, Sept. 2, 1950; children—Darvis Glen, Daryl Arnett. B.S., Ariz. State U., 1951; M. Arch., U. Ariz., 1984. Registered architect Ariz. Asst. mgr. architecture Del E. Webb Corp., Phoenix, 1969-72, sr. draftsman, project coordinator, 1963-69; pvt. practice architecture, Phoenix, 1972—; asst. prof. architecture Ariz. State U., Tempe, 1977—; cons. Murphy Elem. Sch. Dist. 26, Phoenix, 1975-78. Mem. Western Region Nat. Urban Coalition Task Force, 1986; past pres. Citizens adv. com. Phoenix Elem. Sch. Dist. 1975; chmn. Bd. Appeals for Signs, City of Phoenix, 1976, v. chmn. sign code rev. com., 1978; adv. com. SBA, Phoenix, 1973-79. Served to capt. U.S. Army, 1951-58; Korea. Recipient commendation, City of Phoenix, 1979, Phoenix Elem. Sch. Dist. 1, 1977. Mem. AIA (Central Ariz. chpt. outstanding service award 1979), Ariz. Soc. Architects AIA (del. 1978-79, commendation award 1981, pres. 1978-81), Architects Found. Inc. Democrat. Home: 501 W Cocopah St Phoenix AZ 85003

FELSMAN, ANNABETH MATT, social worker; b. St. Ignatius, Mont., Dec. 20, 1954; d. Mark Marion and Gladys Susanne (Matt) F.; 1 child, Ashley Ora. BS, Brigham Young U., 1978; postgrad., Antioch U., 1979-80; MA, Antioch U. West, 1981; postgrad., Gonzaga U., 1982-83. Fin. advisor, counselor Seattle Indian Health Bd., 1978-84; child protective services worker/child welfare specialist Confederated Salish and Kootenai Tribes, Pablo, Mont., 1984—; mem. Confederated Salish and Kootenai tribes. Mem. Lake County Child Protection Team, Polson, Mont., 1984—; commr. Seattle Women's Commn., 1981-82; bd. dirs., vol. Lake County Family Crisis and Resource Ctr., 1984—. Named Outstanding Young Women of Wash., 1981, one of Outstanding Young Women of Am., 1981. Mem. Nat. Indian Social Workers Assn. Inc., Nat. Indian Counselors Assn., Nat. Indian Council on Health Careers, Alpha Phi Omega, Phi Alpha Delta. Democrat. Mormon. Avocations: Native Am. art, genealogy, sports. Home: PO Box 73 Ronan MT 59864 Office: Confederated Salish and Kootenai Tribes PO Box 278 Pablo MT 59855

FELT, RICHARD WAYNE, pulmonologist, internist; b. Seattle, Aug. 12, 1954; s. Wayne George and Wilma (Baldwin) F.; m. Alice Jean Sedgwick, Nov. 6, 1982; 1 child, Edward. BA magna cum laude, Linfield Coll., McMinnville, Oreg., 1976; MD, Oreg. Health Scis. U., 1980. Diplomate Am. Bd. Internal Medicine. Resident in internal medicine Ind. U. Med. Ctr., Indpls., 1980-83; staff internist VA Med. Ctr., Walla Walla, Wash., 1983-84; pulmonary fellow Oreg. Health Scis. U., Portland, 1984—. Physician asthma camp Oreg. Lung Assn., Portland, 1984-85. Summer fellow Am. Cancer Soc., 1978. Mem. ACP, AAAS, AMA, Am. Thoracic Soc., Oreg. Thoracic Soc. Avocations: hiking, biking, skiing, music. Office: Oreg Health Scis U 3181 SW Sam Jackson Park Rd Portland OR 97201

FELT, ROWLAND EARL, chemical engineer; b. Idaho Falls, Idaho, Aug. 3, 1936; s. Walter Irvin and Julia Mathilda (Frei) F.; m. Judith Margaret Lankard, Nov. 26, 1966; children: Scott, Brian, Keith, David, Emily. B-SChemE, U. Idaho, 1958, MSChemE, 1959; PhD, Iowa State U., 1964. Staff engr. Isochem, Inc., Richland, Wash., 1966-67; staff engr. Atlantic Richfield Hanford Co., Richland, 1967-73, mgr. prodn. processes engring., 1973-77; mgr. engring. devel. lab. Rockwell Hanford Co., Richland, 1977-79; mgr. chem. engring. Exxon Nuclear Corp., Richland, 1979-81, mgr. process engring., 1981—. Mem. Am. Nuclear Soc., Am. Inst. Chem. Engrs., Sigma Xi. Avocation: scouting. Home: 619 Lynnwood Loop Richland WA 99352 Office: Exxon Nuclear Corp 2101 Horn Rapids Richland WA 99352

FELTER, EDWIN LESTER, JR., lawyer, agency administrator; b. Washington, Aug. 11, 1941; s. Edwin L. Felter and Bertha (Peters) Brekke; m. Yoko Yamauchi-Koito, Dec. 26, 1969. B.A., U. Tex., 1964; J.D., Cath. U. of Am., 1967. Bar: Colo. 1970, U.S. Dist. Ct. Colo. 1970, U.S. Ct. Appeals (10th cir.) 1971, U.S. Supreme Ct. 1973, U.S. Tax Ct. 1979, U.S. Ct. Claims 1979, U.S. Ct. Internat. Trade 1979. Dep. pub. defender State of Colo., Ft. Collins, 1971-75; asst. atty. gen. Office of the Atty. Gen., Denver, 1975-80; state adminstrv. law judge Colo. Div. of Adminstrv. Hearings, Denver, 1980-83, chief adminstrv. law judge, dir., 1983—; discipline prosecutor Supreme Ct. Grievance Com., 1975-78. Contbg. editor: International Franchising, 1970. Mem. Colo. State Mgmt. Cert. Steering com., 1983—; No. Colo. Criminal Justice Planning council, Ft. Collins, 1973-75; bd. dirs., vice chmn. The Point Community Crisis Ctr., Ft. Collins, 1971-73; mem. Denver County Democratic Party Steering Com., 1978-79; chmn. 12th legis. dist., 1978-79. Mem. Colo. Bar Assn., Arapahoe County Bar Assn., Nat. Assn. of Adminstrv. Law Judges (pres. Colo. chpt. 1982—). Office: Colo Div of Hearing Officers 1525 Sherman St #550 Denver CO 80203

FELTER, JACK LAWDER, optometrist; b. Dayton, Ohio, Dec. 23, 1926; s. Alph and Mae Elizabeth (Lawder) F.; m. Ann L. Fischer, June 4, 1949; children—Nancy, Jeffrey. Student U. Dayton, 1950-52; O.D., Ohio State U., 1956. Pvt. practice optometry, Albuquerque, 1956—; sec., pres. N.Mex. Bd. Examiners in Optometry, 1962-69. Served with USN, 1942-44. Fellow Am. Acad. Optometry; mem. Am. Optometric Assn., N.Mex. Optometric Assn. (pres., 1976, 85, N.Mex. Optometrist of Yr. 1976, 85), Better Vision Inst., Am. Optometric Found., Pub. Health Assn., Epsilon Psi Epsilon. Republican. Club: Masons.

FELTON, SAMUEL PAGE, biochemist; b. Petersburg, Va., Sept. 7, 1919; s. Samuel S. and Pearl (Williams) F.; m. Helen Florence Martin, Dec. 31, 1955; 1 child, Samuel Page. Degree in pharmacy, U.S. Army, San Francisco, 1942; BS in Chemistry, U. Wash., 1951, postgrad., 1954. Chief technician U. Wash., Seattle, 1952-59, research assoc., 1959-62, sr. research assoc., 1969—, dir. cur. facilities lab., 1969-73, dir. water quality lab., 1976-83, dir. biochem. lab. sch. of Fisheries, 1983—; asst. mem., asst. to dir. div. biochemistry Scripps Clinic and Research Found., La Jolla, Calif., 1962-66; asst. biochemist Children's Orthopedic Hosp., Seattle, 1966-68. Mem. bd. of adjustments City of Edmonds, Wash. Served to sgt. MC, U.S. Army 1942-45. Mem. Am. Chem. Soc., Am. Inst. Fishery Research Biologists, N.Y. Acad. of Sci. Avocations: sailing, skiing, camping. Office: U Wash Fisheries Research Inst Seattle WA 98195

FELTY, JAMES DAVID, real estate appraiser; b. Brownsdale, Minn., Oct. 20, 1947; s. Mervin Burton and Cornelia (Bonnes) F.; m. Theresa Nanette Tussing, Sept. 17, 1967; 1 child, Jessica Danielle. BS in Forestry, U. Minn., 1975. Sr. appraiser U.S. Fish and Wildlife Service, Albuquerque, 1976—. Republican. Avocations: hunting, fishing, stained glass, horse racing. Home: PO Box 237 Edgewood NM 87015 Office: US Fish and Wildlife Service PO Box 1306 Albuquerque NM 87103

FELVER, CHARLES STANLEY, English educator, consultant; b. Easton, Pa., Oct. 13, 1916; s. Jacob Paul and Caroline Foote (Stanley); m. Marie Alice McRoberts, Aug. 16, 1941; children: Julia Caroline, Madeline Alice, David Stanley. BA, Lafayette Coll., Easton, 1948; MA, Yale U., 1949; PhD, U. Mich., 1956. Instr. English U. Kansas, Lawrence, 1949-50; teaching fellow U. Mich., Ann Arbor, 1950-52; lectr. and supr. U. Mich., Saginaw, 1952-55; from asst. prof. to assoc. prof. Kent (Ohio) State U., 1955-61; prof. English Calif. State U., Chico, 1961—, chmn. dept., 1961-68; cons. U.S. Office Edn., Washington, 1966-68. Author: Robert Armin Shakespeare's Fool, 1961; (with M.K. Nurmi) Poetry: An Introduction and Anthology, 1967, Joseph Crawhall the Newcastle Wood Engraver, 1972; contbr. articles to profl. jours. Chmn. Chico City Planning Commn., 1972-77; bd. dirs. Chico Mus., 1980—. Served to 1st sgt. U.S. Army Med. Service Corps, 1943-46. W.W. Eddy Meml. scholar 1948, Nathaniel Currier fellow 1948-49, Folger fellow 1961. Mem. Phi Beta Kappa, Phi Alpha Theta. Democrat. Avocations: collecting Victorian illus. books and original prints. Home: 1069 Woodland Ave Chico CA 95928 Office: Calif State U Chico CA 95928

FELVER, LINDA, nurse, educator; b. Tulsa, May 17, 1945; d. Donald L. and Eileen (Heskett) Norling; m. Peter Christ, May 4, 1985; children: Jennifer, John. BS, Ohio State U., 1968; BS in Nursing summa cum laude, Eastern Wash. U., 1977; MA, U. Wash., 1978, PhD, 1986. RN, Wash., Oreg. Nursing advisor Eastern Wash. U., Cheney, 1977; assoc. prof. Washington State U., Spokane, 1978-86; assoc. prof. dept. adult health and illness Oreg. Health Scis. U., Portland, 1986—; cons. chemistry Eastern Wash. U., 1975. Contbg. author three books; contbr. Dispensing Information to U.S. Pharmacopeia, 1980—; contbr. articles to profl. jours. Mem. Met. Opera Guild. Mem. Am. Nurses' Assn. (conv. del. 1984-87, Nat. Candidate award 1982), Wash. State Nurses' Assn. (chmn. gerontol. interest group 1981-83, Excellence in Writing award 1979, 81, 82), Council Nurse Researchers, N.Y. Acad. Sci., Am. Soc. Magnesium Research, AAAS, Western Soc. Research in Nursing, Nat. Audubon Soc. (life), Seattle Opera Assn., Seattle Zool. Assn. Home: 2235 Willida Ln Sedro Woolley WA 98284

FEND, EILEEN, personnel service owner; b. Salt Lake City, Oct. 29, 1927; d. Mark and Louise (Irvine) Warburton; m. Jack Hartman, Oct. 28, 1958 (dec. 1968); children: Pamela Greene, Teri Gervais, Mark Hartman; m. Helmut Fend, June 21, 1975. Student, Utah State U., 1945-49, U. So. Calif., 1985. Purchasing agt. Futurecraft Corp., City of Industry, Calif., 1959-64; dir. Vivian Woodard, Panorama City, Calif., 1964-75; pres., owner On Call Personnel, Manhattan Beach, Calif., 1978—; chmn. bd. dirs. Hour Gang Personnel, Orange County, Calif., 1982—; cons. and lectr. in field. Coordinator, Duologue Vendor Com.; mem. roundtable Calif. State U., Dominguez Hills South Bay Bus. Roundtable; bd. dirs. Women in Mgmt. Career Opportunity Liaison; scholarship bd. Bank of Am., Redondo Beach, El Segundo Rotary Club. Mem. Internat. Assn. Personnel Women (hostess nat. mid-winter bd. meetings), Personnel and Indsl. Relations Assn., Bus. Mgmt. Assn., Women in Mgmt., C. of C. (Calif.), Nat. Assn. Women Bus. Owners (pub. affairs com.), Calif. Assn. Personnel Consultants (temprary services sect.), South Bay Mktg. Network. Club: Leads. Avocation: skiing. Office: On Call Personnel 505 N Sepulveda Manhattan Beach CA 90277

FENICAL, WILLIAM HOWARD, oceanography educator; b. Chgo., June 24, 1941; s. Maurice Andrew and Gertrude Agnes (Adams) F.; m. Frances Louise Riggs, Dec. 17, 1967; one child, Scott William. BS, Calif. State Poly. U., San Luis Obispo, 1963; MS, San Jose State U., 1965; PhD, U. Calif., Riverside, 1968. Mem. faculty Scripps Inst. Oceanography, La Jolla, Calif., 1973—, prof. oceanography, 1984—. Editor: Marine Natural Products, 1979. Sr. Queens fellow Govt. Australia, 1984. Mem. Am. Chem. Soc., Am. Soc. Chem. Ecology. Democrat. Avocation: scuba diving. Home: 1128 Highland Dr Del Mar CA 92014 Office: Scripps Inst Oceanography La Jolla CA 92093

FENILI, MARY LOU, university administrator, lawyer; b. Vineland, N.J., July 7, 1945; d. V. J. and Louise W. (Pennino) F. A.B., Douglass Coll., 1967; M.A., Syracuse U., 1970; J.D., U. Santa Clara, 1977. Bar: Calif. 1977, Wash. 1983. Head resident Syracuse U., N.Y., 1967-69, U. So. Calif., Los Angeles, 1969-70; asst. dean student services Mills Coll., Oakland, Calif., 1970-74; staff counsel Bd. Prison Terms, Sacramento, 1977-82; v.p., dean student life Pacific Luth. U., Tacoma, 1982—. Mem. Human Research Rev. Bd., Olympia, Wash., 1983-85; bd. dirs. So. Sound Woman's Network, Tacoma, 1984-87. Recipient Sr. Service award Douglass Coll., 1967; named to Outstanding Young Women Am., U.S. Jaycees, 1972. Mem. Nat. Assn. Female Execs., Nat. Assn. Student Personnel Adminstrs. (women's taskforce 1983-85), Adminstrv. Women in Edn. (v.p. 1984-86, membership chmn. 1986-87), Am. Assn. Counseling and Devel., Am. Coll. Personnel Assn., N.W. Coll. Personnel Assn. (pres.-elect 1986-87), Nat. Assn. Women Deans (profl. employment practices com. 1986—), Wash. Women Lawyers, Wash. State Bar Assn., State Bar Calif., ACLU, Wash. Council on Crime and Delinquency (bd. dirs. 1986—), Sierra Club, NOW. Democrat. Roman Catholic. Home: PO Box 44602 Tacoma WA 98444 Office: PO Box 7041 Tacoma WA 98407

FENN, GEORGE JUNIOR, government official; b. Gridley, Calif., June 11, 1926; s. George Beck and Angeline Lenora (Watson) F.; m. Jacqueline R. Davis, Aug. 24, 1947; children—Stanley, Janice, Daniel. Student Yuba Coll., 1946-47. Farm mgmt., Yuba City, Calif., 1947-56, Chico, Calif., 1957-67; maintenance supr. U.S. Fish and Wildlife Service, Toppenish, Wash., 1967-76, chief of ops., 1976—; ecol. cons., 1970—. Youth conservation adv., 1978—; mem. Fed. Exec. Bd., Yakima, Wash., 1976. Served with USN, 1944-46, PTO. Named Employee of Yr., Fed. Exec. Bd., 1976; recipient various profl. awards. Mem. Internat. Assn. Chiefs of Police. Democrat. Home: Rt 1 Box 1300 Toppenish WA 98948 Office: Rt 1 Box 1300 Toppenish WA 98948

FENSTERBUSH, BRUCE ERNEST, oil company professional; b. Sunbury, Pa., Nov. 9, 1960; s. Ronald Richard and Lois Jean (Gruneberg) F.; m. Kathleen Louise Anderson, July 21, 1984; 1 child, Erica Michelle. BS in Chemistry, Ursinus Coll., 1982. Cathodic protection technician Sun Exploration and Prodn. Co., Valencia, Calif., 1984—. Staff mem. parish relations com. Meth. Ch., 1987. Mem. Nat. Assn. Corrosion Engrs. (speaker 1987 seminar), So. Calif. Cathodic Protection Com., Cen. Calif. Cathodic Protection Com., Soc. Preservation and Encouragement of Barbershop Quartet Singing in Am. (program v.p. 1987). Republican. Methodist. Club: Channel Island Clippers (mgr. 1986—). Home: 6431 Shearwater St Ventura CA 93003 Office: PO Box 55060 25322 W Rye Canyon Rd Valencia CA 17044

FENTON, DENNIS MICHAEL, research scientist; b. Roslyn, N.Y., Nov. 2, 1951; s. Robert Edward and Catherine (O'Dwyer) F.; m. Linda Marie Owens, June 30, 1974. BS in Biology, Manhattan Coll., 1973; PhD in Microbiology, Rutgers U., 1977. Research scientist Pfizer Co., Groton, Conn., 1977-81; research scientist AmGen, Thousand Oaks, Calif., 1982-84, head lab., 1984-86, dir., 1986—. Contbr. articles to profl. jours.; patentee in field. Mem. Am. Chem. Soc., Soc. Indsl. Microbiology, Am. Soc. Microbiology. Avocations: sports, music, hiking, camping. Office: AmGen 1900 Oak Terrace Ln Thousand Oaks CA 91320

FENTON, JOHN VINCENT, medical association executive; b. N.Y.C., Oct. 24, 1945; s. Robert S. and Catherine (O'Dwyer) F.; m. Stella S. Capon; children—John, Jennifer, Kimberly. B.S. in Pre-Med. and Biology, Manhattan Coll., 1968; M.S. in Phys. Therapy, Columbia U., 1969; M.B.A./M.H.A. in Health Sci. Mgmt., Century U., Beverly Hills, Calif., 1981. Cert. Nursing Home Extended Care Facilities Adminstrn. 1973; lic. phys. therapist, Calif., N.Y., Mich., N.J. Med., recreational asst. in cardiac hosp. St. Frances Hosp., Roslyn, N.Y., 1962-64; emergency med. technician St. Vicent's Hosp., N.Y.C., 1964-69; dir. ctr. services Cerebral Palsy Treatment Ctr., Albany, N.Y., 1964-69; asst. adminstr., dir. rehab. services Menorah Home and Hosp., Bklyn., 1971-73; exec. adminstr. N.Y. Med. Coll., Mental Retardation Inst., Valhalla and N.Y.C., N.Y., 1973-76; adminstr. Jewish Bd. of Guardians, N.Y.C., 1977-78; adminstrv. asst. North Detroit Gen. Hosp., 1978; sr. phys. therapist Brotman Meml. Hosp., Culver City, Calif., 1978-79; corp. officer, exec. dir. profl. services cons. Creative Escapes, Beverly Hills, Calif., 1980-84; cons. of rehab. services, dir. AMI/Westside Hosp., Los Angeles, 1979-82; dir. rehab. services Brotman Med. Ctr., Culver City, 1982-86, asst. adminstr., 1986—; instr. Sch. Phys. Therapy, Russell Sage Coll., Albany, 1969-71; instr. rehab. services Sch. Nursing, Albany Med. Coll., N.Y., 1969-71, instr. human behavior, 1969-74; instr. health care adminstrn. and rehab. medicine N.Y. Med. Coll., 1973-76. Mem. sch. bd. Pleasantville, N.Y., 1977; mem. Willowbrook rev. panel Fed. Govt., N.Y., 1976. Mem. Am. Phys. Therapy Assn., Am. Assn. Mental Deficiency, Am. Hosp. Assn., Am. Coll. Sports Medicine, Am. Coll. Nursing Home Adminstrs., Am. Coll. of Health Care Adminstrs., Assn. Adminstrs. Mental Health and Retardation Facilities. Home: 1144 21st St Apt 4 Santa Monica CA 90403 Office: Brotman Med Ctr 3828 Delmas Terr Culver City CA 90230

FENWICK, JERRY LEE, city safety inspector, risk manager; b. Exeter, Calif., Sept. 20, 1936; s. Omar Thomas and Erma Mae (Weaser) F.; m. Patricia C. Reynolds, June 1, 1958 (div. Oct. 1979); children: Daniel L., Raymond H. BA, U. Nev., 1958. Asst. mgr. Fenwick's, Reno, 1958-76; supply officer Reno Police Dept., 1976-81; revenue officer City of Reno, 1981, safety inspector, risk mgr., 1982—. Active Adv. Bd. Community Coll., Reno, 1976-81; mem. cen. com. Wahoe County Rep. Party, 1984—; chmn. City of Reno Employees United Fund, 1984, 86, Local Bd. 7 Selective Service, Sparks, Nev., 1982—. Mem. Am. Soc. Safety Engrs, Reno Coin Club (pres.), Reno Colorfoto Club (pres.), Nev. Stamp Study Soc. (bd. dirs.). Republican. Methodist. Lodge: Masons. Home: 1024 Bradley Sq Sparks NV 89431 Office: City of Reno 450 S Center Reno NV 89502

FERBER, ROBERT RUDOLF, researcher, educator; b. New Eagle, Pa., June 11, 1935; s. Rudolf F. and Elizabeth J. (Robertson) F.; m. Eileen Merhaut, July 25, 1964; children—Robert Rudolf, Lynne C. B.S. in E.E., U. Pitts., 1958; M.S. in E.E., Carnegie-Mellon U., 1966, Ph.D. in Semiconductor Physics, 1967. Registered profl. engr., Pa. Mgr. engrng. dept. WRS Motion Picture Labs., Pitts., 1954-58, sec., 1959-76, v.p., 1976-79; sr. engr. Westinghouse Research Labs., Pitts., 1956-67; mgr. nuclear effects group Westinghouse Elec. Corp., Pitts., 1967-71, mgr. adv. engr. energy projects, East Pittsburgh, 1971-77; photovoltaic materials and collector research mgr. Jet Propulsion Lab., Pasadena, Calif. 1977-85, SP100 Project contract tech. mgr., 1985—; v.p. Executaire Inc., Pitts., 1960-64; pres. Tele-Cam Inc., Pitts., 1960-78. Editor: Transactions of the 9th World Energy Conf. 1974, Digest of the 9th World Energy Conf., 1974. Contbr. articles to profl. jours. Patentee in field. Mem. Franklin Regional Sch. Dist. Bd., Murrysville, Pa., 1975-77. Fellow Buhl Found., 1965-66, NDEA, 1976-77. Mem. IEEE (sr.), Am. Solar Energy Soc., ASME (chmn. 1986 Solar Energy Div. Conf.). Republican. Lutheran. Home: 5314 Alta Canyada Rd La Canada CA 91011 Office: Jet Propulsion Lab 4800 Oak Grove Dr Pasadena CA 91109

FERDUN, GARETH STANLEY, social service executive; b. Modesto, Calif., Nov. 17, 1937; s. Stanley and Jean (Van Buskirk) F.; m. Georgenne Marie Brann, Feb. 19, 1961; children: Severn, Muir, Destin. Student, UCLA, 1958; BA, U. Calif., Berkeley, 1961; MA, San Francisco State U., 1962. Sr. social research analyst Calif. Youth Authority, Sacramento, 1970-76, project dir. PMES, 1976-83, chief program planning and evaluation, 1983-85, chief mgmt. and policy analysis, 1985—. Contbr. numerous articles to profl. jours. Office: Mgmt and Policy Analysis 4241 Williamsbourgh Dr Sacramento CA 95823

FERENTCHAK, LINDA BURLEIGH, public relations executive; b. Camp Hanford, Wash., Feb. 26, 1955; d. Thomas Dearborn and Nora Beatrice (Reed) B.; m. James A. Ferentchak, Oct. 17, 1986. BA in Tech. Journalism, Colo. State U., 1977, MBA, 1980. Pub. relations dir. Eugene F. Pilz & Co., Denver, 1979-81; pub. relations mgr. Bank Western Fed. Savs., Denver, 1982-87; investor relations coordinator Bates Corp. Communications, Denver, 1987—. Editor: (newletters) Inst. Fin. Edn. 4-Sight, 1984-86 (nat. competition award 1985), Wealth and Health, 1984-85 (Bronze Quill award 1985). Mem. Nat. Investor Relations Inst. (bd. dirs., sec. Colo. chpt. 1986), Pub. Relations Soc. Am. Republican. Avocations: peak walking, skiing, reading, hiking. Home: 3371 E Euclid Ave Littleton CO 80121 Office: Bates Corp Communications 1228 15th St Suite 401 Denver CO 80202

FERGUSON, DAVID MICHAEL, safety administrator; b. Sylva, N.C., Feb. 26, 1947; s. Philetus Samuel and Esther (Margaret) F.; m. Karen Miller, Aug. 7, 1979; children: Cara, Ian. AA, Grossmont Coll., 1974; BA, Calif. State U., San Diego, 1974, MA, 1980. Cert. community coll. tchr., Calif. Sch. bus driver Lemon Grove (Calif.) Sch. Dist., 1970-76; adminstrv. asst. San Diego Community Coll., 1981-82; br. librarian San Diego County, 1976-84; safety adminstr. Nat. Steel Shipbldg., San Diego, 1984—; instr. health San Diego Mesa Coll., 1981—. Commr. Internat. Friendship Commn., Chula Vista, Calif., 1983—; vol. Chula Vista Disaster Council, 1984—, Safety Ethics Regulatory and Aging Comms., Chula Vista, 1980—. Served as sgt. U.S. Army, 1966-70. Mem. Am. Soc. Safety Engrs., Sister Cities Internat. Democrat. Mem. Christ Ch. Unity. Olympic torch relay runner Cities of Chula Vista and Odawara, Japan, 1984; avocations: jogging, golf, gardening. Office: Nat Steel and Ship Building Co 28th and Harbor Dr MS 27 San Diego CA 92113

FERGUSON, DEE ANN, academic director; b. Columbus, Ohio, July 13, 1947; d. Walter Lewis and Rachel Dixon (Stone) Lucas; m. David Elton Ferguson (dec. June 1969); 1 child, Patrick Antonio. B cum laude, Ohio State U., 1966; MBA, U. Exeter, Eng., 1975. Mng. dir. Lori of London, Internat. London, 1973-80; bus. mgr., cons. Los Angeles, 1978-80; adminstr. Gussi Watches, Los Angeles, 1979-82; dir. facilities Marlborough Sch., Los Angeles, 1983—; mem. steering com. Earthquake Preparedness Marlborough Sch., 1984—. Inventor roll-r-shoe, load stabelizer, chem. formulae. Mem. Assn. Phys. Plant Admistrs. of Colls. and Univs., Young Reps. Roman Catholic. Avocations: skiing, horticulture, aerobics, outdoor sports. Home: 1147 N Wilcox Pl Los Angeles CA 90038 Office: Marlborough Sch 250 S Rossmore Ave Los Angeles CA 90004

FERGUSON, EVELYN CLAIRE, educational administrator, consultant; b. Simcoe, Ontario, Can., Oct. 22, 1915; d. Charles Herbert and Leeta Belva (Wood) Fick; came to U.S., 1942; m. Ernest Wayne Ferguson, June 12, 1941 (dec.); children—Donald Wayne, Alan Wood. A.A., Bakersfield Coll., 1964; B.A. with honors (scholar), Fresno State Coll., 1966; M.A., Fresno State U., 1970. Cert. reading specialist, Calif. Elem. tchr., 1966-68; Miller-Unruh reading specialist, 1968-72; adj. lectr. Calif. State Coll.-Bakersfield, 1971-72, coordinator early childhood program, 1972-73, spl. programs coordinator, 1973-74, dir. Calif. Demonstration Program in Reading, 1974—; cons., presenter regional, state confs., program writing. Past pres. Wayside PTA, 1955-56, Bakersfield Council PTA, 1957-58, South High Sch. PTA, 1959-60; past sec., area dir. 7th Dist. PTA, 1958-60; past pres. Kern Council Internat. Reading Assn., 1978-79, dir. 1972—. Mem. Reading Specialists Calif., Internat. Reading Assn. (mem. exec. bd. Kern Council), Fresno Area Reading Council, Assn. Calif. Sch. Adminstrs., Nat. Council Tchrs. English, Assn. Supervision and Curriculum Devel., AAUW, PTA (hon. life), Delta Kappa Gamma (exec. bd.). Democrat. Episcopalian. Office: 1109 Pacheco Rd Bakersfield CA 93307

FERGUSON, HELAMAN ROLFE PRATT, mathematician, sculptor; b. Salt Lake City, Aug. 11, 1940; s. Helaman and Jeanne (Reinhardt) Pratt; adopted Samuel and Dora (Call) Ferguson; m. Claire Eising, Apr. 16, 1963; children: David, Sam, Ben, Noelle, Jonathan, Alexander, Michael Paul. AB, Hamilton Coll., 1962; MS, Brigham Young U., 1966, U. Wash., 1968; PhD, U. Wash., 1971. Prof. math. Brigham Young U., Provo, Utah, 1971-83, 1985—; vis. fellow Princeton (N.J.) U., 1983-84; sr. scientist Geomath, Orem, Utah, 1981-82; cons. algorithms, supercomputers, vector-parallel processors, applied logic, geophysics, geometric design, computer-aided manufacture, biomed. modeling. Contbr. articles to profl. jours.; commd. for numerous sculptures with math. themes; patentee in field. Research grantee Brigham Young U., 1971-85. Mem. Am. Math. Soc., Math. Assn. Am., Soc. Indsl. and Applied Mathematicians, Soc. Exploration Geophysicists, Internat. Jugglers Assn., Internat. Sculpture Ctr. Mormon. Home and Studio: 3895 Quail Run Provo UT 84604-5279 Office: Brigham Young U Dept Math 300 Talmage Provo UT 84602

FERGUSON, JONNY EDWARD, aerospace engineer; b. Kilgore, Tex., Nov. 16, 1942; s. Ralph Edward and Mary Frances (Ray) F.; m. Gloria Lynn Gray, July 17, 1967; children: Wendy Kay, Kristi Gail, Kevin Gray. Assoc. in Engring., Kilgore Coll., 1963; BSEE, U. Tex., 1965. Manned space flight controller Johnson Space Ctr., NASA, Houston, 1966-67, 71-80, mem. Apollo recovery team, 1967-71; space flight ops. engr. Denver Aerospace div. Martin Marietta Corp., 1980-85, lead engr. space sta. ops., 1985—. Author numerous tech. reports. Named Outstanding Ex-Student of Past 50 Yrs., Kilgore Coll., 1984. Baptist. Avocations: camping, music, gardening, skiing. Home: 3807 E Kettle Pl Littleton CO 80122 Office: Martin Marietta Denver Aerospace PO Box 179 Denver CO 80201

FERGUSON, LLOYD NOEL, chemist; b. Oakland, Calif., Feb. 9, 1918; s. Noel Swithin and Gwendolyn Louise (Johnson) F.; m. Charlotte Olivia Welch, Jan. 2, 1944; children—Lloyd Noel, Stephen Bruce, Lisa Annette. B.S., U. Calif. at Berkeley, 1940, Ph.D., 1943; D.Sc., Howard U., 1970, Coe Coll., 1979. Research asst. Nat. Def. Project, U. Calif. at Berkeley, 1941-44; asst. prof. Agr. and Tech. Coll., Greensboro, N.C., 1944-45; faculty Howard U., 1945-65, prof. chemistry, 1955-65, chmn. dept., 1958-65; prof. chemistry Calif. State U., Los Angeles, 1965—; chmn. chemistry dept. Calif. State U., 1968-71; vis. prof. U. Oreg., summers 1958, 60, 63, U. Nairobi, Kenya, 1971-72; govt. chemist Nat. Bur. Standards, Naval Ordnance Lab. and Dept. Agr., summers 1950, 51, 67; vis. scientist, div. chem. edn. Am. Chem. Soc., 1959—; touring lectr. N.Y. State, 1956, Okla., 1974; series lectr., Copenhagen, Denmark, and Lund, Sweden, 1954; cons. Coll. Chemistry Cons.'s Service. Author: Electron Structures of Organic Molecules, 1952, Textbook of Organic Chemistry, 1958, The Modern Structural Theory of Organic Chemistry, 1963, Organic Chemistry: A Science and an Art, 1972, Highlights of Alicyclic Chemistry, Vol. 1, 1973, Vol. 2, 1977, Organic Molecular Structure, 1974; also, numerous articles. Recipient Mfg. Chemists award, 1974; Outstanding Prof. award Calif. State U., Los Angeles, 1974; Oakland Mus. Assn. award, 1973; Distinguished medallion Am. Found. Negro Affairs, 1976; Outstanding Teaching award Nat. Orgn. Black Chemists, 1979; Outstanding Prof. award Calif. State U. and Colls., 1981; Guggenheim fellow Carlsberg Lab., Copenhagen, 1953-54; NSF faculty fellow Swiss Fed. Inst. Tech., Zurich, 1961-62. Fellow Chem. Soc. London, AAAS, Am. Inst. Chemists; mem. Am. Chem. Soc. (award Chem. Edn. 1978, chmn. chem. edn. div. 1980), AAUP, Nat. Inst. Sci., Sigma Xi. Home: 4221 S Cloverdale Ave Los Angeles CA 90008

FERGUSON, PAUL WESLEY, toxicologist; b. Hollywood, Calif., Nov. 20, 1952; s. Jack White and Doris (Lee) F.; m. Grace Muriel Bovey, Nov. 30, 1974; 1 child, David. BA in Biology, Whittier Coll., 1974; PhD in Pharmacology and Toxicology, U. Calif., Davis., 1981. Diplomate Am. Bd. Toxicology. Research specialist Los Angeles County-U. So. Calif. Med. Ctr., 1973-74; research biologist Pennwalt Corp., Monrovia, Calif., 1974-76; asst. prof. toxicology Sch. Pharmacy N.E. La. U., Monroe, 1981-84; sr. toxicologist UNOCAL Corp., Los Angeles, 1984—. Contbr. articles to profl. publs. Mem. Gov.'s Task Force on Environ. Health, Baton Rouge, 1983-84. Jastro-Shields Research scholar U. Calif., Davis, 1979-80; grantee Nat. Inst. Environ. Health Scis., 1979, 80; Stauffer Sci. fellow Whittier Coll., 1972. Mem. Soc. Toxicology (Procter and Gamble Research fellow 1979), Am. Indsl. Hygiene Assn., Soc. Risk Analysis. Office: UNOCAL Corp Med Dept 1201 W 5th St Los Angeles CA 90017

FERGUSON, SHANNON, accountant; b. Chattanooga, Tenn., June 26, 1945; d. William Fleming and Grace Gwendolyn (Marshall) Cargo; student Mount San Antonio Coll., 1963-64; student UCLA, 1966; m. William Clark Ferguson III, Dec. 30, 1967; children—William Jeffrey, Jill. Jr. acct. United Geophys. Corp., Pasadena, Calif., 1964-67; controller, chief fin. officer, corp. sec. Presto-Tek Corp., Los Angeles, 1979-81; corp. sec., chief fin. officer Accessory Supply, Arcadia, Calif., 1981—, also dir. Asst. treas. Holiday Homes Tour, 1981, safety chmn., 1980; chmn. 20th Anniversary Ball Meth. Hosp., 1977; bd. dirs. Arcadia Tournament of Roses, 1985—; mem. U.S. Bus. Adv. Bd., Washington, Republican Presdl. Task Force, Arcadia aux. Meth. Hosp.; sustaining mem. Rep. Nat. Com., Calif. Rep. Com. Mem. Internat. Div. Credit Mgrs., Exec. Female, Office Automation Mgmt. Adv. Bd., Credit Mgrs. So. Calif., Arcadia Bus. Assn., Alpha Aux. Vis. Nurses Assn., Arcadia C. of C. Republican. Club: Altursa (Arcadia). Home: 1230 Oakglen Ave Arcadia CA 91006

FERGUSON, SYBIL RAE, franchise business executive; b. Barnwell, Alta., Can., Feb. 7, 1934; came to U.S., 1938, naturalized, 1976; d. Alva John and Xarissa (Merkley) Clarke; m. Roger N. Ferguson, July 10, 1952; children: Debra Kay, Michael David, Wade Clarke, Lois Christine, Julie Xarissa. Student public schs. Founder Diet Ctr. Inc., Rexburg, Idaho, 1970—; dir. Am. Health Products, Diet Ctr. Counselor Training, Diet Center Inn, Ferguson's Pharm. Labs., Diet Center Shipping and Receiving Co., Diet Center Print Shop, Audio Visual Studio, Sybils, Inc., Ferguson & Assos.; Charter mem. women's aux. Madison Meml. Hosp., Rexburg; dir. Diet Ctr. Counselor Tng., Golden Eagle Ranches, Diamond Mine Ice Plant. Author: The Diet Center Program; Lose Weight Fast and Keep It Off Forever, 1983, Diet Center Cookbook. Recipient Bus. Leader of Yr. award Ricks Coll., 1980. Mem. Rexburg C. of C. (program dir. 1976), Comm. of 200 (founding). Mormon. Clubs: Rexburg Civic, Soroptimists (v.p. Rexburg 1975, award 1979). Office: Diet Center Inc 220 S 2d St W Rexburg ID 83440

FERGUSON, WARREN JOHN, federal judge; b. Eureka, Nev., Oct. 31, 1920; s. Ralph and Marian (Damele) F.; m. E. Laura Keyes, June 5, 1948; children: Faye F., Warren John, Teresa M., Peter J. B.A., U. Nev., 1942; LL.B., U. So. Calif., 1949; LL.D. (hon.), Western State U., San Fernando Valley Coll. Law. Bar: Calif. 1950. Mem. firm Ferguson & Judge, Fullerton, Calif., 1950-59; city atty. for cities of Buena Park, Placentia, La Puente, Baldwin Park, Santa Fe Springs, Walnut and Rosemead, Calif., 1953-59; mcpl. ct. judge Anaheim, Calif., 1959-60; judge Superior Ct., Santa Ana, Calif., 1961-66, Juvenile Ct., 1963-64, Appellate Dept., 1965-66; U.S. dist. judge Los Angeles, 1966-79; judge U.S. Circuit Ct. 9th Circuit, Los Angeles, 1979-86, sr. judge, 1986—; faculty Fed. Jud. Ctr., Practising Law Inst., U. Iowa Coll. Law, N.Y. Law Jour.; sr. judge U.S. Cir. Ct. (9th cir.), Santa Ana, Calif., 1986—; assoc. prof. psychiatry (law) Sch. Medicine, U. So. Calif.; assoc. prof. Loyola Law Sch. Served with AUS, 1942-46. Decorated Bronze Star. Mem. Phi Kappa Phi, Theta Chi. Democrat. Roman Catholic. Office: 34 Civic Ctr Plaza Santa Ana CA 92701

FERGUSON, WAYNE SANDER, sch. supt.; b. Ogden, Utah, Apr. 26, 1926; s. George Cochran and Charlotte (Sander) F.; B.S., Brigham Young U., 1950, M.Ed., 1953; Ed.D., U. So. Calif., 1960; m. Dorothy Jean Curtis, Dec. 19, 1952; children—George Ray, April Lynne, Susan Gaye. Math. tchrs. Tooele County Sch. Dist., Utah, 1950-53; prin. Dugway (Utah) Elem. and High Schs., 1953-55; asst. supt. bus. services Mt. Eden Sch. Dist., Hayward, Calif., 1956-61; asst. supt. instructional services, 1961-63; supt. Orland (Calif.) public schs., 1963-72, Palmdale (Calif.) Sch. Dist., 1972-75, Fremont (Calif.) Unified Sch. Dist., 1975—; instr. San Jose State U., part-time, 1978-80. Served with USN, 1944-46. Mem. Am. Assn. Sch. Adminstrs., Assn. Calif. Sch. Adminstr., Phi Kappa Phi, Phi Delta Kappa, Delta Epsilon. Republican. Mormon. Lodge: Kiwanis (pres. 1980-81, lt. gov. div. 40 Calif.-Nev.-Hawaii 1983-84). Home: 2620 Forrest Ct Fremont CA 94536 Office: 4210 Technology Dr Fremont CA 94538

FERGUSSON, ROBERT GEORGE, retired army officer; b. Chgo., May 20, 1911; s. Archibald Campbell and Anne (Sheehan) F.; m. Charlotte Lawrence, Nov. 18, 1937; 1 son, Robert Lawrence (dec.). Student, Beloit Coll., 1929-32; B.S., U.S. Mil. Acad., 1936; M.A. in Internat. Relations, Boston U., 1959. Commd. 2d lt. U.S. Army, 1936, advanced through grades to maj. gen., 1962; comdg. officer 14th Inf. Regt., Hawaii, 1955-57; chief army adv. group Naval War Coll., Newport, R.I., 1957-61; asst. div. comdr. 24th Inf. Div., Augsburg, Ger., 1961-62; chief staff Hdqrs. Central Army Group (NATO), Heidelberg, Ger., 1962-65; comdg. gen. U.S. Army Tng. Center, Inf., Ft. Ord, 1965-67; comdr. U.S. Forces, Berlin, 1967-70; ret. 1970; corp. group v.p. manpower planning Dart Industries, Inc., Los Angeles, 1970-78; cons., 1978-82, ret., 1982. Decorated D.S.M., Legion of Merit with oak leaf cluster, Bronze Star with 3 oak leaf clusters, Purple Heart (U.S.); knight comdr. Cross with badge and star Order of Merit (W.Ger.); officer Legion of Honor (France). Mem. Clan Fergusson Soc. (Scotland), Beta Theta Pi. Clubs: Cypress Point (Pebble Beach); Old Capitol (Monterey, Calif.). Home: Box 1515 Pebble Beach CA 93953

FERICANO, PAUL FRANCIS, poet, writer, satirist; b. San Francisco, Jan. 16, 1951; s. Frank Paul and Josephine Angelina (Anello) F.; student San Francisco State U., U. Calif.-Berkeley, Calif. State U.-Hayward, Stanford U., U. Calif.-Santa Barbara, Sacramento State U., 1969-76; m. Katherine Judeen Daly, Oct. 14, 1972. Mng. editor Crow's Nest mag., San Francisco, 1973-76; editor The West Conscious Rev., Millbrae, Calif., 1974-77; pub. Scarecrow Books, Millbrae, 1974-78, Poor Souls Press, Millbrae, 1978-84; editor Yossarian Universal News Service, 1984—; dir. The Creative Response Outlet for Writers, 1973-78; asst. field coordinator Calif. Poets-in-the Schs. San Mateo County, 1977-78; chmn. Millbrae Arts Commn., 1976-77. Recipient commendation City of Millbrae, 1977; Howitzer prize, 1982. Author: Beneath the Smoke Rings, 1976; Cancer Quiz, 1977; Loading the Revolver with Real Bullets, 1977; The Condition of Poetry in the Modern World, A Stoogist Manifesto, 1980; Sinatra, Sinatra, 1982; Commercial Break, 1982; editor The Stoogism Anthology, 1977; contbr. poetry and prose to numerous mags., 1970—; author (with E. Ligi) The One Minute President, 1987. Home and Office: PO Box 236 Millbrae CA 94030

FERN, KATHERINE MILLIKEN, garment manufacturing company executive, financial executive, consultant; b. Lafayette, Ind., Apr. 6, 1948; d. Arthur Thomas and Mary June (Thurnau) Weaver; m. Joseph Jacob Fern, June 5, 1982. BA, UCLA, 1971. Controller Mort Ross Enterprises and Carol Ann of Calif., Los Angeles, 1973-82; cons., 1982-84; chief fin. officer Topson Downs Calif., Inc., Los Angeles, 1984—. Contbr. articles to profl. jours. Chmn. physician's com. United Way, 1979. Recipient award of merit United Cerebral Palsy, 1980. Mem. U.S. Ski Writers Assn., So. Calif. Ski Writers. Club: Single Ski (treas. 1981, Snow Queen 1981) (Los Angeles). Avocations: photography, amateur ski racing, skiing, sailing, travel writing. Office: Topson Downs Calif Inc 830 E 14th Pl Los Angeles CA 90021

FERNALD, RUSSELL DAWSON, biologist, researcher; b. Chuquicamata, Chile, Nov. 20, 1941; s. Russel G. and Catherine (Graf) F.; m. Anne Fernald, May 25, 1969; children: Lia, Anya. BSE, Swarthmore Coll., 1963; PhD in Biophysics, U. Pa., 1968; postgrad., Max-Planck-Inst. for Psychiatry, Munich, 1968-71. Postdoctoral fellow Max-Planck-Inst. for Psychiatry, Munich, 1969-71; research scientist Max Planck Inst. for Behavioral Physiology, Seewiesen, Fed. Republic of Germany, 1970-77; asst. prof. biology U. Oreg., Eugene, 1976-80, assoc. prof., 1980—, dir. Inst. Neurosci., 1985—; dir. P.H.S. tng. grant, U. Oreg.; panel mem. and site vis. N.I.G.M.S. NIH; panel mem. N.I.C.H.D. NIH, Nat. Research Council; Fogarty sr. vis. scientist NIH, London, 1984-85; vis. prof. anatomy, U. Colo., 1983; vis. scientist Max-Planck-Inst. for Behavioral Physiology, 1971-73. Mem. edit. bd. Neurobiology and Behavior monographs, 1980—; editor Neuroethology newsletter, 1985—. Recipient Research Career Devel. award NIH; predoctoral fellow Ford Found., predoctoral fellow NIH. Mem. N.Y. Acad. Scis., AAAS, Assn. Research Ophthamology and Vision, Animal Behavior Soc., Internat. Soc. Neurothology. Office: U Oreg Inst Neurosci Dept Biology Eugene OR 97403

FERNANDES, KATHLEEN, research psychologist; b. Hayward, Calif., Jan. 2, 1946; d. Edward Daniel and Lillian May (Silva) F. BA, U. Calif., Santa Barbara, 1967; MA, San Jose State U., 1969; PhD, Stanford U., 1974. Mem. project staff San Jose (Calif.) State U., 1969-71; research asst. Stanford (Calif.) U., 1971-73; assoc. research scientist Am. Inst. Research, Washington, 1973-79; research assoc. Ctr. Study Evaluation, Los Angeles, 1979; supr. personnel research psychologist Navy Personnel Research and Devel. Ctr., San Diego, 1979—; cons. Navy Sci. Assistance Program, Pearl Harbor, Hawaii, 1985-86. Contbr. tech. articles on military personnel to profl. publs. Mem. AAAS, Am. Ednl. Research Assn., Human Factors Soc. (sec.-treas. San Diego chpt. 1985—), U.S. Naval Inst. Home: 3138 Old Bridgeport Way San Diego CA 92111 Office: Navy Personnel Research and Devel Ctr Code 41 San Diego CA 92152

FERNÁNDEZ, CARLOS ALEJANDRO, lawyer; b. Pueblo, Colo., Sept. 3, 1954; s. Carlos Prudencio and Katherine Laurel (Gray) F.; m. Ellen Louise Ekström; 2 children. BA, Calif. State U., Hayward, 1978; JD, Golden Gate U., 1982. Bar: Calif. 1984, U.S. Dist. Ct. (no. dist.) Calif. 1984, U.S. Ct. Appeals (9th cir.) 1985, U.S. Ct. Internat. Trade. Assoc. Law Offices of Nathan Cohn, San Francisco, 1985-86; with I-Pride, Inc., San Francisco, 1985—, sec., 1986, pres., 1987, also bd. dirs.; incorporator Indsl. Fermentation Genetics, Inc., Crockett, Calif., 1982-83, bd. dirs. Mem. Alameda County (Calif.) Community Health Services Adv. Com., 1985—; mayoral candidate City of Berkeley, Calif., 1986. Mem. ABA, Am. Trial Lawyers Assn., San Francisco Bar Assn., Alameda County Bar Assn. Office: I-Pride Inc 1017 Virginia St Berkeley CA 94710-1832

FERNANDEZ, KEITH DAMIEN, public relations executive; b. Keaau, Hawaii, July 25, 1958; s. John Damien and Rose Marie (Mattos) F.; m. Ann Mie Kakugawa, Dec. 19, 1981; 1 child, Justin Damien Takeshi. B in Journalism, U. Mo., 1980. Account exec. Bruce Pozzi Pub. Relations, Anchorage, 1980-84; vis. promotions coordinator Anchorage Conv. and Vis. Bur., 1984—. Dir. Hist. Anchorage Inc., 1986. Mem. Pub. Relations Soc. Am. (dir. Alaska chpt. 1984—, 1st Place feature writing 1981, 1st Place overall pub. relations program 1981, 1st Place other pub. relations program 1983). Home: 251 McCarrey St Unit 11 Anchorage AK 99508 Office: Anchorage Conv & Vis Bur 201 E Third Ave Anchorage AK 99501

FERNANDEZ-IZNAOLA, RICARDO J(AIME), music educator; b. Havana, Cuba, Feb. 21, 1949; came to U.S., 1980; s. Alfonso and Arabia Raquel (Iznaola) Fernandez; m. Maria Victoria Santos Brandys, Aug. 22, 1974; children: Ricardo, Victor. Degree summa cum laude, Lino Gallardo Mus. Sch., Caracas, Venezuela, 1968; MusM, Royal Conservatory, Madrid, 1973, postgrad., 1978. Guitar instr. Normandale Coll., Bloomington, Minn., 1981-83; asst. prof. music U. Denver Lamont Sch. Music, 1983—; adj. assoc. prof. St. Mary's Coll., Winona, Minn., 1980-83; concert artist, lectr. over 1500 concerts, lectures in Europe, North and S.Am., and Japan, 1969—; dir. Internat. Guitar Week, Denver, 1984—. Composer Monologue II, 1983 (Stroud Festival award 1983); contbr. articles to profl. publs. Hon. scholar for Outstanding Performing Achievement, Manuel de Falla Music Course, Granada, Spain, 1974; recipient numerous internat. prizes for performance. Mem. Music Tchrs. Nat. Assn. Office: U Denver Lamont Sch Music 7111 Montview Blvd Denver CO 80220

FERRARI, PAUL ANDREW, structual engineering company executive; b. Reno, Feb. 25, 1948; s. Paul Seraphine and Evelyn (Tacchino) F.; m. Gloria Jean Balsi, Oct. 6, 1979; 1 child, Jennifer Marie. B.S. in Engring., U. Nev., 1971, M.S., 1974. Registered profl. engr., Nev. Chief engr. Reno Bldg. Dept., 1974-77; project engr. Jack A. Means Co., 1977-78; sr. engr. Martin & Cashdan Inc., 1978-79; ptnr. Ferrari-Howard & Assocs., Reno, 1979—. Editor State Engring. Mag., 1971-80; contbr. engring. article to mag. Served to capt. U.S. Army, 1971-80. Recipient U. Nev. Regents award. Mem. ASCE Nat. Soc. Profl. Engrs. (chmn., Young Engr. of Yr., Truckee Meadows Branch 1981, Nev. chpt. 1982), Nat. Acad. Forensic Engrs., Sigma Tau. Republican. Roman Catholic. Club: Optimist. Lodge: Elks. Office: Ferrari-Howard & Assocs Structural Engrs 1000 Bible Way Suite 77 Reno NV 89502

FERRARIO, JOSEPH A., bishop. Educ. St. Charles Coll., Catonsville, Md., St. Mary's Sem., Baltimore, Catholic U., Washington, D.C., U. of Scranton, Pa. Ordained Roman Catholic priest, 1951; ord. aux. bishop of Honolulu, titular bishop of Cuse, 1978, bishop of Honolulu, 1982. Office: Diocese of Honolulu 1184 Bishop St Honolulu HI 96813 *

FERRARO, DOUGLAS PETER, psychologist; b. White Plains, N.Y., Nov. 27, 1939; s. Peter Mario Ferraro and Edith Isabella Lewendon; m. Sandra Jean Odell, Jan. 5, 1980; children: Craig Alan, Kim Elizabeth. AB, Columbia Coll., 1961, MA, 1963, PhD, 1965. Cert. psychologist, N.Mex. Asst. prof. U. N.Mex., Albuquerque, 1965-69, prof. psychology, 1973—, assoc. prof., 1969-73, chmn. dept., 1984—; dist. prof. U. del Noreste, Mex., 1977; adj. prof. Union for Exptl. Colls. and Univs., 1980-84; vis. prof. U. Nacional Auto., Mex., 1981—; cons. forensic psychopharmacology, N.Mex., 1975—; mem. adv. com. Nat. Inst. Drug Abuse, 1979-86. Co-Author (with F.A. Logan) Systematic Analyses of Learning and Motivation, 1978; mem. editorial bd. Exptl. Animal Behavior, 1981—; contbr. articles to profl. jours. Fellow Am. Psychol. Assn.; mem. Soc. Behavioral Medicine, Soc. Psychol. in Substance Abuse, Psychonomic Soc., Am. Soc. Pharmacology. Home: 5016 Grande Vista Ct NW Albuquerque NM 87120 Office: U NMex Dept Psychology Albuquerque NM 87131

FERREIRA, ARMANDO THOMAS, sculptor, educator; b. Charleston, W.Va., Jan. 8, 1932; s. Maximiliano and Placeres (Sanchez) F.; children—Lisa, Teresa. Student, Chouinard Art Inst., 1949-50, Long Beach City Coll., 1950-53; B.A., UCLA, 1954, M.A., 1956. Asst. prof. art Mt. St. Mary's Coll., 1956-57; mem. faculty dept. art Calif. State U., Long Beach, 1957—; prof. Calif. State U., 1967—, chmn. dept. art, 1971-77, now assoc. dean Sch. Fine Arts; lectr., cons. One man shows include, Pasadena Mus.,

1959, Long Beach Mus., 1959, 69, Eccles Mus., 1967, Clay and Fiber Gallery, Taos, 1972, group shows include, Los Angeles County Art Mus., 1948, 66, Wichita Art Mus., 1959, Everson Mus., 1960, 66, San Diego Mus. Fine Arts, 1969, 73, Fairtree Gallery, N.Y.C., 1971, 74; vis. artist, U. N.D., 1974, exhibited widely abroad including, Poland, Portugal, Morocco, Spain, France. Fulbright lectr. Brazil, 1981. Mem. Nat. Assn. Schs. Art (dir.), Internat. Video Network (dir.), Assn. Calif. State Univ. Profs. Office: Calif State U 1250 Bellflower Blvd Long Beach CA 90840

FERREIRA, JACKIE WILMA, company product manager; b. Ont., Can., Oct. 20, 1954; d. William and Margaret Jane (Hunter) Waddell; m. Ronald C. Ferreira, Apr. 16, 1977. Cert. in bus. mgmt. U. Calif.-Hayward, 1983. Adminstrv. asst. Wells Fargo Bank, Oakland, Calif., 1972-75, Mason McDuffe Investment Corp., Berkeley, Calif., 1975-76, Sargent Industries, Oakland, 1976-77; order adminstr. Humphrey Instruments Inc., San Leandro, Calif., 1977-80, product specialist, 1980-82, tng. mgr., 1981-83, product mgr. diagnostic and surg. instrumentation, 1982—. Named Maid of Oakland, 1972; recipient Service Recognition award Humphrey Instruments Inc., 1979. Mem. Am. Soc. Tng. and Devel., Women in Info. Processing. Editor Wheelbarrow Johnny mag., 1976-78. Office: Humphrey Instruments Inc 3081 Teagarden St San Leandro CA 94577

FERRELL, YVONNE SIGNE, state recreation commission administrator; b. Centralia, Wash., Apr. 8, 1936; d. Clifford Francis and Lenora Matilda (Carlson) Battson; m. Richard L. Ferrell, Nov. 5, 1955; 1 child, Linnea Ferrell Bruns. Personnel mgr. Dept. Social and Health Services, Olympia, Wash.; chief personnel and tng. Wash. State Parks, Olympia, asst. dir., dep. dir. Appointed mem. Gov.'s Com. on Status of Women, Olympia, 1980-82; appointed by Sec. of Transp. to Nat. Boating Safety Council, 1986—; bd. dirs. Wash. State Employees Credit Union, Olympia, 1970-79, pres. 1976-77. Mem. Nat. Parks and Recreation Assn., Wash. Parks and Recreation Assn. Republican. Lutheran. Avocations: music, photography, boating, golf. Home: 2366 Seminary Hill Centralia WA 98531 Office: Wash State Parks and Recreation Commn 7150 Cleanwater Ln Olympia WA 98504

FERRER, RAFAEL DOUGLAS PAUL, lawyer; b. Seattle, Apr. 12, 1957; s. Rafael George and Barbara (Gould) F. BA in Acctg., U. Wash., 1979; M in Taxation, Golden Gate U., 1982; JD, U. Puget Sound. Bar: Wash. 1985, U.S. Ct. Appeals (9th cir.) 1986. Acct. Lallman & Feldman, Ketchum, Idaho, 1980; tax profl. Touche Ross & Co., Seattle, 1981-82; securities syndicator Brouner Securities, Seattle, 1983; Ferrer Law Offices P.C. Seattle, 1985—. Mem. Poncho Arts Found., Seattle, 1982, Madroma Community Group, Seattle, 1985; bd. dirs. Westboro Assn., Federal Way, Wash., 1981. Served with U.S. Marine Corps, 1975-80. Mem. ACLU, Wash. State Bar Assn., Assn. Trial Lawyers Am., Seattle King County Bar Assn., Wash. State Trial Lawyers Assn., Constrn. Fin. Mgmt. Assn. Republican. Congregationalist. Avocations: skiing, skydiving, scuba diving, mountain climbing, sailing. Home and Office: 1605 36th Ave Seattle WA 98122

FERREY, EDGAR EUGENE, association executive; b. Columbia City, Ind., May 22, 1920; s. Ralph Roy and Sarah Delilah (Dowell) F.; m. Claudia Sue Leininger, Jan. 29, 1944; 1 son, Steven Edgar. A.B., Ind. U., 1942. Mem. editorial staff Ft. Wayne News-Sentinel, Ind., 1942-43; news dir. Sta. WHAS, Louisville, 1943-46; pub. relations dir. Farnsworth TV and Radio Corp., Ft. Wayne, 1946-48; editor news bur. Ind. U., Bloomington, 1948-52; pub. relations dir. Lenkurt Electric Co., San Carlos, Calif., 1952-60; pres. and chief exec. officer Am. Electronics Assn. (formerly Western Electronic Mfrs. Assn.), Palo Alto, Calif., 1960-85, also vice chmn., bd. dirs., cons.; bd. dirs. VLSI Tech. Inc., Winkler McManus, Micropolis Corp.; mem. adv. bd. Export-Import Bank of U.S., 1985—; bd. govs. El Camino Hosp. Found., 1986—. Bd. dirs. San Mateo County Devel. Assn., 1953-54, Golden Gate chpt. ARC, 1959-60, v.p. Sequoia chpt., 1958-60; v.p., dir. Sequoia YMCA, 1953-60; pres., bd. dirs. San Carlos C. of C., 1956; bd. dirs. Urban Coalition, 1970-73; mem. adv. bd. Leavey Sch. Bus. and Adminstrn., Santa Clara U., 1984—. Recipient Medal of Achievement, Am. Electronics Assn., 1985, Distinguished Alumni Service award Ind. U., 1987. Mem. Am. Soc. Assn. Execs. (dir. 1982-84, chartered assn. exec., Key award 1986), Pub. Relations Soc. Am., Armed Forces Communications and Electronics Assn., Am. Mgmt. Assn., Ind. U. Alumni Assn. (Disting. Alumni Service award 1987), Sigma Delta Chi, Sigma Alpha Epsilon. Republican. Presbyterian. Home: 26350 Espenanza Dr Los Altos Hills CA 94022 Office: Am Electronics Assn 3000 Sand Hill Rd Bldg 1 Bldg 1 Suite 120 Menlo Park CA 94025

FERRIGNO, DANIEL JOSEPH, JR., internist, health care corporation executive; b. Bronx, N.Y., Jan. 23, 1933; s. Daniel J. and Serena (Natarelli) F.; m. Patricia Bettencourt, Feb. 14, 1975; children: Shireen, Janine. AB, NYU, 1954; MD, SUNY, Downstate Bronx, 1960. Intern Bklyn. VA Hosp., 1961-62; resident in internal medicine Bklyn. Jewish Hosp., 1962-64; gen. practice internal medicine Sacramento, Calif., 1966—; med. dir. CAREUnit (adult and adolescent), Starting Point Adolescent, Smokenders Internat., Sacramento; assoc. corp. med. dir. CompCare, Irvine; assoc. clin. prof. med., U. Calif. Med. Sch., Davis, 1975—. Bd. advisors Mercy Hosp. Found., Sacramento, 1975—. Served to capt. USAF, 1964-66. Mem. AMA, Calif. Med. Assn., Am. Soc. Internal Medicine, AMA for Alcoholism and Other Drug Dependencies, Nat. Council Alcoholism. Republican. Avocations: flying, photography, snow and water skiing. Home: Box 178 Clarksburg CA 95612

FERRIN, ALLAN HOGATE, architect; b. N.Y.C., Oct. 24, 1951; s. Allan Wheeler and Barbara (Hogate) F.; m. Barbara Lorayne Weaver, May 1, 1976; children: Leigh, Ellen. Student, Princeton U., 1969-72; BA in Chinese, U. Wis., 1973; MArch, U. N.Mex., 1975. Registered architect, Wash., Fla. Draftsman Amrep. Corp., Albuquerque, 1975-76, Mitchell Assocs., Albuquerque, 1976-77; architect Jorge del la Torre, Albuquerque, 1977-78, John Graham Co., Seattle, 1978-79; project dir. Charles Kober Assocs., Seattle, 1979-85; ptnr. Carlson/Ferrin Assocs., Seattle, 1985—. Bd. dirs. Gainsborough Condominium Assn., Seattle, 1986—. Mem. AIA, Urban Land Inst., Internat. Council Shopping Ctrs. Office: Carlson Ferrin Architects 1928 Pike Place Market Seattle WA 98101

FERRIS, CLIFFORD DURAS, electrical engineer, bioengineer, educator; b. Phila., Nov. 19, 1935; s. Raymond Henry and Edythe (Fisher) F. BSEE, U. Pa., 1957, MSEE, 1958; DSc, George Wash. U., 1962. Registered profl. engr., Wyo. Systems analyst Melpar Inc., Falls Church, Va., 1959; from instr. to assoc. prof. elec. engring. George Wash. U., Washington, 1959-63; assoc. prof. Drexel U., Phila., 1963-64, U. Md., College Park, 1964-68; prof., dir. bioengring. U. Wyo., Laramie, 1968—; cons., vis. scientist Armed Forces Inst. Pathology, Washington, 1961-68, Capitol Radio Engring. Inst., Washington, 1960-69; bd. dirs. Rocky Mountain Bioengring. Symposium Inc., Denver. Author: Linear Network Analysis, 1962, Introduction to Bioelectrodes, 1974, Introduction to Bioinstrumentation, 1978, Guide to Medical Laboratory Instruments, 1980; author/editor (with others) Butterflies of the Rocky Mountain States, 1980; contbr. numerous articles to profl. jours. Indsl. grantee bioengring. research, 1959—. Fellow AAAS; mem. IEEE (sr.), N.Y. Acad. Scis., Lepidopterists' Soc. (pres. 1985-86), Sigma Xi. Home: PO Box 3351 U Station Laramie WY 82071 Office: U Wyo PO Box 3295 Univ Station Laramie WY 82071

FERRIS, EVELYN SCOTT, lawyer; b. Detroit, d. Ross Ansel and Irene Mabel (Bowser) Nafus; m. Roy Shorey Ferris, May 21, 1969 (div. Sept. 1982); children—Judith Ilene, Roy Sidney, Lorene Marjorie. J.D., Willamette U., 1961. Bar: Oreg. 1962, Fed. Dist. Ct. 1962. Law clk. Oreg. Tax Ct., Salem, 1961-62; dep. dist. atty. Marion County, Salem, 1962-65; judge Mcpl. Ct., Stayton, Oreg., 1965-76; ptnr. Brand, Lee, Ferris & Embick, Salem, 1965-82; chmn. Oreg. Workers' Compensation Bd., Salem, 1982—. Bd. dirs. Friends of Deepwood, Salem, 1979-82, Salem City Club, 1972-75; bd. dirs. Marion County Civil Service Commn., 1970-75; com. mem. Polk County Hist. Commn., Dallas, Oreg., 1976-79; mem. Oreg. legis. com. Bus. Climate, 1967-69, Govs. Task Force on Liability, 1986. Recipient Outstanding Hist. Restoration of Comml. Property award Marion County Hist. Soc., 1982. Mem. Oreg. Mcpl. Judges Assn. (pres. 1967-69), ABA, Altrusa, Internat., Mary Leonard Law Soc., Phi Delta Delta. Republican. Episcopalian. Club: Capitol (Salem) (pres. 1977-79). Home: 747 Church St SE Salem OR 97301 Office: Oreg Workers' Compensation Bd 480 Church St SE Salem OR 97310

FERRIS, HARRY, JR., state government official, administrator; b. Muncie, Ill., July 22, 1925; s. Harry and Mary Gray (Young) F.; m. Dorothy Jean Weldon, May 30, 1947; children—Diana Ferris Wilson, Randall. Student Ill. State U., 1944-45, U. Ill., 1945-46; B.S. in Edn., Ill. State U., 1949, postgrad., 1948-49. Clk., U.S. Postal Service, Normal, Ill., 1947-55; asst. actuary State Farm Ins. Co., Bloomington, Ill., 1955-62; claims adjuster State Comprehensive Ins. Fund, Denver, 1962-67, sr. claims adjuster, 1967-75; claims program mgr. Div. of Labor, Denver, 1975—. Editor: Office Procedures, 1976, 84; Workers Comprehension Act, 1976—. Served with USN, 1944-46. Mem. Ins. Inst. Am. Republican. Episcopalian. Clubs: Shrine Clowns (sec. 1970-71), Shrine Keystone Kops (sec.-treas. 1983-85). Home: 6715 S Marion Circle E Littleton CO 80122 Office: Div of Labor 1313 Sherman St Denver CO 80203

FERRIS, ROBERT CLARKE, chemical consultant; b. Vancouver, B.C., Can., Dec. 28, 1919; came to U.S., 1920; s. Robert Chester and Dora Belle (Clarke) F.; m. Elizabeth Irene Lucas, June 19, 1941 (div. Nov. 1965); children: John Mark, Robert Dana; m. Alma Marie Blanchard, Dec. 10, 1965. BSc, U. Wash., 1944; MS, Northwestern U., 1947; PhD, U. Utah, 1949. Pres. Chem. Lab. Products, Downey, Calif., 1959-64; mgr. comml. devel. Monsanto Co., St. Louis, 1964-67; dir. materials mgmt. Stepan Chem. Co., Northfield, Ill., 1967-74; v.p. chem. ops. Sealed Air Corp., Danbury, Conn., 1974-85; cons. Vista, Calif., 1985—. Patentee in field; contbr. articles to profl. jours. Mem. Nat. Spa and Pool Assn. (bd. dirs. 1963-66), Sigma Xi. Republican. Lutheran. Club: Vista Valley Country. Avocation: golf. Home and Office: 2215 Tierra Verde Rd Vista CA 92084

FERRIS, TIMOTHY (THOMAS), journalist, educator, writer; b. Miami, Fla., Aug. 29, 1944; s. Thomas Addis and Jean (Baird) Ferris; m. Carolyn Dinner Zecca, Apr. 20, 1985; 1 child, Patrick Thomas. BS, Northwestern U., 1966, postgrad.; postgrad., Rutgers U. Reporter UPI, N.Y.C., 1967-69, N.Y. Post newspaper, N.Y.C., 1969-71; bur. chief, N.Y. div. Rolling Stone mag., 1971-73; prof. English Bklyn. Coll., N.Y.C., 1974-81; prof. U. So. Calif., Los Angeles, 1984-86; prof. grad. sch. journalism U. Calif., Berkeley, 1986—; commentator Nat. Pub. Radio, 1981-85. Author: The Red Limit, 1977, Galaxies, 1980, SpaceShots, 1984; author and host (TV special) The Creation of the Universe, 1985. Semifinalist Journalist in Space Project NASA, 1986; recipient Sci. Writing awards AAAS and Westinghouse Corp., 1983, 86, Dorothea Klumpke-Roberts prize Astron. Soc. Pacific, 1986, prize Am. Inst. Physics, 1978; Guggenheim fellow 1986, 87. Fellow Brit. Interplanetary Soc.; mem. PEN, The Author's Guild. Democrat. Producer phonograph record, artifact of world cultures launched aboard spacecraft Voyager from Kennedy Space Ctr., 1977. Office: 525 Brannan St #309 San Francisco CA 94107

FERRIS, YVONNE MARIE, manufacturing company executive, statistician; b. East St. Louis, Ill., June 6, 1934; d. Clarence Raymond and Frankye Elizabeth (Bradberry) Clark; m. Livingston Polk Ferris II, July 5, 1967. BS, Iowa State U., 1956; postgrad. Rochester Inst. Tech., 1962, U. Colo., 1964-66. Statistician, Rockwell Internat., Golden, Colo., 1956-63, sr. statistician, 1963-73, mgr. stats. lab., 1973-75, mgr. stats. and nuclear material control, 1975-77, mgr. stats. and systems analysis, 1977-79; group leader safeguards IAEA, Vienna, Austria, 1977-79; chmn. Measurement Control Task Force; mem. speakers bur.; chmn. Standard N15.46, Measurement Control. com. Am. Nat. Standards Inst. Counselor Rocky Flats Personal Assistance Program; mem. Expts. in Friendship; active local programs emotionally disturbed and mentally retarded adults. Recipient Cost Improvement Suggestion awards Rockwell Internat., 1971-73, named Engr. of Yr., 1982. Mem. Inst. Nuclear Materials Mgmt. (chmn., cert. safeguards specialist), Am. Statis. Assn. (adv. com. nuclear regulatory research), Am. Soc. Quality Control, Nat. Mgmt. Assn., LWV, Altrusa Internat. (past pres.). Contbr. articles to profl. jours. Office: Rockwell Internat PO Box 464 Golden CO 80401

FERTIG, TED BRIAN O'DAY, producer, public relations and assn. exec.; b. Miami, May 18, 1937; s. Peter John and Frances Marie (Aswell) F.; A.B., 1960; M.B.A., 1969. Mem. profl. staff Congress U.S., Washington, 1965; dir. mem. relations Nat. Bellas Hess, Inc., Kansas City, 1963-69; mgr. employment/manpower planning Capitol Industries, Inc., 1969-70; pres. Mgmt. Cons. Group, Hollywood, Calif., 1970—, Fertig, Toler & Dumond, Hollywood, 1973; sr. partner Nascency Prodns., Hollywood and Sacramento, 1971—; exec. dir. Soc. Calif. Accts., 1974-83, Ednl. Found., Inc., 1975-80. Pres., Hollywood Community Concert Assn., 1971-72; exec. dir. Hollywood Walk of Fame, 1971-74; sec.-treas. Save the Sign, 1972-73; producer, Santa Claus Lane Parade of Stars, Hollywood, 1971-73; dir. Old Eagle Theatre, Sacramento, Sacramento Film Festival. Trustee, finance chmn. Los Angeles Free Clinics, 1970-71; mem. Calif. Commn. on Personal Privacy. Served with AUS, 1960-62. Cert. assn. exec. Mem. Pub. Relations Soc. Am., Am. C. of C. Execs., Am. Soc. Assn. Execs., Sacramento Soc. Assn. Execs. (pres. 1980). Author: A Family Night to Remember, 1971; Los Ninos Cantores de Mendoza, 1972; (with Paul Yoder) Salute to Milwaukee, 1965. Home: 49 Graham Terr, London SW1W, England Office: 401 Watt Ave Sacramento CA 95825 Office: 1850 N Whitley Los Angeles CA 90028 Office: Honolulu HI Office: London England Office: Sylvania OH

FERY, JOHN BRUCE, forest products company executive; b. Bellingham, Wash., Feb. 16, 1930; s. Carl Salvatore and Margaret Emily (Hauck) F.; m. Delores Lorraine Carlo, Aug. 22, 1953; children: John Brent, Bruce Todd, Michael Nicholas. BA, U. Wash., 1953; MBA, Stanford U., 1955; D of Law, Gonzaga U., 1982, D of Law (hon.), 1982; D of Nat. Resources (hon.), U. Idaho, 1983. Asst. to pres. Western Kraft Corp., 1955-56; prodn. mgr. 1956-57; with Boise Cascade Corp., Idaho, 1957—, pres., chief exec. officer, 1972-78, chmn. bd., chief exec. officer, 1978—; bd. dirs. Albertsons, Inc., Hewlett-Packard Co., The Moore Fin. Group, Inc., Nat. Parks Found., Union Pacific Corp.; mem. adv. council Chase Internat.; grad. mem. Bus. Council, mem. policy com.; sr. mem. Conf. Bd. Mem. adv. council Sch. Bus., Stanford U. Served with USN, 1950-51. Recipient Ernest Arbuckle award Sch. Bus. Stanford U., 1980; named Most Outstanding Chief Exec. Officer Fin. World, 1977, 78, 79, 80. Mem. Am. Paper Inst. (bd. dirs., past chmn., mem. exec. com.), Bus. Roundtable (policy com.). Clubs: Arid, Hillcrest Country, Link's, Arlington. Office: Boise Cascade Corp 1 Jefferson Sq Boise ID 83728

FESHBACH, NORMA DEITCH, education educator, department chairman; b. N.Y.C., Sept. 5, 1926; m. Seymour Feshbach; children: Jonathan Stephan, Laura Elizabeth, Andrew David. BS in Psychology, CCNY, 1947, MS in Ednl. Psychology, 1949; PhD in Clin. Psychology, U. Pa., 1956. Diplomate Am. Bd. Prof. Psychology; cert. in clin. psychology, Phila.; lic. clin. and ednl. psychologist, Calif. Tchr. Betsy Ross Nursery Sch., Yale U., 1947-48; clin. psychologist Yale U. Med. Sch., 1948; teaching asst. dept. psychology Yale U., 1948-51; research asst. human resources research office George Washington U., Washington, 1951-52; psychology intern Phila. Gen. Hosp., 1955-56; research assoc. dept. psychology U. Pa., 1959-61; research assoc. Inst. Behavioral Sci. U. Colo., 1963-64; assoc. research psychologist dept. psychology UCLA, 1964-65; clin. psychologist II UCLA Neuropsychiat. Inst., 1965; prof. Grad. Sch. Edn. UCLA, 1965—, prof. psychology dept., 1975—, chmn. dept. edn., 1985—; lectr. Jr. Coll. Phys. Therapy, New Haven, Conn., 1948-49, dept. psychology, U. Pa., 1956-57, UCLA Neuropsychiat. Inst., Calif. Dept. Mental Hygiene, Los Angeles, 1966-69; vis. asst. prof. Stanford U. dept. psychology, 1961-62, U. Calif. Berkeley, 1962-63; vis. scholar dept. exptl. psychology Oxford U., 1980-81; co-prin. investigator various projects and programs; co-prin. dir. and investigator NIMH Tng. Program in Applied Human Devel., 1986-91; clin. and research cons. Youth Services, Inc., Phila., 1955-61; also cons. various media orgns.; head program in Early Childhood and Devel. Studies, 1968-80; dir. NIMH Tng. Prog. in Early Childhood and Devel. Studies, 1972-82; prog. dir. Ctr. for Study of Evaluation, UCLA Grad. Sch. Edn., 1966-69; co-dir. UCLA Bush Found. Tng. Prog. in Child Devel. and Social Policy, 1978-82; chair grad. faculty UCLA Grad. Sch. Edn., 1979-80. Editorial cons., mem. editorial bd. psychology and ednl. research revs., contbr. numerous articles on child psychology to profl. jours. Mem. adv. council of Women's Clinic, Los Angeles, 1974-76; mem. adv. bd. Nat. Com. to Abolish Corporal Punishment in Schs., 1972-80, Nat. Ctr. for Study of Corporal Punishment and Alternatives in the Schs., 1976—; mem. profl. adv. com. on Child Care, Los Angeles Unified Sch. Dist., 1978-80; trustee EVAN-G Com. to End Violence Against the Next Generation, 1972-80; exec. bd. Internat. Soc. for Research in Agression, 1982-84. Recipient James McKeen Cattell Fund Sabbatical award, 1980, 81, Townsend Harris Medal, Disting. Alumnus award CCNY, 1982, Disting. Sci. Achievement in Psychology award Calif. Psychol. Assn., 1983; named Faculty Mem. Woman of Yr. Nat. Acad. Profl. Psychologists, Los Angeles, 1973; U.S. Pub. Health Tng. Fellow, 1953-56; research grantee NIMH, 1972-77 (co-principal with D. Stipek), 77-82, 1986—, Hilton Found., 1985-86, Spencer Found. 1984-85; Child Help, USA, 1982-84 (co-principal with C. Howes), UCLA Acad. Senate, 1981—, Bush Found., 1978-83, 79-80, 80-81, 81-82, 82-83 (co-dir. with J.I. Goodlad), Adminstrn. for Children, Youth and Families, 1981-82 (co-dir. with J.I. Goodlad), NSF, 1976-77, 77-78, 78-80 (co-prin. with S. Feshbach), Com. on Internat. and Comparative Studies, 1973-74, 77-78. Fellow Am. Psychol. Assn. (officer var. coms.); mem. Assn. Advancement Psychology, AAAS, AAUP, Am. Bd. Profl. Psychologists, Am. Ednl. Research Assn., Calif. Assn. for Edn. Young Children, Nat. Assn for Edn. Young Children, Internat. Assn. Applied Psychology, Internat. Soc. for Research on Aggression, Internat. Soc. Study of Behavioral Devel., Internat. Soc. Prevention Child Abuse and Neglect, Nat. Register of Health Services Providers in Psychology, Soc. for Research in Child Devel., Western Psychol. Assn.; Sigma Xi, Delta Phi Upsilon.

FESHBACH, SEYMOUR, psychology educator; b. N.Y.C., June 21, 1925; s. Joseph and Fannie (Katzman) F.; m. Norma Deitch, Aug. 16, 1947; children: Jonathan, Laura, Andrew. B.S., Coll. City N.Y., 1947; M.A., Yale U., 1948, Ph.D., 1951. Project dir. Army Attitude Assessment Br., 1951-52; from asst. prof. to asso. prof. U. Pa., Phila., 1952-63; prof. U. Colo., Boulder, 1963-64; prof. psychology U. Calif., Los Angeles, 1964—; chmn. dept. U. Calif., 1977-83; dir. Fernald Sch., 1964-73; cons. CBS, Ednl. TV, 1972; vis. fellow Wolfson Coll., Oxford (Eng.) U., 1980-81. Author: Television and Aggression, 1970, Psychology, An Introduction, 1977; also others; co-author: Personality, 1982, Learning to Care, 1983; editor: Aggression and Behavior Change: Biological and Social Processes, 1979; cons. editor: Jour. Abnormal Psychology, 1973—; Contbr. chpts. to books, articles to profl. jours. Served to 1st lt., inf. AUS, 1943-46, PTO. Recipient Ward medal Coll. City N.Y., 1947, Townsend Harris medal, Distinguished Alumnus award, 1972, Fellowship award Found. Fund Advancement of Psychiatry, 1980-81, Disting. Scientist award Calif. Psychol. Assn., 1983; NIMH grantee; NSF grantee. Fellow Am. Psychol. Assn.; mem. Western Psychol. Assn. (pres. 1976-77), AAAS, Soc. for Study of Social Issues, Soc. for Research in Child Devel., Internat. Soc. for Applied Psychology, Internat. Soc. for Study of Aggression (pres. 1984-86), Internat. Soc. for Study of Behavior Devel., ACLU, Phi Beta Kappa. Democrat. Jewish. Home: 743 Hanley Ave Los Angeles CA 90049 Office: Dept Psychology U Calif 405 Hilgard Ave Los Angeles CA 90024

FETTER, WILLIAM ALLAN, computer graphics executive; b. Independence, Mo., Mar. 14, 1928; s. William Herbert and Edna Katherine (Werner) F.; m. Darlene Glea Wyss, Aug. 20, 1950 (div. 1963); 1 child, William Arnold (dec.); m. Barbara Ann Shaffer, Dec. 21, 1963; children: Brant Shaffer, Elena Katherine (twins). Student, Kansas City Jr. Coll., 1945-46, Kansas City U., 1948-49; BFA, U. Ill., 1952. Supr. computer graphics The Boeing Co., Seattle and Wichita, Kans., 1959-69; v.p. Graphcomp. Scis., Newport, Calif., 1969-70; chair design dept., lectr. So. Ill. U., Carbondale, 1970-77; pres. So. Ill. Research Ops. and Corp. Office, Bellevue, Wash., 1977—, also bd. dirs.; owner Office for Research In Graphics and Indsl. Design, Bellevue, 1982—. Author: (book monograph) Human figures for Designers by Computer, 1983, Computer Graphics in Communication, 1964; author (TV program) Computer Graphics, The Accurate Eye, 1975; shows include Mus. Modern Art, N.Y.C., 1976; patentee in field. Bd. dirs. Com. on Handicapped, Park Forest, Ill., 1957-58, Master Resources Council Internat., Seattle, 1980—; mem. UNESCO Tact Task Force, Washington, 1975-85. Served with U.S. Army, 1946-48. Recipient Cert. Merit Internat. Graphic Design, 1967, Letter Commendation USAF, Boeing Airplane Co., 1962, Bronze Medal Nat. Soc. Art Dirs., 1963. Fellow AIAA (assoc.); mem. Internat. Design Conf. (presenter 1976, 78), Soc. Info. Display, Master Resources Council Internat., Indsl. Designers Soc. Am., N.W. Human Factors Soc., Mus. Modern Art Club, Sports Car Club Am., Am. Lancia Club.

FETZ, MARGOT, management consultant; b. Evanston, Ill., Nov. 10, 1935; d. Wesley and Mary (Slater) Hardenbergh; m. James Lawrence Talbot, Nov. 15, 1957 (div. Dec. 1981); children: Katrin, Gretchen, Susan. AB, U. Calif., Berkeley, 1958; MBA, Seattle U., 1986. Cert. systems profl. Dept. mgr. U. Mont. Library, Missoula, 1973-76; exec. asst. Soc. Photo-optical Instrumentation Engrs., Bellingham, Wash., 1977-78; cons. The Organizer, various cities, Wash., 1979-81; analyst Wash. Mut. Savs. Bank, Seattle, 1981-82; info. systems analyst Alpac Corp., Seattle, 1982-85; prin. Focus Cons., Seattle, 1985—. Author: Archival Inventory Washington State Department Civil Defense, 1979; (bibliography) Bibliography of Sir Douglas Mawson, 1958. Chmn. County Parks Feasibility Com., Missoula, 1973-74; vice chmn. drafting com. Missoula Local Govt. Study Commn., 1974-76; bd. dirs. Musica Viva Internat., Bellingham, 1979-81. Recipient Wall Street Jour. award, 1985. Mem. Assn. Records Mgrs. and Adminstrs. (v.p. publicity 1982-83), Assn. Systems Mgt. (chmn. awards 1984—, chmn. membership com. 1985-86, sec. 1986—), Office System Research Assn., Nat. Assn. Female Execs., Women's Network, Seattle U. MBA Assn., Greater Seattle C. of C. Club: City (Seattle). Avocations: hiking, music, art, drama.

FETZER, JOHN CHARLES, research chemist; b. Leesville, La., Apr. 19, 1953; s. Jake Magness and Nina (Takeuchi) F.; m. Lauren Noel Cancilla, May 19, 1984. BS, U. Ark., 1976; PhD, U. Ga., 1980. Research chemist Chevron Research Co., Richmond, Calif., 1980—; mem. adv. bd. Lab Con '84, San Mateo, Calif., 1984. Reviewer Jour. Analytical Chemistry, 1983—; contbr. articles to profl. jours. Henry Richmond fellow U. Ga., 1977. Mem. Am. Chem. Soc. Office: Chevron Research Co PO Box 1627 Richmond CA 94802

FEUERSTEIN, GARY RAY, mechanical and civil engineer; b. Pocatello, Idaho, June 10, 1950; s. Charles F. and Florence (Manfredo) F.; m. Karen Louise Fletcher, June 21, 1971. BSME, Oreg. State U., 1972. Registered mech. and civil engr., Calif., Colo., Idaho, La., Oreg., S.Dak., Tex., Utah, Wash.,. Engr. Gordon Assocs., Corvallis, Oreg., 1976-77; facilities mgr. Benton County, Corvallis, 1977-80; pres. Endex Engring. Inc., Corvallis, 1980—. Mem. Benton County Hist. Resources Commn., Corvallis, 1981—. Mem. ASHRAE, ASME (chmn. local history and heritage com. 1984—), Nat. Trust Hist. Preservation. Office: Endex Engring Inc 813 SW Western Blvd Corvallis OR 97333

FEUERSTEIN, MARCY BERRY, dental health service organization executive; b. Wellsville, N.Y., June 18, 1950; d. Marshall Newton and Miriam May (Lingle) Jones; m. Ronald Glenn Berry, Aug. 7, 1967 (div.) 1 dau., Angelia Lynn; m. Richard Alan Feuerstein, Jan. 8, 1984. Student Chaffey Jr. Coll., Alta Loma, Calif. Jr. clk. N.Y. Life Ins., Los Angeles, 1970-73; jr. acct. FMC Corp., Pomona, Calif., 1973-78; sec. Gen. Med. Ctrs., Anaheim, Calif., 1978-79, service rep., 1979-80; dir. mktg. services Protective Health Providers, San Diego, 1980-81, Dental Health Services, Long Beach, Calif., 1981—; owner Mar-Rich Enterprises, 1985—. Mem. Nat. Assn. Female Execs. Democrat. Home: 9582 Golden St Alta Loma CA 91701 Office: Mar-Rich Enterprises 3833 Atlantic Ave Long Beach CA 90807-3505

FEVOLD, H(ARRY) RICHARD, biochemist; b. Madison, Wis., Jan. 28, 1935; s. Harry Leonard and Agnes Beatrice (Molstad) F.; m. M(arjorie) Jeane Ashley, Aug. 3, 1958; children: Eric David, Karen Lynn, Steven Leonard. Student, St. Olaf Coll., 1952-53; BS, U. Mont., 1956; PhD, U. Utah, 1961. NIH postdoctoral fellow Uppsala U., Sweden, 1961-63; asst. prof. U. Mont., Missoula, 1963-66, assoc. prof., 1966-70, prof., 1971—; project asst. U. Wis., Madison, 1970-71. Author 30 research papers in field. Chmn. service com. Immanuel Luth. Ch., Missoula, 1984-87. Recipient NIH Research Career Devel. award U. Mont., 1965-70; research grantee NIH, 1964-77, NSF, 1964-69. Mem. Am. Chem. Soc., Endocrine Soc., Am. Soc. Biol. Chemists, Fedn. Am. Socs. for Exptl. Biology, AAAS. Avocations: skiing, hiking, hunting, fishing, photography. Home: 3615 Creekwood Rd Missoula MT 59802 Office: Chemistry Dept Univ Mont Missoula MT 59812

FEWELL, ANNE, artist, writer; b. Little Rock, Mar. 26, 1939; d. R.B. and Willimette (Bland) Fewell. B.A., Kansas City Art Inst., 1962. Exhibited in group shows: Anaheim (Calif.) Conv. Ctr., 1976, Calif. Mus. Sci. and Industry, 1979, Los Angeles Celebrity Ctr., 1979, Contemporary Showcase,

Los Angeles, 1979; represented in numerous pvt. collections; author/illustrator: The First Spirit of Christmas as Told by Merrywinkle, 1981. Winner, Ann. Art. Competition, Ark., 1953, 54, W.Va., 1970; Eyes and Ears Found. award, Los Angeles, 1979.

FEYNMAN, RICHARD PHILLIPS, physicist; b. N.Y.C., May 11, 1918; s. Melville Arthur and Lucille (Phillips) F. B.S., Mass. Inst. Tech., 1939; Ph.D., Princeton, 1942. Staff atomic bomb project Princeton, 1942-43, Los Alamos, 1943-45; assoc. prof. theoretical physics Cornell U., 1945-50; prof. theoretical physics Calif. Inst. Tech., 1950—; mem. Presdl. Commn. on Space Shuttle Challenger, 1986. Author: Quantum Electrodynamics, Theory of Fundamental Processes, Character of Physical Law, Statistical Mechanics, QED: The Strange Theory of Light and Matter, 1985, Surely You're Joking, Mr. Feynman, 1985; contbr. theory of quantum electrodynamics, beta decay and liquid helium. Recipient Einstein award, 1954; Nobel prize in physics, 1965; Oersted medal, 1972; Niels Bohr Internat. Gold medal, 1973. Mem. Am. Phys. Soc., AAAS, Royal Soc. (fgn. mem.), Pi Lambda Phi. Address: Physics Dept Calif Inst of Tech Pasadena CA 91125 *

FIALER, PHILIP ANTHONY, research scientist, electronics company executive; b. San Francisco, Nov. 6, 1938; s. Harry A. and Elyse E. (Palin) F.; m. Dianne M. Hater, Mar. 4, 1967 (div. 1982); children: Michele S., Melissa L.; m. Sue Eble, Dec. 14, 1985; 1 stepdaughter, Shannon T. Leinbach. BS, Stanford U., 1960, MS, 1964, PhD, 1970. Engr. Lockheed Corp., Sunnyvale, Calif., 1961-67; research assoc. Stanford (Calif.) U., 1967-70; dep. lab. dir., staff scientist SRI Internat., Menlo Park, Calif., 1970—; pres. Mirage Systems, Sunnyvale, Calif., 1984—; research scientist in ionospheric radiosci. and electromagnetic scattering. Contbr. articles to profl. jours. Mem. IEEE. Democrat. Episcopalian. Avocations: skiing, sailing, tennis. Home: 742 Torreya Ct Palo Alto CA 94303 Office: Mirage Systems 537 Lakeside Dr Sunnyvale CA 94086

FIALKOW, PHILIP JACK, medical educator; b. N.Y.C., Aug. 20, 1934; s. Aaron and Sarah (Ratner) F.; m. Helen C. Dimitrakis, June 14, 1960; children: Michael, Deborah. B.A., U. Pa., 1956; M.D., Tufts U., 1960. Diplomate: Am. Bd. Internal Medicine, Am. Bd. Med. Genetics. Intern U. Calif., San Francisco, 1960-61, resident, 1961-62; resident U. Wash., Seattle, 1962-63, instr. medicine, 1965-66, asst. prof., 1966-69, assoc. prof., 1969-73, prof. medicine, 1973—, chmn. dept. medicine, 1980—; chief med. service Seattle VA Ctr., 1974-81; physician-in-chief Univ. Hosp., Seattle, 1980—; attending physicians Harborview Med. Ctr., Seattle, 1965—; cons. Children's Orthopedic Hosp., Seattle, 1964—. Contbr. articles to profl. jours. Trustee Fred Hutchinson Cancer Research Ctr., Seattle, 1982—. NIH fellow, 1963-65; NIH grantee, 1965—. Fellow ACP; mem. Am. Soc. Clin. Investigation, Assn. Am. Physicians, Assn. Profs. Medicine, Am. Soc. Human Genetics (dir. 1974-77), Alpha Omega Alpha. Office: U Wash Dept Medicine RG 20 Seattle WA 98195

FICK, RONALD GERALD, bank executive; b. San Mateo, Calif., May 25, 1940; s. Harold Albert and Grace (Bovet) F.; m. Valerie Louise Peterson, Aug. 11, 1962; children: Heather Borel, David Bovet, Bradley Borel. BA, San Jose State U., 1963; student, U. Wash. Pacific Coast Banking Sch., 1972-74. V.p., trust officer Wells Fargo Bank, San Francisco, 1962-79; exec. v.p., sr. trust officer, chief fin. officer Borel Bank and Trust Co., San Mateo, 1979—; bd. dirs. Custom Travel Cons. Woodside, Calif., 1982—, New Idria Bank, Firebaugh, Calif., 1985—. Editor: San Francisco is No More, 1963. Pres. San Mateo City Sch. Dist. Bd. Edn., 1971-72. Mem. No. Calif. Trust Co. Assn. (pres. 1985). Republican. Avocations: fly fishing, hunting, collecting mil. antiques. Home: 96 Parkwood Dr Atherton CA 94025 Office: Borel Bank & Trust Co 35 Bovet Rd San Mateo CA 94402

FICKERSON, BERT FREDRICK, chemistry educator; b. Los Angeles, Dec. 20, 1938; s. Bert Henry and Dorothy (Lyden) F.; m. Mary Bernick, July 28, 1969; children: James, Scott. BS, UCLA, 1962, MS, 1965. Instr. chemistry Marshall High Sch., Los Angeles, 1965-70, Ventura (Calif.) Coll., 1970—; life guard Los Angeles County, 1957—; water polo coach Ventura Coll., 1974-85, Buena High Sch., 1985—. Mem. Am. Chem. Soc., Faculty Assn. Calif. Community Colls. Republican. Presbyterian. Avocations: swimming, sailing, body surfing. Home: 2911 Seaview Ave Ventura CA 93001 Office: Ventura Coll 4667 Telegraph Ventura CA 93001

FICKLIN, VICKIE J., social worker; b. Wynnewood, Okla., Sept. 8, 1955; d. Jerry P. Ficklin and LaVona (Kinney) Burmeister. BA in Psychology suma cum laude, Cen. State U., 1978; MSW, U. Okla., 1980. Field rep. Okla. Assn. Retarded Citizens, Oklahoma City, 1980-81; dir. social services Bone and Joint Hosp., Oklahoma City, 1981-82; dir. sch. vol. services Oklahoma City Pub. Schs., 1982-84; home health social worker Family Health Program, Long Beach, Calif., 1985; mental health clinician SIerra Vista, Highland, Calif., 1985; med. social worker County Med. Ctr., San Bernardino, Calif., 1985—; bd. dirs. Generation Interaction for Today, Oklahoma City, 1982-84; mem. edn. com. Planned Parenthood, Oklahoma City, 1983-84. Author (slide presentation) Psychological Aspects of Nuclear Age, 1984. Mem. pub. affairs com. YWCA, Oklahoma City, 1983-84; mem. adv. council Passageway Battered Women's Shelter, Oklahoma City, 1983-84; mem. Okla. Women's Polit. Caucus, Oklahoma City, 1982-84. Mem. Nat. Assn. Social Workers (cert., bd. dirs. 1982-84), Calif. Assn. Hosp. Home Health Agys., NOW. Democrat. Mem. Ch. Religious Sci. Home: 104 W Olive #1 Redlands CA 92373

FIDLER, ROY SHERWIN, marketing professional; b. Bklyn., Aug. 10, 1929; s. Irving and Beatrice (Rubin) F.; m. Annette Bergman, Apr. 3, 1955 (div. 1975); children: Lisa, Matthew; m. Aileen B. Friedman, June 18, 1982. BA, Brown U., 1950. Promotion writer The N.Y. Times, N.Y.C., 1953-57, direct mktg. mgr., 1964-69; writer, group head J. Walter Thompson, N.Y.C., 1957-64; v.p., creative dir. Zipnick and Fidler, Inc., N.Y.C., 1970-71; pres. The Fidler Group, Inc., N.Y.C., 1971-82, Fidler Direct, Inc., San Francisco, 1982—; bd. dirs. Direct Mktg. Creative Guild, San Francisco. Served to sgt. U.S. Army, 1950-51. Mem. N.Y. Civil Liberties Union (coordinator 1964). Democrat. Jewish. Avocations: camping, hiking. Home: 1441 Vallejo St San Francisco CA 94109 Office: Fidler Direct Inc 466 Green St San Francisco CA 94133

FIEDLER, E. VICTORIA, psychotherapist, consultant; b. Urbana, Ill., Nov. 17, 1951; d. Fred E. and Judith Miriam (Joseph) F. BA in Social Sci., U. Wash., 1972; AAS in Recreation, Seattle Cen. Community Coll., 1975; MSW, Eastern Wash. U., 1983. Probation clin. psychotherapist Yakima (Wash.), 1982—; mental health cons. EPIC, Yakima, 1985—; chairperson Yakima County Juvenile Justice Adv. Com. Ednl. com. chmn. Women's Polit. Caucus, Yakima, 1984-86. James scholar U. Ill.-Urbana, 1968-69. Mem. Nat. Assn. Social Workers, Am. Acad. Cert. Social Workers. Jewish. Office: 720 Larson Bldg 6 S 2d St Yakima WA 98901

FIELD, GARY GEORGE, printing technology educator; b. Melbourne, Australia, Feb. 2, 1944; came to U.S., 1970; s. Ralph William and Maisie Maud (GIllam) F.; m. Mary Ann Ashcroft, May 24, 1981. Cert. in Printing, Melbourne Coll. of Printing and Graphic Arts, 1966; diploma in Printing Tech., Trent Polytech., Nottingham, Eng., 1970; MBA, U. Pitts., 1975. Camera dept. foreman Leigh-Mardon, Melbourne, 1965-67; printing technologist Mardon Packaging Internat., Bristol, Eng., 1968-70; supr. color and photo research Graphic Arts Tech. Found., Pitts., 1970-76; asst. prof. La Roche Coll., Pitts., 1977-81, Carnegie-Mellon U., Pitts., 1981-83; assoc. prof. Calif. Polytech. State U., San Luis Obispo, 1984—; cons. CBS Records, N.Y.C., 1980-83. Author: Color and Its Reproduction, 1987, (with others) Test Images for Printing, 1984; editor: Advances in Color Reproduction, 1973; contbr. articles to sci. jours. Scholar Bank of New South Wales, 1964, K.D. MacDougall Overseas, Melbourne Coll. of Printing, 1967-70; recipient Outstanding Apprentice award Victorian Apprenticeship Commn., 1963, Cert. Recognition Edn. Council of Graphic Arts Industry, 1987. Fellow Inst. Printing; mem. Tech. Assn. of Graphic Arts (bd. dirs. 1981-84, fellowship com. chmn. 1986—), Soc. for Imaging Sci. and Tech., Inter Soc. Color Council, Royal Photog. Soc. Anglican. Avocations: photography, travel. Home: 1229 Vista del Lago San Luis Obispo CA 93401 Office: Calif Polytech State U Graphic Communication Dept San Luis Obispo CA 93407

FIELD, REBECCA ANN, psychologist, educator; b. Denver, Dec. 18, 1934; d. Herbert P. White and Marjorie (Sharp) F.; m. Kenneth Gordon, Sept. 5, 1959; children—David B., Robert W. B.A., No. Colo. State U., 1957; M.A., Calif. Inst. Integral Studies, 1977, Ph.D., 1981. Camp counselor Girl Scouts U.S.A., Colorado Springs, Colo., 1955, Flint, Mich., 1956; tchr. Anchorage Pub. Schs., 1957-58, Markham (Ill.) Pub. Schs., 1959-65; sr. citizens coordinator West Valley Coll., Saratoga, Calif., 1977-78; psychol. counselor, Los Gatos, Calif., 1981-85; cons., lectr. in field. Chmn. bd. CONTACT of Santa Clara County; active Speakers Bur., Lupus Found., Child Advocacy Council. Recipient 1st prize Sri Aurobindo Centennial Essay Contest, 1973; Kern Found. grantee, 1979-81. Mem. Assn. Transpersonal Psychology, Am. Futurist Assn., Am. Soc. Tng. and Devel., San Jose C. of C., Alpha Psi Omega. Clubs: Toastmasters (pres., area gov. of yr. award), Rebekah. Contbr. articles to profl. jours. Address: 105 Vista del Campo Los Gatos CA 95030

FIELD, THOMAS WALTER, JR., supermarket chain executive; b. Alhambra, Calif., Nov. 2, 1933; s. Thomas Walter and Pietje (Slagveld) F.; m. Ruth Inez Oxley, Apr. 10, 1959; children: Julie, Sherry, Cynthia, Thomas Walter, III, James. Student, Stanford U., 1951-53. Vice pres. retail ops. Alpha Beta Co., La Habra, Calif., 1972-73, sr. v.p., 1973-75, exec. v.p., 1975-76, pres., chief exec. officer, 1976-81; pres. Am. Stores Co., 1981-85; pres., chief exec. officer McKesson Corp., San Francisco, 1986—, also chief operating officer, dir. Bd. dirs. La Habra Boys' Club. Mem. Calif. Retailers Assn. (dir.), Automobile Club So. Calif. (adv. bd.). Republican. Office: McKesson Corp One Post St San Francisco CA 94104 *

FIELDEN, C. FRANKLIN, III, educator; b. Gulfport, Miss., Aug. 4, 1946; s. C. Franklin and Georgia Freeman F.; children—Christopher Michaux (dec.), Robert Michaux, Jonathan Dutton. Student Claremont Men's Coll., 1964-65; A.B., Colo. Coll., 1970; M.S., George Peabody Coll. Tchrs., 1976, Ed.S., 1979. Tutor Proyecto El Guacio, San Sebastian, P.R., 1967-68; asst. tchr. GET-SET Project, Colorado Springs, Colo., 1969-70, co-tchr., 1970-75, asst. dir., 1972-75; tutor Early Childhood Edn. Project, Nashville, 1975-76; public policy intern Donner-Belmont Child Care Center, Nashville, 1976-77; asst. to urban minister Nashville Presbytery, 1977; intern to prin. Steele Elem. Sch., Colorado Springs, 1977-78, tchr., 1978-86; resource person for gifted students El Paso County Sch. Dist. #11, 1986—; lectr. Arapahoe Community Coll., Littleton, Colo., 1981-82; instr. Met. State Coll., Denver, 1981; cons. Jubail Human Resources Devel. Inst., Saudi Arabia, 1982. Mem. governing bd. GET-SET Project, 1969-79; mem. Nashville Children's Issues Task Force, 1976-77; mem. Tenn. United Meth. Task Force on Children and Youth, 1976-77; mem. ad hoc bd. trustees Tenn. United Meth. Agy. on Children and Youth, 1976-77; mem. So. Regional Edn. Bd. Task Force on Parent-Caregiver Relationships, 1976-77; mem. day care com. Colo. Commn. Children and their Families, 1981-82; mem. El Paso County Sch. Dist. #11 Staff Devel. Coordinating Council, 1982-84, Citizens' Goals Leadership Tng., 1986-87, Child Abuse Task Force, 4th Judicial Dist., 1986—. Recipient Arts/Bus./Edn. award, 1983; Innovative Teaching award, 1984; NIMH fellow, 1976. Mem. Assn. Supervision and Curriculum Devel., Nat. Assn. Edn. Young Children, Colo. Assn. Edn. Young Children (legis. com. 1979-84, governing bd. 1980-84, 85-86, exec. com. 1980-84, sec. 1980-84, research conf. chmn. 1982), Pikes Peak Assn. Edn. Young Children, Am. Film Inst., Colorado Springs Fine Arts Center, Huguenot Soc. Great Britain and Ireland, Nat. Trust Historic Preservation, Phi Delta Kappa. Presbyterian. Club: Country of Colo. Home: PO Box 7766 Colorado Springs CO 80933 Office: 900 E Buena Ventura Colorado Springs CO 80907

FIELDER, EVE PICARDY, research sociologist; b. Lakewood, N.J., Aug. 23, 1941; d. Harrison Thomas Fielder and Adele Theresa (Boglietti) Rawlins; m. Stephen Wein Levine, Aug. 29, 1959 (div. 1969). BA in Sociology, UCLA, 1983, MPH, 1985. Project dir. Facts Consol, Los Angeles, 1964-67, Haug Research Assocs., Los Angeles, 1967-71; research dir. Inst. for Social Sci. Research UCLA, 1971—; ptnr. R&E Research Assocs., Los Angeles, 1982—. Mem. Am. Pub. Health Assn., Am Assn. Pub. Opinion Research. Office: U Calif Inst Social Sci Research Los Angeles CA 90024

FIELDS, HOWARD LINCOLN, neurology and physiology professor; b. Chgo., Dec. 12, 1939; s. Charles and Mae (Pinkert) F.; m. Carol Margaret Felts, Dec. 31, 1966; children: Rima Tamar, Gabriel Charles. Research neurologist Walter Reed Research Inst., Washington, 1967-70; clin. fellow Harvard Med. Sch., Boston, 1970-72; asst. prof. U. Calif., San Francisco, 1973-78, assoc. prof., 1978-82, prof., 1982—; cons. NIH, Bethesda, Md., 1979-84, Inst. of Medicine, Nat. Acad. Scis., Washington, 1985-86; vis. fellow Clare Hall Coll., Cambridge, England, 1979. Editor: (book) Recent Advances in Pain Research and Therapy, 1985, Pain, Mechanisms and Management, 1987; contbr. 85 articles to profl. jours. Recipient Research Career Devel. award NIH. Mem. Internat. Assn. Study of Pain (program chmn. 1981-84), Am. Soc. Clin. Investigation, Am. Acad. Neurology, Am. Neurol. Assn., Soc. for Neurosci. Office: U Calif Dept Neurology M 794 San Francisco CA 94143

FIELDS, JAMES RALPH, lawyer, lobbyist, consultant; b. Los Angeles, Mar. 14, 1943; s. Paul Raymond Fields and Della Louise (Brabb) Klebe; m. Barbara Smith Knudson, May 18, 1985. BS in Bus. Adminstrn., U. Idaho, 1965, JD, 1973. Bar: Idaho 1973, U.S. Dist. Ct. Idaho 1973. Staff counsel U.S. Sen. James McClure, Washington, 1973-76; gen. counsel Idaho Assn. Commerce and Industry, Boise, 1976-83, v.p., gen. counsel, 1983-87; cons. Knudson-Fields Human Devel. Cons., Boise, 1985—. Organizer, pres. Idaho Liability Reform Coalition; mem. Gov.'s Adv. Com. on Workers' Compensation, Idaho, 1978—; pres. Idaho Liability Reform Coalition, 1986. Served to 1st lt. U.S. Army, 1966-71, Vietnam. Mem. ABA, Idaho Bar Assn., Am. Soc. Personnel Adminstrn., Human Resources Assn. Treasure Valley (bd. dirs. 1986). Republican. Baptist. Lodge: Kiwanis (pres. Boise chpt. 1985-86). Avocations: travel, outdoor activities, sports. Home: 1183 Wild Phlox Way Boise ID 83709

FIELDS, JERRY FRANCIS, safety and hazardous materials manager; b. Bloomington, Ill., Oct. 30, 1949; s. Robert F. and Isabella Fields; m. LaDonna C. Courtney, June 12, 1976. BS in Indsl. Tech., Ill. State U., 1975. Loss control rep. Country Cos. Ins., Bloomington, 1977-79, New Hampshire Ins., Springfield, Ill., 1979-80; ophthalmic technician Dr. Newman M.D., St. Louis, 1980-81; loss control rep. Home Ins., St. Louis, 1981-82, Mission Ins., Phoenix, 1983-84; safety specialist Wausau Ins., Phoenix, 1984-86; mgr. safety and hazardous materials M/A Com Omni Spectra, Tempe, Ariz., 1984—. Poster judge Glendale (Ariz.) Fire Dept., 1984-85. Mem. Am. Soc. Safety Engrs. (com. chairperson 1984-85), Nat. Fire Protection Assn. Republican. Avocations: scuba diving, boating. Home: 3313 W Malapai Dr Phoenix AZ 85051

FIELDS, JODY THOMPSON, speech-language pathologist; b. Daytona Beach, Fla., Feb. 17, 1958; d. Rhodes and Lois (Long) Thompson; m. Douglas Roy Fields, May 8, 1982. BS in Speech-Hearing Sci. magna cum laude, Phillips U., 1979; MA in Speech Pathology, U. Ill., 1980. Speech-lang. pathologist Drummond (Okla.) Elem. Sch., 1981, Community Speech and Hearing Ctr., Enid, Okla., 1981-82; asst. prof. U. No. Colo., Greeley, 1983-84; speech-lang. pathologist Highland Sch. Dist., Pierce, Colo., 1984—; pvt. practice speech pathologist Greeley, 1984—. Mem. Am. Speech-Lang. Hearing Assn. (cert.), Colo. Speech and Hearing Assn., League of Women Voters (chmn. memberships 1985—). Democrat. Mem. Disciples of Christ Ch. Avocations: aerobics, reading. Home: 1438 11th St Greeley CO 80631 Office: 1115 11th St Greeley CO 80631

FIELDS, JULIAN FRANK, JR., computer software and hardware consultant; b. Honea Path, S.C.; s. Julian F. Fields. BSEE and Computer Engring., Clemson U., 1980. Design engr. Harris Semiconductor Products, Melbourne, Fla., 1980-82; memory design engr. Nat. Semiconductor Corp., San Jose, Calif., 1982-83; gate array engr. Array Tech., San Jose, 1984-85; cons. computer software and hardware Sunnyvale, Calif., 1985—. Home and Office: 1331 S Wolfe Rd #68 Sunnyvale CA 94087-3625

FIELDS, LEE ARTHUR, manufacturing company executive; b. Greenwood, La., May 27, 1932; s. George and Mary (Birdsong) F.; student Long Beach City Coll., 1966-68; m. Velma Myles, Aug. 5, 1953 (div.); children: Patricia, Gwendolyn, Brenda, Geanell, Lee Arthur, Belinda, DeAndria, Leah Megan; m. 2d, Syvilla Armstrong Pettiford, May 4, 1982. Nurses aide VA, Shreveport, La., 1956-60; urol. asst. VA, Long Beach, Calif., 1960-75, hemodialysis technician, 1975-78; owner, mgr. craft products mfg. bus., Long Beach, 1979—; owner, dir. nursing facility for handicapped; owner, mgr. Bar-B-Que Restaurant, Long Beach; pvt. practice importer/exporter spl. gifts, Los Angeles. Active Nat. Republican Congressional Com., Norman Rockwell Mus. Soc., PTA, NAACP; mem. Rep. Presdl. Task Force. Served with U.S. Army, 1951-54. Decorated Purple Heart. Recipient cert. of recognition Nat. Rep. Congressional Com., 1980; various service awards VA. Mem. Nat. Fedn. Ind. Bus., Nat. Urol. Assn., Long Beach Area C. of C., Calhoun Collectors' Soc. Home: 2041 Caspian Ave Long Beach CA 90810 Office: 1819 W Anaheim St Long Beach CA 90813

FIELDS, NINA SHEPARD, clinical social worker; b. N.Y.C.; d. B. John Shepard and Gladys (Marshall) Salit; m. Maurice B. Fields; children: Abbie, Kenneth, Laura. BA, Roosevelt U., 1953; MSW, Case Western Reserve U., 1956; PhD, Calif. Inst. for Clin. Social Work, 1979. Pvt. practice clin. social work Sherman Oaks, Calif., 1960-84, Encino, Calif., 1985—; lectr. UCLA Extension div., 1979—; supr. cons. San Fernando Valley Child, 1979—; mem. adv. bd. San Fernando Valley Guidance Clinic, 1970—. Author: The Well-Seasoned Marriage, 1986. Recipient Gold Medallion, Founders Guild, 1968. Fellow Soc. Clin. Social Work; mem. Calif. Inst. Clin. Social Work (bd. trustees, treas. 1974-84, bd. dirs. 1979—), Social Work Treatment Service (chmn. bd. trustees 1980-82, bd. dir. 1971—), Acad. Cert. Clin. Social Workers, Profl. Adv. Bd., Psi Chi. Avocations: tennis, photography, piano, ceramics. Office: 5353 Balboa Blvd Suite 311 Encino CA 91316

FIELDS, TERRI SUSAN, freelance writer. BA, U. Ariz., 1970; MA, Ariz. State U., 1975; LHD (hon.), No. Ariz. U., 1986. Tchr. Sunnyslope High Sch., Phoenix; featured speaker Ariz. Press Women Freelance Writer Seminar, 1982, 86, Ariz. Sch. Bds. Assn., 1985, Ariz. Interscholastic Journalism Assn., 1985, Reader's Digest Writing Seminar, 1986, Ariz. Prin.'s Acad., 1986. Author: Help Your Child Make the Most of School, 1987; also articles. Named one of twelve Outstanding Women in Communication, 1985, Ariz. Tchr. of Yr., 1986; recipient 1st Place U.S. Ednl. Writing award Nat. Fedn. Press Women, 1982, 3d Place U.S. Mag. Editorial Writing award Nat. Fedn. Press Women, 1983, Outstanding Writing award Ariz. Press Women, 1982, 84, Golden Bell award Ariz. Sch. Bds. Assn., 1984, Achievement Above All award Glendale Union High Sch. Dist. Bd. Edn., 1985 and others. Home: 8228 N 15th Ave Phoenix AZ 85021

FIENHAGE, JOHN FRANCIS, electrical engineer; b. Buffalo, Mo., June 19, 1958; s. Wilfred Joseph and Rita Agnes (Henry) F. BSEE, Kans. State U., 1981. Task leader Motorola Govt. Electronics Group, Scottsdale, Ariz., 1981—. Mem. Tau Beta Pi, Eta Kappa Nu. Republican. Roman Catholic. Avocations: hunting, target shooting, camping. Home: 6507 N 85th Pl Scottsdale AZ 85253 Office: Motorola Govt Electronics Group 8220 E Roosevelt R1215 Scottsdale AZ 85282

FIERO, G. WILLIAM, geology educator; b. Buffalo, Jan. 16, 1936; s. George William and Helen (Mautz) F.; m. Ellen Cady Clark, Apr. 11, 1959; children: Brad, Scott, Kim. BA, Dartmouth Coll., 1957; MS, U. Wyo., 1959; PhD, U. Wis., 1968. Geologist Texaco, Inc., Midland, Tex., 1959-63; tchr. and asst. dean Mt. Hermon Sch., Mt. Hermon, Mass., 1963-66; prof. geology U. Nev., Las Vegas, 1968-87; pres. Venture Tours, Inc., Boulder City, Nev., 1983—, Fiero Ventures, Boulder City, 1983—. Author: Valley of Fire, 1982, Geology of the Great Basin, 1986; co-author Art and Geology, 1986. Planning commr. Clark County Planning Commn., Las Vegas, 1971-75. Mem. Geol. Soc. Am., Am. Assn. Petroleum Geologists. Avocations: canoeing, hiking. Home: 527 Hotel Plaza Boulder City NV 89005 Office: U Nev Dept Geology Las Vegas NV 89154

FIERO, JAMES KENNETH, diversified manufacturing company executive; b. Fort Worth, Nov. 28, 1943; s. Kenneth and Freda (Slade) F.; m. Mary Munro, Sept. 21, 1984. Student, U. Wyo., 1962-64; BA, San Francisco State U., 1976. X-ray technologist Peninsula Med. Ctr., Burlingame, Calif., 1969-76; dist. comml. mgr. Gen. Electric Med. Systems, Burlingame, 1978-81; regional comml. mgr. Gen. Electric Med. Systems, San Bruno, Calif., 1981—. Served with U.S. Army, 1964-67; served with USPHS, 1976-78. Mem. Am. Mgmt. Assn., Calif. Registry Radiologic Technologists, Calif. Soc. Radiologic Technologists. Republican. Methodist. Avocations: flying, skiing, fishing, gardening. Home: 2015 Monroe Ave Belmont CA 94002 Office: Gen Electric Med Systems 1111 Bayhill Suite 230 San Bruno CA 94066

FIFE, DENNIS JENSEN, military officer, chemistry educator; b. Brigham City, Utah, Feb. 10, 1945; s. Glen Shumway and June (Jenson) F.; m. Metta Marie Gunther, June 22, 1972; children: Kimball, Kellie, Keith, Kurt, Katie, Kenton. BS in Chemistry, Weber State U., Ogden, Utah, 1969; MBA, Inter-Am. U., San German, P.R., 1973; MS in Chemistry, Utah State U., 1978, PhD in Phsy. Chemistry, 1983. Assoc. chemist Thiokol Chem. Corp., Brigham City, 1969; commd. 2d lt. USAF, 1969, advanced through grades to lt. col.; pilot, instr., flight examiner Hurricane Hunters, Ramey AFB, P.R. and Keesler AFB, Miss., 1971-76; test project pilot 6514th Test Squadron, Ogden, Utah, 1979-81; instr. chemistry USAF Acad., Colorado Springs, Colo., 1977-79, asst. prof., 1983-85, assoc. prof., 1985—; pres. Select Pubs., Inc., Colorado Springs, 1985—, also chmn. bd. dirs. Author: How to Form a Colorado Corporation, 1986; contbr. articles to profl. jours. Active Boy Scouts Am., Colorado Springs, 1981—, varsity scout coach, Colorado Springs, 1986; sustaining mem. Rep. Nat. Com., Washington, 1983—. Decorated Air medal with oak leaf cluster: NSF research grantee, 1967-68. Mem. Internat. Union Pure and Applied Chemistry (affiliate), Am. Chem. Soc., Phi Kappa Phi. Republican. Mormon. Avocations: racketball, fly fishing, hunting. Home: 535 Big Valley Dr Colorado Springs CO 80919 Office: USAF Acad Dept Chemistry USAF Acad CO 80840

FIFE, JOHN AUSTIN, computer manager, analyst, programmer, counselor for retarded; b. Westboro, Mass., June 10, 1947; s. Hollis A. and Alice D. (Gagnon) F.; m. Susan V. Knoerlein, 1976 (div. 1977); 1 child, Jessica E. AA, Southwestern U., Chula Vista, Calif., 1972; BA, San Diego State U., 1975. Cert. in electronics, 1967. Social worker County of Santa Cruz, Calif., 1977-78; counselor Kanios Home, Redwood City, Calif., 1983—; customer service mgr. Tex. Instruments, Santa Clara, Calif., 1978-83; system mgr. Dept. Interior, Menlo Park, Calif., 1983—. Served to sgt. USAF, 1966-70. Mem. Decus Computer Users. Lodge: MacDuff Soc. (Scotland) (v.p. 1983—). Avocations: racquetball, hiking, camping, historical research. Home: 340A Orchard Ave Redwood City CA 94061 Office: US Geol Survey 275 Middlefield Rd Menlo Park CA 94025

FIFE, LELAND OLIVER, banker; b. Cedar City, Utah, June 28, 1948; s. Joseph Carlos and Leola (DeMille) F.; m. Colleen Sandberg, Nov. 11, 1972; children—Natalie, Bryan, Andrea, Candace, Angela, Allesha. B.A. in History, So. Utah State Coll., Cedar City, 1972; M. Social Sci. in Pub. Adminstrn., Utah State U., 1984. Exec. dir. C. of C., Cedar City, 1972-74; asst. v.p. Am. Savs. & Loan, Salt Lake City, 1974-78, State Bank of So. Utah, Cedar City, 1978—. Councilman, City of Cedar City, 1980-84; bd. dirs. Utah Shakespearean Festival, Cedar City, 1973—. Recipient Disting. Service award Cedar City Jaycees, 1973; Outstanding Young Man award Utah State Jaycees, 1974; Mayor's award Cedar City, 1983. Mem. Am. Inst. Banking, Utah Bankers Assn. (mem. bank seminar com. 1983—), Cedar City C. of C. (bd. dirs. 1975-77), Phi Kappa Phi. Republican. Mormon. Lodge: Kiwanis (pres. 1984—). Home: 883 S Fountain Dr Cedar City UT 84720 Office: State Bank So Utah 26 N Main St Cedar City UT 84720

FIFE, MICHAEL EDWARD, marketing and research executive; b. Ogden, Utah, May 21, 1945; s. Edward Stratton and Dixie Maxine F.; m. Maureen Joan Dunn, Aug. 14, 1968; children: Jason Michael, Jordan Joseph. BS, San Jose State U., 1967, MBA, 1969. With sales, merchandising depts. Johnson & Johnson, San Jose, Calif., 1967-69; with sales, mktg. depts. Shell Oil Co., San Jose, 1969-71; dir. research Palm Springs (Calif.) Conv. and Visitors Bur., 1971-74, dir. mktg. and research, 1974-86, v.p. communications and fin., 1986—; instr. Skyline Coll., San Bruno, Calif., 1970-71; owner Desert Research Assoc., Palm Springs, 1971—, Marketrends, 1986—. Author numerous profl. publs. Mem. Am. Soc. Assn. Execs., Internat. Assn. Conv. and Visitors Burs., Am. Mktg. Assn., Insearch (bd. dirs.), Western Assn. Conv. and Visitors Burs. (bd. dirs.), Travel and Tourism Research Assn. (bd. dirs.). Home: 633 W Stevens Rd Palm Springs CA 92262 Office: Palm Springs Conv and Vis Bur 255 N El Cielo Rd Suite 315 Palm Springs CA 92262

FIFKOVA, EVA, behavioral neuroscience educator; b. Prague, Czechoslovakia, May 21, 1932; came to U.S., 1968; d. Ivan and Maria (Domalipová) Fifka. MD, Charles U., Prague, 1957; PhD, Inst. Physiology Czechoslovakia Acad. Scis., Prague, 1963. Lectr. Charles U., 1954-60; mem. staff Czechosolvakia Acad. Scis., 1960-68; research assoc. Calif. Inst. Tech., Pasadena, 1968-74; asst. prof. behavioral neuroscis. U. Colo., Boulder, 1974-75, assoc. prof., 1975-78, prof., 1978—; mem. neurobiology adv. panel NSF, Washingotn, 1982-85. Contbr. numerous articles to profl. jours. U. Colo. Faculty fellow, Boulder, 1979, 84; research grantee Nat. Inst. Aging, Bethesda, Md., 1984-86, Nat. Inst. Alcohol, Bethesda, 1983-86. Mem. AAAS, Am. Physiol. Soc., Soc. Neurosci., Am. Assn. Anatomists, Electron Microscopy Soc. Am. Club: Cajal (Denver). Office: U Colo Dept Psychology Campus Box 345 Boulder CO 80309

FIGEARO, FRANK S., computer system analyst; b. Santa Monica, Calif., Oct. 23, 1943; s. Frank S. and Betty (Shepard) F. AA in Bus., Am. River Coll., 1962; BA in Bus., Sacramento State Coll., 1964; M in Pub. Adminstrn., U. Nev., Reno, 1978. Account clk. Aerojet Gen., Sacramento, 1959-61, computer operator, 1961-64, programmer, 1966-67; ops. mgr. State of Nev., Carson City, 1967-72, sr. systems analyst, 1972-84, system mgr., 1984—; prof. data processing Western Nev. Community Coll., Carson City, 1982—. Designer On Line Over the Counter Drivers License System, 1981 (Gov. award 1981). Campaign mgr. Hal Dunn for Sheriff, Carson City, 1982, Pete Rasner for Sheriff, Carson City, 1974, 78; campaign advisor William Burnhaugh City Supt., Carson City, 1978. Served to lt. USMC, 1965-66. Recipient Capt. Commn., Carson City Sheriff's Office, 1979, Comdr. Commn., Carson City Sheriff's Office, 1981. Mem. AAMUA. Democrat. Club: Automators (Carson City) (pres. 1979-81). Avocations: outdoorsmanship, racing cars, motorcycles, teaching. Office: Nev Motor Vehicles and Pub Safety Office 555 Wright Way Carson City NV 89711-0300

FIGHTS, MICHAEL LEWIS, manufacturing company executive; b. Muncie, Ind., Mar. 31, 1954; s. Gerald Lewis and Naomi Ruth (Gasper) F.; m. Cydney Terese Haynes, Feb. 23, 1974; children: Michael Lewis II, Matthew Kirk, Mitchell Alex. Lab. supr. and tech. Ball Meml. Hosp., Muncie, 1972-74; advt. devel. lab. supr. Ball Corp., Muncie, 1974-85; supr. packing maintenance Ball Corp., El Monte, Calif., 1985—. Patentee in field. Republican. Avocations: inventing, flying, volleyball, sports, music. Home: 3235 Merrifield Ave Pomona CA 91767 Office: Ball Corp 4000 N Arden Dr El Monte CA 91734

FIGUEIREDO, HUBERT FERNANDES, aerospace engineer; b. Elizabeth, N.J., Nov. 21, 1958; s. Fernando and Maria Alexandria Figueiredo. BS in Aerospace Engring., Polytech. Inst. N.Y., 1980; postgrad. in systems mgmt., U. So. Calif., 1986—. Prodn. inspector Amax, Inc., Carteret, N.J., 1978; analytical engr. Pratt and Whitney Aircraft Corp., East Hartford, Conn., 1979; space shuttle mech. systems test engr. Rockwell Internat. Space Div., Palmdale, Calif., 1980-84, pub. relations speaker, 1981-84; space shuttle mechanisms/structures engr. Lockheed Space Ops. Co., Vandenberg AFB, Calif. and Kennedy Space Ctr., Fla., 1984-87; sr. structural design engr. Advanced Systems div. Northrop Corp., Palmdale, Calif., 1987—. Recipient Superior Achievement award Rockwell Internat. Space Div. Mem. AIAA. Republican. Roman Catholic. Avocations: sports, traveling, researching Soviet technology. Home: 518 E Ave J-4 Lancaster CA 93535 Office: Northrop Advanced Systems Div AF Plant 42 Site 4 Palmdale CA 93550

FIGUEROA, MICHAEL OTTO, law enforcement official; b. Los Angeles, Dec. 26, 1943; s. Jesse Albert and Elsie (Lea) F.; children—Jeffrey Michael, Noelle Kathryn. A.A. in Bus. Adminstrn., East Los Angeles Coll., 1965; B.A., in Adminstrn., Calif. State Coll.-San Bernardino, 1974; grad. U. So. Calif. Delinquency Control Inst., 1978, Calif. Peace Officers Standards and Tng. Commn. Command Coll., 1985. Cert. peace officer, supr., Calif. Dep. Los Angeles County Sheriff's Dept., 1970-72; patrolman Riverside, Police Dept., Calif., 1972-74, agt., 1974, spl. agt., investigator, 1974-76, sgt., 1976-80, lt. adj. to chief of police, 1980-83, capt., 1983—; cons. on street gangs and graffiti. Bd. dirs. Riverside Area Child Abuse Council, 1980, Riverside Area Rape Crisis, 1977-80; Cub master local Cub Scouts, 1975-77; active local Y-Indian Guides. Served to 1st. lt. AUS, 1966-68. Decorated Bronze Star with oak leaf cluster; named Supr. of Yr., Riverside Police Officers Assn., 1984, Law Enforcement Officer of Yr. VFW, 1986. Mem. Internat. Police Assn., Mex.-Am. Police Command Assn., Latino Peace Officers Assn., Calif. Gang Investigators Assn., Peace Officer Research Assn. Calif., Nat. Police Athletic Fedn., Vietnam Vets. of Am. Republican. Roman Catholic. Club: Athletic Express Track (Male Athlete of Yr. 1985) (Riverside). Office: 4102 Orange St Riverside CA 92501

FILEVICH, BASIL, bishop; b. Jan. 13, 1918. Ord. priest, Roman Catholic church, 1942. Consecrated bishop Ukrainian Eparchy of Saskatoon, Sask., Can., 1984. Office: Bishop's Residence, Eparchy of Saskatoon, 866 Saskatchewan Crescent E, Saskatoon, SK Canada S7N 0L4 *

FILLEY, RICHARD DAVID, writer, industrial engineer; b. Columbus, Ohio, July 28, 1955; s. Laurence Duane and Bette Elaine (Riley) F.; m. Phyllis Jane Carlton, July 14, 1979; children: Derek James, Dena Michelle. BS in Indsl. Engring., U. Wash.-Seattle, 1978. Indsl. analyst, The Boeing Co., Seattle, 1978; indsl. engr. Garrett/AiResearch Mfg. Co., Phoenix, 1979-80; facilities engr. Sperry Flight Systems, Phoenix, 1980-81; people and technologies editor Indsl. Engring. Mag., Norcross, Ga., 1981-85; dir. tech. transfer programs Dept Indsl. and Mgmt. Systems Engring., Ariz. State Univ., Tempe, 1985—. Author: (with Drui, Hairfield and Johnson) Industrial Engineering in the Boeing Company, 1978, (mag. series) Communicate With Graphics, 1981-82; contbr. articles to profl. jours. Founder, pres. AiResearch Employees Aluminum Can Recycling Program, Phoenix, 1979-81. Mem. Inst. Indsl. Engrs. (newsletter editor Cen. Ariz. chpt. 1980-81, pub. 1986—, v.p. Atlanta chpt. 1983-85), Soc. Mfg. Engrs., Coll.-Industry Council Material Handling Edn., Sigma Delta Chi. Republican. Evangelical Christian. Clubs: Seattle Mountaineers, Am. Alpine; Swiss Alpine. Home: 2445 W Pecos Ave Mesa AZ 85202 Office: Arizona State Univ Dept Indsl & Mgmt Systems Engring Tempe AZ 85287

FILOSA, GARY FAIRMONT RANDOLPH DE VIANA, II, financier; b. Wilder, Vt., Feb. 22, 1931; s. Gary F.R. de Marco de Viana and Rosaline M. (Falzarano) Filosa; divorced; children: Marc Christian Bazire de Villadon, III, Gary Fairmont Randolph de Viana, III. Grad., Mt. Hermon Sch., 1950; Ph.B., U. Chgo., 1954; B.A., U. Americas, Mex., 1967; M.A., Calif. Western U., 1968; Ph.D., U.S. Internat. U., 1970. Sports reporter Claremont Daily Eagle, Rutland Herald, Vt. Informer, 1947-52; pub. The Chicagoan, 1952-54; account exec., editor house publs. Robertson, Buckley & Gotsch, Inc., Chgo., 1953-54; account exec. Fuller, Smith & Ross, Inc., N.Y.C., 1955; editor Apparel Arts mag. (now Gentlemen's Quar.), Esquire, Inc., N.Y.C., 1955-56; pres., chmn. bd. Teenarama Records, Inc., N.Y.C., 1956-62; pres., chmn. bd. Filosa Publs. Internat., N.Y.C., 1956-61, Los Angeles, 1974-83, Palm Beach, Fla., 1983—; pres. Montclair Sch., 1958-60, Pacific Registry, Inc., Los Angeles, 1959-61, Banana Chip Corp. Am., N.Y.C., 1964-67; exec. asst. to exec. producer Desilu Studios, Inc., Hollywood, 1960-61; exec. asst. to Benjamin A. Javits, 1961-62; dean adminstrn. Postgrad. Center for Mental Health, N.Y.C., 1962-64; chmn. bd., pres. Producciones Mexicanes Internationales (S.A.), Mexico City, 1957-68, Filosa Films Internat., Hollywood, 1962-74; pres. Filosa Films Internat., Newport Beach, Calif., 1975-83, Palm Beach, Fla., 1984—; pres. Casa Filosa Corp., Palm Beach, Fla., 1982—; dir. tng. Community Savs., F.A., Riviera Beach, Fla., 1983-86; chmn. bd., pres. Cinematografica Americana Internationale (S.A.), Mexico City, 1964-74; v.p. acad. affairs Journey Assocs., Phoenix, 1986-87; v.p. acad. affairs World Acad., San Francisco, 1967-68; asst. headmaster, instr. Latin Bishop Sch., San Diego, 1968-69; asst. to provost Calif. Western U., San Diego, 1968-69; assoc. prof. philosophy Art Coll., San Francisco, 1969-70; v.p. acad. affairs, dean of faculty Internat. Inst., Phoenix, 1968-73; chmn. bd., pres. Universite Universelle, 1970-73; bd. dirs., v.p. acad. affairs, dean Summer Sch., Internat. Community Coll., Los Angeles, 1970-72; v.p. acad. affairs The Journey Assocs., Phoenix, 1986-87; chmn. bd., pres. Social Directory Calif., 1967-75, Am. Assn. Social Registries, Los Angeles, 1970-76; pres. Social Directory U.S., N.Y.C., 1974-76; chmn. bd. Internat. Assn. Social Registers, Paris, 1974—; surfing coach U. Calif. at Irvine, 1975-77; instr. history Coastline Community Coll., Fountain Valley, Calif., 1976-77; v.p. Xerox-Systemic, 1979-80. Pub.: Teenage, Rustic Rhythm mags., Teen Life, Talent, Rock & Roll Roundup, Celebrities Stardust, Personalities, Rustic Rhythm, Campus, N.Y.C., 1956-61; editor: Sci. Digest, 1961-62. Author: (stage play) Let Me Call Ethel, 1955, Technology Enters 21st Century, 1966, musical Feather Light, 1966, No Public Funds for Nonpublic Schools, 1968, Creative Function of the College President, 1969, The Surfers Almanac, 1977, Payne of Florida (TV series), 1985, The Filosa Newsletter, 1986—. Contbr. numerous articles to mags., and profl. jours. and encys. including Sci. Digest, World Book Ency., Ency. of Sports. Trustee Univ. of the Ams., 1986—; candidate for Los Angeles City Council, 1959; chmn. Publishers for John F. Kennedy, 1960, Educators for Reelection of Ivy Baker Priest, 1970; mem. exec. and fin. com. Brown for Gov. Calif., 1974; patron Monterey Peninsula Mus. Art, 1978; mem. So. Calif. Com. for Olympic Games, 1977-84; founder, pres. Am. Cath. Ch., 1978—; Served with AUS, 1954-55. Recipient DAR Citizenship award, 1959; Silver Conquistador award Am. Assn. Social Registers, 1970; Ambassador's Cup U. Ams., 1967; resolution Calif. Legislature, 1977; Duke Kahanamoku Classic surfing trophy, 1977; gold pendant Japan Surfing Assn., 1978. Mem. U.S. Surfing Found. (founder, pres. 1974-76), Internat. Profl. Surfing Fedn. (founder, pres. 1974-77, 83-86), Am. Surfing Assn. (founder, pres. 1960-78, chmn. exec. com. 1974-78, pres. 1980-86), Internat. Amateur Surfing Fedn. (chmn. bd., found, pres. 1960-77, 83-86), Am. Profl. Surfing Assn. (pres., founder 1940-86), Internat. Surfing Com. (founder, pres. 1960—), U.S. Surfing Com. (founder, pres. 1960—), Am. Walking Soc. (founder, pres. 1980), Am. Assn. UN, Authors League, Authors Guild, Alumni Assn. U. Americas (pres. 1967-70, trustee 1986—), United Shareowners Am., Sierra Club, NCAA (bd. dels. 1977-82), AAU (gov. 1978-82), World Affairs Council San Francisco, Am. Cath. Chs. (pres., founder 1970—), Am. Acad. Polit. Sci., Mt. Hermon Sch. Alumni Assn., Coral Soc., U. Chgo. Alumni Assn., Sigma Omicron Lambda (founder, pres. 1965—). Democrat. Mem. Am. Cath. Ch. Clubs: Chapultepec (Mexico City); Embajadores (U. of Americas, Puebla, Mex.); Palm Beach Surf (Fla); Mt. Kenya Safari (Nairobi); Coral Reef Soc. (Palm Beach). Address: PO Box 2174 Palm Beach FL 33480 and: PO Box 1315 Beverly Hills CA 90213

FIMBRES, MARTHA MOLINA, psychiatric social worker; b. Tucson, July 29, 1943; d. John Augustin and Concepcion (Borboa) Molina; m. Carlos V. Fimbres; children: Anna Maria, Christine, Vanessa, Jacqueline, Michele. BS, U. Ariz., 1974; MSW, Ariz. State U., 1978. Adminstrv. asst. U. Ariz., Tucson, 1974-76, lectr. Coll. Medicine, 1978—, researcher, 1978—; pvt. practice clin. social work Tucson, 1984—; dir. bilingual/bicultural track Sonota Desert Hosp., Tucson, 1987—; psychiat. social worker Palo Verde Hosp., Tucson, 1985—; cons. HEW, Washington, 1980-82, Consad Inc., Washington, 1980-82. Contbr. articles to profl. jours. Vol. Nat. Ctr. Orthopsychiatry, 1985—. NIMH scholar, Washington, 1978. Mem. Nat. Assn. Social Workers (pres. Ariz. chpt. 1983—), Exec. Female Assn. Democrat. Roman Catholic. Clubs: La Red, Second Tuesday (Tucson). Avocations: jogging, piano, reading, aerobics. Home: 2014 W Calle Del Reposo Tucson AZ 85745 Office: U Ariz Coll Medicine 1501 N Campbell Tucson AZ 85724

FINAN, ELLEN CRANSTON, English language educator, consultant; b. Worcester, Mass., June 26, 1951; d. Thomas Matthew and Maureen Ann (Moulton) F. BA, U. San Francisco, 1973; MA, U. Calif., Riverside, 1978. ESL specialist U.S. Peace Corps, Finote Selam, Ethiopia, 1974-75; English instr. U. Redlands, Calif., 1977-79; mentor tchr. Jurupa Unified Sch. Dist., Riverside, 1979—; tech. writer Callan Assocs., San Francisco, 1973-74, Wilshire Assocs., Santa Monica, Calif., 1976-77; English instr. U. Pa., Phila., 1979; writing cons. Inland Area Writing Project U. Calif., Riverside, 1980—; tchr., coordinator U. Calif., Riverside, 1982. Author: Prickley Pear, 1981. NEH fellow, 1985; Squaw Valley Community of Writers scholar, 1981. Mem. Nat. Council English Tchrs., Assn. Supervision and Curriculum Devel., Alpha Sigma Nu, Phi Delta Kappa. Democrat. Mem. Unitarian Ch. Avocations: writing, travel. Home: 23607 Whispering Winds Moreno Valley CA 92388 Office: Jurupa Unified Schs 4250 Opal Riverside CA 92509

FINCH, CALEB ELLICOTT, neurobiology, gerontology, researcher, educator; b. London, July 4, 1939; came to U.S., 1939; s. Benjamin F. and Faith (Stratton) Campbell; m. Doris Nossamen, Oct. 11, 1975. B.S., Yale U., 1961; Ph.D., Rockefeller U., 1969. Guest investigator Rockefeller U., N.Y.C., 1969-70; asst. prof. Cornell U. Med. Coll., N.Y.C., 1970-72; asst. prof. biology, gerontology U. So. Calif., Los Angeles, 1972-75, assoc. prof., 1975-78, prof., 1978—; ARCO and William Kieschnick prof. neurobiology of aging U. So. Calif.; mem. cell biology study sect. NIH, Bethesda, Md., 1975-78; prin. investigator co-dir. Alzheimer Disease Research Ctr. So. Calif.; mem. sci. adv. counsil Nat. Inst. Aging, 1987—, sci. adv. bd. Nat. Inst. Aging, 1987—. Editor: Handbook of Biology of Aging, 1977, 85; editorial bd.: Jour. Gerontology, 1979—, Neurobiology of Aging, 1982—; contbr. 150 articles to sci. jours. Cons. Office of Tech. Assessment, U.S. Congress, Washington, 1982-84. NIH research grantee, 1972; postdoctoral fellow, 1969-71; recipient Brookdale award 1985. Fellow AAAS, Gerontol. Soc. Am. (Robert W. Kleemeier award 1984); mem. Endocrine Soc., Neurosci. Soc., Psychoneuroendocrine Soc., Soc. Study Reprodn. Home: 2144 Crescent Dr Altadena CA 91001 Office: U So Calif University Park Los Angeles CA 90089-0191

FINCH, DOUGLAS CARL, aerospace engineer; b. Newark, May 8, 1960; s. Robert Carl and Helen Theresa (Harazda) F. SB in Aero. and Astro. Engring., MIT, 1982, SM in Aero. and Astro. Engring., 1984. Registered profl. engr., Calif. Mem. tech. staff Aerospace Corp., El Segundo, Calif., 1984-86; engring. specialist Composites Horizons Inc., Covina, Calif., 1986-87; gen. mgr. Nuwuvi Composites Techs., Los Vegas, Nev., 1987—; founder, pres. SunTech Cons., Manhattan Beach, Calif., 1985—. Mem. AIAA, Am. Soc. Composites (founder), Soc. Advancement Material and Process Engring., Composites Group of Soc. Mfg. Engrs. Republican. Avocations: golf, scuba diving, personal computers, neon art. Home: 2312 Green Valley Pkwy Apt 3221 Henderson NV 89015 Office: Nuwuvi Composites Techs 6 Paiute Dr Las Vegas NV 89106

FINCH, SAMUEL PRESTLEY, III, systems engineer; b. Pitts., Mar. 31, 1942; s. Samuel Prestley Jr. and Mary Elizabeth (Booth) F.; m. Sarah Weidner, June 3, 1964 (div. Aug. 1974); children: Lucy Garnett, Sarah Elizabeth; m. Andrea Gudahl, Aug. 29, 1975; 1 child, Nicole Samantha. BS in Engring., USAF Acad., 1964; MS in Chemistry, U. Calif., Riverside, 1973. Commd. 2d lt. USAF, 1964, advanced through grades to lt. col., 1980, ret., 1985; asst. prof. chemistry USAF Acad., 1973-77; asst. chief tng. div. 43d Strategic Wing, Anderson AFB, Guam, 1977-79; chief mission devel. 319 Bomb Wing, Grand Forks AFB, N.D., 1979-81; research assoc. Air Power Research Inst., Maxwell AFB, Ala., 1981-83; comdr. det. 3 Field Command Def. Nuclear Agy., Los Alamos, N.Mex., 1983-85; systems engr., ops. research scientist Lockheed Calif. Co., Burbank, 1985—. Mem. Air Force Assn., Ret. Officers Assn., Assn. USAF Acad. Graduates.

FINCH, THOMAS WESLEY, corrosion engineer; b. Alhambra, Calif., Dec. 17, 1946; s. Charles Phillip and Marian Louisa (Bushey) F.; m. Jinx L. Heath, Apr. 1979. Student Colo. Sch. Mines, 1964-68. Assayer, prospector Raymond P. Heon, Inc., Idaho Springs, Colo., 1968; corrosion engr. Cathodic Protection Service, Denver, 1973-80, area mgr., Lafayette, La., 1980-81; area mgr. Corrintec/USA, Farmington, N.Mex., 1981-83; dist. mgr. Gen. Cathodic Protection Services Co., Farmington, 1983—. Served with C.E., U.S. Army, 1968-72. Mem. Nat. Assn. Corrosion Engrs., Soc. Am. Mil. Engrs., U.S. Ski Assn., Am. Security Council (nat. adv. bd. 1978—), Kappa Sigma. Republican. Lutheran. Home: 2628 E 24th St Farmington NM 87401 Office: PO Box 388 Farmington NM 87499

FINCKE, MARY SUSAN, public relations executive; b. Pasadena, Calif., Aug. 4, 1944; d. Robert Theodore and Margaret (Williams) F. Student, Internat. Christian U., Tokyo, 1962-63; BA, U. N.Mex., 1967; MA, U. Minn., 1971; MBA, U. Phoenix, 1983. Dir. unit program ARC, South Vietnam, 1966-67; dir. pubs. Am. Soc. Landscape Architects, Washington, 1969; reporter Idaho State Jour., Pocatello, 1971-72; freelance writer Tucson, 1974-79; coordinator news info. Pima Community Coll., Tucson, 1979-83; account exec. JLTC & Assocs., Tucson, 1983-84; pvt. practice pub. relations Tucson, 1984—. Vice chmn. pub. info. com. Am. Cancer Soc., Tucson, 1985-86. Named Pub. Info. Vol. of Yr., Am. Cancer Soc., Tucson, 1985. Mem. Am. Mktg. Assn., Pub. Relations Soc. Am., Kappa Tau Alpha. Avocations: Latin Am. lit., Mexican folk music and dance. Home and Office: 1227 N Tyndall Tucson AZ 85719

FINDLER, NICHOLAS VICTOR, research computer science educator; b. Budapest, Hungary, Nov. 24, 1930; came to U.S., 1963; s. Otto and Aranka (Hirschkovitz) F.; m. Catherine Ellenbogen, Mar. 5, 1955; children: Marianne N., Michèle C. BE with honors, Budapest U. Tech. Scis., 1953, PhD in Math, Physics, 1956. Research scientist Carnegie Inst. Tech., Pitts., 1963-64; assoc. prof. computer sci. U. Ky., Lexington, 1964-66; prof. SUNY, Buffalo, 1966-82; research prof., dir. artificial intelligence lab. Ariz. State U., Tempe, 1982—; vis. prof., sr. Fulbright scholar Tech. U. Vienna, Austria, 1972-73, Free U. and U. Amsterdam, The Netherlands, 1979-80; mem. staff applied math. The C.S.R. Co. Ltd., Sydney, Australia, 1959-63; participant summer inst. Rand Corp., Santa Monica, Calif., 1963, cons., 1981; cons. AFHRL, Phoenix, 1985. Contbr. numerous articles to profl. jours., chpts. to books. Recipient Centennial award of Merit, Office of Pres. Ariz. State U., 1986, Medal of Merit, Office of Rector U. Helsinki, Finland, 1980. Fellow Brit. Computer Soc.; mem. Assn. Computing Machinery (doctoral dissertation awards com. 1983—, Recognition of Service award 1986), IEEE, Brit. Computer Soc., Assn. Computational Linguistics, Cognitive Sci. Soc., others. Democrat. Jewish. Avocations: classical music, poetry, natural langs., travelling, painting. Office: Ariz State U Computer Sci Dept Tempe AZ 85258

FINDLEY, JAMES SMITH, biology educator, museum director; b. Cleve., Dec. 28, 1926; s. Howard Nevin and Dorothy Georgine (Smith) D.; m. Muriel Thomson, June 18, 1949; children: Stuart Thomson, Heidi Ann, Douglas Smith, Joan Nevin. AB, Western Res. U., 1949; PhD, U. Kans., 1955. Asst. instr. zoology U. Kans., Lawrence, 1950-54; curatorial asst. U. Kans. Mus. Nat. History, 1953-54; instr. zoology U. S.D., Vermillion, 1954-55; from asst. prof. to prof. biology U. N.Mex., Albuquerque, 1955—, chmn. dept. biology, 1978-82; dir. U. N.Mex. Mus. Southwestern Biology, 1982—. Author: Mammals of New Mexico, 1976, Natural History of New Mexican Mammals, 1986; contbr. numerous articles on mammalian systematics, ecology, and biogeography to jours. Served with U.S. Army, 1945-46. Fellow AAAS; mem. Am. Soc. Mammalogists (pres. 1980-82, recipient C. Hart Merriam award 1978), Ecol. Soc. Am., Am. Soc. Naturalists, Soc. for Study Evolution. Democrat. Avocation: farming. Home: PO Box 44 Corrales NM 87048 Office: U NMex Biology Dept Albuquerque NM 87131

FINE, JAMES STEPHEN, physician; b. St. Paul, June 14, 1946; s. Ralph Irving and Beverlee Lois (Rockler) F.; m. Meredith Ann Blehert, June 20, 1970; children: Zachary, Esther, Gabriel. BA in Math., U. Minn., 1968, MD, 1972, MS in Biometry, Health Info. Systems, 1977. Intern in medicine St. Paul-Ramsey Hosp., 1972-73; residency U. Minn., Mpls., 1973-77; dir. info. and spl. procedures div. U. Wash. Hosp., Seattle, 1977—; residency dir. Dept. of Lab. Medicine U. Wash., Seattle, 1981—. Editor: (videodisk) Videolibrary of Laboratory Medicine: Atlas of Hemotology, 1985, Acad. Clin. Lab. Physicians and Scientists Directory, 1977—. Mem. Am. Soc. Clin. Pathologists (mem. bd. registry), Am. Soc. Clin. Chemistry, Acad. Clin. Lab. Physicians and Scientists, Assn. Computint Machinery, Computer Soc. of IEEE. Office: U Wash Hosp SB10 Dept Lab Medicine Seattle WA 98195

FINE, RICHARD ISAAC, lawyer; b. Milw., Jan. 22, 1940; s. Jack and Frieda F.; m. Maryellen Olman, Nov. 25, 1982; 1 child, Victoria Elizabeth. B.S., U. Wis., 1961; J.D., U. Chgo., 1964; Ph.D. in Internat. Law, U. London, 1967; cert., Hague (Netherlands) Acad. Internat. Law, 1965, 66; cert. comparative law, Internat. U. Comparative Sci., Luxembourg, 1966; diplome superiere, Faculte Internat. pour l'Ensignment du Droit Compare, Strasbourg, France, 1967. Bar: Ill. 1964, D.C. 1972, Calif. 1973. Trial atty. fgn. commerce sect. antitrust div. Dept. Justice, 1968-72; chief antitrust div. U.S., Los Angeles City Atty.'s Office, also spl. counsel gov. efficiency com., 1973-74; prof. internat., comparative and EEC antitrust law U. Syracuse (N.Y.) Law Sch. (overseas program), summers 1970-72; individual practice Richard I. Fine and Assocs., Los Angeles, 1974; mem. antitrust adv. bd. Bur. Nat. Affairs, 1981—. Contbr. articles to legal publs. Mem. ABA (chmn. subcom. internat. antitrust and trade regulations, internat. law sect. 1972-77, co-chmn. com. internat. econ. orgn. 1977-79), Am. Soc. Internat. Law (co-chmn. com. corp. membership 1978-83, mem. exec. council 1984-87), Am. Fgn. Law Assn., Internat. Law Assn., Brit. Inst. Internat. and Comparative Law, World Peace Through Law Center, State Bar Calif. (chmn. antitrust and trade regulation law sect. 1981-84, exec. com. 1981—), Retinitis Pigmentosa Internat. (bd. dirs. 1985—), Los Angeles County Bar Assn. (chmn. antitrust sect. 1977-78), Ill. Bar Assn., Am. Friends London Sch. Econs. (bd. dirs. 1984—, co-chmn. So. Calif. chpt. 1984—), Phi Delta Phi. Address: Suite 250 10100 Santa Monica Blvd Los Angeles CA 90067

FINEGAN, WILLIAM ROBERT, public relations executive; b. Cork, Munster, Ireland, Mar. 10, 1927; came to U.S., 1948; s. William Alan and Muriel (Piens) F.; m. Doris Jean Geier, Aug. 15, 1953; children—William, Mark, Roy, John. Student Wesley Coll., Dublin, Ireland, London Sch. Journalism. Newspaper editor, mag. editor, advt. writer various locations in N.J. and N.Y., 1949-65; dir. devel. communications Cornell U., Ithaca, N.Y., 1965-69; dir. pub. relations, editor Wells Coll., Aurora, N.Y., 1969-73, Colgate U., Hamilton, N.Y., 1973-76; dir. pub. info. and editor Pomona Coll., Claremont, Calif., 1976-79; dir. pub. relations and alumni affairs Coll. Osteo. Medicine of the Pacific, Pomona, Calif., 1979—; pres. Central N.Y. Coll. Pub. Relations Council, 1974-75. Contbr. articles to profl. jours. Bd. dirs. Central Bus. Dist., Pomona, 1984-86; chmn. Pomona Communications Com., C. of C., 1983—; co-chmn. C. of C. Ambassadors, Pomona, 1983-85; chmn. maj. gifts YMCA, Pomona Valley, 1984—; bd. dirs. Pomona Valley Chpt. ARC, 1985—, Youth At Risk, Pomona, 1986—. Served with Brit. Army, 1945-48; PTO. Named Ambassador of Yr. C. of C. of Pomona, 1983, Ambassador of Month, 1982. Mem. Council for Advancement and Support of Edn., Nat. Soc. Fund Raising Execs., Compatriots. Republican. Episcopalian. Club: University of Claremont. Lodges: Rotary (bd. dirs. 1985—) (Pomona); Masons (Cork). Home: 1012 Ottawa Dr Claremont CA 91711 Office: Coll Osteo Medicine of the Pacific College Plaza Pomona CA 91766

FINESILVER, SHERMAN GLENN, judge; b. Denver, Oct. 1, 1927; s. Harry M. and Rebecca M. (Balaban) F.; m. Annette Warren, July 23, 1954; children: Jay Mark, Steven Brad, Susan Lynn. B.A., U. Colo., 1949; LL.B., U. Denver, 1952; certificate, Northwestern U. Traffic Inst., 1956; LL.D. (hon.), Gallaudet Coll., Washington, 1970. Bar: Colo. bar 1952, also U.S. Supreme Ct 1952, U.S. Ct. of Appeals 1952, 10th Circuit, U.S. Dist. Ct., Colo 1952. Legal asst. Denver City Atty.'s Office, 1949-52; asst. Denver city atty. 1952-55; judge Denver County Ct., 1955-62; judge Denver Dist. Ct., 2d Jud. Dist., 1962-71, presiding judge domestic relations div., 1963, 67, 68; judge U.S. Dist. Ct., Denver, 1971—; Faculty Denver Opportunity Sch., 1949-54, U. Denver Coll. Law and Arts and Sci. Sch., 1955—; Faculty Westminster Law Sch., 1955-61, Nat. Coll. Judiciary, Reno, 1967—, Atty. Gen.'s Advocacy Inst., Washington, 1974—, seminars for new fed. judges, 1974—; cons. HEW, 1958-62. Author: Model Law for Interpreters in Court Proceedings, 1968, Protect Your Life-Wise Words for Women, 1969, Timely Tips When Disaster Strikes-No Second Chance, 1970; Contbr.: chpt. to Epilepsy Rehabilitation, 1974; Editor: chpt. to Proceedings Nat. Symposium on the Deaf, Driving and Employability, 1964; Contbg. editor: chpt. to Lawyers Coop. Pub. Co, Rochester, N.Y., 1958-60, Teaching Driver and Traffic Safety Education, 1965; Contbr. articles to profl. jours. Founder Denver Driver Improvement Sch., 1959, dir., 1959-71; chmn. Denver Citizenship Day, 1967; organizer Denver Youth Council, 1968; dir. leadership conf. Neighborhood Youth Corps, 1969; mem. Pres.'s Task Force on Hwy. Safety, 1969-71; mem. advisory com. Nat. Hwy. Traffic Safety Adminstrn., Dept. Transp., 1969-72; mem. task force White House Conf. on Aging, 1972; chmn. Gov.'s Adv. Com. on Hwy. Safety, 1960-71; commr. Gov.'s Commn. on Aging, 1967-71; mem. nat. youth commn. B'nai B'rith, 1970-74; Pres. Jewish Family and Childrens Service of Colo., 1962-64; bd. dirs. Nat. Council Orgns. Serving Deaf, Washington, 1968-71; trustee Am. Med. Center, Denver, 1960-72. Decorated Knight Comdr. Ct. of Honor K.C., Rocky Mountain Consistory, 1967; recipient numerous awards including citation Nat. Safety Council, 1958, Paul Gray Hoffman award Automotive Safety Found., 1960, spl. award N.Am. Judges Assn., merit award Colo. Assn. Deaf and Nat. Soc. Deaf, 1966, Service to Mankind award Denver Sertoma Club, 1969, Freedoms Found. award, 1969, medallion for outstanding service by a non-handicapped person to physically disabled Nat. Paraplegia Found., 1972, certificate of commendation Sec. Transp., 1974, numerous others. Mem. ABA (nat. chmn. Am. citizenship com. 1968, award of merit Law Day 1968), Colo. Bar Assn. (chmn. Law Day 1964, chmn. Am. citizenship com. 1963), Denver Bar Assn. (chmn. Law Day 1964), Am.

Judicature Soc., Hebrew Ednl. Alliance, Allied Jewish Community Council, Phi Sigma Delta (trustee 1960-66); mem. B'nai B'rith. Clubs: Mason (Shriner), Am. Amateur Radio. Office: US Dist Ct Room C-236 US Courthouse 1929 Stout St Denver CO 80294 *

FINGARETTE, HERBERT, philosopher, educator; b. Bklyn., Jan. 20, 1921; m. Leslie J. Swabacker, Jan. 23, 1945; 1 dau., Ann Hasse. B.A., UCLA, 1947, Ph.D., 1949. Mem. faculty U. Calif.-Santa Barbara, 1948—, Phi Beta Kappa Romanell prof. philosophy, 1983—; William James lectr. religion Harvard U., 1971; W.T. Jones lectr. philosophy Pomona Coll., 1974; Evans-Wentz lectr. Oriental religions Stanford U., 1977; Gramlich lectr. human nature Dartmouth Coll., 1978; cons. NEH; Raphael Demos lectr. Vanderbilt U., 1985; Disting. tchr. U. Calif.-Santa Barbara, 1985, faculty research lectr., 1977. Author: The Self in Transformation, 1963, On Responsibility, 1967, Self Deception, 1969, Confucius: The Secular as Sacred, 1972, The Meaning of Criminal Insanity, 1972, Mental Disabilities and Criminals Responsibility, 1979. Washington and Lee U. Lewis law scholar, 1980; fellow NEH, NIMH, Walter Meyer Law Research Inst., Battelle Research Ctr., Addiction Research Inst., Royal Coll. Psychiatry; fellow Ctr. for Advanced Studies in Behavioral Sci., Stanford, 1985-86. Mem. Am. Philos. Assn. (pres. Pacific div. 1977-78). Home: 1507 APS Santa Barbara CA 93103 Office: Philosophy Dept U Calif Santa Barbara CA 93106

FINGER, PHILLIP REID, college administrator; b. St. Joseph, Mo., Feb. 9, 1941; s. Henry Reid and Norma Laura (Van Buskirk) F.; BA, U. Wash., 1963; MBA, Central Mo. U., 1974; m. Dorothy Ann Lund, Sept. 4, 1977; children: Derek Reid, Kevin Donald, James Edward. Sr. personnel asst. Seattle City Light, 1969-72; media technician III, Bellevue (Wash.) Community Coll., 1976-77, fin. aid supr., 1977-78, asst. dir.-fin. aid, 1978-79; asst. dir. fin. aid N. Seattle Community Coll., 1979-81; dir. fin. aid Yakima Valley Community Coll., 1981—. Served in USAF, 1964-68; Vietnam. Mem. Wash. Fin. Aid Assn. (exec. com.), Nat. Assn. Student Fin. Aid Adminstrs., Western Assn. Student Fin. Aid Adminstrs., Wash. Assn. Community Coll. Fin. Aid Adminstrs., Assn. Wash. Community Coll. Adminstrs., Wash. Council High Sch. and Coll. Relations. Office: 16th Ave and Nob Hill Blvd Yakima WA 98902

FINGER, THOMAS EMANUEL, neuroscience educator; b. Orange, N.J., Aug. 30, 1949; s. Sidney and Marjorie (Heyman) F.; m. Sheila O'Connell, Dec. 7, 1974; children: Katherine, Sarah, Rebecca. BS, MIT, 1971, MS, 1972, PhD, 1975. Research fellow Washington U., St. Louis, 1975-78; asst. prof. cellular and structural biology U. Colo. Sci. Ctr., Denver, 1978-84; assoc. prof. U. Colo., Denver, 1984—; study sect. mem. NIH, Bethesda, Md., 1984—; organizing com. Internat. Symposium on Olfaction and Taste, 1985-86. Mem. editorial bd. Jour. Comparative Neurology, 1980—, Brain, Behavior, Evolution, 1986—; contbr. numerous articles to profl. jours. Sloan Found. fellow, 1973, Grass Found. fellow, 1976; recipient Research Career Devel. award NIH, 1983—. Mem. Soc. Neurosci., Am. Assn. Anatomy, AAAS, Assn. Chemoreception Research. Office: U Colo Med Sch 4200 E 9th Ave Denver CO 80262

FINK, JAMES BREWSTER, consulting geophysicist; b. Los Angeles, Jan. 12, 1943. BS in Geophysics and Geochemistry, U. Ariz., 1969; MS in Geophysics cum laude, U. Witwatersrand, Johannesburg, Transvaal, Republic of South Africa, 1980. Registered profl. engr., Ariz.; registered land surveyor. Geophysicist Geo-Comp Exploration, Inc., Tucson, 1969-70; geophys. cons. IFEX-Geotechnica, S.A., Hermosillo, Sonora, Mex., 1970; chief geophysicist Mining Geophys. Surveys, Tucson, 1971-72; research asst. U. Ariz., Tucson, 1973; cons. geophysics Tucson, 1974-76; sr. minerals geophysicist Esso Minerals Africa, Inc., Johannesburg, 1976-79; sr. research geophysicist Exxon Prodn. Research Co., Houston, 1979-80; pres. Geophynque Internat., Tucson, 1980—; cons. on NSF research U. Ariz., 1984-85, adj. lectr. geol. engring., 1985-86, assoc. instr. geophysics, 1986—, supr. geophysicist, geohydrologist, 1986—, bd. dirs. Lab. Advanced Subsurface Imaging, 1986; lectr. South African Atomic Energy Bd., Pelindaba, 1979. Contbr. articles to profl. jours. Served to sgt. U.S. Air NG, 1965-70. Named Airman of Yr., U.S. Air NG, 1967. Mem. Soc. Exploration Geophysicists(co-chmn. Houston, 1980, Dallas, 1981), Am. Geophys. Union, European Assn. Exploration Geophysicists, South African Geophys. Assn., South African Council Nat. Scientists, Mineral and Geotech. Logging Soc., Assn. Petroleum Geochem. Explorationists, Ariz. Geol. Soc., Mining Geophysicists Denver, Mensa, Intertel, Triple Nine Soc. Republican. Avocations: reading, computers, natural sciences. Home: 5865 S Old Spanish Trail Tucson AZ 85747 Office: U Ariz Dept Mining and Geol Engring Tucson AZ 85721

FINK, JAMES WILLIAM, international business development executive, consultant; b. Los Angeles, Sept. 11, 1939; s. Frederick G. and Alma Irene (Eslick) F.; m. Linda Reavis, Apr. 22, 1967; children—Christi, Kevin, Andrew. B.A., Azusa Pacific U., 1961; postgrad. Calif. State U.-Los Angeles, Calif. State U.-Fullerton, 1962-63. Various mfg. and operational positions, 1962-76; dir. internat. materials control Revell, Inc., Venice, Calif., 1976-78, v.p. corp. materials mgmt. and quality assurance, 1978-79, v.p. engring., 1979-83, gen. mgr. Revell, Hong Kong, 1980-83, corp. sec., 1982-83; pres., dir. Jalack Enterprises, Garden Grove, Calif., 1984—; lectr. MBA program Azusa Pacific U., asst. prof. Calif. State, Los Angeles, Inst. Entrepreneurship. Mem. Am. Prodn. and Inventory Control Soc., Nat. Assn. Purchasing Mgmt., Internat. Material Mgmt. Soc., Am. Soc. Quality Control, Fgn. Trade Assn. So. Calif. Republican. Office: 12866 Main St Suite 201 Garden Grove CA 92640

FINK, RAYMOND RUSSELL, art educator; b. Long Beach, Calif., July 8, 1922; s. Halsey Hoarse Fink and Eleanor Oma (Jones) Wright; m. Sylvia Jean Sanders, Jan. 26, 1964. BAE, Art Inst. Chgo., 1952; MSAE, Ill. Inst. Design-Ill. Inst. Tech., 1955. Instr. Art Inst. Chgo., 1953-55, Ill. Inst. Design, Ill. Inst. Tech., Chgo., 1953-58; prof. art Ariz. State U., Tempe; 1958—. Executed murals Phoenix City Pub. Library, 1984, Nat. Housing Industry Bldg., Phoenix, 1973. Recipient Walte M. Campana prize Art Inst. Chgo., 1956, George Bright Meml. award Phoenix Art Mus., 1962; Momentum Mid-Continental Mementum, 1952-53; U.S. War Bonds Com. State Dept.,1959. Democrat. Baptist. Home: 7036 N 22d St Phoenix AZ 85020 Office: Ariz State U Sch Art Tempe AZ 85287

FINK, ROBERT JAMES, newspaper editor; b. Tacoma, Mar. 13, 1948; s. Robert J. and Verla Mae (Bates) F.; m. Carol J. Silbernagel, Sept. 2, 1967; children—Melissa, Michael, Stephen. B.S. in Social Sci., St. Cloud State U., 1970. Sports editor Morning Pioneer, Mandan, N.D., 1967-68; Daily Times, St. Cloud, Minn., 1968-70; news editor Gazette-times, Corvallis, Oreg., 1970-73; news editor Press Democrat, Santa Rosa, Calif., 1973-82, mng. editor, 1982—. Office: The Press Democrat PO Box 569 Santa Rosa CA 95402 *

FINKEL, JOEL ROBERTS, anticounterfeiting specialist; b. Chgo., Mar. 10, 1937; s. Max Jay and Dorothy (Roberts) F.; m. Ila Joy Gutter, June 14, 1959; children: Howard Sanford, Leslie Allyn. Student Ill. Inst. Tech., 1954-56; BS in Chemistry, Roosevelt U., 1958; postgrad., Purdue U., 1958-60. Research chemist Beckman Instruments, Fullerton, Calif., 1960-62; research engr. Aerojet Gen., Azusa, Calif., 1962-66; sr. scientist Melpar, Inc., Falls Church, Va., 1966-69; environ. engr. Grumman Aerospace, Bethpage, N.Y., 1969-70; owner J. R. Finkel & Assocs., Oxon Hill, Md., 1969-71; tech. mgr. GTE Labs., Inc., Waltham, Mass., 1970-83; sr. systems engr., mgr. bus. devel., info. security systems dept. Xerox Spl. Info. Systems, Pasadena, Calif., 1983-86; pres. S-P-I Tech, Inc., Calabasas, Calif., 1986—; co-chmn. tech. task force Internat. Anticounterfeiting Coalition, 1984-85; also patents cons., 1984-85. Commr. Wayland, Little League, Mass., 1973-75; CPR instr., trainer, Wayland, 1977-83. Mem. ASTM (counterfeiting subcom. 1985—), N.Y. Acad. Scis., Sigma Xi. Home: 5800-53 N Owensmouth Ave Woodland Hills CA 91367 Office: 23801 Calabasas Rd Suite 2015 Calabasas CA 91302

FINKEL, MARTIN HOWARD, marine chemist; b. Boston, Jan. 13, 1952; s. J. William and Bernice (Kagno) F. BS, U. Calif., 1974; MA, Webster U., 1981. Lab assoc. USDA Salinity Lab., Riverside, Calif., 1975-78; marine safety officer U.S. Coast Guard, St. Louis, 1979-82; cert. marine chemist, cons. Harbor Testing Lab., Wilmington, Calif., 1982—; owner, lab. dir. Finkel Analytical Lab., Lakewood, Calif., 1983—. Served to lt. USCG, 1979-81. Mem. Marine Chemists' Assn., Am. Indsl. Hygiene Assn. Avocations: snow skiing, flying, jazz, reading. Home: 4853 Coldbrook Ave Lakewood CA 90713 Office: Harbor Testing Lab PO Box 703 Wilmington CA 90748

FINKELMAN, JAY MATHEW, marketing professional; b. N.Y.C., Nov. 3, 1945; s. Milton and Florence (Sokolov) F.; m. Carin Lesley Wong, June 29, 1985. BA, CUNY, Bklyn., 1966; MBA, CCNY, 1968; PhD, NYU, 1970. Diplomate Am. Bd. Forensic Psychology, Am. Bd. Profl. Psychology. Lectr. Baruch Coll., N.Y.C., 1967-70, asst. prof. psychology, 1970-73, assoc. prof., 1974-77, prof., dean, 1977-81; exec. v.p. Lenox, Inc., N.Y.C., 1980; mgr. Sta. KTVU-TV, San Francisco, 1980-84; pres. TV Mktg. Co., Seattle, 1985; v.p. mktg. Walt Disney TV-Walt Disney Co., Burbank, Calif., 1985—; mem. doctoral bus. faculty CUNY, N.Y.C., 1974-79; cons. indsl., organizational and human factors engring., N.Y.; profl. assoc. BFS Psychol. Assn., Inc., N.Y.C.;. Co-editor: The Role of Human Factors in Computers, 1977; contbr. articles to profl. jours. Recipient Founders Day award NYU, 1971, Excellence in Teaching award CUNY, 1974, Faculty Research award CUNY, 1971-76. Mem. N.Y. Psychol. Assn. (cert.), Nat. Register Health Service Providers in Psychology (cert.), Am. Psychol. Assn. (pres. Met. chpt. 1978), Assn. Applied Psychology, N.Y. State Psychol. Assn., Acad. TV Arts and Sci. Home: 1735 Crisler Way Los Angeles CA 90069

FINKLEMAN, DAVID, military officer, aerospace engineer; b. N.Y.C., Aug. 31, 1940; s. Irving Solomon and Claire (Barachowitz) F.; m. Edith Fechter; children: Theodore, Daniel. BS, Va. Poly. Inst., 1963; SM, MIT, 1964, PhD, 1967. Asst. project mgr. tech., high energy laser project USN, Washington, 1973-80, dep. program mgr., directed energy weapons program, 1980-83; dir. tech./ systems, ballistic missile def. orgn. U.S. Army, Washington, 1983-85, dir. kinetic energy weapons, strategic def. initiative, 1984-85; dir. analysis U.S. space command, AF space command NORAD, Colorado Springs, Colo., 1985—. Contbr. articles to profl. jours. Docent Nat. Air and Space Mus., Washington, 1978-85. Served to capt. USAF, 1969-73, col. Res., 1973—. Assoc. fellow AIAA (nat. com. mem. 1975-80, Outstanding Young Scientist and Engr. award 1974); mem. AAAS, Am. Phys. Soc., Colo. Mountain Club (instr. mountaineering), Appalachian Trail Club, Washington Apple Pi Club, Sigma Xi, Tau Beta Pi. Lodge: Rotary. Avocations: mountaineering, skiing, radio-controlled aircraft, woodworking, needlepoint. Home: 1620 Big Valley Dr Colorado Springs CO 80919 Office: US Space Com /AN Peterson AFB CO 80914

FINLEY, JEFFREY ROBERT, lawyer; b. Phoenix, Apr. 17, 1959; s. Robert and Rhea Finley; m. Michelle Clair Finley, Sept. 6, 1980. BA in History, Stanford U., 1981; JD, Ariz. State U., 1984. Bar: Ariz. 1984, U.S. Dist. Ct. Ariz. 1984. Assoc. Fresquez & Fresquez, Flagstaff, Ariz., 1984-85, Teilborg, Sanders & Parks, Phoenix, 1985-86, Wisniewski, Surrano & Fendon, Phoenix, 1986—. Mem. ABA, Maricopa County Bar Assn., Phoenix Assn. Def. Counsel, Moot Ct. Bd. (chmn. 1983-84). Democrat. Roman Catholic. Office: Wisniewski Surrano & Fendon 3200 N Central #1550 Phoenix AZ 85012

FINLINSON, FRED WHEELER, lawyer, state senator; b. Murray, Utah, June 27, 1942; s. Fred Lyman and Luella (Wheeler) F.; m. Jeanne Braithwaite, June 13, 1967; children—Scott, Michelle, Laurie Ann, Jami, Robert. B.S. in Acctg., U. Utah, 1967, J.D., 1969. Bar: Utah 1969. Ski instr. Alf Engen Ski Sch., Alta, Utah, 1967-75; law clk. Utah Supreme Ct., 1968; asst. atty. gen. State of Utah, 1969; ptnr. Finlinson & Finlinson, Salt Lake City, 1971-85; dir. Callister, Duncan & Nebeker, 1985—; mem. Utah Senate, Salt Lake City, 1973—, minority whip, 1977-78, majority leader, 1979-80, chmn. energy and natural resources com., 1979—, chmn. ins. task force, 1985, chmn. reapportionment com. 1980-82, chmn. water devel. task force, 1982, chmn. oil and gas policy task force, 1983. Exec. dir. Utah Republican Party, 1969-72; v.p. Nat. Rep. Legislators' Assn., 1981-82, pres., 1983-84; del. to various state and Salt Lake County Rep. convs., 1964—. Mem. ABA, Utah Bar Assn., Salt Lake County Bar Assn., Am. Judicature Soc., Nat. Conf. State Legislatures, Nat. Rep. Legislators Assn. (pres. 1984-85), Natural Resources and Energy (vice chmn. 1980-81, chmn. 1983-84). Office: 720 Shiloh Way Murray UT 84107

FINN, FRANCIS WILLIAM, magazine publishing company executive; b. Washington, June 30, 1950; s. Gerald H. and Dorothy (Covey) F.; m. Hannah M. Lindsay, Apr. 24, 1970; children: Rebecca, Sean. BA in Lit., Coll. William and Mary, 1972. Assoc. editor Door & Hardware Inst., Washington, 1974-75; mng. editor Elec. Contractor, Washington, 1975-78; assoc. group editor 13-30 Corp., Knoxville, Tenn., 1978-83, exec. editor, 1983-84, v.p., editor, 1984-85; editorial dir. Commtek Pub., Boise, Idaho, 1985—. Mem. Am. Soc. Mag. Editors. Office: Commtek Pub PO Box 53 Boise ID 83707

FINN, SARA SHIELS, public relations consultant; b. Cin., July 12; d. Paul Vincent and Freda K. (Kohstall) Shiels; m. Thomas Finn, Nov. 11, 1952; children—Shawn, Paula, Anne-Marie, Sara Louise. B.A. in English, Maryville Coll., 1950. Reporter La Jolla (Calif.) Jour.; advt. and pub. relations rep. San Diego Mag., 1964-71; dir. pub. relations U. San Diego, 1971—; lectr. and cons.; dir. Ptnrs. for Liveable Places, 1984—. Pres. Nat. Assn. Alumnae of Sacred Heart, 1979-81; active San Diego Mus. Art. Inducted into Equestrian Order Holy Sepulchre induction, 1982, lady comdr., 1985; mem. parish council All Hallows Cath. Ch., La Jolla, Calif., 1983—. Mem. Pub. Relations Soc. Am. (accredited, bd. dirs. local and nat. chpts.), San Diego Press Club (charter mem.), Council Advancement and Support Edn., San Diego C. of C. Roman Catholic.

FINNANE, DANIEL F., M. Carol F.; 3 sons, 2 daughters. Grad. Univ. Wis., 1958. CPA. Registered rep. Robert W. Baird and Co., Wis., 1965-68; sr. v.p. Dain Bosworth and Co., Mpls.; pres. First Financial Group, 1975-82; exec. v.p. TOTAL-TV Inc. cable television system, Janesville, Wis., 1980-85; co-owner, now also pres. Golden State Warriors (Nat. Basketball Assn.), Oakland, Calif.; Mem. bd. dirs., Milwaukee Bucks (Nat. Basketball Assn.), 1978-85. Office: Golden State Warriors Oakland Collseum Arena Oakland CA 94621 *

FINNEGAN, WILLIAM GEORGE, chemist; b. Hancock, Mich., Dec. 19, 1923; s. William Michael and Edith Marie (Hoppa) F.; m. Martha Loraine Kautto, Oct. 6, 1952 (div. 1982); children: Timothy Allan, Nancy Marie. BS, U. Calif., Berkeley, 1944; PhD, Ohio State U., 1949. Postdoctoral fellow Calif. Inst. Tech., Pasadena, 1949-50; chemist Eastman Kodak, Rochester, N.Y., 1944-45, Naval Weapons Ctr., China Lake, Calif., 1950-78; research assoc. Colo. State U., 1978-85; research prof. Desert Research Inst., Reno, Nev., 1985—. Contbr. articles to profl. jours.; patentee in field. Mem. AAAS, Am. Chem. Soc., Am. Meteorology Soc., Sigma Xi, Alpha Chi Sigma. Avocation: science. Office: Desert Research Inst Sage Bldg PO Box 60220 Reno NV 89506

FINNIE, C(LARENCE) HERB(ERT), aerospace company executive; b. San Marcos, Tex., Feb. 22, 1930; s. Clarence Herbert and Robbie Mary (Hinkle) F.; B.S., S.W. Tex. State U., 1951; M.A., U. Calif.-Berkeley, 1955; M.B.A., U. Santa Clara, 1968; m. Bruna Rebecchi, June 28, 1955; children—Elisa Gene, John Herbert, Mary Lea, Ann Catherine. Bur. chief, disk jockey KCNY, 1950; with Lockheed Missiles & Space Co., Inc., Sunnyvale, Calif., 1958—, supr. computer programming, systems analyst, mgr. software design and devel., advanced system staff engr. sr; free-lance writer, photographer; pres. Creative Imagineering, Sunnyvale, 1984—; cons. in field. Mem. adv. bd. KRON-TV. Served to capt. USAF, 1951-58. Mem. Assn. Computing Machinery, Nat. Mgmt. Assn., Pentagon Players (charter), Photog. Soc. Am., Air Force Assn., Assn. Old Crows, Alpha Chi, Beta Gamma Sigma, Phi Mu Alpha Sinfonia. Roman Catholic. Club: Marquis. Designed and developed first generally used compiler prepared for a digital electronic computer, computer game package, 1952. Home: 1582 Lewiston Dr Sunnyvale CA 94087-4148 Office: Creative Imagineering 1111 Lockheed Way Sunnyvale CA 94088-3504

FINNIE, PHILLIP POWELL, aerospace engr.; b. Memphis, Dec. 21, 1933; s. Phillip and Daisy L. (Green) F.; B.S.C.E., Howard U., 1956; postgrad. U. Calif., Los Angeles, U. So. Calif.; M.B.A., Pepperdine U., 1979; m. Mary Bebe Clark, Sept. 14, 1968. Stress analyst N.Am. Aviation Corp., Los Angeles, 1956-59; dynamicist RCA, Van Nuys, Calif., 1959-62, Aerojet Gen. Corp., Azusa, Calif., 1962-64, Philco-Ford Corp., Newport Beach, Calif., 1964-67; dynamicist, analyst of radar observables, TRW Inc., Redondo Beach, Calif., 1967—. Mem. Republican Nat. Com. Mem. AIAA, Air Force Assn. Baptist. Home: 20102 Dalfsen Ave Carson CA 90746

FINOCCHIARO, MAURICE ANTHONY, philosophy educator; b. Floridia, Italy, June 13, 1942; s. Biagio and Jane (Mudano) F.; came to U.S., 1957; m. Ramona K. Thomason, Dec. 11, 1966. B.S., MIT, 1964; Ph.D., U. Calif.-Berkeley, 1969. Asst. prof. philosophy U. Nev., Las Vegas, 1970-74, assoc. prof., 1974-77, prof., 1977—. Recipient Barrick Disting. Scholar award U. Nev., 1981-82, 86-87; Nat. Endowment Humanities fellow, 1983-84; NSF grantee, 1976-77. Mem. Am. Philos. Assn., Philosophy of Sci. Assn., History of Sci. Soc., Soc. for Social Study Sci., Am. Hist. Sci. Assn., Am. Soc. Polit. and Legal Philosophy. Author: History of Science as Explanation, 1973; Galileo and the Art of Reasoning, 1980. Office: Dept Philosophy U Nev Las Vegas NV 89154

FINSTAD, LINETTE ARLOINE, speech pathologist; b. Fargo, N.D., Feb. 7, 1956; d. Lawrence Ellsworth and Arloine Mavis (Shern) F. Speech lang. pathologist Fairbanks North Star Borough Sch. Dist., Fairbanks, Alaska, 1981—. Mem. Fairbanks Meml. Hosp. Aux., 1983-86, Northland Chamber Chorale, Fairbanks, 1983—, Fairbanks Luth. Ch. Choir, 1983, PTA, Fairbanks, 1982—; vol. Love, Inc., Fairbanks, 1986—, Ofcl. Spl. Olympics, Fairbanks, 1986; Alaska rep. Nat. Ichthyosis Found., 1986—. Mem. Am. Speech Lang. and Hearing Assn. (cert., pres. No. chpt.1983-84), Friends of Interpreters Referral Line, Fairbanks Edn. Assn. (bldg. rep. 1983, 86—), Golden Heart Reading Council, (recording sec. 1986—), Assn. Children with Learning Disabilities, Alaska Speech Lang. and Hearing Assn. (sec. 1983-84, pres. No. chpt. 1983-84), Farthest North Club for Deaf. Home: 1606 Marika Rd #4 Fairbanks AK 99709 Office: Fairbanks North Star Borough Sch Dist PO Box 1250 Fairbanks AK 99707

FINZEL, LILJA MARIE TOBIE, data processing executive, management consultant; b. Portland, Oreg., Dec. 14, 1947; d. Richard Edward and Lily Ailin (Hakonen) Toban; m. Jack Edward Finzel, July 19, 1974. Student, Bard Coll., 1966; BA, Portland State U., 1969. Cert. info. systems auditor, data processor. Data processing quality assurance officer Western Bancorp, Portland, 1974-78; sr. programmer and analyst U.S. Nat. Bank of Oreg., Portland, 1978-79, info. security officer, 1984-86; EDP tech. systems auditor First Interstate Bank, Portland, 1979-81, data security officer, 1981-84; EDP audit mgr. Am. Savs. and Loan, Portland and Salt Lake City, 1986—; nat. com. mem. Bank Adminstrn. Inst., Chgo., 1984—. 1st v.p., treas. YWCA, Portland, 1980—, fin. chmn., 1985; pres., 1985-86; mem. steering com. Women and Tech. Symposium, Portland, 1985. Mem. EDP Auditors Assn. (pres. 1981-82, asst. region v.p. 1982-83, del. Peoples Republic of China 1986) Data Processing Mgmt. Assn. (bd. dirs., awards chair 1980-83, com. chair 1985-87, individual performance award 1984; com. chair 1985-87). Democrat. Lutheran. Club: Toastmasters (Portland) (pres.). Avocations: travel, reading, hiking. Home: 13707 SE Beech Milwaukie OR 97222 Office: Am Savings and Loan PO Box 40031 Portland OR 97240-0031

FIORINO, JOHN WAYNE, podiatrist; b. Charleroi, Pa., Sept. 30, 1946; s. Anthony Raymond and Mary Louise (Caramela) F.; m. Susan K. Bonnett, May 2, 1984; children—Jennifer, Jessica, Lauren; student Nassau Coll., 1969-70; B.A. in Biology, U. Buffalo, 1972; Dr. Podiatric Medicine, Ohio Coll. Podiatric Medicine, 1978. Salesman, E. J. Korvettes, Carle Place, N.Y., 1962-65; orderly Nassau Hosp., Mineola, N.Y., 1965-66; operating room technician-trainee heart-lung machine L.I. Jewish-Hillside Med. Center, New Hyde Park, N.Y., 1967-69; pharmacy technician Feinmel's Pharmacy, Roslyn Heights, N.Y., 1969-70; mgr., asst. buyer Fortunoffs, Westbury, N.Y., 1972-73; bd. certified perfusionist L.I. Jewish-Hillside Med. Center, New Hyde Park, N.Y., 1973-74; clin. instr. cardiopulmonary tech. Stony Brook (N.Y.) Univ., 1973-74; operating room technician Cleve. Met. Hosp., 1975; lab. technician Univ. Hosp., Cleve., 1976-78; staff podiatrist, 1979—; pvt. practice podiatry, Mesa, 1979—; staff podiatrist Sacaton (Ariz.) Hosp., 1979—, Mesa Gen. Hosp., 1979, Valley Luth. Hosp., Mesa, 1985, Chandler Community Hosp., 1985, Desert Samaritan Hosp., Mesa, 1986, podiatrist U.S. Govt. Nat. Inst., Sacaton, 1980-87, Indian Health Services, Sacaton, 1980-87; cons. staff Phoenix Indian Med. Ctr., 1985. Served with USN, 1966-67. Mem. Am. Podiatry Assn., Ariz. Podiatry Assn. (treas. 1984—), Acad. Ambulatory Foot Surgery, Am. Coll. Foot Surgeons (assoc.), Mut. Assn. Profls., Pi Delta, Alpha Gamma Kappa. Home: 2624 W Upland Dr Chandler AZ 85224 Office: 5520 E Main St Mesa AZ 85205

FIRBY, JAMES RONALD, paleontologist, educator; b. Detroit, Nov. 28, 1933; s. Hugh E. and Jean (Harper) F.; children—Leslie Jean, Rebeca Ruth Firby Aubin. B.A., San Francisco State U., 1960; M.A., U. Calif.-Berkeley, 1963, Ph.D., 1969. From lectr. to assoc. prof. geology and paleontology Mackay Sch. Mines, U. Nev.-Reno, 1966—; cons. to bus. Contbr. articles to profl. jours. Served with U.S. Army and USN, 1956-61; Ger. Mem. Am. Assn. Petroleum Geologists, Soc. Econ. Paleontologists and Mineralogists, Sigma Xi. Republican. Office: U Nev Reno NV 89557

FIRESTONE, CHARLES MORTON, lawyer, educator; b. St. Louis, Oct. 16, 1944; s. Victor and Betty (Solomon) F.; m. Pattie Winston Porter, Apr. 19, 1975; children—Laurel, Asa. B.A., Amherst Coll., 1966; J.D., Duke U., 1969. Bar: D.C. 1969, U.S. Ct. Appeals (D.C. cir.) 1970, U.S. Ct. Appeals (5th cir.) 1972, U.S. Ct. Appeals (9th cir.) 1973, U.S. Ct. Appeals (2d cir.) 1975, U.S. Ct. Appeals (3d cir.) 1976, U.S. Ct. Appeals 8th cir.) 1977, U.S. Supreme Ct. 1977, Calif. 1983. Litigation atty. FCC, Washington, 1969-73; dir. litigation Citizens Communications Ctr., Washington, 1973-77; adj. prof. law, dir. communications law program, UCLA, 1977-86; vis. lectr. UCLA Sch. Law, 1986-87; counsel firm Mitchell, Silberberg & Knupp, Los Angeles, 1983—; faculty adviser Fed. Communications Law Jour., Los Angeles, 1977-86; cons. FTC, Washington, Pub. Agenda Found., N.Y.C., 1978; counsel statewide television debates LWV, Los Angeles, 1978—; pres. Bd. Telecommunications Commrs., City of Los Angeles, 1984-86. Editor case materials, symposia resource manuals on communications; contbr. articles to profl. jours. Bd. dirs. Corp. for Disabilities and Telecommunications, Los Angeles, 1980-82, KCRW Found., Santa Monica, Calif., 1982—; adv. com. campaign Mondale for Pres., Los Angeles, 1984. Recipient Am. Jurisprudence award, 1968, 69; Cert. Commendation award Mayor Los Angeles, 1986; Resolution Commendation award City Council Los Angeles, 1986; Recognition award NOW, Nat. Black Media Coalition, Nat. Latino Media Coalition, Nat. Citizens Com. for Broadcasting, Washington, 1977; Luther Ely Smith scholar and Andrew Laurie scholar Amherst Coll., 1965-66. Mem. ABA (chmn. broadcast and spectrum use com., sect. sci. and tech. 1981-83, chmn. electronic campaigning com. 1984-86), Fed. Communications Bar Assn., Soc. Satellite Profls. (sec. bd. dirs. So. Calif. chpt. 1984—). Democrat. Jewish. Office: Mitchell Silberberg & Knupp 11377 W Olympic Blvd Los Angeles CA 90064

FIRKINS, WALTER WILLIS, JR., health maintenance company executive; b. Canon City, Colo., June 26, 1946; s. Walter W. and Dorothy Marie (Willis) F.; m. B. Anne Villyard, Aug. 18, 1968; children: Brent, Stephani. BA in Bus. and Acctg., Adams State Coll., 1975. Acct. Wall, Smith, Bateman Assocs., Alamosa, Colo., 1975-80; fin. adminstr. San Luis Valley HMO, Inc., Alamosa, 1980-82; ops. dir. HMO Health Plans Inc., Alamosa, 1982-85; v.p. ops. Health Systems Mgmt., Alamosa, 1986; v.p. ops., fin. Health Maintenance Orgn. Wash. Inc., Seattle, 1986—. Served with USN, 1966-70. Republican. Lodge: Masons. Avocations: skiing, fishing, stained glass. Home: 18139 195th Pl NE Woodinville WA 98072 Office: Health Maintenance Orgn Wash Inc 4010 Lake Washington Blvd Kirkland WA 98033

FISCHER, ALFRED GEORGE, geology educator; b. Rothenburg, Germany, Dec. 10, 1920; came to U.S., 1935; s. George Erwin and Thea (Freise) F.; m. Winnifred Varney, Sept. 26, 1939; children: Joseph Fred, George William, Lenore Ruth Fischer Walsh. Student, Northwestern Coll., Watertown, Wis., 1935-37; BA, U. Wis., 1939, MA, 1941; PhD, Columbia U., 1950. Instr. Va. Poly. Inst. and State U., Blacksburg, 1941-43; geologist Stanolind Oil & Gas Co., Kans. and Fla., 1943-46; instr. U. Rochester, N.Y., 1947-48; from instr. to asst. prof. U. Kans., Lawrence, 1948-51; sr. geologist Internat. Petroleum, Peru, 1951-56; prof. geology Princeton (N.J.) U., 1956-84, U. So. Calif., Los Angeles, 1984—. Co-Author: Invertebrate Fossils, 1952, The Permian Reef Complex, 1953, Electron Micrographs of Limestone, 1967; editor: Petroleum and Global Tectonics, 1975. Recipient Verrill medal

Yale U. Fellow Geol. Soc. Am., Soc. Econ. Paleontologists (hon., Twenhofel medal); mem. Am. Assn. Petroleum Geologists, AAAS, Paleontol. Soc., Deutsche Geologische Gesellschaft (Leopold von Buch medal), Geologische Vereinigung, Sigma Xi. Home: 1736 Perch St San Pedro CA 90732 Office: U So Calif Dept Geol Scis University Park Los Angeles CA 90089-0741

FISCHER, CRAIG LELAND, physician; b. Bklyn., Feb. 17, 1937; s. Emil Carl and Ruth Barbara (Minarcik) F.; m. Sandra Lucile Canfield, Feb. 17, 1962; children: Emil Lewis, Lisa Anne. BS, Kans. State U., 1958; MD, U. Kans., 1962. Diplomate Nat. Bd. Med. Examiners, Am. Bd. Family Practice; cert. anatomic and clin. pathology, nuclear medicine. Dir. labs. Eisenhower Med. Ctr., Rancho Mirage, Calif., 1973-78, dir. nuclear med., 1975-78; gen. practice medicine Palm Desert, Calif., 1978-80; chief med. ops. NASA, Houston, 1980-82; dir. labs. J.F. Kennedy Hosp., Indio, Calif., 1982—; asst. clin. prof. U. Calif., Irvine, 1986—; chmn., trustee Diametrix, Inc., Indio, 1985—; mem. sci. adv. bd. Dept. Air Force, Washington, 1986—. Contbr. numerous articles to profl. jours. Served to lt. col. USAFR, 1983—. Recipient Group Achievement award NASA Manned Spacecraft Ctr., 1966, 69, 70, Apollo 7 Flight Ops. Team award NASA Manned Spacecraft Ctr., 1969, Sustained Superior Achievement award NASA Manned Spacecraft Ctr., 1969, Skylab Group Achievement award NASA Johnson Space Ctr., 1974, Group Achievement award NASA, 1982, Presdl. medal of Freedom Apollo 13 Mission Ops. Team, 1970. Fellow Coll. Am. Pathologists, Am. Soc. Clin. Pathologists, Am. Pub. Health Assn., Am. Coll. Nuclear Physicians; mem. AAAS, Aerospace Med. Assn., N.Y. Acad. Scis., Calif. Soc. Pathologists, Riverside County Med. Assn. (councilor 1984—), Calif. Med. Assn., AMA, Palm Springs Acad. Medicine. Republican. Club: The Explorers (N.Y.C.). Avocations: sailing, tennis. Home: 45-800 Cholame Way Indian Wells CA 92260 Office: 47-001 Monroe Suite 104 Indio CA 92201

FISCHER, DOUGLAS ARTHUR, electrical engineer; b. Tokyo, Japan, Oct. 31, 1952; came to U.S., 1958; s. Robert Kay and Maryann (Carter) F. BEE, Mont. State U., 1974; MEE, So. Meth. U., 1983. Mem. staff Campus Crusade for Christ, San Bernardino, Calif., 1974-80; sr. engr. Gen. Dynamics, Ft. Worth, 1980-84; project engr. Honeywell Aeorspace (formerly Sperry Flight Systems), Albuquerque, 1984-86, sr. project engr., 1986—. Mem. IEEE, Tau Beta Pi. Republican. Mem. Evang. Ch. Home: 13404 Auburn NE Albuquerque NM 87112 Office: Honeywell Sperry Def Systems PO Box 9200 Albuquerque NM 87119

FISCHER, EDMOND HENRI, biochemistry educator; b. Shanghai, Republic of China, Apr. 20, 1920; came to U.S., 1953; s. Oscar and Renée (Tapernoux) F.; m. Beverley B. Bullock. Lic. es Sciences Chimiques et Biologiques, U. Geneva, 1943, Diplome d'Ingenieur Chimiste, 1944, PhD, 1947; D (hon.), U. Montpellier, France, 1985. Pvt. docent biochemistry U. Geneva, 1950-53; research assoc. biology Calif. Inst. Tech., Pasadena, 1953; asst. prof. biochemistry U. Wash., Seattle, 1953-56, assoc. prof., 1956-61, prof., 1961—; mem. exec. com. Pacific Slope Biochem. Conf., 1958-59, pres. 1975; mem. biochemistry study sect. NIH, 1959-64; symposium co-chmn. Battelle Seattle Research Ctr., 1970, 73, 78; mem. sci. adv. bd. Biozentrum, U. Basel, Switzerland, 1982-86; sci. adv. bd. Friedrich Miescher Inst., Ciba-Geigy, Basel, 1976-84, chmn. 1981-84; pres. Comite de Direction du Centre de Recherches de Biochimie Macromoleculaire, Montpellier, France, 1986. Contbr. numerous articles to sci. jours. Mem. sci. council on basic sci. Am. Heart Assn., 1977-80, sci. adv. com. Muscular Dystrophy Assn., 1980—, sci. adv. bd. Friedrich Miescher Inst. CIBA-GEIGY, Basel, 1976-84, chmn., 1981-84; pres. Comité de Direction du Centre de Recherches de Biochimie Macromoleculaire, Montpellier, France, 1986. Recipient Lederle Med. Faculty award, 1956-59, Guggenheim Found. award, 1963-64, Disting. Lectr. award U. Wash., 1983; Spl. fellow NIH, 1963-64. Mem. AAAS, AAUP, Am. Soc. Biol. Chemists (council mem. 1980-83), Am. Chem. Soc. (biochemistry div., mem. adv. bd. 1962, exec. com. div. biology 1969-72, monography adv. bd. 1971-73, editorial adv. bd. Biochemistry Jour., 1961-66, assoc. editor 1966—), Swiss Chem. Soc. (Werner medal), Brit. Biochem. Soc., Am. Acad. Arts and Scis., Nat. Acad. Scis., Sigma Xi. Office: U Wash Dept Biochemistry SJ70 Seattle WA 98195

FISCHER, FRED WALTER, physicist, engineer, educator; b. Zwickau, Germany, June 26, 1922; s. Fritz and Louiska (Richter) F.; B.S. in Mech. Engring., Columbia U., 1949, M.S., 1950; M.S. in Physics, U. Wash., 1957; Dr.Engr. in Elec. Engring., Tech. U. Munich, 1966; m. Yongja Kim, Oct. 1, 1970. Analyst, Boeing Co., Seattle, Munich, Bonn, W. Ger., 1950-84; cons. Boeing Co., 1984—; owner Fischer Cons.; instr. physics, math., and engring. North Seattle Community Coll., 1973—. Author: Analysis for Physics and Engineering, 1982. Served with AUS, 1943-46. Boeing scholar, Max Planck Inst. Plasma Physics, Munich, 1964-65. Mem. Sigma Xi (life). Office: North Seattle Community Coll 9600 College Way N Seattle WA 98103

FISCHER, HERMINA SUSANNA, entertainment executive; b. Haarlem, The Netherlands, Feb. 8, 1948; came to U.S., 1957; d. William P. and Susanna H. (Gosen) Vreenegoor; m. Richard A. Fischer, Mar. 7, 1976. Student, Orange Coast Community Coll., Costa Mesa, Calif. From tour guide to guest relations mgr. Disneyland, Anaheim, Calif., 1966-78; mktg. mgr. Pacific Northwest Walt Disney Co., Anaheim, Calif., 1979-84; sales mgr. U.S. tickets Expo 1986, Vancouver, B.C., Can., 1984-86. Recipient Silver Ice Dancing medal. Mem. Seattle Employee Services and Recreation Assn. (sec., membership chmn., chairperson 1987 conf.). Republican. Club: Wash. Athletic (Seattle). Avocations: competitive ice skating, bicycling. Office: The Fischer Co 4038 128th Ave SE Suite 220 Bellevue WA 98006

FISCHER, JEANETTE LUCILLE STOCKETT (MRS. RICHARD ALLEN FISCHER), occupational therapist; b. Albert Lea, Minn., Nov. 13, 1937; d. Stewart Joseph and Bessie Lucille (Junk) Stockett; B.S. in Occupational Therapy, Washington U., St. Louis, 1960; M.A. in Health Facility Mgmt., Webster Coll., St. Louis, 1981; m. Richard Allen Fischer, Oct. 22, 1960; children—Richard Arnold, Robert Andrew. Occupational therapy aide St. Louis State Hosp., 1958-59; dir. occupational therapy Alexian Bros. Hosp., St. Louis, 1960-62. Americana Healthcare Center, Florissant, Mo., 1975-80; coordinator occupational therapy, phys. medicine dept. St. Mary's Health Center, 1980-81; dir. occupational therapy dept. Fullerton (Calif.) Care Convalescent Hosp., 1981-84, Orange (Calif.) Region Coordinator Occupational Therapy Services Intermountain Healthcare Rehab. Services, 1985—. Contbr. to Management Techniques for Physical and Occupational Therapists, 1984. Clinic vol. aide ARC, 1971-73; treas. Midland Valley Estates Improvement Assn., 1966-68, 69-70, v.p., 1971-72, pres., 1972-73, bd. dirs., 1974-81, treas., 1972-73; treas., Marion PTA, carnival chmn., 1968-69, v.p., 1969-71, picnic chmn., 1969-73; sch. talent show dir. Boy Scouts Am., 1971-72; mem. St. Louis Civic Ballet, 1973-78; mem. Sta. KETC-TV Ednl. TV, 1971-78; sec.-receptionist Michael Simms Acad. Dance, St. Louis, 1974-76. Mem. Am., Mo. (public relations chmn. 1965. program chmn. 1979, pres. 1980-81), Calif. (v.p. Orange County chpt. 1983-84) occupational therapy assns., World Fedn. Occupational Therapy, Orange County Dirs. Forum, Los Angeles Occupational Therapy Dirs. Forum, Humane Soc. Mo., Alpha Xi Delta. Lutheran. Home: 4217 Elder Ave Seal Beach CA 90740 Office: 2222 N Harbor Blvd Fullerton CA 92635

FISCHER, JOEL, social work educator; b. Chgo., Apr. 22, 1939; s. Sam and Ruth (Feiges) F.; children—Lisa, Nicole. B.S., U. Ill., 1961, M.S.W., 1964; D.S.W., U. Calif., Berkeley, 1970. Prof. Sch. Social Work U. Hawaii, Honolulu, 1970—; vis. prof. George Warren Brown Sch. Social Work, Washington U., St. Louis, 1977, U. Wis. Sch. Social Welfare, Milw., 1978-79, U. Natal, South Africa, 1982, U. Hong Kong, 1986, Fordham U., 1987—; cons. various orgns. and univs. Author: (with Harvey L. Gochros) Planned Behavior Change: Behavior Modification in Social Work, 1975, Handbook of Behavior Therapy with Sexual Problems, Vol. I, 1977, Vol. II, 1977, Analyzing Research, 1975, Interpersonal Helping: Emerging Approaches for Social Work Practice, 1973, The Effectiveness of Social Casework, 1976, Fundamentals of Social Work Practice, 1982, Effective Casework Practice: An Eclectic Approach, 1978, (with Martin Bloom) Evaluating Practice: A Guide for the Helping Professions, 1982, (with Harvey L. Gochros) Treat Yourself to a Better Sex Life, 1980, Helping the Sexually Oppressed, 1986, (with Kevin Corcoran) Measures for Clinical Practice, 1987, (with Daniel Sanders) Visions for the Future: Social Work and Pacific-Asian Perspectives, 1987; contbr. over 120 articles, revs., chpts. and papers to profl. publs. Mem. Hawaii Com. for Africa. Served with U.S. Army, 1958. Mem. Nat. Assn. Social Workers, Council Social Work Edn., Acad. Cert. Social Workers, Nat. Conf. Social Welfare, AAUP. Democrat. Home: 1449-2 Hunakai St Honolulu HI 96816 Office: U Hawaii 2500 Campus Rd Honolulu HI 96822

FISCHER, KENNETH EDWARD, industrial hygienist; b. Englewood, N.J., June 9, 1940; s. Frank Joseph and Anna Clair (Dettner) F. BA, Fordham U., 1965; MS, Cath. U., 1970. Chmn. dept. phys. scis. Colegio San Ignacio, San Juan, Puerto Rico, 1965-68; resident engr. Western Electric Co., Arlington, Va., 1970-76; program analyst EPA, Washington, 1976-79; indsl. hygienist EPA Nat Enforcement Investigations Ctr., Denver, 1979. Tuition fellow Cath. U., 1968. Mem. Am. Indsl. Hygiene Assn. (hazardous wastes com.), Am. Conf. Govtl. Hygienists (hazardous wastes com.). Avocation: horticulture. Office: US EPA Nat Enforcement Investigations Ctr Box 25227 Bldg 53 Denver CO 80225

FISCHER, LEONARD, electronics executive; b. N.Y.C.. BS (hon.), Moses Holistic Ctr., 1985. Tech. dir. Video Access Ctr., N.Y.C., 1973-80; dir. engring. TRAX Softworks, Inc., Los Angeles, 1981—. Creator software products. Fellow Musical Instrument Digital Interface. Avocation: electronic music.

FISCHER, ROBERT BLANCHARD, university administrator, researcher; b. Hartford, Conn., Oct. 24, 1920; s. Charles Albert and Matilda (Nylen) F.; m. Mary Ellen Mitchell, June 29, 1946; children: Lois, Marcia, Philip, Vivian, Valerie. BS, Wheaton Coll., 1942; PhD, U. Ill., 1946. Research chemist U.S. Army Atomic Bomb Project, Chgo., 1944-46; instr. chemistry U. Ill., Urbana, 1946-48; prof. chemistry Indiana U., Bloomington, 1948-63; dean sch. of sci. Calif. State U.-Dominguez Hills, Carson, 1963-79, dean emeritus, 1979—; provost, sr. v.p. Biola U., La Mirada, Calif., 1979—; research assoc. Calif. Inst. Tech., Pasadena, 1959-60; cons. in field. Contbr. articles to profl. jours. Fellow AAAS, Am. Sci. Affiliation (nat. pres. 1965-66); mem. Am. Chem. Soc. (sect. and region chmn.). Republican. Avocations: theology, amateur radio, sports. Home: 30238 Via Victoria Rancho Palos Verdes CA 90274 Office: Biola U 13800 Biola Ave La Mirada CA 90639

FISCHER, ROBERT EDWARD, meterologist; b. Bethlehem, Pa., Aug. 4, 1943; s. Frederic Philip and Muriel Winifred (Johnson) F. BS cum laude, U. Utah, 1966; MS, Colo. State U., 1969. Meterologist Nat. Weather Service, Fairbanks, Alaska, 1973—. Contbr. articles to profl. jours. Fellow Royal Meteorol. Soc.; mem. Am. Meteorol. Soc. (Charles L. Mitchell award 1985), Nat. Weather Assn., Sigma Xi, Phi Kappa Phi. Avocations: running, photography, astronomy, bird watching. Home: Box 82210 Fairbanks AK 99708 Office: Nat Weather Service Forecast Office 101 12th Ave Box 12 Fairbanks AK 99701

FISCHER, VIRGINIA RIGG, educator, poet; b. Alderson, W.Va.; A.B., Coll. William and Mary; M.A., Northwestern U.; postgrad. W.Va. U., Va. Poly. Inst. and U.; m. Monroe C. Fischer. Chmn. dept. theatre arts Lander Coll., Greenwood, S.C.; hosp. recreation worker ARC, Ft. Campbell, Ky. and Ft. Jackson, Columbia, S.C.; costume designer, radio dir., dept. theatre arts Va. Commonwealth U., Richmond; instr. English dept. Va. Poly. Inst. and U., Blacksburg; costume designer Dock St. Theatre, Charleston, S.C.; founder Blacksburg Thursday Contemporary Book Club. Recipient 1st place prize Nev. Bicentennial Poetry Contest. Mem. Nat. League Am. Pen Women, DAR (state motion picture chmn.), Fedn. Chaparral Poets, World Poetry Soc. Intercontinental, Acad. Am. Poets, Delta Delta Delta, Theta Alpha Phi, Alpha Psi Omega, Zeta Phi Eta. Republican. Methodist. Club: Mesquite. Contbr. poetry to various publs.

FISCHER, ZOE ANN, real estate and property marketing company executive, real estate consultant; b. Los Angeles, Aug. 26, 1939; d. George and Marguerite (Carrasco) Routsos; m. Douglas Clare Fischer, Aug. 6, 1960 (div. 1970); children—Brent Sean Cecil, Tahlia Georgienne Marguerite Bianca. B.F.A. in Design, UCLA, 1964. Pres. Zoe Antiques, Beverly Hills, Calif., 1973—; v.p. Harleigh Sandler Real Estate Corp. (now Merrill Lynch), 1980-81; exec. v.p. Coast to Coast Real Estate & Land Devel. Corp., Century City, Calif., 1981-83; pres. New Market Devel., Inc., Beverly Hills, 1983—; dir. mktg. Mirabella, Los Angeles, 1983, Autumn Pointe, Los Angeles, 1983-84, Desert Hills, Antelope Valley, Calif., 1984-85; cons. Lowe Corp., Los Angeles, 1985. Designer album cover for Clare Fischer Orch. (Grammy award nomination 1962). Soprano Roger Wagner Choir, UCLA, 1963-64. Mem. UCLA Alumni Assn. Democrat. Roman Catholic. Avocations: skiing, designing jewelry, interior design, antique collecting, photography.

FISH, RICHARD HERBERT, staff scientist; b. Providence, Sept. 7, 1939; s. Jerome and Florence (Lang) F.; m. Ann Judith Chandler, Aug. 21, 1961 (div. 1974); children: David E., Michael P. BS, U. R.I., 1961; PhD, U. N.H., 1964. Research chemist U.S. Borax Research Corp., Anaheim, Calif., 1965-67; lectr. U. Calif., Irvine, 1967-68; sr. research chemist ARCO Chem. Co., Anaheim, 1969-70; research chemist USDA, Berkeley, Calif., 1970-73, U. Calif., Berkeley, 1973-79; staff scientist U. Calif. Lawrence Berkeley Lab., 1979—; vis. prof. U. Utrecht, Netherlands, 1978, U. Bordeaux (France), 1984; cons. ARCO Co., Los Angeles, 1983-84; Chevron Chem. Co., Richmond, Calif, 1986. Contbr. articles to profl. jours.; patentee in field. Mem. AAAS, Am. Chem. Soc., N.Y. Acad. Sci., Sigma Xi. Home: 527 Woodmont Ave Berkeley CA 94708 Office: Lawrence Berkeley Lab U Calif Berkeley CA 94720

FISH, RICHARD WAYNE, chemistry educator; b. Gowrie, Iowa, Aug. 27, 1934; s. Albert Lawrence and Myrtle Lulu (Carr) F.; m. Madeleine Paula Fischer, June 14, 1964; children: Brian Charles, Daniel Mark. BS in Chemistry, Iowa State U., 1956; PhD in Organic Chemistry, Mich. State U., 1960. Research chemist Chevron Research subs. Standard Oil Co. Calif., Richmond, Calif., 1960-61; research assoc. Brandeis U., Waltham, Mass., 1961-63; NSF postdoctoral fellow U. Calif., Berkeley, 1963-64; mem. faculty Calif. State U., Sacramento, 1964—, prof. chemistry, 1970. Recipient research award Calif State U., Sacramento, 1968-69, Meritorious Performance Incentive award, Calif. State U., Sacramento, 1985. Mem. Am. Chem. Soc. (chmn. Sacramento sect. 1982-83), Sigma Xi. Democrat. Home: 180 Breckenwood Way Sacramento CA 95864 Office: Calif State U Dept Chem Sacramento CA 95819

FISH, RUBY MAE BERTRAM (MRS. FREDERICK GOODRICH FISH), civic worker; b. Sheridan, Wyo., July 24, 1918; d. Ryan Lawrence and Ruby (Beckwith) Bertram; R.N., St. Luke's Hosp., 1936; postgrad. Washington U., St. Louis, 1941; m. Frederick Goodrich Fish, Apr. 12, 1942; children—Bertram Frederick, Lisbeth Ann Fish Kalstein. Staff nurse Huntington Meml. Hosp., Pasadena, Calif., 1941-42; dr.'s office nurse, Denver, 1943-44; travel cons. Buckingham Travel Agy., Aurora, Colo., 1976—. Bd. dirs. Jefferson County Easter Seal Soc., 1949—, pres., 1952-53, 56-57, 66-67; pres. Colo. Easter Seal Soc., 1960-61; bd. dirs. Nat. Easter Seal Soc., 1968-69, sec. ho. of dels., 1976-77; bd. dirs. Assistance League Denver, 1968-70, 75-76, People to People for Handicapped; mem. Pres.'s Com. on Employing Handicapped, 1976—; active Rehab. Internat. of U.S.A., 1972—, Rehab. Internat., 1960—; v.p. Denver chpt. Freedom Found. at Valley Forge. Mem. Dau. of Nile-El Mejedel. Home: 4646 Bow Mar Dr Littleton CO 80123 Office: 13741 E Mississippi Ave Aurora CO 80012

FISH, WILLIAM, environmental research chemist; b. Dania, Fla., Apr. 26, 1956; s. William and Ethel Matilda (Schoedel) F. BSE, U. Fla., 1979; PhD, MIT, 1984. Post-doctoral fellow Oreg. Grad. Ctr., Beaverton, 1984-85, asst. prof. chemistry, 1986—; cons. Pro-Solve Inc., Cambridge, Mass., 1983-84. Contbr. articles to profl. jours. Grantee U.S. Geol. Survey, 1985-86. Mem. AAAS, Internat. Humic Substances Soc., Am. Soc. Limnology and Oceanography, Sigma Xi. Democrat. Avocations: bicycling, hiking, skiing, gardening. Home: 3142 SE Yamhill St Portland OR 97214 Office: Oreg Grad Ctr 19600 NW Von Neumann Dr Beaverton OR 97006-1999

FISHBEIN, JUSTIN MANTEL, communications specialist, writer, editor; b. Chgo., Apr. 7, 1927; s. Morris and Anna (Mantel) F.; m. Ann Demereckis, July 21, 1951; children: Amy Louise Jackson, Morris Daniel, Anne Marie. AB, Harvard U., 1949. Newsman Chgo. Sun-Times Newspaper, 1949-60; editor and editorial mgr. Sci. Research Assocs., Inc., Chgo., 1960-76; communications specialist IBM, Chgo., 1976-78, Dallas, 1978-81; mgr. communications and community relations IBM Space Shuttle Programs, Houston, 1981-84, IBM, Boulder, Colo., 1984—. Author: Successful Marriage, 1970, A Question of Competence: Language, Intelligence and Learning to Read, 1972, Dr. Fishbein's International Medical Encyclopedia, 1977. Active Lincoln Park Zool. Soc., Field Mus. Natural History, Art Inst. Chgo., Chgo. Hist. Soc., Chgo. Hort. Soc., Internat. Wildlife Fedn. Nat. Audubon Soc., Smithsonian Instn., Am. Mus. Natural History; bd. dirs. Boulder Bach Festival, 1985—, Boulder Hist. Soc., 1985—, Congregation Har Hashem, Boulder, 1986—. Served with USN, 1945-46. Recipient Am. Polit. Sci. Assn. award, 1956, Disting. Service award Highland Park C. of C., 1964. Mem. Pub. Relations Soc. Am. (accredited), Chgo. Newspaper Reporters Assn., Chgo. Press Vets. Assn. Jewish. Clubs: Tavern, Harvard, Mastiff of Am., Old English Mastiff (Eng.); Rocky Mountain Univ. (v.p. 1985—). Home: 3800 Spring Valley Rd Boulder CO 80302

FISHBEIN, MICHAEL CLAUDE, physician, pathologist; b. Brussels, May 25, 1946; came to U.S., 1949; s. Fred F. and Celia (Feldman) F.; m. Astrid Lorette du Mortier, Aug. 11, 1974; children: Danielle Renee, Gregory Andrew. BS, U. Ill., 1967; MD, U. Ill., Chgo., 1971. Diplomate Coll. Am. Pathologists; cert. anatomic and clin. pathology. Intern UCLA/Harbor Gen. Hosp., 1971-72, resident, 1972-75; asst. prof. pathology Harvard U. Sch. Medicine, Boston, 1975-78; assoc. pathologist Peter Bent Brigham Hosp., Boston, 1975-78, Cedars-Sinai Med. Ctr., Los Angeles, 1978—; cons. Beth Israel Hosp., Boston, 1975-78, mem. faculty Harvard U.-MIT program in health scis., Boston, 1975-78; adj. prof. UCLA Sch. Medicine, 1978—. Contbr. articles to profl. jours. Mem. Phi Beta Kappa, Alpha Omega Alpha. Jewish. Avocation: tennis. Office: Cedars-Sinai Med Ctr 8700 Beverly Blvd Los Angeles CA 90048

FISHER, ALAN STEPHEN, physicist; b. Toronto, Ont., Can., Aug. 13, 1953; s. Ralph and Edith Molly (Kruger) F.; m. Barbara Rose Sommer, June 10, 1979. SB in Physics, MIT, 1974, SB in Elec. Engring., 1974, PhD in Physics, 1983. Research assoc. MIT, Cambridge, 1983; sr. scientist research div. Raytheon Corp., Lexington, Mass., 1983-84; research assoc. elec. engring. dept. Stanford (Calif.) U., 1985—. Contbr. articles to profl. jours. Mem. AAAS, IEEE, Am. Phys. Soc., Phi Beta Kappa, Sigma Xi. Office: Stanford U 308 McCullough Bldg Stanford CA 94305

FISHER, ALBERT L., geography educator; b. Meadow, Utah, Sept. 5, 1925; s. Albert Hyrum and Alta Jane (Beckstrand) F.; m. Dorothy Bishop, June 16, 1950; children: Geraldine Fisher Richards, Barbara Fisher Olsen, Douglas Albert. BS, U. Utah, 1951; MA, Johns Hopkins U., 1952, PhD, 1954. Asst. prof. geography Brigham Young U., Provo, Utah, 1954-56, chmn. dept. geography, 1959-60; with U.S. Govt., Washington and overseas, 1956-59; chmn. dept. geography U. Utah, Salt Lake City, 1960-70, prof. geography, 1971—; mem. social studies adv. com., Utah Office Edn., Salt Lake City, 1967—, textbook com., 1967—. Author: (books) World People and Places, latest rev. ed., 1985, Utah Geography, latest rev. ed., 1986; (TV programs) Utah Geography, 1979-82 (Am. Film Festival award 1983), World Cultural Geography. Recipient Disting. Service award Oreg. State U., 1978. Mem. Utah Acad. Scis., Arts and Letters (pres. 1985-87), Western Social Scis. Assn. (pres. 1969-70), Assn. Am. Geographers (div. chmn. 1968-70), Phi Kappa Phi (nat. pres. 1977-80). Mormon. Avocations: boating, hiking, racquetball. Home: 1885 Millcreek Way Salt Lake City UT 84106 Office: U Utah Dept Geography 270 Orson Spencer Hall Salt Lake City UT 84112

FISHER, ALICE EVELYN, univ. official; b. Eldon, Iowa, July 14, 1919; d. John and Olive (Randall) Fisher; student U. Mo., 1937-39; B.A., Parsons Coll., 1940. Wire chief S.W. Daily Times, Liberal, Kans., 1944-45; editor Forum, Eldon, 1947-49; sta. mgr., sec.-treas. KBIZ, KTVO-TV, Ottumwa, Iowa, 1950-57; exec. dir. Ottumwa Community Chest, 1957-63; publs. mgr. U. Calif. Extension, Riverside, 1964-84, coordinator Pub. Relations Programs, 1984—. County chmn. Am. Cancer Soc., 1956-57; mem. communications com. San Gorgonio council Girl Scouts U.S.A., 1974-82, chmn., 1978-81, bd. dirs., 1978-81; sec. Animal Relief League, 1955-63; v.p Ottumwa Community Players, 1957; mem. pub. relations com. San Bernardino YWCA. Recipient Best Acting Female in Minor Role award Ottumwa Community Players, 1959; Pub. Relations Practice certificate U. Calif., 1973. Mem. Pub. Relations Soc. Am. (Most Outstanding Contbn. to Pub. Edn. award Calif. Inland Empire chpt. 1973, 79, 80, 81, award of excellence for outstanding contbn. to pub. relations 1982, 84, 85, disting. award 1986, sec. 1973-75, pres. 1975-76, bd. dirs. 1973—, treas. 1985, del. assembly 1980-81, chmn. profl. devel. 1977—), AAUW (Iowa State editor 1957, v.p. Riverside br. 1985), World Affairs Council, Alpha Chi Omega. Republican. Baptist. Clubs: Soroptimist (assembly del.) Eastern Star. Home: 2900 Pecos Way Riverside CA 92506 Office: U Calif 1161 Adminstrn Bldg Riverside CA 92521

FISHER, BENJAMIN PAUL, architect; b. El Paso, Tex., Apr. 26, 1952; s. Robert Sheldon and Ann Gordon (Clise) F.; m. Margaret Anne Long, July 31, 1976; children: Winston Sheldon, Matthew Stuart, Myles Gordon. BA, Stanford U., 1974; M in Bus. Adminstrn., U. Calif., 1983. Registered architect, Calif.; lic. gen. contractor, Calif. Architect Ron Nunn Assocs., San Francisco, 1975, Wm. Gleckman Assocs., N.Y.C., 1975-76; gen. contractor San Francisco, 1976-78; architect L. Gale Abels Assocs., Boulder, Colo., 1978-80, D.M.J.M., Denver, 1980-81; studio mgr. Kaplan, McLaughlin, Diaz, San Francisco, 1984-86; dir. ops. IDG Architects, Inc., Oakland, Calif., 1986—. Author: Marketing for Architectural Services, 1983. Trustee Stanford Sailing Assn. Mem. Berkeley Real Estate Assn., Soc. Mktg. Profl. Services, Stanford Alumni Assn., Am. Soc. Aging, Nat. Trust Hist. Preservation, Profl. Services Mgmt. Assn., Tau Beta Pi. Republican. Avocations: sailing, backpacking, choral singing, tennis. Home: 792 Mandana Blvd Oakland CA 94610 Office: IDG Architects 1730 Franklin St Oakland CA 94612

FISHER, DELBERT ARTHUR, physician, educator; b. Placerville, Calif., Aug. 12, 1928; s. Arthur Lloyd and Thelma (Johnson) F.; m. Beverly Carne Fisher, Jan. 28, 1951; children: David Arthur, Thomas Martin, Mary Kathryn. B.A., U. Calif., Berkeley, 1950; M.D., U. Calif., San Francisco, 1953. Diplomate: Am. Bd. Pediatrics (examiner 1971-80, mem. subcom. pediatric endocrinology 1976-79). Intern, then resident in pediatrics U. Calif. Med. Center, San Francisco, 1953-55; resident in pediatrics U. Oreg. Hosp., Portland, 1957-58; Irwin Meml. fellow pediatric endocrinology U. Oreg. Hosp., 1958-60; from asst. prof. to prof. pediatrics U. Ark. Med. Sch., Little Rock, 1960-68; prof. pediatrics UCLA Med. Sch., 1968-73; prof. pediatrics and medicine 1973—; research prof. devel. and perinatal biology Harbor-UCLA Med. Ctr., 1975-85, chmn. pediatrics, 1985—; cons. genetic disease sect. Calif. Dept. Health Services, 1978—; mem. organizing com. Internat. Conf. Newborn Thyroid Screening, 1977-82. Co-editor: 5 books including Pediatric Thyroidology, 1985; editor-in-chief: Jour. Clin. Endocrinology and Metabolism, 1978-83; Pediatric Research, 1984—; contbr. 350 articles profl. jours., chpts. to 80 books. Served to capt. M.C. USAF, 1955-57. Recipient Career Devel. award NIH, 1964-68. Mem. Am. Acad. Pediatrics (Borden award 1981), Soc. Pediatric Research (v.p. 1973-74), Am. Pediatric Soc., Endocrine Soc. (pres. 1983-84), Am. Thyroid Assn., Am. Soc. Clin. Investigation, Assn. Am. Physicians, Lawson Wilkins Pediatric Endocrine Soc. (pres. 1982-83), Western Soc. Pediatric Research (pres. 1983-84), Phi Beta Kappa, Alpha Omega Alpha. Home: 4 Pear Tree Ln Rolling Hills Estates CA 90274 Office: Dept Pediatrics Harbor-UCLA Med Center 1000 W Carson St Torrance CA 90509

FISHER, DONALD G., casual apparel chain stores executive; b. 1928; married. B.S., U. Calif., 1950. With M. Fisher & Son, 1950-57; former ptnr. Fisher Property Investment Co.; co-founder, pres. The Gap Stores Inc., San Bruno, Calif., dir. Office: The Gap Stores Inc 900 Cherry Ave Box 60 San Bruno CA 94066 *

FISHER, EVALYN JEAN, interior designer; b. Roswell, N.Mex., Aug. 27, 1943; d. Newel Edward and Genevieve (Kester) Porter; m. Robert Earl Fisher, Apr. 3, 1966. BA in Art and Design, Calif. State U., Los Angeles, 1968. Cert. tchr., Calif.; cert. interior and environ., designer, Calif. Art instr. pub. schs. Baldwin Park and Rialto, Calif., 1969-74; visual arts specialist pub. schs. Riverside, Calif., 1975-79; assoc. designer Maryanne

Levine Interior Designs, Los Angeles, 1982-85; prin. Evalyn Fisher, ASID & Assocs., Redlands, Calif., 1985—; adj. instr. U. Calif., Riverside, Fashion Inst. Design and Merchandising, Los Angeles and Santa Ana, Calif., 1985—. Recipient numerous design awards from area hist. socs. and civic groups. Mem. Am. Soc. Interior Designers (cert.). Democrat. Office: Evalyn Fisher ASID & Assocs 300 E State St Suite 503 Redlands CA 92373

FISHER, FREDERICK HENDRICK, oceanographer; b. Aberdeen, Wash., Dec. 30, 1926; s. Sverre and Astrid (Kristofferson) F.; midshipman U.S. Naval Acad., 1945-47; B.S., U. Wash., 1949, Ph.D., 1957; m. Julie Gay Saund, June 17, 1955; children—Bruce Allen, Mark Edward, Keith Russell, Glen Michael. Research fellow acoustics Harvard, 1957-58; research physicist, research oceanographer Marine Phys. Lab., Scripps Instn. Oceanography, La Jolla, Calif., 1958—, asso. dir., 1975—; dir. research Havens Industries, San Diego, 1963-64; prof., chmn. dept. physics U. R.I., Kingston, 1970-71; mem. environ. sci. panel Naval Research Adv. Com., 1984—; mem. governing bd. Am. Inst. Physics, 1984—; cons., 1964—; lectr. Nat. Acad. Scis., NRC. Contbr. numerous articles to prol. jours.; patentee in field. Mem. San Diego County Dem. Cen. Com., 1956-57, 60-62; NCAA nat. tennis doubles champion, 1949. Served with USNR, 1945. Fellow Acoustical Soc. Am. (assoc. editor jour. 1969-76, v.p. 1980-81, pres. 1983-84, lectr.), Explorers Club; mem. IEEE (sr.), Am. Chem. Soc., U.S. Naval Inst., Am. Inst. Physics (gov. bd. 1985—), Marine Tech. Soc., Am. Geophys. Union, U.S. Naval Inst., Am. Def. Preparedness Assn., Sigma Xi, AAAS, Pi Mu Epsilon. Club: Seattle Tennis. Co-designer research platform FLIP, 1960-62, chief scientist numerous seatrips. Home: 3726 Charles St San Diego CA 92106 Office: U Calif Marine Phys Lab Scripps Inst Oceanography La Jolla CA 92093

FISHER, GERALD SAUL, lawyer, financial consultant, publisher; b. Bronx, N.Y., Mar. 24, 1931; s. Abraham Samuel and Rose (Richards) F.; m. Sue Louise Chidakel, Apr. 7, 1957; children—Steven Lawrence, A. Jody, David Scot. B.B.A., Clark U., 1952; J.D., Boston U., 1955. Bar: Mass. 1955, D.C. 1962, U.S. Supreme Ct. 1962. Atty.-adviser div. corp. finance SEC, 1956-58; with SBA, 1958-67, asst. dep. adminstr. investment, 1963-65, asst. dep. adminstr. procurement and mgmt. assistance, 1965-67; adminstrv. v.p. internat. foods div. Internat. Industries; pres. Copper Penny Family Restaurants (an Internat. Industries Co.), 1969-71; v.p. real estate Internat. Industries, 1971-72; pres. Triota Orgn., 1972—; pres., chmn. Sir Speedy, Inc., 1975-78; pub. Tile & Decorative Surfaces mag., Worldwide Meetings and Incentives mag., Contemporary Dialysis mag., Dimensional Stone mag., Encino, Calif., 1978—; lectr. franchising and small bus. financing Practising Law Inst. Author articles in field.; sr. editor Boston U. Law Rev. Recipient awards for outstanding service to govt. Mem. Am., Fed. bar assns., Phi Theta Kappa. Home: 4450 Callada Pl Tarzana CA 91356 Office: 17901 Ventura Blvd Encino CA 91316

FISHER, GLENN ANDREW, science educator; b. N.Y.C., Sept. 5, 1947; s. Robert Andrews and Glory Ann (Zahradnik) F.; m. Jane Ellen Fisher, May 2, 1971; children: David, Daniel. BS in Chemistry, Harvey Mudd Coll., 1969. Cert. elem. tchr., Calif. Tchr. San Ramon (Calif.) Valley Unified Sch. Dist., 1974-81; computer specialist Alameda County Office Edn., Hayward, Calif., 1981-85; program dir. Lawrence Hall Sci., Berkeley, Calif., 1985—. Co-author: Commodore 64 Data File Programming, 1985; author, editor: Technology in the Curriculum Science Resource Guide, 1986; contbr. articles to profl. jours. Mem. Elem Sch. Sci. Assn., Calif. Math. Council, Computer-Using Educators (pres. 1983-86), Assn. Supervision and Curriculum Devel. Avocations: hiking, sailing, cello, chamber music. Office: U Calif Lawrence Hall Sci Berkeley CA 94720

FISHER, JOEL MARSHALL, political scientist, legal recruiter; b. Chgo., June 24, 1935; s. Dan and Nell (Kolvin) F.; m. Linda Joyce Buss, 1970; children: Sara Melinda, Matthew Nicholas. A.B., U. So. Calif., 1955; LL.B., U. Calif.-Berkeley, M.A.; Ph.D. in Govt., Claremont Grad. Sch., 1968. Orgn. dir. Republican Citizens Com. of U.S., Washington, 1964-65; dir. arts and scis. state legis. divs. Rep. Nat. Com., Washington, 1968-69; asst. dep. counsel to pres. U.S. White House, 1969-70; dep. asst. sec. econ. and social affairs U.S. Dept. State, Washington, 1969-71; vis. prof. comparative and internat. law Loyola U. Sch. Law, Los Angeles, 1972-73; dir. World Bus. Inst., Ctr. Internat. Bus., Pepperdine U., Los Angeles, 1974-75; prof. constl. law Southwestern U. Sch. Law, Los Angeles, 1974-76; dir. World Trade Inst. So. Calif., 1976—; prof. internat. law, asst. dean Whitter Coll. Sch. Law, Los Angeles, 1977-80; prin. Ziskind, Greene and Assocs., 1980-83; v.p. Wells Internat., 1983-84; pres. LawSearch Inc., 1984—; ofcl. visitor The European Communities, 1974, 76; mem. U.S. dels. UN confs., 1969-71; chmn. Strategy for Peace Conf. Panel on U.S. and UN, 1972—; coordinator Series on the Contemporary Am. Presidency, 1972-73; cons. Interconti, Inc., 1975-76, Robert Taft Inst., 1977—, World Trade Inst. N.Y., 1977-80, Woodstock Prodns., 1978-81, Curtis, Hoxter & co., N.Y.C., 1978-83. Co-author two books; contbr. articles on polit. sci. and law to profl. publs. Mem. steering com. Calif. Com. for Reelection of Pres., 1972; nat. chmn. Community Leaders for Ford, 1976; trustee Rep. Assocs., 1978—; mem. vestry, sr. warden St. Michael and All Angeles Ch., Studio City, Calif., 1983-86, mem. diocesan council Los Angeles, 1986—, chmn. budget com. 1987. Fellow Nobel Found., 1958; Falk fellow, 1961-62. Mem. Am. Soc. Internat. Law, Am. Polit. Sci. Assn. (state legis. fellow 1970-73). Home: 4963 Bluebell Ave North Hollywood CA 91607 Office: 16000 Ventura Blvd Encino CA 91436

FISHER, JOHN SERGIO, architect, educator; b. Milano, Italy, May 7, 1934; s. Albert Darius and Elsa Maria (Weinstock) F.; came to U.S., 1939, naturalized, 1952; B.Arch., Carnegie Inst. Tech., 1958; Finnish Inst. Tech., 1959; M.Arch., Carnegie Inst. Tech., 1961; m. Bonnie Jean McIntosh, Jan. 28, 1962; children—Ava, Carina, Matt. Asst. prof. dept. architecture U. Calif., Berkeley, 1963-69; partner Fisher/Jackson Assos., Architects/Urban Designers, Berkeley, N.Y.C., 1964-67; pres. Fisher/Jackson Assos., Inc., Architecture/Systems Development/Urban Planning, Berkeley, Calif., 1967-72; dean Sch. Architecture, Syracuse (N.Y.) U., 1972-75; pres. John Sergio Fisher AIA & Assos., Inc., Tarzana and Oakland, Calif., 1976—; adj. lectr. dept. architecture Calif. Poly. Inst., Pomona, fall 1975, Sch. Architecture and Urban Planning, UCLA, 1979, 80, 82; hearing examiner Calif. Bd. Archtl. Examiners. Shelter analyst, instr. Office of CD, 1962; mem. Com. on Aging, Berkeley, 1966-69; chmn. Fisher Housing Systems, 1977-79; trustee Los Angeles Actors Theatre, 1979—; bd. dirs. Back Alley Theatre, 1986—. Fulbright grantee, 1958; HUD Urban Devel. Action grantee, 1979, 82. Mem. AIA (San Francisco chpt. Spl. Design award 1969, Grand award, 1986, Honor award, 1986), Design Methods Group, Internat. Solar Energy Soc., Inst. Urban Planning, Nat. Trust Historic Preservation. Democrat. Patentee in industrialized housing. Office: 5567 Reseda Blvd #209 Tarzana CA 91356

FISHER, JOSEPH STEWART, diversified electronics company executive; b. Athens, Pa., Mar. 3, 1933; s. Samuel Royer and Agnes Corinne (Smith) F.; m. Anita Ann Coyle, May 15, 1954; 1 child, Samuel Royer. BS in Tech. Mgmt., Regis Coll., 1981. Field engr. IBM Corp., Syracuse, N.Y., 1956-60; qualtiy analyst, engr. IBM Corp., Endicott, N.Y., 1960-68; systems support adminstr. IBM Corp., Boulder, Colo., 1968-72, field support adminstr., 1972-78, systems assurance adminstr., 1978-79, security adminstr., 1979-87; sec. cons. Fisher Enterprises, Boulder, 1980—; bd. dirs. Vervcraft Inc., Boulder, Am. Protective Securities Services, Boulder, Asset Protective Services, Loveland, Colo. Leadership devel. Boy Scouts Am., Boulder, 1975—, chmn. long range planning, 1982-86, mem. bd. Longs Peak Council 1983—; bd. dirs. Colo. Crime Stoppers. Served with USN, 1952-56, Korea. Recipient Silver Beaver award Boy Scouts Am., Boulder, 1978, Wood Badge Beads, Boy Scouts Am., 1975. Mem. Am. Soc. Indsl. Security (cert. CPP 1984, treas. 1985), Colo. Crime Prevention Assn. Republican. Methodist. Lodges: Elks, Optimists, Masons (treas. Columbia lodge 1969-85). Avocations: scouting, fishing, camping. Home and Office: 4645 Bedford Ct Boulder CO 80301

FISHER, KATHLEEN MARY, biology educator; b. Long Branch, Aug. 4, 1938; d. James F. and Katherine E. Flynn; m. L. Karl Fisher, Dec. 4, 1959 (div. 1980); children: Tawn Fisher Dale, Dore. BS, Rugers U., 1960; PhD, U. Calif., Davis, 1969. Professorial series U. Calif., Davis, 1971—; postdoctoral fellow Atomic Energy Commn., Davis, 1970; dir. teaching resources ctr., U. Calif., Davis, 1974-79; program assoc. NSF, Washington, 1980-81; Fulbright lectr., Universiti Sains, Penang, Malaysia, 1980. Contbr. articles to profl. jours.; editor, producer tv programs on genetics and sci. writing. Mem. AAAS, Am. Ednl. Research Assn., Nat. Assn. Research in Sci. Teaching, Sigma Xi. Club: Tradewinds Sailing. Office: U Calif Dept Edn Davis CA 95616

FISHER, KENNETH L., sculptor; b. Tacoma, Apr. 28, 1944; s. Henry John and Anna Mary (Trafford) F. B.S., U. Oreg., 1968, B.F.A., 1969, M.F.A., 1971. Cert. univ. level tchr., Calif. One-man shows include Thelma Pearson Gallery, Lincoln City, Oreg., 1971, Internat. Art Gallery, Pitts., 1971, Jewish Community Ctr., Portland, Oreg., 1971, Howell Street Gallery, Seattle, 1981, Lakewood Ctr. Gallery, Lake Oswego, Oreg., 1983, William Temple House, Portland, 1984, Grants Pass Art Mus., Oreg., 1984, 86, Benton County Hist. Mus., Philomath, Oreg., 1984, Pacific U., Forest Grove, Oreg., 1985, Mondak Hist. & Art Soc., Sidney, Mont., 1986, Umpqua Community Coll., Roseburg, Oreg., 1986, Lower Columbia Coll., Longview, Wash., 1987, Pacific Northwest Art Expo., Seattle, 1987; group shows include Coos Art Mus., Oreg., 1981 (hon. mention), 82, Ga. Inst. Tech., 1982, 83 (cert. of recognition), Painters and Sculptors Soc., N.J., 1982, La. Arts Guild, 1982, Galerie Triangle, Washington, 1982, 83, Alexandria Mus. Arts, La., 1982, Terrance Gallery, N.Y.C., 1982 (hon. mention), Cooperstown Art Assn., N.Y., 1982, Knickerbocker Artists, N.Y.C., 1982, 83, 84, Idaho State U. (1st place award), 1982, Del Mar Coll., (Joseph A. Cain Meml. Purchase award in sculpture), Corpus Christi, Tex., 1982, 83, Goldsboro's 3d Ann. Juried Exhbn., N.C., 1982, Fine Arts League 14th Nat. Show (1st place award), Colo., 1982, Franklin Sq. Gallery (M. Grumbacher Inc. Bronze medallion), N.C., 1982, J.K. Ralston Mus. (1st and 2d Place awards), Mont., 1982, Oreg. State U. (honor award), 1983, Hill Country Arts Found., 11th Ann. Exhbn. (1st place award in sculpture), Tex., 1983, Hill Country Arts Found., Tex., 1983, Art Ann. Four, Okla., 1983, Audubon Artists, N.Y.C., 1983, 86, Salmagundi Club, N.Y.C., 1983, Las Vegas Art Mus., 1984, Nat. Art Appreciation Soc., 1984 (hon. mention), Palm Beach Galleries, La. (grand prize), 1984, NAD, N.Y.C., 1984, Allied Artists Am., N.Y.C., 1984, N.Am. Sculpture Exhbn., Colo., 1986, Audobon Artists Nat. exhbn., 1986, 87; represented in permanent collections Grants Pass Art Mus., Coos Art Mus., U. Oreg. Mus. Art, Oreg. State U., Del Mar Coll., Pacific U., Umpqua Community Coll., U. Portland, also numerous pvt. collections. Mem. Portland Art Assn.

FISHER, KNUTE ADRIAN, biochemistry educator; b. Woodland, Calif., Dec. 2, 1941; s. Daniel Earl Fisher and Karin AnneRose (Peterson) Harvey; m. Sharon Kay Wheeler, June 12, 1965; 1 child, Kurt Adrian. BS, U. Calif., Davis, 1967, MS, 1969; PhD, U. Calif., Berkeley, 1974. Teaching and research asst. U. Calif., Berkeley and Davis, 1967-73; acting instr. electron microscopy U. Calif., Berkeley, 1973; postgrad. researcher biophysics U. Calif., San Francisco, 1974-77, asst. adj. prof. biochemistry, 1977-80, assoc. adj. prof., 1980—; referee grant proposals NIH, NSF, 1970—; study sect. advisor NIH, 1984. Referee manuscripts Jour. Sci., Nature, Jour. Membrane Biology; contbr. articles to profl. jours. Judge sci. fair, Kensington, Calif., 1979-82. Fellow NDEA, 1969; grantee NIH, 1980, 83. Mem. AAAS, Am. Heart Assn., Am. Soc. Cell Biology (edn. com. 1983-86 manuscript referee 1970—), Biophys. Soc., Electron Microscopy Soc. Am. (manuscript referee 1970—), M.W.C.A. (chmn. lease com. 1983-86, rep. 1982-86), Sigma Xi. Democrat. Avocations: folkdance, electronics, computers, photography. Home: 144 Highland Blvd Kensington CA 94708 Office: U Calif Dept Biochemistry Biophysics Cardiovascular Research Inst 1327-M CVRI San Francisco CA 94143-0130

FISHER, LAWRENCE W., public relations company executive; b. Los Angeles, June 5, 1938; s. Gilbert W. and Augusta (Gelsheimer) F.; A.B. magna cum laude, U. So. Calif., 1960; m. Elizabeth Sheridan Burke, July 16, 1966; children—Lawrence Timothy, Lara Elizabeth. Legislative asst. Speaker Assembly, Calif. Legislature, 1960-62; exec. dir. Democratic State Central Com., 1962-66; pres. Braun & Co., Los Angeles, 1966—. Dir. Norris Cancer Hosp. and Research Center. Mem. Town Hall, Phi Beta Kappa, Sigma Delta Chi. Home: 767 Via de la Paz Pacific Palisades CA 90272 Office: 3580 Wilshire Blvd Los Angeles CA 90010

FISHER, MICHAEL EDWARD, electrical engineer, consultant; b. Tulsa, Sept. 24, 1949; s. Edward Thomas and Bertha Lynn (Sanders) F.; m. Phyllis Dilworth, Oct. 6, 1979; children—Marsha Nichole, Marc Elliot, Alicia Joy, Sandra Janelle. Student UCLA, 1969, 71; B.S. in Elec. Engring., Washington U., St. Louis, 1971; MSEE, U. So. Calif., 1985. Broadcast engr. Sta. KVOO-TV, Tulsa, 1966-68; elec. design engr. Rockwell Internat., El Segundo, Calif., 1969-73; elec. design engr. Hughes Aircraft, Fullerton, Calif., 1973-78, staff systems engr., 1981-87, sr. staff systems engr., 1985—; project engr. Technicolor, Costa Mesa, Calif., 1978-79, Interstate Electronics, Anaheim, Calif., 1979-81. Scholar Washington U., 1968-71; Hughes Masters fellow Hughes Aircraft, 1983-85. Mem. Mu Alpha Theta. Republican. Home: 598 Camono De La Cima San Marcos CA 92069 Office: Hughes Aircraft 1901 Malvern PO Box 3310 Fullerton CA 92634

FISHER, NANCY LOUISE, pediatrician, medical geneticist; b. Cleve., July 4, 1944; d. Nelson Leopold and Catherine (Harris) F.; m. Larry William Larson, May 31, 1976; 1 child, Jonathan Raymond. Student, Notre Dame Coll., Cleve., 1962-64; BSN, Wayne State U., 1967; postgrad., Calif. State U., Hayward, 1971-72; MD, Baylor Coll. of Medicine, 1976; M in Pub. Health, U. Wash., 1982. Diplomate Am. Bd. Pediatrics. RN coronary care unit and med. intensive care unit Highland Gen. Hosp., Oakland, Calif., 1970-72; RN coronary care unit Alameda (Calif.) Hosp., 1972-73; intern in pediatrics Baylor Coll. of Medicine, Houston, 1976-77, resident in pediatrics, 1977-78; attending physician, pediatric clinic Harborview Med. Ctr., Seattle, 1980-81; staff physician children and adolescent health care clinic Columbia Health Ctr., Seattle, 1981—, founder, dir. of med. genetics clinic, 1984—; maternal child health policy cons. King County div. Seattle King County Dept Pub. Health, 1983-85; nurses aide psychiatry Sinai Hosp., Detroit, 1966-67; charge nurse Women's Hosp., Cleve., 1967; research asst. to Dr. Shelly Liss, 1976; with Baylor Housestaff Assn., Baylor Coll. Medicine, 1980-81; clin. asst. prof. grad. sch. nursing, U. Wash., Seattle, 1981-85; clin. asst. prof. dept. pediatrics, U. Wash., Seattle, 1982—; com. appointments include Seattle CCS Cleft Palate Panel, 1984—; bd. dirs., first v.p. King County Assn. Sickle Cell Disease 1985—, acting pres. 1986, pres. 1986-87; hosp. affiliation include Childrens Orthopedic Hosp. and Med. Ctr., Seattle, 1981—, Virginia Mason Hosp., Seattle, 1985—, Harborview Hosp., Seattle, 1986—. Contbr. articles to profl. jours. Active Seattle Urban League, 1982—, 101 Balck Women, 1986—; bd. dirs. Seattle Sickle Cell Affected Family Assn., 1984-85. Served to lt. USN Nurse Corps, 1966-70. Mem. Student Governing Body and Graduating Policy Com. Baylor Coll. Medicine (founding mem. 1973-76), Loans and Scholarship Com. Baylor Coll. Medicine (voting mem. 1973-76), Am. Med. Student Assn., Student Nat. Med. Assn., Admission Com. Baylor Coll. Medicine (voting mem. 1974-76), AMA, Am. Med. Women's Assn., Am. Acad. Pediatrics, Am. Pub. Health Assn., Am. Soc. Human Genetics, Birth Defects and Clin. Genetics Soc., Wash. State Assn. Black Providers of Health Care, Northwest Chpt. Soc. Adolescent Medicine, Wash. State Soc. Pediatrics, Sierra Club, Sigma Gamma Rho, Phi Delta Epsilon. Address: 600 Wellington Seattle WA 98122

FISHER, PHYLLIS KAHN, social worker; b. Oakland, Calif., Mar. 30, 1919; d. Sidney Stanwood Kahn and Helen (Rosenberg) Geballe; m. Leon Harold Fisher, Dec. 21, 1941; children: Robert Alan, Lawrence Edgar, Carol Fisher Slotnick, David Bruce. AB, U. Calif., Berkeley, 1940, MSW, 1966. Lic. clin. social worker. Sr. social worker Children's Health Council, Palo Alto, Calif., 1966-79; pvt. clin. practice Atherton, Calif., 1982—; part-time sr. social worker, supr. Tokyo Community Counseling Service, 1979-82, Internat. Sch. Sacred Heart, Tokyo, 1979-82; cons. Aoibashi Clinic, Kyoto, Japan, 1980-81, Albert L. Schultz Jewish Community Ctr., Palo Alto, 1983-84; vis. instr. U. Wash. Sch. Social Work, Seattle, summer 1979; lectr. social work, child abuse Japan, India, New Zealand, Australia, U.S.; leader workshops and presentations. Author: Los Alamos Experience, 1985 (translated into Japanese, 1986); contbr. numerous articles to scholarly and profl. jours. in Japan and U.S. People to people child and family mental health del. to People's Republic China, 1987. Mem. Nat. Assn. Social Workers (diplomate in clin. social work), Prytanean Soc., Nat. Council of Jewish Women (past pres. local chpts.), LWV, Beyond War, New Forum, Pi Phi Delta. Democrat. Jewish. Home and Office: 102 Encinal Ave Atherton CA 94025

FISHER, RICHARD ALLEN, social worker; b. Walker, Minn., Sept. 6, 1939; s. Donald F. and Agnes H. (Dahlgren) F.; m. Phyllis K. Haynes, June 9, 1962; children: Kari Beth, Ann Marie. BA, Mankato State Coll., 1964, MS in Human Services, 1981; MSW, U. Utah, 1969. Lic. social worker II, Colo. Chief clin. services Gerard Schs., Austin, Minn., 1972-80; chief clinician mental health St. Mary Corwin Hosp., Pueblo, Colo., 1980-86; pvt. practice social work Pueblo, 1984-86; dir. behavioral programs Rocky Mountain Hosp., Denver, 1986—; social work cons. Sangre de Cristo Hospice, Pueblo, 1985—. Treas. Dream Weavers So. Colo., Pueblo, 1985-86. Served with U.S. Army, 1958-61. Mem. Nat. Assn. Social Workers (cert., bd. dirs. 1985—). Methodist. Home: 1102 Candytuft Pueblo CO 81001 Office: Rocky Mountain Hosp 4701 E 9th Ave Denver CO 80220

FISHER, RICHARD FORREST, soils educator, academic administrator; b. Champaign, Ill., May 15, 1941; s. Richard Forrest Fisher and Hannah Elizabeth (Ponath) Kistler; m. Karen Dangerfield Fisher, Sept. 4, 1959; children: William Forrest, Marilu, Kevin Royden. BS, U. Ill., 1963; MS, Cornell U., 1967, PhD, 1968. Research scientist Can. Forestry Service, Sault Sainte Marie, Ont., 1968-69; asst. prof. forestry U. Ill., Urbana, 1969-72; assoc. prof. U. Toronto, Ont., 1972-77; prof. U. Fla., Gainesville, 1977-82; prof. and head dept. forest resources Utah State U., Logan, 1982—. Contbr. articles to profl. jours. Fellow Soc. Am. Foresters; mem. Soil Sci. Soc. Am. (assoc. editor journal), Assn. Tropical Biology, Internat. Soc. Tropical foresters, AAAS, Ecol. Soc. Am. Democrat. Avocations: round dance cuer, tchr. Home: 1573 E 1260N Logan UT 84321 Office: Utah State U Forest Resources Dept Logan UT 84322-5215

FISHER, ROBERT FRANCIS, architect; b. Cin., July 9, 1921; s. Robert Howard and Faye (Maple) F.; m. Mary Angeline Marchese, Apr. 8, 1944; children: Elizabeth, Ingrid, Cary. BSCE, Oreg. State U., 1944; BArch, U. Mich., 1946. Registered architect, Oreg., Calif., Idaho. Drafter Pietro Belluschi, Portland, Oreg., 1946-48; pvt. practice architecture Grants Pass, Oreg., 1948—; siesmology collaborator Nat. Earthquake Service, Grants Pass. Prin. works include numerous chs., schs., colls., nursing homes, hosps., comml. indsl., bldgs., Oreg. Chmn. City Planning Com., Grants Pass, 1960-67 (mem. 1954-77), County Great Decisions Study Groups, Josephine County, Oreg., 1958-64; v.p. Josephine County Council Boy Scouts Am., 1955; lay leader Newman Meth. Ch., Grants Pass, 1953-54. Served with U.S. Army, 1943-45, ETO. Decorated EAME Ribbon with 2 Bronze stars. Mem. AIA (held various offices So. Oreg. chpt. 1965-69), Phi Kappa Phi, Tau Sigma Delta. Republican. Club: Active (Grants Pass) (v.p. 1950-51). Avocations: running, tennis, sailing, travel. Home: 220 NE Hillcrest Dr Grants Pass OR 97526 Office: 131 NE B St Grants Pass OR 97526

FISHER, ROBERT JAMES, public relations consultant, advertising executive; b. Kingston, Pa., Oct. 2, 1942; s. Harold Wilson and Esther Luella (Cole) F.; m. Patricia Gail Kelso, May 17, 1975; children: Christian Scott, Tiffany Nicole. Student, Santa Moncia City Coll., 1960-62, Valley State Coll., 1964; BA in Pub. Relations, San Jose State Coll., 1966. Reporter Los Angeles bur. N.Y. Times, 1968; pub. relations dir. Los Angeles Beautiful, 1969; asst. account exec. Harshe-Rotman and Druck, Los Angeles, 1967-70; account exec. Burson-Marsteller, Los Angeles, 1970-71; promotion dir. Atlantic Richfield Plaza, Los Angeles, 1971-73; account supr. Doremus and Co., Los Angeles, 1973-78; ptnr. Fisher and Gillespie, Los Angeles, 1978-80; pres. Fisher and Assocs., Inc., Los Angeles, 1980—. Voluntary probation officer County of Los Angeles, 1970-72; active Big Bros. of Los Angeles, 1974-79; mem. Town Hall Calif., Los Angeles, 1986—. Served with U.S. Army, 1966-68. Mem. Pub. Relations Soc. Am., Publicity Club Los Angeles (bd. dirs.), Pub. Interest Radio and TV Ednl. Soc., Los Angeles Jr. C. of C., Am. Heart Assn. (communications com. mem. 1981—). Republican. Methodist. Avocations: spectator sports, tennis, travel. Office: Fisher and Assocs Inc 15300 Ventura Blvd Suite 514 Sherman Oaks CA 91403-3103

FISHER, ROBERT WILSON, geologist, consultant; b. Chgo., May 11, 1931; s. Clyde and Mary Hannah (Robb) F.; m.. Martha Sue Johnson, Apr. 5, 1952 (div. 1976); children—Thomas R., Richard W., Andrew D., David C.; m., Lauren Huddleston, Apr. 5, 1976. B.S., U. Ill.-Urbana, 1953, M.S., 1956. Cert. prof. petroleum geologist, geol. scientist. Research analyst Ill. Geol. Survey, Champaign, Ill., 1955-56; project geologist Amoco Prodn. Co., New Orleans, 1956-64; chief geologist Estate of William G. Helis, New Orleans, 1964-81; v.p. Lynx Exploration Co., Denver, 1981-83; pres. Bradden Exploration Co., Denver, 1983-86; founder, chmn. Fisher Energy Group, Denver, 1986—. Author: The Fisher Report, 1986, 87; co-author: Visual Estimates of Grain Size Distribution in Some Chester Sandstones, 1959; map compiler Geol. Map of Ill., 1967; contbr. articles to profl. jours. Active Com. for Responsible Devel. of Bergen Park (Colo.), 1983-84. Served to 1st lt. U.S. Army, 1953-55. Mem. Am. Assn. Petroleum Geologists, Am. Inst. Profl. Geologists, Rocky Mountain Assn. Geologists, Internat. Transactional Analysis Assn. (advanced), Ind. Petroleum Assn. Am. (bd. dirs.), Soc. Ind. Earth Scientists. Home: 127 Sawmill Dr Evergreen CO 80439 Office: Fisher Energy Group 1020 15th St Suite 4-L Denver CO 80202

FISHER, STEVEN KAY, neurobiology eductor; b. Rochester, Ind., July 18, 1942; s. Stewart King and Hazel Madeline (Howell) F.; m. Dinah Dawn Marschall, May 2, 1971; children: Jenni Dawn, Brian Andrew, Steven William. BS, Purdue U., 1964, MS, 1966; postgrad., Johns Hopkins U., 1967-69; PhD, Purdue U., 1969. Postdoctoral fellow Johns Hopkins U., Balt., 1969-71; prof. U. Calif., Santa Barbara, 1971—, dir. Inst. Environ. Stress, 1985—; cons. Ultrastructure Tech., Goleta, Calif., 1984—. Contbr. numerous articles to profl. jours. Grantee NIH, 1971—; recipient Devel. award NIH, 1980-84. Mem. AAAS, Assn. Research in Vision and Ophthalmology (mem. program com. 1979-80), Soc. Neurosci., Am. Soc. Cell Biology, Electron Microscopy Soc. Am. Avocations: music, gardening, lit. Home: 6890 Sabado Tarde Rd Goleta CA 93117 Office: U Calif Dept Biol Scis Santa Barbara CA 93106

FISHER, WILLIAM HENRY, education educator; b. York, Pa., July 4, 1912; s. Charles Henry and Mary Naomi (Light) F.; m. Christine Albers, June 25, 1938 (dec. Nov. 1959); 1 child, Charles Albers; m. Ruth Dyer, Dec. 27, 1962. BA in Sociology, Secondary Edn., U. Wash., 1935, MEd, 1943; DEd in Social Studies Edn., Columbia U., 1949. Tchr. social studies Wapato (Wash.) Sr. High Sch., 1936-39, Kirkland (Wash.) Sr. High Sch., 1939-44, Fieldston Sch. of The Ethical Culture Soc., N.Y.C., 1945-47; asst. prof. edn., sociology Eastern Wash. State U., Cheney, 1947-50; asst. prof., supr. student tchrs. U. Ariz., Tucson, 1950-51, Temple U., Phila., 1951-52, Wilkes Coll., Wilkes-Barre, Pa., 1952-53; curriculum dir. Las Vegas (N.Mex.) Pub. Schs., 1953-56, supt. schs., 1956-61; assoc. prof. edn. U. Tex., El Paso, 1961-67, assoc. prof., 1967-71; prof. U. Mont., Missoula, 1971—; vis. prof. (summers) Highlands U., Las Vegas, N.Mex., 1950-55, U. N.Mex., Albuquerque, 1961, Western State Coll., Gunnison, Colo. (summers) 1960, 63, 66, Eastern Ill. U., Charleston, 1967, U. Fla. Gainesville, 1971, U. Tenn., Knoxville, 1976; v.p. student council Tchrs. Coll., Columbia, 1946-47; appointed to commn. to revise the high sch. Phys. Edn. Curriculum, N.Mex., 1954-56; pres. Coop. Program in Ednl. Adminstrn., N.Mex., 1960-61; program chmn. Trans-Pecos Edn. Conf. U. Tex., El Paso, 1963-65; chmn. umbrella com. supporting grad. programs Sch. Edn. U. Mont., 1968-78; instr. in field, Mont. Contbr. numerous articles to profl. jours. Mem. AAUP (pres. Univ. Tex.-El Paso chpt. 1964-65), NEA, Philosophy of Edn. Soc., Am. Edn. Studies Assn., Western Social Sci. Assn., Phi Delta Kappa, Kappa Delta Pi. Home: 604 Plymouth Missoula MT 59801 Office: U Mont Sch Edn Missoula MT 59812

FISHKIN, GERALD LOREN, psychologist, educator; b. Bronx, N.Y., Aug. 16, 1944. A.A., El Camino Jr. Coll., Torrance, Calif., 1965; B.A., Calif. State Coll., Long Beach, 1967; M.S., Brigham Young U., 1969; Ph.D., U.S. Internat. U., 1978. Research asst. psychology dept. Calif. State Coll., Long Beach, 1965-66, dir. research-counseling and testing dept., asst. prof. ednl. psychology, 1969-70, cons. to police officers standards and tng. workshops Center for Criminal Justice, 1975—; clin. psychometrist VA Hosp., Long Beach, 1966-68; clin. intern Brigham Young U. Counseling Center, Provo, Utah, 1968-69; pvt. practice psychology, Long Beach, 1970—; cons. psychologist Long Beach Meml. Hosp., 1970-74; founder, coordinator dept. spl. edn. Long Beach City Coll., 1971-77, instr. applied psychology for law enforcement, dept. adminstrn. of justice, 1972—, assoc. prof. and psychologist, 1978—; pvt. clin. practice, 1978—; cons. Long Beach Police Dept., 1975; dir. Community Rehab. Industries, Inc. Mem. Mayor's Com. for Employment Handicapped, Long Beach; bd. dirs. Long Beach Retarded Children's Found. Mem. NEA, Calif. Tchrs. Assn., Harbor Soc. Clin. Hypnosis, Am. Psychol. Assn., Calif. Assn. Marriage and Family Therapists, Calif. Community and Jr. Coll. Assn. (Task Force on Post-Secondary Ednl.

Programs for Developmentally Disabled), Brit. Psychol. Soc. (fgn. affiliate), Long Beach Police Officers Assn. (hon.), Phi Delta Kappa. Office: 5199 E Pacific Coast Hwy Suite 304 N Long Beach CA 90804

FISHMAN, JOEL LAWRENCE, public relations and marketing executive; b. Los Angeles, Oct. 12, 1947; s. Herman Jerome and Dorothy (Feld) F.; m. Catherine Doubleday, June 23, 1974. BA, U. Calif., Berkeley, 1969; JD, U. So. Calif., 1976. Bar: Calif., 1977. Adminstrv. asst. Congressman Thomas Rees, Washington, 1970-74; sole practice Los Angeles, 1976-83; pres. Joel Fishman & Assocs., Beverly Hills, Calif., 1984—. Dir. Olympic Torch Relay Los Angeles Olympic Organizing Com., 1983-84; chmn. Calif. Lexington Group, Los Angeles, 1986; mem. exec. com. UCLA Govtl. Relations program, 1986; mem. Los Angeles Mayor's 2000 com.; mem. 1991 U.S. Olympic Sports Festival Bldg. Com., Western Regional Corp. Solicitation Com., mem. Los Angeles Conservancy, 1986. Recipient Key to City Indpls., 1984. Mem. Calif. Bar Assn., D.C. Bar Assn., Pub. Relations Soc. Am., Phi Beta Kappa. Democrat. Jewish. Avocations: sailing, tennis, music. Office: 450 N Roxbury Dr Suite 602 Beverly Hills CA 90210

FISHMAN, LINDA KAY, social worker; b. Youngstown, Ohio, Feb. 8, 1939; d. Samuel Richard and Syd Ruth (Hoffman) Zoss; m. Lawrence Shelden Fishman, June 12, 1960 (div. 1975); 1 child, Julie Ann. BA magna cum laude, U. Mich., 1960, MSW, 1961. Clin. social worker VA Hosp., Los Angeles, 1963-65; social work cons. USPHS, Washington, 1965-67; exec. sec. Health Planning div. USPHS, N.Y.C., 1968; social work cons. Jarrett Assocs., Van Nuys, Calif., 1975-84; dir. social services Nat. In Home Health Services, Van Nuys, 1984-87; dir. planning Nat. In-Home Health Services, Van Nuys, 1987—. Recipient Superior Performance award USPHS, 1966, Dirs. Commendation, VA Ctr., 1965. Fellow Soc. Clin. Social Workers; mem. Acad. Clin. Social Work, (cert.), Nat. Assn. Social Workers (Home Health Task Force, 1986—), Am. Pub. Health Assn., Nat. Conf. Social Welfare, Home Health Social Workers (chmn. 1986-87), Phi Beta Kappa, Phi Kappa Phi. Home: 248 S Detroit St Los Angeles CA 90036 Office: Nat In-Home Health Services 14549 Archwood St Van Nuys CA 91405

FISHMAN, ROBERT ALLEN, educator, neurologist; b. N.Y.C., May 30, 1924; s. Samuel Benjamin and Miriam (Brinkin) F.; m. Margery Ann Satz, Jan. 29, 1956 (dec. May 29, 1980); children: Mary Beth, Alice Ellen, Elizabeth Ann.; m. Mary Craig Wilson, Jan. 7, 1983. A.B., Columbia U., 1944; M.D., U. Pa., 1947. Mem. faculty Columbia Coll. Phys. and Surg., 1954-66, asso. prof. neurology, 1962-66; asst. attending neurologist N.Y. State Psychiat. Inst., 1955-66, Neurol. Inst. Presbyn. Hosp., N.Y.C., 1955-61; asso. Neurol. Inst. Presbyn. Hosp., 1961-66; co-dir. Neurol. Clin. Research Center, Neurol. Inst., Columbia-Presbyn. Med. Center, 1961-66; prof. neurology, chmn. dept. U. Calif. Med. Center, San Francisco, 1966—; cons. neurologist San Francisco Gen. Hosp., San Francisco VA Hosp., Letterman Gen. Hosp.; dir. Am. Bd. Psychiatry and Neurology, 1981—, v.p., 1986, pres., 1987. Author: Cerebrospinal Fluid in Diseases of the Nervous System, 1980; Contbr. articles to profl. jours. Nat. Multiple Sclerosis Soc. fellow, 1956-57; John and Mary R. Markle scholar in med. sci., 1960-65. Mem. Am. Neurol. Assn. (pres. 1983-84), Am. Fedn. for Clin. Research, Assn. for Research in Nervous and Mental Diseases, Am. Acad. Neurology (v.p. 1971-73, pres. 1975-77), Am. Assn. Physicians, Am. Soc. for Neurochemistry, Soc. for Neurosci., N.Y. Neurol. Soc., Am. Assn. Univ. Profs. Neurology (pres. 1972-73), AAAS, Am. Epilepsy Soc., N.Y. Acad. Scis., AMA (sec. sect. on nervous and mental diseases 1964-67, v.p. 1967-68, pres. 1968-69), Alpha Omega Alpha (hon. faculty mem.). Home: 61 Cloudview Rd Sausalito CA 94965 Office: U Calif Med Center 794 Herbert C Moffitt Hosp San Francisco CA 94143

FISHMAN, WILLIAM HAROLD, cancer research foundation executive; biochemist; b. Winnipeg, Man., Can., Mar. 2, 1914; s. Abraham and Goldie (Chmelnitsky) F.; m. Lillian Waterman, Aug. 6, 1939; children—Joel, Nina, Daniel. B.S., U. Sask., Can., Saskatoon, 1935; Ph.D., U. Toronto, Ont., Can., 1939; MDhc U. Umea, Sweden, 1983; Dir. cancer research New Eng. Med. Ctr. Hosp., Boston, 1958-72; research prof. pathology Tufts U. Sch. Medicine, 1961-70, prof. pathology, 1970-77, dir. Cancer Research Ctr., 1972-76; pres. La Jolla Cancer Research Found., Calif., 1976—, dir., 1981—; mem. basic sci. programs merit rev. bd. com. VA, 1971-75; mem. pathobiol. chemistry sect. NIH, Bethesda, Md., 1977-81. Author in field. Research Career award NIH, 1962-77; Royal Soc. Can. research fellow, 1939, 17th Internat. Physiol. Congress-U.K. Fedn. fellow, 1947. Fellow AIC; mem. Am. Assn. Cancer Research, Am. Soc. Biol. Chemists, Am. Soc. Cell Biology, Am. Soc. Exptl. Pathology, Histochem. Soc. (pres. 1983-84), Internat. Soc. Clin. Enzymology (hon.). Jewish. Club: University (San Diego). Current work: Basic research on expression of placental genes by cancer cells; monoclonal antibodies; oncodevelopmental markers; immunocytochemistry. Home: 715 Muirlands Vista Way La Jolla CA 92037 Office: La Jolla Cancer Research Found 10901 N Torrey Pines Rd La Jolla CA 92037

FISK, EDWARD RAY, civil engineer, author, educator; b. Oshkosh, Wis., July 19, 1924; s. Ray Edward and Grace O. (Meyer) Barnes; student Marquette U., 1945-49, Fresno (Calif.) State Coll., 1954, UCLA, 1957-58; B.S., M.B.A., Calif.-Western U.; m. Oct. 28, 1950; children—Jacqueline Mary (Mrs. John Joseph Stamp), Edward Ray II, William John, Robert Paul. Engr., Calif. Div. Hwys., 1952-55; engr. Bechtel Corp., Vernon, Calif., 1955-59; project mgr. Toups Engring Co., Santa Ana, Calif., 1959-61; dept. head Perliter & Soring, Los Angeles, 1961-64; Western rep. Wire Reinforcement Inst., Washington, 1964-65; cons. engr., Anaheim, Calif., 1965; asso. engr. Met. Water Dist. So. Calif., 1966-68; chief specification engr. Koebig & Koebig, Inc., Los Angeles, 1968-71; mgr. constrn. services VTN Consol., Inc., Irvine, Calif., 1971-78; pres. E.R. Fisk Constrn., Orange, Calif., 1978-81; corp. dir. constrn. mgmt. James M. Montgomery Cons. Engrs., Inc., Pasadena, Calif., 1981-83; v.p. Lawrance, Fisk & McFarland, Inc., Santa Barbara and Orange, 1983—; pres. E.R. Fisk & Assocs., Orange, 1983—; adj. prof. engring. Orange Coast Coll., Costa Mesa, Calif., 1957-78, Calif. Poly. State U., Pomona, 1974; lectr. U. Calif., Berkeley, internationally for ASCE Continuing Edn.; former mem. Calif. Bd. Registered Constrn. Insps. Served with USN, 1942-43, USAF, 1951-52. Registered profl. engr., Ariz., Calif., Colo., Fla., Idaho, La., Mont., Nev., Oreg., Utah, Wash., Wyo.; lic. land surveyor, Oreg., Idaho; lic. gen. engring. contractor, Calif.; cert. abritator Calif. Constrn. Contract Arbitration Com. Fellow ASCE (past chmn. exec. com. constrn. div.; former chmn. nat. com. inspection 1978—); mem. Orange County Engring. Council (former pres.), Calif. Soc. Profl. Engrs. (past pres. Orange County), Am. Arbitration Assn. (nat. panel), U.S. Com. Large Dams, Order Founders and Patriots Am. (past gov. Calif.), Soc. Colonial Wars (gov.), S.R. (past dir.), Engring. Edn. Found. (trustee), Tau Beta Pi. Republican. Author: Machine Methods of Survey Computing, 1958, Construction Project Administration, 1978, 82, 87, Construction Engineers Form Book, 1981, Contractor's Project Guide, 1987. Home: PO Box 6448 Orange CA 92613-6448 Office: 1224 E Katella Suite 105 Orange CA 92667

FISK, LANNY HERBERT, geology educator, consultant; b. Edmore, Mich., Feb. 24, 1944; s. Paul James and Mildred Pauline (Courser) F.; m. Carolyn Mae McDowell, Jan. 29, 1967. BA with honors, Andrews U., 1971; PhD, Loma Linda U., 1976; postdoctoral, Mich. State U., 1986. From asst. prof. to assoc. prof. Walla Walla Coll., College Place, Wash., 1974-79; assoc. prof. geology Loma Linda U., Riverside, Calif., 1979—, chmn. dept. geology, 1979-85; chief exec. officer, chmn. bd. dirs. F & F GeoResource Assocs., Inc., Riverside, 1982—. Editor: Tertiary Palynology, 1984; contbr. articles to profl. publs. Active So. Calif. Marriage Encounter, 1984—. Served with U.S. Army, 1967-69. Named one of Outstanding Young Men of Am., 1972. Mem. Geol. Soc. Am., Am. Assn. Petroleum Geologists, Tobacco Root Geol. Soc. (charter, v.p. 1979-80, Best Paper award 1980), Inland Geol. Soc. (founder). Republican. Adventist. Avocations: photography. Home: 4620 Ambs Dr Riverside CA 92505 Office: Loma Linda U Dept Geol Scis Riverside CA 92515

FISSER, HERBERT GEORGE, management researcher, educator; b. Ames, Iowa, Mar. 9, 1926; s. Hillerk and Anna (Kaiser) F.; m. Donna L. Helm, Dec. 28, 1952; children: Michele, Pamela, Alan. BS, U. Mont., 1950; MS, Mont. State U., 1961; PhD, U. Wyo., 1962. Supply instr. U. Wyo., Laramie, 1959-62, asst. prof., 1962-66, assoc. prof., 1966-70, prof., 1970—. Contbr. numerous articles and reports on range ecology; editor: Proceedings, Wyo. Shrub Ecology Workshop, 1980-82. Mem. Soc. for Range Mgmt. (named Range Man of Yr. 1971), Ecology Soc. Am., Colo.-Wyo. Acad. Sci., Gamma Sigma Delta, Sigma Xi. Lodges: Elks, Lions. Home: 1072 Duna Dr Laramie WY 82070 Office: Range Mgmt Dept Box 3354 U Station Laramie WY 82071

FITCH, JOHN RICHARD, newspaper executive; b. Newark, Ohio, June 1, 1938; s. John Clyde and Mildred Josephine (Nethers) F.; m. Peggy Spencer, Apr. 17, 1959 (div. Jan. 1983); children: Joanne, Troy, Victoria, Valerie; m. Carol Critchlow, Mar. 24, 1984; 1 child, Megan Nichole. Student, Baylor U., 1958-59, Imperial Valley Coll., 1962. Newspaper advt. salesperson Associated Desert News, El Centro, Calif., 1960-64, advt. mgr., 1964-65, bus. mgr., 1965-66, gen. mgr., 1966-69, pub., 1969—, pres., editor, 1978—; bd. dirs. Schurz Communications, South Bend, Ind.; chmn. govt. affairs Calif. Newspaper Pubs., Sacramento, 1982—, bd. dirs., mem. exec. bd. Mem. adv. bd. El Centro Community Hosp.; charter pres. Regional Econ. Devel. Corp., El Centro. Served with USAF, 1956-60. El Centro C. of C. (past pres.). Republican. Lodge: Kiwanis (past pres. and lt. gov., bd. dirs.). Home: 903 W McCabe Rd El Centro CA 92243 Office: Imperial Valley Press 205 N 8th St El Centro CA 92243

FITZGERALD, GLENN LESLIE, petroleum engineering company executive, consultant; b. Pottsville, Pa., Dec. 12, 1954; s. John Earl and Ethel Louise (Franz) F. BS with high distinction, U. Ariz., 1976. Tchr., coach Lincoln High Sch., San Jose, Calif., 1976-77; sales rep. Century Pipe and Supply Co., Midland, Tex., 1977-79; engring. technician Amoco Prodn. Co. subs. Standard Oil Ind., Andrews, Tex., 1979-81; engring. mgr. Nabla Corp., Bakersfield, Calif., 1981—. Developer oil-related software programs, 1980-86. Mem. Am. Petroleum Inst. Republican. Baptist. Avocations: golf, off-road motorcycling, electronics, classical music. Home: 3605 Sonoita Dr Bakersfield CA 93309 Office: Nabla Corp PO Box 9275 Bakersfield CA 93389

FITZGERALD, JAMES MARTIN, judge; b. Portland, Oreg., Oct. 7, 1920; s. Thomas and Florence (Linderman) F.; m. Karin Rose Benton, Jan. 19, 1950; children: Dennis James, Denise Lyn, Debra Jo, Kevin Thomas. BA, Willamette U., 1950, LLB, 1951; postgrad., U. Wash., 1952. Bar: Alaska 1953. Asst. U.S. atty. Ketchikan and Anchorage, Alaska, 1952-56; city atty. City of Anchorage, 1956-59; legal counsel to Gov. Alaska, Anchorage, 1959; commr. pub. safety State of Alaska, 1959; judge Alaska Superior Ct., 3d Jud. Dist., 1959-69, presiding judge, 1969-72; assoc. justice Alaska Supreme Ct., Anchorage, 1972-75; judge U.S. Dist. Ct. for Alaska, Anchorage, 1975—. Mem. advisory bd. Salvation Army, Anchorage, 1962—, chmn., 1965-66; mem. Anchorage Parks and Recreation Bd., 1965-77, chmn., 1966. Served with AUS, 1940-41; Served with USMCR, 1942-46. Office: US District Court US Courthouse 701 C St Anchorage AK 99513 *

FITZGERALD, JON KEVAN, management consulting company executive; b. South Bend, Ind., Mar. 31, 1945; s. Robert John and Mary Katherine (Veach) F.; m. Carol Ann Arcenian, Jan. 20, 1968; children: Scott, Brett. Student, U. Mass., Amherst, 1963-67, U. Md., 1970; BS in Indsl. Tech., Northeastern U., 1973; MBA, Babson Coll., 1974. Ski instr. Haystack Ski Sch., Vt., 1967-68; asst. v.p. corp. devel. Electro Med. Systems Inc., Englewood, Colo., 1974-76, asst. sales mgr., 1974-76; dir. v.p., co-founder Health Industry Cons. Inc., Englewood, 1976-79, pres., 1979—, also bd. dirs.; chmn. bd. dirs., pres., founder Colo. Venture Group, Englewood; mktg. cons. Capital Cities ABC, N.Y.C., 1985-86; bd. dirs. Neighborhood Ministries Inc., Denver; dir. Silicon Mt. Assocs., Inc., Englewood; mem. bd. advisors Advanced Tech. Products Inc.; Eagle River Ptnrs. Ltd. Bd. dirs., v.p. Normandy Estates Improvement Assn., Littleton, Colo., 1982; referee Columbine Soccer Assn., Littleton, 1982. Served with U.S. Army, 1967-71. Named Eagle Scout, Boy Scouts Am., Hamden, Conn., 1958. Mem. Assn. MBA Execs., Am. Mgmt. Assn., Assn. Venture Clubs (v.p., dir. 1986—), Inc. Assn. Advancement Med. Instrumentation, Amateur Radio Emergency Corps, Nat. Ski Patrol Assn., Pi Lambda Phi (charter bros. 1965-67), Beta Gamma. Avocations: music, skiing, camping, photography, cooking. Home: 5477 W Portland Dr Littleton CO 80123 Office: Health Industry Cons Inc 7353 S Alton Way #200 Englewood CO 80112

FITZGERALD, MARK CHARLES, publisher; b. Greenville, Miss., Oct. 9, 1955; s. James Charles and Alice Catharine (Ffrench) F.; m. Carolyn O'Malley, Aug. 10, 1986. BA in Biology, U. Ariz., 1977; MA in Energy and Environ. Planning, Gov.'s State U., 1980. Community energy mgmt. specialist Nat. Ctr. Appropriate Tech., Butte, Mont., 1979-81; dir. mktg. RES Photovoltaic Engring., Scottsdale, Ariz., 1981-82; publisher PV Internat. mag. PVI Pub. Co., Denver, 1983—. PV Info. Edn. Assn. (bd. dirs., chmn. 1985—). Roman Catholic. Avocations: water polo, masters swimming, skiing. Home: PO Box 4168 Highlands Ranch CO 80126 Office: Photovaltaics Info Edn Assn PO Box 4169 Highlands Ranch CO 80126

FITZ-HENLEY, NORMAN HOWARD, physician; b. Port-au-Prince, Haiti, Sept. 25, 1931; came to U.S., 1961, naturalized, 1968; s. Randolph and Doris (Campbell) Fitz-Henley; children: Onyl Grace, Garnell Dean, John Aldwyn, Orville Jay. Student CCNY, 1967; M.D., George Washington U., 1971. Ofcl. verbatim ct. reporter Supreme Ct. Kingston, Jamaica, 1951-61; freelance ct. reporter Beekman's Reporting Service, N.Y.C., 1962-67; intern D.C. Gen. Hosp., George Washington U. Service, Washington, 1971-72; resident in internal medicine, U. Calif., San Diego, 1972-75; practice medicine specializing in internal medicine, El Centro, Calif., 1975—; chmn. dept. medicine El Centro Community Hosp., 1977, 85, chief-of-staff, 1987—; chmn. dept. medicine Pioneers Meml. Hosp., Brawley, 1986, vice chief-of-staff, 1987—; bd. dirs. Valley Ind. Bank, El Centro, John M. Perkins Found. Active non-denominational religious evang. affairs. Life fellow Royal Soc. Arts (London); mem. AMA, Calif. Med. Assn., Am. Heart Assn., Imperial County Med. Soc., Calif. Heart Assn., Imperial Valley Heart Assn. (bd. dirs.), Alpha Sigma Lambda. Co-inventor Fitz-Henley's All-Curve System of Shorthand, 1962. Home: PO Box 479 El Centro CA 92244 Office: 1745 S Imperial Ave El Centro CA 92243 Office: 126 Main St Brawley CA 92227

FITZMAURICE, LEONA CLAIRE, biotechnologist, researcher; b. Grand Rapids, Minn., Apr. 25, 1945; d. Clair Carlton and Norma Annetta (Behm) P. BA in Biology, U. Chgo., 1967; PhD in Cellular and Molecular Biology, U. So. Calif., 1973. Postdoctoral fellow Nat. Inst. Med. Research, London, 1973-74, U. Glasgow, Scotland, 1974-77, U. Calif., Los Angeles, 1977-79; research expert NIH, Bethesda, Md., 1979-82; research scientist Phytogen, Inc., Pasadena, Calif., 1982-83; staff scientist SIBIA, Inc., La Jolla, Calif., 1983—. Contbr. articles to profl. jours. Bd. dirs. Timberlane Homeowners' Assn., San Diego, 1985—. Scholar Nat. Merit, 1963-67, U. Chgo., 1963-67; fellow NATO postdoctoral, 1973-74, Nat. Cancer Inst., 1973-78; recipient traineeship NSF, 1970-73, Nat. Cancer Inst., 1978-79. Mem. AAAS, N.Y. Acad. Scis., Internat. Soc. Plant Molecular Biology, Sierra Club. Democrat. Episcopalian. Avocations: music, reading, photography, gourmet cooking, hiking. Office: SIBIA Inc 505 Coast Blvd S San Diego CA 92037

FITZSIMONS, PATRICK S., police chief; b. N.Y.C., Apr. 16, 1930; s. Patrick Joseph and Mary (Brabazon) F.; m. Olga Parker, Aug. 18, 1959. B.S., Fordham U., 1954; J.D., 1972; J.D. fellow criminal justice, Harvard U. Law Sch., 1972-73. Adj. prof. John Jay Coll. Grad. Sch., N.Y.C.; mem. N.Y.C. Police Dept.; asst. chief programs and policies; now chief of police City of Seattle; mem. Gov. Wash. Council Criminal Justice, Wash.; Bd. Law Enforcement Tng. and Standards; mem. bd. Nat. Criminal Info. Center, Police Rxecs. Research Forum. Bd. dirs. Chief Seattle council Boy Scouts Am. Served to 1st lt. USMC, 1953-56. Recipient award criminal justice Am. Soc. Public Adminstrn. Mem. Fordham U. Law Sch. Alumni Assn., Harvard U. Law Sch. Alumni Assn. Clubs: Wash. Athletic, 101. Office: Seattle Police Dept 610 3d Ave Seattle WA 98104

FJORDBOTTEN, EDWIN LEROY, government official; b. Claresholm, Alta., Can., Nov. 4, 1938; s. Artun Edwin and Belinda Janet (Enbysk) F.; m. Deanne Marie Perchinsky, Nov. 16, 1962; children—Tracy, Karine. Grad. Camrose Luth. Coll., 1956. Farmer, nr. Granum, Alta., Can., 1960-83; mem. Alta. Legis. Assembly, Edmonton, 1979—, minister of agr., 1982-86, minister of tourism, 1986—. Progressive Conservative. Lutheran. Office: Legislature Bldg, Room 418, Edmonton, AB Canada T5K 2B7

FLACCO, PAUL RICHARD, economics educator; b. Washington, Feb. 19, 1950; s. Richard Anthony and Sidonie Marianne (Alemann) F.; m. Margaret Sue Woodley, June 23, 1972 (div.); 1 dau., April Margaret. A.B., U. Calif.-Santa Cruz, 1975, M.S., Oreg. State U., 1977, Ph.D., U. Oreg., 1980. Research asst. Oreg. State U., 1975-77; grad. teaching fellow U. Oreg., 1977-80; asst. prof. econs. Claremont McKenna Coll. and Claremont Grad. Sch., 1980—. Calif. State scholar 1973-75, Eric England Meml. scholar 1977-78. Mem. Am. Econs. Assn., Western Econs. Assn., So. Econs. Assn. Democrat. Author: A Generalized Theory of Markets: The Demand and Supply of Heterogeneous Commodities, 1980. Office: 314 Bauer Center Claremont McKenna College Claremont CA 91711

FLACH, VICTOR H., designer, educator; b. Portland, Oreg., May 31, 1929; s. Victor H. and Eva (Huget) F. Student of, Jack Wilkinson, W.R. Hovey; B.S., U. Oreg., 1952, M.F.A., 1957; postgrad., U. Pitts., 1959-65. Archtl., elec. engring. and cartographic draftsman with various cos. and U.S. govt. agy. 1948-62; teaching fellow, curator Henry Clay Frick Fine Arts Dept. and Gallery, U. Pitts., 1959-63; docent Frank Lloyd Wright's Fallingwater, Western Pa. Conservancy, 1963-64; prof. art, design, painting, theory and history U. Wyo., Laramie, 1965—; participant R. Buckminster Fuller Geodesic Prototype Projects, 1953, 59; interviewer Heritage series TV program PBS-TV, 1965; cons. Nat. Symposium on Role of Studio Arts in Higher Edn., U. Oreg., 1967. Participant: various TV programs including Arts in Practice series, 1971-77; designer multi-walled murals, U. Oreg., Eugene, 1952, Rainbow Club, 1954, Clear Lake Sch., Eugene, 1956, Sci. Ctr., U. Wyo., Laramie, 1967, one-man and group shows of paintings, photographs, exptl. films and drawings, 1949—; Author and editor: IJHTBIW20 Poems, 1949, 12 New Painters, 1953, IN/SERT Active Anthology for the Creative, 1955-62, Gloss of the Four Universal Forms, 1959, The Anatomy of the Canvas, 1961, The Eye's Mind, 1964, By These Presents, 1975, The Stage, 1978, Contextualist Manifesto, 1982, Displacings & Wayfarings, 1986; contbr. poems, articles and photographs to lit. jours., 1949—. Served with U.S. Army, 1953-55. Office: Dept Art U Wyo Laramie WY 82071

FLACKS, RICHARD ISAAC, sociology educator; b. Bklyn., Apr. 26, 1938; s. David and Mildred Flacks; m. Miriam Hartman, Nov. 20, 1959; children: Charles Wright, Marc Ajay. BA, Bklyn. Coll., 1958; PhD, U. Mich., 1963. Asst. prof. sociology U. Chgo., 1964-69; prof. U. Calif., Santa Barbara, 1969—; chmn. sociology dept. U. Calif., Santa Barbara, 1975-80, vice chmn. academic senate, 1985—. Author: Youth and Social Change, 1971; co-author Persistence and Change, 1967; author/editor Conformity Resistance and Self-Determination, 1973; weekly radio show Culture of Protest, Sta. KCSB-FM. Bd. dirs. Network, Santa Barbara, 1978—. Mem. Am. Sociol. Assn., Soc. for Psychol. Study of Social Issues (council mem. 1971-75). Home: 3758 Brenner Dr Santa Barbara CA 93105 Office: U Calif Dept Sociology Santa Barbara CA 93106

FLAGAN, RICHARD CHARLES, environmental and mechanical engineering educator; b. Spokane, Wash., June 12, 1947; s. Robert George and Frances Cory (Arnold) F.; m. Aulikki Tellervo Pekkala, Aug. 4, 1979; children: Mikko, Suvi, Taru. BME, U. Mich., 1969; MME, MIT, 1971, PhDME, 1973. Research assoc. MIT, Cambridge, 1973-75; asst. prof. mech. engring. Calif. Inst. Tech., Pasadena, 1975-81, assoc. prof., 1981-85, prof., 1986—. Mem. Am. Assn. Aerosol Research, Am. Inst. Chem. Engrs., Combustion Inst. Office: Calif Inst of Tech Dept of Engring Pasadena CA 91125

FLAGLER, WILLIAM LAWRENCE, publisher, purchasing consultant; b. Oakland, Calif., June 13, 1922; s. Albert William and Violet Dorthy (Marris) F.; B.A., San Francisco State U., 1951; degree in Library Sci., San Jose State U., 1963; m. Ruth Greiner Gilbert, Aug. 23, 1970; children by previous marriage—Vickie, David, Michael; stepchildren—Denise Gilbert La Hay, Ethan Gilbert. Pres., LaRu Enterprises, San Jose, Calif., 1975—. Active Boy Scouts Am. Served with U.S. Army, World War II, ETO. Republican. Club: Masons. Office: PO Box 10460 San Jose CA 95157

FLAHAVIN, G. THOMAS, retail executive; b. Canton, Ill., Nov. 10, 1932; s. Paul Otto and Katie Marie (McLouth) F.; m. Marian J. Druffel, Aug. 6, 1960; 1 child, John Thomas. BA, U. Mich., 1956. With sales dept. Westinghouse Co., Peoria, Ill., 1957-60; with sales dept. Columbia Lighting, Inc., Spokane, Wash., 1960-66, nat. mktg. mgr., 1966-68, v.p. mktg., 1971-78, pres., 1978—. Mem. Phi Beta Kappa, Phi Kappa Phi. Republican. Roman Catholic. Club: Spokane Country. Avocations: raising quarter horses, boating, water and snow skiing. Home: Rte 7 Schafer Rd Spokane WA 99206 Office: Columbia Lighting Inc Spokane Indsl Park Spokane WA 99206

FLAHERTY, KELLY MARGUERIETTE, business owner; b. Helena, Mont., Dec. 4, 1957; d. Neil Edward and Elizabeth Louise (Coyle) F. Student, Seattle U., 1976-78; BA in Polit. Sci., U. Mont., 1980. Pres. Leasing, Inc., Helena, Mont., 1980—; pres., owner Firemaster, Inc., Helena, Mont., 1981—. Mem. Nat. Assn. Women in Constrn., Am. Soc. Safety Engrs., Nat. Assn. Fire Equipment Distbrs., Women's Lobbyist Fund, Mont. Contractors' Assn. Democrat. Roman Catholic. Lodge: Soroptimists. Avocations: running, skiing, sewing, knitting, needle work. Home: 710 Harrison Helena MT 59601 Office: Firemaster Inc 1055 N Rodney Helena MT 59601

FLAIM, SILVIO JOSEPH, economist, consultant; b. Augusta, Ga., Feb. 19, 1952; s. Rudolph Alfred and Bernice Marie (Haddock) F.; m. Mary Louise Prosser, May 25, 1974; children—Amanda Leigh, Michael Joseph. B.S. in Agrl. Econs., U. Mo., Columbia, 1973, M.S., 1974; Ph.D. in Resource Econs., Cornell U., 1978. Teaching and research asst., U. Mo., Cornell U., 1970-77; econ. cons., AID, Nicaragua, 1973; sr. economist Solar Energy Research Inst., Golden, Colo., 1977-81; sr. economist, Amoco Prodn. Co., Denver, 1981-83, Argonne Nat. Labs., Chgo., 1985—; cons. on valuation of mineral properties, tax, fin. for litigation and renewable energy applications in agr. Mem. Am. Agrl. Econs. Assn., Am. Econs. Assn., Western Econs. Assn. Contbr. articles to profl. jours. Home: 31808 Quarterhorse Rd Evergreen CO 80439 Office: PO Box 26970 Denver CO 80226

FLAMER, MARY JEAN, advertising executive; b. Orange, N.J., Mar. 2, 1950; d. Vincent Carl and Jean Niven (Breingan) Cuccinello; m. Michael Abraham Flamer, June 7, 1981; 1 child, Joseph Vincent. BA in Theatre Arts, U. Bridgeport, 1972. Media buyer Batten, Barton, Durstine & Osborne Advt., N.Y.C., 1973-75; media supr. Ted Bates Advt., N.Y.C., 1975-78; media dir. Fotomat Corp., San Diego, 1978-81; v.p., dir. network TV and radio Western Internat. Media, Los Angeles, 1982-83; account exec. nat. sales CBS-FM, Los Angeles, 1983-85; account exec. CBS Radio Reps., Los Angeles, 1985—; instr. UCLA. Mem. Holy Spirit Cenacle House. Office: 6121 Sunset Blvd Los Angeles CA 90028

FLAMSON, RICHARD JOSEPH, III, banker; b. Los Angeles, Feb. 2, 1929; s. Richard J. and Mildred (Jones) F.; m. Arden Black, Oct. 5, 1951; children: Richard Joseph IV, Scott Arthur, Michael Jon, Leslie Arden. B.A., Claremont Men's Coll., 1951; cert. Pacific Coast Banking Sch., U. Wash., 1962. With Security Pacific Nat. Bank, Los Angeles, 1955—, v.p., 1962-69, sr. v.p., 1969-70, exec. v.p. corp. banking dept., 1970-73, vice-chmn., 1973-78, pres., chief exec. officer, 1978-81, chmn., chief exec. officer, 1981—, dir., 1981-85; also dir. Security Pacific Corp., Los Angeles; vice-chmn. Security Pacific Corp., 1973-78, pres., 1978-81, chief exec. officer, 1978—, chmn., 1981—; dir. Northrop Corp., Kaufman and Broad. Trustee Claremont Men's Coll. 1st lt. AUS, 1951-53. Mem. Res. City Bankers, Robert Morris Assocs., Town Hall, Stock Exchange Club. Clubs: Caif. Los Angeles Country; Balboa Bay (Newport Beach, Calif.), Balboa Yacht (Newport Beach, Calif.). Office: Security Pacific Corp 333 S Hope St Los Angeles CA 90071 *

FLANAGAN, JOHN DAVID, state agency administrator, data processing executive; b. Chgo., Nov. 16, 1938; s. William Bernard and Mildred (Frazier) F.; m. Virginia Inez Jones, Oct. 17, 1959; children: David, Randall, Brenda, John, Wendy. AA in Social Sci., Centralia Coll., 1980; BBA, The Evergreen State Coll., 1983. Program dept. mgr. Certified Grocers, Chgo., 1959-65; systems engr. RCA Computer Systems, Sacramento, 1965-71; project mgr. Sperry Univac, Riverton, N.J., 1971-76; systems mgr. State Dept. Licensing, Olympia, Wash., 1976-80; asst. dir. State Data Processing Authority, Olympia, 1980—; mem. tech. adv. com. State Supply Mgmt. Adv. Bd.,

Olympia, 1982—; State Career Exec. Adv. Bd., Olympia, 1981-85. Editor Washington Data Processing Authority Pocket Data Book, 1985, 86; contbr. articles to profl. jours. Legis. coordinator PTA, Lacey, Wash., 1984; mem. Wash. State Justice Info. Systems Com., Seattle, 1986—. Served with U.S. Army, 1955-58. Mem. Assn. Computing Machinery, Assn. Data Processing Mgrs. (cert., program chmn. 1984-85), Telecommunications Assn. Republican. Roman Catholic. Home: 8825 Pacific Hwy Olympia WA 98503 Office: Wash State Data Processing Authority 9th & Columbia Bldg Suite 360 Olympia WA 98504

FLANAGAN, TIMOTHY SEAN, county official; b. San Francisco, Mar. 1, 1958; s. Jack Code and Clara (Ehrmann) F. BA in Pub. Policy Econs., U. Calif., Santa Barbara, 1981; M in Pub. Adminstrn., Calif. State U., Hayward, 1986. Staff rep. Calif. State Assembly, Sacramento, 1981; pub. affairs coordinator City of San Mateo, Calif., 1982; material recovery program mgr. City of Palo Alto, Calif., 1982-85; solid waste mgmt. cons. County of Santa Clara, San Jose, Calif., 1985-87; dist. mktg. mgr., spl. services Waste Mgmt. Inc. of N. Am., San Jose, 1987—. Contbr. articles to profl. jours. Mem. San Mateo County Rep. Cen. Com., 1982—; assoc. mem. State Rep. Cen. Com., Sacramento, 1984—. Named Outstanding Vol., Calif. Rep. Com., San Mateo, 1983. Mem. No. Calif. Recycling Assn. (v.p. 1982-83), Nat. Recycling Coalition, Calif. Resource Recovery Assn. Roman Catholic. Avocations: sports, politics, political history, outdoor activities. Home: 1654 Baybridge Way San Mateo CA 94402 Office: Waste Mgmt Inc of N Am 2099 Gateway Place San Jose CA 95110

FLANDERS, GEORGE JAMES, mechanical engineer; b. Bunker Hill, Ind., June 3, 1960; s. Melvin S. and Edith J. (Mason) F. BSME, Bradley U., 1982, MBA, 1984. Lab. engr. Materials Testing & Research Lab., Peoria, Ill., 1982; research design engr. Caterpillar Tractor Co., Peoria, 1982-85; staff engr. Bristol Myers Co., Englewood, Colo., 1985-86, sr. engr., 1986—; cons. in field. Mem. NSPE, ASME, Soc. Automotive Engrs., Sigma Phi Delta (grand v.p. 1985—, several other offices), Tau Beta Pi, Pi Tau Sigma, Omicron Delta Kappa. Avocations: organizing social and profl. activities, basketball, boating, skiing, tae kwon do. Home: 2967 W Centennial Dr Apt M204 Littleton CO 80123 Office: Aspen Labs Inc 181 Inverness Dr W Englewood CO 80112

FLANDERS, LYNN PINARD, marketing and promotional advertising executive; b. Manchester, N.H., June 3, 1947; d. Omer and Beatrice (Grenon) Pinard; 1 child, Keith Lawton Flanders. BA, R.I. Sch. Design, 1969. Chief exec. officer, owner ADPRO Unlimited, Carlsbad, Calif., 1982—. Vol. papa-counselor Trama Intervention Program, Oceanside (Calif.) Police Dept., 1986—. Mem. Am. Mktg. Assn. Office: ADPRO Unlimited PO Box 3194 Newport Beach CA 92663

FLANDERS, STEPHEN L(AWRENCE), stockbroker, investor; b. Boston, July 10, 1942; s. Royal Call and Mildred Grace (O'Brien) F.; m. Robin Lee Lord, Nov. 20, 1963 (div. 1969); 1 son, Bradford; m. 2d, Barbara Ann Randol, Apr. 1, 1971 (div. 1977); children—William Brett, Krystal; m. 3d, Linda Lorraine Skodack, Dec. 1, 1979. B.S. in Bus. Adminstrn. and Econs., U. Denver, 1967; postgrad. Babson Inst., Harvard U., Boston U., C.W. Post Coll. Stockbroker, McDonnell & Co., Denver, 1968-69; mgr. spl. services, stockbroker Wall St. West, Inc., Englewood, Colo., 1982-85; v.p. Marshall Davis, Inc., 1985—; chmn. bd. Denver Penny Stocks, Inc.; lectr., cons. Pres. Heather Ridge Homeowners Assn., 1978-79. Named Salesman of Yr., Townsend, Bauerle, Inc., 1981; winner Stockbrokers Bull and Bear Ski Race, Winter Park, Colo., 1983. Mem. N.Y. Stock Exchange, Nat. Assn. Securities Dealers, Profl. Ski Patrol Assn. Republican. Roman Catholic. Club: Heather Ridge Country (treas., dir. pub. relations 1978-81). Contbr. articles to newspapers and trade mags. Home: 2192 S Victor St Aurora CO 80014 Office: Marshall Davis Inc 7800 E Union Ave Suite 900 Denver CO 80237

FLANDRO, SCOTT COOPER, state official; b. Salt Lake City, Jan. 22, 1932; s. Arthur Louis and Mable Claire (Pendleton) F.; m. Emma Jean Ballard, Aug. 28, 1952; children—Deborah Kay, Arthur Leland, Stephen Wayne, Diana Lynn, Patricia Jean, Michael Scott. B.S. in Bus. Mgmt., U. Utah, 1954; grad. U.S. Army Command and Gen. Staff Coll., 1972. Asst. credit mgr. Phillips Petroleum Co., Salt Lake City, 1956-59; salesman John Hancock Ins. Co., Salt Lake City, 1959-61; sales mgr. Mut. Trust Life Ins. Co., Salt Lake City, 1961-64; v.p. West, Am. Express Co., Salt Lake City and Los Angeles, 1964-67; dep. dir. Utah Dept. Natural Resources Salt Lake City, 1967-79, adminstrn. mgr. div. state lands State of Utah, Salt Lake City, 1979—. Treas., Pine Meadow Service Dist., Salt Lake City, 1982—; treas. Pine Meadow Assn., 1982—; youth leader Boy Scouts Am.; adult leader Ch. Jesus Christ Latter-day Saints; del. Republican State Conv.; state chmn. United Fund, 1972. Served to col. USAR, 1953-84. Mem. Life Underwriters Tng. Council, Utah Pub. Employees Assn. (vice chmn., chmn. 1970-74), Res. Officers Assn. (life; officer), Sons Utah Pioneers. Home: 2974 E 3215 S Salt Lake City UT 84109 Office: Div State Lands and Forestry 3 Triad Center Salt Lake City UT 84180

FLATTÉ, STANLEY MARTIN, physicist, educator; b. Los Angeles, Dec. 2, 1940; s. Samuel and Henrietta (Edelstein) F.; m. Renelde Marie Demeure, June 26, 1966; children: Michael, Anne. B.S., Calif. Inst. Tech., 1962; student, NYU, 1960-61; Ph.D., U. Calif.-Berkeley, 1966. Research particle physicist Lawrence Berkeley Lab., Calif., 1966-71; asst. prof. physics U. Calif.-Santa Cruz, 1971-73, assoc. prof., 1973-78, prof., 1978—; dir. Ctr. for Studies of Nonlinear Dynamics La Jolla Inst., 1982-86, dept. chmn., 1986—; cons. phys. oceanography and underwater sound U.S. Govt.; vis. researcher, Cern, Geneva, 1975, Scripps Inst. Oceanography, 1980, Cambridge U., Eng., 1981. Author: (with others) Sound Transmission Through a Fluctuating Ocean, 1979; contbr. (with others) articles profl. jours. Woodrow Wilson fellow, 1962; NSF fellow, 1962-66; Guggenheim Found. fellow, 1975. Fellow Acoustical Soc. Am.; mem. Am. Phys. Soc., AAAS, Am. Geophys. Union, Sigma Xi. Discovered cusp phenomenon in particle physics; developed methods for probing statis. ocean and earth processes with sound. Home: 678 Spring St Santa Cruz CA 95060 Office: Univ Calif Santa Cruz CA 95064

FLECK, MICHELLE COOPER, geologist; b. Maryville, Tenn., Nov. 26, 1957; d. Graham Dinwiddie and Thelma (Hammontree) C.; m. Kenneth Stewart Fleck, Apr. 7, 1984. BS, Tenn. Tech. U., 1979; MS, U. Mo., Rolla, 1981. Mineralogist, petrographer Internat. Fertilizer Devel. Ctr., Muscle Shoals, Ala., 1981-84; instr. math. Coll. Ea. Utah, Price, 1985—. Mem. AIME, Sigma Xi, Phi Kappa Phi. Presbyterian. Home: 205 N Carbon Ave Price UT 84501 Office: Coll Eastern Utah Price UT 84501

FLEISCHAKER, GORDON HENRY, JR., pediatrician; b. Louisville, July 1, 1928; s. Gordon H. and Agnes Rose (Shatzen) F.; m. Barbara Lorraine Draeger, Aug. 15, 1954; children: Rachel, Judith, James. BA in Zoology, U. Louisville, 1949, MD, 1953. Intern Univ. Hosp., Madison, Wis., 1953-54; resident in pediatrics The Childrens Hosps., Denver, 1956-58; fellow in pediatric rheumatology State U. Iowa, Iowa City, 1958-60; practice medicine specializing in pediatrics Denver, 1960—; assoc. clin. prof. pediatrics U. Colo. Sch. of Med., Denver, 1960—; mem. active med. staff The Children's Hosp., Denver. Served to capt. MC, USAF, 1953-56. Fellow Am. Acad. Pediatrics; mem. AMA, Colo. Med. Soc., Clear Creek Valley Med. Soc. Office: G H Fleischaker MD 4485 Wadsworth Blvd Wheat Ridge CO 80033

FLEISCHAUER, PAUL DELL, physical chemist; b. Buffalo, Sept. 23, 1942; s. Albert Paul and Ella Ruth (Jackson) F.; m. Patricia Diane Slodden, June 12, 1965 (div. 1977); m. Marlene Sumie Awane, Dec. 5, 1978; children: Melissa Ann, Michael Robert. BA in Chemistry, Wesleyan U., Middletown, Conn., 1964; PhD in Phys. Chemistry, U. So. Calif., 1968. NSF postdoctoral fellow U. Rome, 1968-69; mem. tech. staff The Aerospace Corp., El Segundo, Calif., 1969-75, sect. mgr., 1975—; adj. asst. prof. U. So. Calif., Los Angeles, 1975-76. Editor: Concepts of Inorganic Photochemistry, 1975; contbr. articles to profl. jours. Mem. Am. Chem. Soc. (sect. chmn. 1984), Am. Soc. Lubrication Engrs. (assoc. editor Transactions pub. 1986—, Al Sonntag award 1985), Am. Vacuum Soc., Sigma Xi. Republican. Episcopalian. Club: Aerospace Golf. Avocations: stained glass, sports. Home: 2105 Agnes Rd Manhattan Beach CA 90266 Office: The Aerospace Corp PO Box 92957 M2-271 Los Angeles CA 90009

FLEISCHMANN, ERNEST MARTIN, music administrator; b. Frankfurt, Germany, Dec. 7, 1924; came to U.S., 1969; s. Gustav and Antonia (Koch) F.; children: Stephanie, Martin, Jessica. Mus.B., U. Cape Town, South Africa, 1954; postgrad., South African Coll. Music, 1954-56; MusD (hon.), Cleve. Inst. Mus., 1987. Gen mgr. London Symphony Orch., 1959-67; dir. for Europe CBS Records, 1967-69; exec. dir. Los Angeles Philharm. Orch. and Hollywood Bowl, 1969—; mem. French Govt. Commn. Reform of Paris Opera, 1967-68; steering com. U.S. nat. commn. UNESCO Conf. Future of Arts, 1975. Debut as condr., Johannesburg (South Africa) Symphony Orch., 1942, asst. condr., South African Nat. Opera, 1948-51, Cape Town U. Opera, 1950-54, condr., South African Coll. Music choir, 1950-52, Labia Grand Opera Co., Cape Town, 1953-55, music organizer, Van Riebeeck Festival, Cape Town, 1952, dir. music and drama, Johannesburg Festival, 1956, Contbr. music publs. Bd. dirs. Calif. Confedn. of Arts;. Recipient award of merit Los Angeles Jr. C. of C. Mem. Assn. Calif. Symphony Orchs. (bd. dirs.), Major Orch. Mgrs. Conf., Am. Symphony Orch. League (vice chmn. bd. dirs.). Address: Los Angeles Philharmonic Orch 135 N Grand Ave Los Angeles CA 90012

FLEISHER, ARTHUR A., II, physician; b. Phila., Sept. 7, 1932; s. Oscar Teller and Beatrice Naomi (Rosenzweig) F.; m. Francine Queenth, June 26, 1955; children—Rebecca, Martin Q., Arthur III, Carolyn B. B.S., U. Miami, Fla., 1954, M.D., 1958. Diplomate Am. Bd. Obstetrics and Gynecology. Resident in obstetrics and gynecology Jackson Meml. Hosp., Miami, Fla., 1959-62; obstetrician/gynecologist So. Calif. Permanente Med. Group, Panorama City, Calif., 1962—, chief dept. ob-gyn, 1975-81; assoc. clin. prof. ob-gyn U. So. Calif. Med. Ctr., Los Angeles, 1972—; asst. clin. prof. ob-gyn UCLA, 1964-83. Fellow Am. Coll. Ob-Gyn, ACS, Los Angeles Ob-Gyn Soc. Office: So Calif Permanente Med Group 13652 Cantara St Panorama City CA 91402

FLEMING, JOSEPH LANCASTER, infosystems specialist, university administrator; b. Detroit, July 9, 1939; s. Joseph E. and Minota E. (Lancaster) F.; m. Mary E. Householder, Aug. 7, 1965; children: James H.H., David A.L. BA, Albion Coll., 1964; MA, U. Mich., 1967, PhD, 1979. Research chemist Dow Chem. Co., Midland, Mich., 1964-65; mem. faculty physics and astronomy dept. Olivet (Mich.) Coll., 1967-79, registrar, dir. computer services, 1979-82; dir. computer services Western N.Mex. U., Silver City, 1982—, dir. univ. info. services, 1985—. Prin. tuba Silver City Brass Ensemble, 1982—; pres. Silver City Choral Union, 1984—; bd. dir. Silver City Mus. Soc. Served with USN, 1957-60. Mem. AAAS, N.Mex. Collegiate Data Processing Assn. (pres. 1984—). Home: PO Box 253 Silver City NM 88062 Office: Western NMex U PO Box 680 Silver City NM 88062

FLEMING, QUENTIN WALLACE, aircraft manufacturing executive; b. Detroit, Oct. 25, 1931; s. Quentin Ira and Dorothy (Bogus) F.; m. Elaine Lawrence, Oct. 30, 1953; children: Quentin James, Sheldon John, Kirsten. BS, Calif. State U., Long Beach, 1961; LLB, Lasalle Extension U., Chgo., 1973; MA in Mgmt., U. Redlands, 1981. Mgr. Aero. div. Ford Motor Co., Newport Beach, Calif., 1963-68, Northrop Corp., Hawthorne, Calif., 1968-71, 76—; dir. Peace Corps, Tehran, Iran, 1971-76. Author: Doing Business on Arabian Peninsula, 1981, Put Earned Value into Your Management Control System, 1983, Project & Production Scheduling, 1987. Mem. Tustin (Calif.) Parks Commn., 1964-71; founder, pres. Boys Club of Tustin, 1965-68. Named Citizen of Yr. Ford Motor Co., 1967. Mem. Project Mgmt. Inst., Am. Prodn. and Inventory Control Soc. Republican. Avocation: writing. Home: 14001 Howland Way Tustin CA 92680 Office: Northrop Corp #1 Northrop Ave Hawthorne CA 90250

FLEMING, WILLIAM HENRY, medical instrument manufacturing company executive; b. Kansas City, Mo., Dec. 14, 1946; s. Philip George and Josephine Anna Fleming; m. Suzanne Gayle, Apr. 22, 1972; children—David K., Kathryn A. B.A., Calif. State U.-Hayward, 1971, M.B.A., 1973; Ph.D., Calif. Western U., 1981. Asst. quality assurance mgr. Flintkote Co., 1971-73; mgr. wafer fab prodn. Nat. Semicondr. Co., 1973-76; shift supr. Intel Corp., 1977-78; mgr. mfg. Instromedix, Inc., Beaverton, Oreg., 1978-79; v.p., gen. mgr. Cardiac Resuscitator Corp., Lake Oswego, Oreg., 1980-81; pres. Life Sci. Instrumentation, Inc., Portland, Oreg., 1981-86; pres. ITM, Cons.; dir. ops. Noninvasive Tech., Portland, Oreg. 1986—; cons. med. device quality assurance, 1977—. Served with USN, 1966-68. Decorated Air medal with 2 gold stars. Mem. ASTM, Assn. for Advancement of Med. Instruments. Republican. Roman Catholic. Patentee surg. back plate electrode. Office: 4432 SE 16th Ave Portland OR 97123

FLESSATTI, PAULA M., speech pathologist; b. Livermore, Calif., Apr. 2, 1959; d. Paul Andrew and Rosemarie J. (Schenone) F. BS, Calif. State U., Hayward, 1981; MS, U. Wash., 1983. Speech pathologist Communication Concepts, Seattle, 1983-85, Vis. Nurse Services, Seattle, 1985, Profl. Rehab. Assocs., Sacramento, 1986—. Mem. Am. Speech Lang. Hearing Assn. (cert.).

FLETCHER, AARON NATHANIEL, physical chemist, researcher; b. Los Angeles, Dec. 24, 1925; s. Robert Eugene and Mabel Louise Fletcher; m. Edna Delora Stulce, Feb. 23, 1951; children: Clixie, Roberta, Delora, Ronald, Denise. BS, Calif. Inst. Tech., 1949; PhD, UCLA, 1961. Chemist So. Pacific Co., Sacramento, 1949-54; research chemist Naval Weapons Ctr., China Lake, Calif., 1954-86. Contbr. articles to profl. jours.; patentee in field. Served with USAAF, 1944-45. Fellow Naval Ordnance Test Sta., 1959-60. Fellow AAAS; mem. Am. Chem. Soc., Electrochem. Soc. Home: PO Box 1314 Ridgecrest CA 93555

FLETCHER, HON. BETTY B., judge; b. Tacoma, Mar. 29, 1923. B.A., Stanford U., 1943; LL.B., U. Wash., 1956. Bar: Wash. 1956. Former mem. firm Preston, Thorgrimson, Ellis, Holman & Fletcher, Seattle, 1956-1979; judge U.S. Circuit Ct. for 9th Circuit, Seattle, 1979—. Mem. ABA, Wash. Bar Assn., Order of Coif, Phi Beta Kappa. Office: US Court of Appeals 1010 5th Ave Seattle WA 98104

FLETCHER, CLIFF, professional hockey executive; b. 1935; m. Donna Owens; 2 children. With Montreal Canadien Orgn., 1956-66; mgr. Verdun Jr. B team; later mgr. Jr. Canadiens; chief scout St. Louis Blues, 1966-69, asst. gen. mgr., 1969-72; v.p., gen. mgr. Atlanta Flames, Nat. Hockey League, 1972-80; v.p., gen. mgr. Calgary (Alta., Can.) Flames, from 1980, now pres., gen. mgr. Office: Calgary Flames, PO Box 1540, Station M, Calgary, AB Canada T2P 3B9 *

FLETCHER, DONNA LYNNE, association executive; b. Johnson City, N.Y., Aug. 12, 1952; d. Donald Curtis and Elizabeth (Belden) F. B.A. in Pub. Affairs, George Washington U., 1974. Legis. asst. Nat. Fedn. Business and Profl. Women's Clubs Inc., Washington, 1974-75; asst. to exec. dir. No. Calif. Service League, San Francisco, 1976-78; asst. to program funding dir. Sierra Club, San Francisco, 1978-79, dir. gen. giving, 1979—, dir. mem. donor devel., 1984—. Bd. dirs. Gray Panthers met. group, Washington, 1974-75. Mem. Nat. Soc. Fundraising Execs. Democrat. Office: Sierra Club 730 Polk St San Francisco CA 94109

FLETCHER, HOMER LEE, librarian; b. Salem, Ind., May 11, 1928; s. Floyd M. and Hazel (Barnett) F.; m. Jacquelyn Ann Blanton, Feb. 7, 1950; children—Deborah Lynn, Randall Brian, David Lee. B.A., Ind. U., 1953; M.S. in L.S, U. Ill., 1954. Librarian Milw. Pub. Library, 1954-56; head librarian Ashland (Ohio) Pub. Library, 1956-59; city librarian Arcadia (Cal.) Pub. Library, 1959-65, Vallejo (Calif.) Pub. Library, 1965-70, San Jose, Calif., 1970—. Contbr. articles to profl. jours. Pres. S. Solano chpt. Calif. Assn. Neurol. Handicapped Children, 1968-69. Served with USAF, 1946-49. Mem. ALA (intellectual freedom com. 1967-72), Calif. Library Assn. (pres. pub. libraries sect. 1967), Phi Beta Kappa. Democrat. Mem. Christian Ch. Disciples of Christ (elder, chmn. congregation 1978-79). Club: Rotarian. Home: 7921 Belknap Dr Cupertino CA 95014 Office: San Jose Public Library 180 W San Carlos St San Jose CA 95113

FLETCHER, JAMES ALLEN, electronic engineer; b. Toledo, Sept. 18, 1947; s. Allen Rae and Ruth Helen (Scharf) F.; m. Kathy Jane Barrett, Jan. 25, 1975. AS, West Coast U., 1977, BS, 1979. Electronic technician Hughes Aircraft Co., El Segundo, Calif., 1970-72; engring. technician Altec Corp., Anaheim, Calif., 1972-75, Magna Corp., Santa Fe Springs, Calif., 1975-76; engring. technician Odetics Inc., Anaheim, 1976-79, electronic engr., 1979-86; owner, founder Gaslight Video, Orange, Calif., 1980—. Served as sgt. U.S. Army, 1967-69. Mem. Soc. Motion Picture and TV Engrs., Internat. TV Assn., Mensa. Libertarian. Club: Bikecentennial. Avocations: bicycling, record collecting. Home: 281 N Park Ln Orange CA 92667 Office: Gaslight Video 281 N Park Ln Orange CA 92667

FLETCHER, JESSIE LOUISE, social service director; b. Fairmont, W.Va., Oct. 28, 1943; d. Robert Frederic and Lillian Louise (Shackelford) Larosa; m. Phillip E. CaPece, Jan. 30, 1965 (div. Nov. 1974); children: Rebecca Louise CaPece, Melissa Anne CaPece; m. Mark Stephen Fletcher, July 24, 1976. B in Sociology, Calif. State U., Long Beach, 1965; MSW, Calif. State U., Fresno, 1985. Personnel rep. Allstate Ins. Co., Santa Ana, Calif.; personnel mgr. Pacific T&T, Los Angeles; personnel rep. Walt Disney Prodns., Burbank, Calif.; co-owner Sunrise Builders, Clovis, Calif., 1983—; dir. alcohol services Kings County Community Action Orgn., Hanford, Calif., 1986—; vol. counselor Fresno Vet. Ctr., 1985—. Chair City of Fresno Affirmative Action Commn., 1980-81; vice-chair citizen's adv. commn. Fresno Employment Tng. Commn., 1980-82; appointed mem. Mayor's Commn. on Fresno Unification, 1982; mem. Fresno County Alcohol Commn.; sec. United Way of Fresno County, 1984-85, v.p., 1985—, also bd. dirs; chairperson City of Clovis Personnel Commn., 1985—; vol. counselor Fresno Family Service Ctr., 1985-86, Fresno Vet. Ctr. 1985—; block capt. Clovis Neiborhood Watch, 1985—; bd. dirs. Fresno Community Council, 1980-82. Mem. Nat. Assn. Realtors, Fresno Bd. Realtors, Nat. Assn. Social Workers, Am. Soc. Tng. and Devel., Sales Execs. and Mktg. Assn., Fresno C. of C., Clovis C. of C., Cap and Gown. Democrat. Avocations: reading, travel, boating. Home: 540 Pierce Dr #263 Clovis CA 93612 Office: Sunrise Builders 141 Sunnyside Clovis CA 93612 Office: 1222 W Lacey Hanford CA 93230

FLETCHER, LELAND VERNON, artist; b. Cumberland, Md., Sept. 18, 1946; s. Kenneth L. and Marjorie L. (Benecke) F.; B.S., U. Minn., 1972; m. Janis Traub, July 19, 1978; children—Nathan Fletcher, Joshua Traub. One man shows include: U. Minn. Exptl. Gallery, 1972, La Mamelle Art Center, San Francisco, 1976, San Jose State U. Union Gallery, 1978; group exhbns. include: Mus. Contemporary Art, Sao Paulo, 1977, Urbanart '77, Vancouver, Can., 1977, Los Angeles Inst. Contemporary Art, 1978, Inst. Modern Art, Brisbane, 1978, Hansen Gallery, N.Y.C., 1978, Fendrick Gallery, Washington, 1979, 8th Internat. Print Bienale, Cracow, Poland, 1980, Cooper-Hewitt Mus., N.Y.C., 1980 Sch. Art Inst. Chgo., 1981, Metronome Gallery, Barcelona, 1981, 16th Bienal de Sao Paulo, Brazil, 1981, Neue galerie der Stadt Linz, 1982, Bienal de Pontevedra, Spain, 1983, Lyng by Kunstbibliotek, Denmark, 1984, Otis Art Inst./Parsons Sch. Design, Los Angeles, 1984, 10th Internat. Print Bienale, Cracow, Poland, 1984, Museu de Arte da Universidade Federal de Mato Grosso, Brazil, 1984, 11th Biennal Internacional, Museu d'Art Contemporani d'Eivissa, Spain, 1984, Intergrafik '84 Triennale, Berlin, Fiatel Muveszek Klubja Budapest, 1985, Intersection Gallery, San Francisco, 1985, Musee de Petit Format, Couvin, Belgium, 1985, 9th British Internat. Print Biennale, Bradford, Eng., 1986, Sculpt 87/3, Maubeuge, France, 1987, Fundacio la Caixa, Valencia, Spain, 1987, Richards Gallery, Northwestern U., Boston, 1987, Montserrat Coll. Art, Beverly, Mass., 1987; 11 Internat. Print Biennale, Krakow, 1986; others; represented in permanent collection at Mus. Contemporary Art, Sao Paulo, Mpls. Inst. Arts, Art Mus. of Calif. State U., Long Beach, deSaisset Mus., U. Santa Clara (Calif.), Art Inst. Chgo., Victoria and Albert Mus., London, Museen der Stadt Koln, Ludwig Mus., Cologne, Mus. Plantin-Moretus, Antwerp, Mus. de Arte Moderno, Barcelona, Bradford Mus., Eng., Kunsthalle, Hamburg, Galleria D'Arte Moderna, Trieste, Ecole des Beaux-Arts, Maubeuge, others. Address: PO Box 335 San Geronimo CA 94963

FLETCHER, ROSE MARIE, mortgage banker, consultant; b. Oakland, Calif., Dec. 8, 1940; d. Martin George Maher and Gertrude Elizabeth (Noe) Maher McCarthy; m. Jamie Franklin Fletcher, Aug. 1, 1960; children—Roberta JoAnne, Rebecca Louise, Jamie Suzanne. Student San Jose State U., 1958-60, West Valley Coll., 1972-76. Lic. real estate broker, Calif. Formerly br. mgr. Sutro Mortgage Co., San Jose, Calif., 3 yrs.; sr. v.p. Unified Mortgage Co., Cupertino, Calif., 1981-85; owner, pres., cons. Processing Place, San Jose, 1985—; dir. ops. Mortgage Loans Am., Campbell, Calif., 1986—; cons., lectr., trainer in lending field. Mem. Calif. Assn. Residential Lenders (1st v.p. 1985, pres. 1986), Assn. Profl. Mortgage Women (regional gov. 1980-81, Woman of Yr. 1979). Democrat. Roman Catholic. Avocations: water skiing; swimming; dancing. Home: 3704 Heppner Ln San Jose CA 95136 Office: Mortgage Loans Am 62 San Thomas Rd Campbell CA 95008

FLETCHER, SHERRY LYN, elementary school principal; b. Ashland, Kans., Dec. 29, 1947; d. James Thomas Fletcher and Maxine (Lane) Cecil; m. Baxter Barnard Brown, Nov. 1, 1982. BA in Edn., N.Mex. State U., 1968, MA in Edn., 1975, endorsement in edn]. adminstrn., endorsement in early childhood, 1984; Montessori cert., St. Nicholas Tng. Cen., London, 1976. Elem. tchr. pub. schs. pub. schs., Las Cruces, N.Mex., 1969-75; dir., founder Montessori Unltd., Las Cruces, 1976; tchr. Truth or Consequences (N.Mex.) Pub. Schs., 1983-85, elem. prin., 1983—; cons. in field, 1981—; mem. steering com. State Bd. Edn., Santa Fe, 1985-86, mem. adv. com. early childhood, 1985-86. Mem. Elephant Butte/Caballo Leaseholders' Assn. (sec. 1985—), N.Mex. Assn. for the Edn. Young Children, Assn. Supervision and Curriculum Devel., Assn. Sch. Adminstrs. Republican. Home: Star Route N Box B Truth or Consequences NM 87901 Office: Truth or Consequences Schs Box 952 Truth or Consequences NM 87901

FLICK, ROBERT JAMES (BOB ROBERTS), broadcasting executive; b. Butte, Mont., Sept. 9, 1952; s. Raymond P. and Marie B. Flick; diploma Brown Inst. Broadcasting, Mpls., 1973; Journeyman, Bert's Car Triming, Butte, 1969-73; with Sta. KOPR, Butte, 1974, Sta. KBOW, Butte, 1974-75; with Sta. KXLF, Butte, 1975—, program dir., music dir., 1976-80; program dir., music dir. Sta. KXTL-AM, Butte, 1982-84; ops. dir. air talent KXTL-KQUY-FM, Butte, 1984—; music cons., 1977—. Mem. Nat. Assn. Broadcasters, Mont. Assn. Broadcasters, Nat. St. Rod Assn., Internat. Hot Rod Assn., Pioneer St. Rods of Butte, Southwest Corvette Club, Am. Drag Racing Assn., Nat. Drag Racing Assn., United Comml. Travellers, Butte Jaycees, Nat. Hot Rod Assn. Lodge: Elks. Home: 428 Colorado St Butte MT 59701 Office: KQUY-FM 3219 Harrison Ave PO Box 3788 Butte MT 59701

FLIEGE, STEWART EDWARD, finance educator, management consultant; b. Alhambra, Calif., Oct. 8, 1927; s. J. Stewart and Mary G. (Nysewander) F.; m. Mary Jo Perry, Sept. 13, 1952; children: Malcolm, Kevin, Heather. BA, UCLA, 1950; MA, U. Mich., 1952, PhD, 1956. Lic. psychologist, Calif. Sect. head Rand Corp., Santa Monica, Calif., 1955-57; dept. mgr. Systems Devel. Corp., Santa Monica, 1957-64; v.p. Computer Scis. Corp., El Segundo, Calif., 1964-71, UMF Systems, Inc., Los Angeles, 1971-72; pres. Westwind Travel, Los Angeles, 1973-80; prof. fin. and quantitative methods Pepperdine U., Malibu, Calif., 1972—; chmn. Cory Computers, Inc., Costa Mesa, Calif., 1981-82; exec. dir. Calif. Inst. Bus. Mgmt., Los Angeles, 1980—. Served with U.S. Army, 1945-47. Mem. Am. Psychol. Assn., Psychometric Soc., Assn. Computing Machinery, Phi Beta Kappa, Sigma Xi. Home: 12115 San Vicente Blvd 409 Los Angeles CA 90049 Office: Pepperdine U 3415 Sepulveda Blvd Malibu CA 90265

FLINT, LOU JEAN, state education official; b. Ogden, Utah, July 11, 1934; d. Elmer Blood and Ella D. (Adams) F.; children—Dirk Kershaw Brown, Kristie Susan Brown Felix, Flint Kershaw Brown. B.S., Weber State Coll., 1968; M.Ed., U. Utah, 1974, Ed.S, 1981. Cert. early childhood and elem. edn., Utah Bd. Edn., 1968, edn. adminstrn., 1981. Master tchr. Muir Elem., Davis Sch. Dist., Farmington, Utah, 1968-77; edn. specialist Dist. I, Dept. Def., Eng., Scotland, Norway, Denmark, Holland, Belgium, 1977-79; ednl. cons. Office Higher Edn. State of Utah, Utah System Approach to Individualized Learning, Tex., S.C., Fla., Utah, 1979—; research analyst Office Commr. Higher Edn. State of Utah, Salt Lake City, 1982—; mem. Equity Vocat. Edn. Bd.; adv. Women and Bus. Conf. Bd. State bd. dirs. Am. Council Edn. Named Exemplary Tchr., Utah State Bd. Edn., 1970-77; Outstanding Educator, London Central High Sch., 1979; recipient Appreciation award, Gov. of Utah, 1983, 84, 85, Woman of Achievement award Utah Bus. and Profl. Women, 1985. Mem. AAUW (Edn. Found. award given in her honor, 1986, com. mem. Nat. Assn. Women's Work/Women's Worth, Disting. Woman award 1987), Am. Council Edn. (Nat. Identification Program 1982, Susa Young Gates award 1987), Consortium Women in Higher Edn., Nat. Assn. Edn. Young Children, Utah Assn. Edn. Young Children (past pres.), Women Concerned About Nuclear War, Utah Jaycee Aux. (past pres. Centerville), Phi Delta Kappa, Delta Kappa Gamma. Mormon. Author: The Comprehensive Community College, 1980; others. Office: Office Commr Higher Edn State Utah 355 W North Temple #3 Triad Suite 550 Salt Lake City UT 84180

FLINT, ROBERT THOMAS, psychologist; b. Los Angeles, Sept. 16, 1935; s. Thomas and Louise (Jones) F.; m. Winifred LaVonne, Aug. 29, 1955 (div.); m. 2d Gayla Kaibel, May 21, 1972; children—Jerretta Villines, Sean Flint, Kathleen Flint, Deirdre Flint. B.A., San Francisco State Coll., 1961, M.A., 1963; Ph.D. (USPHS fellow), U. Minn., 1970. Lic. psychologist, Calif. Research psychologist Am. Rehab. Found., Mpls., 1966-68; instr. Student Counseling Bur., U. Minn., 1968-70, asst. prof., 1970-74, assoc. prof., 1974-77; v.p. Judson Family Ctr., Mpls., 1977-80; chief psychol. services Ashby Med. Group, Berkeley, Calif., 1980-83; staff psychologist Paul S. D. Berg and Assocs., Oakland, Calif., 1983-85; pres. Robert T. Flint and Gayla Kaibel, Inc., Lafayette, Calif., 1986—; cons. law enforcement, 1968—; pvt. practice psychotherapy; trainer psychotherapists; forensic psychologist; tchr. in field; founder Minn. Health Careers Council, 1965; sec., bd. dirs. Central Contra Costa County (Calif.) Rape Crisis Service, 1982-83. Served with USN, 1954-58. Mem. Am. Psychol. Assn., Calif. Psychol. Assn., Internat. Assn. Chiefs of Police (assoc.). Democrat. Contbr. articles on psychology as related to occupational therapy, dental hygiene, nursing, dentistry and law enforcement to profl. jours.; script writer, cons. tng. films for law enforcement on psychology of crime victims, especially sexual assault victims. Home: 3690 Sun View Ct Concord CA 94520 Office: 985 Moraga Rd Lafayette CA 94549

FLOCKS, MILTON, physician, ophthamologist, researcher; b. N.Y.C., Nov. 12, 1914; s. Morris and Rose (Blackman) F.; m. Jean Harris Rosenthal, Dec. 6, 1946 (div. 1966); m. Jean Jones, Nov. 29, 1969 (div. 1979). Student, George Washington U., 1932-34; BA, La. State U., 1938; MD, La. State U., New Orleans, 1940. Diplomate Am. Bd. Ophthalmology. Clin instr., research assoc. Stanford (Calif.) U., 1955-57, asst. clin. prof., 1957-60, assoc. clin. prof., 1960-79, assoc. clin. prof emeritus, 1979—, assoc. clin. prof. surgery div. ophthalmology; practice medicine specializing in ophthalmology Midpeninsula Ophthalmologic Med. Group, Palo Alto, Calif. Contbr. articles to profl. jours. Mem. Portola Valley (Calif.) Sch. Bd., 1960-64. Served to lt. col. U.S. Army, 1941-46. Recipient Heed Found. award, 1968. Mem. AMA, Am. Acad. Ophthalmology, Pacific Coast Acad. Ophthalmology and Otolaryngology. Avocations: tennis, swimming, bridge. Home: 1380 Oak Creek Dr Apt 215 Palo Alto CA 94304 Office: Midpeninsula Ophthalmol Med Group 1101 Welch Rd Suite B-8 Palo Alto CA 94304

FLOOD, JAMES JOSEPH, airline executive; b. Joliet, Ill., Sept. 3, 1923; s. Joseph P. and Rose Marie (Kwasneski) Lencioni; m. Joan Lydia Dahlquist, Jan. 31, 1948; children: James W. (dec.), Janice K., Jody Ann. B.A., Beloit Coll., 1949. Pricing adminstr. Sundstrand Corp., 1952-61; pres., chief exec. officer Alaska Brick Co. Inc., 1961-76, Wien Air Alaska, Anchorage, 1976—; chmn. Wien Air Alaska, 1978—, also dir.; dir. Alaska Pacific Bank. Bd. dirs. YMCA Anchorage, from 1968, pres., 1971; bd. dirs. Anchorage Fine Arts Museum Assn., from 1977. Served with USAAF, 1943-45. Decorated Air medal; recipient Community Service award YMCA, 1977. Mem. Airline Transport Assn., Beloit Coll. Chapin Soc., Assn. Local Transport Airlines, Sigma Alpha Epsilon. Republican. Methodist. Clubs: Petroleum of Anchorage, Washington Athletic, Elks. Office: Wien Air Alaska Inc 301 W Northern Lts Blvd #502 Anchorage AK 99503

FLOOD, JAMES TYRRELL, broadcasting executive, public relations consultant; b. Los Angeles, Oct. 5, 1934; s. James Joseph and Teresa (Rielly) F.; m. Bonnie Carolyn Lutz, Mar. 25, 1966; children: Hilary C., Sean L. BA in Sociology, U. Calif., Santa Barbara, 1956; MA in Communications, Calif. State U., Chico, 1981. Cons. pub. relations, Beverly Hills, Calif., 1964-72; pub. relations, advt. dir. Jerry Lewis Films, 1964-72; pub. relations cons. Medic Alert Found. Internat., Paradise, 1976-83; owner, mgr. Sta. KRIJ-FM, Paradise, 1983—; instr. Calif. State Sch. Communications, Chico, 1982—. Calif. media cons. Carter/Mondale campaign, 1976; mem. Calif. Dem. Fin. Com., 1982-83. Served with USNR, 1956-58. Mem. Calif. Broadcasters Assn. (bd. dirs. 1986—), Pub. Relations Soc. Am. Lodge: Rotary (Paradise).

FLOOR, EMANUEL ANDREW, land development executive; b. Salt Lake City, Dec. 3, 1935; s. Andrew W. and Marie A. (Trakas) F.; Nan Hansen, June 6, 1964; children: David Emanuel, Gina Marie, Michael Patrick. BS, U. Utah, 1957. Pres., bd. dirs. Triad Properties, Salt Lake City, 1975—; exec. v.p., bd. dirs. Triad Am., Salt Lake City; bd. dirs. Utah Travel Council; dir. instl. devel. Utah State U., Logan, 1966-68. Cons. vol. program. ARC, 1950-66; chmn. Western Gov.'s Travel Council, 1966-69; bd. dirs. Cath. Charities, Salt Lake City, Utah Symphony, Pine Canyon Ranch for Boys. Mem. Salt Lake Area C. of C., Pi Kappa Alpha. Club: Ft. Douglas. Home: 2205 Country Club Dr Salt Lake City UT 84109 Office: Lakeside Plaza I Suite 500 Wiley Post Way Salt Lake City UT 84116

FLOR, LOY LORENZ, chemist, corrosion engineer, consultant; b. Luther, Okla., Apr. 25, 1919; s. Alfred Charles and Nellie M. (Wilkinson) F.; B.A. in Chemistry, San Diego State Coll., 1941; m. Virginia Louise Pace, Oct. 1, 1946; children—Charles R., Scott R., Gerald C., Donna Jeanne, Cynthia Gail. With Helix Water Dist., La Mesa, Calif., 1947-84, chief chemist, 1963—, supr. water quality, 1963—, supr. corrosion control dept., 1956—. Served to 1st. lt. USAAF, 1941-45. Registered profl. engr., Calif. Mem. Am. Chem. Soc. (chmn. San Diego sect. 1965—), Am. Water Works Assn. (chmn. water quality div. Calif. sect. 1965—), Nat. Assn. Corrosion Engrs. (chmn. western region 1970). Republican. Presbyterian. Club: Masons. Office: 11315 Manzanita Rd Lakeside CA 92040

FLORATOS, WILLIAM ANDREW, lawyer; b. Mt. Shasta, Calif., May 15, 1957; s. Nick D. and Billie Jean (Sumrall) F. BA in Polit. Sci., Pepperdine U., 1979, JD, 1982. Bar: Calif. 1983, U.S. Dist. Ct. (No., Cen., Ea. So.) Calif. Atty. E.C. Leleus, a Profl. Corp., Bakersfield, Calif., 1983-84, Morinello, Barone, Holden, Narduli, Newport Beach, Calif., 1984-86; lawyer Greenbaum and Ferentz, Newport Beach, 1986; sole practice Newport Beach, 1986—. Mem. ABA, Am. Trial Lawyer Assn., Calif. Trial Lawyer Assn., Orange Cutny Petroleum Assn. Office: 4400 MacArthur Blvd Fifth Floor Newport Beach CA 92660

FLORENCE, KENNETH JAMES, lawyer; b. Hanford, Calif., July 31, 1943; s. Ivy Owen and Louella (Dobson) F.; m. Verena Magdalena Demuth, Dec. 10, 1967. B.A., Whittier Coll., 1965; J.D., Hastings Coll. Law, U. Calif.-San Francisco, 1974. Bar: Calif. 1974, U.S. Dist. Ct. (cen. dist.) Calif. 1974, U.S. Dist. Ct. (ea. and so. dists.) Calif., 1976, U.S. Dist. Ct. (no. dist.) Calif. 1980, U.S. Ct. Appeals (9th cir.) 1975, U.S. Supreme Ct. 1984. Dist. mgr. Pacific T&T, Calif., 1969-71; assoc. Parker, Milliken, et al, Los Angeles, 1974-78; ptnr. Dern, Mason, et al, 1978-84, Swerdlow & Florence, A Law Corp., Beverly Hills, 1984—; pres. Westside Legal Services, Inc., Santa Monica, Calif., 1982-83. Served to lt. USNR, 1966-69, Vietnam. Col. J.G. Boswell scholar, 1961. Mem. ABA (co-chmn. state labor law com. 1982-83). Democrat. Home: 1124 21st St #2 Santa Monica CA 90403 Office: Swerdlow & Florence 9401 Wilshire Blvd Suite 828 Beverly Hills CA 90212

FLORENCE, VERENA MAGDALENA, legal administrator; b. Interlaken, Switzerland, Nov. 4, 1946; came to U.S., 1967; d. Paul Robert and Marie (Raess) Demuth; m. Kenneth James Florence, Dec. 10, 1967. BA, U. Calif., Berkeley, 1974; MS, UCLA, 1979, PhD, 1982. Research scientist Procter & Gamble, Cin., 1983; adminstr. Swerdlow & Florence, Beverly Hills, Calif., 1984—. Contbr. articles to profl. jours. Democrat. Home: 1063 Stradella Rd Los Angeles CA 90077 Office: Swerdlow & Florence 9401 Wilshire Blvd Suite 828 Beverly Hills CA 90212

FLORES, DAVID ALFONSO, development scientist personal computer consultant; b. Los Angeles, July 21, 1959; s. Angel Alfonso and Martha Terrazas (Granado) F. BS in Chemistry, Calif. Poly. U., 1982. Assoc. chemist Beckman Instruments, Brea, Calif., 1982-85, scientist, 1986; co-owner, cons. PC-Compatibles Plus, Stanton, Calif., 1986. Mem. Am. Chem. Soc. Republican. Roman Catholic. Avocations: photography, music. Office: Beckman Instruments Inc 200 S Kraemer Blvd Brea CA 92622

FLORES, HECTOR MOSES, marine corps officer; b. Houston, July 6, 1958; s. Moses and Carol (Moreno) F. Student, Brown U., 1976-78; BA, Nat. U., 1987. Enlisted USMC, 1979, advanced through grades to staff sgt., 1985; infantryman USMC, Kailua, Hawaii, 1979-81, tng. non-commd. officer, 1981-83; guard non-commd. officer USMC, Charleston, S.C., 1983-85; instr. USMC, San Diego, 1985—. Mem. U.S. Naval Inst. (assoc.), Nat. Rifle Assn. (life, instr./coach 1986—), Nat. Geographic Soc., San Diego Zool. Soc., Marine Corps Assn., SMithsonian Assocs., Nat. Audobon SOc., Internat. Shooting Assn., Calif. Rifle and Pistol Assn. Republican. Club: Team U.S. Avocations: coaching shooting sports, fishing, hunting. Home: 10445 Mast Blvd Apt 50 Santee CA 92071 Office: USMC Sea Sch San Diego CA 92140

FLORES, THOMAS L., savings and loan executive, consultant; b. Alhambra, Calif., Aug. 8, 1932; s. Charles John and Alta Chloe (Scott) F.; m. Colleen Patricia Scharp, June 15, 1963; children: Leslie Ann, Tracy Lynn. BBA, Calif. State U., Los Angeles, 1959; postgrad., Ind. U., 1971. Lic. real estate broker. Treas. Quaker City Fed. Savs. and Loan, Whittier, Calif., 1967-78; sr. v.p. Orange Coast Savs. & Loan, Costa Mesa, Calif., 1978-79, San Clemente (Calif.) Savs. & Loan, 1979-80; pres. Placentia (Calif.) Linda Savs. & Loan, 1980-82; pres. Perpetual Savs. Bank, Santa Ana, Calif., 1982—, also bd. dirs.; bd. dirs. Case Mgmt. Services Inc., Fountain Valley, Calif., Tomco Enterprises Inc., Fountain Valley, Art Leasing Inc., Newport Beach, Calif. Assoc. mem. Rep. State Cen. Com., Calif., 1962-63; mem. Mayor's Adv. Com., City of Los Angeles, 1966. Served with USAF, 1952-56. Mem. Fin. Mgrs. Soc. (pres. Los Angeles chpt. 1976-77, cert. of merit 1977), Orange County Antique Soc. (pres. 1976-78). Republican. Lodge: Kiwanis (pres. East Whittier club 1967-78). Avocations: coin collecting, travel. Office: Perpetual Savs Bank PO Box 25859 Santa Ana CA 92799

FLORES, THOMAS R., professional football coach; b. Fresno, Calif., Mar. 21, 1937; s. Tom C. and Nellie (Padilla) F.; m. Barbara Ann Fridell, Mar. 25, 1961; children: Mark and Scott (twins), Kim. BA, Coll. Pacific, 1959. Quarterback Oakland Raiders, 1960-66; quarterback Buffalo Bills, 1967-68, Kansas City (Mo.) Chiefs, 1969-70; asst. coach Oakland (now Los Angeles) Raiders, 1972-78, head coach, 1979—; player rep. AFL, 1966-68. Nat. hon. chmn. Lung Assn. Named Man of Yr. No. Calif. Lung Assn., 1979; Latino of Yr. City of Los Angeles, 1981. Democrat. Roman Catholic. Coached team to Super Bowl victories 1981, 84. Office: Los Angeles Raiders 332 Center St El Segundo CA 90245 *

FLOREY, MARY JO, microbiologist; b. Oregon City, Oreg., Sept. 22, 1928; d. Sidney and Lorena (Kleinsmith) W.; m. Robert D. Florey, July 2, 1950 (dec.). BA in Biology, Linfield U., 1950; MS, Oreg. Health Sci. U., 1968; MS in Microbiology, U. Mont., 1970. Cert. med. technician, Calif. Microbiologist Palo Alto (Calif.) Clinic, 1953-58, U. Oreg. Med. Sch., Portland, 1958-62, Oreg. State Pub. Health Services, Portland, 1968-69; research assoc. Pacific N.W. Red Cross, Portland, 1974-86, Pacific N.W. Research Found., Seattle, 1986-87, The Biomembrane Inst., Seattle, 1987—. NIH scholar, 1962-68. Mem. AAAS, Am. Assn. Clin. Pathologists, N.Y. Acad. Scis., Sigma Xi. Democrat. Avocations: hiking, photography. Home: 4920 242nd St SW Mountlake Terrace WA 98043 Office: The Biomembrane Inst 201 Elliot Ave Suite 305 Seattle WA 98119

FLORINE, DAGNE LU, biologist; b. Glencoe, Minn., Mar. 6, 1953; d. Arthur William and Mary Marvin (Coons) F. BS, U. Minn., Mpls., 1975; PhD, U. Minn., Rochester, 1980. Project investigator M D Anderson Hosp., Houston, 1981-83; research scientist Triton Bioscis., Inc., Alameda (Calif.) and Houston, 1983-85; project leader, sr. research scientist Triton Bioscis., Inc., Alameda, 1985—, project leader cancer diagnostics tumor marker project, 1985—, project leader cancer diagnostics infectious disease project, 1986—. Mem. N.Y. Acad Sci., Am. Soc. Cell Biology, Phi Beta Kappa. Home: 29 Corte Yolanda Moraga CA 94556 Office: Triton Bioscis Inc 1501 Harbor Bay Pkwy Alameda CA 94501

FLOWER, LAWRENCE MARONEY, engineer; b. Denver, Apr. 11, 1923; s. Ludlow and Mary (Maroney) F.; m. Mary Lee Paulson, Sept. 8, 1948; children—Mary Susan, Lawrence Lee, David Ludlow, Ann Maroney. B.S. in Mech. Engring., U. Colo., 1947, M.S., 1952. Registered profl. engr., Wyo., Colo. Project engr. Atomics Internat., Canoga Park, Calif., 1958-68, Litton Industries, Culver City, Calif., 1968-72; chief engr. Dixson Inc., Grand Junction, Colo., 1972-73, Western Sales, Grand Junction, 1973-78, Grand Junction Steel, Grand Junction, 1978-84; cons. engr., Grand Junction, 1971—. Mem. Mayor's Adv. Com., Los Angeles, 1968. Served to 1st lt. USAAF, 1943-45. Mem. AIME, Pi Tau Sigma, Chi Psi. Republican. Roman Catholic. Club: Petroleum and Mining (Grand Junction), Rocky Mountain Ghost Squadron. Home: 1820 O Rd Fruita CO 81521

FLOYD, BARTOW WILLIAM, advertising, public relations executive; b. Meigs, Ga., Jan. 6, 1930; s. Leonard Ivy and Mattie Lou (Golden) F.; m. Janice Irene Bigler, May 29, 1969; children: Terri, Heather. Student, Beauty Coll., San Diego. Lic. cosmetologist. Hair stylist James Hall, San Diego, 1954-59; instr. Chula Vista (Calif.) Beauty Coll., 1959-61; owner, instr. 2 Corp. Beauty Colls., Chula Vista and Lemon Grove, Calif., 1961-69; owner, then pres. 7 Corp. Beauty Colls., 18 Beauty Salons, San Diego County, 1969-74; v.p. McAdams System Inc., San Diego, 1974-78, owner, pres., 1978-84; exec. dir. mktg. and advt. Calif. Consumer Automobile Protection Assn., Bonita, 1984—. Author: Crime Prevention, 1977, For You and Your Community, 1976. Bd. dirs. ch., Lemon Grove, Calif., chmn. fin. 1974—; youth club dir., Lemon Grove, 1969-71. Served with USN, 1948-53. Mem. Cosmetology Assn. (pres. 1966-68). Republican. Lodge: Kiwanis (campaign chmn. Lemon Grove club 1975). Avocations: golf, singing. Office: Calif Consumer Automobile Protection Assn 3130 Bonita Rd Bonita CA 92010

FLOYD, MARY ALICE, counselor, educator; b. Fairhope, Ala., Feb. 27, 1928; d. Walter S. and Nell Palmer; student San Francisco U., 1945-47; B.A., Ala. U., 1949; postgrad. Tulane U., 1951-52, San Jose State U., 1958, U. Calif., Santa Barbara, 1966-72; M.A., U. So. Ala., 1969; m. Gerald L. Floyd, Mar. 22, 1952; 1 son, Jonathan Curran. Guidance cons. and coordinator Careers for Women project Santa Barbara (Calif.) Sch. Dist., 1973-74; counselor terminally ill Life Acceptance unit Pinecrest Hosp., Santa Barbara, 1975-77; counselor-dir. Women's Center, Santa Barbara City Coll., 1977-78; tchr. adult edn., Santa Barbara, 1972—, pvt. practice cons., counseling; cons., coordinator Alienated Youth Program, 1971; mem. faculty U. Calif. at Santa Barbara Extension, 1976; bd. dirs. Calif. Luth. U. Grad. Studies, 1984-85. Mem. Am. Personnel and Guidance Assn., Nat. Vocat. Guidance Assn., Calif. Personnel and Guidance Assn., Santa Barbara C. of C., Council Internat. Students (pres. 1983-85), Calif. Coll. Personnel Assn., South Coast Bus. Network. Democrat. Unitarian.

FLOYD, ROBERT W., computer scientist, educator; b. N.Y.C., June 8, 1936; s. Darwin and Mary F.; (divorced); children: Susan, Michael, Sean. A.B., U. Chgo., 1953, B.S. in Physics, 1958. Elec. engr. Westinghouse Co., Elmira, N.Y., 1955-56; computer operator, programmer Armour Research Found., Chgo., 1956-62; analyst Computer Assocs., Wakefield, Mass., 1962-65; assoc. prof. computer sci. Carnegie-Mellon U., 1965-68; assoc. prof. Stanford U., 1968-70, prof., 1970—, chmn. dept. computer sci., 1974-77. Guggenheim fellow, 1976-77. Fellow Am. Acad. Arts and Scis.; mem. Assn. Computing Machinery (asso. editor Jour. 1966-67, A.M. Turing award 1978), AAAS. Avocation: tournament backgammon. Home: 895 Allardice Way Stanford CA 94305 Office: Stanford U Computer Sci Dept Stanford CA 94305

FLOYD, RODNEY WAYNE, computer specialist, system analyst; b. Crosby, Miss., Nov. 6, 1938; s. Hoyt Williams Jennings and Lillian Estelle (Smith) F.; m. Mary Jo Porch, Feb. 19, 1966; children—Rodney Wayne, William Douglas. B.S., U. So. Miss., 1959; diploma Armed Forces Staff Coll., 1985. Cert. in data processing. Computer specialist U.S. Army Missile Command, Huntsville, Ala., 1964-71, U.S. Army Safeguard System Command, Huntsville, 1971-73, U.S. Army Info. Systems Command, Fort Huachuca, Ariz., 1973—. Served with U.S. Army, 1961-67. Mem. Armed Forces Communications and Electronics Assn. Methodist. Home: 1969 Chantilly Dr Sierra Vista AZ 85635 Office: US Army Info Systems Command AS-OPS-CC Fort Huachuca AZ 85613

FLUECK, JOHN ALBERT, statistician, researcher; b. Cin., Apr. 13, 1933; s. Walter John and Bernice H. (Weber) F.; children: Alex, David, Michael. BS, Beloit Coll., 1955; MBA, U. Chgo., 1958, PhD, 1967. Tutorial lectr. U. Chgo., 1962-64, lectr. in stats., 1964-67, vis. lectr., 1967-68; prof. stats. Temple U., Phila., 1968-85; sr. research fellow, chief statistician U. Colo.-Coop. Inst. Research Environ. Scis., Boulder, 1984—; cons. numerous cos., N.Y.C., Phila., Washington, 1967—, UN, Rome, Geneva; vis. statistician, White House, Washington, 1959-60, 70-71; pres. Flueck Assocs., Phila., Boulder, 1974-85. Contbr. articles to profl. jours., chpts. to books. Served with U.S. Army, 1955-57. Fellow Ford Found., U. Chgo., 1958, Walgreen Found., 1960-62, NAS-NRC, Washington, 1982-84. Fellow Am. Statis. Assn. (counsel chmn. 1975); mem. AAAS, Soc. Internat. Devel. (program chmn. 1986—), Biometrics Soc., Sigma Xi. Clubs: Lake Eldora Ski Team (Netherland, Colo.); F.C. Boulder (bd. dirs. 1983-85). Home: 3140 3d St Boulder CO 80302 Office: U Colo-Coop Inst Research Environ Scis 3100 Marine St Boulder CO 80303

FLUETSCH, PETER JAY, insurance company executive; b. Merced, Calif., Nov. 17, 1934; s. John Jay and Helen Katherine (Shaffer) F.; A.A., Menlo Coll.; m. Mary Catherine Bacciarini, Nov. 10, 1957; children—Kathleen, John, Christine, Jeanette, Douglas. Partner, Fluetsch Ins. Agy., Merced, 1960-67, v.p., 1967-80; pres. Fluetsch & Busby Ins., 1980—. Past pres. Merced-Mariposa bd. Am. Cancer Soc. Central Calif. Bd. Rev.; active Yosemite Area council Boy Scouts Am., pres., 1976-78, area v.p. Western region com., 1980-83, recipient Silver Beaver award, 1967, Silver Antelope award, 1981; v.p. Merced United Way, 1976-79, pres., 1979—; adv. com. Calif. State U., State Bus. Week. Served with Calif. N.G. Mem. Merced Mariposa Ind. Ins. Agts. (past pres.), Merced County Life Underwriters Assn. (past pres.) Calif., Merced City (past pres.), Merced County chambers commerce. Democrat. Club: Merced Boosters, (past pres.), Merced Trade (past pres.) Kiwanis (past dist. lt. gov., past. pres.) Elks, Masons. Home: 1012 Wyoming Dr Merced CA 95340 Office: 725 W 18th St Merced CA 95340

FLUHARTY, ARVAN LAWRENCE, biochemistry educator, research administrator; b. Haines, Oreg., June 10, 1934; m. Claire L. Boyd, June 24, 1961; children: Michael, Lawrence, Colleen. BS in Chemistry magna cum laude, U. Wash., 1956; PhD in Biochemistry, U. Calif., Berkeley, 1959. Asst. prof. biochemistry U. So. Calif., Los Angeles, 1962-66, assoc. prof., 1966-68; research specialist biochemistyr, research dept. Pacific State Hosp., Pomona, Calif., 1968-73, assoc. research biochemist UCLA/Mental Retardation Research Ctr. Research Group, 1973-75, adj. prof., 1975-79; prof. in residence UCLA/Mental Retardation Research Ctr. Research Group Lanterman State Hosp., Pomona, 1979—, research group coordinator, 1980—; vis. assoc. prof. biomedicinal chemistry Sch. Pharmacy, U. So. Calif., 1969, adj. assoc. prof. biochemistry Sch. Medicine, 1969-72, adj. prof., 1972-75; cons. various sci. projects; lectr. numerous schs. and confs. nationally; reviewer grant proposals Nat. Found., NSF, Research Corp., Petroleum Research Fund, Am. Chem. Soc. Mem. editorial bd. Biochem. Medicine, 1980—; reviewer manuscripts for various profl. jours.; contbr. numerous articles and abstracts to profl. jours. Vice pres. Claremont North Swim Club, 1976-78; sr. referee Am. Youth Soccer Orgn., 1977-87; chief umpire Claremont Am. Little League, 1978. Served with USPHS, 1959-62. Research grantee USPHS, 1962-68, 64-68, State of Calif., 1981-82, Calif. Dept. Mental Hygiene, 1969-70, Nat. Inst. Child Health and Human Devel., 1970-77, Nat. Inst. Neurol. Diseases and Strokes, 1969-83, 86—; predoctoral fellow NSF, 1956-59. Mem. AAAS, Am. Soc. Biol. Chemistry, Biochem. Soc., Am. Chem. Soc. (divs. biol. and carbohydrate chemistry), Am. Soc. Neurochemistry, Phi Beta Kappa, Sigma Xi. Office: UCLA/MRRC Lanterman Devel Ctr PO Box 100 R Pomona CA 91769

FLUHARTY, JESSE ERNEST, lawyer, former judge; b. San Antonio, Tex., July 25, 1916; s. Jesse Ernest and Gwendolyn (Elder) F.; m. Ernestine Gertrude Corlies, Oct. 25, 1945; 1 son, Stephen Robert. Student Calif. State U.-San Diego, 1935-36, Art Ctr. Sch. Design Los Angeles, 1938-39; J.D. with distinction, U. Pacific, 1951; grad. Nat. Jud. Coll. Adminstrv. Law 1982. Bar: Calif. 1952, U.S. Dist. Ct. (no. dist.) Calif. 1952, U.S. Ct. appeals (9th cir.) 1952, U.S. Dist. Ct. (cen. dist.) Calif. 1979, U.S. Supreme Ct. 1983. Sole practice, Sacramento, 1952-60; referee in charge Indsl. Accident Commn., Stockton, Calif., 1960-67; presiding referee so. Calif. Workers Compensation Appeals Bd., Los Angeles, 1967-71, workers compensation Judge, Los Angeles, 1971-79; presiding judge, Los Angeles, 1979-81, Long Beach, 1981-83; of counsel Law Office of Stephen Fluharty, Glendale, Calif., 1984—. Pres. Family Service Agy., Sacramento, 1958, 59, Community Council Stockton and San Joaquin County, 1965, Service Club Council Los Angeles, 1973-74, Glendale Hills Coordinating Council, 1976-78, Chevy Chase Estates Assn., 1971-77; chmn. San Joaquin County Recreation and Park Commn., 1963-67. Served with U.S. Army, 1943-45. Decorated Bronze Star, Philippine Liberation medal; recipient Meritorious citation Calif. Recreation Soc., 1967. Mem. Calif. State Bar, Los Angeles County Bar Assn., Glendale Bar Assn., Am. Judicature Soc., Lawyers Club Los Angeles (pres. 1980, Judge of Yr. 1982). Republican. Congregationalist. Clubs: Chevy Chase Country, Verdugo. Lodges: Lions (pres. Los Angeles 1971-72), Masons. Home: 3330 Emerald Isle Dr Glendale CA 91206 Office: 501 N Central Ave Suite B Glendale CA 91203

FLUKE, JOHN MAURICE, JR., electrical equipment manufacturing company executive; b. 1942; s. John Maurice and Lyla (Schram) F., Sr. BS in elec. engring., Univ. of Wash., 1964; MS in elec. engring., Stanford Univ., 1966. With John Fluke Mfg. Co. Inc., 1966—, gen. mgr. Central Products Group, 1978-82, gen. mgr. Indsl. Measurement & Control Div., 1982, vice-chmn., 1982-84, chief exec. officer, 1983—, chmn., 1984—. Office: John Fluke Mfg Co Inc 6920 Seaway Blvd Box C 9090 Everett WA 98206 *

FLUKE, LYLA SCHRAM, publisher; b. Maddock, N.D.; d. Olaf John and Anne Marie (Rodberg) Schram; B.S. in Zoology and Physiology, U. Wash., Seattle, 1934, teaching diploma, 1935; m. John M. Fluke, June 5, 1937; children—Virginia Fluke Gabelein, John M., David Lynd. High sch. tchr., 1935-37; tutor Seattle schs., 1974-75; pub. Portage quar., mag. of Hist. Soc. of Seattle and King County, 1980—. Founder, N.W. chpt. Myasthenia Gravis Found., 1953, pres., 60-63; obtained N.W. artifacts for destroyer tender Puget Sound, 1966; mem. Seattle Mayor's Com. for Seattle Beautiful, 1968-69; sponsor Seattle World's Fair, 1962; charter mem. Seattle Youth Symphony Aux., 1974; bd. dirs. Cascade Symphony, Salvation Army, 1985—; mem. U.S. Congl. Adv. Bd.; benefactor U. Wash., 1982—, nat. chmn. ann. giving campaign, 1983-84; benefactor Stanford U., 1984; mem. condr.'s club Seattle Symphony, 1978—. Fellow Seattle Pacific U., 1972—. Mem. Wash. Trust for Historic Preservation, Nat. Trust for Historic Preservation, English Speaking Union, Northwest Ornamental Hort. Soc. (life, hon.), Smithsonian Assocs., Nat. Assn. Parliamentarians (charter mem., pres. N.W. unit 1961), Wash. Parliamentarians Assn. (charter), IEEE Aux. (chpt. charter mem., past pres.), Seattle C. of C. (women's div.), Seattle Symphony Women's Assn. (life mem.; sec. 1982-84, pres. 1985-86), Hist. Soc. Seattle and King County (exec. com. 1975-78, pres. women's mus. league 1975-78, pres. Moritz Thomsen Guild of Hist. Soc., 1978-80, 84-87), Highlands Orthopedic Guild (life), Wash. State Hist. Soc., Antiquarian Soc. (v.p. 1986—), N.W. Pres.'s Club, Stanford Assocs., Sterling Circle. Republican. Lutheran. Clubs: Women's U., Rainier, Seattle Golf, Seattle Tennis, U. Wash. Pres.'s. Author articles on history. Address: 1206 NW Culbertson Dr Seattle WA 98177

FLY, CLAUDE LEE, soil and water resource development consultant; b. Fulbright, Tex., June 23, 1905; s. Anderson Bureaugard and Emmeline Josephine (Lowry) F.; m. Miriam Rector, Aug. 21, 1927; children: Maurita Fly Kane, John M. B.S. in Soils and Chemistry, Okla. State U., 1927, M.S. in Soils and Chemistry, 1928; Ph.D. in Soil Chemistry and Plant Physiology, Iowa State U., 1931. Head sci. dept., prof. chemistry Panhandle State Coll., Goodwell, Okla., 1931-35; soil scientist, asst. regional adminstr. soil surveys Dept. of Agr. Soil Conservation Service, 1935-52; chief agronomist Morrison-Knudsen, also Internat. Engrng. Co., 1952-58; asst. adminstr., project leader Agrl. Research Service, USDA, 1958-63; pres. Claude L. Fly & Assocs., Ft. Collins, Colo., 1963—; dir. Lower Lower Brule Farm Corp. Nat. adv. bd. Am. Security Council; mem. U.S. Def. Com.; mem. Ams. Against Union Control of Govt., Conservative Caucus, Nat. Right to Work Com., Nat. Taxpayers Union, Coalition for Peace through Strength, Nat. Congl. Club, Republicans of Colo., Rep. Nat. Com., Rep. Presdl. Task Force, U.S. Senatorial Club, Nat. Fedn. Decency, Salvation Army. Named hon. mayor City of Oklahoma City, 1972; recipient Gold medal of Good Citizenship, SAR, 1972, Disting. Service to Agr. award Gamma Sigma Delta, 1972, Alumni Ambassadors Hall of Fame award Panhandle State Coll., 1974, 4-H Alumni award Nat. and Colo. 4-H, 1976, Disting. Service awards, Am. Soc. Agrl. Cons., 1971, 81. Fellow Soil Conservation Soc. Am. (citation Kans. chpt. 1972), Am. Inst. Chemists; mem. Am. Soc. Agrl. Cons. (pres. 1975), Am. Soc. Agrl. Engrs., Internat. Soc. Soil Sci., Am. Soc. Agronomy (hon. life), Soil Sci. Soc. Am., Sigma Xi, Phi Lambda Upsilon, Gamma Sigma Delta, Alpha Chi Sigma. Methodist. Club: Lions. Author: No Hope But God, 1971; contbr. numerous articles to profl. jours. Home and Office: 415 S Howes St Apt 1107 Fort Collins CO 80521

FLYNN, DALE TIMOTHY, audiologist; b. Detroit, May 12, 1949; s. Clifford Earl and L. Ilene (Nickerson) F. AB, U. Calif., Berkeley, 1970; BS, U. Wash., 1975, M in Speech Pathology and Audiology, 1978. Cert. clin. competence in audiology; lic. hearing aid dispenser, Wash. Inspector Bur. Alcohol, Tobacco and Firearms, U.S. Dept. Treas., Seattle, 1971-74; audiologist Puget Sound Otolaryngology, Inc., Edmonds, Wash., 1978—. Contbr. articles to sports mag. Treas. Pacific Northwest Chamber Chorus, Seattle, 1977-84, Hellinki Greek Tavern Dancers, Seattle, 1979-85. Recipient Bank Am. Achievement award in Fine Arts, Oakland, Calif., 1966; scholar U. Calif. Berkeley, 1966-69; Kiwanis Found. scholar, 1966-70. Mem. Am. Speech and Hearing Assn., Wash. Speech and Hearing Assn., Wash. Soc. Audiology, Seattle Marathon Assn. (v.p. 1986—), The Mountaineers (Six Major Peaks Pin 1977), The Athletics Congress, Club Northwest (pres. 1986—). Avocations: running, mountain climbing, skiing, ethnic dancing, writing. Home: 4219 Latona Ave NE Seattle WA 98105 Office: Puget Sound Otolaryngology Inc 7935 216th St SW Suite B Edmonds WA 98020

FLYNN, ELIZABETH ANNE, advertising and public relations company executive; b. Washington, Aug. 21, 1951; d. John William and Elizabeth Goodwin (Mahoney) F. A.A., Montgomery Coll., Rockville, Md., 1972; B.S. in Journalism, U. Md., 1976; postgrad. San Diego State U., 1976. Writer, researcher, Sea World, Inc., San Diego, 1977-79; sr. writer Lane & Huff Advt., San Diego, 1979-80; account exec. Kaufman, Lansky, Baker Advt., San Diego, 1980-82; mng. dir. Excelsior Enterprises, Beverly Hills, Calif., 1983-84; sr. account exec. Berkhemer & Kline, Inc., Los Angeles, 1985; pres. Flynn Advt. & Pub. Relations, Los Angeles, 1985—; cons. Coca-Cola Bottling Co. Los Angeles, 1982-84. Bd. dirs. Friends of Reconstructive Surgery, Beverly Hills, 1983—. Recipient Cert. of Distinction, Art Direction Mag., 1982. Mem. Nat. Assn. Female Execs., Beverly Hills C. of C., Republican. Roman Catholic. Avocations: screenwriting; short stories; painting; horseback riding. Office: Flynn Advt & Pub Relations 1440 Reeves St Suite 104 Los Angeles CA 90035

FLYNN, JACK CHRISTIAN, teleprocessing professional; b. Nevada City, Calif., Mar. 28, 1936; s. Barney and Ila Elizabeth (Barnson) F.; m. Rosalind Olsen, Nov. 20, 1954; children—Debra, Jack Kelly, Kevin Barney, Kathleen Elizabeth, Michael O'Riley, Shannon, Patrick O'Brian, Sean Christian. A.S.E.E., Phoenix Coll., 1969; student U. Utah, 1963. System engr. IBM Corp., Rochester, Minn., 1964-65; computer instruction RCA, Inc., Cape Kennedy, Fla., 1965-67; engr. computers Gen. Electric, Phoenix, 1967-69; sales mgr. Calcomp, Inc., Anaheim, Calif., 1969-75; v.p. mktg. N.W. Germania, Salem, Oreg., 1975-78, E.T.P. Corp., Salt Lake City, 1978-81; nat. mktg. mgr. Questronics, Inc., Salt Lake City, 1981—; dir. edn. Weltech Coll., Salt Lake City, 1959-64; dir. mktg. Wesco Pub., Inc., Salt Lake City, 1960-67, N.W. Germania, 1975-78. Author: Fundamentals of Electronics, vols. 1-6, 1960-64; Fundamental of Computers, 1964; Telecommunication Performance Analysis, vols. 1 and 2, 1982. Served with U.S. Army, 1955-59. Space Pioneer, Cape Kennedy NASA Assocs., 1957; named Top Profl. Salesman, Calcomp, Inc., Anaheim, Calif., 1975; Top Salesman, N.W. Germania, 1976, 77, 78. Mem. Vets. Assn., Am. Legion, inst. Process Engrng. Technologists. Mormon. Lodge: Elks. Home: 5007 Marilyn Dr Holladay UT 84117 Office: Questronics Inc 3570 S West Temple St Salt Lake City UT 84115

FLYNN, JAMES BERNARD, monsignor; b. Portland, Oreg., Feb. 17, 1924; s. Michael J. and Teresa (Ginty) F. BA, St. Patrick's Coll., 1944; MTh, St. Patrick's Sem., 1948; MSW, Cath. U. Am., 1952. Ordained priest Roman Cath. Ch., 1948, named Monsignor, 1964. Pastor St. Gabriel's Ch., San Francisco, St. Peter's Ch., San Francisco; faculty St. Patrick's Sem., Menlo Park, Calif., 1987—. Contbr. numerous articles to profl. jours. Gen. dir. Cath. Charities of San Francisco, Social Justice Commn., San Francisco. Named Young Man of Yr., San Francisco Jaycees, 1957. Mem. Nat. Assn. Social Workers (cert.). Home: 2535 40th Ave San Francisco CA 94116

FLYNN, MICHAEL DAVID, marketing executive; b. Balt., Aug. 7, 1951; s. Robert Paul and Jean (Rhudy) F.; m. Melanie Jane Dougherty, Dec. 15, 1973; children: Matthew David, Brett Michael. BS, LaSalle Coll., 1973, MBA, 1981. CPA, Md. Staff acct. Arthur Anderson & Co., Balt., 1973-74; line controller Browning-Ferris Industries, Inc., Glen Burnie, Md., 1974-76; fin./forecast analyst, sales rep. BBL Microbiology Systems, Cockeysville, Md., 1976-81, assoc. product mgr., 1981-82; product mgr. Hynson, Westcott & Dunning, Balt., 1982-84; product licence mgr. Quidel, La Jolla, Calif., 1984-85, dir. sales and mktg., 1985-86; prin. Profl. Services Cons., San Diego, 1986—. Mem. Am. Inst. CPAs, Biomed. Mktg. Assn., Md. Assn. CPAs. Home and Office: 13375 Samantha Ave San Diego CA 92129

FLYNN, THOMAS CHARLES, banker; b. Pittsfield, Mass., July 27, 1950; s. Charles Edward and Angelina Mary (Cicurello) F.; m. Susanne Carin Ifcher. B.S. in Mgmt., U. Bridgeport, 1972; M.B.A. in Fin., St. John's U., N.Y.C., 1975. Nat. bank examiner internat. div. Comptroller of Currency, Washington, 1973-75; asst. v.p., div. controller Citibank N.A., N.Y.C., 1975-79; mgr. mgmt. adv. services Price Waterhouse & Co., N.Y.C., 1979-81; v.p., dir. corp. mgmt. acctg. and reporting Bank of Am., San Francisco, 1981-85; nat. dir. cons. services to fin. intitutions Touche Ross, San Francisco, 1985-87; dir. ops. U.S. Leasing, San Francisco, 1987—. Career profl. advisor St. John's U. Recipient cert. of exceptional performance Comptroller of Currency, 1975. Mem. Am. Mgmt. Assn. Home: 36 Willow Ln Sausalito CA 94965

FLYNT, LARRY CLAXTON, publisher; b. Magoffin County, Ky., Nov. 1, 1942; s. Larry Claxton and Edith (Arnett) F.; m. Althea Leasure, Aug. 21, 1976; children: Tonya, Lisa, Teresa, Larry Claxton, III. Student public schs., Saylersville, Ky. Factory worker Gen. Motors, Dayton, Ohio, 1958, 64-65; owner, operator Hustler Club, Dayton, Columbus, Toledo, Akron and Cleve., 1970-74; owner, pub. Hustler and Chic mags., Los Angeles, 1974—; owner, operator Flynt Distbg. Co., Los Angeles, 1976—. Served with U.S. Army, 1958; Served with USN, 1959-64. Office: 2029 Century Park E Suite 3800 Los Angeles CA 90067

FOCH, NINA, actress, educator; b. Leyden, Netherlands, Apr. 20, 1924; came to U.S., 1928; d. Dirk and Consuelo (Flowerton) F.; m. James Lipton, June 6, 1954; m. Dennis de Brito, Nov. 27, 1959; 1 child, Dirk de Brito; m. Michael Dewell, Oct. 31, 1967. Grad., Lincoln Sch., 1939. adj. prof. drama U. So. Calif., 1966-68, 78-80, adj. prof. film directing, 1987—; artist-in-residence U. N.C., 1966, Ohio State U., 1967, Calif. Inst. Tech., 1969-70; mem. sr. faculty Am. Film Inst., 1973-77; founder, tchr. Nina Foch Studio, Hollywood, Calif., 1973—; a founder, actress Los Angeles Theatre Group, 1960-65; Bd. dirs. Nat. Repertory Theatre, 1967-75. Appeared in: motion pictures Nine Girls, 1944, Return of the Vampire, 1944, Shadows in the Night, 1944, Cry of the Werewolf, 1944, Escape in the Fog, 1945, A Song to Remember, 1945, My Name Is Julia Ross, 1945, I Love a Mystery, 1945, Johnny O'Clock, 1947, The Guilt of Janet Ames, 1947, The Dark Past, 1948, The Undercover Man, 1949, Johnny Allegro, 1949, An American in Paris, 1951, Scaramouche, 1952, Young Man with Ideas, 1952, Sombrero, 1953, Fast Company, 1953, Executive Suite, 1954, Four Guns to the Border, 1954, You're Never Too Young, 1955, Illegal, 1955, The Ten Commandments, 1956, Three Brave Men, 1957, Cash McCall, 1959, Spartacus, 1960, Such Good Friends, 1971, Salty, 1973, Mahogany, 1976, Jennifer, 1978, Rich and Famous, 1981; appeared in: Broadway plays including John Loves Mary, 1947, Twelfth Night, 1949, A Phoenix Too Frequent, 1950, King Lear, 1950, Second String, 1960; appeared with Am. Shakespeare Festival in Taming of the Shrew, Measure for Measure, 1956, San Francisco Ballet and Opera in, The Seven Deadly Sins, 1966; also many regional theatre appearances including, Seattle Repertory Theatre (All Over, 1972 and The Seagull, 1973); actress on TV, 1947—, including, Playhouse 90, Studio One, Pulitzer Playhouse, Playwrights 56, Producers Showcase, Lou Grant, Mike Hammer, Shadow Chasers, 1985, War and Remembrance, 1986; many other series, network spls. and TV films; TV panelist and guest on The Dinah Shore Show, Merve Griffin Show, The Today Show, Dick Cavett, The Tonight Show; TV moderator: Let's Take Sides, 1957-59; asso. dir.: film The Diary of Ann Frank, 1959; dir.: nat. tour and on Broadway Tonight at 8:30, 1966-67; asso. producer re-opening nat. tour and on Broadway, Ford's Theatre, Washington, 1968; (nominated for Emmy award for supporting performance Lou Grant 1980). Hon. chmn. Los Angeles chpt. Am. Cancer Soc., 1970. Recipient Film Daily award, 1949, 53; nominated for Acad. Award for supporting performance Executive Suite, 1954. Mem. Acad. Motion Pictures Arts and Scis. (co-chmn. exec. com. fgn. film award, exec. com. student film award, com. mem. spl. projects), Hollywood Acad. TV Arts and Scis. (gov. 1976-77). Address: PO Box 1884 Beverly Hills CA 90213

FOERCH, BRUCE FREDERICK, social studies educator; b. St. Johns, Mich., Mar. 20, 1949; s. Berl L. and Doris Foerch; m. Elena Wassillie, May 22, 1982; children: Frederick Bruce, John Berl, Eugene Frederick. BA, Western Mich. U., 1972; MA, Mich. State U., 1976. Cert. elem. tchr. Tchr. St. Johns Pub. Schs., 1972-78; prin., tchr. Southwest Region Schs., Dillingham, Alaska, 1978—; cons. Bristol Bay curriculum project U. Alaska, Dillingham, 1983—. Advisor: (newspaper) Togiak Times, 1984—; producer, dir. (video) Togiak Village Profile. Mem. exec. bd. East Olive PTO, St. Johns, 1976; chmn. Sjea Profl. Rights and Responsibility Com., St. Johns, 1977 (editor newsletter, 1973-75), SRS Social Studies Com., Dillingham, 1984; mem. exec. com. Togiak (Alaska) Com. on Future Edn., 1986. Mem. NEA, Social Studies Educators of Alaska, Nat. Alaska Assn. Curriculum Devel. and Supervision. Avocations: pvt. pilot, fishing, photography, outdoor activities. Home: 454 Bayview Dr Togiak AK 99678 Office: Togiak Sch Togiak AK 99678

FOGARETTE, LOUIS P., manufacturing company executive; b. Chgo., Jan. 29, 1925; s. Louis Phillip and Jennie (Prete) F.; B.A., Wabash Coll., 1948; postgrad Stanford U., 1951-54. Chemist, W.P. Fuller Co., San Francisco, 1948-49; asst. chief chemist Nat. Industries, Los Angeles, 1950-60; tech. writer N.Am. Aviation Corp., Downey, Calif., 1961-64, sr. project staff engr. parent co. N.Am. Rockwell, 1965-69; supr. subcontractor configuration mgmt. Litton Ship Systems, Los Angeles, 1969-72; v.p. Stic-Adhesive Products Co., Los Angeles, 1972—; head configuration mgmt. program office Hughes Aircraft Co., Los Angeles, 1974-82, dept. configuration mgr., 1982—; tech. cons. Tannenbaum & Assocs., Ft. Lauderdale, Fla., 1975-82. Served to lt. USNR, 1943-46. Home: 8254 Telegraph Rd Downey CA 90240 Office: Hughes Aircraft Co Long Beach CA

FOGGIATO, G. (JOHN) A., electrical engineer; b. Yreka, Calif., Feb. 16, 1940; s. Giuseppe and Luigia A. (Zanotto) F.; m. Antoinette Marie Sofo, May 9, 1964; children: Mark E., Joseph A., John G. BSEE, Chico State U., 1961; MSEE, Stanford U., 1964, PhD in Elec. Engrng., 1972. Mgr., engr. Hewlett Packard, Palo Alto, Calif., 1969-73, Fairchild Corp., Mountain View, Calif., 1973-76; mgr. tech. Amdahl Corp., Sunnyvale, Calif., 1976-84; dir. tech. mktg. Flex Mfg. Systems, Los Gatos, Calif., 1984—; instr. Foothill Coll., Los Altos, Calif., 1970-77, Mission Coll., Santa Clara, Calif., 1977-80; cons. Venture Capital Group, Sunnyvale, 1982—. Patentee in field; contbr. articles to profl. jours. Active Parks Commn., Cupertino, Calif., 1975; mem. Sch. Improvement Com., Morgan Hill, Calif., 1978-81. Mem. IEEE, Sigma Xi, Phi Kappa Phi. Democrat. Roman Catholic. Club: Men's (sec. 1985). Avocations: teaching, gardening, outdoor sports. Home: 16340 Oakwood Ln Morgan Hill CA 95037 Office: Flex Mfg Systems 16780 Lark Ave Los Gatos CA 95030

FOGLEMAN, HARRY FRANK, development company executive; b. Johnson City, Tenn., May 21, 1931; s. E. Carl F.; m. Keturah Carroll, Oct. 15, 1960. B.S.E.E., Tenn. State U. Engr. Gen. Dynamics, San Diego, 1955-57; mgr. Arnoux, Los Angeles, 1957-60; pres. Aeromarine, San Diego, 1960-69, Gremlin Industries, San Diego, 1969-80; vice chmn. Sega Electronics, San Diego, 1980-83; chmn., chief exec. officer Omnar Technologies, Inc., San Diego, 1985—; dir. Cerprobe, Phoenix, AGMA, Washington, Penduflo, Scottsdale, Ariz. Patentee temperature apparatus, solid state switch, electronic game panel, underwater release, electronic safe. Served with USN, 1951-55. Home: 9955 Lemonwood Ln San Diego CA 92124 Office: Omnar Techs Inc 9938 Via Pasar San Diego CA 92126

FOK, AGNES KWAN, cell biologist; b. Hong Kong, British Crown Colony, Dec. 11, 1940; d. Sun and Yau (Ng) Kwan; m. Fok, June 8, 1965; children: Licie Chiu-Jane, Edna Chiu-Joan. BA, Coll. Great Falls, 1965; MS, Utah State U., 1966; PhD, U. Tex., Austin, 1971. Asst. researcher U. Hawaii, Honolulu, 1975-82, assoc. researcher, 1982—; assoc. researcher U. Hawaii, Honolulu, 1982—. Contbr. articles to profl. jours. Mem. Am. Soc. Cell Biology, Soc. Protozoologists, Sigma Xi (treas. Hawaii chpt. 1980—). Avocations: reading, sewing, hiking.

FOLAND, RICKEY LEE, social worker; b. Cin., July 24, 1948; s. James Ray Foland and Onlee Omega (Partin) Davis. BA in Psychology, U. Cin., 1977; MSW, Loyola U., 1980. Cert. vocat. rehab. counselor, Oreg., Wash. Drug rehab. technician VA Hosp., Cin., 1976-78; adolescent counselor Response Ctr., Chgo., 1978-79; clin./med. social worker Lakeside Vets. Hosp., Chgo., 1979-80; vocat. rehab. counselor Ingram & Assocs., Portland, Oreg., 1981-83; vocat. rehab. cons. Bland, Funk, Obara & Thompson Assocs., Portland, 1983-86; exec. dir. Kinship Rehab. and Counseling, Portland, 1987—. Mem. adv. bd. Quest Schs., Portland, 1984—; chmn. Washington County com. Citizen Involvement, Hillsboro, 1985-87, Aloha/Reedville Community Planning Orgn., 1985-87; mem. Washington County Pub. Adv. Com. Transp., Hillsboro, 1985-86, Washington County Carter Rev. com., Hillsboro, 1986. Served as sgt. U.S. Army, 1968-70. Mem. Nat. Assn. Social Workers (chmn. occupational council 1983-86), Nat. Rehab. Assn., Nat. Rehab. Counseling Assn., Nat. Rifle Assn., Hillsboro C. of C. (alumni mem. leadership tng. program 1984-85), Sigma Chi. Avocations: ancient history, motorcycles. Home: 2030 SW 203d Aloha OR 97006

FOLBERG, HAROLD JAY, mediator, educator; b. East St. Louis, Ill., July 7, 1941; s. Louis and Matilda (Ross) F.; m. Diana L. Taylor, May 1, 1983; children: Lisa, Rachel, Ross. B.A., San Francisco State U., 1963; J.D., U. Calif., Berkeley, 1968. Bar: Oreg. 1968. Assoc. Rives & Schwab, Portland, Oreg., 1968-69; dir. Legal Aid Service, Portland, 1970-72; exec. dir. Assn. Family and Conciliation Cts., Portland, 1974-80; prof. law Lewis and Clark Law Sch., Portland, 1972—; clin. asst. prof. child psychiatry U. Oreg. Med. Sch., 1976—; judge pro-tem Oreg. Trial Cts., 1974—; vis. prof. U. Wash. Sch. Law, 1985-86; mem. vis. faculty Nat. Jud. Coll., 1975—; mem. Nat. Commn. on Accreditation for Marriage and Family Therapists. Contbr. articles to profl. jours. Author: Joint Custody and Shared Parenting, 1984; (with Taylor) Mediation-A Comprehensive Guide to Resolving Conflicts without Litigation, 1984. Mem. editorial bd. Conciliation Cts. Rev., Jour. of Divorce, Mediation Quar. Mem. Oreg. State Bar Assn. (chmn. family and juvenile law sect. 1979-80), Am. Bd. Trial Advocates, Legal Aid Service Multnomah Bar Assn. (chmn. 1973-76), Internat. Soc. Family Law, ABA (chmn. mediation and arbitration com. family law sect. 1980-82), Assn. Family and Conciliation Cts. (pres. 1983-84), Assn. of Marriage and Family Therapists (disting. mem.), Acad. of Family Mediators (bd. dirs.), Soc. of Profls. in Dispute Resolution, Am. Arbitration Assn. (panel arbitrators). Am. Assn. Law Schs. (chmn. alternative dispute resolution sect. 1988). Office: 10015 SW Terwillger St Portland OR 97219

FOLDVARY, SHERRY LEE, speech pathologist; b. Guatemala City, Guatemala, July 24, 1960; d. Fritz Charles and Miriam Elena (Barrera) F. BS, Loma Linda U., 1982; MA, Calif. State U., Northridge, 1985. Cert. in rehabilitative service, Calif. Speech pathologist Glendale (Calif.) Adventist Med. Ctr., 1984—, coordinator head injury program, 1987—. Mem. Am. Speech-Lang.-Hearing Assn. (cert.), Nat. Assn. for Female Execs., Calif. Speech-Lang.-Hearing Assn. Republican. Adventist. Avocations: volleyball, swimming, piano, reading. Home: 7760 Jaydee Circle Tujunga CA 91402 Office: Glendale Adventist Med Ctr 1509 Wilson Terr Glendale CA 91206

FOLEY, CRAY LYMAN, mechanical engineer; b. Tulsa, Apr. 15, 1927; s. Lyndon Lyman and Margaret Clark (Cray) F.; student U. Tulsa, 1945-46, 47-48; B.S., Okla. State U., 1951, M.S., 1957; children—Kelly Ann, Jill, Cray, Seth. Jr. research engr. Lockheed Aircraft Corp., Burbank, Calif., 1951-52; engr. Sperry Gyroscope Co., Great Neck, N.Y., 1953-57; advanced systems staff engr. Lockheed Missile & Space Co., Sunnyvale, Calif., 1957-82, sr. staff engr., 1982—. Pres. Homeowners Assn., 1964-66; Cub Scout com. chmn. Santa Clara County council Boy Scouts Am., 1971-72. Mem. Nat., Okla. socs. profl. engrs., Soc. Automotive Engrs., Am. Def. Preparedness Assn., Lockheed Mgmt. Assn., Okla. State U. Alumni Assn., Lambda Chi Alpha. Republican. Home: 7090 Galli Dr San Jose CA 95129 Office: Lockheed Missile & Space Co 7090 Galli Dr San Jose CA 95129

FOLEY, DANIEL EDMUND, real estate devel. exec.; b. St. Paul, Mar. 1, 1926; s. Edward and Gerry (Fitzgarld) F.; student U. Minn., 1941-43; m. Paula Evans, Apr. 1, 1946. Chmn. bd. Realty Ptnrs. Ltd., Los Angeles; pres. Alpha Property Mgmt. Served with AUS, 1943-46. Office: 523 W 6th St Suite 385 Los Angeles CA 90014

FOLEY, JAMES JOSEPH, electronics executive; b. Worcester, Mass., Dec. 20, 1935; s. Charles Joseph and Mary Margaret (Markley) F.; m. Annemarie Elizabeth McNally, June 24, 1961; children: Anne Marie, Patricia Marie, James Joseph. BSEE, Northeastern U., 1963. Research engr. Space Scis., Inc., Waltham, Mass., 1963-69; subcontract mgr. Grumman Aerospace, Hicksville, N.Y., 1969-74; asst. program mgr. Raytheon Corp./ESD, Goleta, Calif., 1974-80; prin. Western Digital Repairs, Santa Barbara, Calif., 1980-81; program ops. mgr. Raytheon Co., Goleta, 1981-86, program mgr. AN/ALQ-142, 1986—; chmn. bd. dirs. Marymount Acad., Santa Barbara, 1985—. Author: Feasibility...Turbine Inlet Temperatures, 1968; inventor in field. Served with USAF, 1954-58. Mem. Assn. Old Crows. Roman Catholic. Home: 722 San Roque Rd Santa Barbara CA 93105 Office: Raytheon Co 6380 Hollister Ave Goleta CA 93117

FOLEY, MICHAEL GLEN, geologist, research company executive; b. Independence, Mo., July 23, 1945; s. Roy Eugene and Joyce Helen (Luken) F.; m. Katherine Elizabeth Reynolds, June 1, 1968. Cert. profl. geologist; cert. profl. hydrologist. B.S. in Engrng., Calif. Inst. Tech., 1967, M.S. in Aeros., 1968, Ph.D. in Geology, 1976. Research engr. Boeing Corp., Houston, 1968-69; engr. Jet Propulsion Lab., Pasadena, Calif., 1969-70; asst. prof. geology U. Mo., Columbia, 1976-80; sr. geologist Battelle-Northwest, Richland, Wash., 1980-85, staff scientist, 1985—. Served to capt. USAF, 1972. Mem. Am. Geophys. Union, Am. Quaternary Assn., Brit. Geomorphological Research Group, Geol. Soc. Am. Office: Battelle-Pacific NW Labs PO Box 999 Richland WA 99352

FOLEY, ROGER D., judge; b. 1917; s. Roger T. and Helen (Drummond) F. LL.B., U. San Francisco. Bar: Nev. bar 1946. Former atty. gen. Nev.; chief judge U.S. Dist Ct. Nev., Las Vegas, to 1980; judge U.S. Dist Ct. Nev., 1980—. Office: US Dist Ct Nev 300 Las Vegas Blvd S Room 3-305 Las Vegas NV 89101 *

FOLEY, THOMAS MICHAEL, lawyer; b. Glendive, Mont., June 6, 1947; s. Raymond Paul Foley and Shirley Lorriane (Kostic) Mizel; m. Marylouise Hata, Aug. 31, 1968; children: Michael, Malia. BA, U. Wash., 1969, JD, 1973. Bar: Hawaii 1973. Sr. tax acct. Ernst & Ernst, Honolulu, 1973-74; mng. ptnr. Mukai, Ichiki, Raffetto & MacMillan, Honolulu, 1976-81, Foley, Maehara, Judge, & Nip, Honolulu, 1982—; commr. Hawaii Tax Review Commn., Honolulu, 1983-85; trustee Tax Found. Hawaii, Honolulu, 1983—. Bd. dirs. Small Bus. Council Am., Honolulu, 1984—, Goodwill Vocat. Tng. Ctrs. Hawaii, Honolulu, 1985—, Kuakini Dialysis Ctr., Honolulu, 1982—, Honolulu C. of C., 1981—, chmn. taxation com. 1982-83. Mem. ABA, Hawaii Bar Assn., Hawaii Hotel Assn. (tax com.). Episcopalian. Club: Pacific (Honolulu). Office: Foley Maehara Judge Nip 737 Bishop St Suite 2700 Honolulu HI 96813

FOLEY, THOMAS STEPHEN, congressman; b. Spokane, Wash., Mar. 6, 1929; s. Ralph E. and Helen Marie (Higgins) F.; m. Heather Strachan, Dec. 1968. B.A., U. Wash., 1951, LL.B., 1957. Bar: Wash. Partner Higgins & Foley, 1957-58; dep. pros. atty. Spokane County, Spokane, 1958-60; asst. atty. gen. State of Wash., Olympia, 1960-61; spl. counsel interior and insular affairs com. U.S. Senate, Washington, 1961-64; mem. 89th-100th Congresses from 5th Dist. Wash.; chmn. Com. Agr., 1975-81, vice chmn., 1981—; chmn. House Democratic Caucus, 1976-80, House majority whip, 1981—; instr. law Gonzaga U., 1958-60. Mem. Phi Delta Phi. Democrat. Office: 1201 Longworth Bldg Washington DC 20515

FOLEY-SHAFFER, PEG ANNE, social service center coordinator; b. Buffalo, Feb. 20, 1958; d. Kenneth Charles and Lois Ann (Argy) Foley; m. Daniel Lynn Shaffer, Aug. 27, 1983. AS, SUNY, Canton, 1978; BA in Social Welfare, Pacific Luth. U., 1983, MA in Marriage and Family Therapy, 1983. Supr. Young Adult Conservation Corps Monroe County Parks, Rochester, N.Y., 1979-81; diversion supr. Remann Hall, Tacoma, 1981-84; police-social worker Pierce County Sheriff, Tacoma, 1982-84; contract therapist Greater Lakes Mental Health Clinic, Tacoma, 1983—; clinic coordinator Marriage and Family Therapy Ctr. Pacific Luth. U., Tacoma, 1983—. Mem. Nat. Assn. Social Workers, Am. Assn. Marriage and Family Therapy (region 5 communicator 1986—), Soil Conservation Soc. Am. (pres. 1987, participant Olympic View chpt. 1986), N.W. Family Tng. Inst. Democrat. Roman Catholic. Avocations: hiking, swimming, reading. Home: 509 Sixth Ct PO Box 94 Fox Island WA 98333 Office: Pacific Luth U East Campus Marriage Family Therapy Ctr Tacoma WA 98447

FOLK, LEE EDWARD, mechanical engineer; b. Kirtland, Ohio, Dec. 10, 1928; s. William Edward and Myrtle Irene (McEldowney) F.; m. Gloria Mae Leibfreid, June 10, 1950; children: Anita, Thomas, James. AA in Engrng., Phoenix Coll., 1964; student, Ariz. State U., 1965-75. Tool and die maker various companies, Cleve., 1948-59; engrng. aide Motorola, Inc., Phoenix, 1959-64, mech. engr., 1964-68, sect. mgr., 1968-73, mgr. equipment engrng., 1973-82, prin. staff engr., scientist, 1982—. Patentee in field. Served as cpl. USMC, 1946-48. Recipient MEIP award Motorola, Inc., 1980. Mem. Robots Internat. div. of Soc. Mfg. Engrs., Am. Soc. Metals, Motorola Sci. Tech. Soc. (charter). Republican. Avocations: swimming, hiking, reading, fishing. Home: 6812 N 23d Pl Phoenix AZ 85016 Office: Motorola Inc 5005 E McDowell Phoenix AZ 85008

FOLK, RICHARD DALE, Canadian provincial legislator; b. Saskatoon, Sask., Can., Mar. 5, 1950; s. Alex Martin and Janet Kerr (Bell) F.; m. Elizabeth Ann Short, Aug. 5, 1978; children—Kevin, Andrea. Mgr. Nutana Curling Club, Saskatoon, 1975-76; real estate salesman, Saskatoon, 1979-81; owner, mgr. Rich Folk Sports Centre, Saskatoon, 1981-83; mem. Legis. Assembly, Govt. Sask., Saskatoon, 1982—, minister of culture and recreation, 1983—, minister of govt. ins., 1985—. Home: 34 Riel Crescent, Saskatoon, SK Canada S7N 2W6 Office: 30 Legislative Bldg, Regina, SK Canada S4S 0B3

FOLKMAN, DAVID H., department store executive; b. Jackson, Mich., Nov. 6, 1934; s. Jerome D. and Bessie (Schomer) F.; m. Susan Kleppner, June 22, 1958; children: Louis, Sarah, Karen, Jeffrey. A.B., Harvard U., 1957, M.B.A., 1960. Mdse. mgr. Foley's, Houston, 1957-69; v.p. dir. stores Famous-Barr, St. Louis, 1969-74; sr. v.p., gen. mdse. mgr. Macy's Calif., San Francisco, 1974-82; pres., chief exec. officer Emporium Capwell, San

Francisco, 1982—; lectr. U. Houston, 1965-68; instr. Washington U., St. Louis, 1970-73; dir. Golden West Fin. Corp., World Savs. & Loan Assn. Clubs: Olympic (San Francisco); Harvard (N.Y.C.). Office: Emporium Capwell Co 835 Market St San Francisco CA 94103

FOLLICK, EDWIN DUANE, chiropractic physician, legal educator, educational administrator; b. Glendale, Calif., Feb. 4, 1935; s. Edwin Fulfford and Esther Agnes (Catherwood) F. BA Calif. State U., Los Angeles, 1956, MA, 1961; MA Pepperdine U., 1957, MPA, 1977; PhD, D in Theology St. Andrews Theol. Coll., Sem. of the Free Protestant Episcopal Ch., London, 1958; MS in Literary Sci., U. So. Calif., 1963, MEd, 1964, AdvMEd, 1969; Calif. Coll. Law, 1965; LLB Blackstone Law Sch., 1966, JD, 1967; DC Cleve. Chiropractic Coll., Los Angeles, 1972; PhD, Academia Theatina, Pescara, 1978. Tchr., library adminstr. Los Angeles City Schs., 1957-68; law librarian Glendale U. Coll. Law, 1968-69; coll. librarian Cleveland Chiropractic Coll., Los Angeles, 1969-74, dir. edn. and admissions, 1974-84, prof. jurisprudence, 1975—, dean student affairs, 1976—, chaplain, 1985— ; assoc. prof. Newport U., 1982—; extern prof. St. Andrews Theol. Coll., London, 1961; dir. West Valley Chiropractic Health Ctr., 1972—. Contbr. articles to profl. jours. Served as chaplain's asst. U.S. Army, 1958-60. Decorated Cavaliere Internat. Order legion of Honor of Immacolata (Italy); knight of Malta, Sovereign Order of St. John of Jerusalem; chevalier Ordre Militaire et Hospitalier de St. Lazare de Jerusalem, numerous others. Mem. ALA, NEA, Am. Assn. Sch. Librarians, Los Angeles Sch. Library Assn., Calif. Media and Library Educators Assn., Assn. Coll and Research Librarians, Am. Assn. Law Librarians, Am. Chiropractic Assn., Internat. Chiropractors Assn., Nat. Geog. Soc., Internat. Platform Assn., Phi Delta Kappa, Sigma Chi Psi, Delta Tau Alpha. Democrat. Episcopalian. Home: 6435 Jumilla Ave Woodland Hills CA 91367 Office: 590 N Vermont Ave Los Angeles CA 90004 also: 7022 Owensmouth Ave Canoga Park CA 91303

FOLONIS, MICHAEL WILLIAM, architect, educator; b. Sioux City, Iowa, June 12, 1947; s. Vincent Edward and Marie (Peterson) F.; m. Julie Jean Chambers, Feb. 14, 1982; children: Michele, Christopher Chambers, Jonathan. AA, Chaffey Coll., 1972; BArch, So. Calif. Inst. Architecture, 1978. Registered profl. architect, Calif. Draftsman Frank Gehry, Architect, Santa Monica, Calif., 1974-75, Kahn, Kappe, Architects, Santa Monica, 1975-76; prin. Michael W. Folonis, AIA, and Assocs., Santa Monica, 1977—; faculty mem. Santa Monica Coll., 1977-83; assoc. prof. Calif. State Poly. U., Pomona, 1983—; lectr. and critic various Calif. schs. architecture, 1978-85. Mem. editorial bd. Los Angeles Architect, 1983—; contbr. articles to profl. jours. and newspapers in U.S., France, Italy, Japan, Eng.; exhibited work Calif. State Poly. U., 1984, Inst. Francais d'Architecture, Paris, 1985, U. Argentina, 1985, A.A. Sch. Architecture, London, 1983, Pacific Design Ctr., Los Angeles, 1985, Mus. Sci. and Industry, Los Angeles, 1984. Served to 2d lt. U.S. Army, 1968-69, Vietnam. Decorated Bronze Star; recipient cert. commendation, Mayor, City of Los Angeles, 1984. Mem. A.I.A. (design awards, Los Angeles chpt., 1977, 84). Democrat. Lutheran. Avocations: golf, travel. Office: 2520 18th St Santa Monica CA 90405

FOLSOM, BRUCE AMES, psychiatric social worker; b. Palo Alto, Calif., Dec. 11, 1952; s. Rolfe Ames and Jeanne (Rose) F. AA, DeAnza Coll., 1974; BA, U. Calif., Santa Cruz, 1977; MSW, San Francisco State U., 1984. Cts. alternative specialist Adult Probation Dept., San Francisco, 1977-81; counselor Hospitality House, San Francisco, 1982-83; therapist Family Service Agy., San Francisco, 1983-84; disability cons. Operation Concern, San Francisco, 1984-85; psychiat. social worker Community Mental Health Ctr., San Francisco, 1985—. Oboist Calif. Youth Symphony, Palo Alto, 1967-71; mem. exec. bd. Friends Com. on Legis., 1976-79; clk. San Francisco Friends Meeting, 1979-84. Prin. oboist Internat. Festival of Youth Orch., Lausanne, Switzerland. Mem. Nat. Assn. Social Workers, Inst. Consciousness and Music (profl.), Folsom Family Assn. Democrat. Mem. Soc. of Friends. Avocations: music, genealogy, history. Home: 2690 Great Hwy #107 San Francisco CA 94116 Office: Southeast Mission Geriatric Services 3905 Mission St San Francisco CA 94112

FOLSOM, TYLER CLEVELAND, JR., oral and maxillofacial surgeon; b. Cripple Creek, Colo., Aug. 12, 1921; s. Tyler Cleveland and Edith Esther (Christiansen) F.; m. Phyllis Emily Greer, Mar. 6, 1942; children—Tyler Cleveland III, Thomas C., Bruce W., Robert J. B.S., Northwestern U., 1945, D.D.S., 1947, M.S., 1957. Dentist, USPHS, Wash., Ohio and Ill., 1948-54, oral surgeon, S.I., N.Y. and San Francisco, 1954-67; chief dental service USPHS Hosp., S.I., 1962-67; assoc. chief dental service, chief oral surgery USPHS Hosp., Seattle, 1967-72; practice dentistry specializing in oral surgery, Seattle, 1972-83; faculty U. Wash., Seattle, 1948-51, 67-72, Case Western Res. U., Cleve., 1951-53. Fellow Am. Coll. Dentists, Internat Assn. Oral Surgeons, Am. Soc. Oral and Maxillofacial Surgeons; mem. ADA, Wash. State Dental Assn., Seattle-King County Dental Assn., Wash. State Soc. Oral and Maxillofacial Surgeons, Western Soc. Oral Surgeons, Commd. Officers Assn. USPHS. Republican. Roman Catholic. Club: Ft. Lewis Golf (Tacoma, Wash.). Home: 15016 SE 51st St Bellevue WA 98006

FOLSOM, VIVIAN LEE, clinical social worker; b. Mpls., Nov. 29, 1954; d. Robert P. Folsom and Claudia (Bigelow) Ranis. BA, Evergreen State Coll., 1976; MS, Bryn Mawr Coll., 1979. Clin. social worker Kaiser Permante, San Francisco, 1980-84, Assn. Adolescent, Albuquerque, 1985-86; clin. cons. USPHS, San Fidel, N.Mex., 1985, U. N.Mex., Albuquerque, 1985; pvt. practice social work Albuquerque, 1986—. Editor Adolescent Abuse and Neglect Study for Youth Devel. Bur., HEW, 1979, Adolescent Abuse and Neglect, 1985. Grad. study scholar, Bryn Mawr Coll., 1979. Mem. Nat. Assn. Social Workers. Home: 1028 Stanford NE Albuquerque NM 87106

FOLSOME, CLAIR EDWIN, microbiology educator; b. Ann Arbor, Mich., June 26, 1935; s. Clair Edwin and Leah (Carter) F.; m. Jo Grubawicz, Sept. 26, 1956 (div. Oct. 1980); children: Russell S., Wyn, Alexander, Theodore; m. Geraldine DeBenedetti, June 20, 1982; children: Cassandra, Grant. AB, Harvard U., 1956, MA, 1959, PhD, 1960. Research asst. prof. Boston U., 1960-62; sr. lectr. Melbourne (Australia) U., 1962-64; prof. microbiology U. Hawaii, Honolulu, 1964—; v.p. Biofoods Inc., Honolulu, 1981—; pres. Ecoculture Assn., Honolulu, 1980—; bd. dirs. Islenet Inc., Honolulu. Author: Origins of Life, 1979, rev. edit. 1982; editor: Genetics and the Origins of Life, 1956-86; contbr. articles to profl. jours. Research grantee NASA, Honolulu, 1971—; sr. research fellow Nat. Acad. Sci., Honolulu, 1971. Fellow Brit. Interplanetary Soc.; mem. AAAS, Am. Chem. Soc., Internat. Soc. Study Origin Life, Mensa, Sigma Xi. Clubs: Waikiki Yacht, Outrigger Canoe, Honolulu (Honolulu). Avocations: open ocean sailing, distance running. Home: 916 Kana Pl Honolulu HI 96816 Office: U Hawaii 2538 The Mall SNY201 Honolulu HI 96822

FOLTZ, MELVYN LEROY, counselor; b. Barstow, Calif., July 21, 1940; s. Raymond Edwin and Ethel Gertrude (Wright) F.; student N.W. Christian Coll., Eugene, Oreg., 1959-60; B.S., U. Oreg., 1964, M.S., 1966; m. Mary Jane Gabriel, June 20, 1964 (dec. Jan. 1971); 1 dau., Melody. Vocat. rehab. counselor Oreg. Div. Vocat. Rehab., Eugene, 1965-66, Calif. Dept. Rehab., Vallejo, 1966-71, Napa, 1971-77, Fairfield, 1977-79; pvt. practice counseling, specializing in hypnosis, Napa, 1980—; pvt. practice group co-counseling, 1976; vocat. rehab. counselor Mirfak Assocs., Santa Rosa, 1986—. Mem. Health Manpower Com., 1973-75, Napa County Comprehensive Health Planning Council, 1975, Napa County Manpower Planning Council, 1974-77; founder, pres. Napa New Age Enterprises; alt. mem. Napa County Democratic Central Com., 1976; bd. dirs. Napa County chpt. Am. Cancer Soc., 1978-80. Lic. marriage, family and child counselor, Calif. Mem. Am. Soc. for Psychical Research, Am. Assn. Counseling and Devel., Am. Rehab. Counselors Assn., Mental Health Assn. of Napa County. Democrat. Club: Single Parents (founder, pres. 1973-79). Home: 1698 San Vicente Napa CA 94558 Office: 2025 Redwood Rd Suite 6A Napa CA 94558

FONCK, HUGO KARL HERMANN, structural engineer; b. Bunzlau, Fed. Republic of Germany, Dec. 13, 1922; came to U.S., 1956; s. Hermann Arthur and Elvira Franziska (Markel) F.; m. Adelaida Margarita Fonck, Mar. 23, 1963; children: Ingeborg Claudia, Heinrich Hermann. Diploma, Engr. Tech. U., Graz, Austria, 1950. Project architect H.T.H. Holthey Archtect, Hamburg, Fed. Republic of Germany, 1950-51; pvt. practice architecture Graz, 1951-53; architect Mathers & Haldenby Architects, Toronto, Ont., Can., 1953-54; plan checker Aluminum Co. Can., Montreal, Que., 1954-56; structural engr. Chin & Hensolt Engrs., San Francisco, 1956—. Patentee in mech. engring.; mem. redesign and reconstrn. team San Francisco cable car system. Mem. Calif. Tax Reduction Movement, Los Angeles, 1985—, Fedn. Am. Immigration Reform, Washington, 1985—. Avocation: theoretical physics research. Home: 200 Richardson Dr Mill Valley CA 94941 Office: Chin & Hensolt Engrs Inc 246 First St San Francisco CA 94105

FONG, HAROLD MICHAEL, federal judge; b. Honolulu, Apr. 28, 1938; m. Judith Tom, 1966; children—Harold Michael, Terrence Matthew. A.B. cum laude, U. So. Calif., 1960; J.D., U. Mich., 1964. Bar: Hawaii 1965. Dep. pros. atty. City and County of Honolulu, 1965-68; assoc. Mizuha and Kim, Honolulu, 1968-69; asst. U.S. atty. dist. Hawaii, 1969-73; U.S. atty. 1973-78; ptnr. Fong and Miho, Honolulu, 1978-82; judge U.S. Dist. Ct., Dist. of Hawaii, 1982-84, chief judge, 1984—. Office: PO Box 50128 Honolulu HI 96850

FONKALSRUD, ERIC WALTER, physician, educator; b. Balt., Aug. 31, 1932; s. George and Ella (Fricke) F.; m. Margaret Ann Zimmermann, June 6, 1959; children: Eric Walter, Margaret Lynn, David Loren, Robert Warren. B.A., U. Wash., 1953; M.D., Johns Hopkins U., 1957. Diplomate Am. Bd. Surgery, Am. Bd. Thoracic Surgery, Am. Bd. Pediatric Surgery. Intern Johns Hopkins Hosp., Balt., 1957-58; asst. resident Johns Hopkins Hosp., 1958-59, U. Calif. Med. Center, Los Angeles, 1959-62; chief resident surgery U. Calif. Med. Center, 1962-63, asst. prof. surgery, chief pediatric surgery, 1965-68, assoc. prof., 1968-71, prof., 1971—, vice chmn. dept. surgery, 1982—; resident pediatric surgery Columbus (Ohio) Childrens Hosp. and Ohio State U., 1963-65; practice medicine specializing in pediatric surgery Los Angeles, 1965—; Mem. surg. study sect. NIH; James IV surg. traveller to, Gt. Britain, 1971. Mem. editorial bd. Jour. Surg. Research, Archives of Surgery, Annals of Surgery, Surgery, Current Problems in Surgery, Am. Jour. Surgery, Current Surgery; author book, chpts. in textbooks; contbr. over 350 articles to med. jours. Recipient Mead Johnson award for grad. tng. surgery A.C.S., 1963; Golden Apple award for teaching UCLA Sch. Medicine, 1968; John and Mary R. Markle scholar in acad. medicine, 1963-68. Fellow ACS (surg. forum com., bd. govs. 1978-84), Am. Acad. Pediatrics (exec. bd., chmn. surgical sect. 1986-87); mem. Soc. Univ. Surgeons (sec. 1973-76, pres. 1976-77), Assn. Acad. Surgeons (pres. 1972), AMA, Calif., Los Angeles County med. assns., Am. Surg. Assn., Pan Pacific Surg. Assn., Pacific Coast Surg. Assn. (recorder 1979-85), Am. Pediatric Surg. Assn. (gov. 1975-78), Pacific Assn. Pediatric Surgeons (pres. 1983-84), S.W. Pediatric Soc., Los Angeles Pediatric Soc., Soc. for Clin. Surgery, Transplantation Soc., Pediatric Surgery Biology Club, Am. Thoracic Surg. Assn., Bay, Los Angeles surg. socs., Am. Acad. Sci., Sigma Xi, Alpha Omega Alpha. Methodist. Club: Pithotomy (pres.). Home: 428 24th St Santa Monica CA 90402 Office: U Calif Med Ctr Dept Surgery Los Angeles CA 90024

FONSHILL, IRA WILLIAM, III, real estate and securities broker, construction company executive; b. Balt., May 16, 1930; s. Ira William II and Irma Marie (Gardner) F.; m. Pamela W. Leavitt, June 1, 1955; children: Ira William IV, Susan B., Peter B., Pamela Hope. BS, NYU, 1955; MBA, U. Wash., Seattle, 1957. Grad. Realtors Inst. Indsl. engr. Boeing Aerospace, Seattle, 1956-59; long-range planner Monsanto Co., N.Y.C., 1960-65; fin. planner Boise (Idaho) Cascade, 1965-70; officer Devco, Inc., Boise, Idaho, 1971-82; pres. Intermountain Realty, Boise, Idaho, 1974—; proprietor, broker Fonshill & Co., Boise, Idaho, 1977—; v.p., sec. Silver Maple Devel. Co., Inc., Bullhead, Ariz., 1986—; bd. dirs. DLB Inc., Boise, 1983—. Bus. dir. United Way, Boise chpt., 1977-78. Served with USAF, 1950-54. Mem. Real Estate Securities Inst. (pres. 1978-81, Specialist Real Estate Securities award 1980), Realtor Mktg. Inst. (Cert. Comml. Investment Mem. 1979), NW Investment Soc. (vice-chmn. 1978-79), Nat. Assn. Securities Dealers, Inc. Republican. Lutheran. Avocations: scuba diving, archery, photography. Home: 200 Coston St Boise ID 83712 Office: Fonshill & Co 331 W Idaho St PO Box 1288 Boise ID 83701

FOOTE, LOREN DEWAINE, chemical company executive; b. Ontario, Oreg., Apr. 16, 1944; s. Loren William and Margaret Ellen (George) F.; m. Lucille Carol Dickerson, July 18, 1964; children: Paul Thomas, Adam Michael, Noah William. AA in Quality Scis., Glendale (Ariz.) Community coll., 1985. Night mgr. Safeway Stores, Scottsdale, Ariz., 1962-63; framer Ariz. Booth, Phoenix, 1963-64; quality assurance dir. Chemresearch, Phoenix, 1964—; bd. dirs. Guarantee Mut. Life Ins. Co., Omaha; cons. Travenol, Phoenix, 1983—. Pres., co-founder The Patrick Murphy Found. for Pediatric Care, Glendale, 1980—; coach Baseball Majors Glendale Recreation, 1978—. Recipient Assisting Police Officer award Glendale Police Dept., 1978, Community Service award Glendale Community Coll., 1981-82. Mem. Am. Soc. Quality Control, Am. Soc. Nondestructive Testing, Am. Soc. Metals, Facilities and Health Care Com., Ariz. Assn. Industries, Phi Theta Kappa. Republican. Lodge: Kiwanis. Avocations: hunting, fishing, skiing, restoring Mustangs, coin collecting. Home: 6325 W Garden Dr Glendale AZ 85304

FOOTMAN, GORDON ELLIOTT, ednl. adminstr.; b. Los Angeles, Oct. 10, 1927; s. Arthur Leland and Meta Fay (Neal) F.; B.A., Occidental Coll., 1951, M.S., 1954; Ed.D., U. So. Calif., 1972; m. Virginia Rose, Aug. 7, 1954; children—Virginia, Patricia, John. Tchr., Arcadia, Calif., 1952, Glendale, Calif., 1956; psychologist Burbank (Calif.) Schs., 1956-64, supr., 1964-70, dir. pupil personnel services, 1970-72; dir. div. ednl. measurement, evaluation and research Office Los Angeles County Supt. Schs., Downey, Calif., 1972—. Lectr. ednl. psychology U. So. Calif., 1972-75, asst. prof. ednl. psychology, 1976—. Pres. Council for Exceptional Children, 1969-70; pres. Burbank Coordinating Council, 1969-70; mem. Burbank Family Service Bd., 1971-72. Served with AUS, 1945-47. Mem. Am. Edn. Research Assn., Am. Assn. for Counciling and Devel. (senator 1983—, western regional br. assembly publs. editor 1985-87), Calif. Personnel and Guidance Assn. (pres.), Calif. Assn. Sch. Psychologists and Psychometrists, Nat., Calif. (monograph editor 1977—) assns. pupil personnel adminstrs., Calif. Assn. Counselor Educators and Suprs. (trustee), Calif. Assn. Sch. Adminstrs., Calif. Soc. Ednl. Program Auditors and Evaluators (sec. 1975-76, v.p. 1976-77, pres.), Calif. Assn. Measurement and Evaluation in Guidance (sec. 1976, pres.), Council Exceptional Children (pres. Foothill chpt. 1969-70), Phi Beta Kappa, Phi Alpha Theta, Psi Chi. Republican. Presbyn. Home: 1259 Sherwood Rd San Marino CA 91108 Office: 9300 E Imperial Hwy Downey CA 90242

FOOTT, ROGER, civil engineer; b. Bingley, Eng., Sept. 30, 1946; s. Albert B. and Dorothy (Whitaker) F.; m. Jacqueline G. Richards, Sept. 1, 1969; children: Christopher B., Helen C. BS, U. Birmingham, Eng., 1967; Sc.D., MIT, 1973. Profl. engr.; chartered engr. Engr. Binnie and Ptnrs., London, 1967-69; dir. Louis Berger Inc. Subs., Nigeria, 1973-75; pvt. practice cons. engring. Boston, 1975-80; prin. in charge Dames and Moore, Boston and Hong Kong, 1980-83; ptnr. Dames and Moore, San Francisco, 1983-86; pres. Roger Foott Assoc., Inc., San Francisco, 1986—. Contbr. articles to profl. jours. Recipient Kenwood S. Oliphant Meml. award for excellence in engring. Cons. Engrs. Assoc. of Calif., 1983. Mem. ASCE (Norman Medal 1981), Inst. Civil Engrs., Hong Kong Inst. Engring. Avocations: cars, fly fishing, wine. Home: 3644 B Happy Valley Rd Lafayette CA 94549 Office: Roger Foott Assocs Inc 94 Natoma St San Francisco CA 94105

FORAKER-THOMPSON, JANE, criminology educator, researcher; b. Alhambra, Calif., Oct. 23, 1937; d. Field and Margaret Hall (Foraker) Thompson; m. Laurence E. Lynn, Aug. 24, 1958; m. Edwin W. Stockly, July 22, 1979; children—Stephen, Daniel, Diana, Julia Lynn. Student U. N.Mex., 1955-56; BA, U. Calif.-Berkeley, 1959, MA, 1965; PhD, Stanford U., 1985; postgrad. U. Leiden (Netherlands), summer 1973. A founder, active Stanford/Soledad Teaching Project, 1971-74; criminal justice specialist Bernalillo County Mental Health Ctr., Albuquerque, 1974-75; chief planner N.Mex. State Police, Santa Fe, 1975-78; project mgr. N.Mex. restitution project N.Mex. Criminal Justice Dept., Santa Fe, 1978-80; pres. Analysis, Innovation, Devel., Inc., human services cons., Santa Fe, 1980-81; asst. prof. criminal justice Boise State U., 1981-86, assoc. prof., 1986—; mem. N.Mex. Task Force on Victims of Sex Crimes, 1974-81, pres., 1978-80; chairwoman N.Mex. Gov.'s Task Force on Family Policy, 1979-80; first pres., chairwoman bd. Alternatives, Inc., treatment program for offenders, 1974-75; mem. ABA Jail Incapacitation and Prisons Com., 1982-83; mem. planning com. workshop leader N.W. Regional New Call to Pacemaking Conf., 1983; mem. N.Mex. Council Community Mental Health Services, 1974-81, mem. exec. com., 1979-80; mem. adv. bd. Albuquerque Rape Crisis Ctr., 1974-75; mem. adv. bd. N.Mex. Bar Assn. Com. Criminal Justice System, 1975; pres. Citizens for Prison Change, Inc., N.Mex., 1980-81; clk. Santa Fe Religious Soc. Friends, 1976-78, N. Mex. quar. meetings, 1978-80, clk. Boise Valley Worship Group, 1982-83; mem. peace and justice com. Idaho Diocese Episcopal Ch., 1983—; mem. Ada County Citizens for Peace (Idaho). Canadian govt. grantee, 1986. Mem. Western Assn. Sociologists and Anthropologists (pres. 1986-87), U.S. and Can. Acad. Soc., Am. Polit. Sci. Assn., Am. Soc. Pub. Adminstrn., ABA, Nat. Orgn. Victim Assistance, Acad. Criminal Justice Scis., Am. Soc. Criminology, Internat. Soc. Law Enforcement and Criminal Justice Instrs., Snake River Alliance. Contbr. articles to profl. jours. Office: Boise State U Dept Anthropology Sociology and Criminal Justice Boise ID 83725

FORBES, KENNETH ALBERT FAUCHER, urological surgeon; b. Waterford, N.Y., Apr. 28, 1922; s. Joseph Frederick and Adelle Frances (Robitaille) F.; m. Eileen Ruth Gibbons, Aug. 4, 1956; children: Michael, Diane, Kenneth E., Thomas, Maureen, Daniel. BS cum laude, U. Notre Dame, 1943; MD, St. Louis U., 1947. Diplomate Am. Bd. Urology. Intern St. Louis U. Hosp., 1947-48; resident in urol. surgery VA Hosp., Washington U., St. Louis. U. schs. medicine, St. Louis, 1948-52; fellow West Roxbury (Harvard) VA Hosp., Boston, 1955; asst. chief urology VA Hosp., East Orange, N.J., 1955-58; practice medicine specializing in urology Green Bay, Wis., 1958-78, Long Beach, Calif., 1978-85; mem. cons. staff Fairview State Hosp. U. Calif. Med. Ctr., Irvine, VA Hosp., Long Beach; asst. clin. prof. surgery U. Calif., Irvine, 1978-85; cons. Vols. in Tech. Assistance, 1986—. Contbr. articles to profl. jours. Served with USNR, 1944-46; capt. U.S. Army, 1952-54. Fellow ACS, Internat. Coll. Surgeons; mem. AMA, Calif. Med. Assn., Am. Urol. Assn., AAAS, Royal Soc. Medicine (London), N.Y. Acad. Scis., Santa Barbara County Med. Soc., Urologists Corr. Club, Phi Beta Pi. Republican. Roman Catholic. Clubs: Notre Dame (Los Angeles); Great Lakes Cruising. Home and Office: 15 Langlo Terr Santa Barbara CA 93105

FORBES, LEONARD, engineering educator; b. Grande Prairie, Alta., Can., Feb. 21, 1940; came to U.S., 1966; s. Frank and Katie (Tschetter) F.; B.Sc. with distinction in Engring. Physics, U. Alta., 1962; M.S. in E.E., U. Ill., 1963, Ph.D., 1970. Staff engr. IBM, Fishkill, N.Y. and Manassas, Va., 1970-72; IBM vis. prof. Howard U., Washington, 1972; asst. prof. U. Ark., Fayetteville, 1972-75; assoc. prof. U. Calif.-Davis, 1976-82; prof. Oreg. State U., Corvallis, 1983—; with Hewlett-Packard Labs., Palo Alto, Calif., 1978; cons. to Telex Computer Products, D.H. Baldwin, Hewlett-Packard, Fairchild United Epitaxial Tech.; organizer Portland Internat. Conf. and Exposition on Silicon Materials and Tech., 1985—. Served with Royal Can. Air Force, 1963-66. Mem. IEEE. Contbr. articles to profl. jours. Home: 537 Mountain View Ave Santa Rosa CA 95407 Office: Dept Elec Engring Oreg State U Corvallis OR 97331

FORCE, JACK KEITH, manufacturing executive; b. Fremont, Nebr., Oct. 19, 1946; s. Keith B. and Paula (Walther) F.; m. Marti Broussard, Aug. 1, 1970 (div. June 1980); children: Brian Christopher, Robin Elise. BSChemE, U. Nebr., 1969. Constrn. engr. E.I. DuPont deNemours, La Porte and Orange, Tex., 1969-72; process engr., maint. supr. E.I. DuPont deNemours, Richmond, Va., 1972-75; plant engr. MRI Corp. div. M&T Chems., South San Francisco, 1975-76, west regional mgr., 1981-82; plant mgr. MRI Corp. div. M&T Chems., Seattle, 1976-81, plant mgr. and mgr. mktg., 1982—, sec., treas., 1982—, also chmn. bd. dirs.; treas. and cons. Constrn. Devel. Services, Inc., Seattle, 1982—. Asst. scoutmaster Seattle council Boy Scouts Am., 1985—; also troop chmn. Mem. Wash. State Recycling Assn. (pres. 1985—, bd. dirs. 1984-85). Avocations: mountain climbing, water and snow skiing, backpacking, river rafting, bicycling. Office: MRI Corp 6000 W Marginal Way SW Seattle WA 98105

FORCE, JO ELLEN, forestry educator; b. Marshalltown, Iowa, May 17, 1943; d. George Henry and Ruth Alice (Willits) Hitch; m. Ronald Wayne Force, May 31, 1964; children: Emily, Alicia. BS, Iowa State U., 1965; MS, Ohio State U., 1973, PhD, 1978. Teacher pub. schs. Mpls. and Columbus, Ohio, 1966-71; asst. prof. forest resources U. Idaho, Moscow, 1979-85, assoc. prof., 1985—; cons. extension forestry tng. U.S. Agy. Internat. Devel., New Delhi, 1985, mem. evaluation team, 1986. Contbr. articles to profl. jours. Named Outstanding Faculty Mem., U. Idaho Coll. Forestry, Wildlife and Range Scis., 1984. Mem. Soc. Am. Foresters (local chair 1984, working group chair 1984-86), Gamma Sigma Delta, Alpha Pi Mu. Democrat. Unitarian Universalist. Avocations: travel, gourmet cooking, reading, hiking. Home: NW 1430 Orion Dr Pullman WA 99163 Office: U Idaho Dept Forest Resources Moscow ID 83843

FORD, BETTY (ELIZABETH) BLOOMER, wife of former Pres. U.S.; b. Chgo., Apr. 8, 1918; d. William Stephenson and Hortence (Neahr) Bloomer; m. Gerald R. Ford (38th Pres. U.S.), Oct. 15, 1948; children: Michael Gerald, John Gardner, Steven Meigs, Susan Elizabeth. Student, Sch. Dance Bennington Coll., 1936, 37; LL.D. hon., U. Mich., 1976. Dancer Martha Graham Concert Group, N.Y.C., 1939-41; model John Powers Agy., N.Y.C., 1939-41; fashion dir. Herpolscheimer's Dept. Store, Grand Rapids, Mich., 1943-48; dance instr. Grand Rapids, 1932-48; pres., bd. dirs. The Betty Ford Ctr., Rancho Mirage, Calif. Author: autobiography The Times of My Life, 1979. Bd. dirs. Nat. Arthritis Found. (hon.); formerly active Cub Scouts Am.; program chmn. Alexandria (Va.) Cancer Fund Drive; chmn. Heart Subday, Washington Heart Assn., 1974; pres. ARC Senate Wives Club; supporter Nat. Endowment Arts; mem. Nat. Commn. Observance Internat. Women's Year, 1977; bd. dirs. League Republican Women, D.C.; trustee Eisenhower Med. Ctr., Rancho Mirage; advisory bd. Rosalind Russell Med. Research Fund; hon. chmn. Palm Springs Desert Mus.; nat. trustee Nat. Symphony Orch.; trustee Nursing Home Advisory and Research Council Inc.; mem. Golden Circle Patrons Ctr. Theatre Performing Arts; bd. dirs. The Lambs, Libertyville, Ill. Episcopalian (tchr. Sunday sch. 1961-64). Home: Rancho Mirage CA 92270

FORD, GERALD RUDOLPH, JR., former president U.S.; b. Omaha, July 14, 1913; s. Gerald R. and Dorothy (Gardner) F.; m. Elizabeth Bloomer, Oct. 15, 1948; children—Michael, John, Steven, Susan. A.B., U. Mich., 1935; LL.B., Yale U., 1941; LL.D., Mich. State U., Albion Coll., Aquinas Coll., Spring Arbor Coll. Bar: Mich. bar 1941. Practiced law at Grand Rapids, 1941-49; mem. law firm Buchen and Ford; mem. 81st-93d Congresses from 5th Mich. Dist., elected minority leader, 1965; v.p. U.S., 1973-74, pres., 1974-77; del. Interparliamentary Union, Warsaw, Poland, 1959, Belgium, 1961; del. Bilderberg Group Conf., 1962; dir. Santa Fe Internat., GK Technologies, Shearson Loeb Rhoades, Pebble Beach Corp., Tiger Internat. Served as lt. comdr. USNR, 1942-46. Recipient Grand Rapids Jr. C. of C. Distinguished Service award, 1948; Distinguished Service Award as one of ten outstanding young men in U.S. by U.S. Jr. C. of C., 1950; Silver Anniversary All-Am. Sports Illustrated, 1959; Distinguished Congressional Service award Am. Polit. Sci. Assn., 1961. Mem. Am., Mich. State, Grand Rapids bar assns., Delta Kappa Epsilon, Phi Delta Phi. Republican. Episcopalian. Clubs: Masons (Kent County), Univ. (Kent County), Peninsular (Kent County). Home: PO Box 927 Rancho Mirage CA 92262 *

FORD, GLENN MARCUS, ophthalmologist; b. Chgo., Mar. 1, 1951; s. Edwin Levi and Hazel Eileen (Smith) F.; m. Jeannette Therese Chambers, Feb. 15, 1986. BA, Cornell U., 1973; MD, U. Ill., Chgo., 1978; postgrad., UCLA, 1986—. Diplomate Am. Bd. Ophthalmology, Am. Bd. Med. Examiners. Intern Los Angeles County/U. So. Calif. Med. Ctr.; resident Martin Luther King Hosp.; fellow in ophthalmology U. Ill., Chgo., 1982-83; ophthalmologist Eye Care Physicians, Chgo., 1983-84; chief vision care dept. Watts Health Found. Inc., Los Angeles, 1984—; chmn. vision care quality assurance com. United Health Plan, Los Angeles, 1984—. Named one of Outstanding Young Men of Am., 1981. Mem. AAAS, Calif. Med. Assn., Los Angeles County Med. Assn., Physicians for Social Responsibility. Democrat. Presbyterian. Avocations: photography, chess, tennis, jogging. Office: Watts Health Found Inc 10300 S Compton Ave Los Angeles CA 90002

FORD, GRACE RIDDELL, educator; b. Montgomery, Ala., Oct. 11, 1921; d. Glenn Ernest and Neva (Mitchum) Riddell; m. Gerald M. Ford, June 9, 1948; children: Pamela Jane, Douglas Roy. Student, George Washington U., 1942-43; BA, Tex. Women's U., 1944; postgrad., Gonzaga U., 1970-72. Cert. sch. tchr., Wash. Identification clk. FBI, Washington, 1942; research chemist Nat. Bur. Standards, Washington, 1943-48; sci. tchr. pub. schs. Spokane, Wash., 1970—. Author: (with others) This We Believe, 1977; patentee metalls.; contbr. articles to profl. jours. Delegate gen. assembly Nat. Council Chs., Miami, Fla., 1966; bd. dirs. Internat. Conv. Christian Chs., Indpls., 1961-67; pres. bd. dirs. Calif. Christian Home, Rosemead, 1964-66. Named Tchr of Yr., Cen. Valley Sch. Dist., 1985. Mem. Am. Chem. Soc., Nat. Sci. Tchrs. Assn., Wash. Sci. Tchrs. Assn. (sec. 1978-79), LWV, Peace and Justice Action League, Alpha Delta Kappa (local pres., Wash. bd. dirs. 1978-80). Democrat. Avocations: swimming, bicycling. Home: E 1628 35th Spokane WA 99203 Office: Cen Valley High Sch S 821 Sullivan Rd Spokane WA 99037

FORD, JUDITH ANN, natural gas distribution company executive; b. Martinsville, Ind., May 11, 1935; d. Glenn Leyburn and Dorotha Mae (Parks) Tudor; m. Walter L. Ford, July 25, 1954 (div. 1962); children—John Corbin, Christi Sue. Student, Wichita State U., 1953-55; student, U. Nev.-Las Vegas. Legal sec. Southwest Gas Corp., Las Vegas, 1963-69, adminstrn. sec., 1968-79, asst. corp. sec., 1969-72, corp. sec., 1972-82, v.p., 1977-82, sr. v.p., 1982—, also bd. dirs., dir. 7 subs. Trustee Nev. Sch. Arts, Las Vegas, 1979—, chmn. bd. dirs., 1985-86; trustee Disciples Sem. Found., Claremont Sch. Theology, Calif., 1985—. Mem. Am. Soc. Corp. Secs., Greater Las Vegas C. of C. (bd. dirs. 1979-85), Pacific Coast Gas Assn. (bd. dirs. 1984—), Ariz. Bus. Women Owners (exec. com. 1985—). Democrat. Mem. Christian Ch. (Disciples of Christ). Office: Southwest Gas Corp 5241 Spring Mountain Rd Las Vegas NV 89102

FORD, LINDA MARIA, lawyer, educator; b. Oil City, Pa., Feb. 7, 1949; d. Matthew Stanley and Theresa (Malvaso) Moran; m. James Ray Ford, Mar. 20, 1971. AA, Chaffey Jr. Coll., 1972; BA, Calif. State Poly. U., Pomona, 1974; MA, Sonoma State U., 1982; JD, Empire Coll., 1985. Bar: Calif. 1985. Loan officer Ontario (Calif.) Inland Bank, 1969-72; library aid Ontario Library, 1971-72; research aid Calif. State Poly. Tech., 1972-74; tchr. Chino (Calif.) High Sch., 1975-76, Analy High Sch., Sebastopol, Calif., 1976—; sole practice Santa Rosa, Calif., 1985—. Author: Folklore of Wine Country, 1982. Mem. Calif. Trial Lawyers Assn. Republican. Roman Catholic. Avocations: writing, skiing, swimming. Home and Office: PO Box 477 Sebastopol CA 95472

FORD, PATRICIA, interior designer; b. Warsaw, N.Y., Feb. 17, 1947; d. Homer James and Ellen Louise (Dixon) F.; B.A. in Fine Arts, UCLA, 1969, M.A. in Fine Arts, 1971. Designer, Herb Rosenthal & Assos., Los Angeles, 1973; sr. designer Charles Kratka Planning and Design, Los Angeles, 1973-75; ptnr The Ford Wilson Partnership, Los Angeles, 1975-78; pres. Ford Design Group Inc., Los Angeles, 1978-82; dir. interior design Bobrow Thomas & Assocs., architects, Los Angeles, 1982-84; ptnr. Kaneko Ford Design, Los Angeles, 1985—; cons. to Los Angeles Olympic Organizing Com., 1984—. Mem citizens adv. council Los Angeles Olympics of 1984, 1980—; mem. Los Angeles Hdqrs. City Assn. 1980—. Mem. Assn. Women in Architecture (v.p.), Am. Soc. Interior Designers, AIA, Town Hall. Episcopalian. Contbr. articles to profl. jours. Office: Kaneko Ford Design 2200 Michigan Ave Santa Monica CA 90404

FORD, RICHARD FISKE, marine ecology educator; b. Los Angeles, Mar. 7, 1934; s. Harold Harrison and Grace Elizabeth (Hoskins) F.; m. JoAnn Louise Dickinson, June 16, 1957; children: Joanna Lynn, Michael Ian. BA in Zoology, Pomona Coll., 1956; MA in Biology, Stanford U., 1959; PhD in Biol. Oceanography, Scripps Instn. Oceanography, 1965. Asst. prof. marine ecology San Diego State U., 1964-68, assoc. prof., 1968-71, prof., 1971—, coordinator biol. grad. program, 1971-73, dir. Ctr. Marine Studies, 1974-86; vis. scientist Commonwealth Sci. and Indsl., Research Orgn., Perth, Australia, 1980-81; ecol. cons. San Diego Gas & Electric Co., 1968—, Calif. Water Quality Control Bd., San Diego, 1968—, San Diego Port Dist., 1970—, Irvine Co., Calif., 1978—, David Smith & Assocs., 1978—, Phillips, Brandt, Redick, Inc., 1986—. Editor: Readings in Aquatic Ecology, 1972; contbr. articles to profl. jours. Active Citizens Coordinate for Century III, San Diego, 1970—. Eli Lilly fellow, 1957-58, U.S. Bur. Comml. Fisheries fellow, 1962-64; grantee NSF, Nat. Sea Grant Program, Calif. Dept. Fish and Game, Calif. Water Quality Control Bd. Mem. AAAS, Am. Soc. Limnology and Oceanography, Ecol. Soc. Am., World Mariculture Soc., Zool. Soc. San Diego, Sigma Xi (pres. San Diego chpt. 1983-84). Office: San Diego State U Dept Biology San Diego CA 92182

FORD, ROBERT WHARTON HENDRIE, educator; b. Stamford, Conn., Jan. 28, 1933; s. Wharton Hendrie and Marian (Humphries) F.; m. Diane Hughes Ford, Dec. 29, 1956; children: Gary, Jill, Rob. BSEd, U. Ariz., 1961, MEd, 1962. Cert. secondary tchr., Ariz. Tchr. Tucson Sch. Dist. #1, 1962—; instr. U. Ariz., Tucson, 1980—; commd. reserve law officer, Ariz. Dept. Pub. Safety. Served with USN, 1953-55, Korea. Named Reserve Officer of Yr. Ariz. Dept. Pub. Safety, 1978. Mem. Ariz. Driver Edn. and Safety Assn. (pres. 1976-78), Tchr. Edn. Assn., Am. Edn. Assn., NEA, VFW, Phi Delta Kappa. Republican. Lodge: Moose. Participant diving 1955 Pan Am. Games Trials, 1956 Olympic Trials. Home: 4940 N Calle Bosque Tucson AZ 85718 Office: Palo Verde High Sch 1302 S Avenida Vega Tucson AZ 85710

FORD, RONALD EDWARD, communications executive; b. Omaha, Apr. 26, 1943; s. Ralph Andrew and Martha (Gadeken) F.; m. Nancy Lee Hendrix, Apr. 23, 1965 (div. 1979); children—Don Andrew, John Edward. Student U. Omaha, 1965—. Sales rep. U.S. Check Book, Omaha, 1965-77; gen. mgr. Sta. KDGO, Durango, Colo., 1977—. Pres. S.W. Colo. Mental Health Ctr., Durango, 1982—; v.p. Colo. Assn. Community Mental Health Ctrs. and Clinics, Denver, 1984—; bd. dirs. Nat. Council of Community Mental Health Ctrs., Region VIII, 1984—. Office: KDGO 730 Main Durango CO 81301

FORD, VICTORIA, public relations executive; b. Carroll, Iowa, Nov. 1, 1946; d. Victor Sargent and Gertrude Francis (Headlee) F.; m. John K. Frans, July 4, 1965 (div. Aug. 1975); m. David W. Keller, May 2, 1981 (div. Nov. 1985). AA, Iowa Lakes Community Coll., 1973; BA summa cum laude, Buena Vista Coll., 1974; postgrad., U. Nev., 1981—. Juvenile parole officer Iowa Dept. Social Services, Sioux City, 1974-78; staff reporter Feather Pub. Co., Quincy, Calif., 1978-80; tng. counselor CETA, Quincy, 1980; library pub. info. officer U. Nev., Reno, 1982-84; pub. relations exec. Brodeur Martin Co., Reno, 1984—. Contbr. articles to profl. jours. Mem. adv. bd. Reno Philharm., 1985—, Reno-Sparks Conv. and Visitors Authority, 1985—. Mem. ALA, Reno Women in Advt., Pub. Relations Soc. Am. (charter v.p. Sierra Nevada chpt. 1986—), NOW, Sigma Delta Chi. Democrat. Home: 1218 Searchlite Ct Reno NV 89503 Office: Brodeur/Martin Pub Relations 50 Washington St Reno NV 89503

FORHAN, WILLIAM EDWARD, accountant; b. Butte, Mont., Mar. 20, 1947; s. Rudi and Alice (Mehrens) F.; m. Carol Lynn Johnson, Nov. 25, 1967; children—David John, Michael Scott. B.S. in Bus. Adminstrn., U. Mont., 1969. C.P.A., Mont. Staff acct. Krausman & Assocs., Englewood, Colo., 1972-74; controller, I.T.T. Auto. Distbrs., Colo.-Utah ops., 1974-78, Iowa-Ill. ops., 1978-80; controller Billings (Mont.) Gazette, 1980—. past pres. community adv. bd. Sch. Bus. and Econs., Eastern Mont. Coll., 1981-83. Served to 1st lt. U.S. Army, 1969-72. Mem. Internat. Newspaper Fin. Execs. (mem. ins. and benefits com., info. systems com., membership com.), Mont. Soc. CPAs (mem. continuing edn. com.). Republican. Episcopalian. Office: 401 N Broadway Billings MT 59101

FORKERT, CLIFFORD ARTHUR, civil engr.; b. Verona, N.D., Oct. 16, 1916; s. Arthur Louis and Bessie (Delamater) F.; grad. N.D. State Coll., 1940; postgrad. M.I.T.; m. Betty Jo Erickson, July 1, 1940; children—Terry Lynn Forkert Williamson, Michael, Debra. Hwy. engr., N.D., Tex., 1937-40; hydraulic engr. Internat. Boundary Commn. Tex. on Rio Grande and Tributaries, 1940-43; constrn., topographic and cons. engr., Calif. 1946—; now civil engr., prin. Clifford A. Forkert, Civil Engr.; pres. Calif. Poly. Pomona Assos. Served as capt. USMCR, 1943-46. Registered civil engr. Calif., Oreg., Ariz., profl. engr., Nev.; lic. land surveyor, Nev. Fellow Am. Congress and Mapping (life); mem. ASCE (life), Land Surveyors Assn. Calif. (dir.), Alumni Assn. N.D. State Coll. Home: 20821 Skimmer Ln Huntington Beach CA 92646 Office: 22311 Brookhurst St Huntington Beach CA 92646

FORMEISTER, RICHARD BRUNO, electronics engineer, consultant; b. Chgo., Jan. 14, 1946; s. Bruno and June Patricia (Kelly) F.; m. Jonille Denise Fay, July 20, 1968 (div. Jan. 1980); 1 child, Tiffany R.; m. Jacqueline Ann Martin, Mar. 5, 1983; 1 child, Christopher R. BSEE, U. Ill., 1968; MSEE, Ariz. State U., 1978. With Sperry Flight Systems, Phoenix, 1968-79, engring. sect. head, 1979-84; mem. tech. staff Fairchild Data Corp., Scottsdale, Ariz., 1984—; cons. Deer Valley High Sch., 1983-84, pvt. practice cons., Glendale, Ariz., 1984—. Author: Non-Linear Devices and System Bandwidths, 1978; patentee in field. mem. adv. bd. Glendale Community Coll., 1984; mem. Assn. for Fathers and Children Together, 1980-82. Fulbright-Hayes grantee Ariz. State U., 1978. Mem. IEEE, Eta Kappa Nu. Republican. Home: 6407 W Yucca St Glendale AZ 85304 Office: Fairchild Data Corp 350 N Hayden Rd Scottsdale AZ 85257

FORMHALS, ROBERT WILLARD YATES (SANGUSZKO), ret. ednl. adminstr.; b. Los Angeles, June 14, 1919; s. Carl Wright and Muriel (Yates) (Sanguszko) Formhals; LLB, JD, Welch Coll. Law, Los Angeles, 1943; cert. pub. adminstrn. Sacramento State Coll., 1959; DCL, Sheffield Coll., 1965; m. Elaine Mary Peters, Apr. 4, 1947; 1 child, Robert Arthur Clinton. Personnel mgr. Warman Steel Casting Co., Vernon, Calif., 1943-47; dep. labor commr. Calif., 1948; adminstrv. asst. to state architect Calif., 1948-59; No. Calif. mgr. William L. Aldrich Co., 1960-61; exec. sec.-treas. Calif. Sch. Bds. Assn., 1961-67; dir. bd. policies services Ednl. Service Bur., 1967; pres. Assos. Mgmt. Service, 1967-70; mcpl. employee relations officer City of San Jose (Calif.), 1970-74; program mgr. West Valley Coll., Saratoga, Calif., 1975-76, also instr. labor relations and mgmt., 1972-75; dir. employer-employee relations Conejo Valley Unified Sch. Dist., 1976-81. Commr. Calif. Commn. Sch. Dist. Orgn., 1961-64; chmn. Gov. Calif. Edn. and Tng. Adv. Com. Civil Def., also mem. Calif. Disaster Council, 1961-67; personnel commr. Pleasant Valley Sch. Dist., 1979-81, trustee, 1981— ; exec. vice chmn. Young Dems. Calif., 1941-44; mem. Nat. Com. Dems. for Dewey, 1944; Calif. chmn. Dems. for Knowland, 1946; vice chmn. Sacramento County Com. for Nixon, 1960. Chmn. bd. Pacific Maritime Acad., 1950-52; trustee St. John Found., 1972—. Served with AUS, 1943-44. Created knight by King Peter II of Yugoslavia; decorated grand officer White Eagle, grand officer Crown (Yugoslavia); grand master, grand cross St. John Jerusalem; grand cross Constantine the Gt.; knight comdr. St. Laszlo (Hungary). Mem. Am. Soc. Safety Engrs. (past nat. exec. bd.), Am. Arbitration Assn. (nat. labor panel), Am. Legion, SAR (pres. Palo Alto chpt., pres. Patton chpt., state exec. sec. 1978-79, state pres. 1979-80 nat. trustee 1980-81, nat. v.p. gen. 1981-82, 84-85), KP, Eagles. Clubs: Commonwealth (San Francisco); Severance (Los Angeles). Author: Handbook of Armed Forces of the World, 1948, Book of Precedence, 1965, White Cross, 1980; also articles. Address: 5609 E Willow View Dr Camarillo CA 93010

FORMWALT, WILLIAM ALEXANDER, military officer, civil engineering educator; b. Balt., June 24, 1951; s. William Swan and Florence Tait (Dornin) F.; m. Incha Pak, May 8, 1982; children: Cynthia Florence, Lucie Dornin. BS in Architecture, U. Va., 1974; diploma in Russian, Def. Lang. Inst., 1976; MS in Archtl. Engring., Pa. State U., 1982. Commd. 2d lt. USAF, 1976, advanced through grades to capt., 1980; chief of programs USAF, Pope AFB, N.C., 1976-79; project engr. Pacific Air Forces USAF, Taegu AFB, Republic of Korea, 1979-80; mgr. commd. facility energy program USAF, Europe, 1982-85; instr. archtl. and solar engring. U.S. Air Force Acad. USAF, Colorado Springs, Colo., 1985—; mem. energy conservation task group U.S. Air Force Acad., 1985—, personnel officer dept. civil engring., 1986. Coach lacrosse Rampart High Sch., Colorado Springs, 1986. Mem. ASHRAE, Soc. Am. Mil. Engrs., Am. Solar Energy Soc., Phi Kappa Phi, Theta Tau. Republican. Episcopalian. Avocations: sports, chess, micro computing. Office: HQ USAF Acad/DFCE Colorado Springs CO 80840

FORNEY, CHARLES FREDERICK, research plant physiologist; b. Bellefonte, Pa., Nov. 21, 1956; s. Charles Binkley and Miriam Irene (Meyer) F.; m. Jane Ellen Bollinger, Aug. 9, 1980; children: Andra Louise, Paul Meyer. BS in Horticulture, BS in Biology, Pa. State U., 1978, MS in Horticulture, 1980; PhD in Horticulture, Oreg. State U., 1984. Research asst. Pa. State U., University Park, 1978-80, Oreg. State U, Corvallis, 1980-84; research scientist Agrl. Research Service USDA, Fresno, Calif., 1984—. Contbr. articles to profl. jours. Mem. Am. Soc. Hort. Sci., Am. Soc. Plant Physiol., Sigma Xi, Alpha Gamma Rho (v.p. 1977), Gamma Sigma Delta. Republican. Presbyterian. Avocations: gardening, hiking, camping, photography. Home: 5397 E Turner Fresno CA 93727 Office: USDA Agrl Research Service Market Quality and Transp Unit 2021 S Peach Ave Fresno CA 93727

FOROUZAN, BEHROUZ A., computer programming educator; b. Arak, Iran, Oct. 15, 1944; came to U.S., 1981; s. Ahmad A. Forouzan and Soror Mina; m. Faezeh Golboo, June 4, 1971; one child, Setareh. BS in Elec., Tehran (Iran) U., 1967; MS in Elec., U. Calif., Irvine, 1984. Chmn. bd. dirs. Techno Frigo, Tehran, 1969-79; project engr. Memco, Zurich, Switzerland, 1979-81; computer instr. Navajo Community Coll., Shiprock, N.Mex., 1984—. Served to lt. Army of Iran, 1967-69. Mem. IEEE, BYTE. Home: 2800 N Dustin Apt #205 Farmington NM 87401 Office: Navajo Community Coll Dept Sci Shiprock NM 87420

FORREST, GARY GRAN, psychologist, consultant, author; b. New Castle, Pa., Dec. 1, 1943; s. Granville Hamilton and Florence Ruth (Cox) F.; m. Sandra G. Della-Giustina, Dec. 28, 1974; children—Sarah Ellen, Allison Giustina. B.A. (Coll. scholar), Westminster Coll., 1965; M.Ed. (Vocat. Rehab. Assn. stipendee), U. Mo.-Columbia, 1967; Ed.D. (Univ. higher edn. grantee), U. N.D., 1970; diploma U. Okla., Norman, 1971; Ph.D., Columbia Pacific U., 1984. Lic. clin. psychologist, Colo.; diplomate in profl. psychotherapy Internat. Acad. Profl. Counseling and Psychotherapy. Clin. dir. alcohol rehab. program, dept. psychiatry Alcohol and Drug Rehab. Ctr., Ft. Gordon, Ga., 1971-73, ct. clin. dir., 1973-76; instr. dept. psychology Augusta Coll., 1971-73; mem. dept. psychiatry Community Mental Health Ctr., Med. Coll. Ga., 1973; vis. prof. psychology, counseling and guidance U. No. Colo., 1975-81; exec. dir. Psychotherapy Assocs. and Inst. for Addictive Behavioral Change, Colorado Springs, Colo., 1976—; cons. psychologist alcohol services div. Pikes Peak Mental Health Ctr., Colorado Springs, 1982-85. Mem. adv. bd. Nat. Council on Alcoholism, Colorado Springs, 1975—; bd. dirs. Riegel Ctr., Penrose Community Hosp., Colorado Springs, 1980-83. Recipient Nat. Service award Nat. Council Alcoholism, 1981, Alumni Achievement award Westminster Coll. 1986. Mem. Am. Psychol. Assn., Colo. Psychol. Assn., Assn. for Counselors and Devel., Nat. Register Health Service Providers in Psychology, Assn. for Advancement Profl. Psychology, Phi Delta Kappa, Delta Tau Delta. Republican. Methodist. Author books, the most recent being: Confrontation in Psychotherapy With Alcoholics, 1982; Alcoholism and Human Sexuality, 1982; How to Cope with a Teenage Drinker, 1983; Alcoholism, Narcissism and Psychopathology, 1983; Intensive Psychotherapy of Alcoholism, 1984; Alcoholism and Substance Abuse: Clinical Intervention Strategies, 1985. Home: 935 War Eagle Dr N Colorado Springs CO 80919 Office: 3208 N Academy Blvd Suite 160 Colorado Springs CO 80907

FORREST, KENTON HARVEY, science educator, historian; b. Fort Lauderdale, Fla., Oct. 3, 1944; s. Harvey William and Marjorie A. (Boxrud) F. B.A., Colo. State Coll., 1968; M.A., U. No. Colo., 1981. Science tchr. Dunstan Jr. High, Jefferson County Pub. Schs., Lakewood, Colo., 1968—; pres. Tramway Press, Inc., 1983—. Author: Denver's Railroads, 1981; (with William C. Jones) Denver-A Pictorial History, 1973; (with others) The Moffat Tunnel, 1978; Rio Grande Ski Train, 1984. Trustee Colo. Railroad Hist. Found., Golden, 1975—; mem., 1st pres. Lakewood Hist. Soc. (Colo.), 1976. Mem. NEA (life) Rocky Mountain Assn. Geologists, Colo. Sci. Soc., Nat. Railway Hist. Soc. (Intermountain chpt. pres. 1980-83), Mobile Post Office Soc., Mile High Ry. Club. Home: PO Box 15607 Lakewood CO 80215 Office: Dunstan Jr High Sch 1855 S Wright St Lakewood CO 80226

FORRESTER, ALVIN THEODORE, physicist; b. Bklyn., Apr. 13, 1918; s. Joseph D. and Rose (Kissen) F.; m. Joy Levin, 1948 (dec. 1956); children—Bruce H., Cheri J.; m. June Doris Berg, Oct. 5, 1956 (div. 1972); children—William C., Susan J. A.B., Cornell U., 1938, A.M., 1939, Ph.D., 1942. Research asso. U. Calif. at Berkeley, 1942-45; physicist RCA Labs., Princeton, N.J., 1945-46; asst. prof. physics U. So. Calif., Los Angeles, 1946-51; asso. prof. U. So. Calif., 1951-54; vis. asso. prof. physics U. Pitts., 1954-55; physicist Westinghouse Research Labs., Pitts., 1955-58; nuclear spl. Atomics Internat., Los Angeles, 1958-59; dept. mgr. Electro-Optical Systems, Pasadena, Calif., 1959-65; prof. U. Calif.- (Irvine), 1965-67, U. Calif.-(Los Angeles), 1967—; Vis. prof. astronomy U. Utrecht, Netherlands, 1971; asso. Culham Lab., Eng., spring 1974; vis. prof. physics Technion, Haifa, Israel, fall 1977. Fellow Am. Phys. Soc., IEEE; mem. AIAA (Research award 1962, chmn. electrostatic propulsion panel 1960-61), AAAS, AAUP, Am. Assn. Physics Tchrs., Sigma Xi, Phi Kappa Phi. Research in photoetoelectric mixing of light, ion propulsion, isotope separation, superconductivity, plasma physics, high power neutral beams. Home: 11525 Ohio Ave Los Angeles CA 90025 Office: Room 7731 BH U Calif Los Angeles CA 90024

FORRESTER, PATRICK JAMES, JR., public policy consultant; b. Portsmouth, Va., July 22, 1949; s. Patrick James Forrester and Virginia Belle (Hatch) Cook; m. Victoria Sparks, July 22, 1972 (div. Sept. 1980); m. Pamela Gene Cosby, Mar. 20, 1982; 1 child, Nicole Sparks. BA in Polit. Sci., U. Nev., 1975; M in Pub. Adminstrn., Harvard U., 1978. Staff mem. U.S. House Reps., Washington, 1977; research assoc. Harvard U., Cambridge, Mass., 1977-78; asst. to gov. Commonwealth of Mass., Boston, 1978-80; pres. Equinox Assn. Inc., Carson City, Nev., 1980—; polit. columnist Tribune, Reno, Nev. 1985. Del. Dem. Nat. Conv., N.Y.C., 1976; mem. Carson City Dem. Cen. Com.; exec. dir. Common Cause/Nev., 1986—; bd. dirs. Great Basin Zool. Soc., Reno, 1982-85. Served to lt. U.S. Army, 1970-72. Recipient Juvenile Justice award Nat. Council Juvenile Ct. Judges, 1975, Am. Legion Gold medal, 1975. Club: Harvard (Nev. pres.). Home: 3785 Meadow Wood Rd Carson City NV 89701

FORSBERG, KEVIN JOHN, consulting company executive; b. Oakland, Calif., July 20, 1934; s. Ted Otto and Gladys (Reid) F.; m. Edna Dorles, Apr., 1966 (div. Nov. 1979); m. Cindy Jane Beason, Jan. 1, 1981; children: Ian, Chenoa. BSCE, MIT, 1956; MS in Engring. Mechanics, Stanford U., 1958, PhD in Engring. Mechanics, 1961, postgrad., 1979. Mem. tech. staff Lockheed Missiles & Space Co., Sunnyvale, Calif., 1956-61, program mgr., 1973-84; mgr. solid mech. Lockheed Missiles & Space Co., Palo Alto, Calif., 1963-71, asst. dir., 1971-73; v.p. Consulting Resources, Inc., Santa Clara, Calif., 1984—; lectr. grad. sch. Santa Clara U., 1984—, U. Calif. Santa Cruz, 1985—. Co-author: (handbook) Project Management and Project Leadership, 1985; regional editor Jour. Computers and Structures, Washington, 1970-80; contbr. articles to profl. jours. Chmn. Citizens' Com. on High Sch. Edn., Redwood City, Calif., 1969-70. Served to capt. U.S. Army, 1961-63. Recipient Pub. Service award NASA, 1981. Fellow ASME; mem. AIAA. Home: 1225 Vienna Dr Sunnyvale CA 94089 Office: Consulting Resources Inc 5333 Betsy Ross Santa Clara CA 95052

FORSEN, HAROLD KAY, engineering executive; b. Sept. 19, 1932; s. Allen Kay and Mabel Evelyn (Buehler) F.; m. Betty Ann Webb, May 25, 1952; children: John Allen, Ronald Karl, Sandra Kay. AA, Compton Jr. Coll., 1956; BS, Calif. Inst. Tech., 1958, MS, 1959; PhD, U. Calif., Berkeley, 1965. Research assoc. Gen. Atomic, San Diego, 1959-62; research assoc., elec. engr. U. Calif., Berkeley, 1962-65; assoc. prof. nuclear engring. U. Wis., Madison, 1965-69, prof., 1969-73, dir. Phys. Sci. Lab., 1970-72; mgr. engring. Exxon Nuclear Co., Bellevue, Wash., 1973-75, v.p., dir., 1975-80, exec. in charge laser enrichment, 1981; exec. v.p. Jersey-Avco Isotopes, Inc., 1975-80, pres., 1981, dir., 1975-81; mgr. engring. and materials Bechtel Group, Inc., San Francisco, 1981-83, dep. gen. mgr. advanced systems, 1984-85, mgr. research and devel., 1986—, dep. mgr. research and engring, 1983-84; v.p. Bechtel Nat. Inc., 1983-86, sr. v.p., 1986—; mem. fusion power reactor sr. rev. com. Dept. Energy, 1977, magnetic fusion adv. com., 1982-86; chmn. U.S. del. of AEC on Ion Sources to Soviet Union, 1972; cons. Oak Ridge Nat. Lab., Tenn., 1969-72, Argonne Nat. Lab., Ill., 1970-72, Exxon Nuclear Co., 1970-73, Battelle N.W. Lab., 1971-72; mem. sci. and tech. adv. com. Argonne Nat. Lab., 1983-85; mem. fusion energy adv. com. Oak Ridge Nat. Lab., 1977-84. Contbr. articles to tech. jours. Patentee fusion and laser isotope separation. Vice pres., trustee Pacific Sci. Ctr. Found., 1977, pres., 1978-80, chmn., 1981; mem. dean's vis. com. Coll. Engring., U. Wash., 1981—. Served with USAF, 1951-55. Fellow Am. Phys. Soc.; mem. Am. Nuclear Soc. (Arthur H. Compton award 1972, chmn. tech. group controlled nuclear fusion 1973), IEEE (sr.), Sigma Xi. Home: 255 Tim Ct Danville CA 94526 Office: Bechtel Nat Inc PO Box 3965 San Francisco CA 94119

FORSIAK, WALTER WILLIAM, publishers' representative; b. Detroit, Apr. 30, 1935; s. John J. and Patricia (Jurek) F.; m. Ella Eggers, July 27, 1963; children—Erica, Christa. B.S. in Bus. Adminstrn., Wayne State U., 1957. Advt. sales McGraw-Hill Pub. Co., various locations, 1957-83; v.p. Bus. Times, Inc., TV show, 1983-85; pres. Forsiak & Assocs., Inc., 1985—. Bd. dirs. Switzer Ctr. Ednl. Therapy, 1979-81, Timber Cove Homes Assn. Served in USAFR, 1958-64. Mem. San Francisco Advt. Club, Los Angeles Advt. Club. Roman Catholic. Clubs: Trail Ride of N.Mex.; The Guardsmen (San Francisco). Office: PO Box 2649 San Anselmo CA 94960

FORSLUND, SCOTT WILHELM, journalist, editor; b. Seattle, June 25, 1957. BA in English, U. Wash., 1980. Assoc. editor Pacific N.W. mag., Seattle, 1982-85; publs. dir. Bonneville Power Adminstrn., Portland, Oreg., 1985-86; exec. editor Pacific N.W. Mag., Seattle, 1986—. Recipient Excellence in Journalism award Soc. Profl. Journalists, 1980-85. Office: Pacific Northwest Mag 222 Dexter Ave N Seattle WA 98109

FORSTE, NORMAN LEE, management consultant; b. Carthage, Mo., Aug. 18, 1935; s. John Edward and Lula Mae (Martin) F.; m. Catherine Jean Culver, July 20, 1958; children: Patricia, Diana, John II, Karl. AA, Am. River coll., 1961; BA, Calif. State U., 1964, MA, 1971; MBA, Golden Gate U., 1973; PhD in Higher Edn., U. Wash., 1984. Adminstrv. analyst State of Calif., Sacramento, 1962-64, sr. data processing systems analyst, 1966-67, supr. info. systems devel., 1967-68; sr. adminstrv. analyst County of Sacramento (Calif.), 1964-66, dir. systems and data processing dept., 1968-74; dir. adminstrv. data processing div. U. Wash., Seattle, 1974-76; mgr. mgmt. adv. services Deloitte Haskins & Sells, 1976-81, dir. mgmt. adv. services, 1981-85; pvt. practice mgmt. cons., Carmichael, Calif., 1985—; instr. mgmt. scis. program U. Calif. at Davis, 1968; professorial lectr. mgmt. info. systems Golden Gate U., Sacramento, 1971-74, 79—; instr. info. systems Calif. State U.-Sacramento, 1982-83; instr. systems analysis and introduction to data processing Am. River Coll., Sacramento, 1968-71. Mem. curriculum adv. com. for data processing Am. River Coll., Sacramento, 1969-74, mem. com. to evaluate vocational and tech. edn. program for accreditation, 1972-73. Served with USAF, 1954-57, 62, maj. USAFR, Ret. Mem. Am. Soc. Pub. Adminstrn. (dir. 1969-71, 84-85), Data Processing Mgmt. Assn. (chpt. pres. 1968-69), Methods and Procedure Assn. (pres. 1969), Calif. Assn. County Data Processors (1st v.p. 1973-74), Air Force Res. Officers Assn. (chpt. v.p. 1971-74, 79-82), Air Force Calif. Dept. Res. Officers Assn. (jr. v.p. 1971). Home and Office: 5401 Valhalla Dr Carmichael CA 95608

FORSTER, WILLIAM OWEN, federal agency official, marine radioecologist; b. Dearborn, Mich., July 2, 1927; s. Clarence William and Florence Veda (Spencer) F.; m. Ruth Lynn Austin, Sept. 4, 1948; children: Vicki Lynn Forster Harris, Suki Mari Forster Mayami, Janis Kaye Forster Koch. BS, Mich. State Coll., 1951; MA, Mich. State U., 1953; PhD, U. Hawaii, 1966. Chem. oceanographer Oreg. State U., Corvallis, 1966-69; head marine biology P.R. Nuclear Ctr., Mayaguez, 1969-72; marine researcher ERDA, AEC, Germantown, Md., 1972-77; sr. environ. officer IAEA, Vienna, Austria, 1977-81; head marine research U.S. Dept. Energy, Germantown, 1981-85; head subseabed disposal U.S. Dept. Energy, Albuquerque, 1985—. Contbr. chpts. to books. Active Germantown Civic Assn., 1974-77; lay leader Covenant Meth. Ch., Gaithersburg, Md., 1981-84. Served as aviator USN, 1945-47. Named Expert in Marine Pollution, UN Food and Agriculture Orgn., 1976; recipient Nat. Geog. Soc. award, 1977. Mem. Am. Chem. Soc., Am. Soc. Limnology and Oceanography, Am. Geophys. Union., Sigma Xi. Avocations: golf, tennis, travel, automobiles. Office: DOE/ALU/WMTDD Box 5400 Albuquerque NM 87115

FORSYTH, JOSEPH, transportation executive; b. County Durham, Eng., Aug. 15, 1942; emigrated to Can., 1966; s. James Frederick and Maisie (Appleby) F.; m. Kay Frances Appleby, Oct. 3, 1964; children: Julian Alastair, Andrew Stuart. Asso. of Library Assn., Newcastle (Eng.) Sch. Librarianship, 1963; M.A. in Library Sci., U. London, 1976, Fellow of Library Assn., 1971. Library asst. Durham County Library, 1960-62; coll.

librarian Easington (Eng.) Tech. Coll., 1962-63; regional librarian North Riding County (Eng.) Library, 1964-66; reference librarian Calgary (Alta., Can.) Public Library, 1966-70; library devel. officer Govt. Alta., Edmonton, 1970-77; dir. library services Alta. Dept. Culture, Edmonton, 1977-86; regional supt. air navigation programming and adminstrn. Transport Can., 1986—. Author: Government Publications Relating to Alberta, 1972. Mem. Library Assn. Alta. Anglican. Home: 15211 83d Ave, Edmonton, AB Canada T5R 3T5 Office: 9th Floor Fed Bldg, 9820 107 St, Edmonton, AB Canada T5W 2Z5

FORSYTH, RAYMOND ARTHUR, civil engr.; b. Reno, Mar. 13, 1928; s. Harold Raymond and Fay Exona (Highfill) F.; B.S., Calif. State U., San Jose, 1952; M.C.E., Auburn U., 1958; m. Mary Ellen Wagner, July 9, 1950; children—Lynne, Gail, Alison, Ellen. Jr. engr., asst. engr. Calif. Div. Hwys., San Francisco, 1952-54; assoc. engr., sr. supervising, prin. engr. Calif. Dept. Transp., Sacramento, 1961-83, chief geotech. br., 1972-79, chief soil mechanics and pavement br., 1979-83, chief Transp. Lab., 1983—; cons., lectr. in field. Served with USAF, 1954-56. Fellow ASCE (pres. Sacramento sect., chmn. Calif. council 1980-81); mem. Transp. Research Bd. (chmn. embankments and earth slopes com. 1976-82, chmn. soil mechanics sect. 1982—), ASTM. Contbr. articles to profl. publs. Home: 5017 Pasadena Ave Sacramento CA 95841

FORT, TOMLINSON, JR., chemist, chemical engineering educator; b. Sumter, S.C., Apr. 16, 1932; s. Tomlinson and Madeline A. Kean (Scott) F.; m. Martha Kirby, Oct. 13, 1956; children: Tomlinson, III, Frances Clare. B.S. in Chemistry, U. Ga., 1952; M.S., U. Tenn., 1957, Ph.D. in Phys. Chemistry, 1957; A.E. and F.A.Q. Stephens postdoctoral fellow, U. Sydney, Australia, 1957-58; cert., Inst. Ednl. Mgmt., Harvard U., 1978. Instr. surface chemistry U. Sydney, 1957-58; research chemist, then sr. research chemist and project leader duPont Co., 1958-65; mem. faculty Case Western Res. U., 1965-73, prof. chem. engring., dir. surfaces research lab., 1971-73; prof. chem. engring. and chemistry, head dept. chem. engring. Carnegie-Mellon U., 1973-80, adj. prof., 1980-83; prof. chemistry and chem. engring., provost U. Mo., Rolla, 1980-82; v.p. acad. affairs Calif. Poly. State U., San Luis Obispo, 1982-83, provost, 1983—; summer vis. prof. Nat. U. Mex., 1973, U. Copenhagen, 1978, 80; pres. Frances Fort Brown Realty Co., Chattanooga, 1970—. Author papers on surface and colloid sci. Mem. Am. Chem. Soc., Am. Inst. Chemists, Catalysis Soc., Am. Soc. Engring. Edn., Mo. Acad. Sci., Am. Inst. Chem. Engrs., AAAS, N.Y. Acad. Sci., Sigma Xi, Gamma Sigma Epsilon, Alpha Chi Sigma, Sigma Chi. Home: 966 Vista del Collados San Luis Obispo CA 93401 Office: Calif Poly State U San Luis Obispo CA 93407

FORTH, KEVIN BERNARD, beverage distributing executive; b. Adams, Mass., Dec. 4, 1949; s. Michael Charles and Catherine Cecilia (McAndrews) F.; m. Alice Jane Farnum, Sept. 14, 1974; children: Melissa, Brian. AB, Holy Cross Coll., 1971; MBA, NYU, 1973. Div. rep. Anheuser-Busch, Inc., Boston, 1973-74, dist. sales mgr., Los Angeles, 1974-76, asst. to dir. mktg. staff, St. Louis, 1976-77; v.p. Straub Distbg. Co., Ltd., Orange, Calif., 1977-81, pres., 1981—, chmn., chief exec. officer, 1986—, also bd. dirs. Adv. bd. Rancho Santiago Community Coll. Dist. 1978-83; bd. dirs. Children's Hosp. of Orange County, 1980-84, Orange County Sports Hall of Fame, 1982—, Citizens for Am.; exec. com., bd. dirs. Nat. Council on Alcoholism, 1980-84; pres. Titan Athletic Found., 1984, Olympia Brewing Co. Wholesaler Forum; v.p. Freedom Bowl Found. of Calif. State U. at Fullerton, 1984-85, pres., 1986—, chmn., 1987—; bd. dirs. Citizens for Am. Com., 1986-87; mem. Rep. Silver Circle. Benjamin Levy fellow, 1971-73. Mem. Nat. Beer Wholesalers Assn. (bd. dirs.), Calif. Beer Wholesalers Assn. (bd. dirs., exec. com., pres. 1985), Industry Environ. Council, Holy Cross Alumni Assn., Nat. Assn. Stock Car Auto Racing, Beta Gamma Sigma. Roman Catholic. Club: Lincoln. Home: 4333 Mahagony Circle Yorba Linda CA 92686 Office: Straub Distbg Co Ltd 410 W Grove Ave Orange CA 92667

FORTHMANN, ANDREW KEATING, lawyer; b. Los Angeles, Aug. 27, 1910; s. John A. and Elvira (Keating) F.; A.B., U. So. Calif., 1933, M.A., 1934, LL.B., 1939; m. Gertrude Ingli, Apr. 26, 1947; children—Andrea Marie, Andrew Keating, Christopher, DruAnne, Angele. Admitted to Calif. bar, 1946; with firm Dockweiler & Dockweiler, Los Angeles, 1946; with Los Angeles Soap Co., 1942, chmn. bd., 1956, also dir.; with White King Soap Co., Los Angeles, 1947, pres., 1955, also dir.; pres., dir. Calif. Rendering Co., 1947-62, chmn. bd., 1962-66; v.p., sec. Forthmann Estate Co., 1950-74, pres., 1974. Served from 1st lt. to capt. USAAF, 1942-46. Decorated knight comdr. Equestrian Order of Holy Sepulchre of Jerusalem. Mem. Am., Calif., Los Angeles bar assns., Soap and Detergent Assn. (v.p. Western div. 1954-58, 61-65, nat. pres. 1958-61), So. Calif. Wine and Food Soc. Clubs: Los Angeles Country, California (Los Angeles), Chevaliers du Tastevin. Office: PO Box 2198 TA Los Angeles CA 90051

FORTMANN, STEPHEN PAUL, medical educator, researcher, epidemiologist; b. Burbank, Calif., Oct. 13, 1948; s. Daniel John and Mary (Van Halteren) F.; m. Lindy Barocchi, Mar. 11, 1984; children: Nicolas, Michele. AB, Stanford U., 1970; MD, U. Calif., San Francisco, 1974. Diplomate Am. Bd. Internal Medicine, Am. Coll. Epidemiology. Clin. instr. Stanford (Calif.) U. Sch. Medicine, 1979-83, asst. prof., 1983—; advisor World Health Orgn., Geneva, 1980-86. Contbr. articles to profl. jours. Fellow Am. Heart Assn. (council on epidemiology), ACP; mem. Am. Coll. Epidemiology. Avocations: photography, running. Office: Stanford U Sch Medicine 1000 Welch Rd Stanford CA 94305

FORTNER, ROBERT WILLIAM, medical facility administrator; b. Leavenworth, Wash., Nov. 9, 1939; s. Elmer L. and Marjorie C. (Holland) F.; m. Vicky Allison, 1963 (div. 1973); children: Allison N., Robert W. Jr.; m. Nancy J. Gibbs., Nov. 5, 1977: 1 child, Meredith H. BA in Zoology, U. Wash., 1962, MD, 1967. Diplomate Am. Bd. Internal Medicine, Am. Bd. Nephrology. Intern. U. So. Calif. Med. Ctr., Los Angeles, 1967-68; resident in internal medicine Walter Reed Gen. Hosp., Washington, 1968-69; chief, nephrology service William Beaumont Army Med. Ctr., El Paso, Tex., 1971-73; cons. nephrology Hotel Dieu Hosp., El Paso, Tex., 1972-73; clin. assoc. in medicine U. N.Mex. Sch. Medicine, Albuquerque, 1974; dir. artificial kidney unit El Camino Hosp., Mountain View, Calif., 1974—, med. staff, 1974—; clin. instr. in medicine Stanford (Calif.) U. Med. Ctr., 1974-77; med. staff Santa Clara County Med. Ctr., San Jose, Calif., 1974-83; instr. Foothil Community Coll., Los Altos Hills, Calif., 1975-80. Contbr. articles to profl. jours. Pres. Kings Mountain Assn., Woodside, Calif., 1984. Served to maj. USMC, 1968-73. Mem. Soc. Nephrology, Am. Soc. Artificial Internal Organs, Internat. Soc. Nephrology, Calif. Dialysis Council (pres. 1984-85), Renal Physicians Assn., Nat. Dialysis Assn. (founding mem.). Office: El Camino Dialysis Services 2500 Grant Rd, PO Box 7025 Mountain View CA 94039-7025

FORTUNE, JAMES MICHAEL, stock brokerage house executive; b. Providence, Sept. 6, 1947; s. Thomas Henry and Olive Elizabeth (Duby) F.; m. G. Suzanne Hein, July 14, 1973. Student, Pikes Peak Community Coll., 1983. Owner Fortune Fin. Services, Colorado Springs, Colo., 1975-79; ptnr. Robert James and Assocs., Colorado Springs, 1979-81; pres. Fortune & Co., Colorado Springs, 1981—; bd. dirs. Colorado Springs Computer Systems, 1985—, Perfect Printer Inc., Colorado Springs, 1986—, Am. Discount Securities, Inc., 1987—; radio talk show host Sta. KRCC; fin. commentator Wall Street Report Sta. KKHT, 1983-84. Editor Fortune newsletter, 1981-85, The Can. Market News, 1981-83; editor, pub. Penny Fortune newsletter, 1981—, The Low Priced Investment newsletter, 1986—, Women's Investment Newsletter, 1987—; contbr. articles to profl. jours. Cons. Jr. Achievement bus. project, Colorado Springs, 1985. Served as sgt. U.S. Army, 1968-70, Vietnam. Mem. Internat. Assn. Fin. Planners (pres. 1977-78), Newsletter Assn., Nat. Assn. Securities Dealers Inc., Securities Investor Protection Corp. Lodge: Elks. Avocations: skiing, hiking, backpacking. Home: 3465 Hickory Hill Dr Colorado Springs CO 80906 Office: Fortune & Co PO Box 2B Colorado Springs CO 80901-0670

FORWARD, ROBERT L(ULL), physicist, consultant; b. Geneva, N.Y., Aug. 15, 1932; s. Robert Torrey and Mildred (Lull) F.; m. Martha Neil Dodson, Aug. 29, 1954; children—Robert Dodson, Mary Lois, Julie Elizabeth, Eve Laurel. BS in Physics, U. Md., 1954, PhD, 1965; MS in Applied Physics, UCLA, 1958. With Hughes Aircraft Co., 1956—, assoc. mgr. theoretical studies dept., 1966-67, mgr. exploratory studies dept., 1967-74; sr. scientist Hughes Aircraft Co., Malibu, Calif., 1974—; popular sci. writer and lectr. Author, science fiction: Dragon's Egg, 1981; The Flight of the Dragonfly, 1983; Starquake, 1985; contbr. articles to profl. jours. Builder 1st gravitational radiation antenna; patentee in field. Served to capt. USAF, 1954-56. Hughes Masters and Doctoral fellow, 1956-62. Fellow AIAA (assoc.), Brit. Interplanetary Soc.; mem. Am. Phys. Soc., IEEE (sr. mem), Am. Astron. Soc. (sr.), Sci. Fiction Writers of Am., Sigma Xi, Sigma Pi Sigma. Home: PO Box 2783 Malibu CA 90265-7783 Office: Hughes Research Labs 3011 Malibu Canyon Rd Malibu CA 90265

FOSHA, GEORGE MALCOLM, civil engineer, water resources consultant; b. Colorado Springs, Colo., Feb. 16, 1951; s. Henry Kenneth and Margaret Ann (Gammon) F. BSCE, U. Denver, 1973. Registered profl. engr., Colo., N. Mex. Jr. engr. W.W. Wheeler & Assocs. Inc., Englewood, Colo., 1973-75, assoc. engr., 1976-78, proj. engr., 1978-85, v.p., sr. project engr., 1986—; water resources cons. AMAX Inc., Golden, Colo., 1974-85, Colo.-Ute Electric Assn., Montrose, 1976-82, Denver Water Dept., 1982-86, Gov. Lamm's Met. Water Roundtable, Denver, 1983-84. Mem. ASCE, Am. Cons. Engrs. Council, Nat. Fedn. Ind. Businessmen, Tau Beta Pi. Republican. Methodist. Home: 2620 S Ivy St Denver CO 80222 Office: WW Wheeler & Assocs Inc 3700 S Inca Englewood CO 80110

FOSS, FRANK WILLIAM, electronics design engineer; b. St. Louis, Oct. 4, 1947; s. Frank William Foss Jr. and Betty Lee (Ammon) Elliot; m. Helga Karoline Mayer, May 15, 1968(div. Oct. 1973); m. Nancy Elaine Marshall, June 2, 1979; children: Frank William IV, Bridget Lee. BSEE, Jackson State U., 1985. Prodn. engr. Electronic Processors, Englewood, Colo., 1973-76; v.p. engring. Solar Electric, Westminster, Colo., 1978-79; pres. Foss Engring., Englewood, 1979-; test design engr. Ampex, Wheatridge, Colo., 1981-83; systems engr. Custom Engring., Englewood, 1983-; v.p. engring. Electronic Solutions, Lakewood, Colo., 1985-; ptnr. Solar Techs., Englewood, 1985. Contrb. articles to profl. jours.; inventor line operated switcher supply (design award 1981), 5W CW krypton laser, room temperature heat camera, computer axis tracker for solar collectors, low cost tracking solar collector. served as sgt. USAF, 1965-69. Dept. Energy and Clearance grantee, Sandia, N.Mex., 1983. Avocations: camping, hiking. Home: 2928 S Clarkson Englewood CO 80110 Office: Custom Engring 2640 S Raritan Ctr Englewood CO 80110

FOSS, THEODORE NICHOLAS, historian; b. Juneau, Alaska, Nov. 25, 1950; s. Harold Byron and Helen Johansen (Hunsbedt) F. BA, Pomona Coll., Claremont, Calif., 1972; MA, U. Chgo., 1974, PhD, 1979. Research asst. U. Chgo., 1973-78; instr. Loyola U., Chgo., 1978-79; research historian Archdiocese of Chgo., 1980-81, planning cons. Office fo Cath. Edn., 1982; asst. prof. U. Ill., Chgo., 1982-83; research assoc. China Jesuit History Project, Los Gatos, Calif., 1983-84; assoc. dir. Inst. Chinese-Western Cultural History U. San Francisco, 1984—. Contbr. articles to profl. jours. Mem. Assn. Asian Studies, Am. Hist. Assn., Am. Cath. Hist. Assn., Am. Soc. Eighteenth Century Studies, Soc. for the History of Discoveries, Soc. for Ch'ing Studies. Club: Univ. Club of Chgo. Office: U San Francisco 2130 Fulton St San Francisco CA 94117

FOSSELIUS, GEORGE ANDERS, chemistry educator; b. San Francisco, May 18, 1942; s. Carl Einar and Florence (Talbot) F.; m. Cynthia Ruth Lane, June 20, 1964; children: Kristin, Eric, Peter. BS in Chemistry, U. Calif., Berkeley, 1964. cert. secondary tchr., Calif. Chemist Shell Devel., Emeryville, Calif., 1964-69; tchr. Albany (Calif.) Schs., 1970—; chmn. Mentor Tchr. Com., Albany, 1984—. Mus. dir. North East Bay Choir Festival, Albany-El Cerrito, Calif., 1976-86; leader Boy Scouts Am., Contra Costa County, Calif. 1978—; mem. policy bd. dirs. Tchr. Edn. and Computer Ctr., Alameda County, Calif., 1986—, chmn. 1987—. Recipient Dist Award of Merit, Boy Scouts Am., 1981, Hon. Service award Calif. Congress of Parents, Tchrs and Stu., 1983, 85; fellow Industry Initiatives for Sci. and Math. Edn., 1986. Mem. Albany Tchrs. Assn. (pres. 1978-80), Am. Chem. Soc., Calif. Sci. Tchrs. Assn., Computer Using Educators, Alpha Chi Sigma (trustee 1966—, appreciation award 1980), Sierra Club. Democrat. Lutheran. Avocations: backpacking, trail repair, cross-country skiing, folk singing. Home: 1232 Everett El Cerrito CA 94530 Office: Albany High School 603 Key Rt Blvd Albany CA 94706-1498

FOSSUM, KENT CARLTON, insurance agent; b. Hollywood, Calif., Sept. 30, 1946; s. Alvin Einar and Berniece (Manor) F.; m. Lana Jean Dollar, Apr. 6, 1968; children: Kevin Christopher, Nolan Neil. AA, Mt. San Antonio Coll., 1967; BS, Calif. Poly. State U., Pomona, 1969. Premium fin. mgr., sales rep., comml. and personal lines underwriter Am. Res. Ins. Co., Los Angeles, 1969-78; from mktg. rep. to br. mktg. mgr. Safeco Ins. Co., Fountain Valley, Calif., 1978-85; property and casual inst. agt. Armstrong-Robitaille Ins. Services, Inc., Orange, Calif., 1985—; pres., treas. Ins. Field Assn. Orange County, Calif., 1980-81. Com. chmn. Cub Scouts Am., Huntington Beach, Calif., 1980-85; troop leader Boy Scouts Am., Huntington Beach, 1982-83; team mgr. Ocean View Nat. Little League, Huntington Beach, 1984; choir mem. Redeemer Luth. Ch., Huntington Beach, 1984—. Mem. CPCU Soc. (cert.), Collector's Club. Democrat. Avocations: collecting olympic pins and memorabilia, swimming, fishing, tennis, golf. Home: 17172 Friml Ln Huntington Beach CA 92649 Office: Armstrong-Robitaille Ins Service Inc 2211 W Orangewood Ave Orange CA 92668

FOSTER, ALLEN VAUGHN, biotechnology company executive; b. Stockton, Calif., Sept. 25, 1953; s. Albert Vaughn and Mona (Lund) F. BS in Biology, U. Calif., Davis, 1975. Researcher Research Inst. Scripps Clinic, La Jolla, Calif., 1979-82; purchasing mgr. Med. Biology Inst., La Jolla, 1982—; purchasing materials mgr. Quidel, La Jolla, 1982—. Office: Quidel 11077 N Torrey Pines Rd La Jolla CA 92037

FOSTER, CHARLES THOMAS, elementary educator; b. Fremont, Ohio, Apr. 17, 1921; s. Charles Lincoln and Lucy Elizabeth (Rooney) F.; m. Evelyn May Foster, Jan. 1, 1942; children—Charles Thomas, Stephanie. B.G.E., U. Nebr., 1964; M.A., Chapman Coll., 1974. Cert. elem., secondary, and coll. tchr., Calif. Asst. to sales mgr. Henkel Clauss Co., Fremont, Ohio, 1945-50; commd. U.S. Air Force, 1950, advanced through grades to lt. col., 1964, ret., 1967; tchr. Los Padres Elem. Sch., Lompoc, Calif., 1968-85. Mem. exec. bd. PTA, 1974-75; mem. site com. Calif. Sch. Improvement Program, 1974-75; mem. instructional evaluation panel Curriculum Devel. & Supplemental Materials Commn. of Calif. State Bd. Edn., 1978-79. Served to capt., U.S. Army, 1942-45. Decorated Bronze Star, Army Commendation medal, Air Force Commendation medal with two oak leaf clusters; Recipient Hon. Service award PTA. Mem. Air Force Assn., Ret. Officers Assn. (scholarship com. 1979-83), PTA. Republican. Lutheran. Clubs: Officers, Thousand Trails, Elks. Home: 2155 Fallen Leaf Dr Santa Maria CA 93455

FOSTER, DUDLEY EDWARDS, JR., musician, educator; b. Orange, N.J., Oct. 5, 1935; s. Dudley Edwards and Margaret (DePoy) F.; student Occidental Coll., 1953-56; A.B., UCLA, 1957, M.A., 1958; postgrad. U. So. Calif., 1961-73. Lectr. music Immaculate Heart Coll., Los Angeles, 1960-63; dir. music Holy Faith Episcopal Ch., Inglewood, Calif., 1964-67; lectr. music Calif. State U., Los Angeles, 1968-71; assoc. prof. music Los Angeles Mission Coll., 1975-83, prof., 1983—, also chmn. dept. music, 1977—; dir. music First Lutheran Ch., Los Angeles, 1968-72; organist, pianist, harpsichordist; numerous recitals; composer O Sacrum Convivium for Trumpet and Organ, 1973, Passacaglia for Brass Instruments, 1969, Introduction, Arioso & Fugue for Cello and Piano, 1974. Fellow Trinity Coll. Music, London, 1960. Mem. Am. Guild Organists, Am. Musicol. Soc., Town Hall Calif., Los Angeles Coll. Tchrs. Assn. (pres. Mission Coll. chpt. 1976-77, v.p., exec. com. 1982—), Mediaeval Acad. Am. Republican. Anglican. Office: Los Angeles Mission Coll Dept Music 1212 San Fernando Dr San Fernando CA 91340

FOSTER, EDWARD E., educational adminisrator; b. West New York, N.J., Nov. 19, 1939; s. John Conroy and Helen (Fischbach) F.; m. Jan Kennedy, June 4, 1956; children: John Conroy, James Kennedy. A.B., St. Peter's Coll., 1961; Ph.D., U. Rochester, 1965. Prof. English Grinnell Coll., Iowa, 1964-73; dean arts and sci. U. San Diego, 1973-76; chmn. humanities dept. St. Mary's Coll. of Md., St. Mary's City, 1976-79; dean faculty Whitman Coll., Walla Walla, Wash., 1979—; commr. Northwest Assn. Schs. and Colls., Seattle, 1982—. Author: Modern Lexicon of Literary Terms, 1968; contbr. articles on English lit. to profl. jours. Vice pres. Walla Walla Symphony Bd., 1982-84; trustee Wash. Commn. for the Humanities, 1985—. Mem. MLA, Medieval Acad. Am., Am. Assn. Colls., Am. Conf. Acad. Deans. Home: 220 Newell St Walla Walla WA 99362 Office: Whitman Coll Office of the Dean Walla Walla WA 99362

FOSTER, FRANCES SMITH, English educator; b. Dayton, Ohio, Feb. 8, 1944; m. Warren Reed; children: Krishna, Warren. BS, Miami U., Oxford, Ohio, 1964; MA, U. So. Calif., 1971; PhD, U. Calif., San Diego, 1976. Tchr. Western Hills High Sch., Cin., 1964-66, Cass Tech. High Sch., Detroit, 1966-68; lectr. Calif. State U., Northridge, 1970-71; prof. English San Diego State U., 1971—, asst. dean, 1976-79. Author: Witnessing Slavery, 1979; mng. editor Pacific Coast Philology, 1981-84; contbr. articles to profl. jours. Mem. La Mesa (Calif.) Spring Valley GATE Com, 1984-85, La Mesa Counicl United Ch. of Christ, 1985—, KPBS Humanities Adv. Bd., 1976-82. NEH research grantee, 1980. Mem. MLA (assembly del. 1980-83, exec. bd. ethnic div. 1983—), Danforth Assocs., Coll. Lang. Assn., Children's Lit. Assn., East County Performing Arts Ctr., Jack and Jills of Am., Phi Beta Kappa, Phi Kappa Phi, Alpha Kappa Alpha. Office: San Diego State U Dept English San Diego CA 92182-0295

FOSTER, HELEN LAURA, geologist; b. Adrian, Mich., Dec. 15, 1919; d. Stanley Allen and Alice Mary (Osborn) F. BS, U. Mich., 1941, MS, 1943, PhD, 1946. Registered profl. geologist, Calif. Tchr. Blissfield (Mich.) High Sch., 1941-42; instr. geology Wellesley (Mass.) Coll., 1946-48; instr. field geology U. Mich. Field Camp, Jackson, Wyo., 1947; geologist U.S. Geol. Survey, Tokyo, 1948-55, Ishigaki-shima, Tokyo (Japan) and Washington, 1955-65, Menlo Park (Calif.) and Alaska, 1965—. Contbr. articles to profl. jours. Recipient Outstanding Achievement award U. Mich., 1976, Meritorious Service award U.S. Dept. Interior, 1984. Fellow AAAS, Geol. Soc. Am. (various com. memberships); mem. Am. Geophys. Union, Am. Assn. Petroleum Geologists, Penisula Geol. Soc. (v.p. 1977-78), U. Mich. Alumni Assn. (corr. sec.), Eagle Hist. Soc. Club: Potomac Appalachian Trail (Washington). Avocations: stamp collecting, hiking, skiing, traveling, music. Home: 270 O'Keefe St Apt. H Palo Alto CA 94303 Office: US Geol Survey 345 Middlefield Rd Menlo Park CA 94025

FOSTER, JERRY ROBERT, transportation educator; b. Wichita, Kans., Feb. 2, 1942; s. Leo Mark and Lydia Rose (Federer) F.; m. Karen L. Kelly, Dec. 27, 1964; children: Damon, Kellie. BA, U. Wyo., 1968; M in Pub. Adminstrn., U. Colo., 1969; PhD, Syracuse U., 1973. Transp. analyst Atchison, Topeka & Santa Fe R.R., Houston, 1969-70; from asst. prof. to assoc. prof. transp. U. Colo., Boulder, 1973—, assoc. dean, 1978-85; assoc. dir. Colo. Grad. Sch. Bank, Boulder, 1979—; cons. Burlington North R.R., Ft. Worth, 1985, Anheuser-Busch, St. Louis, 1982-83, Tiger Internat. Air, Los Angeles, 1982, Tex. Internat. Air, Houston, 1979. Author: Small Business Administration, 1981. Chmn. transp. com. Colo. Outlook Forum, Denver, 1980-84; mem. edn. adv. com. E. Griffith, Denver, 1981—; examiner Dept. Regulatory Agys., Denver, 1983; dir. transp. council Boulder C. of C., 1976-84. Served with U.S. Army, 1961-63. Recipient C. of C. Service award Boulder, 1977. Mem. Nat. Def. Transp. Assn. (editorial rev. com.), Am. Soc. Transp. and Logistics (examiner, 1981—), Council of Logistics Mgmt., Colo. Dist. Export Council, Delta Nu Alpha (transp. leadership award 1983, nat. edn. com. 1979-81). Republican. Avocations: golf, skiing, tennis. Office: Univ Colo Coll Bus Adminstrn Office of the Assoc Dean Boulder CO 80309

FOSTER, MARY FRAZER (LECRON), anthropologist; b. Des Moines, Feb. 1, 1914; d. James and Helen (Cowles) LeCron; B.A., Northwestern U., 1936; Ph.D., U. Calif., Berkeley, 1965; m. George McClelland Foster, Jan. 6, 1938; children—Jeremy, Melissa Foster Bowerman. Research asso. dept. anthropology U. Calif., Berkeley, 1955-57, 75—; lectr. in anthropology Calif. State U., Hayward, 1966-75; mem. faculty Fromm Inst. Lifelong Learning, U. San Francisco, 1980. Fellow Am. Anthropol. Assn.; mem. Linguistic Soc. Am., Internat. Linguistic Assn., Southwestern Anthrop. Assn., AAAS, Soc. Woman Geographers. Democrat. Author: (with George M. Foster) Sierra Popoluca Speech, 1948; The Tarascan Language, 1969; editor: (with Stanley H. Brandes) Symbol As Sense: New Approaches to the Analysis of Meaning, 1980, (with Robert A. Rubinstein) Peace and War=Cross-Cultural Perspectives, 1986. Home: 790 San Luis Rd Berkeley CA 94707

FOSTER, MICHAEL WILLIAM, librarian; b. Astoria, Oreg., June 29, 1940; s. William Michael and Margaret Vivian (Carlson) F. BA in History, Willamette U., 1962; MA, U. Oreg., 1965; postgrad., So. Oreg. Coll., 1976. Tchr. Astoria High Sch., 1963-66, librarian, 1970—; tchr. Am. Internat. Sch. of Kabul (Afghanistan), 1966-70; bd. dirs. Astoria High Sch. Scholarships, Inc., 1976—. Commr. Oreg. Arts Commn., Salem, 1983—; bd. dirs. Am. Cancer Soc., Clatsop County, Oreg., 1980—; bd. dirs., treas. Astoria Community Concert Assn., 1964—. Mem. NEA, Oreg. Edn. Assn., Oreg. Edn. Media Assn., Clatsop County Hist. Soc. (pres. 1983—, bd. dirs.), Ft. Clatsop Hist. Assn. (treas. 1974—, bd. dirs.), Ed and Eda Ross Scholarship Trust (bd. dirs. 1980—), Astoria C. of C. (bd. dirs. 1982—, George award 1985, pres. 1987), Beta Theta Pi. Republican. Roman Catholic. Lodge: Rotary (pres. Astoria club 1986—). Avocations: antique dealer, art collector, oil painter, golf, tennis. Home: 1636 Irving Ave Astoria OR 97103 Office: Astoria High Sch Library 1001 W Marine Dr Astoria OR 97103

FOSTER, PAUL JOSEPH, architect, urban designer; b. Denver, Oct. 1, 1941; s. Bernard Edmund and Lucille (Brush) F.; m. Marilyn Ann Marranzino, Jan. 8, 1966; 1 child, Tania Sheilagh. BArch, Cath. U., 1964; MArch, U. Calif., Berkeley, 1967. Registered architect, Colo., Wyo. Asst. project dir. New Town Study U. Colo., Denver, 1967-68; dir., prin. T.H.K. Assn., Denver, 1968-72; pres. Morgan & Foster, Denver, 1972-76; pvt. practice architecture, owner Paul J. Foster Assocs., Denver, 1976—; assoc. prof. architecture U. Colo., Denver, 1986—. Vice chmn. Denver Landmark Preservation Commn., 1984-85, chmn. rev. com. 1984-85, chmn. 1985-86; chmn. Speer Blvd. Task Force, 1986-87; trustee Denver Urban Forest Project, 1985. Recipient Honor award Coll. Design and Planning, U. Colo., 1984, Honor award from Hist. Denver, 1986. Mem. AIA (chmn. Urban Design Commn., 1984, Denver chpt. AIA (treas. 1983, v.p. 1984, bd. dirs. 1985—, Leadership and Disting. Service award 1983,86, named Outstanding Member 1984), Colo. Soc. Architects, Denver Urban Design Forum, Inst. for Urban Design. Republican. Roman Catholic. Avocations: photography, golf, Denver history. Home: 657 Lafayette St Denver CO 80218 Office: Paul J Foster Assocs 1730 Blake St Suite 301 Denver CO 80202

FOSTER, ROBERT JOE, biochemist; b. Glendale, Calif., June 6, 1924; s. Joel Pierce and Lorena (Garner) F.; m. Helen Dorothy Hemestray, July 7, 1951; children: Robin Ann, Robert Louis. BS, Calif. Inst. Tech., 1948, PhD in Chemistry, 1952. Biochemist Wash. State U., Pullman, 1955—. Contbr. articles to profl. jours. Served to 1st lt. USAAF, 1943-46. European Molecular Biology Orgn. fellow, 1970-71. Mem. AAAS, Am. Soc. Biol. Chemists, Sigma Xi. Democrat. Avocations: skiing, personal computer.

FOSTER, ROBERT LEE, retired aerospace company executive, realtor; b. Murphysboro, Ill., Feb. 7, 1922; s. Moses Franklin and Ethel Gladys (Hendrickson) F.; m. Antoinette Tomlin Hayne, June 12, 1950 (div. 1981); children—Robert Lee, Jr., Sarah Amanda, William Ashley. Student, Tulane U., 1939-40; student Washington U., St. Louis, 1940; B.S. in Elec. Engring., Ga. Inst. Tech., 1952. With McDonnell Aircraft Co., St. Louis, 1953, sr. engr., F101 Fighter Airplane, 1953-57; group engr. advanced design, Project Mercury, Cape Kennedy, Fla., 1958-59, sr. group engr., 1959-60, engring. mgr., 1960-65, ops. mgr. Project Gemini, 1965-67; base mgr. McDonnell Astronautics Co., Vandenberg AFB, Calif., 1967-68; dep. dir. McDonnell Douglas Thor-Delta project, Vandenberg Test Center, 1968, dir. test center, 1969-74, guidance systems mgr., Huntington Beach, Calif., 1975-79. Served with U.S. Army, 1942-43, to capt., 1943-50, to maj., NG, 1950-59. Decorated Am. Campaign medal, European African Middle Eastern Campaign medal with two battle stars, WW II Victory medal. Mem. Nat. Mgmt. Assn., Phi Kappa Phi. Republican. Presbyterian. Club: Rotary of Santa Ynez Valley (Solvang, Calif.) Home: 2831 Quail Valley Rd Solvang CA 93463 Office: 435 1st St Suite 23 Solvang CA 93463

FOSTER, RODNEY PATRICK, personnel executive; b. San Antonio, Apr. 30, 1951; s. Cecil Glenn and Margaret Mary (Frazar) F.; m. Lynell Porritt, June 6, 1974; children—Alisa, Paul, Melinda, Emily. B.A. cum laude, Brigham Young U., 1974. Missionary to Norway, 1970-72; adminstrv. asst. First Presidency's Office, Mormon Ch., Salt Lake City, 1974-80, mgr. tng.

and pre-dedication services, Temple Dept., 1980—. Mem. Mormon Youth Symphony and Chorus, 1978-81. Mem. Am. Soc. Tng. and Devel. Republican. Office: 50 E North Temple Salt Lake City UT 84150

FOSTER, STEPHEN GLEN, nuclear engineering educator; b. Memphis, Feb. 12, 1952; s. Laurence Brock and Bertie Mae (Hale) F.; m. Sally Irene Snode, May 9, 1970 (div. Apr. 1981); children: Sarah Irene, Stephen Brock. Assoc. in Nuclear Engring., Saddleback Community Coll., 1984. Enlisted USN, 1969, advanced through grades to interior communications chief electrician, 1979, resigned, 1978; freelance constrn. worker various locations, Calif., 1979-81; maintenance planner So. Calif. Edison Co., Rosemead, 1981-83; instr. nuclear engring. dept. So. Calif. Edison, San Clemente, Calif., 1983—; peer evaluator Inst. Nuclear Power Ops., Atlanta, 1986—. Mem. Rep. Nat. Com., Washington, 1978; com. chmn. Boy Scouts Am., San Juan Capistrano, Calif., 1985. Mem. Am. Nuclear Soc., VFW. Avocations: photography, cooking, travel. Home: 29333 Edgewood Rd San Juan Capistrano CA 92675 Office: So Calif Edison PO Box 128 San Clemente CA 92672

FOSTER, THEODORE DEAN, oceanographer, physicist; b. Plainfield, N.J., July 25, 1929; s. Ronald Martin and Annabel (Conover) F. ScB, Brown U., 1952; MS, U. Colo., 1958, MA, 1960; PhD, U. Calif., San Diego, 1965. Physicist Reaction Motors Inc., Denville, N.J., 1952-55; instr. U. Colo., Boulder, 1955-60; physicist Scripps Inst. Oceanography, La Jolla, Calif., 1960-65, oceanographer, 1969-77; asst. prof. Yale U., New Haven, 1965-69; prof. marine scis. U. Calif., Santa Cruz, 1977—, dean natural scis., 1979-80; chief scientist U.S. Antarctic Research Program, Antarctica, 1973, 75, 76, 78, 80, 81, 85; comdg. officer USNR Research Program, Pasadena, Calif., 1982-84. Contbr. articles to profl. jours. Served as midshipman USN, 1948-50, capt. Res. 1953—. Recipient Antarctic Service medal NSF, 1973. Mem. Am. Phys. Soc., Am. Geophys. Union, Philosophy Sci. Assn., Arctic Inst. N.Am., Internat. Glaciol. Soc., Am. Meteorol. Soc., Sigma Xi. Avocations: swimming, hiking, skiing. Office: U Calif 273 Applied Scis Santa Cruz CA 95064

FOSTER, WANELL BAIZE, oncology social worker; b. Hartford, Ky., May 7, 1928; d. Charles Ellis and Viola (Simpson) Baize; children: Charles Keaton, Don Franklin, Susan Kay. AA, U. Ky., 1975; MS in Social Work, U. Louisville, 1977. Tchr. Jefferson County Pub. Schs., Louisville, 1978-79; social worker Dept. Human Services, Louisville, 1979-80, VA Med. Ctr., Long Beach, Calif., 1980—; adj. prof. Calif. State U., Long Beach, 1986—; cons. at large, 1981—. Author: Health & Social Work Jour., 1981. Named to Hon. Order of Ky. Cols. Mem. Nat. Assn. Social Workers, Nat. Assn. Oncology Social Workers. Avocations: world travel, music, reading, sponsoring families from foreign countries. Home: PO Box 90031 Long Beach CA 90809 Office: VA Med Ctr 5901 E 7th St Long Beach CA 90822

FOTINE, P. NICHOLAS, II, freelance editor, writer; b. Phila., Aug. 9, 1941; s. Lawrence Constantine and Dorothy Barber (Owens) Fotinakis; 1 child. BA in Journalism, Calif. State U., Northridge, 1973; M Pub. Adminstrn., U. So. Calif., 1978; postgrad. in geography, Calif. State U., Northridge. Copy editor Los Angeles Times, 1968-75; systems officer Seattle-First Nat. Bank, 1975-76; sr. systems analyst Kaiser Found. Health Plan, Los Angeles, 1976-78; methods & forms mgr. Sears Savings Bank, Glendale, Calif., 1978-82; documentation specialist Cedars-Sinai Med. Ctr., Beverly Hills, Calif., 1982-83; prodn. editor Glencoe Press, Encino, Calif., 1983; tech. writer Flying Tiger Line, Los Angeles, 1984; sr. editor Poly Tone Press, Sepulveda, Calif., 1984-85; prodn. editor Matrix Publs., Lawndale, Calif., 1986-87, Times-Mirror Press, Los Angeles, 1987. Editor: Contemporary Musician's Handbook and Dictionary, 1984; contbg. editor Jour. Forms Mgmt., 1976-78; freelance editor high sch. and coll. textbooks. Res. officer Glendale (Calif.) Police Dept., 1981—; non-partisan candidate in gen. election for corp. governing bd. Health Systems Agy. for Los Angeles County, 1977. Served with USNR, 1969-71, 79-81, 84-86. Mem. Bus. Forms Mgmt. Assn. (chpt. pres. 1980-81, editor FormuLA chpt. newsletter 1977-79, chpt. v.p. 1979-80, lectr. Pacific N.W. chpt. 1975, Grand prize 1978, Los Angeles chpt. mem. yr. 1979-80), Soc. Colonial Wars, SAR (life), Police Marksman Assn., Naval Enlisted Res. Assn., Calif. State U. Northridge Alumni Assn. (charter life, journalism alumni), Sierra Club, Sigma Delta Chi. Home: 16027 Sunburst St Sepulveda CA 91343-3024

FOTINOS, KATHERINE, educator; b. San Francisco, Apr. 12, 1926; d. Christ Anastasios and Ageliki George (Pilarinos) F. B.A., San Francisco State Coll., 1948; M A., Stanford U., 1955. Life diploma tchr. Calif. Tchr. Excelsior Sch., San Francisco, 1948-53, Ridgepoint III, San Francisco, 1953-54, Jedediah Smith Sch., San Francisco, 1954-55; head tchr. Washington Irving Sch., San Francisco, 1955-60, Jean Parker Sch., San Francisco, 1960—; curriculum designer 1951—; cons. Calif. Geog. Alliance. Co-author: Curriculum Guide for Language Arts, Curriculum Guide for Music, Curriculum Guide for Social Studies and Science (all for grades K-6 in San Francisco Unified Sch. Dist.). Designer Deaf Scrabball, 1981. Vol. Assn. for Deaf and Blind, 1980—; docent Calif. Hist. Soc., Sonoma; festival decoration chmn. Greek Orthodox Ch., Solono County 1982; vol. Sonoma Rep. Com., 1982; U.S. senatorial candidate campaign chmn. Sonoma County. Mem. AAUW, Calif. PTA (hon. life), Calif. Tchrs. Assn., Stanford Edn. Club (sec. 1972-74), Sonoma Valley Chorale, Sonoma County Ballet Guild, Am. Chorale Dirs. Assn., Sonoma Valley Rep. Women (charter mem.), Nat. Fedn. Rep. Women (fed. regent), Alpha Delta Kappa (life; pres. 1962-64). Lodge: Daus. Penelope (v.p. 1974-76). Avocations: travel, archaeology, dance, art, gardening. Home: 150 El Portola Dr Sonoma CA 95476

FOTSCH, DAN ROBERT, physical education educator; b. St. Louis, May 17, 1947; s. Robert Jarrel and Margaret Louise (Zimmermann) F.; m. Jacquelyn Sue Rotter, June 12, 1971; children: Kyla Michelle, Jeffrey Scott, Michael David. BS in Edn. cum laude, U. Mo., 1970; MS in Edn., Colo. State U., 1973. Cert. tchr. Tchr. phys. edn., coach North Callaway Schs., Auxvasse, Mo., 1970-71; grad. teaching asst., asst. track coach Colo. State U., Ft. Collins, 1971-73; tchr. elem. phys. edn., coach Poudre R-1 Sch. Dist., Ft. Collins, 1973-85; co-dir. Colo. State U. Handicapped Clinic, Ft. Collins, 1973-87; dir. Moore Elem. Lab. Sch., Ft. Collins, 1979—, Colo. State U. Super Day Camp, 1979—. Contbr. articles to profl. jours. State dir. Jump Rope for Heart Project, Denver, 1981. Recipient Scott Key Acad. award, Sigma Phi Epsilon, 1969, Honor Alumni award, Coll. of Profl. Studies of Colo. State U., 1983; grantee Colo. Heart Assn., 1985. Mem. NEA, Poudre Edn. Assn., Colo. Edn. Assn., Colo. Assn. of Health, Phys. Edn., Recreation and Dance (pres. 1979-82, Tchr. award 1977, Honor award 1985), Am. Alliance for Health, Phys. Edn., Recreation and Dance (exec. bd. mem. council on phys. edn. for children 1983-85, fitness chairperson, convention planner 1986), Phi Delta Kappa (found. rep. 1985), Phi Epsilon Kappa (v.p. 1969, pres. 1970). Republican. Avocations: marathons, triathlons, racketball, volleyball, soccer. Home: 3042 Appaloosa Ct Fort Collins CO 80526 Office: Moore Elem Sch 1905 Orchard Pl Fort Collins CO 80521

FOUDRAY, SAMUEL HOUSTON, real estate appraiser, consultant, executive; b. Long Beach, Calif., Sept. 14, 1935; s. Charles William and Norma Aldine (Cook) F.; m. Martha Nellie Siggson, Apr. 26, 1959; children—Robin Wayne, Linda Grace. A.A., Compton Coll., 1956. Real estate sales agt. various firms, So. Calif., 1964-73; owner, opr. appraisal co., Paramount, Calif., 1973-80; pres. Samartha Corp., Paramount, 1980—. Author: Competitive Market Analysis Techniques, 1980; host (cable TV series) This is Real Estate. Mem. Paramount C. of C. (pres. 1977-78, bd. dirs.), Soc. Real Estate Appraisers (pres. chpt. 94 1981-82), Am. Inst. Real Estate appraisers, Nat. Assn. Rev. Appraisers, Rancho Los Cerritos Bd. Realtors (bd. dirs. 1976-78). Republican. Lutheran. Lodge: Lions (pres. Paramount 1977-78). Home: 9856 Hoback St Bellflower CA 90706 Office: Samartha Corp 15726 Paramount Blvd Paramount CA 90723

FOUQUETTE, MARTIN JOHN, JR., zoology educator; b. Phila., June 14, 1930; s. Martin John and Ruby (Lowry) F.; m. Carol Lynn Legett, 1962 (div. 1972); children: David Brian, Hyla Ann. BA, U. Tex., 1951, MA, 1953, PhD, 1959. Interim asst. prof. biology U. Fla., Gainesville, 1959-61; asst. prof. U. Southwestern La., Lafayette, 1961-65; assoc. prof. zoology Ariz. State U., Tempe, 1965—, dir. undergrad. studies dept. zoology, 1985—. Contbr. articles to profl. jours. Served to capt. USAF, 1953-58. Grantee NSF, 1963-64, 68-69, 72-78, Am. Philosophy Soc., 1960. Fellow Herpetologists League (past gov.); mem. Am. Soc. Ichthyologists and Herpetologists (past gov.), Am. Soc. Zoologists, Am. Soc. Naturalists, Soc. Study of Amphibians and Reptiles, Soc. Systematic Zoology, Soc. Study of Evolution, Southwestern Assn. Naturalists, Ariz. Apple Users Group (sec. 1981-82, editor 1982-85, bd. dirs. 1983—), Sigma Xi. Office: Ariz State U Dept Zoology Tempe AZ 85287

FOURNEY, MICHAEL E., engineering educator, consultant; b. Blue Jay, W.Va., Jan. 30, 1936; m. Patricia; 1 dau., Michelle. B.S., W. Va. U., 1958; M.S., Calif. Inst. Tech., 1959, Ph.D., 1963. Registered profl. engr., Wash., Calif. Engr. Gen. Electric Co., Cin., 1957, Douglas Aircraft Co., Santa Monica, Calif., 1958; engr. Boeing Aircraft Co., Seattle, 1959, research engr., 1961, 63-64; engr. Boelkow Entwicklungen KG, Munich, W. Germany, 1963-64; asst. prof. U. Wash., Seattle, 1964-69, assoc. prof., 1969-72; dir. engring. Math. Scis. Corp., Seattle, 1965-72; assoc. prof. UCLA, 1972-76, prof., 1976—, chmn. dept. mechanics and structures, 1979-83; cons. engr. Southwest Engrs., Seattle, Rocket Research Corp., Washington, U.S. Army, N.H., USN, Port Hueneme, Army Missile Commander, Ala., Math. Scis. Corp., Seattle, U. Wash., Seattle. Contbr. articles to profl. publs. Recipient B.S. Lazan award Soc. for Exptl. Stress Analysis, U. Wash. faculty; research grantee NASA, NSF, U.S. Army, USAF, U. Wash., NASA Ames, Hubbes Sea World; Fulbright fellow, Australia, 1986. Fellow Soc. of Exptl. Mechanics; mem. ASME, Optical Soc. Am., Soc. for Exptl. Stress Analysis (nat. past pres.), 8th U.S. Nat. Congress Applied Mechanics (treas.), Reunion Internationale des Laboratoires d'Ensais des Materianx Com., Sigma Xi, Sigma Gamma Tau, Tau Beta Pi. Home: 32060 1/2 Pacific Coast Hwy Malibu CA 90265 Office: UCLA 405 Hilgard Ave Los Angeles CA 90265

FOUSHEE, CYNTHIA LOUISE, info systems specialist; b. Monterey Park, Calif., May 8, 1956; d. Thomas Lewis and Evon Jeannette (Frederickson) Weaver; m. Richard Foushee. B.A. cum laude in Math., U. Calif.-Irvine, 1978; M.S. in Biostats., UCLA, 1980. Biostatistician, Sch. Pub. Health, UCLA, 1980-84, Dept. Neurology, U. Calif., Irvine, 1984-85; user devel. ctr. specialist Shiley Inc., 1986—. Mem. Planetary Soc.

FOUST, RICHARD DUANE, JR., academic administrator; b. Windber, Pa., Dec. 3, 1945; s. Richard Duane and Edna Larue (Pebley) F.; m. Lorriane Beverly Felt, June 24, 1967 (div. Oct. 1983); children: Richard Duane III, Barbara Anne, Cynthia Marie; m. Glenda Earle Swanner, Oct. 29, 1983. BS, Pa. State U., 1967; PhD, U. Calif., Santa Barbara, 1971. Chemist Westvaco, Luke, Md., 1966-67; asst. prof. No. Ariz. U., Flagstaff, 1972-75, assoc. prof., 1975-87, prof., 1987—, dir. Bilby Research Ctr., 1981—; state dir. Am. Energy Week, Washington, 1982. Author: Arizona Energy Education Activities, 1982; mem. edit. bd. Jour. Coll. Sci. Teaching, 1983—; contbr. articles to profl. jours. Bd. dirs. Arizonans for Jobs and Energy, Pheonix, 1977-82; mem. Ariz. Adv. Council on Energy Edn., Pheonix, 1977—; mem. The Ariz. Acad., 1981—. Recipient Excellence in Coll. Teaching award Danforth Found., St. Louis, 1980. Mem. Internat. Soc. Chem. Ecology, Soc. Applied Spectroscopy, NSF (peer rev. psnel 1977—), Nat. Sci. Teachers Assn. (Search for Excellence in Sci. Edn. award 1984), Am. Chem. Soc., Ariz. Sci. Teachers Assn. (pres. 1982-83), Sigma Xi (pres. 1982-83). Democrat. Methodist. Avocations: large format monochrome photography, fly fishing. Home: 3430 Fox Lair Flagstaff AZ 86004 Office: No Ariz U Ralph M Bilby Research Ctr Flagstaff AZ 86011

FOUTCH, RAYMOND ALAN, oil company executive; b. Muskogee, Okla., July 13, 1951; s. Raymond Doyle and Alma Sue (Romback) F.; m. Kathryn Gibbs, May 11, 1973; children—Laura Alecia, Stephany. B.S. in Geology, U. Tex., 1976; M.S. in Petroleum Engring., U. Houston, 1982. Cert. profl. geol. scientist. Mgr. exploration Keplinger & Assocs., Houston, 1976-80; v.p., gen. mgr. Yates Energy Co., Houston, 1980; Rocky Mountain regional mgr. Anschutz Corp., Denver, 1981—. Fellow Soc. Petroleum Engrs., Am. Assn. Petroleum Geologists, Rocky Mountain Assn. Geologists, Dallas Geol. Soc., Houston Geol. Soc., Ind. Petroleum Assn. Mountain States; mem. Am. Inst. Petroleum Geologists.

FOUTS-HOAG, BOBBI JEAN, interior designer; b. Hawthorne, Calif., Oct. 26, 1960; d. John Earl and Adelina (Ortega) Fouts; m. Robert Dowell Hoag, May 25, 1985; 1 child, Erica Reneé. Student, No. Ariz. U., 1978-79; BS, So. Ill. U., 1983. Interior designer Johnson's Furniture, Tucson, 1983-84, PIMA County Facilities Mgmt., Tucson, 1984-87. Leader 4-H Club, Tucson, 1983-85. Mem. Inst. Bus. Designers. Avocation: gardening.

FOUTZ, PAUL BECK, corporate financial executive; b. Westminster, Md., Jan. 17, 1946; s. Carl B. and Nellie Foutz; m. Rae Shermeyer, June 1, 1968. BS, Lebanon Valley coll., 1968; MBA in Acctg., U. Wash., 1970. CPA, Wash., Alaska. Sr. acct. Arthur Andersen, Seattle, 1970-75; asst. adminstr. fin. Providence Hosp., Anchorage, 1975-77; sr. mgr. Price Waterhouse, Anchorage, 1977-83; dir. fin. Pingo Corp., Anchorage, 1983-85; v.p. fin. Aleut Corp., Anchorage, 1985—; bd. dirs., treas. Hope Cottages, Anchorage. Bd. dirs. Southcen. Counseling Ctr., Anchorage, 1983—, past treas.; pres. Southcen. Health Planning and Devel., Anchorage, 1976-82, Mcpl. Health Commn., Anchorage, 1976-78. Mem. Nat. Assn. Accts. (pres. Alaska chpt. 1980-82, nat. bd. dirs. 1984-86.), Am. Inst. CPA's, Am. Acctg. Assn. Club: Tower (Anchorage). Avocations: hiking, reading, travelling, microcomputers. Home: 3919 Geneva Pl Anchorage AK 99508

FOWBLE, ROBERT HENRY, architect, educator; b. El Centro, Calif., Jan. 11, 1921; s. James Raymond Sr. and Robbie Lou (Estes) F. B.S. in Engring., Econs., San Diego State U., 1949; M.Arch., MIT, 1952. Registered architect, Calif. Engr., draftsman Consol. Aircraft Co., San Diego, 1940-44; sr. designer Kistner, Wright & Wright, Los Angeles, 1952-53; architect., engr. Frank L. Hope & Co., San Diego, 1954-56; prin. Robert H. Fowble, architect, San Diego, 1956-68, Neuman-Riddle & Fowble (J.V.), El Centro, Calif., 1963-68, Robert H. Fowble & Assocs., Inc., San Diego, 1968—; instr. San Diego City Coll., 1956-63, U. Calif. Extension, San Diego, 1956. Co-author: Mass Produced Housing, 1952. Bd. dirs. Mesa Coll. Adv. Council, San Diego; pres., bd. dirs. San Diego County Citizens Scholarship Found.; pres. Mesa Coll. Found.; chmn. Joint Adv. Bd. on Open Space, 1969-78. Served with USN, 1944-46; PTO. Mem. AIA, Am. Soc. Mil. Engrs., Am. Soc. Indsl. Security, Greater San Diego Industry-Edn. Council, Nat. Classification Mgmt. Soc., San Diego C. of C. (chmn. met. planning com.), MIT Alumni (pres., treas., dir. San Diego chpt.). Democrat. Baptist. Lodge: Masons. Home: 3416 Bunker Hill St San Diego CA 92117 Office: Robert H Fowble & Assocs Inc 3416 Bunker Hill St San Diego CA 92117

FOWLER, BETTY JANMAE, dance company director, editor; b. Chgo., May 23, 1925; d. Harry and Mary (Jacques) Markin; student Art Inst., Chgo., 1937-39, Stratton Bus. Coll., Chgo., 1942-43, Columbia U., 1945-47; B.A., Eastern Wash. U., 1984; 1 dau., Sherry Mareth Connors. Mem. public relations dept. Girl Scouts U.S.A., N.Y.C., 1961-63; adminstrv. asst. to editor-in-chief Scholastic Mags., N.Y.C., 1963-68; adminstrv. dir. Leonard Fowler Dancers, Fowler Sch. Classical Ballet, Inc., N.Y.C., 1959-78, tchr. ballet, 1959-61; editor Bulletin, Kiwanis weekly publ., Spokane, Wash., 1978-82, also adminstrv. sec. Kiwanis Club; instr. Spokane Falls Community Coll., 1978. Cert. metabolic technician Internat. Health Inst. Address: W 5615 Lyons Ct Spokane WA 99208

FOWLER, CHARLES ANTHONY, computer company executive; b. Los Angeles, Dec. 14, 1944; s. Charles Anthony and Marion Jurgens (Joslin) F.; m. Joyce Lillian Stiltts, May 16, 1965 (div. Oct. 1968); m. Sharon Dian, Nov. 1, 1969; children: Michele Renee, Charles Anthony. Student, U. Pacific, 1964, Ventura Jr. Coll., 1965; cert., Electronic Tech. Inst., San Diego, 1971. Electrician Explorer Motor Homes Co., San Marcos, Calif., 1975-78; test technician Nat. Semiconductor Corp., San Diego, 1978-80, Datagrafix Inc., El Cajon, Calif., 1980-84; owner Chuck's Robots, El Cajon, 1983-85, Craziness Inc., El Cajon, 1985—. Mem. San Diego Atari Computer Enthusiasts (librarian 1982-85), San Diego Model R.R. Club (electrician 1983—). Avocations: model railroading, electronics, robots, jazz, classical music. Home and Office: 1535 Clarke Dr El Cajon CA 92021

FOWLER, CHARLES WINSOR, large mammal population dynamicist; b. Loup City, Nebr., Apr. 21, 1941; s. Ervon Winsor and Merna Dorothy (Kee) F.; m. Jean Forsyth, June 10, 1967; 1 child, Catherine Marie. BA, Hastings Coll., 1963; MS, U. Wash., 1966, PhD, 1973. With Peace Corps; prof. La Universidad Javeriana, Bogota, Colombia, 1967-69; research asst. prof. Utah State U., Logan, 1973-79; mgr. fur seal research program Nat. Marine Mammal Lab., Seattle, 1979—; cons. Food and Agriculture Orgn., Africa, U.S. Marine Mammal Commn.; prin. investigator for prodn. Internat Conf. on Population Dynamics of Large Mammals, 1978. Editor: (with T.D. Smith) Dynamics of Large Mammal Populations, 1981; mem. editorial bd. Current Mammalogy jour., 1986—; contbr. numerous articles and papers to profl. jours. Mem. Ecol. Soc. Am., AAAS, Am. Inst. Biol. Scis. Unitarian. Office: Nat Marine Mammal Lab 7600 Sand Point Way NE Seattle WA 98115

FOWLER, FRANK AUSTIN, computer science professional; b. Richland, Wash., Nov. 22, 1947; s. Herbert Austin and Barbara Regina (Purdy) F. BS in Computer Sci., Wash. State U., 1973. Cert. data processor. Programmer U. Idaho, Moscow, 1972-73, sr. programmer, 1973-75, programmer/analyst I, 1975-76, programmer, analyst II, 1976-78, tech. analyst, 1978—; systems programmer Boeing Computer Services, Renton, Wash., 1973; v.p. Integrated Systems Tech., Inc., Moscow, 1983—. Vol. Am. Heart Assn., Am. Cancer Soc. Republican. Episcopalian. Clubs: Toastmasters (pres. 1985, competent toastmaster award 1985), P.M. Investors (Moscow) (treas. 1986). Home: 500 Queen Rd #34 Moscow ID 83843 Office: U Idaho Office Computer Services Moscow ID 83843

FOWLER, NANCY CROWLEY, government economist; b. Newton, Mass., Aug. 8, 1922; d. Ralph Elmer and Margaret Bright (Tinkham) Crowley; m. Gordon Robert Fowler, Sept. 11, 1949; children—Gordon R., Nancy P., Betty Kainani, Diane Kuulei. A.B. cum laude, Radcliffe Coll., 1943; Grad. Cert., Harvard-Radcliffe Mgmt. Tng. Program, 1946; postgrad. U. Hawaii, 1971-76. Econ. research analyst Dept. Planning & Econ. Devel., Honolulu, 1963-69; assoc. chief research Regional Med. Program, Honolulu, 1969-70; economist V and VI, Dept. Planning and Econ. Devel., Honolulu, 1970-78, chief policy analysis br., 1978-85, tech. info. services officer, 1985—; staff rep. State Energy Functional Plan Adv. Com., Honolulu, 1983—, Hawaii Integrated Energy Assessment, 1978-81. Contbr. articles to profl. jours. Com. mem. Kailua Com. to Re-elect Mayor Eileen Anderson, 1984. Recipient Employee of Yr. award Dept. Planning and Econ. Devel., Honolulu, 1977, others. Mem. Hawaii Econs. Assn. (various offices). Democrat. Clubs: Radcliffe of Hawaii, Propeller of Honolulu (pres.). Avocations: gardening; surfing. Home: 203 Aumoe Rd Kailua HI 96734 Office: Dept Planning and Econ Devel 250 S King St Honolulu HI 96813

FOWLER, NATHANIEL EUGENE, ophthalmologist; b. Rochester, N.Y., Dec. 19, 1922; s. John Denison and Lettie (Oliver) F.; student U. Wis., summers 1940, 41, U. Mich., 1940-43; M.D., U. Rochester, 1946; postgrad. Northwestern U., 1947-48; m. Norma Pammenter, Dec. 27, 1944; children—Leigh Pammenter, James Nathaniel, Richard Edward. Intern Genesee Hosp., Rochester, N.Y., 1946-47; commd. lt. (j.g.), M.C., USN, 1946, advanced through grades to lt. comdr., 1956; chief eye, ear, nose throat dept. U.S. Naval Hosp., Key West, Fla., 1948-51, 54-56; resident in ophthalmology U.S. Naval Hosp., Bethesda, Md., 1951-53; sr. med. officer in U.S.S. Baltimore, 1953-54; practice medicine specializing in ophthalmology, Casper, Wyo., 1956—; chief of staff Natrona County (Wyo.) Meml. Hosp., 1964-66. Trustee Natrona County Sch. Bd., 1963-70, pres., 1967-68; mem. Natrona County Commn., 1971-82, chmn., 1980; bd. dirs. Natrona County Parks and Pleasure Grounds. Diplomate Am. Bd. Ophthalmology. Fellow ACS, Am. Acad. Ophthalmology; mem. Casper C. of C. (dir. 1962-64), Natrona County Med. Soc. (pres. 1959), AMA, Pan Am. Med. Assn., Pan Am. Assn. Ophthalmology, Wyo. Sch. Bds. Assn., N.Am. Yacht Racing Union. Clubs: Elks, Lions (dir. 1961-64), Masons, Shriners, Casper Mountain Ski, Casper Boat (commodore 1960-62), Nat. Ski Patrol. Home: 3338 Monte Vista Dr Casper WY 82601 Office: 111 S Jefferson Casper WY 82601

FOWLER, THOMAS KENNETH, physicist; b. Thomaston, Ga., Mar. 27, 1931; s. Albert Grady and Susie (Glynn) F.; m. Carol Ellen Winter, Aug. 18, 1956; children—Kenneth, John, Ellen. B.S. in Engring, Vanderbilt U., 1953, M.S. in Physics, 1955; Ph.D. in Physics, U. Wis., 1957. Staff physicist Oak Ridge Nat. Lab., 1957-65, group leader plasma theory, 1961-65; staff physicist Gen. Atomic Co., San Diego, 1965-67; head plasma physics div. Gen. Atomic Co., 1967; group leader plasma theory Lawrence Livermore Lab., Livermore, Calif., 1967-69; div. leader Lawrence Livermore Lab., 1969—, asso. dir., 1970—. Fellow Am. Phys. Soc. (chmn. plasma physics div. 1970); mem. Sigma Xi, Sigma Nu. Home: 221 Grover Ln Walnut Creek CA 94596 Office: Lawrence Livermore Lab PO Box 5511 L-640 Livermore CA 94550 *

FOWLER, WILLIAM ALFRED, physicist, educator; b. Pitts., Aug. 9, 1911; s. John McLeod and Jennie Summers (Watson) F.; m. Ardiane Olmsted, Aug. 24, 1940; children: Mary Emily, Martha Summers Fowler Schoenemann. B of Engring. Physics, Ohio State U., 1933, DSc (hon.), 1978; PhD, Calif. Inst. Tech., 1936; DSc (hon.), U. Chgo., 1976, Denison U., 1982, Ariz. State U., 1985, Georgetown U., 1986, U. Mass., 1987; Doctorat hc, U. Liège (Belgium), 1981, Observatoire de Paris, 1981. Research fellow Calif. Inst. Tech., Pasadena, 1936-39; asst. prof. physics Calif. Inst. Tech., 1939-42, asso. prof., 1942-46, prof. physics, 1946-70, Inst. prof. physics, 1970—; Recipient Sullivant medal Ohio State U., 1985; Fulbright lectr. Cavendish lab. U. Cambridge, 1954-55; Guggenheim fellow, 1954-55; Guggenheim fellow St. John's Coll. and dept. applied math. and theoretical physics U. Cambridge, 1961-62; vis. fellow Inst. Theoretical Astronomy, summers 1967-72; vis. scholar program Phi Beta Kappa, 1980-81; asst. dir. research, sect. L NDRC, 1941-45; tech. observer, office of field service OSRD, South Pacific Theatre, 1944; sci. dir., project VISTA, Dept. Def., 1951-52; mem. nat. sci. bd. NSF, 1968-74; mem. space sci. bd. Nat. Acad. Scis., 1970-73, 77-80; chmn. Office of Phys. Scis., 1981-84; mem. space program adv. council NASA, 1971-73; mem. nuclear sci. adv. com. Dept. Energy/NSF, 1977-80; Phi Beta Kappa Vis. scholar, 1980-81, named lectr. univs., colls. Contbr. numerous articles to profl. jours. Bd. dirs. Am. Friends of Cambridge U., 1970-78. Recipient Naval Ordnance Devel. award U.S. Navy, 1945, Medal of Merit, 1948; Lammé medal Ohio State U., 1952; Liège medal U. Liège, 1955; Calif. Co-Scientist of Yr. award, 1958; Barnard medal for contbn. to sci. Columbia, 1965; Apollo Achievement award NASA, 1969; Vetlesen prize, 1973; Nat. medal of Sci., 1974; Bruce gold medal Astron. Soc. Pacific, 1979; Nobel prize for physics, 1983; Benjamin Franklin fellow Royal Soc. Arts. Fellow Am. Phys. Soc. (Tom W. Bonner prize 1970, pres. 1976, William A. Fowler award for excellence in physics So. Ohio sect. 1986), Am. Acad. Arts and Scis., Royal Astron. Soc. (assoc., Eddington medal 1978); mem. Nat. Acad. Scis. (council 1974-77), AAAS, Am. Astron. Soc., Am. Inst. Physics (governing bd. 1974-80), AAUP, Am. Philos. Soc., Soc. Royal Sci. Liège (corr. mem.), Brit. Assn. Advancement Sci., Mark Twain Soc. (hon.), Naturvetenskapliga Foreiningen (hon.), Sigma Xi, Tau Beta Pi, Tau Kappa Epsilon. Democrat. Clubs: Athenaeum (Pasadena); Cosmos (Washington). Research on nuclear forces and reaction rates, nuclear spectroscopy, structure of light nuclei, thermonuclear sources of stellar energy and element synthesis in stars and supernovae; study of gen. relativistic effects in quasar and pulsar models. Office: Calif Inst Tech Kellogg 106-38 Pasadena CA 91125 also: care Anthony Sheil Assocs Ltd., 2/3 Morwell St., London WCIB 3AR England *

FOWLES, ROY RONALD, mental health administrator, psychotherapist; b. Chgo., Mar. 30, 1944; s. James A. and Agnes M. (Bruha) F.; m. Sally Anne Hammon, Dec. 18, 1980; children: Amy, Matthew, Jonathan. BS, U. Oreg., 1968; MSW, U. Denver, 1970, PhD, 1978. Lic. social worker Colo. Bd. Social Work Examiners. Program dir. Western Inst. Human Resources, Denver, 1973-75; adminstrv. social worker Suburban Community Tng. and Services, Englewood, Colo., 1975-76; asst. prof. Metro State Coll., Denver, 1977-81; pvt. practice psychotherapy Denver, 1973—; clin. adminstr. Ft. Logan Mental Health Ctr., Denver, 1981—; cons. dept. gerontology Denver U., 1979-81. Mem. Nat. Assn. Social Workers. Avocations: cooking, gardening, fitness, model rail roading. Home: 3009 Ames Wheat Ridge CO 80214 Office: Ft Logan Mental Health Ctr 3520 W Oxford Denver CO 80236

FOX, HAROLD LAVAR, computer execituve; b. Provo, Utah, Aug. 24, 1923; s. George James and Jennie (Holdaway) F.; m. Lucy Grant, May 16, 1942 (dec. Apr. 1968); children: James Harold, Nancy Jane, Kathleen, Caroline; m. Joyce Benson, Aug. 20, 1968. BS, U. Utah, 1951, MBA, 1972; cert. in meterology, UCLA, 1952; PhD, Found. for Advancement and Mastery of Edn., 1984. Commd. USAF, 1951-59, advanced through grades to capt., resigned, 1959; missile system engr. Hughes Aircraft Corp., Sperry Corp., Los Angeles and Salt Lake City, 1959-71; dir. project ops. IRMP U. Utah, Salt Lake City, 1972-73; founder D.C.P.S., Salt Lake City, 1973-83; pres. CAI & Video Vantage, Salt Lake City, 1983-87; founder CITE Nat., Inc., 1987—; cons. hydroponics industry, 1960-80, tar sand processing, 1975-84, advanced computer software devel., 1973—. Co-author: Modern Science and Technology, 1965, Fluidic Systems Design Guide, 1966; contbr. articles to profl. jours.; patentee in field. Mormon. Avocations: writing sci. fiction, poetry, gardening, inventing. Office: CAI 2171 E 3300 S Salt Lake City UT 84109

FOX, HOWARD NEAL, museum curator; b. Atlantic City, Oct. 4, 1946; s. Jerry and Rose (Zuck) F. BA, U. Md., 1968; MA, U. Wis., 1970. Instr. U. Md., College Park, 1970-75; assoc. curator Hirshhorn Mus. Smithsonion Inst., Washington, 1976-85; curator of contemporary art Los Angeles County Mus. Art., 1985—; mem. exhbn. adv. com. Ind. Curators Inc., N.Y.C., 1982—. Author (exhbn. catalogue) Directions, 1979, Metaphor: New Projects by Contemporary Sculptors, 1982, Content: A Contemporary Focus 1974-84, 1984, A New Romanticism: Contemporary Italian Art, 1985, Avant-Garde in the Eighties, 1987. Research travel grantee Smithsonian Instn., 1984. Home: 750 S Spaulding Ave #112 Los Angeles CA 90036 Office: Los Angeles County Mus Art 5905 Wilshire Blvd Los Angeles CA 90036

FOX, JACK, retired clinical psychologist; b. Vienna, Austria, Nov. 1, 1917; came to U.S. 1939; s. Abraham and Regina (Gerlich) F.; m. M. Ruth Howard, Apr. 8, 1962; children: Eric Russell, Julian Randolph. BA summa cum laude, UCLA, 1949, MA, 1952, PhD, 1959. Lic. psychologist, Calif.; diplomate Am. Bd. Profl. Psychology, Am. Bd. Psychol. Hypnosis. From acting sr. psychologist to sr. psychologist Patton (Calif.) State Hosp., 1959-68, chief psychologist, cons., 1968-81; clin. prof. psychology Fuller Theol. Sem. Grad. Sch. Psychology, Pasadena, Calif. Contbr. chpts. to books and articles to jours. Served to master sgt. U.S. Army, 1941-46. NIMH grantee, 1951-52. Fellow Am. Psychol. Assn.; mem. Western Psychol. Assn., Sigma Xi. Avocation: photography.

FOX, JAMES JULIAN, state social service administrator; b. Alexandria, La., Oct. 21, 1942; s. James Lawrence and Helen Marie (Buckmaster) F.; m. Jeanette Clara Cox, Apr. 10, 1965; children: Kristina Marie, James Abrim. BS in Psychology, La. State U., 1964, MSW, 1968. Supr. casework Dept. Pub. Welfare, Lafayette, La., 1968-70; social worker Bur. Indian Affairs, San Carlos, Ariz., 1970-72; supr. social work Bur. Indian Affairs, Juneau, 1972-73, Nome, Alaska, 1973-77; coorrdinator interstate placement Alaska Div. Family and Youth Services, Juneau, 1977-79; regional mgr. Alaska Div. Family and Youth Services, Fairbanks, 1979—. Co-founder Arctic Alliance for People Programs, Fairbanks, 1981-82, Fairbanks Child Sexual Abuse Task Force, 1984. Mem. Nat. Assn. Social Workers, Am. Pub. Welfare Assn., Am. Assn. Child Protection Adminstrn., Tanana Valley Sportsman Assn. Club: Tanana Valley Sportsman Rifle and Pistol (Fairbanks) (treas. 1983-84). Avocations: shooting, camping. Home: PO Box 58153 Fairbanks AK 99711 Office: No Region Div Family Youth Services 1001 Noble St Suite 400 Fairbanks AK 99701

FOX, JONATHAN RANDALL, banker, real estate broker, insurance agent; b. Pueblo, Colo., June 2, 1958; s. Joseph Marlin and Maxine (Randall) F. B.S., U. Colo., 1980. Asst. cashier Fowler State Bank, Colo., 1980-82, asst. v.p., 1983-84, v.p., 1985—, ptnr., 1980—, also dir.; sec., treas. Ark. Valley Clearing House, Southeast Colo., 1983. Mem. governing bd. Pioneers Meml. Hosp. and Nursing Home, Rocky Ford, Colo., 1982-86; trustee Pioneers Meml. Hosp. Health Ins. Fund, Rocky Ford, 1983-86; bd. dirs. Ark. Valley Regional Med. Ctr., 1986—; treas. Mo. Day Assn., Fowler, Colo., 1983—; bd. dirs. Ark. Valley 4-H Found., Rocky Ford, 1984—, La Junta Med. Ctr. and Nursing Home, 1986—; adv. council Future Bus. Leaders Am., Fowler, 1983—, chmn. 1985—; active in Colo. Soc. Sons Am. Revolution, Colo., 1983—; chmn. pub. relations Fowler Community Assn. Chs., 1982-84; pres. Kittredge Community Bd. U. Colo., Boulder, 1977. Mem. Fowler C. of C. (v.p. 1983-84, pres. 1985-86, and bd. dirs. 1983—), Am. Bankers Assn., Colo. Bankers Assn., Independent Bankers Assn. Am., Bank Adminstrn. Inst., Nat. Assn. Realtors, Ark. Valley Bd. Realtors (G.R.I. award, 1981), Colo. Hosp. Assn. (bd. dirs., mem. panel trustees 1987—). Republican. United Methodist. Home: 606 Main St Fowler CO 81039 Office: Fowler State Bank 201 Main St Fowler CO 81039

FOX, JOSEPH MARLIN, bank executive, insurance executive; b. Longford, Kans., July 23, 1915; s. Hurley Wellington and Eva Kathryn (Marty) F.; m. Mildred Maxine Randall, Aug. 25, 1946; children—Lynette, Jonathan. B.A., U. Colo., 1937. With Fowler (Colo.) State Bank, 1937—, v.p., cashier, dir., 1945-54, pres., dir., 1955—, chmn. bd., 1986—; co-owner Fox Agy., Fowler. Treas. bd. edn. Sch. Dist. 26 Otero County, Colo., 1945—; treas. Local Rodeo Assn.; active Ark. Valley Fair Assn., Colo. Arkansas Valley, Inc.; regional chmn. for banks Colo. 4-H Club Found., 1964; mem. 16th Jud. Dist. Nominating Commn. for Judges, 1967; dist. chmn. Rocky Mountain council Boy Scouts Am. Served with U.S. Army, 1941-44. Mem. Am. Bankers Assn., Colo. Bankers Assn., Ind. Bankers Am., Bank Adminstrn. Inst., Ark. Valley Clearing House Assn. (pres.), Am. Legion (local service officer). Democrat. Methodist. Clubs: Pueblo (Colo.) Country, Lions. Home: 3308 Rd KK 75/100 Fowler CO 81039 Office: Fowler State Bank 201 Main St Fowler CO 81039

FOX, JOSEPH MICKLE, III, process technology manager, chemical engineer; b. Phila., Nov. 20, 1922; s. Joseph Mickle II and Ruth Louise (Martin) F.; m. Elizabeth Jane Larkin, Oct. 16, 1948; children: Joseph Larkin, Elizabeth Amelia Fox Royston, Martha Anne, Thomas Downing, Harry Lay, Justin Mickle. BSChemE, Princeton U., 1943, MSChemE, 1947. Tech. service engr. Am. Oil Co., Texas City, Tex., 1943-45; research engr. M.W. Kellogg Co., Jersey city, 1947-58; research section head Pullman Kellogg Co., Piscataway, N.J., 1958-66; process design mgr. Bechtel Inc., San Francisco, 1966—; del. Calif. Legis. Council for Profl. Engrs., Sacramento, 1968-72, Bay Area Engring. Council, San Francisco, 1972-83. Contbr. articles to profl. jours.; patentee in field. Fellow Am. Inst. Chem. Engrs. (chmn. no. Calif. sect. 1971-72, bd. dirs. 1975-78, Profl. Progress award 1985); mem. Am. Chem. Soc., Am. Petroleum Inst. (tech. data com. 1984, 86). Democrat. Roman Catholic. Club: Orindawoods Tennis (Orinda, Calif.) (TAC Com. 1980-82). Avocations: outdoor sports, music, opera. Home: 3396 Angelo St Lafayette CA 94549 Office: Bechtel Nat Inc Research and Devel Div PO Box 3965 50 Beale St San Francisco CA 94119

FOX, LAWRENCE, III, forestry and computer systems educator, consultant; b. Salt Lake City, June 16, 1947; s. Lawrence Jr.and Ruth (Everett) F.; m. Brooke Marie Hanlon, June 21, 1968; children: Justin, Joshua, Aaron, Benjamin, Joseph. BS in Forestry, Humboldt State U., 1970; MS in Remote Sensing, U. Mich., 1974, PhD in Natural Resources, 1976. Mgmt. trainee Georgia Pacific Corp., Eureka, Calif., 1970-72; with dept. forestry and computer info. systems Humboldt State U., Arcata, Calif., 1976-85, prof., 1985—; curriculum coordinator Asian Inst. Tech., Bangkok, 1982-84, mem. NASA Remote Sensing Sci. Council, 1979-80, Calif. Integrated Remote Sensing System Task Force, 1979-81. Contbr. articles to profl. jours. Recipient Meritorious Performance and Profl. Promise award Humboldt State U., 1984, Coop. Agreement award Calif. Dept. Forestry, Sacramento, 1985-87; McIntire-Stennis Forestry Research grantee, Washington, 1984-85. Mem. Am. Soc. Photogrammetry and Remote Sensing, Soc. Am. Foresters. Republican. Baptist. Avocations: Christian philosophy, psychology, history. Home: 1783 Hyland st Bayside CA 95524 Office: Humboldt State U Forestry Dept Arcata CA 95521

FOX, LORRAINE ESTHER, consulting psychologist in human services; b. S.I., N.Y., Aug. 27, 1941; d. Charles Frederick and Dorothy Elizabeth (Clohessy) F. BA, Northeastern Ill. U., 1973, MA, 1976; postgrad., Profl. Sch. Psychol. Studies, San Diego. Cert. in child care; cert. counselor and instr., Calif. Community Colls. Exec. dir. The Harbour, Des Plaines, Ill., 1975-81; asst. prof. Coll. St. Francis, Joliet, Ill., 1981-84; dir. clin. services Casa de Amparo, San Luis Rey, Calif., 1984-86; cons. Profl. Growth Facilitators, San Clemente, Calif., 1986—; vis. lectr. U. Ill. Chgo., 1983-84; cons. Arthur D. Little, Washington, 1979-82. Author tng. tapes on child care info.; various media appearances; pub. speaker; contbr. articles to profl. jours. Mem. Calif. Assn. Child Care Workers (com. mem. 1984—, pres. Ill. chpt. 1982-84), ACLU, NOW, AAUW, Psi Chi. Avocations: outdoor activities, camping, reading. Home: 1402 Buena Vista #2 San Clemente CA 92672 Office: Profl Growth Facilitators PO Box 5981 San Clemente CA 92672

FOX, MICHAEL HENRY, radiation biologist; b. Great Bend, Kans., Mar. 19, 1946; s. Robert Loren and Wilma Mae (Ulrich) F.; m. Mary Ann Ryser, May 24, 1975; children: Nathan Michael, Jennifer Marie. BS cum laude, McPherson Coll., 1968; MS, Kans. State U., 1972; postdoctoral fellow, Colo. State U., 1977-79, PhD, 1977, asst. prof., 1979—, faculty grad. sch. cell and molecular biology, 1981—. cons. NIH, Bethesda, Md., 1985. Contbr. articles to sci. jour. Active Wellington (Colo.) Vol. Fire Dept., 1981-84; active Amigos de las Americas, Ft. Collins, 1980-81; mem. exec. com. Larimer County Dems., Ft. Collins, 1980—; mem. ch. bd. Foothills Unitarian Ch., Ft. Collins, 1980-83; bd. dirs. Larimer County Bd. Adjustment, Ft. Collins, 1983—, chmn., 1987—. Named one of Outstanding Young Men Am., 1981, 82. Mem. Radiation Research Soc., Soc. Analytical Cytology (chmn. publs. com. 1984—, counselor 1985—), N.Am. Hyperthermia Group. Democrat. Avocations: fishing, skiing, piano, reading, woodworking. Home: 901 Eggleston Fort Collins CO 80524

FOX, NEIL STEWART, chemical company executive; b. Detroit, July 21, 1945; s. David and Bertha (Merkowitz) F.; m. Linda Kaye Mazur; children: Melanie, Aaron. BS in Chemistry, Wayne State U., 1967; MS in Chemistry, Iowa State U., 1970, PhD in Chemistry, 1973. Sr. research chemist 3M Corp., St. Paul, 1973-77; tech. mgr. Dynachem. Corp., Tustin, Calif., 1977-85; tech. dir., v.p. Chemline Industries Inc., Carson City, Nev., 1985—, also bd. dirs. Author: (book chpt.) Polymers in Electronics, 1984; contbr. articles to profl. jours. Mem. Am. Chem. Soc., Inst. Printed Circuits (mem. task force on solden masks 1980—), Goldengate Coating Soc., Brewery Arts Ctr., Sigma Xi. Avocations: jogging, hiking, sailing, traveling. Office: Chemline Industries Inc 4650 Wagon Wheel Rd Carson City NV 89701

FOX, RICHARD BRYCE, chemist, instrument repairman; b. LaGrange, Ind., Apr. 2, 1956; s. Allen John and Marian Frances (McCullough) F.; m. Joyce Marie Hanson, June 31, 1982; children: Amy Jo, Kyle Stephen. AA, Glendale (Ariz.) Community Coll., 1977; BS, Ariz. State U., 1978. Chemist Phelps Dodge Corp., Morenci, Ariz., 1979-85; lab. technician Ross Labs., Casa Grande, Ariz., 1985-86; materials engr. Garrett Turbine, Phoenix, 1986—. Mem. ACS, Am. Inst. Mining Engrs. Republican. Presbyterian. Avocations: fishing, hunting, hiking, woodworking, gardening. Home: 704 E Manor Dr Casa Grande AZ 85222

FOX, ROBERT AUGUST, food company executive; b. Norristown, Pa., Apr. 24, 1937; s. August Emil and Elizabeth Martha (Deimling) F.; m. Linda Lee Carnesale, Sept. 19, 1964; children: Lee Elizabeth, Christina Carolyn. B.A. with high honors, Colgate U., 1959; M.B.A. cum laude, Harvard U., 1964. Unit sales mgr. Procter & Gamble Co., 1959-62; gen. sales mgr. T.J. Lipton Co., 1964-69; v.p. mktg. Can. Dry Corp., 1969-72; pres., chief exec. officer, dir. Can. Dry Internat., 1972-75; exec. v.p., dir. Hunt-Wesson Foods, Inc., 1975-78; pres., chief exec. officer, dir. R.J. Reynolds Tobacco Internat. S.A., 1978-80; chmn., chief exec. officer, dir. Del Monte Corp., San Francisco, 1980-85; vice chmn. Nabisco Brands, Inc., East Hanover, N.J., 1986—; bd. dirs. New Perspective Fund, Growth Fund Am., Income Fund Am., Am. Balanced Fund, Indsl. Indemnity Co.; trustee Euro-Pacific Growth Fund. Trustee Colgate U. Mem. San Francisco C. of C. (dir.), Colgate U. Alumni Assn. (dir.). Office: Del Monte Corp PO Box 3575 San Francisco CA 94119

FOX, STUART IRA, physiologist; b. Bklyn., June 21, 1945; s. Sam and Bess Fox; m. Ellen Diane Fox; 1 dau., Laura Elizabeth. BA, UCLA, 1967; MA, Calif. State U., Los Angeles, 1967; postgrad., U. Calif., Santa Barbara, 1969; PhD, U. So. Calif., 1978. Research assoc. Children's Hosp., Los Angeles, 1972; prof. physiology Los Angeles City Coll., 1972-85, Calif. State U., Northridge, 1979-84, Pierce Coll., 1986—; cons. William C. Brown Co. Pubs., 1976—; project dir. NSF. Author: Computer-Assisted Instruction in Human Physiology, 1979, Laboratory Guide to Human Physiology, 2d edit., 1980, 3d edit., 1984, 4th edit., 1987, Textbook of Human Physiology, 1984, 2d edit., 1987, Concepts of Human Anatomy and Physiology, 1986, Laboratory Guide to Human Anatomy and Physiology, 1986. Named Outstanding Tchr. Los Angeles City Coll., 1978. Mem. AAAS, So. Calif. Acad. Sci., Am. Physiol. Soc., Sigma Xi. Home: 10525 Encino Ave Granada Hills CA 91344 Office: Pierce Coll 6201 Winnetka Ave Woodland Hills CA 91371

FOX, TERRY JAMES, architect, remodeling contractor; b. Olympia, Wash., June 30, 1946; s. Earnest Robert and Helene Marie (O'Meara) F. B.A. in Econs., U. Wash., 1968, M.Arch. summa cum laude, 1978. Registered architect, Oreg. Foreman Hawaiian Improvement Corp., Honolulu, 1975-78; architect Skidmore Owings & Merrill, Portland, Oreg., 1979, Army C.E., Portland, 1979—. Restorer Portland's historic Osbeck house, 1979-84. Served with U.S. Army, 1968-71. Mem. AIA, Am. Soc. Mil. Engrs., Portland Opera Assn., Phi Kappa Psi. Republican. Roman Catholic. Clubs: U. Wash. Alumni, Princeton Athletic.

FOX, WARREN HALSEY, academic administrator, consultant; b. Loma Linda, Calif., Apr. 20, 1945; s. Gaylord Hollis and Helen Elizabeth (Halsey) F.; Candace A. Evart, June 7, 1970. BA, U. Calif., Berkeley, 1967; PhD, U. So. Calif., 1973. Program mgr. U. Calif., Berkeley, 1970-72; vis. prof. U. Tex., Austin, 1973-74; prof. polit. sci. U. Nev., Reno, 1974-79, assoc. dean, 1979-82; vice chancellor U. Nev. system, Reno, 1982—; Chmn. Burroughs' Project "Reducing the Risk", U. Consortium, Detroit, 1984-85. Contbr. articles to jours. Commr. Gov.'s Com. Future of Nev., 1980; mem. Gov.'s Task Force on MX Missile, 1981, Gov.'s Com. Econ. Devel., 1984; vice chmn. Truckee Meadows Adv. Bd., 1984; chmn. exec. com. Nat. Forum for System Chief Acad. Officers, 1985-86. Named Faculty Speaker of Yr., U. Nev., 1975; Econ. Devel. grantee Nev. Commn., 1984; Am. Council Edn. fellow, 1981, NASA fellow, 1968-71. Mem. Am. Soc. Pub. Adminstrn. (pres. Reno chpt. 1978), Internat. Indsl. Relation Assn., Acad. Polit. Sci., Western Govt. Research Assn. Democrat. Presbyterian. Office: Office of Chancellor 405 Marsh Ave Reno NV 89509

FOX, WILLIAM WALTER, psychiatrist; b. Winnipeg, Man., Can., June 24, 1924; came to U.S., 1952, naturalized, 1957; s. William Joseph and Edith (MacDonald) F.; m. Margaret Elizabeth Livingston, Dec. 16, 1949; children—Tannis Lillian, Jennifer Colleen. M.D., U. Man., 1948; M.S. in Adminstrv. Medicine, Columbia, 1965. Diplomate: Am. Bd. Psychiatry and Neurology. Intern Winnipeg Gen. Hosp., 1947-48; resident Winnipeg Gen. Hosp., also Norton Psychiat. Unit, Louisville, 1952-54; practice medicine specializing in psychiatry Winnipeg, 1950-51, Louisville, 1954-65, New Orleans, 1965-66, Mt. Pleasant, Iowa, 1966-72; staff psychiatrist Winnipeg Psychopathic Hosp., 1951-52; cons. (psychiatry); Ky. Dept. Mental Health, 1954-55, Ky. Dept. Mental Health (research on problems of aged), 1955; clin. dir. Central Hosp., Louisville, 1955-56; supt. Central Hosp., 1956-65; asst. prof. dept. psychiatry Faculty Medicine, U. Louisville, 1952-65, Tulane Med. Sch., 1965-66; supt., area dir. mental health Mental Health Inst., Mt. Pleasant, 1966-72; asst. commr. for mental health Ariz. Dept. Health, Phoenix, 1972-75; dir. Camelback Hosp. Mental Health Center, Scottsdale, Ariz., 1975-78; practice medicine specializing in psychiatry Phoenix, 1978—; lectr. dept. psychiatry U. Ariz. Sch. Medicine, 1972-80; spl. cons. NIMH; mem. tech. com. health White House Conf. on Aging, 1971; field rep. Accreditation Council for Psychiat. Facilities, Joint Commn. on Accreditation of Hosps., 1973-78. Fellow Am. Psychiat. Assn.; mem. Assn. Med. Supts. Mental Hosps. (past pres.), A.M.A., Ariz. Med. Assn., Ariz. Psychiat. Soc., Maricopa County Med. Assn. Home: 5313 N 43d St Phoenix AZ 85018 Office: 5051 N 34th St Suite 6 Phoenix AZ 85018

FOX, WILLIAM WALTER, business consultant; b. Ft. Morgan, Colo., Oct. 3, 1921; s. Eugene And Cora Irene (Gerkin) F.; m. Mary Gregg Rea, July 15, 1943; children: William Walter, Arthur Gregg, James Henry. BME, U. Va., 1943; postgrad. Exec. Program, UCLA, 1959, Stanford U., 1969. With Convair div. Gen. Dyamics, 1939-72; chief engr. San Diego, 1960-62; founder, dir. U.S. Fin., San Diego, 1962-77, pres., 1975-77; bus. cons. San Diego, 1977—. Served with A.C., U.S. Army, 1945-46. Mem. Inst. Aero. Scis., Soc. Automotive Engrs. Lodge: Optimists. Home: 1264 Santa Barbara St San Diego CA 92107 Office: PO Box 6805 San Diego CA 92106

FOXHOVEN, MICHAEL JOHN, retail/wholesale company executive, retail merchant; b. Sterling, Colo., Mar. 2, 1949; s. Mark John and Mary Kathryn (Hagerty) F.; m. Catherine Marie Carricaburu, Feb. 16, 1980; children—Patrick Michael, Rachel Marie. Student U. Colo., 1967-70, U. San Francisco, 1971-72. Comml. sales mgr. Goodyear Tire & Rubber Co., Denver, 1978-80, area sales mgr., 1980-81, store mgr., 1981-83, wholesale mgr., 1983-84, appeared in TV commls., 1972; v.p. Foxhovens, Inc., Sterling, 1984—; cons. Foxhoven Bros., Inc., Sterling, 1984—; participant deale. mgmt. seminar, Akron, Ohio, 1973, 85. Mem. mgmt. adv. com. Northeastern Jr. Coll., Sterling, 1976-78; sec. Highland Park Sanitation Dist., Sterling, 1984—. Mem. Logan County C. of C. Republican. Roman Catholic. Club: Sterling Country. Lodges: Elks, Kiwanis. Home: 107 Highland Ave Sterling CO 80751 Office: Foxhovens Inc 1100 W Main St Sterling CO 80751

FOY, CYNTHIA BIDDLE, real estate company executive; b. Hanover, Pa., Oct. 15, 1949; d. Berl William and Lorna Mae (Diviney) Biddle: m. Ron Eddie Foy, June 17, 1968 (div. Sept. 1984); 1 child, Anthony Stewart. Student, Ohio State U., 1967-68, 72-73; BA, Boston U., 1976; postgrad., Golden Gate U., 1981-82; MBA, U. Calif., Berkeley, 1984. Real estate legal asst. Pettit & Martin, San Francisco, 1978-80; adminstrv. asst. The Travelers Cos., San Francisco, 1980-83; supr. investments The Travelers, San Francisco, 1983-85; chief analyst mortgages Indsl. Indemnity Fin. Corp., San Francisco, 1986—. Fellow Acad. Liberation Studies; mem. No. Calif. Mortgage Bankers Assn. (sec. 1985), Women in Real Estate (co-founder 1983). Office: Indsl Indemnity Fin Corp 3 Embarcadero Ctr 9th Floor San Francisco CA 94111

FRADKIN, DAVID BARRY, aerospace research executive; b. Washington, Aug. 14, 1941; s. William Stanley and Gertrude (Hoffeld) F.; m. Judith Park, Jan. 2, 1964 (div. June 1976); children: Sheryl Lynn, Jonathan Matthew, Jesse Dor; m. Stacey Ann, Dec. 30, 1979; children: Jennifer Lynn, Benjamin M. BS in Engring., U. Md., 1963; MS in Engring., Princeton U., 1965, MA, 1970, PhD, 1972. Staff mem. Los Alamos (N.Mex.) Nat. Lab., 1965-74, asst. group leader, 1974-77, dep. group leader, 1977-78, group leader, 1978-85, program mgr., 1985—; participated as program mgr. spl. isotope separation, Los Alamos Lab., 1985-86. Patentee isotope separation apparatus and method; contbr. over 20 articles to profl. jours. Religious chmn. Los Alamos Jewish Ctr., 1972-74, bd. dirs. 1972-74, 1983-84. Guggenheim fellow Princeton U., 1964. Mem. AAAS, AIAA, Am. Chem. Soc., N.Y. Acad. Scis., Sigma Xi, Tau Beta Pi, Omicron Delta Kappa. Democrat. Jewish. Clubs: Los Alamos Ski, Sports Car del Valle Rio Grand. Avocations: sports car racing, tennis, skiing. Home: 162 Chamisa Los Alamos NM 87544 Office: Los Alamos Nat Lab MS E-581 Los Alamos NM 87545

FRAKER, MARK ARNOTT, environmental scientist; b. Columbus, Ind., Dec. 13, 1944; s. Ralph Waldo and Carol (Arnott) F.; m. Pamela Norton, May 27, 1967 (div. Feb. 1985); 1 child, Russell; m. Donice Horton, Aug. 23, 1986. BA with honors, Ind. U., 1967, MA, 1969. Biologist, project mgr. F.F. Slaney and Co., Vancouver, Can., 1972-78; biologist, project dir. LGL Ltd., Sidney, B.C., Can., 1978-82; sr. environ. scientist Standard Alaska Prodn. Co., Anchorage, 1982—; broadcaster CBC, Vancouver, 1970-72; mem. sci. com. Internat. Whaling Com., Cambridge, Eng., 1982—; instr. U. Alaska, 1985—. Author: Balaena mysticetus, 1984; also articles; mem. editorial bd. Biol. Papers of the U. of Alaska. Ambassador to Peru, Anchorage Olympic Com., 1986—. Woodrow Wilson fellow, Princeton, N.J., 1967. Mem. AAAS, Nat. Acad. Scis. (appointed to com. panel 1987-1991), Am. Soc. Mammalogists, Can. Soc. Zoologists, Soc. for Marine Mammalogy, The Wildlife Soc. Avocations: Latin Am. affairs, bird watching, backpacking, hunting, Spanish. Office: Standard Alaska Prodn Co PO Box 196612 Anchorage AK 99519

FRAKES, ROD VANCE, plant geneticist, educator; b. Ontario, Oreg., July 20, 1930; s. Wylie and Pearl (Richardson) F.; m. Ruby L. Morey, Nov. 27, 1952; children:Laura Ann, Cody Joe. BS, Oreg. State U., 1956, MS, 1957; PhD, Purdue U., 1960. Instr. dept. agronomy Purdue U., West Lafayette, Ind., 1959-60; asst. prof. dept. crop sci. Oreg. State U., Corvallis, 1960-64, assoc. prof., 1964-69, prof., 1969—, assoc. dean research, 1981—. Author numerous papers and abstracts; contbr. to books in field. Served with USCG, 1950-53. Named Man of Yr., Pacific Seedsmen's Assn., 1972; recipient Elizabeth P. Ritchie Disting. Prof. award Oreg. State U., 1980. Fellow Am. Soc. Agronomy, Crop Sci. Soc. Am.; mem. AAAS, Soc. Research Adminstrs., Nat. Council Univ. Research Adminstrs., Western Soc. Crop Sci. (pres. 1978). Club: Corvallis Historic Auto. Lodge: Rotary. Avocations: antique autos, Am. history, amateur radio. Home: 2625 NW Linnan Circle Corvallis OR 97330 Office: Research Office Oreg State Univ Corvallis OR 97331

FRAKNOI, ANDREW, astronomical society executive, educator; b. Budapest, Hungary, Aug. 24, 1948; came to U.S., 1959; s. Emery I. and Katherine H. (Schmidt) F.; m. Beverly Carol McMillan, Apr. 23, 1983. B.A. in Astronomy, Harvard U., 1970; M.A. in Astrophysics, U. Calif.-Berkeley, 1972. Instr. astronomy and physics Cañada Coll., Redwood City, Calif., 1972-78; exec. officer Astron. Soc. of Pacific, San Francisco, 1978—; part-time prof. San Francisco State U., 1980—; fellow Com. for Sci. Investigation of Claims of Paranormal, Buffalo, 1984—; dir. Search for Extra Terrestrial Intelligence Inst., Palo Alto, Calif., 1984—; host radio program Exploring the Universe, KGO-FM, San Francisco, 1983-84. Author: Resource Book for the Teaching of Astronomy, 1978, Universe in the Classroom, 1985; (with others) The Planets, 1985, (with R. Robert Robbins) The Universe at Your Fingertips, 1985; (with others) Universe, 1987; editor Mercury Mag., 1978—, The Universe in the Classroom Newsletter, 1985—; assoc. editor The Planetarian, 1986—; contbr. syndicated column on astronomy to newspaper, 1975-80; author monthly column on astronomy to San Francisco Examiner, 1986—. Bd. dirs. Bay Area Skeptics, San Francisco, 1982—. Recipient award of merit Astron. Assn. No. Calif., 1980. Mem. Am. Astron. Soc., Astron. Soc. Pacific, Am. Assn. Physics Tchrs., Nat. Assn. Sci. Writers, No. Calif. Sci. Writers Assn. (program chmn. 1983-85). Avocations: music and astronomy; sci. and lit. Office: Astron Soc of Pacific 1290 24th Ave San Francisco CA 94122

FRALEY, GAIL JEAN, administrative trainer; b. Talullah, La., June 17, 1946; d. Jame Edward and Erma (Dautel) Smith; m. Theodore R.E. Fraley, July 11, 1972; 1 child, Ty. BS, U. Northwestern La., 1967, MEd, 1969. Cert. tchr. Tchr. Sumter (S.C.) Sch. Dist. 17, 1970-74; real estate broker Tompkins Realty, Tucson, 1974-78; instr. Miami-Jacobs Jr. Coll., Dayton, Ohio, 1980-83; adminstrv. trainer Gas Co. of N.Mex., Albuquerque, 1983—. Ops. mgr. Youth for Understanding, Albuquerque, 1983-86, area mgr., 1986—. Named Mother of Yr. PTA, Yorktown, Va., 1979. Mem. Am. Soc. Tng. and Devel., Desk and Derrick, LWV, Albuquerque Fedn. Rep. Women, Albuquerque Coordinating Council for Internat. Friendship (bd. dirs., v.p. 1985—). Methodist. Club: Officer's Wives (Kirtland AFB). Avocations: camping, bowling, stained glass. Home: 4019 Calle Pino NE Albuquerque NM 87111 Office: Gas Co of NMex PO Box 1692 Albuquerque NM 87103

FRAME, TED RONALD, lawyer; b. Milw., June 27, 1929; s. Morris and Jean (Lee) F.; student UCLA, 1946-49; A.B., Stanford U., 1950, LL.B., 1952; m. Lois Elaine Pilgrim, Aug. 15, 1954; children—Kent, Lori, Nancy, Owen. Bar: Calif. 1953. Gen. agri-bus. practice, Coalinga, Calif., 1953—; sr. ptnr. Frame & Courtney, 1965-82; prin. Ted R. Frame, Inc., 1982—. Trustee, Baker Mus. Mem. ABA, Calif. Bar Assn., Fresno County Bar Assn., Coalinga C. of C. (past pres.). Clubs: Masons, Shriners, Elks. Home: 1222 Nevada St Coalinga CA 93210 Office: 201 Washington St Coalinga CA 93210

FRANCE, JOHN LYONS, air force officer; b. Forest City, Mo., Sept. 11, 1933; s. Calvert Glen and Gertrude May (Lyons) F.; B.A. in English, U. Denver, 1963, J.D., 1966; m. Carole Jean Denton, Sept. 16, 1961; children—Allison Lisa, Amy Denton. Commd. 2d lt. USAF, advanced through grades to maj. gen.; now adj. gen., State Colo., Denver; flight leader Colo. Air N.G., later squadron comdr., group comdr., wing comdr. Mem. Air Res. Forces Policy Com.; mem. Tactical Air Command Res. Forces Policy Counil. Decorated D.F.C., Air medal with ten oak leaf clusters. Mem. ABA, Colo. Bar Assn., Air Force Assn. Office: Office of the Adjutant General 300 Logan St Denver CO 80203

FRANCESCHI, ERNEST JOSEPH, JR., lawyer; b. Los Angeles, Feb. 1, 1957; s. Ernest Joseph and Doris Cecilia (Beluche) F.; m. Jeannean Lynn Baker, Oct. 27, 1983. BS, U. So. Calif., 1978; JD, Southwestern U., Los Angeles, 1980. Bar: Calif., 1984, U.S. Dist. Ct. (cen. dist.) Calif., 1984, U.S. Dist. Ct. (ea. dist.) Calif., 1986, U.S. Dist. Ct. (no. dist.) Calif., 1987, U.S. Ct. Appeals (9th cir.) 1984. Sole practice Seal Beach, Calif., 1984—. Mem. Assn. Trial Lawyers Am., Calif. Trial Lawyers Assn., Los Angeles Trial Lawyers Assn. Republican. Roman Catholic. Office: 500 Pacific Coast Hwy Suite 212 Seal Beach CA 90740

FRANCIS, MARC BARUCH, pediatrician; b. Rochester, N.Y., Mar. 3, 1934; s. Nathan and Beverly (Salsburg) F.; A.B., U. Rochester, 1955; M.D., N.Y. U., 1959; m. Janet Irene Harding, Sept. 21, 1960; children—Josephine, Teresa, Jacqueline, Wallace. Intern, Los Angeles County Harbor Gen. Hosp., 1959-60; resident in pediatrics Children's Hosp. of Los Angeles, 1960-62; practice medicine specializing in pediatrics, Salt Lake City, 1962-65; clin. instr. pediatrics U. Utah Med. Sch., 1962-70; chief dept. pediatrics Cottonwood Hosp., 1963-65; partner dept. pediatrics Permanente Med. Group Inc., Napa, Calif., 1971—, chief dept., 1982-86. Served to capt. M.C., USAF, 1966-68. Diplomate Am. Bd. Pediatrics. Fellow Am. Acad. Pediatrics; mem. Calif. Med. Assn., Napa County Med. Soc. Clubs: NYU, U. Rochester Alumni. Office: Permanente Med Group Inc 3284 Jefferson St Napa CA 94558

FRANCIS, TIMOTHY LLOYD, chemical engineer; b. McAlester, Okla., Jan. 29, 1952; s. Lloyd Franklin and Joyce Geneva (Moye) F.; m. Elaine Barlow, May 26, 1976; children: William David and Matthew MacKenzie. BSChemE, N.Mex. State U., 1975. From research engr. to sr. research engr. Dow Chem. Co., Freeport, Tex., 1975-80; mgr. separation dept. Western Zirconium, Inc. div. Westinghouse Elec., Ogden, Utah, 1980-82, mgr. reduction dept., 1982—. Bd. dirs. Kids at Home Nat. Pediat. Home Care, Ogden, 1985—; mem. Parents Assn. Weber County Handicap Tng. Ctr., Ogden, 1982—. Recipient Spl. Achievement award Westinghouse Elec. Co., 1981. Mem. Am. Inst. Chem. Engrs. Home: 2679 Fillmore Ave Ogden UT 84001 Office: Western Zirconium PO Box 3208 Ogden UT 84409

FRANCISCO, WAYNE M(ARKLAND), petroleum marketing company executive; b. Cin., June 14, 1943; s. George Lewis and Helen M. (Markland) F.; student Ohio State U., 1962-63; B.S. in Mktg. and Acctg., U. Cin., 1967; div.; children: Diana Lynn, W. Michael; m. Inez Francisco. Unit sales mgr. Procter & Gamble, Cin., 1967-69; mktg. mgr. Nat. Mktg. Inc., Cin., 1969-70; pres. Retail Petroleum Marketers, Inc., Cin., 1970-72, chmn. bd., chief exec. officer, Phoenix, 1972-85; chmn. bd., chief exec. officer DMC Industries, Inc., 1985-87; pres., chief exec. officer Cassia Petroleum Corp., Vancouver, B.C., Can., 1980-84; bd. dirs. P.F.K. Enterprises, F.I.C. Inc., Internat. Investment and Fin. Enterprises, Inc., Alpha Realty, Inc. Mem. Phoenix Bd. Appeals, 1978-80; v.p. Cuervanaca Homeowners Assn., 1982, pres., 1983-86. Recipient Image Maker award Shell Oil Co., 1979; Top Performer award Phoenix dist. Shell Oil Co., 1979, 80. Mem. Petroleum Retailers Ariz. (pres. 1977-79), Nat. Congress Petroleum Retailers (adv. bd.), Nat. Inst. Automotive Service Excellence (cert.), Culver Legion (life), Studebaker Drivers Club (zone coordinator Pacific Southwest 1983, 84, 85,86; nat. v.p. 1986-87; Grand Canyon chpt. pres. 1986), Avanti Owners Assn. (nat. bd. dirs. 1975-86, internat. pres. 1986-87). Republican. Lodge: Optimists (bd. dirs. Paradise Valley club 1984, sec.-treas. 1984). Office: 21824 N 19th Ave Phoenix AZ 85027

FRANCL, WALTER JOSEPH, engineering company executive; b. Vienna, Austria, Oct. 18, 1922; came to Can., 1952; m. Maria Anna Uchatius, Oct. 6, 1951; children—Walter, Susan, Tony, Elisabeth. B.S.C.E., U. Vienna, 1948. Lic. profl. engr. Alta., B.C., Ont., Yukon. Chief engr. D.R. Stanley & Assocs., Edmonton, Alta., Can., 1954-65; pres. W.J. Francl Cons. Ltd., Edmonton, 1965—. Mem. Environ. Council Alta., Edmonton, 1981-83. Mem. Can. Water Resources Assn. (v.p. 1977-80), Edmonton C. of C. (fgn. trade com. 1979-81, chmn. resources div. 1981-83, exec. com. 1983-84). Roman Catholic. Office: WJ Francl Counsulting Ltd, 11710 Kingsway Ave, Edmonton, AB Canada T5G 0X5

FRANCO, JORGE, physician; b. Ica, Peru, June 9, 1929; s. Fortunato and Sabina (Cabrera) F.; B.S., San Marcos U., 1947, M.D., 1955; m. Mary Loretta Jones, Sept. 19, 1957; children—Mary Pat, Lori, Ann Marie, Raymond Joseph, Stephen Michael. Came to U.S., 1955. Intern, Bon Secours Hosp., Balt., 1955-56; fellow medicine Stanford Med. Sch., 1956-58, asst. clin. prof. nuclear medicine, 1969-76, assoc. clin. prof., 1976—; resident pathology O'Connor Hosp., San Jose, Calif., 1958-62, assoc. pathologist, 1963—, chief clin. pathology, dir. nuclear medicine, 1968—. Diplomate Am. Bd. Pathology, Am. Bd. Nuclear Medicine. Mem. Am. Fedn. Clin. Research, Am. Soc. Clin. Pathologists, Am. Soc. Hematology, Am. Assn. Blood Banks, Soc. Nuclear Medicine, Am. Inst. Ultrasonics in Medicine, AMA, Calif. Med. Assn., Calif. Soc. Pathologists, Am. Thermographic Soc., Calif. Acad. Medicine, N.Y. Acad. Scis. Contbr. articles to profl. jours.; also clin. and lab. research. Home: 1259 Central Ave San Jose CA 95128 Office: O'Connor Hosp Tumor Center San Jose CA 95128

FRANDEN, BLANCHE M., nursing educator; b. N.Y.C., June 9, 1923; d. Samuel and Rebekah (Stern) Randall; m. Robert Jacob Franden, Aug. 20, 1950; children—Richard Jules, Peter Herb, Daniel Ethan. Grad. Mass. Meml. Hosp. Sch. Nursing (now U. Hosp.), 1945; B.Vocat. Edn., Calif. State U.-Los Angeles, 1980. Registered nurse, Calif. dir. student health Mass. Meml. Hosp., Boston, 1947-49; staff nurse various hosps., N.Y., Calif., 1949—; instr. Baldwin Park Unified Sch. Dist. Adult Sch. (Calif.), 1983—, East San Gabriel Valley Regional Occupational Program, West Covina, Calif., 1973—, La Puente Valley Regional Occupational Program, 1984—; CPR instr.-trainer; mem. CPR com. Am. Heart Assn. Mem. Calif. Assn. Regional Occupational Ctrs./Programs, Calif. Council of Adult Edn., Am. Vocat. Assn., Calif. Assn. Health Career Educators, Orange County Profl. and Bus. Jewish Women, AAUW, Women's Aux., VFW. Democrat. Jewish. Author student manual. Home: 15111 Mystic St Whittier CA 90604 Office: East San Gabriel Valley Regional Occupation Program 1024 Workman St West Covina CA 91790

FRANK, ALAN, psychiatry educator; b. N.Y.C., May 16, 1922; s. Lawrence Kelso and Alice Vermandoir (Bryant) F.; m. Louise Thompson, 1956 (dec. 1964); children: Alexandra, Margaret, Lucia; m. Anita Magnus, May, 1969; 1 child, Loren. BA, Columbia U., 1944, MD, 1949. Diplomate Am. Bd. Med. Examiners; cert. Am. Bd. Psychiatry and Neurology. Head psychiat. div. Student Health Service U. Colo., Boulder, 1956-67; psychiatrist Health Service Pa. State U., State College, 1967-68; asst. prof. psychiatry U. N.Mex., Albuquerque, 1968—; cons. in field, 1969—. Fellow Am. Psychiat. Assn. (life), Am. Orthopsychiat. Assn., AAAS, ACP; mem. N.Y. Acad. Scis. Office: U NMex Dept Psychiatry Albuquerque NM 87131

FRANK, ALFRED LOUIS, endodontist; b. Cleve., July 17, 1922; s. Jacob and Yetta (Bergman) F.; m. Teri Frank, Dec. 16, 1951; children: Clifford, Robert, Bradley, Jeffrey, David. Student, Case Western Res. U., 1940-42, Ohio State U., 1942; DDS, U. So. Calif., 1945. Clin. prof. U. So. Calif., Los Angeles, 1956—; cons. Long Beach (Calif.) Vets. Hosp., Hudson comprehensive Health Ctr., Los Angeles, ADA Council on Dental Edn.; lectr. Loma Linda (Calif.) U., UCLA. Author: Clinical and Surgical Endodontics, 1983; contbr. articles to profl. jours., chpts. to books. Bd. dirs. U. West Los Angeles, 1980-85, Jewish Big Bros., Los Angeles, 1960-70. Served to capt. U.S. Army, 1946-48. Internat. Coll. Dentistry fellow, 1968. Fellow Am. Coll. Dentistry; mem. Am. Assn. Endodontics (pres. 1974-75, Edgar A. collidge award 1981, Ralph Sommer award 1985), Internat. Assn. Dental Research, Am. Bd. Endodontists (pres. 1972), So. Calif. Acad. Endodontists (pres. 1962), Alpha Omega (pres. Los Angeles chpt. 1969, internat. trustee 1970). Alpha Tau Epsilon, Omicron Kappa Epsilon, Sigma Xi. Democrat. Avocations: downhill and water skiing, boat racing, sailing. Home: 701 Walden Dr Beverly Hills CA 90210 Office: U So Calif 2080 Century Park E #1710 Los Angeles CA 90067

FRANK, CHRISTOPHER LYND, mechanical engineer; b. Chesterton, Ind., Dec. 26, 1949; s. Clarence Edward and Marie Caroline (Saylor) F.; m. Deborah Lynn Tanner, July 3, 1971; 1 child, Erin Marie. BS in Engring., Calif. State U., Sacramento, 1983; cert. injection molding, U. Lowell, 1986. Plant mgr. Redelco Plastics, Clouis, Calif., 1975-79; owner, designer The Energy Factory, Fresno, Calif., 1977-79, Solar Utility Network, Yuba City, Calif., 1979-81; engr., designer Houston Fearless 76, Carson, Calif., 1983-86, Air FOrce Advanced Composites Program, Sacramento, 1986—. Served to sgt. USAF, 1970-74. Mem. Soc. Automotive Engrs., ASME. Avocations: flying, rock climbing, coastal sailing. Office: SM-ALC/MMEP Bldg 243-E McClellan AFB CA 95652

FRANK, LYNN ELLEN, communications executive; b. Detroit, June 14, 1953; d. Phillip Harrison and Leota (Presley) F.; m. Timothy James Alldridge, Oct. 31, 1983. BA, Mich. State U., 1975. Creative advisor San Jose (Calif.) Mercury News, 1975-78, advt. sales rep., 1978-80, NIE coordinator, 1980-81, CIS mgr., 1981-82, circulation mgr., 1982-83, safety, telecommunications mgr., 1983—. Bd. dirs. Opera San Jose, 1985—. Mem. Am. Soc. Safety Engrs., Nat. Safety Council: Printing and Pub. (exec. com. 1986), Nat. ROLM Users Group, San Jose Women in Advt. (founder, pres. 1979-80). Office: San Jose Mercury News 750 Ridder Park Dr San Jose CA 95190

FRANK, ROBERT GREGG, JR., medical historian, educator; b. Topeka, Dec. 17, 1943; s. Robert Gregg and Patricia W. (Shoaf) F.; m. Myra L. Lampman, Sept. 3, 1966; children—Elisabeth VanWaggoner, Katharine Cosgrove. A.B., Stanford U., 1965; M.A., Harvard U., 1967, Ph.D., 1971; student Oxford (Eng.) U., 1968-69. Teaching fellow and tutor Harvard U., Cambridge, Mass., 1966-68, 69-70; asst. prof. history Tufts U., Medford, Mass., 1970-71, U. Mass., Amherst, 1971-72; asst. prof. med. history UCLA Sch. Medicine, 1972-79, assoc. prof., 1979—, chief Med. History Div., 1986—. Author: (with B. Shapiro) English Scientific Virtuosi in the 16th and 17th Centuries, 1979; Harvey and the Oxford Physiologists: Scientific Ideas and Social Interaction, 1981, Italian edit., 1983; assoc. editor Jour. History of Biology, 1973-81; editorial bd. Jour. History of Medicine, 1979-82; contbr. articles to profl. jours. Trustee, San Marino (Calif.) Schs. Found., 1984—. Nat. Library Medicine grantee, 1975-77, 77—; Woodrow Wilson fellow, 1965-66. Mem. History of Sci. Soc., Am. Assn. History of Medicine (William Henry Welch medal 1983), Phi Beta Kappa, Sigma Xi. Democrat. Roman Catholic. Home: 780 Granada Ave San Marino CA 91108 Office: UCLA Sch Medicine Los Angeles CA 91108

FRANK, SANDERS THALHEIMER, physician, educator; b. Middletown, Conn., May 11, 1938; s. Harry S. and Pauline (Thalheimer) F.; B.A., Amherst Coll., 1959; M.D., N.Y. Med. Coll., 1963; m. Marta Santoyo, Jan. 7, 1981; children by previous marriage—Geoffrey Brooks, Susan Kimberly, Jonathan Blair, Adam. Intern, Sinai Hosp., Balt., 1963-64; resident Wilford Hall Med. Center, San Antonio, 1965-68; practice medicine, specializing in pulmonary disease, Monterey Park, Calif., 1971—; dir. respiratory care Garfield Hosp., Monterey Park, 1974—, Beverly Hosp., Montebello, Calif., 1975-78; assoc. prof. medicine U. So. Calif., Los Angeles, 1972—. Served to maj. USAF, 1964-71. Decorated USAF Commendation medal; recipient Philip Hench award for demonstrating relationship of rheumatoid arthritis to lung disease, 1968; award of merit Los Angeles County Heart Assn., 1974. Fellow Royal Soc. Medicine (London), Am. Coll. Chest Physicians, A.C.P.; mem. Am. Thoracic Soc., Calif. Thoracic Soc., Nat. Assn. Dirs. Respiratory Care, Respiratory Care Assembly Calif., Alpha Omega Alpha. Contbr. articles in field to med. jours. Recorded relationship of ear-lobe crease to coronary artery disease, 1973. Home: 891 E Grandview Sierra Madre CA 91024 Office: 500 N Garfield Ave Monterey Park CA 91754

FRANK, STEPHEN RICHARD, lawyer; b. Portland, Oreg., Dec. 13, 1942; s. Richard Sigmund Frank and Paula Anne (Latz) Lewis; m. Cornelia Mills Brookhart, Aug. 13,1966 (div. Jan. 1978); children: Richard Sigmund II, Theresa Anne. AB in Econs., U. Calif., Berkeley, 1964; JD, Willamette U., 1967. Bar: Oreg., U.S. Ct. Appeals (9th cir.), U.S. Supreme Ct. Assoc. Tooze, Marshall, Shenker, Holloway & Duden, Portland, 1967-72, ptnr., 1972—; mem. audit com. Seligman & Latz NYSE, 1981-85, bd. dirs. 1976-85. Editor Willamette Law Jour., 1967. Trustee, sec. Oreg. High Desert Mus., 1977-86; sec., bd. dirs. Palatine Hill Water Dist., 1973-77; bd. dirs. Emanuel Hosp. Found., 1980-83, Portland Ctr. for Visual Arts, 1977-82. Mem. ABA, Assn. Trial Lawyers Am., Oreg. Trial Lawyers Assn., Oreg. State Bar Assn. (dir., sec. minority scholarship program 1981—, sec.-chmn. com. worker's compensation 1974-77), Oreg.Assn. Ins. Def. Counsel, Oreg. Assn. Workers Compensation Def. Counsel. Clubs: Multnomah Athletic; City (Portland). Avocations: snow skiing, bicycling, running, mountain climbing, sailing. Home: 3103 SW Cascade Dr Portland OR 97201 Office: Tooze Marshall Shenker Holloway & Duden 333 SW Taylor St Portland OR 97204

FRANKE, EILEEN DIANE, parasitologist, naval officer; b. Bklyn., Nov. 10, 1956. BS, SUNY, Albany, 1978; PhD, U. Notre Dame, 1982. NIH predoctoral trainee U. Notre Dame, Ind., 1979-82; NRC postdoctoral research assoc. Walter Reed Army Inst. of Research, Washington, 1982-84; commd. lt. USN, 1984; head dept. parasitology USN Med. Research Unit #2, Jakarta, Indonesia, 1985—; advisor Onchocerciasis Chemotherapy Project, World Health Orgn., Geneva, 1984—. Contbr. articles on parasitology. Recipient NIH predoctoral stipend, 1979-82; NRC postdoctoral assoc., 1982-84. Mem. AAAS, Am. Soc. Parasitologists, Am. Soc. Tropical Medicine & Hygiene, Royal Soc. Tropical Medicine & Hygiene, Helminthological Soc. Washington, Sigma Xi. Avocations: swimming, running, bicycling, hiking. Home and Office: NAMRU #2 Jakarta Detachment APO San Francisco CA 96356

FRANKE, WILLIAM AUGUSTUS, corporate executive; b. Bryan, Tex., Apr. 15, 1937; s. Louis John and Frances (Hanna) F.; m. Carolyn D. Walker, July 16, 1977; children: Catherine Anne, Paige Estelle, Brian Hanna, David Parker, Rebecca Ann Walker. BA, Stanford, 1959, LLB, 1961. Bar: Wash. 1961. Assoc. MacGillivray, Jones, Clark & Schiffner, Spokane, 1962-67, ptnr., 1967-70; v.p., sec., corp. counsel S.W. Forest Industries, Phoenix, 1970-72, sr. v.p., sec., 1972-73, exec. v.p., asst. chief exec. officer, 1973-75, pres., 1975—, chief operating officer, 1977-78, chief exec. officer, 1978, chmn. bd. dirs., 1986—, also bd. dirs., chmn. exec. com., also bd. dirs. subs. cos.; bd. dirs. Phelps Dodge Corp., Circle K Corp., Valley Nat. Bank, Am. Paper Inst. Mem. dean's council Stanford U. Law Sch., Ariz. State U. Served to capt. U.S. Army, 1961-62. Mem. ABA, Wash. Bar Assn., Spokane County Bar Assn., Young Pres.'s Orgn. Episcopalian. Clubs: Stanford, Paradise Valley Country, Phoenix Country, Mansion (Phoenix); Plaza. Home: 7701 N Saguaro Dr Paradise Valley AZ 85253 Office: Southwest Forest Industries Inc 6225 N 24th St Phoenix AZ 85016

FRANKEL, CHARLES LOUIS, travel agency executive; b. Chgo., Dec. 5, 1932; s. Louis and Thelma (Cohn) F.; m. Diane Francine Bejosa, July 10, 1966; children: Matthew, Alexander. AB, Harvard U., 1954, MBA, 1956. Asst. U.S. Senator from Calif., 1966-68; v.p. Ruder & Finn, San Francisco, 1968-70; asst. regional dir. U.S. HUD, San Francisco, Boston, 1971-73; country dir. U.S. Peace Corps, Gaborone, Botswana, 1973-75; ptnr. Gulliver's Travel Agy., San Francisco, 1976—; mem. adv. bd. PanAm Travel Agy., northern Calif., 1976—. Co-chmn. campaign Ford for Pres., San Francisco, 1976; vice chmn., bd. dirs. Mt. Zion Hosp., San Francisco, 1980—. Named Hon. Consul Republic Botswana, 1982. Mem. African Travel Assn. (pres. northern Calif. sect. 1982-83, bd. dirs. internat. div. 1984-85), Friends of Ethnic Art, (pres. 1978-79), Soc. Internat. Devel. (v.p. 1977-78), Wofld Affairs Council (trustee northern Calif. div. 1985—), Am. Soc. Travel Agts., Assn. Retail Travel Agts. Club: Harvard (N.Y.C.).

FRANKISH, BRIAN EDWARD, film producer, director; b. Columbus, Ohio, July 28, 1943; s. John (Jack) Fletcher Frankish and Barbara Aileen (Tondro) Gray; m. Tannis Rae Benedict, Oct. 13, 1985; children: Merlin L. Reed III, Michelle Lynn Reed. AA, Chaffey Coll., 1964; BA, San Francisco State U., 1967. Freelance producer Los Angeles; prin. Frankish Inc., Los Angeles. Producer film Vice Squad, 1981, Max Headroom, 1987; assoc. producer films Elephant Parts, 1981, Strange Brew, 1982, The Boy Who Could Fly, 1985, In the Mood, 1986; 1st asst. dir. (TV shows) Big Shamus, 1979, Skag, 1979, Why Me?, 1983, Making Out, 1984, Berrengers, 1984; (films): Strange Brew, 1982, Uncle Joe Shannon, 1978, Savage Harvest, 1980, Dead and Buried, 1980, Spring Break, 1982, Brainstorm, 1982-83, The Last Starfighter, 1983, The New Kids, 1983, Hanauma Bay, 1984, The Best of Times, 1985, Odd Jobs, 1985; unit prodn. mgr. Second Serve, 1986; distbr.'s rep. and completion bond rep. Made in Heaven, 1986; other prodn. credits include: Play it Again, Sam, 1971, Everything You Always Wanted to Know About Sex..., 1972, Time to Run, 1972, Haunts, 1975, Mahogany (Montage), 1975, King Kong, 1976, The Betsy, 1977. Mem. Dirs. Guild Am. Republican. Home: 8162 Kirkwood Dr Los Angeles CA 90046

FRANKL, KEITH E., lawyer; b. N.Y.C., July 12, 1956; s. Kenneth R. and Connie P. Frankl. BA in Polit. Sci., U. Denver, 1979. Bar: Colo. 1982, U.S. Dist. Ct. Colo., 1982. Assoc. Quiat Bucholtz, Denver, 1983-87, Podoll & Podoll, Denver, 1987—; sec. and chairperson Colo. Grievance Policy Commn., Denver, 1985. Author: Continuing Liability for Corporate Debts: The Colorado Lawyer, vol. 14, 1985. Mem. Colo. Bar Assn., Denver Bar Assn. Avocation: karate. Home: 9725 E Harvard BB 459 Denver CO 80231 Office: Podoll & Podoll 3530 Republic Plaza 370 17th St Denver CO 80231

FRANKLE, ALLAN HENRY, psychologist; b. Des Moines, Nov. 5, 1921; s. Harry Raymond and Ruth (Cohen) F.; m. Esther Alpern, June 22, 1947; children: Katherine, Jonathan. Student U. Chgo., 1939, Ph.D., 1953; student U. Minn., 1943. Dir. Des Moines Child Guidance Ctr., 1947-52; pvt. practice clin. psychology, Des Moines, 1952-85, clin. research, 1985—; Univ. fellow Drake U., 1970—; vis. clin. assoc. prof. psychology U. Iowa, 1969-70; cons. clin. psychology Broadlawns Polk County Hosp., 1967-81; cons. VA Hosp., Knoxville, Iowa, 1976-81; supervising psychologist N.Am. Mensa, 1966-78. Served with U.S. Army, 1943-45. Decorated Bronze Star. Diplomate Am. Bd. Profl. Psychology. Contbr. articles to profl. jours. Fellow Am. Orthopsychiat. Assn.,; mem. Am. Psychol. Assn., Iowa Psychol. Assn. (pres. 1960-61, Disting. Service award 1973), Am. Acad. Psychotherapists, Internat. Neuropsychology Soc., Brit. Psychol. Soc. (fgn. mem.), Sigma Xi, Psi Chi, Mensa. Democrat. Jewish. Home: 7931 Caminito Del Cid La Jolla CA 92037

FRANKLIN, CHARLES ELLSWORTH, social worker, sociologist, educator; b. Washington, Apr. 1, 1947; s. William McHenry and Alicelia (Hoskins) F.; m. Cynthia Jean Beattie, Nov. 22, 1975; children—Nathan Charles, Andrew Warner. B.A. in Psychology and Sociology, Earlham Coll., 1969; M.S.W., U. Wash., 1973; Ph.D. in Sociology, U. Colo., 1981. Trainee Eastern State Hosp., Medical Lake, Wash., 1972-73; therapist Bethesda Mental Health Ctr., Denver, 1973—; ptnr. Colo. Discourse Cons.; assoc. Arvada Psychol. and Family Service, 1982-84; pvt. practice specializing in psychotherapy, Denver; research assoc. TOSCO Found., Boulder, Colo., 1977-78; assoc. Greenwood Psychotherapy and Counseling Assocs., Englewood, Colo., 1979-81; mem. faculty family therapy cert. program Grad. Sch. Social Work, U. Denver, 1984—. Contbr. articles to profl. publs. Vol., Am. Friends Service Com., 1966-71. Recipient Amigos de las Americas Service award, 1976, 78. Mem. Am. Sociol. Assn., Nat. Assn. Social Workers, Acad. Cert. Social Workers. Home: 2217 Elm St Denver CO 80207 Office: 425 S Cherry St Suite 570 Denver CO 80222

FRANKLIN, DELANCE FLOURNOY, horticulture educator; b. Yakima County, Wash., Apr. 9, 1909; s. Watson Miller Taylor and Hattie Belle (Flournoy) F.; m. Florence Rebecca Kooser, Sept. 3, 1935; children: DeLance Flournoy Jr., Eleanor Gay. BS in Agriculture, U. Idaho, 1942, MS in Agriculture, 1955. Food products inspector Idaho State Dept. Agriculture, 1928-39; asst. horticulturist U. Idaho, Parma, 1942-45, assoc. horticulturist, 1945-50; supr. Agricultural Research and Extension Ctr., Parma, 1942-74; research prof. horticulture U. Idaho, Parma, 1950-74, research prof. emeritus, 1974—; collaborator USDA, 1942-74, cons. 1974—; cons. to U.N., Cairo, 1974; chmn., co-founder Nat. Carrot and Onion Improvement Program, 1960; originator numerous F, hybrid onions and carrots; sec. Idaho Seed Council, 1955-73. Contbr. numerous articles to profl. jours. Trustee Parma Devel. Corp., 1955-60, Sch. Bd., Parma, 1945-50, Idaho State Redevel. Bd., Boise, 1968-74. Named Disting. Citizen, Idaho Statesman Newspaper, 1968, Man-of-Yr., Pacific Seedsmen's Assn., 1968; recipient Disting. Service award Idaho-Eastern Oreg. Seed Assn., 1971, U. Idaho Gold and Silver award, 1985. Mem. Idaho Seed Council (hon.), Idaho Seed Assn. (hon.), Parma C. of C. (pres. 1943-45), Am. Soc. Hort. Scis., Nat. Carrot and Onion Confs., SW Idaho-Eastern Oreg. Onion Assn. (Hall of Fame 1987), Nat. Soc. Horticulturists, Entomologists and Plant Pathologists (pres. 1958-59), Sigma Xi, Alpha Zeta (Chancellor 1941—), Phi Gamma Delta, Gamma Sigma Delta. Republican. Lodge: Shriners, Lions (pres. Parma club 1949—). Avocations: photography, golfing, fishing, travel. Home: 227 N 10th St Parma ID 83660

FRANKLIN, MICHAEL HAROLD, orgn. exec.; b. Los Angeles, Dec. 25, 1923; children—Barbara, John, James, Robert. A.B., UCLA, 1948; LL.B., U. So. Calif., 1951. Bar: Calif. bar 1951. Practiced in Los Angeles, 1951-52; pvt. practice 1951-52; atty. CBS, 1952-54, Paramount Pictures Corp., 1954-58; exec. dir. Writers Guild Am. West, Inc., 1958-78; nat. exec. dir. Dirs. Guild Am., Inc., 1978—; Mem. Fed. Cable Adv. Commn. Served with C.E. AUS, 1942-46. Mem. ACLU, Los Angeles Copyright Soc., Order of Coif. Office: Dirs Guild Am Inc 1129 Maybrook Dr Beverly Hills CA 90210

FRANKOVICH, TOM BERNARD, artist, art educator; b. Belleville, Ill., Sept. 19, 1951; s. Bernard Michael and Bernadine Mary (Behrman) F. AA, Sch. Tech. Careers, 1971; BA, So. Ill. U., 1974; postgrad., George Washington U., 1975-76, Corcoran Sch. Art, 1976; MA, San Diego State U., 1979. Cert. community coll. tchr., Calif. Graphic artist Sta. KPBS TV and Radio, San Diego, 1977-78; art dir. County of San Diego PLU, 1978-82; dir. corp. design Ziggy's Restaurants Inc., Newport Beach, Calif., 1979; prof. art U.S. Internat. U., San Diego, 1983-86, Mesa Coll., San Diego, 1980—; curator exhibitions San Diego County Artist Exhibition, 1980; dir. univ. gallery U.S. Internat. U., 1984-86; juror San Diego Art Inst., 1986, Clairemont (Calif.) Artist Guild, 1986, Sculptor's Guild, Calif., 1986. One-man shows include Installation Gallery, San Diego, 1981, Fed. Bldg., San Diego, 1981, Gallery 38, San Diego, 1980, San Diego State U. Gallery, 1979, Unicorn Gallery, La Jolla, Calif., 1979, Beasley Gallery, San Diego, 1986, Univ. Gallery U.S. Internat. U., 1984, Keller Gallery Point Loma Coll., San Diego, 1983, Boehm Gallery, Palomar Gallery, San Marcos, Calif., 1983, San Diego Art Inst., 1983; exhibited in group shows at Maple Creek Gallery, San Diego, 1982, Lenten Art Exhibition, San Diego, 1982, 81 (award 1982), Small Image VII, San Diego, 1982, San Diego Art Inst., 1981, A.R.T. Beasley Gallery, San Diego, 1981-82, So. Calif. Contemporary Art Galleries, Los Angeles, 1979-82, Riverside (Calif.) Art Mus., 1979-82, San Diego Art Inst., 1979-82, The Drawing Gallery, Pozan, Poland, 1981, La Jolla Art Assn., 1981, Gaslamp Gallery, San Diego, 1981, San Diego County Adminstrn. Ctr., 1980, Gallery 21, San Diego, 1980, So. Calif. Expo., Imperial Valley, 1980, San Diego Art Inst., 1979, Los Angeles Art Assn. Galleries, 1979, Knowles Art Ctr., La Jolla, 1979, San Diego Mus. Art, 1979, 1983-86, U.S. Fed. Bldg., San Diego, 1979, Sheraton Park Hotel Gallery, Washington, 1978, So. Calif. Expo, Del Mar, 1978, Inter-Cultural Art Gallery, San Diego, 1977-79, Muth Gallery, Washington, 1976, Capital for the Age of Enlightenment, N.Y.C., 1975, So. Ill. U. Gallery, Carbondale, 1973-74, UNNA Gallery, Chgo. and Seoul, Republic of Korea, 1986; contbr. articles to profl. jours. Bd. dirs. San Diego Mus. Art, 1985—, San Diego Art Inst., 1972-74. Recipient 1st award Mayor San Diego County, 1980, 1st award La Jolla Art Assn. Ann., 1986, Best Exhibition of Yr. award USIU Creative Soc., San Diego, 1984, NAEB Graphics award, Washington, 1978, AWard for Excellence in Art, U.S. Info. Agy., Washington, 1976, Distinctive Merit award So. Ill. U., 1974. Mem. San Diego Artist Guild (bd. dirs. 1984—), San Diego Art Inst. (bd. dirs. 1972-74), La Jolla Mus. Contemporary Art., Los Angeles Mus. Contemporary Art, Fed. Design Council, Bullmoose Group (founder 1981). Home: 2034 29th St San Diego CA 92104 Office: Mesa Coll Fine Arts Dept 7250 Mesa Coll Dr San Diego CA 92111-4998

FRANKS, LARRY ALLEN, technical company executive; b. Chesterland, Ohio, July 22, 1934; s. Edward Ewald and Margaret Muriel (Bartlett) F.; m. Donna Adell, Aug. 27, 1960; children: Gregory Allen, Gwendolyn Marie. AB, Hiram Coll., 1958; MS, Vanderbilt U., 1960, PhD, 1968. Sci. specialist EG&G, Inc., Santa Barbara, Calif., 1972-76, head sect., 1976-83, mgr. dept., 1985, asst. program mgr., 1985—. Contbr. articles to profl. jours.; patentee in field. AEC fellow. Mem. Am. Phys. Soc. Office: EG&G/EM 130 Robin Hill Rd Goleta CA 93017

FRANSON, LESLIE ORAL, podiatrist; b. Payson, Utah, Jan. 23, 1945; s. Oral Maxwell and Nelda Ann (Johnson) F.; m. Linda Darlene Whitten, Dec. 15, 1967; children: Angelique, Tad, Christopher. BS, Brigham Young U., 1970; Doctor of Podiatric Medicine, Calif. Coll. of Podiatric Medicine, 1976. Diplomate Nat. Bd. Podiatry Examiners. Practice medicine specializing in podiatry Portland, Oreg., 1976—. Chmn. Crime Prevention Task Force, Gresham, Oreg., 1983-84. Served with USN, 1970. Named Eagle Scout Boy Scouts Am., 1963. Mem. Am. Podiatric Med. Assn., Oreg. Podiatric Med.

Assn., Gateway Boosters, Alpha Gamma Kappa. Mormon. Avocations: oil painting, carpentry, hunting, white water rafting. Home: 1924 SE 139th Portland OR 97233 Office: 1701 NE 122d Portland OR 97230

FRANTZ, JOHN CORYDON, librarian; b. Seneca Falls, N.Y., Aug. 25, 1926; s. John Clark and Cora May (Gilbert) F.; m. Vivien May Rowan, Dec. 31, 1947; children—Sheila Heather, Keith Hunter, Jay Corydon. A.B., Syracuse (N.Y.) U., 1950, B.S., 1951, M.S., 1952. Cons. Wis. State Library, 1954-58; dir. Green Bay (Wis.) Pub. Library, 1958-61; dir. pub. library grants U.S. Office Edn., 1961-67; dir. Bklyn. Pub. Library, 1967-70, Nat. Book Com., 1970-75; exec. chmn. Pahlavi Nat. Library, Tehran, Iran, 1975-77; librarian San Francisco Pub. Library, 1977-87; bd. dirs. Reading is Fundamental, Bookmobile Services Trust, Am. Reading Council, Metro Research Libraries Council. Served with U.S. Army, 1945-47. Mem. Am., N.Y. State, Calif. library assns. Club: Coffee House (N.Y.C.). Home: 1390 Market St San Francisco CA 94102 Office: Public Library Civic Center San Francisco CA 94102

FRANTZ, PAUL LEWIS, lawyer; b. Bozeman, Mont., Sept. 11, 1955; s. Walter Kirke and Charlotte Catherine (Caldwell) F. BS in Bus. and Fin., Mont. State U., 1978; JD, U. Mont., 1983; M in Internat. Mgmt., Am. Grad. Sch. Internat. Mgmt., 1985. Bar: Mont. 1983, U.S. Dist. Ct. Mont. 1983, U.S. Ct. Internat. Trade 1984, U.S. Ct. Appeals (9th cir.) 1986. Law clk. to U.S. magistrate Billings, 1983-84; law clk. to judge U.S. Dist. Ct., Helena, 1985; assoc. Morrow, Sedivy & Bennett, Bozeman, 1985—. Mem. Mont. Bar Assn. Baptist. Lodge: Kiwanis. Home: 112 Sunset Blvd Bozeman MT 59715 Office: Morrow Sedivy & Bennett 1st Security Bank Bldg PO Box 1168 Bozeman MT 59771-1168

FRANTZ, THEODORE CLAUDE, fisheries biologist; b. Reno, Jan. 27, 1922; s. Theodore and Alma Natalia (Swanson) F.; B.S. in Biology, U. Nev., 1951. Researcher stream and lake surveys Nev. Dept. Wildlife, 1951-58, mgr. fisheries Eastern Nev., 1958-60, researcher interstate fisheries study, Lake Tahoe, Nev., 1960-65, mgr. fisheries Western Nev., Smith, 1965—. Mem. Lake Tahoe Basin Environ; Coms., 1970-72; mem. tech. resource team Lake Tahoe Regional Planning Agy., 1982-85. Served with USNR, 1942-45. Recipient Nev. Fish and Game Fisheries Project, 1964, Shikar Safari Internat. award, 1981; commended by Lake Tahoe Area Council, 1972. Mem. Am. Fisheries Soc., Wildlife Soc. Contbr. articles on fisheries research to tech. jours. Home and office: PO Box 50 Smith NV 89430

FRANZ, DONALD NORBERT, pharmacology educator; b. Indpls., Sept. 23, 1932; s. Norbert John and Henrietta P. (Bluemel) F.; m. Barbara L. Stiver, Sept. 14, 1958 (div. Nov. 1984); children: Diane Valerie, Beth Lorraine. BS, Butler U., 1954, MS, 1961; PhD, U. Utah, 1966. Research assoc. Edinburgh U., Scotland, U.K., 1966-68; asst. prof. U. Utah, Salt Lake City, 1968-75, assoc. prof., 1975-85, prof., 1985—; medico-legal cons., Salt Lake City, 1984—. Contbg. author: Pharmacological Basis of Therapeutics, 1975, 80, 85; contbr. numerous research articles to other books and profl. jours. Served with U.S. Army, 1954-56. USPHS, NIH fellow, Edinburgh, 1966-68, David P. Gardner fellow U. Utah, 1981; NIH, Nat. Heart, Lung and Blood Inst. research grant, 1979-86. Mem. AAAS, Am. Soc. Pharmacology and Exptl. Therapeutics, Soc. for Neurosci., Am. Heart Assn. (high blood pressure council). Lutheran. Office: Univ Utah Dept Pharmacology Salt Lake City UT 84132

FRANZ, KAY B(URTA), nutrition educator; b. Walkermine, Calif., Oct. 30, 1936; d. John Cahoon and Eva (Burton) F. BS, U. Calif., Berkeley, 1958, PhD, 1978; MS, Brigham Young U., 1968. Registered dietitian. Lab. technician U. Calif., Davis, 1958-59, U. Wash., Seattle, 1959-63; research asst. Sch. Pub. Health Harvard U., Boston, 1963-65; instr. food sci., nutrition Brigham Young U., Provo, Utah, 1966-78, asst. prof., 1978-83, assoc. prof., 1983—; cons. Oak Ridge Nat. Lab. Mem. AAAS, Am. Dietetic Assn., Inst. Food Technologists, Am. Coll. Nutrition, Am. Soc. Magnesium Research, Sigma Xi (bd. dirs. 1986—), Phi Kappa Phi. Mormon. Office: Brigham Young U Dept Food Sci and Nutrition Provo UT 84602

FRANZMANN, ALBERT WILHELM, wildlife veterinarian, consultant; b. Hamilton, Ohio, July 19, 1930; s. Wilhelm Heinreich and Louise Marie (Schlichter) F.; m. Donna Marie Grueser, Dec. 13, 1953; children: Karl Wilhelm, Louise Ann. DVM, Ohio State U., 1954; PhD, U. Idaho, 1971. Veterinarian Tiffin (Ohio) Animal Hosp., 1956-59; gen. practice vet. medicine Hamilton, 1959-68; NDEA research fellow U. Idaho, Moscow, 1968-71; wildlife cons. F-2 Wildlife Cons., Moscow, 1971-72; dir. moose research ctr. Alaska Dept. Fish and Game, Soldotna, 1972—; bd. dirs. Hamilton Tool Co., 1986—; cons. in field. Contbr. 85 articles to profl. jours. Served to capt. USAF, 1954-56. Named Disting. Moose Biologist, N.Am. Moose Conf., Prince George, B.C., Can.,1983. Mem. AVMA, Am. Assn. Wildlife Veterinarians (pres. 1979-81), Wildlife Disease Assn. (council 1980-81), Am. Assn. Zoo Veterinarians, The Wildlife Soc. (cert. wildlife biologist), Phi Zeta, Xi Sigma Pi. Republican. Lodge: Elks. Avocations: photography, hunting, fishing, travel, exploration. Home: PO Box 666 Soldotna AK 99669 Office: Alaska Dept Fish and Game Moose Research Ctr Box 3150 Soldotna AK 99669

FRANZONE, ALBERT DAVID, manufacturing company executive; b. Rockville Centre, N.Y., July 9, 1954; s. John Peter and Vivian Ruth (Lawton) F.; m. Carol Bisson, June 4, 1976. BS, USCG Acad., 1976; MS, U. So. Calif., 1980. Commd. lt. USCG, Washington, 1976; resigned USCG, 1981; prodn. mgr. Pepsico, Los Angeles, 1981-83; engring. mgr. Am. Hosp. Supply Corp., Los Angeles, 1983-85; project mgr. Optical Radiation Corp., Los Angeles, 1985-86; dir. advanced tech. Unitek Corp., Los Angeles, 1986-87; dir. mfg. United Corp., Los Angeles, 1987—. Republican. Methodist. Avocations: sailing, scuba diving. Home: 2322 Clark Ave Venice CA 90291 Office: Unitek Corp 2724 S Peck Rd Monrovia CA 91016

FRASCO, DAVID LEE, chemistry educator; b. Brush, Colo., Apr. 8, 1931; s. Anthony Eric and Elma Arlene (Bartram) F.; m. Nancy Ann Morrison, Aug. 29, 1954 (dec. Oct. 1975); children: Michael, Eric; m. Emilie Gwyn Williams, Oct. 8, 1976; stepchildren: Bradley, Barry. BA, No. Colo. U., 1953; MS, Wash. State U., 1955, PhD, 1958. Teaching asst. Wash. State U., Pullman, 1953-56, research asst., 1956-58; cons. Battelle Northwestern Labs., Richland, Wash., 1966-75; prof. chemistry Whitman Coll., Walla Walla, Wash., 1958—, chmn. dept. chemistry, 1984—. Contbr. articles to profl. jours. Mem. Sigma Xi.

FRASER, ROBERT HENRY, marketing executive; b. Washington, Apr. 30, 1939; s. Havelock F. and Dorothy (Cassel) F. B.A., U. Ky., 1962; B.A. in Bus., Mich. State U., 1963. Dir. advt. John R. Thompson Co., Chgo., 1963-69; v.p. David W. Evans Advt., Los Angeles, 1969-76; v.p. mktg. Lyon's Restaurants, Inc., Foster City, Calif., 1976—. Republican. Presbyterian. Office: 1165 Triton Dr Foster City CA 94404

FRASER-SMITH, ELIZABETH BIRDSEY, microbiologist; b. Pasadena, Calif., Apr. 19, 1938; s. William Canvin and Elizabeth Armstrong (Creswell) Birdsey; m. Antony Charles Fraser-Smith, Apr. 6, 1968; children: Julie Gaye, William Antony. BA, Stanford U., 1960, MA, 1962. From assoc. scientist to sr. scientist Lockheed Missiles and Space Co., Palo Alto, Calif., 1960-69; biologist Enviros, Los Altos, Calif., 1973-77; from biologist II to staff researcher II Syntex Research Corp., Palo Alto, 1977—; tchr. exploratory experience program Palo Alto Unified Sch. Dist., 1966-68; tchr. Lyceum for Gifted Students, Palo Alto, 1978-80. Author: Child Ecology: A Resource for the Elementary School Teacher, 1974; contbr. articles to profl. jours.; patentee in field. Mem. AAAS, Am. Soc. Microbiology, Assn. Research in Vision and Ophthalmology. Avocations: sailing, piano, organ, swimming, running. Home: 71 Alma Ct Los Altos CA 94022 Office: Syntex Research Corp 2375 Charleston Rd Mountain View CA 94043

FRASURE, CARL C., history educator; b. Spokane, Wash., Aug. 4, 1944; s. Carl and Harriet (Hartford) F.; m. Patricia Day, Nov. 2, 1978. BA, Eastern Wash. U., 1968, MA, 1972. Prof. history U. Alaska, Anchorage, 1974—; pres. Campus Assembly, Anchorage, 1980-84. Editor: (oral history) Gold Rush, 1980. Active Alaska Vietnam Vets. Task Force, Anchorage, 1982-84. Served to capt. MI, 1969-72. Decorated Bronze Star. Mem. Alaska Fedn. of Tchrs. (pres. 1981-83). Democrat. Home: 2715 N Pines #1 Spokane WA 99206

FRAZER, CLOYCE CLEMON, retired educator; b. Warren, Ark., Jan. 2, 1919; s. Charles Columbus and Maude Mae (Jones) F.; m. Beverley Jane Mundorff, Apr. 10, 1942. B.A., Calif. State U.-San Jose, 1952, M.A., Calif. State U.-Sacramento, 1961. Cert. spl. secondary life diploma in indsl. arts, 1959, gen. secondary life diploma, 1960, standard teaching credentials life, 1971, services, 1971 (all Calif.); FAA comml. pilot lic. with flight instr. cert., 1949, aircraft and power plant lic., 1948. Aircraft mechanic, flight instr., Oakland, Calif., 1946-50; tchr. Folsom (Calif.) Unified Sch. Dist., 1953-54, Sacramento City Unified Sch. Dist., 1954-63; tchr. San Mateo (Calif.) Union High Sch. Dist., 1963-83, dept. head, 1963-73, program evaluator, 1976-77. Pres., Crestmoor High Sch. Faculty Assn., 1965-66; treas. Calif. Aerospace Edn. Assn., 1983—, pres. No. sect., 1978-79; mem. advocacy com. San Mateo County Commn. on Aging. Served to major USAF, 1941-79. Recipient honorable mention for sculpture San Mateo County Fair and Floral Fiesta, 1967. Mem. NEA, Calif. Tchrs. Assn., Calif. Ret. Tchrs. Assn. (pres. San Mateo County div. 1986—), Calif. Aerospace Edn. Assn., Air Force Assn., Calif. Indsl. Edn. Assn., Vocat. Edn. Assn., Am. Craft Council, Aircraft Owners and Pilots Assn., Exptl. Aircraft Assn. (Individual Achievement award 1982), Res. Officers Assn. U.S., Epsilon Pi Tau. Democrat. Club: Caterpillar. Contbr. articles to profl. jours.; co-author curriculum materials. Home: 620 Alameda Belmont CA 94002

FRAZER, GREGORY JAMES, audiology researcher; b. Sacramento, Sept. 28, 1952; s. Wilbur Robert and Miriam Dorothy (Quinn) F. BA in Speech Pathology and Audiology, Calif. State U., Sacramento, 1974; MS in Audiology and Counseling of Deaf/Hearing Impaired, U. Utah, 1976; PhD in Audiology, Wayne State U., 1981. Cert. audiologist, hearing aid dispenser, Calif. Intern U. Utah Med. Ctr., Salt Lake City, 1974-76, Detroit Med. Ctr., 1976-78, Henry Ford Hosp., Detroit, 1978-81; dir. audiology Midwest Health Ctr., Dearborn, Mich., 1981, Pulec Ear Clinic, Los Angeles, 1982, Olive View Med. Ctr., Van Nuys, Calif., 1984-85, Auditory-Vestibular Ctr., Panorama City, Calif., 1982—; clin. prof. audiology UCLA Sch. Medicine Head and Neck Surgery, 1986—. Bd. dirs. Citizens for Health Care Rights, Van Nuys, 1985—. Scholar Calif. State U., Sacramento, 1970-71, Wayne State U. Grad. Profl., Detroit, 1979-80; grantee Rehab. Services U. Utah, 1974-76. Mem. Am. Speech Lang. Hearing Assn., Calif. Speech Lang. Hearing Assn., Internat. Electric Response Audiometry Study Group, Acad. Dispensing Audiologists, Am. Tinnitus Assn., Am. Auditory Soc., Centurions of Deafness Research Found., Assn. Research in Otolaryngology, Nat. Hearing Aid Soc., Caif. Speech Pathologists and Audiologists in Pvt. Practice, Nat. Assn. Hearing and Speech Action, Calif. Hearing Aid Assn., San Fernando Valley Speech Pathologists and Audiologists (bd. dirs. 1985—), Phi Kappa Phi, Sigma Alpha Epsilon (pres. 1973-74). Republican. Roman Catholic. Avocations: snow and water skiing, golf, tennis, backpacking, jogging. Home: 4116 Perlita Ave Los Angeles CA 90039 Office: Auditory-Vestibular Ctr 14427 Chase St #103 Panorama City CA 91402

FRAZER, JOAN ROSE, association executive, writer; b. Rutland, Vt., Aug. 28, 1930; d. Harry and Ethel Mintzer; m. David Ray Frazer, July 26, 1953; children: Douglas, Thomas. BA with honors, U. Mich., 1952; MA with honors, Ariz. State U., 1966. Speech clinician pub. schs. Mich. and Va., 1952-63; speech clinician Madison Sch., Phoenix 1 Schs., Creighton (Ariz.) Schs., 1963-82; pres. Contacts and Connections, Inc., Phoenix, 1982—; cons. speech and lang. Headstart programs, Phoenix, 1972-75; v.p. Communication Skill Builders Pub. Co., 1966-86; bd. dirs. Ariz. Bus. Alliance. Co-author: Peel 'n Put Book series, 1968-77, Star Trails Workbooks (McMillan Book of Month, 1978, 80), Shape Up Your Language (Macmillan Book of month) 1983, 40,000 Selected Words (Macmillan Book of Month, 1987). Bd. dirs. Jewish Fedn. Community Relations Com., 1984—, Jewish Bus. and Profl. Women, 1983—. Recipient Woman of Yr. award Women's Council of Jewish Fedn., 1984—, Histadrut award AFL-CIO, 1980, Headstart award LEAP Edn. Council, 1976. Mem. Am. Speech and Hearing Assn., Ariz. Speech and Hearing Assn., Charter 100, Jewish Bus. and Profl. Women (pres. 1983-85, Achievement award 1985). Democrat. Jewish. Clubs: Plans (Scottsdale, Ariz.), Sales Profls. (Phoenix), U. Mich. (Phoenix) (pres. 1967). Avocations: gardening, baking, aerobics. Office: Contacts and Connections for Singles 2001 E Campbell Suite 203 Phoenix AZ 85018

FRAZIER, JANICE DIANNE, chemist, researcher; b. San Mateo, Calif., Jan. 15, 1956; d. Melvin Sidney and Wilma Frazier. Student, U. London, 1976-77; ScB in Chemistry with honors, U. Calif., Berkeley, 1978; ScM in Chemistry, U. Calif. San Diego, La Jolla, 1980, PhD, 1984. Research asst. U. Calif., Berkeley, 1978; research and teaching asst. U. Calif. San Diego, La Jolla, 1978-84, synthetic chemist, 1984; postdoctoral fellow IBM Research Facilities, San Jose, Calif., 1984-86, research staff mem., 1986—. Contbr. articles to profl. jours. Chevron fellow, 1981-82. Mem. Am. Chem. Soc. Avocations: equestrian activities, river rafting, windsurfing, softball, dancing. Office: IBM Research K91/802 650 Harry Rd San Jose CA 95120-6099

FRAZIER, J(OHN) PHILLIP, manufacturing company executive; b. Beech Grove, Ind., Mar. 2, 1939; s. Stanley C. and Dorothy E. Frazier; m. Carole Gilbert, Aug. 15, 1964; children: Gregory and Bradley (twins), Natalie. BS, Butler U., 1965; MBA, Harvard U., 1969. Acct. Wolf & Co., Indpls., 1962-65; acct. Cummins Engine Co., Inc., Columbus, Ind., 1965-73, controller, 1970-73; pres., chief exec. officer Hyster Co., Portland, Oreg., 1973—; bd. dirs. Guy F. Atkinson Co. Calif. Bd. dirs. United Way-Columbia Willamette. Served with USAR, 1957-61. Mem. Harvard U. Bus. Sch. Assn. (past pres., chmn. Oreg. chpt). Republican. Presbyterian. Clubs: Portland Golf, Arlington (Portland). Avocations: golf, tennis. Home: 722 NW Albemarle Terr Portland OR 97210 Office: Hyster Co PO Box 2902 700 NE Multnomah 16th Floor Portland OR 97208

FRAZIER, KENDRICK CROSBY, writer, editor; b. Windsor, Colo., Mar. 19, 1942; s. Francis Elliott and Sidney Lenore (Crosby) F.; m. Ruth Toelle, Sept. 10, 1964; children—Christopher, Michele. B.A. in Journalism, U. Colo., 1964; M.S., Columbia U., 1966. Reporter Greeley (Colo.) Daily Tribune, 1962; news editor Golden (Colo.) Transcript, 1963-64; newsman Denver bur. UPI, 1964-65; editor News Report, Nat. Acad. Scis., Washington, 1966-69; earth scis. editor Sci. News mag., Washington, 1969-70; mng. editor Sci. News mag., 1970-71, editor, 1971-77, contbg. editor, 1977-82; sci. writer Sandia Nat. Labs., Albuquerque, 1983—; editor The Skeptical Inquirer, 1977—; freelance sci. writer 1977—; adj. instr. U. Mo. Sch. Journalism, 1975-77; guest lectr. George Washington U., 1974-77; mem. com. pub. affairs Am. Geophys. Union, 1976-78. Author: The Violent Face of Nature, 1979, Our Turbulent Sun, 1982, Solar System, 1985, People of Chaco, 1986; also numerous articles on sci. topics; editor: Paranormal Borderlands of Science, 1981, Science Confronts the Paranormal, 1986. Boettcher Found. scholar, 1960-64; Pulitzer traveling fellow, 1966; Robert E. Sherwood scholar, 1966. Mem. Nat. Assn. Sci. Writers, Com. for Sci. Investigation of Claims of the Paranormal (editor 1977—, exec. council 1977—, dir. 1978—), Am. Astron. Soc. (hist. astronomy div.), Am. Polar Soc., Soc. South Pole, Planetary Soc. Home: 3025 Palo Alto Dr NE Albuquerque NM 87111

FREAS, GEORGE CRAIG, civil engineer, consultant; b. New Brunswick, N.J., Mar. 23, 1947; s. George Edwin and Virginia Grace (Woolnough) F.; m. Carol Louise Lease, June 22, 1969 (div. 1980); children: Miriam Rebekah, Virginia Elizabeth; m. Nancy Jean Cliff, May 21, 1983. BSCE, Pa. State U., 1969. Registered profl. engr., Alaska, Alta. Project engr. Wince-Corthell & Assocs., Kenai, Alaska, 1972-78; prin. Wince-Corthell-Bryson-Freas, Kenai, 1978-80; mgr. civil engring. Tryck Nyman & Hayes, Anchorage, 1980-84, ptnr., 1984—. Served with USN, 1970-72. Mem. ASCE, Am. Concrete Inst., Soc. Am. Mil. Engrs., Prestressed Concrete Inst., Assn. Profl. Engrs., Geologists and Geophysicists of Alta. Avocations: watercolor painting, photography. Home: 1004 Potlatch Circle Anchorage AK 99503 Office: Tryck Nyman & Hayes 911 W 8th Ave Anchorage AK 99501

FRECH, HARRY EDWARD, III, economics educator, consultant; b. St. Louis, Nov. 11, 1946; s. Harry Edward Jr. and Margaret Byrne (O'Reilly) F.; m. Carol Ann Vouga, June 8, 1968 (div. Aug. 1980); children: Jon Clayton, Justin Tyler; m. Elizabeth Chen, Apr. 9, 1983; 1 child, Michael Anthony. BS in Indsl. Engring., U. Mo., 1968; MA in Econs., UCLA, 1970, PhD in Econs., 1974. Economist HEW, Rockville, Md., 1970-72; asst. prof. econs. U. Calif., Santa Barbara, 1973-77, assoc. prof. econs., 1977-81, prof., 1981—; vis. asst. prof. econs. Harvard U., Cambridge, Mass., 1976-77; vis. prof. U. Chgo., 1982; sr. economist The Econs. Group, Santa Barbara, 1982—; econs. cons. FTC, Washington, 1977—, HHS, Washington, 1973-78; expert witness U.S. Dept. Justice, Washington, 1984—. Co-author: Public Insurance in Private Medical Markets, 1978; assoc. editor Economic Inquiry, 1975-78; mem. editorial bd. Am. Economic Review, 1980-82; contbr. articles to profl. jours. Bd. dirs. Christ Luth. Ch., Goleta, Calif., 1978. Research grantee HEW, 1976, Found. for Research in Econs. and Edn., 1974. Mem. Am. Econ. Assn., So. Econ. Assn., Western Econ. Assn., Pacific Inst. (co-editor health policy series, 1982—). Republican. Avocations: skiing, sports car racing, sailing, softball, reading. Home: 438 Pitzer Ct Goleta CA 93117 Office: U Calif Econs Dept Santa Barbara CA 93106

FREDELL, CONRADT HERBERT, biology educator, sports coach; b. Alamogordo, N.Mex., Nov. 2, 1951; s. C. Herbert and Eleanor (Shafer) F.; m. Jeri Lyn Wedgworth, June 12, 1976; children: Heidi Kirsten, Karl Gustaf. BS in Edn., No. Ariz. U., 1973, MA in Biology Edn., 1976. Cert. secondary tchr., Mont., Ariz., Colo., community coll. tchr., Ariz. Sci. tchr. Kingman (Ariz.) Jr. High, 1973-81, football coach, 1973-81, softball coach, 1978-81, basketball coach, 1980; biology tchr. Mohave Community Coll., Kingman, 1978; sci. tchr., varsity ski coach, asst. varsity football coach Clear Creek High Sch., Idaho Springs, Colo., 1981—. Del. Rep. Com., Idaho Springs, 1986. Named Eagle Scout Boy Scouts Am., 1965. Mem. NEA, Nat. Assn. Biology Tchrs., Nat. Assn. Sci. Tchrs., Colo. Edn. Assn., Clear Creek Edn. Assn., U.S. Ski Coaches Assn. Presbyterian. Avocations: music, hunting, fishing, photography, gardening. Home: PO Box 360 2101 Riverside Dr Idaho Springs CO 80452 Office: Clear Creek High Sch PO Box 3369 Idaho Springs CO 80452

FREDERICKS, WARD ARTHUR, manufacturing company executive; b. Tarrytown, N.Y., Dec. 24, 1939; s. Arthur George and Evelyn (Smith) F.; BS cum laude, Mich. State U., 1962, M.B.A., 1963; m. Patricia A. Sexton, June 12, 1960; children—Corrine E., Lorrine L., Ward A. Assoc. dir. Technics Group, Grand Rapids, Mich., 1964-68; gen. mgr. logistics systems Massey-Ferguson Inc., Toronto, 1968-69, v.p. mgmt. services, comptroller, 1969-73, sr. v.p. fin., dir. fin. Americas, 1975—; comptroller Massey-Ferguson Ltd., Toronto, Ont., Can., 1973-75; cons. W.B. Saunders & Co., Washington, 1962—; sr. v.p. mktg. Massey/Ferguson, Inc., 1975-80, also sr. v.p., gen. mgr. Tractor div., 1978-80; v.p. ops., Rockwell Internat., Pitts., 1980-84; v.p. Fed. MOG., 1983-84; pres. MixTec Corp., 1984—, also dir., chmn.; dir. Badger Northland Inc., Tech-Mark Inc., Mixtec Corp., Compu-Kore Ltd., Unicorn Corp., Harry Ferguson Inc., M.F. Credit Corp., M.F. Credit Co. Can. Ltd. Bd. dirs., mem. exec. com. Des Moines Symphony, 1975-79; exec. com. Conejo Symphony, Alliance for Arts.; mem. Constn. Bicentennial Com., 1987—, Gov.'s Task Force on Tech. Am. Transp. Assn. fellow, 1962-63; Ramlose fellow, 1962-63. Mem. Am. Mktg. Assn., Nat. Council Phys. Distbn. Mgmt. (exec. com. 1974), IEEE, Soc. Automotive Engrs., Toronto Bd. Trade, Westlake Village C. of C., Community Leaders Club, Pres.'s Club Mich. State U., Beta Gamma Sigma. Rotarian. Author: (with Edward W. Smykay) Physical Distribution Management, 1974. Contbr. articles to profl. jours. Home: 1640 Aspenwall Rd Westlake Village CA 91361 Office: 32123 Lindero Canyon Rd Westlake Village CA 91361

FREDERICKSEN, RICK STEWART, geologist; b. Pocatello, Idaho, Aug. 16, 1949; s. Stanley Stewart and Betty Ann (Dowling) F.; m. Melinda Jane Law, Oct. 4, 1980 (div. 1982). B.S., Idaho State U., 1971; M.S., U. Ariz., 1974. Engr.'s aide J.R. Simplot Co., Pocatello, 1969-71; geologist Dural Corp., Salt Lake City, 1971, Heinrich's Geoexploration, Tucson, 1972, Texasgulf, Inc., Denver, 1974-78; sr. geologist, v.p. WGM Inc., Anchorage, Alaska, 1978—, dir., 1983—. Contbr. articles to profl. jours. Mem. Alaska Miners Assn., N.W. Mining Assn., Am. Inst. Mining Engrs. Republican. Lutheran. Clubs: Internat. Mining (Anchorage); Investment. Home: 3105 Delta Dr Anchorage AK 99502 Office: WGM Inc 718 L St Anchorage AK 99510

FREDRICKS, WILLIAM JOHN, chemistry educator; b. San Diego, Sept. 18, 1924; s. William and Jenney (Cunnion) F.; m. Lola M. Dacy, Sept. 20, 1942. BS, San Diego State Coll., 1951; PhD, Oreg. State U., 1955. Technician, planner USN, San Diego, 1942-46; electronics technician Waldorf Appliance Co., San Diego, 1946-47; jr. civil engr. Calif. Div. Architecture, San Diego, 1947-51; phys. chemist, solid state mgr. Stanford Research Inst., Menlo Park, Calif., 1956-62; mem. faculty Oreg. State U., Corvallis, 1962—, prof. chemistry, 1967—; vis. acad. Atomic Research Establishment, Harwell, Eng., 1973-74; sr. vis. fellow U. Western Ont. Ctr. Chem. Physics, 1982; cons. in field. Contbr. articles to profl. jours. Chmn. Corvallis Airport Commn., 1979—. Fulbright fellow 1955-56. Mem. Am. Assn. Crystal Growth (mem. exec. bd. West Sect. 1976—), Am. Chem. Soc., Am. Phys. Soc., AAAS, Materials Research Soc., Oreg. State U Flying Club. Democrat. Avocations: flying, fishing, bonzai. Home: 641 NW 36th St Corvallis OR 97330 Office: Oreg State U Dept Chemistry Corvallis OR 97331

FREED, LEONARD ALAN, biology and zoology educator; b. Cleve., July 17, 1947; s. Irwin and Alice Jane (Winkelman) F.; m. Jean Dixon Barks, June 15, 1974 (div. Dec. 1980); 1 child, Rebecca. BA, Northwestern U., 1969, MS, PhD, U. Iowa, 1981. Postdoctoral fellow Smithsonian Instn., Republic of Panama, 1982-83; asst. prof. zoology, biology U. Hawaii, Honolulu, 1983—. Contbr. articles to profl. jours. Served to lt. USN, 1969-72. Recipient Research award NSF, 1978, 86, Nat. Geog. Soc., 1984-86. Mem. AAAS, Am. Ornithologists' Union, Animal Behavior Soc. (W.C. Allee award 1981), Ecol. Soc. Am., Sigma Xi. Avocations: hiking, woodworking. Office: U Hawaii Dept Zoology Honolulu HI 96822

FREED, PETER QUENTIN, amusement park executive; b. Salt Lake City, Jan. 8, 1921; s. Lester David and Jasmine (Young) F.; B.A. with honors, U. Utah, 1947; children—David Wicker, Michael Stahle, Howard Eldred, Anne, Kristen, Jennifer. Pres., Freed Corp., 1952-74; v.p., sec., Freed Co., 1952-74; exec. v.p. Amusement Service, Salt Lake City, 1947—; v.p. Terrace Co., Salt Lake City, from 1952; exec. v.p. Patio Gardens, Farmington, Utah, from 1956; v.p. Westworld Corp., Salt Lake City, from 1974, Pioneer Village Campground, Farmington, from 1975; dir. Pioneer Village, Farmington; pres. Lagoon Corp., Salt Lake City, 1974—. Mem. Union Sta. Theatre Bd. Served with USNR, 1942-45. Mem. Nat. Assn. Amusement Parks, Utah Mus. Assn. Republican. Christian Scientist. Clubs: Salt Lake Tennis, New Yorker. Home: 642 Aloha Rd Salt Lake City UT 84103 Office: Box N Farmington UT 84025

FREED, THOMAS ALEXANDER, radiologist; b. Cleve., Sept. 27, 1935; s. Alexander Norbert and Catherine Evelyn (Balogh) F.; m. Sally Joanna Catherine Twist, Aug. 8, 1963; children: Eric, Andrew. AB, Harvard U., 1957; MD, Case Western Res. U., 1961. Diplomate Am. Coll. Radiology. Resident Stanford (Calif.) U., 1962-66; asst. prof. radiology Med. Coll. Va., Richmond, 1966-67; sr. surgeon NIH, Bethesda, Md., 1967-69; radiologist Marin Gen. Hosp., Greenbrae, Calif., 1969—; assoc. prof. radiology Stanford U., 1969—; pres. Marin Radiology, Larkspur, Calif. 1982—. Contbr. articles to profl. jours. Served with USPHS, 1967-69. Mem. Am. Coll. Radiology, Radiol. Soc. N.Am., Western Angiography Soc. Club: Marin Tennis (San Rafael, Calif.). Avocations: reading, walking, tennis. Home: 14 Tamal Vista Ln Kentfield CA 94904 Office: Marin Radiology 900 Larkspur Landing Circle Larkspur CA 94939-1723

FREEDLAND, RICHARD ALLAN, biological researcher, educator; b. Pitts., May 9, 1931; s. Milton and Gertrude (Davis) F.; m. Beverly Jane Pachefsky, June 22, 1958; children: Howard M., Judith L., Stephen J. BS, U. Pitts., 1953; MS, U. Ill., 1955; PhD, U. Wis., 1958. Research assoc. U. Wis., Madison, 1958-60; lectr. U. Calif., Davis, 1960-61, asst. prof., 1961-65, assoc. prof., 1965-69, prof. physiol. chemistry, 1969-74, prof., chmn. physiol. scis., 1974—. Author: A Biochemical Approach to Nutrition, 1977; mem. editorial bd. Archives Biochemistry and Biophysics, 1978—, Jour. Biol. Chemistry, 1985—; assoc. editor Jour. of Nutrition, 1984—. Fellow AAAS; mem. Am. Soc. Biol. Chemists, Am. Inst. Nutrition, Am. Physiol. Soc., Biochem. Soc. (Eng.). Office: Univ of Calif Dept of Physiol Scis Davis CA 95616

FREEDMAN, DANIEL X., psychiatrist, educator; b. Lafayette, Ind., Aug. 17, 1921; s. Harry and Sophia (Feinstein) F.; m. Mary C. Neidigh, Mar. 20, 1945. B.A., Harvard U., 1947; M.D., Yale U., 1951; grad., Western New Eng. Inst. Psychoanalysis, 1966; D.Sc. (hon.), Wabash Coll., 1974, Indiana U., 1982. Intern pediatrics Yale Hosp., 1951-52, resident psychiatry, 1952-55; from instr. to prof. psychiatry Yale U., 1955-66; chmn. dept. U. Chgo., 1966-83, Louis Block prof. biol. scis., 1969-83; Judson Braun prof. psychiatry and pharmacology UCLA, 1983—; career investigator USPHS, 1957-66; dir. psychiatry and biol. sci. tng. program Yale U., 1960-66; cons. NIMH, 1960—, U.S. Army Chem. Center, Edgewood, Md., 1965-66; chmn. panel psychiat. drug efficacy study Nat. Acad. Sci.-NRC, 1966; mem. adv. com. FDA, 1967-78; rep. to div. med. scis. NRC, 1971-82, mem. com. on brain scis., 1971-73, mem. com. on problems of drug dependence, 1971—; mem. com. problems drug dependence Nat. Inst. Medicine, 1971-76, com. substance abuse, and habitual behavior, 1976-84; advisor Pres.'s Biomed. Research Panel, 1975-76; mem. selection com., coordinator research task panel Pres.'s Commn. Mental Health, 1977-78; mem. Jt. Commn. Prescription Drug Use, Inc., 1977—. Author: (with N.J. Giarman) Biochemical Pharmacology of Psychotomimetic Drugs, 1965, What Is Drug Abuse?, 1970, (with F.C. Redlich) The Theory and Practice of Psychiatry, 1966, (with D. Offer) Modern Psychiatry and Clinical Research, 1972; editor: (with J. Dyrud) American Handbook of Psychiatry, Vol. V, 1975, The Biology of the Major Psychoses: A Comparative Analysis, 1975; chief editor: Archives Gen. Psychiatry, 1970—. Bd. dirs. Founds. Fund for Research in Psychiatry, 1969-72, Drug Abuse Council, 1972-80; vice chmn. Drug Abuse Council Ill., 1972—. Served with AUS, 1942-46. Recipient Distinguished Achievement award Modern Medicine, 1973; William C. Menninger award ACP, 1975; McAlpin medal for research achievment, 1979; Vestermark award for edn., 1981. Fellow Am. Acad. Arts and Scis., Am. Psychiat. Assn. (chmn. commn. on drug abuse 1971—), Am. Coll. Neuropsychopharmacology (pres. 1970—); mem. Inst. Medicine Nat. Acad. Scis., A.C.P. (William C. Menninger award 1975), Ill. Psychiat. Soc. (pres. 1971-72), Social Sci. Research Council (dir. 1968-74), Chgo. Psychoanalytic Soc., Western New Eng. Psychoanalytic Inst., Am. Soc. Pharmacology and Exptl. Therapeutics, AAAS, Am. Assn. Chairmen Depts. Psychiatry (pres. 1972-73), Am. Psychiat. Assn. (v.p. 1975-77, pres.-elect 1980-81, pres. 1981-82), Group Advancement Psychiatry, Psychiat. Research Soc., Am. Psychosomatic Soc. (councillor 1970-73), Assn. Research in Nervous and Mental Disease (pres. 1974), Soc. Biol. Psychiatry (pres. 1985-86), Sigma Xi, Alpha Omega Alpha. Home: 806 Leonard Rd Los Angeles CA 90049 Office: Univ of CA Los Angeles Sch of Medicine 760 Westwood Plaza Los Angeles CA 90024

FREEDMAN, KENNETH DAVID, lawyer; b. N.Y.C., Dec. 25, 1947; s. Samuel and Ethel Roberta (Myers) F.; m. Maxine Lantin, July 25, 1976; children—Jill Rose-Sophia, Robert Lantin. B.S., Ariz. State U., 1970; M.Ed., U. Ariz., 1973; J.D., Calif. Western Sch. Law, San Diego, 1979. Bar: Ariz. 1980, D.C. 1985, U.S. Dist. Ct. Ariz. 1980, U.S. Ct. Internat. Trade, 1980, U.S. Ct. Mil. Appeals 1980, U.S. Ct. Appeals (9th cir.) 1980, U.S. Tax Ct. 1981, U.S. Supreme Ct. 1983, D.C. 1985. Grad. asst. U. Ariz., Tucson, 1972-73; adminstr. So. Colo. State Coll., Pueblo, 1973-74; adult probation officer Maricopa County Superior Ct., Phoenix, 1974-76, judge pro tem, 1986—, law clk. to chief presiding justices Maricopa County Superior Ct., 1979-80; assoc. Hocker, Yarbrough & Gilcrease, Tempe, Ariz., 1980-81; sole practice, Phoenix, 1981—; commr. pro tempore Juvenile div. Maricopa County Superior Ct., 1980—, instr. Park Coll., Williams AFB, 1976, Phoenix Coll., 1981—, U. Phoenix, 1985—; mem. disciplinary panel Ariz. State Bar, def. rep. exec. counsel criminal justice sect., mem. coms. legal edn., criminal and continuing legal edn. Served to 1st lt. U.S. Army, 1970-72. Mem. Nat. Assn. Criminal Def. Lawyers, Am. Arbitration Assn. (arbitration panel, 1986—), Ariz. State Univ. Greater Phoenix Alumni Assn. (bd. dirs.), Maricopa County Bar Assn. (chmn. com. on continuing legal edn. 1983-84, speakers bur.), Phi Alpha Delta. Republican. Jewish. Office: 11 W Jefferson St #16 Phoenix AZ 85003

FREEDMAN, LAWRENCE RAPHAEL, medicine educator; b. N.Y.C., Dec. 1, 1927; s. Hyman and Hannah (Epstein) F.; m. Rina Esther Stahl, Apr. 3, 1955; children: Julia, Leora. BS, Yale U., 1947, MD, 1951. Diplomate Am. Bd. Internal Medicine. Intern in internal medicine, asst. resident Yale New Haven (Conn.) Hosp., 1951-532, chief resident in internal medicine, 1956-57; asst. in pathology Johns Hopkins Hosp., Balt., 1955-56; prof. medicine Yale U., New Haven, Conn., 1970-73; prof. medicine, chmn. dept. U. Lausanne, Switzerland, 1973-80; prof. medicine UCLA Sch. Medicine, 1980—; chief med. services VA Wadsworth Med. Ctr., Los Angeles, 1980-86, assoc. chief of staff for edn., 1986—. Author: Infective Endocarditis, 1982; contbr. articles to profl. jours. Served to 1st lt. U.S. Army, 1953-55. Mem. Sociètè Suisse de Medecine Interne, Assn. Am. Physicians, Am. Soc. Clin. Investigation, We. Assn. Physicians, Sigma Xi, Alpha Omega Alpha. Jewish. Office: VA Wadsworth Med Ctr Wilshire and Santelle Blvds Los Angeles CA 90073

FREEDMAN, MERVIN BURTON, psychologist, educator; b. N.Y.C., Mar. 6, 1920; s. Eli and Rose (Weithorn) F.; m. Marjorie Ellingson, Feb. 16, 1952; children: Eric, Kristin, Rolf, Anne Marie. B.S., Coll. City N.Y., 1940; Ph.D., U. Calif. at Berkeley, 1950. Lectr. dept. psychology U. Calif. at Berkeley, 1950-53; research asso. Mellon Found. for Advancement Edn., Vassar Coll., 1953-58; dir. Mellon Found., 1958-60; research asso. Inst. for Study Human Problems, Stanford, 1962-63; asst. dean undergrad. edn. Inst. for Study Human Problems, 1963-65; chmn. dept. psychology San Francisco State U., 1965-68, prof. psychology, 1968—; dean grad. sch. Wright Inst., Berkeley, 1969-79; sr. Fulbright research scholar U. Oslo, 1961-62; fellow Center for Advanced Study Behavioral Sci., 1960-61. Author: The College Experience, 1967; (with others) Search for Relevance, 1969, Academic Culture and Faculty Development, 1978, Human Development in Social Settings, 1983, Personality and Social Change, 1986; Assoc. editor: Polit. Psychology. Vice pres. San Francisco Am.-Scandinavian Found. Served with AUS, 1941-45. Decorated Bronze Star. Fellow Am. Psychol. Assn.; mem. Western Psychol. Assn., Internat. Soc. Polit. Psychology. Home: 866 Spruce St Berkeley CA 94707 Office: Dept Psychology San Francisco State U San Francisco CA 94132

FREEDMAN, MICHAEL HARTLEY, mathematician, educator; b. Los Angeles, Apr. 21, 1951; s. Benedict and Nancy (Mars) F.; 1 child by previous marriage, Benedict C.; m. Leslie Blair Howland, Sept. 18, 1983; 1 child, Hartley. Ph.D., Princeton U., 1973. Lectr. U. Calif., 1973-75; mem. Inst. Advanced Study, Princeton, N.J., 1975-76; prof. U. Calif., San Diego, 1976—; Charles Lee Powell chair math. U. Calif., 1985—. Author: Classification of Four Dimensional Spaces, 1982; assoc. editor Jour. Differential Geometry, 1982—, Annals of Math., 1984—. MacArthur Found. fellow, 1984-89; named Calif. Scientist of Yr., Calif. Mus. Assn., 1984; recipient Veblen prize Am. Math. Soc., 1986, Fields medal Internat. Congress of Mathematicians, 1986. Mem. Nat. Acad. Scis., Am. Assn. Arts and Scis. Avocation: technical rock climber (soloed Northeast ridge Mt. Williamson 1970, Great Western boulder climbing champion 1979). Office: U Calif Dept Math C-012 La Jolla CA 92093

FREEDMAN, STANLEY DAVID, physician; b. Pitts., Oct. 12, 1935; s. Joseph and Mary (Shelkrot) F.; m. Saralyn Cohen, Aug. 11, 1957; children: Joseph Andrew, Eric Lewis, Douglas Marc. AB, Harvard U., 1957; MD, NYU, 1961. Cert. Am. Bd. Internal Medicine, Am. Bd. Infectious Diseases. Intern U. Pitts., 1961-62, resident, 1962-63, fellow, 1965-69; chief div. infectious disease York (Pa.) Hosp., 1969-76; asst. prof. medicine U. Md., Balt., 1972-76; head div. infectious disease Scripps Clinic, La Jolla, Calif., 1976—, vice chmn., dept. medicine, dir. GME, 1984—; assoc. clin. prof. medicine U. Calif., San Diego, 1976—; mem. dept. pathology Scripps Clinic, 1977—, bd. dirs., 1985-87; pres. med. staff Green Hosp. Scripps Clinic, 1985-87. Contbr. chpts. to books; contbr. articles to profl. jours. Served to capt. USAF, 1963-65. Fellow Infectious Diseases Soc. Am.; mem. ACP, Am. Soc. Microbiology, Calif. Med. Soc. Avocations: hiking, photography. Office: Scripps Clinic Head div. Infectious Diseases 10666 N Torrey Pines Rd La Jolla CA 92037

FREEL, MARLIN JAMES, manufacturing executive; b. Glendive, Mont., Feb. 27, 1924; s. Amos F. and Beatrice (Polen) F.; children—Michael, Cynthia. B.S., U. So. Calif., 1948; postgrad. Woodbury Coll., 1955, UCLA, 1973, LaVerne U. Law, 1974. Pres., Sproco Mfg. Inc., 1949-58; v.p. Tasker Instruments, 1958-63, mgr. contracts TRW Systems Group, 1964-68, Litton Data Systems, 1968-72; legal asst. Ingram, Baker & Griffiths Law Office, Covina, Calif., 1972-78; pres. Ricon Corp., Ricon Internat., Inc. and Ricon Sales, Sun Valley, Calif., 1978—, Freel Enterprizes, Inc., 1984—, M. Freel and Assocs., 1968—. Chmn. Park and Recreation Dept. City of San Dimas (Calif.), 1979—; PTA sch. bd. rep. Bonita Sch. Dist.; scoutmaster Boy Scouts Am., Troop 106, Pomona, Calif. Served with USN, 1942-46. Mem. U. So. Calif. Assocs. Co-inventor wheelchair lift, 1982. Office: Ricon Corp 11684 Tuxford St Sun Valley CA 91352

FREELAND, DARRYL CREIGHTON, psychologist, educator; b. Omaha, Feb. 22, 1939; s. Elverson Lafayette and Lauretta Joyce (Coffelt) F.; m. Tina Anne Richmond, July 21, 1979; children—Adam Daniel, Noah Nathan, Sarah Eileen. B.S., U. Nebr., 1961; S.T.B., Fuller Theol. Sem., 1965; M.A., Calif. State U.-Fullerton, 1966; Ph.D., U. So. Calif., 1972. Lic. psychologist, Calif.; lic. marriage, family and child therapist, Calif. Tchr. elem. schs., Calif., 1961-66; instr. Glendale Community Coll., Calif., 1966-67, Citrus Community Coll., Glendora, Calif., 1967-79; pvt. practice psychology, Laguna Niguel, Calif., 1969—; field faculty and vis. prof. Calif. State U.-Los Angeles, 1970, San Marino Community Presbyterian Ch., 1972, Calif. Sch. Profl. Psychology, Los Angeles, 1972-73, U. Calif.-Riverside, 1973, Humanistic Psychology Inst., San Francisco, 1976-79, Profl. Sch. Humanistic Studies, San Diego, 1983—; asst. dir. clin. tng. U.S. Internat. U., 1986-87, assoc. prof. psychology, 1986-87. Finisher, Newport Beach-Irvine Marathon, 1981, San Francisco Marathon, 1982. Office: 30131 Town Center Dr Suite 298 Laguna Niguel CA 92677

FREELAND, ROBERT FREDERICK, librarian; b. Flint, Mich., Dec. 20, 1919; s. Ralph V. and Susan Barbara (Goetz) F.; m. June Voshel, June 18, 1948; children: Susan Beth Visser, Kent Richard. BS, Eastern Mich. U., 1942; postgrad., Washington & Lee U., 1945; MS, U. So. Calif., 1948, postgrad., 1949; postgrad., U. Mich., 1950-52, Calif. State U., 1956-58, UCLA, 1960; LittD (hon.), Linda Vista Bible Coll., 1973. Music supr. Consol. Schs. Warren, Mich., 1946-47; music dir. Carson City (Mich.) Pub. Schs., 1948-49; librarian, audio-visual coordinator Ford Found., Edison Inst., Greenfield Village, Dearborn, Mich., 1950-52, Helix High Sch. Library, 1952—; librarian, prof. library sci. Linda Vista Bible Coll., 1976—; guest prof. Calif. State U., San Diego, 1963-66, U. Calif., San Diego, 1969-71, Linda Vista Bible Coll., 1970-72; lectr. San Diego City Coll., 1954-65, Grossmont Coll., El Cajon, 1966-68; librarian San Diego City Coll., 1953-54, San Diego County Library, 1955-56, San Diego Pub. Library, 1968—. Editor book and audio-visual aids review, Sch. Musician, Dir. and Teacher, 1950—. Former deacon and elder Christian Reform Ch., librarian, 1969-72. Served with USAAF, 1942-46. Named Scholar Freedoms Found., Valley Forge, Pa., 1976-80. Mem. NEA (life), ALA, Assn. for Ednl. Communication and Tech., Western Ednl. Soc. for Telecommunications, Calif. Tchrs. Assn., Music Library Assn. So. Calif. (adviser exec. bd.), Calif. Library Assn. (pres. Palomar chpt. 1972-73), Sch. Library Assn. Calif. (treas. 1956-58), Calif. Media and Library Educators (charter mem.), Am. Legion (Americanism chmn. 22d dist. San Diego County, chmn. oratorical contest com. La Mesa post), Ret. Officers Assn., San Diego Aero Space Mus., San Diego Mus. Art. Home: 4800 Williamsburg Ln Apt 223 La Mesa CA 92041 Office: 7323 University Ave La Mesa CA 92041

FREEMAN, CURTIS JAMES, geologist; b. Warren, Ohio, Apr. 4, 1956; s. Claude R. and Clara M. (DiMuzio) F.; m. Patricia DeLong, Mar. 26, 1983. BA in Geology, Coll. Wooster, 1978; MS in Econ. Geology, U. Alaska, 1980. Cert. geologist, Alaska. Geologist Exxon Minerals Co., Silver City, N.Mex., 1980-82; sr. geologist Nerco Minerals Co., Fairbanks, Alaska, 1982-85; pres. Onyx Exploration Inc., Fairbanks, 1985—; pres. Fairbanks Exploration Inc., 1985—, also bd. dirs. Grantee Chugach Gem and Mineral Soc., Anchorage, 1980. Mem. Alaska Miners Assn. (bd. dirs. 1985—), Am. Inst. Profl. Geologists (cert.), Sigma Xi, Phi Kappa Phi. Avocations: outdoor sports, basketball, hunting. Home: PO Box 74261 Fairbanks AK 99707 Office: Fairbanks Exploration Inc PO Box 82549 Fairbanks AK 99708

FREEMAN, DONNA RHEA, small business owner; b. Waldron, Ark., Apr. 18, 1937; d. Oliver Raymond and Lura Edna (Doyle) Cook; m. Clarence Lee Freeman, Jan. 24, 1954; children—Scott, Kevin, Steven, Melissa, Melinda. Student Humphrey's Bus. Coll., Stockton, Calif., U. So. Calif. Sec., Bodega Bay Sch. (Calif.), 1973-75; staff aquaculture dept. U. Calif. Bodega Marine Lab., 1976-77; real estate assoc., 1978-82; ptnr. Freeman's Union 76 Service, Bodega Bay, 1983—; co-owner fishing vessel Noyo Belle, 1981-84. Vice chmn. Shoreline Trust Ednl. Program Services, 1981—; bd. dirs. Bodega Bay Area Rescue, 1973-74; chmn. Bodega Bay Fisherman's Festival, 1973, 74, 83; alt. mem. Democratic Central Com., 1982; mem. local bd. SSS, 1982—; chmn. Spud Point Adv. Bd., 1985—; bd. dirs. Sonoma County Fair, 1985—, Costal Fisheries Found., 1986—; mem. Calif. Dem. Cen. Com.; Sonoma County grand juror; 1983-84; mgr. polit. campaign, 1984. Mem. Bodega Bay Fisherman's Aux., Bodega Bay C. of C. (pres. 1979-81, dir. 1982-86), Bodega Bay Community Assn., Bodega Bay Grange. Home: 1060 Bay View St Bodega Bay CA 94923

FREEMAN, HERBERT JAMES, educational administrator; b. Raleigh, N.C., May 14, 1941; s. Hurley Lee and Annie Lee (Upchurch) F.; m. Ollie Faye Mack, Aug. 23, 1965 (div.). B.A., Shaw U., 1963; M.A., U. Nev., 1978. Cert. elem. tchr., spl. edn. tchr., elem. prins., Elem. tchr., 1963-65, 70-72; spl. edn. tchr. emotionally disturbed, 1965-70; program specialist Clark County Sch. Dist., Las Vegas, Nev., 1972-79, adminstrv. asst., 1979-80, coordinator basic adult edn. program, 1984—; prin. Rex Bell Elem. Sch., Las Vegas, 1980—; mem. Nev. State Bd. for Child Care. Choir dir. Zion United Methodist Ch., 1977—, So. Nev. Mass Meth. Chs.; registrar voter registration. Named Boss of Yr., Clark County Assn. Office Personnel, 1982. Mem. Assn. Supervision and Curriculum Devel., Nat. Alliance Black Sch. Educators, Clark County Elem. Prins. Assn., Clark County Assn. Sch. Adminstrs., NAACP, Phi Delta Kappa, Kappa Alpha Psi. Democrat. Home: 1101 Sharon Rd Las Vegas NV 89106 Office: 2900 Wilmington Way Las Vegas NV 89102

FREEMAN, HOWARD E., sociology educator; b. N.Y.C., May 28, 1929; s. Herbert M. and Rose H. (Herman) F.; m. Sharon W. Kleban, Apr. 20, 1952 (div. 1977); children—Seth R., Lisa J.; m. Marian A. Solomon, Feb. 2, 1979. B.A., NYU, 1948, M.A., 1950, Ph.D., 1956. Asst. social scientist Rand Corp., Santa Monica, Calif., 1955-56; research assoc. Harvard U. Sch. Pub. Health, Boston, 1956-62; Morse prof. urban studies Brandeis U., Waltham, Mass., 1960-72; social sci. advisor Ford Found., Mexico City, Mex., 1972-74; prof. sociology UCLA, 1974—, chmn. dept. sociology, 1986—; sociologist Russell Sage Found., N.Y.C., 1967-77; research advisor Robert Wood Johnson Found., Princeton, N.J., 1976—; advisor Inst. Nutrition C.Am. and Panama, 1965—, U.S.-Mex. Border Health Assn., San Antonio, 1981-82; cons. NIMH, Washington, 1971-76; mem. panel on social indicators HEW, Washington, 1966-69. Author: (with others) The Mental Patient Comes Home, 1963 (Hofheimer prize, 1967), The Middle Income Negro Family Faces Urban Renewal, 1965, The Clinic Habit, 1967, Social Problems, 1957, 3rd edit., 1967, Academics and Entrepreneurial Research, 1975, Evaluation Research, 1971, 3rd edit, 1986; editor Evaluation Review, Los Angeles, 1976—, Health and Social Behavior, Washington, 1969-72, Policy Studies Review Annual, 1987; (with others) Handbook of Medical Sociology, 1963, 4th edit., 1988, The Social Scene, 1972, America's Troubles, 1973, The Dying Patient, 1982, Applied Sociology, 1983, Collecting Evaluation Data, 1985, others; contbr. articles to profl. jours. Served to capt. USAF, 1952-53. Mem. Am. Sociol. Assn., Am. Psychol. Assn., Am. Assn. Pub. Opinion Research, Am. Pub. Health Assn., Nat. Acad. Scis. (Inst. Medicine). Avocation: sailing. Home: 7911 Hillside Ave Los Angeles CA 90046

FREEMAN, MELVIN IRWIN, ophthalmic surgeon, educator, municipal official; b. Seattle, Mar. 17, 1935; s. Joseph and Rally (Arensberg) F.; m. Nanette Jean Dreyfuss, Feb. 17, 1979; children—Robert Eliot, Jacqueline Dreyfuss, Joseph Dreyfuss. B.S., U. Wash.-Seattle, 1957, M.D., 1960. Intern VA Hosp., Los Angeles, 1960-61; resident Washington U., St. Louis, 1961-66; fellow Retina Found., Boston, 1966-69, Mass. Eye and Ear Infirmary, Boston, 1967-69; head sect. ophthalmology The Mason Clinic, Seattle, 1974—; dir. continuing med. edn. Virgina Mason Med. Ctr., Seattle, 1984—; head contact lens clinic, clin. assoc. prof. ophthalmology U. Wash., Seattle, 1969—; cons. Madigan Gen. Hosp., U.S. Army, Tacoma, 1969-74; cons. to various mfrs. contact lenses; chmn. Tel-Med Trust of King County, Seattle, 1977—; nat. commissionaire The Joint Commn. on Allied Health Personnel in Ophthalmology, St. Paul, 1986—. Author, co-author numerous sci. papers, book chpts. and presentations. Mayor pro tempore, councilman Town of Yarrow Point, Wash., 1974—; trustee, treas., v.p., pres. Temple De Hirsch Sinai, Seattle, 1976—; trustee Virginia Mason Research Found., Seattle and Bellevue, 1978-84. Served to capt. M.C., U.S. Army, 1961-63. Fellow USPHS, 1957, 58, 59, NSF, 1959, Nat. Inst. Neurol. Disease and Blindness 1961, 64-69, Fight for Sight, 1966; recipient Williams prize in med. research U. Wash., 1960. Fellow ACS, Am. Acad. Ophthalmology (honors award 1984), Wash. State Acad. Ophthalmology (officer, trustee 1976—), Pacific Coast Oto-Ophthal. Soc., Seattle Surg. Soc. Club: Washington Athletic (Seattle). Home: 4625 Yarrow Point Rd Bellevue WA 98004 Office: The Mason Clinic 1100 9th Ave Seattle WA 98101

FREEMAN, MILTON MALCOLM ROLAND, anthropology educator; b. London, Apr. 23, 1934; came to Can., 1958; s. Louis and Fay (Bomberg) F.; m. Mini Christina Aodla; children: Graham, Elaine, Malcolm. BS, Reading U., Eng., 1958; postgrad., U. Coll., London, 1962-64; PhD, McGill U., 1965. Research scientist No. Affairs Dept., Ottawa, Ont., Can., 1965-67; asst. prof. Meml. U., St. John's, Nfld., Can., 1967-71, assoc. prof., 1971-72; dir. Inuit Land Use Study, Hamilton, Ont., 1973-75; prof. anthropology McMaster U., Hamilton, 1976-81; Henry Marshall Tory prof. U. Alta., Edmonton, Can., 1982—; adj. prof. environmental studies U. Waterloo, Ont., 1977-81; sr. sci. advisor Indian and No. Affairs, Ottawa, 1979-81; bd. dirs. Sci. Inst. N.W.T. Author: People Pollution, 1974; editor: Inuit Land Use and Occupancy Report, 1976, Proceedings International Symposium on Renewable Resources and the Economy of the North, 1981. Sr. Research scholar Boreal Inst. No. Studies, U. Alta, 1984—. Fellow Am. Anthropol. Assn., Arctic Inst. N.Am., Soc. Applied Anthropology; mem. Soc. Applied Anthropology Can. (pres. 1984-85), Can. Ethnology Soc. Home: 10650-11 Ave, Edmonton Can T6J 5M3 Office: U Alta, Dept Anthropology, Edmonton, AB Canada T6G 2H4

FREEMAN, NEIL, accounting and computer consulting firm executive; b. Reading, Pa., Dec. 27, 1948; s. Leroy Harold and Audrey Todd (Dornhecker) F.; m. Janice Lum, Nov. 20, 1981. BS, Albright Coll., 1979. Cert. systems profl.; cert. data processing specialist. Acct. Jack W. Long & Co., Mt. Penn, Pa., 1977-78; comptroller G.P.C., Inc., Bowmansville, Pa., 1978-79; owner Neil Freeman Cons., Bowmansville, 1980-81; program mgr., systems cons. Application Systems, Honolulu, 1981-82; instr. Chaminade U., Honolulu, 1983—; owner Neil Freeman Cons., Kaneohe, Hawaii, 1982—. Author: (computer software) NFC Property Management, 1984, NFC Mailing List, 1984; (book) Learning Dibol, 1984. Served with USN, 1966-68, Vietnam. Mem. Nat. Assn. Accts., Am. Inst. Cert. Computer Profs., Data Processing Mgmt. Assn., Assn. Systems Mgmt. Office: 45-449 Hoene Pl Kaneohe HI 96744

FREEMAN, PATRICIA ELIZABETH, library and education specialist; b. El Dorado, Ark., Nov. 30, 1924; d. Herbert A. and M. Elizabeth (Pryor) Harper; m. Jack Freeman, June 15, 1949; 3 children. B.A., Centenary Coll., 1943; postgrad. Fine Arts Ctr., 1942-46, Art Students League, 1944-45; B.S.L.S., La. State U., 1946; postgrad. Calif. State U., 1959-61, U. N.Mex., 1964-74; Ed.S., Peabody Coll., Vanderbilt U., 1975. Librarian, U. Calif.-Berkeley, 1946-47, U.S. Air Force, Barksdale AFB, 1948-49, Albuquerque Pub. Schs., 1964-67; ind. sch. library media ctr. cons., 1967—. Painter lithographer; one-person show La. State Exhibit Bldg., 1948; author: Pathfinder: An Operational Guide for the School Librarian, 1975; compiler, editor: Elizabeth Pryor Harper's Twenty-One Southern Families, 1985. Mem. task force Goals for Dallas-Environ., 1977-82; pres. Friends of Sch. Libraries, Dallas, 1979-83. Honoree AAUW Ednl. Found., 1979; vol. award for outstanding service Dallas Ind. Sch. Dist., 1978; AAUW Pub. Service grantee 1980. Mem. ALA, AAUW (dir. Dallas 1976-82, Albuquerque 1983—), LWV (sec. Dallas 1982-83, editor Albuquerque 1984—), Nat. Trust Historic Preservation, Friends of Albuquerque Pub. Library, N.Mex. Symphony Guild, Alpha Xi Delta. Home: 3016 Santa Clara SE Albuquerque NM 87106

FREEMAN, PAUL DOUGLAS, symphony conductor; b. Richmond, Va., Jan. 2, 1936; s. Louis H. and Louise (Willis) F.; m. Cornelia Perry; 1 son, Douglas Cornel. MusB, Eastman Sch. Music, 1956, MusM, 1957; PhD, 1963; PhD Fulbright scholar, Hochshule fûr Musik, Berlin, Germany, 1957-59. Dir. Hochstein Music Sch., Rochester, N.Y., 1960-66; First v.p. Nat. Guild Community Music Schs., 1964-66; bd. dirs. N.Y. State Opera League, 1963-66, Detroit Community Music Sch.; music adv. com. San Francisco chpt. Young Audiences, 1966—; mem. Calif. Framework Com. for Arts and Humanities, 1967-68. Founder, conductor, Faculty-Community Orch., also music dir., Opera Theatre, Rochester, 1961-66, dir., San Francisco Community Music Center, 1966-68, conductor, San Francisco Conservatory Orch., 1966-67, music dir., San Francisco Little Symphony, 1967-68, asso. conductor, Dallas Symphony, 1968-69, 69-70, conductor-in-residence, Detroit Symphony Orch., 1970-79, condr., music dir., Victoria (B.C., Can.) Symphony, 1979—, music dir., Saginaw Symphony, artistic dir., Delta Fstival Music and Art, 1977-79, numerous guest appearances with maj. orchs. in, U.S. and Europe; recording artist, Columbia Records, Vox Records, Orion Records. Recipient prize Dimitri Mitropolous Internat. Conductor's competition, 1967—; Spoleto award Festival of Two Worlds, 1968. Office: Victoria Symphony, 631 Superior St, Victoria, BC Canada V8V 1V1

FREEMAN, PETER KENT, chemist, educator; b. Modesto, Calif., Nov. 25, 1931; s. Russell Arthur and Helen Aleth (Surryhne) F.; m. Marilyn Taber, June 15, 1955; children: Diane, Irene, Theodore, Michael. BS, U. Calif., Berkeley, 1953; PhD, U. Colo., 1957. Research assoc. Pa. State U., University Park, 1958; asst. prof. chemistry U. Idaho, Moscow, 1959-62, assoc. prof., 1962-65, prof., 1965-68; prof. Oreg. State U., Corvallis, 1968—. Contbr. articles to profl. jours. Mem. Am. Chem. Soc., Sigma Xi, Phi Kappa Phi, Phi Lambda Upsilon.. Home: 3335 Chintimini Ave Corvallis OR 97333 Office: Oreg State U Dept Chemistry Corvallis OR 97331

FREEMAN, PHILIP CONRAD, JR., computer systems company executive; b. Santa Barbara, Calif., Jan. 1, 1937; s. Philip and Mabel (Linville) F.; student Ventura (Calif.) Jr. Coll., 1955-57; B.S. in Bus. Adminstrn, U. So. Calif., 1960, M.B.A., 1964; m. Virginia Ann Bramham, June 14, 1959; children—Jon Allen, Kym Michelle. Sr. cons. Peat, Marwick, Mitchell & Co., Los Angeles, 1961-68; pres., F.A.C.T., Inc., Los Angeles, 1968-71; v.p., western regional mgr. Intercontinental Computer Inc., Los Angeles, 1971-73; exec. v.p. Kimberly Devel., Inc., Los Angeles, 1973-75; v.p., gen. mgr. Met. Computer Center, Glendale, Calif., 1975-82; pres., chmn. bd. Data Select Systems Inc., Woodland Hills, Calif., 1982—; dir. Constrn. Bank Systems, Inc., San Francisco, 1982—; asst. treas., asst. sec. Forest Lawn Co., Glendale, 1978-82. Bd. dirs., treas. Hidden Hills (Calif.) Homeowners Assn., 1976-81; pres. Bill Bryant So. Calif. Jr. Golf Assn., 1979-80; bd. dirs. Greater Los Angeles County council Boy Scouts Am.; ptnr. Crystal City Devel., Solano County, Calif. Mem. Calif. Savings and Loan League, Nat. Mortgage Bankers Assn., U.S. Savs. and Loan League, Am. Bankers Assn. Republican. Presbyterian. Clubs: Calabasas Park (Calif.) Country, Hidden Hills Horseman Assn., Calif. Poly Rodeo Boosters, Pepperdine U. Assocs., Hidden Hills Vaulting Assn., Hidden Hills Tennis Assn. Home: 24333 Long Valley Rd Hidden Hills CA 91302 Office: Data Select Systems Inc 6400 Canoga Ave Suite 305 Woodland Hills CA 91367

FREEMAN, RICK ALLEN, corporate executive; b. Lansing, Mich., Oct. 4, 1951. BA in Pub. Adminstrn. and Laws, U. Washington, 1977. Mgr. subcontracts and purchasing Sci. Applications Internat. Corp., McLean, Va., 1980-82; dir. contracts internat. ops. Electronic Data Systems Corp., Dallas, 1982-85; pres. Mastery, Inc., Hillsboro, Oreg., 1986—. Avocations: hiking, running, camping, swimming, writing. Office: Mastery Inc 2401 NE Cornell Rd Suite 131 Hillsboro OR 97124

FREEMAN, RONALD GENE, hospital administrator; b. Muskogee, Okla., Apr. 3, 1945; s. Isparhecher and Juanita Fawn (Horner) F.; m. Linda Rae Cordell, Mar. 21, 1980. B.S., Northeastern State U., Tahlequah, Okla., 1971; M.P.H., U. Calif.-Berkeley, 1974. Dir. planning and evaluation Miss. Band of Choctaw, Philadelphia, 1975-77; dir. Ft. Yuma USPHS Indian Health Service Hosp. Ariz., 1977—; mem. health planning and devel. commn. Western Ariz. Health Systems Agy., Yuma, 1978-79; bd. dirs. Valley Health Ctr.,

Word & Data Processing Adv. Imperial Valley R.O.P. Served with U.S. Army, 1966-69, Vietnam. Recipient citation USPHS, Indian Health Service, 1983, unit commendation, 1984. Mem. USPHS Commd. Officers Assn., Am. Pub. Health Assn., Fed. Health Care Execs. Inst. (bd. dirs.). Democrat. Home: PO Box 821 Yuma AZ 85364 Office: USPHS Ft Yuma Indian Hosp PO Box 1368 Yuma AZ 85364

FREEMAN, VAL LEROY, geologist; b. Long Beach, Calif., June 25, 1926; s. Cecil LeRoy and Marjorie (Austin) F.; B.S., U. Calif. at Berkeley, 1949, M.S., 1952; m. June Ione Ashlock, Sept. 26, 1959 (div. June 1962); 1 dau., Jill Annette Freeman Michener; m. 2d, Elizabeth Joann Sabia, Sept. 4, 1964 (div. Oct. 1972); 1 dau., Rebecca Sue; 1 stepson, Jeffrey David. Geologist, U.S. Geol. Survey, 1949-85, Fairbanks, Alaska, 1955-57, Denver, 1957-70, 74-85, Flagstaff, Ariz., 1970-74, dep. chief coal resources br., until 1985. Served with USNR, 1943-45. Fellow Geol. Soc. Am. Contbr. articles to profl. jours. Home: 65 Clarkson St Apt 508 Denver CO 80218

FREIMANN, JOHN RAYMOND, theater educator; b. Yakima, Wash., Nov. 10, 1926; s. Raymond Christopher and Elsie Mary (Doyle) F. BS, NYU, 1951; MFA, Fordham U., 1955. Tchr. drama NYU, 1954-59; tchr. Whitman Coll., Walla Walla, Wash., 1962—, chmn. drama dept., 1967—; actor, designer, dir. Forestburgh (N.Y.) Playhouse, 1982-85, Berkeley (Calif.) Repertory Theatre, 1974-82. Mem. United Scenic Artists, Scenic and Title Artists, Actors Equity Assn., Soc. Stage Dirs. and Choreographers, Dramatists Guild, Screen Actors Guild. Office: Whitman Coll Harper Joy Theatre Walla Walla WA 99362

FREISER, LEONARD H., library director; b. N.Y.C., Feb. 9, 1925; s. Abraham and Henrietta (Graubard) F.; m. Helen Hammer, Dec. 13, 1950; children: Leslie, Erik. MusB, Manhattan Sch. Music, 1948; MA, Columbia U., 1948, MLS, 1955. Instr. music U. Sask., Can., 1948, Hunter Coll., N.Y.C., 1949, Evansville (Ind.) Coll., 1950; asst. prof. San Jose (Calif.) State Coll., 1951; trainee, br. librarian Bklyn. Pub. Library., 1954-57; chief librarian Glens Falls (N.Y.) City Library, 1957-60, Toronto (Ont., Can.) Bd. Edn., 1960-69, Franklin Inst., Phila., 1981-83; dep. chief librarian Chgo. Pub. Library, 1970-72; dir. Wilmette (Ill.) Pub. Library, 1972-73; with Nat. Coll. Edn., Evanston, Ill., 1972-78; pub. Am. Families Pub., 1978-81; dir. libraries, media, acad. support services Oreg. Inst. Tech., Klamath Falls, 1985—; vis. assoc. prof. library sci. SUNY, Albany, 1959-60; pres. Chgo. Conservatory Coll., 1979-81; trustee Klamath County Public Library, 1985—; bd. govs. Shaw Hist. Library, 1985—; cons. in field. Contbr. articles to mags., newspapers. Conductor Klamath Youth Symphony, 1985—. Mem. ALA (councillor 1963-68, chmn. spl. resolutions 1978). Office: Oreg Inst Tech Klamath Falls OR 97601

FREITAS, BEATRICE B(OTTY), opera theatre artistic director, musician, educator; b. Youngstown, Ohio, Aug. 28, 1938; d. John and Pauline (Esterhay) Botty; m. Lewis P. Freitas, Nov. 30, 1963; children—Roslyn K., John B. B.A., Oberlin Coll., 1958; M.Mus., Boston U., 1959; spl. student Juilliard Sch. Music, 1959-62. Artistic dir. Hawaii Opera Theatre, Honolulu; pianist, organist, harpsichordist, tchr. Recipient Outstanding Achievement in Area of Arts award YMCA, 1983.

FREITAS, RICHARD JOSEPH, speech pathologist; b. Castro Valley, Calif., Feb. 27, 1958; s. Leonard Joseph and Jaqueline Rae (Rose) F. BA, San Jose State U., 1981; MS, U. Mich., 1983. Cert. clin. competence. Speech pathologist N.W. Speech and Hearing Ctr., Seattle, 1983—. Mem. Am. Speech/Hearing Assn., Wash. State Speech/Hearing Assn. Roman Catholic. Avocations: skiing, tennis. Office: NW Hosp Speech & Hearing Ctr 1530 N 115th Seattle WA 98115

FREMMING, HAL ERIC, safety engineer, consultant; b. Alameda, Calif., Mar. 21, 1950; s. Harley Sether and Birgit Gertrude (Jerner) F.; m. Leyla Jane Parug, Mar. 3, 1979; children: Eric Michael, Emily Jane, Joel Edward. BA in Biol. Environ. Studies, U. Calif., Berkeley, 1973; M in Adminstrv. Systems Analysis, Calif. State U., Hayward, 1975. Inspector Ins. Cos. Inspection Bur., San Francisco, 1975-77; loss control rep. Republic Indemnity, San Francisco, 1978-80; sr. loss control rep. Mission Ins., Campbell, Calif., 1981-84, CIGNA, Inc., San Jose, Calif., 1985; sr. loss control specialist Nationwide Ins., Walnut Creek, Calif., 1986; sr. loss control cons. Argonaut Ins., San Jose, Calif., 1987—. Treas. Pioneer Gospel Chapel, Inc., San Leandro, 1985-86. Mem. Am. Soc. Safety Engrs. (cert.). Democrat. Club: Toastmasters (mem. Hayward chpt. 1973-75). Avocations: Bible study, guitar, vegetable gardening, sailing, bicycling. Home: 5725 Medallion Ct Castro Valley CA 94552 Office: Argonaut Ins 100 Homeland Ct Suite 200 San Jose CA 95109-3610

FREMOUW, EDWARD JOSEPH, physicist; b. Northfield, Minn., Feb. 23, 1934; s. Fred J. and Marion Elizabeth (Drozda) F.; m. Rita Lorraine Johnson, June 26, 1960; children: Thane Edrik, Sean Fredrik. BSEE, Stanford U., 1957; MS in Physics, U. Alaska, 1963, PhD in Geophysics, 1966. Asst. prof. geophysics U. Alaska, College, 1966-67; physicist Stanford Research Inst., Menlo Park, Calif., 1967-70, sr. physicist, 1970-75; program mgr. SRI Internat., Menlo Park, 1975-77; v.p. Phys. Dynamics, Inc., Bellevue, Wash., 1977-86; pres. Northwest Research Assocs., Inc., Bellevue, Wash., 1986—, also bd. dirs.; cons. Geophys. Inst., College, 1967-68; assoc. La Jolla (Calif.) Inst., 1981—. Contbr. articles to profl. jours. Trustee East Shore Unitarian Ch., 1984-86. Geographic feature Fremouw Peak named in his honor, 1968. Mem. IEEE, Am. Geophys. Union (Excellence in Refereeing award 1984), Union Radio Sci. Internat. Democrat. Unitarian Universalist. Clubs: Stanford of Western Wash. (trustee 1984-86), Mercer Island Beach. Avocations: hiking, climbing, skiing, sailing. Home: 8232 E Mercer Way Mercer Island WA 98040 Office: Northwest Research Assocs Inc PO Box 3027 Bellevue WA 98009

FRENCH, CLARENCE LEVI, JR., shipbuilding company executive; b. New Haven, Oct. 13, 1925; s. Clarence L. and Eleanor (Curry) F.; m. Jean Sprague, June 29, 1946; children: Craig Thomas, Brian Keith, Alan Scott. B.S. in Naval Sci., Tufts U., 1945, B.S. in Mech. Engring., 1947. Registered profl. engr., Calif. Foundry engr. Bethlehem Steel Corp., 1947-56; staff engr., asst. supt. Kaiser Steel Corp., 1956-64; supervisory engr. Bechtel Corp., 1964-67; with Nat. Steel & Shipbldg. Co., San Diego, 1967—; exec. v.p., gen. mgr. Nat. Steel & Shipbldg. Co., to 1977, pres., chief operating officer, 1977-84, chmn., chief exec. officer, 1984—; mem. maritime transp. research bd. NRC. Bd. dirs. United Way, San Diego, YMCA, San Diego; past chmn., bd. dirs. Pres. Roundtable; chmn. bd. trustees Webb Inst. Served to lt. USN, 1943-53. Fellow Soc. Naval Architects and Marine Engrs. (hon., past pres.); mem. Shipbuilders Council Am. (dir., past chmn. exec. com.), ASTM, Am. Bur. Shipping (bd. mgrs., tech. com.), Am. Soc. Naval Engrs., U.S. Naval Inst., Navy League U.S., Propeller Club U.S. Office: Nat Steel and Shipbldg Co 28th St and Harbor Dr San Diego CA 92138

FRENCH, FRANCES ELIZABETH, broadcasting company executive; b. Los Angeles, Sept. 16, 1947; d. William Baxter and Frances Olin (Porter) French; 1 child, George Joseph Zawalonka, Jr. AA, Glendale (Calif.) Community Coll., 1975. Video tape scheduling coordinator NBC, Burbank, Calif., 1967-72, unit mgr., 1976-81, sr. unit mgr., 1982-85; prodn. mgr., 1985—; prodn. coordinator KNBC, Burbank, 1972-74, supr. film editing, 1974-75, unit mgr., 1975-76; chief fin. officer, bd. dirs. Zawa & Son, Inc., 1980—. Mem. Am. Women in Radio and TV, LWV, DAR, Delta Theta Tau. Republican. Episcopalian. Office: 3000 W Alameda St Burbank CA 91523

FRENCH, GEORGINE LOUISE, guidance counselor; b. Lancaster, Pa., May 15, 1934; d. Richard Franklin and Elizabeth Georgine (Driesbach) Beacham; B.A., Calif. State U., San Bernardino, 1967; M.S., No. Ill. U., 1973; D.D., Am. Ministerial Assn., 1978; m. Barrie J. French, Feb. 4, 1956; children—Joel B., John D., James D., Jeffrey D. Personnel counselor Sages Dept. Store, San Bernardino, 1965-66; asst. bookkeeper Bank Calif., San Bernardino, 1964-65; tchr. Livermore (Calif.) Sch. Dist., 1968-69; guidance counselor Bur. Indian Affairs, Tuba City, Ariz., 1974-80, Sherman Indian High Sch., Riverside, Calif., 1980-82, Ft. Douglas Edn. Ctr., U.S. Army, Salt Lake City, 1982-86; guidance counselor Los Angeles Air Force Sta., USAF, 1986—; extension tchr. Navajo Community Coll., Yavapai Jr. Coll.; personnel counselor USNR, 1976-86; ordained to ministry Am. Ministerial Assn., 1979. Served with USAF, 1954-56. Cert. guidance counselor, secondary tchr. Mem. Am. Assn. for Counselor Devel., Am. Assn. Retired Assn. Home: 1721 Aviation Blvd #38 Redondo Beach CA 92078 Office: 6592 ABG/DPE PO Box 92960 Los Angeles CA 90009-2960

FRENCH, HERBERT SARGENT, health care executive; b. Decatur, Ill., Nov. 14, 1935; s. Arthur Herbert and Julia Marlowe (White) F.; divorced; children: Stephanie, Stephen, Caroline. Student, U. Ala., 1954-59; BS, Portland State U., 1977; MBA, U. Phoenix, 1986. Banker various banks, Tuscaloosa, Ala., 1959-72; v.p. First Nat. Bank, Portland, Oreg., 1977-81; family counselor Parkview-Meadows, Wickenburg, Ariz, 1982-83; family program coordinator Parkview-Meadows, Chattanooga, 1983-84; adminstrv. dir., corp. sec. Sierra Tucson, Inc., 1984—. Pres. YMCA, Tuscaloosa, 1961-63. Served with USAFR, 1958-64. Mem. Am. Mgmt. Assn., Health Care Fin. Mgmt. Assn., Nat. Assn. Social Workers. Republican. Episcopalian. Club: Can. Hills Country. Lodge: Rotary (Tuscaloosa, chpt. sec., treas., 1961-63). Avocations: running, downhill skiing, writing, golf. Home: 3350 W Starfall Pl Tucson AZ 85741 Office: Sierra Tucson Inc 16500 N Lago Del Oro Pkwy Tucson AZ 85704

FRENCH, JOHN STORRS, biochemistry educator; b. Phila., Jan. 17, 1949; s. Arthur Bancroft and Margaret (Storrs) F.; m. Margaret Warlikowski, June 5, 1983. AB in Chemistry, Oberlin Coll., 1971; PhD in Biochemistry, U. Mich., 1979. With Peace Corps, Melaka, Malaysia, 1971-74; postdoctoral fellow U. Calif., Berkeley, 1979-80; asst. prof. biochemistry U. Alaska, Anchorage, 1980-85, assoc. prof., 1985—; cons. Alaska Ctr. for Environment, 1982-84; prin. investigator Alaska Sea Grant Program, 1983-85, Alaska Council Sci. and Tech., 1982. Contbr. articles to profl. jours. Sec. South Fork Community Council, Eagle River, Alaska, 1984. Recipient traineeship NIH, U. Mich., 1974-79; NIH dir. MARC honors program, U. Alaska, 1982-85. Mem. Am. Chem. Soc. (sect. pres. 1984-85), Am. Fisheries Soc., Inst. Food Technologists, Internat. Soc. for Study Xenobiotics. Lodge: Rotary. Office: U Alaska FITC 202 Center St #201 Kodiak AK 99615

FRENCH, RICHARD HARRY, desert researcher, educator; b. Wheeling, W.Va., Jan. 5, 1947; s. Clyde Leslie and Florence (McComb) F.; m. Darlene Gates, May, 1975; 1 child, Mercedes. Student, Ga. Inst. Tech., 1965-68; BCE, Ohio State U., 1971, MS, 1972; PhD, U. Calif., Berkeley, 1975. Registered profl. engr., Calif., Nev. Asst. prof. Vanderbilt U., Nashville, 1975-79; assoc. prof. Water Resources Ctr., Desert Research Inst., Las Vegas, Nev., 1979-84, research prof. and assoc. exec. dir., 1984—; vis. prof. Nat. Def. Acad. Yokosuka, Japan, 1983; cons. Div. Environ. Protection Carson City, Nev., 1983-84. Author: Open-Channel Hydraulics, 1985, Hydraulic Processes on Alluvial Fans, 1986; editor: Salinity in Watercourses and Reservoirs, 1984. Boris A. Bakhmeteff research fellow Columbia U., 1973. Mem. ASCE, Internat. Assn. Hydraulic Research, Am. Water Resources Assn., Nev. Water Resources Assn. Home: 2268 E Hacienda Ave Las Vegas NV 89119 Office: Desert Research Inst Water Resources Ctr 2505 Chandler Ave Las Vegas NV 89120

FRENZL, STEPHEN JOHN, marketing consultant; b. Akron, Colo., Apr. 9, 1947; s. Frank J. and Esther M. (Casey) F.; divorced; children: Mary Jayne, John David, Stephan Joseph. BSBA in Mktg and Advt., U. Colo., 1970. Media buyer Leo Burnett USA, Chgo., 1970-71; media dir. JFP & Assocs., Duluth, Minn., 1971-72; mktg. research mgr. Jenos Inc., Duluth, 1973-75; advt. mgr. Carefree of Colo., Broomfield, 1976-79; v.p. mktg. Mktg. Tours, Denver, 1980-84; pres., cons. Performance Resources Group Inc., Boulder, Colo., 1985—. Author: Incentive Marketing, 1984; editor, pub. Travel-Talk mag., 1982-83; contbr. articles to profl. jours. Media dir. Dem. for Nixon Nat. Com., Duluth and Washington, 1972. Mem. Soc. Incentive Travel Execs., Am. Mktg. Assn. Republican. Roman Catholic. Avocations: singing groups, hiking, sailing, reading, cooking. Office: Performance Resources Group Inc 1221 Pearl St Mall Boulder CO 80302

FRESCHI, RICHARD ALBERT, medical supply company executive; b. Oakland, Calif., Feb. 11, 1937; s. Albert P. and Marie F.; student U. Calif. at Berkeley, 1955-57; B.S., Armstrong Coll., Berkeley, 1959; m. Joy Sylvia Ritter, Feb. 26, 1961; children—Paula J., Lisa M. Salesman, Don Baxter Inc. div. Am. Hosp. Supply Co., Glendale, Calif., 1962-65, Western area mgr. Coverters div., Santa Ana, Calif., 1965-71; founder, pres. Sentinel Disposables Co., Los Angeles, 1971-74; v.p. mktg. Plasta-Medic div. Bergen Brunswig Corp., Los Angeles, 1974-78, gen. mgr., 1978-80; pres. Plasta-Medic div. Hadley Industries, Inc., v.p. Hadley Industries, Inc., 1980-82; pres. Jordan/Plasta Medic, Romalite Corp., Union Plastics Calif., 1982-1983; v.p. Jordan Group, 1982-83; pres. Paulisa Inc., Reno, Nev., 1983-86; pres., chief exec. officer Insta-Cool of N. Am., 1986. Bd. dirs. Providence Speech and Hearing Ctr., Orange, Calif. Mem. Soc. Plastics Industry, Native Sons Golden West, Kappa Sigma Kappa, Alpha Sigma Rho. Club: Elks. Home: 10151 Phelan Dr Villa Park CA 92667 Office: Insta-Cool of N Am 1 Waters Park Dr Suite 108 San Mateo CA 94403

FRESTON, NORMA PATRICIA, energy company executive; b. Brigham City, Utah, July 2, 1939; s. Lawrence and Norma Josephine (Wight) Robinson; 1 child, Mitchel Wade. BS, Weber State Coll., 1966; MA, Utah State U., 1968; MS, U. Tex., 1971; PhD in Indsl. Psychology, U. Utah, 1978. Teaching asst. U. Tex., Austin, 1969-71; assessment counselor U. Utah, Salt Lake City, 1971-72, program specialist, 1972-74, dir. acad. programming, 1974-77; asst. dir. manpower planning and devel. Mountain Fuel Supply, Salt Lake City, 1977-80; mgr. personnel services Questar Corp., Salt Lake City, 1980—; cons. Ore-Ida Foods Inc., Boise, Idaho, Star-Kist Inc., Los Angeles, Gagliardi Bros. Inc., Phila. Contbr. articles to profl. jours. Commr. Salt Lake City Corp. Recipient Gold Medal award Pacific Coast Gas Assn., 1985, Silver Medal award Pacific Coast Gas Assn., 1981, 83, Argyle-Linberg award Am. Soc. Tng. and Devel., 1979. Mem. Salt Lake City C. of C. Mormon. Lodge: Zonta (pres. Salt Lake City club). Home: 1907 S 2600 E Salt Lake City UT 84108 Office: Questar Corp 180 E 100 S Salt Lake City UT 84147

FRETER, MARK ALLEN, marketing and public relations executive, consultant; b. Chgo., Oct. 31, 1947; s. John Maher and Christopher Patricia (Allen) F. BA, U. Calif., Santa Barbara, 1969; MBA, U. Calif., Berkeley, 1971. V.p. affiliate relations X-Press Info. Services, Denver, 1984-85; v.p. mktg. Telecrafter Corp., Denver, 1985-86; mktg. dir. Computer Services Corp., Boulder, Colo., 1986-87; dir. pub. relations services MultiMedia, Inc., Denver, 1987—; lectr. Internat. Council Shopping Ctrs., N.Y.C., 1977; conf. planner ICSC-West, San Francisco, 1978-79; training program devel. HBO, N.Y.C., 1982. Youth coach South Suburban YMCA, Littleton, Colo., 1984-86. Recipient First Place cert. for Retail Ad Campaign San Diego Advt. Assn., 1980. Mem. Calif. Cable TV Assn., No. Calif. Promotion Mgrs. Assn. (v.p. 1977-78), So. Calif. Promotion Mgrs. Assn. (sec., treas. 1976-77). Democrat. Mem. Soc. Friends. Avocations: skiing, ice hockey, reading, coaching youth sports. Home: 6363 S Dexter St Littleton CO 80121

FREY, CHARLES FREDERICK, surgeon, educator; b. N.Y.C., Nov. 15, 1929; s. Charles N. and Julia (Leary) F.; m. Jane Louise Tower, July 20, 1957; children: Jane Elizabeth, Susan Ann, Charles Frederick, Robert Tower, Nancy Louise. BA, Amherst Coll., 1951; MD, Cornell U., 1955. Diplomate Am. Bd. Surgery. Intern Cornell Med. Ctr., N.Y.C., 1955-56, asst. resident, 1956-57, 59-61, 1st asst. resident, 1962, chief resident, 1963; instr. surgery U. Mich., Ann Arbor, 1964-65, asst. prof. surgery, 1965-68, assoc. prof., 1968-72, prof., 1972-76; prof. U. Calif., Davis, 1976—, vice. chmn. dept. surgery, 1976-81, exec. vice-chmn. dept., 1981—; mem. staff VA Hosp., Martinez, Calif., chief surg. service, 1976-80; surg. cons. U. Mich., 1966-76, VA, 1971—, Highway Safety Research Inst., 1973-76. Assoc. editor: The Pancreas; contbr. numerous articles to profl. jours. Served to capt. USAF, 1957-59. Fellow ACS (chief regional com. on trauma 1976—, disaster preparedness com. 1978—, med. motion pictures com. 1981—, allied health com. 1981-82, program com. No. Calif. chpt. 1981—, credentials com. No. Calif. chpt. 1982—), Am. Assn. Surgery Trauma; mem. AMA, Calif. Med. Assn., Contra Costa Med. Assn., Am. Fedn. Clin. Research, Am. Assn. Automotive Medicine (bd. dirs. 1970-74), Internat. Assn. Accident and Traffic Medicine, Am. Trauma Soc. (founding, standards devel. com. 1978—, v.p. Calif. div. 1979—, bd. dirs. 1980—), Calif. Trauma Soc. (trustee 1977—), Nat. Trauma Com. of ACS (chmn. membership com. 1980-84, exec. com. 1981-85) Assn. Acad. Surgery, Am. Surg. Assn., Brazilian Surg. Soc., Western Surg. Assn., Cen. Surg. Assn. (membership com. 1971-73), Pacific Coast Surg. Assn., Sacramento Surg. Soc., Assn. VA Surgeons (publs., program coms. 1981—), Soc. Univ. Surgeons, Soc. Surgery Alimentary Tract (constn. and by-laws com. 1969—, chmn. 1972-76), Internat. Assn. Pancreatology (mem. editorial bd. 1986), Internat. Biliary Assn., Am. Gastroenterology Assn., Pancreas Club (chmn. 1975—). Home: 52 Charles Hill Rd Orinda CA 94563 Office: U Calif Med Ctr Dept Surgery 4301 X St Sacramento CA 95817

FREY, JULIA BLOCH, French language educator; b. Louisville, July 25, 1943; d. Oscar Edgeworth and Jean Goldthwaite (Russell) B.; m. Roger G. Frey, Dec. 27, 1968 (div. Mar. 1976). BA, Antioch Coll., 1966; MA, U. Tex., 1968; MPhil, Yale U., 1970, PhD, 1977. Instr. Brown U., Providence, 1972-73; chargé de cours U. de Paris, 1974-75; lectr. Yale U., New Haven, 1975-76; prof. French, Inst. Internat. Comparative Law U. San Diego, Paris, 1979-86; assoc. prof. U. Colo., Boulder, 1976—; guest prof. Sarah Lawrence Coll., Bronxville, N.Y., 1983. Editor: Gustave Flaubert's La Lutte du Sacerdoce et de L'Empire (1837), 1981; contbr. articles and monographs to profl. publs., chpts. to books; translator: Réné. Recipient Conn. Grad. Study award, 1970-73; grantee NDEA, 1967, Brown U. Research and Travel, 1973, Boulder Arts Com., 1979, 80, Ctr. for Applied Humanities, 1985, S.W. Inst. for Research on Women, 1985-86; fellow NDEA, 1966-68, Yale U., 1968-72, Gilbert Chinard, Inst. Français de Washington, 1977. Mem. Unitarian Ch. Club: Yale (Denver). Home: 1505 Bluebell Ave Boulder CO 80302 Office: U Colo Campus Box 238 Dept French and Italian Boulder CO 80309

FREY, WILLIAM CARL, bishop; b. Waco, Tex., Feb. 26, 1930; s. Harry Frederick and Ethel (Oliver) F.; m. Barbara Louise Martin, June 12, 1952; children: Paul, Mark, Matthew, Peter, Susannah. B.A., U. Colo., 1952; Th.M., Phila. Div. Sch., 1955, D.D. (hon.), 1970. Ordained to ministry Episcopal Ch.; vicar Timberline Circuit (Colo.) Missions, 1955-58; rector Trinity-on-the-Hill Ch., Los Alamos, 1958-62; missionary priest Episcopal Ch., Costa Rica, 1962-67; bishop Episcopal Ch., 1967, Diocese of Guatemala, 1967-72; chaplain U. Ark., Fayetteville, 1972; bishop Diocese of Colo., Denver, 1972—; chmn. Epsicopal Ch.'s Joint Commn. on Peace, 1979-85. Contbr. articles to religious mags. Office: PO Box M Capitol Hill Sta Denver CO 80218

FREYBERG, DEREK PETER, lawyer; b. Auckland, New Zealand, Oct. 2, 1948; came to U.S., 1972; s. Peter Stuart and Winifred Edith (Allen) F.; m. Susan Violeta Ramos, June 1, 1974; 1 child, Frances May. MSc with honors, Victoria U., Wellington, New Zealand, 1970; PhD, U. Va., 1977; JD, Santa Clara U., 1982. Bar: Calif. 1982, U.S. Dist. Ct. (no. dist.) Calif. 1982, U.S. Ct. Appeals (fed. cir.) 1983, U.S. Patent and Trademark Office 1979. Postdoctoral fellow U. Calif., Berkeley, 1977-79, Lawrence Berkeley (Calif.) Lab., 1979; patent agt., atty. Raychem Corp., Menlo Park, Calif., 1979-83; patent atty. Chevron Research Corp., San Francisco, 1983-84, Syntex (U.S.A.) Inc., Palo Alto, Calif., 1984—. Contbr. articles to profl. jours. DuPont fellow, 1973; Japanese Ministry Edn. scholar, 1970-72. Mem. ABA, Am. Chem. Soc., Chem. Soc. London, Am. Intellectual Property Law Assn., San Francisco Patent and Trademark Law Assn., Peninsula Patent Law Assn. Home: 408 Shirley Way Menlo Park CA 94025 Office: Syntex (USA) Inc 3401 Hillview Ave A2-200 Palo Alto CA 94304

FRICHETTE, JIM, design engineering company executive; b. Ellensburg, Wash., Apr. 5, 1935; s. Theodore and Florence (Holmes) F.; m. Florence Haight, Mar. 2, 1957; children—James G., Janean D. B.S., Central Wash. State U., 1958; M.B.A., U. Wash., 1963; postgrad. Northwestern U., 1965-68. Research chemist Am. Marietta, Seattle, 1958-60, tech. service and prodn. mgr., 1960-64; worldwide mktg. mgr. Morton Chem. Co., Chgo., 1964-68, gen. mgr., 1968-75; divisional gen. mgr. Nat. Semicondr., Santa Clara, Calif., 1975-81; pres., chief exec. officer Paktec Inc., San Jose, Calif., 1981—; Contbr. articles to profl. jours.; patentee plastics and electronics. Officer, Lombard Baseball League, Ill., 1967-73; pres. Almaden Valley Tennis Assn., San Jose, 1981—. Served to cpl. U.S. Army, 1953-55; Central and South Am. Mem. Soc. Plastics Engr. (pres. 1966-67), Semicondr. Equipment and Materials Inst., IEEE. Republican. Episcopalian. Office: Paktec Inc San Jose CA 95120

FRICK, OSCAR LIONEL, physician, educator; b. N.Y.C., Mar. 12, 1923; s. Oscar and Elizabeth (Ringger) F.; m. Mary Hubbard, Sept. 2, 1954. A.B., Cornell U., 1944, M.D., 1946; M.Med. Sci., U. Pa., 1960; Ph.D., Stanford U., 1964. Diplomate: Am. Bd. Allergy and Immunology (chmn. 1967-72). Intern Babies Hosp., Columbia Coll. Physicians and Surgeons, N.Y.C., 1946-47; resident Children's Hosp., Buffalo, 1950-51; pvt. practice medicine specializing in pediatrics Huntington, N.Y., 1951-58; fellow in allergy and immunology Royal Victoria Hosp., Montreal, Que., Can., 1958-59; fellow in allergy U. Calif.-San Francisco, 1959-60, asst. prof. pediatrics, 1964-67, assoc. prof., 1967-72, prof., 1972—, dir. allergy tng. program, 1964—; fellow immunology Inst. d'Immunobiologie, Hosp. Broussais, Paris, France, 1960-62. Contbr. articles papers to profl. publs. Served with M.C., USNR, 1947-49. Mem. Am. Assn. Immunologists, Am. Acad. Pediatrics (chmn. allergy sect. 1971-72, Bret Ratner award 1982), Am. Acad. Allergy (exec. com. 1972—, pres. 1977-78), Internat. Assn. Allergology and Clin. Immunology (exec. com. 1970-73, sec. gen. 1985—), Am. Pediatric Soc. Club: Masons. Home: 370 Parnassus Ave San Francisco CA 94117

FRICKLE, ROGER WILLIAM, social worker; b. Hardin, Mont., July 6, 1951; s. William and Mary (Lind) F.; m. Jodie Elizabeth Knerr, June 18, 1982; children: Travis, Jared. BA, Ea. Mont. Coll., 1976. Research assoc. Ea. Mont. Coll., Billings, 1975-76; historian U.S. Bur. Land Mgmt., Lewistown, Mont., 1977; title examiner Title Co., Lewistown, 1978-80; social worker Mont. State, Lewistown, 1980—; coordinator Fergus County Child Protection Team, Lewistown, 1980—, Fergus County child Sexual Abuse Team, Lewistown, 1984—. Author: Socio-Economic Profile, 1975. Named Social Worker of Yr., Mont. State Foster Parents Orgn., 1985. Lodge: Eagles. Avocations: hunting, camping, fishing, skiing, trail bike riding. Office: Fergus County Welfare Dept 308 Bank Electric Bldg Lewistown MT 59457

FRIDEGER, SISTER MARCIA ANN, organizational behavior consultant, educator; b. San Francisco, Oct. 21, 1945; d. Edward James and Lenore Ann (Makelim) F. BA, Holy Names Coll., 1969; M in Organizational Behavior, Brigham Young U., 1981. Joined Sisters of the Holy Names of Jesus and Mary, 1963; cert. secondary tchr., Calif. Tchr. St. Ignatius Sch., Sacramento, 1968-70, Holy Names High Sch., Oakland, Calif., 1970-73, 75-78; organizational cons. Sisters of Holy Names, Calif., 1973-78; tchr. Holy Names Coll., Oakland, 1981—; cons. Diocese of Oakland, Blue Cross of Calif. and various Catholic parishes and religious communities in Calif., 1981—. Vice chmn. Clergy Edn. Bd., Diocese of Oakland, 1981-85. Mem. Acad. Mgmt., Orgnl. Behavior Teaching Soc., Beta Gamma Sigma. Democrat. Avocations: hiking, reading, yoga. Office: Holy Names Coll 3500 Mountain Blvd Oakland CA 94619

FRIDLEY, SAUNDRA LYNN, internal audit manager; b. Columbus, Ohio, June 14, 1948; d. Jerry Dean and Esther Eliza (Bluhm) Fridley. BS, Franklin U., 1976; MBA, Golden Gate U., 1980. Accounts receivable supr. Internat. Harvester, Columbus, Ohio, San Leandro, Calif., 1972-80; sr. internal auditor Western Union, San Francisco, 1980; internal auditor II, County of Santa Clara, San Jose, Calif., 1980-82; sr. internal auditor Tymshare, Inc., Cupertino, Calif., 1982-84, div. controller, 1984; internal audit mgr. VWR Scientific, Brisbane, Calif., 1984—. Mem. Internal Auditors Speakers Bur., Inst. Internal Auditors (pres., founder), Nat. Assn. Female Execs. Avocations: woodworking; gardening; golfing. Home: 862 Bellflower St Livermore CA 94550 Office: VWR Scientific 3745 Bayshore Blvd Brisbane CA 94005

FRIED, BURTON DAVID, physicist, educator; b. Chgo., Dec. 14, 1925; s. Albert O. and Bertha (Rosenthal) F.; m. Sally Rachel Goldstein, Aug. 17, 1947; children—Joel Ethan, Jeremy Steven. B.S., Ill. Inst. Tech., 1947; M.S., U. Chgo., 1950, Ph.D., 1952. Instr. physics Ill. Inst. Tech., 1947-52; research physicist Lawrence Berkeley Lab. of U. Calif., 1952-54; sr. staff physicist TRW Systems, Los Angeles, 1954-86; dir. research lab. (Ramo-Wooldridge Computer Div.), Los Angeles, 1961-63; prof. physics U. Calif. at Los Angeles, 1963—. Served with USNR, 1944-46. Fellow Am. Phys. Soc. (chmn. plasma physics div. 1978-79); mem. Sigma Xi. Research and publs.

on theoretical elementary particle and plasma physics. Home: 1119 Las Pulgas Pl Pacific Palisades CA 90272 Office: Physics Dept U Calif at Los Angeles 405 Hilgard St Los Angeles CA 90024

FRIED, ELAINE JUNE, business executive; b. Los Angeles, Oct. 19, 1943; grad. Pasadena (Calif.) High Sch., 1963; various coll. courses; m. Howard I. Fried, Aug. 7, 1966; children: Donna Marie, Randall Jay. Agt., office mgr. Howard I. Fried Agy., Alhambra, Calif., 1975—; v.p. Sea Hill, Inc., Pasadena, Calif., 1973—. Publicity chmn., unit telephone chmn. San Gabriel Valley unit; past chmn. Am. Diabetes Assn.; past publicity chmn. San Gabriel Valley region Women's Am. Orgn. for Rehab. Tng. (ORT); chmn. spl. events publicity, past v.p. membership Temple Beth Torah, Alhambra; former mem. bd. dirs., pub. relations com., personnel com. Vis. Nurses Assn., Pasadena and San Gabriel Valley, Recipient Vol. award So. Calif. affiliate Am. Diabetes Assn., 1974-77; co-recipient Ner Tamid award Temple Beth Torah. Contbr. articles to profl. jours. Clubs: B'nai B'rith Women, Hadassah, Temple Beth Torah Sisterhood. Speaker on psycho-social aspects of diabetes, insurance and the diabetic. Home: 404 N Hidalgo Ave Alhambra CA 91801

FRIED, LOUIS LESTER, information systems, artificial intelligence and management consultant; b. N.Y.C., Jan. 18, 1930; s. Albert and Tessie (Klein) F.; m. Haya Greenberg, Aug. 15, 1960; children: Ron Chaim, Eliana Ahuva, Gil Ben. BA in Pub. Adminstrn., Calif. State U., Los Angeles, 1962; MS in Mgmt. Theory, Calif. State U., Northridge, 1965. Mgr. br. plant data processing Litton systems, Inc., Woodland Hills, Calif., 1960-65; dir. mgmt. info. systems Bourns, Inc., Riverside, Calif., 1965-68, Weber Aircraft Co., Burbank, Calif., 1968-69; v.p. mgmt. services T.I. Corp. of Calif., Los Angeles, 1969-75; dir. advanced computer systems dept. Stanford Research Inst., Menlo Park, Calif., 1976-85, dir. ctr. for infor. tech., 1985-86, exec. dir. info. industries div., 1986—; cons. editor Auerbach Pubs., 1978—, Reston Pubs., 1979—; lectr. U. Calif., Riverside, 1965-69, lectr. mgmt. and EDP. Contbr. numerous articles to profl. jours., textbooks. Mem. Assn. Systems Mgmt. Home: 788 Loma Verde Ave Palo Alto CA 94303 Office: Stanford Research Inst Menlo Park CA 94025

FRIED, NORMAN ZANDER, retired public relations executive; b. Chgo., Sept. 18, 1920; s. Philip Edward and Fannie (Grazenda) F.; m. Zelda Lasky, Feb. 6, 1944; children: Leslie Fried Rice, Gayle Fried Friedlander, Kenneth J. Freed. BEd, No. Ill. U., 1942; postgrad., U. Colo., 1970-72. Owner Norman Fried Advt., Denver, 1954-65; v.p. communications KWAL Paints Inc., Denver, 1965-84; lectr. advt. U. Denver, 1956-70; lectr. pub. relations U. Colo., Boulder and Denver, 1963-71; adj. faculty Columbia Coll., Aurora, Colo., 1986—; cons. Benjamin Moore Paint Co., Denver, 1986. Contbr. articles to profl. jours.; numerous watercolor and acrylic artworks. Docent Denver Zoo Assocs., 1984—; active Denver Mus. Natural History, 1985—, Denver Art Mus. Served to 2d lt. USAF, 1942-46, lt. col. Res. ret. Mem. Pub. Relations Soc. Am., Denver Artists Guild, Soc. Profl. Journalists. Jewish. Clubs: Denver Press; Pinery Country (Parker, Colo.). Avocations: travel, photography, golf, flyfishing, classical music. Home: 2966 S Paris St Aurora CO 80014

FRIED, STEPHEN MARK, fishery scientist; b. N.Y.C., Sept. 18, 1950; s. Alexander and Dolores (Greenberg) F.; m. Marie Philippon, Mar. 27, 1977; 1 child, David Alexander. BS in Biology, CCNY, 1971; MS in Zoology, U. Maine, 1973, PhD in Zoology, 1977. Research and teaching asst. U. Maine, Orono, 1971-77; fisheries biologist Oreg. Dept. Fish and Wildlife, Corvallis, 1977; dir., fisheries ecologist Alaska Trollers Assn., Ketchikan, 1977-78; area biologist Bristol Bay Fishery Rehab. Enhancement and Devel. Div. Alaska Dept. Fish and Game, Dillingham, 1978-80; project leader Bering Sea Herring Research-Comml. Fish Div. Alaska Dept. Fish and Game, Anchorage, 1980-83, project leader Bristol Bay Salmon Research-Comml. Fish Div., 1983—; reviewer grants NSF, Alaska Sea Grant. Contbr. articles to profl. jours.; reviewer Can. Jour. Fish and Aquatic Scis. Recipient Antarctic Service medal NSF, 1980. Mem. AAAS, Am. Fisheries Soc. (cert. fisheries scientist), Am. Inst. Fishery Research Biologists. Avocations: boating, hunting, fishing, cross country skiing, weight tng. Office: Alaska Dept Fish and Game Div Comml Fishing 333 Raspberry Rd Anchorage AK 99518

FRIEDBERG, THOMAS FRANKLIN, lawyer; b. Los Angeles, June 3, 1958; s. Herman R. and Phyllis (Shapiro) F.; m. Sarah L. Bunge, Oct. 7, 1984. BA in Edn., U. Ariz., 1980; JD, U. San Diego, 1983. Bar: Calif., 1983, U.S. Dist. Ct. (so. dist.) Calif., 1983. Lawyer Roseman and Mann (formerly Frank, Roseman, Freedus & Mann), San Diego, 1983—; instr. appellate advocacy, U. San Diego, 1982-83. Intern U.S. Senator Dennis DiConcinni, Tucson, 1978-79. Recipient Am. Jurisprudence award in Torts U. San Diego, 1981. Mem. ABA, Am. Trial Lawyers Assn., San Diego Trial Lawyers Assn., San Diego Bar Assn., Order of Barristers. Democrat. Jewish. Avocations: bicycling, theatre, sports activities. Home: 1224 Clove St San Diego CA 92106 Office: Roseman and Mann 101 W Broadway Suite 1100 San Diego CA 92106

FRIEDEL, CAROL ANN, dentist; b. Seattle, Oct. 23, 1945; d. John Earl and Darlene Cecelia (McDonnell) Gorman; m. Thomas Stinnette Friedel Jr. B.S. in Biology, U. Wash., 1975, D.D.S., 1978. Gen. practice dentistry, Seattle, 1978—. Author: (with others) (manual) Wheelchair Transfers in the Dental Office, 1976. Mem. ADA, Wash. State Dental Assn., Am. Assn. Women Dentists, Am. Acad. Gold Foil Operators, Phi Beta Kappa. Office: 6319 24th Ave NW Seattle WA 98107

FRIEDL, RICK, college president; b. Berwyn, Ill., Aug. 31, 1947; s. Raymond J. and Ione L. (Anderson) F.; BA, Calif. State U., Northridge, 1969; MA (Calif. State Grad. fellow 1970-72), UCLA, 1976; PhD candidate UCLA, 1984; JD Western State U., 1987; m. Diane Marie Guillies, Sept. 2, 1977; children: Richard, Angela, Ryan. Dept. mgr. Calif. Dept. Indsl. Relations, 1973-78; mem. faculty dept. polit. sci. U. So. Calif., 1978-80; pres. Pacific Coll. Law, 1981—; bd. dirs. Calif. State U., Northridge, 1979. Mem. Los Angeles County Bar Assn., Am. Polit. Sci. Assn., Latin Am. Studies Assn., Acad. Polit. Sci., Pacific Coast Council Latin Am. Studies, L.A. County Bar Assn. Author: The Political Economy of Cuban Dependency, 1982; tech. editor Glendale Law Rev., 1984; contbr. articles to profl. jours. Home: PO Box 3908 Chatsworth CA 91313

FRIEDLANDER, CHARLES DOUGLAS, investment company executive, consultant; b. N.Y.C., Oct. 5, 1928; s. Murray L. and Jeane (Sottosanti) F.; m. Diane Mary Hutchins, May 12, 1951; children: Karen Diane, Lauren Patrice, Joan Elyse. BS, U.S. Mil. Acad., 1950; exec. mgmt. program, NASA, 1965; grad., Command and Staff Coll. USAF, 1965, Air War Coll. USAF, 1966. Commd. 2d lt. U.S. Army, 1950, advanced through grades to 1st lt.; officer inf. U.S. Army, Korea, 1950-51; resigned U.S. Army, 1954; mem. staff UN Forces, Trieste, Italy, 1953-54; chief astronaut support office NASA, Cape Canaveral, Fla., 1963-67; space cons. CBS News, N.Y.C., 1967-69; exec. asst. The White House, Washington, 1969-71; pres. Western Ranchlands Inc., Scottsdale, Ariz., 1971-74; pres. Fairland Co. Inc., Scottsdale, 1974—, also bd. dirs.; space program cons., various cos., Boca Raton, Fla., 1967-69; mem. staff First Postwar Fgn. Ministers Conf., Berlin, 1954; radio/TV cons. space program. Author: Buying & Selling Land for Profit, 1961, Last Man at Hungnam Beach, 1952. V.p. West Point Soc., Cape Canaveral, Fla., 1964. Served to lt. col. USAFR. Decorated Bronze Star, Combat Inf. badge; recipient Emmy award CBS TV Apollo Moon Landing, 1969. Mem. Nat. Space Club, Nat. Exec. Service Corps, Explorer's Club, West Point Soc., Chosin Few Survivors Korea, Internat. Exec. Service Corps. Avocations: fishing, travel.

FRIEDLANDER, MARCI COX, insurance and financial services sales specialist; b. Lynwood, Calif., Apr. 7, 1948; d. Billie Lea and Marcille (Gunther) Cox; m. Jack H. Friedlander, June 7, 1981. B.A., UCLA, 1970, M.Ed., 1976, Ph.D., 1980. Adminstrv. analyst UCLA, 1972-78, research analyst, 1978-80; resource mgr. Pacific Telephone, Buena Park, Calif., 1980; pension adminstr. TSP Assocs., Inc., Los Angeles, 1980-81; pension specialist Litton Industries, Inc., Beverly Hills, Calif., 1981-83; ins. and pension specialist Sun Fin. Group, Walnut Creek, Calif., 1983—; assoc. Aravil Ins. Services, Inc., Walnut Creek, 1984—; sales rep. Alamar Fin. Services, Inc., Santa Barbara, Calif., 1987—; condr. seminars. Author: Characteristics of Students Attending Proprietary Schools and Factors Influencing Their Institutional Choice, 1978. Recipient Outstanding Student award B'nai B'rith, 1966, Dana Hart Meml. award Assn. Ind. Schs. and Colls., 1981; UCLA grantee, 1979. Mem. Nat. Assn. Life Underwriters, Sun Life Sales Leaders Conf. Democrat. Home: 4017 B Via Diego Santa Barbara CA 93110 Office: Alamar Financial Services Inc 40k E Alamar Santa Barbara CA 93105

FRIEDMAN, BRUCE A., lawyer; b. Los Angeles, June 6, 1935; s. Samuel L. and Irene L. (Oreck) F.; children—David, Julie, Stephen. B.A., UCLA, 1957; J.D., U. Calif.-Berkeley, 1960. Bar: Calif. 1961, U.S. Superior Ct. 1976. Research atty. Calif. Ct. Apl. 4th App. Dist., 1960-61; sole practice, Los Angeles, 1961—; instr. Southwestern U., Los Angeles, 1965; arbitrator Los Angeles Superior Ct., 1980—. Mem. Assn. Trial Lawyers Am., Calif. Trial Lawyers Assn., Los Angeles Trial Lawyers Assn., ABA, Los Angeles County Bar Assn. Office: 2029 Century Park E Suite 2610 Los Angeles CA 90067

FRIEDMAN, JONATHAN MARK, lawyer; b. Highland Park, Ill., June 13, 1958; s. Daniel Richard and Veronica (Simundza) F.; m. Michele Durham, Nov. 16, 1985. BA, Carleton Coll., 1980; JD, Lewis and Clark Coll., 1984. Bar: Oreg., 1984, U.S. Dist. Ct. Oreg., 1984. Ptnr. Dixon, Nicholls and Friedman, Portland, Oreg., 1984-86, Portland, 1986—; flight instr., pilot Vancouver (Wash.) Aviation, 1981—. Mem. ABA, Assn. Trial Lawyers Am., Oreg. Trial Lawyers Assn., Oreg. Criminal Def. Lawyers Assn., Multnomah Bar Assn. Democrat. Club: Willamette Athletic, Tualitian. Avocations: golf, flying. Office: 1020 SW Taylor Suite 430 Portland OR 97205

FRIEDMAN, MAURICE STANLEY, religious educator; b. Tulsa, Dec. 29, 1921; s. Samuel Herman and Fanny (Smirin) F.; m. Eugenia Chifos, Jan. 1947 (div. 1974); children: David Michael, Dvora Lisa; m. Aleene Marie Wright Dorn, Sept. 29, 1986. SB in Econs. magna cum laude, Harvard U., 1943; MA in English, Ohio State U., 1947; PhD in History of Culture, U. Chgo., 1950; LLD (hon.), U. Vt., 1961; MA in Psychology, Internat. Coll., 1983; LHD (hon.), Profl. Sch. Psychol. Studies, San Diego, 1986. Prof. philosophy and lit. Sarah Lawrence Coll., 1951-54, prof. philosophy, 1954-64; prof. philosophy and religion Manhattanville Coll. of the Sacred Heart, Purchase, N.Y., 1966-67, Vassar Coll., Poughkeepsie, N.Y., 1967; prof. religion Temple U., Phila., 1966-73, also dir. PhD programs in religion and psychology and religion and lit.; prof. religious studies, philosophy and comparative lit. San Diego State U., 1973—; tutor Internat. Coll., Los Angeles, 1976-86, William Lyon U., 1986—; vis. prof. religious philosophy Hebrew Union Coll.-Jewish Inst. Religion, Cin., 1956, Union Theol. Sem., N.Y.C., 1965, 67; mem. faculty New Sch. for Social Research, N.Y.C., 1954-66, Pendle Hill, Quaker Ctr. for Study, Wallingford, Pa., 1959-60, 64-65, 67-73; lectr. univ. research San Diego State U., 1984-85; fellow com. on the history of culture U. Chgo., 1947-49. Author: Martin Buber: The Life of Dialogue, 1965, Problematic Rebel: Melville, Dostoievsky, Kafka, Camus, 1963, rev. edit. 1970, The Worlds of Existentialism, 1964, To Deny Our Nothingness: Contemporary Images of Man, 1967, Touchstones of Reality: Existential Trust and the Community of Peace, 1972, The Hidden Human Image, 1974, The Human Way: A Dialogical Approach to Religion and Human Experience, 1982, The Confirmation of Otherness: In Family, Community and Society, 1983, Martin Buber's Life and Work: The Early Years 1878-1923, 1982, The Middle Years, 1945-65, 1983, The Later Years 1945-65, 1984 (Nat. Jewish Book award for biography 1985), Contemporary Psychology: Revealing and Obscuring the Human, 1984, The Healing Dialogue In Psychotherapy, 1985 (main selection of Psychotherapy and Social Sci. Book Club, Mar. 1985), Martin Buber and The Eternal, 1986, Abraham Joshua Heschel and Elie Wiesel: "You are my Witnesses", 1987; contbr. numerous articles to profl. jours. Recipient Outstanding Faculty award San Diego State U., 1980. Mem. Religious Edn. Assn. (past bd. dirs., past edit. bd.), Am. Philol. Assn., Am. Acad. Religion, Am. Soc. Study Religion, Fellowship of Reconciliation, Jewish Peace Fellowship, Assn. Humanistic Psychology (edit. bd. Jour. Humanistic Psychology and Person-Centered Rev.), Inst. Dialogical Psychotherapy (co-dir.). Home: 421 Hilmen Pl Solana Beach CA 92075 Office: San Diego State U Dept Religious Studies San Diego CA 92182-0304

FRIEDMAN, MILTON, economist, educator; b. Bklyn., July 31, 1912; s. Jeno Saul and Sarah Ethel (Landau) F.; m. Rose Director, June 25, 1938; children: Janet, David. AB, Rutgers U., 1932, LLD, 1968; AM, U. Chgo., 1933; PhD, Columbia, 1946; LLD, St. Paul's (Rikkyo) U., 1963, Kalamazoo Coll., 1968, Lehigh U., 1969, Loyola U., 1971, U. N.H., 1975, Harvard U., 1979, Brigham Young U., 1980, Dartmouth Coll., 1980, Gonzaga U., 1981; SD, Rochester U., 1971; LHD, Rockford Coll., 1969, Roosevelt U., 1975, Hebrew Union Coll., Los Angeles, 1981; LittD, Bethany Coll., 1971; PhD (hon.), Hebrew U., Jerusalem, 1977; DCS (hon.), Francisco Marroquin U., Guatemala, 1978. Assoc. economist Nat. Resources Com., Washington, 1935-37; mem. research staff Nat. Bur. Econ. Research, N.Y., 1937-45, 1948-81; vis. prof. econs. U. Wis., 1940-41; prin. economist, tax research div. U.S. Treasury Dept., 1941-43; assoc. dir. research, statis. research group, war research div. Columbia U., 1943-45; assoc. prof. econs. and statistics U. Minn., 1945-46; assoc. prof. econs. U. Chgo., 1946-48, prof. econs., 1948-62, Paul Snowden Russell disting. service prof. econs., 1962-82, prof. emeritus, 1983—; Fulbright lectr. Cambridge U., 1953-54; vis. Wesley Clair Mitchell research prof. econs. Columbia, 1964-65; fellow Ctr. for Advanced Study in Behavioral Sci., 1957-58; sr. research fellow Stanford U., 1977—; mem. Pres.'s Commn. All-Vol. Army, 1969-70, Pres.'s Commn. on White House Fellows, 1971-74, Pres.'s Econ. Policy Adv. Bd., 1981—; vis. scholar Fed. Res. Bank, San Francisco, 1977. Author: (with Carl Shoup and Ruth P. Mack) Taxing to Prevent Inflation, 1943, Income from Independent Professional Practice, (with Simon S. Kuznets), 1946, Sampling Inspection, (with Harold A. Freeman, Frederic Mosteller, W. Allen Wallis), 1948, Essays in Positive Economics, 1953, A Theory of the Consumption Function, 1957, A Program for Monetary Stability, 1960, Price Theory: A Provisional Text, 1962, (with Rose D. Friedman) Capitalism and Freedom, 1962, Free To Choose, 1980, Tyranny of the Status Quo, 1984, (with Anna J. Schwartz) A Monetary History of the United States, 1867-1960, 1963, Inflation: Causes and Consequences, 1963, The Great Contraction, 1965, Monetary Statistics of the United States, 1970, Monetary Trends in the U.S. and the United Kingdom, 1982, Bright Promises, Dismal Performance, 1983, (with Robert Roosa) The Balance of Payments: Free vs. Fixed Exchange Rates, 1967, Dollars and Deficits, 1968, The Optimum Quantity of Money and Other Essays, 1969, (with Walter W. Heller) Monetary vs. Fiscal Policy, 1969, A Theoretical Framework for Monetary Analysis, 1972, (with Wilbur J. Cohen) Social Security, 1972, An Economist's Protest, 1972, There Is No Such Thing As A Free Lunch, 1975, Price Theory, 1976, Milton Friedman's Monetary Framework, 1974, Tax Limitation, Inflation and the Role of Government, 1978; editor: Studies in the Quantity Theory of Money, 1956; bd. editors: Am. Econ. Rev, 1951-53, Econometrica, 1957-69; adv. bd.: Jour. Money, Credit and Banking, 1968—; columnist: Newsweek mag, 1966-84, contbg. editor, 1971-84; contbr. articles to profl. jours. Recipient Nobel prize in econs., 1976, Pvt. Enterprise Exemplar medal Freedoms Found., 1978, Grand cordon of the Sacred Treasure Japanese Govt., 1986; named Chicagoan of Yr., Chgo. Press Club, 1972, Educator of Yr., Chgo. United Jewish Fund, 1973. Fellow Inst. Math. Stats., Am. Statis. Assn., Econometric Soc.; mem. Nat. Acad. Scis., Am. Econ. Assn. (mem. exec. com. 1955-57, pres. 1967; John Bates Clark medal 1951), Am. Enterprise Inst. (adv. bd. 1956-79), Western Econ. Assn. (pres. 1984-85), Royal Economic Soc., Am. Philos. Soc., Mont Pelerin Soc. (bd. dirs. 1958-61, pres. 1970-72). Club: Quadrangle. Office: Stanford U Hoover Instn Stanford CA 94305-6010

FRIEDMAN, RON, TV and performing arts producer; b. Pitts., Aug. 1, 1932; s. Louis and Mina (Hirschfield) F.; divorced; children: Ian C., Liza P.; m. Valerie Clare Fidgeon, Aug. 15, 1973; 1 child, Ashley R. BArch, Carnegie-Mellon U., 1955; postgrad., UCLA, 1983. Registered architect, Pa., Ohio, W.Va. Writer (TV series) The Odd Couple, Fantasy Island, Starsky and Hutch, The Fall Guy, Chico and the Man, Bewitched, All in the Family, and others, 1962—; headwriter (TV dramas, comedies, animated spls.) The Jonathan Winters Show, Danny Kaye Show, Betty Boop-CBS; author: Minnie's Boys, 1969, Fair Game'39, 1986. Mem. AFTRA, Writers Guild Am. West, Dramatists Guild. Office: ILI Prodns Inc 9171 Wilshire Blvd Suite 627 Beverly Hills CA 90210

FRIEDMAN, SHELLY ARNOLD, physician, cosmetic surgeon; b. Providence, Jan. 1, 1949; s. Saul and Estelle (Moverman) F.; m. Andrea Leslie Falchook, Aug. 30, 1975; children: Bethany Erin, Kimberly Rebecca. BA, Providence Coll., 1971; DO, Mich. State U., 1982. Diplomate Nat. Bd. Med. Examiners. Intern Pontiac (Mich.) Hosp., 1982-83, resident in dermatology, 1983-86; assoc. clin. prof. dept. internal med. Mich. State U., 1984—; med. dir. Inst. Cosmetic Dermatology, Scottsdale, Ariz., 1986—. Contbr. articles to profl. jours. Mem. B'nai B'rith Men's Council, 1973, Jewish Welfare Fund, 1973. Am. Physicians fellow for medicine, 1982. Mem. AMA, Am. osteopathic Assn., Am. Assn. Cosmetic Surgeons, Am. Acad. Cosmetic Surgery, Internat. Soc. Dermatologic Surgery, Internat. Acad. Cosmetic Surgery, Am. Acad. Dermatology, Am. Soc. Dermatol. Surgery, Frat. Order Police, Sigma Sigma Phi. Jewish. Avocations: karate, horseback riding. Office: Scottsdale Inst Cosmetic Dermatology 10603 N Hayden Rd Suite 112 Scottsdale AZ 85260

FRIEDMAN, TERRY WILLIAM, banker; b. Los Angeles, July 21, 1947; s. Morris L. and Lillian (Shank) F.; m. Nancy Lynn Jackson, Oct. 24, 1970; 1 child, Todd Richard. A.A. in Bus. Adminstrn., Long Beach City Coll., 1967; B.A. in Polit. Sci., Calif. State U.-Long Beach, 1970; M.B.A., Pepperdine U., 1981. Vice pres. Goldstein Samuelson, Beverly Hills, Calif., 1972-78; v.p. Fidelity Fed. Savs., Stanton, Calif., 1978-81; v.p. First Nationwide Savs., Long Beach, Calif., 1981-83; v.p. Signal Savs. & Loan, Signal Hill, Calif., 1983—; dir. mktg. D.I.C.O., Anaheim, Calif.; owner T.N.T. Enterprises, Rossmoor, Calif., 1980—, The Works, Rossmoor, 1981—; pres. U.S. Trade Co.; ptnr. Townsend and Friedman; cons. mktg. and mgmt.; bd. dirs. Natat, Inc.; host Sta. KWHY-TV show Pit Talk, 1973. Contbr. articles to profl. jours. Mem. Gov. Reagan's Student Adv. Com., 1970; bd. dirs. Orange County Regional Occuptation Program, Calif., Stanton Boys and Girls Club; chmn. Rossmoor Sch. Site Council; leader cub pack, Boy Scouts Am. Mem. Stanton C. of C. (v.p.). Republican. Lodge: Kiwanis (v.p.). Home and Office: 3151 Kempton Dr Rossmoor CA 90720

FRIEDMANN, PERETZ PETER, aerospace engineer, educator; b. Timisoara, Romania, Nov. 18, 1938; came to U.S., 1969; s. Mauritius and Elisabeth (Gross) F.; m. Esther Sarfati, Dec. 8, 1964. DSc, MIT, 1972. Engring. officer Israel Def. Force, 1961-65; sr. engr. Israel Aircraft Industries, Ben Gurion Airport, Israel, 1965-69; research asst. dept. aeronautics and astronautics MIT, Cambridge, 1969-72; asst. prof. mech., aerospace and nuclear engring. dept. UCLA, 1972-77, assoc. prof., 1977-80, prof., 1980—. Editor-in-chief Vertica-Internat. Jour. Rotorcraft and Powered Lift Aircraft; contbr. numerous articles to profl. jours. Grantee NASA, U.S. Army Research Office, NSF. Fellow AIAA (assoc.); mem. ASME (Structures and Materials award 1983), Am. Helicopter Soc., Sigma Xi. Jewish. Home: 221 N Bowling Green Way Los Angeles CA 90049 Office: UCLA Dept Mech Aerospace Nuclear Engring Los Angeles CA 90024

FRIEDRICH, LIESEL CHARLOTTE, real estate corporation executive; b. Frankfurt, Fed. Republic Germany, July 21, 1951; came to U.S., 1954; d. Otto Alva and Priscilla (Boughton) F.; m. James B. Lucas, Dec. 21, 1985. AB, Kenyon Coll., 1973. TV news researcher ABC, N.Y.C., 1978-80; producer NBC, N.Y.C., 1980-81; writer CBS-TV, N.Y.C., 1982-84; producer TV news Metromedia, Los Angeles, 1984-85, Telepictures Corp., Los Angeles, 1984-85; v.p. D.R. Mgmt. Co., Los Angeles, 1985—. Assoc. producer VW Beetles, 1979 (Emmy award 1979), Am. Women in the 20th Century, 1981 (Peabody award 1981). Fundraiser Holy Apostles Soup Kitchen, N.Y.C., 1983; lay minister St. Augustine's by the Sea, Santa Monica, Calif., 1984-86. Democrat. Episcopalian. Avocations: cooking, reading, sailing. Home: 440 Raymond Ave Santa Monica CA 90405 Office: DR Mgmt Co 924 Westwood Blvd #615 Los Angeles CA 90024

FRIEL, THOMAS JOHN, JR., software executive; b. Oxnard, Calif., May 5, 1954; s. Thomas John and Anna Marie (Nobel) F.; m. Kathleen Carol Lakes, Oct. 19, 1985. BS in Math., Loyola Marymount U., 1976; MSEE, U. Calif., Irvine, 1978. With Spectra Research Corp., Irvine, 1976-78; mem. aircraft group Northrop Corp., Los Angeles, 1978-80; with Grumman Corp., Point Mugu, Calif., 1980-83; tech. software support dir. Quadratron Systems, Encino, Calif., 1983—; pres. Macrosoft Co., Oxnard, 1981-84. Republican. Roman Catholic. Avocations: pilot, automobiles. Office: Quadratron Systems 15260 Ventura Blvd Sherman Oaks CA 91403

FRIEMAN, EDWARD ALLAN, university administrator, educator; b. N.Y.C., Jan. 19, 1926; s. Joseph and Belle (Davidson) F.; m. Ruth Paula Rodman, June 19, 1949 (dec. May 1966); children: Jonathan, Michael, Joshua; m. Joy Fields, Sept. 17, 1967; children: Linda Gatchell, Wendy. B.S., Columbia U., 1945, M.S. in Physics, 1948; Ph.D. in Physics, Poly. Inst. Bklyn., 1951. Prof. astrophys. scis., dep. dir. Plasma Physics Lab. Princeton U., N.J., 1952-79; dir. energy research Dept. Energy, Washington, 1979-81; exec. v.p. Sci. Applications Internat. Corp., La Jolla, Calif., 1981-86; dir. Scripps Instn. Oceanography, La Jolla, 1986—; vice chancellor marine scis. Scripps Instn. Oceanography, San Diego, 1986—; vice chmn. White House Sci. Council, 1981—, Def. Sci. Bd., Washington, 1984—. Contbr. articles to profl. jours. Served with USN, 1943-46, PTO. Recipient Disting. Service medal Dept. Energy; Disting. Alumni award Poly. Inst. Bklyn.; NSF sr. postdoctoral fellow; Guggenheim fellow. Fellow Am. Phys. Soc. (Richtmyer award); mem. AAAS, Nat. Acad. Scis. Club: Cosmos (Washington). Avocations: piano; tennis; literature. Home: 6425 Muirlands Dr La Jolla CA 92037 Office: Scripps Instn Oceanography Dirs Office A-010 La Jolla CA 92093

FRIEND, DAVID ROBERT, chemist; b. Vallejo, Calif., Aug. 10, 1956; s. Carl Gilbert and Roberta (Schwarzrock) F.; m. Carol Esther Warren, Dec. 17, 1983. BS in Food Biochemistry, U. Calif., Davis, 1979; PhD in Agrl. Chemistry, U. Calif., Berkeley, 1983. Polymer chemist SRI Internat., Menlo Park, Calif., 1984—. Patentee in field. Mem. Am. Chem. Soc., N.Y. Acad. Scis., Controlled Release Soc., Sigma Xi. Democrat. Jewish. Avocations: piano, swimming. Home: 429 Concord Dr Menlo Park CA 94025 Office: SRI Internat 333 Ravenswood Ave Menlo Park CA 94025

FRIES, DOUGLAS WILHELM, aerospace engineer; b. Madison, Mar. 5, 1960; s. Richard Otto and Marjory Sherwood (Fifield) F.; m. Mary Davidson Limbach, June 28, 1986. BS, MS, MIT, 1983. Assoc. mem. tech. staff The Aerospace Corp., El Segundo, Calif., 1980-83; research engineer Lockheed Missiles and Space Corp., Inc., Sunnyvale, Calif., 1983—. Fellow The Aerospace Corp., 1982. Mem. AIAA, Sigma Xi, Tau Beta Pi. Home: 20183 Beatty Ridge Rd Los Gatos CA 95030

FRIESE, ROBERT CHARLES, lawyer; b. Chgo., Apr. 29, 1943; s. Earl Matthew and Laura Barbara (Mayer) F.; m. Chandra Ullom. A.B. in Internat. Relations, Stanford U., 1964; J.D., Northwestern U., 1970. Admitted to Calif. bar, 1972; dir. Tutor Applied Linguistics Center, Geneva, Switzerland, 1964-66; atty. Bronson, Bronson & McKinnon, San Francisco, 1970-71, SEC, San Francisco, 1971-75; atty., partner Shartsis, Friese & Ginsburg, San Francisco, 1975—; dir., co-founder Internat. Plant Research Inst., Inc., San Carlos, Calif., 1978—. Chmn. Bd. Suprs. Task Force on Noise Control, 1972-78; chmn. San Franciscans for Cleaner City, 1977; exec. dir. Nob Hill Neighbors, 1972-81; bd. dirs. Nob Hill Assn., 1976-78, Calif. Heritage Council, 1977-78, San Francisco Beautiful, 1986—; mem. major gifts com. Stanford U. Mem. Am. Bar Assn., Calif. Bar Assn., Bar Assn. San Francisco, (chmn. bus. litigation com., 1978-79, chmn. state ct. civil litigation com. 1983—), Lawyers Club of San Francisco, Mensa, Calif. Hist. Soc. Clubs: Commonwealth; Swiss-American Friendship League (chmn. 1971-79). Office: Shartsis Friese & Ginsburg 1 Maritime Plaza 18th Floor San Francisco CA 94111-2204

FRIESECKE, RAYMOND FRANCIS, management consultant; b. N.Y.C., Mar. 12, 1937; s. Bernhard P. K. and Josephine (De Tomi) F.; B.S. in Chemistry, Boston Coll., 1959; M.S. in Civil Engring., MIT, 1961. Product specialist Dewey & Almy Chem. div. W. R. Grace & Co., Inc., Cambridge, Mass., 1963-66; market planning specialist USM Corp., Boston, 1966-71; mgmt. cons., Boston, 1971-74; dir. planning and devel. Schweitzer div. Kimberly-Clark Corp., Lee, Mass., 1974-78; v.p. corp. planning Butler Automatic, Inc., Canton, Mass., 1978-80; pres. Butler-Europe Inc., Greenwich, Conn. and Munich, Fed. Republic Germany, 1980; v.p. mktg. and planning Butler Greenwich Inc., 1980-81; pres. Strategic Mgmt. Assocs., San Rafael, Calif., 1981—; bd. dirs. Calif. Acad., Kentfield, 1986—; Butler-

Europe, Inc., Greenwich; corp. clk., v.p. Bldg. Research & Devel., Inc., Cambridge, 1966-68. State chmn. Citizens for Fair Taxation, 1972-73; vice chmn. Kentfield Med. Hosp. Found., 1986—; state co-chmn. Mass. Young Reps., 1967-69; chmn. Ward 7 Rep. Com., Cambridge, 1968-70; vice chmn. Cambridge Rep. City Com., 1966-68; Rep. candidate Mass. Ho. of Reps., 1964, 66; pres. Marin Rep. Council, 1986—; chmn bd. Calif. Acad., Kentfield, 1986—. Served to 1st lt. U.S. Army, 1961-63. Mem. Am. Chem. Soc., The Planning Forum, Am. Mktg. Assn., Navy League (v.p. council Marin County), Am. Rifle Assn. Author: Management by Relative Product Quality; contbr. articles to profl. jours. Clubs: MIT, Commonwealth of Calif. Home and Office: 141 Convent Ct San Rafael CA 94901

FRIGON, JUDITH ANN, electronics executive, office systems consultant; b. Wisconsin Rapids, Wis., Feb. 11, 1945; d. Harold Leslie and Muriel Alice (Berard) Neufeld; m. Gene Roland Frigon, June 17, 1967; children: Shane P., Shannon M., Sean M. Sec., office mgr. George Chapman D.D.S., Fairfax, Va., 1971-75; owner, operator Sunset Motel, Havre, Mont., 1976-78; sec. Wash. State U. Social Research Ctr., Pullman, 1978-80; administrv. sec. Wash. State U. Systems and Computing, Pullman, 1980-85, office automation cons., word processing trainer, IBM profl. office system administrt., 1983—; systems analyst, programmer Wash. State U. Computing Ctr, Pullman, 1985—. Pres. Pullman Girl Scout Service Unit, 1983—; v.p. Inland Empire Girl Scout Council, Spkane, Wash., 1985-88; mem. Pullman Civic Trust, 1986. Mem. Profl. Secs. Internat., Jaycees (Jayceen of Yr. 1975). Roman Catholic. Home: NW 1235 Davis Way Pullman WA 99163 Office: Wash State U Computing Ctr 2072 Computer Sci Bldg Pullman WA 99164-1220

FRISBEE, DON CALVIN, utilities executive; b. San Francisco, Dec. 13, 1923; s. Ira Nobles and Helen (Sheets) F.; m. Emilie Ford, Feb. 5, 1947; children: Ann, Robert, Peter, Dean. B.A., Pomona Coll., 1947; M.B.A., Harvard U., 1949. Sr. investment analyst, asst. cashier investment analysis dept. 1st Interstate Bank Oreg., N.A., Portland, 1949-52, now dir.; with PacifiCorp, Portland, 1953—, treas., 1958-60, then v.p., exec. v.p., pres., 1966-73, chmn., chief exec. officer, 1973—; bd. dirs. First Interstate Bancorp, Weyerhaeuser Co., Standard Ins. Co., Portland, Precision Castparts Corp., Portland, First Interstate Bank of Oreg., Portland, Pacific Credit, Inc. Trustee Reed Coll., Com. for Econ. Devel.; pres., bd. dirs. Oreg. Community Found.; bd. dirs. Oreg. Bus. Council; chmn Portland Boy Scouts council Boy Scouts Am. Served to 1st lt. AUS, 1943-46. Clubs: Arlington, University, Multnomah Athletic. Office: PacifiCorp 851 SW 6th St Portland OR 97204

FRISHMAN, RICHARD ALLEN, photographer; b. Chgo., May 12, 1951; s. Alvin and Sherley Betty (Vender) F.; m. Brenda Alane Hartman, Sept. 24, 1983. BS, U. Ill., 1973. Photographer Pioneer Press, Wilmette, Ill., 1973-76; freelance photographer Chgo., 1976-77; photographer Everett (Wash.) Herald, 1977-84; freelance photographer Everett, 1984—; videographer Video Verite, Everett, 1984—. Named Regional Photographer of Yr. Nat. Press. Photographer's Assn., 1978, 79, New Face in Photography Am. Photographer Mag., 1980. Mem. Nat. Press Photographers Assn. (Photographer of Yr. runner up 1976), Ill. Pres. Photographer's Assn. (cochmn. Pictures of Yr. 1976-77, Ill. Press Photograher of Yr. 1977). Avocations: documentary videography, blues harmonica, backpacking, fishing. Office: Video Verite 3005 Panaview Rd Everett WA 98203

FRISK, JACK EUGENE, recreational vehicle mfg. co. exec.; b. Nampa, Idaho, Jan. 22, 1942; s. Steinert Paul and Evelyn Mildred (Letner) F.; m. Sharon Rose Caviness, Aug. 3, 1959; 1 dau., Toni. With Ideal of Idaho, Inc., Caldwell, purchasing mgr., 1969-75, gen. mgr., sec.-treas., 1975-82; sales mgr. Travelez Industries (div. Thor Industries), Sun Valley, Calif., 1982—. Mem. adv. bd. Ctr. for Employment Tng. Mem. Recreational Vehicle Industry Assn. Episcopalian. Home and Office: 2527 Marisa Pl Simi Valley CA 93065

FRITSCH-HEISELT, BRENDA JOYCE, temporary help company executive; b. Loma Linda, Calif., July 11, 1951; d. L.C. Causey and Connie June Cooper; m. Mike Jacobson, Mar. 29, 1968 (div.); children: Richard L., Andrew M.; m. John Fritsch, Sept. 11, 1976 (div.); m. Jim L. Heiselt, Feb. 23, 1985. With data processing and acctg. depts. So. Calif. Savs. & Loan, 1971-74; with customer service, tng., data entry and computer ops. depts. Met. Computer Co., 1974-78; mgr. data placement and sales Data Overload, 1978-81; mgr., sales Career Data Personnel, 1981-83; v.p. data processing and personal computer tng. divs., sales United Temporary Services, 1983—; subject specialist office automation, data entry and computer ops. Creativ mgr. Data Mgmt. mag., 1982. Mem. Nat. Assn. Tech. and Trade Schs. (west coast), Data Entry Mgrs. Assn. (pres. Greater Los Angeles chpt.). Home: 613 E Bonnie View Dr Rialto CA 92376 Office: United Temoporary Services 5757 Wilshire Blvd Suite 270 Los Angeles CA 90036

FRITTS, HAROLD CLARK, dendochronology educator, researcher; b. Rochester, N.Y., Dec. 17, 1928; s. Edwin Coulthard and Ava Lee (Washburn) F.; m. Barbara Smith, June 11, 1955 (dec.); children: Marcia L., Paul T.; m. Miriam Colson, July 19, 1982. AB, Oberlin Coll., 1951; MS, Ohio State U., 1953, PhD in Botany, 1956. Asst. prof. botany Eastern Ill. U., Charleston, 1956-60; asst. prof. dendochronology U. Ariz., Tucson, 1960-64, assoc., 1964-69, prof., 1969—; dir., founder Internat. Tree-Ring Data Bank, 1975—; NSF faculty, mem. Task Group 3 adv. com. on paleoclimatology, Climate Dynamics Program, 1978—; lectr. NATO Advanced Study Inst. on Climatic Variability, Sicily, 1980; vis. dr. U. Wyo. Summer Sci. Camp, summer 1956; mem. U. Ariz del. to People's Republic of China, 1976; participant Nat. Def. Univ., 1978—; mem. organizing group internat. conf. on dendroclimatology, England, 1980. Author: Tree Rings and Climate, 1976; edit. adv. bd. Quaternary Research, 1977-82; contbr. articles to profl. jours. Mem. local sch. bd., 1971-72. Grad. fellow Ohio State U., 1954-56, NSF fellow Oreg. Inst. Marine Biology, summer 1957, Guggenheim fellow, 1968-69; grantee NSF 1971—; U. Calif. Lawrence Livermore Lab., 1978-79, State of Calif., 1979-80, 85-86. Mem. Am. Assn. Quaternary Environment (council 1978-82, adv. com. paleoclimatology), Ecol. Soc. Am. (edit. bd. 1964-66, council rep., chmn. paleoecology sect 1984), AAAS, Am. Inst. Biol. Scis., Tree-Ring Soc., Am. Meteorol. Soc. (Oustanding Achievement in Bioclimatology award 1982), Am. Quaternary Assn. (mem. council 1978—), Internat. Assn. for Ecology, Internat. Soc. Ecol. Modeling, Internat. Union Quaternary Research, Sigma Xi. Home: 5703 N Lady Ln Tucson AZ 85704 Office: U Ariz Bldg 58 Lab of Tree-Ring Research Tucson AZ 85721

FRITZ, DOYL M., consulting engineering executive; b. Hot Springs, S.D., Oct. 12, 1945; s. Marvin L. and Venida P. (Prentice) F.; m. Jacqueline Patricia Eaton, Aug. 27, 1966; children: Jennifer Eaton, Jack William. BCE, U. Wyo., 1968; MCE, Ariz. State U., 1969. Registered profl. engr., Wyo., Colo., Mont. Water resources engr. State of Wyo., Cheyenne, 1970-73; cons. engr. HKM Assocs., Billings, Mont., 1973-76; dist. engr. Wyo. Dept. Environ. Quality, Sheridan, 1976-78; prin., co-owner Western Water Cons., Inc., Sheridan, 1978—. Bd. dirs. County Planning Commn., Sheridan County. Mem. ASCE (v.p. state sect. 1986, pres. 1986-87), Nat. Water Well Assn., Wyo. Engring. Soc., Wyo. Water Devel. Assn., Assn. Environ. Scientists and Administrs. Republican. Lodge: Masons. Avocations: horseback riding, horse training, fly fishing. Home: 217 Sheridan WY 82801 Office: Western Water Cons Inc 2 N Main Suite 405 Sheridan WY 82801

FRITZ, JAMES JOHN, retired chemistry educator; b. Sunbury, Pa., Sept. 21, 1920; s. John Milton and Laura Frances (Kline) F.; m. Helen Marie Morris, Feb. 14, 1943; children: Catherine E., James H., Phebe A., Charles H. BS in Chemistry, Pa. State U., 1939; MS in Chemistry, U. Chgo., 1940; PhD in Chemistry, U. Calif., Berkeley, 1948. Research assoc. Ohio State U. Columbus, 1948-49; from asst. prof. to full prof. chemistry Pa. State U., University Park, 1949-85. Co-author: Chemical and Statistical Thermodynamics, 1968; contbr. articles to profl. jours. Guggenheim fellow Oxford U., 1961-62, Japan Soc. for Promotion of Sci. fellow, 1970. Mem. Am. Chem. Soc. N.Y. Acad. Scis. Democrat. Avocation: chess. Home: 217 Holiday Way Oceanside CA 92056

FRITZEMEIER, LESLIE GENE, aerospace materials engineer; b. Mitchell, S.D., Feb. 23, 1955; s. William and Rilla Mae (Anderson) F.; m. Marilyn Lee Randall, June 21, 1986. BA, Augustana Coll., Sioux Falls, S.D., 1977;

BS, Columbia U., 1978, MS, 1979, PhD in Engring. Sci., 1984. Engr. Rockwell Internat., Canoga Park, Calif., 1984—; cons. Westinghouse, Chester, Pa., 1982-84, Rolls Royce, Eng., 1983. Contbr. articles to profl. jours. Mem. Am. soc. Metals, The Metall. Soc., Sigma Xi. Democrat. Lutheran. Avocations: downhill skiing, ultimate flying disk, woodworking. Home: 19169 Erwin St Reseda CA 91335 Office: Rockwell Internat Rocketdyne Div 6633 Canoga Ave Canoga Park CA 91307

FROEHLICH, DODY (JEANNINE), industrial chemicals company executive; b. Denver, Aug. 20, 1935; d. Douglas James and Ruth Snowden (Johnston) Izett; m. Fred Froehlich, Oct. 26, 1934. Student U. Colo., 1953-54, Colo. State U., 1955-56. GS-5 and div. sec. Air Res. Records Ctr., Denver, 1954-55; stewardess various airlines, N.Y.C. and San Francisco, 1957-61; asst. to fashion salon dir. Gump's, San Francisco, 1961-62; sec. Z.W. Wong Esq., San Francisco, 1961-62; exec. sec., asst. David Nelson Pub. Relations Co., San Francisco, 1962-65; sec. to mayor San Francisco, 1965-68; reservationist, then mgr. Silver Tree Inn & Eldorado Lodges, then asst. mgr. Crestwood Condominiums, Snowmass-at-Aspen, Colo., 1968-78; owner, pres. D. Froehlich Indsl. Co., Anchorage, 1978—. Mem. Anchorage Mayor's Adv. Bd. Animal Control, 1979-84; mem. Alaska State Bd. Veterinary Examiners, 1981-84. Recipient Dog World award German Shepherd Dog Club of Alaska, 1985; winner Top Alaskan Showdog Kennel Rev. System, 1978, 80, 82, 83; Gov.'s Recognition award for community vol. work, 1983. Mem. Am. Dog Owners Assn. (dir.), Alaska Kennel Club (pres. 1985-86, Dog World award 1979), CARE Alaska (founding), Puget Sound Norwegian Elkhound Assn., Norwegian Elkhound Assn. Am. (dir.), Delta Gamma. Episcopalian. Home and Office: PO Box 110849 Anchorage AK 99511

FROELICH, DEBORAH ANN HWA, speech pathologist; b. Rome, Ga., Mar. 7, 1954; d. Eugene Ching Hwa and Margaret Ann Zia; m. Dana Alan Froelich, July 31, 1976; children: Jason Paul, Mark Alan. BS, U. Kans., 1976, MA, 1978. Speech/lang. pathologist Pub. Sch. System, Lawrence, Kans., 1978, Highbee, Renick, and Clark, Mo., 1978-79, Columbia, Mo., 1979-80; speech/lang. pathologist La Junta (Calif.) Med. Ctr., 1981-86; speech/lang. pathologist Ark. Valley Community Ctr. Bd. Infant Stimulation Class, La Junta, 1984-86; chmn. Acute-care Rehab. and Extended Care Facility Long-term Care Rehab., La Junta, 1985-86; spl. educator Early Childhood Edn. Toddler Class, La Junta, 1986—. Mem. Am. Speech-Lang. and Hearing Assn. (cert.), Phi Kappa Phi. Avocations: skiing, tennis, aerobics. Home: 1616 Cimarron La Junta CA 81050 Office: La Junta Med Ctr 1100 Carson Ave La Junta CA 81050

FROHLICH, ALI CAN, career military officer; b. Wright-Patterson AFB, Ohio, Aug. 30, 1958; s. Donald Ralph and Leyla (Yalcin) F.; m. Serra Gül Giray, June 7, 1980; 1 child, Danyal Sibel. BS, USAF Acad., 1980. Commd. 2d. lt. USAF, 1976, advanced through grades to capt., 1984; student pilot 82d flying tng. wing, Williams AFB, Ariz., 1980-81; liaison officer and O-2A forward air controller 24th composite wing, Howard AFB, Republic of Panama, 1981-84; flight commdr. 24th composite wing, Republic of Panama, 1983-84; F-16 pilot 56th tactical tng. wing, Macdill AFB, Fla., 1984-85; F-16 pilot, mobility and plans officer 4th tactical fighter squadron, 388 tactical fighter wing, Hill AFB, Utah, 1985—, chief readiness div., 1985—. Mem. Air Force Assn., Hill AFB Officers Club, Order of Daedalions. Republican. Mem. Moslem Co. Avocations: powerlifting, skiing, hunting. Home: 1184 Cistena Circle Layton UT 84041 Office: USAF 4th Tactical Fighter Squadron Hill AFB UT 84056

FROHNEN, RICHARD GENE, educator; b. Omaha, Mar. 26, 1930; s. William P. and Florence E. (Rogers) F.; student U. Nebr., Omaha, Mo. Valley Coll., 1948-52; B.A., Calif. State U., 1954; M.S., UCLA 1961; Ed.D., Brigham Young U., 1976; grad. Army War Coll., 1982 m. Harlene Grace LeTourneau, July 4, 1958; children—Karl Edward, Eric Eugene. Bus. mgr. athletics and sports publicity dir. U. Nebr., Omaha, 1951-52; pub. relations dir. First Congl. Ch. Los Angeles, 1953-54, 58-59; writer Los Angeles Mirror News, 1959; gen. assignment reporter, religion editor Los Angeles Times, 1959-61; prof. journalism, dean mem Eastern Mont. Coll., Billings, 1961-65; N.W. editor, editorial writer Spokesman-Review, Spokane, 1965-67, also editor Sunday mag.; prof. journalism U. Nev., Reno, 1967-79; exec. dir. devel. Coll. of Desert/Copper Mountain, 1982-85, Ariz. Health Scis. Ctr., Tucson, 1986—; pub. relations devel. officer Sch. Med. Scis. U. Nev., 1969-75; adj. prof. mgmt., dir. grad. prois. in Mgmt. U. Redlands (Calif.), 1979-85; cons. pub. relations. Mem. exec. bd. Nev. area council Boy Scouts Am., 1968-76, council commn., 1973-74, v.p., 1975-76; mem. exec. bd. Yellowstone Valley council Boy Scouts Am., 1961-65, council pres. 1963-64; v.p. Catalina Council Boy Scouts Am., 1987—; founder, mng. dir. Gt. Western Expdns., 1958—; administrv. asst. to Gov. of Nev., 1985. Served to 1st lt. USMC, 1954-58; now col. Res. Recipient Silver Beaver award Boy Scouts Am., 1974, Pres.' Vol. Action award Coll. Desert/Copper Mountain, 1984, Outstanding Faculty award U. Redlands, 1984. Mem. Assn. Edn. Journalism, Am. Legion, Res. Officers Assn. U.S., Marine Corps Assn., Marine Corps Res. Officers Assn., Am. Humanics Found., Internat. Platform Assn., Nat. Soc. Fund Raising Execs., Planning Execs. Inst., Internat. Communication Assn., Religion Newswriters Assn., Navy League, Smoker Fidelis Soc., Kappa Tau Alpha, Alpha Phi Omega, Sigma Delta Chi (sec.-treas. chpt.). Episcopalian. Kiwanian, Lion, Rotarian. Home: 6631 N Cibola Ave Tucson AZ 85718 Office: U Ariz 1501 N Campbell Ave Tucson AZ 85724

FROHNMAYER, DAVID BRADEN, state attorney general; b. Medford, Oreg., July 9, 1940; s. Otto J. and Marabel (Fisher) B.; m. Lynn Diane Johnson, Dec. 30, 1970; children: Kirsten, Mark, Kathryn, Jonathan, Amy. A.B. magna cum laude, Harvard U., 1962; B.A., Oxford (Eng.) U., 1964, M.A. (Rhodes scholar), 1971; J.D., U. Calif. Berkeley, 1967. Bar: Calif. 1967, Oreg. 1971. Assoc. firm Pillsbury, Madison & Sutro, San Francisco, 1967-69; asst. to sec. Dept. HEW, 1969-70; prof. U. Oreg. Law Sch., 1971-81, spl. asst. to pres., 1971-79; atty. gen. State of Oreg., 1981—; mem. Oreg. Ho. of Reps., 1975-81; chmn. Conf. Western Attys. Gen., 1985-86; pres.-elect Nat. Assn. Attys. Gen., 1986—. Recipient awards Weaver Constl. Law Essay competition Am. Bar Found., 1972, 74. Mem. ABA (Ross essay winner 1980), Oreg. Bar Assn., Calif. Bar Assn., Assn. Attys. Gen. (v.p. 1985-86, pres. elect 1986—), Round Table Eugene, Order of Coif, Phi Beta Kappa. Republican. Presbyterian. Club: (). Home: 2875 Baker St Eugene OR 97403 Office: Office of Atty Gen 100 State Office Bldg Salem OR 97310

FROMM, CARL HENRY, engineering company executive. BS in Chem. Engring., Wayne State U., 1973. Registered profl. engr., Calif. Research and devel. engr. Lee Pharm., South El Monte, Calif., 1974-76; process engr. Ralph M. Parsons Co., Pasadena, Calif., 1976-79, Procon Inc., El Monte, 1979-81; sr. project engr. Jacobs Engring., Pasadena, 1981—, project mgr., 1985—. Author: Waste Minimization, 1986. Mem. Am. Inst. Chem. Engrs. (profl. devel. recognition cert. 1984), Sci. Research Soc., Sigma Xi. Office: Jacobs Engring 251 S Lake Ave Pasadena CA 91101

FROMM, HANNA, educational administrator; b. Nuremberg, W.Ger., Dec. 20, 1913; d. David and Meta (Stiebel) Gruenbaum; m. Alfred Fromm, July 4, 1936; children—David, Caroline Fromm Lurie. Grad. in choreography and music Folkwang Sch. Dancing and Music, Essen, Gemany, 1934; D.Pub. Service (hon.), U. San Francisco, 1979. Served with ARC, World War II; exec. dir. Fromm Inst. Lifelong Learning, U. San Francisco, 1975—. Cofounder Music in the Vineyards, Saratoga, Calif.; bd. dirs. Amnesty Internat., Nat. Council of Fine Arts Museums; former bd. dirs. Young Audiences, Community Music Ctr., Legal Aid to Elderly, San Francisco Chamber Music Soc.; coordinating com. geriatric curriculum and program U. Calif.-San Francisco; dir. Nat. Council on Aging. Mem. Gerontology Assn. Psychoanalytic Inst. of San Francisco Jewish. Club: Met. (San Francisco). Home: 850 El Camino del Mar San Francisco CA 94121 Office: 538 University Center 2130 Fulton St San Francisco CA 94117

FRONAPFEL, HAROLD JOHN, structural engineer; b. Feb. 28, 1929; s. John Henry and Rose Jean (Tuchek) F.; m. Bonita Marie Schuman; children: Thomas, Steven, James, Karen, Michael, Gretchen, Lori, Edward, Eric, Paul. BSCE, Colo. State U., 1952; postgrad., U. Colo., 1956. Registered profl. engr. Colo., Calif.; Fla.; registered structural engr. Nev. Engr. A.J. Ryan & Assocs., Denver, 1954-61; engr. and supt. Stearns-Roger Engring. Corp., Denver, 1961-82; staff structural engr. Stearns Catalytic Corp. div. Stearns-Roger Engring. Corp., Denver, 1982—. Served to 1st lt. U.S. Army,

1952-54. Recipient Structural-Welding Innovation award Lincoln Arc Welding, Colo., 1978. Mem. NSPE (pres. Jefferson County, Colo. chpt. 1985-86). Club: Republican. Home: 9750 W 77th St Arvada CO 80005 Office: Stearns Catalytic Corp 4500 Cherry Creek Dr S Denver CO 80217

FRONSKE, ROBERT DEAN, architect, industrial designer; b. Flagstaff, Ariz., Oct. 17, 1943; s. Robert Martin and Threse Marie (Jakle) F.; m. Donnielle Sisti, Apr. 15, 1969 (div. 1974); children: Thresa Louise, Joan Avie; m. Jeanne Alice Edmonds, Feb. 26, 1976. BArch., U. Ariz., 1969. Registered architect, Ariz. Designer Balsiger Assocs., Wilsonville, Oreg., 1969-72, VSS Assocs., Phoenix, 1972-74, O/H/G Assocs., Phoenix, 1974-76; prin. Fronske Assocs., Tempe, Ariz., 1976—. Inventor clay mixer, dental fob. Avocations: archery, golf, philosophy, poetry, nature. Office: Fronske and Assocs Ltd 525 S Mill Ave Tempe AZ 85281

FRONTIERE, GEORGIA, professional football team executive; m. Carroll Rosenblum, July 7, 1966 (dec.); children—Dale Carroll, Lucia; m. Dominic Frontiere. Pres. Los Angeles Rams, NFL, 1979—. Bd. dirs. Los Angeles Boys and Girls Club, Los Angeles Orphanage Guild, Los Angeles Blind Youth Found. Named Headliner of Yr., Los Angeles Press Club, 1981. Office: Los Angeles Rams 2327 W Lincoln Ave Anaheim CA 92801 *

FROST, BRENT HIXSON, financial executive; b. Glendale, Calif., Oct. 26, 1945; s. Donald Ernest and Elizabeth B. (Hixson) F.; m. Janet Susan Bright, Aug. 1, 1969; children—Todd, Ryan, Jared, Darren, Chanel. B.S. cum laude, Brigham Young U., 1969. C.P.A., Calif., 1973. Staff acct., tax mgr. Peat, Marwick, Mitchell & Co., Los Angeles, 1969-78; sr. v.p., dir. taxes Fin. Corp. Am., Los Angeles, 1978—; exec. v.p., dir. taxes Am. Savs. & Loan, 1978—. Missionary, Ch. of Jesus Christ of Latter-day Saints, Eng., 1965-67; pres. Elders Quorum, Glendale, Calif., 1973-80; Cub Scout leader Boy Scouts Am., La Canada, Calif., 1980-84. Mem. Calif. League Savs. Instns., Am. Inst. C.P.A.s, Calif. Soc. C.P.A.s. Republican.

FROST, HAROLD MAURICE, physician; b. Boston, May 21, 1921; s. Harold M. and Lucy (Church) F.; m. Elsa Claudius, Oct. 21, 1956; children—Harold Maurice III, Mary Jean, Michael, Patricia, Robert, Eric. B.A., Dartmouth Coll., 1943; M.D., Northwestern U., 1945. Intern Mary Hitchcock Meml. Hosp., Hanover, N.H.; resident Worcester (Mass.) City Hosp. 1948-50, Buffalo Gen. Hosp., 1950-52, Buffalo Children's Hosp., 1952-53; clin. instr. orthopaedic surgery Buffalo U. Med. Sch., 1953-55; asst. prof. orthopaedic surgery Yale U. Sch. Medicine, 1955-57; assoc. orthopaedic surgeon Henry Ford Hosp., Detroit, 1957-73; dir. orthopedic research lab. Henry Ford Hosp., 1957—, chmn. dept. orthopedic surgery, 1966-72; clin. prof. surgery U. Mich., Ann Arbor, 1970-73; adj. prof. anatomy Purdue U. Author: Clinical Fundamentals of Orthopaedic Surgery, 1953, Bone Remodeling Dynamics, 1963, Mathematical Elements of Bone Remodeling, 1964, Laws of Bone Structure, 1964, Bone Biodynamics, 1964, Dynamics in Osteoporosis and Osteomalacia, 1966, Introduction to Biomechanics, 1966, Orthopedic Surgery in Spasticity, 1972, Physiology of Cartilaginous, Fibrous and Bony Tissue, 1972, Bone Remodeling and Its Relationship to Metabolic Bone Disease, 1972, Bone Modeling and Skeletal Modeling Errors, 1973, Orthopaedic Biomechanics, 1973, Intermediary Organization of the Skeleton, 1986; assoc. editor: Clin. Orthopaedics; contbr. over 400 articles to profl. jours. Served to lt. (j.g.), M.C. USNR, 1946-48. Mem. AMA (Hektoen gold medal award basic research 1963), Am. Acad. Orthopaedic Surgeons, Orthopaedics Research Soc., Am. Geriatric Soc., Am. Gerontol. Soc., Am. Rheumatism Soc., Detroit Physiol. Soc., Detroit Surg. Soc., Detroit Acad. Orthopaedic Surgery, Assn. Bone and Joint Surgeons, Mich. Orthopaedic Soc., Am. Acad. Cerebral Palsy, Clin. Orthopaedic Soc., N.Y. Acad. Scis., Soc. for Cerebral Palsy, Sigma Xi. Spl. research on biomechanics bone physiology and cell dynamics.

FROST, JOHN ROOT, indsl. and mfg. engr.; b. Oakland, Calif., Sept. 29, 1906; s. George Booth and Ruth (Godfrey) R.; student San Francisco Sch. Bus., 1933-34, San Francisco Sch. Law, 1934-37; spl. postgrad. U. Calif. at Berkely, 1936-50; m. Esther M. Foster, June 19, 1932; children: Lisa E. (Mrs. Robert L. Smythe) (dec.), John Hunnicutt. With Calif. & Hawaiian Sugar Co., Crockett, Calif., 1932-70; developer curricula, organizer Engring. Sch., John F. Kennedy U., Martinez, Calif., 1977-70, administrv. v.p., 1970-73, dean. Sch. Engring., 1968-70; vis. prof. dept. indsl. sci. Korea Advanced Inst. Sci., Seoul, 1973-75; exec. dir. Productivity Ctr. of S.W. at Los Angeles, 1977-86; expert examiner Calif. State Bd. Registration for Profl. Engrs., 1968-70; pvt. cons. indsl. engring., 1969—; mem. Internat. Exec. Service Corps., 1969—. Active Boy Scouts Am., ARC, mem. Senator Alan Cranston's State of Calif. Productivity Bd., 1985—. Named Indsl. Engr. of Year, Am. Inst. Indsl. Engrs., San Francisco and Oakland, Calif., 1968. Registered profl. engr.; Calif. Fellow Am. Inst. Indsl. Engrs. (pres. 1946-47, chmn. edn. com. 1948-53); mem. NSPE, Calif. Soc. Profl. Engrs. Soc. Mfg. Engrs., Korean Inst. Indsl. Engrs. (hon.), Alpha Pi Mu (hon.). Club: Commonwealth. Contbr. articles to profl. jours. Address: 3173 Buckingham Rd Glendale CA 91206

FROST, S. NEWELL, telecommunications company executive; b. Oklahoma City, Dec. 21, 1935; s. Sterling Johnson and Eula Dove (Whitford) F.; m. Patricia Joyce Rose, Aug. 18, 1957; children—Patricia Diane Wiscarson, Richard Sterling, Lindy Layne Wasilko. B.S. Indsl. Engring., U. Okla., Norman, 1957; M.S. Indsl. Engring., Okla. State U., 1966. Registered profl. engr., Okla. Calif. asst. mgr. acctg Western Electric, Balt., 1972-73, mgr. indsl. engring., Chgo., 1973-75, mgr. devel. engring., 1975-76, mgr. acct. mgmt., San Francisco, 1976-78, dir. staff, Morristown, N.J., 1978-79; distbn. & repair AT&T Techs., Sunnyvale, Calif., 1979-85, ops. gen. mgr., 1979-85; dir. Contract Office Group, San Jose, Calif., 1983—, chmn., 1984—; with material mgmt. services AT&T Info. Systems, Oakland, Calif., 1985—, area v.p., 1985—. Bd. dirs. Santa Clara County YMCA, San Jose, Calif., 1981-84. Recipient Man of Day citation Sta. WAIT Radio, Chgo. Mem. Nat. Soc. Prof. Engrs. (chmn. edn. com. 1969-70), Am. Inst. Indsl. Engrs. (pres. bd. dirs. 1966-68), Okla. Soc. Profl. Engrs. (v.p. 1968-69), San Jose C. of C. Republican. Baptist. Home: 4144 Paradise Dr Tiburon CA 94920 Office: AT&T 1000 Broadway Oakland CA 94607

FROST, WILLIAM, English educator; b. N.Y.C., June 8, 1917; s. John William and Christina (Gurlitz) F.; m. Marjorie Hayes Pangburn, Aug. 5, 1942; children—Marjorie Augusta Frost McCracken, Christina Emily, Clifford William. A.B., Bowdoin Coll., 1938, D.Litt. (hon.), 1980; M.A., Columbia U., 1942; Ph.D., Yale U., 1946. Instr. Carnegie Inst. Tech., 1942-44; instr. Yale U., 1946-47, vis. assoc. prof., 1958-59; asst. prof. U. Calif., Santa Barbara, 1951-55, assoc. prof., 1955-58, 1947-51; asst. prof. U. Calif., Santa Barbara, 1951-55, assoc. prof., 1955-58, 59-61, acting chmn. dept. English, 1965-66, chmn., 1974-79, prof. English, 1961—, coeditor Works of John Dryden, Vol. IV, 1974. Guggenheim fellow, 1959, 79-80, Am. Council Learned Socs. fellow, 1966-67, Nat. Endowment for Humanities fellow, 1972-73; Am. Philos. soc. grantee, 1982-83. Mem. MLA, Philol. Assn. of Pacific Coast, Medieval Acad. Am., Calif. State Employees Assn., Phi Beta Kappa. Club: Elizabethan (Yale U.). Author: Fulke Greville's Caelica: An Evaluation, 1942; Dryden and the Art of Translation, 1955, 69; Dryden and Future Shock, 1976; editor, co-editor, assoc. editor: English Masterpieces, 1950, 61; Selected Works of Dryden, 1953, 71; Pope's Homer, 1967; Dryden's Juvenal and Persius and Other Poems, 1974, Dryden's Virgil, 1987; contbr. articles on Chaucer, Shakespeare, Pope, Persius, others to publs. Office: English Dept Univ Calif Santa Barbara CA 93106

FROULA, BARBARA SUE, artist, architect; b. Hot Springs, Ark., Nov. 30, 1955; d. James C. and Helen B. (Tanana) F.; m. Timothy W. Adams, Sept. 3, 1983. B.Arch., Auburn U., 1978; Cert. Royal Danish Acad. Fine Arts, Copenhagen, 1976-77. Registered architect, Colo. Instr. Auburn U., Ala., 1978-79; architect Baer & Hickman, Denver, 1979-80; project administr. U. Colo. Dept. Adminstrn., Denver, 1980-81; instr. U. Colo., Boulder, 1981; owner Barbara Froula Studio Gallery, Denver. One-woman shows Trinity Place, 1983, Women's Bank, Denver, 1983, Boetcher Concert Hall, Denver, 1983, 84, Denver Ctr. Cinema, 1984; exhibited in group shows Driscol Gallery, Denver, 1984, 85, Foothills Art Ctr., Golden, 1984, 85, Royce Galleries, Denver, 1984, 85, Temple Ctr., Denver, 1985, Art by Architects, 1981, 82, Cogswell Gallery, Vail, Colo., 1987. Author: (with Engelken and Huth) Undiscovered Denver Dining, 1982; illustrator: Beyond Undiscovered Denver Dining, 1983; (posters) Historic Denver, 1983, 84, 85 (Award of Honor, 1985), Temple Ctr., 1985; The Mayan, 1985; An Afternoon in the City, 1985; Westin Hotel, Tabor Ctr., 1985, Historic Boulder, 1985, Westin La Paloma, Tucson, 1986, Rotary Club of Golden, 1986, A Visit to 17th Avenue, 1986; (bookcover) Denver: The City Beautiful, 1987. Co-sponsor, instr. Hmong Refugee Program, Denver, 1980. Recipient best of show award Denver Symphony Guild, 1983; scholar Rotary Internat. Found., 1976. Mem. Foothills Art Ctr., AIA (medal award 1978, juror's award 1982), Colo. Lawyers for Arts (poster composite award 1983), Denver Art Mus., Hist. Denver, Inc., Nat. Trust for Hist. Preservation, Colo. Hist. Soc., Friends of the Mayan. Democrat. Roman Catholic. Studio: 108 W Byers Pl 208 Denver CO 80223

FRUCHTER, JONATHAN SEWELL, research scientist, geochemist; b. San Antonio, June 5, 1945; s. Benjamin and Dorothy Ann (Sewell) F.; m. Cecelia Ann Smith, Mar. 31, 1973; children: Diane, Daniel. BS in Chemistry, U. Tex., 1966; PhD in Geochemistry, U. Calif., San Diego, 1971. Research assoc. U. Oreg., Eugene, 1971-74; research scientist Battelle Northwest, Richland, Wash., 1974-79, research and devel. mgr., 1979—. Contbr. numerous articles to profl. jours. Mem. AAAS, Am. Chem. Soc., Phi Beta Kappa, Phi Kappa Phi. Avocations: fishing, skiing, boating. Office: Battelle Northwest PO Box 999 Richland WA 99352

FRUMKIN, GENE, author, educator; b. N.Y.C., Jan. 29, 1928; s. Samuel and Sarah (Blackman) F.; B.A. in English, UCLA, 1951; m. Lydia Samuels, July 3, 1955 (dec.); children—Celena, Paul. Exec. editor Calif. Apparel News, Los Angeles, 1952-66; asst. prof. English, U. N.Mex., Albuquerque, 1967-71, assoc. prof., 1971—. Mem. Rio Grande Writers Assn., Associated Writing Programs, Hawaii Literary Arts Council. Author: The Hawk and the Lizard, 1963; The Orange Tree, 1965; The Rainbow-Walker, 1968; Dostoevsky and Other Nature Poems, 1972; Locust Cry: Poems 1958-65, 1973; The Mystic Writing-Pad, 1977; Loops, 1979; Clouds and Red Earth, 1982, A Sweetness in the Air, 1987; co-editor San Marcos Rev., 1976-83; The Indian Rio Grande: Recent Poems from 3 Cultures (anthology), 1977; editor: Coastlines Lit. Mag., 1958-62, N.Mex. Quar., 1969. Home: 3721 Mesa Verde NE Albuquerque NM 87110

FRUSH, JAMES CARROLL, JR., health services cons.; b. San Francisco, Oct. 18, 1930; s. James Carroll and Edna Mae (Perry) F.; BA, Stanford, 1953; postgrad. U. Calif. at San Francisco, 1957-58; MA, Saybrook Inst., 1981; PhD, 1985; m. Patricia Anne Blake, Oct. 29, 1960 (div. 1977); children—Michael, Gloria; m. 2d, Carolyn Fetter Bell, Aug. 23, 1978; 1 child, Stephen. Partner, James C. Frush Co. San Francisco, 1960-70; v.p., dir. research Retirement Residence, Inc., San Francisco, 1964-70, pres., 1970—; pres. Nat. Retirement Residence, San Francisco, 1971—, Casa Dorinda Corp., 1971—; lectr. Pres., Marin Shakespeare Festival, 1971-73, James C. Frush Found., 1972-78. Bd. dirs. San Francisco Sr. Center, 1973-78. Mem. Gerontol. Soc., Informational Film Producers Am., Internat. Hosp. Assn., Am. Geriatrics Soc., Assn. for Anthropology and Gerontology, Stanford Alumni Assn. Author (with Benson Eschenbach): The Retirement Residence: An Analysis of the Architecture and Management of Life Care Housing, 1968, Self-Esteem in Older Persons Following a Heart Attack: An Exploration of Contributing Factors, 1985. Contbr. articles to profl. jours.; producer ednl. films. Office: care T Pimsleur 2155 Union St San Francisco CA 94123 Home: 990 Bay Esplanade Clearwater Beach FL 33515

FRY, HELEN NADHERNY, medical technologist; b. Oak Park, Ill., Apr. 23, 1932; d. Victor John and Helen Johnna (Moser) Nadherny; m. Kenneth B. Fry, June 27, 1953 (div. 1962). BS in Chemistry, U. Redlands, 1953. Lic. med. technologist, Calif. Biochemist Bioferm Corp., Wasco, Calif., 1957-59; biochem. researcher Childrens Hosp., Los Angeles, 1959-82; med. technologist Glendale (Calif.) Meml. Hosp., 1982—. Mem. AAUW (treas. 1978-80), Am. Chem. Soc., Calif. Assn. Med. Lab. Technologists, Am. Soc. Med. Technology. Lodge: PEO (corresponding sec. 1984—, continuing edn. grantee 1980). Office: Glendale Meml Hosp 1420 S Central Ave Glendale CA 91204

FRY, KIRK ELLIOTT, molecular biologist; b. Waterloo, Iowa, Aug. 14, 1946; s. Charles and Doris Fry; m. Pamela Jo Bock; children: Christopher, Emily. PhD, UCLA, 1974. Postdoctoral fellow Stanford (Calif.) U. Med. Sch., 1975-78, research assoc., 1978-83, acting dir. Cancer Biology REsearch Lab., 1983-84; molecular biologist Genelabs, Inc., Redwood City, Calif., 1984—. Contbr. numerous articles to profl. jours.; patentee cloning immunoglobulins. Grantee NIH, 1985—. Mem. AAAS, Am. Soc. Microbiology. Office: Genelabs Inc 505 Penobscot Redwood City CA 94063

FRYE, JUDITH ELEEN MINOR (MRS. VERNON LESTER FRYE), editor; b. Seattle; d. George Edward and Eleen G. (Hartelius) Minor; student U. Cal. at Los Angeles, evenings 1947-48, U. So. Calif., 1948-53; m. Vernon Lester Frye, Apr. 1, 1954. Accountant, office mgr. Colony Wholesale Liquor, Culver City, Calif., 1947-48; credit mgr. Western Distbg. Co., Culver City, 1948-53; partner in restaurants, Palm Springs, Los Angeles, 1948, partner in date ranch, La Quinta, Calif., 1949-53; partner, owner Imperial Printing, Huntington Beach, Calif., 1955—; editor New Era Laundry and Cleaning Lines, Huntington Beach, 1962—; registered lobbyist, Calif., 1975-84. Mem. Laundry and Cleaning Allied Trades Assn., Laundry and Dry Cleaning Suppliers Assn., Calif. Coin-op Assn. (exec. dir. 1975-84), Cooperation award 1971, Dedicated Service award 1976), Nat. Automatic Laundry and Cleaning Council (Leadership award 1972), Women in Laundry/Drycleaning (past pres.; Outstanding Service award 1977), Printing Industries Assn., Master Printers Am., Nat. Assn. Printers and Lithographers, Huntington Beach C. of C. Office: 22031 Bushard St Huntington Beach CA 92646

FRYE, RAYMOND EARL, computer company executive; b. Toledo, Aug. 23, 1944; s. William Raymond and Mary Cathrine (Pullen) F.; m. Margaret Ann Harvey, July 22, 1967; children: Jason Todd, Jonathan David. BS in Bus. Mgmt., Grand Canyon Coll., 1975. Hardware test engr. Computer Div. Gen. Electric, Syracuse, N.Y., 1968-69; software programmer Honeywell, Phoenix, 1970-76, software test mgr., 1977-81, file system mgr., 1981-84, release planner, mgr., 1984—. Coach Moon Valley Soccer team, Phoenix, 1980-85, Shaw Butte Little League, Phoenix, 1981-85, v.p. 1984, safety dir. 1986. Served with USAF, 1962-66. Republican. Methodist. Home: 402 E Deepdale Rd Phoenix AZ 85022 Office: Honeywell PO Box 8000 Phoenix AZ 85005

FRYER, CHARLES WILLIAM, gemologist; b. Springfield, Mo., May 4, 1928; s. Rufus Lester and Elsamae (Johnson) F.; m. Helen Pearl King, Sept 7, 1953 (dec. 1974); 1 child, Kathleen Ann; m. Janet Ingall Macfarlane, Dec. 31, 1976; stepchildren: Michael, Russell, Frasier. Grad., Gemol. Inst., 1963. Cert. gemologist, Calif. Mgr. field measurements W.P. Fuller and Co., San Diego, 1947-62; mgr. C. Holle Glass, San Diego, 1962-64, R&B Art Craft, San Diego, 1964-66; supr. lab. Gemol. Inst. Am., Los Angeles, 1966-75; tour dir. Gemol. Inst. Am., Australia, New Zealand and Fiji Islands, 1975; dir. gem. trade lab. Gemol. Inst. Am., Santa Monica, Calif., 1975-80, chief gemologist, 1980-86; dir. gem identification gem trade lab. Gemol. Inst. Am., N.Y., Santa Monica and Los Angeles, 1986—; researcher Smithsonian Inst., Washington, 1970. Editor: Gems and Gemology mag.; contbr. articles to profl. jours. Active gem council Los Angeles County Mus. Natural History, cons. Bogota, Colombia, 1981. Served as cpl. U.S. Army, 1950-52. Fellow Gemol. Assn. Great Brit.; mem. Am. Gem. Soc. (conclave instr. 1968—), San Diego Gemol. Soc. (life). Republican. Presbyterian. Club: PMYC. Avocations: sailing, golf, model ship bldg. Home: 1153 Stanford Santa Monica CA 90403 Office: Gemol Inst Am 1660 Stewart Santa Monica CA 90404

FRYER, GLADYS CONSTANCE, convalescent center director, medical educator; b. London, Mar. 28, 1923; came to U.S., 1967; d. William John and Florence Annie (Dockett) Mercer; m. Donald Wilfred Fryer, Jan. 20, 1944; children: Peter Vivian, Gerard John, Gillian Celia. MB, BChir, U. Melbourne, Victoria, Australia, 1956. Resident Box Hill Hosp., 1956-57; cardiologist Assunta Found., Petaling Jaya, Malaysia, 1961-64; clin. research physician U.S. Army Clin. Research Unit, Malaysia, 1964-66; intern Hawaii Permanente Kaiser Found., Honolulu, 1968-73; practice medicine specializing in internal medicine Honolulu, 1973—; med. dir. Hale Nani Health Ctr., Honolulu, 1975—, Beverly Manor Convalescent Ctr., Honolulu, 1975—; asst. clin. profl. medicine John Burns Sch. Medicine U. Hawaii, 1968—; med. cons. Salvation Army Alcohol Treatment Facility, Honolulu, 1975-81; physician to skilled nursing patients VA, Honolulu, 1984—; preceptor to geriatric nurse practitioner program U. Colo., Honolulu, 1984-85; lectr. on geriatrics, Alzheimer's disease, gen. medicine and profl. women's problems, 1961—; mem. ad hoc due process bd. Med. Care Evaluation Com., 1982—, Hospice Adv. Com., 1982—; mem. pharmacy com. St. Francis Hosp. Clin. Staff, 1983—, chmn. 1983-84. Contbr. articles to profl. jours. Mem. adv. com. Honolulu Home Care St. Francis Hosp., Honolulu, 1974—; mem. adv. bd. Honolulu Gerontology Program, 1983—, Straub Home Health Program, Honolulu, 1984—; mem. sci. adv. bd. Alzheimers Disease and Related Disorders Assn., Honolulu, 1984—; mem. long term care task force Health and Community Services Council Hawaii, 1978-84. Recipient Edgar Rouse Prize in Indsl. Medicine, U. Melbourne, 1955. Mem. AAAS, ACP, Hawaii Med. Assn. (councillor 1984—), Honolulu County Med. Soc. (chmn., mem. utilisation rev. com. 1973—), World Med. Assn., Am. Geriatrics Soc., Gerontol. Soc. Am., N.Y. Acad. Scis. Episcopalian. Avocations: reading, lit. search, work processing, classical music, needlepoint. Office: Hale Nani Health Ctr 1677 Pensacola St Honolulu HI 96822-2699

FRYER, MICHAEL OWEN, computer engineer; b. Los Angeles, Dec. 12, 1942; s. Robert Owen Fryer and Orpha Marie (Kiethley) Newton; m. Stephanie Ann Le Lesch, Sept. 6, 1963; children: Douglas, Samantha, Benjamin, David, Jennifer, Johanna. BS in Engring. Physics, U. Calif., Berkeley, 1965; PhD in Physics, U. Wash., 1972. Mem. tech. staff Logicon Inc., San Pedro, Calif., 1972-77; systems analyst Fed. Electric Corp., Vandenberg AFB, Calif., 1977-79; engring. specialist EG & G Idaho Inc. subs. EG & G Inc., Idaho Falls, 1979—; instr. Golden Gate U., Vandenberg AFB, 1978; adj. prof. computer sci. U. Idaho, Idaho Falls, 1979—. Contbr. articles to profl. jours.; developer computer software and nuclear tech. Textbook cons. Jefferson County Sch. Bd., Rigby, Idaho, 1985. NDEA fellow, 1965. Mem. IEEE, Assn. Computing Machinery (local pres. 1976), Arabian Horse Assn. (local pres. 1986), Phi Beta Kappa. Avocations: skiing, horse showing, home computing. Home: Rt 1 Box 139 Roberts ID 83444 Office: EG & G Idaho Inc PO Box 1625 Idaho Falls ID 83415

FRYER, ROBERT SHERWOOD, theatrical producer; b. Washington, Nov. 18, 1920; s. Harold and Ruth (Reade) F. B.A., Western Res. U., 1943. Asst. to mng. dir., Theatre Inc., 1946, casting dir., 1946-48, asst. to exec., CBS, 1949-51, casting dir., 1951-52; Broadway co-producer: A Tree Grows in Brooklyn, 1951, By the Beautiful Sea, 1954; producer: Wonderful Town, 1953, The Desk Set, Shangri-La, Auntie Mame, Redhead, There Was a Little Girl, Advise and Consent, A Passage To India, Hot Spot, Roar Like a Dove, Sweet Charity, Chicago, 1975, The Norman Conquests, 1976, California Suite, 1976, On the Twentieth Century, 1977, Sweeney Todd, 1978, Merrily We Roll Along, The West Side Waltz, 1981, Brighton Beach Memoirs, Noises Off, 1983, Benefactors, 1985, Wild Honey, 1986; producer films: The Boston Strangler, 1963, Abdication, 1973, Mame, 1973, Great Expectations, 1974, Voyage of the Damned, 1976, The Boys from Brazil, 1978, Prime of Miss Jean Brodie 1969, Travels with My Aunt, 1973, The Shining 1979 ; artistic dir. Ahmanson Theatre, Ctr. Theatre Group, Los Angeles; author: Professional Theatrical Management New York City, 1947. Bd. dirs. Kennedy Ctr., Ctr. Theatre Group, Music Ctr., Los Angeles; trustee, exec. com. John F. Kennedy Ctr., Washington. Served as capt. AUS, 1941-46; maj. Res. Decorated Legion of Merit.; Rockefeller Found. fellow. Mem. Episcopal Actors Guild (v.p.), League of N.Y. Theatres (bd. govs.). Office: 135 N Grand Ave Los Angeles CA 90012

FRYMER, MURRY, theater critic and columnist; b. Toronto, Ont., Can., Apr. 24, 1934; came to U.S., 1945; s. Dave and Sylvia (Spinrod) F.; m. Barbara Lois Grown, Sept. 4, 1966; children—Paul, Benjamin, Carrie. B.A., U. Mich., 1956; M.A., NYU, 1964. Viewpoints editor, critic Newsday, L.I., N.Y., 1964-72; asst. mng. editor Rochester Democrat & Chronicle, N.Y., 1972-75; Sunday and feature editor Cleve. Plain Dealer, 1975-77; editor Sunday Mag., Boston Herald Am., 1977-79; film and TV critic San Jose Mercury News, Calif., 1979-83, theater critic, 1983—, columnist, 1983—; instr. San Jose State U., Cleve. State U., judge Emmy awards Nat. Acad. TV Arts and Scis., 1968. Author, dir. musical revue Four by Night, N.Y.C., 1963; author (play) Danse Marriage, 1955 (Hopwood prize 1955). Served with U.S. Army, 1956-58. Mem. Bay Area Theater Critics Assn. Jewish. Home: 1060 Moongate Pl San Jose CA 95120 Office: San Jose Mercury News 750 Ridder Park Dr San Jose CA 95190

FUCHS, ROLAND JOHN, geography educator; b. Yonkers, N.Y., Jan. 15, 1933; s. Alois L. and Elizabeth (Weigand) F.; m. Gaynell Ruth McAuliffe, June 15, 1957; children: Peter K., Christopher K., Andrew K. B.A., Columbia U., 1954, postgrad., 1956-57; postgrad., Moscow State U., 1960-61; M.A., Clark U., 1957, Ph.D., 1959. Asst. prof. to prof. U. Hawaii, Honolulu, 1958—; chmn. dept. geography U. Hawaii, 1964-86, asst. dean to assoc. dean Coll. Arts and Scis., 1965-67, dir. Asian Studies Lang. and Area Center, 1965-67, adj. research assoc. East West Ctr., 1980—, spl. asst. to pres., 1986; vis. prof. Clark U., 1963-64, Nat. Taiwan U., 1974; mem. bd. internat. orgns. and programs Nat. Acad. Scis., 1976—, chmn., 1980—, mem. bd. sci. and tech. in devel., 1980-85; mem. U.S. Nat. Commn. for Pacific Basin Econ. Coop., 1985—; sr. advisor United Nations U., 1986, vice rector, 1987. Asst. editor Econ. Geography, 1963-64; mem. editorial adv. com. Soviet Geography; Review and Translation, 1966—; author, editor: Theoretical Problems of Geography, Geographical Perspectives on the Soviet Union, Population Distribution Policies in Development Planning, Urbanization: The Urban Policies in the Asian-Pacific Region. Ford Found. fellow, 1956-57; Fulbright Research scholar, 1966-67. Mem. Internat. Geog. Union (U.S. nat. commn. 1969-80, chmn. 1973-80, v.p. 1980-84, 1st v.p. 1984—), AAAS, Assn. Am. Geographers, (honors award 1982), Am. Assn. Advancement Slavic Studies (dir. 1976-81), Pacific Sci. Assn. (council 1978—, mem. exec. com. 1986—). Home: 5136 Maunalani Circle Honolulu HI 96816

FUCHSER, FAY EUGENE, commercial electrical engineer, consultant; b. Gordon, Nebr., July 31, 1926; s. Emil I. and Jeanette (Hathorn) F.; m. Helen Irene Adams, Nov. 11, 1961; children: Cheryl, Keith, Catherine. BEE, U. Nebr., 1951. Chief comml. engr. Behrent Engring. Co., Denver, 1960—. Served as sgt. USAF, 1945-47. Mem. NSPE, IEEE, Illuminating Engring. Soc. Republican. Methodist. Avocations: travel, sports. Office: Behrent Engring Co 2680 18th St Denver CO 80211

FUERSTENAU, DOUGLAS WINSTON, mineral engineering educator; b. Hazel, S.D., Dec. 6, 1928; s. Erwin Arnold and Hazel Pauline (Karterud) F.; m. Margaret Ann Pellett, Aug. 29, 1953; children: Lucy, Sarah, Stephen. B.S., S.D. Sch. Mines and Tech., 1949; M.S., Mont. Sch. Mines, 1950; Sc.D., MIT, 1953; Mineral Engr., Mont. Coll. Mineral Sci. and Tech., 1968. Asst. prof. mineral engring. MIT, 1953-56; sect. leader, metals research lab. Union Carbide Metals Co., Niagara Falls, N.Y., 1956-58; mgr. mineral engring. lab Kaiser Aluminum & Chem. Corp., Permanente, Calif., 1958-59; asso. prof. metallurgy U. Calif.-Berkeley, 1959-62, prof. metallurgy, 1962-86, Plato Malozemoff prof. of mineral engring., 1987—, Miller research prof., 1969-70, chmn. dept. materials sci. and mineral engring., 1970-78; dir. Homestake Mining Co.; chmn. Engring. Found. Research Conf. on Comminution, 1963; mem. adv. bd. Sch. Earth Scis., Stanford, 1970-73; mem. Nat. Mineral Bd., 1975-78; Am. rep. Internat. Mineral Processing Congress Com., 1978—. Editor: Froth Flotation-50th Anniversary Vol, 1962; co-editor-in-chief: Internat. Jour. of Mineral Processing, 1972—; Mem. editorial adv. bd.: Jour. of Colloid and Interface Sci, 1968-72, Colloids and Surfaces, 1980—; Contbr. articles to profl. jours. Recipient Disting. Teaching award U. Calif., 1974; Alexander von Humboldt Sr. Am. Scientist award Fed. Republic Germany, 1984. Fellow Instn. Mining and Metallurgy, London. Mem. Nat. Acad. Engring., Am. Inst. Mining and Metall. Engrs. (chmn. mineral processing div. 1967, Robert Lansing Hardy Gold medal 1957, Rossiter W. Raymond award 1961, Robert H. Richards award 1975, Antoine M. Gaudin award 1978, Mineral Industry Edn. award 1983), Soc. Mining Engrs. (dir. 1968-71, Distinguished mem.), Am. Chem. Soc., Am. Inst. Chem. Engrs., Sigma Xi, Theta Tau. Congregationalist. Home: 1440 LeRoy Ave Berkeley CA 94708

FUHLENDORF, CHARLENE LEE, Persian cat breeder; b. Turlock, Calif., July 27, 1949; d. Amilcar and Ima Jean (Hoard) Martins; m. Michael Edward Fuhlendorf, Nov. 9, 1974; children—Erik Michael and Allan John (twins). Grad. Valley Comml. Coll., 1967-69, 70; student Modesto Jr. Coll., 1981. Breeder Persian cats, Modesto, Calif.; pres. Adriel Persians, Modesto, 1982—. Author: Evangelica Light, 1984, Raising Pampered Pets, 1983. Author: Evangelical Light, 1984. Mem. Republican Party Victory Fund, Washington, 1982, 83; pres. Evang. Light. Soc., 1983—. Recipient Bronze award, Grace M. Davis Honor Band, 1967, 66. Mem. County Faire Cat Fanciers. Republican. Club: Bible Study Fellowship. Home: 3117 Nightingale Dr Modesto CA 95356 Office: Adriel Persians 3117 Nightingale Dr Modesto CA 95356

FUHRMAN, FREDERICK MICHAEL, electrical engineer; b. Santa Monica, Calif., Jan. 31, 1945; s. Harold Leroy and Harriette Nell (Harrison) F.; m. Susan Laurene Webb, Jan. 1, 1962 (div. June 1966); 1 child, Hallie Marie; m. Gail Ann Wilbur, Dec. 14, 1973; 1 child, Michael Thomas. AA, Santa Monica Coll., 1975; BSEE, Calif. State U., Long Beach, 1978. Cable splicer Dept. Water and Power, Los Angeles, 1966-78; elec. engr. Met. Water Dist., Los Angeles, 1978—; cons. in field, Los Angeles, 1978—. Served with USN, 1962-66, Vietnam. Mem. IEEE, Tau Beta Pi, Eta Kappa Nu. Republican. Lutheran. Avocations: flying, scuba diving. Home: 5625 Busch Dr Malibu CA 90265 Office: Met Water Dist 1111 Sunset Blvd Los Angeles CA 90012

FUHRMAN, ROBERT ALEXANDER, aerospace company executive; b. Detroit, Feb. 23, 1925; s. Alexander A. and Elva (Brown) F. B.S., U. Mich., 1945; M.S., U. Md., 1952; postgrad., U. Calif., San Diego, 1958; Exec. Mgmt. Program, Stanford Bus. Sch., 1964. Project engr. Naval Air Test Center, Patuxent River, Md., 1946-53; chief tech. engring. Ryan Aero. Co., San Diego, 1953-58; mgr. Polaris 1958-64, chief engr. MSD, 1964-66; v.p., asst. gen. mgr. missile systems div. Lockheed Missiles & Space Co., Sunnyvale, Calif., 1966-68; v.p., gen. mgr. Lockheed Missiles & Space Co., 1969, v.p., 1973-76, pres., 1976-83, chmn., 1979—; v.p. Lockheed Corp., Burbank, Calif., 1969-76; sr. v.p. Lockheed Corp., 1976-83, group pres. Missiles, Space & Electronics System, 1983-85, pres., chief operating officer, 1986—; also dir., pres. Lockheed Ga. Co., Marietta, 1970-71; pres. Lockheed Calif. Co., Burbank, 1971-73; chmn. bd. Ventura Mfg. Co., 1970-71; bd. dirs. Bank of the West; mem. FBM Steering Task Group, 1966-70. Mem. adv. bd. Sch. Bus., U. Santa Clara; bd. govs. Federated Employees of Bay Area; trustee United Way of Santa Clara County, 1975-85; bd. dirs. Atlanta Jr. Achievement; mem. adv. council Sch. Engring., Stanford U.; mem. adv. bd. Coll. Engring., U. Mich., 1981—; mem. adv. council Coll. Engring. Found. U. Tex.-Austin, 1983-86; mem. Def. Sci. Bd., chmn. task force on indsl. responsiveness, 1980; mem. exec. com. San Jose Mgmt. Task Force; mem. sci. adv. com. Ala. Space and Rocket Center; bd. dirs. Bay Area Council. Served to ensign USNR, 1944-46. Recipient Silver Knight award Nat. Mgmt. Assn., 1969, John J. Montgomery award, 1964; award Soc. Mfg. Engrs., 1973; Disting. Citizen award Boy Scouts Am., 1983; Donald C. Burnham award Soc. Mfg. Engrs., 1983; Recipient Eminent Engr. award Tau Beta Pi, 1983. Fellow AIAA (hon., dir.-at-large, Von Karman 1978), Soc. Mfg. Engrs.; mem. Nat. Acad. Engring., Am. Astron. Soc. (sr.), Nat. Aero. Assn., Ga. C. of C. (dir.), Am. Def. Preparedness Assn. (dir., exec. com.), Navy League U.S. (life), Air Force Assn., Assn. U.S. Army, Soc. Am. Value Engrs. (hon.), Santa Clara County Mfrs. Group (past chmn.), Beta Gamma Sigma. Clubs: Los Altos Country (Calif.),Burning Tree (Bethesda, Md.), N. Ranch Country (Westlake Village). Office: Lockheed Corp 4500 Park Granada Blvd Calabasas CA 91399

FUHS, ALLEN EUGENE, engineer, physicist, educator; b. Laramie, Wyo., Aug. 11, 1927; s. Michael Allen and Grace Emeline (Terrill) F.; m. Emily Ann Large, Dec. 22, 1951; 1 child, Susan Elizabeth. B.S.M.E., U. N.Mex., 1951; M.S.M.E., Calif. Inst. Tech., 1955, Ph.D., 1958. Owner service sta. Gallup, N.Mex., 1944-46; asst. prof. Northwestern U., Evanston, Ill., 1958-59; mem. tech. staff TRW Systems, El Sequndo, Calif., 1959-60; staff scientist Aerospace Corp., El Segundo, Calif., 1960-66; prof., chmn. aeros. Naval Postgrad. Sch., Monterey, Calif., 1966-68; disting prof. Naval Postgrad. Sch., 1970—, chmn. dept. mech. engring., 1975-78, chmn. space systems, 1982—; chief scientist Air Force Aeropropulsion Lab., Dayton, Ohio, 1968-70; cons. TRW Systems, Aerospace Corp., others. Author: Instrumentation for High Speed Plasma Flow, 1965; editor 4 books; editor-in-chief: Jour. of Aircraft, 1974-79; contbr. articles to profl. jours.; patentee in field. Served with USN, 1951-54, Korea. recipient SAE Ralph R. Teetor award; named Disting. Alumnus, U. N.Mex. Coll. Engring., 1985; Guggenheim fellow, 1957-58. Fellow AIAA (v.p. publs. 1979-81, dir. 1982-85, pres. 1986-87), ASME; mem. Soc. Automotive Engrs., Am. Phys. Soc., Am. Soc. Naval Engrs., Soc. Naval Architects and Marine Engrs., Am. Optical Soc., Sigma Xi. Office: Naval Postgrad Sch Monterey CA 93943

FUHS, G(EORG) WOLFGANG, state agency administrator; b. Cologne, Fed. Republic Germany, May 19, 1932; came to U.S., 1964; s. Friedrich Karl and Lisette I. (Stayen) F.; children: Lisette I., H. Georg, Dagmar A. Diploma in biology, D in Nat. Scis., U. Bonn, Germany, 1956; postdoctoral, Tech. U. Delft, The Netherlands, 1956-57. Sci. employee dept. botany U. Frankfurt, Fed. Republic Germany, 1957-58; research assoc. dept. hygiene U. Bonn Sch. Medicine, 1958-63; fellow dept. genetics U. Cologne, 1963-64; sr., prin. research scientist div. labs. and research N.Y. State Dept. Health, Albany, 1964-72, dir. environ. health labs., 1973-85; chief div. labs. Calif. Dept. Health Services, Berkeley, 1985—; vis. prof. U. Wis., Milw., 1973; research assoc. U. Minn. Sch. Pub. Health, Mpls., 1970-74; adj. prof. dept. biology SUNY, Albany, 1984-86; mem. exptl. com. on human health effects of Great Lakes water Quality U.S./Can. Internat. Joint Commn., 1978—, co-chmn. 1983—. Contbr. articles to profl. jours. (Inst. Sci. Info. award 1969); mem. editorial bd. Jour Phycology, 1972-74, Limnology and Oceanography, 1973-76, Microbial Ecology, 1974—. Mem. AAAS, Am. Soc. Microbiol. (past chmn. Eastern N.Y. br.), Internat. Assn. Theoretical Applied Limnology, Am. Pub. Health Assn., Water Pollution Control Fedn., Am. Water Works Assn. Office: Calif Dept Health Services Div Labs 2151 Berkeley Way Berkeley CA 94704

FUITEN, JOSEPH BENJAMIN, minister; b. Medford, Oreg., Nov. 21, 1949; s. John Harold and Florence (Moyer) F.; m. Linda Marie Vanden Bos, Dec. 31, 1971; children: Rosalind, Sandra, Benjamin, Zachary. BA, Willamette U., 1972. Ordained to ministry Assemblies of God Ch., 1971. Assoc. pastor Aloha (Oreg.) Assembly, 1972-73, Life Ctr., Tacoma, 1973-79; dir. Christian edn. N.W. Dist. Assemblies of God, Kirkland, Wash., 1979-81; pastor Cedar Park Ch., Kirkland, 1981—; v.p. Mainstream Ministries, Tacoma, 1976—; v.p. bd. dirs. Calcutta Mission of Mercy, Tacoma; sec. Family Broadcasting Co., Tacoma, 1979-85. Republican. Avocation: stamp collecting.

FUJII, JACK KOJI, university administrator; b. Phoenix, June 9, 1940; s. Richard Masuo and Chiye (Wada) F.; m. Gail M. Fujii; children: Scott, Todd, Jeff. BS in Entomology, U. Calif., Berkeley, 1963; MS in Entomology, U. Hawaii, Manoa, 1968; PhD in Entomology, U. Hawaii, 1975. Entomologist Hawaii Div. Forestry, Honolulu, 1974-76; assoc. prof. entomology U. Hawaii Coll. Agriculture, Hilo, 1976-83, dean, 1983—. Served with U.S. Army, 1963-65. Mem. Entomol. Soc. Am., Hawaiian Entomol. Soc., Soc. Invertebrate Pathology, Sigma Xi. Office: U Hawaii Coll Agriculture 523 W Lanikaula St Hilo HI 96720

FUJII, KIYO, pharmacist; b. Portland, Oreg., July 1, 1921; s. Kanji and Mitoyo (Kurata) F.; student U. Wash., 1939-42; B.S., St. Louis Coll. Pharmacy, 1943. Pharmacist, C.F. Knight Drug, St. Louis, 1943-48, Sargent Drug, Chgo., 1950-52, Mt. Sinai Hosp., Chgo., 1953-54, Campus Pharmacy, Los Angeles, 1973—; chief pharmacist Evang. Hosp., Chgo., 1948-49, Am. Hosp. Clinic, Los Angeles, 1958-60. Mem. Am., Calif. pharm. assns., Am. Soc. Hosp. Pharmacists, St. Louis Coll. Pharmacy Alumni Assn., Rho Chi, Sigma Epsilon Sigma. Democrat. Presbyterian. Home: 7913 Kentwood Ave Los Angeles CA 90045

FUJIKAWA, DENSON GEN, neurologist, researcher; b. Denson, Ark., Oct. 23, 1942; s. Yoshihiko Fred and Alice May (Aoki) F.; m. Christine Margaret Nelson, Dec. 2, 1964 (div. 1967); m. Lilla Rose Smithline, Dec. 12, 1976. AB magna cum laude, Harvard U., 1964; MD, U. So. Calif., 1969. Diplomate Am. Bd. of Psychiatry and Neurology. Intern surgery Columbia Presbyn. Med. Ctr., N.Y.C., 1969-70; resident in surgery Columbia Presbyn. Med. Ctr., N.Y.C., 1970-71; resident in neurosurgery UCLA Med. Ctr., 1971-73; resident in neurology Harbor UCLA Med. Ctr., Torrance, 1978-81; asst. adj. prof. neurology UCLA Sch. Medicine, 1981—; co-dir. EEG and evoked potentials lab. VA Med. Ctr., Sepulveda, Calif., 1983—, head of seizure clinic, 1983—. Contbr. articles to profl. jours. Grantee VA,

1984-85, 87—, Epilepsy Found. Am., 1985-87, biomed. research support grantee NIH, 1986-87. Mem. Am. Acad. Neurology, Soc. for Neurosci., Am. EEG Soc., Am. Epilepsy Soc., Los Angeles Soc. Neurology and Psychiatry (councillor 1985-88). Club: Harvard of So. Calif. (Los Angeles). Office: Neurology Service (127) VA Med Ctr 16111 Plummer St Sepulveda CA 91343

FUJIMOTO, REBECCA YAE, microbiologist; b. Wailuku, Hawaii, Jan. 9, 1958; d. Masakazu Robert and Takako (Oka) F. Student, U. Hawaii, Manoa, 1976-77; BS, Colo. State U., 1980. Lab. asst. Colo. State U., Ft. Collins, 1979-80; microbiologist Foster Farms, Livingston, Calif., 1980-81, Hawaii Dept. Health, Lihue, 1981—. Mem. Hawaii Dept. Health, Lihue, 1981-86, Honolulu, 1986—. Mem. AAAS, Am. Soc. Microbiology (Hawaii chpt.), Nat. Registry of Microbiologists, Hawaii Pub. Health Assn. Club: Brown Bag (Lihue) (pres. 1985-86). Avocations: tennis, fishing, golf, jogging. Home: 1503 Emerson St Apt 5 Honolulu HI 96813 Office: Hawaii Dept Health Lab 1250 Punchbowl St Honolulu HI 96813

FUJIMURA, ROBERT KANJI, biochemist; b. Seattle, July 28, 1933; s. Tatsuo and Tamiko Ruth Fujimura; m.Shigeko Ichikawa, Dec. 1, 1962; children: Dan, Tomi, Kei. BS, U. Wash., 1956; MS, U. Wis., 1959, PhD, 1961. Sr. staff mem. biology div. Oak Ridge (Tenn.) Nat. Lab., 1963—; 1st sec. Am. Embassy, Tokyo, 1985-86; biotechnologist Fgn. Comml. Service div. Am. Embassy, Tokyo, 1985-86; lectr. U. Tenn. Grad. Sch., Oak Ridge, 1970—. Contbr. articles to profl. jours. Fellow Japan Soc. Promotion Sci., 1981. Mem. AAAS, Am. Soc. Biol. Chemists. Methodist.

FUJIOKA, MASANOBU RICHARD, consulting engineer; b. Hakata, Fukuoka, Japan, June 5, 1950; came to U.S., 1955; s. George Isami and Momoe (Fukuda); m. Amy Ai Isobe, July 28, 1973 (div. Nov. 1986); 1 child, Michael Minoru. BS, U. Hawaii, 1973, MS, 1978. Registered profl. engr., Hawaii. Research U. Hawaii, Honolulu, 1972-74; asst. engr. Dames and Moore, Honolulu, 1973-76, staff engr., 1976-79, project engr., 1979-83, sr. engr., 1983-85, prin.-in-charge, 1986—. Contbr. articles to profl. jours. Mem. ASCE (treas. Hawaii sect. 1985-86, sec. 1986—), Engring. Assn. Hawaii (bd. dirs. 1982-86, v.p. 1986—), Am. Geophys. Union, Soc. Am. Mil. Engrs., Nat. Water Well Assn., Am. Inst. Hydrology (cert. profl., pres. Hawaii sect. 1987—, cert. profl. hydrologist), Internat. Soc. Soil Mechanics and Found. Engring., Internat. Assn. Engring. Geology, S.E. Asian Geotech. Soc., Res. Officers Assn., Hawaii Army Mus. Soc. Avocations: golfing, travelling. Home: 7242 Naohe St Honolulu HI 96825 Office: Dames and Moore 1144 10th Ave Suite 200 Honolulu HI 96816

FUJIOKA, ROGER SADAO, research microbiology educator; b. Pearl City, Hawaii, May 11, 1938; s. Nobuichi and Hisayo (Iboshi) F.; m. Ruby Nanaye Yamashita, July 2, 1966; 1 child, Ryan Makoto. BS in Med. Tech., U. Hawaii, 1960, MS in Microbiology, 1966; PhD in Virology, U. Mich., 1970. Assoc. research U. Hawaii, Honolulu, 1963-66, research microbiologist, 1972—; predoctoral fellow U. Mich., Ann Arbor, 1966-70; postdoctoral fellow Baylor Coll. Medicine, Houston, 1970-71; sec.-treas. Hawaii Water Pollution Control, Honolulu, 1986—; mem. com. Standard Methods, Washington, 1986—. Contbr. articles to profl. jours. Served to capt. USAR, 1960-66. Grantee Sea Grant Coll. Program, 1976-84, Office Water United States Geol. Survey, 1978—, Office Naval Research, 1985—, Dept. Health, 1986—, all in Honolulu. Mem. AAAS, Am. Soc. Microbiology, Water Pollution Control Fedn., Am. Water Works Assn., Internat. Assn. Advancement Aquatic Mammals. Avocation: tennis. Office: U Hawaii Water Resources Research Ctr 2540 Dole St Honolulu HI 96822

FUJIWARA, ELIZABETH JUBIN, lawyer, social worker; b. New Orleans, Dec. 20, 1945; d. Otha Ernest and Yvette Marie (Jubin) Barron; m. Ronald Toshio Fujiwara, Jan. 7, 1978; children: Jean Paul Jubin Toshiro, Maria Sachiko, Cathleen Sumiko Yonahara. Student, U. Tex., Irving, 1963-64; BA in Sociology, Loyola U., New Orleans, 1967; MSW, U. Hawaii, 1971, JD, 1983. Exec. dir. ACLU of Hawaii, Honolulu, 1975-77; specialist in equal edn. opportunity Dept. Edn., Honolulu, 1978; asst. dir. Inst. Productive Behavior, Honolulu, 1978-80; faculty research asst. William S. Richardson Sch. Law, U. Hawaii, Honolulu, 1981; law clk. to presiding justice Intermediate Ct. Appeals Hawaii, Honolulu, 1984-86; sole practice Honolulu, 1986—. Mng. editor Handbook Women's Legal Rights in Hawaii, 1987. Active Hawaii Women's Polit. Action League, 1983—, Ad Hoc Com. Abortion Rights, 1977-79; organizer Coalition Against Capital Punishment, 1976-78; Peace Corps trainee in Puerto Rico and Guatemala, 1968. Named one of Outstanding Young Women of Yr. State Commn. on Status of Women, 1976. Mem. ABA, Hawaii Bar Assn., Assn. Trial Lawyers Am., Hawaii Women Lawyers (co-chair pay equity com. 1985-87, spouse abuseand women prisoners legal penal project 1985—, mem. legis. com. 1985—, bd. dirs.), Clark Hatch Health Club, Women's Support Group, Kappa Beta Gamma. Democrat. Buddhist. Avocations: swimming, stained glassmaking, sewing, painting, music. Office: Cen Pacific Plaza 220 S King St Suite 1501 Honolulu HI 96813

FUJIYAMA, RODNEY MICHIO, lawyer; b. Honolulu, Aug. 1, 1945; s. Wallace Sachio Fujiyama and Jean (Osumi) Shin; m. Vicki Ann Yamaguchi, Dec. 28, 1968; children—Christopher, Laurie, Sandra, Jonathan, Shannon. Student Oberlin Coll., 1963-64; B.A. with high honors, U. Hawaii, 1967; J.D., U. Calif.-San Francisco, 1970. Bar: Hawaii 1970, U.S. Dist. Ct. Hawaii 1970, U.S. Ct. Appeals (9th cir.) 1971. Assoc., Chuck & Fujiyama, Honolulu, 1970-74; assoc. Law Offices of Wallace S. Fujiyama, Honolulu, 1974; ptnr. Fujiyama, Duffy, Fujiyama, Honolulu, 1975-78, Fujiyama, Duffy, Fujiyama & Koshiba, Honolulu, 1979, Fujiyama, Duffy & Fujiyama, Honolulu, 1979—; per diem judge Dist. Ct. of 1st Cir., State of Hawaii, Honolulu, 1979-85. Mem. ABA, Hawaii State Bar Assn., Assn. Trial Lawyers Am., Phi Beta Kappa. Office: Fujiyama Duffy & Fujiyama 1001 Bishop St 2650 Pacific Tower Honolulu HI 96813

FUKUDA, HAROLYN GLENEICE, product manager; b. Honolulu, Nov. 2, 1945; d. Harold S. and Gladys Y. (Morimoto) Toma; B.Edn., U. Hawaii, 1967; m. Keith Hideo Fukuda, Oct. 19, 1974. With Meadow Gold Dairies, Honolulu, 1967—, sales/advt. coordinator, 1975-77, mktg. coordinator, 1977-84, product mgr., 1984—. Recipient Jaycee of Yr. award Honolulu Chinese Jaycees, 1980; named Friend of 4-H, State of Hawaii, 1980. Mem. Am. Mktg. Assn., Hawaii Food Mfrs. (sec. 1980-82, pres. 1982-84), Hawaii Fashion and Products Assn. (sec. 1980—), Pres.'s Honor Club for Beatrice Foods Cos., Inc. Office: 925 Cedar St Honolulu HI 96814

FUKUDA, MINORU, cancer research scientist; b. Hiroshima, Japan, July 6, 1945; came to U.S., 1975, naturalized, 1980; s. Iwao and Sueko (Fujiwara) F.; m. Michiko Nishida, Apr. 8, 1970; children—Ko, Shun. B.S. in Biochemistry, U. Tokyo, 1968, M.S., 1970, Ph.D., 1973. Research assoc. U. Tokyo, 1973-75; postdoctoral assoc. Yale U., 1975-77; assoc. Hutchinson Cancer Research Ctr., Seattle, 1977-81; asst. prof. U. Wash., Seattle, 1980-81; staff scientist La Jolla (Calif.) Cancer Research Found., 1982—, dir. carbohydrate chemistry lab., 1984—. Author: Biology of Glycoproteins, 1984; also chpts. and articles in profl. publs. Nat. Cancer Inst. grantee, 1981—; NSF grantee, 1983. Mem. Am. Soc. Cell Biology, N.Y. Acad. Scis., Am. Soc. Biol. Chemists. Home: 2818 Passy Ave San Diego CA 92122 Office: La Jolla Cancer Research Found 10901 N Torrey Pines Rd La Jolla CA 92037

FUKUMOTO, FLORENCE MAE, lawyer; b. Sacramento, Nov. 16, 1957; d. Clarence G.C. Leong and Carmen Luke; m. Steve H. Fukumoto, June 14, 1986. AA, Sacramento City Coll., 1977; BS, U. Calif., Berkeley, 1979; JD, U. Pacific, 1982. Bar: Calif. 1982. Atty. Chin & Leong, Sacramento, 1983-84; legal asst. San Francisco Tax Collector, 1984—. Mary Phlegher scholar U. Calif., Berkeley, 1979; recipient William James Found. award U. Pacific, 1981. Mem. ABA, Asian Am. Bar Assn. Democrat. Methodist.

FUKUNAGA, GEORGE JOJI, corporate executive; b. Waialua, Oahu, Hawaii, Apr. 13, 1924; s. Peter H. and Ruth (Hamamura) F.; B.A., U. Hawaii, 1948; certificate Advanced Mgmt. Program Harvard U. Hawaii, 1955; m. Alice M. Tagawa, Aug. 5, 1950; 1 son, Mark H. Adminstrv. asst., dir. Service Motor Co., Ltd. (named changed to Servco Pacific Inc. 1969), Honolulu, 1948-50, v.p., 1952-60, pres., 1960—; chmn., dir. 10 subsidiaries of Service Fin., Ltd. (name now Servco Financial Corp.), 1960—, Servco Services Corp., Am. Ins. Agy. Inc., Intercontinental Servco Service Ins. Agy. Inc., Servco Securities Corp., Servco Investment Corp., Hawaiiana Advt. Agy., Pacific Internat. Co. Inc. (Guam), Pacific Fin. Corp. (Guam), Pacific Motors Corp. (Guam), Pacific Internat. Marianas Inc., Saipan, Pacific Marshalls Inc., Majuro; dir. Am. Trust of Hawaii Inc., Island Ins. Ltd., Hawaiian Pacific Resorts, Inc. Bd. govs. Iolani Sch.; trustee Fukunaga Scholarship Found.; trustee Hawaii Pacific Coll., Contemporary Arts Found., U.S. Army Mus.; bd. govs. U. Hawaii Found., East-West Ctr. Found. Served to 2d lt. AUS, 1945-47, to 1st lt., 1950-52. Mem. Hawaii (v.p. 1970, 83-84, dir. 1970-75, 82—), Honolulu Japanese (pres. 1969, dir. 1963—) chambers commerce, Hawaii Employers Council (dir.), Better Bus. Bur. (v.p. 1963-66, dir. 1977—), Hawaii Econ. Study Club (pres. 1962), Hawaii-Japan Econ. Council, U.S.-Japan Soc. (dir. 1983—). Methodist. Clubs: Pacific, Plaza (dir.), 200 Rotary, Deputies, Oahu Country. Office: 900 Fort St Mall Honolulu HI 96813 *

FUKUSHIMA, BARBARA NAOMI, accountant; b. Honolulu, Apr. 5, 1948; d. Harry Kazuo and Misayo (Kawasaki) Murakoshi; B.A. with high honors, U. Hawaii, 1970; postgrad. Oreg. State U., 1971, 73, U. Oreg., 1972; m. Dennis Hiroshi Fukushima, Mar. 23, 1974; 1 son, Dennis Hiroshi Jr. Intern, Coopers & Lybrand, Honolulu, 1974; auditor Haskins & Sells, Kahului, Hawaii, 1974-77; pres. Book Doors, Inc., Pukalani, 1977—; pres. Barbara N. Fukushima C.P.A., Inc., Wailuku. 1979—; sec. treas. Target Pest Control, Inc., Wailuku, 1979—; internal auditor, acct. Maui Land & Pineapple Co., Inc., Kahului, 1977-80; auditor Hyatt Regency Maui, Kaanapali, 1980-81; ptnr. D & B Internat., Pukalani, 1980—; instr. Maui Community Coll., Kahului, 1982-85; fin. cons. Merrill Lynch, Pierce, Fenner & Smith, Inc., 1986—. Recipient Phi Beta Kappa Book award, 1969. Mem. Am. Inst. C.P.A.s, Hawaii Soc. C.P.A.s, Nat. Assn. Accts., Hawaii Assn. Public Accts., Bus. and Profl. Women's Club. Tenrikyo. Home: 200 Aliiolani St Pukalani HI 96768 Office: 270 Hookahi St Suite 210 Wailuku HI 96793

FUKUTA, NORIHIKO, professor in meteorology, researcher; b. Tokoname, Aichi-ken, Japan, May 11, 1931; came to U.S., 1966; s. Teizo and Haru (Takeuchi) F.; m. Yoko Kuriyama, Mar. 3, 1966. BS, Nogoya (Japan) U., 1954, MS, 1956, PhD, 1959. Lab. dirs. Meteorology Research, Inc., Pasadena, Calif., 1966-68; lab. Head U. Denver, 1968-75, prof., 1968-75, adj. prof., 1976-77, div. head, 1968-77; prof. U. Utah, Salt Lake City, 1977-86; dir. atmospheric physics lab. U. Utah Research Inst., 1986—. Recipient Huffsmith award U. Denver, 1971, Sesquicentennial medal Leningrad U., 1980. Mem. Am. Meteorol. Soc. (assoc. editor J. Atmos. 1976-83, J. Appl. 1972-79, Editor's award 1974), Japanese Meteorol. Soc., Am. Geophys. Union, Am. Phys. Soc., Sigma Xi. Office: Dept Meteorology U Utah 819 WBB Salt Lake City UT 84112

FULCO, ARMAND JOHN, biochemist; b. Los Angeles, Apr. 3, 1932; s. Herman J. and Clelia Marie (DeFeo) F.; m. Virginia Loy Hungerford, June 18, 1955 (div. July 1985); children: William James, Lisa Marie, Linda Susan, Suzanne Yvonne. B.S. in Chemistry, UCLA, 1957, Ph.D. in Physiol. Chemistry, 1960; postdoctoral work, Lipid Labs., U. Calif. Med. Sch., Los Angeles, 1960-61. NIH postdoctoral fellow Lipid Labs. UCLA, 1960-61; research fellow dept. chemistry Harvard U., Cambridge, Mass., 1961-63; biochemist, prin. investigator Lab. Nuclear Medicine and Radiation Biology, UCLA, 1963-80; asst. prof. dept. biol. chemistry UCLA (Med. Sch.), 1965-70, assoc. prof., 1970-76, prof., 1976—, prin. investigator, lab. biomed. and environ. scis., 1981—; cons. biochemist VA, Los Angeles, 1968—. Author: (with J.F. Mead) The Unsaturated and Polyunsaturated Fatty Acids in Health and Disease, 1976; contbr. over 75 articles to sci. jours. Served with U.S. Army, 1952-54. Mem. Am. Chem. Soc., Am. Soc. Biol. Chemists, Am. Oil Chemists Soc., AAAS, Am. Soc. Microbiology, Harvard Chemists Assn., Sigma Xi. Office: U Calif Lab Biomed and Environ Scis 900 Veteran Ave Los Angeles CA 90024

FULGHUM, BRICE ELWIN, cons.; b. Fredonia, Kans., Aug. 27, 1919; s. Byron Harmon and Myrtle (Broderick) F.; student U. Kansas City, San Francisco State Coll.; married; 1 dau., Linda Lee Fulghum McDonald. Asst. to sales mgr. Gas Service Co., Kansas City, Mo., 1939-41, sales mgr. Ace Auto Rental & Sales Co., Kansas City, 1945-48; asst. mgr. Owl Drug Co., San Francisco, 1948-50; mgr. Pacific Mut. Life Ins. Co., 1950-61; v.p. Gordon H. Edwards Co., 1961-64; v.p. Federated Life Ins. Co. Calif., 1964-66; gen. mgr. Los Angeles Fulghum agy. Pacific Mut. Life Ins. Co., 1966-71; v.p. Hendrie Bonding & Ins. Corp., Huntington Beach, Calif., 1976-77; chmn. bd. PGA Ins. Services, Inc., Torrance, Calif., 1976—; cons. Am. Health Profiles, Inc., Nashville; sr. fin. cons. Shearson Hayden Stone Inc., Newport Beach, Calif., 1977-79; cons. Penn Gen. Agys., Los Angeles and Employee Benefit Cons.'s, Santa Ana, Calif., 1979-80; cons. Assn. Calif. State U. Profs., Profl. Sponsoring Fund, 1979—. Chmn. Cancer drive; active Community Chest, Am. Heart Assn., founder Opera Pacific. Served with Q.M.C., U.S. Army, 1941-43. C.L.U. Mem. Am. Soc. C.L.U.s (Golden Key Soc.), Leading Life Ins. Producers No. Calif. (life mem., pres. 1955), San Francisco Peninsula (charter), Los Angeles-San Fernando Valley (life) estate planning councils, Orange County Life Underwriters Assn. Republican. Clubs: Commonwealth, Town Hall of So. Calif. (charter mem. charitable giving council, Orange County), El Niguel Country. Mem. editorial advisory bd. Western Underwriter. Contbr. articles to ins. publs. Home: 31201 Calle Villa Clara San Juan Capistrano CA 92675 Office: PO Box 1198 San Juan Capistrano CA 92673-1198 *

FULKERSON, LARRY RAY, mechanical engineering executive; b. China Lake, Calif., Nov. 28, 1945; s. William Ray and Edith Marie (Bartlett) F.; m. Vicki Jo Wold, Feb. 18, 1966; children: Donald, Douglas, David. BSME, Calif. State Poly. U., San Luis Obispo, 1967. Registered profl. engr., Utah. Engr. Allis-Chalmers Inc., Springfield, Ill., 1967-72; design engr. Dart Truck Co., Kansas City, Mo., 1972-73; project engr. EIMCO Mining Machinery Co., Salt Lake City, 1973-78; mgr. Norton Christensen, Inc., Salt Lake City, 1978—. Inventor wireline borehole packer, anti-jamming core barrel. Mem. Soc. Petroleum Engrs. (jr.). Republican. Home: 1663 E Hidden Valley Club Dr Sandy UT 84092

FULLER, GENE BOB, reproductive physiologist, researcher; b. Overton, Tex., Aug. 4, 1939; s. Jones Branch and Winnie Arlene (Villyard) F.; m. Margaret Ann Mc Laughlin, Aug. 6, 1960; children: Robert, Michael, Melissa. BS with honors, Sam Houston State U., 1962; MS, Okla. State U., 1964; PhD, Purdue U., 1968. Postdoctoral researcher Cornell U., Ithaca, N.Y., 1968-69; asst. prof. biol. scis., animal behavior, toxicology U. N.H., Durham, 1969-71, U. So. Miss., Hattiesburg, 1971-74; asst. research prof. Primate Research Inst., Holloman AFB, N.Mex., 1974-77, assoc. research prof., 1977—, chief, reproductive biology div., 1980—, dir. research, 1984—. Named Outstanding Tchr. U. N.H., 1970-71; Nat. Inst. Child Health and Human Devel. research grantee, 1973-77. Mem. Soc. for Study of Reprodn., AAAS, Am. Soc. Primatologists, Alpha Chi. Republican. Mem. Christian Ch. Lodges: Lions (pres. 1980-81), Rotary, Elks. Avocations: softball, hunting, fishing. Home: Haynes Canyon High Rolls NM 88325 Office: Primate Research Inst Box 1027 Holloman AFB NM 88330

FULLER, JEFFERY BRYAN, civil engineer; b. Torrington, Wyo., Nov. 18, 1951; s. James Henry and Jo Ann (Flanders) F.; m. Judith Anne McMillan, Dec. 27, 1980. BSc, U. Wyo., 1975, postgrad., 1975-78. Asst. track and field coach U. Wyo., Laramie, 1975-80, head track and field coach, 1980-84; civil engr. Banner Assocs., Inc., Laramie, 1984—; state coordinator track and field. Spl. Olympics, Laramie, 1984. Mem. com. Laramie Sports Devel., 1986. Named Coach of Yr. High County Athletic Conf., Provo, Utah, 1984. Democrat. Methodist. Avocations: fishing, hunting. Home: 414 Canby Laramie WY 82070 Office: Banner Assocs Inc 620 Plaza Ct Laramie WY 82070

FULLER, MARY FALVEY, management consultant; b. Detroit, Oct. 28, 1941; d. Lawrence C. and Mathilde G. Falvey; m. James W. Fuller, Aug. 22, 1981. B.A. with honors in Econs., Cornell U., 1963; M.B.A., Harvard U., 1967. Systems engr. IBM Corp., N.Y.C., 1963-65; mgmt. cons. McKinsey & Co., Inc., N.Y.C., 1967-75; v.p. Citibank, N.A., N.Y.C., 1975-78, head asset servicing div., 1977-78; sr. v.p., dir., head adminstrn. div., mem. exec. com., mem. operating com. Blyth Eastman Dillon & Co., Inc., N.Y.C., 1978-80; pres. M.C. Falvey Assocs., Inc., N.Y.C., 1980-81; v.p. fin. Shaklee Corp., San Francisco, 1981-82; pres., dir. Falvey Autos, Inc., Troy, Mich., 1978—; trustee Fed. Hosp. Ins. Trust Fund, Fed. Old Age and Survivors Ins. Trust Fund, Fed. Disability Ins. Trust Fund; dir. Tech. Funding Inc., 1983—; mem. regional dealer adv. council Toyota Motor Sales Corp. Mem. Com. for N.Y. Philharmonic, 1975-77; mem. 1979 Adv. Council on Social Security, 1979-80, Pres. Reagan's Transition Task Force on Social Security, 1979-80, Nat. Commn. on Social Security Reform, 1982-83; adminstrv. bd. Cornell U. Council, 1984-86; mem. adminstrn. and legal processes adv. council Mills Coll., 1982-85; chmn. bd. trustees San Francisco Performances, 1982—. Harvard Bus. Sch. grantee, 1965-67. Republican. Episcopalian. Club: Commonwealth of Calif. (chmn. Asia Pacific study sect., program com. 1983-85, chmn. Asia-Pacific study sect.). Home and Office: 2584 Filbert St San Francisco CA 94123

FULLER, RICKI SUE, social worker; b. Detroit, Aug. 28, 1959; d. Arnold Meyer and Terry Lois (Keywell) F. BA in Psychology, U. Ariz., 1981; MSW, Ariz. State U., 1984. Extended childcare worker Casa De Los Ninos, Tucson, 1981-82; intern Tucson Job Corps, 1982-83; intern Cigna Health Plan, Phoenix, 1983-84, clin. social worker, 1984-85; med. social worker Boswell Hosp., Sun City, Ariz., 1985-86, Boswell Extened Care Ctr, Sun City, Ariz., 1986—. Vol. Info. and Referral, Tucson, 1981-82; active Valley Big Brothers/Big Sisters. Mem. Nat. Orgn. Social Workers, Employee Assistance Relations Assn. Jewish. Lodge: B'Nai Brith Women. Avocations: racquetball, aerobic dancing, biking, hiking, jazz dancing. Office: Boswell Extended Care Ctr Sun City AZ 85372

FULLER, ROBERT KENNETH, architect, urban designer; b. Denver, Oct. 6, 1942; s. Kenneth Roller and Gertrude Ailene (Heid) F.; m. Virginia Louise Elkin, Aug. 23, 1969; children: Kimberly Kirsten, Kelsey Christa. BArch, U. Colo., 1967; MArch and Urban Design, Washington U., St. Louis, 1973. Archtl. designer Fuller & Fuller, Denver; architect, planner Urban Research and Design Ctr., St. Louis, 1970-72; pres. Fuller & Assocs., Denver, 1972—. prin. works include Pattonsburg New Town, Mo., 1972. del. Aspen Design Conf., 1966, bd. dirs. Cherry Creek Improvement Assn., Greater Cherry Creek Steering com., Colo. Arlberg Club; past pres. Denver East Cen. Civic Assn. Served with USMCR, 1964-70. Mem. AIA (pres. Denver chpt. 1987, traveling scholar to Gt. Britain, Colo. chpt., 1972), Phi Gamma Delta, Delta Phi Delta. Home: 2244 E 4th Ave Denver CO 80206 Office: 3320 E 2d Ave Denver CO 80206

FULLER, RONALD IVAN, chemical computing consultant; b. Riverton, Wyo., July 20, 1950; s. Ivan Lauchie and Colleen (Dalley) F.; m. Joyce Deanne Henderson, May 30, 1972; children: Sean Cameron, Karey Rae-Ann. BS, Brigham Young U., 1974. Chief chemist Hartley Research Labs., Provo, Utah, 1972-75; v.p., lab. supr. Western Standard Labs., Orem, Utah, 1975-77; lab supr. Core Labs., Inc., Casper, Wyo., 1977-80; lab. supr. II Core Labs., Inc., Aurora, Colo., 1980-84, mgr. computer ops., 1984—; computer curriculum advisor Parks Bus. Coll., 1984-85; computer cons. Local Real Estate, Denver, 1986—. Scouting coordinator Boy Scouts Am., Aurora, 1984-85; eastern chmn. Citizens Com. Jewell Overpass, Aurora, 1984; del. Aurora Pub. Schs. Regional Conf. on Edn., Denver, 1985. Mem. Am. Chem. Soc., Digital Equipment Users Soc. (chmn LUG 1984-85). Republican. Mormon. Avocations: camping, target shooting, photography. Home: 1483 S Yampa Ct Aurora CO 80017 Office: Core Labs Inc 1300 S Potomac St #130 Aurora CO 80012

FULLERTON, CHARLES MICHAEL, meteorologist, physics educator; b. Oklahoma City, Mar. 10, 1932; s. Joseph Austin and Rose Marsh (Ingraham) F.; m. Jane Jo Wyatt, Dec. 27, 1954; children: Stephanie Malia, Christopher Damien, Amy Juliet. BS in Math., U. Okla., 1954; postgrad., U. N.Mex., 1957-61; MS in Physics, N.Mex. Inst. Mining and Technology, 1964, PhD, 1966. Instr. math, physics Coll. St. Joseph, Albuquerque, 1957-61; from asst. prof. to full prof. U. Hawaii, Hilo, 1966—, dean arts and scis., 1984—; dir. Cloud Physics Obs., Hilo, 1966-84; dir. mgmt. services State Dept. Health and Social Services, Santa Fe, 1972, dir. personnel services, 1975. Contbr. articles to profl. jours. Served to 1st lt. U.S. Army, 1954-57. Grantee NSF, 1964-66, U.S. Dept. Interior, 1971-77. Mem. Am. Meteorol. Soc., Am. Geophys. Union, Hawaiian Acad. Sci., N.Mex. Acad. Sci., Sigma Xi (local pres. 1975-76). Republican. Roman Catholic. Lodge: Rotary. Office: U Hawaii Coll Arts and Scis Hilo HI 96720-4091

FULLERTON, GAIL JACKSON, university president; b. Lincoln, Nebr., Apr. 29, 1927; d. Earl Warren and Gladys Bernice (Marshall) Jackson; m. Stanley James Fullerton, Mar. 27, 1967; children by previous marriage—Gregory Snell Putney, Cynde Gail Putney. B.A., U. Nebr., 1949, M.A., 1950; Ph.D., U. Oreg., 1954. Lectr. sociology Drake U., Des Moines, 1955-57; asst. prof. sociology Fla. State U., Tallahassee, 1957-60; asst. prof. sociology San Jose (Calif.) State U., 1963-67, assoc. prof., 1968-71, prof., 1972—, dean grad. studies and research, 1972-76, exec. v.p. univ., 1976-78, pres., 1978—; Bd. dirs. EUDUCOM, Assoc. Western Univs., Inc., 1980—; mem. sr. accrediting commn. Western Assn. Schs. and Colls., 1982—, chmn., 1985-86. Author: Survival in Marriage, 2d edit, 1977, (with Snell Putney) Normal Neurosis: The Adjusted American, 2d edit, 1966. Carnegie fellow, 1950-51, 52-53; Doherty Found. fellow, 1951-52. Mem. Am. Sociol. Assn., Western Coll. Assn. (exec. com., past pres.), San Jose C. of C. (bd. dirs.), Phi Beta Kappa. Home: 226 Wave Crest Ave Santa Cruz CA 95060 Office: San Jose State U Office of Pres San Jose CA 95192

FULMER, CHARLES VIRGIL, geologist; b. Council Bluffs, Iowa, Nov. 15, 1920; s. Fred Roy and Lula B. (Cluphf) F.; m. Carol L. Smith, Sept. 18, 1947; children: Charles Jr., Steven, Clark, John. BS, MS, U. Wash., 1947; PhD, U. Calif., Berkeley, 1956. Geologist Standard Oil of Calif., San Fransicso, 1951-62; research engr. Boeing Co., Seattle, 1962-72; earth scientist King County, Seattle, 1972-85; cons. geologist Geometrotec, Seattle, 1985—. Served to 1st lt. U.S. Army, 1942-46. Fellow Geol. Soc. Am.; mem. Am. Assn. Engring. Geologists. Home: 6174 NE 187 Pl Seattle WA 98155

FULMER, RUSSELL FRANCIS, librarian; b. Birmingham, Ala., Nov. 28, 1946; s. John A. and Agnes E. (Parker) F. AB, Dickinson Coll., 1968; MLS, U. Ala., 1972. Cataloger, U. Ala., Tuscaloosa, 1971-74; coordinator tech. services Jackson Met. Library System, Miss., 1974-83; asst. dir. tech. services Colo. Sch. Mines, Golden, 1983—; mem. data base quality adv. com. Southeastern Library Network, 1979-81; cons. Miss. Library Assn., 1983. Asst. editor Miss. Libraries, 1980-81. Vol., Easter Seals Miss., 1975-76; mem. mission com. St. Christopher's Episcopal Ch., Jackson, 1981-83. Mem. ALA, Library Sch. Alumni Assn. (pres. 1972), Miss. Library Assn. (resolution 1983), Southeastern Library Assn., Colo. Library Assn. (chmn. tech. services and automation div. 1987-88), Beta Phi Mu. Episcopalian. Home: 1612 Secrest St Golden CO 80401 Office: Colo Sch Mines Library Golden CO 80401

FULTON, GLORIA JEAN, librarian, educator; b. Sterling, Ill., Nov. 20, 1940; d. Reese H. and Aldine (Hansen) Hinton; m. Lloyd Griffiths Fulton, Mar. 26, 1977 (div. 1984); 1 child, Alexander. BA, UCLA, 1963, MLS, 1968; MA, Humboldt State U., 1976. Cons. RAND Corp., Santa Monica, Calif., 1965-66; librarian Santa Monica Pub. Library, 1969-70; librarian Humboldt State U., Arcata, Calif., 1970—, prof. Russian lang., 1979—; librarian Coll. Redwoods, Eureka, Calif., 1970-72. Fellow CLR, 1976-77, NDEA, 1963, HEA, 1967-68, Woodrow Wilson Found, 1963, Inst. Internat. Edn. U. Zagreb, Yugoslavia, 1964-65. Mem. ALA, Chinese Lang. Computer Soc., Phi Beta Kappa. Avocations: folk dancing, cooking, travel. Home: 879 Union St Arcata CA 95521 Office: Humboldt State U Library Catalog Dept Arcata CA 95521

FULTON, NORMAN ROBERT, home entertainment co. exec.; b. Los Angeles, Dec. 16, 1935; s. Robert John and Fritzi Marie (Wacker) F.; A.A., Santa Monica Coll., 1958; B.S., U. So. Calif., 1960; m. Nancy Butler, July 6, 1966; children—Robert B., Patricia M. Asst. v.p. Raphael Glass Co., Los Angeles, 1960-65; credit adminstr. Zellerbach Paper Co., Los Angeles, 1966-68; gen. credit mgr. Carrier Transicold Co., Montebello, Calif., 1968-70, Virco Mfg. Co., Los Angeles, 1970-72, Superscope, Inc., Chatsworth, Calif., 1972-79; asst. v.p. credit and adminstrn. Inkel Corp., Carson, Calif., 1980-82; corp. credit mgr. Gen. Consumer Electronics, Santa Monica, Calif., 1982-83; br. credit mgr. Sharp Electronics Corp., Carson, Calif., 1983—. Served with AUS, 1955-57. Fellow Nat. Inst. Credit; mem. Credit Mgrs. So. Calif., Nat. Notary Assn. Home: 31820 Cottontail Ln Malibu CA 90265

FULWILER, DAN ORAL, audio-visual media company executive; b. Seattle, May 4, 1951; s. Oral and Eleanor (Sinclair) F.; m. Nancy Rae, March 17, 1973. BA in Psychology, Seattle U., 1973; AAS in Tech. Photography, Seattle Cen. Coll., 1976; AA Biol. Photography, Bellevue (Wash.) Coll., 1977; postgrad. in bus. adminstrn., Seattle U., 1986. Supr. photography Good Samaritan Hosp., Portland, Oreg., 1977-81; mgmt. cons. Seattle, 1981-83; gen. mgr. VisionWorks, Portland, 1983—. Contbr. articles and photo. series to profl. jours. Recipient Med. Edn. award Biocommunications mag., 1979, 81. Mem. Biol. Photog. Assn. (chpt. chmn. 1979-81, photog. awards), Portland C. of C. Democrat. Club: President's. Lodge: Lions. Home: 1500 SW 5th #2006 Portland OR 97201 Office: VisionWorks 221 NW 2d Ave Suite 221 Portland OR 97209

FUNCH, FRED BERGMAN, II, designer; b. Fresno, Calif., Apr. 15, 1953; s. James H. and Nancy D. (Downs) F.; m. Linda R. Kelley, Feb. 3, 1973 (div. 1981); children: Anastasia Lynn, Christopher Bergman, Catheryn Suzanne; m. Kim Anne Cuccurullo, June 10, 1984; 1 child, Nancy Daniel. BA, Ariz. State U., 1975, Calif. State Poly. U., Pomona, 1979. Pvt. practice designer Fresno, 1971-75; v.p. Amco, Orange, Calif., 1975-76, P.N.P.E., Santa Ana, Calif., 1976-77, L.D. King Archtl. Engrs., Newport Beach, Calif., 1977-79; prin. F.B. Funch & Assocs., Newport Beach, 1979-85; pres. Heritage Archtl. Group, Fair Oaks, Calif., 1985-86; prin. U.A. Architect Assocs., Rancho Cordova, Calif., 1986—. Avocations: music, artist, flying, scuba diving, coaching soccer. Office: UA Architect Assocs 12161 Folsom Blvd Suite C Rancho Cordova CA 95670

FUNG, KEE-YING, engineering educator, researcher; b. Hunan, Peoples Republic of China, Dec. 20, 1948; came to U.S., 1972; s. Yuk-Kowng and Nam-Hing (Tam) F.; m. E.E. Ho, Jan. 18, 1976 (div. Apr. 1985); m. Ivy Wang, Mar. 15, 1987. BS, Nat. Taiwan (Republic of China) U., 1972; PhD, Cornell U., 1976. Research assoc. aerospace and mech. engring. dept. U. Ariz., Tucson, 1976-79, asst. prof., 1979-85, assoc. prof., 1985—; vis. scientist DFVLR, Göttingen, Fed. Republic of Germany, 1981; cons. Ariz. State U., Phoenix, 1985—, Zonatech., 1985—. Contbr. articles to profl. jours. A.V. Humboldt fellow, 1981. Mem. AIAA, Tucson Soaring Club. Home: 121 Los Pinos Vista Tucson AZ 85704 Office: U Ariz Areospace and Mech Engring Dept Aero Bldg #16 Tucson AZ 85721

FUNK, DAVID CHARLES, design firm executive; b. Los Angeles, Feb. 4, 1947; s. Charles Deane and Joanne Katherine (McElroy) F.; m. Duane Donise Morrison, Mar. 21, 1971; children: McKenzie, Grace. BA, Calif. State U., Los Angeles, 1970. Dir. art Ad Creations, Eugene, Oreg., 1973-76; dir. art Advt. Services, Eugene, 1976-77, creative dir., 1977-80; ptnr. Rubick and Funk, Eugene, 1980-85; pres. Funk and Assocs., Eugene, 1985—; adj. prof. design Lane Community Coll., Eugene, 1984-85. Del. Community Goals Conf., Eugene, 1985. Recipient Desi award, 1981. Fellow Am. Inst. Graphic Arts; mem. Designers Forum (founder, v.p. 1985), Designers Roundtable, Sacramento Art Dir. Club (assoc.). Democrat. Club: Mid-Oreg. Ad. Avocations: white water rafting, backpacking, fishing, camping, climbing. Home: 30806 Blanton Rd Eugene OR 97405 Office: Funk and Assocs 1234 Pearl St Eugene OR 97401

FUNK, DONALD DWAIN, physician, consultant; b. Caddo, Okla., May 20, 1933; s. Lloyd Donald and Sadie Opal (Welch) F.; m. Betty Lou Hudson, Mar. 16, 1958; children: Carolyn, Thomas, Elizabeth, John. Undergrad., Tex. Tech. U., 1951-54; MD, Baylor U., 1958. Diplomate Am. Bd. Internal Medicine. Resident in internal medicine USPHS Hosp., Seattle, 1960-63, chief of hematology, 1965-73; fellow in hemotology U. Wash., Seattle, 1963-65; clin. dir. Mt. Edgecumbe Hosp., Sitka, Alaska, 1973-86; pvt. practice specializing in internal medicine Sitka Community Hosp., 1986—; bd. dirs. Sitka Diabetic Assn.. Mem. AMA. Avocations: fishing, computer applications in medicine. Home: Box 1589 Sitka AK 99835 Office: Moore Clinic 814 Halibut Point Rd Sitka AK 99835

FUNK, MILTON ALBERT, real estate broker; b. Cantonement, Okla., Oct. 12, 1918; s. John Anton and Cornelia Elizabeth (Schwake) F.; m. Earline Myrtle Burkholder, Feb. 15, 1937; children: DeAnne Funk Kiralla, Gary Milton. Cert. in real estate, UCLA, 1960. Owner Realty Sales & Exchange Co., South Gate, Calif., 1961—; sec.-treas. Apt. Investments, Inc., South Gate, 1961—; dir. Apple Valley View Water Assn., cons. to Los Angeles Apartment Assn. Directory, 1987. Served with arty. AUS, 1944-46, PTO. Mem. Calif. Assn. Realtors (regional v.p. 1969, dir.), S.E. Bd. Realtors (pres. 1966, dir. 1980), Los Angeles County Apt. Assn. (dir., sec.), Laguna Shores Owners Assn. (pres.), VFW, Downey and South Gate C. of C's. Home: 11714 Bellflower Blvd Downey CA 90242 Office: 3947 Tweedy Blvd South Gate CA 90280

FUNK, WARREN KEITH, retired military officer, consultant; b. Minneapolis, Kans., Apr. 8, 1943; s. Leslie Ivan and Charlotte Aline (Rogers) F.; m. Linda Joan Dickerson, Aug. 15, 1965 (div. Sept. 1976); children: Ryan Adam, Rachel Regan; m. Lesley Jean Bartman, Feb. 4, 1979. BA in Tech. Journalism, Kans. State U., 1966; MS in Human Resource Mgmt., Gonzaga U., 1978. Commd. 2d lt. USAF, 1966, advanced through grades to maj., 1977; squadron section comdr 21st Supply Squadron, Elmendorf AFB, Alaska, 1973-75; chief of protocol Alaskan Air Command Hdqrs., Elmendorf AFB, Alaska, 1975-76; dir. adminstrn USAF Survival Sch., Fairchild AFB, Wash., 1976-78; chief base adminstr 2nd Combat Support Group, Barksdale AFB, La., 1979-84; chief base adminstr 60th Air Base Group, Travis AFB, Calif., 1984-86, cons., 1984-86; ret. 1986; cons. Fairfield, Calif., 1986-87; support services mgr. City of Monterey Park, Calif., 1987—. Counselor Rape Crisis Network Luth. Family and Child Service, Spokane, Wash., 1977-79, counselor and trainer Rape Crisis Ctr., YWCA, Shreveport, La., 1980-84. Mem. Am. Mgmt. Assn., Air Force Assn., Assn. of Info. Systems Profls. (v.p. Shreveport chpt. 1978-79). Republican. Presbyterian. Club: Officers (Travis AFB). Avocations: fishing, canoeing, chess, reading, coin collecting. Home: 677 E Colorado Blvd Pasadena CA 91101

FUNK, WILLIAM HENRY, civil engineer, educator; b. Ephraim, Utah, June 10, 1933; s. William George and Henrietta (Hackwell) F.; m. Ruth Sherry Mellor, Sept. 19, 1964; 1 dau., Cynthia Lynn. B.S. in Biol. Sci, U. Utah, 1955, M.S. in Zoology (USPHS trainee), 1963, M.S. in Zoology, 1963, Ph.D. in Limnology, 1966. Tchr. sci., math. Salt Lake City Schs., 1957-60; research asst. U. Utah, Salt Lake City, 1961-63; head sci. dept. N.W. Jr. High Sch., Salt Lake City, 1961-63; mem. faculty Wash. State U., Pullman, 1966—; assoc. prof. civil engring. Wash. State U., 1971-75, prof., 1975—, chmn. environ. sci./regional planning program, 1979-81; dir. Environ. Research Center, 1980-83, State of Wash. Water Research Ctr., 1981—; cons. Harstad Engrs., Seattle, 1971-72, Boise Cascade Corp., Seattle, 1971-72, U.S. Army C.E., Walla Walla, Wash., 1970-74, ORB Corp., Renton, Wash., 1972-73, State Wash. Dept. Ecology, Olympia, 1971-72, U.S. Civil Service, Seattle, Chgo., 1972-74; mem. High Level Nuclear Waste Bd., State of Wash. Author publs. on water pollution control and lake restoration. Served with USNR, 1955-57. Recipient President's Disting. Faculty award Wash. State U., 1984. Grantee NSF Summer Inst., 1961, Office Water Resources Research, 1971-72, 73-76, EPA, 1980-83, U.S. Geol. Survey, 1983-87, Nat. Parks Service, 1985-87. Mem. Naval Res. Officers Assn. (chpt. pres. 1969), Res Officers Assn. (U.S. Naval Acad. info. officer 1973-76), N.Am. Lake Mgmt. Soc. (pres. 1984-85), Pacific N.W. Pollution Control Assn. (editor 1969-77, pres.-elect 1982-83, pres. 1983-84), Water Pollution Control Fedn. (Arthur S. Bedell award Pacific N.W. assn. 1976, nat. dir. 1978-81), Nat. Assn. Water Inst. Dirs. (chair 1985-86), Am. Soc. Limnology and Oceanography, Am. Micros. Soc., N.W. Sci. Assn., Sigma Xi, Phi Sigma. Home: SW 330 Kimball Ct Pullman WA 99163

FUREDY, JOHN PETER, insurance company executive; b. Yugoslavia, May 2, 1910; came to U.S., 1941, naturalized, 1943; s. Jaco and Jenny (Schrank) F.; student Pazmany Peter U., Budapest, 1929-30; grad. Life Ins. Agts. Mgmt. Assn. Sch. Mgmt., 1955; m. Lila Anne Moore, Mar. 31, 1978. Vice pres., dir. life agys. Beneficial Standard Life Ins. Co., Los Angeles, 1950-58; pres., chmn. bd. Nat. Security Ins. Agy., Inc., Los Angeles, 1958-83; pres. T.W.A. Ins. Agy., Los Angeles, 1979—, Furedy Ins. Agy., Inc., 1983—. Served with U.S. Army, 1943. Mem. Life Ins. Agts. Mgmt. Assn. (research com., ins. co. com.), Gen. Agts. Mgmt. Corp. (charter), Life Underwriters Assn., Fgn. Affairs Council. Club: TownHouse. Home: 8364 Mulholland Dr Los Angeles CA 90046 Office: 3660 Wilshire Blvd Penthouse E Los Angeles CA 90010

FUREY, KIT, court administrator, lawyer; b. Salmon, Idaho, Apr. 6, 1950; s. Jack and Nancy (Stafford) Furey; m. Leo Edward Miller, Dec. 18, 1976. B.S., U. Idaho, 1972, J.D., 1975. Law clk. U.S. Cts., Boise, 1976-77; dep. pros. atty. Canyon County Prosecutor's Office, Caldwell, Idaho, 1977-78; referee Idaho Indsl. Commn., Boise, 1978-80; jud. edn. officer Idaho Supreme Ct., Boise, 1980-84; asst. dir. Adminstrv. Office of Cts., Boise, 1984—; mem. citizens juvenile justice adv. com. 4th Dist. Ct., 1983-84. Bd. dirs. LWV of Boise, 1985, St. Joseph's Sch. Found.; bd. dirs. YWCA, Boise, 1983-85, v.p. 1985, chmn. program planning com., 1984, mem. personnel com., 1986; mem. Gov.'s Comm. on Child Support Enforcement, 1985-86. Mem. Am. Soc. Tng. and Devel. (bd. dirs.), Idaho Bar Assn., Boise Com. on Fgn. Relations (exec. com. 1985—), Jr. League of Boise (mktg. v.p. 1987—). Roman Catholic. Club: Ada Toastmaters (v.p. 1984, pres. 1985). Address: 3120 Crane Creek Rd Boise ID 83702

FURGASON, SAMUEL LAWSON, lawyer; b. Benham, Ky., Feb. 13; s. Samuel Lawson and Jo Francis (Steely) F.; m. Joanne Margaret Furgason, May 5, 1984; 1 child. BA, U. Fla., 1969; JD, U. Idaho, 1976. Bar: Wash., U.S. Dist. Ct. (we. dist.) Wash., U.S. Ct. Appeals (9th cir.). Assoc. Clay Nixon Law Offices, Seattle, 1977; prin. Hansen & Furgason (name changed to Hansen, Furgason and Leonardson), Woodinville, Wash., 1978-85; chmn., chief operating officer Hansen & Furgason, Woodinville, Wash., 1985—. Pres. Woodinville C. of C., 1979-80, bd. dirs., 1980-81, 86-87; bd. dirs. EKC Estate Planning Council, Bellevue, Wash., 1983-85. Mem. Wash. State Bar Assn. (trial practice sect., corp. bus. and banking law sect.), N.W. Venture Group. Lodge: Rotary (bd. dirs. Woodinville 1986—). Office: 18106 140th Ave NE Woodinville WA 98072

FURMAN, ERIC BERTRAM, pediatric anesthesiologist; b. Johannesburg, South Africa, Nov. 27, 1934; came to U.S., 1965, naturalized, 1976; s. Solomon and Milly (Dinkin) F.; M.B., B.Ch., U. Witwatersrand, Johannesburg, 1958; m. June Elizabeth Abrams, Dec. 16, 1958; children—Terrence, Joanne Peta, Nicola Millicent. Intern in family practice, resident in anesthesiology U. Witwatersrand Hosps., Johannesburg, 1964; fellow in pediatric anesthesia Hosp. Sick Children, Toronto, 1965; fellow in anesthesiology, then instr. U. Vt. Hosps., 1965-68; dir. pediatric anesthesia Mass. Gen. Hosp., Boston, instr. anesthesia Harvard U. Med. Sch., Boston, 1968-71; prin. anesthesist Children's Hosp., Johannesburg, 1972-74; dir. anesthesia Children's Orthopedic Hosp. and Med. Center, Seattle, 1974—, clin. asso. prof. anesthesia and pediatrics U. Wash. Med. Sch., Seattle, 1974-86, prof. anesthesia, 1987—. Trustee, Bush Sch., Seattle, 1977-83, v.p., 1978. Recipient African Oxygen Gold medal in anesthesia, 1963. Mem. Am. Soc. Anesthesiologists (chmn. com. pediatric practice 1978-81), Am. Acad. Pediatrics (chmn. sect. anesthesia 1980-82), AMA, Wash. Med. Soc., Wash. Soc. Anesthesiologists (pres.-elect 1984). Jewish. Author articles in field; editor: International Anesthesia Clinics, 1975. Home: 4416 54th St NE Seattle WA 98105 Office: Children's Hosp and Med Center Seattle WA 98105

FURMAN, ROBERT HOWARD, pharmaceutical company consultant; b. Schenectady, Oct. 23, 1918; s. Howard Blackall and Jane Blessing (MacChesney) F.; m. Mary Frances Kilpatrick, Feb. 10, 1945; children: Carol K. Furman Friedman, Jane C. Furman Dougherty, Robert Howard, Hugh Patrick. AB (Allison prize 1939), Union Coll., Schenectady, 1940; MD, Yale U., 1943. Diplomate Am. Bd. Internal Medicine. Intern, then asst. resident in medicine New Haven Hosp., 1944-45; asst. in medicine Yale U. Med. Sch., 1944-45; asst. resident physician, then resident physician Vanderbilt U. Hosp., 1948-50; from research asst. in medicine to asst. prof. Vanderbilt U. Med. Sch., 1946-52; assoc. prof., then prof. research medicine U. Okla. Med. Sch., 1952-70; prof. medicine Ind. U. Med. Sch., 1970—; head cardiovascular sect. Okla. Med. Research Found. and Hosp., 1952-70, assoc. dir. found., 1957-70; exec. dir. clin. research Eli Lilly and Co., Indpls., 1970-73, v.p. corp. med. affairs, 1976-83; v.p. Lilly Research Labs., 1973-76; clin. research cons. Walker Clin. Research, Indpls.; mem. vis. staff Wishard Meml. Hosp., Indpls., 1971; pres. Okla. Heart Assn., 1967-68; mem. cardiovascular study sect. Nat. Heart Inst., NIH, 1960-63, heart spl. projects com., 1963-66; bd. mgrs., sci. adv. com. Wistar Inst., 1972-78; sci. adv. com. Hormel Inst., Austin, Minn., 1973-83; mem. clin. scis. panel NRC, 1978-83; mem. clin. pharmacology adv. com. PMAF, 1977-83. Contbr. to med. jours.; mem. editorial bds. jours. Mem. council Inst. Adminstrn. and Mgmt.; mem. adv. bd. Union Coll., trustee, 1982; bd. dirs. Cathedral Arts, Indpls.; assoc. trustee U. Pa.; bd. dirs., exec. com. Indpls. Symphony Orch. Served to comdr., M.C. USNR, 1945-46, 55-57. Fellow Am. Coll. Cardiology, A.C.P., N.Y. Acad. Scis., Royal Soc. Medicine; mem. Am. Assn. World Health (dir. 1974-83), AAAS, Am. Clin. and Climatol. Assn., Am. Fedn. Clin. Research, Am. (fellow council arteriosclerosis, nat. bd. dirs., exec. and central coms.; chmn. research com. 1964-65), Ind. (dir.), Marion County heart assns.), Am. Physiol. Soc., Am. Soc. Clin. Pharmacology and Therapeutics, Am. Soc. Internal Medicine, Assn. Yale Alumni in Medicine, Central Soc. Clin. Research (council 1963-66), Endocrine Soc., Ind., Marion County med. assns., Soc. Exptl. Biology and Medicine, So. Soc. Clin. Research, Southwestern Soc. Naturalists, Wilson Ornithol. Soc., Nat. Audubon Soc., Sigma Xi, Alpha Omega Alpha, Delta Upsilon. Clubs: Cosmos, Capitol Hill (Washington); Confrerie des Chevaliers du Tastevin; Mohawk (Schenectady); Garden of the Gods, Colorado Springs Country, Plaza (Colorado Springs). Home: 2734 Foxgrove Ct Colorado Springs CO 80609

FURMANSKI, PHILIP, cancer research scientist; b. Fed. Republic Germany, July 26, 1946; came to U.S., 1947, naturalized, 1954; s. Ed and Rose (Warsawski) F.; m. Elizabeth Ann Fremer, Oct. 5, 1968; children: Lisa Anne, Jonathan David. BA, Temple U., 1966, PhD, 1969. Research assoc. Albert Einstein Med. Ctr., Phila., 1970; research assoc., instr. Dartmouth Coll. Med. Sch., Hanover, N.H., 1970-72; chmn., asst. dir. Mich. Cancer Found., Detroit, 1974-81; asst. prof., then assoc. prof. Wayne State U. Sch. Med., Detroit, 1974-81; assoc. dir., sci. dir. AMC Cancer Research Ctr., Denver, 1981—; mem. virus working group WHO/Food and Agriculture Orgn., 1977-80; mem. rev. com. Nat. Cancer Inst., Bethesda, Md., 1981—; cons. numerous indsl. and acad. concerns, 1975—. Editor: Biological Carcinogenesis, 1982, Understanding Breast Cancer, 1983, RNA Tumor Viruses, Oncogenes, Human Cancer, and AIDS, 1985; mem. editorial bd. Leukemia Revs. Internat., 1980—; also articles. Damon Runyon Meml. fellow NIH, 1967-72; Nat. Cancer Inst. grantee, 1969—. Mem. Internat. Soc. Exptl. Hematology, Internat. Assn. Breast Cancer Research, Am. Soc. Cell. Biology, AAAS, Am. Assn. Cancer Research. Office: AMC Cancer Research Ctr 1600 Pierce St Denver CO 80214

FURNAS, DAVID WILLIAM, plastic surgeon; b. Caldwell, Idaho, Apr. 1, 1931; s. John Doan and Esther Bradbury (Hare) F.; m. Mary Lou Heatherly, Feb. 11, 1956; children: Heather Jean, Brent David, Craig Jonathan. A.B., U. Calif.-Berkeley, 1952, M.S., 1957, M.D., 1955. Diplomate: Am. Bd. Surgery, Am. Bd. Plastic Surgery (dir. 1979-85). Intern, U. Calif. Hosp., San Francisco, 1955-56; asst. resident in surgery U. Calif. Hosp., 1956-57; asst. resident in psychiatry, NIMH fellow Langley Porter Neuropsychiat. Inst., U. Calif., San Francisco, 1959-60; resident in gen. surgery Gorgas Hosp., C.Z., 1960-61; asst. resident in plastic surgery N.Y. Hosp., Cornell Med. Center, N.Y.C., 1961-62; chief resident in plastic surgery VA Hosp., Bronx, N.Y., 1962-63; registrar Royal Infirmary and Affiliated Hosps., Glasgow, Scotland, 1963-64; asso. in hand surgery U. Iowa, 1965-68, asst. prof. surgery, 1966-68, asso. prof., 1968-69; asso. prof. surgery, chief div. plastic surgery U. Calif., Irvine, 1969-74; prof., chief div. plastic surgery U. Calif., 1974-80, clin. prof., chief div. plastic surgery, 1980—; surgeon East Africa Flying Doctors Service, African Med. and Research Found., Nairobi, Kenya, 1976-86; plastic surgeon S.S. Hope, Nicaragua, 1966, Ceylon, 1968, Sri Lanka, 1969; mem. Balakbayan med. mission, Mindanao and Sulu, Philippines, 1980, 81, 82. Contbr. chpts. to textbooks, articles to med. jours.; author/editor 4 textbooks; assoc. editor Jour. Hand Surgery, Annals of Plastic Surgery. Served to capt. M.C., USAF, 1957-59. Recipient Golden Apple award for teaching excellence U. Calif.-Irvine Sch. Medicine, 1980, Kaiser-Permanente award U. Calif.-Irvine Sch. Medicine, 1981, Humanitarian Service award Black Med. Students, U. Calif. Irvine, 1987, Sr. Scholarship award Plastic Surgery Ednl. Found., 1987; named Orange County Press Club Headliner of Yr., 1982. Fellow ACS, Royal Coll. Surgeons Can., Royal Soc. Medicine, Explorers Club, Royal Geog. Soc.; mem. AMA, Calif., Orange County med. assns., Am. Soc. Plastic and Reconstructive Surgeons, Am. Soc. Reconstructive Microsurgery, Soc. Head and Neck Surgeons, Am. Cleft Palate Assn., Am. Soc. Surgery of Hand, Soc. Univ. Surgeons, Am. Assn. Plastic Surgeons (trustee 1983-86), Am. Soc. Aesthetic Plastic Surgery, Am. Soc. Maxillofacial Surgeons, Assn. Acad. Chmn. Plastic Surgery (bd. dirs. 1986—), Assn. Surgeons East Africa, Pacific Coast Surg. Assn., Internat. Soc. Aesthetic Plastic Surgery, Internat. Soc. Reconstructive Microsurgery, Pan African Assn. Neurol. Scis., Assn. of Acad. Chmn. of Plastic Surgeons (bd. dirs. 1986—), Phi Beta Kappa, Alpha Omega Alpha. Clubs: Muthaiga, Center. Office: U Calif Div Plastic Surgery Irvine Med Ctr 101 City Dr S Orange CA 92625

FURNIVAL, GEORGE MITCHELL, petroleum and mining consultant; b. Winnipeg, Man., Can., July 25, 1908; s. William George and Grace Una (Rothwell) F.; B.Sc., U. Man., 1929; M.A., Queens U., 1933; Ph.D., MIT, 1935; m. Marion Marguerite Fraser, Mar. 8, 1937; children—William George, Sharon (Mrs. John M. Roscoe), Patricia M., Bruce A. Field geologist in Man., Ont., N.W.T., and Que., 1928-36; asst. mine supt. Cline Lake Gold Mines, Ltd., 1936-39; geologist Geol. Survey Can., No. and Southwestern Sask., 1939-42; sr. geologist Standard Oil Co. of Calif. (Chevron Standard, Ltd.), Calgary, Alta., 1942-44, asst. to chief geologist, 1944-45, field supt. So. Alta., 1945-46, mgr. land and legal dept., 1948-50, v.p. land and legal, dir., 1950-52, v.p. legal, crude oil sales, govt. relations, dir., 1952-55; dir. mines Dept. Mines and Natural Resources, Man., 1946-48; pres., dir. Dominion Oil, Ltd., Trinidad and Tobago, 1952-60; v.p. exploration, dir. Calif. Exploration Co. (Chevron Overseas Petroleum, Inc.), San Francisco, 1955-63; staff asst. land to v.p. exploration and land Standard Oil Co. of Calif., 1961-63; chmn. bd., mng. dir. West Australian Petroleum Pty., Ltd., Perth, 1963-70; v.p., dir. Newport Ventures, Ltd., Calgary, 1971-72; v.p. ops., dir., mem. exec. com. Brascan Resources, Ltd., Calgary, 1973-75, sr. v.p., dir., 1975-77, sr. cons., 1977-78; pres., chief exec. officer, dir. Western Mines Ltd., 1978-80, exec. v.p., gen. mgr. mining div. Westmin Resources Ltd., also dir., mem. exec. com., 1981-82; dir. Western Mines Inc., 1978-82; pres., acting gen. mgr. Coalition Mining, Ltd.; pres., chief operating officer, dir. Lathwell Resources Ltd., 1983-84; cons. petroleum and mining, 1982—; dir. Cretaceous Pipe Line Co., Ltd., Austen & Butta Pty., Ltd., Western Coal Holdings, Inc., Quest Explorations Ltd., San Antonio Resources Inc.; del. Interprovincial Mines Ministers Conf., several years; sec. Winnipeg Conf., 1947. Elected to Order of Can., 1982. Fellow Royal Soc. Can., Geol. Soc. Am., Geol. Soc. Can.; mem. Am. Assn. Petroleum Geologists, Engring. Inst. Can. (hon. life), Canadian Inst. Mining and Metallurgy (hon. life mem., past br. chmn., dist. councillor, v.p., chmn. petroleum div., Distinguished Service award 1974, Selwyn G. Blaylock gold medal 1979), Australian Petroleum Exploration Assn. (hon. life mem., chmn. com. West Australian petroleum legislation, councillor, state chmn. for Western Australia), Australian Am. Assn. in Western Australia (councillor), Australian Geol. Soc., Soc. Econ. Geologists, Assn. Profl. Engrs., Geologists and Geophysicists of Alta. (hon. life mem., Centennial award 1985), Coal Assn. of Can. (bd.dirs.). Clubs: Calgary Golf and Country, Calgary Petroleum, Ranchmen's. Author numerous govt. papers, reports, reference guides, also sci. articles to profl. jours. Home: 1315 Baldwin Crescent SW, Calgary, AB Canada T2V 2B7

FURR, COLEMAN, college president; b. Lincoln, Nebr., Feb. 22, 1925; s. Archie and Mattie (Houghton) F.; B.S., U. Nebr., 1950; Ed.D., U.S. Internat. U.; m. Lois Stewart, July, 1952; children—Jean Elizabeth, Lisa Martin, Kevin Clark, Colette Marie, Martina. Buyer, Archie Furr Co., Lincoln, 1946-51; dir. ops. S&W Foods, San Francisco, 1951-59; computer cons. Govt. of P.R., 1959-61; pres. Union Distbg. Co., San Diego, 1961-62; founder, pres. Coleman Coll., San Diego, 1963—. Served with AUS, 1943-46. Mem. Assn. Ind. Colls. and Schs. (chmn. accrediting commn. 1977), Inst. Certification Computer Profls. (founder, chmn. 1979-86), Data Processing Mgmt. Assn., Automation I Assn. Republican. Unitarian. Home: 6014 Sierra View Way San Diego CA 92120 Office: 7380 Parkway Dr La Mesa CA 92041

FURST, ARTHUR, toxicologist, educator; b. Mpls., Dec. 25, 1914; s. Samuel and Doris (Kolochinsky) F.; m. Florence Wolovitch, May 24, 1940; children: Carolyn, Adrianne, David Michael, Timothy Daniel. A.A., Los Angeles City Coll., 1935; A.B., UCLA, 1937, A.M., 1940; Ph.D., Stanford U., 1948; Sc.D., U. San Francisco, 1983. Mem. faculty, dept. chemistry San Francisco City Coll., 1940-47; asst. prof. chemistry U. San Francisco, 1947-49, asso. prof. chemistry, 1949-52; asso. prof. medicinal chemistry Stanford Sch. Medicine, 1952-57, prof., 1957-61; with U. Calif. War Tng., 1943-45, San Francisco State Coll., 1945; research assoc. Mt. Zion Hosp., 1952-82; clin. prof. pathology Columbia Coll. Physicians and Surgeons, 1969-70; dir. Inst. Chem. Biology; prof. chemistry U. San Francisco, 1961-80, prof. emeritus, 1980—, dean grad. div., 1976-79; Vis. fellow Battelle Seattle Research Center, 1974; Michael vis. prof. Weizmann Inst. Sci., Israel, 1982; cons. toxicology, 1980—; cons. on cancer WHO; mem. com., bd. mineral resources NRC. Contbr. over 225 articles to profl. and ednl. jours. Bd. trustees Pacific Grad. Sch. Psychology. recipient Klaus Schwartz Commemorative medal Internat. Toxological Congress, Tokyo, 1986. Fellow AAAS, N.Y. Acad. Scis.; mem. Am. Soc. Pharmacology and Exptl. Therapeutics, Am. Chem. Soc., Am. Assn. Cancer Research, Soc. Toxicology, Am. Coll. Toxicology (nat. sec., pres. 1985), Sigma Xi, Phi Lambda Upsilon. Research activities on organic synthesis, chemotherapy cancer, carcinogenesis of metals and hydrocarbons. Home: 3736 La Calle Ct Palo Alto CA 94306 Office: U San Francisco Inst Chem Biology San Francisco CA 94117-1080

FURTH, ALAN COWAN, transportation company executive, lawyer; b. Oakland, Calif., Sept. 16, 1922; s. Victor L. and Valance (Cowan) F.; m. Virginia Robinson, Aug. 18, 1946; children: Andrew Robinson, Alison Anne. A.B., U. Calif. at Berkeley, 1944, LL.B., 1949; grad., Advanced Mgmt. Program, Harvard U., 1959. Bar: Calif., U.S. Supreme Ct. With So. Pacific Co., San Franciso, 1950—, gen. counsel, from 1963, v.p., 1966, exec. v.p. law, 1976-79, pres., 1979—, also dir. and mem. exec. com.; chmn., dir. Fed. Res. Bank; dir. So. Pacific Land Co., Indsl. Indemnity Co., Ticor of San Francisco. Trustee Merritt Hosp., Oakland, Calif.; trustee Pacific Legal Found.; bd. dirs. U. Calif. at Berkeley Found. Served to capt. USMCR, 1944-46, 51-52. Mem. Am. Bar Assn., Calif. State Bar Assn. Clubs: Bohemian (San Francisco), Pacific-Union (San Francisco), San Francisco Golf (San Francisco); Met., Burning Tree (Washington). Office: So Pacific Co One Market Plaza Stewart St San Francisco CA 94105 *

FURU, KAREN LEE, nurse, counselor; b. Ft. Riley, Kans., May 3, 1950; d. Jack Alvin and Mabel Lee (Zirk) Stanturf; m. Robert Llaird Furu, June 30, 1971; children—Robert B., Sandra R. Student Idaho State U., 1968-70, U. Idaho, 1970; grad. Walter Reed Army Inst. Nursing, 1972; B.S.N., U. Md., 1972; M.Ed. in Counseling and Guidance, Mont. State U., 1981, postgrad., 1981-82. R.N., Idaho, 1972, Mont., 1973. Head nurse U.S. Army Res. 396th Sta. Hosp., Helena, Mont., 1973—; asst. dir. nursing Hillcrest Retirement Ctr., Bozeman, Mont., 1974-77; staff nurse, team leader/supr. Bozeman Deaconess Hosp., 1977-83; pub. health nurse Gallatin County, 1983-86; pvt. counselor, 1987—; tchr., cons. Mont. Law Enforcement Acad., Bozeman. Den leader Cub Scouts, Boy Scouts Am., 1981-83, cubmaster, 1983-84, troop leader Girl Scouts U.S.A. Served in U.S. Army, 1968-72, with Army Nurse Corps, 1972-73; to maj. USAR, 1973—. Decorated Army Commendation medal with oak leaf cluster. Mem. Am. Nurses Assn., Mont. Nurses Assn., Res. Officers Assn., Mil. Surgeons U.S., Am. Assn. Counseling and Devel., Mont. Personnel and Guidance Assn., Am. Mental Health Counselors Assn. (chpt. adv.), Alpha Omicron Pi (chpt. relations advisor; honored alumnus 1982). Democrat. Presbyterian. Clubs: United Presbyterian Women, Order Eastern Star.

FURUKAWA, DAVID HIROSHI, consulting chemical engineer; b. San Pedro, Calif., Mar. 26, 1938; s. James T. and Frances F. (Kamei) F.; BSChemE, U. Colo., 1960; m. Natchi Natsumi Matsunami, June 21, 1964; children: Douglas, Ross, Gregg, Derek, Ryan. Desalting sect. head Bur. Reclamation, Denver, 1960-69; mgr. research and devel. Havens Internat., San Diego, 1969-71; mgr. comml. devel. Calgon Corp., Pitts., 1971-73, UOP, Inc., San Diego, 1973-75; cons. Furukawa & Assos., Poway, Calif., 1975-78; prin. chem. engr. Boyle Engring. Corp., San Diego, 1978-81; dir. mktg. Resources Cons. Co., San Diego, 1981-83; v.p. western ops Filmtec Corp., San Diego, 1983—; cons. on reverse osmosis, ultrafiltration, desalination and water pollution control. Recipient Meritorious Service award U.S. Govt., 1968. Mem. Am. Inst. Chem. Engrs., Water Pollution Control Fedn., Internat. Desalination and Environ. Assn., Water Supply Improvement Assn. (dir.), Am. Water Works Assn., Am. Chem. Soc. Patentee in field. Home: 13511 Willow Run Rd Poway CA 92064 Office: 10919 Technology Pl San Diego CA 92127

FURUKAWA, SHIRO BRUCE, data processing administrator; b. Pasadena, Calif., June 7, 1953; s. Shiro and Matsuko (Miyamoto) F.; B.S. in Biol. Scis. (Edmondson fellow in pathology), U. So. Calif., 1975. Research technician U. So. Calif. Med. Center, Los Angeles, 1973-74, supervising research technician, 1975-76; research chemist Rancho Los Amigos Hosp., Downey, Calif., 1976-79, phlebotomist, 1979-80, asst. data systems analyst, 1980-81; computer programmer Hughes Aircraft Corp., Fullerton, Calif., 1981-83; data processing mgr. Irwin Industries Inc./Westinghouse, 1983-85; v.p. Flair Data Services, Inc., South El Monte, Calif, 1985—. Mem. Am. Mgmt. Assn., Inst. Cert. Fin. Planners, So. Calif. Data Point Users Group, Assn. MBA Execs., Pacific Slopes Biochem. Soc. Republican. Contbr. writings to profl. publs. in field. Home: 2004 Driftstone Dr Glendora CA 91740 Office: 1170 N Durfee Suite H South El Monte CA 91733

FURUMOTO, AUGUSTINE SADAMU, geophysics educator; b. Honolulu, Aug. 12, 1927; s. Kitaru and Shizuko (Okita) F.; m. Chieko Abe, Sept. 12, 1965; children: Anne, Gregory. EdB, U. Dayton, 1949; MS in Geophysics, U. Tokyo, 1955; PhD in Geophysics, St. Louis U., 1961. Tchr. St. Joseph High Sch., Hilo, Hawaii, 1949-51, St. Louis High Sch., Honolulu, 1951-53; asst. prof. U. Hawaii, Honolulu, 1961-67, assoc. prof., 1968-72, prof. geophysics, 1972—; cons. in field, Honolulu, 1965—. Editor: Utilization of Volcano Energy, 1974; contbr. articles to profl. jours. Chmn. Hawaii Kai Neighborhood Bd., Honolulu, 1978; pres. Hawaii Kai Homeowners Ltd., Honolulu, 1978-80, 82—. Fulbright scholar U.S. Dept. State, 1953-55; NSF fellow, 1958-61. Mem. Am. Geophys. Union, Seismol. Soc. Am., Seismol. Soc. Japan, Volcanol. Soc. Japan, St. Louis Alumni Assn., Sigma Xi. Democrat. Roman Catholic. Avocations: golf, carpentry, computer programming. Home: 349 Kekupua St Honolulu HI 96822 Office: U Hawaii Inst Geophysics 2525 Correa Rd Honolulu HI 96822

FURUTO, SHARLENE BERNICE CHOY LIN, social work educator; b. Honolulu, Sept. 29, 1947; d. Harry Tadao and Bernice Lan (Young) Maeda; m. David Masaru Furuto, Apr. 1, 1977; children: Linda, Matthew, Michael, Daniel. BS, Brigham Young U., 1969, EdD, 1981; MSW, U. Hawaii, 1972. Social worker I Hawaii Dept. Social Services, Honolulu, 1969; sch. social worker Hawaii Dept. Edn., Honolulu, 1972-73; coordinator services ctr. Progressive Neighborhood Program, Maile, Hawaii, 1973-74; coordinator social work program Hawaii campus Brigham Young U., Laie, 1975—; cons. Rodriguez Agrl. Vocat. Sch., Philippines, 1986—. V.p. Laie PTA, 1985—; chmn. Koolauloa (Hawaii) Community Council, 1986—. Mem. Nat. Assn. Social Workers (cert., v.p., chmn. program com. 1977—), Am. Asian Social Work Educators (sec.-treas. 1986—), Am. Bus. Women's Assn. (v.p. 1980-82), Council Social Work Edn. Democrat. Mormon. Avocations: reading, baking. Home: PO Box 84 Laie HI 96762 Office: Brigham Young U Hawaii Campus Laie HI 96762

FUSCALDO, ANTONIO FRANK, educational administrator; b. Greenwich, Conn., Feb. 8, 1919; s. Joseph Mario and Anna Maria (Columbo) F.; m. Marie V. Green, Nov. 5, 1982. B.B.A., Pace Coll., 1948; M.A., U. Ariz., 1965, M.Ed., 1970; postgrad. Ariz. State U., 1965-68, Cochise Coll., 1965-67, U. Nev., 1974, Phoenix Coll., 1981, N.Y.C. Fashion Mdse. Workshop, 1981. Practice acctg., Cos Cob, Conn., 1948-58; comptroller Superior Elec. Industries, Hollywood, Fla., 1958-59; asst. sales mgr. PESCO, Ft. Lauderdale, Fla., 1959-62, v.p., 1962-63; tchr. adult edn., distributive edn. tchr.-coordinator pub. schs., Douglas, Ariz., 1965-67; distributive edn. tchr. coordinator Pueblo High Sch., Tucson, 1967-83; pvt. practice acctg, tax, mktg. cons., Tucson, 1983—; leader Tony Francis Orchestras, Tucson, 1983—. Mem. Tucson Distributive Edn. Adv. Com. Served with USAAF, 1942-45. Recipient Ariz Kidney Found. award Pima County Chpt., 1972; Distributive Edn. Dir. award Ariz. Dept. Edn., 1972; cert. of appreciation Future Bus. Leaders Am., 1983; Service award Ariz. Dept. Edn., 1983; Outstanding Service award Tucson Mktg./Distributive Educators, 1983; others. Mem. Ariz. Assn. Distributive Edn. Tchrs. (pres. 1972-73), Nat. Assn. Distributive Edn. Tchrs. (chmn. com. pub. relations 1970-71), Tucson Distributive Edn. Tchr-Coordinators Assn., Tucson Bus. Edn. Assn., Ariz. Bus. Edn. Assn., Nat. Bus. Edn. Assn., Tucson Musicians Assn. (v.p., sec.-treas. 1986—), Douglas Bus. Edn. Assn., Distributive Edn. Clubs Am. (dir. chpt.), Council Distributive Tchr. Educators Assn., Am. Vocat. Assn., Ariz. State Vocat. Assn. (dir. 1970-72), Nat. Soc. Pub. Accts., Am. Legion, VFW, Am. Fedn. Musicians (life), Beta Alpha Psi. Clubs: Elks, Lions, Eagles/Moose, Ariz. Diamond, Ariz./Nat. DECA. Contbr. articles to profl. jour. Home: 2510 W Calle Tonala Tucson AZ 85745-2507 Office: 3500 S 12th Ave Tucson AZ 85713

FUSCO, STEVEN MICHAEL, environmental executive, consultant; b. Tacoma; s. Steven George and Marie B. (Willey) F.; m. Barbara Call, June 12, 1976; children: Stephanie, Scott. BA, Wash. State U., 1971; M in Urban Planning, U. Wash., 1973. Planner City of Seattle, 1972-73, Lee Johnson and Assocs., Everett, Wash., 1973-74; environ. studies mgr. URS Co., Seattle, 1974-84, Santa Barbara, Calif., 1984—; cons. in architecture, Seattle, 1972-84. Served to capt. USAF, 1972-80. Mem. Acacia. Republican. Mem. Unity Ch. Avocations: swimming, bicycling, building construction. Home: 3739 Lincolnwood Dr Santa Barbara CA 93110 Office: URS Co 111 W Micheltorena Santa Barbara CA 93101

FUSSELL, ROBERT ALLEN, publishing company executive, marketing director; b. Port Angeles, Wash., Aug. 17, 1946; s. John and Sylvia Hazel (Asphors) F.; m. Janet Lynn Sorick, June 11, 1966; children: Robin Lynn, Kelly Rex. BS in Edn., Eastern Oreg. State Coll., 1968; MS in Edn., Western Oreg. State Coll., 1973. Edn tch., adminstr. Pendleton (Oreg.) Schs., 1968-70; edn. exec. Umetilla (Oreg.) County Schs., 1971-73, Oreg. State Edn. Dept., Salem, 1974-77; proprietor Rob Fussell and Assocs., Salem, 1977-80; pub. Bus. Success mag., Portland, Oreg., 1980-81, Oreg. Bus. mag., Portland, 1981-82; v.p. mktg. MEDIAmerica (formerly Oreg. Bus. mag.), Portland, 1982—, also bd. dirs., 1980—. Mem. communications com. Columbia Willamette YMCA, Portland, 1985-86; mem. pub. relations com. Oreg. Ctr. Credit Union., Portland, 1985-86. Served to sgt. USNG, 1972-78. Mem. Associated Oreg. Industries, Portland Advt. Fedn., Greater Portland Vis. and Conv. Bur. Republican. Avocation: outdoor activities. Office: Oreg Bus Mag 208 SW Stark St Portland OR 97204

GAARDER, THOMAS DWIGHT, cardiologist; b. Leon, Iowa, Mar. 24, 1938; s. Olaf Gustavsen and Ruth (Ellen) G.; m. Ann Austin Kidder, Dec. 6, 1966; children: Kirsten Lee, Kelly Lynn. AA, Graceland Coll., 1958; BA, U. Iowa, 1960, MD, 1965. Diplomate Am. Bd. Internal Medicine, Am. Bd. Cardiovascular Diseases. Resident U. So. Calif. Sch. Medicine, Los Angeles, 1965-69, fellow in cardiology, 1971-74, asst. prof. medicine, 1974-86, clin. assoc. prof., 1986—; practice medicine specializing in cardiology Whittier, Calif., 1981—; acting chief sec. cardiology Rancho Los Amigos USC Med. Ctr., Downey, Calif., 1986—. Served to capt. USAF, 1969-71. Fellow Am. Coll. Cardiology. Home: 1124 Glenview Dr Fullerton CA 92635 Office: 12433 E Lambert Rd Suite A Whittier CA 90606

GABBITA, KASI VISWANATH, agricultural researcher, consultant; b. Machilipatnam, India, July 26, 1943; came to U.S., 1980; s. Soma Sundaram and Vara (Lakshmi) G.; m. Geetha Viswanath, June 22, 1972; children—Soma Kiran, Siva Ranjani. B.S. in Botany, Zoology and Chemistry, Andhra U., Waltair, India, 1961; M.S. in Soil Sci. and Agrl. Chemistry, Indian Agrl. Research Inst., New Delhi, 1963; Ph.D., Indian Inst. Sci., Bangalore, 1972. Sr. research asst. Indian Inst. Sci., Bangalore, 1970-78; tech dir. CIERS Research & Consultancy Pvt. Ltd., Bangalore, 1978-80; project assoc. U. Wis.-Milw., 1980-81; asst. research engr. Nat. Ctr. Intermedia Transport Research, UCLA, 1981—; cons. in field. Recipient award Bangalore Water Supply and Sewerage Bd., 1975, Ramineni Ranga Rao Transport Contractors, 1976, AMCO Batteries, 1977; Indian Ministry Food and Agr. merit scholar, 1962-63; Council Sci. and Indsl. Research grantee, 1963-65; Indian Dept. Atomic Energy grantee, 1965-68. Mem. Am. Soc. Agronomy, Internat. Assn. Humic Substances. Contbr. articles to profl. jours.; mem. editorial adv. bd. Internat. Jour. Environ. Monitoring and Assessment, Toxicological and Environ. Chemistry. Home: 1610 Preuss Rd Apt 6 Los Angeles CA 90035 Office: UCLA 2066 Engring I Los Angeles CA 90024

GABE, DEBORAH ANN LARKINS, audiologist; b. Honolulu, July 21, 1950; d. Gerald Gregory and Elaine Tomiko (Tachibana) L.; m. Matthew John Gabe, Aug. 7, 1983; 1 child, Stephanie Tomiko Larkins. BA in Speech Pathology and Audiology, Case Western Res. U., 1972, MA in Audiology, 1973. Audiologist Kaiser Health Found., Cleve., 1973-75, Cleve. Clinic, 1975-78; audiologist Kapiolani Women's and Children's Med. Ctr., Honolulu, 1980—, coordinator Ho'opa Ola project, 1984—. Mem. Am. Speech Lang. Hearing Assn. (cert. clin. competence), Hawaii Speech Lang. Hearing Assn. (dir. at large 1983-84), Am. Soc. Deaf Children, Alexander Graham Bell Assn. for Deaf. Home: 180-3 Noke St Kailua HI 96734 Office: Kapiolani Womens and Childrens Med Ctr 1319 Punahou St Honolulu HI 96826

GABERSON, HOWARD AXEL, mechanical engineer; b. Detroit, Apr. 11, 1931; s. Axel Rudolph and Lillian (Quatherine) G.; B.S.M.E., U. Mich., 1955; M.S., MIT, 1957, Ph.D., 1967; m. Dale Virginia Maitland, Apr. 27, 1969. Stress analysis engr. Raytheon Co., Wayland, Mass., 1957-59; asst. prof. mech. engring. Lowell (mass.) Tech. Inst., 1959-60; asst. prof. Boston U., 1960-64; asso. prof. mech. engring. U. Hawaii, 1967-68; shock and vibration research mech. engr. Naval Civil Engring. Lab., Port Hueneme, Calif., 1968-82; div. dir. mech. systems div., 1982—. NSF fellow, 1964; Wilfred Lewis fellow, 1966. Mem. Am. Acad. Mechanics, ASME (chpt. pres. 1973, 80, region IX operating bd., nat. mem. interests com. 1985—), Soc. Exptl. Mechanics, Soc. Automotive Engrs. (G-5 shock and vibration com.), NSPE, Inst. Noise Control Engrs., U. Mich. Alumni Assn., MIT Alumni Assn., UCLA Alumni Assn., Rare Bird Preservation Soc. (pres. 1980-81), West Valley Bird Soc., Ventura County Bird Soc., Am. Fedn. Aviculture, Aviculture Soc. Am., Bromeliad Soc., Alpha Sigma Phi, Sigma Xi, Tau Beta Pi, Pi Tau Sigma. Patentee in field. Home: 234 Corsicana Dr Oxnard CA 93030 Office: US Naval Civil Engring Lab Port Hueneme CA 93043

GABLE, JAMES G., electrical engineering executive, consultant; b. Phila., Mar. 26, 1918; s. James F. and Stella (Gingrich) G.; m. Ruth Ann Goetz, Oct. 14, 1940; (dec. 1977); children—Suzanne R. Tognazzini, Mary C. Price, James E. BSEE, Carnegie-Mellon U., 1940. Registered profl. engr., Calif. Design engring. mgr. Westinghouse Electric Corp., Buffalo, 1951-54, div. gen. mgr., 1954-62; mgr. orgn. devel. Lockhead Missiles & Space Co., Sunnyvale, Calif., 1962-70; pvt. cons., 1970-74; v.p. Micro Power Systems, Inc., Santa Clara, Calif., 1974-85, ret., 1985. Patentee 4 control systems. Chmn. Town Long Range Fiscal Planning Commn.; engr. mem. Town Drainage Com., Los Altos Hills, Calif. Served to 1st lt. U.S. Army, 1943-45, ETO. Mem. Nat. Soc. Profl. Engrs., Calif. Soc. Profl. Engrs. Lodges: Masons (32 degree), KT (past cmdr.), Shriners, Jesters. Home: 7251 Via Mimosa San Jose CA 95135

GABRIEL, HOWARD WAYNE, III, publishing executive, health administrator; b. Berkeley, Calif., Dec. 28, 1946; s. Howard Wayne Jr. and Lorraine Celia (Novak) G.; m. Mona Beth Prather; children: Anna, Howard IV. BA, Eastern Wash. U., 1969; MA, No. Mich. U., 1970; PhD, U. Utah, 1972. Instr. No. Mich. U., Marquette, 1969-70; research assoc. U. Utah Med. Ctr., Salt Lake City, 1970-72; assoc. dir. S. Cen. Kans. Health Council, Wichita, 1973-75; mgmt. cons. Gabriel Assocs., Sacramento, Calif., 1975-76; exec. dir. Southeast Alaska Health Systems, Ketchikan, 1976-82; propr. M&H Enterprises, Sacramento, 1982—; preceptor U. Okla. Sch. Pub. Health, Norman, 1973-74. Author: Growing Up With Character, 1986, Loving Memories From Dog to Dog, 1987, Adventures with Shivers the Hamster, 1987, Natural Procreation Alternatives for Men with Low Sperm Counts--A Guide for Laypersons Under Medical Supervision and Consultation, 1987, Hypothermic Vectors as Etiological Factors in Oligospermia, 1972. Counselor Rancho San Antonia Boys Town, Chatsworth, Calif., 1966; chmn. Ketchikan(Alaska) Health Council, 1982, Valley Park Sch. Parent Bd., Ketchika, 1982; bd. trainer United Way, Sacramento, Calif., 1985. Mem. AAAS, Internat. Soc. Edn. Health Scis. (charter), Northwest Health Assn. (pres. 1980-82), Am. Rural Health Assn. (mem. exec. adv. bd. mem. 1978-82), Am. Pub. Health Assn., Nat. Rural Health Assn., Calif. Public Health Assn., The Nat. Writers Club. Avocations: sports, jogging, music, reading. Office: M&H Enterprises PO Box 26374 Sacramento CA 95826

GABRIELE, SHERRY LEE SOSKIN, accountant; b. Cleve., Jan. 1, 1943; d. Zelman and Molly (Miller) Soskin; B.S., UCLA, 1964; M.Bus. Taxation, U. So. Calif., 1976. Acct. various firms, Calif., 1960-69; acct. Wolf and Co., Los Angeles, 1969-75, mgr., 1969-73, partner in charge tax dept., 1973-75; pvt. practice acctg. specializing in tax planning and compliance, Los Angeles, 1975—; substitute instr. acctg. UCLA, 1965-66. C.P.A., Calif. Mem. Am. Inst. C.P.A.s, Calif. Soc. C.P.A.s, Am. Women's Soc. C.P.A.s, Calif. Scholarship Soc. (seal bearer life mem.). Contbr. articles to profl. publs. Office: 5567 Reseda Blvd Suite 218 Tarzana CA 91356

GABRIELLI, DOROTHY DONOHUE, language arts educator; b. Newark; d. Morton P. and Regina (Muller) Donohue; m. Ralph B. Gabrielli, Sept. 5, 1964; children: Ralph Martin, Jennifer Kathryn. BS, SUNY, New Paltz, 1956, MS, 1969. Art tchr. Averill Park (N.Y.) Jr. High Sch., 1966-68, Tully (N.Y.) Cen. Sch., 1968-72, Elizabethtown (N.Y.) Lewis Cen. Sch., 1972-82; lang. arts, arts and crafts tchr. Nome (Alaska) Pub. Schs., 1982—; tchr., leader Alaska State Writing Consortium Summer Inst., 1985, 86; instr. art Northwest Community Coll., Nome, 1983-86. Artist: (painting) Proud Diomede Carver, 1986 (2d pl. award Kevatorak moses regional art show); presenter poetry workshop Alaska State Reading Conf., 1984. Mem. Alaska State Writing Consortium (bd. dirs. 1984-86), Alaska Council Tchrs. of English, (regional rep. 1984-86), Alaska Arts in Edn. Avocations: aerobics, camping, canoeing, travel. Home: Box 1024 Nome AK 99762

GABRINI, PHILIPPE JEAN, academic administrator; b. Albi, France, Dec. 21, 1940; came to U.S., 1984; s. André and Simone (Roger) G.; m. Anne-Marie Elisabeth Lanniel, May 1, 1967; children: Karine, Céline, Audrey. Ingénieur, Ensam, Paris, 1964; MS, U. Pa., 1966; Docteur Ingénieur, U. Grenoble, France, 1970. Assoc. prof. U. Quebec, Montreal, Can., 1971-80, program dir., 1976-79, prof. computer sci., 1980-84, dept. dir., 1982-84; head dept. computer sci. N.Mex. State U., Las Cruces, 1984—; cons. Multitek, Montreal, 1979-84; dir. CRIM, Montreal, 1983-84. Author: Structures D'Information, 1982, Informatique De Gestion, 1982, Problem Solving with Modula-Q, 1986; contbr. articles to profl. jours. Grantee Fulbright Found., 1964-67, Can. Internat. Devel. Agy., 1982-84. Mem. Assn. Computing Machinery. Presbyterian. Avocations: long distance running. Home: 2940 Huntington Dr Las Cruces NM 88001 Office: NMex State U Dept Computer Sci Box 3CU Las Cruces NM 88003

GAC, FRANK DAVID, materials engineer; b. Granite City, Ill., Mar. 26, 1951; s. Frank John and Betty Marie (Kasprovich) G.; m. Christina Lynn McMullen, Aug. 12, 1973; children: Jessie Lynn, Benjamin Thomas. BS in Ceramic Engring., U. Ill., 1973; MS in Ceramic Engring., U. Mo., Rolla, 1975; postgrad., U. N.Mex., 1982-83, U. Wash. Registered profl. engr., N.Mex. Mem. staff Los Alamos (N.Mex) Nat. Lab., 1975-78, sect. leader, 1980-83, staff mem., 1983-84, advanced study candidate, 1984-85, project leader, 1986—; research engr. U. Wash., Seattle, 1979-80; mem. steering com. Advanced Composites Working Group, Cocoa Beach, Fla., 1981—. Contbr. articles to profl. jours. Father helper Aspen Elem. Sch., Los Alamos, 1983-84; Sunday sch. supt. Trinity Bible Ch., Los Alamos, 1986, elder, 1987—; deacon, youth leader Sangre de Cristo Covenant Ch., Los Alamos, 1975-79; scoutmaster Boy Scouts Am., Granite City, 1967-69. Fellow A.P. Green Refractories Co., 1973-74; named Knight of St. Pat 100 Club, U. Ill., Champaign, 1973, one of Outstanding Young Men Am., 1986. Mem. Am. Ceramic Soc. (div. chmn. 1985-86, Cert. 1986), Nat. Inst. Ceramic Engrs. (coordinator 1979-80), Gideons Internat. (pres. 1976), Young Life (leader 1975-79). Democrat. Home: 901 Tewa Loop Los Alamos NM 87544 Office: Los Alamos Nat Lab MST 6 MS G770 Los Alamos NM 87545

GACHUPIN, ROSALIND, speech pathologist; b. Albuquerque, Sept. 29, 1954; d. Gregorio and Marie (Fragua) G. BS, N.Mex. State U., 1979; MS, U. Ariz., 1983. Cert. speech-lang. pathologist. Speech-lang. pathologist Tuba City (Ariz.) Pub. Health Service Hosp., 1980, Southwest Speech and Hearing Clinic, Albuquerque, summer 1981, Pueblo Infant Parent Edn. Project & Five Sandoval Headstart Project, Bernalillo, N.Mex., 1982-83, Bur. Indian Affairs-Eastern Navajo Agy. and So. Pueblos Agy., Albuquerque, 1984-86, BIA-Eastern Navajo Agy., Crownpoint, N.Mex., 1984—. Mem. Am. Speech Lang. Hearing Assn. Avocations: reading, softball, camping. Home: PO Box 185 San Ysidro NM 87053

GADBOIS, RICHARD A., JR., judge; b. Omaha, June 18, 1932; s. Richard Alphonse Gadbois and Margaret Ann (Donahue) Bartlett; m. Jeanne E. Roach, Dec. 15, 1956; children: Richard, Gregory, Guy, Geoffrey, Thomas. A.B., St. John's Coll., Camarillo, Calif., 1955; J.D., Loyola U., Los Angeles, 1958; postgrad. in law, U. So. Calif., 1958-60. Bar: Calif. 1959, U.S. Dist. Ct. (cen. dist.) Calif. 1959, U.S. Supreme Ct. 1966. Ptnr. Musick, Peeler & Garrett, Los Angeles, 1962-68; v.p. Denny's Inc., La Mirada, Calif., 1968-71; judge Mcpl. Ct., Los Angeles, 1971-72, Superior Ct., Los Angeles, 1972-82, U.S. Dist. Ct. (cen. dist.) Calif., Los Angeles, 1982—. Decorated knight Order of Holy Sepulchre (Pope John Paul II). Mem. ABA, Los Angeles County Bar Assn. (trustee 1966-67), State Bar Calif. (profl. ethics com. 1965-70). Republican. Roman Catholic. Home: 2155 El Molino Ave San Marino CA 91108 Office: US Dist Ct 176 US Courthouse 312 N Spring St Los Angeles CA 90012

GADDY, MICHAEL ROGERS, psychiatric technician; b. Los Angeles, July 17, 1945; s. Buddy Rogers Gaddy and Mary Belle (Gaines) Aminoff; divorced; children: Ginger Marie, Kristina Michele. Lic. psychiat. technician, Calif. Program psychiat. technician Development Service, Pomona, Calif., 1969-70, research psychiat. technician, 1970-75, program supr., 1975-80; health program evaluator State Dept. Health, Fresno, Calif., 1980-84; cert. specialist State Dept. Health, Sacramento, 1984—; cons. Friends of Handicapped Children, San Diego, 1975-76. Served with USAF, 1962-66. Mem. Calif. Assn. Human Services Technologists (2d v.p. 1978—, regional dir. 1970-78, Outstanding Individual in the Human Services 1975), Calif. State Employees Assn., Iris Soc., BMW Am. Republican. Avocations: scuba diving, Koi skiing, stunt kiting. Office: Dept Health Services Provider Cert Unit 2422 Arden Way B-35 Sacramento CA 95825

GAEDEKE, RALPH MORTIMER, business administration educator; b. Nadrau, Germany, May, 25, 1941, came to U.S. 1953. s. Horst Friederich and Margot Hanna (Boltz) G.; m. Johanna Vivian House, June 19, 1965; children—Jolene R., Michael C. B.A., U. Washington, 1964, M.A., 1965, Ph.D., 1969. Instr. U. Sask. (Can.), 1965-66, U. Wash., 1967-69; assoc. prof. Calif. State U. Sacramento, 1969-71, U. Alaska, Anchorage, 1971-73; prof. bus. adminstrn. Calif. State U.-Sacramento, 1974—; also cons. Scholar study tour grantee W.Ger., 1977. Mem. Am. Mktg. Assn. (pres. Sacramento chpt. 1974-75), Acad. Internat. Bus., Delta Sigma Pi. Author: Marketing: Principles and Applications, 1983; co-author: Marketing Management: Cases and Readings, Small Business Management; Small Business Management: Operations & Profiles; Marketing in Private and Public Non-Profit Organizations, Cases and Classics In Marketing Management 1986; Consumerism. Home: 237 Hartnell Pl Sacramento CA 95825 Office: Calif State U-Sacramento Coll Bus Adminstrn 6000 J St Sacramento CA 95819

GAER, ERIC W., computer industry executive; b. Bklyn., June 21, 1948; s. Joseph and Rena (Weiss) G.; m. Tamara Hess, Sept. 21, 1975; 1 child, Christopher. BA, Calif. State U., Northridge, 1970. Pres. Gaer & Assoc., Inc., Westlake Village, Calif., 1974-78; pub. Songwriter Mag., Hollywood, Calif., 1978-80; assoc. pub. Reese Pub., N.Y.C., 1980-81; dir. mktg. Softsel Computer Products, Ingelwood, Calif., 1981-82; v.p., gen. mgr. The Barth Group, Encino, Calif., 1982-84; pres. Venture Software, Encino, Calif., 1984—; guest lectr. Loyola Mgmt. U., Los Angeles, 1984. Contbr. articles to profl. jours. Active Woodland Hills Sunrise Little League. Served to pfc. U.S. Army, 1970-73. Mem. Am. Mktg. Assn., Sofware Pubs. Orgn., Utah State C. of C. Jewish. Avocations: outdoor sports, writing. Home: 21040 Ave San Luis Woodland Hills CA 91364 Office: Venture Sofware 16200 Ventura Blvd Encino CA 91436

GAFFNEY, JEFFREY STEVEN, chemistry researcher; b. San Bernardino, Calif., July 28, 1949; s. Jack Paul and Jeanette Theodosia (Heistand) G.; m. Linda Marie Myers, Mar. 27, 1971; children: Colleen Marie, Juliet Hope, Ryan Michael. BS in Chemistry, U. Calif., Riverside, 1971, MS in Chemistry, 1973, PhD in Chemistry, 1975. Research assoc. Brookhaven Nat. Lab., Upton, N.Y., 1975-77, assoc. chemist, 1977-80, chemist, 1980-85; staff mem. INC-7 Los Alamos (N.Mex.) Nat. Lab., 1985—. Contbr. articles to profl. jours. Sci. advisor Boces Summer Program for the Gifted and Talented, Brookhaven Nat. Labs., 1979-85; troop leader Girl Scout Am., Sound Beach, N.Y. 1981-84; program chmn. Parent-Tchr. Orgn., Miller Place, N.Y., 1984-85. Mem. Am. Chem. Soc., Am. Assn. Aerosol for Research. Democrat. Roman Catholic. Avocations: basketball, softball. Home: 195 El Rayo Los Alamos NM 87544 Office: Los Alamos Nat Lab Group INC-7 MS-J514 Los Alamos NM 87545

GAGLIANO, VINCENT, diversified consumer products manufacturing company executive; b. Chgo., Jan. 17, 1931; s. Salvatore and Phyllis Rose (Monaco) G.; m. Janet Rose Terrafino, Sept. 25, 1954; children: Phyllis Marie, Madeline Rose. Student, U. Ill., Chgo., 1948-49, Wright Jr. Coll., 1950-51; BS in Indsl. Engring., Indls. Engring. Coll., Chgo., 1956. Indsl. engr. U.S. Steel Corp. (now called USX Corp.), Chgo., 1954-56, Motorola Corp., Chgo., 1956-58; dir. procurement Webcor Dormeyer Corp., Chgo., 1958-62; div. v.p. Thomas Div. Whirlpool, Sepulveda, Calif., 1962-81; v.p. ops. Forecast Lighting Co., Inglewood, Calif., 1981-82; group v.p. Kidde Consumer Durables Corp., Compton, Calif., 1982-85; pres. Yigon Lighting Co. subs. Kidde. Chmn. Elk Grove (Ill.) Cancer Soc., 1970; pres. Jaycees, Elk Grove, 1959-60. Lifetime bd. mem. (hon.) Elk Grove Boys Baseball, 1968. Republican. Roman Catholic. Club: Porter Valley Country. Avocation: golf. Home: 9403 Vanalden Ave Northridge CA 91324 Office: Kidde Consumer Durables Corp 201 W Carob St Compton CA 90220

GAHRE, TERI LEA, speech pathologist; b. Upland, Calif.. BA, Calif. State U., Fullerton, 1980; MS in Communicative Disorders with honors, U. La Verne, 1983. Speech-lang.-hearing specialist Ontario (Calif.) Montclair Schs., 1981-84, Fontana (Calif.) Unified Schs., summer 1983; speech pathologist Almansor Edn. Ctr., Alhambra, Calif., summer 1984, Kaiser Permanente Med. Ctr., Anaheim, Calif., 1984—; clin. fellowship supr. Ontario Montclair Schs., 1983-84, Almansor Edn. Ctr., Alhambra, summer 1984, Kaiser Permanente Med. Ctr., 1984—. Sec. Rialto (Calif.) Christian PreSch. bd. dirs., 1984—; mem. ch. council-Luth. Ch. of the Cross, Rialto, 1984—. Mem. Am. Speech Lang. Hearing Assn. (cert. clin. competence), Calif. Speech and Hearing Assn. Avocations: crafts, needlework, jazz exercise. Home: 17576 Vine Fontana CA 92335 Office: Kaiser Permanente Med Ctr 411 N Lakeview Anaheim CA 92807

GAILER, ROBERT JOHN, computing consultant, electrical engineer; b. N.Y.C., Aug. 1, 1940; s. John and Katherine (Priwitzer) G.; m. Virginia Lee Rumsey, June 3, 1963 (div. Sept. 1980). BSEE, Rensselaer Poly. Inst., 1962; MDiv, Asbury Theol. Sem., 1967. Software engr. Kuhlman Electric Co., Versailles, Ken., 1969-70; software, hardware engr. various cos., Boulder, Colo., 1970-72; telecommunication engr. Boeing Computer Service, Seattle, 1974-75, software engr., 1975-78, sr. instr., 1978-84; cons. Seattle, 1984—; chmn. spl. interest group in A Programming Lang. Conf., Seattle, 1985. Recipient Spl. Achievement award Boeing Computer Services, Seattle, 1984. Mem. Assn. Computing Machinery (Recognition of Service award 1985). Mem. Unity Ch. of Truth. Avocation: African marimba. Home: 2416 E Madison St Suite C Seattle WA 98112-5437

GAILLARD, MARY KATHARINE, physics educator; b. New Brunswick, N.J., Apr. 1, 1939; d. Philip Lee and Marion Catharine (Wiedemayer) Ralph; children: Alain, Dominique, Bruno. BA, Hollins (Va.) Coll., 1960; MA, Columbia U., 1961; Doctorat du 3eme cycle, U. Paris, Orsay, France, 1964, Doct-es-Sciences d'Etat, 1968. With Centre National de Recherche Scientifique, Orsay and Annecy-le-Vieux, France, 1964-84; maitre de recherches Centre National de Recherche Scientifique, Orsay, 1973-80; maitre de recherches Centre National de Recherche Scientifique, Annecy-le-Vieux, 1979-80, dir. research, 1980-84; prof. physics U. Calif., Berkeley, 1981—; Morris Loeb lectr. Harvard U., Cambridge, Mass., 1980; Chancellor's Disting. lectr., U. Calif., Berkeley, 1981; Warner-Lambert lectr. U. Mich., Ann Arbor, 1984; cons., mem. adv. panels U.S. Dept. Energy, Washington, and various nat. labs. Editor: Gauge Theories in High Energy Physics, 1983; contbr. numerous articles to profl jours. Recipient Thibaux prize U. Lyons (France) Acad. Art & Sci., 1977. Fellow Am. Phys. Soc. (mem. various coms.); mem. Assn. Women in Sci., AAAS. Office: U Calif Dept Physics Berkeley CA 94720

GAINES, HAYDON DECATUR, data processing executive; b. Moline, Ill., Jan. 19, 1943; s. Jay Haydon and Betty Louise (McDannell) G.; m. Suzanne Taylor Lee, Oct. 13, 1979 (div. Aug. 1983); m. Kendra Jeanne Roby, Feb. 11, 1984; stepchildren: Jeffery Hagedorn, Jennifer Hagedorn. BS, U. Ariz., 1965, postgrad., 1967-68. Programmer Wallgreen's Inc., Chgo., 1965-67; sr. programmer So. Ariz. Bank, Tucson, 1967-69; systems div. mgr. Computer Scis. Corp., San Francisco, 1970-76; dir. program devel. Electronic Data Systems, San Diego, 1978-81; systems devel. mgr. San Diego City Schs., 1981-83; data adminstrn. mgr. Equitable Life Leasing, San Diego, 1983-86; pres. The Delphi Group, San Diego, 1986—; cons. A.G. Aguilar, Mexico city, 1977-78, Coast Community Coll., Costa Mesa, Calif., 1985-86; chmn. IDEAL CADRE User Group, Princeton, N.J., 1985-86. Contbr. articles to profl. jours. Mem. Zoolog. Soc. San Diego, LaJolla Mus. Contemporary Art, San Diego Hall of Sci., 1986. Recipient SPOKE award Tucson Jaycees, 1968. Mem. Data Processing Mgmt. Assn., Soc. Info. Mgmt. REpublican. Methodist. Club: Berkeley (Calif.) Yacht. Avocations: sailing, golf, skiing. Home: 12760 Larchmont St Poway CA 92064 Office: The Delphi Group 17155 W Bernardo Dr Suite 102 San Diego CA 92127

GAITHER, GANT, artist, sculptor, designer, producer; b. Hopkinsville, Ky., Aug. 1, 1917; s. Joseph Gant and Jane Eskridge (Lum) G. Student U. Mex., Mexico City, 1933-34; B.A., U. of South, 1938; postgrad. Yale Sch. Architecture, 1938-39. Owner, producer Miami Beach Playhouse, Fla., 1940-43; producer Broadway Theater, N.Y.C., 1947-56; exec. producer Paramount Pictures Corp., Hollywood, Calif., 1960-64; artist-designer, licensor Shedrain Umbrella Co., Portland, Oreg., 1977—, Lilli Ann Corp. Ladieswear, San Francisco, 1986—, Berggren-Trayner Porcelains, Libertyville, Ill., 1981—, Artex-Green Corp., Bklyn., 1976—, Schreter Mens Neckwear, Balt., 1977—, Art Guild Greeting Cards, Glendale, Calif., 1980—. Artist-sculptor The Zoophisticates Collection, New York, Paris, Chgo., Mexico City, other locations. Author: Princess of Monaco, 1957. Author/illustrator: Sally Seal, 1964. Trustee Princess Grace Found.; bd. dirs. Baar & Beades Inc. Scarves, N.Y.C., Jewelmark Originals Ltd., N.Y.C. Served as sgt. USAF, 1943-46, PTO. Decorated Bronze Star; recipient Bronze Sculpture award Loews Monte-Carlo Hotel, Monaco, 1984. Republican. Episcopalian. Club: Yale (N.Y.C.). Home and Studio: The Zoophisticates Collection 1411 Buena Vista Dr Palm Springs CA 92262

GAJDORUS, CARL, 2ND, architect; b. Endicott, N.Y., May 17, 1952; s. Carl and Katherine (Constantinou) G.; B.Arch., U. Ariz., 1976. Registered architect, Ariz. Programmer Studio 3, Ltd., Tucson, 1977-78; project architect R.M. Reif Assocs., Tucson, 1978-82, 83—; job capt. CNWC Architects, Tucson, 1983; mem. adv. com. City of Tucson Floodplain, 1981-82. Pres. So. Ariz. Environ. Council, Tucson, 1981. Mem. AIA (exec. com. Ariz. Soc. 1985-86). Home: 4467 E Dianthus Pl Tucson AZ 85712 Office: RM Reif Assocs Architects 1636 N Swan Rd Suite 200 Tucson AZ 85712

GALANE, MORTON ROBERT, lawyer; b. N.Y.C., Mar. 15, 1926; s. Harry J. and Sylvia (Schenkelbach) G.; m. Rosalind Feldman, Dec. 22, 1957; children: Suzanne Galane Duvall, Jonathan A. B.E.E., CCNY, 1946; LL.B., George Washington U., 1950. Bar: D.C. 1950, Nev. 1955, Calif. 1975. Patent examiner U.S. Patent Office, Washington, 1948-50; spl. partner firm Roberts & McInnis, Washington, 1950-54; practice as Morton R. Galane, P.C., Las Vegas, Nev., 1955—; spl. counsel to Gov. Nev., 1967-70. Contbr. articles to profl. jours. Chmn. Gov.'s Com. on Future of Nev., 1979-80. Fellow Am. Coll. Trial Lawyers; mem. Am. Law Inst., IEEE, Am. Bar Assn. (council litigation sect. 1977-83), State Bar Nev., State Bar Calif., D.C. Bar. Home: 2019 Bannies Ln Las Vegas NV 89102 Office: 302 E Carson Suite 1100 Las Vegas NV 89101

GALBRAITH, OLIVER, III, business educator, management consultant; b. Mpls., Mar. 17, 1926; s. Oliver Jr. and Maybelle Ruth (Hauswirth) G.; m. Nanette Elaine Gerks, Dec. 18, 1948; children: Craig Scott, Diane Frances. BS, Northwestern U., 1949, MBA, 1951; PhD, UCLA, 1968. Cons. engr. Cyrus G. Hill, Chgo., 1949-50; systems engr. Abbot Labs., North Chicago, Ill., 1951-53; instr. U. Okla., Norman, 1953; asst. prof. San Diego State U., 1955-68, assoc. prof. bus., 1968-72, prof., 1972—, dir. Bur. Bus. Econ. Research, 1982—; v.p. Galbraith Forensic and Mgmt. Scis., Ltd., San Diego, 1982—; cons. Office Naval Research, San Diego Zoo, 1955—; litigation cons. Steres Alpert & Carne, CPA, San Diego, 1982—; chmn. adv. bd. Minority Bus. Devel. Ctr., Los Angeles, 1983—, San Diego, 1982—; vis. prof. UCLA, 1955, U. Mich., Ann Arbor, 1963, Northeastern U., Boston, 1969. Author: Starting and Managing a Small Business of Your Own, 1982; co-author: Manual for Project Directors of the SBI, 2d rev. edit., 1978; contbr. articles to profl. publs. Mem. adv. council, chmn. Small Bus. Assn., 1979—. Served to sgt. inf. U.S. Army, 1943-46, ETO. Fellow Ford Found., 1956, Gen. Electric, 1957. Fellow Small Bus. Adminstrn. Dirs. Assn. Republican. Episcopalian. Club: Southwestern Yacht (San Diego). Avocation: sailing. Office: San Diego State U Coll Bus Adminstrn San Diego CA 92182

GALBREATH, MARTI J., marketing professional; b. Evansville, Ind., Oct. 21, 1947; d. Leroy Dewitt Higdon and Vonda Belle (Griffon) Wilhite; divorced; 1 child, Mitchell Dewitt Andrews. Student, Tulsa Jr. coll., 1971-73, Shoreline Community Coll., 1973-74, U. Wash., 1974-75, Evergreen State Coll., 1986-87. Propr. Budget Tapes & Records, Olympia and Bellingham (Wash.), Portland, Oreg., 1975-81; exec. dir. Olympia Downtown Assn., 1981-82; propr. Advt. Design Services, Olympia, 1982-84; dir. mktg. Intercity Transit, Olympia, 1984—; chmn. mktg. Thurston County econ. devel. council, Olympia, 1986—. Producer, co-author (video) Good News for Kids Totally Transit Show, 1985. Pres. Olympia Downtown Assn., 1980; bd. dirs. Wash. State Downtown Assn., 1980-81, Econ. Devel. Council, 1982-85; mem. Mayor's task force on downtown devel., 1983; sales commn. Visitor and Conv. Bur., 1986. Recipient Mktg. Excellence newsletter design award Nat. Credit Union Conf., Hawaii, 1983. Republican. Baptist. Club: Ad (founding mem. bd. dirs. 1986). Avocations: sailing, swimming, travel. Office: Intercity Transit PO Box 659 Olympia WA 98507

GALE, DANIEL BAILEY, architect; b. St. Louis, Nov. 6, 1933; s. Leone Caryll and Gladys (Wotowa) G.; student Brown U., 1951-53, Ecole Des Beaux Arts, Paris, 1954-55; BArch., Washington U., 1957; m. Nancy Susan Miller, June 15, 1957; children: Caroline Hamilton, Rebecca Fletcher, Daniel Bailey With Gale & Cannon, Architects and Planners, Hellmuth, Obata & Kassabaum, Inc., Architects, St. Louis, and exec. v.p. corp. devel., dir. HOK, Inc., St. Louis, 1961-79; ptnr. Heneghan and Gale, architects and planners, Aspen, Colo., 1967-69; pres., chief exec. officer Gale Kober Assocs., San Francisco, 1979-83; pvt. practice architecture, Belvedere, Calif., 1984—; pres. Program Mgmt. Inc., Belvedere, 1984—. Recipient Henry Adams prize Washington U., 1957. Mem. AIA, Singapore Inst. Architects. Home and Office: 280 Belvedere Ave Belvedere CA 94920

GALE, ROBERT PETER, physician, medical educator, scientist, researcher; b. N.Y.C., Oct. 11, 1945; s. Harvey Thomas and Evelyn (Klein) G.; m. Tamar Tishler, June 2, 1976; children—Tal, Shir, Elan. B.A., Hobart Coll., 1966; M.D., SUNY-Buffalo, 1970; Ph.D., UCLA, 1976. Diplomate Am. Bd. Internal Medicine, Am. Bd. Med. Oncology. Postdoctoral studies UCLA Med Ctr.; assoc. prof. medicine UCLA, 1974—; chmn. Internat. Bone Marrow Transplant Registry, Milw., 1982—; Meyerhoff vis. prof. Weizmann Inst. Sci., Israel, 1983; vis. prof. Excerpta Medica Found., Amsterdam, 1979; pres. Armand Hammer Ctr. for Advanced Studies in Nuclear Energy Medicine. Author 13 books, numerous articles on hematology, oncology and transplantation. Recipient Presdl. award N.Y. Acad. Sci., 1986, Olander Peace Prize, 1986; Leukemia Soc. Am. scholar, 1976-81. Fellow ACP; mem. Transplantation Soc., Am. Soc. Hematology, Am. Assn. Immunologists, Internat. Soc. Hematology, Internat. Soc. Exptl. Hematology, Am. Soc. Clin. Oncology, Am. Assn. Cancer Research. Home: 2316 Donella Circle Bel Air CA 90077 Office: UCLA Sch Medicine Los Angeles CA 90024

GALEF, ANDREW GEOFFREY, investment and management corporations executive; b. Yonkers, N.Y., Nov. 3, 1932; s. Gabriel and Anne (Fruchter) G.; m. Suzanne Jane Cohen, June 26, 1954 (div. Feb. 1963); children—Stephanie Anne Galef Streeter, Marjorie Lynn, Michael Lewis; m. Billie Ruth Medlin, Nov. 7, 1964; children—Phyllis Anne, Catherine Marie. B.A., Amherst Coll., 1954; M.B.A., Harvard U., 1958. Vice pres. Kamkap, Inc., N.Y.C., 1958-60; pres. Kemline Calif., San Jose, 1960-61, Zeigler Harris Corp., San Fernando, Calif., 1961-63; v.p. Fullview Industries, Glendale, Calif., 1963-65; cons. Mordy & Co., Los Angeles, 1965-68; prin. Grisanti & Galef, Inc., Los Angeles, 1968-84; pres. Spectrum Group, Inc., Los Angeles, 1978—; chmn., chief exec. officer MagneTek, Inc., Milw., 1984—; chmn. bd. dirs. Midland Color, Inc. (formerly Roberts & Porter, Inc.), Chgo., Exide Corp., Horsham, Pa., Warnaco Inc., Los Angeles; bd. dirs. Post Group, Inc., Hollywood, Calif. Mem. nat. adv. bd. Childhelp, USA, Woodland Hills, Calif., 1984—; bd. dirs. Pacific Homes, Encino, Calif. Served to capt. USAF, 1956-58. Office: Spectrum Group Inc 11111 Santa Monica Blvd Los Angeles CA 90025

GALEHOUSE, JON SCOTT, geology educator; b. Doylestown, Ohio, Feb. 16, 1939; s. Jack Henry and Doris Elaine (Bush) G.; m. Barbara Ann Adams, June 6, 1959; children: Scott, Jennifer. BA, Coll. of Wooster, 1962; PhD, U. Calif., Berkeley, 1966; postgrad., Scripps Inst. Oceanography, 1966-67. Asst. prof. geology San Francisco State U., 1967-70, assoc. prof., 1970-75, prof., 1975—, chmn. dept., 1973-76; sedimentologist Deep Sea Drilling Project, San Diego, 1969, 71, 75; mem. governing bd. Moss Landing (Calif.) Marine Labs., 1970—. Mem. Friends of Pacifica, Calif., 1980—, former chmn.; mem. Pacifica City Council, 1984—; mem. San Mateo County Dem. Cen. Com., 1985—; bd. dirs. West Point Inn Assn., Mt. Tamalpais, Calif., 1982-84. Grantee Am. Chem. Soc., 1967-69, U.S. Geol. Survey, 1979—; fellow NSF, 1966-67. Fellow Calif. Acad. Scis., Geol. Soc. Am.; mem. Internat. Assn. Sedimentologists, Am. Geophys. Union, Sierra Club, Phi Beta Kappa (local chpt. pres. 1981-83). Avocations: backpacking, jogging. Home: 937 Oddstad Blvd Pacifica CA 94044 Office: San Francisco State U 1600 Holloway Ave San Francisco CA 94132

GALES, SAMUEL JOEL, army logistics specialist; b. Dublin, Miss., June 14, 1930; s. James McNary McNeil and Alice Francis (Smith) Broadus-Gales; m. Martha Ann Jackson; children: Samuel II, Martha Diane, Katherine Roselein, Karlmann Von, Carolyn B., Elizabeth Angelica. BA, Chapman Coll., 1981, MS, 1986. Ordained Eucharistic minister. Enlisted U.S. Army, 1948, advanced through grades to master 1st sgt., 1969, ret., 1976; tchr. Monterey (Calif.) Unified Sch. Dist., 1981-82; civilian U.S. Army Directorate of Logistics, Ft. Ord, Calif., 1982—. Active Family Service Agy., Monterey, 1979-85; rep. Episc. Soc. for Ministry on Aging, Carmel, Calif., 1980—, Task Force on Aging, Carmel 1983—. Decorated Air medal. Mem. Am. Legion (post comdr. 1973-74), Forty and Eight (chef-de-gare 1979, 80), Monterey Chess Club. Republican. Avocation: classical music, peer counseling. Home: 1617 Lowell St PO Box 919 Seaside CA 93955-0919 Office: Self-Service Supply Ctr 2080 Quartermaster Ave Fort Ord CA 93941

GALICIAN, MARY-LOU, broadcasting educator; b. New Bedford, Mass., Apr. 5, 1946; d. Benn and Evelyn Nancy (Scott) G. BA magna cum laude, L.I. U., 1966; MS, Syracuse U., 1969; EdD, Memphis State U., 1978. Writer, N.Y. corr. Standard Times, New Bedford, 1961-66; producer, dir., talk show host Sta. WCMU-TV, Mt. Pleasant, Mich., 1967-70, dir. programming, 1968-70; v.p., dir. Evelyn-Nancy Cosmetiques, Inc., New Bedford, 1970-73; nat. advt. mgr. Maybelline Co./Schering-Plough, Memphis, 1973-75; pres., creator FUN-dynamics!, Memphis, Little Rock, Phoenix, 1976—; prof. journalism Memphis State U., 1978-80; nat. mktg. mgr. Fedn. Am. Hosps., Little Rock and Washington, 1980-82; prof. broadcasting Ariz. State U., Tempe, 1983—; motivation, communication cons. various nat. pub. and pvt. orgns., 1966—; speaker, performer nat. convs. and co., 1966—; mem. broadcast services subcom. FCC Industry Adv. Com., Grand Rapids, Mich., 1967-70; mem. adv. bd. Cen. Mich. Ednl. Resources Council, Mich., 1967-70; anchor nat. TV fund drives, 1984—. Writer, producer No Miracles Here, 1967, Witch is it?, 1969-70, Saturday's Child: 20 Years of Network TV Children's Programs, 1969; editor: The Coming Victory, 1980; radio hostess To Broadway with Love, 1967, TV hostess Interview with Mary-Lou Galician, 1967-70; scriptwriter, songwriter, presenter FUN-dynamics! The FUN-damentals of DYNAMIC Living, 1976—; contbr. articles to profl. pubs. Charter mem. Symphony League of Cape Cod, Mass., 1972-73; adviser Boy Scout Explorer Post, Cape Cod, 1972-73; mem. exec. bd. Tenn.-Ark.-Miss. Girl Scouts U.S., Memphis, 1973-75; patron Memphis Ballet Co., 1974-75; mem. steering com. Make Today Count, Memphis, 1976; Health Systems Agy. Council mem. MidSouth Med. Ctr. Council, Memphis, 1976-78. Recipient Cert. Achievement, S.W. Edn. Council for Journalism, 1985 ; named Mich.'s Woman of Yr., Outstanding Ams. Found., 1969; Conolly Coll. scholar L.I. U., 1963-66; grantee Ariz. State U., 1984, 85; Syracuse U. fellow, 1966-67. Mem. AAUW (bd. dirs. Mich. and Mass. chpts. 1967-73), Am. Advt. Fedn. (pyramid awards com. 1980), Am. Women in Radio and TV (com. chair Tenn. chpt. 1979), Ariz. State U. Faculty Women's Assn., Assn. Edn. in Journalism and Mass Communication, Broadcast Edn. Assn. (promotion com. 1985), Pub. Relations Soc. Am. (faculty adviser Ariz. State U. 1983-84), Sales and Mktg. Execs. Internat. (com. chair Ark. chpt. 1981-83), Women in Communications Inc. (founding faculty adviser Cen. Mich. U. 1969-70, Memphis State U. 1979-80, Ariz. State U. 1985—, Outstanding Adv. award 1985-86), Zeta Tau Alpha (gen. faculty adviser 1968-70, membership adviser 1974-75). Club: Phoenix Advt. Avocations: tennis, music, dancing. Home: 1008 E Laguna Dr Tempe AZ 85282 Office: Ariz State U Walter Cronkite Sch Journalism Tempe AZ 85287

GALIDO, PROSPERO GUMATO, mechanical engineer, machinery and equipment appraiser; b. Loreto, Philippines, May 28, 1950; came to U.S., 1981; s. Odon and Gualberta (Gumato) G.; m. Nora Cruz, Jan. 14, 1979; children: Paolo Rommel, Cristina Noelle. BSME, Cebu Inst. Tech., Cebu City, Philippines, 1970. Registered profl. engr., Philippines. Mech. engr. machinery and equipment appraiser Asian Appraisal Co., Manila, 1975-81, Am. Appraisal Assocs., Pasadena, Calif., 1982—. Active Nat. Trust for Hist. Preservation. Mem. Am. Soc. Appraisers (sr., cert.). Office: Am Apparaisal Assocs 150 E Colorado Blvd Pasadena CA 91105

GALINSKY, RAYMOND ETHAN, pharmacy educator; b. Hartford, Conn., Jan. 27, 1948; s. Max and Cecille Marie (Smith) G. BA, U. Calif., Berkeley, 1970; PharmD, U. Calif., San Francisco, 1975. Lic. pharmacist, Calif. Resident in clin. pharmacy U. Calif. Med. Ctr., San Francisco, 1975-76; research assoc. Children's Hosp., U. Pa., Phila., 1977-78; postdoctoral fellow Sch. Pharmacy SUNYAB, Amherst, N.Y., 1978-80; research asst. prof. SUNYAB, Amherst, 1980-83; asst. prof. Coll. Pharmacy U. Utah, Salt Lake City, 1983—. Mem. Am. Soc. Clin. Pharmacology and Therapeutics, Am. Coll. Clin. Pharmacy, AAAS, N.Y. Acad. Scis., Am. Fedn. Clin. Research. Office: Dept Pharmaceutics U Utah Salt Lake City UT 84112

GALL, MEREDITH DAMIEN, education educator, author; b. New Britain, Conn., Feb. 18, 1942; s. Theodore A. and Ray (Ehrlich) G.; m. Joyce Pershing, June 12, 1968; 1 child, Jonathan. AB, Harvard U., 1963, EdM, 1963; PhD, U. Calif., Berkeley, 1968. Sr. research assoc. Far West Lab. for Ednl. Research and Devel., San Francisco, 1968-75; assoc. prof. edn. U. Oreg., 1975-79, prof., 1980—. Author: (with K.A. Acheson) Techniques in the Clinical Supervision of Teachers, 1980; Handbook for Evaluating and Selecting Curriculum Materials, 1981; (with Borg) Educational Research: An Introduction, 4th edit., 1983; co-author: Study for Success: the Most Essential Study Skills for School and College, 1985; editor: (with B.A. Ward) Critical Issues in Educational Psychology, 1974; cons. editor Jour. Ednl. Research. U.S. Pub. Health fellow, 1963-64. Fellow Am. Psychol. Assn.; mem. Am. Ednl. Research Assn., Assn. Supervision and Curriculum Devel., Nat. Soc. Performance and Instrn., Oreg. Ednl. Research Assn. (pres. 1985-86), Nat. Soc. for Study of Edn., Phi Delta Kappa (Dist. I Meritorious award 1978). Home: 4810 Mahalo Dr Eugene OR 97405 Office: U Oreg Coll Edn Eugene OR 97403

GALLAGHER, DENNIS JOSEPH, state senator, educator; b. Denver, July 1, 1939; s. William Joseph and Ellen Philomena (Flaherty) G.; B.A., Regis Coll., 1961; M.A., Cath. U. Am., 1968; postgrad. (Eagleton fellow) Rutgers U., 1972, 86; m. Joanne Ruth Froling, July 8, 1973; children—Meaghan Kathleen, Daniel Patrick. With locals of Internat. Assn. Theatrical and Stage Employees, Denver and Washington, 1956-63; tchr. St. John's Coll. High Sch., Washington, 1964-66, Heights Study Center, Washington, 1965-67, Regis Coll., 1967; mem. Colo. Ho. of Reps from 4th Dist., 1970-74; mem. Colo. Senate, 1974—, chmn. Dem. Caucus, 1982-84, Dem. Whip, 1985—. Mem. Platte Area Reclamation Com., 1973—; mem. Denver Anti-Crime Council, 1976-77; trustee Denver Art Mus.; bd. dirs. Cath. Community Services; mem. Colo. Commn. on Aging; mem. Colo. State Adv. Council on Career Edn.; mem. Victim Assistance Law Enforcement Bd., Denver, 1984—; Named Gates Found. fellow Harvard U. Mem. Colo. Fedn. Tchrs. (pres. local 1333, 1972-74), Colo. Calligrapher's Guild, James Joyce Reading Soc. Democrat. Roman Catholic. Home: 2511 W 32d Ave Denver CO 80211 Office: Regis Coll Dept Communication W 50th Ave and Lowell Blvd Denver CO 80221

GALLAGHER, JACK PAUL, health science facility executive; b. Buffalo, June 18, 1946; s. Francis J. and Kathleen (Crotty) G.; Jean Rozmus, July 29, 1967; children: Michelle, Melissa, Patrick. BBA, Coll. Gt. Falls, 1982. Sales mgr. Beacon Sales Co., Billings, Mont., 1977-78; cen. supply asst. mgr. St. Vincent Hosp., Billings, 1978-80, supply mgr., 1980-86; owner Rainbow Photo, Billings, 1986—; gen. mgr. Med-Link Homecare Services, Billings, 1985—. Served to sgt. USAF, 1966-73. Mem. Am. Hosp. Assn., Mont. Hosp. Assn., Mont. Hosp. Assn. Material Mgrs. (pres. 1986-87). Club: Toastmasters (Billings) (v.p. 1984-85, pres. 1985-86). Avocations: photography, golf. Office: St Vincent Hosp Supply Distbn Dept PO Box 35200 Billings MT 59107-5200

GALLAGHER, JAMES STEPHEN, stock exchange executive; b. N.Y.C., Mar. 7, 1943; s. John James and Catherine (Morrissey) G.; m. Veronica Redding, May 13, 1967; children: Sean, Geoffrey, Marc. B.A., Fordham U., 1965; M.B.A. summa cum laude, St. John's U., 1976. Asst. v.p. facilities upgrade N.Y. Stock Exchange, 1978, v.p. operating systems, 1979-80; v.p. market ops. N.Y. Futures Exchange, 1980; pres. Pacific Stock Exchange, 1981—. Mem. exec. council Regis High Sch., 1971-80. Served with U.S. Army, 1967-69. Republican. Roman Catholic. Clubs: Stock Exchange (San Francisco), Bankers (San Francisco). Office: Pacific Stock Exchange 301 Pine St San Francisco CA 94104

GALLAGHER, JOHN JOSEPH, cardiologist; b. Bklyn., Mar. 3, 1943. B.S. in Physics, Coll. of Holy Cross, 1964; M.D. cum laude, Georgetown U., 1968. Diplomate: Am. Bd. Internal Medicine. Intern Duke U. Med. Center, Durham, N.C., 1968-69; resident in medicine Duke U. Med. Center, 1969-70, fellow in cardiology, 1972-74, asst. prof. medicine, 1974-77, asso. prof., 1977-80, Edward S. Orgain prof. medicine, 1980—; dir. Clin. Electrophysiology Lab., 1974—; practice medicine specializing in cardiology Durham, 1974—; cons. cardiopulmonary div. USPHS Hosp., S.I., N.Y., 1974—. Mem. editorial bd.: Jour. of Pacing and Clin. Electrophysiology; contbr. over 125 articles on cardiology and electrophysiology to profl. jours. Served with USPHS, 1970-72. Recipient Ray C. Fish award for sci. achievement in cardiovascular disease Tex. Heart Inst., 1979. Fellow Am. Coll. Cardiology, Am. Heart Assn. (council on Clin. cardiology); mem. Am. Soc. Clin. Investigation, N.Y. Heart Assn., Am. Fedn. Clin. Research, Alpha Omega Alpha. Office: Heineman Med Research Ctr 1960 Randolph Rd Charlotte NC 28207

GALLAGHER, MARIAN GOULD, librarian, educator; b. Everett, Wash., Aug. 29, 1914; d. John H. and Grace (Smith) Gould; m. D. Wayne Gallagher, Oct. 1, 1942 (dec. 1953). Student, Whitman Coll., 1931-32; A.B., U. Wash., 1935, LL.B., 1937, M.L.S., 1939. Law librarian, instr. law U. Utah, Salt Lake City, 1939-44; law librarian U. Wash., Seattle, 1944-81; asst. prof. law U. Wash., 1944-48, asso. prof., 1948-53, prof., 1953-81, prof. emeritus, 1981—, adj. prof., 1944-84; vis. prof. law and disting. law librarian, Hastings Law Sch., San Francisco, 1982; cons. various law schs. and govt. law libraries. Mem. Gov.'s Commn. on Status of Women, 1964-71, Pres.'s Nat. Adv. Com. on Libraries, 1967-68; mem. adv. com. White House Conf. on Library and Info. Services, 1976-80; mem. council sect. on legal edn. and admissions to bar Am. Bar Assn., 1979-83. Named Disting. Alumna U. Wash. Sch. of Librarianship, 1970, Disting. Alumna U. Wash. Sch. Law, 1980, Disting. Alumna Whitman Coll., 1981. Fellow Am. Bar Found.; mem. Am. Bar Assn., Am. Assn. Law Libraries (pres. 1954-55, Disting. Service award 1966, 84), Wash. State Bar Assn., Seattle-King County Bar Assn., PEO, Mortar Bd., Order of Coif, Delta Delta Delta, Phi Alpha Delta. Presbyterian. Office: 900 University St Seattle WA 98101-2765

GALLAR, JOHN JOSEPH, mechanical engineer, educator; b. Poland, July 3, 1936; came to U.S., 1981; s. Joseph and Sophie (Gallar) Filipecki; m. Christina B. Wilczynski, June 30, 1962; 1 child, Darek A. BSME, State U. Poland, 1957, MSME, 1958; PhD in Tech. Scis., M & M Acad., 1966; professorship, Ahmadu Bello U., Zaria, Nigeria, 1980. Dir., prof. engring. Acad. State U., Poland, 1957-72; dir., prof. engring. Ahmadu Bello U., 1973-81, dir. postgrad. studies, 1976-81; with module design Timex Co., Cupertino, Calif., 1981-82; sr. mfg. Computer Research Co., Santa Clara, Calif., 1982-84; mgr. hardware devel. Nat. Semiconductor Co., Santa Clara, 1984-85; chief robotics engr. Varian Corp., Palo Alto, Calif., 1986—; dep. vice-chancellor State U., Poland, 1970-71; cons. Enplan Corp., Kaduna, Nigeria, 1980-81, Criticare Tech., Sparks, Nev., 1985-86, also bd. dirs.; mgr. mfg. engring. Retro-Tek Co., Santa Clara, 1986. Contbr. articles to profl. jours.; patentee in field. Trustee, charter mem. Presdl. Task Force, Washington, 1984; mem. Nat. Conservative Polit. Action Com., Washington, 1981. Recipient U.S. Ceremonial Flag Presdl. Task Force; Medal Merit from Pres. Ronald Reagan, Washington, 1985. Mem. Calif. State Sheriff's Assn., Nat. Rifle Assn. Roman Catholic. Avocations: playing classical violin music, listening to Country-Western music. Home: 5459 Entrada Cedros San Jose CA 95123 Office: Varian Corp 611 Hansen Way Palo Alto CA 95051

GALLEGLY, ELTON, congressman; b. Huntington Park, Calif., Mar. 7, 1944; married; four children. Grad., Calif. State U., Los Angeles. Businessman, real estate broker Simi Valley, Calif., from 1968; mem. Simi Valley City Council, 1979; mayor Simi Valley, 1980-86; mem. 100th Congress from the 21st dist. of Calif., 1986—; vice chmn. Calif. Rep. delegation, mem. interior & insular affairs and small bus. coms. U.S. Ho. of Reps.; formerly vice chmn., chmn. Ventura County Assn. Govts., Calif. Bd. dirs. Moorpark Coll. Found.; chmn. Tri-City YMCA Drive, 1986, Ventura County Heart Assn. Drive, 1982, Boys & Girls Club Auction, 1981, 84.

GALLEGO GARCIA, JOSE MIGUEL, chemist, researcher; b. Mexicali, Mexico, Nov. 5, 1955; s. Waldemar and Josefina (Garcia) G.; m. Leticia Osuna, Jan. 10, 1981; 1 child, Kimberly. Preparatoria Federal Lazaro Cardenas, Mexico, 1971-73; BS in Chemistry, Universidad Autonoma de Guadalajara, 1977, postgrad., 1977. Ops. supr. State Water Commn., Tijuana, Mex., 1978-79; research chemist Quimica Organica de Mexico, Mexicali, Mex., 1979-81; v.p., chief chemist, part-owner Laboratorios Industriales y Servicios Internacionales, Tijuana, Mex., 1981-84; tchr. Universidad Autonoma de Baja Calif., Tijuana, 1983-84; owner G.C. Systems, Chula Vista, Calif., 1983-85; research chemist Chemical Energy of Calif., San Diego, 1984—; founder, gen. mgr., ptnr. Innovative Computer Accessories, Imperial Beach, Calif., 1985—; Rep. State Water Commn. of Tijuana, San Diego, 1979-80, Quimica Organica de Mexico S.A., 1980; tchr. Universidad Autonoma de Guadalajara, 1978, Quimica Organica de Mexico S.A., Mexicali and Little Rock, 1980, Universidad Autonoma de Baja Calif, 1981-84, 82. Patentee in field. Served with Mex. Army, 1973-74. Recipient spl. award Tex. Instruments, Inc., 1979, 6th-pl. award in laser constrn., Mexicali, 1973. Mem. Soc. Exptl. Scis. (founder and pres. 1972-73), Chem. Soc. Mex., Am. Chem. Soc., South Bay Commodore Users Group (v.p. 1983-85), San Diego Computer Soc. Roman Catholic. Avocations: computer programming and hardware experimentation, coin collecting. Home: 1844 D Ave National City CA 92050 Office: Innovative Computer Accessories 1249 Downing St Imperial Beach CA 92032

GALLEGOS, ALPHONSE, bishop; b. Albuquerque, Feb. 20, 1931; s. Jose Angel and Caseana (Apodaca) G. B.S., St. Thomas Aquinas Coll., 1971; M.S., St. John's U., Jamaica, N.Y., 1972; M.E., Loyola U., Los Angeles, 1979. Ordained priest Roman Catholic Ch., 1958. Pastor San Miguel Ch., Los Angeles, Our Lady of Guadalupe Ch., Sacramento; vicar Hispanics in Sacramento area; first hispanic bishop Sacramento; Aux. bishop of Sacramento 1981—; Vicar gen. Roman Catholic Ch., Sacramento, vicar for Hispanics; active campaign for human devel. U.S. Catholic Conf., Washington. Mem. Calif. Govs. Com.; bd. dirs. Sacramento Concilio, Boy Scouts Am. Home: 1119 K St Sacramento CA 95808 Office: PO Box 1706 Sacramento CA 95808

GALLEGOS, CATHERINE ZACHMAN, fiscal analyst; b. Toledo, Dec. 18, 1947; d. John Wesley and Anne Gaylord (Morley) Zachman; m. Edward Bailey Wickes III, June 21, 1969 (div. Sept. 1979); m. Robert Alan Gallegos, Apr. 27, 1985. BA, Briarcliff Coll., 1970. Draftsman, planner Toledo-Lucas County Planning Com., 1970-71; research planner Samborn-Steketee, Toledo, 1971-73; tech. service asst. Toledo Met. Area Council of Govts., 1973-74; from planner III to dep. dir. N.Mex. State Planning Office, Santa Fe, 1974-79; dir. adminstrv. services div. N.Mex. Natural Resources Dept., Santa Fe, 1979-82; sr. fiscal analyst N.Mex. Legislative Fin. Com., Santa Fe, 1983-86; planning and program devel. chief environ. improvement div. N.Mex. Health and Environment Dept., Sante Fe, 1986—. Contbr. articles to profl. jours. Pres. Chorus of Santa Fe, 1979-85, sec., bd. dirs. Mem. Gamma Theta Upsilon, Pi Gamma Mu. Republican. Episcopalian. Avocations: singing, gardening, hiking, sailing, biking. Home: PO Box 1133 Santa Fe NM 87504-1133 Office: NMex Health and Environment Dept Environ Improvement Div PO Box 968 Santa Fe NM 87504-0968

GALLEGOS, FREDERICK, auditor; b. San Bernardino, Calif., June 10, 1947; s. Frederick Reyna and Guadalupe (Aceves) G.; m. Susan Melina Carney, Apr. 17; children: David F., Christopher R. AA, San Bernardino Valley Coll., 1970; BS in Data Processing, Calif. State Poly. U., Pomona, 1972, MBA, 1973. Cert. info. systems auditor. Evaluator GAO, Los Angeles, 1972—; lectr. computer info. systems Calif. State Poly. U., 1975—. Co-author: MEDCO Inc., 1973, Audit and Control of Information Systems, 1986; contbr. articles to profl. jours. Served with U.S. Army, 1966-68, Vietnam. Recipient Disting. Alumnus award Calif. State Poly. U., 1982, Meritorious Service award GAO, Washington, 1978, 84, Stanley D. Halper award for Excellence DP Audit Report, N.Y.C., 1985, Outstanding Alumni award Calif. State Poly. U., 1980. Mem. EDP Auditor's Found. Inc. (sec. 1978-79, exec. v.p. 1979-80, trustee 1978-86), EDP Auditor's Assn., Soc. Data Educators. Democrat. Roman Catholic. Office: GAO 350 S Figueroa St Suite 1010 Los Angeles CA 90071

GALLET, RENE CHARLES, marketing executive; b. Chgo., June 19, 1941; s. Charles J. and Joyce T. (Distel) G.; m. Marilyn J. Croak, Sept. 24, 1966. BA, DePaul U., 1962; BBA in Mktg., Nat. U., 1985. Mgr. nat. mktg. Datagraphix, San Diego, 1970-85; mgr. product mktg. Xidex Corp., Mountain View, Calif., 1983-85; dir. mktg. Alta Chem. Corp., San Diego, 1985-86, pres., 1987—. Bd. dirs. Jr. Achievement, San Diego, 1982-83; com. mem. Boy Scouts Am., Chgo., 1960-62. Served with USAF, 1962-67. Mem. Printer Inst. Am., Photographic Mfrs. Am., Internat. Microfilm Council, Am. Mgmt. Assn., Soc. Photographic Scis. and Engrs. Avocations: creative photography, landscaping, computer science, hiking, travel. Office: Alta Chem Corp 11526 Sorrento Valley Rd San Diego CA 92121

GALLETTA, JOSEPH LEO, physician; b. Bessemer, Pa., Dec. 21, 1935; s. John and Grace (Galletta) G.; student U. Pitts., 1953-56; M.D., U. Santo Tomas, Manila, Philippines, 1962; m. Teresita Suarez Soler, Feb. 19, 1961; children—John II, Angela, Eric, Christopher, Robert Francis, Michael Angelo. Intern, St. Elizabeth Hosp., Youngstown, Ohio, 1963-64; family practice medicine, 29 Palms, Calif., 1967-77, Hemet, Calif., 1977—; chief of staff 29 Palms Community Hosp., 1970-71, 73-76; vice chief of staff Hi-Desert Med. Center, Joshua Tree, Calif., 1976-77; chmn. dept. family practice Hemet Valley Hosp., 1981-83; pres. Flexisplint, Inc.; founding mem. Hemet Hospice; former cons. Morongo Basin Mental Health Assn. Hon. mem. 29 Palms Sheriff's Search and Rescue, 1971-77. Bd. dirs. 29 Palms Community Hosp. Dist., Morongo Unified Sch. Dist. Served with M.C. USN, 1964-67. Diplomate Am. Bd. Family Practice. Founding fellow West Coast div. Am. Geriatric Soc.; fellow Am. Acad. Family Practice; mem. AMA, Calif. Med. Assn., Am. Holistic Med. Assn. (charter), Am. Med. Soc. on Alcoholism and Other Drug Dependencies, Calif. Soc. Treatment Alcoholism and Drug Dependencies, Riverside County Med. Assn., Am. Acad. Family Practice, Calif. Acad. Family Practice. Roman Catholic. Established St. Anthonys Charity Clinic, Philippines, 1965; inventor Flexisplint armboards. Home: 27691 Pochea Trail Hemet CA 92344 Office: 850 E Latham Ave Suite B Hemet CA 92343

GALLI, DARRELL JOSEPH, mgmt. cons.; b. Ft. Bragg, Calif., Nov. 10, 1948; s. Joseph Germain and Esther Edith (Happajoki) G.; B.A., San Francisco State U., 1975; M.B.A., Golden Gate U., 1980, postgrad., 1980-81; m. Rondus Miller, Apr. 23, 1977 (div. 1981); 1 dau., Troyan Hulda. With Pacific Gas & Electric Co., Santa Cruz, Calif., 1972-73; with Calif. Western R.R., Ft. Bragg, 1975-77, Sheldon Oil Co., Suisun, Calif, 1978-80; mgr. House of Rondus, Suisun, 1974-79; mgmt. cons., Suisun City, 1979—; instr. Solano Coll., 1979-81, Golden Gate U., 1981; mem. faculty U. Md. European div., Heidelberg, W.Ger., 1982—; coordinator Small Bus. Mgmt. Seminar, 1980. Asst. coordinator Sr. Citizens Survey for Solano Coll. and Sr. Citizens Center, 1980. Served with U.S. Army, 1969-71. Lic. Calif. real estate agt. Mem. Am. Assn. M.B.A. Execs., World Trade Assn., Bay Area Elec. R.R. Assn. Republican. Episcopalian. Club: Odd Fellows. Home: 321 Morrow St Fort Bragg CA 95437 Office: U Md APO New York NY 09102

GALLIGAN, DAVID, columnist, interviewer, critic; b. San Francisco, July 1, 1940; s. Henry and Patricia (Galligan) Mozzetti. Student, schs. San Francisco. Actor, roles including appearance on Med. Center, Batman, Margie, The Lieutenant, 1962-68; juvenile lead nat. tour of The Impossible Years, with George Gobel, 1968; theatre and movie critic for Fashion Week, Men's Week, Drama Logue, 1972-83; personality interviewer, movie reviewer Drama-Logue, 1977-83, also Photoplay, Liberty, Coronet, Andy Warhol's Interview mags. Mem. Los Angeles Drama Critics Circle.

GALLIN, JOEL GARY, food company executive; b. Boston, Oct. 4, 1936; s. Henry Daniel and Rose (Shaler) G.; m. Ingrid Goldstein, Dec. 30, 1956; children: Deborah, Lisa, Stacy. B.A. in Biochemistry, U. Calif.-Berkeley, 1958. Asst. research pharmacologist Cutter Lab., Berkeley, 1958-61; quality control mgr. Hunt-Wesson Foods (now Beatrice Hunt/Wesson), Hayward, Calif., 1961-67, quality assurance technologist, Fullerton, 1969-71, mgr. research and devel. project planning, 1971-72, quality assurance mgr., 1972-78, dir. quality assurance, 1978—; assoc. divisional dir. quality assurance Gen. Foods, Chgo., 1967-69; instr. Chapman Coll. Served with USCGR, 1954-62. Mem. Inst. Food Technologists. Author (with R.J. Moshy) Factors Affecting Quality-Consumer, Cost and Government, 1980. Office: Beatrice Hunt/Wesson 1645 W Valencia Dr Fullerton CA 92633

GALLIVAN, JOHN WILLIAM, publisher; b. Salt Lake City, June 28, 1915; s. Daniel and Frances (Wilson) G.; m. Grace Mary Ivers, June 30, 1938; children—Gay, John, William, Michael D., Timothy. B.A., U. Notre Dame, 1937. With Salt Lake Tribune, 1937—, promotion mgr., 1942-48, asst. pub., 1948-60, pub., 1960—; pres. Kearns-Tribune Corp., 1960—; v.p., dir. Telemation, Inc., 1963—, Tele-Communications, Inc., 1965—; pres. Silver King Mining Co., 1960—. Pres. Utah Symphony, 1964-65; exec. com. Pro-Utah, 1964—. Mem. Sigma Delta Chi. Clubs: Nat. Press (Washington); Alta (Salt Lake City), Salt Lake Country (Salt Lake City), Rotary (Salt Lake City). Home: 17 S 12th E Salt Lake City UT 84102 Office: Kearns-Tribune Corp 143 S Main St Salt Lake City UT 84110 *

GALLO, MARTA IRENE, Spanish educator; b. Córdoba, Argentina, Oct. 20, 1926; d. Gregorio and María Luisa (Teodoro) G. Grad., U. Buenos Aires, 1951. Researcher Inst. de Filologia, Univ. de Buenos Aires, 1960-61, asst. prof. Lit. Theory, 1961-66; vis. prof. U. Puerto Rico, 1967-68; prof. U. Calif., Santa Barbara, 1968—. Author: Novela Hispanoamericana del siglo XIX; also articles. Mem. MLA, Asociación Española de Semiótica, Inst. Internat. de Literatura Iberoamericana, Asociación Inernat. de Hispanistas, Internat. Assn. Semiotic Studies. Home: 2948 Kenmore Pl Santa Barbara CA 93105 Office: U Calif Dept Spanish Santa Barbara CA 93106

GALLOP, JEFFREY RICHARD, media company executive; b. Boston, June 15, 1962; s. Richard Charles and Ann Morris (McEldowney) G. BA in Drama, BS in Journalism, U. Ariz., 1985. Producer McCann-Erickson Inc., N.Y.C., 1984; creative writer McCann-Erickson Inc., London, 1985, Dailey & Assocs., Los Angeles, 1985—; producer Film Creations Ltd., Tucson, 1984; ind. producer Heights Films, N.Y.C., 1984—. Creative writer McCann Erickson, London and N.Y.C., 1984—. Chmn. Mondale for Pres. Campaign, Tucson, 1984. Mem. Phi Delta Theta. Democrat. Episcopalian. Clubs: Sleepy Hollow Country (Scarborough, N.Y.); Tucson Racquet. Avocations: squash, tennis, golf, photography.

GALLUP, LEE, theatre educator, director, actress, coach; b. St. Louis; d. Michael M. and Eva C. G. Gallup; m. Arthur Feldman; 1 child, Amy Nina. Student, Northwestern U.; BA, U. Ill., MA; PhD, U. Denver, 1969. Freelance dir. and actress Denver, 1969—, freelance acting coach, 1978—; instr. Arvada (Colo.) Ctr. for Performing Arts, 1978—; assoc. prof. theatre Loretto Heights Coll., Denver, 1981—; dir. Evergreen (Colo.) Chorale, 1983—; founder Theatre Under Glass, Denver, 1974-78; theatre design cons. Max Saul & Assocs., Denver, 1970's. Author: (play) The Moose Hangs High, 2d rev. edit., 1981, The Green Witch, 1971. Bd. dirs. Greater Denver Council for Arts and Humanities, Denver; performer Community Arts Symphony, Englewood, Colo., 1971-75; judge Am. coll. Theatre Play Festival, 1974, local Miss Am. Contest, Lakewood (Colo.) Players Award Season, 1980-81. Recipient Best Actress award Bonfils Theatre, 1978. Mem. AFTRA, Am. Theatre Assn., Brecht Soc. Am., Zeta Phi Eta. Office: Loretto Heights Coll Dept Fine Arts 3001 S Federal Blvd Denver CO 80236

GALLUP, MARC RICHMOND, biology educator, paleontologist; b. Glendale, Calif., Sept. 25, 1949; s. Donald Ray and Gloria Muriel (Grimes) G.; m. Susan Holly Smith, Dec. 30, 1971. BA in Zoology, UCLA, 1971, PhD in Biology, 1982; MA in Zoology, U. Tex., 1974. Instr. biology Santa Monica (Calif.) Coll., 1980-84; instr. Calif. State U., Northridge, 1981-83, Los Angeles Mission Coll., San Fernando, Calif., 1981-84, South Pasadena (Calif.) High Sch., 1984-86, Rowland High Sch., Rowland Heights, Calif., 1986—; cons. Jet Propulsion Lab., Pasadena, 1985—. Cons. Los Angeles Libraries, 1974-76, Los Angeles County Mus. Natural History, 1975-84. Grantee Sigma Xi, 1977, Karl Schmidt Field Mus. Natural History, 1977, UCLA Patent, 1975, 77. Mem. NEA, AAAS, Am. Soc. Zoologists, Nat. Sci. Tchrs. Assn., Planetary Soc. Democrat. Home: 1466 S Sherbourne Dr #6 Los Angeles CA 90035 Office: Rowland High Sch Rowland Heights CA 91748

GALT, DIANE CARRITHERS, social worker; b. Bakersfield, Calif., June 23, 1941; d. Ray Carlton and Frances (Bartlett) Carrithers; m. Warren Lee Whitnah, June 26, 1960 (div. 1975); children: Tymmera Rae, Robert Warren; m. Richard Kelly Galt, Oct. 1, 1977. BS, Eastern Oreg. State Coll., 1964; MSW, U. Wash., 1977. Caseworker, supr. casework State of Oreg. Pub. Welfare, Portland and Baker, 1964-71; dir. in-patient alcoholism treatment Monticello Med. Ctr., Longview, Wash., 1980-81; pvt. practice social worker Longview, 1982—; vice chmn. bd. dirs. Lower Columbia Mental Health Ctr., Longview, 1982-84; bd. dirs., vice chmn. subcom. Cowlitz County Social Services Coordinating Bd., Longview, 1984—. Vice chmn. Cowlitz County Rep. Com., Longview, 1984; sr. warden St. Matthews Episcopal Ch., Castle Rock, Wash., 1984. Mem. Nat. Assn. Social Workers (cert.). Avocations: skiing, painting, bridge. Office: 1044 11 Suite B Longview WA 98632

GALT, JOHN KIRTLAND, physicist, laboratory administrator; b. Portland, Oreg., Sept. 1, 1920; s. Martin Happer and Elsie (Lee) G.; m. Marguerite VanNest, Dec. 30, 1949; children: James Michael (dec.), Lloyd Anthony. A.B., Reed Coll., 1941; Ph.D., MIT, 1947. Mem. tech. staff Bell Labs., Murray Hill, N.J., 1948-57; head solid state and plasma physics dept. Bell Labs., 1957-61, dir. solid state electronics lab., 1961-74; dir. solid state scis. research orgn. Sandia Nat. Labs., Albuquerque, 1974-78; v.p. Sandia Nat. Labs., 1978-85; prin. scientist Aerospace Corp., 1985—; mem. Air Force Studies Bd., Nat. Acad. Sci., 1971-76, Air Force Sci. Adv. Bd., 1975-82. Cons. editor: McGraw-Hill Ency. Sci. and Tech., 1965-86. NRC fellow Bristol, Eng., 1947-48. Fellow Am. Phys. Soc., IEEE, AAAS, Nat. Acad. Engring. Office: Aerospace Corp PO Box 92957 Los Angeles CA 90009

GALTON, SIDNEY ALAN, administrative law judge; b. Portland, Oreg., Jan. 9, 1947; s. Herbert B. and Ida Mae G.; m. Cynthia Weintraub Weber, Aug. 6, 1970 (div. Dec. 1980); children—Amy Louise, Allen Weintraub. AB in German, Polit. Sci., Stanford U., 1969; JD U. Calif.-Berkeley, 1972. Assoc. Galton, Popick & Scott, Portland, 1972-81; adminstrv. law judge Oreg. Workers Compensation Bd., Salem and Portland, 1982—; attys.' fee arbitrator Oreg. State Bar, 1977, 78, 81, 84; chmn. disciplinary trial bd. Oreg. State Bar, 1984; judge Northwestern Regional Moot Ct. Competition, 1977.Rev. editor: Ecology Law Quar., U. Calif., 1971-72; contbr. articles in field to profl. jours. Chmn. adv. com. Bridlemile Elem. Local Sch., Portland, 1978-80; pres., gen. mgr. Rose City Performing Arts, 1984-86; treas. GALA Choruses, 1985-86, also pres., 1986-87. Named Florence-Virginia K. Wilson scholar, 1969-70. Mem. Oreg. State Bar Assn., Multnomah Bar Assn., Oreg. Workers Compensation Attys. Assn. (pres. 1976-78), Order of Coif, Phi Beta Kappa. Democrat. Jewish. Office: 2525 SW 3rd AVe Portland OR 97201

GALVAN, ELIAS G., clergyman; b. Puebla, Mexico, Apr. 9, 1938; came to U.S., 1956, naturalized; s. Elias and Olga (Peralta) G. B.A., Calif. State U.; D.Religion, Sch. Theology Claremont. Ordained to ministry, Methodist Ch. Asst. pastor Asbury United Meth. Ch., Los Angeles, 1963-66; pastor City Ter. United Meth. Ch., Los Angeles, 1966-69, All Nations United Meth. Ch., Los Angeles, 1969-71; exec. dir. ethnic planning dept. United Meth. Ch., Los Angeles, 1971-74, dist. supt. Santa Barbara Dist., 1974-80, council dir. Pacific and Southwest Conf., 1980-84, bishop, Desert Southwest Conf., 1984—. : AZ 85012 Office: 5510 N Central Ave Phoenix AZ 85012 *

GALVAN, SABINO, public school business officer; b. Kyle, Tex., Oct. 27, 1934; s. Paul R. and Mary A. Galvan; student Trinity U., 1954; A.A., Sacramento Community Coll., 1960; B.S., Sacramento State U., 1967; m. Jo Ana K., June 12, 1981; children by previous marriage—Gregory P., Jeanette K.; stepchildren—Jimmy, Peggy, Donna, Steve, Todd. Auditor trainee dept. fin. State of Calif., Sacramento, 1962; tax examiner IRS, Sacramento, 1962-63; auditor-appraiser Sacramento County Assessor's Office, 1963-64; acct. Sacramento County Office Edn., 1965-67, adminstrv. asst., 1967-68; chief acct. San Juan Unified Sch. Dist., Carmichael, Calif., 1968-76, sr. fin. analyst, 1976-78, asst. dir. fin., 1978-80, dir. acctg. services, 1980—, San Juan United Dir. Compensation and Benefits, 1983—; chmn. payroll task force, 1977-78. Troop treas. Golden Empire council Boy Scouts Am., 1968-69, chmn. membership com., 1969-70; bd. dirs. Superior Calif. Sch. Employees Credit Union, 1977—, chmn. nominating com., 1979, chmn. planning com., 1979-80; mem. Sacramento County Acad. Decathalon Scholarship com., 1986-87. Served with USAF, 1954-58. Mem. Calif. Assn. Sch. Bus. Ofcls. (dir. 1972-73, 75-76, pres. 1976-77, chmn. acctg. research and devel. com. 1980—), Assn. Calif. Sch. Adminstrs. (dir. 1982-83), San Juan Adminstrs. Assn. (dir. 1979—, pres. 1982-83), Assn. Calif. Sch. Adminstrs. Region III (v.p. programs, pres. 1985-86), Calif. Assn. Purchasing Officers. Democrat. Home: 8215 Scarlet Oak Circle Citrus Heights CA 95610 Office: San Juan Unified Sch Dist 3738 Walnut Ave Carmichael CA 95608

GAMBARO, ERNEST UMBERTO, lawyer, consultant; b. Niagara Falls, N.Y., July 6, 1938; s. Ralph and Teresa (Nigro) G.; m. Winifred Sonya Gambaro, June 3, 1961. B.A. in Aero. Engring. with honors, Purdue U., 1960, M.S. with honors, 1961; Fulbright scholar, Rome U., 1961-62; J.D. with honors, Loyola U., Los Angeles, 1975. Bar: Calif. 1975, U.S. Tax Ct. 1976, U.S. Supreme Ct. 1979, U.S. Ct. Appeals (9th cir.). With Aerospace Corp., El Segundo, Calif., 1962-80, counsel, 1975-80; asst. gen. counsel, asst. sec. Computer Scis. Corp., El Segundo, 1980—; cons. bus. fin. and mgmt., 1968—. Recipient U.S. Air Force Commendation for contbns. to U.S. manned space program, 1969; Purdue U. Pres.'s scholar, 1959-60. Mem. ABA (internat., taxation sects.), Los Angeles Bar Assn. (exec. com. 1976—, founder chmn. sect. law and tech. 1976-78, chmn. bar reorgn. com. 1981-82), Am. Arbitration Assn. Los Angeles Ctr. Internat. Comml. Arbitration (founder, bd. dirs.), Internat. Law Inst. (faculty), St. Thomas More Law Soc., Phi Alpha Delta, Omicron Delta Kappa (past pres.), Tau Beta Pi, Sigma Gamma Tau (past pres.), Phi Eta Sigma. Republican. Newspaper columnist Europe Alfresco; contbr. articles to profl. publs. Home: 4221 Rousseau Ln Palos Verdes CA 90274 Office: 2100 E Grand Ave El Segundo CA 90245

GAMBINO, JEROME JAMES, nuclear medicine educator; b. N.Y.C., Sept. 13, 1925; m. Jacquelyn Ann Mazzola, Mar. 27, 1948; children: Charles, John, Mary Ellen, Jacquelyn. BA, U. Conn., 1950, MS, 1952; PhD, U. Calif., 1957. Asst. prof. natural scis. SUNY, New Paltz, 1957-59; research radiobiologist UCLA, 1959-61; mem. research staff Northrop Corp., Hawthorne, Calif., 1961-69; dir. edn. nuclear medicine dept. VA Med. Ctr., Los Angeles, 1969—; lectr. anatomy U. So. Calif., Los Angeles, 1963—, radiol. scis. UCLA, 1978—. Mem. Radiation Research Soc., Soc. Nuclear Medicine (pres. So. Calif. chpt. 1981-82). Avocations: watercolor painting, pen and pencil sketching. Office: VA Med Ctr W Los Angeles Wadsworth Div Nuclear Med W115 Wilshire and Sawtelle Blvds Los Angeles CA 90073

GAMBLE, DOUGLAS SCHIBSBY, food company executive; b. Waterloo, Iowa, 1925; married. BA Williams Coll., 1947, MBA Stanford U., 1949. With Pacific Gamble Robinson Co., Inc., Kirkland, Wash., 1949—, v.p. distbn. brs. from 1965, pres., chief exec. officer, 1974—, also dir. Served to lt. (j.g.) USN. Office: Pacific Gamble Robinson Co Inc 10829 NE 68th St Kirkland WA 98033 *

GAMBLE, FREDERICK GEORGE, lawyer; b. Willimantic, Conn., Jan. 17, 1948; s. George Walter and Nancy (Webb) G.; BEE magna cum laude, Ariz. State U., 1969, JD cum laude (Phelps Dodge fellow), 1974; m. Joyce Dionne, July 18, 1975; 1 dau., Heather Dionne. Design engr. Omnitec Corp., Phoenix, 1967-70; pvt. practice engring. cons., Phoenix, 1972-75; admitted to Ariz. bar, 1974; assoc. Fennemore, Craig, von Ammon & Udall, Phoenix, 1973-77, Gust, Rosenfeld, Divelbess & Henderson, Phoenix, 1977-83; prin. Frederick G. Gamble, P.C., 1984-86, Oplinger and Gamble, 1986—. Named Collegiate All Am. Archer, 1969. Mem. ABA, Ariz. Bar Assn., Maricopa County Bar Assn. (jud. evaluator state com.), Ariz. State U. Law Sch. Alumni Assn. (treas. 1977-78), Eta Kappa Nu, Tau Beta Pi. Presbyterian. Office: 4015 S McClintock Dr Suite 101 Tempe AZ 85282

GAMBLE, WALTER RANDOLPH, construction engineer, contractor; b. San Jose, Calif., July 23, 1946; s. William Harold Gamble and Brenda Ruth (Moody) Wales; m. Jacqueline Irene Robinson, Aug. 6, 1966; children: Stuart Walter, Patrick William. BS, Oreg. State U., 1969. Registered civil engr., Oreg., Wash. Engr. and mgr. Gibbons and Reed, Portland, Oreg., 1969-76; constrn. mgr. Columbia West, Portland, 1976-80; prin. W.R. Gamble Engring., Portland, 1980-87, Gamble & Pyritz Constrn. Co., Portland, 1987—. Served to 1st. lt. C.E. U.S. Army, 1972-78. Mem. ASCE, Assn. Gen. Contractors (bd. dirs.). Avocations: hunting, camping, skiing. Office: WR Gamble Engring 0324 SW Abernethy Portland OR 97201

GAMBOA, GEORGE CHARLES, oral surgeon; b. King City, Calif., Dec. 17, 1923; s. George Angel and Martha Ann (Baker) G.; pre-dental certificate Pacific Union Coll., 1943; D.D.S., U. Pacific, 1946; M.S., U. Minn., 1953; A.B., U. So. Calif., 1958; Ed.D., U. So. Calif., 1976; m. Winona Mae Collins, July 16, 1946; children—Cheryl Jan Gamboa Williams, Jon Charles, Judith Merlene Gamboa Hiscox. Fellow oral surgery Mayo Found., 1950-53; assoc. prof. grad. program oral surgery U. So. Calif., Los Angeles, 1954—; assoc. prof. Loma Linda (Calif.) U., 1958—, chmn. dept. oral surgery, 1960-63; pvt. practice oral surgery, San Gabriel, Calif., 1955—. chmn. first aid com. West San Gabriel chpt. ARC; dir. Calif. Dental Soc. Anesthesiology. Diplomate Am. Bd. Oral and Maxillofacial Surgery. Fellow Am. Coll. Oral and Maxillofacial Surgeons, Am. Assn. Oral and Maxillofacial Surgeons; mem. Internat. Assn. Oral Surgeons, So. Calif. Soc. Oral and Maxillofacial Surgeons, Western Soc. Oral and Maxillofacial Surgeons, Am. Acad. Dental Radiology, Marsh Robinson Acad. Oral Surgeons, So. Calif. Acad. Oral Pathology, Profl. Staff Assn. Los Angeles County-U. So. Calif. Med. Ctr. (exec. com. 1976—), Am. Cancer Soc. (Calif. div., profl. edn. subcom. 1977—), San Gabriel Valley Dental Soc. (past pres.), Xi Psi Phi, Omicron Kappa Upsilon, Delta Epsilon. Seventh-day Adventist. Home: 1102 Loganrita Ave Arcadia CA 91006 Office: 132 S Mission Dr San Gabriel CA 91776

GAMLEN, SARA JEANNE, mathematics educator; b. Seattle, Aug. 7, 1934; d. Richard Shepard and Opal Mae (Moore) Trumbull; m. Earl Ray Kelley, Sept. 4, 1956 (div. 1960); 1 child Opal Kathleen; m. John William Gamlen, Nov. 26, 1975;. BEd, Linfield Coll., 1958; MA, Bowling Green State U., 1962; PhD in Number Theory, Wash. State U., 1967; postgrad., Oberlin Coll., 1954, 56, 60. Instr. Olympic Community Coll., Bremerton, Wash., 1962-64; teaching asst. Wash. State U., Pullman, 1964-65, instr., 1965-66, research asst., 1966-67; asst. prof. Western Wash. U., Bellingham, 1967-71, assoc. prof., 1971—; Cons. Bermerton (Wash.) Sch. Dist., 1962-64, Coupeville (Wash.) Sch. Dist., 1968-69, 79, N. Kitsap Sch. Dist, Poulsbo, Wash., 1969-70, Anacortes (Wash.) Sch. Dist., 1982-83. Author: Learning Mathematics Through Activities, 1973, The Math Fair, 1978. Foster parent Sate of Wash., Bellingham, 1980-85. Grantee Western Wash. U., 1969, Faculty Devel. Western Wash. U., 1985; recipient Disting. Teaching award Western Wash. U., 1978. Mem. Wash. State Math. Council, Oreg. Council Tchrs. Math., Nat. Council Tchrs. Math., Delta Kappa Gamma. Lodges: Order of the Rainbow for Girls (worthy advisors 1951) Order of Eastern Star. Avocation: raising horses. Home: PO Box 17 Maple Falls WA 98266 Office: Western Wash U Bond Hall Bellingham WA 98225

GAMMILL, DARRYL CURTIS, financier; b. Milw., Jan. 20, 1950; s. Lawrence H. and Eunice G. (Birkett) G.; B.S., U. Colo., 1973; m. Maureen Mulcahy, Sept. 16, 1972; children—Rebecca, Bridgett, Maureen, Bryann. Lic. Gen. Prin., Fin. Prin., Registered Options Prin., Sr. Compliance Officer, Registered Rep., SEC, registerd investment advisor, broker dealer, SEC. Stockbroker, Douglas, Stanat, Inc., Denver, 1974; dir. research Pittman Co., Denver, 1975; option specialist B.J. Leonard & Co., Denver, 1976; v.p. research, corp. fin. Neidiger, Tucker Bruner, Denver, 1977; chmn., pres., chief exec. officer G.S. Omni Corp., 1979-82; chmn., chief exec. officer Gammill and Co., 1981—, chief exec. officer, DiMarchi, Gammill & Assocs., 1986—; mng. ptnr. G.S. Oil, G.S. Leasing; dir. Valudyne, Inc., 1973-79; pres. Chalton Investment Services; chmn., pres. Fusion Mgmt. Corp., 1981-83; chmn. Applied Fusion Research & Tech. Corp., 1982, Pres. Research Mgmt., 1984; gen. partner Fusion Ltd. Trustee Gammill Found.; pres. Platinium Club Inc., 1985—; founder AudioOptics. Founder Nicholas R. Massano Ednl. Scholarship, 1985; co-founder Opera Colo. Mem. Fin. Analysts Fedn., Nat. Assn. Security Dealers, Denver Soc. Security Analysts, IEEE, Am. Nuclear Soc., Nat. Energy Assn. (nat. chmn.), U.S. Ski Assn. Clubs: Optimists, Elks. Contbr. articles to profl. jours. Home: 9770 W Frost Pl Littleton CO 80123

GAMMON, MATTIE JEAN, comptroller; b. Los Angeles, Aug. 11, 1924; d. Roy E. and Mary Lucille (Slack) Gould; m. Robert R. Gammon, Dec. 18, 1948; children: Mark R., Greg B. BS, U. Calif., Berkeley. Comptroller Nat. Council Juvenile and Family Ct. Judges, Inc., Reno, 1971—; bd. dirs. Fallon Mobile Homes, Inc., Reno, 1972—, Internation Inst. Youth, Inc., Mt. Vernon, Ind., 1984—. Mem. AAUW, Calif. Alumni, Alpha Xi Delta. Clubs: Croesus, Inc. Home: 1455 Vulgamore Pl Reno NV 89509

GANAPOL, BARRY DOUGLAS, nuclear engineering educator, consultant; b. San Francisco, May 15, 1944; s. Manny Mervin and Miriam (Comar) G.; m. Starr Storms Schroeder, Nov. 7, 1982; 1 child, Joshua Storms. BS, U. Calif., Berkeley, 1962-66, PhD, 1971; MS, Columbia U., 1967. Engr. Swiss Fed. Inst., Switzerland, 1971-72, Saclay, France, 1972-77; engr. Argonne Nat. Lab., Chgo., 1977-78, cons., 1977-79; prof. U. Ariz., Tucson, 1976—; cons. Los Alamos (N.Mex.) Nat. Labs., 1979, Sci. Application Inc., Albuquerque, 1979-82. Contbr. articles to profl. jours. Mem. Soc. Indsl. and Applied Math., Am. Nuclear Soc., Sigma Xi. Avocations: guitar, model building. Home: 4012 Calle Chica Tucson AZ 85711 Office: U Ariz Dept Nuclear Engring Room 106 Tucson AZ 85721

GANCHER, DAVID ARTHUR, editor; b. Augusta, Ga., Feb. 17, 1943; s. Ralph and Anita Frances (Sosno) G.; m. Betty Lynn Moulton, Sept. 29, 1973; children: Sarah, Elizabeth. BA, U. Calif., Berkeley, 1964; MA, San Francisco State U., 1969. Editor Friends of the Earth, 1974-79; sr. editor Sierra Mag., San Francisco, 1979-84; asst. dir. pub. affairs Sierra Club, San Francisco, 1980-84; editor in chief Computerland Corp., Oakland, Calif., 1984—. Office: Computerland Corp 2901 Peralta Oaks Ct Oakland CA 94605 Other Address: Computerland Magazine Computerland Corp 30985 Santana St Hayward CA 94544

GANCHER, STEPHEN THEO, neurologist; b. Berkeley, Calif., May 23, 1955; s. Ralph and Anita (Susno) G.; m. Susan Elizabeth Graham, Aug. 22, 1981; 1 child, Nathan Holmes. Student, Stanford U., 1972-73; BA in Music, U. Calif., Berkeley, 1976; MD, Bowman Gray, 1980. Diplomate Am. Bd. Psychiatry and Neurology. Intern VA Med. Ctr., Marinez, Calif., 1980-81;

resident in neurology Oreg. Health Scis. U., Portland, 1981-84, fellow in movement disorders, 1984-86, asst. prof. neurology, 1987—; cons. neurologist Western Med. Cons., Portland, 1984-86, asst. prof., 1987—; cons. Parkinson Disease VA Med. Ctr., Boise, Idaho, 1986—; dir. movement disorder clinic VA Med. Ctr., Portland, 1986—. Contbr. articles to profl. jours. Tarter Trust fellow, Portland, 1984; recipient Nat. Research Service award Nat. Inst. Neurol. and Communicative Disorders and Stroke, Bethesda, Md., 1985—. Mem. AAAS, Am. Acad. Neurology, AMA. Democrat. Jewish. Avocations: gardening, music, camping, cooking. Home: 1124 SE Malden St Portland OR 97202

GANDHI, OM PARKASH, electrical engineer; b. Multan, Pakistan, Sept. 23, 1934; came to U.S., 1967, naturalized, 1975; s. Gopal Das and Devi Bai (Patney) G.; m. Santosh Nayar, Oct. 28, 1963; children: Rajesh Timmy, Monica, Lena. B.S. with honors, Delhi U., India, 1952; M.S.E., U. Mich., 1957, Sc.D., 1961. Research specialist Philco Corp., Blue Bell, Pa., 1960-62; asst. dir. Cen. Electronics Engring. Research Inst., Pilani, Rajasthan, India, 1962-65, dep. dir., 1965-67; prof. elec. engring., research prof. bioengring. U. Utah, Salt Lake City, 1967—; cons. U.S. Army Med. Research and Devel. Command, Washington, 1973-77; cons. to industry and govtl. organizing; mem. Internat. URSI Commn. B., 1976—; mem. study sect. on diagnostic radiology NIH, 1978-81. Author: Microwave Engineering and Applications, 1981; editor Engineering in Medicine and Biology mag., Mar., 1987; contbr. over 150 articles on biol. effects and med. applications of electromagnetic energy, microwave semicondr. devices and microwave tubes to profl. jours. Recipient Disting. Research award U. Utah, 1979-80; grantee NSF, NIH, EPA, USAF, U.S. Army, USN, N.Y. State Dept. Health, others. Fellow IEEE (editor Procs. of IEEE Spl. Issue, 1980 ; Tech. Achievement award Utah sect. 1975); mem. Bioelectromagnetics Soc. (dir. 1979-82). Office: U Utah Elec Engring Dept 3053 Merrill Engineering Salt Lake City UT 84112

GANDILHON, CATHERINE (CANOE) JEAN, professional cultural society administrator; b. Algers, Algeria, Mar. 18, 1943; came to U.S., 1967, naturalized, 1974; d. Jean Marie and Gevevieve (Berger) G.; m. Erik C. Pfeiffer, Dec. 24, 1983. Baccalaureat, State Exam, Paris, 1962; Dante Alighieri, State Exam, Rome, 1964; BA, Columbia U., 1975, MA, 1976. Asst. editor Vogue mag., Paris, Los Angeles, N.Y.C., 1964-71; head of office Cultural Services French, Embassy in N.Y.C., 1976-79; with city and county of Albuquerque, 1979-85; exec. dir. Albuquerque United Artists Assn., 1985—; mem. translations com. Franco-Am. Inst., N.Y.C., 1976-78, official Archaeolog. Resources Planning Adv. Com., Albuquerque, 1985. Sustaining mem. Rep. Nat. Com., Washington; sponsor GOP Victory Fund; mem. Rep. Party N.Mex., 1983—; Nat. Fedn. Rep. Women, 1984—; active bd. N.Mex. Mus. Nat. History, 1985-86. Mem. ZIA Federated Women (hospitlity chmn. 1983—). Roman Catholic. Avocations: skiing, needlepoint, ballet, jazz exercises. Home: 209 Ortega Rd NW Albuquerque NM 87114

GANDLER, JOSEPH RUBIN, chemistry educator; b. Bklyn., Dec. 2, 1949; s. Benjamin and Mary (Levine) G.; m. Marlene Ryba, Mar. 24, 1974; children: Rachel Karen, Alan Jeremy. BS in Chemistry, Bklyn. Coll., 1971; PhD in Chemistry, U. Calif., Santa Cruz, 1978. NIH fellow SUNY, Buffalo, 1978-79, Brandeis U., Waltham, Mass., 1979-81; asst. prof. chemistry Calif. State U., Fresno, 1981-84, assoc. prof., 1985—. Contbr. articles to profl. jours. Asst. dir. Cen. Valley Sci. and Engring. Fair, Fresno, 1981-84. Research grantee Petroleum Research Fund, 1985—. Mem. Am. Chem. Soc. (chmn. San Joaquin Valley sect. 1984, program chmn. 1982-84, sec.-treas. 1981). Jewish. Office: Calif State U Chemistry Dept Fresno CA 93740

GANER, PATRICIA MARIAN, forensics educator; b. Stephenville, Tex., Dec. 4, 1948; d. George Joseph and Erika Johanna (Zeus) G. AA, Cypress Coll., 1968; BA, U. So. Calif., 1970; MA, UCLA, 1971, Calif. State U., Fullerton, 1976. Prof., dir. forensics Cypress (Calif.) Coll., 1971—; cons. NOW, Los Angeles, 1982-84, Nat. Women's Edn. Fund., Washington, 1982—, Calif. Dept. Edn., Sacramento, 1986. Contbr. articles to profl.jours. Cons. So. Calif. Democrats, 1984—. Recipient Disting. Coaching award U. Utah, 1984. Mem. Am. Forensic Assn. (pres. 1986—, editor jour. 1982-84, 86-88), Speech Communications Assn. (mem. legis. council. 1984—), Western Forensic Assn. (pres. 1983-85), Phi Rho Pi (Disting. Service award 1981). Avocation: travelling. Home: 5600 Cajon Ave Buena Park CA 90621 Office: Cypress Coll 9200 Valley View St Cypress CA 90630

GANN, HELAINE GOLDFIELD, health services coordinator; b. Chgo., Feb. 25, 1940; d. Samuel and Anita Sonja (Mosko) Goldfield; m. Larry Dean Knight, June 7, 1963 (div. Dec. 1970); 1 child; Andrew; m. Galen Dean Gann, July 28, 1974 (dec.); children: Michael, Kenneth. AA, U. Calif., Berkeley, 1959; BS, U. So. Calif., Los Angeles, 1963; postgrad., U. Calif. Med. and Dental Schs., San Francisco and Davis, 1969-73, 76. Dental asst. San Leandro, Calif., 1957-61; occupational therapist Altedena (Calif.) Therapy, 1962, Supulveda (Calif.) Vet. Hosp., 1963; tutor community coll. students Richmond, Calif., 1964-67; tchr. Temple Beth Sholem, Richmond, 1967-71; dental asst., tchr. Oakland (Calif.) Coll. Dental and Med. Assts., 1969-70; coordinator Head Start Health Services, Concord, Calif., 1970—; cons., trainer Am. Acad. Pediatrics, Oakland, 1972-74, Regional Tng. Office Region IX, San Francisco, 1971-74, Devel. Assocs., San Francisco, 1985-86; cons., planner Early Childhood Edn. Program Los Medanos Coll., Pittsburg, Calif., 1973-74; cons., evaluator Health and Human Services Region IX, San Francisco, 1973—; mem. Tricounty Nutrition Bd., Calif., 1971-75; mem. sch. health com. State of Calif., 1971-76; chmn. handicap cluster Head Start Bay Area, 1973-75; regional rep. food rebate program Nat. Head Start, 1972-73; rep. Econ. Opportunity Office to Bay Area Comprehensive Health Assn., 1972-76; mem. adv. com. Resource Access Project, Los Angeles, 1976; chmn. Maternal, Child and Adolescent Health Bd., Contra Costa County, 1986—. Block capt. Heart Assn., Richmond, 1966-71. Mem. Calif. Assn. Neurogically Handicapped, Child Passenger Safety Assn. (parliamentarian, bd. dirs. 1985-86), Am. Pub. Health Assn., Beta Sigma Phi (various postitions held 1966-71), Phi Sigma Sigma (alumni liason officer 1965-66). Democrat. Jewish. Club: Richard III Soc. Avocations: painting, reading, collecting music boxes, sports, history. Home: 1731 Pine St Martinez CA 94553 Office: Contra Costa County Community Services 2425 Bisso Ln Suite 120 Concord CA 94520

GANN, JO RITA, social services administrator; b. Talihina, Okla., June 2, 1940; d. Herbert and Juanita Rita (Fields) G. BS, Okla. Bapt. U., 1962; M Theatre Arts, Portland State U., 1970. Tchr. Oklahoma City Pub. Schs., 1962-64; teen dir., dir. health edn. YWCA, Oklahoma City, 1964-67; camp dir., teen dir. YWCA, Portland, Oreg., 1967-72; asst. dir., program coordinator YWCA, Flint, Mich., 1972-75; exec. dir. YWCA, Salem, Oreg., 1975—; chair N.W. regional staff YWCA, Portland, 1983. Co-author: A New Look at Supervision, 1980. Del. UN Conf. for Non-Govtl. Orgns.; internat. study del. on world econ. interdependence to Ghana, Africa; speaker Global Concerns, Salem and Portland, 1981—; mem. pres.'s council Salem Summerfest, 1985—. Mem. Exec. Dirs. YWCA of U.S., Nat. Orgn. Female Execs. Democrat. Chistian Scientist. Avocations: photography, hiking, swimming, travel. Office: YWCA 768 State St Salem OR 97301

GANNATAL, JOSEPH PAUL, mechanical engineer; b. Ventura, Calif., Sept. 9, 1955; s. Paul and Janet Mae (Carpenter) G.; m. Sandy Jean Lincoln, Jan. 14, 1984; children: Leonard Troy Garcia, Jennfier Lynn Garcia, Sarah Jean Gannatal. BSME, Calif. Polytech. Inst., San Luis Opisbo, 1979; postgrad. in space systems technology, Naval Postgrad. Sch., 1986—. Indsl. engr. Nat. Semiconductor, Santa Clara, Calif., 1979-81; spl. projects engr. Pacific Missile Test Ctr., Point Mugu, Calif., 1981—; mgr. devel. program Pacific Missile Test Ctr., Port Mugu, Calif., 1986—. Mem. bldg. com. Camarillo Baptist Ch., 1984—. Recipient Spl. Achievement award USN, 1982, 84, Letter of Commendation USN, 1983, Outstanding Service award USN, 1985, 86. Mem. AIAA, ASME. Republican. Avocations: ch. constrn., water sports, photography, space systems ops.

GANONG, WILLIAM F(RANCIS), physician, physiologist; b. Northampton, Mass., July 6, 1924; s. William Francis and Anna (Hobbet) G.; m. Ruth Jackson, Feb. 22, 1948; children: William Francis III, Susan B., Anna H., James E. A.B. cum laude, Harvard U., 1945, M.D. magna cum laude, 1949. Intern, jr. asst. resident in medicine Peter Bent Brigham Hosp., Boston, 1949-51; asst. in medicine and surgery Peter Bent Brigham Hosp., 1952-55; research fellow medicine and surgery Harvard U., 1952-55; asst. prof. physiology U. Calif., San Francisco, 1955-60; asso. prof. U. Calif., 1960-64, prof., 1964-82, Jack D. and Deloris Lange prof., 1982—, faculty research lectr., 1968, vice chmn. dept., 1963-68, chmn., 1970-87; cons. Calif. Dept. Mental Hygiene. Author: Review of Medical Physiology, 12th edit., 1985; editor: (with L. Martini) Neuroendocrinology, vol. I, 1966, vol. II, 1967, Frontiers in Neuroendocrinology, 1969, 71, 73, 76, 78, 80, 82, 84, 86; editor-in-chief: Neuroendocrinology, 1979-84. Served with U.S. Army, 1943-46; served to capt. M.C. 1951-52. Recipient Boylston Med. Soc. prize Harvard U., 1949; A.A. Berthold medal, 1985. Fellow AAAS; mem. Am. Physiol. Soc. (pres. 1977-78), Assn. Chairmen Depts. Physiology (pres. 1976-77), Am. Soc. for Gravitational and Space Biology, Soc. Exptl. Biology and Medicine, Endocrine Soc., Chilean Endocrine Soc. (corr.), Internat. Brain Research Orgn., Nat. Soc. Med. Research, Soc. for Neurosci., Internat. Soc. Neuroendocrinology (v.p. 1976-80). Home: 710 Hillside Ave Albany CA 94706 Office: Dept Physiology U Calif San Francisco CA 94143

GANS, WILLIAM LEO, civil servant, electronics engineer; b. Springfield, Mass., Feb. 10, 1943; s. Leo Hubert and Barbara (Powers) G.; m. Sharon K. Malczyk, March 21, 1974 (div. Feb. 1978). BSEE magna cum laude, Northrop U., 1970; MSEE, U. Colo., 1975. Electronics engr. Nat. Bur. Standards, Boulder, Colo., 1970—. Contbr. articles to profl. jours. Chmn. Louisville (Colo.) Housing Authority, 1973-75; mem. Boulder County (Colo.) Housing Authority, 1975-81. Served with U.S. Navy, 1961-66. Mem. IEEE (sr.), Internat. Radio Sci. Union, Sigma Xi, Tau Beta Pi (life). Avocations: swimming, Japanese studies. Home: PO Box 1013 Lyons CO 80540 Office: Nat Bur Standards 325 Broadway Boulder CO 80303

GANT, JOSEPH ERWIN, chemist, former state senator; b. Altamahaw, N.C., Feb. 4, 1912; s. Joseph Erwin and Mary (Banner) G.; B.S., U. N.C., 1934; m. Opal Martin, Feb. 11, 1938 (dec. June 1982); children—Joseph Erwin III, Mary Martin; m. Margaret Minter Doss, Dec. 28, 1985. With U.S. Potash Co., Carlsbad, N.Mex., 1934-56, U.S. Borax & Chem. Co., Carlsbad, 1956-67; chmn. N.Mex. Bd. Eddy Commrs., 1967-68; mem. N.Mex. Senate, 1969-84, mem. judiciary com., 1969-72, rules com., 1973-84, chmn. conservation com., 1973-84, chmn. majority caucus, 1973-84, also vice chmn. legis. univ. study com., 1971-75, mem. local govt. com., 1974-75, chmn. legis. higher edn. admissions standards com., 1976-77, legis. energy com., 1976-77, mem. legis. council, 1978-84, chmn. joint interim radioactive waste consultation com., 1979-84, vice chmn. com. on coms.; dir. Glen Raven Mills, Inc. (N.C.). Pub. mem. N.Mex. State Investment Council, 1959-60; v.p. N.M. Assn. Counties, 1969; dir. Southeastern N.Mex. Econ. Devel. Dist.; mem. Southwestern Regional Energy Council, 1975-84; mem. nat. resources task force intergovtl. com. Nat. Conf. State Legislatures, 1973-77; mem. state-fed. relations energy com., 1977-84; mem. Roswell Dist. Land Use Com., Bur. Land Mgmt., 1978-82, N.Mex. Water Resources Adv. Com., 1982-84; chmn., Eddy County Democratic Com., 1948-60; mem. N.Mex. Dem. Exec. Com., 1953-54. Mem. Am. Chem. Soc., Alpha Tau Omega. Episcopalian. Elk. Home: 602 Riverside Dr PO Box 909 Carlsbad NM 88220 Office: 111 W Menmod PO Drawer DD Carlsbad NM 88220

GANTZ, NANCY ROLLINS, nurse; b. Buffalo Center, Iowa, Mar. 7, 1949; d. Troy Gaylord and Mary (Emerson) Rollins; diploma in Nursing, Good Samaritan Hosp. and Med. Center, Portland, Oreg., 1973; BSBA, City Univ., 1986; MBA, Kennedy-Western U., 1987; m. Aug. 1981. Nurse ICU, Good Samaritan Hosp., 1973-75; charge nurse Crestview Convalescent Hosp., Portland, 1975; dir. nursing services Roderick Enterprises, Inc., Portland, 1976-78, Holgate Center, Portland, 1978-80; nursing cons. in field of adminstrn., 1980-84; coordinator CCU; mgr. ICU/CCU Tuality Community Hosp., Hillsboro, Oreg., 1984-86; head nurse intensive care unit, cardiac surgery unit, Good Samaritan Hosp. & Med. Ctr., Portland, 1986—; mem. task force Oreg. State Health Div. Rules and Regulations Revision for Long Term Health Facilities and Hosps., 1978-79. Mem. Am. Nurses Assn. (cert.), Oreg. Nurses Assn., Nat. League Nursing, Am. Assn. Critical Care Nurses (pres. elect greater Portland chpt. 1985-86, pres. 1986-87), Am. Heart Assn., Oreg. Heart Assn., Geriatric Nurses Assn. Oreg. (founder, charter pres.), Clackamus Assn. Retarded Citizens. Adventist. Home: 2670 NW Eastway Ct Beaverton OR 97006

GARA, ROBERT IMRE, research forest entomology educator; b. Santiago, Chile, Dec. 16, 1931; came to U.S., 1941; s. Emery Imre and Marina G. (Briones) G.; m. Ola Olivia Alexander, Sept. 31, 1958 (div. Jan. 1979); children: Jennifer Gail, Kathryn Alexis; m. Marcela B. Garcia-Huidobro, Sept. 1, 1980; children: Robert Imre, Marcela Bernarda Marina. BS, Utah State U., 1953; MS, Oreg. State U., 1962, PhD, 1964. Forester Kirby Lumber Corp., Houston, 1957-60; scientist Boyce Thompson Inst., Grass Valley, Calif., 1960-64; project leader Boyce Thompson Inst., Beaumont, Tex., 1964-66; assoc. prof. forest entomology State Coll. Forestry, Syracuse, N.Y., 1966-68; prof. U. Wash., Seattle, 1968—; course dir. Orgn. Tropical Studios, Cen. Am., 1969; cons. FAO, Costa Rica, 1970, Peace Corps, Chile, 1970-76, USAID, Ecuador, 1983—. Contbr. articles to profl. jours. Served to capt. USAF, 1953-57. Mem. AAAS, Entomol. Soc. Am., Can. Entomol. Soc., Soc. Am. Foresters. Avocations: swimming, hiking. Home: 1335 NE 106th St Seattle WA 98125 Office: U Wash Coll Forest Resources AR-10 Seattle WA 98195

GARAMENDI, JOHN R., state legislator; m. Patricia Garamendi; 6 children. Grad., U. Calif.-Berkeley; M.B.A., Harvard U. Rancher nr. Sacramento County, Calif.; former mem. Calif. Assembly, now mem. Calif. Senate, chmn. revenue and taxation Joint Com. on Sci. and Tech., mem. energy and pub. utilities com., govt. orgn. com., natural resources com., wildlife com. Served with Peace Corps. Office: State Capitol Room 4081 Sacramento CA 95814

GARBARINI, EDGAR JOSEPH, civil engineer, engineering company executive; b. Jackson, Calif., Aug. 1, 1910; s. Henry Casamero and Elvira (Gardella) G.; m. Lillian Rosemarie Arata, Nov. 14, 1936; children—Paul Henry, Ann Elisabeth. B.S., U. Calif. at Berkeley, 1933. Registered profl. engr., several states. Jr. research engr. U. Cal. at Berkeley, 1933-34, research engr., 1934-38; field engr. W.A. Bechtel & Six Cos. Calif., San Francisco, 1934; civil engr. Calif. Commn., Golden Gate Internat. Expn., 1938-39, Dewell & Earl (cons. engrs.), San Francisco, 1939, Pacific Gas & Electric Co., San Francisco, 1939-40; with Bechtel Group of Cos., San Francisco, 1940—; now sr. exec. cons. Bechtel Group of Cos. Fellow ASCE; mem. Nat. Acad. Engring., Structural Engrs. Assn. No. Calif., Mining and Metall. Soc. Am., Order of Golden Bear, U. Calif. Alumni Assn., Sigma Xi, Tau Beta Pi, Chi Epsilon. Clubs: Family (San Francisco), World Trade (San Francisco), Pacific Union (San Francisco). Office: PO Box 3221 San Francisco CA 94119

GARBARINO, JOSEPH WILLIAM, economics and business educator; b. Medina, N.Y., Dec. 7, 1919; s. Joseph Francis and Savina M. (Volpone) G.; m. Mary Jane Godward, Sept. 18, 1948; children: Ann, Joan, Susan, Ellen. B.A., Duquesne U., 1942; M.A., Harvard U., 1947, Ph.D., 1949. Faculty U. Calif., Berkeley, 1949—; prof. U. Calif., 1960—, dir. Inst. Bus. and Econ. Research, 1962—; cons. in field; vis. lectr. Cornell U., 19S9-60, UCLA, 1949, SUNY, Buffalo, 1972; Fulbright lectr. U. Glasgow, Scotland, 1969; vis. scholar U. Warwick; mem. staff Brookings Instn., 1959-60; vis. lectr. U. Minn., 1978; labor arbitrator. Author: Health Plans and Collective Bargaining, 1960, Wage Policy and Long Term Contracts, 1962, Faculty Bargaining: Change and Conflict, 1975. Served with U.S. Army, 1942-45, 51-53. Decorated Bronze Star. Mem. Am. Econs. Assn., Indsl. Relations Research Assn. Democrat. Roman Catholic. Home: 7708 Ricardo Ct El Cerrito CA 94530 Office: 350 Barrows Hall Sch Bus Adminstrn U of Calif Berkeley CA 94720

GARBER, JANICE WINTER, advertising executive; b. N.Y.C., July 25, 1950; d. Irving and Frances (Edelman) Winter; stepdau. of Daniel Friedman; m. Dale Wayne Garber, Nov. 30, 1978. B.A., Queens Coll., 1979. Prodn. asst. P & F Graphics, N.Y.C., 1969-73; guest service mgr. Sheraton Corp., N.Y.C., 1973-76; advt. mgr. Am. Specialty Corp., N.Y.C., 1976-79; mng. editor VPO Industry News, 1979; advt. mgr. B & M Automotive Products, 1980-81; advt. mgr. Toyota Indsl. Equipment div. Toyota Motor Sales, U.S.A., Inc., Torrance, Calif., 1981—. Mem. Bus./Profl. Advt. Assn. (dir. Los Angeles chpt. 1981), Am. Mktg. Assn. (Marsy award So. Calif. chpt. 1983).

GARBER, JEROLD ALLAN, broadcast executive, educator; b. Peoria, Ill., Aug. 10, 1942; s. Allan Edward and Mary Maxine (King) G.; m. Judith Jane Clause, June 18, 1966 (div.); m. Susan Annette Colonese, May 21, 1982; children—Sara, Timothy, Seth, Jason. B.S.E., No. Ill. U., 1964; M.A., U. Mich., 1969. Tchr., mgr. Sta. WHFH-FM, Homewood-Flossmoor High Sch., Flossmoor, Ill., 1964-79; tchr. Prairie State Coll., Chgo., 1970-79; dir. telecommunications Central Wyo. Coll., Riverton, 1979—; gen. mgr. Sta. KCWC-FM, KCWC-TV, Riverton, 1979-85; gen. mgr. Idaho Ednl. Pub. Broadcasting System, 1985—; dir. Rocky Mountain Corp. Pub. Broadcasting; cons. in pub. radio and T.V. NDEA fellow, 1969. Mem. Western Ednl. Soc. Telecommunications (bd. dirs. Wyo. 1979—, pres. 1985). Democrat. Methodist. Office: Idaho Ednl Pub Broadcasting System 1910 University Dr Boise ID 83725

GARBER, JOSEPH RENÉ, management consultant; b. Phila., Aug. 16, 1943; s. Joseph Michael and Margaret Anne (de Grasse) G.; m. Janice McGuire, Apr. 16, 1969. BA; grad. exec. program, Stanford U. With AT&T, N.Y.C., 1969-73, Booz, Allen & Hamilton, N.Y.C., 1973-84, SRI Inc., Menlo Park, Calif., 1984-85, A.T. Kearney Tech. Inc., Redwood City, Calif., 1985—. Contbr. articles to profl. jours. Served with U.S. Army, 1963-66. Office: A T Kearney Tech 1 Lagoon Dr Redwood City CA 94065

GARBER, MORRIS JOSEPH, statistical consultant, computer programmer; b. N.Y.C., Nov. 6, 1912; s. Isidor and Ethel (Shevack) G.; m. Gloria Ruth Routman, Mar. 7, 1943; children: David I., Diana L. Garber-McCarthy. BS in Zoology, Columbia U., 1933; PhD in Genetics, Tex. A&M U., 1951. Asst. prof. genetics Tex. A&M U., College Station, 1947-56; prof. statistics, biometrician U. Calif., Riverside, 1956-80, emeritus, 1980—; statistician, head statis. lab. Inst. Tropical Agr., 1974-76; cons. research planning and statistics Inter-Am. Inst. Agrl. Scis., Brazilian Enterprise for Agrl. Research, Nat. Ctr. Research in Rice and Beans, 1980-81. Served with Med. Service Corps, AUS, 1941-45. Fellow AAAS, Tex. Acad. Sci.; mem. Am. Genetics Assn., Am. Statis. Assn., Assn. Computing Machinery, Biometric Soc., Sigma Xi. Democrat. Jewish. Club: B'nai B'rith. Home: 3504 Bryce Way Riverside CA 92506 Office: U Calif Riverside Dept Stats Riverside CA 92521

GARBER, RAYMOND ALAN, geologist, researcher; b. Schenectady, N.Y., July 11, 1951; s. William and Laura Sarah (Coplon) G.; m. Barbara Ruth Miretzky, May 25, 1980; children: Jonathan, Joshua. BA, U. Rochester, 1973; MS, Rensselaer Poly. Inst., 1976, PhD, 1980. Prodn. geologist Sun Oil Co., Houston, 1980-81; geologist Gulf Oil Exploration and Prodn., Houston, 1981-84; research geologist Gulf Research and Devel., Houston, 1984-85, Chevron Oil Field Research Co., La Habra, Calif., 1985—. Mem. Am. Assn. Petroleum Geologists, Internat. Assn. Sedimentologists, Soc. Econ. Paleontologists and Mineralogists, Sigma Xi. Democrat. Jewish. Avocations: hiking, gardening. office: Chevron Oil Field Research Co PO Box 446 La Habra CA 90631

GARCIA, BERNIE ISIDORE, real estate appraiser, consultant; b. Taos, N.Mex., June 8, 1939; s. Bernabe and Maria Faustina (Romero) G.; m. Nancy Carolyn Walker, Oct. 29, 1960 (div. 1979); children—Shelley Marie, Bernie Douglas, Susan Therese; m. Cynthia Therese Moraga, June 18, 1983; children: Erik Wayne, Alec Casey. B.S. in Civil Engring., Loyola U., Los Angeles, 1960. Pres. BIG & Assocs., Inc., Covina, Calif., 1968—; v.p. Leegar Inc., Monterey Park, Calif., 1983—; sr. appraiser Ashby Appraisals, Los Angeles, 1978—; instr. Citrus Coll., Azusa, Calif., 1978-82. Recipient award San Gabriel Valley Human Relations Com., 1982. Mem. Am. Soc. Appraisers (sr. mem., editor newsletter 1976), Nat. Assn. Ind. Fee Appraisers, Manufactured Housing Appraisal Inst. Democrat. Home: 3748 Woodhurst Dr Covina CA 91724 Office: Bernie I Garcia & Assocs Inc 267 E Badillo St Covina CA 91723

GARCIA, BONIFACIO BONNY, lawyer; b. Fresno, Calif., Oct. 27, 1956; s. Bonifacio Mata and Corrine (Miranda) G. B.A. magna cum laude, Loyola Marymount U., Los Angeles, 1978; J.D., Harvard U., 1981. Bar: Calif. 1981, U.S. Dist. Ct. (cen. dist.) Calif. 1982. Assoc., Fulop & Hardee, Beverly Hills, Calif., 1981-82; assoc. law firm Leff & Stephenson, Beverly Hills, Calif., 1983-84; assoc. Allen Matkins, Leck, Gamble & Mallory, Los Angeles, 1984-85; assoc. Lillick McHose & Charles, Los Angeles, 1985—; adj. prof. history Loyola Marymount U., 1984. Recipient Loyola Marymount U. Pres.'s citation, 1978. Mem. Los Angeles County Bar Assn., Alpha Sigma Nu; Phi Alpha Theta. Democrat. Roman Catholic. Home: 1440 Veteran Ave #538 Los Angeles CA 90024

GARCIA, DAVID MARTIN, public relations executive; b. Montebello, Calif., Aug. 23, 1956; s. Nick and Laura (Frontino) G.; m. Laura Velez, Apr. 23, 1983. B.A. in Pub. Relations, U. So. Calif., 1978. Spl. project participant Carnation Co., 1978; dir. Student News Bur. U. So. Calif., Los Angeles, 1978; pub. relations rep. TigerAir, Inc., Los Angeles, 1978; asst. pub. info. officer Bank Am., Los Angeles, 1978-80, pub. info. officer, 1980-82, sr. pub. relations officer, 1982-84; account exec. Fleishman-Hillard Inc., 1985, account supr., 1986—. Mem. Altadena Mountain Rescue Team, Los Angeles County Sheriff's Dept.; participant Mex.-Am. Legal Def. and Edn. Fund Leadership Devel. and Advocacy Program. Named Outstanding Grad. USC, 1978; mem. Outstanding Squad, U. So. Calif. Trojan Marching Band, 1978; acad. honors Los Angeles County Sheriff's Acad., 1982. Mem. Publicity Club Los Angeles, Pub. Relations Soc. (Los Angeles chpt.) (vice chmn. task force on minority affairs), Hispanic Pub. Relations Assn. (pres. 1985), U. So. Calif. Alumni Assn., U. So. Calif. Mexican Am. Alumni Assn., Skull and Dagger (men's honor soc.). Republican. Roman Catholic. Office: Fleishman-Hillard 444 S Flower St Los Angeles CA 90071

GARCIA, F. CHRIS, academic administrator, political science educator, public opinion researcher; b. Albuquerque, Apr. 15, 1940; s. Flaviano P. and Crucita A.G.; m. Sandra D.; children—Elaine L., Tanya C. B.A., U. N.Mex., 1961, M.A. in Govt., 1964; Ph.D. in Polit. Sci., U. Calif.-Davis, 1972. Asst. prof. polit. sci. U. N.Mex., Albuquerque, 1970-74, assoc. prof., 1975-78, prof. polit. sci., 1978—, asst. dir. div. govt. research, 1970-72, assoc. dean Coll. Arts and Scis., 1975-80, dean Coll. Arts and Scis., 1980-86; chmn. Zia Research Assocs., Inc., Albuquerque, 1973—. Author: Political Socialization of Chicano Children/1973, La Causa Politica: A Chicano Politics Reader, 1974; The Chicano Political Experience, 1977; State and Local Government in New Mexico, 1979; New Mexico Government, 1976, 1981. Served with N.Mex. Air N.G., 1957-63. Mem. Western Polit. Sci. Assn. (pres. 1977-78), Am. Polit. Sci. Assn. (exec. council 1984-86), Am. Assn. Pub. Opinion Research, Council of Colls. of Arts and Sci. (bd. dirs. 1982-85), Western Social Sci. Assn. (exec. council 1973-76), Phi Kappa Phi, Phi Beta Kappa. Democrat. Roman Catholic. Home: 1409 Snowdrop PL NE Albuquerque NM 87112 Office: U New Mex Scholes Hall 226 Albuquerque NM 87131

GARCIA, HECTOR THOMAS, accountant; b. San Juan Bautista, Calif., Oct. 28, 1926; s. Tomás Jose Garcia y Espinosa and Aurelia María Esparza y Terrazas; B.S., U. Calif.-Berkeley, 1950; M.B.A., Santa Clara U., 1966; M.S., Golden Gate U., San Francisco, 1978; m. Leah Adele Mumm, Nov. 3, 1951; children—Thomas R., Carolyn A., Daniel C., Susan L. Cost acct. Bethlehem Steel Corp., South San Francisco, Calif., 1951-54; supr. cost acctg. Western Gear Corp., Belmont, Calif., 1954-56; supr. microwave cost acctg. Varian Assos., Palo Alto, Calif., 1956-62; sr. budget analyst Lockheed Missiles & Space Co., Sunnyvale, Calif., 1962-66; supr. auditing Calif. Dept. Finance, Sacramento, 1966-70; chief acct. San Jose State U., 1971-72; prin. acct., Office of Pres., U. Calif., Berkeley, 1972-80; dir. Internal audit U. Calif., Davis, 1980—. Served as sgt. U.S. Army, 1944-46; PTO, ETO. CPA, Calif. Mem. Am. Inst. CPA's, Calif. Soc. CPA's, Inst. Internal Auditors (cert.). Home: 630 Cleveland St Davis CA 95616 Office: U Calif Davis Internal Audit Office Orchard Park Dr Davis CA 95616

GARCIA, MARTHA ELAINE, legal secretary; b. Silver City, N.Mex., June 10, 1955; d. G. Rawley and Shirley E. (Leach) Jackson; m. Ronald Joseph Garcia, Sept. 12, 1975; children; Houston Bradley, Ryan Joseph. Student N.Mex. State U. Cert. profl. legal sec. Nat. Assn. Legal Secs. Legal sec. Pickett and Holmes, Las Cruces, N.Mex., 1974—, now also office mgr. Mem. Dona Ana County Legal Secs. Assn. Office: 500 N Church St PO Box 1239 Las Cruces NM 88004

GARCIA, MARTI, interior designer; b. Marrakech, French Morocco, Sept. 28, 1942; d. Meyer and Sabine (Corcos) Sabbah; children—Anthony Martin, Mark Othon. B.P.A. cum laude in Interior Design, Woodbury Coll., Los Angeles, 1965. Interior designer Robinsons, Los Angeles, 1972-74, Bullocks, Santa Ana, 1975-77; prin. Interiors By Marti, Huntington Beach, Calif., 1977-85; sr. adminstr. design and facilities Pacific Mutual, Newport Beach, Calif., 1985— . Mem. Am. Soc. Interior Designers (dir.). Office: Pacific Mutual 700 Newport Center Dr Newport Beach CA 92660

GARCIA, PRISCILLA LORRAINE, speech language pathologist; b. Ogden, Utah, Sept. 25, 1954; d. Dan J. and Clara R. (Gonzales) G. Student, Weber State Coll., 1971-73; BS, Utah State U., 1977; MS, U. Utah, 1981; postgrad., U. N.Mex., 1982, 84. Speech lang. pathologist Park City (Utah) Sch. Dist., 1978; speech aide U. Utah Med. Ctr., Salt Lake City, 1980, Matheson Headstart and U. Utah, Salt Lake City, 1980, Cen. City Headstart, Salt Lake City, 1980-81; speech lang. pathologist Albuquerque Pub. Schs., 1981-86; speech lang. pathologist Mt. Bell Grant for Rural Speech and Hearing Outreach Program U. N.Mex., Albuquerque, 1986—; cons. AT&T Pioneers, Albuquerque, 1985-86. Vol. Spl. Olympics, Albuquerque, 1985-86. Vocat. Rehab. grantee U. Utah, 1979-81; Ethnic Studies Weber State Coll., Ogden, Utah, 1972-73. Mem. Am. Speech Lang. and Hearing Assn. (cert.), N.Mex. Speech Lang. and Hearing Assn., Sch. Improvement Team. Avocations: needlework, knitting, crocheting, water color, running.

GARCIA, SOLEDAD SOTRES, educational adminstrator; b. Gering, Nebr., Sept. 29, 1930; d. Macedonia Lopez and Soledad Penafiel (Sotres) G. B.A., UCLA, 1954; M.A., Calif. State U.-Los Angeles, 1958; Ph.D., U. So. Calif., 1975. Sr. high sch. tchr. Los Angeles Unified Sch. Dist., Hamilton High Sch., 1955-68, tchr. adult edn. Venice Adult Sch., 1958-69; prof. Spanish dept. Calif. State U.-Dominguez Hills, 1975-76; prof. orgn./adminstrn., secondary edn. Calif. State U.-Northridge, 1977-80; secondary girls' vice prin. Los Angeles Unified Sch. Dist., Hollenbeck Jr. High Sch., 1968-71, dir. ednl. services central office East/N.E. Model Cities, 1971; secondary prin. Los Angeles Unified Sch. Dist., Wilmington Jr. High Sch., 1971-76, asst. dir. Tax Revenue Limit Info. Office, 1976, secondary prin. Northridge Jr. High Sch., 1976-80, secondary prin. Webster Jr. High Sch., 1980-83, Gage Jr. High Sch., 1983—; cons. Mount St. Mary's Dept. Edn., 1982. Mem. Calif. State Behavioral Sci. Bd. Examiners, 1979-83; dir. So. Calif. Met. Water Dist., 1976-86; mem. exec. com. and adv. council U. Calif. Water Resources Ctr., 1980; mem. Sch. Community Adv. Council, 1980-83, West Los Angeles Coordinating Council, 1980-83. Recipient Mayor of Wilmington Spl. award, 1976; named Dep. Mayor, Los Angeles City Employees Orgn., 1975; Educator of Yr., Los Angeles County Bd. Edn., 1982. Mem. Assn. Mexican-Am. Educators, Mexican-Am. Women Educators, So. Calif. Assn. for Edn. Young Children, Assn. Calif. Sch. Adminstrs., MLA Calif., Los Angeles Jr. High Sch. Prins. Assn., Associated Adminstrs. Los Angeles, Hon. Assn. Women in Edn., Sigma Delta Phi. Democrat. Roman Catholic. Office: Los Angeles Unified Sch Dist 450 N Grand Ave Los Angeles CA 90012

GARCIA-BORRAS, THOMAS, oil co. exec.; b. Barcelona, Spain, Feb. 2, 1926; came to U.S., 1955, naturalized, 1961; s. Thomas and Teresa (Borras-Jarque) Garcia-Julian; M.S., Nat. U. Mex., 1950; postgrad. Rice U., 1955-56; m. Alia Castellanos Lima, Apr. 30, 1952; children—Erik, Angelica, Laureen, Cliff. Chief chemist Petroleos Mexicanos, Veracruz, Mex., 1950-55; research engr. Monsanto, Texas City, Tex., 1956-60; pilot plant mgr. Cabot and Foster Grant Co., 1960-69; engring. mgr. Signal Chem. Co., Houston, 1969-71; mgmt. and engring. cons., Covina, Calif., 1971-73; project mgr. Occidental Petroleum Co., Irvine, Calif., 1973-79; fleet and indsl. mgr. internat. ops. Wynn Oil Co., Fullerton, Calif., 1979—. Mem. Internat. Mktg. Assn., Am. Inst. Chem. Engrs., Am. Chem. Soc. Author: Manual for Improving Boiler and Furnace Performance, 1983; contbr. articles to profl. jours. Home: 1430 E Adams Park Dr Covina CA 91724 Office: 2600 E Nutwood Ave Fullerton CA 92631

GARCIA-BUNUEL, LUIS, neurologist; b. Madrid, Spain, Feb. 24, 1931; s. Pedro Garcia and Concepcion Bunuel; came to U.S., 1956, naturalized, 1965; B.A., Universidad de Zaragoza, 1949, B.S., 1949, M.D., 1955; m. Virginia M. Hile, June 30, 1960. Intern, Universidad De Zaragoza Hosp. Clinico, 1955-56 resident in neurology Georgetown U., Washington, 1956-59; NIH fellow in neurochemistry dept. pharmacology, Washington U., St. Louis, 1959-61; practice medicine specializing in neurology St. Louis, 1959-61; instr. neurology Jefferson Med. Coll., Phila., 1961-64, asst. prof. neurology, 1964-67; asst. prof. neurology U. N.Mex., Albuquerque, 1967-72; chief neurology service VA Hosp. Portland, Oreg., 1972; asso. prof. neurology, U. Oreg. Health Center, 1972-84; chief staff Phoenix VA Med. Ctr., 1984—. Diplomate Am. Bd. Neurology and Psychiatry. Fellow Am. Acad. Neurology; mem. AAAS, Am. Soc. Neurochemistry, Oreg. Neuropsychiat. Soc., Portland Myasthenia Gravis Assn. (med. adv. bd.), Sigma Xi, Phi Kappa Phi. Contbr. articles to profl jours. Office: VA Med Ctr 7th St and Indian School Rd Phoenix AZ 85012

GARDENSWARTZ, LEAH ELLEN, mgmt. cons. co. exec.; b. Denver, May 12, 1943; d. Nathan William and Rosyne Miriam (Bloom) G. BA, U. Colo., 1965; MA, Calif. Luth. Coll., 1977; PhD, U.S. Internat. U., 1981. Tchr., Los Angeles Sch. Dist., 1965-77, various positions, 1977-80; cons., trainer, ptnr. Tng. and Cons. Assocs., Los Angeles, Calif., 1980—. Author: Beyond Sanity and Survival: A Stress Management Workbook. Mem. Am. Soc. Tng. and Devel., Calif. Women Bus. Owners, Nat. Assn. Female Execs. Contbr. articles to profl. jours. Address: 12720 Bonaparte Ave Los Angeles CA 90066

GARDESKI, THOMAS FRANK, chemical research executive, consultant; b. Milw., June 1, 1945; s. Frank Dominic and Joyce Marie (Fedrizzi) G.; m. Carole Ann Champion, June 18, 1966; children: Dawn Marie, Shawn Thomas. BS ChemE, U. N.D., 1964; BS in Chemistry, U. Minn., 1966. Chemist Sheldahl Inc., Northfield, Minn., 1964-67; dir. Sheldahl Inc., Northfield, 1979-84; polymer chemist 3M Co., St. Paul, 1967-69, advanced chemist, 1969-73, sr. chemist, 1973-79; v.p. Gila River Products, Chandler, Ariz., 1984—. Patentee in field. Fellow Am. Inst. Chemistry; mem. AAAS, Soc. Advancement Materials and Process Engring., Am. Mgmt. Assn., N.Y. Acad. Scis. Republican. Roman Catholic. Avocations: golf, marathon running, tennis. Home: 1259 E Louis Way Tempe AZ 85284 Office: Gila River Products 6615 W Boston St Chandler AZ 85226

GARDIN, JULIUS MARKUS, cardiologist; b. Detroit, Jan. 14, 1949; s. Abram and Fania (Toba) G.; m. Susan Deanne Kelemen, Dec. 19, 1982; 1 child, Adam Lev. BS with high distinction, U. Mich., 1968, MD cum laude, 1972. Diplomate Am. Bd. Internal Medicine. Intern then resident in medicine U. Mich., Ann Arbor, 1972-75; fellow in cardiology Georgetown U., Washington, 1975-77; dir. cardiology noninvasive lab., staff cardiologist Lakeside VA Med. Ctr., Chgo., 1977-79; staff cardiologist, asst. prof. Northwestern U. Med. Sch., Chgo., 1977-79; dir. cardiology noninvasive lab. U. Calif. Irvine Med. Ctr., Orange, 1979—, assoc. prof., 1984—; acting chief cardiology Long Beach (Calif.) Med. Ctr., 1982-84. Co-editor: Textbook of Two-Dimensional Echocardiography, 1983; editor: Update on Cardiovascular Diagnostics, 1982; assoc. editor Am. Jour. Cardiac Imaging, 1985—; mem. editorial bd. Archives of Internal Medicine and Chest, 1978-, Echocardiography, Am. Jour. Noninvasive Cardiol., 1985—, Am. Jour. Cardiol., 1987—; contbr. articles to profl. jours. Served to maj. Med. Service Corps, USAR. Am. Heart Assn. grantee, 1980-82, 83-84. Fellow ACP, Am. Coll. Cardiology, Am. coll. Chest Physicians, Am. Heart Assn. (council Clin. cardiology), Am. Geriatrics Soc.; mem. Internat. Cardiac Doppler Soc. (chmn. 1986, bd. dirs. Pan-Am. sect. 1984—), Am. Soc. Echocardiography (bd. dirs. 1985—, mem. subcom. doppler tng. and edn.), Am. Inst. Ultrasound Med. (sr.), U. Mich. Med. Ctr. Alumni Assn. (bd. govs. 1979-81), Phi Beta Kappa, Alpha Omega Alpha, Phi Delta Epsilon. Jewish. Office: U Calif Irvine Med Ctr Div Cardiology Bldg 53 Rt 81 101 City Dr S Orange CA 92668

GARDINER, LESTER LLEWELYN, municipal government official, real estate associate; b. Nassau, The Bahamas, Dec. 17, 1959; came to U.S., 1962; s. Nathaniel Branford and Myrtle Violet (Hamilton) G. BSBA, Biola U., 1982. Lic. in real estate sales, Calif. Gen. mgr. U-Haul Co., Los Angeles, 1985—; sales agt. Larry Porchia Estates, Los Angeles, 1986—; mgmt. asst. community devel. dept. City of Los Angeles, 1986—, asst. mgr. Mem. City of Los Angeles Community Devel. Democrat. Avocations: martial arts, reading, jazz music, real estate investment, religion. Home: 751 W 124th St Los Angeles CA 90044

GARDIS, GILDA J., quality analyst; b. Jersey City, Jan. 16, 1944; d. William Patrick and Gilda Esther (Weber) Cornett; m. David Richard Gardis, Oct. 8, 1966 (div. 1981). Student Oceanside-Carlsbad Jr. Coll., Santa Monica City Coll. Prin. typist clk. UCLA, 1966-69, adminstrv. asst., 1969-73, acctg. asst., 1973-75, mgmt. services officer, UCLA, 1975-79; mgmt. services officer U. Calif., San Diego, La Jolla, 1979-85; quality analyst Teledyne Kinetics, Solana Beach, Calif., 1986—; part-time sales rep. Mervyn's, Oceanside, Calif., 1986—. Active Oceanside High Sch. Booster Club, 1980-83. Recipient Tiffany award, Manpower, Carlsbad, Calif., 1985. Mem. Am. Mgmt. Assn. (assoc.), Nat. Assn. Female Execs., Am. Mgmt. Assn. (assoc.), Network Exec. Women, NEW. Roman Catholic. Avocations: Tennis; bicycling; art; bowling. Home: 3559 Guava Way Oceanside CA 92054 Office: Teledyne Kinetics 410 S Cedros Solana Beach CA 92075 Mailing Address: PO Box 1401 Oceanside CA 92054

GARDNER, A. BARCLAY, state employment services executive; b. Spanish Fork, Utah, Jan. 25, 1930; s. Archibald Barclay and Virginia (Williams) G.; m. Renee Wilkey, Feb. 16, 1951; children—Kristie Gardner Mikstas, Gregory Barclay, Janeanne. B.S., Brigham Young U., 1954, M.S., 1956. Supr., mgr. Utah Dept. Employment Security, Provo, Vernal, and Salt Lake City, 1954-75, dir. adminstr. services, Salt Lake City, 1975-78, adminstr., 1978-86; gov.'s adminstrv. asst. Office Leadership, Mgmt. and Orgn. Devel., State of Utah, 1986-87. Pres. Interstate Conf. Employment Security Agencies, 1982-83, bd. dirs., 1979-84. Mem. Utah Job Tng. Coordinating Council, 1983-86, Utah Gov.'s Council Econ. Advisers, 1981-84, Nat. Vets. Council, 1982-85, Utah Commn. on Efficiency and Effectiveness in Govt., 1985-86, Practitioners Task Force, 1984-86; bd. dirs. Utah br. Nat. Alliance Bus., 1979-80. Mem. Nat. Commn. Employment Policy, Am. Legion. Mormon. Served with U.S. Army, 1950-52; Korea. Home: 2805 Marcus Rd Salt Lake City UT 84119 Office: 2100 State Office Bldg Salt Lake City UT 84114

GARDNER, AUTREY THADDEUS, JR., industrial technology educator; b. Scottsboro, Ala., Aug. 5, 1939; s. Autrey Thaddeus and Faye Louise (Kennamer) G.; m. Joyce Elva Keel; children: Tracey Anne, Autrey Thaddeus III. BSBA, U. Ala., 1962; postgrad., U. N.D., 1967-70; MA in Communications, U. No. Colo., 1983. Commd. 2d lt. USAF, Amarillo AFB, Tex., 1962; advanced through grades to major USAF, various locations, 1972; chief of plans 351st Strategic Missile Wing, Whiteman AFB, Mo., 1973-74, supr. maintenance, 1974-76; maintenance staff officer 3901st Strategic Missile Squadron, Vandenberg AFB, Calif., 1976-80; dir. tng. 90th Strategic Missile Wing, F.E. Warren AFB, Wyo., 1980-83; ret. USAF, 1983; asst. prof. So. Ill. U., F.E. Warren AFB, Wyo., 1983—, faculty rep., 1983—. Contbr. articles to profl. jours. Mem. Nat. Assn. Indsl. Technologists, Inst. Indsl. Engrs., Am. Soc. Safety Engrs., Speech Communications Assn., Western Speech Assn., Air Force Assn., Ret. Officers Assn. Republican. Mem. Ch. Christ. Clubs: Warren AFB Officers (bd. dirs. 1982-83), Rocky Mountain Health. Avocations: golf, raquetball, woodworking, calligraphy. Home: 3300 Carey Ave Cheyenne WY 82001 Office: So Ill U 90 CSG/DPE FE Warren AFB WY 82005

GARDNER, BARBARA ELAINE, system analyst; b. Sandia Base, N.Mex., Sept. 5, 1950; d. Orville Kenneth and Gladys (Hancock) G.; B.S., U. Colo., M.B.A., 1978. Instr. adult basic edn., Independence, Iowa, 1971; merit grad. asst. U. Colo., Boulder, 1976, 77, 78, grad. adminstr. simulated production game, 1977, grad. teaching asst., 1976-77, research asst. to Bur. Econ. Research, 1977, computer lab. advisor, statis. tutor, 1977-78, instr. prodn. mgmt., 1980-81; devel. programmer IBM, Boulder, 1979-82, analyst, 1983—. Organizer, coordinator legal aid program Welfare Rights Orgn.; protective payee and conservator Social Service Dept.; worker Drug Councils, Planned Parenthood, Probation Office, Council on Alcoholism, 1970-72. Mem. Am. Prodn. and Inventory Control Soc., Sigma Iota Epsilon, Beta Gamma Sigma. Home: 209 29th St Boulder CO 80303 Office: IBM 5600 N 63d St Boulder CO 80314

GARDNER, BOOTH, governor of Washington; b. Tacoma, Aug. 21, 1936; m. Jean Gardner; children—Doug, Gail. B.A. in Bus., U. Wash., 1958; M.B.A., Harvard U., 1963. Asst. to dean Sch. Bus. Adminstrn., Harvard U., Cambridge, Mass., 1966; dir. Sch. Bus. and Econs., U. Puget Sound, Tacoma, 1967-72; pres. Laird Norton County, 1972-80; mem. Wash. Senate, 1970-73; county exec. Pierce County, Tacoma, 1981; gov. State of Wash., 1984—. Co-founder Central Area Youth Assn. Seattle; trustee Central City Learning Ctr. Tacoma, Wash. Commn. for Humanities, Seattle Mental Health Inst., Troubleshooters advocacy for developmentally disabled, Pvt. Industry Council, U. Puget Sound. Office: Legislative Bldg Olympia WA 98504 *

GARDNER, DAVID PIERPONT, university president; b. Berkeley, Calif., Mar. 24, 1933; s. Reed S. and Margaret (Pierpont) G.; m. Elizabeth Fuhriman, June 27, 1958; children: Karen, Shari, Lisa, Marci. BS, Brigham Young U., 1955, DH (hon.), 1981; MA, U. Calif., Berkeley, 1959, PhD, 1966; DLitt (hon.), U. Utah, 1983; LLD (hon.), U. of the Pacific, 1983, U. Nev., Las Vegas, 1984. Dir. Calif. Alumni Found., U. Calif. at Berkeley, 1962-64; asst. to the chancellor, asst. prof. higher edn. U. Calif. at Santa Barbara, 1964-67, asst. chancellor, asst. prof. higher edn., 1967-69, vice chancellor, exec. asst., assoc. prof. higher edn., 1969-70; v.p. U. Calif. System, Berkeley, 1971-73, pres., 1983—; pres., prof. higher edn. U. Utah, Salt Lake City, 1973-83; vis. fellow Clare Hall, Cambridge U., 1979, assoc., 1979—. Author: The California Oath Controversy, 1967; mem. editorial bd. Higher Edn. Quarterly; contbr. articles to profl. jours. Bd. dirs. First Security Corp., George S. and Dolores Dore Eccles Found., The Nature Conservancy, Calif. C. of C., Calif. Econ. Devel. Corp.; trustee Tanner Lectures on Human Values; chmn. Southwestern Dist. Rhodes Scholarship Selection Com.; mem. Bay Area Internat. Forum of World Affairs Council of No. Calif. Decorated Legion d'Honneur (France), 1985; recipient Benjamin P. Cheney medal East Wash. U., 1984, James Bryant Conant award, 1985; named Pres. Emeritus, U. Utah, 1985, 40th Anniversary Disting. Fellow, Fulbright Found., 1987. Fellow Am. Acad. Arts and Scis.; mem. Nat. Assn. State Univs. and Land Grant Colls., Nat. Acad. Pub. Adminstrn., Assn. Am. Univs., Higher Edn. Forum (mem. exec. com. bus.), Phi Beta Kappa, Phi Kappa Phi. Home: 70 Rincon Rd Kensington CA 94707 Office: Office of the Pres Univ of Calif 714 University Hall Berkeley CA 94720 *

GARDNER, DEE RAY, radio broadcasting executive; b. Delta, Utah, Nov. 27, 1925; s. William Nelson and Alice Laura (Iverson) G.; m. Virginia Lea Humphries, Dec. 10, 1949; children—Danna Gayle, Joanne, Laura Marie, Paul Galen. Student, U. of Utah, 1952-54. Radio prodn. KLUB-KALLKNAK radio stations, Salt Lake, 1951-61; TV dir. KUTV, Inc., Salt Lake City, 1961-68; owner KWNA Radio, Winnemucca, Nev., 1977-81; sta. mgr. KELK Radio, Elko, Nev., 1968-74; owner and chief exec. officer ELKO Broadcasting, Elko, Nev., 1974—. Served to staff sg., USAF, 1948-52. Mem. Elko C. of C. (pres. 1977-79). Democrat. Mormon. Lodge: Elks (Elko) (exalted ruler 1970-72), Elks (North Nevada). Home: 1240 Hannah Dr Elko NV 89801 Office: Elko Broadcasting Co 1800 Idaho St Elko NV 89801 *

GARDNER, EDWARD EUGENE, electrical engineering educator; b. Somerset, Pa., Aug. 3, 1923; s. Lloyd Calvin and Ethel Mae (Weyand) G.; m. Betty Bondesen, Sept. 18, 1948; children: Katherine, William, Gregory, Cynthia. SB, MIT, 1948; MA, U. Minn., 1950; PhD, Cath. U. Am., 1955. Asst. prof. Va. Poly. Inst., Blacksburg, 1950-51, U.S. Naval Acad., Annapolis, Md., 1951-55, Lehigh U., Bethlehem, Pa., 1955-58; project leader Whirlpool Corp., St. Joseph, Mich., 1958-62; engring. mgr. IBM Corp., Burlington, Vt., 1962-85; prof. elec. engring. U. Colo., Boulder, 1985—. Patentee in field; contbr. articles to profl. jours. Mem. Am. Phys. Soc., Electrochem. Soc., IEEE, ASTM (subcom. chmn. 1978, Service award 1985), Sigma Xi. Republican. Avocations: duplicate bridge, skiing, tennis, hiking, computers. Home: 81 Benthaven Boulder CO 80303 Office: U Colo Campus Box 425 ECE Dept Boulder CO 80309

GARDNER, FREDERICK BOYCE, reference librarian; b. Hopkinsville, Ky., Mar. 12, 1942; s. Boyce and Alleen Louise (Brown) G. BA, U. Ky., 1964; MA, Ind. U., 1966; postgrad., CUNY, 1970-71, Calif. State U., Northridge, 1973-76, UCLA, 1982-85. Head librarian U. Ky. Hopkinsville Community Coll., 1966-69; head, reader's services Manhattan Community Coll. CUNY, N.Y.C., 1969-71; reference librarian Calif. Inst. Arts, Valencia, 1971-74, head pub. services, 1974-75, dir. computer services, 1974-85, 1984—; cons. Total Interlibrary Exchange, Ventura, Calif., 1984-85, v.p. 1980-81, pres. 1981-82, chmn. tech. task force 1983—. Sec. Sequoia String Quartet Found., Los Angeles, Calif., 1977—. Served to capt. USAF, 1968-69. Mem. Calif. Conf. on Networking (del. 1985), So. Calif. Online User's Group, Calif. Library Assn. Avocations: music, computer games, hiking, camping, space. Office: Calif Inst Arts 24700 McBean Pkwy Valencia CA 91355

GARDNER, GENTRY GARY, computer software engineer; b. El Paso, Tex., Oct. 14, 1961; s. Kenneth Willard and Mayola (Kent) Jantz; m. Gayleen Ruth. BS in Math. Sci., Biola U., 1983. Cert. artificial intelligence UCLA; cert. ada programming lang. Computer programmer XOR Data Sci., Huntington Beach, Calif., 1982-84; software engr. Rockwell Internat., Downey, Calif., 1984—. Mem. speaker's bur. Right to Life League of So. Calif., Los Angeles, 1985-86; tchr. Sunday Sch. Evangelical Free Ch., Huntington Beach, 1986—. Republican. Avocations: basketball, skiing, tennis, mountaineering, painting. Home: 8300 Chapman Ave #42 Stanton CA 90680 Office: Rockwell Internat 12214 Lakewood Blvd MC FA94 Downey CA 90241

GARDNER, JACK IRVING, librarian; b. Seattle, Oct. 7, 1934; s. Irving and Florence Florine (Morgan) G.; m. Carroll Sutherland, June 12, 1963. B.A., U. Wash., 1959, M.L.S., 1960. Br. librarian Bklyn. Pub. Library, 1960-62; librarian, coordinator Sno-Isle Regional Library, Everett, Wash., 1963; librarian, cataloger U. Nev., Reno, 1963-65; documents librarian Nev. State Library, Carson City, 1965-72; adminstr. Clark County Library, Las Vegas, 1972—. Author: Gambling: a bibliography, 1980; contbr. articles, revs. and indices to profl. publs. Served with U.S. Army, 1954-56. Mem. ALA, Nev. Library Assn. (pres. 1974-75), Calif. Library Assn., Friends of Library. Republican. Lodge: Rotary Internat. Office: Las Vegas Library 1726 E Charleston St Las Vegas NV 89104

GARDNER, JAMES HARKINS, insurance executive; b. Evanston, Ill., July 15, 1943; s. James Floyd and Charlotte (Hoban) G.; m. Shirley Jane Bisset, June 22, 1968 (div. 1980); 1 child, Warren Lee; m. Shannon Lee Greer, Nov. 19, 1982; 1 child, Charlotte Greer. BS, Purdue U., 1965; MBA, Harvard U., 1968. V.p. Geomet, Inc., Rockville, Md., 1970-78; pres. Risk Mgmt. Resources, San Francisco, 1979—; dir. Practical Elegance, Sausalito, Calif. Del. White House Conf. on Small bus., 1986; treas. No. Calif. Del. Served with USPHS, 1968-70. Club: Commonwealth Calif. (San Francisco). Lodge: Masons. Office: Risk Mgmt Resources Inc 500 Sansome St San Francisco CA 94111

GARDNER, JOHN DARRELL, mining engineering educator; b. San Francisco, Mar. 16, 1929; s. Darrell and Mary Canice (Sullivan) G.; m. Ruth Ann Richmond; children: Shannon, Jean. BS in Mining Engring., U. Ariz., 1956, (hon.) Mining Engr. degree, 1968; MBA, Harvard U., 1961; PhD in Mining Engring., U. Utah, 1981. V.p. Howmet Corp., N.Y.C., 1961-70; pres. Mgmt. Vectors, Blue Bell, Pa., 1970-76, Tintic Western Mining, Salt Lake City, 1978-86; gen. mgr. Mullen Engring., Casper, Wyo., 1976-79; asst. prof. mining engring. U. Wyo., Laramie, 1981-83, assoc prof., 1984—; cons. Benchmark Engrs., Laramie, 1979—. Author: Mine Evaluation and Design Opti., 1981; contbr. articles to profl. publs. Served to 1st lt. U.S. Army, 1951-53. Mem. N.W. Mining Assn., Soc. Mining Engrs., Sigma Xi, Tau Beta Pi, Theta Tau. Republican. Club: Harvard (N.Y.). Avocations: S.W. mining history, astronomy, pilot. Home: Box 3101 University Station Laramie WY 82071 Office: U Wyo Dept Mining Engring Laramie WY 82071

GARDNER, LEONARD BURTON, II, industrial automation engineer; b. Lansing, Mich., Feb. 16, 1927; s. Leonard Burton and Lillian Marvin (Frost) G.; m. Barbara Jean Zivi, June 23, 1950; children: Karen Sue, Jeffrey Frank. B.Sc. in Physics, UCLA, 1951; M.Sc., Golden State U., 1953, Sc.D. in Engring, 1954; M.Sc. in Computer Sci, Augustana Coll., Rock Island, Ill., 1977. Registered profl. engr.; cert. mfg. engr. Instrumentation engr. govt. and pvt. industry 1951—; prin. engr. computerized systems Naval Electronic Systems Engring. Center, San Diego, 1980-82; founder, dir. Automated Integrated Mfg., San Diego, 1982—; prof. and dir. Center for Automated Integrated Mfg.; cons. govt. agys. and industry, lectr., adj. prof. vaious univs. and colls., sci. advisor state and nat. legislators, 1980—, speaker in field. Author: Computer Aided Robotics Center; editor: Automated Manufacturing. Contbg. author: Instrumentation Handbook, 1981; contbr. numerous articles to tech. jours. Recipient award U.S. Army. Fellow IEEE; sr. mem. Soc. Mfg. Engrs. (Pres.'s award 1984); mem. ASTM, Nat. Soc. Profl. Engrs., Calif. Soc. Profl. Engrs., Sigma Xi. Office: PO Box 1523 Spring Valley CA 92077

GARDNER, NORD ARLING, management consultant; b. Afton, Wyo., Aug. 10, 1923; s. Arling A. and Ruth (Lee) G.; B.A., U. Wyo., 1945; M.S., Calif. State U., Hayward, 1972, M.P.A., 1975; postgrad. U. Chgo., U. Mich., U. Calif.-Berkeley; m. Thora Marie Stephen, Mar. 24, 1945; children—Randall Nord, Scott Stephen, Craig Robert, Laurie Lee. Commd. 2d lt. U.S. Army, 1945, advanced through grades to lt. col., 1964; ret., 1966; personnel analyst Univ. Hosp., U. Calif.-San Diego, 1966-68; coordinator manpower devel. U. Calif.-Berkeley, 1968-75; univ. tng. officer San Francisco State U., 1975-80, personnel mgr., 1976-80; exec. dir. CRDC Maintenance Tng. Corp., non-profit community effort, San Francisco, 1980-85; pres., dir. Sandor Assos. Mgmt. Cons., Pleasant Hill, Calif., 1974-86; gen. mgr. Verićlean Janitorial Service, Inc.; in-charge bus. devel. East Bay Local Devel. Corp., Oakland, Calif., 1980-85; incorporator and pres. Indochinese Community Enterprises, USA, Ltd., Pleasant Hill, Calif., 1985-87; freelance writer, grantsmanship cons., 1987—; instr. Japanese, psychology, supervisory courses, 1977-78. Adv. council San Francisco Community Coll. Dist. Decorated Army Commendation medal. Mem. Ret. Officers Assn., Am. Soc. Tng. and Devel., No. Calif. Human Resources Council. Am. Assn. Univ. Adminstrs., Internat. Personnel Mgrs. Assn., Internat. Platform Assn., Coll. and Univ. Personnel Assn. Republican. Clubs: Commonwealth of Calif., U. Calif.-Berkeley Faculty, Univ. (San Francisco). Author: To Gather Stones, 1978. Home and Office: 2995 Bonnie Ln Pleasant Hill CA 94523 Office: 310 8th St Suite 100 Oakland CA 94607

GARDNER, RICK MICHAEL, psychology educator; b. Fresno, Calif., Aug. 10, 1943; s. Joseph Howard and Edna Mae (Shull) Jensen; m. Elizabeth Ann Miller, June 4, 1967; children: Michael, Lisa. BA, Humboldt State U., 1965; MA, U. Nev., 1967, PhD, 1969. Instr. U. Nev., Reno, 1968; from asst. to full prof. psychology U. So. Colo., Pueblo, 1969—, asst. v.p. for research, 1980-81, chmn. dept. psychology, 1981—; cons. in field, 1969—. Author: Exercises for General Psychology, 1980; contbr. articles to profl. jours. Grantee NIH, 1980—. Mem. Am. Psychol. Assn., Sigma Xi. Avocation: pvt. piloting. Home: 10 Hasting Dr Pueblo CO 81001 Office: U So Colo 2200 N Bon Forte Pueblo CO 81001

GARDNER, ROBERT, judge; b. Arlington, Wash., Dec. 27, 1911; s. Frank M. and Kate H. (Hamilton) G.; m. Kathryn H., Feb. 14, 1942; children—Nancy, Patty. A.B., U. So. Calif., 1933, LL.B., 1936. City judge City of Newport Beach, Calif., 1938-41, 45-47; superior ct. judge Orange County, Calif., 1947-70; judge U.S. Ct. Appeals (4th dist.), San Bernardino, Calif., 1970-82; chief justice High Ct. of American Samoa, Pago Pago, 1982—. Contbr. articles to profl. pubs. Served to lt. comdr. USN, 1941-45; PTO. Decorated Bronze Star. Republican. Avocation: body surfing. Home: 320 Evening Canyon Rd Corona del Mar AS 92625 Office: Am Samoa High Ct, Pago Pago 96799, American Samoa

GARDNER, WILBERT LEE, JR., fire and safety inspector; b. Kansas City, Mo., May 31, 1956; s. Wilbert Lee and Permeila Jane (Barton) G.; m. Elizabeth Kay Cox, Nov. 12, 1977; 1 child, Amy Elizabeth. BS, Cen. Mo. State U., 1977, MS, 1981. Cert. safety profl. Fire fighter Kansas City Fire Dept., 1977-78, 1979-81; safety trainee B.F. Goodrich Chem. Co., Henry, Ill., 1978-79; safety engr. Olin Chem. Co., Lake Charles, La., 1981-82; safety technician U. Tex., Houston, 1982-83; fire and safety insp. Unocal Corp., Parachute, Colo., 1983—; fire fighter Rifle (Colo.) Fire Protection Dist., 1981—. Mem. Am. Soc. Safety Engrs. Presbyterian. Avocation: fishing.

Home: 508A E 7th Rifle CO 81650 Office: Unocal Corp 2712 County Rd 215 Parachute CO 81635

GARDNER, WILFORD ROBERT, physicist, educator; b. Logan, Utah, Oct. 19, 1925; s. Robert and Nellie (Barker) G.; m. Marjorie Louise Cole, June 9, 1949; children: Patricia, Robert, Caroline. B.S., Utah State U., 1949; M.S., Iowa State U., 1951, Ph.D., 1953. Cert. profl. agronomist-soil scientist. Physicist U.S. Salinity Lab., Riverside, Calif., 1953-66; prof. U. Wis., Madison, 1966-80; physicist, prof., head dept. soil and water sci. U. Ariz., Tucson, 1980-87; dean coll. natural resources U. Calif., Berkeley, 1987—. Author: Soil Physics, 1972. Served with U.S. Army, 1943-46. NSF sr. fellow, 1959; Fulbright fellow, 1971-72; Soil Sci. Soc. Am. Research awardee, 1962. Fellow AAAS, Am. Soc. Agronomy; mem. Internat. Soil Sci. Soc. (pres. physics commn. 1968-74), Nat. Acad. Scis. Office: U Calif Coll Natural Resources Berkeley CA 94720

GARDNER, WILLIAM ALLEN, electrical engineering educator; b. Palo Alto, Calif., Nov. 4, 1942; s. Allen Frances McLean and Francis Anne (Demma) Gardner Hodge; m. Nancy Susan Lenhart Hall, June 19, 1966. MS, Stanford U., 1967; PhD, U. Mass., Amherst, 1972. Engr. Bell Telephone Labs., North Andover, Mass., 1967-69; asst. prof. U. Calif., Davis, 1972-77, assoc. prof., 1977-82, prof. elect. engring., 1982—; pres. Statis. Signal Processing Inc. Author: Introduction to Random Processes with Applications to Signals and Systems, 1985; contbr. numerous articles to profl. jours.; patentee in field. Grantee Air Force Office Sci. Research, 1979-82, NSF, 1983-84, Electromagnetic Systems Labs., 1984—. Mem. IEEE, Am. Math. Soc., Sigma Xi, Eta Kappa Nu. Office: U Calif Dept Elec and Computer Engring Davis CA 95616

GARDNER-LOCKETT, MARCELLA LYNN, marketing executive; b. Centralia, Ill., July 16, 1954; d. Joe Marshall and Ernestine (Vaughn) Gardner; m. Jeffery C. Lockett. B.A. in Bus. Adminstrn. and Communication, U. Pacific, 1976; M.B.A., U. Wash., 1978. Systems engr. trainee IBM, Seattle, 1977-78; mktg. engr. customer relations Hewlett-Packard Co., Cupertino, Calif., 1978, mktg. engr. sales devel., major account program, bus. devel. group, 1979-81, mktg. engr. third party program, 1981-82, V2 vertical market devel. mgr., 1982-84; govt. and edn. mgr., 1984—; prin. Lynn Gardner & Assocs. Advisor Jr. Achievement, Santa Clara County (Calif.), 1979-81. Mem. Nat. Assn. Female Execs., Nat. Assn. M.B.A.s, Internat. Fedn. Female Execs., Delta Sigma Theta. Democrat. Office: Hewlett Packard Co 19091 Pruneridge Ave Cupertino CA 95104

GAREY, CHARLES THOMSON, theatre educator; b. Balt., Nov. 22, 1947; s. Thomas Irwin Buchanan and Elizabeth Carroll (Thomson) G.; m. Judith Ann Freeman, June 27, 1971; children: Kirsten Anne, Scott Charles. BA, U. Md., 1971; MA, U. Calif., Santa Barbara, 1975; postgrad., U. Ill., 1981-83. Cert. community coll. tcht. (life), Calif. Asst. theatre carpenter U. Theatre, College Park, Md., 1968-69; theatre technician Tawes Fine Arts Theatre, College Park, 1969-73; lighting designer Lakewood Mus. Playhouse, Barnesville, Pa., 1970; designer, tech. dir. Diner's Playhouse, Lexington, Ky., 1974-75; assoc. prof., design dir. Santa Barbara City Coll., 1975—; v.p. Academic Senate Santa Barbara City Coll., 1985-86, pres., 1987—; del. Academic Senate Calif. Community Colls., Sacramento, 1985-87; mem. nat. adv. com. Design by Motley, Urbana, Ill., 1985—; gen. mgr. Santa Barbara Theatre Group, 1986-87. U. Ill. fellow, 1981-82. Mem. U.S. Inst. Theatre Tech., Omicron Delta Kappa, Nat. Collegiate Players. Democrat. Avocation: computer applications. Office: Santa Barbara City Coll Theater Dept 721 Cliff Dr Santa Barbara CA 93109

GAREY, DONALD LEE, pipeline executive; b. Ft. Worth, Sept. 9, 1931; s. Leo James and Jessie (McNatt) G.; B.S. in Geol. Engring., Tex. A. and M. U., 1953; m. Elizabeth Patricia Martin, Aug. 1, 1953; children—Deborah Anne, Elizabeth Laird. Reservoir geologist Gulf Oil Corp., 1953-54, sr. geologist, 1956-65; v.p., mng. dir. Indsl. Devel. Corp. Lea County, Hobbs, N.Mex., 1965-72, dir., 1972-86, pres., 1978-86; v.p., dir. Minerals, Inc., Hobbs, 1966-72, pres., dir., 1972-86, chief exec. officer, 1978-82; mng. dir. Hobbs Indsl. Found. Corp., 1965-72, dir., 1965-76; v.p. Llano, Inc., 1972-74, exec. v.p., chief operating officer, 1974-75, pres., 1975-86, chief exec. officer, 1978-82, also dir.; pres., chief exec. officer, Pollution Control, Inc., 1969-81; pres. NMESCO Fuels, Inc., 1982-86; chmn., pres., chief exec. officer Estacado Inc., 1986—; pres. Llano Co2, Inc., 1984-86; cons. geologist, geol. engr., Hobbs, 1965-72. Chmn., Hobbs Manpower Devel. Tng. Adv. Com., 1965-72; mem. Hobbs Adv. Com. for Mental Health, 1965-67; chmn. N.Mex. Mapping Adv. Com., 1968-69; mem. Hobbs adv. bd. Salvation Army, 1967-78, chmn., 1970-72; mem. exec. bd. Conquistador council Boy Scouts Am., Hobbs, 1965-75; vice chmn. N.Mex. Gov.'s Com. for Econ. Devel., 1968-70; bd. regents Coll. Southwest, 1982-85. Served to capt. USAF, 1954-56. Registered profl. engr., Tex. Mem. Am. Inst. Profl. Geologists, Am. Assn. Petroleum Geologists, AIME, N.Mex., Roswell geol. socs., N.Mex. Amigos. Club: Rotary. Home: 315 E Alto Dr Hobbs NM 88240 Office: Broadmoor Bldg PO Box 5587 Hobbs NM 88241

GARFIELD, KIM HONEY, public relations executive, writer; b. N.Y.C., Feb. 18, 1934; d. Leon and Celia (Schwartz) G.; m. Douglas Lambert, Mar. 5, 1986. BA, Hunter Coll., 1962. Sr. publicist MGM Pictures, N.Y.C., 1956-64; pres. Kim Garfield, Inc., N.Y.C., 1965-74; v.p. West coast region John Springer Assocs., N.Y.C., 1976-86; free lance unit publicist Los Angeles, 1986—. Contbr. articles to United Features Syndicate, N.Y.C., 1975-84, Los Angeles Times newspaper, 1976—, Dramalogue mag., Los Angeles, 1978—, The Advocate mag., Los Angeles, 1978—, Ladies Home Jour. Mag., 1987—. Mem. Women in Film, Am. Film Inst. Democrat. Mem. Ch. Religious Sci. Avocations: theatre, films, sports, reading, travel. Home and Office: 6363 Orange St Los Angeles CA 90048

GARFIN, DAVID EDWARD, biochemist, researcher; b. Mpls., July 7, 1940; s. Rudolph and Beatrice (Katz) G.; m. Susan Carol Bettelheim, Aug. 3, 1969; children: Phillip Michael, Daniel Alan. BS, U. Minn., 1962, MSEE, 1964; PhD in Biophysics, U. Calif., Berkeley, 1972. Research assoc. U. Calif., San Francisco, 1972-78, asst. research biochemist, 1978-79; mgr. product devel. Tago, Inc., Burlingame, Calif., 1979-80; head immunol. devel. Hana Biologics, Inc., Emeryville, Calif., 1981-82; sr. research biochemist Bio-Rad Labs., Inc., Richmond, Calif., 1983-84, group leader, 1984—. Contbr. chpts. to books, articles to profl. jours.; patentee in field. Mem. AAAS, Biophys. Soc., Am. Chem. Soc., Am. Soc. Microbiology, Eta Kappa Nu, Tau Beta Pi. Home: 112 Kenyon Ave Kensington CA 94708 Office: Bio-Rad Labs Inc 1414 Harbour Way S Richmond CA 94804

GARGAN, THOMAS JOSEPH, plastic surgeon; b. Denver, Sept. 28, 1952; s. Thomas Joseph and Maria Augusta (Casagranda) G.; m. Nancy Lee Hall, Jan. 20, 1979; children: Daniel Thomas, John William. BA summa cum laude, Colo. Coll., 1974; MD, U. Colo., 1978. Diplomate Am. Bd. Plastic Surgery. Intern Presbyn. Med. Ctr., Denver, 1978-79, resident in surgery, 1978-79; resident in surgery Beth Israel Hosp., Boston, 1979-81, instr. gen. surgery, 1979-82, sr. resident in surgery, 1981-82, chief resident in plastic surgery, 1983-84; sr. resident in plastic surgery Cambridge (Mass.) City Hosp., 1982-83; resident in plastic surgery Children's Hosp. and Brigham and Women's Hosp., Boston, 1983, Newton-Wellesley Hosp., Mass., 1983; clin. fellow in surgery Harvard U. Med. Sch., Boston, 1979-84; clin. instr. plastic surgery U. Colo. Sch. Med., Denver, 1984; chief plastic surgery div. Rose Med. Ctr., 1987—; instr. plastic surgery Cambridge Hosp., Children's Hosp., and Beth Israel Hosp., Boston, 1982-84, Harvard Med. Sch., Boston, 1984. Contbr. articles to profl. jours. Recipient George B. Packard award for excellence in surgery U. Colo. Med. Ctr., 1978; Eagle Scout; Barnes Chemistry scholar Colo. Coll. Mem. AMA, Denver Med. Soc. (Pres. Gold Star award), Colo. Med. Soc., Colo. State Soc. Plastic and Reconstructive Surgeons, Rocky Mountain Hand Surgery Soc., Rocky Mountain Soc. of Reconstructive Plastic Surgeons. Lodge: Ancient Order Hibernians in Am. Avocations: skiing, fly fishing, mountaineering. Home: 10 Blackmer Rd Englewood CO 80110 Office: 4545 E 9th Ave Denver CO 80220

GARGANTA, NARCISO MERIOLES, librarian; b. Masbate, Philippines, Sept. 18, 1932; s. Francisco Legaspi and Leonor (Merioles) G. B.L.S., Arellano U., 1956; M.L.S., Pratt Inst., 1971; cert. profl. pub. librarian N.Y. Dir. tech. library United Drug Co., Inc., United Labs. Inc., Manila, Philippines, 1960-67; serials librarian Norris Med. Library, U. So. Calif. Med. Ctr., 1967-68; med. librarian Milton Helpern Library Legal Medicine, N.Y.C., 1970-72; curriculum devel. specialist RCA Resource Ctr., N.Y.C., 1972-77; asst. librarian VA Med. Ctr., Brentwood, Calif., 1978-79, dir. med. library, 1984—; dir. med. library Burbank (Calif.) Community Hosp., 1979-84; cons. Calif. Acupuncture Coll. Mem. Calif. Local Bd. 113, 1982—, chmn., 1985—. Mem. Med. Library Assn., Am. Soc. Info. Sci., Med. Group So. Calif. and Ariz., N.Y.C. Geneal. Soc. Mng. editor Philippine Library Jour., 1959, Internat. Microform Jour. of Legal Medicine, 1970. Home: 4914 York Blvd Los Angeles CA 90042

GARGUILO, JOSEPH CHRISTOPHER, communications executive; b. Bklyn., June 23, 1952; s. Joseph Patrick and Kathleen (Armstrong) G.; m. Jean Mangin (dec. May 1982); m. Karrie Skonier, Aug. 23, 1986. BA in Econs. cum laude, SUNY, New Paltz, 1974; degee in TV prodn., Colo. State U., 1976. Tchr. speech Colo. State U., Ft. Collins, 1974-76; owner, mgr. Frontier Fence Co., Boulder, Colo., 1976-81; ptnr., mgr., cons. Media, Ft. Collins, 1979—; mgr. facilities Visual Communications Group, Boulder, 1985-86; now with Media, Inc., Boulder; chief fin. officer, corp. sec. New West Tech., Boulder, 1983-84. Scriptwriter TV and radio commls., 1979—. Cons. Office City Mgr., Ft. Collins, 1981. Mem. Nat. Assn. Broadcasters, Internat. TV Assn. Democrat. Roman Catholic. Club: BMW Car. Avocations: weight lifting, skiing, gourmet cooking, travel videos, bus. planning. Home: 2612 Blue Mt. Ave Berthoud CO 80513 Office: Media Inc PO Box 843 Boulder CO 80306

GARIN, EUGENE, artist; b. Odessa, USSR, Nov. 30, 1922; came to U.S., 1959; s. Vasilij and Martha (Drokov) G.; m. Raisa Peredelsky, Mar. 24, 1958 (dec. Aug. 1977); m. Rita Seljavin, Dec. 27, 1978; children: Irene, Tanja, Stella. Art student, Novomoskowsk, USSR, 1936-39, Comml. Coll., Odessa, 1940-41; cert., Chgo. Tech. Coll., 1962. Freelance artist Buenos Aires, 1948-59. Exhibited at H. Morseburg Galleries, Los Angeles, 1962-78, G. Livingston Galleries, Monterey, Calif., 1965-80, Old Main Gold Gallery, Bellevue, Wash., 1970-82, Lyon Gallery, San Francisco, 1970-83, Simic Galleries, Carmel, Calif., 1982. Editor in chief (newspaper) Our Days, 1974—; editor Golden Weath, 1984—. Sec. Slavic Bapt. Assn., Sacramento, 1976-84. Home: 1002 La Jolla Ct Roseville CA 95678 Office: care Simic Galleries attention Jessica Haynes PO 5687 Carmel CA 93921

GARLAND, ROBERT LEE, educator, writer; b. Chgo., Feb. 26, 1932. BA, UCLA, 1953; MA, Calif. State U., 1962; postgrad., U. Calif., Berkeley, Nat. U. Mex., Mexico City, Stanford U. Educator Los Angeles Sch. Dist., 1957—; mem. various coms. Los Angeles Schs., 1970—. Contbr. articles on travel and edn. to jours. Served with U.S. Army, 1955-57. Nat. Def. Edn. Act scholar U.S. Govt., 1966, Fulbright scholar, U.S. Govt., 1967, Freedoms Found. scholar, 1982, 86; Robert Taft fellow, 1977, 81, 86. Mem. Nat. Council Social Studies (com. chmn. 1980—), Fulbright Alumni Assn., Navy League of U.S., Nat. Edn. Assn., Steamship Hist. Soc., Am. Film Inst. Club: Travelers Century. Office: Los Angeles Unified Sch Dist 13000 Oxnard St Van Nuys CA 91401

GARLOUGH, WILLIAM GLENN, marketing executive; b. Syracuse, N.Y., Mar. 27, 1924; s. Henry James and Gladys (Killam) G.; m. Charlotte M. Tanzer, June 15, 1947; children: Jennifer, William, Robert. BEE, Clarkson U., 1949. With Knowlton Bros., Watertown, N.Y., 1949-67, mgr. mfg. services, 1966-67; v.p. planning, equipment systems div. Vare Corp., Englewood Cliffs, N.J., 1967-69; mgr. mktg. Valley Mould div. Microdot Inc., Hubbard, Ohio, 1969-70; dir. corp. devel. Microdot Inc., Greenwich, Conn., 1970-73, v.p. corp. devel., 1973-76, v.p. adminstrn., 1976-77, v.p. corp. devel., 1977-78; v.p. corp. devel. Am. Bldg. Maintenance Industries, San Francisco, 1979-83; pres. The Change Agts., Inc., Walnut Creek, Calif., 1983—; mem. citizens adv. com. to Watertown Bd. Edn., 1957. Bd. dirs. Watertown Community Chest, 1958-61; ruling elder Presbyn. ch. Served with USMCR, 1942-46. Mem. Am. Mgmt. Assn., Profl. and Tech. Cons. Assn., Bldg. Service Contractors Assn., Internat. Sanitary Supply Assn., Mensa, Am. Mktg. Assn., TAPPI, Assn. Corp. Growth (pres. San Francisco chpt. 1984-85, v.p. chpts. west 1985—), Lincoln League (pres. 1958), Am. Contract Bridge League (life master), Clarkson Alumni Assn. (Watertown sect. pres. 1955), Tau Beta Pi. Clubs: Olympic; No. N.Y. Contract (pres. 1959), No. N.Y. Transp. Home: 2557 Via Verde Walnut Creek CA 94598 Office: The Change Agts 1990 N California Blvd Walnut Creek CA 94596

GARMAN, JOHN ALAN, military officer; b. Fairchild AFB, Wash., Aug. 29, 1960; s. Harold Meade and Laura Loretta (Laplante) G. BS in Computer Sci., N.Mex. State U., 1982; MS in systems mgmt., U. So. Calif., 1986. Commd. 2d lt. USAF, 1982, advanced through grades to capt., 1986. Mem. Air Force Assn., Res. Officers Assn., Mil. Order of the World Wars, San Jose State U. Jaycees. Democrat. Club: Toastmasters (asst. lt. gov. for edn. 1985, Humorous Speaker award, Sunnyvale 1984, 85, Internat. Speaker award 1986).

GARN, EDWIN JACOB (JAKE), Senator; b. Richfield, Utah, Oct. 12, 1932; s. Jacob Edwin and Fern (Christensen) G.; m. Hazel Rhae Thompson, Feb. 2, 1957 (dec. 1976); children: Jacob Wayne, Susan Rhae, Ellen Marie, Jeffrey Paul; m. Kathleen Brewerton, Apr. 8, 1977; children: Matthew Spencer, Christopher Brook, Jennifer Kathleen. B.S., U. Utah, 1955. Spl. agt. John Hancock Mut. Life Ins. Co., Salt Lake City, 1960-61; asst. mgr. Home Life Ins. Co. N.Y., Salt Lake City, 1961-66; gen. agt. Mut. Trust Life Ins. Co., Salt Lake City, 1966-68; city commr. Salt Lake City, 1968-72, mayor, 1972-74; dir. Met. Water Dist., 1968-72; mem. U.S. Senate from Utah, 1974—. Chmn. joint bd. commrs. Salt Lake Model Cities Agy., 1973—; Bd. dirs. Salt Lake Community Action Program, 1968—; pres. Salt Lake County unit Am. Cancer Soc., 1970-72, chmn. county crusade, 1967, bd. dirs. Utah div., 1968—; mem. advisory bd. Salvation Army; bd. dirs. Utahns for Effective Govt., Columbus Community Center; Mem. Utah Republican party fin. com., 1965-68; chmn. Rep. voting dist., 1960-64, Rep. legis. dist., 1962-66; bd. dirs. Salt Lake County Young Reps., 1960-66; co-chmn. Coalition Peace Through Strength. Served to lt. (s.g.) USNR, 1956-60; col. Utah Air N.G., 1963-79; payload specialist, spae shuttle mission 51D, 1985. Recipient Tom McCoy award Utah League Cities and Towns, 1972. Mem. Utah League Cities and Towns (pres. 1971-72, dir. 1968—), Nat. League Cities (1st v.p. 1973-74, hon. pres. 1975), Sigma Chi. Mormon. Club: Kiwanian. Office: 505 Dirksen Senate Bldg Washington DC 20510 *

GARNER, ESTHER RUTH, state agency director; b. Rochester, N.Y., July 27, 1936; d. William G. and Minnie (Sorge) Jaster; m. Wilbur T. Garner, April 22, 1956; children: Marlene, Treva, Jody. BS in Pub. Adminstrn., City U., Bellevue, Wash., 1977, MPA, 1985. Office mgr. M&S Maintenance Co., Orange, Calif., 1960-65; ct. clk. Thurston County Superior Ct., Olympia, Wash., 1967-70; adminstrv. asst. State Adminstr. for Cts., Olympia, 1971-80; program auditor Dept. Social and Health Services, Olympia, 1980-81; exec. dir. State Jud. Qualifications Commn., Olympia, 1981—. Author: Agency Annual Report, 1981; contbr. articles to profl. jours. Fellow Ctr. for Jud. Conduct Orgns., Inst. Ct. Mgmt. (cert.); mem. Nib n' Ink Club. Seventh-day Adventist. Clubs: Altrusa (Olympia) (1st v.p. 1986—, pres. 1987-88). Avocations: music, sewing, calligraphy, travel, tennis. Office: Jud Qualifications Commn 12th and Jefferson Bldg Suite 9 Olympia WA 98504

GARNER, GIROLAMA THOMASINA, educational administrator, educator; b. Muskegon, Mich., Sept, 15, 1923; d. John and Martha Ann (Thomas) Funaro; student Muskegon Jr. Coll., 1941; B.A., Western Mich. U., 1944, M.A. in Counseling and Guidance, 1958; Ed.D., U. Ariz., 1973; m. Charles Donald Garner, Sept. 16, 1944 (dec.); 1 dau., Linda Jeannette Garner Blake. Elem. tchr., Muskegon and Tucson, 1947-77; counselor Erickson Elem. Sch., Tucson, 1978-79; prin. Hudlow Elem. Sch., Tucson, 1979—, adj. prof. U. Ariz., 1973—, Pima Community Coll., 1981—; mem. Ariz. Com. Tchr. Evaluation and Cert., 1976-78; del. NEA convs. Active ARC, Crippled Children's Soc., UNESCO, DAV Aux., Rincon Renegades; bd. dirs. Hudlow Community Sch., 1973-76. Recipient Apple award for teaching excellence Pima Community Coll., 1982. Mem. Nat. Assn. Sci. Tchrs., Tucson Edn. Assn., Ariz. Edn. Assn., NEA, Assn. Supervision and Curriculum Devel., AAUW, Delta Kappa Gamma, Kappa Rho Sigma, Kappa Delta Pi. Democrat. Christian Scientist. Home: 6922 E Baker St Tucson AZ 85710 Office: 502 N Caribe St Tucson AZ 85710

GAROUTTE, BILL CHARLES, neurophysiologist; b. Absarokee, Mont., Mar. 15, 1921; s. Bernard Clark and Anna Kosir G.; m. Sally Jeter, July 18, 1948; children—Brian, Susanna, David, Katherine. Student, San Diego State Coll., 1939-42; A.B., U. Calif., Berkeley, 1943, M.D., 1945, Ph.D., 1954. With U. Calif. Med. Sch., San Francisco, 1949—; from lectr. to prof. anatomy and nuerology U. Calif. Med. Sch., 1949-66, prof. anatomy and neurology, 1966-86, prof. emeritus, 1986—; vis. asst. prof. U. Indonesia, Jakarta, 1956-57; electromyography and electroencephalography U. Calif., San Francisco, 1953—; vis. investigator Brain Research Inst. U. Tokyo, 1963; external examiner anatomy Nat. U. Malaysia, 1978, Sci. U. Malaysia, 1984. Author: Survey of Functional Neuroanatomy, 1981, 2d edit., 1987. Served as lt. (j.g.), M.C. USNR, 1946-47. Fulbright scholar London, 1950-51. Mem. Western Inst. on Epilepsy (pres. 1962), Am. Assn. Anatomists, Am. Acad. Neurology, Am. Electroencephalography Soc., Western Electroencephalography Soc. (pres. 1961-62), Hist. Soc. Pa., San Francisco Neurol. Soc. (pres. 1969-70). Research on elec. activity of central nervous system. Home: 105 Molino Ave Mill Valley CA 94941 Office: U Calif San Francisco CA 94143

GARRETT, EDWARD O'BANION, advertising agency executive; b. Long Beach, Calif., June 19, 1951; s. Frank O'Banion and Marie Louise (Goodman) G. B.B.A., U. Notre Dame, 1973; M.A., Mich. State U., 1976. Asst. media planner Campbell-Mithun Advt. Co., Chgo., 1976-77; ops. supr. Ackerley Airport Advt. Co., Seattle, 1981—; v.p. Seattle Book Co. Club: Notre Dame of Western Wash. Office: Ackerley Airport Advt Co 2001 6th Ave Seattle WA 98121

GARRETT, JOHN ALLEN, JR., insurance claims professional; b. Kearny, N.J., Aug. 4, 1944; s. John Allen and Anne (Spieker) G.; m. Marie Elaine Delourey, June 20, 1970; children: Megan D., Ryan D. Assoc. in Claims, Ins. Inst. Am., 1975; Assoc. in Casualty Claims Law, Am. Edn. Inst., 1977. Trainee adjuster Fireman's Fund Ins. Co., Newark, 1968-69; from adjuster to sr. adjuster Fireman's Fund Ins. Co., Newark and Denver, 1969-78; claims supr. Fireman's Fund Ins. Co., Denver, 1978-79; sr. supr. home office Fireman's Fund Ins. Co., San Francisco and Novato, Calif., 1979-85; br. claims mgr. Fireman's Fund Ins. Co., Pleasant Hill, Calif., 1985-86; litigation specialist Fireman's Fund Ins. Co., Petaluma, Calif., 1986—; speaker Western Ins. Info. Service, Denver and San Francisco, 1976-80. Coach Petaluma Youth Soccer League, 1985-86. Served with USN, 1964-70. Democrat. Avocations: reading, travelling, auto repair and restoration, photography. Home: 412 Casa Verde Circle Petaluma CA 94952 Office: Fireman's Fund Ins Co 3700 Lakeville Hwy Petaluma CA 94952

GARRETT, JOYCE LYNN, education educator; b. Prineville, Oreg., Oct. 17, 1946; d. James Edward and Bettye Jeanne (Forbes) G. BA, U. Oreg., 1968, MS, 1973, MA, 1981, PhD, 1982; BS, Oreg. State U., 1970. Interim tchr. Colo. Sch. Deaf and Blind, Colorado Springs, 1969; tchr. phys. edn. Lincoln County Schs., Newport, Oreg., 1970-76; grad. teaching fellow U. Oreg., Eugene, 1977-82; supr. spl. edn. Creswell (Oreg.) Pub. Schs., 1978-80; asst. prof. edn. Weber State Coll., Ogden, Utah, 1982-84; assoc. prof. edn. Calif. State U., Chico, 1984—, coordinator spl. edn. programs, 1986—; dir. resource specialist tchr. tng. project Calif. State U., Chico, 1985—; program specialist cons. Modoc County Schs., Alturas, Calif., 1984—; cons. classroom mgmt. various local sch. dists., 1980—. Contbr. articles to profl. jours. Vol. Spl. Olympics, Ogden, 1982-84. Recipient Profl. Promise award Calif. State U., Chico, 1985. Mem. NEA, Am. Edn. Research Assn., Assn. Supervision and Curriculum Devel., Council Exceptional Children (v.p. Eugene chpt. 1979-80), Assn. Retarded Citizens (v.p. 1982-84). Avocations: out-door edn., skiing, hiking, reading. Office: Calif State U Dept Edn Chico CA 95929-0222

GARRETT, KENNETH JAMES, marketing executive; b. Casper, Wyo., Jan. 21, 1953; s. James Robert and Mary Agnes (Colby) G.; m. Kristin Hatlen, Sept. 25, 1985. AS, Casper Coll., 1973; BS with honors, U. Wyo., 1975, M Computer Sci., 1977, MBA, 1979. Mktg. rep. IBM Corp., Denver, 1978-79; account exec. Mountain Bell, Boulder, Colo., 1979-81; tng. mgr. AT&T, Denver, 1981-83; dir. product mktg. U.S. West, Denver, 1983-85; dir. bus. planning U.S. West Info. Systems, Englewood, Colo., 1985-86; dir. planning Norand Corp., Boulder, 1986-87; dir. mktg. EI Corp., Boulder, 1987—; pres. K. Garrett and Assoc. 1982—. Contbr. articles to profl. jours. Named to Achievers Club, Mountain Bell, 1981. Mem. Phi Beta Kappa, Phi Kappa Psi. Roman Catholic. Lodge: Kiwanis. Avocations: skiing, golf, bicycling. Home: 4232 Quince Ct Boulder CO 80302 Office: EI Corp 5797 Central Ave Boulder CO 80301

GARRETT, ROBERT STEPHENS, public relations executive; b. Bell, Calif., July 12, 1937; s. Sammie Jacob and Martha Ethelwynn (Dench) G.; m. Mary Lynn Harris, Sept. 9, 1955 (div. July 1972); children: Lisa, Julie, Kim; m. Camille Ann Priestley, Feb. 15, 1975; children: Lee Ann, Nikki, Grant. Grad. high sch., Downey, Calif. From machinist to head shipping dept. Axelson Mfg. Co., Vernon, Calif., 1955-60; prodn. control planner, methods analyst autonetics div. Rockwell Internat., Downey, Compton and Anaheim, Calif., 1960-70; pub. relations mgr., property mgr., clinic coordinator, investigator, property researcher and chief adminstr. bd. UMEDCO Inc., Long Beach, Calif., 1970-77; dir. ops. Regency Mgmt. Service, Anaheim, 1977-78; cons. med. pub. relations Garden Grove, Calif., 1978—. Bd. dirs. Boys Club of Garden Grove, 1978—, Girls Club of Garden Grove, 1980—, v.p. 1984-86, pres. 1986—; traffic commr. City of Garden Grove, 1981—. Republican. Lodges: Rotary (bd. dirs. Garden Grove club 1978-79), Elks. Avocations: rock collecting, archtl. and landscape design, tropical fish, coin collecting, designing and building model cars and planes. Office: PO Box 1221 Garden Grove CA 92642

GARRETT, STEVEN LURIE, physicist; b. Los Angeles, Apr. 3, 1949; s. Fred Ellis and Vivian Dorothy (Lurie) G.; m. Gloria Kalisher, Nov. 26, 1975. BS in Physics, UCLA, 1970, MS in Physics, 1972, PhD in Physics, 1977. Asst. prof. Naval Postgrad. Sch., Monterey, Calif., 1981-85, assoc. prof., 1985—; Rosen prof. Technion, Haifa, Israel, 1985. Contbr. articles to profl. jours.; patentee in field. Fellow Miller Inst. Basic Research in Sci., 1978-81. Mem. Acoustical Soc. Am. (Hunt fellow 1978), Optical Soc. Am., Am. Phys. Soc., Am. Assn. Phys. Tchrs., Sigma Xi. Avocation: aviation. Home: 4153 El Bosque Dr Pebble Beach CA 93953 Office: Naval Postgrad Sch Physics Dept 61GX Monterey CA 93943

GARRETT, SUSAN AVIVA DOSHAY, technical writer; b. Los Angeles, Jan. 23, 1953; d. Martin Joseph and Selma (Tarr) Garrett; m. David Doshay, Aug. 28, 1983. BA in Chemistry, U. Calif., Santa Cruz, 1975; MS in Pub. Health Nutrition, UCLA, 1979. Editor Zilog Inc., Cupertino, Calif., 1980-81; tech. writer Tymshare Inc., Cupertino, 1981-82; tech. writer, writing supr. Gavilan Computers, Campbell, Calif., 1982-84; sr. tech. writer Saber Tech., San Jose, Calif., 1984-85, Excelan Inc., San Jose, 1985—. Avocations: raising rabbits, spinning, volleyball, reading, knitting. Home: C4 Koshland Way Santa Cruz CA 95064 Office: Excelan Inc 2180 Fortune Dr San Jose CA 95131

GARRIGUES, GAYLE LYNNE, lawyer; b. Anchorage, Aug. 7, 1955; s. James Martin and Julia Ann (Harris) G. B.A. in Polit.Sci., U. Alaska, 1977; J.D., U. Idaho, 1980. Bar: Alaska 1981, U.S. Dist. Ct. Alaska 1982. Atty. Alaska Legal Services Corp., Kotzebue, 1980-82; assoc. Settles, Kalamarides & Assocs., P.C., Anchorage, 1982; sole practice, Kotzebue, 1982-84; asst. dist. atty. Dept. of Law 2d Jud. Dist., Kotzebue, 1984—; instr. criminal justice Chuckchi Community Coll., 1985-86. Bd. dirs. Kotzebue Womens Crisis Project, 1982-84; del. Alaska State Dem. Conv., 1974, 84; leader Girl Scouts U.S., 1981-83, 86. Mem. ABA, Assn. Trial Lawyers Am., Alaska Bar Assn., Anchorage Women Lawyers, Phi Alpha Delta.

GARRIGUES, JOHN SHARPLESS, geophysicist; b. East Orange, N.J., Apr. 30, 1941; s. Henry Haydock and Elizabeth (Russell) G.; m. Vivien Monica Sexton, June 30, 1979; 1 son, John-Paul Henry. B.S.C. in Math., N.Mex. Tech. 1963; postgrad. in math., Purdue U., 1963-64. Seismologist, Geosource, Middle East, 1965-71; geophysicist, London, 1971-79; advanced geophysicist Marathon Oil Co., Littleton, Colo., 1979—. Mem. Union Concerned Scientists, Soc. Exploration Geophysicists, AAAS, Am. Geophys. Union, European Assn. Exploration Geophysicists. Office: Marathon Oil Co PO Box 269 Littleton CO 80122

GARRISON, LESTER BOYD, chemist; b. Eureka, Calif., May 7, 1948; s. Lester Boyd and Marian (Weamer) G.; m. Sandra Marie Ryan, June 21,

1980; children: Jay Patrick, Kaye Camille, Brian Lee. AA in Gen. Edn., Coll. of the Redwoods, 1971-73; BA in Chemistry, Humboldt State U., 1973-76; postgrad. in chemistry, Portland State U., 1978-79; student in sales and mktg., Portland Community Coll., 1983-84. Research asst. Oreg. Health Scis. U., Portland, 1976-78, sr. research asst., 1978-79; systems engr. Alpkem Corp, Clackamas, Oreg., 1979-81; sr. lab. technician Qatar Gen. Petroleum Corp., Doha, 1981-82; diagnostics prodn. mgr. Alpkem Corp., Clackamas, 1982-85; plant mgr. Alpkem Corp., Orchards, Wash., 1985-86; chief operating officer Intersect, Inc., Longview, Wash., 1987—. Co-author, contbr. articles to profl. jours. Served with USMC, 1967-71. Decorated Nat. Def. Service medal. Mem. AAAS, Am. Chem. Soc., Alexander von Humboldt Marine Sciences Assn. (life) (chmn. marine lab and open house com. 1975), Humboldt State U. Oceanographic Soc. (chmn., co-founder). Avocations: judo, canoeing, timber ranching. Home: 26802 Archibald Ln Deer Island OR 97054 Office: Intersect Inc 1606 E Kessler Blvd #100 Longview WA 98632

GARROD, PETER VINCE, agriculture and resource economics educator; b. San Jose, Calif., Aug. 12, 1943; s. Vince Stolte and Jane (Whiteman) G.; m. Nora Naomi Wakayama, Jan. 18, 1979. BS, U. Calif., Davis, 1965; MS, U. Calif., Berkeley, 1966, PhD, 1972. Prof. agrl., resource econs. U. Hawaii, Honolulu, 1972—, grad. chmn. dept. agrl. econs., 1983-86; cons. Ford Found., Chile, 1970-71, Masi Internat., Inc., Portugal, 1978-79, IRI, Inc., Peru, 1985, Hawaii Agronomic, Honolulu, 1985. Contbr. articles to profl. jours. Mem. Am. Agrl. Econ. Assn., Am. Econ. Assn., Western Agrl. Econ. Assn. Home: 826 19th Ave Honolulu HI 96816 Office: U Hawaii at Manoa Dept Agrl & Resource Econs 2545 The Mall Honolulu HI 96822

GARRUTO, JOHN ANTHONY, cosmetic research chemist; b. Johnson City, N.Y., June 18, 1952; s. Paul Anthony and Katherine Helen (DiMartino) G.; m. Denise Kitty Conlon, Feb. 19, 1971 (div. May 1978); 1 child, James Joseph; m. Anita Louise, May 12, 1979 (div. Sept. 1984); 1 child, Christopher Russell; m. Debra Lynn Brady. BS in Chemistry, SUNY, Binghamton, 1974; AAS in Bus. Adminstrn., Broome Coll., 1976. Research chemist Lander Co. Inc., Binghamton, 1974-77; research dir. Lander Co. Inc., St. Louis, 1977-79, Olde Worlde Products, High Point, N.C., 1979-81; v.p. research and devel. LaCosta Products Internat., Carlsbad, Calif., 1981—; cons. Trans-Atlantic Mktg., Binghamton, 1975-78. Mem. AAAS, Am. Chem. Soc., Soc. Cosmetic Chemists (newsletter editor 1980-81, publicity chmn. 1984—). Democrat. Roman Catholic. Avocations: acting, telecommunications, ski-diving, jet skiing. Home: PO Box 793 Carlsbad CA 92008 Office: La Costa Products 2251 Las Palmas Dr Carlsbad CA 92008

GARRY, JACQUELYNN LEE, holding corporation executive; b. Salem, N.J., Mar. 11, 1957; d. Henry Edward Klingler and Josephine Sarah (Poulson) Parker. Student, Delcastle Vocat. Tech. Inst., 1975; AA, AS, Fort Steilacoom Community Coll., AS in Bus., AS in Broadcasting; student, L.H. Bates Vocat. Tech. Inst., 1979-80. Mgr. inventory control, pub. relations McDonalds of Wilmington, Del., 1974-77; sales account rep. Rainbow of Tacoma/Auburn, Wash., 1977-80; mgmt. trainee Agy. Rent-A-Car, Wash., 1980; sales mgr. Puget (Wash.) Mobilex Inc., 1980-82; planning specialist Bus. Ins. Assocs., 1982, Target Ins. Bus. Service, 1982-84; chief exec. officer Just Like Gold, Inc., San Diego, 1983—. Dir. TV including The Music Hour, Meet the Candidates; co-dir. film The Great Am. Masacare; producer TV The Fashinable Female, (co-producer) Condomania; author newspaper columns The Fashionable Female, 1984-85. Served with USAF, 1974-77. Mem. Ch. Religious Sci. Avocations: swimming, reading, jogging, sailing, horseback riding. Office: Just Like Gold Inc PO Box 86993 San Diego CA 92138

GARSON, G. PAUL, magazine editor; b. Washington, Mar. 7, 1946; s. Harry Gilbert and Rae Garson. BA, Tulane U., 1968; MA, Johns Hopkins U., 1970; MFA, U. So. Calif., 1979. Periodical editor The McMullen Pub. Co., Anaheim, Calif., 1982-86, Petersen Pub. Co., Los Angeles, 1986—; instr. writing Calif. State U., Fullerton, 1980-81. Author: (novel) The Great Quill, 1972; author numerous short stories and non-fiction articles; screenwriter films Cyclone, Huntress. Mem. Jaguar Owners Club, Classic Car Club Am. Avocations: karate instr., photography, travel, classic cars and motorcycles. Home: 733 N Kings Rd #250 Los Angeles CA 90069

GARSTANG, ROY HENRY, astrophysicist, educator; b. Southport, Eng., Sept. 18, 1925; came to U.S., 1964; s. Percy Brocklehurst and Eunice (Gledhill) G.; m. Ann Clemence Hawk, Aug. 11, 1959; children—Jennifer Katherine, Susan Veronica. B.A., U. Cambridge, 1946, M.A., 1950, Ph.D., 1954, Sc.D., 1983. Research assoc. U. Chgo., 1951-52; lectr. astronomy U. Coll., London, 1952-60; reader astronomy U. London, 1960-64, asst. dir. Obs., 1959-64; prof. astrophysics U. Colo., Boulder, 1964—; chmn. Joint Inst. for Lab. Astrophysics, 1966-67; cons. Nat. Bur. Standards, 1964-73; v.p. commn. 14 Internat. Astron. Union, 1970-73, pres., 1973-76; Erskine vis. fellow U. Canterbury, New Zealand, 1971; vis. prof. U. Calif., Santa Cruz, 1971. Editor: Observatory, 1953-60; Contbr. numerous articles to tech. jours. Fellow Am. Phys. Soc., AAAS, Optical Soc. Am., Brit. Inst. Physics, Royal Astron. Soc.; mem. Am. Astron. Soc., Royal Soc. Scis. Liege (Belgium). Research on atomic physics and astrophys. applications. Home: 830 8th St Boulder CO 80302 Office: Joint Inst for Lab Astrophysics U Colo Boulder CO 80309

GARTH, JOHN S., marine zoologist educator, entomologist researcher; b. Los Angeles, Oct. 3, 1909; s. James Gray and Jessie Florence (Imlach) G.; m. Isla Lora Detter, June 25, 1940; 1 child, Linda Jean (dec.). BMus., U. So. Calif., 1932, MS, 1935, PhD in Zoology, 1941; postgrad., Cornell U., 1937, U. Pa., 1940. Research assoc. Allan Hancock Found., Los Angeles, 1937-42, 46-52, chief curator, 1963-75, chief curator emeritus, 1975—; assoc. prof. biology U. So. Calif., Los Angeles, 1952-67, prof. biology, 1967-75, prof. emeritus, 1975—; seasonal naturalist Glacier Nat. Park, Belton, Mont., 1935; Marine Biologist Eniwetok Marine Biology Lab., Marshall Islands, 1957, 59, U.S. Program in Biology Internat. Indian Ocean Expedition, 1964. Author: Calif. Butterflies, 1986, (booklet) Butterflies of Yosemite National Park, 1963, (booklet) Butterflies of Grand Canyon National Park, 1950; contbr. articles to profl. jours. Bd. dirs. Am. Cancer Soc., Los Angeles, 1965-66. Served to capt. AUS, 1944-46. Grantee NSF, 1956-68; recipient Cert. Appreciation Am. Cancer Soc., 1965-66, John Adams Comstock award Lepidopterists' Soc., 1987, Disting. Emeriti award U. So. Calif., 1987. Fellow AAAS (Councillor 1952-53), Calif. Acad. Scis., So. Calif. Acad. Scis.; mem. Carcinol. Soc. Japan (hon.), Soc. Systematic Zoology (pres. Pacific sect. 1952-53). Republican. Presbyterian. Avocations: music, butterfly collecting. Home: 515 Nebraska Ave Long Beach CA 90802 Office: U So Calif Allan Hancock Found Los Angeles CA 90089-0372

GARTLAND, MARGARET-ANN DELIA, speech pathologist; b. Hackensack, N.J.; d. Aloysius J. and Kathleen (Boyle) G. BS in Speech Correction, Nazareth Coll., Rochester, N.Y., 1970; MA in Speech Patholgy, SUNY, Geneseo, 1974, MS in Spl. Edn., 1975; PhD in Speech Pathology and Audiology, U. Utah, 1983. Cert. elem. tchr., spl. edn., N.Y. Intinerant speech therapist B.O.C.E.S., Mexico, N.Y., 1970-73, 75-77; instr. SUNY, Geneso, 1977-80; clin. assistantship U. Utah, Salt Lake City, 1980-83; asst. prof. No. Ariz. U., Flagstaff, 1983—; cons. Bur. Indian Affairs, Kayenta, Dennehotso, Navajo Nation, Ariz., 1985—. Grantee Minority Biomed. Research. Mem. Am. Speech Lang. Assn., Ariz. State Speech Hearing Assn., Utah State Speech Hearing Assn. (student rep. 1982-83), Internat. Assn. Oral Myologists, Pi Delta Kappa.

GARTLER, STANLEY MICHAEL, geneticist, educator; b. Los Angeles, June 9, 1923; s. George David and Delvira (Cupferberg) G.; m. Marion Ruth Mitchelson, Nov. 7, 1948. B.S., UCLA, 1948; Ph.D., U. Calif.-Berkeley, 1952. Research assoc. Columbia U., N.Y.C., 1952-57; research asst. prof. U. Wash., Seattle, 1957-60, assoc. prof., 1960-64, prof. genetics, 1964—; dir. NATO meeting on mosaicism, Venice, Italy, 1972. Author: (with R.E. Cole) Inactivation Sexual Differentiation, 1978. Grantee NIH and NSF, 1956—; merit scholar NIH. Mem. Am. Soc. Human Genetics (dir. 1970, pres.-elect 1986, pres. 1987), Genetics Soc. Am., Soc. Cell Biology, Am. Soc. Naturalists. Home: 9009 42d St NE Seattle WA 98115 Office: Dept Genetics U Wash Seattle WA 98195

GARTNER, CHARLES HARRISON, obstetrician, gynecologist; b. Covington, Ky., June 24, 1942; s. Joseph Charles and Mary Aleen (Stamper) G.; m. Eileen Shirlee Mann, Jan. 26, 1968 (div. Jan. 1974); 1 child, Gayle Marie. BS, Xavier U., 1964; MD, Northwestern U., 1968. Diplomate Am. Bd. Ob-Gyn. Practice medicine specializing in ob-gyn Denver, 1972—. Fellow Am. Coll. Obstetricians Gynecologists, Am. Assn. Gynecol. Laparoscopists, Am. Fertility Soc.; mem. Colo. Med. Soc., Clean Creek Valley Med. Soc. Democrat. Office: 1145 S Denver CO 80219

GARTRELL, WILLIAM GEORGE, academic administrator; b. Sterling, Colo., Oct. 27, 1948; s. Percy Barnett and Ruth Ann (Lundholm) G.; m. Deborah Rachel Stine, Aug. 29, 1975. BA in Social Sci., Biola Coll., 1977; postgrad., Calif. State U., Fullerton, 1979, Colo. State U., Ft. Collins, 1983. Computer operator Biola Coll., La Mirada, Calif., 1971-74, programmer, analyst, 1974-78, registrar, 1978-82; registrar, dir. admissions, dir. computer services Denver Seminary, 1982—. Served with U.S. Army, 1968-71, Vietnam. Mem. Am. Assn. Collegiate Registrars and Admissions Officers (presenter seminars1984, 86). Baptist. Office: Denver Seminary PO Box 10000 Denver CO 80210

GARVEY, BARBARA HARMAN, clothing design executive, publisher; b. Champaign, Ill., Nov. 10, 1934; d. Harry Jones and Helen Betty (Rosenblatt) Harman; m. Albert Garvey; children: Megan, Samantha. BA, Oberlin Coll., 1956. Systems service rep. IBM, Chgo., 1956-59; artist's agt. Al Garvey Designs, Fairfax, Calif., 1966-74; ptnr. Folkwear, Forestville, Calif., 1975-79; pres. Folkwear Inc., San Rafael, Calif., 1979—. Democrat. Avocations: travel, ballroom dancing. Home: 281 Scenic Rd Fairfax CA 94930 Office: Folkwear Inc 21A Golden Gate Dr San Rafael CA 94901

GARVEY, STEVEN PATRICK, professional baseball player; b. Tampa, Fla., Dec. 22, 1948; s. Joseph Patrick and Mildred Emma (Winkler) G.; m. Cynthia Ann, Oct. 29, 1971 (div.); children: Krisha Lee, Whitney Alyse. BS, Mich. State U., 1971. First baseman Los Angeles Dodgers; now with San Diego Padre, asst. player rep., 1972-76; mem. Nat. League All-Star Team, 1974-81, 84-85; operator Garvey Mktg. Group, San Diego; pub. relations for Pepsi-Cola Bottling Co., Los Angeles, 1974—, Allegretti Co., 1976—, Head Shampoo Co., 1977—. Trustee U. San Diego, Cath. U. Am., Scripps Clinic and Research Inst.; bd. dirs. Profl. Athletes Career Enterprises. Named Most Valuable Player Nat. League, 1974, Most Valuable Player, All Star Game, 1974, 78, Outstanding Young Man of Calif., 1976. Mem. Baseball Players Assn. Am., North Hills Jr. C. of C. Democrat. Roman Catholic. Address: San Diego Padres PO Box 2000 San Diego CA 92120 *

GARVIN, RICHARD WADE, banker; b. Pocatello, Idaho, May 27, 1940; s. Robert C. and Carmen J. (Salisbury) G.; m. Peggy Lee Freckleton, May 27, 1964; children—Cori Lynn, Adrienne Cheri. B.B.A., Idaho State U., 1963; grad. Pacific Coast Banking Sch., Seattle, 1975. Installment loan officer First Security Bank, Pocatello, 1966-67, mgr. East Pocatello office, 1967-70, real estate loan officer, 1970-73, v.p., asst. mgr., 1973-77, v.p., mgr., 1977-83, sr. v.p., 1983—; instr. real estate Idaho State U., 1971-72, Am. Inst. Banking, 1971-77, Idaho Real Estate Edn. Council, 1977-78; dir. First Security Bank Idaho, Boise. Chmn. Pocatello Housing Authority, 1979, Idaho State U. Vocat.-Tech. Adv. Council, 1982; appointed to Gov.'s Council on Vocat. Edn., 1986—. Served as 1st lt. U.S. Army, 1963-65. Recipient Disting. Service award Pocatello Jaycees, 1974; Meritorious Service award Idaho State U. Alumni Assn., 1975; award of appreciation Idaho Civic Symphony, 1983. Mem. Am. Inst. Banking, Idaho Bankers Assn., State Council Vocat. Tech. Edn., Pocatello C. of C. (pres. 1978). Club: Pocatello Golf and Country. Lodges: Lions (pres. 1970), Rotary. Avocation: painting. Home: 77 Cedar Hills Dr Pocatello ID 83204 Office: First Security Bank PO Box 1729 Pocatello ID 83204

GARY, JAMES FREDERICK, business executive; b. Chgo., Dec. 28, 1920; s. Rex Inglis and Mary Naomi (Roller) G.; m. Helen Elizabeth Gellert, Sept. 3, 1947; children: David Frederick, John William, James Scott, Mary Anne. BS, Haverford (Pa.) Coll., 1942. With Wash. Energy Co. and predecessors, Seattle, 1947-67; v.p. Wash. Energy Co., 1956-67; pres., chief exec. officer Pacific Resources Inc., Honolulu, 1967-79, chmn.; chief exec. officer, 1979-84, chmn., 1985, chmn. emeritus, 1986—, also bd. dirs.; bd. dirs. Bancorp. Hawaii, Inc., Bank of Hawaii, Castle & Cooke, Inc., Flexi-Van, Inc., N.Y., Wash. Energy Co., Seattle, Wash. Nat. Gas Co., Airborne Freight Corp., Seattle, GDC, Inc., Chgo., Petroleum Industry Research Found., Inc., N.Y. Pres. Chief Seattle council Boy Scouts Am., 1966-67, Aloha council, 1973-74; mem. Nat. Council, 1964—, v.p. western region, 1978-85, pres., 1985—, also bd. dirs.; chmn. Aloha United Way, 1978, pres., 1979, chmn., pres., 1980; bd. regents U. Hawaii, 1981—; trustee Linfield Coll., McMinnville, Oreg.; bd. mgrs. Haverford Coll.; adv. bd. Kamehameha Schs., Honolulu; bd. dirs. Research Corp. of U. Hawaii, 1971-77, chmn., 1974-77; bd. dirs., officer and trustee Oahu Devel. Conf., Hawaii Employers Council, Hawaii Loa Coll., Friends of East-West Ctr., Honolulu Symphony Soc., East-West Ctr. Internat. Found. Served to capt. AUS, 1942-46. Recipient Distinguished Eagle award Boy Scouts Am., 1972, Silver Beaver award Boy Scouts Am., 1966, Silver Antelope award Boy Scouts Am., 1976. Mem. Am. Gas Assn. (bd. dirs. 1970-74), Pacific Gas Assn. (pres. 1974; Basford trophy 1960), Nat. LP-Gas Assn. (bd. dirs. 1967-70), Inst. Gas Tech. (trustee 1975-86), Hawaii Econ. Council, Nat. Petroleum Council, Hawaii Dist. Export Council, Japan-Calif. Assn., Japan-Western Assn., Japan-Hawaii Econ. Council, Pacific Basin Econ. Council (chmn. Am. com. 1984-86), Japan-Am. Soc. Honolulu, Pacific Forum Honolulu com. fgn. relations, Hawaii C. of C. (chmn. 1979). Episcopalian. Clubs: Pacific Union (San Francisco); Oahu Country, Waialae Country, Outrigger Canoe, Pacific, Plaza (Honolulu); Seattle Tennis, Wash. Athletic (Seattle). Office: Pacific Resources Inc 733 Bishop St PO Box 3379 Honolulu HI 96842

GARY, JAMES HUBERT, chemical engineer, university research administrator; b. Victoria, Va., Nov. 18, 1921; s. James Edward and Jessie (DuPriest) G.; m. Jane Zerbee, July 18, 1945; children: Jane Lynne, Sue Ellen, Robert James, John Stephen. BS, Va. Poly. Inst., 1942, MS, 1946; PhD, U. Fla., 1951. From jr. engr. to group engr. tech. service div. Standard Oil Co., Ohio, 1946-52; asst. prof. chem. engring. U. Va., Charlottesville, 1952-56, research dir. engring. exptl. sta., 1952-56; assoc. prof. U. Ala., 1956-59, prof., 1959-60; chem. engr. So. Research Lab. U.S. Bur. Mines, 1957-60; prof., head chem. and petroleum refining engring dept. Colo. Sch. Mines, Golden, 1960-72, v.p. acad. affairs, 1972-79, dean faculty, 1977-79, dir., trustee Research Inst., 1970-72, 81-84; mem. tech. adv. com. Regional Air Pollution Control Adminstrn., Denver, 1967-74; mem. supply/delivery panel com. nuclear and alt. energy systems, chmn. subcom. on subecon. resources-shale oil NRC, 1976-78; mem. materials adv. com., chmn. oil shale tech. adv. com. Office Tech. Assessment, 1977-80; mem. adv. consortium U. Petroleum and Minerals, Saudi Arabia, 1975-85. Author: (with G. Handwerk) Technology and Economics, 1975, 2d rev. ed., 1984; contbr. articles to profl. jours. Patentee in field. Mem. Colo. Gov.'s Sci. and Tech. Adv. Council, 1970-72. Served to maj. CAC AUS, 1942-46. Decorated Bronze Star. Fellow AAAS, Am. Inst. Chem. Engrs. (sect. vice-chmn. 1962, chmn. 1963, Halliburton award 1981); mem. Am. Chem. Soc., Am. Soc. Engring. Edn. (sect. chmn.-elect 1978), Am. Inst. Mining Engring., Sigma Xi, Tau Beta Pi. Home: 1021 18th St Golden CO 80401 Office: Colo Sch Mines Chem Engring Dept Golden CO 80401

GARY, JUDSON EMMET, magazine editor, designer; b. Nashville, June 25, 1954; s. Laurence and Bernice Olivia (Berry) G.; m. Maria Olga Aleu, May 21, 1978; children: David Judson, Christine Elizabeth. BS of Indsl. Mgmt., Ga. Inst. Tech., 1976; MEd, Calif. State U., 1983. Campus minister Campus Crusade for Christ, Phila., 1976-78; adminstrv. dir. Inst. Internat. Studies, Pasadena, Calif., 1978-82; exec. editor World Christian Mag., Chatsworth, Calif., 1982—; tng. cons. Inst. Internat. Studies, Pasadena, 1982; curriculum writer Harvest, Scottsdale, Ariz., 1985; lectr. William Carey Internat. U., Pasadena, 1983—. Editor, writer features and articles Internat. Jour. Frontier Missions, 1984, World Christian Mag., 1986. Tchr., com. member First Bapt. Ch., Pasadena, 1982—. Mem. Nat. Soc. Performance and Instrn. Republican. Baptist. Avocation: jogging. Home: 1869 Galbreth St Pasadena CA 91104 Office: World Christian Mag PO Box 5199 Chatsworth CA 91313

GARY, KATHLEEN NOLAND, pharmaceutical company public relations executive; b. Long Beach, Calif.; d. Richard Lee and Grace Irene Noland; m. Richard N. Gary. B.A., U. Wash., 1967. Assoc. editor Kaiser News, Kaiser Aluminum & Chem. Corp., Oakland, Calif., 1968-73; dir. communications Kaiser Engrs., Oakland, 1973-74; mgr. internal communications Kaiser Industries Corp., Oakland, 1975-77; dir. pub. relations and advt. Kaiser Steel Corp., Oakland, 1977-80, v.p. pub. affairs, 1979-80; corp. v.p. pub. affairs and communications Syntex Corp., Palo Alto, Calif., 1981—. Mem. steering com. St. Mary's Coll. Exec. Seminar.; mem. San Francisco Mus. Modern Art, Nat. Investor Relations Inst. Mem. Pub. Relations Soc. Am., World Affairs Council, Calif. Mfrs. Assn., Pharm. Mfrs. Assn., Forum West. Clubs: Silverado Country, San Francisco Tennis, World Trade. Author: (with Don Fabun) Dimensions of Change, 1971, Children of Change, 1970. Office: Syntex Corp 3401 Hillview Ave Palo Alto CA 94304

GASKILL, HERBERT LEO, accountant, engineer; b. Seattle, July 1, 1923; s. Leo Dell and Vesta Rathbone (Dahlen) G.; m. Margaret Helen Jenkins, Mar. 1, 1944 (div.); children—Margaret V., Herbert Leo. B.S. and M.S. in Chem. Engring., U. Wash., 1949, M.B.A., 1976. C.P.A., Wash. Asst. prof. dental materials, exec. officer dept. dental materials Sch. Dentistry, U. Wash., 1950-56; ops. analyst The Boeing Co., Seattle, 1958-71, mktg. cons. govt. programs, 1972-74; pvt. practice acctg., Seattle, 1976-80; hazardous waste mgr. Boeing Co., Seattle, 1980—. Active Seattle Art Mus., Pacific Northwest Aviation Hist. Found. Served to lt. (j.g.) USNR, 1941-46. TAPPI fellow, 1956; U. Wash. Engring. Expt. Sta. fellow, 1957. Mem. Wash. Soc. C.P.A.s. Contbr. articles to profl. jours. Home: 1100 University St 15 K Seattle WA 98101

GASKILL, LISA SHARIDAN, mechanical engineer; b. Cheyenne, Wyo., Apr. 27, 1960; d. John Franklin and Marcia Mae (Schoening) G. BSME, Colo. State U., 1983; postgrad. in Mktg., U. Denver, 1984—. Cert. engr.-in-tng. Design mech. engr. Johnson & Johnson Ultrasound, Englewood, Colo., 1983-84; design mech. engr. Honeywell Inc., Littleton, Colo., 1984-85, quality engr., 1985—. Inventor in field. Republican. Presbyterian. Home: 2575 S Syracuse Way #M205 Denver CO 80231 Office: Honeywell Inc 4800 E Dry Creek Rd MS 101 Littleton CO 80112

GASPARI, RUSSELL ARTHUR, electronic engineer, educator; b. Redding, Calif., Jan. 15, 1941; s. Richard Anthony and Elena Adelaide (Biancalana) G.; B.S., U. Calif., Berkeley, 1963; M.S., San Diego State U., 1965; Ph.D., U. Calif., Los Angeles, 1970; m. Carole Anne Sterni, Feb. 20, 1965; children—Heather Elizabeth, Catherine Annette. Electronic engr. astronoautics div. Gen. Dynamics, San Diego, 1963-65; instr. engring. No. Ariz. U., Flagstaff, 1965-67; engring. specialist data systems div. Litton Systems, Van Nuys, Calif., 1968-71; sr. staff scientist microwave applications group Chatsworth, Calif., 1971-72; vis. prof. engring. Calif. State U., San Diego, 1972-73; sr. scientist Hughes Space & Communications Group, Los Angeles, 1973—. Litton fellow, 1969-70. Registered profl. engr., Calif. Mem. IEEE (sr. mem., officer, Outstanding Engr. award San Diego computer chpt. 1973, outstanding engr. award Los Angeles Harbor Sect. 1980, mgr. winter communications conf.; Region 6 achievement award 1984, Centennial medal 1984). Patentee in field. Home: 6656 W 87th Pl Los Angeles CA 90045

GASSER, ROBERT EUGENE, archaeologist, archaeobotanist; b. Berkeley, Calif., Nov. 11, 1944; s. Vincent Eugene Martell and Bernice Betty (Thomas) G. BS, Ariz. State U., 1975, MA, 1978. Casualty underwriter Alexander and Alexander, San Francisco, 1968-71; archaeologist Ariz. State U., Tempe, 1971-78; archaelogy specialist II Ariz. State Mus., Tucson, 1984-86; supr. archaeologist Mus. No. Ariz., Flagstaff, 1978-86; project dir. Soil Systems, Inc., Phoenix, 1986—. Contbr. 30 articles on southwestern archaelogy to profl. jours. E. Blois du Bois scholar Ariz. State U., 1977-78. Mem. Soc. Am. Archaeology, Ariz. Archaeology Council, Ariz. Archeol. and Hist. Soc. Democrat. Avocations: desert landscaping, photography. Home: 2662 S Elm St Tempe AZ 85282 Office: Soil Systems Inc 521 E Portland St Phoenix AZ 85004

GAST, MONTE W., media executive; b. Dec. 21, 1947; s. Rudi Kurt and Reli Victoria Gast; B.A. in Journalism, Humboldt State U., 1969; M.Journalism, UCLA, 1971. Writer, editor Tarcher Pub., Los Angeles, 1971-72; reporter KRLA Radio, Pasadena, Calif., 1972-74; account exec. KMET Radio, Los Angeles, 1974-75; sales mgr. KWST Radio, Los Angeles, 1975-77, gen. mgr., 1977-79; pres. JAM Advt., Culver City, Calif., 1980-82; creative cons./assoc. producer for nationally syndicated TV show, MV3, 1983-84; exec. producer TV Show Video Beat on KTLA, 1985; exec. producer and producer-Image West for all ednl.-appeal segments and spl. animation for Live Aid World Wide Broadcast, 1985; pres. Monte Gast & Assocs., Malibu, Calif., 1982—. Recipient Gold medal Internat. Film and TV Festival N.Y.C., 1981, Silver medal, 1982. Author: Getting the Best of L.A., 1972.

GAST, NANCY LOU, chemical company executive; b. Appleton, Wis., Aug. 13, 1941; d. Harvey William Gast and June Louella (Mohr) Webster. Med. technologist Palo Alto/Stanford (Calif.) Hosp., 1963-65; med. technologist St. Vincent Hosp., Portland, Oreg., 1965-70, chemistry supr., 1970-81; tech. rep. DuPont-Diagnostic Systems, Claremont, Calif., 1981-83, sales rep., 1983-85, account rep., 1985-87, acct. mgr., 1987—. Vol. med. technologist Health Help Ctr., Portland, 1984—; assoc. Sisters of HolyNames of Jesus and Mary, Marylhurst, Oreg., 1984—. Mem. Am. Soc. Med. Tech., Assn. Oreg. Med. Technologists. (treas. 1976-78), Am. Soc. Clin. Pathologists (cert. med. technologist, assoc.). Republican. Roman Catholic. Office: EI DuPont Diagnostic Systems 1480 N Claremont Blvd Claremont CA 91711-9990

GASTEL, BARBARA JEAN, medical writer; b. Washington, Sept. 26, 1952; d. Joseph P. and Sophie (Bergman) G. BA, Yale, 1974; MD, Johns Hopkins, 1978, MPH, 1978. Spl. asst. office of dir. Nat. Inst. Aging, Bethesda, Md., 1978-80; spl. asst. to dir. Nat. Ctr. for Health Care Tech., Rockville, Md., 1980-81; asst. prof. sci. writing MIT, Cambridge, 1981-84; vis. prof. tech. communication Beijing (People's Republic of China) Med. U., 1983-85; adjunct asst. prof. epidemiology internat. health U. Calif. Sch. Med., San Francisco, 1985—, asst. dean teaching and teaching evaluation, 1985—; lectr., cons. Chinese Med. Jour., Beijing, 1983-85. Author: Presenting Science to the Public, 1983; asst. editor: Johns Hopkins Medical Journal, 1976-82; contbr. articles to profl. and popular jours. AAAS mass media internship Newsweek, N.Y.C., 1978. Mem. AAAS, Assn. Tchrs. Preventive Medicine, Council Biology Editors, Am. Med. Writers Assn., Phi Beta Kappa. Office: Office of Dean U Calif Sch Med 513 Parnassus Ave Room S-224 San Francisco CA 94143-0410

GASTELUM, SYLVIA ROCHIN, union official; b. Nogales, Ariz., Aug. 13, 1937; d. Mario L. and Maria Jesus (Puchi) Rochin; m. James J. Gastelum, Sept. 16, 1957 (div. 1980); children—Anthony James, Therese Marie, Sandra Rosina. Student Flagstaff Coll., 1955-57. Main cashier Capins Mdse., 1955-56; sec. Schrader Ins. Agy., 1956; rep. Avon Corp., 1955-58; sec. to dir. Walt Disney Prodns., Burbank, Calif., 1958-59; U.S. postal clk., Nogales, Ariz., 1968—, postmaster service, Tumacacari, Ariz., 1979—; officer in charge U.S. Postal Service, Patagonia, Ariz. Leader 4-H, 1969-79; treas. Nogales Women's Aglow Internat. Fellowship. C.C. Cheshire Scholar, 1955. Mem. Am. Bus. Women's Assn. (membership chair, pres. La Amistad charter chpt. 1987), Am. Postal Workers Union (past sec., local #658, pres.), Better Govt. Assn., Womens' Aglo Internat. (treas. Nogales chpt.), Gamma Chi Beta. Republican. Mem. Assembly of God. Club: Newman (Flagstaff). Office: US Post Office Morley Ave Nogales AZ 85621

GATEKA, FREDRICK ALAN, engineering executive; b. Chickasha, Okla., Aug. 15, 1929; s. Floyd Fredrick and Odla Irene (Caldwell) G.; m. Helen Jo Bolton, Jan. 28, 1958; children—Renee, Stephen. B.S.E.E., Okla. State U., 1955; M.B.A., Calif. Luth. Coll., 1984. Field engr. Western Electric Co., Long Beach, Calif., Fort Walton Beach, Fla., Whippany, N.J., 1955-60; mem. tech. staff Bell Telephone Labs., Reading, Pa., Whippany, N.J., 1960-67; engring. Semtech Corp, Newbury Park, Calif., 1967—. Republican. Mem. Christian Ch. Club: Rotary Internat. Patentee semiconductor magnetron modulator. Office: 652 Mitchel Rd Newbury Park CA 91320

GATER, DAVID WINFIELD, diversified aerospace company executive, editor; b. Council Bluffs, Iowa, Feb. 6, 1933; s. Roy Winfield and Hazel Leona (Bays) G.; m. Eva Bertine Hollingsworth, June 1, 1958; children: Elizabeth, Roy, Michael, Susan, Catherine. BA in Physics, Math., Simpson Coll., 1959. Tech. writer Collins Radio Co., Cedar Rapids, Iowa, 1959-61; engring. writer Hughes Aircraft Co., Fullerton, Calif., 1961-65, mem. tech. staff, 1965-68, mng. editor, 1968-80, head publs. automation, 1980-84, mgr.

publs. prodn., 1984—; instr. tech. writing Fullerton Coll., 1980—. Author: The Grass-Roots Campaign Handbook, 1969. Chmn. Rep. Speakers Bur., Orange County, Calif., 1968-69; pres. Calif. Rep. Assembly, 1970-71; bd. dirs. So. Calif. dist. BEME, 1979-81. Served as sgt. U.S. Army, 1950-54. Mem. Am. Mgmt. Assn., So. Calif. Users Com. Automated Publs. (founder, chmn. 1984—), Mensa. Baptist. Avocations: writing, teaching, polit. consultancy. Home: 998 S Chantilly St Anaheim CA 92806

GATES, CECIL RAYMOND, agricultural engineer; b. Morgantown, W.Va., Mar. 25, 1927; s. Cecil R. and Margaret (Scott) G.; m. Francis J. Gates, May 25, 1968 (div. 1984); children: Margaret, Scott. BS, W.Va. U., 1950. Registered profl. engr., W.Va., Calif. Pres. Miller Mfg., Turlock, Calif., 1970-74; dist. mgr. Reynolds ALU, Los Angeles, 1974-76; v.p. Assn. Commerce and Industry, Albuquerque, 1976-77; prin. Gates Co. Inc., Albuquerque, 1977—. Served to sgt. U.S. Army, 1945-47, ETO. Mem. Am. Soc. Agrl. Engrs. Republican. Presbyterian. Club: Albuquerque Press. Lodges: Lions (pres. Albuquerque club 1985-86), Elks. Home: 163 Ravin Rd PO Box 430 Tijeras NM 87059 Office: Gates Co Inc 3013 Edith NE Albuquerque NM 87107

GATES, CHARLES CASSIUS, rubber company executive; b. Morrison, Colo., May 27, 1921; s. Charles Cassius and Hazel LaDora (Rhoads) G.; m. June Scowcroft Swaner, Nov. 26, 1943; children: Diane, John Swaner. Student, MIT, 1939-41; B.S., Stanford U., 1943; D.Eng. (hon.), Mich. Tech. U., 1975, Colo. Sch. of Mines, 1985. With Copolymer Corp., Baton Rouge, 1943-46; with Gates Rubber Co., Denver, 1946—, v.p., 1951-58, exec. v.p., 1958-61, chmn. bd., 1961—; chmn. bd., chief exec. officer The Gates Corp., 1982—; chmn. bd. Gates Learjet Corp., Wichita, Kans.; dir. Hamilton Bros. Petroleum Corp., Denver, Robinson Brick Co., Denver. Pres., trustee Gates Found.; pres. bd. trustees Denver Mus. Natural History. Recipient Community Leadership and Service award Nat. Jewish Hosp., 1974; Mgmt. Man of Year award Nat. Mgmt. Assn., 1965; named March of Dimes Citizen of the West, 1987. Mem. Conf. Bd. (dir.), Conquistadores del Cielo. Clubs: Denver Country, Cherry Hills Country, Denver, Outrigger Canoe, Waialae Country, Boone and Crockett, Club Ltd, Country Club of Colo, Roundup Riders of Rockies, Shikar-Safari Club Internat. (dir.), Augusta Nat. Golf, Castle Pines Golf. Office: The Gates Corp 900 S Broadway Denver CO 80209

GATES, DARYL FRANCIS, police chief; b. Aug. 30, 1926. B.S. in Pub. Adminstrn., U. So. Calif., also postgrad. in Pub. Adminstrn. With Dept. Police City of Los Angeles, 1949—, lt., 1959-63, capt., 1963-65, comdr., 1965-68, dep. chief, 1968-69, asst. chief, 1969-78, chief, 1978—. Bd. councilors U. So. Calif. Inst. Saftey and Systems Mgmt.; bd. dirs. YMCA, Los Angeles; mem. Children's Village Adv. Bd. Served with USN, World War II. Mem. Calif. Peace Officers Assn., Internat. police Assn., Calif. Police Chief Assn., Internat. Assn. Chiefs of Police, Women's Peace Officers Assn. Calif., Los Angeles C. of C. Lodge: Rotary. Office: City of Los Angeles Police Dept 150 N Los Angeles St Los Angeles CA 90012 *

GATES, GLODEAN KENT KERKMANN, education administrator; b. St. Louis, May 6, 1934; d. H. Warren and Glodean (Warthen) Kerkmann; m. Armand H. Hemon, May 25, 1957 (div.); children—Angela Hemon Baker, Charles; m. Philip W. Gates, May 22, 1976 (div.). Student U. Mich., 1955-56; B.A., UCLA, 1958. Tchr. Pub. Schs. Lancaster (Calif.), 1965-69; sales rep. Sta. KBVM-AM, Lancaster, 1967-69; account exec. Sta. KOTE-FM, Lancaster, 1970-71, sales mgr., 1971-73; gen. sales mgr. Sta. KOTE-FM, Sta. KKZZ-AM, Lancaster, 1973, v.p., gen. mgr. Lancaster-Palmdale Broadcasting Co., Lancaster, 1974-77; regional affairs dir. Sta. KFWB News 98, Westinghouse Broadcasting & Cable, Inc., Los Angeles, 1978-85; coordinator satellite ctr. UCLA Extension, 1985—; guest lectr. broadcasting UCLA Extension. Mem. communications, exec. heart health coms. Los Angeles affiliate Am. Heart Assn.; bd. dirs. Hollywood Human Services, Recipient Martin R. Gainsbrugh citation Econ. News Broadcasters Assn., 1981; citation Disting. Service, Am. Heart Assn., 1981; Community Service award United Way, 1980; Achievement award Credit Counselors Los Angeles, 1982; Champion Media award for Econ. Understanding, Amos Tuck Sch. Bus., Dartmouth Coll., 1982. Mem. Pub. Relations Soc. Am., Pub. Info. Radio and TV Edn. Soc., So. Calif. Broadcasters Assn. Pub. Affairs Dirs., Women's Council Greater Los Angeles C. of C. (dir. 1979-80), Women in Pub. Affairs, Coro Found. Assocs., UCLA Alumni Club (life), Nat. Assn. Broadcasters (chmn. small market radio com.), Pi Beta Phi. Office: UCLA Extension 10995 LeConte Ave Suite 514 Los Angeles CA 90024

GATES, JANE CAROL, artist, writer, referral service proprietor; b. Providence, Aug. 6, 1948; d. Robert Leonard Schwartz and Grace Adrian Black. BFA, R.I. Sch. Design, 1970; cert., Academia Di Perugia, Italy, 1971. Cert. community coll. instr., Calif. Songwriter, performer Red Bus Internat. Music Pub., London, 1971-76; freelance writer, illustrator various advt. and pub. relations agys., London, Boston, San Diego, 1975-82; project mgr. Ctr. Human Resources, Irvine, Calif., 1983-84; pres., tng. program developer Gates & Croft, Los Angeles, 1983—; founder, pres. Createmps Inc., Los Angeles, 1985—. Composer numerous recorded and pub. popular songs, 1971-76 (grand prize composition Yamaha World Popular Song Festival, Tokyo, 1972, 3d prize best song internat. Luxembourg Radio Festival, 1973); author: (children's book series) Adventures of Dat and Sidney, 1976; exhibited paintings and prints London, Boston, Los Angeles, 1971-81. Mem. Artists Equity Assn., The Performing Right Soc. (Eng.). Avocations: swimming, horticulture.

GATES, MADI, interior designer; b. Salix, Iowa, Aug. 13, 1938; d. Ralph Fredrick Madison and Joyce Elaine (Rugger) King; m. James Roland Gates, Dec. 30, 1962; children: Kirsten Ann. BS in Nursing Edn., U. Minn., 1963; student interior design program, Calif. Poly. State U., 1983. Staff nurse Winnebago (Nebr.) Indian Reservation, 1959-60; intensive care nurse U. Minn. Hosp., Mpls., 1960-63; head nurse Sierra Vista Hosp., San Luis Obispo, Calif., 1963-64, "float" nurse, 1966-80; owner, designer Madi Gates Interiors, San Luis Obispo, Calif., 1983—. Mem./seamstress Altar Guild St. Stephen's Episc. Ch., San Luis Obispo, 1968-80; mem. Children's Home Soc., San Luis Obispo, 1971—; chmn. Achievement House Workshop for the Disabled, San Luis Obispo, 1980-81, bd. dirs.; pres. Rep. Women, San Luis Obispo, 1969-70. Recipient scholarship Sioux City (Iowa) Med. Aux., 1956-59; named Nurse of Yr., U. Minn., 1962. Mem. Cen. Coast Interior Designers, Am. Soc. Interior Designers (assoc., cert. masters level), San Luis Obispo C. of C. Clubs: Ninety-nines (San Luis Obispo) (treas. 1979-80), Pharmacy Aux. (pres. 1963-64). Avocations: karate, nordic and alpine skiing, knitting and sewing, flower arranging, flying (7th place finisher Palms to Pines Air Race, Santa Monica, Calif., 1972). Home and Office: 125 Serrano Heights San Luis Obispo CA 93401

GATES, THEODORE ALLAN, JR., data processing executive; b. Washington, May 24, 1933; s. Theodore Allan and Margaret (Camp) G.; m. Anne Bissell, Sept. 8, 1955; children: Virginia Anne, Nancy Bissell, Theodore Allan III, Margaret Kenyon. Student, U. Md., 1951-53, 56-57, 68-69. Mem. staff Arthur D. Little Systems, Burlington, Mass., 1976-77, Corp. Tech. Planning, Portsmouth, N.H., 1977-78; project mgr. Honeywell Info. Systems, Phoenix, 1978-81; tech. mgr. Honeywell Info. Systems, Seattle, 1981-83; mgr. data and software engring. ISC Systems Corp., Spokane, Wash., 1983—. Served with U.S. Army, 1953-56, Korea. Recipient Superior Performance award Census Bur., 1958. Mem. IEEE, Assn. Computing Machinery, Data Processing Mgmt. Assn., Am. Mgmt. Assn. Democrat. Lutheran. Club: Commodores (Boston). Lodge: Shriners, Masons. Avocations: photography, sailing, music. Home: S 4505 Farr Rd Spokane WA 99206 Office: ISC Systems Corp Box TAF-C8 Spokane WA 99220

GATES, THOMAS J., chemical dependency specialist; b. San Diego, July 29, 1950; s. Delton O. and Violet B. (Barone) G.; m. Karla D. Schutt, Nov. 24, 1984. BA in Humanities, Seattle U., 1974, BA in Edn., 1977; MA in Applied Behavioral Sci., Whitworth Coll., 1985. Laborer Todd Shipyards, Inc., San Pedro, Calif., 1968-69; janitor Seattle U., 1974-76; custodian John F. Kennedy Meml. High Sch., Seattle, 1975-77; groupworker Toutle River Boys Ranch, Castle Rock, Wash., 1978-84; substance abuse counselor Community Alcohol Ctr., Longview, Wash., 1984—; family counselor Cowlitz County Family Ct., Longview, Wash., 1983; supr. candidate Cons. ALCOA Aluminum, Vancouver, Wash., 1983-84. reading tutor Wash. State Literacy Council, Seattle, 1974-76; subscirber Child Welfare League of Am., Washington, 1978; core team mem. Longview/Kelso (Wash.) Sch. Dists., 1984—. Recipient Pres. award Scholar, Pepperdine Coll., 1968. Mem. Alliance for Children, Youth and Families, Lower Columbia Personnel & Guidance Assn., League of Schs. Adolescent Care Unit, Alcoholism Profl. Staff Soc., Nat. Assn. Alcoholism and Drug Abuse Counselors. Presbyterian. Club: Toastmasters Internat. (Toastmaster of Month 1985-86). Avocations: collections of books, outdoor sports & activities, sponsoring youth. Office: Lower Columbia Community Alcohol & Drug Ctr 1260 Commerce Ave Suite 213 Longview WA 98632

GATES, WILLIAM HENRY, software company executive; b. Seattle, Oct. 28, 1955; s. William H. and Mary M. (Maxwell) G. Grad. high sch., Seattle, 1973; student, Harvard U., 1975. Chmn. bd. Microsoft Corp., Redmond, Wash., 1976—. Recipient Howard Vollum award, Reed Coll., Portland, Oreg., 1984. Office: Microsoft Corp 16011 NE 36th Way Redmond WA 98073-9717 *

GATLIN, LILA LEE, scientist, writer; b. Hutchinson, Kans., Aug. 23, 1928; d. Henry and Anna (Schoenhoff) Krause; m. Carl Gatlin, Sept. 3, 1947 (dec. Jan. 1977); children: Amy, Jeff, Laura, Jennifer. BS in Zoology with honors, U. Tulsa, 1957; MS in Phys. Chem. with honors, Pa. State U., 1961; PhD in Phys. Chem. with honors, U. Tex., 1963. NIH postdoctoral fellow Gnentics Found., U. Tex., Austin, 1964-65; asst. prof. chemistry Drexel Inst. Tech., Phila., 1965-66; vis. lectr. Bryn Mawr (Pa.) Coll., 1967-68; assoc. research geneticist U. Calif., Davis, 1974-77; Thomas W. Stanford psychology research fellow Stanford (Calif.) U., 1977-78, research assoc. psychology dept., 1978—; Author: Information Theory and the Living System, 1972; mem. editorial bd. Jour. Molecular Evolution, 1973-78; contbr. articles to profl. jours. Mem. AAAS, Soc. Sci. Exploration, Parapsychol. Assn. Avocation: yoga. Home: 706 Tolman Dr Stanford CA 94305 Home: 129 E 16th Newton KS 67114

GATZEK, LEO ELLNER, engineering consultant; b. N.Y.C., Nov. 25, 1911; s. Maxwell Thorton and Sadell Catherine (Ellner) G.; m. Beatrice Sandler, June 20, 1943; children: Jesse Ellis, Deborah Gatzek Kratter. BS, U. Chgo., 1933; MS, MIT, 1935; PhD, UCLA, 1963; PhD (hon.), U. Houston, 1965. Registered profl. engr. Sr. research engr. Internat. Harvester Co., Chgo., 1947-50; supt. and mgr. tech. lab. Bendix Aviation, N. Hollywood, Calif., 1950-58; mgr. materials engr. Aerospace Corp., El Segundo, Calif., 1958-68; space research scientist Rockwell Internat., Downey, Calif., 1962-68; chief quality engr. Lockheed Aircraft, Burbank, Calif., 1968-77; dir. Advanced Engring. Technologies, N. Hollywood, Calif., 1977—; instr. engring. dept. Los Angeles and Valley Colls., 1953-63, engring. UCLA, 1960-72, U. Houston, 1965-70; cons. space div. USAF, El Segundo, 1958-62. Author: Space Structures, 1965; patentee in field. Served to lt. USN, 1943-46. Fellow AIAA; mem. Am. Soc. Metals (tech. chmn. 1979-80), Nat. Assn. Corrosion Engrs., ASME. Avocations: swimming, hiking.

GAUGLER, WILLIAM MATHIAS, archaeology educator; b. Highland Park, Mich., Aug. 5, 1931; s. Mathias Regine (Hilzinger) Gaugler; m. Gladys Bernice Utchenik; 1 child, Laura Martha. B.A., Roosevelt U., 1954; Litt.D., U. Florence, 1965. Lectr. European div. U. Md., 1966-69; prof. classical archaeology San Jose State U., Calif., 1969—. Author: Fechten, 1983. Contbr. articles to profl. jours. Mem. Archeol. Inst. Am., Soc. for Promotion Hellenic Studies, Soc. for Promotion Roman Studies, Brit. Inst. Archeology at Ankara. Office: Dept Art San Jose State U One Washington Sq San Jose CA 95192

GAULKE, MARY FLORENCE, library administrator; b. Johnson City, Tenn., Sept. 24, 1923; d. Gustus Thomas and Mary Belle (Bennett) Erickson; m. James Wymond Crowley, Dec. 1, 1939; 1 son, Grady Gaulke (name legally changed); m. 2d, Bud Gaulke, Sept. 1, 1945 (dec. Jan. 1978); m. 3d, Richard Lewis McNaughton, Mar. 21, 1983. B.S. in Home Econs., Oreg. State U., 1963; M.S. in L.S., U. Oreg., 1968, Ph.D. in Spl. Edn., 1970. Cert. standard personnel supr., standard handicapped learner, Oreg. Head dept. home econs. Riddle Sch. Dist. (Oreg.), 1963-66; library cons. Douglas County Intermediate Edn. Dist., Roseburg, Oreg., 1966-67; head resident, head counselor Prometheus Project, So. Oreg. Coll., Ashland, summers 1966-68; supr. librarians Medford Sch. Dist. (Oreg.), 1970-73; instr. in psychology So. Oreg. Coll., Ashland, 1970-73; library supr. Roseburg Sch. Dist., 1974—; resident psychologist Black Oaks Boys Sch., Medford, 1970-75; mem. Oreg. Gov.'s Council on Libraries, 1979. Author: Vo-Ed Course for Junior High, 1965; Library Handbook, 1967; Instructions for Preparation of Cards For All Materials Cataloged for Libraries, 1971; Handbook for Training Library Aides, 1972. Coordinator Laubach Lit. Workshops for High Sch. Tutors, Medford, 1972. Mem. So. Oreg. Library Fedn. (sec. 1971-73), ALA, Oreg. Library Assn., Pacific N.W. Library Assn., Delta Kappa Gamma (pres. 1980-82), Phi Delta Kappa (historian, research rep.). Republican. Methodist. Clubs: Lodge: Order Eastern Star (worthy matron 1956-57). Home: 10407 Tiller Trail Hwy Canyonville OR 97417 Office: Roseburg Pub Schs 1419 Valley View Dr Roseburg OR 97470

GAUSTAD, EDWIN SCOTT, historian; b. Rowley, Iowa, Nov. 14, 1923; s. Sverre and Norma (McEachron) G.; m. Helen Virginia Morgan, Dec. 19, 1946; children—Susan, Glen Scott, Peggy Lynn. B.A., Baylor U., 1947; M.A., Brown U., 1948, Ph.D., 1951. Instr. Brown U., 1951-52, Am. Council Learned Socs. scholar in residence, 1952-53; dean Shorter Coll., 1953-57; prof. humanities U. Redlands, 1957-65; asso. prof. history U. Calif., Riverside, 1965-67; prof. U. Calif., 1968—. Author: The Great Awakening in New England, 1957, Historical Atlas of Religion in America, 2d edit, 1976, A Religious History of America, rev. edit, 1974, Dissent in American Religion, 1973, Baptist Piety: The Last Will and Testimony of Obadiah Holmes, 1978, George Berkeley in America, 1979; editor books, most recent being: Documentary History of Religion in America, 2 vols., 1982, 83; editor: Arno Press, 1970-79; editorial bd.: Jour. Ch. and State, 1970—; contbr. articles to profl. publs. Served to 1st lt. USAAC, 1943-45. Decorated Air medal; Am. Council Learned Socs. grantee, 1952-53, 72-73; Am. Philos. Soc. grantee, 1972-73. Mem. Am. Hist. Assn., Am. Acad. Religion, Am. Soc. Ch. History (pres.), Phi Beta Kappa. Democrat. Baptist. Office: Dept History Univ Calif Riverside CA 92521

GAUTHIER, MARJORIE ANN, educator; b. Franklin, N.H.; d. Ernest J. and Beatrice E. (Sorette) G. B.A. in Humanities, Mt. St. Mary Coll., 1960; M.Ed., Boston Coll., 1969. Life teaching credential, Calif. Mem. Sisters of Mercy, 1953-74; tchr. elem. schs. Diocese of Manchester (N.H.), 1960-70; prin. elem. sch. Archdiocese Los Angeles, 1970-74; tchr. Paramount (Calif.) Unified Sch. Dist., 1974-79, 81—, mentor tchr., 1983-87; tchr. Dept. Def. Dependent Schs., Worms, Ger., 1979-81. Spl. minister of Eucharist, master catechist, lay missionary Roman Catholic Diocese Orange (Calif.), 1982-84. Mem. Assn. Supervision and Curriculum Devel., Calif. Council Social Studies, Calif. Tchrs. Assn., Paramount Tchrs. Assn. (dir. 1982-84), Los Coyotes Council Social Studies (v.p. southeastern county 1984-85, pres. 1985-86), Internat. Assn. for Mentoring, Nat. Council for Social Studies, NEA, PTA, Delta Kappa Gamma, Kappa Delta Pi. Democrat. Home: 4900-84 E Chapman Ave Orange CA 92669

GAVIOLA, CARLOS DOMINGO, transportation engineer; b. Helsinki, Finland, Apr. 21, 1952; came to U.S., 1980; s. Carlos Armando and Cecile Doris Amanda Karen (Rampin) G.; m. Laurence Jacqueline Meillat, June 25, 1981; 1 child, Nicolas Thierry. BSE, Catholic U., Buenos Aires, 1978; MSE, U. Calif., Berkeley, 1981. Registered profl. engr., Tex. Jr. engr. De Lavallaz, Buenos Aires, 1977; civil engr. Latino Consult, Buenos Aires, 1977-80; research asst. U. Calif., Berkeley, 1980-81; assoc. engr. Kaiser Engrs., Houston, 1981-83, sr. transp. engr., 1983-85; project mgr. Kaiser Engrs., Oakland, Calif., 1985—; Contbr. numerous photojournalistic articles to pubs.; photographer documentaries in S. Am. mags. Mem. ASCE (co-chmn. transp. com. Houston chpt., 1984-85), Inst. Transp. Engrs. Avocations: photojournalism, offshore sailing races. Office: Kaiser Engrs Inc 1800 Harrison St Oakland CA 94623

GAY, E. LAURENCE, lawyer; b. Bridgeport, Conn., Aug. 10, 1923; s. Emil D. and Helen (Mihalich) G.; m. Harriet A. Ripley, Aug. 2, 1952; children: L. Noel, Peter C., Marguerite S., Georgette A. B.S., Yale U., 1947; J.D., Harvard U., 1949. Bar: N.Y. 1950, Conn. 1960, Calif. 1981. Atty. Root, Ballantine, Harlan, Bushby & Palmer, N.Y.C., 1949-51; legal staff U.S. High Commr. for Germany, 1951-52; law sec., presiding justice appellate div. 1st dept. N.Y. Supreme Ct., 1952-53; atty. Debevoise, Plimpton & McLean, 1953-58; v.p., sec.-treas. Hewitt-Robins, Inc., Stamford, Conn., 1958-65; pres. Litton Gt. Lakes Corp., N.Y.C., 1965-67; sr. v.p. finance AMFAC, Inc., Honolulu, 1967-73; vice chmn. AMFAC, Inc., 1974-78; fin. cons. Burlingame, Calif., 1979-82; of counsel Pettit & Martin, San Francisco, 1982—. Pres. Honolulu Symphony Soc., 1974-78; trustee Loyola Marymount U., 1977-80, San Francisco Chamber Soloists, 1982-86. Served to 2d lt. AUS, 1943-46. Mem. Phi Beta Kappa. Roman Catholic. Home: 580 Arastradero Rd #407 Palo Alto CA 94306 Office: 101 California St 35th Floor San Francisco CA 94111

GAY, JAMES EDWARD, manufacturing executive; b. Richmond, Calif., Oct. 7, 1949; s. Raymond L. and Jennie Lee (Gillock) G.; m. Bonnie S. Werth, Oct. 10, 1976; 1 child, Courtney Anne. BS, U. Calif., Berkeley, 1972; M in Bus., St. Mary's Coll., Moraga, Calif., 1979. Merchandise mgr. Lucky Stores, Inc., Dublin, Calif., 1972-79; assoc. A.T. Kearney Inc., Chgo., 1979-83, Slavin Assocs., San Francisco, 1982-83; mgr. Amdahl Corp., Santa Clara, Calif., 1983—. Mem. Am. Prodn. and Inventory Control Soc. (cert. mgmt. 1983, coll. liaison 1983-85), St. Mary's Coll. Grad. Sch. Alumni Assn. (bd. dirs. 1983-84). Avocations: jogging, racquetball. Home: 11867 W Vomac Rd Dublin CA 94568 Office: Amdahl Corp MS #190 1250 E Arques Ave Sunnyvale CA 94086

GAYLORD, EDWARD LEWIS, publishing company executive; b. Denver, May 28, 1919; s. Edward King and Inez (Kinney) G.; m. Thelma Feragen, Aug. 30, 1950; children: Christine Elizabeth, Mary Inez, Edward King II, Thelma Louise. A.B., Stanford U., 1941; LL.D., Oklahoma City U., Okla. Christian Coll., Pepperdine U., 1984. Chmn., chief exec. officer, dir. Gaylord Broadcasting Co.; WKY, Oklahoma City; chmn., chief exec. officer, dir. WSM-AM-FM, Nashville, WTVT, Tampa-St., Petersburg, KTVT, Dallas-Ft. Worth, KHTV, Houston, WVTV, Milw., KSTW-TV, Seattle-Tacoma, WVUE-TV, New Orleans, WUAB-TV, Cleve.-Lorain; pres., gen. mgr., dir. Okla. Pub. Co.; editor, pub. Daily Oklahoman, Sunday Oklahoman; Pubs. Petroleum, Okla. Graphics; pres. Sun Resources, Inc., Greenland (Colo.) Ranch, OPUBCO Resources, Inc., OPUBCO Devel. Co.; chmn. Opryland USA Inc., Nashville; chmn. bd. Gayno, Inc., Denver, Farmer-Stockman, Dallas, Gaylord Prodn. Co. Calif.; partner Cimarron Coal Co., Denver, Lazy E Ranch, Saint Jo, Tex., Westwind Ranch, San Saba, Tex. Chmn., trustee Okla. Industries Authority; chmn. bd. govs. Okla. Christian Coll.; bd. dirs. Okla. State Fair, pres., 1961-71; bd. dirs., pres. Nat. Cowboy Hall of Fame and Western Heritage Center; bd. dirs. Okla. Eye Found.; vice chmn. bd. govs. Am. Citizenship Center; trustee S.W. Research Inst., San Antonio; chmn. Okla. Med. Research Found., 1983—; past trustee Casady Sch., Oklahoma City U. Served with AUS, 1942-46. Recipient Brotherhood award NCCJ named to Okla. Hall of Fame, 1974; first recipient Spirit of Am. award U.S. Olympic Com., 1984; Disting. Service award U. Okla., 1981; Golden Plate award Am. Acad. Achievement, 1985. Mem. Oklahoma City C. of C. (dir., past pres.), So. Newspaper Pubs. Assn. (past pres.). Conglist. Home: 1506 Dorchester Dr Oklahoma City OK 73120 Office: Daily Oklahoman Okla Pub Co 500 N Broadway PO Box 25125 Oklahoma City OK 73125

GAYMAN, PATRICIA GYNETH, chiropractor; b. San Pedro, Calif., Aug. 16, 1938; d. Norman Alan and Olive Delone (Jensen) Smith; m. Robert Dale May, Jan. 13, 1956 (div. Nov. 1968); children: Cheryl, Robert, Karla, Kym, Leland, Deirdre, Stacy; m. Merrill Gene Gayman, Mar. 29, 1969. Student Monterey Peninsula Coll., 1958-59, Shasta Coll., 1971-73; D.C., Palmer Coll. of Chiropractic, 1964. Chiropractor, Monterey, Calif., 1964; assoc. in chiropractic practice, Hayward, Calif., 1968-69, Redding, Calif., 1974—; owner, operator Gayman Chiropractic Ctr., Redding, 1979-87; owner, operator The Whole Approach, Redding, 1987—; founder Metaphys. Exploration Ctr., Redding, 1973-83; dir. Wellness Resource Ctr., Redding, 1979—; founder, sponsor Holistic Health Fair, 1979—; speaker. Contbr. articles to profl. jours. Personnel chmn. Family Planning Inc., Redding, 1972-77; regent Pacific States Chiropractic Coll., San Leandro, 1979-81; sec. Jazz Soc., Redding, 1985-86. Mem. Nat. Assn. Female Execs., Bus. and Profl. Women's Club, C. of C. (bd. dirs. 1987—, Bus. Woman of Yr. 1985). Avocations: continuing education, metaphysical studies, jazz. Home: 7252 Churn Creek Rd Redding CA 96001 Office: The Whole Approach 2551 Park Marina Dr Suite I Redding CA 96001

GAYNOR, JOSEPH, marketing professional; b. Phila., Dec. 10, 1939; s. Joseph Charles Gaynor and Regina Dolores (Foley) Evans; m. Lonnie Louise Lee Boris, Aug. 10, 1959 (div. Feb. 1972); children: Daniel Joseph, Valerie Ann, William Charles; m. Nancy Louise Fairlie, July 28, 1974. BA, U. Calif., Berkeley, 1962. With sales dept. Bergen Brunswig Drug Co., San Jose, Calif., 1960-73; with regional sales div. Western Union Telegraph Co., San Francisco, 1974-76; mgr. western region Worldcom Communications, Mt. View, Calif., 1976-77; mgr. nat. sales Pioneer Tex. Corp., Dallas, 1977-79; v.p. mktg. and sales Micro-Baud, Inc., Santa Clara, Calif., 1980-83; pres. Tek Com Corp., San Jose, 1984—, also chmn. bd. dirs.; asst. sec. Prentice T-C Acquisitions, San Jose, 1985-86. Pres. Valley Homeowners Assn., San Jose, 1969-71. Named Salesman of Yr. Bergen Brunswig Corp., 1972, Mgr. of Yr. Worldcom, 1977. Republican. Roman Catholic. Club: Chess of Am. (San Francisco). Lodge: Elks. Avocations: auto mechs., chess, golf. Office: Tek Com Corp 120 Charcot Ave San Jose CA 95131

GAYNOR, WILLIAM LYNCH, healthcare executive; b. Sioux City, Iowa, Feb. 4, 1947; s. Frederick Bicknell and Phoebe Helen (Foot) G.; m. Carol Phyllis Hemke, Dec. 29, 1968; children: Alexa Hemke, Emily Glidden. BA, U. Oreg., 1969; M in Pub. Adminstrn., Portland State U., 1980. Chief technician dialysis unit Portland (Oreg.) State U. Hosp., 1975-79; adminstrv. dir. dialysis services Good Samaritan Hosp., Portland, 1980-83, adminstrv. dir. ambulatory care, 1983-85; v.p. satellite devel. Good Samaritan Health Enterprises, Portland, 1985-86, v.p. ops., 1986—; cons. health care, Oreg., Wash., 1983—; bd. dirs. Good Samaritan Hosp. Fed. Credit Union. Editor quar. mag. Oreg. Foresight, 1979-80. Mem. Am. Hosp. Assn., Assn. Western Hosps. Democrat. Avocations: music, literature, travel. Office: Good Samaritan Health Enterprises 1015 NW 22d Ave Portland OR 97210

GEBHARD, DAVID, museum director, educator; b. Cannon Falls, Minn., July 21, 1927; s. Walter J. and Ann (Olson) G.; m. Patricia Peeke, July 7, 1954; children: Ellen Jean, Tyra Ann. B.A., U. Minn., 1949, M.A., 1951, Ph.D., 1957. Curator, instr. art U. N.Mex., 1953-55; dir. Roswell (N.Mex.) Mus., 1955-61; prof. art, dir. art galleries U. Calif. at Santa Barbara, 1961-80; curator archtl. drawing collection Art Mus., 1980—; field research in archeology, summers 1949-57; Fulbright prof. Tech. U. Istanbul, Turkey, 1960-61; cons. hist. preservation, 1970—. Author: Prehistoric Cave Paintings of the Diablo Region of Texas, 1960, A Guide to the Architecture of Purcell and Elmslie, 1960, A Guide to Architecture in Southern California, 1964, R.M. Schindler: Architect; Architecture in California, 1868-1968, 1968, Kem Weber and the Moderene, 1969, The Richfield Building, 1928-1968, 1969, Charles F.A. Voysey, Architect, 1970, Architecture in Los Angeles, A Complete Guide, 1985, An Arcadian Landscape: The Gardens of A.E. Hanson, 1920-31, 1985, Santa Barbara: El Pueblo Viejo, 1986; co-author: Lloyd Wright, Architect, 1972, High Style Design, Whitney Museum American Art, 1985, A Guide to Architecture in San Francisco and Northern California, 1973, 2d edit., 1986, Indian Art of the Northern Plains, 1974, Los Angeles in the 30's; Bay Area Houses, 1976, A Guide to Architecture in Los Angeles and Southern California, 1977, A Guide to Architecture in Minnesota, 1977, 200 Years of American Architectural Drawing, 1977, A View of California Architecture, 1960-1976, 1977, Picturesque California Homes, 1978, The Architecture of Samuel and J.C. Newsom, 1878-1908, 1979, The Architecture of Gregory Ain, 1980, California Crazy, 1980, Tulsa Art Deco, 1980, Santa Barbara, the Creation of a New Spain in America, 1980, Legacy of Minneapolis, 1983; co-author: Frank Lloyd Wright in California, 1987; editor: California Architects & Architecture Series; mem. com. Montecito Archtl. Rev.; contbr. articles to profl. jours. Pres. Citizens Planning Assn. Santa Barbara County, Inc., 1970-76; vice chmn. Historic Landmark Commn., Santa Barbara, 1973—, Citizens Planning Assn., 1980—; Bd. dirs. Regional Plan Assn., So. Calif., Western Found. Served with AUS, 1945-47. Research grantee NSF; Research grantee NEA; Research grantee Nat. Endowment Humanities; Nat. Park Service grantee; Ford found. grantee study Turkish architecture, 1965; Guggenheim Found. fellow, 1980-81. Mem. AIA (hon., M. Riggs award), Soc. Am. Archaeology, Am. Anthrop. Assn., Coll. Art Assn., Soc. Archtl. Historians (pres. 1980-81, dir.), Archtl. Found. Santa

Barbara (bd. dirs.). Home: 895 E Mountain Dr Santa Barbara CA 93103 Office: Archtl Drawing Collection U Calif Santa Barbara CA 93106

GEBO, EMMA MARIE JOKI, academic administrator, education instructor; b. Billings, Mont., Jan. 1, 1945; d. Waino August and Vera H. (Luoma) Joki; m. David Ray Gebo, Sept. 12, 1964; children: Lorri D., Paul A., Robyn J. BS in Home Econs., Mont. State U., 1966; MEd, U. Mont., 1971; postgrad., Colo. State U., 1986—. Cert. secondary tchr., Idaho. Substitute tchr. various cities, Idaho, Mont., 1967-74; adult instr. Fashion Fabrics, Pocatello, Idaho, 1975-76; clothing instr., tchr. edn. Idaho State U., Pocatello, 1975-80, dept. chmn., tchr. edn., 1980—. Editor: Idaho Adult Living/Teen Living, 1986, Idaho Cooperative Vocational Education, 1984, 86. Named one of Outstanding Young Women of Am., 1978-81, Pocatello Disting. Young Woman, Jaycettes, 1981. Mem. Idaho Home Econs. Assn. (pres. 1983-85, disting. home economist 1985), Home Econs. Edn. Assn. (publs. bd. 1986, 87), Nat. Assn. Tchr. Educators Vocat. Home Econs. (newsletter editor 1986), Am. Home Econs. Assn. (by-laws com. 1983-85), Am. Vocat. Assn., Nat. Future Homemakers Am. (tchr. task force, 1984—, hon. mem. Idaho chpt.). Methodist. Avocations: whitewater rafting, skiing, backpacking, reading. Home: 2409 S Fairway Pocatello ID 83201 Office: Home Econs Vocat Tchr Edn Idaho State U Campus Box 8081 Pocatello ID 83209

GECHMAN, RONALD STUART, diversified electronics company communications executive; b. Oskaloosa, Iowa, Mar. 19, 1934; s. Nathan and Dorothy (Bush) G.; m. Rosalie Small, July 1, 1962; children: Stacy, Eric. AS, Milw. Sch. Engring., 1958; BS in Adminstrv. Sci., Pepperdine U., 1975, MBA, 1977. Engring. writer Gen. Dynamics Corp., San Diego, 1959-61, Hughes Aircraft Co., Fullerton, Calif., 1961-62; supr. pubs. Lear Siegler Inc., Anaheim, Calif., 1962-66; west coast editor Electronic Design Mag., Los Angeles, 1966-68; mgr. communication services Xerox Corp., Pasadena, Calif., 1968—. Editor: Language Without Speech, 1978. Served as staff sgt. USAF, 1953-57. Office: Xerox Corp 250 N Halstead St Pasadena CA 91107

GEDDES, BARBARA SHERYL, communications consultant, publications specialist; b. Poughkeepsie, N.Y., May 27, 1944; d. Samuel Pierson and Dorothy Charlotte (Graham) Brush; m. James Morrow Geddes, Feb. 24, 1968 (div. Dec. 1980); 1 child, Elisabeth. Project leader Four-Phase Systems, Cupertino, Calif., 1976-77, Fairchild Co., San Jose, Calif., 1979-80; mgr. tech. publs. Mohawk Data Scis., Los Gatos, Calif., 1977-79, Sytek Inc., Mountain View, Calif., 1981-83; project mgr. Advanced Micro Computers, Santa Clara, Calif., 1980-81; v.p. communications systems Strategic Inc., Cupertino, 1983-86; pres., mng. ptnr. Computer and Telecommunicatios Profl. Services, Mountain View, Calif., 1986—; cons. H-P, Varian, Aydin Energy, Chemelex, also others, 1972—; v.p. Conf. Recorders, Santa Clara, 1975-77; advisor Tele-PC, Morgan Hill, Calif., 1983—. Editor: Mathematics/Science Library, 7 vols., 1971. Contbr. numerous articles to mags. Mem. Santa Clara County Adoptions Adv. Bd., 1971-73, Las Cumbres Archtl. Control Commn., Los Gatos, 1983; advisor Los Altos Hills Planning Commn., Calif., 1978-79. N.Y. State Regents merit scholar, 1962. Mem. Assn. for Computing Machinery (editor 1970-72), Nat. Soc. for Performance and Instrn., Bus. and Profl. Advt. Assn., Women in Communications (pres. San Jose 1983—). Democrat. Home: 1052 Colorado Pl Palo Alto CA 94303 Office: Computer Telecommunications Profl Services 2672 Bayshore Pkwy #1050 Mountain View CA 94043

GEDDES, GARY LEE, wildlife park director; b. Peoria, Ill., Aug. 23, 1950; s. Robert and Mary O. (McCartney) G.; m. Debbie L. Lush, Sept. 7, 1974; children: Jake Austin, Cody Robert, Katelyn Jane. AS, Ill. Cen. Jr. Coll., 1970; BA in Zoology, So. Ill. U., 1972. Dir. Wildlife Prairie Park, Hanna City, Ill., 1973-81, NW Trek Wildlife Park, Eatonville, Wash., 1981—; co-chmn. bd. dirs. Region 6 Tourism Council, Olympia, Wash., 1984-86; vice-chmn. Mt. Rainier/St. Helens Mountain Connection, Ashford, Wash., 1984-87; exec. bd. mem. Regional Tourism Council, Olympia, Wash., 1983—. Fellow Am. Assn. Zool. Parks and Aquariums. Club: Mountaineers (Tacoma). Avocations: mountain climbing, camping, cross-country skiing, gardening. Home: 6502 255th St Ct E Graham WA 98338 Office: NW Trek Wildlife Park 11610 Trek Dr E Eatonville WA 98328

GEE, ELAINE, psychotherapist; b. Oakland, Calif., Feb. 14, 1949; d. Bing J. and Kam M. (Lee) G. BA, U. Calif., Berkeley, 1969; MA, U. Chgo., 1971; postgrad., Georgetown U. Family Ctr., 1976-79. Lic. clin. social worker. Tchr. Death Valley (Calif.) Elem. Sch., 1971-72; social worker, supr. Gouverneur Hosp., N.Y.C., 1973-81; pvt. practice social work Rafa Counseling Assocs., Hayward, Calif., 1981-85, Castro Valley, Calif., 1982—; educator adult schs. Fremont and San Lorenzo, Calif., 1982-85; mgr. employee services Mervyn's, Hayward, 1985-86. HEW fellow U. Chgo., 1969-71; Regents scholar U. Calif., Berkeley, 1966-69. Fellow Am. Orthopsychiat. Assn.; mem. Assn. Labor Mgmt. Adminstrs. and Cons. on Alcoholism, Acad. Cert. Social Workers, Nat. Assn. Social Workers (Bay Area Counseling and Psychotherapy Referral Service), Am. Assn. Marriage and Family Therapy. Democrat. Avocations: singing, piano, writing, hiking. Home: 1315 Culver Pl San Lorenzo CA 94580 Office: 20600 John Dr Castro Valley CA 94546

GEE, ELWOOD GORDON, university president; b. Vernal, Utah, Feb. 2, 1944; s. Elwood A. and Vera (Showalter) G.; m. Elizabeth Dutson, Aug. 26, 1968; 1 dau., Rebekah. B.A., U. Utah, 1968; J.D., Columbia U., 1971, Ed.D., 1972. Asst. dean U. Utah, Salt Lake City, 1973-74; jud. fellow U.S. Supreme Ct., Washington, 1974-75; assoc. dean Brigham Young U., Provo, Utah, 1975-79; dean W.Va. U., Morgantown, 1979-81, pres., 1981-85; pres. U. Colo., Boulder, 1985—. Author: Education Law and Public Schools, 1978, Law and Public Education, 1980, Violence, Values and Justice in American Education, 1982, Fair Employment Practice, 1982. W.K. Kellogg fellow, 1971-72; Mellon fellow, 1977-78. Mem. ABA, Adminstrv. Conf. U.S., Phi Delta Kappa, Phi Kappa Phi. Mormon. Home: Univ Colorado Residence of the President Boulder CO 80309 Office: Univ of Colorado 914 Broadway Campus Box B-35 Boulder CO 80309

GEERY, MICHAEL JAMES, electronics company executive; b. Missoula, Mont., July 15, 1937; s. Glenn Leroy and Rhye (Ward) G.; B.S. in Aero. Engring., Northrop U., 1960; m. Michelle A. Decrow, July 9, 1983; children—Laura Lynn, Angela, Jill, Holly, Michelle, Laura, Melanie, Jeff, Coleen. Electronic design engr. N. Am. Aviation, Los Angeles, 1960-62; electronic project engr. Lockheed Electronics, Los Angeles, 1962-64; biomed. electronic design engr. Space Labs Inc., Chattsworth, Calif., 1964-65; mktg. staff exec. TRW, Los Angeles, 1965-73; western area mgr. Gates Energy Products Co., Los Angeles, 1973-78; chief exec. officer Xenotronix Inc., Valencia, Calif., 1978—; cons. Mem. Ch. of Scientology. Home: 27167 Sena Ct Valencia CA 91355 Office: 25520 Ave Stanford Suite 305 Valencia CA 91355

GEHLAR, PAUL MARK, food processing executive; b. Salem, Oreg., July 30, 1950; s. Mark Gale and Paula Irma (Trommlitz) G. B.A., Linfield Coll., 1975. With Oreg. Fruit Products Co., Salem, 1962—, dir., 1974—, treas., 1978-80, pres., gen. mgr., 1980—; dir. Northwest Packers Indsl. Relations Assn., 1981—, vice chmn., 1983-84, chmn., 1984-86; dir. Northwest Food Processors Assn., 1982-85, exec. com., 1984-85; dir. Capital Improvement Inc., Salem, 1973—, pres., 1974—. Mem. Salem Airport Adv. Com., 1977-80. Mem. Am. Bonanza Soc., Western Bonanza Soc., Aircraft Owners and Pilots Assn., Oreg. Pilots Assn. Lic. private pilot, Oreg. Home: PO Box 5398 Salem OR 97304 Office: PO Box 5283 Salem OR 97304

GEHRES, JAMES, lawyer; b. Akron, Ohio, July 19, 1932; s. Edwin Jacob and Cleora Mary (Yoakam) G.; m. Eleanor Agnew Mount, July 23, 1960. B.S. in Acctg., U. Utah, 1954; M.B.A., U. Calif.-Berkeley, 1959; J.D., U. Denver, 1970, LL.M. in Taxation, 1977. Bar: Colo. 1970, U.S. Dist. Ct. Colo. 1970, U.S. Tax Ct. 1970, U.S. Supreme Ct. 1973, U.S. Ct. Appeals (10th cir.) 1978. Atty. IRS, Denver, 1965-80, atty. chief counsel's office, 1980—. Served with USAF, 1955-58, capt. Res. ret. Mem. ABA, Colo. Bar Assn., Am. Inst. C.P.A.s, Colo. Soc. C.P.A.s, Am. Assn. Atty.-C.P.A.s, Am. Judicature Soc., Am. Acctg. Assn., Order St. Ives, Beta Gamma Sigma, Beta Alpha Psi. Democrat. Contbr. articles to profl. jours. Address: 935 Pennsylvania St Denver CO 80203

GEHRIG, ALLEN JOHN PETER, finance and marketing executive; b. N.Y.C., Nov. 4, 1944; BA, U. N.Mex., 1968; MPA, Golden Gate U., 1980, MBA, 1983. Regional v.p. Mastercard Internat., Inc., San Francisco. Pres., San Francisco Spl. Olympics, 1977-81, chmn. bd., 1981-82; state treas. Calif. Spl. Olympics, 1981—; trustee St. Francis Hook and Ladder Soc., San Francisco, 1981-83; mem. Civil Grand Jury, City and County of San Francisco, 1982-83; active Rep. Nat. Com.; chmn. San Francisco Spl. Olympics Ann. Golf Tournament, 1986—. Recipient cert. of commendation U.S. Senator S.I. Hayakawa, 1978, 81; KABL Citizen of Day, 1978; joint resolution of commendation Calif. State Legislature, 1979; San Francisco Mayoral Proclamation of Commendation, 1979; letter of commendation U.S. Senator Alan Cranston, 1979, 81; cert. of appreciation Joseph P. Kennedy Jr. Found., 1979; plaque of appreciation San Francisco Spl. Olympics, 1980, 82, 83, 85; President's award for social service Wells Fargo Bank, 1981, Outstanding Vol. award, 1981; resolution San Francisco Bd. Suprs., 1979; communications award Easter Seals Soc. San Francisco, 1979; San Francisco Vol. Activist award Bay Area Vol. Bur. and Macy's Calif., 1981; recognition of valuable contbn. to community through vol. service cert. No. Calif. Council Vol. Burs., 1981; Nat Commendation for vol. service in the community Pres. Reagan; award of merit City and County of San Francisco, 1981; resolution Bd. Suprs. City and County of San Francisco, 1981; San Francisco mayor's commendation for public services, 1981; commendation resolution Calif. Spl. Olympics, 1981; resolution Calif. Senate, 1981; letter of commendation Eunice Kennedy Shriver/Spl. Olympics, Inc., Washington, 1981, numerous others. Mem. San Francisco Jaycees (pres. 1977-79, chmn. bd. 1979-80, Mem. of Yr. 1978, Officer of Yr. 1978, Disting. Service award 1979), Smithsonian Instn., Am. Mus. Nat. History. Clubs: Olympic, Commonwealth of Calif. Roman Catholic. Home: 1550 Bay St #340 San Francisco CA 94123

GEHRING, GEORGE JOSEPH, JR., dentist; b. Kenosha, Wis., May 24, 1931; s. George J. and Lucille (Martin) G.; D.D.S., Marquette U., 1955; m. Ann D. Carrigan, Aug. 2, 1982; children—Michael, Scott. Pvt. practice dentistry, Long Beach, Calif., 1958—. Author: The Happy Flosser. Chmn. bd. Long Beach affiliate Calif. Heart Assn.; mem. Long Beach Grand Prix com. of 300. Served with USNR, 1955-58. Mem. Harbor Dental Soc. (dir.), Pierre Fauchard Acad., Delta Sigma Delta. Club: Rotary. Home: 1230E Ocean Blvd #603 Long Beach CA 90802 Office: 532 E 29th ST Long Beach CA 90860

GEHRY, FRANK OWEN, architect; b. Toronto, Ont., Can., Feb. 29, 1929; came to U.S., 1947; s. Irving and Thelma (Caplan) G.; children—Leslie, Brina; m. Berta Aguilera, Sept. 11, 1975; children—Alejandro, Samuel. B. in Architecture, U. So. Calif., 1954; postgrad., Harvard U., 1956-57. Registered profl. architect, Calif. Designer Victor Gruen Assn., Los Angeles, 1953-54, planning, design and project dir., 1958-61; project designer, planner Pereira & Luckman, Los Angeles, 1957-58; prin. Frank O. Gehry & Assocs., Venice, Calif., 1962—. Architect, California Aerospace Mus., 1984, Loyola Law Sch., 1981-84, Mus. of Contemporary Art, 1983, Frances Howard Goldwyn Regional Br. Library, 1986, Info. and Computer Sci. Engring. Research Facility-U. Calif. Irvine, 1986. Trustee Hereditary Disease Found., Santa Monica, Calif., 1970—. Recipient Arnold W. Brunner Meml. Architecture prize, 1983, Eliot Noyes Desigh Chair award Harvard U., 1984; awarded Charlotte Davenport Chair, Yale U., 1982, 85. Fellow AIA. Office: Frank O Gehry & Assocs 11 Brooks Ave Venice CA 90291

GEIDUSCHEK, E(RNEST) PETER, biophysics and molecular biology educator; b. Vienna, Austria, Apr. 11, 1928; came to U.S., 1945, naturalized, 1946; s. Sigmund and Frieda (Tauber) G.; m. Joyce Barbara Brous; 2 children. B.A., Columbia U., 1948; A.M., Harvard U., 1950, Ph.D., 1952. Instr. chemistry Yale U., New Haven, 1952-53, 55-57; asst. prof. chemistry U. Mich., Ann Arbor, 1957-59; asst. prof. biophysics U. Chgo., 1959-62, assoc. prof., 1962-64, prof., 1964-70; prof. biology U. Calif.-San Diego, 1970—, chmn. dept., 1981-83; cons. USPHS, 1963-69. Editorial bd. Biphys. Jour., 1967-69, Ann. Revs. Biophysics and Bioengring., 1971-74, Virology, 1972—, Science, 1977-84. Served with U.S. Army, 1953-55. Recipient research award Am. Postgrad. Med. Assn., 1962, USPHS, 1962; Guggenheim fellow, 1964-65. Fellow Am. Acad. Arts and Scis.; mem. Nat. Acad. Scis., Am. Soc. Biol. Chemists, Biophys. Soc. (council 1964-66), AAAS, Am. Soc. Microbiology, Am. Soc. Virology (council 1985—). Office: U Calif Dept Biology LaJolla CA 92093

GEIGER, ALLEN RICHARD, research physicist; b. Sayre, Pa., Dec. 31, 1951; s. Richard A. and Francis M. (Aumick) G. BS in Physics, N.Mex. State U., 1975. Research aid N.Mex. State U., Las Cruces, 1975-76; research physicist Deep Space Systems, Las Cruces, 1977-79; chmn. bd. dirs. G.E.I., Las Cruces, 1979-81, PetroLaser, Inc., El Paso, Tex., 1987—; research physicist Atmospheric Sci. Lab., White Sands Missile Range, N.Mex., 1980—; cons. to petroleum industry, 1981—. Patentee in field. Mem. U.S. Naval Inst. (assoc.), World Space Found. (charter), Planetary Soc. (charter). Republican. Home: PO Box 2425 Las Cruces NM 88004 Office: Atmospheric Sciences Lab White Sands Missile Range NM 88002

GEIGER, ARTHUR LEE, corporate professional, consultant; b. Billings, Mont., Aug. 25, 1942. BA, Coll. of Great Falls, 1966; postgrad., U. Wis., 1968, U. Notre Dame, 1969. Assoc. dir. Kans. Regional Council on Higher Edn., 1966-67; dir. devel. Viterbo Coll., La Crosse, Wis., 1967-69; fin. underwriter, mgr. short-term money B.C. Ziegler Co., West Bend, Wis., 1969-72; regional mgr., nat. dir. mktg. and admissions Bell & Howell Edn. Group, Chgo., 1972-84; dir. sales Nat. Edn. Corp., Irvine, Calif., 1984-85; founder, owner Geiger-Felker, Ltd., Phoenix, 1985—. Named to Ariz. State Regulatory Bd., 1984, U.S. Congl. Advisory Bd., Ariz., 1985, chmn. Arix. State Bd. for Private Postsecondary Edn., 1986. Recipient Community Service award U.S. Jaycees, 1968, Achievement of Excellence award Bell & Howell, 1976; named one of Outstanding Young Men of Am., 1973, one of Disting. Ams., 1983. Home: 8331 N 21st Dr#208 Phoenix AZ 85021

GEIGER, WILLIAM ANDREW, JR., English educator; b. Los Angeles, Jan. 25, 1941; s. William Andrew and May Elizabeth (Koch) G.; m. Janice Lee Barker, Aug. 18, 1962; children: Thomas Lawrence, Anne Elizabeth. BA, Whittier Coll., 1962; MA, U. So. Calif., 1964, PhD, 1973. Instr. English Whittier (Calif.) Coll., 1965-73, asst. prof., 1973-75, assoc. prof., 1975-82, prof., 1982—; cons. Hunt-Wesson Foods, Fullerton, Calif., 1976-77, Occidental Petroleum, San Dimas, Calif., 1978. Author: Inventing, Ordering, and Communicating, 1984, Making Sense, 1986; contbr. articles to profl. jours. Recipient Elizabeth Pleasants award U. So. Calif., Los Angeles, 1963, Graves award Pomona (Calif.) Coll., 1975. Mem. MLA, Nat. Council Tchrs. English, So. Calif. Renaissance Soc. (at large bd. dirs. 1973). Democrat. Episcopalian. Avocation: stamp collecting. Office: Whittier Coll Dept English 13406 E Philadelphia Whittier CA 90608

GEISELMAN, PAULA J., physiological psychologist; b. Ohio, June 30, 1944; d. Paul and Rosemary (Dawson) Parsley; m. R. Edward Geiselman, Mar. 20, 1976. AB in Psychology with honors, Ohio U., 1971, MS in Exptl. Psychology, 1976; PhD in Physiol. Psychology, UCLA, 1983. Adj. asst. prof. UCLA, 1986—; lectr. in field. Reviewer for Sci. Jour., Am. Jour. Physiology, Physiology and Behavior, Brain Research Bulletin, Appetite: Determinants and Consequences of Eating and Drinking; contbr. numerous articles to profl. jours. Mem. Soc. Neurosci., AAAS, N.Am. Assn. Study of Obesity, Women in Neurosci., Assn. Acad. Women, Am. Psychol. Assn., Am. Psychol. Assn., Eastern Psychol. Assn., Western Psychol. Assn. (head of physiol. psychol., chair. Animal Feeding and Behavior paper session 1981), Assn. Advancement Psychology, Internat. Brain Research Orgn., World Fedn. Neuroscientists, Brit. Brain Research Assn. (hon.), European Brain and Behavior Soc. (hon.), N.Y. Acad. Scis., Sigma Xi, Psi Chi. Avocations: opera, ballet, early music, Italian Renaissance, Mesoamerica. Office: UCLA Dept Psychology Franz Hall 405 Hilgard Ave Los Angeles CA 90024

GEISSERT, KATY, mayor. Mayor, city of Torrance, Calif. Office: Office of the Mayor 3031 Torrance Blvd Torrance CA 90503 *

GEIST, HAROLD, psychologist; b. Pitts., July 22, 1916; s. Alexander and Edna (Liebhaber) G. AB, Cornell U., 1936; AM, Columbia U., 1937; PhD, Stanford U., 1951. Lic. psychologist, Calif. Advisor edn. vocat. Community Cen. Office, Patterson, N.J., 1946-47; pvt. practice psychology Va., 1947-48; chief psychologist Mare Island Naval Hosp., Vallejo, Calif., 1947-48; pvt. practice psychology Berkeley, Calif., 1955—; sr. clin. psychologist Napa State Hosp., Imola, Calif., 1971-80; vis. prof. U. Puerto Rico, Rio Piedras, 1953-55; lectr. San Francisco State U., 1966-82; adj. prof. U. San Francisco, 1980-82. Author: Etiology of Idiopathic Epilepsy, 1962, Psychological Aspects of Diabetes, 1964, Tennis Psychology, 1976, Bahian Adventure, 1985, others; contbr. numerous articles to profl. jours. Served with M.C., U.S. Army, 1942-46. Fellow Internat. Council Psychologists; mem. Am. Psychol. Assn. (life), AAAS (life), Calif. State Psychol. Assn. (chmn. div. edn. and tng. 1960—, editor newsletter), Phi Sigma Delta. Home: 2255 Hearst Ave Berkeley CA 94709 Office: 2380 Ellsworth St Berkeley CA 94704

GEIST, JERRY DOUGLAS, electric utility company executive; b. Raton, N.Mex., May 23, 1934; s. Jacob D. and Jessie Kathleen (Wadley) G.; m. Sharon Ludell Kaemper, June 12, 1956; children: Douglas, Bruce, Robert. Student, U. Mo., 1952-54; BEE, U. Colo., 1956. Registered profl. engr., N.Mex. With Pub. Service Co. N.Mex., Albuquerque, 1960—, v.p. engring. and ops., 1970-71, v.p. corporate affairs, 1971-73, exec. v.p., 1973-76, pres., 1976-82, chmn., pres., 1982—, also bd. dirs., mem. exec. com.; bd. dirs. Fed. Res. Bank of Kansas City, Lectrosonics Inc., Venture Advisors Investment Funds, Aegis Ins. Services, Inc.; chmn. Utech Venture Capital Corp. Ltd.; mem. Pres.'s Export Council. Bd. dirs. Resources for the Future, Nat. Symphony, S.W. Community Health Services; chmn. adminstrv. bd. First United Meth. Ch. Served with USN, 1952-59. Mem. Edison Electric Inst. (chmn.), Albuquerque C. of C. (pres. 1972-73), Bus. Roundtable, Tau Beta Pi, Sigma Tau, Eta Kappa Nu, Pi Mu Epsilon. Clubs: Four Hills Country, Albuquerque Country, Albuquerque Petroleum; Tanoan Country, Links. Home: 1312 Cuatro Cerros Trail SE Albuquerque NM 87123 Office: Pub Service Co N Mex Alvarado Sq Albuquerque NM 87158

GEIST, WILLIAM SIDNEY, SR., architectural engineer; b. Spokane, Wash., Dec. 8, 1936; s. Walter Louise and Helen Lee (Donovan) G.; m. Sharon Joyce Schaffert, Mar. 12, 1961 (div. Mar. 1975); children—William Sidney, Christina Lee, Timothy Patrick. B.S. in Architecture, Wash. State U., 1960. Facilties engr. Sylvania Electronics Co., Mountain View, Calif., 1960-66; engr. planning dept. Boeing Co. Seattle Facilities, 1966-69; engr. bldgs. Pacific N.W. Bell Telephone Co., Seattle, 1969-84; cons. engr., 1984-86; engring. cons. Wetherhold & Assocs., 1986—; photographer. Chmn. Wash. State Big Game Council, 1974-78, treas., 1976-77; sec. Pacific N.W. Bell Community Relations Team, Seattle, 1978-82; mem. Nat. Rep. Congl. Com., 1981—. Served with USNR, 1953-63. Mem. Constrn. Specifications Inst. (chmn. membership 1981-82). Lutheran.

GELBER, DON JEFFREY, lawyer; b. Los Angeles, Mar. 10, 1940; s. Oscar and Betty Sheila (Chernitsky) G.; m. Jessica Jeasun Song, May 15, 1967; children—Victoria, Jonathan, Rebecca, Robert. Student UCLA, 1957-58, Reed Coll., 1958-59; A.B., Stanford U., 1961, J.D., 1963. Bar: Calif. 1964, Hawaii 1964, U.S. Dist. Ct. (cen. and no. dists. Calif.) 1964, U.S. Dist. Ct. Hawaii 1964, U.S. Ct. Appeals (9th cir.) 1964. Assoc. Greenstein, Yamane & Cowan, Honolulu, 1964-67; reporter Penal Law Revision Project, Hawaii Jud. Counsel, Honolulu, 1967-69; assoc. H. William Burgess, Honolulu, 1969-72; ptnr. Burgess & Gelber, Honolulu, 1972-73; prin. Law Offices of Don Jeffrey Gelber, Honolulu, 1974-78; prin., pres. Gelber & Wagner, Honolulu, 1978-83; prin., pres. Gelber & Gelber, Honolulu, 1984—; legal counsel Hawaii State Senate Judiciary Com., 1965; adminstrv. asst. to majority floor leader Hawaii Senate, 1966, legal csl. Edn. Com., 1967, 68; majority counsel Hawaii Ho. of Reps., 1974. Contbr. articles to legal publs. Mem. State Bar Calif., ABA (sect. corp., banking, bus. law), Am. Bankruptcy Inst., Hawaii Bar Assn. (sect. corps. and securities), Am. Bankruptcy Inst., Hawaii Estate Planning Council. Clubs: Pacific, Plaza. (Honolulu). Office: Gelber & Gelber 745 Fort St Suite 1400 Honolulu HI 96813

GELBERD, HOWARD H., educational association administrator; b. Cleve., Sept. 25, 1949; s. Sam and Ann Gelberd. Student, Hebrew U., Jerusalem, 1967-68, 70-71; BA, Calif. State U., Northridge, 1971; EdM, U. So. Calif., 1972; BA, U. Judaism, Los Angeles, 1973. Cert. secondary tchr., Calif. Adminstr. schs. Sinai Temple, Los Angeles, 1972-75; asst. dir. Bur. Jewish Edn., Los Angeles, 1975-85; exec. dir. Bur. Jewish Edn., San Francisco, 1985—; chmn. community adv. council Fairfax Adult Sch., Los Angeles, 1975-78. Mem. Assn. Supervision and Curriculum Devel., Nat. Council Social Studies, Phi Delta Kappa. Home: 350 7th Ave #320 San Francisco CA 94118 Office: Bur Jewish Edn 639 14th Ave San Francisco CA 94118

GELFAND, MARSHALL M., accountant; b. Claremont, N.H., Dec. 14, 1927; s. I.N. and Annie (Senoff) G.; m. Judy Jaffe, Dec. 17, 1955; children: Todd, Elizabeth, Dean. BS, Syracuse U., 1950; JD, NYU, 1955. CPA, N.Y., Calif. Bar: N.Y. 1958. Ptnr. H.H. Lawin & Co., N.Y.C., 1958-67; mng. ptnr. Gelfand Rennert & Feldman, CPA's, Los Angeles, 1967—; dir. Palm Springs Savs. Bank, Calif. Trustee Syracuse U., N.Y., 1983—; bd. dirs. Palm Springs Friends of Los Angeles Philharm., 1981—, Jewish Community Ctr., Palm Springs, 1981—, Bob Hope Cultural Ctr. Inc., 1985—, Desert Mus., Palm Springs. Mem. Calif. CPA Soc., Sigma Alpha Mu (trustee 1979—). Democrat.

GELLER, FLOYD STUART, optometrist; b. Portland, Oreg., Oct. 16, 1933; s. Jack J. and Gussie (Frager) G.; m. Dorothy Ruth Jermulowske, June 10, 1956; children—Carol Sue, Cynthia Sharon, Craig Steven. B.S., Pacific U., 1958, O.D., 1958. Mgr., Columbian Optical of Gateway (Oreg.), 1964-77, owner, mgr., 1977-83; optometrist Mall 205 Optical, Portland, 1981—. Commr. Multnomah County Parks; pres. Greater Gateway Boosters; mem. adv. com. Portland Community Coll. Jewish. Lodges: Elks, Masons, Shriners, Lions (pres. Parknose chpt. 1987—). Home: 13209 SE Ankeny Ct Portland OR 97233 Office: 9978 SE Washington Portland OR 97216

GELL-MANN, MURRAY, theoretical physicist; b. N.Y.C., Sept. 15, 1929; s. Arthur and Pauline (Reichstein) Gell-M.; m. J. Margaret Dow, Apr. 19, 1955 (dec. 1981); children: Elizabeth, Nicholas. BS, Yale U., 1948; PhD, Mass. Inst. Tech., 1951; ScD (hon.), Yale U., 1959, U. Chgo., 1967, U. Ill., 1968, Wesleyan U., 1968, U. Turin, Italy, 1969, U. Utah, 1970, Columbia U., 1977, Cambridge U., 1980. Mem. Inst. for Advanced Study, 1951, 55, 67-68; instr. U. Chgo., 1952-53, asst. prof., 1953-54, assoc. prof., 1954; assoc. prof. Calif. Inst. Tech., Pasadena, 1955-56; prof. Calif. Inst. Tech., 1956—, now R.A. Millikan prof. physics.; vis. prof. MIT, spring 1963, CERN, Geneva, 1971-72, 79-80; mem. Pres.'s Sci. Adv. Com., 1969-72; mem. sci. and grants com. Leakey Found.; chmn. bd. trustees Aspen Ctr. for Physics, 1973-79. Author: (with Y. Ne'eman) Eightfold Way. Regent Smithsonian Instn., 1974—; bd. dirs. J.D. and C.T. MacArthur Found., 1979—. NSF post doctoral fellow, vis. prof. Coll. de France and U. Paris, 1959-60; recipient Dannie Heineman prize Am. Phys. Soc., 1959; E.O. Lawrence Meml. award AEC, 1966; Overseas fellow Churchill Coll., Cambridge, Eng., 1966; Franklin medal, 1967; Carty medal Nat. Acad. Scis., 1968; Research Corp. award, 1969; Nobel prize in physics, 1969. Fellow Am. Phys. Soc.; mem. Nat. Acad. Scis., Royal Soc. (fgn.), Am. Acad. Arts and Scis. (v.p., chmn. Western ctr. 1970-76), Council on Fgn. Relations, French Phys. Soc. (hon.). Clubs: Cosmos (Washington); Century Assn., Explorers (N.Y.C.); Athenaeum (Pasadena). Office: Dept Physics Calif Inst Tech Pasadena CA 91125

GELMAN, HERBERT, lawyer; b. Bklyn., Feb. 17, 1933; s. Jack and Sarah (Aberman) G.; m. Barbara L. Jensen, Apr. 11, 1959; children—Mark, Dana, Sarah, Megan. B.A., Bklyn. Coll., 1954; J.D., U. Wash., 1962. Asst. atty. gen. Office Atty. Gen., Olympia, Wash., 1963-66, spl. asst. atty. gen., Tacoma, 1966-67; prin. Gelman, Couture & Pate, Tacoma, 1967—. Trustee, chmn. Evergreen State Coll., Olympia, 1979—; bd. dirs., chmn. Lakewood Gen. Hosp., Tacoma, 1974-81, Franklin-Pierce Sch. Bd., Tacoma, 1965-73; bd. dirs. Family Counseling Service, Tacoma, 1973-79; active Pub. Employee Collective Bargaining Com., Olympia, 1969-76. Served to capt. USAF, 1955-59. Mem. ABA, Wash. State Bar Assn., Am. Trial Lawyers Assn. Democrat. Jewish. Home: 1509 S 138th Tacoma WA 98444 Office: Gelman Couture & Pate 1101 S Fawcett Tacoma WA 98402

GEMMELL, GERALD WILLIAM, non-commissioned military officer; b. Pontiac, Mich., Aug. 31, 1941; s. Melvin Russel and Joyce Olive (Newman) G.; m. Sylvia Pacheco, Sept. 8, 1963; children: Gary Anthony, Stanley William, Erin Denise, Gayle Kristen. AA, East Los Angeles Coll., 1968; BS,

Calif. State U., Los Angeles, 1971; MA, Pepperdine U., 1979; postgrad., U.S. Internat. U. Enlisted USMC, 1961-65, 76—; criminal investigator USMC, Camp Pendleton, Calif., 1980-83, supr. mil. police, 1984-86, chief mil. intelligence, 1986—; criminal investigator USMC, Okinawa, Japan, 1983-84; pub. safety officer, commd. Detroit Police officer Wayne State U., Detroit, 1971-73; res. dep. sheriff Los Angeles County, 1966-68; police officer Stanton, Calif., 1968-69; instr. Los Angeles Metro Coll., Iwakuni, Japan, 1979-80; tchr. Chapman Coll., Camp Pendleton, 1980-83, Cen. Tex. Coll., Okinawa, Japan, 1983-84. Lector Cath. Chapel, Iwakuni, 1979-80, Camp Pendleton Base Chapel, 1980-83; lay eucharistic minister St. Margaret's Ch., Oceanside, Calif., 1984—; v.p. PTO Camp Lejeune, 1978. Mem. U.S. Aikido Fedn. (Sho-dan award 1982), Fraternal Order of Police, Lambda Alpha Epsilon. Republican. Roman Catholic. Avocations: Aikido. Home: 3546 San Piper Pl Oceanside CA 92056

GENCHUR, PATRICIA ANN, bank executive; b. Evanston, Ill., May 25, 1949; d. Robert John and Florence (Nightengale) Kehe; m. John Arthur Genchur, Nov. 27, 1971; 1 child, Brian Jeffrey. BS, MS, U. Ill., 1971. Officer 1st Interstate Bank, Seattle, 1972-77; sr. mktg. officer Seafirst Bank, Seattle, 1977-79; mktg. officer Rainier Nat. Bank, Seattle, 1979-82, v.p., mgr. electronic banking, 1982-86, v.p., mgr. consumer fin. services, 1987—; speaker at local, nat. convs. and orgns. regarding electronic banking; instr. Am. Inst. Banking, Seattle, 1974-81. Past dir. Widowed Info. and Cons. Services, Seattle, 1983; active YMCA membership drive, Seattle, 1982—. Recipient Presdl. citation Am. Bankers, 1984. Mem. Nat. Assn. Bus. Women (officer 1974-85), Am. Mktg. Assn. (officer 1974-85), Women's Bus. Exchange, Women's Network. Office: Rainier Nat Bank PO Box 3966 Seattle WA 98124

GENENSKY, SAMUEL MILTON, visual rehabilitation center administrator; b. New Bedford, Mass., July 26, 1927; s. Maurice and Jessie Marion (Kaufman) G.; m. Marion Malis, Nov. 26, 1953; children: Marsha Lynn, Judy Mara. BS in Physics magna cum laude, Brown U., 1949, PhD in Applied Math., 1958; MA in Math., Harvard U., 1951; LHD (hon.), Ill. Coll. Optometry, 1979. Mathematician Nat. Bur. Standards, Washington, 1951-54; sr. mathematician Rand Corp., Santa Monica, Calif., 1958-76; exec. dir. Ctr. for Partially Sighted, Santa Monica, 1976—; mem. adv. com. on services to blind and partially sighted Calif. Dept. Rehab., 1972-81, mem. study group on services to blind and partially sighted, 1981; mem. adv. com. low vision services Am. Found. for Blind, 1975-77, 80-81; cons. Rand Corp., 1976—; mem. nat. implementation adv. com. White House Conf. on Handicapped Individuals, 1979; mem. ad hoc com. on standards for low vision clinics Nat. Accreditation Council, 1980; mem. long term care planning group Calif. Health and Welfare Agy., 1981; lectr. dept. ophthalmology Sch. Medicine, UCLA, 1982—; mem. NRC Commn. Aging Workers and Visual Impairment, 1985-86; task force Low Vision Am. Found. Blind, 1985—. Contbr. articles on visual research and rehab. to profl. jours; patentee underground boring equipment. Bd. dirs., past pres. Council Citizens with low vision; trustee So. Calif. Coll. Optometry, Fullerton, 1972-86. Recipient Meritorious Service award South Bay Mayor's Com. on Employment for Handicapped, 1972, Paul Yarwood award Calif. Optometric Assn., 1972, Disting. Services award NCCJ, 1979, Mainstream Milestones award Los Angeles Jaycees, 1980, Pub. Affairs award Coro Found., 1986, Low Vision Disting. Achievement award Am. Optometric Assn., 1985; fellow Brown U., 1954-55; Francis Wayland scholar Brown U., 1946. Fellow Am. Acad. Optometry; mem. AAAS, Am. Math. Soc., Sigma Xi. Home: 826 Jacon Way Pacific Palisades CA 90272 Office: Ctr for Partially Sighted 919 Santa Monica Blvd Suite 200 Santa Monica CA 90401

GENG, SHU, agronomy educator; b. Sichung, People's Republic of China, Sept. 3, 1942; s. Mei-Chang and S.Q. (Ho) G.; m. Hai-Yen Wong, June 29, 1968; children: Elvin H., Joy J. BS, Nat. Taiwan U., Taipei, 1964; MS, Kans. State U., 1969, PhD, 1972. Biostatistician The Upjohn Co., Kalamazoo, 1972-76; asst. prof. U. Calif., Davis, 1976-78, assoc. prof., 1978-84, prof., 1984—. Contbr. articles to profl. jours. Mem. AAAS, Am. Soc. Agronomy, Crop Sci. Soc. Am., Biometrics Assn., Am. Statis. Assn. Home: 425 Grande Ave Davis CA 95616 Office: U Calif Dept Agronomy and Range Sci Davis CA 95616

GENGOR, VIRGINIA ANDERSON, financial planning executive, financial services educator; b. Lyons, N.Y., May 2, 1927; d. Axel Jennings and Marie Margaret (Mack) Anderson; m. Peter Gengor, Mar. 2, 1952 (dec.); children—Peter Randall, Daniel Neal, Susan Leigh. A.B., Wheaton Coll., 1949; M.A., U. No. Colo., Greeley, 1975, 77. Cert. fin. planner. Chief hosp. intake service County of San Diego, 1966-77, chief Kearny Mesa Dist. Office, 1977-79, chief Dependent Children of Ct., 1979-81, chief child protection services, 1981-82; registered rep. Am. Pacific Securities, San Diego, 1982-85; assoc. Pollock & Assocs., San Diego, 1985-86; pres. Gengor Fin. Advisors, 1986—; cons. instr. Nat. Ctr. for Fin. Edn., San Diego, 1986—; instr. San Diego Community Coll., 1985—. Mem. allocations panel United Way, San Diego, 1976-79; chmn. com. Child Abuse Coordinating Council, San Diego, 1979-83; pres. Friends of Casa de la Esperanza, San Diego, 1980-85; 1st v.p. The Big Sister League, San Diego, 1985-86, pres., 1987—. Mem. Inst. Cert. Fin. Planners, Internat. Assn. Fin. Planning, Inland Soc. Tax Cons., AAUW (bd. dirs.), Nat. Ctr. Fin. Edn., Am. Bus. Women's Assn., Nat. Assn. Female Execs. Presbyterian. Avocations: community service; traveling; reading. Home: 6462 Spear St San Diego CA 92120 Office: Gengor Fin Advisors 4950 Waring Rd Suite 7 San Diego CA 92120

GENIN, GRACE-ANN, speech and language pathologist; b. London, Nov. 11, 1937; came to U.S., 1959; d. G. Edwin and Carole Fisher (Waldron) G.; m. Joseph Genin, July 11, 1964; children: Kent E., Guy M., Hugh S. BA with honors, U. London, 1959; MS, Purdue U., 1979. Speech therapist Wabash Ctr., Lafayette, Ind., 1979-80; speech-lang. pathologist Monticello (Ind.) Healthcare, 1980-81, Children's Med. Services, Las Cruces, N.Mex., 1982-85, Associated Home Health Services, Las Cruces, 1983—. Mem. Am. Speech-Lang.-Hearing Assn. (cert. clin. competence in speech pathology), N.Mex. Speech and Hearing Assn., El Paso Speech and Hearing Assn. Home: 2012 Crescent Dr Las Cruces NM 88005 Office: Associated Home Health Services PO box 576 Las Cruces NM 88005

GENNARO, ANTONIO, biology educator; b. Raton, N.Mex., Mar. 18, 1934; s. Paul and Mary Lou (Gasperetti) G.; m. Virginia Marie Sullivan, May 15, 1955 (div. 1979); children—Theresa Ann, Carrie Marie, Janelle Elizabeth; m. Marjorie Lou Cox, Sept. 27, 1980. B.S., N.Mex. State U., 1957; M.S., U. N.Mex., 1961, Ph.D., 1965. Tchr. biology Las Cruces High Sch., N.Mex., 1957-58; asst. prof. biology St. John's U., Collegeville, Minn., 1964-65; prof. biology Eastern N.Mex. U., Portales, 1965—. Contbr. articles to sci. jours. Served to capt. U.S. Army, 1958-59; mem. Res., 1959-66. Recipient Presdl. Faculty award Eastern N.Mex. U., 1970; Outstanding Sci. award N.Mex. Acad. Sci., 1975. Mem. Southwestern Naturalists (treas. 1974-78), Am. Soc. Mammalogists, Herpetologists League, Sigma Xi, Phi Kappa Phi (pres. 1970-74). Roman Catholic. Office: Eastern NMex U Portales NM 88130

GENOVESE, ANTHONY (BUD), JR., auditor; b. Cleve., Sept. 17, 1947; s. Anthony Sr. and Bernice (DiVita) G.; m. Carla Jane Batchelder, Dec. 14, 1969; children: Gregory, Erin. BBA in Fin., Ohio U., 1969; MBA in Mgmt., Golden Gate U., 1978; postgrad., U. Wis., 1982. Chartered bank auditor; cert. internal auditor; cert. info. systems auditor. Engring. analyst Memorex Corp., Santa Clara, Calif., 1970-72; prodn. analyst Am. Microsystems, Santa Clara, 1972-74; EDP auditor Federal Home Loan Bank of San Francisco, 1974-78; v.p., chief auditor County Bank & Trust, Santa Cruz, Calif., 1978—, now sr. v.p., chief auditor. Mem. EDP Auditors Assn. (v.p. 1985, pres. 1987), Bank Auditors Roundtable (chmn. 1983-84, bd. dirs. 1985—), Inst. Internal Auditors, Bank Adminstrn. Inst., Ohio U. Alumni Assn., Bay Area Browns Backers Assn. (founder). Democrat. Avocations: photography, spectator sports, hockey, bicycling. Office: County Bank & Trust PO Box 1260 Santa Cruz CA 95061

GENTRY, JAMES WILLIAM, state official; b. Danville, Ill., Aug. 14, 1926; s. Carl Lloyd and Leone (Isham) G.; A.B., Fresno State Coll., 1948; M.J., U. Calif., Berkeley, 1956; m. Dorothie Shirley Hechtlinger, Mar. 18, 1967; 1 stepdau., Susan Mushkin. Field rep. Congressman B.W. Gearhart, Fresno, Calif., 1948, Assemblyman Wm. W. Hansen, Fresno, 1950, sec., 1953-56; exec. asst. Calif. Pharm. Assn., Los Angeles, 1956-69, editor, pub. jour., 1956-69; pub. relations dir. PAID Prescriptions, 1963-64; dir. pub. info. comprehensive Health Planning Council, Los Angeles County, 1969; asst. adminstr., dir. pub. info. So. Calif. Comprehensive Health Planning Council, 1969-71, acting adminstr., 1971-72; exec. sec. Calif. State Health Planning Council, 1972-73, Calif. Adv. Health Council, 1973-85, fed. cons., 1986—; Calif. Health Care Commn., 1973-75; acting public info. officer Calif. Office Statewide Health Planning and Devel., 1978-79; interim dir. Calif. Office Statewide Health Planning and Devel., 1983; mem. Los Angeles Civil Service Police Interview Bd., 1967-72; asst. sgt.-at-arms Calif. State Assembly, 1950; exec. sec. Calif. Assembly Interim Com. on Livestock and Dairies, 1954-56; mem. adv. bd. Am. Security Council; mem. Calif. Health Planning Law Revision Commn.; former mem. Calif. Bldg. Safety Bd. Mem. Fresno County Republican Central Com., 1950; charter mem. Rep. Presdl. Task Force. Served to col. AUS, 1949-50, 50-53; Korea. Decorated Legion of Merit, Bronze Star medal, Commendation Ribbon with metal pendant; recipient pub. awards Western Soc. Bus. Publns. Assn., 1964-67. Mem. Am. Assn. Comprehensive Health Planning, Pub. Relations Soc. Am., Ret. Officers Assn., Allied Drug Travelers So. Calif., Los Angeles Press Club, Mil. Police Assn., Res. Officers Assn. (life), Assn. U.S. Army, Pi Gamma Mu, Phi Alpha Delta. Sigma Delta Chi. Club: U.S. Senatorial. Editor: Better Health, 1963-67; Orientation Conf. Comprehensive Health Planning, 1969; Commentary, 1969-71. Editorial adv. Pharm. Services for Nursing Homes: A Procedural Manual, 1966. Editor: Program and Funding, 1972; Substance Abuse, 1972. Home: 902 Commons Dr Sacramento CA 95825

GENTRY, RICHARD ELLSWORTH, fabric company executive; b. Oakland, Calif., Jan. 28, 1944; s. Richard and Amalie (Browne) G.; m. Marla Jaclyn Weiss, Aug. 4, 1968; children—Lisa, Stacy. B.A., U. Pacific, 1966. Indsl. engr. Fibreboard Corp., Stockton, Calif., 1967-68; with Wesco Fabrics Inc., Denver, 1968—, pres., 1984—; dir. Shalomar Corp., Denver. Bd. dirs., v.p. Colo. Ballet, Denver, 1981-82. Mem. Fabric Distbrs. Assn. Am. (bd. dirs.). Republican. Unitarian. Clubs: Triathlon, Denver Track (Denver). Office: Wesco Fabrics Inc 4001 Forest St Denver CO 80216

GENTRY, SUSAN KAY, librarian; b. Glendale, Calif., July 30, 1957; d. William Jerry and Jean (Lederer) G. AA, Ventura Coll., 1977; BA, U. Calif., Santa Barbara, 1979; MLS, San Jose State U., 1980. Tech. librarian Santa Barbara Research Ctr., Goleta, Calif., 1980—. Mem. Spl. Libraries Assn. Democrat. Presbyterian. Clubs: Santa Barbara Research Ctr. Mgmt. (sec. 1983-86), Toastmasters (adminstrv. v.p. 1985-86) (Goleta). Office: Santa Barbara Research Ctr 75 Coromar Dr Goleta CA 93117

GENTRY, WARREN MILLER, art and antique gallery executive; b. Manville, Wyo., Oct. 3, 1921; s. William George and Ina Ella (Miller) G.; m. Billie Jean Axline, Aug. 15, 1948; children—Edward, Thomas, Bradley. A.A., Curtiss Wright Tech. Inst. Aeronautics, 1940; B.A. with distinction, Ariz. State U., 1950, M.A., 1955. Tchr., Miami High Sch., Ariz., 1950-53; art supply salesman Elquest & Son, Phoenix, 1953-55; tchr. Phoenix Union High Sch. Dist., 1955-63; from asst. prof. to prof. humanities Glendale Community Coll., Ariz., 1963-83, founding dir. art collection, 1963—, founding chmn. dept. art, 1963-68; owner, operator Gentry Gallery, Scottsdale, Ariz., 1984—; cons. art silk screen U.S. Army, Ft. Huachuca, Ariz. One-man shows: Phoenix Art Mus., 1954, Sombrero Playhouse, 1955, Phoenix Coll., 1963; group shows include Artists U.S.A., Wynnewood, Pa., 1970-71. First Chmn. Scottsdale Beautification Com., 1960s; mem. first Scottsdale Fine Arts Com., 1960s; mem. West Coast Air Tng. Command. Recipient Painting awards Ariz. State Fair, 1950s, Purchase award Valley Bank Sister City, Orange, France, 1958. Mem. Ariz. State U. Order of Red Rose, Internat. Netsuke Collectors Soc., Humanities Council Western Colls. and Univs. Republican. Lodge: Masons. Office: Gentry Gallery 7135 Main PO Box 4082 Scottsdale AZ 85261

GENUIT, DAVID WALTER, podiatrist; b. Stockton, Calif., May 12, 1949; s. Walter Morales and Betty Alice (Behney) G. BS in Biology, U. Calif., Davis, 1971; BS in Med. Sci., Calif. Coll. Podiatric Medicine, 1973, D in Podiatric Medicine, 1975. Diplomate Am. Bd. Podiatric Surgery, Nat. Bd. Podiatry Examiners. Practice medicine specializing in podiatry Bremerton, Wash., 1975—; clin. instr. Edmonds (Wash.) Community Coll., 1979-84, Bremerton Naval Hosp., 1981—. Contbr. articles to profl. jours.; patentee in field. Med. mem. Olympic Mountain Rescue, Bremerton, 1978—, Explorer Search and Rescue, Bremerton, 1981—; mem. Nat. Assn. for Search and Rescue, 1980—. Fellow Am. Acad. Podiatric Sports Medicine; mem. Am. Podiatric Med. Assn., Wash. State Podiatric Med. Assn., Am. Pub. Health Assn., Am. Coll. Sports Medicine, Wilderness Med. Assn., Am. Assn. Trauma Specialists. Office: 1935 Wheaton Way Bremerton WA 98310

GEOFFROY, CHARLES HENRY, retail executive; b. Longford, Ireland, Sept. 24, 1926; came to U.S., 1927, naturalized, 1945; s. Francis Louis and Kathleen Elizabeth (Fetherston) G.; m. Alida Baird McClenahan, Apr. 24, 1954; children: Evan Lloyd, Mark Lee, Douglas Baird. B.A., Haverford Coll., 1949; postgrad., U. Pa., 1950. With Gen. Motors Ins. Corp., Phila., 1950-51; mgr. research dept. Ward Wheelock Co., Phila., 1951-54; assoc. research dir., account exec. Lennen & Newell, Inc., N.Y.C., 1954-59; account exec. Young & Rubicam, Inc., N.Y.C., 1959-64; v.p. Young & Rubicam, Inc., Los Angeles, 1965-67; pres., mng. dir. Young & Rubicam, Ltd., Toronto, Ont., Can., 1968-74; pres., dir. J.K. Gill Co. Ltd., Portland, Oreg., 1974-80; pres., chief operating officer Grantree Corp., Portland, 1980-83; pres. Rathcline Corp., Portland, 1984-86; chmn. Wide Travel Internat., Portland, 1986—. Served with AUS, 1945-46. Fellow Inst. Can. Advt.; mem. Portland Execs. Assn. Clubs: Riverside (Conn.) Yacht; Waverley Country, University (Portland). Office: Wide Travel Internat Inc 1001 SW Fifth Ave rm 140 Portland OR 97204

GEORGE, DANIEL MCCALL, mental health center program director; b. Vermillion, S.D., Aug. 10, 1953; s. Boyd Winston and Barbara Jean (Woods) G.; m. Doris Ann Southworth, Sept. 4, 1983; 1 stepdaughter, Amy Jean Richardson. Student, U. Mont., 1971-74; BA in Sociology, Wash. State U., 1975; MSW, Eastern Wash. State Coll., 1977. Lic. social worker, Mont. Dir. Block Watch YMCA, Spokane, Wash., 1977-78; clin. supr. Spokane Mental Health, 1978-82; dir. Lamplighter House Western Mont. Regional Community Mental Health, Kalispell, Mont., 1982—. Youth group leader 1st Presbyn. Ch., Kalispell, 1983-86, Active Big Brothers and Big Sisters, Kalispell, 1985, ch. leader Inter-denominational Peace Movement, Kalispell, 1985—; bd. dirs. Kalispell Youth Soccer League, 1986—. Named Outstanding Employee West Mont. Mental Health Ctr., Missoula, Mont., 1984, 85. Mem. Nat. Assn. Social Workers (bd. dirs. Mont. chpt. 1987—), Mont. Mental Health Assn. (Outstanding Adminstr. 1985), Nat. Assn. Social Workers (Mont. chpt.), Glacier Natural Hist. Assn., Glacier Philatelic Soc. Democrat. Avocations: sports, collecting stamps and records, photography. Home: 804 2nd Ave E Kalispell MT 59901 Office: Lamplighter House 146 3rd Ave W Kalispell MT 59901

GEORGE, DICK, Pres. Sav-On Drugs Inc, Anaheim, Calif. Office: Sav-On-Drugs 1500 S Anaheim Blvd Anaheim CA 92805 *

GEORGE, G. WORTH, retirement center administrator; b. Goshen, Ind., Apr. 7, 1933; s. Gilbert W. and Alfie (Jasper) G.; m Mary Lou Smith, Nov. 24, 1956; children: Diane, Lawrence, Lynda. BA, Manchester Coll., 1955; MDiv, Bethany Theol. Sem., 1958; postgrad., U. Chgo., 1958-61; M in Pub. Adminstrn., Calif. State U., Fullerton, 1983; cert. health care facilities mgmt., UCLA Sch. Pub. Health, 1977. Lic. marriage counselor, family counselor, nursing home adminstr.; ordained to ministry United Ch. of Christ, 1960. Hosp. chaplain, instr. Bethany Hosp. and Sem., Chgo., 1957-60; minister Morgan Park Congl. Ch., Chgo., 1960-62; assoc. minister Bryn Mawr Community Ch., Chgo., 1962-66; sr. minister Ch. of the Oaks, Thousand Oaks, Calif., 1966-72; exec. dir. Pilgrim Place, Claremont, Calif., 1973—; adj. instr. master of nonprofit adminstrn. U. San Francisco. Vice chmn., bd. dirs. Pomona Valley Community Services, 1976-78, United Way Planning Council. Fellow Am. Coll. Health Care Adminstr.; mem. Calif. Assn. Homes for the Aging (pres. 1979-80), Am. Assn. Pub. Adminstrn., Acad. Ind. Scholars, Acad. Mgmt., Nat. Soc. Fund Raising Execs. (cert.), Assn. Voluntary Action Scholars, World Future Soc., Non Profit Mgmt. Assn., Am. Soc. on Aging. Club: University (Claremont). Office: Pilgrim Pl 660 Avery Rd Claremont CA 91711

GEORGE, GERALD EUGENE, high school distict administrator; b. St. Paul, Kans., July 21, 1935; married; 6 children. BS in Edn., Kans. State Coll., 1959, MS in Edn., 1962; EdD in Adminstrn. and Supervision, Ariz. State U., 1970. Assoc. prin. Moon Valley High Sch., Phoenix, 1972-73; adminstr. fed., state and vocat. programs Glendale (Ariz.) Union High Sch. Dist., 1973-74, adminstr. ednl. mgmt. system, from 1974, supt. of schs., 1982—. Office: Glendale Union High Sch Dist Office of the Supt of Schools 7650 N 43rd Ave Glendale AZ 85301 *

GEORGE, JOHN, lawyer; b. Palatka, Fla., Sept. 16, 1928; s. Claude Clarence and Claudia (Johnson) G.; m. Anabella Whitaker, June 15, 1958; children: Pamela, Reginald, Angela. AB, U. Calif., Berkeley, 1956; LLB, Hastings Coll., 1961. County supr. Office of Alameda County Bd., Oakland, Calif. Office: Office of the Alameda County Bd 1221 Oak Oakland CA 94612

GEORGE, LLOYD D., federal judge; b. 1930. Attended Brigham Young U. and U. Calif., Berkeley. Ptnr. Albright, George, Johnson & Stephen, 1969-71, George, Steffen & Simmons, 1971-74; judge, U.S. Bankruptcy Ct. Dist. Nev., 1974-84, U.S. Dist. Ct. Nev., 1984—. Served with USAF, 1955-58. Office: US Courthous 300 Las Vegas Blvd S Room 3-632 3rd Floor Las Vegas NV 89101 *

GEORGE, MARY SHANNON, state senator; b. Seattle, May 27, 1916; d. William Day and Agnes (Lovejoy) Shannon; B.A. cum laude, U. Wash., 1937; postgrad. U. Mich., 1937, Columbia U., 1938; m. Flave Joseph George; children—Flave Joseph, Karen Van Hook, Christy, Shannon Lowrey. Prodn. asst., asst. news editor Pathe News, N.Y.C., 1938-42; mem. fgn. editions staff Readers Digest, Pleasantville, N.Y., 1942-46; columnist Caracas (Venezuela) Daily Jour., 1953-60; councilwoman City and County of Honolulu, 1969-74; senator State of Hawaii, 1974—, asst. minority leader, 1978-80, minority policy leader, 1983-84, minority floor leader, 1987, minority leader, 1987—, chmn. transp. com., 1981-82; mem. Nat. Air Quality Adv. Bd., 1974-75. Vice chmn. 1st Hawaii Ethics Commn., 1968; mem. budget com. Aloha United Fund, 1970; co-founder Citizens Com. on Constl. Conv., 1968; vice-chmn. platform com. Republican Nat. Conv., 1976, co-chmn., 1980; bd. dirs. Hawaii Planned Parenthood, 1970-72, 79-86, Hawaii Med. Services Assn., 1972-86; mem. adv. bd. Hawaii chpt. Mothers Against Drunk Driving, 1984—. Recipient Jewish Men's Club Brotherhood award, 1974; Outstanding Legislator of Yr. award Nat. Rep. Legislators Assn., 1985; named Woman of Yr., Honolulu Press Club, 1969, Hawaii Fedn. Bus. and Profl. Women, 1970; Citizen of Yr., Hawaii Fed. Exec. Bd., 1973, 76. Mem. LWV (pres. Honolulu 1966-68), Mensa, Phi Beta Kappa, Kappa Alpha Theta. Episcopalian. Author: A Is for Abrazo, 1961. Home: 782-G N Kalaheo Ave Kailua HI 96734 Office: Hawaii State Capitol Honolulu HI 96813

GEORGE, PETER T., orthodontist; b. Akron, Ohio; s. Tony and Paraskeva (Ogrenova) G.; B.S. Kent State U., 1952; D.D.S., Ohio State U., 1956; cert. in orthodontics Columbia U., 1962; children—Barton Herrin, Tryan Franklin. Pvt. practice orthodontics, Honolulu, 1962—; cleft palate cons. Hawaii Bur. Crippled Children, 1963—; asst. prof. Med. Sch., U. Hawaii, Honolulu, 1970—. Mem. Hawaii Gov.'s Phys. Fitness Com., 1962-68; mem. Honolulu Mayor's Health Council, 1967-72; mem. med. com. Internat. Weightlifting Fedn., 1980-84; chmn. bd. govs. Hall of Fame of Hawaii, 1984. Served to capt. Dental Corps, U.S. Army, 1956-60. Olympic Gold medallist in weightlifting, Helsinki, 1952, Silver medallist, London, 1948, Melbourne, 1956; six times world champion; recipient Disting. Service award Hawaiian AAU, 1968; Gold medal Internat. Weightlifting Fedn., 1976; named to Helms Hall of Fame, 1966. Diplomate Am. Bd. Orthodontics. Fellow Am. Coll. Dentistry, Internat. Coll. Dentistry; mem. Hawaii Amateur Athletic Union (pres. 1964-65), U.S. Olympians (pres. Hawaii chpt. 1963-67, 80—), Am. Assn. Orthodontists, Honolulu Dental Soc. (pres. 1967-68), Hawaii Dental Assn. (pres. 1978), Hawaii Soc. Orthodontists (pres. 1972). Editor Hawaii State Dental Jour., 1965-67. Inventor appliance to prevent sleep apnea. U.S. weightlifting coach USSR, 1979, asst. coach Olympic weightlifting team, 1980. Home: 400 Hobron Ln #814 Honolulu HI 96815 Office: 1441 Kapiolani Blvd Room 520 Honolulu HI 96814

GEORGE, WESTON WILLIAM, JR., advertising manager; b. Hutchinson, Kans., Mar. 21, 1935; s. Weston William and Marie (Craven) G.; m. Jennie Lee Chaney, June 15, 1957; children: Denise, James, Robert. BFA, U. Kans., 1957. Indsl. designer Hamilton Mfg., Two Rivers, Wis., 1959-62, Franz Wagner Assocs., Chgo., 1962-63, Warwick Electronics, Niles, Ill., 1963-65; mgr. product devel. Hubbard Sci., Northbrook, Ill., 1965-73, Creative Pubs., Palo Alto, Calif., 1973-75; advt. mgr. Meda Sonics Inc., Mountain View, Calif., 1975—. Author: Kites for all Seasons, 1978; also articles. Founder North Shore Ecology Ctr., Highland Park, Ill., 1971. Served to 1st lt. USAF, 1957. Mem. Internat. Customer Service Assn., Early Ford V8 Club. Avocations: antique automobiles, drawing and painting, photography. Office: Meda Sonics Inc 340 Pioneer Way Mountain View CA 94039

GERBA, CHARLES PETER, microbiologist, educator; b. Blue Island, Ill., Sept. 10, 1945; s. Peter and Virginia (Roulo) G.; m. Peggy Louise Scheitlin, June 9, 1970; children: Peter, Phillip. BS in Microbiology, Ariz. State U., 1969; PhD in Microbiology, U. Miami, 1973. Postdoctoral fellow Baylor Coll. Medicine, Houston, 1973-74, asst. prof. microbiology, 1974-81; assoc. prof. U. Ariz., Tucson, 1981-85, prof., 1985—; cons. EPA, Tucson, 1980—; advisor CRC Press, Boca Ratan, Fla., 1981—. Editor: Methods in Environmental Virology, 1982, Groundwater Pollution Microbiology, 1984; contbr. numerous articles to profl. and sci. jours. Advisor Pima County Bd. Health, 1982—. Named Outstanding Research Scientist U. Ariz., 1984; environ. science and engring. fellow AAAS, 1984. Mem. Am. Soc. Microbiology (div. chmn. 1982-83, pres. Ariz. br. 1984-85, councilor 1985—), Inst. Food Technologists, Internat. Assn. Water Pollution Research (sr. delegate 1985-88). Home: 1980 W Paseo Monserrat Tucson AZ 85704 Office: U Ariz Dept Microbiology and Immunology Tucson AZ 85721

GERBER, DONALD LINDAHL, ergotect; b. N.Y.C., June 16, 1930; s. Stephen Ward and Hilma Louise (Lindahl) G.; ed. San Francisco Jr. Coll., Stanford U., Pacific Western U.; B.S.I.E.; M.B.A. Pres. Mgmt. Research Frontiers, Inc.; v.p. Mgmt. Research Found. Registered indsl. engr., profl. engr., Calif.; cert. systems profl. Mem. Am. Inst. Indsl. Engrs., Assn. Systems Mgmt., The Mgmt. Inst., Mensa. Club: Commonwealth. Home: 160 Caldecott Ln Apt 214 Oakland CA 94618 Office: 160 Caldecott Ln Suite 214 Oakland CA 94618

GERBER, SANFORD EDWIN, audiologist; b. Chgo., June 16, 1933; s. Leon and Rose (Ely) G.; m. Sharon R. Doyle; children: Howard M., Michael B., Naomi R., Sharon R. B.A., Lake Forest Coll., 1954; M.S., U. Ill., 1956; Ph.D., U. So. Calif., 1962. Sr. human factors specialist System Devel. Corp., Santa Monica, Calif., 1958-60; head speech and hearing research Hughes Aircraft Co., Fullerton, Calif., 1960-65; asst. prof. audiology U. Calif., Santa Barbara, 1965-69; assoc. prof. U. Calif., 1969-75, prof., 1975—, coordinator speech and hearing scis., 1974-79, chmn. dept. speech and hearing scis., 1979-84; mem. sci. bd. Audio-Metric Labs. Inc., Stamford, Conn., 1979-82; cons. CBS Tech. Center, Stamford, 1969-80. Author: Introductory Hearing Science, 1974, Audiometry in Infancy, 1977, Early Diagnosis of Hearing Loss, 1978, Auditory Dysfunction, 1980, Early Management of Hearing Loss, 1981, The Development of Auditory Behavior, 1983, The Multiply-Handicapped Hearing-Impaired Child, 1983; contbr. numerous articles to profl. jours. Pres. Congregation B'nai B'rith, Santa Barbara, 1972-74; pres. Univ. Religious Conf., 1974-76; trustee Santa Barbara Council for Retarded, 1973-78, 80—, treas. 1977-78; trustee Santa Barbara Jewish Fedn., 1974-84. Fellow Soc. Ear, Nose, Throat Advances in Children (pres. 1976-77), Am. Acad. Otolaryngology Head and Neck Surgery (assoc.), Am. Speech-Lang.-Hearing Assn.; mem. Internat. Soc. Audiology (exec. com. 1982—), Am. Auditory Soc., AAUP, Sigma Xi. Lodge: B'nai B'rith. Home: 126 Loureyro Rd Santa Barbara CA 93108 Office: U Calif Dept Speech and Hearing Scis Santa Barbara CA 93106

GERBERDING, WILLIAM PASSAVANT, university president; b. Fargo, N.D., Sept. 9, 1929; s. William Passavant and Esther Elizabeth Ann (Habighorst) G.; m. Ruth Alice Albrecht, Mar. 25, 1952; children: David Michael, Steven Henry, Elizabeth Ann, John Martin. B.A., Macalester Coll., 1951; M.A., U. Chgo., 1956, Ph.D., 1959. Congl. fellow Am. Polit.

Sci. Assn., Washington, 1958-59; instr. Colgate U., Hamilton, N.Y., 1959-60; research asst. Senator E.J. McCarthy, Washington, 1960-61; staff Rep. Frank Thompson, Jr., Washington, 1961; faculty UCLA, 1961-72, prof., chmn. dept. polit. sci., 1970-72; dean faculty, v.p. for acad. affairs Occidental Coll., Los Angeles, 1972-75; exec. vice chancellor ULCA, 1975-77; chancellor U. Ill., Urbana-Champaign, 1978-79; pres. U. Wash., Seattle, 1979—; dir. Wash. Mut. Savs. Bank, Pacific Northwest Bell, Safeco Corp., Seattle; cons. Def. Dept., 1962, Calif. Assembly, 1965. Author: United States Foreign Policy: Perspectives and Analysis, 1966; co-editor, contbg. author: The Radical Left: The Abuse of Discontent, 1970. Trustee Macalester Coll., 1980-83. Served with USN, 1951-55. Recipient Distinguished Teaching award U. Calif., Los Angeles, 1966; Ford Found. grantee, 1967-68. Mem. Am. Polit. Sci. Assn. Office: U Wash Pres Office 301 Administrn Bldg AH-30 Seattle WA 98195

GERDING, ROBERT BRUCE, diversified company executive; b. Glenside, Pa., Sept. 23, 1947; s. George Henry and Kathryn Elizabeth (Evleth) G.; m. Roberta Marsha Kohm, Dec. 20, 1970; children: Matthew Darin, Erica Lauren. BS in Aerospace Engring., U. Mich., 1969; MS in Engring., UCLA, 1972, D in Environ. Scis. and Engring., 1976, diploma in exec. mgmt., 1983. Mgr. sci. and tech. planning Def. and Space Systems Group TRW, Redondo Beach, Calif., 1976-77, mgr. MX environ., geotech. and siting activities Ballistic Missile div., 1978-80, dir. maj. programs Energy Devel. Group, 1981-85, dir. combustion bus. unit Energy Product Group, 1986—; cons., asst. to chmn. U.S. Pres.'s Com. on Sci. and Tech., Washington, 1976-77. Contbr. articles to profl. jours. Mem. Los Angeles Town Hall, 1981-86. Named one of Outstanding Young Men Am. U.S. Jaycees, 1981. Mem. AAAS, Environ. Scis. and Engring. Soc. (founding). Avocations: tennis, scuba diving, painting. Home: 26721 Hawkhurst Dr Rancho Palos Verdes CA 90274 Office: TRW Combustion Bus Unit 2111 Rosecrans Ave El Segundo CA 90278

GERDTS, DONALD DUANE, TV sta. mgr.; b. Janesville, Minn., Oct. 18, 1932; s. Ernest William and Gertrude Louise (Bartsch) G.; B.S., Mankato (Minn.) State U., 1957; postgrad. UCLA, 1958-59; M.A., Calif. State U., Fullerton, 1970; m. Marilyn June Anderegg, June 15, 1957; children—James, Paul, Julie. Chmn. fine arts El Rancho High Sch., Pico Rivera, Calif., 1959-66; sr. producer, dir. ITV Center, Santa Ana, Calif., 1967-70; dir. prodn. Sta. KOCE-TV, Huntington Beach, Calif., 1971-75, asst. sta mgr., exec. producer, 1976-78, exec. v.p., sta. mgr., 1978—; exec. producer Bill Alexander's Magic of Oil Painting TV series; lectr. in field. Served with USMC, 1951-54. Recipient Emmy award (2) Acad. TV Arts and Scis., 1978, 1979. Mem. Acad. TV Arts and Scis. Conglist. Exec. producer 12 ednl. television series used by 800 colls. and univs., also 21 documentary films for Pub. Broadcasting Service. Office: Sta KOCE TV Box 2476 Huntington Beach CA 92647

GERE, JAMES MONROE, educator; b. Syracuse, N.Y., June 14, 1925; s. William S. and Carol (Hixson) G.; m. Janice M. Platt, June 1, 1946; children—Susan M., William P., David S. B.S., Rensselaer Poly. Inst., 1949, M.S., 1951; Ph.D., Stanford, 1954. Registered profl. engr., Calif., N.Y. Instr. Rensselaer Poly. Inst., 1949-51; faculty Stanford, 1954—; prof. civil engring. 1962—; asso. dean Sch. Engring., 1960-67, exec. head dept. civil engring., 1967-72; cons. and lectr. in field, 1954—. Author 7 textbooks in field, also tech. papers. Served with USAAF, 1943-46, ETO. Fellow ASCE; mem. Am. Soc. Engring. Edn., Earthquake Engring. Research Inst., Sigma Xi, Tau Beta Pi. Home: 932 Valdez Pl Stanford CA 94305

GERHARDT, GREG ALLEN, educator, neuroscience researcher; b. La Harpe, Ill., July 3, 1957; s. Gene Arnold and Violet Elaine (Kirchner) G. BS in Chemistry, N.E. Mo. State U., 1979; PhD in Analytical Chemistry and Neurosci., U. Kans., 1983. Lab asst. Adolph Coors Co., Golden, Colo., 1977; research asst. N.E. Mo. State U., Kirksville, 1977-79; teaching asst. U. Kans., Lawrence, 1979-80, research asst., 1980-83; researcher U. Colo. Med. Ctr., Denver, 1983-85, instr. in psychiatry, 1985-87, asst. prof., 1987—; bd. dirs. Wickford Patio Townhomes, Denver. Contbr. numerous articles to profl. jours. Instr. Colo. Assn. Continuing Med. Lab. Edn., Denver, 1985-86. Recipient H.P. Cady award U. Kans. 1980; fellow Phillipe Petroleum, 1981, Am. Chem. Soc., 1981, Nat. Research Service, 1984-85. Mem. Am. Chem. Soc. (pres. student affiliates Kirksville, Mo., 1977-79, summer fellowship 1981—), Am. Aging Assn., N.Y. Acad. Sci., Soc. for Neurosci., Phi Kappa Phi. Republican. Home: 1475 S Quebec Way #D16 Denver CO 80231

GERHARDT, ROBERT ALLAN, savings and loan association executive; b. Porterville, Calif., Oct. 19, 1935; s. Walter Theodore and Edna Jane (Coe) G.; m. Arlene Rae Peterson, Nov. 10, 1960 (div. Aug. 1973); 1 child, Lorrane; m. Lynda Dale Thompson, Oct. 10, 1980. AA, Calif. State U., Fresno, 1955, BS, 1958. Right of way agt. CALTRANS, Redding, Calif., 1958-65; v.p. Jessie Love Co., San Francisco, 1965-67; pvt. practice real estate broker Sacramento, 1967-72; real property agt. San Diego County, 1972-82; sr. acquisitions officer Home Fed. Savs. and Loan, San Diego, 1982—. Mem. Internat. Right of Way Assn. (designated Sr. Right of Way Agt. 1980). Republican. Lodge: Elks. Avocations: travel, hunting, fishing. Home: 5707-A Adobe Falls Rd San Diego CA 92120 Office: Home Fed Savs and Loan Assn 625 Broadway Room 515 San Diego CA 92101

GERHART, JAMES BASIL, physics educator; b. Pasadena, Calif., Dec. 15, 1928; s. Ray and Marion (van Deusen) G.; m. Genevra Joy Thomesen, June 21, 1958; children: James Edward, Sara Elizabeth. B.S., Calif. Inst. Tech., 1950; M.A., Princeton, 1952, Ph.D., 1954. Instr. physics Princeton, 1954-56; asst. prof. physics U. Wash., Seattle, 1956-61; asso. prof. U. Wash., 1961-65, prof., 1965—; Exec. officer Pacific Northwest Assn. for Coll. Physics, 1972—, bd. dirs., 1965—, chmn., 1970-72; governing bd. Am. Inst. Physics, 1973-76, 78-81. Recipient Disting. Teaching award U. Wash. Regents and Alumni Assn., 1983. Fellow Am. Phys. Soc, AAAS; mem. Am. Assn. Physics Tchrs. (sec. 1971-77, v.p. 1977, pres.-elect 1978, pres. 1979, Millikan medal 1985). Home: 2134 E Interlaken Blvd Seattle WA 98112

GERHEIM, EARL CLARENCE, sports writer; b. Albuquerque, July 24, 1944; s. Earl B. and Julia K. (Fritz) G.; m. Sherrie M. Worthington, Oct. 11, 1969; children: Earl D., Lara. Student, Wayne State U., 1962-63; BA, Pacific Luth. U., 1966; BE, Eastern Wash. U., 1975, MA, 1976. Sports editor Evening News, Port Angeles, Wash., 1969; newsman AP, Spokane, Wash., 1970-71; sports writer AP, N.Y.C., 1971-74, Spokesman Rev./Spokane Chronicle, 1977—. Co-author: Sports Immortals, 1972, Of Guts and Glory, 1968; contbr. articles to newspapers, mags. Served with USMC, 1966-68, Vietnam. Decorated Purple Heart with gold star; Gallantry Cross (Rep. Vietnam); fellow Eastern Wash. U., 1975. Mem. Marine Combat Correspondents Assn., Inland Empire Sports Writers, Am. Philatelic Soc., Sigma Delta Chi (sports feature award 1985). Avocations: stamp collecting, travel. Home: W3716 Lyons Spokane WA 99208 Office: Spokesman Rev/Spokane Chronicle W999 Riverside Spokane WA 99210

GERKEN, WALTER BLAND, insurance company executive; b. N.Y.C., Aug. 14, 1922; s. Walter Adam and Virginia (Bl) G.; m. Darlene Stolt, Sept. 6, 1952; children—Walter C., Ellen M., Beth L., Daniel J., Andrew P., David A. B.A., Wesleyan U., 1948; M. Pub. Adminstrn., Maxwell Sch. Citizenship and Pub. Affairs, Syracuse, 1958. Supr. budget and adminstrv. analysis Wis., Madison, 1950-54; mgr. investments Northwestern Mut. Life Ins. Co., Milw., 1954-67; v.p. finance Pacific Mut. Life Ins. Co., Los Angeles, 1967-69; exec. v.p. Pacific Mut. Life Ins. Co., 1969-72, pres., 1972-75, chmn. bd., 1975—, also dir.; bd. dirs. Whittaker Corp., Carter Hawley Hale Stores, So. Calif. Edison Co., Times Mirror Co. Bd.; mem. bd. overseers Rand/Ulla Ctr. for Study of Soviet Internat. Behavior. Dirs. Automobile Club. So. Calif., Keck Found., James Irvine Found., Hoag Meml. Presbyn. Hosp.; chmn. bd. overseers U. Calif.-Irvine, trustee Occidental Coll., Los Angeles, Wesleyan U., Middletown, Conn., United Way, Los Angeles, Calif. Round Table. Served to capt. USAAF, 1942-46. Decorated D.F.C., Air medal. Clubs: California, Stock Exchange (Los Angeles); Pacific Union (San Francisco); Balboa Bay (Newport Beach, Calif.); Dairymen's Country (Boulder Junction, Wis.); Metropolitan (Washington); Pauma Valley Country. Office: Pacific Mutual Life Ins Co 700 Newport Center Dr Newport Beach CA 92660

GERKIN, KATHERINE PIKE, audiologist; b. Morgantown, W.Va., June 2, 1950; d. Richard Dunkin and Mary Agnes (Cavanaugh) Pike; m. John Michael Gerkin, July 10, 1971 (divorced); children: Erin Christine, Hayley. BA, U. Denver, 1976, MA, 1978. Audiologist, dir. newborn screening U. Colo. Health Scis. Ctr., Denver, 1978—; dist. mgr. Audiotone, Denver, 1982-86; pvt. practice audiologist Denver, 1986—; mem. profl. adv. bd. Infant Hearing Program, Concord, Calif., 1984—; cons. infant screening Rose Med. Ctr., Denver, 1986—; instr. otolaryngology. V.p. bd. dirs. Hear at Home. Mem. Am. Speech-Lang.-Hearing Assn. (cert. clin. competence), Colo. Speech-Lang.-Hearing Assn. Avocation: skiing. Office: U Colo Health Scis Ctr 4200 E 9th Ave B-210 Denver CO 80262

GERMAN, WILLIAM, newspaper editor; b. N.Y.C., Jan. 4, 1919; s. Sam and Celia (Norack) G.; m. Gertrude Pasenkoff, Oct. 12, 1940; children: David, Ellen, Stephen. B.A., Bklyn. Coll., 1939; M.S., Columbia U., 1940; M.S. Nieman fellow, Harvard U., 1950. Reporter, asst. fgn. editor, news editor, mng. editor, exec. editor San Francisco Chronicle, 1940—; editor Chronicle Fgn. Service, 1960-77; mng. editor KQED, Newspaper of the Air, 1968; lectr. U. Calif., Berkeley, 1946-47, 68-70. Editor: San Francisco Chronicle Reader, 1962. Served with AUS, 1943-45. Mem. Am. Soc. Newspaper Editors, A.P. Mng. Editors Assn. Home: 150 Lovell Ave Mill Valley CA 94941 Office: San Francisco Chronicle 901 Mission St San Francisco CA 94103

GERMERAAD, DONALD POUND, aerospace company executive, consultant; b. Billings, Mont., July 18, 1921; s. John Henry and Jane Holland (Blake) G.; m. Esther Pietrina, Mar. 6, 1946; children—Paul Blake, Ann Germeraad Swain. B.S. with honors in Aero. Engring., MIT, 1950; M.S. in systems Mgmt., U. So. Calif., 1971. Airline transport pilot cert., airframe and propulsion cert. FAA; profl. mgr. cert. Nat. Mgmt. Assn. Chief engring. test pilot Convair, Gen. Dynamics Co., San Diego, 1947-62, chief crew performance, astronautics, 1962-66; mgr. ocean systems advanced programs Lockheed Missiles & Space Co., Inc., Sunnyvale, Calif., 1966-69, dir. test ops. spacecraft program, 1969-72, program mgr. high speed ships, 1972-76, dir.-mgr. ocean systems program devel., 1976-83; now pres. Mid-Columbia Small Woodlands Bus. Assocs., Stevenson, Wash.; cons.; aerospace lectr. Stanford U., Palo Alto, Calif. Pres. Tollgate Homeowners Assn., Saratoga, Calif., 1980-81; chmn. bd. deacons Saratoga Federated Ch., 1981-82; chmn. Yoking com. Bethel Congl. Ch. and United Ch. Christ, Cascade Locks; col. Oreg. CAP, also mission pilot, Hood River Squadron CAP, 1984—; bd. dirs. Wash. Farm Forestry Assn. Served to capt. AC, USNR, 1941-46. Recipient aviation award San Diego C. of C., 1961; Man of Yr. award Gen. Dynamics Co., 1961. Fellow Soc. Exptl. Test Pilots; assoc. fellow AIAA, Royal Aero. Soc.; hon. life mem. Survival and Flight Equipment Assn., Deep Subergence Pilots Assn. Republican. Club: Naval Officers (Moffett Field, Calif.). Home: Star Route 86B Underwood WA 98651

GERRARD, KEITH, lawyer; b. Malden, Mass., Feb. 8, 1935; s. William Francis and Mary Ethel (Compton) G., A.B., Harvard U., 1956, LL.B., 1963; m. Linda Jane Fay, Apr. 16, 1974; children by previous marriage: Jessica, Elizabeth; stepchildren—Elizabeth Perera, Jonathan Perera. Admitted to Wash. bar, 1963; mem. firm Perkins Coie, Seattle, 1963-70, partner, 1970—. Served to 1st lt. USAF, 1956-59. Mem. Am., Wash. State, Seattle-King County bar assns. Club: Rainier (Seattle). Home: 618 W Highland Dr Seattle WA 98119 Office: Perkins Coie 1900 Washington Bldg 1325 4th Ave Seattle WA 98101

GERRINGER-BUSENBARK, ELIZABETH JACQUELINE, systems analyst, consultant; b. Edmund, Wis., Jan. 7, 1934; d. Clyde Elroy and Matilda Evangeline Knapp; student Madison Bus. Coll., 1952, San Francisco State Coll., 1953-54, Vivian Rich Sch. Fashion Design, 1955, Dale Carnegie Sch., 1956, Murray Sch. Modern Dance, 1956, Biscayne Acad. Music, 1957, Los Angeles City Coll., 1960-62, Santa Monica (Calif.) Jr. Coll., 1963; Hastings Coll. of Law, 1973, Wharton Sch., U.Pa., 1977, London Art Coll., 1979; Ph.D., 1979; m. Roe Devon Gerringer-Busenbark, Sept. 30, 1968 (dec. Dec. 1972). Actress, Actors Workshop San Francisco, 1959, 65, Theatre of Arts Beverly Hills (Calif.), 1963, also radio; cons, and systems analyst for banks and pub. accounting agys.; artist, singer, songwriter, playwright, dress designer. Pres., Environ Improvement, Originals by Elizabeth, Dometrik's, JIT-MAP, San Francisco, 1973—; ordained minister, 1978. Author: New Highways, 1967; Happening - Impact-Mald, 1971; Seven Day Rainbow, 1972; Zachary's Adversaries, 1974; Fifteen from Wisconsin, 1977; Bart's White Elephant, 1978; Skid Row Minister, 1978; Points in Time, 1979; Special Appointment, A Clown in Town, 1979; Happenings, 1980, Votes from the Closet, 1984, Wait for Me, 1984, The Stairway, 1984, The River is a Rock, 1985, Happenings Revisted, 1986, Comparative Religion in the United States, 1986, Summer Thoughts, 1987; mem. Unitarian Soc. (steering com. explorations in worship). Address: PO Box 1640 7th and Mission Station San Francisco CA 94101

GERSHENGORN, KENT NORMAN, physician; b. N.Y.C., Oct. 17, 1940; s. Victor and Anna (Friedman) G.; m. Rita Lynne Milkman, Aug. 25, 1962; children: Susan Joy, Jeffrey Andrew. BA, Cornell U., 1961; MD, SUNY, Buffalo, 1965. Diplomate Am. Bd. Internal Medicine. Intern in medicine Mt. Sinai Hosp., N.Y.C., 1965-66, resident in medicine, 1968-71; staff assoc. NIH, Bethesda, Md., 1966-68; trainee in cardiology U. Calif., San Francisco, 1971-72, asst. clin. prof. medicine, 1972-81, assoc. clin. prof., 1981—. Fellow Am. Coll. Cardiology, Am. Heart Assn. (council clin. cardiology). Jewish. Home: 5 Fairway Dr San Rafael CA 94901 Office: U Calif 400 Parnassus Ave San Francisco CA 94143

GERSHENZON, MURRAY, electrical engineering educator; b. N.Y.C., Nov. 17, 1928; s. Joseph and Dora (Otchet) G.; m. Rosalie Grayer, Nov. 22, 1952; children: Jonathan, Ruth, Leora. BS, CCNY, 1949; MA, Columbia U., 1954, PhD, 1957. Mem. tech. staff Bell Labs., Murray Hill, N.J., 1957-66; prof. U. So. Calif., Los Angeles, 1966—. Editor: (regional) Jour. of Luminescence, 1966-71, (assoc.) Materials Letters, 1981—. Served with U.S. Army, 1953-55. Mem. IEEE, Am. Phys. Soc., Electrochem. Soc. (divisional editor 1974-84). Jewish. Home: 5433 Red Oak Dr Los Angeles CA 90068 Office: U So Calif Materials Sci Dept Los Angeles CA 90089-0241

GERSHOW, JAY, hematologist; b. Bklyn., May 28, 1931; s. Irving Jay and Sophie (Kramer) G.; m. Karen Ruth Singer, Mar. 6, 1958 (div. May 1968); children: Jeffrey Mark, Wendy Sue, Ira James; m. Odile Catherine Chauvet, Dec. 14, 1975; 1 child, Anne Marie. BS, Ark. State U., 1953; MS, U. Ark., 1954; MD, U. Chgo., 1958. Diplomate Am. Bd. Hematology, Am. Bd. Internal Medicine. Intern R.I. Hosp., 1958-60; resident in internal medicine Mt. Zion Hosp., San Francisco, 1960-63, assoc. chief medicine, 1966—, assoc. dir. oncology dept., 1968—; practice medicine specializing in hematology and internal medicine San Francisco, 1964—; cons. hematology and oncology VA Hosp., Livermore, Calif., 1963-84; pres. Mt.Zion Med. Group, San Francisco, 1983—; co-dir., treas. Tumor Immunology Program, San Francisco, 1976-82; med. bd. dirs. Mt. Zion Hosp.; bd. dirs. Preferred Providers Am.. Contbr. articles to profl. jours. Mem. Am. Soc. Hematology, AAAS, N.Y. Acad. Sci., Sierra Club. Avocation: wine collecting. Office: 2320 Sutter San Francisco CA 94115

GERSTEN, JEROME WILLIAM, physician; b. N.Y.C., Apr. 20, 1917; s. Louis and Bessie (Abrams) G.; m. Rhoda Rich, Nov. 8, 1941; children: Steven, Wendy, Christopher, Dennis, Madeleine. B.S., CCNY, 1935; M.D., N.Y. U., 1939; M.S. in Physiology, U. Minn., 1949. Diplomate: Am. Bd. Phys. Medicine and Rehab. Intern Morrisania City Hosp., N.Y.C., 1939-40; resident in internal medicine Montefiore Hosp., N.Y.C., 1940-41; fellow M.I.T., 1946, Columbia U. Coll. Phys. and Surg., 1946-47; resident in phys. medicine Mayo Clinic, Rochester, Minn., 1947-49; mem. faculty U. Colo. Med. Sch., 1949—, prof. phys. medicine and rehab., 1957—, chmn. dept., 1955-81. Editorial bd.: Am. Jour. Phys. Medicine; contbr. numerous articles med. jours. Served as officer M.C. AUS, 1941-46. Mem. Am. Inst. Ultrasonics in Medicine (pres. 1956-59), Am. Assn. Electromyography (pres. 1959), Am. Congress Rehab. Medicine (pres. 1969), Am. Physiol. Soc., Am. Acad. Phys. Medicine and Rehab., Soc. Exptl. Biology and Medicine, Am. Assn. Electromyography and Electrodiagnosis, Am. Heart Assn., Phi Beta Kappa, Sigma Xi, Alpha Omega Alpha. Home: 1370 Forest St Denver CO 80220 Office: 4200 E 9th Ave Denver CO 80262

GERSTER, JOSEF JACOB, cardiologist; b. Saarbrücken, Germany, Aug. 29, 1923, naturalized, 1961; s. Jacob Martin and Maria Anna (Köhl-Rosch) G.; m. Carolyn Frances Taylor, Feb. 22, 1958; children—John Alan, Eric Josef, Kurt Andrew, Mark Steven, Karl Matthew. MD, U. Mainz, Duesseldorf and Göttingen Fed. Republic Germany, 1953. Intern Fitkin Meml. Hosp., Asbury Park, N.J., 1954-55; resident in cardiology Western Res. U. Huron Road Hosp., Cleve., 1957-59; chief resident in medicine St. Joseph's Hosp., Phoenix, 1959-60; practice medicine specializing in cardiology, Scottsdale, Ariz., 1960—; dir. non-invasive cardiovascular lab. Scottsdale Meml. Hosp. Bd. dirs. Maricopa Heart Assn., Phoenix, 1973-79, 83—, pres., 1979-80. Fellow Am. Coll. Cardiology; mem. AMA, Am. Heart Assn., Am. Soc. Echocardiography, N.Am. Soc. Pacing and Electrophysiology. Republican. Episcopalian. Office: Scottsdale Internal Medicine Assocs 7350 E Stetson Dr Scottsdale AZ 85251

GERSTLE, MARK LEWIS, III, public relations professional, writer; b. San Franicsco, Feb. 12, 1919; s. Mark Lewis Jr. and Marion (Mercier) G.; m. Elizabeth Bunker, Apr. 30, 1922; children—Judith Gerstle Mayhew, M. Philip. Student pvt. schs., Lawrenceville, N.J. Prodn. mgr. Sta. KLX-AM-FM, 1947-52; pub. relations mgr. San Francisco Internat. Airport, 1952-59; press sec. to mayor, San Francisco, 1959-63; exec. asst. to Bishop James Pike, San Francisco, 1963-64; dir. info. Episcopal Diocese of Washington, 1966-71; ptnr. Freeman & Gerstle, San Francisco, 1964-66; pub. and press relations rep. Calif. State Automobile Assn., San Francisco, 1971-84. Served with O.S.S., U.S. Army, 1940-45. Mem. Pub. Relations Soc. Am., San Francisco Bay Area Publicity Club (past pres.).

GERTH, DONALD ROGERS, university president, educator; b. Chgo., Dec. 4, 1928; s. George C. and Madeleine (Canavan) G.; m. Beverly J. Hollman, Oct. 15, 1955; children: Annette Childs, Deborah A. Hougham. BA, U. Chgo., 1947, AM in Polit. Sci, 1951, PhD in Polit. Sci, 1963. Field rep. S.E. Asia World Univ., 1950; asst. to pres. Shimer Coll., 1951; Admissions counselor U. Chgo., 1956-58; assoc. dean students, admissions and records, mem. dept. polit. sci. San Francisco St. U., San Francisco, 1958-63; assoc. dean instnl. relations and student affairs Calif. State Univ., 1963-64; chmn. commn. on extended edn. Calif. State Univs. and Colls., 1977-82; dean of students Calif. State U., Chico, 1964-68, prof. polit. sci., 1964-76, assoc. v.p. for acad. affairs, dir. internat. programs, 1969-70, v.p. acad. affairs, 1970-76; co-dir. Danforth Found. Research Project, 1968-69; coordinator Inst. Local Govt. and Public Service, 1968-70; pres., prof. polit. sci. and public adminstrn. Calif. State U., Dominguez Hills, 1976-84; pres., prof. govt. and polit. sci. Calif. State U., Sacramento, 1984—; assoc. West Coast coordinator Higher Edn. Exec. Assos. of Chgo., 1967-71; bd. dirs. Ombudsman Found., Los Angeles, 1968-71; com. continuing edn. Calif. Coordinating Council for Higher Edn., 1963-64; lectr. U. Philippines, 1953-54, Claremont Grad. Sch. and Univ. Ctr., 1965-69. Co-author, The Learning Society, 1969, co-ed., An Invisible Giant, 1971, contbd. numerous articles to profl. journals. Mem. personnel commn. Chico Unified Sch. Dist., 1969-76, chmn., 1971-74; adv. com. on justice programs Butte Coll., 1970-76; mem. Varsity Scouting Council, 1980-84; mem., bd. dirs. Golden Empire Council, Boy Scouts of Am., 1984-; chmn. United Way campaign Calif. State Univs., Los Angeles Co., 1981-82, mem. Sacramento area bd. dirs., 1984-; mem. bd. dirs., South Bay Hospital Found., 1979-82; delegate, Commiss. of the Californias, 1979-;mem., The Cultural Commiss., Los Angeles, 1981-84; dir., Metropol. Chamber of Commerce, Sacramento, 1984-; served to capt., USAF, 1952-56. Mem. Soc. Coll. and Univ. Planning, Town Hall of Los Angeles, Am. Polit. Sci. Assn., Am. Soc. Pub. Adminstrn., Western Govtl. Research Assn., World Affairs Council Los Angeles, Calif. Assn. Pub. Adminstrn. Edn. (chmn. 1973-74), Nat. Assn. Schs. Pub. Affairs and Adminstrn, Western Polit. Sci. Assn., Comstock Club. tennis, skiing. Office: Calif State U Pres's Office 6000 J St Sacramento CA 95819-2694

GERTHOFFER, WILLIAM THOMAS, pharmacology educator; b. Latrobe, Pa., Aug. 16, 1952; s. Lawrence Charles and Jeanne (Poerstel) G.; m. Elizabeth Ann Tharp, Aug. 27, 1977; children: Justin Thomas, Michael Edward. BS cum laude, Waynesburg Coll., 1974; PhD, W.Va. U., 1978. Research assoc. U. Va., Charlottesville, 1980-82; asst. prof. pharmacology U. Nev., Reno, 1982-86. Contbr. articles to profl. jours. Grantee Nat. Heart Lung and Blood Inst., Am. Lung Assn. Mem. The Biophys. Soc., Am. Heart Assn. (research com. 1984—, mountain west sect. peer rev. group 1984-87, grantee 1984-87). Democrat. Roman Catholic. Avocations: cross country skiing, microcomputers, reading. Office: U Nev Sch Medicine Dept Pharmacology Reno NV 89557

GERTLER, ALAN WILLIAM, atmospheric chemist; b. Far Rockaway, N.Y., July 20, 1952; s. Stanley Gertler and Rickley Politziner; m. Camille Caracappa, June 7, 1981; 1 child, Courtney Celia. BS, SUNY, Albany, 1974; PhD, UCLA, 1979. Asst. research prof. Desert Research Inst., Reno, 1979—. Contbr. articles to profl jours. Mem. Air Pollution Control Assn., Am. Chem. Soc. (environ. div.), Sigma Xi, Sigma Pi Sigma. Democrat. Jewish. Avocations: cooking, stained glass. Home: 973 Gear St Reno NV 89503 Office: Desert Research Inst PO Box 60220 Reno NV 89506

GERWICK, BEN CLIFFORD, JR., construction engineer, educator; b. Berkeley, Calif., Feb. 22, 1919; s. Ben Clifford and Bernice (Coultrap) G.; m. Martelle Louise Beverly, July 28, 1941; children: Beverly (Mrs. Robert A. Brian), Virginia (Mrs. Roy Wallace), Ben Clifford III, William. B.S., U. Calif., 1940. With Ben C. Gerwick, Inc., San Francisco, 1939-70, j1pres, 1952-70; exec. v.p. Santa Fe-Pomeroy, Inc., 1968-71; prof. civil engring. U. Calif. at Berkeley, 1971—; sponsoring mgr. Richmond-San Rafael Bridge substructure, 1953-56, San Mateo-Hayward bridge, 1964-66; lectr. constrn. engring. Stanford U., 1962-68; cons. major bridge and marine constrn. projects; cons. constrn. engr. for ocean structures and bridges, also offshore structures in North Sea, Arctic Sea, Japan, Australia, Indonesia, Arabian Gulf, Southeast Asia, South Am.; mem. Commn. on Engring. and Tech. Systems, past chmn. marine bd., past mem. polar research bd. NRC. Author: Russian-English Dictionary of Prestressed Concrete and Concrete Construction, 1966, Construction of Prestressed Concrete Structures, 1971; Construction and Engineering Marketing for Major Project Services, 1981, Construction of Offshore Structures, 1986; contbr. articles to profl. jours. Served with USN, 1940-46; comdr. Res. ret. Recipient Lockheed award Marine Tech. Soc., 1977. Fellow ASCE (hon. mem.; Karp award 1976), Am. Concrete Inst. (dir. 1960, hon. mem., Turner award 1974, Corbetta award 1981); mem. Federation Internationale de la Precontrainte (pres. 1974-78, now hon. pres., Freyssinet medal 1982), Prestressed Concrete Inst. (pres. 1957-58, hon.), Deutscher Beton Verein (hon., Emil Mörsch medal 1979), Concrete Soc. U.K. (hon.), Association Francaise pour Constrn. (hon.), Verein Deutscher Ingenieure (hon.), Royal Swedish Acad. Tech. Sci. (hon.), Norwegian Acad. of Tech. Sci., Royal Acad. Tech. Sci. (Sweden), Nat. Acad. Engring., Moles, Soc. Naval Architects and Marine Engrs. (Blakely Smith award 1981), Beavers (Engring. award 1975), Phi Beta Kappa, Tau Beta Pi, Sigma Xi, Chi Epsilon, Kappa Sigma. Conglist. Clubs: Bohemian (San Francisco); Claremont Country (Oakland). Home: 5874 Margarido Dr Oakland CA 94618 Office: U Calif 217 McLaughlin Hall Berkeley CA 94720 Office: 500 Sansome St San Francisco CA 94111

GERWICK-BRODEUR, MADELINE CAROL, marketing and sales professional; b. Kearney, Neb., Aug. 29, 1951; d. Vern Frank and Marian Leila (Bliss) Gerwick; m. David Louis Brodeur; 1 child, Maria Louise. Student, U. Wis., 1970-72, U. Louisville, 1974-75; BA in Econs. magna cum laude, U. N.H., 1979. Indsl. sales rep. United Radio Supply Inc., Seattle, 1980-81; mfrs. rep. Ray Over Sales Inc., Seattle, 1981-82; sales engr. Tektronix, Inc., Kent, Wash., 1982-83; mktg. mgr. Zepher Industries, Inc., Burien, Wash., 1983-85, Microscan Systems Inc., Portland, Oreg., 1986—; market devel. URS Electronics, Inc., Portland, 1986—; bd. dirs., sec. Starfish Enterprises Inc., Tacoma, 1984—; com. chmn. Northcon, Seattle and Portland, 1984-86; speaker to Wash. Women's Employment and Edn., Tacoma, 1983—. Mem. Electronic Mfrs. Assn., Phi Kappa Phi. Avocations: writing, hiking, house restoration, antiqueing. Office: URS Electronics Inc 123 NE 7th Ave PO Box 14040 Portland OR 97214

GESSEL, STANLEY PAUL, emeritus soil science educator; b. Providence, Utah, Oct. 14, 1916; s. Gottlieb and Esther (Heyrend) G.; m. Beverly Ann Pfieffer, June 29, 1974; children—Susan, Paula, Patti, Pamela, Michael. B.S., Utah State Agr. Coll., 1939; Ph.D., U. Calif.-Berkeley, 1950. Instr. Coll. Forest Resources, U. Wash., Seattle, 1948-50, asst. prof., 1950-56, assoc. prof., 1965-60, prof. forest soils, 1960-84, prof. emeritus, 1984—; with atomic weapons testing program Coll. Forest Resources, U. Wash., Marshall Islands, 1958-64; assoc. dean Coll. Forest Resources, U. Wash., Seattle, 1965-82, dir. spl. programs, 1982-84; cons. soil, water and forestry problems, New South Wales Forestry Commn., 1983-85, Research div. New Zealand Forest

Service, 1986—, New South Wales Forest Commn., 1987, Bikini and Rongelap Island Rehab. Lawrence Libermore Lab., 1986; bd. dirs. Coniferous Biome IBP, 1976-84; chmn. Site Group IUFRO, 1970-86. Contbr. articles to sci. publs., chpts. to books. Mem. Lake City Citizens Adv. Group. Served to capt. USAAF, 1942-45. Recipient citation N.W. Sci. Assn.; named to hon. alumnus Foresters Alumni Assn. U. Wash., 1976. Fellow AAAS, Soil Sci. and Agronomy Soc. Am., Soc. Am. Foresters; mem. Internat. Forestry Assn., Tropical Forestry Soc., Internat. Union Forest Research Orgns. Home: 8521 Latona St NE Seattle WA 98115 Office: Coll Forest Resources U Wash Seattle WA 98195

GETCHES, DAVID HARDING, law educator, state environmental executive, lawyer; b. Abington, Pa., Aug. 17, 1942; s. George Winslow Getches and Ruth Erskine (Harding) Fossette; m. Ann Marks, June 26, 1964; children: Matthew, Catherine, Elizabeth. AB, Occidental Coll., 1964; JD, U. So. Calif., 1967. Bar: Calif. 1968, U.S. Supreme Ct. 1971, D.C. 1972, Colo. 1973. Assoc. Luce, Forward, Hamilton & Scripps, San Diego, 1967-69; directing atty. Calif. Indian Legal Services, Escondido, 1969-70; founding dir. Native Am. Rights Fund, Boulder, Colo., 1970-76; ptnr. Getches & Greene, Boulder, 1976-78; prof. U. Colo. Sch. Law, Boulder, 1978—; exec. dir. Colo. Dept. Natural Resources, Denver, 1983-87. Co-author: Cases and Materials on Federal Indian Law, 1986; author: Water Law in a Nutshell, 1984; mem. editorial bd. Felix S. Cohen's Handbook on Federal Indian Law, 1982, Am. Law Mining, 1985; contbr. articles to profl. jours. Chmn. state govt. campaign United Way, Denver, 1984; mem. Colo. River Basin Salinity Control Forum, Salt Lake City, 1983-87, Colo. Water Conservation Bd., Denver, 1983-87, Colo. Groundwater Commn., Denver, 1983-87, Colo. Mined Land Reclamation Bd., Denver, 1985-87. Mem. Colo. Bar Assn., D.C. Bar Assn., Calif. Bar Assn. Democrat. Home: 627 Pine St Boulder CO 80302 Office: Univ Colo Sch Law Boulder CO 80309-0401

GETREU, IAN E(DWIN), electronics engineer; b. Melbourne, Australia, Sept. 14, 1943; s. Leo and Matylda Getreu; m. Beverly S. Salmenson, June 5, 1983. BE with honors, U. Melbourne, 1965, M Engring. Sci., 1967; postgrad., UCLA, 1966-67; PhD, U. Calif., Berkeley, 1972. Sr. engr. Tektronix Inc., Beaverton, Oreg., 1972-79, mgr. integrated cir. computer aided design devel., 1979-83, mgr. advanced products mktg., 1983-85, scientist advanced products, 1985-86; dir. research and devel., modeling Analogy, Inc. (formerly Inner-Product Simulation), Beaverton, 1986—; also bd. dirs. Analogy Inc., Beaverton; lectr. U. New South Wales, Sydney, Australia, 1974-75; chmn. ComputerAided Network Design Com., 1980-82. Author: Modeling the Bipolar Transistor, 1976. Bd. dirs. Jewish Fedn. of Portland, 1986—. Mem. IEEE (sr.), Internat. Conf. Computer Aided Design (chmn. 1986). Home: PO Box 1356 Beaverton OR 97075

GETREU, SANFORD, city planner; b. Cleve., Mar. 9, 1930; s. Isadore and Tillie (Kuchinsky) G.; B.A. in Architecture, Ohio State U., 1953; M.A. in Regional Planning, Cornell U., 1955; m. Gara Eileen Smith, Dec. 8, 1952 (div. Feb. 1983); children—David Bruce, Gary Benjamin, Allen Dana. Resident planner Mackesey & Reps., consultants, Rome, N.Y., 1955-56; planning dir., Rome, 1956-57; dir. gen. planning, Syracuse, N.Y., 1957-59, dep. commr. planning, 1959-62, commr. planning, 1962-65; planning dir. San Jose, Calif., 1965-74; urban planning cons., 1974—; pres. Sanford Getreu, AICP, Inc., vis. lectr., critic Cornell U., 1960-65, Syracuse U., 1962-65, Stanford, 1965—, San Jose State Coll., 1965—, Santa Clara U., Calif. State Poly. Coll., DeAnza Coll., San Jose City Coll., U. Calif. at Berkeley; pres. planning dept. League of Calif. Cities, 1973-74; advisor State of Calif. Office of Planning and Research. Past bd. dirs. Theater Guild, San Jose, Triton Mus., San Jose. Mem. Am. Soc. Cons. Planners, Am. Planning Assn., Am. Inst. Cert. Planners, Bay Area Planning Dirs. Assn. (v.p. 1965-74, mem. exec. com. 1973-74), Assn. Bay Area Govts. (regional planning com. 1967-74). Club: Rotary. Home: 105 Coronado Ave Los Altos CA 94022 Office: 925 Regent St San Jose CA 95110

GETTELL, LINDA WONG, textile professional; b. Los Angeles, Apr. 10, 1949; d. Nom S. and Gouie (Shee) Wong; m. Richard William Gettell, Nov. 1, 1979; children: Eryk, Oliver. BA, Calif. State U., Los Angeles, 1970. Colorist Aaronson Textiles, Los Angeles, 1970-72; designer Stanton-Kutasi, Los Angeles, 1972-74; designer Citation-Langley, Los Angeles, 1974-76, stylist, 1976-84; stylist Darlington Fabrics, Los Angeles, 1985—. Office: S Edward Darlington 117 W 9th St #210 Los Angeles CA 90015

GETTO, MICHAEL HUTSON, hotel executive; b. Lawrence, Kans., June 8, 1934; s. Michael James and Virginia Francis (Hutson) G.; m. Clare Elenora Donmoyer, Aug. 5, 1956 (div. Sept. 1974); children: Michael Hutson II, Mary Virginia; m. Marsha Lea Rogers, Apr. 26, 1975 (div. Aug. 1983); children: Jarin Hutson, Jeremy Marshall; m. Eliabeth Ann Velez, Jan. 29, 1986; 1 child, Jon Todd. Student, U. Kans., 1952-54, Mich. State U., 1956. V.p. Holiday Inns, Inc., San Francisco, 1976-78, High Country Corp., Denver, 1978-81; sr. v.p. Ramada Inns, Inc., Phoenix, 1971-76, Brock Hotel Corp., Irving, Tex., 1981-84; pres. Spectrum Hotels, Inc., Denver, 1984—. Planning commr. City of Lawrence, Kans., 1962-64, commr., 1964-66; mem. Colo. Tourism Council, Denver, 1981; dir. AMC Cancer Bd., Denver, 1986. Served to 1st lt. U.S. Army, 1956-58. Named Young Man of Yr., Lawrence Jaycees, 1964, Innkeeper of Yr., Kans. Hotel-Motel Assn., 1969, Disting. Jayhawker, Gov. Kans., 1964. Mem. Colo. Wyo. Hotel-Motel Assn. (bd. dirs. 1979—, Disting. Service award 1981), Am. Hotel-Motel Assn. (bd. dirs. 1964-66), Bus. and Econ. Council. Democrat. Roman Catholic. Lodge: Rotary. Avocations: skiing, mountain climbing, swimming, gardening. Home: 470 Race Denver CO 80206 Office: Spectrum Hotels Inc 303 E 17th Ave Suite 610 Denver CO 80203

GETTY, DONALD ROSS, provincial premier; b. Westmount, Que., Can., Aug. 30, 1933; s. Charles Ross and Beatrice (Hampton) G.; m. Margaret Inez Mitchell, Aug. 18, 1955; children: Dale, David, Darin, Derek. BBA, U. Western Ont., 1955. With Imperial Oil Natural Gas Ltd., 1955-61; with Midwestern Indsl. Gas Ltd., 1961-63; pres., mng. dir. Baldonnel Oil & Gas Ltd., 1964-67; ptnr. Doherty Roadhouse & McCuaig Ltd., 1967; minister fed. and intergovtl. affairs Province of Alta., 1971-75, minister energy and natural resources, 1975-79, premier, 1985—; past pres. D. Getty Investments Ltd.; chmn. bd. dirs. Ipsco, 1981-85; former chmn. Nortek Energy Corp. Former mem. Alta. Legislature, mem., 1985—; active Alta. No. Lights Wheelchair Basketball Team. Recipient Outstanding Can., Western Canada Football League award. Conservative. Clubs: Edmonton Petroleum (bd. govs.), Derrick Golf and Winter (bd. dirs.). Avocations: golfing, horse-racing, hunting. Home: 52 Westbrook Dr, Edmonton, AB Canada T6J 2C9 Office: Office of the Premier, 307 Legislature Bldg, Edmonton, AB Canada T5K 2B6

GETZ, GEORGE FULMER, JR., business executive; b. Chgo., Jan. 4, 1908; s. George Fulmer and Susan Daniel (Rankin) G.; m. Olive Cox Atwater, Jan. 17, 1933 (dec. Sept. 22, 1980); children: George Fulmer, III (dec.), Bert Atwater. Pres. Eureka Coal & Dock Co., 1935-45; chmn. bd., chief exec. officer Globe Corp.; chmn. bd. Getz Coal Co., 1939-48, pres., 1948-53; dir. Chgo. Nat. League Ball Club, 1940-72; mem. exec. com., dir. A.T. & S.F. Ry., 1955-80, Sante Fe Industries, Inc., 1968-80; dir. Upper Ave. Nat. Bank, Chgo., 1936-74, Chgo. Transit Authority, 1945-47. Mem. United Republican Fund Ill.; mem. citizens bd. U. Chgo., 1956-71; bd. dirs. Jr. Achievement Chgo., 1939—, v.p., 1947-49; v.p. Met. Jr. Achievement, 1942-44; mem. Pres.'s Commn. White House Fellowships, 1982, 83; bd. dirs. Getz Found., Ind. U. Found.; pres., dir. Arthur R. Metz Found.; hon. trustee Chgo. Zool. Soc.; past v.p. finance, treas. Nat. Safety Council; pres. Geneva Lake Water Safety Com., Inc., 1949-54, bd. dirs., 1949-69, hon. dir., 1969—; mem. Ill. Com. Crusade for Freedom, Inc., 1957, 58; pres., dir. Nat. Hist. Fire Found., Globe Found.; bd. dirs. Ariz. Zool. Soc., 1966-81, 84—; trustee Am. Grad. Sch. Internat. Mgmt., vice chmn. bd., 1976-78; mem. organizing com., mem. Chgo. Rotary Found., 1936-45; mem. Nat. Rep. Fin. Com., 1976—; trustee Grand Cen. Art Galleries, N.Y.C., 1982—; bd. dirs. Scottsdale Meml. Health Found., 1984—. Mem. Chgo. Assn. Commerce and Industry (com. mem. govtl. affairs council); emeritus mem. Phoenix 40. Episcopalian. Clubs: Chicago, Tavern, Chicago Yacht, Economic (Chgo.); Los Rancheros Visitadores (Santa Barbara, Calif.); Paradise Valley Country (Ariz.); Circumnavigators; Phoenix Symphony Assn. 400; Valley Field Riding and Polo (Ariz.); Balboa (Mazatlan, Mexico). Home: 80 Mountain Shadows W Scottsdale AZ 85253 Office: Globe Corp 3634 Civic Center Plaza Scottsdale AZ 85251 also: 16555 W Hwy 120 Libertyville IL 60048

GETZ, WAYNE MARCUS, biomathematician, researcher, educator; b. Johannesburg, Africa, Apr. 26, 1950; came to U.S., 1979; m. Jennifer Bryna Gonski, Feb. 15, 1972; children: Stacey Lynn, Trevor Russell. BSc. with honors, U. Witwatersrand, South Africa, 1972, PhD, 1976. Research scientist Council for Sci. and Indsl. Research, Pretoria, South Africa, 1974-79; biomathematician U. Calif., Berkeley, 1979—; cons. Nat. Marine Fisheries Service, 1980—. Editor MacMillan book series on biological resource mgmt., 1983—; contbr. articles to profl. jours. Mem. AAAS, Internat. Soc. for Ecol. Modelling, Am. Entomol. Soc. Office: U Calif Div Biol Control Berkeley CA 94720

GEVINS, ALAN STUART, neuroscientist; b. N.Y.C., Feb. 4, 1946; s. Michael S. and Rose (Master) G.; B.S., M.I.T., 1967; postgrad., Calif. Inst. Asian Studies, 1968-71. Sr. systems analyst Berkeley (Calif.) Sci. Labs., 1968-69; sr. ops. analyst Langley Porter Neuropsychiat. Inst., San Francisco, 1971-72; dir. EEG Systems Lab, Inc. U. Calif. Med. Sch., San Francisco, 1972-81, chief scientist, pres., 1981—; pres. SAM Tech., Inc., 1986—; regents prof. U. Calif.; cons. in field. Grantee NIMH, 1978-80, Nat. Inst. Neurol. Diseases, 1972-79, 84—, Office Naval Research, 1980-85, Air Force Office Sci. Research, 1981—, Air Force Sch. Aerospace Medicine, 1981-85, NSF, 1983—. Fellow Am. EEG Soc.; mem. AAAS, Soc. Biol. Psychiatry, Am. Epilepsy Soc., IEEE (sr.), Soc. Neurosci., Psychophysiology Soc., N.Y. Acad. Scis., Internat. Neuropsychology Soc. Contbr. articles in field to profl. jours. Office: 1855 Folsom San Francisco CA 94103

GEYER, STANLEY JAMES, physician; b. Pitts., July 25, 1949; s. George Shadrach and Helen Dorothy (Hawley) G.; m. Kathleen Frey, June 27, 1970; 1 child, Christopher Scott. MD, Jefferson Med. Coll., 1974. Diplomate Am. Bd. Pathology. Research fellow U. Pitts., 1976-77; staff pathologist VA Med. Ctr., Pitts., 1977-79, chief of labs., 1979-82, chief of staff, 1982-84; chief of staff VA Med. Ctr., Seattle, 1984—; assoc. prof., assoc. dean U. Wash., Seattle, 1984—. Recipient Golden Apple award for excellence in teaching Am. Med. Student Assn., 1979, 81; VA research grantee, 1977-86. Democrat. Presbyterian. Avocation: squash. Office: VA Med Ctr 1660 S Columbian Way Seattle WA 98101

GEYMAN, JOHN PAYNE, physician, educator; b. Santa Barbara, Calif., Feb. 9, 1931; s. Milton John and Betsy (Payne) G.; m. Emogene Clark Deichler, June 9, 1956; children: John Matthew, James Caleb, William Sabin. A.B. in Geology, Princeton U., 1952; M.D., U. Calif., San Francisco, 1960. Diplomate: Am. Bd. Family Practice. Intern Los Angeles County Gen. Hosp., 1960-61; resident in gen. practice Sonoma County Hosp., Santa Rosa, Calif., 1961-63; practice medicine specializing in family practice Mt. Shasta, Calif., 1963-69; dir. family practice residency program Community Hosp. Sonoma County, Santa Rosa, 1969-71; asso. prof. family practice, chmn. div. family practice U. Utah, 1971-72; prof., vice chmn. dept. family practice U. Calif., Davis, 1972-77; prof., chmn. dept. family medicine U. Wash., 1977—. Author: The Modern Family Doctor and Changing Medical Practice, 1971, Family Practice: Foundation of Changing Health Care, 1980, 2d edit., 1985; editor: Content of Family Practice, 1976, Family Practice in the Medical School, 1977, Research in Family Practice, 1978, Preventive Medicine in Family Practice, 1979, Profile of the Residency Trained Family Physician in the U.S, 1970-79, Funding of Patient Care, Education and Research in Family Practice, 1981, The Content of Family Practice: Current Status and Future Trends, 1982, Archives of Family Practice, 1980, 81, 82; founding editor: Jour. Family Practice, 1973—; co-editor: Behavioral Science in Family Practice, 1980; editor: Family Practice: An International Perspective in Developed Countries, 1983. Served to lt. (j.g.) USN, 1952-55, PTO. Recipient Gold-headed Cane award U. Calif. Sch. Medicine, 1960. Mem. Am. Acad. Family Physicians, AMA, Soc. Tchrs. Family Medicine, Inst. Medicine of Nat. Acad. Scis. Republican. Unitarian. Home: 2325 92d Ave NE Bellevue WA 98004 Office: Dept Family Medicine RF 30 U Wash Sch Medicine Seattle WA 98195

GHARRETT, ANTHONY JOHN, fishery genetics educator; b. Seattle, Dec. 23, 1945; s. John T. and Elizabeth Mary (Campbell) G.; m. Jessica Ann Romm, Aug. 21, 1976. BS in Biology, Calif. Inst. Tech., 1967; MS in Fisheries, Oreg. State U., 1973, PhD in Genetics, 1975. NIH postdoctoral trainee U. Min., Mpls., 1974-76; asst. prof. U. Alaska, Juneau, 1976-80, assoc. prof. fishery genetics, 1980—; vis. assoc. prof. U. Mich., Ann Arbor, 1985-86. Contbr. articles to profl. jours. Alaska Sea Grant Coll. Program grantee, 1977—; named one of Outstanding Young Men in Am., 1979. Mem. Am. Inst. Fisheries Research Biologists, Am. Fisheries Soc. Avocations: fishing. Office: U Alaska 11120 Glacier Hwy Juneau AK 99801

GHOLSTON, HELEN ALBERTA, educator; b. Lawrence, Mass., May 13, 1923; d. Albert Clinton and Helen Gertrude (Mitchell) McIlwain; B.A. in English with distinction, San Diego State U., 1976, M.A. in Edn., 1980; m. Andrew J. Gholston, Apr. 25, 1944; children—Andrea, Juanita, Corale, Wendy, Michael, Andrew J. Microfilm operator San Diego City Civil Service, 1957-58; engaged in real estate, 1961-70; tutor EEO program San Diego Community Colls., 1971-75; tchr. San Diego Unified Sch. Dist., 1977—, tchr. English secondary div. Abraham Lincoln Sr. High Sch., 1979-86, chmn. dept., 1980-82, mem. textbook com. San Diego city schs. Mem. Nat. Council Tchrs. English, Assn. Supervision and Curriculum Devel., Nat. Council Negro Women (chmn. edn. 1984-85), Am. Bus. Women's Assn. (chmn. edn. 1983-84), San Diego State U. Alumni Assn., Browning Soc. Baptist. Author articles, curriculum materials. Home: 5322 Hilltop Dr San Diego CA 92114 Office: San Diego City Schs 4100 Normal St San Diego CA 92103

GHORMLEY, JOHN HARNED, bldg. contractor; b. Greenfield, Iowa, Aug. 11, 1936; s. Clarence E. and Dorothy (Harned) G.; student Purdue U., 1954; B.S., U. Wis., 1959; m. Anne Doran, May 25, 1960; children—Dorothy Lynne, Rebecca Anne. Assoc. engr. Douglas Aircraft Co., El Segundo, Calif., 1959; civil engring. assoc. City of Torrance, Calif., 1959-62; dir. pub. works-city engr. City of Gardena, Calif., 1962-66, adminstrv. officer, 1966-70; cons. civil engring. practice, Gardena, 1962-66; ptnr. Benner and Ghormley, Santa Paula, Calif., 1970-75; v.p. Ervin, Ghormley, Johnson & Assocs., Los Angeles, 1975-77; pres. Bonita Homes, Inc., 1977—, Bonita Am., 1986—, Computer Terminal, 1986—. Adviser, Boy Scout Splty. Explorer Post, 1968-70; bd. mgrs. Gardena Valley YMCA; pres. South County Econ. Devel. Assn., 1984-85. Recipient award for outstanding service Gardena Valley C. of C., 1968. Registered profl. engr., Calif., Fla., Ind. Mem. Sigma Phi. Republican. Presbyterian. Clubs: Masons, Ojai Optimist (pres. 1976), Kiwanis. Home: 980 Branch Mill Rd PO Box 356 Arroyo Grande CA 93420 Office: 550 Camino Mercado PO Drawer FF Arroyo Grande CA 93420

GIACOBBI, PETER DOMINIC, engineering company executive, mechanical engineer; b. San Francisco, July 6, 1939; s. Elvin Albert Giacobbi and Roberta (Searls) Giacobbi Eastman; m. Lesslie Jean Avery, June 17, 1961; children: Sara Lisa, Celia Jean. BME, Cornell U., 1962, MBA, 1963. Chief engr. Eaton Livia, Turin, Italy, 1963-67; gen. mgr. Safety Systems Europe, Turin, 1967-75; corp. mgr. research and devel. Eaton Corp., Southfield, Mich., 1975-77; dir. engring. DeLorean Motor Co., Bloomfield Hills, Mich., 1977-78; v.p. engring. Gen. Valve Co., Glendora, Calif., 1978-87; v.p. ops. Hunter Engring. Co., Riverside, Calif., 1987—. Mem. Soc. Automotive Engrs. Home: 9761 Janice Circle Villa Park CA 92667 Office: Hunter Engring Co 1455 Columbia Ave Riverside CA 92507

GIALANELLA, PHILIP THOMAS, newspaper publisher; b. Binghamton, N.Y., June 6, 1930; s. Felix and Frances (Demuro) G.; 1 son, Thomas Davis. B.A., Harpur Coll., 1952; M.A., State U. N.Y., 1955. Promotion dir. Evening Press and Sta. WINR-TV, Binghamton, 1957-62; v.p., gen. mgr. Daily Advance, Dover, N.J., 1962-66; v.p. Hartford (Conn.) Times, 1966-70; pres., pub. Newburgh (N.Y.) News, 1970-71; exec. v.p. Hawaii Newspaper Agy., Honolulu, 1971-73; pres. Hawaii Newspaper Agy., 1974-86; pub. Honolulu Star-Bull., 1975-86, Honolulu Advertiser, 1986—; v.p. Persis Corp., Honolulu, 1986—, pres. Persis Media div., 1986—; pres., chief exec. officer Longview Pub. Co., Bellevue, Wash., 1986—; bd. dirs. Capital Investment Co., Hawaii Newspaper Agy., Inc., Waterhouse Properties. Past chmn., exec. com. mem. Nat. Alliance Businessmen for Hawaii and Micronesia; v.p. Hawaii Newspaper Agy. Found.; bd. dirs. Aloha United Way, AP Assn., Calif., Ariz., Hawaii and Nev.; mem. Japan Hawaii Econ. Council; bd. govs. Pacific Asian Affairs Council; bd. dirs. Hawaii Theatre Ctr., Honolulu Boy Choir, Honolulu Symphony; mem. adv. group Western Command U.S. Army. Served with U.S. Army, 1952-54. Mem. Am. Newspaper Pubs. Assn., Hawaii Pubs. Assn., Sigma Delta Chi. Roman Catholic. Office: The Honolulu Advertiser Honolulu HI 96802

GIANG, BENJAMIN YUNWEN, research chemist; b. Clear Water Bay, Hong Kong, July 7, 1941; came to U.S., 1959; s. Tsung Guang and Chen Hwa (Tan) G.; m. Virginia Wai-ping Liang, Aug. 22, 1965; children: Vernon Lloyd, Andrew Bernard, Leslie Brian. BA in Chemistry, Columbia Union Coll., 1963; MS in Analytical Chemistry, U. Md., 1967; PhD in Agrl. Chemistry, U. Calif., Davis, 1972. Staff research assoc. U. Calif., Davis, 1966-69, research asst., 1970-71; prin. research chemist Stauffer Chem. Co., Richmond, Calif., 1971—. Contbr. articles to profl. jours. Pres. Fairfield (Calif.)-Suisun Chinese Assn., 1981. Mem. Am. Chemical Soc., Am. Soc. Mass Spectrometry, Internat. Union Pure and Applied Chemistry (affiliate). Avocations: home gardening, tennis, fishing. Home: 1789 Barton Dr Fairfield CA 94533 Office: Stauffer Chem Co 1200 S 47th St Richmond CA 94804

GIANTURCO, PAOLA, advertising executive; b. Urbana, Ill., July 22, 1939; d. Cesare and Verna Bertha (Daily) Gianturco; B.A., Stanford U., 1961; postgrad. U. So. Calif., 1971; children—Scott Sangster. Pub. relations dir. Joseph Magnin, San Francisco, 1961-67; pub. relations dir., account exec. Hall & Levine Advt. Agy., Los Angeles, 1968-73, v.p., account supr., 1973-76, sr. v.p., 1977-82; v.p. Dancer Fitzgerald Sample, 1982—. Past mem. bd. dirs. The Country Schs. Mem. Women in Communications, Stanford Profl. Women (past mem. bd. dirs.), Women in Communications, Internat. Assn. Bus. Communicators, Bus. and Profl. Advt. Assn. Home: 74 Wellington Ave Ross CA 94960 Office: DFS Corporate Advertising 1010 Battery St PO Box 7166 San Francisco CA 94111

GIAP, NGHIA CHI, software systems engineer; b. Hai-Phong, Socialist Republic of Vietnam, Oct. 17, 1949; came to U.S., 1975; s. Thap Van and Thuc Le Giap; divorced; children: Evelyn Minh, Steven Doan. BS in Computer Sci., San Diego State U. Software engr. Nat. Semiconductor Corp., Santa Clara, Calif., 1981-83; sr. software engr. NSC/Data Checker, Santa Clara, 1983—; software system cons. NCG Software Ctr., Sunnyvale, Calif., 1984—. Served to lt. USN, 1969-75. Mem. Assoc. Computing Machine, Navy Officer Club. Republican. Buddhist. Avocations: tennis, swimming, skiing. Home: 3232 El Sobrante St Santa Clara CA 95051 Office: Datachecker/DTS 800 Center Expressway Santa Clara CA 95052

GIBB, DOUGLAS GLENN, police chief; b. Makaweli, Hawaii, June 5, 1940; s. Douglas Stormont and Gwendolyn Elizabeth (Bedell) G.; m. Melanie Ululani Hardy, Nov. 16, 1963; children—Diane Nalani, Glenn Kale. BS in Bus. Adminstrn., U. Denver, 1966; cert., Nat. Execs. Inst., FBI, 1984. Patrolman Honolulu Police Dept., 1967-71, sgt., 1971-76, lt., 1976-80, capt., 1980-83, chief police, 1983—; cons. on sting projects Office Justice Assistance, Dept. Justice, 1983—; mem. Hawaii Gov.'s Planning Commn. on Crime, 1983—, Juvenile Justice Interagy. Bd., 1983—. Bd. dirs. ARC, Honolulu, 1983—; mem. exec. bd. Boy Scouts Am., Honolulu, 1983—; mem. sr. adv. council CAP, Honolulu, 1983—. Recipient cert. of merit Law Enforcement Assistance Adminstrn., Washington, 1979; named Police Officer of Yr., 200 Club, Honolulu, 1982. Mem. Hawaii Law Enforcement Officer Assn. (pres. 1983-85), Internat. Assn. Chiefs of Police (membership com. 1985), Major City Chiefs, Honolulu C. of C. (crime com. 1983—). Episcopalian. Avocations: golf; volleyball; skin diving. Home: PO Box 510 Kaawa HI 96730 Office: Honolulu Police Dept 1455 S Beretania Honolulu HI 96814 *

GIBB, RICHARD DEAN, university president; b. Smithshire, Ill., Dec. 6, 1928; s. Edward Dale and Anna Marie (Anderson) G.; m. Betty G. Epperson, Dec. 22, 1951; children: Richie William, Connie Marie. Student, Western Ill. U., 1947-50; B.S., U. Ill., 1951, M.E., 1955; Ph.D., Mich. State U., 1958. Faculty agrl. econs. Western Ill. U., Macomb, 1958-68; prof. Western Ill. U., 1965-68, adminstrv. asst. to pres., 1964-67, dean adminstrn., 1967-68, acting coordinator internat. programs, 1964-65; S.D. commr. for higher edn. Pierre, 1968-74; Ind. commr. for higher edn. Indpls., 1974-77; pres. U. Idaho, 1977—. Served with AUS, 1952-53. Mem. Am. Assn. Higher Edn., Statewide Higher Edn. Assn., Am. Agrl. Econs. Assn., Delta Sigma Phi. Home: 1026 Nez Perce Dr Moscow ID 83843 Office: Office of the President U Ida Moscow ID 83843

GIBBLE, WALTER PAUL, oil and gasindustry consultant; b. Atglen, Pa., July 26, 1916; s. Walter Paul and Mabel Teresa (Wise); m. Jeanne A. van Dyck, Dec. 31, 1960. BS, U. Pa., 1941; MS, U. Ariz., 1951, PhD, 1956. Dir. research Vegetable Oil Products, Wilmington, Calif., 1955-57, VA Hosp., Tucson, 1957-62; sr. chemist Hunt-Wesson Foods, Fullerton, Calif., 1962-76; tech. cons. Govt. of India, New Delhi, 1979-80; indsl. cons. Edible Oil Cos., 1980—; cons. Hunt-Wesson Foods, Fullerton, Wilsey Food Inc., City of Industry, Calif., Surya Agroils Ltd., New Delhi, Modipon Ltd., Modingar, India. Contbr. articles to sci. jours.; patentee in field. Served to commdr. USN, 1942-49. Recipient Highest Merit award Hunt-Wesson Foods, Fullerton, 1971. Mem. Service Corps Retired Execs. (chmn. local satellite chpt. 1983—), Am. Chem. Soc., Am. Oil Chemists Soc., Sigma Xi. Lutheran. Avocations: fishing, photography. Home and Office: 2931 Viking Way Carson City NV 89701

GIBBONS, ANDREW H., library science educator; b. Central, Ariz., Sept. 18, 1926; s. Andrew Gibbons and Lola Heaton; m. Claron Gardner, Apr. 15, 1951 (div. Apr. 1976); children: Ann, Wallace, Lorrain, Ronda, Kenneth, Carolyn, Marie; m. Janice Schrib Olmsted, July 2, 1977. BA in Music Edn., Utah State U., 1952, ME in Ednl. Adminstrn., 1962; MLS, East Carolina U., 1971; Doctor in Edn. Curriculum, U. No. Colo., 1977. Commd. 2d lt. USAF, 1962, advanced through grades to maj., 1971, resigned, 1971; adminstr. computer activities USAF, various locations, 1962-71; tchr. music Idaho Pub. Schs., 1952-59; tchr. music, social studies Utah Pub. Schs., Providence, 1959-62; instr. AFROTC East Carolina U., Greenville, N.C., 1968-71; prof. ednl. media U. No. Colo., Greeley, 1971—, prof. in ednl. technology, 1971—. Author: Bibliography of Thomas Crapper, 1982, (with others) Dictionary of Patchwork Patterns, 1976, Shhh is a 4 Letter Word, 1984. Vol. Weld Library Dist., Greeley, 1971—; active Colo. Council for Library Devel. Colo. State Bd. Edn., Denver, 1978-83, Republican caucus, Greeley, 1971—. Mem. Colo. Ednl. Media Assn. (convention program chmn. 1978, 85, editor state profl. mag. 1984—), Mt. Plains Library Assn. (fin. com. 1978-80, grants com. 1983-84), Am. Library Assn. (bibiotherapy com. 1977-85), MENSA, Phi Kappa Phi. Avocations: Louis Armstrong recordings and memorabilia. Home: 2500 15 Ave Ct Greeley CO 80631 Office: U No Colo Greeley CO 80639

GIBBONS, BENJAMIN FRANKLIN, safety engineer; b. Wilmington, Del., Mar. 29, 1953; s. Donald Merritt and Elizabeth Jane (Weyl) G.; m. Rosemarie Yoshiko Markgraf, Aug. 2, 1980; 1 child, Ryan Benjamin. B.A. in Psychology, Ind. U., 1979; M.S. in Indsl., Organizational Psychology, Purdue U., 1984. Sr. med. technician, instr. Dept. Def., Ft. Harrison, Ind., 1978-81; sr. med. instr. Ind. Vocat. Sch., Indpls., 1977-80; sr. safety engr. Hosp. Shared Service of Colo., State of Colo., Denver, 1981-84; safety and worker compensation adminstr. Am. Med. Internat. Rocky Mountain div., Denver, 1984—; cons. in field. Instr. CPR, Am. Heart Assn., ARC, 1975—. Served with U.S. Army, 1972-78. Recipient cert. Patriotic Civilian Service, U.S. Army, 1981, Service award ARC, 1978. Mem. Am. Psychol. Assn., Am. Soc. Safety Engrs., Colo. Hosp. Assn., Colo. Hosp. Safety Assn. (pres.). Republican. Home: 1305 S Joplin St Aurora CO 80017 Office: Am Med Internat Rocky Mountain Div 601 E 19th Ave Denver CO 80203

GIBBONS, GARY EUGENE, investment counseling executive; b. Tucson, May 5, 1949; s. Lawrence Lee and Naomi (Price) G.; m. Amy Smith, Sept. 1, 1979; children: Lawrence Smith, Ryan Smith. B.S., U. Ariz., 1973; M.S., Calif. State U.-Carson, 1982. Prin. Gibbons, Meihaus, Seal Beach, Calif., 1975-86; chief exec. officer Advanced Telephone Communications, 1986—; v.p. Fin. Hanseatic Corp., Albuquerque; dir. Richmark Corp., Los Angeles; lectr. fin. Calif. State U.-Fullerton, 1983—, U. So. Calif., Los Angeles, 1984—. Editor: Strokes and Strategies, 1973; contbr. numerous articles on econs., investments to publs. Mem. Fin. Mgmt. Assn., U.S. Profl. Tennis Assn., Coll. Fin. Planning (adj. faculty), Calif. State U. Alumni Assn. and Bus. Alumni Council. Republican. Episcopalian. Clubs: Santa Monica Yacht,

Old Ranch Country. Home: 861 Rancho Dr Long Beach CA 90815 Office: 110 Pine Ave #300 Long Beach CA 90802

GIBBONS, JERRY LEE, advertising executive; b. Coalinga, Calif., Feb. 10, 1936; s. James A. and Hazel Bernice (Drummond) G.; m. Alba Valdez, Feb. 22, 1963; children: Jeffery Scott, Cristin Lyn, Trisha Leigh. BA, San Jose State U., 1958. Trainee Young & Rubicam, San Francisco, 1957; account exec. McCann-Erickson, San Francisco, 1960-63; asst. to pres. Western Outdoor Markets, San Francisco, 1964; v.p., sales mgr. Naegele Outdoor Advt., Oakland, Calif., 1965-67; account exec. Blair Radio Co., San Francisco, 1968, Campbell-Ewald, San Francisco, 1969; v.p., account supr. Dailey & Assocs., San Francisco, 1970-71; co-founder, pres. Pritikin & Gibbons Communications, San Francisco, 1971-73; pres. Ayer, Pritikin & Gibbons, San Francisco, 1973-81; pres., chief exec. officer DDB Needham, San Francisco, 1981-87; sr. v.p. Foote, Cone and Belding, San Francisco, 1987—; guest lectr. San Jose State U. and San Francisco State U., 1970-73. Mem. adv. bd. Nat. Assn. Visually Handicapped, 1968-72; bd. dirs., mem. exec. com. Oakland Symphony Orch. Assn., 1980-83; elder Montclair Presbyn. Ch., Oakland, 1974-84. Served with U.S. Army, 1958-60. Recipient Profl. Achievement award San Jose State U., 1984. Mem. Am. Assn. Advt. Agys. (bd. govs. No. Calif. chpt., chmn. Western region), Sales and Mktg. Assn. San Francisco (chmn. publicity com. 1975-76, past pres.), San Francisco Soc. Communicating Arts (pres., dir. 1975-78), San Francisco C. of C., Alpha Delta Sigma (past pres., dir.). Clubs: San Francisco Advt. Avocation: ranching. Office: Foote Cone and Belding 1255 Battery St San Francisco CA 94111

GIBBONS, MARIBETH VIVIAN, environmental consulting company executive; b. Teaneck, N.J., Apr. 19, 1952; d. Stephen John and Veronica Marie (Henke) Hanussak; m. Harry Lawrence Gibbons, Aug. 4, 1973; children: Ryan, Michael. BA in Math., Wash. State U., 1977, MS in Environ. Sci., 1980, MS in Environ. Engring., 1984. Cert. engr.-in-tng., Wash. Lab. technician Wash. State U., Pullman, 1977-84, research asst. civil and environ. engring., 1979-82; pres. Water Environ. Services, Inc., Bainbridge Island, Wash., 1984—. Contbr. articles to profl. jours. Mem. N.Am. Lake Mgmt. Soc., Aquatic Plant Mgmt. Soc., Sigma Xi, Phi Kappa Phi, Tau Beta Pi. Roman Catholic. Avocations: swimming, backpacking, stamp collecting, gardening, fishing. Home: 9515 Windsong Loop NE Bainbridge Island WA 98110

GIBBONS, STEVEN VAN, lawyer; b. Bremerton, Wash., May 5, 1955; s. John Farrell and Catherine Gennette (Cooper) G.; m. Darla Denise Recknagle, Oct. 20, 1976; children: Heather, Garrett Wesley, Morgan Rhys, John Weylin. BA with high honors, Brigham Young U., 1980; JD, George Washington U., 1983. Bar: Wash. 1984, U.S. Dist. Ct. (we. dist.) Wash. 1984, U.S. Ct. Appeals (9th cir.) 1984. Assoc. Diamond & Sylvester, Seattle, 1984-85, Lane, Powell, Moss & Miller, Seattle, 1985—. Mem. Maritime Law Assn. U.S., Seattle King County Bar Assn. (chmn. maritime and fisheries 1986—), Asia-Pacific Lawyers Assn., Assn. Trial Lawyers Am. Democrat. Mormon. Avocations: sailing, mountaineering. Home: 15011 Skogen Ln Bainbridge Island WA 98110 Office: Lane Powell Moss Miller 3800 Ranier Bank Tower Seattle WA 98101

GIBBS, ALAN NORMAN, test engineer; b. Marlboro, Mass., June 25, 1946; s. Norman Eugene Gibbs and Ruth Anne (Williams) Strom; m. Chiumin Michelle Tsong, Dec. 22, 1981. BBA, Nat. U., San Diego, 1982, MS in Edn., 1984. Career counselor USN, 1964-82; electronics instr. ITT, San Diego, 1982-84; test engr., sr. specialist electronics div. Gen. Dynamics, San Diego, 1984—; prof. Learning Tree U., Thousand Oaks, Calif., 1986—; pres. Profl. Tng. Cons. Recipient Outstanding Achievement award Gen. Dynamics, 1985. Mem. Nat. Soc. for Performance and Instrn., Am. Radio Relay League (life), Fleet Res. Assn., Non-commd. Officers Assn. Republican. Roman Catholic. Avocations: amateur radio, golf. Home: 4505 N Canyonlands Rd Moorpark CA 93021 Office: Gen Dynamics Electronics Div c/o Eaton IMS 31717 La Tienda Dr Westlake Village CA 91359

GIBBS, BARBARA KENNEDY, art museum director; b. Newton, Mass., Feb. 15, 1950; d. Frederic Alexander and Jane Jarvis (Ensinger) K. A.B. magna cum laude, Brown U., 1972; M.B.A., UCLA, 1979. Dep. dir. Portland Art Assn., Oreg., 1979-83; dir. Crocker Art Mus., Sacramento, 1983—. Guggenheim intern fellow Solomon R. Guggenheim Mus., 1978. Mem. Assn. Art Mus. Dirs., Am. Assn. Mus. Home: 1036 56th St Sacramento CA 95819 Office: Crocker Art Mus 216 O St Sacramento CA 95814

GIBBS, GORDON EVERETT, pediatrician, medical educator; b. Cordova, Ill., Sept. 25, 1911; s. George Eugene and Mabel Melissa Alvira (Ewell) G.; m. Gertrude Elise Fleischmann, Dec. 19, 1941; children—Gale Roeder, Gwen Stone, Gerald, Greta. A.B., U. Redlands, 1932; Ph.D., U. Calif.-Berkeley, 1939; M.D., U. Calif.-San Francisco, 1942. Intern, U. Calif. Hosp., San Francisco, 1942-43, resident in pediatrics, 1945-47, NRC fellow in pediatrics, 1947-49; NRC fellow U. Ill., Chgo., 1949-50; assoc. prof. in pediatric research, U. Md., Balt., 1950-54; assoc. prof. pediatrics U. Nebr., 1954-56, prof., chmn. dept. pediatrics, 1956-66, research prof. pediatrics, 1966-81, sr. cons. pediatrics, 1981—; practice medicine specializing in diabetes, Omaha, 1981-84, Thermal, Calif., 1985—. Contbr. numerous articles to profl. jours. Served with U.S. Army, 1943-45, USAR, 1945-56, USAFR, 1956-70. Recipient Bronze Star, Meritorious Service medals, NIH awards, 1960-68. Mem. AMA, Am. Pediatric Soc., Am. Diabetes Assn., Soc. Pediatric Research, Soc. Exptl. Biology and Medicine, Am. Acad. Pediatrics, Res. Officers Assn., Sigma Xi, Phi Chi. Republican. Baptist. Home: 88120 Ave 73 Thermal CA 92274

GIBBS, JERRY W., city official; b. Mt. Pleasant Iowa, Feb. 23, 1950; s. Orval R. and Vivian (Lear) G.; m. Stacey E. Frieze, Jan. 21, 1984. B.S.C.E., U. Mo. Registered profl. engr., Mo., Colo., Utah. Jr. design engr. Cooper Communities, Inc., Bella Vista, Ark., 1973-74; dir. pub. works City of Nevada, Mo., 1974-83, Park City Mcpl. Corp., Park City, Utah, 1983—. Mem. Nat. Soc. Profl. Engrs., Am. Pub. Works Assn. (exec. bd. 1981-83, treas. 1983). Methodist. Lodges: Rotary, Elks. Home: PO Box 4483 Park City UT 84060 Office: Park City Mcpl Corp PO Box 1480 Park City UT 84060

GIBBS, MARY HANNAH, publishing executive; b. Ames, Iowa, Aug. 27, 1944; d. Clifford and Kathryn Louise (Carter) Hach.; m. Keith Lowell Dobbs, June 7, 1967 (div. July, 1976); m. Charles Russell Gibbs, July 16, 1976; children: David Linnaeus, Rebecca Nicole. Student, Pratt Inst., 1969-70; BA, Drake U., 1967. Pres., owner Micro Environ., Bklyn., 1971-75, Art Service, Inc., Loveland, Colo., 1980-85; pres., editor In House Graphics, Inc., Loveland, 1985—; Author/editor: (newsletters) In House Graphics, 1984—, The Desktop, 1986—. Home: 535 W 5th St Loveland CO 80537 Office: In House Graphics 342 E 3d St Loveland CO 80537

GIBBS, SUSAN ELIZABETH, medical technology administrator; b. Mare Island, Calif., Jan. 29, 1942; d. Burton Cook Jr. and Therese (Moisan) Lillis; m. Roy L. Gibbs, Aug. 16, 1965; children: Deidre, Chandra, Je-Nel. BA, Calif. State U., Los Angeles, 1969. Cert. med. technologist, Calif. Intern in med. tech. St. Joseph Med. Ctr., Burbank, Calif., 1969-70, med. tech. supr. I, 1970-72, med. tech. supr. II, 1973-79, asst. chief tech., computer mgr., 1979—; computer cons. Am. Hosp. Supply Corp., Chgo., 1981-82, Arcadia (Calif.) Meth. Hosp., 1985, Hemet (Calif.) Valley Hosp., 1985—. Author: (with others) Standard Guide for Computer Automation in the Clinical Laboratory, 1981. Mem. Am. Soc. Clin. Pathology. Republican. Roman Catholic. Avocations: reading, swimming, family activities. Office: St Joseph Med Ctr Buena Vista and Alameda Burbank CA 91505

GIBILISCO, JOHN MICHAEL, electrical engineer, electronics engineering consultant; b. Omaha, Dec. 20, 1949; s. Sebistino and Grace Lucille (Battiato) G. B.S.E.E. with high distinction, U. Nebr., 1972. Electronics design engr. Tektronix, Inc., Beaverton, Oreg., 1973-76; project engr. Valleylab, Inc., Boulder, Colo. 1976-79; systems engr. Rockwell-Collins, Inc., Cedar Rapids, Iowa, 1979-80; sr. staff engr. ADR Ultrasound, Inc., Tempe, Ariz., 1980-82; research engr. Life Imaging, Inc., Boulder, 1982-83; group mgr., sr. engr. Reference Tech., Inc., Boulder, 1983-85; pres., owner Analog Solutions-Electronics Engring. Cons., Boulder, 1983—. Patentee in field. Mem. Rocky Mountain Inventors Congress. Office: Analog Solutions 5484 White Pl Boulder CO 80303

GIBLETT, ELOISE ROSALIE, hematology educator; b. Tacoma, Wash., Jan. 17, 1921; d. William Richard and Rose (Godfrey) G. B.S., U. Wash., 1942, M.S., 1947, M.D. with honors, 1951. Mem. faculty U. Wash. Sch. Medicine, 1957—, research prof., 1967-87, emeritus research prof., 1987—; asso. dir., head immunogenetics Puget Sound Blood Center, 1955-79, exec. dir., 1979-87, emeritus exec. dir., 1987—; former mem. several research coms. NIH. Author: Genetic Markers in Human Blood, 1969; Editorial bd. numerous jours. including Blood, Am. Jour. Human Genetics, Transfusion, Vox Sanguinis; Contbr. over 190 articles to profl. jours. Recipient fellowships, grants, Emily Cooley, Karl Landsteiner, Philip Levine and Alexander Wiener immunohematology awards. Fellow AAAS; Mem. Nat. Acad. Scis., Am. Soc. Human Genetics (pres. 1973), Am. Soc. Hematology, Am. Assn. Immunologists, Brit. Soc. Immunology, Internat. Soc. Hematologists, Am. Fedn. Clin. Research, Western Assn. Physicians, Assn. Am. Physicians, Sigma Xi, Alpha Omega Alpha. Home: 6533 53d St NE Seattle WA 98115 Office: Puget Sound Blood Ctr Terry and Madison Sts Seattle WA 98104

GIBLETT, PHYLIS LEE WALZ, educator; b. Denver, July 17, 1945; d. Henry and Leah (Pabst) Walz; B.S.B.A. (Estelle Hunter scholar 1963, Denver Classroom Tchr.'s scholar 1963, Outstanding Bus. Edn. Student scholar 1967), U. Denver, 1967, M.B.A., 1969; m. Thomas Giblett, May 31, 1975; children—Leann Ruth, Douglas Henry, John Peter. Tchr. bus. Aurora (Colo.) South Middle Sch., Aurora Pub. Schs., 1967-80, 82-86, on leave, 1980-82, 86—, chmn. bus. dept., 1972-79; evening tchr. S.E. Met. Bd. Coop Services, 1967-68, post secondary/adult classes Aurora Pub. Schs., 1972-75, Community Coll. Denver, North Campus, 1973, Aurora Pub. Schs. Adult Edn., 1983-84; mem. Dist. Tchr. Adv. Com., 1975-79; adviser chpt. Future Bus. Leaders Am., 1976-78; mem. Colo. Curriculum Specialist Com., 1976-77. Named Miss Future Bus. Tchr., Phi Beta Lambda of Colo., 1965. Mem. Nat., Mountain-Plains (participant leadership conf. 1977), Colo. (pres. 1976-77) bus. edn. assns., Colo. Educators for/About Bus., Am., Colo. vocat. assns., NEA, Colo., Aurora edn. assns., Delta Pi Epsilon (pres.-elect Eta chpt. 1978, pres. 1980-81). Republican. Lutheran.

GIBSON, BRUCE, executive recruiter; b. Hartford, Sept. 24, 1940; s. Nelson and Helen Mary (Janek) G.; B.S., UCLA, 1964; m. Barbara Anne Bares, Nov. 25, 1961; children—William, Robert, Leslie. Vice pres. Hergenrather, Gibson, Hanrahan & Assocs., Los Angeles, 1969-71; founder, sr. v.p. N.W. Gibson Assocs., Los Angeles, 1971-80; pres., chmn. Gibson & Co., Los Angeles, 1980—. Roman Catholic.

GIBSON, DARYL RAYMOND, publishing executive; b. Nephi, Utah, Nov. 19, 1954; s. Roy E. and Emma Zoe (Powell) G. BA, Brigham Young U., 1982. Systems mgr. Brigham Young U., Provo, Utah, 1979-84, ops. mgr., 1984—. Mem. Bedford Users Group, Newspaper Computer Users Group. Mormon. Avocations: photography, writing, editing, computers. Home: 315 East 600 South 2 Springville UT 84663 Office: Brigham Young U 538 ELWC Provo UT 84602

GIBSON, DOROTHY ELIZABETH, social worker, psychotherapist; b. Columbus, Ohio, Feb. 9, 1923; d. James William and Grace Theresa (Wallace) G. BS in Social Adminstrn., Ohio State U., 1944; MS in Social Work, Smith Coll., 1952. Field worker Childrens Home Soc., San Francisco, 1952-55; supr. Calif. Dept. Mental Hygiene, 1958-62; field work supr., cons. U. Calif., Berkeley, 1962-67; instr. Yale U. Psychiatry, New Haven, 1967-70; dir. counseling Planned Parenthood, San Francisco, Oakland, Calif., 1970-72; pvt. practice specializing in clin. social work San Francisco, 1972—; bd. dirs., co-founder Family Survival Project for Brain Damaged Adults, San Francisco; co-founder Marin Counseling Service, San Rafael, Calif., 1955; 74—; instr. Sch. Social Work San Francisco State U., 1978-81. Contbr. articles to profl. jours. chmn. Planning Commn., Sausalito, Calif., 1972-76, Design Rev. Bd., Sausalito, 1983—. Nat. Inst. Mental Health scholar, 1951-52. Fellow Soc. Clin. Social Work (bd. dirs. 1980-82), Am. Orthopsychiat. Assn.; mem. Nat. Assn. Social Workers (bd. dirs. Golden Gate Redwood Empire Region 1983—, editor newsletter, bd. dirs. Calif. chpt. 1978-83), Mt. Tamalpais Interpretive Assn. (v.p. 1986), Sausalitoans Against Nuclear Destruction, Greenpeace, Sierra. Democrat. Clubs: Sausalito Rowing. Avocations: traveling, hiking, rowing, cycling, gourmet cooking. Home: 429 1/2 Johnson St Sausalito CA 94965 Office: 2105 O'Farrell St Suite 206 San Francisco CA 94115

GIBSON, DWAIN LEE, II, computer programmer, real estate developer; b. Ransomville, N.Y., Oct. 13, 1953; s. Dwain Lee and Clara Rachel (Drinkwater) G. BS, U. Wash., 1976; AAS in Chem. Sci., U. Alaska, 1979, AA in Computer Info. Systems, 1981; AAS in Electronics Tech., Tanana Valley Community Coll., 1979, AAS in Petroleum Tech., 1980. Computer operator Fairbanks (Alaska) North Star Borough, 1981-83, jr. computer programmer, 1983-84, computer programmer, 1984—. Home: Box 74725 Fairbanks AK 99707 Office: Fairbanks N Star Borough PO Box 1267 Fairbanks AK 99707

GIBSON, EDWARD FERGUS, physicist, educator; b. Colorado Springs, Colo., Apr. 2, 1937; s. George Merrick and Elsie Ida (Schnurr) G.; m. Harriette Graham DuShane, June 1, 1963; children: Sascha, Graham, Clark, Eileen. B.A., U. Colo., 1959, M.A., 1964, Ph.D., 1966. Physicist Nat. Bur. Standards, Boulder, Colo., 1958-64; research asst., research assoc. U. Colo., Boulder, 1964-66; postdoctoral research assoc. U. Oreg., Eugene, 1966-68; scientist-in-residence Naval Radiol. Def. Lab., San Francisco, 1968-69; prof. physics Calif. State U., Sacramento, 1969—, chmn. dept., 1979—; cons. on alternative energy sources Calif. Energy Commn., 1977-78; cons. computer-assisted instrn. Control Data Corp., 1981—. Assoc. Western Univs. fellow, 1971- 72, 73. Mem. Am. Phys. Soc., Phi Beta Kappa, Sigma Xi, Sigma Pi Sigma. Home: 527 Blackwood St Sacramento CA 95815 Office: Dept Physics Calif State U Sacramento 6000 J St Sacramento CA 95819

GIBSON, ELISABETH JANE, principal; b. Salina, Kans., Apr. 28, 1937; d. Cloyce Wesley and Margaret Mae (Yost) Kasson; m. William Douglas Miles, Jr., Aug. 20, 1959; m. Harry Benton Gibson, Jr., July 1, 1970. A.B., Colo. State Coll., 1954-57; M.A. (fellow), San Francisco State Coll., 1967-68; Ed.D., U. No. Colo., 1978; postgrad. U. Denver, 1982. Cert. tchr., prin., Colo. Tchr. elem. schs., Santa Paula, Calif., 1957-58, Salina, Kans., 1958-63, Goose Bay, Labrador, 1963-64, Jefferson County, Colo., 1965-66, Topeka, 1966-67; diagnostic tchr. Cen. Kans. Diagnostic Remedial Edn. Ctr., Salina, 1968-70; instr. Loretto Heights Coll., Denver, 1970-72; co-owner Ednl. Cons. Enterprises, Inc., Greeley, Colo., 1974-77; resource coordinator Region VIII Resource Access Project Head Start Mile High Consortium, Denver, 1976-77; exec. dir. Colo. Fedn. Council Exceptional Children, Denver, 1976-77; asst. prof. Met. State Coll., Denver, 1979; dir. spl. edn. Northeast Colo. Bd. Coop. Edn. Services, Haxtun, Colo., 1979-82; prin. elem. jr. high sch., Elizabeth, Colo., 1982-84; prin., spl. projects coordinator Summit County Schs., Frisco, Colo., 1985—; prin. Frisco Elem. Sch., 1985—; cons. Colo. Dept. Edn., 1984-85; cons. Colo. Dept. Edn., 1984-85, Montana Dept. Edn., 1978-79, Love Pub. Co., 1976-78, Colo. Dept. Inst., 1974-75; pres. Found. Exceptional Children, 1980-81; pres. bd. dirs. Northeast Colo. Services Handicapped, 1981-82; bd. dirs. Dept. Ednl. Specialists, Colo. Assn. Sch. Execs., 1982-84; mem. Colo. Title IV Adv. Council, 1980-82; mem. Mellon Found. grant steering com. Colo. Dept. Edn., 1984-85. Mem. Colo. Dept. Edn. Data Acquisition Reporting and Utilization Com., 1983, Denver City County Commn. for Disabled, 1978-81; chmn. regional edn. com. 1970 White House Conf. Children and Youth. Recipient Ann. Service award Colo. Fedn. Council Exceptional Children, 1981. Mem. Colo. Assn. Retarded Citizens, Assn. Supervision Curriculum Devel., Nat. Assn. Elem. Sch. Prins., Kappa Delta Pi, Pi Lambda Theta, Phi Delta Kappa. Republican. Methodist. Club: Order Eastern Star. Author: (with H. Padzensky) Goal Guide: A minicourse in writing goals and behavioral objectives for special education, 1975; (with H. Padzensky and S. Sporn) Assaying Student Behavior: A minicourse in student assessment techniques, 1974. Contbr. articles to profl. jours. Home: 2443 S Colorado Blvd Denver CO 80222 Office: Frisco Elem Sch PO Box 7 Frisco CO 80443

GIBSON, EMILY FULLER, English educator, writer; b. Litchfield, Ill., Sept. 27, 1940; d. Edward Lucious and Mildred Mae (Lamb) F.; m. Melvin Gibson, June 15, 1958 (div. 1974); children: Melvin Gibson Jr., Michelle Reneé, Melanie Rae. Student, No. Ill. U., 1958, Aurora Coll., 1961, 63, Aurora Coll., 1961, 63; AA cum laude, Los Angeles Southwest Coll., 1980; BA in English magna cum laude, Calif. State U., Dominguez Hills, 1981, MA in English, 1982, secondary teaching credential, 1984. Cert. single subject tchr. English secondary; cert. Calif. community college tchr. Free-lance writer 1969—; instr. English Calif. State U., Dominguez Hills, 1982; tchr. English Manuel Dominguez High Sch., Compton, Calif., 1982—; coordinator Gifted-Talented Program Manuel Dominguez High Sch., 1984-85; writing coach Manuel Dominguez High Sch., 1983—. Contbr. numerous articles to newspaper and mags. U.S. Del. World Conf. Peace Forces, Moscow, 1973; U.S. Del. U.N. Conf. of Women, Berlin, 1975; co-founder, Com. Justice in So. Africa, Los Angeles, 1978-79, vice chmn.; active Ward African Meth. Episc. Ch., Los Angeles, 1981—; active Trans-Africa, Los Angeles, 1984—. Recipient Gold Clock "Great Gal" award Sta. WGRT, 1968, Community Service award Black Caucus Resthaven Mental Health Ctr., 1974; fellow Calif. Lit. Project UCLA Grad. Sch. Edn., 1986; named One of Outstanding Young Women Am., 1968. Mem. Nat. Council Tchrs. English, Conf. Coll. Composition and Communication, 1982—. Democrat. Avocation: performing dramatic recitations. Home: 181 E 47th Pl Los Angeles CA 90011 Office: Manuel Dominguez Sr High Sch 15301 San Jose Compton CA 90221

GIBSON, FRANCES, nurse; b. Junction, Tex., Sept. 28, 1936; d. August and Juanita (Corpus-Garcia) Rehwold; m. Richard Gibson, July 4, 1954 (dec. July 25, 1962); children: Kenneth, Rene, Allison. AA, East Los Angeles Coll. Lic. vocat. nurse, 1969; registered nurse 1976, operating room technician, 1971; cert. adult edn. tchr. Instr., profl. expert East Los Angeles Coll., Monterey Park, Calif., 1971-74; hostess talk show (in Spanish) Sta. KMEX-TV, Los Angeles, 1970-76; tchr. adult edn. Garvey Sch. Bd., Rosemead, Calif., 1976-77; clinical nurse Los Angeles County/U. So. Calif. Med. Ctr., 1981—; vol. nurse Lung Assn., Los Angeles, 1970-76, ARC, Los Angeles, 1969—; instr. health classes, ARC, also instr. Spanish to ARC personnel, mgr. info. booths at health fairs and conventions, provide first aid at various gatherings, immunization clinics, etc., chmn. adv. bd., 1971-72, bd. dirs., 1972-75, 80-82; med. review/legal asst. Ivie & McNeill, Los Angeles, 1986—. Author: Spanish for English-Speaking Personnel, 1972. Recipient Spotlight award ARC, 1972, Clara Barton award, 1976; named one of Ten Prettiest Chicanas in East Los Angeles, 1970. Mem. Nursing Edn. Associates, Chicana Nurses Assn., AFL CIO, ACLU, Alpha Gamma Sigma. Democrat. Roman Catholic. Avocations: gardening, crafts. Home: 2241 Charlotte Ave Rosemead CA 91770

GIBSON, JAMES ISAAC, chemical manufacturing company executive; b. Golden, Colo., Mar. 22, 1925; s. Fred Daniel and May Emma (Borsberry) G.; m. Audrey June Brinley, June 23, 1947; children: James Brinley, David Scott, Robin Lee, Terry Lynn, Cynthia Rae, Holly Jo. BS, U.S. Naval Acad., 1947; BCE, MCE, Rensselaer Poly. Inst., 1950. Registered profl. engr., Nev., Ariz. Ensign C.E., USN, 1947, advanced through grades to lt., 1953, resigned, 1953; asst. chief engr. Western Electro-Chem. Co., Henderson, Nev., 1953-56; chief engr. Am. Potash and Chem. Corp., Henderson, 1956-61; chief engr. Pacific Engring. and Prodn. Co. Nev., Henderson, 1961-66, exec. v.p., 1966-85, pres., 1985—, also bd. dirs.; pres. Henderson Ventures, Inc., 1968—. Mem. assembly Nev. Legis., Carbon City, 1958-66, mem. senate, 1966—; majority leader Nev. Senate, 1976—; chmn. council state govts., Lexington, Ky., 1985, vice chmn., 1984, governing bd., 1968—. Recipient Silver Beaver award Boulder Dam Area council Boy Scouts Am., 1970; named Disting. Nevadan, U. Nev., 1973. Mem. NSPE, Nev. Soc. Profl. Engrs., Sigma Xi. Democrat. Mormon. Avocation: sports. Home: 806 Park Ln Henderson NV 89015 Office: Pacific Engring Prodn Co Nev PO Box 797 Henderson NV 89015

GIBSON, JAMES ROBERT, JR., architectural restorer, designer; b. Lakeland, Fla., Dec. 19, 1951; s. James Robert and Joyce Ramona (Ford) G. AA, Southwestern Coll., Chula Vista, Calif., 1971. Designer Met. Mus. Art, N.Y.C., 1973-78; conservator decorative arts De Young Mus., San Francisco, 1978-80; designer, archtl. restorer Design, Chula Vista, 1980—; founder Artistic Lic. in San Francisco. Prin. works include Timken House, San Diego, Livingston House, Coronado, Calif., Graham Meml. Presbyn. Ch., Coronado (SOHO Restoration of Yr. award Save Our Heritage Orgn., 1984) and others. Recipient Residential Restoration SOHO Award, San Diego, 1985, Residential Restoration Fulford Bungalow #2 award, 1985, Comml. Restoration award St. Matthews Ch., 1985. Home: 356 Palm Ave Chula Vista CA 92011 Office: Design 348 Palm Ave Chula Vista CA 92011

GIBSON, JENNIE, marketing executive; b. Beardstown, Ill.; d. Howard J. and Ethyl J. (Divvers) Tucker; m. Robert W. Gibson; children: Deborah K. Cooper, David J. Exec. sec. Wheeler Realty, Greeley, Colo., 1976-78, administrv. asst., 1978-81; office mgr. Cornerstone Builders, Greeley, 1981—, dir. mktg., 1983—. Mem. Soc. Mktg. Profl. Services. Avocations: music, gardening. Office: Cornerstone Builders Inc PO Box 204 Greeley CO 80632

GIBSON, JOANNE EVE, econometrician; b. Utica, N.Y., Dec. 12, 1946; d. Lawrence Ronald and Eve Maribe (Mar) Broderick; m. Carl Hunter Gibson, June 7, 1976. BA, U. Miami, 1968, MS, 1970. Prof. Fla. Internat. U., Miami, 1972-75; econometrician Copley Press, La Jolla, Calif., 1980-85; pres. Triadic Research, San Diego, 1985—. Author, editor: Review of San Diego Economic Activity, 1985; editor: Memoirs of Director of Scripps Instution of Oceanography, 1986. Mem. San Diego C. of C. (city council new library com. 1985). Avocations: chess, jewelry design. Home: 4412 Camrose Ave San Diego CA 92122

GIBSON, KEITH PATRICK, pharmacist, lawyer; b. Tulane, Calif., Feb. 26, 1953; s. Floyd M. and Martha Yvonne (Ribail) G. PharmD, U. So. Calif., 1980; JD, U. Pacific, 1985. Bar: Calif., 1986; lic. profl. pharmacist, Calif., Nev. Pharmacist Los Angeles New Hosp., 1974-81, Kaufman Pharmacies, Sacramento, 1981, Sutter Meml. Hosp., Sacramento, 1981—; sole practice Sacramento, 1986—. Mem. AAAS, Am. Soc. Law and Medicine, Am. Soc. Hosp. Pharmacists, Am. Soc. Pharmacy Law, Calif. Soc. Hosp. Pharmacists, Sacramento Valley Soc. Hosp. Pharmacists, Rho Pi Phi. Democrat. Avocation: home computers. Home: 7363 Perera Circle Sacramento CA 95831

GIBSON, MARGARET I(MOGENE), Russian language educator; b. Lincoln, Nebr., July 13, 1923; d. Hillory and Linnie Hazel (Truex) Bohannan; m. Ray V. Gibson, Aug. 21, 1943 (div. Oct. 3, 1973); children: Roy William, Ann Christine Gibson Gastelum. BS in Chemistry, U. Ariz., 1946, MA in Russian, 1970; PhD in Slavis Linguistics, U. Wash., 1978. Instr. chemistry U. Ariz., Tucson, 1946-49, lectr. Russian, 1976-78, asst. prof., 1978-84, assoc. prof., 1984—. Author: The Roots of Russian Through Chekhov: A Study in Word-formation; contbr. articles to profl. jours. Mem. Am. Assn. Tchrs. Slavic and Eastern European Langs.; Rocky Mountain Modern Lang. Assn. Avocations: Russian folk music and creative dance. Home: 1260 W Las Lomitas Tucson AZ 85704 Office: U Ariz Tucson AZ 85721

GIBSON, MELVIN ROY, pharmacognosy educator; b. St. Paul, Nebr., June 11, 1920; s. John and Jennie Irene (Harvey) G. B.S., U. Nebr., 1942, M.S., 1947, D.Sc. (hon.), 1985; Ph.D., U. Ill., 1949. Asst. prof. pharmacognosy Wash. State U., Pullman, 1949-52; assoc. prof. Wash. State U., 1952-55, prof., 1955-85, prof. emeritus, 1985—. Editor: Am. Jour. Pharm. Edn, 1956-61; editorial bd., co-author: Remington's Pharm. Sci, 1970, 75, 80, 85; editor, co-author: Studies of a Pharm. Curriculum, 1967; author over 100 articles. Served as arty. officer AUS, 1942-46. Decorated Bronze star, Purple Heart; sr. vis. fellow Orgn. for Econ. Cooperation and Devel., Royal Pharm. Inst., Stockholm, Sweden and U. Leiden (Holland), 1962; recipient Rufus A. Lyman award, 1972, Wash. State U. Faculty Library award, 1984; named Wash. State U. Faculty Mem. of Yr., 1985. Founder, charter mem. Am. Diplomates in Pharmacy.; fellow AAAS; assoc. fellow Am. Coll. Apothecaries; mem. N.Y. Acad. Sci., Am. Pharm. Assn., Am. Soc. Pharmacognosy (pres. 1964-65), Am. Assn. Coll. Pharmacy (exec. com. 1961-63, bd. dirs. 1977-79, chmn. council of faculties 1975-76, pres. 1979-80, Disting. Educator award 1984), U.S. Pharmacopeia (revision com. 1970-75), Am. Found. Pharm. Edn. (hon. life, bd. dirs. 1980-85, exec. com. 1981-85, vice chmn. 1982-85), AAUP, Acad. Pharm. Sci., Am. Public Health Assn., Fedn. Internat. Pharm., Am. Inst. History of Pharmacy, Am. Acad. Polit. and Social Sci., Sigma Xi, Kappa Psi (Nat. Service citation 1961), Rho

Chi, Phi Kappa Phi, Omicron Delta Kappa. Democrat. Presbyterian. Club: Spokane. Home: W 707 6th Ave Apt 41 Spokane WA 99204

GIBSON, PAUL RAYMOND, international trade and investment development executive; b. Cathay, Calif., Apr. 10, 1924; s. Otto and Louella (Vestal) G.; m. Janice Elizabeth Carter, Dec. 19, 1952; children—Scott C., Paula S. B.S. in Internat. Commerce, Georgetown U., 1956. Export mgr. Asia Philip Morris Co., San Francisco, 1952-54; founder, v.p., gen. mgr. McGregor and Werner Internat. div., Washington, 1954-62, v.p., dir. McGregor and Werner Corp., 1955-62; v.p. fin. Parsons & Whittemore, Inc., N.Y.C., 1962-65; founder, pres. Paul R. Gibson and Assocs., Washington, 1965-70; mng. dir. Black Clawson Pacific Co., Sydney, Australia, 1970-72; pres. Envirotech Asia Pacific, Sydney, 1972-74, pres. Envirotech Internat., Menlo Park, Calif., 1975-80; founder, pres. INTERACT, Burlingame, Calif., 1980—; pres. The Manchester Group, Ltd., Washington, 1987—. dir. Eimco K.C.P., Ltd., India. Mem. Pacific Basin Econ. Council v.p. program and vice chmn. govt. liaison U.S. Sect., 1976—; trustee World Affairs Council No. Calif., 1978—; mem. San Francisco Com. Foreign Relations, 1980—. Served to sgt. USMC, 1941-45. Mem. U.S. C. of C. (chmn. Asia-Pacific council Am. C. of C. 1974, mem. adv. com. 1975—). Clubs: Internat. (Washington); Am. Nat. (Sydney, Australia). Home: 1202 Sharon Park Drive #70 Menlo Park CA 94025 Office: INTERACT 1340 Old Bayshore Hwy Suite 750 Burlingame CA 94010

GIBSON, ROBERT DANIEL, academic administrator; b. Tacoma, July 1, 1925; s. Ray and Madeline Alice (Roberts) G.; m. Helen Marie Sigismund, Aug. 31, 1951; (div. Oct. 1971); children: Dana Alice, Barton Ray, Todd David; m. Aurora Helen Cromer, June 9, 1979; children: Debra Helen, Kim Dianne. BA in Chemistry, U. Oreg., 1949; BS in Pharmacy, U. Calif., San Francisco, 1954, PharmD, 1958; DSc (hon.), Mass. Coll. Pharmacy, 1984. Mem. faculty Sch. Pharmacy U. Calif., San Francisco, 1962—, dir. pharm. tech. lab., 1970-81, assoc. dean Sch. Pharmacy, 1972-82, assoc. vice chancellor student acad. affairs, 1982—; cons. HEW, 1969-70, Shaklee Corp., Emeryville, Calif., 1974-75, Boericke & Runyon, El Cerrito, Calif., 1970-74; bd. dirs. Am. Found. Pharm. Edn., 1986—. Author: Introduction to Ethnic Related Diseases, 1975, Hypertension, 1977; contbr. articles to profl. publs. Mem. Med., Therapeutic and Drug Adv. Com., Sacramento, 1966-70, statewide adv. com. Area Health Edn. Ctr. System, Fresno, Calif., 1979—. Served to sgt. U.S. Army, 1944-46. Named Man of Yr., Pharmacists Planning Service Inc., 1983, Disting. Alumnus, U. Calif., 1983; Fulbright-Hayes scholar 1965-66. Mem. Am. Colls. Pharmacy (pres. 1984-85), Federacione Internationale Pharmaceutique, Am. Pharm. Assn., AAAS. Avocations: flying, golf, fishing. Home: 7 Wentworth Ln Novato CA 94947 Office: U Calif 520 Parnassus Ave Upper Level San Francisco CA 94947

GIBSON, RONALD FRANKLIN, mechanical engineering educator; b. Macon, Ga., Nov. 7, 1942; s. James Madison and Lora (Peek) G.; m. Mary Anne Schmidt, June 12, 1965; 1 child, Tracy Ellen. BS, U. Fla., 1965; MS, U. Tenn., 1971; PhD, U. Minn., 1975. Devel. engr. Union Carbide Nuclear, Oak Ridge, Tenn., 1965-72; asst. research, teaching U. Minn., 1972-75; asst. prof. engring. sci., mechanics Iowa State U., Ames, 1975-78; assoc. prof. U. Idaho, Moscow, 1978-84, prof. mech. engring., 1984—; cons. Union Carbide Nuclear, 1972-84; vis. prof. U. Fla., Gainesville, 1980-81; fellow NASA Langley Research Ctr., Hampton, Va., 1981. Contbr. numerous articles on composite materials to profl. jours. Research grantee USAF Office Sci. Research, 1983-85. Mem. ASME, AIAA, Am. Soc. Engring. Edn., ASTM, Soc. Exptl. Mechanics (chmn. composites com. 1983-85). Avocations: running, biking, reading, travel. Office: U Idaho Mech Engring Dept Moscow ID 83843

GIBSON, ROY BERRETT, educator; b. North Ogden, Utah, Feb. 17, 1924; s. John William and Hazel (Berrett) G.; B.F.A., U. Utah, 1949; m. Bena Le Bowring, Mar. 22, 1948; children—Robert Barrett, Kathy Danielle, Cory Denise, Wendy Jo, Laurie Lee, Susan Kaye. Comml. announcer sta. KTVT-TV, Salt Lake City, 1952-57; newscaster KDYL Radio, Salt Lake City, 1957; news dir. KTVT-TV, 1958-62, KCPX-TV, Salt Lake City, 1962-72; guest lectr. U. Utah Sch. Journalism, 1968-72, vis. prof., 1972-73, asso. prof. communication, 1973—. Served with AUS, 1943-46. Mem. Radio-TV News Dirs. Assn., Assn. Edn. in Journalism, Nat. Broadcast Editorial Assn., Sigma Delta Chi (chpt. pres. 1965, regional dir. 1970-72). Club: Exchange (pres. Salt Lake City 1968-69). Home: 561 Northmont Way Salt Lake City UT 84103

GIBSON, SAMANTHA LIVINGSTON, sales representative; b. Mesa, Ariz., Dec. 9, 1941; d. Burr and Gwendolyn (Porter) Webb; student No. Ariz. U., Flagstaff, 1961, Coll. San Mateo, Calif., 1969, U. Ariz., Tucson, 1977; m. David Kent Gibson, June 2, 1981; children by previous marriage—Laurence, Donald and Danielle Livingston. Public relations ofcl. Sahara Tahoe Hotel, Stateline, Nev., 1969-71; with South Lake Tahoe C. of C., 1972-75; mgr. Winslow (Ariz.) C. of C., 1975-76; preventive maintenance analyst S.W. Forest Industries, Snowflake, Ariz., 1976-82, Brown & Root, 1985, Weyerhauser Paper Mill, Vallient, Okla., 1986; cons. troubleshooting mech. problems through vibration analysis. Mem. Snowflake Planning and Zoning Commn., 1977-78. Mem. Paper Industry Mgmt. Assn., Ariz. Assn. Indsl. Devel. (dir. 1975-76), Indsl. Devel. Endeavor Assn. (dir. 1975-76), Snowflake-Taylor C. of C. Republican. Research on trending in vibration analysis, analyzing mech. problems in rotating equipment. Home: PO Box 997 Snowflake AZ 85937 Office: Country Club at Fairway Snowflake AZ 85937

GIBSON, WILLIAM G., accountant; b. Salt Lake City, Aug. 22, 1946; s. William M. and Katherine T. Lupas; m. Christine Scothern, Feb. 15, 1974. B.S. in Acctg., U. Pacific, 1970; LL.B., La Salle U., 1974; C.P.A., Utah. Area dir. Person-Wolinsky C.P.A. Rev. Course, Salt Lake City, 1979-81; gen. ptnr., mgr. Gibson Investment Fund., 1980—; owner William Gibson, C.P.A.s, 1979—; tchr. Bryman Sch.; fin. cons. Mem. Am. Inst. C.P.A.s. Contbr. articles to profl. jours. Office: 3700 S 900 E Salt Lake City UT 84117

GICLAS, HENRY LEE, astronomer; b. Flagstaff, Ariz., Dec. 9, 1910; s. Eli and Hedwig Herminna (Leissling) G.; m. Bernice Francis Kent, May 23, 1936; 1 child, Henry Lee. BS, U. Ariz., 1937; postgrad., U. Calif., Berkeley, 1939-40; PhD with honors, No. Ariz. U., 1980. Research asst. Lowell Obs., Flagstaff, 1931-44, astronomer, 1944-79, exec. sec., 1952-75; adj. prof. Ohio State U., Columbus, 1968-79, No. Ariz. U., 1972—. Mem. Flagstaff Freeholder's Com., 1959; exec. v.p. Raymond Ednl. Found., 1971-77, pres., 1977—. Fellow AAAS; mem. Am. Astron. Soc., Ariz. Acad. Sci., Astron. Soc. Pacific (dir. 1959-61), No. Ariz. Pioneers Hist. Soc. (pres. 1972-80), Internat. Astron. Union. Clubs: Coconino Country (pres 1962), Continental Country (adv. bd. 1972-75). Lodge: Elks. Home: 120 E Elm Ave Flagstaff AZ 86001 Office: Lowell Obs Flagstaff AZ 86001

GIEDT, BRUCE ALAN, paper company executive; b. Fargo, N.D., May 7, 1937; s. Alexander and Alice Mildred (Rognaldson) G.; m. Suzanna Tae Abbott, Apr. 30, 1963; children: Alex, Jeffrey, Marybeth. BA, U. Wash., 1959; MBA, Harvard U., 1965. From regional sales mgr. to v.p. service products bus. units Crown Zellerbach Corp., San Francisco, 1965—; pres. Champion Paper Distbrs., Inc., Riverside, Calif., 1981-87, Pioneer Packaging, Phoenix, 1987—. Author: The Future of Commercial Arbitration, 1965. V.p. exec. com. Keep Riverside AHead, econ. devel. com., bd. dirs.; exec. com. mem. Riverside C. of C., devel. com. Served to Capt. USAF, 1959-63. Evans scholar Western Golf Assn., 1967. Mem. Am. Paper Inst. (past com. chmn.). Republican. Lutheran. Club: Victoria. Lodge: Elks. Home: 4811 E Beryl Ave Paradise Valley AZ 85253 Office: 4022 S 20th St Phoenix AZ 85040

GIELNIAK, CARY FRANK, industrial applications engineer; b. Gary, Ind., Aug. 1, 1957; s. William Hubert and Mary Ann Elizabeth (Bocca) G.; m. Judy Novoa, Aug. 16, 1985. BSEE, Purdue U., 1979. Power applications engr. No. Ind. Pub. Service Co., Hammond, 1980-84; indsl. applications engr. Salt River Project, Phoenix, 1984—. Mem. IEEE, Assn. Energy Engrs. (sr. mem.). Republican. Lodge: Elks. Avocations: golf, computers. Home: 1060 E Louis Way Tempe AZ 85251 Office: Salt River Project PO Box 52025 Phoenix AZ 85072

GIEM, ROSS NYE, JR., physician-surgeon; b. Corvallis, Oreg., May 23, 1923; s. Ross Nye and Goldie Marie (Falk) G.; student U. Redlands, Walla Walla Coll.; B.A., M.D., Loma Linda U.; children—John, David, Paul, James, Ross Nye, Matthew, Julie. Intern, Sacramento Gen. Hosp., 1952-53; resident in ob-gyn, Kern County Gen. Hosp., Bakersfield, Calif., 1956-57, in gen. surgery, 1957-61; practice medicine specializing in gen. surgery, Sullivan, Mo., 1961-70; staff emergency dept. Hollywood Presbyn. Med. Center, 1971-73, Meml. Hosp., Belleville, Ill., 1973—, St. Luke Hosp., Pasadena, Calif., 1973—; instr. nurses, physicians, paramedics, emergency med. technicians, 1973—. Served with AUS, 1943-46. Diplomate Am. Bd. Surgery. Fellow ACS, Am. Coll. Emergency Physicians; mem. AMA, Ill. Med. Assn., Pan Am. Med. Assn., Pan Pacific Surg. Assn., Royal Coll. Physicians (Eng.)

GIER, DENNIS MICHAEL, civil engineering consultant; b. Navarre, Ohio, Apr. 7, 1950; s. Thomas B. an Stella G. (Beazel) G.; m. Judith V. Wilson, Aug. 28, 1976; 1 child, Justin. BSCE, U. Dayton, 1972, MS in Engring., 1977; MS in Mgmt., U. So. Calif., 1975. Registered profl. civil engr. Project engr. Armbruster Constrn. Co., Kaiserlautern, Fed. Republic Germany, 1975-76; research engr. U. Dayton Research Inst., 1976-77; project engr. Ted Forsi and Assocs., Anchorage, 1978-80, Little Susitna Co., Anchorage, 1980-82; prin. engr. D.M. Gier & Co., Homer, Alaska, 1982—; cons. City of Homer, 1983—, City of Kachemak, Alaska, 1983—, Alaska Dept. Transp., 1982—. Contbr. articles to profl. jours. Scoutmaster Boy Scouts Am., Republic Korea, Fed. Republic Germany; mem. Homer Council on Arts, 1983—, Friends of the Library, Homer, 1983—. Served to 1st lt. C.E., U.S. Army, 1972-75. Named Eagle Scout Boy Scouts Am. Mem. ASCE, NSPE, Am. Mgmt. Assn., Homer C. of C. Roman Catholic. Clubs: Ski, Yacht (Homer) (bd. dirs. 1985-86). Avocations: hiking, fishing, skiing, reading, sailing. Home: 2146 Frisbee Ct Homer AK 99603 Office: PO Box 3670 3691 Ben Walters Ln Homer AK 99603

GIESEN, KENNETH M., wildlife research biologist; b. New Prague, Minn., Nov. 1, 1950; s. Raymond C. and Cecilia (Meger) G. BS in Wildlife Mgmt., U. Minn., 1972; MS in Wildlife Biology, Colo. State U., 1977. Wildlife laborer Minn. Dept. Nat. Resources, St. Paul, 1969-72; research asst. Coop. Wildlife Research Unit, Ft. Collins, Colo., 1975-77; wildlife technician Colo. Div. Wildlife, Ft. Collins, 1977-79, wildlife researcher, 1980—; affiliate faculty Colo. State U., Ft. Collins, 1985—. Contbr. articles to sci. jours. Served with U.S. Army, 1973-74. Mem. AAAS, The Wildlife Soc. (compiler of current lit. for The Wildlife Soc. Bull. 1983-85), Am. Ornithol. Union (life), Wilson Ornithol. Soc. (life), Cooper Ornithol. Soc., Ft. Collins Audubon Soc. (bd. dirs. 1982—), Sigma Xi, Alpha Zeta. Roman Catholic. Club: Ft. Collins Running. Avocations: photography, birding, road racing, biking. Office: Wildlife Research Ctr 317 W Prospect Rd Fort Collins CO 80526

GIFFORD, BECKY JENSEN, infosystems specialist; b. Akron, Ohio, Apr. 30, 1947; d. Henry Hartwig and Dorothy Myrtle (Surber) Jensen; m. James Roy Gifford, Jan. 18, 1986. BA, U. Nebr., 1970; MLS, UCLA, 1977. Cert. info. scientist. Librarian Instructional Materials Ctr. for Spl. Edn., U. So. Calif., Los Angeles, 1970-73; cons. Los Angeles, 1972-77; mgr. info. services NASA Indsl. Application Ctr., Los Angeles, 1977-81; dir. info. systems Savage Info. Services, Rolling Hills, Calif., 1981-85, v.p., 1985—. Mem. So. Calif. Online User Group (founding), Spl. Libraries Assn., Assn. Records Mgrs. and Adminstrs. Avocations: travel, computers, river rafting, reading. Office: Savage Info Services 608 Silver Spur Rd Rolling Hills Estates CA 90274

GIFFORD, GERALD FREDERIC, academic program director; b. Chanute, Kans., Oct. 24, 1939; s. Gerald Leo and Marion Lou (Browne) G.; m. Cinda Jean Lowman, June 26, 1982. Student, Kans. U., 1957-60; BS in Range Mgmt., Utah State U., 1962, MS in Watershed Mgmt., 1964, PhD in Watershed Sci., 1968. Asst. prof. watershed sci. Utah State U., Logan, 1967-72, assoc. prof., 1972-80, prof., 1980-84, chmn. watershed sci. unit, 1967-84, dir. Inst. Land Reclamation, 1982-84; head range, wildlife and forestry U. Nev., Reno, 1984—; exchange scientist NSF, Canberra, Australia, 1974; cons. Smithsonian Inst., Nat. Park Service, Office of Tech. Assessment, Tex. Tech U., U. Minn., Bur. Land Mgmt. AMAX Coal Co., Nat. Commn. Water Quality, 1967—. Author: Rangeland Hydrology, 1981; assoc. editor Arid Soil Research and Rehab., 1985—; contbr. papers to profl. publs. Mem. Am. Water Resources Assn., Soc. Range Mgmt. (assoc. editor 1982—), Soil Conservation Soc. Am. Avocations: racquetball, antiques, garage sales. Home: 3880 Squaw Valley Circle Reno NV 89509 Office: U Nev Range Wildlife and Forestry 1000 Valley Rd Reno NV 89512

GIGES, BOB ELI, academic administrator; b. N.Y.C., Mar. 14, 1955; s. Gerald Giges and Devera (McCoy) Black. Student, Wesleyan U., 1973-75; BA with honors, U. Calif., Santa Cruz, 1977. Acad. preceptor Porter Coll. U. Calif., Santa Cruz, 1979—, assoc. fellow, 1981—. Mem., com. chmn. Mental Health Adv. Bd., Santa Cruz, 1977-82; mem. Health Systems Agy. Mental Health Com., Salinas, Calif., 1977; founder and coordinator Psychiat. Inmates Rights Collective, Santa Cruz, 1976-80; coordinator YM & YWHA Drug Hotline, Scarsdale, N.Y., 1971-73; mem. Santa Cruz Action Network, Santa Cruz AIDS Project. Fellow Porter Coll. Faculty U. Calif. Santa Cruz (assoc.); mem. Amnesty Internat. Jewish. Office: U Calif Porter Coll Santa Cruz CA 95064

GILBAUGH, JAMES HERBERT JR., urologist; b. Portland, Oreg., Feb. 23, 1937; s. James Herbert Sr. and Lillian D. (Zeller) G.; m. Linda Montgomery, June 25, 1960 (div. Feb. 1981); children: James H. III, Mollie, Wendy; m. Marilyn L. Jenkinson, Oct. 28, 1983; children: Rogan, Molly, Annie. BS, U. Oreg., 1958; MS in Anatomy, MD, U. Oreg., Portland, 1963. Diplomate Am. Bd. Urology. Intern Ancker Hosp., St. Paul, 1963-64; fellow in urology Mayo Clinic, Rochester, Minn., 1964-68; practice medicine specializing in urology St. Vincent's Med. Ctr., Portland, 1978—. Contbr. articles on urology to profl. and sci. jours. Served as maj. M.C., USAF, 1968-70. Fellow ACS; mem. Oreg. Med. Assn., Sigma Xi. Republican. Roman Catholic. Clubs: Portland Golf, Multnomah Athletic. Lodge: Rotary. Avocations: furniture making, skiing, golf, fishing, writing. Home: 2902 SW Canterbury Ln Portland OR 97201 Office: St Vincent's Med Ctr 9155 SW Barnes Rd Suite 422 Portland OR 97225

GILBERT, HEATHER CAMPBELL, manufacturing company executive; b. Mt. Vernon, N.Y., Nov. 20, 1944; d. Ronald Ogston and Mary Lodivia (Campbell) G.; B.S. in Math. (Nat. Merit scholar), Stanford U., 1967; M.S. in Computer Sci. (NSF fellow), U. Wis., 1969. With Burroughs Corp., 1969-82, sr. mgmt. systems analyst, Detroit, 1975-77, mgr. mgmt. systems activity, Pasadena, Calif., 1977-82; mgr. software product mgmt. Logical Data Mgmt. Inc., Covina, Calif., 1982-83, dir. mktg., 1983, v.p. bus. devel., 1983-84; v.p. profl. services, 1984-85; mgr. software devel. Burroughs Corp., Lake Forest, Calif., 1985-86, Unisys Corp., El Toro, Calif., 1986—. Mem. Assn. Computing Machinery, Am. Prodn. and Inventory Control Soc., Stanford U. Alumni Assn. (life), Stanford Profl. Women Los Angeles County (pres. 1982-83), Nat. Assn. Female Execs., Town Hall. Republican. Home: 21113 Calle de Paseo El Toro CA 92630 Office: Unisys Corp 21113 Calle de Paseo El Toro CA 92630

GILBERT, JAMES FREEMAN, geophysics educator; b. Vincennes, Ind., Aug. 9, 1931; s. James Freeman and Gladys (Paugh) G.; m. Sally Bonney, June 19, 1959; children: Cynthia, Sarah, James. BS, MIT, 1953, PhD, 1956. Research assoc. MIT, Cambridge, 1956-57; asst. research geophysicist Inst. Geophysics and Planetary Physics at UCLA, 1957, asst. prof. geophysics, 1958-59; sr. research geophysicist Tex. Instruments, Dallas, 1960-61; prof. Inst. Geophysics and Planetary Physics at U. Calif. San Diego, La Jolla, 1961—, assoc. dir., 1976—; chmn. steering com. San Diego Supercomputer, 1984-86, Nat. Research Council Com. on Seismology, 1976-78, Nat. Acad. Scis. Panel on U.S.-USSR Exchange Program of the Bd. of Internat. Sci. Exchange, 1978-81; mem. NSF adv. com. Advanced Sci. Computing, 1983-85, NSF network subcom., 1985. Contbr. numerous articles to profl. jours. Recipient Arthur L. Day medal Geol. Soc. Am., 1985; Fairchild scholar Calif. Inst. Tech., Pasadena, 1987; fellow NSF, 1956, Guggenheim, 1964-65, 72-73, Overseas fellow Churchhill Coll. U. Cambridge, Eng., 1972-73. Fellow AAAS, Am. Geophys. Union; Nat. Acad. Scis., European Union Geoscis. (hon.); mem. Seismology Soc. Am., Soc. Exploration Geophysicists, Am. Math. Soc., Royal Astron. Soc. (recipient Gold medal 1981), Nat. Research Council (mem. ad hoc com. of Govt./Univ. Round Table, 1986), Sigma Xi. Home: 780 Kalamath Dr Del Mar CA 92014 Office: U Calif San Diego Inst Geophysics & Planetary Physics A-025 La Jolla CA 92093

GILBERT, KIM EILEEN, lawyer; b. Berkeley, Calif., June 20, 1947; d. Charles R. and Elvyna J. (Waller) G. B.A., U. Calif.-Davis, 1967; M.A., Rutgers U., 1969; J.D., U. Pacific, 1974. Bar: Calif. 1974, U.S. Dist. Ct. (ea. and cen. dists.) Calif. 1974, U.S. Supreme Court 1979. Legis. asst. Calif. State Legislature, Sacramento 1967-68; prin. research cons. Eagleton Inst. Politics, New Brunswick, N.J., 1969; econ. budget analyst Calif. State Dept. Fin., Sacramento, 1970-72; govtl. program analyst Calif. State Dept. Health, Sacramento, 1973; asst. to v.p. and gen. counsel HMO Internat., Los Angeles, 1973-74; sole practice, Beverly Hills, Calif., 1974—; judge pro tem Superior Ct., Los Angeles, 1980—, Mcpl. and Small Claims Ct., 1980—. House analyst desk Am. Broadcasting Co., N.Y.C., 1968; campaign staff Citizens for Unruh Com., Sacramento, 1970; Sacramento County com. Common Cause, Sacramento, 1972-73. Calif. State scholar, 1964, Eagleton fellow, Rutgers U., 1968. Mem. Los Angeles County Bar Assn., Beverly Hills Bar Assn., Los Angeles Trial Lawyers Assn., Women Lawyers Assn. of Los Angeles, Westside Women Lawyers Assn., San Fernando Valley Women Lawyers Assn., ABA, ACLU. Democrat. Roman Catholic. Office: 9100 Wilshire Blvd Suite 501 E Tower Beverly Hills CA 90212-3408

GILBERT, MARJORIE JEAN, stockmarket advisor, investment execuitve, artist; b. Englewood, Colo., Dec. 27, 1936; d. Lonzo E. and Dorothy Imogene (Fowler) Cox; m. Donald L. Gilbert, Sept. 4, 1955; children—David Lee, Daniel Leigh, Dawna Lea. Owner, v.p. Escondido Foods, 1960-82, also freelance writer, 1975-80; artist, 1976—; investment counselor, 1980—; organizer investment clubs; tchr. classes on stock market. Area chmn. San Diego Light Opera Assn.; mem. San Diego Zool. Soc. Named Escondido Mother of Yr., 1966. Mem. Nat. Assn. Investment Clubs (pres. San Diego council). Republican. Methodist. Clubs: Toastmasters (pres.), Expressions. Home and Office: 1603 Skyhawk Rd Escondido CA 92025

GILBERT, NEIL ROBIN, social work educator; b. N.Y.C., Sept. 18, 1940; s. Alan and Ida (Bedzin) G.; m. Barbara Diane Feinstein, June 2, 1963; children: Evan Mallory, Jesse Arthur. BA, Bklyn. Coll., 1963; MSW, U. Pitts., 1965, PhD, 1968. Caseworker Interdepartmental Service Ctr., N.Y.C., 1963; dir. research Mayor's Com. on Human Resources, Pitts., 1967-69; prof. sch. social welfare U. Calif., Berkeley, 1969—, chmn. doctoral program, 1983—, acting dean sch. social welfare, 1986. Author: Clients or Constituents, 1970, Capitalism and the Welfare State, 1983, (with others) Dimensions of Social Welfare Policy, 1974, 2d rev. edit. 1986, Dynamics of Community Planning, 1978; editor: Social Welfare Series, 1977, Series of Social Services, 1977-82, (advisor) Jour. Social Policy, 1982—. Fellow NIMH, 1966, U.N. Research Inst. for Social Devel., 1975; Fulbright scholar, U.S. Info. Agy, 1981; Fulbright Western European scholar, 1987. Mem. Nat. Assn. Social Workers, Assn. Pub. Policy Analysis and Mgmt. Avocations: skiing, moutaineering. Home: 57 Hill Rd Berkeley CA 94708 Office: Univ of Calif Sch of Social Welfare Haviland Hall Berkeley CA 94720

GILBERT, RICHARD GENE, research plant pathologist, research microbiologist; b. Holdenville, Okla., Dec. 3, 1935; s. Myron Lee and Martha Viola (Cates) G.; m. Sharon Lee Smith, Sept. 7, 1959 (div.); children: Mark Dean, Jill Susanne; m. Sallie Arambula, July 22, 1978 (div.). BS in Phys. and Biol. Scis., Colo. State U., 1961, MS in Plant Pathology, 1963, PhD in Plant Pathology, 1964. Research asst. dept. plant pathology U. Calif., Berkeley, 1964; research microbiologist U.S. Soils Lab. div. USDA, Beltsville, Md., 1965-70, U.S. Water Conservation Lab., Phoenix, 1970-82; research plant pathologist Irrigated Agrl. Research and Extension Ctr., Prosser, Wash., 1982—. Contbr. numerous articles to tech. jours. With U.S. Army, 1954-57. Recipient Unit award U.S. Dept. Agr., 1973. Mem., Am. Phtopathol. Soc., Am. Soc. Agronomy, Soil Sci. Soc. Am., Phi Beta Kappa, Sigma Xi, Phi Kappa Phi. Mem. Unity Ch. Lodge: Kiwanis. Home: 623 3d St Grandview WA 98930 Office: USDA Agrl Research Service PO Box 30 Prosser WA 99350

GILBERT, ROBERT WOLFE, lawyer; b. N.Y.C., Nov. 12, 1920; s. L. Wolfe and Katherine L. (Oestreicher) Wolfe; m. Beatrice R. Frutman, Dec. 25, 1946; children—Frank Richard, Jack Alfred. B.A., UCLA 1941; J.D., U. Calif., Berkeley, 1943. Bar: Calif. 1944, U.S. Ct. Apls. (9th cir.) 1944, U.S. Ct. Apls. (D.C. cir.) 1976, U.S. Sup. Ct. 1959. Pres. Gilbert & Sackman, P.C. and predecessors, Los Angeles, 1944—; judge pro tem Los Angeles Mcpl. Ct., Beverly Hills Mcpl. Ct. Commr. City of Los Angeles Housing Authority 1953-63; bd. dirs. Calif. Housing Council 1955-63. Mem. Internat. Bar Assn., Interam. Bar Assn. (co-chmn. labor law and social security com.), ABA (co-chmn. internat. labor law com.), Fed. Bar Assn., Beverly Hills Bar Assn., Los Angeles Bar Assn. (chmn. labor law sect.), Am. Judicature Soc., Order of Coif, Pi Sigma Alpha. Club: Nat. Lawyers. Contbr. articles to profl. jours. Home: 7981 Hollywood Blvd Hollywood CA 90046 Office: 6100 Wilshire Blvd Suite 700 Los Angeles CA 90048-5107

GILBERT, RUSSELL JAMES, electronics executive; b. Flushing, N.Y., Sept. 18, 1952; s. James William and Veronica Gilbert; B.S. in Mgmt., St. John's U., 1974; postgrad in bus. C.W. Post Coll., 1976; J.D., Western State U., 1980. Planning analyst Grumman Aerospace Corp., Bethpage, N.Y., 1974-76; with electronics div. Gen. Dynamics Co., San Diego, 1976—, sr. systems analyst, 1980-83 , sr. project mgr., 1983—; mem. Automated Data Collection working group with Gen. Dynamics Corp.; engring. cons. for small high tech. cos. Cert. on Ramis II. Mem. Nat. Mgmt. Assn.(1st v.p. gen. dynamics electronics div. 1986—) Clubs: Harbor Lions (dir. 1982-83, Internat. award 1981); San Diego Mission Bay Boat and Ski (bd. dirs. 1986-87, 1st vice commodore 1987—). Author: Manufacturing and Material Control Systems for an Integrated Environment, 1977; Planning Management Information System, 1981; Parts Labor History; Automated Data Collection System Utilizing Bar Code High Technology. Home: 6361 Rancho Mission Rd Unit 8 San Diego CA 92108 Office: Gen Dynamics Electronics Div 5011 Kearny Villa Rd PO Box 85039 Mail Zone 8232-C San Diego CA 92138

GILBERT, WILLIAM ALLAN, agronomist, consultant; b. Batavia, N.Y., Sept. 6, 1954; s. Reed Davies and Frances (Owens) G.; m. Lucinda Russell, June 2, 1973; children—Seth, Jesse, Caleb. B.S., Cornell U., 1976; M.S., Colo. State U., 1978. Cert. profl. agronomist. Research asst. agronomic research Colo. State U., 1976-78; asst. scientist, room control supr. Castle & Cooke Inc., East Windsor, Conn., 1978-80; cons. agronomist Inter-Am. Labs., Ft. Collins, Colo., 1980-82; owner Applied Agronomics, Ft. Collins, 1982—. Med. Colo. Dry Bean Adv. Bd. 1986-87. Gt. Western Sugar Co. grantee Colo. State U., 1976-78. Mem. Am. Soc. Agronomy, Crop Sci. Soc. Am., Soil Sci. Soc. Am., Nat. Alliance Ind. Crop Cons. (sec./treas. 1986-87). Democrat. Contbr. articles to profl. jours.

GILBERTSON, OSWALD IRVING, marketing executive; b. Bklyn., Mar. 23, 1927; s. Olaf and Ingeborg (Aase) Gabrielsen; m. Magnhild Hompland, Sept. 11, 1954; children—Jan Ivar, Eric Olaf. Electrotechnician, Sorlandets Tekniske Skole, Norway, 1947; B.S. in Elec. Engring., Stockholms Tekniska Institut, Stockholm, Sweden, 1956. Planning engr. test equipment design and devel. Western Electric Co., Inc., Kearny, N.J., 1957-61, planning engr. new prodn., 1963-67, engring. supr. test equipment, 1963-67, engring. supr. submarine repeaters and equalizers, 1967-69; engring. mgr. communication cables ITT Corp., Oslo, Norway, 1969-71, mktg. mgr. for ITT's Norwegian co., Standard Telefon og Kabelfabrik A/S, 1971—, div. mgr. Eswa Heating Systems. Hon. Norwegian consul, 1981. Served with AUS, 1948-52. Registered profl. engr., Vt. Mem. IEEE, Norwegian Soc. Profl. Engrs., Soc. Norwegian Am. Engrs., Sons of Norway. Patentee in field. Home: 6240 Brynwood Ct San Diego CA 92120 Office: Standard Telefon OG Kabelfabrik A/S 591 Camino de la Reina Suite 500 San Diego CA 92108

GILCHRIST, DORIS IRENE, interior designer; b. Camrose, Alta., Can., 1960; came to U.S., 1960; d. Bernard Leo and Valara Alberta (Sissons) Nugent; m. James Douglas Gilchrist, May 21, 1960; children: Jeffrey, David, Sharon. B in Interior Design, U. Man., Winnipeg, Man., Can, 1959. Pvt. practice interior design Rancho Palos Verdes, Calif., 1976-81; designer Robinson Dept. Store, Torrance, Calif., 1981; owner, operator Design II, Rolling Hills Estates, Calif., 1982—. Mem. adv. bd. So. Calif. Regional Occupational Ctr., Torrance, 1986—; speaker Career Day, Manhattan Beach (Calif.) Pub. Schs., 1986. Mem. Women in Mgmt. (chmn. job bank 1984-86), Creative Services Network (pres., program chmn. 1984—, mem. adv. bd.

1983—), South Bay Mktg. Networks I and II (founder 1986), Creative Connections (leader 1984—), The Assembly, Beta Sigma Phi (v.p., pres., program chmn. ways & means com.). Avocations: reading, biking. Office: Design II 916 Silver Spur Rd #305 Rolling Hills Estates CA 90274

GILE, JANICE ANN, elementary educator; b. Richland, Wash., Jan. 16, 1948; d. John Alexander and Sarah Helen (Grant) G. AA, Columbia Basin Coll., 1968; BA in Edn., Eastern Wash. State Coll., 1970, MA in Edn., 1979, MS in COmputer Sci., 1987. Tchr. Keene-Riverview Regular Kindergarten, Prosser, Wash., 1970-75, Bilingual Title VII Kindergarten, Keene-Riverview Elem. Sch., Prosser, 1975-81; tchr. first grade Whitstran Elem. Sch., Prosser, 1981-83, chpt. 1 migrant tchr. math., 1983-85; chpt. 1 migrant tchr. Whitstran Elem. Sch. and Heights Elem. Sch., Prosser, 1985-86; title 1 summer migrant tchr., Prosser, 1971, 80-84; title 1 remedial summer math. program tchr., Prosser, 1973; participant NSF Math. workshop, summer 1974, Bilingual-Bicultural Inst., summer 1977. Co-leader Bluebirds, 1972-73; mem. choir Luth. Ch., 1970—. Mem. NEA, Wash. Edn. Assn., Prosser Edn. Assn. (sec. 1972-74, bldg. rep. 1971-72, 82-83, negotiator 1977-78), Wash. Assn. Supervision and Curriculum Devel. (mini-grant award 1986), Nat. Assn. Supervision and Curriculum Devel., Phi Delta Kappa, Alpha Delta Kappa. Home: 1026 Hemlock Prosser WA 99350

GILES, GERALD LYNN, mathematics, psychology, computer educator; b. Manti, Utah, Jan. 2, 1943; s. Bert Thorne and Sarah Jenett (Carlen) G.; m. Sharon Ruth Bleak, June 12, 1967; children: Kim, David, Kristie, Becky, Michael, Andrew, Brent. BA, U. Utah, 1968, MA, 1971. Tchr. Granite Sch. Dist., Salt Lake City, 1968-72; prof. Utah Tech. Coll., Salt Lake City, 1972—; adj. prof. U. Utah, 1985—; cons. QUE Enterprises, Salt Lake City, 1976—; mem. faculty U. Phoenix, Salt Lake City, 1986. Author: The Vicious Circle of Life, 1986. Chmn. Rep. voting dist., Salt Lake City, 1984-86. Recipient Teaching Excellence award, 1986; named Outstanding Tchr. of Yr., 1986. Mem. Am. Math. Assn. Two Yr. Colls., Assn. Coll. Unions Internat. Mormon. Avocations: photography, computer programming. Home: 4342 Beechwood Rd Salt Lake City UT 84123 Office: Utah Tech Coll PO Box 30808 Salt Lake City UT 84130-0808

GILFILLAN, GEORGE WILLIAM, construction and engineering company executive; b. San Francisco, Jan. 29, 1938; s. Harold M. and Alberta (Horan) G.; m. Mona Ann Kelso; children: Dana, Chris, Brett. BCE, Sacramento State U., 1960. Engr. Morrison-Knudsen Co., Inc., Boise, Idaho, 1954-66, mgr., 1966-72, v.p., 1973-85, pres., 1985—. Mem. Soc. Am. Mil. Engrs. (nat. dir.). Roman Catholic. Clubs: Beavers, Moles; Arid (Boise); Pacific (Hawaii); World Trade (San Francisco); Internat. (Washington). Lodge: Elks. Avocation: boating. Office: Morrison-Knudsen Co Inc One Morrison-Knudsen Plaza PO Box 7808 Boise ID 83729

GILJE, JOHN WINTON, chemistry educator; b. Elkader, Iowa, Feb. 24, 1939; s. Lorimer A. and Eleanor (Winton) G.; m. Julia Zartman, May 8, 1971. B in Chemistry with distinction, U. Minn., 1961; PhD, U. Mich., 1965. Asst. prof. chemistry U. Hawaii, Honolulu, 1965-69, assoc. prof., 1969-75, prof., 1975—; vis. prof. U. Tex., Austin, 1972-73; acad. visitor Imperial Coll. Science and Techn., London, 1979-80; guest prof. Techn. U., Braunschweig, Fed. Republic of Germany, 1980-81. Contbr. technical articles in inorganic chemistry to profl. jours. Recipient medal Am. Inst. Chemists, 1961, Forschungsstipendium Alexander von Humboldt Found., Fed. Republic Germany, 1981. Mem. Am. Chem. Soc., Phi Lambda Upsilon, Sigma Xi. Office: U Hawaii Chemistry Dept 2545 The Mall Honolulu HI 96821

GILL, DAVID WALTER, theology educator; b. Omaha, Feb. 2, 1946; s. Walter Leonard and Vivian Erna (Wurz) G.; m. Lucia Lynn Paulson, Sept. 9, 1967; children: Jodie Lynn, Jonathan Christopher. BA in History, U. Calif., Berkeley, 1968; MA in History, San Francisco State U., 1971; PhD in Religion and Social Ethics, U. So. Calif., 1979. Co-editor Radix Mag., Berkeley, 1971-73; founder, project dir. New. Coll. Berkeley, 1977-79, dean and asst. prof. Christian Ethics, 1979-82, dean and assoc. prof., 1982-86, pres., prof., 1986—. Author: The Word of God in the Ethics of Jacques Ellul, 1984, Peter the Rock, 1986. Mem. Am. Acad. Religion, Pacific Coast Theol. Soc., Soc. Christian Ethics, Evang. Theol. Soc., Conf. on Faith and History. Mem. Evang. Covenant Ch. Avocations: tennis, golf, travel, music. Office: New Coll Berkeley 2600 Dwight Way Berkeley CA 94704

GILL, GEORGE WILHELM, anthropologist; b. Sterling, Kans., June 28, 1941; s. George Laurance and Florence Louise (Jones) G.; B.A. in Zoology with honors (NSF grantee), U. Kans., 1963, M.Phil. Anthropology (NDEA fellow, NSF dissertation research grantee), 1970, Ph.D. in Anthropology, 1971; m. Pamela Jo Mills, July 26, 1975; children—George Scott, John Ashton, Jennifer Florence, Bryce Thomas. Mem. faculty U. Wyo., Laramie, 1971—, prof. anthropology, 1985—; forensic anthropologist law enforcement agencies, 1972—; sci. leader Easter Island Anthrop. Expdn., 1981. Served to capt. U.S. Army, 1963-67. Recipient J.P. Ellbogen meritorious classroom teaching award, 1983; research grantee U. Wyo., 1972, 78, 82, Nat. Geog. Soc., 1980, Center for Field Research, 1980; Diplomate Am. Bd. Forensic Anthropology (bd. dirs. 1985—). Fellow Am. Acad. Forensic Scis. (sec. phys. anthropology sect. 1985—); mem. Am. Assn. Phys. Anthropologists, Current Anthropology (assoc.), Plains Anthrop. Soc., Wyo. Archael. Soc. Republican. Presbyterian. Author articles, chpts. in books. Home: 649 Howe Rd Laramie WY 82070 Office: Dept Anthropology Univ Wyo Laramie WY 82071

GILL, LAWRENCE GORDON, III, obstrician-gynecologist; b. Atlanta, Nov. 6, 1950; s. Lawrence G. Jr. and Jonnie Evelyn (Cochran) G.; m. Elizabeth Litt, June 17, 1972 (div. 1981); children: Molly Chana, Zachary Whitman. BA, Yale U., 1973; MD, NYU, 1977. Cert. Bd. Ob-Gyn. From intern to chief resident U. Calif., San Diego, 1977-81; obstetrician-gynecologist Lander (Wyo.) Med. Clinic, 1984—. Bd. dirs. Wyo. Wilderness Experience, Lander, 1985—; vol. Boy Scouts Am., Lander, 1985—. Served as maj. USPHS, 1981-84, with USAR, 1984—. Fellow Am. Coll. Obstetricians and Gynecologists; mem. Am. Fertility Soc., Wyo. Med. Soc., Nat. Rifle Assn. (life), Alpha Omega Alpha. Lodge: Am. Mountain Men. Office: Lander Med Ctr 745 Buena Vista Dr Lander WY 82520

GILL, REBECCA SHARMA, engineering executive; b. Brownsboro, Tex., Sept. 17, 1944; d. Milton and Dona Mildred (Magee) La Losh; BS in Physics, U. Mich., 1965; MBA, Calif. State U., Northridge, 1980; m. Peter Mohammed Sharma, Sept. 1, 1965 (div.); m. James Frederick Gill, Mar. 9, 1985; children: Erin, Melissa, Ben. Tchr., Derby, Kans., 1966; weight analyst Beech Aircraft, Wichita, Kans., 1966; weight engr. Ewing Tech. Design, assigned Boeing-Vertol, Phila., 1966-67, Bell Aerosystems, Buffalo, 1967; design specialist Lockheed-Calif. Co., Burbank, 1968-79; sr. staff engr. Hughes Aircraft Missile Systems, Canoga Park, Calif., 1979-82, project mgr. AMRAAM spl. test and tng. equipment, 1982-85, project mgr. GBU-15 guidance sect., IR Navy Maverick Missile, Tucson, 1985—; sec. Nat. Cinema Corp. Com. chmn. Orgn. for Rehab. through Tng., 1971-75; speaker ednl. and civic groups. Active NOW; pres. Briarcliffe East Homeowners Assn. Recipient Lockheed award of achievement, 1977. Mem. Soc. Allied Weight Engrs. (dir., sr. v.p., chmn. pub. relations com.), Aerospace Elec. Soc. (dir.), Nat. Assn. Female Execs, Hughes Mgmt. Club (bd. dirs., chmn. spl. events). Republican. Club: Tennis Racquet. Contbr. articles to tech. pubs. Office: Hughes Aircraft Missile Systems Bldg 801 MSF6 Tucson AZ 85734

GILL, ROGER WILLIAM THOMAS, management specialist; b. Whitehaven, Eng., Oct. 3, 1945; came to U.S., 1978; s. Wilfred Henry and Marie Eleanor (Gilmore) G.; children: Victoria Louise, Julian Charles. BA, Oxford (Eng.) U., 1968, MA, 1971; BPhil, Liverpool (Eng.) U., 1969; PhD, U. Bradford, Eng., 1980. Personnel asst. English Electric Co., Liverpool, 1965-66; personnel officer English Electric Computers/ICL, Winsford, 1968-69; mgmt. cons. Inbucon, Birmingham, Eng., 1969-71; personnel mgr. De La Rue Co., London, 1971-72; manpower mgr. Associated Weavers, Bradford, Eng., 1972-74; lectr. U. Bradford Mgmt. Centre, 1974-78; asst. prof. orgnizational behavior, human resources mgmt., dir. mgmt. programs Sch. Mgmt. SUNY, Binghamton, 1979-82; mng. dir., prin. cons. Roger Gill and Assocs. Pte, Ltd., 1982—; pres. Internat. Mgmt. Devel. Corp.; bd. dirs. Heslegrave Gill Ltd., U.K.; advisor to Nat. Productivity Bd., Singapore; cons. to industry, govt., U.K., U.S., , Malaysia, Brunei, Hong Kong, Indonesia, UAE. Fellow Found. for Mgmt. Edn., 1978; grantee Prodn. Mgmt., 1977-78, SUNY, 1979-80. Mem. Am. Soc. Tng. and Devel. (pres. So. Tier, N.Y., 1980-81), Am. Psychol. Assn., Acad. Mgmt., Internat. Assn. Applied Psychology, British Psychol. Assn., Inst. Personnel Mgmt., British Inst. Mgmt., Singapore Psychol. Soc., Singapore Inst. Mgmt., Internat. Council Small Bus., Singapore Nat. Productivity Assn. (1st v.p. 1985—). Clubs: Cambridge U., United Oxford (London). Address: 4614 Kilauea Ave Suite 524 Honolulu HI 96816 Address: PO Box 3047 Maxwell Rd, Singapore 9050, Singapore

GILLAND, BRUCE, guidance counselor, education officer; b. Marion, Ky., Mar. 8, 1933; s. Roy T. and Francis A. (Horning) G.; m. Anita D. Hendrickson, Jan. 31, 1959; children—Cynthia Ann, Brent Stuart, Kristi Faye. B in Gen. Studies, Rollins Coll., 1973. B.S., 1976; BA, SUNY-N.Y.C., 1977; MA, Calif. State U. Consortium-Sacramento, 1979, postgrad. U. So. Calif., 1987. Enlisted U.S. Air Force, 1950; ret., 1974; guidance counselor U.S. Army, Korea, 1977-78, U.S. Air Force, Malstrom AFB, Mont., 1979, edn. officer, Sunnyvale AFS, Calif., 1980-81, guidance counselor, Travis AFB, Calif., 1982—. Mem. Am. Personnel and Guidance Assn., Nat. Vocat. Guidance Assn., Am. Vocat. Assn., Am. Mgmt. Assn. Republican. Baptist. Club: DAV. Office: 60th ABG/DPE Travis AFB CA 94535

GILLARD, ELIZABETH BARTLETT, educator; b. Vernal, Utah, June 21, 1923; d. Charles Owen and Caroline Mabel (Jones) Bartlett; m. Don C. Hall, June 1, 1945 (dec.); m. 2d Hyrum Earl Carlson, June 12, 1956 (dec.); m. 3d, Virgil Roy Gillard, July 1, 1960 (dec.); 1 dau., Jean Hall Chiovaro. B.S., Brigham Young U., 1950; stenographical cert. LDS Bus. Coll., Salt Lake City, 1944; postgrad. U. Utah, Utah State U., Brigham Young U. Gen. secondary edn. teaching cert., Utah. Bookkeeper, Lyman Gas & Oil Co., Vernal, Utah, 1942; dep. county clk., Vernal, 1943-44; mem. steno pool RFC, Salt Lake City, 1944-45; sec. Alterra High Sch., Roosevelt, Utah, 1947-48; tchr. bus. Twin Falls (Idaho) Bus. Coll., 1950-51, Parowan (Utah) High Sch., 1951-54, Cyprus High Sch., Magna, Utah, 1954-59, Wasatch Jr. High Sch., Salt Lake City, 1959-63, Skyline High Sch., Salt Lake City, 1963-81; tchr. bus., chmn. dept. Taylorsville High Sch., Salt Lake City, 1981-84; bus. and mktg. edn. supr., Granite Sch. Dist., 1984—; mem. Utah Bus. and Office Edn. Adv. Bd., 1977-80; bd. dirs. Utah Future Bus. Leaders Am., 1978-81. Recipient Scroll of Honor, Sal Ute chpt. Nat. Secs. Internat., 1969; named Outstanding Tchr., Utah Bus. Edn. Newsletter, 1975, Bus. Tchr. of Yr., Delta Pi Epsilon, 1983. Mem. Internat. Soc. Bus. Edn., Nat. Bus. Edn. Assn., Western Bus. Edn. Assn. (sec. 1979-80), NEA, Utah Bus. Edn. Assn. (pres. 1976-77, research award 1980), Granite Edn. Assn., Classroom Educators of Bus. and office Edn., Am. Vocat. Assn., Utah Vocat. Assn. (Bus. Educator of Yr. 1976, mem. exec. bd. 1975-77, pres. 1985-86), Profl. Secs. Internat. Mormon. Home: 3784 S 3145 E Salt Lake City UT 84109 Office: Taylorsville High Sch 5225 S Redwood Rd Salt Lake City UT 84107

GILLE, JOHN CHARLES, scientific researcher; b. Akron, Ohio, Oct. 12, 1934; s. Merrill Charles and Marjorie Ruth (Tragler) G.; m. Ellen Cole Fetter, Aug. 24, 1963; children: Sarah T., Edward P. BS, Yale U., 1956; BA, Cambridge U., 1958, MA, 1966; PhD, MIT, 1964. Postdoctoral researcher Harvard U., Cambridge, Mass., 1964; from asst. to assoc. prof. Fla. State U., Tallahassee, 1964-72; sr. scientist, sect. head Nat. Ctr. Atmospheric Research, Boulder, Colo., 1972—; mem. coms. Nat. Acad. Scis., Washington, 1970—; mem. adv. groups NASA, Washington, 1969—; mem. Com. on Space Research, 1974—. Contbr. articles to profl. jours. Recipient Tech. Achievement award Nat. Ctr. Atmospheric Research, 1978, Exceptional Sci. Achievement award NASA, 1982. Fellow AAAS (electorate nominating com. 1986—), Am. Meteorol. Soc. (assoc. editor Jour. Atmospheric Sci., 1974-79); mem. Am. Geophys. Union (assoc. editor Jour. Geophys. Research 1980-83), Internat. Union Geology and Geophysics (internat. com. meteorol. upper atmosphere 1976-84, internat. radiation commn. 1980—), Phi Beta Kappa, Sigma Xi. Office: Nat Ctr Atmospheric Research PO Box 3000 Boulder CO 80307

GILLESPIE, DANIEL THOMAS, physicist; b. Springfield, Mo., Aug. 15, 1938; s. Kenneth Thomas Gillespie and Betrix Dorothy (Frazier) Evans; children: Mark Thomas, Christopher Ewan; m. Carol Ann Clarke, Feb. 28, 1976. BA, Rice U., 1960; PhD, Johns Hopkins U., 1968. Research assoc. U. Md., College Park, 1968-71; research physicist Naval Weapons Ctr., China Lake, Calif., 1971-81, supervisory mathemetician, 1981—. Author: A Quantum Mechanics Primer, 1970; contbr. articles to profl. jours. Mem. Am. Phys. Soc., Phi Beta Kappa, Sigma Xi. Home: 812 W Vicki Ave Ridgecrest CA 93555 Office: Naval Weapons Ctr Research Dept China Lake CA 93555

GILLESPIE, DAVID ELLIS, distributing company executive; b. Chgo., Dec. 18, 1933; s. David Ellis and Helen Leota (Andrews) G. B.A., Wayne State U., 1955; postgrad., U. Tex. Market research mgr. Gen. Steel Wares, London, Ont., Can., 1955-58; market research mgr. KLM Royal Dutch Airlines, Montreal, Que., 1958-60; media dir. Comcore Communications Ltd., Toronto, Ont., 1960-61; v.p. Comcore Communications Ltd., 1961-62, exec. v.p., 1963-65, pres., chief exec. officer, 1965-73; chief exec. officer Core-Mark Distbrs. Inc. (formerly Glaser Bros.), Los Angeles, 1974—, Core Mark Internat., Vancouver; dir. Core Mark Midcontinent Inc., Denver, CM Products Inc., Los Angeles, Bingo Cash'n Carry Inc., Los Angeles, SJL Products Inc., Los Angeles, Davlin Bus. Systems, Inc., Toronto, ASI Telesystems, Los Angeles, Sandy's Fast & Fresh Inc., Los Angeles. Bd. dirs. Pritiken Research Found., Santa Monica, Calif., Vancouver Symphony Orch. Mem. Nat. Assn. Tobacco Distbrs. (dir.), Calif. Assn. Tobacco and Candy Distbrs. (dir.). Republican. Episcopalian. Club: Ontario (Toronto). Home: 135 N Rossmore Los Angeles CA 90004 Home: Pym Island, Sidney, BC Canada V8L 3R9 Office: 1800 N Vine St Hollywood CA 90028 also: 13951 Bridge Port Rd, Richmond, BC Canada V6V 1J6

GILLESPIE, MICHAEL GORDON, safety engineer; b. Great Falls, Mont., Sept. 12, 1945; s. Elmer W. and Ruth (Rosedall) G.; m. Judy Lynn Barnicoat, Oct. 3, 1970 (div. Oct. 1976); 1 child, Eric Sean. EdB, U. Mont., 1969. Cert. assoc. safety profl. Bd. Cert. Safety Profls., 1986. Safety officer Boulder (Mont.) River Sch., 1969-74; asst. safety dir. Zidell Inc., Portland, Oreg., 1975-83; safety dir. Tube Forgings Am., Portland, 1983-85; safety specialist Tri-Met., Portland, 1986—. Vol. ARC, Portland, chpt. chmn., Boulder, 1970-74. Mem. Am. Soc. Safety Engrs. Roman Catholic. Home: 3027 NE 117th Portland OR 97226 Office: Tri-Met 4012 SE 17th Ave Portland OR 97203

GILLETTE, DEAN, mathematician, educator, consultant; b. Chgo., Aug. 11, 1925; s. Frank Kenneth and Ruth (Whitmore) G.; m. Helen Klamt, Dec. 19, 1949; 1 child, Troy. B.S. in Chemistry, Oreg. State U., 1948; M.A. in Math., U. Calif.-Berkeley, 1950, Ph.D. in Math., 1953. Mem. tech. staff Bell Labs., Holmdel, N.J., 1953-84; exec. dir. labs. Bell Labs., 1966-84; prof. Harvey Mudd Coll., Claremont, Calif., 1984—; Henry R. Luce prof. info. technology and soc. Harvey Mudd Coll.; prof. Claremont McKenna Coll., Calif., 1984—; mem. various coms. Dept. Def.; mem. com. Office Tech. Assessment; mem. adv. com. Internat. Tele-Communications Research Inst., U. Houston; mem. coms. Nat. Research Council. Author papers on math., systems engring., mgmt.; editorial com. Newtworks, Telecom. Policy. Served with USN, 1944-46; PTO. Mem. IEEE , Am. Math. Soc., Soc. Indsl. and Applied Math. Repubican. Office: Harvey Mudd Coll Claremont CA 91711

GILLETTE, EDWARD LEROY, oncology educator; b. Coffeyville, Kans., May 21, 1932; s. Harold R. and Laura Belle (McLaughlin) G.; m. Carol J. Peterson, June 2, 1956 (div. Oct. 1981); children: William R., Jeffrey S., Timothy E., Jennifer L. BS, DVM, Kans. State U., 1956; MS, Colo. State U., 1961, PhD, 1965. Cert. Am. Coll. Vet. Radiology. From instr. to assoc. prof. radiology and radiation biology Colo. State U., Ft. Collins, 1959-71, prof., 1972—, dir. comparative oncology, 1974—; bd. dirs. The Children's Hosp. Kempe Research Ctr., Denver. Assoc. editor Radiation Research, 1986—; contbr. articles to profl. jours. Mem. Am. Cancer Soc., exec. com. Colo. div. 1978-82; pres. Larimer County chpt. , 1977-81, bd. dirs. Colo. div., 1984—, Colo. State Sci. Fair, 1984—. Served to 1st lt. U.S. Army, 1956-58. U. Tex. fellow 1968-69; recipient Outstanding Service to the Vet. Profession, Am. Animal Hosp. Assn., 1984. Mem. Am. Coll. Vet. Radiology (pres. 1973-74), Vet. Cancer Soc. (pres. 1982-84), Radiation Research Soc., Am. Soc. Therapeutic Radiology and Oncology, Am. Assn. Cancer Research, Am. Vet. Medicine Assn., Colo. State U. Alumni Assn. (Honor Alumnus award 1985). Republican. Avocation: reading. Office: Colo State U Vet Teaching Hosp Comparative Oncology Unit 300 West Drake Fort Collins CO 80523

GILLETTE, JAY MICHAEL, film, theatre educator; b. Iowa City, Oct. 18, 1939; s. Arnold Simpson and Josephine (Jay) G.; m. Joyce Ann Shaffer, Nov. 1, 1979; children: Michael Christopher, Lauren Hope, Kathleen Joanne, John Alton. BA, U. Iowa, 1963; MFA, Ohio U., 1965. Instr. Southeast Mo. State U., Cape Girardeau, 1967-68; from asst. prof. to assoc. prof. U. Fla., Gainesville, 1968-73; assoc. prof. W.Va. U., Morgantown, 1973-74; prof. film, theatre U. Ariz., Tucson, 1974—; chmn. Tucson Film Commn., 1986; exec. dir. Ariz. Ctr. for Media Arts, 1986—. Author: The Cortes Letter, 1983, Designing with Light, 1978; co-author: Stage Scenery: Its Construction and Rigging, 1981, Theatrical Design and Production, 1987. Served to capt. U.S. Army, 1965-67. Mem. U.S. Inst. Theatre Tech. (bd. dirs. 1981-85). Avocations: golf, fishing, restoring automobiles, travel. Office: U Ariz Dept Drama 104 Tucson AZ 85721

GILLETTE, (PHILIP) ROGER, physicist, systems engineer; b. Mt. Vernon, Iowa, May 12, 1917; s. Clinton Edgar and Celia (Rogers) G.; m. Bettelaine Dunbar, April 26, 1947 (dec. Mar. 1986); children: Kenneth Lee, Sandra Jo. B.A., in Physics, Cornell Coll., 1937; B.S. in Engring. Physics, U. Ill., 1938, M.S. in Physics, 1939, Ph.D. in Physics, 1942. Staff mem. Radiation Lab. MIT, Cambridge, Mass., 1942-45; research engr. Sperry Gyroscope Co., Great Neck, N.Y., 1945-48; physicist Hanford Works Gen. Electric Co., Richland, Wash., 1948-50; sr. research physicist SRI Internat. Menlo Park, Calif., 1950—. Co-author: Pulse Generators, 1948. Bd. dirs. West Bay Opera Assn., Palo Alto, Calif., 1959-64, 1977-79. Mem. AAAS, IEEE (life mem.), Am. Phys. Soc. (life), Sigma Xi, Phi Beta Kappa, Tau Beta Pi, Phi Kappa Phi. Home: 151 Canada Cove Ave Half Moon Bay CA 94019 Office: SRI Internat 333 Ravenswood Ave Menlo Park CA 94025

GILLIAM, EARL BEN, federal judge; b. Clovis, N.Mex., Aug. 17, 1931; s. James Earl and Lula Mae G.; m. Barbara Jean Gilliam, Dec. 6, 1956; children—Earl Kenneth, Derrick James. B.A., Calif. State U., San Diego, 1953; J.D., Hastings Coll. Law, 1957. Bar: Calif. 1957. Dep. dist. atty. San Diego, 1957-62; judge San Diego Mcpl. Ct., 1963-74, Superior Ct. Calif., San Diego County, 1975-80, U.S. Dist. Ct. (so. dist.) Calif., San Diego, 1980—. Office: US Courthouse 940 Front St San Diego CA 92189

GILLIAM, JACKSON EARLE, bishop; b. Heppner, Oreg., June 20, 1920; s. Edwin Earle and Mary (Perry) G.; m. Margaret Kathleen Hindley, Aug. 11, 1943; children—Anne Meredith, Margaret Carol, John Howard. A.B., Whitman Coll., 1942; B.D., Va. Theol. Sem., 1948, S.T.M., 1949, D.D., 1969. Ordained to ministry Episcopal Ch., 1948; rector in Hermiston, Ore., 1949-53; canon St. Mark's Cathedral, Mpls., 1953-55; rector Ch. Incarnation, Great Falls, Mont., 1955-68; bishop Episc. Diocese Mont., 1968-86; chmn. com. on pastoral devel., mem. council on ministry, mem. program, budget and fin. com. Episc. Ch., 1978, pres. Province VI. Served to 1st lt. AUS, World War II. Decorated companion Order of Cross of Nails, companion Coventry Cathedral, Eng., 1974. Club: Rotary. Home: Shoreline Route Polson MT 59860

GILLILAND-MALLO, DAVID, social worker; b. Syracuse, N.Y., May 19, 1954; s. John and Mary (Fedele) Mallo; m. Sylvia Bartholomew, July 19, 1976 (div. June 1982); m. Gay Gilliland, June 6, 1982; children: Eric, Drake, Nichole. AS, Monroe Community Coll., 1974; BS, Rochester Inst. Tech., 1982; MSW, U. Denver, 1984. Social worker Crossroads Halfway House, Rochester, N.Y., 1981-82, Lakewood (Colo.) Youth Services, 1982-83, Colo. Boys Ranch, Denver, 1983-86, Spl. Child Placement Agy., Denver, 1984—, S.W. Denver Mental Health Ctr., 1986—. Author: Discipline: The Art of Teaching Self Control, 1985, The Effectiveness of Residential Care Facilities for Adolescent Boys, 1986. Mem. Family Life Task Force, United Ch. Christ, 1984-86. Grantee United Ch. Christ Bd. Homeland Ministries, Denver, 1985. Mem. Nat. Assn. Social Workers, Stepfamily Assn. Democrat. Home: 6970 W Calahan Lakewood CO 80226 Office: SW Denver Mental Health Ctr 1611 S Federal Blvd Denver CO 80219

GILLILAND-MALLO, GAY, social worker; b. Boulder, Colo., Sept. 27, 1952; d. Vail R. and Ethel Irene (Rounds) Gilliland; m. Michael Scott, June 6, 1971 (div. Nov. 1981); m. David Mallo, June 5, 1982; children: Eric, Drake, Nichole. AA in Spl. Edn., Empire State Coll., 1979; B in Social Work, Rochester Inst. Tech., 1982; MSW, U. Denver, 1983; postgrad., Iliff Sch. Theology, 1983—. Braille transcriber Nat. Braille Assn., Rochester, N.Y., 1977-78; aide Monroe Devel. Ctr., Rochester, 1978-79; interpreter, tutor BOCES, Fairport, N.Y., 1980; notetaker, tutor Rochester Inst. Tech., 1979-82; home-sch. counselor Primary Prevention Project, Seneca Falls, N.Y., 1980-81; dir. foster care Spl. Child, Denver, 1982-86; dir. Touchstone Child Placement Agy., 1986—. Supt. ch. sch. First Bapt. Sch., Fairport, 1979-80, Greece (N.Y.) Bapt. Ch., 1977-79; bd. Christian edn. Christ Congl. Ch., Denver, 1984-86; mem. conf. family life task force Rocky Mountain United Ch. Christ, 1984—; vol. presch. Eastside Community Ctr., Rochester, 1977-78; Dem. Precinct Chmn., Lakewood, Colo., 1984-85. Mem. Nat. Assn. Social Workers, Am. Assn. Mental Defiency, Step Family Assn. Avocations: Am. sign lang., sewing.

GILLIN, PHILIP HOWARD, lawyer; b. Council Bluffs, Iowa, Apr. 11, 1937; s. Nathan E. and Louise (Herzoff) G.; student U. Ariz., 1955-57, U. Calif., San Francisco, 1957-59; J.D., U Santa Clara, 1960; m. Joycelyn Hall, July 4, 1977; children—Jamie Lynn, Julia Ann. Andrea Leigh. Admitted to Calif. bar, 1961; mem. firm Gillin & Scott, Hollywood, Calif., 1959-60; sole practice law, Hollywood, 1970-75; mem. firm Gillin, Gottesman & Menes, Los Angeles, 1975-81; sole practice, 1981—; tchr. real estate law Calif. Continuing Edn. for the Bar; pres. Church Lane Music Inc., Berkeley Square Music Inc., Kings Road Music; pres. Scott Gillin Ltd. Chmn. March of Dimes, Sherman Oaks, 1964-69. Mem. Am. (nat. sec. student assn. 1958-59), Hollywood (dir. 1963-66, sec. 1967-68, pres. 1971) bar assns., Century City Bar Assn., Los Angeles Bar Assn., Calif. Copywright Conf. Office: 1901 Ave of Stars #1240 Century City CA 90067

GILLIO, CAROLYN IRENE, psychotherapist; b. Wells, Minn., Jan. 1, 1931; d. William Frederick and Antonia Willemina (Augst) Moll; m. Cesar Padilla, June 28, 1953 (div. 1967); children: Paula, Mark, Julie; m. Frank Gillio, May 24, 1969. BA, Gustavus-Adolphus Coll., 1952; postgrad., U. Chgo., 1952-53; MSW, U. Calif., Berkeley, 1955. Psychotherapist Agnews St. Hosp., San Jose, Calif., 1955-56; supr. San Jose Family Services, 1956-68; Psychotherapist Mid-Peninsula Psychotherapy Clinic, Sunnyvale, Calif., 1968-76; pvt. practice psychotherapy Sunnyvale, 1976—; adj. instr. U. Calif.-Santa Cruz Extension, Sunnyvale, 1979-80; cons. Santa Clara County (Calif.) Mental Health, 1975-78, other orgns. in field. Mem. Cen. Core Comprehensive Mental Health Planning Commn., Santa Clara, Calif., 1965-67; chmn. Sunnyvale Coordinating Council, 1968; bd. dirs. No. County Social Planning Council, Santa Clara, 1968-69. Recipient Disting. Service award Santa Clara County Family Service, 1968; named Disting. Woman on Mid-Peninsula, Girls Club of the Mid-Peninsula, 1973. Fellow Nat. Assn. Social Workers (bd. dirs. 1970-71), Soc. Clin. Social Workers (legis. com. 1975-77), Soc. Clin. Social Work (bd. dirs. 1977-81); mem. AAUW, Alphas. Home and Office: 869 Cumberland Dr Sunnyvale CA 94087

GILLIS, KENNETH ROBERT, real estate company executive; b. Ithaca, N.Y., Aug. 15, 1950; s. Marvin Bob and Helen (Reed) G.; B.S., Colo. State U., 1972; M.A., U. Colo., 1973; m. Ann Louise Conde, Oct. 26, 1974; children—Reed Kenneth, Robert Conde. Econ. analyst Great Western Sugar Co., Denver, 1974-76, mgr. fin. planning, 1977-78; mgr. fin. planning Foxley & Co. and Flavorland Industries, Denver, 1978-79, v.p. fin. 1979-81; stockbroker A.G. Edwards & Sons, 1981-84; v.p. La Salle Ptnrs. Inc., Denver, 1984—. Mem. Am. Econs. Assn., Am. Agrl. Econs. Assn. Club: Denver Athletic. Home: 12659 E Villanova Aurora CO 80014 Office: La Salle Ptnrs Inc 1225 17th St Suite 2420 Denver CO 80202

GILLIS, WILLIAM FREEMAN, information resource company executive; b. Henderson, Ky., July 9, 1948; s. James Edward and Florida Ann Gillis; m. Gwendolyn Elizabeth Slaughter, Aug. 8, 1969 (div. Mar. 1979); children: Jeffrey, Janeen, Kevin. BSEE, Purdue U., 1970. Mgr. mktg. Consumer Electronics div. RCA, Indpls., 1970-78, Bell System, 1978-81; v.p. mktg. Mattel Electronics, Hawthorne, Calif., 1981-83; exec. v.p. Charles

Schwab & Co. Inc., San Francisco, 1983-85; pres. Tsunami Info. Resources, Sausalito, Calif., 1985—. Author: Technological Financial Planning, 1986. Bd. nominee San Francisco YMCA, 1985. Served to lt. USAF, 1969. Named Businessman to Watch, Fortune Mag., 1985. Democrat. Baptist. Avocations: skydiving, martial arts, piano, bd. games. Home: 350 S Fuller Ave Los Angeles CA 90036 Office: Tsunami Info Resources 1525 Aviation Blvd Suite B302 Redondo Beach CA 90278

GILLMAR, STANLEY FRANK, lawyer; b. Honolulu, Aug. 17, 1935; s. Stanley Eric and Ruth (Scudder) G.; m. Constance Joan Sedwick; children—Sara Tamsin, Amy Katherine. A.B. cum laude with high honors, Brown U., 1957; LL.B., Harvard U., 1963. Bar: Calif. 1963. Ptnr. Graham & James, San Francisco, 1970—. Sec., Calif. Council Internat. Trade, 1973—; mem. Mayor San Francisco Adv. Council Econ. Devel., 1976-82; mem. Title IX Loan Bd., 1982—, sec. 1986—. Served with USNR, 1957-60. Mem. ABA, Calif. State Bar, Bar Assn. San Francisco. Clubs: Bankers (San Francisco); Villa Taverna, Inverness Yacht. Co-author: How To Be An Importer and Pay For Your World Travels, 1979; co-pub. Travelers Guide to Importing, 1980. Office: 300 One Maritime Plaza San Francisco CA 94111

GILLON, DAVID STEPHEN, cardiologist; b. Chester, Pa., June 23, 1943; s. David Stephen Gillon and Margaret (Rawlings) Smith; m. Diane Doreen Guenst, May 31, 1969; children: Jennifer, Zachary, Stephanie, Kathryn. BA, Rutgers U., 1965; MD, Hahnemann Med. Coll. and Hosp., 1969. Lic. cardiologist, Calif; cert. Am. Bd. Internal Medicine, Am. Bd. Cardiovascular Disease. Intern Santa Barbara (Calif.) Cottage and Gen. Hosps., 1969-70; resident in internal medicine Orange County Med. Ctr. and Long Beach VA Hosp., Calif., 1970-71; resident in internal medicine New Eng. Deaconess Hosp., Boston, 1971-72, cardiology fellow, 1972-74; cardiologist Santa Barbara Cardiovascular Med. Group, 1974—; asst. prof. medicine U. So. Calif., Santa Barbara, 1981—. Fellow Am. Coll. Cardiology; mem. ACP, AMA, Calif. Med. Soc., Am. Heart Assn., Santa Barbara County Med. Soc. (bd. dirs.). Avocations: flying, skiing, scuba diving, reading. Home: 130 E Padre St Santa Barbara CA 93105 Office: Santa Barbara Cardiovascular Med Group 221 W Pueblo St Santa Barbara CA 93105

GILLOW, GEORGE BRACEY, electrical engineer; b. Potrerillos, Chile, Oct. 27, 1945; s. Joseph Robert and Annie Rachel (Taylor) G.; came to U.S., 1957; B.S. in Elec. Engring., San Diego State U., 1970, M.S. in Elec. Engring., 1973; m. Pamela Jean Kennedy, Sept. 24, 1982. Project leader, design central processing units for computer, advanced devel. dept. Data Processing div. NCR Corp., San Diego, 1970-78; group mgr., design of large central processing units for computer Nat. Semi-condr. Corp., San Diego, 1978-80; with JRS Industries, San Diego, 1980-82; mgr. engring. DDG Corp., San Diego, 1982—; v.p. Digidyne Corp., San Diego, 1983—; dir. engring. Questron Corp., 1984-86; instr. Southwestern Coll., evenings, 1974, 75. Chmn. Environ. Control Commn. Chula Vista, 1975-78, chmn. Hist. Sites Bd., 1975-78; mem. Chula Vista City Council, 1978—, vice mayor, 1979-80. Mem. Tau Beta Pi. Democrat. Home: 250 Camino Del Cerro Grande Bonita CA 92002 Office: 10220 Sorrento Valley Rd San Diego CA 92121

GILLPATRICK, THOMAS RUSSELL, marketing educator; b. Cedar Rapids, Iowa, Aug. 8, 1953; s. Thorald David Gillpatrick and G. Lonetta (Joeger) Armstrong. BS, Calif. State U., Bakersfield, 1975; MBA, Utah State U., 1977; PhD, U. Oreg., 1985. Research assoc. Utah State U., Logan, 1976-77, instr. mktg., 1977-79; instr. mktg. U. Oreg., Eugene, 1977-82; asst. prof. mktg. Portland (Oreg.) State U., 1983-86, assoc. prof., 1986—; cons. electronics industry, CAE Systems, software and components. Contbr. articles to profl. jours. Active YMCA, City Club of Portland, 1985—, 1,000 Friends of Oreg., 1985—. Grantee U. Oreg., Eugene, 1982, Utah State U., 1977, Portland State U., 1985. Mem. Am. Mktg. Assn., Product Mgmt. Assn., Assn. Consumer Research Assn. Advancement Health Care (program com. 1986), Acad. Mktg. Sci, Phi Kappa Phi, Beta Gamma Sigma (chpt. sec. 1983—). Avocations: U.S. History, antique autos, skiing, internat. traveling. Home: 4034 NE Laddington Ct Portland OR 97232 Office: Portland State U Dept Mktg PO Box 751 Portland OR 97207

GILMAN, CHRISTOPHER JOHN, radiologist; b. Watertown, N.Y., May 21, 1949; s. Ralph C. and Mary J. (LeVasseur) G.; m. Lynn Margules, Mar. 16, 1973; 1 child, Joshua M. AB, U. Rochester, 1971; MD, U. Ill., Chgo., 1975. Diplomate Am. Bd. Family Practice, Am. Bd. Radiology. Asst. prof. radiology U. N.Mex., Albuquerque, 1981-82, Baylor Coll. Medicine, Houston, 1982-85, Loma Linda (Calif.) U., 1986—. Mem. Am. Roentgen Ray Soc., Am. Radium Soc., N.Y. Acad. Scis., Am. Acad. Family Physicians, Am. Soc. Clin. Hypnosis. Republican. Roman Catholic. Avocations: fgn. travel, bicycling, badminton. Home: 1221 San Ildefonso Rd Los Alamos NM 87544

GILMAN, JAMES IRVING, physician, director intensive care unit; b. Hartford, Conn., Jan. 31, 1934; s. Ralph Lawrence and Ruby Gertrude (Weaver) G.; m. Patricia Anne Crane, Mar. 2, 1968; children: Jason, Timothy, Nicholas, Alison. BA, Harvard U., 1956; MD, Yale U., 1960. Diplomate Am. Bd. of Anesthesiology. Intern U. Colo., Boulder, 1960-61; resident in anesthesiology Yale U., New Haven, Conn., 1963-66; instr. to assoc. prof. Yale U. Sch. Medicine, New Haven, Conn., 1966-74; assoc. clin. prof. to prof. U. Colo. Health Sci. Ctr., Denver, 1974-86; anesthesiologist Children's Hosp., Denver, 1974—; exec. v.p., med. dir. Children's Emergency Transport Service, Denver, 1984-87. Served to lt. comdr. USNR, 1961-63. Fellow Am. Acad. Pediatrics; mem. Am. Soc. Anesthesiologists, Am. Soc. Critical Care Medicine, Assn. Advancement Med. Instrumentation, AAAS. Office: Childrens Hosp 1056 E 19th Ave Denver CO 80218

GILMAN, JOHN JOSEPH, national laboratory research director; b. St. Paul, Dec. 22, 1925; s. Alexander Falk and Florence Grace (Colby) G.; m. Pauline Marie Harms, June 17, 1950 (div. Dec. 1968); children: Pamela Ann, Gregory George, Cheryl Elizabeth; m. Gretchen Marie Sutter, June 12, 1976; 1 son, Brian Alexander. B.S., Ill. Inst. Tech., 1946, M.S., 1948; Ph.D., Columbia, 1952. Research metallurgist Gen. Electric Co., Schenectady, 1952-60; prof. engring. Brown U., Providence, 1960-63; prof. physics and metallurgy U. Ill., Urbana, 1963-68; dir. Materials Research Center Allied Chem. Corp., Morristown, N.J., 1968-78; dir. Corp. Devel. Center, 1978-80; mgr. corp. research Standard Oil Co. (Ind.), Naperville, Ill., 1980-85; assoc. dir. Lawrence Berkeley Lab., Calif., 1985—; mem. solid state scis. com. Nat. Acad. Scis., 1979-82. Author: Micromechanics of Flow in Solids, 1969; Editor: The Art and Science of Growing Crystals, 1963, (with D.C. Drucker) Fracture of Solids, 1963, Atomic and Electronic Structures of Metals, 1967; editorial bd.: Jour. Applied Physics, 1969-72; Contbr. papers, articles to tech. jours. Served as ensign USNR, 1943-46. Recipient Mathewson gold medal Am. Inst. Metal Engrs., 1959, Application to Practice award, Distinguished service award Alumni Assn. Ill. Inst. Tech., 1962. Fellow Am. Phys. Soc., Am. Soc. for Metals (Campbell lectr. 1966); mem. Nat. Acad. Engring., Phi Kappa Phi, Tau Beta Pi. Home: 780 Spruce St Berkeley CA 94707 Office: Lawrence Berkeley Lab Berkeley CA 94720

GILMAN, NELSON JAY, library director; b. Los Angeles, Mar. 30, 1938; s. Louis L. and Alice (Cohen) G.; m. Virginia L. Ford, May 27, 1961 (div. Sept. 1970); children: Justine C., Seth F.; m. Lelde B. Trapans, Nov. 23, 1970. BS, U. So. Calif., 1959, MS, 1960; MLS, U. Calif., Berkeley, 1964. Tchr. math. dept. Pasadena (Calif.) High Sch., 1960-61, Tamalpais High Sch., Mill Valley, Calif., 1962-63; intern library adminstrn. UCLA, 1964-65, asst. to librarian, 1965-66, asst. to biomedical librarian, 1966-67, asst. biomedical librarian, 1967-69; assoc. dir. Pacific Southwest Regional Med. Library Service, UCLA, 1969-71; dir. Los Angeles County/U. So. Calif. Med. Ctr. Libraries, 1974-79; asst. prof. dept. med. edn. U. So. Calif. Sch. Med., 1971—, dir. Norris Med. Library, 1971—, dir. health scis. library system, 1984—, assoc. dir. devel. and demonstration ctr., 1981—; cons. HEW, San Francisco, 1973-76, NIH, Washington, 1970-71. Assoc. editor U. So. Calif. Sch. Medicine Info. Systems Research Program, 1984—; contbr. articles to profl. jours. Served with USAR, 1961-67. Mem. Am. Library Assn., Am. Soc. Info. Sci., Assn. Acad. Health Scis. Library Dirs. (bd. dirs. 1980-83), Med. Library Assn. (bd. dirs. 1977-79), Spl. Library Assn. Democrat. Jewish. Avocation: gardening. Home: 615 22d St Santa Monica CA 90402 Office: U So Calif Norris Med Library 2003 Zonal Ave Los Angeles CA 90033

GILMAN, RICHARD CARLETON, college president; b. Cambridge, Mass., July 28, 1923; s. George Phillips Brooks and Karen Elise (Theller) G.; m. Lucille Young, Aug. 28, 1948 (dec. June 1978); children: Marsha, Bradley Morris, Brian Potter, Blair Tucker; m. Sarah Gale, Dec. 28, 1984 (dec. 1986). B.A., Dartmouth, 1944; student, New Coll., U. London, Eng., 1947-48; Ph.D. (Borden Parker Bowne fellow philosophy), Boston U., 1952, L.H.D., 1969; LL.D., Pomona Coll., 1966, U. So. Calif., 1968, Coll. Idaho, 1968; L.H.D., Chapman Coll., 1984. Teaching fellow religion Dartmouth, 1948; mem. faculty Colby Coll., 1950-56, assoc. prof. philosophy, 1955-56; exec. dir. Nat. Council Religion Higher Edn., New Haven, 1956-60; dean coll., prof. philosophy Carleton Coll., 1960-65; pres. Occidental Coll., 1965—; bd. dirs. Ind. Colls. So. Calif., pres., 1983-84; bd. dirs. Assn. Ind. Calif. Colls. and Univs., Los Angeles World Affairs Council; mem. Intergovtl. Adv. Council on Edn., 1980-82; mem. policy planning commn. Nat. Assn. Ind. Colls. and Univs.; past bd. dirs. Am. Council Edn., Assn. Am. Colls., Nat. Council Ind. Colls. and Univs., Council Fin. Aid to Edn., Council on Post-secondary Edn., Ind. Coll. Funds Am., Calif. Mus. Found., Westridge Sch.; mem. Exec. Service Corps So. Calif., Cape of Good Hope Found., mem. pres.' commn. NCAA; past bd. dirs. Assn. Governing Bds., mem. council of pres.'. Served with USNR, 1944-46. Fellow Soc. Values in Higher Edn.; mem. Newcomen Soc., Calif. C. of C. (dir.), Phi Beta Kappa. Clubs: Univ. (N.Y.C.); Calif. (Los Angeles). Home: 1852 Campus Rd Los Angeles CA 90041

GILMER, MARY GRACE, speech pathologist; b. La Grange, Ill., Aug. 14, 1960; d. Paul Joseph and Lorraine Blanch (Stolzer) Schlesinger; m. Robert Louis Gilmer, Dec. 29, 1981. BA, Calif. State U., Northridge, 1983, MA, 1984. Lic. bd. med. quality assurance; cert. clin. competence Am. Spl. Hearing Assn. Intern in speech pathology Cedars-Sinai, Los Angeles, 1983; assoc. tchr. Stagg St. Elem. Sch., Los Angeles, 1984, Miller High Sch., Los Angeles, 1984; speech pathologist Villa Serena, Long Beach, Calif., 1984-85, Bernard Landes PhD. Assocs., Long Beach, 1985—. Mem. Calif. Speech-Lang.-Hearing Assn., Am. Speech-Lang.-Hearing Assn. Republican. Roman Catholic. Avocations: piano, golf. Home: 356 E Yale Loop Irvine CA 92714 Office: 1240 W La Habra Blvd La Habra CA 90631

GILMORE, LARRY ALLAN, software engineer; b. Colorado Springs, Colo., Mar. 10, 1937; s. Oliver Franklin and Mable Alice (Archibald) G.; m. Lois Ruth Bleier, Nov. 21, 1965 (div. Feb. 1978); children: Jonathan Allan, Catherine Ruth; m. Victoria Emily Warlop, Apr. 1978. BSEE, West Coast U., 1968, MS in Systems Engring., 1970, MS in Computer Sci., 1974. Mem. tech. staff The Marquardt Co., Van Nuys, Calif., 1963-70; sr. mem. tech. staff Xerox Corp., El Segundo, Calif., 1970-75; mem. tech. staff Ball Aerospace, Gardena, Calif., 1975-79; sect. head TRW, Redondo Beach, Calif., 1979—. Served with U.S. Army, 1960-63. Republican. Home: 21210 Broadwell Torrance CA 90502 Office: TRW 1 Space Park MS M5/1216 Redondo Beach CA 90278

GILMORE, SUSAN ASTRID LYTLE, speech and language pathologist; b. Phila., July 12, 1942; d. Ford Bertrand and Astrid Elizabeth (Hammerstrom) Lytle; m. Stuart Irby Gilmore, June 6, 1970 (div. Dec. 1981); 1 child, Ford Lytle. BA, U. Pacific, 1964, MA, 1965; PhD, Ohio U., 1968. Cert. pub. sch. adminstr., elem. tchr., speech-lang. pathologist, Calif. Asst. prof. spl. edn., speech-lang. pathology La. State U., Baton Rouge, 1968-76, assoc. prof., 1976-79; supr. spl. edn. Sacramento City Unified Sch. Dist., 1979—; cons. State Dept Health, Baton Rouge, 1970-75, State Dept. Hosps., Baton Rouge, 1973-75; instr. U. Pacific, Stockton, Calif., 1979, ind. examiner Sacramento City Unified Sch. Dist., 1979. Editor: (asst.) Lang., Speech and Hearing Services in Schs., 1983—; contbr. articles to profl. jours. Vestry mem. Trinity Episcopal Cathedral Ch., Sacramento, 1983-85, altar guild mem. 1980—; bd. dirs. Friends of People With Chronic Mental Illness, Sacramento, 1983-85. Mem. Assn. Calif. Sch. Adminstrs., Am. Speech-Lang.-Hearing Assn., Calif. Speech-Lang.-Hearing Assn. (cert. of appreciations 1985—), Council for Exceptional Children (sec.), Am. Assn. Mental Deficiency, Kappa Alpha Theta (pres. 1961-62), Phi Delta Kappa. Republican. Avocations: crossword puzzles, walking, photography. Home: 6333 Driftwood St Sacramento CA 95831 Office: Sacramento City Unified Sch Dist 1901 60th Ave Sacramento CA 95822

GILMORE, TIMOTHY JONATHAN, foundation executive officer; b. Orange, Calif., June 24, 1949; s. James and Margaret (Swanson) G.; m. Blanche Jean Panter, Sept. 3, 1984; 1 child, Erin. BA, St. Mary's Coll., Moraga, Calif., 1971. Adminstrv. asst. Gov. Ronald Reagan, Sacramento, Calif., 1971-73; salesman Penn Mutual, Anaheim, Calif., 1973-76; asst. devel. dir. St. Mary's Coll., Moraga, 1976-81; devel. dir. St. Alphonsus Hosp., Boise, Idaho, 1981-83; adminstr. Blaine County Hosp., Hailey, Idaho, 1983-86; exec. dir. Poudre Hosp. Found., Ft. Collins, Colo., 1986—. Mem. Nat. Assn. Hosp. Devel. Republican. Roman Catholic. Lodge: Kiwanis (pres. Moraga club 1980-81, sec. Boise club 1982-83). Avocation: fishing. Home: 2200 W Elizabeth St Fort Collins CO 80521 Office: Poudre Hosp Found 1024 Lemay Fort Collins CO 80524

GILPATRIC, (PATRICIA ANNE) TRISH, marketing professional; b. Casper, Wyo., July 13, 1945; d. Warren James and Nella Marie (Hammack) Ullery; m. Royce Edward Gilpatric, Aug. 31, 1968; children: Royce Edward II, Eric Wynn, Michael Thomas. AA summa cum laude, Oakland Community Coll., 1978; student, Oakland U., 1978-79, Regis Coll., 1981-82. With Continental Oil Co., Casper and Denver, 1963-67, Chrysler Corp., Denver, 1967-68; editor The Cider Press, Auburn Hills, Mich., 1976-79; dir. pub. relations Oakland County Youth Assistance, Auburn Hills, 1977-79; div. editor Richardson-Vick Inc., Phila., 1979-81; corp. editor Van Schaack & Co., Denver, 1981-82; dir. mktg. Rocky Mountain Region Flack & Kurtz, Denver, 1982-87; dir. mktg. Western Region M.D. Mortenson Co., Lakewood, Colo., 1987—. Freelance reporter The Oakland Press, Pontiac, Mich., 1979; editor: (newspaper) Van Schaack Talk, 1982, (newsletter) Update, 1985. Mem. C. of C. Mil. Affairs Com., Denver, 1985—, Lower Downtown Task Force Denver Comprehensive Plan, 1985—; bd. dirs. Urban Design Forum, Denver, 1985-87. Recipient Merit for Outstanding Bus. Communications award Internat. Assn. Bus. Communicators, 1982. Mem. Soc. Mktg. Profl. Services (mem. nat. editorial bd. 1985—; named Mktg. Profl. of Yr., Rocky Mountain chpt. 1986, Leonardo award 1985, 86), Nat. Assn. Indsl. and Office Parks (sec. 1986—), Pub. Relations Soc. Am. (gold pick com.), Nat. Assn. Corp. Real Estate Execs. (membership com. 1984—), Bldg. Owners and Mgrs. Assn. (Outstanding Allied Mem. of Yr. 1986-87). Republican. Methodist. Club: City Club of Denver (bd. dirs. 1985—). Avocations: piano, bicycling, jogging, gardening. Home: 7536 W Ottawa Pl Littleton CO 80123 Office: MD Mortenson Co 143 Union Blvd Lakewood CO 80228

GILPIN, GARY (DAYNE), engineering and architectural company executive, mayor; b. Grand Island, Nebr., Jan. 30, 1939; s. Oral D. and Lilliam (Williams) G.; m. Mary Lou Johnson, July 19, 1964; children: Michelle D., Nicole D., Noelle D., Gina D. BArch, U. Nebr., 1963. Registered architect, Colo., Wyo., N.Mex.; cert. Nat. Council Archtl. Registration Bds. Mgr. Geo. E. Clayton & Assoc., Brighton, Colo., 1969-74; ptnr. Geo. E. Clayton & Assoc., Brighton, 1974-79; mktg. rep. Greiner Engring., Denver, 1979-81, v.p., dir. architecture, 1981-84, v.p., project dir., 1984-85, v.p., mgr. Denver office, 1985—. Mem. Planning and Zoning Com., City of Brighton, 1974-77, Adams County Bd. Adjustments, 1987—; councilman City of Brighton, 1974-86; mayor pro tem City of Brighton, 1976-82; mayor City of Brighton, 1982-86. Recipient Jaycee Internat. Senatorship award, 1973; named Outstanding Citizen of Yr., Brighton C. of C., 1976, Boss of Yr., Brighton Jaycees, 1977, Boss of Yr., Brighton High Sch. Future Bus. Leaders of Am., 1974. Mem. AIA, Brighton Jaycees (pres. 1972-73), Colo. Jaycees (dist. v.p. 1973-74). Democrat. Presbyterian. Lodge: Eagles. Avocations: fishing, hunting, tennis, pen and ink sketching, carpentry. Office: Greiner Engring Scis Inc 570 W 44th Ave Denver CO 80216

GIMA, JOE MARTIN, electronic technician, real estate consultant; b. Naha, Japan, Apr. 15, 1949; came to U.S., 1969; s. Leo E. and Maria (Gima) Martin. AS in Electronics, Monterey Peninsula Coll., 1973. Radar/computer tech. RCA Corp. USAF Early Warning Radar Sta., Alaska, 1978-79; electronic technician civil service Naval Weapon Ctr. Civil Service, China Lake, Calif., 1980—. Served with U.S. Army, 1973-76. Mem. FCC (lic.). Home: 532 Garis Ridgecrest CA 93555 Office: Naval Weapon Ctr Code 3525 China Lake CA 93555

GIMA, STANLEY SHINKI, architect; b. Kahului, Hawaii, Feb. 17, 1934; s. Shinyu and Ushi (Kakinohana) G.; m. Sally S. Katena, July 22, 1961; children: Stephen, Charlene, Cheryl. BS in Chem. Engring., Colo. Sch. of Mines, 1957; BArch, Calif. Poly. U., 1964. Registered architect, Hawaii, Calif. Deputy planning dir. County of Maui, Wailuku, Hawaii, 1969-70; assoc. Architects Hawaii, Ltd., Wailuku, Hawaii, 1970-73, ptnr., 1973-84; pres. Gima, Yoshimori and Assocs., AIA, Inc., Wailuku, Hawaii, 1984—; past pres. Urban Design Rev. Bd., Maui County, 1978-84. Bd. dirs. Boy Scouts of Am., 1976—, Maui Philharm. Soc., 1973-80. Mem. AIA (pres. Maui sect., 1976), Planners, Architects and Landscape Architects of Maui (pres. 1974), C. of C. (bd. dirs. 1979-81). Buddhist. Club: Pukalani Golf (Hawaii) (pres. 1978). Lodge: Rotary (pres. 1974-75). Avocations: golf, art, music. Office: Gima Yoshimori and Assocs Inc 2145 Wells St Suite 303 Wailuku HI 96793

GIMBEL, GILBERT WILLIAM, accountant, lawyer; b. Hazelton, N.D., Oct. 28, 1937; s. Milbert Walter and Myrtle May (Beseler) G.; student Jamestown Coll., 1955-57; B.S. in Bus. Adminstrn. magna cum laude, U. N.D., 1959, LL.B., 1962; m. Lynda Marie Holdren, May 19, 1979; children—John William, Robert Karl, LaVone Alice. Auditor, GAO, Washington, 1961; instr. U. Nebr., 1962-63; admitted to N.D. bar, 1962, Oreg. bar, 1975; pvt. practice pub. accounting, Omaha, 1964-65, Corvallis, Oreg., 1966-69, Hillsboro, Oreg., 1969—; C.P.A., Oreg. Mem. Hillsboro C. of C. Oreg. Soc. C.P.A.s, Oreg. State Bar, Phi Delta Phi, Sigma Nu, Beta Gamma Sigma (award 1959), Beta Alpha Psi. Republican. Lutheran. Rotarian. Author: (with Glen A. Mumey) An Analysis of North Dakota Trust Funds, 1960. Home: 532 NE Birchwood Terr Hillsboro OR 97123 Office: 238 SE 2d Ave Hillsboro OR 97123

GINN, SANDRA LUENN, audiologist; b. Slayton, Minn., Apr. 16, 1959; d. Chester and Idalia (Pacheco) G. BS, Mankato State U., 1982; MA, U. S.D., 1983. Cert. clin. competence audiology; lic. hearing aid dispenser, Wash. Audiology supr. Siouxland Easter Seal Soc., Sioux City, Iowa, 1984-85; dir. clin. audiology Hearing Healthcare Ctr., Seattle, 1985—. Mem. Am. Speech-Lang.-Hearing Assn. Avocations: photography, golf, scuba diving, skiing, piano. Home: 10923 SE 255th Pl #L-101 Kent WA 98031 Office: Hearing Healthcare Ctr PS 1023 SW 136th Seattle WA 98166

GINSBERG, BERNARD LAWRENCE, medical marketing and management company executive; b. Albany, N.Y., May 9, 1946; s. Nathan David and Sylvia Dorothy (Schwartz) G. B.S., Southern Ill. U., 1970; M.A., Wayne State U., 1974; M.P.A., U. So. Calif., Los Angeles, 1981. Pres., Speech, Hearing Ctr., Hollywood, Fla., 1974-79; dir. audiology Centinela Hosp. Med. Ctr., Inglewood, Calif., 1979-80; chief exec. officer Norwalk Community Hosp., Calif., 1982-83, Chalmette Gen. Hosp., New Orleans, 1984-85; assoc. exec. dir. Doctors Hosp. Santa Ana, Calif., 1983-84; pres., owner M3 Med. Mktg. & Mgmt. Co., Los Angeles, 1985—. Cons. Health Adv. Com., 1982-83; bd. govs. Fedn. Am. Hosp. Adv., 1984—. Mem. Am. Coll. Hosp. Adminstrs., Am. Speech and Hearing Assn., U. So. Calif. Alumni Assn. Republican. Lodges: Lions, Kiwanis, B'Nai B'Rith. Avocations: piano; jogging; baseball; racquetball; coin and stamp collecting. Home: 1018 Pacific St Apt A Santa Monica CA 90405 Office: M3 Med Mktg & Mgmt Co 12304 Santa Monica Blvd Suite 30 0 West Los Angeles CA 90025

GINZTON, EDWARD LEONARD, engineering corporation executive; b. Dnepropetrovsk, Ukraine, Dec. 27, 1915; came to U.S., 1929; s. Leonard Louis and Natalie P. (Philipova) G.; m. Artemas A. McCann; children: Anne, Leonard, Nancy, David. BS, U. Calif., 1936, MS, 1937; EE, Stanford U., 1938, PhD, 1940. Research engr. Sperry Gyroscope Co., N.Y.C., 1940-46; asst. prof. applied physics and elec. engring. Stanford U., 1946-47, assoc. prof., 1947-50, prof., 1951-68; dir. Microwave Lab., 1949-59; with Varian Assocs., Palo Alto, Calif., 1948—, chmn. bd. dirs., 1959-84, chief exec. officer, 1959-72, pres., 1964-68, chmn. exec. com., 1984—, also bd. dirs.; dir. project M Stanford Linear Accelerator Ctr., 1957-60; mem. commn. 1 U.S. nat. com. Internat. Sci. Radio Union, 1958-68; mem. Lawrence Berkeley Lab. Sci. and Adv. Com., 1972-79; chmn. adv. bd. Sch. Engring., Stanford, 1968-70; bd. dirs., mem. exec. com. co-chmn. Stanford Mid-Peninsula Urban Coalition, 1968-72; bd. dirs. Nat. Bur. Econ. Research, 1981—; mem. com. on animal research NRC; mem. Stanford Synchrotron Radiation Lab. Sci. Policy Bd., 1985—. Author: Microwave Measurements, 1957; contbr. articles to tech. jours. Bd. dirs. Mid-Peninsula Housing Devel. Corp., 1970—, Stanford Hosp., 1975-80; trustee Stanford U., 1977-86. Recipient Morris Liebmann Meml. prize I.R.E., 1958, Calif. Manufacturer of Yr. award, 1974. Fellow IEEE (bd. dirs. 1971-72, chmn. awards bd. 1971-72, medal of Honor 1969); mem. Nat. Acad. Scis. (chmn. com. on motor vehicle emissions 1971-74, co-chmn. com. nuclear energy study 1975-80, com. on sci. and nat. security 1982-84, com. on use of lab. animals in biomed. and behavioral research 1985—), Am. Acad. Arts and Scis. (mem. exec. com. Western Ctr. 1985—), Nat. Acad. Engring. (mem. council 1974-80), Sigma Xi, Eta Kappa Nu, Tau Beta Pi. Patentee in field. Home: 28014 Natoma Rd Los Altos Hills CA 94022 Office: Varian Assocs 611 Hansen Way Palo Alto CA 94303

GINZTON, LEONARD EDWARD, cardiologist, educator; b. Mineola, Y.Y., Oct. 2, 1953; s. Edward Leonard and Artemas Alma (McCann) G.; m. Cheryl Lynn Mathe, June 20, 1964; 1 child, Katherine. AB, Stanford U., 1965; MD, U. So. Calif., 1969. Diplomate Am. Bd. Internal Medicine, Cardiovascular Diseases. Intern in internal medicine Los Angeles County U. So. Calif. Med. Ctr., 1969-70, resident in internal medicine, 1970-73; practice medicine specializing in internal medicine Watsonville, Calif., 1973-78; dir. noninvasive cardiology Harbor UCLA Med. Ctr., Torrance, 1980—. Editorial cons. Chest, 1983—, Am. Jour. Cardiology, 1984—, Archives of Internal Medicine, 1986—; contbr. articles to profl. jours. Fellow Am. Heart Assn., 1979, UCLA Med. Ctr., 1978-80. Fellow Am. Coll. Cardiology; mem. Am. Soc. Echocardiography, Am. Inst. Ultrasound, Am. Fedn. Clin. Research, Los Angeles Soc. Echocardiography (pres. 1984-85). Democrat. Avocations: horseback riding, bicycling, photography, sailing, gardening. Home: 5042 Hook Tree Rd La Canada-Flintridge CA 91011 Office: Harbor UCLA Med Ctr 1000 W Carson St Torrance CA 90509

GIOMI, THELMA ANNE, clinical psychologist; b. Albuquerque, Feb. 26, 1947; s. James E. and Esma Anne (Snyder) G. BA cum laude, U. N.Mex., 1969, MA, 1972, PhD, 1974. Diplomate Am. Bd. Psychotherapy. Psychometrician Albuquerque Pub. Schs., 1969-70; intern Pitts. Child Guidance, 1974-75; clin. psychologist U. N.Mex., Albuquerque, 1975-81; pvt. practice clin. psychologist Albuquerque, 1981—; dir. Psychology Internship Program, U. N.Mex., 1979-81; adj. asst. prof. psychology, U. N.Mex., 1980, clin. assoc. Nat. Sci. Found. grantee, 1968. Mem. AAAS, Am. Psychol. Assn., N.Mex. Psychol. Assn., Nat. Register of Health Care Providers, Southwest Writers Workshop, Albuquerque Conservation Assn., Phi Beta Kappa, Phi Kappa Phi. Club: Rio Grande Writers Assn. (Albuquerque). Avocations: photography, gourmet cooking, herbalism. Office: 406 San Mateo Blvd NE Suite 8B Albuquerque NM 87110

GIORDANO, PAUL JOSEPH, financial planner; b. Rome, Sept. 25, 1955; came to U.S., 1955; s. Modesto Felix and Giovanna (Morelli) G. BA in Bus. Law, U. Calif., Berkeley, 1978; postgrad., Golden Gate U., 1978—. Cert. fin. planner. Fin. analyst Inst. Econ. Analysis, San Francisco, 1977-79; 1st v.p. mktg. Am. Software Corp., San Rafael, Calif., 1979-82; mgr. mktg. SimuCad, Incline Village, Nev., 1982-85; fin. planner Waddell & Reed, San Jose, 1985—. Contbr. articles to profl. jour. Vol. Spl. Olympics, Incline Village, 1984, United Way, Incline Village, 1984. Mem. Nat. Speaker Assn., Incline Village C. of C., Cadillac/Lasalle Club, Alfa Romeo Owners Club, Ferrari Owners Club, Phi Kappa Phi (named alumnus of yr. 1980). Lodge: Rotary. Home: 1505 Fairway Dr Los Altos CA 94022 Office: Waddell & Reed 1150 N First San Jose CA 89450

GIPSTEIN, ROBERT MALCOLM, physician; b. Springfield, Mass., Mar. 29, 1936; s. Benjamin Louis and Dorothy (Weitzman) G.; 1 child, Jason Harold. BA, Wesleyan U., 1957; MD, Tufts U., 1961. Diplomate Am. Bd. Internal Medicine, Am. Bd. Nephrology. Research assoc. U. N.C., 1965-66; clin. assoc. UCLA Med. Ctr., 1964-65, clin. instr. medicine, 1968-75, asst. clin. prof., 1975-83, assoc. clin. prof., 1983—; dir. hemodial unit St. John's Hosp., Santa Monica, Calif., 1976-78; chief nephrology Santa Monica Hosp., 1975-82, dir. plasmapheresis unit, 1980-87, dir. hemodialysis unit, 1978—, chief dept. medicine, 1987—; also mem. exec. bd.; cons. plasmapheresis Wadsworth VA, Los Angeles, 1982. Contbr. articles to med. jours. Served to capt. M.C., U.S. Army, 1966-68. Nat. Kidney Found. grantee, 1980. Fellow ACP; mem. AMA, AAAS, Calif. Med. Assn., Los Angeles County Med. Assn., Am. Soc. Nephrology, Internat. Soc. Nephrology, Am. Soc. Internal Medicine. Office: Pacific Med and Nephrology 11860 Wilshire Blvd Los Angeles CA 90025

GIRARDEAU, MARVIN DENHAM, physics educator; b. Lakewood, Ohio, Oct. 3, 1930; s. Marvin Denham and Maude Irene (Miller) G.; m. Susan Jessica Brown, June 30, 1956; children—Ellen, Catherine, Laura. B.S., Case Inst. Tech., 1952; M.S., U. Ill., 1954; Ph.D., Syracuse U., 1958. NSF postdoctoral fellow Inst. Advanced Study, Princeton, 1958-59; research assoc. Brandeis U., 1959-60; staff mem. Boeing Sci. Research Labs., 1960-61; research assoc. Enrico Fermi Inst. Nuclear Studies, U. Chgo., 1961-63; assoc. prof. physics, research asso. Inst. Theoretical Sci., U. Oreg., Eugene, 1963-67; prof. physics, research assoc. Inst. Theoretical Sci., U. Oreg., 1967—, dir., 1967-69, chmn. dept. physics, 1974-76. Contbr. articles to profl. jours. Recipient Humboldt Sr. U.S. Scientist award, 1984-85. NSF research grantee, 1965-79; ONR research grantee, 1981—. Fellow Am. Phys. Soc.; mem. AAUP. Research on quantum-mech. many-body problems, statis. mechanics, atomic, molecular and chemical physics. Home: 2398 Douglas Dr Eugene OR 97405 Office: Dept Physics U Oreg Eugene OR 97403

GIRARDI, LAURENCE LEONARD, graphic designer; b. Sewickly, Pa., Sept. 23, 1953; s. Leonard and Annabella Helen (Yurcak) G.; m. Carol Lyn Hernandez, Aug. 1986. A.A., Los Angeles Pierce Coll., 1975. Art dir. Wine World Mag., Van Nuys, Calif., 1975-76, La Rose Graphics, Van Nuys, 1976-77; pres. Girardi Design, Canoga Park, Calif., 1977-78, Grafica, Woodland Hills, Calif., 1978—; design cons. Fiberworks, Center for Textile Arts, Berkeley, Calif., 1981—. Bd. dirs. Monte Nido Valley Property Owners Assn., 1987 (corresponding sec.). Recipient Community Recognition award Los Angeles Pierce Coll., 1980. Mem. Nat. Fedn. Ind. Bus., Graphic Artists Guild, Alpha Gamma Sigma. Republican. Roman Catholic. Office: 7529 Remmet Ave Canoga Park CA 91303

GIRAUDI, GARY STEPHEN, school system administrator; b. Porterville, Calif., July 19, 1942; s. Stephen Vincent and Katherine (Della) G.; m. Karlin Sue Johnson, May 2, 1964; children: Michelle Ruth, Lisa Karlin. BA, Calif. State U., Fresno, 1976; MA, Calif. State U., Bakersfield, 1980. Tng. officer Bank Am., San Francisco, 1964-72; prin. Saucelito Sch. Dist., Terra Bella, Calif., 1976-80; supt. Columbine Sch. Dist., Delano, Calif., 1980—. Dir. Sequoia Youth Football Assn., Porterville, 1978-82. Named Outstanding Dir., Sequoia Youth Football Assn., 1980; recipient Outstanding Supporter award Sequoia Youth Football Cheerleaders, 1979. Mem. Calif. Sch. Bds. Assn. Republican. Roman Catholic. Lodges: K.C. (Grand Knight 1983-85, award 1986, named Man of Yr. 1985), Sons of Italy. Avocations: traveling, gardening. Home: 23508 Ave 178 Porterville CA 93257 Office: Columbine Sch Dist 2240 Rd 160 Delano CA 93215

GIRAULT, LAWRENCE JOSEPH, aircraft engineer; b. Washington, Aug. 27, 1915; s. Alexandre Arsene and Elizabeth Jeanette (Pilcher) G.; m. Lenora Josephine Keahey, Jan. 19, 1946 (dec. 1981); m. 2d, Lois Ione Rasmussen, Aug. 5, 1984. Ground engr. Q.A.N.T.A.S., Brisbane, Queensland, Australia, 1932-41; engrng. test operator Commonwealth Aircraft, Port Melbourne, Australia, 1941-42; aircraft insp. Douglas Aircraft Corp., Park Ridge, Ill., 1944; design engr. Belmont Radio Corp., Chgo., 1944-45; engr.-in-charge liaison engrng. dept. Aeronca Aircraft Corp., Middletown, Ohio, 1945-46; designer Waco Aircraft Corp., Troy, Ohio, 1946; self-employed airplane and power plant mechanic, Williams, Calif., 1946-47; asst. mech. engr. Phelps Dodge Corp., Ajo, Ariz., 1947-48; designer Fairchild Aircraft Corp., Hagerstown, Md., 1948-50; lead designer Chance Vought Aircraft Corp., Dallas, 1950-60; lead designer The Boeing Co., Renton, Wash., 1960-63, sr. engr., 1967-71; mem. staff N.Mex. State U., Las Cruces, 1963-67, 84-86, VOH, INc., 1986-87; self-employed gen. aviation aircraft mechanics insp., Las Cruces, 1971—; broker O'Donnell Realty, Las Cruces, 1971-83; owner, founder Shoestring Airport Realty, 1983-87. Served with USAAF, 1942-44. Lic. ground engr., Australia; lic. pilot; real estate broker, N.Mex.; lic. aircraft mechanic. Mem. U.S. Naval Inst., Aircraft Owners and Pilots Assn. Adventist. Inventor main landing gear uplock, outer panel-wing and wing fold prototype, other inventions in field of aircraft mechanics. Home: Courtney Rd PO Box 666 Bingen WA 98605

GIRON, EDWARD DAVID, health care management executive; b. Los Angeles, July 28, 1955; s. John F. and Carol Marian (Bliss) G.; m. Linda R. Hebrank, Jan. 13, 1979. V.p. Staff Builders Inc., N.Y.C., 1976-81, Superior Care Inc., Great Neck, N.Y., 1982-86; chief operating officer Superior Care of Calif. Inc., Hawthorne, 1983-86; chief exec. officer Med-Eval Services, Inc., Sherman Oaks, Calif., 1986—; pres., cons. diagnostic radiology Magnetic Resonance Imaging Ctrs., 1986—; lectr. med. seminars, 1986—; sec. bd. dirs. Indsl. Med. Specialists Inc., Los Angeles, Lawndale (Calif.) Pharmacy; cons. Nursing Care at Home, Los Angeles, 1985—; mgmt. cons. Assn. Med. Group Specialists, Hawthorne, 1982—. Mem. Calif. Applicants Attys. Assn., Calif. Soc. Indsl. Medicine and Surgery, Am. Hosp. Assn. Democrat. Lutheran. Office: Med-Eval Services Inc 4910 Van Nuys Blvd Sherman Oaks CA 91403

GIRTCH, CLARENCE MARVIN, municipal official; b. White City, Kans., May 28, 1933; s. Clarence Joshua and Beulah Norma (Edwards) G.; m. Margaret S. Stansfield, Aug. 21, 1955; children—Charles Andrew, Jon Michael. B.S., U. Ill., 1956, M.S., 1957; postgrad. U. Calif.-San Francisco, 1960-62; Ed.D. in Exec. Devel., Ind. U., 1971. Registered recreator, cert. in adminstrn., Calif. Bd. Parks and Recreation Personnel. With Ford Found. Interagy. Project, City of Oakland (Calif.), 1959-62; recreation coordinator, assoc. dean of students U. Calif.-Santa Barbara, 1962-68; dep. dir. Indpls. Dept. Parks and Recreation, 1968-69, chief adminstrv. officer, 1969-75; dep. supt. Seattle Dept. Parks and Recreation, 1975-77, chief operating officer, 1975—; adj. prof. Cen. Wash. U. Bd. regents Pacific N.W. Maintenance Mgmt. Sch., 1976-8, Pacific Revenue Sources Mgmt. Sch., 1984—; pres. bd. trustees Univ. Unitarian Ch. of Seattle, Camp Conestoga, Inc., 1964—; mem. planning commn. Seattle Sch. Dist., 1979-81. Served with AUS, 1957-59. Named Profl. of Yr., Ind. Parks and Recreation Assn., 1973. Mem. Ind. Parks and Recreation Assn. (pres. 1974-75), Nat. Recreation and Park Assn. (council Gt. Lakes Dist. 1974-75), Nat. Sports Governing Bd., Am. Park and Recreation Soc. Club: Evergreen Aqua (v.p., dir.). Author series of monographs; contbr. numerous articles to profl. jours. Office: 210 Municipal Bldg 600 4th Ave Seattle WA 98104

GISH, DUANE TOLBERT, research facility administrator; b. White City, Kans., Feb. 17, 1921; s. Tolbert Charles and Mattie (Brittain) G.; m. Lorraine Jeanette Gibson, June 15, 1946; children: Sandra Rae Gish Slaughter, Duane Randolph, Darrell Gregory, Laurie Jean. BS, UCLA, 1949; PhD, U. Calif., Berkeley, 1953. Eli Lilly postdoctoral fellow Cornell U. Med. Coll., N.Y.C., 1953-55, asst. prof. biochemistry, 1955-56; asst. research assoc. Virus Lab. U. Calif., Berkeley, 1956-60; research assoc. The Upjohn Co., Kalamazoo, Mich., 1960-71; v.p. Inst. Creation Research, El Cajon, Calif., 1971—. Author: Evolution—The Fossils Say NO!, 1972, Dinosaurs—Those Terrible Lizards, 1975, Evolution—The Challenge of the Fossil Record, 1985; co-author: Manipulating Life, 1981; also articles. Served to capt. U.S. Army, 1940-46, PTO. Mem. Am. Chem. Soc., Creation Research Soc. (exec. bd. 1963—), Phi Beta Kappa, Phi Lambda Upsilon. Republican. Baptist. Avocations: golf. Home: 4300 Summit Dr La Mesa CA 92041 Office: Inst Creation Research 10946 Woodside Ave N Santee CA 92071

GITZ, MITCHELL, business executive; b. Phila., Mar. 16, 1946; s. Irving and Isabel (Fienman) G.; m. Virginia Ann Sublett, Nov. 21, 1981; children—Michael, Robert. A.S. in Elec. Engring., Philco Tech. Inst., 1966; B.A. in Bus. Adminstrn., Nat. U., 1976, M.B.A., 1978. Field engr. Burroughs Corp., Paoli, Pa., 1966-67; electronic warfare repairman U.S. Air Force, 1967-71; field engr. Raytheon Service Co., Burlington, Mass., 1971-72; equal opportunity officer U.S. Navy, San Diego, 1972-82; owner/mgr. Gitz Electronics, 1975-84; dist. mgr. Starcom Enterprise, San Diego, 1984—; pres. Fed. EEO Council San Diego County, 1981-83. Treas. Cub Scout Pack 1210, Boy Scouts Am., 1978—, scout leader, 1980-83; Sunday sch. tchr. St. James By-the-Sea Episcopal Ch.; bd. dirs. Pacific Chamber Opera.; chmn. sch. improvement com. Walker Sch., San Diego, 1981-83. Served with USAF, 1967-71; Vietnam. Mem. Federally Employed Women, Assn. Retarded Citizens San Diego. Club: Toastmasters. Home: 8628 Perseus Rd San Diego CA 92126 Office: Exec Ctr Suite A 9560 Black Mountain Rd San Diego CA 92126

GIUDICI, JIM CARL, lawyer; b. Weaverville, Calif., Aug. 6, 1952; s. Silvio and Catherine Giudici. BA, Gonzaga U., 1974; JD, Gonzaga Sch. Law, 1979. Bar: Nev. 1979, U.S. Dist. Ct. Nev. 1980, U.S. Ct. Appeals (9th cir.) 1982, U.S. Supreme Ct. 1983. Judicial law clk. U.S. Dist. Ct., Las Vegas, Nev., 1979-81; dep. atty. gen. gaming div. Nev. Atty. Gen.'s Office, Carson City, Nev., 1981—. Contbr. articles to law revs. Scholar Sons of Italy, 1970, John Ascuaga U. Nev., 1970. Mem. ABA, Nat. Assn. Gaming Atty.'s. Roman Catholic. Avocations: snow skiing, trout fishing, duck hunting. Home: 500 W Graves Apt Y-398 Carson City NV 89701 Office: Atty Gen's Office 1150 E Williams Carson City NV 89710

GIULIANELLI, JAMES LOUIS, chemist, educator; b. Beverly, Mass., Aug. 7, 1940; s. Guerino Louis and Janet (Cormier) G.; m. Elisabeth Ann Hansen, Aug. 26, 1966; children: Karma, Derek. BS, U. Mass., 1962; PhD, U. Wis., 1969. Robert Welch fellow U. Tex., 1969-71; asst. prof. chemistry U. Los Andes, Merida, Venezuela, 1971-77, Colo. Sch. Mines, Golden, 1977-85; assoc. prof. chemistry Regis Coll., Denver, 1985—. Contbr. articles to profl. jours. Rep. Youth Exchange Service, Los Angeles, 1985—. Dept. Energy Am. Soc. Engring. Edn. research grantee Jet Propulsion Lab., Pasadena, Calif., 1980, 81. Mem. Am. Chem. Soc. Avocations: skiing, tennis, golf. Home: 2193 Creighton Dr Golden CO 80401 Office: Regis Coll Dept Chemistry W 50th and Lowell Blvd Denver CO 80221

GIVENS, JEANETTE MARLENE, corporate professional; b. St. Joseph, Mich., Feb. 22, 1948; d. Anthony and Ida Mary (Sarao) Mansueto; m. Bart Joel Givens, Feb. 16, 1985. BA, St. Louis U., 1970. Dept. mgr. Howard Life Ins., Lakewood, Colo., 1971-76, office mgr., 1976-82, corp. sec., 1981-86, v.p. adminstrn., sec., 1986—. Bd. dirs. Fla. Park Homeowners Assn., Lakewood, 1981-83; bd. govs., Lakewood on Parade, 1979—, bd. dirs., 1984—, sr. v.p., 1977—, pres., 1984—. Named Lakewood Woman of Yr., Lakewood Sentinel newspaper, 1983. Mem. Lakewood C. of C. (bd. dirs. 1983-84, bus. fair task force 1985—). Office: Howard Life Ins Co 12265 W Bayaud Ave Lakewood CO 80228

GIVENS, MICHAEL ROY, development company executive, researcher; b. Munich, W.Ger., Mar. 16, 1958 (parents Am. citizens); came to U.S., 1966; s. Roy Eugene and Gertraud Maria (Altenried) G. B.B.A., Pacific Lutheran U., 1983. Asst. Tacoma Country and Golf Club, 1978-83; project mgr. Hemisphere N.W. Inc., Tacoma, 1983—. Mem. Am. Mktg. Assn., Sanford C. of C., Seminole County C. of C. Republican. Roman Catholic. Home: 14200 SE 63rd St Bellevue WA 98006 Office: Hemisphere NW Inc 1775 12th NW Suite 109 Issaquah WA 98027

GIVI, PEYMAN, research scientist; b. Tehran, Iran, June 26, 1958; came to U.S., 1977; s. Ali and Aghdas (Gheblehgahi) G.; m. Suzanne Pellarin, July 2, 1983. BE, Youngstown State U., 1980; ME, Carnegie Mellon U., 1982, PhD, 1984. Research asst. Carnegie Mellon U., Pitts., 1980-84, teaching asst., 1984; research scientist Flow Research Inc., Kent, Wash., 1985—. Contbr. articles to profl. jours. Mem. ASME, AIAA Combustion Inst., Sigma Xi, Phi Kappa Phi, Tau Beta Pi. Avocations: guitar, football, softball. Home: 2630 S 256th St #1-205 Kent WA 98032 Office: Flow Research Co 21414 68th Ave S Kent WA 98032

GLAD, DAIN STURGIS, aerospace engineer; b. Santa Monica, Calif., Sept. 17, 1932; s. Alma Emanuel and Maude La Verne (Morby) G.; B.S. in Engring., U. Calif. at Los Angeles, 1954; M.S. in Elec. Engring., U. So. Calif., 1963. Registered profl. engr., Calif. m. Betty Alexandra Shainoff, Sept. 12, 1954 (dec. 1973); 1 dau., Dana Elizabeth; m. 2d, Carolyn Elizabeth Giffen, June 8, 1979. Electronic engr. Clary Corp., San Gabriel, Calif., 1957-58; with Aerojet Electro Systems Co., Azusa, Calif., 1958-72; with missile systems div. Rockwell Internat., Anaheim, Calif., 1973-75; with Aerojet Electrosystems, Azusa, 1975-84; with support systems div. Hughes Aircraft Co., 1984—. Contbr. articles to profl. jours. Served as ensign U.S. Navy, 1954-56; lt. j.g. Res., 1956-57. Mem. IEEE, Calif. Soc. Profl. Engrs., Soc. Info. Display. Home: 1701 Marengo Ave South Pasadena CA 91030 Office: Hughes Aircraft Co 1100 W Hollyvale St Azusa CA 91702

GLADISH, LEROY ELMER, publ. specialist; b. St. Paul, Mar. 15, 1924; s. John Joseph and Jeanette Emeline (Klug) G.; B.A. cum laude, U. Minn., 1957; m. Sharrell Joan Robertson, Feb. 2, 1960 (div., 1977). Account exec., copywriter Advt., Inc., Boulder, Colo., 1958-61; publ. specialist Western Interstate Commn. for Higher Edn., Boulder, 1961-76; exec. editor Colo. Quar., U. Colo., Boulder, 1977-80; editor, book coordinator Geol. Soc. Am., Boulder, 1980—; program cons. Boulder Civic Opera Assn.; promotion cons. Boulder Public Library Commn. Mayor, Gold Hill, Colo., 1962-63. Served with USN, 1942-48, 51-52. Recipient award of merit, Soc. Illustrators, 1979. Republican. Presbyterian. Home: 900 Hartford Dr Boulder CO 80303 Office: Geol Soc Am 3300 Penrose Pl Boulder CO 80301

GLASCOCK, RAY D., engineering services and furniture and equipment company executive; b. Auxausse, Mo., Apr. 1, 1922; s. Joseph Ewing and Mildred Hazel (Thomas) G.; m. Martha G. Greene, Nov. 18, 1977; children: Barbara Joan (Mrs. Jerry Bourland), Donald Ray. BS, U. Ill., 1949, MS, 1950. Group leader Norair div. Northrop Corp., Hawthorne, Calif., 1951-59; sect. leader communications div. Hughes Aircraft Co., Los Angeles, 1959-63; sect. head aeronutronic div. Philco Ford Corp., Newport Beach, Calif., 1964-65; owner, mgr. Engring. Corp. of Am.-Orange County, Anaheim, Calif., 1966—; owner Glascock Enterprises, Anaheim, 1976—. Served with U.S. Maritime Service, 1943-46. Mem. IEEE, Eta Kappa Nu. Home: 111 S Broadview St Anaheim CA 92804 Office: Engring Corp of Am-Orange County 210 A and B N Crescent Way Anaheim CA 92801

GLASER, CAROL GROVEMAN, therapist; b. Bronx, N.Y., June 30, 1949; d. M. Arnold and Margaret (Moskowitz) Groveman; m. Donald Howard Glaser, Aug. 5, 1979; children: Ryan Elizabeth, Morgan Alexandra. BA, CUNY, 1971; MA, Calif. Sch. Profl. Psychology, 1977, PhD, 1979. Tchr. pub. schs. Bronx, 1971-73; tchr., ednl. coordinator Southwood Mental Health Ctr., Chula Vista, Calif., 1973-75; pvt. practice psychotherapy San Diego, 1978—. Mem. Am. Psychol. Assn., Calif. Psychol. Assn., Acad. San Diego Psychologists (assoc.), Calif. Assn. Marriage and Family Therapists. Home: 5430 Pacifica Dr La Jolla CA 92037 Office: 2710 Health Ctr Dr Suite C San Diego CA 92123

GLASER, DONALD A(RTHUR), physicist; b. Cleve., Sept. 21, 1926; s. William Joseph Glaser. B.S., Case Inst. Tech., 1946, Sc.D., 1959; Ph.D., Cal. Inst. Tech., 1949. Prof. physics U. Mich., 1949-59; prof. physics U. Calif. at Berkeley, 1959—, prof. physics and molecular biology, 1964—. Recipient Henry Russel award U. Mich., 1955; Charles V. Boys prize Phys. Soc., London, 1958; Nobel prize in physics, 1960; NSF fellow, 1961; Guggenheim fellow, 1961-62. Fellow Am. Physics Soc. (prize 1959); mem. Nat. Acad. Scis., Sigma Xi, Tau Kappa Alpha, Theta Tau. Office: Molecular Biology Dept Univ of Calif Berkeley CA 94720 *

GLASER, EDWARD MAYNARD, psychologist; b. N.Y.C., Apr. 8, 1911; s. Martin and Teresa (Schmeling) G.; m. Mildred Carlson, Apr. 24, 1943. B in Social Sci., MS, City U. N.Y., 1936; PhD, Columbia U., 1940. Diplomate Am. Bd. Profl. Psychology. Psychologist USPHS, Chillicothe, Ohio, 1940-42; cons. psychologist Rohrer, Hibler & Replogle, Los Angeles, 1946-52; mng. assoc. Edward Glaser & Assocs., Los Angeles, 1952—; pres. Human Interaction Research Inst., Los Angeles, 1961-86, founder and chmn. bd. dirs., 1987—. Author: An Experiment in the Development of Critical Thinking, 1941, Productivity Gains Through Worklife Improvement, 1976; co-author: Putting Knowledge to Use, 1983; contbr. numerous articles to profl. jours. Served to lt. comdr. USN, 1942-46. Recipient Myrdal prize Evaluation Research Soc., 1978. Fellow Am. Psychol. Assn. (pres. div. cons. psychology 1963-64, chmn. ethics com. 1964-65, 1st prize cons. psychology research, Perry L. Rohrer award for profl. excellence 1985), AAAS, So. Calif. Psychol. Assn. (pres. 1957-58). Methodist. Club: Los Angeles Athletic. Avocation: tennis. Office: Edward Glaser and Assocs Human Interaction Research Inst 1849 Sawtelle Blvd #102 Los Angeles CA 90025

GLASER, HAROLD, physicist, university administrator; b. Kurseni, Lithuania, Aug. 28, 1924; s. Joseph and Emma G.; m. Margaret Stoney, Dec. 29, 1945; children: Roberta L., Miriam L., Ruth H. M.S., Northwestern U., 1949, Ph.D., 1953. Sr. staff physicist Applied Physics Lab., Johns Hopkins U., 1952-54; head theoret. analysis sect. Applications Research div. Naval Research Lab., Washington, 1954-57; physicist Electronics br. Applications Research div. Naval Research Lab., 1957-59; physicist Physics br. Office Naval Research, Washington, 1959-65; spl. asst. div. math., phys. and engring. scis. NSF, Washington, 1962; head Nuclear Physics br. 1964-66; acting chief solar physics NASA, Washington, 1966-68; chief NASA, 1968-70; chief long-range planning Nat. Bur. Standards, Washington, 1970-71; detailed Office of Sci. and Tech.; Exec. Office of President, Washington, 1971-72; acting dir., dep. dir. Exptl. Tech. Incentives Program Nat. Bur. Standards, Washington, 1972; dep. dir. sci. and tech. office nat. research and devel. assessment NSF, Washington, 1972-75; dir. solar terrestrial div. NASA, Washington, 1975-80; cons. Office of Mgmt. and Budget, 1980-81; cons. U. Colo.; asst. to pres. U. Calif., 1981-84; cons. Lawrence Livermore Nat. Lab. Served with AUS, 1943-46. Fellow Washington Acad. Sci.; Mem. Am. Phys. Soc., Am. Geophys. Union, Am. Astronom. Soc., Internat. Astronom. Union, N.Y. Acad. Scis., Sigma Xi. Address: 1346 Bonita Berkeley CA 94709

GLASER, PAUL FRANKLYN, engineer; b. N.Y.C., Apr. 17, 1926; s. Philip and Bertha (Rosenfeld) G.; m. Florence Hellman, June 1, 1947; children—Stephanie Tracy, Wendy. B.E.E., NYU, 1949, M.E.E., 1952. Chief engr. Am. Chronoscope, Mount Vernon, N.Y., 1949-55; dir. engring. Gruen Watch Co., Cin., 1955-58; project mgr. TRW, Redondo Beach, Calif., 1958-61, dept. mgr., 1961-64, lab. mgr., 1964-68, v.p., gen. mgr., 1968-73; pres. TRW Colo. Electronics, Colorado Springs, 1970-73; chmn. Transaction Tech., Inc. subs. Citibank, N.A., 1973-85; sr. v.p., mem. policy com., chmn. corp. tech. com. Citibank, N.A., 1982—; lectr., speaker in field. Contbr. articles to profl. jours.; patentee automated teller machine, 1979, high speed oscillograph, 1954. Spl. chmn. United Crusade, Los Angeles, 1965-66; chmn. new tech. subcom. United Way, 1984-85; mem. elec. engring. adv. council Calif. State Long Beach, 1985—. Served with USN, 1944-46, PTO. Mem. IEEE (group chmn. 1963-64), Am. Nat. Standards Inst. (bd. dirs. 1985—), Tau Beta Pi, Eta Kappa Nu. Clubs: Brentwood Country (Los Angeles); Indian Wells Country (Palm Desert, Calif.). Avocations: golfing; cabinetmaking. Office: Citicorp 3100 Ocean Park Blvd Santa Monica CA 90405

GLASER, ROBERT JOY, physician, foundation executive; b. St. Louis, Sept. 11, 1918; s. Joseph and Regina G.; m. Helen Louise Hofsommer, Apr. 1, 1949; children: Sally Louise, Joseph II, Robert Joy. SB, Harvard U., 1940, MD magna cum laude, 1943; DS (hon.), U. Health Scis.-Chgo. Med. Sch., 1972, Temple U., 1973, U. N.H., 1979, U. Colo., 1979; LHD, Rush Med. Coll., 1973; BS, Mt. Sinai Med. Sch., 1984. Med. intern Barnes Hosp., St. Louis, 1944, asst. resident physician, 1945-46, resident physician, 1946-47, asst. physician, 1949-57; asst. resident physician Peter Bent Brigham Hosp., Boston, 1944-45; NRC fellow med. scis. Wash. U. Med. Sch., 1947-49, instr. medicine, 1949-50, asst. prof., 1950-56, asst. dean., 1947, 53-55, assoc. prof., 1956-57, assoc. dean, 1955-57; dean, prof. medicine Med. Sch. U. Colo., 1957-63, v.p. for med. affairs, 1959-63; vis. physician Washington U. Med. Service, St. Louis City Hosp., 1950, chief service, 1950-53, cons., 1953-57; attending physician Colo. Gen. Hosp., Denver, 1957-63; prof. social medicine Harvard, Boston, 1963-65; pres. Affiliated Hosps. Ctr., Inc., 1963-65; v.p. med. affairs, dean Sch. Medicine, prof. medicine Stanford U., 1965-70, acting pres., 1968, cons. prof., 1972—; bd. dirs. Henry J. Kaiser Family Found., 1970-83, pres., chief exec. officer, 1972-83; attending physician Columbia-Presbyn. Med. Ctr., N.Y.C., 1971-72, clin. prof. medicine, 1971-72; dir. for med. sci. Lucille P. Markey Charitable Trust, 1984—; bd. dirs. Hewlett-Packard Co., Alza Corp., First Boston Inc., Calif. Water Service Co.; cons. medicine VA Hosp., Denver, 1957-63, Fitzsimons Army Hosp., Aurora, Colo., 1957-63, Lowry AFB, Denver, 1957-63; mem. nat. adv. council NIMH, 1970-72, Harvard Fund Council, 1953-56, Harvard Med. Alumni Council, 1956-59; assoc. mem. streptococcal commn. Armed Forces Epidemiologic Bd., 1958-61; chmn. com. study nat. needs biomed. and behavioral research personnel Nat. Acad. Scis.-NRC, 1974-77; mem. vis. com. Med. Sch. Harvard U., 1968-74, Sch. Pub. Health, 1971-77; bd. visitors Charles Drew Postgrad. Med. Sch., 1972-79; mem. com. on med. affairs Yale U., 1969-82, adv. bd. Sch. Orgn. and Mgmt., 1976-84; vis. com. Tufts Med. Sch., 1974-84. Editor: Pharos, 1962—; contbr. articles to sci. jours. and chpts. to books. Bd. regents Georgetown U., 1976-78; bd. dirs. Kaiser Found. Hosps., Kaiser Found. Health Plan, 1967-79, Council on Founds., 1974-79; trustee Commonwealth Fund, 1969—, v.p., 1970-72; trustee David and Lucille Packard Found., 1984—, Pacific Sch. Religion, 1972-77, Washington U., St. Louis, 1979—; mem. Sloan Commn. on Govt. in Higher Edn., 1977-79. Fellow AAAS, Am. Acad. Arts and Scis. (exec. bd., v.p. 1972-76); mem. Am. Clin. and Climatological Assn. (pres. 1982-83), Am. Fedn. Clin. Research (chmn. midwestern sect. 1954-55), Central Soc. Clin. Research (councillor 1955-58), Am. Soc. Clin. Investigation, Assn. Am. Med. Colls. (asst. sec. 1956-59, chmn. com. edn. and research 1958-62, mem. exec. council 1959-63, 76-79, v.p. 1963-64, chmn. exec. council and assembly 1968-69), Assn. Am. Physicians, Western Assn. Physicians (councillor 1960-63), Am. Soc. Exptl. Pathology, Nat. Inst. Allergy and Infectious Disease (tng. grant com. 1957-60), Inst. Medicine, Nat. Acad. Sci. (mem. exec. com. 1971-73, chmn. membership com. 1970-72, acting pres. 1971-72), Sigma Xi, Alpha Omega Alpha (bd. dirs. 1963-77). Clubs: Harvard (N.Y.C.), Century (N.Y.C.). Office: 525 Middlefield Rd Suite 130 Menlo Park CA 94025

GLASGOW, MARY ANN, agency administrator; b. Meadville, Pa., July 18, 1935; d. John Glenn and Mary (Mull) Lewis; m. Lowell A. Glasgow, June 16, 1956 (dec. Feb. 1982); children: Russell Lowell, Lauren Sue, Scott Lewis. Student, Coll. of Wooster, 1952-54; BS in Elem. Edn., U. Rochester, 1956; MSW, U. Utah, 1980, postgrad., 1983—. Cert. social worker, clin. social worker. Therapist Family Support Ctr., Salt Lake City, 1981-82, dir., 1982—; adj. instr. dept. pediatrics U. Utah Med. Ctr., Salt Lake City, 1982—; mem. clin. field faculty U. Utah Grad. Sch. Social Work, Salt Lake City, 1982—; pvt. practice counseling Three Fountains, Salt Lake City, Denver, Alburquerque, Chgo., Hawaii, 1986—; workshop facilitator, developer Phoenix Inst., Salt Lake City, 1980-82; co-dir. Pediatrics Honors Program, U. Utah, Salt Lake City, 1982-84. Bd. dirs. Alumni Bd. Grad. Sch. Social Work, U. Utah, 1982-85; task force mem. Human Family Task Force, United Ch. of Christ, Denver, 1984—, self sufficiency Task Force, Dept. Human Services, Salt Lake City, 1985—. Mem. Nat. Assn. Social Workers, Internat. Transactional Analysis Assn. (TAU adv. bd. chairperson 1984-86, mountain states conf. chairperson 1984, membership com. 1986), Utah Assn. Children's Therapy, Ontario Soc. Utah, Phi Kappa Phi. Democrat. Clubs: Cottonwood Study (pres. 1978-79), Wasatch Mountain. Lodge: Zonta (adv. bd. 1985-87). Home: 4258 Mount Olympus Way Salt Lake City UT 84124 Office: Family Support Ctr Satellite 75 W Center St Midvale UT 84047

GLASKY, ALVIN JERALD, medical research scientist; b. Chgo., June 16, 1933; s. Oscar and Bessie (Akwa) G.; m. Rosalie Anne Hanfling, Aug. 25, 1957; children: Michelle S., Karen R., Mark J., Ira D. BS in Pharmacy, U. Ill., Chgo., 1954, PhD in Biochemistry, 1958. Dir. biochem. research Michael Reese Hosp., Chgo., 1959-61; research pharmacologist Abbott Labs., North Chicago, Ill., 1961-66; v.p. research ICN, Burbank, Calif., 1966-68; pres., chief executive officer Newport Pharms., Inc., Newport Beach, Calif., 1968-86; pres. Glasky Assoc., Inc., Santa Ana, Calif., 1983—. Contbr. articles to profl. jours. Active Am.-Jewish Com., World Affairs Council of Orange County. Mem. AAAS, Am. Pharm. Assn., Calif. Pharm. Assn., Am. Soc. Microbiology, Am. Chem. Soc., Rho Chi. Republican. Jewish. Lodge: B'nai Brith. Avocations: tennis, swimming, theater. Home and Office: Glasky Assocs Inc 9902 Brier Ln Santa Ana CA 92705

GLASS, CHARLES EDWIN, geological engineering educator; b. Loma Linda, Calif., Jan. 23, 1944; s. David Eugene and Arline (Powers) G.; m. Josie Mary Ritchey, Jan. 31, 1967; children: Aaron James, Shelyse Maureen. Student, Coll. of Marin, 1965-70; BS in Geophysics, U. Nevada, 1970; MS in Geol. Engring., U. Calif., Berkeley, 1971, PhD in Geol. Engring., 1974. Registered profl. engr., Ariz. Research asst. U. Nevada, Reno, 1967, U. Calif., Berkeley, 1970; instr. dept. mining and geol. engring. U. Ariz., Tucson, 1973-74, asst. prof. dept. mining and geol. engring., 1974-80, assoc. prof. dept. mining and geol. engring., 1980—, head dept. mining and geol. engring., 1982—; cons. U.S. Army Corps Engrs. Waterways Experiment Station and New England div., Wash. Pub. Power Supply System,

Weston Geophys. Corp., Woodward-Clyde Cons., Pincock, Allen and Holt, Inc., Call, Nicholas, Inc., Exxon Minerals, Inc., Dames & Moore, Inc., U.S. Nat. Com. for Rock Mechanics Nat. Research Council, 1979-81; lectr. Engring. Found. Conf. on Earthquakes and Lifeline Systems, 1974, Ariz. Emergency Services Assn., 1975, U.S. Army Corps Engrs., 1977-78, Stanford U., 1978. Contbr. numerous articles to profl. jours. Bd. dirs. Ariz. Innovation Network, 1986—, v.p. univ. relations, 1986—; pres. Terragraf Inc., 1986—. Served with USN, 1961-64. Soc. Exploration Geophysicists scholar, 1968-69, Max E. Fleischman scholar; Jane Lewis fellow, 1971-72, 72-73; also various research grants. Mem. ASCE (Nuclear Structures and Materials Com., Subcom. on Influence Siting Concepts on Structural Design Criteria, 1974-75), Western Interstate Commn. Higher Edn. (Sci. Tech. Task Force), Western Tech. Manpower Council, U. Ariz. coms. Natural Hazards, Remote Sensing, 1974—; Cooperative Edns. Com., Press Release Com., Curriculum and Accreditation Com., Exec. Com., Hon. and Profl. Degree Nominating Com., Scholarships and Awards Com., Student Counseling, Discipline and Guidance Com., Grad. Study Com., Seismol. Soc. Am., Assn. Engring. Geologists, Soc. Exploration Geophysicists (assoc.), Am. Soc. Photogrammetry, Internat. Assn. Math. Geology, AAAS, Ariz. Geol. Soc. (sec. 1974), Sigma Xi. Democrat. Roman Catholic. Office: U Ariz Dept Mining and Geol Engring Tucson AZ 85721

GLASS, DOUGLAS ALAN, lawyer; b. Columbus, Ohio, Sept. 4, 1954; s. Bernard and Jeannette (Shapiro) G.; m. Diane Oakes, Mar. 17, 1979. BS, San Diego State U., 1977; JD, Calif. Western Sch. Law, 1982. Bar: Calif. 1982, U.S. Dist. Ct. (so. dist.) Calif. 1983. Assoc. Gibson & Kennerson, San Diego, 1983; sole practice San Diego, 1984—; bd. dirs. Fifth Ave. Ins., San Diego, 1985—; lectr. Anthony Real Estate Sch., San Diego, 1986; talk show guest Sta. KFMB Radio, San Diego, 1986. Mem. ABA, San Diego County Bar Assn., San Diego Trial Lawyers Assn., Calif. Western Alumni (bd. dirs. 1984—). Democrat. Jewish. Avocations: karate, soccer. Office: 2350 Fifth Ave San Diego CA 92101

GLASS, JULIE KAY, public relations executive; b. Oklahoma City, Aug. 27, 1960; d. Rex M. and Marge E. (Crowley) Ball; m. John Edward Glass, May 24, 1986. BA in Sociology, Pomona Coll., 1983; postgrad., UCLA, U. So. Calif., 1983-86. Exhibit floor mgr. Omniplex Sci. Ctr., Oklahoma City, 1977-80; intern Michael Levine Pub. Relations, Los Angeles, 1983; columnist Tower Records' Pulse!, Sacramento, 1984-85, Goldmine mag., Iola, Wis., 1984-85; acct. exec. New Image Pub. Relations, Los Angeles, 1983-86; account exec. Brocato & Kelman Inc., Public Relations, Los Angeles, 1986—. Contbr. articles to mags. Vol. alcohol and drug abuse programs, Pasadena, Calif., 1985—, Los Angeles County probation camps, 1982-83, ERA, Oklahoma City, Los Angeles, 1982-83. Mem. Nat. Acad. Video Arts and Scis., Pub. Relations Soc. Am. (membership com., 1985). Democrat. Episcopalian. Club: Hollywood Women's Press (co-editor newsletter 1986). Avocations: making stained glass windows, sports, reading. Home: 146 N Holliston Pasadena CA 91106 Office: New Image Pub Relations 3151 Cahuenga Blvd W Suite 225 Los Angeles CA 90068

GLASS, PAUL WILLIAM PARSONNET, accounting corporation executive; b. Newark, June 27, 1945; s. William Burton and Doris (Parsonnet) G.; m. Susan Volpe, Dec. 9, 1967; children—Andrew Parsonnet, William Shane, Joshua Michael. B.S. in Bus. Adminstrn., Boston U., 1967; postgrad. U. R.I.-Kingston, 1967-68. C.P.A., R.I., N.Y., Mass., Calif. Staff acct. Glass, Dittelman & Co., C.P.A.s, Providence, 1969; supr. Laventhal & Horwath, C.P.A.s, N.Y.C., 1969-73, audit mgr., Boston, 1973-77, continuing edn. faculty Am. Inst. C.P.A.s, 1976-77; ptnr. Glass, Karp, Warburg & Perera, C.P.A.s, Beverly Hills, Calif., 1977-80; ptnr., pres. Glass & Rosen, An Accountancy Corp., Encino, Calif., 1981—. Active Free Arts Clinic, Malibu, Calif. Served with Army N.G., 1968-74. Mem. Am. Inst. C.P.A.s, Calif. Soc. C.P.A.s, Mass. Soc. C.P.A.s, Boston U. Alumni Assn. Jewish. Club: B'nai B'rith (v.p., treas. Framingham, Mass. 1976-77). Co-designer computerized acctg. system for non-profit orgns., 1977.

GLASSBERG, ALAN BURNETT, physician; b. Charleston, S.C., Jan. 23, 1937; s. Joseph and Helen (Bebergal) G.; m. Lissa Marie Rohrberg, June 13, 1979; children: Jordan Joseph, Lauren Marie-Helene. BS, Coll. Charleston, 1958; MD, Med. U. S.C., 1962. Diplomate Am. Bd. Internal Medicine, Am. Bd. Hematology, Am. Bd. Med. Oncology. Intern U. Pa. Hosp., 1962-63, resident, 1963-69; practice medicine San Francisco, 1969-80; dir. med. oncology Mt. Zion Med. Ctr., San Francisco, 1980—; clin. prof. medicine U. Calif., San Francisco, 1983—; trustee Am. Cancer Soc., San Francisco, 1980—, Norcal Cancer Program, Palo Alto, Calif., 1980—. Fellow ACP; mem. AMA, Calif. Med. Assn., Calif. Acad. Medicine, San Francisco Med. Soc., Am. Soc. Hematology, Am. Soc. Clin. Oncology. Office: 1515 Scott St San Francisco CA 94111

GLASSMEYER, JAMES MILTON, aerospace and electronics engineer; b. Cin., Mar. 31, 1928; s. Howard Jerome and Ethel Marie (Nieman) G.; m. Anita Mary Tschida, Apr. 21, 1979. Student U. Cin., 1947-49; BSEE with spl. honors, U. Colo., Boulder, 1958, MS in Aeronautics and Astronautics, MIT, 1960. Commd. 2d lt. U.S. Air Force, 1950, advanced through grades to lt. col., 1971; astron. engr. Air Force Space Systems Div. Hdqrs., Los Angeles, 1960-64, astronautical engr. and astronautics tech. intelligence analyst Air Force Rocket Propulsion Lab., Edwards AFB, Calif., 1967-73; ret., 1973; pvt. practice aerospace and electronics research and analysis, 1973—. Contbr. articles to jours. in field. Recipient Air Force Inst. Tech. scholarship, U. Colo., 1956-58, MIT, 1958-60, USAF Master Missileman badge, Air Force Rocket Propulsion Lab., 1970. Mem. AIAA, Air Force Assn., Planetary Soc., Ret. Officers Assn., Tau Beta Pi (1st grand prize Greater Interest in Govt. Nat. Essay Contest 1957), Eta Kappa Nu, Sigma Tau, Sigma Gamma Tau, Sigma Xi. Roman Catholic. Home: 5801 E North Wilshire Dr Tucson AZ 85711 Office: 5610-B E Glenn St Tucson AZ 85712

GLASSY, MARK CHARLES, research biologist; b. Tacoma, Wash., July 2, 1952; s. Frank Joseph and Lorraine Mary (Gay) G.; m. Donna Marie McCarthy, June 8, 1974; children: Jason, Matthew, Dawn. BS in Biology and Chemistry, U. San Francisco, 1974; postgrad., Ind. U., Indpls., 1974-75; PhD in Biochemistry, U. Calif., Riverside, 1978; postdoc., Scripps Clinic & Research Found., La Jolla, Calif., 1978-81. Teaching asst. dept. biochemistry U. Calif., Riverside, 1975-78; research fellow dept. molecular immunology Scripps Clinic & Research Found., La Jolla, 1978-81; asst. research immunologist dept. medicine div. hematology, oncology U. Calif. San Diego, 1980-86; staff U. Calif. San Diego Cancer Ctr., 1981-86, dir. Cancer Ctr. Hybridoma CORE lab., 1986—; sr. staff scientist Biotherapeutics, Inc., La Jolla, 1986—; cons. Travenol-Hyland Diagnostics, Deerfield, Ill., 1982-83, Kureha Chem. Industry, Ltd., Tokyo, 1983-84, Hagiwara Inst. Health, Osaka, Japan, 1984-85; lectr. various industries and labs. Editor Jour. Immunology, Cancer Research, Hybridoma; contbr. numerous articles to profl. jours., mags. and textbooks. Recipient Chancellor's Patent Fund, 1978; Nat. Research Service award Pub. Health Service NIH, 1978-79, NIH New Investigator Research award, 1983-86; grantee NIH Program Project, 1984-87, Am. Cancer Soc., 1981-82, U. Calif. Cancer Research Coordinating Com., 1981-82; fellow Earle C. Anthony, 1976-77, NIH Postdoc., 1979-81. Mem. Am. Chem. Soc., AAAS, N.Y. Acad. Sci., Fedn. Am. Scientists, Am. Assn. Immunologists. Democrat. Roman Catholic. Avocation: collecting science fiction publications. Office: Biotherapeutics Inc 11025 N Torrey Pines Rd La Jolla CA 92037

GLATHE, JOHN PARSONS, psychiatrist; b. Bklyn., Nov. 22, 1926; s. Henry Bernhard and Alice Elizabeth (Parsons) G.; m. Jean-Karlin Johnson, Dec. 26, 1953 (div. Jan. 1973); children: Jeffrey, Susan, Caroline. AB, Stanford U., 1949, MD, 1953. Diplomate Am. Bd. Psychiatry and Neurology. Intern U. Mich. Hosp., Ann Arbor, Mich., 1952-53; resident Max Found., Rochester, Minn., 1957-60; practice medicine specializing in psychiatry Palo Alto, Calif., 1960—; clin. assoc. prof. dept. psychiatry Stanford (Calif.) U., 1960—; bd. dirs. Found. Med. Care of Santa Clara County, San Jose, Calif. Served to capt. USAF, 1953. Fellow Am. Phychiat. Assn.; mem. Calif. Med. Assn., Biofeedback Soc. Am., Med. Friends of Wine. Home: 13801 La Paloma Rd Los Altos Hills CA 94022 Office: 780 Welch Rd Palo Alto CA 94304

GLATZER, ROBERT ANTHONY, marketing and sales executive; b. N.Y.C., May 19, 1932; s. Harold and Glenna (Beaber) G.; m. Paula Rosenfeld, Dec. 20, 1964; m. 2d, Mary Ann Murphy, Dec. 31, 1977; children—Gabriela, Jessica, Nicholas. B.A., Haverford Coll., 1954. Br. store dept. mgr. Bloomingdale's, N.Y.C., 1954-56; media buyer Ben Sackheim Advt., N.Y.C., 1956-59; producer TV commls. Ogilvy, Benson & Mather Advt., N.Y.C., 1959-62; dir. broadcast prodn. Carl Ally Advt., N.Y.C., 1962-63; owner Chronicle Prodns., N.Y.C., 1963-73; dir. Folklife Festival, Smithsonian Inst., Washington, 1973, Expo 74 Corp., Spokane, Wash., 1973-74; pres. Robert Glatzer Assocs., Spokane, 1974—; ptnr. Delany/Glatzer Advt., Spokane, 1979-84; dir. sales/mktg. Pinnacle Prodns., Spokane; adj. faculty Ea. Wash. U., 1987—. Bd. dirs. Riverfront Arts Festival, 1977-78; bd. dirs. Comprehensive Health Planning Council, 1975-78, Spokane Quality of Life Council, 1976-82, Allied Arts of Spokane, 1976-80, Art Alliance Wash. State, 1977-81, Spokane chpt. ACLU, 1979-83, Wash. State Folklife Council, 1983—; commr. Spokane Arts, 1987—. Recipient CINE Golden Eagle award (2). Mem. Dirs. Guild Am. Democrat. Jewish. Author: The New Advertising, 1970; co-scenarist Scorpio and other TV prodns. Office: W 905 Riverside Ave Spokane WA 99201

GLAU, GREGORY ROBERT, writer, small business owner; b. Phoenix, Oct. 28, 1945; s. Robert Henry and Gertrude Margaret (Kohl) G.; m. Courtney Ann Fields, June 5, 1966; children: Robert G., Tracy C., Kohl M. Student, Regis Coll., 1963-65; BA in English Edn., U. Ariz., 1968. Field underwriter N.Y. LIfe, Phoenix and Prescott, Ariz., 1968-69; pres. Glau Gas Equipment, Prescott, 1969—. Author: Business Power for Your Apple, 1985, Business Graphics for the Macintosh, 1985, Business Graphics with the IBM PC/XT/AT, 1986, Controlling Your Cash Flow with 1-2-3 or Symphony, 1986; contbr. numerous articles to mags. Cubmaster Boy Scouts Am., Prescott, 1985—. Republican. Roman Catholic. Home: 461 Canyon Springs Prescott AZ 86301 Office: Glau Gas Equipment Co 1052 E Willow Creek Rd Prescott AZ 86301

GLAUNER, FREDERICK WILLIAM, financial planner; b. Columbus, Ohio, July 29, 1931; s. Frederick Earl and Grace Morgan (Busey) G.; m. Gertrud Louise Plambeck, May 21, 1955; children—Frederick, Jr., Nancy, Joanna Glauner Gruntmeir, Linda. B.S., U.S. Mil. Acad., 1953; M.S., Frostburg State Coll., 1974; Assoc. Sci., Regis Coll., 1976. Commd. 2d lt. U.S. Army, advanced through grades to major, 1965; ret., 1973; agt. Montgomery Ward Life, Colorado Springs, Colo., 1973-76; gen. ins. agt., Colorado Springs, 1976-85; registered rep. Waddell & Reed, 1985—. Pres. PTA, Frankfurt Elem. Sch., Ger., 1966; jr. warden St. Michael's Episcopal Ch., Colorado Springs, 1980-81. Decorated Bronze Star; recipient Meritorious Service medal Mil. Dist. Washington, 1973. Republican. Episcopalian. Lodges: Masons (Master), Al Kaly Temple (Pueblo, Colo.); Al Kaly Drum Corps (Colorado Springs) (pres. 1982-83); Actual Past Masters (El Paso County). Home: 14150 Wyandott Dr Colorado Springs CO 80908

GLAVIS, ANTHONY WILLIAM, social worker; b. Cardena, Calif., Apr. 26, 1957; s. George Glavis Barela and Zaida Ramona Sotela Quijano. Student, El Camino Coll., 1977-84; BA in Social Work, Calif. State U., Long Beach, 1986. Computer operator Sunset House, Los Angeles, 1975-80; keypunch supr. Banking Data Services, Los Angeles, 1980-84; social worker Children of the Night, Hollywood, Calif., 1983-84, AIDS Project, Los Angeles, 1984—, Harbor Regional Ctr., Torrance, Calif., 1985—. Mem. Nat. Assn. Social Workers. Avocations: jogging, aerobics, swimming.

GLAZE, WILLIAM HOWARD, environmental educator; b. Sherman, Tex., Nov. 21, 1934; s. Homer Ray and Leta Leota (Scott) G.; m. Erma Lee Smith, Jan. 28, 1956 (div. Jan. 1976); children: David, Amy; m. Jean Adel Stevenson, Aug. 6, 1976. BS, Southwestern U., Georgetown, Tex., 1956; MS, U. Wis., 1958, PhD, 1961. Asst. prof. North Tex. State U., Denton, 1961-63, assoc. prof., 1963-65, prof. chemistry, 1965-80, assoc. dean Coll. Letters and Sci., 1973-75; prof. U. Tex. Dallas, Richardson, 1980-84, head grad. program environ. scis., 1980-84, dir. Ctr. Energy and Environ. Studies, 1980-84; prof. pub. health, dir. Environ. Sci. and Engring. Program UCLA, 1984—; cons. EPA, Washington, 1980—, Los Angeles Dept. Water and Power, 1984—, James Montgomery Engrs., Pasadena, Calif., 1985—; lectr. Okla. Dept. Health, Okalhoma City, 1983. Mem. editorial bd. Environ. Sci. Tech., 1980-86. Organizer, lectr. Tex. Pub. Health Assn., Arlington, 1982. Recipient Analyst of Yr. award Dallas Soc. Analytical Chemists, 1979, Zimmerman award, 1986. Mem. Am. Chem. Soc. (chmn., treas., del. to nat. council, nat. environ. analytical chemistry div., symposium organizer 1979), Am. Water Works Assn., Am. Inst. Chem. Engrs., Southwestern U. Alumni Assn. (exec. v.p. 1979-80), NRC (safe drinking water com. 1978-79, 85-87, chmn. water treatment chems. com. 1980-85), Sigma Xi, Al pha Chi. Home: 10439 Colina Way Los Angeles CA 90077 Office: U Calif Sch Pub Health 650 Circle Dr S Los Angeles CA 90024

GLEASON, A. M., electric utility and telecommunications company executive; b. 1930; married. Student, U. Oreg. With Pacific Power & Light Co. Inc., Portland, Oreg., from 1949, asst. to v.p., 1952-65, mgr. pub. accounts, 1965-68, v.p., 1968-73; pres. Pacific Telecom, Inc. (formerly Telephone Utilities, Inc.), 1973-82; chmn. Pacific Telecom, Inc., Vancouver, Wash., 1982—, chief exec. officer, 1973-82, also dir.; also pres. Pacificorp (parent), Portland. Office: Pacificorp 851 SW 6th Ave Portland OR 97204

GLEASON, BERNARD ALLEN, business educator; b. Riverton, Iowa, Aug. 6, 1929; s. Edward Vincent and Freda Lucille (Savage) G.; m. Barbara Lee Nay, Aug. 7, 1955; children: Kevin Lee, Kelly Ann. BS, U. Nebr., 1956, MS, 1959; EdD, So. Calif. U., 1969. Tchr. Washington Jr. High Sch., Long Beach, Calif., 1956-62, chmn. dept. bus., 1960-62; tchr. Jordan High Sch., Long Beach, 1962-68, chmn. dept. bus., 1965-68; prof. bus. Long Beach City Coll., 1962—, chmn. dept. bus., 1972-86; bd. dirs. Long Beach Tchrs. Credit Union. Commr. City Parks Commn., Long Beach, 1984—, Pub. Safety Adv. Commn., Long Beach, 1987—; bd. dirs. Boy Scouts Am., Long Beach, 1972-76, Pacific Hosp., Long Beach, 1985—. Served to staff sgt. USMC, 1948-52. Mem. Calif. Bus. Edn. Assn. (sec. 1974-76, com. mem.), Calif. Tchrs. Assn., (treas. Long Beach, 1974-80, pres. Long Beach 1980-82), Long Beach City Coll. Academic Senate (pres, 1983-85), Phi Kappa Lambda, Theta Chi (pres Lincoln, Nebr., 1955-56). Democrat. Roman Catholic. Lodge: Elks. Avocations: running, collecting Railroadiana. Home: 4556 Graywood Ave Long Beach CA 90808 Office: Long Beach City Coll Dept Office Adminstrn 4901 E Carson St Long Beach CA 90808

GLEASON, CAROL CREPS, training and development professional; b. Cleve., May 25, 1926; d. John A. Creps and Dorothy (Hunter) Severns; m. Richard Arlington Gleason, June 29, 1948; children: Lynn Hunter, Richard A. Jr. BA in English and Journalism, Ohio State U., 1948; postgrad., Ariz. State U., 1974. Cert. tchr., Ariz. Mem. advt. direct mail dept. Gen. Electric, Schenectady, N.Y., 1948-51; mktg. dir. WR Schulz Co., Phoenix, 1975; mgmt. trainee Goldwaters, Phoenix, 1974; dir. tng. devel. Goldwaters, Scottsdale, Ariz., 1976—. Mem. Am. Soc. Tng. Devel., Alpha Phi (pres. 1947-48), Phi Lambda Theta. Democrat. Presbyterian. Office: Goldwaters 4500 N Scottsdale Rd Scottsdale AZ 85251

GLEASON, CYNTHIA S., public relations company executive, public relations educator; b. Portage, Wis., Mar. 2, 1949; d. Walter E. and Arleen (Slette) G.; m. William J. Kostka, Jr., Apr. 6, 1974; children—Jennifer Kostka, William Kostka III. B.A. in Journalism, U. Wis., 1972. Intern, U. Wis.-Madison Med. Ctr. Office of Pub. Info., 1970, State of Wis. Dept. Natural Resources, Madison, 1971; writer-researcher, jr. account exec. William Kostka & Assocs., Denver, 1972—, sr. account exec., 1974-77, v.p., 1977-79, sr. v.p., 1979-81, exec. v.p., 1981—; instr. dept. journalism U. Colo. Bd. dirs. Juvenile Offenders In Need, Inc., Denver; active Guardians Ad Litem. Recipient Pub. Relations Person of Year award Southland Corp., 1976. Mem. Pub. Relations Soc. Am. (accredited; counselors acad.), Denver Press Club. Home: 13955 E Hamilton Dr Aurora CO 80014 Office: William Kostka & Assocs 1407 Larimer Sq Denver CO 80202

GLEASON, DOUGLAS RENWICK, marketing professional; b. Worcestor, Mass., Oct. 27, 1956; s. Sherman M. and Dolores E. (Murad) G. BA, Stanford U., 1978; MBA, UCLA, 1982. Asst. product mgr. Pepsico, Purchase, N.Y., 1982-83, assoc. product mgr., 1983-85; product mgr. Carnation Co., Los Angeles, 1985—. Mem. Beta Gamma Sigma. Avocations: tennis, skiing, piano, singing. Office: Carnation Co 5045 Wilshire Blvd Los Angeles CA 90036

GLEIM, KIMBERLY ANN, social worker; b. Yokosuka, Japan; d. Thomas Gilroy and Loretta Lois (Herron) Bond.; m. John William Gleim, Feb. 5, 1977; children: Robert Alan, Laura Ann. Student, Humboldt State U., 1974-76; BSW, Dakota Wesleyan U., 1978; MSW, U. Louisville, 1980. Dir. social services Gregory (S.D.) Hosp., 1978-79; team leader, social worker R.XIV Mental Health Ctr., Burkesville, Ky., 1980-82; sch. social worker Boundary County Sch. Dist., Bonners Ferry, Idaho, 1982—; cons. social work Community Hosp., Bonners Ferry, 1982—. Mem. Acad. Cert. Social Workers (cert.), Nat. Assn. Social Workers, Boundary County Mental Health Assn., Region 1 Mental Health Adv. Bd. (vice chmn. 1983—), Jaycees. Democrat. Roman Catholic. Avocations: tennis, cross country skiing, camping, fishing, needlework. Home: Rural Rt 1 Box 532 AC Bonners Ferry ID 83805 Office: Boundary County Sch Dist PO Box 899 Bonners Ferry ID 83805

GLENDENNING, NORMAN KEITH, theoretical physicist; b. Galt, Ont., Can., Jan. 17, 1931; came to U.S., 1956; m. Laura Louis. BSc, McMaster U., Hamilton, Ont., 1954, MSc, 1955; PhD, Ind. U., 1959. Sr. scientist Lawrence Berkeley Lab., Calif., 1958—; guest prof. U. Franfurt, Fed. Republic Germany, Laboratoire Physique Theorique, Orsay, France, U. Pierre and Marie Curie, Paris; chmn. sr. staff com. nuclear sci. div. Author: Direct Nuclear Reactions, 1983; contbr. articles to sci. jours. Named Disting. Alumni Lectr., McMaster U., 1978. Fellow Am. Phys. Soc. Home: 1304 Campus Dr Berkeley CA 94708 Office: Lawrence Berkeley Lab Berkeley CA 94708

GLENN, GUY CHARLES, physician; b. Parma, Ohio, May 13, 1930; s. Joseph Frank and Helen (Rupple) G.; B.S., Denison U., 1953; M.D., U. Cin., 1957; m. Lucia Ann Howarth, June 13, 1953; children—Kathryn Holly, Carolyn Helen, Cynthia Marie. Intern, Walter Reed Army Med. Center, Washington, 1957-58; resident in pathology Fitzsimons Army Med. Center, Denver, 1959-63; commd. 2d lt. U.S. Army, 1956, advanced through grades to col., 1977; demonstrator pathology Royal Army Med. Coll., London, 1970-72; chief dept. pathology Fitzsimons Army Med. Center, Denver, 1972-77; pres. med. staff St. Vincent Hosp.; mem. governing bd. Mont. Health Systems Agy. Diplomate Am. Bd. Pathology. Fellow Coll. Am. Pathologists (sustaining; chmn. chemistry resources com., chmn. sci. resources com., mem. budget program and review com., council on quality assurance), Am. Soc. Clin. Pathology, Soc. Med. Cons. to Armed Forces, Colo. Assn. Continuing Lab. Edn., Midland Empire Health Assn. (past pres.). Contbr. to profl. jours. Home: 3225 Jack Burke Ln Billings MT 59102 Office: St Vincent Hosp Billings MT 59102

GLENN, JAMES D., JR., lawyer; b. Oakley, Idaho, July 1, 1934; s. Vernal D. and Vilate H. Glenn; student U. Utah, 1952-57, J.D., 1960; m. Alice Rexine, Dec. 14, 1956; children—Sheilagh Ann Glenn Thornock, Michelle Glenn Larson, James D. III, Deirdre, David R., Alison. Assoc. counsel Fed. Trade Commn., San Francisco, 1960-61; admitted to Utah bar, 1960, Calif. bar, 1961, Idaho bar, 1978; ptnr. firm Ferguson & Vohland, 1961-63; ptnr. firm Ferguson & Glenn, 1963-65; individual practice law, Oakland, Hayward and Fremont, Calif., 1965-77; ptnr. firm Webb, Burton, Carlson, Pedersen & Paine, Twin Falls, Idaho, 1977-83; sr. ptnr. Glenn & Henrie, Twin Falls, 1983—; sec. Virga Land Corp., Calif.; counsel Norton Enterprises, Inc., A & B Bean & Grain, Inc., Haney Seed Co., Klein Bros., Ltd., Beta Western, Inc., Loughmiller Farm, Inc. Bd. dirs. So. Alameda County (Calif.) Legal Services Corp., 1969-73. Mem. Am. Judicature Soc., Idaho Trial Lawyers Assn., Phi Kappa Phi. Republican. Mormon. Office: Glenn & Henrie 155 2d Ave N PO Box 1768 Twin Falls ID 83301

GLENNEY, LYNN HARREN, manufacturing company executive; b. Marshalltown, Iowa, Feb. 8, 1934; s. Paul McClean and Edith Banff (Harren) G.; student Iowa State Coll., 1951-53; B.S. with honors, UCLA, 1960, M.B.A., 1961; m. Fumie Morimoto, Mar. 24, 1958; children—Paul Masaya, Kathleen Mizuho. Asst. to v.p. sales Flying Tiger Lines, Inc., Burbank, Calif., 1960-62; market analyst Douglas Aircraft Co., Inc., Santa Monica, Calif., 1962-64; sr. assoc. Planning Research Corp., Los Angeles, 1964-69; dir. corp. planning Lear Siegler, Inc., Santa Monica, 1969—; expositor planning and strategy Instituto de Aministración Científica de las Empresas, Republic of Mex., 1981; tech. expert on planning Asian Productivity Orgn., Tokyo, 1979. Chmn. priorities com. Western Region, United Way, 1974-78, 80-81, chmn. planning council, 1982-84, bd. dirs. Western region, 1982—; bd. dirs. Westside Ind. Services for Elderly, 1981—; mem. West Los Angeles Coll. Found., 1984—; mem. Ad hoc com. on productivity City of Los Angeles, 1984-85; mem. strategic process com., United Way, 1985—. Served with USMC, 1954-58. Recipient Outstanding Vol. Service award United Way, 1976. Mem. N.Am. Soc. Corp. Planning, Inc. (v.p. 1981-83), The Planning Forum, So. Calif. Corp. Planners Assn. (pres. 1976-77), Assn. Asian Studies, Marine Corps Assn., Internat. Affiliation Planning Socs. (v.p. 1977-80), Acacia. Republican. Presbyterian. Home: 428 Gretna Green Way Los Angeles CA 90049 Office: Lear Siegler Inc 2850 Ocean Park Blvd Santa Monica CA 90405

GLICK, ANDREW JUSTUS, computer systems consulting executive; b. Culver City, Calif., Oct. 25, 1948; s. George Gordon and Josephine (Griner) G. BA in Music Composition, Calif. State U., Long Beach, 1969; BSEE, U. So. Calif., 1977. Quality engr. supr. Thomas Organ Co., Sepulveda, Calif., 1974-75; sr. systems analyst Tektronix, Inc., Woodland Hills, Calif., 1978-80; supr. computer graphics Lockheed CALAC, Burbank, Calif., 1980-82; regional tech. support mgr. Digital Research, Los Angeles, 1982-84; pres. Justus Engring., La Canada, Calif., 1984—; prof. computer sci. Northrop U., Inglewood, Calif., 1984-86; cons. Glenray Prodns., Pasadena, Calif., 1985-86, Teledyne Camera, Arcadia, Calif., 1985, Hughes Aircraft, Conoga Park, Calif., 1980. Musical composer Cosmogony Oratorio, 1979; inventor, video encoder. V.p. Mus. Arts Soc. Los Angeles, 1986; librarian Cambridge Singers, Los Angeles, 1984—, commd. composer, 1986; dir. services and music Throop Meml. Unitarian Ch., Pasadena, 1982-84. Served with U.S. Army, 1969-71. Performance grantee Meet the Composer, 1986. Mem. AAAS, Assn. Computing Machinery, Audubon Soc. Democrat. Office: Justus Engring PO Box 1451 La Canada CA 91011-5451

GLICK, BETTY JANE, accountant; b. Carlisle, Pa., Sept. 15, 1935; d. Benjamin Burns and Margaret Irene (Brinkerhoff) Bailey; student pub. schs., Carlisle; m. Carl Samuel Glick, Jr., Sept. 4, 1953; children—Elizabeth Rose, Carl Samuel III (dec.), John Robert, William Joseph. Sec., Bedford Shoe Co. div. G.R. Kinney Co., Carlisle, 1953-54, bookkeeper, 1956-57, lacer pre-fit room, 1959; acct. M.G. Riley, C.P.A., Kenai, Alaska, 1966-82. Program chmn. Kenai PTA, 1968-69, pres., 1969-70; mem. Kenai Planning & Zoning Adv. Com., 1974-76, chmn., 1976; mem. Kenai City Council, 1976-83, vice mayor, 1979-82; mem. Kenai Peninsula Borough Assembly, 1982—, v.p., 1984-85, pres., 1985-86; parliamentarian Kenai Peninsula Borough Planning and Zoning Com., 1976-77, vice chmn., 1977-81, chmn., 1981-82; workshop speaker Kenai Peninsula Community Coll., 1984. Treas., Jr. Achievement, Kenai, 1978-81, chmn., 1981-82; bd. dirs. Jr. Achievement Alaska, 1982-85; bd. dirs. Cook Inlet Council on Alcohol and Drug Abuse, 1983-85; chmn. steering com. for sheltered workshop/residential care facility for handicapped People Count, Inc., 1983—. Named Citizen of Month, Kenai C. of C., 1977. Mem. Alaska Mcpl. League (dir. 1980-81, 2d v.p. 1981-82, 1st v.p. 1982-83, pres. 1983-84), Nat. League Cities (small cities adv. council 1983-84), Nat. Assn. Counties (bd. dirs. western region 1984—), Billiken Bus. and Profl. Women's Club (named Woman of Yr. 1978), LWV (parliamentarian Alaska ann. meeting 1983). Club: Peninsula Petroleum Wives. Home: 1601 E Aliak St Kenai AK 99611

GLICKMAN, HARRY, athletics executive; b. Portland, Oreg., May 13, 1924; s. Sam and Bessie (Karp) G.; m. Joanne Carol Matin, Sept. 28, 1958; children: Lynn Carol, Marshall Jordan, Jennifer Ann. B.A., U. Oreg., 1948. Press agt. 1948-52; pres. Oreg. Sports Attractions, 1952—, Portland Hockey Club, 1960-73; exec. v.p. Portland Trail Blazers (Nat. Basketball Assn.), from 1970, now pres. Trustee B'nai B'rith Jr. Camp, 1965; bd. dirs. U. Oreg. Devel. Fund. Served with AUS, 1943-46. Mem. Portland C. of C. (dir. 1968-72), Sigma Delta Chi, Sigma Alpha Mu. Jewish. Office: Lloyd Bldg Suite 950 700 NE Multnomah St Portland OR 97232 •

GLIHA, JOHN LEE, management information consultant, researcher; b. Sidney, N.Y., Feb. 18, 1953; s. Edward Richard and Agnes (Bennett) G. BA, SUNY, Oswego, 1976; postgrad., Ariz. State U., 1977—. Grad.

asst. Boulton Collection Mus. Instruments, Ariz. State U., 1977-78; supr. research info. ctr. music library Ariz. State U., 1979-83, cataloger music library, 1979-83, project coordinator collection devel. music library, 1983-84, dir. devel. research devel. office, 1984—; cons. AT&T, Phoenix, 1985—. Contbr. book reviews to library jour. Mem. Grievance com. Ariz. State U., 1983-84, ombudsman, chmn. staff personnel com., 1980-84, adv. bd. aux. services, 1981-82, also platform speaker univ. inauguration commn., 1981-82. Mem. Am. Mgmt. Assn. Assoc. Records Mgrs. and administrs., Ariz. State Library Assn., Ariz. State U. Friends Music, Ariz. State U. Library Assn., Friends KAET. Republican. Home: PO Box 1009 Tempe AZ 85281 Office: Ariz State U Devel Office Tempe AZ 85287

GLINES, ALAN CLAIR EDWIN, space systems manager, consultant; b. Independence, Kans., Jan. 1, 1943; s. Lewis Clair and Mary Ellen (Patty) G. B.S. in Elec. Engring., U. Kans., 1966 M.S. in Systems Mgmt., U. So. Calif., 1983. With NASA Johnson Space Ctr., Houston, 1966-79, asst. flight dir. mission control Apollo-Soyuz test project, Apollo and Skylab programs, astronaut rep. Space Shuttle Checkout, Palmdale, Calif., 1976-79; sub-project mgr. payload integration TRW Space and Tech. Group, Redondo Beach, Calif., 1979-84, subproject mgr. space shuttle payload integration orbital maneuvering vehicle and gamma ray obs. projects, 1984-85; subproject mgr. Space Station Ops., 1985—; part-time prof. U. So. Calif. Grad. Sch. in Systems Mgmt.; instr. TRW After Hours Program. Recipient Presdl. Medal of Freedom for contbns. to NASA Apollo 13. Mem. Am. Space Found., Planetary Soc. Nat. Space Council. Republican. Home: 1136 3d St Hermosa Beach CA 90254 Office: TRW 1 Space Park Redondo Beach CA 90278

GLINES, STEPHEN WAYNE, computer systems executive; b. Ogden, Utah, Nov. 19, 1949; s. Lawrence T. and Eilene L. (Rudolph) G.; m. Barbara J. Bingham, Aug. 26, 1973; children: Richard, James. BS, Weber State Coll., 1973; MS, Utah State U., 1974. Asst. mgr. S.S. Kresge, Denver, 1974-75; info. system mgr. Utah Dept. Pub. Safety, Salt Lake City, 1975-79; computer cons. Matteson Byrd Cons., Salt Lake City, 1979-81; sr. system analyst Browning Arms Co., Morgan, Utah, 1981-83, data processing ops. mgr., 1983-87; v.p. info. systems C.R. England, Inc., 1987—. Avocations: racquetball, skiing, weight lifting, camping. Home: 4275 W 5700 N Morgan UT 84050 Office: CR England Inc 975 W 21005 Salt Lake City UT 84119

GLODAVA, MILAGROS GARCIA, entrepreneur, consultant; b. Bauan, Batangas, Philippines, May 27, 1945, came to U.S., 1972, naturalized, 1976; d. Francisco Ramos and Rosalia Manalo (Coronel) Garcia; m. Mark Jeffrey Glodava, Jan. 29, 1972; children—Kirsten Angela, Kevin Marc. B.S. in Edn., St. Paul Coll., Manila, 1969. Tchr. Mt. Carmel High Sch., Polillo, Quezon, P.I., 1969-72; bookkeeper First Nat. State Bank of N.J., Newark, 1972-74; pres. Glodava Bus. Services, Arvada, Colo., 1980—. Active in Filipino-Am. community affairs; rep. to first White House briefing on Asian/Pacific women, 1985. Mem. Arvada C. of C., Nat. Assn. Female Execs., Nat. Network of Asian and Pacific Women (rep., editor), Colo. Network of Asian and Pacific Women (founder, chmn., Philippine Week com.). Democrat. Roman Catholic. Author: In Search of a Dream, 1980. Editor, Filipino-Am. News. Home and Office: 7350 Braun Way Arvada CO 80005

GLODE, LEONARD MICHAEL, medical oncologist; b. Chadroc, Neb., July 19, 1947; s. Leonard Michael and Millicent Gretta (Roe) G.; m. Mary Patricia Rose, Dec. 21, 1969; children: Elizabeth, Christopher, Thatcher. Student, U. Nebr.; MD, Washington U., St. Louis. Asst. prof. U. Colo., Denver, 1978-83; assoc. prof. medicine U. Colo., 1983—. Contbr. articles to profl. jours. Bd. dirs. Am. Cancer Soc. Mem. Am. Assn. Cancer Research, Am. Soc. Clin. Oncology. Presbyterian. Office: U Colo Health Scis Ctr 4200 E 9th Ave B-171 Denver CO 80262

GLOGOW, ELI, public health educator, health services administrator; b. Bklyn., Mar. 8, 1924; s. Selig and Mollie (Nissenson) G.; m. Gloria Spiegel (div. June 1968); children: Steve, Nancy Pickett; m. Christine Drilling, Sept. 3, 1978. BS, UCLA, 1949, DPH, 1968; MPH, U. Calif., Berkeley, 1951. Pub. health sanitarian Oakland (Calif.) Health Dept., 1949-50; field rep. Los Angeles County Tuberculosis Assn., 1951-54; supr. health edn. San Francisco Tuberculosis Assn., 1954-55; dir. grad. programs health administrn. U. So. Calif., Los Angeles, 1969-70, 73-75, assoc. prof. pub. health, 1968—; cons. U.S. VA, Los Angeles, 1969-73, State Dept. Mental Health, Calif., 1966-76, Hosp. Council So. Calif., Los Angeles, 1985. Served as cpl. U.S. Army, 1943-46. Recipient Teaching Excellence award U. So. Calif. Sch. Pub. Adminstrn., 1977, Outstanding Community Service award Los Angeles PTA, 1961. Mem. Am. Soc. Pub. Adminstrn., Am. Pub. Health Assn., Am. Cancer Soc. (workplace subcom. Calif. sect.), Los Angeles Pub. Health Found. (bd. dirs. 1981—), Calif. Hosp. Ctr. Health Edn., Delta Omega. Office: U So Calif Sch Pub Adminstrn Los Angeles CA 90089-0041

GLORE, CHARLES FOSTER, III, college administrator, educator; b. Lake Forest, Ill., Sept. 29, 1944; s. Charles Foster Glore Jr. and Dolores (Mummert) Preston; m. Lorraine Ann Nudell, Dec. 15, 1985. BA, U. Denver, 1967; MA, La Universidad de Las Americas, Mex. City, 1972; PhD, U. Colo., 1981. Cert. tchr., Colo. Teaching asst. Universidad de Las Americas, 1970; tchr. English Arvada (Colo.) Sr. High Sch., 1973-76; tchr. Spanish Pomona Sr. High Sch., Arvada, 1976-77; teaching asst. U. Colo., Boulder, 1980; chmn. dept. edn. Colo. Women's Coll., Denver, 1981-82, tennis coach, 1981-82; dir. secondary edn., asst. prof. Westminster Coll., Salt Lake City, 1983-85, tennis coach, 1984-85; mem. Utah State Bd. Edn. Task Force for High Sch. Accreditation, 1984—; mem. steering com. 1984—. Recipient Cert. Appreciation Colo. Children's Meml. Hosp., 1983, Colo. Women's Coll. award Distinction in Teaching and Service, 1982. Mem. Colo. Council Deans of Edn., Colo. Assn. Tchr. Educators, Colo./Wyo. Dirs. Field Experiences (host spring meeting 1981-82), Utah State Adv. Com. on Tchr. Edn., U.S. Profl. Tennis Assn., Utah Assn. for Supervision and Curriculum Devel., Profl. Ski Instrs. Am. (assoc.), Phi Delta Kappa. Avocations: fgn. langs., skiing, tennis. Office: Glore & Co PO Box 24752 Denver CO 80224

GLOUDEMAN, JOSEPH FLOYD, mechanical engineer; b. West Allis, Wis., Oct. 19, 1935; s. Martin Peter and Anna Marie (Kieweg) G.; m. Jeanette Therese Markert, June 14, 1958; children: Mike, Mark, John. BSME, Marquette U., 1958; MSME, U. So. Calif., 1962; Dr.-Ing., U. Stuttgart, Republic of Germany, 1970. Engring. trainee Kearney & Trecker, Milw., 1955-58; engr. Northrop Corp., Los Angeles, 1958-61; sect. mgr. The Aerospace Corp., Los Angeles, 1961-67; dir. data mgmt. Rockwell Internat., Los Angeles, 1967-83; v.p. mktg. MacNeal-Schwendler, Los Angeles, 1978-83, pres., chief exec. officer, 1983—; also bd. dirs. Contbr. articles to profl. jours. Mem. Pres. Council, Loyola Marymount U., Los Angeles, 1985, Pres. Adv. Council, U. La Verne, 1985; active Newcomen Soc., 1985, Town Hall of Calif., 1985. Recipient Spl. Achievement award USAF Space Systems Div., The Aerospace Corp., 1966, Apollo Achievement award NASA, 1969, Significant Achievements to Space Div. Program, N.Am. Rockwell, 1973. Fellow: AIAA (assoc.); mem. Structural Mechanics in Reactor Tech. (dept. orgn. chmn. 1977—), Computer Aided Engring. Reactor Structures (seminar co-organizer 1977—). Republican. Roman Catholic. Avocations: racquetball, running. Home: 731 Hillcrest La Canada Flintridge CA 91011 Office: MacNeal-Schwendler Corp 815 Colorado Blvd Los Angeles CA 90041

GLOVER, JOEL FRANCISCO, dentist; b. Bakersfield, Calif., Mar. 22, 1943; s. Torrance Summers and Lydia (Francisco) G.; m. Mary Eleanor Haines, Aug. 20, 1966; children: Joel Torrance, Jeffie Clare. Student U. Nev., 1961-64; DDS, Northwestern U., 1968. Gen. practice dentistry, Reno, 1971—; bd. Nev. Bd. Dental Examiners, 1979—, pres. Bd. dirs. YMCA, Sparks, Nev., 1972-73; mem. health council Washoe County Sch. Dist., 1979; bd. dirs. Wolfpack Boosters, U. Nev. Alumni Assn., 1981. Served to lt. Dental Corps, USN, 1968-71. Fellow Am. Coll. Dentists, Internat. Coll. Dentists, Acad. Gen. Dentistry, Acad. Dentistry Internat: mem. ADA (council 1984—, pres. council on dental edn.), No. Nev. Dental Soc. (pres. 1979), Nev. Acad. Gen. Dentistry (pres. 1976), Nev. Acad. Dentistry for Children (pres. 1974). Republican. Lodge: Rotary (pres. Reno South 1979-80). Office: 3605 Grant Dr Reno NV 89509

GLOWNIAK, JERRY VINCENT, nuclear medicine physician, researcher; b. Detroit, Aug. 10, 1948; s. Henry and Hattie (Peters) G. BS, U. Mich., 1970, MS, 1972; MD, Wayne State U., 1976. Diplomate Am. Bd. Internal Medicine, Am. Bd. Nuclear Medicine, Am. Bd. Endocrinology. Intern Wil-

liam Beaumont Hosp., Royal Oaks, Mich., 1976-77; resident in internal medicine William Beaumont Hosp., Royal Oak, Mich., 1976-79; fellow in endocrinology U. Mich., Ann Arbor, 1980-82, fellow in nuclear medicine, 1982-84; asst. chief, nuclear medicine dept. VA Hosp., Portland, Oreg., 1984—. Mem. Phi Beta Kappa, Home: 9824 SW 6th Ave Portland OR 97219 Office: VA Med Ctr PO Box 1034 Portland OR 97219

GLUCK, HENRY, resort complex executive; b. 1928; married. BS, U. Pa., 1950. Former pres., chief operating officer Monogram Industries, Inc.; chmn., pres., chief exec. officer Magnasync-Moviola, Inc.; chmn. Standun, Inc., 1978—; chief exec. officer Caesars World, Inc., 1982—, now also chmn., bd. dirs. Served with U.S. Army, 1950-53. Office: Caesars World Inc 1801 Century Park East Los Angeles CA 90067 *

GLUSHIEN, ARTHUR SAMUEL, physician, educator; b. Bklyn., July 15, 1911; s. Isaac and Minnie (Hoffman) G.; m. Edith Risk, Dec. 25, 1938 (dec. July 1978); 1 son, Thomas Michael. B.S. cum laude, N.Y. U., 1930, M.D., 1936. Intern, Kings County Hosp., Bklyn., 1936-37, Ellis Hosp., Schenectady, 1937-38; physician VA Hosp., Pitts., 1939-44, cardiologist, 1944-55, chief med. service, 1955-59; pvt. practice medicine, Pitts., 1959-64; chief cardiology sect. VA Hosp., East Orange, N.J., 1964-74; pvt. practice medicine specializing in cardiology, San Diego, 1974-78; council Inst. Continued Learning U. Calif.-San Diego, 1978—; assoc. clin. prof. medicine U. Pitts. Sch. Medicine, 1952-64; assoc. prof. medicine N.J. Coll. Medicine, 1965-74; chief staff Russellton Med. Group, 1959-64. Pres. Western Pa. Heart Assn., 1961-62. Served to maj. U.S. Army, 1944-46. Recipient Distinguished Service award Western Pa. Heart Assn., 1962; Superior Performance award East Orange VA Hosp., 1969. Diplomate Am. Bd. Internal Medicine. Fellow A.C.P., Am. Coll. Cardiology; mem. Am. Heart Assn., Phi Beta Kappa, Alpha Omega Alpha. Independent. Jewish. Contbr. articles to med. jours. Home: 6761 Caminito del Greco San Diego CA 92120

GLUSKER, PETER (DUCHAN), neurologist; b. N.Y.C., Sept. 3, 1936; s. David Sims and Anita (Brenner) G.; m. Gretchen Knapp, 1958 (div. 1963). Student, Reed Coll., 1954-57; BA, U. Calif., Berkeley, 1959; postgrad., Oxford (Eng.) U. 1960; MD, U. Okla., Oklahoma City, 1974, PhD, 1975. Diplomate Am. Bd. Psychiatry and Neurology. Intern U. Calif., Irvine, 1974-75; resident in neurology U. Calif., San Diego, 1975-78; dir. neurophysiology lab. Mendocino Coast Dist. Hosp., Fort Bragg, Calif., 1979—, mem. exec. com., 1983—, sec. med. staff, 1985—, chief of staff, 1986-87. Contbr. poems to several pubs., 1950-83. Mem. citizens adv. com. Coll. of the Redwoods, Fort Bragg, 1984—; handicapped students adv. com., 1985—; advisor People First, Fort Bragg, 1984—. Fellow Am. Acad. Neurology; mem. Am. EEG Soc., Fedn. Am. Scientists, AAAS, Physicians for Social Responsibility, Am. Assn. Electromyography and Electrodiagnosis. Avocations: bicycling, kayaking. Office: 442 N McPherson St Fort Bragg CA 95437

GNEHM, MAX WILLI, financial consultant; b. Switzerland, July 15, 1943; s. Max Hans and Frieda Gnehm; m. Henrietta D. Schwarz, July 1, 1984; children: Alexandra Barbara, William Anthony. MBA, Swiss Sch. Bus., 1963; postgrad. Swiss Inst. Mktg. and Fgn. Trade Research. Asst. mgr. Maxwell Sci. Internat. Book Co., 1964-66; mgr. book and periodical div. Internat. Univ. Booksellers, N.Y.C., 1966-69; dir. Internat. div. Richard Abel Co., 1969-74; v.p. mktg. Blackwell of N.Am., Inc., Beaverton, Oreg., 1974-76, pres., 1976-79, also bd. dirs.; pres., chmn. bd. Swiss-Am. Investment Group Inc.; pres. Hongkong Fin. Group, Ltd.; bd. dirs. Swiss Am. Data Net, Swiss Am. Data Exchange, Atlin Investment Group, Inc. Author: New Reference Tools for Librarians, 1965. Mem. ALA, Pres.'s Assn. Home: Route 2 Box 376 Forest Grove OR 97116 Office: Hong Kong Fin Group Ltd 42066 Avenida Alvarado Suite S Temecula CA 92390

GOAD, JOHN DAVID, social worker; b. Bowling Green, Ky., Aug. 11, 1946; s. James Clifton and Myrtle Lee (Chaney) G.; m. Judith Ann Yates, May 28, 1972; children: Brian, Jeremy, Brandon. BA in Sociology, Ind. U., 1970; MSW, Ariz. State U., 1975, D Pub. Adminstrn., 1987. Social worker Ariz. Dept. Econ. Security, Phoenix, 1975—. Mem. Nat. Assn. Social Workers (cert.), Am. Humane Assn., Phi Alpha Alpha. Democrat. Methodist. Home: 4232 W Harmont Dr Phoenix AZ 85051 Office: Dept Econ Security 3727 E McDowell Rd Phoenix AZ 85008

GOBAR, ALFRED JULIAN, economic consultant, educator; b. Lucerne Valley, Calif., July 12, 1932; s. Julian Smith and Hilda (Millbank) G.; B.A. in Econs., Whittier Coll., 1953, M.A. in History, 1955; postgrad. Claremont Grad. Sch., 1953-54; Ph.D. in Econs., U. So. Calif., 1963; m. Sally Ann Randall, June 17, 1957; children—Wendy Lee, Curtis Julian, Joseph Julian. Asst. pres. Microdot Inc., Pasadena, 1953-57; regional sales mgr. Sutorbilt Corp., Los Angeles, 1957-59; market research assoc. Beckman Instrument Inc., Fullerton, 1959-64; sr. marketing cons. Western Mgmt. Consultants Inc., Phoenix, Los Angeles, 1964-66; ptnr., prin., chmn. bd. Darley/Gobar Assocs., Inc., 1966-73; pres., chmn. bd. Alfred Gobar Assocs., Inc., Brea, Calif., 1973—; asst. prof. finance U. So. Calif., Los Angeles, 1963-64; assoc. prof. bus. Calif. State U.-Los Angeles, 1963-68, 70-79, assoc. prof. Calif. State U.-Fullerton, 1968-69; mktg., fin. adviser 1957—; pub. speaker seminars and convs. Contbr. articles to profl. publs. Home: 1100 W Valencia Mesa Dr Fullerton CA 92633 Office: 201 S Brea Blvd Brea CA 92621

GOBAR, SALLY RANDALL, school principal; b. Santa Maria, Calif., Nov. 27, 1933; d. Vernon Blythe Randall and Leona Margaret (Jackson) Batchman; m. Alfred Julian Gobar, June 17, 1957; children—Wendy Lee, Curtis Julian, Joseph Julian B.A., Whittier Coll., 1955; M.A., Claremont Grad. Sch., 1967, Ph.D., 1979. Tchr., So. San Francisco High Sch., 1956-57, Santa Ana High Sch., Calif., 1957-61; counselor Sunny Hills High Sch., Fullerton, Calif., 1961-66; head counselor Troy High Sch., Fullerton, 1967-83; asst. prin. Buena Park High Sch., Calif., 1983-84; prin. Fullerton High Sch., 1984—; cons. Coll. Bd., N.Y., 1972-77. Mem. Pres.'s Assocs., Calif. State U.-Fullerton. Recipient Golden Book award Exchange Club, 1978, Outstanding Service award Calif. Personnel and Guidance Assn., 1980. Mem. Assn. Calif. Sch. Adminstrs., Whittier Coll. Alumni Assn., Claremont Grad. Sch. Alumni, Fullerton C. of C. Republican. Avocations: travel; classical music; piano. Home: 1100 Valencia Mesa Dr Fullerton CA 92633 Office: Fullerton Union High Sch 201 E Chapman Fullerton CA 92634

GOBRECHT, ROBERT WILLIAM, retired retail toy store executive; b. Waukegan, Ill., July 8, 1923; s. Edwin Rudolph and Ruth Maria (Parmenter) G.; m. Betty Barbara Cazel, Apr. 15, 1944; children: Janet Claire, Robert Edwin, Carol Ruth. BS, U. So. Calif. Underwriter Firemans Fund Ins. Co., Los Angeles, 1946-48; with exec. tng. program Sears Roebuck & Co., Calif., 1948-60, operating supt., 1959-60; founder, owner, pres. Macabob Toys Co., Inc., Pasadena, Calif., 1961-87; cons. to toy cos. and factories throughout U.S. and Far East. Dep. sheriff Los Angeles County; former pres. Los Angeles County Sheriff Rhythm Posse, 1973-74. Served with USAAF, 1951-45, USAF, 1951-54. Named to Hon. Order Ky. Cols. Mem. Family Motor Coach Assn. (nat. exec. bd., nat. treas.). Republican. Presbyterian. Club: U. So. Calif. Trojans. Lodges: Masons, Maestros. Home: 3575 Newhaven Rd Pasadena CA 91107

GODAGER, JANE ANN, social worker; b. Blue River, Wis., Nov. 29, 1943; d. Roy and Elmyra Marie (Hood) G. BA, U. Wis., 1965; MSW, Fla. State U., 1969. Social worker III State of Wis. Dept Corrections, Wales, 1965-71; supervising psychiat. social worker I State of Calif., San Bernardino, 1972-75, La Mesa, 1975-77; psychiat. social worker State of Calif., San Bernardino, 1978-85; supr. mental health services Riverside (Calif.) County Dept. Mental Health, 1985-86; mental health counselor Superior Ct. San Bernardino County, 1986—. Mem. Nat. Assn. Social Workers, Acad. Cert. Social Workers, Kappa Kappa Gamma Alumnae Assn. Avocations: travel, reading, music. Office: Office Mental Health Counselor 700 E Gilbert St Bldg 1 San Bernardino CA 92415

GODBOLD, WILFORD DARRINGTON, JR., enclosure manufacturing company executive, lawyer; b. Honolulu, Apr. 3, 1938; s. Wilford Darrington and Virginia Mae (Ehlert) G.; m. Sheri Gene Coburn, Feb. 7, 1961; children: Sheila Tiari, Bryan Darrington, Lauri Fairchild. AB, Stanford U., 1960; JD, UCLA, 1966, grad. exec. mgmt. course, UCLA Grad. Sch. Bus. 1983. Bar: Calif., 1967. Ptnr. Gibson, Dunn, & Crutcher, Los Angeles, 1967-82; exec.

v.p. Zero Corp., Burbank, Calif., 1982-84, pres., chief exec. officer, 1984—, mem. exec. com., 1982—, also bd. dirs.; instr. securities law U. West Los Angeles, 1976-1982; bd. dirs. Winchell's Donut Houses, L.P.; bd. advisors Paul-Munroe Hydraulics Co., Inc., 1982-86; lectr. in field. Formerly bd. dirs. Ctr. Theater Group, Los Angeles Music Ctr.; trustee Marlborough Sch., Los Angeles; mem. Los Angeles Adv. Olympic Com. Served to lt. (j.g.) USN, 1960-63. Mem. Los Angeles County Bar Assn. (exec. com.), State Bar of Calif., ABA, Order of Coif, Phi Delta Phi, Delta Upsilon. Republican. Clubs: Verdugo (Glendale, Calif.); Jonathan (Los Angeles); Outrigger Canoe (Honolulu). Office: Zero Corp 444 S Flower St Los Angeles CA 90071

GODDARD, BRENT LEE, marketing professional; b. Salt Lake City, Feb. 21, 1954; s. Benjamin Orson and D. Bernice (Wallace) G.; m. Joyce Ellen Johnson, Mar. 11, 1986; children: Tiffany, Jared, Kelli, Travis. BA, U. Utah, 1978; MBA, Harvard U., 1980. Asst. product mgr. Gen. Mills, Mpls., 1980-82; exec. v.p. Matrix Minerals, Salt Lake City, 1982-83; product mgr. Gourmet Brands, Salt Lake City, 1983-85, Oral-B Labs., Redwood City, Calif., 1985—. Mem. Harvard Bus. Sch. Club (pres. 1984-85, com. chmn. Minn. chpt. 1981-82, Utah chpt. 1984-85). Mormon. Avocations: skiing, lit. Office: Oral-B labs #1 Lagoon Dr Redwood City CA 94065

GODDARD, HAZEL BRYAN, religious organization administrator; b. Mineral, Ill., Aug. 17, 1912; d. Thomas Benton and Maude Carrie (Riley) B.; m. John Howard Goddard; children: David Bryan, Joan Kathryn. BA, Judson Coll., 1966; MS, No. Ill. U., 1973; LittD (hon.), Calif. Grad. Sch. Theology, 1981. Lic. Marriage and family therapist, Fla. Clin. counselor Warrenville (Ill.) Med. Clinic, 1958-78; pres. Christian Counseling Ministries, Buena Vista, Colo., 1978—; lectr., cons., 1978—. Auhtor: Can I Hope Again, 1971, Somebody Else's Girl, Connie, Bob Bronson; contbr. articles to jours. Mem. Am. Assn. Marriage and Family Therapists (clin.), Nat. Assn. Social Workers, Am. Assn. Counseling and Devel. Republican. Baptist. Avocations: writing, music, hiking, fishing, travel. Home: PO Box 789 Buena Vista CO 81211

GODDARD, TERRY, mayor. Mayor, City of Phoenix. Office: Office of the Mayor 251 W Washington St Phoenix AZ 85003§

GODDARD, WILLIAM ANDREW, III, chemist, applied physicist, educator; b. El Centro, Calif., Mar. 29, 1937; s. William Andrew and Barbara Worth (Bright) G.; m. Yvonne Amelia Correy, Oct. 27, 1957; children: William Andrew, Susan Yvonne, Cecelia Monique, Lisa Sharéll. B.S. in Engring. with highest honors, UCLA, 1960; Ph.D. in Engring. Sci, Calif. Inst. Tech., 1964. Mem. faculty Calif. Inst. Tech., Pasadena, 1964—; asso. prof. theoretical chemistry Calif. Inst. Tech., 1971-75, prof. theoretical chemistry, 1975-78, prof. chemistry and applied physics, 1978-84, Charles and Mary Ferkel prof. chemistry and applied physics, 1984—, dir. Caltech-NSF materials research group, 1985—; vis. staff mem. Los Alamos Sci. Lab., 1973—; cons. Gen. Motors Research Labs., 1978—, Argonne Nat. Lab., 1978-82, Sandia Labs., 1979-84, Bell Labs., 1979-83, Gen. Electric Research and Devel. Labs., 1982—, Shell Devel., 1982—, Triton Bioscis. Inc., 1984—, Signal-UOP Research Ctr., 1984—, also Exxon, Sohio; mem. adv. com. for chemistry NSF, 1984-86, chmn., 1985-86; mem. council Gordon Research Confs., 1985-87. Mem. adv. editorial bd. Chem. Physics, 1972—, Jour. Phys. Chemistry, 1976-80, Langmuir, 1984—, Jour. Am. Chem. Soc., 1985—. Recipient Buck-Whitney medal for major contbns. in chemistry, 1978; NSF fellow, 1960-61, 62-64; Shell Found. fellow, 1961-62; Alfred P. Sloan Found. fellow, 1967-69. Fellow Am. Phys. Soc.; Mem. Nat. Acad. Scis., Materials Research Soc., Am. Chem. Soc., Am. Vacuum Soc., Calif. Catalysis Soc., Sigma Xi, Tau Beta Pi. Home: 955 Avondale Dr San Marino CA 91108 Office: Calif Inst Tech Mail Code 127-72 Pasadena CA 91125

GODFREY, ANDREW ELLIOTT, land management planner, geomorphologist; b. Phila., May 31, 1940; s. Ellwood Watson and Sophia (Moore) G.; m. Marie Lorraine St. Pierre, Sept. 1, 1968; children: Sabrina Lorraine, Alida Margaret. AB, Franklin and Marshall Coll., 1964; PhD, Johns Hopkins U., 1969. Asst. project geology Vanderbilt U., Nashville, 1968-72; geologist Ashley Nat. Forest, Vernal, Utah, 1972-79; land mgmt. planner Fishlake Nat. Forest, Richfield, Utah, 1979—; cons. geologist Nat. Ecol. Found., Nashville, 1972-73, Brigham Young U. Mus. Peoples and Cultures, Provo, Utah, 1984—. Contbr. articles to profl. jours. Recipient NDEA Title IV, U.S. Govt., Balt., 1964-68, Cert. Merit, Ashley Nat. Forest, 1979, Fishlake Nat. Forest, 1987. Mem. Geol. Soc. Am., Utah Geol. Assn., Geol. Soc. Wash., Sigma Xi. Presbyterian. Lodge: Kiwanis (pres. Vernal club 1977), Elks (house com. Richfield club 1980). Avocations: fishing, cross country skiing. Home: 523 Valley View Dr Richfield UT 84701 Office: Fishlake Nat Forest 115 E 900 N Richfield UT 84701

GODFREY, DOROTHY DOUD, home economist in business; b. Chattanooga; d. John Veeder and Georgie Louellen (Vest) Doud; m. Chester O. Godfrey, (div.) 1 dau., Jane Godfrey Rhinehart. B.S. in Foods and Nutrition, U. Tenn., 1948, postgrad., 1952. Central regional home economist Westinghouse Electric Corp., 1948-52, southeastern regional home economist, 1953-57; instr. foods and home mgmt. Ohio Wesleyan U., Delaware, 1952-53; home econs. dir. Rena Ware Distbrs., Opportunity, Wash., 1957-66, internat. home econs. dir., Bellevue, Wash., 1966-84, home econs. cons., 1984—. Mem. Internat. Fedn. Home Econs., Am. Home Econs. Assn., Home Economists in Bus., Inst. Food Technologists, Nat. Assn. Parliamentarians, Nat. Assn. Miniature Enthusiasts, Chi Omega Alumnae, Phi Kappa Phi, Omicron Nu. Author Rena Ware use and care books, cookbooks, sales articles for profl. publs. Home: 3035 125th Ave NE Bellevue WA 98005

GODFREY, JANA RHOADS, advertising art director, designer, consultant; b. Pocatello, Idaho, Feb. 27, 1954; d. Steve C. and Betty June (Olson) Rhoads; m. Jeffrey Keith Dudley, July 21, 1974 (div.); m. Emil William Godfrey, June 22, 1981; children: Jason Rhoads, Logan Elizabeth, J. Tyler. BFA in Advt. Design, Utah State U., 1981. Dir. transition gallery Idaho State U., Pocatello, 1976-78; advt. dir., bus. mgr. Utah Statesman, Logan, 1978-80; art dir. Klein/Richardson Advt., Beverly Hills, Calif., 1981-82, Calif. Cable Systems, LaMirada, Calif., 1982; pres., owner, art dir. Good Godfree Prodns., Westminster, Calif., 1982—. Active Rep. Task Forces, 1982. Recipient gen. excellence in ad campaign award Rocky Mountain Collegiate Press Assn., 1980, award Orange County Advt. Fedn., 1984, Ad award Sales Kits and Dealers Aids, 1984, Creativity award Stationery Packages Internat., 1985, Art Dir.'s award, 1985, Lulu award 1986, Internat. Advt. award, 1986. Mem. Los Angeles Art Dirs. Club, Los Angeles Creative Club (bd. dirs.). Episcopalian. Exhibitor: one woman show Idaho State U. 1981; several group shows. Home: 6661 Sutton Ave Westminster CA 92683

GODFREY, PAUL GANNON, surgeon; b. Evanston, Ill., Feb. 14, 1944; s. Paul Rochette and Mary Frances (Gannon) G.; B.S. in Physics, M.I.T., 1966; M.D., U. Ill., 1970; m. Maureen Ann Kelly, June 7, 1969; 1 dau., Kelly Kristine. Diplomate Am. Bd. Surgery. Intern, Rush Presbyn.-St. Luke's Hosp., Chgo., 1970-71, resident in surgery, 1970-75; surg. asst. N.W. Community Hosp., Arlington Heights, Ill., 1975-76; gen. surgeon San Bernardino (Calif.) Med. Group, 1977—; attending staff St. Bernardine Hosp., San Bernardino Community Hosp. Fellow ACS; mem. AMA, Calif. Med. Assn., San Bernardino County Med. Soc., Tri-County Surg. Soc. Office: 1700 N Waterman Ave San Bernardino CA 92404

GODFREY, RICHARD GEORGE, real estate appraiser; b. Sharon, Pa., Dec. 18, 1927; s. Fay Morris and Elisabeth Maguerite (Stefanak) G.; m. Golda Fay Goss, Oct. 28, 1951; children: Deborah Jayne, Gayle Rogers, Bryan Edward. BA, Ripon Coll., 1949. V.p. 1st Thrift & Loan Assn., Albuquerque, 1959-61; pres. Richard G. Godfrey & Assocs., Inc., Albuquerque, 1961—. Mem. Am. Inst. Real Estate Appraisers (v.p. 1981-82), Valuation Network, Inc., Am. Right of Way Assn., Am. Soc. Real Estate Counselors (cert.). Baptist. Lodge: Elks. Home: 1700 Columbia Dr NE Albuquerque NM 87106 Office: 523 Louisiana Blvd SE Albuquerque NM 87108

GODI, DONALD HARRY, landscape architect; b. St. Louis, Feb. 3, 1940; s. Joseph John and Mabel Irene (Andrews) G.; m. Barbara Elizabeth Linville, Aug. 18, 1962; children: Jeanette Elizabeth, Michelle Lynn. BAgr, U. Mo. 1961; M in Landscape Arch., U. Ill., 1967. Landscape architect

Clyde E. Williams Assocs., Indpls., 1967-69, Harmon, O'Donnell, Henninger, Denver, 1969-71; assoc. Phelps, Brauer & Assocs., Denver, 1971-72; prin. D.H. Godi & Assocs., Lakewood, Colo., 1972—; bd. dirs. Colo. Hort. Research, Inc., Denver, Colo. Xeriscape Task Force, Denver; mem. exec. bd. Colo. State U. Dept. Agrl. Sci., Ft. Collins, also mem. adv. bd. Prin. works include urban design Bannock Ctr. (Am. Soc. Land Architects Merit award 1983), landscape Crestwood Restaurant (ALCA Env. award 1978). Mem. adv. council Jefferson County (Colo.) Community Planning com., 1986. Served to 1st lt. USAF, 1961-64. Mem. Am. Arbitration Assn. (panel arbitrators 1985—), Lakewood-S. Jeffco C. of C. (task force com. community planning, 1985-86), Am. Soc. Land Architects (chmn. govt. affairs com. 1983—), Colo. Park and Recreation Assn., Pi Alpha Xi, Gamma Sigma Delta, Delta Chi. Office: D H Godi & Assocs 7805 W Hampden Lakewood CO 80227

GODWIN, JOYCE, health and business services executive; b. Washington, July 25, 1943; m. Earl R. Godwin. BA in Govt., Fla. State U., 1965; MA in Polit. Sci. and Pub. Adminstrn., George Washington U., 1967. Dir. inquiry service Nat. League Cities, Washington, 1965-68; mem. polit. sci. faculty Calif. State Coll., San Jose, 1968-71; mgr. govtl. and pub. affairs San Jose (Calif.) C. of C., 1968-69, gen. mgr., 1969-70, acting exec. v.p., 1970-71; dir. staff devel. Meml. Med. Ctr., Corpus Christi, Tex., 1971-73; dir. edn. Southwest Community Health Services, Albuquerque, 1973-74, dir. personnel, 1974-79, v.p. mgmt. services, 1979-85, v.p. diversification, 1985-86, sec. corp., bd. dirs., 1982—; pres. Southwest Bus. Ventures Inc., 1986—, Vanguard Properties Inc., 1986—; v.p. Southwest Health Found., 1981—; pres., chmn. bd. dirs. MedWest, Inc., 1984—, Total Bus. Systems, Inc., 1981—. Contbr. articles to profl. publs. Chmn. orchestra relations com. N.Mex. Symphony Orch., 1985—, exec. com., 1985-86, bd. dirs., 1983—; assoc. gen. chmn. United Way, 1987. Mem. Greater Albuquerque C. of C. (chmn. roadrunners, bd. dirs., exec. com. 1984, chmn. statewide econ. devel. task force 1985, officer 1985-86, v.p. econ. affairs div. 1985, v.p. ednl. affairs div. 1986, v.p. membership 1987). Avocations: psychology, religion, music, travel. Office: Southwest Bus Ventures Inc PO Box 26027 Albuquerque NM 87125-6027

GODWIN, RALPH RAY, computer software company executive; b. Cleve., July 27, 1948; s. Ralph Rene and Alice Mae (Pretzer) G.; m. Brenda Joy Buttrell, Jan. 14, 1972 (div. 1974); m. Phyllis Ann Fast, June 6, 1977. BBA, U. Alaska, Anchorage, 1977. Data processing mgr. Anchorage Times, 1969-73; analyst Bomhoff & Assocs., Anchorage, 1973-74; chief exec. officer Computer Cons. Alaska Inc., Anchorage, 1974-83; dir. Aardvark Word Processing Systems Inc., Anchorage, 1978—; chief exec. officer Aviation Software Cons. Inc., Anchorage, 1983—; mem. adj. faculty Anchorage Community Coll., 1981-84. Recipient Charles Palmer Davis award Balt. Sch. Dist., 1963. Mem. Ind. Computer Cons. Assn., Anchorage C. of C. (econ. devel. commn. 1985—), Mensa (proctor 1982—). Avocations: writing fiction, skiing, fishing, photography, travel. Home: 6944 Fountain Dr Anchorage AK 99502 Office: Aviation Software Cons Inc 701 W 41st Suite 102 Anchorage AK 99503-6604

GODWIN, ROBERT PAUL, physicist; b. Harvey, Ill., Apr. 4, 1937; s. Paul Stafford and Marguerite Anita (Probst) G.; m. Patricia Elaine Zwickel, June 11, 1960; children: Alan, Susan. AB, DePauw U., 1959; MS, U. Ill., 1961, PhD, 1966. Post-doctoral fellow Deutsches Elektronen Synchrotron, Hamburg, Fed. Republic Germany, 1966-68; mem. staff Los Alamos (N.Mex.) Nat. Lab., 1968—; guest researcher Max-Planck Institut für Plasma Physik, Garching, Fed. Republic Germany, 1976-77. Contbr. articles to profl. jours. Active Nat. Ski Patrol, Los Alamos, 1974—; active N.Mex. Emergency Services Council, Los Alamos, 1980—. Volkswagen fellow Deutsches Elektronen Synchrotron, 1966-68; grantee Fulbright Found., 1976-77. Mem. IEEE, Am. Phys. Soc., Am. Assn. Physics Tchrs., Sigma Xi. Avocations: skiing, sailing, search and rescue.

GOELDNER, CHARLES RAYMOND, business educator; b. Fort Dodge, Iowa, Mar. 21, 1932; s. Leslie Raymond and Beulah (Bohrer) G.; m. Jacquelyn Rae Anderson, Dec. 31, 1954; children: Jo Lynn, Bradley Allen, Deborah Kay. B.A., State U. Iowa, 1954, M.A., 1958, Ph.D., 1961. Asst. prof. Calif. State U., Northridge, 1959-63; assoc. prof., dir. Bur. Bus. Research and Services, 1963-67; prof., dir. bus. research div. U. Colo., Boulder, 1967—; head mktg. div. U. Colo., 1976-79, assoc. dean Coll. Bus., 1985—; Mem. faculty UCLA, summer 1963, 65; lectr. Grad. Sch. Bus., U. So. Calif., Los Angeles, 1963-66. Editor: Jour. Travel Research, 1967—; author: Bibliography of Tourism and Travel Research Studies, Reports and Articles, 9 vols, 1980, Travel Trends in the United States and Canada, 1981, 2d edit., 1984, Automatic Merchandising, A Selected and Annotated Bibliography, 1964, Business Facts: Where to Find Them, 1976, Economic Analysis of North American Ski Areas, 18th edit., 1986, (with Robert McIntosh) Tourism: Principles, Practices, Philosophies, 5th edit., 1986, (with J.R. Brent Ritchie) Travel, Tourism and Hospitality Research, 1987. Trustee U.S. Travel Data Center, 1972—. Served with AUS, 1954-56. L.R. Fairall scholar; Ford Found. Mktg. Research Workshop fellow. Mem. Western Council Travel Research (1st vice chmn. 1970-71), Travel Research Assn. (pres. 1974), Assn. Univ. Bus. and Econ. Research (sec.-treas. 1970-73), Assn. U. Bus. and Econ. Research (v.p. 1973-74, pres. 1974-75), Am. Econ. Assn., Am. Acad. Advt., Inst. Cert. Travel Agts. (acad. council 1974—), Am. Mktg. Assn. (reprints editor 1970-73), Phi Beta Kappa. Home: 3147 Westwood Ct Boulder CO 80302

GOELTZ, JUDITH LENZ, corporate executive, writer; b. Boscobel, Wis., Nov. 23, 1940; d. Sheridan Lee and Bernice Angeline (Graf) Lenz; m. Francis S. Goeltz, Dec. 7, 1968; stepchildren—Marshall Link, Dianna, Shaun, Robert. BS, U. Wis., 1962; postgrad. Adelphi U., Garden City, N.Y., 1963, U. San Francisco, Valencia, Spain, 1964; MS U. N.Mex., 1987. Cert. tchr. Spanish, Wis., N.Y. Tchr., Huntington (N.Y.) Schs., 1962-65; purser/flight attendant Pan Am. Airways, Miami and San Francisco, 1965-70; sales woman Castleton's Stores, Salt Lake City, 1971-72; mgr. organic farm Fightmaster Farms, Fairview, Utah, 1973-78; owner Tony B. Enterprises, San Francisco, 1980-83; asst. mktg. dir. Leach Research, Santa Fe, N.Mex., 1984-85; corp. sec., treas., bus. mgr. Gibraltar, Inc.; hostess radio show Sta. KEST, San Francisco, 1980; pvt. practive psychotherapy, 1987—. Author: Beginner's Natural Food Guide, 1975; Jet Stress: What It Is & How to Cope with It, 1980; contbr. articles on health to profl. jours. Mem. Nat. Assn. Female Execs., Bus. and Profl. Women, Nat. Speakers Assn., Marin Self-Pubs., Orthomolecular Med. Soc., AAUW, Phi Beta Kappa, Phi Kappa Phi, Sigma Delta Pi, Pi Lambda Theta, Eta Kappa Lambda. Home: 2168 Candelero St Santa Fe NM 87505

GOELTZ, PAUL LOUDS, small business owner; b. Taipei, Republic of China, Sept. 12, 1958; (parents Am. citizens); s. James Donald and Sheila Ann (Westbury) G. Student, San Jose State U., 1986—. Engr. WAH Sound, Sacramento, 1982-83, NASA Ames Research Ctr., Moffett Field, Calif., 1984-85; prin. P&G Sound, Santa Clara, Calif., 1984—; stage dir. One Step Beyond, Santa Clara, 1985—; program dir. Spartan Pub, San Jose (Calif.) State U., 1985—; concert chmn. A.S. Program bd., 1986—. Served as sgt. USAF, 1979-82. Mem. Audio Engring. Soc. Avocations: sound systems, coins.

GOERING, LEONARD LOWELL, clergyman, philosophy educator; b. McPherson, Kans., June 22, 1938; s. Ellis Elbert and Esther Elva (Wedel) G.; m. Imogene Helen Ediger, June 10, 1957 (div. 1969); children: Preston, Angela; m. Jane Ellen Kurtz, Dec. 15, 1979; children: David, Jonathan, Rebecca. PhB, Northwestern U., 1964; postgrad., Northeastern Ill. U., 1969-71; MDiv, McCormick Theol. Sem., 1973; postgrad., Vanderbilt U., 1975-77. Ordained to ministry Presbyn. Ch., 1977. Campus minister United Ministries in Higher Edn., Emporia, 1973-75; instr. philosophy, coll. chaplain Coll. Emporia, Kans., 1973-74, Univ. Christian Ministries, Carbondale, Ill., 1977-80; pastor United Presbyn. Ch., Trinidad, Colo., 1981—; instr. philosophy Trinidad State Jr. Coll., 1983—; pres. Family Guidance Services, Trinidad, 1985—. Congl. dist. coordinator Bread for the World, Illinois, 1979-81; chmn. local bd. Emergency Food and Shelter Program of Fed. Emergency Mgmt. Agy., Las Animas County, Colo., 1983—. Mem. Acad. Parish Clergy, Assn. Mental Health Clergy, United Assn. Christian Counselors, Am. Assn. Profl. Hypnotherapists, Trinidad Ministerial Assn., Internat. Platform Assn. Lodge: Kiwanis. Avocations: sailing, hiking, wilderness camping. Home: 721 Pine St Trinidad CO 81082 Office: United Presbyn Ch 224 N Commercial Trinidad CO 81082

GOERING, STEVEN DONALD, air traffic controller; b. Newport Beach, Calif., Aug. 25, 1960; s. Rollie Keith and Celia Helen (Galles) G. Lic. air traffic controller FAA. Air traffic controller FAA, Salt Lake City, 1982—. Served as sgt. USAF, 1978-82. Fellow Nat. Air Traffic Controllers Assn. Republican. Roman Catholic. Avocations: jet skiing, snow and water skiing, camping. Home: 21 Gray Ave Salt Lake City UT 84103

GOETTLICH RIEMANN, WILHELMINA MARIA ANNA, scientist, chemist; b. Jaworow, Poland, June 25, 1934; came to U.S., 1965; d. Jan Stanislaw Goettlich and Kazimiera Henryka (Smielowska) Goettlich-Glazewska; m. Stanislaw Alexander Salomon, Mar. 28, 1958 (div. Nov. 1964); m. Hans Peter Yerndorff Storm Riemann, Aug. 28, 1965. BS in Food Chemistry, Warsaw Agrl. U., Poland, 1954, MS in Food Chemistry, 1957; PhD in Chemistry, Gdansk (Poland) Poly. Inst., 1977. Research asst. Dairy Research Inst., Warsaw, 1957-62; asst. prof. Meat Research Inst., Warsaw, 1961-65; staff research assoc. U. Calif., Davis, 1966-83, researcher, 1986-87; chief coordinator Comecon Meat Research Inst., Warsaw, 1962-65; cons. Polish Patent Commn., Warsaw, 1963-65; lectr. U. Calif., Davis, 1974-75, Meat Research Inst., Warsaw, 1965. Contbr. articles to profl. jours.; patentee in field. Mem. Am. Dairy Sci. Assn., Inst. Food Technologists, Am. Fedn. Tchrs., Sigma Xi. Lodge: Soroptomists. Avocations: piano, literature, history, china painting, sports.

GOETZEL, CLAUS GUENTER, metallurgical engineer; b. Berlin, July 14, 1913; came to U.S., 1936; s. Walter and Else (Baum) G.; m. Lilo Kallmann, Nov. 19, 1938; children: Rodney G., Vivian L. Dipl.-Ing., Technische Hochschule, Berlin, 1935; PhD, Columbia U., 1939. Registered profl. engr., Calif. Research chemist, lab. head Hardy Metall. Co., 1936-39; tech. dir., works mgr. Am. Electro Metal Corp., 1939-47; v.p., dir. research Sintercast Corp. Am., 1947-57; adj. prof. NYU, N.Y.C., 1945-57, sr. research scientist, 1957-60; cons. scientist Lockheed Missiles & Space Co., Sunnyvale, Calif., 1960-78; cons. metall. engring. Portola Valley, Calif., 1978—; lectr., vis. scholar Stanford (Calif.) U., 1961—. Author: Treatise on Powder Metallurgy, 5 vols., 1949-63; contbr. articles to profl. jours. Recipient Alexander von Humboldt Sr. U.S. Scientist award, Fed. Republic Germany, 1978. Fellow Am. Soc. Metals, AIAA (assoc.); mem. AIME (life), Am. Powder Metallurgy Inst. (sr.), Metal Sci. Club N.Y. (life, past pres.), Inst. Metals (life, London).

GOETZKE, GLORIA LOUISE, medical social worker; b. Monticello, Minn.. BA, U. Minn., 1964; MSW, U. Denver, 1966; MBA, Coll. St. Thomas, 1977. Med. social worker VA Med. Ctr., Los Angeles, 1980—; income tax cons. and instr. H&R Block, Santa Monica, Calif., 1980—; preceptor for grad. social work students at UCLA and U. So. Calif. Mem. Nat. Assn. Social Workers (cert.), Acad. Cert. Social Workers.

GOFF, HARRY RUSSELL, manufacturing company executive; b. San Francisco, May 24, 1915; s. Harry Roy and Ethel S. (Ludwigsen) G.; B.A., Stanford U., 1937; M.B.A., Harvard U., 1939; m. Kathleen K. Kloster, Feb. 10, 1940; children—Kathleen, Karen, Betsi. With Nat. Lead Co., San Francisco, 1939-41; partner James D. Dole & Assos., San Francisco, 1946-60; pres. James Dole Corp., San Francisco, 1955-79; chmn. bd., Pacific Sci. Co., Anaheim, Calif., 1979—; dir. Newport Corp. Vice chmn. bd. Stanford U. Library Assn., 1979—. Served with USNR, 1941-46. Mem. Inst. Food Technologists. Republican. Clubs: Bohemian, University (San Francisco); Los Altos Golf and Country; California (Los Angeles). Home: 868 Southampton Dr PO Box 50095 Palo Alto CA 94303 Office: Pacific Scientific Co 172 Constitution Dr Menlo Park CA 94025

GOFF, ROBERT E., business executive; b. Grant City, Mo., Sept. 8, 1935; s. Elvis G. and Gladys G.; m. Donna Lee Peters, June 27, 1964; children—Laura L., Launa L. B.S., San Jose State U., 1972; M.B.A. U. Santa Clara, 1977; regional mgr. Signetics Corp., 1966-70, mktg. mgr., 1970-73; dir. mktg. Avantek Inc., 1973-78, v.p., gen. mgr., 1978-84, sr. v.p., group exec., 1984—. Mem. adv. bd. internat. bus. studies U. Santa Clara. Served with U.S. Army, 1958-60. Mem. IEEE, Assn. of Old Crows, Beta Gamma Sigma. Republican. Episcopalian. Clubs: Saratoga Country. Mem. editorial rev. bd. Jour. Electronics Def. Office: Avantek Inc 3175 Bowers Ave Santa Clara CA 95051

GOFFMAN, JERRY M., psychologist, publisher; b. Bklyn., Feb. 6, 1940; s. Ben and Esther (Bregman) G.; m. Patricia S. Akers, June 10, 1964 (div. May 1972); 1 child, David M.; m. Dora E. Casas, Dec. 29, 1983 (div. 1986). B.A., San Diego State Coll., 1964, M.S. 1969; Ph.D., U.S. Internat. U., San Diego, 1972. Lic. psychologist, marriage, family and child counselor, Calif. Research psychologist med. Neuropsychiat. research unit U.S. Navy, San Diego, 1963-69; research dir. Ctr. for P.O.W. Studies, San Diego, 1970-73; head psychiat. epidemiology br. Naval Health Research Ctr., San Diego, 1973-75; program mgr. San Bernardino County Mental Health Dept., Calif., 1977-82; pvt. practice clin. psychology, San Bernardino, 1980—; founder, coordinator Batterers/Molesters Anonymous, San Bernardino, 1980—, Molesters Anonymous, San Bernardino, 1986—; pub. B.A. Press, San Bernardino, 1982—. Author: (manual) Mutual Support Counseling for Women Batterers, 1980; Self-Help Counseling for Men Who Batter Women, 1984; Self-Help Counseling for Men Who Molest Children, 1986. Contbr. articles to profl. jours. Chmn., San Bernardino County Sch. Attendance Rev. Bd., 1980. Served with U.S. Army, 1963-69. Mem. Inland Psychol. Assn. Jewish. Lodge: Elks. Office: Lawrence Psychological Ctr 407 E Gilbert St Suite 6 San Bernardino CA 92404

GOGOLIN, MARILYN TOMPKINS, educational administrator, language pathologist; b. Pomona, Calif., Feb. 25, 1946; d. Roy Merle and Dorothy (Davidson) Tompkins; m. Robert Elton Gogolin, Mar. 29, 1969. BA, U. LaVerne, Calif., 1967; MA, U. Redlands, Calif., 1968; postgrad., U. Washington, 1968-69; MS, Calif. State U., Fullerton, 1976. Cert. clin. speech pathologist; cert. teaching and sch. adminstrn. Speech/lang. pathologist Rehab. Hosp., Pomona, 1969-71; diagnostic tchr. Los Angeles County Office of Edn., Downey, Calif., 1971-72, program specialist, 1972-75, cons. lang., 1975-76, cons. orgns. and mgmt., 1976-79, asst. to supt., 1979—; cons. lang. sch. dists., Calif., 1975-79; cons. orgn. and mgmt. and prof. assns., Calif., 1976—; exec. dir. Los Angeles County Sch. Trustees Assn., 1979—. Founding patron Desert chpt. Kidney Found., Palm Desert, Calif., 1985. Doctoral fellow U. Washington, 1968; named One of Outstanding Young Women Am., 1977. Mem. Am. Mgmt. Assn., Am. Speech/Hearing Assn., Calif. Speech/Hearing Assn., Am. Edn. Research Assn. Baptist. Avocation: tennis. Home: 15 Sweetwater Irvine CA 92715 Office: Los Angeles County Office Edn 9300 E Imperial Hwy Downey CA 90242

GOHEEN, STEVEN CHARLES, biochemist, researcher; b. Seattle, May 14, 1951; s. Joseph Warner and Margaret Elizabeth (Lange) G.; m. Diane Louise Kent, Mar. 6, 1981; children: Rebecca Elizabeth, Katherine Helen. BS, U. Wash., 1973; PhD, Northwestern U., 1978. Research chemist VA Med. Ctr., Martinez, Calif., 1977-84; sr. mktg. specialist Bio-Rad Labs., Richmond, Calif., 1984—; exec. dir. Membrane Protein Symposium, Richmond, 1986—. Contbr. articles on chromatography and biochemistry to sci. jours. Mem. N.Y. Acad. Sci., AAAS, Am. Inst. Nutrition, Sigma Xi, Tau Beta Pi. Home: 2260 Spring Lake Dr Martinez CA 94553 Office: Bio-Rad Labs 1414 Harbour Way S Richmond CA 94804

GOHIL, PUNIT, physicist, researcher; b. Bhullarai, India, Apr. 8, 1957; came to U.S., 1983; s. Chaman Lal and Mohinder (Kuar) G. BSc in Physics, Imperial Coll., London, 1978, PhD and diploma Imperial Coll. in Physics, 1982. Research fellow Sci. Research Council, Swindon, Eng., 1982-84; staff scientist II Lawrence Berkeley (Calif.) Lab., 1984-85; sr. scientist GA Techs., San Diego, 1985—. Mem. AAAS, Am. Phys. Soc. Avocations: squash, soccer. Home: 3913 Carmel Brooks Way San Diego CA 92130 Office: G A Techs MS13-413 PO Box 85608 San Diego CA 92138

GOING, MARY ELIZABETH, mine safety professional; b. Ft. Benning, Ga., Sept. 12, 1943; d. Richard Louis and Elizabeth Anne (Armstrong) Hennessy; m. David Lawrence Going, Aug. 4, 1984; 1 child, Robert Armstrong Hopkins. BS, Iowa State U., 1966; MS, Marshall U., 1981. Environ. cons. Tenneco Inc., Hawthorne, Nev., 1981-82; sr. safety and health rep. Nev. Occupational Safety and Health Adminstrn., Reno, 1983-85; asst. adminstr. Nev. Div. Mine Inspection, Carson City, Nev., 1985—. Mem. Am. Conf. Govt. Indsl. Hygienists, Am. Soc. Safety Engrs. Avocations: archaeology, oil painting, skiing. Office: Dept Indsl Relations 1380 S Curry St Carson City NV 89701

GOLBECK, AMANDA LORRAINE, mathematics educator, researcher, statistical consultant; b. Milw., May 25, 1952; d. Harvey Fred and Gladys Amanda (Mateer) G.; m. Craig Allen Molgaard, Aug. 11, 1979. BA in Anthropology with honors, Grinnell Coll., 1974; MA in Anthropology, U. Calif., Berkeley, 1977, MA in Stats., 1979, PhD in Biostats., 1983. Research analyst Planned Parenthood, St. Paul, Minn., 1980-81; asst. prof. math. San Diego State U., 1983—; statis. cons. Wash. State U., Pullman, 1979-80, U. Calif., San Francisco, 1981-82, Pacific SW Forest, Berkeley, 1982-84, Ctr. Neurologic Study, San Diego, 1985, Corp. Decisions Systems, San Diego, 1985. Contbr. articles to profl. jours. U. Calif. fellow, Berkeley, 1976-77, 81-83. Research Support grantee HEW, 1983. Mem. Am. Statis. Assn., Population Assn. Am. Office: San Diego State U Dept Math Scis San Diego CA 92182

GOLD, ALBERT, university adminstrator; b. Phila., July 2, 1935; s. Charles and Ida (Nades) G.; m. Martina Basilio, July 9, 1960 (div. July 1977); children: Anthony C., Joseph E., Josephine I. BS in Engring. Physics, Lehigh U., 1956; PhD in Physics, U. Rochester, 1960. Research assoc. U. Ill., Urbana, 1960-62; asst. prof. U. Rochester, N.Y., 1962-65, assoc. prof., 1965-69, assoc. dean Coll. Engring., 1966-68; spl. asst. to pres., dir. postdoctoral affairs Rockefeller U., N.Y.C., 1969-73, v.p., 1973-78; provost Poly. Inst., N.Y.C., 1978-82; v.p. fin., adminstrn. Desert Research Inst., Reno, 1982—. Author: (with R.S. Knox) Symmetry in the Solid State, 1964; contbr. articles to profl. jours. Trustee Jewish Community Council of No. Nev., 1985; trustee Sierra (Nev.) Mus. Art, 1982-85; mem. Provincial Sch. Bd., Order Sacred Heart, N.Y.C., 1973-78; trustee Cheshire (Conn.) Acad., 1975-77. Mem. Am. Phys. Soc., AAAS, Nat. Assn. Coll. Univ. Bus. Officers, Sigma Xi, Phi Beta Kappa, Tau Beta Pi. Avocations: soaring, music. Office: Desert Research Inst 7010 Dandini Blvd Reno NV 89512

GOLD, BREENA FAY, advertising executive; b. Harrisburg, Pa., Aug. 12, 1956; d. Stanley M. and Edith C. (Goldberg) G. BA in Speech Communication and Radio/TV Broadcasting, Pa. State U., 1978. Asst. press sec. Pa. Office of Gov., Harrisburg, 1978-79; dep. press sec. Office Pa. State Sec. Commerce Dept. Commerce, Harrisburg, 1979-82; exec. Dancer Fitzgerald Sample, Inc., Torrance, Calif., 1984—. Club: Advt. (Los Angeles). Office: DFS Dorland So Calif 3501 Sepulveda Blvd Torrance CA 90505

GOLD, MICHAEL, lawyer, litigation consultant; b. N.Y.C., Nov. 17, 1935; s. Nat and Sylvia (Price) G.; m. Lucienne Kacew, July 14, 1957 (div. May 1979); children: Pamela, Katrine, Jennifer; m. Virginia D'Andrade, May 13, 1979; children: David, Anne. AB, Columbia U., 1957; JD, Rutgers U., 1962. Atty. N.J. Office Atty. Gen., Trenton, 1962-65, dep. atty. gen., 1965-67; ptnr. Gold & Gold, Flemington, N.J., 1967-80; v.p. John Day Mgmt. Corp., Santa Monica, Calif., 1980-83; ptnr. M.G. Harrington Co., Pasadena, Calif., 1983—; bd. dirs. HSA Tech. Corp., Los Alamitos; cons. N.J. Fedn. Planning Ofcls., 1975-79. Contbr. articles to profl. jours. Chmn. advancement comm. Boy Scouts Am., Flemington, 1970, Hunterdon County (N.J.) Dem. Com., Flemington, 1972; treas. Hunterdon Legal Services Corp., Flemington, 1974; trustee Trenton State Coll., 1975. Served as sgt. USNG, 1959-65. Mem. Am. Judicature Soc., Los Angeles Bar Assn. (law mgmt. sect.), N.J. Bar Assn. (chmn. criminal sect. 1978), Supreme Ct. Criminal Com., Alpha Epsilon Pi (pres. 1964-67). Lodge: Lions (pres. local chpt. 1968-69). Home: 187 S Catalina Pasadena CA 91106 Office: MG Harrington Co PO Box 60308 Pasadena CA 91106

GOLD, MICHAEL NATHAN, technology and finance manager, biomedical engineer; b. Chgo., May 3, 1952; s. Julius and Sarah (Blitzblau) G.; m. Cynthia Bilicki, June 19, 1976; 1 child, Aaron Michael. B.A., Kalamazoo Coll., 1976. Research fellow Sinai Hosp., Detroit, 1976; research assoc. Molecular Biological Inst., UCLA, Los Angeles, 1976-77; lab mgr., adminstr. Biomed. Engring. Ctr., U. So. Calif., Los Angeles, 1977-80; asst. dir. Crump Inst., UCLA, 1980-84, assoc. dir. Crump Inst. for Med. Engring., UCLA, Los Angeles, 1984—. Mem. IEEE, Assn. for Advancement of Med. Instrumentation, Clin. Ligand Assay Soc., Am. Assn. for Med. Systems and Informatics, Sea Edn. Soc. Office: UCLA Crump Inst for Med Engring 405 Hilgard Ave Los Angeles CA 90024-1654

GOLD, MITZI, psychotherapist; b. Pensacola, Fla., July 30, 1952; d. Sam Harold and Margaret Ann (Cook) G. BA, Western Wash. U., 1974; MPH, U. Hawaii, 1980, MSW, 1981; postgrad., Saybrook Inst., 1987—. Cert. social worker. Program coordinator Po'Ailani, Inc., Honolulu, 1982—; TV hostess Gold Mind, Channel 20, Honolulu, 1985-87. Mem. Hawaii Psychol. Assn., Nat. Assn. Social Workers (cert.), Hawaii Assn. Humanistic Psychology, Ptnrs. in Health. Club: Toastmasters (pres. 1984). Avocations: holistic health studies, healing, music, dance. Home: 2957 Kalakaua Ave #312 Honolulu HI 96815 Office: Po'Ailani Inc 1111 Hala Dr Honolulu HI 96817

GOLD, ROBERT CARLYLE, communications executive; b. New Rochelle, N.Y., June 3, 1955; s. Reuben Robert Gold and Lucille Ellen (Edelson) Holliday; m. Marcia Ann Friedman, Feb. 14, 1986. AA, Hebrew Union Coll., 1975; BS in Psychology, Guilford Coll., 1977; MA in Communications, U. So. Calif., 1979. Asst. to unit publicist Universal Studios, Universal City, Calif., 1979-80; account exec. Ruder Finn & Rotman, Los Angeles, 1980-82; pub. relations specialsit Cable Health Network, Beverly Hills, Calif., 1982-83; instr. Calif. State U., Dominguez Hills, Carson, Calif., 1982-84; mgr. affiliate pub. relations Home Box Office, Inc., Los Angeles, 1983—; cons. Kamar Toys, Torrance, Calif., 1982; ptnr. Cable Reports, Burbank, Calif., 1982-83, MAFGRAFIX, Los Angeles, 1985—. Bd. dirs. Varsity Socuts Steering Com., 1984—. Mem. Calif. Cable TV Assn. (pub. affairs com.), Pub. Relations Soc. Am. (chmn. community services com.), Annenberg West Alumni Assn. (exec. bd.), So. Calif. Cable Assn. Avocation: scuba diving. Home: 1364 N Ave 46 Eagle Rock CA 90041 Office: Home Box Office Inc 2049 Century Park E Los Angeles CA 90067

GOLD, ROBERT J., inventor; b. N.Y.C., Mar. 10, 1953; s. E. Frank and Etta (Hirsch) G.; m. Susan Patricia Bland, Sept. 5, 1981. Student, Queens Coll., 1971-73. Pres. Gold Research and Devel., N.Y.C., 1973-81; dir. research Neoteric Inc., N.Y.C., 1981-83; pres. Neoteric Inc. name changed to Power Staf Inc. in 1985, Phoenix, 1983—, also bd. dirs.; cons. Law Enforcement Tech. Mag., N.Y.C., 1985—; speaker Nat. Orgn. Wardens, San Antonio, 1984, Am. Def. Preparedness Assn., Virginia Beach, Va., 1986, others. Contbg. editor L.E.T. mag.; contbr. articles to profl. jours.; patentee non-lethal equipment. Mem. Internat. Non-Lethal Weapons Assn., Tactical Response Assn. Avocations: inventing, writing, skiing, hang gliding, target shooting. Office: Power Staf Inc 21617 North 9th Ave Phoenix AZ 85027

GOLD, RUSSELL STUART, psychologist; b. Chgo., Jan. 7, 1949; s. Irving Louis and Victoria (Saltzman) G.; m. Andrea Marie Bofinger; children—Celia, Kristofer, Kristen. B.A., U. Ill., 1970; M.A., Northwestern U., 1973; Ph.D., Calif. Sch. Profl. Psychology, San Diego, 1978. Intern, postdoctoral fellow Mercy Hosp. and Med. Center, San Diego, 1977-79; pvt. practice psychology, San Diego, 1979—; police psychologist San Diego County, 1985—. Mem. Am. Psychol. Assn., Calif. Psychol. Assn., Acad. San Diego Psychologists (sec. 1981-83, pres. 1984), Council Exceptional Children. Office: 4060 4th Ave San Diego CA 92103

GOLD, WILLIAM, microbiologist; b. Buffalo, Jan. 2, 1923; s. Paul and Merle (Stirberg) G.; m. Aida Sara Frank, Dec. 21, 1952; children: Avram Reuben, Morris Samuel, Rebecca Rose, Hannah Star. BS, Cornell U., 1943; MS, U. Wis., 1948, PhD, 1950. Fellow Rutgers (N.J.) U., 1950-51; research assoc. E.R. Squibb, New Brunswick, N.J., 1951-57; microbiologist Bzura, Inc., Keyport, N.J., 1957-63; supr. biochemistry dept. Beechnut/Lifesavers Co., Portchester, N.Y., 1963-67; asst. prof. NYU Coll. Dentistry, N.Y.C., 1967-73; mgr. pharmacology Cooper Labs., Mountain View, Calif., 1973-81; supr. devel. of biologics Am. Microscan, Sacramento, 1982—. Contbr. articles to profl. jours.; patentee in field. Served with U.S. Army, 1943-46,

ETO. Grantee John Hartford Found., NYU Coll. Dentistry, 1968-73. Mem. Am. Chem. Soc., Am. Soc. Microbiology, Sigma Xi. Jewish. Avocations: religious studies. Home: 3121 Hempstead Rd Sacramento CA 95864

GOLDAPER, GABRIELE GAY, clothing executive, consultant; b. Amsterdam, The Netherlands, May 4, 1937; came to U.S., 1949; d. Richard and Gertrud (Sinzheimer) Mainzer; married, 1957; children: Carolyn, Julie, Nancy. BA in Econs., Barnard Coll., 1959; BS in Edn., U. Cin., 1960; postgrad. in Econs., Xavier U., 1962. V.p. planning, systems and material control High Tide Swimwear div. Warnaco, Los Angeles, 1974-79; v.p., customer support cons. Silton AMS, Los Angeles, 1979-80; exec. v.p., ptnr. Prisma Corp., Los Angeles, 1980-84; exec. v.p. Mindstar Prods., Los Angeles, 1984-85; gen. mgr. Cherry Lane, Los Angeles, 1985-86; dir. inventory mgmt. Barco Uniforms, Los Angeles, 1986; mgmt. cons. to clothing industry 1986—; instr. Calif. State U., 1978-79, UCLA Grad. Bus. Mgmt. Sch., 1979—, Fashion Inst. Design and Merchandising. 1985—; chmn. data processing com. Calif. Fashion Creators, 1980; lectr. various colls. Author: A Results Oriented Approach to Manufacturing Planning, 1978, Small Company View of the Computer, 1979; also articles. Elected mem. Commn. on Status Women, 1985—. Mem. Apparel Mfrs. Assn. (mgmt. systems com. 1978-80), Calif. Apparel Industries Assn. (exec. com., bd. dirs. 1980), Am. Arbitration Assn. Home: 37 Village Pkwy Santa Monica CA 90405

GOLDBERG, ALFRED, metallurgist; b. Montreal, Quebec, Can., Oct. 2, 1923; s. Morris and Mary (Zimmerman) G.; m. Tanna Guadalupe de la Torre, Nov. 4, 1950; children: John M., Teresa Ann Goldberg Diaz, Edward T. B in Engring., McGill U., Montreal, 1946; MS, Carnegie Mellon U., 1947; PhD, U. Calif., Berkeley, 1955. Research engr. U. Calif., Berkeley, 1947-50; from asst. to assoc. prof. U.S. Naval Postgrad. Sch., Monterey, Calif., 1953-64; metallurgist Lawrence Livermore (Calif.) Nat. Lab., 1964-80, project leader, 1980—; Fulbright prof. Nat. Engring. U., Lima, Peru, 1961; Internat. AEA prof. Inst. Physics, Bariloche, Argentina, 1962. Contbr. articles to profl. jours. Chmn. Livermore-Quezaltenango Sister City Orgn., Livermore, 1972-73. Fellow Internat Nickel Co., 1950; Univ. scholar Que. (Can.) Bur. of Mines, 1944-46; recipient Best Paper award, Internat. Metall. Soc., First in Class awards Metallographic Exhibit, Internat. Metall. Soc., 1972, 73. Fellow Am. Soc. for Metals; mem. Am. Soc. for Metals, InterAm. Confs. on Materials Tech. (exec. com. 1973—), Sigma Xi. Home: 1220 Glenwood St Livermore CA 94550 Office: Lawrence Livermore Nat Lab End East Ave PO Box 808 Livermore CA 94550

GOLDBERG, CARYN, psychologist; b. Jersey City, Jan. 12, 1954; d. Walter and Elayne (Schwartz) Goldberg. BA, U. Colo., 1975; MEd, U. Ariz., 1976; PhD, Calif. Sch. Profl. Psychology, 1980. Lic. psychologist. Therapist, Fremont (Calif.) Youth Service Ctr., 1977-78, Vallejo (Calif.) Mental Health Ctr., 1978-80; pvt. practice psychotherapy, Denver, 1980—; therapist Inst. Motivational Devel., Denver, 1983-84; instr. U. Colo. Continuing Edn., 1983—, Met. State Coll., 1986—; psychologist Ctr. for Eating Disorders Rocky Mountain Hosp., Denver, 1986—. Mem. Colo. Psychol. Assn., Am. Psychol. Assn., N.Am. Soc. for Adlerian Psychology. Jewish. Contbr. articles to profl. jours.

GOLDBERG, DAVID CHARLES, computer maintenance executive; b. Los Angeles, Feb. 26, 1940; s. David and Hazel Madeline (Lucatorta) G.; m. Jolane Kay Bjork, Aug. 11, 1962 (div. Jan. 1979); children—Deborah Dawn, Jennifer Lyn. B.S. in Bus. Adminstrn., Sacramento State Coll., 1972; A.A. in Math./Sci., Santa Monica Coll., 1969. Technician Gen. Plastics, Los Angeles, 1961-62, Honeywell Computer Control Co., Los Angeles, 1962-65; mgr. br. customer engring. Sperry Univac, RCA, Sacramento, Calif., 1965-74; mgr. gen. services communication systems and services TRW, Hawthorne, Calif., 1974-79; mgr. west region Info. Internat. Inc., Culver City, Calif., 1979-81; v.p. field engring. Data Systems Services div. Eaton Corp., Culver City, 1981—. Pres., Gates Square Homeowners Assn., Redondo Beach, Calif., 1982-84; mem. adv. com., high tech. dept. Indian Hills Community Coll., Ottumwa, Iowa. Served with U.S. Army, 1957-66. Mem. Assn. Field Service Mgrs., Am. Def. Preparedness Assn. Republican. Club: Aza. Lodge: Masons. Home: 2511 Gates Ave Redondo Beach CA 90278 Office: Eaton Corp DSSD 5875 Green Valley Circle Culver City CA 90230

GOLDBERG, DONALD MICHAEL, speech pathology and audiology educator; b. N.Y.C., Jan. 17, 1955; s. Irving and Emilie Marie (Berg) G. AB, Lafayette Coll., Easton, Pa., 1977; MA, U. Fla., 1979, PhD, 1985. Speech pathologist Wakeland Elem. Sch., Bradenton, Fla., 1979-80; therapist, intern Beebe Speech and Hearing Ctr., Easton, 1980-81; clin. supr., instr. speech pathology and aural rehabilitation U. Fla., Gainesville, 1981-85; asst. prof. U. Mont., Missoula, 1985—. Mem. Am. Speech Lang. and Hearing Assn. (cert.), Acad. Rehabilitative Audiology, Alexander Graham Bell Assn. for the Deaf, Sigma Xi, Phi Gamma Delta. Jewish. Avocations: swimming, skiing. Home: 409 McLeod #5 Missoula MT 59801 Office: U Mont Missoula MT 59812

GOLDBERG, EDWARD DAVIDOW, geochemist, educator; b. Sacramento, Aug. 2, 1921; s. Edward Davidow and Lillian (Rothholz) G.; m. Kathe Bertine, Dec. 26, 1973; children—David Wilkes, Wendy Jean, Kathi Kiri, Beck Bertine. B.S., U. Calif.-Berkeley, 1942; Ph.D., U. Chgo., 1949. Mem. faculty Scripps Instn. Oceanography, La Jolla, Calif., 1949—; prof. chemistry Scripps Instn. Oceanography, 1960—; provost Revelle Coll., U. Calif. at San Diego, 1965-66. Author: (with J. Geiss) Earth Sciences and Meteorites, 1964, Guide to Marine Pollution, 1972, North Sea Science, 1973, The Sea: Marine Chemistry, Vol. V, 1974, The Health of the Oceans, 1976; Black Carbon in the Environment, 1985. Contbr. numerous articles to profl. jours. Guggenheim fellow, 1961; NATO fellow, 1970. Fellow Am. Geophys. Union, AAAS; mem. Geochem. Soc., U.S. Acad. Scis., Sigma Xi. Research, publs. primarily on marine pollution, chem. composition sea water, sediments, marine organisms, environmental mgmt.; radioactive dating techniques in marine environment and glaciers. Home: 750 Val Sereno Dr Encinitas CA 92024

GOLDBERG, JEROLD MARTIN, TV, advt., promotion executive; b. N.Y.C., Nov. 29, 1938; s. Murray Lyon and Ruth Alice (Margolis) G. BFA, Syracuse U., 1960. Art dir. House Beautiful mag., N.Y.C., 1961-71; with talent and casting div., program dept. CBS, Los Angeles, 1972, on-air graphic artist, advt. and promotion dept., 1973-74, on-air writer, producer, 1975-76, mgr. promotions, 1977-78; mgr. on-air promotion CBS, N.Y.C., 1979-83, dir. advt., 1984-85; v.p. on-air promotion CBS/Entertainment, Los Angeles, 1985—. Democrat. Jewish. Office: 7800 Beverly Blvd Los Angeles CA 90036

GOLDBERG, JERRY DAVID, city planner, urban designer; b. St. Louis, Oct. 12, 1934; s. Joseph D. and Idale (Glass) G.; m. Katherine E. Farnsworth, Mar. 25, 1967; 1 dau., Jennifer. A.B. magna cum laude, Harvard U., 1957; B.Arch., Washington U., St. Louis, 1962. Assoc. ptnr. Skidmore, Owings & Merrill, Chgo., 1963-66, San Francisco, 1966—; lectr. U. Tex., Austin, 1974, 76, UCLA, 1977, U. Calif., Berkeley, 1980, Stanford U., 1980. Author: Collective Form, 1961. Mem. planning com. San Francisco Planning and Urban Research, 1970; trustee French Am. Internat. Sch., 1981—. Fulbright scholar, Netherlands, 1962-63. Mem. Am. Inst. City Planners, Assn. Collegiate Schs. Architecture, Bay Area Council, Amnesty Internat., ACLU, Sunday Afternoon Watercolor Soc. Democrat. Jewish. Club: Harvard of San Francisco. Office: Skidmore Owings & Merrill 333 Bush St San Francisco CA 94104

GOLDBERG, LEE WINICKI, furniture co. exec.; b. Laredo, Tex., Nov. 20, 1932; d. Frank and Goldie (Ostrowiak) Winicki; student San Diego State U., 1951-52; m. Frank M. Goldberg, Aug. 17, 1952; children—Susan Arlene, Edward Lewis, Anne Carri. With United Furniture Co., Inc., San Diego, 1953-83, corp. sec., dir., 1963-83, dir. environ. interiors, 1970-83; founder Drexel-Heritage store Edwards Interiors, subs. United Furniture, 1975; founding ptnr., v.p. FLJB Corp., 1976—, founding ptnr., sec. treas., Sea Fin., Inc., 1980, founding ptnr., First Nat. Bank San Diego, 1982. Den mother Boy Scouts Am., San Diego, 1965; vol. Am. Cancer Soc., San Diego, 1964-69; chmn. jr. matrons United Jewish Fedn., San Diego, 1958; del. So. Pacific Coast region Hadassah Conv., 1960, pres. Galilee group San Diego chpt., 1960-61; supporter Marc Chagall Nat. Mus., Nice, France, Smithsonian Instn., Los Angeles County Mus., La Jolla (Calif.) Mus. Contemporary Art, San Diego Mus. Art. Recipient Hadassah Service award San Diego chpt., 1958-59. Democrat. Jewish.

GOLDBERG, MORRIS, physician; b. N.Y.C., Jan. 23, 1928; s. Saul and Lena (Schanberg) G.; B.S. in Chemistry cum laude, Poly. Inst. Bklyn., 1951; M.D., SUNY, Bklyn., 1956; m. Elaine Shaw, June 24, 1956; children—Alan Neil, Seth David, Nancy Beth. Intern, Jewish Hosp. Bklyn., 1956-57, resident, 1957-58, 61-62, renal fellow, 1958-59; practice medicine, specializing in internal medicine, N.Y.C., 1962-71, Phoenix, 1971—; instr. to asst. clin. prof. internal medicine State U. N.Y. Coll. Medicine, Bklyn., 1962-71; clin. investigator, metabolic research unit Jewish Hosp. Bklyn., 1962-71; cons. in field; mem. staff Phoenix Bapt., Maryvale Samaritan, Good Samaritan, St. Joseph's hosps. Served to capt. M.C., U.S. Army, 1959-61. Diplomate Am. Bd. Internal Medicine. Fellow ACP; mem. Am. Soc. Internal Medicine, AMA, Am. Coll. Nuclear Physicians, Internat. Soc. Internal Medicine, Am. Soc. Nephrology, Am. Soc. Hypertension, Internat. Soc. Nephrology, 38th Parallel Med. Soc. S. Korea, Ariz., Maricopa County med. assns., N.Y. Acad. Sci., Sigma Xi, Phi Lambda Upsilon, Alpha Omega Alpha. Jewish. Contbr. articles to med. jours. Home: 24 E Wagonwheel Dr Phoenix AZ 85020 Office: 5310 W Thunderbird Rd Glendale AZ 85306

GOLDBERG, NORMAN JOEL, gastroenterologist, educator, health facility administrator; b. Montreal, Que., Can., Mar. 27, 1934; s. Joseph and Anne (Scott) G.; m. Barbara Jane Usher, June 25, 1957; children: David, Judy, Jonathan. BSc, McGill U., Montreal, 1955, MD, 1959. Diplomate Am. Bd. Internal Medicine. Intern Jewish Gen. Hosp., Montreal, 1959-60; resident in internal medicine Montreal Gen. Hosp., 1960-61, 63-64, research fellow Med. Research Council Can., 1961-62; resident in gastroenterology Grad. Hosp. U. Pa., 1962-63; asst. prof. medicine McGill U., Montreal, 1970-77; adj. assoc. prof. UCLA, Los Angeles, 1977-83, adj. prof., 1983—; dir. gastroenterology San Bernardino County (Calif.) Med. Ctr., 1977—. Contbr. articles to profl. jours. Fellow Royal Coll. Physicians and Surgeons, Am. Coll. Gastroenterology; mem. ACP, Am. Gastroenterological Assn., So. Calif. Soc. Gastroenterology, San Bernardino County Med Soc. (bd. dirs.). Jewish. Home: 1580 Franklin Ave Redlands CA 92373 Office: San Bernardino County Med Ctr 780 E Gilbert St San Bernardino CA 92415

GOLDBERG, ROBERT M., lawyer; b. Chgo., Jan. 23, 1941; s. Arthur Joseph and Dorothy (Kurgans) G.; m. Barbara Sproston, Feb. 13, 1966; children—Esther Fiona, Angus Ephraim, Duncan Abraham. B.A. with honors, Amherst Coll., 1963; postgrad. London Sch. Econs., 1964; J.D., Harvard U., 1967. Bar: Alaska 1969, Ill. 1969, U.S. Ct. Appeals (9th cir.) 1973, U.S. Ct. Appeals D.C. Cir. 1978, U.S. Sup. Ct. 1978, D.C. 1979. Law clk. presiding justice U.S. Ct. Appeals for D.C., 1967-68; assoc. Kay, Miller & Libby, Anchorage, 1969-70; assoc. prof. law sea grant program U. Alaska, 1970-72, adj. prof., 1980—; ptnr. Goldberg & Elliott, Anchorage, 1976-78, Goldberg, Breckberg, & Gottstein, Anchorage, 1978-80, Goldberg & Gottstein, Anchorage, 1980-82, Robert M. Goldberg & Assocs., Anchorage, 1982—; adj. prof. law U. Denver, 1973-75; adj. prof. govt. and econs. Alaska Pacific U., Anchorage, 1970-73. Trustee, Alaska Pacific U., 1975—; del. Democratic Nat. Conv., 1974, 76; chmn. Alaska Assn. for Hist. Preservation, 1981-85. Recipient Best Non-Fiction Book award Alaska Press Club, 1970. Mem. ABA, Ill. State Bar Assn., D.C. Bar Assn., Alaska Bar Assn., Fed. Bar Assn., Am. Soc. Internat. Law. Jewish. Editor: Alaska Survey & Report, Vols. I and II, 1970-72. Home: 1130 S St Anchorage AK 99501 Office: 1107 W 7th St Anchorage AK 99501

GOLDBERGER, MARVIN L., educator, physicist, institute technology president; b. Chgo., Oct. 22, 1922; s. Joseph and Mildred (Sedwitz) G.; m. Mildred Ginsburg, Nov. 25, 1945; children: Samuel M., Joel S. B.S., Carnegie Inst. Tech., 1943; Ph.D., U. Chgo., 1948. Research asso. Radiation Lab., U. Calif., 1948-49; research asso. Mass. Inst. Tech., 1949-50; asst.-asso. prof. U. Chgo., 1950-55, prof., 1955-57; Higgins prof. physics Princeton U., 1953-54, 57-78, chmn. dept., 1970-76, Joseph Henry prof. physics, 1977-78; pres. Calif. Inst. Tech., Pasadena, 1978-87; dir. Inst. Advanced Study, Princeton U., N.J., 1987—; Mem. President's Sci. Adv. Com., 1965-69; Chmn. Fedn. Am. Scientists, 1971-73; dir. Gen. Motors Corp., Haskel, Inc., Interactive Systems Corp., Internat. Tech. Corp. Fellow Am. Phys. Soc., Am. Acad. Arts and Scis.; mem. Nat. Acad. Scis., Am. Philos. Soc., Council on Fgn. Relations, Internat. Tech. Corp. Club: Princeton, Calif., Bohemian (N.Y.C.), Calif.

GOLDBLATT, STEVEN MELVIN, construction management educator; b. Sacramento, Jan. 24, 1950; s. Walter Irving and Shirley Ann (Marcus) G.; m. Joan Leventhal, June 20, 1982; 1 child, Sarah Kate. BSEE, U. Calif., Berkeley, 1971; JD, Golden Gate U., 1977. Bar: Calif. 1977, U.S. Dist. Ct. (no. dist.) Calif., 1977. Engr. Los Angeles Dept. Water and Power, 1971-74, Pacific Gas and Electric Co., San Francisco, 1974-78; asst. mgr. regional counsel Western Caissons, Inc., Concord, Calif., 1978-79; sr. cons. Wagner-Hohns-Inglis, Inc., La Crescenta, Calif., 1979-80; asst. prof. bldg. constrn. and contracting Purdue U., West Lafayette, Ind., 1980-82; assoc. prof., chmn. dept. bldg. constrn. U. Wash., Seattle, 1982—. Editor Constrn. Edn. Quar. newsletter, 1983—. Mem. Wash. State Council Faculty Reps., Olympia, 1984—, Wash. State Sch. Facilities Cost Adv. Bd., Olympia, 1982—; precinct com. man King County Dems., Seattle, 1982—. Mem. ABA, Calif. Bar Assn., ASCE, Am. Inst. Constructors, Council Edn!. Facility Planners, Nat. Orgn. Legal Problems of Edn., Am. Arbitration Assn. Jewish. Club: City (Seattle), U. Wash. Pres.'s. Avocations: college sports, travel. Home: PO Box 85420 Seattle WA 98145 Office: U Wash Dept Bldg Constrn 208 Gould JO-24 Seattle WA 98195

GOLDE, DAVID WILLIAM, physician, educator; b. N.Y.C., Oct. 23, 1940. B.S. in Chemistry, Fairleigh Dickinson U., 1962; M.D., McGill U., 1966. Diplomate: Am Bd. Internal Medicine, Am. Bd. Med. Oncology, Nat. Bd. Med. Examiners. Asst. research chemist Gen. Foods Corp., 1962; intern. U. Calif. Hosps., San Francisco, 1966-67, resident in medicine, 1970-71, fellow Cancer Research Inst., 1971-72; staff cons. continuing edn. and tng. br. div. regional med. program (NIH), 1967-68; hematology fellow, resident in clin. pathology NIH, 1969-70; instr. medicine U. Calif., San Francisco, 1972-73, asst. prof., 1973-74; asst. prof. medicine UCLA, 1974-75, assoc. prof., 1975-79, prof., 1979—; co-dir. Clin. Research Ctr. (UCLA), 1974—; chief div. hematology-oncology UCLA, 1981—, dir. AIDS ctr., 1986—. Mem. editorial bd.: Blood, 1978, Peptides, 1979-83, 1981, Leukemia, 1986—, Scand. Jour. Hematology, 1986, Blood Revs., 1986; contbr. numerous articles to profl. jours. Served with USPHS, 1967-70. N.J. Coll. Surgeons Med. scholar, 1963-65. Mem. Am. Assn. Cancer Research, AAAS, ACP, Am. Fedn. Clin. Research, Am. Soc. Clin. Investigation, Am. Soc. Clin. Oncology, Am. Soc. Hematology, Am. Assn. Physicians, Internat. Soc. Exptl. Hematology, Reticuloendothelial Soc., Soc. Exptl. Biology and Medicine, Western Soc. Clin. Research, Phi Omega Epsilon, Alpha Omega Alpha. Home: 10718 Lindbrook Ave Los Angeles CA 90024

GOLDEN, CONSTANCE JEAN, aerospace executive; b. Highland Park, Ill., June 8, 1939; d. Herman William and Chrystle O'Linda Leuer; BS Beloit Coll. summa cum laude, 1961; AM, Harvard, 1962; PhD in Math., Stanford U., 1966, MS, 1970; m. Charles Joseph Golden, June 13, 1962; 1 dau., Kerri Lynn. Scientist/engr. research and devel. div. Lockheed Missiles & Space Co., Sunnyvale, Calif., 1962-68, sr. scientist/engr. Palo Alto research labs., 1968-74, mgr. planning requirements and mgmt. control, missile systems div., Sunnyvale, 1975-78; program mgr. manned space ops. studies Ford Aerospace, Palo Alto, 1978-79, corp. strategy mgr., Detroit, 1980-81, mgr. mission ops. and tech. devel., Sunnyvale, Calif., 1982-84, mgr. adv. programs, 1984—; mem. comml. satellite survivability task force. Nat. Security Telecommunications Adv. Com., 1982-84; mem. Nat. Def. Exec. Res.-Fed. Emergency Mgmt. Agy.; mem. adv. council for sci. and math. Mills Coll., 1976-80. NSF fellow, 1961-62; recipient Tribute to Women in Industry award, 1985-86; named Disting. Woman of Yr. Lockheed, 1976. Mem. AIAA (space systems tech. panel 1982-83), Armed Forces Communications and Electronic Assn. (sect. dir. 1979-80), Am. Astronautical Soc. (chmn. San Francisco Bay Area sect. 1984), Soc. Women Engrs. (fellow 1982, past pres. San Francisco Bay Area sect., past nat. scholarship chmn.), Military Space Systems Tech. Plan, Jr. Achievement, Phi Beta Kappa (award 1960-61). Club: Toastmasters (past pres., ATM). Contbg. author: Second Careers for Women, 1975. Office: Ford Aerospace 1260 Crossman Ave Sunnyvale CA 94089

GOLDEN, JOSEPH MICHAEL, JR., bank executive; b. San Francisco, May 21, 1937; s. Joseph Michael Sr. and Lorraine Alice (Hamilton) G.; m. Ione Mary McIver, Aug. 27, 1960; children: Veronica Ann, Maureen Alice, Joanna Lorraine, Joseph Michael III. BS in Money and Banking, U. Santa Clara. Teller, trainee Bank of Am. Nat. Trust and Savs. Assn., San Jose, Calif., 1958-60; asst. inspector Bank of Am. Nat. Trust and Savs. Assn., San Francisco, 1960-62; asst. cashier regional office Bank of Am. Nat. Trust and Savs. Assn., San Jose, 1962-63; asst. br. mgr. Bank of Am. Nat. Trust and Savs. Assn., East Los Gatos, Calif., 1963-66; asst. mgr. main office Bank of Am. Nat. Trust and Savs. Assn., San Jose, 1966-72; asst. br. mgr. Bank of Am. Nat. Trust and Savs. Assn., Christiansted, St. Croix, Virgin Islands, 1972-73, mgr. island ctr. br., 1973-76; asst. v.p. Latin Am./Caribbean div. Bank of Am. Nat. Trust and Savs. Assn., Caracus, Venezuela, 1976-79; asst. v.p. consumer loan services Bank of Am. Nat. Trust and Savs. Assn., San Francisco, 1979-84, asst. v.p., sr. product mgr. retail fin. services, consumer loan adminstrn., 1983-84, v.p., sr. product mgr. retail fin. services, consumer loan adminstrn., 1984-85, v.p. BA acceptance group, 1985—. Capt., tng. officer CAP, Santa Clara (Calif.) County, 1955-58; treas. March of Dimes, Los Gatos, 1963-65; mem. fin. com., parish council St. Lucy's Cath. Ch., Campbell, Calif., 1970-72; capt., sr. officer Campbell Police Res., 1962-72; trustee Good Hope Sch., V. I., 1973-75, pres. 1975-76; fin. com. chmn. St. Ann's Ch., St. Croix, 1974-76; bd. dirs. Christian Community Conscience Ctr., V. I., 1973-76; 1st v.p. St. Croix C. of C., 1975; treas. Santa Rosa de Lima Cath. Ch., Caracus, 1977-79. Mem. V. I. Bankers Assn. (sec. 1975-76), USN League, Aircraft Owners and Pilots Assn., Nat. Marine Bankers Assn. (bd. dirs. 1984—), Calif. Manufactured Housing Inst. (bd. dirs. 1984—). Republican. Club: Olympic (San Francisco). Office: Bank Am Nat Trust & Savs Assn 555 California St San Francisco CA 94104

GOLDEN, JULIUS, advertising/public relations firm executive, lobbyist, investor in developing companies; b. N.Y.C., Feb. 25, 1929; s. Nathan and Leah (Michlin) G.; m. Constance Lee Carpenter, Dec. 31, 1954 (div. Mar. 1965); children—Andrew Mitchell, Juliet Deborah; m. Diana Zana George, Apr. 30, 1973; 1 child, Jeremy Philip. B.A., U. N.Mex., 1952. Asst. dir. info. U. N.Mex., Albuquerque, 1952-53; writer AP, Albuquerque, part-time 1952-53, staff writer, 1953-55, fgn. corr., S.Am., 1956-59; pres. Group West Advt./Pub. Relations Albuquerque, 1959—; dir. Comparative Annuity Reports, Albuquerque, Tax Deferred Savs., Inc., Albuquerque, Diagnostek, Inc., Albuquerque, Galaxy Broadcasting Co., Albuquerque, Triad Communications Inc., Albuquerque. Author: A Time to Die, 1975. Active Bernalillo County Lung Assn., 1961-64; mem. Met. Crime Commn., Albuquerque, 1967-71; chmn., 1970-71. Served with AUS, 1945-48, PTO, Korea. Recipient Nat. Feature Writing award Sigma Delta Chi, 1952, E.H. Shaffer award N.Mex. Press Assn., 1953. Mem. Pub. Relations Soc. (pres. N.Mex. chpt. 1972), Profl. Journalism Soc. (pres. 1969-70), Pub. Relations Soc. N.Mex. pres. 1972), Am. Advt. Fedn., Sigma Delta Chi. Democrat. Jewish. Clubs: Overseas Press of Am., Albuquerque Press, Petroleum, 4 Hills Country. Home: 1408 Stagecoach Ln SE Albuquerque NM 87123 Office: Group West 7005 Prospect Pl NE Albuquerque NM 87110

GOLDEN, LAURIE RUTH, public relations executive; b. Santa Monica, Calif., Oct. 17, 1945; d. Mort Wolson and Ruth Mary (Sykes) Thieme; m. Alan Golden, July 23, 1966 (div.); 1 child, Michael. Student, U. Calif., Northridge, 1965-68. Dir. mktg. JL&A, Woodland Hills, Calif., 1983-84; prin. Jacob's Well, Woodland Hills, 1984—; cons. Ctr. Bus. Devel., Calif. Luth. U. Bd. dirs. Girl Scouts U.S. San Fernando Valley, 1985—; mem. enterprise com. Pacific Lodge Boys' Home, Woodland Hills, 1984—; mem. Police Activity League Supporters, Woodland Hills, 1985—; mem. ACLU. Mem. Radio TV News Assn., San Fernando Valley Pub. Relations Roundtable, Woodland Hills C. of C., Valley Industry and Commerce Assn., Latin Bus. Assn., Town Hall of Calif. Republican. Club: The Lincoln. Avocations: lit., opera, ballet, theater. Office: Jacob's Well 21777 Ventura Blvd Suite 256 Woodland Hills CA 91364

GOLDEN, MORTON JAY, museum director; b. Bklyn., Apr. 11, 1929; s. Sam C. and Anna (Denmark) G.; m. Evelyn Gould, Oct. 6, 1956; children: Caron, Linda, Jay. BS, U. So. Calif., 1952. Dep. dir. Los Angeles County Mus. Art, 1972-82; dir. Palm Springs (Calif.) Desert Mus., 1982—. Bd. dirs. Convention and Visitors Bur., Palm Springs, 1985—. Honor of Republic, nation of Egypt, 1979. Mem. Calif. Assn. Mus. (bd. dirs. 1978—, chmn. 1978-82), Am. Assn. Mus. (cons. 1984). Home: 1830 El Alameda Palm Springs CA 92262 Office: Palm Springs Desert Mus Inc PO Box 2288 101 Museum Dr Palm Springs CA 92263

GOLDEN, RALPH WILARD, electrical engineer; b. Superior, Wis., Sept. 24, 1937; s. Floyd W. and Ruth M. (Harper) G.; m. Mary Jane Sethre, Aug. 13, 1961 (dec. Jan. 1985); childen: Gloria G., Jeffery T.; m. Coy M. Peterson, Apr. 4, 1987; children: Linda M. Peterson, Kathleen D. Peterson Miller, Steven O., Eric G. AAS in electronic tech., Milw. Tech. Coll., 1968; BSEE, U. Idaho, 1975; MEE, U. Idaho, Idaho Falls, 1981. Registered profl. engr., Idaho. Grain inspector Wis. State Grain Commn., Superior, 1959; material handler Am. Motor Corp., Milw., 1959-61, painter, 1962-67; receiving inspector AC Electronics of Gen. Motor Corp., Oak Creek, Wis., 1967-68; sr. engr. EG&G Idaho, Inc., Idaho Falls, 1968; instrument technician Idaho Nat. Engring. Lab., 1968-70, assoc. engr. Idaho Nuclear Corp./ Aerojet Nuclear Corp., 1970-74, engr. Aerojet Nuclear Corp., 1975, sr. engr. Aerojet Nuclear Corp./EG&G Idaho, Inc., 1975—. Contbr. articles to profl. jours. Asst. scoutmaster Boy Scouts Am., Idaho Falls, 1982—; camp pres. Gideons Internat., Idaho Falls, 1980—, bistate sec. Idaho-Utah Gideons, Idaho and Utah, 1987—. Served with USNG, 1955-62. Mrm. Inst. Soc. Am. (sr., sec.-pres. 1981-82). Mem. Christian Ch. Club: Idaho Alpine (Idaho Falls). Avocations: backpacking, fishing, hunting, photography, woodworking. Home: Rt 7 PO Box 185 Idaho Falls ID 83401 Office: EG&G Idaho Inc PO Box 1625 Idaho Falls ID 83415

GOLDFARB, SAUL HOWARD, health care company executive, consultant; b. N.Y.C., Jan. 5, 1940; s. George and Miriam (Press) G.; m. Judy K. Jacobs, June 16, 1963; children—Stephanie, Jennifer. A.B., Hunter Coll., 1961; cert. phys. therapy Columbia U., 1962, M.S. in Hosp. Adminstrn., 1968; cert. exec. mgmt. program UCLA, 1976. Phys. therapist Inst. Rehab Medicine, 1962-66; asst. v.p. Lutheran Med. Ctr., 1968-70; asst. adminstr. Cedars-Sinai Med. Ctr., 1970-71; adminstr. Van Nuys Psychiat. Hosp. Calif., 1971-73, Beverly Glen Hosp., Am. Medicorp, 1973-74, West Hills Med. Ctr., 1974-76; adminstr. Queen of Angels Hosp., Hosp. Affiliates Internat., 1976-78, regional dir., Hosp. Affiliates Internat., 1978-79; mng. dir. Hosp. Affiliates Australia P/L, Sydney, 1979-80; hosp. adminstr. Valley Park Med. Ctr., Nu-Med, Inc., Canoga Park, Calif., 1981-86, regional dir. Nu-Med, Inc., 1984-86; v.p. ops. Delano Med. Mgmt. Corp., 1986—. Mem. Am. Coll. Hosp. Adminstrn., United Hosp. Assn. (treas. 1982-83, v.p. 1983-84, exec. v.p. 1985, pres. 1987). Home: 27081 Esward Dr Agoura CA 91301 Office: Valley Park Med Ctr 7011 Shoup Ave Canoga Park CA 91307

GOLDIE, RAY ROBERT, lawyer; b. Dayton, Ohio, Apr. 1, 1920; s. Albert S. and Lillian (Hayman) G.; student U. So. Calif., 1943-44, J.D., 1957; student San Bernardino Valley Coll., 1950-51; m. Dorothy Roberta Zafman, Dec. 2, 1941; children—Marilyn, Deanne, Dayle, Ron R. Elec. appliance dealer, 1944-54; teaching asst. U. So. Calif. Law Sch., 1956-57; admitted to Calif. bar, 1957; dep. atty. gen. State of Calif., 1957-58; individual practice, San Bernardino, 1958—. Pres., Trinity Acceptance Corp., 1948-53. Mem. World Peace Through Law Center, 1962—; regional dir. Legion Lex, U. So. Calif. Sch. Law, 1959-75; chmn. San Bernardino United Jewish Appeal, 1963; v.p. United Jewish Welfare Fund San Bernardino, 1964-66, Santa Anita Hosp., Lake Arrowhead, 1966-69. Bd. dirs. San Bernardino Med. Arts Corp. Served with AUS, 1942-43. Fellow Internat. Acad. Law and Sci.; mem. Am., San Bernardino County bar assns., State Bar Calif., Am. Judicature Soc., Am. Soc. Hosp. Attys., Calif. Trial Lawyers Assn. (v.p. chpt. 1965-67, pres. 1967-68), Am. Arbitration Assn. (nat. panel arbitrators), Order of Coif, Nu Beta Epsilon (pres. 1956-57). Club: Lake Arrowhead Country (pres. 1972-73, 80-81), Lake Arrowhead Yacht, Club at Morningside. Home: 1 Hampton Ct Rancho Mirage CA 92270 Office: 432 N Arrowhead Ave San Bernardino CA 92401 also: 1111 Tahquitz E Palm Springs CA 92262

GOLDIN, ROBERT W., aerospace engineer; b. Phila., Nov. 7, 1919; s. Solomon and Marcia (Agrons) G.; children: Patricia Gail, Robert Wayne. BS, U. Pa., 1941; MS, Calif. Inst. Tech., 1942. Cartographic engr.

U.S. Coast and Geodetic Survey, Washington, 1942-43; stress analyst Curtiss Wright Corp., Columbus, Ohio, 1943-44; group engr. applied loads USN, Washington, 1945-49; asst. chief engr. Bell Aerosystems Co., Niagara Falls, N.Y., 1950-60; cons. engr. Lockheed Missiles & Space Co., Sunnyvale, Calif., 1960—; flight safety counselor FAA; instr. Evening Sch., De Anza Coll.; cons. engr. Aircraft Owners and Pilots Assn. Air Safety Found. Co-author: Aircraft Owners and Pilots Assn. Mountain Flying Course, 1971; patentee aircraft flight instruments. Served to lt. USN, 1944-46. Named Flight Instr. of Yr.; grantee Aircraft Owners and Pilots Assn. Air Safety Found., 1971; recipient Group Achievement award NASA, 1979. Assoc. fellow AIAA; mem. Soc. Automotive Engrs., Nat. Assn. Flight Instrs., Tau Beta Pi. Home: 1372 Sydney Dr Sunnyvale CA 94087 Office: Lockheed Missiles & Space Co 1111 Lockheed Way Sunnyvale CA 94086

GOLDING, EVAN ELDEN, interior designer; b. Price, Utah, June 8, 1934; s. Elden Barton and Ruth (Branch) G.; m. Kay Petersen, Sept. 2, 1952; children: Debra, Rachelle, Bary, GeriLin, Thad. Grad. high sch., Provo, Utah. Interior designer Taylor Bros., Provo, 1952-55, Sears Roebuck & Co., Salt Lake City, 1955-58, J.C. Penney & Co., Salt Lake City, 1958-63, Christiansen Furniture Co., Salt Lake City, 1963-77; owner Barbara Jenson Interiors, Salt Lake City, 1977-84; mgr. showroom Pearsons Galleries, Inc., Phoenix, 1984—. Named Eagle Scout Boy Scouts Am., Provo, 1953. Mem. Interior Design Soc. (pres. Utah chpt. 1975-76, nat. chpt. 80-81, v.p. nat. chpt. 1976-80, chmn. bd. examiners 1977-80, chmn. exec. com. 1981-82). Mormon. Avocations: pianist, organist, choir dir., painting, swimming. Office: Pearsons Galleries Inc 12404 N Paradise Village Pkwy E Phoenix AZ 85032

GOLDING, GEORGE EARL, journalist; b. Oakdale, Calif., Aug. 26, 1925; s. Herbert Victor and Elva M. (Leydecker) G.; A.A., Modesto Jr. Coll., 1950; B.A., San Francisco State Coll., 1959; m. Joyce Mary Buttner, July 15, 1948; children—Earlene Golding Brown, Brad Leslie, Dennis Lee, Frank Edwin, Charlton Kenneth, Daniel Duane. Advt. salesman Riverbank News, 1949; galley bank boy, cub reporter San Bernardino Sun, 1951; editor Gustine Standard, 1952; photographer-reporter Humboldt Times, 1952-56; reporter, asst. city editor San Mateo (Calif.) Times, 1956-63; corr. UPI; contbg. writer, photographer Nat. Motorist mag.; aviation writer, columnist Flight Log. Pub. relations adviser Powder Puff Derby start. 1972. Served with U.S. Maritime Service, 1943, USAAF, 1944-46, AUS, 1950. Recipient John Swett award Calif. Tchrs. Assn., 1964; nominee McQuaid award Cath. Newsmen, 1965, 68; A.P. and Ency. Brit. photography awards, 1954-55, A.P. newswriting award, 1964. Mem. Am. Newspaper Guild, San Francisco-Oakland News Guild, Aviation/Space Writers Assn. (regional writing awards), Peninsula Press Club (founding dir., pres. 1976, co-chmn. awards and installation 1986-87), San Mateo County Arts Council (charter). Home: 1625 Ark St San Mateo CA 94403 Office: 1080 S Amphlett Blvd San Mateo CA 94402

GOLDMAN, AARON SAMPSON, statistician; b. Red Lion, Pa., Feb. 8, 1932; s. William and Lilly (Slotkovich) G.; m. Peggy Ann Hopkins, Sept. 13, 1963; children: Kathy, William, Keith. BS, Okla. State U., 1954, MS, 1958, PhD, 1961. Statistician Los Alamos (N.Mex.) Lab., 1960-65, 79—; prof. math., stats. Gonzaga U., Spokane, Wash., 1965-69, U. Nev., Las Vegas, 1970-79. Served to 1st lt., USAF, 1954-56. Home: 4723 Sandia Los Alamos NM 87544 Office: Los Alamos Nat Lab N-1 MS E 540 Los Alamos NM 87545

GOLDMAN, HENRY HOWARD, management consultant; b. Los Angeles, July 17, 1936; s. Herman Henry and Leonore (Soghor) G.; m. Kathryn Ellen Shotton, Jan. 27, 1961; children: James, Christopher. BA, UCLA, 1958; MA, U. Iowa, 1960. Mgr. budget Norris Industries, Los Angeles, 1972-79; mgr. fin. ops. Leighton & Assocs., Irvine, Calif., 1979-80; prin., cons. Goldman Group, Huntington Beach, Calif., 1981—; adj. instr. U. Phoenix, 1983—, Nat. U., Los Angeles, 1984—, Webster U., St. Louis, 1985—. Player agt., bd. dirs. Seaview Little League, Huntington Beach, 1985; mem. supt.'s fin. adv. com. Huntington Beach City Schs., 1986. Mem. Planning Forum (treas. 1977-78, v.p. 1978-79, pres. 1979-80, fellow 1978). Republican. Mem. Reorganized Ch. Jesus Christ Latter-day Saints. Home and Office: 20531 Paisley Ln Huntington Beach CA 92646

GOLDMAN, MARVIN, biophysicist, educator; b. N.Y.C., May 2, 1928; s. Sidney Albert and Mary (Wind) G.; m. Joyce T. Weiss, Aug. 30, 1953; children—David Lee, Beth Lisa, Robert Sidney. A.B., Adelphi U, N.Y., 1949; M.S., U. Md, College Park, 1951; Ph.D., U. Rochester, NY, 1957. Biologist NIH, Bethesda, Md., 1951-52; jr. scientist U. Rochester, N.Y., 1957-58; adj. assoc. prof. U. Calif., Davis, 1958-72; biophysicist U.S. AEC, Washington, D.C., 1972-73; dir. Energy Lab.-Health Research Lab., Davis, Calif., 1973-85; prof. U. Calif., Davis, Calif., 1973—; cons. NRC, Washington, 1972—, WHO, Copenhagen, 1982—; biomed. panel chair Dept. Energy, NASA, U.S. Air Force, Washington, 1973—. Editor: Radiostrontium Effects, 1972; contbr. articles to profl. jours. Inventor: X-Ray Fluorescence, 1968. Recipient E.O. Lawrence award U.S. AEC, 1972; Cert., NASA, 1977. Mem. Nat. Council Radiation Protection, Radiation Research Soc., Health Physics Soc., AAAS, Sigma Xi. Home: 1122 Pine Ln Davis CA 95616 Office: U Calif Lab Energy Related Health Research Davis CA 95616

GOLDMAN, RALPH, physician, educator; b. N.Y.C., June 11, 1919; s. Henry and May (Hoffman) G.; m. Helen C. Wolfson, Jan. 15, 1941; children—Paul, Richard, Elizabeth. A.B., U. Calif. at Berkeley, 1939; M.D., U. Calif. at San Francisco, 1942. Intern Los Angeles County Gen. Hosp., 1942-43, resident internal medicine, 1943-44; resident internal medicine VA Center Los Angeles, 1946-48, chief metabolic and renal disease sect., 1948-55; chief med. service VA Hosp., Sepulveda, Calif., 1955-58; prof. medicine U. Calif. at Los Angeles Med. Sch., 1958-77, prof. medicine/geriatrics in residence, 1980—, asst. dean allied health Professions, 1971-75; chief intermediate care and geriatric med. sect. VA Center Los Angeles, 1975-77; asst. chief med. dir. for extended care VA Central Office, Washington, 1977-80; asso. chief staff for edn. VA Wadsworth Med. Center, Los Angeles, 1980—; clin. prof. medicine George Washington U., 1979-80. Contbr. articles to profl. jours. Served to lt., M.C. USNR, 1944-46. Fellow A.C.P., Gerontol. Soc., Geriatrics Soc.; mem. Internat. Assn. Gerontology, Am. Geriatric Soc. (Willard O. Thompson award 1970), Internat., Am. socs. nephrology. Home: 10501 Wilshire Blvd Los Angeles CA 90024

GOLDMAN, ROGER O., banker; b. N.Y.C., Mar. 9, 1945; s. Erwin and Dorothy G.; m. Randye Jill Farmer; children—Jodi Frances, Cindy Lynn. B.S. in Mktg., NYU, 1966; J.D., Am. U., 1969. Bar: D.C. 1969, N.J. 1970. Congl. liaison officer U.S. Dept. Agr., Washington, 1967-69; mem. corporate planning dept. Citibank, 1971-72, account mgr., dir. mktg., mgr. account mgmt. group Citicorp Bus. Credit, 1972-76, South Bronx area dir., 1976-79, Bronx area dir., 1979-81, regional bus. mgr. Bronx/Westchester/Mid-Hudson region, 1981-83; pres., chief exec. officer Redwood Bank, San Francisco, 1983-86; mng. prin. Consulting for Bus. Growth, Inc., 1986—. Chmn. fin. com. Juvenile Diabetes Found., 1976-78, v.p. field services, 1978-80, chmn. bd., 1980-83; mem. bd. N.Y.C. Cadet Corps., 1980-83; campaign dir. U.S. Congressman, 1970-72, candidate for N.J. State Assembly, 1973. Recipient Humanitarian awards Albert Einstein Med. Ctr., 1981, Bronx council of Am. Jewish Congress, 1982, Gold medal N.Y.C. Mission Soc. Cadet Corps, 1982. Office: Consulting for Bus Growth Inc 3641 Sacramento St Suite G San Francisco CA 94111

GOLDSCHMIDT, NEIL EDWARD, governor of Oregon; b. Eugene, Oreg., June 16, 1940; s. Lester H. and Annette (Levin) G.; m. Margaret Wood; children: Joshua, Rebecca. A.B. in Polit. Sci., U. Oreg., 1963; LL.B., U. Calif., 1967. Atty. Legal Aid Oreg., 1967-70; commr. City of Portland, 1971-72, mayor, 1973-79; sec. transp. Washington, 1979-81; v.p. internat. mktg. NIKE/BRS, Inc., Beaverton, Oreg., from 1981; gov. State of Oreg., 1987—; dir. Nat. Semi-Condr. Corp., Gelco Corp. Civil rights worker, Miss., 1964; Former chmn. transp. com. U.S. Conf. Mayors, also chmn. housing and community devel. com.; former co-chmn. energy task force Nat. League Cities; bd. dirs. Kaiser Permanente Found. Health Plan, 1981—. Named Outstanding Young Man Am., 1972. Address: 3900 SW Murray Blvd Beaverton OR 97005 Office: Governors Office 254 State Capitol Bldg Salem OR 97310

GOLDSCHMIDT, WALTER ROCHS, educator, anthropologist; b. San Antonio, Feb. 24, 1913; s. Hermann and Gretchen (Rochs) G.; m. Beatrice Lucia Gale, May 27, 1937; children: Karl Gale, Mark Stefan. B.A., U. Tex., 1933, M.A., 1935; Ph.D., U. Calif. at Berkeley, 1942. Social scientist Bur. Agrl. Econs., 1940-46; mem. faculty UCLA, 1946—, prof. anthropology, 1956—, chmn. dept., 1964-69, prof. anthropology and psychiatry, 1970-83, prof. emeritus, 1983—; Vis. lectr. Stanford, summer 1945, U. Calif. at Berkeley, 1949, Harvard, 1950. Dir. radio program: Ways of Mankind, 1951- 53, Culture and Ecology in E. Africa, 1960-68. Spl. editor: World of Man Series, Aldine Pub. Co., 1966-75. Author: Small Business and the Community, 1946, As You Sow, 1947, 2d edit., 1978, Nomlaki Ethnography, 1951, Ways to Justice, 1953, Man's Way, 1959, Exploring the Ways of Mankind, 1960, 3d edit., 1977, Comparative Functionalism, 1966, Sebei Law, 1967, Kambuya's Cattle, The Legacy of an African Herdsman, 1968, On Being an Anthropologist, 1970, Culture and Behavior of the Sebei, 1976, The Sebei: A Study in Cultural Adaptation, 1986. Editor: The U.S. and Africa, rev, 1963, French edit., 1965, The Anthropology of Franz Boas, 1959, (with H. Hoijer) The Social Anthropology of Latin America, 1970, The Uses of Anthropology, 1979, Anthropology and Public Policy: A Dialogue, 1986, Am. Anthropologist, 1956-59; founding editor: Ethos, 1972-79. Fulbright scholar U.K., 1953; grantee Social Sci. Research Council, 1953; grantee Wenner-Gren Found., 1953; NSF postdoctoral fellow, 1964-65; fellow Center Advanced Study Behavioral Scis., 1964-65; sr. sci. fellow NIMH, 1970-75. Fellow Am. Anthrop. Assn. (pres. 1975-76), African Studies Assn. (founding, bd. dirs. 1957-60); mem. AAAS, Southwestern Anthrop. Assn. (pres. 1950-51), Am. Ethnol. Soc. (pres. 1969-70), Phi Beta Kappa, Sigma Xi. Home: 978 Norman Pl Los Angeles CA 90049

GOLDSMITH, BRAM, banker; b. Chgo., Feb. 22, 1923; s. Max L. and Bertha (Gittelsohn) G.; m. Elaine Maltz; children: Bruce, Russell. Student, Herzl Jr. Coll., 1940, U. Ill., 1941-42. Asst. v.p. Pioneer-Atlas Liquor Co., Chgo., 1945-47; pres. Winston Lumber and Supply Co., East Chicago, Ind., 1947-50; v.p. Medal Distilled Products, Inc., Beverly Hills, Calif., 1950-75; pres. Buckeye Realty and Mgmt. Corp., Beverly Hills, 1952-75; exec. v.p. Buckeye Constrn. Co., Inc., Beverly Hills, 1952-75; chmn. bd., chief exec. officer City Nat. Corp., Beverly Hills, 1975—; dir. City Nat. Bank, Beverly Hills, 1964—, chmn. bd., chief exec. officer, 1975—; past dir. Los Angeles br. San Francisco Fed. Res. Bank. Pres. Jewish Fedn. Council of Greater Los Angeles, 1969-70; nat. chmn. United Jewish Appeal, 1970-74; regional chmn. United Crusade, 1976; co-chmn. bd. dirs. NCCJ. Served with Signal Corps U.S. Army, 1942-45. Jewish. Clubs: Hillcrest Country, Masons (Los Angeles), Balboa Bay. Office: 400 N Roxbury Dr Beverly Hills CA 90210 *

GOLDSMITH, DONALD WILLIAM, lawyer, astronomer, writer; b. Washington, Feb. 24, 1943; s. Raymond William and Selma Evelyn (Fine) G.; m. Rose Marien, Apr. 10, 1975 (div. 1978); 1 child, Rachel Evelyn. BA, Harvard U., 1963; PhD, U. Calif., Berkeley, 1969, JD, 1983. Asst. prof. earth and space sci. SUNY, Stony Brook, 1972-74; vis. prof. Niels Bohr Inst., Copenhagen, 1977; vis. instr. physics Stanford (Calif.) U., 1983; vis. lectr. astronomy U. Calif., Berkeley, 1980-85; assoc. Pillsbury, Madison and Sutro, San Francisco, 1985-87; cons. Cosmos TV program, Los Angeles, 1978-80; pres. Interstellar Media Publs., Berkeley, 1978—. Author: Nemesis, 1985, The Evolving Universe, 1985; (with others) The Search for Life in the Universe, 1980, Cosmic Horizons, 1982; co-writer (TV program) Is Anybody Out There, 1986. Recipient 1st prize popular essays in astronomy Griffith Obs./Hughes Aircraft Corp., Los Angeles, 1983, Best Popular Writing by a Scientist award Am. Inst. Physics, 1986. Home: 2153 Russell St Berkeley CA 94705

GOLDSMITH, FRANK, executive, real estate developer, marina owner; b. Mulheim, W.Ger., Oct. 13, 1949; came to U.S., 1950, naturalized, 1954; s. Henry L. and Ellen H. (Baldeschwiler) G. BSEE, CCNY, 1972. Master electrician, Colo. Electrician, Elec. Union, N.Y., 1972-74; electrician Aspen Highlands Ski Corp. (Colo.), 1974-76; propr. pres. Aspen Elec., Inc. (Colo.), 1976-86; pres. MGM Imports, 1986—; pres. Lake George Marina, Inc.; faculty Colo. Mountain Coll. Home: PO Box 3126 Aspen CO 81612 Office: Aspen Elec Inc 465 N Mill St Aspen CO 81611

GOLDSMITH, SUSAN AMY, social work and health care consultant, writer; b. Portland, Oreg., Oct. 26, 1952; d. Gerson F. and Mathilda (Fischl) G.; m. John W. Clarke, Sept. 14, 1985 (dec. Oct. 1986); stepchildren: Kevin G., Catherine R. Student, Oreg. State U., 1970-72; BS in Sociology, Psychology summa cum laude, Portland State U., 1975, MSW, 1977. Social worker Children's Services Div. State of Oreg., 1977-79; trust social worker U.S. Nat. Bank Oreg., Portland, 1979-83, trust officer, 1983-85; founding ptnr. Resource Connectors, Portland, 1985—; bd. dirs. Hospice House, Inc., Portland. Contbr. articles to profl. jours. Grantee NIMH, 1975. Mem. Nat. Assn. Social Workers, Am. Soc. Aging, Portland C. of C., ARC (bd. dirs. guardianship, adv. and protective services 1981—). Democrat. Jewish. Club: Profl. Women Investors (Portland) (founder 1983, pres. 1984-85). Avocations: skiing, sailing, reading, writing, houseboats. Home: 7720 SW Macadam Ave Portland OR 97219 Office: Resource Connectors 1400 SW Montgomery Portland OR 97201

GOLDSTEIN, AVRAM, pharmacology educator; b. N.Y.C., July 3, 1919; s. Israel and Bertha (Markowitz) G.; m. Dora Benedict, Aug. 29, 1947; children—Margaret, Daniel, Joshua, Michael. A.B., Harvard, 1940, M.D., 1943. Intern Mt. Sinai Hosp., N.Y.C., 1944; successively instr., assoc., asst. prof. pharmacology Harvard, 1947-55; prof. dept. pharmacology Stanford, 1955—, exec. head dept., 1955-70; dir. Addiction Research Found., Palo Alto, Calif., 1973—. Author: Principles of Drug Action. Served from 1st lt. to capt., M.C. AUS, 1944-46. Mem. Nat. Acad. Scis., Am. Soc. Pharmacology and Exptl. Therapeutics, AAAS, Am. Soc. Biol. Chemists. Home: 735 Dolores St Stanford CA 94305 Office: Dept Pharmacology Stanford U Stanford CA 94305

GOLDSTEIN, BARRY BRUCE, biologist, researcher; b. N.Y.C., Aug. 2, 1947; s. George and Pauline (Kolodner) G.; m. Jacqueline Barbara Aboulafia, Dec. 21, 1968; children: Joshua, Jessica. BA, Queens Coll., 1968; MA, CCNY, N.Y.C., 1974; PhD, CUNY, N.Y.C., 1980. Microbiologist CPC Internat., Yonkers, N.Y., 1968-71; research scientist U. Tex., Austin, 1977-80; v.p. Systems Culture Inc., Honolulu, 1980-83; bioenergy program mgr. N.Mex. Solar Energy Inst., Las Cruces, 1983—; pres. Managed Food Chains, Inc., Las Cruces, 1985—. Contbr. articles to profl. jours. Recipient Nat. Energy Innovation award Dept. Energy, Washington, 1985; Grad. fellow CUNY, 1971, Jesse Smith Noyes fellow, 1975, Regents scholar, N.Y. State U., 1964. Mem. World Aquaculture Soc., Am. Soc. Microbiology, AAAS. Avocations: aquaculture, gardening, reading, inventing. Office: NMex Solar Energy Inst Box 3 SOL Las Cruces NM 88003

GOLDSTEIN, DONALD AARON, engineering company executive; b. N.Y.C., May 11, 1934; s. Joachim and Anna G.; B.B.A., CCNY, 1955; M.S., Pa. State U., 1957, Ph.D., 1961; m. Audrey Pearl Buonocore, May 5, 1968; children—Carla, Seth, Liza. Dir. indsl. engring. electric boat div. Gen. Dynamics, Groton, Conn., 1973-76; mgmt. cons., Waterford, Conn., 1976-77; exec. v.p., gen. mgr. Health Physics Systems, Gainesville, Fla., 1979-80; dir. adminstrn. and personnel Quadrex Corp., Campbell, Calif., 1977-79, 80; pres. Project Assistance Corp., San Jose, Calif., 1981—. Mem. Am. Soc. Quality Control, Am. Psychol. Assn. Contbr. articles in field to profl. jours. Home: 2261 Elkhorn Ct San Jose CA 95125 Office: Project Assistance Corp 100 N Winchester Blvd San Jose CA 95128

GOLDSTEIN, ELLIOTT STUART, geneticist, educator; b. Bklyn., July 7, 1942; s. William and Lottie (Roth) G.; m. Suzanne Kussner, July 7, 1963; children: Andrew Richard, Hyla Lynn. BS, U. Hartford, 1967; MS, U. Minn., 1970, PhD, 1972. Postdoctoral fellow Mass Inst. Tech., 1972-76; asst. prof. Ariz. State. U., 1974-78; asso. prof. Ariz. State. U., 1978—; vis. assoc. prof. Calif. Inst. Tech., 1980. Past pres. Temple Beth Sholom Mesa, Ariz. NIH fellow, Nat. Cancer Ins., 1972; NIH grantee 1976, Del E. Webb Found. grantee, 1984. Mem. AAAS, Soc. Devel. Biology, Genetics Soc. Am. Jewish. Home: 2342 E Alameda Tempe AZ 85282

GOLDSTEIN, HOWARD, illustrator, graphic designer; b. N.Y.C., Dec. 21, 1931; s. Fred Philip and Kay (Oleck) G.; m. Susan Frye, Jan. 22, 1961; children—Lisa Fawn, Amanda Rose. B.A., CCNY, 1953, postgrad., 1956-57; postgrad. Hunter Coll., 1956-57. Pub. Decorator's Directory Greater N.Y., 1955-57; with Am. Visuals Corp., N.Y.C., 1957-58; artist, prodn. mgr. Petersen Publs., Los Angeles, 1958-59; art dir. Dave Beck & Co., Los Angeles, 1959-60, Datamation Inc., Los Angeles, 1961-63, Missile Systems Corp., Los Angeles, 1961-63, Revell Inc., Los Angeles, 1963-65, Howard Goldstein/Artist, Van Nuys, Calif., 1969-82; ptnr. The Howard Group Inc., Woodland Hills, Calif., 1981-82; pres. Howard Goldstein Design, cons. in graphic art and computer graphics, Van Nuys, 1982—; mem. faculty Otis Inst. Parsons Sch. Design, Los Angeles, 1981-83. Assoc. editor Studio Systems Jour. Mem. UCLA Alcohol Research Ctr. Com. Served with AUS, 1953-55. Recipient Western Publs. Assn. Eddie awards, 1975, 76, Maggie awards 1978, 80-83; over 65 awards for graphic design and illustration. Mem. Soc. Illustrators Los Angeles (pres. 1979-80), Artists Equity, Graphic Artists Guild Los Angeles (co-founder, chmn. bd. 1980-81), Art Dirs. Los Angeles (bd. dirs.), Am. Inst. Graphic Arts. Jewish. Creator over 300 pub. illustrations, paintings and mag. covers, numerous metal sculptures and constrns.

GOLDSTEIN, JANET HOLLIS KIRSH, speech-language pathologist; b. Bklyn., Jan. 14, 1957; d. Lawrence and Pauline (Goldberg) Kirsh; m. Sam Goldstein, Dec. 5, 1976; children: Allyson Rose, Ryan Mitchell. BS, U. Utah, 1978, MS, 1980. Lic. speech pathologist, Utah. Speech-hearing aide Salt Lake City Sch. Dist., 1979-80; speech-language pathologist Primary Children's Med. Ctr., Salt Lake City, 1980-84, mgr. clin. services, 1984—. Fellow Am. Speech and Hearing Assn. (cert.), Utah Speech and Hearing Assn., Phi Kappa Phi. Jewish. Avocations: skiing, bike riding. Office: Primary Childrens Med ctr 320 12th Ave Salt Lake City UT 84103

GOLDSTEIN, MICHAEL STUART, systems executive; b. N.Y.C., Apr. 22, 1945; s. David and Anne (Klotz) G.; B.A., UCLA, 1966; m. Penelope Donaldson, May 4, 1968; children—David, Darren. Promotions mgr. Transamerica Fin., Los Angeles, 1966-70; Western regional mgr. Trans Union Systems, Corp., Los Angeles, Chgo., 1970-78; pres. Mutogo Data Corp., Irvine, Calif., 1978—; condr. seminars in field; cons. in field. Mem. Am. Mgmt. Assn., Data Processing Mgmt. Assn., Data Entry Mgmt. Assn. Office: 1801 Newport Circle Santa Ana CA 92705

GOLDSTEIN, NORMAN, dermatologist; b. Bklyn. July 14, 1934; s. Joseph H. and Bertha (Docteroff) G.; B.A., Columbia Coll., 1955; M.D., SUNY, 1959; m. Ramsay, Feb. 14, 1980; children—Richard, Heidi. Intern, Maimonides Hosp., N.Y.C., 1959-60; resident Skin and Cancer Hosp., 1960-61, Bellevue Hosp., 1961-62, NYU. Postgrad. Center, 1962-63 (all N.Y.C.); partner Honolulu Med. Group, 1967-72; practice medicine specializing in dermatology, Honolulu, 1972—; asso. clin. prof. dermatology U. Hawaii Sch. Medicine, 1973—; bd. dirs. Pacific Laser. Trustee, Hawaii Jewish Welfare Bd., 1976-79; bd. dirs. Skin Cancer Found., 1979—; trustee Dermatol. Found., 1979-82; pres. Hawaii Theater Ctr., Hawaii Med. Library, 1987—; mem. Oahu Heritage Council, 1986—. Recipient Henry Silver award Dermatol. Soc. Greater N.Y., 1963; Husik award NYU, 1963; Spl. award Acad. Dermatologia Hawaiiana, 1971. Served with U.S. Army, 1960-67. Fellow Am. Acad. Dermatology (Silver award 1972), ACP, Royal Soc. Medicine; mem. Internat. Soc. Tropical Dermatologists (Hist. and Culture award), Soc. Investigative Dermatologists, Assn. Mil. Dermatologists, AAAS, Am. Soc. Photobiology, Environ. Health and Light Research Inst., Internat. Soc. Cryosurgery, Am. Soc. Micropigmentation Surgery, Nat. Fedn. Ind. Bus., Small Bus. Council Am. (bus. adv. council), Pacific and Asian Affairs Council, Navy League, Assn. Honolulu Artists, Nat. Stereoscopic Soc., Am. Assn. Clin. Oncology, Biol. Photog. Assn., Internat. Solar Energy Soc., Photog. Soc. Am., Societe Internationale de la Photographie, Friends of Photography, Health Sci. Communication Assn., Internat. Pigment Cell Soc., Am. Med. Writers Assn., Physicians Exchange of Hawaii, N.Y. Acad. Sci., Am. Coll. Cryosurgery, Internat. Soc. Dermatol. Surgery, Am. Soc. Preventive Oncology, Soc. for Computer Medicine, Am. Assn. for Med. Systems and Info., computer Security Inst., Pacific Telecom Council, Hawaii State Med. Assn. (mem. public affairs com.), Hawaii Dermatol. Soc. (sec.-pres.), Hawaii Public Health Assn., Pacific Dermatol. Assn., Pacific Health Research Inst., Honolulu County Med. Soc. (gov.), Nat. Wildlife Fedn., Am. Forestry Assn., C. of C., Preservation Action, Pan Pacific Surg. Assn., Am. Coll. Sports Medicine. Jewish. Clubs: Outrigger Canoe, Rotary, Plaza, Honolulu, Chancellor's, Japan-Am., Oahu Country. Contbr. articles to profl. jours. Office: Historic Stangenwald Bldg 119 Merchant St Honolulu HI 96813

GOLDSTEIN, RICHARD HAROLD, audio and video consultant; b. Manhattan, N.Y., May 19, 1949; s. Harold I. and Julia S. (Deutsch) G.; m. Pamela Barkentin, Sept. 29, 1974 (div. Sept. 1980). BA, U. Ill., 1971. Artist mgr. Spirit Prodns., Los Angeles, 1972-74; audio systems designer Trancus Music, Los Angeles, 1976-80; audio cons. The Federated Group, Los Angeles, 1977-79; audio visual cons. Trancus Industries Internat., Los Angeles, 1980—; audio visual cons. CBS Records, Los Angeles, 1978-79, MCA Records, Los Angeles, 1980-81, Lawrence Gordon Prodns., Los Angeles, 1983—, Twentieth Century Fox Film Corp., Los Angeles, 1984—. Author (mag.) Town Moon, 1979. Republican. Eschatologist. Avocations: wine, cooking, rare book collecting, metaphys. research.

GOLDSTEIN, SAMUEL JACK, pediatric and developmental psychologist, educator; b. Jersey City, May 13, 1952; s. Nathan and Sarah G.; m. Janet Hollis, Dec. 5, 1976. B.S., Bklyn. Poly. Inst., 1973; M.S., Montclair State Coll., 1976; Ph.D., U. Utah, 1980. Lic. psychologist, cert. sch. psychologist, and cert. devel. disabilities educator, Utah; cert. sch. psychologist, N.Y. State, N.J. Clin. psychology intern Children's Ctr., Salt Lake City, 1978-79; sch. psychologist Jordon Resource Ctr., Salt Lake City, 1979-82; clin. dir. Neurology, Learning and Behavior Ctr., Salt Lake City, 1982—; Author: A Parent's Guide to ADD in Children, 1986; media psychologist weekday talk show Sta. KSTU-TV. Mem. Am. Psychol. Assn., Utah Sch. Psychologist Assn., Nat. Register Health Service Providers in Psychology. Office: Neurology Learning and Behavior Ctr 670 E 3900 S Suite 100 Salt Lake City UT 84107

GOLDSTEIN, STEVEN EDWARD, psychologist; b. Bronx, N.Y., Nov. 25, 1948; s. Maurice and Matilda (Weiss) G.; B.S. in Psychology, CCNY, 1970, M.S. in Sch. Psychology, 1971; Ed.D. in Sch. Psychology, U. No. Colo., 1977. Tchr., N.Y.C. Public Schs., 1970-71, 72-73, tchr., counselor, 1974; extern in sch. psychology N. Shore Child Guidance, 1972; sch. psychologist Denver Public Schs., 1975; asst. prof. psychology Northeastern Okla. State U., Tahlequah, 1976-78; coordinator inpatient, emergency services Winnemucca (Nev.) Mental Health Center, 1978-80; dir. Desert Devel. Ctr., Las Vegas, Nev., 1980-82; sr. psychologist Las Vegas Mental Health Ctr., 1982—; pvt. practice psychology, Las Vegas, 1983—; participant NSF seminar on biofeedback, 1977. Sec. grad. council CUNY, 1971; pres. grad. council in edn. CCNY, 1971. Lic. psychologist, Nev.; cert. sch. psychologist, N.Y., Calif. Mem. Am. Psychol. Assn., Nat. Assn. Sch. Psychologists, Biofeedback Soc. Nev. (membership dir. 1982—), Nev. Soc. Tng. and Devel. (dir. 1982-83), Biofeedback Soc. Am., So. Nev. Soc. Cert. Psychologists (pres. 1984—). Presenter papers to profl. confs. Office: 6161 W Charleston Blvd Las Vegas NV 89158 also: 2225 E Flamingo Suite 200 Las Vegas NV 89119

GOLDSTEIN-SAULTER, RITA, psychologist; b. N.Y.C., Jan. 4, 1929; d. Joel Herbert and Pauline Birns; children—Michael Alan Goldstein, Robert Steven Goldstein; m. Leon Saulter, May 7, 1982. A.A., Santa Monica Coll., 1966; B.A., Calif. State U.-Northridge, 1970, M.A., 1974; PhD Profl. Sch. for Psychol. Studies, San Diego, 1984. Cert. marriage family and child counselor, Calif. Group facilitator campus problems, reform, and innovations Hamilton High Sch., Los Angeles, 1969; dir. new counseling program So. Calif. Counseling Ctr., 1971-76; group facilitator city-wide conf. on youth and sr. citizens services Mayor Bradley's office, 1974; supr. mental health ctr. for young adults Beverlywood Board and Care, 1976; supr. families with battered children Anando Marga Family Unity Ctr., 1977; pvt. psychotherapy, Beverly Hills, Westwood and Van Nuys, Calif., 1974—. Recipient service awards So. Calif. Counseling Ctr., Calif. Assn. Marriage and Family Therapists, Group Psychotherapy Assn. of So. Calif., Mar Vista Optomist Club. Mem. Am. Psychol. Assn., Am. Assn. Marriage and Family Therapists, Nat. Council Family Relations, Assn. Humanistic Psychology, Los Angeles Mental Health Assn., Western Psychol. Assn., Assn. Women in Psychology. Contbr. articles to profl. jours. Office: 921 Westwood Blvd Suite 212 Los Angeles CA 90024

GOLDSTON, HUGH W., communications executive, consultant; b. Roscoe, Tex., May 2, 1948; s. Hubert Willis and Pansye Laverne (Harrison) G.; m. Lynette Ruth Hughes, Nov. 3, 1973 (div. May 1985); children: Erika Naomi, Cameron Hughes. AAS, Utah Tech. Coll., 1980; BS in Computer Sci., Weber State Coll., 1985. Dir. nat. project mgmt. Bonneville Telecommunications Co., Salt Lake City, 1983—; v.p., chief ops. officer Integrated Communication Techs., Salt Lake City, 1986—, also bd. dirs., 1986—. Avocations: snow and water skiing, restoration of classic autos.

GOLDSTONE, JOHN CHARLES-DAVID, marketing executive; b. Everett, Wash., Mar. 1, 1958; s. Herbert Eugene and Helen Ann (Shaffer) G.; m. Laura Irene French, Feb. 14, 1981. BABA magna cum laude, U. Wash., 1986. Night dispatcher Seattle Post-Intelligencer, 1976-78, dist. sales mgr., 1978-79; asst. dist. advisor Seattle Times, 1979, dist. adviser, 1979—; treas. Prosperous Growth Inc., Seattle, 1982-83; ptnr. French and Goldstone Inc., Edmonds, Wash., 1980—. Contbr. articles to profl. jours. Named Dist. Adv. of Yr., 1985. Mem. Phi Beta Kappa (researcher ednl. issues com. 1985—), Beta Gamma Sigma. Avocations: skiing, running, swimming, chess.

GOLDTHWAITE, RONALD OLMSTED, behavioral systems analyst; b. Aug. 17, 1951. AS, West Valley Coll., 1971; BS, U. Calif., Santa Cruz, 1973; postgrad., U. Calif., Davis. Mgr. user services Calif. State U., San Francisco, 1977-79; research asst. Calif. Dept. Food and Agrl., Sacramento, 1979-85; research assoc. dept. psychology U. Calif., Davis, 1985—. Scholar No. Calif. Achievement Rewards for Coll. Scientists Soc., San Francisco, 1982, 83, 85. Mem. Sigma Xi. Democrat. Home: 805 E 11th St #7 Davis CA 95616 Office: U Calif Dept Psychology Davis CA 95616

GOLDWARE, DAVID, insurance company executive; b. Omaha, Aug. 22, 1916; s. Joseph and Fannie Goldware; m. June Goldware; 2 children. BS in Acctg., U. Nebr., 1937. Pvt. practice acctg. Omaha, 1937-39; with Govt. Printing Office, Washington, 1939-42; store mgr. 1946-56; pvt. practice ins. agt. Riverside, Calif., 1956-64; ins. agt., founder David Goldware Ins. Services, Riverside, 1964—; bd. dirs. Inland Empire Nat. Bank. Bd. dirs. Temple Beth El Congregation, Riverside, past pres., past chmn. fin. com., past chmn. fund raising com., past mem. archtl. com.; mem. Parkview Community Found., past sec. bd. dirs., chmn. long-range planning com., endowment com.; mem. founders club Riverside Community Hosp. Found., 1979—; mem. citizens adv. com. Loma Linda (Calif.) U. Hosp., bd. dirs. So. Calif. div. St. Jude's Children's Research Hosp. Found., 1977—, past. v.p.; mem. City of Hope, 1957-59, past. v.p. Riverside chpt.; founding bd. dirs., v.p. exec. com. Janet Goeske Ctr. Srs. and Handicapped Persons; past bd. dirs. YMCA; mem. chancellor's assocs. U. Calif. Riverside, town and gown com., boosters club; v.p. World Affairs Council Inland So. Calif.; active United Way, 1956—, Monday Morning Group; past. pres., past. chmn. mil .affairs com. Greater Riverside C. of C.; pres. Riverside Civic Ctr. Authority, past mem.; vol. Mayor's Council on Human Relations; mem. Mayor's com. Housing, 1976—, Mayor's Com. Establish Performing Arts Ctr., 1976—, Mayor's Com. UN Mgmt. Com., 1964; past mem. mgmt. com., devel. com., Mission Inn Found.; bd. dirs., past fin. com. mem. Riverside Citizens Goals Com. Named So. Calif. Man of Yr., St. Jude Children's Research Hosp. Found., 1976, Man of Yr., Inland Empire Mag., 1980, Man of Yr. So. Calif. Inland Area Boy Scouts Am., 1982. Mem. Air Force Assn. (chmn. bd. dirs. Riverside chpt.). Lodges: Kiwanis (past pres. Univ. Area), B'nai Brith (past pres.), Masons (active various coms.). Home: 3815 Westwood Dr Riverside CA 92504

GOLDWATER, BARRY MORRIS, former U.S. senator; b. Phoenix, Jan. 1, 1909; s. Baron and Josephine (Williams) G.; m. Margaret Johnson, Sept. 22, 1934 (dec. 1985); children: Joanne, Barry, Michael, Margaret (Mrs. Bob Clay). Student, Staunton Mil. Acad., U. Ariz., 1928. With Goldwater's, Inc., 1929—, pres., 1937-53; U.S. senator from Ariz., 1953-65, 69-87; chmn. Armed Services Com.; mem. Commerce Com.; former chmn. Select Com. on Intelligence; mem. Select Com. Indian Affairs; Councilman, Phoenix, 1949-52; mem. adv. com. Indian affairs Dept. Interior, 1948-50. Author: Arizona Portraits (2 vols.), 1940, Journey Down the River of Canyons, 1940, Speeches of Henry Ashurst, The Conscience of a Conservative, 1960, Why Not Victory?, 1962, Where I Stand, 1964, The Face of Arizona, 1964, People and Places, 1967, The Conscience of the Majority, 1970, Delightful Journey, 1971, The Coming Breakpoint, 1976, Barry Goldwater and the Southwest, 1976, With No Apologies, 1979. Bd. dirs. Heard Mus., Mus. No. Ariz., St. Joseph's Hosp. Served as pilot USAAF, 1941-45; col., chief staff Ariz. NG, 1945-52; maj. gen. Res. Recipient award U.S. Jr. C. of C., 1937; named Man of year Phoenix, 1949. Mem. Royal Photog. Soc., Am. Assn. Indian Affairs (dir.), Am. Legion, V.F.W., Municipal League (v.p.), Am. Inst. Fgn. Trade (dir.), Eta Mu Pi, Sigma Chi. Lodges: Masons, Shriner, Elks. Republican candidate for President of the U.S., 1964. *

GOLDWYN, RALPH NORMAN, fin. co. exec.; b. Chgo., Jan. 24, 1925; s. Herman and Rissie F. Goldwyn; B.S., U. Calif. at Los Angeles, 1948; m. Joan J. Snyder, Dec. 25, 1954; children—Bob, Greg, Lisa. Partner, Arc Loan Co., Los Angeles, 1948-52; v.p. Arc Discount Co., Los Angeles, 1952-73; pres. Arc Investment Co., Los Angeles, 1952-73; partner First Factors, Los Angeles, 1960-78; pres. First Comml. Fin., Los Angeles, 1978—; dir. Roy J. Maier, Inc. trustee UCLA Found. Served to lt. (j.g.) USN, 1943-46. Mem. U. Calif. at Los Angeles Chancellor Assos., Anti-Defamation League. Jewish. Clubs: Town Hall of Calif. (life), Brentwood Country, Los Angeles. Office: First Comml Fin 4221 Wilshire Blvd Suite 470 Los Angeles CA 90010

GOLIGHTLY, MAX CHATTERTON, drama educator; b. 1924; m. Beverly Keith. BA, Brigham Young U., 1950, MA, 1959; PhD, So. Ill. U., 1980; PhD in Arts, hon., World U., 1981. Tchr. Provo (Utah) High Sch., 1951-53; with instr. Citrus Jr. Coll., Citrus High Sch., Glendora, Calif., 1953-57; with Brigham Young U. Lab. Sch., Provo, 1957-61, Brigham Young U. Dept. Speech and Dramatic Arts, Provo, 1961; Active in civic theatre in Calif., Idaho. Actor in films including Knocking on Heaven's Door, Run, Joe, Run. Served with U.S. Army, 1943-46, ETO. Named Utah Poet of Yr., 1970; recipient Fine Arts Creative award, 1987, Nat. prizes in playwrighting, poetry. Mem. Blue Key Frat. Nat. Honorary, Nat. Fedn. State Poetry Socs. Am. (officer 1964, 66, pres. 1967, 68), Utah Poetry Soc., Thespian Nat. Drama Soc., Theta Alpha Phi, Alpha Epsilon Rho. Office: Brigham Young U Dept Theatre Arts Provo UT 84602

GOLIGHTLY, VELVETA PATRICE, lawyer; b. Tuscaloosa, Ala., July 7, 1957; d. Lonnie William and Marie (Brown) Golightly; m. John Luckett Howell, May 7, 1983. B.S., Tuskegee Inst., 1978; J.D., U. Colo.-Boulder, 1981; M in Pub. Adminstrn. U. Colo.-Denver, 1986. Bar: Colo. 1982, U.S. Dist. Ct. Colo. 1982. Student asst. Congressman Bill Nichol, Tuskegee, Ala., 1976; law clk. U.S. Atty.'s Office, Denver, 1979; dep. dist. atty. City of Denver, 1980-86; asst. city atty., 1986—. Vol., Democratic Party, Denver, 1983—. Mem. Sam Cary Bar Assn., Denver Bar Assn., Colo. Bar Assn., ABA, Am. Trial Lawyers Assn., Phi Beta Kappa. Democrat. Baptist. Office: Office of Denver City Atty 1445 Cleveland Pl #303 Denver CO 80020

GOLITZ, LOREN EUGENE, dermatologist, pathologist, clinical administrator, educator; b. Pleasant Hill, Mo., Apr. 7, 1941; s. Ross Winston and Helen Francis (Schupp) G.; MD, U. Mo., Columbia, 1966; m. Deborah Burd Frazier, June 18, 1966; children: Carrie Campbell, Matthew Ross. Intern, USPHS Hosp., San Francisco, 1966-67, med. resident, 1967-69; resident in dermatology USPHS Hosp., Staten Island, N.Y., 1969-71; dep. chief dermatology, 1972-73; vis. fellow dermatology Columbia-Presbyn. Med. Ctr., N.Y.C., 1971-72; asst. in dermatology Coll. Physicians Surgeons, Columbia, N.Y.C., 1972-73; vice chmn. Residency Rev. Com. for Dermatoloby, 1983—. Earl D. Osborne fellow dermal. pathology Armed Forces Inst. Pathology, Washington, 1973-74; assoc. prof. dermatology pathology U. Colo. Med. Sch., Denver, 1974—; chief dermatology Denver Gen. Hosp., 1974—; attending physician dermatology Denver VA Hosp., 1974—; Diplomate Am. Bd. Dermatology. Nat. Bd. Med. Examiners. Mem. Am. Soc. Dermatopathology (sec.-treas. 1985—), Am. Acad. Dermatology (chmn. council on clin. and lab. services, council sci. assembly 1987—), Soc. Pediatric Dermatology (pres. 1981), Am. Soc. Dermatopathology (sec.-treas. 1985—), Soc. Investigative Dermatology, Pacific Dermatol. Assn. (exec. com. 1979—, sec.-treas. 1984-87, pres.-elect 1987), Noah Worcester Dermatol. Soc. (publs. com. 1980), Colo. Dermatol. Soc. (pres. 1978), Am. Bd. Dermatology Inc. (bd. dirs. 1987—), Colo. Med. Soc., Denver Med. Soc., AMA (residency rev. com. for dermatology 1982—, dermatopathology test com. 1979-85), Denver Soc. Dermatopathology, Am. Dermatol. Assn. Editorial bd. Jour. Pediatric Dermatology, editorial bd. Jour. Am. Acad. Dermatology, Current Issues in Dermatology. Contbr. articles to med. jours. Home: 11466 E Arkansas Ave Aurora CO 80012

GOLL, DARREL EUGENE, biochemistry educator; b. Garner, Iowa, Apr. 19, 1936; s. Leon Oscar and Marie Eleanor (Nonnweiller) G.; m. Rosalie Elaine Bullock, Jan. 12, 1958; children: Laurene Elaine, Jeffrey Eugene, Kathleen Kay. BS, Iowa State U., 1957, MS, 1959; PhD, U. Wis., 1962. Asst. prof. biochemistry Iowa State U., Ames, 1962-65, assoc. prof., 1965-70, prof., 1970-76; prof. U. Ariz., Tucson, 1976—, head dept., 1976-84; mem. NRC com. on Animal Products of Adv. Bd. Mil. Personnel Supplies, 1975-78. Mem. editorial bd. Jour. Animal Sci., 1969-72, Jour. Food Sci., 1970-75, Jour. Food Biochemistry, 1976—; contbr. articles to profl. jours. NIH fellow UCLA, 1966-67, Oxford (Eng.) U., 1971-72; NSF Found. scholar, 1974; recipient Gastwissenschaftler, German Cancer Research Inst., Heidelberg, Disting. Research award Am. Meat Sci. Assn., 1972, Meats Research award Am. Soc. Animal Sci., 1973. Mem. AAAS, Am. Chem. Soc., Am. Soc. Biol. Chemists, Inst. Food Technologists (Samuel Cate Prescott Research award 1970). Presbyterian. Avocations: sports, cycling, reading. Home: 3940 E Alvernon Circle Tucson AZ 85718 Office: U Ariz Muscle Biology Group Tucson AZ 85721

GOLTZ, ROBERT WILLIAM, physician, educator; b. St. Paul, Sept. 21, 1923; s. Edward Victor and Clare (O'Neill) G.; m. Patricia Ann Sweeney, Sept. 27, 1945; children: Leni, Paul Robert. B.S., U. Minn., 1943, M.D., 1945. Diplomate: Am. Bd. Dermatology (pres. 1975-76). Intern Ancker Hosp., St. Paul, 1944-45; resident in dermatology Mpls. Gen. Hosp., 1945-46, 48-49, U. Minn. Hosp., 1949-50; practice medicine specializing in dermatology Mpls., 1950-65; clin. instr. U. Minn. Grad. Sch., 1950-58, clin. asst. prof., 1958-60, clin. assoc. prof., 1960-65, prof., head dept. dermatology, 1971-85; prof. medicine/dermatology U. Calif.-San Diego,, 1985—; prof. dermatology, head div. dermatology U. Colo. Med. Sch., Denver, 1965-71. Former editorial bd.: Archives of Dermatology; editor: Dermatology Digest. Served from 1st lt. to capt., M.C. U.S. Army, 1946-48. Mem. Am. Dermatol. Assn. (dir. 1976-79, pres. 1985-86), Am. Soc. Dermatopathologists (pres. 1981), Am. Dermatology Soc. Allergy and Immunology (pres. 1981), AMA (chmn. sect. on dermatology 1973-75), Dermatology Found. (past dir.), Minn. Dermatol. Soc., Soc. Investigative Dermatology (pres. 1972-73), Histochem. Soc., Am. Acad. Dermatology (pres. 1978-79, past dir.), Brit. Assn. Dermatology (hon.), Chilean Dermatology Soc. (hon.), Colombian Dermatol. Soc. (corr. mem.), Can. Dermatol. Soc. (hon. mem.), Pacific Dermatol. Soc. (hon.-mem.), S. African Dermatol. Soc. (hon. mem.), N.Am. Clin. Dermetol. Soc., Chgo. Dermatol. Soc., Assn. Profs. Dermatology (sec.-treas. 1970-72, pres. 1973-74). Home: 6097 Avenida Chamnez La Jolla CA 92037 Office: Div Dermatology H-811 J U Calif-San Diego Med Ctr 225 Dickinson St San Diego CA 92103

GOLUB, MORTON ALLAN, polymer chemist; b. Montreal, Que., Can., June 11, 1925; came to U.S. 1947, naturalized, 1954; s. Michael and Fanny (Gold) G.; m. Joanna Belle Hoffmaster, Feb. 12, 1954; children: Kevin King (dec.), Erik Norman. BSc, McGill U., Montreal, 1944; MSc, U. N.B., Can., 1947; PhD, U. Mo., 1951. From research chemist to research assoc. The B.F. Goodrich Co., Akron and Brecksville, Ohio, 1951-60; sr. polymer chemist Stanford Research Inst., Menlo Park, Calif., 1960-68; research scientist NASA, Ames Research Ctr., Moffett Field, Calif., 1970—; instr. math. Foothill Coll., Los Altos Hills, Calif., 1963-68. Mem. adv. bd. Jour. Applied Polymer Sci., 1979—; contbr. articles to profl. jours., chpts. to books. Bd. dirs. Peninsula Symphony Assn., Los Altos, 1981—, pres., 1984-86. Sr. Postdoctoral Resident Research associateship NRC, 1968-70. Mem. AAAS, Am. Chem. Soc. Avocation: music appreciation. Home: 1726 Kinglet Ct Sunnyvale CA 94087 Office: Ames Research Ctr MS 230-3 Moffett Field CA 94035

GOLUBIC, THEODORE ROY, sculptor, designer, inventor; b. Lorain, Ohio, Dec. 9, 1928; s. Ivan and Illonka (Safar) G.; m. Rose Andrina Ieraci-Golubic, Nov. 27, 1958; children—Vincivan, Theodore E., Victor, Georjia. Student Ohio State U., Columbus, 1947-48; B.F.A. in Painting, Miami U., Oxford, Ohio, 1951; student Syracuse U., 1955; M.F.A. in Sculpture, U. Notre Dame, 1957. Asst. to Ivan Mestrovic, 1954-60; guest tchr. U. Notre Dame, 1959; urban planner redevel. dept., South Bend, Ind., 1960-65; sculpture cons., Rock of Ages Corp., 1965-67; instr. Central Mo. State U., 1969; instr. San Diego Sculptors' Guild, 1970-71; artist-in-residence Roswell (N.Mex.) Mus. and Art Ctr., 1971-72; sculptor, designer, inventor, 1958—; works include: Limestone relief sculpture Cathedral of the Nativity, Dubuque, Iowa, 4 dimensional sun environ. design, South Bend, Ind., 3 dimensional interconnected integrated cir., Phoenix. Served in U.S. Army, 1951-53. Mem. Artists Equity Assn., Coll. Art Assn. Am., Internat. Sculpture Ctr. Contbr. articles to profl. jours.

GOLUM, ROBERT BRUCE, journalist; b. Long Beach, Calif., May 6, 1956; s. Abraham and Irma (Berman) G.; m. Pamela Joan Ruben, Sept. 4, 1983. BA in Journalism, San Diego State U., 1978. Reporter Chula Vista (Calif.) Star News, 1978-79, Women's Wear Daily, N.Y.C., 1979-84, Investor's Daily, Los Angeles, 1984—. Mem. ACLU, Los Angeles, 1985-86. Democrat. Jewish. Avocation: fly fishing.

GOLZE, ALFRED RUDOLF, civil engineer; b. Washington, July 6, 1905; s. Rudolph Leon and Blanche (Wenderoth) G.; B.S.C.E., U. Pa., 1930, C.E., 1940; m. Gladys Louise Whitney; children—Gretchen Wenderoth, Peter Wenderoth. Engr. subways, Phila., 1925-27; valuation engr. ICC, Washington, 1930-33; designing engr. U.S. Bur. Reclamation, Denver, 1933-35; supervising engr. in charge Civilian Conservation Camps on reclamation projects Bur. of Reclamation, Washington, 1936-43; budget examiner public works Bur. of Budget, San Francisco and Washington, 1943-45; asst. dir. operations and maintenance Bur. of Reclamation, 1945-47, dir. of programs and finance, 1947-53, chief, program coordination and finance div., 1953-58, asst. commr., 1958-61; chief engr. Calif. Dept. Water Resources, 1961-67, Sacramento, dep. dir., 1967-71; chief hydroelectric engr. Burns and Roe, Inc., Los Angeles, 1971-73, chief water resources engr., 1973-74; pvt. practice as cons. engr., 1975-87; cons. Govt. Turkey, 1960, AID, Pakistan, 1964; mem. exec. com. U.S. Com. on Large Dams, 1969-74, chmn. com. model law on safety of dams, 1968-71; mem. exec. com. U.S. Com. on Irrigation, Drainage and Flood Control, 1967-72. Recipient Distingished Service award U.S. Dept. Interior, 1962; Toulmin medal Soc. Am. Mil. Engrs., 1964; Outstanding Service Engring. Profession award Engring. Council Sacramento Valley, 1966; Dir.'s Service award Calif. Dept. Water Resources, 1966; Dr. Robert Yarnall award Alumni Soc. U. Pa., 1979. Fellow ASCE (hon. mem.; pres. nat. capital sect. 1958-59, chmn. com. engring. edn. 1959-60, chmn. nat. water policy com. 1972-73, pres. Sacramento sect. 1968-69, mem. jury to select outstanding civil engring. achievement of 1979); mem. Fed. Govt. Accountants Assn. (Washington chpt. pres. 1960-61), Soc. Am. Mil. Engrs., Earthquake Engring. Research Inst., Sigma Xi (asso.), Tau Beta Pi, Sigma Tau, Chi Epsilon (hon. U. Colo. chpt.), Theta Xi (pres. Washington alumni 1956-57). Clubs: Cosmos (Washington); Commonwealth, (San Francisco). Author: Reclamation in the United States, 1961; Your Future in Civ l Engineering, 1965; contbr. to Applied Sedimentation, 1950. Editor: Handbook of Dam Engineering, 1977. Contbr. numerous articles in engring. and other mags. Deceased Feb. 1987.

GOMENA, JOHN EDWARD, food products company executive; b. 1927; married. BS, U. R.I., 1951; postgrad., Carnegie-Mellon U., 1972. Indsl. engr. U.S. Rubber Co., 1951-52, Bostitch Inc., 1952-54; area mfg. and engring. mgr. Birds Eye div. Gen. Foods Corp., 1964-66; with Amfac Inc., 1966—; v.p. ops. Lamb-Weston, 1966-73, pres., 1973-80; vice chmn. Amfac Foods Group, 1980-81, chmn., 1981; now exec. v.p. Amfac Inc. Served with USNR, 1945-46. Mem. Am. Frozen Food Assn. (past chmn.), Frozen Foods Assn. (past v.p.). Office: Amfac Inc 81 Blue Ravine Rd Folsom CA 95630 *

GOMER, RICHARD HANS, cell biologist, astronomer; b. Chgo., Oct. 11, 1956; s. Robert and Anne (Olah) G. BA in Physics, Pomona Coll., 1977; PhD in Biology, Calif. Inst. Tech., 1983. Electronics engr. U. Chgo., 1977; vis. scientist Mount Wilson and Las Campanas Obs., Pasadena, Calif., 1983, Carnegie Inst. Wash., 1983; postdoctoral fellow U. Calif., San Diego, 1983—. Contbr. articles to profl. jours. Fellow NIH, 1983, Am. Cancer Soc., 1986. Mem. Am. Soc. Cell Biology. Democrat. Methodist. Club: Cypress (Calif.) Soaring. Avocations: automotive repair, electronics, bicycling. Home: 3407 Mt Armour Place San Diego CA 92111 Office: U Calif San Diego Dept Biology B-022 La Jolla CA 92093

GOMEZ, ANTHONY ANTONIO, sales and marketing executive; b. Upland, Calif., Jan. 21, 1945; s. Jose and Maria (D'Anda) G.; m. Susie Browning, June 10, 1967; children: Scott, Amiee. AA, Chaffey Coll., 1976; cert., U. So. Calif., 1977; BS, U. Redlands, 1981. Retail devel. mgr. Quaker Oats Co., Anaheim, Calif., 1968-81; regional mgr. Sunshine Biscuits, Santa Fe Springs, Calif., 1981-83; gen. sales mgr., mktg. Carnation Co., Los Angeles, 1983-84; regional sales Early Calif. Foods, Los Angeles, 1984-86; sales, mktg. mgr. Cen. 'de Abastos, Los Angeles, 1986-87; dir. Hispanic products div. Ross-Billings Thunderbird Cos., Buena Park, Calif., 1987—. Quaker Oats Co. scholar, 1976. Mem. Sales-Mktg. Execs. Club, Food Industry Sales Mgrs., Mexican-Am. Assn. (publicity chmn. 1981-85). Avocations: golfing, gardening, reading. Home: 604 W La Deney Dr Ontario CA 91762 Office: Ross-billings Thunderbird Cos 6250 Caballero Blvd Buena Park CA 90620

GOMEZ, ARMANDO, sales executive; b. Manhattan, N.Y., Aug. 1, 1948; s. Armando and Raquel (Perez) G. AS, CUNY, 1971; BS, L.I. U., 1975. Lab. rep. Smith Kline Lab., Burlingame, Calif., 1979; pres. Leasing Services, Santa Clara, Calif., 1979-81; v.p. sales Telemark, San Jose, Calif., 1981-83; salesman Western region Micropolis Corp., Chatsworth, Calif., 1983-84; dist. sales mgr. Nissei Sangyo Am., Mountain View, Calif., 1985—. Lodge: Kiwanis. Avocations: world travel, tennis, scuba diving, reading, skiing. Home: 1102 Prevost Ct San Jose CA 95125 Office: Nissei Sangyo Am Ltd 460 E Middlefield Rd Mountain View CA 94043

GOMPERTZ, CHARLES BATES, management consulting executive, priest; b. Phila., Sept. 13, 1935; s. John Langdon and Margaret (Bates) G.; m. Leslie Lynne Ross, July 5, 1985; children—Pamela, Margaret, John. B.A., U. Calif., 1959; M.Div., CDSP Episcopal Sem., 1962. Ordained to ministry Episcopal Ch., 1962. Curate St. John's Ch., Ross., Calif., 1962-65; vicar Ch. in Ignacio, Novato, Calif., 1965-70; with sales dept. Land Investors Research Co., Larkspur, Calif., 1970-71; mental health educator, chief community services, County of Marin, San Rafael, Calif., 1971-74; mgr. Human Service Ctr. Ross Valley, San Rafael, 1975-78; pres. Gompertz Mgmt. Group, San Anselmo, Calif., 1980—; mem. staff St. John's Ch., Ross, Calif., 1970—; dir. Maxon Industries, Huntington Park, Calif.; instr. Lay Acad., Diocese of Calif., San Francisco, 1984—. Author: Mend a Broken Heart, 1977; Personal Productivity Log, 1983. Served with USNR, 1956-58, ETO. Mem. Am. Soc. Tng. and Devel., Marin Amateur Radio Soc., Soc. Calif. Pioneers. Club: University (San Francisco). Office: The Gompertz Mgmt Group PO Box 454 San Anselmo CA 94960

GONICK, HARVEY CRAIG, nephrologist; b. Winnipeg, Man., Can., Apr. 10, 1930; s. Joseph Wolfe and Rose (Chernick) G.; m. Gloria Granz, Dec. 16, 1967; children: Stephan, Teri. BS in Chemistry, UCLA, 1951; MD, U. Calif., San Francisco, 1955. Diplomate Am. Bd. Internal Medicine, Am. Bd. Nephrology. Intern Peter Bent Brigham Hosp., 1955-56; fellow in nephrology Mass. Meml. Hosp., 1956-57; fellow in nephrology, resident in internal medicine Wadsworth VA Hosp., Los Angeles, 1959-61, clin. investigator, 1961-64, chief metabolic balance unit, 1964-67; instr. medicine Sch. Medicine, UCLA, 1961-64, asst. prof., 1964-69, assoc. prof., 1969-72, adj. assoc. prof., 1972-76, adj. prof., 1976—, assoc. chief div. nephrology, 1965-72, co-dir. Bone and Stone Clinic,, 1972-76, coordinator postgrad. nephrology edn., 1975-78; mem. staff Santa Monica (Calif.) Hosp., St. John's Hosp., Santa Monica; mem. staff Century City Hosp., Los Angeles, med. dir. dialysis unit, 1972-79, chief medicine, 1978-79; mem. staff Cedars-Sinai Med. Ctr., Los Angeles, dir. trace element lab., 1979—, clin. chief nephrology, 1983-85; practice medicine specializing in nephrology Los Angeles, 1972—; co-founder, med. dir. Berkeley East Dialysis Unit, Santa Monica, 1971-75; co-founder, cons. Kidney Dialysis Care Units Inc., Lynwood, Calif., 1971-78; mem. numerous adv. coms. to state and fed. agys., 1969-83. Contbr. articles to profl. jours.; editor: Current Nephrology, 1977—. Served to capt. M.C., USAF, 1957-59. Fellow Charles Nelson Fund, Kaiser Found., NIH; recipient Oliver P. Douglas Meml. award Los Angeles County Heart Assn., 1959, Vis. Scientist award Deutscher Academischer Austauschendienst, 1978. Fellow ACP; mem. Internat. Soc. Nephrology (organizing com. internat. cong. 1984), Am. Soc. Nephrology, European Dialysis and Transplant Assn., Los Angeles Transplant Soc., Soc. Exptl. Biology and Medicine, AAAS, AMA, Pan-Am. Med. Assn., Calif. Med. Assn., Los Angeles County Med. Assn. (legis. com.), Nat. Kidney Found. (active ann. conf. 1963-65, sec. nat. med. adv. council 1969-70, regional rep. and legis com. nat. med. adv. council 1970-73, grantee 1963), So. Calif. Kidney Found. (chmn. sci. adv. council 1968-70, co-chmn. legis. com. 1970-73, bd. dirs. 1974-83, honoree 1979), Am. Soc. Bone and Mineral Research, Am. Coll. Toxicology, Soc. Toxicology, Am. Heart Assn. (renal sect. of council on circulation), Am. Fedn. Clin. Research, Western Soc. Clin. Research, Western Assn. Physicians, Los Angeles Soc. Internal Medicine, Phi Beta Kappa, Sigma Xi, Alpha Omega Alpha, Phi Eta Sigma, Alpha Mu Gamma, Phi Lambda Upsilon. Avocation: tennis. Office: 2080 Century Pk E #707 Los Angeles CA 90067

GONSALVES-WENDT, DIANA LYNN, medical center administrator, speech pathologist; b. Wahiawa, Hawaii, Nov. 1, 1951; d. Alfred T. and Leonora (Timario) Gonsalves; m. David G. Wendt. Student, U. Hawaii, 1970-73; BA, Chaminade U., d1973; MA, U. Colo., 1976. Lic. speech-lang. pathologist, N.Mex. Speech-lang. pathologist Sheridan Head Start, Denver, 1975-76, The Rehab. Ctr. Inc., Albuquerque, 1976-78; dir. speech pathology San Juan Regional Med. Ctr., Farmington, N.Mex., 1978—; cons. Farmington Cleft Palate Team, 1978—. Mem. San Juan Animal League, Farmington, 1985—. Mem. Am. Speech & Hearing Assn. (cert.), Nat. Head Injury Found., N.Mex. Speech & Hearing Assn. Avocations: mountain and river sports, tennis. Home: 3420 Monterey Circle Farmington NM 87401 Office: San Juan Regional Med Ctr 801 W Maple Farmington NM 87401

GONZALES, JOHN GREG MICHAEL, sanitary engineer; b. Reno, Nev., Apr. 5, 1948; s. John C. and Lorreine (Fitzjerell) G.; m. Barbara Fay Andrulli, Feb. 9, 1974; B.S. in Civil Engring., U. Nev., 1971; M.S., 1972. Registered profl. engr., Calif., Nev.; cert. water and waste water operator, Calif., Nev. Systems engr. South Tahoe P.U.D., South Lake Tahoe, Calif., 1972-76; project mgr. Pillsbury Engrs., So. Lake Tahoe, 1976-77; instr. Tahoe Coll., 1975-77; sanitary engr. City of Sparks, Nev., 1977—. Contbr. articles to profl. jours. Bd. dirs. Nev. Humane Soc., Sparks, 1981—; chmn. Select Soc. of Sludge, 1981—. Served to 2d lt., U.S. Army, 1971—. Named Young Engr. of Year., Nev. Soc. Profl. Engrs., 1982. Mem. Nev. Water Polution Control (pres. 1981), ASCE (dir. 1983). Democrat. Roman Catholic. Home: PO Box 250 Sparks NV 20250 Office: PO Box 857 431 Prater Way Sparks NV 89432

GONZALES, NANCY ALDERETE, mathematics educator, consultant, researcher; b. Albuquerque, Nov. 28, 1948; d. Delfino and Crucita (Alderete) G.; 1 child, Miguel Angel. BA in Math. and Spanish, Eastern N.Mex. U., 1970; MEd, U. Wash., 1974; EdD, Harvard U., 1986 Dir. Child Devel. Program, Eastern Plains Community Action Agy., Tucumcari, N.Mex., 1970-71; instr. South Seattle Community Coll., 1972-73; legis. analyst Wash. State Senate Com. on Edn., Olympia, 1974-75; child devel. program dir. Isleta Pueblo, (N.Mex.), 1975-76; curriculum devel. specialist Eastern N.Mex. U., Roswell, 1976-77; instr. U. Albuquerque, 1981-82; lectr. dept. math. and stats. U. N.Mex., Albuquerque, 1982-86, asst. prof., 1986—. Nat. Inst. Edn. research fellow, Women and Minorities Project, Washington, 1980; guest lectr. Border Coll. Consortium, Brownsville, Tex., 1983; speaker Ford Found. Comprehensive Math. Project, Santa Fe, 1984. Elected mem. Hispanic Study Task Force, Harvard Grad. Sch. Edn., 1979-81, apptd. mem. Steering Com. for Study Caribbean Migration, 1980-81; Congl. intern, 98th Congress, Senator Bingaman, 1983; apptd. mem. N.Mex. Dem. State Platform Com., 1982, elected mem. State Cen. Com., 1983-85. Radcliffe grantee for Grad. Women at Harvard U., 1979, 80, 82; grad. sch. fellow U. Wash., 1972-74; acad. scholar Eastern N.Mex. U., 1966. Mem. Math. Assn. Am., Nat. Council Tchrs. of Math. (reactor, discussion leader annual conf. 1981, speaker S.W. regional conf. 1985), Phi Delta Kappa. Roman Catholic.

GONZALES, RICHARD ROBERT, college counselor; b. Palo Alto, Calif., Jan. 12, 1945; s. Pedro and Virginia (Ramos) G.; A.A., Foothill Coll., 1966; B.A., San Jose (Calif.) State U., 1969; M.A., Calif. Poly. State U., San Luis Obispo, 1971; grad. Dept. Def. Equal Opportunity Mgmt. Inst., U.S. Army Adjutant Gen. Officer Advanced Course. Cert. counselor. Counselor student activities Calif. Poly. State U., San Luis Obispo, 1969-71, instr. ethnic studies, 1970-71; counselor Ohlone Coll., Fremont, Calif., 1971-72, coordinator coll. readiness, 1971; counselor De Anza Coll., Cupertino, Calif., 1972-78, mem. community speakers bur., 1975-78; counselor Foothill Coll., Los Altos Hills, Calif., 1978—, mem. community speakers bur., 1978—; instr. Def. Equal Opportunity Mgmt. Inst., 1984—. Mem. master plan com. Los Altos (Calif.) Sch. Dist., 1975-76; vol. worker, Chicano communities, Calif.; fellow Masters and Johnson Inst.; Served with Calif. Army N.G., now capt. Adj. Gen. Corps, USAR. Recipient Counselor of Year award Ohlone Coll., 1971-72; lic. marriage family child counselor, Calif. Mem. Am. Calif. personnel and guidance assns., Am. Coll. Personnel Assn., Calif. Assn. Marriage and Family Therapists, Calif. Community Coll. Counselor Assn., Calif. Assn. Counseling and Devel.- Hispanic Caucus, Res. Officers Assn., La Raza Faculty Assn. Calif. Community Colls., Phi Delta Kappa. Democrat. Roman Catholic. Office: Foothill Coll Los Altos Hills CA 94022

GONZALES, RON, city mayor; b. San Francisco; m. Alvina Gonzales; 3 children: Miranda, Rachel, Alejandra. BA in Urban Studies, U. Calif., Santa Cruz. Formerly with Sunnyvale (Calif.) Sch. Dist., City of Santa Clara, Calif.; then human resource mgr. Hewlett-Packard Co.; market program mgmt. cons. state and local govts.; mem. city council City of Sunnyvale, 1979-81, 83-87, mayor, 1981-83, 87—. Coordinator city programs in transp., housing and regional land use planning; Sunnyvale rep. Golden Triangle Task Force, 1985-87; bd. dirs. League of Calif. Cities, Nat. League of Cities and Pub. Tech., Inc. Office: Office of the Mayor PO Box 60607 Sunnyvale CA 94088

GONZALEZ, ALEJANDRO GERMAN, advertising agency executive; b. New Orleans, Nov. 27, 1961; s. Alfredo Francisco and Lourdes Leticia (Hernandez) G. BA, Baker U., 1983. Sales, mktg. asst. US Hispanic C. of C., Kansas City, Mo., 1984; info. asst. ERC Life Cos., Overland Park, Kans., 1984; asst. to personnel J. Walter Thompson Co., Los Angeles, 1984-85, account coordinator, 1985-86, asst. account exec., 1986—; cons. Goal Inc., Tampa, Fla., 1985—. Mem. Sigma Phi Epsilon (local v.p. 1984-85). Republican. Roman Catholic. Avocations: writing, reading, tennis, golf, baseball. Home: 3861 Mentone Ave Apt 41 Culver City CA 90230 Office: J Walter Thompson Co 10100 Santa Monica Blvd Los Angeles CA 90067

GONZALEZ, ALEXANDER, psychologist, educator; b. Los Angeles, Sept. 14, 1945; s. William and Altagracia (Medina) G.; m. Gloria Martinez, June 12, 1971; children—Alejandro, Michael. B.A., Pomona Coll., Claremont, Calif., 1972; postgrad. Harvard Law Sch., 1972-74; M.A., U. Calif.-Santa Cruz, 1977, Ph.D. in Psychology, 1979. Research asst. U. Calif.-Santa Cruz, 1970-72, acad. preceptor, 1975-78, fellow in psychology, 1975-79; assoc. prof. Calif. State U.-Fresno, 1979—; cons., participant profl. confs. Served with USAF, 1963-67. Ford Found. fellow, 1974-79; NRC fellow, 1982. Mem. Am. Psychol. Assn., Calif. Psychol. Assn., Internat. Assn. for Advancement of Cooperation in Edn., Phi Beta Kappa. Contbr. articles to profl. jours. and chpts. to books. Home: 181 N Karen Ave Clovis CA 93612 Office: Dept Psychology Calif State U Fresno CA 93740

GONZALEZ, RAMON R(AFAEL), JR., physiology educator; b. Los Angeles, May 25, 1940; s. Ramon Rafael and Lydia (Navarrete) G.; m. Nickole Ursula Meidell, June 14, 1964; 1 child, Ramon R. III. BS, Walla Walla Coll., 1962, MA, 1965; PhD, Wake Forest U., 1973. Physiologist Virginia Mason Research Ctr., Seattle, 1965-68; NIH predoctoral trainee Wake Forest U., Winston-Salem, N.C., 1968-73; asst. prof. physiology Loma Linda (Calif.) U., 1975-85, assoc. prof., 1985—; cons. Delalande Internationelle, Paris, 1974-75, Carolina Med., King, N.C., 1983—. Contbr. articles to profl. jours.; patentee computer software for ultra sound process. Hoffman-LaRoche Delalande fellow, U. Basel, 1973-75. Mem. Am. Physiol. Soc.,Am. Inst. Ultrasound in Med., Am. Heart Assn. (council on basic sci.), Sigma Xi. Avocations: bicycling, skiing, backpacking, music, reading. Home: 12844 Oriole Ave Grand Terrace CA 92324 Office: Loma Linda U Sch Medicine Dept Physiology Loma Linda CA 92350

GONZALEZ, WILLIAM G., hospital administrator, educator; b. Hackensack, N.J., Mar. 28, 1940; s. William G. and Blanche (Saffery) G.; m. Shirley Ann Mos, Aug. 15, 1964; children: Dana Lynn,Liane Renee. B.A., Rutgers U., 1964; M.B.A., Cornell U., 1966; cert., Sloan Inst. Hosp. Adminstrn., 1966; M.P.A., N.Y. U., 1980. Bus. adminstr. U. Calif.-San Francisco Med. Ctr., 1966-68, asst. dir., various positions, 1968-74; dep. dir. Capital Dist. Psychiat. Ctr., Albany, N.Y., 1974-79; instr. Albany Med. Coll., 1974-79; adj. asst. prof. SUNY-Albany, 1978-79; dir. U. Calif.-Irvine Med. Ctr., Orange, 1979-85; sr. lectr. U. Calif.-Irvine Grad. Sch. Mgmt., 1980-85; bd. dirs. Hosp. Council So. Calif., Orange, 1983-85; pres., chief exec. officer Butterworth Health Corp. and Butterworth Hosp., Grand Rapids, Mich., 1985—. Active Health Professions Council, San Francisco, 1971-74; active Planned Parenthood-World Population, Alameda,Calif. and San Francisco, 1972-74. Served with M.C. U.S. Army, 1961-64, ETO. William Stout scholar, 1964; Alfred P. Sloan scholar, 1964-65; N.Y. State Regents scholar, 1964-65; Rotary Internat. exchange fellow in hosp. adminstrn. Australia, summer 1982. Mem. Am. Coll. Health Care Adminstrs., Health Care Execs. No. Calif. (pres. 1973-74).

GOO, EDWARD KWOCK WAI, materials science educator; b. Honolulu, Nov. 25, 1956; s. See Hong and Rose Sheung (Liu) G. BS, Cornell U., 1978; MS, U. Calif., Berkeley, 1980; PhD, Stanford U., 1984. Research engr. Fairchild Cameria and Instrument Corp., Palo Alto, Calif., 1980-81; staff scientist Lawrence Berkeley (Calif.) Nat. Lab., 1984-85; asst. prof. U. So. Calif., Los Angeles, 1985—. Mem. AAAS, AIME, Electron Microscopy Soc. Am., Am. Phys. Soc., Am. Ceramic Soc. Office: U So Calif Los Angeles CA 90089-0241

GOOD, JANET LOIS, occupational health nurse; b. Coudersport, Pa., Mar. 18, 1938; d. Warren Worth and Jeannette (Britton) Ohlman; m. Robert Jack Good, Feb. 14, 1960; children: Diana Ivy, Robert Warren. Diploma in nursing, Pa. Hosp., 1958; cert. in alcohol studies, U. N.D., 1970; cert. in nurse practition, U. Colo., 1973; BS in Health Care Adminstrn., St. Joseph Coll., 1981—. Cert. instr. CPR, cert. audiometry, spirometry. Staff and recovery room nurse Children's Hosp., Phila., 1958-60; supr. male div. Pennhurst State Sch. for Mentally Retarded, Spring City, Pa., 1961-65; office nurse Pediatric Clinic, Denver, 1966-69; nurse practitioner mgr. Mountain Bell, Denver, 1969-82; adminstrv. nurse Atlantic Richfield Co., Denver, 1982—; presenter health care topics 1978—. Rep. com. woman Adams County, Northglenn, Colo., 1980; del. Rep. State Conv., Denver, 1980; counselor merit badges Boy Scouts Am., Northglenn, 1984-85. Mem. Am. Nurses Assn. (cert.), Am. Nurses Assn. Primary Council Nurse Practitioners, Am. Assn. Occupational Health Nurses (bd. dirs. 1983-87, sec. 1987—), Colo. Assn. Occupational Health Nurses (corr. sec. 1975-76, pres. elect 1977-78, pres. 1978-79, named Occupational Health Nurse of Yr. 1979, Schering Occupational Health Nurse 1985), Denver Assn. Occupational Health Nurses. Lodge: Order Eastern Star. Office: Atlantic Richfield Co 555 17th St Room 711 Denver CO 80202

GOOD, JOHN HENRY, advertising executive; b. Orange, Calif., Jan. 20, 1965; s. John Henry Sr. and Dorothy Helen (Fricke) G. Student, Orange Coast Coll., 1983-85. Pres. Good-Koupal Advt., Irvine, Calif., 1984—. Mem. Orange County Advt. Fedn., Advt. Fedn., Los Angeles Advt. Communications Network, Desert Bus. Assn., Pub. Relations Soc. Am. Republican. Roman Catholic. Avocation: photography. Office: Good Koupal Advt Pub Relations 18013 Sky Park Circle Suite A Irvine CA 92714

GOOD, SUSAN PAULINE, banker; b. Sanger, Calif., Aug. 17, 1953; d. Alfred Anton and Elsbeth (Grimm) Good; A.A., Reedley Coll., 1973; B.A. summa cum laude, Calif. State U., Fresno, 1975. Advt. asst. Bell Public Relations Agy., Fresno, Calif., 1976-77; account exec. Meeker Advt., Fresno, Calif., 1977-78; dir. advt. Coast Savs. and Loan, Fresno, Calif., 1978-81 (merger with Central Savs. and Loan 1981), asst. v.p., br. promotions mgr., br. mgr., 1981-84, br. mgr., 1984—. Mem. mktg. com. U.S. League Savs. Assn., 1980-81; chmn. Fresno City-County Commn. on Status Women, 1979; chmn. Fresno County Democratic Central Com., 1985-86; pres. Calif. State U. Fresno Alumni Assn., 1981; sec., bd. dirs. Fresno Rape Counseling Service, 1981; mem. Leadership Fresno Alumni Exec. Bd., 1986; mem. Charter Leadership Fresno Class, 1984. Recipient cert. of achievement Inst. Fin. Edn., 1982, Silver medal Am. Advt. Fedn., 1982. Mem. Fresno Advt. Fedn. (pres. 1982), Inst. Fin. Edn., C. of C. (past chmn. ambassadors, Leadership of Fresno Alumni). Roman Catholic. Office: 1930 E Shields St, Fresno CA 93726

GOODACRE, KENNETH ROBERT, real estate executive; b. San Antonio, Jan. 21, 1943; s. Robert Edward and Lorraine Allison G.; B.S., Ariz. State U., 1970; m. Cinda C. Poarch, Sept. 9, 1972; 1 stepson, Donald Ray Bouthillier. Asst. dir. property mgmt. O'Malley Investment Co., Phoenix, 1970; mgr. residential properties Del E. Webb Realty & Mgmt., Phoenix, 1970-76, gen. mgr. Dewguard div., 1974-76; pres., chief exec. officer, co-founder Camelback Mgmt. Co., Phoenix, 1976-82; v.p. Murdock Realty Services, Inc., 1982-83; pres., chief exec. officer, founder Ventura Properties, Inc., 1983—; adv. bd. mem. 1st Bus. Bank Ariz. Mem. Ariz. Gov.'s Sport Council, 1978—; bd. dirs. Phoenix Symphony; mem. legal arbitration panel State Bar Ariz., 1979—. Served with AUS, 1966-68. Mem. Inst. Real Estate Mgmt. (cert. property mgr., nat. faculty mem. 1984—), Nat. Assn. Realtors, Phoenix Bd. Realtors, Am. Mgmt. Assn., Phoenix C. of C., Omega Tau Rho. Republican. Club: Guardian Angels Ariz. State U. Home: 5124 E Desert Park Ln Paradise Valley AZ 85253

GOODALL, JACKSON WALLACE, JR., restaurant company executive; b. San Diego, Oct. 29, 1938; s. Jackson Wallace and Evelyn Violet (Koski) G.; m. Mary Esther Buckley, June 22, 1958; children—Kathleen, Jeffery, Suzanne, Minette. B.S., San Diego State U., 1960. With Foodmaker, Inc., San Diego, 1965-70, pres., 1970—, chief exec. officer, 1979—, chmn. bd., 1985—; founder, dir. Grossmont Bank, La Mesa, Calif. Bd. dirs. Faith Chapel, La Jolla Acad. of Advt. and Graphics, Greater San Diego Sports Assn.; assoc. chmn. Laymen's Nat. Bible Com.; chmn. Athletes in Action Worldwide Basketball. Recipient Disting. Alumni of Year award San Diego State U., 1974, Golden Chain award, 1982, Silver Plate award Internat. Foodservice Mfg. Assn., 1985. Mem. Am. Restaurant Assn., San Diego State U. Alumni Assn. (bd. dirs.). Republican. Club: Fairbanks Ranch Country (founder). Office: Foodmaker Inc 9330 Balboa San Diego CA 92123

GOODALL, LEONARD EDWIN, public administration educator; b. Warrensburg, Mo., Mar. 16, 1937; s. Leonard Burton and Eula (Johnson) G.; m. Lois Marie Stubblefield, Aug. 16, 1959; children: Karla, Karen, Greg. B.A., Central Mo. State U., 1958; M.A., U. Mo., 1960; Ph.D. (Kendrick C. Babcock fellow), U. Ill., 1962; A.A. (hon), Schoolcraft Coll., 1977. Asst. prof. polit. sci., asst. dir. Bur. Govt. Research, Ariz. State U., Tempe, 1962-65; dir. Bur. Bur. Govt. Research, Ariz. State U., 1965-67; assoc. prof. polit. sci., assoc. dean faculties U. Ill. at Chgo. Circle, 1968-69, vice chancellor, 1969-71; chancellor U. Mich., Dearborn, 1971-79; pres. U. Nev., Las Vegas, 1979-85; prof. mgmt. and pub. adminstrn. U. Nev., 1985—; cons. Ariz. Acad., Phoenix, 1964-67; dir. Peace Corps tng. program for Chile, 1965. Author: The American Metropolis: Its Governments and Politics, 1968, rev. edit., 1975, Gearing Arizona's Communities to Orderly Growth, 1965, State Politics and Higher Education, 1976, When Colleges Lobby States, 1987; editor: Urban Politics in the Southwest, 1967. Mem. univ. exec. com. United Fund, 1966-67; v.p. Met. Fund, Inc.; mem. Mich. Gov.'s Commn. Long Range Planning, 1973-75, Tempe Planning and Zoning Commn., 1965-67, New Detroit Com., 1972-79; mem. Wayne County (Mich.) Planning Commn., 1973-79, vice chmn., 1976-79; mem. exec. bd. Clark County chpt. NCCJ, 1979—; bd. dirs. Nev. Devel. Authority, 1980', Boulder Dam council Boy Scouts Am., 1980—, Nev. Power Co. Consumer Adv. Council, 1984—. Served with AUS, 1959. Mem. Am. Polit. Sci. Assn., Am. Soc. Pub. Adminstrn., Western Govtl. Research Assn. (exec. council 1966-68), Dearborn C. of C. (dir. 1974-79), Phi Sigma Epsilon, Phi Kappa Phi. Club: Las Vegas Country. Home: 6530 W Darby Ave Las Vegas NV 89102 Office: U Nev Las Vegas NV 89154

GOODE, JOHN WOLFORD, technology management consultant; b. Paxton, Ill., Apr. 19, 1939; s. Frank Wolford and Dorothy (Phillips) G.; 1 child, John. Student, U. Ill. Med. Ctr., 1961-63; BS, U. Ill., 1962; MS, Loyola U., Chgo., 1966, PhD, 1968; MBA, Duquesne U., 1981. Lab. dir. Nalco Chem., Chgo., 1967-78; fellowship dir. Carnegie-Mellon Inst., Pitts., 1978-80; dir. research Gulf-Oil Corp., Pitts., 1980-85; sr. mgmt. cons. in tech. and research Stanford Research Inst., Menlo Park, Calif., 1985-86; mgmt. cons. AtKearney, Redwood City, Calif., 1987—; assoc. prof. U. Pitts., 1981-85. Contbr. articles to profl. jours. Mem. Managerial Accts. Soc., Coll. Toxicology, Am. Chem. Soc., Am. Indsl. Hygiene Soc., Soc. Risk Analysis. Home: 1903 Somersworth Dr San Jose CA 95124 Office: Atkearney 3 Lagoon Dr Redwood CA 94065

GOODE, WILLIAM JOSIAH, sociology educator; b. Houston, Aug. 30, 1917; s. William J. and Lillian Rosalie (Bare) G.; m. Josephine Mary Cannizzo, Dec. 22, 1938 (div. 1946); children: Brian Erich, Rachel (dec.), Barbara Nan; m. Ruth Siegel, Oct. 20, 1950 (div. 1971); 1 son, Andrew Josiah. B.A., U. Tex., 1938, M.A., 1939; Ph.D., Pa. State U., 1946; D.Sc. (hon.), Upsala U., 1970. Instr. sociology Pa. State U., 1941-43; social sci. analyst Inter-Am. Statis. Inst., 1943-44; asst. prof. Wayne State U., 1946-50; asso. research dir. Columbia U., 1950-52, asso. prof. sociology, 1952-56, prof., 1956-74; Giddings prof. sociology Stanford U., 1975-77, prof., 1977-86; prof. Harvard U., 1986—; prof. Free U. Berlin, 1954; vis. fellow Wolfson Coll., Oxford U., 1980; U.S. del. UN Conf. Aid to Tech. Undeveloped Nations, 1963; bd. dirs., sec. Social Sci. Research Council; gov., asso. dir. Bur. Applied Social Research; mem. behavioral scis. tng. com. Nat. Inst. Gen. Med. Scis., NIMH, 1966-67; vis. scholar Nat. Acad. Scis., People's Rep. China, 1986. Author: Religion Among the Primitives, 1951, Methods in Social Research, 1952, After Divorce, 1956, Struktur Der Familie, World Revolution and Family Patterns, 1963, The Family, 1964, 82, Family and Society, 1965, Dynamics of Modern Society, 1966, (with L. Mitchell and F. Furstenberg) Willard Waller: On the Family, Education and War, 1970, Principles of Sociology, 1977, The Celebration of Heroes: Prestige as a Social Control Process, 1979; co-author: The Other Half, 1971, Explorations in Social Theory, 1973, Social Systems and Family Patterns, 1971; editor: series Sociol, 1953; assoc. editor: Marriage and Family Living, 1956; contbr. articles to profl. jours. Served with USNR, 1944-45. Guggenheim fellow, 1965-66, 83-84; sr. scientist career grantee NIMH, 1969-74; Russell Sage Found. fellow, 1983-84; recipient MacIver award Am. Sociol. Soc., 1965, Burgess award Nat. Council Family Relations, 1969. Fellow Am. Acad. Arts and Scis.; mem. Am. Sociol. Soc. (exec. com., council 1959-62, pres. 1971-72), Eastern Sociol. Soc. (pres. 1959-60, exec. com. 1959-61), ACLU (dir.), Sociol. Research Assn. (exec. council, pres. 1967—). Home: 77 Francis Ave Cambridge MA 02138 Office: Harvard U Dept Sociology Cambridge MA 02138

GOODELL, CAROL GUYTON, educational administrator, consultant; b. River Forest, Ill., Feb. 18, 1936; d. Robert Harmar and Margaret (Thomas) Guyton; m. William Dudley Goodell, Dec. 20, 1958; children—Douglas Sewall, Elizabeth Ormond. B.S., B.A., Ohio State U., 1958; M.A. in Ednl. Adminstrn., Stanford U., 1969, M.A. in Anthropology, 1974, Ph.D., 1979. Tchr., pub. schs., DeCoto, San Mateo, Hillsborough, Calif., 1958-67; pres. Real World Learning, Inc., San Carlos, Calif., 1968-72; co-ordinator Early Childhood Project, Mass. State Dept. Edn., Boston, 1977-79; dir. Nueva Learning Ctr., Hillsborough, Calif., 1979-84; pres. Carol Goodell and Associates, Coll. Campus Tours, 1984—. Quaker. Editor: The Changing Classroom, 1973, 75, 79.

GOODELL, PETER BEASANT, entomologist, research agriculturalist; b. Covina, Calif., Jan. 29, 1952; s. Robert Baily and Beth (Stirdivant) G.; m. Nancy Catherine Wells, Oct. 9, 1976. BA, San Francisco State U., 1974; MS, U. Calif., Riverside, 1978; PhD, U. Calif., 1986. Registered profl. entomologist. Area integrated pest mgmt. advisor Coop. Extension U. Calif., Bakersfield, 1981—. Mem. Soc. Nematologists, Entomol. Soc. Am., Assn. Registered Entomologists.

GOODEN, DAVID CLAYTON, psychotherapist; b. Lexington, Ky., Dec. 21, 1948; s. Elmer Clayton and Mabel Doris (Lumpkin) G.; m. Anne Haney, July 17, 1976; children: Andrea, Cristina. BA, U. Ariz., 1976; MSW, Ariz. State U., 1978. Cert. social worker. Psychotherapist Desert Community Mental Health Ctr., Indio, Calif., 1978-79, La Frontera Ctr., Tucson, 1979-81, So. Ariz. Mental Health Ctr., Tucson, 1981—; adv. to bd. dirs. Community Orgn. for Personal Enrichment, Tucson, 1983—; pvt. practitioner, Tucson, 1981—. Nat. Assn. Social Workers, Phi Beta Kappa, Phi Eta Sigma. Democrat. Presbyterian. Avocations: photography. Office: So Ariz Mental Health Ctr 1930 E 6th St Tucson AZ 85719

GOODEY, ILA MARIE, psychologist; b. Logan, Utah, Feb. 1, 1948; d. Vernal P. and Leona Marie (Williams) Goodey. BA with honors in English and Sociology, U. Utah, 1976; Grad. Cert. Criminology, U. Utah, 1976, MS in Counseling Psychology, 1984, PhD in Psychology, 1985. Speech writer for dean of students U. Utah, Salt Lake City, 1980—, psychologist Univ. Counseling Ctr., 1984—; cons. Dept. Social Services, State of Utah, Salt Lake City, 1983—; pvt. practice psychology Consult West, Salt Lake City, 1985—; pub. relations coordinator Univ. Counseling Ctr., 1985—; cons. Aids Project, U. Utah, 1985—; writer civic news Salt Lake City Corp., 1980—. Author book: Love for All Seasons, 1971; play: Validation, 1979; musical drama: One Step, 1984. Contbr. articles to profl. jours. Chmn. policy bd. Dept. State Social Service, Salt Lake City, 1986—; campaign writer Utah Dem. Party, 1985. Recipient Creative Achievement award Utah Poetry Soc., 1974, English SAC, U. Utah, 1978. Mem. Am. Psychol. Assn., Utah Psychol. Assn., AAUW, Internat. Platform Assn., Mortar Board, Am. Soc. Clin. Hypnosis, Utah Soc. Clin. Hypnosis, Soc. Psychol. Study Social Issues, League of Women Voters, Phi Beta Kappa, Phi Kappa Phi, Alpha Lambda Delta. Mormon. Clubs: Mormon Theol. Symposium, Utah Poetry Assn. Avocations: theatrical activities, creative writing, travel, political activities. Office: University Counseling Center 450 SSBUtah Salt Lake City UT 84112

GOODFIELD, REGINA KAHN, social services administrator; b. Chgo., Feb. 15, 1942; d. Milton Merrill and Elizabeth (Lewin) K. BA in Sociology, U. Ariz., 1964; MSW, San Francisco State U., 1968. Licensed clin. social worker, Calif. Child welfare worker Pima County Dept. Pub. Welfare, Tucson, 1964-65; social worker San Francisco Dept. Social Services, 1965-66, supr. child welfare, 1968-70; psychiat. social worker So. Ariz. Mental Health Ctr., Tucson, 1970; social work coordinator San Francisco Boy's Home, 1970-72; social worker Children's Garden, San Rafael, Calif., 1973-75, program dir., 1975-79, asst. dir., 1979-83, exec. dir., 1983—; commr. oral exams. Calif. State Bd. Behavioral Sci. Examiners, 1983-86; spl. adv. bd. Calif. Children's Lobby adv. com. project on Instl. Child Abuse. Author: (video presentation) Setting Goals and Objectives in the Helping Professions, 1980; co-author Attachment Impairment in Latency Aged Children, 1983, Outcome of Older Child Adoptions, 1986, Children's Garden Attachment Model, 1987. Recipient Meritorious Service award Children's Garden Bd. Dirs., 1983. Mem. Nat. Assn. Social Workers, Calif. Assn. Services for Children. Office: Children's Garden 7 Mt St Lassen Dr #B256 San Rafael CA 94903

GOODFRIEND, MARK EDWARD, management holding company executive; b. N.Y.C., May 17, 1943; s. Samuel and Ibi Goodfriend; m. Barbara Schreiner, Aug. 28, 1977; 1 child, Alexander S. BSEE, CUNY, 1966; MS in Aeros. and Astronautics, NYU, 1968. Systems project engr. Grumman Aerospace Corp., L.I., N.Y., 1965-70; gen. mgr. eastern ops. Standard Bus. Research, Chgo., 1970-72; pres., chief exec. officer I.S. English, Inc., N.Y.C., 1972-75; exec. v.p., chief ops. officer Orelube Corp., L.I., 1975-80; v.p. stategic planning and expansion DHL Corp., Redwood City, Calif., 1980-82; managing dir. Mgmt. Resources Internat., San Francisco, 1982—, also bd. dirs.; sr. v.p., bd.dirs. Bank of Saipan; pres., chief exec. officer, bd. dirs. Cocos Lagoon Devel. Corp.; bd. dirs. Net Express, Inc. Mem. AIAA, Sigma Gamma Tau. Home: 3063 Washington San Francisco CA 94115 Office: Mgmt Resources Internat Ltd 582 Market St #2000 San Francisco CA 94104

GOODIN, WILLIAM CHARLES, oil company consultant; b. Louisville, Sept. 18, 1917; s. Edward C. and Bertha (Vorhies) G.; m. Emily Ellen Percefull, Sept. 8, 1946; children: Sue Ellen Goodin Bach, Charles W. B.A. in Econs., U. Colo., 1941. Owner, operator Petroleum Info. Corp., Denver, 1946-68; ptnr., v.p. Petroleum Info. Corp., subs. A.C. Nielsen Co., Denver, 1968-75, pres., 1975-79; chmn. bd., chief exec. officer Petroleum Info. Corp., subs. A.C. Nielsen Co., Littleton, Colo., 1979-83, chmn. bd., 1983-85; ret. 1986; mem. Colo. Oil and Gas Commn., 1972-76, Interstate Oil Compact Commn.; cons. oilcompanies. Bd. dirs. Swedish Med. Ctr. Found., Englewood, Colo., 1979—, U. Colo. Found., Inc., Boulder, 1983—. Served to 1st lt. CIC, AUS, 1942-46, Philippines, Korea. Recipient Betty McWhorter award Denver chpt. Desk & Derrick, 1979. Mem. Rocky Mountain Oil and Gas Assn. (dir. 1982—), Denver Landmen's Assn., Soc. Petroleum Engrs., Am. Assn. Petroleum Geologists, Rocky Mountain Petroleum Pioneers, Assn. Petroleum Writers, Ind. Petroleum Assn. Mountain States; hon. life mem. Rocky Mountain Assn. Petroleum Geologists. Republican. Presbyterian. Clubs: Denver Petroleum (bd. dirs. 1958-62, v.p. 1961, pres. 1962), Cherry Hills Country (Englewood, Colo.); Garden of God's (Colorado Springs, Colo.); 25 Yr. Club of Petroleum Industry (Solvang, Calif.). Home: 11 Parkway Dr Englewood CO 80110 Office: Petroleum Info Corp 600 Denver Club Bldg Denver CO 80202

GOODKIN, SANFORD RONALD, real estate analyst; b. Passaic, N.J., Feb. 8, 1929; s. Robert and Lillian (Ellman) G. Pres., chmn. bd. The Goodkin Group, Sanford R. Goodkin Research Corp., 1956; pub., writer The Goodkin Report (23 yrs.), also real estate editor Calif. Bus. Mag.; contbg. editor, columnist writer column Real Estate Dynamics in Profl. Builder Mag., Frontier Mag. (Pacific Basin 1986), Daily Pacific Builder, frequent contbr. L.A. Times, S.D. Union, Fin. News Network; syndicated columnist Visions; cons. to industry; author Web Apt. Reporter; chmn. Asian Pacific Protocal, producing first Taiwan Productivity Tour, 1987, The Goodkin Group; condr. real estate seminars; lectr. series Japan, Hong Kong, Australia, Can., 1982-86; advisor Nat. Inst. Bldg. Scis. Fgn. Influences Task Force; sr. fellow Hubert Humphrey Sch. Social Ecology, Ben Gurion U., Israel. Contbr. articles to The Los Angeles Times, other newspapers. Mem. San Diego County Housing Adv. Com.; advisor San Diego World Trade Ctr.; founder, bd. govs. Ben-Gurion U., Negev, Israel; exec. bd. and internat. adv. bd. World Congress of Engrs. and Architects. Recipient Medal of Valor, State Israel, 1975, Max C. Tipton Meml. award for mktg. excellence, 1974; named one of West's most disting. citizens Sunset Mag., 1973. Mem. Urban Land Inst. (vice chmn. exec. council), Nat. Assn. Homebuilders (v.p., trustee sales and mktg. council, pres.), Inst. Residential Mktg. (past pres.), Lambda Alpha (founder). Author: The Goodkin Guide to Winning in Real Estate, 1977, Higher Density Housing, 1986; contbg. author Land Economics, 1983, Higher Density Housing, 1986. Address: 3252 Holiday Ct #108 La Jolla CA 92037

GOODLEY, PAUL HARVEY, physician; b. Bklyn., Feb. 6, 1932; s. Israel Harry and Ruth (Reiter) G.; m. Dolores Henrietta Ledfors, Apr. 2, 1955; children—Mark David, Pamela Susan, Diane Deborah, Caryn Lynn, Lisa Louise. B.A. cum laude, U. So. Calif., 1955; M.D., UCLA, 1959. Diplomate Am. Bd. Phys. Medicine and Rehab., Am. Bd. Family Practice. Intern, Harbor Gen. Hosp., Torrance, Calif., 1959-60; gen. practice indsl. medicine, Torrance, 1960, Wilmington, Calif., 1961-72; resident phys. medicine and rehab. U. So. Calif.-Los Angeles County Med. Ctr., 1972-73, U. Calif.-Davis, 1974; practice medicine specializing in phys. medicine and rehab., Los Angeles, 1975—; med. dir. rehab. ctr. Glendale Adventist Med. Ctr., Calif., 1975-76; med. cons. orthopedic medicine U.S. VA, 1981-84; founder Pain Diagnostics and Rehab. Inst., Los Angeles, 1977, dir., 1977-84; adj. prof. orthopedic medicine Coll. Osteo. Medicine of Pacific; exam. physician Los Angeles County Sheriff's Dept., 1962-79; exec. dir. Am. Coll. Orthopaedic Medicine, 1987—. Inventor Goodley Polyaxial Cervical Traction System; (with others) Goodley/Shemet Lumbar Lift. Mem. Founders Club of Music Ctr. Performing Arts; Recipient Award of Valor, Los Angeles County Sheriff's Dept., 1968. Mem. Am. Assn. Orthopedic Medicine (founding, 1st pres., pres. emeritus), Am. Acad. Phys. Medicine and Rehab. (chmn. task force and spl. interest group musculoskeletal medicine), Internat. Rehab. Medicine Assn. (chmn. com. musculoskeletal medicine), AMA, Los Angeles County Med. Assn., Am. Assn. Electromyography and Electrodiagnosis, Am. Congress Rehab. Medicine, Soc. Orthopedic Medicine, Internat. Assn. Study of Pain, Am. Pain Soc., Am. Thermographic Soc., Nat. Rifle Assn. (life master, Gold medal Calif. championships 1968), Phi Delta Epsilon. Office: PO Box 317 Fawnskin CA 92333

GOODMAN, GARY E., oncologist; b. Chgo., Oct. 15, 1948; s. Joseph I. and Dorothy G. (Grossman) G.; m. Joanna Beckley, Nov. 19, 1983. BS in Biochemistry magna cum laude, Mich. State U., 1970; MD, U. Ill., Chgo., 1974, MS in Pharmacology, 1974. Diplomate Am. Bd. Internal Medicine, Med. Oncology. Intern U. Oreg. Health Scis. Ctr., Portland, 1974-75, resident, 1975-77; staff oncologist Swedish Hosp. Tumor Inst., Seattle, 1981—; affiliate investigator Fred Hutchinson Cancer Research Ctr., Seattle, 1981—; clin. asst. prof. medicine, U. Wash., Seattle, 1981—; cons. Oncogene Co., Seattle, 1985—. 7ontbr. numerous articles to profl. jours., chpts. to books. Nat. Cancer Inst. grantee, 1983, 86; hematology, oncology fellow U. Ariz., 1978-81. Office: Swedish Hosp Tumor Inst 1221 Madison Seattle WA 98104

GOODMAN, GERALD, marketing consultant; b. Bklyn., Oct. 30, 1916; s. Charles and Freda Goodman; m. Florence Rothlein, Oct. 12, 1939 (div. May 1982); children: Len Hunt, Roger Wyck. BS, CUNY, 1937, MS, 1939. Exec. v.p. Tower Chems., Butler, Pa., 1959-60, ABCO, Inc., Irwin, Pa., 1960-68; dir. mktg. Chemtrust Industries, Chgo., 1968-69, v.p. mktg., 1970-71; chief exec. officer Mktg. Counselors Internat., Inc., Santa Fe, 1971—. Co-author: Institutional Laundry, 1970; contbr. articles to profl. jours.; mem. mgmt. adv. bd. Chem. Week mag., 1981—. Exec. dir. Santa Fe Council Soviet Jews, 1986. Sales Letter Roundtable award Sales & Mktg. Mgmt. Mag., N.Y.C., 1964, 65. Mem. Am. Mktg. Assn., Internat. Sanitary Supply Assn., Am. Cons. League. Democrat. Jewish. Avocations: art, music. Home and Office: Mktg Counselors Internat Inc 330 Calle Loma Norte Santa Fe NM 87501

GOODMAN, GWENDOLYN ANN, nursing educator; b. Davenport, Iowa, Aug. 7, 1955; d. Merle Erwin and Loraine Etta (Mahannah) Langfeldt; m. Mark Nathan Goodman, Oct. 24, 1982; 1 child, Zachary Aaron. BS in Nursing, Ariz. State U., 1977. RN, Ariz. Staff nurse surgical floor and intensive care unit St. Luke's Hosp. and Med. Ctr., Phoenix, 1977-81; staff nurse intensive care unit Yavapai Regional Med. Ctr., Prescott, Ariz., 1981-82; instr. nursing Yavapai Coll., Prescott, 1982—, cons., 1986; part time staff nurse Ariz. Poison Control Ctr., Phoenix, 1980-81. Mem. community ethics com. Prescott Health Decisions, 1986—. Mem. Am. Nurses Assn. (Ariz. Constituent). Democrat. Home: PO Box 450 Prescott AZ 86302 Office: Yavapai Coll 1100 E Sheldon Prescott AZ 86301

GOODMAN, JANE, lawyer, psychologist, consultant; b. Johannesburg, Republic of South Africa, Feb. 17, 1952; came to U.S., 1976; d. Roy and Myrtle Ianthe (Meyer) Fraser; m. Oscar Goodman, Oct. 11, 1976. BA, U. Witwatersrand, Johannesburg, 1972, TTHD, 1973; JD cum laude, U. Puget Sound, 1983; PhD, U. Wash., 1986. Bar: Wash. 1983, U.S. Dist. Ct. (we. dist.) Wash. 1983. Tchr. English and French Transvaal Edn. Dept., Johannesburg, 1973-75; owner Plain English, Seattle, 1981-86; assoc. Bricklin & Gendler, Seattle, 1983-84; trial atty. EEOC, Seattle, 1984—; research assoc., psychology dept. U. Wash., Seattle, 1986—. Editor: Washington Lawyer's Practice Manual for Seattle-King County Bar Assn., 1984—; contbr. chpts. to books, articles to trial mags., book reviews to various profl. jours. Active com. Grad. and Profl. Student Sen. Com. on Black S. African Study Aid, Seattle, 1985-86. Grantee NSF, 1986-88, Am. Jurisprudence, 1982-83; Nat. Inst. Justice fellow, 1985-86. Mem. ABA (cons. Chgo. chpt.), Wash. State Bar Assn., Law and Soc. Assn., Am. Judicature Soc., Assn. Trial Lawyers Am., Am. Psychol. Assn. (research grantee 1984). Office: U Wash Dept Psychology N1-25 Seattle WA 98195

GOODMAN, JOEL HARRY, JR., university administrator; b. Seattle, Apr. 18, 1944; s. Joel H. and Edith (Kullmann) G.; m. Barbara Guzofsky, May 8, 1976; 1 child, Elliott James. BA with distinction, Stanford U., 1966; MAT, Harvard U., 1967; MA, Stanford U., 1973 and 76; postgrad., U. Chgo., 1975-76. Asst. dir. admissions Stanford U., Palo Alto, Calif., 1972-74; mktg. services mgr. Bell & Howell Edn. Group, Chgo., 1974-80; dir. planning and devel. Western State U., Fullerton, Calif., 1980-83, dean of admissions, 1983—; v.p. adminstrn. Western State U., 1984—. Bd. dirs., sec. Orange County chpt. Am. Diabetes Assn., also Calif. affiliate. Clubs: Stanford of Orange County (bd. dirs.). Office: 1111 N State College Blvd Fullerton CA 92631

GOODMAN, JOHN KESTNER, investment company executive, rancher; b. Kansas City, Mo., Aug. 1, 1920; s. Barney and Sophia (Kestner) G.; m. Beatrice Gardiner Prescott, Apr. 1, 1948 (div. 1958); 1 dau., Lucy Prescott; m. 2d, Aline Lees Bragg, Aug. 6, 1966; 1 son, John K. II. Student U. of Pa., 1938-40; B.A. summa cum laude, Yale U., 1942. Owner, operator, H Bar A Ranch, Mammoth, Ariz., 1944-46; dir. Goodman Properties, Tucson, 1946—; ptnr. Ashton Goodman Properties, Tucson, 1948—; ptnr. Kittle, Goodman Hook Bar Ranch, Show Low, Ariz., 1955-66; founding dir. Catalina Savings and Loan Co., Tucson 1959-82; owner, dir. ranch, Australia, 1970—. Bd. dirs., Tucson Mus. of Art, 1968-83; dir. Friends of Western Art, 1970—; mem. Ariz. Racing Commn., 1965-85, chmn., 1982-83; chmn. Rillito Race Track Hist. Com., Tucson, 1987. Served with U.S. Army, 1942-43. Recipient Wrangler award, Best Western Art Book, Cowboy Hall of Fame, 1978. Mem. Nat. Assn. State Racing Commrs. (pres. 1979, exec. bd. mem. 1980—), U.S. Polo Assn. (del.). Clubs: Mountain Oyster, Tucson Country, La Paloma Country (Tucson), Los Charros del Desierto (Tucson); Jockey, Yale (N.Y.C.), Rancheros Visitadores (Santa Barbara, Calif.), Rolls Royce Owners (Mechanicsville, Pa.). Author: Ross Stefan-An Impressionistic Painter of the Southwest, 1977. Office: 283 N Stone Ave Tucson AZ 85701

GOODMAN, JOSEPH WILFRED, electrical engineering educator; b. Boston, Feb. 8, 1936; s. Joseph and Doris (Ryan) G.; m. Hon Mai Lam, Dec. 5, 1962; 1 dau., Michele Ann. B.A., Harvard U., 1958; M.S. in E.E., Stanford U., 1960, Ph.D., 1963. Postdoctoral fellow Norwegian Def. Research Establishment, Oslo, 1962-63; research assoc. Stanford U., 1963-67, asst. prof., 1967-69, assoc. prof., 1969-72, prof. elec. engring., 1972—; vis. prof. Univ. Paris XI, Orsay, France, 1973-74; dir. Info. Systems lab., dept. elec. engring., Stanford U., 1981-83; cons. to govt. and industry, 1965—; v.p. Internat. Comm. for Optics, 1984—; mem. internat. adv. com. on phys. scis. and engring. Sci. Council Singapore. Author: Introduction to Fourier Optics, 1968, Statistical Optics, 1985; contbr. articles to profl. jours. Recipient F.E. Terman award Am. Soc. Engring. Edn., 1971; research grants NSF; Air Force Office Sci. Research Office Naval Research. Fellow Optical Soc. Am. (dir. 1977-83, editor jour. 1978-83, Max Born award 1983), IEEE (edn. medal 1987), Soc. Photo-optical Instrumentation Engrs. (bd. govs. 1979-82); mem. AAAS, Nat. Acad. Engring., Sigma Xi. Home: 570 University Terrace Los Altos CA 94022 Office: Dept Elec Engring Durand 127 Stanford U Stanford CA 94305

GOODMAN, JULIUS, nuclear engineer, consultant, researcher; b. Odessa, USSR, July 19, 1935; came to U.S., 1979, naturalized, 1986; s. Isaac and Eugenia (Lusher) Guttmann; m. Rachel Bezpalko, July 4, 1959; 1 dau., Marina. M.S. in Theoretical Physics, State U., Odessa, 1958, Ph.D., Inst. Nuclear Physics, Tashkent, USSR, 1962, Inst. Tech. Odessa, 1965. Sr. researcher Inst. Nuclear Physics, Tashkent, Acad. Sci., USSR, 1958-63; prof. Inst. Tech., Odessa, 1963-70, Poly U., 1970-76; sr. engr. Bechtel Power Corp., Norwalk, Calif., 1980-86; prof. Calif. State U. Long Beach, 1986—. Author: Professional Education, 1975, (with P.U. Arifov) Positron Diagnostic, 1978; contbr. numerous articles to profl. jours. Pres. Hatchiya (Revival), Orange County, Calif., 1982—. Mem. Am. Nuclear Soc., Internat. Soc. Reliability Engrs., Internat. Platform Assn., Com. on Internat. Freedom of Scientists, AAAS, N.Y. Acad. Scis., Los Angeles Council Engrs. and Scientists (publicity chmn. 1983-84). Club: Toastmasters (Fullerton, Calif.). Lodge: B'nai B'rith. Research on probabilistic risk assessment, reliability, statistics, artificial intelligence, simulation; gen. relativity, atomic and nuclear physics, physics of space nuclear reactors. Patentee nuclear reactor with UF-6. Home: 1630 Via Linda Fullerton CA 92633 Office: Calif State U Sch Engring 1250 Bellflower Blvd Long Beach CA 90840

GOODMAN, MURRAY, chemistry educator; b. N.Y.C., July 6, 1928; s. Louis and Frieda (Bercun) G.; m. Zelda Silverman; Aug. 26, 1951; children: Andrew, Joshua, David. BS magna cum laude, Bklyn. Coll., 1949; PhD, U. Calif., Berkeley, 1952. NRC fellow Cambridge (Eng.) U., 1955-56; asst. prof. Polytechnic Inst., Bklyn., 1956-60, assoc. prof., 1960-64, prof. chemistry, 1964-71, dir. polymer research inst., 1967-71; chmn. U. Calif.-San Diego, La Jolla, 1971-76, prof. chemistry, 1971—; vis. prof. U. Alta., Can., 1981, Lady Davis Vis. Prof., Hebrew U., Jerusalem, 1982; Goldberg chmn. biomed. engring. Technion-Israel Inst. Tech., 1982; William H. Rauscher lectr. Rensselaer Poly. Inst., 1982. Editor Biopolymers Jour., 1963—; contbr. numerous articles to profl. jours. Recipient Disting. Alumnus Medal Bklyn. Coll., 1965, Scoffone Medal U. Padova, 1980, Humboldt award, 1985. Mem. AAAS, Am. Chem. Soc., Am. Soc. Biol. Chemists, The Chem. Soc. Eng., Biophys. Soc., Council for Chem. Research (sci. adv. bd.), U.S. Nat. Commn., Sigma Xi. Home: 9760 Blackgold Rd La Jolla CA 92037 Office: U Calif San Diego Dept Chemistry La Jolla CA 92093

GOODMAN, SEYMOUR EVAN, computer science and international studies educator, researcher, consultant; b. Chgo., June 19, 1943; s. Paul S. and Shirley (Young) G.; m. Diane Margot Samuel, Dec. 18, 1966; children—Richard Michael, Steven Neal. B.S., Columbia U., 1965, M.S., 1966; Ph.D., Calif. Inst. Tech., 1970. Asst. prof. applied math. U. Va., Charlottesville, 1970-75, assoc. prof. applied math. and computer sci., 1975-81; vis. prof. pub. and internat. affairs, Princeton (N.J.) U., 1977-79, research fellow, 1978-79; vis. scholar U. Chgo., 1979; prof. mgmt. info. systems U. Ariz., Tucson, 1981—; mem. adv. com. Internat. Trade Adminstrn., Dept. Commerce, 1979—; mem. adv. com. Def. Sci. Bd., Dept. Def., 1981-84, Def. Intelligence Agy., 1983—, NRC coms., 1985—; cons. govtl. agys. Danforth Assoc., 1977-82; Sesquicentennial Assoc. State of Va., 1977; NSF grantee, 1978-79, 83; numerous grant and research contracts Office Tech. Assessment, U.S. Congress, 1979-81, Los Alamos Nat. Lab., U.S. Air Force, Battelle Meml. Labs., IBM, Nat. Council for Soviet and East European Research. Mem. Assn. for Computing Machinery (nat. lectr. 1981-82, com. computing and pub. policy 1981-83), Am. Assn. for Advancement Slavic Studies, IEEE. Contbr. numerous articles to profl. jours. Office: Univ of Arizona MIS BPA Tucson AZ 85721

GOODMAN, WILLIAM LEE, commercial pilot; b. Butte, Mont., May 15, 1946; s. William Lonzo and Phyllis Helen (White) G.; m. Susan Margaret Thompson, Nov. 29, 1969; children: Kathryn, Margaret, William. BS in Computer Sci., Oreg. State U., 1968; MBA, City U., Seattle, 1982; postgrad., Seattle U.; postgrad. in def. econs., U.S. Naval War Coll., 1986. Cert. airline transport pilot, flight engr., control tower operator, flight instr., FAA. Systems analyst Mohawk Data Scis. Corp., Portland, Oreg., 1974-76; air traffic controller FAA, Pendleton, Oreg., 1976-78; pilot Trans Internat. Airlines, Oakland, Calif., 1978; aerospace engr. Boeing Comml. Airplane Co., Seattle, 1978-86; pilot Pacific Southwest Airlines, San Diego, 1986—. Editor Boeing Tng. Ctr. newsletter Intercom, 1980-82; contbg. editor Boeing Customer Service mag. Advisor, 1982-86. V.p. Homeowners Assn., Auburn, 1982-85. Served to comdr. USN, 1968-73, Vietnam, with USNR. Mem. Airline Pilots Assn., Naval Res. Officers Assn., Soaring Soc. Am. Republican. Avocations: skiing, auto restoration. Home: 33720 135th Ave SE Auburn WA 98002

GOODMAN, WOODROW I., academic administrator; b. Olive Hill, Ky., Aug. 21, 1918; s. William Preston and Myrtie Viola (Martt) G.; m. Evelyn Marie Everest, Sept. 30, 1939; children: Annetta Marie, Dennis Ray (dec.), Sandra Kae. AB, BS in Edn., Marion Coll., 1939; MA in Bibl. Lit., Wheaton Coll., 1947; DD (hon.), Taylor U., 1952; LittD(hon.), Houghton Coll., 1956. Tchr. pub. schs. Ohio, Ind., Mich., 1939-40, 42-43, 44-45; pastor United Missionary Ch., Bremen, Ind., 1940-43, Bronson, Mich., 1943-45; pres. Bethel Coll., Mishawaka, Ind., 1946-59; registrar Houghton (N.Y.) Coll., 1959-60; pres. Marion (Ind.) Coll., 1960-76; researcher, planner Friends U., Wichita, Kans., 1976—. Editor, writer Sunday sch. lit., 1952-56. Chmn. Com. Sch. Bd. Election, Marion, 1970; dir. Marion Easter Pageant, 1960-76. Named Disting. Alumnus, Marion Coll., 1966, Hon. Alumnus, Friends U., 1983. Lodge: Lions (pres. Marion club 1970-71). Avocations: photography, golfing, gardening. Home: 1922 Belmar Way Upland CA 91786

GOODNEY, DAVID EDGAR, chemistry educator; b. Wilmington, Del., Dec. 2, 1949; s. Robert F. and Barbara C. (Ahn) G.; m. Susan M. Albrecht, Jan. 1, 1971; children: Christina, Andrew. BA, Austin Coll., 1971; PhD, U. Hawaii, 1977. Asst. prof. chemistry Willamette U., Salem, Oreg., 1977-82, assoc. prof., 1982—; adj. prof. Oreg. Grad. Ctr., Beaverton, Oreg., 1986—. Mem. AAAS, Am. Chem. Soc., Northwest Assn. Environ. Studies (chmn. scholarship com. 1983—). Avocations: reading, hiking, traveling. Home: 4065 Copper Glen Ct SE Salem OR 97302 Office: Willamette U 900 State St Salem OR 97301

GOODRICH, JOY BENTON, service executive, educator; b. Yellville, Ark., Mar. 4, 1937; d. Floyd Dewey and Myrtle Ruth (Baughman) Benton; m. Paul Thomas Peckman, June 17, 1956; children: Thomas Michael, Martin Roy, Douglas Benton, Virginia Ruth; m. Quentin Allan Goodrich, Nov. 23, 1978; stepchildren: Lynn Elizabeth, Dean Vernon. Student, Ark. Poly. U., 1954-55, Yakima Valley Jr. Coll., 1955; AA, Green River Community Coll., 1976; BA, Evergreen State Coll., 1978. Stenographer FBI, Little Rock, 1955; sec., bookkeeper Firemans Fund Ins., Seattle, 1958-60; sec. Boeing Co., Renton, Washington, 1961-63; supr. Avis Rent-a-Car, SeaTac Airport, Seattle, 1970-75; adminstrv. asst. Luth. Community Services, Tacoma, 1975-77; owner Speedy Office Services, Port Townsend, Wash., 1978—; instr. typing Peninsula Community Coll., Port Townsend, 1986—. Bd. dirs. North Olympic Health Planning Council, Clallam and Jefferson Counties, Wash.; Pub. chmn. Jefferson County United Good Neighbors, 1982-86, sec. exec. com. 1985—; mem. vocat. adv. com. Port Townsend High Sch., 1984—, citizen's adv. com. Townsend Br. Peninsula Coll., 1986—; pres. bd. trustees Community United Meth. Ch., Hadlock, Wash., 1986—, sec. adminstrv. council, 1984-85; chmn. communications com. Jefferson County United Good Neighbors, 1987. alt. del. state Dem. conv., 1984. Mem. AAUW (pres. Port Townsend br.), Nat. Assn. Quick Printers, Nat. Fedn. Ind. Bus., Port Townsend C. of C. (chair edn. com. 1984-85, 85-86, trustee 1987), Rhody-O's Square Dance Club. Club: Port Ludlow (Wash.) Yacht. Avocations: sewing/tailoring, swimming, square dancing, boating. Home: 70 Keefe Ln Port Ludlow WA 98365 Office: Speedy Office Services 712 Washington Port Townsend WA 98368

GOODSON, JOHN F., lawyer; b. Phoenix, Nov. 4, 1931; s. J. Melvin and Carol (Angeny) G.; m. Siglinde R. Goodson, Sept. 27, 1956; children: Melvin A., Colleen Goddson Manley, Christine. BA, U. Ariz., 1953, MD, 1961. Assoc. Jennings, Stzous, Salmond and Trask, Phoenix, 1961-63; founding ptnr. Goodson & Rose, Phoenix, 1963-69, Cunningham, Godson & Tiffany, Phoenix, 1969-80, Goodson and Allen, Phoenix, 1980—. Author: Gift of an Elephant, 1974; co-author: Legal Aspects of Doing Business in Arizona, 1968. Chmn. bd. dirs. Prescott (Ariz.) Coll., 1976-80; founding dir. PAK Found., Phoenix, 1968—; founding trustee Reevis Mountain Sch. for Self Reliance, Globe, Ariz.; bd. dirs. Aspen (Colo.) Acad. Martial Arts, 1978-82; campaign mgr. Ralph A. Watkins for Congress, Phoenix, 1974; Dem. dist. chmn., Phoenix, 1972. Served to 1st lt. U.S. Army, 1953. Mem. Friends of Ariz. Hwy. Mag. Found. (founding atty.). Presbyterian. Club: Toastmasters (Roundup, Ariz.), (pres. 1972, winner state evaluation contest 1974). Lodges: Rotary, Masons. Avocations: martial arts, mountain climbing, marksmanship, writing, speaking. Home: 1117 W Coronado Phoenix AZ 85007 Office: Goodson and Allen Ltd 2025 N 3d St Phoenix AZ 85004

GOODSON, MARK, TV producer; b. Sacramento, Jan. 24, 1915; s. Abraham Ellis and Fannie (Gross) G.; children (by previous marriages): Jill, Jonathan, Marjorie. A.B., U. Calif., 1937. Announcer, newscaster, dir. Radio Sta. KFRC, San Francisco, 1938-41; radio announcer, dir. N.Y.C., 1941-43; radio dir. U.S. Treasury War Bond Drive, 1944-45; 1st v.p. Mid-Atlantic Newspapers, Inc.; chmn. bd. Central States Pub. Co.; 1st v.p. Capitol City Pub. Co.; v.p. New Eng. Newspapers, Inc.; dir. Am. Film Inst. Formed, Goodson-Todman Prodns., 1946; originated: radio shows Winner Take All, 1946, Stop the Music, 1947, Hit the Jackpot, 1947-49; creator: TV game programs What's My Line, It's News to Me, The Name's the Same, I've Got a Secret, Two for the Money, The Price is Right, Password, Match Game, What's My Line, To Tell the Truth, Password, Price is Right, Family Feud, others, Child's Play; others; TV film series The Web, The Rebel, Richard Boone Theater, Branded. Recipient nat. television award Great Britain, 1951; Emmy award Acad. TV Arts and Scis., 1951, 52; Sylvania award. Mem. Acad. TV Arts and Sci. (pres. N.Y.C. 1957-58), Phi Beta Kappa. Office: 375 Park Ave New York NY 10152 : 6340 Sunset Blvd Hollywood CA 90028

GOODSTEIN, JUDITH RONNIE, archivist; b. Bklyn., July 8, 1939; d. Sigmund and Fanny (Wingrad) Koral; m. David Louis Goodstein, June 30, 1960; children: Marcia Barrie, Mark Alexander. BA, Bklyn. Coll., 1960; PhD, U. Wash., 1969. Inst. archivist Calif. Inst. Tech., Pasadena, 1968—; bd. dirs. Pasadena Oral History Project. Author: (with Alice Stone) Caltech's Throop Hall, 1981; contbr. artictles to profl. jours. Grantee U.S. Geol. Soc., 1980-84, Haynes Found., 1980-86, NEH, 1976-78, Accademia Nazionale dei Lincei, 1975. Mem. History of Sci. Council, West Coast History of Sci. Soc. (pres. 1976), Sigma Xi. Office: Calif Inst Tech 1201 E Calif Blvd Pasadena CA 91125

GOODWIN, ALFRED THEODORE, judge; b. Bellingham, Wash., June 29, 1923; s. Alonzo Theodore and Miriam Hazel (Williams) G.; m. Marjorie Elizabeth Major, Dec. 23, 1943 (div. 1948); 1 son, Michael Theodore; m. Mary Ellin Handelin, Dec. 23, 1949; children—Karl Alfred, Margaret Ellen, Sara Jane, James Paul. B.A., U. Oreg., 1947; J.D., 1951. Bar: Oreg. bar 1951. Newspaper reporter Eugene (Oreg.) Register-Guard, 1947-50; practiced in Eugene until, 1955; circuit judge Oreg. 2d. Jud. Dist., 1955-60; assoc. justice Oreg. Supreme Ct., 1960-69; U.S. dist. judge Dist. Oreg., 1969-71; judge U.S. Ct. Appeals 9th Circuit, 1971—. Contbr.: articles to Oreg. Law Rev, 1949-51; student editor articles to, 1950-51. Bd. dirs. Central Lane YMCA, Eugene, 1956-60, Salem (Oreg.) Art Assn., 1960-69; adv. bd. Eugene Salvation Army, 1956-60, chmn., 1959. Served to capt., inf. AUS, 1942-46, ETO. Mem. Am. Judicature Soc., Am. Law Inst., ABA (ho. of dels. 1986-87), Order of Coif, Phi Delta Phi, Sigma Delta Chi, Alpha Tau Omega. Republican. Presbyn. Club: Multnomah Athletic (Portland, (Oreg.). Home: 311 E Glenarm St #6 Pasadena CA 91106 Office: US Court of Appeals PO Box 91510 Pasadena CA 91109-1510

GOODWIN, BRUCE MERRIMAN, architect; b. Hartford, Conn., Apr. 12, 1954; s. William Thomas and Elizabeth (Vernlund) G. BA, Stanford U., 1976; MArch, UCLA, 1979. Registered profl. architect, Calif. Asst. prof. architecture Tulane U., New Orleans, 1981-87; prin. Bruce M. Goodwin, Architect, San Francisco, 1985—; vis. prof. U. Calif., Berkeley, 1985. Contbr. articles to profl. jours. Recipient Sch. Medal AIA, 1979; Henry Luce Found. scholar, Tokyo, 1979-80. Mem. Phi Beta Kappa. Avocations: small plane pilot, karate, scuba diving. Home: 116 Lundys Ln San Francisco CA 94110

GOODWIN, FELIX LEE, retired educational administrator, former army officer; b. Lawrence, Kans., Nov. 24, 1919; s. Felix and Lucille Marie (Lee) G.; m. Esther Brown, Nov. 1, 1941 (dec.); children—Cheryl Washington, Sylvia, Judith Barnes. B.S., U. Md., 1958; M.Pub. Adminstrn., U. Ariz., 1965; Ed.S., U. Ariz., 1974, Ed.D., 1979. Enlisted in U.S. Army, 1939, advanced through grades to lt. col., 1963; ret., 1969; asst. prof. army mil. sci. dept. U. Ariz., Tucson, 1968-69, asst. to pres., 1969-83. Chmn., Pima County Merit System Commn., 1977-82, Pima County Law Enforcement Merit Council, 1973-82; mem. Ariz. Bicentennial Commn., 1974-77, chmn., 1976-77. Decorated Legion of Merit, Army Commendation medal with oak leaf cluster, Meritorious Service medal; recipient Cert. of Appreciation, City of Tucson, 1967, Pima County (Ariz.), 1975, Man of Yr. award Una Noche Plateada, Tucson, 1976, Leadership award Tucson Urban League, 1975, IRS award, 1981; named Hon. Citizen, Sierra Vista, Ariz. Mem. Nat. Alliance Black Sch. Educators (life), NEA, Soc. Ethnic and Spl. Studies, Assn. U.S. Army, NAACP (life), Am. Legion, DAV, Nat. Rifle Assn., Amvets, Phi Delta Kappa, Alpha Phi Alpha (Outstanding Service award 1985, Sr. Disting. Service award 1984), Pi Lambda Theta, Alpha Delta Delta (Tucson com. on fgn. relations), Beta Gamma Sigma. Roman Catholic. Lodge: Kiwanis, K.C.

GOODWIN, JAMES JEFFRIES, lawyer; b. San Juan, P.R., Aug. 24, 1949; s. David Badger and Elizabeth Ann (Ryan) G.; m. Mary Ann Schweikert, Nov. 29, 1981; 1 child, David Charles. B.A., U. Ky., 1971; M.P.A., Golden Gate U., 1977; J.D., U. Pacific, Sacramento, 1981. Bar: Calif. 1981, U.S. Dist. Ct. (ea. dist.) Calif. 1981, U.S. Ct. Appeals (9th cir.) 1983, U.S. Supreme Ct. 1984. Atty. Sacramento Pub. Defender's Office, 1980-82; sole practice, Sacramento, 1982—; legis. advocate Aircraft Owners and Pilots Assn., Washington, 1982—; legal counsel Emergency Med. Services, Sacramento, 1984. Served to capt. U.S. Army, 1971-77. Mem. Assn. Trial Lawyers Am., Calif. Trial Lawyers Assn. Episcopalian. Office: 2300 Bell Executive Ln Sacramento CA 95825

GOODWIN, JOHN ROBERT, lawyer, educator; b. Morgantown, W.Va., Nov. 3, 1929; s. John Emory and Ruby Iona G.; m. Betty Lou Wilson, June 2, 1952; children—John R., Elizabeth Ann Paugh, Mark Edward, Luke Jackson, Matthew Emory. B.S., W.Va. U., 1952, J.D., 1964. Bar: W.Va., U.S. Supreme Ct. Formerly city atty., county commr., spl. pros. atty., then mayor City of Morgantown; prof. bus. law W.Va. U.; prof. hotel and casino law U. Nev., Las Vegas; Author: Legal Primer for Artists, Craftspersons, 1987, Hotel Law, Principles and Cases, 1987. Served with U.S. Army; Korea. Recipient Bancroft-Whitney award in Constl. Law. Democrat. Author: Twenty Feet From Glory; Business Law, 3d edit.; High Points of Legal History; Travel and Lodging Law; Desert Adventure; Gaming Control Law; editor Hotel and Casino Letter; past editor Bus. Law Rev., Bus. Law Letter. Home: 241 Sands Ave Apt 201B Las Vegas NV 89109 Office: 5250 E Lake Mead Blvd Las Vegas NV 89115

GOODWIN, MARCY, architectural coordinator, consultant; b. San Diego, Mar. 11, 1948; d. Don and Beverly (Stern) G. BFA, Chouinard Art Sch., 1965-69; MFA in Painting, Claremont Grad. Sch., 1969-71. Exhibition coordinator Office of Charles & Ray Eames, Venice, Calif., 1977-79, curator Inventions exhibit, 1977-79; exhibition cons. IBM, Armonk, N.Y., 1980-81, R. Meier & Assocs. Architect, N.Y.C., 1982; bldg. project dir. Mus. Contemporary Art, Los Angeles, 1980-86, Tech. Ctr. Silicon Valley, San Jose, Calif., 1986—; curator Automobile and Culture exhibit Mus. Contemporary Art, Los Angeles, 1982-83; design cons. San Diego Arts Ctr., 1984-86, curator On the Drawing Bd. exhibit, 1984-85, J. Jerde exhibit, 1985-86; panelist, speaker Nat. Conf. on Arts and the Handicapped, Washington, 1975, West Week conf. Pacific Design Ctr., Los Angeles, 1984; panel moderator conf. on architecture and art AIA, Los Angeles, 1985; panel moderator annual meeting Am. Assn. Mus., Los Angles, 1986. Author: LA/ACCESS, 1980-81; contbr. articles to Los Angeles Mag. Calif. Arts Commn. grantee, 1974, 75. Home: 5026 Fulton St San Francisco CA 94121 Office: Tech Ctr Silicon Valley 2880 Zanker Rd Suite 103 San Jose CA 95134

GOODWIN, SANDRA JOAN, mcpl. official, state and local govt. industry rep.; b. St. Louis, Sept. 30, 1937; d. Robert Earl and Irma Josephine (Modray) Balencia; m. Richard Allen Hughes, 1963 (div. 1978); m. Earl Victor Goodwin II, July 22, 1980; children: Kathleen Anne, Kristine Annette. Student, Wash. U.; MS in exec. mgmt., U. Calif., Riverside, 1986. Adminstrv. aide Wash. U., St. Louis, 1955-65; mgmt. cons. Hughes Heiss & Assocs., San Mateo, Calif., 1975-79; budget analyst San Bernardino (Calif.) County, 1979-80, mgmt. cons., 1980-82, data processing projects mgr., 1982-83, chief edn. and info. services, 1983-87, exec. post dep. county admnstr. office, 1987—; ptnr. Mgmt. Assocs. Tng. and Cons. Services, San Bernardino, 1982—. State chairperson Calif. Regional Criminal Justice Planning Bd., San Mateo, 1974-78, regional vice chairperson; San Mateo Bd. Suprs., 1978. Coro Found. scholar, 1976. Mem. Am. Soc. Pub. Adminstrn., Nat. Acad. Polit. Scientists, Am. Soc. Tng. Devel., LWV (chairperson fin., tng. bur. 1973-78), Bus. and Profl. Women, League of Women Voters. Democrat. Lutheran. Home: 648 Palo Alto Redlands CA 92373 Office: Mgmt Assocs PO Box 8505 San Bernardino CA 92412

GOODWIN, WILLARD ELMER, urologist; b. Los Angeles, July 24, 1915; s. Willard and Olive (Belt) G.; m. Mary Pearson Josephs, Feb. 21, 1942; children—Mary Devereux (Mrs. E.B. Cabot), Peter Colt (dec.), Willard II. A.B., U. Calif. at Berkeley, 1937; M.D., Johns Hopkins U., 1941; M.D. (hon.), Frei Universitat Berlin, 1978. Diplomate: Am. Bd. Urology. Mem. faculty Johns Hopkins Med. Sch., 1948-51; assoc. prof. urology UCLA, 1951-53, prof., 1953-86, prof. emeritus, 1986—; cons. urology Wadsworth VA Hosp., Los Angeles; physician VA Hosp., Sepulveda, Calif. Named Disting. Physician VA, 1983-86, 86—. Fellow ACS, Am. Acad. Pediatrics; mem. AMA, Am. Urol. Assn., Pacific Coast Surg. Assn., Am. Surg. Assn., Am. Assn. Genito-urinary Surgeons (Keyes Medal), Clin. Soc. Genito-urinary Surgeons, Assn. Univ. Surgeons. Research and numerous publs. on urol. surgery, kidney transplantation, pediatric urology. Home: 254

Bronwood Ave Los Angeles CA 90049 Office: UCLA Sch Medicine Div Urology 66-138 Los Angeles CA 90024

GOOKIN, THOMAS ALLEN JAUDON, civil engineer; b. Tulsa, Aug. 5, 1951; s. William Scudder and Mildred (Hartman) G.; m. Leigh Anne Johnson, June 13, 1975 (div. Dec. 1977); m. Sandra Jean Andrews, July 23, 1983. BS with distinction, Ariz. State U., 1975. Registered profl. engr., Calif., Ariz. Civil engr., treas. W.S. Gookin & Assocs., Scottsdale, Ariz., 1968—. Chmn. Ariz. State Bd. Tech. Registration Engring. adv. com., 1984—. Mem. NSPE, Ariz. Soc. Profl. Engrs. (sec. Papago chpt. 1979-81, v.p. 1981-84, pres. 1984-85, named Young Engr. of Yr. 1979), Ariz. Congress on Surveying and Mapping, Am. Soc. Civil Engrs., Ariz. Water Works Assn., Tau Beta Pi, Delta Chi (Tempe chpt. treas. 1970-71, sec. 1970, v.p. 1971), Phi Kappa Delta (pres. 1971-73). Republican. Episcopalian. Avocations: Roman history, sci. fiction, computer gaming. Home: 10760 E Becker Ln Scottsdale AZ 85259 Office: W S Gooking & Assocs 4203 N Brown Ave Scottsdale AZ 85251

GOOKIN, WILLIAM SCUDDER, consulting engineer, hydrologist; b. Atlanta, Sept. 8, 1914; s. William Cleveland and Susie (Jaudon) G.; m. Mildred Hartman, Sept. 4, 1937; children: William Scudder Jr., Thomas Allen Jaudon. BSCE, Pa. State U., 1937. Registered profl. engr. and hydrologist. Engr. U.S. Geol. Survey, Tucson, 1937-38; inspector City of Tucson, 1938-49; steel designer Allison Steel Mfg. Co., Phoenix, 1939-40; engr. Bur. Reclamation, various locations, 1940-53; chief engr. San Carlos Irrigation and Drainage Dist., Coolidge, Ariz., 1953-58; dist. engr. Ariz. Interstate Stream Commn., Phoenix, 1956-62, state water engr., 1961-68; adminstr. Ariz. Power Authority, Phoenix, 1958-60; cons. engr. Scottsdale, Ariz., 1968—; bd. dirs. Cen. Ariz. Project Assn., Phoenix, 1985—. Contbr. articles to profl. jours. Dem. committeeman State of Ariz., 1979-84. Served to 2d lt. C.E., U.S. Army, 1938-42. Fellow Am. Soc. Civil Engrs.; mem. NSPE (bd. dirs.), Nat. Water Resources Assn. (small projects com.), Colo. River Water Users' Assn., State Bar Ariz. (assoc., environ. natural resources sect.), Culver Legion, Order of the Engr., Chi Epsilon. Home: 9 Casa Blanca Estates Paradise Valley AZ 85253

GOOLSBY, JE Y., advertising executive; b. Livingston, Tenn., Jan. 25, 1936; s. John Y. and Nina Elizabeth (Bullock) G.; m. Ingeborg F. Rabe, Oct. 30, 1969 (div. 1979); children—Ellen F., Desiree Monique, Cjaer Zorba. B.A., U. Calif.-Santa Barbara, 1963; postgrad. Santa Barbara Bus. Coll., 1963-64. Publs. mgr. Human Factor Research, Inc., Santa Barbara, 1965-70; art dir. KVZK-TV, Govt. Am. Samoa, Pago Pago, 1970-72; publs. mgr. U. Calif.-Santa Barbara, 1972-76; advt. mgr. Sloan Tech. Corp., Santa Barbara, 1981-84; documentation mgr. Essex Corp., Santa Barbara, 1984—. Served with U.S. Army, 1955-56. Recipient Best Archtl. Graphics award Am. Fedn. Advt., 1976, Best Trade Mag. Design award, 1976. Mem. Advt. Club Tri-County. Democrat. Unitarian.

GORANS, GERALD ELMER, accountant; b. Benson, Minn., Sept. 17, 1922; s. George W. and Gladys (Schneider) G.; m. Mildred Louise Stallard, July 19, 1944; 1 child, Gretchen. B.A., U. Wash., Seattle, 1947. C.P.A., Wash. With Touche, Ross & Co., C.P.A.s, and predecessor, Seattle, 1947—; ptnr. Touche, Ross & Co., 1957—, in charge Seattle office, 1962-82, mem. policy group, adminstrv. com., 1964-69, dir., 1974-83, sr. partner, 1979—, chmn. mgmt. group, 1982—. Vice pres. budget and fin. Seattle Worlds Fair, 1962; chmn. budget and fin. com. Century 21 Center, Inc., 1963-64; mem. citizens adv. com. Seattle License and Consumer Protection Com., 1965; head profl. div. United Way King County, Seattle, 1963-64, head advanced gifts div., 1965, exec. v.p., 1966, pres., 1967; trustee United Way Endowment Fund, 1984—; adv. bd. Seattle Salvation Army, 1965-80, treas., 1974-80; fin. com. Bellevue Christian Sch., 1970-77; citizens adv. bd. public affairs sta. KIRO-TV, 1970-71; treas., bd. dirs., exec. com. Scandinavia Today in Seattle, 1981-83; treas., bd. dirs. Seattle Citizens Council Against Crime, 1972-80, pres., 1976, 77; bd. dirs. U. Wash Alumni Fund, 1967-71, chmn., 1971; trustee U. Wash. Pres.'s Club, 1980-83; bd. dirs., chmn. devel. com. Northwest Hosp. Found., 1977-83, trustee hosp., 1980—, treas. bd., 1981-84, vice chmn. bd. hosp., 1984—; chmn. fin. com. Com. for Balanced Regional Transp., 1981—; co-chmn. United Cerebal Palsy Seattle Telethon, 1986; chmn. fin. com. fund raising Mus. Flight, 1983—. Served to lt. (j.g.) USNR, 1943-45. Mem. Am. Inst. C.P.A.s, (chmn. nat. def. com. 1969-75, mem. spl. investigation com. 1984—), Nat. Office Mgmt. Assn. (past pres.), Wash. Soc. C.P.A.s, Seattle C. of C. (chmn. taxation com. 1970-71, bd. dirs. 1971-74, 76-79, 80-81, 85—, mem. exec. com. 1980-83, v.p. 1981-84, 1st vice chmn. 1983-84, chmn. 1984-85, vice chmn. facilities fund drive, 1982-84, bd. dirs. 1985—), Nat. Def. Exec. Res., Nat. Club Assn. (bd. dirs. 1984—), Japanese/Am. Conf. Mayors and C. of C. Pres. (exec. com. 1984—). Clubs: Harbor, Seattle Golf, Wash. Athletic (pres. 1975—), Rainier (treas. 1976-77), Quarterback, 101; Family (San Francisco). Home: 9013 NE 37th Pl Bellevue WA 98004 Office: Touche Ross & Co 1111 3d Ave Seattle WA 98101

GORANSON, REX WALDEMAR, physicist, consultant; b. Washington, Nov. 25, 1932; s. Roy Waldemar and Nan Nell (Mullins) G.; m. Sheila Bernadette Kelly, June 11, 1955; children: Mark Christian, Kevin Jon, David Eric. BS, U. N.Mex., 1961. Chief engr. Grafix Inc., Albuquerque, 1963-64; staff physicist EG&G Inc., Albuquerque, 1964-72, Gulton Industries, Albuquerque, 1972-74; chief scientist Dynalectron Corp., Albuquerque, 1974-80; tech. dir. BDM Internat., Albuquerque, 1980-85; prin. investigator Rockwell Internat., Albuquerque, 1985—; cons. Rocketdyne, Canoga Park, Calif., 1984-85, Scott Sci. and Tech., Albuquerque, 1982-84, Titan Systems Inc., Albuquerque, 1985, Union Carbide, Tonawanda, N.Y., 1976-77. Contbr. articles to profl. jours.; inventor IR beam vergence instrument; co-inventor bolometer. Treas. Active 20/30 Internat., West Covina, Calif., 1970-71; bishop's deacon St. Francis Episcopal Mission, Placitas, N.Mex., 1964-83. Served to sgt. USAF, 1952-56. Mem. Optical Soc. Am. (handbood of optics award 1978), Soc. Photogramic Instrumentation Engrs. (complimentary membership 1983), IEEE, Laser Inst. Am. (bd. dirs. 1977), Soc. Am. Inventors. Republican. Avocations: hunting, fishing, skiing, woodworking, electronics. Home: Star Rt Box 14 Placitas NM 87043 Office: Rockwell Internat 2309 Renard SE Albuquerque NM 87106

GORBIS, BORIS ZINOVJEVICH, lawyer; b. Odessa, USSR, Aug. 29, 1950; came to U.S., 1975; s. Zinoviy R. and Nelli (Goldenstein) G.; m. Eda Jacobashvili, Nov. 29, 1981. Student Odessa Inst. Tech., 1967-80; M.A., U. Odessa, 1972; J.D., U. Calif.-Berkeley, 1980. Bar: Calif. 1980, U.S. Dist. Ct. (cen. dist.) Calif. 1981. Vis. prof. Stanford U., 1976; assoc. Graham & James, Los Angeles, 1980-82; prin. Boris Z. Gorbis, Los Angeles and San Francisco, 1982—; gen. counsel Almanac-Panorama, Russian weekly, Los Angeles, 1980—. Contbr. articles to profl. jours. Bd. dirs. Am. Jewish Congress, San Francisco, 1977, Jewish Community Ctr., Los Angeles, 1982-84. Mem. ABA, Assn. Trial Lawyers Am., Calif. Trial Lawyers Assn., Los Angeles Trial Lawyers Assn. Republican. Clubs: New Times, Guardians (Los Angeles). Office: 7080 Hollywood Blvd Suite 518 Los Angeles CA 90028

GORDAN, GILBERT SAUL, physician, educator; b. San Francisco, July 8, 1916; s. Gilbert Saul and Sadie (Joseph) G.; m. Cynthia Vaughan, Feb. 2, 1978. A.B., U. Calif., 1937, M.D., 1941, Ph.D., 1947. Intern U. Calif. Hosp., San Francisco, 1940-41; resident U. Calif. Hosp., 1941-42; mem. faculty U. Calif., San Francisco, 1946-85; prof. medicine U. Calif., 1962-85, prof. emeritus, 1985—; prof. medicine U. Calif., Davis, 1985—; Lady Davis vis. prof. Hebrew U., Jerusalem, 1978; assoc. chief of staff for edn. VA Med. Ctr., Martinez, Calif., 1985—; cons. in field. Author: Endocrinology in Clinical Practice, 1953, The Parathyroids, 1971, Clinical Management of the Osteoporoses, 1976; editor: Yearbook of Endocrinology, 1951-63; contbr. numerous articles to profl. jours. Served with M.C. AUS, 1942-45. Decorated Bronze Star.; Commonwealth fellow, 1947-48, 62-63; Guggenheim fellow, 1967-68. Fellow ACP, AAAS; mem. Assn. Am. Physicians, Am. Soc. Clin. Investigation, Endocrine Soc., Royal Soc. Medicine (hon.). Democrat. Jewish. Office: VA Med Ctr Martinez CA 94553

GORDANINEJAD, FARAMARZ, mechanical engineering educator; b. Tehran, Iran, Nov. 1, 1953; came to U.S., 1978; s. Ghasem Gordaninejad and Mahin-Banoo Sepanloo; m. Roya Sadeghy Lahijany, Sept. 26, 1977. BSME, U. Tehran, 1977; MSME, U. Okla., 1980, PhD, 1983. Instr. mech. engring. U. Okal., Norman, 1979-83, research assoc., 1984, vis. asst. prof., 1984; asst. prof. U. Nev., Reno, 1984—; research engr. XEBEC Corp., Reno, 1985. Contbr. articles to profl. jours. R.L. Disney scholar U. Okla., 1981-82, Iran Atomic Energy Orgn. scholar 1979-81. Mem. AIAA, ASME (assoc.), Soc. Engring. Sci., Soc. Advancement of Material and Process Engring., Am. Acad. Mechanics, Sigma Xi (Research award 1984), Pi Tau Sigma. Office: U Nev Dept Mech Engring Reno NV 89557

GORDON, BARRY MONROE, metallurgist, corrosion scientist; b. N.Y.C., July 15, 1947; s. Sydney Irving and Selma (Van Gelderen) G.; m. Aldene E. Stoner, Jan. 4, 1981. BS, Carnegie-Mellon U., 1969, MS, 1971. Registered profl. engr., Calif., corrosion specialist. Corrosion and material engr. Westinghouse Electric, West Mifflin, Pa., 1969-70, material engr. Steam Generators, 1975-81; tng. asst., fellow NSF, Carnegie-Mellon U., Pitts., 1970-71; program mgr. stress corrosion crackling Gen. Electric, San Jose, Calif., 1975-81, prin. engr. corrosion performance, 1981—; lectr. corrosion engring. Evergreen Coll., San Jose, Calif., 1985—. Author: Corrosion and Corrosion Control in Boiling Water Reactors; contbr. articles to profl. jours. Mem. West Valley Coll. Symphony, Los Gatos Chamber Orch. Fellow NSF, 1970; recipient Waldemar Cancer Research Sci. Award, 1965, French Medal of Honor, 1985. Mem. Nat. Assn. Corrosion Engrs. (com. chmn.), Am. Soc. for Metals, Almaden Cycle Touring Club, Colnago Assn. Am., Radsport Brügelmann, League of Am. Wheelman, Phi Kappa Phi. Avocations: bicycling, music. Home: 16230 W Ellenwood Ave Monte Sereno CA 95030 Office: Gen Electric 175 Curtner Ave MC 785 San Jose CA 95125

GORDON, C(HESTER) DUNCAN, chemistry consultant; b. Ankerton, Alta., Can., Oct. 13, 1920; came to U.S., 1949; s. Robert John and Emma Mae (McIntyre) G.; m. Sybil Margaret MacLeod, Aug. 22, 1950; children: Robert Hugh, John Duncan, Susan Pamela. BSc, U. Alta., Edmonton, 1949; PhD, U. Notre Dame, Notre Dame, Ind., 1952. Research chemist Calif. Research Corp., Richmond, 1952-60, sr. research chemist, 1960-65; sr. research assoc. Chevron Research Co., Richmond, 1965-84; cons. Lubrizol Corp., Cleve., 1986—; chmn. research and devel. ASTM, Phila., 1981-84. Pres. Boys Club El Sobrante, Calif. chpt., 1962, treas., 1963-85; treas. Girls Club El Sobrante, Calif. chpt., 1984—. Served as flight lt. RCAF, 1941-45. Mem. Am. Chem. Soc. Republican. Episcopalian. Club: Richmond Country (bd. dirs.). Avocations: golf, bridge. Home: 2579 Patra Dr El Sobrante CA 94803

GORDON, DAVID BUDDY, physiologist, medical researcher; b. Chgo., Dec. 17, 1918; s. Louis Eleazer and Lena (Etshokin) G.; m. Lili Plutalov, Oct. 30, 1948; children: Valentin, Anatole, Dmitri. Student, U. Mich., 1936-39; BS, U. Chgo., 1945; MS, U. So. Calif., 1949, PhD, 1951. Instr. physiology U. So. Calif., Los Angeles, 1951-55; asst. prof. physiology U. Miami Sch. Med., Coral Gables, Fla., 1956-62; chief physiol. research VA Med. Ctr., San Francisco, 1967-71, Livermore, Calif., 1973-81. Editor: Hypertension, The Renal Basis, 1980. Served with U.S. Army, 1946-48, ETO. Fellow Am. Heart Assn., 1955-56, 62-64. Mem. Am. Physiol. Soc., Am. Heart Assn., Soc. for Exptl. Biology and Medicine, Internat. Soc. Hypertension, Am. Soc. Hypertension. Home: 567 Amber Ct Livermore CA 94550

GORDON, DONALD HOWARD, podiatrist; b. Ft. Smith, Ark., Nov. 16, 1954; s. Halton Howard and M. Janelle (Carter) G.; m. Carol Ann Miller, Aug. 15, 1975; children: Stephanie, Andrew. BS in Chemistry, Okla. Christian Coll., 1977, BSE in Science, 1977; BS in Basic Medicine, Calif. Coll. Podiatric Medicine, 1981, D in Podiatric Medicine, 1983. Tchr. chemistry, football coach Midwest City (Okla.) High Sch., 1977-79; resident in surgery Calif. Podiatry Hosp., San Francisco, 1983-84, sr. resident in surgery, 1984-85; podiatrist Ambulatory Family Podiatry Group, Daly City, Calif., 1985-87; pvt. practice podiatry Pacifica, Calif., 1987—. Named one of Outstanding Young Men of Am., 1985. Mem. Am. Podiatric Med. Assn., Calif. Podiatric Med. Assn., San Francisco/San Mateo County Podiatry Assn., Am. Coll. Foot Surgeons (assoc.), Pacifica (Calif.) C. of C. (dir. membership com., edn. com. 1985-86, chmn. edn. com. 1986-87). Mem. Ch. of Christ. Avocations: woodworking, weightlifting, racquetball. Office: 320 Eureka Square Pacifica CA 94044

GORDON, FRANK X., JR., judge; b. Chgo., Jan. 9, 1929; s. Frank X. and Lucille (Gburek) G.; m. Joan C. Gipe, Sept. 17, 1950; children: Frank X., Candace Gordon Lander. BA, Stanford U., 1951; LLB, U. Ariz., 1954. Bar: Ariz. 1954. Assoc. Gordon and Gordon, Kingman, Ariz., 1954-62; atty. City of Kingman, 1955-57; judge Superior Ct. Mohave County (Ariz.), Kingman, 1962-75; justice Ariz. Supreme Ct., Phoenix, 1975—, now chief justice; mem. various coms. Ariz. State Bar; Ariz. rep. to Council for State Ct. REps., Nat. Ctr. State Cts. Bd. visitors U. Ariz. Law Sch., 1972-75; trustee Chester H. Smith Meml. Scholarship Fund; past bd. dirs., pres. Mohave County Mental Health Clinic, Inc.; past mem. Gov.'s Commn. Mental Health; state bd. dirs. Ariz. Heart Assn.; active Boulder Dam Area council Boy Scouts Am. Mem. ABA, Ariz. Bar Assn. Maricopa County Bar Assn., Am. Judicature Soc., Mohave County C. of C. (past pres.). Democrat. Methodist. Lodges: Rotary, Elks. Office: Ariz Sup Ct State Capitol Bldg Phoenix AZ 85007 *

GORDON, HOWARD, accountant, educator; b. Chgo., July 19, 1938; s. Maurice J. and Doris (Smutok) G.; m. Gerda Halbreich, July 10, 1960; children—Renee, Jeffrey. B.S.B.A., Roosevelt U., Chgo., 1960. CPA, Ill., Calif. Controller, Joseph Stern & Co., Northbrook, Ill., 1959-72; tax ptnr. Maryanov, Madsen, Gordon & Campbell, Palm Springs, Calif., 1972—; mem. faculty U. Calif.-Riverside Extension, Chapman Coll., Palm Springs Adult Edn. Dist., Calif. CPAs Found., Coll. of Desert. Monthly columnist Palm Springs Life mag., 1977—. Bd. dirs. Palm Springs Sr. Citizens Ctr., 1978, Lyceum of the Desert, 1979-82, Arthritis Found., Palm Springs, 1977-81; mem. planning com. Eisenhower Hosp., Rancho Mirage, Calif., 1977-80. Mem. Am. Inst. CPAs, Calif. Soc. CPAs, Desert Estate Planning Council (charter), Internat. Assn. Fin. Planners. Club: Palm Springs Bicycle (treas. 1982-82). Office: 801 E Tahquitz Way Palm Springs CA 92262

GORDON, JACK, professional ice hockey executive. Dir. hockey ops., gen. mgr. Vancouver (B.C.) Canucks, Can. Office: Vancouver Canucks, 100 N Renfrew St, Vancouver, BC Canada V5K 3N7 *

GORDON, JACK FRANCIS, assn. exec.; b. Portland, Oreg., June 30, 1921; s. James Samuel and Mabel Ann (Ratchford) G.; grad. Seattle U., 1950, U. Wash., 1955; m. Roberta M. Gordon, May 1, 1948; children—John, Mary, Ann, Joseph. City editor Catholic NW Progress, Seattle, 1947-48; dir. pub. relations Seattle U., 1948-50, Greater Seattle, Inc., 1950-64; commr. employment security State of Wash., 1964-65; dir. spl. events Seattle Ctr., 1965; exec. v.p. Restaurant Assn. Wash., Seattle, 1966—, Wash. Lodging Assn., 1981—; spl. asst. to gov. Wash., 1973-74, spl. agt., 1980; v.p., bd. dirs. Wash. Trade Fair, 1950-78; mem. Seattle Human Rights Commn., 1966-79, Wash. Am. Bicentennial Commn., 1975-76; bd. dirs. Seattle-King County Conv. and Visitors Bur., 1976—; mem. Wash. State Personnel Appeals Bd., 1981-82. Pres., Providence Med. Found., 1980-81; bd. dirs. Seattle Youth Symphony Orch.; pres. Pacific Internat. Hospitality Indsl. Expn., 1982—. Served with USNR, World War II; maj. NG. Named Alumnus of Year, Seattle U., 1969, Newsmaker of Tomorrow, Time Mag., 1953. Mem. Am. Soc. Assn. Execs., AGVA, Seattle C. of C., Internat. Platform Assn., Am. Security Council, U.S. Security and Intelligence Fund, Musicians Assn., Am. Legion (past post comdr.). Roman Catholic. Clubs: Rainier, Wash. Athletic, Rotary, KC. (Seattle). Home: 6814 44th Pl NE Seattle WA 98115 Office: 722 Securities Bldg Seattle WA 98101

GORDON, LAURENCE, rehabilitation company executive; b. Peabody, Mass., Aug. 30, 1943; s. Abraham Lewis and Esther (Goldenberg) G.; m. Madelyn Marie Buonocore, Feb. 25, 1972; children—Rachel, Sarah. B.S. in Edn., State Coll. Salem, Mass., 1965, Ed.M., 1968; postgrad. Boston U., 1969-73. Tchr. Newburyport High Sch., (Mass.), 1965-68; counselor Mass. Rehab. Commn., 1968-72, supr., 1972, area mgr., 1973, regional dir., 1974, dir., 1975-78; mem. faculty dept. psychology Mass. Community Coll., Beverly, 1971-78; pvt. practice rehab. 1978-79; v.p. CRS Inc., Arcadia, Calif.; v.p. Rehab Data, Inc.; pres. BIS, Inc., Northridge, Calif. Recipient service and leadership award State of Mass. Mem. Nat. Rehab. Counseling Assn. of Calif. (mem. bd. dirs.), Nat. Rehab. Assn. (cert. rehab. counselor). Home: 19001 Kilfinan St Northridge CA 91326

GORDON, LEONARD, sociology educator; b. Detroit, Dec. 6, 1935; s. Abraham and Sarah (Rosen) G.; m. Rena Joyce Feigelman, Dec. 25, 1955; children: Susan Melinda, Matthew Seth, Melissa Gail. B.A., Wayne State U., 1957; M.A., U. Mich., 1958; Ph.D., Wayne State U., 1966. Instr. Wayne State U., Detroit, 1960-62; research dir. Jewish Community Council, Detroit, 1962-64; dir. Mich. area Am. Jewish Com., N.Y.C., 1964-67; asst. prof. Ariz. State U., Tempe, 1967-70, assoc. prof., 1970-77, prof., 1977—, chmn. dept. sociology, 1981—; cons. OEO, Maricopa County, Ariz., 1968. Author: A City in Racial Crisis, 1971, Sociology and American Social Issues, 1978; co-author: (with A. Mayer) Urban Life and the Struggle to Be Human, 1979, (with others) Confronting Social Problems, 1984. Sec. Conf. on Religion and Race, Detroit, 1962-67; mem. exec. bd. dirs. Am. Jewish Com., Phoenix chpt., 1969-70. Grantee NSF, 1962, Rockefeller found., 1970, 84. Fellow Am. Sociol. Assn.; mem. Pacific Sociol. Assn. (v.p. 1978-79, pres. 1980-81), AAUP, Ariz. State U. Alumni Assn. (faculty dir. 1981-82). Democrat. Jewish. Home: 5262 N Woodmere Fairway Scottsdale AZ 85253 Office: Ariz State U Dept Sociology Tempe AZ 85287

GORDON, MALCOLM STEPHEN, biology educator; b. Bklyn., Nov. 13, 1933; s. Abraham and Rose (Walters) G.; m. Diane M. Kestin, Apr. 16, 1959 (div. Sept. 1973); 1 son, Dana Malcolm; m. Marjorie J. Weinzweig, Jan. 28, 1976. B.A. with high honors, Cornell U., 1954; Ph.D. (NSF fellow), Yale, 1958. Instr. UCLA, 1958-60, asst. prof., 1960-65, assoc. prof., 1965-68, prof. biology, 1968—, dir. Inst. Evolutionary and Environ. Biology, 1971-76, chmn. interdept. com. Environ. Sci. Engring. Program, 1984—; asst. dir. research Nat. Fisheries Ctr. and Aquarium, U.S. Dept. of Interior, Washington, 1968-69; vis. prof. zoology Chinese U. Hong Kong, 1971-72; Mem. panel on marine biology, panel on oceanography Pres.'s Sci. Adv. Com., 1965-66; mem. nat. adv. com. R/V Alpha Helix, Scripps Inst. Oceanography, 1969-73; mem. com. on Latimeria Nat. Acad. Scis., 1969-72. Author coll. textbooks.; Contbr. articles to sci. jours. Active community orgns. on environ. Fulbright fellow U.K., 1957-58; Guggenheim fellow Italy and Denmark, 1961-62; Sr. Queen's fellow in marine sci. Australia, 1976. Fellow AAAS; mem. Am. Physiol. Soc., Am. Soc. Ichthyologists and Herpetologists, Am. Soc. Zoologists (chmn. div. ecology 1979-80, chmn. div. comparitive physiol. biochemistry 1988-89), Soc. for Exptl. Biology. Home: 2801 Glendower Ave Los Angeles CA 90027 Office: UCLA Dept Biology Los Angeles CA 90024

GORDON, PAUL GENE, consulting chemist; b. Denver, Oct. 2, 1928; s. Morris Charles and Anna (Katz) G.; m. Beverly Olken, June 12, 1951; children: Bradley Malcolm, Shana Mendel. BS, U. Denver, 1950; MS, U. Ill., 1951, PhD, 1954. Chief chemist Chem. Sales Co., Denver, 1954-55, mgr. customer service, 1955-59, mgr. purchasing, 1959-61, mgr. chem. div., 1961-67, gen. mgr., 1967-78, pres., chief exec. officer, 1978-84; pres. Chem. Cons. Inc., Englewood, Colo., 1985—. Mem. Am. Chem. Soc. (employment chmn. 1984-87), Colo. Chem. Club (pres.), The Expert Witness Network, Sigma Xi, Phi Lambda Upsilon, Phi Sigma Delta (chpt. pres. 1948-49). Avocations: photography, war memorabilia, stamps, coins, walking. Home and Office: 6047 E Briarwood Circle Englewood CO 80112-1023

GORDON, RANDY WAYNE, business executive, consultant; b. Big Timber, Mont., Apr. 17, 1952; s. Bill Willim and Ruth Opel (Thompson) G.; m. Susan Stover, Aug. 11, 1971 (div. June 1973); 1 child, Cherie. Student Mont. State U., 1973. Licensed real estate broker. Salesman ABC Realty, Sheridan, Wyo., 1980-82; mgr. Big Sky Airlines, Sheridan, 1978-80; owner Sunshine Clean/K-B Chem., Sheridan, 1982-84; asst. mgr. Sugarland Estates, Sheridan, 1984—; bldg. cons. Tri-Steel Structures, Sheridan. Mem. Sheridan C. of C. Home: 3950 Coffeen Ave Sheridan WY 82801-9112

GORDON, REX BLACKSTOCK, system safety engineer; b. San Luis Obispo, Calif., July 7, 1932; s. Rexford Lewis and Jeannette (Blackstock) G.; m. Alice Constance Lehman, June 20, 1954; children: Susan, Carolyn, Linda. BA, San Jose State U., 1954; MPH, U. Calif., Berkeley, 1958. Registered profl. engr., Calif.; cert. safety profl. Environ. engr. Santa Clara County Health Dept., San Jose, Calif., 1954-55; system safety engr. Rocketdyne, Canoga Park, Calif., 1958-66; supr. system safety Gen. Electric Co., Phila., 1966-72; mgr. system safety Ford Aerospace Corp., Newport Beach, Calif., 1972-85; pres. R&C Enterprises, Irvine, Calif., 1985—; pres. System Safety Found., Los Angeles, 1984—; gen. chmn. 2d Internat. System Safety Conf., San Diego, 1955. Co-author: Loss Control Management, 1972, Automotive Engineering and Litigation, 1985; tech. editor Hazard Prevention Jour., 1985—; contbr. articles to profl. jours. Served to capt. USAFR, 1955-58. Fellow System Safety Soc. (pres. 1975-77); mem. Am. Soc. Safety Engrs. (profl.), Acad. Product Safety Mgmt. (charter), Am. Soc. Profl. Engrs., Soc. for Risk Analysis. Republican. Avocations: tennis, sailing, skiing, World and Biblical history. Home and Office: 621 Fuller Ave San Jose CA 95125

GORDON, RONALD DOUGLAS, communications educator; b. Los Angeles, Feb. 21, 1944; s. Douglas Gordon and Clarice Marie (Fega) Christner; m. Judith Cardle Katch, Aug. 20, 1965 (div. 1974); one child, Liahna Elise. AA, Los Angeles City Coll., 1964; BA with distinction, San Jose State U., 1966, MA, 1968; PhD, U. Kans., 1971. Grad. instr. U. Kans., Lawrence, 1968-71; asst. prof. Calif. State U. Humboldt, Arcata, 1971-74; instr. West Valley Coll., Saratoga, Calif., 1975-77; asst. to the personnel mgr. Omaha World-Herald, 1978-80; counselor The Motivational Ctr., Omaha, 1980-81; vis. asst. prof. Tex. A&M U., College Station, 1982, U. Hawaii, Manoa, 1982-83; asst. prof. U. Hawaii, Hilo, 1984—. Co-author: (in Japanese) Communicating with the West, 1985; contbr. articles to profl. jours. Mem. World Communication Assn., Speech Communications Assn., Communications Assn. Pacific, Hawaii Council Tchrs. of English. Democrat. Office: U Hawaii Hilo HI 96720-4091

GORDON, ROSE MARIA ELIZABETH, counselor-therapist, consultant, lecturer; b. Camden, N.J., Aug. 27, 1931; d. Rocco and Mary Antonio Theresa (Sartarella) Locantore; m. Irving Gordon, Feb. 29, 1952 (div.); children—Rocky, Maia, Heidi, Aaron. B.S. in Secondary Edn. and Sociology, U. Nev.-Las Vegas, 1978, M.S. in Rehab. Counseling, 1981. Cert. substance abuse counselor, Nev. Counselor-therapist Verdun Trione, Ph.D., Las Vegas, Nev., 1971-85, North Las Vegas Hosp. Care Unit, part-time 1975-85; therapist, care unit Community Hosp. North Las Vegas, 1984-85; owner, exec. dir. Nev. Growth Ctr., 1985—; cons.-lectr. Raleigh Hills Hosp., Las Vegas, 1982-83; faculty Clark County Community Coll., 1984—; cons. in field; expert witness in substance abuse; rape crisis counselor; vol. counselor-therapist Clark County Jail, Las Vegas, 1982—. Founder, bd. dirs. August Found., Cocaine Outreach Network, 1984—; past pres. Counselors-Community Action Against Rape. Mem. Am. Personnel and Guidance Assn., Am. Counseling & Devel., Nev. Rehab. Assn., Am. Psychol. Assn. (assoc.), Nev. Psychol. Assn. Office: Nev Growth Ctr 3376 S Eastern Ave Suite 130 Las Vegas NV 89102

GORDON, TED HOWARD, lawyer; b. Oakland, Calif., May 2, 1946; m. Sharon J. Gordon, July 2, 1972; 1 child, Matthew. BS, San Jose State U., 1969, MBA, 1971; JD, Hastings Coll., 1973. Title asst. Transam. Title Ins. Co., 1967; mortgage clk. Commonwealth Mortgage Corp., 1968; research analyst Boise Cascade Bldg. Co., 1969; real estate broker Van Vleck Realtors, 1970; assoc. Graham, Gordon, McFarlan & Stewart, San Rafael, Calif., 1974-79, Gordon, McFarlan, Stewart & Blecher, San Rafael, 1979-86, Gordon, McFarlan & Blecher, San Rafael, 1987—; instr. Ju-Jitsu, San Francisco, 1964-71, Golden Gate U., San Francisco, 1976—; profl. lectr. Golden Gate U., 1985—. Author: California Real Estate Law: Text & Cases, 2d edit., 1985; co-author: Real Estate Principles in California, 5th ed., 1987. Recipient Disting. Person's award San Jose State U.; Real Estate Personality of Week, San Jose Mercury News. Mem. Nat. Real Estate Fraternity (pres. 1967-68, named Mem. of Yr.), Soc. Advancement Mgmt. (asst. to pres. 1969), Fin. Mgmt. Assn. (asst. to pres. 1969). Office: Gordon McFarlan & Blecher 1050 Northgate Dr Suite 475 San Rafael CA 94903

GORDON, WILLIAM P., neuroscience educator; b. Los Angeles, Feb. 10, 1945; s. Irving and Claire (Phillips) G. BA, Northridge State U., 1966; MA, Rice U., 1972; PhD, U. Houston, 1973. Postdoctoral fellow Stanford U., Stanford, Calif., 1973-75; instr. Foothill Coll., Los Altos, Calif., 1975-80; lectr. Stanford U., Stanford, 1980—; pres. research and devel. Inst. for Cortext Research and Devel., Palo Alto, 1984—; cons. VA Med. Ctr., Palo Alto, 1977-78, NSF, Washington, 1980, Nat. Inst. Mental Health, Washington, 1983. Contbr. articles profl. jours. Mem. AAAS, Internat. Neuropsychol. Soc., Am. Speech, Hearing and Lang. Assn., Inner Quad, Stanford

U., Union for Concerned Scientists, 1985. Avocations: tennis, musical composition. Home: 3903 D Middlefield Rd Palo Alto CA 94303 Office: Stanford U Dept Psychology Jordan Hall Room 400 Stanford CA 94305

GORE, DARCIE ADRIENNE, social worker; b. Pomona, Calif., Jan. 29, 1954; d. Dwight Harold Click and Linda Lee (Akin) Wheat; m. James Paul Gore, Mar. 30, 1972; children: Laura Ann, Jeffrey Wade. AA, Fullerton Coll., 1973; BA in Sociology, Calif. State U., Fullerton, 1974; MSW, Calif. State U., Sacramento, 1987. Coordinator progarm USO, Oxnard, Calif.; co-dir. Crisis Lines, Ventura, San Luis Obispo, Calif., 1972-80; exec. dir. Help, Inc., Redding, Calif., 1982-84; job developer Brown & Farley, Redding, 1985-86; owner Rehab. Support Service Assn., Redding, 1986—; cons., presenter communty workshops, Redding, 1982—. Mem. Nat. Assn. Social Workers, AAUW, NOW, Women's Forum, Beyond War. Office: Rehab Support Service Assn PO Box 720335 Redding CA 96099

GORHAM, CHRISTINE JEANETTE, bank librarian; b. Santa Monica, Calif., July 13, 1952; d. Wayne Kenneth and Jeanette Idell (Mathis) G. BA in Polit. Sci., Calif. State U., Northridge, 1977, MA in Spl. Edn. and Communication Handicapped, 1983. Customer service rep. Lincoln Savs. & Loan, Sherman Oaks, Calif., 1976-83; bank librarian Coast Savs. & Loan, Granada Hills, Calif., 1984—. Mem. AAUW, Nat. Assn. Deaf. Office: Coast Savs & Loan 18000 Chatsworth Granada Hills CA 91344

GORMEZANO, KEITH S., publisher; b. Madison, Wis., Nov. 22, 1955; s. Isadore and Miriam (Fox) G.; BS U. Iowa, 1977; BGS Yeshiva Aish Ha-Torah, 1977; postgrad. U. Puget Sound, 1984—. Pub. relations dir. Hillel Found., Iowa City, Iowa; pub. Le Beacon Presse, Seattle, 1980—; owner Keith Gormezano, Effective PR, 1983—; Op. Improvement Found., 1980-81; pub. info. officer Op chmn. Iowa City Young Ams. for Freedom, 1979-81; vol. VISTA, 1982-83; dir. ACJS, Inc., 1981-82. Vice chmn. Resource Conservation Commn., Iowa City, 1979-80; chmn. Iowa City Young Ams. for Freedom, 1979-81; pres. Downtown Neighborhood Assn., 1980—; bd. dirs. Seattle Mental Health Inst., 1981-83, Youth Advocates, Seattle, 1984, Atlantic St. Ctr., 1984; mem. City of Seattle Animal Control Commn., 1984-86, vice chmn., 1985-86, chmn. 1986; mem. Selective Service System, 1982—, vice chmn. civilan rev. bd. 742, 1985—. Mem. Mcpl. League, Com. of Small Mag. Editors and Pubs., Cityclub, NOW, Sigma Delta Chi. Republican. Jewish. Club: Wash. Athletic. Editor, M'godolim, 1979-81, Le Beacon Rev., 1979-81; author (poetry) 36 Flavours, 1980. Home: PO Box 15945 Seattle WA 98115-0945 Office: 2921 E Madison St Suite 7WWW Seattle WA 98112-4242

GORMLEY, FRANCIS XAVIER, JR., social worker; b. Boston; s. Francis Xavier and Catherine Caroline (Ireland) G. Student, Massasoit Community Coll., 1973; BA in Psychology, U. Mass., Boston, 1981; MSW, U. Wash., 1984. Coordinator Gerontology Career Program Elder Fest, Chico, Calif., 1981; mgr. Arnold's Restaurant, Cardiff, Wales, 1981-82; med. social worker Harborview Med. Ctr., Seattle, 1983-84; psychotherapist Seattle Counseling Service, 1982—; clin. social worker Pain Ctr. Swedish Hosp., Seattle, 1984—; speaker U. Wash. Sch. Social Work Graduation Class, 1984, Social Sensitivity in Health Care U. Wash, 1985—; coordinator Coping with AIDS Swedish Hosp. Tumor Inst., 1985; guest speaker Sta. KIRO-TV, Seattle, 1985, Sta. KPLZ, Seattle, 1985; cons. Assn. Workers Resources, Seattle, 1985—. Editor abstract form Comprehensive Multi-Disciplinary Documentation, Western U.S.A. Pain Soc., 1986. Mem. Seattle Aids Network, 1985—. Mem. Acad. Cert. Social Workers, Nat. Assn. Social Workers, Occupational Social Work Orgn. of Nat. Assn. Social Workers, Social Work Coalition Swedish Hosp., U. Wash. Alumni Assn., U. Mass. Alumni Assn., Green Key Soc. Democrat. Avocations: travel, reading, swimming. Home: 235 13th Ave E #203 Seattle WA 98102

GORMLEY, MYRA DEVEE, newspaper columnist, genealogist; b. Muskogee, Okla., Feb. 7, 1940; d. John Oscar and Doris Jean (Fricks) Vanderpool; m. John Carl Goerges, Nov. 9, 1958 (div. Oct. 1966); m. Leo Claude Gormley, Mar. 1, 1975; stepchildren: Kirk, Rick, Kyle. Student, Muskogee Jr. Coll., 1957-58, Okla. U., 1960-61, U. Md. extension, Darmstadt, Fed. Republic Germany, 1962. Copy editor, proofreader, typesetter Stars & Stripes, Darmstadt, 1961-64; proofreader, typesetter San Antonio Light, 1964-65, Seattle Times, 1965-66, News Tribune, Tacoma, 1966—; syndicated columnist Los Angeles Times, 1985—. Loaned exec. United Way, Tacoma, 1984. Mem. Nat. Geneal. Soc., Assn. Profl. Genealogists, Oral History Assn., Fedn. Geneal. Socs., Wash. State Hist. Soc., Tacoma/Pierce County Geneal. Soc. (v.p. 1979-80), DAR. Democrat. Avocations: writing family histories. Home: 8402 57th St W Tacoma WA 98467 Office: Los Angeles Times Syndicate Times Mirror Sq Los Angeles CA 90053

GORMLY, WILLIAM MOWRY, financial consultant; b. Pitts., Mar. 15, 1941; s. Thomas Wilson and Lourene (Blaine) G.; m. Barbara Diesner, Aug. 21, 1965; children: Kirsten Eve, Kellie Blaine. BA in Econs., Dickinson Coll., Carlisle, Pa., 1963; postgrad. Northwestern U., 1967, DePaul U., 1968; grad. banking degree Stonier Grad. Sch. Banking Rutgers U., 1978. Regional mgr. Harris Bank, Chgo., 1967-69; corp. banking officer Wells Fargo Bank N.A., San Francisco, 1969-73; v.p. 4th Nat. Bank of Wichita, 1973-74, Union Nat. Bank of Pitts., 1974-79; v.p., sr. nat. accts. officer Ariz. Bank, Phoenix, 1979-82; pres. Cons. in Pub. Fin., Ltd., Scottsdale, Ariz., 1982—. Mem. Dickinson Coll. Alumni Council, 1975-80; bd. dirs. Ariz. Theatre Co., Phoenix, 1980-83; trustee Northland Pub. Library, Pitts., 1975-79. Served to 1st lt. U.S. Army, 1963-65. Mem. Assn. Corp. Growth, Am. Hosp. Assn., Phi Delta Theta. Republican. Methodist. Club: Plaza (Phoenix). Office: Cons in Pub Fin Ltd 23150 N Pima Rd Suite 1 Scottsdale AZ 85255

GORNEY, RODERIC, psychiatry educator; b. Garnd Rapids, Mich., Aug. 13, 1924; s. Abraham Jacob Gorney and Edelaine (Roden) Harburg; m. Carol Ann Sobel, Apr. 13, 1986. BS, Stanford U., 1948, MD, 1949; PhD in Psychoanalysis, So. Calif. Psychoanalytic Inst., 1977. Cert. psychiatrist, Calif. Pvt. practice psychiatry San Francisco, 1952-62; asst. prof. UCLA, 1962-71, assoc. prof., 1971-73, prof. psychiatry, 1980—, dir. psychosocial adaption and the future program, 1971—. Author: The Human Agenda, 1972. Served with USAF, 1943-46. Recipient Gold medal Soc. Academique of L'Academie Francaise, 1976. Fellow AAAS, Acad. Psychoanalysis, Am. Psychiatric Assn. (essay prize 1971); mem. Group for Advancement of Psychiatry, So. Calif. Psychoanalytic Inst. Avocations: trail riding, guitar, singing. Office: UCLA Neuropsychiatric Inst 760 Westwood Plaza Los Angeles CA 90024

GORONKIN, HERBERT, physicist; b. Pitts., Jan. 9, 1936; s. Sander (Tammie) and Mae (Shulman) G.; children: David, Jeffrey, Michael; m. Pamela Louise Cooper, Oct. 4, 1980; children: Rebecca Louise, Theresa Louise, James David. AB, Temple U., 1961, AM, 1962, PhD, 1973. Physicist Internat. Resistance Co., Phila., 1963-65; sr. research physicist Honeywell Inc., Ft. Washington, Pa., 1965-66; sect. head Am. Electronic Labs., Colmar, Pa., 1966-69; project engr. Gen. Electric Co., Syracuse, N.Y., 1969-75; mgr. semiconductor ops. Varian Assocs., Beverly, Mass., 1975-77; from mgr. high speed devices to chief scientist compound semiconductors Motorola Inc., Phoenix, 1977—; chmn. Workshop on Compound Semiconductor Microwave Materials and Devices, 1984-86, Quantum Electronics and Compound Semiconductor Devices, 1986; mem. various tech. meeting coms., 1980—. Contbr. articles to profl. jours., chpts. to books; patentee in field. Served with USAF, 1954-57. Mem. IEEE (sr., IEDM compound semiconductor tech. program com. 1983-86), Am. Phys. Soc., Sigma Xi. Republican. Avocations: hiking, golf, Japanese, cooking. Home: 1849 N 77 St Scottsdale AZ 85257 Office: Motorola Inc 5005 E McDowell Rd Phoenix AZ 85008

GORSUCH, NORMAN CLIFFORD, law educator; b. Pitts., Oct. 3, 1942; s. Clifford Lee and Helen (Berzac) G.; m. Marjorie Jean Menzi, Sept. 10, 1966 (div. Sept. 1985); children—Elizabeth, Kieth, Jennifer, Deborah, David; m. Lenore W. Boston, Oct. 18, 1985. B.A. with honors, U. N.C., 1964; J.D., Columbia U., 1967. Bar: Alaska 1968, U.S. Dist. Ct. Alaska 1968, U.S. Ct. Internat. Trade 1968, U.S. Ct. Appeals (9th cir.) 1969, U.S. Supreme Ct. 1973. Assoc. Ely, Guess & Rudd, Anchorage, 1967-70, ptnr., 1970-71; ptnr. Ely, Guess & Rudd, Juneau, Alaska, 1974-82; dep. atty. gen. State of Alaska, Juneau, 1971-73, atty. gen., 1973-74, 82-85; assoc. prof. law and pub. adminstrn. U. Alaska, Juneau, 1985—; of counsel Guess & Rudd, Juneau, 1986—. Contbr. articles to profl. jours. Trustee Alaska Permanent Fund, Juneau, 1982—, 85; mem. Alaska Democratic Central Com., 1982; commr. Alaska Fed.-State Land Use Planning Commn., 1977-79. Mem. Alaska Bar Assn., Alaska C. of C. (bd. dirs. 1980-81, Juneau C. of C. (bd. dirs. 1979-82), Phi Beta Kappa. Democrat. Methodist. Lodge: Rotary.

GORSUCH, RICHARD LEE, graduate school educator; b. Wayne, Mich., May 13, 1937; s. Culver C. and Velma L. (Poe) G.; m. Sylvia Sue Coalson, Aug. 18, 1961; children: Eric, Kay. AB, Tex. Christian U., 1959; MA, U. Ill., 1962, PhD, 1965; MDiv., Vanderbilt U., 1968. Ordained to ministry Ch. Disciples of Christ, 1968. Asst. prof. psychology Vanderbilt U., Nashville, 1966-68; asst., then assoc. prof. George Peabody Coll., Nashville, 1968-73; assoc. prof. Tex. Christian U., Ft. Worth, 1973-75; assoc. prof. U. Tex., Arlington, 1975-76, prof., 1976-79; prof. Fuller Theol. Sem., Pasadena, Calif., 1979—. Author: Factor Analysis (rev. 2d edit., 1983); co-author: Nature of Man, 1976; Psychology of Religion, 1984; contbr. numerous articles to profl. jours.; cons. editor religious, ednl. and psychol. jours. Fellow NIMH, 1960-61. Fellow Am. Psychol. Assn., Soc. for Sci. Study Religion; mem. Am. Men and Women Sci., Soc. Multivariate Exptl. Psychology, Religious Research Assn., Sigma Chi. Home: 3367 Ellington Villa Dr Altadena CA 91001

GORTATOWSKI, MELVIN JEROME, chemist; b. Chgo., Oct. 30, 1925; s. Walter Harry and Anna Martha (Santowski) G. BS, U. Ill., 1950, PhD, 1955; MS, Wash. State U., 1952. Research instr. biochemistry U. Utah, Salt Lake City, 1955-58, research assoc. psychiatry, 1958-59, research instr. biochemistry, chemist VA Hosp., 1959-65; assoc. investigator, asst. prof. pediatrics, biochemistry U. So. Calif. Children's Hosp., Los Angeles, 1965-71; dir. bur. clin. chemistry Utah State Health Lab., Salt Lake City, 1971—, safety officer, 1980—. Contbr. articles to jours. Served with U.S. Army, 1944-46. Eastman Kodak fellow U. Ill., 1954. Mem. Am. Chem. Soc., Mineral Collectors Utah, Utah Numismatic Soc. (bd. dirs. 1976-77), Sigma Xi, Phi Lambda Upsilon. Roman Catholic. Avocations: photography, philatelics, music, tennis, swimming. Home: 4045 Foubert Ave Salt Lake City UT 84124 Office: Utah State Health Lab 44 Medical Dr Salt Lake City UT 84113

GORTNER, WILLIS ALWAY, nutritional biochemist, author; b. Cold Spring Harbor, N.Y., Dec. 20, 1913; s. Ross Aiken and Catherine (Willis) G.; m. Susan Leet Reichert, Aug. 25, 1960; children—Willis Alway II, David Allen, Catherine Willis, Frederick Aiken. B.A. magna cum laude, U. Minn., 1934; Ph.D., U. Rochester, 1940. Research chemist Gen. Mills, Inc., Mpls., 1934-37, 40-42; teaching asst. biochemistry U. Rochester Med. Sch., 1937-40; asst. prof. biochemistry and chem. engring. Cornell U., 1943-45, asso. prof. biochemistry, 1945-48; head chemistry dept. Pineapple Research Inst., Hawaii, Honolulu, 1948-64; dir. human nutrition research div. Agrl. Research Service, USDA, Beltsville, Md., 1964-72; mem. nat. program staff coordinating human nutrition and family living Agrl. Research Service, USDA, 1972-76; exec. officer Am. Inst. Nutrition, Bethesda, Md., 1976-78; Hoffman LaRoche lectr. Canadian Nutrition Soc., 1971; with Bikini Sci. Resurvey Team, 1947, Bjorksten Research Found., Madison, Wis., 1953, NRC-Nat. Acad. Sci., 1957, Nat. Canners Assn. Research Lab., 1960-61; dept. nutritional scis. U. Calif. at Berkeley, 1963; affiliate grad. faculty U. Hawaii, 1956-64; chmn. Nat. Acad. Scis. com. Internat. Union Nutritional Scis., 1973-76; secretariat Internat. Congress Food Sci. and Tech., 1970; adv. com. Honolulu County Air Pollution Control, 1957-64, State Hawaii Radiol. Health, 1958-64, Nutrition Found., 1968-79, Cornell U. Inst. Food Sci., 1971-76, Am. Health Found., 1973-76, Fedn. Am. Socs. Exptl. Biology Life Scis. Research Office, 1974-77, Diet, Nutrition and Cancer Program, Nat. Cancer Inst., 1975-77, Office Biochem. Nomenclature, NRC, 1976-77; bd. dirs. Nat. Nutrition Consortium, 1973-78. Author: Ancient Rock Carvings of the Central Sierra: The North Fork Indian Petroglyphs, 1984, The Martis Indians: Ancient Tribe of the Sierra Nevada, 1986; Co-author: Principles of Food Freezing, 1948, The Food Additives Book, 1982; co-editor, author: Outlines of Biochemistry, rev. edit, 1949; Contbr. articles to profl. jours. Recipient Thomas Andrews award for undergrad. research U. Minn., 1934, 1st Hoffman LaRoche Nat. Lectr. award Nutrition Soc., Can., 1971. Fellow AAAS, Inst. Food Technologists (mem. com. on constn. 1947, councilor 1955-57, editorial bd. 1965-70); mem. Am. Soc. Biol. Chemists, Am. Soc. for Clin. Nutrition, Am. Chem. Soc. (Cornell exec. com. 1946-47, Hawaii exec. com. 1948-53, 56-59, Hawaii chmn. 1949-50, councilor 1950-53, 56-59), Soc. Am. Archaeology, Am. Rock Art Research Assn., Am. Inst. Nutrition (exec. officer 1976-78), Sigma Xi (Hawaii pres. 1955-56), Phi Lambda Upsilon, Alpha Chi Sigma. Patentee in field. Home: 470 Cervantes Rd Portola Valley CA 94025

GORTON, SLADE, senator; b. Chgo., Jan. 8, 1928; s. Thomas Slade and Ruth (Israel) G.; m. Sally Jean Clark, June 28, 1958; children: Tod, Sarah Jane, Rebecca Lynn. AB, Dartmouth Coll., 1950; LLB with honors, Columbia U., 1953. Bar: Wash. 1953. Assoc. law firm, Seattle, 1953-65; ptnr. law firm 1965-69; atty. gen. State of Wash., Olympia, 1969-80; U.S. Senator from Wash. 1981-87; ptnr. Davis, Wright & Jones, Seattle, 1987—; Mem. Wash. Ho. of Reps., 1959-69, majority leader, 1967-69. Trustee Pacific Sci. Center, Seattle, found. mem., 1977-78; mem. Pres.'s Consumer Adv. Council, 1975-77; mem. Wash. State Law and Justice Commn., 1969-80, chmn., 1969-70; mem. State Criminal Justice Tng. Commn., 1969-80, chmn., 1969-76. Served with AUS, 1945-46; to 1st lt. USAF, 1953-56; col. Res. Mem. ABA, Wash. Bar Assn., Nat. Assn. Attys. Gen. (pres. 1976-77, Wyman award 1980), Phi Delta Phi, Phi Beta Kappa. Clubs: Seattle Tennis, Wash. Athletic (Seattle). Address: 2600 Century Square Seattle WA 98101

GOSE, RICHARD VERNIE, lawyer; b. Hot Springs, S.D., Aug. 3, 1927; s. Vernie O. and Mame K. (Thompson) G.; B.S., U. Wyo., 1950; M.S. in Engring., Northwestern U., 1955; LL.B., George Washington U., 1967; J.D., George Washington U., 1968; children—Beverly Marie, Donald Paul, Celeste Marlene. Bar: N.Mex. 1967, U.S. Supreme Ct. 1976, Wyo. 1979. Exec. asst. to U.S. Senator Hickey, Washington, 1960-62; mgr. E.G. & G., Inc., Washington, 1964-66; asst. atty. gen. State of N.Mex., Santa Fe, 1967-70; sole practice law, Santa Fe, 1967—; assoc. prof. engring. U. Wyo., 1957-60, owner, mgr. Gose & Assocs., Santa Fe, 1967-78; sole practice law, Casper, Wyo., 1978-83; co-chmn. Henry Jackson for Pres., M.Mex., 1976, Wyo. Johnson for Pres., 1960. Served with U.S. Army, 1950-52. Registered profl. engr., N.Mex., Wyo.; Mem. 1st Jud. Dist. Bar Assn. (past pres.), N.Mex. Bar Assn., Wyo. Bar Assn., Phi Delta Theta, Pi Tau Sigma, Sigma Tau. Methodist. Lodge: Masons. Home and Office: PO Box 8301 Santa Fe NM 87504

GOSLIN, IVAL VINTON, civil engineer; b. Pullman, Wash., May 7, 1911; s. Raymond L. and Zelma (Gustin) G.; m. Glenda Marcelyn Bridal, Mar. 2, 1963. Student U. Oreg., 1929-30; B.A., U. Utah, 1934, M.A., 1935; postgrad. U. Idaho, 1940-42; B.S. in C.E., Utah State U., 1944. From asst. to project engr. U.S. Geol. Survey, Logan, Utah, 1943-46; gen. mgr. Aberdeen-Springfield Canal Co., Abderdeen, Idaho, 1946-52; asst. chief engr. Upper Colorado River Commn., Grand Junction, Colo., 1953-55, acting sec., 1955, exec. dir., Salt Lake City, 1955-79; pvt. cons. civil engring., 1979—. Treas., Aberdeen Bd. Edn., 1948-52; v.p. Snake River Com. of 9; pres. Upper Snake River Valley Water Users Protective Assn., 1948-52; mem. Snake River Compact Commn., 1949-50; mem. Columbia River Basin Compact Commn., 1950-52; mem. Wyo. Reclamation Projects Survey Team, 1962-63; charter mem. adv. com. on Water Data for Pub. Use, U.S. Geol. Survey, 1965—; exec. dir. Colo. Water Resources and Power Devel. Authority, 1982—. Recipient Citizens award U.S. Dept. Interior, 1976; Water Leader of Yr. award Colo. Water Congress, 1981; Outstanding Pub. Service award Water for Colo., 1982, others. Mem. Water Resources Congress (chmn. 1981), ASCE, Nat. Rifle Assn., Beta Theta Pi. Clubs: Masons, (32 deg.), Shriners. Address: 340 Lorey Dr Grand Junction CO 81505

GOSLING, JOHN THOMAS, space plasma physicist, researcher; b. Akron, Ohio, July 10, 1938; s. Arthur Warrington and Wilhelmina (Bell) G.; m. Marie Ann Turner, Dec. 21, 1963; children: Mark Raymond, Steven Arthur. BS in Physics, Ohio U., 1960; PhD in Physics, U. Calif., Berkeley, 1965; postdoctoral studies, Los Alamos (N.Mex.) Nat. Lab., 1965-67. Staff mem. Nat. Ctr. Atmospheric Research, Boulder, Colo., 1967-75, Los Alamos Nat. Lab., 1975—. Contbr. articles to profl. jours. Recipient Tech. Achievement award Nat. Ctr. Atmospheric Research, Boulder, 1974. Mem. Am. Geophys. Union, AAAS. Democrat. Avocations: sports, hiking, music. Home: 1420 45th Los Alamos NM 87544 Office: Los Alamos Nat Lab ESS8 MS D438 Los Alamos NM 87545

GOSS, ANN LUCILLE GODFREY, infosystems specialist, consultant; b. Mpls., June 14, 1946; d. Roy Ira and Roselyn Lizetta (Johnson) G.; m. Roger Roland Goss, June 14, 1969; children: Daniel Lee, Malia Fay. BA in Anthropology, Lawrence U., 1968. Women's editor Norman (Okla.) Transcript, 1971-72; women's editor, legal editor Weatherford (Okla.) Daily News, 1972-73; office mgr., prodn. asst. InterGraphics Press, Norman, 1974-76; coordinator graphic arts Bendix Field Engring. Corp., Grand Junction, Colo., 1977-79, publications coordinator, 1979-84, microcomputer coordinator, 1984—; cons. Mus. Western Colo., Grand Junction, 1983—, St. Matthew's Episc. Ch., Grand Junction, 1985—; owner The Right Type, Grand Junction, 1980-84. Compiler, editor annual reports U.S. Dept. Energy, GJPO, NURE, 1978-81; creator graphics, video Vietnam Vets. Am., Grand Junction, 1983. Den and Troop Leader Western Colo. Council Boy Scouts Am., Grand Junction, 1982—; instr. Little Maverick Ski Sch. Powderhorn, Mesa, Colo., 1984—. Recipient Best Feature Photo award Okla. Press Assn., 1972. Episcopalian. Avocations: singing, music, camping, archeoastronomy, skiing. Home: 2519 Arroyo Dr Grand Junction CO 81503 Office: UNC Tech Services Inc 2597 B-3/4 Rd PO Box 14000 Grand Junction CO 81502-5504

GOSS, GEORGIA BULMAN, translator; b. N.Y.C., Dec. 1, 1939; d. James Cornelius and Marian Bright (McLaughlin) Bulman; m. Douglas Keith Goss, Dec. 21, 1957; children—Kristin Anne, David. B.A., U. Mich., 1961. Librarian, High Altitude Obs., Boulder, Colo., 1963-64, U.S. Bur. Standards, Boulder, 1964-65; cons. editor Spanish lang. pilots' tng. manual, 1981-82; freelance translator, Englewood, Colo., 1982—. Mem. Internat. Trade Assn. Colo., Phi Sigma Iota. Republican. Episcopalian. Home and Office: 5091 S Boston St Englewood CO 80111

GOSS, JAMES ARTHUR, technical writer; b. Brigham City, Utah, May 19, 1924; s. Archie James and Mary Alberta (Pulsipher) G.; m. Lucille Woolley, Mar. 21, 1947; children: Lawrence Arthur, Raymond Lynn, Linda Lucille, Gerald Lee, Liana, Lori. BS, Utah State U., 1951; PhD, UCLA, 1957. Research asst. UCLA Sch. Medicine, 1955-56; prof. Kans. State U., Manhattan, 1956-76; chemist Scott Pro., Inc., Scott City, Kans., 1979-83; tech. writer Jana, Inc., Concord, Calif., 1984-86; freelance writer Fairfield, Calif., 1986—; cons. in field Calif., 1984—. Author: Physiology of Plants, 1972; contbr. articles to profl. jours. Served to 2d lt. Infantry, 1943-68. Mem. Am. Assn. Feed Microscopists, Sigma Xi (pres. 1968-69). Mormon. Home: 1109 Worley Rd Suisun City CA 94585

GOSS, JEROME ELDON, cardiologist; b. Dodge City, Kans., Nov. 30, 1935; s. Horton Maurice and Mary Alice (Mountain) G.; m. Lorraine Ann Sanchez, Apr. 20, 1986. BA, U. Kans., 1957; MD, Northwestern U., 1961. Diplomate Am. Bd. Internal Medicine, Am. Bd. Cardiology (fellow, bd. govs. 1981-84). Intern Met. Gen. Hosp., Cleve., 1961-62; resident Northwestern U. Med. Ctr., Chgo., 1962-64; fellow in cardiology U. Colo., Denver, 1964-66; asst. prof. medicine U. N.Mex., Albuquerque, 1968-70; practice medicine specializing in cardiology Albuquerque Cardiovascular Assn., 1970—; mem. bd. alumni counsellors Northwestern U. Med. Sch., 1977—; chief dept. medicine Presbyn. Hosp., Albuquerque, 1978-80, mem. exec. com. 1980-82, bd. dirs. cardiac diagnostic services; cons., cardio-pace med. lectr., Marion Labs., Kansas City (Mo.) and Mpls. Contbr. articles to profl. jours. Served to lt. comdr. USN, 1966-68. Nat. Heart Inst. research fellow, 1965-66; named one of Outstanding Young Men Am., Jaycees, 1970; recipient Alumni Service award Northwestern U. Med. Sch., 1986. Fellow ACP, Council Clin. Cardiology of Am. Heart Assn., Soc. Cardiac Angiography; mem. Albuquerque-Bernalillo County Med. Soc. (sec. 1972, treas. 1975, v.p. 1980), Alpha Omega Alpha. Republican. Methodist. Lodge: Rotary. Office: Albuquerque Cardiovascular Assocs 201 Cedar SE Suite 604 Albuquerque NM 87106

GOSS, L. BLAINE, speech educator, academic director; b. San Mateo, Calif., Oct. 13, 1943; s. Louis Harold and Erma Ruthlee (Stewart) G.; m. Carol Jeanne Hillberg, June 20, 1965; children: Angela Suzanne, Melissa Diane. BA, San Jose State U., 1967, MA, 1968; PhD, Mich. State U., 1971. Asst. prof. speech San Jose (Calif.) State U., 1971-72; from asst. prof. to assoc. prof. U. Okla., Norman, 1972-84; prof., head dept. speech N.Mex. State U., Las Cruces, 1984—. Author: Communication at Work, 1975, Processing Communication, 1982, Communication in Everyday Life, 1983; contbr. articles to profl. publs. Mem. Speech Communication Assn. (div. chmn. 1976), Internat. Communication Assn., Western Speech Communication Assn., World Communication Assn. Avocations: photography, horseback riding, fishing. Home: 150 Horseshoe Circle Las Cruces NM 88005 Office: NMex State U Dept Speech Box 3W Las Cruces NM 88001

GOTO, KENJI, former hosp. adminstr. and cons., cultural society executive; b. Puako, Hawaii, Oct. 10, 1904; s. Unokichi and Yana (Inaba) G.; B.A. in Bus. and Econs., U. Hawaii, 1927, postgrad., 1930-31; m. Hagino Mikami, Feb. 23, 1935; children—Irving Ken, Alan Jiro. Salesman, Theodore H. Davies & Co., Honolulu, 1927-29; mgr. U. Goto Store, Kona, Hawaii, 1929-30; tchr. Konawaena High Sch., 1931-42; prin. Hookena Elementary Sch., 1942-43; supr. On-Job Tng. Program for Vets., Honolulu, 1947-48; adminstr. Kuakini Hosp. and Home, 1948-69, cons., 1970-73. Pres., Oahu Health Council, 1959-61; mem. Mayor's Adv. Com. on Community Renewal Program, 1964-65; vice chmn. Hawaii Adv. Council Hosp. and Med. Facilities, 1965-76; mem. Honolulu Com. on Aging, 1970-78, chmn., 1976-78; chmn. adv. com. Honolulu Heart Research Programs, 1964-77, state and Oahu chmn. Com. for Centennial Celebration of Japanese Immigration to Hawaii, 1967-68; chmn. Centennial Celebration Arrival of Govt.-contract (Kanyaku)Japanese Immigrants to Hawaii, 1983-86; leader U.S. Army Pacific Friendship Mission to Japan, 1968; chmn. adv. com. Japan-Hawaii Cancer Study, 1971-77; mem. Crown Prince Akihito Scholarship Fund, 1972—, chmn., 1980—; treas., chmn. membership com. Japanese Immigrant Heritage Preservation Ctr., 1975-86, sec., 1980-85, v.p., 1985—; bd. dirs. Kuakini Med. Center, 1973-79; chmn. bd. Hawaii Sr. Services, Inc., 1977-79. Served with AUS, 1943-45. Decorated Order of Rising Sun Fourth Class, Japanese Govt., 1983; named Hawaii Man of Year, 1970; recipient Outstanding Older Am. award for County of Honolulu, 1979. Mem. United Japanese Soc. Hawaii (pres. 1967-68, adviser 1969—), Am. Coll. Hosp. Adminstrs. (life), Hosp. Assn. Hawaii (pres. 1957, 67), Japan-Am. Soc. Honolulu (trustee 1976-84, sr. advisor 1984—), Teiko Kai (pres. chpt. 1978—). Home: 99-869 Lalawai Dr Aiea HI 96701

GOTTFRIED, EUGENE LESLIE, physician, educator; b. Passaic, N.J., Feb. 26, 1929; s. David Robert and Rose (Chill) G.; m. Phyllis Doris Swain, Aug. 16, 1957. AB, Columbia Coll., 1950, MD, 1954. Cert. Nat. Bd. Med. Examiners, Am. Bd. Internal Medicine. Intern Presbyn. Hosp., N.Y.C., 1954-55, asst. resident in medicine, 1957-58; resident Bronx (N.Y.) Mcpl. Hosp. Ctr., 1958-59, fellow in medicine, 1959-60; asst. instr. medicine Albert Einstein Coll. Medicine Yeshiva U., N.Y.C., 1959-60, instr., 1960-61, assoc. prof., 1961-65, asst. prof., 1965-69; assoc. prof. medicine Cornell U. Med. Coll., N.Y.C., 1969-81; assoc. prof. pathology Cornell U. Med. Coll., Ithaca, N.Y., 1975-81; clin. prof. dept. lab. medicine U. Calif., San Francisco, 1981—, vice chmn. dept. lab. medicine, 1981—; hosp. appointments include asst. vis. physician Bronx Mcpl. Hosp. Ctr., 1960-66, assoc. attending physician, 1966-69; assoc. attending physician N.Y. Hosp., N.Y.C., 1969-81, assoc. attending pathologist, 1975-81, dir. lab. clin. hematology, 1969-81; chief lab. medicine San Francisco Gen. Hosp. Med. Ctr., 1981—, dir. clin. labs., 1981—. Assoc. editor Jour. Lipid Research, 1971-72, 75-77; mem. editorial bd. Jour. Lipid Research, 1972-77. Served to lt. comdr. USNR, 1955-57. Recipient Career Scientist award Health Research Council City of N.Y., 1964-72. Fellow Am. Soc. Hematology (com. clin. lab. standards 1984-86), Internat. Soc. hematology, ACP, Acad. Clin. Lab. Physicians and Scientists; mem. AAAS, Phi Beta Kappa, Alpha Omega Alpha. Office: San Francisco Gen Hosp Clin Labs 1001 Potrero Ave San Francisco CA 94110

GOTTFRIED, IRA SIDNEY, management consulting and accounting executive; b. Bronx, N.Y., Jan. 4, 1932; s. Louis and Augusta (Champagne) G.; m. Judith Claire Rosenberg, Sept. 19, 1954; children: Richard Alan, Glenn Steven, David Aaron. B.B.A., CCNY, 1953, M.B.A., U.S.C., 1956. Sales mgr. Kleerpak Plastics, North Hollywood, Calif., 1956-57; head systems and procedures Hughes Aircraft Co., Culver City, Calif., 1957-60; mgr. corp. bus. systems The Aerospace Corp., El Segundo, Calif., 1960-61; dir. adminstrn. Eldon Industries, Inc., Hawthorne, Calif., 1962; mgr. info. systems Litton Industries Inc., Woodland Hills, Calif., 1963-64; exec. v.p. Norris & Gottfried, Inc., Los Angeles, 1964-69; pres. Gottfried Cons., Inc., 1970-85; exec. ptnr. Coopers & Lybrand, CPA's, 1985—; chmn., dir. Mgmt. Adv. Services, Inc., 1968—; vice chmn. ACME Inc., 1984-85; dir., mem. exec. com. Blue Cross of S. Calif., 1968-77; instr. UCLA; cons. in field. Contbr. articles in field to prof. jours. Bd. dirs. ARC, 1980—. Served with USNR, 1953-56. Recipient Pres.'s award United Hosp. Assn. Mem. Inst. Mgmt. Cons. (cert.), Am. Arbitration Assn., Data Processing Mgmt. Assn. (life), Alpha Phi Omega (life). Jewish. Clubs: Brentwood Country, Palm Desert Resort Country; Los Angeles Athletic. Lodge: Rotary. Home: 12118 La Casa Ln Los Angeles CA 90049 Office: 1000 W 6th St Los Angeles CA 90017

GOTTLIEB, ALAN MERRIL, association executive; b. Los Angeles, May 2, 1947; s. Seymour and Sherry (Schutz) G.; m. Julie Hoy Versnel, July 27, 1979; children: Amy Jean, Sarah Merril. BS in Nuclear Engring., U. Tenn., 1971; postgrad. Georgetown U. Inst. Comparative Econ. and Polit. Systems. Nat. dir. Young Ams. for Freedom, Washington, 1971-72; nat. treas. Am. Conservative Union, Washington, 1971—; chmn. Citizens Com. for Right to Keep and Bear Arms, Bellevue, Wash., 1974—; pres. Ctr. Def. of Free Enterprise, Bellevue 1976—; pres. Second Amendment Found., Bellevue, 1974—; pub. Gun Week, 1985—. Served with U.S. Army, 1968-74. Recipient Good Citizenship award Citizens Home Protective Assn., 1978, Cicero award Nat. Assn. Federally Licensed Firearms Dealers, 1982; Second Amendment award Scope, 1983, Roy Rogers award 1987. Mem. Direct Mail Mktg. Assn. Wash., Nat. Rifle Assn. Republican. Author: The Gun Owners Political Action Manual, 1976; The Rights of Gun Owners, 1981, The Gun Grabbers, 1986.

GOTTLIEB, WERNER, clinical social worker; b. Frankenwinheim, Fed. Republic Germany, Sept. 12, 1925; came to U.S., 1937; s. Max and Jennie (Nussbaum) G.; m. Shirley Belle Unger, June 12, 1949; children: Debra Gottlieb Looks, Leonard, David. BS, CCNY, 1949; MS, Columbia U., 1951. Lic. clin. social worker, Calif. Clin. social worker Community Service Soc., N.Y.C., 1951-53; child care dept. dir. Jewish Community Service Soc., Buffalo, 1953-54; supr., asst. dir. casework Family Service Assn. of Cleve., 1954-69; exec. dir. Youth Service, Cleve., 1969-71; dir. counseling, asst. exec. dir. Ctr. Human Services, Cleve., 1971-79; exec. dir. Jewish Family & Children's Services of San Francisco, 1979-85; cons. San Francisco, 1985—; cons. Univ. Hosps., Cleve., 1970-74, Family Service Assn. Am., Mid-West region, 1968-79, chairperson dirs. profl. services, 1975-76; adj. faculty Case Western Res. U., Cleve., 1968-79. Contbr. articles to profl. jours. Served with U.S. Army, 1944-46, ETO. Mem. Nat. Assn. Social Workers (local bd. dirs. 1967-74, v.p. 1972-74), Nat. Assn. Jewish Family and Children's and Health Profls. (bd. dirs. 1983-85), Assn. Jewish Family and Children's Agys. (exec. council 1983-85). Democrat. Home: 2261 Colonial Ct Walnut Creek CA 94598 Office: 2477 Washington St San Francisco CA 94115

GOTTLOBER, ABRAHAM BER, psychologist; b. Cleve., May 28, 1912; s. Alexander and Helen (Alkow) G.; B.A., Western Res. U., 1933, M.A., 1935; Ph.D., State U. Iowa, 1937; m. Helen R. Rabinowitz, Apr. 12, 1940; children—Alexandra Jean, Dale Lynn. Chief, Psychophysiol. Clinic, 1932-40, vis. psychologist, 1940-46; psychologist, psychiat. ward Cleve. City Hosp., 1934-46; dir. Cleve. Speech Correction Clinic, 1937-46; pvt. practice clin. psychology and psychotherapy, Los Angeles, 1946—, marriage counselor, sex therapist. Diplomate Am. Bd. Profl. Psychology. Mem. Am. Psychol. Assn., Calif. State Psychol. Assn., Los Angeles Soc. Clin. Psychologists, Sigma Xi. Jewish. Condr. research in electroencephalography; co-discovered individuality and constancy of EEG; contbr. Understanding Stuttering, 1953. Office: 134 S Gunston Dr Los Angeles CA 90049

GOTTSCHALK, LOUIS AUGUST, psychiatrist, psychoanalyst; b. St. Louis, Aug. 26, 1916; s. Max W. and Kelmie (Mutrux) G.; m. Helen Reller, July 24, 1944; children—Guy H., Claire A., Louise H., Susan E. A.B., Washington U., St. Louis, 1940, M.D., 1943; Ph.D., So. Calif. Psychiat. Inst., 1977. Asst. in neuropsychiatry Washington U. Sch. Medicine, 1944-46; commd. asst. surgeon USPHS, 1946, advanced through grades to med. dir., 1979; instr. psychiatry S.W. Med. Coll., Dallas, 1947-48; research psychiatrist NIMH, Bethesda, Md., 1950-53; coordinator research, research prof. psychiatry U. Cin. Coll. Medicine, 1953-67; attending psychiatrist Cin. Gen. Hosp., 1953-67; faculty Inst. Psychoanalysis, Chgo., 1957-67, So. Calif. Psychiat. Inst., Los Angeles, 1970—; chmn. research com. Hamilton County (Ohio) Diagnostic Center, 1958-67; prof. psychiatry, social sci. and social ecology, dept. psychiatry and human behavior U. Calif. - Irvine Coll. Medicine, 1967—, chmn. dept., 1967-78; also program dir. psychiat. residency tng.; dir. psychiat. services U. Calif. - Irvine Med. Center, 1967-78, dir. cons. and liaison program, 1978—; sci. co-dir. U. Calif. - Irvine Med. Center (Nat. Alcoholism Research Center), 1978-84; Mem. clin. psychopharmacology study sect. NIMH, 1968-71; mem. research rev. com. Nat. Inst. Drug Abuse, 1973-77, Mental Health Study Center, 1978-84. Author: (with G. C. Gleser) The Measurement of Psychological States through the Content Analysis of Verbal Behavior, 1969, How to Understand and Analyze Your Own Dreams, 1975, Greek edit., 1978, Spanish edit., 1981, 3d rev. edit., 1985; editor: Comparative Psycholinguistic Analysis of Two Psychotherapeutic Interviews, 1961, (with A. H. Auerbach) Methods of Research in Psychotherapy, 1966, (with S. Merlis) Pharmacokinetics of Psychoactive Drugs: Blood Levels and Clinical Responses, 1976, Pharmacokinetics of Psychoactive Drugs: Further Studies, 1979, The Content Analysis of Verbal Behavior: Further Studies, 1979, (with F.L. McGuire and others) Drug Abuse Deaths in Nine Cities: A Survey Report, 1980; (with R. Cravey) Toxicological and Pathological Studies on Psychoactive Drug-Involved Deaths, 1980; (with Winget, Gleser and Lolas) Analisis de la Conducta Verbal, 1984; The Tree of Knowledge, 1985, (with F. Lolas and L.L. Viney) The Content Analysis of Verbal Behavior: Significance in Clinical Medicine and Psychiatry, 1986; editorial bd.: Psychosomatic Medicine, 1960-70, Psychiatry, 1967—, Am. Jour. Psychotherapy, 1975—; others; contbr. numerous articles to tech. lit. Recipient Hofheimer Research award, 1955, Franz Alexander Essay prize So. Calif. Psychoanalytic Inst., Los Angeles, 1973; Disting. Research award U. Calif. Irvine Alumni Assn., 1974; named Disting. Practitioner, Nat. Acad. Med. Practice, 1984; Rockefeller fellow Bellagio Study Ctr., Italy, 1985; Hofheimer Research award, 1955; NIMH Research Career award, 1960-67. Fellow AAAS, Am. Psychiat. Assn. (Found. Fund prize research 1978), Am. Coll. Neuropsychopharmacology, Am. Coll. Psychiatrists; mem. Assn. for Research Nervous and Mental Diseases, Am. Psychosomatic Soc., Cin. Soc. Neurology and Psychiatry (past pres.), Am. Psychoanalytic Assn., AMA, Orange County Med. Assn., So. Calif. Psychiat. Soc., Am. Assn. Child Psychoanalysts, So. Calif. Psychoanalytic Soc., Phi Beta Kappa, Sigma Xi, Alpha Omega Alpha., Omicron Delta Kappa. Club: Cosmos. Home: 4607 Perham Rd Corona Del Mar CA 92625 Office: Dept Psychiatry and Human Behavior Coll Medicine U Calif Irvine CA 92717

GOTTSCHALK, MAX JULES, new development specialist, industrial designer; b. St. Louis, Dec. 14, 1909; s. Max William and Kelmie (Mutrux) G.; m. Josephine Pipkin, 1933 (div. 1940); children—Sandra, Jules; m. Cecil Cornsweet, June 8, 1979. B.A. in Design, Washington U., St. Louis, 1933, postgrad. in psychology and history of art, 1936-38, Sch. Engring., 1942-44. With Knapp Monarch Elec. Co., St. Louis, 1934-36; chief tech. advisor govt. Nfld., Can., 1938-42; chief devel. engr. Hussman Co., St. Louis, 1942-44; sr. engr. devel. Walter Dorwin Teague, N.Y.C., 1942-44; chief engr. Gerald C. Johnson Assocs., N.Y.C., 1946-48; sr. engr. in charge field handling equipment Hughes Aircraft, Tucson, 1952-60; sr. research product design engr. Bell Aerosystems Co., Buffalo, 1962-64; pres. Max's Enterprises, 1986; instr. in design, drafting, perception, electronics, coordinator design and drafting dept., cons. sound recording systems Pima Coll., Tucson, 1967-77; cons. Mark A. Simpson Mfg. Co., L.I., N.Y., 1944-52, Plymold Corp., Lawrence, Mass., Wheeldex Corp., White Plains, N.Y., Simpla Research and Mfg. Co., N.Y.C., 1944-52; cons. engr. Burr-Brown Research Corp., Lee Supply, 1964-67; lectr. Coop. Summer Coll., St. John's and Corner Brook, Nfld., 1937-39; cons. art and design Sullivan, Stauffer, Colwell and Bayless, Foote, Cone, and Belding, Gardner Advt., Darcy Advt.; 1948-52; indsl. designs and devels. include: new modular chassis systems, electronic test equipment, paper towel holder, rotary card file, 1st open case frozen food refrigeration, 1st self service electronic checkout, use of cellophane for wrapping cheeses and meats, lunar escape vehicle, air cushion vehicle, curtain wall air cooling, intensive care cooling systems, electronics packaging systems; pres. Imagineering, Tucson, 1960—; chief engr. Godesca and Gottschalk Engring., 1970—; owner Max's Enterprises, 1980—; work exhibited St. Louis Artist Guild, 1935, St. Louis Art Mus., 1936, St. John's U., 1940-42, Mus. Modern Art, N.Y.C., 1948-50, Internat. Canvas Exhibit, Tokyo, 1975, Pima Coll., Rosequist Wohlheim Gallery, Tucson, 1970—, Udinotti Gallyer, Scottsdale, Ariz. Mem. Radio Engring. Soc., Plastic Engring. Soc., Audio Engring Soc. (life). Home: 5620 N Campbell St, Tucson, AZ 85718

GOTTSCHALK-GRAFMAN, CAROLE MARCIA, audiologist; b. Detroit, Aug. 11, 1946; d. Eric Sherman and Bertha Mildred (Weisbrot) Gottschalk; m. Richard Dale Grafman, Aug. 11, 1974 (dec. Oct. 1986); 1 child, Russell Douglas. BA, U. Mich., 1968, MS, 1969, cert. edn., 1968. Clin. audiologist UCLA Med. Ctr., 1969-71; dir. Century Speech and Hearing Ctr., Los Angeles, 1971-77; cons. audiologist Los Angeles, 1977-80, Audio-Vestibular Lab., Santa Monica, Calif., 1981—; mem. field faculty Goddard Coll., Los Angeles, 1973—. Mem. Am. Speech-Lang. Hearing Assn. (cert., congressional action contract 1980-83), Calif. Speech Pathologists and Audiologists in Pvt. Practice, Soc. Med. Audiology, Variety Club So. Calif., Guardians of Courage (founders circle 1980—). Jewish. Avocations: tennis, golf. Home and Office: 3411 Merrimac Rd Los Angeles CA 90049

GOTTSTEIN, BARNARD JACOB, retail and wholesale food company executive, real estate executive; b. Des Moines, Dec. 30, 1925; s. Jacob B. and Anna (Jacobs) G.; children—Sandra, James, Ruth Anne, David, Robert; m. Rachel Landau Heisiger, July, 1986. B.A. in Econs. and Bus., U. Wash., 1949. Pres. J.B. Gottstein & Co. Inc., Anchorage, 1953—; chmn. bd. Carr Gottstein Co., Anchorage, 1974—; dir. United Bank Alaska, Anchorage, 1975-86. Commr. Alaska State Human Rights Commn, 1963-68; del. Democratic Nat. Conv., 1964, 68, 76; committeeman Dem. Nat. Com., 1976-80; v.p. State Bd. Edn., Alaska Served with USAF, 1944-45. Jewish. Office: J B Gottstein & Co Inc 6411 A St Anchorage AK 99518

GOUD, NAGANA AGASALADINNI, chemist; b. Agasaladinni, India, July 11, 1937; came to U.S., 1973; s. Veerana and Ramalingamma Goud; m. Reddy Rajeswari, May 17, 1968; children: Sunitha, Anitha, Anil. BSc, P.C. Jabin Sci. Coll., Hubli, India, 1962; MSc, Karnatak U., India, 1964, cert. in German, 1966, PhD, 1968. Assoc. lectr. Regional Engring. Coll., Warangal, India, 1967-68, postdoctoral research assoc., 1968-69; research chemist CIBA Research Ctr., Bombay, 1969-73; postdoctoral fellow U. N.C., Chapel Hill, 1973-77; sci. dir. Bachem, Inc., Torrance, Calif., 1977—. Contbr. articles to profl. jours. Mem. Am. Chem. Soc. Avocations: photography, jogging. Home: 21914 Ladeene Ave Torrance CA 90503

GOUGH, HARRISON GOULD, psychologist, educator; b. Buffalo, Minn., Feb. 25, 1921; s. Harry B. and Aelfreda (Gould) G.; m. Kathryn H. Whittier, Jan. 23, 1943; 1 dau., Jane Kathryn Gough Rhodes. A.B. summa cum laude, U. Minn., 1942, A.M. (Social Sci. Research Council fellow 1946-47), 1947, Ph.D., 1949. Asst. prof. psychology U. Minn., 1948-49; asst. prof. U. Calif.-Berkeley, 1949-54, assoc. prof., 1954-60, prof., 1960—, assoc. dir. Inst. Personality Assessment and Research, 1964-67, dir., 1973-83, chmn. dept. psychology, 1967-72; cons. VA, 1951—; dir. cons. Psychologists Press, Inc., 1956—; mem. research adv. com. Calif. Dept. Corrections, 1958-64, Calif. Dept. Mental Hygiene, 1964-69, Gov.'s Calif. Adv. Com. Mental Health, 1968-74, citizens adv. council Calif. Dept. Mental Hygiene, 1968-71; clin. projects research review com. NIMH, 1968-72. Served to 1st lt. AUS, 1942-46. Recipient U. Calif. the Berkeley citation, 1986, Bruno Klopfer Research award, 1987; Fulbright research scholar, Italy, 1958-59, 65-66; Guggenheim fellow, 1965-66. Mem. Am., Western psychol. assns., Soc. Personality Assessment, Internat. Assn. Cross-Cultural Psychology, Académie National de Psychologie, Soc. Mayflower Desc., Phi Beta Kappa, Sigma Xi. Club: Commonwealth (San Francisco). Author: Adjective Check List, California Psychological Inventory, other psychol. tests; chmn. bd. editors U. Calif. Publs. in Psychology, 1956-58; cons. editor Jour. Cons. and Clin. Psychology, 1956-74, 77-84, Jour. Abnormal Psychology, 1964-74, Jour. Personality and Social Psychology, 1981-84, Med. Tchr., 1978-84, Cahiers d'Anthropologie, 1978—, Population and Environment: Behavioral and Social Issues, 1977-80; Current Psychol. Research and Revs., 1985—, Pakistan Jour. Psychol. Research, 1985—, Jour. Personality Assessment, 1986—; assoc. editor Jour. Cross-Cultural Psychology, 1969-81. Home: PO Box 909 Pebble Beach CA 93953 Office: U Calif Dept Psychology Berkeley CA 94720

GOUGH, ROBERT GEORGE, operations research and national security analyst; b. Abington, Pa., Apr. 15, 1941; s. Harold B. and Ruth M. (Dupert) G.; m. Jean B. Craig, Apr. 6, 1963; 1 son, Steven R. B.S. in Chem. Engring., Lehigh U., 1962; M.B.A. with honors, U. Chgo., 1966; M.S., Stanford U., 1972; Ph.D., 1974. Commd. officer U.S. Air Force, 1963, advanced through grades to lt. col., 1983, asst. to dir. net assessment Immediate Office of Sec. of Def., Washington, 1976-79, chief Electronic Systems Div., Air Force Test and Evaluation Ctr., N.Mex., 1979-83; mem. tech. staff Sandia Nat. Labs., 1983—; adj. prof. mgmt., statistics and econs. U. Md., 1969-70, U. Colo., 1968, 75-76, George Washington U., 1976-79, N.Mex. Highland U., 1981-82, U. N.Mex., 1982—; cons. in field. Bishop's warden, vestryman, treas. ch. bldg. com. Episcopal Ch., 1970—; mem. U.S. Delegation to United Nations Conf. on Disarmament, Geneva; dept. energy rep. to U.S. Delegation to UN. Bd. dirs. PTO, 1974-76. Mem. Am. Inst. Decision Sci. (v.p. 1976), Mil. Ops. Research Symposium (founding chmn. Decision Analysis Working Group), Alpha Iota Delta, Beta Gamma Sigma, Omicron Delta Epsilon. Contbr. articles to prof. jours.s. Home: 8912 Camino Osito NE Albuquerque NM 87111 Office: Sandia Nat Labs Orgn 9111 Albuquerque NM 87185

GOULD, CLIO LAVERNE, electric utility and irrigation dist. exec.; b. Madison, S.D., Feb. 20, 1919; s. Howard Bennett and Moneta Kay (Herrick) G.; student Walla Walla Coll., 1948, U. Wash. Extension, 1954, U. Calif. at San Diego Extension, 1962, Capital Radio Engring. Inst. Corr., 1958-62; diploma elec. engring. Internat. Corr. Schs., 1958; m. Mildred May Newell, Apr. 13, 1942; children—George Marcus, Deanna May (Mrs. Terry L. Paxton). With astronautics div. Gen. Dynamics Corp., San Diego, 1957-66, sr. design engr. research and devel. Atlas and Centaur space vehicles, 1958-66; supt. power and pumping depts. Wellton Mohawk Irrigation & Drainage Dist., Wellton, Ariz., 1966-76, gen. mgr., 1976—. treas. Liga Internat., Inc., San Diego, 1964-65. Served with AUS, 1941-45; PTO. Recipient Performance award Gen. Dynamics Corp., 1963. Registered profl. engr., Ariz. Mem. IEEE (sr.), AIAA, Nat., Ariz. (pres. chpt. 1977-78) socs. profl. engrs., Photog. Soc. Am., Nat. Water Resources Assn., Ariz. State Reclamation Assn., Colorado River Water Users Assn. (bd. dirs. 1982—), Ariz. Agri-Bus. Council (exec. bd. 1980—, v.p. 1981). Republican. Seventh-day Adventist (elder 1956—, chmn. bldg. com. 1970-73). Home: Route 1 Box 4 Wellton AZ 85356 Office: Route 1 Box 19 Wellton AZ 85356

GOULD, DONALD ERNEST, insurance and investment company executive; b. Portland, Oreg., Dec. 10, 1942; s. LaVerne E. and Veeda (Spencer) G.; m. Charan R. Earl, June 24, 1961; children—Julie Anne, Dawn LeAnn. A.S., Lane Community Coll., 1974; B.S., Eastern Oreg. State Coll., 1986. Registered fin. planner, 1979. Br. mgr. Budget Fin. Plan, Seattle, 1965-71, Granning & Treece Fin. Services, Eugene, Oreg., 1971-75; fin. and ins. mgr. Betz Chevrolet-Pontiac-Oldsmobile Inc., Cottage Grove, Oreg., 1975-77; prin. Western-Pacific Ins. Mgmt., Gresham, Oreg., 1977—. Mem. sch. bd. Clackamas Dist. 107, Boring, Oreg., 1979-80, Mt. Hood Christian Sch., Gresham, Oreg., 1983—. Served with USMC, 1962-65, USNR, 1985—. Mem. Internat. Assn. Registered Fin. Planners, Nat. Assn. Life Underwriters, Gresham C. of C., Am. Legion, Phi Theta Kappa. Democrat. Mem. Assembly of God Ch. Lodge: Kiwanis. Home: 2281 SE Kelly Ave Gresham OR 97030 Office: Western-Pacific Ins Mgmt 1217 E Burnside Ave Suite 204 Gresham OR 97030

GOULD, GARY HOWARD, state official; b. Dayton, Oreg., Apr. 1, 1938; s. Calvin J. and Alice Viola G.; student North Idaho Coll., 1957-59; B.A. in Govt., Idaho State U., 1965, M.A. in Edn., 1971; m. Marcella Jean Gould, July 24, 1963; children—Susan Marie, Jon Calvin. Dir. fin. aids and scholarships Idaho State U., 1969-78, spl. asst. to v.p. for adminstrn., 1978-79; ins. agent, realtor Paul Smith Agy., Pocatello, Idaho, 1979—; mem. Idaho Ho. of Reps., 1977-80, Idaho Senate, 1980-84; dir. Idaho Dept. Labor and Indsl. Services, 1984—. Precinct committeeman, Bannock County, Idaho, 1972-74; chmn. Democratic Central Com., 1974-77. Served with U.S. Army, 1959-61. Mem. Idaho Realtors Assn., Ind. Ins. Agts. Assn., Western Council State Legislators, Phi Delta Kappa. 116 Clubs: Masons (Scottish Rite 32 deg.), Elks. Office: Idaho Dept Labor Statehouse Mall 2401 Ellis Ave Boise ID 83720

GOULD, JAMES WARREN, international relations educator; b. Boulder, Colo., May 14, 1924; s. Douglas W. and Elsa (Dohne) G.; m. Anne Garrison, Jan. 5, 1951; children: Robert D., Steven C., Christopher W., C. Linn, Elizabeth A. Cert. des etudes, U. Paris, 1946; AB, U. Pa., 1946; MA, Fletcher Sch. Law and Diplomacy, 1947, PhD, 1955. Fgn. service officer U.S. Fgn. Service, Sumatra and Hong Kong, 1947-52; internat. oil legislator Mobil Oil Co., N.Y.C., 1955; asst. prof. internat. relations Claremont (Calif.) Men's Coll., 1955-60; assoc. prof. Scripps Coll., Claremont, 1960-64, prof., 1967—; Fulbright prof. U. Munich, 1960-61. Author: The U.S. and Malaysia, 1969, Americans in Sumatra, 1960, America Interests in Sumatra, 1955, Altruistic Statecraft, 1986. Chmn. Coalition for Peace with Justice, Pomona Valley, Calif., 1985, 86; coordinator Interfaith Peace Ctr., Pomona Valley, 1986; sec. Interfaith Legis. Action, Pomona Valley, 1985-86; bd. dirs. Council of Chs., Pomona Valley, 1979—. Served to sgt. inf. U.S. Army, 1941-45, ETO. Fellow Asia Found., 1953; Fulbright Found., 1959, Danforth Found., 1963. Mem. Consortium on Peace Research and Edn., Conf. Peace Research in History, Internat. Peace Research Assn., UN Assn. (v.p. 1965—). Mem. Soc. of Friends. Interests: nonviolence, human rights. Office: Scripps Coll Dept History Claremont CA 91711

GOULD, MARTHA B., librarian; b. Claremont, N.H., Oct. 8, 1931. BA in Edn., U. Mich., 1953; MS in Library Sci., Simmons Coll., 1956; cert., U. Denver Library Sch. Community Analysis Research Inst., 1978. Childrens librarian N.Y. Pub. Library, 1956-58; adminstr. library services act of demonstration regional library project Pawhuska, Okla., 1958-59; cons. N.Mex. State Library, 1959-60; childrens librarian then sr. childrens librarian Los Angeles Pub. Library, 1960-72; acctg. dir. pub. srvices, reference librarian Nev. State Library, 1972-74; pub. services librarian Washoe County (Nev.) Library, 1974-79, asst. county librarian, from 1977, now county librarian. Contbr. articles to jours. Pres. United Jewish Appeal, 1981; bd. dirs. Temple Sinai, RSVP; trustee N. Nevadans for ERA. Recipient Nev. State Library Letterof Commendation, 1973, Washoe County Bd. Commrs. Resolution of Appreciation, 1978. Mem. ALA (bd. dirs. intellectual freedom round table 1977-79, intelledtual freedom com. 1979-83), Nev. Library Assn. (chmn. pub. info. com. 1972-73, internat. freedom com. 1975-78, govt. relations com. 1978-79, v.p., pres.-elect 1980, pres. 1981, Spl. Citation 1978). Office: Washoe Country LIbrary 301 S Center St PO Box 2151 Reno NV 89505 *

GOULD, MAXINE LUBOW, administrator, consultant; b. Bridgeton, N.J., Feb. 28, 1942; d. Louis A. and Bernice L. (Goldberg) Lubow; B.S., Temple U., 1962, J.D., 1968; m. Sam C. Gould, June 17, 1962 (div. Dec. 1984); children—Jack, Herman, David. Head resident dept. student personnel Temple U., 1962-66; dir., treas. Hilltop Interest Program, Inc., Los Angeles, 1973-74; law clk. law firms, Los Angeles, 1975-77; with Buffalo Resources Corp., Los Angeles, 1978-82, corp. sec., 1979-82; corp. sec., securities prin. Buffalo Securities Corp., Los Angeles, 1979-82; corp. sec. LaMaur Devel. Corp., Los Angeles, 1979-82; contracts analyst, land dept. Texaco Inc., Los Angeles, 1982-83; exec. dir. Sinai Temple, West Los Angeles, 1983-85; pres. Cutting Edge, Los Angeles, 1986; adminstr. law firm Robinson, Wolas & Diamant, Century City, 1986, acctg. firm Roth, Beckstein & Zaslow, Los Angeles, 1986-87. Mem. Roscomare Valley Assn. Edn. Com., Bel Air, Calif., 1975-76; subcom. chmn. Roscomare Rd. Sch. Citizens Adv. Council, Bel Air; active various community drives. Recipient Joseph B. Wagner Oratory award B'nai B'rith, 1959, Voice of Democracy award, 1958-59, award Commentator Club, 1959. Mem. ABA (law office econs. sect.), Los Angeles Bar Assn. (assoc., law office econs. sect.), Nat. Assn. Legal Adminstrs. (Beverly Hills chpt.), Nat. Assn. Female Execs. (network dir.), Nat. Assn. Law Firm Mktg. Adminstrs., Calif. Women Lawyers, Women in Bus., Calif. CPA Soc. (adminstr. com.), Nat. Assn. Synagogue Adminstrs., Am. Assn. Petroleum Landmen, Los Angeles Assn. Petroleum Landmen, Phi Alpha Theta, Alpha Lambda Delta. Jewish. Home: 2501 Roscomare Rd Bel Air CA 90077

GOULD, ROBERT WILLIAM, JR., software engineer; b. State College, Pa., Sept. 17, 1956; s. Robert W. and Marcia (Rodes) G.; m. Linda Flewellen, June 19, 1982. Student, U. Fla., 1982, BS in Engring., Computer, Info. Scis., 1982. Software specialist Digital Equipment Corp., Colorado Springs, Colo., 1982-84; pres. Contemporary Software Systems, Inc., Colorado Springs, 1984—.

GOULD, STANLEY FARRELL, physician, educator; b. Detroit, Jan. 27, 1949; m. Ann Marie Makowski, Aug. 16, 1980; children: Matthew Adam, Mark Andrew, Gregory Aaron. BS, U. Mich., 1970; PhD, Wayne State U., 1974, MD, 1975. Diplomate Am. Bd. Ob-Gyn. Intern U. Mich, Ann Arbor, 1975; intern Wayne State U., Detroit, 1976, resident in ob-gyn, 1975-79; asst. prof. ob-gyn and anatomy, dir. med. student edn. ob-gyn U. Colo. Health Sci. Ctr., Denver, 1979-85, assoc. prof., dir. ambulatory clinics in ob-gyn, 1985—; vis. asst. prof. biology Oakland U., Rochester, Mich., 1974-75; adj. asst. prof. anatomy Wayne State U., 1974-79; chief gynecologist VA Hosp., Denver, 1983—. Contbr. articles and revs. to profl. jours.; mem. editorial bd. Archives of Andrology, 1984—. Fellow Am. Coll. Ob-Gyns, ACS; mem. AAAS, Am. Fertility Soc., Am. Assn. Anatomists, Am. Soc. Cell Biology, Mich. Electron Microscopy Forum, Soc. Study Reprodn., Am.Coll. Ob-Gyn, Am. Soc. Andrology. Roman Catholic. Avocation: piano. Home: 8919 E Colorado Dr Denver CO 80231 Office: U Colo Health Scis Ctr Dept Ob-Gyn 4200 E 9th Ave B-198 Denver CO 80262

GOULD, STEVEN JAMES, chemistry educator; b. N.Y.C., Feb. 18, 1946; s. Robert T. and Ruth M. (Singer) G. BS, UCLA, 1966; PhD, MIT, 1970. Postdoctoral fellow Eidgenossische Technische Hochschule, Zurich, Switzerland, 1970-72; sr. research chemist Syva Research Inst., Palo Alto, Calif., 1972-74; asst. prof. pharmacology U. Conn., Storrs, 1974-80, assoc. prof. chemistry, 1980-82; assoc. prof. Oreg. State U., Corvallis, 1982-86, prof., 1986—; cons. ARCO, Kali Inc., 1978-80, Antivirals Inc., 1983—. Contbr. articles to profl. jours. Pres. Mid-Willamette Valley Jewish Community Ctr., Corvallis, 1985-87. Mem. Am. Chem Soc., Royal Soc. Chem. (Eng.), AAAS, Am. Soc. Pharmacognosy, Sigma Xi. Avocations: skiing, hiking, tennis, golf. Office: Oreg State U Dept Chem Corvallis OR 97331

GOULDEY, GLENN CHARLES, controls manufacturing company executive; b. N.Y.C., July 28, 1952; s. George Howard and Jeannette Ruth Williamson; m. Leslie Jeanne Ruth, Oct. 2, 1982; children: Jeremy Charles, Nicholas Glenn. B.S. in Bus., Trenton State Coll., 1976; postgrad. Portland State U., 1980; M.B.A., Rider Coll., 1981. Cert. in purchasing mgmt. Purchasing Mgrs. Assn. Sr. planner Eaton Corp., Flemington, N.J., 1975-77, pricing mgr., distbn., 1977-79, inventory control mgr., 1979-80, materials mgr., purchasing, Beaverton, Oreg., 1980-81, mfg. and materials mgr., 1981-83, mktg. and materials mgr., 1983-87; plant and gen. mgr., 1987—. Patentee in field. Mem. Am. Prodn. Inventory Control Soc. (cert. in prodn. and inventory control). Republican. Presbyterian. Home: 17688 NW Dogwood Ct Beaverton OR 97006 Office: Eaton Corp 13725 SW Millikan Way Beaverton OR 97005

GOULDING, MERRILL KEITH, consulting engineer; b. Erie, Pa., Jan. 21, 1933; s. Forest Clute and Felicita Clara (Johnson) G.; BS, UCLA, 1968, PhD, 1979; children: Merrill, Robert, Nida, Gina, Asst. to v.p. Internat. Controls Corp., 1963-69; chmn. bd. Village Verde Corp., 1963-64; pres. Merrill K. Goulding & Assocs., Inc., Los Angeles, 1974—; chief exec. officer Coin Cop Electronics Co., 1975—; bd. dirs. Mid City Travel Industry; cons. FAA, DOT, DNA. Bd. dirs. Rio Hondo Area Action Com., 1970; guiding counselor Inst. Cultural Affairs; past pres. Request Computer Users Group. Served with USMC, 1953. Registered profl. engr., N.Y., Calif. Mem. ASME, IEEE, AIAA, NSPE, Calif. Soc. Profl. Engrs., Am. Soc. Metals, Constrn. Specifications Inst., Soc. Material and Process Engrs., Vols. in Tech. Assistance, Mensa, Am. Legion, Blue and Gold Circle Alumni Assn. UCLA. Republican. Clubs: Shriners, Calif. Yacht. Address: PO Box 577 Glendale CA 91209

GOULDTHORPE, KENNETH ALFRED PERCIVAL, publisher; b. London, Jan. 7, 1928; s. Alfred Edward and Frances Elizabeth Finch (Callow) G.; came to U.S., 1951, naturalized, 1956; m. Judith Marion Cutts, Aug. 9, 1975; children: Amanda Frances, Timothy Graham Cutts. Student U. London, 1948-49, Bloomsbury Tech. Inst., 1949-50; diploma City and Guilds of London, 1949; student, Washington U., 1951-53. Staff photographer St. Louis Post-Dispatch, 1951-55, picture editor, 1955-57; nat. and fgn. corr. Life mag., Time, Inc., N.Y.C., 1957-65, regional editor Australia-New Zealand, 1966-68, editorial dir. Latin Am., 1969-70; editor Signature mag., N.Y.C., 1970-73; mng. editor Penthouse mag., N.Y.C., 1973-76, pub. cons., 1976-79; editor, exec. pub. Adventure Travel mag., Seattle, 1979-80; sr. ptnr. Pacific Pub. Assocs., Seattle, 1981-83; editor, pub. Washington mag., 1984—; v.p. Evergreen Pub. Co., 1984—; tchr. design, editorial techniques Parsons Sch. Design, N.Y.C.; lectr., mem. seminar faculty Writer's Digest. Served with Royal Navy, 1946-48. Decorated Naval Medal and bar; recipient awards of excellence Nat. Press Photographers Assn., AP and UP, 1951-57; certs. excellence, Am. Inst. Graphic Arts, 1971, 72, 73, Communication Arts, 1980, 81, 84; spl. award, N.Y. Soc. Publs. Designers, 1980. Mem. Regional Pubs. Assn. (v.p., pres., Best Typography award 1985), Western Publs. Assn. (Best Consumer Mag. award, Best Travel Mag. awards, 1980, Best Regional and State Mag. award 1985, 86, Best New Publ. award 1985, Best Column award 1985, Best Signed Essay 1986, Best Four-Color Layout 1985, Best Four Color Feature Design), City and Regional Mag. Assn. (William Allen White Bronze awards), Time/Life Alumni Soc., Sigma Delta Chi. Episcopalian. Nominated for Pulitzer Prize for coverage of Andrea Doria disaster, 1956; contbr. articles, photographs to nat. mags., books by Life mag. Home: 3049 NW Esplanade Seattle WA 98117 Office: 901 Lenora St Seattle WA 98121

GOULET, WILLIAM DAWSON, marketing professional; b. Hartford, Conn., Sept. 24, 1941; s. Henry J.K. and Elizabeth Bryne (Dawson) G. BA in English, Marietta Coll., 1963. Field service rep. Conn. Gen. Life Ins. Co., Hartford, 1963-65; sales promotion assoc. Phoenix Mut. Life Ins. Co., Hartford, 1965-69; dir. sales promotion Pacific Nat. Life Ins. Co., San Francisco, 1969-70; v.p. sales and mktg. E.F. Hutton Life Ins. Co., San Francisco, 1970-79; sr. v.p., fin. planning Prudential-Bache, San Francisco, 1979; v.p. GUMP's, San Francisco, 1980—; dean ins. faculty Life Ins. Industry Sch., Williamsburg, Va., 1974; mktg. cons. U. of the Pacific, Stockton, Calif., 1972-80. bd. dirs. Mus. Soc. San Francisco; v.p. bd. Friends of Recreation and Parks, 1986—; mem. adv. bd. The McLean Home, Simsbury, Conn., 1985—. Served to sgt. USAR, 1963-69. Recipient Lawrence award Life Advertisers Assn., Vancouver, B.C., Can., 1979, Disting. Alumni Lectr. award Marietta Coll., 1985. Mem. San Francisco Grand Prix Assn. (adv. bd. 1986—). Democrat. Roman Catholic. Avocations: gardening, travel. Home: PO Box 155 Ross CA 94957 Office: GUMP's 250 Post St San Francisco CA 94108

GOWER, MARK ALLEN, oil company executive; b. Denver, Dec. 20, 1953; s. Frank Herbert Jr. and Marie Patricia (Pedersen) G.; m. Helen Kathleen Dunn, Apr. 23, 1975; children—Jeffrey Bryan, Jill Elizabeth. Student Santa Barbara City Coll., 1972-74, U. Calif.-San Diego, 1974-75, Scripps Inst., 1974-75; B.S. in Geology, San Diego State U., 1977. Exploration geologist ECHO Oil Co., Casper, Wyo., 1977-80; exploration geologist Gower Oil Co. Denver, 1980-81, exploration mgr., pres., 1981—; owner Mark Gower Oil Properties, Denver, 1983—; v.p. Garske Energy Corp., Denver, 1984—. Mem. Wyo. Geol. Assn., Am. Assn. Petroleum Geologists, Am. Inst. Profl. Geologists, Rocky Mountain Oil and Gas Assn., Internat. Oceanographic Found. Republican. Roman Catholic. Clubs: Metropolitan (founding mem. 1983-84) (Englewood, Colo.); Denver Petroleum, Mt. Vernon Country, Las Verdes Golf (Denver). Office: Gower Oil Co 5600 S Quebec Suite 315-A Englewood CO 80111

GOYER, ROBERT STANTON, communication educator; b. Kokomo, Ind., Oct. 7, 1923; s. Clarence V. and Genevieve M. (Sober) G.; m. Patricia Ann Stutz, Aug. 12, 1950; children—Karen, Susan, Linda, Amy. B.A., DePauw U., 1948; M.A., Miami U., Oxford, Ohio, 1950; Ph.D., Ohio State U., 1955. Instr. Miami U., Oxford, 1949-51; instr., then asst. prof. Ohio State U., Columbus, 1955-58; research assoc., research cons. research found. Ohio State U., 1956-63; from asst. to assoc. to prof. Purdue U., Lafayette, Ind., 1958-66; prof. Ohio U., Athens, 1966-81; dir. ctr. communications studies Ohio U., 1966-74, 79-81, assoc. dean grad. coll., 1978, dean grad. coll., acting dir. research, 1979, acting assoc. provost grad. and research programs, 1979; prof., chmn. dept. communication Ariz. State U., Tempe, 1981—; cons. in field. Author books; contbr. articles to profl. jours. Served to 1st lt. U.S. Army, 1943-46, 52-53. Decorated Bronze Star. Fellow Internat. Communication Assn. (past pres.), AAAS; mem. Am. Psychol. Assn., Acad. Mgmt., Speech Communication Assn. Presbyterian. Home: 517 W Summit Pl Chandler AZ 85224 Office: Dept Communication Ariz State U Tempe AZ 85287

GRAB, LAWRENCE ANDRE, bioorganic chemist; b. Paris, Aug. 15, 1957; s. Ernest Oscar and Francoise Odett (Scomogué) G. BS, Fordham U., 1979; PhD, Brown U., 1984. Postdoctoral fellow U. Calif., San Francisco, 1984—. Contbr. articles to profl. jours. Recipient Am. Inst. Chemists award, Am. Inst. of Chemists, 1979. Mem. Am. Chem. Soc. Avocations: squash, softball. Home: 1721 Kirkham St San Francisco CA 94122 Office: U Calif Dept Pharm Chem San Francisco CA 94143

GRABARZ, DONALD FRANCIS, health care industry consultant; b. Jersey City, Sept. 18, 1841; s. Joseph and Frances (Zotynia) G.; m. Joan Isoldi, Aug. 13, 1966; children: Christine, Robert, Danielle. BPharm, St. Johns U., N.Y.C., 1964. Lic. pharmacist, N.Y., Vt. Dir. qualtiy control and assurance Johnson and Johnson Co., New Brunswick, N.J., 1965-72; asst. dir. regulatory affairs and quality assurance Becton Dickinson, Franklin Lakes, N.J., 1972-80; dir. regulatory affairs, quality assurance C.R. Bard Inc., Murray Hill, N.J., 1980-85; v.p. regulatory affairs, qualtiy assurance Symbion Inc., Salt Lake City, 1985-86; cons. DFG & Assocs., Salt Lake City, 1986—. Bd. dirs. v.p., asst. treas. Am. Lung Assn., N.J., 1972-75; chmn. Drug Edn., DuPage County, Ill., 1968. Mem. Health Industry Mfg. Assn. (chmn. Legal and Regulatory commn. 1983), Regulatory Affairs Profl. Soc., Am. Soc. Quality Control, Am. Mfr. Med. Instrumentation Assn., Am. Pharm. Assn. Avocations: soccer, tennis, baseball.

GRACE, EDWARD EVERETT, mathematics educator; b. Gulfport, Miss., Apr. 15, 1927; s. Herbert Landrum and Florence Estell (Kennedy) G.; m. Joan Marie Combs, Dec. 26, 1954; children: Geoffrey Robert, Elizabeth Ann, David Scott. BS, U. N.C., 1951, PhD, 1956. Asst. prof. Emory U., Atlanta, 1956-62; vis. assoc. prof. U. Ga., Athens, 1962-63; prof. math. Ariz. State U., Tempe, 1963—. Editor: Arizona State University Topology Conference, 1968; contbr. articles to profl. jours. Served with USN, 1945-46. Sci. Faculty fellow NSF, 1961-62. Mem. AAAS, AAUP, Am. Math. Soc., Math. Assn. Am., Sigma Xi. Democrat. Home: 1119 E Broadmor Dr Tempe AZ 85282 Office: Ariz State U Dept Math Tempe AZ 85287

GRACE, GEORGE EDWIN, market research executive, consultant; b. Montgomery, Ala., May 2, 1938; s. George Edwin and Mary Ruth (Head) G. B.A., Tulane U., 1960. Systems engr. IBM Corp., New Orleans, 1963-70; mgr. software mktg. Dynamic Computer Services, Houston, 1970-71; dir. computer services Ochsner Med. Found., New Orleans, 1971-74; pres. The Research Ctr., Torrance, Calif., 1974-75; pres., owner Grace Market Research, Los Angeles, 1975—; dir. Star World Prodns., Los Angeles; cons. in field. Author screenplay (with others) Amigoes, 1981. Mem. state com. McGovern presdl. campaign, New Orleans, 1972; created computer based donor info. system Jerry Brown for U.S. Senate, Los Angeles, 1982. Democrat. Office: Grace Market Research Inc 3902 Wilshire Blvd Los Angeles CA 90010

GRACE, JOHN WILLIAM, elec. co. exec.; b. Swissville, Pa., May 29, 1921; s. Joseph and Ruth Margaret (Bailey) G.; student Am. TV Inst. Tech., 1950; BEE, Drexel U., 1960; m. Ruth Delores Schroeder, Nov. 25, 1950; children: Martha, Joan, Nancy, John William. Technician missiles and surface radar div. RCA, Moorestown, N.J., 1950-56, design engr., 1956-60, project engr., 1960-66; mgr. engring. and sci. exec. EG & G, Inc., Las Vegas, Nev., 1966-73, mgr. bus. devel. operational test and evaluation, Albuquerque, 1973-77; engring. mgr. Instrumentation div., Idaho Falls, Idaho, 1977-79, mgr. systems project office, 1979, mgr. instrumentation program office, 1979-82, mgr. engring. spl. products div., 1982-84, mgr. tech. resources, 1984—. Active Boy Scouts Am., 1969-71. Served with USNR, 1941-45. Mem. IEEE, Instrument Soc. Am. (dir. sci. instrumentation and research div.), Assn. Old Crows, Am. Legion (post adj. vice comdr. 1950). Episcopalian (pres. couples retreat 1969-70). Patentee contradirectional waveguide coupler. Home: 2900 S Valley View 154 Las Vegas NV 89102 Office: EG&G Spl Projects Div 2755E Desert Inn Las Vegas NV 89121

GRACE, LINDA BRALEY, interior designer; b. Houston, Mar. 27, 1945; d. Ralph Stanley and Beverly (Sparks) Braley; m. Thomas Gladson Grace, Mar. 29, 1969; children: Thomas Jonathan, Brian Braley. AA, Stephens Coll., 1965; student, Tulane U., 1965-68, U. Tex., 1968-69. V.p. sales Braley Travel, Bryan, Tex., 1969-70, sales rep., 1970-72; prin. Linda Grace Interiors, Albuquerque, 1977—, Grace Investments, Albuquerque, 1985—, Young at Heart Gallery, Albuquerque, 1985—. Author (booklet) Coming to Terms with Antiques, 1980. Chmn. com. N.Mex. Symphony Bd., Albuquerque, 1983—; 2d v.p. N.Mex. Symphony Guild Exec. Bd., Albuquerque, 1982-83; chmn. bd. dirs. March of Dimes Gourmet Gala, Albuquerque, 1984; mem. Albuquerque Med. Aux. Bd., 1979-80; bd. dirs. N.Mex. Symphony. Episcopalian. Avocations: skiing, needlepoint, reading, investing. Office: 8301 Spain NE Albuquerque NM 87111

GRACE-CHARRY, LORRAINE LOUISE, travel company executive, educator; b. N.Y.C., Nov. 14, 1950; d. Oliver Russell and Lorraine (Graves) Grace; married, 1984. BA, Antioch U. West, 1976; MA in Psychology, Sonoma State Coll., 1979. Therapist, group leader San Francisco, 1969-79, wilderness expdn. leader, cross cultural exchange leader, 1976—; founder, bd. dirs. Sunrise Ctr. Inc., San Francisco, 1976—; founder, owner Return to the Earth Inc., San Francisco, 1980—; therapist, group leader Haiku, Hawaii, 1983—. Mem. Women's Found., Friends of Right Livelihood; bd. dirs. Threshold Found. Mem. Air Travel Assn., Internat. Assn. Travel Agts., Pacific Cruise Conf. Unitarian. Office: Star Rt One Box 161 Haiku HI 96708

GRACIDA, JOAQUIN CHAUSSEE, marine corps officer, information systems specialist; b. Mexico City, June 14, 1940; came to U.S., 1958, naturalized, 1962; s. Joaquin O. and Esperanza (Chaussee) G.; m. Ann Marie Smith, May 11, 1963; children: Joaquin Gerard, Leon Edward. BS in Math., U. Idaho, 1966; MA in Counseling, Pepperdine U., 1976; MS in Computer Sci., Naval Postgrad. Sch., 1978. Enlisted USMC, 1958, advanced through grades to col., 1987; programming analyst, hdqrs. USMC, Washington, 1978-81; sr. analyst, fin. ctr. USMC, Kansas City, Mo., 1981-83; dep. dir. Regional Automated Services Ctr. USMC, Camp Pendleton, Calif., 1983-86, dir., 1986—; instr. data processing Johnson County (Kans.) Community Coll., 1981-83, Miracosta Coll., Oceanside, Calif., 1983-84. Mem. Cardiff (Calif.) Town Council, 1986-87. Mem. Data Processing Mgmt. Assn. Republican. Roman Catholic. Lodge: Elks. Home: 1618 Falcon Hill Ct Cardiff-by-the-Sea CA 92007 Office: Regional Automated Services Ctr Camp Pendleton CA 92055

GRADIE, JONATHAN CAREY, planetary scientist; b. Putnam, Conn., June 20, 1951; s. Robert Richmond and Avis Leona (Gregg) G.; m. Nancy Hunter Adams, Oct. 20, 1977; 1 child, Hunter Carey Adams. BS, U. Ariz., 1973, PhD, 1978. Research scientist Cornell U., Ithaca, N.Y., 1978-84; planetary scientist U. Hawaii, Honolulu, 1984—. Contbr. sci. articles and abstracts to profl. publs. Asteroid named in honor, 1987. Mem. AAAS, Am. Astron. Soc. (div. planetary scis.), Am. Geophys. Union, Internat. Astron. Union. Office: Hawaii Inst Geophysics Planetary Geoscis Div 2525 Correa Rd Honolulu HI 96822

GRADY, JOAN BUTTERWORTH, school administrator; b. N.Y.C., May 4, 1929; d. Roderick Gerard and Pearl (Levy) Butterworth; m. George Edward Grady, Nov. 24, 1954; children: Alicia Grady Sukle, Glen Andrew. BA, CUNY, 1951; MA, Columbia U., 1953; PhD, U. Colo., 1977. Cert. elem. sch. prin., Colo., secondary sch. prin., Colo., elem. sch. supt., Colo., secondary sch. supt., Colo. Adminstrv. asst. St. Mary's Acad., Englewood, Colo., 1963-75; from asst. prin. to prin. Cherry Creek Pub. Schs., Englewood, 1975—; cons. Coll. Bd., Princeton, N.J., 1970-80. Contbr. articles to profl jours. Vol. ARC, Denver, 1951—; Bd. dirs. Mile-Hi council Girl Scouts U.S., Denver, 1980-83. Fulbright scholar Italy, 1986. Fellow Inst. Devel Ednl. Activities (Disting. Educator 1983, 84, 85); mem. Nat. Assn. Secondary Sch. Prins. (Disting. Service 1980), Assn. Supervision and Curriculum Devel., Nat. Middle Sch. Assn., Aurora Stamp Club, Aurora Geneal. Soc., Phi Delta Kappa. Avocations: travel, genealogy, philately.

GRADY, WILLIAM G. (BING), banker; b. Cambridge, Mass., Nov. 22, 1932; m. Carmoline A. Annicelli. B.B.A., U. N.Mex., 1955, M.A. in Econs., 1959. With Sunwest Bank Albuquerque, N.A., 1951—, trust investment officer, 1961-72, chief investment officer, 1972-78, pres., 1978—; chmn. bd. Sunwest Bank of Sandoval County. Past pres. N.Mex. Symphony Orch.; bd. dirs., v.p. Albuquerque Econ. Devel., Inc., N.Mex. Bus. Devel. Corp.; mem. exec. com. Albuquerque Ctr., Inc.; past mem. bd. dirs. United Way, Albuquerque. Mem. Greater Albuquerque C. of C. (past pres.), N.Mex. Bankers Assn. (past bd. dirs.). Avocations: reading; singing; golf. Home: 14 Link NW Albuquerque NM 87120 Office: Sunwest Bank Albuquerque NA PO Box 1344 Albuquerque NM 87103

GRAF, ERVIN DONALD, municipal administrator; b. Crow Rock, Mont., Mar. 9, 1930; s. Emanuel and Lydia (Bitz) G.; m. Carolyn Sue Robinson, Mar. 15, 1956 (div. 1958); m. Eleanor Mahlein, Apr. 13, 1959; children: Debra, Belinda, Corrina, Melanie, Ervin Jr. Enlisted U.S. Army, 1948, ret., 1972; with office and maintenance staff Greenfields Irrigation Dist., Fairfield, Mont., 1972-77, sec. to Bd. Commrs., 1977—. Mem. Am. Legion. Democrat. Lutheran. Avocations: bowling, coin collecting, fishing, camping. Home: 211 6th St N Fairfield MT 59436 Office: Greenfields Irrigation Dist Central Ave W Fairfield MT 59436

GRAF, KARL-HEINZ GUENTER, electronics company executive, consultant; b. Vienna, Austria, Dec. 8, 1941; came to U.S., 1954, naturalized, 1960; s. Ignaz Gunter Graf and Hildegard (Kuhfusz) Lutz; m. Edith Martha Guddat, Feb. 28, 1969 (div. Jan. 1986); children: Stephen, Thomas, Monika. Student, Colo. State U., 1961. Communications specialist AT&T Long Lines, Tucson, 1961-63; communications engr. Herman Kaets TS Co, Frankfurt, Germany, 1968-72; customer service rep. Magnavox System Inc., Denver, 1972-73; customer service specialist 3M BPSI, Denver, 1973-74; field engr. Rapicom, Denver, 1974-84; advanced product specialist Rapicom/Ricoh Corp., Denver, 1984-85; internat. tech. mgr. mgr. Ricoh Corp., Denver, 1985—; communication cons., Denver, 1972—; product tchr. Rapicom/Ricoh, Worldwide, 1978—. Developer product test equipment Protocol Decoder, 1983. Exec. officer CAP, Tucson, 1963; active PTA, Denver, 1984. Served with U.S. Army, 1964-68. Recipient Disting. Service award Rapicom Inc., 1983. Mem. Denver Amateur Computer Soc., Amateur Radio Soc., Denver Kaypro Assn. (bd. dirs. 1986-87). Republican. Home: PO Box 19388 1356 S Tennyson St Denver CO 80219 Office: Ricoh Corp PO Box 19388 Denver CO 80219

GRAF, OTTO WALTER, JR., retired entomologist, acarologist, biologist, educator; b. San Francisco, May 26, 1925; s. Otto Walter and and Mildred Ilyne (Morrison) G.; m. Anne Marie Minaker, Mar. 7, 1953; children—Catherine, David, Paul, Lloyd, John, Walter, Matthew, Robert. A.B., San Francisco State Coll., 1952; M.A., U. San Francisco, 1979; postgrad. Stanford U., Duke U., U. Calif.-Berkeley, Calif. State U.-Hayward. Secondary teaching credential, Calif. Profl. asst. San Francisco State Coll., 1950-51; film librarian, supr. student sect. Calif. Acad. Scis., 1954-62; instr. U. Calif.-Berkeley, 1956-61, Washington High Sch., Fremont, Calif. 1955-84. Active Boy Scouts Am., Republican Party. Served with USN, 1943-46; to 1st lt., U.S. Army, 1951-54. Decorated Pacific Theatre ribbon, Am. Theatre ribbon, Korean ribbon, 2 Presidential Unit citations, Presidential citation, Korean Merit citation; recipient Silver Beaver award, Boy Scouts Am., 1971; Outstanding Secondary Tchr. award, 1974; NSF grantee; Biol. Scis. Curriculum Studies grantee. Mem. Pan Pacific Entomol. Soc., Nat. Sci. Tchrs. Assn., Korean War Vets. Assn., Nat. Assn. Biology Tchrs., E. Africa Wild Life Soc., Internat. Wildlife Fedn., Nat. Wildlife Fedn., VFW, Am. Legion. Roman Catholic. Author: Key to the Mosquitos of Korea, 1951, Flies of Medical and Veternary Importance of Japan & Korea, 1952; Nature Games for the Secondary School, 1979; designed trap for live mice in Korea. Home: 5151 Tenaya Ave Newark CA 94560-2653

GRAFE, WARREN BLAIR, television executive; b. N.Y.C., June 22, 1954; s. Warren Edward and Maree Lee (Ahn) G.; m. Pamela Arden Rearick, Mar. 8, 1980 (div. 1982). Student Kendall Coll., 1974-75, U. Wis.-Platteville, 1975-76; B.A., Ind. U., 1979. Part-time announcer sta. WTTS-WGTC, Bloomington, Ind., 1978-79, sales rep., sta. WGTC-FM, 1979-80, account exec., coop. coordinator, 1980-84; nat. sales rep. Sta. WTTS-WGTC, 1984; account exec. Sta. KLFF-KMZK, Phoenix, 1985, Rita Sanders Advt. and Pub. Relations Agy., Inc., 1985, Times Mirror Cable TV Dimension Media Services (formerly Am. Cable TV), 1985—. Recipient Nat. Sales award Cable Advt. Bur., 1986. Home: 2146 W Isabella Ave #241 Mesa AZ 85202 Office: Dimension Media Services 2331 W Royal Palm Rd #111-112 Phoenix AZ 85021

GRAFF, EVERETT EDWARD, hospital official; b. Lincoln, Nebr., Sept. 23, 1925; s. John Henry and Juliana (Gloucer) G.; m. Betty Louise Jamesson, July 20, 1951; children—Gretchen Juliana, Valerie Lyn Graff Flannery, Courtney Jon Graff. Grad., Gen. Motors Inst. Tech., 1943; student U. Denver, 1947; B.A. summa cum laude, Park Coll., 1975; M.A., Central Mich. U., 1980. City clk., treas. City of York (Nebr.), 1949-51; prin. and sr. acct. W.D. Messenger & Co., C.P.A.s, 1951-53, 55-57; tax. acct. No. Natural Gas, 1953-55; controller Refinite Corp., 1957-59; asst. adminstr. adminstrv. services Nebr. Meth. Hosp., Omaha, 1959-70; chief fin. officer North Kansas City (Mo.) Meml. Hosp., 1971-76; asst. adminstr. for fin. St. Mary's Hosp. and Health Center, Tucson, 1976-78; asst. exec. dir. fin. Lawrence (Kans.) Meml. Hosp., 1978-80; asst. exec. dir. adminstrn. services Riverside (Calif.) Community Hosp and Med. Center, 1980-83; v.p. fin., treas. St. Joseph's Hosp. of Orange (Calif.), 1983; corp. v.p. fin., Hillcrest Med. Ctr., Tulsa, 1983—; mem. Tulsa Med. Edn. Found.; treas. Hillcrest Servico Co., Hillcrest, Hillcrest Mobile Diagnostics and Mammography, Slimcrest, Inc., East Tulsa Med. Group, Healthcrest Care Group, Hillcrest Fin. Services; dir. Trujillo Water Co., Riverside; bd. dirs. Hosp. Casualty Co., Oklahoma City Mem. Riverside Pub. Utilities Commn.; bd. dirs. Riverside chpt. ARC. Served with USAAF, 1946-47. Mem. Am. Coll. Hosp. Adminstrs., Fin. Execs. Inst., Hosp. Fin. Mgmt. Assn. (past pres. Nebr. chpt., past mem. bd. dirs. Nebr. and Kansas City chpts., nat. dir. 1966-69, dir. So. Calif. chpt. 1981—, former mem. nat. inst. com., nominating com., past chmn. nat. data processing com., William G. Follmar Individual Achievement award 1968, Robert H. Reeves award 1974), Sigma Iota Epsilon. Republican. Presbyterian. Contbr. articles to profl. publs. Office: St Joseph's Hospital 1100 W Stewart Dr Orange CA 92667

GRAFF, LLOYD LEE, advertising agency executive, writer, broadcast journalist; b. Dalton, Nebr., June 2, 1933; s. Raymond August and Alice Clara (Martin) G.; m. Elizabeth E. Wray, May 1, 1954; children—Sharon Lee Graff Crable, Steven Wray, Martin Joseph, Michael Edward. B.A. in Journalism and Drama, U. Nebr., 1956. Writer, performer, producer, dir. radio and TV sta., Iowa and Nebr., 1956-60; writer, account exec., gen. mgr. Bozell & Jacobs, Inc., Sioux City and Omaha, 1960-69; account supr. Standard Oil-McCann Eickson, Inc., San Francisco, 1969-75; dir. corp. communications Barnes Hind, div. Revlon, Inc., Sunnyvale, Calif., 1975-82; pres., owner Graff Advt., Inc., Palo Alto, Calif., 1982—; direct distbr. Amway Corp. Active Iowa Democratic Campaign Com., 1968-69, Pres.'s Council Youth Opportunity, 1968; chmn. first day of issue Post Office Dept., 1966; mem. mayor's com. on communications, Sioux City, 1964-68; cub master, com. chmn. Boy Scouts Am., 1965-75. Served with U.S. Army, 1954-56. Recipient spl. recognition Pres.'s Council on Youth Opportunity, 1968. Mem. Nat. Agrl. Mktg. Assn. (pres. 1970, 72), Med. Mktg. Assn. (v.p. 1978-79), Med. Writers Assn. Democrat. Roman Catholic. Club: KC (past grand knight). Home: 1478 Valcartier Dr Sunnyvale CA 94087 Office: Graff Advt Inc 4151 Middlefield Rd Suite 209 Palo Alto CA 94303

GRAFIUS, GUY ALBERT BOYER, research engineer; b. Shamokin, Pa., Feb. 4, 1933; s. Guy Elliott and Melba (Boyer) G.; m. Ruth Marian Ressler, Aug. 30, 1958; children: I. Kurt Ressler, Guy William. BS, U.S. Naval Acad., 1955. Commd. ensign USN, 1955, advanced through grades to capt., 1976, ret., 1985; commdg. officer USS Mauna Kea USN, Concord, Calif., 1971-72; commdg. officer USS Camden USN, Bremerton, Wash., 1977-80; commdg. officer Naval Sta. USN, Seattle, 1982-85; sr. engr. Sci. and Engring. Assocs., Inc., Seattle, 1985—. Decorated Legion of Merit with gold V, 2 Bronze Stars. Mem. IEEE, U.S. Naval Acad. Alumni Assn. (trustee 1985), U.S. Naval Submarine League, U.S. Naval Inst. Republican. Presbyterian. Club: Seattle Yacht. Avocations: boating, fly fishing. Home: 4408 170th Ave SE Issaquah WA 98027-9069 Office: Sci and Engring Assocs Inc 701 Dexter Ave N Suite 400 Seattle WA 98109

GRAHAM, BILL, producer; b. Berlin, Germany, Jan. 8, 1931; came to U.S., 1941, naturalized, 1953; s. Jacob and Frieda (Zess) Grajonca; m. Bonnie McLean, June 1967 (div. 1969); 1 son, David. B.A. in Bus. Adminstrn, City Coll. N.Y., 1955. Statistician Pace Motor Trucking Co., from 1955; paymaster Guy F. Atkinson Constructors; office mgr. Allis-Chalmers Mfg. Co., to 1965. Concert promoter producer/mgr. maj. rock music artists, Santana, Ronnie Montrose, Eddie Money, Van Morrison; creator, Fillmore Auditoriums East, N.Y.C., 1968-71, and West, San Francisco, 1965-71, pres. FM Prodns., San Francisco, 1966—, Bill Graham Presents, San Francisco, 1976—, Bill Graham Mgmt., 1976—, Wolfgang Records, San Francisco, 1976—; producer outdoor musical events including, Watkins Glen, N.Y., 1974, country-wide tours, Bob Dylan, Crosby, Stills, Nash and Young and George Harrison and Rolling Stones, 1975, 30 maj. outdoor concerts at, Oakland (Calif.) Stadium, 1974-79; originator: Bill Graham's World of Plants, 1976, 77; actor, producer: concert for film A Star Is Born, 1976; actor: Apocalypse Now, Cotton Club; concert prodn. cons. Organizer, producer maj. benefit concerts for causes including, Center for Self-Determination, 1975, Save Our Cities, 1976, San Francisco Sch. Dist., 1976, Live Aid, Amnesty Internat.; (commendation of excellence Broadcast Music Inc. 1975, St. Francis of Assisi award City of San Francisco 1975, Billboard Conv. award as promoter of the Year 1975, 76, 77, others.). Served with U.S. Army, 1951-53. Decorated Bronze Star medal, Purple Heart.; Recipient B'nai B'rith Lodge award, 1973. Office: 260 Fifth St San Francisco CA 94103

GRAHAM, CELESTE MARILYN GOTCHER, business executive; b. Santa Monica, Calif., July 12, 1937; d. Leslie Louis and Winnie Viola (Miller) Gotcher; B.A. in Sociology, Calif. State U., Los Angeles, 1974; divorced; children—Leslie Dawn, Cindy Celeste, Wendy Ione, Linda Marie. Propr., C. Graham Graphics, Santa Monica, 1977—; editor Illumination mag., 1979—; adminstrv. dir. Inst. Psycho-Dynamics, Inc., Fla., 1975—; pres. Hawk Diversified; dir. Celestial Visions Software Pub. Corp.; instr. Fla. Dept. Recreation, 1976-77; dir. info. mgmt. and graphics U. So. Calif. Sch. Music, 1983-86; pres., Coll. Fin. Aid Found. Author: Layman's Guide to Enlightenment, or Cosmic Consciousness on the American Plan, 1980; Residential Treatment System for the Chronically Mentally Ill, 1981; The Utilization of Graying America, 1981; (fiction) Love in High Places, 1986, Dos Does It, 1987; co-author: American Square Dancing, 1961. Originator techniques for meditation. Home and Office: 3175 S Hoover St 513 Los Angeles CA 90007

GRAHAM, DENIS DAVID, vocational education specialist, marriage and family counselor; b. Santa Rosa, Calif., Oct. 21, 1941; s. Elbert Eldon and Mildred Bethana (Dyson) G.; m. Margaret Katherine Coughlan, Aug. 31, 1968; children—Kathleen Ann, Todd Cameron. B.S. in Edn., U. Nev., 1964, M.Ed., 1973, M.A., 1982. Cert. for ednl. personnel; lic. marriage and family counselor, Nev.; nat. cert. counselor Nat. Bd. for Cert. Counselors. Tchr. vocat. bus. edn. Earl Wooster High Sch., Reno, 1964-66, chmn. dept. bus. edn., 1966-67; state supr. bus. and office edn. Nev. Dept. Edn., Carson City, 1967-70, adminstr. vocat. edn. field services, 1970-74, asst. dir., 1974-78, vocat. edn. cons., 1978-85; vocat. edn. curriculum specialist Washoe County Sch. Dist., Reno, 1985—; marriage and family counselor Severance & Assocs., Carson City, 1983-85, Mountain Psychiat. Assocs., 1985—; mem. tng. and youth employment council S.W. Regional Lab. for Ednl. Research and Devel., Los Alamitos, Calif., 1982, mem. career edn. council, 1980-81. Editor Council of Chief State Sch. Officers' Report: Staffing the Nation's Schools: A National Emergency, 1984. Contbr. articles to profl. jours. Mem. Gov.'s Crime Prevention Com., Carson City, 1979-83, Atty. Gen.'s Anti-Shoplifting Com., Carson City, 1974-78, Gov.'s Devel. Disabilities Planning Council, Carson City, 1977-79. Recipient award for service Bus. Edn. Assn. of No. Nev., 1973; Service award YMCA, 1962, 63. Mem. Am. Vocat. Assn., Nat Assn Vocat. Edn. Spl. Needs Personnel (Outstanding Service award region V 1982), Am. Assn. for Counseling and Devel., Am. Mental Health Counselors Assn., U. Nev. Reno Alumni Assn. (exec. com. 1971-75), Phi Delta Kappa, Phi Kappa Phi. Democrat. Presbyterian. Office: 425 E 9th St Reno NV 89520

GRAHAM, DOUGLAS JOHN, museum administrator, poet, banker; b. Dunfermline, Scotland, July 6, 1934; came to U.S., 1959, naturalized, 1965; s. Hugh Merton and Ellen Charlotte (Podmaniczky) G.; children: Robert, Christopher, Anabel, Isis. BA, N.Y. Inst. Fin., 1961. Ptnr. Mitchell, Hutchins & Co., N.Y.C., William D. Witter Inc., N.Y.C., 1959-72; founder, dir. The Turner Mus., Denver, 1973—; pres. Internat. Bank Holdings Ltd., Denver, 1979—. Life mem. St. Andrew's Soc. Colo. Served with M.I., Brit. Army, 1952-59. Mem. Unity Ch. Office: The Turner Mus 773 Downing Denver CO 80218

GRAHAM, JON FREDRICK, neurosurgeon, hospital administrator; b. Wahiawa, Hawaii, Nov. 15, 1952; s. Neff William and Jane Ellen (Wilder) G. BS, Mich. State U., 1974; MD, Wayne State U., 1978. Diplomate Nat. Bd. Med. Examiners, Am. Bd. Neurol. Surgery; lic. physician, Md., Hawaii. Commd. 2d lt. U.S. Army, 1975, advanced through grades to maj., 1984; intern Walter Reed Army Med. Ctr. U.S. Army, Washington, 1978-79, resident physician Walter Reed Army Med. Ctr., 1979-84; asst. chief neurosurgery Tripler Army Med. Ctr. U.S. Army, Honolulu, 1984-86, chief dept. neurosurgery Tripler Army Med. Ctr., 1986—; instr. surgery U. Hawaii, Honolulu, 1985—; clin. asst. prof. surgery F. Edward Hebert Sch. Medicine, Bethesda, Md., 1986—. Mem. AAAS, AMA, Congress Neurol. Surgeons, Alpha Omega Alpha. Republican. Presbyterian. Club: Mililani (Hawaii) Orchid. Avocations: golf, swimming, growing orchids. Office: Tripler Army Med Ctr Chief Neurosurgery Services Honolulu HI 96859-5000

GRAHAM, LOIS LAVERNE, academic administrator, educator; b. Muscogee, Okla., Jan. 19, 1933; d. Louis G. and Bonnie (Hill) Reed; children: Harold Gibson, Kathryn Ann Jayson. BA in English, Calif. State U., Sacramento, 1974, M in Pub. Adminstrn., 1978. Cert. community coll., standard elem. tchr., Calif.; lic. nurse. Nurse various hosps., San Diego, 1953-63; adminstrv. asst. Joseph Bonnheim Sch., Sacramento, 1963-74; tchr., adminstr. Creative Careers, Sacramento, 1974-78; tchr. Mark Hopkins Elem. Sch., Sacramento, 1978-84; secondary tchr. Fern Bacon Jr. High, Sacramento, 1984—; instr. Los Rios Community Coll., Sacramento, 1978-85; bd. dirs. Ynobe Internat., Sacramento, 1984—; participant in state tchr. roundtable, Sacramento, 1983—; appointed by Gov. Calif. to Fair Employment and Housing Commn., 1984—. Contbr. articles to profl. jours. Named Tchr. of Yr. Sacramento Sch. Dist. 1984-85, Outstanding Educator Mexican Am., 1984-85; Calif. Tchr. grantee State/Sch. Dist., 1985-86, Outstanding Woman award YWCA, 1985. Mem. Black Educators (pres. 1984—, named Outstanding Educator), River City Rep. Assembly, sec., bd. dirs. 1985-86, Outstanding Work), AAUW (bd. dirs. 1983-84, 86—, pres. Capitol br. 1986—, multi-cultural award), Sacramento City Tchrs. Assn. (chmn., pub. adminstrn., bd. dirs. 1980-84, Mentor tchr. 1985-86, Spl. Media award Outstanding Work), Delta Sigma Theta. Unitarian. Home: 7408 Toulon Ln Sacramento CA 95828

GRAHAM, ROGER JOHN, photography and journalism educator; b. Phila., Feb. 16; s. William K. and Peggy E. (Owens) G.; divorced; children; John Roger, Robb Curt. AA, Los Angeles Valley Coll., 1961; BA, Calif. State U., Fresno, 1962, MA, 1967; postgrad, UCLA, 1976. Tchr. Riverdale (Calif.) Sch., 1963, Raisin City (Calif.) Sch., 1964; tchr., counselor Calif. State Prison, Jamestown, 1966; tchr. trainer UCLA's Western Ctr., 1967; chmn. media arts dept. Los Angeles Valley Coll., Van Nuys, Calif., 1968—; vis. prof. Pepperdine U., Malibu, Calif., 1976, Calif. Luth. Coll., Thousand Oaks, 1973. Author: Observations on the Mass Media, 1976, (jour) Jr. Coll. Jour., 1972; photo illustrator: The San Fernando Valley, 1980; contbr. articles to profl. jours.; display advertiser Turlock (Calif.) jour., 1962, Fresno Guide, 1963. Mem. Hayden's Com. for Schs., Santa Monica, Calif., 1984, YMCA, Pacific Palisades, Calif. Served with USN, 1957. NEH scholar 1981; recipient Mayor's Outstanding Citizen award Los Angeles Mayor's Office, 1974, Extraordinary Service award UCLA, 1971; named one of Outstanding Young Men Am., 1971. Mem. Community coll. Journalism Assn. (nat. pres. 1978—, Nat. Dedication Journalsim award 1972-76), Journalism Assn. Community Colls. (pres. Calif. sect. 1972—), Los Angeles Prof's. Club, Am. Legion (sgt. at arms 1986—), Sigma Delta Xi, Phi Delta Kappa, Pi Lambda Theta. Democrat. Avocation: hiking. Home: 438 E Rustic Rd Santa Monica CA 90402 Office: Los Angeles Valley Coll 5800 Fulton Ave Van Nuys CA 91401

GRAHAM, STEPHEN MICHAEL, lawyer; b. Houston, May 1, 1951; s. Frederick Mitchell and Lillian Louise (Miller) G.; m. Joanne Marie Sealock, Aug. 24, 1974; children: Aimee Elizabeth, Joseph Sealock, Jessica Anne. BS, Iowa State U., 1973; JD, Yale U., 1976. Bar: Wash. 1977. Assoc. Perkins Coie, Seattle, 1976-83, ptnr., 1983—. Bd. dirs. Wash. Spl. Olympics, Seattle, 1979-83, pres., 1983; mem. Seattle Bd. Ethics, 1982—, chmn., 1983-87, Seattle Fair Campaign Practices Commn., 1982—; trustee Cornish Coll. of the Arts, 1986—, Epiphany Sch., 1987—. Mem. ABA, Wash. State Bar Assn., Seattle-King County Bar Assn. Episcopalian. Clubs: Wash. Athletic, Columbia Tower. Office: Perkins Coie 1900 Washington Bldg Seattle WA 98101

GRAHAM, SUE BARTHOL, computer literacy educator; b. San Francisco, July 13, 1948; d. Robert George and Jane (Wanamaker) Barthol; m. Thomas Spencer Graham, Mar. 27, 1981. BA, Calif. State U., Chico, 1970; MA, San Jose State U., 1981; computer cert., U. Calif., Santa Cruz, 1986. Phys. edn. instr. East Side Union High Sch. Dist., San Jose, Calif., 1971-79, 83-85, counselor, 1980-83, computer literacy tchr., 1985—, coordinator staff devel in computer literacy, 1985—. Author: Self Defense for Women, 1981. Recipient Outstanding Service award, Independence High Sch., 1986. Mem. Calif. Tchrs. Assn., East Side Tchrs. Assn. Roman Catholic. Avocations: jogging. Home: 1126 Telfer Ave San Jose CA 95125 Office: East Side Union High Sch Dist 1776 Educational Park Dr San Jose CA 95133

GRAHAM, TAD LAURY, computer systems analyst; b. Wichita, Kans., May 12, 1943; s. Robert Virgil and Jeana Ardath (Black) g.; married (div.); children: Carol Lynn, Peter Mark; m. Judith Anne Hathaway, Sept. 1, 1972; 1 child, Geoffrey Todd. BA, U. Ariz., 1969; MS, U. Ill., 1974; BS, Chapman Coll., 1981. Dir. info. services Intrec, Inc., Santa Monica, Calif., 1974-77; mem. tech. staff Computer Scis. Corp., San Diego, 1977-79, sr. mem. tech. staff, 1979-81, sect. mgr., 1981-85, dept. mgr., 1985—; part-time instr. computer sci. Chapman Coll., Orange, Calif., 1983—. Served with USN, 1960-64. Mem. Nat. Mgmt. Assn. (dir. chpt. 1981-83), IEEE, Assn. Computing Machinery. Democrat. Episcopalian. Office: Computer Scis Corp 4045 Hancock St San Diego CA 92110

GRAHAM, WALTER, painter, sculptor; Toledo, Ill., Nov. 17, 1903; s. Elijah and Florence (Cramer) G.; m. Alma L. Raber, May 5, 1952; 1 son, David. Student Chgo. Art Inst., Chgo. Acad. Art, also pvt. instrn., 1924-30. Owner, operator, Nugent Graham Studios, 1939-49; fine arts painter murals, sculptor; pres. Central Wash. Mus., 1960; mem. Wash. State Arts Commn., 1960; former illustrator Street and Smith Pubs., Western Story, Western Life; one man show of over 50 paintings Frye Mus., Seattle, 1986. Recipient 1st prizes Chgo. Galleries, 1937, 38, 42, Bronze medal Nat. Advt. Assn., 1954, 55, 56. Mem. Palette Chisel Acad. (Gold medal 1940), Soc. Animal Artists N.Y., North Central Wash. Mus. (past pres.), Seattle Art Dirs. Soc. (hon. mention). Prin. works include murals Rocky Reach Dam, Wenatche, Wash.; fountain sculpture for Lincoln Savs. Bank, Spokane; Paintings on Alaskan steamships; commd. paintings for Northwest banks; paintings in TV and films, including Exploration Northwest, Chief Joseph's War Trail. Home and Studio: 201 S Elliott Apt 9 Wenatchee WA 98801

GRAHAM, WARREN KIRKLAND, dentist; b. Albuquerque, July 22, 1938; s. Warren Reno and Alice Barbara (Eller) G.; m. Nancy Lou White, Apr. 2, 1966; children—John Warren, Jason Kirkland. B.S., U. N.Mex., 1960; D.D.S., Baylor U., 1964. Pvt. practice dentistry, Albuquerque, 1965—; clin. instr. dental programs U. N.Mex., 1968-73. Bd. dirs. N.Mex. Council on Smoking and Health, 1969-71; mem. N.Mex. Medicaid Adv. Bd., 1972-77, Mid Rio-Grande Health Planning Council, 1972-76; chmn. N.Mex. Health Systems Agy. Subarea Council, Dist. II, 1977-78. Served as capt. USAF, 1964-65. Fellow Am. Coll. Dentists, Acad. Gen. Dentistry (pres. Albuquerque chpt. 1976); mem. ADA, N.Mex. Dental Assn. (sec.-treas. 1982-86, v.p. 1986-87), Albuquerque Dist. Dental Soc. (pres. 1976), Pierre Fouchard Acad., Sigma Chi, Delta Sigma Delta. Republican. Mem. Ch. of Jesus Christ of Latter-day Saints. Home: 8216 Delwood NE Albuquerque NM 87111 Office: 7520 D-11 Montgomery NE Albuquerque NM 87109

GRAHAM, WILLIAM ERRETT, clinical social worker; b. Tucson, Oct. 1, 1947; s. Kenneth Errett and M. Natalie (Koehler) G.; m. Mary Catherine Grenier, June 14, 1973; children: Matthew, Joseph. BA in Psychology, U. Ariz., 1975; MSW, Ariz. State U., 1977. Clin. social worker Ariz. Children's Home, Tucson, 1977—; pvt. practice psychotherapy Tucson, 1985—; mem. youth services adv. com. Pima Coll., Tucson, 1979—; field instr. Sch. Social Work, Ariz. State U., Tempe, 1979—. Workshop chmn. Am. Assn. Psychiat. Services for Children Conv., Chgo., 1979; sports ofcl. Ariz. Interscholastic Assn., Tucson, 1982; bd. dirs. Enrichment for Parents, Tucson, 1986. Named Outstanding Field Instr. Sch. Social Work Ariz. State U., 1985. Mem. Nat. Assn. Social Workers (cert., diplomate, registered clin. social worker). Avocations: high sch. sports ofcl. Office: Ariz Children's Home PO Box 7277 Tucson AZ 85725

GRAICHEN, ALFRED CARL, data processing executive; b. Lawrence, Mass., Apr. 28, 1949; s. Carl Otto and helen Alfreda (Walker) G.; m. Tannissee Anne Laufenburg, June 4, 1976; 1 child, Carla. BA in Biology, Gordon Coll., 1970; cert. data processing, Andover Inst., 1971, Lowell Inst. Tech., 1971. With computer ops. Liberty Mut. Ins., Burlington, Mass., 1970-72; computer tech. supr. Electronic Data Systems, Camp Hill, Pa., 1972-73; computer tech. supr. Electronic Data Systems, San Francisco, 1973-79, system software supr., 1979-83; data ctr. mgr. Electronic Data Systems, Sunnyvale, Calif., 1983-85; dir. tech. services Electric Power Research Inst., Palo Alto, Calif., 1985—. Campaign mgr. Friends for Freeman, Hercules, Calif., 1979, Measure G., Hercules, 1980; mem. Nat. Ski Patrol, Heniker, N.H., 1968-72. Republican. Presbyterian. Lodges: Lions Internat. (treas. Pinole, Calif. 1984-86), Masons. Home: 4047 Eagle Nest Ln Danville CA 94526 Office: Electric Power Research Inst 3412 Hillview Ave Palo Alto CA 94103

GRAMBLING, JEFFREY ARTHUR, geologist; b. Milw., Apr. 1, 1953; s. F. Arthur and Lois (Goodwin) G.; m. Gail E. Johnston, June 14, 1975; 1 child, Lara Harding. BA, Colgate U., 1975; PhD, Princeton U., 1979. Asst. prof. U. Okla., Norman, 1979-80; asst. prof. U. N.Mex., Albuquerque, 1980-85, assoc. prof., 1985—; mem. exec. com. N.Mex. Geol. Soc., Socorro, 1982-85. Contbr. articles to profl. jours.; editor: Albuquerque Country II, 1982. NSF fellow, 1976-79, grantee, 1982-86. Mem. Mineral. Soc. Am., Geol. Soc. Am., Am. Geophys. Union, Mineral. Assn. Can., N.Mex. Geol. Soc. (pres. 1985). Democrat. Presbyterian. Avocation: backpacking. Home: 505 Wellesley Dr SE Albuquerque NM 87106 Office: U N Mex Dept Geology Albuquerque NM 87131

GRAMS, THEODORE CARL WILLIAM, librarian, educator; b. Portland, Oreg., Sept. 29, 1918; s. Theodore Albert and Emma Elise (Boehne) G. B.A., U. Wash., 1947; postgrad. Harvard Law Sch., 1947-48; M.S. in L.S., U. So. Calif., 1951. Land title asst. U.S. Bonneville Power Adminstrn., Portland, 1939-45, accountant, 1948-50, librarian, 1951-52; head cataloger, lectr. Portland State U. Library, 1952-59, dir. processing services, 1960-83, prof., 1969—. Panelist on community action N.W. Luth. Welfare Assn. Conf., 1969; mem. adv. council Area Agy. on Aging, 1974-75; commr. City-County Commn. Aging, Portland-Multnomah County, 1975-80. Bd. dirs. Hub-Community Action Program, Portland, 1967-70, Project ABLE, 1972-74. HEW Inst. fellow, 1968-69. Mem. Am., Oreg., Pacific N.W. library assns., AAUP, Am. Soc. for Info. Sci. (panelist on impact new technologies on info. sci. 1974, Library of Congress services 1976), Portland Area Spl. Librarians (pres. 1954-55), Spl. Libraries Assn., Beta Phi Mu. Lutheran. Clubs: Multnomah Athletic, University, Portland. Author: Allocation of Joint Costs of Multiple-Purpose Projects, 1952; Textbook Classification, 1968. Editor: Procs. 4th Am. Soc. Info. Sci. Midyear Meeting, 1975; Special Collections in Libraries of the Pacific Northwest, 1979; Disaster Preparedness and Recovery 1983; Technical Services: The Decade Ahead, in Beyond 1984: The Future of Technical Services, 1983. Home: 1000 SW Vista Ave Portland OR 97205

GRAND, MARCIA, civic worker; b. N.Y.C., Aug. 9, 1933; d. Irving and Dorothy (Miller) Kosta; m. Richard Grand, Jan. 27, 1952; 1 child, Cindy Deborah. Student U. Ariz., 1950-52, 59-60. Docent, coordinator, docent trainer Tucson Mus. Art, 1965-71, chmn. edn. com., 1975-79, bd. dirs., 1972-79; v.p., sec. Richard Grand Found. for Legal Research and Edn., 1966-80, pres., 1980—; bd. dirs. Greenfields Schs., 1977-82; bd. dirs., sec. U. Ariz. Found., 1979—; bd. fellows Ctr. Creative Photography, 1983—; mem.-at-large, bd. dirs. Tucson Mus. Art League, 1977-78. Recipient YWCA Woman on the Move award, 1982; Community Service award Mortar Board, 1978; Disting. Citizen award U. Ariz. Coll. Fine Arts, 1979. Office: 127 W Franklin St Tucson AZ 85701

GRANGE, LARRY WILLIAM, electro-mechanical engineer electronics executive; b. Topeka, Kans., Nov. 19, 1937; s. William Frank and Edna Laverne (Sales) G. AACE, Los Angeles Harbor Coll.; BA in Math., U. Calif., Long Beach; MBA, Pepperdine U. Sr. draftsman Douglas Aircraft Co., El Segundo, Calif., 1958-59; designer Ramo-Woolridge, Canoga Park, Calif., 1959-60; engr. Nortronics, Northrop Corp., Hawthorne, Calif., 1960-64; sr. design engr. Northrop Aircraft Co., Hawthorne, 1966; sr. engring. designer Hughes Aircraft Co., Culver City, Calif., 1964-66; product engr. TRW Systems, Redondo Beach, Calif., 1966-70; asst. mgr., sr. engr. Ampex Computer Products Div., El Segundo, 1970-75; mgr. Xerox Corp., El Segundo, 1975—; bd. dirs. Crane Electronics; pres. Gramor Property Investments. Mem. Electric Connector Study Group (chmn. membership). Office: Xerox Corp 701 S Aviation Blvd El Segundo CA 90245

GRANT, CHERYL, producer, syndicator TV; b. Phoenix, Mar. 1, 1944; d. William Edward and Mary Louise (Weldon) Grant; m. Louis Tancredi, Nov. 27, 1976; children—John Francis, Jennifer Grant. Student U. Fribourg, Switzerland, 1963-64; B.A., Coll. of Notre Dame of Md., 1965; M.S., Syracuse U., 1966. Assoc. producer Girl Talk ABC Films, N.Y.C., 1968-70, New Jersey Speaker for Itself, WNDT-TV, N.Y.C., 1966-68, Communications and Education, WNDT-TV, N.Y.C., 1967, The Virginia Graham Show, RKO, Los Angeles, 1970-71, Manhattan Townhouse, Source Internat., N.Y.C., 1971-72, Collision Course, Wolper Prodns., Los Angeles, 1972, Living Easy with Dr. Joyce Brothers, Capricorn Prodns., N.Y.C., 1972-73, Mike Douglas Show, Westinghouse, Phila., 1974, Beverly & Vidal Sassoon, Sta. KCOP, Los Angeles, 1975, Dinah, 20th Century Fox, Los Angeles, 1975; hostess A.M. Miami, Sta. WPLG-TV, Miami, Fla., 1972; exec. producer/pres. Carter-Grant Prodns., Inc., Los Angeles, 1976—, Sherry Grant Enterprises, Inc., Los Angeles, 1982—. Programs have been honored by the Freedom Found. award, Internat. Film and TV Festival of N.Y. Gold Award and Calif. Motion Picture Assn. Golden Halo award. Mem. Acad. T.V. Arts and Sci., Women in Bus., Women in Film, Am. Women in Radio and TV, AFTRA, Women in Cable. Roman Catholic. Home: 18120 Sweet Elm Dr Encino CA 91316 Office: Sherry Grant Enterprises 17915 Ventura Blvd Suite 208 Encino CA 91316

GRANT, DAVID MORRIS, chemistry educator; b. Salt Lake City, Mar. 24, 1931; s. David Lewis and Mary Lucille (Greenwood) G.; m. Reva Luella Carlow, Sept. 11, 1953; children: David James, Linda Grant Halling, Heidi Grant Cox, Karen Grant Lindstrom, John Carlow Grant. BS in Chemistry, U. Utah, 1954, PhD in Chemistry, 1957. Du Pont instr. chemistry U. Ill., Champaign-Urbana, 1957-58; asst. prof. U. Utah, Salt Lake City, 1958-62, assoc. prof., 1962-65, prof., 1965-85, disting. prof., 1985—, chmn. dept. chemistry, 1962-73, dean coll. sci., 1976-85; adj. prof. fuels engring., U. Utah, 1985-86; co-investigator study to improve mgmt. of costly instrumentation trs., 1974-75; lectr. numerous univs., sci. and tech. assns. and confs., 1963—. Mem. editorial bd. Jour Am. Chem. Soc., 1975-76, Jour. Magnetic Resonance, 1969-84; mem. editorial adv. bd. Spectrochimica Acta, 1976-84. Named Sherman Fairchild Disting. Vis. Scholar Calif. Inst. Tech., 1973-74; recipient U. Utah Disting. Research award, 1971-72, Willard Gardner prize Utah Acad. Scis., Arts and Letters, 1971. Mem. AAAS, Am. Chem. Soc. (assoc. editor jour. 1975-76, accreditation rev. com. 1985, Gold Medal award Calif. sect. 1969, Utah sect. award 1973), Am. Phys. Soc., Sigma Xi (Ann. award Utah chpt. 1957), Phi Beta Kappa, Phi Kappa Phi. Mormon. Avocation: crafts. Office: U Utah Dept Chemistry Salt Lake City UT 84112

GRANT, DONALD WEBSTER, insurance executive; b. Essex, Eng., Sept. 24, 1924; s. John Webster and May Sarah (Perkins) G.; m. Jean Margaret Brooke, Sept. 10, 1949; children—Gary, John, Donna; m. 2d Gigi Boschy, Oct. 4, 1974. Student London U., 1940-41; Keyman, dir. Fairfield, Ellis & Grant Ltd., Montreal, 1947-60; mgr. indsl. risk ins., dir. Grant & Russell Ltd., Montreal, 1960-64; exec. v.p. M.B. Buettner & Co., Inc., Los Angeles, 1964-70; pres. Western Reins. Brokers Inc., Los Angeles, also exec. v.p. Western Brokers Ins. Services, 1971—. Served with Brit. Mcht. Marine, 1941-46. Decorated campaign medals. Mem. Am. Assn. Mng. Gen. Agts., Calif. Surplus Line Assn., (mem. exec. com.), Calif. Fair Plan (del.). Republican. Clubs: Los Angeles (past pres.), Riviera Tennis. Home: 10501 Wilshire Blvd Apt 1010 Los Angeles CA 90024 Office: 3460 Wilshire Blvd Suite 400 Los Angeles CA 90010

GRANT, GARY FERRILL, broadcasting engineer; b. Hollywood, Calif., May 10, 1936; s. Ferrill George and Emma Elizabeth (Holmberg) G.; m. Elizabeth Emily Jones, Mar. 30, 1963; children—Jennifer Ann, Nicholas Ferrill. A.A., Glendale Community Coll., 1978; B.A., Calif. State U.-Chico, 1980, M.P.A., 1984; student Pasadena City Coll., 1955. Lab. specialist Collins Radio Co., Newport Beach, Calif., Cedar Rapids, Iowa, 1960-62; TV engr. Sta. KCRL TV, Reno, 1962-77; engr., owner Sierra Electronics Co., Reno, 1964-68; project dir. State of Nev., Reno, 1977-79; engr. U. Nev., Reno, 1979—; cons. engr. KBUB Inc., Reno, 1963—; instr. Truckee Meadows Community Coll., Reno, 1971—. Bd. dirs. Sr. Edn. Council U. Nev., 1980. Mem. Soc. Broadcast Engrs., Nev. Amateur Radio Assn. (pres. 1964)., Nat. Assn. Radio and Telecommunications Engrs., Sierra Nev. Amateur Radio Soc. (bd. dirs. 1972-74). Democrat. Episcopalian. Home: 11040 Broken Hill Rd Reno NV 89511 Office: U Nev Instructional Media Services Reno NV 89557

GRANT, HOWARD W., symphony orchestra executive. Exec. dir. Honolulu Symphony Orch. Office: Honolulu Symphony Orchestra 1441 Kapiolani Blvd Suite 1515 Honolulu HI 96814 *

GRANT, JAMES LUCIUS, civil engineer, consultant; b. Jasper, Ga., Jan. 26, 1942; s. Lucius Lanier and Ora (Wood) G.; m. Susan Leigh McCubbin, July 4, 1981. BS in Math., Ga. Inst. Tech., 1964, MS in Math., 1967, BSCE, 1968, PhD, 1973. Registered profl. engr., Ga., K., Colo., Wyo., Nev., Ill.; land surveyor, Ga. Mathematician Lockheed-Ga. Co., Marietta, 1964-68; engr. Urban Engrs., Inc., Atlanta, 1968-73; hydrologist Law Engr. Testing Co., Atlanta, 1973-77; cons. Law Engr. Testing Co., Denver, 1979-83; chief engr. Nuclear Engring. Co., Louisville, 1977-79; prin. James L. Grant & Assocs., Englewood, Colo., 1983—. Contbr. articles to profl. jours. Campaign worker Colo. Dems., Denver, 1982, Butterworth for Congress, Marietta, 1976. Mem. Am. Water Works Assn., Nat. Water Well Assn., Am. Geophys. Union, Sigma Xi. Baptist. Avocations: reading, fishing, hunting. Home: 8134 E Phillips Circle Englewood CO 80112 Office: 8301 E Prentice Ave Englewood CO 80111

GRANT, JOHN CARRINGTON, advertising agency executive; b. St. Louis, Feb. 2, 1937; s. George Nelson Whitfield and Mary Frances (Tissier) G.; m. Judith Ann Thompson, Oct. 20, 1962; children: Christopher, Susan. Student Westminister Coll., 1960; BS, Washington U., St. Louis, 1969. Account mgr. Darcy, McManus & Masius, St. Louis, N.Y.C. and San Francisco, 1960-68; with Gardner Advt., St. Louis, 1963-66, McCann-Erickson, Seattle, 1974-75; stockbroker Dean Witter, San Francisco, 1968-74; with Tracy-Locke/BBDO, 1975-80; pres. Grant Pollack Advt., Denver, 1980-85; v.p. Brock & Assocs., Denver, 1985-86; dir. Univ. relations U. Denver, 1987—; mem. faculty Met. State Coll., Denver, 1981-82. Mem. Denver Advt. Fedn. Clubs: Denver Athletic, Oxford. Home: 8506 E Mineral Circle Englewood CO 80112

GRANT, PATRICK MICHAEL, chemist; b. Oakland, Calif., Sept. 20, 1944; s. Dudley-Francis Patrick and Mary Grace (Zugnoni) G.; m. Joni Marie Bryan, June 28, 1969; children: Lori Lyn, Crystal-Lyn, Patricia. BS, U. Calif., Santa Barbara, 1967; PhD, U. Calif., Irvine, 1973. Teaching and research asst. U. Calif., Irvine, 1967-73, sr. reactor operator, 1969-73; research radiochemist Sch. Medicine U. N.Mex., Albuquerque, 1973-74, adj. asst. prof. chemistry, 1977-81; mem. staff Los Alamos (N.Mex.) Nat. Lab., 1974-80, assoc. group leader, 1980-81, cons., 1981-83; research chemist Chevron Research Co., Richmond, Calif., 1981-83; radiochemist Livermore (Calif.) Nat. Lab., 1983—. Contbr. numerous articles to profl. jours.; patentee in field. Recipient Louis B. Silverman Meml. award Health Physics Soc., So. Calif., 1972. Mem. AAAS, Am. Chem. Soc., Am. Phys. Soc., Am. Nuclear Soc. Avocations: sports, music. Office: Livermore Nat Lab Nuclear Chemistry Div L-234 Livermore CA 94550

GRANT, RICHARD EARL, nursing educator; b. Spokane, Wash., Aug. 27, 1935; s. Conrad Morrison and Sylva Celeste (Sims) G.; m. Susan Kimberly Hawkins, Mar. 17, 1979; children: Aaron Sahmie Q., Camber Do'otsie O. BSc cum laude, U. Wash., 1961; MEd, Whitworth Coll., 1974; PhD, Wash. State U., 1980. Supr. nursing Providence Hosp., Seattle, 1970-72; asst. prof. nursing Wash. State U., Spokane, 1972-78; dir. nursing Winslow (Ariz.) Meml. Hosp., 1978-79; adminstr. psychiat. nursing Ariz. State Hosp., Phoenix, 1979-80; asst. prof. Ariz. State U., Tempe, 1980-83; assoc. prof. Linfield Coll., Portland, Oreg., 1983-86, Intercollegiate Ctr. for Nursing Edn., Spokane, 1986—; cons. Ariz. State Hosp., 1980-82, Pres.'s Commn., Washington, 1981-83, U. No. Colo., Greely, 1985-86. Author: The God-Man-God Book, 1976, Publications of the Membership (Conaa), 1983, 2d rev. edit., 1985; contbr. articles to profl. jours. Judge Student Space Shuttle Project, Portland, 1983—, Northwest Sci. Expo, Portland, 1983—. Served with U.S. Army, 1953-56. Grantee NIMH, U. Wash., 1961; named one of top Hopi Scholars, Hopi Tribe, Second Mesa, Ariz., 1981. Mem. AAAS, N.Y. Acad. Scis., Nat. League for Nursing, Council on Nursing and Anthropology (editor 1982—), Sigma Theta Tau. Avocations: painting, scuba diving.

GRANT, SCOTT, ophthalmologist, educator; b. Bklyn.; s. Milton and Sylvia Grant; m. S. Raenele Cote, Jan. 25, 1980; children—Andrew Benjamin, Michael Raymond. B.S., Cooper Union, 1969; M.S., Stanford U., 1970, M.D., 1975. Diplomate Am. Bd. Ophthalmology. Resident in ophthalmology Jules Stein Eye Inst., UCLA, 1976-79; fellow in vitreo-retinal disease Washington Hosp. Ctr., 1979-80; fellow retinal diseases Moorfields Eye Hosp., London, 1980; asst. clin. prof. ophthalmology U. Calif.-Irvine Med. Sch., 1980-81, 84—, asst. prof.-in-residence, 1981-83; retinal cons. Kaiser Hosp., Anaheim, Calif., 1984—, Long Beach Vets. Hosp., Calif., 1980—. Contbr. articles to profl. jours. Fellow Am. Acad. Ophthalmology. Club: Mensa. Office: 100 E Valencia Mesa Dr Fullerton CA 92635 Office: Anaheim Eye Med Group 1211 W La Palma Ave Anaheim CA 92801

GRANT, SURLENE GEORGETTE, legislative aide; b. Redwood City, Calif., Apr. 25, 1959; d. George Gene and Surlene (Jackson) G. BS in Journalism, Northwestern U., 1981. Multicultural edn. dir. YWCA, Palo Alto, Calif., 1981-83; pub. relations dir. Bay Area Urban League, Oakland, Calif., 1983-85; legis. aide Calif. State Senate, Sacramento, 1985-86; asst. press sec. speakers office Calif. Assembly, 1986—. Author: Chronological History of Jerusalem Baptist Church, 1986. Mem. YWCA, Palo Alto, 1986; campaign worker Bradley for Gov., Sacramento, 1986. Named Employee of Yr., Bay Area Urban League, Oakland, 1985. Mem. Pub. Relations Soc. Am. Democrat. Baptist. Avocations: photography, sports. Office: State Capitol Room 217 Sacramento CA 95816

GRANTHAM, DONALD JAMES, engineering educator, author; b. Grantham, N.C., Aug. 1, 1916; s. James Clarence and Nannie (Rose) G.; children—David S., Philip L. B.A. in Chemistry, U. N.C., 1939. Radio announcer, 1940-42, 46; radio programmer, sta. gen. mgr., 1947-50; founder, pres. Grantham Coll. of Engring., Los Alamitos, 1951—. Mem. IEEE, ASEE.70. Served with U.S. Army, 1942-46. Mem. IEEE, ASEE. Office: 10570 Humbolt St Los Alamitos CA 90720

GRANTHAM, LEROY FRANCIS, chemist; b. Chadron, Nebr., Nov. 23, 1929; s. Charles Clint and Frances (Vogle) G.; m. Fay A. Walker, June 29, 1952; children: Connie, Theresa, Becky. BS, Nebr. State Coll., 1951; MS, Iowa State U., 1954; PhD, Kans. State U., 1959. Postgrad. Dowell fellow Kans. State U., Manhattan, 1957-58; mem. tech. staff Rockwell Internat., Canoga Park, Calif., 1959-75, mem. tech. staff VI, 1975-81, sr. scientist,

1981—. Contbr. tech. reports to profl. publs.; patentee in field. Named Engr. of Yr., Rockwell Internat., 1978. Mem. Am. Chem. Soc., Am. Nuclear Soc., Sigma Xi (pres. Rockwell West Valley chpt. 1962-63). Republican. Baptist. Avocations: photography, hiking. Office: Rockwell Internat 6633 Canoga Ave Canoga Park CA 91304

GRANTHAM, THAD O., aerospace systems engineer; b. Corsicana, Tex., Dec. 17, 1958; s. Thelbert O. and Catherine Elizabeth (Holcomb) G. BS in Engring. Analysis, Clemson U., 1982. Systems engr. Trident II Missiles Systems Div. Lockheed Missiles and Space Co. Inc., Sunnyvale, Calif., 1982—. Mem. Am. Soc. Safety Engrs., System Safety Soc. Republican. Methodist. Avocations: kenpo karate, waterskiing, snow skiing, wind surfing. Home: PO Box 70483 Sunnyvale CA 94086 Office: Lockheed Missiles and Space Co Inc 1111 Lockheed Way O/81-74 B/157 Sunnyvale CA 94088-3504

GRANZOW, OTTO JOACHIM, psychiatrist; b. Burg Stargard, Germany, Aug. 16, 1923; s. Wilhelm and Margarete (Peters) G.; student U. Berlin, 1941-42, 43-44, U. Wuerzburg, 1942-43, 44-45; M.D., U. Hamburg, 1946; m. Inge Johanna Stephan, 1970; children—Joachim Wilhelm, Christian Lars. Came to U.S., 1950, naturalized, 1955. Intern internal medicine U. Hamburg, 1947-48; resident ob-gyn, surgery St. Georg Hosp., Hamburg, 1948-50; course in tropical medicine Inst. Tropical Diseases, Hamburg, 1948; psychiat. tng. Mass. Dept. Mental Health, 1950-52; rotating intern St. John's Hosp., Santa Monica, Calif., 1952-53; child psychiatry fellow Pasadena (Calif.) Child Guidance Clinic, 1953-54; fellow child psychiatry Harvard U., 1954-55; surgeon Grace Line, 1955-56; practice medicine specializing in psychiatry, child psychiatry, Los Angeles, 1956—; mem. staff St. John's, Santa Monica, Serra Meml. hosps.; clin. instr. psychiatry UCLA, 1956-64; cons. Los Angeles Sch. Guidance Clinic, 1956-65, Calif. Dept. Rehab., 1970—; med. examiner Workmen's Compensation Appeals Bd., 1972—; med. cons. German Consulates Gen., Los Angeles and San Francisco. Served with M.C., German Air Force, 1940-45. Mem Calif., Los Angeles County med. assns. Republican. Lutheran. Office: 2021 Santa Monica Blvd Santa Monica CA 90404

GRATSON, DAVID ALAN, chemical analyst; b. Englewood, Colo., Apr. 3, 1959; s. Walter Gratson and Nancy Jane (Doverspike) Heath. BS in Biology, Allegheny Coll., 1981; student, Met. State Coll. Analyst Free-Col. Environ. Lab., Meadville, Pa., 1980; darkroom technician Community Press, Denver, 1981-82, Hoflin Publ. Ltd., Wheatridge, Colo., 1982-84; analyst Rocky Mtn. Analytical Lab., Arvada, Colo., 1984—. Mem. AAAS, Rocky Mountain Chromatography Discussion Group, Am. Chem. Soc. Democrat. Lutheran. Avocations: fly fishing, skiing, hiking. Home: 17611 W 16th Ave 3-211 Golden CO 80401 Office: Rocky Mountain Analytical Labs 4955 Yarrow Arvada CO 80002

GRATT, LAWRENCE BARRY, engineer, educator; b. Chgo., Sept. 20, 1940; s. Jack J. and Bette V. (Goldbloom) G.; m. Dona Jean Janecek, Aug. 21, 1963; children—Robyn, Gambyl, Alexis, Natalee. B.S. in Engring. with honors, UCLA, 1962, M.S. (Hughes Fellow), 1964, Ph.D. (AEC fellow), 1969. Mem. tech. staff Hughes Aircraft Co., 1962-65; sect. head TRW, Inc., 1965-73; asst. v.p. Sci. Applications Inc., La Jolla, Calif., 1973-79; pres. IWG Corp., San Diego, 1979—; instr. West Coast U., UCLA. Mem. Am. Nuclear Soc., AIAA, AAAS, Am. Chem. Soc., Geothermal Resource Council, Soc. for Risk Analysis, Tau Beta Pi. Contbr. articles to profl. jours. Office: 3065 Rosecrans Pl Suite 210 San Diego CA 92110

GRATZ, REED HOWE, music educator, composer; b. Bluffton, Ohio, June 30, 1950; s. James Leonard and Jane Louise (Howe) G.; m. Deborah Anne Waas, Aug. 12, 1972; children: Erin, Ian. BA in Music Theory, Manchester Coll., 1973; MM in Jazz Composition, New England Conservatory, 1975; DMA in Composition, U. Miami, Coral Gables, Fla., 1977; studies with George Russell, Boston, 1973-75; studies with Dennis Kam, Miami, 1975-77; studies with Gunther Schuller, Boston, 1975. Asst. prof. music U. La Verne, Calif., 1977-79, assoc. prof. music, 1980—, men's varsity tennis coach, 1985—; jazz pianist, keyboardist, Los Angeles, 1977—; vis. prof. music Wash. State U., Pullman, 1979-80. Composer: (ballet) Dance of Returning, 1985, numerous Jazz Compositions, 1977-78, With Whom Shall I Begin for guitar soloist, 1977. Named one of Outstanding Young Men Am., Jaycees, 1979, 82; Nat. Endowment for Arts Fellowship, 1984; NEH grantee, 1982. Mem. Am. Fedn. Musicians, Coll. Music Soc., Nat. Assn. Jazz Educators. Mem. Ch. of Brethern. Home: 2147 E St La Verne CA 91750 Office: U La Verne 1950 3d St La Verne CA 91750

GRAVEL, CLIFFORD RICHARD-HILAIRE, educator, writer; b. Passaic, N.J., Mar. 5, 1939; s. Raoul Donat and Edith (Shaw) G.; grad. various tax, sales, and ins. schools; Bradstreet, 1982; BS in Phys.Sci. teaching, N.Mex., 1986; 1 child, Genevieve. Chemist various cos., 1959-72; sales rep. Benjamin Moore Co., Los Angeles, 1973-81; sales mgr. Western Auto, 1981-82. Editor: Menzia, Touchups, Turning Point; contbr. articles to various pubs. Fellow Internat. Soc. Philos. Inquiry; mem. Am. Mensa, Mensa Internat. (news service rep. 1982-83), Am. Judo Assn., Internat. Platform Assn., Golden Key, U. N.Mex. Advisory Council, Returning Students Assn. (coordinator), Sigma Pi Sigma, Kappa Delta Pi, Pi Lambda Theta, Phi Eta Sigma. Office: 1709 Vail Pl SE Albuquerque NM 87106

GRAVES, MARSHALL WILLIAM, insurance representative; b. Seattle, Feb. 26, 1933; s. Clifford William and Annette Elizabeth (Bryant) G. BS in Physics, U. Wash., 1960. Cert. hazard control mgr., assoc. safety profl. Tchr., mgr. ranch Ann Graves Sch., Seattle, 1960-65; surveyor Wash. Surveying and Rating Bur., Seattle, 1965-75; owner Fire Ins. Research and Evaluation, Seattle, 1975-77; loss control specialist Warner Ins. Group, Chgo., 1977-85; loss control rep. City-County Ins. Services, Salem, Oreg., 1985—. Served with U.S. Army, 1955-57. Mem. Am. Soc. Safety Engrs. Avocations: underwater photography. Office: City County Ins Services PO Box 928 Salem OR 97308

GRAVES, NATHAN ALAN, hazardous waste consultant; b. Alexandria, Va., Sept. 21, 1957; s. Jacob D. and Frances E. (Ketterman) G.; m. Amy R. Borenstein; 1 child, Rebecca Ann. BS, U. Richmond, 1979. Biologist, chemist Versar Inc., Springfield, Va., 1979-82; environ. scientist TetraTech Inc., Seattle, 1982-84; regional mgr. indsl. services Kennedy, Jenks, Chilton, Federal Way, Wash., 1984—; mem. Metro Citizens Water Quality Com., Seattle, 1984—. Mem. Am. Chem. Soc., Tacoma C. of C. (environ. task force 1985—), Assn. Wash. Bus. (hazardous task force 1985—), Beta Beta Beta, Gamma Sigma Epsilon. Home: 25735 117th Pl SE Kent WA 98031 Office: Kennedy Jenks Chilton 33301 9th Ave S Federal Way WA 98003

GRAVES, RANDY KEITH, science educator; b. Madison, Tenn., Nov. 21, 1956; s. William Eugene Graves and Laveta Faye (Herber) Piper; m. Mary Ann Wines, Aug. 7, 1978; 1 child, Byron Keith. BS in Biology, Southwestern Adventist Coll., 1978; cert., Eastern Wash. U., 1980-82. Cert. tchr., Wash. Asst. boy's dean Upper Columbia Acad., Spangle, Wash., 1979-83, sci. tchr., 1979—, attendance officer, 1984—, also curriculum com. chmn., 1986—; sponsor assoc. student body, Upper Columbia Acad. Office: Upper Columbia Acad Biology Dept Spangle WA 99031

GRAVES, TIMOTHY LEE, architect, civil engineer; b. San Bernardino, Calif., Aug. 5, 1955; s. Olin Ray and Betty Jo (Coyle) G.; m. Emmy Lynne Yanaga, Apr. 7, 1984. Student San Bernardino Valley Coll., Calif., 1972-75; B.S. in Architecture and Archtl. Engring. with highest honors, Calif. Poly. State U.-San Luis Obispo, 1979. Registered profl. engr., Calif.; registered architect, Calif. Designer, draftsman Baldwin-Graphic Engrs., San Bernardino, 1976-77; structural engr. J.E. Bondamin & Assocs., San Bernardino, 1978; structural engr. Austin Co., Irvine, Calif., 1979-80, structural estimator, 1980-83, project estimator, 1982-83, project mgr., 1983-85; devel. coordinator Santa Fe Pacific Realty Corp., Brea, Calif., 1985-86, constrn. mgr., 1986—; missionary constrn. worker Inter-Varsity Christian Fellowship, Honduras, C.Am., 1981; cons. Arro Archtl. Prodn., Van Nuys, Calif., 1982—. Mem. missions com. Mariners Ch., Newport Beach, Calif., 1979—, vice-chmn. short-term missionary guidance com., 1986, chmn. 1987; chmn. service and outreach com. The Salt Co., 1980-84; asst. scoutmaster Santa Lucia Area council Boy Scouts Am., 1975, scoutmaster, 1976, mate Calif. Inland Empire council, Arrowhead council, 1973-75; charter mem., Republican Presdl. Task Force, trustee 1986—; permanent mem. Nat. Rep. Senatorial Com. Recipient Eagle Scout Bronze Palm Boy Scouts Am., 1970, God and Country award Boy Scouts Am., 1971, Adult Leader Tng. award Boy Scouts Am., 1976. Mem. ASCE, Am. Assn. Cost Engrs., AIA, Structural Engrs. Assn., Calif. Poly. State U. Alumni Assn., Phi Kappa Phi. Home: 22 Melodylane Irvine CA 92714 Office: Santa Fe Pacific Realty Corp 3230 E Imperial Hwy Suite 100 Brea CA 92621

GRAVLEE, GRADY JACKSON, SR., history educator; b. Birmingham, Ala., May 31, 1930; s. Gaines Grady and Olathe (Parsley) G.; m. Rhonda Lynn Cooley, Oct. 10, 1953; 1 child, Grady Jackson Jr. (dec.). Student, William Jewell Coll., 1952-53; BA, Samford U., 1955; MA, La. State U., 1958, PhD, 1963. Instr. U. Houston, 1959-61; asst. prof. U. N.Mex., Albuquerque, 1962-64; assoc. prof. Auburn (Ala.) U., 1964-65; mem. faculty Colo. State U., Ft. Collins, 1965—, prof. rhetorical history, 1974—, chmn. dept. speech communication, 1975—. Editor: (with James R. Irvine) Pamphlets and the American Revolution, 1976, Speech Coursebook, 1977; contbr. articles to various publs. Served with USAF, 1948-52. Recipient Lory Disting. Service award Colo. State U., 1975, faculty research grantee, 1972, 76, 78. Mem. Speech Communication Assn., So. Speech Communication Assn., Western Speech Communication Assn., Conf. Brit. Studies, Rhetoric Soc. Am., Colo. Broadcasters Assn., Hist. Soc. Episcopal Ch. Democrat. Home: 1409 Country Club Rd Fort Collins CO 80524 Office: Colo State U Dept Speech Communication Fort Collins CO 80523

GRAY, ALFRED ORREN, journalism educator, research and communications consultant; b. Sun Prairie, Wis., Sept. 8, 1914; s. Charles Orren and Amelia Katherine (Schadel) G.; m. Nicolin Jane Plank, Sept. 5, 1947; children—Robin, Richard. B.A., U. Wis.-Madison, 1939, M.A., 1941. Reporter-intern U. Wis.-Madison and Medford newspapers, 1937-39; freelance writer 1938-41, 51-57; intelligence investigator U.S. Ordnance Dept., Ravenna, Ohio, 1941-42; hist. editor, chief writer U.S. Office Chief Ordnance Service, ETO, Paris and Frankfurt, Germany, 1944-46; asst. prof. journalism Whitworth Coll., Spokane, Wash., 1946-48, assoc. prof., 1948-56, prof., 1958-80, prof. emeritus, 1980—, head dept. journalism, 1946-80, chmn. div. bus. and communications arts, 1958-66, chmn. div. applied arts, 1978-79; cons. research and communications Spokane, 1980—; dir. Whitworth News Bur., 1952-58; dir. numerous research projects. Author: The History of U.S. Ordnance Service in the European Theater of Operations, 1942-46, Not by Might, 1965, Eight Generations from Gondelsheim: a Genealogical Study, 1980; co-author: Many Lamps, One Light: A Centennial History, 1984; editor: The Synod Story, 1953-55; contbr. articles to newspapers, mags., jours.; advisor All-Am. college newspaper, 1946-80. Chmn. Pinewood Addition Archtl. Com., Spokane, 1956—; dir. Inland Empire Publs. Clinic, Spokane, 1959-74; mem. ho. of dels. Greater Spokane Council of Chs., 1968-71; judge Goodwill Worker of Yr. awards Goodwill Industries Spokane County; vice-moderator Synod Wash.-Alaska, Presbyterian Ch. (U.S.A.), 1966-67; bd. dirs. Presbyn. Hist. Soc., 1984—, exec. com., 1986—, chmn. hist. sites com., 1986—; mem. Am. Bd. Mission Heritage Commn. for Sesquicentennial of Whitman Mission, 1986; elder, clk. of session Presbyn. Ch., 1984-86. Served as warrant officer (j.g.) U.S. Army, 1942-46. Decorated Bronze Star and Army Commendation medal; recipient Spl. Teaching Recognition award Whitworth Coll. Alumni Assn., 1972, Printers Ink trophy Advt. Assn. West, 1953, citation Nat. Council Coll. Publ. Advisers, 1967, Outstanding Tchr. of Journalism award Whitworth Coll Alumni Assn., 1979; named Disting. Newspaper Adviser, Nat. Council Coll. Publ. Advisers, 1979. Mem. Assn. for Edn. in Journalism, Eastern Wash. Hist. Soc., Eastern Wash. Geneal. Soc., Coll. of Media Advisers (hon.), Soc. Profl. Journalists, N.Am. Mycol. Assn., Phi Beta Kappa (pres. profl. chpt. 1949-50, 67-68, 70-71). Democrat. Presbyterian (elder, clk. session 1984-86). Avocations: genealogy; travel. Home: W 304 Hoerner Ave Spokane WA 99218

GRAY, BETTY HOWELL, business and marketing education consultant; b. Goldsboro, N.C., Apr. 3, 1942; d. Vasco Herbert and Adell (Ford) H.; children: Frederick and Cedric (twins), Kimberly. BS, N.C. Agrl. and Tech. State U., 1963; MA, U. Wash., 1975; prin. cert., Western Wash. U., 1983. Dept. head, tchr. SOIC Vocat. Schs., Seattle, 1966-71; bus. tchr. Seattle Pub. Schs., 1971-86, curriculum cons., 1986—; mem. ednl. task force Wash. Vocat. Assn., Seattle, 1966—. Mem. Presch. Bd., chairperson Personnel com. Mt. Zion Bapt. Ch., Seattle, 1979—; vol. Jesse Jackson for Pres., 1984. Recipient Outstanding Educator award N.C. Agrl. and Tech. State U., 1978, Outstanding Bus. Educator award Iota Phi Lambda, 1985; nominee Outstanding Tchr. for Excellence in Edn. award Seattle Pub. Schs., 1986. Mem. NEA, Nat. Bus. Edn. Assn., Western Wash. Bus. Edn. Assn., Wash. Vocat. Assn., Black Profl. Assn. (publicity chmn. 1970—), N.C. Agrl. and Tech. State U. Alumni Assn. (pres. 1982—), Alpha Kappa Alpha (chair various coms.). Democrat. Avocations: reading, modeling, community events.

GRAY, GARY DAVID, communications engineer; b. Orange, Calif., Nov. 7, 1942; s. Albert Eldred and Wilda Minerva (Fender) G.; m. Mary Irene Reilly; children: David Christian, Holly Anne. AA, Fullerton Jr. Coll., 1963; BS in Engring. cum laude, Calif. State U., Long Beach, 1969, MSEE, 1974. Registered profl. engr., Calif., D.C.; lic. comml. and amateur radio operator. Communications engring. asst. Gen. Services Agy. Communications div. County of Orange, Calif., 1969-71, communications project engr., 1971-76, communications engr., communications dir., 1976-82, chief communications engr., 1982-85, prin. telecommunications engr., 1985-86, chief telecommunications engr., 1986—. Fellow Radio Club Am., Inst. Advancement Engring; mem. NSPE, IEEE (sr., chmn. Orange County sect. 1974-75), Instn. Electronic and Radio Engrs. Eng., Calif. Soc. Profl. Engrs., Associated Pub.-Safety Communications Officers (pres. So. Calif. chpt. 1980, 84, 1st nat. v.p. 1986-87), Calif. Fire Chiefs Assn., Eta Kappa Nu, Tau Beta Pi. Republican. Clubs: Orange County Communicators. Lodge: Masons. Office: Orange County Communications Ctr 481 The City Dr S Orange CA 92668

GRAY, GEORGE WALTER, city official; b. Oakland, Calif., Aug. 23, 1927; s. Walter Joseph and Elsie M. (Gefkin) G.; m. Dorothy Florence Damon, Aug. 16, 1953; children—Gordon W., Linda J. A.A. in Fire Service, Merritt Coll., 1967; B.A. in Pub. Mgmt., St. Mary's Coll., Moraga, Calif., 1976; postgrad. Exec. Devel. III, Nat. Fire Acad., 1982. Firefighter, Oakland Fire Dept., 1949-56, fire engr., 1956-58, fire lt., 1958-68, fire capt., 1968-78, bn. chief, 1978-82; asst. chief, 1982, dep. fire chief, 1982—; instr. mcpl. fire adminstrn. Merritt Coll., Chabot Coll., Hayward, Calif.; mem. adv. com. fire curriculum; Participant rail rapid transit safety workshop, Washington, 1982. Dist. commr. San Francisco Bay Area Council, 1968-70, dist. chmn. bd. dirs., 1975-77; scoutmaster San Francisco Bay Area council Boy Scouts Am., 1970-79, leader 7th & 10th Nat. Scout Jamborees, 13th World Jamboree, Shizuoka, Japan, 1971. Served with U.S. Army, 1946-47. Recipient Silver Beaver award Boy Scouts Am., 1972; Steven R. O'Day award Oakland Fire Dept., 1980. Mem. Nat. Fire Protection Assn. (charter Fire Service Sect.), Internat. Assn. Fire Chiefs, Bay Area Fire Protection Forum (v.p. 1966). Club: Rotary (pres. East Oakland 1981-82, Paul Harris award 1978). Home: 3518 Rubin Dr Oakland CA 94602-4146 Office: Oakland Fire Dept 1605 Martin Luther King Jr Way Oakland CA 21393

GRAY, JAMES E., electrical engineer; b. Santa Barbara, Calif., June 3, 1932; s. Percival Allen and Mary (Foster) G.; m. Evelyn Lorriane Muhlhauser (div. 1971); m. Penney Mae Hobbs, Apr. 18, 1976. BA with honors, U. Calif., 1954, MA, 1960. Physicist Nat. Bur. of Standards, Boulder, Colo., 1960-73, engr., 1973—. Mem. Am. Radio Relay League, Radio Soc. of Great Britain, Sigma Xi. Avocations: music, amateur radio. Home: 942 Seventh St Boulder CO 80302 Office: Nat Bur Standards 325 Broadway Boulder CO 80303

GRAY, JAMES EDWARD, real estate executive; b. Chgo., Jan. 17, 1949; s. Winton S. and Anita (McCahey) G.; m. Constance Anne Kemmerer, June 10, 1972 (div. Oct. 1983); children: James Edward Jr., Carolyn Kemmerer; m. Frances Lyon Hoppen, Nov. 16, 1985. BA, U. Denver, 1973, MA, 1978. Headmaster St. Anne's Episcopal Sch., Denver, 1973-78; exec. dir. Sun Valley (Idaho)/Ketchum C. of C., 1978-80; ptnr. Sun Valley (Idaho) Assocs., 1980—. Commr. Sun Valley Planning and Zoning Bd., 1980-84; pres. Pioneer Montessori Sch., Ketchum, 1980—, chmn.; bd. dirs. EAR Internat. Found., Los Angeles, 1980—, past. chmn.; packmaster Boy Scouts Am., Ketchem, 1980—. Mem. Nat. Assn. Realtors, Idaho Assn. Realtors, Sawtooth Bd. Realtors. Republican. Roman Catholic. Club: Sun Valley Ski (pres.). Avocations: skiing, hunting, fishing, white water rafting, competitive biking. Home: PO Box 2700 Sun Valley ID 83353 Office: Sun Valley Assocs PO Box 326 Sun Valley ID 83353

GRAY, JAN CHARLES, lawyer; b. Des Moines, June 15, 1947. s. Charles Donald and Mary C. Gray; m. Anita Marie Ringwald, June 6, 1987. B.A. in Econs., U. Calif.-Berkeley, 1969; M.B.A., Pepperdine U., 1986, J.D., Harvard U., 1972. Bar: Calif. 1972, D.C. 1974. Law clk. Kindel & Anderson, Los Angeles, 1971-72; assoc. Halstead, Baker & Sterling, Los Angeles, 1972-75; sr. v.p., gen. counsel external affairs Ralphs Grocery Co. div. Federated Dept. Stores, Inc., Los Angeles, 1975—; judge pro tem Los Angeles Mcpl. Ct., 1977—; instr. bus. UCLA, 1976—, Pepperdine MBA Program, 1985—; arbitrator Am. Arbitration Assn., 1977—; media spokesman So. Calif. Grocers Assn., Calif. Grocers Assn.; real estate broker, Los Angeles, 1973—. Trustee, South Bay U. Coll. Law, 1978-79; mem. bd. visitors Southwestern U. Sch. Law, 1983—; mem. Los Angeles County Pvt. Industry Council, 1982—, exec. com. 1984—, chmn. econ. devel. task force, 1986—; mem. Los Angeles County Martin Luther King, Jr. Gen. Hosp. Authority, 1984—; mem. Los Angeles County Aviation Commn, 1986—; Los Angeles Police Crime Prevention Adv. Council, 1986—; Los Angeles Plaza Adv. Bd., 1983—; bd. dirs. RecyCAL of So. Calif., 1983—; bd. trustees Santa Monica Hosp., 1986—; mem. Los Angeles County Democratic Central Com., 1980-82 ; del. Dem. Nat. Conv., 1980. Recipient So. Calif. Grocers Assn. award for outstanding contbns. to food industry, 1982; Calif./Nev. Soft Drink Assn. appreciation award for No on 11 Campaign, 1983. Mem. ABA, Calif. Bar Assn., Los Angeles County Bar Assn. (exec. com. corp. law depts. sect. 1974-76, 79—, exec. com. barristers sect. 1974-75, 79-81, treas. 1986—), San Fernando Valley Bar Assn. (chmn. real property sect. 1975-77, Los Angeles Pub. Affairs Officers Assn., Los Angeles World Affairs Council, Calif. Retailers Assn. (supermarket com.), Food Mktg. Inst. (govt. relations com., govt. affairs council), So. Calif. Businessmen's Assn. (bd. dirs. 1981—, mem. exec. com. 1982—, sec. 1986—), Town Hall Los Angeles, U. Calif. Alumni Assn., Ephebian Soc. Los Angeles, Phi Beta Kappa. Club: Harvard of So. Calif. Contbg. author: Life or Death, Who Controls?, 1976; contbr. articles to legal jours. Home: PO Box 407 Beverly Hills CA 90213 Office: PO Box 54143 Los Angeles CA 90054

GRAY, JOHN DELTON, retired manufacturing company executive; b. Ontario, Oreg., July 29, 1919; s. Elmer R. and Mabel (Ridgley) G.; m. Elizabeth Neuner, Jan. 4, 1946; children—Anne, Joan, Janet, John Richard, Laurie. B.Secretarial Sci., Oreg. State Coll., 1940; M.B.A., Harvard U., 1947; LL.D., Lewis and Clark Coll., 1967. Asst. to pres. Pointer-Willamette Co., Portland, 1947; asst. gen. mgr. Oreg. Saw Chain Corp. (now Omark Industries, Inc.), Portland, 1948-50; gen. mgr. Oreg. Saw Chain Corp. (now Omark Industries, Inc.), 1950-53, pres., gen. mgr., 1953-67, chmn. bd., 1961-83, vice chmn. bd., 1983-85; chmn. Textronix, Inc., Grayco Resources, Inc.; dir. Precision Castparts Corp., First Interstate Bank Oreg., N.A., Standard Ins. Co. Past pres. Portland area council Boy Scouts Am., 1959-61; past mem. exec. bd., also past pres. Columbia-Pacific council; trustee Com. Econ. Devel., 1967-81; mem. Chief Execs. Orgn., 1969—; trustee Reed Coll., Portland, 1961—, chmn., 1968-82, chmn. steering com. capital campaign, 1983—; trustee Oreg. Grad. Center. Served from 2d lt. to lt. col. AUS, 1941-46. Decorated Bronze Star medal; recipient Silver Beaver award Portland Area council Boy Scouts Am. Republican. Episcopalian. Lodge: Rotary. Office: 5331 SW Macadam Ave Suite 200 Portland OR 97201

GRAY, KARL ALAN, electrical engineer, consultant; b. Wakefield, Va., July 20, 1958; s. Edward Elonce and Melvin Louise (King) G. BS in Indsl. Tech., Va. State Coll., 1979. Mfg. support engr. Ford Aerospace, Newport Beach, Calif., 1979-81; plant engr. Westinghouse Aerospace, Compton, Calif., 1981-84; cons., owner Venture Engring., Anaheim, Calif., 1984—. Co-founder Uplift Youth Employment Program, Anaheim, 1986. Mem. Los Angeles Council Black Profl. Engrs. (editor newsletter 1985-86), Black Bus. Alliance Orange County. Avocations: auto racing, motorcycles, computers, bowling. Home and Office: Venture Engring 2434 W Theresa Ave Anaheim CA 92804

GRAY, KATHERINE, marriage and family counselor and support therapist; b. Los Angeles, July 6, 1941; d. Edward David and Marjorie (Graves) Ross; m. Daniel C. Gray, Feb. 5, 1965; children—Michael, Lisa. B.A., Calif. State U.-Sacramento, 1983, MS, 1987. Instr. Shasta Coll., Redding, Calif., 1965-69; owner Water Ojai Valley Chapel, Ojai, Calif., 1971-77, Lipp & Sullivan, Marysville, Calif., 1978—; cons. and organizer various community outreach programs in edn. Contbr. articles to profl. jours., newspapers. County coordinator, bd. dirs. Am. Cancer Soc., Marysville, 1980—; mem. exec. com., bd. dirs., com. chairperson Gateway Projects, Yuba City, Calif., 1980—; bd. dirs. Mercy Guild, Yuba City, 1980—, Easter Seals, Rainbow for Girls, 1985-87; past bd. dirs., com. chairperson Campfire Inc., Yuba City and Morro Bay, Calif., 1979-80; past pres. Ojai Valley-Oxnard Symphony Orch. Assn., Ventura County, Calif., 1975; Sacramento focus program coordinator 4-H, Yuba and Sutter Counties, 1985—; exec. officer, bd. dirs. Gateway Projects, 1985-87. Grantee in field. Mem. Calif. Funeral Dirs. Assn., Calif. Assn. for Counseling and Devel., Sacramento Area Gifted Assn. Lodges: Soroptimists (bd. dirs.), Rainbow for Girls (bd. dirs. 1985-87). Avocations: music; art, travel; historical studies. Home: PO Box 611 Yuba City CA 95992 Office: PO Box 148 629 D St Marysville CA 95901

GRAY, NORMAN EUGENE, fire chief; b. Helena, Mont., Nov. 3, 1937; s. Eugene F. and Gladys I. (Lippert) G.; student public schs., Helena, Mont.; m. Sharon A. Weed, Nov. 21, 1959; children—Debra A., Norman Dean. Clk., IRS, Helena, Mont., 1959; firefighter, Helena, 1960—, fire chief, 1979—, tng. officer, 1973-79. Served with USN, 1955-58. Mem. Internat. Assn. Fire Chiefs, Western Fire Chiefs Assn., Mont. State Fire Chiefs Assn. Republican. Club: Elks. Office: City of Helena Office of Fire Chief Helena Fire Dept Helena MT 59623 *

GRAY, PHILIP HOWARD, psychologist, educator; b. Cape Rosier, Maine, July 4, 1926; s. Asa and Bernice (Lawrence) G.; m. Iris McKinney, Dec. 31, 1954; children: Cindelyn Gray Eberts, Howard. M.A., U. Chgo., 1958; Ph.D., U. Wash., 1960. Asst. prof. dept. psychology Mont. State U., Bozeman, 1960-65; assoc. prof. Mont. State U., 1965-75, prof., 1975—; vis. prof. U. Man., Winnipeg, Can., 1968-70; pres. Mont. Psychol. Assn., 1968-70; chmn. Mont. Bd. Psychologist Examiners, 1972-74; speaker sci. and geneal. meetings on ancestry of U.S. presidents. Organized exhbns. folk art in Mont. and Maine, 1972-79; author The Comparative Analysis of Behavior, 1966, (with F.L. Ruch and N. Warren) Working with Psychology, 1963, A Directory of Eskimo Artists in Sculpture and Prints, 1974, The Science that Lost its Mind, 1985; contbr. numerous articles on behavior to psychol. jours., poetry to lit. jours. Served with U.S. Army, 1944-46. Recipient Am. and Can. research grants. Fellow Am. Psychol. Assn., AAAS, Internat. Soc. Research on Aggression; mem. History of Sci. Soc., Nat. Geneal. Soc., New Eng. Hist. Geneal. Soc., Gallatin County Geneal. Soc. (charter), Deer Isle-Stonington Hist. Soc., Psychonomic Soc., Internat. Soc. for Human Ethology, Descs. of Illegitimate Sons and Daus. of Kings of Britain, Piscataqua Pioneers, Animal Behavior Soc.; Flagon and Trencher, SAR (trustee Mont.), Sigma Xi. Home: 1207 S Black Ave Bozeman MT 59715 Office: Montana State U Dept Psychology Bozeman MT 59717

GRAY, RANDALL JOSHUA, information services administrator; b. Santa Monica, Calif., Sept. 30, 1949; s. Joshua and Eunice M. (Serr) G.; B.A. in English, San Fernando Valley State Coll., 1972; M.L.S., UCLA, 1974, cert. law librarianship, 1974; m. Roberta Christine Johnson, June 15, 1973. Intern, Los Angeles County Law Library, 1973-74; asst. librarian O'Melveny & Myers, Los Angeles, 1974-76; law librarian Adams, Duque & Hazeltine, Los Angeles, 1976-82, dir. info. services, 1982-84; sales rep. Callaghan & Co. Law and Tax Publs., 1984-85; mgr. info. services Haight, Dickson, Brown & Bonesteel, Santa Monica, Calif., 1986— instr. Inst. Pvt. Law Librarians, Biltmore Hotel, Los Angeles, 1980, UCLA Extension, 1980, Practising Law Inst., 1981; participant Calif. State Colls. Internat. Studies Program, Uppsala, Sweden, 1971; chmn. 10th Ann. Inst. on Calif. Law, 1982. Cert. law librarian, 1980—. Mem. Am. Assn. Law Libraries, Def. Research Inst., So. Calif. Assn. Law Libraries (chmn. cons. com. 1980, v.p. 1981-82, pres. 1982-83), Spl. Libraries Assn., UCLA Grad. Sch. Library and Info. Sci. Students Assn. (pres. 1973-74). Author: Effective Administration: Better Decisions through Information, 1981. Home: 521 Ramona Ave Sierra Madre CA

91024 Office: Haight Dickson Brown & Bonesteel 201 Santa Monica Blvd PO Box 680 Santa Monica CA 90406

GRAY, ROBERT DANA, electrical engineer, consultant; b. Spokane, Wash., Nov. 13, 1934; s. George Robert and Emma Carolyn (Morrill) G.; m. Beverly Jean Harty, July 31, 1954; children: Robert R., Daniel E., Jeanette C., Caryn M. BSEE, Wash. State U., 1959. Sr. engr. United Nuclear Industries, Richland, Wash., 1970-76; cons. Richland, 1972-75, Elk, Wash., 1981-83, 84—; sr. staff engr. Kaiser Aluminum Corp., Spokane, 1976-81; sr. elec. engr. ASC Machine Tool Co., Spokane, 1983-84; tech. tng. mgr. Transtector Systems Inc., Hayden, Idaho, 1984—; prin. R-B Mktg., Elk, 1980—; pres. R.O. Assocs., Ltd., 1986—. Mem. IEEE, Instrument Soc. Am. (sr.). Avocations: catamaran sailing, hiking, running. Home: Rt 1Box 131B Elk WA 99009 Office: RA Assocs Ltd 10701 Airport Dr Suite 86 Hayden Lake ID 83835

GRAY, RUSSELL WILLIAM, manufacturing engineer; b. New Kensington, Pa., Apr. 3, 1959; s. John Robert and Bernice Marie (Heasley) G.; m. Kathryn Anne Spear, July 10, 1982. BS in Indsl. Engrin., Geneva Coll., Beaver Falls, Pa. Indsl. engr. Storage TEK, Louisville, Colo., 1981-83; mfg. engr. Storage TEK, 1983-84, Woodward Gov., Ft. Collins, Colo., 1984—; cons. Front Range Systems, Boulder, Colo., 1984. Mem. Inst. Indsl. Engrs., Soc. Mfg. Engrs. Republican. United Presbyterian. Avocations: flyfishing, model building, golfing, reading. Home: 612 Armstrong Ave Fort Collins CO 80521 Office: Woodward Gov Co 1000 E Drake Rd Fort Collins CO 80526

GRAY, THOMAS STEPHEN, newspaper editor; b. Burbank, Calif., Aug. 22, 1950; s. Thomas Edgar and Lily Irene (Ax) G.; m. Barbara Ellen Bronson, Aug. 27, 1977; children: Jonathan Thomas, Katherine Marie. B.A., Stanford U., 1972; M.A. in English, UCLA, 1976. Teaching assoc. UCLA, 1976-77; reporter Los Angeles Daily News, 1977-79, editorial writer, 1979-84, editorial page editor, 1984—. Recipient Editorial Excellence award Greater Los Angeles Press Club, 1980, 81. Mem. Nat. Conf. Editorial Writers, Phi Beta Kappa. Office: Daily News Editorial Pages 14539 Sylvan St Van Nuys CA 91411

GRAY, WILLIAM PERCIVAL, judge; b. Los Angeles, Mar. 26, 1912; s. Jacob L. and Catherine (Percival) G.; m. Elizabeth Polin, Nov. 8, 1941; children—Robin Marie, James Polin. A.B., U. Calif. at Los Angeles, 1934; LL.B. cum laude, Harvard, 1939. Bar: Calif. bar 1941. Legal sec. to judge U.S. Ct. Appeals, Washington, 1939-40; with firm O'Melveny & Myers (lawyers), Los Angeles, 1940-41; pvt. practice Los Angeles, 1945-49; partner Gray, Pfaelzer & Robertson, Los Angeles, 1950-66; U.S. dist. judge Central Dist. Calif., 1966—; spl. asst. to atty. gen. U.S., 1958-64; chmn. Calif. Conf. State Bar Dels., 1952. Trustee Ch. of Lighted Window, La Canada. Served from 1st lt. to lt. col. AUS, 1941-45. Fellow Am. Bar Found.; mem. Am. Law Inst., Am. Bar Assn., Los Angeles County Bar Assn. (pres. 1956), State Bar Calif. (bd. govs. 1960-63, pres. 1962-63). Office: US Court House Los Angeles CA 90012

GRAY, WILLIAM THOMAS, urban designer, consultant; b. Oakland, Calif., May 31, 1954; s. Robert James and Merle Lois (Cullen) G. BArch., U. Calif., Berkeley, 1981. Researcher environ. simulation lab. Inst. Urban & Regional Devel. U. Calif., Berkeley, 1981-85; planning cons. Devel. Planning Assocs., Oakland, Calif., 1985—; cons. Dept. City Planning, San Francisco, 1981-85, Fed. Highway Safety Adminstrn., Washington, 1983, Calif. State Coastal Conservancy, 1984. Expert witness Planning Commn., San Francisco, 1981—, Bd. Appeals, San Francisco, 1986—. Recipient Merit award Downtown Plan Dept. City Planning, San Francisco, 1985, Outstanding Achievement award U. Calif., Berkeley, 1984, award of Merit USDA, 1984, Design Merit award NEA, 1983. Mem. Am. Planning Assn. Democrat. Avocations: book collecting, bowling, travel. Home: 5816 Morpeth St Oakland CA 94618 Office: Devel Planning Assocs 5410 Broadway Suite 205 Oakland CA 94618

GRAYBILL, DAVID WESLEY, foundation executive; b. Council Bluffs, Iowa, Apr. 8, 1949; s. John Donald and Dorothy Lorraine (King) G.; m. Kortney Loraine Steinbeck, Aug. 17, 1974; 1 child, Darcy Lorraine. BA in Journalism, U. Iowa, 1971. Cert. indsl. econ. developer. Adminstrv. asst. Iowa City C. of C., 1972-74; exec. v.p. Brighton (Colo.) C. of C., 1974-77; pres. Fremont (Nebr.) C. of C., 1977-83; pres., chief exec. officer Tacoma-Pierce County C. of C., 1983—; pres. Nebr. C. of C. Execs., 1981-82; treas. NE Nebr. Econ. Devel. Dist., 1980-83. Mem. Gov.'s Small Bus. Improvement Com., Wash., 1984—. Mem. Am. C. of C., Am. Econ. Devel. Council (bd. dirs. 1985-87), Wash. C. of C. Execs. (bd. dirs. 1984—), Econ. Devel. Execs. Wash., Pacific NW Indsl. Devel. Council. Mem. Reorganized Ch. Jesus Christ Latter-day Saints. Lodge: Rotary. (bd. dirs. Tacoma club 1985-87). Office: Tacoma-Pierce County C of C PO Box 1933 Tacoma WA 98401

GRAYSON, DOLORES ANN (DEE), educator, writer, consultant; b. Quincy, Ill., May 9, 1939; d. James Clinton and Stella Florine (Summers) G. BS, U. N.C., Greensboro, 1961; MS, Calif. State U., Fullerton, 1976. Cert. tchr., Calif. Tchr., adminstr. Rowland Unified Sch. Dist., Rowland Heights, Calif., 1971-78; title IX staff tng. specialist Midwest Race & Sex Desegregation Assistance Ctr., Manhattan, Kans., 1978-79; cons. title IX Calif. State Dept. Edn., Sacramento, 1979-82; cons. and program dir. Los Angeles County Office Edn., Downey, Calif., 1982—; cons. to state, regional and local ednl. agys. nationwide, 1975—. Author: The Equity Principal, 1986, (with Mary D. Martin) Gender Expectations and Student Achievement, 1984, Infusing an Equity Agenda into School Districts, 1984; contbr. articles to profl. jours. Pres. bd. dirs. Alcoholism Ctr. for Women, Los Angeles, 1982-84. Named Outstanding Tchr. of Yr., Los Angeles County, 1976-77; Outstanding Tchr. of Yr. Rowland Unified Sch. Dist., 1976-77; Tchr. of Yr. Placentia (Calif.) Unified Sch. Dist., 1966-67; Tchr. of Yr. Bellflower (Calif.) Unified Sch. Dist., 1965. Mem. Nat. Coalition for Sex Equity in Edn. (founding mem.), Women Educators (chair nat. steering com. 1980-83), Am. Edn. Research Assn., Assn. Calif. Sch. Adminstrs., Phi Kappa Phi (life). Democrat. Episcopalian. Avocations: golf, skiing, reading. Home: 329 Termino Ave Long Beach CA 90814 Office: Los Angeles County Office Edn 9300 E Imperial Hwy Rm 246 Downey CA 90242-2890

GRAYSON, DONALD KENNETH, archaeologist, educator; b. N.Y.C., Apr. 10, 1945; S. S.A. and Marion Grayson; m. Barbara E. Proller, Mar. 24, 1968. BA, SUNY, Buffalo, 1966; MA, U. Oreg., 1969, PhD, 1973. Asst. prof. anthropology Kirkland Coll., Clinton, N.Y., 1971-74; archaeologist Bur. Land Mgmt., Portland, Oreg., 1974-75; asst. prof. U. Wash., Seattle, 1975-78, assoc. prof., 1978-83, prof., 1983—; adj. asst. prof. Quaternary Research Ctr., U. Wash., 1975-78, adj. assoc. prof., 1978-82; vis. assoc. prof. NYU, 1981; adj. asst. curator environ. archaeology Thomas Burke Meml. Mus., U. Wash., 1977-78, adj. assoc. curator 1978-83, adj. curator 1983—; research assoc. dept. anthropology, Am. Mus. Nat. History, 1979—; cons. U. Oreg. archaeol. crew, 1973; dir. Kirkland Coll. archaeol. crew, 1973, Bur. Land Mgmt. archaeol. crews, 1975, U. Wash. archaeol. field sch., 1978, 79, 80; dir. various small mammal censuses throughout Oreg., Nev., Calif., 1975-84. Author: The Establishment of Human Antiquity, 1983 (Book of Yr. in anthropology, Am. Library Assn., 1983), Quantitative Zooarchaeology, 1984; editor Volcanic Activity and Human Ecology, 1979, Studies in Archaeological Science, 1985; assoc. editor Quaternary Research, 1983—; mem. editorial bd. Advances in Archaeolog. Method and Theory, 1983—; contbr. articles to profl. jours. Grantee NSF 1977-80, 80-82, 81-83, 83-84, U. Oreg. 1969, Wenner-Gren Found. 1971, Mellon Found. 1973, Am. Philosophical Soc. Penrose Fund 1976, Am. Mus. Nat. History 1977-78, Mr. Bingham's Trust for Charity 1982-83, U.S. Forest Service 1983-84. NDEA Title IV fellow, 1966-69. Fellow Am. Anthropol. Assn.; mem. Am. Orinthologists' Union, NSF (archaeology panel 1985—), Soc. Am. Archaeology (exec. officer 1979-81, Fryxell award for Interdisciplinary Research 1986), Am. Soc. Conservation Archaeology (v.p. 1977-78, pres. 1978-79), Am. Soc. Mammalogists, Council for Mus. Anthropology, Soc. Systematic Zoology, History of Sci. Soc., Internat. Council Archaeozoology, Sigma Xi. Office: U Wash Dept Anthropology Seattle WA 98195

GRAYSON, JOHN WESLEY, business consultant, computer science educator; b. N.Y.C., Sept. 7, 1941; s. Roger Henry and Dorothy Mae (Kenny) G.; children—John Wesley Jr., Carleton Avery. M.A., SUNY-Stony Brook, 1974; postgrad. U. West Los Angeles Sch. Law, 1979. Programmer, Data Stats., Inc., N.Y.C., 1961-62; sr. programmer Computech, Inc., N.Y.C., 1962-65; systems analyst Nat. Shoes, Inc., Bronx, N.Y., 1965-68; sr. systems analyst Acad. Press, Inc., N.Y.C., 1968-69; sr. systems cons. Grumman Aerospace Corp., 1969-71; sr. mgmt. cons. FRB, N.Y.C., 1971-72; coll. lectr., mgr. mgmt. info. systems SUNY-Stony Brook, 1972-76; communications cons. Gen. Telephone Calif., Los Angeles, 1976-79; v.p. Security Pacific Nat. Bank, Los Angeles, 1980; owner, pres. Bus. Cons. Firm, Glendale, Calif., 1981—; assoc. prof. computer sci. Compton (Calif.) Coll.; lectr. SUNY-Stony Brook. Treas., Sunset Baseball Little League, Redondo Beach, Calif.; pres. 147th Bd. Election Dist. Insps., N.Y.; trustee Middle Island (N.Y.) Pub. Library; SBA pres. U. West Los Angeles Sch. Law, 1979; com. examiner Glendale (Calif.) Unified Sch. Dist.; mem. usher bd. St. Francis Episcopal Ch., also mem. choir; scoutmaster Cub Scouts Am., St. James, N.Y.; mem. West High Sch. Band Assn., Torrance, Calif., West High Sch. PTA. Mem. Data Processing Mgmt. Assn., Assn. Systems Mgmt., ACM (treas.). Republican. Clubs: Suffolk County Republican (Brook Haven, N.Y.); Pioneer Track (N.Y.); Los Verdes Men's Golf; Masons, Shriners. Home: 1533 S Pearl Ave Compton CA 90221 Office: 1533 S Pean Ave Canton CA 90221

GRAYSON, ROBERT ALLEN, marketing executive, educator; b. N.Y.C., Oct. 8, 1927; s. Julius and Lillian (Davidson) G.; m. Suzanne B. Bomse, June 18, 1960; children: Peter, Jocelyn, Andrea. B.S., U. Ill., 1948; M.B.A., NYU, 1962, Ph.D., 1968. Vice pres. Henry S. Harris Assos. (mgmt. cons.), 1952-58; v.p. mktg. I. Rokeach & Sons, 1958-62; new products mgr. Lever Bros., 1962-68; sr. v.p., mem. exec. com. Daniel & Charles, Inc., N.Y.C., 1968-71; chmn. Grayson Assos., Inc., mgmt. cons. and trade show producers, Santa Barbara, Calif., 1971—; prof. bus. adminstrn. NYU Grad. Sch., 1966-85; prof. bus. policy Fordham U., 1972-75. Author: Introduction to Marketing, 1971, Resumes that Get Interviews, Interviews that Get Jobs, 1973; editor: Marketing and the Computer, 1967; pub.: Jour. Consumer Mktg., Jour. Bus. and Indsl. Mktg., Jour. Services Mktg. Mem. Am. Marketing Assn. (pres. 1969-70), Inst. Mgmt. Sci., AAUP, Acad. Mgmt. Office: 108 Loma Media Rd Santa Barbara CA 93103

GRAZIANO, JOHN, broadcast executive; b. Los Angeles, Mar. 22, 1951; s. William D. and Mary Joyce (Plourde) G.; m. Wendy Ann Willing, Apr. 2, 1977 (div. June 1978). Student, Loyola U., Los Angeles. Dir. sales promotions Jeans West, Los Angeles, 1970-73; v.p. dir. advt. Integrity Advt., Los Angeles, 1973-75; gen. mgr. Sta. KNAC Radio, Long Beach, Calif., 1975-80; v.p. H-R Stone Radio, Los Angeles, 1980-82; sr. v.p. Torbet Radio, Beverly Hills, Calif., 1982—; pres. John Graziano Advt., Torrance, Calif., 1975—. Graphic designer Pro Am Sports, 1977 (Best Ad award South Bay mag.); producer radio spot comml. Leo's Stereo, 1978 (Best Ad award Sta. KNAC). Mem. So. Calif. Broadcasting Assn., Calif. Broadcasters. Club: Los Angeles Ad. Avocations: golf, photography, design. Home: 4024 Mesa St Torrance CA 90505 Office: Torbet Radio 11111 Santa Monica Blvd #1820 Los Angeles CA 90025

GREASER, CONSTANCE UDEAN, research organization executive; b. San Diego, Jan. 18, 1938; d. Lloyd Edward and Udean Greaser; B.A., San Diego State Coll., 1959; postgrad. U. Copenhagen Grad. Sch. Fgn. Students, 1963, Georgetown U. Sch. Fgn. Service, 1967; M.A., U. So. Calif., 1968; Exec. M.B.A., UCLA, 1981. Advt., publicity mgr. Crofton Co., San Diego, 1959-62; supr. Mercury Publs., Fullerton, Calif., 1962-64; supr. engring. support services div. Arcata Data Mgmt., Hawthorne, Calif., 1964-67; mgr. computerized typesetting dept. Continental Graphics, Los Angeles, 1967-70; v.p., editorial dir. Sage Publs., Inc., Beverly Hills, Calif., 1970-74; head publs. Rand Corp., Santa Monica, Calif., 1974—. Mem. Women in Bus. (pres. 1977-78), Soc. for Scholarly Pubs. (nat. bd. dirs.), Women in Communication, World Future Soc., Brahma Kumaris World Spiritual Orgn. Co-author: Quick Writer—Build Your Own Word Processing Users Guide, 1983; Quick Writer—Word Processing Center Operations Manual, 1984; editor: Urban Research News, 1970-74; mng. editor Comparative Polit. Studies, 1971-74; contbr. articles to various jours. Office: The Rand Corp 1700 Main St Santa Monica CA 90406

GREAVES, JAMES LOUIS, art conservator; b. Middletown, Conn., Jan. 25, 1943; s. Wellington North and Mabel (Frazer) G.; divorced; 1 child, Stephen Frazer. BS in Biology, Coll. William and Mary, 1965; MA in Art History, Diploma in Art Conservation, Inst. Fine Arts, NYU, 1970. Conservation intern Los Angeles County Mus., 1968-70, conservator, 1970, asst. head conservator, 1977-79, acting head conservator, 1979-81, sr. paintings conservator, 1981-85; owner, cons. Conservation Services, Santa Monica, 1985—; chief conservator Detroit Inst. Arts, 1970-77; cons. conservator Art Gallery of Huntington Library, San Marino, Calif., 1979—; part-time instr. art conservation for sr. and grad. level art historians, UCLA and Calif. State U., Fullerton, 1979—. Fellow Internat. Inst. Conservation, Am. Inst. Conservation; mem. Western Assn. Art Conservators.

GREBEL, KEN WALTER, industrial electronics executive; b. Torrance, Calif., Feb. 2, 1947; s. Robert Walter and Betty Jane (pearsall) G.; m. Linda Marie Dowling; children: Cari, CHristy, Brad. Student pub. schs., Calif. Warehouse mktg. Hamilton, Culver City, Calif., 1967-70; mktg., sales Wyle, El Segundo, Calif., 1970—; v.p. Wyle, Irvine, Calif., 1982—. Served with USCG, 1965-71. Republican. Club: Balboa Bay (Newport Beach, Calif.). Avocations: water and snow skiing, deep sea fishing, raising horses. Office: Wyle 17872 Cowan Irvine CA 92714

GREEGOR, ROBERT B., II, research scientist; b. Tarentum, Pa., May 10, 1947; s. Robert B. and Carrie Irene (Romberger) G.; m. Dixie Kay Kackley, Aug. 2, 1969; children: Jennifer, Joshua. BS, Muskingum Coll., 1969; MS, U. Wyo., 1973. Research scientist Boeing Aerospace, Seattle, 1973—; cons. faculty Nat. Inst. for Occupational Safety and Health, 1974—, USC, Los Angeles, 1981—; x-ray cons. USS, Gen. Electric, Exxon, 1978—, Los Alamos (N.Mex.) Nat. Lab., 1986—; mem. exec. com. Stanford (Calif.) Synchrotron Radiation Lab., 1986—. Contbr. articles to profl. jours. Mem. AAAS, Materials Research Soc., Kappa Sigma. Republican. Presbyterian. Office: Boeing Aerospace MS 2T-05 Seattle WA 98124

GREELY, MICHAEL TRUMAN, attorney general of Montana; b. Great Falls, Mont., Feb. 28, 1940; s. Myril Jay and Laura Harriet (Haugh) G.; m. Marilyn Jean Myhre, Dec. 1, 1972; children: Winston Truman, Morgen. B.A., Yale U., 1962; J.D., U. Mont., 1967. Bar: Mont. 1967. Tchr. pub. schs. Oklahoma City, 1962-63; asst. atty. gen. Mont., 1968-70; atty. gen. 1977—; chmn. Mont. Justice Project, 1975; dep. county atty. Cascade County, Mont., 1970-74. Mem. Mont. Ho. of Reps., 1971-74; mem. Mont. Senate, 1975-77; Pres. 8th Dist. Youth Guidance Home, Great Falls, 1971-72. Mem. Nat. Assn. Attys. Gen. (pres. 1983-84), Mont., Cascade County bar assns. Democrat. Office: Justice Bldg 215 N Sanders St Helena MT 59620

GREEN, ALLEN THEODORE, electronics manufacturing executive; b. Chgo., Mar. 30, 1934; s. Carl M. and Gertrude C. (Lerman) G.; m. Shirley M. Grundstein, Feb. 12, 1956; children: Keri, Lorie, Bowie. BS in Aerospace Engring., U. Ill., 1956. Registered prof. engr., Calif. Flight test engr. G-D Convair, San Diego, 1956-58, structures test engr., 1958-61; project engr. Aerojet, Sacramento, 1961-70; v.p. sales and mktg. Dunegan Research Co., Livermore, Calif., 1970-72; pres. Acoustic Emission Tech. Corp., Sacramento, 1972—, also bd. dirs. Contbr. articles to profl. jours.; patentee in field. Organizer Big Bros. of San Diego, 1958, Sacramento, 1963. Named Outstanding Alumnus U. Ill. Dept. Aerospace Engring., 1981. Fellow Am. Soc. Nondestructive Testing, Acoustic Emission Working Group (Gold Medal 1983); mem. ASTM, Soc. Exptl. Mechs., Instrument Soc. Am. (sr.). Avocations: racquetball, tennis, swimming, sailing, hiking. Office: Acoustic Emission Tech Corp 1824 J Tribute Rd Sacramento CA 95815

GREEN, ARTHUR FREDRICK, logistics engineer; b. Cleve., Sept. 14, 1934; s. Arthur Abraham and Mary Elizabeth (Davidson) G.; m. Iva Jean Hairston, July 2, 1960; children: Arthur F. Jr., Bret Allan. BS in Adminstrv. Sci., Pepperdine U., 1976. Design draftsman Reliance Electric Co., Cleve., 1957-62; engr. technician, gen. engr. Long Beach (Calif.) Naval Shipyard, 1962-71, adminstrv. officer, 1971-74, br. head workload coordination, 1974-79, repairables mgmt. officer, 1979—; prin. Cypress, Calif., 1985—. Contbr. articles Naval Engrs. Jour., 1983 (Cert. 1983). Served with USN, 1953-57. Mem. Naval Civilian Adminstrs. Assn. (pres. 1974-76), Fed. Mgrs. Assn., Am. Cons. League, Soc. Logistics Engrs. Democrat. Methodist. Home: 4559 Blanca Dr Cypress CA 90630 Office: Long Beach Naval Shipyard Planning Dept Code 224 Long Beach CA 90822

GREEN, BARRY, lawyer; b. Bklyn., Oct. 24, 1957; s. Joseph and Anne (Polsky) G. BA, Brandeis U., 1978; JD, Tulane U., 1982. Bar: N.Mex. 1982, U.S. Dist. Ct. N.Mex. 1986. Asst. dist. atty. Dist. Atty.'s Office, Santa Fe, 1983; sole practice Santa Fe, 1983—. Mem. N.Mex. Trial Lawyers Assn., Am. Trial Lawyers Assn., N.Mex. Bar Assn. Democrat. Avocations: sense of humor, high country mountaineering. Office: 150 Washington Ave Suite 300 Santa Fe NM 87501

GREEN, BENSON ARTHUR, film/TV executive; b. N.Y.C. B.A., Dartmouth Coll., 1956; postgrad. UCLA, 1957. Pres., chief exec. officer N. Lee Lacy Assocs., Los Angeles, N.Y., Chgo., London, Paris, 1971—; pres., chief exec. officer Greenbriar Prodns., Los Angeles, N.Y.C., 1973—; pres., chief exec. officer Greenhouse Properties, Los Angeles, N.Y.C., 1980—; pres., chief exec. officer Photon Pub., Los Angeles, 1981—; pres., chief exec. officer LBA Inc., N.Y.C., 1981—. Mem. Assn. Ind. Comml. Producers (founding pres. 1976-81, bd. dirs.). Office: 8446 Melrose Pl Los Angeles CA 90069

GREEN, CAROL H., lawyer, journalist; b. Seattle, Feb. 18, 1944; B.A. summa cum laude in History and Journalism, La. Tech. U., 1965; L.L.M. (Ford Found. fellow), Yale U., 1977; J.D., U. Denver, 1979. Intern, Shreveport (La.) Times, 1964, reporter, 1965-66; reporter Guam Daily News, 1966-67; city editor Pacific Jour., Agana, Guam, 1967-68; reporter, editorial writer, Denver Post, 1968-75, legal affairs reporter, 1977-79, asst. editor editorial page, 1979-81, house counsel, 1980-83, labor relations mgr., 1981-83; assoc. Holme Roberts & Owen, 1983-85; v.p. human resources and legal affairs Denver Post, 1985—; mem. corrections task force Colo. Criminal Justice Standards and Goals, 1985 speaker for USIA, India, Egypt. Bd. dirs. YWCA, Trans. Council, Denver C. of C. Recipient McWilliams award for juvenile justice, Denver, 1971; award for interpretive reporting Denver Newspaper Guild, 1979. Mem. ABA (forum on communications law), Colo. Women's Bar Assn., Colo. Bar Assn. (bd. govs. 1985-86, chairperson BAR-press com. 1980), Denver Bar Assn. (co-chairperson jud. selection and benefits com. 1982-85, 1st v.p. 1986), Alliance Profl. Women (exec. com.), Women's Forum, Leadership Denver. Clubs: Denver Press, Denver Athletic. Episcopalian. Office: The Denver Post 650 15th St Denver CO 80202

GREEN, CHARLES ELIAS, sonar specialist, engineering physicist; b. San Diego, Mar. 27, 1912; s. David Elias and Veva Fanny (Kent) G.; m. Emily G. Haddan, Nov. 26, 1937; children: Gerald C., Marilyn E. AB, UCLA, 1936, EdB, 1937, BS, 1942; PhD (hon.), AAAS, 1982. Registered profl. engr., Calif. Tchr., counselor San Diego Pub. Schs., 1937-46; with War Research div. U. Calif., 1944-46; from research physicist to supervisory physicist Naval Ocean Sci. Ctr. (formerly Navel Undersea Lab. formerly Naval Electronics Lab.), San Diego, 1946-75, retired., 1975; cons. sonar and naval ships San Diego and Washington, 1975—. Contbr. articles to profl. jours.; patentee sonar transducers. Mem. planning bd. San Diego North Park Community, 1975—, chmn. 1976-77. Recipient Presdl. Citation, Pres. Lyndon Johnson, 1964. Fellow AAAS; mem. Acoustical Soc. Am. (chmn. San Diego 1968-69, nat. meeting program planner, Calif. noise control com.), Phi Delta Kappa. Avocation: electronics. Home and Office: 3427 Florida St San Diego CA 92104

GREEN, CHRISTOPHER JOHN, architect; b. Denver, May 4, 1954; s. John Elliot and Mildred Gladys (Witt) G.; m. Gay Ninette Gardner, Nov. 9, 1985; 1 child, Rebecca Lee Gardner Green. BArch in Environ. Design, U. Colo., 1976; MArch, Ill. Inst. Tech., 1982. Registered architect, Wash. Interior designer State of Ohio, Columbus, 1978-79, Skidmore Owings & Merrill, Chgo., 1979-81; space planning, interior designer Swanke Hayden Connell, Chgo., 1982; mktg. coordinator ECI Interiors, Spokane, Wash., 1982-84; pres. Archtl. Concepts, PS, Spokane, Wash., 1984—. Bd. dirs. Future Spokane, also liaison to river com. Mem. AIA, Spokane C. of C. Office: Archtl Concepts PS W 412 Riverside Suite 504 Spokane WA 99201

GREEN, CYRIL KENNETH, retail company executive; b. Portland, Oreg., June 11, 1931; s. Lionel and Nora Evelyn G.; m. Beverly Ann Hutchinson, July 24, 1950; children: Kenneth James, Teri Ann, Tamara Jo Green Easton, Kelly Denise Green Van Horn. Student pub. schs., Portland. With Fred Meyer, Inc., Portland, 1947—, food dept. mgr., supr. food stores, grocery buyer, until 1967, mgr. Spokane wholesale div., 1967-70, v.p., dir. ops., 1970-72, pres., chief operating officer, 1972—. Office: Fred Meyer Inc 3800 SE 22d Ave Portland OR 97202

GREEN, DOUGLAS ROSS, immunologist; b. N.Y.C., Feb. 15, 1955; s. Warren Sawyer and Lila Dorothea (Eichel) G.; m. Rona Janis Mogil, May 22, 1982. BS magna cum laude, Yale U., 1977, PhD, 1981. Postdoctoral fellow Yale U., New Haven, 1981-83, research biologist, 1984-85; asst. prof. U. Alta., Edmonton, Can., 1985—. Contbr. articles to profl. jours. Mem. Am. Assn. Immunologists, N.Y. Acad. Scis. Avocations: music, songwriting. Office: U Alberta, Dept Immunology 8-63MSB, Edmonton, AB Canada T6G 2M7

GREEN, FRANCIS WILLIAM, investment consultant; b. Locust Grove, Okla., Mar. 17, 1920; s. Noel Francis and Mary (Lincoln) G.; B.S., Phoenix U., 1955; M.S. in Elec. Engring., Minerva U., Milan, Italy, 1959; M.S. in Engring., West Coast U., Los Angeles, 1965; m. Alma J. Ellison, Aug. 26, 1950 (dec. Sept. 1970); children—Sharmon, Rhonda; m. Susan G. Mathis, July 14, 1973 (div. July 1979). With USN Guided Missile Program, 1945-49; design and electronic project engr. Falcon missile program Hughes Aircraft Co., Culver City, Calif., 1949-55; sr. electronic engr. Atlas missile program Convair Astronautics, San Diego, 1955-59; sr. engr. Polaris missile program Nortronics div. Northrop, Anaheim, Calif., 1959-60; chief, supr. electronic engr. data systems br. Tech. Support div. Rocket Propulsion Lab., USAF, Edwards AFB, Calif., 1960-67, dep. chief tech. support div., 1967-69; tech. adviser Air Force Missile Devel. Center, Holloman AFB, N.Mex., 1969-70, 6585 Test Group, Air Force Spl. Weapons Center, Holloman AFB, from 1970; pvt. investment cons., 1978—. Bd. examiners U.S. CSC; mem. Pres.'s Missile Site Labor Relations Com.; cons. advanced computer and data processing tech. and systems engring.; mem. USAF Civilian Policy Bd. and Range Comdrs. Council. Served as pilot USAAF, 1941-45. Mem. IEEE, Am. Inst. Aeros. and Astronautics; Nat. Assn. Flight Instrs. Contbr. articles to profl. jours. Home and Office: 2345 Apache Ln Alamogordo NM 88310

GREEN, GEORGE, radio executive; b. N.Y.C., May 23; m. Mim, Aug. 23, 1958; children—Jeff, Randy, Jamie. B., UCLA, 1955. Acct. exec. Sta. KPAL, Palm Springs, Calif., 1956-57, KDAY-KRHM, Los Angeles, 1957-59; salesman Sta. KABC-TV, Los Angeles, 1959-60, acct. exec. Sta. KABC, Los Angeles, 1960-65, gen. sales mgr., 1965-79, gen. mgr., 1979—, v.p., 1979-86, pres., 1986—. Mem. exec. com. United Cerebral Palsy/Spastic Children's Found., Los Angeles, 1980—. Recipient Lifesaver award Advt. Industry Emergency Fund, Los Angeles, 1983. Mem. So. Calif. Broadcaster's Assn. (chmn. 1983—), Ad Club (bd. dirs. 1980—). *

GREEN, JACK LAMARS, judge; b. Kalispell, Mont., May 18, 1922; s. Leonard L. and Artie M. (Naud) G.; m. Patsy Jane Cohe, June 21, 1944; children: Susan Jane, Jack Leonard, Linda Luanne. BA, U. Mont., 1947, LLB, 1948, JD, 1970. Bar: Mont. 1949. Atty. City of Missoula, Mont., 1959-61; judge Dist. Ct. Missoula, 1963—; Faculty adviser Nat. Coll. State Judiciary, U. Nev., 1971, 75; chmn. meeting Five State Jud. Conf., Missoula, 1960; Mont. rep. Nat. Conf. State Trial Judges, 1973-78; mem. sentence rev. div. Mont. Supreme Ct., 1973-77; chmn. Mont. Jud. Standards Commn., 1973-77. Chmn. Missoula County chpt. Nat. Found., 1953-60, Missoula County Rep. Cen. Com., 1955-61; mem. State Rep. com., 1962-63; del. Rep. Nat. Conv., 1960; alderman 4th ward Missoula City Council, 1962-63; bd. dirs. Missoula ARC, 1960-64, Missoula council Camp Fire Girls, 1963-69, pres. 1966-67. Served with inf. AUS, 1943-46. Decorated D.S.M. Mem. Mont. Bar Assn., Western Mont. Bar Assn. (pres. 1960), Mont. Judges Assn. (pres. 1973-74), Mont. Dist. Judges Assn. (pres. 1967-68), Theta Chi, Phi Delta Phi. Lodges: Elks, Masons, Shriners. Home: 127 Hastings Ave Missoula MT 59801 Office: Missoula County Courthouse Missoula MT 59801

GREEN, JAMES CRAIG, data systems company executive; b. Gladstone, Mich., Apr. 19, 1933; s. Albert Keene and Margaret Josephine (Craig) G.; student Coll. of Gt. Falls, 1951-53, UCLA, 1962; m. Catherine Maxwell, Nov. 1, 1957; children—Cindi, Shelley, Nancy, James W., Robert. Clk., carrier U.S. Post Office, Gt. Falls, Mont., 1951-57; clk. office and sales Mont. Liquor Control Bd., Gt. Falls, 1957-59; payroll clk. Herald Examiner, Hearst Publs., Los Angeles, 1959-67, data processing mgr., 1967-75, data processing ops. mgr. corp. hdqrs. Hearst Publs., N.Y.C., 1975-78; gen. mgr., v.p. Computer/Data Inc., Billings, Mont., 1978-83; mgr. customer service Big Sky Data Systems, Billings, Mont., 1983-84; pres. FACTS, Inc., 1985—; tax cons., Los Angeles, 1962-75. Cub Scout leader, com. chmn., Los Angeles council Boy Scouts Am., 1973-75; pres. Bus. Office Employees Assn. Los Angeles, 1963-66. Area commr. Black Otter Council Boy Scouts Am., 1982-84, com. chmn., 1982-84. Served with USNR, 1951-59. Recipient degree of Chevalier, Order De Molay, 1951; cert. data processing mgr. Mem. Data Processing Mgrs. Assn., Los Angeles Masonic Press Club. Clubs: Masons, Blue Lodge, York Rite, Shrine (Grotto charter mem. Gt. Falls), DeMolay (chpt. advisor 1983—, state publs. advisor 1982—). Writer, negotiator contract Bus. Office Employees Assn., Los Angeles, 1965. Office: 2110 Wiligate Ln Billings MT 59102

GREEN, JANET MARY, business, marketing educator; b. Pitts., Nov. 6, 1933; d. Lawrence John and Agnes Petronella (Lanzine) Yoest; m. Donald Marion Stoops, Aug. 6, 1959 (div. 1970); m. Cecil Dennis Green, July 27, 1977; children: Donald Lawrence, Denise Lynn. Diploma in nursing, Braddock Gen. Hosp., 1954; B. U. Redlands, 1974; M in Bus., Calif. State U., Long Beach, 1978. Cert. nursing, bus., and pub. adminstrn. tchr., Calif. Head nurse Riverside (Calif.) Gen. Univ. Med. Ctr., 1966-77; assoc. prof. bus. and econs. San Bernardino (Calif.) Valley Coll., 1977—; lectr. Calif. State U., San Bernardino, 1985—; cons. in field, 1977—. Officer Pub. Employees Assn., Riverside County, 1972-74, Riverside Emblem Club, 399, 1983-84. Served to 1st lt., 1958-60. Mem. Am. Bus. Women Assn. (chmn. edn. assoc. boos night 1986, Woman of Yr. 1986). Republican. Roman Catholic. Lodge: Rotary. Avocations: golfing, dancing, fishing. Home: 17334 Ranchero Rd Riverside CA 92504 Office: San Bernardino Community Coll 701 S Mt Vernon Ave San Bernardino CA 92410

GREEN, JON ALLEN, physician, educator; b. N.Y.C., May 7, 1942; s. George and Ethel (Cohen) G.; m. Janet Ann Rutstein, July 19, 1970; children: Jason, Daniel, Laurence. BA, Clark U., 1963; PhD, Boston U., 1971, MD cum laude, 1972. Diplomate Nat. Bd. Med. Examiners, Am. Bd. Internal Medicine. Intern then resident U. Utah, Salt Lake City, 1972-74, fellow in infectious diseases, 1977-78, asst. prof. medicine, 1978-84, assoc. prof., 1984-86; research assoc. NIH, Bethesda, Md., 1974-77; assoc. prof. U. Calif., Davis, 1986—; chief Ambulatory Care VA Med. Ctr., Martinez, Calif., 1986—, cons. infectious disease, 1986—. Contbr. articles to profl. jours. Served to comdr. USPHS, 1974-77. NIH fellow, 1964-67; NIH grantee, 1978-81. Mem. AAAS, Am. Assn. Microbiology, Am. Fedn. Clin. Research (regional councillor 1980-83). Avocations: swimming, hiking, skiing. Home: 122 Venado Corte Walnut Creek CA 94598 Office: VA Med Ctr 11C 150 Muir Rd Martinez CA 94553

GREEN, KENNETH CHARLES, education educator, researcher; b. N.Y.C., Feb. 2, 1951; s. Gilbert and Shirley (Milter) G.; m. Rika Rosemary van Dam, June 29, 1980; children: Aaron Hans, Mara Claire. BA, New Coll., 1973; MA, Ohio State U., 1977; PhD, UCLA, 1982. Research assoc. Higher Edn. Research Inst., Los Angeles, 1979-83; assoc. dir. Higher Edn. Research Inst. UCLA, 1984—; lectr., various colls. and universities. Author: (with F.R. Kemerer and J.V. Baldridge) Strategies for Effective Enrollment Management, 1982, Government Support for Minority Participation in Highter Education, 1982, (with W. Zumeta, V. Melloff) The States and Independent Institutions, and numerous research publs.; reviewer Jour. Higher Edn., also monograph series. Mem. Am. Assn. Higher Edn., Assn. for Study of Higher Edn., Am. Edn. Research Assn., Fund for Improvement of Postsecondary Edn. (reviewer), Policy Studies Orgn. Office: UCLA Higher Edn Research Inst 320 Moore Hall 405 Hilgard Ave Los Angeles CA 90024

GREEN, KENNETH EDWARD, ceramic materials engineer, researcher; b. Denver, Jan. 4, 1948; s. James Milton and Mae Lucille (Miner) G.; m. Mary Elizabeth Ewell, June 17, 1967; children: Pamela Mae, Annette Elizabeth, Kenneth James. BS in Engring. Physics, Colo. Sch. Mines, 1976. Research technician Coors Porcelain Co., Golden, Colo., 1966-77, jr. research engr., 1977-78, research engr., 1978-81, sr. research engr., 1981—. Served to lt. USN 1965, Vietnam, with Res. Mem. Am. Ceramic Soc., Am. Radio Relay League, Mensa, Colo. State Hist. Soc., Smithsonian Inst. Lodges: AF&AM, RAM (high priest 1986—), KT (commdr. 1986—). Avocations: ham radio, history, photography, outdoor recreation, classical music. Home: 6139 Routt St Arvada CO 80004 Office: Coors Porcelain Co 17750 W 32d Ave Golden CO 80401

GREEN, MARJORIE BILLER, nonprofit organization adminstrator; b. Boston, Nov. 5, 1939; d. David Wolfe and Martha S. (Rosenthal) Biller; m. Jason I. Green, Mar. 17, 1963; children: Nancy Elke, David Charles, Matthew Adam. AB cum laude, Boston U., 1961, MA, 1964; postgrad., U. Calif., Berkeley, 1961-62, UCLA, 1973-78. Ednl. cons. Rand Corp., Los Angeles, 1977-78; coordinator Wilshire Community Edn. Complex, Los Angeles, 1979-80; cons. Los Angeles Unified Sch. Dist., 1980-83; exec. dir. Calif. Coalition Pub. Edn., Los Angeles, 1985—. Mem. Mayor Bradley's Edn. Adv. Com., Los Angeles, 1979—; del. Dem. Nat. Conv., San Francisco, 1984; chairperson 24th Congl. Dist. Women-to-Women campaign, Los Angeles, 1984; mem. Los Angeles Commn. Sex Equity, 1984—; bd. dirs. Community Relations Conf. So. Calif., 1984, bd. dirs., 1985—; bd. dirs. Para los Niños, Los Angeles, 1984—; bd. dirs. community relations com. Jewish Fedn. Council So. Calif., 1986, chmn. edn. commn., 1986—. Recipient Outstanding Service award Los Angeles Unified Sch. Dist., 1981-82, Outstanding Contbn. award Los Angeles Commn. Sex Equity, 1983, citation Calif. Assembly, 1986, Euclan award U. Calif., 1986. Mem. LWV, Phi Beta Kappa, Phi Delta Kappa. Avocations: literature, music, swimming. Home: 218 S Lorraine Blvd Los Angeles CA 90004 Office: Calif Coalition Pub Edn 4034 Buckingham Rd Suite 212 Los Angeles CA 90008-2398

GREEN, MICHAEL JOSEPH, clinical social worker; b. Stockton, Calif., Jan. 26, 1951; s. Earl Adolphe and Hattie Rebecca (Smith) G.; m. Gwendolyn Sue Davis, Dec. 8, 1979; 1 child, Christopher Michael. AA, Delta Jr. Coll., 1971; BA, San Francisco State U., 1974; MSW, Calif. State U., Fresno, 1976. Social worker Luth. Care, San Francisco, 1971-74; social worker Fresno (Calif.) County Ednl. Opportunity Commn., 1974-76, vol. coordinator, 1974-76; psychiat. social worker State of Calif., Chico, 1977-78, Stockton, 1978-81; clin. social worker Valley Mountain Regional Ctr., Stockton, 1981—, Outreach Ministries, Stockton, 1986—. Fellow Am. Orthopsychiat. Assn.; mem. Nat. Assn. Social Workers (lic.), Gideons Internat. Republican. Mem. Pentecostal Ch. Avocations: running, model ship bldg.

GREEN, STANLEY JOSEPH, chemical engineer, researcher; b. N.Y.C., Mar. 11, 1920; s. Maurice and Ada (Silverstein) G.; m. Alice B. Denenholz, Apr. 8, 1951; children: David P., Douglas M., Ronald F. BSChemE, CCNY, 1940; MSChemE, Drexel Inst. Tech., 1953; PhDChemE, U. Pitts., 1968. Registered profl. engr., Pa. Assoc. chem. engr. U.S. Bur. Mines, College Park, Md., 1942-45; chem. engr. Fercleve Corp., Oak Ridge, Tenn., 1945, Acme Coppersmithing & Machine Co., Oreland, Pa., 1945-54; mgr. reactor devel. and analysis Bettis Atomic Power Lab. div. Westinghouse, West Mifflin, Pa., 1954-77; dir. steam generator project Electric Power Research Inst., Palo Alto, Calif., 1977—. Contbr. articles to profl. jours. Recipient Donald & Kern award Am. Inst. Chem. Engring., 1985. Fellow ASME (chmn. ditto-heat transfer div. 1973, centennial medallion 1980). Democrat. Jewish. Home: 3348 Middlefield Rd Palo Alto CA 94306 Office: Electric Power Research Inst 3412 Hillview Ave Palo Alto CA 94303

GREEN, THERESA DIANE, social worker; b. Port Angelas, Wash., Oct. 10, 1939; d. Walter Arnold and Edna Katherine (Lanich) Vickery; m. Norman Edward Green, Sept. 5, 1964 (div. June 1983); children: Darrin Scott, Brian Allen. BS in Psychology, Wash. State U., 1961; MSW, U. Denver, 1969. Child welfare worker Spokane (Wash.) County State Dept Pub Assistance, 1962-64, State Dept Pub Assistance, Colfax, Wash., 1970-72; asst. prof. social work Wash. State U., Pullman, 1970-76; diagnostic intake worker Whitman County Mental Health, Pullman, 1974-76; child abuse psychiat. social worker Humboldt Child Care Council, Eureka, Calif., 1978-84; pvt. practice in social work Arcata, Calif., 1984—; Cons. Hoffman Inst., San Francisco, 1984—, Humboldt and Del Norte Counties, Eureka, 1985—, State Dept. Alcoholism Prevention, Calif., 1986—, Benamor Inst., Eureka, 1986—, Rural Human Services Domestic Violence Program Services to Children, 1986., Humboldt Women for Shelter-Therapist to Child Victims of Domestic Violence. Mock com. dist. atty. reform, Eureka, 1986. Recipient Redwood Broadcasting Heroism award, 1982; named Outstanding Faculty Mem. of Yr. Wash. State U., 1974. Mem. Nat. Assn. Social Workers (cert.), Acad. Cert. Social Workers, Common Cause, Women Against Pornography, Serious Legis. Against Molesters, Psi Chi. Democrat. Methodist. Avocations: water skiing, art, music, creative visualization. Home and Office: 1179 Stromberg Ave Arcata CA 95521

GREEN, TYLER SCOT, architect; b. Marshall, Mich., Dec. 6, 1960; s. Richard M. and Carolyn J. Green. BArch, Ariz. State U., 1985. Assoc. Lawrence Enyart & Assoc., Phoenix, 1984-85, William Bruder Architect, Ltd., New River, Ariz., 1985—; pvt. practice architecture Carefree, Ariz., 1985—. Home: PO Box 1088 Carefree AZ 85377 Office: Box 4575 New River St New River AZ 85029

GREEN, WILLIAM HOWARD, entrepreneur; b. Cedar Rapids, Apr. 24, 1915; s. Howard Ruggles and Stella Juliette (Wolfe) G.; m. Louise Henrietta Chandler, Dec. 24, 1937; children: Dianne Elizabeth Boons, Howard Ruggles II, Julie Anne, Deborah Chandler, Cecily Ellen Green Douglass. BSEE, Iowa State U., 1937. Editor Gen. Electric Co., Schenectady, N.Y., 1937-43; v.p. Kenyon & Eckhardt, Inc., N.Y.C., 1943-61; owner, mgr. Radio KLOV subs. Evergreen Enterprises, Loveland, Colo., 1962-70, Greentree Ranch Wools subs. Evergreen Enterprises, Loveland, Colo., 1965—, Rocky Mt. Pottery, Loveland, Colo., 1980-86, Greentree Ranch Morgan Horses, Loveland, Colo., 1962—. Co-author: Help for Your Headaches, 1950; contbr. over 500 editorials for radio broadcast; contbr. articles on mktg. to jours. and mags. Mem. Valhalla (N.Y.) Bd. Edn., 1945-48. Mem. Morgan Horse Breeders Assn. (pres., Morgan Horse Trotting Assn. (bd. dirs.), Continental Divide Horse Morgan Assn. (bd. dirs. 1965—), Circle J. Morgan Horse Assn. (bd. dirs. 1984—), Sigma Alpha Epsilon, Tau Beta Pi, Eta Kappa Nu, Sigma Delta Chi. Republican. Avocation: amateur radio. Home and Office: 163 N Carter Lake Rd Loveland CO 80537

GREEN, WILLIAM PORTER, lawyer; b. Jacksonville, Ill., Mar. 19, 1920; s. Hugh Parker and Clara Belle (Hopper) G.; m. Rose Marie Hall, Oct. 1, 1944; children: Hugh Michael, Robert Alan, Richard William. B.A., Ill. Coll., 1941; J.D., Northwestern U., 1947. Bar: Ill. 1947, Calif. 1948, U.S. Dist. Ct. (so. dist.) Tex. 1986, Ct. Customs and Patent Appeals 1948, U.S. Patent and Trademark Office 1948, U.S. Ct. Appeals (fed. cir.) 1982, U.S. Ct. Appeals (5th and 9th cirs.), U.S. Supreme Ct. 1948, U.S. Dist. Ct. (cen. dist.) Calif., U.S. Dist. Ct. (so. dist.) Tex., 1986. Practice patent, trademark and copyright law Los Angeles, 1947—; mem. firm Wills, Green & Mueth, 1974-83; of counsel Nilsson, Robbins, Dalgarn, Berliner, Carson & Wurst, Los Angeles, 1984—; del. Calif. State Bar Conv., 1982-87, delegation chair 1986. Bd. editors Ill. Law Rev, 1946. Mem. Los Angeles World Affairs Council, 1975—; del., chmn. Calif. State Bar Conv., 1986 Served lt. USNR, 1942-46. Mem. ABA, Calif Bar Assn., Los Angeles County Bar Assn (trustee 1986-87), Am. Intellectual Property Law Assn., Los Angeles Patent Law Assn. (past sec.-treas., bd. govs.), Lawyers Club Los Angeles (past treas., past sec., bd. govs., pres.-elect 1983 84, pres. 1985-86), Los Angeles County Bar Assn (trustee 1986-87), Am. Legion (past post comdr.), Phi Beta Kappa, Phi Delta Phi, Phi Alpha. Republican. Presbyn. (deacon 1961-63). Clubs: Big Ten of So. Calif, Northwestern U. Alumni of So. Calif, Phi Beta Kappa Alumni of So. Calif, Town Hall of Calif. Home: 3570 E Lombardy Rd Pasadena CA 91107 Office: Nilsson Robbins Dalgarn Berliner Carson & Wurst 201 N Figueroa St 5th Floor Los Angeles CA 90012

GREENAWALT, DAVID FRANKLIN, dairy and agricultural company executive; b. 1933. B.S. in Econs., U. Pa., 1955. Dist. operating mgr. Sealtest Foods div. Dart-Kraft Co., 1959-67; v.p. ops. Farmbest Inc., 1967-73; exec. v.p. Dairylea Coop. Inc., 1973-77; v.p. prodn. and engring. William Underwood Co., 1977-79; sr. v.p. mfg. Knudsen Corp., 1979, exec. v.p. ops., 1980, pres., chief operating officer, bd. dirs., 1982-86; pres., chief operating officer Santee Dairies, Inc., Los Angeles, 1986—; owner Nev. Dairies, Inc., 1986—. Bd. dirs. Los Angeles chpt. Nat. Safety Council, 1986—. Mem. Merchants and Mfrs. Trade Assn. (bd. dirs.), Internat. Ice Cream Assn. (chmn. bd. dirs.). Served to capt. USMC, 1956-59. Office: Santee Dairies Inc 60310 Terminal Annex Los Angeles CA 90060

GREENBERG, BARRY DAVID, molecular biologist; b. Waterbury, Conn., Dec. 29, 1955; s. Alvin Ira and Sally (Behar) G.; m. Renee Grossman, June 19, 1977; children: Devora Zahava, Avigal Naomi. BA, Northwestern U., 1977, MS, 1977; PhD, U. N.C., 1982. Cert. molecular geneticist. Biologist Nat. Inst. Environ. Health Scis., Research Triangle Park, N.C., 1979-82; postdoctoral scholar Stanford (Calif.) U., 1982-83; assoc. Calif. Biotechnology, Inc., Mountain View, 1983-84, staff scientist, 1984—; cons. and sci. adv. Bioresearch, Inc., San Rafael, Calif. 1983-86. Contbr. articles to profl. jours. Nat. vice-chairperson student adv. bd. United Jewish Appeal, N.Y.C., 1981-82; nat. chairperson, 1982-83. Mem. N.Y. Acad. Scis., Soc. Neurosci. (assoc.), Union Concerned Scientists. Democrat. Avocations: carpentry, guitar. Office: Upjohn Co 7242-267-5 301 Henrietta St Kalamazoo MI 49001

GREENBERG, IRA ARTHUR, clinical psychologist, mgmt. cons.; b. Bklyn., June 26, 1924; s. Philip and Minnie (Seligman) G.; B.A. in Journalism, U. Okla., 1949; M.A. in English, U. So. Calif., 1962; M.S. in Counseling, Calif. State U.-Los Angeles, 1963; Ph.D. in Psychology, Claremont (Calif.) Grad Sch., 1967. Editor, Ft. Riley (Kans.) Guidon, 1950-51; reporter, copy editor Columbus (Ga.) Enquirer, 1951-55; reporter Louisville Courier-Jour., 1955-56, Los Angeles Times, 1956-62; free-lance writer, Los Angeles, Montclair, Camarillo, Calif., 1960-69, 76—; counselor Claremont Coll. Psychol. Clinic and Counseling Ctr., 1964-65; lectr. psychology Chapman Coll., Orange, Calif., 1965-66; psychologist Camarillo State Hosp., 1967-69, supervising psychologist, 1969-73, part time psychologist, 1973—; part time asst. prof. edn. San Fernando Valley State Coll., Northridge, Calif., 1967-69, lectr. psychodrama, social welfare U. Calif. Extension Div., Santa Barbara, 1968-69; vol. psychologist Free Clinic, Los Angeles, 1968-70; staff dir. Calif. Inst. Psychodrama, 1969-71; tng. cons. Topanga Ctr. for Human Devel., 1970-75, bd. dirs., 1971-74, faculty Calif. Sch. Profl. Psychology, 1970—; founder, exec. dir. Behavioral Studies Inst., mgmt. cons., Los Angeles, 1970—; pvt. practice cons. in psychology, psychodrama, hypnosis, 1970—; founder, exec. dir. Psychodrama Center for Los Angeles, Inc., 1971—, Group Hypnosis Ctr., Los Angeles, 1976—; producer, host TV talk show Crime and Pub. Safety, Century Cable, Channel 3, 1983—. Vol. humane officer State of Calif., 1979—; res. officer Los Angeles Police Dept., 1980-86; capt. Calif. State Mil. Res., 1986—. Served with AUS, 1943-46; ETO; USAR, 1950-51. Fellow Am. Soc. Clin. Hypnosis; mem. Am. Soc. Group Psychotherapy and Psychodrama, Am., Calif. personnel and guidance assns., Assn. Research and Enlightenment, Los Angeles Soc. Clin. Psychologists (dir. 1975), Am., Western, Calif., Los Angeles psychol. assns., Am. Soc. for Psychical Research, Group Psychotherapy Assn. So. Calif. (dir. 1974-76, 82—, pres. 1987—), Soc. for Clin. and Exptl. Hypnosis, Am. Mgmt. Assn., Am. Soc. Bus. and Mgmt. Cons. (nat. adv. council 1977—), So. Calif. Soc. Clin. Hypnosis (dir., exec. v.p. 1973-76, pres. 1977-78), So. Calif. Psychotherapy Affiliation (dir. 1976-85), Assn. for Humanistic Psychology, Mensa, Am. Zionist Fedn., Nat. Rifle Assn., Calif. Rifle and Pistol Assn., S.W. Pistol League, Animal Protection Inst. Am., Humane Educators Council (bd. dirs. 1982-86), Soc. Sci. Study Sex, Airport Psychol. Assocs., Sigma Delta Chi. Clubs: Sierra, Greater Los Angeles Press; B'nai B'rith; Beverly Hills Gun. Author: Psychodrama and Audience Attitude Change, 1968. Editor: Psychodrama: Theory and Therapy, 1974; Group Hypnotherapy and Hypnodrama, 1977. Address: Camarillo State Hosp Box A-369 Camarillo CA 93011 Address: BSI 11692 Chenault St Suite 206 Los Angeles CA 90049

GREENBERG, MARVIN, educator; b. N.Y.C., June 24, 1936; s. Samuel and Rae (Sherry) G.; B.S. cum laude, N.Y.U., 1957; M.A., Columbia U., 1958, Ed.D., 1962. Tchr. elem. schs., N.Y.C., 1957-63; prof. music edn. U. Hawaii, Honolulu, 1963—, research cons. Center for Early Childhood Research, 1969-71; edn. adminstr. Model Cities project for disadvantaged children Family Services Center, Honolulu, 1971-72. Cons. western region Volt Tech. Services, Head Start program, 1969-71; Head Start worker, 1972-75; Child Devel. Assoc. Consortium rep., 1975—. Recipient several fed. and state grants for ednl. research and curriculum projects. Mem. Hawaii Music Educators Assn., Music Educators Nat. Conf., Soc. for Research in Music Edn., Council for Research in Music Edn., Nat. Assn. for Edn. Young Children. Author: Teaching Music in the Elementary School: Guide for ETV Programs, 1966; Preschool Music Curriculum, 1970; Music Handbook for the Elementary School, 1972; Staff Training in Child Care in Hawaii, 1975; Your Child Needs Music, 1979; also articles. Home: 2575 Kuhio Ave 19-2 Honolulu HI 96815 Office: 2411 Dole St MB203 Honolulu HI 96822

GREENBERG, MORTON PAUL, lawyer, insurance broker, advanced underwriting consultant; b. Fall River, Mass., June 2, 1946; s. Harry and Sylvia Shirley (Davis) G.; m. Louise Beryl Schindler, Jan. 24, 1970; 1 dau., Alexis Lynn. BSBA, NYU, 1968; JD, Bklyn. Law Sch., 1971; chartered life underwriter Am. Coll., 1975. Bar: N.Y. 1972. Atty., Hanner, Fitzmaurice & Onorato, N.Y.C., 1971-72; dir., counsel, cons. on advanced underwriting The Mfrs. Life Ins. Co., Toronto, Ont., Can., 1972—; mem. sales ideas com. Million Dollar Roundtable, Chgo., 1982-83; speaker on law, tax, and advanced underwriting to various profl. groups, U.S., Can. Author: (tech. jour.) ManuBriefs. Mem. ABA, N.Y. State Bar Assn., Assn. for Advanced Life Underwriting, Internat. Platform Assn., NYU Alumni Assn., Nat. Assn. of Life Underwriters, Denver Assn. Life Underwriters, Am. Soc. CLU. Office: 7617 E Sunrise Trail Parker CO 80134

GREENE, ALVIN, service company executive, management consultant; b. Pitts., Aug. 26, 1932; s. Samuel David and Yetta (Kroff) G.; B.A., Stanford U., 1954, M.B.A., 1959; m. M. Louise Sokol, Nov. 11, 1977; children—Sharon, Ami, Ann, Daniel. Asst. to pres. Narmco Industries, Inc., San Diego, 1959-62; adminstrv. mgr., mgr. mktg. Whittaker Corp., Los Angeles, 1962-67; sr. v.p. Cordura Corp., Los Angeles, 1967-75; chmn. bd. Sharon-Sage, Inc., Los Angeles, 1975-79; exec. v.p., chief operating officer Republic Distbrs., Inc., Carson, Calif., 1979-81, also dir.; chief operating officer Memel, Jacobs & Ellsworth, 1981-87; pres. SCI Cons., Inc.; dir. Sharon-Sage, Inc., True Data Corp.; vis. prof. Am. Grad. Sch. Bus., Phoenix, 1977-81. Chmn. bd. commrs. Housing Authority City of Los Angeles, 1983—. Served to 1st lt., U.S. Army, 1955-57. Mem. Direct Mail Assn., Safety Helmet Mfrs. Assn., Bradley Group. Office: 1801 Century Park East Suite 2500 Los Angeles CA 90067

GREENE, ARTHUR EDWARD, physicist; b. Chgo., Dec. 10, 1945; s. Shirley Edward and Ellen Catherine (Tweedy) G.; m. Nancy Ellen Green, Sept. 12, 1970; 1 child, Ellen Dorothy. Student, Doane Coll., 1963-65; B.S. cum laude, Ohio State U., 1967, Ph.D. in Astronomy, 1971. Staff mem. theoretical chemistry and molecular physics group Los Alamos Nat. Lab., 1975-81, staff mem. thermonuclear application group, 1981-86, staff mem. pulsed energy application group, 1986—. Contbr. articles to profl. jours. Served to capt. USAF, 1971-75. Recipient award of Excellence Dept. Energy, 1986. Mem. Am. Phys. Soc., Phi Beta Kappa. Clubs: Road Runner Cycling, Pajarito Astromoners. Office: Los Alamos Nat Lab X-10 MS B259 Los Alamos, NM 87545

GREENE, BENJAMIN PHILIP, symphony association director; b. Middletown, Conn., Oct. 16, 1953; s. Raymond Franklin and Concetta (Cariri) G. MusB, Manhattanville Coll., 1975; MA, Ind. U., 1980. Adminstrv. asst., opera prodn. mgr. San Antonio Symphony, 1976-79, orch. mgr., 1979-84; exec. dir. Sacramento Symphony, 1984—. Mem. Am. Symphony Orch. League, Assn. Calif. Symphony Orchs. (bd. dirs. 1985-86). Office: Sacramento Symphony Orch 2848 Arden Way Suite 210 Sacramento CA 95825

GREENE, FRANK S., JR., business executive; b. Washington, Oct. 19, 1938; s. Frank S. and Irma O. (Swygert) G.; m. Phyllis Davison, Jan. 1958 (dec. 1984); children: Angela, Frank; m. Nilene D. Fitzpatrick, Sept. 1985; children: Christopher, David. BS, Washington U., St. Louis, 1961; MS, Purdue U., 1962; PhD, U. Santa Clara (Calif.), 1970. Part-time lectr. Washington U., Howard U., Am. U., 1959-65; dir., chmn. Tech. Devel. Corp., Arlington, Tex., 1985—; pres. ZeroOne Systems, Inc. (formerly Tech. Devel. of Calif.) Santa Clara, Calif., 1971—; asst. chmn., lectr. Stanford U., 1972-74; dir. Comsis Corp. Author two indsl. textbooks; also articles; patentee in field. Bd. dirs. NCCJ, Santa Clara, 1980—; bd. regents U. Santa Clara, 1983—. Served to capt. USAF, 1961-65. Mem. Assn. Black Mfrs. (dir., 1974-80), Am. Electric Assn. (indsl. adv. bd., 1975-76), Fairchild Research and Devel. (tech. staff, 1965-71), IEEE, IEEE Computer Soc. (governing bd., 1973-75), Bay Area Purchasing Council (dir. 1978-84), Security Affairs Support Assn. (dir. 1980-83), Sigma Xi, Eta Kappa Nu. Office: ZeroOne Systems Inc 2431 Mission Coll Blvd Santa Clara CA 95054

GREENE, GERALD R., physician; b. Los Angeles, Dec. 6, 1941; s. Joseph L. and Mignon (Rubenstein) G.; m. Marcia Layton, Mar. 21, 1969 (div. Apr. 1982); children: Allison, Benjamin. BS, UCLA, 1962; MD, U. So. Calif., 1966; MPH, Johns Hopkins, 1971. Diplomate Am. Bd. Pediatrics. Intern. Los Angeles County/U. So. Calif. Med. Ctr., Los Angeles, 1971-72, resident in pediatrics, 1971-72; resident in pediatrics The Johns Hopkins Hosp., Balt., 1969-70; with USPHS, Balt., 1967-69; epidemic intelligence service officer Ctr. for Disease Control, Balt., 1967-69; asst. adj. prof. pediatrics U. Calif. Med. Ctr., Irvine, 1974-80, assoc. adj. prof. pediatrics, 1980-82, asst. prof. pediatrics, 1982—, dir. div. of pediatric infectious diseases, 1974—; cons. FDA adv. com. on ob-gyn. drugs and contraception, 1975-79; lectr. in field. Active Health Com. Orange County Southeast Asian Refugee Forum. Named Outstanding Tchr., Pediatric Housestaff, 1979-80, 82-83. Fellow Am. Acad. Pediatrics (chmn. com. on health care for spl. groups), Am. Coll. Epidemiology; mem. Am. Pub. Health Assn., AAAS, Am. Fedn. Clin. Research, Am. Soc. Microbiology, Infectious Disease Soc. Am., Western Soc. Pediatric Research, Lancefield Soc., Los Angeles Pediatric Soc., Orange County Pediatric Soc. Democrat. Jewish. Avocations: fishing. Home: 1844 N Ridgewood St Orange CA 92668 Office: U Calif-Irvine Med Ctr 101 City Dr Rt 81 Bldg 27 Orange CA 92668

GREENE, HARMON KAYTON, sales professional; b. Evanston, Ill., Dec. 24, 1943; s. Harmon Kayton and Mari Bertha (Koretz) G.; m. Louise Marie Leavitt, Mar. 5, 1965; children: Lorelei, Wendy, Terranee, Dolly. Student, Purdue U., 1966. Acctg. supr. Allstate Ins., Northbrook, Ill., 1966-69; salesman Pitney Bowes/A. Bazzoni, Arlington Heights, Ill., 1969-72; mktg. dir., sales mgr. Alcon Labs., Ft. Worth, 1972-81; mktg. dir. beauty div. Syntex Labs., Palo Alto, Calif., 1981; owner Salon Mgmt. Services, Arlington, Tex., 1982-83; nat. sales mgr., gen. mgr. Sebastian Internat., Woodland Hills, Calif., 1983-86, dir. sales, 1986—; cons. H.H. Kayton, Arlington, 1982. Avocations: reading, skiing, traveling. Home: 3904 Daguerre Woodland Hills CA 91364 Office: Sebastian Internat 6160 Variel Woodland Hills CA 91367

GREENE, JOHN CLIFFORD, dentist, university dean; b. Ashland, Ky., July 19, 1926; s. G. Norman and Ella R. G.; m. Gwen Rustin, Nov. 17, 1957; children: Alan, Lisa, Laura. A.A., Ashland Jr. Coll., 1947; student, Marshall Coll., 1948; D.M.D., U. Louisville, 1952, Sc.D. (hon.), 1980; M.P.H., U. Calif., Berkeley, 1961; Sc.D. (hon.), U. Ky., 1972, Boston U., 1975. Diplomate: Am. Bd. Dental Public Health (pres.). Intern USPHS Hosp., Chgo., 1952-53; staff USPHS Hosp., San Francisco, 1953-54; asst. regional dental cons. Region IX, San Francisco, 1954-56; asst. to chief dental officer Region IX, Washington, 1958-60; chief epidemiology program Dental Health Center, 1961-66; dep. dir. Div. Dental Health, 1966-70, acting dir., 1970, dir., 1970-73; acting dir. Bur. Health Resources Devel., 1973-74, dir., 1974-75; chief dental officer USPHS, 1974-81, dep. surgeon gen., 1978-81; with Epidemic Intelligence Service, Communicable Disease Center, Altanta and Kansas City, Mo., 1956-57; epidemiology and biometry br. Nat. Inst. Dental Research, NIH, Bethesda, Md., 1957-58; dean. Sch. Dentistry, U. Calif., San Francisco, 1981—; spl. cons. WHO, India, 1957; faculty Calif., U. Mich., U. Pa.; cons. Am. Dental Assn. Council, Nat. Health Professions Placement Network. Contbr. writings to profl. publs. Served with USN, 1945-46. Recipient citation Sch. Grad. Dentistry Boston U., 1971, citation U. of the Pacific, 1977, Meritorious and Disting. Service awards HEW, 1972, 75, Outstanding Alumnus award U. Louisville, 1980, award of merit FDI, 1978; Alumnus of Yr. award U. Calif. Sch. Pub. Health, Berkeley, 1984.

Fellow Am. Coll. Dentists; mem. ADA, Calif. Dental Assn., San Francisco Dental Soc., Internat. Assn. Dental Research, Am. Assn. Dental Research (pres.), Am. Assn. Public Health Dentists, Am. Acad. Periodontology, Am. Assn. Dental Schs. (v.p.), Inst. of Medicine of Nat. Acad. Sci., Federation Dentaire Internationale (chmn. commn. on public dental health, mem. WHO panel of experts on dental health), Omicron Kappa Upsilon, Delta Omega. Home: 103 Peacock Dr San Rafael CA 94901 Office: U Calif Sch Dentistry 513 Parnassus Ave Room S-630 San Francisco CA 94143-0430

GREENE, JOHN THOMAS, JR., judge; b. Salt Lake City, Nov. 28, 1929; s. John Thomas and Mary Agnes (Hindley) G.; m. Kay Buchanan, Mar. 31, 1955; children: Thomas B., John B., Mary Kay. B.A., U. Utah, 1952, J.D., 1955. Bar: Utah 1955. Law clk. Supreme Ct. Utah, Salt Lake City, 1954-55; asst. U.S. atty. Dist. Utah, Salt Lake City, 1957-59; partner firm Marr, Wilkins & Cannon, Salt Lake City, 1959-69, Cannon, Greene & Nebeker, Salt Lake City, 1969-74, Greene, Callister & Nebeker, Salt Lake City, 1974-85; judge U.S. Dist. Ct. Utah, 1985—; spl. asst. atty. gen. State of Utah, 1965-69; spl. grand jury counsel Salt Lake County, 1970; pres. Utah Bar Found., 1971-74, trustee, 1971—. Author: sect. on mining rights American Law of Mining, 1965; contbr. articles to profl. jours. Pres. Community Services Council, Salt Lake City area, 1971-73; Republican chmn. Voting Dist. 47, Salt Lake County, 1969-73; chmn. Utah Bldg. Authority, 1980-85; mem. Utah State Bd. Regents, 1983-86. Mem. Utah Bar Assn. (pres. 1970-71, chmn. judiciary com. 1971-76, chmn. com. post. law sch. tng. 1985—), ABA (Utah del. to ho. of dels. 1975-81, 82—, mem. spl. com. delivery legal service 1975-81, council gen. practice sect. 1974-82, chmn. spl. com. on environ. law 1971-75, mem. adv. com. Nat. Legal Service Corp. 1975-81, mem. standing com. on jud. selection, tenure and compensation 1985—), Am. Inn Ct. II (pres. 1983-84), U. Utah Alumni Assn. (dir. 1968-69), Order of Coif, Phi Beta Kappa, Phi Kappa Phi. Mormon. Clubs: Ft. Douglas Country, Salt Lake Tennis. Office: Fed Bldg 350 S Main St #222 Salt Lake City UT 84101

GREENE, MONROE MALCOLM, process chemical engineer, consultant; b. Slatington, Pa., June 26, 1921; s. Herbert and Matilda A. (Holben) G.; m. June Frances Valenteen, Apr. 11, 1943; children: Jacqueline Louise Greene Thomas, Peggy Jo Greene Sahlman, Mary Alice Greene Gaster, Andrew Monroe. BS in Chemistry, Muhlenberg Coll., 1942; postgrad., U. Pa., Claymont-Del., 1942, 44, Lehigh U., 1953-55. Process engr., chemist Gen. Chem. Co., Pa., W.Va., Va., 1942-53; project engr., ops. and engring. mgr. Air Products and Chemicals, Allentown, Pa., 1953-66, gen. engr. indsl. gas div., 1960; Europe tech. mgr. indsl. gases Air Products and Chemicals, London, Brussels, Dusseldorf and Milan, 1966; gen. mgr. Europe Gardner Cryogenics Europe, Brussels, 1966-69; cons. and exec. v.p., bd. dirs. KRG Chem. Services, Mertztown, Pa., 1969-74; sr. process engr. Cunningham-Limp Co., Birmingham, Mich., 1974-79; process chem. engr. MultiTech div. MSE, Inc., Butte, Mont., 1980—. Inventor various chem. procedures. Served with USNR, 1944-46. Mem. Am. Chem. Soc. Republican. Presbyterian. Home: 5380 Saddle Rock Rd Butte MT 59701 Office: MultiTech div MSE Inc 505 Centennial Butte MT 59702

GREENE, VAUGHN MAYNARD, utility company executive, controller; b. Anaheim, Calif., Nov. 2, 1929; s. Maynard Ellesworth and Verona Myrtle (Teitsort) G.; m. Shizuko Chiba; 1 child, Sterling Hiroshi. Student, San Diego Coll. With Ryan Aircraft, San Diego, 1949-51, Convair Aircraft Co., San Diego, Calif., 1953-55, Dept. Def. USN, 1955-60; controller Pacific Gas and Electric Co., San Francisco, 1960—. Author: Underwater Prospecting Techniques, 1960, Astronauts of A. Japan, 1978, 6000 Year Old Spacesuit, 1985. Served with U.S. Army, 1951-53. Served with USN, 1955-60. Mem. Cousteau Soc., U.S. Naval Inst. Avocations: pre-history research, aviation. Home: 548 Elm Ave San Bruno CA 94066

GREENE, WAYNE MARK, chemical engineer; b. Queens, N.Y., Feb. 21, 1963; s. Stanley Lawrence and Renée (Handler) G. BS, MIT, 1984. Research asst. MIT, Cambridge, Mass., 1982-84; research intern IBM, Yorktown Heights, N.Y., 1984; research asst. U. Calif., Berkeley, 1984—; cons. Stone & Webster Corp., Boston, 1983. Mem. Am. Inst. Chem. Engrs., Material Research Soc., Electrochem. Soc. Am., Sigma Xi, Tau Beta Pi. Avocations: racquetball, shotokan karate, tennis, softball. Home: 2427 Durant Ave #6 Berkeley CA 94704 Office: U Calif 201G Golman Hall Berkeley CA 94720

GREENFIELD, PATRICIA ANN MARKS, psychology educator; b. Newark, July 18, 1940; d. David and Doris Jeannette (Pollard) Marks; m. Sheldon Greenfield, Mar. 13, 1965 (div.); children; Lauren, Matthew Michael. AB summa cum laude, Radcliffe Coll., 1962; PhD in Social Psychology, Harvard U., 1966. Research fellow in psychology Ctr. for Cognitive Studies Harvard U., Cambridge, Mass., 1968-72; vis. asst. prof. psychology Stanford (Calif.) U., 1972-73; asst. prof. U. Calif., Santa Cruz, 1973-74; assoc. prof. UCLA, 1974-78, prof., 1978—; bd. dirs. Westside Women's Clinic; external examiner U. Lagos, 1977-79; collaborating scientist Yerkes Regional Primate Ctr., Emory U., 1979—. Contbr. articles to profl. jours. Recipient 1st award Am. Insts. Research, 1967, award div. 2 Am. Psychol. Assn., 1986; named Sci. scholar Bunting Inst. Radcliffe Coll., 1986-87. Fellow AAAS, Am. Psychol. Assn.; mem. Soc. Research in Child Devel. Home: 42 Park Ave Venice CA 90291 Office: UCLA Dept Psychology Los Angeles CA 90291

GREENLAND, DAVID EDWARD, geography educator; b. Bournemouth, Eng., Aug. 19, 1940; came to U.S., 1965; s. Edward Henry and Grace Ada (Haggar) G.; m. Risa I. Palm, June 28, 1976; 1 child, John. BS, U. Birmingham, Eng., 1963, MS, 1965; PhD, U. Canterbury, Christchurch, New Zealand, 1971. Sr. lectr. U. Canterbury, 1966-75; prof. geography U. Colo., Boulder, 1976—. Author: Guidelines for Modern Resource Management, 1983; co-author: The Earth inProfile, 1977. Research grantee USDA Forest Service, 1978, NSF, 1980—. Mem. Assn. Am. Geographers, Am. Meteorol. Soc., Am. Geophys. Union, Royal Meteorol. Soc., Internat. Mountain Soc. Episcopalian. Avocations: lit., astronomy, mountain activities. Office: U Colorado Dept Geography Campus Box 260 Boulder CO 80302-0260

GREENLAW, ROGER LEE, interior designer; b. New London, Conn., Oct. 12, 1936; s. Kenneth Nelson and Lyndell Lee (Stinson) G.; children—Carol Jennifer, Roger Lee. B.F.A., Syracuse U., 1958. Interior designer Cannell & Chaffin, 1958-59, William C. Wagner, Architect, Los Angeles, 1959-60, Gen. Fireproofing Co., Los Angeles, 1960-62, K-S Wilshire, Inc., Los Angeles, 1963-64; dir. interior design Calif. Desk Co., Los Angeles, 1964-67; sr. interior designer Bechtel Corp., Los Angeles, 1967-70; sr. interior designer, project mgr. Daniel, Mann, Johnson, & Mendehall, Los Angeles, 1970-72, Morganelli-Heumann & Assos., Los Angeles, 1972-73; owner, prin. Greenlaw Design Assos., Glendale, Calif., 1973—; lectr. UCLA; mem. adv. curriculum com. Mt. San Antonio Coll., Walnut, Calif., Fashion Inst. Design, Los Angeles. Scoutmaster Verdugo council Boy Scouts Am.; past pres. bd. dirs. Unity Ch., La Crescenta, Calif. Mem. Am. Soc. Interior Designers (treas. Pasadena chpt. 1983-84, pres. 1986, 1st v.p. 1985, chmn. So. Calif. regional conf. 1985, nat. com. legis., nat. com. jury for catalog award, speaker ho. dels.), Adm. Farragut Acad. Alumni Assn., Delta Upsilon. Republican. Lodge: Kiwanis. Home: 2100f Valderas Dr Glendale CA 91208 Office: 3901 Ocean View Blvd Montrose CA 91020

GREENLEAF, GRACEMARY BOOTH, lawyer, writer; b. Mineola, N.Y., Aug. 24, 1939; d. John Edwards and Katherine (Keeler) B.; m. Henry D. James, Aug. 8, 1970 (div. 1978); m. Emile Edgar Greenleaf, Feb. 14, 1981 (dec. Aug. 1985). AB, Bryn Mawr Coll., 1961; JD, Fordham U., 1967. Bar: N.Y., 1967, Colo., 1972, U.S. Dist. Ct. Colo., 1972. Assoc. Harry Lipsig, esq., N.Y.C., 1967-68; adminstr. personal trust Chase Manhattan Bank, N.Y.C., 1971; officer personal trusts United Bank of Denver, 1972-78, trust counsel, 1978-84; lectr. law U. Denver, 1986; presenter seminars Personal Transitions Seminars Co., Aurora, Colo., 1986—. Bd. dirs., trustee Patten Inst. for Arts, Denver, 1981-84, Animal Assistance Assn., Denver, 1978—; trustee Colo. Episcopal Found., Denver, 1986—; vestry mem. St. Gregory's Episcopal Ch., Littleton, Colo., 1983-87. Recipient Community Challenge award United Bank Denver, 1983. Mem. Colo. Bar Assn., Colo. Mountain Club (Denver) (councillor 1981-84). Avocations: hiking, cross-country skiing, gardening, photogrpahy. Home and Office: 9767 W Nova Ave Littleton CO 80127

GREENLEAF, JOHN EDWARD, research physiologist; b. Joliet, Ill., Sept. 18, 1932; s. John Simon and Julia Clara (Flint) G.; m. Carol Lou Johnson, Aug. 28, 1960. BA in Phys. Edn., U. Ill., 1955; MA, N.Mex. Highlands U., 1956; MS, U. Ill., 1962, PhD in Physiol., 1963. Teaching asst. N.Mex. Highlands U., Las Vegas, 1955-56; engring. draftsman Allis-Chalmers Mfg. Co., Springfield, Ill., 1956-57; teaching asst. in phys. edn. U. Ill., Urbana, 1957-58, research asst. in phys. edn., 1958-59, teaching asst. in human anatomy and physiology, 1959-62; summer fellow NSF, 1962; pre-doctoral fellow NIH, 1962-63; research physiologist Life Scis. Directorate, NASA, Ames Research Ctr., Moffett Field, Calif., 1963-66, 67—; postdoctoral fellowship Royal Gymnastic Ist., Stockholm, 1966-67. Contbr. numerous articles to profl. jours; patentee in field. Recipient George Huff award for Scholarship, U. Ill. 1954-55, NASA Spl. Achievement award, 1973. Served with U.S. Army, 1952-53. Exchange fellow Nat. Acad. Scis., 1973-74, 77, NIH, 1980. Fellow Am. Coll. Sports Medicine (trustee 1984-87), Aerospace Med. Assn. (Harold Ellingson award 1981); mem. Am. Physiol. Soc. (mem. com. on coms. 1984-87), Am. Inst. Nutrition, Shooting Sports Research Council (internat. shooters devel. fund 1984—), Sigma Xi. Home: 12391 Farr Ranch Ct Saratoga CA 95070 Office: NASA Ames Research Ctr Space Physiology Br MS 239A-1 Moffett Field CA 94035

GREENLEE, RICHARD WESLEY, social worker; b. Canton, Ohio, Dec. 7, 1954; s. Ralph Wesley and Mary Jane (Lupton) G.; m. Cynthia Ann Bechtold, June 14, 1975; children: Melissa Ann, Ryan Wesley. BS magna cum laude, U. Md., College Park, 1978; post-master's cert., U. Md., Balt., 1984; MSW, U. Pitts., 1980. Social work supr. Mental Health Devel. Ctr., Cambridge, Ohio, 1980-81; rehab. cons. Ohio Indsl. Commn., Cambridge, 1981-82; dep. dir. alcohol rehab. ctr. Malcolm Grow Med. Ctr., Andrews AFB, Md., 1982-84; dir. alcohol rehab. ctr. USAF Regional Hosp., March AFB, Calif., 1984—; adj. instr. Muskingum Area Tech. Coll., Zanesville, Ohio, 1981; cons. Applied Sci. Assoc., Pitts., 1979-80. Vol. football coach St. Catherine's Grade Sch., Riverside, Calif., 1986, head basketball coach, 1986. Served to capt. USAF, 1982—. Named one of Outstanding Young Men of Am., 1984. Mem. Acad. Cert. Social Workers, Nat. Assn. Social Workers, Phi Kappa Phi. Democrat. Roman Catholic. Avocations: folk music performer, running, sports. Home: 7073 New Mexico Dr Riverside CA 92506 Office: USAF Regional Hosp Alcohol Rehab Ctr March AFB CA 92518

GREENSPAN, DOUGLAS HOWARD, financial executive, consultant; b. Perth Amboy, N.J., Apr. 10, 1951; s. Walter Mortimer and Harriet Rose (Shusterman) G.; m. Priscilla Rose Milliren, Aug. 4, 1984. BS in Chemistry, U. Miami, 1974; MBA, U. Colo., 1981. Lic. real estate broker, Colo. Chemist Accu-Labs Research Co., Wheat Ridge, Colo., 1974-75; field engr. Dow Chem. Co., Denver, 1975-76; mktg. cons. Glaxon Mktg. Assocs., Denver, 1976-79, v.p. fin., 1980—; also bd. dirs. Glaxon Mktg. Assocs., Metuchen, N.J.; prin. The GreenSpan, Boulder, Colo.; bd. dirs. Youthink Found., Denver; cons. State of Colo., 1983-85. Advisor Moffat County Econ. Devel. Council, Craig, Colo., 1983-85, Colo. Title IX Loan Program, 1984; mem. Gov.'s High-Tech Cabinet Council, Boulder, 1985; comptroller Gt. Am. Beer Festival, Denver, 1983-84. Mem. Am. Mgmt. Assn., Aircraft Owners & Pilots Assn., Am. Homebrewers Assn. (comptroller Gt. Am. Beer Festival 1983-84), Small Bus. Council of Boulder C. of C. Jewish. Avocations: flying, skiing, scuba diving, sailor. Home: 200 Lois Circle Louisville CO 80027 Office: PO Box 4656 Boulder CO 80306

GREENWELL, ROGER ALLEN, scientist; b. Santa Maria, Calif., Dec. 4, 1941; s. George C. and Bessie Florence (Sutton) G.; m. Jeannine Pendleton, July 25, 1969; 1 son, George Eli. A.A., Hancock Jr. Coll., 1961; B.S., Calif. Poly. Coll., 1968; M.S., U.S. Internat. U., 1974, D.B.A., 1981. Mathematician Naval Weapons Ctr., China Lake, Calif., 1968, ops. research analyst, Corona, Calif., 1969-70; ops. research analyst Comdr. Naval Forces, Vietnam, 1968-69; mathematician Naval Electronics Lab. Ctr., San Diego, 1970-77; scientist Naval Ocean Systems Ctr., San Diego, 1977-84; sr. scientist Sci. and Engring. Assoc., Inc., 1984—; cons. fiber optics and econ. analysis. Served with U.S. Army, 1964-67. Decorated Bronze Star. Mem. Ops. Research Soc. Am., Inst. Mgmt. Sci., AIAA, Soc. Allied Weight Engrs., Soc. Photo Optical and Instrumentation Engrs. Contbr. chpts. to books, govt. publs., and movies in field. Home: 3778 Eagle St San Diego CA 92103 Office: 3838 Camino del Rio North Suite 120 San Diego CA 92108

GREENWOOD, ROBERT WALTER, actor, director educator, performing arts adminstr.; b. Hanover, N.H., Mar. 1, 1941; s. Clayton H. and Lillian F. (Bliss) G.; B.A. cum laude (Rufus Choate scholar) with honors, Dartmouth, 1963; M.F.A. with honors, Yale Sch. of Drama, 1964-67. Actor, Columbia Repertory Theatre, N.Y.C., 1967-69; actor-tchr. Dartmouth Repertory Theatre, Hanover, 1969-70; asst. prof. acting, stage movement U. Okla., Norman, 1970-72; dir. Southwest Repertory Theatre, Norman, 1971; actor-dir. Contemporary Arts Found., Oklahoma City, 1971-73; asst. prof. U. Calgary, Alta., 1973-77, chmn. acting-directing, 1973-75; reviewer theatre, dance, films for CBCR and The Albertan, 1977-78; adminstrv. mgr. Arete Contemporary Mime Troupe, 1977-78; actor, dir. Ensemble Players, 1976-77; actor Alta. Show Case on Stage, CBC-TV, 1977, Theatre Calgary, 1978—, Access TV, 1975, 77-79; artistic and mng. dir. Sun-Ergos, 1977—; communications officer Dance and the Child Internat., 1978-82; commentator CBC radio and TV. Mem. Southwest Theatre Conf., 1970, Alta. Theatre Conf., 1974; poet, poetry-in-the-schs. program, Okla. Arts and Humanities Council, Oklahoma City, 1972-73; mem. World Vision of Can., 1973—; adjudicator Calgary High Sch. Drama Festival, 1974, 75, 76, Alta. Provincial Drama Festival, 1976, Red Deer Provincial Drama Workshop, 1976, 77; bd. dirs. Theatre Can., 1974-78, Festival Calgary, 1975-77; participant Cultural Resources Mgmt. Programme, Banff, 1975, Canadian Council-Touring Office Conf., Red Deer, 1976, Laban Inst. Movement Studies, 1979, Edinburgh Fringe Festival, 1980-86, Swansea (Wales) Festival, 1981-86. Recipient Marcus Heiman award, 1962, Adelbert Ames award, 1963, Citizen of the Age of Enlightenment award, 1976, du Maurier Search for Stars award, 1980, Alta. Cultural Assistance award, 1980; named Actor of Yr., Albertan, 1976. Okla. Arts and Humanities Council grantee, 1973. Mem. Okla. Community Theatre Assn., Canadian Child and Youth Drama Assn., Dance in Can. Assn. (exec. sec. 1976-78, 1st vice chmn. 1978-79), Dance and Theatre Arts Calgary Soc. (pres. 1975-77), Internat. Meditation Soc., Internat. Platform Assn., Humanities Assn. Can., Univ. and Coll. Theatre Assn., Am. Theatre Assn., ACTRA, Can. Actors Equity. Home: 2205-700 9th St SW, Calgary, AB Canada T2P 2B5

GREER, MONTE ARNOLD, physician, educator; b. Portland, Oreg., Oct. 26, 1922; s. William Wallace and Rose (Rasmussen) G.; m. Margaret Johnson, Dec. 31, 1943; children: Susan Elizabeth, Richard Arnold. Student, Oreg. State U., 1940-43; A.B., Stanford U., 1944, M.D., 1947. Intern San Francisco Gen. Hosp., 1946-47; research fellow endocrinology New Eng. Med. Center, Boston, 1947-49; resident internal medicine Mass. Meml. Hosp., Boston, 1949-50; research assoc. in endocrinology New Eng. Med. Center Hosp., 1950-51; sr. investigator, sr. asst. surgeon USPHS, Nat. Cancer Inst., NIH, Bethesda, Md., 1951-55; chief radioisotope unit VA Hosp., Long Beach, Calif.; clin. asst. prof. medicine UCLA, 1955-56; faculty, head div. endocrinology U. Oreg. Med. Sch., Portland, 1956-80; prof. medicine U. Oreg. Med. Sch., 1962—; head div. endocrinology, metabolism and clin. nutrition Oreg. Health Scis. U., 1980-84, head sect. endocrinology, 1984—. Author: (with H. Studer) The Regulation of Thyroid Function in Iodine Deficiency, 1968, (with P. Langer) Antithyroid Drugs and Naturally Occurring Goitrogens, 1977; Editor: (with D.H. Solomon) The Thyroid, 1974; Mem. editorial bd.: Endocrinology, 1960-72, Neuroendocrinology, 1965-76; Contbr. articles to profl. jours. Recipient Ciba (Oppenheimer) award Endocrine Soc., 1958, Research Career award NIH, 1962-81; Discovery award Med. Research Found. Oreg., 1985. Mem. Am. Fedn. for Clin. Research (chmn. Western sect. 1958-59), Western Soc. for Clin. Research (v.p. 1963-64, pres. 1967-68), Endocrine Soc. (mem. council 1965-68, v.p. 1976-77), Am. Thyroid Assn. (past v.p., dir. 1974-77, pres. 1980, Disting. Service award 1985), Am. Soc. Clin. Investigation, Soc. Exptl. Biology and Medicine, Western Assn. Physicians (sec.-treas. 1974-77), Assn. Am. Physicians, Internat. Brain Research Orgn., Internat. Soc. Neuroendocrinology, AAAS, European Thyroid Assn., Japan Endocrine Soc. (hon.), Czechoslovak Endocrine Soc. (hon.), Sigma Chi. Home: 2706 Glen Eagles Rd Lake Oswego OR 97034 Office: Oreg Health Scis U Portland OR 97201

GREER, WILLIAM THOMAS, military officer; b. Madrid, Aug. 2, 1960; s. William Thomas and Marian Freda (Buesing) G. BSME, Syracuse U., 1983. Commd. 2d lt. USAF, 1983, advanced through grades to capt., 1987; ordnance project officer USAF, Norton AFB, Calif., 1983-84, stage project officer, 1984-85, chief ordnance br., 1985-87; ptnr., gen. mgr. Greer Bros. Mobile Homes, Sterling, N.Y., 1984—; ptnr., field supr. Penn-Tex Real Estate, San Bernardino, Calif., 1984—. Mem. ASME, AAAS, Air Force Assn., Am. Mgmt. Assn., Soc. Automotive Engrs. Methodist. Club: Officer's (Norton AFB). Avocations: restoration, carpentry, woodwork. Home: PO Box 385 Lake Arrowhead CA 92352-0385 Office: BMO/ENMP Norton AFB CA 92409-6468

GREEVER, MARGARET QUARLES, mathematics educator; b. Wilkensburg, Pa., Feb. 7, 1931; s. Lawrence Reginald and Ella Mae (LeSueur) Quarles; m. John Greever, Aug. 29, 1953; children: Catherine Patricia, Richard George, Cynthia Diane. Cert. costume design, Richmond Profl. Inst., 1952; student, U. Va., 1953-56; BA in Math., Calif. State U., Los Angeles, 1963; MA in Math., Claremont Grad. Sch., 1968. Cert. tchr. specializing in Jr. Coll. math., Calif. Tchr. math. Chaffey Unified High Sch. Dist., Alta Loma, Calif., 1963-64, Los Angeles Unified Sch. Dist., 1964-65, Chino (Calif.) Unified Sch. Dist., 1965-81; from asst. prof. to assoc. prof. Chaffey Coll., Alta Loma, 1981—, phys. sci. div. chmn., 1985—; mem. Matrix Test Team, Chino, 1973. Mem. Nat. Council Tchrs. Math., Calif. Math. Council, Calif. Tchrs. Assn., LWV (bd. dirs. 1969-72), Pi Lambda Theta. Avocations: quilting, cooking, sewing. Home: 135 W 12th St Claremont CA 91711 Office: Chaffey Coll 5885 Haven Ave Alta Loma CA 91701

GREFF, RICHARD JOSEPH, medical company executive; b. N.Y.C., Apr. 8, 1944; s. Joseph and Helen G.; m. Jeullee K. Johnson; children: Jill, Daniel. BS, Wagner Coll., 1965; PhD, Poly. Inst. N.Y., 1969. Research chemist Union Carbide Corp., Bound Brook, N.J., 1969-73; polymer physicist Medtronic, Mpls., 1973-74; dir. chem. devel. Renal Systems, Mpls., 1974-76; mgr. advanced devel. Baxter Travenol, Deerfield, Ill., 1976-81; dir. technology Am. Pharmaseal div. Baxter Travenol, Valencia, CA, 1981—; dir. cardiovascular implants Edwards Labs. div. Baxter Travenol, Mission Viejo, Calif., 1987—. Patentee in field. Mem. Am. Chem. Soc., Health Industry Mfrs. Assn. (rep.), Am. Assn. Med. Instrumentation (rep.), N.Y. Acad. Sci. Home: 22282 Canaveras Mission Viejo CA 92691 Office: Edwards Labs Red Hill Ave Irvine CA 92714

GREFRATH, RICHARD WARREN, librarian; b. Greenwich, Conn., Aug. 7, 1946; s. Warren Paul and Dorothy Lee (Von Bieberstein) G.; m. Valentina Mary Lyntkowski, Dec. 23, 1971; children—Jason Richard, David Jonathan. Student Carnegie Inst. Tech., 1964-66; B.A. in English cum laude, NYU, 1968; M.A. in English, Temple U., 1971; M.L.S., U. Md., 1972. Research librarian Coll. Library and Info. Services, U. Md., 1973; reference librarian Pacific Luth. U. Library, Tacoma, Wash., 1973-78; instructional services librarian U. Nev., Reno, 1978—, instr. library sci., 1978—. Served with U.S. Army, 1968-70. Decorated Bronze Star, Army Commendation medal, Vietnamese Commendation medal, Nat. Def. Service medal, Vietnam Service medal. Recipient NYU Founder's Day scholar award, 1968. Mem. ALA, Nev. Library Assn., AAUP, 101st Airborne Div. Assn., Vietnam Vets. Am., ACLU, VFW, Am. Rose Soc., Phi Beta Kappa. Democrat. Author: Use of the Library: A Self-Paced Workbook in Library Skills, 1981; book reviewer Library Jour., Am. Reference Books Annual; contbr. articles to profl. jours. Office: U Nev Library Reno NV 89557-0044

GREGG, FRANK MELVIN, programmer analyst, guitarist, singer, songwriter; b. Lake Wales, Fla., June 3, 1948; s. Frank Melvin Gregg and Olivene Marie (Browning) Matchette; m. Kathryn Ann Pefferman, Jan. 28, 1968 (div. Jan. 74) m. Linda Louise Norman, July 23, 1975; children—Kelly Marie, Aaron Russell. Grad. high sch., Sarahsville, Ohio; grad. with honors U.S. Air Force Leadership Sch., 1970. EKG technician Presbyn. Hosp., Denver, 1976-78; staff programmer analyst Storage Tech. Corp., Louisville, Colo., 1978-84; gen. mgr. Boulder Printing Service, Colo., 1984; programmer Applied Microbotics Corp., Boulder, 1984-85; dir. software engring. Carrox Systems, Inc., Denver, 1982-84. Commr. Lafayette Charter Commn., 1982, Planning Commn., 1983-85; Republican candidate for city council City of Lafayette, 1984. Served to staff sgt. USAF, 1967-75. Republican. Club: Grange (Kennonsburg, Ohio). Home: PO Box 301 Lafayette CO 80026

GREGG, MARC BOYCE, computer programmer/analyst; b. Woonsocket, R.I., Feb. 8, 1955; s. Boyce and Jeanne Marie (Plasse) G. BS in Biology, Lowell Tech. Inst., 1977; BA in Computer Sci., U. Calif., San Diego, 1981; MS in Computer Sci., West Coast U., 1984. Programmer Sci. Applications, San Diego, 1979-81; programmer/analyst NCR Corp., San Diego, 1982—. Mem. NRA (life), Nat. Assn. Fed. Licensed Firearms Dealers, Escondido Fish and Game Assn., Sigma Xi (assoc.). Republican. Roman Catholic. Avocations: shooting, golf, computers, fitness, reading. Home: 721 Fresca St Solana Beach CA 92075 Office: NCR Corp 16550 W Bernardo Dr San Diego CA 92127

GREGG, NANCY VAN SANT, retail/wholesale executive; b. Fostoria, Ohio, Oct. 19; d. Lester A. and Nella C. (Mellott) Van Sant; m. R. Calvin Gregg, Apr. 24, 1960; children—Roger C., Christian V. Student North Central Coll., Naperville, Ill., 1957-58, Ripon Coll., 1958-59, U. Calif.-Santa Barbara, 1962-64; Otis Art Inst., 1968-69. Med. sec. to gen. physician, Fostoria, 1959-60; med. transcriber Oxnard (Calif.) Community Hosp., 1969-72; sales, mktg. rep. Tiny's, Inc., Oxnard, 1972—, v.p. mktg. and advt., 1974-84, pres., 1984—; lectr. in field. Editor: Focal Points Newsletter. Mem. Nat. Assn. Female Execs., Ventura County Bus. Profl. Women's Network (bd. dirs.), Oxnard C. of C., Point Hueneme C. of C., Nat. Assn. Ind. Businesses, Better Bus. Bur., Am. Bus. Women's Assn., Nat. Assn. Retail Dealers of Am., Internat. Platform Assn. Republican. Office: Tiny's Inc 1237 Saviers Rd Oxnard CA 93033

GREGGS, ELIZABETH MAY BUSHELL (MRS. RAYMOND JOHN GREGGS), librarian; b. Delta, Colo., Nov. 7, 1925; d. Joseph Perkins and Ruby May (Stanford) Bushell; m. Raymond John Greggs, Aug. 16, 1952; children: David M., Geoffrey B., Timothy C., Daniel R. BA, U. Denver, 1948. Children's librarian Grand Junction (Colo.) Pub. Library, 1944-46, Chelan County Library, 1948, Wenatchee Pub. Library, 1948-52, Seattle Pub. Library, 1952-53; children's librarian Renton (Wash.) Pub. Library, 1957-61, dir., 1962, br. supr. and children's services supr., 1963-67; area children's supr. King County Library, Seattle, 1968-78, asst. coordinator childen's services, 1978-86; head librarian Valley View Library of King County Library System, Seattle, 1986—; cons., organizer Tutor Ctr. Library, Seattle South Community Coll., 1969-72; mem. Puget Sound (Wash.) Council for Reviewing Children's Media, chmn. 1974—; cons. to children's TV programs. Editor: Cayas Newsletter, 1971-74; cons. to Children's Catalog, Children's Index to Poetry. Chmn. dist. advancement com. Kloshee dist. Boy Scouts Am., 1975-78; mem. Bond Issue Citizens Group to build new Renton Library, 1958, 59. Recipient Hon. Service to Youth award Cedar River dist. Boy Scouts Am., 1971, award of merit Kloshee dist., 1977. Mem. ALA (Newbery-Caldecott com. 1978-79, com. chmn. 1983-84; membership com. 1978-80, Boy Scouts com. children's services div. 1973-78, chmn. 1976-78, exec. bd. dirs. Assn. for Library Service to Children 1979-81, mem. council 1985—, chmn. nominating com. Assn. Library Service to Children 1986-87), Wash. Library Assn. (exec. bd. children's and young adult services div. 1970-78, chmn. membership com. 1983—), King County Right to Read Council (co-chmn. 1973-77), Pierce-King County Reading Council, Wash. State Literacy Council (exec. bd. 1971-77), Wash. Library Media Assn. (jr. high levels com. 1980-84), Pacific NW Library Assn. (young readers' choice com. 1981-83, chmn. div. 1983-85, exec. bd. 1983-85), Puget Sound Orton Soc., Council for Reviewing Children's Media (chmn. 1974-76). Methodist. Home: 800 Lynnwood Ave NE Renton WA 98056 Office: Valley View Library 17850 Military Rd S Seattle WA 98188

GREGORY, BARBARA JEAN, editor; b. Geneva, N.Y., Mar. 14, 1954; d. Philip Keith Gregory and Ruth Shirley (Harding) Zamory. BA, Alfred U., 1972-76. Med. illustrator U. Rochester, N.Y., 1976-78; typesetter, proofreader TypeGraphics, Syracuse, N.Y., 1979-80; prodn. editor Am. Numismatic Assn., Colorado Springs, Colo., 1981—; cons. Random House Unabridged Dictionary, 1985. Contbr. articles to jour. Avocation: home renovation. Office: Am Numismatic Assn 818 N Cascade Ave Colorado Springs CO 80903-3279

GREGORY, CALVIN, insurance service executive; b. Bronx, N.Y., Jan. 11, 1942; s. Jacob and Ruth (Cherchian) G.; m. Rachel Anna Carver, Feb. 14, 1970 (div. Apr. 1977); children—Debby Lynn, Trixy Sue; m. 2d, Carla Deane Deaver, June 30, 1979. A.A., Los Angeles City Coll., 1962; B.A., Calif. State U.-Los Angeles, 1964; M.Div., Fuller Theol. Sem., 1968; M.R.E., Southwestern Sem., Ft. Worth, 1969; Ph.D. in Religion, Universal Life Ch., Modesto, Calif., 1982; D.Div. (hon.), Otay Mesa Coll., 1982. Notary pub., real estate lic., casualty lic., Calif.; ordained to ministry Am. Baptist Conv., 1970. Youth minister First Bapt. Ch., Delano, Calif., 1964-65, 69-70; youth dir. St. Luke's United Meth. Ch., Highland Park, Calif., 1969-70; tchr. polit. sci. Maranatha High Sch., Rosemead, Calif., 1969-70; aux. chaplain U.S. Air Force 750th Radar Squadron, Edwards AFB, Calif., 1970-72; pastor First Bapt. Ch., Boron, Calif., 1971-72; ins. agt. Prudential Ins. Co., Ventura, Calif., 1972-73, sales mgr., 1973-74; casualty ins. agt. Allstate Ins. Co., Thousand Oaks, Calif., 1974-75; pres. Ins. Agy. Placement Service, Thousand Oaks, 1975—; head youth minister Emanuel Presbyn. Ch., Los Angeles, 1973-74; owner, investor real estate, U.S., Wales, Eng., Can., Australia. Counselor YMCA, Hollywood, Calif., 1964, Soul Clinic-Universal Life Ch., Inc., Modesto, Calif., 1982. Mem. Apt. Assn. Los Angeles, Life Underwriter Tng. Council. Republican. Clubs: Forensic (Los Angeles); X32 (Ventura). Lodge: Kiwanis (club speaker 1971). Home: 3307 Big Cloud Circle Thousand Oaks CA 91360 Office: Ins Agy Placement Service PO Box 4407 Thousand Oaks CA 91359

GREGORY, ELEANOR ANNE, artist, educator; b. Seattle, Jan. 20, 1939; d. John Noel and Eleanor Blanche G.; BA, Reed Coll., 1963; MFA, U. Wash., 1966; MEd, Columbia U., 1978, EdD., 1978. Art tchr. Seattle Public Schs., 1970-75; instr. N.Y.C. Community Coll., 1977, Manhattan Community Coll., N.Y.C., 1978; asst. prof. N.Mex. State U., Las Crucas, 1978-79; asst. prof. art Purdue U., West Lafayette, Ind., 1979-82, West Tex. State U., Canyon, 1982-84; lectr. Calif. State U., Long Beach, 1985—; one woman shows: Columbia U. Tchrs. Coll., 1976, Watson's Crick Gallery, West Lafayette, 1980, 81, Gallery I, Purdue U., 1980, W. Tex. State U., 1983, Amarillo Art Ctr., 1984, Sch. Visual Concepts, Seattle, 1985; group shows include: El Paso (Tex.) Art Mus., 1979, Ind. State Mus., Indpls., 1980, Lafayette (Ind.) Art Mus., 1982, T. Billman Gallery, Long Beach, 1987; represented in permanent collection: Portland (Oreg.) Art Mus.; mgr. Watson's Crick Gallery, West Lafayette, 1982-83. Mem. Nat. Art Edn. Assn., N.Y. Soc. Scribes, Chgo. Calligraphy Collective, Internat. Soc. Edn. Through Art. Episcopalian. Office: Calif State U Dept Art 1250 Bellflower Blvd Long Beach CA 90840

GREGORY, JAMES MCKANNA, bank executive; b. Los Angeles, Apr. 16, 1939; s. Bert Oswald and Christine (McKanna) G.; m. Laura Anne White, July 7, 1961; children: David James, Brent Loren. BSEE, Stanford U., 1961, MBA, 1963, MS, 1965, PhD, 1967. Tech. mgr. Stanford Research Inst., Menlo Park, Calif., 1963-67; dir. econometrics Bunker-Ramo Corp., Chgo., 1967-76; v.p. cons. Chem. Bank, N.Y.C., 1976-83; v.p. research and devel. Bank Am., San Francisco, 1983—. Mem. Ops. Research Soc. Am., Inst. Mgmt. Scis. Office: Bank Am #5377 555 California St San Francisco CA 94104

GREGORY, RICK DEAN, lawyer; b. Edmond, Okla., Feb. 22, 1954; s. Jerry D. and Elaine (Hall) G. B.A. in History, Central State U., 1977; J.D., Oklahoma City U., 1981. Bar: Okla. 1982, U.S. Dist. Ct. (ea. and we. dist.) Okla. 1982, U.S. Ct. Appeals (10th cir.) 1982. Juvenile parole officer dept. human services State of Okla., Oklahoma City, 1977-81; law clk. Jess Horn, Inc., Oklahoma City, 1981-82; atty. in sole practice, Oklahoma City, 1982—. Editor: Policy Options on Political Reform, 1974; author: A Historical, Legal and Moral Analysis of Unauthorized Audio Duplication in the United States, 1975. Mem. ABA, Am. Trial Lawyers Assn., Am. Judicature Soc., Okla. Bar Assn., Okla. Trial Lawyers Assn., Okla. County Bar Assn., Can. County Bar Assn., Okla. Criminal Defense Lawyers Assn. Democrat. Methodist. Avocations: skiing, tennis, swimming.

GREGORY, WILLIAM A., college dean, theatre educator and director; b. Williamston, Mich., Aug. 20, 1924; s. William Alfred and Erna Mae (Roeser) G.; m. JoAnn Alvestrom, June 11; children—Kay, Erna. B.S., Central Mich. U., 1946; M.A., Mich. State U., 1950; Ph.D., U. Minn., 1957. Founder, dir. Lake Michigan Playhouse, Grand Haven, Mich., Vanguard Equity Theatre, Detroit; tchr. high schs., Mich., 1946-50; mem. faculty Alma (Mich.) Coll., 1951-53; prof. theatre Western Wash. U., Bellingham, 1957-60, 69—, dean Coll. Fine and Performing Arts, also theatre dir. Fulbright scholar, Taipei, Taiwan, 1983-84; named Outstanding Alumnus, Central Mich. U., 1981. Mem. Internat. Council Fine Arts Deans, Am. Theatre Assn. Democrat. Author: The Director. Office: Coll Fine and Performing Arts Western Wash U Bellingham WA 98225

GREINER, MAURICE LUTHER, loss control consultant; b. Assiniboia, Sask., Can., Jan. 4, 1931; came to U.S., 1971, naturalized, 1979; s. William Morris and Daisy (Weightman) G.; diploma Briercret Bible Coll., 1952; adminstrn. diploma U. Toronto Extension Program, 1966; grad. Inst. of Fire Engrs., 1968; m. Zelma Alma Ross, June 30, 1951; children—Blayne Maurice, Brenda Gail. Firefighter, instr. City of Regina (Sask., Can.), 1952-66; dir. Regina Emergency Measures Orgn., 1966-68; safety tng. supr. Simplot Chem. Co., Brandon, Man., Can., 1968-71, corp. dir. tng. and safety, Pocatello, Idaho, 1971-86; founder, dir. ann. Intermountain Fertilizer Safety Sch., 1974—; mem. safety health task force Fertilizer Inst., Washington, 1975-86, vice chmn., 1980-83, chmn., 1983-86; loss control cons. Johnson & Higgins, Seattle, 1986—. Bd. dirs. Idaho State Symphony; mem. Community Task Force on Geriatric Health Care, 1984. Recipient Queen's Commendation for brave conduct in fire service, 1966; Disting. service to safety award Nat. Safety Council, 1981; cert. hazard control mgr. Mem. Inst. Fire Engrs., Am. Soc. Tng. and Devel., Am. Soc. Safety Engrs., Am. Inst. Chem. Engrs., Vets. of Safety Internat., SAR, Delta Epsilon Chi. Republican. Mem. Ch. of Nazarene. Club: Order St. John. Lodge: Rotary. Author: The Greiners of Amityville, Pa., 1700-1900, 1982; editor fertilizer sect. Newsletter for Nat. Safety Council, 1972; contbr. articles to profl. jours.; co-author: Self-Evaluation Manual for Fertilizer Industry, HHS, NIOSH, 1980.

GREMBAN, JOE LAWRENCE, utilities executive; b. Goodman, Wis., June 3, 1920; s. Joseph and Anna (Kryzyak) G.; m. V. June Smith, June 8, 1945; children: Ronald D., Keith D., Brian D. BBA, U. Wis., 1948; postgrad., U. Mich., 1973. Spl. acct. Cen. Ill. Electric & Gas Co., Rockford, 1949-62; asst. treas. Sierra Pacific Power Co., Reno, 1962-63, corp. sec., 1963-69, v.p., 1969-71, v.p., sec., treas., 1971-72, fin. v.p., treas., 1972-73, exec. v.p., 1973-75, pres., 1975-76, pres., chief exec. officer, 1976-80, chmn., pres., chief exec. officer, 1980-86, chmn., chief exec. officer, 1986-87; chmn. bd. Sierra Pacific Power Co., 1987—; chmn., pres. Sierra Pacific Resources, Reno, 1984—; mem. faculty industry adv. com. Pub. Utilities Edn., U. Mich., 1974; bd. dirs. WEST Assocs., Western Regional Council, Econ. Devel. Authority of Western Nev., Pacific Coast Elec. Assn., also pres.; mem. adv. bd. Coll. Bus. Adminstrn. U. Nev., Reno. Past pres., past commr., mem. exec. bd. Nev. Area council Boy Scouts Am.; past dir. Reno Better Bus. Bur.; dir., past pres. United Way of No. Nev. Served as pilot USAAF, 1942-45. Mem. Nat. Assn. Accountants (past pres. Reno chpt.), Reno Execs. Club (past pres.), Edison Electric Inst., Pacific Coast Gas Assn. (past dir.), Pacific Coast Elec. Assn. (past pres., past dir.), Greater Reno-Sparks C. of C. Lodge: Rotary. Home: 2865 Juliann Way Reno NV 89509 Office: Sierra Pacific Power Co 100 E Moana Ln Reno NV 89520

GREMBOWSKI, EUGENE, insurance company manager; b. Bay City, Mich., July 21, 1938; s. Barney Thomas and Mary (Senkowski) G.; m. Teresa Ann Frasik, June 27, 1959; children: Bruce Allen, Debora Ann. AA, Allan Hancock U., 1963; BA, Mich. State U., 1967; MBA, George Washington U., 1972. Enlisted USAF, 1955, commd. 2d lt., 1968, advanced through grades to capt., 1971; personnel officer USAF, Goldsboro, N.C., 1968-70; chief of procurement USAF, Cheyenne, Wyo., 1971-73; contract analyst USAF, Omaha, 1973-76; chief of contracting USAF, Atwater, Calif., 1976-79; ret. USAF, 1979; office supr. Farmers Ins. Group of Cos., Merced, Calif., 1980-85, office mgr., 1985-86; fleet mgr. Los Angeles, 1986—. Author: Governmental Purchasing: Its Progression Toward Professional Status, 1972. Cubmaster Boy Scouts Am., Goldsboro, 1968; com. chmn. Am. Heart Assn., Merced-Mariposa, Calif., 1985, sec.-treas., 1986. Recipient Meritorious Service medals Office of the Pres., 1973, 76. Mem. Nat. Contract Mgmt. Assn. Avocations: home movies, travel, coin and stamp collecting. Home: 14633 Mountain Spring St Hacienda Heights CA 91745 Office: Farmers Ins Group Leasing Co 4680 Wilshire Blvd Los Angeles CA 90010

GRENKO, SUELLEN MARY, educator; b. Dunsmuir, Calif., Apr. 12, 1946; d. Joseph J. and Maureen B. (Roney) G. B.A. in English, Calif. State U.-Chico, 1968; M.A. in Ednl. Adminstrn., Calif. State U.-Rohnert Park, 1982. Cert. secondary tchr., cert. in adminstrv. services, Calif. Tchr. secondary English lit. Livermore (Calif.) Unified Sch. Dist., 1969-71; tchr. English, history and journalism Santa Rosa (Calif.) City Secondary Schs., 1971-79, project coordinator/designer CARMS Vocat. Edn. Project, 1980-84; tchr. English as a Second Language, 1984—; journalism tchr. for newspaper and yearbook, 1972-78; student/family counselor; tchr. English as a Second Language, Mexico. Active youth work activities; travel Mexico and Europe vol. missionary work, 1981-87. Mem. Profl. Educators Group, Journalism Edn. Assn., Assn. Supervision and Curriculum Devel., Nat. Right to Work Com. Republican. Office: Santa Rosa City Secondary Schs 1916 Genoa Pl Santa Rosa CA 95401

GRENLEY, PHILIP, physician; b. N.Y.C., Dec. 21, 1912; s. Robert and Sara (Schrader) G.; B.S., N.Y.U., 1932, M.D., 1936; m. Dorothy Sarney, Dec. 11, 1938; children—Laurie (Mrs. John Hallen), Neal, Jane (Mrs. Eldridge C. Hanes), Robert. Intern, Kings County Hosp., Bklyn., 1936-38, resident, 1939; resident in urology L.I. Coll. Hosp., Bklyn., 1939-41; practice medicine specializing in urology, Tacoma, Wash., 1946—; urologist Tacoma Gen. Hosp., St. Joseph Hosp., Drs. Hosp., Mary Bridge Children's Hosp. (all Tacoma), Good Samaritan Hosp., Puyallup, Wash.; pres. med. staff St. Joseph Hosp., Tacoma, 1968-69, mem. exec. bd., 1950-54, 67-68; cons. urologist to Surgeon Gen., Madigan Army Med. Center, Tacoma, 1955—, USPHS McNeil Island Penitentiary, 1955-82, Good Samaritan Rehab. Center, Puyallup, 1960—; lectr. in sociology U. Puget Sound, Tacoma, 1960—. Trustee Wash. Children's Home Soc., 1951-60, Charles Wright Acad., 1961-69, Wash. State Masonic Home, 1984—; trustee Pierce County Med. Bur., 1949-51, 59-61, 71-73, pres., 1973-74, mem. exec. bd., 1975-77. Served with AUS, 1941-46. Diplomate Am. Bd. Urology. Fellow ACS; mem. Am. Urol. Assn., AMA, Wash., Pan Am. med. assns., Pierce County Med. Soc. Lodges: Masons, Shrine (med. dir. 1965-78, imperial council 1982-85, potentate 1983), Royal Order Jesters (dir. 1986, 87), Lions, Elks, Red Cross of Constantine (knight). Home: 40 Loch Ln SW, Tacoma, WA 98499 Office: 721 S Fawcett Ave, Tacoma, WA 98402

GRENNAN, CYNTHIA, superintendent schools; b. Sterling, Ill., Jan. 4, 1938; d. Francis John and Elza (Pippert) G. B.S., Ill. State U., 1959; M.A., Ariz. State U., 1964. Tchr. Palatine Sch. Dist., Ill., 1959-61, Chandler Sch. Dist., Ariz., 1961-64, Anaheim Union High Sch. Dist., Calif., 1964-67, counselor, 1972-76, psychologist, 1972-76, asst. prin. to asst. supt., 1976-79, supt., 1979—; state supt. com. Assn. Calif. Sch. Adminstrs., Burlingame, Calif., 1984—. Episcopalian. Office: PO Box 3520 Anaheim CA 92803 *

GRETHEL, THOMAS EARL, mechanical engineer; b. Denver, May 15, 1947; s. Earl Frederick and Agnes Elizabeth (Hansen) G.; m. Martha Louise Lidke, May 8, 1983. Graduate, U.S. Naval Nuclear Power Sch. and Engring. Lab. Tech., 1968; BSME, Colo. State U., 1981; postgrad., U. Phoenix, 1986—. Marine machinist Mare Island Naval Shipyard, Vallejo, Calif., 1972-74; nuclear equipment operator Pub. Service Co. Colo., Platteville, 1974-79, radio-chemistry lab. asst., 1979-80; lead software quality assurance analyst Pub. Service Co. Colo., Denver, 1983—; technician Solar Energy Research Inst., Golden, Colo., 1980; engr. Stone and Webster Engring. Corp., Denver, 1981-83. V.p. Highlands Luth. Ch. Council, Denver, 1984, chmn. bldg. com., 1984-85; chmn. Ecumenical Youth Group Adult Com., Denver, 1984. Served with USN, 1966-72. Mem. ASME, Am. Nuclear Soc., Colo. Soc. Engrs. (bd. govs. 1985-86), Am. Legion, Pi Tau Sigma. Republican. Lodge: Masons. Avocations: cross country skiing, racquetball, collecting antiques, working with the elderly and youth. Home: 1960 Yarrow St Lakewood CO 80215 Office: Pub Service Co of Colo 18201 W 10th Ave Golden CO 80401

GRETHER, DAVID MACLAY, economics educator; b. Phila., Oct. 21, 1938; s. Ewald T. and Carrie Virginia (Maclay) G.; m. Susan Edith Clayton, Mar. 24, 1961; children: Megan Elizabeth, John Clayton. B.S., U. Calif., Berkeley, 1960; Ph.D., Stanford U., 1969. Research staff economist Cowles Found., Yale U., 1966-70; lectr. econs. Yale U., 1966-68, asst. prof., 1968-70; assoc. prof. econs. Calif. Inst. Tech., Pasadena, 1970-75; prof. econs. Calif. Inst. Tech., 1975—, exec. officer for social scis., 1978-82, chmn. Humanities and Social Scis. div., 1982—. Author: (with M. Nerlove and J.L. Carvalho) Analysis of Economic Time Series: A Synthesis, 1979; contbr. articles to profl. jours. Mem. Econometric Soc., Am. Statis. Assn., Am. Econ. Assn. Home: 2116 N Craig Ave Altadena CA 91001 Office: Calif Inst Tech Pasadena CA 91125

GRETZKY, WAYNE, professional hockey player; b. Brantford, Ont., Can., Jan. 26, 1961; s. Walter and Phyllis G. Center Peterborough Petes, Jr. Ont. Hockey Assn., 1977-78, Sault Ste. Marie Greyhounds, 1977-78, Indpls. Racers, World Hockey Assn., 1978-79, Edmonton Oilers (Alta., Can.), NHL, 1979—. Player NHL All-Star Game, 1980-87; named Rookie of Yr. World Hockey Assn., 1979, Most Valuable Player NHL, 1980-87, Sportsman of Yr. Sports Illus., 1982; recipient Lady Byng Meml. Trophy NHL, 1980, Art Ross trophy NHL, 1986. Adress: care Edmonton Oilers, Northlands Coliseum, Edmonton, AB Canada T5B 4M9 *

GRIEK, MARTIN RICHARD, construction company executive; b. Newark, Feb. 4, 1943; s. Martin M. and Elisabeth K. (Berner) G.; m. Lynda M. Schmidt, May 6, 1967 (div. May 1982); 1 dau., Melissa. B.S.C.E., U. Denver, 1965, M.S. in Bus. Mgmt., 1966. Supt. Peter Kiewit Sons Co., Denver, 1966-67; staff engr. Internat. Engring. Co., Denver, 1967-71; constrn. mgr. Suburban Devel. Corp., Clinton, Md., 1972-74; project mgr. John Driggs Co., Capital Heights, Md., 1974-79; dept. mgr. PCL Constrn. Inc., Denver, 1979-84; pres. Westbrook Constrn. Inc., Denver, 1984—; ptnr. SCM Devel. Co., Boulder, 1967—, RE Investments, Boulder, 1983—. Pres., Home Owners Assn., Newberg, Md., 1976-79; bd. dirs. So. Md. Marching Band, Newberg, 1975-78. Mem. Pi Kappa Alpha (chmn. frat. house corp. 1967-72, dist. pres. 1969-72, Disting. Service award 1972). Roman Catholic. Home: 200 Fox Dr Boulder CO 80303 Office: Westbrook Constrn Inc 455 Sherman St Suite 460 Denver CO 80203

GRIESINGER, DONALD WILLIAM, business educator; b. Los Angeles, Aug. 8, 1932; s. William Fred and Mildred Mae (Strohm) G.; m. Judith Annette Miller, Dec. 27, 1960; children: Kathryn, John. BS in Physics, U. So. Calif., 1954; MS in Applied Physics, UCLA, 1960; PhD in Psychology, U. Calif., Santa Barbara, 1970. Assoc. scientist Westinghouse Bettis Atomic Power Labs., Pitts., 1958-59; project mgr. Gen. Electric Co. TEMPO, Santa Barbara, 1962-71; prof. mgmt. Union Coll., Schenectady, N.Y., 1971-79; v.p. ops. Ray Wilson Co., Los Angeles, 1979-82; prof. mgmt. Claremont (Calif.) Grad. Sch., 1982—, chmn. faculty of mgmt. Grad. Mgmt. Ctr., 1983—; cons. in field. Contbr. articles to tech. jours. Served to lt. USN, 1954-58. Mem. Acad. Mgmt., Phi Beta Kappa, Sigma Xi. Republican. Episcopalian. Home: 876 Wabash Ct Claremont CA 91711 Office: Claremont Grad Sch Claremont CA 91711

GRIESMER, GERARD JOSEPH, chemical company executive; b. N.Y.C., June 22, 1928; s. Joseph and Theresa (Hereth) G.; m. Ursula A. Demuth, Sept. 23, 1977; 1 child, Alexandra. BS in Chem. Engring., Notre Dame U., 1950; MS in Chem. Engring., MIT, 1952. Registered profl. engr. Comml. developer Union Carbide Corp., Buffalo, 1952-64; bus. dir. Union Carbide Europa, Geneva, 1964-74; pres., chief exec. officer Liquichimica Inc., N.Y.C., 1974-79; cons. G.J. Griesmer, N.Y.C., 1980; v.p. Filtrol Corp., Los Angeles, 1981-82; pres., chief exec. officer Atec Inc., Riverton, Wyo., 1982-86, also bd. dirs.; pres., chief exec. officer Mitrix Medica Inc., Denver, 1986—; also bd. dirs. Mitral Med. Inc., Denver. Contbr. articles to profl. jours.; patentee in field. Recipient Chem. Engring. Acheivement award Chem. Engring. Publ., 1961, John C. Vaalor award Chem. Processing Publ., 1964. Mem. Am. Inst. Chem. Engrs. Roman Catholic. Avocations: skiing, bowling. Home: 629 Humboldt St Denver CO 80218 Office: Matrix Medica Denver CO 80206

GRIEVE, HAROLD WALTER, retired interior designer; b. Los Angeles, Feb. 1, 1901; s. Alexander and Maria (Chapman) G.; m. Jetta Goudal, Oct. 11, 1930. Student Los Angeles art schs., 1920-21, Chouinard Sch. Art, 1920-21, Camillo Innocentie, Rome, 1923-24. Art dir. M.P. Studios, 1920-28; art dir. for motion pictures including: Dorothy Vernon of Haden Hall, Lady Windemer's Fan, So This is Paris; interior designer, Los Angeles, now ret.; decorated Colleen Moore Doll House interiors, 1935; interior design work includes homes of George Burns, Jack Benny, Bing Crosby, Erving Thalberg, Norma Schearer, others. Fellow Am. Inst. Interior Designers (life mem., past nat. pres., past local pres.), Acad. of Motion Pictures (founder mem., life mem.), Hist. Soc. So. Calif. Republican. Clubs: Los Angeles Athletic; Beach (Santa Monica, Calif.).

GRIEVE, MICHAEL JOSEPH, banker; b. Richmond, Va., Jan. 18, 1934; s. Harry Logan and Irene (Taylor) G.; m. Ona Pearl Phipps, July 31, 1956; 1 child, Michael Logan. A.S. in Banking, N.M.M.I., 1974. Served to master sgt. USAF, 1952-72; mgr. Otero Credit Union, Roswell, N.Mex., 1972-77; ops. officer Dominion Bank, Richmond, Va., 1977-79; treas.-mgr. Govt. Employees Credit, Roswell, N.Mex., 1979-81; v.p. mktg. 1st Interstate Bank, Roswell, 1981—. Chmn. United Way, 1984—. Recipient Wood Badge award Boy Scouts Am., 1971, Silver Beaver award Boy Scouts Am., 1986 . Mem. Sertoma (pres., gov., Greater Rocky Mountain Regional Sertoman of Yr., 1986), Roswell C. of C. (bd. dirs.), N.Mex. Bankers Assn., Bankers Adminstrn. Inst. (past sec.). Republican. Methodist. Office: PO Box 2057 128 W 2nd St Roswell NM 88201

GRIFFIN, DON LEWIS, electrical engineer; b. Ogden, Utah, Feb. 26, 1934; s. Ellis Byron and Gwendolyn (Jenkins) G.; m. Marilyn Kunz, Aug. 9, 1962; children: Karla, Kent, Tana, Donette, Jacqui. BSEE, Utah State U., 1965, MSEE, 1969. Test equipment fabricator Hill AFB, Ogden, 1952-62; research engr. Utah State U., Logan, 1965-74; sr. engr. Idaho Nat. Engring. Lab., Idaho Falls, 1974—. Served with USN, 1956-57. Recipient Bronze Signature award Westinghouse, 1986. Republican. Mormon. Avocations: mountaineering, tech. rock climbing, sailing, ham radio. Home: 19 S 675 W Blackfoot ID 83221 Office: Westinghouse-ECF PO Box 2068 Idaho Falls ID 83401

GRIFFIN, DONALD JAMES, minister; b. Redwood City, Calif., Apr. 8, 1958; s. John and Joan Mae (Leonard) G.; m. Martha Marie Crown, June 27, 1981; children: Annie Bricole, Aaron James. Student, Oreg. Coll. Edn., 1976-79; BA, N.W. Coll. of the Assemblies of God, 1982. Ordained minister Assembly of God Ch., 1985. Pastor Cen. Park Assembly of God, Aberdeen, Wash., 1982—; layworker Cen. Assembly of God, Seattle, 1980-82. Fellow Gen. Council Assemblies of God (pastor 1982). Avocations: archery, golfing, gardening. Home and Office: 516 7th St Hood River OR 97031

GRIFFIN, HERSCHEL EMMETT, educator, administrator; b. Valley City, N.D., July 28, 1918; s. Herschel Raymond and Olive Buckley (Whalian) G.; m. Frances Helen Nye, June 6, 1943; children—Bruce Nye, Karen Lynn. A.A., Chaffey Jr. Coll., Ontario, Calif., 1937; B.A., Stanford U., 1939; M.D., U. Calif.-San Francisco, 1943. Diplomate Am. Bd. Preventive Medicine (sec., treas. 1978-79). Intern in surgery U. Calif. Hosp., 1944; resident surgery San Francisco Hosp., 1945; practice medicine Upland, Calif., 1947-50; became 1st lt., M.C. U.S. Army, 1943, advanced through grades to col., 1962; regtl. surgeon, div. preventive medicine officer Calif., comdg. officer med. br. Japan; div. surgeon Korea (40th Inf. Div.), 1950-52; comdg. officer (U.S. Army Hosp.), Sasebo, Japan, 1952-53; fellow in epidemiology Walter Reed Army Research and Grad. Sch., 1954-55; chief communicable disease br. Office Surgeon Gen., Dept. Army, 1955-58; theater epidemiologist U.S. Army, Europe; dep. for profl. services U.S. Army (9th Hosp. Center), Germany, 1959-62; asst. for profl. services Office Dep. Asst. Sec. Def., 1963-65; exec. officer Office Surgeon Gen., Dept. Army, 1965-66, chief preventive medicine div., 1966-69; ret. 1969; prof. epidemiology, dean Grad. Sch. Pub. Health, U. Pitts., 1969-80; prof. epidemiology Grad. Sch. Public Health, San Diego State U., 1980—; U.S. Army rep. Gorgas Meml. Inst., 1966-69, Leonard Wood Meml., 1966-69; cons. Walter Reed Army Inst. Research, 1972-77, WHO, 1972-77, chmn. expert com. on recommended requirements for schs. pub. health, 1972; del. Pa. Health Conf. Com., U. Health Center of Pitts., 1970-73, Pa. Health Council, 1972-74; sci. adviser U.S. EPA, 1973-87; pres. Pa. Health Council, 1973-74; cons. Uniformed Services U. of Health Scis., 1975-84; chmn. Pa. Health Conf. Com., 1973-74; chmn. com. on med. and biol. effects of environ. pollutants NRC/Nat. Acad. Scis., 1972-76; chmn. infectious disease adv. com. Nat. Inst. Allergy and Infectious Diseases, NIH, 1974-76; mem. Gov.'s Task Force on Health Edn. in Pa., 1974-76; mem. adv. com. Gov.'s Energy Council, 1974-79; bd. dirs. Pa. Health Research Inst., 1973-75; mem. Armed Forces Epidemiological Bd., 1973-84, pres., 1977-79, chmn. ad hoc study team on procurement standards, 1974-75; chmn. com. to study health effects of air pollution Allegheny County Bd. Health/Allegheny County Health Dept., 1974-76; mem. sci. adv. bd. and environ. health com. EPA, 1982-87, chmn. environ. health com., 1982-85, mem. exec. com., 1983-85, mem. drinking water com., 1985-87. Contbr. articles to profl. jours. Decorated Legion of Merit, Bronze Star medal, Army Commendation medal; recipient Comdr.'s award for pub. service Dept. Army. Fellow ACP, Am. Coll. Preventive Medicine, Am. Pub. Health Assn.; mem. AMA (mem. Ho. Dels.), Assn. Schs. of Pub. Health (pres. 1971-73, exec. com. 1973-75), Internat. Health Soc. (pres.-elect 1985), Soc. Med. Cons. to Armed Forces (chmn. preventive medicine com. 1970-73, pres. 1975-76). Home: 11274 Pabellon Ct San Diego CA 92124 Office: Grad Sch Pub Health San Diego State U San Diego CA 92182

GRIFFIN, JOHN HENRY, medical researcher; b. Seattle, June 26, 1943; s. John Henry and Lillian Louise (O'Connell) G.; m. Antonia Lastreto, 1965 (div. 1984); children—John, Deanna, Paul; m. Arlene LaPlante, 1985. B.S., U. Santa Clara, 1965; Ph.D., U. Calif.-Davis, 1969. Teaching asst. U. Calif., 1967-69; research fellow Harvard U. Med. Sch., 1969-71; guest worker NIH, 1971-73; on staff Service de Biochimie Centre d'Etudes Nucleaires, Saclay, France, 1973-74; asst. dept immunopathology Scripps Clinic and Research Found., La Jolla, Calif., 1974-75, assoc. depts. immunopathology and molecular biology, 1975-80, assoc. mem. dept. immunology, 1980—; peer rev. com. NIH, 1979—. Contbr. articles to profl. jours. Treas. San Diego Assn. Gifted Children, 1978-81; active Pub. Sch. Cluster Com., University City, S.D., 1984-85; mem. adv. com. High Sch. Community, University City, 1979-82, 86—. Recipient Research Career Devel. award NIH, 1976-81. RCA physics scholar 1961-64; fellow NIH, 1966-69, 72-73, Helen Hay Whitney Found. 1969-72. Mem. Am. Chem. Soc., Am. Soc. Biol. Chemists, Am. Assn. Pathologists, Am. Assn. Immunologists, Internat. Soc. Thrombosis and Hemostasis, Am. Heart Assn., Sigma Xi, Alpha Sigma Nu, Phi Kappa Phi. Current work: Basic and clinical research on regulation of hemostasis and thrombosis. Subspecialties: Biochemistry (medicine); Hematology.

GRIFFIN, JOHN LAWRENCE, martial arts and Oriental exercise instr., writer, lectr.; b. Butler, Pa., Mar. 16, 1942; s. William and Rose G.; student Wakayama U., Japan, 1964-65; B.A., Calif. State U., Fresno, 1971; postgrad. Calif. State U., Dominguez Hills; pvt. studies psychology and parapsychology Dr. L.J. Bendit; m. Ann Avery (div.); 1 dau., Erin Marie. Ednl. cons. Laucks Found., 1970-73; instr. Oriental exercise and martial arts, public and pvt. instns., 1965—; mem. faculty phys. edn. U. Calif., Santa Barbara, 1974-78, head coach karate team, 1974-79; lectr. in psychology and parapsychology U. Calif. Extension, 1971-73; lectr. Oriental culture. People-to-People cultural exchange student to Japan, 1964-65; vice chair Tobu City (Japan)-Santa Barbara Sister City Com. Mem. Screenwriters Assn. Santa Barbara, Pacific Ctr. Contbr. articles on Asian cultural arts and parapsychology to periodicals. Home: 2834 Foothill Rd Santa Barbara CA 93105

GRIFFIN, KENYON NEAL, academic administrator; b. Natoma, Kans., Aug. 8, 1939; s. Leslie Tillman and Elizabeth Alice (Hobrock) G.; m. Leah Gwen Sharp, Mar. 2, 1962; children: Karol Rene, Shari Lene. BA in History, Ft. Hays (Kans.) State U., 1961; MA in Polit. Sci., Kans. State U., 1968; PhD in Polit. Sci., U. Ky., 1972. Edn. officer Govt. Tanzania, Dodoma, 1961-63; tchr. Garden City (Kans.) Pub. Schs., 1964-66; prof. polit. sci. U. Wyo., Laramie, 1970-83, dir. extended credit program, 1983—; cons. Wyo. State Bar, Cheyenne, 1978-86; mem. Wyo. Jud. Supervisory Commn., Cheyenne, 1982-85. Contbr. articles to profl. jours. Mem. Western Polit. Sci. Assn., Western Social Sci. Assn., Western Assn. Summer Session Adminstrs. (chmn. ann. meeting 1985-87). Avocations: photography, hiking, camping, horseback riding. Office: U Wyo Extended Credit Programs Box 3106 Laramie WY 82071

GRIFFIN, SUSAN ELIZABETH, clinical psychologist; b. Holyoke, Mass., Dec. 11, 1944; d. Cornelius John and Elizabeth Cecilia (Hickson) Griffin; m. Neal Kenton Baker, June 15, 1968; 1 dau., Anne Elizabeth. B.A. cum laude, Seton Hill Coll., 1967; M.S., Pa. State U., 1973, Ph.D., 1976. Lic. psychologist, Calif.; lic. marriage, family and child counselor, Calif. USPHS trainee dept. psychology Pa. State U., State College, 1971-75; intern in clin. psychology Kaiser Pemenente Med. Care Program, Los Angeles, 1975-76, psychol. asst. Kaiser Permanente Med. Ctr., West Los Angeles, 1976-77; staff psychologist Long Beach Neuropsychiat. Inst., Calif., 1976-77; sr. clin. psychologist div. clin. neurology City of Hope Nat. Med. Ctr., Duarte, Calif., 1977-80; clin. psychologist Beck Psychiat. Med. Group, Santa Monica, Calif., 1983-86. Contbr. articles to sci. jours., chpts. to book Chronic Pain, 1979. Mem. Am. Psychol. Assn., Am. Pain Soc., Calif. State Psychol. Assn., Internat. Soc. Study of Pain, Sigma Xi.

GRIFFIN, THOMAS W., physician; b. Omaha, Feb. 16, 1945; s. Charles Ward and Nellie Forrest (Gaden) G.; m. Vickie Jo McCabe, Oct. 8, 1973; 1 child, Andrea Lynn. BS, U. Nebr., 1966, MD, 1970. Cert. Am. Coll. Radiology. Instr. U. Wash., Seattle, 1976-77, asst. prof., 1977-79, assoc. prof., 1979-83, prof., 1983—, chmn. dept. radiology and oncology, 1979—; bd. dirs. U. Wash. Cancer Ctr. Editor High LET Radiation Therapy, 1986; contbr. articles to profl. jours. Served to capt. U.S. Army, 1971-73. Mem. Am. Soc. Therapeutic Radiologists and Oncologists, Am. Coll. Radiology, Am. Radium Soc., Radiation Research Soc., Soc. Chmn. Acad. Radiation Oncology Programs, AAAS. Avocations: skiing, mountain climbing. Office: U Wash Dept Radiation Oncology 1959 Pacific St Seattle WA 98195

GRIFFITH, CARL DAVID, civil engineer; b. Hill City, Kans., Mar. 1, 1937; s. Wilfred Eugene and Veda May (Jackson) G.; m. Tillie Sargoza Luna, Aug. 12, 1967 (div.). BSCE summa cum laude, West Coast U., 1978; MSCE and Water Resources, U. So. Calif., 1980, MS in Engring. Mgmt., 1983. Profl. engr., Calif. Chief draftsman Bear Creek Mining Co., Spokane, Wash., 1959-64; right-of-way technician So. Calif. Edison Co., Los Angeles, 1964-65; engr. treatment plant design and spl. projects sect. Metropolitan Water Dist. So. Calif., Los Angeles, 1965—, com. chmn. employees assn.; lectr. Sch. Engring., West Coast U. Sustaining mem. Calif. Republican party. Served with USAF, 1957-58. Mem. ASCE, NSPE, Am. Water Works Assn., Nat. Mgmt. Assn., Metropolitan Water Dist. Mgmt. Club. Lodge: Masons. Home: PO Box 4324 Sylmar CA 91342 Office: PO Box 54153 Los Angeles CA 90054

GRIFFITH, JAMES SEAVEY, folklorist, writer; b. Santa Barbara, Calif., July 30, 1935; s. Richard Matthews (Griffith) and Eleanor (Seavey) Tilt; m. Loma Claire Kimball, June 22, 1963; children: Catherine Eleanore, Richard David. BA, U. Ariz., 1960, MA, 1967, PhD, 1974. Dir., coordinator U. Ariz. Southwest Folklore Ctr., Tucson, 1979—; weekly appearance on Sta. KUAT-TV discussing Southern Ariz. traditions, 1985—; weekly radio presentation Sta. KUAT-AM, 1986—. Author: Mexican Masks from the Cordry Collection, 1983, Respect and Continuity, 1985; co-author: Old Men of the Fiesta, 1981. Recipient Cultural Service award Una Noche Plateada, 1983; co-recipient Jefferson award, 1984. Mem. Am. Folklore Soc., Calif. Folklore Soc. Democrat. Avocation: music. Home: Rural Rt 11 Box 624 Tucson AZ 85746 Office: U Ariz Southwest Folklore Ctr 1524 E 6th St Tucson AZ 85721

GRIFFITH, JOHN ALFRED, psychologist; b. Redlands, Calif., Sept. 29, 1939; s. John E. and Emily B. G.; student Hanover Coll., 1958-60; A.B., San Diego State Coll., 1966; M.Ed., U. Hawaii, 1969, Ph.D., 1973. Field assessment officer U. Hawaii Peace Corps Tng. Center, Hilo, 1967-69, counseling psychologist Counseling and Testing Center, Honolulu, 1970-72; psychologist U.S. Army Support Command Hawaii, Honolulu, 1972-74, alcohol and drug abuse program specialist, 1974-76; pvt. practice psychology, Honolulu, 1976—; dir. Pain Ctr. Rehab. Hosp. of Pacific, 1984—; instr. U. Hawaii, Pepperdine U.; cons. Hawaii Dept. Edn. Mem. State of Hawaii Commn. on Drug Abuse and Controlled Substances, 1973—; mem. City and County of Honolulu Oahu Substance Abuse Adv. Bd., 1975-76. Lic. psychologist, Hawaii; certified mental health care provider Nat. Register of Health Service Providers in Psychology; lic. instr. Effectiveness Tng. Assos. Mem. Am., Western, Hawaii (pres. 1979) psychol. assns., Am., Hawaii personnel and guidance assns., Nat. Council on Family Relations, Assn. Labor-Mgmt. Adminstrs. and Cons., Am. Soc. Tng. and Devel., Honolulu Marathon Assn. Clubs: Hawaii Masters Track, Honolulu, Kailua Racquet. Home: 920 Ward Ave #7C Honolulu HI 96814 Office: 226 N Kuakini St Honolulu HI 96817

GRIFFITH, MICHAEL LYNN, neurosurgeon; b. Dayton, Ohio, Nov. 27, 1951; s. Floyd and Charlotte Gail (Waggoner) G.; m. Mary Ann Howard, Aug. 31, 1974; children: Breland Ann, Adam Michael. BS in Chemistry, Auburn U., 1975; MD, U. Ala., Birmingham, 1981; disting. grad., Sch. Aerospace Medicine, San Antonio, 1983. Diplomate Nat. Bd. Med. Examiners. Intern gen. surgery Wilford Hall Med. Ctr., San Antonio, 1981-82; resident neurosurgery U. Ala., Birmingham, 1982-83; chief aerospace medicine USAF, F.E. Warren AFB Cheyenne., Wyo., 1983-85, flight surgeon, 1983-85; resident neurosurgery U. Colo., Denver, 1985—. Served to capt. USAF, 1981—. Mem. Am. Acad. Sci., Rocky Mountain Elk Found., Alpha Omega Alpha. Methodist. Avocation: bow hunting. Home: 11967 E Ford Dr Denver CO 80012 Office: Dept Neurosurgery 4200 E Ninth Ave Campus Box C-307 Denver CO 80262

GRIFFITH, VALRIE QUARNBERG, electronic manufacturing company executive; b. Salt Lake City, July 17 1956; d. David Ray and Janice Robins Quarnberg; m. Robert Wayne Griffith, Jan. 4, 1975. Student public schs. Kearns, Utah. With MSI, Murray, Utah, 1973-75; prodn. mgr. SSC, Murray, 1973-75; v.p., mgr. Microtek of Utah, Salt Lake City, 1978-82, pres., West Valley City, Utah, 1982-86; mfg. and purchasing mgr. Cirris Systems, Inc., Salt Lake City, 1986—. Recipient Speech award Sertoma Club, 1970. Avocations: Ceramics; quarterhorses. Office: Cirris Systems Inc 1864 S State St #90 Salt Lake City UT 84115

GRIFFITH, WILLIAM ALEXANDER, mining co. exec.; b. Sioux Falls, S.D., Mar. 28, 1922; s. James William and Adeline Mae (Reid) G.; m. Gratia Frances Hannan, Jan. 27, 1949; children—Georgeanne Reid, James William, Wade Andrew. B.S. in Metall. Engring., S.D. Sch. Mines and Tech., 1947; M.S. in Metallurgy, M.I.T., 1950; Mineral Dressing Engr. (hon.), Mont. Coll. Mineral Sci. and Tech., 1971; D in Bus. Adminstrn. (hon.), S.D. Sch. Mines & Tech., 1986. With N.J. Zinc Co., 1949-57, chief milling and maintenance, 1956-57; metallurgist Rare Metals Corp. Am., Tuba City, Ariz., 1957-58; dir. research and devel. Phelps Dodge Corp., Morrenci, Ariz., 1958-68; with Hecla Mining Co., Wallace, Idaho, 1968—, exec. v.p., 1978, pres., chief exec. officer, 1979-86, chmn., 1985—; chmn., chief exec. officer Hecla Mining Co., 1986-87, also bd. dirs.; dir. Granduc Mines Ltd., Consol. Silver Corp. Bd. dirs. Kootonai Med. Ctr. Found. Served with USNR, 1943-46. Mem. AIME (Gaudin award 1977, Richards award 1981, Disting. Mem. 1977, Hon. 1987), Am. Mining Congress (dir.), Idaho Mining Assn. (past pres.), Idaho Assn. Commerce and Industry (past bd. dirs., Western Regional Council chmn. 1986-87), Nat. Strategic Materials and Minerals Adv. Com. to Sec. Interior (mem.), Silver Inst. (past pres., past chmn.), Sigma Tau, Theta Tau. Republican. Lodge: Rotary. Home: 630 S 14th St Coeur d'Alene ID 83814 Office: 6500 Mineral Dr Box C-8000 Coeur d'Alene ID 83814-1931

GRIFFITHS, ARTHUR MELVIN, small business owner, executive; b. Denver, July 6, 1945; s. Thomas Melvin and Rose Barbara (Hitchings) G.; m. Karen Rae Stonemets, Dec. 23, 1967; children: Travis, Everett, Anne. BA in Econs., Denver U., 1967; MS in Oceanography, U. Wash., 1972. Research asst. U. Wash., Seattle, 1970-75; prin. investigator Stearns-Roger Engr., Denver, 1975-80, program mgmt., 1980-82; farm and ranch mgr. Johnstown, Colo., 1980—; pres., owner Hillsboro Inc., Denver, 1984—; cons. AG Comtec, Denver, 1982—; outside salesperson, Greeley, Colo., 1983-85. Contbr. articles to profl. jours.; inventor water test equipment, 1979. Scout leader Boy Scouts Am., Denver and Johnstown, Colo., 1963, 85. Mem. Am. Chem. Soc. Republican. Christian Scientist. Lodge: Lions (v.p. Johnstown club 1983-84, sec. 1985-87). Avocations: outdoor sports, book collecting. Office: Hillsboro Inc 8774 Yates Dr Suite 100 Westminster CO 80030

GRIFFITHS, DONALD JAMES, logistics engr.; b. S.I., Nov. 16, 1929; s. Joseph and Teresa Ann (Horenberg) G.; m. Emily Margaret Chrzczonowski, Apr. 25, 1947; children—Eve, Monica, Mark, Donna, Jennifer, Rodger. B.S., NYU, 1952; postgrad. Columbia U., 1955; M.B.A. N.Mex. Highlands U., 1979. Commd. U.S. Navy, 1950, advanced through grades to comdr., 1969, ret., 1980; dir. material mgmt. U. N.Mex. Hosp., Albuquerque, 1980-81; sr. logistics analyst Tracor Internat., Albuquerque, 1981-82; material mgr. Frank Basil, Inc. Internat., 1983-85, Royal Saudi Navy, Saudi Arabia, 1986—. Decorated Legion of Merit, Army and Navy Service Commendation medal with oak leaf cluster. Mem. Soc. Logistics Engrs., Alpha Kappa Psi. Republican. Roman Catholic. Clubs: Kiwanis, Kirtland AFB.

GRIFFITHS, FRANK A., professional sports team executive. Chmn. bd. Vancouver Canucks, Nat. Hockey League, B.C., Can. Office: Care Vancouver Canucks, 100 N Renfrew St, Vancouver, BC Canada V5K 3N7 *

GRIGGS, JOHN WILBUR, Spanish language educator; b. Three Rivers, Mich., Oct. 5, 1948; s. Kenneth C. and Erma R. (Hadden) G.; m. Virginia Jean Roberts, Jan. 23, 1971. BA in Edn., Ariz. State U., 1970, MA in Spanish, 1971, PhD in Spanish, 1982. From asst. prof. to full prof. Spanish Glendale (Ariz.) Community Coll., 1972—. Mem. Am. Assn. Tchrs. of Spanish and Portuguese, Ariz. Fgn. Lang. Assn., Rocky Mountain Modern Lang. Assn. Avocations: racquetball, weightlifting, aerobics. Office: Glendale Community Coll 6000W Olive Ave Glendale AZ 85302

GRIGGS, JOSEPH FRANKLIN, physician, surgeon; b. Tacoma, Jan. 30, 1908; s. Joseph Franklin and Alice Emily (Van Gorder) G.; m. Jeannette Speiden, Aug. 8, 1936 (dec. Dec. 1975); children: Joseph Jr., David Norman, Sylvia Jean Baker. MD, U. Mich., 1933. Diplomate Nat. Bd. Med. Examiners. Intern Alameda County Hosps., Calif., 1933-34; coll. physician The Claremont (Calif.) Colls., 1937-40; researcher, educator Claremont, 1947-71; clin. physician Planned Parenthood Clinics, Claremont and Pomona, Calif., 1962-78; mng. dir. Claremont Med. Research Found., Inc., 1948-62; pres. The Claremont Found., Inc., 1962-85; vis. prof. biolog. scis. Scripps Coll., Claremont, 1949, 59-69. Contbr. articles to profl. jours. Mem. AAAS, Union of Concerned Scientists, Physicians for Social Responsibility, Assn. Planned Parenthood Physicians. Mem. Soc. of Friends. Avocations: theater, book revs., continuing edn. Home: 900 E Harrison Ave K-3 Pomona CA 91767

GRILL, LAURENCE KAY, molecular biologist; b. Ogden, Utah, Dec. 19, 1949; s. George Charles and Geraldine (Carroll) G.; m. Terry Gayle Malone, Oct. 3, 1976. BA, Calif. State U., Fullerton, 1973, MS, 1976; PhD, U. Calif., Riverside, 1979. Research scientist Zoecon Research Inst., Palo Alto, Calif., 1979-84, mgr. research, 1985—. Contbr. 20 articles to sci. jours.; editor Plant Molecular Biology Reporter, 1982, Plant Cell Reports, 1986. Mem. Internat. Soc. Plant Molecular Biology, Am. Soc. Virology. Democrat. Club: Pedali Alpini (Los Altos, Calif.) (sec. 1986—). Avocations: bicycle racing, sailing.

GRILLO, JAMES THOMAS, marketing executive; b. Warren, Pa., July 17, 1950; s. Carl Charles and Rita Evelyn (Manfrey) G.; m. Lorrie Webb, Dec. 29, 1984. BA, Edinboro U., 1975. Prin. Grillo Assocs., Warren, 1979-81; market dir. Continental Cablevision, Boston, 1979-85; v.p. mktg. Jones Group, Englewood, Colo., 1985—. Contbr. various papers to cable TV trade publs. Chmn. mayors com. Tourism, Rochester, N.Y., 1979; bd. dirs. Big Bros. of Denver. Mem. Cable TV Adminstrn. and Mktg. Soc. (mktg. dir. com.), Sales and Mktg. Execs. Assn. (bd. dirs.). Avocations: running, fly fishing, landscape.

GRIM, CLARENCE EZRA, medical educator, internist, researcher; b. Kirksville, Mo., July 28, 1938; s. Clarence Foncannon and Gladys Susan (Stronger) G.; m. Carlene Margaret Minks, Jan. 27, 1962; children: Christopher Adrian, Jonathon Ezra. BS in Chemistry, Northeast Mo. State Tchrs. Coll., 1959; MS in Biochemistry, U. Mo., 1963, MD, 1964. Diplomate Am. Bd. Internal Medicine. Intern Duke U., Durham, N.C., 1964-65, resident, 1965-67; fellow in endocrinology U. Mich., Ann Arbor, 1969; asst. prof. medicine U. Mo., Columbia, 1970-73; assoc. prof. Ind. U., Indpls., 1973-78, prof., 1978-84; prof. medicine, dir. hypertension research Charles R. Drew Postgrad. Med. Sch.-Martin Luther King Hosp., Los Angeles, 1984—. Contbr. numerous articles on high blood pressure to med. jours. Served to lt. comdr. USPHS, 1977-79. Australian Nat. Heart Found. internat. fellow, 1983; NIH grantee, 1982—. Mem. Am. Heart Assn. (council high blood pressure research), Internat. Soc. Twin Research, Am. Coll. Cardiology, Am. Soc. Hypertension, Am. Soc. Internal Medicine, Endocrine Soc. Presbyterian. Home: 25 Coveview Dr Rancho Palos Verdes CA 90274

GRIM, DOUGLAS PAUL, lawyer; b. Bellingham, Wash., May 12, 1940; s. Paul R. and Vivian I. (McMillen) G.; m. Catherine Powers, Dec. 28, 1968; children—Caryn, Devin. B.A., Lawrence Coll., 1962; LL.B., Stanford U., 1965; LL.M., N.Y.U., 1966. Bar: Calif. 1966, U.S. Supreme Ct. 1985. Assoc. Hanna and Morton, Los Angeles, 1966-72; of counsel Harris, Noble, Uhler & Gallop, Los Angeles, 1972-75; ptnr. Nicholas, Kolliner, Myers, D'Angelo and Givens, Los Angeles, 1975; sole practice, Los Angeles, 1975—; instr. Golden Gate U. Sch. Law, 1975; dir. Am. Internat. Seaview Properties, Inc., 1976—; chmn. bd. Agri-Feeds, Inc., 1981—. Chmn. exec. com. Troop 35 Los Angeles Area Council Boy Scouts Am., 1967-72; v.p., dir. Los Angeles Jaycees, 1966-75. Recipient Michael F. Tobey award Los Angeles Jr. C. of C., 1972; named Outstanding Young Man of Am., 1972. Mem. State Bar of Calif., Los Angeles County Bar Assn., ABA. Methodist. Clubs: Jonathan, Riviera Tennis (Los Angeles), Wilshire Kiwanis (bd. dirs.), Uptown Investment (pres. 1978). Author: Drafting a 1244 Plan; Medical Reimbursement Plans. Home: 247 S Lorraine Blvd Los Angeles CA 90004 Office: 523 W Sixth St Los Angeles CA 90014

GRIMM, LARRY LEON, school psychologist; b. Goshen, Ind., Aug. 16, 1950; s. Warren Arden and Elizabeth Ann (Rassi) G.; m. Ann Mae Nelson, July 16, 1977; 1 dau., Kirsten Ann. B.S. in Elem. Edn., No. Ariz. U., 1975, M.A., 1977, Ed.D. in Ednl. Psychology, 1983. Cert. psychologist, sch. psychologist, cert. elem. tchr. Ariz. Tchr. elem. sch. Page (Ariz.) Unified Dist., 1975-76; grad. asst. Coll. Edn., No. Ariz. U., Flagstaff, 1976; tchr. elem. sch. Litchfield Sch. Dist., Litchfield Park, Ariz., 1976-80; grad. assoc. dept. ednl. psychology No. Ariz. U., Flagstaff, 1980-81; sch. psychologist intern Peoria (Ariz.) Unified Dist., 1981-82; adj. faculty Grand Canyon Coll., Phoenix, 1982; sch. psychologist Child Study Services, Prescott (Ariz.) Unified Sch. Dist., 1982-87; adj. faculty No. Ariz. U., Flagstaff, 1984-87, asst. prof. , 1987—; cons. in field; presenter at convs. Mem. Am. Psychol. Assn. (publications com.), Ariz. Assn. Sch. Psychologists (bd. dirs. No. Ariz., pres. 1986-87), Nat. Assn. Sch. Psychologists (del. fiscal adv. com.). Republican. Contbr. articles to profl. jours. Home: 660 Dragonfly Dr Prescott AZ 86301 Office: No Ariz U Flagstaff AZ 86011

GRIMM, NANCY BETH, research ecologist; b. Huron, S.D., Oct. 11, 1955; d. Robert Elmer and Roberta (Johnson) G.; m. Stuart Gordon Fisher, Dec. 19, 1981; 1 child, Ian Brook. BA, Hampshire Coll., 1978; MS, Ariz. State U., 1980, PhD, 1985. Faculty assoc. Hampshire Coll., Amherst, Mass., 1978; grad. research asst. Ariz. State U., Tempe, 1978-80, grad. research assoc., 1980-84, faculty assoc., 1984—. Contbr. articles to profl. jours. NSF fellow, 1987—. Mem. Ecol. Soc. Am., N.Am. Benthol. Soc., Am. Soc. Limnology and Oceanography, Desert Fishes Council. Home: 1714 Kings Ranch Apache Junction AZ 85219 Office: Ariz State U Dept Zoology Tempe AZ 85287

GRIMM, ROYDEN ARCHIE, editor; b. Roseburg, Oreg., Aug. 5, 1925; s. Royden Alexandria and Sylvia Ada (Myers) G.; m. Joanne Rossmann, Apr. 11, 1954; children—Margaret Sylvia Rose, Scott Thomas, Joseph Conrad. Student, U. Calif.-Berkeley, 1950. Reporter, city editor Daily Rev., Hayward, Calif., 1953-56; from reporter to mng. editor The Tribune, Oakland, Calif., 1956—; instr. Laney Coll., Oakland, 1969-70. Served with U.S. Army, 1951-53. Mem. Am. Soc. Newspaper Editors, Associated Press Mng. Editors, Soc. Profl. Journalists, Calif. Freedom Info. Com., Calif. Soc. Newspaper Editors. Democrat. Office: The Tribune PO Box 24304 Oakland CA 94623

GRIMMETT, TOM ROGER, tax consultant, state bankruptcy trustee; b. Pocatello, Idaho, Nov. 24, 1942; s. Francis Benson and Margaret Vira (Adams) G.; m. Renee Belnap, Feb. 16, 1963; children—Michelle, Melissa, Michael, Melanie. BS, Utah State U., 1965. Registered rep. N.Y. Stock Exchange, 1969. With U.S. Steel, 1965-68; with A.G. Edwards & Sons, 1968-70; with Texaco, Inc., 1970-78; pres. Desert Fin. Group, Inc. Las Vegas, T.R. Grimmett, Inc., Las Vegas; dir. numerous cos.; U.S. Bankruptcy trustee so. dist. Nev.; Nev. field rep. Intermountain Oil Marketers Assn., 1984; tchr. tax and investment seminars. Active Boulder Dam Council Boy Scouts Am., Youth Soccer, Las Vegas. Republican. Mormon. Lodge: Lions. Office: 1700 E Desert Inn Suite 205 Las Vegas NV 89109

GRIMSHAW, DONALD HARVEY, logistics engineer; b. Turtlecreek Twp., Ohio, June 22, 1923; s. Percy and Louella Rose (Harvey) G.; m. Jean Dolores Mrazek, Nov. 18, 1950; children—Randall, Kimberley, Stuart, Paul, Heather, Matthew. A.B. in Govt., Calif. State U.-Los Angeles, 1959; postgrad. in pub. adminstrn. U. So. Calif., 1960-62. Research asst. Hughes Aircraft, Culver City, Calif., 1951-54, Douglas Aircraft, Santa Monica, Calif., 1954-57; research engr. Northrop Corp., Hawthorne, Calif., 1957-62; research writer Calif. Dept. Water Resources, Los Angeles, 1962-65; mgr. logistics TRW Def. Systems Group, Redondo Beach, Calif., 1965—. Mem. exec. com. Calif., Los Angeles County and 53d Assembly dist. Republican Party, 1978—; Rep. nominee for U.S. Rep. from Calif.'s 31st Dist., 1978, 80. Served with USN, World War II; Korea. Mem. Soc. Logistics Engrs. (mng. editor SPECTRUM 1966-68), AIAA, Soc. Tech. Communications, U.S. Naval Inst., VFW. Office: TRW 1 Space Park Redondo Beach CA 90278

GRIMSKE, TIMOTHY JAY, marketing and management professional; b. Flint, Mich., Sept. 23, 1953; s. Frank and Lois Evelyn (FredBerg) G.; m. Valerie Eve Bellino. BA in Advt., BA in Mktg., Ferris State U., 1975. Dir. mktg. The Taubman Co., Grand Rapids, Mich., 1976-78; dir. promotion The Taubman Co., Ann Arbor, Mich., 1978-80; asst. mgr. The Taubman Co., Short Hills, N.J., 1980-82; property mgr. The Ctr. Cos., Flint, Mich., 1982-84; group mgr. The Ctr. Cos., Las Vegas, Nev., 1984-86; dir. mgmt. services The Ctr. Cos., Los Angeles, 1986—. Office: The Ctr Cos 404 S Figueroa Suite 606 Los Angeles CA 90071

GRINBERG, MICHAEL MARK, psychiatrist; b. Kansas City, Mo., May 26, 1950; s. Robert H. and Shirley (Sandler) G.; m. Sherry L. Silver, Apr. 1, 1985. BA, Brandeis U., 1972; MD, U. Calif, San Diego, 1976. Diplomate Am. Bd. Psychiatry and Neurology. Practice medicine specializing in psychiatry San Diego, 1979—. Fellow Am. Coll. Forensic Psychiatry; Am. Psychiat. Assn., Am. Assn. Sex Educators, Counselors, Therapists (cert.), San Diego Soc. for Sex Therapy and Edn. (pres. 1985-86). Jewish. Office: 5252 Balboa Ave Suite 400 San Diego CA 92117

GRINDLEY, JUNE NADINE, biologist, researcher; b. Wimbledon, Eng., June 24, 1943; d. Geoffrey Arthur Mayhew and Margaret (Herbert) M. BS in Biology, Leicester (Eng.) U., 1964; Diploma Imperial Coll. in Microbiology, London U., 1965, PhD in Genetics, 1973. Research assoc. Ctr. Pub. Health Services, London, 1966-73, U. Pitts., 1973-75, 1978-80, Yale U., New Haven, 1975-78, Biogen, Inc., Cambridge, Mass., 1981-84; mgr. extramural research Triton Bioscis., Inc., Alameda, Calif., 1984—. Patentee in field. Grantee U. Pitts., 1973, 79, NIH, 1979. Avocations: painting, gardening. Office: Triton Bioscis Inc 1501 Harbor Bay Pkwy Alameda CA 94501

GRINSTEIN, GERALD, transportation executive; b. 1932; married. B.A., Yale U., 1954; LL.B., Harvard U., 1957. Bar: D.C., Wash. Counsel to merchant marine and transp. subcoms., chief counsel U.S. Senate Commerce Com., Washington, D.C., 1958-67; adminstrv. asst. U.S. Senator Warren G. Magnuson, Washington, D.C., 1967-69; ptnr. Preston Thorgrimson Ellis & Holman, 1969-83; chmn. bd. Western Air Lines Inc., Los Angeles, 1983-84, pres., chief operating officer, 1984-85, chief exec. officer, 1985-86, chmn., chief exec. officer, 1986-87; vice chmn. Burlington Northern, Inc., Ft. Worth, 1987—; bd. dirs. Gen. Telephone Co. of Calif., Seattle-First Nat. Bank, Gen. Telephone Co. of Calif., Delta Airlines; vice chmn. Burlington Northern, Inc., 1987—. Office: Burlington Northern Inc 3800 Continental Plaza Fort Worth TX 76102

GRISHAM, CAROLE JEAN, museum director; b. Seattle, Nov. 21, 1949; d. George Yoshio and Alyce Fuysia (Hiyama) Kumasawa; m. Raymond Luther Grisham, Aug. 21, 1967; 1 child, Amy. BA in Econs., U. Wash., 1984. Dist. sales supr. Westinghouse Corp., Seattle, 1968-74; edn. supr. Pacific Sci. Ctr., Seattle, 1975-76, bus. mgr., 1976-77, dir. adminstrn., 1977-83, assoc. dir., 1983—; pres. Evergreen Trading Co., Seattle, 1984—. Bd. dirs. Totem Council Girl Scouts U.S., Seattle, 1983—. Mem. AAAS. Office: Pacific Sci Ctr 200 2d N Seattle WA 98109

GRISMORE, ROGER, physics educator, researcher; b. Ann Arbor, Mich., July 12, 1924; s. Grover Cleveland and May Aileen (White) G.; m. Marilynn Ann McNinch, Sept. 15, 1950; 1 child, Carol Ann. BS, U. Mich., 1947, MS, 1948, PhD, 1957; BS in Computer Sci., Coleman Coll., 1979. From asst. to assoc. physicist Argonne (Ill.) Nat. Lab., 1956-62; assoc. prof. physics Lehigh U., Bethlehem, Pa., 1962-67; specialist in physics Scripps Inst. Oceanography, La Jolla, Calif., 1967-71, 75-78; prof. physics Ind. State U., Terre Haute, 1971-74; sr. scientist JAYCOR, San Diego, 1979-84; lectr. Calif. Poly. State U., San Luis Obispo, 1984—. Contbr. numerous articles to profl. jours. Served as ensign USNR, 1944-46, PTO. Mem. Am. Phys. Soc., Am. Geophys. Union, N.Y. Acad. Scis., Sigma Xi. Republican. Avocations: reading, walking, sailing, amateur radio. Home: 4640 Obispo Rd Atascadero CA 93422 Office: Calif Poly State U Dept Physics San Luis Obispo CA 93407

GRISSOM, LEE ALAN, association executive; b. Pensacola, Fla., Sept. 7, 1942; s. Levi Aaron and Virginia Sue (Olinger) G.; m. Sharon Kay Hasty, May 14, 1966; children: David, Jonathon, Matthew, Andrew. B.A., San Diego State U., 1965, M.City Planning, 1971. Sr. research assoc. Western Behavioral Scis. Inst., La Jolla, Calif., 1965-73; mgr. planning div., then gen. mgr. San Diego C. of C., 1973-75, exec. v.p., gen. mgr., 1975-81, pres., 1981—; instr. urban planning U. Calif.-San Diego, 1973; host TV program The City Game, 1972-75; mem. San Diego County Internat. Trade Commn., NFL Super Bowl '88 Task Force, 1988; mem. bd. and exec. com. San Diego Holiday Bowl. Chmn. Boy Scouts Am. Fair, San Diego, 1977-78; chmn. San Diego council Boy Scouts Am.; trustee Calif. State U.; bd. dirs. Armed Forces YMCA; bd. dirs. Econ. Devel. Corp.; chmn. San Diego Housing Commn., 1983-86, Pres.'s Adv. Bd., San Diego State U., 1983—; mem. Calif. Econ. Devel. Task Force, 1983—; adv. com. Fed. Home Loan Mortgage Corp. Named Outstanding Young Citizen San Diego Jaycees, 1976; named Outstanding Young Citizen Calif. Jaycees, 1977, Outstanding Young Citizen U.S. Jaycess, 1978, Outstanding Alumnus San Diego State U., 1987. Mem. Calif. Assn. C. of C. Execs., Greater San Diego Sports Assn. (bd. dirs.). Lodge: Rotary. Office: San Diego C of C 110 W C St Suite 1600 San Diego CA 92101

GRISWOLD, DANIEL HALSEY, retired engineering geologist; b. Colorado Springs, Colo., Jan. 10, 1909; s. Clyde Tyler and Grace (Halsey) G.; Geol. Engr., Colo. Sch. Mines, 1930; m. Maud Walton Mays, June 2, 1931; children—Miriam Griswold Miller, Julia Douglas (Mrs. Jude W. Barry). Geophysicist, asst. geologist U.S. Smelting Refining & Mining Co., 1930-31; asst. engr. C.T. Griswold, Mining 1931-32; lessee Magnolia Petroleum Co., 1932-33; instrumentman Mid Rio Grande Conservancy Dist., 1933; jr. topog. engr. Conservation br. U.S. Geol. Survey, 1933-35; jr. agrl. engr. Soil Conservation Service, U.S. Dept. Agr. (N.Mex.), 1935-38, asst. agrl. engr. (Utah), 1938-40, asso. geologist (N.Mex.), 1941-46, soil conservationist, 1946-49, geologist (N.Mex.), 1949-56, Portland, Oreg., 1956-69; geologist ground water div. Oreg. Engr.'s Office, 1969; sr. geologist Found. Scis., Inc., Portland, 1969-72, assoc. 1972-84. Served to lt. col. C.E., AUS, 1941-45. Recipient 20 year service award Soil Conservation Service, Dept. Agr., 1956; 35 years service as fed. employee, 1969. Registered profl. engr., land surveyor, N.Mex.; registered profl. engr., Oreg., Ga.; registered engring. geologist, Oreg., Calif. Fellow Geol. Soc. Am.; mem. Soil Conservation Soc. Am., Geol. Soc. Oregon County, Res. Officers Assn., Assn. Engring. Geologists, AIME, Am. Inst. Profl. Geologists, Soc. Am. Mil. Engrs., Alpha Tau Omega, Theta Tau. Mem. Evangelical Covenant Ch. Mason. Home: 6656 SW Miles Ct Portland OR 97223

GRISWOLD, GEORGE BULLARD, geology educator, geologist; b. Ponca City, Okla., Dec. 9, 1928. B.S. in Mining Engring., N.Mex. Inst. Mining and Tech., 1955; M.S. in Mining Engring., U. Ariz., 1957, Ph.D. in Geol. Engring. 1967. Vice pres., mgr. Getty Mines, Ltd., Vancouver, B.C., 1970-73; sr. staff mem. Sandia Labs., Albuquerque, 1974-77; pres. Tecolote Corp., N.Mex., 1978-83; mining and geol. engring. dept. chmn. N.Mex. Inst. Mining and Tech., Socorro, 1983—. Office: N Mex Inst Mining and Tech Socorro NM 87801

GRISWOLD, MARTHA KERFOOT, social worker; b. Oklahoma City, Mar. 22, 1930; d. John Samuel III and Frances (Mann) Kerfoot; m. George Littlefield Griswold, Jan. 28, 1967. AB, Occidental Coll., 1951; MRE, U. So. Calif., 1956, postgrad., 1962. Cert. social worker. Teen dir. Toberman Settlement, San Pedro, Calif., 1954-56; social worker County of Los Angeles, 1956-62, 1969-72; dir. program to integrate disabled children Internat. Inst., Los Angeles, 1979-80; cons. community orgn. Los Angeles, 1980-84; dir. L.I.V. Disability Resources Ctr., Altadena, Calif., 1984—; instr. Calif. State U., Los Angeles, 1966-68, 1983-84; chair Childrens' Adv. Com. Los Angeles County Dept. Mental Health, 1985-86; coordinator So. Calif. Conf. on Living Long Term with Disability, 1985. Mem. Pasadena (Calif.) City Disability Issues Com., 1984-86, Pasadena Strategic Planning Task Force, 1985-86; mem. task force on aging, long term care United Way Region 2, Los Angeles. Recipient 1986 award So. Calif. Rehab. Assn. Mem. Nat. Assn. Soc. Workers, Nat. Assn. for Edn. Young Children, Calif. Assn. Physically Handicapped. Congregationalist. Office: LIV Ctr 943 E Altadena Dr Altadena CA 91001

GRISWOLD, WILLIAM, pediatric researcher; b. Seattle, Sept. 25, 1942; s. Norris Rockwell and Margaret Moore (Kennedy) G.; m. Sharon Fitzpatrick, Feb. 21, 1963; children: James, Erik. AB, Stanford U., 1964; MD, UCLA, 1968. Diplomate Am. Bd. Pediatrics; cert. sub-bd. Pediatric Nephrology. Intern UCLA, 1968-69, resident Harbor Gen. Hosp., 1969-70, sr. resident, 1970-71; USPHS postdoctoral fellow in nephrology and immunology dept. pediatrics Columbia U., N.Y.C., 1971-73; pediatric nephrologist and immunologist Naval Regional Med. Ctr., San Diego, 1973-75, lectr. cons., 1975—; pediatric nephrologist Children's Hosp., San Diego, 1974—, sr. staff pediatrician nephrology, 1978—, chief div. pediatric nephrology, 1985—; pediatric nephrologist U. Calif. San Diego Med. Ctr., 1975—, acting dir. pediatric nephrology, 1978-79, dir. pediatric ICU, 1978-82, dir. pediatric Lupus Clinic, 1978—, dir. pediatric dialysis, 1982—; asst. clin. prof. U. Calif. San Diego, 1973-75, asst. prof. pediatrics, 1975-79, assoc adj. prof. pediatrics, 1979-83, assoc. prof. pediatrics, 1983—. Contbr. numerous articles to profl. jours. Served to lt. comdr. USN, 1973-75. Jolliffee Found. fellow, 1972; recipient grants for clin. and basic research, 1974—; scholar Stanford U., 1960-64, UCLA, 1965-66. Mem. AAAS, Am. Fedn. Clin. Research, Am. Heart Council on Kidney Disease, Western Soc. Pediatric Research, Soc. Pediatric Research, Soc. Exptl. Biology and Medicine, Am. Soc. Pediatric Nephrology, Internat. Soc. Nephrology, Internat. Soc. Pediatric Nephrology, Sigma Xi. Democrat. Avocations: photography, piano, collecting fossils. Office: U Calif Dept Pediatrics T-008-E San Diego CA 92103

GRITTON, EUGENE CHARLES, nuclear engineer; b. Santa Monica, Calif., Jan. 13, 1941; s. Everett Mason and Matilda (Benne) G.; m. Sandra Jennie Kelley (div.); children: Dennis Mason, Kathleen Wanda; m. Betty Jane Verdick (div.); m. Gwendolyn Owen, Jan. 1, 1980. B.S., UCLA, 1963, M.S., 1965, Ph.D., 1966. Research engr. environ. simulation modelling and power systems engring. Rand Corp., Santa Monica, Calif., 1966-73, project leader advanced undersea tech. program, 1973-76, program dir. marine tech., 1974-76, head phys. scis. dept., 1975-77, head engring. and applied scis. dept., 1977-86; dep. v.p. Nat. Security Research Div., 1986—, Research Ops. Group, 1986—; vis. lectr. dept. mech. engring. U. So. Calif., Los Angeles, 1967-72; vis. lectr. dept. energy and kinetics UCLA, 1971, 73. Recipient Engring. Alumnus of Yr. award UCLA Sch. Engring. and Applied Sci., 1985-86; AEC fellow, 1963, NSF Coop. Grad. fellow, 1964-66. Mem. Am. Nuclear Soc. (mem. exec. com. aerospace and hydrospace div. 1974-75), AIAA. Home: 3616 The Strand #C Manhattan Beach CA 90266 Office: The Rand Corp 1700 Main St Santa Monica CA 90406

GROBE, WILLIAM HOWARD, retired state government official; b. Winnett, Mont., Feb. 19, 1916; s. Wesley H. and Leota H. (Smith) G.; m. Jane Singleton, May 7, 1967; stepchildren: John C. Singleton (dec.), Linda G. Moore; children from previous marriage: William H., Robert. Student, Simpson Coll., Indianola, Iowa, 1934-37, Mo. State U., 1937-39, Mont. State Tchrs. Coll., 1940-41; BS, Mont. State U., 1948; BS in Health and Phys. Edn., Miss. Coll., 1951; postgrad., U. Nev., summers 1958-62. Clk. N.P. Ry., Livingston, Mont., 1946-47; student and line coach Mont. State U., Bozeman, 1947-48; coach, phys. edn. tchr. Edgar (Mont.) High Sch., 1948-51; athletic dir., coach, phys. edn. tchr., guidance counselor Bridger (Mont.) High Sch., 1951-57, Lassen Union High Sch. Dist., Herlong, Calif., 1957-62; supt. recreaton and phys. edn. Calif. Conservation Ctr., State Dept. Corrections, Susanville, 1962-75, ret., 1975. Served with USAAF, 1941-45. Mem. Calif. Employees Assn., Nat. Recreation Assn., Calif. Correctional Assn. Lodge: Masons. Home: 3485 Lakeside Dr Apt 300 Reno NV 89509

GROBELCH, MICHAEL RICHARD, computer sales professional; b. Waukegan, Ill., July 25, 1954; s. Robert Richard and Carole Diane (Fisher) G.; m. Sheryl Lynne Yonkers, Sept. 23, 1983; children: Melanie Patrice, Natalie Nicole. BSBA in Acctg., BS in Mgmt. Info. Systems, U. Ariz., 1975. Systems engr. Electronic Data Systems, San Francisco, 1977-78; systems analyst Optimum Systems, Santa Clara, Calif., 1978-80; systems engr. Boole & Babbage, Larkspur, Calif., 1980-81; salesman Boole & Babbage, Culver City, Calif., 1981-83, Candle Corp., Marina del Rey, Calif., 1983—. Bd. dirs. property 1st Luth. Ch. Culver City and Palms, 1986, asst. ch. dir., 1986—. Recipient 1 Million award ICP, 1986, 1 Million club award Candle Corp., 1985, Pres.'s Club award Boole & Babbage 1981, 82. Republican. Lutheran. Avocation: water skiing. Home: 8507 Bleriot Ave Westchester CA 90291 Office: Candle Corp 4676 Admirality Way Marina del Rey CA 90291

GRODIN, JOSEPH R., state supreme court justice; b. Oakland, Calif., Aug. 30, 1930; m. Janet G.; children—Sharon, Lisa. B.S., U. Calif., Berkeley, 1951; LL.B. cum laude, Yale U., New Haven, 1954. Atty. San Francisco, 1955-72; assoc. judge Calif. Ct. Appeals (1st dist.), 1979-82; justice Calif. Supreme Ct., San Francisco, 1982—. Office: Calif Supreme Ct 350 McAlister St San Francisco CA 94102 *

GRODINS, SYLVIA VIOLA, interior designer; b. DeKalb, Ill., May 7, 1916; d. Andrew Yaehon and Ann Henrika (Anderson) Johnson; m. Fred Sherman Grodins, Mar. 28, 1942. Student, No. Ill. U., 1934-35; RN, Augustana Sch. Nursing, Chgo., 1939; degree, N.Y. Sch. Interior Design, 1954. Pvt. duty nursing Chgo., 1939-41; interior designer Pond's Interiors, Evanston, Ill., 1948, Interior Design Inc., Chgo., 1956-58; owner Creative Studio, Chgo., 1958—, Palos Verdes, Calif., 1968—. Contbr. articles to newspapers and mags. Avocations: painting, piano. Home: 26 Chuck Wagon Rd Rolling Hills CA 90274 Office: Creative Studio 2325 Palos Verdes Dr W Palos Verdes CA 90274

GROFER, EDWARD (TED) JOSEPH, publisher, marketing communications corporation executive, newspaper consultant; b. Cin., Sept. 20, 1934; s. Edward Joseph and Margaret Mary (McGinley) G.; m. Mary Janet Procissi, Aug. 18, 1962; children—Catherine Mary, Laura Marie, Daniel McGinley. B.A., U. Cin., 1957; M.A., U. Iowa, 1959. Asst. dir. pub. relations Champion Paper, Hamilton, Ohio, 1959-61; mktg. dir. The Jam Handy Orgn., Detroit, 1961-69; dir. promotion and research Detroit News, 1969-74; v.p., pub. Desert Sun, Palm Springs, Calif., 1974-80; pres. Ted Grofer Assocs., Inc., Palm Springs, 1980—; pub. Desert Community Newspapers, Inc., Palm Desert, Calif., 1981-85; v.p. Desert Mailing Services, Inc., Cathedral City, Calif., 1982—; gen. ptnr. The Graphic Arts Ctr., Cathedral City, 1985—; cons. to several major newspapers; compiler of Newspaper Market Analysis Report, 1980—. Bd. dirs., pres. Palm Springs chpt. Am. Cancer Soc. Mem. Calif. Newspaper Pubs. Assn. (bd. dirs. 1978-80), Internat. Newspaper Promotion Assn. (bd. dirs. 1972-74), Palm Springs C. of C. (pres. 1979-80), Pi Kappa Alpha (nat. v.p. 1982-86). Republican. Roman Catholic. Clubs: The Springs (Rancho Mirage); Palm Springs. Lodge: Rotary. Home: 584 Fern Canyon Dr Palm Springs CA 92264 Office: The Graphic Arts Ctr 68-816 Summit Dr Cathedral City CA 92234 Address: Ted Grofer Assocs Inc PO Drawer 1763 Palm Springs CA 92263

GROGINSKY, CHARLES MICHAEL, chemist, technical administrator; b. Denver, Aug. 12, 1943; s. Jack Hyman and Gertrude Frances (Dashut) G.; m. Barbara Helen Schor, Aug. 29, 1965 (div. Nov. 1975); children: Scott Alan, Lynne Merritt; m. Kathleen I. Keith, June 3, 1977; children: Matthew Keith, Lauren Paige. BA in Chemistry cum laude, U. Colo., 1965; PhD in Chemistry, U. Kans., 1970. Research assoc. U. Ariz., Tucson, 1970-72; research scientist Armour Pharm. Co., Kankakee, Ill., 1972-77, process mgr., 1977-79; mgr. lab. Vega Biotech., Inc., Tucson, 1979-83, dir. tech. service and support, 1983—; local com. mem. 8th Am. Peptide Symposium, Tucson, 1983; co-chmn. 7th Marvel Symposium. Contbr. articles to profl. jours. NIH fellow, 1971-72. Mem. Am. Chem. Soc. (local exec. bd. 1982-87, chmn. 1986), N.Y. Acad. Sci., Kans. U. Alumni Assn. and Chem. Soc., The Planetary Soc., Phi Beta Kappa, Sigma Xi. Republican. Avocations: jogging, racquetball, softball, astronomy, tennis. Office: Vega Biotech Inc 1250 E Aero Park Blvd Tucson AZ 85706

GROHMAN, ROBERT T., business executive; b. 1924; student S.D. State Coll., U. Nebr., U. Calif., Davis; married. Gen. mgr. weaving ops. Duplan, 1946-57; v.p. gen. mgr. ops. Internat. Playtex Corp., 1957-69; pres. BVD Co., 1969-74; v.p. parent co., pres. internat group Levi Strauss & Co., from 1974—, exec. v.p., chief operating officer, from 1976, pres., chief exec. officer, until 1984; v.p., gen. mgr. ops. Internat. Playtex Corp., 1984—; dir. Clorox Co., Bank of Calif. Tri-State Corp., Calmount Techs., Inc.; cons. Henkel of Am.; bus. cons. Address: 1100 Larkspur Landing Circle Suite 275 Larkspur CA 94939

GROMAN, FERN ROGOW, speech therapist; b. N.Y.C., Oct. 17, 1953; d. Robert and Sally Muriel (Levine) Rogow; m. Richard Paul Groman, Mar. 27, 1982; 1 child, Rachel Tova. BA with honors, U. B.C., Vancouver, Can., 1975; MS, U. Tex., 1977. Speech therapist Cons. Speech Pathology Services, Seattle, 1978-79, N.W. Hosp., Seattle, 1979—; lectr. in field, 1978-84. Mem. Am. Speech Lang. and Hearing Assn. Avocations: Flamenco, gardening, hiking. Office: NW Speech and Hearing Ctr 1530 N 115th St Seattle WA 98133

GROMAN, NEAL BENJAMIN, microbiology educator; b. Chisholm, Minn., May 21, 1921; s. Raphael Simon and Jenny Rebecca (Levine) G.; m. Elaine Ruth Spigle, Nov. 19, 1943; children: Jo Ann Tamarin, Nancy (Mrs. Meir Sheffer), Richard, Ellen. B.S., U. Chgo., 1947, Ph.D., 1950. Instr. U. Wash., Seattle, 1950-53; asst. prof. U. Wash., 1953-58, assoc. prof., 1958-63, prof. microbiology, 1963—, dir. office biology edn., 1971-75, acting chmn. dept. microbiology, 1981-82. Contbr. articles to profl. pubs. Served with AUS, 1942-46. John and Mary Markle Found. scholar, 1955-60; John Simon Guggenheim fellow, 1958-59; USPHS fellow, 1966-67. Fellow Am. Acad. Microbiology; mem. Am. Soc. Microbiology (chmn. virology sect. 1963-64), N.Y. Acad. Scis., Sigma Xi. Home: 4805 NE 40th Seattle WA 98105 Office: Dept Microbiology Univ Wash Seattle WA 98195

GRONSKY, RONALD, materials scientist; b. Pitts., July 9, 1950; s. Andrew John Gronsky; m. Andrea Hritz; children: Kristin, Damian, Stefan, Ryan. BS, U. Pitts., 1972; MS, U. Calif., Berkeley, 1974, PhD, 1977. Staff sr. scientist Lawrence Berkley Lab., 1978—; assoc. prof. dept. materials sci. U. Calif., Berkeley, 1982—. Contbr. chpts. to books; articles to profl. jours. Mem. AAAS, The Metallurgical Soc. of AIME (chmn. No. Calif. sect., R.L. Hardy medal 1979), Electron Microscopy Soc. Am. (Burton medal 1983), Materials Research Soc., Am. Soc. Metals (Bradley Stoughton award 1985). Avocation: photography. Home: Lawrence Berkeley Lab Nat Ctr Electron Microscopy Berkeley CA 94720

GROOTHUIS, DOUGLAS RICHARD, minister; b. Anchorage, Jan. 3, 1957; s. Harold Fred and Lillian (Cominetto) G.; m. Rebecca Merrill, Aug. 4, 1984. BS in Philosophy, U. Oreg., 1979; MA in Philosophy, U. Wis., 1986. Instr., writer McKenzie Study Ctr., Eugene, Oreg., 1979-84; research assoc. Probe Ministries, Seattle, 1986—. Author: Unmasking the New Age, 1986, The New Age Movement, 1986; contbr. articles to profl. jours. Grantee, Fieldstead, 1983, 84, 87. Mem. Soc. Christian Philosophers, Evang. Ministries to New Religions. Mem. Evang. Ch. Avocation: book collecting. Office: Probe Study Ctr NW 4750 18th Ave NE Seattle WA 98105

GROSBAYNE, FRANKLIN CHARLES, dean of student services; b. N.Y.C., May 27, 1946; s. Benjamin R. and Freda Sadie (Spitz) G.; m. Madeline Isaacson, July 10, 1973; children: Marjorie, Brian. Student, Western Md. Coll., 1963-65; BA, U. Md., 1968; MA, U. Minn., 1973; EdD, No. Ariz. U., 1985. Cert. community coll. tchr., Ariz. Asst. coordinator student activities Ariz. Western Coll., Yuma, 1974-76, coordinator student activities, 1976-78, dir. student life, 1978-84, dean student services, 1984—. Bd. mem. El Toro Athletic Booster Assn., Yuma, 1984—. Recipient Pres.' Cup Ariz. Western Coll., Yuma, 1978, numerous state, nat. music awards. Mem. Consortium for Student Unions (cons., charter), Ariz. Assn. Student Personnel Adminstrs. (pres.-exect 1985-86, sec.-treas. 1984-85), Ariz. Community Coll. Athletic Assn. Republican. Lodge: Optimists (local scholarship chmn. 1981-84). Avocations: cello, travel, reading, statistics, baseball. Home: 1935 Naples Ave Yuma AZ 85364 Office: Ariz Western Coll PO Box 929 Yuma AZ 85364

GROSE, ANDREW PETER, state official; b. Washington, July 16, 1940; s. Peter Andrew and Mildred (Holsten) G.; m. Jacqueline Stamm, Aug. 17, 1963; children—Peter Andrew II, Tracey Christine. B.S. with high honors, U. Md., 1962, M.A., 1964. Mem. legis. staff Fla. Ho. of Reps., Tallahassee, 1972-74; research dir. Nev. Legislature, Carson City, 1974-83; chief of staff Office of Gov. Nev., Carson City, 1983-84, dir. econ. devel., 1984—; mem. exec. com. Nat. Conf. State Legislatures, Denver, 1982-83. Author: Florida Model City Charter, 1974; mem. editorial bd. Nev. Rev. of Bus. and Econs., Reno, 1976—. Chmn. adminstrv. bd. 1st United Meth. Ch., Carson City, 1979-81. Served to capt. USAF, 1964-70, to col. Res. Recipient spl. citation Nev. Library Assn., Carson City, 1981. Mem. Air Force Assn., Res. Officers Assn., Nat. Assn. State Devel. Agys. (1st v.p.), Am. Polit. Sci. Assn., Western Polit. Sci. Assn. Democrat. Lodge: Kiwanis (pres. 1981-82). Home: 4801 Bryce Dr Carson City NV 89701 Office: Commn Econ Devel Capitol Complex Carson City NV 89710

GROSE, KARL R., nutritional research associate; b. San Luis Obispo, Calif., Jan. 4, 1951; s. Raymond Reich and Janka (Brugger) G.; m. Katalin Markus, Aug. 9, 1971; children: Zoltan, Tibor. BS, U. Calif., 1973. Staff research assoc. dept. nutritional scis. U. Calif., Berkeley, 1979—. Contbr. articles to profl. jours. Mem. Am. Chem. Soc., AAAS. Home: 623 Sonoma St Richmond CA 94805-1971 Office: U Calif Dept Nutritional Scis Berkeley CA 94720

GROSECLOSE, JAY C., civil engineer, consultant; b. Roswell, N.Mex., Aug. 10, 1951; s. J.C. and V. Faye (Owen) G.; m. Earlene Sue Clay, May 28, 1977. B.S.C.E., N.Mex. State U., 1974; student Kans. U., 1978-80. Registered profl. engr., Mo., N.Mex. Project engr. Black & Veatch Cons. Engrs., Kansas City, Mo., 1974-80; project engr., mgr. Scanlon & Assocs. Inc., Santa Fe, 1980-82; staff profl. engr. N.Mex. Interstate Stream Commn., Santa Fe, 1982—. Ofcl. Kansas City Baptist Assn. Youth Basketball League, 1976-80. Named One of Outstanding Young Men Am., 1980. Mem. ASCE, Am. Water Works Assn., Gideons Internat. (pres. Santa Fe 1983, v.p. Santa Fe 1984-86, treas. Santa Fe 1987), Phi Kappa Tau. Democrat. Home: 120 Calle Don Jose Santa Fe NM 87501 Office: NMex Interstate Stream Commn State Capitol Bataan Bldg Santa Fe NM 87501

GROSHONG, LAURA WOLF, psychotherapist, researcher; b. Chgo., Oct. 24, 1947; d. Henry Peter and Janyce Faye (Gluck) Wolf; m. Geoffrey Groshong, June 8, 1969; children: Joseph, Jacob. AM, U. Rochester, 1969; MusB, U. Chgo., 1974. Psychiat. social worker Harborview Med. Ctr., Seattle, 1974-77; pvt. practice in psychotherapy Seattle, 1977—; research coordinator Freud group, PATHS research project U. Wash, Seattle, 1984-86. Mem. Nat. Assn. Social Workers, Wash. State Soc. Clin. Social Workers. Democrat. Jewish. Avocations: music, hiking. Home: 3413 NE 193d Seattle WA 98155 Office: 801 Broadway Suite 830 Seattle WA 98155

GROSS, FRED ALFRED, JR., physicist; b. Fulton, Mo., Apr. 2, 1923; s. Fred Alfred Sr. and Florence Marie (Hutsel) G.; m. Susan Kist, July 2, 1943; children—Joyce D. Gross Freiwald, Cheryl A. Gross Boone, Fred Alfred III, Nara S. Gross Garver. Student Westminster Coll., 1942-43, U. N.Mex., 1952-53, Indsl. Coll. Armed Forces, 1959-60; B.S. in Physics, U. Wis., 1951, M.S. in Nuclear Physics, 1952. Enlisted U.S. Air Force 1942, commd. officer, advanced through grades to lt. col., 1958, ret., 1963; supr. Sandia Corp., Albuquerque, 1963-67; v.p. Nuclear Def. Research Corp., Inc., Albuquerque, 1967-76; assoc. dir. Western Interstate Nuclear Bd., Denver, 1976-78; mem. budget div. Los Alamos Nat. Lab., 1978-83, staff mem. defense systems engring., analysis and assessment div., 1983—; vis. scientist N.Mex. Acad. Scis., 1960-67; wildlife mem. dist. adv. bd. Bur. Land Mgmt., 1968-71; mem. nat. adv. bd. council Dept. Interior, 1968-72; wildlife mem. N.Mex. Multiple-Use Adv. Bd., Bur. of Land Mgmt., 1968-72, 75-76; vice chmn. N.Mex. Policy Bd. Air and Water Pollution, 1969-71; advisor Gov.'s Tech. Excellence Com., 1969-76; N.Mex. alternate mem. Western Interstate Nuclear Bd., 1970-76; mem. Legis. Environ. Health Study Com., 1971-73; environ. com. advisor Western Systems Coordinating Council, 1971-76; v.p. research, dir. Regional Edn. Energy Research and Industry Orgn., 1972-76; mem. N.Mex. Land Use Adv. Council, 1973-75; mem. energy com. Western Council State Govts., 1973-75; mem. elec. utility adv. com. FEA, 1973-78. Contbr. articles to profl. jours. Bd. dirs. Chaparral council Girl Scouts U.S., 1958-62, Keep N.Mex. Beautiful, 1970-74; cubmaster, scoutmaster, explorer advisor Kit Carson council Boy Scouts Am., 1960-68, exec. bd., 1971-76; v.p. Albuquerque Wildlife Fedn., 1965, pres., 1966-67, bd. dirs., 1965-76; v.p. N.Mex. Wildlife Fedn., 1968, 86, bd. dirs. 1966-71, 73-76, 80—; mem. Albuquerque Civic Beautification Com., 1967-74; mem. N.Mex. State Senate, 1968-77, N.Mex. State Trails Adv. Com., 1972-73; N.Mex. del. Nat. Wildlife Fedn., 1969-72, alt. del., 1982-83; v.p., mem. exec. com. bd. dirs., 1972-81; sec. energy task force Nat. Conf. State Legislators, 1973-76; mem. N.Mex. Joint Legis. Interim Energy Com., 1975-77; bd. dirs. Rocky Mountain Ctr. Environment, 1976-82; trustee Thorne Ecol. Inst., 1979-80; vice chmn. Los Alamos County Planning and Zoning Commn., 1979-81; chmn. fin. com., bd. dirs. Sangre de Cristo council Girl Scouts U.S., 1980-83; chmn. Los Alamos County Pub. Utility Bd. Mem. Ret. Officers Assn. (bd. dirs. roadrunner chpt. 1983-85), Nat. Rifle Assn., Western Hist. Soc., Pi Kappa Delta. Republican. Methodist. Club: Los Alamos Sportsmen's (pres. 1984-85). Home: 9 La Rosa Ct White Rock NM 87544 Office: Los Alamos Nat Lab PO Box 1663 Los Alamos NM 87544

GROSS, JOSEPH FRANCIS, chemical engineering educator; b. Plauen, Fed. Republic of Germany, Aug. 22, 1932; s. Joseph and Helen (Doelling) G. BSChemE, Pratt Inst., 1953; PhDChemE, Purdue U., 1956. Research engr., staff mem. Rand Corp., Santa Monica, Calif., 1958-72; prof. chem. engring. U. Ariz., Tucson, 1972—, head chem. engring. dept., 1975-81, prof. Ariz. research labs., 1981—. Editor: Mathematics of Microcirculation Phenomena, 1980; co-editor: Finite Elements in Biomechanics, 1982; contbr. articles to profl. jours. Bd. dirs. Tucson Mus. Art, 1984. Recipient Humboldt U.S. Sr. Scientist award Alexander von Humboldt Found., 1979. Fellow AIAA (assoc.), Am. Inst. Chem. Engrs.; mem. ASME, Am. Physiol. Soc., Microcirculatory Soc. (pres. 1976-77), Internat. Inst. Microcirculation (sec., treas. 1983—), Internat. Soc. Biorheology (treas. 1982-86). Home: PO Box 41445 Tucson AZ 85717 Office: U Ariz Dept Chem Engring Tucson AZ 85721

GROSS, LESLIE ANN, communications services executive, speech and language pathologist; b. Abington, Pa., Mar. 20, 1954; d. Donald Howard and Marjorie Louise (Breniser) Burrell; m. Charles Howard Gross, May 15, 1981. BS in Edn., Bloomsburg State U., 1976, MS, 1977. Cert. clin. competence in speech. Staff speech pathologist Soc. Crippled Children and Adults, Lansdale, Pa., 1977-79, Devel. Ctr. for Autistic Children, Phila., 1979-80; multi-handicapped deaf children tchr. Tex. State Sch. for Deaf, Austin, 1980-81; speech pathologist Dept. Def. Dependent Schs., Brindisi, Italy, 1982-84; speech pathologist pediatrics Alaska Treatment Ctr., Anchorage, 1984-85, dir. communication services program, 1985—; cons. San Vito Air Sta. Clinic, Brindisi, 1981-84; pvt. practice speech pathology, Brindisi, 1981-82. Sec. PTO, Brindisi Am. Schs., 1983-84, curriculum com., 1983-84; mem. San Vito Telethon, San Vito Sta., Italy, 1981-84. Mem. Am. Speech Hearing Lang. Assn., Alaska State Speech Hearing Lang. Assn. Republican. Lutheran. Avocations: reading, hiking, horseback riding. Office: Alaska Treatment Ctr 3710 E 20 Ave Anchorage AK 99508

GROSSETETE, GINGER LEE, gerontology administrator, consultant; b. Riverside, Calif., Feb. 9, 1936; d. Lee Roy Taylor and Bonita (Beryl) Williams; m. Alec Paul Grossetete, June 8, 1954; children: Elizabeth Gay Blech, Teri Lee Zeni. BA in Recreation cum laude, U. N.Mex., 1974, M in Pub. Adminstrn., 1978. Sr. ctr. supr., Office of Sr. Affairs, City of Albuquerque, 1974-77, asst. dir. Office of Sr. Affairs, 1977—; conf. coordinator Nat. Consumers Assn., Albuquerque, 1978-79; region 6 del. Nat. Council on Aging, Washington, 1977-84; conf. chmn. Western Gerontol. Soc., Albuquerque, 1983. Contbr. articles to mags. Pres. Albuquerque Symphony Women's Assn., 1972; exec. com. mem. Jr. League Albuquerque, 1976; campaign dir. March of Dimes N.Mex., 1966-67. Recipient N.Mex. Disting. Pub. Service award N.Mex. Gov.'s Office, 1983, Disting. Woman on the Move award YWCA, 1986. Fellow Nat. Recreation and Park Assn. (bd. dirs. Southwest Regional Council, pres. N.Mex. chpt. 1983-84, Outstanding Profl. 1982); mem. U. N.Mex. Alumni Assn. (bd. dirs. 1978-80, Disting. Alumni award 1985), Southwest Soc. on Aging (pres. 1984-85, bd. dirs.), Am. Soc. Pub. Adminstrn. (pres.-elect N.Mex. Council, 1986), Pi Alpha Alpha, Chi Omega (pres. alumni 1959-60). Club: Las Amapolas Garden (Albuquerque) (pres. 1964). Avocations: tennis, water skiing, snow skiing, jogging, arts and crafts. Home: 517 La Veta NE Albuquerque NM 87108 Office: Office of Sr Affairs 714 7th St SW Albuquerque NM 87102

GROSSMAN, GARY MICHAEL, broadcasting exec.; b. Santa Barbara, Calif., Dec. 5, 1950; s. Emil and Yvonne Anne (Prophet) G.; B.S. in Speech Communications and Theatre Arts cum laude, S. Oreg. State Coll., 1973; m. Barbara Ann Kalin, Sept. 12, 1971; children—Joshua Michael, Brittany Dawn. Program dir. KBOY Broadcasters, Medford, Oreg., 1973-74; salesman, mgr. KRKT-Radio, Albany, Oreg., 1974-76, gen. mgr., 1976—; v.p. broadcasting, chief operating officer M3X Corp., Albany. Bd. dirs. YMCA, 1982-84; mem. Albany City Budget Com., 1987—. Mem. Nat. Radio Broadcasters Assn. (state dir. 1978-82, v.p. West 1985-86), Mid-Willamette Valley Broadcasters Assn. (pres. 1977-82), Nat. Assn. Broadcasters (bd. dirs. 1986—), Oreg. Assn. Broadcasters (dir. 1979-81, v.p., 1982-83, pres. 1983-84), Greater Albany C. of C. (bd. dirs. 1986—). Republican. Methodist. Club: Jaycees. Lodges: Rotary, Optimists. Home: 2477 SE 25th St Albany OR 97321 Office: M3X Corp 1207 E 9th St Albany OR 97321

GROSSMAN, JOHN ALAN, plastic surgeon; b. N.Y.C., Oct. 1, 1941; s. William Milton and Beatrice (Netzer) G.; m. Sylvia Haszard, Oct. 1, 1966 (div. May, 1985); children: Galen Haszard, Kyle Mills, Caroline Parr. AB summa cum laude, Princeton U., 1963; MD, Cornell U., 1967. Diplomate Am. Bd. Plastic Surgery, Am. Bd. Surgery; lic. plastic surgeon Colo., N.Y., Mass., Calif. Resident Harvard Surgical Unit Boston City Hosp., 1967-73; terminable lectr. in surgery U. Aberdeen, Aberdeen Royal Infirmary, Scotland, 1970-71; fellow in surgery Harvard Med. Sch., 1971-73; resident in plastic surgery U. Colo. Med. Ctr., Denver, 1973-75; chmn. div. plastic surgery Rose Med. Ctr., Denver, 1976-85; dir. The Clinic for Plastic Surgery, Denver, 1985—; clin. instr. plastic surgery U. Colo. Health Scis. Ctr., Denver, 1975—; attending surgeon VA Hosp., Denver, 1975-80; vice chmn. dept. surgery Rose Med. Ctr., 1979-82, chmn. surgical audit com., 1979-81, 83-85; chmn. and dir. Rose Emergency Symposium, 1982-85; bd. dirs. The Rose Found., Denver, The Found. for Edn. in Plastic Surgery, Denver; guest speaker PM Mag., Phil Donohue Show, The Today Show and other radio and TV talk shows; TV host Let's Talk Health. Author: Minor Injuries and Disorders, 1984; contbr. articles to profl. jours., mags. Mem. AMA, Colo. Med. Soc., Denver Med. Soc. (assoc.), Adams County-Aurora Med. Soc. (v.p. 1977-78), Colo. State Soc. Plastic and Reconstructive Surgeons, Am. Soc. Plastic and Reconstructive Surgeons, Denver Acad. Surgery, Rocky Mountain Hand Soc., Am. Burn Assn., Harvard Med. Alumni Assn., Sigma Xi, Phi Beta Kappa. Republican. Jewish. Clubs: Princeton (N.Y.); Met. (Denver). Office: The Clinic for Plastic Surgery 310 Steele St Denver CO 80206

GROSSMAN, PATRICIA ANN, lawyer, lecturer, law educator; b. Cleve., Feb. 11, 1942; d. John Francis and Josephine Rose (Leonti) Klepacki; m. Arthur John Grossman, Jr., Aug. 24, 1963; 1 child, Arthur John Grossman, III, B.A., Marquette U., 1962; M.A., U. Hawaii, 1967; J.D., Lincoln U., 1979. Bar: Calif., 1979, U.S. Dist. Ct. (no. dist.) Calif. 1979. Tchr. Hawaii Dept. Edn., Honolulu, 1966-67; underwriter, claims adjuster St. Paul Fire & Marine Ins. Co., San Jose, Calif., 1974-79; assoc. atty. Van Loucks & Hanley, San Jose, 1980-81, Eagle & Courtney, San Jose, 1982-84; sole practice, San Jose, 1984—; law instr. Lincoln U., San Jose, 1980—; judge pro tem Santa Clara County Superior Ct., San Jose, 1984—, arbitrator civil litigation, 1984—; adminstr. child advocacy project Santa Clara County Bar Assn., 1983—; lectr. Brinkerhoff & Assocs. life planning seminars, San Jose, 1984—. Author: Introduction to Estate Planning, 1984. Editor: Handbook of Immigration Law, 1979. Recipient Outstanding Law Sch. Achievement award Bancroft Whitney Pub. Co., 1978. Mem. Santa Clara County Bar Assn. (mem. various panels 1980—, mem. law exec. com. 1984—), Calif. State Bar Assn., Peninsula Profl. Women's Network. Office: 210 N 4th St Suite 101 San Jose CA 95112

GROSSMAN, THEODOR A., JR., architect; b. Denver, Mar. 2, 1939; s. Theodor A. Sr. and Ruthe (Swab) G.; m. Martha Nelle Hudson, Sept. 10, 1961; 1 child, Naomi Wright. BA, U. Colo., 1961, BArch, 1969. Registered architect, Colo., N.M., Utah. Prin. TAG Assocs., Denver, 1970-72, 79—; guest lectr. Arapahoe Community Coll., Denver, 1980—, also mem. adv. bd., 1986—; adj. assoc. prof. U. Colo., 1987—. Contbr. articles on architecture and design to profl. jours. (award citation 1973). vol. U.S. Peace Corps, Columbia, S.Am., 1964-66. Recipient Outstanding Facility Design award U.S. Tennis Assn., 1981. Mem. AIA (bd. dirs. Colo. chpt. 1980, Denver chpt. 1981, Honor award 1980, Award of Merit 1977, 71, Arthur Fisher fellowship 1969), U. Colo. Alumni C Club. Republican. Club: Denver Tennis (bd. dirs. 1974). Former nationally-ranked tennis player and Colo.-ranked veteran bicycle racer. Avocations: cycling, tennis, basketry, pottery, jewelry. Home: 51 Village Rd Parker CO 80134 Office: TAG Assocs Architects 6551 S Revere Pkwy Englewood CO 80111

GROSSO, DAVID SPENCER, biochemist; b. Grand Coulee, Wash., Feb. 13, 1944; s. J.W. and Gladys G. (Beeman) G.; m. Patricia M. Washburn, June 14, 1968; children: Jennifer L., Kendra M. BS, Wash. State U., 1967; MS, U. Mass., Amherst, 1970; PhD, U. Mass., 1974. Postdoctoral fellow U. Ariz., Tucson, 1975-77, adj. asst. prof. ob-gyn, 1977—. Recipient Nat. Research Service award NIH, 1976. Mem. AAAS, Am. Chem. Soc., Endocrine Soc., Sigma Xi. Avocations: photography, bicycling, youth softball coaching. Home: 5262 E Rosewood St Tucson AZ 85711 Office: U Ariz Dept Ob-Gyn Ariz Health Sci Ctr Tucson AZ 85724

GROTH, ALEXANDER JACOB, political science educator; b. Warsaw, Poland, Mar. 7, 1932; came to U.S., 1947; s. Jacob and Maria (Hazenfuss) Goldwasser; m. Marilyn Ann Wineburg, Dec. 15, 1961; children: Stevin James, Warren Adrian. BA magna cum laude, CCNY, 1954; MA, Columbia U., 1955, PhD, 1960. Instr. polit. sci. Trinity Coll., Hartford, Conn., 1957-58, CUNY, 1960-61; asst. prof. Harpur Coll., Binghamton, N.Y., 1961-62, U. Calif., Davis, 1962—; cons. Ency. Am., Danbury, Conn., 1966—. Author: Comparative Politics, 1971, Major Ideologies, 1971, 2d rev. edit., 1983, People's Poland, 1972, Progress and Chaos, 1984; co-author: Contemporary Politics: Europe, 1976, Comparative Resource Allocation, 1984, Public Policy Across Nations, 1985; contbr. numerous articles to encys., scholarly jours. Recipient Ward medal dept. govt. CCNY, 1954; grantee Am. Co. Learned Socs. and Social Sci. Research Council, 1965-66. Mem. Western Polit. Sci. Assn., Policy Studies Assn., Far West Slavic Assn., Jewish Fellowship of Davis. Republican. Jewish. Avocations: baseball, baseball history, research and writing. Home: 603 Georgetown Pl Davis CA 95616 Office: U Calif Dept Polit Sci Davis CA 95616

GROTHE, PETER (JOHN), political scientist, educator; b. San Francisco, May 28, 1931; s. Walter and Dorothy Swaey (Bromberg) G.; B.A., Stanford U., 1953, M.A. in Communications, 1954; Ph.D. with distinction, George Washington U., 1970. Fgn. relations advisor to Se. Hubert Humphrey of Minn., Washington, 1960; dep. dir. UN br. Peace Corps, Washington, 1961; research asso. George Washington U., 1968; asst. prof. polit. sci. San Jose State U., 1969-74; vis. prof. Odense U., Denmark, 1976-78; asst. prof. internat. studies Monterey (Calif.) Inst. Internat. Studies, 1979-81, asso. prof., 1981-84; dir. Internat. Student Office, Monterey Inst. Internat. Studies, 1984—; lectr. USIA, 25 countries in Europe, Africa, Latin Am., and Australia; cons. to Peace Corps and USIA, 1969; vis. prof. N.Y. U., Stony Brook, 1973, 74; vis. research scholar Norwegian Inst. Internat. Affairs, Oslo, and Stockholm U., 1970-71. Pres. Hillsborough Democratic Club, 1959; campaign aide to Sen. Claire Engle of Calif., and State Atty. Gen. Stanley Mosk, 1958; del. Dem. Nat. Conf., 1972; active NAACP, Amnesty Internat., Am. Field Service. Served with AUS, 1955-56. Am.-Scandinavian Found. fellow, 1971—; Office of Edn. and Epworth Fund grantee, 1968. Mem. Am. Polit. Sci. Assn., Internat. Studies Assn., Soc. Intercultural Edn., Tng. and Research, No. Calif. Polit. Sci. Assn. (bd. councillors, pres. 1983-84), No. Calif. World Affairs Council. Episcopalian. Club: Sierra. Author: Great Moments in Stanford Sports, 1953; To Win the Minds of Men, 1958; Attitude Change of American Tourists in the Soviet Union, 1969; contbr. numerous articles and book revs. to profl. jours., Washington Post, New York Times, Christian Sci. Monitor. Home: 966 Fremont St Menlo Park CA 94025 Office: Monterey Inst Internat Studies Monterey CA 93940

GROTJAHN, MARTIN, medical writer, retired psychiatrist and analyst; b. Berlin, July 8, 1904; s. Alfred and Charlotte (Hartz) G.; M.D., Kaiser Friedrich U., Berlin, 1929; came to U.S., 1936, naturalized, 1942; m. Etelka Gross, Aug. 18, 1927; 1 son, Michael. Intern, Hosp. Reinikendaf, Berlin; resident Charité Hosp., Berlin, 1933-36, Menninger Clinic, Topeka, 1936-38, Chgo. Psychoanalytic Inst.; head physician Berlin U. dept. psychiatry and neurology, 1933-36; mem. staff Chgo. Inst. Psychoanalysis, 1938-46; mem. faculty U. So. Calif., 1946-86, now prof. emeritus, tng. analyst emeritus; practice psychiatry, Topeka, Chgo., now Los Angeles, Calif. Served with M.C., AUS, 1942-46. Recipient Sigmund Freud award Psychoanalytic Physicians, 1976. Mem. Am. Psychoanalytic Assn. (life), Am. Psychiat. Assn. (life), So. Calif. Psychiat. Assn. (life), So. Calif. Psychoanalytic Soc. (life). Author: Beyond Laughter, 1957; Psychoanalysis and the Family Neurosis, 1960; A Celebration of Laughter, 1970; The Voice of the Symbol, 1972; The Art and the Technique of Analytic Group Therapy, 1977; My Favorite Patient: The Memoirs of an Analyst, 1987; author, co-editor Psychoanalytic Pioneers, 1966. Contbr. 400 articles to profl. jours. Home: 2169 Century Hill Los Angeles, CA 90067

GROVE, ANDREW S., electronics company executive; b. Budapest, Hungary, 1936; married; 2 children. B.S., CCNY, 1960; Ph.D., U. Calif.-Berkeley, 1963. With Fairchild Camera and Instrument Co., 1963-67; pres., chief operating officer Intel Corp., Santa Clara, Calif., 1967-87, pres., chief exec. officer, 1987—; also dir. Recipient Medal award, Am. Inst. Chemists, 1960; cert. of merit, Franklin Inst.,1975; Townsend Harris medal, CCNY, 1980. Mem. Nat. Acad. Engring.; fellow IEEE (achievement award 1969, J. J. Ebers award 1974). Office: Intel Corp 3065 Bowers Ave Santa Clara CA 95051

GROVE, DAVID THOMAS, orthodontics educator; b. Alturas, Calif., Mar. 19, 1941; s. David Irvin and Kathleen (Wylie) G.; m. Kathy Arnold; 1 child, David Patrick. AB in Zoology, Calif. State U., Humboldt, 1965; DMD, U. Louisville, 1969; MS in Orthodontics, St. Louis U., 1971; MSEd, U. So. Calif., 1976. Mem. dental staff Washoe Med. Ctr., Reno; past dir. No. Nev. Craniofacial Anomalies Clinic U. Nev., Reno; past dir. TMJ Clinic U. Nev. Sch. Medicine, Reno, asst. clin. prof. orthodontics, past research dir.; asst. prof. sch. dentistry dept. growth and devel., past clin. dir. orthodontics U. Calif., San Francisco; gen. practice dentistry specializing in orthodontics Reno, 1971-74, 77-85. Served to maj. U.S. Army, 1974-77. U. Louisville Sch. Dentistry Meml. Fund scholar 1967; research fellow Oral Pathology Cleft Palate Research U. Louisville, 1967-68, Bristol Growth Study St. Louis U., 1970-71; recipient Best Table Clinic award Ann. Alumni Seminar U. Tenn., 1968, 3d Place award Postgrad. Clinic, D.S., 1968, 1st Place award Ky. Sect. Am. Coll. Dentists, Am. Acad. Oral Medicine award, Am. Soc. Dental Anesthesiology award, Outstanding Sr. award U. Louisville, Mosby award. Mem. ADA (student clinicians sect.), Am. Assn. Orthodontists, Orthodontic Edn. and Research Found., Nev. Dental Assn., No. Nev. Dental Soc. (past sec.), Am. Pain Soc., Royal Soc. Medicine, Greater Reno Acad. Dentistry (organizer), Nev. Orthodontic Soc. (pres.), Phi Kappa Phi, Omicron Kappa Upsilon, Beta Delta, Phi Delta, Psi Omega (Scholastic Achievement award). Republican. Roman Catholic. Lodge: Masons. Avocations: computers, marine biology, research, traveling. Mailing: 581 12th St Elko NV 89801

GROVER, MARTELL R., watchmaker, jeweler; b. Sugar City, Idaho, Sept. 29, 1916; s. Daniel Wells and Martha May (Ricks) G.; B.A. B.S., Ricks Coll., 1937; diploma as master watchmaker Am. Acad. Horology, 1948; m. Zell Stevenson, Mar. 21, 1942; children—Fred M., Gail S. Owner, mgr. Grover Jewelry, Rexburg, Idaho, 1948—. Mem. Latter Day Saints Mission to Germany, 1937-39. Served with U.S. Army, 1940-45. Recipient Silver Beaver award Boy Scouts Am., 1977; Outstanding Businessman of Yr. award Rexburg C. of C., 1982. Mem. Intermountain Retail Jewelers (bd. dirs. 1967-73), Rexburg C. of C. (past bd. dirs., past v.p., named Outstanding Businessman of Yr. 1983), Am. Watchmakers Inst., Ret. Jewelers Am., Am. Numismatic Assn. (life), Nat. Assn. Watch and Clock Collectors, Gem State Watchmakers Assn. (dir. 1978-79, pres. 1980-81), Am. Def. Preparedness Assn. (life), Am. Legion, VFW. Clubs: Lions, Rotary. Home: 500 E 350th S Rexburg ID 83440 Office: 58 E Main St Rexburg ID 83440

GROVES, KAY ALLEN, hospice program director; b. Chgo., Feb. 26, 1930; d. Harland Hill and Florence (Brooks) Allen; divorced; children: Michael Allen, Susan Kay Groves French, Jay Patrick and Sharon Patricia (twins), William Kevin. AA in Home Econs., San Bernardino Valley Coll., 1955; BA in Social Welfare, Calif. State U., Chico, 1973; MEd in Counseling and Guidance, U. Ariz., 1979; MSW, Ariz. State U., 1984. Parking control officer Police Dept., Riverside, Calif., 1957-60; social worker County Welfare Dept., Riverside, 1960-63; activity dir., social worker Hermiston (Oreg.) Good Samaritan Ctr., 1979-80; social worker Flower Sq., Tucson, 1980-82; program dir., social worker, vol. coordinator Lawrence Meml. Hospice, Cottonwood, Ariz., 1984—. Treas. Verde Village (Ariz.) Property Owners Assn. Inc., 1986—. Served to sgt. USAF, 1950-51. Mem. Nat. Assn. Social Workers (dist. rep. 1984), Ariz. Hospice Orgn., VFW. Democrat. Unitarian. Club: Mothers of Twins (Riverside) (v.p. 1965-66). Home: PO Box 1823 4600 Oxbow Trail E Cottonwood AZ 86326 Office: Lawrence Meml Hospice 202 S Willard PO Box 548 Cottonwood AZ 86326

GROW, ANN ELIZABETH, chemist; b. Omaha, Apr. 9, 1950; d. John Nolan Baker and Dorothy Alma (Dixon) B.; m. Stephen Warren Grow, June 9, 1971 (div.). B.A., Grinnell Coll., 1973; postgrad. in embryology, cell physiology, phys. chemistry U. Iowa, 1973-74. Research asst. Grinnell Coll. (Iowa), 1971-73, U. Iowa, Iowa City, 1974-76; chemist Thompson-Hayward Chem. Co., Kansas City, Kans., 1977-79; asst. biochemist Midwest Research Inst., Kansas City, Mo., 1979-80, assoc. chemist, 1980-84, program mgr., 1980-84; staff engr., mgr. analytical systems GA Technologies Inc., San Diego, 1984—. Active Lyric Opera Guild, 1979-80, Friends of the Zoo, 1978—. Mem. Am. Chem. Soc., San Diego Zool. Soc., Phi Beta Kappa. Club: Spaulding Racquetball (Kansas City, Kans.). Patentee processes and devices for detection of substances such as enzyme inhibitors, 1983; contbr. articles to profl. jours. Office: PO Box 85608 San Diego CA 92138

GROW, GERALD DALE, coal company executive; b. Oakland, Calif., July 7, 1942; s. Walter Dale and Betty Lou (Cowan) G.; m. Mary Ann Mills, Apr. 18, 1970. BS, U. Utah, 1966. V.p. sales Peabody Devel. Co., Flagstaff, Ariz., 1979—. Bd. dirs. Flagstaff Festival of Arts, 1985-86. Served as sgt. USAR, 1964-70. Republican. Mormon. Home: 1330 N LaCosta Way Flagstaff AZ 86001 Office: Peabody Devel Co 1300 S Yale Flagstaff AZ 86001

GRUCHALLA, MICHAEL EMERIC, electronics engineer; b. Houston, Feb. 2, 1946; s. Emeric Edwin and Myrtle (Priebe) G.; m. Elizabeth Tyson, June 14, 1969; children: Kenny, Katie. BSEE, U. Houston, 1968; MSEE, U. N.Mex., 1980. Registered profl. engr., Tex. Project engr. Tex. Instruments Corp., Houston, 1967-68; group leader EG&G Washington Analytical Services Ctr., Albuquerque, 1974—; cons. engring., Albuquerque; lectr. in field, 1978—. Contbr. articles to tech. jours; patentee in field (2). Judge local sci. fairs, Albuquerque, 1983—. Served to capt. USAF, 1968-74. Mem. IEEE, Instrumentation Soc. Am., Planetary Soc., N.Mex. Tex. Instruments Computer Group (pres. 1984-85), Sigma Xi, Tau Beta Pi, Eta Kappa Nu. Avocations: electro-optics, photography, woodworking. Office: EG&G WASC Inc 2450 Alamo Ave SE Albuquerque NM 87119

GRUENEWALD, PAUL JULIUS, statistical analyst; b. Mineola, N.Y., Jan. 19, 1951; s. John F. and Ethel L. (Eklund) G.; m. Vivian Alvarez, June 24, 1982 (div.). BS, U. Ga., 1973; PhD, Duke U., 1978. Sr. research technician Ctr. for Study Aging and Human Devel. Duke U., Durham, N.C., 1979-80; statistician, programmer Pacific Inst. Research Evaluation, Walnut Creek, Calif., 1980-84, sr. psychometrician, 1985—; statistician U.S. Pub. Health Mgmt., Santa Monica, Calif., 1986. Author: The Organization of Language, 1981, National Evaluation New Pride Replication Program, 1985; contbr. articles to publs. HEW research fellow, 1980; Horace B. Russell scholar, U. Ga., 1973. Mem. Sci. Research Soc. N.Am., Am. Statis. Assn., So. Calif. Skeptics. Democrat. Avocations: cooking, photography, bicycling. Office: Pacific Inst Research Evaluation 1777 N California Blvd Walnut Creek CA 94596

GRUENFELD, LEE, management consultant; b. Bklyn., Feb. 10, 1950; s. Martin and Helen (Faust) G.; m. Cherie Andresen, Dec. 30, 1982. BA cum laude, SUNY, Stony Brook, 1972. Cert. computer programer, data processing and systems profl. Mgr. systems devel. Tymshare, Inc., N.Y.C., 1973-79; mgmt. cons. Touche Ross & Co., Los Angeles, 1979—; nat. tech. task force advisor Touche Ross & Co., 1983—. Contbr. articles to profl. jours. Mem. Soc. Cert. Data Processors (bd. dirs. 1977-79). Avocations: airplane racing, skiing, music, photography. Office: Touche Ross & Co 3700 Wilshire Blvd Suite 50 Los Angeles CA 90010

GRUENWALD, GEORGE HENRY, new products management consultant; b. Chgo., Apr. 23, 1922; s. Arthur Frank and Helen (Duke) G.; m. Corrine Rae Linn, Aug. 16, 1947; children: Helen Marie Gruenwald Orlando, Paul Arthur. B.S. in Journalism, Northwestern U., 1947; student, Evanston Acad. Fine Arts, 1937-38, Chgo. Acad. Fine Arts, 1938-39, Grinnell Coll., 1940-41. Asst. to pres. Uarco, Inc., Chgo., 1947-49; creative dir., mgr. mdse. Willy-Overland Motors Inc., Toledo, 1949-51; brand and advt. mgr. Toni Co., Chgo., 1951-53; v.p., creative dir., account supr. E.H. Weiss Agy., Chgo., 1953-55; exec. v.p., supr. mgmt. North Advt., Chgo., 1955-71; pres., treas., dir. Pilot Products, Chgo., 1964-71; pres., dir. Advance Brands, Inc., Chgo., 1963-71; exec. v.p., dir. Campbell Mithun Inc., Mpls. and Chgo., 1971-72; pres., dir. Campbell Mithun Inc., 1972-79, chmn., dir., 1980-81, chief exec. officer, dir., 1981-83, chief creative officer, dir., 1983-84; vice-chmn., dir. Ted Bates Worldwide, N.Y.C., 1979-80; mgmt. cons. new products 1984—. Editor-in-chief Oldsmobile Rocket Circle mag., 1956-64, Hudson Family mag., 1955; author: New Product Development—What Really Works, 1985; contbr. articles to profl. jours.; creator numerous packaged consumer products. Trustee Chgo. Pub. TV Assn., 1969-73, Mpls. Soc. Fine Arts, 1975-83, Linus Pauling Inst. Sci. and Medicine, Palo Alto, 1984—; chmn., v.p., chmn. class reps. Northwestern U. Alumni Fund Council, Chgo., 1965-68; trustee, chmn., pres., chief exec. officer, chmn. exec. com. Twin Cities Pub. TV Corp., 1971-84; trustee Minn. Pub. Radio Inc., 1973-77, vice chmn., 1974-75; bd. dirs., exec. com. Pub. Broadcasting Service, Washington, 1978-86; bd. dirs. St. Paul Chamber Orch., 1982-84,. San Diego Chamber Orchestra, 1986—; mem. adv. bd. San Diego State U. Pub. Broadcasting Community, 1986—. Served with USAAF, 1943-45, MTO. Recipient Hermes award Chgo. Federated Advt. Clubs, 1963; Ednl. TV awards, 1969, 71. Mem. Am. Assn. Advt. Agys. (mgmt. com. 1976-84), The Am. Inst. Wine and Food (bd. dirs. 1985—). Office: PO Box 1696 Rancho Santa Fe CA 92067

GRUENWALD, JANICE VALEE, marketing and public relations consultant; b. Beaver Dam, Wis., Feb. 14, 1948; d. Kenneth Walther and Loira Magdalena (Radtke) Squires; m. Jon Ray Gruenwald, Jan. 25, 1969; 1 child, Jordan Jon. Student, Oshkosh State U., 1966-67; BS, U. Wis., 1970. Media specialist Edn. Resources Health Scis., Madison, Wis., 1973-76; pub. relations dir. Appleton (Wis.) Mills, 1976-80; community affairs dir. devel. Calif. State U., Northridge, 1981-84; pres. IMAGE, Valencia, Calif., 1984—. Editor: Listen to Yourself-Again, 1984. Bd. dirs. Appleton Taxpayers Alliance Com., 1978. Recipient Nat. 4-H Photography award Kodak Corp. 1966, Tri-State Tercentenary Design award, 1976. Mem. Internat. Assn. Bus. Communicators, Pub. Relations Soc. Am., U. Wis. Alumni Assn. (life), Calif. State Alumni Assn. (life). Avocations: drawing, hiking, interior decoration. Office: IMAGE 25570 Rye Canyon Rd Unita Valencia CA 91355

GRUHL, JAMES, energy scientist; b. Milw., Apr. 9, 1945; s. Alfred and Helen (Vanderveer) G.; m. Nancy Lee Huston, July 4, 1974; children—Amanda Natalie, Steven Christopher. S.B., MIT, 1968, S.M., 1968, Ph.D., 1973. Lectr., MIT, 1969-83; research scientist MIT. Energy Lab., Cambridge, 1973-83, program mgr., 1978-83, research affiliate, 1984, U.S. Environ. Protection Agy., sci. adv. bd., 1986—; energy cons. U.S. Congress, research insts. energy industries, 1973—. Ednl. counselor MIT, 1978—. Recipient Silver Beaver award Boy Scouts Am., 1986. NSF grantee. Mem. IEEE, AAAS, Math. Programming Soc., MIT Alumni Assn. (officer 1978—), Tau Beta Pi, Eta Kappa Nu. Research on uncertainties and validity of analytic models, validity of govt. and industry energy policy models, econ. and health impacts of energy sources, design of advanced coal combustion techniques. Office: Gruhl Assocs PO Box 36524 Tucson AZ 85740

GRUNANDER, CARL L., retailing educator; b. Logan, Utah, June 29, 1947; s. Edward Ray and Ila Jane (Smith) G.; m. Christine Van Orden, Dec. 19, 1969; children—Carl Jason, Todd Ryan, Jennifer Christine. Mgmt. trainee Sears, Roebuck and Co., Ogden, Utah, 1971, dept. mgr., 1971-76; coop. edn. coordinator Weber State Coll., Ogden, Utah, 1976-79, asst. prof. distributive tech., 1979-84, assoc. prof., 1984—; pres. Assn. Coop. Educators and Employers Utah, 1981; Utah adviser Delta Epsilon Chi div. Distributive Edn. Clubs Am., 1981—, chmn. exec. com. Western region bd., 1982-83. Fund-raiser United Way, Ogden, 1972-74; mem. North Ogden City Planning Commn., 1985—. Recipient Outstanding Tchrs. award Dept. Distributive Tech., Weber State Coll., 1981. Mem. Am. Vocat. Assn., Distributive Edn. Clubs Am., Utah Vocat. Assn. (Tchr. of Yr. 1985), Utah Mktg. and Distributive Edn. Assn. Republican. Mormon. Home: 943 E 2850 N Ogden UT 84404 Office: 3750 Harrison Blvd Ogden UT 84408

GRUNDY, GEORGE HENRY (BEN), association executive; b. Estelline, Tex., Jan. 8, 1912; s. Jesse Lee and Cora Anne (Findley) G.; m. Lena Christine Holwick, June 29, 1945; children—Betty Louise Brown, Sharon Ruth Biloff, Sandra Bartlett. City councilman City of Shafter (Calif.), 1950-74, mayor, 1958-62; mgr., sec.-treas. Shafter C. of C., 1980—. Mem. exec. bd. South San Joaquin League Cities, 1958-60; trustee, chmn. bd. Pub. Cemetery Dist. 1 Kern County (Calif.); dir. Calif. Assn. Spl. Dist.; gen. chmn. Shafter Potato and Cotton Festival. Served with U.S. Army, 1942-45. Decorated Purple Heart with Bronze Star medal; recipient Kern County Bd. Trade award of merit, 1960; Community Service award Shafter C. of C., 1983; named Shafter Citizen of Yr., 1976. Mem. Calif. Assn. Pub. Cemeteries (past pres. Cemeterian of Yr. 1979). Clubs: Kiwanis (pres. 1965, lt. gov. Div. 33, 1978-79), VFW, Am. Legion, DAV (Shafter). Office: PO Box 1088 Shafter CA 93263

GRUNER, GEORGE FRANK, editor; b. Alameda, Calif., Feb. 13, 1925; s. George F. and Alberta (Potter) G.; m. Irene Obermiller, May 8, 1949; 1 son, Richard. Reporter Oakland (Calif.) Tribune, 1942, 45-52; desk man Stars and Stripes (U.S. Army daily newspaper), Darmstadt, Germany, 1952-55; with Fresno (Calif.) Bee, 1955—, asst. mng. editor, 1970, mng. editor, 1971-81, exec. editor, 1981—. Served with AUS, 1943-45. Mem. Am. Soc. Newspaper Editors. Office: 1626 E St Fresno CA 93786

GRUNEWALD, LYNN CHRISTINE, psychiatric social worker; b. Virginia, Minn., Feb. 18, 1953; d. Arthur W. and Judith K. Grunewald. BA in Social Welfare, English, U. Minn., 1979; MSW, U. Calif., Berkeley, 1983. Adult protection worker Steele County Welfare Dept., Owatonna, Minn., 1979-80; social worker Hennepin County Welfare Dept., Mpls., 1980-81; psychiatric social worker Crystal Springs Rehab. Ctr., San Mateo, Calif., 1983—; creator program for employment assistance, 1980. Served with USN, 1972-74. Mem. Nat. Assn. of Social Workers, Calif. Specialists on Aging. Avocations: jogging, aerobics, swimming, reading, jazz music. Office: Crystal Springs Rehab Ctr Gero-Psychiat Program 35 Tower Rd San Mateo CA 94402

GRUSH, JULIUS SIDNEY, lawyer; b. Los Angeles, Dec. 4, 1937; s. Rose (Ida) Yankovitz; m. Eileen, June 14, 1963 (div.); children: Robin, Randi, Ronna, Rodney. BS, UCLA, 1960; postgrad., U. Calif., San Francisco, 1960-62; LLB, Southwestern U., 1964. Bar: Calif. 1965. Dep. city atty. City of Los Angeles, 1965-67; sole practice Los Angeles, 1967—; prof. Bar-Bri Harcourt Brace Pubs. Bar Course, Los Angeles, 1986—. Pres. Lockhurst Booster Club; mem. City of Hope (past pres.). Mem. ABA, Los Angeles Bar Assn., Beverly Hills Bar Assn., Century City Bar Assn., Phi Alpha Delta. Republican. Lodge: Money of Brotherhood. Office: 1880 Century Park E Suite 1400 Los Angeles CA 90067

GRUSH, PAUL LEE, software engineer; b. Ft. Wayne, Ind., July 15, 1961; s. John Fredrick and Helen Ilene (Minniear) G. BS in Computer Sci., Rose-Hulman Inst. Tech., 1983. Jr. programmer, analyst SCS, Inc., Ft. Wayne, 1983-84, programmer, analyst, 1984-85, engr., analyst, 1985-86, acting treas., 1986—; mgr. SCS, Inc., Reston, Va., 1986—, also bd. dirs., 1986—. class agt. Rose-Hulman Inst. Tech., Terre Haute, Ind., 1984—. Mem. IEEE, Armed Forces Communications and Electronics Assn., Assn. Computing Machinery, Lambda Chi Alpha. Republican. Methodist. Avocations: water sports, cars, wood refinishing.

GRYCE, DAVID CONRAD, lawyer; b. Danbury, Conn., Jan. 16, 1955; s. Walter I. and Barbara Ann (Bacon) G.; m. Patricia Ann Brown, Aug. 13, 1983. BA, Brown U., 1977; JD, U. Denver, 1983. Bar: Colo. 1983, U.S. Dist. Ct. (Colo.) 1983, U.S. Ct. Appeals (10th cir.) 1983. Assoc. Karansky, McCullough and Friedman, P.C., Denver, 1983-85; sole practice Evergreen and Lakewood, Colo., 1985—. Named one of Outstanding Young Men Am. by Outstanding Young Men Am., 1984, Order of St. Ives for Outstanding Scholarly Achievement in the Study of Law, 1983. Mem. ABA, Colo. Bar Assn., Denver Bar Assn., Assn. Trial Lawyers Am., Nat. Assn. Counsel for Children, Evergreen C. of C., Bear Creek Rodeo Assn., Colo. Lawyers for the Arts (dir., lectr.), Entertainment Law Soc. (founder, also editor and writer quarterly newsletter). Republican. Lodge: Elks. Avocations: music, horseback riding, basketball. Home: 24757 Red Cloud Dr Conifer CO 80433 Office: 6949 Hwy 73 Evergreen CO 80439 Address: 44 Union Suite 610 Lakewood CO 80228

GRYCZ, CZESLAW JAN, publishing executive. BA in Philosophy with honors, U. San Francisco, 1966; postgrad., Stanford U., 1967, U. Santa Clara, 1967. With Lane Mag. & Book Co., 1966-71; ptnr. The Oldstyle Press, 1971-75; art and preparatory dept. foreman Stanford (Calif.) U. Press, 1974-76; design, prodn. mgr. U. Calif. Press, 1976—; lectr., cons. various seminars and confs. on pub. Contbr. articles to profl. jours. Bd. dirs. Arts in Process. Mem. Am. Assn. Pubs. (panelist conf. on smaller pubs. 1980), Assn. Am. Univ. Presses (book show com. 1980, book show chmn. 1981, systems and tech. com. chmn. 1982), Bookbuilders West (bd. dirs., edn. com. 1977-80), Book Club Calif., Graphic Arts Tech. Found., Soc. Scholarly Publ. (program com. 1986), Assocs. of U. Calif. Press (founding mem., bd. dirs. 1980—), Western Univ. Presses (panelist 1979, program com. chmn. 1980), U. San Francisco Alumni Assn. (bd. dirs. 1977-79, publs. adv. bd. 1978-79). Home: 8637 Arbor Dr El Cerrito CA 94530

GRZYBOWSKI, PAUL MICHAEL, robotics-mechanical engineer; b. New Brunswick, N.J., Jan. 29, 1958; s. Thomas Joseph and Constance Elizabeth (Bondzio) G. AAS in Mech. Engring. Tech., Middlesex County Coll., 1980; BS in Mech. Engring. Tech., Trenton State Coll., 1982. Facilities engr. IBM, Dayton, N.J., 1980-82; mech. design engr. Shuttle Launch Umbilical Systems Rockwell Internat., Downey, Calif., 1982-84; teleoperator design engr. Rockwell Internat., Downey, 1984-85, teleoperator, robotics lab. mgr. space station systems div., 1985—; drafting instr. advanced career tng. program Rockwell Internat., Downey, 1985. Creator software program for collision avoidance. Mem. R.I. Flying Club Inc., Phi Theta Kappa. Republican. Roman Catholic. Avocation: piloting small aircraft, restoring classic cars.

Home: 703 S Valinda West Covina CA 91790 Office: Rockwell Internat 12214 Lakewood Blvd Downey CA 90241

GU, ALSTON LEE-VAN, mechanical engineer; b. Chengtuh, Szechwan, China, Apr. 7, 1941; came to U.S., 1964; s. Wan-Yin and Man-Yin (Hsu) G.; m. Judy Y. Wu, Apr. 12, 1969; children—Arthur, Alice. B.S., Nat. Taiwan U., 1963; S.M., MIT, 1966, M.E., 1967, Sc.D., 1969. Research asst. MIT, Cambridge, 1964-69; mem. tech. staff Bell Telephone Labs., Whippany, N.J., 1967; sr. research scientist Mech. Tech., Inc., Latham, N.Y., 1969-76; adj. assoc. prof. Union Coll., Schenectady, 1972-75; grad. lectr. Calif. State U., Long Beach, 1978-79; project engr. AiResearch Mfg. Co., Torrance, Calif., 1976—. Patentee foil bearing rubbing surface coating application methods, foil thrust bearings. Recipient Appreciation award Design Engring. Conf., 1975, 77, Western Design Engring. Conf., 1978, 82. Mem. ASME, Sigma Xi. Home: 5832 Sunmist Dr Rancho Palos Verdes CA 90274 Office: AiResearch Mfg Co 2525 W 190th St Torrance CA 90509

GUALTIERI, VINCENT, urologist; b. Reggio Calabria, Italy, Jan. 5, 1934; s. Joseph Anthony and Victoria (Cartizano) G.; A.B., UCLA, 1955; M.D., U. Calif., Irvine, 1962; m. Gina Mirella Coggi, May 19, 1963; children—Lisa, Joseph, Stephen. Resident in urology, Los Angeles County Gen. Hosp., 1962-66; urologist Ross-Loos Med. Group, Los Angeles, 1966-68; practice medicine specializing in urology, Sherman Oaks, Calif., 1968—; chief of staff Sherman Oaks Community Hosp., 1986—; clin. instr. urology Calif. Coll. Medicine, 1966-68. Diplomate Am. Bd. Urology. Fellow A.C.S.; mem. AMA, Calif. Med. Assn. (ho. dels.), Los Angeles County Med. Assn. (pres. E. San Fernando Valley chpt. 1986-87), Los Angeles Urol. Soc., Am. Urol. Assn. Republican. Office: 4955 Van Nuys Blvd Sherman Oaks CA 91403

GUARD, DONALD EUGENE, meat company executive; b. Plymouth, Ind., Nov. 18, 1928; s. Orville L. and Lois Erdene (Cramer) G.; student Purdue U., 1949-50, Alexander Hamilton Inst. Bus., 1953-56; m. Dolores Eileen Garber, Sept. 5, 1948; children—Pamela, David, Janet, Richard. Indsl. products mgr. Kraft Foods, Chgo., 1953-60; div. mgr. Leo's Quality Foods, Los Angeles, 1960-68; pres. GRD Food Brokers, Portland, Oreg., 1968-73; regional mgr. R.B. Rice Sausage Co., Lee's Summit, Mo., 1973-77, Jimmy Dean Meat Co., Dallas, 1977—; dir. Casco Devel. Co., Portland, 1972—. Mem. Deshler (Ohio) City Council, 1954-58. Served with AUS, 1946-48. Mem. Nat. Food Distbrs. Assn., So. Calif. Deli Council. Republican. Methodist. Clubs: Elks, Masons.

GUAY, GORDON HAY, postal service executive; b. Hong Kong, Aug. 1, 1948; came to U.S., 1956; s. Daniel Bock and Ping Gin (Ong) G. AA, Sacramento City Coll., 1974; BS, Calif. State U., Sacramento, 1976, MBA, 1977; PhD, U. So. Calif., 1981. Mgmt. assoc. U.S. Postal Service, Sacramento, 1980-82, br. mgr., 1982-83, fin. mgr., 1983-84, mgr. quality control, 1984-86, mgr. tech. sales and services div., 1986—; assoc. prof. bus. adminstrn., mktg. and mgmt. Calif. State U., Sacramento, 1981-85; prof. Nat. U., San Diego, 1984—; sr. cons. Gordon Guay & Assocs., Sacramento, 1979—; cons. Mgmt. Cons. Assocs., Sacramento, 1977-79. Author: Marketing: Issues and Perspectives, 1983; also articles to profl. jours. Served with U.S. Army, 1968-70. Recipient Christopher Columbus award U.S. Postal Service, Potomac, Md., 1982, Cert. Accomplishments, U.S. Postal Service, Los Angeles, 1983, Outstanding Merits award U.S. Postal Service, Sacramento, 1985, Cert. of Appreciation, U.S. Postal Service, Sacramento, 1986, Patriotic Service award U.S. Treasury Dept., San Francisco, 1985. Mem. NEA, AAUP, Soc. Advancement Mgmt. (Outstanding Mem., 1976), Am. Mgmt. Assn., Am. Mktg. Assn., Assn. MBA Execs., Am. Soc. Pub. Adminstrn. Democrat. Avocations: photography, golf, tennis, fishing, camping. Office: US Postal Service 555 capitol Mall Suite 550 Sacramento CA 95814-4560

GUDE, ARTHUR JAMES, III, research geologist; b. Eagle Grove, Iowa, Sept. 25, 1917; s. Arthur James Jr. and Blanche (Kimmey) G.; m. Bertha Theresa Truscolaska, Sept. 21, 1942; 1 child, Christina K. Student, Colo. Sch. Mines, 1939-41, 45-48, MSc in Geology, 1949. Geochem. advisor Geol. Survey Pakistan U.S. Geol. Survey, Quetta, 1959-60; research geologist U.S. Geol. Survey, Lakewood, Colo., 1949-86. Contbr. articles to profl. jours.; inventor 3-dimension crystal model constrn. kits (2), 1949, 57. Vice chmn. Lakewood Permanent Com., 1965-86; mem. Lakewood Home Rule Charter Commn., 1970-71. Served as chief petty officer, USN, 1941-45. Fulbright research fellow, Brazil, 1986; recipient Meritorious Service award U.S. Geol. Survey, 1965. Fellow Mineral. Soc. Am., Geochem. Soc.; mem. AAAS, Am. Assn. Petroleum Geologists, Am. Crystallographic Assn., Internat. Commn. Properties and Utilization of Natural Zeolites. Democrat. Avocations: skiing, violin, history, gardening, cooking. Home: 845 Dudley St Lakewood CO 80215-5410

GUENTHER, NANCY STEPHENSON, school district administrator; b. Omaha, Apr. 26, 1936; d. Robert Kirk and Lucile Helen (Dailey) Stephenson; m. Alfred Walter Guenther, Dec. 13, 1958. BS, U. Wis., 1958; MS, U. So. Calif., 1963, EdD, 1979. Cert. tchr., Calif. Tchr. coordinator Van Deene Ave. Elem. Sch., Los Angeles, 1960-68; chmn. art dept. White Jr. High Sch., Los Angeles, 1968-80; asst. prin. Bellflower (Calif.) Unified Sch. Dist., 1980-83; prin. Hawthorne (Calif.) High Sch., 1983-86; dir. instructional services Centinela Valley Union High Sch. Dist., Lawndale, Calif., 1985—; cons. in field. Author: Guess Who's Not Hiding Behind the Classroom Door, 1981; co-editor Take Five: A Methodology for the Humane School, 1979. Pres. Palos Verdes (Calif.) Jr. Womans Club; mem. com. for incorp. of Rancho Palos Verdes; founder LaCresta Homeowners Assn.; bd. dirs. Palos Verdes Community Arts Assn.; sec. South Bay Young Reps., Palos Verdes Rep. Club; cen. com. mem. Calif. State Reps.; trustee Little Co. of Mary Hosp. Recipient Outstanding Personal Contbns. award Palos Verdes Community Arts Assn., 1981-83, Outstanding Jr. award Palos Verdes Jr. Womans Club. Mem. Dist. Art Textbook Evaluation Com., Assn. Calif. Sch. Adminstrs. (chmn. area IX curriculum leaders com., mem. state curriculum leaders com.), Assn. Supervision and Curriculum Devel., Nat. Assn., Secondary Sch. Prins., Hon. Assn. Women Educators, Educare, Trojan League of South Bay, Delta Epsilon, Delta Kappa Gamma, Phi Delta Kappa. Office: Centinela Valley Union High Dist 14901 S Inglewood Ave Lawndale CA 90260

GUERRA, CÁSTULO, actor; b. Córdoba, Argentina, Aug. 24, 1945; came to U.S., 1971; s. Cástulo and María (Sola) G.; m. Christy Claire Risska, Dec. 15, 1972. Licenciado en Inglés, Universidad Nacional, Tucumán, Argentina, 1971. Creator, dir. Free Theatre Lab., N.Y.C., 1973-74; appeared in stage prodns. with N.Y. Shakespeare Festival, N.Y.C., 1979, Ctr. Stage, Balt., 1979-81, Arena Stage, Washington, 1980-82; films include Two of a Kind, 1983, Stick, 1984, Where the River Runs Black, 1985, Nuts, 1987; stage Mark Taper Forum, Los Angeles, 1986. Fellow Fulbright-Hayes Found., Kans. U., 1971-72, Ford Found., N.Y.C., 1973-74. Mem. Actor's Equity Assn., Am. Fedn. TV And Radio Actors, Screen Actors Guild. Avocations: langs., music, travelling. Office: STE Representation Ltd 211 S Beverly Dr Beverly Hills CA 90212

GUERRASIO, DOMINIC EDWARD, chemical engineer; b. McKees Rocks, Pa., Feb. 6, 1943; s. Dominic Peter and Tessie (Trombetta) G.; m. Patricia Garvey, Dec. 3, 1966; children: Dominic Edward Jr., Nicole, Damon Patrick. BSChemE, N.Mex. State U., 1969, MBA, 1972. Cost engr. Bechtel Corp., San Francisco, 1972-73, Arabian Am. Oil Co., Dhahran, Saudi Arabia, 1975-78; ops. mgr. F.M. Qahtani Constrn., Abqaiq, Saudi Arabia, 1978-79; program engr. Lockheed Corp., Las Cruces, N.Mex., 1979-83; sr. test engr. Martin Marietta Aerospace Corp., Vandenberg AFB, Calif., 1983—. Mem. AIAA. Democrat. Roman Catholic. Avocations: skiing, swimming, jogging, golfing. Home: 2240 Caballero Ln Santa Maria CA 93454 Office: Martin Marietta Corp PO Box 1681 Vandenberg AFB CA 93437

GUERRERO, REUBEN CASTRO, med. oncologist, internist; b. Manila, Philippines, Aug. 22, 1935; came to U.S., 1962, naturalized, 1978; s. Jacobo Tolentino and Francisca Claravall (Castro) G.; A.A., U. Philippines, Manila, 1952, M.D. (Univ. scholar, 1955-56; United Drug Co. scholar, 1956-57), 1957; m. Celina V. Sison, June 18, 1962; children—Chiarina, Leonora, Anthony Paul. Intern, Philippine Gen. Hosp., Manila, 1956-57; mem. faculty Coll. of Medicine, U. Philippines, 1957-62; resident in medicine, Ch. Home and Hosp., Balt., 1962-64, chief resident, 1965-66; postdoctoral fellow in medicine Johns Hopkins Hosp., Balt., 1964-65, postdoctoral fellow in med. oncology, 1966-68; asst. prof. medicine, chief chemotherapy div. U. Philippines and Cancer Inst., 1968-73; med. oncologist, chmn. cancer com. Straub Clinic and Hosp., Honolulu, 1973—; clin. assoc. prof. John A. Burns Sch. Medicine, U. Hawaii; chmn. research Philippine Cancer Soc., 1969-73; chmn. service and rehab. com., bd. dirs. Hawaii div. Am. Cancer Soc., 1973—. Served with Philippine Army Res., 1957-58. Fellow ACP; mem. Am. Soc. Internal Medicine, Am. Soc. Clin. Oncology, Philippine Soc. Med. Oncology, Honolulu County Med. Soc., Hawaii Med. Assn. (cancer commn.), AMA, Am. Geriatric Soc., Aerospace Med. Assn., Honolulu Marathon Assn. Republican. Roman Catholic. Club: Honolulu. Contbr. articles to profl. jours. Home: 1424 Ohialoke St Honolulu HI 96821 Office: Straub Clinic and Hosp 888 S King St Honolulu HI 96813

GUERRIERI, TERESA ELLEN, transportation company executive; b. Espanola, N.Mex., Nov. 22, 1934; d. George M. and Irma P. (Muth) Witzke; m. Gasper J. Guerrieri, May. 13, 1950; children: Gasper L., Jimmy George, Robin B. Grad. high sch. Pres., treas. G&G Truck Leasing Inc., Thornton, Colo., 1967—. Recipient Golden Poet award World of Poetry, 1985, 86. Republican. Avocations: writing fiction and poetry, bowling, computers, reading, book collecting. Office: G&G Truck Leasing Inc 5974 Marion Dr Denver CO 80216

GUEST, BERNETTE PARKER, oil company executive; b. Salt Lake City, May 18, 1952; d. Robert Farnsworth and Ilona Leiola (Wiebke) Parker; m. Russel Paul Guest, Sept. 15, 1973; children—Forrest Farnsworth, Robert Russel. B.S. in Fin., Colo. State U., 1973. Transfer agt., sec.-treas. Am. Stock Transfer, Inc., Denver, 1969-70; v.p., dir. 1971-74; corp. sec., controller Golden Oil Co., Denver, 1974-78, treas., 1977—, dir., 1976—, v.p., 1978—; sec.-treas., dir., cons. G & S Service Co., Inc., Tulsa, 1977-79. Mem. Nat. Fedn. Ind. Bus., Ind. Petroleum Assn. Mountain States, Ind. Petroleum Assn. Am., Petroleum Accts. Soc. Colo., Nat. Assn. Female Execs., Inst. Energy Devel., Am. Mgmt. Assn. Office: 372 Denver Club Bldg Denver CO 80202

GUGAS, CHRIS, criminologist; b. Omaha, Aug. 12, 1921; s. Nicholas and Vera (Henas) G.; student U. So. Calif., 1946-49, U. Calif. at Northridge, 1955-56; B.A., M.A. in Pub. Adminstrn., U. Beverly Hills, 1977; D.Div., Ch. Living Sci., 1968; Ph.D., U. Beverly Hills, 1983; m. Anne Claudia Setaro, June 27, 1942; children—Chris, Steven Edward, Carol Ann Gugas Hawker. Asst. dir. security Los Angeles Bd. Edn., 1948-49; spl. agt. CIA, Washington, 1950-54; criminol. cons., Los Angeles, 1955-61; pub. safety dir., Omaha, 1962-65; dir. polygraph services Profl. Security Cons., Los Angeles, 1966—; exec. dir. Calif. Acad. Polygraph Scis., Los Angeles, 1974-76, The Truthseekers, 1975—; instr. Los Angeles Inst. Polygraph, 1979—, Gormac Polygraph Sch., Los Angeles, 1972-73; chief instr. Las Vegas Acad. Polygraph Sci., 1982-83; columnist Los Angeles Daily Jour., Security World mag., The Truthseekers. Mem. advisory bd., sec. Calif. Dept. Consumer Affairs, 1971-76. Served with USMCR, 1940-45, 47-49. Mem. Marine Corps League (comdr. 1946), Marine Corps Combat Corr.'s Assn. (pres. Los Angeles chpt. 1975-77), Nat. Bd. Polygraph Examiners (pres. 1958), Security Officers Assn. (pres. 1968), Am. Polygraph Assn. (pres. 1971, exec. dir. 1972-73), Am. Soc. Indsl. Security. Club: Los Angeles Press. Author: The Silent Witness; co-author: The National Corruptors; Pre-Employment Polygraph; The Polygraphist in Court; Our National Rebellion, 1982; contbr. numerous articles to various jours. Home: 4018 Dixie Canyon Sherman Oaks CA 91403 Office: 1680 Vine St Ste 400 Hollywood CA 90028

GUGGENHIME, RICHARD JOHNSON, lawyer; b. San Francisco, Mar. 6, 1940; s Richard F. and Charlotte Guggenhime; m. Emlen Hall, June 5, 1965 (div.); children—Andrew, Lisa, Molly. A.B. in Polit. Sci. with distinction, Stanford U., 1961; LL.B., Harvard U., 1964. Bar: Calif. 1965, U.S. Dist. Ct. (no. dist.) Calif. 1965, U.S. Ct. Appeals (9th cir.) 1965. Assoc. Heller, Ehrman, White & McAuliffe, 1965-71, ptnr., 1972—; spl. asst. to U.S. Senator Hugh Scott, 1964; bds. dir. Comml. Bank of San Francisco, global Savings Bank, San Francisco. Mem. San Francisco Bd. Permit Appeals, 1978-86; bd. dirs. Marine World Africa USA, 1980-86; mem. San Francisco Fire Commn., 1986—; trustee San Francisco U. High School, St. Ignatius Prep. Sch., San Francisco. Mem. Am. Coll. Probate Counsel, San Francisco Opera Assn. (dir.). Clubs: Bohemian, University, Wine and Food Soc., Olympic, Chevaliers du Tastevin (San Francisco); Silverado Country (Napa, Calif.); Vintage (Palm Springs). Home: 115 Presidio Ave San Francisco CA 94115 Office: Heller Ehrman White & McAuliffe 333 Bush St San Francisco CA 91104

GUICE, TERRY L., oil jobber, warehouse executive; b. Jonesboro, Ark., May 27, 1955; s. Lyndol P. and Betty C. (Gibson) G.; m. Jane A. Hodge, Mar. 8, 1980; 1 child, Brian. BS, U. Wyo., 1978. Salesman Four "G" Enterprises, Laramie, Wyo., 1974-78, sales mgr., 1978-82, v.p., 1982—; mem. Wyo. Legislature, 1986—. Mem. Cen. Rep. Com. Albany County, Laramie, 1984—, Cen. Rep. Com. Wyo., 1985—; mem. bd. advisors Wyo. Coll. Reps., 1986—; bd. dirs. Laramie Jubilee Days Com., 1985—; mem. Albany County Blood Donors, Laramie, 1984—. Mem. Wyo. Oil Jobber Assn., Nat. Fed. Ind. Bus., Laramie C. of C., Wyo. Petroleum Marketers Assn., Laramie Internat. fedn. League (pres. 1982-83). Baptist. Clubs: Laramie Country, Wheel and Whale (pres. 1984-85). Lodges: Rotary (bd. dirs.), Masons, Shriners. Home: 1714 Palmer Dr Laramie WY 82070 Office: Four "G" Enterprises Inc PO Box 359 Laramie WY 82070

GUIDRY, SUSAN DIANE ARNOLD, finance executive; b. Denver, Apr. 1, 1953; d. William J. and M. Lucille (Tell) Arnold; m. Dwight J. Guidry, Feb. 14, 1981. B.A., Colo. Women's Coll., 1976; M.B.A., So. Meth. U., 1977; M.Internat. Mgmt., Am. Grad. Sch. Internat. Mgmt., Glendale, Ariz., 1977; postgrad. in Fin. Mgmt., Stanford U., 1985-86. Documentation supr. Internat. Air Transport Assn., Geneva, 1974-75; mgmt. candidate PACCAR Inc, Bellevue, Wash., 1978-79, collections specialist/region fin. mgr./credit mgr. PACCAR Internat., Inc., Bellevue, 1979-82, asst. to v.p. and treas., 1982-83; credit mgr., dir. credit and treasury, PACCAR Leasing Corp., Bellevue, 1983-87; mgr. internat. fin. cos. PACCAR Inc., 1987—. Fin. adv. Jr. Achievement, 1979-81, coordinator, 1982-83; alumni coordinator Am. Grad. Sch. Internat. Mgmt., 1978—. Recipient Elaine Miller award Colo. Women's Coll., 1976. Republican. Methodist. Mem. Association Internationale des Etudiants en Sciences Economiques et Commerciales (adv. bd. U. Wash. chpt. 1982-84), Seattle Met. Softball Umpires' Assn. (bd. dirs. 1984-85), Nat. Assn. Credit Mgrs. Home: PO Box 40 Carnation WA 98014 Office: PO Box 1518 Bellevue WA 98009

GUILD, DAVID WILLIAM, information services executive; b. Blue Island, Ill., Oct. 1, 1944; s. William Miller and Delores Jean (Kay) G.; m. Janice Lee Munson, Sept. 3, 1966; children: Wendy L., Jeffrey A. BA, Knox Coll., 1966. Mgr. accounts Electronic Data Systems, San Francisco, 1971-78; v.p. info. services McKesson Corp., San Francisco, 1978-84; prin. Ernst & Whinney, San Francisco, 1984-86; sr. v.p. info. services Calif. Blue Cross, Woodland Hills, 1986—. Pres. Cowell Homeowners Assn., Concord, Calif., 1981-84, treas. 1980-81; mem. San Quentin Adv. Council, San Francisco, 1980-84. Served to lt. USN, 1966-71. Avocations: tennis, running, reading, motorcycle touring. Home: 1574 Wynnefield Ave Westlake Village CA 91362 Office: Calif Blue Cross 21555 Oxnard St Woodland Hills CA 91367

GUILD, STEPHEN EVES, management consultant, educator; b. Oklahoma City, Aug. 21, 1941; s. Carl Earl and Frances Beatrice (Eves) G.; m. Patricia Ann O'Rourke Burke, Nov. 25, 1985; children: Darren Michael, Sue Anne Jeong. BA, Washington and Lee U., 1963; EdD, U. Mass., 1973. With Peace Corps, Sierra Leone, 1963-64; liason officer Peace Corps, Washington, 1964-67; tng. project dir. Peace Corps, St. Thomas, V.I., 1967-68; dir. Global Survival Freshman Yr. Program U. Mass., Amherst, 1973-77, assoc. dir. Office to Coordinate Energy Research and Edn., 1977-80; pres. The Teaching Advisory, Seattle, 1981—; ptnr. Results Plus, Seattle, 1986—; adj. prof. dept. environ. scis., U. Mass., Amherst, 1973-75, Sch. Edn., 1975-80;faculty human resources extension U. Wash., Seattle, 1984—; adj. prof. Seattle Pacific U., 1986; adj. faculty sch. of bus. Seattle U., 1987—; bd. dirs. Ploughshares, 1984—. Author: Effective Training Skills, 1986; (with others) Instructional Skills for the "Occasional Teacher", 1984, Developing Effective Instructional Skills, 1983; editor: Directory of the Five College Faculty Colloquium on Ethics, the Environment and Energy, 1980, University Energy Update, 1979-80; contbr. articles to profl. jours. Pres. and bd. dirs. The Carriage Towne Players, Belchertown, Mass., 1979-80, Hitchcock Ctr. for Environment, Amherst, 1973-79. Mem. Am. Soc. Tng. and Devel. (dir. publs. Puget Sound chpt., 1984-86, v.p. fin., 1983-84). Home: 2632 40th Ave W Seattle WA 98199 Office: The Teaching Advisory PO Box 99131 Seattle WA 98199 also: Results Plus 1932 1st Ave Suite 301 Seattle WA 98101

GUILES, ROBERT EMERSON, artist; b. Addison, N.Y., Oct. 14, 1917; s. Lester E. and Amelia (Kreja) G.; student U. Rochester, 1939, Acad. Art, San Francisco, 1945-46; A.A. cum laude in Art Indian Valley Colls., Novato, Calif., 1981-84; m. Hazel Mae Anderson, June 7, 1947; children—William Alan, Frank Emerson. Asst. art dir. Ruthrauf & Ryan, Advt., 1948; staff artist San Francisco News, 1948-60, News-Call Bull., 1960-65, San Francisco Newspaper Agy., 1965-80; advt. cons., freelance graphic designer, 1980—; polit. cartoonist various labor publs., artist, 1958—; civic art commr., Novato, 1985—. Mem. Black Raven Pipe Band San Francisco, 1966-67. Publicity chmn. Marin Citizens for Responsible Firearms Control. Served to capt. AUS, 1940-45. Mem. Newspaper Guild (pres. local 52 1964, 75-76, treas. 1978-79). Clubs: Sierra. Democrat. Contbr. articles to profl. jours. Home and Office: 1265 Parkwood Dr Novato CA 94947

GUILES-FELLEZ, ROBIN ELLEN, social worker; b. East Orange, N.J., May 15, 1955; s. William Leonard and Lois Agnes (Weiboldt) Guiles; m. Cynthia Lynn Fellez, Oct. 12, 1977; 1 child, Sarah Michael. AS in Recreation, Pa. State U., 1975; BSW, U. Hawaii, 1981, MSW, 1982. Cert. social worker. Crisis worker Rape Cirsis Ctr., Honolulu, 1981-83; intake dir. Salvation Army Addiction Ctr., Honolulu, 1981-83; substitute care worker, cons. Oreg. Children's Services Div., Albany, 1983-84; juvenile liason, cons. Oreg. Children's Services Div., Eugene, 1984—; cons. Human Sexuality Class, Honolulu, 1979-83. Mem. Com. to Elect Jean King, Honolulu, 1982. Mem. Nat. Assn. Social Workers. Democrat. Roman Catholic. Avocations: camping, fishing, child rearing. Home: 477 W 27th Pl Eugene OR 97405 Office: Children's Services Div 1102 Lincoln St Eugene OR 97401

GUILFORD, WILLIAM JOSEPH, chemical researcher; b. Oakland, Calif., July 8, 1954; s. Adrian Peter and Frances Mary (Salel) G. BS, U. Calif., Berkeley, 1976; PhD, U. Ill., 1982. Research fellow Swiss Fed. Inst. Tech., Zurich, 1981-83, Harvard U., Cambridge, Mass., 1984-85; sr. research chemist Sogetal, Inc., Hayward, Calif., 1985—. Contbr. articles to profl. jours. Fellow NIH, 1982-83, Merck, 1979-80, Eastman Kodak, 1978-79, 3M, 1977-78. Mem. AAAS, Am. Chem. Soc., Calif. Acad. Sci. Avocations: bicycling, camping, photography. Office: Sogetal Inc 3872 Bay Ctr Place Hayward CA 94545

GUILLEMIN, ROGER, physiologist; b. Dijon, France, Jan. 11, 1924; came to U.S., 1953, naturalized, 1963; s. Raymond and Blanche (Rigollot) G.; m. Lucienne Jeanne Billard, Mar. 22, 1951; children—Chantal, Francois, Claire, Helene, Elizabeth, Cecile. B.A., U. Dijon, 1941, B.Sc., 1942; M.D., Faculty of Medicine, Lyons, France, 1949; Ph.D., U. Montreal, 1953; Ph.D. (hon.), U. Rochester, 1976, U. Chgo., 1977, Baylor Coll. Medicine, 1978, U. Ulm, Germany, 1978, U. Dijon, France, 1978, Free U. Brussels, 1979, U. Montreal, 1979, U. Man., Can, 1984, U. Turin, Italy, 1985. Intern, resident univs. hosps. Dijon, 1949-51; asso. dir., asst. prof. Inst. Exptl. Medicine and Surgery, U. Montreal, 1951-53; asso. dir. dept. exptl. endocrinology Coll. de France, Paris, 1960-63; prof. physiology Baylor Coll. Medicine, 1953—; adj. prof. medicine U. Calif. at San Diego, 1970—; resident fellow Salk Inst., 1970—. Decorated chevalier Legion of Honor (France), 1974, officier, 1984; recipient Gairdner Internat. award, 1974; U.S. Nat. Medal of Sci., 1977; co-recipient Nobel prize for medicine, 1977; recipient Lasker Found. award, 1975; Dickson prize in medicine, 1976; Passano award med. sci., 1976; Schmitt medal neurosci., 1977; Barren gold medal, 1979; Dale medal Soc. for Endocrinology U.K., 1980. Fellow AAAS; Mem. Am. Physiol. Soc., Endocrine Soc. (pres.) 1986), Soc. Exptl. Biology and Medicine, Internat. Brain Research Orgn., Internat. Soc. Research Biology Reprodn., Soc. Neuro-scis., Nat. Acad. Scis., Am. Acad. Arts and Scis., Académie nationale de Médecine (fgn. assoc.), Swedish Soc. Med. Scis. (hon.), Académie des Scis. (fgn. assoc.), Académie Royale de Médecine de Belgique (corr. fgn.), Club of Rome. Office: Salk Inst Box 85800 San Diego CA 92138

GUINN, AL F., fund raising director, former music company executive; b. Parkersburg, W.Va., Mar. 25, 1928; s. Alva Foster and Garnett (Creel) G.; B.Sc. in Music Edn., U. Cin., 1952, postgrad., 1960-63; M.Mus. Edn., Miami U., Oxford, Ohio, 1956; Ed.D., East Coast U., 1969; 1 dau., Caryl Joscelyn. Band dir. Mt. Healthy (Ohio) City Schs., 1950-57; band dir., chmn. dept. music Princeton City Schs., Cin., 1957-63; acting dir. U. Cin. Bands, 1963; band dir., chmn. dept. mus. Fine Arts div., assoc. prof. Rocky Mountain Coll., Billings, Mont., 1963-69, 76-78; band dir., assoc. prof. music edn. Wright State U., Dayton, Ohio, 1969-73; owner Al Guinn's Music, Billings, 1973-78; Western Sales rep. L.D. Heater Music Co., Portland, Oreg., 1978-79; band and orch. dir. Butte (Mont.) High Sch., 1979-85; fund raising dir. Ward, Dreshman & Reinhardt, Inc., Worthington, Ohio, 1986—; flutist Billings Symphony Orch., 1963-69, 73-78; flutist Billings Chamber Orch.; dir. South Cen. Mont. Tri-County Honor Band, 1974-76; instr. flute Rocky Mountain Coll., 1974-78; assoc. prof. Eastern Mont. Coll., 1976; dir., founder Billings Concert Band, 1975-78; assoc. condr. Butte Symphony Orch., 1980-85; adjudicator Dist., Region and State Music Festival, Mont., Wyo., N.D., Ohio, Ill.; marching band adjudicator, Mont., Wyo., Ohio. Served as flutist USMC Band, 1946-48. Mem. Music Educators Nat. Conf. (past dist. pres., chpt. sponsor), Mont. Bandmasters Assn., Coll. Band Dirs. Nat. Assn., Ohio Music Educators Assn., Nat. Band Assn., Am. Sch. Band Dirs. Assn., Phi Beta Mu. Clubs: Antique Automobile Am., Rolls-Royce Owners; Rolls-Royce Enthusiasts, Bently Drivers (Eng.). Office: 902 S 30th Ave Yakima WA 98902

GUINN, DONALD EUGENE, telephone company executive; b. Wellington, Kans., Oct. 26, 1932; s. Cecil William and Avis Velma (Scoles) G.; m. Marlene Darhl, Mar. 21, 1953; children: Debra Michele, Damon Jeffrey, David Leslie. B.S. in Civil Engring, Oreg. State U., 1954. Various mgmt. positions Pacific Tel. & Tel., Portland, Oreg., 1954-75; v.p. engring. and network sers. Pacific N.W. Bell, 1976; asst. v.p. engring., asst. v.p. customer sers. AT&T, 1976-78, v.p. customer services, v.p. network services, 1978-80; now chmn., chief exec. officer Pacific Tel & Tel (now Pacific Telesis Group), San Francisco; chmn. Pacific Bell, San Francisco, 1984—. Bd. dirs. Pacific Sci. Ctr., Seattle, 1975-76. Mem. Profl. Engrs. Oreg., IEEE (communications policy bd.). Republican. Lutheran. Office: Pacific Telesis Group 140 New Montgomery St San Francisco CA 94105 *

GUINN, HENRY ALAN, consultant; b. Bristol, Va., Mar. 22, 1952; s. Henry Virgil and Alsace Lorraine (Jones) G.; B.S., Tenn. Tech. U., 1975, postgrad., 1976; m. Carla Denise Austin Highfill, Sept. 5, 1980; children—Daniel Joseph, Elizabeth Lorraine. Unit mgr. Pizza Hut, Inc., Cookeville, Tenn., 1974-76, Lebanon, Tenn., 1976, area gen. mgr., Waycross, Ga., 1976-77; field service rep. Franchise Services, Inc., Atlanta, 1977-78; nat. mgr. Equipment Sales, Wichita, Kans., 1978-79; franchise ops. rep. Pepsico Food Service Internat., Wichita, 1980-81; dir. francise devel. Can., 1981; gen. mgr. PM Foods Ltd., Calgary, Alta., Can., 1981-82; franchise area dir. Wendy's Internat., Inc., Lake Oswego, Oreg., 1982-83; pres. AVM Mgmt. Cons., Ltd., Calgary, Alta., 1982-84; sr. ptnr. Tri-Am, Tigard, Oreg., 1982-84; v.p., dir. ops. N.W. TAG Enterprises, Inc., Redding, Calif., O'Cal Corp., Bay Cities Restaurant, Inc. Recipient Pub. Service awards Am. Radio Relay League, 1969-74. Mem. Am. Radio Relay League, Shasta Cascade Amateur Radio Soc., Omicron Delta Kappa. Episcopalian. Lodge: Rotary (Redding). Home: 600 Rafael Redding CA 96002 Office: 3609 Bechelli Ln Suite D Redding CA 96002

GUINN, SUZANNE KAY, speech language pathologist; b. Kalamazoo, Mar. 4, 1944; d. Kenneth Jeremiah and Ruth Minnie (Baker) Yeomans; m. Howard Christopher Guinn, Apr. 26, 1968; 1 child, Ian Christopher. BS, Western Mich. U., 1966; MS, U. Wis., 1967. Presch. supr. Kalamazoo Valley Intermediate Sch. Dist., 1967-68; speech-lang. pathologist State operated schs., Eielson AFB, Alaska, 1968-74; coordinator speech-lang. and presch. services Fairbanks (Alaska) North Star Borough Sch. Dist., 1974—. Recipient DiCarlo award Am. Speech and Hearing Found., 1983. Mem. NEA, Alaska Speech Lang. Hearing Assn. (pres. 1974-75, 80-81), Am. Speech and Hearing Assn., Delta Kappa Gamma (pres. Fairbanks chpt. 1978-80). Home: 1438 Dupont Ln Fairbanks AK 99709 Office: Fairbanks North Star Borough Sch Dist PO Box 1250 Fairbanks AK 99707

GUINN, VINCENT PERRY, chemistry educator, consultant; b. Los Angeles, Nov. 9, 1917; s. Walter C. and Marie Martha (Mortensen) G.; m. Thora Marjorie Offersen, Sept. 2, 1938; children: Marjorie Cheryl, Terry Walter. AA, Pasadena Jr. Coll., 1937; AB, U. So. Calif., 1939, MS, 1941; PhD, Harvard U., 1949. Research chemist Shell Devel. Co., Emeryville, Calif., 1941-46, 1949-61, radiochemistry head, 1956-61; tech. dir. activation analysis Gen. Atomic Co., San Diego, 1961-70; prof. chemistry U. Calif., Irvine, 1970—. Contbr. numerous articles to profl. jours. Recipient George Hevesy medal Jour. Radioanalytic Chemistry, Budapest, 1979. Fellow AAAS, Am. Nuclear Soc. (Spl. award 1964), Am. Acad. Forensic Scis.; mem. Am. Chem. Soc., Forensic Sci. Soc. (Eng.), Calif. Assn. Criminalists, Phi Beta Kappa, Sigma Xi, Phi Kappa Phi, Phi Lambda Upsilon. Avocations: hiking, mountain climbing. Home: 1141 Muirlands Vista Way La Jolla CA 92037 Office: U Calif Chemistry Dept Irvine CA 92717

GULBERG, E(DWARD) LAWRENCE, JR., chemistry educator, technical sales professional; b. Bremerton, Wash., Apr. 6, 1949; s. Edward Lawrence Gulberg and Aileen Marguerite (Bellinger) Epling; m. Deborah Lou Fine, June 7, 1974; children: Edward Robert, Sunny Deanna. BS in Chemistry, Stanford U., 1971; cert. in teaching, Seattle Pacific Col., 1972; MEd, U. Wash., 1977, PhD in Analytic Chemistry, 1980. Assoc. faculty mem. Shoreline Jr. Coll., Seattle, 1980; tchr. chemistry Northshore Schs., Bothell, Wash., 1972-86; instrument sales specialist Fisher Sci., Kent, Wash., 1986—; participant Oreg. Sci., Math. Inst. for Teaching Excellence, Eugene, Oreg., 1985. Contbr. articles to profl. jours. Active AFS, travel rep., interviewer, Seattle, 1975-76. Mem. Am. Chem. Soc., Wash. Sci. Tchrs. Assn., Christian Youth Ministry. Avocation: whitewater rafting guid. Home: 19720 65th Ave SE Snohomish WA 98290 Office: Fisher Sci Co 8030 S 228th St Kent WA 98032

GULBRANDSON, L.C., justice Montana Supreme Court; b. Vida, Mont., Oct. 28, 1922; s. E.O. and May (Farnham) G.; m. Wilma Loomans, Apr. 20, 1976; 1 son by previous marriage, Stephen. B.S.L., U. Minn., 1950, LL.B., 1952. Bar: Mont. 1953. Judge U.S. Dist. Ct. 7th Dist. Mont., 1959-83; justice Mont. Supreme Ct., Helena, 1983—. Served to capt. USAAF, 1942-48, PTO. Home: 2034 Gold Rush Ave Helena MT 59601 Office: Montana Supreme Court Sanders St Helena MT 59601 *

GULDHAMMER, B(ENTE) ANETTE, university administrator; b. Give, Denmark, July 10, 1944; came to U.S., 1959, naturalized, 1977; d. David Hjorth and Edith (Clausen) G. m. Mitchell Eric Beaven, June 3, 1962 (div.); 1 dau., Michelle Lisa. B.S., Columbia Union Coll., Takoma Park, Md., 1965; M.Music Edn., So. Ill. U., 1967, Ph.D., 1982. Asst. to dean Coll. Edn., So. Ill U., Carbondale, 1967-68, fgn. student adviser Internat. Student Ctr., 1968-69, grad. asst. learning resources, 1978-79, research asst. career guidance handbook project, 1980, cons., 1981; music tchr. Blue Mountain Elem. Sch., Hamburg, Pa., 1975-78; lang. and music instr. ednl. instns. in Iceland, 1981; assoc. dean student affairs Loma Linda U., Riverside, Calif., 1982—, dir. placement service, 1982—. Univ. rep. Riverside Arts Council, 1982-83; choir dir. Corona Seventh-day Adventist Ch., Calif., 1983—. Mem. Am. Coll. Personnel Assn., Nat. Assn. Fng. Student Affairs, Am. Assn. Counseling and Devel., Coll. Placement Council, Western Coll. Placement Assn., Assn. for Sch. Coll. and Univ. Staffing (profl. growth com. 1983-84), Am.-Scandinavian Found. Los Angeles, Kappa Delta Phi. Home: 5005 Sierra Vista Ave Apt 11 Riverside CA 92505 Office: Loma Linda Univ Student Affairs 4700 Pierce St Riverside CA 92515

GULICK, LLOYD RUSSELL, JR., computer scientist, educator; b. Charles City, Iowa, Feb. 18, 1936; s. Lloyd Russell Sr. and Gladys Audrey (Lambert) G.; m. Virginia Ann Bengochea, Aug. 5, 1957 (div. May 1971); children: Matthew Scott, Darcy Ellen, Victoria Ann; m. Maryann McBee O'Kane, Sept. 5, 1980. AA, Orange Coast Coll., 1956. Cert. data processor. Dept. mgr. Linbrook Hardware, Anaheim, Calif., 1956-66; data processing tech. cons. Hughes Aircraft Co., Fullerton, Calif., 1966-79; systems analyst Mendcino County Office Edn., Ukiah, Calif., 1980—. Republican. Morman. Avocation: ranching. Home: PO Box 336 Talmage CA 95481 Office: Mendocino County Office Edn 2240 Eastside Rd Ukiah CA 95482

GULLAND, MELINDA BETH, speech pathologist; b. Clearwater, Fla.; d. Frederick Bethel and Vallie Mae (Reed) McMullen; m. James Edward Gulland, Dec. 23, 1977; children: Amanda Bethel, Megan Eileen. AA, St. Petersburg Jr. Coll., 1971-73; student, U. Fla., 1974-75; MS, U. S. Fla., 1977. Speech pathologist Polk County Schs., Lakeland, Fla., 1978-79, Los Angeles County Schs., 1980-81; v.p. Marina Profl. Services, Long Beach, Calif., 1981—; pres., chief exec. officer Gulland & Assocs., La Palma, Calif., 1986—; bd. dirs. Creative Quality of Life Found., Glendale, Calif. 1984—. V.p. Pomona (Calif.) Continuity of Care Council, 1986—; mem. Rep. Nat. Com., Washington, 1983—. Mem. Am. Speech-Lang.-Hearing Assn., Calif. Speech-Lang.-Hearing Assn., Occupational Therapy Assn. Calif., Calif. Assn. Speech Pathologists and Audiologist in Pvt. Practice, So. Calif. Hosp. Dirs. Council, Calif. Assn. Health Facilities. Presbyterian. Avocations: waterskiing, weight lifting, jogging, reading. Home: 5082 Malaga Dr La Palma CA 90623 Office: Marina Profl Services 3938 E 4th St Long Beach CA 90814

GULLEY, EDWIN D., data processing executive; b. Wellington, Tex., Jan. 6, 1940; s. Carl Shell and Mary Wilma (Alexander) G.; m. Suzann Robison, Mar. 1, 1963; children: Gregory Edwin, Jeffrey Shell, Bradley Norman. Grad. high sch., Amarillo, Tex. Cert. in data processing. Computer operator Pioneer Natural Gas, Amarillo, 1958-59; sr. programmer Mason and Hanger-Silas Mason Co., Amarillo, 1962-66; data processing mgr. Mason and Hanger-Silas Mason Co., Grand Island, Nebr., 1966-70; sr. programmer, analyst T.I.M.E.-DC Inc., Lubbock, Tex., 1970-82; data processing mgr. N.W. Transport Service, Inc., Denver, 1982—. Adv. mem. Nebr. Vocat. Tech. Sch., Hastings, Nebr., 1968-69; pres. Lubbock Soccer Assn., 1980-81. Recipient Individual Performance award, Data Processing Mgmt. Assn., 1976, 80. Republican. Methodist. Avocations: golf, reading. Home: 12908 N Roundup Rd Parker CO 80134 Office: NW Transport Service Inc PO Box 5001 Commerce City CO 80037

GULLIXSON, CRAIG ALAN, research astronomist; b. Idaho Falls, Idaho, Sept. 11, 1956; s. Lawrence Orville and Elinor Marie (Slagle) G. BS in Physics, Idaho State U., 1979; MS in Physics, U. Wyo., 1983. Instrumentation applications specialist Lowell Obs., Flagstaff, Ariz., 1983—. Contbr. articles to profl. jours. Mem. AAAS, Am. Astron. Soc., Astron. Soc. Pacific, Sigma Xi. Republican. Methodist. Avocations: photography, wookworking, golf. Home: 3670 S Walapai #3 Flagstaff AZ 86001 Office: Lowell Obs Mars Hill Rd 1400 West Flagstaff AZ 86001

GUMBERT, MATTHEW THOMAS, savings and loan company executive; b. Phila., Aug. 21, 1956; s. Ralph Emerson and Patricia Ann (McMahon) G. BA in Social Sci., Pa. State U., Middletown. Asst. v.p. Time Savs. and Loan Co., San Francisco, 1981—. Democrat. Roman Catholic. Office: Time Savs and Loan Co 2142 Fillmore St San Francisco CA 94115

GUMM, LINLEY FORD, electronics engineer; b. Spokane, Wash., Jan. 30, 1942; s. Ford and Florence Jeanett (Smith) G.; m. Celia Frances Larson, June 6, 1964; children: Elisabeth Frances, Deborah Elaine. BSEE, Wash. State U., 1964; MSEE, U. Wash., 1970. Registered profl. engr., Oreg. Electronics engr. Tektronix, Inc., Beaverton, Oreg., 1964-76, sr. engr., 1976-81, prin. engr., 1981-85, chief engr., 1985—; cons., Beaverton, 1976—. Contbr. articles to profl. jours.; patentee in field. Chmn. tech. adv. com. Oreg. Commn. Pub. Broadcasting, Portland, 1985—. Recipient Disting. Service award Tektronix Communications Group, 1977. Mem. IEEE. Office: Tektronix Inc PO Box 500 MS 58-204 Beaverton OR 97077

GUMS, DENISE ADELE, social services administrator; b. Oakland, Calif.; d. Louis and Thelma (Derosans) G. BA in Sociology, Polit. Sci., Holy Names Coll., 1975; postgrad. studies in pub. adminstrn., Calif. State U., Hayward, 1986—. Exec. and research planning asst., then dir., then urban analyst Oakland (Calif.) Concerned Citizens for Urban Renewal, 1978-81; adminstrv. asst. Oakland Community Housing Inc., 1981-83; Bay area regional coordinator Mission Safe Shelter for the Homeless, Oakland, 1984—, asst. dir., 1986—; vice chmn., bd. dirs. Oakland Shelter, 1986—. Mem. Councilman Carter Gilmore's Adv. Com., Oakland, 1986, Oakland Homeless Council, 1985, Black Cath. Vicariate; vice-chair Oakland community bd. Oakland Ind. Support Ctr., 1987. Named Outstanding Woman of Yr., 1984; recipient Youth Citizens award EOYDC, 1984, Youth award Congl. Black Caucus, 1986. Mem. Free South Africa Movement (chair women's com.). Club: Niagara Dem. Office: Mission Safe 5406 E 14th St Oakland CA 94601

GUMUCIO, FERNANDO RAUL, foods and beverage company executive; b. Bolivia, Sept. 9, 1934; s. Julio F. G.; children: Linda, Julie, Cynthia, Beverly. B.S., U. San Francisco, 1957; M.B.A., St. Mary's Coll., 1977. Dir. mktg. Latin Am. Del Monte, Mexico, 1963-68; group product dir. Del Monte Corp., San Francisco, 1971-73, dir. sales and product mgmt., 1973-74, v.p. mktg., 1973-80, pres. dry grocery and beverage products group, 1980-85, group v.p., 1985—, pres. Del Monte U.S.A. operating group, 1985—; dir. Basic Am. Foods, San Francisco; mem., exec. bd. Nat. Food Producers Assn., Washington. Active Boy Scouts Am.; bd. regents St. Mary's Coll. Republican. Roman Catholic. Clubs: St. Francis Yacht; World Trade (San Francisco). Office: Del Monte Corp PO Box 3575 1 Market Plaza San Francisco CA 94119 *

GUNAWARDENA, SHANTI, engineer; b. Colombo, Sri Lanka, Aug. 15, 1946; came to U.S., 1971; s. Dionicious Ratnapala and Mildred (Rajapakse) G.; m. Delmi Barreto, Apr. 7, 1983; 1 child, Delani. BS in Engring., U. Ceylon, Sri Lanka, 1968; MSME, Cleve. State U., 1973; PhD, U. Calif., Berkeley, 1977. Exec. engr. Colombo Port Commn., 1968-71; teaching asst. U. Calif., Berkeley, 1973-75, research asst., 1976-77; sr. mem. research staff AT&T Technologies, Princeton, N.J., 1977-83; project leader Hewlett-Packard Labs., Palo Alto, Calif., 1983—. Recipient Maurice Simpson Tech. Editor's award Inst. Environ. Scis., 1985. Office: Hewlett-Packard Labs 3500 Deer Creek Rd Palo Alto CA 94304

GUNBERG, DAVID LEO, anatomy educator; b. Mpls., May 1, 1922; s. David and Brita Sophia (Ness) G.; m. Jorraine Aileen Jacobson, June 23, 1946; children: David, Robert, Nancy, Rebecca. AB magna cum laude, U. Redlands, 1949; MS, U. Calif., Berkeley, 1952, PhD, 1954. Instr. anatomy U. So. Calif. Sch. Medicine, Los Angeles, 1954-55; asst. prof. Oreg. Health Sci. U. Sch. Medicine, Portland, 1955-60, assoc. prof., 1960-66, prof., 1966-72; prof., chmn. dept. anatomy Oreg. Health Sci. U. Sch. Dentistry, Portland, 1975—. U. Malaya Sch. Medicine, Kuala Lumpur, Malaysia, 1972-75; vis. prof. anatomy Airlangga U., Surabaja, Indonesia, 1962-64, U. W.I., Kingston, Jamaica, 1984; external examiner U. Kebangsaan, Kuala Lumpur, 1980, U. W.I., 1982, 83, 87—. Contbr. articles to profl. jours. Pres. bd. dirs. West Hills Unitarian Fellowship, Portland, 1955—, lay minister; vis. speaker Portland schs., chs., social groups, 1955—. Served as cpl. U.S. Army, 1943-46, ETO. Named Hon. Alumnus Airlangga U. Med. Faculty, 1964. Mem. Am. Assn. Anatomists, Teratology Soc. (exec. bd. dirs. 1960-62, 66-68), European Teratology Soc., Japanese Teratology Soc. Democrat. Unitarian. Clubs: Lawn Tennis and Cricket (Surabaja(; Lake (Kuala Lumpur). Avocations: gardening, remodeling, fishing, ice hockey, squash. Home: 23950 SW Murdock Rd Sherwood OR 97140 Office: Oreg Health Scis U Sch Dentistry Dept Anatomy 611 SW Campus Dr Portland OR 97201

GUND, GEORGE, III, financier; b. Cleve., May 7, 1937; s. George and Jessica (Roesler) G.; m. Mary Theo Feld, Aug. 13, 1966; children—George, Gregory. Student, Western Res. U., Menlo (Calif.) Sch. Bus. Engaged in personal investments San Francisco, 1967—; cattle ranching Lee, Nev., 1967—; partner Calif. Seals, San Francisco, 1976-77; pres. Ohio Barons, Inc., Richfield, 1977-78; chmn. bd. Northstar Fin. Corp., Bloomington, Minn., 1978—, Minn. North Stars, Bloomington; dir. Ameritrust Cleve.; vice-chmn. Gund Investment Corp., Princeton, N.J.; chmn. North Stars Met Center Mgmt. Corp., Bloomington; v.p. hockey Sun Valley Ice Skating, Inc., Idaho. Chmn. San Francisco Internat. Film Festival, 1973—; mem. sponsors council Project for Population Action; adv. council Sierra Club Found.; mem. internat. council Mus. Modern Art, N.Y.C.; collectors com. Nat. Gallery Art; bd. dirs. Calif. Theatre Found., Bay Area Ednl. TV Assn., San Francisco Mus. Art, Cleve. Health Museum, George Gund Found., Cleve. Internat. Film Festival, Sun Valley Center Arts and Humanities, U. Nev. Reno Found., Sundance Inst. Served with USMCR, 1955-58. Clubs: Calif. Tennis (San Francisco), University (San Francisco), Olympic (San Francisco); Union (Cleve.), Cleve. Athletic (Cleve.), Kirkland Country (Cleve.), Rowfant (Cleve.); Ranier (Seattle). Office: 1821 Union St San Francisco CA 94123

GUNDERSEN, MARTIN ADOLPH, physicist, educator; b. Glenwood, Minn., May 19, 1940; s. Gilbert Theodore and Frances (Iverson) G.; m. Roberta McShirley, Dec. 20, 1963; children: Gilbert, Martin. BA, U. Calif., Berkeley, 1965; PhD in Physics, U. So. Calif., 1972. Asst. prof. elec. engring. and physics Tex. Tech U., Lubbock, 1973-77, assoc. prof., 1977-80; assoc. prof. U. So. Calif., Los Angeles, 1980-83, prof., 1983—. Contbr. numerous articles in field of quantum electronics, pulsed power and laser physics to profl. jours. Mem. IEEE, Am. Phys. Soc., Optical Soc. Am. Office: U So Calif Dept Elec Engring and Physics Los Angeles CA 90089

GUNDERSEN, WAYNE CAMPBELL, oil company executive, aluminum and chemical company executive; b. Elgin, Ill., May 27, 1936; s. LeRoy Arthur and Jean Ellen (Campbell) G.; m. Gail Andrews, Mar. 21, 1959; children—Thomas Dexter, Lori Ann, Kathy Lee. B.S., U. Nebr., 1959, M.S., 1961. Advisor fgn. ops. Standard Oil of Calif., San Francisco, 1974-76; asst. to v.p. Chevron Overseas Petroleum, San Francisco, 1976-80; dir. oil and gas Kaiser Aluminum & Chem. Corp., Oakland, Calif., 1980-81; v.p., gen. mgr. Kaiser Energy, Inc., Oakland, 1983-85, pres., 1985—; v.p. Kaiser Aluminum and Chem. Corp., Oakland, 1983—; pres. Kaiser Aluminum Exploration Co., Oakland, Kaiser Exploration and Mining Co., Oakland, 1985—; dir. Halbouty Energy Co., Houston; mem. geology adv. bd. U. Nebr., Lincoln, 1984—. Co-author articles in field. Pres. Parents Club Foothill Sch., Walnut Creek, Calif., 1978-79. Named Man-of-Yr., New Orleans Jaycees, 1973; Shell fellow, 1960-61. Mem. Am. Assn. Petroleum Geologists. Republican. Methodist. Office: Kaiser Energy Inc 300 Lakeside Dr Oakland CA 94643

GUNDERSON, ELMER MILLARD, state justice; b. Mpls., Aug. 9, 1929; s. Elmer Peter and Carmaleta (Oliver) G.; m. Lupe Gomez, Dec. 29, 1967; 1 son, John Randolph. Student, U. Minn., U. Omaha, 1948-53; LL.B., Creighton U., 1956; LL.M., U. Va., 1982; LL.D., Calif. Western Sch. Law; student appellate judges seminar, N.Y. U., 1971; LL.D., U. Pacific. Bar: Nebr. bar 1956, Nev. bar 1958. Atty.-adviser FTC, 1956-57; pvt. practice Las Vegas, 1958-71; justice Nev. Supreme Ct., 1971—, now chief justice; instr. bus. law So. regional div. U. Nev.; lectr., author bulls. felony crimes for Clark County Sheriff's Dept.; counsel Sheriff's Protective Assn.; mem. legal staff Clark Council Civil Def. Agy.; legal counsel Nev. Jaycees. Compiler, annotator: Omaha Home Rule Charter; project coordinator: Jud. Orientation Manual, 1974. Chmn. Clark County Child Welfare Bd., Nev. central chpt. Nat. Multiple Sclerosis Soc.; hon. dir. Spring Mountain Youth Camp. Served with U.S. Army. Recipient A.J.S. Herbert Harley award. Mem. Am., Nebr., Nev. bar assns.; Mem. Inst. Jud. Adminstrn., Am. Law Inst., Am. Trial Lawyers Assn., Am. Judicature Soc., Phi Alpha Delta, Alpha Sigma Nu. Office: Supreme Ct Bldg Carson City NV 89710 *

GUNDERSON, TED LEE, security consultant; b. Colorado Springs, Colo., Nov. 7, 1928. BBA, U. Nebr. Sales rep. George A. Hormel Co., Austin, Minn., 1950-51; spl. agt. in charge U.S. Dept. Justice FBI, Los Angeles, Dallas, Memphis, Phila., 1951-79; internat. security cons. Ted L. Gunderson & Assocs., Santa Monica, Calif., 1979—; cons. Calif. Narcotic Authority. Mem. Bel Air U.S. Navy League (pres.), Internat. Assn. Chiefs of Police, Am. Soc. Indsl. Security, Internat. Footprinters Assn., Nat. Football Found. and Hall of Fame, Philanthropic Soc. (Los Angeles chpt.), Sigma Alpha Epsilon. Avocations: golf, racquetball, tennis, swimming.

GUNDERSON, THOMAS JOHN, social service agency executive, consultant; b. Eureka, Calif., Dec. 10, 1943; s. Lowell Gunhart and Ruth Ann (Hayes) G.; m. Marian D'Arcy, Feb. 17, 1970; children: Thomas, Eric, William. BA, Calif. State U., Fullerton, 1967; MA, U. Chgo., 1970. Registered clin. social worker, Oreg. Psychiat. soc. worker Jewish Bd. Guardians, N.Y.C., 1970-73; dir. residential treatment Lincoln Child Ctr., Oakland, Calif., 1973-78; dir. clin. services Ala. Children's Services, Anchorage, 1978-86; exec. dir. Luth. Family Service of Oreg. and Southwest Wash., Portland, 1986—; peer reviewer Council on Accreditation of Services to Families and Children, 1982—. Active Child Care Task Force, Anchorage, 1979-80. NIMH grantee, 1969. Fellow Am. Orthopsychiat. Assn. (residential treatment task force); mem. Ala. Assn. Homes for Children (sec. 1982-85), Luth. Native Outreach (bd. dirs. 1984-85), Nat. Assn. Social Workers (sec. Ala. chpt. 1985), Ala. Soc. Clin. Social Work (sec.-treas. 1983-85), Acad. Cert. Social Workers. Democrat. Avocations: skiing, fishing, hiking, map collecting, gardening. Home: 18135 NW Clarno Ct Portland OR 97229

GUNN, GILES BUCKINGHAM, English educator, religion educator; b. Evanston, Ill., Jan. 9, 1938; s. Buckingham Willcox and Janet (Fargo) G.; m. Janet Mears Varner, Dec. 29, 1969 (div. July 1983); 1 child, Adam Buckingham; m. Deborah Rose Sills, July 9, 1983; 1 child, Abigail Rose. BA, Amherst Coll., 1959; student, Episc. Theol. Sch., Cambridge, Mass., 1959-60; MA, U. Chgo., 1963, PhD, 1967. Prof. religion and lit. U. Chgo., 1966-74; prof. religion and Am. studies U. N.C., Chapel Hill, 1974-85; prof. English and Religion U. Fla., 1984-85; prof. English U. Calif., Santa Barbara, 1985—; vis. asst. prof. religion Stanford U., Palo Alto, Calif., 1973; Benedict Disting. vis. prof. Religion Carleton Coll., Northfield, Minn., 1977; William R. Kenan Disting. vis. prof. Humanities Coll. William and Mary, Williamsburg, Va., 1983-84; dir. NEH summer sems. for coll. and univ. tchrs., 1979, 81, 85, 87. Author: F.O. Matthiessen: The Critical Achievement, 1975, The Interpretation of Otherness: Literature, Religion and the American Imagination, 1979, The Culture of Criticism and the Criticism of Culture, 1987; editor: Literature and Religion, 1971, Henry James, Senior: A Selection of His Writings, 1974, New World Metaphysics: Readings on the Religious Meaning of the American Experience, 1981, The Bible and American Arts and Letters, 1983, Church, State, and American Culture, 1984; contbr. numerous articles to profl. jours. Edward John Noble Leadership grantee, 1959-63; Amherst-Doshisha fellow, Kyoto, Japan, 1960-61, Kent fellow, Danforth Found., 1963-65, Guggenheim fellow, 1978-79. Mem. MLA, Am. Acad. Religion (dir. research and pubs. 1974-77), Am. Studies Assn., Soc. Religion, Arts and Contemporary Culture, Soc. Am. Phil. Democrat. Avocations: walking, sailing. Home: 931 W Campus Ln Goleta CA 93117 Office: Univ of Calif Dept of English Santa Barbara CA 93106

GUNSALUS, ROBERT PHILIP, microbiologist, educator, molecular geneticist; b. Ithaca, N.Y., Aug. 24, 1947; s. Irwin and Merle G. BS, S.D. State U., 1970; MS, U. Ill., 1972, PhD, 1977. Postdoctoral fellow Stanford (Calif.) U., 1978-80; asst. prof. microbiology UCLA, 1981—; mem. Moclecular Biology Inst. UCLA, Los Angeles, 1981—. Mem. AAAS, Am. Soc. Microbiology, Am. Chem. Soc, Am. Soc. Biol. Chemists. Office: UCLA Microbiology Dept 5304LS Los Angeles CA 90024

GUNSON, DIANE LEE, interior designer, consultant; b. Mpls., Oct. 4, 1947; d. Elmer Eugene and Nancy Louise (Thom) Engelbert. BA, U. Colo., 1969. Interior designer St. Paul Book and Stationery, 1966, Hal Lipstein's Design Forum, Denver, 1969, Howard Lorton Inc., Denver, 1969-84, First Impressions, Denver, 1984—. Chmn. bd. dirs. Olympics of the Mind, 1985—. Mem. Am. Soc. Interior Designers (accredited, sec. 1983-84), Phi Beta Kappa. Republican. Presbyterian. Avocations: skiing, tennis, hiking, cooking, golf.

GUNSUL, DIANE VERN, air force logistician; b. Seattle, Mar. 7, 1939; d. Frank Justus and Phyllis Emmerette (Webster) G.; m. Roy Earl Hicks, May 10, 1976 (dec. Mar. 1986). BA in Mgmt., St. Mary's Coll., Moraga, Calif., 1982. With adminstrv. dept. U.S. Govt., Washington, 1963-70; with clerical dept., HQ MAAG U.S. Govt., Taipei, Republic of China, 1971-73; adminstrv. officer U.S. Embassy, Saigon, Republic of Vietnam, 1973-75; logistics mgmt. specialist USAF, Sacramento, 1975—; chief plans and programs sect. 1982. Contbr. articles to China News newspaper. Judge annual student speakers program Lions Clubs Internat., Sacramento, 1984. Recipient Spl. Achievement award USAF, 1980, 2 Sustained Superior Performance awards USAF, 1984, 85. Mem. Soc. Logistics Engrs. (sr., publicity chmn. Sacramento chpt. 1983-85). Avocations: vegetable gardening, biking, reading. Office: Sacramento Air Logistics Ctr Plans and Programs sect McClellan AFB CA 95652

GUPTA, ANSHOO SUDHIR, marketing professional; b. Kota, Rajasthan, India, Dec. 5, 1946; came to U.S., 1968; s. Dwarka Das and Vimla (Jain) G.; m. Jyotsna Anshoo Prasad, Dec. 24, 1973; children: Ankur Sudhir, Roli. BSEE with honors, Indian Inst. Tech., Kharagpur, 1968; MSEE, U. Rochester, 1969, MBA, 1971. V.p. fin. Systems Mktg. div. Xerox Corp., El Segundo, Calif., 1983-84, v.p. mktg. Bus. Systems Group, 1985—; dir. Xerox Employees Fed. Credit Union, El Segundo, 1978-82. Home: 30104 Via Victoria Rancho Palos Verdes CA 90274 Office: Xerox Corp 101 Continental Blvd ES-XC15J El Segundo CA 90274

GUPTA, BIMLESHWAR PRASAD, mechanical engineer, researcher; b. Jaipur, Raj, India, May 17, 1946; s. Hari Prasad and Sarla D. (Agarwal) G.; m. Rajni Garg, Dec. 10, 1974; children: Anjli, Neeraj. BSME, U. Jodhpur, India, 1968; MSME, U. Minn., 1971, MBA, 1974. Registered profl. engr., Colo. Engr. Honeywell Inc., Mpls., 1974-76, sect. mgr., 1976-78; program mgr. Solar Energy Research Inst., Golden, Colo., 1978—; lectr. in field. Contbr. articles to profl. jours. Mem. ASME (assoc. editor jour. 1983-85), Internat. Solar Energy Soc., India Assn. Colo. (exec. com. 1983-84). Club: Toastmasters (Lakewood, Colo.) (pres. 1985). Home: 14373 W Bayaud Pl Golden CO 80401 Office: Solar Energy Research Inst 1617 Cole Blvd Golden CO 80401

GURBUZ, ERGIN, quality engineer; b. Istanbul, Turkey, Feb. 27, 1944; came to U.S., 1968; s. Muharrem and Fatma (Kaptan) G.; m. Katherine Eddy, Jan. 7, 1969 (div. Feb. 1975); 1 child, Eriz; m. Theresa Marie Franco, June 25, 1976. Tchr. Gedikpasa Jr. High, Istanbul, 1965-66; bacteriologist DEVA, Istanbul, 1968; quality control tech. Coors Porcelain Co., Golden, Colo., 1969-72; inspector Sundstrand Aviation, Denver, 1972-84, quality planner, 1984-87, quality engr., 1987—. Served as 1st lt. Army Turkey, 1966-68. Mem. Am. Soc. Quality Control (cert.), U.S. Soccer Fedn. (state referee), Soccer Officials Assn. Colo. Office: Sundstrand Aviation 2480 W 70th Ave Denver CO 80221

GURZI, WILLIAM ROBERT, advertising and public relations company executive; b. Long Beach, Calif., July 14, 1947; s. Dominic F. and Carmela M. (Bongiorno) G. BS in Journalism, Calif. Poly. State U., San Luis Obispo, 1971. mem. pub. relations com. Calif. State U., Dominguez Hills. On-air and various mgmt. positions various radio stas., Calif., Iowa, Idaho, 1971-77; account exec. KID-TV div. CBS, Pocatello, Idaho, 1977-79; dir. mktg. and pub. relations Long Beach YMCA, 1979-81; dir. pub. relations Greg Smith & Assocs. Advt. Agy., Santa Ana, Calif., 1981-82; prin. Gurzi & Assocs. Advt./Pub. Relations, Long Beach, 1982—. Bd. dirs. YMCA, Long Beach, 1983-86, Goodwill Industries of So. Los Angeles County, 1984-85; sec., Downtown Long Beach Assocs.; chmn. Downtown Long Beach Assocs. Polit. Action Com., 1986—; co-founder Karing For Kids, Long Beach, 1984; emcee Miss Idaho-USA Pageant, Pocatello and Boise, 1979-85; mem. mayor's adv. com. Downtown Long Beach Urban Design Study. Named one of Outstanding Young Men in Am., Jaycees, 1981, 84; recipient Addy award Des Moines Ad Club., 1974. Mem. Advt. Club. Los Angeles. Republican. Lodge: Kiwanis (Best Newsletter Gold div. award 1985, El toro award 1985). Avocations: running, weightlifting, racquetball, travel. Office: 320 Pine Ave Suite 610 Long Beach CA 90802

GUSKE, JACK DEAN, educator; b. Tacoma, June 11, 1951; s. Fred and Evelyn Maude (Lowell) G.; m. Alura Colleen O'Keefe, Aug. 25, 1979; 1 child, Brett. BS in Psychology, BA in Communications, Wash. State U., 1974, MA in Edn., 1983; postgrad., U.S. Army Commd. and Gen. Staff Coll., 1986. Tchr. Washtucna (Wash.) Sch. Dist., 1979—; engr. Sta. KNOI-KO, Pullman, Wash., 1977-79. Pub. Tucna Times, 1979— (2d pl. Quill and Scroll award), Wildcat (Showcase award 1984, Gallup award 1985). Trustee Adams County Hist. Soc., Ritzville, Wash., 1985—; commr. Adams County Centennial, Ritzville, 1985—. Served to commdr. USAR, 1974—. Grantee Wash. State Commn. Humanities, 1983, 85. Mem. Wash. Edn. Assn., Wash. Library Media Assn., Wash. Journalism Edn. Assn., Wash. State Research Counicl, N.G. Assn. Lodge: Lions (v.p. 1983-84). Avocations: woodworking, hunting, amateur radio.

GUSMAN, SAMUEL, chemist; b. N.Y.C., Oct. 14, 1925; s. Frank and Bella (Slote) G.; m. Carolyn Strauss, June 29, 1947; children: John Frank, David Morris. SB, MIT, 1946, SM, 1947; PhD, Brown U., 1950. Research mgr. Rohm & Haas Co., 1950-76; pres. Warrenteed Pharm., 1950-76; cons., sr.

assoc. The Conservation Found., 1976-84, policy dialogue cons., 1984-86, sr. fellow, 1984—; mem. program steering com. Dubos Ctr., N.Y.C.; com. mem. Nat. Acad. Scis., Nat. Research Council; chmn. Adminstrs. Pesticide Adv. Com., EPA. Author: Public Policy for Chemicals, 1980; contbr. articles to profl. jours.; patentee in field. Founding pres. Taos (N.Mex.) Community Orch., 1985-86, bd. dirs. 1986—; mem adv. bd. Millicent Rogers Mus., Taos, 1986—. Recipient Environ. Regeneration award Rene Dubos Ctr., 1984. Mem. Am. Chem. Soc., Tau Beta Pi, Sigma Xi. Avocations: photography, sculpting, painting, skiing, hiking. Home: PO Box 1876 Taos NM 87571

GUST, (JOHN) DEVENS, JR., chemist, educator; b. Phoenix, Nov. 28, 1944; s. John Devens and Mary Elizabeth (Montgomery) G.; m. Elaine Alice Leachman, Dec. 26, 1969; children: Karen Alison, John Devens III. BS in Chemistry, Stanford U., 1967; MA in Chemistry, Princeton U., 1972, PhD in Chemistry, 1974. Postdoctoral assoc. Calif. Inst. Tech., Pasadena, 1974-75; asst. prof. Ariz. State U., Tempe, 1975-80, assoc. prof., 1980-85, prof., 1985—; vis. prof. biophysics Muséum Nat. d'Histoire Naturelle, Paris, 1982, 85; vis. scientist CEN Saclay, Paris, 1982-83, 84. Contbr. articles to profl. jours. Served to sgt. U.S. Army, 1969-71. Mem. Am. Chem. Soc., Am. Soc. Photobiology, Phi Beta Kappa, Sigma Xi, Phi Lambda Upsilon. Office: Ariz State U Dept Chemistry Tempe AZ 85287

GUSTAFSON, ALBERT KATSUAKI, lawyer, engineer; b. Harimachida, Tokyo, Dec. 5, 1949; came to U.S., 1951; s. William A. and Akiko (Osada) G.; m. Helen Melissa Laird, July 31, 1971 (div. 1975); m. Karen Jane Ekblad, Dec. 31, 1978. B.A. with distinction, Stanford U., 1972; J.D., U. Wash., 1980. Bar: Wash. 1981, U.S. Dist. Ct. (we. dist.) Wash. 1981, U.S. Ct. Appeals (9th cir.) 1984. Acoustics analyst Boeing Co., Seattle, 1973-74, materiel buyer, 1974; legal editor, book pub. co., Seattle, 1975-76; research analyst Batelle Inst., Seattle, 1975-76; legal intern Office of U.S. Atty., Seattle, 1976; engr. U.P.R.R., 1977-85; corp. counsel Ansette Fin. Corp., Inc., Seattle, 1987—; pres. Albert K. Gustafson, P.S., Seattle, 1981—; corp. counsel Dorden, Inc., Centralia, Wash., 1984—, Ansette Fin. Corp., Inc., Seattle, 1987. Sec. local 117-E, United Transp. Union, 1984, local vice-chmn., 1984; Dem. precinct chmn., 1984. Kraft scholar, 1968; Calif. State scholar, 1968-72. Mem. Assn. Trial Lawyers Am., Wash. State Trial Lawyers Assn., ABA, Fed. Bar Assn., Seattle-King County Bar Assn., Seattle C. of C. Democrat. Presbyterian. Club: College. Lodges: Masons, Shriners, Order of DeMolay (master councilor 1968), Rotary. Home: 3971 Evanston Ave N Seattle WA 98103 Office: 804 First Interstate Ctr 999 Third Ave Seattle WA 98104 Office: Fuji Bldg 8F, 3-18-6 Hatchbori Chuo-ku, Tokyo 104, Japan

GUSTAFSON, CARL ROHN, management consultant; b. Bklyn., June 6, 1939; s. Richard Melker and Alette (Inger) G.; m. Joanne C. Rinse. Artium degree, Kingsyard Coll., Stavanger, Norway, 1960; B.Sc. in Bus. Adminstrn., U. Calif.-Berkeley, 1963; cert. in internat. bus., Strathclyde U., Glasgow, Scotland, 1961. Prodn. planner Crown Zellerbach, 1963-65; with Carl Gustafson Advt., pub. Businessmen's Newsletter and Australia Newsletter, 1965-76; pres. Gustafson & Assocs., Walnut Creek, Calif., Newport Beach, Calif., Dallas, Denver, Chgo., Atlanta, N.Y.C., 1976—; pub. The Gustafson Report, 1984—. Bd. regents John F. Kennedy U., Orinda, Calif., 1978—. Served with Army NG, 1963-69. Address: Box 309 Lafayette CA 94549

GUSTAFSON, JAMES ARTHUR, architect; b. Oak Park, Ill., Nov. 12, 1943; s. Arthur Elias and Anne Gizelle (Plaza) G.; m. Mary Brent Childers, May 30, 1970; children—Britta Anne, Kalli Anelia, Sonya Marie. B.Arch., U. Ill., 1966. Registered architect, Colo. Draftsman, designer Caudill Assocs., Aspen, Colo., 1970-74, project architect, 1975-79, prin., Caudill Gustafson & Assocs., Aspen, 1980-84, pres., 1984—. Chmn. Snowmass Village Planning commn., Colo., 1981-86, Snowmass Village Bd. of Examiners, 1979-86; architect Snowmass Design Rev. Bd., 1980-86; v.p. bd. dirs. Homeowners, Snowmass Village. Served as 1st lt. U.S. Army, 1966-69; Vietnam. Decorated Bronze Star. Recipient Aspen Community Service award City of Aspen, 1980-86. Mem. Am. Arbitration Assn. (panel mem. Colo. 1983-86), AIA, Colo. Soc. Architects, Council of Ednl. Facility Planners Internat. Home: PO Box 6067 Snowmass Village CO 81615 Office: Caudill Gustafson & Assocs Box FF Aspen CO 81612

GUSTAFSON, LEIF VALENTINE, consulting engineer; b. Gothenburg, Sweden, Dec. 31, 1911; s. Oscar Gustaf and Olga Alida (Anderson) G.; B.S. in Civil and Structural Engring., Chalmers Inst. Tech. (Sweden), 1934; post-grad. in bus. adminstrn. Alexander Hamilton Inst., 1969; m. Joan Miller, Nov. 15, 1969; children—Glenn Nordhal, Linda Margaret. Registered profl. engr., engring. contractor. Chief structural engr. Elec. Bond & Share Co., N.Y.C., 1947-52; supervising engr. Bechtel Corp., Los Angeles, 1952-61; pres., owner Leif Engring. & Constrn. Corp., Studio City, Calif., 1961-67; mgr. engring. Western Precipitation, Los Angeles, 1967-69; pres., gen. mgr. Esco Internat., Guam, Saipan, 1969-74; dep. dir. pub. works Govt. Am. Samoa, Pago Pago, 1974-76; cons. ballistics and space systems div. U.S. Army, 1962-65; bd. Project 75 Dept. Def. Served with U.S. Army, 1943-45. Mem. Nat. Soc. Profl. Engrs. Republican. Clubs: Swedish (past pres. Los Angeles); Showboat Country. Maj. designer minute man and Atlas launching systems; inventor hydrolaunch system, sonic electrostatic precipitator, acid applications electrostatic precipitator, knob conveyor; contbr. articles on missile launching designs. Home: 17902 Hyacinth Dr Sun City West AZ 85375

GUSTAVSON, DEAN LEONARD, architect; b. Salt Lake City, June 27, 1924; s. Ernest L. and Leona (Hansen) G.; m. Barbara Knight, Apr. 28, 1944; children—Mark Steven, Lisa Ann, Clint Knight. Student, U. Utah, 1946-47; B.Arch., U. Calif-Berkeley, 1951. Individual practice architecture Salt Lake City, 1953—; pres. Gustavson Assocs., Inc. (formerly Dean L. Gustavson Assos. architects and planners), Salt Lake City, 1957-86, Gustavson, Nelson and Panushka, Inc. (architects), Salt Lake City, 1976-82, Gustavson Group Inc. (design and constrn. mgrs.), 1978—; mng. architect U. Utah Med. Center Additions Project, 1975-82; pres. Nat. Council Archtl. Registration Bds., 1969-70; project mgr. U. Calif.-Berkeley Bioscis. Additions Complex, 1982—; co-chmn. Internat. Com. Archtl. Registration, 1970—; chmn. World Conf. on Edn. and Reciprocity of Architects, Amsterdam, Holland, 1971; Chmn. planning Salt Lake City's Second Century Plan, 1960-62; mem. Utah Air Travel Commn., 1987—. Mem. Utah Air Travel Commn., 1987—. Served with USAAF, 1942-46. Fellow A.I.A. (pres. Utah chpt. 1959-60, chmn. chpt. task force on objectives and means 1974); mem. Salt Lake C. of C. (chmn. econ. devel. steering com. 1980-85, com. of 100), U.S. C. of C. Clubs: Ft. Douglas (Salt Lake City); Bloomington (Utah) Country. Dean L. Gustavson award established in his honor NCARB, 1974. Home: 5775 Highland Dr Salt Lake City UT 84121 Office: 630 E South Temple Salt Lake City UT 84102

GUSTIN, NELSON SAGE, manufacturing co. exec.; b. Detroit, July 7, 1919; s. Nelson Sage and Florence (Sharp) G.; B.A., Pomona Coll., 1943; m. Yvonne Sheridan, July 14, 1943; children—Sheridan, Christopher, David. Pres., N.S. Gustin Co., 1947—, Design Craft Corp., Los Angeles, 1947—. Mem. Young Pres.'s Orgn. Republican. Episcopalian. Office: 1933 S Broadway Los Angeles CA 90007

GUSTINE, DIXIE LEE ALMS, speech pathologist; b. Mattoon, Ill., Nov. 30, 1952; d. Everett Roy and Hilda Lee (Jenkins) Alms; m. Thomas Harold Gustine, Aug. 9, 1975. BS in Edn., Eastern Ill. U., 1974, MS, 1975. Cert. tchr. Ill. Speech and lang. pathologist Hoopeston (Ill.)-Rankin Schs., 1975-77; speech and lang. pathologist Big Sky Spl. Edn. Coop., Conrad, Mont., 1977—, supr. speech and lang. pathology, 1981—. Mem. Am. Speech, Lang. and Hearing Assn. (cert. clin. competence, continuing edn. award 1985), Mont. Speech, Lang. and Hearing Assn., Council for Exceptional Children, Conrad Jaycee Women (bd. dirs. 1978-79, treas. 1980-81, pres. 1982-83) Conrad Jaycees (sec.-treas. 1985—). Republican. Lutheran. Avocations: reading, sewing, camping, hiking. Home: 518 S Wisconsin St Conrad MT 59425 Address: Meadowlark Sch 215 S Maryland St Conrad MT 59425

GUTAI, LASZLO SANDOR, research physicist; b. Budapest, Hungary, Oct. 7, 1936; came to U.S., 1979; s. Istvan and Ilona (Glatter) G.; m. Anna Maria Becsi, Aug. 11, 1965; 1 child, Sophie Alexandra. BS, L. Eotvos U., Budapest, 1959; diploma, L. Eotvos U., 1960; PhD, Acad. Scis., 1975. Asst. prof. L. Eotvos U., 1960-62; from research physicist to sr. physicist Research Inst. for Tech. Physics, Budapest, 1962-79; sr. mem. tech. staff Signetics/Philips, Sunnyvale, Calif., 1980—. Contbr. articles to profl. jours. Mem. ASTM, IEEE. Avocations: camping, gardening, reading. Office: Signetics Co 811 Arques Sunnyvale CA 94088

GUTENBERG, ARTHUR WILLIAM, mechanical engineer, business policy educator; b. Darmstadt, Republic of Germany, Nov. 10, 1920; came to U.S., 1930; s. Beno and Hertha (Dernburg) G.; m. Natalie Maxine Shapiro, Feb. 7, 1946 (div. Oct. 1972); children: Jeff S., Arlan P., Lee F., Susan B., Diane H.; m. Barbara Ann Franklin, Aug. 8, 1974. BAS, U. Calif., Berkeley, 1942, BS, 1946, MBA, 1947; PhD, Stanford U., 1955. Registered mechanical engr., Ariz., indsl. engr., Calif. Head econ. research Pan Am. Airlines, S. San Francisco, Calif., 1947-48; instr. Fresno (Calif.) State U., 1948-51; from. asst. to assoc. prof. Ariz. State U., Tempe, 1951-60; prof. U. So. Calif., Los Angeles, 1960—; cons., lectr. A.W. Gutenberg, Inc., Pasadena, Calif., 1949—. Author books in bus. mgmt. Chmn. productivity adv. com., Los Angeles Bd. Supervision, 1982-84; active Town Hall Sect. of Systems and Procedures, 1982—. Served to 1st lt. Mil. Intelligence, 1942-45. Fellow Standard Oil of Calif., 1953. Fellow Aurisa-Australian Land Info. Assn.; mem. Am. Acad. Mgmt., Am. Stats. Assn. (nat. bd. dirs. 1974-76), Inst. Indsl. Engrings. (local officer 1978-84). Home: 1105 Mesita Rd Pasadena CA 91107 Office: U So Calif Univ Park Peter Stark Program Los Angeles CA 90089-0111

GUTENBERG, DIANE HELEN, social worker; b. Phoenix, Mar. 29, 1959. BA in Psychology, U. Calif., Davis, 1981; MSW, UCLA, 1984. Clin. social worker Los Angeles County Rancho Los Amigos Med. Ctr., Downey, Calif., 1984—; expert jury solicited witness, Calif., 1985. Mem. Nat. Kidney Found. (So. Calif. chpt.), Nat. Assn. Social Workers. Avocations: cooking, entertaining, music, racquetball. Office: Rancho Los Amigos Med Ctr 7601 E Imperial Hwy Downey CA 90242

GUTHRIE, JAMES WILLIAMS, educator; b. Chgo., Aug. 28, 1936; s. James Williams and Florence (Harvey) G.; m. Paula Humphreys Skene, Feb. 26, 1976; 1 son, James Kyle; children by previous marriage: Sarah Virginia, James Williams, Shannon Louise. B.A., Stanford U., 1958; M.A., 1960, Ph.D., 1968. High sch. tchr. Arcata, Calif., 1960-61, Palo Alto, Calif., 1961-64; asst. to dean Sch. Edn. Stanford U., 1965-66; spl. asst. to sec. Dept. HEW, Washington, 1966-67; prof. U. Calif., Berkeley, 1967-70; Alfred North Whitehead postdoctoral fellow Harvard U., 1970; dep. dir. N.Y. State Edn. Commn., 1971-72; edn. specialist U.S. Senate, Washington, 1972-73; prof. edn. U. Calif., Berkeley, 1973-80; chmn. dept. edn. U. Calif., 1981-83; cons. HEW, AID, also state legislatures Chile, N.J., N.Y., Fla., Calif., Alaska, Oreg., Wash. Author: Schools and Inequality, 1970, New Models for American Education, 1971, State School Finance Alternatives, 1975, School Finance: Economics and Politics of Public Education, 1978, School Finance Policies and Practices, 1980, Educational Administration and Policy, 1986, Ed School: A Brief for Professional Education, 1987; editor: Educational Evaluation and Policy Analysis. Mem. City of Berkeley Bd. Edn., 1975-82, pres., 1976-77; mem. City of Berkeley Transp. Commn., 1987—, Calif. Commn. on Tchr. Credentialing, 1982-84; chmn. bd. dirs. Berkeley-Albany YMCA, 1977—; bd. dirs. Alta Bates Hosp., 1981-85. Recipient cert. of merit Am. Public Adminstrn. Assn., 1976; grantee U.S. Office of Edn., 1968-69, Ford Found., 1970-73, Hewlett Found., 1982—, Clark Found., 1986—. Mem. Am. Ednl. Research Assn., Phi Delta Kappa. Episcopalian. Home: 52 Oakvale St Berkeley CA 94705 Office: U Calif Room 3659 Tolman Hall Berkeley CA 94720

GUTHRIE, LYNDA LAYTON, corporate professional; b. Seattle, Mar. 16, 1940; divorced; 3 children. BA in History and Govt., Mills Coll., 1963; M in Pub. Adminstrn., U. San Francisco, 1983. Dir. coll. events Mills Coll., Oakland, Calif., 1973-75; coordinator community edn. Indian Valley Colls., Marin Community Coll. Dist., Novato, Calif., 1975-80; exec. dir. Richmond (Calif.) Art Ctr., 1980-83; assoc. dir. conv. and assoc. mem. services Western States Meat Assn., Oakland, 1983—. Home: 1018 Mariposa Ave Berkeley CA 94707 Office: Western States Meat Assn 1615 Broadway Suite 1200 Oakland CA 94612-2115

GUTHRIE, SALLY RECORD, publishing executive; b. Jan. 19, 1929; d. Harry Evans and Marian J. (Looney) Record; m. Donald L. Guthrie, Aug. 19, 1950; children: Jessica, J. Benjamin, Daniel, Donald Jr., Mary Scott. BA, Elmira Coll., 1950, MS, 1964. Editor Homelite div. Textron, Port Chester, N.Y., 1970-72; editor, dir. publications Jonathan Club, Los Angeles, 1973—. Editor Probable Cause, 1980. Mem. Town Hall, Los Angeles, 1980—. Recipient Mark of Excellence, Kimberly Clark, Los Angeles, 1975. Mem. Internat. Assn. Bus. Communicators (sec. bd. dirs. 1977-78, Bronze Quill award 1983). Republican. Roman Catholic. Avocations: reading, bicycling, flower arranging.

GUTHRIE, ZACHARY O'NIEL, safety engineer; b. Tyler, Tex., Sept. 16, 1956; s. Johnie Ruth and Dollie Dimple (King) G.; m. Carolyn Ann Williams, Feb. 2, 1984. BS Indsl. Arts, Tex. A&M U., 1980. Profl. football player Cin. Bengals, 1980-81; safety engr. Amoco Prodn. Co., Hobbs, N.Mex., 1981-86; with Tyler (Tex.) Ind. Sch. Dist., 1986—. Mem. Am. Soc. Safety Engrs. (v.p. 1983-84, sec. 1984-85), ARC (chmn. 1983-84), Iota Lambda, Iota Sigma. Democrat. Methodist. Club: Aggie (fund raiser 1984-85). Lodge: Lions. Avocations: football, auto racing, hunting, fishing, reading.

GUTIERREZ, FRANCISCO XAVIER, lawyer; b. El Paso, Tex., Jan. 18, 1957; s. Candelario and Guadalupe (Saenz) G.; m. Eugenia Garcia, Dec. 10, 1977; children: Trina Marie, Manuel Javier, Vanessa Monique. BS, Ariz. State U., 1980, JD, 1983. Bar: Ariz. 1984, U.S. Dist. Ct. Ariz. 1984. Assoc. Daniel Ortega, P.C., Phoenix, 1982—; ptnr. Gutierrez, Contreras, Padilla & Salaiz, P.C., Phoenix, 1984—; bd. dirs. State of Ariz. Bd. Psychologist Examiners; hearing officer S. Phoenix Justice Ct., 1986—. Mem. Assn. Trial Lawyers Am., Ariz. Trial Lawyers Assn., Maricopa County (Ariz.) Bar Assn., Los Abogados Hispanic Bar Assn. Ariz., South Mountain C. of C. Democrat. Roman Catholic. Lodge: Kiwanis. Office: Gutierrez Contreras et al 6033 S Central Ave Phoenix AZ 85040

GUTIERREZ, RALPH, engineering educator; b. Los Angeles, Dec. 23, 1931; s. Jose and Antonia (Acosta) G.; m. Lorene Mae Kesler, Aug. 21, 1954; children: Dennie, Denise, Jolie, Ralph. BA in Vocat. Edn., Calif. State U., Los Angeles, 1972. Coll. work study, fin. aids advisor Pasadena (Calif.) City Coll., 1971-73, coordinator coop. edn. and student placement services, 1973-78, coordinator, assoc. prof. coop. work experience edn., 1978-83, assoc. prof. engring. and tech., 1983—. Bd. dirs. Mid-Valley Mental Health, 1979—; mem. Cable TV Selection Adv. Com., El Monte Calif., 1980; adv. com. mem. Mexican-Am. Cultural Inst. Rio Hondo Coll., Whittier, Calif., 1978—. Nat. Ctr. Vol. Action, 1976-80, Women's Equity Action League, 1976-80; vice pres. Alumni Assn. Roosevelt High Sch., Los Angeles, 1966—; ednl. liaison Am. GI Form, 1982—. Served as cpl. U.S. Army, 1952-54. Mem. Pasade Am. Legion. Lodge: Masons. Avocations: product devel., recreation. Home: 10021 Brockway El Monte CA 91733 Office: Pasadena City Coll 1570 E Colo Blvd Pasadena CA 91106

GUTJAHR, ALLAN LEO, mathematics educator; b. Hosmer, S.D., Mar. 20, 1938; s. Christian E. and Emma Preszler; m. Ellen Troxel, Nov. 21, 1959, (div. 1978); children: Kurt, Eric, Kristin; m. Margaret Rae Sjostedt, Aug. 15, 1981; children: Ted, Meghan. Student, Cen. Wash. Coll., 1958-59; BS in Math., U. Wash., 1962; MSE, Johns Hopkins U., 1963; PhD in Stats., Rutgers U., 1970. Mem. tech staff Bell Labs., Holmdel, N.J., 1962-71; prof. math. N.Mex. Tech. U., Socorro, 1971—, chmn. dept. math., 1985—; vis. researcher Ecole Des Mines, Paris, 1978, U.S. Geol. Survey, Denver, 1978. Contbr. articles to profl. jours. Served with U.S. Army, 1956-58. Mem. Am. Geophys. Union, Math. Assn. Am., Sigma Xi, Pi Mu Epsilon. Avocations: reading, writing. Home: 445 Aquina Ct Belen NM 87002

GUTJAHR, HAROLD CALVIN, oil company executive; b. Hosmer, S.D., Mar. 24, 1930; s. Chris C. and Ann B. (Sayler) G.; m. Ilene M. Jermiason, July 12, 1957; children—Karen, Paul. B.S. in Bus. Adminstrn., U. Denver, 1952; M.B.A., 1952. C.P.A. Treas., Fin. Consol. Oil & Gas, Inc., Denver, 1961-72, v.p., 1972-79, sr. v.p. fin., 1979—, bd. dirs., 1974—. Served with U.S. Army, 1952-54. Republican. Home: 2741 S Fillmore St Denver CO 80210 Office: Consol Oil & Gas Inc 1860 Lincoln St Denver CO 80295

GUTTMANN, KARL, consulting mechanical engineer; b. Vienna, Austria, May 11, 1919 came to U.S., 1949; s. Otto and Friederike (Kraus) G.; m. Clarice Brown, Jan. 18, 1954 (div. May 1955); m. Ethel Weiner, Jan. 31, 1958; 1 child, Steven O. M.E. with honors, Vienna State Coll. Engring., 1938. Registered profl. engr., Calif., Oreg., Wis., D.C., Utah. Vice pres. Kasin, Guttmann & Assocs., San Francisco, 1956-77; pres. Guttmann & MacRitchie, San Francisco, 1977—; mem. Calif. Bldg. Safety Bd., 1986—; mem. San Francisco Seismic Hazard Evaluation Com., 1978—; tech. adviser Calif. Energy Commn., 1981—. Fellow ASHRAE (life mem.; pres. Golden Gate chpt. 1960-61); mem. Am. Assn. Energy Engrs. Club: Engineers (San Francisco). Home: 389 Upper Terr San Francisco CA 94117 Office: Guttmann & MacRitchie 1300 Sutter St San Francisco CA 94109

GUY, RICHARD HENRY, pharmacy educator; b. London, Nov. 27, 1954; came to U.S., 1980; s. Richard Henry and Olive Marjorie (Newberry) G.; m. Anna Helen Read, Aug. 20, 1977; children: Elizabeth Anna, Philip Richard. MA with honors, U. Oxford, Eng., 1977; PhD, U. London, 1980. Asst. prof. pharmacy and pharm. chemistry U. Calif., San Francisco, 1980—; cons. various pharm. cos., 1982—; mem. sci. adv. bd. HERCON, South Plainsfield, N.J., 1986—. Contbr. articles to profl. jours. Grantee EPA, Nat. Inst. Gen. Med. Scis., Nat. Inst. Child Health and Human Devel., Nat. Inst. Occupational Safety and Health; named Hon. Prof. U. Wales Inst. Sci. and Tech., 1986. Mem. Am. Chem. Soc., Royal Soc. Chemistry, AAAS, Am. Assn. Pharm. Scientists, Controlled Release Soc. (Pennwalt award 1983), Soc. Investigative Dermatology. Office: U Calif Sch Pharmacy San Francisco CA 94143

GUYNN, STEFANIE CAROL, social worker; b. N.Y.C., Apr. 25, 1938; d. David L. and Beatrice (Gould) Blum; m. William Howard Guynn, July 31, 1965; children: Jessica Rachel, Noah David. BA magna cum laude, Barnard Coll., 1959; Student, Harvard U. and Radcliffe Coll., 1959-61; MSW, U. Calif., Berkeley, 1970. Lic. clin. social work, Calif. Librarian U. Calif., Berkeley, 1961-66; psychiat. social worker Calif. State Dept. Mental Hygiene, Oakland, 1972-74; social casework specialist II Social Service Dept., Richmond, Calif., 1974-84; social work supr. II Social Service Dept., Martinez, Calif., 1984—; field work supr. U. Calif. Sch. Social Welfare, Berkeley, 1985—. Woodrow Wilson fellow, 1959-60; Radcliffe Coll. grantee, 1960-61, NIMH, 1966-67, Calif. State Dept. Mental Hygiene, 1967-68. Mem. Nat. Assn. Social Workers (cert.), Phi Beta Kappa. Jewish. Home: 643 Vincente Ave Berkeley CA 94707 Office: Social Service Dept Contra Costa County 30 Muir Rd Martinez CA 94553

GUZIEC, FRANK STANLEY, JR., chemistry educator; b. Chgo., Sept. 16, 1946; s. Frank Stanley and Jean (Swiniuch) G.; m. Joan McClure, Apr. 15, 1972; 1 child, Daniel. BS with honors, Loyola U., Chgo., 1968; PhD, MIT, 1972. Research assoc. Imperial Coll., London, 1972-74, MIT, Cambridge, Mass., 1975-76, Wesleyan U., Middletown, Conn., 1976-77; asst. prof. Tufts U., Medford, Mass., 1977-81; assoc. prof. N.Mex. State U., Las Cruces, 1981—. Mem. Am. Chem. Soc. (sect. chmn. 1984). Episcopalian. Office: NMex State U Chemistry Dept Las Cruces NM 88003

GUZMAN, DIANNE BELLE, county government official; b. El Paso, Tex., July 9, 1944; d. Caswell MacIntyre Hunter. BS, U. Ariz., 1966. Planner San Bernardino County (Calif.) Planning Dept., 1967-79; asst. dir. San Diego County Planning Dept., 1980-81; dir. Santa Barbara County (Calif.) Resource Mgmt. dept., 1981—; mem. Calif. Planning Roundtable, Sacramento, 1981—. Mem. Am. Planning Assn. (sect. pres. 1981-82), Urban Land Inst. Office: Resource Mgmt Dept 123 E Anapamu Santa Barbara CA 93101

GUZMAN, PABLO MONZON, beer company executive; b. El Paso, Tex., Sept. 26, 1956; s. Leopoldo and Socorro (Monzon) G. BBA, Coll. Santa Fe, 1979. Auditor State of N.Mex., Santa Fe, 1979-80; sales rep. Adolph Coors Co., Denver, 1980-81, area mgr., 1981-82, project mgr., 1982-83; asst. div. mgr. Adolph Coors Co., San Francisco, 1983-84; div. mgr. Adolph Coors Co., Denver, 1985-86; mgr. regional nat. accts. Adolph Coors Co., Chgo., 1986—; cons. San Jose (Calif.) GI Forum, 1983-84. Mem. Am. Mgmt. Assn. Club: Pace (Golden, Colo.). Avocations: basketball, golf, young adult seminars to teach about drug and alcohol abuse.

GUZOFSKY, MICHAEL ROBERT, advertising executive; b. Denver, Sept. 22, 1955; s. Harold and Vivian E. (Cohn) G. m. Cheryl A. Biasella, Sept. 1, 1983. BS, U. Tex., 1977. Mgr. Samsonite Corp., Denver, 1978-80; pres., creative dir. Guzofsky Communications, Denver, 1980—; owner PageWorks, Denver, 1987—; chief exec. officer, gen. ptnr. Intuitive Solutions Ltd., 1986—. Mem. Antidefamation League, Denver Advt. Fedn., Art Dirs. Club of Denver. Jewish. Avocations: tennis, cycling, photography, music. Office: Guzofsky Communications Inc 8801 E Hampden Suite 210 Denver CO 80231

GUZY, MARGUERITA LINNES, educator; b. Santa Monica, Calif., Nov. 19, 1938; d. Paul William Robert and Margarete (Rodowski) Linnes; m. Stephen Paul Guzy, Aug. 25, 1962; 1 child, David Paul. AA, Santa Monica Coll., 1959; student, U. Mex., 1959-60; BA, UCLA, 1966, MA, 1973. Cert. secondary tchr., Calif. Tchr. Inglewood (Calif.) Unified Sch. Dist., 1967—, chmn. dept., 1972-82, mentor, tchr., 1985—; tchr. Santa Monica Coll., 1975-76; cons. bilingual edn. Inglewood Unified Sch. Dist., 1975—; mem. ednl. teaching com. Monroe Jr. High Sch., 1985-86, staff devel. com., 1985—, chmn. drug and alcohol awareness com., 1986—. Author: English Mechanics Workbook, 1986. Named Tchr. of Yr., 1973. Mem. NEA, Calif. Tchrs. Assn., Inglewood Tchrs. Assn. (local rep. 1971-72, tchr edn. and profl. services com. 1972-78), UCLA Alumnae Assn. (life), Prytanean Alumnae Assn. Republican. Club: Westside Alano (Los Angeles)(bd. dirs., treas. 1982-83). Lodge: Masons. Avocations: reading, travel, swimming, dancing, cooking. Office: Monroe Jr High Sch 10711 10th Ave Inglewood CA 90303

GUZY, PETER MICHAEL, cardiologist, educator; b. Monongahela, Pa., Oct. 30, 1940. BS in Chemistry, U. Notre Dame, 1962; PhD in Biochemistry, U. Ky., 1970; MD, Med. Coll. of Ohio, 1973. Resident McMaster U., Hamilton, Ont., Can., 1973-75, U. Toronto, Ont., Can., 1975-76; fellow in cardiology UCLA Sch. Medicine, 1976-79; asst. prof. medicine UCLA div. Cardiology, 1979-83, assoc. prof. medicine, 1984—; dir. UCLA Pacemaker Clinic, 1980—. Bd. dirs. Am. Heart Assn. Recipient Tchr. of Yr. award UCLA Dept. Medicine, 1981-82. Fellow Am. Coll. Cardiology, Royal Coll. Physicians, Surgeons of Can. Office: UCLA Div Cardiology CHS 47-123 Los Angeles CA 90024

GWILYM, ROBERT DAVID, environmental department executive; b. Neath, Wales, Apr. 3, 1945; s. William Aubrey and Leila Margaret (Evans) G. BSC, U. Wales, Swansea, 1969; MES, York U., Ont., Can., 1976. Cert. profl. geol. scientist, environ. profl. Geologist INCO Ltd., Sudbury, Ont., 1969-72; environ. design officer Fed. Govt. Can., Toronto, Ont., 1974-76; environ. coordinator Watts, Griffis, McOuat, Toronto, 1976-80, Anaconda Canada, Bathurst, N.B., Can., 1980-82; environ. advisor Anaconda Minerals, Denver, 1982-83; environ. mgr. Fox and Assocs., Wheat Ridge, Colo., 1983-86; waste div. mgr. Steffen, Robertson and Kirsten, Lakewood, Colo., 1986—. Contbr. articles to profl. jours. Mem. Am. Inst. Profl. Geologists, Nat. Assn. Environ. Profls. (v.p. Rocky Mt. region 1985-87), Can. Inst. Mining and Metallurgy (dir. Maritime region 1981-82), Geol. Assn. Can. Avocations: auto mechanics, hiking. Home: 5733 Santa Clara Box 571 Indian Hills CO 80454 Office: Steffen Robertson and Kirsten 3232 S Vance St Lakewood CO 80227

GWYNN, ANTHONY KEITH (TONY), professional baseball player; b. Los Angeles, Calif., May 9, 1960; m. Alicia; children: Anthony, Anisha Nicole. Educ. San Diego State U. Player San Diego Padres, Nat. League, 1982, 1983—. Player All-Star game, 1984-86, 1984 World Series. Holder Nat. League batting title, 1984, recipient Gold Glove, 1986. Office: San Diego Padres PO Box 200 San Diego CA 92120 *

GYLSETH, DORIS (LILLIAN) HANSON, librarian, educator; b. Helena, Mont., May 26, 1934; d. Richard E. and Lillie (Paula) Hanson; m. Arlie Albeck, Dec. 26, 1955 (div. Apr. 1964); m. Hermann M. Gylseth, Apr. 29, 1983 (dec. Aug. 1985). BS in Edn., Western Mont. Coll. Edn., 1958; MLS,

U. Wash., 1961. Tchr. Helena Sch. Dist., 1955-56, Dillon (Mont.) Elem. Sch., 1957-59, Eltopia (Wash.) Unified Sch. Dist., 1959-60; sch. librarian Shoreline Sch. Dist., Seattle, 1960-64, Dept. of Defense, Chateauroux, France, Hanau, Fed. Republic Germany, Tachikawa, Japan, 1964-68, Long Beach (Calif.) Unified Sch. Dist., 1968-70; br. librarian Long Beach Pub. Library, 1970-74, coordinator children's services, 1974-85; part-time librarian Long Beach (Calif.) Unified Sch. Dist., 1986—. Bd. dirs. Children's Services Div. Calif. Library Assn., 1985; co-chmn. Long Beach Authors Festival, 1978-86; mem. planning council Third Pacific Rim Conf. on Children's Lit., UCLA, 1986. Mem. So. Calif. Council on Lit. for Children and Young People (bd. dirs. 1974—, pres. 1982-84), Helen Fuller Cultural Carrousel (bd. dirs. 1985—). Lodges: Zonta (pres. 1978-80), Sons of Norway. Avocations: cats, traveling. Home: 2700 Panorama Dr #304 Signal Hill CA 90806

HAAG, CAROL ANN GUNDERSON, marketing professional, consultant; b. Mpls.; d. Glenn Alvin and Genevieve Esther (Knudson) Gunderson; m. Lawrence S. Haag, Aug. 30, 1969; 1 child, Maren Anne. BJ, U. Mo., 1969; postgrad., Roosevelt U., Chgo., 1975—. Pub. relations writer, advt. copywriter Am. Hosp. Supply Corp., Evanston, Ill., 1969-70; asst. dir. pub. relations Rush-Presbyn. St. Luke's Med. Ctr., Chgo., 1970-71; asst. mgr. pub. and employee communications Quaker Oats Co., Chgo., 1971-72, mgr. editorial communications, 1972-74, mgr. employee communications programs, 1974-77; dir. pub. relations Shaklee Corp., San Francisco, 1978-82; pres. CH & Assocs., San Francisco, 1982-84; dir corp. communications BRAE Corp., San Francisco, 1984; dir. mktg. St. Francis Meml. Hosp., San Francisco, 1985—; cons. in field. Bd. dirs. Calif. League Handicapped; mem. adv. bd. San Francisco Spl. Olympics; mem. pub. relations com. San Francisco Recreation and Parks Dept., San Francisco Vol. Bur. Recipient 1st Place cert. Printing Industry Am., 1972, 74, 1st Place Spl. Communication award Internat. Assn. Bus. Communicators, 1974; 1st Place citation Chgo. Assn. Bus. Communicators, 1974. Mem. Nat. Acad. TV Arts and Scis., Indsl. Communication Council, Pub. Relations Soc. Am., San Francisco C. of C. Club: San Francisco Press. Home: 133 Fernwood Dr Moraga CA 94556 Office: Saint Francis Meml Hosp 900 Hyde St San Francisco CA 91409

HAAG, CARRIE ANN, non-profit association executive; b. Chgo., July 7, 1950; d. Arthur L. and Janice (Tidmarsh) H. BA, Purdue U., 1972; MA, Eastern Ky. U., 1977, EdS, 1978; postgrad., U. N.C., 1978-79. Dir. nat. championships Assn. for Intercollegiate Athletics for Women, Washington, 1979-82; asst. dir. athletics Darthmouth Coll., Hanover, N.H., 1982-84; exec. dir. U.S. Field Hockey Assn., Inc., Colorado Springs, Colo., 1984—. U.S. Olympic Found. grantee, 1986, 87. Mem. Am. Alliance for Health, Phys. Edn., Recreation and Dance. Home: 405 Bear Creek Pl Colorado Springs CO 80906 Office: US Field Hockey Assn Inc 1750 E Boulder St Colorado Springs CO 80909

HAAG, NANCY MARIE, real estate developer; b. Dayton, Ohio, Mar. 27, 1956; d. Jerry Richard and Buelah Faye (Carson) H. BA, Ohio U., 1978; M in Community Planning, U. Cin., 1980. Cons. Cress-Bandy Assocs., Ft. Mitchell, Ky., 1979-80; planner Summa Corp., Los Angeles, 1980-82, sr. planner, 1982-84; project dir. Howard Hughes Properties, Los Angeles, 1984—. Council appointee West Hollywood (Calif.) Gen. Plan Adv. Com., 1986. U. Cin. scholar, 1978-80. Mem. Urban Land Inst. (assoc.). Avocations: bicycling, reading, spectator sports, traveling. Home: 837 W Knoll Dr #320 West Hollywood CA 90069 Office: Howard Hughes Properties 6167 Bristol Pkwy #330 Culver City CA 90230

HAAGENSON, KEITH ALAN, agronomist, researcher; b. Denver, Oct. 29, 1955; s. Clifford Pershing and Marjorie Mae (Benson) H.; m. Mary Elizabeth Schmidt, Mar. 14, 1981; 1 child, Erik Clifford. BS, Colo. State U., 1978, MS, 1987. Research technician Great Western Sugar, Longmont, Colo., 1979-82, sr. agronomist, 1984-85; sr. agronomist Monohy Seed Inc., Longmont, 1985—. Mem. Western Soc. Weed Sci., Council for Agrl. Sci. and Tech., Am. Soc. Sugar Beet Technologists, Am. Chem. Soc. (affiliate, agrochems. sect.). Office: Monohy Seed Inc 11939 Sugarmill Rd Longmont CO 80501

HAAK, HAROLD HOWARD, university president; b. Madison, Wis., June 1, 1935; s. Harold J. and Laura (Kittleson) H.; m. Betty L. Steiner, June 25, 1955; children—Alison Marie, Janet Christine. B.A., U. Wis., 1957, M.A., 1958; Ph.D., Princeton U., 1963. From asst. prof. to assoc. prof. polit. sci., pub. adminstrn. and urban studies San Diego State Coll., 1962-69, dean coll. profl. studies, prof. pub. adminstrn. and urban studies, 1969-71; acad. v.p. Calif. State U., Fresno, 1971-73; pres. Calif. State U., 1980—; v.p. U. Colo., Denver, 1973, chancellor, 1974-80; mem. joint council on food and agrl. scis. U.S. Dept. Agr., 1985—. Trustee William Saroyan Found., 1981—; chmn. AASCU Com. on Agr. Renewable Resources and Rural Devel., 1985—; mem. NCAA Pres.' Commn., 1987—; bd. dirs. Fresno Econ. Devel. Corp., 1981—, Found. for the 21st Century, 1987—. Recipient U. Colo. medal, 1980. Mem. Phi Beta Kappa, Phi Kappa Phi. Office: Calif State U-Fresno Office of Pres Fresno CA 93740

HAAPALA, DAVID ANDREW, behavioral scientist administrator, psychologist, consultant; b. Tacoma, June 13, 1949; s. Andrew A. and Shirley Teresa (Shannon) H.; m. Jill McCleave Kinney, July 26, 1976; 1 child, Scott McCleave. AA, Tacoma Community Coll., 1969; BS, Wash. State U., 1971, MA, 1975; PhD, Saybrook Inst., 1983. Youth counselor Dept. Human Devel., Tacoma, 1974-75; child and family therapist Comprehensive Mental Health Ctr., Tacoma, 1975-76; co-founder, dir. tng., cons. Homebuilders Program Cath. Community Service, Tacoma, 1974-77; co-dir. Homebuilders Cath. Community Service, Tacoma, 1977-82; pvt. practice psychotherapy, con. Tacoma, 1975-82; co-founder, exec. dir. Behavioral Scis. Inst., Fed. Way, Wash., 1981—; co-dir. pilot project N.Y.C. Homebuilders, 1987—. Research grantee U.S. Dept. Health and Human Services, Wash., 1979, 84, 86, Utah, 1984. Mem. Am. Orthopsychiat. Assn., Alliance for Children, Youth and Families, Western Psychol. Assn. Lutheran. Home: 1901 Markham Ave NE Tacoma WA 98422 Office: Behavioral Scis Inst 1717 S 341st Pl Federal Way WA 98003

HAARSAGER, DENNIS LEE, broadcasting executive; b. Wadena, Minn., Apr. 18, 1947; s. Ralph Oliver and Doris Blanche (Johnson) H.; m. Julie Carol Wince, July 16, 1966 (div. 1976); 1 child, Jennie Ella; m. Sandra Lynn Smith Watkinson, Jan. 1, 1977; children: Anna Lynn, Andrew Lee. BS, U. S.D., 1972, MA, 1975. Dir. adminstrn. S.D. Pub. TV Network, Vermillion, S.D., 1972-75; state coordinator Broadcasting State Bd. Edn., Boise, Idaho, 1975-78; gen mgr. radio-TV, Wash. State U., Pullman, 1978—; pres. Wash. Ednl. Network, 1980-82, 83-84; telecommunications cons. to numerous orgns., 1977—. Served with USAF, 1966-69. Home: SW 310 Skyline Dr Pullman WA 99163 Office: Wash State U KWSU/Radio-TV Services Pullman WA 99164-2530

HAAS, DEBORAH LYNN, bank officer; b. Chgo., June 11, 1952; d. William Hermann and Elizabeth Dorothy (Badali) H. B.A., U. Dayton, 1973; M.A., U. Ariz., 1976; M.I.M., Am. Grad. Sch. Internat. Mgmt., 1979. Advt. mgr. Flyer News, U. Dayton (Ohio), 1970-73; instr. U. Ariz., Tucson, 1974-79; consumer lending officer Valley Nat. Bank, Phoenix, 1980-82, comml. lending officer, 1982-83, asst. mgr., med. banking specialist, 1984—; tchr. ESL, 1975-79; tchr. German, U. Ariz., 1974-76. Mem. Ariz. Sonora Desert Mus., 1984—, Nat. Wildlife Fedn.; sec. Friends of Refugees, 1982; instr. Vols. for Refugee Self-Sufficiency, 1982-83. Mem. Am. Assn. Tchrs. German, Phoenix T-Bird Alumni Assn. (sec. steering com. 1983-85, balloon race com. 1986—, pres. 1987), Friends of Thunderbird (coordinator fgn. student luncheons, 1986), Delta Phi Alpha, Phi Beta Alpha. Lodge: Civitan (bd. dirs. local chpt. 1984—, pres.-elect 1985—, pres. 1985-86). Address: 15015 N 7th Pl Phoenix AZ 85022

HAAS, GALEN KENT, dentist; b. Torrington, Wyo., Mar. 14, 1949; s. Howard Adolph and Joyce (Hacker) H.; m. Maryann Precht, Sept. 21, 1973; children—Cody Kent, Desiree Sommer. B.A., U. Wyo., 1971; D.D.S., U. Wash., 1975. Pvt. practice dentistry, Lewiston, Idaho, 1975—. Mem. ADA, Lewis-Clark Dental Soc., Am. Equilibration Soc., Fin. Arts Inst., Am. Assn. Nutritional Cons., Ironskull, Alpha Epsilon Delta. Office: 1639 23d Ave Lewiston ID 83501

HAAS, PETER E., manufacturing company executive; b. San Francisco, Dec. 20, 1918; s. Walter A. and Elise (Stern) H.; m. Josephine Baum, Feb. 1, 1945; m. Mimi Lurie, Aug., 1981; children: Peter E., Michael Stern, Margaret Elizabeth. Student, Deerfield Acad., 1935-36; A.B., U. Calif., 1940; MBA, Harvard, 1943. With Levi Strauss & Co., San Francisco, 1945—; exec. v.p. Levi Strauss & Co., 1958-70, pres., 1970-81, chief exec. officer, 1976-81, chmn. bd., 1981—; dir. AT&T. Former mem. Golden Gate Nat. Recreation Area Adv. Com.; Former pres. Jewish Welfare Fedn.; former trustee Stanford U.; former v.p., trustee San Francisco Bay Area Council, United Way of San Francisco Bay Area; currently bd. govs. United Way of Am. Office: Levi Strauss & Co Levi's Plaza 1155 Battery St San Francisco CA 94106 *

HAAS, ROBERT DOUGLAS, apparel manufacturing company executive; b. San Francisco, Apr. 3, 1942; s. Walter A. and Evelyn (Danzig) H.; m. Colleen Gershon; 1 child, Elise Kimberly. BA, U. Calif.-Berkeley, 1964; MBA, Harvard U., 1968. With Peace Corps, Ivory Coast, 1964-66; with Levi Strauss & Co., San Francisco, 1973—; sr. v.p. corp. planning Levi Strauss & Co., 1978-80, pres. new bus. group, 1980, pres. operating groups, 1980-81, exec. v.p., chief operating officer, 1981-84, pres., chief exec. officer, 1984—, also dir. Mem. Bay Area Com.; bd. dirs. Levi Strauss Found., San Francisco A.I.D.S. Found. Baker scholar Harvard U., 1968; White House fellow, 1968-69. Mem. Brookings Inst. (trustee), Conf. Bd., Council Fgn. Affairs, Phi Beta Kappa. Office: Levi Strauss & Co 1155 Battery St San Francisco CA 94120

HAAS, WALTER J., professional sports team executive. s. Walter A. Haas, Jr., and Evelyn Danzig H. Exec. v.p. Oakland A's, Am. League, Oakland, Calif. Office: Care Oakland A's Oakland-Alameda County Coliseum Oakland CA 94621 *

HABA, LEONARD ALLEN, manufacturing company executive; b. Carrington, N.D., Aug. 11, 1931; s. Martin and Agnes (Zebd) H.; m. Sherry Marie Kearney, May 19, 1962; children—Linda, Cindy, Matthew, Steven. B.A. in Acctg., U. Wash., 1956. CPA, Wash. Sr. auditor Ernst & Ernst, Seattle, 1956-65; chief internal auditor PACCAR Inc., Renton, Wash., controller Kenworth div., Seattle, v.p., corp. controller, Bellevue, Wash., 1965-83, sr. v.p., 1983—; dir. various PACCAR subs. Bd. dirs. Am. Diabetes Assn., N.Y.C., 1982-83, also Wash. affiliate, Seattle; trustee Diabetic Trust Fund, Seattle. Mem. Am. Inst. CPAs, Wash. Soc. CPAs, Fin. Execs. Inst. Office: PACCAR Inc 777 106th Ave NE Bellevue WA 98004

HABER, HOWARD ELI, physicist; b. Bklyn., Feb. 3, 1952; s. Leo Max and Sylvia (Bittkower) H.; m. Marjorie Anne Gorker, Aug. 21, 1980. SB in Physics, SB in Math., SM in Physics, MIT, 1973; PhD in Physics, U. Mich., 1978. Postdoctoral research assoc. Lawrence Berkeley (Calif.) Lab., 1978-80, U. Pa., Phila., 1980-82; postdoctoral research assoc. U. Calif., Santa Cruz, 1982-84, adj. asst. prof., 1984—. Editor: (conf. proceedings) Proceedings of Theoretical Symposium on Intense Medium, 1983, Proceedings of the Theoretical Advanced Study Inst., 1986; contbr. articles to profl. jours. Outstanding Jr. Investigator grantee Dept. of Energy, 1985—. Mem. Am. Phys. Soc., Am. Assn. Physics Tchrs., Sigma Xi. Democrat. Jewish. Office: U Calif Dept Physics Santa Cruz CA 95064

HABERMAN, CHARLES MORRIS, mechanical engineer, educator; b. Bakersfield, Calif., Dec. 10, 1927; s. Carl Morris and Rose Marie (Braun) H. BS, UCLA, 1951; MS in Mech. Engring., U. So. Calif., 1954, ME, 1957. Lead, sr. and group engr. Northrop Aircraft, Hawthorne, Calif., 1951-59, cons., 1959-61; from asst. prof. to prof. mech. engring. Calif. State U., Los Angeles, 1959—; cons. Royal McBee Corp., 1960-61. Author: Engineering Systems Analysis, 1965, Use of Computers for Engineering Applications, 1966, Vibration Analysis, 1968, Basic Aerodynamics, 1971. Served with AUS, 1946-47. Mem. Am. Acad. Mechanics, Am. Soc. Engring. Edn., AIAA, AAUP. Democrat. Roman Catholic.

HACHTEN, RICHARD ARTHUR, II, hospital administrator; b. Los Angeles, Mar. 24, 1945; s. Richard A. and Dorothy Margaret (Shipley) H.; m. Jeanine Hachten, Dec. 12, 1970; children—Kristianne, Karin. B.S. in Econs., U. Calif.-Santa Barbara, 1967; M.B.A., UCLA, 1969. Mgmt. intern TRW Systems Group, Redondo Beach, Calif., 1969-72; adminstrv. asst. Methodist Hosp., Arcadia, Calif., 1972-73, asst. adminstr., 1973-74, assoc. adminstr., 1974-76, v.p. adminstrn., 1976-80, exec. v.p., adminstr., 1980-81, pres., adminstr., 1981-84; chief exec. officer Tri-City Hosp. Dist., Oceanside, Calif., 1984—; instr. health care mgmt. Pasadena City Coll. Bd. dirs., pres. Hospice of Pasadena, Inc. Bd. dirs. ARC, Arcadia. Mem. Am. Coll. Hosp. Adminstrs., Healthcare Execs. So. Calif., Hosp. Council So. Calif., Beta Gamma Sigma. Republican. Methodist. Club: Rotary. Home: 1130 Sugarbush Dr Vista CA 92084 Office: 4002 Vista Way Oceanside CA 92056

HACK, DALLAS CHRISTIAN, anesthesiologist; b. Neudorf, Sask., Can., Aug. 7, 1952; s. Christian and Elsie Wilhemina Emelia (Jahnke) H.; came to U.S., 1970, naturalized, 1977; m. Linda Nay Rutschow; children—Dana Marie, Melissa Jane, John Wayne, Terri Renea. Student Can. Union Coll., 1968-70, Walla Walla Coll., 1970-71, U. Winnipeg, 1971-72; B.A., Andrews U., 1972; M.D., Loma Linda U., 1975. Pres. Profl. Data Systems, Loma Linda, Calif., 1974-77; intern Loma Linda U., 1975-76, resident in anesthesiology, 1976-77, fellow in cardiology and biomath., 1977-78; v.p. Data Compass Corp., Costa Mesa, Calif., 1977-79; v.p. Algorithmic Design Services, San Diego, 1979-81, Star Techs., Irvine, Calif., 1981-85, Hack Enterprises, Santa Ana, Calif., 1985-86, Basic Time, Carson, Calif., 1985-86; med. dir. Community Health Projects, West Covina, Calif., 1986—; cons. Point 4 Data Corp., Coopervision. Mem. AMA, Calif. Med. Assn., Orange County Med. Assn., IEEE Computer Soc., Am. Acad. Family Practice. Home: 2231 D East Santa Clara Ave Santa Ana CA 92705

HACK, MAURICE CHARLES, JR., dentist; b. Indpls., Jan. 7, 1935; s. Maurice Charles and Cornelia Gurtrude (Hirsch) H.; D.D.S. (Mosby scholar), Loyola U., Chgo., 1959; m. Barbara Ann Moore, Nov. 25, 1970; children—Patricia, Paul. With Pub. Health Service, Oslo, Norway, 1963-64; gen. practice dentistry, Las Vegas, 1964—; adviser Vita Plus Corp. Served to lt. comdr. USNR, 1959-62. Named hon. Ky. Col. Mem. Am., Nev., Clark County dental assns., Acad. Gen. Dentistry, Pierre Fachard Acad., Internat. Analgesia Soc., Blue Key, Sigma Chi, Xi Psi Phi. Democrat. Roman Catholic. Clubs: Desert Inn Country. Home: 3105 Cabachon Ave Las Vegas NV 89121 Office: 1500 E Desert Inn Rd Las Vegas NV 89109

HACKER, HERBERT F., architect, planner; b. Joliet, Ill., June 5, 1937; s. Christian and Eva Marie (Feulner) H.; m. Judith Kay, June 29, 1963; 1 child, Dirk. BArch, Ill. Inst. Tech., 1960, MBA, 1969. Registered architect Ariz, Ill., Ind., Wis.; cert. Nat. Council Archtl. Registration Bds. Chief architect Friedman, Alschuler & Sincere, Chgo., 1966-80; sr. architect MTOY, Chgo., 1980-81; project mgr. McDonalds' Office-Campus, Oakbrook, Ill., 1981-83; pvt. practice architecture Chgo., 1983-84; planner, architect Ariz. Pub. Service Co., Phoenix, 1984—. Mem. AIA. Lutheran. Office: Ariz Pub Service Co 411 N Central PO Box 53999 Sta 1575 Phoenix AZ 85072-3999

HACKER, NIGEL PATRICK, research chemist; b. Bristol, England, Nov. 17, 1951; came to U.S., 1978; s. Dennis Henry and Beatrice Jane (McIntyre) H.; m. Victoria Florence Lysakowski, July 1, 1977. BSc with honors, U. Coll., Cardiff, Wales, 1973, MSc, 1974; PhD, Bristol U., England, 1977. Postdoctoral research assoc. Newcastle (Eng.) U., 1976-78; lectr. Northwestern U., Evanston, Ill., 1978-80; postdoctoral research assoc. Columbia U., N.Y.C., 1980-82; sr. organic chemist Eli Lilly & Co., Lafayette, Ind., 1982-85; research staff mem. IBM Research, San Jose, Calif., 1985—. Contbr. articles to profl. jours. Recipient scholarship, Sci. Research Council, England, 1974-76, county major scholarship, 1970-73; postdoctoral fellow Sci. Research Council, 1976-78. Mem. Am. Chem. Soc. Office: Almaden Research Ctr K91/802 IBM Research Div 650 Harry Rd San Jose CA 95120

HACKER, ROBERT WILLIAM, consulting engineer, computer company executive, educator; b. Milw., Oct. 9, 1923; s. Emil Henry and Lillian Meta (Strothoff) H.; m. Caroline Elizabeth Adams, June 12, 1949; children—William, Linda. Student Milw. Sch. Engring., 1941-42, Washington U., St. Louis, 1943; B.S.E.E., U. Wis.-Madison, 1949; M.S. in Engring. Adminstrn., Syracuse U., 1966. Registered profl. engr., N.Y., Ariz. Constrn. engr. Gen. Motors Co., Danville, Ill., 1949-51; plant engr. Bell Aircraft Corp., Niagara Falls, N.Y., 1951-55; facilities engr., mgr. plant facilities Gen. Electric Co., Utica, N.Y., 1955-66, Phoenix, 1966-70; mgr. plant engring. Honeywell Info. Systems, Phoenix, 1970-86; owner, pres. R.W. Hacker Cons. Engrs., Inc., Phoenix, 1986—, mem. energy conservation steering com., 1975-86; instr. Utica Coll., Mohawk Valley Community Coll. Bd. dirs. Golden Gate Settlement House, 1968-71; chmn. facilities rev. com., dir. Maricopa County Comprehensive Health Planning Council, 1970-76; mem. Deer Valley Planning Com., 1974-76; 1st v.p., dir. Central Ariz. Health Systems Agy., 1976-78; mem. Gov.'s Commn. Ariz. Environ., 1973-86; trustee First United Meth. Ch., 1986. Served with U.S. Army, 1943-46; ETO, PTO. Recipient Community Service award Honeywell, 1976. Mem. Assn. Energy Engrs., Ariz. Assn. Industries, (chmn. Facilities com., rate intervention com.), Ariz. C. of C. (chmn. hazardous waste com.). Lodge: Kiwanis. Home and Office: 750 E Winter Dr Phoenix AZ 85020

HACKETT, CAROL ANN HEDDEN, physician; b. Valdese, N.C., Dec. 18, 1939; d. Thomas Barnett and Zada Loray (Pope) Hedden; B.A., Duke, 1961; M.D., U. N.C., 1966; m. John Peter Hackett, July 27, 1968; children—John Hedden, Elizabeth Bentley, Susanne Rochet. Intern. Georgetown U. Hosp., Washington, 1966-67, resident, 1967-69; clinic physician DePaul Hosp., Norfolk, Va., 1969-71; chief spl. health services Arlington County Dept. Human Resources, Arlington, Va., 1971-72; gen. med. officer USPHS Hosp., Balt., 1974-75; pvt. practice family medicine, Seattle, 1975—; mem. staff, chmn. dept. family practice Overlake Hosp. Med. Ctr., 1985-86; clin. instr. U. Wash. Bd. dirs. Mercer Island (Wash.) Preschool Assn., 1977-78; coordinator 13th and 20th Ann. Inter-profl. Women's Dinner, 1978, 86; trustee Northwest Chamber Orch., 1984—. Mem. Wash. Med. Soc., King County Med. Soc. (chmn. com. TV violence), DAR, Bellevue C. of C., NW Women Physicians (v.p. 1978), Seattle Symphony League, Eastside Women Physicians (founder, pres.), Sigma Kappa. Episcopalian. Club: Wash. Athletic. Home: 4304 E Mercer Way Mercer Island WA 98040 Office: 1128 112th Ave NE Bellevue WA 98004

HACKETT, JOHN PETER, dermatologist; b. N.Y.C., Feb. 10, 1942; s. John Thomas and Helen (Donohue) H.; m. Carol A. Hedden, July 27, 1968; children: John, Elizabeth, Susanne. AB, Holy Cross Coll., 1963; MD, Georgetown U., 1967. Diplomate Am. Bd. Internal Medicine, Am. Bd. Dermatology. Intern Georgetown U. Hosp., 1967-68, resident, 1968-69; fellow Johns Hopkins Hosp., 1972-75, chief resident, 1975; practice medicine specializing in dermatology Seattle, 1975—; asst. prof. dermatology U. Wash., 1975; active staff Swedish Hosp.; active staff Providence Hosp.; pres. Psoriasis Treatment Ctr., Inc., 1978-80; cons. physician Children's Orthopedic Hosp. Contbr. articles to profl. jours. Bd. dirs. Mercer Island Boys and Girls Club, 1976-81, Seattle Ctr. for Blind, 1979-80. Served to lt. condr. USNR, 1969-71. Mem. Am. Acad. Dermatology, Seattle Dermatol. Soc. (pres. 1981-82), Soc. Investigative Dermatology, Wash. State Med. Soc., King County Med. Soc. (chmn. media relations com. 1977-80), Wash. Physicians Ins. Assn. (adv. bd., chmn. actuarial com.). Club: Wash. Athletic. Lodge: Rotary. Home: 4304 Mercer Way Mercer Island WA 98040 Office: 1500 Cabrini Tower 901 Boren Ave Seattle WA 98104

HACKETT, ROSEMARY REYNOLDS, computer consultant; b. Detroit, Feb. 18, 1941; d. Sydney Herbert and Mary Jane (Kirchman) Reynolds; m. Robert Swain Young, June 7, 1963 (div. June 1972); children: Anthony, Patrick; m. Charles Milton Hackett, Mar. 23, 1985; stepchildren: Cheryl, Linda, Dan. BA in Sociology, Whittier Coll., 1963. Cert. systems profl., data processor. Supr. computer ctr. Rockwell Internat., Anaheim, Calif., 1966-70; mgr. EDP Rohm Corp., Santa Ana, Calif., 1972-75; mgr. mgmt. info. systems Armstrong Pacific Corp., Santa Fe Springs, Calif., 1975-85; owner RYH Systems, Irvine, Calif., 1985—; cons., Irvine, Santa Fe Springs, 1984—. Mem. Tustin Meadows Homeowners Assn., 1982-84, civic liaison, mem. fin. com. long term planning; vol. hosp. aide Tustin (Calif.) Community Hosp., 1970-71. Mem. Data Processing Mgmt. Assn., Assn. Systems Mgmt. (editor 1981-83, sec. 1980-81), Assn. Cert. Computer Profls., Sierra Club (dance chmn. 1984-85), Alpha Kappa Delta. Avocations: hiking, tennis, original cartoon strip collections of Pogo. Home and Office: 38 Farragut Irvine CA 92720

HACKNEY, HENRY, sales executive; b. Chgo., Sept. 21, 1953; s. Henry and Inez (Hamilton) H.; m. Darwin Lylee, July 26, 1986. BA, Morehouse Coll., 1975; MBA, Roosevelt U., 1979. Sales rep. Life Savers, Inc., Chgo., 1975-80, dist. sales mgr., 1980-84; key acct. mgr. Internat. Playtex, Mpls., 1984-86; broker area sales mgr. Barnes-Hind, Chgo., 1986—. Dem. precinct capt., Chgo., 1980-84. Mem. Assn. MBA Execs., Morehouse Coll. Alumni Assn., Chgo. Tobacco Round Table, Omega Psi Phi. Roman Catholic. Avocations: golf, swimming, basketball, tennis. Home: 5421 NE River Rd Chicago IL 60656 Office: Barnes Hind Inc 895 Kifer Rd Sunnyvale CA 94086

HACKNEY, ROBERT WARD, plant pathologist, nematologist, parasitologist; b. Louisville, Dec. 11, 1942; s. Paul Arnold and Ovine (Whallen) H.; m. Cheryl Lynn Hill, June 28, 1969; 1 child, Candice Colleen. B.A., Northwestern U., 1965; M.S., Murray State U., 1969; Ph.D., Kans. State U., 1973.; Postgrad. research nematologist U. Calif., Riverside, 1973-75; plant nematologist Calif. Dept. Food and Agr., Sacramento, 1975-85, sr. plant nematologist, 1985—. chmn. Calif. Nematode Diagnosis Adv. Commn., Sacramento, 1981—. Contbr. articles to profl. jours. Hon. dep. Sheriff, Sacramento, 1982—. Served with USMC, 1966. NSF grantee, 1974. Mem. Soc. Nematologists, Internat. Council Study of Viruses and Virus Diseases of the Grape, Am. Arbitration Assn. (comml. arbitrator), Delta Tau Delta. Democrat. Methodist. Home: 2024 Flowers St Sacramento CA 95825 Office: Calif Dept Food and Agr 1220 N St Room 340 Sacramento CA 95814

HACKWOOD, SUSAN, electrical and computer engineering educator; b. Liverpool, Eng., May 23, 1955; came to U.S., 1980; d. Alan and Margaret Hackwood. BS with honors, Leicester Poly., Eng., 1976, PhD in Solid State Electrochemistry, 1979. Research fellow Leicester Poly., Eng., 1976-79; postdoctoral research fellow AT&T Bell Labs., Homdel, N.J., 1980-81, mem. tech. staff, 1981-83, supr. robotics tech., 1983-84, dept. head robotics tech., 1984-85; prof. elec. and computer engring. U. Calif., Santa Barbara, 1985—, dir. Ctr. Robotic Systems in Microelectronics, 1985—. Editor: Jour. of Robotic Systems, 1983, Recent Advances in Robotics, 1985; contbr. 51 articles to tech. jours.; 7 patents in field. Mem. IEEE, Electrochem. Soc. (treas. 1985-87). Office: U Calif Ctr Robotic Systems 6740 Cortona Santa Barbara CA 93106

HACKWORTH, THEODORE JAMES, JR., city official; b. Denver, Nov. 7, 1926; s. Theodore James and Thelma B. (Hill) H.; m. Doris Evelyn Larson, Dec. 31, 1947; children—James Robert, Joan Evelyn Grady, Linda Jean Hoffman. B.A., U. Denver, 1955. Sales mgr. Continental Baking Co., Denver, 1950-64; mktg. exec. Sigman Meat Co., Denver, 1964-76; v.p. sales Pierce Packing Co., Billings, Mont., 1976-79; city councilman City of Denver, 1979—, pres., 1983-84; cons. EPA. Mem. Denver pub. schs. bd. edn., 1971-77; dir. Urban Drainage and Flood Control Dist., 1981-84; dir. Met. Sewer dist., 1982—, sec., 1984-85; mem. Denver Regional Council Govts., 1979—, vice chmn., 1981-83, chmn., 1984-86; neighborhood commr. Boy Scouts Am., 1968-69, Western Dist. commr., 1970-71; pres. Harvey Park Improvement Assn., 1969; chmn. Denver Met. Library Task Force, 1982. Served with USAF, 1945-47. Mem. Nat. Assn. Regional Council (bd. dirs. Region VIII, mem. environ. energy policy com., chmn. trans. task force). Republican. Club: Mt. Vernon Country. Contbr. articles to EPA jours. Home: 3955 W Linvale Pl Denver CO 80236 Office: 1601 S Federal Blvd Denver CO 80219

HADAYA, BASSAM ABDUL, nephrologist; b. Damascus, Syria, Dec. 4, 1945; s. Abdul-Sattar and Bashira (Nwaylati) H.; m. Kamar Rabbat, June 13, 1970; children: Bassel, Kinan, Dena Suzanne. Sci. diploma, Damascus U., 1964, MD, 1970. Diplomate Am. Bd. Internal Medicine, Am. Bd. Nephrology. Intern Mt. Carmel Mercy Hosp., Detroit, 1971; resident William Beaumont Hosp., Royal Oak, Mich., 1971-73; nephrology fellow Cleve. Clinic, 1973-75; asst. clin. prof. Mich. State U. Med. Sch., Lansing, 1975-77; co-dir. Lancaster (Calif.) Dialysis Unit, 1977-78; dir. Antelope Valley Dialysis Ctr., Lancaster, 1978—; internal medicine coordinator family practice div. UCLA, Lancaster, 1978-84; chief med. services Antelope Valley Med. Ctr., Lancaster, 1980-84; head infection control com. Antelope Valley Hosp.

Med. Ctr., Lancaster, 1982—, Lancaster Community Hosp., 1982—. Office: Antelope Valley Nephrology Med Group 44725 10th St #240 Lancaster CA 93534

HADDEN, PATRICIA ANN, advertising copywriter; b. N.Y.C., Oct. 26, 1955; d. Edward and Ann (Ratushenko) Bradbury; m. Robert Berwick Hadden, Dec. 5, 1982. BA in English, Drama, Publ. magna cum laude, Hofstra U., 1977; postgrad., N.Y. Inst. Tech., 1983-84. Administrv. asst. EDP/Temps-TAC, N.Y.C., 1979-80; promotional writer Exposition Press, Smithtown, N.Y., 1980-82; sr. copywriter Histacount/SCM, Melville, N.Y., 1982-84, Comfortably Yours/Myron, Maywood, N.J., 1984-85; sr. copywriter Wakeman & deForrest Direct Response Mktg., Newport Beach, Calif., 1985-87, copy chief, 1987—. Author: (anthologies) Inclusion All Around the Mulburry Bush, 1976, Inclusion Pegasus, 1976, poetry rev., 1980. Recipient Best Advertisement award Case and Comment Mag., 1983. Mem. Direct Mktg. Assn. (cert., contbr. chpt. newsletter). Avocations: writing poetry and short fiction, Reggae dancing, deep sea fishing. Home: 23262-B La Mar Mission Viejo CA 92691 Office: Wakeman & deForrest Direct Response Mktg 4770 Campus Dr Newport Beach CA 92660

HADDIX, CHARLES E., legislative and regulatory consultant; b. Astoria, Oreg., Nov. 23, 1915; s. Charles H. and Mattie Lee (Wilson) H.; grad. U.S. Maritime Officers Sch., 1943; grad. in traffic mgmt. Golden Gate U., 1951; m. Betty Lee Wylie, Aug. 22, 1948; children—Bruce W., Anne C., C. Brian. Nat. sales mgr. Radio Sta. KLX, Oakland, Calif., 1953-55; West Coast mgr. Forjoe & Co., 1955-60; v.p. Calif. Spot Sales, 1958-60, Radio Calif., KLIP, Fowler, Calif., 1961-63; med. sales rep. Ives Labs., Inc., Sanger, Calif., 1964-73; state govt. relations cons. Marion Labs., Inc., 1973—; Calif. legis. advocate, 1968-85; Ariz., Nev., N.Mex., Oreg., Wash., Idaho, Utah and Mont. legis. advocate, 1975-85. Mem. Central Calif. Forum on Refugee Affairs, 1983—. Served with Marina Mercante Nat., Republic of Panama, 1945, U.S. Mcht. Marine, 1939-50. Mem. U.S. Naval Inst., Internat. Oceanographic Found., Am. Mus. Natural History, Oreg. Hist. Soc., Manuscript Soc., Columbia River Maritime Mus. Club: Commonwealth of Calif. (San Francisco). Address: 3218 N McCall Sanger CA 93657

HADEN, BILLY HARPER, research biochemist; b. Jackson, Miss., Mar. 8, 1940; s. Billy Sunday and Fannie Lou (Ware) H.; m. Linda Lee Mims, Feb. 23, 1963; children: Billy, Stacey, Andrew. BS in Chemistry, Miss. State U., 1963; MS in Chemistry, U. Notre Dame, 1968, postgrad., 1968-71; postgrad., Mich. State U., 1971-72. Researcher Ames Co. div. Miles Labs., Inc., Elkhart, Ind., 1963-68, assoc. research biochemist, 1968-72; applications and customer service chemist Analytical Systems Mktg. div. Bausch and Lomb, Rochester, N.Y., 1972-74; mgr. applications Syva Co., Palo Alto, Calif., 1974-77, Beckman Instruments, Inc., Carlsbad, Calif., 1977—. Patentee in field; contbr. articles to profl. jours. Advisor Boy Scouts Am./Cub Scouts, Elkhart and Rochester, 1971-74;chief, asst. chief Y Indian Guides/Princesses, Elkhart and Rochester, 1970-82, com. mem., 1972-73; v.p. bd. dirs. Elkhart Civic Theater, 1969-72. Recipient Career Devel. award Syntex Corp., Palo Alto, 1975, Mgmt. Supervisory Devel. U. Calif., 1982, Excellence in Leadership award Beckman Instruments, Inc., Brea, Calif., 1985. Mem. Am. Chem. Soc., Am. Assn. Clin. Chemists. Avocations: outdoor activities, traveling, coin collecting. Office: Beckman Instruments Inc 6200 El Camino Real Carlsbad NM 92008

HADLEY, HELEN RUTH RICHMOND, school counselor, social worker; b. Pocatello, Idaho, Apr. 20, 1926; d. William Cleve and Emma (Deeg) Richmond; m. Russell J. Hadley, Nov. 3, 1946 (div. May 1970); children: Douglas Russell, Paul Richard, James Kelly, William Richard, Mary Frances, Russell Robert. BS in Sociology, U. Utah, 1974, MSW, 1976. Elem. counselor Granite Sch. Dist., Salt lake City, 1977—. Ednl. grantee NIMH, 1974-75, 75-76; named Counselor of Yr. Granite Sch. Dist., 1985-86. Mem. ACLU, Nat. Assn. Social Workers, Granite Sch. Dist. Counselors Assn., Am. Assn. Retired Persons, Utah Women's Polit. Caucus. Avocations: music, reading, bridge, travelling. Office: Granite Sch Dist 340 E 3545 S Salt Lake City UT 84106

HADLEY, HENRY THEODORE, engineering consultant; b. Wenatchee, Wash., July 21, 1922; s. Theodore Henry and Inger Pauline (Liland) H.; m. Bette Rae Graves, June 30, 1946; children—Mark Henry, Victoria Rae. B.E.M.E., U. So. Calif., 1948. Registered profl. engr., Calif. Metallurgist, U.S. Steel Corp., Pittsburg, Calif., 1948-51; project mgr. PACCAR, Inc., Renton Wash., 1951-60, plant metall. engr., 1960-64, chief materials engr., 1964-73, chief welding engr., 1973-76, engring. mgr., 1976-85; cons. in field. Contbg. author metals handbooks. Served with USMC, 1943-46. Mem. Am. Soc. Metals (life, chmn., circuit speaker 1965), Am. Welding Soc., ASTM, AIME, Am. Def. Preparedness Assn., Assn. U.S. Army. Republican. Club: U.S. Marine Meml. Home and Office: 4418 137th Ave SE Bellevue WA 98006

HADLEY, LAWRENCE N(ATHAN), physics educator; b. Valley Center, Kans., Oct. 14, 1916; s. Lawrence N. and Daisy B. (Zaring) H.; m. Jean Ogden, Dec. 23, 1939 (div. Aug. 1968); children: Kathe Weathers, Janet Brody; m. Lucienne Celine De Simplaire, June 12, 1970. AB, Friend's U., 1937; MS, U. Okla., 1939; PhD, U. Mich., 1947. Instr. physics No. Okla. Jr. Coll., Tomkawa, 1937-39; from asst. prof. to assoc. prof. Dartmouth Coll., Hanover, N.H., 1947-55; from asst. prof. to prof. Colo. State U., Ft. Collins, 1955—, chmn. dept. physics, 1965-68, prof. emeritus, 1987—; pres. Colo. State Research Found., 1961-64. Fellow Rackham Sch. Grad. U. Mich., Ann Arbor, 1945-46, Ford Found., 1954-55. Fellow Optical Soc. Am. (pres. Rocky Mountain sect. 1972-73); mem. Colo.-Wyo. Acad. Sci. (pres. 1969-70), Am. Phys. Soc., Am. Assn. Physics Tchrs. (pres. local sect. 1960), Sigma Xi. Democrat. Home: 3417 Canadian Pkwy Fort Collins CO 80524 Office: Colo State U Physics Dept Fort Collins CO 80523

HADLEY, RUTH BANDY POWELL, educator; b. Honolulu, Mar. 28, 1925; d. Edwin R. and Ruth Bandy (Powell) Millikan; B.A., U. Ariz., 1958; M.A., Calif. State Poly. U., 1967; m. John Calvin Hadley, Oct. 9, 1948; children—John Craige, Ruth Bandy Priest. With Lompoc (Calif.) Unified Sch. Dist., 1959-85; mem. Calif. Math. Framework Com.; math. coordinator publ. Calif. State Bd. Edn.; active Calif. Math. Model Curriculum Guide Com., Curriculum Devel. and Supplemental Materials Commn., 1978-84, Calif. Instrnl. Materials Evaluation Panel for Math., 1986; chairperson Calif. Legal Compliance Com., 1984—, Calif. Math. Initiative Cadre, Calif. assessment program Math. Adv. Com., Calif. Basic Ednl. Skills Test Math. Com. Recipient Presdl. award for Excellence in Sci. and Math. Teaching, 1985; named Lompoc Unified Sch. Dist. Tchr. of Yr., 1963. Mem. NEA, Nat. Council Tchrs. Math., Calif. Math. Council, Assn. for Supervision and Curriculum Devel., Nat. Council Suprs. Math., Calif. Tchrs. Assn., Delta Delta Delta, Delta Kappa Gamma. Episcopalian. Home: 1414 S Wallis St Santa Maria CA 93454

HADLEY, WILLIAM KEITH, laboratory medicine educator, microbiology laboratory director; b. Eugene, Oreg., Nov. 12, 1928; s. Olin Clair and Elma Ruby (Paulsen) H.; m. Marilyn JoAnn Norville, Nov. 15, 1952; Joan Elizabeth, Ruth Sarah. AB, U. Calif., Berkeley, 1950, PhD, 1967; MD, Yale U., 1959. Diplomate Am. Bd. Pathology. From asst. prof. to prof. lab. medicine U. Calif., San Francisco, 1967-77, prof., 1977; chief microbiology div. San Francisco Gen. Hosp., 1967—. Contbr. articles to profl. jours. Fellow Am. Soc. Clin. Pathology, Acad. Clin. Lab. Physicians Scientists; mem. Am. Soc. Microbiology (nat. counselor 1980). Home: 18 Reed Ranch Rd Tiburon CA 94920 Office: San Francisco Gen Hosp Microbiology Div 1001 Potrero Ave San Francisco CA 94110

HADLICH, ROGER LEE, Spanish language educator; b. St. Paul, Jan. 10, 1930; s. Walter Henry Hadlich and Dorothy (Dodge) Noble; m. Shirley Grail, Dec. 30, 1952 (div. July 1973); children: Heidi Chrisman, Rex C.; m. Elizabeth Matson Foster, Jan. 31, 1982. BA, Yale U., 1951; diploma, U. Madrid, 1956; MA, Middlebury Coll., 1957; PhD, U. Mich., 1961. Instr. Spanish U. Mich., Ann Arbor, 1960-61; asst. prof. linguistics Cornell U., Ithaca, N.Y., 1961-65; vis. prof. English U. Rome, 1964-65; assoc. dean U. Hawaii, Honolulu, 1968-77, prof. Spanish, 1965—. Author: The Phonological History of Vegliote, 1964, A Transformational Grammar of Spanish, 1971; co-author: A Drillbook of Spanish Pronunciation, 1968, A Spanish Review Grammar: Theory and Practice, 1977; editor MLA newsletter, 1963-65. Served to lt. USNR, 1952-55. Avocations: sports, choral singing, carpentry. Home: 2333 Kapiolani Blvd Apt 1914 Honolulu HI 96826 Office: U Hawaii European Langs Dept 1890 East West Rd Honolulu HI 96821

HADZERIGA, PABLO, metallurgical engineer, chemist; b. Buenos Aires, Dec. 25, 1929; came to U.S., 1957; s. Zacarias and Xenia (Antoniuc) H.; m. Azucena Alcira Tumburus, Jan. 3, 1957; children: Pablo Jr., Madeleine Carmen, Anthony Ruy. BS, U. La Plata, Argentina, 1951; MS, U. Buenos Aires, 1955, PhD, 1956. Chemist Bonneville, Ltd., Wendover and Salt Lake City, Utah, 1957-60, chief chemist, 1960-61, dir. research and devel., 1961-64; sr. process engr. Hazen Research, Inc., Golden, Colo., 1964-78; cons. Arvada, Colo., 1978—. Contbr. articles to profl. jours.; patentee in field. Mem. Am. Chem. Soc., Argentine Chem. Soc., Am. Soc. Metals, Soc. Mining Engrs of AIME, Can. Inst. Mining and Metallurgy. Avocations: music, numismatics, philately. Home: 6058 Owens St Arvada CO 80004

HADZIIOANNOU, GEORGES, polymer engineer; b. Kavala, Greece, Oct. 21, 1953; came to U.S., 1980; s. Panayotis and Marouda (Vrana) H.; m. Evelyne Bourdin, Oct. 11, 1980; 1 child, Celine. BS, U. Thessaloniki, Greece, 1975; M DEA, U. Louis Pasteur, Strasbourg, France, 1976, PhD in Phys. Chemistry, 1977, DSc in Physics, 1980. Research assoc. Centre Nat. de la Recherche Sci., Strasbourg, 1975-80, U. Mass., Amherst, 1980-82; research staff mem., Almaden Research Ctr. IBM, San Jose, Calif., 1982—. Mem. Am. Phys. Soc., Am. Chem. Soc., Soc. Rheology, Greek Chem. Assn., Synergy (bd. dirs. 1983—). Office: IBM Almaden Research Ctr K64 802 650 Harry Rd San Jose CA 95120-6099

HAEG, MARQUE RICHARD, vocational and psychological assessment specialist, consultant; b. Missoula, Mont., June 3, 1949; s. Leo Thomas and Gloria Aleta (Peirce) H.; m. Cheryl Leah Martsch, Feb. 28, 1969 (div. May 1978); m. Christene Mae Edgerton, May 24, 1981. B.A., Idaho State U., 1972, M.Ed., 1975. Cert. vocat. evaluator. Rehab. specialist State of Idaho, Pocatello, 1972-73; rehab. coordinator New Day Products, Inc., Pocatello, 1973-75, dir. rehab., 1975-79; coordinator assessment service Mid-Willamette Consortium, Salem, Oreg., 1980—. Bd. dirs. United Campaign, Pocatello, 1977-79. Mem. Am. Assn. Individual Investors, Nat. Rehab. Assn., Oreg. Employment and Tng. Assn., Bannock County Assn. Retarded Citizens (bd. dirs. 1977-80), Oreg. Assn. Rehab. Profls. in the Pvt. Sector. Lutheran. Home: 1280 Elser Ct SE Salem OR 97302 Office: Mid Willamette Consortium 1495 Edgewater NW Suite 225 Salem OR 97304

HAEGER, JOHN WINTHROP, academic administrator; b. Washington, Sept. 4, 1944; s. Leonard George and Nancy (Leigh) H. AB, Princeton U., 1966; PhD, U. Calif., Berkeley, 1971. Asst. prof. Asian Studies Pomona Coll., Claremont, Calif., 1968-73; dir. corp. and found. relations The Asia Found., San Francisco, 1973-78; v.p. Research Libraries Group, Inc., Stanford, Calif., 1979—. Editor: Crisis and Prosperity in Sung China, 1974; contbr. articles to profl. jours. Mem. Assn. Asian Studies, Am. Council of Learned Socs. (dir. east Asian library program 1977-80). Home: 335 Olive St Menlo Park CA 94025 Office: Research Libraries Group Inc Jordan Quadrangle Stanford CA 94305

HAFEMEISTER, DAVID WALTER, physics educator; b. Chgo., July 1, 1934; s. Lester David and Alma Doris (Schmidt) H.; m. Elsa Georgene Rohlander, June 10, 1961; children: Andrew, Jason, Heidi. MS in Physics, U. Ill., 1959, PhD in Physics, 1964. Asst. prof. physics Carnegie-Mellon U., Pitts., 1966-69; prof. physics Calif. Poly. State U., San Luis Obispo, 1969—; vis. scientist U. Groningen, The Netherlands, 1971, 80, Program Sci. Tech. and Soc., MIT, Cambridge, 1983-84, Energy and Bldgs. dept. Lawrence Berkley (Calif.) Lab., 1985-86, Office Strategic Nuclear Policy U.S. Dept. State, 1987. Co-author: Physics of Modern Architecture, 1983, Arms Control Verification, 1986, Energy Sources: Conservation and Renewables, 1985. Sci. advisor Sen. John Glenn U.S. Senate, Washington, 1975-77; spl. asst.to Under Sec. State Benson and Nye U.S. State Dept., Washington, 1977-79. Grantee Levinson Found. Mem. AAAS (congl. fellow 1975-76, arms control fellow 1987), Am. Phys. Soc. (chmn. forum on physics and soc. 1985-86), Fedn. Am. Scientists, Arms Control Assn., Am. Inst. Physics (co-editor jours.). Home: 553 Serrano San Luis Obispo CA 93401 Office: Calif Poly U Dept Physics San Luis Obispo CA 93407 Mailing: 3743 Aplleton NW Washington DC 20016

HAFEY, EDWARD EARL JOSEPH, precision tool company executive; b. Hartford, Conn., June 7, 1917; s. Joseph Michael and Josephine (Pyne) H.; B.S. in Mech. Engring., Worcester Poly. Inst., 1940; postgrad. Johns Hopkins U., 1943, 44; m. Loyette Lindsey, Oct. 21, 1971; children—Joseph M., Barbara Hafey Beard, Edward F. Instr. dept. mech. enging. Worcester Tech. Inst., 1940-41; mgr. Comfort Air Inc., San Francisco, 1946-47; owner, mgr. Hafey Air Conditioning Co., San Pablo, Calif., 1947—, pres. Hafey Precision Tool, Inc., Laguna Beach, Calif., 1982—; cons. air conditioning U.S. Navy, C.E., Japan, Korea, Okinawa. Served to comdr. USNR, 1941-46. Registered profl. engr., Calif.; named Man of Year, San Pablo, 1962. Mem. ASHRAE, Assn. Energy Engrs., Calif. Air Conditioning Service Engring. Soc., World Trade Center Orange County, Am. Legion, Ret. Officers Assn., Sigma Alpha Epsilon. Republican. Roman Catholic. Clubs: Exchange of Laguna Beach, Marine's Meml. Office: PO Box 417 Laguna Beach CA 92652

HAFFEY, JOHN DANIEL, state senator, utility company executive; b. Anaconda, Mont., Sept. 19, 1945; s. John Daniel and Clara (Kloker) H.; m. Susan Marie McGinley, 1968; children: Kelly Ann, John Francis, Daniel Joseph Patrick. BA in Math., Carroll Coll., Helena, Mont., 1967; MBA, U. Notre Dame, 1972. Gen. mgr. revenue requirements and regulatory affairs Mont. Power Co., Butte, 1978-85, exec. asst. to pres., 1986—; mem. Mont. State Senate, Dist. 45, 1981-85, Dist. 33, 1985—. Democrat. Roman Catholic. Lodge: KC. Home: 709 W 4th St Anaconda MT 59711 Office: Montana State Senate Helena MT 59620

HAGA, ENOCH JOHN, educator, author; b. Los Angeles, Apr. 25, 1931; s. Enoch and Esther Bouncer (Higginson) H.; student Sacramento Jr. Coll., 1948-49; A.A., Grant Tech. Coll., 1950; student U. Colo., Denver, 1950, U. Calif., Berkeley, 1954, Midwestern U., 1950-54; A.B., Sacramento State Coll., 1955, M.A., 1958; Ph.D., Calif. Inst. Integral Studies, 1972, diploma tchr. Asian Culture, 1972; m. Elna Jo Wright, Aug. 22, 1957. Tchr. bus. Calif. Med. Facility, Vacaville, 1956-60; asst. prof. bus. Stanislaus State Coll., Turlock, Calif., 1960-61; engring. writer, publs. engr. Hughes Aircraft Co., Fullerton, Calif., 1961-62, Lockheed Missiles & Space Co., Sunnyvale, Calif., 1962, Gen. Precision, Inc., Glendale, Calif., 1962-63; sr. adminstrv. analyst Holmes & Narver, Inc., Los Angeles, 1963-64; tchr., chmn. dept. bus. and math. Amador Valley Dist., Pleasanton, Calif., 1964—, coordinator computer services, adminstrn. and instrn., 1984-85; vis. asst. prof. bus. Sacramento State Coll., 1967-69; instr. bus. and computer sci. Chabot Coll., Hayward, Calif., 1970—; instr. bus. and philosophy Ohlone Coll., Fremont, Calif., 1972; prof., v.p., mem. bd. govs. Calif. Inst. Asian Studies, 1972-75; pres., prof. Pacific Inst. East-West Studies, San Francisco, 1975-76, also mem. bd. govs.; dir. Certification Councils, Livermore, Calif., 1975-80; mem., chmn. negotiating team Amador Valley Secondary Educators Assn., Pleasanton, Calif., 1976-77, pres., 1984-85. Served with USAF, 1949-52, with USNR, 1947-49, 53-57. Mem. Soc. Data Educators (exec. dir. 1970-74). Coordinating editor: Total Systems, 1962; editor: Automation Educator, 1965-67; Automated Educational Systems, 1967; Data Processing for Education, 1970-71; Computer Techniques in Biomedicine and Medicine, 1973; contbg. editor Jour. Bus. Edn., 1961-69, Data Processing mag., 1967-70. Author and compiler: Understanding Automation, 1965. Author: Simplified Computer Arithmetic, Simplified Computer Logic, Simplified Computer Input, Simplified Computer Flowcharting, 1971-72. Editor: Data Processor, 1960-62, Automedica, 1970-76, FBE Bull., 1967-68. Home: 983 Venus Way Livermore CA 94550 Office: 4375 Foothill Rd Pleasanton CA 94566

HAGAN, BARRY JOSEPH, priest, educator, archivist; b. Glendive, Mont., May 31, 1931; s. Paul Joseph and Aimee Burke (Barry) H. BA in Philosophy, U. Portland, 1953; MA in Sacred Doctrine, Holy Cross Coll., 1960; MA in History, U. Notre Dame, 1964. Instr. history U. Portland, Oreg., 1961-67, asst. prof., 1967—, univ. archivist, 1983—. Contbr. articles to profl. jours. Mem. Council on Am.'s Mil. Past (nat. pres. 1981-86), Order of Indian Wars (founding companion), Fort Phil Kearny/Boseman Trail Assn. (dir. at large 1985—). Democrat. Roman Catholic. Office: U Portland 5000 N Willamette Blvd Portland OR 97203-5798

HAGAN, PATRICIA KITTREDGE, medical administrator; b. Milo, Maine, May 12, 1935; d. Milton Donald and Beatrice Alma (Ingalls) Kittredge; B.S., U. Maine, 1961; M.P.A., Calif. State U., 1982. Food service mgr. U. Maine, Orono, 1961-62, Ind. U., 1962-64, U. Tex., Austin, 1965; adminstr. dietary services Cabrillo Med. Center, San Diego, 1965-69, adminstr. gen. services, 1969-70, adminstr. for ops., 1970-73, assoc. adminstr., 1973-76, adminstr., 1976-82; health services con. Cons. Health Services Adminstrn., San Diego, 1982—; chief exec. officer Specialty Med. Clinic, La Jolla, Calif., 1986—. Served with USAF, 1954-58. Mem. Am. Coll. Hosp. Adminstrs., Am. Acad. Med. Adminstrs., Am. Hosp. Assn., Med. Group Mgmt. Assn., Am. Dietetic Assn., Asso. Western Hosps. Episcopalian. Club: Altrusa Internat. Home: 1275 Alexandria Dr San Diego CA 92107 Office: 351 Santa Fe Dr Suite 200 Encinitas CA 92024

HAGAN, WILLIAM LEONARD, plant breeder, plant pathologist, researcher; b. Atkinson, Ill., Mar. 21, 1936; s. Delmar Harlan and Marsellia (Hall) H.; m. Janet Helen McKenzie, July 27, 1957; children: Kent William, Kimberly Ann. BS, U. Ill., 1959, MS, 1960, PhD, 1963; MBA, John F. Kennedy U., 1985. Research asst. U. Ill., Urbana, 1959-63; mgr., plant breeder, corp. agrl. research dir. Del Monte Corp., San Leandro, Calif., 1963—. Served with AUS, 1954-56. Mem. Am. Soc. Agronomy, Am. Soc. Hort. Sci., Am. Soc. Phytopathology, Sigma Xi, Gamma Sigma Delta. Home: 628 Broadmoor Blvd San Leandro CA 94577 Office: 850 Thornton St PO Box 36 San Leandro CA 94577

HAGAN-CHUN, ADRIENNE JOYCE, communicative disorders specialist; b. Bloomington, Ind., Mar. 28, 1951; m. Daniel Anthony Chun; children: Cristin Erin, Corey Michael. BS, Eastern N.Mex. U., 1972; MS, North Tex. State U., 1974; postgrad., La. State Med. U., 1976. Instr., cons. Research and Evaluation Ctr. U. New Orleans, 1975-78; speech and lang. cons. Mesa County Sch. Dist., Grand Junction, Colo., 1978-82; speech and lang. pathologist Hilltop Rehab. Hosp., Grand Junction, 1982-85, VA Med. Ctr., Grand Junction, 1983-85; pvt. practice speech pathology Grand Junction, 1983-85; dir. Grand Junction Regional Ctr., 1985—; speech, lang. cons. Mesa Devel. Services, Grand Junction, 1986—. Mem. Am. Speech-Lang. Hearing Assn. (cert. clin. competence), Colo. Speech-Lang. Hearing Assn., Phi Kappa Phi. Home: 447 E Scenic Dr Grand Junction CO 81503 Office: Grand Junction Regional Ctr 2800 D Rd Grand Junction CO 81501

HAGBERG, CHRIS ERIC, lawyer; b. Steubenville, Ohio, Dec. 19, 1949; s. Rudolf Eric and Sara (Smith) H.; m. Viola Louise Wilgus, Feb. 19, 1978. B.S., Duke U., 1975; J.D., U. Tulsa, 1978; postgrad. Nat. Law Ctr., George Washington U. Bar: Va. 1979, Okla. 1978, U.S. Ct. Appeals (4th cir.), Calif. 1986. Law clk. to presiding justice U.S. Dist. Ct. (no. dist.) Okla.; asst. counsel ADP Selection Office, Dept. Navy, Navy Regional Contracting Ctr., Washington; counsel Naval Supply Ctr., Pearl Harbor, Hawaii; Pacific area counsel Naval Supply Systems Command, Dept. Navy, Makakilo, Hawaii, assoc. counsel Naval Supply Systems Command, Washington; now atty. Pettit & Martin, Los Angeles. Served to lt. USN, 1970-74. Recipient David I. Milsten award, 1978, 7 Am. Jurisprudence awards, 1976-78, First prize Dept. Navy Legal Writing Contest, 1981. Mem. ABA, Fed. Bar Assn., Nat. Contract Mgmt. Assn., Order of Coif. Democrat. Presbyterian. Contbr. articles to legal jours. Address: 4200 Ironwood Ave Seal Beach CA 90740

HAGE, STEPHEN JOHN, radiology administrator, consultant; b. Chgo., July 22, 1943; s. Steve and Irene (Lewandowski) H.; m. Constance Louise Simonis, June 10, 1967. AAS, YMCA Community Coll., Chgo., 1970. Registered radiol. tech. Staff tech. Highland Park (Ill.) Hosp., 1966-68; chief radiotherapy tech. VA Hines (Ill.) Hosp., 1968-70; chief radiology tech. Gottlieb Meml. Hosp., Melrose Park, Ill., 1970-71; radiology adminstr. S. Chgo. County Hosp., 1971-79; adminstrv. dir. radiology Cedars-Sinai Med. Ctr., Los Angeles, 1979—; cons. Computer Sci. Corp., El Segundo, Calif., 1983—. Contbr. articles to profl. jours. Served with USMC, 1961-64. Recipient 1st pl. Essay award Ill. State Soc. Radiol. Technicians, 1966. Mem. Am. Hosp. Radiology Adminstrs. (charter), Am. Soc. Radiol. Technologists, AAAS, Phi Theta Kappa. Avocations: motorcycling, Tai Chi Chuan. Home: 22115 Halsted St Chatsworth CA 91311 Office: Cedars Sinai Med Ctr 8700 Beverly Blvd Los Angeles CA 90048

HAGEL, JOHN, III, management consultant; b. Berlin, N.H., Sept. 14, 1950; s. John Jr. and Evelyn Gertrude (Parent) H. BA, Wesleyan U., 1972; PhB, Oxford U., 1974; MBA, Harvard U., 1978, JD, 1978. Bar: Mass. 1978. Cons. Boston Cons. Group, 1978-80; pres. Sequoia Group, Larkspur, Calif., 1980-82; v.p. Atari, Inc., Sunnyvale, Calif., 1982-83, sr. v.p., 1983-84, sr. engagement mgr. McKinsey and Co., N.Y.C., 1984—. Author: Alternative Energy Strategies, 1976; co-editor: Assessing The Criminal, 1977; contbr. articles to profl. jours. Mem. ABA, Mass. Bar Assn. Episcopalian.

HAGEN, CHARLES ALFRED, microbiologist; b. East Rutherford, N.J., Feb. 1, 1925; s. Charles Alfred and Lina Dorothea (Scharch) H.; m. Alice Diana Wiltse, Dec. 14, 1951; children: Erich Christoph, Kristine Ann, Susan Lynn. AB, U. Chgo., 1952, MS, 1956. Microbiologist U. Chgo., 1954-55; sr. med. technologist Inst. Tb Research, Chgo., 1955-56; research microbiologist Kraft Inc., Glenview, Ill., 1956-62; microbiologist Ill. Inst. Tech., Chgo., 1962-69; lab. mgr. Avco Jet Propulsion Lab., Pasadena, Calif., 1967-72, Bionetics Corp. Jet Propulsion Lab., Pasadena, 1972-76; chief bacteriologist Becton Dickinson Lab., Oxnard, Calif., 1976-79, regulatory affairs officer, 1976-86; quality assurance engr. Spectramed Inc., Oxnard, 1986—. Contbr. articles to profl. jours. Served with USN, 1943-46. Mem. AAAS, Am. Assn. Lab. Animal Sci., Am. Soc. Microbiology, Soc. Indsl. Microbiology, Am. Soc. Quality Control, Assn. Advancement Med. Instrumentation. Republican. Lutheran. Home: 2085 Lyndhurst Ave Camarillo CA 93010

HAGEN, CYNTHIA WINN, home economics educator; b. Hayden Colo., Mar. 4, 1950; d. Gordon C. and Caroline (Winder) Winn. B.S. in Vocat. Home Econs. Edn., Oreg. State U., 1972; M.A. in Home Econs. Edn., U. No. Colo., 1976. Cert. tchr., Colo. Tchr. home econs. and bus., McKenzie High Sch., Blue River, Oreg., 1972-73; tchr. home econs. Helen McCune Jr. High Sch., Pendleton, Oreg., 1973-76, Isaac Newton Jr. High Sch., Littleton, Colo., 1976-78; chmn. home econs. dept., tchr. Powell Jr. High Sch., Littleton, 1981—, chair dist. writing team, mem. dist. steering com., 1983-85, dist. home econs. chair, 1984-85. Steering com. mem. Bethany Lutheran Ch. Singles, 1979-81. Mem. NEA, Littleton Edn. Assn., Am. Home Econs. Assn., Colo. Home Econs. Assn., Delta Kappa Gamma. Republican.

HAGEN, LARRY WILLIAM, retail executive; b. Pyote, Tex., May 5, 1945; s. Lawrence Herbert and Marjorie Fern (MacFarland) H.; m. Jean Carol Horton, June 19, 1965 (div. Apr. 1986); 1 child, Bret William. AA, Highline Coll., 1965; BS cum laude, Seattle U., 1969; postgrad., City Coll., Seattle, 1985—. Dir. ops. group III The Bon Marche, Seattle, 1967-75; dir. distbn. Brittania Sportswear, Seattle, 1975-77; sr. v.p. ops. Schoenfeld Neckwear, Seattle, 1977—, also bd. dirs., 1984—; bd. dirs. Mallory & Church Ltd., London, 1985—; cons. Jeans Warehouse, Seattle, 1979-81. Loaned exec. United Way, Seattle, 1966-69; collector YMCA Disadvantaged Youth, Seattle, 1983-86. Served with USNG, 1964-74. Mem. Am. Prodn. Inventory Control Soc., Pacific NW Personnel Mgmt. Assn., Am. Soc. Personnel Adminstrn. (v.p. Seattle chpt. 1970-71, pres. Columbian Basin 1981-82). Democrat. Lutheran. Avocations: golf, fishing, music. Home: 5021 Ripley Ln N Renton WA 98056 Office: Schoenfeld Neckwear Corp 676 S Industrial Way Seattle WA 98108

HAGEN, RONALD HENRY, publisher; b. Gettysburg, S.D., Aug. 11, 1941; s. Henry William and Otilla Marie (Trefz) H.; children: Ronda Anne, Racquel Kristie. B.S., Drake U., 1963; M.A., U. San Francisco, 1965. Nat. sales mgr. Berkley Pub. Co., 1963-64; sales mgr. Sunset mag., San Francisco, 1964-68; v.p., gen. mgr. KoraCorp Industries, San Francisco, 1968-70; pres. The Hagen Group, San Francisco, 1970—; also chmn. Hagen Mktg. and Communications div. The Hagen Group; pub. Arts and Leisure Publs., San Francisco, 1974—, U.S. Football League mag. Kickoff, 1983—; pres., editor The Exec. mag., 1983—; editor-in-chief San Francisco Mag., 1983-86; mktg. dir. Major League Volleyball, 1986—; pub. Bus. West, the mag. of the Pacific Rim; dir. Performing Arts Services. Bd. dirs. Performing Arts Services.; bd. dirs. Los Angeles Theater Alliance; nat. bd. dirs., chmn. spl. fundraising Aid to Adoption Spl. Kids; bd. trustees San Francisco Archives for the Performing Arts, 1984. Served with USAF, 1964-65. Mem. Western Pubs. Assn., San Francisco C. of C. Republican. Home: 101 Lombard San

Francisco CA 94111 Office: The Hagen Group 450 Sansoine St San Francisco CA 94111

HAGENSTEIN, WILLIAM DAVID, consulting forester; b. Seattle, Mar. 8, 1915; s. Charles William and Janet (Finigan) H.; m. Ruth Helen Johnson, Sept. 2, 1940 (dec. 1979); m. Jean Kraemer Edson, June 16, 1980. B.S. in Forestry, U. Wash., 1938; M. Forestry, Duke, 1941. Registered profl. engr., Wash., Oreg. registered forester, Calif. Field aid in entomology U.S. Dept. Agr., Hat Creek, Calif., 1938; logging supt. and engr. Eagle Logging Co., Sedro-Woolley, Wash., 1939; tech. foreman U.S. Forest Service, North Bend, Wash., 1940; forester West Coast Lumbermen's Assn., Seattle and Portland, Oreg., 1941-43, 45-49; sr. forester FEA, South and Central Pacific Theaters of war and Costa Rica, 1943-45; mgr. Indsl. Forestry Assn., Portland, 1949-80; exec. v.p. Indsl. Forestry Assn., 1956-80, hon. dir., 1980—; pres. W. D. Hagenstein & Assos., Inc., Portland, 1980—; H.R. MacMillan lectr. forestry U. B.C., 1952, 77; Benson Meml. lectr. U. Mo., 1966; S.J. Hall lectr. indsl. forestry U. Calif. at Berkeley, 1973; cons. forest engr. USN, Philippines, 1952, Coop. Housing Found., Belize, 1986; mem. U.S. Forest Products Trade Mission, Japan, 1968; del. VII World Forestry Congress, Argentina, 1972, VIII Congress, Indonesia, 1978; mem. U.S. Forestry Study Team, West Germany, 1974; mem. sec. Interior's Oreg.-and Calif. Multiple Use Adv. Bd., 1975-76; trustee Wash. State Forestry Conf., 1948—, Keep Oreg. Green Assn., 1957—, v.p., 1970-71, pres., 1972-73; adv. trustee Keep Wash. Green Assn., 1957—; dir. World Forestry Ctr., 1965—, v.p., 1965-79. Author: (with Wackerman and Michell) Harvesting Timber Crops, 1966; Assoc. editor: Jour. Forestry, 1946-53; columnist Wood Rev., 1978-82; contbr. numerous articles to profl. jours. Trustee Oreg. Mus. Sci. and Industry, 1968-73. Served with USNR, 1933-37. Recipient Forest Mgmt. award Nat. Forest Products Assn., 1968; Western Forestry award Western Forestry and Conservation Assn., 1972, 79. Fellow Soc. Am. Foresters (mem. council 1958-63, pres. 1966-69); mem. Am. Forestry Assn. (life, hon. v.p. 1966-69, 74—), Commonwealth Forestry Assn. (life), Internat. Soc. Tropical Foresters, Portland C. of C. (mem. forestry com. 1949-79, chmn. 1960-62), Nat. Forest Products Assn. (mem. forestry adv. com. 1949-80, chmn. 1972-74, 78-80), West Coast Lumbermen's Assn. (v.p. 1969-79), Lang Syne Soc., Hoo Hoo Club, Xi Sigma Pi (named outstanding alumnus Alpha chpt. 1973). Republican. Home: 3062 SW Fairmount Blvd Portland OR 97201 Office: 225 SW Broadway Room 412 Portland OR 97205

HAGER, HAROLD EDWARD, chemical engineering educator; b. Reno, Feb. 27, 1953; s. Edward Harold and Yvonne Antonette (Siard) H.; m. Sarah Ann Sheahan, June 16, 1979; 1 child, Elizabeth Ann. BSChemE with highest honors, U. Calif., Berkeley, 1975; MAChemE, Princeton U., 1976, PhDChemE, 1979. Engring. asst. Occidental Petroleum, La Verne, Calif., 1973, 74; research asst. Princeton (N.J.) U., 1975-79; asst. prof. chem. engring. U. Wash., Seattle, 1979—; cons. in field, 1980—; advosor environ. issues Wash. State U., 1984—. Contbr. articles to profl. jours.; inventor in field. Mem. AAAS, Am. Chem. Soc. (acad. editor N.W. sect. 1982—), Am. Inst. Chem. Engrs. (edn. com. 1981—), Electrochem. Soc., Sierra Club, Phi Beta Kappa, Tau Beta Pi. Democrat. Roman Catholic. Avocations: hiking, biking, fishing, tennis, squash. Home: 6837 26th NE Seattle WA 98115 Office: U Wash Dept Chem Engring BF-10 Seattle WA 98195

HAGER, THOMAS ARTHUR, editor, writer; b. Portland, Oreg., Apr. 18, 1953; s. Donald Preston and Betty Jeanne (Buehner) H.; m. Lauren Jeanne Kessler, July 7, 1984; 1 child, Jackson Kessler. BS in Biology, Portland State U., 1976; MS in Microbiology, Oreg. Health Scis. U., 1978; MS in Journalism, U. Oreg., 1981. Writer Eugene, Oreg., 1981-82, 83-85; editor Aster Pub., Eugene, 1982-83, U. Oreg., Eugene, 1985—; dir. Univ. Relations, Eugene, 1985—;. Author: Staying Young, 1987; founding editor LC mag., 1983; editor Old Oreg. mag. (Case 1 award 1986), 1985—; contbr. articles to mags. Mem. U. Oreg. Alumni Assn. (ex-officio mem. bd.). Office: U Oreg Old Oreg Mag 101 Chapman Eugene OR 97403

HAGEY, DALES WILLIS, JR., biologist, ecologist; b. Union, Oreg., Sept. 4, 1937; s. Dale Willis and Louisa Fay (Mayfield) H.; m. Glorietta May Bond, June 7, 1957; children: Daletta, David, Meleah, Darin. BS, Oreg. State Coll., 1960. Biologist Oreg. Fish Commn., Coos Bay, 1960, ORE Fish Commn., Blue River, Oreg., 1963-67; biologist-ecologist Eugene (Oreg.) Water and Electric Bd., 1968—; chmn. utility environ. com. Pacific N.W. Utilities Conf. Com., Portland, Oreg., 1986-87; mem. environ. com. Western Systems Coordinating Council, 1974-86. Served with U.S. Army, 1960-62. Mem. Am. Fisheries Soc., Pacific Fisheries Biologists, Associated Power Biologists, FWC. Republican. Baptist. Avocations: fishing, hunting, hiking, woodworking, writing. Home: 41909 McKenzie Hwy Springfield OR 97478 Office: Eugene Water and Electric Bd 500 E 4th Ave Eugene OR 97440

HAGGARD, BETTY ANN, nurse, educator, author; b. Cin., Nov. 8, 1945; s. Roy and Katherine (Detweiler) Haggard. R.N., Michael Reese Hosp., Chgo., 1966; B.S. in Nursing, Pittsburg State U. (Kans.), 1976; M.S. in Health Care Mgmt., Calif. State U.-Los Angeles, 1980; Ph.D., Columbia Pacific U., 1984. Staff nurse, Chgo., 1966-68; head nurse Weiss Meml. Hosp., Chgo., 1968-71; instr. nursing program Franklin Tech. Sch., Joplin, Mo., 1971-74, Valley Coll. Med. Careers, North Hollywood, Calif., 1976-77; coordinator nursing edn. Hosp. of Good Samaritan, Los Angeles, 1977-79; mgmt. devel. coordinator Huntington Meml. Hosp., Pasadena, Calif., 1979—. Recipient Writing award Scholastic Mags., 1962. Mem. Am. Soc. Healthcare Edn. and Tng. (sec. So. Calif. chpt.), Am. Soc. Tng. and Devel., Phi Kappa Phi. Contbr. articles to profl. jours. Home: 12 Maverick Circle Pomona CA 91766 Office: Huntington Meml Hosp Edn Dept 100 Congress St Pasadena CA 91105

HAGGARD, CLAUDE COLLINS, electrical engineering consultant; b. Ranfurly, Alta., Can., Feb. 6, 1908; s. Joshiah Collins and Adella Elizabeth (Prescott) H.; m. Yvonne May Pickell, Oct. 11, 1933; children—Gloria, Merrill. Student Oreg. schs. With Mountain States Power Co., Tillamook, Oreg., 1926-29; elec. plant operator Calif. Oreg. Power Co., North Bend, Oreg., 1929-39; dir. safety Calif.-Oreg. Power Co., 1939-63; safety specialist Pacific Power and Light Co., 1963-73; elec. cons. and internat. lectr. on safe use of electricity Haggard's Seminars, Medford, Oreg., 1973—; instr. War Manpower Commn. Recipient Oreg. Accident Commn. award, 1965; Oreg. Workmen's Compensation award, 1967; named to Hall of Fame, Internat. Assn. Elec. Insps., 1974. Mem. Edison Electric Inst. (cardiopulmonary resuscitation com.), IEEE (sr. mem.; Contbn. award 1972), Am. Soc. Safety Engrs., NW Electric Light and Power Assn., Nat. Fire Protection Assn., Vets. of Safety. Republican. Mem. Christian Ch. Producer TV programs; developer safety devices. Home and Office: 2607 Eastover Terr Medford OR 97501

HAGGERTY, ALLEN CHARLES, transportation company executive; b. Bklyn., Apr. 23, 1936; s. Charles Joseph and Florence G. (Cohn) H.; m. Iris May Parkinson, Aug. 13 ,1960; children: Robert, Kathryn, Kenneth. BS in Aero. Engring., Princeton U., 1958; MS in Mgmt., Rensselaer Poly. Inst., 1962; postgrad., Harvard U., 1974. Dir. ops. Boeing Vertol Co., Ridley Park, Pa., 1976-79, dir. comml. helicopter program, 1979-80; sr. v.p. ops. McDonnell Douglas Helicopter Co., Culver City, Calif., 1981, exec. v.p. ops., 1981-85; exec. v.p. engring and ops. McDonnell Douglas Helicopter Co., Mesa, Ariz., 1986—; mem. rotorcraft adv. group Aerospace Industries Assn. Am., 1986—. Co-inventor snap-ring grommet for elec. wiring. Trustee Del. County Community Coll., Media, Pa., 1978-80; pres. bd. of deacons Media Presbyn. Ch., 1977-80, pres. Indian Ln. Jr. High Sch., Media, 1976. Served to lt. USN, 1958-61. Named Mfg. Mgr. of Yr., Soc. Mfg. Engrs., 1984. Mem. Am. Helicopter Soc., Am. Defense Preparedness Assn., Assn. U.S. Army, Soc. Mfg. Engrs. (sr. mem.). Club: McDonnell Douglas Helicopter Mgmt. Avocations: sailing, tennis, jogging. Home: 30600 N Pima Rd Scottsdale AZ 85262 Office: McDonnell Douglas Helicopter Co 5000 E McDonnell Rd Mesa AZ 85205

HAGGITT, RODGER C., pathology educator; b. Detroit, Aug. 28, 1942; s. Russell Phillip and Eldora Emma (Reynolds) H.; m. Mary Jane Dugan, May 18, 1985; children: Kathryn, Scott. Student, East Tenn. State U., 1960-63; MD, U. Tenn., 1967. Diplomate Am. Bd. Pathology, Anatomic and Clin. Pathology. Pathologist New Eng. Deaconess Hosp., Boston, 1974-77; dir. surg. pathology Bapt. Meml. Hosp., Memphis, 1977-84; dir. hosp. pathology U. Wash., Seattle, 1984—, prof. pathology, 1984—, adj. prof. medicine; instr. pathology Harvard Med. Sch., Boston, 1974-77; clin. assoc. prof. U. Tenn., Memphis, 1977-84. Author book chapters; contbr. articles to profl. jours. Served to maj. U.S. Army, 1972-74. Recipient Disting. Teaching award U. Tenn. Coll. Medicine, 1981, Outstanding Teaching award U. Tenn. Med. Student Exec. Council, 1983. Fellow Am. Soc. Clin. Pathology (mem. council on anatomic pathology 1980-86, chmn. 1982-85), Coll. Am. Pathologists; mem. Gastrointestinal Pathology Club (pres. 1981), Am. Gastroenterol. Assn. (mem. abstract rev. com. 1985—), Alpha Omega Alpha. Home: 1427 39th Ave East Seattle WA 98112 Office: U Wash Univ Hosp RC-72 Seattle WA 98195

HAGLUND, WILLIAM ARTHUR, plant pathologist; b. Mpls., May 3, 1930; s. Knute Martin and Corinne Annette (Carlson) H.; m. Jean Christine Rallis, June 21, 1952; children: Michael Martin, Lynne Ann. BS, U. Minn., 1953, MS, 1958, PhD, 1960. Plant pathologist Wash. State U., Mt. Vernon, 1960—; plant pathologist, nematologist Cascade Agrl. Service, 1963—. Contbr. articles to profl. jours.; patentee plant variety protection. Bd. dirs. Mt. Vernon Sch., 1968—. Served to cpl. U.S. Army, 1953-55. Mem. Am. Phytopath. Soc., Am. Soc. Nematologists, Canadia Soc. Plant Pathology, Bean Improvement Council, Nat. Pea Improvement Assn. (pres. 1982-83). Republican. Lutheran. Club: Skagit Golf and Country (Burlington). Lodges: Lions, Masons. Home: 110 Claremont Pl Mount Vernon WA 98273 Office: Wash State U NWREC 1468 Memorial Hwy Mount Vernon WA 98273

HAGUE, JOHN BRIAN, energy company executive; b. Lethbridge, Alta., Can., Aug. 15, 1944; s. John Rayson and Rose (Inowlden) H.;. BA in Honors Econs., U. B.C., 1965; postgrad., U. Minn., 1965-66. Bus. analyst Pacific Region Office Imperial Oil Ltd., 1966-69; asst. dir. price rev. div. Prices & Income Commn., Ottawa, Ont., Can., 1969-72; fin. analyst Can. Devel. Corp., Toronto, Ont., 1972-75, mgr. fin. analysis, 1976, v.p., 1976-79, exec. v.p., 1979-86; dir. gen. grices and profits br. Anti-Inflation Bd., Ottawa, 1975-76; pres., chief operating officer Canterra Energy Ltd., Calgary, Atla., Can., 1986—; also bd. dirs. Canterra Energy Ltd., Calgary, Alta., Can.; bd. dirs. Cansulex Ltd., Vancouver, B.C., Can., Polysar Ltd., Sarnia, Ont. Avocations: boating, travelling. Office: Canterra Energy Ltd, PO Box 1051, Calgary, AB Canada T2P 2K7

HAHESY, WILLIAM CARRICK, lawyer; b. Tulare, Calif., Oct. 31, 1932; s. William Martin and Roberta Carrick (Clarke) H.; children—William Carrick, Cynthia Ellen. B.A., Fresno State Coll., 1954; J.D., U. Calif.-Berkeley, 1957. Bar: Calif. 1957. Dep. dist. atty. Tulare County, 1958-59; individual practice, 1959—; jud. dist. judge, 1969-76. Pres. Kings Canyon Savs. & Loan Assn., 1968-69; sec., dir. Kaweah Savs. and Loan Assn., 1973-82; mem. adv. com. Gt. Am. Fed. Savings & Loan Assn., 1982—; chmn. bd. dirs. Visalia Community Bank, 1976—. Mem. Tulare Plaza Project, 1964-66; mem. Tulare City Planning Commn., 1960-69; chmn. Task Force Com., Tulare, 1967; chmn. Tulare Redevel. Agy., 1967-81. Chmn., Stanley Mosk for Atty.-Gen., Tulare County, Calif., 1958, 62, Edmund G. Brown for Gov., 1966. Bd. dirs. Tulare County Legal Services, 1964-67, Tulare County Tng. Center for Handicapped, 1962-72, Tulare County Alcoholism Council, 1971-72; bd. dirs., v.p. Tulare Local Devel. Co. Mem. Tulare County Bar Assn. (treas. 1965-68, pres. 1985-86), State Bar Assn. Calif., Lambda Chi Alpha, Pi Gamma Mu, Phi Delta Phi. Democrat. Congregationalist. Club: Elks. Home: 3738 Millcreek Dr Visalia CA 93277 Office: 225 N M St Tulare CA 93274

HAHN, ELLIOTT JULIUS, lawyer; b. San Francisco, Dec. 9, 1949; s. Leo Wolf and Sherry Marion (Portnoy) H. BA cum laude, U. Pa., 1971, JD, 1974; LLM, Columbia U., 1980. Bar: N.J. 1974, U.S. Dist. Ct. N.J. 1974, Calif. 1976, U.S. Dist. Ct. (cen. dist.) Calif. 1976, D.C. 1978, U.S. Supreme Ct. 1980. Assoc. von Maltitz, Derenberg, Kunin & Janssen, N.Y.C., 1974-75; law clk. to presiding justice Los Angeles County Superior Ct., 1975-76; atty. Atlantic Richfield Co., Los Angeles, 1976-79; assoc. prof. law Calif. Western Sch. of Law, San Diego, 1980-85; assoc. Morgan, Lewis & Bockius, Los Angeles, 1985-87, Milbank, Tweed, Hadley & McCloy, Los Angeles, 1987—; prof. in Tokyo program Santa Clara Law Sch., 1981-83, Hong Kong program Santa Clara Law Sch., 1982; vis. scholar Nihon U., Tokyo, 1982; vis. lectr. Internat. Christian U., Tokyo, 1982; adj. prof. law Southwestern U., 1986—, Pepperdine U., 1987—. Author: Japanese Business Law and the Legal System, 1984. Vice chmn. San Diego Internat. Affairs Bd., 1981-85; bd. dirs. San Diego-Yokohama Sister City Soc., 1982-85, Los Angeles Nagoya Sister City Soc., 1986—. Mem. ABA, Assn. Asian Studies, U. Pa. Alumni Club (pres. San Diego chpt. 1982-85, pres. council Phila. 1983-85), Japan-Am. Soc. of So. Calif., Calif. Bar Assn., Japanese-Am. Soc. Legal Studies. Jewish. Home: 11411 Ohio Los Angeles CA 90025 Office: Milbank Tweed Hadley McCloy 515 S Figueroa St #1800 Los Angeles CA 90071

HAHN, ERWIN LOUIS, physicist, educator; b. Sharon, Pa., June 9, 1921; s. Israel and Mary (Weiss) H.; m. Marian Ethel Failing, Apr. 8, 1944 (dec. Sept. 1978); children: David L., Deborah A., Katherine L.; m. Natalie Woodford Hodgson, Apr. 12, 1980. B.S., Juniata Coll., 1943, D.Sc., 1966; M.S., U. Ill., 1947, Ph.D., 1949; D.Sc., Purdue U., 1975. Asst. Purdue U., 1943-44; research assoc. U. Ill., 1950; NRC fellow Stanford, 1950-51, instr., 1951-52; research physicist Watson IBM Lab., N.Y.C., 1952-55; assoc. Columbia U., 1952-55; faculty U. Calif.-Berkeley, 1955—, prof. physics, 1961—, assoc. prof. Miller Inst. for Basic Research, 1958-59, 1966-67, 1985-86, prof., 1966-67, 85-86; vis. fellow Brasenose Coll., Oxford (Eng.) U., 1981-82; Eastman vis. prof. Oxford U., 1987—; cons. Office Naval Research, Stanford, 1950-52, AEC, 1955—; spl. cons. USN, 1959; adv. panel mem. Nat. Bur. Standards, Radio Standards div., 1961-64; mem. Nat. Acad. Sci./NRC com. on basic research; adv. to U.S. Army Research Office, 1967-69. Author: (with T.P. Das) Nuclear Quadrupole Resonance Spectroscopy, 1958. Served with USNR, 1944-46. Recipient Oliver E. Buckley prize Am. Phys. Soc., 1971; prize Internat. Soc. Magnetic Resonance, 1971; award Humboldt Found., Germany, 1976-77; co-winner Wolf Found. prize in physics, 1983-84; named to Calif. Inventor Hall of Fame, 1984; Guggenheim fellow, 1961-62, 69-70; NSF fellow, 1961-62; vis. fellow Brasenose Coll., Oxford, 1969-70; lifetime hon. fellow Brasenose Coll., Oxford, 1984, Alumni Achievement award, Juanita Coll., 1986. Fellow Am. Phys. Soc. (past mem. exec. com. div. solid state physics); mem. Am. Acad. Arts and Scis., Nat. Acad. Scis., Slovenian Acad. Scis. and Arts (fgn.). Home: 69 Stevenson Ave Berkeley CA 94708 Office: Dept Physics U Calif Berkeley CA 94720

HAHN, GARY WILLIAM, environmental manager; b. Buffalo, Apr. 19, 1951; s. William Henry and Margaret Rose (Martin) H. BS in Chemistry, Case Western Res. U., 1973. Chemist Ohio EPA, Youngstown, 1976-79; hazardous waster specialist Oreg. Dept. Environ. Quality, Portland, 1980; project mgr. Chem-Security Systems, Portland, 1981-83; environ. mgr. McCall Oil and Chem. Corp., Portland, 1983-86; environ. scientist Century Environ. Scis., Portland, 1986; prin. SRH Assocs. Inc., Portland, 1986-87, Hahn and Assocs., Inc., Portland, 1987—. Mem. Am. Chem. Soc., Nat. Assn. Environ. Profls., Air Pollution Control Assn. Home: 2918 NE Hancock St Portland OR 97212 Office: Hahn and Assocs Inc 2918 NE Hancock St Portland OR 97212

HAHN, GLENN ALLEN, engineer; b. Houston, Nov. 9, 1956; s. Richard Allen and Florence (Wright) H.; m. Sylvie Marie Galerneau, June 13, 1984. BS, U. Mo., 1978; MS in Engring., Stanford U., 1986. Engr. ROLM Corp., Santa Clara, Calif., 1980-85; sr. engr. Silicon Solutions Corp., Menlo Park, Calif., 1985—. Mem. IEEE, AAAS, Assn. Computing Machinery, Sigma Xi. Home: 231 Oakhurst Place Menlo Park CA 94025 Office: Silicon Solutions Corp 1380 Willow Rd Menlo Park CA 94025

HAHN, HAROLD THOMAS, physical chemist, chemical engineer; b. N.Y.C., May 31, 1924; s. Gustave Hahn and Lillie Martha (Thomas) H.; m. Bennie Joyce Turney, Sept. 5, 1948; children: Anita Karen, Beverly Sharon, Carol Linda, Harold Thomas Jr. Student, Hofstra U., 1941-43; BSChemE, Columbia U., 1943-44; PhD in Chemistry, U. Tex., 1950-53. Chem. engr. Manhattan Dist. U.S. Army, Los Alamos, N.Mex., 1945-47; chem. engr. U. Calif., Los Alamos, 1947-50; sr. scientist Gen. Electric Co., Hanford, Wash., 1953-58; sect. chief, chem. research dept. Phillips Petroleum Co., Idaho Falls, Idaho, 1958-64; sr. staff scientist Lockheed Missiles & Space Co., Palo Alto, Calif., 1964—. Contbr. articles to profl. jours.; patentee in field. Pres. Edgemont Gardens PTA, Idaho Falls, 1963-64; commr. cub scout div. Stanford area council Boy Scouts Am., Palo Alto, 1973-76, also cubmaster pack 36, 1973-80, chmn. troops 36 and 37, 1975-77; mem. adminstrv. bd. Los Altos Meth. Ch. Served to col. U.S. Army, 1944-46, with res., 1946-84, col. res. ret. Humble Oil Co. fellow, 1952, Naval Bur. Ordnance fellow, 1953. Fellow Am. Inst. Chemists; mem. Calif. Acad. Scis., Internat. Platform Assn., Am. Chem. Soc., AIAA, Sigma Xi, Phi Lambda Upsilon, Kappa Rho. Republican. Avocations: fishing, skiing, backpacking, philately, photography. Home: 661 Teresi Ln Los Altos CA 94022 Office: Lockheed Research Lab Dept 93-50 Bldg 204 3251 Hanover St Palo Alto CA 94304

HAHN, JOAN CHRISTENSEN, drama educator, travel agent; b. Kemmerer, Wyo., May 9, 1933; d. Roy and Bernice (Pringle) Wainwright; m. Milton Angus Christensen, Dec. 29, 1952 (div. Oct. 1, 1971); children—Randall M., Carla J. Christensen Teasdale; m. Charles Henry Hahn, Nov. 15, 1972. B.S., Brigham Young U., 1965. Profl. ballroom dancer, 1951-59; travel dir. E.T. World Travel, Salt Lake City, 1969—; tchr. drama Payson High Sch., Utah, 1965-71, Cottonwood High Sch., Salt Lake City, 1971—; dir. Performing European Tours, Salt Lake City, 1969-76; dir. Broadway theater tours, 1976—. Dir. Salem City Salem Days, Utah, 1965-75; regional dir. dance Latter-day Saints Ch., 1954-72. Named Best Dir. High Sch. Musicals, Green Sheet Newspapers, 1977, 82, 84; recipient 1st place award Utah State Drama Tournament, 1974, 77, 78; Limelight award, 1982; Exemplary Performance in teaching theater arts Granite Sch. Dist., Salt Lake City, 1982. Mem. Internat. Thespian Soc. (sponsor 1968—, internat. dir. 1982-84, trustee 1978-84), Utah Speech Arts Assn. (pres. 1976-78), NEA, Utah Edn. Assn., Granite Edn. Assn., Profl. Travel Agts. Assn., Utah High Sch. Activities Assn. (drama rep. 1972-76), AAUW (pres. 1972-74). Republican. Mormon. Avocations: reading; travel; dancing. Home: 685 S 1st E Box 36 Salem UT 84653 Office: Cottonwood High Sch 5715 S 1300 E Salt Lake City UT 84121

HAHN, LIDA, healthcare services executive, hospital administrator; b. Oakland, Calif.; d. James Dyer and Cora Mildred (Helfrich) H.; m. Donald Richard Rasmussen (div.); children—Marina Ann, Donald Richard Jr.; m. Paul B. Henne, Jan. 12, 1974. R.N., Samuel Merritt Sch. Nursing, Oakland, 1941; student U. Munich (Germany), 1951, U. Calif.-Berkeley, 1969; student in bus. adminstrn., U. Calif-Santa Clara, 1970. Registered nurse. Chief nurse Oakland Army Base, Calif., 1944-48, Darmdstadt Infirmary, Germany, 1949-50; dir. nursing Civic Ctr. Hosp., Oakland, 1953-63, adminstr., 1960-63; sec., treas. and corp. owner Psychiat. Contract Services, Oakland, 1981—; v.p., exec. adminstr. E.A. Gladman Meml. Hosp., Oakland, 1967—; v.p. Telecare Corp., Oakland. Organized 21 health care dispensaries in Oakland and Richmond, Calif., chief nurse Oakland Army Base. Mem. Calif. State Legislature Com. Mental Health, Sacramento, 1968, Alameda County Mental Health Assn., Oakland, Alameda County Comprehensive Health Planning Council, Oakland, 1974-76. Recipient Meritorious Service by a Civilian award U.S. War Dept., 1948, Merit award Hosp. Council No. Calif., 1980, 86. Fellow Am. Coll. Hosp. Adminstrs.; mem. East Bay Hosp. Conf. (pres.; Meritorious award 1981), Calif. Hosp. Assn., Women's Network (award of merit, life mem. exec. bd.), Assn. Western Hosps., Am. Hosp. Assn., ARC Nursing Service-1st Res. Club: Soroptimist. Office: Everett A Gladman Meml Hosp 2633 E 27th St Oakland CA 94601

HAHN, ROGER, historian, educator; b. Paris, Jan. 5, 1932; came to U.S., 1941, naturalized, 1953; s. John P. and Thérèse E.L. (Lévy) H.; m. Ellen Isabel Leibovici, Sept. 11, 1955; children: Elisabeth L., Sophie A. B.A. magna cum laude, Harvard U., 1953, M.A. in Teaching, 1954; certificate, Ecole Pratique des Hautes Etudes, Paris, 1955; Ph.D., Cornell U., 1962. Instr. history U. Del., 1960-61; mem. history faculty U. Calif. at Berkeley, 1961—, prof., 1974—; spl. asst. to dir. sci. affairs Bancroft Library, Berkeley, 1972—; chief U.S. del. XVth Internat. Congress History of Sci., Edinburgh, 1977, co-chmn. XVIIth Internat. Congress, Berkeley, 1985; bd. dirs. Centre de Synthèse, Paris, 1976—; vis. prof. Collège de France, 1984. Author: L'Hydrodynamique au XVIIIe Siècle, 1965, Laplace as a Newtonian Scientist, 1967, The Anatomy of a Scientific Institution: The Paris Academy of Sciences 1666-1803, 1971, paperback edit., 1986; A Bibliography of Quantitative Studies on Science and Its History, 1980, Calendar of the Correspondence of Laplace, 1982; (with R. Taton) Ecoles Techniques et Militaires au XVIIIe Siècle, 1986; adv. editor: Isis, 1971-75, 18th-Century Studies, 1976-80; cons. editor: History of Sci, 1972—; editorial advisor: Social Studies of Science, 1974—. Served with AUS, 1955-57. Fulbright scholar, 1954-55, 83-84; NSF fellow, 1959-60, 64-65; Am. Council Learned Socs. fellow, 1973-74; decorated chevalier Ordre des Palmes Académiques, 1977; recipient book prize Pacific Coast br. Am. Hist. Assn., 1972. Fellow AAAS (council 1967-73); mem. History Sci. Soc. (council 1967-70, 77-80), Am. Soc. 18th Century Studies (pres. 1982-83), Western Soc. 18th Century Studies (pres. 1977-78), West Coast History of Sci. Soc. (pres. 1982-84), Acad. Internat. d'Histoire des Scis.

HAIGHT, FULTON WILBUR, lawyer; b. Los Angeles, July 9, 1923; s. Raymond Leroy and Heloise Marie (Davis) H.; m. Dorothy Cornelia Fitger, Oct. 4, 1952; children—Fulton Wilbur, Maureen Elizabeth, Hilary Josephine, Talis Susanne. LL.B., U. So. Calif., 1948. Bar: Calif. bar 1949. Practiced in Los Angeles, 1949-50; sr. dep. city atty. City of Los Angeles, 1950-52; asso. mem. law firm Moss, Lyon & Dunn (name changed to Haight, Lyon & Smith 1967, now Haight, Dickson, Brown & Bonesteel, 1976), Los Angeles, 1952-59; partner Moss, Lyon & Dunn (name changed to Haight, Lyon & Smith 1967, now Haight, Dickson, Brown & Bonesteel, 1976), 1959-67, sr. partner, 1967—; lectr. Mem. Calif. Jud. Council Arbitration Adv. Com., 1972; organizer, def. chmn. Los Angeles Attys. Spl. Arbitration Plan, 1972; mem. bench and bar com. Los Angeles Superior Ct., 1970-72; mem. adminstrv. com. Arbitration Com., 1976—. Author: (with Cotchett) California Courtroom Evidence, 1972. Served to 1st lt. USAF, 1943-45. Decorated Air medal with 3 oak leaf clusters. Fellow Am. Coll. Trial Lawyers (state chmn. So. Calif. 1984-85, regent 1985—); mem. Assn. So. Calif. Def. Counsels (pres. 1970-71), State Bar Assn. Calif. (bd. govs. 1977-81, chmn. com. on arbitration 1974-77, v.p., bd. govs. 1977-78, 81—, com. bar examiners 1986—), Los Angeles Bar Assn. (chmn. co. for rev. jury procedure 1976—). Home: 1725 San Vicente Blvd Santa Monica CA 90402 Office: 201 Santa Monica Blvd Santa Monica CA 90406

HAIGHT, GARY WAYNE, lawyer, electronics company executive; b. Trail, B.C., Can., July 25, 1942; s. Kenneth Charles and Violet Honeyborn (Butler) H.; m. W. Deanna Elliott, Oct. 23, 1963; children: Dawn, Carey. BA, U. Idaho, 1966, JD, 1968. Bar: Idaho 1968, Minn. 1976, Wis. 1976. Law clk. to presiding justices Idaho Supreme Ct., Boise, 1968-69; atty. SEC, Washington, 1969-71, Internat. Multifoods Co., Mpls., 1971-75; asst. gen. counsel A.O. Smith Corp., Milw., 1976-83; v.p. Key Tronic Corp., Spokane, Wash., 1983—. Rep. precinct chmn., Minn., 1972; founding officer Cursillo Movement, Wis., 1976-80; del. and officer AMOR, Wis., 1977-82. Recipient Superior Performance award SEC, Washington, 1971. Mem. Idaho Bar Assn., Minn. Bar Assn., Wis. Bar Assn., Phi Alpha Delta. Episcopal. Club: Toastmasters. Lodge: Fraternal Order Eagles. Avocations: sailing, jogging, cycling, hunting, fishing. Home: E2155 Cherry Hill Rd Coeur d'Alene ID 83814 Office: Key Tronic Corp N4424 Spokane WA 99216

HAIGHT, JACQULYN A., secondary teacher; b. Emporia, Kans., Aug. 2, 1935; d. Roscoe Edward and Geneva Louise (Timmons) LeGresley; m. David Dee Haight, Aug. 14, 1954 (div. Mar. 1972); children: Karen, Terrie, Sandra, Michael. BA, U. Idaho; BS, Lewis Clark State Coll. Drama coach Lewiston (Idaho) High Sch., 1976, Clarkston (Wash.) High Sch., 1977; tchr. Tammany Elem. Sch., Lewiston, 1978, Nez Perce Tribal Sch., Lapwai, Idaho, 1979-84; tchr. drama Potlatch (Idaho) High Sch., 1984—. Active Lewiston Civic Theatre, 1972—. Sandra Reed drama scholar Lewis-Clark State Coll., 1974. Mem. NEA.

HAIGHT, JAY DALE, animal manager; b. Galesburg, Ill., May 13, 1952; s. Jack Howard and Billie Jeane (Hansbrough) H.; m. Jane Elizabeth Altier, Aug. 27, 1978 (div. June 1981). Student, Knox Coll., 1970-72, Portland State U., 1976-78. Research coordinator Washington Park Zoo, Portland, Oreg., 1976, exhibit design technician, 1978-79, elephant keeper, 1980—. Contbr. articles to profl. jours. Cons. Oreg. Archtl. Preservation Resource Ctr., Portland, 1984. Recipient Excellence in Journalism award Am. Assn. Zoo Keepers, 1980. Mem. AAAS, Animal Behavior Soc.; Am. Assn. Zoological Parks and Aquariums (affiliate). Avocations: hiking, poetry, video. Home: 5827 SW Vermont St Portland OR 97219 Office: Washington Park Zoo 4001 SW Canyon Rd Portland OR 97221

HAIKALIS, SUSAN W(ILLIAMS), social worker; b. Montclair, N.J., Oct. 20, 1941; d. Richard Sugden and Helen Faith (Fellows) Williams; m. Peter Dennis Haikalis, May 27, 1967; 1 child, Joanna. BA, U. Mich., 1963; MSW, NYU, 1965. Cert. social worker; lic. clin. social worker, Calif. Dir. social work Riverside (Calif.) Community Hosp., 1968-70; med. social work cons. Vis. Nurse Assn. Riverside County, Riverside, 1970-75; case mgmt. specialist Riverside County Assn. Retarded Citizens, Riverside, 1975-77; program dir. Assn. for the Advancement of Mentally Handicapped, Princeton, N.J., 1977-79; assoc. dir. social work Mt. Zion Hosp. and Med. Ctr., San Francisco, 1980-86, dir. social work, 1986—; med. social work cons. Riverside, 1970-77. Author: (with Epke and Meadows) How Discharge Planning Works and Can Work for You Under Prospective Payment, 1985. Sec., bd. dirs. Hellenic Devel. Corp., Oakland, Calif., 1984—; pres. bd. dirs. East Bay Regional Ctr., 1986; v.p., bd. dirs. Berkeley (Calif.) Pub. Edn. Found., 1986—. Recipient O.E. Nelson Service award Am. Cancer Soc., Riverside, 1971. Mem. Soc. Hosp. Social Work Dirs. (pres. no. Calif. chpt. 1983, chmn. state polit. action com. 1984—, mem. nat. nominating com. 1986—). Democrat. Episcopalian. Avocations: choral singing, skiing, swimming, reading. Home: 1118 Park Hills Rd Berkeley CA 94708 Office: Mt Zion Hosp and Med Ctr 1600 Divisadero St San Francisco CA 94115

HAIL, JAMES ARTHUR, II, newspaper executive; b. St. Louis, July 10, 1949; s. James Arthur and Frances Elizabeth (Koziatek) H.; m. Cynthia Joy Henthorn, May 27, 1972; children—James Arthur III, Laura Elizabeth. Reporter Ft. Scott (Kans.) Tribune and Pittsburg (Kans.) Sun, 1970-73; copy editor Bradenton (Fla.) Herald, 1973-74, sports editor, 1974-75, met. editor, 1975-77; mng. editor Junction City (Kans.) Daily Union, 1977-79; editor, gen. mgr. Golden (Colo.) Daily Transcript, 1979-80; v.p. North Idaho Pub. Co., editor pub. North Idaho Press, Wallace Miner newspapers, Wallace, Idaho, 1980-85; editor North Idaho Newspaper Group of Hagadone Communications, Coeur D'Alene, Idaho, 1986—; founder, ptnr. HRM Investments, Inc., Osburn, Idaho, 1985—; ptnr. The Profit Co., Coeur D'Alene, 1985—. Mem. Geary County (Kans.) Tourism and Conv. Com., 1978-80; bd. dirs. George Smith Library, Junction City, Kans., 1978-79; bd. dirs. Colo. Jr. Miss program, 1979. Mem. , Idaho Newspaper Assn. (bd. dirs. 1986—). Republican. Roman Catholic.Club: Idaho Press. Home: 1534 Lookout Dr Coeur d'Alene ID 83814 Office: 201 Second Coueur d'Alene ID 83814

HAILE, LAWRENCE BARCLAY, lawyer; b. Atlanta, Feb. 19, 1938; m. Ann Springer McCauley, March 28, 1984; children: Gretchen Vanderhoof, Eric McKenzie, Scott McAllister. B.A. in Econs, U. Tex., 1958, LL.B., 1961. Bar: Tex. 1961, Calif. 1962. Law clk. to U.S. Judge Joseph M. Ingraham, Houston, 1961-62; pvt. practice law San Francisco, 1962-67, Los Angeles, 1967—; mem. firm Simon, Buckner, Haile & Migdal, Marina Del Rey, Calif., 1977—; instr. U. Calif. at Los Angeles Civil Trial Clinics, 1974, 76; lectr. law Calif. Continuing Edn. of Bar, 1973-74, 80-87; mem. nat. panel arbitrators Am. Arbitration Assn., 1965—. Asso. editor: Tex. Law Rev, 1960-61; Contbr. articles profl. publs. Mem. adv. bd. Inglewood Gen. Hosp. Mem. State Bar Calif., Tex., U.S. Supreme Ct. bar assns., Internat. Assn. Property Ins. Counsel (founding mem., pres. 1980), ASTM, London World Trade Centre Assn., Phi Delta Phi, Delta Sigma Rho. Club: Marine (London). Office: 4551 Glencoe Ave #300 Marina Del Rey CA 90292 Office: 1910 Huntington Dr South Pasadena CA 91030

HAILE, MARCUS ALFRED, chemistry educator; b. Haviland, Kans., Oct. 14, 1930; s. William Oral and Myrna May (Stotts) H.; m. Lynne Helene Hunsucker, Mar. 20, 1964; children: Marta Helene, Cavan William. BS, Pepperdine U., 1955; Master, U. No. Iowa, 1968. Cert. secondary tchr., Calif. Tchr. chemistry Hamilton High Sch., Los Angeles, 1957-67; prof. chemistry Los Angeles City Coll., 1969—, also pres. acad. senate, 1972-73. Author: Experimental General Chemistry, 1973, 76, Gen. Analytical Chemistry, 1987; contbr. articles to profl. jours. Chmn. Amateur Athletic Union So. Calif. Swimming U.S. Swim, Los Angeles, Ventura and Santa Barbara Counties, Calif., 1980-81. Served with U.S. Army, 1950-52. NSF grantee, 1967-68. Mem. Am. Chem. Soc., Am. Fedn. Tchrs., Calif. Thoroughbred Breeders Assn. Democrat. Avocations: race horse owner, skiing, fishing. Home: 22404 Kearny St Woodland Hills CA 91364 Office: Los Angeles City Coll 855 N Vermont Ave Los Angeles CA 90026

HAIMES, FLORENCE CATHERINE, chemistry educator; b. San Jose, Calif., June 10, 1917; d. Robert Archibald and Clara Mae (Burk) H. BA, San Jose State U., 1938; MA, Stanford U., 1940, EdD, 1952. Tchr. secondary schs. Calif., 1940-47; prof. chemistry San Francisco State U., 1947—. Fellow AAAS; mem. Calif. Assn. Chemistry Tchrs. (pres. 1968-69), Calif. Acad. Scis. Democrat. Home: 785 Burnett Ave Apt 10 San Francisco CA 94131 Office: San Francisco State U Dept Chemistry 1600 Holloway San Francisco CA 94132

HAINES, CLARA JOSEPHINE, hospital administrator; b. Denver, Sept. 24, 1924; d. Frank Anthony and Eva (Gonzales) Lucero; m. Edward Rolen Haines, Oct. 17, 1959; children—Mark, Susan. B.A., U. Calif.-Berkeley, 1950; postgrad. U. So. Calif., 1951-57. Hosp. adminstr. Los Angeles County U. So. Calif. Med. Ctr., 1978-79, hosp. adminstr., assoc. exec. dir., 1979—, chief ops. officer, assoc. exec. dir., 1985—; asst. clin. prof. U. So. Calif. Grad. Sch. Health Care Adminstrn., Los Angeles, 1980—; career advisor U. Calif.-Berkeley. Active LWV, So. Pasadena. Recipient Clin. Faculty Excellent Service award U. So. Calif., 1984. Mem. Am. Hosp. Assn., Calif. Hosp. Assn., Women in Health Adminstrn., Nat. Assn. Female Execs. Democrat.

HAINES, JIM ALLEN, architect; b. Escondido, Calif., Apr. 28, 1946; s. Allen Ray and Arlene Haines; m. Margaret Amanda Howell, Apr. 4, 1982; 1 child, Amanda Christine. BArch with distinction, Wash. State U., 1972. Lic. architect, Wash.; cert. bldg. inspector, Wash. Structural draftsman Aiwood-Hinzman Cons. Structural Engrs., Spokane, Wash., 1972-74; archtl. draftsman Tan-Brookie Kundig Architects, Spokane, 1974-76; architect E.M. Hicks Architects, Spokane, 1976-78; bldg. tech. Spokane County Bldg. Dept., 1979-84; prin. Haines Archtl. Services, Spokane, 1985—. Served with U.S. Army, 1967-69, Vietnam. Mem. Constrn. Specifications Inst. (program chmn. 1985-86), Phi Kappa Phi. Presbyterian. Avocations: snow skiing, painting, stamp collecting. Office: Haines Archtl Services W 3121 8th Ave Spokane WA 99204

HAINSWORTH, DAVID JAMES, high technology company executive; b. St. Louis, Nov. 29, 1941; s. Joseph C. and Anna M. Hainsworth; student Coll. of Sch. Ozarks, 1960-63, Forest Park Community Coll., 1967-68, U. Mo., 1968-69; m. Beverly Ann Berner, Oct. 25, 1969 (div. 1985); children—Lorry Ann, Jessica Nicole. Purchasing agt. Anheuser-Busch, Inc., St. Louis, 1967-70; asst. to v.p. mktg. D & D Bean Co., Greeley, Colo., 1970-77; asst. mgr. Outwest Bean, Inc., regional mktg. coop., Littleton, Colo., 1977-78, gen. mgr. and treas., 1978-81, pres., 1981-85, Glenn L. Cogil and Assocs., 1984-86; v.p. ops. Internat. Power Techs., Inc., Littleton, 1986—; dir. Nat. Council Farmers Coops., Washington, 1981-82; sec. adv. bd. Wichita (Kans.) Bank for Coops., 1980-82; participant Mktg. and Internat. Trade Conf., 1980; mem. nat. adv. bd. Farm Credit Adminstrn., Washington, 1983-85. Active choirs and youth orgns. Oak Hill Presbyn. Ch., St. Louis, 1958-69, First United Meth. Ch., Greeley, 1969-78; supply pastor Hollister (Mo.) Presbyn. Ch., 1961-63; mem. citizen's budget rev. com. Arapahoe County Dist. 6 Sch. Dist., 1980-81; area leader Republican Com. Arapahoe County. Served with USAF, 1963-67; Vietnam. Mem. Rocky Mountain Bean Dealers Assn. (dir. 1979-83, v.p. 1981-83), Englewood C. of C., HIspanic C. of C. (corp. rep. 1986—), Traffic Club of Denver. Methodist. Club: Rotary. Home: 5955 S Sycamore St #101 Littleton CO 80120 Office: Internat Power Techs Inc 5965 S Prince St Littleton CO 80120

HAIR, KITTIE ELLEN, secondary teacher; b. Denver, June 12, 1948; d. William Edward and Jacqueline Jean (Holt) H. BA, Brigham Young U., 1971; postgrad. in history, U. Nev. cert. tchr., Nev. Health educator Peace Corps, Totota, Liberia, 1971-72; tchr. Clark County Sch. Dist., Las Vegas, Nev., 1972-77, 1979—; missionary Ch. Jesus Christ Latter-Day Saints, Alta., Can., 1977-79. Mem. NEA, Nat. Council for Social Scis., Clark County Tchr.'s Assn., ACLU, Phi Kappa Phi, Phi Alpha Theta. Democrat. Avocations: collecting western and Indian art, gardening.

HAIRABEDIAN, MARTIN, JR., protective services official, lawyer; b. Chgo., Aug. 18, 1932; s. Martin and Tamara (Kacutoff) H.; m. Pauline Galewick, Mar. 15, 1953; children: Pamela Jane, Penny, Patricia. Student, East Los Angeles Coll., 1950-63, U. So. Calif., 1963, Southwestern U., Los Angeles, 1963-66; JD, So. Bay U., 1976. Police officer Los Angeles Police Dept., 1954-77, sgt., 1959-64, lt., 1964-69, capt., 1969-77; chief of police Fullerton (Calif.) Police Dept., 1977—; mem. Calif. state crime resistance task force, 1984—. Mem. steering com. for gov. to elect George Deukmejian, Orange County, Calif., 1984; mem. Civil Air Patrol, Elmonte, Calif., 1980-85; commr. Orange County Human Relations Commn., 1982-85. Mem. Internat. Assn. Chiefs Police, Calif. Police Chiefs Assn. (pres. Orange County chpt. 1985), Police Mgmt. Assn., Calif. Peace Officers Assn. Republican. Lodge: Rotary. Office: Fullerton Police Dept 237 W Commonwealth Ave Fullerton CA 92632

HAIRE, MICHAEL JOSEPH, chemist, researcher; b. Kansas City, Mo., Jan. 18, 1947; s. Joseph M. and Agnes L. (Gatton) H.; m. Theresa M. Asher, Oct. 25, 1968; children: MIchael J., Christopher A., Matthew J. Student, St. Benedict's Coll., 1965-67; BS in Chemistry, U. Kans., 1969; PhD in Organic Chemistry, U. Wis., 1974. Research chemist E.I. DuPont de Nemours and Co., Wilmington, Del., 1974-79; research chemist Chevron Chem. Co., Richmond, Calif., 1979-83, sr. research chemist, 1983-85, asst. to dir. research, 1985-87, sr. formulations chemist, 1987—; mem. State of Del. Med. Malpractice Rev. Bd., Wilmington, 1978. Referee Jour. of Organic Chemistry, 1976—; contbr. articles to profl. jours.; patentee in field. Pres. Casa Grande Music Assn., Petaluma, Calif., 1985-86, student grants chmn., 1984-85. Mem. Am. Chem. Soc., Sierra Club. Avocations: cross country ski racing, running, backpacking. Office: Ortho Research Ctr 15049 San Pablo Ave Richmond CA 94804

HAIRSTON, JAMES JOSEPH, JR., safety engineer; b. Jacksonville, Fla., Sept. 30, 1937; s. James Joseph and Elsie (Verlie) H.; m. Carole Kaye Acker, June 1, 1963; children: James Joseph, Christopher M., Leah Kaye. BS in Math., Jacksonville U., 1962; MS in Safety, U. So. Calif., 1977. Marine electrician Merrell Stevens Shipyard, Jacksonville, Fla., 1957-62; commd. 2d lt. USAF, 1962, advanced through grades to capt., 1966, served radar navigator bombardier, ret., 1978; system safety/reliability engr. Boeing Aerospace Co., Houston, 1978-84; prin. engr. Boeing Mil. Airplane Co., Seattle, 1984—; instr., cons. in field. Co-author: Nuclear Safety Analysis Computer Code, 1981; contbr. articles to profl. jours. Cubscout master Boy Scouts Am., Sacramento, 1976; tchr. So. Bapt. Ch., 1966-76. Decorated 40 medals including Air Medal with nine oak leaf clusters. Mem. Am. Soc. Safety Engrs., System Safety Soc. Democrat. Home: 2223 224th Pl NE Redmond WA 98053 Office: The Boeing Co PO Box 3707 Seattle WA 98124

HAISCH, BERNHARD MICHAEL, astronomer; b. Stuttgart-Bad Canstatt, Fed. Republic Germany, Aug. 23, 1949; s. Friedrich Wilhelm and Gertrud Paula (Dammbacher) H.; m. Pamela S. Eakins, July 29, 1977 (div. 1986); children: Katherine Stuart, Christopher Taylor; m. Marsha A. Sims, Aug. 23, 1986. Student, St. Meinrad (Ind.) Coll., 1967-68; BS in Astrophysics, Ind. U., 1971; PhD in Astrophysics, U. Wis., 1975. Research assoc. Joint Inst. Lab. Astrophysics, U. Colo., 1975-77, 78-79; vis. scientist space research lab. U. Utrecht, The Netherlands, 1977-78; research scientist Lockheed Research Lab., Palo Alto, Calif., 1979-83, staff scientist, 1983—; guest investigator NASA programs, Internat. Ultraviolet Explorer,Einstein obs., EXOSAT obs., 1980—. Contbr. numerous articles to profl. jours. Fellow Royal Astron. Soc.; mem. Internat. Astron. Union, Am. Astron.Soc., Astron. Soc. of Pacific, Phi Beta Kappa, Sigma Xi, Phi Kappa Phi. Avocations: Tae Kwon Do, internat. folk dance, downhill skiing. Office: Lockheed Palo Alto Research Lab Div 91-20 Bldg 255 3251 Hanover St Palo Alto CA 94304

HAISLEY, FAY BEVERLEY, academic dean; b. Sydney, Australia, Feb. 20, 1933; came to U.S., 1971; d. Reginald Charles and Edna Irene (Kidd) Sambrook; m. Ian George Haisley, May 11, 1963 (div. 1973). BA, U. Papua New Guinea, Port Moresby, 1970; MEd with honors, U. Oreg., 1971, PhD, 1973. Cert. elem. tchr., spl. edn., Oreg., New South Wales, Australia. Tchr., prin. Dept. Edn., Australia, 1952-70; prin., lectr. Dept. Edn., Port Moresby, Papua New Guinea, 1969-70; lectr. early childhood U. Calif., Santa Barbara, 1973-75; from asst. prof. to assoc. prof. learning disabilities and elem. edn. U. Oreg., Eugene, 1975-80, assoc. dean tchr. edn., 1981-84; dean Sch. of Edn. U. Pacific, Stockton, Calif., 1984—, dir. dean's grant, 1977-83; commr. Calif. Commn. on Tchr. Credentialling, 1985—; dir. spl. project Am. Nepalese Edn. Found., Eugene, 1982-84; dir. doctoral dept. edn. program U. Guam, 1983-84; bd. dirs. Far West Ednl. Labs. Contbr. articles to profl. jours. Trustee Stockton Civic Theatre, 1986. Grantee U.S. Office Edn., 1979-82, Nat. Inst. Edn., 1981, Oreg. State Dept. Edn., 1978. Mem. Am. Ednl. Research Assn., Assn. Tchr. Educators, Am. Assn. Colls. Tchr. Edn., Calif. Assn. Tchr. Educators, Phi Delta Kappa. Anglican. Office: Univ Pacific Sch Edn Pacific Ave Stockton CA 95211

HAITH, MARSHALL MYRON, psychology educator; b. Chilicothe, Mo., Apr. 23, 1937; s. Nathan and Frances (Rabicoff) H.; m. Sue Ann Schneider, June 8, 1962; children: Michael, Brian, Gary. BA, U. Mo., 1959; MA, UCLA, 1962, PhD, 1964. Predoctoral fellow UCLA, 1962-64; postdoctoral fellow Yale U., New Haven, 1964-66; asst. prof. Harvard U., Boston, 1966-72; prof. psychology U. Denver, 1972—. Author: Rules that Babies Look By, 1980; editor: Infancy and Developmental Psychology, 1983; contbr. articles to profl. jours. Recipient Research Scientist award NIMH; grantee NIH, 1985—, NIMH, 1972—; Guggenheim Found. fellow, 1978-79. Fellow Am. Psychol. Assn., AAAS, Soc. Research in Child Devel., Internat. Soc. Study of Behavioral Devel. (editorial bd.). Home: 39 Viking Dr Englewood CO 80110 Office: U Denver Psychology Dept Denver CO 80208

HAKKILA, EERO ARNOLD, nuclear safeguards technology chemist; b. Canterbury, Conn., Aug. 4, 1931; s. Jack and Ida Maria (Lillquist) H.; children: Jon Eric, Mark Douglas, Gregg Arnold. BS in Chemistry, Cen. Conn. State U., 1953; PhD in Analytical Chemistry, Ohio State U., 1957. Staff mem. Los Alamos (N.Mex.) Nat. Lab., 1957-78, assoc. group leader safeguard systems, 1978-80, dep. group leader, 1980-82, group leader, 1982-83, project mgr. internat. safeguards, 1983—. Editor: Nuclear Safeguards Analysis, 1978; contbr. numerous articles to profl. jours. Fellow Am. Inst. Chemists; mem. N.Mex. Inst. Chemists (pres. 1971-73), Am. Chem. Soc., Am. Nuclear Soc. (exec. com. fuel cycle and waste mgmt. div. 1984-86), Inst. Nuclear Materials Mgmt. Avocations: skiing, fishing, rockhounding. Office: Los Alamos Nat Lab PO Box 1663 Los Alamos NM 87545

HAKOMORI, SEN-ITIROH, immunochemist, biochemist, researcher, educator; b. Sendai, Japan, Feb. 13, 1929; came to U.S., 1963, naturalized, 1978; s. Shinichiro and Kiku (Amae) H.; m. Mitsuko Ito, June 16, 1956; children—Yoichiro, Kenjiro, Naoko. M.D., Tohoku U., Sendai, 1952, D. Med. Sci., Inst. Biochemistry, 1957. Intern, Sendai City Hosp., Japan, 1952-53, asst. prof. Tohoku U., 1957-59, prof. Coll. Pharmacy, 1959-63; research assoc. Med. Sch., Harvard U., Boston, 1963-66; vis. prof. Brandeis U., Waltham, Mass., 1966-68; assoc. prof., then prof. U. Wash., Seattle, 1968-75; program head, prof. pathobiology and microbiology F. Hutchinson Cancer Ctr. and U. Wash., Seattle, 1975-86; scientific dir. The Biomembrane Inst., Seattle, 1986—; mem. study sect. NIH, Bethesda, Md., 1975-78, mem. adv. com., 1984. Author: Sphingolipid Biochemistry, 1983; contbr. numerous articles to profl. publs. Recipient Philip Levin award Am. Soc. Clin. Pathology, 1984, Outstanding Investigator Nat. Cancer Inst., 1986. Mem. Am. Soc. Biol. Chemists, Am. Assn. Cancer Research, Am. Soc. Immunology.r Research, Am. Soc. Immunology. Office: F Hutchinson Cancer Research Ctr 1124 Columbia St Seattle WA 98104

HALADYNA, LINDA JOY, academic administrator; b. Vallejo, Calif., Feb. 15, 1947; d. Donald Ferald and Ruth Louise (Haire) Gregory; m. John Theodore Haladyna, June 29, 1974; children: Donald Paul, John Ryan. BA in Edn., Eastern Wash. U., 1969; MEd, cert. sch. prin., Whitworth Coll., 1979. Elem. tchr. Spokane (Wash.) Pub. Schs., 1969-74, program specialist, 1974-75, tchr. of gifted, 1975-78, 80-81, adminstr., 1978-80, elem. prin., 1981—; ptnr. Gt. Western Savs. Bank, Spokane, 1984—. Bd. dirs. Mulcular Dystrophy Assn., Spokane, 1978-80. Recipient Outstanding Leadership award YWCA, Spokane, 1985-86. Mem. Elem. Prin.'s Assn. Wash. (conv. com. 1985-86), Spokane Prin.'s Assn., Altrusa, Delta Kappa Gamma (chmn. program com. 1983-84), Phi Delta Kappa (scholarship com. 1985-87), Pi Lambda Theta (pres. 1986—). Democrat. Presbyterian. Lodge: Eagles. Avocations: sewing, writing, reading, traveling, collecting antiques. Home: S 5518 Willamette Spokane WA 99223 Office: Balboa Elem Sch W 3010 Holyoke Spokane WA 99223

HALBERT, ROBERT ORLAF, insurance company executive; b. Denver, May 9, 1937; s. Harold Nolan and Dorothy Irene (Swanson) H.; m. Jean Anne Billigmeier, June 20, 1959; children: John Gregory, Mark Bradford. BA in Sociology, Dartmouth Coll., 1959. CLU, chartered fin. cons. Asst. gen. agt. Equitable of Iowa, Denver, 1962-71; trust officer United Bank of Denver, 1971-75; chmn., pres., chief exec. officer Fidelity Nat. Life Ins. Co., Denver, 1975—; mem. ins. com. Assn. Bank Holding Cos. 1976-85, chmn. 1983-84; speaker Am. Bankers Assn., Colo. Bankers Assn., Colo. Brokerage Assn., 1975—; bd. dirs. Lincoln Agy., Inc., Denver, 1975—. Contbr. numerous articles to publs. Chmn. Denver Metro Sports Com., 1984—. Served to capt. USMC, 1959-62. Mem. Am. Soc. Chartered Life Underwriters, Colo. Assn. Life Underwriters, Colo. Heart Assn. (bd. dirs. 1975-86, Vol. of Yr. 1985), Am. Cancer Soc. (bd. dirs. 1972-85), Colo. Sports Hall of Fame (dir. 1983—), Denver C. of C., Dartmouth Alumnae Assn. (pres. 1972-74). Republican. Club: Valley Country (Aurora, Colo.). Avocations: golfing, reading, racquetball, woodworking. Home: 6657 E Dartmouth Ave Denver CO 80224 Office: Fidelity Nat Life Ins Co Three United Bank Ctr 1700 Broadway Denver CO 80274

HALCROMB, VERNON CORTEZ, coll. dean; b. Kansas City, Kans., May 18, 1929; s. Ray Reed and Almeta Frances (Adkins) H.; B.Vocat.Edn., Calif. State U., Long Beach, 1971; M.A., UCLA, 1972, Ed.D., 1975; m. Odessa Marlene Pettis, Sept. 10, 1949; children—Gail, Kent, Brian, Craig, Mark. Instr., counselor Los Angeles Unified Sch. Dist., 1966-69; dir. SE Area Manpower Inst. Devel. Staff, 1969-72; dir. inservice edn. UCLA, 1972-76; dean occupational edn. Pasadena (Calif.) Area Community Coll. Dist., 1976—; adv. com. Pasadena Unified Sch. Dist.; staff Turner Sch. Learning, Pasadena. Mem. Calif. Gov.'s Com. on Employment of Handicapped; mem. planning council Pasadena United Way, 1980-81; mem. Pasadena Pvt. Industry Council, 1980. Served with USNR, 1948-53. Grantee Calif. Dept. Edn., 1972-73, Edn. Professions Devel. Act, 1974; Mem. Am. Vocat. Assn., NEA, Calif. Tchrs. Assn., NAACP. Democrat. Home: 5532 Bedford Ave Los Angeles CA 90056 Office: 1570 E Colorado Blvd Pasadena CA 91106

HALE, CARL DENNIS, electronics company materials manager; b. Oakland, Calif., July 12, 1949; s. William Francis and Irene Helegard (Knoth) H.; children: Telissa, Desiree, Michael. BS, San Jose State U., 1974; mfg. studies program, Gen. Electric Co., San Jose, 1976. Prodn. planner Gen. Electric, San Jose, Calif., 1974-77; mfg. engr. Gen. Electric, Paterson, N.J., 1977-78; advisor, prodn. mgr. Gen. Electric Co., San Jose, 1978-79; materials mgr. Spectra Physics, Mountain View, Calif., 1979-81; factory parts mgr. Hewlett-Packard, Mountain View, 1981-82; materials mgr. Hewlett-Packard, Santa Clara, 1982-86; mgr. prodn. sect. Hewlett-Packard, San Jose, 1986—; part time instr. San Jose State U., 1985—. Author: (manuals) Material Requirements Planning, 1981, Conceptual Manufacturing, 1983. Mem. Am. Prodn. and Inventory Control Soc. (cert. prodn. and inventory mgmt.). Republican. Roman Catholic. Club: Schobers. Avocations: jogging, softball, gardening, reading. Home: 7821 Foothill Knolls Dr Pleasanton CA 94566 Office: Hewlett-Packard 370 W Trimble Rd San Jose CA 95131

HALE, DEAN EDWARD, social services administrator; b. Balt., Aug. 4, 1950; s. James Russell and Marjorie Elinor (Hoerman) H.; B.A.S.W., U. Pa., 1975; postgrad. U. Oreg., 1976, U. London, 1974, U. Mont., 1968-71; m. Lucinda Hoyt Muniz, 1979. Dir. recreation Hoffman Homes for Children, Gettysburg, Pa., 1970; social worker Holt Adoption Program, Inc., Eugene, Oreg., 1975-78; supr. social services Holt Internat. Children's Services, Eugene, 1978-84, Asia rep., 1984—; lectr. U. Oreg.; cons. internat. child welfare, 1982—; co-founder Family Opportunities Unltd. Inc., 1981—. Author: Adoption, A Family Affair, 1981, When Your Child Comes Home, 1986. Pres. Woodtique Heights Homeowners Assn., 1980—, Our Saviour's Lutheran Ch., 1981—; bd. dirs. Greenpeace of Oreg., 1979-84. Named Outstanding New Jaycee, Gettysburg Jaycees, 1971. Mem. Nat. Assn. Social Workers (bd. dirs. 1978-80, sec. 1979-80), Nat. Assn. Christian Social Workers. Home: 931 Taylor Ave Eugene OR 97402 Office: PO Box 2880 1195 City View St Eugene OR 97402

HALE, HARRY WILLIAM, surgeon, educator; b. N.Y.C., Feb. 3, 1917; s. Harry William and Caroline Bridgman (Noyes) H.; m. Mary Augustine Slusher, May 25, 1946; children: Nancy D., Harry W. III, Daniel L., Robert H., Alice M. BS in Biology, Rensselaer Poly Inst., 1938; MD, U. Rochester, 1943. Diplomate Am. Bd. Surgery. Intern in surgery Strong Meml. Hosp., Rochester, N.Y., 1943; resident in surgery E.J. Meyer Meml. Hosp., Buffalo, 1946-52; from instr. to prof. surgery SUNY, Buffalo, 1952-69; chmn. dept. surgery Maricopa Med. Ctr., Phoenix, 1969-86, attending surgeon, 1986—; clin. prof. surgery U. Ariz., Tucson, 1979—; chmn. bd. dirs. Ariz. Emergency Med. Services, Phoenix, 1976-81. Contbr. chpts. to books and articles to profl. jours. Served to lt. commdr., USNR, 1944-46, 50-51. Fellow ACS (gov. 1963-69), Am. Assn. for Surgery of Trauma, Soc. Surgery of Alimentary Tract; mem. AMA, Cen. Surg. Assn., Western Surg. Assn., Southwestern Surg. Congress. Avocations: photography, carpentry. Home: 3220 E Stanford Dr Scottsdale AZ 85253 Office: Maricopa Med Ctr 2601 Roosevelt St Box 5099 Phoenix AZ 85010

HALE, IRVING, investment executive, writer; b. Denver, Mar. 22, 1932; s. Irving Jr. and Lucile (Beggs) H.; B.A. with distinction, U. Colo., 1964; m. Joan E. Domenico, Dec. 29, 1954; children—Pamela Joan, Beth Ellen. Security analyst Colo. Nat. Bank, Denver, 1955-58; asst. sec. Centennial Fund, Inc., Second Centennial Fund, Inc., Gryphon Fund, Inc., Meridian Fund, Inc., 1959-68; portfolio mgr. Twenty Five Fund, Inc. (formerly Trend Fund, Inc.), Denver, 1969-72; v.p. Alpine Corp., Denver, 1971-72; dir. research Hanifen, Imhoff & Samford, Inc., Denver, 1973-77; v.p. research First Fin. Securities, Inc., 1977-82; contbg. editor Nat. OTC Stock Jour., 1982-83; exec. v.p. research/corp. Fin. R. B. Marich, Inc., 1983—. lectr., Community Talent, 1975—; bd. dirs. Community Denver Public Schs. Resources, Inc., 1981—. Fellow Fin. Analysts Fedn.; mem. Denver Soc. Security Analysts, Radio Hist. Assn. Colo. (pres. 1977-78), Mensa, Beta Sigma Tau. Republican. Episcopalian. Club: Denver Press (assoc. mem.). Columnist, Denver Post; contbr. articles to profl. jours. Home: 1642 Ivanhoe St Denver CO 80220 Office: R B Marich Inc 1512 Larimer St Suite 800 Denver CO 80202

HALE, JILL JANETTE, legal administrative assistant; b. Wakefield, Nebr., Feb. 13, 1950; d. Robert Yates and Gail Harrielle (Warner) Goodell; m. Richard Seth Hale, June 1, 1974. Student Ariz. State U., 1968, Phoenix Coll., 1969-70, Yavapai Coll., 1970, Lamson Bus. Coll., 1971; diploma, Paralegal Inst., 1979. Legal sec. Law Offices Richard Walraven, Prescott, Ariz., 1971-80; legal sec. Walraven, Lange & Mabery, Prescott, 1980-82, legal asst., 1982-83; legal asst. Walraven & Roberts, 1983—; speaker at local schs.; mem. bus. div. adv. council Yavapai Coll., Prescott. Mem. chamber singers Yavapai Coll. Chamber Choir; recording sec. Rep. Women Prescott. Mem. Yavapai County Legal Secs. Assn. (past pres., Legal Sec. of Yr. 1981-82), Ariz. Assn. Legal Secs. (pres., Legal Sec. of Yr. 1981-82), Nat. Assn. Legal Secs. (Continuing Legal Edn. award 1983, bd. dirs.), Nat. Assn. Legal Assts., Prescott Shakespeare Soc. Contbr. articles to profl. jours. Home: 705 Maricopa Dr Prescott AZ 86303 Office: 239 S Cortez St Prescott AZ 86301

HALE, KAYCEE, research marketing professional; b. Mount Hope, W.Va., July 18, 1947; d. Bernard McFadden and Virginia Lucille (Mosley) H. AA, Compton Coll., 1965; BS, Calif. State U., Dominguez Hills, 1981. Faculty mem. Los Angeles Trade-Tech. Coll., 1969-71, Fashion Inst., Los Angeles, 1969-77, 1975—; pres. The Fashion Co., Los Angeles, 1970-75; co-host The Fashion Game TV Show, Los Angeles, 1982-85; exec. dir. Fashion Inst. Design and Merchandising Mus. and Library, Los Angeles, 1979—; lectr. in field, internat., 1969—. Mem. Spl. Libraries Assn. (pres. elect 1986—, pres. 1987-88, bd. dirs. 1985—), Spl. Libraries Adv. Council (pub. relations com. 1987—), Textile Assn. Los Angeles (bd. dirs. 1985—), Calif. Media and Library Educators Assn., Am. Library Assn., Am. Mktg. Assn., Western Mus. Conf., Am. Mus. Assn., Costume Soc. Am. Office: Fashion Inst Design and Merchandising 818 West Seventh St Los Angeles CA 90017

HALE, ROBERT STARLING, signal processing specialist, mathematician; b. Seattle, Dec. 31, 1929; s. Robert Henry and Jessie Lawson (Osman) H.; m. Patricia Louise Colvard, Feb. 15, 1953; children: Paul David, Barbara

Jane. BSEE, U. Wash., 1951, MSEE, 1960; MS in Applied Math, U. Santa Clara, 1971, degree in elec. engring., 1980. Sr. mem. tech. staff GTE Govt. Systems, Mountain View, Calif., 1962—. Served with U.S. Army, 1955-57. Mem. IEEE, Am. Statis. Assn., Soc. Ind. Applied Math., Am. Math Assn., Sigma Xi (v.p. local chpt. 1963-65). Avocations: tennis, running. Office: GTE Products Corp Western Div Box 7188 100 Ferguson Mountain View CA 94039

HALE, VERLE QUINN, agronomist; b. Pocatello, Idaho, July 25, 1927; s. Lyman Maeser and Luella Susan (Quinn) H.; m. Verna Swann, Nov. 26, 1948; children: David, Luann, Elaine, Nolan, Eloise, Carol, Alma, James, Lorin. BS, Utah State U., 1953, MS, 1958; PhD, UCLA, 1963. Asst. agronomist U. Calif., Davis, 1962-66; staff research specialist Geigy Agr., Ardsley, N.Y., 1966-68; assoc. soil scientist UCLA, 1968-71; sr. researcher Battelle Columbus (Ohio) Labs., 1971-78, Battelle N.W. Labs., Richland, Wash., 1978-81; staff engr. Rockwell Hanford Ops., Richland, 1981—. Contbr. articles to profl. jours. Served with U.S. Army, 1945-47. Mem. Am. Soc. Agronomy Cert. Profls., Am. Registry of Cert. Profls. in Agronomy Crops and Soils (bd. dirs. 1981—, chmn. agronomy sub-bd. 1984-85), Sigma Xi. Republican. Mormon. Avocations: genealogy, translating German and Latin records. Home: 4504 W Henry Pasco WA 99301 Office: Rockwell Hanford Ops PO Box 800 Richland WA 99352

HALES, ALFRED WASHINGTON, mathematics educator, consultant; b. Pasadena, Calif., Nov. 30, 1938; s. Raleigh Stanton and Gwendolen (Washington) H.; m. Virginia Dart Greene, July 7, 1962; children—Andrew Stanton, Lisa Ruth, Katherine Washington. B.S., Calif. Inst. Tech., 1960, Ph.D., 1962. NSF postdoctoral fellow Cambridge U., Eng., 1962-63; Benjamin Peirce instr. Harvard U., 1963-66; faculty mem. UCLA, 1966—, prof. math., 1973—; cons. Jet Propulsion Lab., La Canada, Calif., 1966-70, Inst. for Def. Analyses, Princeton, N.J., summers 1964, 65, 76, 79-84, 86; vis. lectr. U. Wash., Seattle, 1970-71; vis. mem. U. Warwick Math. Inst., Coventry, Eng., 1977-78, Math. Sci. Research Inst., Berkeley, 1986-87. Co-author: Shift Register Sequences, 1967, 82; contbr. articles to profl. jours. Mem. Am. Math. Soc., Math. Assn. Am., Soc. Indsl. and Applied Math. (Polya prize in combinatorics 1972), Sigma Xi. Clubs: Pasadena Badminton. Office: Dept Math UCLA 405 Hilgard Ave Los Angeles CA 90024

HALES, D(EAN) WILSON, otolaryngic surgeon; b. Rexburg, Idaho, May 9, 1920; s. Wayne B. and Belle (Wilson) H.; m. Anne Danvers, June 24, 1942; children: Robert D., Stephen W., John R., Mary Anne. AB, Brigham Young U., 1941; MD, U. Wis., 1945; MA in Medicine, Coll. Med. Evangelists, 1952. Diplomate Am. Bd. Otolaryngology. Intern Calif. Hosp., Los Angeles, 1945-46; resident in surgery VA Hosp., Los Angeles, 1949-51; head physician Harbor Gen. Hosp., Torrance, Calif., 1951; head dept. otolaryngology Ogden (Utah) Clinic, 1952—; mem. med. staff McKay-Dee and St. Benedict Hosp., Ogden, 1952—; asst. clin. surgeon U. Utah Med. Sch., Salt Lake City, 1954—; cons. Hill AFB, Ogden, 1960-86. Served to lt. USNR, 1942-53. Fellow Am. Coll. Surgeons; mem. AAAS, Am. Laryngol. Rhinol. and Otol. Soc., Utah Soc. Otolaryngology-Head Neck Surgery (pres. 1959, 75), AMA, Am. Acad. Otolaryngology-Head and Neck Surgery, Brigham Young U. Alumni Assn. (bd. dirs. 1976-79). Republican. Mormon. Home: 1460 36th St Ogden UT 84403 Office: The Ogden Clinic 4650 Harrison Blvd Ogden UT 84403

HALES, RALEIGH STANTON, JR., mathematics educator, college dean; b. Pasadena, Calif., Mar. 16, 1942; s. Raleigh Stanton and Gwendolen (Washington) H.; m. Diane Cecilia Moore, July 8, 1967; children—Karen Gwen, Christopher Stanton. B.A. Pomona Coll., 1964; M.A., Harvard U., 1965, Ph.D., 1970. Teaching fellow Harvard U., Cambridge, Mass., 1965-67; instr. math. Pomona Coll., Claremont, Calif., 1967-70, asst. prof., 1970-74, assoc. prof., 1974-85, prof., 1985—, assoc. dean of coll., 1973—; pres. Claremont Computations, 1983—; cons. Calif. Div. Savs. and Loan, 1968-70, Econs. Research Assocs., Los Angeles, 1969, Devel. Econs., Los Angeles, 1971, Fed. Home Loan Bank Bd., Washington, 1971-72. Author computer software. Contbr. articles to profl. jours. Patentee calculator. Bd. dirs. U.S. Badminton Assn., 1967-73, 1978—, pres., 1985—; trustee Polytech. Sch., Pasadena, Calif., 1973-79; trustee Foothill Country Day Sch., Claremont, Calif., 1985—, sec., 1986—. Named Wig Disting. Prof., Pomona Coll., 1971. Mem. Am. Math. Soc. Math. Assn. Am., Phi Beta Kappa (treas. 1986—). Republican. Episcopalian. Club: Pasadena Badminton (pres. 1978-85). Home: 1421 Niagara Ave Claremont CA 91711 Office: Pomona Coll Claremont CA 91711

HALES, ROBERT H., ophthalmologist. BS, Brigham Young U., 1954; MD, U. Utah, 1957. Diplomate Am. Bd. Ophthalmology. Intern Lackland AFB, San Antonio, 1957-58; resident in ophthalmology U. Calif., San Francisco, 1969-63; pvt. practice medicine specializing in ophthalmology Provo, Utah, 1963—; instr. Brigham Young U. Coll. of Nursing, Salt Lake City, 1963—; clin. instr., clin. prof. dept. ophthalmology U. Utah, Provo, 1966—; mem. staff Utah Valley Hosp., 1963—, chmn. dept. ophthalmology, 1967-70, 85-88, pres. staff, 1970. Author: Contact Lenses: A Clinical Approach to Fitting, 1978; contbr. numerous articles to profl. jours. Fellow ACS; mem. Am. Acad. Ophthalmology (bd. of councillors 1981-84), Am. Assn. Automotive Medicine, Am. Intra-Ocular Implant Soc. (founding mem.), AMA (del. 1980), Assn. Research in Ophthalmology, Contact Lens Assn. Ophthalmologists, Fredrick C. Cordes Eye Soc. (pres. 1976-77), Kerato-Refractive Soc., Pacific Coast Oto-Ophthal. Soc., Utah Ophthal. Soc. (exec. com. 1981-84, pres. 1982-83), Utah Profl. Rev. Orgn. (bd. dirs. 1976-80, 82—, exec. com. 1976-79, v.p. 1977-78), Utah State Med. Assn. (trustee (1974-80, exec. com. 1976-79, pres. 1977-78), Sigma Xi. Address: 1275 N University Ave Provo UT 84604

HALEY, JOHN DAVID, petroleum consulting executive; b. Denver, Mar. 16, 1924; s. Peter Daniel and Margaret Dorothy (O'Haire) H.; m. Annie Loretta Breeden, June 20, 1951; children—Laura, Patricia, Brian, Sharon, Norine, Kathleen. Profl. engr. Colo. Sch. Mines, 1948. Registered profl. engr., Colo., Okla. Petroleum engr. Creole Petroleum, Venezuela, 1948-50, Texaco Corp., 1950-52; staff engr. Carter Oil (Exxon), Tulsa, 1954-56; petroleum cons. Earlougher Engring., Tulsa, 1956-61, resident mgr., Denver, 1961-62; v.p. prodn. Anschutz Corp., Denver, 1962-86; dir. Circle A Mud, Denver, 1983-86; pres. Greylock Pipeline, Denver, 1983-86, Anschutz Pipeline, Denver, 1984-86; chief exec. officer H.K. van Poollen and Assocs., Inc., Littleton, Colo., 1986-87; pres., chief exec. officer, Van Poollen & Haley, 1987—; bd. dirs. Future Devel., 1985—, Polar III, 1986—. Rep. committeeman, Littleton. Served to lt. comdr. USNR, 1943-46, 52-54. Mem. Soc. Petroleum Engrs. (dir. Denver chpt.), Soc. Petroleum Evaluation Engrs., Ind. Petroleum Assn. Am., Ind. Petroleum Assn. Mountain States, Am. Petroleum Inst. (citation for service), Internat. Assn. Drilling Contractors, Soc. Profl. Well Log Analysts. Petroleum Club (Denver chpt.). Roman Catholic. Home: 561 E Caley Dr Littleton CO 80121

HALEY, TENISON, college administrator. Student, Calif. Poly. State U., San Luis Obispo, 1948-50, U. Colo., 1951-52; BS, Washington U., St. Louis, 1954; MEd, U. Oreg., 1958, DEd in Higher Edn. and Counseling Psychology, 1963. Lic. psychologist, Oreg.; cert. marriage and family therapist, Oreg. Tchr., counselor, dir. guidance services The Dalles (Oreg.) Pub. Schs., 1955-61; counseling psychologist, asst. prof. Oreg. State U., Corvallis, 1963-64; assoc. prof., dir. counseling and testing Cen. Oreg. Community Coll., Bend, 1964-67; assoc. prof., dean of student services Southwestern Oreg. Community Coll., Coos Bay, 1967-71; mem. faculty dept. psychology Rogue Community Coll., Grants Pass, Oreg., 1971-75, dean of student services, 1971—; coll. evaluator Northwest Assn. Schs. and Colls. Regional Accreditation Assn., 1978—; chmn. student personnel services adv. com., Oreg. State Dept. Edn., 1976-78, Oreg. Am. Coll. Testing Council, 1982-83, ann. conf. Oreg. Community Coll. Student Personnel Services, 1973; mem. regional adv. bd. So. Oreg. State Coll., 1976—; practicum dir. CAUSE II tng. program paraprofl. counselors, Oreg. State U., 1965; cons. Am. Assn. Community and Jr. Colls., 1969-73, State Oreg. Vocat. Rehab. div., 1970-71, Nat. Alliance Businessmen, Josephine County, Oreg., 1972-73; ednl. tour organizer to People's Republic China, 1984, 86; mem. ednl. tours Japan, 1984, 86, Mex., Cuba, 1960; bd. dirs. Am. Coll. Testing Program. Contbr. articles to profl. bulls., jours., revs. Exec. dir. Rogue Community jColl. Found., 1986—; bd. dirs. Rogue Valley Council Govts. Area Agy. on Aging. Adv. Council, 1982—, chmn., 1984-86; bd. dirs. Josephine County Council on Alcoholism, 1977—, pres., 1980-82; bd. dirs. Josephine County Council on Drug Abuse, 1973-75; mem. gov.'s adv. com. on Vocat. Rehab., Oreg., 1967-68; mem. State Oreg. Selective Service System Appeals Bd., 1972-74; vol. dir. staff tng. and devel. Southwestern Oreg. Community Action Com., Coos Bay, 1967-70; chmn. bd. dirs. Northwest Social Systems, Inc., Seattle, 1970-71; mem. mental health adv. bds. various programs, Josephine, Coos and Deschutes counties, 1965-75; active in Boy Scouts Am., 1955-82. Served as sgt. USAF, 1951-54. Recipient Bold Journey award, 1959. Mem. NEA (life), Nat. Assn. Student Personnel Adminstrs., Nat. Vocat. Guidance Assn. (cert. profl.), Am. Coll. Personnel Assn. (life), Am. Assn. Counseling and Devel. of Am. Personnel and Guidance Assn. (life, sen. 1973-76, chmn. western region br. assembly 1970-71), Am. Psychol. Assn. (Counseling Psychology div.), Am. Assn. Marriage and Family Therapy (clin.), Am. Coll. Personnel Assn. (commr. student devel. in 2-yr. colls. 1967-70, commr. counseling 1971-74), Northwest Coll. Personnel Assn., Oreg. Personnel and Guidance Assn. (life, cert. sch. counselor, pres. 1970-71), Oreg. Psychol. Assn., Oreg. Assn. Marriage and Family Therapy, Oreg. Council Student Services Adminstrs. (chmn. 1986-87), Phi Delta Kappa (life, pres. So. Oreg. region chpt. 1974-75), Oreg. Community Coll. Deans of Students Consortium (chmn. The Displaced Worker 1982-83), Psy Chi, Alpha Phi Omega. Office: Rogue Community Coll 3345 Redwood Hwy Grants Pass OR 97527

HALFORD, RICHARD EUGENE, architect; b. Ventura, Iowa, July 10, 1924; s. Robert Sidney and Christine (Edmundson) H.; m. Monica Christine Sosaya, June 21, 1963; children: Vikki, Felicia, Richard Jr., Raquel, James. BArch, Iowa State U., 1952. Registered architect, N.Mex.; registered profl. engr., N.Mex.; lic. real estate broker, N.Mex. Project architect W.C. Kruger & Assocs., Santa Fe, 1952-58; pvt. practice architecture Santa Fe, 1958-85; staff architect Office Mil. Affairs State of N.Mex., Santa Fe, 1985—; pres. Madonna Corp., Santa Fe, 1962-67; bd. dirs. Guadalupe Resources Corp., Santa Fe. Prin. works include La Casa Loma, Santa Fe, Las Vistas, Santa Fe (Hon. Mention, Mich. Soc. Architects), Wilner Office Bldg., Albuquerque, State of N.Mex. Lab., Albuquerque. Councilman City of Santa Fe, 1964-68. Served to capt. C.E., U.S. Army, 1943-46. Mem. AIA. Democrat. Methodist. Lodge: Elks. Avocations: golf, hunting, stamp collecting, wood working. Home: 850 El Caminito Box 2386 Santa Fe NM 87504 Office: Office Mil Affairs 2600 Cerrillos Rd Santa Fe NM 87502

HALFPENNY, JAMES C., scientist, educator; b. Shreveport, La., Jan. 23, 1947; s. Donald Frazier and Dorothy (Carson) H. BS, U. Wyo., 1969, MS, 1970; PhD, U. Colo., 1980. Various positions govt. conservation agys., parks and univ. conservation programs, 1966-80; coordinator long term ecol. research program U. Colo., Boulder, 1980—; research assoc. Inst. Arctic and Alpine Research, U. Colo., 1980—; instr. Teton Sci. Sch., Moran, wyo., 1980—, Aspen (Colo.) Ctr.for Environ. Studies, 1984—, Yellowstone (Wyo.) Inst., 1984—; pres. A Naturalist's World, Boulder, 1985—; staff trainer Colo. Div. Wildlife, Sterling, 1979, 83, sci. advisor 1982-85; staff trainer Yellowstone Nat. Park, 1985-86; grant proposal rev. bd. NSF, 1984—, Nat. Geog. Sci., 1984—; trustee Thorne Ecol. Inst., Boulder, 1982-84; mem. Indian Peaks Wilderness Area Adv. Panel, Boulder, 1982-86, others. Author: A Field Guide to Mammal Tracking, 1986; editor (booklets) Mountain Research Sta.; its environment and research, 1982, Long Term Ecol. Research in the U.S.; a network of research sites, 1982, 83, 84; contbr. articles to profl. jours. Mem. Sci. Adv. Panel to EOP Program U. Colo., 1982-84; bd. advisors Teton Sci. Sch., Moran, 1985—; bd. dirs. Nat. Outdoor Leadership Sch., Lander, Wyo., 1975-80, chmn. 1978-79. Served with USNR, 1969-71, Vietnam. Decorated Navy Achievement medal with combat "v", Vietnamese Gallantry Cross with palm (Republic Vietnam); recipient Roosevelt Meml. grant Am. Mus. Natural History, 1979, Walker Van Riper grant U.Colo., 1979, Kathy Lichty Fund grant U. Colo., 1979. Mem. AAAS, Am. Soc. Mammalogists, Southwestern Assn. Naturalists, Northwest Sci. Assn., Colo.-Wyo. Acad. Sci., Orgn. Biol. Field Stas., Sigma Xi. Avocations: nature photography, cross country skiing, hiking, country and folk dance. Office: U Colo Inst Arctic/Alpine Research PO Box 450 Boulder CO 80309

HALL, ADRIENNE ANN, advertising agency executive; b. Los Angeles; d. Arthur E. and Adelina P. Kosches; m. Maurice Hall; children: Adam, Todd, Stefanie, Victoria. B.A., UCLA. Founding ptnr. HaLL & Levine Advt., Los Angeles, 1960-80; vice chmn. bd. Eisaman, Johns & Laws Advt. Inc., Los Angeles, Houston, Chgo., N.Y.C., 1980—; founding mem. Advt. Industry Emergency Fund, Los Angeles; vice chmn. bd. dirs. Eisaman, Johns & Laws Advt. Inc., Los Angeles; founder, dir. Advt. Industry Emergency Fund. Trustee UCLA; bd. regents Loyola-Marymount U., Los Angeles; mem. Blue Ribbon of Music Ctr., Press. Circle, Los Angeles County Mus. Art, Calif. Gov.'s Commn. on Econ. Devel.; bd. dirs. Wonder Women Found., N.Y.C.; mem. adv. council Girl's Clubs Am., Girl Scouts U.S.; mem. adv. bd. Asian Pacific Women's Network, Downtown Women's Ctr. and Residence; mem. exec. bd. Greater Los Angeles Partnership for Homeless; mem. Nat. Network for Hispanic Women. Recipient Nat. Headliner award Women in Communications, 1982; recipient Profl. Achievement award UCLA Alumni, 1979; named Woman of Yr. Am Advt. Fedn., 1973, Ad Person of the West award Mktg. and Media Decisions, 1982; Bus. Woman of Yr. award Boy Scouts Am., 1983; Women Helping Women award Soroptimist Internat., 1984; Bullock's 1st ann. portfolio award for exec. women, 1985; Communicator of yr. award Ad Women, 1986; Leader award YWCA, 1986; named One of 20 Top Corp. Women, Savry mag., 1983. Mem. Nat. Women's Forum, Am. Assn. Advt. Agys. (bd. dirs., chmn. bd. govs. western region), Western States Advt. Agys. Assn. (pres.), Hollywood Radio and TV Soc. (dir.), Overseas Edn. Fund, Com. 200 (western chmn.), Women in Communications, Orgn. Women Execs., Nat. Women's Forum (v.p.), Calif. Women's Forum (chmn. trusteeship). Clubs: Calif. Yacht; Stock Exchange, Los Angeles Advt. (pres.) (Los Angeles). Office: Eisaman Johns & Laws Advt 6255 Sunset Blvd Los Angeles CA 90028

HALL, ANTHONY ELMITT, plant physiologist; b. Tickhill, Yorkshire, Eng., May 6, 1940; came to U.S., 1964; s. Elmitt and Mary Lisca (Schofield) H.; m. Bretta Reed, June 20, 1965; children: Kerry, Gina. Student, Harper Adams Agrl. Coll., Eng., 1958-60; student in agrl. engring., Essex Inst. Agrl. Engring., Eng., 1960-61; BS in Irrigation Sci., U. Calif., Davis, 1966, PhD in Plant Physiology, 1970. Farmer Dyon House, Austerfield, Eng., 1955-58; extension officer Ministry of Agrl. Scis., Tanzania, 1961-63; research asst. U. Calif., Davis, 1964-70, asst. research scientist, 1971; research fellow Carnegie Inst., Stanford, Calif., 1970; prof. U. Calif., Riverside, 1971—; cons. in field. Editor: Agriculture in Semi-Arid Environments, 1979; adv. editor: (jour.) Irrigation Sci.; mem. editorial adv. bd. Field Crops Research, Vigna Crop Adv. Com. USDA; contbr. articles to profl. jours. Mem. Am. Soc. Plant Physiologists, Am. Soc. Agronomy, Crop Sci. Soc. Am., Scandinavian Soc. Plant Physiology, Alpha Zeta, Gamma Sigma Delta, Phi Beta Kappa, Phi Kappa Phi. Avocations: camping, fishing. Office: U Calif Dept Botany and Plant Scis Riverside CA 92521

HALL, BRETT GERARD, marketing executive; b. Great Bend, Kans., Apr. 10, 1954; s. Luke Charles and Lila Magdalen (Weber) H.; m. Beverly Jean Lovald, Oct. 12, 1974; children: Gram Matthew and Shea Patrick (twins). Cert. in graphic arts, Colo. Inst. Art, 1974; student, Met. State Coll., 1974; cert. of merit, Famous Artist Sch., Westport, Conn., 1970. Prodn. artist Southeast Pub., Denver, 1974-75; mgr. prodn. Brighton (Colo.) Pub., 1975-76; art dir. Community Publs., Denver, 1976-78; mgr. graphics The Printery at Vail, Colo., 1978-79; art dir. Widdico Advt., Denver, 1979-81; product mgr. Rocky Mountain Bank Note, Denver, 1981—. Designer/contbr. Colo. Guest Guide, 1977. Vol. designer Anderson Presdl. Campaign, Denver, 1980. Mem. Graphic Arts Prodn. Club, Art Dirs. Club of Denver (cert. Merit 1984, 85). Roman Catholic. Avocation: photography. Home: 1285 E Goldsmith Highlands Ranch CO 80126 Office: Rocky Mountain Bank Note PO Box 17727 10455 W 6th Ave Denver CO 80215

HALL, CHARLES ADDISON SMITH, research biologist; b. Hingham, Mass., May 3, 1943; s. Addison Smith and Frances Winston (Ivey) H. AB, Colgate U., 1965; MS, Pa. State U., 1966; PhD, U. N.C., 1970. Research assoc. Brookhaven Nat. Lab., Upton, N.Y., 1970-73; research scientist II Marine Biol. Lab., Woods Hole, Mass., 1973-75; vis. asst. prof. Cornell U., Ithaca, N.Y., 1973-76, asst. prof., 1976-85; research assoc. prof. U. Mont. Biol. Sta., Polson, 1985—; research assoc. prof. Dept. Zoology U. Mont., Missoula, 1986—. Author: Ecosystem Modeling in Theory and Practice, 1977, Energy and Resource Quality: The Ecology of the Economic Process, 1985; contbr. numerous articles to profl. jours. Recipient Outstanding Publ. of Yr. award Nat. Wildlife Soc., 1985, Outstanding Publ. of Yr. award Sigma Xi, 1985; Fullbright fellow, 1986. Mem. Ecol. Soc. Am. (rep. to AAAS), Am. Soc. Limnology and Oceanography, Internat. Soc. Ecol. Modeling. Avocations: fishing, hunting, ice hockey. Home: Yellow Bay Big Fork MT 59911 Office: U Mont Biol Sta and Dept Zoology Yellow Bay Flathead Lake Polsen MT 59911

HALL, CHARLES LESLIE, diversified financial services company executive; b. Geneva, Ohio, Apr. 30, 1943; s. George Edward and Monta Victoria (Markham) H.; m. Diane G. Thayer, Jan. 7, 1964; children: Kevin Charles, Jason Edward. BS, Ariz. State U., 1970. Internal auditor Western Union Corp., N.Y.C., 1970-72; mgr. data services Am. Express, Phoenix, 1972-79; mgr. revenue acctg. Tex. Internat. Airlines, Houston, 1979-80; v.p. ops. Harlequin Books, Tempe, Ariz., 1980-86, Intercorp Internat. Inc., Phoenix, 1986—. Curriculum advisor Maricopa Coll., Phoenix, 1974; advisor Jr. Achievement, Phoenix, 1978; mem., advisor Ariz. Legis. Blue Ribbon Com. Served with USN, 1961-66. Mem. Direct Mktg. Assn., VFW. Republican. Methodist. Club: Amateur Radio (Phoenix). Lodge: Masons. Home: 7728 S Willow Dr Tempe AZ 85284 Office: Intercorp Internat Inc 9830 S 51st St Suite A 124 Phoenix AZ 85044

HALL, CLARENCE HERBERT, quality engineer; b. Shillington, Pa., Dec. 20, 1931; s. Herbert Hickman and Stella Matilda (Umbenhouer) H.; m. Nancy Carol Fries, Oct. 12, 1957; children: Andrea Jean, Anita Michell. BS, Albright Coll., 1957. Analytical research chemist Atlas Chem. Industry Inc., Wilmington, Del., 1957-62; supr. analytical devel. lab. Stuart Pharm., Pasadena, Calif., 1962-70; mgr. quality assurance Stuart Pharm., Newark, 1970-74; staff spl. quality assurance Riker Lab. div. 3M, Northridge, Calif., 1974-80, spl. quality engr., 1980—. Mem. Am. Soc. Quality Assurance (sr.), Am. Chem. Soc., Am. Pharm. Assn., Am. Assn. Pharm. Sci. Republican. Lutheran. Avocations: tennis, camping. Home: 11549 Doral Ave Northridge CA 91326 Office: Riker Labs div 3M 19901 Nordhoff St Northridge CA 91324

HALL, CLYDE MATTHEW, lawyer, advocate; b. Pocatello, Idaho, Apr. 8, 1951; s. William Mckinley and Charlotte Rose (Truchot) H. Student Idaho State U., 1968-75; Broadcasting Cert, Career Acad.-San Francisco, 1970; J.D., Utah State U., 1980. Bar: Idaho 1981, Tribal 1981. Park ranger Grand Teton Nat. Park, Moose, Wyo., 1975-79; art instr. Sho-Ban High Sch., Ft. Hall, Idaho, 1979-80; chief judge Ft. Hall Tribal Ct., 1980-83; Indian art cons. Grant Teton Nat. Park, 1983—; performer Am. Indian Art Exchange, Seattle, 1983—; lawyer Ft. Hall Tribes, 1983—; cons. D.T. Vernon Indian Arts Mus., Denver Mus. Natural History; others. Contbr. articles to profl. jours. Chmn. bd. dirs. Alcohol Adv. Bd., Ft. Hall, 1981—. Mem. Shoshone Bannock Tribal Bar Assn., Am. Indian Broadcasters Assn. Democrat. Mem. Native American Ch. Clubs: Imperial Gem. Ct. of Idaho (ambassador to native Ams.), G.A.I. of San Francisco. Home: PO Box 135 West Agency Rd Fort Hall ID 83203 Office: Fort Hall Tribal Ct PO Box 306 Fort Hall ID 83203

HALL, CYNTHIA HOLCOMB, judge; b. Los Angeles, Feb. 19, 1929; d. Harold Romeyn and Mildred Gould (Kuck) Holcomb; m. John Harris Hall, June 6, 1970 (dec. Oct. 1980); 1 child, Harris Holcomb; 1 child by previous marriage, Desma Letitia. A.B., Stanford U., 1951, J.D., 1954; LL.M., NYU, 1960. Bar: Ariz. 1954, Calif. 1956. Law clk. to judge U.S. Ct. Appeals 9th Circuit, 1954-55; trial atty. tax div. Dept. Justice, 1960-64; atty.-adviser Office Tax Legis. Counsel, Treasury Dept., 1964-66; mem. firm Brawerman & Holcomb, Beverly Hills, Calif., 1966-72; judge U.S. Tax Ct., Washington, 1972-81, U.S. Dist. Ct. for central dist. Calif., Los Angeles, 1981-84; U.S. circuit judge 9th Circuit, Pasadena, Calif., 1984—. Served to lt. (j.g.) USNR, 1951-53. Office: 125 S Grand PO Box 91510 Pasadena CA 91109-1510

HALL, DAVID, newspaper editor; b. Lebanon, Tenn., Mar. 7, 1943; s. Hal Turner Hall and Mildred (Durham) Hall Carson; m. Suzanne Lovell, Sept. 5, 1964; children: Carson, Matthew, Amanda. BJ, U. Tenn., 1965, MA in Econs., 1966. Fin. news reporter, asst. fin. editor, Middle East corr., editorial writer, asst. mng. editor Chgo. Daily News, 1966-78; asst. mng. editor Chgo. Sun-Times, 1978; mng. editor St. Paul Pioneer Press, 1978-82; exec. editor St. Paul Pioneer and Dispatch, 1982-84; editor, v.p. The Denver Post, 1984-86, editor, sr. v.p., 1986—. Mem. Denver Com. Fgn. Relations, 1984—; mem. Trinity United Meth. Ch., Denver. Served with U.S. Army, 1967-69, Vietnam. Recipient Disting. Alumni award Castle Heights Mil. Acad., Lebanon, 1984. Mem. Am. Soc. Newspaper Editors, Soc. Profl. Journalists. Clubs: Denver, Denver Athletic; Columbine Country (Littleton, Colo.). Office: The Denver Post 650 15th St Denver CO 80202

HALL, EARL, accountant, educator; b. Bertha, Minn., May 13, 1946; s. Lloyd E. and Esther M. (Fraedrich) H.; m. Lisa Coe Boyce, Aug. 24, 1968; children—Jonathan, Marc. B.A., U. Wash., 1971. C.P.A., Calif. Staff acct. Arthur Andersen & Co., San Francisco, 1971-72; prin. George Hamilton, C.P.A., San Jose, Calif., 1972-73; tax sr. Alexander Grant, San Jose, Calif., 1973-75; tax ptnr. Roberts, McMains, Sellman, Lewiston, Idaho, 1975-80; dir. taxation Boyd, Olofson & Co., Yakima, Wash., 1980-83; pres. Earl Hall, C.P.A., Inc., Yakima, 1983—; instr. Heritage Coll., Toppenish, Wash., 1984-85. Chmn. radio day Yakima Kiwanis Club, 1984; del. Wash. State Republican Conv., 1982; mem. fin. com. Wesley United Methodist Ch., Yakima, 1982-85, young adult coordinator, 1985, pastor parish com., 1986—. Served with USAF, 1965-68; PTO. Recipient Haskins & Sells award U. Wash., 1970. Mem. Wash. Soc. C.P.A.s (estate planning com. 1981-83), Am. Inst. C.P.A.s (hon. mention Elijah Watt Sells award 1971), Idaho Soc. C.P.A.s, Greater Yakima C. of C. (tax legis. com. 1981—). Lodge: Apple Valley Kiwanis (v.p. 1985-86, pres. elect 1986—). Home: 350 N 24th Ave Yakima WA 98902 Office: Earl Hall CPA PO Box 10883 Yakima WA 98909

HALL, FRANCES GLORIA, biology educator; b. Bessemer, Ala., Nov. 4, 1939; d. Ulysses and Mary Frances (Robinson) H. BA, Clark Coll., 1961; MA, U. San Francisco, 1979. Buyer Sears Roebuck & Co., Los Angeles, 1964-65; sci. educator Columbus (Miss.) Pub. Schs., 1961-64; probation counselor Los Angeles County, 1973-75; sci. educator Los Angeles Unified Sch. Dist., 1965—, sci. dept. head, 1974-77, spl. edn. coordinator, 1976-78, dir. Magnet Sch., 1978-83; cons. urban edn. Calif. State U., Fullerton, 1974-76; sec. dean's adv. council Charles R. Drew Med. Sch., Los Angeles, 1979; mem. adv. council Calif. State U., Long Beach, 1980. Fundraiser United Way, Los Angeles, 1977—. Fellow NSF, 1985-86, Los Angeles Ednl. Partnership, 1985-86. Mem. NEA, Calif. Tchrs. Assn., Calif. Assn. for Gifted, Nat. Assn. Female Execs., Assn. for Supervision and Curriculum Devel., Clark Coll. Alumni Assn. Democrat. Methodist. Avocations: writing, reading, traveling, interior decorating. Office: Los Angeles Unified Sch Dist Hamilton High Sch 2955 S Robertson Blvd Los Angeles CA 90034

HALL, GORDON R., state supreme court chief justice; b. Vernal, Utah, Dec. 14, 1926; s. Roscoe Jefferson and Clara Maud (Freestone) H.; m. Doris Gillespie, Sept. 6, 1947; children: Rick Jefferson, Craig Edwin. B.S., U. Utah, 1949, LL.B., 1951. Bar: Utah 1952. Sole practice Tooele, Utah, 1952-69; city atty. City of Grantsville, Utah, 1954-69; town atty. Town of Wendover, Utah, 1955-69, Town of Stockton, Utah, 1955-69; legal adviser Tooele Army Depot, 1953-58; county atty. Tooele County, 1958-69; judge 3d Jud. Dist. Utah, 1969-77; assoc. justice Supreme Ct. Utah, 1977-81, chief justice, 1981—; pres. Utah Assn. Counties, 1965; mem. Pres's. Adv. Com. OEO, 1965-66. Served with U.S. Maritime Service, 1944-46. Mem. ABA, Utah Bar Assn. Office: Supreme Ct Utah 332 State Capitol Salt Lake City UT 84114

HALL, GWENDOLYN LOUISE, communication specialist; b. Washington, July 14, 1948; d. Baxter Austin and Virginia Dare (Dunston) Yarborough; m. Ronald E. Hall, June 5, 1976 (dec. July 1979). Student, U. D.C., 1973-79, Alameda Coll., 1982, Laney Coll., 1983; cert. tchr., Calif. State Poly. U., Pomona, 1985. Stenographer FCC., Washington, 1966-73; adminstrv. asst. Bd. Trustees U. D.C., Washington, 1973-77; spl. asst. to pres. U. D.C., Washington, 1978-80; prin. Gwendolyn Hall & Assocs., Alameda, Calif., 1980—; bd. dirs. DaMontel Engrs., Oakland; adminstrv. asst. Dani Perkins & Assocs., Oakland, Calif., 1984—; workshop facilitator on career devel. crown Zellerbach Paper Co. MVO Personnel Services, San Francisco, 1986; computer instuction adminstr. MAC Bus. Inst., Fairfield, Calif., 1987; guest speaker BET (Black Entertainment TV). Contbg. poet Widow-Hearts of

Fire, 1980, 85; announcer Pub. Affairs Program Sta. KJAZ-FM, Alameda, 1981; choreographer Lord's Prayer, 1983. Bd. dirs. Everybody's Creative Art Ctr., Oakland, 1982. Recipient Appreciation award Flag of U.S. at request of Congressman Fortney H. Stark, 1985, Vet. award U. D.C., 1979, Outstanding Service award U. D.C. Bd. Trustees, 1978; recipient Recognition award Anacostia High Sch., 1986, Appreciation award Holy Land Reunion Allen Temple Baptist Ch., 1987; named one of Outstanding Young Women of Am., 1984. Mem. Widows Network, Bay Area Black Journalist Assn., YMCA, Black Filmmakers Hall of Fame, Women in Telecommunications (charter), Soc. Humanistic Mgmt., Nat. Bus. Edn., Nat. Assn. Trade and Tech. Schs., Am. Fedn. State, County and Mcpl. Employees. Baptist. Avocations: reading, computers, dancing, writing, music. Office: Gwendolyn Hall & Assocs 2515 Santa Clara Ave Suite 103 Alameda CA 94501

HALL, HAL, businessman; b. Colby, Kans., June 7, 1911; s. Robert Ellsworth and Sarah (Myers) H.; m. Liane Hanft, May 23, 1947; children: Robert Eric, Alan Rae, Ronald Frederick. BA U. Ill., 1939. Journeyman welder Shipyards, Oakland and Alameda, Calif., 1941-43; mechanic U.S. Army, 1943-46; journeyman carpenter Kaiser, San Jose, Calif., 1946-49; house designer and builder, Calif., Colo., 1949-53; lodge owner and operator Red Mountain Lodge, Ouray, Colo., 1953-80; farmer, ranch owner, 1980—. Author: The Great Conflict, 1943, Even to the Last Man, 1960, The Wealth of Persons, 1968, Collectivism and Freedom, 1976, The Sleeping Dragon, 1981, 2d rev. edit., 1986; also polit., econ. and religious critic, various pubs. Served with U.S. Army, 1943-46. Mailing Address: Red Mountain Trading Post Box 129 Ouray CO 81427

HALL, HAROLD ROBERT, computer engineer; b. Bakersfield, Calif., Feb. 7, 1935; s. Edward Earl and Ethel Mae (Butner) H.; m. Tenniebee May Hall, Feb. 20, 1965. BS, U. Calif., Berkeley, 1956, MS, 1957, PhD, 1966. Chief engr. wave-filter div. Transonic, Inc., Bakersfield, 1957-60; chief design engr. Circuit Dyne Corp., Pasadena and Laguna Beach, Calif., 1960-61; sr. devel. engr. Robertshaw Controls Co., Anaheim, Calif., 1961-63; research engr. Naval Ocean Systems Ctr. Navy Research Lab., San Diego, 1966—; bd. dirs. Circuit Dyne Corp., Pacific Coil Co. Recipient Thomas Clair McFarland award U. Calif., Berkeley, 1956, NSF fellow, 1957. Mem. IEEE, Acoustical Soc. Am., Phi Beta Kappa. Home: 5284 Dawes St San Diego CA 92109 Office: Naval Ocean Systems Ctr San Diego CA 92152

HALL, HARRIET LOUISE, mental health center adminstr.; b. Los Angeles, Oct. 9, 1947; d. Donald Moore and Ethyl Louise (Hartsough) Hall; B.A., Coll. of Wooster, 1969; M.A., U. Wis., Madison, 1971, Ph.D., 1973; m. Randy C. Stith, Nov. 26, 1977; children—Carolyn Annaliese Hall-Stith, Daniel Dag Hall-Stith, Timothy Vernon Hall-Stith. Psychologist, dir. inservice tng. Weld Mental Health Center, Greeley, Colo., 1974-78; child advocacy team mgr. Adams County Mental Health Center, Commerce City, Colo., 1978-80; dep. dir. clin. programs, 1980-81; assoc. dir. programs Jefferson County Mental Health Center, Wheat Ridge, Colo., 1981-84, exec. dir., 1984—. Mem., Adams County Placement Alternative Commn., 1980-81, Adams County Child Protection Team, 1979-80; mem. handicapped child subcom. Colo. Gov.'s Commn. for Children and Families, 1979-80; bd. dirs. Centennial Area Health Edn. Center, 1978, Partners Inc., Greeley, Colo., 1977-78; mem. Jefferson County Community Corrections Bd., 1984—. Cert. psychologist, Colo. Mem. Colo. Psychol. Assn., Colo. Women Psychologists, NOW, Jefferson County Govts. Assn. (v.p. 1986), Colo. Com. for Status of Women in Mental (treas. 1981-86, Outstanding Woman in Mental Health award 1982). Democrat. Office: care Jefferson County Mental Health 6195 W 38th Ave Wheat Ridge CO 80033

HALL, JACK HENRY, TV executive; b. South Gate, Calif., Sept. 29, 1926; s. Lamont Dupere and Mildred Elizabeth (Hooker) H.; B.A., Calif. State U., Fresno, 1949; m. Peggy Jean Walterscheid, Dec. 27, 1974; children—Julie Anne, Jeffrey Adams; stepchildren—Robert, Jeffrey, April, Steven. Radio singer Sta. KECA, Los Angeles, summer 1938; announcer Sta. KARM, Fresno, 1943-44; asst. theatre mgr. Fox West Coast Ltd., 1944, 46-48; announcer Sta. KSGN, Sanger, Calif., 1949-50, Sta. KMJ, Fresno, 1950-53; dir., announcer Sta. KMJ-TV, Fresno, 1953-81, sta. KSEE, 1981—, community affairs mgr., 1979—; performer, stage dir. Fresno Community Theater, 1960-85, pres., 1963-64, 73-74; mem. Fresno Community Chorus, 1952-60, pres., 1959-60. Mem. Easter Seal Soc. Central Calif., 1980—, pres., 1982-84, sec. Easter Seal Soc. Calif., 1984-86, pres. 1986—. Served with AUS, 1944-45. Recipient Best Actor award Fresno Community Theater, 1965, Pres.'s award, 1971, 72, 77, J.U. Berry award, 1987. Mem. Am. Community Theatre Assn. Producer TV documentary Opus 20, 1974; producer, narrator film documentary Lost, 1976. Home: 1435 Park St Sanger CA 93657 Office: 5035 E McKinley Ave Fresno CA 93727

HALL, JAMES C(HRIS), clinical social worker, psychiatric program administrator; b. San Francisco, July 30, 1950; s. Thomas Milton and Mary Jane (Hughes) H.; m. Rena Lorraine Whitelock, Aug 3, 1973 (div. Mar. 1982); children: Sarah Lorraine. BS in Psychology, U. Utah, 1975, MSW, 1978. Lic. clin. social worker, Utah. Social worker pub. schs. Idaho Falls, Idaho, 1978-79; mental health specialist Cen. Utah Mental Health Ctr., Fillmore, 1979-82; clin. social worker Mountain View Hosp. subs. Hosp. Corp. Am., Payson, Utah, 1982-83, psychiat. services program dir., 1982-85, seniority coordinator, 1985—; pvt. practice outpatient therapy Payson, 1983—; cons. geriatric social work Fillmore Hosp., 1983—, Gunnison (Utah) Hosp., 1985—; mem. governing bd. Ctr. for Women and Children in Crisis, Provo, Utah, 1984—. Mem. Nat. Assn. Social Workers. Mormon. Avocations: antique furniture, doll house and miniature furniture building, travel. Home: PO Box 4 Payson UT 84651 Office: Mountain View Hosp 1000 E Hwy 6 Payson UT 84651

HALL, JEROME WILLIAM, research engineering educator; b. Brunswick, Ga., Dec. 1, 1943; s. William L. and Frances K. (Wickie) H.; m. Loretta E. Hood, Aug. 28, 1965; children: Jennifer, Bridget, Bernadette. BS in Physics, Harvey Mudd Coll., 1965; MS in Engring., U. Wash., 1968, PhDCE, 1969. Registered profl. engr., Washington, N.Mex., Va. Asst. prof. civil engring. U. Md., College Park, 1970-73, assoc. prof., 1973-77; assoc. prof. U. N.Mex., Albuquerque, 1977-80, prof., 1980—, dir. bur. engring. research, 1981—, asst. dean engring., 1985—; cons. in field, 1971—. Contbr. articles to profl. jours. Recipient Teetor award Soc. Automotive Engrs., 1975. Fellow Inst. Transp. Engrs. (sect. pres. 1984-86); mem. Transp. Research Bd. (com. chmn. 1986—), Am. Soc. Engring. Educators, Am. Road and Transp. Builders Assn. Republican. Roman Catholic. Office: U NMex Bur Engring Research FEC 124 Albuquerque NM 87131

HALL, JOHN CHARLES, electronics company executive; b. Santa Fe, July 21, 1949; s. Jody C. and Elizabeth Nelle (Bissell) H.; m. Mary Edith Simmons, June 10, 1972; children: Jeremy Colin, Megan Michele. Student, Mich. State U., 1967-68; BS in Engring. Mgmt., BS in Humanities, USAF Acad., 1972; MBA in High Tech. Mgmt., City U., Bellingham, Wash., 1985. Commd. 2d lt., chief of radarstrike USAF, 1972-78, advanced through grades to capt.; sr. indsl. engr. Crown-Zellerbach, Camas, Wash., 1978-80; project mgr. Crown-Zellerbach, Camas and San Francisco, 1980-82, mgr. napkin and printing, 1982-84; major Oreg. Air N.G., Portland, 1978—; programs mgr. OECO Corp., Portland, 1984—; owner, ptnr. Check Six Co., Portland, 1985—. Contbr. articles to profl. jours. Mem. Mensa, USAF Acad. Assn. Grads. Lodge: Toastmasters (Vancouver, Wash.) (area gov. 1984). Home: 13508 NE 21st St Vancouver WA 98684 Office: OECO Corp 4607 SE Internat Way Milwaukie OR 97222

HALL, JOHN DAVID, III, marine resources biologist, consultant; b. Berkeley, Calif., Oct. 7, 1944; s. John David Jr. and Betty (MacMannus) H.; m. Linda Lee Faville, June 5, 1968 (div. Dec. 1977); children: Scott, Joel, Kevin; m. Holly Jo Erlandson, Jan. 21, 1984. BA, Humboldt State U., 1966, MA, 1967; MA, U. Calif., Santa Cruz, 1974, PhD, 1981. Marine biologist Naval Undersea Ctr., San Diego, 1967-72; research specialist U. Calif., Santa Cruz, 1972-75; sr. biologist U.S. Fish and Wildlife, Anchorage, 1975-79; pres. Solace Enterprises, Anchorage, 1979-85; research scientist Sea World, Inc., San Diego, 1986—. Contbr. articles to profl. jours. Mem. Soc. Marine Mammology (charter), Am. Fisheries Soc., Am. Assn. Zool. Parks and Aquaria. Republican. Lutheran. Avocations: reading, diving, surfing, fly fishing. Office: Sea World Inc 1720 S Shores Rd San Diego CA 92109

HALL, KATHRYN LAURIE, pediatrician; b. Oakland, Calif., May 8, 1953; d. Harold Hershey and LaVon (Doner) H.; m. Lawrence Wayne Ginsberg, May 18, 1975; children—Corinne, David, Rachel. B.S., Pa. State U., 1973; M.D., Jefferson Medical Coll., 1975. Diplomate Am. Bd. Pediatrics. Intern Bridgeport Hosp., Conn., 1975-76, resident, 1976-78; practice medicine specializing in pediatrics, Lindsay, Calif., 1978-83, Lindsay Med. Group, Calif., 1983—; dir. medical edn. Lindsay Hosp. Med. Ctr., 1983—. Trustee sch. bd. Lindsay Unified Sch. Dist., 1985—. Fellow Am. Acad. Pediatrics; mem. Physicians for Social Responsibility, Calif. Med. Assn., Tulare County Med. Soc., Am. Med. Women's Assn., AAUW. Jewish. Home: 21620 Ave 247 Lindsay CA 93247 Office: Lindsay Medical Group 833 N Sequoia Ave Lindsay CA 93247

HALL, KATHY WELCH, medical technologist; b. Lexinton, Ky., Dec. 29, 1947; d. Porter Prather and Betty Jane (Price) Welch; m. Charles Noel Hall, May 30, 1970; 1 child, Amanda Jane. BS, U. Louisville, 1969. Staff technologist Welborn Meml. Hosp., Evansville, Ind., 1969-70, Clin. Lab., Inglewood, Calif., 1970-72; staff technologist Torrance (Calif.) Meml. Hosp., 1972-76, chemistry supr., 1976—. Recipient South Bay Panhellenic, 1985. Mem. Am. Soc. Clin. Pathologists, Calif. Assn. Med. Lab. Technologists, Pi Beta Phi Alumnae (v.p. 1981-82, pres. 1982-84). Democrat. Episcopalian. Office: Torrance Meml Hosp 3330 Lomita Blvd Torrance CA 90509

HALL, LARRY D., energy company executive; b. Hastings, Nebr., Nov. 8, 1942; s. Willis E. and Stella W. (Eckoff) H.; m. Jeffe D. Bryant, Sept. 5, 1985; children: Scott, Jeff, Mike, Bryan. BA in Bus., Kearney (Nebr.) State Coll.; JD, U. Nebr. Bar: Nebr., Colo. Ptnr. Wright, Simmons, Hancock & Hall, Scottsbluff, Nebr., 1967-71; atty., asst. treas. KN Energy Inc., Hastings, Nebr., 1971-76; v.p. law div. KN Energy Inc., Lakewood, Colo., 1976-82, sr. v.p., 1982-85, exec. v.p., 1985—, also bd. dirs.; bd. dirs. Midwest Gas Assn., Mpls., 1985—. Mem. ABA, Fed. Energy Bar Assn., Nebr. Bar Assn., Colo. Bar Assn., Pres. Assn. Democrat. Presbyterian. Club: Columbine Country. Lodges: Elks, Masons. Avocations: skiing, golf, photography. Home: 6537 Vesuvius Rd Evergreen CO 80439 Office: KN Energy Inc 12055 W Second Pl Lakewood CO 80228

HALL, LOIS RIGGS, symphony orchestra administrator, state senator; b. Beeville, Tex., May 22, 1930; d. Ira Franklin and Pearl Ophelia (McCoy) Riggs; student Tex. Women's U., 1947-49, U. Tex., Austin, 1949-50; m. Walter William Hall, Dec. 28, 1950 (dec.); children—Robert Macfarlane, Elaine Denise, Judith Lea. Exec. sec. N.Mex. Symphony Orch., Albuquerque, 1975—; mem. N.Mex. Senate, 1980-85. Active Boy Scouts Am., Girl Scouts U.S.A., Officers Wives Clubs; 2d v.p. Albuquerque Symphony Women's Assn.; bd. dirs. Friends of Music, 1986—; treas., publicity dir. N.Mex. Aviation Assn. Republican. Home: 620 Ortiz NE Albuquerque NM 87108 Office: PO Box 769 Albuquerque NM 87103

HALL, NANCY SUSAN, media buyer; b. Phoenix, Feb. 23, 1958; d. Arlin Earl and Marie June (Zarorek) Ehlers; m. Thomas Franklin Hall, Dec. 27, 1985. Sales asst. Sta. KDKB Radio, Mesa, Ariz., 1979-83; pub. relations sec. Pointe Communications, Phoenix, 1983-85, media buyer, 1985—. Mem. AD2. Office: Pointe Communications 7500 N Dreamy Draw Dr #215 Phoenix AZ 85020

HALL, RADFORD SKIDMORE, II, civil engineer, planner; b. Denver, Sept. 10, 1941; s. Radford Skidmore and Florence (Fulton) H.; m. Geraldine M. Bissell, Sept. 3, 1966; children—Romany S., Radford Skidmore III. B.S.C.E., Denver U., 1965; M.S. in Natural Resources Policy, Colo. State U., 1977, PhD in Natural Resources Policy, 1986 . Civil engr. trainee FAA, 1959-65; jr. civil engr. Corps Engrs., San Francisco, 1965-71, sr. civil engr./planner navigation, beach erosion, and water resources, San Francisco, 1971-76, supervisory civil engr., chief permits sect. San Francisco Dist., 1977—; lectr./instr. Colo. State U. Coll. Forestry and Natural Resources, 1980-81; mem. Tech. Com. Susiun Marsh, Calif. Mem. Hillside Preservation Bd., City of Pacifica (Calif.), 1975-78, mem. planning commn., 1978-80, 83—, chmn. planning commn., 1979. Recipient Outstanding Performance award Corps Engrs., 1981, 84, 85; Office of Chief of Engrs. civil works fellow, 1976-77. Mem. Am. Planning Assn., Sierra Club, Am. Inst. Cert. Planners, Phi Kappa Phi, Sigma Chi. Author: Water Use and Management in an Arid Region, 1977.

HALL, RALPH CORBIN, forest entomologist, consultant; b. Ellenville, N.Y., May 7, 1899; s. James Harvey and Anna (Newkirk) H.; m. Dorothy Dane Colby, Sept. 7, 1930 (dec. Aug. 1981); children: James Dane, Judith Gilmore Thomson, John Colby, Joanne Newkirk Parrish (dec.). BS, Syracuse U., 1925; MF, Harvard U., 1927; PhD, U. Mich., 1931. Registered profl. entomologist, U.S.; registered profl. forester, Calif. Research forest entomologist Bur. Entomology and Plant Quarantine, Columbus, Ohio, 1931-38, Berkeley, Calif., 1938-53; with U.S. Forest Service, 1953-64; entomologist San Francisco, 1961-64; v.p., dir. Natural Resources Mgmt. Corp., Orinda, Calif., 1970-74; cons. forest entomology Orinda, 1974—; cons. research grants NSF, 1951—. Mem. nat. council Boy Scouts Am., 1955-66, mem. exec. council Mt. Diablo Council, 1947-71; bd. dirs. Wildernees Found., Calif. Forestry Found., Forest Landowners Calif. Named Man of Yr. by City of Orinda, 1949; recipient Silver Beaver award Boy Scouts Am., 1957; award of Merit SUNY, award of Merit Calif. Acad. Scis., award of Merit N.Y. Acad. Scis. Fellow Soc. Am. Foresters (Golden Membership award 1978), AAAS, Internat. Platform Assn., Fedn. Am. Scientists, Explorers Club; mem. Assn. Cons. Foresters, Wildlife Soc., Wilderness Soc., Am. Forestry Assn., Entomol. Soc. Am., Sierra Club, Sigma Xi, Gamma Sigma Delta, Phi Sigma. Address: 72 Davis Rd Orinda CA 94563

HALL, RAYMOND CLARENCE, safety engineer; b. Durhamville, N.Y., June 23, 1920; s. Ellsworth Roscoe and Blanche Dora (Ferguson) H.; m. Edna Julia Pirog, Dec. 4, 1946; children: Susan Blanche, Deborah Francis Ferguson, Pamela Joyce. BS in Ceramic Engring., Alfred U., 1942; postgrad., SUNY, Buffalo, 1950-51, U.S. Army Command and Gen. Staff Coll., 1965. Cert. safety profl.; registered profl. engr., Calif. Indsl. relations engr. Martin Co., Denver, 1960-62, mfg. research engr., 1962-64; safety cons. Colo. Safety Assn., Denver, 1964-68; safety engr. U. Colo., Boulder, 1968-82; pres. Hazard Control Assn., Inc., Boulder, 1982—; safety cons. Associated Gen. Contractors of Minn., St. Paul, 1983—. Contbr. articles to profl. jours. Served with C.E., USAAF, 1942-54; col. Res. Recipient Cert. Excellence Colo. Div. Labor and Employment, 1979, Outstanding Service award Coll. and U. Sect. Nat. Safety Council, 1977-79. Mem. Am. Soc. Safety Engrs. (pres. Colo. chpr. 1968-69, Vets. Safety Tech. Publs. award 1968), Soc. Am. Mil. Engrs., Nat. Campus Safety Assn. (chmn. 1976-77), Nat. Fire Protection Assn., Safety Inst. Australia, Ednl. Resources div. Nat. Safety Council (hon., life). Avocations: travel, golf, sailing. Home and Office: Hazard Control Assocs Inc 3193-8th St Boulder CO 80302

HALL, ROBERT EMMETT, JR., investment banker, realtor; b. Sioux City, Iowa, Apr. 28, 1936; s. Robert Emmett and Alvina (Faden) H.; m. Marna Thiel, 1969. BA, U. S.D., 1958, MA, 1959; MBA, U. Santa Clara, 1976; grad. Am. Inst. Banking, Realtors Inst. Grad. asst. U. S.D., Vermillion, 1958-59; mgr. ins. dept., asst. mgr. installment loan dept. Northwestern Nat. Bank of Sioux Falls, S.D., 1959-61, asst. cashier, 1961-65; asst. mgr. Crocker Nat. Bank, San Francisco, 1965-67, loan officer, 1967-69, asst. v.p., asst. mgr. San Mateo br., 1969-72; v.p., Western regional mgr. Internat. Investments & Realty, Inc., Washington, 1972—; owner Hall Investment Co., 1976—; pres. Almaden Oaks Realtors, Inc., 1976—; instr. West Valley Coll., Saratoga, Calif., 1972-82, Grad. Sch. Bus., U. Santa Clara (Calif.), 1981—. Treas., Minnehaha Leukemia Soc., 1963, Lake County Heart Fund Assn., 1962, Minnehaha Young Republican Club, 1963. Mem. Am. Inst. Banking, San Mateo C. of C., Calif. Assn. Realtors (vice chmn.), Beta Theta Pi. Republican. Roman Catholic. Clubs: Elks, Rotary (past pres.), K.C., Almaden Country, Mercedes Benz Calif. Home: 6951 Castlerock Dr San Jose CA 95102 Office: 6501 Crown Blvd 100 San Jose CA 95120

HALL, ROBERT WHITNEY, airline executive; b. Upper Derby, Pa., Feb. 9, 1934; s. Arthur Franklin and Ruth Whitney (Flewelling) H.; m. Bertha S. Hall, May 14, 1961; 1 son, Keith T. Student Towson State Coll., U Md., 1951-54; BGS with distinction, Chaminade U. of Honolulu, 1984; MS in Psychology, 1986. Pilot, Mohawk Airlines, 1959-60, Hawaiian Airlines, 1960, Internat. Air Service Co. (Japan Airlines), 1962-63; asst. to pres. E.L. Forde Ltd. Honolulu, 1960-61; mgr. Hawaii Transp. Co., Hilo, Hawaii, 1961-62; pres. Royal Hawaiian Trading Co. Inc., Honolulu, 1963-67; pres., dir. Robert W. Hall Assocs. Inc. (Hawaii Air Cargo Inc.), 1962-82, Island Airlines Hawaii Inc., 1977-82; chmn., chief exec. officer, dir. Airlines Capital Corp., Inc., 1982—; exec. dir. Hawaii Inst. Biosocial Research, 1981—. Served to capt. USAFR, 1954-59. Mem. Am. Acad. Environ. Medicine (assoc.), Am. Assn. Counseling and Devel., Am. Arbitration Assn. (panel of arbitrators 1987—). Republican. Methodist. Clubs: Plaza, Honolulu Press, Honolulu Internat. Country, Shriners (Honolulu). Contbr. articles to profl. jours.

HALL, ROBERTA LOUISE, anthropologist; b. Ft. Wayne, Ind., Mar. 19, 1939; d. David W. and Florence (Kendrick) Bash; m. Don Alan Hall, Apr. 30, 1960; children: Alice Leigh, Nancy Elizabeth. BA in Journalism, Ind. U., 1963; MA in Anthropology, U. Oreg., 1969, PhD in Anthropology, 1970. Asst. prof. anthropology U. Victoria, B.C., Can., 1970-74; asst. prof. anthropology Oreg. State U., Corvallis, 1974-78, assoc. prof., 1978-84, chmn. dept. anthropology, 1984—; postdoctoral fellow U. Conn. Health Ctr., Farmington, 1981-83. Contbg. editor: Wolf and Man: Evolution in Parallel, 1978, Sexual Dimorphism in Homo Sapiens, 1982; author: The Coquille Indians, 1984; author, editor Male-Female Differences: A Bio-Cultural Perspective, 1985; book rev. editor Am. Jour. Phys. Anthropology, 1986—. Mem. Am. Assn. Phys. Anthropologists, Human Biology Council (exec. com. 1979-81). Home: 1257 NW Van Buren Ave Corvallis OR 97330 Office: Oreg State U Dept Anthropology Corvallis OR 97331

HALL, STANTON HARRIS, dental educator; b. Boise, Idaho, Apr. 8, 1940; s. Perce and Orpha (Harris) H; m. Sharon Viola Price, June 30, 1962; children: Jennifer Ann, Camille Elaine, Matthew Ridd. MS, DDS, Northwestern U., 1967; PhD, U. Wash., 1974. Cert. orthodontist. Research ass c. Nat. Inst. Health, Bethesda, Md., 1974-77; assoc. prof. dept. orthodontics U. Wash., Seattle, 1979—. Contbr. articles to profl. jours. Mem., counselor stake presidency Ch. Jesus Christ Latter-day Saints, 1984—; councilman Aurora Dist. Boy Scouts Am., Seattle, 1984—. Served to commdr. USPHS, 1964-67; recipient C.V. Mosby award for scholarship, Northwestern U. Dental Sch., 1967. Mem. ADA, Wash. State Soc. Orthodontists (bd. dirs., publ. chmn. 1982-86, bd. dirs., sec.-treas. 1986—), Internat. Assn. Dental Research, Am. Soc. for Bone and Mineral Research, AAAS, Am. Assn. Orthodontists, Omicron Kappa Upsilon. Home: 4549 Thackeray Pl NE Seattle WA 98105 Office: U Wash Dept Orthodontics Seattle WA 98195

HALL, STUART CAMPEN, lawyer, public affairs and travel consultant; b. San Jose, Calif., June 18, 1935; s. Marshall Spencer and Helen Bernice (Campen) H. B.A., U. Calif. at Berkeley, 1957; M.A., Stanford U., 1961; J.D., Harvard U., 1964. Legis. asst. Calif. Legislature Assembly, 1958-59, asst. clk. 1960, 1st asst. clk., 1961; adminstrv. analyst Office of Pres., U. Calif. at Berkeley, 1960, grad. research analyst, 1960; investigator Office of Dist. Atty., County of Santa Clara, San Jose, 1962-63; cons. Calif. Constn. Revision Commn., Calif. Legislature, San Francisco, 1964-65; lectr. polit. sci., dept. polit. sci. San Jose State Coll., 1965-69; cons. com. on elections and constl. amendments Calif. Assembly, 1969-70; adminstrv. asst. to Calif. State Senator John A. Nejedly, 1970-71; legis. counsel, legis. affairs, agy. Alaska Legislature, 1971-75, sr. legis. counsel, 1975-76; mem. Alaska Pub. Utilities Commn., 1976-83; adj. lectr. pub. adminstrn. U. Alaska, Juneau, 1973-76; adj. lectr. polit. sci. Anchorage Community Coll., U. Alaska, Anchorage, 1984-85. Mem. Rep. Cen. Com. Santa Clara County, 1967-70. Trustee Jr. Statesmen Found., 1970-80; bd. dirs. S. Cen. Alaska chpt. ARC, 1986—. Served with USAFR, 1959—, now lt. col. Woodrow Wilson fellow, 1957-58. Mem. ABA, Alaska Bar Assn., Calif. Hist. Soc., Nat. Mcpl. League, Am. Soc. for Pub. Adminstrn., Western Govtl. Research Assn., Am. Philatelic Soc., Harvard Law Sch. Assn., Stanford U. Alumni Assn., U. Calif. Alumni Assn., Ripon Soc. (nat. governing bd. 1979-81), Sigma Delta Chi. Episcopalian. Clubs: Masons, Rotary, Lions, Commonwealth (San Francisco). Home: 815 Colwell St PO Box 300 Anchorage AK 99510 Office: 308 G St Suites 308-310 Anchorage AK 99510

HALL, THOMAS CHRISTOPHER, physician, educator; b. N.Y.C., Nov. 26, 1921; s. John Clarence and Theresa (McDonald) H.; m. Lorina Amanda Friesen, July 30, 1978; children: Christopher, Thomas, Seth, Amity, Bronwen, Nathan, Jinny, Nicholas. Student, Harvard U., 1944, MD magna cum laude, 1949. Diplomate Am. Bd. Internal Medicine, Am. Bd. Med. Oncology; lic. physician Calif., N.Y., Mass., Hawaii. Intern Peter Bent Brigham Hosp., Boston, 1949-50; resident Mass. Gen. Hosp., Boston, 1951-53, asst. resident, 1954; asst. Harvard Med. Sch., Boston, 1955, instr., 1957; dir. oncology Lemuel Shattuck Hosp., Boston, 1957-62; sr. research assoc. in biochemistry Brandeis U., Waltham, 1959, adj. assoc. prof. biochemistry, 1961; dir. Harvard Cancer Chemotherapy Unit Pondville Hosp., 1959-68; asst. physician Children's Hosp. Med. Ctr., 1961, research assoc. in pathology, 1961, sr. assoc. in medicine, 1963, asst. prof. medicine, 1965; co-chmn. eastern coop. oncology group NIH, 1961; sr. assoc.in tumor therapy div. Children's Cancer Research Found., 1961, chief clin. and biochemicalpharmacology, 1964; assoc. in medicine Peter Bent Brigham Hosp., Boston, 1964; teaching assoc. Newton-Wellesley Hosp., 1967; physician Boston Hosp. for Women, 1967; dir. div. of oncology U. Rochester, N.Y., 1968-72; assoc. dir. therapeutics, prof. medicine and biochemistry USC Cancer Hosp. and Research Ctr. U. So. Calif., Los Angeles, 1972-75; affiliate staff mem. Hosp. of Good Samaritan Med. Ctr., Los Angeles, 1973-75; dir. Cancer Control Agy. of B.C., Can., 1975-76; prof. faculty of medicine Univ. B.C., Vancouver, 1975-77; scientist Pasadena Found. for Med. Research, Calif., 1977-78; clinician Tumor Clinic Med. Group, Inc., 1977-78; clin. prof. medicine U. Calif., Irvine, 1978—; prof. medicine, pharmacology U. Hawaii, Honolulu, 1978; physician Queen's Med. Ctr., Honolulu, 1983; dir. cancer ctr.Programs in Cancer Control Edn. and Outreach U. Hawaii, Honolulu, 1978; prof. U. Rochester, 1968-72; physician Strong Meml. Hosp., Rochester, 1968-72; cons. oncology Long Beach VA Hosp., 1979; medical staff, cons. oncology Queen's Med. Ctr., 1980, cons. St. Francis Hosp., Honolulu, 1980, Kuakini Med. Ctr., Honolulu, 1983. Contbr. articles to profl. jours. and numerous chpts. to books. Named hon. mem. USPHS Research Soc., Royal Coll. of Physicians and Surgeons of Can., Life Res. Prof. of the Am. Cancer Soc., First K.D. Allen Prof. Presbyterian Med. Ctr., Denver, Sixth Hubert Lectr. Brit. Assocs. for Cancer Research, Second Winfield Meml. Prof. St. Vincent Hosp. and Med. Ctr., Portland, Oreg., hon. mem. Western Assn. of Gynecologists. Named to Royal Coll. of Physicians and Surgeons of Can., Life Research Prof. First K.D. Allen Professor Presbyterian Med. Ctr., Denver, Sixth Hubert Lectr. Brit. Assocs. for Cancer Research, Second Winfield Meml. Prof. Fellow AAAS, Am. Assn. for Cancer Edn., Am. Soc. of Clin. Pharmacology and Chemotherapy, AAUP, Endocrine Soc., Internat. Soc. of Chemotherapy, Mass. Med. Soc., Soc. for Cryobiology, Western Assn. of Physicians, Can. Oncologic. Soc., Sigma Xi. Avocations: travel, camping. Office: U Hawaii Cancer Ctr 2456 Lauhala St Honolulu HI 96813

HALL, THOMAS JAMES, lawyer; b. Glendale, Calif., Mar. 25, 1943; s. Donald T. and Peggy (Townsend) H.; m. Arlene H. Kaastrup, Sept. 2, 1967; children: Greg, Scott, Justin, Kelly. BS, U. Nev., 1965; JD, Northwestern U., 1971. Bar: Nev. 1971, U.S. Ct. Appeals (9th cir.) 1974, U.S. Supreme Ct. 1975; lic. contractor, Nev. Law clk. to chief justice Nev. Supreme Ct., Carson City, 1971-72; assoc. Guild, Hagen & Clark, Reno, 1972-85, ptnr., 1975-85; sole practice Reno, 1985—; lectr. law U. Nev., 1972; trustee Hall Trust, Stateline, Nev., 1972—. Pres. Washoe County (Nev.) Citizens' Adv. Bd., 1984, 86, Tahoe-Sierra Preservation Council, Lake Tahoe, Nev., 1986-87. Mem. ABA, State Bar of Nev., Washoe County Bar Assn. (pres. 1981-82, sgt.-at-arms 1977-78, treas. 1978-79, sec. 1979-80, v.p. 1980-81), U. Nev.-Reno Alumni Assn. (pres. 1983-85, Outstanding Alumnus 1980), Ducks Unltd. Republican. Presbyterian. Avocations: soaring, racquetball, skiing, hunting, fishing. Home: 4000 Old Ranch Rd Carson City NV 89701

HALL, WARREN SEIYU, chemist; b. Toledo, Nov. 17, 1957; s. Raymond Ward and Akiko (Akasaki) H.; m. Mira Park Cuevas, Nov. 17, 1984. BS in Chemistry, U. Hawaii, Manoa, 1980. Chem. salesman Chem. Systems Inc., Honolulu, 1980-83, Dearborn Chem. div. W.R. Grace and Co., Honolulu, 1983-86; chemist Unitek Environ. Co., Honolulu, 1986—. Mem. Am. Chem. Soc., ASHRAE (assoc.). Republican. Avocations: ocean sports, running. Home: 3050 Ala Poha Pl #W-3 Honolulu HI 96818 Office: Unitek Environ Services 2889 Mokumoa St Honolulu HI 96819

HALLADAY, ROBERT EUGENE, assn. exec.; b. Provo, Utah, Apr. 19, 1917; s. Thomas Eugene and Fern Elizabeth (Peters) H.; BS, Brigham Young U., 1942; m. Geraldine Steedman, Dec. 17, 1943; children: Kathie H. (Mrs. Antonio Cano), Robert Greg, Anne H. (Mrs. Virgil Latimer), Thomas Eugene, Paul Andrew, Michael. Missionary to Brazil, Ch. of Jesus Christ of Latter-day Saints, 1937-40; with Utah Welfare Dept., 1942-45; parole agy. Utah Dept. Corrections, 1945-51; mem. staff Provo C. of C., 1951-58, mgr., 1954-58; mgr. Utah Mfrs. Assn., 1958-64, exec. v.p., 1964-82, pres., 1982—. Chmn. Utah Adv. Council on Tech. Edn., 1964-70; mem. exec. com. Utah Com. on Indsl. and Employment Planning, 1958-68; mem. State Adv. Council Unemployment Compensation, 1958—; mem. exec. com. Conf. State Mfrs. Assns.; pres. Utah C. of C. Execs., 1956; mem. N.A.M. Task Force, 1972; vice chmn. NIC, 1974, chmn., 1975—. Mem. alumni bd. Brigham Young U., 1964-67, mem. nat. adv. council Coll. Bus., 1960-78; mem. instnl. council Utah Tech. Coll. at Provo, 1978-86; chmn. Utah State Accreditation Com. for Vocat. Edn., 1985—. Recipient Outstanding Citizens award City of Provo, 1958, Legis. commendation to State of Utah and personal integrity; named Man of Integrity Utah State Ho. Reps./Utah State Senate. Republican. Mem. Ch. of Jesus Christ of Latter-day Saints (bishop 1955-59, mem. high council 1953-55, 61-67). Kiwanian. Home: 5947 Lakeside Dr Salt Lake City UT 84121 Office: Utah Mfrs Assn 136 S Main St Salt Lake City UT 84101

HALLBERG, DALE MERTON, sculptor; b. Spokane, Wash., Aug. 30, 1927; s. Gustaf Philip and Thelma (Bauman) H.; student U. Idaho, 1947-49, Wash. State U., 1949-50, U. Oreg., 1952-54; B.S. in Landscape Architecture, U. Calif., Berkeley, 1955; B.A. in Art, B.Ed., Eastern Wash. State Coll., 1956; postgrad. Claremont Grad. Sch., 1960-62, 62-67; M.A., Calif. State Coll. at Long Beach, 1967; m. Mildred May Lemmon, May 1, 1955. Tchr. art LaHabra (Calif.) High Sch., 1956-62; instr. landscape architecture Calif. State Poly. Coll., 1962-64; art instr. Troy High Sch., Fullerton, Calif., 1964-84; pvt. practice landscape architecture, Orange, Calif., 1955-78, Fullerton, 1978—; exhibited sculpture Muckenthaler Cultural Center, Fullerton, 1966, Calif. State Coll. at Long Beach, 1967, Galleria Numero, Venice, 1971, Galleria Fiamma Vigo, Rome, 1971, Art Alliance Safari for Calif. State U. at Fullerton, 1975, Common Ground Artists' Coop., Fullerton, 1978, 79, 80, others. Served with USMC, 1945-47, 50-52. Recipient certificate of merit Am. Soc. Landscape Architects, 1968; prin. works include Art in Pub. Places, Brea, Calif., 1985. Mem. Am. Soc. Landscape Architects, Art. Alliance of Fullerton State U., Laguna Beach Art Assn., Orange County Orchid Soc. (dir.), Specie Orchid Soc. (dir.). Republican. Presbyterian. Address: 1630 Skyline Dr Fullerton CA 92631

HALLER, HOWARD EDWARD, investment banker; b. Balt., Mar. 30, 1947; s. Howard Earl and Clemence Anne (Young) H.; B.A. with honors in Polit. Sci., Calif. State U., Northridge, 1970; grad. Am. Inst. Banking, 1970; postgrad. U. So. Calif., 1968-75; M.S. in Mgmt., U. Redlands, 1981; m. Terri Lynne Koster, June 20, 1969; children—Jennifer Louise, Justin Douglas, Jason Davis. Lic. real estate broker, Calif. Corp. officer Bank of Am., Los Angeles, 1969-71; mgr. Mgmt. Advisory Services, sr. cons. Matthew Wolfson & Co., C.P.A.s, Los Angeles, 1971-73; dist. mgr. U.S. Leasing Corp., Los Angeles, 1973-75; dist. mgr. Chem. Bank of N.Y., Santa Monica, Calif., 1976-77; v.p. Patagonia Leasing Co., Phoenix, 1977; regional leasing mgr. Prime Computer Inc., Woodland Hills, Calif., 1977-81; pres. Haller Co., Woodland Hills, Calif., 1974—; pres., dir. Leasing Dept. Inc., 1981-85; chmn. bd., chief exec. officer IFC Capital Corp., 1981-85; prof. fin. Calif. State U., Northridge, 1981-84, 1st v.p., pres., trustee univ. trust fund; pres., chief exec. officer, dir. Haller, Koster & Haller Corp. Served with USAFR, 1968-70. Lic. comml. pilot. Mem. Am. Mktg. Assn., Am. Mgmt. Assn., Nat. Assn. Corp. Dirs., Practising Law Inst., Nat. Eagle Scout Assn., Am. Assn. Equipment Lessors, Inst. Mgmt. Cons., Nat. Assn. Accts., Nat. Assn. Realtors, Am. Legion. Republican. Mormon. Office: 20750 Ventura Blvd Suite 300 Woodland Hills CA 91364

HALLETT, JOSEPH LEWIS, electronics company executive; b. Quincy, Mass., Sept. 23, 1932; s. Joseph Lewis and Helen McKay (Handy) H.; m. M. Isabelle Thomas, Jan. 7, 1953 (div. 1972); children: Kathy, Christopher, Carole, Karen, Virginia, Teresa; m. V. Linda Holland, July 11, 1980; children: Alison Marie, Sara Elizabeth. BSEE, Northeastern U., 1955, postgrad., 1966-68. Registered profl. engr., Mass. Instr. Lincoln Coll., Boston, 1957-70; engr. Sylvania Electric, Waltham, Mass., 1955-70; engring. mgr. GTE Sylvania, Seneca Falls, N.Y., 1970-79; product mgr. Tektronix Inc., Beaverton, Oreg., 1980-82, engring. mgr., 1982—. Contbr. articles to profl. jours. Patentee in field. Mem. Soc. Info. Display (chpt. officer), Nat. Computer Graphics Assn. (charter mem.), Soc. Motion Picture and TV Engrs.

HALLFORD, DENNIS MURRAY, animal science educator; b. Abilene, Tex., Feb. 11, 1948; s. Tommy Lamoine and Tiny Elizabeth (Stockton) H.; m. Marilyn Williams, Sept. 13, 1971; 1 child, Amy Denise. BS, Tarleton State U., 1970; MS, Okla. State U., 1973, PhD, 1975. Instr. Tarleton State U., Stephenville, Tex., 1970-71; grad. asst. Okla. State U., Stillwater, 1971-75; asst. prof. animal sci. N.Mex. State U., Las Cruces, 1975-80, assoc. prof., 1980-84, prof., 1984—; advisor Aggie Rodeo Assn., Las Cruces, 1975-80, Block and Bridle Club, Las Cruces, 1980-82, Animal and Range Sci. Grad. Student Orgn., Las Cruces, 1984—; mem. Univ. Research Council N.Mex. State U., 1984—, chmn., 1987—. Contbr. articles to profl. jours. Named Outstanding Tchr., N.Mex. State U., 1977, Outstanding Researcher, Univ. Research Council N.Mex. State U., 1986; recipient Disting. Teaching award Agrl. Coll. N.Mex. State U., 1980, Burlington No. Found. Faculty Achievement award N.Mex. State U., 1985. Mem. Am. Soc. Animal Sci. (pres. Western sect. 1987—), Am. Soc. Animal Scis. (pubs. com. 1986—, teaching award com.)Sigma Xi, Gamma Sigma Delta (pres. 1985-86, Grad. Teaching/Advising award 1983), Alpha Zeta, Alpha Chi. Methodist. Avocation: photography. Home: 1135 Calle del Encanto Las Cruces NM 88005 Office: NMex State U Dept Animal and Range Scis Box 30003 Las Cruces NM 88005

HALLIDAY, JOHN MEECH, investment company executive; b. St. Louis, Oct. 16, 1936; s. William Norman and Vivian Viola (Meech) H.; m. Martha Layne Griggs, June 30, 1962; children: Richard M., Elizabeth. BS, U.S. Naval Acad., 1958; MBA, Harvard U., 1964. Dir. budgeting and planning Automatic Tape Control, Bloomington, Ill., 1964-66; dir. planning Ralston-Purina, St. Louis, 1966-67, v.p. subsidiary, 1967-68, dir. internat. banking, 1967-68; v.p. Servicetime Corp., St. Louis, 1968-70; assoc. R.W. Halliday Assocs., Boise, Idaho, 1970-87; v.p. Sawtooth Communications Corp., Boise, 1970-73, Commander Corp., 1979-81; pres. Sonoma Internat., San Francisco, 1971-77, also chief exec. officer, ML Ltd., San Francisco, 1974—, Halliday Labs., Inc., Reno, 1980—, also dir.; exec. v.p., dir. Franchise Fin. Corp. Am., Phoenix, 1980-85. bldg. com. YMCA, 1965; pres. Big Bros. of San Francisco, 1978-81. Served to lt. comdr. USNR, 1958-66. Mem. Nat. Restaurant Assn., Soc. Advancement Food Research, Heart Ill. Restaurant Assn. (v.p. 1969-70), Nat. Assn. Accountants. Republican. Episcopalian. Clubs: Family, Olympic (San Francisco), Scott Valley Tennis (Mill Valley, Calif.), Harvard Bus. Sch. No. Calif. (v.p., dir.). Home: 351 Corte Madera Ave Mill Valley CA 94941 Office: 625 Market St Suite 602 San Francisco CA 94105

HALLIDAY, WILLIAM ROSS, physician, author, speleologist; b. Emory U., Ga., May 9, 1926; s. William Ross and Jane (Wakefield) H.; m. Eleanore Hartvedt, July 2, 1951; children: Marcia Lynn, Patricia Anne, William Ross III. B.A., Swarthmore Coll., 1946; M.D., George Washington U., 1948. Diplomate Am. Bd. Vocat. Experts. Intern Huntington Meml. Hosp., Pasadena, 1948-49; resident King County Hosp., Seattle, Denver Childrens Hosp., L.D.S. Hosp., Salt Lake City, 1950-57; practice medicine Seattle, 1957-65, 83-84; with Wash. Dept. Labor and Industries, 1965-76; med. dir. Wash. Div. Vocat. Rehab., 1976-82, Middle Tenn. Bank Care Ctr., 1984—; dep. coroner, King County, Wash., 1964-66; med. dir. Comprehensive Med. Rehab. Ctr., 1976-82. Author: Adventure Is Underground, 1959, Depths of The Earth, 1966, 76, American Caves and Caving, 1974, 82; Editor: Jour. Spelean History, 1968-73; contbr. articles to profl. jours. Mem. Gov.'s North Cascades Study Com., 1967-76; mem. North Cascades Conservation Council, v.p., 1962-63; Dir. Western Speleological Survey, Seattle, 1955-81; pres., 1981—; Internat. Speleological Found. asst. dir. Internat. Glaciospeleological Survey, 1972—. Served to lt. comdr. USNR, 1949-50, 55-57. Fellow Am. Coll. Chest Physicians, Am. Acad. Compensation Medicine, Nat. Speleological Soc., Explorers Club; mem. Soc. Thoracic Surgeons, AMA, Am. Congress Rehab. Medicine, Am. Coll. Legal Medicine, Wash. State Med. Assn., King County Med. Soc., Am. Fedn. Clin. Research, Am. Spelean History Assn. (pres. 1968), Brit. Cave Research Assn., Nat. Trust (Scotland), Am. Pain Soc., Internat. Soc. for the Study of Pain, Am. Acad. Algology. Clubs: Mountaineers (past trustee), Seattle Tennis. Home: 1117 36th Ave E Seattle WA 98112

HALLIGAN, THOMAS WALSH, construction company executive; b. Davenport, Iowa, Oct. 20, 1922; s. Eugene Joseph and Gertrude (Walsh) H.; m. Mary E. McClelland, Apr. 17, 1947; children: Carol, Mary Beth, Susan, Nancy, Timothy, Kathleen. A.B., Georgetown U., 1943. With Walsh Constrn. Co., Trumbull, Conn., 1946-80; pres. Walsh Constrn. Co., 1975-80; now chmn., chief exec. officer Guy F. Atkinson Co., South San Francisco, former pres. Office: Guy F Atkinson Co 10 W Orange Ave South South San Francisco CA 94080 *

HALLMAN, BOB EVERETT, electrical engineer; b. Orlando, Fla., June 10, 1952; s. Joseph A. and Ida L. (Castleberry) H. BSEE, U. Fla., 1974. Registered profl. engr., Fla., La. Elec. engr. Chevron Corp., San Ramon, Calif., 1975—. Mem. Instrument Soc. Am. (local pres. 1981), Fla. Engring. Soc., Tau Beta Pi. Avocations: jogging, golf, tennis, sailing. Home: 2605 Fountainhead Dr San Ramon CA 94583 Office: Chevron Corp PO Box 5045 San Ramon CA 94583

HALLORAN, JAMES VINCENT, III, business analyst; b. Greenwich, Conn., May 12, 1942; s. James Vincent and Rita Lucy (Keator) H.; m. Barbara Sharon Case, Sept. 7, 1974. BME, Cath. U. Am., 1964; MBA, U. Chgo., 1973. Mktg. rep. Rockwell Internat., El Segundo, Calif., 1973-76, bus. area mgr., 1976-80, bus. analysis mgr., 1980-84; asst. dir. market analysis H. Silver & Assocs. Inc., Torrance, Calif., 1984-87, dir. mktg., 1987—. Commr. Redondo Beach Housing Adv. and Appeals Bd., 1985—; mem. citizens adv. bd. South Bay Union High Sch. Dist., Redondo Beach, 1983. Served to capt. USAF, 1964-68. Mem. Am. Def. Preparedness Assn., Internat. Windsurfer Class Assn., Alfa Romeo Owners Club. Libertarian. Avocations: cycling, photography, windsurfing, traveling abroad. Home: 612 S Gertruda Ave Redondo Beach CA 90277 Office: H Silver & Assocs Inc 3420 Kashiwa St Torrance CA 90505-4025

HALOPOFF, WILLIAM EVON, industrial designer, consultant; b. Los Angeles, May 31, 1934; s. William John Halopoff and Dorothy E. (Foote) Lawrence; m. Nancy J. Ragsdale, July 12, 1960; children: Guy William and Carolee Nichole. BS, Art Ctr. Coll. Design, 1968. Internat. indsl. design cons. FMC Corp. Cen. Engring. Lab., Santa Clara, Calif., 1969-81; mgr. indsl. design Tandem Computers, Cupertino, Calif., 1981-84; design cons. Halopoff Assocs., Palo Alto, Calif., 1984—. Patentee in field. Served with U.S. Army, 1957-59. Mem. Indsl. Designers Soc. Am., Soc. Automotive Engrs. (chmn. subcom. 29 1979-85). Avocation: fine art. Home: 17544 Holiday Dr Morgan Hill CA 95037

HALPER, RITA MACK, science facility administrator; b. St. Paul, Feb. 9, 1929; d. Harry Isaac and Betty (Brodsky) Mack; m. Stanley Benjamin Halper, Mar. 30, 1952; children: Judith, Roxanne, Orrin. BS, U. Minn., 1951. With Minn. State Bd. Health, 1951-53; quality control microbiologist Hamms's Brewery, 1953-54; with dept. phys. med. and rehab. U. of Minn. Hosp., Mpls., 1954-57; supr. quality assurance Advanced Cardiovascular Systems, Mt. View, Calif., 1984—. Fin. sec. Congregation Beth David, chmn. 1983-85. Mem. Am. Soc. Safety Engrs., Am. Soc. for Safety Control, Regulatory Affairs Profl. Soc., Jewish Fedn. of San Jose (bd. dirs. women's div., pres. career women sect., 1985-86), Hadassah (pres. Huntsville chpt. 1970-72, v.p. San Jose chpt. 1972-74). Democrat. Avocations: gardening, hiking, gourmet cooking, reading.

HALPERIN, ROBERT MILTON, electrical machinery company executive; b. Chgo., June 1, 1928; s. Herman and Edna Pearl (Rosenberg) H.; m. Ruth Levison, June 19, 1955; children: Mark, Margaret, Philip. Ph.B., U. Chgo., 1949; B.Mech. Engring., Cornell U., 1949; M.B.A., Harvard U., 1952. Engr. Electro-Motive div. Gen. Motors Corp., La Grange, Ill., 1949-50; trust rep. Bank of Am., San Francisco, 1954-56; adminstr. Dumont Corp., San Rafael, Calif., 1956-57; pres. Raychem Corp., Menlo Park, Calif., 1957—; dir. Raychem Corp., 1961—; bd. dirs. Molecular Design Ltd. Trustee U. Chgo.; bd. dirs. Harvard Bus. Sch. Assocs., Stanford U. Hosp. Served to lt. USAF, 1952-53. Club: Harvard of New York City. Home: 80 Reservoir Rd Atherton CA 94025 Office: Raychem Corp 300 Constitution Dr Menlo Park CA 94025

HALPERIN, WARREN LESLIE, management consultant; b. Bklyn., Apr. 12, 1938; s. Abraham and Bertha Gertrude (Aronowitz) H.; m. Sherry Lee Weshner, Mar. 31, 1968; children: Jonathan David, Justin Edward. PhB, Adelphi U., 1959. Dir. mktg. Faust-Day Inc., Los Angeles, 1969-71; product mgr. Hunt-Wesson Foods, Fullerton, Calif., 1972-74; sr. v.p. Searchmasters Inc., Newport Beach, Calif., 1975-79; ptnr. MCS Assocs., Newport Beach, 1979-83; pres. The Halperin Co. Inc., Newport Beach, 1983—; also bd. dirs.; bd. dirs. West Helena (Ariz.) Savings. Contbr. articles to profl. jours. Mem. nat. bd. trustees Leukemia Soc. Am., N.Y.C., 1980-85; trustee Amigos De Las Americas, Irvine, Calif., 1975-78; chmn. Jewish Nat. Fund., Orange City, 1987; pres. Leukemia Soc. Am. Tri-City chpt., Garden Grove, Calif., 1979. Recipient Exec. of Yr. Exec. Mag., 1986. Mem. U.S. League of Savings Insts., Mortgage Bankers Assn. Am., Bank Adminstrn. Inst. Home: 23 South Peak Laguna Niguel CA 92677 Office: The Halperin Co Inc 23041 Avenida De La Carlotta Suite 360 Laguna Hills CA 92653

HALPERN, DAVID, physical oceanographer; b. Montreal, Que., Can., June 24, 1942; came to U.S., 1964; s. Harry and Rachel (Cohn) H.; m. Tema Kovack, May 29, 1966; children: Michael Adam, Lisa Jennifer. BSc with honors, McGill U., Montreal, 1964; PhD, MIT, 1969. Research assoc. MIT, Cambridge, 1969; research oceanographer NOAA, Seattle, 1969-85; from affiliate asst. prof. to full prof. oceanography and atmospheric scis. U. Wash., Seattle, 1969-85, research prof., 1985-86; sr. oceanographer Jet Propulsion Lab., Calif. Inst. Tech., Pasadena, 1986—; chmn. and convenor numerous nat. and internat. oceanographic and air-sea interactio coms., Paris, 1979-86. Contbr. numerous articles to profl. publs. Mem. AAAS, Marine Tech. Soc., Can. Meteorol. Oceanographic Soc., Am. Meteorol. Soc., Am. Geophys. Union. Office: Jet Propulsion Lab MS 169-236 4800 Oak Grove Dr Pasadena CA 91109

HALPERN, GEORGES MAURICE, physician, consultant; b. Warsaw, Poland, Sept. 7, 1935; came to France, 1935, came to U.S., 1981; s. Bernard Neftali and Renee Rachel (Nysenholc) Halpern Gelbard; m. Marie Catherine Guillard, 1958 (div. 1963); m. Genevieve Bourineau, 1965 (div. 1969); m. Emiko Oguiss, May 14, 1971; children: Emmanuelle Miyoko, Emilie Hideko. Baccalaureate summa cum laude, Lycee Henri IV, Paris, 1953; BS in physics, chemistry, biology, Faculty of Scis., Paris, 1954; degree in nuclear medicine, Institut National des Science et Techniques Nucleaires, Saclay, France, 1965; MD silver medal, Faculty of Medicine, Paris, 1964; med. diplomate, U. Paris, 1964. Practicing internist, allergist Allergy and Clinical Immunology Clinic, Paris, 1964-83; dir. program research Inst. ImmunoBiologie, Paris, 1966-78; chief sci. advisor 3M Diagnostic Systems, Mountain View, Calif., 1983—; pres. BioDelta, Frame, Medintern, Portola Valley, Calif., 1985—; adj. prof. medicine U. Calif. Sch. Medicine, Davis, 1986—; med. dir. French Pharmacy Hong Kong, Kowloon, 1970-77; cons. Lab. Cassenne, Paris, 1970-78, Pharmacia, Bois d'Arcy, France, 1971-83, Vittel U.S.A., San Francisco, 1983—; vis. research scholar Stanford U., Palo Alto, Calif., 1981-83. Author: L'Allergie et la Peau, 1976 (gold medal 1977), Allergies, 1985; editor in chief (med. jour.) Allergie et Immunologie, 1969-84; contbr. recipes to cooking mag., 1969-71 (merite agricole 1974); inventor IgG4 FAST. Recipient Prix Auguste Becard, Soc. de Gastronomie Medicale, Paris, 1969, Medal of Honor, Czech. Soc. J.E. Purkynje, Prague, 1977, Medal of Vermeil, City of Paris, 1985. Fellow European Acad. of Allergy, The Royal Soc. Medicine, Am. Acad. Allergy; mem. Colombian Acad. Medicine (corresponding mem.), GAILL (gen. sec.), Internat. Congress Food and Health (co-pres.). Lodge: Pacifica GODF (venerable). Avocations: cooking, wine tasting, journalism (food, wine, travel). Home: 9 Hillbrook Dr Portola Valley CA 94025

HALPERN, KATHERINE SPENCER, educator; b. Reading, Mass., Aug. 7, 1913; d. Carl Mason and Elizabeth Bertha (Beaudry) Spencer; m. Abraham Meyer Halpern, Nov. 16, 1968 (dec. 1985). BA, Vassar Coll., 1935; MA, U. Chgo., 1944, PhD, 1952. Research asst., fellow Harvard U., Cambridge, Mass., 1939-40, 46-50; social sci. analyst Office War Info., Washington, 1944-46; research assoc. Harvard Sch. Pub. Health and Med. Sch., Boston, 1953-56; assoc. prof., then prof. Boston U. Sch. of Social Work, 1954-70; prof. anthropology Am. U., Washington, 1970-78; researcher Wheelwright Mus. of Am. Indian, Santa Fe, N.Mex., 1979—; cons. in field Columbia U. Sch. Social Work, N.Y.C., 1950-52, Indian Health Service U.S. Pub. Health Service, Washington, Window Rock, Ariz., 1964-71. Author: Social Reflection in Navaho Origin Myth, 1947, Navaho Chantway Myths, 1957 (Chgo. Folklore prize, 1957). Fellow Am. Anthropol. Assn., Soc. Applied Anthropology; mem. NIMH (review coms. 1963-76), Soc. Med. Anthropology, Nat. Assn. Social Workers. Office: Wheelwright Mus Box 5153 Santa Fe NM 87502

HALPERN, LAWRENCE MAYER, pharmacologist, educator; b. N.Y.C., July 3, 1931; s. Jacob and Clara Deborah (Solomon) H.; m. Frances Weingart (div. 1976); children—Gordon Neil, Sharon Lee, Lisa Ann; m. 2d, Gail Arshon, July 12, 1981. B.S. in Biology and Chemistry, Bklyn. Coll., 1953; Ph.D. in Neuropharmacology, Albert Einstein Coll. Medicine, 1961. Neuropharmacologist, Merck Inst. Therapeutic Research, West Point, Pa., 1962-65; prof. U. Wash. Sch. Medicine, Seattle, 1965—, also dir. drug abuse info. service., 1967-75, cons. pain clinic, 1968—; cons. Nat. Inst. Neurol. Disease, Bethesda, Md., 1967-68. Contbr. articles to profl. jours; chpts. to books. Served with USN, 1950-58. Mem. Am. Soc. Pharmacology and Exptl. Therapeutics, Internat. Assn. Study Pain, Intractable Pain Soc. Gt. Britain and Ireland, Soc. Neurosci. Democrat. Jewish. Club: Seattle.

HALPIN, CHARLES AIME, archbishop; b. St. Eustache, Man., Can., Aug. 30, 1930; s. John S. and Marie Anne (Gervais) H. B.A., U. Man., 1950; B.Th., U. Montreal, 1956; Licentiate Canon Law, Gregorian U., Rome, 1960. Ordained priest Roman Catholic Ch., 1956; named monsignor Roman Cath. Ch., 1969, consecrated bishop, 1973; asst. St. Mary's Cathedral, Winnipeg, Man., 1956-58; vice chancellor, sec. to archbishop Archdiocese Winnipeg, 1960; officialis Archdiocesean Matrimonial Tribunal, 1962; vice-officialis Regional Matrimonial Tribunal, Regina, Sask.; chaplain to Pope, 1969-73; archbishop of Regina, 1973—. Mem. Western Cath. Conf. Bishops (past pres.), Can. Conf. Cath. Bishops (past dir.). Home: 2522 Retallack St, Regina, SK Canada S4T 2L3 Office: 3225 13th Ave, Regina, SK Canada S4T 1P5

HALSEY, ROBERT HARRY, controller, communications executive; b. St. Louis, Apr. 6, 1950; s. Robert and Dorothy (Stephens) H.; m. Anita C. Crafts, Oct. 19, 1985. BBA, Lincoln U., Jefferson City, Mo., 1972. Sr. acct. Ole's Home Ctrs., Pasadena, Calif., 1978-82; asst. controller Corona (Calif.)-Foothill Co., 1982-84; ptnr. Bookkeeping Plus, San Dimas, Calif., 1984; controller Pasadena Media, Inc., 1984—; pres. Macro Media, Inc., Pasadena, 1986—, also bd. dirs. Republican. Avocation: record production. Office: Pasadena Media Inc 300 S Raymond Ave Suite 12 Pasadena CA 91101

HALSTEAD, BRUCE WALTER, biotoxicologist; b. San Francisco, Mar. 28, 1920; s. Walter and Ethel Muriel (Shanks) H.; m. Joy Arloa Mallory, Aug. 3, 1941; children: Linda, Sandra, David, Larry, Claudia, Shari. A.A., San Francisco City Coll., 1941; B.A., U. Calif.-Berkeley, 1943; M.D., Loma Linda U., 1948. Research asst. in ichthyology Calif. Acad. Scis., 1935-43; instr. Pacific Union Coll., 1943-44; mem. faculty Loma Linda (Calif.) U., 1948- 58; research assoc. Lab. Neurol. Research, Sch. Medicine, 1964—; dir. World Life Research Inst., Colton, Calif., 1959—, Internat. Biotoxicol. Center; research assoc. in ichthyology Los Angeles County Mus., 1964—; instr. Walla Walla Coll., summers 1964—; Cons. to govt. agys., pvt. corps; mem. editorial staff Exerpta Medica, 1959—, Toxicon, 1962—; mem. joint group experts on sci. aspects marine pollution UN; Dir. Nat. Assn. Underwater Instrs., Internat. Underwater Enterprises, Internat. Bots., Inc. Author: Poisonous and Venomous Marine Animals of the World, 5 vols., 1966; others.; contbr. 280 articles to profl. jours. Fellow AAAS, Internat. Soc. Toxicology (a founder), N.Y. Acad. Scis., Royal Soc. Tropical Medicine and Hygiene; mem. Am. Inst. Biol. Scis., Am. Micros. Soc., Am. Soc. Ichthyologists and Herpetologists, Am. Soc. Limnology and Oceanography, numerous others. Republican. Adventist. Office: World Life Research Inst 23000 Grand Terrace Rd Colton CA 92324

HALSTEAD, LARRY ALVIN, computer manufacturing executive; b. Tulsa, Feb. 5, 1944; s. Virgil Alvin and Alo-Jean (Barksdale) H.; m. Laine Virginia Johnson, Feb. 5, 1966; children—Dean Sheridan, Jeffrey John, Jennifer Laine. A.A., Ventura Coll., 1966; B.S., U. Calif.-Irvine, 1977. Mgr. data processing I/O Computing Co., Long Beach, Calif., 1972-77; mgr. planning EECO, Inc., Santa Ana, Calif., 1977-79, mgr. mktg. services, 1979-82; v.p. mktg. Standard Logic, Inc., Corona, Calif., 1982-84, v.p. property mgmt. systems, 1984—. Served with U.S. Army, 1966—; Germany; to col. USAR. Mem. Res. Officers Assn. (chpt. pres. 1975, 87), Am. Mktg. Assn., Nat. Assn. Scuba Diving Schs. Republican. Episcopalian.

HALVER, JOHN EMIL, nutritionist; b. Woodinville, Wash., Apr. 21, 1922; s. John Emil and Helen Henrietta (Hansen) H.; m. Jane Loren, July 21, 1944; children: John Emil, Nancy Lee Halver Hadley, Janet Halver Fix, Peter Loren, Deborah Kay. B.S., Wash. State U., 1944, M.S. in Organic Chemistry, 1948; Ph.D. in Med. Biochemistry, U. Wash., 1953. Plant chemist Asso. Frozen Foods, Kent, Wash., 1946-47; asst. chemist Purdue U., 1948-49; instr. U. Wash., Seattle, 1949-50; affiliate prof. U. Wash., 1960-75, prof. Sch. Fisheries, 1975—; dir. Western Fish Nutrition Lab., U.S. Fish and Wildlife Service, Dept. Interior, Cook, Wash., 1950-75, sr. scientist, nutrition, Seattle, 1975-78; cons. FAO, UNDP, Internat. Union Nutrition Scientists, Nat. Fish Research Inst., Hungary, World Bank, Euroconsult, UNDP, IDRC; affiliate prof. U. Oreg. Med. Sch., 1965-69; vis. prof. Marine Sci. Inst., U. Tex., Port Arkansas; pres. Fisheries Devel. Technology, Inc., 1980—, Halver Corp., 1978—. Served from pvt. to capt. U.S. Army, World War II; col. USAR. Decorated Purple Heart, Bronze Star with oak leaf cluster, Meritorious Service Conduct medal. Fellow Am. Inst. Fishery Research Biologists; mem. AAAS, Nat. Acad. Sci., Am. Sci. Affiliation, Am. Chem. Soc., Am. Fishery Soc., Am. Inst. Nutrition, Phi Lambda Upsilon, Pi Mu Epsilon, Alpha Chi Sigma. Methodist (lay leader). Club: Rotary. Determined vitamin and amino acid requirements for fish; identified aflatoxin B1 as specific carcinogen for rainbow trout hepatoma; identified vitamin C2 for fish. Home: Box 116 Underwood WA 98651 Office: U Wash Sch Fisheries Seattle WA 98195

HALVERSEN, GARY LANE, physician; b. Salt Lake City, Oct. 2, 1939; s. Leon Lemon and Nisha (Seamons) H.; m. Ann Elizabeth Woolstenhulme, Aug. 7, 1964; children: Lane, Lisa, Julie Ann, Matthew Gary, Ashley Anne. BA, U. Utah, 1963, MD, 1967. Intern William Beaumont Army Hosp., El Paso, Tex., 1967-68; resident in radiology Tripler Army Hosp., Honolulu, 1968-70; fellow in neuroradiology and angiography Walter Reed Army Hosp., Washington, 1970-71, resident, 1971-72; chief Angiography Fitzsimons Army Hosp., Denver, 1973-74; chief neuroradiology, ultrasound Fresno (Calif.) Community Hosp., 1974-75; chief spl. procedures/ultrasound Sierra Hosp., Fresno, 1975-78; radiology staff St. Mark's Hosp., Salt Lake City, 1978—; with Western Neurol. Assocs., Salt Lake City, 1979—; clin. teaching faculty U. Utah Coll. Medicine, Salt Lake City, 1984—. Co-author: Interpretation of Lumbar Spine CAT Scans, 1982, High Resolution CT of Cervical Spine, 1985. Served to maj. U.S. Army, 1967-72. Mem. Am. Med. Soc., Am. Coll. Radiology, Utah State Med. Soc., Salt Lake County Med. Soc. (treas. 1984-85, sec. 1986). Republican. Mormon. Club: Ft. Douglas Hidden Valley Golf. Avocations: swimming, water skiing, skiing, painting, music. Home: 299 Fairfax Circle Salt Lake City UT 84103 Office: Western Neurolo Assocs 1151 E 3900 S Suite B199 Salt Lake City UT 84124

HALVORSEN, WILLIAM JOHN, mining engineering consultant; b. Phila., Jan. 26, 1921; s. William John and Eugenia (Worsham) H.; m. Betty Jane Toothman, Sept. 3, 1948; children: Darwin John, Kirsten Jane, Walter Lee. BSChemE, Va. Poly. Inst., 1942; MSChemE, Ill. Inst. Tech., 1948, MS in Gas Tech., 1948. Registered profl. engr., Pa. Process engr. Standard Oil of La., Baton Rouge, 1942-46; research fellow Inst. Gas Tech., Chgo., 1947-48; research engr. Consolidation Coal Co., Pitts., 1948-56; mgr. coal pipeline Consolidation Coal Co., Cadiz, Ohio, 1957-63; dir. process design Consolidation Coal Co., Pitts., 1964-82; engring. cons. Consolidation Coal Co., Sedona, Ariz., 1983—; cons. iron ore pipeline, Bechtel, San Francisco, 1966, also coal pipeline, 1982-84; coal preparation China Coal Ministry, Bejing, 1981, 83, Consol Rio of Australia, Brisbane, 1985, various U.S. cos. Contbr. articles on coal pipelining and preparation to profl. jours. Mem. Am. Inst. Chem. Engring., AIME, Service Corps Retired Execs. Republican. Lodge: Kiwanis. Home and Office: PO Box 3914 West Sedona AZ 86340

HAMACHEK, TOD RUSSELL, manufacturing executive; b. Jan. 3, 1946; m. Barbara Callister, 1969; children: Mark, Elizabeth. BA, Williams Coll., 1968; MBA, Harvard U., 1970. Nat. sales mgr. Harris Corp., Westerly, R.I., 1970-74; asst. to pres. Gt. Western Malting Co., Vancouver, Wash., 1974-76; v.p. sales Gt. Western Malting Co., Vancouver, Oreg., 1976-79, pres., chief exec. officer, 1979-84; pres., chief ops. officer Penwest, Ltd., Bellevue, Wash., 1984-85, pres., chief exec. officer, 1985—; sr. v.p. Univar Corp., Seattle, 1982-84; bd. dirs. N.W. Natural Gas Co., First Internat. Bank of Wash. Trustee Lewis and Clark Coll., Portland, Oreg., Pacific NW Arts and Crafts Assn., Bellevue, Wash. Research Council, Olympia, Seattle Found.; past trustee Portland Opera Assn., Pacific Crest Outward Bound Sch., Outward Bound, Inc. Mem. Young Pres.' Orgn. Office: Penwest Ltd 411 108th Ave NE Bellevue WA 98004

HAMADA, HAROLD SEICHI, civil engineer, educator; b. Honolulu, Nov. 1, 1935; s. Kihachi and Tsuruyo (Hamada) H.; m. Lucy Tachiko Igawa, Aug. 24, 1958; children: Kyle Hideo, LeeAnn Hiroko. BS, U. Hawaii, 1957; MS, U. Ill., 1958, PhD, 1962. Registered profl. engr, Hawaii. Project officer Air Force Weapons Lab., Kirtland AFB, N.Mex., 1962-65; engr. Lawrence (Calif.) Radiation Lab., 1965-67; prof. civil engring. U. Hawaii, Honolulu, 1967—. Served with USAF, 1962-65. Mem. ASCE, Structural Engrs. Assn. Hawaii, Sigma Xi. Home: 2084 Alaeloa St Honolulu HI 96821 Office: Univ Hawaii Dept Civil Engring 2540 Dole St Honolulu HI 96822

HAMAMURA, DENNIS TSUYOSHI, optometrist; b. Honolulu, Jan. 31, 1947; s. Ronald A. and Doris T. (Yamamura) H.; m. Dixie B. Hardy, Aug. 20, 1972 (separated). B.A. in Biology, U. Calif.-Riverside, 1970; O.D., So. Calif. Coll. Optometry, 1975; postgrad. Calif. State U.-Fullerton, 1982—. Lic. optometrist, Calif. Lab. technician U. Calif.-Riverside, 1967-70, lab. asst. dept. entomology, 1967-70; lab. technician Salinity Lab., Dept. Agr., Riverside, 1968-70; assoc. R.A. Wilmer O.D., Santa Monica, Calif., 1975-77, R.J. Anelle, O.D., Colton, Calif., 1977—; asst. prof. optometry So. Calif. Coll. Optometry, 1982—; dir. optometry Sherman Indian High Sch., 1979-81, El Progreso del Desierto Family Health Ctr., Inc., 1984-86; cons. Toiyabe Indian Health Project, 1981; faculty adv. Gamma chpt. Omega Delta. Japanese Am. Optometric Soc. scholar, 1975; Evening Kiwanis Club scholar, 1965. Mem. Am. Pub. Health Assn., Am. Optometric Assn., Calif. Optometric Assn., Orange Belt Optometric Soc., Japanese Am. Optometric Soc., Nat. Rifle Assn., Calif. Rifle and Pistol Assn., Calif. Golden State Trapshooting Assn. (life; So. Circle 5 Champion 1978, So. Zone Class A Champion 1981, Calif. State Zone Champion 1982). Clubs: Upland (Calif.) Gun; Inland Fish and Game (Redlands, Calif.). Office: 190 W H St Suite 105 Colton CA 92324

HAMBER, HERBERT WALTER, physics educator; b. Milan, Italy, Feb. 1, 1953; came to U.S., 1977; s. Heinz Arthur and Vittoria (Emiliani) H.; m. Franca Filippucci, July 28, 1977; 1 child, Jane Alessandra. Laurea in Physics, U. Milan, 1977; PhD in Physics, U. Calif., Santa Barbara, 1980. Research assoc. U. Calif., Santa Barbara, 1980, Brookhaven Nat. Lab., Upton, N.Y., 1980-82; staff mem. Inst. Advanced Study, Princeton, N.J., 1982-85; asst. prof. physics U. Calif., Irvine, 1985—. Contbr. articles to sci. jours. Fulbright fellow, 1977-81. Mem. AAAS, Am. Phys. Soc., N.Y. Acad. Sci. Roman Catholic. Office: U Calif Physics Dept Irvine CA 92717

HAMBY, JAMES ALLAN, university administrator; b. Oakland, Calif., May 16, 1943; s. Walter B. Hamby and Jane E. (Harvey) Petrie; children: Jean Marie, Deborah Suzanne, Tracey Gail. BA in Humanities, So. Oreg. State Coll., 1965, MA in English, 1969. Dir. Oreg. Mus. Natural History, Ashland, 1964-66; asst., writer So. Oreg. State Coll., Ashland, 1965-66; mem. faculty Medford (Oreg.) High Sch., 1967-70, Utah State U., Logan, 1970-71, Coll. of the Redwoods, Eureka, Calif., 1971-77; adminstr. Humboldt State U., Arcata, Calif., 1971—; bd. govs. Humboldt Area Found., Eureka, 1973-76, Nielson Inst., Arcata, 1975—; judge Calif. Writing Competition, Arcata, 1979-84, Humboldt History Day, Arcata, 1983—. Co-author: Principles & Issues in Nutrition, 1985; contbr. articles to profl. jours. Co-chmn. United Way of Humboldt County, Eureka, 1972-73, Baywood Golf & Country Club Ball, Arcata, 1973. Elk's Club scholar, 1960-61; recipient Creative Writing award Utah Inst. Fine Arts, 1971. Mem. Poets and Writers Inc., Acad. Am. Poets, Council for Advancement and Support of Edn., Arcata C. of C. (bd. dirs.). Republican. Club: Eureka Pacers Track & Field Club (pres. 1980-82). Home: PO Box 1124 Arcata CA 95521 Office: Humboldt State U Found PO Box 1185 Arcata CA 95521

HAMILTON, ALAN RAY, chemistry educator; b. Chickasha, Okla., Apr. 30, 1944; s. John Woodrow and Willie Mae (Hambleton) H.; m. Laurie Ann Shaffer, Jan. 22, 1966; children: Chesa Dawn, Jason Todd. BA in Chemistry, McMurry Coll., 1966; MEA, U. Mont., 1974. Tchr. chemistry, physics, math. Anson High Sch., Anson, Tex., 1966-68; tchr. sci., math. East Jr. High Sch. Dist. 1, Great Falls, Mont., 1968-70, North Jr. High Sch., Great Falls, 1970-76, C.M. Russell High Sch., Great Falls, 1976—; tchr. chemistry Coll. Great Falls, 1985-86. Mem. Calvary Community Ch. Named Most Inspirational Tchr. Mont. State U., Bozeman, 1984, 85; recipietn Doctor of Service award C.M. Russell High Sch., 1981. Mem. NEA (life), Mont. Edn. Assn. (life), Great Fall Ed. Assn. (exec. bd. 1978-79), Am. Chem. Soc. Republican. Avocations: tennis, racquetball, fly fishing, fly tying. Home: 1112 20th Ave SW Great Falls MT 59404 Office: CMR High Sch 228 17th Ave NW Great Falls MT 59404

HAMILTON, BRANDON LESLIE, systems engineer, mathematician; b. Chgo., Nov. 26, 1947; s. Eugene Alexander Hamilton and Gloria Lee (Gladney) Hamilton Atkins; m. Linda Jean Gholson, Dec. 22, 1967 (div. 1971); 1 son, Brandon Hamilton. A.A., Kennedy-King Coll., 1975; B.S., U. Ill.-Chgo., 1979. Engring. cons. Stone & Webster Engring., Boston, 1972-74; tutor/instr. Inroads Inc., Chgo., 1975-78; physics lab. asst. Ill. Inst. Tech., Chgo., 1977; strategic analyst Analytic Services Inc., Arlington, Va., 1979-80; nuclear-computer engr. So. Calif. Edison, San Clemente, 1980-84; sr. mem. tech. staff Aerojet ElectroSystems Co., Azusa, Calif., 1984—; bus. cons., 1986-87. Contbr. articles to profl. publs. Bus. cons. Jr. Achievement, 1986-87. Served with USN, 1968-72. Mem. Math. Assn. Am., D.C. Student Math. Soc. (editor newsletter 1979-80), Soc. Indsl. and Applied Mathematicians, Am. Soc. Computer Simulation, Los Angeles Council of Black Profl. Engrs. Home: 410 S Hobart Apt 312 Los Angeles CA 90020 Office: Aerojet ElectroSystems Co 1100 W Hollyvale St Azusa CA 91702

HAMILTON, CHARLES HOWARD, metallurgist; b. Pueblo, Colo., Mar. 17, 1935; s. George Edwin and Eva Eleanor (Watson) H.; m. Joy Edith Richmond, Sept. 7, 1968; children: Krista Kathleen, Brady Glenn. BS, Colo. Sch. Mines, 1959; MS, U. So. Calif., 1965; PhD, Case Western Res. U., 1968. Research engr. Space div. Rockwell Internat., Downey, Calif., 1959-65; mem. tech. staff Los Angeles div. Rockwell Internat., 1968-75; tech. staff, phys. metallurgy Sci. Ctr., Thousand Oaks, Calif., 1975-77, group mgr. metals processing, 1977-79, prin. scientist, 1979-81, dir. materials synthesis and processing dept., 1982-84; assoc. prof. Washington State U., Pullman, 1984-87, prof., 1987—; chmn. corp. tech. panel, materials research and engring; co-organizer 1st Internat. Symposium Superplastic Forming, 1982. Sr. editor Jour. Materials Shaping Tech.; contbr. tech. articles to profl. publs.; patentee advanced metalworking and tech. Named Rockwell Engr. of Yr., 1979; recipient IR 100 award Indsl. Research mag., 1976, 80. Fellow Am. Soc. Metals; mem. AIME (shaping and forming com.), Sigma Xi. Home: 410 SE Crestview Pullman WA 99163

HAMILTON, CLAYTON CORRELL, municipal official; b. Tucson, Jan. 15, 1945; s. Gordon Brown and Zilpha (Correll) H.; m. June Diane Sawyer, Apr. 4, 1970 (div. 1986); children: Jennifer, Margaret, April. Student, U. Ariz., 1965-71, 84-86. V.p. Hamilton Aircraft Co., Tucson, 1972-80, Integrated Data Corp., Tucson, 1980-84; cable TV adminstr. City of Tucson, 1984—; ex-officio bd. dirs. Tucson Community Cable Corp. Pres. state bd. dirs. Very Spl. Arts Ariz., 1985—. Served with U.S. Army, 1968-70. Mem. Nat. Assn. Telecommunications Officers and Advisors (pres. Rocky Mountain States region 1985—), Nat. Fedn. Local Cable Programmers. Republican. Avocations: classical piano, flying, restoring autos. Office: City of Tucson Office Cable Adminstrn 255 W Alameda Tucson AZ 85726-7210

HAMILTON, DARDEN COLE, flight test engineer; b. Pitts., Nov. 28, 1956; s. Isaac Herman Hamilton and Grace Osborne (Fish) Thorp; m. Linda Susanne Moser, Aug. 8, 1976; children: Christopher Moser Hamilton, Elijah Cole Hamilton. BS in Aeronautics, St. Louis U., Cahokia, Ill., 1977; postgrad. in aeronautical tech., Ariz. State U. Licensed comml. pilot; licensed airframe and power mechanic. Engr. McDonnell Douglas Aircraft Co., St. Louis, Mo., 1977-80; group leader, engring. Cessna Aircraft Co., Wichita, Kans., 1980-83, sr. flight test engr., 1983-85; sr. flight test engr. Garrett Turbine Engine Co., Phoenix, 1986—. Mem. Soc. Flight Test Engrs. Republican. Lodge: Masons. Avocations: horses, target shooting, camping. Home: 4501 W Paradise Ln Glendale AZ 85306 Office: Garrett Turbine Engine Co 111 S 34th St Phoenix AZ 85010

HAMILTON, DAVID MIKE, publishing company executive; b. Little Rock, Feb. 25, 1951; s. Ralph Franklin and Mickey Garnet (Chappell) H.; m. Carol Nancy McKenna, Oct. 25, 1975; children: Elisabeth Michelle, Caroline Ellen. BA, Pitzer Coll., 1973; MLS, UCLA, 1976. Cert. tchr. library sci., Calif. Editor Sullivan Assocs., Palo Alto, Calif., 1973-75; curator Henry E. Huntington Library, San Marino, Calif., 1976-80; mgr. prodn., mktg. William Kaufmann Pubs., Los Altos, Calif., 1980-84; pres. The Live Oak Press, Palo Alto, 1984—; pub. cons. Am. Assn. Artificial Intelligence, Menlo Park, Calif., 1984—; cons. editor, gen. ptnr. Sensitive Expressions Pub. Co., Palo Alto, 1985—. Author: To the Yukon with Jack London, 1980, The Tools of My Trade, 1986; contbg. author (jour.) Small Press, 1986; (books) Book Club of California Quarterly, 1985, Research Guide to Biography and Criticism, 1986. Sec. Vestry of Trinity Parish, Menlo Park, 1986, bd. dirs., 1985-87; trustee Jack London Ednl. Found., Las Vegas, Nev. Mem. ALA, Bookbuilder's West (book show com. 1983), Author's Guild, Soc. Tech. Communication (judge 1984), Assn. Computing Machinery (chmn. pub. com. 1984), Book Club of Calif. Democrat. Episcopalian. Avocations: backpacking, camping, hiking, book collecting. Home: 2620 Emerson St Palo Alto CA 94306 Office: The Live Oak Press PO Box 60036 Palo Alto CA 94306

HAMILTON, DOUGLAS HOLMES, geologist, executive; b. Pasadena, Calif., July 12, 1934; s. Everett L. and Verlyn (Weatherford) H.; m. Joyce Johnson, Nov. 7, 1972; children: James E., Colin D. BS, Stanford U., 1956, MS, 1962, PhD, 1984. Registered geologist, Calif.; cert. engring. geologist, Calif. Geologist Utah Constrn. Co., San Francisco, 1956, Phillips Mining Co., Grants, N.Mex., 1960; engring. geologist W.A. Wahler & Assocs., Palo Alto, Calif., 1961-69; pres., prin. geologist Earth Scis. Assocs., Palo Alto, 1969—. Served with USN, 1957-60, with Res. 1960-68. Mem. Am. Geophys. Union, Geol. Soc. Am., Soc. Econ. Geologists, Assn. Engring. Geologists, Soc. Mining Engrs. Avocations: vintage sports cars, backpacking, numismatics, shooting. Home: 2 Bassett Ln Atherton CA 94025 Office: Earth Scis Assocs Inc 701 Welch Rd Palo Alto CA 94304

HAMILTON, JAMES MARVIE, automotive research and development executive; b. Blythe, Calif., Jan. 2, 1950; s. D.L. Hamilton and Mary Elizabeth (Dekens) Charboneau; m. Tracy Parks, Mar. 16, 1985. BSEE, Loyola U., Los Angeles, 1972; MS in Computer Sci., UCLA, 1974. Cert. Engineering Indsl. Technician. Mem. tech. staff Hughes Aircraft, Los Angeles, 1972-76, group head, 1976-80; sect. head Hughes Aircraft, Irvine, Calif., 1980-84; pres., chief exec. officer Coast Tech., San Diego, 1984—, also bd. dirs.; gen. ptnr. Spectrum Investments, San Diego, 1976-82. Contbr. articles to tech. jours.; patentee integrated circuits and computerized suspension. Bd. dirs. MSJH, Inc. Home for Handicapped Children, San Diego, 1984-86. Mem. IEEE, Loyola Engring. Alumni Assn. (v.p. 1977-78, pres. 1978-79), Sigma Phi Delta, Tau Beta Pi, Alpha Sigma Nu. Republican. Avocations: inventing, physics, skiing. Office: Coast Tech Inc PO Box A6-297 Laguna Niguel CA 92677

HAMILTON, JUNE DIANE, computer company executive; b. Gainsville, Fla., June 10, 1946; d. Clarence Weeks and Pearl Marie (Brackett) Sawyer; m. Clayton Correll Hamilton, Apr. 4, 1970. B. U. Md., 1968. Analyst RCA, Washington, 1969-71; cons. RCA, Tucson, 1971-72; project supr. Pima County, Tucson, 1973; cons. Honeywell, Tucson, 1974, Hamilton Systems, Tucson, 1975-78; pres. Integrated Data Corp., Tucson, 1978—. Republican. Club: Women's Aglow (treas.). Lodge: Soroptimists. Office: IDC 2424 E Broadway Suite 106 Tucson AZ 85719

HAMILTON, MADRID TURNER, sociologist, consultant; b. Greensboro, Ga., May 14; s. Paul and Mary Lillyan (Hubert) Turner; m. Norman Woodrow Hamilton, June 9, 1948 (dec. July 1964); one child, Alexander Turner. AB, Spelman Coll., 1943; MSW, Atlanta U., 1946; PhD, Union for Experimenting Colls. and Univs., 1979. Cert. tchr.; lic. social worker; lic. real estate agt. Asst. prof. sociology Morehouse Coll., Atlanta, 1946-48; sch. social worker N.Y.C. Bur. Child Guidance, 1954-56; cons., social worker N.Y.C. Dept. Pub. Health, 1958-64; regional dir. Planned Parenthood, N.Y.C. and San Francisco, 1964-69; regional rep. Family Services Assn. Am., N.Y.C. and San Francisco, 1969-72; pres. M.T. Hamilton Enterprises Inc., San Francisco, 1973—; assoc. prof. sociology U. Redlands, Calif., 1974-77; adj. assoc. prof. social work San Francisco State U., 1966-67; counties coordinator West Bay Health Systems Agy., San Francisco, 1977-78; mem. leased housing staff San Francisco Housing Authority, 1979-81. Author: Erosive Health, 1986, Rural Health Education; Family Planning, Prejudice and Politics, How to Give a Health Fair; editor The Dem. Wome's Forum, 1984—; contbr. articles on health in the black community to newspapers. Mem. Gov.'s Population Study Commn., Calif., 1966-67, western region v.p. YWCA of U.S., 1979-82, loc. treas., 1976-77, 80; v.p. Dem. Women's Forum of San Francisco, 1984—; loc. pres. Coalition of 100 Black Women, 1983—; pres. Dem. Women's Forum of San Francisco, 1987. Mem. Am. Assn. Polit. and Social Scis., Nat. Assn. Social Workers, Spelman Coll. Alumnae Assn. (founding mem., pres., award 1985, 1st Regional coordinator), Am. Inst. Research Biographical Assn. (life, grand ambassador of achievement), Ct. Appointed Spl. Advocate for Children. Democrat. Avocations: crewel and needlepoint, beekeeping, gardening, traveling. Home: 136 Geneva Ave San Francisco CA 94112 Office: PO Box 12413 San Francisco CA 94112

HAMILTON, MARIAN JOAN ETTER, arts consultant, designer; b. Dorris, Calif., June 21, 1938; d. Benjamin Walter and Eva Louise (Larson) Etter; m. William John Hamilton III, Nov. 23, 1956; children: John Douglas, Susan Marie. BA, Dominican Coll., San Rafael, 1954; teaching cert., Notre Dame Coll., San Bruno, Calif., 1956; student in Fine Arts, U. Calif., Davis. Exec. dir. Davis Art Ctr., 1972-80; african travel specialist U. Pacific, Stockton, Calif., 1981-83; owner Hamilton Design, Winters, Calif., 1983—. Mem. Civic Arts Commn., Davis, 1976-82; chmn. Yolo County Arts Council, Woodland, Calif., 1982-83. Democrat. Avocations: bird watching, tennis, flying. Home and Office: Blue Oak Ranch Winters CA 95694

HAMILTON, MARILYN STANLEY, immunology educator; b. Honolulu, Apr. 30, 1948; d. Emory Day and Mary Jane (Gotshall) Stanley; m. Brian Lukens, Aug. 28, 1971; 1 child, Amy. BS in Microbiology cum laude, U. Wash., 1971, MS in Microbiology, 1973, PhD in Microbiology, Immunology, 1976. Postdoctoral fellow U. Tex. Health Sci. Ctr., Dallas, 1976-78; postdoctoral fellow transplantation unit Mass. Gen. Hosp. Transplantation Unit Dept. Surgery, Boston, 1978-80; research assoc. Harvard U. Med. Sch., Boston, 1980-81, Children's Hosp. Med. Cen., Boston, 1980-81; research asst. prof. biol. structure U. Wash., Seattle, 1981—. Contbr. articles to profl. jours. Mem. AAAS, Internat. Soc. Immunology of Reprod., Soc. Study Reprod., Am. Soc. Immunology of Reprod., Phi Beta Kappa. Episcopalian. Home: 2207 Federal Ave E Seattle WA 98102 Office: U Wash Dept Biological Structure Seattle WA 98195

HAMILTON, NANCI, marketing professional; b. Phila., June 19, 1954; d. William Porter Hamilton and Joyce Arlene (Stubbe) Leech; m. Terry Lee Hansen, Oct. 30, 1976 (div. 1978); m. John Louis Reel, Sept. 18, 1982 (div. 1987). BA in Interpersonal Behavior, Knox Coll., 1975. Instructional writer Deterline Assocs., Palo Alto, Calif., 1977-80; mgr. tech. tng. Friden-Alcatel, Hayward, Calif., 1980-82; chief exec. officer Reeltech, San Lorenzo, Calif., 1982-83; mgr. mktg. communications Teneron, Beaverton, Oreg., 1983-85, Cycomm, Portland, Oreg., 1985—. Author books on Macintosh personal computer; contbr. articles to profl. jours. and mags. Served with USN, 1975-76. Democrat. Episcopalian. Home: 12326 SW 60th Ave Portland OR 97219 Office: Cycomm 6665 SW Hampton Portland OR 97223

HAMILTON, NANCY JEANNE, structural engineer; b. Rochester, Minn., Jan. 1, 1959; d. Michael Joseph and Joanne Marguerite (Brunger) H.; m. Robert Scott Edwards; 1 child, Sarah Marie Hamilton Edwards. BS in Archtl. Engring., Calif. Poly. State U., San Luis Obispo, 1981; MSCE, MIT, 1984. Registered profl. civil engr., Calif. Project engr. KPFF Cons. Engrs., Los Angeles, 1984-85, project mgr., 1986—; vis. critic architecture Calif. Poly. State U., 1986. Recipient scholarships Rotary Club Redding, Calif. chpt., 1977, Women's Archtl. League So. Calif., 1980. Mem. Am. Concrete Inst., ASCE, Sigma Xi, Tau Beta Pi. Republican. Roman Catholic. Home: 9523 Lucerne Ave Culver City CA 90230 Office: KPFF Cons Engrs 2121 Cloverfield Blvd #200 Santa Monica CA 90404

HAMILTON, PHILLIP DOUGLAS, lawyer; b. Pasadena, Calif., Oct. 16, 1954; s. Ivan and Annette O. (Brown) H.; m. Gerry Messner, Sept. 17, 1976 (div. Feb. 1984); m. Janet L. Hester, Apr. 22, 1984; children: Melissa, John. B.A., U. Pa., 1976; J.D., Pepperdine U., 1979. Bar: Calif. 1979, U.S. Dist. Ct. (cen. dist.) Calif. 1980. Assoc., Offices of James J. DiCesare, Santa Ana, Calif., 1979-84; sole practice, Newport Beach, Calif., 1984—. Recipient Am. Jurisprudence award, 1980. Mem. Assn. Trial Lawyers Am., Orange County Trial Lawyers Assn., Calif. Trial Lawyers Assn., Calif. Trial Lawyers Polit. Action Com., Orange County Bar Assn. Republican. Presbyterian. Office: 610 Newport Center Dr Suite 300 Newport Beach CA 92660

HAMILTON, RICHARD SCOTT, chemist, researcher; b. Brigham City, Utah, May 9, 1953; s. Richard Max and Lou Jeanne (Christensen) H.; m. Laura Lee Wheelwright, Nov. 6, 1975; children: Ryan, Khara, Kirk, Teresa, Jenny. BS in Chemistry, Weber State Coll., 1983. Chemist Morton-Thiokol, Inc., Brigham City, 1984—. Mem. Am. Chem. Soc. (hon., cert.). Republican. Mormon. Avocations: camping, hiking, fishing, golfing, home remodeling. Home: 6095 N 4600 W PO Box 118 Bear River City UT 84301 Office: Morton Thiokol Inc M/S 241 PO Box 524 Brigham City UT 84302

HAMLIN, RONALD CRAIG, physicist, consultant executive; b. Rapid City, S.D., Oct. 27, 1946; s. Robert Thomas and Barbara June (Price) H. BS in Physics with high honors, U. Calif., Riverside, 1968; MS in Physics, U. Calif. at San Diego, La Jolla, 1970, PhD in Physics, 1975. Research asst. U. Calif. at San Diego, La Jolla, 1970-75, asst. research physicist, 1975-81, assoc. research physicist, 1981-86; pres. Area Detector Systems Corp., San Diego, 1986—, also chmn. bd. dirs.; cons. U. Calif. San Diego, 1986—. Developer 1st successful position sensitive area x-ray detector for protein crystallography; contbr. articles to profl. jours. Recipient NSF 2 yr. traineeship, U. Calif. San Diego, 1968-70; grantee Small Bus. Innovation Research, NIH, 1986. Mem. Am. Inst. Physics, Am. Crystallographic Assn. (editor and contbg. author transcations rev. 1982), AAAS, Phi Eta Sigma. Democrat. Congregationalist. Avocations: tennis, sailing. Home: 7776 Camino Glorita San Diego CA 92122 Office: Area Detector Systems Corp 7343 Ronson Rd Suite L San Diego CA 92111

HAMM, DAVID ROBERT, chemist; b. Ventura, Calif., 1957; s. Robert Lee H.; m. Rochelle L. Simpson. BA in chemistry, U. Calif. San Diego, 1980. Research assoc. U. Calif. San Diego, La Jolla, 1980-81; research scientist Catalytica, Inc., Mountain View, Calif., 1981-84, research fellow, 1984—. Contbr. articles to profl. jours.; patentee in field. Treas. Crestview Homeowner's Assn., Mountain View, 1986. Mem. Am. Chem. Soc., Catalysis Soc. (Calif. chpt., organic reactions catalysis soc. chpt.). Home: 1033 Crestview Dr #306 Mountain View CA 94040-3448 Office: Catalytica Inc 430 Ferguson Dr Bldg 3 Mountain View CA 94043

HAMM, GEORGE ARDEIL, educator, hypnotherapist, consultant; b. San Diego, Aug. 13, 1934; s. Charles Ardeil and Vada Lillian (Sharrah) H.; m. Marilyn Kay Nichols, July 1, 1972; children—Robert Barry, Charles Ardeil II, Patricia Ann. B.S. in Music, No. Ariz. U., 1958, M.A. in Music Edn., 1961; M.A. in Ednl. Adminstrn., Calif. Lutheran Coll., 1978, M.S. in Guidance and Counseling, 1981. Cert. secondary sch. tchr., adminstr. pupil personnel services, Calif. Tchr. music Needles (Calif.) High Sch., 1958-61; tchr. career guidance and psychology, counselor Hueneme High Sch., Oxnard, Calif., 1961—; cons. applied sport psychology. Served with USMC, 1953-55; Korea. Mem. Am. Personnel and Guidance Assn., N.Am. Soc. Psychology of Sport and Phys. Activity, Am. Fedn. Tchrs., Assn. for Humanistic Edn. and Devel., Am. Council Hypnotist Examiners, U.S. Judo Assn. Inc. (5th Degree Black Belt; named sr. level coach of Judo, 1980), Phi Delta Kappa, Kappa Delta Pi. Republican. Mormon. Contbr. numerous articles to nat. and internat. Judo jours. Pioneer ednl. hypnosis. Home: 1864 S Bearden Ct Oxnard CA 93033 Office: Hueneme High Sch 500 Bard Rd Oxnard CA 93033

HAMM, PATRICIA MALIZIA, medical technologist; b. Dearborn, Mich., June 15, 1945; d. Vincent Adam and Jeana (Bruno) Malizia; m. Vance Edgar Hamm, Nov. 28, 1971 (div.); 1 child, Christy Jean. B.A. in Biology, Calif. State U.-Northridge, 1967. Lic. med. technologist, Calif. Tchr. St. Genevieve High Sch., Panorama City, Calif., 1967-69; intern in med. tech. Valley Presbyn. Hosp., Van Nuys, Calif., 1969-71; evening lab. supr. Palm Harbor Gen. Hosp., Garden Grove, Calif., 1971-72; med. technologist La Habra (Calif.) Community Hosp., 1972-75, microbiologist, epidemiologist, 1975-84; infection control practitioner-microbiologist U. Calif.-Irvine Med. Ctr., 1984—; adult edn. tchr.; cons. in field. Mem. AIDS Coalition to Identify Orange County Needs, speaker's bur.; program mgr., dir. Ctr. for Disease Control programs Mgmt. Skills for Infection Control, Applied Epidemiology. Mem. AAAS, Am. Soc. Microbiologists, Orange County Assn. Practitioners Infection Control (sec. chpt. 1983, pres. 1985, by-laws chair 1986), Calif. Assn. Practitioners Infection Control (coordinating council 1986-87). Contbr. articles to profl. publs. Home: 2549 Branch Ln Brea CA 92621 Office: 101 City Dr Rt 171 Orange CA 92668

HAMM, THOMAS EDWARD, JR., veterinarian; b. Denver, Dec. 26, 1942; s. Thomas Edward and L. Lorraine (Nelson) H.; m. Diane Lynn Mauck, June 17, 1967; 1 child, Jonathan Thomas. BA, U. Colo., 1964; DVM, Colo. State U., 1968, MS, 1972; PhD, Wake Forest U., 1980. Diplomate Am. Coll. Lab. Animal Medicine. Asst. prof. U. Colo. Med. Ctr., Denver, 1975-78; expert cons. Nat. Cancer Inst., Bethesda, Md., 1978-80; head. toxicology dept. Chem. Industry Inst. of Toxicology Research, Triangle Park, N.C., 1980-84; dir. DLAM Stanford (Calif.) U., 1984—; cons. AAALAC, Schaumburg, Ill., 1978—, VA Hosp., Palo Alto, Calif., 1984—; bd. dirs. Nat. Assn. Biomed. Research, Washington, 1983—. Editor: Complications of Viral and Mycoplasmal Infections in Rodents to Toxicology Research and Testing, 1986, mem. editorial bd. Drug & Chem. Toxicology Jour., 1983—; contbr. articles to profl. jours. Served to capt. U.S. Army, 1968-70. Fellow NIH, 1972-75; named Hon. Alumnus, N.C. State U., 1983. Mem. AVMA (mem. Animal Welfare com. 1985—), AAAS, Am. Assn. Lab. Animal Sci. (legis. com. 1984—), Am. Coll. Lab. Animal Medicine, Am. Assn. Pathologists, Sigma Xi, Phi Kappa Phi. Avocations: genealogy, stamp and coin collecting. Office: Stanford U Med Sch Div Lab Animal Medicine Quad 7 Bldg 330 Stanford CA 94305

HAMMER, ARMAND, petroleum company executive, art patron; b. N.Y.C., May 21, 1898; s. Julius and Rose (Robinson) H.; m. Olga von Root, Mar. 14, 1927; m. Angela Zevely, Dec. 19, 1943; m. Frances Barrett, Jan. 26, 1956. B.S., Columbia U., 1919, M.D., 1921, LL.D., 1978; LL.D., Pepperdine U., 1978, Southeastern U., Washington, 1978, U. Aix-en-Provence, 1981; D.Public Service, Salem (W.Va.) Coll., 1979; H.H.D., U. Colo., Boulder, 1979. Pres. Allied Am. Corp., N.Y.C., 1923-25, A. Hammer Pencil Co., N.Y.C., London and Moscow, 1925-30, Hammer Galleries, Inc., N.Y.C., 1930—, J. W. Dant Distilling Co., N.Y.C. and Dant, Ky., 1943-54; pres., chmn. bd. Mut. Broadcasting System, N.Y.C., 1957-58; chmn. bd., chief exec. officer Occidental Petroleum Corp., Los Angeles, 1957—; chmn. M. Knoedler & Co., Inc., N.Y.C., 1972—; dir. Nat. State Bank, Perth Amboy, N.J., 1949-56, City Nat. Bank, Beverly Hills, Calif., 1962-71, Can. Occidental Petroleum Ltd., Calgary, Alta.; dir. Raffinerie Belge de Petroles, Antwerp, Belgium, 1968-79, Cities Service Co., Tulsa; hon. dir. Fla. Nat. Bank of Jacksonville, 1966-72; mem. Nat. Petroleum Council, 1968—, Com. on Arctic Oil and Gas Resources, 1980—. Author: The Quest of the Romanoff Treasure, 1936; subject of biography: The Remarkable Life of Dr.

Armand Hammer (Robert Considine), 1975; Brit. edit. Larger than Life, 1976. Pres. N.J. Aberdeen Angus Assn., 1948-49; Bd. govs. Monmouth County Orgn. Social Service, Red Bank, N.J., 1949-61, Monmouth Meml. Hosp., Long Branch, N.J., 1946-58, Eleanor Roosevelt Cancer Found., N.Y.C., 1960—, Ford's Theatre Soc., 1970—, UN Assn. U.S.A., 1976—; trustee U. North Africa Assn., 1968-71, Los Angeles County Mus. Art, 1968—, UCLA Found., 1973-76, Nat. Symphony, 1977—, United for Calif., 1977—, Capitol Children's Mus., 1978—; chmn. wine and spirits div. Vis. Nurse Service Greater N.Y., 1946, Am. Aid to France, 1947; mem. Citizens Food Com., 1946-47, Cardinal Spellman's Com. of Laity for Catholic Charities, 1946-48, Public Adv. Com. on U.S. Trade Policy, 1968-69, Am. Com. for Nat. Archives, 1974-76, Los Angeles County-U. So. Calif. Cancer Assos., 1975—, George C. Marshall Assos., James Smithson Soc. of Smithsonian Nat. Assos., 1977—, U. Okla. Assos., 1981—, Bus. Adv. Commn. for 1984 Olympics, 1981—, Los Angeles Olympic Citizens Adv. Commn., 1981—; hon. trustee Denver Art Mus., 1980—; mem. adv. bd. Inst. of Peace, 1950-54, Los Angeles Beautiful, Inc., 1969-75, Com. for a Greater Calif., 1969—, Fogg Art Mus. and Fine Arts Library, Cambridge, Mass., 1977—, The Friendship Force, 1977—, Am. Longevity Assn., Inc., 1980—, Center Strategic and Internat. Studies, Georgetown U., 1981—; mem. fine arts com. U.S. Dept. State, 1981—; chmn. Pres.'s Cancer Panel, 1981—; mem. exec. com. Econ. Devel. Bd. City of Los Angeles, 1968-73; trustee, chmn. exec. com. Salk Inst. Biol. Studies, San Diego, 1969—; bd. dirs. Los Angeles World Affairs Council, 1969—, Planned Parenthood World Population/Los Angeles, 1970—, U.S.-USSR Trade and Econ. Council, 1973—, Assos. Harvard Bus. Sch., 1975—, Calif. Roundtable, 1976—, Century City Cultural Commn., 1977—, Corcoran Gallery Art, Washington, 1978—, Keep Am. Beautiful, Inc., 1979—, Bus. Com. for Arts, N.Y.C., 1980—; bd. visitors Grad. Sch. Mgmt., UCLA, 1957—, UCLA Sch. Medicine Center for Health Scis., 1980—; exec. mem. Energy Research and Edn. Found., 1978—; charter mem. Nat. Visiting Council of Health Scis. Faculties, Columbia U., 1978—; mem. univ. bd. Pepperdine U., 1979—; mem. fellows for life New Orleans Mus. Art, 1980—; mem. nat. support council U.S. Com. for UNICEF, 1980—; founder mem. Pepperdine Assos., 1976—; pres. Found. of Internat. Inst. Human Rights, Geneva, 1977—; mem. exec. bd. dirs. UN Assn. Los Angeles; mem. Bd. Mcpl. Arts Commrs. Los Angeles, 1969-73; mem. budget and fin. com. of bd. trustees Los Angeles County Mus. Art, 1972-74; sponsor Internat. Inst. Human Rights Peace Conf., Oslo, 1978, Campobello Peace Park, 1979,, 1981. Served with M.C. U.S. Army, 1918-19. Endowed Armand Hammer Center for Cancer Biology, Salk Inst., 1969; Armand Hammer prof. bus. and public policy UCLA, 1968; Frances and Armand Hammer wing Los Angeles County Mus. Art, 1969; Armand Hammer Animal Facility Salk Inst., 1976; Calif. Inst. Cancer Research UCLA, 1976; Ann. Armand Hammer Cancer Conf. and Fund Salk Inst., 1976; Harvard/Columbia Russian Study Fund, 1977; Julius and Armand Hammer Health Scis. Center Columbia U., 1977; Five-Yr. Funding Program UN Assn., 1978; Five-Yr. Funding Program Corcoran Gallery Art, 1979; Five-Yr. Funding Program Jacquemart-André Mus., Paris, 1979; Ann. Armand Hammer Award Luncheon Los Angeles, 1980; recipient Humanitarian award Eleanor Roosevelt Cancer Found., 1962; city commendation Mayor of Los Angeles, 1968; decorated comdr. Order of Crown Belgium, 1962; comdr. Order of Andres Bellos Venezuela, 1975; Order of Aztec Eagle Mex., 1977; officer Legion of Honor France, 1978; Order of Friendship Among Peoples USSR, 1978; Disting. Honoree of Yr. Nat. Art Assn., 1978; Golden Plate award Am. Acad. Achievement, 1978; Aztec award Mexican-Am. Opportunity Fond., 1978; Appeal of Conscience award N.Y.C., 1978; Spirit of Life award Oil Industry Council of City of Hope, 1979; Royal Order of Polar Star Sweden, 1979; award Antique Monthly, 1980; Entrepreneur of Yr. award U. So. Calif., 1980; Maimonides award Los Angeles Jewish Community, 1980; Golden Achievement award Andrus Gerontology Center, U. So. Calif., 1981; Ambassador of Arts award State of Fla., 1981; officer Grand Order of Merit Italy, 1981. Mem. Los Angeles Petroleum Club, Royal Acad. Arts (London), hon. corr., Am. Petroleum Inst. (dir. 1975—), Navy League U.S. (Los Angeles council 1980—), Fifty-Yr. Club Am. Medicine, Royal Scottish Acad. (hon.), AMA (life), N.Y. County Med. Assn., Internat. Inst. Human Rights, Alpha Omega Alpha, Mu Sigma, Phi Sigma Delta. Office: Occidental Petroleum Corp 10889 Wilshire Blvd Suite 1500 Los Angeles CA 90024

HAMMER, FRANK JORGEN, consulting psychologist; b. Appleton, Wis., Jan. 19, 1918; s. Frank Joseph and Marie (Rasmussen) H.; m. Joyce Frances Waldhaus, Apr. 7, 1968; children—Mark, Laurel, Dan, Frank, Aaron, Michelle, Matthew; m. 2d., Emily Sue Speed, Apr. 9, 1983. B.A., Lawrence U., 1942; Ph.D., U. Chgo., 1952. Lic. psychologist, Wash. Chief psychologist Madigan Army Hosp., 1952-55, Community Psychiat. Clinic, Seattle, 1955-64; pvt. practice cons. psychology, Seattle, Mountlake Terrace, Wash., 1964—; cons. Everett Ctr. Youth Services, Seattle Police Dept., King County Juvenile Ct., Valley Gen. Hosp., Snohomish County Family and Juvenile Cts., Seattle Sch. Dist.; clin. instr. U. Wash. Med. Sch. Mayor Mountlake Terrace, 1960-64; chmn., bd. dirs. Source Found. Mentally Retarded Children; bd. dirs. Snohomish County Alcoholism, Mental Health Services; mem. Snohomish County Bd. Freeholders, 1968-69. Served to lt. col. U.S. Army, 1942-55. Recipient football scholarship Lawrence U., 1938-42. Mem. Wash. State Psychol. Assn., Am. Psychol. Assn., Western Psychol. Assn., Am. Group Psychotherapy Assn., Assn. Labor-Mgmt. Adminstrs. and Cons. Alcoholism, Mace, Sigma Xi, Beta Theta Pi. Home and Office: 22506 66th Ave West Mountlake Terrace WA 98043

HAMMER, LOUIS EUGENE, educator; b. Lusk, Wyo., Oct. 17, 1955; s. Malcolm I. and Viola L. (Payne) H.; B.A. in Math. and Stats., U. Wyo., 1978, M.S. in Stats., 1980. Head math. dept. Glendo (Wyo.) Pub. Sch., 1980-86; community edn. tchr. computer literacy. Vol. Emergency med. tech. Glendo Ambulance Service. Mem. Am. Statis. Assn., Nat. Council Tchrs. Math. Home: Box 913 Lusk WY 82225 Office: Glendo Pub Sch PO Box 68 Glendo WY 82213

HAMMER, RONALD PAGE, JR., neuroscientist, educator; b. Phila., Feb. 21, 1953; s. Ronald Page and Doris G. (Gold) H.; m. Sandra Ann Jacobson, Nov. 14, 1986. AB, U. Calif., Berkeley, 1974; PhD, U. Calif., Los Angeles, 1980. Staff fellow NIMH, Bethesda, Md., 1980-84; assoc. prof. U. Hawaii, Honolulu, 1984—. Contbr. articles to profl. jours. Recipient New Investigator award NIH, 1984. Mem. Soc. Neurosci., Am. Assn. Anatomists. (com. on nomenclature), Internat. Soc. Developmental Neurosci., NOW. Avocation: windsurfing. Office: Dept Anat Reprod Biol 1960 E West Rd Honolulu HI 96822

HAMMERBACK, JOHN CLARK, communications educator; b. San Francisco, Oct. 6, 1938; s. William Joseph and Susan (Ridzik) H.; m. Jean Melton, Aug. 29, 1965; children: Kristen, Karen. BA, San Francisco State Coll., 1962; MA, U. Okla., 1965; PhD, Ind. U., 1970. Teaching asst. dept. speech communication U. Okla., Norman, 1963-65, Ind. U., Bloomington, 1965-68; prof. speech communication Calif. State U., Hayward, 1968-71, 79—, chmn. dept. speech and drama, 1972-79, affirmative action liason officer, 1986—; lectr. U. N.Mex., Albuquerque, 1977, to local Rotary, Kiwanis and Lions clubs; speech writer for local polit. candidates, Fremont, Calif., 1978—. Author: A War of Words: Chicano Rhetoric of the 1960s and 1970s, 1985, In Search of Justice: Studies in Speech Communication in the Indiana Tradition, 1987; contbr. articles, papers, and book reviews to profl. publs. Faculty Research grantee Calif. State U., Hayward, 1975; Meritorious Service award, 1985. Mem. Western Speech Communication Assn. (2d v.p. 1979-80, chmn. legis. assembly 1980, 1st v.p. 1981-82, chief conv. planner 1982-83, pres. 1983-84, assoc. jour.editor 1979-81, 84—, disting. service award com. 1985, nominating com. 1984, chmn. membership com. 1980, mem. legis. assembly 1974-77), Rhetoric Soc., Speech Communication Assn. (nominating com. 1984, com. on coms. 1984), Calif. Speech Assn. (com. on intercultural communication 1976), Greater Kimber Area Homeowners' Assn. (v.p. 1984). Lodges: Rotary, Kiwanis, Lions, Speedies. Home: 203 Fisalia Ct Fremont CA 94539 Office: Calif State U Hayward CA 94539

HAMMERS, OLIVER BERTRAND, mechanical contracting company executive; b. St. Joseph, Mo., Nov. 23, 1924; s. Earl E. and Lola M. (Hetherington) H.; B.S. in Elec. Engring., U. Kans., 1950; m. Patricia Ruth Dillman, Nov. 27, 1954; children—Patrick James, David Earl. With Natkin & Co., 1950-84, v.p. spl. assignments, Omaha, 1966-68, exec. v.p., mgr. S. Central div., Dallas, 1968-80, res., chief exec. officer, Denver, 1980-84, chmn. bd., 1980-84, also pres.; dir. Natkin Service Co., Johansen Co., Colo. pres., chief exec. officer Natkin Group, Inc., 1984—; Colo. Nat. Bank S.W.; officer, dir. Charter Page, Inc. Served with AUS, 1942-46. Mem. Mech. Contractors Assn. (Man of Year award Tex. chpt. 1979), Denver C. of C. Clubs: Denver Athletic; Columbine Country. Office: Natkin Group Inc 2700 S Zuni St Englewood CO 80150

HAMMETT, BENJAMIN COWLES, psychologist; b. Los Angeles, Nov. 18, 1931; s. Buell Hammett and Harriet (Cowles) Graham; m. Ruth Finstrom, June 18, 1957; children: Susan, Sarah, Carol, John. BS, Stanford U., 1957; PhD, U. N.C., 1969. Lic. psychologist, Calif. Staff psychologist Children's Psychiat. Ctr., Butner, N.C., 1965-67; sr. psychologist VA Treatment Ctr. for Children, Richmond, Va., 1968-71; asst. prof. child psychiatry Va. Commonwealth U., Richmond, 1968-71; instr. psychology Western Grad. Sch. Psychology, 1980—; pvt. practice psychology Palo Alto, Calif., 1972—; affiliate staff mem. O'Connor Hosp., San Jose, Calif., 1980—; v.p. bd. dirs. Mental Research Inst., Palo Alto, 1982-83, pres. bd. dirs., 1983-85. Co-author chpts. to two books. Vol. Boy Scouts Am., 1952-54, Peninsula Conservation Ctr., Palo Alto, 1983—; treas. Cary Sch. PTA, Richmond, 1969-70. Named Eagle Scout, 1947; grantee NIMH, 1970. Mem. Am. Psychol. Assn., Am. Group Psychotherapy Assn., Internat. Transactional Analysis Assn., Biofeedback Soc. Am. (BCIA cert.), Biofeedback Soc. Calif., Calif. State Psychol. Assn. Republican. Unitarian. Club: El Tigre (Stanford) (sec. 1954). Avocations: videotaping, photography, computers, environ. geology. Home: 301 Lowell Ave Palo Alto CA 94301 Office: 555 Middlefield Rd Palo Alto CA 94301

HAMMING, RICHARD WESLEY, computer scientist; b. Chgo., Feb. 11, 1915; s. Richard J. and Mabel G. (Redfield) H.; m. Wanda Little, Sept. 5, 1942. B.S., U. Chgo., 1937; M.A., U. Nebr., 1939, Ph.D. in Math, 1942. With Manhattan Project, 1945-46; with Bell Telephone Labs., 1946-76; mem. faculty Naval Postgrad. Sch., Monterey, Calif., 1976—; adj. prof. computer sci. Naval Postgrad. Sch., 1976—. Author books, papers in field. Fellow IEEE (Piore award 1979, $10,000 Prize Medal named in his hon.); mem. Assn. Computing Machinery (Turing prize 1968), Nat. Acad. Engring., Am. Math. Assn., AAAS. Office: Naval Postgrad Sch Code 52 Hdqrs Monterey CA 93940

HAMMOND, DAVID GREENE, engineering company executive, consultant; b. Paterson, N.J., Sept. 8, 1913; s. Nelson Davis and Frances Edna (Greene) H.; m. Joan Constance Morse, Jan. 7, 1947; children—David, Peter, Victoria. B.S. in Civil Engring., Pa. State U., 1934; M. of Civil Engring., Cornell U., 1939; postgrad., Army-Navy Staff Coll., 1945, Army War Coll., 1957. Registered profl. engr., Md., Calif. Instr. civil engring. Pa. State U., University Park, 1934-37; commd. 2d lt. C.E. U.S. Army, 1937, advanced through grades to col., 1952, ret., 1964; dist. engr. Omaha Dist. C.E., 1957-60; chief installations Continental Army Command, Fortress Monroe, Va., 1963-64; asst. gen. mgr. ops. and engring. San Francisco Bay Area Rapid Transit Dist., 1964-73; v.p. Daniel, Mann, Johnson & Mendenhall (DMJM), Balt., 1973—, Los Angeles; chmn. U.S. Nat. Com. on Tunneling Tech. Contbr. articles to profl. jours. Recipient Award of Merit, San Francisco Bay Area Rapid Transit Dist.; named Man of Yr., Kiwanis Internat. and Am. Pub. Works Assn., 1969. Fellow ASCE (co-chmn. specialty conf. on risks and liability), Nat. Soc. Profl. Engrs., Soc. Am. Mil. Engrs.; mem. Am. Pub. Transit Assn. (elected Transit Hall of Fame 1986), Am. Pub. Works Assn., Nat. Acad. Engring. Republican. Clubs: Center (Balt.); The Moles, Athletic (Los Angeles). Avocations: swimming; reading. Home: 364 Noren St La Canada CA 91011 Office: DMJM 3250 Wilshire Blvd Los Angeles CA 90010

HAMMOND, JUDY MCLAIN, business services executive; b. Downey, Calif., June 24, 1956; d. Ernest Richard and Bernice Elaine (Thompson) McLain; m. Dennis Francis Hammond, Aug. 15, 1981. BS in Mgmt., Pepperdine U., 1982; MBA, U. So. Calif., 1986. Br. mgr. Kelly Services, Encino, Calif., 1978-83; mktg. mgr. Payco Am. Corp., Encino, 1981-83, GC Services Corp., Santa Ana, Calif., 1983-86; pres. Resource Mgmt. Services, Norwalk, Calif., 1986—; qualified mgr. Bur. Collection & Investigative Systems. Mem. adv. com. Cerritos Coll. Mem. Am. Soc. Tng. Devel., Women in Mgmt. Club: Toastmasters. Avocations: scuba diving, underwater photography, public speaking. Home: 11528 Leibacher Ave Norwalk CA 90650

HAMMOND, MARK STEVEN, health care executive; b. San Diego, Sept. 10, 1956; s. Clyde Newewll and Gloria Genevieve (McKinstry) H. A.A. in Bus. and Psychology, Mesa Coll., 1976; B.A. in Indsl. Psychology, San Diego State U., 1980; M. Bus. Mgmt., U. Redlands, 1984; lic. hosp. adminstr., Calif. Acctg., Delta Automotive, San Diego, 1976-78; service asst. dept. personnel Price Co., San Diego, 1978-80; adminstr. Longer Life Found. Ocean View Hosp., Encinitas, Calif., 1980-82; exec. v.p. Indsl. Med. Corp., Inc., San Diego, 1982-84; v.p. Mktg. Marine Med. Services San Diego, 1984-85; pres. Indsl. Plus Health Network, Carson, Calif., 1985—. Mem. Nat. Soc. Med. Mgmt. Cons., Am. Mgmt. Assn., Med. Group Mgmt. Assn., Emergency Medicine Mgmt. Assn. Republican. Methodist. Home: 2640 Angell Ave San Diego CA 92122

HAMMOND, PHILIP C., anthropology educator; b. Bklyn., May 5, 1924; s. Philip C. and Julia (Metz) H.; children: Asenath, Sharon, Kristian, Gregory. BA summa cum laude, Drew U., 1948, BD summa cum laude, 1951; MA, Yale U., 1953, PhD, 1957. Asst. prof. anthropology Lycoming Coll., Williamsport, Pa., 1957-60; asst. prof. religion Princeton (N.J.) Theol. Sem., 1960-66; assoc. prof. Brandeis U., West Newton, Mass., 1966-69; prof. U. Utah, Salt Lake City, 1969—; dir. expdns., Petra, Jordan, 1961, 62, 73—, Hebron, Jordan, 1963, 64, 67, Tell El-Shuqafiya, Egypt, 1977—. Author: A Study of Nabataean Ceramics, 1958, Archaeological Techniques, 1963, Petra, Excavations. . ., 1966, History of Nabataeans, 1975. Served to 1st lt. inf. U.S. Army, 1942-46, ETO. Decorated Bronze Star, Purple Heart. Mem. Am. Anthropol. Assn., Archaeol. Inst. Am., Assn. Internat. Egyptologues, Explorers Club. Democrat. Avocations: horses, martial arts, electronics. Office: U Utah Dept Anthropology Salt Lake City UT 84112

HAMMOND, ROBERT DEAN, accountant; b. Denver, Sept. 10, 1935; s. James Delbert and Erna (Fillenberg) H.; m. Margaret Murphy Gorrie; children—Lind Ruth Toldness, James Dean, Steven Leroy. CPA, Colo. Ptnr. Charles A. Taylor & Assocs. (merged into Clifton, Gunderson & Co.), Denver, 1971—, regional dir. ops., govt. services dir., 1981-84, dir fin. ops., 1987—. Pres. Northglenn Recreation Dist., 1970; sec.-treas. Adams County Polit. Action Com. Served as sgt. USAF, 1952-57. Named Boss of Yr., Northglenn Jaycees, 1978. Mem. Am. Inst. CPA's (council, chmn. state and local govt. acctg. com. 1985-87), Colo. Soc. CPA'.s (contining edn. award, pres.), Mcpl. Fin. Officers Assn., Adams County C. of C. (pres.). Republican. Club: Northglenn Rotary. Office: Clifton Gunderson & Co 10190 Bannock St Suite 140 Denver CO 80221

HAMMOND, RONALD ALBERT, artificial intelligence researcher; b. Belleville, Ill., Feb. 11, 1938; s. Albert A. and Herma V. (Dewoody) H.; m. Barbara Jane Dorward, June 14, 1959; children: Bruce R., Kathryn B., Margaret L., Matthew T. BSEE, Purdue U., 1959, MSEE, 1961. Engr. Boeing Airplane Co., Seattle, 1961-64, Boeing Aerospace, Seattle, 1965-69; engr. mgr. Boeing Co., Seattle, 1974-84; researcher Boeing Computer Services, Seattle, 1984—; engr. IBM Corp., Huntsville, Ala., 1964-65, Cornell Aero Lab., Buffalo, 1969-74. Contbr. articles to profl. jours. Chmn. bd. dirs. East Shore Unitarian Ch., Bellevue, Wash., 1983-84, trustee, 1981-83. Recipient Cert. Recognition NASA, 1984; named Instr. of Yr. Boeing Tng. Unit, 1980, Mgr. Yr. Boeing Adv. Tech. Div., 1985. Mem. IEEE, Am. Assn. Artificial Intelligence, Soc. Computer Simulation (chmn. NW region 1982-85), Sigma Xi, Eta Kappa Nu. Democrat. Avocations: photography, model railroading. Office: Boeing Computer Services PO Box 24346 Seattle WA 98124

HAMON, KENNETH L., accountant; b. Delta, Colo., Dec. 18, 1948; s. Kenneth and Dorothy J. (Davis) H.; m. Catherine L. Le Bar, Dec. 22, 1967; children—Morgan, Clark. A.S., Mesa Coll., Grand Junction, Colo., 1968; B.S.B.A., Denver U., 1971. C.P.A., Colo. Sr. acct. Price Waterhouse & Co., Denver, 1971-76; mgr. Dalby Wendland & Co., Grand Junction, 1976-79, prin., 1979-81, pres., 1981—. Bd. dirs. Indsl. Devel., Inc., Grand Junction, 1984—, Cen. Bank Grand Junction, 1987—; pres. Community Services, Inc., Grand Junction, 1980; bd. dirs. officer West Colo. Ctr. for Arts, 1984-85; bd. dirs., treas. Mesa County Econ. Devel. council, 1985—. Bus. scholar Mesa Coll., 1969; acctg. scholar Denver U., 1970. Mem. Am. Inst. C.P.A.s, Colo. Soc. C.P.A.s (pres. Western Colo. chpt. 1979-80, pres., trustee Ednl. Found. 1982—), Grand Junction C. of C. (bd. dirs., pres. 1985—). Republican. Congregationalist. Lodge: Rotary. Home: 667 Roundhill Dr Grand Junction CO 81506 Office: Dalby Wendland & Co PO Box 430 Grand Junction CO 81502

HAMPE, KEITH ROBERT, process equipment company executive; b. Dryden, Ont., Can., Sept. 10, 1941; came to U.S., 1960; s. Leo and Zoelle M. (Merrill) H.; m. Suzanne Runden, Dec. 3, 1960; children: Robert, Margret. B.S. in Chemistry, Ariz. State U., 1963. Engr. Motorola Co., Phoenix, 1961-64; engring. supr. Fairchild Camera Co., Mt. View, Calif., 1965-67; with Nat. Semicondr. Co., 1968-79; group dir. Nat. Semicondr. Co., Santa Clara, Calif., 1975-79; pres. Sertech Co., Salem, Mass., 1980, Temescal div. BOC Group, Inc., Berkeley, Calif., 1981—. Republican. Episcopalian. Office: 2850 7th St Berkeley CA 94710

HAMPLEMAN, RICHARD ALLEN, architect; b. Denver, Oct. 26, 1946; s. LeRoy Albert and Ethel Gertrude (Peyton) H.; m. Judith Kay Wolvington, Jan. 7, 1967 (div.); children: Jason Allen, Kim Elizabeth, Bria Lauren. BArch, U. Colo., 1971. Registered architect, Colo. Architect Haertling Architecture, Boulder, Colo., 1967-68, U. Colo., Boulder, 1968-69, URS Co., Denver, 1969-76, Hampleman Architects, Denver, 1976-86, Hampleman/Braun, Denver, 1986—; tchr. Career Edn., Colo., 1985-86. Prin. works include Fire Station, Denver, 1976 (design award 1976), Fire Hdqrs., Denver, 1976, Dixon Residence, Genesee, Colo., 1983, Hampleman Residence, Golden, Colo., 1984. Democrat. Lodge: Rotary (bd. dirs. 1979-86). Avocations: flyfishing, golf, cooking, backpacking, tennis. Home: 828 Cheyenne St Golden CO 80401 Office: Hampleman & Braun Assocs 25107 Genesee Trail Rd Golden CO 80401

HAMPTON, JAMES C., anatomist, educator, retired; b. Julietta, Idaho, Sept. 20, 1921; s. Joseph D. and Mary Ruth (Horn) H.; m. Erma Dean Law, Mar. 28, 1942; children: Susan Carol, Connie Lou, Joseph Douglas, Walter William. Student, San Francisco State Coll., 1947-49; BS, U. Idaho, 1951, MS in Zoology, 1952; PhD in Anatomy, U. Wash., 1957. Assoc. prof. anatomy and research assoc. prof. pathology, med. br. U. Tex., Galveston, 1961-62; mem. faculty coll. medicine Baylor U., Houston, 1959-61, assoc. prof. exptl. biology and anatomy, 1960-61; mem. faculty U Wash., Seattle, 1957-59, instr. anatomy, 1957-59; prof. anatomy, chmn. dept. Northwestern U., Evanston, Ill., 1962-69; mgr. cytology sect., dept. biology Battelle Meml. Inst., Pacific N.W. Lab., Richland, Wash., 1969-77; assoc. dean acad. programs Joint Ctr. Grad. Study, Richland, 1977-86. Served with USNR, 1942-45. Mem. AAAS, Am. Soc. Cell Biology, Am. Assn. Anatomists, Biophys. Soc., Electron Microscope Soc. Am., N.Y. Acad. Sci., Radiation Research Soc., Sigma Xi. Home: 649 Lynnwod Loop Richland WA 99352 Office: 100 Sprout Rd Richland WA 99352

HAMPTON, REX HERBERT, gold mining company executive; b. Chgo., Aug. 3, 1918; s. John William and Alice Grace (Melling) H.; m. Ruth Lorraine Gibbons, Sept. 30, 1940; children: Hope, Rex Herbert, Robin Virgil, Maryalice. B.S. in Forest Mgmt, Utah State U., 1942; M.A. in Internat. Affairs, George Washington U., 1963; student, U.S. Air Force War Coll., 1963. Real estate broker, Colo. Commd. 2d lt. U.S. Army, 1942, advanced through grades to brig. gen., 1968; ret. 1972; mgr. Bennett Shellenberger Realty, Colorado Springs, Colo., 1975-80; pres., chief exec. officer Golden Cycle Gold Corp., Colorado Springs, 1980—. Decorated D.S.M., Legion of Merit with cluster, Bronze Star, others. Mem. Nat. Realtors Assn., Ret. Officers Assn. (pres. chpt.), VFW, DAV. Republican. Mormon. Clubs: Peterson Field Officers, Eisenhower Golf; Plaza, Broadmoor Golf (Colo. Springs). Office: Golden Cycle Gold Corp 228 N Cascade St Colorado Springs CO 80903

HAMRDLA, GEORGE ROBERT, university administrator; b. Kansas City, Kans., Nov. 8, 1937; s. George Lawrence and Elizabeth Anne (Lundy) H. BS, Stanford U., 1960, MA, 1964. Dir. German br. Stanford U., Fed. Republic. Germany, 1964-66; asst. dir. overseas campuses Stanford (Calif.) U., 1966-70, asst. undergrad. dean, 1970-77, asst to pres. for trustees, 1977-81, asst. to pres., 1981—. Nat. ednl. advisor, Sigma Alpha Epsilon, Evanston, Ill., 1971-85, faculty mem. Leadership Sch., Evanston, Ill., 1970-85. Served to 1st lt. U.S. Army, 1962. Mem. Assn. Governing Bds. Colls. and Univs. Republican. Episcopalian. Avocations: travel, World War II, extensive teaching and lecturing on The German Dem. Republic. Office: Stanford U Office of Pres Bldg Ten Stanford CA 94305

HAMRICK, CLAUDE ARTHUR STUART, patent lawyer; b. Tampa, Fla., Sept. 11, 1939; s. Claude Stuart and Louise Magnolia (Brown) H.; m. Sandra Faye Whitehead, Dec. 24, 1959 (div. Apr. 1982); children: Debra Louise, David Stuart; m. Sandra Lee Lewandowski, Apr. 18, 1982. AA, U. Fla., 1961, BSEE, 1963; JD, George Washington U., 1967. Bar: Calif. 1970, U.S. Dist. Ct. (no. dist.) Calif. 1970, U.S. Ct. Appeals (9th cir.) 1970, U.S. Patent Office 1970, U.S. Ct. Appeals (D.C. cir.) 1975, U.S. Supreme Ct. 1976. Examiner U.S. Patent Office, Washington, 1963-64; patent agt. Gen. Motors Corp., Washington, 1965-67; patent lawyer Varian Assocs., Palo Alto, Calif., 1967-68; ptnr. Louhurst & Hamrick, Palo Alto, 1969-70, Schatzel & Hamrick, Santa Clara, Calif., 1971-78; sole practice patent law Santa Clara, 1979-81; ptnr. Hamrick, Hoffman, Guillot & Kazubowski, San Jose, Calif., 1982—; bd. dirs. Omni Signal Corp., Santa Cruz, Calif., SI Valley Metals, San Jose. Patentee automatic closure apparatus. Named Man of Yr., Sunnyvale Jaycees, 1971, Outstanding Pres., Sunnyvale Jaycees, 1973. Mem. ABA, Calif. State Bar, Santa Clara County Bar Assn. Clubs: Santa Clara County Barristers (San Jose)(pres. 1973). Lodge: Rotary (local pres. 1979, internat. exchange scholar 1973). Avocations: flying, softball, computer programming. Home: 1560 Silacci Dr Campbell CA 95008 Office: Hamrick Hoffman et al 777 N 1st St Suite 444 San Jose CA 95112

HAN, ITTAH, political economist, high technology and financial strategist; b. Java, Indonesia, Jan. 29, 1939; came to U.S., 1956, naturalized, 1972; s. Hongtjioe and Tsuiying (Chow) H. BS in Mech. Engring. and Elec. Engring., Walla Walla Coll., 1960; MA in Math., U. Calif., Berkeley, 1962; BA in French, U. Colo., 1965, MS in Elec. Engring., 1961; MSE in Computer Engring., U. Mich., 1970; MS in Computer Sci., U. Wis., 1971; MBA in Mgmt., U. Miami (Fla.), 1973; BA in Econs., U. Nev., 1977; MBA in Tax, Golden Gate U., 1979, MBA in Real Estate, 1979, MBA in Fin., 1980, MBA in Banking, 1980, MPA in Adminstrv. Orgn. and Mgmt., 1984. Cert. fin. planner. Salesman, Watkins Products, Walla Walla, Wash., 1956-60; instr. Sch. Engring. U. Colo., Denver, 1964-66; systems engr. IBM Corp., Oakland, Calif., 1967-69, Scidata Inc., Miami, Fla., 1971-72; chief of data processing Golden Gate Bridge, Hwy. and Transp. Dist., San Francisco, 1973-74; mgr. info. systems tech. and advanced systems devel. Summa Corp., Las Vegas, Nev., 1975-78; mgr. systems devel. Fred Harvey Inc., Brisbane, Calif., 1978-80; chmn. corp. systems steering com., mgr. systems planning Amfac Hotel & Resorts, Inc., 1978-80; tax strategy planner, innovative turnaround fin. strategy planner, chief exec. Ittahhan Corp., 1980—; exec. v.p. Developers Unltd. Group, Las Vegas, 1982-84; v.p. Fidelity Fin. Co., Las Vegas, 1984-85; exec. v.p. John H. Midby and Assocs., Las Vegas, 1982-84; sec., treas., dir. River Resorts Inc., Las Vegas, 1983-84; sec., treas. Goldriver Ltd., Las Vegas, 1983-84; pres. Weststar Gen. Ptnr. Co., 1984-85, Developers Group Service Co., 1984-86; chief exec. officer, pres. High Tech. Polit. Economy Turnaround Strategist, Inc., 1986—; chief exec. officer, pres. Innovative Artificial Intelligence Computer Engring., Inc., 1986—; pres. Orion Land Devel. Co., Las Vegas, 1987—; instr. U. Nev. Sch. Elec. Engring., Reno, 1981; systems designer, cons. in field. Mem. IEEE, Assn. Computing Machinery, Am. Assn. Artificial Intelligence, Am. Math. Assn., Inst. Cert. Fin. Planners, Am. Contract Bridge League. Republican. Home and Office: PO Box 27025 Garside Station Las Vegas NV 89126

HANAVAN, GWENDOLYN MAE, accountant; b. Washington, Jan. 21, 1943; d. Arthur N. and Esther J. (Spady) Shane; m. Louis Wayne Hanavan Jr., May 28, 1965; 1 dau., Lisa Dawn. B.S. magna cum laude in Bus. Adminstrn., U. No. Colo., 1978. C.P.A., Oreg. Mem. staff C.P.A. firms in Colo. and Oreg., 1978-80; ptnr. Erickson & Hanavan, C.P.A.s, Eugene, Oreg., 1981-86; pvt. practice acctg., Eugene, 1986—. Bd. dirs. Maude Kern's Art Ctr., v.p., 1981-82; treas. Lane County chpt. ARC, 1982-84; bd. dirs. Oreg. Repertory Theatre, 1983-84; bd. dirs. Western Rivers council Girl Scouts U.S.A., treas., 1983-86. Recipient Gold Key award Colo. Soc.

C.P.A.s, 1978. Mem. Oreg. Soc. C.P.A.'s, Am. Inst. C.P.A.'s, Profl. Women's Network of Oreg., AAUW. Office: 235 W 10th Eugene OR 97401

HANCE, ANTHONY JAMES, pharmacologist, educator; b. Bournemouth, Eng., Aug. 19, 1932; came to U.S., 1958; s. Walter Edwin and Jessie Irene (Finch) H.; m. Ruth Anne Martin, July 17, 1954; children—David, Peter, John. B.Sc., Birmingham U., 1953, Ph.D., 1956. Research fellow in electrophysiology Birmingham U., Eng., 1957-58; research pharmacologist UCLA, 1959-62; research assoc. pharmacology Stanford U., Palo Alto, Calif., 1962-65, asst. prof., 1965-68; assoc. prof. U. Calif., Davis, 1968—. Contbr. articles to profl. jours. Mem. AAAS, Am. Soc. for Pharmacology and Exptl. Therapeutics, Biomed. Engring. Soc., Assn. for Computing Machinery. Home: 1103 Radcliffe Dr Davis CA 95616 Office: U Calif Med Sch Dept Pharmacology Davis CA 95616

HANCHETT, WILLIAM A. BARTON, mechanical engineer, designer; b. San Francisco, June 11, 1928; s. William A. Barton Sr. and Tempest Caroline (Wilder) W.; m. Jane Elizabeth Connell, Apr. 6, 1948; children: William A. Barton III, Barbara Lee, Marc Connell. BSBA, SUNY, 1976; BSME, Cath. U. Am., 1980, MSME, 1981. Cert. sr. safety engr. Commd. 2d lt. U.S. Army, 1952, advanced through grades to col., 1971, retired, 1975; dir. Hanchett Engring., Springfield, Va., 1975-81, Ojai, Calif., 1981—; program dir. Advanced Tech., Camarillo, Calif., 1982—. Named hon. mayor Bretten-Badden, Fed. Republic of Germany, 1964-66. Mem. ASME, Soc. Am. Mil. Engrs. (bd. govs. 1986-88), Am. Soc. Safety Engrs., Systems Safety Soc., Am. Soc. Indsl. Security. Republican. Club: Mil. Officer (bd. govs.). Avocations: woodworking, inventions, remodeling houses, German shepard show dogs. Home: 2585 Valley Meadow Ct Oak View CA 93022 Office: Advanced Tech Inc 1000 Paseo Camarillo Suite 215 Camarillo CA 93010

HANCOCK, JOHN CHARLES, general contractor; b. Reno, Aug. 22, 1945; s. Melville Davis and Gretchen Louise (Mock) H.; m. Susan Beth Mahood, June 18, 1977; children: Chase, Evan. BSBA, U. Nev. Asst. planner City of Dallas, 1968-70; carpenter Hancock & Hancock, Reno, 1970-76, foreman, 1976-79, v.p., 1979-83, pres., 1984—. Avocations: tennis, snow skiing, photography, gardening. Office: Hancock & Hancock Inc 115 Linden St Reno NV 89502

HANCOCK, LONI, city mayor; b. N.Y.C., 1940; children: Leita, Mara. BA, Ithaca Coll.; MA, Wright Inst. Mem. Berkeley City Council, 1971-79, co-sponsor Fair Representation Ordinance, introduced affirmative action program, mem. subcom. for creation of Ohlone Park; mem. Berkeley's Waterfront Adv. Commn., 1984-86; mayor City of Berkeley, 1986—. Mem. Berkeley Parent Nursery Schs., 1964-68, Berkeley Citizens Action Com., 1975—; mem., past pres. New Dem. Forum, 1982—; mem. adv. bd. Working Assets, 1984—; bd. dirs., v.p. Berkeley Office of Econ. Opportunity, 1969-71, Local Gov. Commn., Literacy Vols. of Am., Youth Project; past regional dir. of ACTION; exec. dir. Shalan Found., San Francisco, 1981—; mem., cofounder LeConte Neighborhood Assn., 1969-71. Mem. Sierra Club, Nat. Women's Polit. Caucus. Office: Office of the Mayor Martin Luther King Jr Civic Ctr 2180 Milvia St Berkeley CA 94704

HANCOCK, N(EWELL) LES(LIE), accountant; b. Pitts., Apr. 13, 1943; s. Newell Francis and Mildred Helen (Bouveroux) H.; m. Margaret Ann Kendrick, Nov. 30, 1968; children: Michelle Lynn, Jennifer Ann, Marie Noelle. BSBA, U. Denver, 1966; postgrad., various schs., 1969—. CPA, Colo., Nev. Supr. Pannell, Kerr, Forster, Denver and Atlanta, 1969-78; mgr. Wolf & Co. of Colo., Inc., Denver, 1978-79, 83-84; supr. Kafoury, Armstrong & Co., Reno, 1979-82; mgr. Ashby, Armstrong & Co., Denver, 1984-87; pvt. practice acctg. Arvada, Colo. and Reno, 1982—. Served to 1st lt. U.S. Army, 1966-69. Mem. Am. Inst. CPA's, Colo. Soc. CPA's (mem. report rev. com. 1984—), Nev. Soc. CPA's (bd. dirs. Reno chpt. 1982-83, mem. auditing standards com. 1981-82, vice chmn. acctg. prins. com. 1981-83), Hospitality Accts. Assn. (sec. 1976-77). Republican. Baptist. Avocations: summer sports, restoring 1967 Mustang, collections. Office: PO Box 968 Arvada CO 80001-0968

HANCOCK, PETER ADRIAN, safety science educator, researcher, consultant; b. Berkley, Eng., Mar. 9, 1953; s. Ronald and Winifred Mary (Digby) H.; m. Frances A. Martinez, Oct. 1, 1979; children: Susan A., Gabriella M. BEd, Loughborough U., Leicestershire, Eng., 1976; MSc, Loughborough U., Leistershire, Eng., 1978; PhD, U. Ill., 1983. Asst. prof. dept safety sci. U. So. Calif., Los Angeles, 1983—, asst. prof. human factors dept., 1984—; cons. TRW, Pacific Bell. TPS scholar Loughborough U., 1977-78, U. Ill. scholar, 1982-83; Pacific Bell grantee, 1984-85, NASA, 1985-88. Mem. Psychonomic Soc., N.Y. Acad. Scis., Am. Soc. Safety Engrs., Am. Conf. Govt. Indsl. Hygienists. Avocations: soccer, rugby, skiing. Office: U So Calif Dept Safety Sci University Park Los Angeles CA 90089

HANCOCK, VERN G., architect, planner; b. Malad, Idaho, May 27, 1942; s. Carl Bennett and Ella (Bybee) H.; m. Elouise Randall, June 3, 1966; children: Jerry Vern, Chad Randall, Tera, Erin, Wendy. BS, Idaho State U., 1969. Registered architect, Idaho, Utah, Calif. Archtl. draftsman Utah State U., Logan, 1969-71; planner Ronald L. Molen, Salt Lake City, 1970-71; instr. in architecture Idaho State U., Pocatello, 1971-75; ptnr. The Architects Studio, Pocatello, 1975-78; pvt. practice architecture Pocatello, 1978—. Chmn. Community Devel. Commn., 1984—, Mayor's select com. on Handicap Accessibility, Pocatello, 1984; regional architect for no. Calif. Mormon Ch., 1986—; councilor in state presidency Mormon Ch., 1978-85, Bishop, 1986—. Served with USNR, 1966-68. Mem. AIA, Am. Planners Assn., Council Ednl. Facilities Planners. Home: 1127 Malibu Pocatello ID 83201 Office: 315 W Center Pocatello ID 83204

HAND, CADET HAMMOND, JR., marine biologist, educator; b. Patchogue, N.Y., Apr. 23, 1920; s. Cadet Hammond and Myra (Wells) H.; m. Winifred Werdelin, June 6, 1942; children—Cadet Hammond III, Gary Alan. B.S., U. Conn., 1946; M.A., U. Calif. at Berkeley, 1948, Ph.D., 1951. Instr. Mills Coll., 1948-50, asst. prof., 1950-51; research biologist Scripps Inst. Oceanography, 1951-53; mem. faculty U. Calif. at Berkeley, 1953—, prof. zoology, 1963-85, prof. emeritus, 1985—; dir. Bodega Marine Lab., 1961-85; Cons. NIH, 1964-66, NSF, 1964-69; mem. atomic safety and licensing bd. panel Nuclear Regulatory Commn., 1971—, adminstrv. judge atomic safety and licensing bd. panel, 1980—; NSF sr. postdoctoral fellow, 1959-60; Guggenheim fellow, 1967-68. Contbr. articles to profl. jours. Fellow Calif., Wash. acads. scis.; mem. No. Calif. Malacozool. Soc. (pres. 1963—), Soc. Systematic Zoology, Ecol. Soc. Am., Ray Soc. (Gt. Britain), Am. Soc. Zoologists (chmn. div. invertebrate zoology 1977-78), Soc. Limnology and Oceanography. Home: Star Rt Bogeda Bay CA 94923 Office: Bodega Marine Lab Bodega Bay CA 94923

HANDEL, WILLIAM KEATING, sales executive; b. N.Y.C., Mar. 23, 1935; s. Irving Nathaniel and Marguerite Mary (Keating) H.; m. Margaret Inez Sitton; children: William Keating II, David Roger. BA in Journalism, U. S.C., 1959, postgrad., 1959-60. With Packaging div. The Mead Corp., Atlanta, 1960-64, Ketchum, MacLeod & Grove, Pitts., 1964-67, Rexall Drug & Chem. Corp., Los Angeles, 1967-68; owner Creative Enterprises/Mktg. Communications, Los Angeles, 1968-71; creative dir., sales promotion mgr. Beneficial Standard Life Ins., Los Angeles, 1971-72; mgr. advt. and public relations ITT Gen. Controls, Glendale, Calif., 1972-80; mgr. corp. recruitment advt. Hughes Aircraft Co., Los Angeles, 1980-81; mgr. corp. communications Fairchild Camera and Instrument Corp., 1981-83; dist. mgr. Cahners Pub. Co., 1984—; pub. relations counsel Calif. Pvt. Edn. Schs., 1978—; chmn. exhibits Mini/Micro Computer Conf., 1977-78. Bd. dirs. West Valley Athletic League; dir. Los Angeles chpt. USMC Scholarship Found.; public relations cons. Ensenada, Mexico Tourist Commn., 1978; chmn., master of ceremonies U.S. Marine Corps Birthday Ball, Los Angeles, 1979-82. Served with USMC, 1950-53. Decorated Silver Star, Bronze Star, Purple Heart (4), Navy Commendation medal with combat V.; recipient Public Service award Los Angeles Heart Assn., 1971-73. Mem. Bus. and Profl. Advt. Assn. (cert. bus. communicator, past pres.), 1st Marine Div. Assn., Navy League (dir.), Sigma Chi (chpt. adv.). Republican. Roman Catholic. Clubs: Nueva España Boat, Baiamar Country, Ensenada Country, Ensenada Fish and Game (Baja, Mexico). Home: 4443 Ventura Canyon Ave Sherman Oaks CA 91403

HANDLER, HARRY, educational administrator. Suprt. Los Angeles Pub. Sch. System. Office: Office of Supt PO Box 3307 Terminal Annex Los Angeles CA 90051 *

HANDSCHUMACHER, ALBERT GUSTAVE, corporate executive; b. Phila., Oct. 20, 1918; s. Gustave H. and Emma (Streck) H.; m. Inger Stratton, Apr. 11, 1970; children by previous marriage: Albert, David W., Megan, Karin, Melissa. B.S., Drexel Inst. Tech., 1940; diploma, U. Pitts., 1941, Alexander Hamilton Inst., 1948. Prodn. mgr. Jr. Motors Corp., Phila., 1938-40; sales engr. Westinghouse Electric Co., Pitts., 1941; with Lear, Inc., Grand Rapids, Mich., 1945-57; beginning as sales mgr. central dist., successively asst. to pres., asst. gen. mgr., v.p. and gen. mgr., sr. v.p., dir. sales, pres., dir. Lear, Inc., 1959-62; v.p., gen. mgr. Rheem Mfg. Co., 1957-59; pres., dir. Lear Siegler, Inc., 1962-65; chmn. bd. Aeronca, Inc.; dir. First Exec. Corp., Lear Siegler, Inc., Exec. Life Ins. Co., Flight Dynamics Inc.; underwriting mem. Lloyd's of London; chmn. exec. com. First Fin. Group, Inc. Trustee Drexel U.; trustee City of Hope; nat. adv. chmn. Am. Heart Assn.; mem. bus. adv. council UCLA Internat. Student Center; trustee Nat. Asthma Assn. Served to maj. USAAF, 1942-45. Recipient 60th Anniversary Alumni award for outstanding achievements and services field of indsl. mgmt. Drexel U., 1951, Outstanding Alumni award, 1971; Man of Year award City of Hope, 1970; Man of Year award Nat. Asthma Assn., 1978. Mem. Am. Mgmt. Assn., ASHRE. Clubs: Jonathan, Calif. Yacht, Bel Air (Calif.) Country; Wings (N.Y.C.), Metropolitan (N.Y.C.); Confrerie de la Chaine des Rotisseurs, Beverly Hills; Le Mirador Country (Switzerland); Astro (Phila.). Home: 1100 Stone Canyon Rd Los Angeles CA 90077 Office: 844 Morago Dr Los Angeles CA 90049

HANDWERKER, WINSTON PENN, anthropologist; b. Memphis, Oct. 3, 1944; s. Winston P. and Joy (Skillman) H.; m. Leslie Zondervan-Droz; children: Merry Katherine, PennElys Ruth; m Sybil Ann Reed (div.); children: Mishael Penn, Liesl Ann Elizabeth. BA in Sociology, Willamette U., 1966; MA in Anthropology, U. Oreg., 1969, PhD in Anthropology, 1971. Instr. U. Oreg., Eugene, 1969; asst prof. Wash. State U., Pullman, 1971-72; asst. prof. Humboldt State U., Arcata, Calif., 1972-76, assoc. prof., 1976-81, prof., 1982—; cons., lectr. in field. Contbr. articles and revs. to profl. jours. Grantee Ford Found. 1968, NIMH, 1969, U. Oreg. Dept. Anthropology, 1970, Humboldt State U. Found., 1973, 76, 80-81, NSF, 1974, 85-86, NIH, 1977-79; fellow NIMH, 1969-70, Fulbright-Hayes, 1980; recipient Best in Show Photography award North Coast Women's Ctr., 1979. Fellow Am. Anthropol. Assn., Soc. Applied Anthropology, Human Biology Council, Current Anthropology (assoc.); mem. Am. Assn. Phys. Anthropology, Soc. Med. Anthropology, Council on Nutritional Anthropology, Council on Anthropology and Reproduction, Anthropol. Study Group on Agrarian Systems, Am. Ethnol. Soc., AAAS, Wash. Assn. Profl. Anthropologists. Office: Humboldt State U. Anthropology Arcata CA 95521

HANDY, ARTHUR ALVIN, JR., management consultant; b. Springfield, Mass., Jan. 8, 1926; s. Arthur Alvin and Lillian Jeanette (Rhoades) H.; B.S. in Bus. Adminstrn., Am. Internat. Coll., Springfield, 1949; m. Joan F. Reilly, Dec. 18, 1959; children—Arthur Alvin, III, Christopher J., Keith B., Leigh P. Underwriter, personnel asst. Springfield Fire & Marine Ins. Co., 1949-57; wage and salary adminstr. MITRE Corp., Bedford, Mass., 1957-62; mgr. compensation and personnel prgrams data processing div. Honeywell, Inc., Wellesley Hills, Mass., 1962-67; dir. compensation and benefits Kaiser Aluminum & Chem. Corp., Oakland, Calif., 1967-72; dir. orgn. planning, compensation and benefits, then dir. personnel Kaiser Industries Corp., Oakland, 1972-77; dir. personnel Kaiser Steel Corp., Oakland, 1977-79; pres. Handy & Wajda Cons. Group, Inc., Oakland, 1979-81; mng. prin. A.S. Hansen, Inc., 1981—; cons., seminar leader in field, 1957—. Served with USAAF, 1943-45. Life mem. Am. Compensation Assn. (chmn. bd. 1979—); mem. Am. Soc. Personnel Adminstrn., Calif. Compensation Assn., No. Calif. Indsl. Relations Soc., Calif. Inst. Tech. Mgmt. Compensation Group. Republican. Home: 9415 Alcosta Blvd San Ramon CA 94583 Office: 900 Larkspur Landing Circle Larkspur CA 94939

HANEY, WILLIAM SAMUEL, JR., aerospace executive; b. Vanceburg, Ky., June 28, 1934; s. William Samuel and Mary Louise (Moore) H.; m. Sandra Capone, Aug. 14, 1954; 1child: William Charles. BSE, U. Md., 1957. Dir. advanced strategic systems McDonnell Douglas Astronautics Co., Huntington Beach, Calif., 1957—. Fellow AIAA (assoc.); mem. Am. Radio Relay League, Tau Beta Pi. Republican. Avocations: amateur astronomy, amateur radio. Office: McDonnell Douglas Astronautics Co 5301 Bolsa Ave Huntington Beach CA 92647

HANF, JAMES ALPHONSO, poet, government official; b. Chehalis, Wash., Feb. 3, 1923; s. William G. and Willa DeForest (Davis) H.; grad. Centralia Jr. Coll., 1943, DLitt (hon.) World U. Ariz.; m. Ruth G. Eyler, Aug. 16, 1947; children—Maureen Ruth. Naval architect technician P.F. Spaulding, naval architects, Seattle, 1955-56, Puget Sound Bridge & Dredge Co. (Wash.), 1953-55, Puget Sound Naval Shipyard, 1951-53, 56—; cons. Anderson & Assocs., ship bldg.; cons. The Research Bd. Advs., Am. Biographical Inst., Inc.; guest lectr. on poetry and geneal. research methods to various lit. socs., 1969—; contbr. hundreds of poems to lit. jours., anthologies and popular mags.; poetry editor Coffee Break, 1977-82. Recipient Poet Laureate award, 1978, Poet Laureate Wash. State award Internat. Poetry Soc. India and World, 1981, grand prize World Poetry Soc. Conv., 1985, 86, Golden Poet award World of Poetry in Calif., 1985, 86, numerous other awards. Judge poetry contest, Australia and India, 1985. Mem Internat. Poetry Soc., World Poetry Soc., Kitsap County Writers Club (pres. 1977-78), Internat. Fedn. Tech. Engrs., Nat. Hist. Locomotive Soc., Kitsap County Hist. Soc., Puget Sound Geneal. Soc., Western World Haiku Soc., Olympic Geneal. Soc. (pres. 1974-75), N.Y. Poetry Forum, World Poets Resource Center, Literarische Union, Internat. Platform Assn., Calif. Fedn. Chaparral Poets, Internat. Biog. Assn., Am. Biog. Inst. Baptist. Home: PO Box 374 Bremerton WA 98310

HANGE, DONALD WAYNE, JR., architect; b. Elyria, Ohio, Aug. 4, 1959; s. Donald Wayne Sr. and Glendora Marie (Clouser) H. BS in Architecture, Ohio State U., 1981. Registered profl. architect, Ariz., Minn., Calif. With records project Ohio Hist. Soc., Columbus, 1980; project coordinator P.A. Burns, Architect, Columbus, 1981; archtl. draftsman William W. Gilfillen, Architect, Columbus, 1981-82; project mgr., project architect D.T. Whitneybell, Architect, Phoenix, 1982-86; prin. New Metropolis Architects (formerly D.W. Hange, AIA), Phoenix, 1986—. Prin. works include Ariz. Recreation Ctr. for Handicapped, 1985. Recipient Robert Merle Maffit award in Architecture Ohio State U., Columbus, 1981. Mem. AIA, Nat. Trust for Hist. Preservation (contbg.), Constrn. Specification Inst. (profl. mem.). Democrat. Mem. Ch. Disciples of Christ. Avocations: hiking, traveling, fgn. langs, art, architecture. Home and Office: 5309 W Almeria Rd Phoenix AZ 85035

HANIFEN, RICHARD CHARLES, bishop; b. Denver, June 15, 1931; s. Edward Anselm and Dorothy Elizabeth (Ranous) H. B.S., Regis Coll., 1953; S.T.B., Cath. U., 1959, M.A., 1966; J.C.L., Pontifical Lateran U., Italy, 1968. Ordained priest Roman Catholic Ch., 1959; asst. pastor Cathedral Parish, Denver, 1959-66; sec. to archbishop Archdiocese Denver, 1968-69, chancellor, 1969-76; aux. bishop of Denver, 1974-83; 1st bishop of Colorado Springs, Colo., 1984—. Office: 29 W Kiowa St Colorado Springs CO 80903

HANKE, DIETMAR HELGE, marketing professional; b. Los Angeles, Feb. 13, 1958; s. Julius Anton and Ingeborg (Novosad) Charlotte; m. Karen Roney, Aug. 11, 1985. BS in Physics, U. So. Calif., 1981; student in Mktg. and Internat. Bus., Loyola Marymount U., 1987. Sr. mgr. King's Restaurants, Los Angeles, 1979-81; instrumentation engr. Filtroc Corp., Los Angeles, 1982; optical engr. Hughes Aircraft Co., El Segundo, 1982-86; mktg. mgr. Pilkington Electro Optics Inc., Costa Mesa, Calif., 1986—. Republican. Home: 23192 Abeto Mission Viejo CA 92691 Office: Pilkington Electro Optics Inc 1239 Victoria St Costa Mesa CA 92627

HANKINS, HESTERLY G., III, computer systems analyst; b. Sallisaw, Okla., Sept. 5, 1950; s. Hesterly G. and Ruth Faye (Jackson) H. BA in Sociology, U. Calif., Santa Barbara, 1972; MBA in Info. Systems, UCLA, 1974; postgrad., Golden Gate U., 1985-86. Cert. community coll. tchr., Calif. Applications programmer Xerox Corp., Marina Del Rey, Calif., 1979-80; computer programmer Naval Ship Weapon Systems Engring. Sta. of Port Hueneme, Oxnard, Calif., 1980-84; spl. asst. to chief exec. officer Naval Air Sta. of Moffett Field, Mountain View, Calif., 1984-85; computer analyst Pacific Missile Test Ctr., Oxnard, 1985—; instr. bus. West Coast U., Camarillo, Calif., 1987—, De Anza Coll., Sunnyvale, Calif., 1985; lectr. bus. Golden Gate U., Los Altos, Calif., 1984; instr. computer sci. Chapman Coll., Sunnyvale, 1984, Ventura (Calif.) Coll., 1983-84; cons. City of Los Angeles Police Dept., Allison Mortgage Trust Investment Co.; minority small bus. assn. cons. UCLA. Author: Campus Computer, 1983. Mem. St. Paul United Meth. Ch., Oxnard, Calif., 1986-87. Named one of Outstanding Young Men in Am. U.S. Jaycees, 1980. Mem. Nat. Assn. Accts., Calif. Assn. Accts. (sec. 1980), Intergovtl. Council on Tech. Info. Processing, Assn. Computing Machinery, Alpha Kappa Psi (sec. 1972-73). Office: Camarillo Airport Bldg 248 Camarillo CA 93010

HANKS, EUGENE RALPH, land developer, retired naval officer; b. Corning, Calif., Dec. 11, 1918; s. Eugene and Lorena B. Hanks; m. Frances Elliot Herrick, Mar. 4, 1945; children: Herrick, Russell, Stephen, Nina. Student, Calif. Poly. Coll., 1939-41, U. So. Calif., 1949-50, Am. U., 1958-59; grad., Command and Staff Coll., Norfolk, Va., 1960. Served as enlisted man USN, 1941-42, commd. ensign, 1942, advanced through grades to capt., 1963; carrier fighter pilot, test pilot Naval Air Test Ctr., 1946-48; mem. Navy Flight Exhbn. Team Blue Angels, 1950; comdg. officer fighter squadrons, San Diego, 1957-58; ops. officer U.S.S. Constellation, 1961-62; dir. ops. Naval Missile Ctr., 1963-66; test dir. Joint Task Force Two, Albuquerque, 1966-69; ret. Joint Task Force Two, 1969; owner, developer Christmas Tree Canyon, Cebolla Springs and Mountain River subdivs., Mora, N.Mex., 1969—. Decorated Legion of Merit, Navy Cross, D.F.C. with star (2), Air medal (7). Mem. Ret. Officers Assn., Am. Fighter Aces Assn., Combat Pilots Assn., Assn. Naval Aviation, Am. Forestry Assn., Nat. Rifle Assn. Democrat. Home and Office: Christmas Tree Canyon Box 239 Mora NM 87732

HANKS, JOHN WARREN, social work educator; b. Stratton, Nebr., Mar. 14, 1918; s. John Earl and Ocie Nell (Evans) H.; m. Marion Greene Chapman, July 30, 1944; children: John Earl, Gardner Coe. BA, Antioch Coll., 1941; AM, U. Chgo., 1947; PhD, Mich. State U., 1965. Exec. dir. Family Service Agy., Jackson, Mich., 1949-54; psychiat. social worker Mich. State U., East Lansing, 1954-67; prof., dir. social work program U. Wyo., Laramie, 1967-76, prof. social work, 1976-81. Editor: Toward Human Dignity, Social Workers in Politics, 1982. Dir. Sr. Lyceum, Laramie, 1986; founder Wyo. Human Resources Conf., 1970, first pres.; active ACLU (Laramie chpt.), 1942—; active Nuclear Freeze Campaign; coordinator U.S./USSR Bridges for Peace, 1986. Recipient Cert. Appreciation U.S. Dept. Transp., 1985, Outstanding Community Vol. award Daily Boomerang/Lions Club, 1986. Mem. Wyo. Chpt. Nat. Social Workers Assn. (pres. 1970-71), Gov.'s Conf. Aging (Cert. Appreciation 1983), Council on Social Work Edn. (chmn. accreditation teams 1975-81, cons. 1979-82, nat. bd. dirs. 1976-80), Am. Assn. Retired Persons (chpt. pres. 1985, state legis. rep 1981-84), U of Wyo. Retirees Orgn. (founder, officer 1981—), Nat. Retired Tchr.'s Assn. (chpt. pres. 1987). Democrat. Avocations: photography, writing. Home: 1007 Sheridan St Laramie WY 82070

HANKS, LARRY BERKLEY, life insurance company executive; b. Idaho Falls, Idaho, Sept. 25, 1940; s. Victor Franklin and Marjorie (Burke) H.; A.B., Brigham Young U., 1964; M.Fin. Sci., Am. Coll., 1982; C.L.U.; chartered fin. cons.; m. Georgia Lee Gammett, Dec. 29, 1965; children—Tiffany, Berkley, Colli, Andrea, Rachel, Jared, Cyrus. Owner, mgr. Larry B. Hanks, C.L.U., ins. and employee benefits, Salt Lake City, 1969—; pres. Am. Pension Adminstrs. Inc., Salt Lake City 1978—, Integrated Fin. Designs, Inc., 1982—; gen. agt. Mass. Mut. Life Ins. Co., Salt Lake City, 1980—; instr. C.L.U. classes Am. Coll., Bryn Mawr, Pa., 1975—. Served with C.E., U.S. Army, 1968-69. Mem. Am. Soc. C.L.U. (dir. Magic Valley chpt.), Nat. Assn. Life Underwriters, Am. Soc. Pension Actuaries, N.E. Idaho Assn. Life Underwriters (dir., officer), Million Dollar Roundtable, Estate Planning Council Boise, Gen. Agts. and Mgrs. Assn. Republican. Mormon. Home: 7628 Riverwood Dr Sandy UT 84092 Office: 5 Triad Ctr Suite 550 Salt Lake City UT 84180

HANLIN, RUSSELL L., citrus products company executive; b. Sioux Falls, S.D., 1932; married. Student, U. Wash., Los Angeles City Coll. With Sunkist Growers, Inc., Van Nuys, Calif., 1951—, advt. mgr., 1964-72, v.p. mfg., mkt. research and devel., products group, 1972-78, pres., 1978—, now also chief exec. and chief operating officer, also dir. Served with U.S. Army, 1953-55. Office: Sunkist Growers Inc PO Box 7888 Van Nuys CA 91409 *

HANLON, CHARLES JOSEPH, former state senator; b. Pa., Sept. 15, 1918; s. Charles Hugh and Anna (Darby) H.; student public schs., Greensburg, Pa.; m. Neila Margaret Gaines, Mar. 11, 1943; children—Kathy, Jeffrey. With rock, sand and gravel industry, 1946-58; rancher, Cornelius, Oreg., 1958—; mem. Oreg. Senate, 1975-86. Served with Aviation Engrs., AUS, 1941-46; PTO. Democrat. Polit. writer for state newspapers.

HANNA, BOYD EVERETT, artist, engraver; b. Irwin, Pa., Jan. 15, 1907; s. Roscoe Elton and Grace Belle (Boyd) H.; m. Hazel Mae Bauman, Mar. 20, 1930; children—Sylvia Parr, Philip, Kristina Clark. Student, U. Pitts., 1925-28, Carnegie-Mellon U., 1928-30. Graphic artist Pullman, Inc., Pitts., 1950-70; architect City of Pitts. Water Plant, 1960-65; dir. Hanna Studios, Tucson, 1971—; one man shows: Print Club of Albany, 1975, Murphy Gallery, Tucson, 1975; group shows: Color Print U.S.A., 1972. Audubon Artists, 1974, Arena 76 Art Open, Print Club of Albany, 1972-82, Sander Gallery, Chgo., 1982, Soc. Illustrators, 1985, Salmagundi Club, 1985; works represented in permanent collections: Met. Mus. N.Y., Library of Congress Pennell Collection, Carnegie Inst., Pitts., N.Y. Pub. Library, Boston Pub. Library, Life Mag., Readers Digest, Print Club of Albany, Hunt Inst., Pitts. Illustrator: Longfellow's Poems, 1943-44; Leaves of Grass, Story of Nativity, Compleat Angler, Dreamthorp, 1947-58; Bell Telephone Almanac, 1948; Wild and Wily, 1980. Home: 1475 S Jones St Apt G-16 Tucson AZ 85713

HANNA, JOHN ROBERT, attorney; b. San Diego, May 17, 1951; s. Wallace John and Gloria L. (Schotz) H.; m. Jan E. Kitchen, June 16, 1984. BA, Calif. State U., Fullerton, 1974; JD, Loyola U., Los Angeles, 1979. Bar: Calif. 1980. Congl. aide Rep. Jerry Patterson, Santa Ana, Calif., 1976-80; pub. info. officer Ho. of Reps., Washington, 1979-80; ptnr. Horton, Barbaro & Reilly, Santa Ana, 1980—. V.p. St. Joseph Ballet Co., Santa Ana, 1984—; pres. Dem. Assocs., Orange County, 1985; mem. Calif. Dem. Cen. Com., 1975—; mem. Orange County Dem. Cen. Com., 1976—, chmn. 1986—. Mem. ABA, Calif. State Bar Assn., Orange County Bar Assn. Roman Catholic. Avocations: basketball, skiing. Office: Horton Barbaro & Reilly 200 N Main 2d Floor Santa Ana CA 92701

HANNA, KEITH LAWRENCE, photographer; b. Washington, Oct. 19, 1942; s. Keith Lazell and Virginia Victoria (Poston) H.; m. Peggy Lynn Welling, Sept. 25, 1983; 1 child, Brandon Keith. B.S. in Biology and Chemistry, Lynchburg Coll., 1965, postgrad., 1965-66; M.S. in Biochemistry and Nutrition, Va. Poly. Inst. and State U., 1968; postgrad. in physiology Vanderbilt U., 1971; M in Photography, Profl. Photographers Am., 1986. Chemist Nat. Bur. Standards, Washington, summers 1964-66; research biochemist Sch. Medicine, Vanderbilt U., 1969-71; food technologist Pet Food div. Star-Kist Foods, Inc., 1971-76; prin. Larry Hanna Photography, Las Vegas, Nev., 1976—. Mem. Profl. Photographers Am. (cert. profl. photographer, master of photography degree 1986, qualified for comml. studio, Craftsman Photographer award 1983), Profl. Photographers Nev. (Photographer of Yr. award 1981, 83, 84, pres. 1980, 83—, chmn. bd. dirs.). Episcopalian. Home: 4305 Jodi Ave Las Vegas NV 89120 Office: Larry Hanna Photography 3347 S Highland Suite 303 304 Las Vegas NV 89109

HANNA, ROBERT CECIL, lawyer, construction company executive; b. Albuquerque, July 28, 1937; s. Samuel Gray and Orvetta (Cecil) H.; B.A., U. N.Mex., 1959, J.D., 1962. Admitted to N.Mex. bar, 1962; practiced in Albuquerque, 1962-70, 72—; organizer, dep. dir. Micronesian Legal Services Corp., Trust Ter. Pacific Islands, 1970-71; practiced in Hilo; Hawaii, 1974; partner Cotter, Atkinson, Kelsey & Hanna, Ortega, Snead, Dixon & Hanna, Albuquerque, 1975-77; owner, pres., prin. Robert C. Hanna & Assocs., Albuquerque, 1978-80; pres. Sedco Internat. USA, Inc., Albuquerque, 1977-79, Suncastle Builders, Inc., Albuquerque, 1978—; pres. Am. Legal Consortium, 1984—; N.Mex. Real Estate Consortium Ltd., 1986—; mem. Bd. Bar Commrs., Trust Ter. Pacific Islands, 1971-72. Recipient award Rocky Mountain Mineral Law Found., 1962; Public Service award Micronesian Legal Services Corp. Bd. Dirs., 1972. Mem. Hawaii Bar Assn., N.Mex. Bar Assn., Albuquerque Bar Assn. Home: 310 Rio Grande Blvd SW Albuquerque NM 87104 Office: Am Legal Consortium 1840 Lomas Blvd NE Albuquerque NM 87106 also: 150 Lahainaluna Rd Lahaina Maui HI 96761

HANNA, STANLEY SWEET, physicist, educator; b. Sagaing, Burma, May 17, 1920; s. Alexander Carson and Hazel (Ames) H.; m. Jane Reeves Martin, Dec. 27, 1942; children: David Stanley, Peter Alexander, Susan Lee. A.B., Denison U., 1941, D.Sc., 1970; Ph.D., Johns Hopkins U., 1947. Mem. faculty Johns Hopkins U., 1943-55, asst. prof. physics, 1948-55; asso. physicist Argonne Nat. Lab., 1955-60, sr. physicist, 1960-63, cons., 1963-68; prof. physics Stanford U., 1963—; cons. Los Alamos Sci. Lab., 1967-74. Chmn. nuclear physics panel, com. on physics Nat. Acad. Scis., 1964-65. Served with AUS, 1945-46. Guggenheim fellow, 1958-59; Humboldt awardee, 1977; fellow Inst. for Advanced Study, Ind. U., 1983. Fellow Am. Phys. Soc. (organizing com. nuclear physics div. 1966-67, exec. com. 1967-68, 75-82, vice chmn. 1975-76, chmn. 1976-77, nuclear physics councillor 1978-82, publ. com. 1980-83, chmn. com. 1981-83, mem. exec. com. 1979-82); mem. Phi Beta Kappa, Sigma Xi, Omicron Delta Kappa. Spl. research on nuclear structure, giant resonances, polarizations of nuclear radiations, positron polarization, lifetimes of nuclear states, resonance absorption, analogue states, electron scattering, nuclear moments, intermediate energy physics, weak and hyperfine interactions, Mössbauer effect. Home: 784 Mayfield Ave Stanford CA 94305

HANNA, TERRENCE LEE, advertising executive; b. Ogden, Utah, Oct. 14, 1947; s. Robert William and Wanna Mae (Moore) H.; m. Barbara Noyes, Sept. 10, 1970 (div. Sept. 1978); 1 child, Linda Mae; m. Sally Ann Fordham, June 14, 1980. AS, Coll. Eastern Utah, 1972; BS, U. Utah, 1984. Mgr. Sta. KDBM FM, Dillon, Mont., 1973-74; announcer Sta. KYSS AM-FM, Missoula, Mont., 1974-75; news dir. Sta. KWOR AM, Worland, Wyo., 1975-77, Sta. KOWB AM, Laramie, Wyo., 1978; mgr. Taco Time, Missoula, 1977-78; news dir. Sta. KVOC AM, Casper, Wyo., 1978-79; freight rate asst. Hill AFB, Utah, 1980—; pres. Tamarack Advt., North Salt Lake, Utah, 1983—. Mormon. Avocations: camping, fishing, photography, computers, stamps. Office: Tamarack Advt PO Box 444 North Salt Lake UT 84054

HANNAN, CECIL JAMES, school system administrator; b. Sydney, Mont., Oct. 3, 1925; s. Cecil George and Isabelle Mary (Finch) H.; m. Molly M. Roberts, Dec. 16, 1974; children: Matthew G., Kelley J., Marguerite M. BA, Western Wash. State U., 1947, MS, 1948; DEd, Wash. State U., 1961. Exec. sec. Wash. State Edn. Assn., Seattle, 1959-67; assoc. exec. sec. NEA, Washington, 1967-71; pres. NTL Learning Resources Co., Washington, 1971-75; exec. sec. Colo. Edn. Assn., Denver, 1975-77; vice chancellor San Diego Community Coll. Dist., 1977-85; chmn., chief exec. officer Edn. Systems Tech. Co., San Diego, 1985—; pres. Tchrs. Services Corp., Washington, 1968-71. Author: Teach Spelling By All Means, 1952, Merit Pay for Teachers, 1953, Cross Value Dialog, 1963, Twenty Exercises for Classroom, 1966. Chmn. Educators Humphrey for Pres., Washington 1964, Educators Jackson for Pres., Washington, 1968. Served to lt. USAF, 1943-46. Recipient Disting. Service award Wash. State Legis., 1967. Mem. NEA (exec. com. 1964-68, bd. dirs. 1960-64), Nat. Tng. Labs. (exec. com. 1964-72), Fla. Edn. Assn. (life), Mass. Tchrs. Assn. (life), Nat. Congress PTA (life). Democrat. Methodist. Home: 2433 7th St Olivenhain CA 92024 Office: Edn Systems Tech Corp 5230 Carroll Canyon Rd San Diego CA 92121

HANNI, GERALDINE MARIE, therapist; b. Salt Lake City, Nov. 14, 1930; d. John Henry and Theresa Justine (Keirce) Gold; m. Kenneth J. Hanni, Mar. 14, 1951; children: Debra, Valerie, Kathleen, Cynthia, Kristine. BS, U. Utah, 1951, MSW, 1983. Lic. clin. social worker. Tchr. Hillside Jr. High Sch., Salt Lake City, 1970-73; intern Davis County Schs., Farmington, Utah, 1981-82, Westside Mental Health, Salt Lake City, 1982-83; group leader LDS Social Services, Salt Lake City, 1985; therapist ISAT, Salt Lake City, 1983—, clin. dir., 1987—; clin. instr. U. Utah, Salt Lake City, 1986—; mem. bd. Salt Lake County Sexual Abuse Task Force, Salt Lake City; cons. LDS Social Services, Salt Lake City, 1984-86. Sect. dir. Mortar Bd. Honor Soc., western U.S., 1970; pres. Highland High PTA, Salt Lake City, 1980; chairperson Highland High Community Sch. Orgn., Salt Lake City, 1981. Mem. Nat. Assn. Social Workers (Utah chpt.). Democrat. Mormon.

HANNON, WILLARD JAMES, seismologist; b. Jacksonville, Ill., July 9, 1938; s. Willard James and Virginia Josephine (Seifert) H.; m. Mary Ann Freihaut, Aug. 20, 1960; children: Patricia Gerad, Kathleen Ann, Michael John. BS in Geophys. Engring., St. Louis U., 1959, PhD in Geophysics, 1964. Instr. St. Louis (Mo.) U., 1961-64; post-doctoral fellow Calif. Inst. Tech., Pasadena, 1964-65; asst. prof. Wash. U., St. Louis, Mo., 1965-69; physicist, group leader, program mgr. Lawrence Livermore (Calif.) Nat. Lab., 1969—; mem. seismic rev. panel, U.S. Gov't., Washington, 1984—, tech. advisor test ban negotiations, 1980. Mem. Growth Rate Rev. Com., Livermore, 1986. Mem. Am. Geophys. Union, Seismol. Soc. Am., Soc. Exploration Geophysicists, Sigma Xi. Roman Catholic. Avocations: jogging, hiking. Home: 309 Pearl Dr Livermore CA 94550 Office: Lawrence Livermore Nat Lab PO Box 808-L205 Livermore CA 94550

HANOVER, PAUL NORDEN, speaker; b. Hartford, Conn., Sept. 13, 1927; s. Adrian Norden and Ruth (Seide) H.; m. Margaret Manning, Sept. 11, 1954; children: Nancy Gay, Diane Ruth. BEE, Rensselaer Poly. Inst., 1952. Missile engr. Douglas Aircraft Co., Santa Monica, Calif., 1952-54; project engr. Hughes Aircraft Co., Culver City, Calif., 1954-64; sr. project engr. Hughes Aircraft Co., Tucson, 1964-85; profl. speaker Space Programs Am., Tucson, 1985—. Co-author: Star Spangled Speakers, 1982. Fund raiser Jr. Achievement, Tucson, 1985; mem. Tucson Conv. Bur., 1985—; campaign dir. United Way, Tucson, 1981. Served with USN, 1946-48. Fellow AIAA (assoc., dep. dir. 1983-85, Disting. Lectr., 1985-86, recipient Space Plaque, 1984); mem. IEEE (sr., S.W. area chmn. 1973-75), Nat. Speakers Assn. (profl.), Hughes Mgmt. Club (pres. 1982-83), Nat. Space Inst., 1-5 Soc. Mem. Christian Sci. Ch. Lodge: Masons. Avocations: boating, hiking. Home and Office: 3551 Winslow Dr Tucson AZ 85715

HANOWELL, ERNEST GODDIN, physician; b. Newport News, Va., Jan. 31, 1920; a. George Frederick and Ruby Augustine (Goddin) H.; m. Para Jean Hall, June 10, 1945; children: Ernest D., Daborah J. Hanowell Orick, Leland H., Dee P. Hanowell Martinmaas, Robert G. Diplomate Am. Bd. Internal Medicine. Intern USPHS Hosp., Norfolk, Va., 1948-49; resident in internal medicine USPHS Hosp., Seattle, 1952-55; chief medicine USPHS Hosp., Ft. Worth, 1955-57; dept. chief medicine USPHS Hosp., Boston, 1957-59; chief medicine USPHS Hosp., Memphis, 1964-65, Monterey County Gen. Hosp., 1969-70; mem. IM and Cardiology staff Kaiser Permanente Med. Group, Sacramento, 1971—; clin. asst. Tufts Med. Sch., 1960-61; cons. chest disease Phila. Gen. Hosp., 1960-61; asst. prof. U. Md. Med. Sch., 1961-64; instr. U. Tenn. Med. Sch., 1964-65; asst. clin. prof. Sch. Medicine, U. Calif., Davis, 1973-81; mem. attending staff Cardiac Clinic Stanford U. Med. Sch. 1967-69. Mem. sch. bd. Salinas, Calif., 1968-69; bd. dirs. Am. Heart Assn., Tb and Health Assn. Served with AUS, 1943-46. Fellow ACP, Am. Coll. Chest Diseases; mem. AWA, Crocker Art Mus. Assn., Phi Chi. Clubs: Commonwealth (San Francisco), Comstock (Sacramento). Home: 1158 Racquet Club Dr Auburn CA 95603 Office: Kaiser Permanente Found Hosp 2025 Morse Ave Sacramento CA 95825 Office: Kaiser Permanente Roseville Clinic Riverside Dr Roseville CA 95678

HANSBURY, ELIZABETH, chemist, technical writer; b. Las Vegas, N.Mex., Mar. 15, 1925; d. Arthur Henry and Dorothy (Wayland) H. Student, Colo. Women's Coll., 1943-44; BA, U. Colo., 1947; MA, N.Mex. Highlands U., 1950. Assoc. prof. chemistry Moravian Coll. Women, Bethlehem, Pa., 1951-53; research asst. biochemistry Lovelace Found. Med. Edn. and Research, Albuquerque, 1953-56; technician, research asst., staff mem. Los Alamos (N.Mex.) Nat. Lab., 1956-70, staff mem., 1980—; research assoc. biochemistry dept. U. N.Mex., 1971-80. Contbr. articles to profl. jours., chpt. to book. Mem. Am. Chem. Soc., AAAS, Women's Atomic Bowling Assn. Democrat. Presbyterian. Avocations: bowling, tennis, gardening, travel, photography, hiking. Home: 16 San Juan Los Alamos NM 87544 Office: Los Alamos Nat Lab PO Box 1663 Mail Stop E501 Los Alamos NM 87545

HANSEN, CASSANDRA WINN, speech-language pathologist; b. Brawley, Calif., Dec. 14, 1953; d. David Griffin and Shirley (Shreeve) Winn; m. John Michael Hansen, Mar. 18, 1976. BA magna cum laude, U. Utah, 1976, MS, 1978. Speech-lang. pathologist Granite Sch. Dist., Salt Lake City, 1978—; pvt. practice specializing in speech-lang. pathology Salt Lake City, 1981—. Del. Salt Lake Council Women, 1984-86; bd. dirs. Salt Lake County Bar Auxiliary, 1983-84, 1st v.p. 1984-85, pres. 1985-86; bd. trustees Legal Aid Soc. Salt Lake, 1986—; mem. Salt Lake City Ballet Guild, 1985—. Mem. Am. Speech-Lang.-Hearing Assn. (cert. clin. competence), Internat. Assn. Orofacial Myology, Utah Speech and Hearing Assn., Alpha Lambda Delta, Phi Kappa Phi. Democrat. Avocations: ballet, aerobics, tennis, reading, skiing. Home and Office: 1363 Millstream Ln Salt Lake City UT 84106

HANSEN, DAVID ALEXANDER, business educator; b. Portland, Oreg., Mar. 16, 1944; s. Donald Eugene and Florence Ellen (Kearney) H.; m. Sharron Jane Hansen, Aug. 28, 1965; children: Debra Jane, Amy Beth. BA, Willamette U., 1966; MS, Portland State U., 1973. Instr. bus. Linfield Coll., McMinnville, Oreg., 1969, asst. prof., 1970-78, assoc. prof., 1978-86, prof., 1986—, chmn. dept. econs. and bus., 1976-84, chmn. div. social scis., 1979-81; trustee Linfield Coll., 1976-79. Youth leader McMinnville Covenant Ch., 1984-85. Mem. Boy Scout Alums. Avocations: bridge, sports broadcasting. Home: 428 Baker Creek Rd McMinnville OR 97128 Office: Linfield Coll Dept Bus Econ Studies McMinnville OR 97128

HANSEN, EVERETT MATHEW, forest pathologist; b. Portland, Oreg., Sept. 8, 1946; s. George Mathew and Betty Queen (MacDaniels) H.; m. Linda Marie Oster, Dec. 17, 1978; children: Holly, Heather, Anna. BS, Oreg. State U., 1968; MS, U. Wis., 1970, PhD, 1972. Postdoctoral study Oreg. State U., Corvallis, 1972-75, asst. prof., 1975-81, assoc. prof. forest pathology, 1981—. Mem. Am. Phytopathol. Soc. (chmn. forest pathology com. 1987, assoc. editor phytopathology 1985—), Western Forest Disease Work Conf. (program chmn. 1980), Brit. Mycol. Soc. Home: 3130 NW McKinley Corvallis OR 97330 Office: Oreg State U Dept Botany and Plant Pathology Corvallis OR 97331

HANSEN, FLORENCE MARIE CONGIOLOSI (MRS. JAMES S. HANSEN), social worker; b. Middletown, N.Y., Jan. 7, 1934; d. Joseph James and Florence (Harrigan) Congiolosi; B.A., Coll. New Rochelle, 1955; M.S.W., Fla. State U., 1960; m. James S. Hansen, June 16, 1959; 1 dau., Florence M. Caseworker, Orange County Dept. Pub. Welfare, N.Y., 1955-57, Cath. Welfare Bur., Miami, Fla., 1957-58; supr. Cath. Family Service, Spokane, Wash., 1960, Cuban Children's Program, Spokane, 1962-66; founder, dir. social service dept., 1967-85, Spokane and Inland Empire Artificial Kidney Ctr., 1967—, Sacred Heart Med. Ctr., Spokane, 1967-85, adminstrv. supr., 1967—. Asst. in program devel. St. Margaret's Hall, Spokane, 1961-62; trustee Family Counseling Service Spokane County, 1981—, also bd. dirs.; mem. budget allocation panel United Way, 1964-76, mem. planning com., 1968-77, mem. admissions com., 1969-70, chmn. projects com. 1972-73, active work with Cuban refugees; mem. kidney disease adv. com. Wash.-Alaska Regional Med. Program, 1970-73. Mem. Spokane Quality of Life Commn., 1974-75. Mem. Nat. Assn. Social Workers (chpt. pres. 1972-74), Acad. Cert. Social Workers (charter). Roman Catholic. Home: 5609 Northwest Blvd Spokane WA 99205 Office: Sacred Heart Med Ctr W 101 8th St Spokane WA 99204

HANSEN, HANS WILLIAM, engineer, consultant; b. Berkeley, Calif., Sept. 27, 1920; s. Hans William and Banna Alma (Petteys) H.; m. Mary Lee Morris, June 30, 1950 (div. June 1972); m. Inez Justine Kruzewski, Sept. 15, 1972. BS, U. Calif., 1942; MS, Santa Clara U., 1986. Registered profl. engr., Calif. With Westinghouse Electric Corp., Sunnyvale, Calif., 1947-57, 59-60, Beckman Instruments, Richmond, Calif., 1958; sr. engr. Aetron, Blume & Atkinson, Palo Alto, Calif., 1961-62; adv. devel. engr. Sylvania GTE, Mountain View, Calif., 1962-80; design engr. ESL div TRW, Sunnyvale, 1981-84, Westinghouse Electric Corp., Sunnyvale, 1985—. Served with U.S. Army, 1942-46, France. Mem. IEEE (life). Home: 4321 Faraday Dr San Jose CA 95124 Office: Westinghouse Electric Corp 401 E Hendy Ave Sunnyvale CA 94088

HANSEN, JAMES EDWARD, medical educator, researcher; b. Green Bay, Wis., Sept. 4, 1926; s. James Christian and Helen Dorothy (Terp) H.; m. Beverly May Kapke, June 5, 1948; children: Barbara Parry, Patricia Begley, Linda DeGroot, James H. Student, St. Norbert's Coll., 1942-43, U. Wis., 1943-44, Marquette U., 1944-45; MD, Johns Hopkins U., 1945-49. Diplomate Am. Bd. Internal Medicine. Intern, then resident Letterman Army Med. Ctr., San Francisco, 1949-53; commd. 1st lt. U.S. Army, 1949; advanced through grades to col. U.S. Army, Kans., Colo., London, Japan, France, and Jordan, 1975, physician, 1950-62; chief physiology div. U.S. Army Med. Research and Nutrition Lab., Denver, 1962-65; sci. dir. U.S. Army Research Inst. Environ. Medicine, Natick, Mass., 1965-71; chief clin. investigation services Tripler Army Med. Ctr., Honolulu, 1971-75; assoc. prof. dept. medicine UCLA, Torrance, 1976-78, prof. dept. medicine, 1978—; instr., asst. prof. U. Colo., 1961-65; liaison mem. applied physiology study sect. NIH, 1965-71; cons. environ. medicine U.S. Army Surgeon Gen., Washington, 1965-73; lectr. environ. medicine Johns Hopkins U., Balt., 1966-71; clin. prof. physiology U. Hawaii, 1972-75. Co-author: Principles of Exercise Testing and Interpretation, 1986; contbr. numerous articles to profl. jours. Chmn. congregation St. Matthew's Luth. Ch., Aurora, Colo., 1962-64, Gloria Dei Luth. Ch., Pearl City, Hawaii, 1972-74; sch. supt. Luth. Ch., Natick, 1967-69. Pulmonary fellow Fitzsimons Army Med. Ctr., 1960, UCLA Ctr. Health Scis., 1975-76; recipient sustaining membership award Assn. Mil. Surgeons, 1970. Fellow ACP, Am. Coll. Chest Physicians; mem. Am. Physiol. Soc., Am. Thoracic Soc. (sci. adv. bd. 1983—), Calif. Thoracic Soc. (pulmonary chmn. 1980-83, physiology com). Avocations: piano, tennis. Home: 1692 Morse Dr San Pedro CA 90732 Office: Harbor-UCLA Med Ctr PO Box 24 1000 W Carson St Torrance CA 90509

HANSEN, JAMES V., congressman; b. Salt Lake City, Aug. 14, 1932; s. J. Vear and Sena C. H.; m. Ann Burgoyne H., 1958; children—Susan, Joseph James, David Burgoyne, Paul William, Jennifer. B.S., U. Utah, 1961. Mem. Utah Ho. of Reps., 1973-80, speaker of house, 1979-80; mem. 97th-100th Congresses from 1st Utah dist., Washington, 1981—; pres. James V. Hansen Ins. Agy., Woodland Springs Devel. Co. Office: 1113 Longworth HOB Washington DC 20515

HANSEN, JANIS TIM, English educator; b. Jerome, Idaho, Apr. 2, 1934; s. Andrew J. and Elizabeth (Whittier) H.; m. Sharon McGee, Sept. 2, 1956; children: Andrew John, Matthew T. BA, Whitman Coll., 1956; MA, U. Wash., 1960; PhD in English, U. Oreg., 1965. Asst. prof. Mankato (Minn.) State Coll., 1965-68; assoc. prof. U. Puget Sound, Tacoma, 1968-72, prof. English, 1973—; Fulbright lectr. Nat. U., Tehran, Iran, 1976-77. Mem. exec. com. Mcpl. League, Tacoma, 1974-76. Mem. MLA, Assn. Depts. English (exec. com.), Phi Kappa Phi. Democrat. Office: U Puget Sound Dept English Tacoma WA 98416

HANSEN, JOHN WILLIAM, hosp. adminstr.; b. Cin., Dec. 7, 1928; s. Hans Christian and Laura Marie (Deppe) H.; m. Wilma Alice Squires, Dec. 9, 1979; children—John William, Carol, Diane, Steven, Richard, Pamela, Laura, David; stepchildren: Joan Ketzenbarger, Sandra Ketzenbarger. Cert. in acctg., U. Cin., 1952. Cost acct. Stearns & Foster Co., Lockland, Ohio, 1949-62; v.p., chief fin. officer Tucson Med. Center, 1962—. Bd. dirs. ARC, Tucson, 1977-82, also treas. Mem. Nat. Assn. Accts., Hosp. Fin. Mgmt. Assn., Ariz. Hosp. Assn. (dir. 1976-82, treas. 1980-82, 83-85). Episcopalian. Home: 8260 E Rockgate Rd Tucson AZ 85715 Office: PO Box 42195 Tucson AZ 85733

HANSEN, JUDITH EVELYN, research center administrator, consultant; b. San Francisco, May 18, 1947; d. Norton Alexander and Katherine Olive (Simpson) Forsyth; m. John Curt Hansen, Dec. 16, 1968 (div. Oct. 1983); children: Jenny Katherine, Alex. BA, Calif. State U., Fresno, 1969, MA, 1971; PhD, U. Calif., Santa Cruz, 1976. Instr. Moss Landing Marine Lab. San Jose (Calif.) State U., 1975-76; research assoc., instr., faculty mem. U. Calif., Santa Cruz, 1976-78, 83-85, research assoc., 1985—; postdoctoral research assoc. Stanford U., Pacific Grove, Calif., 1978-81; research assoc. Marine Bioassay Lab., Watsonville, Calif., 1981-83; dir. plant culture lab. Plant Scis., Inc., Watsonville, 1985—; cons. Nat. Acad. Scis., Washington, 1985, Monterey (Calif.) Bay Aquarium, 1983—. Mem. steering com. County Childcare Devel., Santa Cruz, 1986. Grantee Calif. Sea Grant Coll. Program, NOAA, 1976-81, 83-85. Mem. Phycol. Soc. Am., Internat. Phycol. Soc., Western Soc. Naturalists, Rare Fruit Growers Assn., Internat. Tissue Culture Assn., Kappa Alpha Theta. Democrat. Avocations: hiking, swimming, fishing, reading. Office: Plant Scis Inc 514 Calabasas Rd Watsonville CA 95076

HANSEN, LEONARD JOSEPH, writer, editor, publisher, marketing consultant; b. San Francisco, Aug. 4, 1932; s. Einar L. and Margie A. (Wilder) H.; A.B. in Radio-TV Prodn. and Mgmt., San Francisco State Coll., 1956, postgrad. 1956-57; cert. IBM Mgmt. Sch., 1967; m. Marcia Ann Rasmussen, Mar. 18, 1966; children—Barron Richard, Trevor Wilder. Jr. writer (part-time) Sta. KCBS, San Francisco, 1952-54; assoc. producer and dir. Ford Found. TV Research Project, San Francisco State Coll., 1955-57; air promotion dir. and writer Sta. KPIX-TV, San Francisco, 1959-60, crew chief on live and remote broadcasts, 1957-59; pub. relations mgr. Sta. KNTV-TV, San Jose, Calif., 1961; radio and TV promotion mgr. Seattle World's Fair, 1962; pub. relations and promotion mgr. Century 21 Ctr., Inc., Seattle, 1963-64; pub. relations dir. Dan Evans for Gov. Com., Seattle, 1964; propr., mgr. Leonard J. Hansen Pub. Relations, Seattle, 1965-67; campaign mgr. Walter J. Hickel for Gov. Com., Anchorage, 1966; exec. cons. to Gov. of Alaska, Juneau, 1967; gen. mgr. No. TV, Inc., Anchorage, 1967-69; v.p. mktg. Sea World, Inc., San Diego, 1969-71; editor and publisher Sr. World Publs., Inc., San Diego, 1973-84; pres. Sr. Publishers Group, 1984—; speaker and mktg. cons. to sr. citizens, 1984—; panelist, pub. affairs radio programs, 1971—; lectr. journalism San Diego State U., 1975-76. Writer weekly syndicated column Mainly for Seniors, 1984—, syndicated column Travel for Adults, 1984—; Founding mem. Housing for Elderly and Low Income Persons, San Diego, 1977-78; mem. Mayor's Ad Hoc Adv. Com. on Aging, San Diego, 1976-79; vice chmn. Housing Task Force, San Diego, 1977-78; bd. dirs. Crime Control Commn., San Diego, 1980, San Diego Coalition, 1980-83; del. White House Conf. on Aging, 1981. Served with U.S. Army, 1953-55. Recipient numerous service and citizenship awards from clubs and community orgns. Mem. Public Relations Soc. Am. (accredited), Soc. Profl. Journalists (Best Investigative Reporting award 1979), San Diego Press Club (Best Newswriting award 1976-77, Headliner of Yr. award 1980), Am. Assn. Travel Editors (profl. mem.). Home: 704-A Asbury Ct San Diego CA 92109 Office: 2117 Garnet Ave San Diego CA 92109

HANSEN, MARK DOUGLAS, human factors engineer; b. Port Arthur, Tex., Oct. 3, 1956; s. Henry Arnold and Evelyn Inez (Young) H. BS in Psychology, Tex. A&M U., 1980, MS in Indsl. Engring., 1982. Registered profl. engr., Tex. Engr. human factors Ford Aerospace and Communications Corp., Houston, 1982-84; lead, human factors and systemssafety engr. Ford Aerospace and Communications Corp., Colorado Springs, Colo., 1984—; sr. human engr. Harris Corp., Melbourne, Fla., 1984; cons. Computer Software Assocs., Inc., Houston, 1982-84. Contbr. research articles to tech. jours. Aide Reps., Houston, 1982-84, Colorado Springs, 1984—. Selected for Citizen Ambassador Program People to People Internat., 1985. Mem. Human Factors Soc., System Safety Soc., Tex. Soc. Profl. Engrs., Am. Soc. Safety Engrs., Inst. Indsl. Engrs., Am. Psychol. Assn., Assn. Aviation Psychologists. Lutheran. Lodge: Sons of Norway. Home: 4960 Artistic Circle Colorado Springs CO 80917 Office: Ford Aerospace and Communications Corp 10440 State Hwy 83 Colorado Springs CO 80908

HANSEN, MARK H., speech pathologist, director special education services; b. Milford, Nebr., Sept. 5, 1936; s. Burdette and Belva (Harrold) H.; m. Sally Jo High, May 14, 1958; children: Laurie, Mark. AB, U. Redlands, 1958, MA, 1959. Cert. spl. edn. and elem. tchr., Calif.; lic. speech pathologist, family and marriage counselor, Calif. Pvt. practice marriage and family counseling Newport Beach, Calif.; pvt. practice speech pathology Newport Beach; speech cons. San Gabriel (Calif.) Sch. Dist., 1960-61; speech cons. Newport-Mesa Unified Sch. Dist., Newport Beach, 1961-68, dir. spl. edn., 1968—; vis. prof. Calif. State Coll., Fullerton, 1970-72; cons. in field. Bd. dirs. U. Redlands, Calif. Mem. Calif. Council Adminstrn. Spl. Edn. (pres. 1985-87), Am. Speech Hearing Assn. (clin. cert., alumni bd. dirs.), Council for Exception Children, Phi Delta Kappa (v.p. 1984-86), Omicron Delta Kappa. Avocations: golf, fishing, travel. Home: 2024 Aliso Ave Costa Mesa CA 92627 Office: Newport-Mesa Unified Sch Dist 1601 16th St Newport Beach CA 92663

HANSEN, RAY SAMUEL, civil engineer; b. Bell, Calif., Feb. 20, 1927; s. Herman and Mable Hansen; m. Mary Bethel, June 6, 1950; children—Mary, Nancy, Thomas, William, Kay, Robert, Douglas, Stephen, Paul. B.S., U.S. Mil. Acad., 1950; M.S., MIT, 1955. Registered profl. engr., Tex. Enlisted U.S. Army, 1944, commd. lt., 1950, advanced through grades to Col., 1968; staff engr. Office Chief of Staff U.S. Army, Washington, 1967-68; dist. engr. Buffalo Dist. U.S. Corps Engrs., N.Y., 1969-72; dep. engr., Central Army Group NATO, Mannheim, Germany, 1972-76; dir. engring. Fort Bliss, Tex., 1976-78; dir. port & ocean engring. CH2M Hill, Bellevue, Wash., 1978—. Chmn., Oreg. Sea Grant Council, Corvallis, 1979—. Pres. PTA, Niagara Falls, N.Y., 1972; active in Political Action Com. Edn., Arlington, Va., 1970; scoutmaster European Council Boy Scouts Am., 1970; mem. U.S. Army rep. Goals El Paso, Tex., 1976-78. Decorated Legion Merit with oak leaf clusters (2), Vietnamese Medal of Honor (Vietnam). Recipient Liberty Bell award Judge Advocate Gen. Hdqrs. European Command, 1976. Mem. Soc. Am. Mil. Engrs. (pres. 1976-78), ASCE, Wash. Pub. Ports Assn., Pacific N.W. Waterways Assn. (v.p. 1982—), Internat. Assn. Navigation Congresses. Club: Seattle Engrs. Office: CH2M Hill Box 91500 Bellevue WA 98009

HANSEN, ROBERT DENNIS, educational administrator; b. San Francisco, July 17, 1945; s. Eiler Cunnard and Muriel Lenore (Morrison) H.; B.A., U. San Francisco, 1967, M.A. in Counseling and Guidance, 1971, M.A. in Supervision and Adminstrn., 1973; m. Diane Armstrong Messinger, Aug. 14, 1971; children—April Michelle, Alison Nicole. Tchr., dept. chmn., counselor, dir. student affairs, attendance officer South San Francisco Unified Sch. Dist., 1968-74, coordinator, asst. prin. Jurupa Unified Sch. Dist., Riverside, Calif., 1974-78; prin., asst. supt. San Gabriel (Calif.) Sch. Dist., 1978—. Exec. bd. South San Francisco PTA, 1968-74. Named hon. chpt. farmer Future Farmers Am.; recipient Hon. Service award Calif. State PTA. Mem. U. San Francisco Edn. Alumni Soc. (pres. 1972-73), U. San Francisco Alumni Assn., Am. Assn. Sch. Adminstrs., Assn. Calif. Sch. Adminstrs., Assn. for Supervision and Curriculum Devel., Nat. Assn. Secondary Sch. Prins., Phi Delta Kappa. Democrat. Episcopalian. Mason (32 deg.). Home: 2010 Cobblefield Way Glendora CA 91740 Office: 102 E Broadway San Gabriel CA 91776

HANSEN, ROBERT GUNNARD, scientist, philatelist, numismatist; b. Chgo., Aug. 16, 1939; s. Earl F. and Mildred E. (Hargrave) H.; A.A., Lincoln Coll., 1960; B.A., Culver Stockton Coll., 1962; M.B.A., U. So. Calif., 1966; postgrad. UCLA Extension, 1962-67; m. Bertha Golds, Aug. 10, 1960; children—Karin Lee, Lisa Marie. With Litton Industries, 1962-63, Sterer Engring., 1963-69; mktg. and contracts ofcl. Santa Barbara Research Ctr., 1969-73; pres., chief exec. officer, R.G. Hansen & Assocs., Santa Barbara, 1964—; pres., owner The Silver Penny and Santa Barbara Stamp & Coin, 1969—; guest lectr. Santa Barbara City Coll. Mem. Am. Vacuum Soc., Am. Philatelic Soc. (life), Am. Numismatic Assn., Hawaii Numismatic Assn., Token and Medal Soc. Republican. Presbyterian. Clubs: Masons, York Rite, Scottish Rite, Shriners, Royal Order of Scotland, Channel City, Royal Arch Masons, Toastmasters, Rotary Internat. Research and publs. on cryogenics, electro-optics, infrared radiation; patentee in field. Office: 631 Chapala St Santa Barbara CA 93101

HANSEN, RONALD GREGORY, civil engineer; b. Waipahu, Hawaii, Aug. 22, 1929; s. Erling M. and Geraldine J. (Nettleton) H.; m. Theresa J. Cunningham, Feb. 5, 1955; children: Eric L., Karen A., Maureen A., Timothy E. BCE, U. Santa Clara, 1952; MSCE, U. So. Calif., 1958, postgrad., 1958-66; M in Pub. Adminstrn., U. Alaska, 1981. Registered civil engr., Alaska, Wash., Oreg., Calif. Engr. Calif. Dept. Water Resources, Los Angeles, 1957-67; sr. engr. Water Quality Control Bd., Los Angeles, 1967-71; chief water pollution control State of Alaska, Juneau, 1971-79; sr. engr. KCM Inc. and EMPS Engring, Juneau, 1980-85; pres. Hansen Engring., Juneau, 1985—.

Former scoutmaster, now mem. bldg com. S.E. Alaska, Boy Scouts Am. Served to lt. col., C.E., U.S. Army. Mem. Am. Water Works Assn., ASCE, Water Pollution Control Fedn., Am. Acad. Environ. Engrs., Am. Water Resources Assn., Internat. Water Resources Assn., NSPE. Republican. Roman Catholic. Home and Office: Hansen Engring 4117 Birch Ln Juneau AK 99801

HANSEN, SIGVARD THEODORE, JR., orthopaedic surgeon, medical educator; b. Spokane, Wash., Nov. 30, 1935; s. Sigvard Theodore and Beverly Esther (Means) H.; m. Mary Jane Weinmann, Aug. 20, 1960; children—Christopher Michael, Eric Theodore. B.A. cum laude, Whitman Coll., 1957; M.D., U. Wash., 1961. Diplomate Am. Bd. Orthopaedic Surgery. Intern, King County Hosp., Seattle, 1961-62; resident in surgery U. Wash., Seattle, 1965-69, asst. prof. orthopaedic surgery 1971-75, assoc. prof., 1975-79, prof., 1979—, chmn. dept., 1981-85; cons. Madigan Army Hosp., 1975—. Served with USN, 1962-65. NIH summer research fellow, 1957, 58. Mem. Am. Acad. Orthopaedic Surgery, Am. Orthopaedic Assn., Assn. Bone and Joint Surgeons, Western Orthopaedic Assn., Am. Orthopaedic Foot and Ankle Soc., AO-NA Found. (pres. N.Am. 1986—), Am. for Study Internal Fixation (bd. dirs. 1984—), M.E. Mueller Found. (bd. dirs. 1986—), Phi Beta Kappa. Club: Sand Point Golf and Country. Contbr. articles to med. jours., chpts. to books. Home: 1 W Highland Dr Seattle WA 98119 Office: 325 9th Ave Suite 6S Seattle WA 98104

HANSEN, STANLEY SEVERIN, II, astrophysicist, aerospace engineer, computer scientist; b. St. Joseph, Mo., Sept. 16, 1945; s. Stanley Severin and Gertrude (Campbell) H. BS in Physics, U. Mo., 1967; MS in Astrophysics, U. Mass., 1972, PhD, 1980. Researcher Oak Ridge Associated Univs., 1966; systems devel. staff IBM, Poughkeepsie, N.Y., 1967-70; faculty Mt. Holyoke Coll., South Hadley, Mass., 1971-73, U. Mass., Amherst, 1974; astronomer Onsala Space Obs. Rao, Onsala, Sweden, 1973, Nat. Radio Astronomy Obs., Charlottesville, Va., 1974-81; mem. tech. staff Aerospace Corp., El Segundo, Calif., 1982—. Contbr. articles to profl. jours. Advisor to Aerospace Corp.'s Explorer Scout Post, 1982—. NSF grantee, 1966. Mem. Am. Astron. Soc., Sierra Club, Tau Beta Pi, Phi Kappa Phi, Sigma Pi Sigma, Sigma Phi Epsilon. Home: 420 S Catalina Ave Apt 208 Redondo Beach CA 90277 Office: The Aerospace Corp 2350 E El Segundo Blvd El Segundo CA 90245

HANSEN, STANLEY WAYNE, computer systems design engineer; b. Long Beach, Calif., Mar. 16, 1940; s. Royal John and Emma Lois (Mackay) H.; B.S., U. Utah, 1964; m. Lorraine Mitchell, Sept. 3, 1965; children—Jeffrey Kent, Gregory Kirk, Michael Wayne. With Ford Aerospace and Communications Corp., Colorado Springs, Colo., 1965—, project engr. JSC Real Time Computer Complex for Apollo lunar landings, now prin. engr. in charge research/devel. and new computer systems design; co-founder Hyper-Tech. Devel. Corp.; cons. in field. Active Boy Scouts Am., 1951—. Served with USNG, 1957-65. Recipient Eagle with Palms award, Boy Scouts Am., 1953, Silver Explorer award, 1956. Mormon. Contbr. articles to profl. jours.; patentee several mini/microcomputer designs. Office: 10440 State Hwy 83 Colorado Springs CO 80908

HANSEN, STEPHEN ALLEN, transportation company executive; b. Shelton, Wash., May 29, 1955; s. Donald LeRoy and Audrey Myrtle (Putvin) H.; m. Barbara Lynne Wiggins, Mar. 26, 1983; 1 child, Emily Grace. BBA, U. Wash., 1977. Lic. pvt. pilot. Interline supr. Kerr Steamship Co. Inc., Seattle, 1977-80; depot controller Container Services Inc., Seattle, 1980-81; mktg. rep. Sea Containers West Inc., Seattle, 1981—. Mem. steering com. Crisis Pregnancy Ctr. of King County, Wash., 1985—. Mem. Transp. Club of Seattle. Office: Sea Containers West Inc 2033 Sixth Ave Suite 1050 Seattle WA 98121

HANSEN, STEVEN ALAN, construction executive; b. Key West, Fla., July 5, 1949; s. Baron Lewis Hansen and June Marie (Ferree) Correll; m. Sally Jo Cooper, Nov. 13, 1976; children: Blake, Carter, Reid. BA in Govt. and Religion, Ind. U., 1972. V.p. Hansen-Haberman Constrn., Aspen, Colo., 1978-82; pres. Hansen Constrn. Inc., Aspen, 1982—. Avocations: oil painting, sketching. Office: Hansen Constrn Inc PO Box 10493 Aspen CO 81612

HANSEN, VERNON HENRY, banker; b. Carroll, Iowa, Feb. 23, 1953; s. Alvan Henry and Elaine Eldora (Schroeder) H.; m. Julie Ann Cota, Aug. 3, 1974; children: Daniel, Mary, Elizabeth, Eric. B.B.A., U. Iowa, 1975. Bank examiner FDIC, Omaha, 1975-78; sr. credit officer Central Nat. Bank, Des Moines, 1978-80; asst. mgr. United Bank of Denver, 1980-81, exec. banking officer, 1981-82; v.p. United Bank of South Park, Littleton, Colo., 1982-83; sr. v.p. United Bank Arapahoe, Englewood, Colo., 1983—. Exec. mem. Muscular Dystrophy Assn., Denver, 1982-84. Mem. Robert Morris Assocs. Independent. Lutheran. Home: 1171 S Joplin St Aurora CO 80017 Office: United Bank of Arapahoe 9350 E Arapahoe Rd Englewood CO 80112

HANSEN, WILFORD NELS, physics and chemistry educator, research consultant; b. Cardston, Alta., Can., May 30, 1928; came to U.S., 1930; s. Nels X. and Maggie Ann (Pritchett) H.; m. Vada Louine Johnson, Feb. 21, 1951; children—Wilford N., Galen J., Vaylene, Loreita, Dwayne Maxwell, Cynthia Louine. B.S., Brigham Young U., 1950; Ph.D., Iowa State U., 1956. Research scientist Atomics Internat., Los Angeles, 1956-57; research assoc. Iowa State U., Ames, 1957-58; asst. prof. chemistry Brigham Young U., Provo, Utah, 1958-60; researcher, cons. N.Am. Aviation, Los Angeles, 1959-68; prof. physics Utah State U., Logan, 1968-73, prof. physics and chemistry, 1973—; organizing chmn. Internat. Conf. on Electronic and Molecular Structure of Electrode-Electrolyte Interfaces, Logan, 1982-83; guest prof. Fritz Haber Inst., Berlin, 1977-78, 84; collaborator Los Alamos Nat. Lab., N.Mex., 1982—. Editor: Proc. International Conference on Electronic and Molecular Structure of Electrode-Electrolyte Interfaces, Elsevier, N.Y., 1983. Patentee in field. Mem., pres. Timber Sch. Dist., Thousand Oaks, Calif., 1963-68. Named Researcher of Yr., Utah State U., Logan, 1984. Mem. Am. Phys. Soc., Am. Chem. Soc., Optical Soc. Am., Electrochem. Soc., Sigma Xi. Mormon. Home: 855 S 600 E Logan UT 84321 Office: Physics Dept UMC 41 Utah State U Logan UT 84322

HANSER, PHILIP, econometrician; b. Ft. Lauderdale, Fla., Jan. 8, 1951; s. Edward and Nettie (Ornstein) H.; m. Suzanne Bonnie Blottner, Aug. 8, 1971; children—Leora B., Samuel B. B.A., Fla. State U., Tallahassee, 1972; M.Phil., Columbia U., 1975. Research asst. in econometrics Bur. Applied Social Research, Columbia U., 1972-74, cons. Center for Computing Activities, 1974-75; lectr. dept. math. U. Pacific, 1975-77; asst. prof. dept. econs., 1977-80; econometrician resource planning dept. Sacramento Mcpl. Utility Dist., 1980-86; project mgr. Electric Power Research Inst., 1986—; vis. lectr. dept. econs. U. Calif.-Davis, 1982-83; industry cons. Electric Power Research Inst. NSF fellow, 1972-74; recipient Teaching Incentive award U. Pacific, 1979; Outstanding Young Men of Am. award Jr. C. of C. Am., 1980. Mem. Econometric Soc., Am. Statis. Assn., Internat. Assn., Energy Economists, Inst. Math. Stats., Internat. Soc. Forecasters. Author: (with D. Christianson and D. Hughes) Statistics Through Laboratory Experiences, 1977; contbr. articles to profl. jours. Home: 749 Matadero Ave Palo Alto CA 94306 Office: PO Box 15830 Sacramento CA 95813

HANSON, DAVID GORDON, physician; b. Seattle, Nov. 16, 1943; m. Terri Dangerfield, Jan. 22, 1976. BS, Wheaton Coll., 1966; MD, U. Wash., 1970; MS, U. Minn., 1976. Intern Hennepin County Gen. Hosp., Mpls., 1970-71; resident in surgery and otolaryngology U. Minn., Mpls., 1972-76; sr. surgeon NIH, Nat. Inst. Neurol. and Communicative Disorders and Stroke, USPHS, Bethesda, Md., 1975-78; asst. prof. surgery UCLA Sch. Medicine, 1978-83, assoc. prof., 1983—, vice chief div. head and neck surgery, 1983—; chief sect. head and neck surgery VA Med. Ctr., West Los Angeles, 1983—. Contbr. articles to profl. jours. Served to comdr. USPHS, 1975-78. NIH grantee, 1983—. Fellow ACS, Am. Broncho-Esophagol. Assn., Am. Soc. Head and Neck Surgery, Am. Acad. Otolaryngology (Award of Honor, 1985); mem. AMA. Avocations: skiing, sailing. Office: UCLA Sch Medicine CHS 62-215 Los Angeles CA 90024

HANSON, DOUGLAS EUGENE, accountant; b. Glenwood, Minn., June 7, 1945; s. Ferdinand Julius and Hazel Josephine (Skarsten) H.; m. Judith Kay Thompson, Jan. 1, 1968; children—Thomas, Timothy, Erika, Denise, Krista (twins). A.A., Contra Costa Coll., San Pablo, Calif., 1963-66; B.S., Calif. Poly. State U., 1973. C.P.A., Alaska. Various positions to supr. Peat, Marwick, Mitchell & Co., C.P.A.s, 1973-79; sole practice acctg., Anchorage, 1979—. Served with USAF, 1966-70. Mem. Am. Inst. C.P.A.s, Alaska Soc. C.P.A.s. Mem. Ch. of God. Office: 3400 Spenard Rd Suite 6 Anchorage AK 99503-3738

HANSON, EUGENE WILLIAM, JR., sales administrator; b. St. Louis, June 11, 1950; s. Eugene William Sr. and Mary Jayne (Drummond) H.; m. Linda Kelley, Apr. 17, 1982; children: Eugene W. III, Jennifer, Marc. BSBA in Acctg., Calif. State Coll., Bakersfield, 1977. Br. systems coordinator Coca-Cola Bottling Co., Los Angeles, 1976-81, mgr. br. controls, 1981-83, mgr. sales adminstrn., 1983—. Democrat. Roman Catholic. Avocations: snow skiing, memorabilia collecting. Office: Coca-Cola Bottling Co 1334 S Central Los Angeles CA 90021

HANSON, GEORGE PETER, real estate investor, retired research botanist; b. Conde, S.D., July 20, 1933; s. George Henry and Rosa Wilhelmina (Peterson) H.; m. Barbara Jean Graves, Aug. 20, 1958; children—David, Carole, Heather, Peter; m. 2d, Gloria Ann Gauntt, June 1, 1969. B.S. in Agronomy, S.D. State U., 1956, M.S. in Plant Breeding, 1958; Ph.D. in Genetics, Ind. U., 1965. Asst. prof. biology Thiel Coll. Greenville, Pa., 1962-65; asst. prof. botany Butler U., Indpls., 1965-67; sr. biologist Los Angeles State and County Arboretum, Arcadia, Calif., 1968-82; real estate investor, 1971—. Mem. Apt. Assn. of Greater Los Angeles. Methodist. Contbr. numerous articles in field to profl. jours. Home: 1345 W Haven Rd San Marino CA 91108

HANSON, LARRY KEITH, plastics company executive; b. Hawkins, Wis., Aug. 14, 1932; s. Harold and Clara Pauline (Lund) H.; m. Patricia Rosalie Sammarco, Aug. 6, 1955; children: Lawrence Keith, John Steven, James Paul. BS, U.S. Mcht. Marine Acad., 1955. Engr. Curtis-Wright Corp., Woodridge, N.J., 1955-58; sales engr. Gits Bros. Mfg. Co., Chgo., 1958-66, Aeroquip Corp., Burbank, Calif., 1966-70; group v.p. Fluorocarbon Co., Laguna Niguel, Calif., 1970—; also bd. dirs. Fluorocarbon SA/NV subs. Fluorocarbon Co., Wilrijk, Belgium, 1983—; bd. dirs. Fluorocarbon SA/NV subs. Fluorocarbon Co., Wilrijk, Belgium. Patentee in field. Avocations: fly fishing, drawing, inventions. Office: Fluorocarbon Mech Seal Div 10871 Kyle PO Box 520 Los Alamitos CA 90720

HANSON, NOEL RODGER, management consultant; b. Los Angeles, Jan. 19, 1942; s. Albert and Madelyne Gladys (Pobanz) H.; B.S. in Indsl. Mgmt., U. So. Calif., 1963, M.B.A. in Fin., 1966; m. Carol Lynn Travis, June 17, 1967; 1 son, Eric Rodger. Asst. dir. alumni fund, then dir. ann. funds U. So. Calif., 1964-66; asst. to Walt Disney for Cal-Arts, Retlaw Enterprises, Glendale, Calif., 1966-68; asst. dir. joint devel. Claremont U. Center, 1968-69; v.p. adminstrn. Robert Johnston Co., Los Angeles, 1969-70; partner Hale, Hanson & Co., Pasadena, Calif., 1970-82, Hanson, Olson & Co., 1982—; pres. Pasadena Services, Inc., 1977—; dir. Pasadena Fin. Cons., Inc., Freeway Motors Ford, Pacific BanCorp, Pacific Inland Bank. Trustee Oakhurst Sch., Pasadena, 1973-75; bd. advisers Girls Club Pasadena, 1977—; mem. U. So. Calif. Assos., 1979—, U. So. Calif. Commerce Assos., 1965—. Republican. Presbyterian. Club: Jonathan (Los Angeles). Address: 1051 LaLoma Rd Pasadena CA 91105

HANSON, ROBERT JOHN, educator; b. Dubuque, Iowa, Oct. 30, 1918; s. Peter John and Esther Anna (Flynn) H.; m. Josephine Corpstein, June 30, 1943; children—Robert John, David J., Peter T., Christina A. B.S.E.E., U.S. Naval Acad., 1941; M.B.A., U. So. Calif., 1967; postgrad. George Washington U., 1959, U. Va., 1962, UCLA, 1963-64. Commd. ensign U.S. Navy, 1941, advanced through grades to capt., 1963, ret., 1968; with McDonnell Douglas, Huntington Beach, Calif., 1968-70; faculty Los Angeles Harbor Coll., 1970—, prof. acctg., 1974—; prof. naval sci. U. So. Calif., Los Angeles, 1964-67. Mem. Assn. Naval Aviation, Ret. Officers Assn., Naval Acad. Alumni Assn., Skull and Dagger Soc. Roman Catholic. Clubs: So. Calif. Golf Assn., K.C. Home: 30803 Rue Valois Rancho Palos Verdes CA 90274 Office: 111 Figueroa Pl Wilmington CA 90744

HANSON, SERGIUS NELS, engineering geologist, consulting engineer; b. Rhinelander, Wis., Oct. 22, 1950; s. Walter Carlton and Ludmilla Bernadette (Chesna) H.; m. Deborah Ann Dunham, Feb. 29, 1984. B.S., U. Wis.-Eau Claire, 1972. Registered profl. engr., Colo. Geotech. geologist Geotech. Engring. Corp. St. Paul, 1973-74; engring. geologist Owen Ayres and Assoc., Inc., Eau Claire, Wis., 1974-78, U.S. Fed. Hwy. Adminstrn., Denver, 1978-81, U.S. Bur. Reclamation, Denver, 1981-86; project mgr. Hydro-Search Inc., Golden, Colo., 1986—; pres. Hanson Engring. Co., Lakewood, Colo., 1982—; USCOLD vol. post-disasters study team com. NRC. Author: (with others) Great Lakes Shore Erosion Protection: A General Review with Case Studies, 1977; Great Lakes Shore Erosion Protection: Structural Design Examples, 1978. Recipient Performance award U.S. Bur. Reclamation, 1982, 85. Mem. Geol. Soc. Am., Assn. Engring. Geologists, ASCE, Soc. Mining Engrs., U.S. Com. on Large Dams. Home: 380 Zang St #6-106 Lakewood CO 80228 Office: Hydro-Search Inc 350 Indiana St Suite 415 Golden CO 80401

HANSON, STANLEY DEAN, optometrist, educator; b. Boulder, Colo., Apr. 23, 1950; s. Russell Howard and Lois Helene H.; m. Janenne Marie Wall, Jan. 6, 1979; children: Christina, Janenne, Catherine. Student Union Coll., 1968-71, U. Tenn., 1974; BS, OD, So. Coll. Optometry, 1975. Cert. optometrist Nat. Bd. Optometric Examiners, Colo., Minn., Tenn. Asst. optometrist C. Vance Bergvall, Optometrists, Littleton, Colo., 1975-77; staff optometrist City and County of Denver Dept. Health and Hosps., 1976-81; pvt. practice optometry, Denver, 1977—; instr. Community Coll. Denver, 1977-79; staff optometrist Kaiser-Permanente Med. Found., Denver, 1981-86; assoc. optometrist Thomas P. Larkin, M.D., Denver, 1981—. Contbr. articles to med. jours. Mem. Am. Optometric Assn., Colo. Optometric Assn. (trustee 1979-82, pres. 1984-85, award of merit 1979, 80). Home: 11869 E Bates Cir Aurora CO 80014 Office: 2465 S Downing St No 209 Denver CO 80210

HANSON, WAYNE CARLYLE, ecologist, consultant; b. Kennewick, Wash., Sept. 5, 1923; s. Oscar Martinius and Gladys Leone (Duffy) H.; m. Delma Ruth Duffy, Apr. 6, 1947 (div. May 1970); children: Christian Martin, Eric Everett; m. Mary Ann Moser, Sept. 4, 1970. BS, Wash. State U., 1949; MS, Colo. State U., 1971, PhD, 1973. Cert. wildlife biologist, sr. ecologist. Sr. research scientist Battelle Pacific Northwest, Richland, Wash., 1949-70, sr. scientist IV, 1978-81; alt. group leader Los Alamos (N.Mex.) Nat. Lab., 1973-78; environ. sci. mgr. Earth Tech., Anchorage, 1981-82; assoc. Dames & Moore, Anchorage, 1982-84; ptnr. Hanson Envireserv, Bellingham, Wash., 1984—. Editor: Transuranic Element, 1980; contbr. articles to profl. jours. Served to sgt. USAF, 1943-45, CBI. Recipient Hapo Gen. Mgr. award Gen. Electric, 1955. Mem. AAAS, Am. Inst. Biol. Scis., Arctic Inst. N.Am., Ecol. Soc. Am., The Wildlife Soc. (Arthur S. Einarsen award 1980). Home and Office: 1902 Yew St Rd Bellingham WA 98226-8909

HANSON, WILLIAM ALBERT, engineering executive; b. Boston, May 12, 1921; s. Albert J. and Reina Ellen (Brackett) H.; m. Jeannine C. Roth, Aug. 1, 1941 (div. Aug. 1980); children: Maren Hoshan, Priscilla Silverman, Royal Hanson. MS, Calif. Coast U., 1977, PhD, 1979. Registered profl. engr., Calif., Wis. Lab. asst. Lee Found., Waukesha, Wis., 1940-44; devel. engr. Lee Engring. Co., Milw., 1946-51; prin. Hanson Research Corp., Northridge, Calif., 1951—; pres. Acad. Aquatic Ecosystems, Westlake Village, Calif., 1974-77; mem. dissolution panel Nat. Formulary, Washington, 1980. Author: Dissolution Technology, 1983; co-author: Cell Autoregulation, 1947, The Westlake Story, 1975; contbr. articles to profl. jours. Pres. Westlake Mgmt. Assn., Westlake Village, 1974-76. Served with Signal Corps, U.S. Army, 1944-46. Mem.NSPE, IEEE, Acad. Environ. Engrs., Am. Chem. Soc. Libertarian. Unitarian. Club: Westlake Yacht (Westlake Village) (commodore 1979). Avocations: sailing, horseback riding. Home: 2546 Northlake Circle Westlake Village CA 91361 Office: Hanson Research Corp 19727 Bahama St Northridge CA 91328

HANTOS, PETER, electrical engineer; b. Budapest, Hungary, Apr. 13, 1949; came to U.S., 1979; s. Andor and Terry (Graf) H. MSEE, Tech. U. Budapest, 1973, PhD, 1980. Asst. prof. Tech. U. Budapest, 1973-79, U. Calif., Santa Barbara, Calif., 1979-82. Contbr. articles to profl. jours. Mem. IEEE (sr.), Assn. Computing Machinery. Home: 8570 Hollywood Blvd Los Angeles CA 90069 Office: Xerox Corp Microelectronics Ctr 701 S Aviation El Segundo CA 90245

HAPPEL, JERALD ROBERT, health care facility administrator; b. Sioux City, Iowa, Jan. 22, 1943; s. Robert John and Glovana Marie (Bennett) H.; m. Barbara Jean Carper, June 30, 1982 (div. July 1978); children: Anthony Allan, Amy Sue. B, Morningside Coll., 1965; MS, Trinity U., San Antonio, 1967. Asst. adminstr. Colo. Gen. Hosp., Denver, 1967-72, adminstr., 1972-77; adminstr. Rose Med. Ctr., Denver, 1977-86; pres. Aricana Resources, Vancouver, B.C., Can., 1986—; faculty mem. U. Colo., Denver, 1967-77. Mem. Am. Coll. Health Adminstrs., Colo. Hosp. Assn. (chmn. 1979-80, bd. dirs. 1977—, mem. legis. council, 1977-85, chmn. Long Range Planning Commn. 1983-84), Colo. Found. (bd. dirs. 1977-79), Denver Metro. Hosp. Council (pres. 1974-75), Am. Hosp Assn. (mem. regulatory adv. bd.). Republican. Lutheran. Lodge: Optimists (Boulder, Colo.) (pres. 1970-71). Avocations: biking, skiing, fishing, boating. Office: Aricana Resources, 625 Howe, Vancouver, BC Canada V6C 2T6

HARADON, PENNI PAUL, interior designer; b. Washington, Oct. 10, 1943; d. Philip Franklin and Dorothy (Hite) Paul; m. Fritz Howard Haradon, Sept. 12, 1964; children—Hollie Elizabeth, David Howard. Student U. So. Calif., 1961-62, Chouinard Art Inst., 1961; B.Profl. Arts, Woodbury Coll., 1964. With Country Cousin Interiors, Los Angeles, 1962—, partner, after 1970—, pres., owner, 1979—; tchr. interior design Western Home Furnishing Assn., 1965-81. Mem. Decorative Arts Council, Los Angeles County Mus. Assn. Recipient Certificates of Merit, Scholastic Mag., 1959, 60, 61, Am. Inst. Interior Design, 1964, Los Angeles County Fair, 1969, Am. Soc. Interior Designers, 1975. Mem. Am. Soc. Interior Designers (bd. mem.). Office: 8687 Melrose Ave Suite M48 Los Angeles CA 90069

HARAWAY, DONNA JEANNE, history educator; b. Denver, Sept. 6, 1944; d. Frank O. and Dorothy Jeanette (Maguire) H. BA, Colo. Coll., 1966, D, 1986; M in Philosphy, Yale U., 1969, PhD, 1972. Asst. prof. U. Hawaii, Honolulu, 1970-74, Johns Hopkins U., Balt., 1974-80; assoc. prof. U. Calif., Santa Cruz, 1980-84, prof. history, 1984—. Author: Crystals, Fabrics and Fields, 1976; mem. editorial bd. Signs, History of Anthropology; contbr. articles to profl. jours. Fellow Danforth Found., 1966, Humanities Inst., 1984. Mem. History Sci. Soc., Nat. Women's Studies Assn., Soc. Social Studies Sci., Soc. Values in Higher Edn. Office: U Calif Kresge Coll Santa Cruz CA 95064

HARBAUGH, DANIEL P., lawyer; b. Wendell, Idaho, May 18, 1948; s. Myron and Manuelita (Garcia) H. BA, Gonzaga U., 1970, JD, 1974. Asst. atty. gen. State of Wash., Spokane, 1974-77; ptnr. Richter, Wimberley & Ericson, Spokane, 1977-83, Harbaugh & Bloom, Spokane, 1983—; bd. dirs. Spokane Legal Services, 1982-86; bd. govs. LAWPAC, Seattle, 1982—. Bd. dirs. Spokane Ballet, 1983—; chpt. dir. Les Amis du Vin, Spokane, 1985—. Mem. ABA, Wash. State Bar Assn., Spokane County Bar Assn., Wash. State Trial Lawyers Assn., Am. Trial Lawyers Assn., Nat. Orgn. Social Security Claimants Reps. Democrat. Roman Catholic. Clubs: Spokane, Spokane Country. Office: Harbaugh & Bloom N 9 Post Spokane WA 99201

HARBER, DARRELL M., real estate broker; b. St. Louis, July 2, 1952; s. Darrell L. and Georgia J. Harber; m. Betty Bosch, Apr. 28, 1973; children—Angela Jean, Matthew Michael. Student SE Mo. State U., 1972. Real estate agt., Wash., 1975-78; owner Ponderosa Land Co., 1978—; pres. Harber Land & Cattle Co., Northwest Investment Strategies, Inc.; v.p. Mgmt. Resources, Inc. Served with U.S. Army, 1972-75. Office: Ponderosa Land Co 9703 Meridian S Puyallup WA 98373

HARBOUR, ANITA SUSAN, speech pathologist; b. Wenatchee, Wash., June 17, 1954; d. Theodore Robert and Phyllis Darlene (Patterson) Homchick; m. William Michael Harbour, Dec. 19, 1981; 1 child, Michael Theodore, Lisa June. BA, Wash. State U., 1976, MA, 1979. Cert. tchr., Wash.; cert. ednl. staff assoc., Wash. Spl. edn. tchr. Olympia (Wash.) Pub. Schs., 1976-77, communication disorders specialist, 1979—; cons. Olympia Sch. Dist., 1984—. Author: (with others) Kindergarten Information Delivery System language screening test, 1985. Mem. Am. Speech and Hearing Assn. (cert.), Wash. Speech and Hearing Assn., NEA, Olympia Edn. Assn. (rep. 1983-84), Pi Lambda Theta, Alpha Lambda Delta, Phi Kappa Phi (scholarship 1974). Roman Catholic. Avocations: swimming, dance, racquetball, sewing. Home: 1903 Thornton St NW Olympia WA 98502 Office: Olympia Pub Schs Spl Services 1113 E Legion Way Olympia WA 98501

HARBOUR, DAVID FRANKLIN, III, public relations executive; b. Coleman, Tex., Sept. 4, 1942; David Franklin and Selma (Koehler) H.; B.A. in English, Colo. State U., 1965; grad. Def. Info. Sch., 1968; M.S., Murray State U., 1971; children Todd Douglas, Benjamin Conrad. Dir. Alaskan affairs Alaskan Meth. U., Anchorage, 1971-72; dir. public relations Murray, Kraft, and Rockey, Inc., Anchorage, 1972-73; dir. public affairs Alaskan Arctic Gas Pipeline Co., Anchorage, 1973, Washington, 1977; regional dir. govt. relations Atlantic Richfield Co., Anchorage, 1978; v.p. univ. relations Alaska Pacific U., Anchorage, 1985; pres. The Harbour Co., Anchorage, 1987—; instr. fin. public relations and mktg. U. Alaska, 1975. Bd. dirs., pres. Common Sense for Alaska; trustee, chmn. Alaska Council on Econ. Edn., Commonwealth North; bd. dirs. Coalition Alaska Vets., Resource Devel. Council Alaska. Served to capt. U.S. Army, 1966-70. Mem. Pub. Relations Soc. of Am. (accredited), Alaska C. of C. (dir.), Alaska Press Club (pres.), Alaska Visitors Assn. Contbr. articles to profl. jours. Office: Box 11360 Anchorage AK 99510

HARCINSKE, JOHN CARL, aerospace engineer; b. Wisconsin Rapids, Wis., July 7, 1949; s. Carl John and Estelle M. (Klonowski) H. BS in Physics, U. Wis., Stevens Point, 1972. Tng. rep. Ford Aerospace Co., Sunnyvale, Calif., 1976-81; ops. lead Martin Marietta Corp., Denver, 1981-85, advanced extravehicular activity systems lead, 1985—. Served as sgt. USAF, 1972-75. Mem. Smithsonian Assocs. Avocations: carpentry, photography, computers, electronic design, gardening. Home: 4192 S Laredo Way Aurora CO 80013 Office: Martin Marietta PO Box 179 MS TO426 Denver CO 80201

HARCOURT, ROBERT NEFF, educational administrator, author; b. East Orange, N.J., Oct. 19, 1932; s. Stanton Hinde and Mary Elizabeth (Neff) H. B.A., Gettysburg Coll., 1958; M.A., Columbia U., 1961. Cert. guidance, secondary edn., career and vocat. guidance, N.Mex. Social case worker N.J. State Bd. Child Welfare, Newark and Morristown, 1958-61; asst. registrar Hofstra U. and asst. to evening dean of students CCNY, 1961-62; housing staff U. Denver, 1962-64; fin. aid and placement dir. Inst. Am. Indian Arts, Santa Fe, 1965—, appointed by corp. pres. to adv. bd. Genre Ltd. Art Pubs., Los Angeles, 1985—; nat. color ad participant The Bradford Exchange, Chgo., 1986—. Donor Am. Indian Library collection Gettysburg (Pa.) Coll. Served with U.S. Army, 1954-56; Ger. Named hon. Okie, Gov. Okla., 1970; decorated Nat. Def. medal; postmasters fellow U. Denver, 1962-64; col. a.d.c. to N.Mex. Gov. David F. Cargo, 1970. Mem. Am. Contract Bridge League (exec. bd. Santa Fe unit; advance sr. master), Safari Club Internat., SAR, Santa Fe Council Internat. Relations, Am. Personnel and Guidance Assn., Assn. Specialists in Group Work (charter), Adult Student Personnel Assn. (charter), Southwestern Assn. Indian Affairs, Phi Delta Kappa (holding exec. bd. membership), bd.), Alpha Tau Omega, Alpha Phi Omega. Club: Safari Internat. Home: 720 Acequia Madre #7 Santa Fe NM 87501 Office: Inst Am Indian Arts CSF Campus Santa Fe NM 87501

HARD, ARTHUR ROBERT, retired metallurgical engineer; b. White Sulphur Springs, Mont., Mar. 10, 1917; s. Jaspar William and Elisa Ann (Brown) H.; m. Margaret Aileen McGregor; children: Peggy Jean, Robert. BS in Metall. Engring., Mont. Sch. Mines (now called Mont. Coll. Mineral Sci. and Tech.), 1940. Engr. Boeing Aircraft Corp., Seattle, 1941-45; research engr. Wash. State U., Pullman, 1945-81, scientist emeritus, 1981—. Co-Author: Wind Induced Conductor Motion, 1979; contbr. articles on welding to profl. jours. Mem. IEEE (mem. working group on vibration), Internat. Conf. Large High-Tension Electric Systems (mem. study com. 22). Republican. Episcopalian. Avocations: photography, boating, fishing, travel. Home and Office: SE 1000 Spring St Pullman WA 99163

HARDAWAY, JOHN EVANS, mining company executive; b. Phila., Mar. 2, 1937; s. Harold Luther and Elsie Mae (Bruder) H.; m. Ann Madison Tilson, Feb. 23, 1963; children: Robert G., James L. BSE with honors, Princeton U., 1959, MSE, 1963. Sr. assoc. scientist Teledyne Isotopes, Westwood, N.J., 1964-69; adminstr. phys. scis., hydrologist Fed. Water Pollution Control Adminstrn., EPA, Dept. Interior, Denver, 1969-78; asst. regional dir. Office of Surface Mining, Dept. Interior, Denver, 1978-81; mgr. regulatory affairs Tosco Corp., Denver and Concord, Calif., 1981-83; scientist KamanTempo, Denver, 1983-84; tech. mgr., environ. affairs Homestake Mining Co., Golden, Colo., 1984—. Chmn. Mass Transit Com., Wheat Ridge, Colo., 1970-81. Served with U.S. Army, 1960-62. Recipient Gold medal EPA, 1978. Mem. AIME, Soc. Petroleum Engrs., Geol. Soc. Am., Am. Geophys. Union, Sigma Xi, Tau Beta Pi. Republican. Home: 3590 Moore St Wheat Ridge CO 80033 Office: Homestake Mining Co 1726 Cole Blvd Golden CO 80401

HARDEN, DAVID GUY, ecological statistician; b. Long Beach, Calif., Aug. 19, 1943; s. Cleo Eugene Oliver Harden and Pauline Marjorie (Blake) Sewell; m. Glenda Ann Edwards, June 16, 1964 (div. 1976); children: Dianne Michelle, Donna Gail, Debra Janette; m. Michele Louise Tegeler, July 23, 1977; children: Laura Louisa Marie, Christopher David. BS in Zoology, San Diego State U., 1966, MS in Biology, 1969; PhD in Biol. Scis., Ill. State U., 1979. Acting pres. Permi-Arts Inc., Coalinga, Calif., 1969-71; teaching fellow Ill. State U., Normal, 1971-75; instr. U. Calif. Extension, San Diego, 1975-76; sr. biologist Marine Biol. Cons., Costa Mesa, Calif., 1976-77; sr. scientist Interstate Electronics Corp., Anaheim, Calif., 1978-83; data quality engr. Marine Rev. Com., Encinitas, Calif., 1983—; gorgonian taxonomist Calif. Acad. Scis, San Francisco, 1966—, Los Angeles County Mus., 1966-69, San Diego Mus. Natural Hist., 1964-69. Editor, contbr. articles to profl. jours. Recipient Achievement award Figgie Internat. Interstate Electronics, 1979, 82. Mem. AAAS, Coelenterate Colloquium, Phi Sigma. Republican. Mormon. Avocations: hiking, geneal. research. Home: 276 Aspenwood Ln Encinitas CA 92024 Office: Marine Review Com Inc 531 Encinitas Blvd Suite 105 Encinitas CA 92024

HARDEN, MARVIN, artist, educator; b. Austin, Tex.; s. Theodore R. and Ethel (Sneed) H. B.A. in Fine Arts, UCLA, also M.A. in Creative Painting. Tchr. art Calif. State U., Northridge, 1968—, Santa Monica (Calif.) City Coll., 1968; mem. art faculty UCLA Extension, 1964-68; mem. visual arts fellowship/painting panel Nat. Endowment Arts, 1985. One-man shows include, Ceeje Galleries, Los Angeles, 1964, 66, 67, Occidental Coll., Los Angeles, 1969, Whitney Mus. Am. Art, N.Y.C., 1971, Eugenia Butler Gallery, Los Angeles, 1971, Irving Blum Gallery, Los Angeles, 1972, Los Angeles Harbor Coll., 1972, David Stuart Galleries, Los Angeles, 1975, Coll. Creative Studies, U. Calif., Santa Barbara, 1976, James Corcoran Gallery, Los Angeles, 1978, Newport Harbor Art Mus., 1979, Los Angeles Mcpl. Art Gallery, 1982, Conejo Valley Art Mus., 1983, Simard Gallery, Los Angeles, 1985; group shows include, U.S. State Dept. Touring Exhbn., USSR, 1966, Oakland (Calif.) Mus. Art, 1966, UCLA, 1966, Mpls. Inst. Art, 1968, San Francisco Mus. Art, 1969, Phila. Civic Center Mus., 1969, Mus. Art, R.I. Sch. Design, 1969, N.S. State Mus., 1969, Everson Mus. Art, Syracuse, 1969, La Jolla (Calif.) Mus., 1969, 70, High Mus. Art, Atlanta, 1969, Flint (Mich.) Inst. Arts, 1969, Ft. Worth Art Center Mus., 1969, Contemporary Arts Assn., Houston, 1970, U. N.Mex., 1974, U. So. Calif., 1975, Bklyn. Mus., 1976, Los Angeles County Mus. Art, 1977, Newport Harbor Art Mus., 1977, Frederick S. Wight Gallery, UCLA, 1978, Cirrus Editions, Ltd., Los Angeles, 1979, Franklin Furnace, N.Y.C., 1980, Art Ctr. Coll. Design, Los Angeles, 1981, Alternative Mus., N.Y.C., 1981, Laguna Beach Mus. (Calif.), 1982, Los Angeles Inst. Contemporary Art, 1982, Mus. Contemporary Art, Chgo., 1983, Mint Mus., Charlotte, N.C., 1983, DeCordova and Dana Mus. and Park, Lincoln, Mass., 1983, Equitable Gallery, N.Y.C., 1984, Los Angeles Municipal Art Gallery, 1984, 1985, Cirrus, Los Angeles, 1986; represented in permanent collections, Whitney Mus. Am. Art, N.Y.C., Mus. Modern Art, N.Y.C., Los Angeles County Mus. Art, Atlantic Richfield Co. Corp. Art Coll., Grunwald Ctr. Graphic Arts UCLA, City of Los Angeles, Metromedia, Inc., Los Angeles, San Diego Jewish Community Center, Berkeley (Calif.) U. Mus., Home Savs. & Loan Assn., Los Angeles, also pvt. collections. Bd. dirs. Images & Issues, 1980—; mem. artists adv. bd. Los Angeles Mcpl. Art Gallery Assn., 1983—. Recipient UCLA Art Council award, 1963, Disting. Prof. award Calif. State U. Northridge, 1984, Exceptional Merit Service award Calif. State U. Northridge, 1984; Nat. Endowment Arts fellow, 1972; awards in Visual Arts, 1983; Guggenheim fellow, 1983. Mem. Los Angeles Inst. Comtemporary Art (co-founder 1972). Home: PO Box 3353 Chatsworth CA 91313-3353 Office: Calif State U Northridge 18111 Nordhoff St Northridge CA 91330

HARDER, ELSIE RUTH, technical information specialist; b. Knippa, Tex., Oct. 28, 1938; d. Alvin Gerhardt and Elsie (Schroeder) Dornbusch; m. Charles Arthur Harder, June 22, 1957; children: Debra Ruth Harder Penny, Coleen Marie, Charles Arthur Jr. AA in Library Tech., Chabot Coll., 1977; BA in English, Calif. State U., Hayward, 1986. Librarian Lawrence Livermore (Calif.) Nat. Lab, 1977—. Lutheran. Avocation: thimble collecting.

HARDER, VIRGIL EUGENE, educator; b. Ness City, Kans., July 19, 1923; s. Walter J. and Fern B. (Pausch) H.; m. Dona Maurine Dobson, Feb. 4, 1951; children—Christine Elaine, Donald Walter. B.S., U. Iowa, 1950, M.A., 1950; Ph.D., U. Ill., 1958. Instr. bus. adminstrn. U. Ill., Urbana, 1950-55; asst. prof. U. Wash., Seattle, 1955-59, assoc. prof., 1959-67, prof., 1967-86, prof. emeritus, 1986—, asso. dean sch. bus. adminstrn., 1966-74; dir. Inst. Fin. Edn. Sch. for Exec. Devel., Seattle, 1974-83. Served with AUS, 1943-45. Fellow Am. Bus. Communications Assn. (pres. 1965). Club: Trail Blazers. Home: 6025 50th Ave NE Seattle WA 98115 Office: Sch Bus Adminstrn U Wash Seattle WA 98195

HARDIN, RALPH ARTHUR, fireman, city official; b. Los Angeles, Feb. 22, 1930; s. Ralph Edward and Ruth Leota (Weidman) H.; m. Sarah McGrew (Schmertz), Mar. 1960 (div. Aug. 1963); m. Patsy Nell Griffin, Jan. 19, 1966; children—Michael, Mitchell, Mark. B.A. in Pub. Adminstrn., Calif. State U., 1971. Firefighter to bn. chief West Covina Fire Dept., Calif., 1954-71; fire chief Hawthorne Fire Dept., Calif., 1971—; adv. to fire marshall Calif. State Bd. Fire Services, Sacramento, 1980-85. Bd. dirs. South Bay dist. ARC, San Pedro, Calif., 1980—. Served to sgt. U.S. Army, 1950-52, Korea. Mem. Calif. Fire Chiefs Assn. (dir. 1977—); Western Fire Chiefs Assn. (state v.p. 1980-85). Republican. Presbyterian. Lodges: Elks, Kiwanis (dir. Hawthorne club 1979—). Home: 2122 W 183d St Torrance CA 90504 Office: Hawthorne Fire Dept 4475 El Segundo Blvd Hawthorne CA 90250

HARDING, MARK MAYENS, materials engineer; b. Portland, Oreg., Mar. 11, 1947; s. Herbert Claggett and Vera Imogene (Mayens) H.; m. Janis Kay Pruitt, Nov. 1, 1974; children: Richard L. Johnson, Bill E. Johnson, Richelle L. Johnson. BS, Portland State U., 1970. Electron gun mgf. mgr. Tektronix, Inc., Beaverton, Oreg., 1972-75, cathode mgf. mgr., 1975-76, assembly test mgr., 1977-82, bus. unit prodn. mgr., 1982-84, MRP project mgr., 1984-85, mfg. site mgr., 1985-86; mgr. Advanced Microelectronics Lab., Hillsboro, Oreg., 1986—. Mem. Am. Soc. Quality Control, Robotics Internat. Soc. Mfg. Engrs. (sr.), Machine Vision Assn. Soc. Mfg. Engrs. (charter), Naval Inst. Republican. Lutheran. Home: 23055 Johnson Ct Hillsboro OR 97123 Office: Lab Instruments div Tektronix Inc PO Box 500 Del: 64-000 Beaverton OR 97077

HARDING, RICHARD SWICK, engineering executive; b. San Antonio, May 27, 1923; s. Robert J. and Louise (Swick) H.; m. Victoria Banning, Sept. 11, 1947 (div. Sept. 1972); children: Robert B., Victoria Grier, Richard S. Jr., Karen Louise; m. Louise McIntyre, Sept. 23, 1972. BSCE, U. Tex., 1950. Registered profl. engr., Calif., Tex., Nev., Oreg., Alaska, Hawaii, Guam. Project engr. Dames & Moore, San Francisco, 1951-55; v.p. Merwin-Harding Inc., San Francisco, 1955-57; pres., founder Harding-Lawson Assocs., Novato, Calif., 1957—. Bd. dirs. Redevel. Agy. Marin County, Calif., 1968-74; commr. Human Rights Commn., Marin County, 1965-73. Served to sgt. U.S. Army, 1943-46, ETO, 1950-51, Korea. Mem. ASCE, Cons. Engrs. Assn. Calif. (bd. dirs. 1965-68), Structural Engrs. Assn. Calif., Tau Beta Pi, Chi Epsilon. Republican. Episcopalian. Clubs: Silverado Country (Napa, Calif.) (bd. dirs. 1983-86); Engineers (San Francisco). Avocations: golfing, hiking, mountaineering. Home: 142 Milliken Creek Dr Napa CA 94558 Office: Harding Lawson Assocs 7655 Redwood Blvd Novato CA 94948

HARDING, ROBERT WILLIAM, economics educator; b. Columbus, Ohio, Dec. 24, 1947; s. Robert Baselt and Dorothy Elaine (Brown) H.; m. Cielo Violante Fajardo, Oct. 6, 1974; 1 child Michael. A.B., Stanford U., 1970; M.A., UCLA, 1980. Instr. Calif. State U., Northridge, Calif., dept. econs., 1981—. Served to lt., USN, 1971-78, to comdr. USNR, 1978—. Mem. Phi Beta Kappa. Democrat. Club: Nat. Rifle Assn.

HARDING, WAYNE EDWARD, III, accountant; b. Topeka, Sept. 29, 1954; s. Wayne Edward and Nancy M. (Gean) H.; B.S. with honors in Bus. Adminstrn., U. Denver, 1976, M.B.A., 1983; m. Janet Mary O'Shaughnessy, Sept. 5, 1979 (div. Mar. 1985). Partner, HKG Assos., Denver, 1976-77; staff auditor Peat, Marwick, Mitchell & Co., Denver, 1976-78; auditor Marshall Hornstein, P.C., Wheat Ridge, Colo., 1978-79; sr. auditor Touche Ross & Co., Denver, 1979-80; controller Mortgage Plus Inc., 1980-81; sec.-treas. Sunlight Systems Energy Corp., 1980-81; partner Harding, Newman, Sobule & Thrush, Ltd., Denver, 1981-82; pvt. practice acctg. specializing in multifamily real estate and acctg. systems, venture capital, 1982—; dir. Harding Transp., Harding Tech. Leasing, Crown Parking Products. Class agt., mem. alumni council Phillips Exeter Acad., Exeter, N.H., 1973-83; bd. dirs., treas. Legal Center for Handicapped Citizens, Denver, 1979-80; vol. Denver Bridge, 1984-85. Mem. Am. Inst. CPA's, Colo. Soc. CPA's, Beta Alpha Psi, Pi Gamma Mu, Beta Gamma Sigma. Republican. Contbr. articles in field of real estate to profl. jours. including Jour. Acctg. on Micro Computers. Home: 6029 S Kenton Way Englewood CO 80111 Office: 6000 E Evans Penthouse Suite 1-425 Denver CO 80222

HARDS, ROBERT GEORGE, biochemist; b. Winnipeg, Manitoba, Can., July 5, 1954; came to U.S., 1983; s. George Sidney Thomas and Ethel Maria (Harju) H.; m. Ann Charlotte Lenich, Oct. 26, 1985. BS (with honors), U. Manitoba, Can., 1977; PhD, U. Manitoba, 1983. Postdoctoral fellow B.F. Stoninsky Research Labs., Denver, 1983; postdoctoral fellow Eleanor Roosevelt Inst., Denver, 1983-86, jr. fellow, 1987—. Scholar Nat. Downs Syndrome Soc., 1985; NATO fellow Natural Sci. Research Council of Can., 1983; fellow Natural Scis. and Engring. Research Council of Can., 1977. Mem. Can. Soc. Cell Biology, AAAS, Sigma Xi. Office: Eleanor Roosevelt Inst 1899 Gaylord St Denver CO 80206

HARDWICKE, SUSAN BOHANNON, industrial and organizational psychologist, consultant; b. Richmond, Va., Jan. 8, 1953; d. David Warren and Evelyn Mae (Sipp) H.; m. Leonard Lee Wouters, July 18, 1981. B.A., U. Va., 1973; M.Ph., George Washington U., 1982, Ph.D., 1983. Interior designer, W & J Sloane, Washington, 1973-75, Hardwicke Interiors, Arlington, Va., 1976-78; grad. teaching asst. George Washington U., Washington, 1979-81; personnel research psychologist U.S. Office Personnel Mgmt., Washington, 1980-81; project mgr., sr. scientist Rehab Group, Inc., San Diego, 1982-84; sr. analyst Logicon, Inc., San Diego, 1984—, tech. contract mgr., 1986—; lectr. in psychology George Washington U., 1982. Contbr. articles to profl. publs. Active Country Friends, No. San Diego County; sr. warden St. Peter's Episcopal Ch., Del Mar, Calif. Mem. Am. Psychol. Assn., U. Va. Alumni Assn., Phi Beta Kappa. Republican. Club: U. Va. Alumni Club of San Diego (pres. 1983-85). Home: 668 Marsolan Ave Solana Beach CA 92075 Office: Logicon Inc 4010 Sorrento Valley Blvd PO Box 85158 San Diego CA 92138

HARDY, ALICE JOAN, postal service official; b. Corvallis Oreg., Mar. 20, 1949; d. John Pickett and Mary Lorine (Barnes) Williams; m. Michael Hardy, Oct. 11, 1967 (div. Feb. 1984); children—Taraleen Annette, Shawn Michael. Clk. substitute U.S Postal Service, Chgo., 1970; part-time clk, postmaster replacement, Tangent, Oreg., 1973-75, rural letter carrier, Tangent, 1975—; mem. women's adv. bd. Salem Post Office, 1982-83. Leader Girl Scouts U.S.A. Troop 209, Corvallis, Oreg., 1981-84; mem. adv. bd. gifted student program Corvallis Sch. Bd., 1981-83. Mem. Oreg. Rural Letter Carrier Assn. (Dist. 7, pres. 1982-85, state bd. dirs. 1983-86, 1st v.p. 1986—, nat. conv. del. 1984-86). Republican. Baptist. Home: 1825 NE Noble Ave Corvallis OR 97330 Office: Main Post Office Tangent OR 97389

HARDY, BEN (BENSON B.), orchid nursery executive; b. Oakland, Calif., Nov. 22, 1920; s. Lester William and Irene Isabell (Bliss) H.; student pub. schs., Oakland, Calif., Concord, Calif.; grad. photo Intelligence Sch., Denver, 1949. Served as enlisted man U.S. Navy, 1942-48; joined USAF, 1948, advanced through grades to capt., 1957; with 67th Reconnaisance Squadron, Korea, 1951-52, Hdqrs. Squadron, Thule AFB, 1956, resigned, 1957; material requirements analyst-coordinator Teledyne Ryan Aero. Co., San Diego, 1958-73, 83-87; dispatcher-coordinator Cubic Western Data Co., San Diego, 1977-80; owner-partner orchid nursery. Pres. San Diego County Orchid Soc., 1972-73, 75-76, Exotic Plant Soc., 1976-78, 81-84, San Diego Gesneriad Soc., 1978; dir. 23d Western Orchid Congress, 1979. Decorated Bronze Star; recipient Letter of Commendation NASA, also others. Mem. Am. Orchid Soc., N.Z. Orchid Soc., Orchid Soc. SE Asia, Pacific Orchid Soc. Hawaii, Hoya Soc. Internat. (pres. 1981-83), Mexicana de Orquideologia, Sociedad Colombiana de Orquideologia, Cymbidium Soc. Am., Orchid Digest Corp. Contbr. articles to orchid jours.; pub. Western Gesneriad Gazette, 1978-79. Home: 9443 E Heaney Circle Santee CA 92071

HARDY, DUANE HORACE, federal agency administrator, educator; b. Ogden, Utah, June 8, 1931; s. Willis and Julia Mary (Garder) H.; m. Janet Myrnel Slater, Aug. 3, 1951; children: Rochelle Anne Leishman, Leslie Kaye Woolston, Kathy Korinne Davis. AA, Weber State Coll., 1951. Cert. EEO investigator. Enlisted U.S. Army, 1951, advanced through grades to lt. col., 1967, ret., 1971; EEO investigator U.S. Postal Service, San Bruno, Calif., 1978—, EEO instr., 1982—. Mem. EEO civic council, Salt Lake City, 1978—. Republican. Mormon. Lodge: Kiwanis. Avocations: watch, clock and jewelry making, engraving. Home: 120 W 5200 S Ogden UT 84405 Office: US Postal Service 3680 Pacific Ave Ogden UT 84401

HARDY, FRANK MCNAIRY, psychiatrist; b. Yakima, Wash., Nov. 20, 1920; s. Frank McNairy and Inez Opal (Frye) H.; m. Doris Arlene Haworth, May 31, 1942 (div. 1970); children—John McNairy, Katherine Marie; m. Mary Elizabeth Astle, Apr. 20, 1970. B.S., U. Oreg., 1945; M.D., George Washington U., 1945. Gen. practice medicine, Yakima, 1948-50, 1951-59; resident in psychiatry U. Wash., 1959-62; practice medicine specializing in psychiatry, 1962—. Served to capt. USAF, 1946-48, 1950-51. Mem. Yakima County Med. Soc., Wash. State Med. Assn., No. Pacific Soc. Neurology and Psychiatry, Am. Psychiat. Assn., Nat. Rifleman's Assn. Lodge: Elks. Home: 802 S 22nd Ave Yakima WA 98902 Office: 412 S 12th Ave Yakima WA 98902

HARDY, JOEL ALLEN, microbiologist, educator; b. Los Angeles, Dec. 1, 1952; s. Allen Williams and Ina Carolyn (Cobia) H.; B.S., Weber State Coll., 1977; M.S., Idaho State U., 1979; m. Vicki Lynn Nickens, Dec. 20, 1974; children—Thomas Joel, Lucas Allen, Janna Marie, Jonica Anne. Chemist, Firestone Tire & Rubber Co., Salinas, Calif., 1980; instr. microbiology and chemistry Hartnell Coll., Salinas, 1980-82; microbiologist Internat. Shellfish Enterprises, Moss Landing, Calif., 1980-82; research specialist U. Utah Sch. Medicine, Salt Lake City, 1982-84, Gull Labs, Salt Lake City, 1984—. Idaho State U. research grantee, 1979. Mem. AAAS, Am. Soc. for Microbiology, Sigma Xi. Republican. Mormon. Home: 78 W 2550 S Bountiful UT 84010 Office: Gull Labs 1011 E 4800 S Salt Lake City UT 84117

HARDY, WILLIAM EVERETT, III, hospital social services director; b. Cheyenne, Wyo., Aug. 6, 1949; s. William E. Jr. and Mary (Brueggemann) H., m. Toni Rae Horton, Sept. 28, 1975; children: Dylan, Anja, Paul. BS in Psychology, U. Wyo., 1975; MA in Sociology, Fordham U., 1980. Cert. addiction specialist. probation and parole agt. State of Wyo., Lander, 1975-83; dir. community social services Pine Ridge and Lander Valley hosps., Lander, 1984—; bd. dirs. Bishop Randall House, Lander. Bd. dirs. Wyo. Wilderness Corp.; co-founder Fremont County Group Homes, Wyo., 1976, co-founder State of Wyo. Wilderness Experience Program for Troubled Youth, 1979; supr. Sr. Companion Program, Lander, 1985—. Served with USN, 1970-72. Mem. Clin. Sociology Assn., Am. Sociol. Soc., Nat. Assn. Social Workers, Wyo. Assn. Addiction Specialists. Avocations: backpacking, carpentry, cross country skiing, canoeing. Home: 636 Cliff St Lander WY 82520 Office: Pine Ridge Hosp 150 Wyoming St Lander WY 82520

HARDYCK, CURTIS DALE, psychology and education professor; b. Mitchell, S.D., July 5, 1929; s. Henry Bernard and Helen (Ensminger) H.; 1 child, Allyn Henry. AB, U. Calif., Berkeley, 1952, PhD, 1960. Asst. prof. psychology U. Calif., San Francisco, 1960-67; from assoc. prof. to prof. U. Calif., Berkeley, 1968—. Author: Introduction to Statistics for the Behavioral Sciences, 1969, Understanding Research in the Social Sciences, 1975; contbr. numerous articles to profl. jours. Recipient Career Dev. award Nat. Inst. Child Health, 1968-72. Mem. AAAS, Internat. Neuropsychology. Office: U Calif Sch Edn Tolman Hall Berkeley CA 94720

HARE, JAMES ALAN, aerospace engineer; b. Sioux Falls, Idaho, Jan. 10, 1961; s. William James and Arlone Delores (Christman) H.; m. Katherine Lynn Miller, June 22, 1985. BS in Aero. Engring., U. Colo., 1983. Engr. Martin Marietta Aerospace, Denver, 1984-85, El Segundo, Calif., 1985—. Mem. AIAA, Am. Astronautical Soc., Soc. Automotive Engrs. (sec. 1985—), Sigma Gamma Tau. Republican. Avocation: tae kwon do. Office: Martin Marietta Aerospace 185 S Douglas El Segundo CA 90245

HARGETT, LOUIE THOMAS, agricultural chemistry corporation executive, entomologist; b. Wilmington, N.C., Oct. 19, 1932; s. Louie Fulton and Catherine Cordelia (Thomas) H.; m. Anna Catherine Hazel, June 26, 1954; children—Cheryl Ann, Robert Thomas, Catherine Lynn. B.A., Bridgewater (Va.) Coll., 1953; M.S., Va. Poly. Inst., 1958; Ph.D., Oreg. State U., 1962; A.M.P., Harvard Bus. Sch., 1976. Cert. profl. entomologist. Mem. faculty dept. entomology Va. Poly. Inst., Blacksburg, 1955-58, Oreg. State U., Corvallis, 1958-60; dir. field devel., asst. to v.p. mktg. Geigy, Inc., N.Y.C., 1961-70; dir. devel., gen. mgr. Rhodia, Inc., Monmouth Junction, N.J., 1970-77; asst. to pres. Environ. Research and Tech., Concord, Mass., 1977-78; dir. research, devel. crop protection Sandoz, Inc., San Diego, 1979-84; dir. product devel. Zoecon Corp. div. Sandoz Co., Palo Alto, 1984-86, dir. product devel. Sandoz Crop Protection, 1986—. Served with AUS, 1953-55. NIH fellow, 1960-61. Mem. Am. Inst. Biologists, Entomology Soc. Am., Weed Sci. Soc. Am., Sigma Xi. Republican. Protestant.

HARING, JOSEPH EMERICK, economist; b. Mansfield, Ohio, July 19, 1931; s. Joseph and Kathryn (Woerner) H.; m. Loreen Carolyn Stuber, June 2, 1956; children—Crystal Janine, Arianne Denise, Elisa Jo, Peter Joseph. B.S., Ohio State U., 1952; Ph.D., Columbia U., 1959. Instr. econs. Columbia U., 1958-59; mem. faculty Occidental Coll., Los Angeles, 1959-77, Richard W. Millar prof. econs. and fin., 1965-77, chmn. dept. econs., 1962-73; econ. planning mgr. Gen. Telephone Co. Calif., Thousand Oaks, 1977-80, planning systems dir., 1980-87; Brookings Nat. research prof. econs. S.E. Asia, 1961-62; vis. prof. econs. U. So. Calif., 1964-66, UCLA, 1965, U. Vienna (Austria), 1974, U. Munich (W.Ger.), 1974-75; cons. Govt. Thailand, 1963-64; mem. steering com. So. Calif. Research Council, 1959-73; pres. Pasadena Research Inst., 1959—; moderator TV series Inside Business, 1970. mem. Calif. State Adv. Com. on Sch. Dist. Budgeting and Fin., 1967-71; pres. Econ. Literacy Council Calif., 1982-86; bd. dirs. Calif. State Univ. Found., 1984—; mem. Calif. Mining and Geology Bd., 1971-74. Author: Utility Regulation During Inflation, 1970; The New Economics of Regulated Industries, 1968; Urban and Regional Economics, 1972. Assoc. editor: Jour. Fin. and Quantitative Analysis, 1965-68; Contbr. articles to profl. jours. Served with U.S. Army, 1953-55. Mem. Planning Execs. Inst., N.Am. Soc. Corp. Planners, Am. Econs. Assn., Western Econ. Assn., So. Calif. Econ. Assn. (past pres.), Western Fin. Assn. Econometric Soc., Regional Sci. Assn., So. Calif. Acad. Scis. (editorial bd.), Lambda Alpha. Office: 607 Laguna Rd Pasadena CA 91105

HARLAN, JAMES HERBERT, medical librarian; b. Indpls., Mar. 18, 1934; s. Fay Herbert and Daisy Edith (Risk) H.; m. Marian Audrey Cummins, July 11, 1972; children—Ardis Lorraine, Albert Warren. B.A., UCLA, 1957; M.S., U. So. Calif., 1959. Librarian Met. State Hosp., Norwalk, Calif., 1959-60; chief librarian Jefferson Twp. Pub. Library, Ind., 1961-62; tech. documents cataloguer Aerospace Corp., El Segundo, Calif., 1962-64; field Librarian U.S. Air Force, Korea, 1964-65, br. librarian, Tokyo, 1965-66, chief librarian, Korea, 1966-67; supr. catalog librarian TRW Systems Group, Redondo Beach, Calif., 1967-68; tech. info. spec. III Lawrence Radiation Lab, Livermore, Calif., 1968-69; base librarian U.S. Air Force, Thailand, 1969-71; dir. library services San Pedro Peninsula Hosp., Calif., 1973—. Bd. dirs. Community Chest, Jeffersonville, Ind., 1961. Mem. Med. Library Assn. (scholar 1959), Am. Soc. of Indexers, Nat. Mgmt. Assn. (chpt. sec. 1981-82), Med. Library Group of So. Calif. and Ariz. Office: Med Library San Pedro Peninsula Hosp 1300 W 7th St San Pedro CA 90732

HARLAN, KATHLEEN T. (KAY), business consultant, professional speaker and seminar leader; b. Bremerton, Wash., June 9, 1934; d. Floyd K. and Rosemary (Parkhurst) Troy; m. John L. Harlan, Feb. 16, 1952 (div. 1975); m. 2d, Merlin Habig, June 30, 1979; children: Pamela Kay, Kenneth Lynwood, Lianna Sue. Owner, operator Safeguard N.W. Systems, Tacoma, 1969-79; devel., mgr. Poulsbo (Wash.) Profl. Bldg., 1969-75; pres. Greenapple Graphics, Inc., Tacoma, 1976-79; owner, mgr. Iskrem Hus Restaurant, Poulsbo, 1972-75; pres. Bus. Seminars, Tacoma, 1977—; mem. Orgnl. Renewal, Inc., Tacoma, 1978-81; assoc. mem. Effectiveness Resource Group, Inc., Tacoma, 1979-80; pres. New Image Confs., Tacoma, 1979-82; owner, mgr. Safeguard Acctg. and Data Systems, Bremerton, Wash., 1982—, Safeguard by Harlan, Port Angeles, 1982—, Safeguard Computer Ctr., Tacoma, 1982—; owner Total Systems Ctr., Tacoma, 1983—; speaker on mgmt. and survival in small bus. Contbg. author: Here is a Genius!, 1980; author small bus. manuals. Mem. Wash. State Bd. Boundary Rev. for Kitsap County, 1970-76, Selective Service Bd. #19, 1971-76; co-chair Wash. State Small Bus. Improvement Council, 1986 apptd. sec. by gov., 1987; del. to White House Conf. on Small Bus., 1986; chair Wash. State Conf. on Small Bus., 1987. Recipient Nellie Cashman award; named Woman Entrepreneur of Yr. for Wash. State, 1986, 87. Mem. Nat. Speakers Assn., Nat. Assn. Female Execs., Better Bus. Bur. (exec. bd.), Tacoma-Pierce County C. of C. (exec. bd. 1985—, chair spl. task force on small bus. for Pierce County, 1986—). Office: Old City Hall Suite 210 625 Commerce St Tacoma WA 98402

HARLAN, NANCY MARGARET, lawyer; b. Santa Monica, Calif., Sept. 10, 1946; d. William Galland and Betty M. (Miles) Plett; B.S. magna cum laude, Calif. State U., Hayward, 1972; J.D., U. Calif., Berkeley, 1975; m. John Hammack, Dec. 1, 1979; children—Laryssa Maria Rebello, Leea Elyce Harlan. Admitted to Calif. bar, 1975, Fed. bar, U.S. Dist. Ct. for Central Dist., 9th Circuit, 1976; assoc. firm Poindexter & Doutré, Los Angeles, 1975-80; residential counsel Coldwell Banker Residential Brokerage Co., Fountain Valley, Calif., 1980-81; sr. counsel for real estate subs. law dept. Pacific Lighting Corp., Santa Ana, Calif., 1981—. Exec. v.p. student body U. Calif., Berkeley, 1974-75; bd. dirs. La Casa. Mem. State Bar Calif., Am. Bar Assn., Los Angeles County Bar Assn., Orange County Bar Assn. (dir. corp. counsel sect. 1982—), Calif. Women Lawyers Assn., Orange County Women Lawyers Assn., Los Angeles Women Lawyers Assn., Nat. Assn. Female Execs., Bus. and Profl. Women. Office: Pacific Lighting Corp 48 Brookhollow Dr Santa Ana CA 92705

HARLAN, NEIL EUGENE, consumer products company executive; b. Cherry Valley, Ark., June 2, 1921; s. William and Mary Nina (Ellis) H.; m. Martha Almlov, Sept. 27, 1952; children: Lindsey Beth, Neil Eugene, Sarah Ellis. Student, U. Edinburgh, Scotland, 1946; B.S., U. Ark., 1947, LL.D., 1969; M.B.A., Harvard U., 1950, D.B.A., 1956. Mem. faculty Grad. Sch. Bus. Adminstrn. Harvard, 1951-62, asst. prof., 1954-58, assoc. prof., 1958-61, prof., 1962; asst. sec. Air Force Washington, 1962-64; v.p., chief fin. officer, dir. Anderson, Clayton & Co., 1964-66, exec. v.p., 1966-67; dir. McKinsey & Co., Inc., 1967-74; with McKesson Corp., San Francisco, 1974—, chmn., 1979—, chief exec. officer, 1984-86, also dir.; chief exec. officer 1984-86; dir. U.S. Leasing Internat., Inc. Author: Management Control in Air Frame Subcontracting, 1956, (with R.H. Hassler) Cases in Controllership, 1958, (with R.F. Vancil) Cases in Accounting Policy, 1961, (with Christenson and Vancil) Managerial Economics, 1962. Trustee San Francisco Ballet, World Affairs Council; bd. dirs. Bay Area Council, Nat. Park Found.; bd. govs. San Francisco Symphony; mem. Calif. Com. on Campaign Fin., Calif. Roundtable San Francisco Bay Area Leadership Task Force; mem. nat. adv. com. YMCA. Sch. Served with AUS, 1943-46. Mem.

Am. Inst. CPA's, Conf. Bd., San Francisco C. of C. (bd. dirs., trustee). Clubs: Congressional Country (Bethesda, Md.); Webhannet Golf, Edgecomb Tennis (Kennebunk Beach, Maine); Bankers, Bohemian, Pacific Union (San Francisco); Menlo Country (Woodside, Calif.); Links (N.Y.C.). Home: 1170 Sacramento St #13 D San Francisco CA 94108 Office: McKesson Corp Crocker Plaza One Post St San Francisco CA 94104

HARLAN, RIDGE LATIMER, corporate executive; b. Pilot Grove, Mo., Feb. 25, 1917; s. George B. and Dale (Latimer) H.; m. Barbara Hawley, Oct. 7, 1939 (div.); children: Brooke, Holly Ann, Robert Ridge; m. Marjory Folinsbee, June 4, 1976. BJ, U. Mo., 1939; postgrad. Harvard, 1943, Colo. U., 1945-46, Stanford U. Grad. Sch. Bus., 1965. Pres. Barnes-Hind Pharms., Inc., 1972-76; prin. Harlan & Clucas, Inc., San Francisco, 1968—; pres. Charila Found., 1969-73; chmn. bd., pres. Flores de las Americas, 1979-81; chmn. Millenium Systems, Inc., 1978-82; pres. Velo-Bind, Inc., 1983-85, chmn., chief exec. officer 1985-87, chmn. 1987—, also dir.; dir. Impulflor de Mexico, Velo-Bind Inc. Served to lt. (j.g.) USNR, 1943-46. Mem. Nat. Investor Relations Inst. (dir.), Assn. Corp. Growth (dir.), Alpha Delta Sigma, Kappa Tau Alpha. Clubs: Olympic, Family (San Francisco). Home: 839 Seabury Rd Hillsborough CA 94010 Office: 650 Almanor Ave Sunnyvale CA 94086

HARLETT, JOHN CHARLES, marine geologist; b. Tiffin, Ohio, Apr. 7, 1936; s. Alphonse Henry and Edna (Geiermann) H.; m. Therese Marie Huddleston, Nov. 28, 1963; children: Maria, Jennifer, Sarah. BS, Ohio State U., 1960; MS, Navy Postgrad. Sch., 1967; PhD, Oreg. State U., 1971. Commd. USN, 1960, advanced through grades to capt., 1982, ret., 1984; asst. dir. programs Applied Physics Lab. U. Wash., Seattle, 1984—. Contbr. articles to profl. jours. Mem. Am. Geophys. Union, Naval Inst., Sigma Xi. Avocation: sailing. Office: U Wash Applied Physics Lab 1013 NE 40th St Seattle WA 98105

HARLEY, ROBISON DOOLING, JR., lawyer, educator; b. Ancon, Panama, July 6, 1946; s. Robison Dooling and Loyde Hazel (Gochenauer) H.; m. Suzanne Purviance Bendel, Aug. 9, 1975; children—Arianne Erin, Lauren Loyde. B.A., Brown U., 1968; J.D., Temple U., 1971; LL.M., U. San Diego, 1985. Bar: Pa. 1972, U.S. Ct. Mil. Appeals 1972, Calif. 1976, N.J. 1978, U.S. Supreme Ct. 1980, D.C. 1981, U.S. Dist. Ct. N.J., U.S. Dist. Ct. (cen. and so. dists.) Calif., U.S. Ct. Appeals (9th cir.) 1982. Cert. criminal law specialist Calif. Bd. Legal Specialization; cert. criminal trial adv. Nat. Bd. Trial Advocacy. Asst. agy. dir. Safeco Title Ins. Co., Los Angeles, 1975-77; ptnr. Cohen, Stokke & Davis, Santa Ana, Calif., 1977-85; sole practice, Santa Ana, Calif., 1985—; instr. Orange County Coll. Trial Advocacy, paralegal program U. Calif.; judge pro-tem Orange County Cts. Bd. dirs. Orange County Legal Aid Soc. Served to lt. col. JAGC, USMCR, 1971—; trial counsel, def. counsel, mil. judge, asst. staff judge adv. USMC, 1971-75, asst. regional def. counsel Western Region, 1986—. Mem. Orange County Bar Assn. (judiciary com., criminal law sect., adminstrn. of justice com.), Orange County Trial Lawyers Assn., Calif. Trial Lawyers Assn., Assn. Trial Lawyers Am., Calif. Attys. for Criminal Justice, Calif. Pub. Defenders Assn., Nat. Assn. for Criminal Def. Attys., Assn. Specialized Criminal Def. Advs., Orange County Criminal Lawyers Assn. (found. com.), Res. Officers Assn., Marine Corps Reserve Officers Assn. Republican. Home: 12 Bayberry Way Irvine CA 92715 Office: 825 N Ross St Santa Ana CA 92701

HARMAN, WARD ALLEN, scientist; b. Seattle, July 3, 1922; s. Fred Dean and Marguerite Frances (Dresser) H.; m. Cleona May Opgrand, Aug. 7, 1949; children: Sharon, Lynda, Fredric. BSEE magna cum laude, U. Wash. 1946; MSEE, Stanford U., 1948, PhD in Elec. Engring., 1954. Research assoc. N.Am. Aviation, Downey, Calif., 1948-50, Stanford U., Palo Alto, Calif., 1953-55; tech. staff mem. Gen. Electric, Palo Alto, 1955-65; sr. scientist VARIAN, Palo Alto, 1965-75, Hughes Aircraft, Co., Torrance, Calif., 1975—. Patentee in field. Served with U.S. Army, 1943-46. Mem. IEEE (chmn. IEDM subcom. on electron tubes 1979), Sigma Xi, Tau Beta Pi. Democrat. Lutheran. Avocations: music, amateur astronomy, horseshoe pitching. Home: 3748 Coolheights Dr Rancho Palos Verdes CA 90274 Office: Hughes Aircraft Co 3100 W Lomita Blvd Torrance CA 90509

HARMAN, WILLIS W(ALTER), research laboratory administrator; b. Seattle, Aug. 16, 1918; s. Fred Dean and Marguerite Frances (Dresser) H.; m. Charlene Cary Reamer, July 20, 1941; children: Charlene Cecelia, Mary Elizabeth, Susan Lorraine, Walter Dean. BSEE, U. Wash., 1939; MS in Physics, PhDEE, Stanford U., 1948. Assoc. prof. elec. engring. U. Fla., Gainesville, 1949-52; prof. Stanford (Calif.) U., 1952-66, prof. engring. and econ. systems, 1966—; sr. social scientist SRI Internat., Menlo Park, Calif. 1967-84; pres. Inst. Noetic Scis., Sausalito, Calif., 1978—. Author: An Incomplete Guide to the Future, 1979; co-author: Changing Images of Mind, 1980, Higher Creativity, 1984. Bd. Regents U. Calif., Berkeley, 1980—. Served to lt. comdr. USN, 1941-45, PTO. Home: 831 Santa Fe Ave Stanford CA 94305 Office: Inst Noetic Scis 475 Gate Five Rd #300 Sausalito CA 94965

HARMON, BARBARA NELLE, controller; b. Marion, Ohio, Oct. 25, 1944; d. Charles Debusman and Marjory June (Potter) H.; m. James Nash, Dec. 27, 1974 (div. Dec. 1977). BA, Lake Erie Coll., 1966; MS in Acctg., Colo. State U., 1980. CPA. Sr. acct. Touche Ross & Co., Denver, 1980-84; fin. analyst Ideal Basic Industry, Denver, 1984-85; supr. acctg. and control Stearns Catalytic, Denver, 1985-86; from asst. controller to controller Wood Bros. Homes subs. MDC Holdings, Denver, 1986—; controller MDC Land Co. and MDC Constrn. Co., Denver, 1986. Mem. Am Inst. CPA's, Colo. Soc. CPA's, Beta Alpha Psi (acctg. chpt.). Democrat.

HARNER, ROBERT EDWARD, safety consultant; b. Taneytown, Md., Nov. 12, 1933; s. George Lamar and Esther Catherine (Ibach) H.; m. B. Lemee Robbins, May 30, 1959; children: Rebecca, Lamar, Scott, Douglas. BS in Indsl. Tech., S.E. La. U., 1960. Cert. safety profl.; registered profl. engr., Calif. Sr. engring. cons. Travelers Ins. Co., Hartford, Conn., 1961-81; safety dir. Gulf Mineral Resources, Denver, 1981-83; pvt. practice safety cons. Littleton, Colo., 1983—; guest lectr. Colo. Sch. Mines, Golden, Colo., 1976-80. Contbr. articles to profl. jours. Mem. Am Soc. Safety Engrs., Systems Safety Soc., Nat. Safety Council, Human Factors Soc. Republican. Lutheran. Home and Office: 2892 E Geddes Pl Littleton CO 80122

HARNSBERGER, THERESE COSCARELLI (MRS. FREDERICK OWEN HARNSBERGER), librarian; b. Muskegon, Mich.; d. Charles and Julia (Borrell) Coscarelli; B.A. cum laude, Marymount Coll., 1952; M.L.S., U. So. Calif., 1953; postgrad. Rosary Coll., River Forest, Ill., 1955-56, UCLA Extension, 1960-61; m. Frederick Owen Harnsberger, Dec. 24, 1962; 1 son, Lindsey Carleton. Free-lance writer, 1950—; librarian San Marino (Calif.) High Sch., 1953-56; cataloger, cons. San Marino Hall, South Pasadena, Calif., 1956-61; librarian Los Angeles State Coll., 1956-59; librarian dist. library Covina-Valley Unified Sch. Dist., Covina, Calif., 1959-67; librarian Los Angeles Trade Tech. Coll., part-time 1972—; Pasadena City Coll. Library, 1973—; librarian, evening instr. East Los Angeles Coll., 1970—; tumor registrar, med. librarian Alhambra Community Hosp., 1975-79; med. library cons., 1978—; pres. Research Unltd., 1980—; freelance reporter L.A.'s Best Bargains Newsletter, 1981—. Chmn. spiritual values com. Covina Coordinating Council, 1964-66; telephone chmn. Fremont Sch. PTA, Alhambra. Mem. Calif. Assn. Sch. Librarians (chmn. legis. com.), Covina Tchrs. Assn., Book Publicists of So. Calif., AAUW (historian 1972-73), U. So. Calif. Grad. Sch. Library Sci. (life), Nat. Tumor Registrars Assn., So. Calif. Med. Library Group (jobs com. 1972—), LWV, Am. Nutrition Soc. (chpt. Newsletter chmn.), Calif. State Poetry Soc., Pi Lambda Theta. Author poetry. Office: 2809 W Hellman Ave Alhambra CA 91803

HARPER, DONALD JACQUES, holding company executive; b. Knoxville, Tenn., June 30, 1928; s. Raymond James and Pauline Jean (Huffstutler) H.; m. Jayne C. Combs; children—Nancy Lynn (Mrs. Norman Mehl), Danial Ray, Larry F., Lenny G., Lindsay J. Student Wichita (Kans.) State U., 1946-47, Kansas City Coll. Engring., 1948; Indsl. Engr., U. Okla., 1950. Indsl. engr. Coleman Co., Inc., Wichita, 1953-56; agt. Penn Mut. Life Ins. Co., Wichita, 1956-60; gen. agt. Crown Life Ins. Co., Wichita, 1960-62; pres. Fin. Unification Corp., Mark V group of cos., holding co.'s, Scottsdale, Ariz., 1963—. Bd. dirs. Scottsdale Symphony. Served with USNR, 1942-45. Mem. Ariz. Law Soc., Am. Mgmt. Soc., Profl. Consultants. Nat. Soc. Bus. Consultants, Scottsdale C. of C. Home: 5320 E Camelback Rd Phoenix AZ 85018 Office: 6060 E Thomas Scottsdale AZ 85251

HARPER, JAMES CARHART, accounting educator, former army officer; b. Geneva, Ala., July 22, 1924; s. Malcolm Henry and Fannie Pearl (Grimes) H.; m. Barbara Jean Baddley, Aug. 19, 1951 (div. 1977); children—Jane, James Carhart, Robert; m. Raeola Miller, Dec. 17, 1977. B.S., U. Ala., 1947, M.B.A., 1958; Ph.D., U. Utah, 1975. C.P.A., Colo., Utah. Commd. 1st lt. U.S. Army, 1948, advanced through grades to lt. col.; 1964; served as comptroller Ft. Worth Army Depot, 1962-63, chief budget br., asst. chief of staff Hdqrs. U.S. Army, Washington, 1963-66, ret., 1966; assoc. prof. Weber State Coll., Ogden, Utah, 1966-78; assoc. prof. U. Nev.-Las Vegas, 1978-86, chmn. acctg. dept., 1982-84; cons. edn. and experience Utah Assn. C.P.A.s, 1974-75. Author: Education and Experience Requirements for Certified Public Accountants, 1975. Vestry mem. Episcopal Ch. of Good Shepherd, Ogden, 1975-78; troop chmn. Bonneville Council Boy Scouts Am., 1968-69, facilities chmn. Scout-a-Rama, 1969. Served with Aus, 1943-46. Decorated Legion of Merit. Mem. Am. Acctg. Assn., Nat. Assn. Accts. (chpt. v.p. 1980), Internat. Soc. Hospitality Accts., SAR, Pi Kappa Phi, Delta Sigma Pi, Beta Gamma Sigma, Phi Kappa Phi, Beta Alpha Psi. Club: Exchange (Ogden). Lodges: Masons, Shrine. Home: 5020 Pacific Grove Dr Las Vegas NV 89130 Office: Univ Nev Las Vegas Dept Acctg 4505 Maryland Pkwy Las Vegas NV 89154

HARPER, MELINDA MARION, accountant; b. Vancouver, B.C., Can., Nov. 18, 1943; d. David Robert and Sadie Marion (White) Nichols. Student Colo. Women's Coll., 1962, U. Ariz., 1975-76; B.S.B.A., W.Va. U., 1977. C.P.A., Colo., W.Va. Asst. buyer Bon Marche, Seattle, 1965-68; office mgr. K-T Textiles, Denver, 1968-71; asst. to treas. U.S. Natural Resources, Menlo Park, Calif., 1973-74; dir. litigation support services, KMG Main Hurdman, Denver, 1977—. Mem. Am. Inst. C.P.A.s (Sells award 1978), Alliance Profl. Women (co-founder 1984, pres. 1985—), Colo. Soc. C.P.A.s (chmn. litigation support services com. 1985—), Denver Women's Soc. C.P.A.s (founding bd. 1981, treas., bd. dirs. 1981-82), Am. Women's Soc. C.P.A.s, Colo. Optometric Soc. (bd. dirs. 1981-82). Avocations: Reading; travel; investing. Home: 274 Vine St Denver CO 80206 Office: KMG Main Hurdman 1675 Broadway Suite 1800 Denver CO 80202

HARPER, MICHAEL ALLEN, planner, consultant; b. Portland, Oreg., June 13, 1951; s. John Norman and Alice Louise (Holroyd) H.; m. Vickie Jo Latimore, July 25, 1971; children: Paul Michael, Joel David. BA, U. Nev., Reno, 1973, M in Pub. Adminstrn., 1977. Planning cons. community devel. dept. City of South Lake Tahoe, Calif., 1977-78; cons. Reno, 1978-79; forecast analyst Bentley Nev., Minden, 1979; planner Washoe County Dept. Regional Planning, Reno, 1980; asst. dir. Washoe County Dept. Comprehensive Planning, Reno, 1981—; Chmn. State of Nev. Commn. for the Acquisition of Land in the Lake Tahoe Basin, 1986-87. Author: An Introduction to Growth Management, 1977. Mem. community devel. block grant Citizen's Adv. Bd., Reno, 1979-83, adv. planning commn. Tahoe Regional Planning Agy. S. Lake Tahoe, 1982—, chmn. 1982-85. Mem. Am. Planning Assn. (no. Nev. sect. sec. 1985-86, dir. 1986—, Chgo. planning threatened com. 1985—), Am. Soc. Pub. Adminstrn. (bd. dirs. Sierra chpt. 1985—, pres. 1986—), Internat. City Mgmt. Assn. Republican. Mem. United Ch. Christ. Club: University (Reno sec. 1982-83). Avocation: photography. Home: 3040 Oreana Dr Reno NV 89509 Office: Washoe County Dept Comprehensive Planning 241 Ridge St Reno NV 89520

HARPER, SHEILA ROSE, speech and language pathologist; b. Elwood, Ind., Dec. 31, 1943; d. Melvin M. and Dorothy Helen (Blake) Eikenberry; m. William Harold Harper, Mar. 4, 1967; children: Scott William, Andrew Blake. Student, Purdue U., 1965-66; BS in Edn., Ball State U., 1969; MS in Edn., Western Oreg. State Coll., 1985. Speech hearing therapist Blue River Valley Schs., Mt. Summit, Ind., 1969-71, Celina (Ohio) City Schs., 1971-80; speech lang. pathologist Lebanon (Oreg.) Elem. Schs., 1980-85, Salem (Oreg.) Keizer Schs., 1985—. Mem. Am. Speech and Hearing Assn. (cert. clin. competency-speech pathology), Oreg. Edn. Assn., NEA, Salem Edn. Assn. Club: Univ. Women's (Celina). Home: 3588 Dogwood Dr S Salem OR 97302 Office: Salem Keizer Sch Dist 245 4868 Buffalo Dr SE Salem OR 97301

HARPER, WILLIAM HAROLD, architect; b. Kokomo, Ind., Aug. 2, 1947; s. Harold Wilbur and Betty Marjorie (Johnston) H.; m. Sheila Rose Eikenberry, Mar. 4, 1967; children—Scott William, Andrew Blake. B.Arch., Ball State U., 1971. Registered architect Ohio, Ind., Oreg.; cert. Nat. Council Archtl. Registration Bds. Pbr. design Fanning/Howey Assocs., Celina, Ohio, 1971-78; owner William Harper Assocs., Celina, 1978-80; mgr. design constrn. Oreg. Dept. Gen. Services, Salem, 1980—; design cons. Salem Group Architects, Oreg., 1980-83. Player agt. Salem Babe Ruth, 1981-83; coach football, baseball Celina City Recreation, 1975-80; mem. Oreg. Archtl. Barriers Adv. Com., 1985—; mem. drafting and design adv. com. Wright State U., Western Ohio Br. Campus, 1979-80. Recipient 6 AIA/AASA Sch. Design awards, 1972-78. Mem. AIA (assoc. 1968-71), Constrn. Specifications Inst., Oreg. State Mgmt. Assn., Sigma Tau Gamma. Lodge: Rotary (charter mem. Celina 1979-80). Home: 3588 Dogwood Dr S Salem OR 97302 Office: Oreg Dept Gen Services 1225 Ferry St SE Salem OR 97310

HARRIMAN, CHARLES JARVIS, JR., international cultural organization administrator; b. Newport, R.I., Sept. 3, 1922; s. Charles Jarvis and Kathryn (Cocroft) H.; m. Nancy Anne Dole, Dec. 10, 1966. BA, Trinity Coll., 1943. Gen. prodn. mgr. Moral Re-Armament, N.Y.C., 1946-56, staff mem., 1956-68; staff mem. Up With People, Tucson, 1968; exec. dir. Tucson Festival Soc., 1970-86; exec. v.p. Westerners Internat., Tucson, 1973-86, chmn. bd. dirs., 1986—. mem. Tucson Mus. Art, Ariz-Sonora Desert Mus.; bd. dirs. St. Lukes in the Desert, Tucson, 1980-84, Friends of Western Art, 1980—, Tucson Trade Bur., 1980—, Ariz.-Mex. Commn., Phoenix, 1983-86. Served to sgt. Med. Dept., U.S. Army, 1943-46. Mem. Internat. Festivals Assn. (pres. 1984-85, bd. dirs. 1981-86), Southwestern Mission Research Ctr. Republican. Episcopalian. Home: 6941 E Third St Tucson AZ 85710 Office: Westerners Internat PO Box 3845 Coll Sta Tucson AZ 85722

HARRINGTON, JOHN ALAN, physician, obstetrician-gynecologist; b. La Jolla, Calif., Aug. 2, 1943; s. Glen Peter and Mary C. (Galleger) H.; m. Sheila A. Harrington, Sept. 21, 1974; children: Sean, Liern. AA, El Camino Coll., 1963; BS, U. Utah, 1965; D in Obstetrady, Kirksville Coll. Osteo. Medicine, 1971. Diplomate Am. Bd. Ob-gyn. Gen. med. officer USAF, Riverside (Calif.) and Guam, 1972-73; advanced through ranks to maj. USAF Med. Corps; resident Tripler Hosp. Army Med. Ctr., Honolulu, 1973-76; ob-gyn physician F.E. Warner AFB, Cheyenne, Wyo., 1976-77, Carwell AFB, Ft. Worth, 1977-79; major and gen. surgeon USAR Med. Corps, 1979—; pvt. practice ob-gyn Denver, 1979—. Co-author: Don't Take Two Aspirin, 1982. Fellow Am. Coll. Ob-gyn; mem. Colo. Med. Soc., Colo. Ob-gyn Soc.; Colo. Osteo. Medicine Soc., Colo. Perinatal Council (chmn. 1985—). Office: 11245 Huron St Westminster CO 80234

HARRINGTON, NANCY JO, tourism office administrator; b. Spokane, Wash., Aug. 6, 1948; s. Robert Louis and Patricia Elizabeth (Seavitt) H.; m. Patrick Warren McIntyre, May 26, 1973 (div. Sept. 1976). Adminstrv., secretarial staff various cos., Wash., 1966-78; adminstrv. coordinator, bookkeeper Spokane (Wash.) Area Conv. and Visitors Bur., 1978-79; v.p. ops. Anchorage Conv. and Visitors Bur., 1979-82; prin. Bus. Services, Anchorage, 1983; controller Allen Nelson & Co. Inc., Seattle, 1983-84; pres. Ketchikan (Alaska) Conv. and Visitors Bur., 1984—; adj. faculty Ketchikan Community Coll., 1984—. Mem. Nat. Assn. Female Execs., Alaska Visitors Assn., SE Alaska Tourism Council bd. dirs.), Am. Mgmt. Assn. Avocations: fishing, camping, hiking, boating, swimming. Home: 709 Cook St Ketchikan AK 99901

HARRINGTON, PETER FRANCIS, group engineer; b. Buffalo, Oct. 31, 1941; s. Francis Vincent and Ruth Frances (Nelson) H.; m. Gloria Rosemary Hitzges, Jan. 5, 1963; children: Markham John, Julie Ann, Peter Jacob. AAS, Bryant & Stratton Coll., 1979; AS, Victor Valley Coll., 1986. Functional test technician Bell Aerospace Textron, Wheatfield, N.Y., 1964-78; test engr. Gen. Dynamics, Pomona, Calif., 1978-82; lab. supr. Gen. Dynamics, Cucamonga, Calif., 1982—; pub. relations dir. Score Internat. East, Springville, N.Y., 1978. Foster parent Cath. Charities, Buffalo, 1969-78, San Bernardino County Social Services, Cucamonga, 1979-81, Apple Valley, Calif., 1982—. Served with USN, 1960-64, USNR 1964-66. Mem. AAAS, Inst. Environ. Mental Scis. (sr.), Western N.Y. Autocross Trail (chmn. 1972-73), San Diego Asebring Assn., Nat. Mgmt. Assn. Lodge: Elks. Home: 18923 Symeron Rd Apple Valley CA 92307 Office: Gen Dynamics Valley Systems Div 11000 4th St MS 600-42 Ontario CA 91761-1085

HARRINGTON, WALTER HOWARD, JR., municipal judge; b. San Francisco, Aug. 14, 1926; s. Walter Howard and Doris Ellen (Daniels) H.; B.S., Stanford, 1947; J.D., Hastings Coll., U. Calif., 1952; m. Barbara Bryant, June 1952 (div. 1973); children—Stacey Doreen, Sara Duval; m. 2d, Hertha Bahrs, Sept. 1974. Admitted to Calif. bar, 1953; dep. legislative counsel State of Calif., Sacramento, 1953-54, 55; mem. firm Walner & Harrington, Sacramento, 1954; dep. dist. atty. San Mateo County, Redwood City, Calif., 1955-62; asso. firm Wagstaffe, Daba & Hulse, Redwood City, 1962-67; practiced in Redwood City, 1967-84; judge San Mateo County Mcpl. Ct., 1984—. Chmn., San Mateo County Criminal Justice Council, 1971-76, San Mateo County Adult Correctional Facilities Com., 1969-71; pro tem referee San Mateo County Juvenile Ct., 1967-72. Served as ensign USNR, 1944-46. Mem. San Mateo County Bar Assn. (pres. 1969, editor publs. 1964-74), State Bar Calif. (editorial bd. 1968-81, vice chmn. 1969, 74-75, chmn., editor 1975-76), San Mateo County Legal Aid Soc. (pres. 1971-72), Order of Coif, Delta Theta Phi. Republican. Episcopalian. Office: Court House 750 Middlefield Rd PO Box 1064 Redwood City CA 94064

HARRIS, ARLO DEAN, chemistry educator; b. Dayton, Ohio, Sept. 17, 1934; s. William Lester and Charlotte Harris. BS, U. Dayton, 1961; PhD, Tulane U., 1964. Instr. U. Dayton, Ohio, 1959-61; teaching asst. Tulane U., New Orleans, 1961-64, instr., 1964; instr. U. New Orleans, 1963; asst. prof. Calif. State U., Fullerton, 1965-67; asst. prof. Calif. State U., San Bernardino, 1967-69, assoc. prof., 1970-79, prof. chemistry, 1980—; programmed instruction cons. Litton Ednl. Industries, 1965-67; textbook cons. various Am. Book Cos.; lectr. U. Nottingham, England, 1969-70; sci. news reporter Sta. KVCR-FM, 1976-78; vis. prof. U. Khartoum, Sudan, 1980, U. Queensland, Brisbane, Australia, 1982, 84, 87; research chemist U. London Kings Coll., England, 1978-79. Photography cons.: General Chemistry, Principles and Modern Applications, 4th rev. edit.; 1985; contbr. articles to profl. jours. Recipient Meritorious Performance and Profl. Promise award, 1984-85. Fellow Am. Inst. Chemists; AAAS, AAUP, Am. Chem. Soc., Chem. Soc. London, Calif. Assn. Chemistry Tchrs. N.Y. Acad. Scis., Am. Acad. Arts and Scis., Nat. Sci. Tchrs. Assn., Sigma Xi. Avocation: music. Home: 3488 North D St San Bernardino CA 92405 Office: Calif State U Dept Chemistry 5500 University Pkwy San Bernardino CA 92407-2397

HARRIS, BARBARA HULL (MRS. F. CHANDLER HARRIS), social agy. adminstr.; b. Los Angeles, Nov. 1, 1921; d. Hamilton and Marion (Eimers) Baird; student UCLA, 1939-41, 45-47; m. F Chandler Harris, Aug. 10, 1946; children—Victoria, Randolph Boyd. Pres., Victoria Originals, 1955-62; partner J.B. Assos., cons., 1971-73; statewide dir. vols. Children's Home Soc. Calif., 1971-75. Los Angeles County Heart Sunday chmn. Los Angeles County Heart Assn. (recipient Outstanding Service award 1965), 1965, bd. dirs., 1966-69; mem. exec. com. Hollywood Bowl Vols., 1966-84, chmn. vols., 1971, 75; chmn. Coll. Alumni of Assistance League, 1962; mem. exec. com. Assistance League So. Calif. (mem.1964-71, 72-80, 83—, pres., 1976-80; bd. dirs. Nat. Charity League, Los Angeles 1965-69, 75, sec., 1967, 3d v.p. 1968; ways and means chmn., dir. Los Angeles Am. Horse Show, 1969; dir. Coronet Debutante Ball, 1968, ball bd. chmn., 1969-70, 75, 84, mem. ball bd., 1969—; pres. Hollywood Bowl Patroness com., 1976; v.p. Irving Walker aux. Travelers Aid, 1976, 79; pres. So. Calif. alumni council Alpha Phi, 1961, fin. adviser to chpts. U. So. Calif., 1961-72, UCLA, 1965-72; benefit chmn. Gold Shield, 1969, 1st v.p. 1970-72; chmn. Golden Thimble III Needlework Exhbn., Hosp. of Good Samaritan, 1975; bd. dirs. UCLA Affiliates, 1976-78, KCET Women's Council, 1979-83, Region V United Way, 1980-83; pres. Jr. Philharmonic Com., 1981-82; bd. dirs. Los Angeles Founder chpt. Achievement Rewards for Coll. Scientists, 1980—, pres. 1984-85. Recipient Ivy award as outstanding Alpha Phi alumna So. Calif., 1969; outstanding alumni award for community service UCLA, 1978; Mannequin's Eve award, 1980. Mem. Hollywood C. of C. (dir. 1980-81). Home: 7774 Skyhill Dr Hollywood CA 90068

HARRIS, BETTY WRIGHT, research chemist; b. Monroe, La., July 29, 1940; d. Henry Hudson and Legertha Evelyn (Thompson) Wright; m. Alloyd A. Harris, July 18, 1960 (div. Feb. 1970); children: Selita Nicole Lucas, Jeffrey L., Alloyd A. Jr. BS, So. U., Baton Rouge, 1961; MS, Atlanta U., 1963; PhD, U. N.Mex., 1975. Asst. prof. chem. So. U., New Orleans, 1964-79, Miss. Valley State U., Itta Bena, 1963, Colo. Coll., Colorado Springs, 1974-75; mgr. chem. div. Solar Turbine, Inc., San Diego, 1982-84; research chem. Los Alamos (N.Mex.) Nat. Lab., 1970—; mem. bd. dirs. Self-Help Inc., Los Alamos. 1985-86. Contbr. articles to sci. jours.; author numerous papers. Chmn. Office of Gov. Ministry com., Los Alamos, 1986—; mem. ch. council Bethelehem Luth., 1981-82; catechism tchr. local Sunday Sch., 1970—. Mem. AAAS, Am. Chem. Soc. (sec., chmn. co-chmn. 1978-81), Nat. Tech. Assn., Bus. and Profl. Women, Sigma Xi, Delta Sigma Theta. Democrat. Club: Toastmasters (disting. dist. 23 gov. 1980-81, named Toastmaster of Yr. 1982-83, Area Gov. of Yr., 1978-79). Avocations: movies, opera concerts, reading, hiking, swimming. Office: Los Alamos Nat Lab PO Box 1663 MS C920 Los Alamos NM 87545

HARRIS, CHARLES JEWETT, periodical editor-in-chief, publishing consultant; b. Rochester, N.Y., Jan. 9, 1949; s. Joseph and Nancy (Bickelhaupt) H.; m. Jean M. Davis, Dec. 17, 1979; 1 child, Jody L. King. AB, Princeton U., 1970. Tchr. sci. Taft Sch., Watertown, Conn., 1975-78; mgr. long. Am. Radio Relay League, Newington, Conn., 1975-78; freelance writer Montserrat, B.W.I., 1978-81; pub. Pacific Woodworker, Santa Rosa, Calif., 1982-85; DX editor 73 mag., Peterborough, NH, 1982—; pres. Popular Woodworking mag., Concord, Calif., 1985—; editor DX Bull., Santa Rosa, 1986—. Author: Tune in the World, 1977, ARRL Code Kit, 1978 (Best Children's Book award Sci. Am. mag. 1978); contbr. articles to profl. jours. Mem. REDXA (sec.-treas. Penngrove, Calif. chpt. 1982—), Mensa (coordinator Sonoma County, Calif. chpt. 1981—). Avocations: amateur radio, photography, travel. Home: 3529 Deer Park Dr Santa Rosa CA 95404 Office: DX Bull 816 4th St Suite 1001 Santa Rosa CA 95404

HARRIS, CYNTHIA VIOLA, educational administrator; management consultant; b. San Francisco, Aug. 18, 1948; d. Gilbert and Mary Lee (Barnes) H. BA in Speech, San Francisco State U., 1970, MA in Counseling, 1975; EdD, Nova U., 1987. U. Cert. tchr., adminstr., Calif. Tchr. Martin L. King Elem. Sch., Oakland, Calif. 1971-74; teaching v.p. Peralta Year Round Sch., Oakland, 1974-80, prin. 1980-86, coordinator staff devel., 1986—; part-time mgmt. cons. year-round educ., leadership; guest lectr. Mills Coll., LaVerne U. Bd. dirs. Wiley Manuel Law Found., Charles Harrison Mason Scholarships. Nominated Outstanding Woman of Am., Alpha Kappa Alpha, 1981; recipient Capwell's Networker award, 1985; named Outstanding Youth

Leader, Nat. Bus. and Profl. Bd., 1981. Mem. Nat. Assn. Female Execs., Nat. Assn. Prins., United Adminstrs. Oakland, Alliance Black Educators, Glamor Working Women's Panel, Phi Delta Kappa. Democrat. Mem. Pentecostal Ch. Club: Coalition of 100 Black Women. Author: (teaching manual) All about Us, 1980.

HARRIS, DALE RAY, lawyer; b. Crab Orchard, Ill., May 11, 1937; s. Ray B. and Aurelia M. (Davis) H.; m. Toni K. Shapkoff, June 26, 1960; children—Kristen Dee, Julie Diane. B.A. in Math., U. Colo., 1959; LL.B., Harvard U., 1962. Bar: Colo. 1962, U.S. Dist. Ct. Colo. 1962, U.S. Ct. Appeals (10th cir.), 1962, U.S. Supreme Ct. 1981. Assoc. Davis, Graham & Stubbs, Denver, 1962-67, ptnr., 1967—, chmn. mgmt. com., 1982-85; speaker, instr. various antitrust seminars. Mem. cabinet Mile High United Way campaign, 1986-87; mem. devel. council U. Colo. Arts and Scis. dept., 1985—; trustee The Spaceship Earth Fund, 1986—; area chmn. Harvard Law Sch. Fund, 1978-81. Served with USAR, 1962-68. Fellow ABA, Am. Bar Found.; mem. Colo. Bar Assn. (chmn. antitrust com. 1980-84; council corp. banking and bus. law sect. 1978-83), Denver Bar Assn., Colo. Assn. Corp. Counsel (pres. 1973-74), Denver Law Club (pres. 1976-77), Phi Beta Kappa. Clubs: University, Union League (Chgo.). Lodge: Denver Rotary. Home: 2032 Bellaire St Denver CO 80207 Office: 370 17th St Denver CO 80201

HARRIS, DARRYL WAYNE, publishing executive; b. Emmett, Idaho, July 29, 1941; s. Reed Ingval and Evelyn Faye (Wengreen) H.; m. Christine Sorenson, Sept. 10, 1965; children: Charles Reed, Michael Wayne, Jason Darryl, Stephanie, Ryan Joseph. B.A., Brigham Young U., 1966. Staff writer Deseret News, Salt Lake City, 1965, Post-Register, Idaho Falls, 1966-67; tech. editor Idaho Nuclear Corp., Idaho Falls, 1967-68; account exec. David W. Evans & Assos. Advt., Salt Lake City, 1968-71; pres. Harris Pub., Inc., Idaho Falls, 1971—; pub. Potato Grower of Idaho mag., 1972—, Snowmobile West mag., 1974—, Sugar Producer mag., 1974—, Blue Ribbon mag., 1987—. Campaign mgr. George Hansen for Congress Com., 1974, 76; campaign chmn. Mel Richardson for Congress Com., 1986; 1st counselor to pres. Korean Mission, Ch. Jesus Christ of Latter-day Saints, Seoul, Korea, 1963, area public communications dir., Eastern Idaho, 1976-86; High Priest, Ch. Jesus Christ of Latter-Day Saints, 1987—; founder Blue Ribbon Coalition, 1987. Mem. Agr. Editors Assn., Internat. Snowmobile Industry Assn. (Best Overall Reporting journalism award 1979, 80), Western Publs. Assn., World Champion Cutter and Chariot Racing Assn. (historian 1966-80), Kappa Tau Alpha. Lodge: Idaho Falls Kiwanis (pres. 1978, Disting. Club Pres. award 1978). Office: Harris Pub Inc 520 Park Ave Idaho Falls ID 83401

HARRIS, DOROTHY LIPP, psychology educator; b. Phila., Mar. 15, 1922; d. Samuel Larue and Pamela (Clarke) Lipp; m. Philip R. Harris, July 3, 1965. BS in Social Scis., Edn., U. Pa., MS, 1945; PhD in Psychology, Northwestern U., 1952. Communications specialist, dir. pub. relations Main Chance Camp div. Elizabeth Arden Corp., Chgo., 1947-48; instr. Northwestern U., Evanston, Ill., 1951, U. Utah, Salt Lake City, 1945-47; dean women, assoc. prof. psychology U. Wis., River Falls, 1952-54, U. N.D., Grand Forks, 1954-59; dean women, spl. asst. v.p. Pa. State U., University Park, 1959-70; prof., assoc. dean Sch. Human Behavior U.S. Internat. U., San Diego, 1971-75, prof., assoc. dean Sch. Bus. and Mgmt., 1976-85, prof., dir. human resource devel., mgmt. Sch. Edn., 1986—; v.p. Harris Internat. Ltd., La Jolla, Calif., 1971—; mem. faculty comm. on peace officiating standards and tng. Command Coll. of Calif. Dept. Justice, 1986—; del. UNESCO, Israel, 1961, Paris, 1963, Geneva, 1964. Author: (with P.R. Harris) Improving Management Communication Skills, 1978, Leadership Effectiveness with People, 1978; A Day to Day Key to Successful Employee Negotiations, 1978. Northwestern U. Carnegie fellow. Mem. AAUW, Acad. Mgmt., Am. Personnel and Guidance Assn., Mortar Bd., Alpha Lambda Delta, Pi Lambda Theta. Republican. Club: La Jolla Beach and Tennis. Home: 2702 Costebelle Dr La Jolla CA 92037 Office: US Internat U Sch Edn 10455 Pomerado Rd San Diego CA 92131

HARRIS, EDWARD A., producer, writer, dir.; b. Elizabeth, N.J., Dec. 14, 1946; s. Howard E. and Bernice W. H.; student in music composition and theory U. Okla., 1964-67, Los Angeles Community Coll., 1977, UCLA, 1978. Singer, songwriter, 1962—; pres., exec. producer Myriad Prodns., a multi-media entertainment prodn. co., Los Angeles, 1965—; creative dir. Myriad Graphics, Los Angeles, 1976—; producer, assoc. dir. Columbia Music Hall, Hartford, Conn., 1972-75; film and TV producer, 1971—; multi-media entertainment cons., Los Angeles, 1977—; field producer Good Morning Am., also Good Night Am.—ABC-TV, 1975-77; exec. producer, dir. The Act Factory, a performing arts services and indsl. show prodn. co., Los Angeles, 1977-83; sr. ptnr. Myriad-Fritz Prodns., Los Angeles, 1977-83; v.p. Sports Prodns., Am. Videogram, Inc., Los Angeles, 1986—; exec. producer Gateway Group, San Francisco, 1974-75; Composer over 30 songs; dir. Performance Evaluation Workshop, Los Angeles Songwriter's Expo, 1978-83; co-dir. SPVA Performing Arts Workshop, Los Angeles, 1980; producer (TV sports mag.) The Clubhouse, 1982—. Pres. Wintonbury Mall Mchts. Assn., Bloomfield, Conn., 1971-72. Mem. Am. Fedn. Musicians, Am. Guild Variety Artists, Soc. for Preservation of Variety Arts, Alpha Epsilon Pi, Kappa Kappa Psi.

HARRIS, ELLEN STERN, public policy educator, writer; b. Los Angeles, Nov. 2, 1929; d. Herman Jastro Stern and Geraldine (Rosenberg) Wayne; divorced; children—Tom, Jane. Pub. affairs workshop instr. Communications Workers Am., Los Angeles, 1977-78; instr., program coordinator, moderator, guest lectr. UCLA, 1972—; exec. dir. Pub. Access Producers Acad., Beverly Hills, Calif., 1983—; consumer advocate columnist Los Angeles Times, 1971-78; consumer advisor Times Mirror Satellite Cable/Apple Prodns, 1981; producer, host TV program Who's In Charge, Sta. KPFK-TV, 1979-80, Consumer Connection program Sta. KCRW-TV, 1979; co-host consumer edn. TV series NBC, 1975. Trustee Sta. WETA-TV-AM, Washington, 1975-78; coordinator Calif. Friends of Pub. Broadcasting, 1976-80; exec. sec. Council for Planning and Conservation, 1967-73, Friends of Santa Monica Mountains Parks, 1965-66; asst. founder Ctr. for Study Democratic Insts., 1964; bd. dirs. Bay Inst. of San Francisco, 1982-86, Friends of Beverly Hills Pub. Library, 1982-83; mem. cable adv. com. Beverly Hills City council, 1986, Mayor's adv. com. on Beverly Hills Water, 1986; adv. bd. Calif. Tomorrow, 1967-83, Urban Environment Found., 1977-79, Town Hall of Calif., 1976—, Los Angeles Conservancy, 1978—; mem. AIA Land Use Task Force, 1972-74; bd. dirs. Met. Water Dist. So. Calif., 1978-81; chmn. Mayor's Adv. Com. on cable TV, City of Beverly Hills, 1982-83, 85; vice chmn. Calif. Coastal Zone Conservation Commn., 1972-76; mem. Fed. Coastal Zone Mgmt. Adv. Com., 1973-75, Los Angeles County Environ. Quality Control Com., 1970-73, Los Angeles County Beach Adv. Com., 1970-73, Los Angeles-Ventura Regional Water Quality Control Bd., 1966-70, Dist. Atty's. Community Adv. Council for Los Angeles County, 1976-82, Calif. Atty. Gen's Environ. Task Force, 1970-79, others. Named Woman of Yr., Los Angeles Times, 1969; honored by Sierra Club, 1969, Audubon Soc., 1969; Clarence Darrow Found., 1978; recipient Am. Motors Conservation award, 1970; World Communications award UN Assn., 1983. Home and Office: PO Box 228 Beverly Hills CA 90213

HARRIS, EMMA EARL, nurse, nursing home executive; b. Viper, Ky., Nov. 6, 1936; d. Andrew Jackson and Zola (Hall) S.; m. Ret Haney Marten Henis Harris, June 5, 1981; children—Debra, Joseph, Wynona, Robert Walsh. Grad. St. Joseph Sch. Practical Nursing. Staff nurse St. Joseph Hosp., Bangor, Maine, 1973-75; office nurse Dr. Eugene Brown, Bangor, 1975-77; dir. nurses Fairborn Nursing Home, Ohio, 1977-78; staff nurse Hillhaven Hospice, Tucson, 1979-80; asst. head nurse, 1980; co-owner Nu-Life Elderly Guest Home, Tucson, 1980—. Vol. Heart Assn., Bangor, 1965-70, Cancer Assn., Bangor, 1965-70. Mem. Nat. Assn. Female Execs., Assn. of Better Living for the Elderly (cons. 1983—). Democrat. Avocations: theatre; opera. Home: 1082 E Seneca Tucson AZ 85719

HARRIS, F. CHANDLER, emeritus university administrator; b. Neligh, Nebr., Nov. 5, 1914; s. James Carlton and Helen Ayres (Boyd) H.; A.B., U. Calif. at Los Angeles, 1936; m. Barbara Ann Hull, Aug. 10, 1946; children—Victoria, Randolph Boyd. Assoc. editor Telegraph Delivery Spirit, Los Angeles, 1937-39; writer, pub. service network radio programs University Explorer, Sci. Editor, U. Calif., 1939-61; pub. information mgr. UCLA, 1961-75, dir., 1975-82, dir. emeritus, 1982—. Mem. pub. relations com., western region United Way, 1972-75; bd. dirs. Am. Youth Symphony, Los Angeles, 1978—, v.p., 1983—; bd. dirs. Hathaway Home for Children, 1982—. Recipient 1st prize NBC Radio Inst., 1944; Harvey Hebert medal Delta Sigma Phi, 1947, Mr. Delta Sig award, 1972; Adam award Assistance League Mannequins, 1980, Univ. Service award UCLA Alumni Assn., 1986. Mem. Western Los Angeles Regional C. of C. (dir. 1976-80), U. Calif. Retirees Assn. Los Angeles (pres. 1985-87), Sigma Delta Chi, Delta Sigma Phi (nat. pres. 1959-63). Club: UCLA Faculty (sec. bd. govs. 1968-72). Editor Interfraternity Research Adv. Council Bull., 1949-50, Carnation, 1969-80. Home: 7774 Skyhill Dr Hollywood CA 90068

HARRIS, FREDERICK EARL, II, investment adviser; b. Los Angeles, Aug. 9, 1940; s. Frederick F. and Maxine (Solomon) H.; UCLA, 1960. Real estate salesman Santa Monica Investment Co. (Calif.), 1964-66; underwater archaeologist Council Underwater Archaeology, Mediterrean Sea, 1966-69; land developer Mustique Island and St. Vincent West Indies, 1969-71; investment adviser for various trusts and pvt. sector, 1972-86; Commr. Santa Monica Dept. Parks and Recreation; past bd. dirs. Am. Cancer Soc.; trustee Santa Monica Heritage Sq. Mus. Served with USCGR, 1958-66. Recipient award of Honor, Compagne Gen. Transalantic, 1971. Mem. Palisades Beach Property Owners Assn. (pres.), Coast Guard Aux. (past flotilla and div. staff officer), U.S. Yacht Racing Union, West Indian Yachting Assn., Screen Actors Guild. Clubs: Calif. Yacht (advisor amateur radio group), Ocean Cruising, Los Angeles Yacht; Grenada Yacht; Transpacific Yacht; Royal Ocean Racing, Lahana Yacht. Patentee color adaptable bandages. Lic. amateur radio operator. Office: PO Box 1859 Santa Monica CA 90406

HARRIS, GODFREY, public policy consultant; b. London, June 11, 1937; s. Alfred and Victoria H.; came to U.S., 1939, naturalized, 1945; B.A. with gt. distinction, Stanford U., 1958; M.A. (disting. mil. grad.), UCLA, 1960; m. Linda Berkowitz, Dec. 21, 1958 (div. 1982); m. Barbara DeKovner-Mayer, Nov. 5, 1984; children—Gregrey, Kennith, Mark. Fgn. service officer U.S. State Dept., Washington, Bonn, Germany and London, 1962-65; mgmt. analyst Office Mgmt. and Budget, Washington, 1965-67; spl. asst. to pres. IOS Devel. Co., Geneva, 1967-68; pres. Harris/Ragan Mgmt. Corp., Los Angeles, 1968—; lectr. Rutgers U., 1960-61. Mem. adv. com. on gifted Santa Monica Unified Sch. Dist. (chmn. 1978-79); mem. Los Angeles World Affairs Council, Town Hall Los Angeles; former W. Coast rep. Panamanian Export Promotion and Investment Devel. Center. Served to 1st lt. U.S. Army, 1958-60. Decorated Commendation medal. Fellow Am. Acad. Cons.'s; mem. Assn. Mgmt. Cons.'s, Stanford U. Alumni Assn. (membership sec. N.Am. chpt.), London C. of C. and Industry. Democrat. Jewish. Author: History of Sandy Hook, N.J., 1961; (with F. Fielder) The Quest for Foreign Affairs Officers, 1966; Panama's Position, 1973; (with C. Sonabend) Commercial Translations, 1985; (with B. DeKovner-Mayer) From Trash to Treasure, 1985; (with K. Katz) Promoting International Tourism, 1986; founder, editor Almanac of World Leaders, 1957-62, Consultants Directory, 1975-76. Office: 9200 Sunset Blvd Los Angeles CA 90069

HARRIS, GRANT ANDERSON, forester, educator; b. Logan, Utah, July 13, 1914; s. Joseph Smith and Hilda (Anderson) H.; m. Jennabee Ballif, Oct. 18, 1939; children: Judith (Mrs. Gaylon Sanford Campbell), Patricia Florence (Mrs. Harold Davis Oak), Joseph Ballif, Halli H. (Mrs. Mark Lee Stone). B.S., Utah State U., 1939, Ph.D., 1965; M.S., U. Idaho, 1941. Cert. Sr. ecologist, range mgmt. cons. Supt., Vigilante exptl. range U.S. Forest Service Research Br., Alder, Mont., 1941-48; project leader Upper Columbia Research Center, Spokane, Wash., 1948-51; asst. prof., extension forester, research Utah State U., 1951-56; assoc. prof., research forester Wash. State U., Pullman, 1956-67; prof., chmn. dept. forestry and range mgmt. Wash. State U., 1967-80; cons. 1980—; chmn. bd. Decagon Devices Inc., 1983—; cons. West Pakistan Agrl. U. Mem. editorial bd. N.W. Sci.; book rev. editor Jour. Range Mgmt., 1984—; contbr. articles to profl. jours. Active Boy Scouts Am.; mem. exec. bd. Pullman United Way. Served to lt. (j.g.) USNR, 1944-46. Recipient Silver Beaver award, 1977; Disting. Alumni award Utah State U. Dept. Range Sci., 1983. Fellow AAAS, Am. Soc. Range Mgmt. (Pacific N.W. sect. pres. 1964); mem. Soc. Am. Foresters (chmn. range ecology working group 1975-77), Am. Forestry Assn., N.W. Sci. Assn., Wash. Farm Forestry Assn., Wash. State Forestry Conf. (trustee, exec. com., Outstanding Service award 1980), Assn. State Colls. and Univs. Forestry Research Orgn. (chmn. Western region 1975—, exec. com. 1975—), Assn. Coll. Honor Socs. (council 1985—), Sigma Xi, Xi Sigma Pi (nat. sec., fiscal agt. 1984-86). Mem. Ch. of Jesus Christ of Latter-day Saints (bishop Pullman ward 1965-73, stake patriarch 1980—). Home: NE 1615 Upper Dr Pullman WA 99163

HARRIS, H. FREEMAN, physician; b. Wynne, Ark., Oct. 2, 1946; s. James Harold and Mildred Merrill (Freeman) H.; m. Karen Mirium Mendelson, June 16, 1968; children—Merrill Gwyn, James Michael. B.A. in Psychology, U. Calif.-Berkeley, 1968; M.D., U. Ark.-Little Rock, 1973. Diplomate Am. Bd. Internal Medicine. Intern, resident in internal medicine U. Oreg., Portland, 1973-76; practice medicine, specializing in internal medicine Oakridge Med. Clinic, Lake Oswego, Oreg.; v.p., dir. Care Mark Services, Portland, 1984; pres. med. staff Meridian Park Hosp., Tualatin, Oreg., 1981. Mem. Am. Soc. Internal Medicine, Alpha Omega Alpha. Democrat. Home: 740 Briercliff Lake Oswego OR 97034 Office: Oakridge Med Clinic 4309 Oakridge Rd Lake Oswego OR 97034

HARRIS, HOWARD JEFFREY, marketing and printing company executive; b. Denver, June 9, 1949; s. Gerald Victor and Leona Lee (Tepper) H.; B.F.A. with honors, Kansas City Art Inst., 1973; M. of Indsl. Design with honors, Pratt Inst., 1975; postgrad. Graphic Arts Research Center, Rochester Inst. Tech., 1977; m. Michele Whealen, Feb. 6, 1975; children—Kimberly, Valerie. Indsl. designer Kivett & Myers, Architects, 1970-71; indsl. designer United Research Corp., Denver, 1971-72; indsl. designer, asst. to v.p., pres. JFN Assos., N.Y.C., 1972-73; dir. facility planning Abt & Assos., Cambridge, Mass., 1973-74; v.p. design, prodn., and research Eagle Lithographics, Denver, 1974—; pres. HSR Corp., Denver. Bd. dirs. Friends of C. Henry Kemp Ctr., Denver. Mem. Indsl. Designers Soc. Am., Graphic Arts Tech. Found., Design Methods Group, The Color Group, Nat. Assn. Counsel for Children, Am. Advt. Fedn. Democrat. Jewish. Office: 5105 E 41st Ave Denver CO 80216

HARRIS, JAMES DOUGLAS, career military officer; b. Rome, June 26, 1947; came to U.S., 1947; s. Merrill Jackson and Mary Madeline (Tousley) H.; m. Pamela J. Bohrnstedt; 1 stepdaughter, Erin. BS in Naval Sci., U.S. Naval Acad., 1969; MS in Systems Mgmt., U. So. Calif., 1983. Commd. ensign USN, Annapolis, 1965; advanced through grades to commdr. USN, 1984; with 100 combat missions in Southeast Asia, 1972; pilot fighter squadron 143 USN, San Diego, 1972-74, top gun instr. pilot, 1974-77, reserve fighter pilot, fighter squadron 301, 1977-84, exec. officer, then commanding officer, 1986—; airline pilot Continental Airlines, Los Angeles, 1977—; test engr. Titan Systems Incorp., La Jolla, Calif., 1984—. Decorated Air medals. Republican. Avocations: snow skiing, tennis, running. Office: Titan Systems Inc 9191 Towne Ctr Dr La Jolla CA 92122

HARRIS, JEFFREY DWIGHT, biologist; b. Prairie du Chien, Wis., Aug. 30, 1947; s. Glenn Forrest and Margie Alice (Hess) H.; m. Pamela Anne Ellis, June 22, 1968; children: Danielle Michele, Sean Gabriel. BA in Biochemistry, U. Calif., Berkeley, 1971, PhD in Molecular Biology, 1978. Postdoctoral fellow U. Calif. Med. Ctr., San Francisco, 1979-81, staff virologist, 1981-83; research scientist Microgenics Corp., Concord, Calif., 1983-85, group leader, 1985—. Contbr. articles to profl. jours. Mem. AAAS. Democrat. Avocations: history, sports. Office: Microgenics Corp 2341 Stanwell Dr Concord CA 94520

HARRIS, KATHLEEN RENEE, computer programmer, seamstress; b. Los Angeles, Nov. 30, 1954; d. William Rogiere Harris and IdaBelle (Norman) Rivers. AA, Chabot Coll., 1980. Lic. pilot. Gen. clk. sec. Western Girl Temp. Agy., San Leandro, Calif., 1973-75; mag card II operator Bechtel Inc., San Francisco, 1975-76; data entry operator Bechtel Corp., San Francisco, 1976-79, office asst., 1979-80; adminstrv. asst. II Bechtel Power Corp., Walnut Creek, Calif., 1980-82, computer programmer I, San Francisco, 1982—; designer, seamstress, owner Feline Fit Weddings, Etc., Calif., 1984. Mem. Better Bus. Bur. Mem. Nat. Assn. Female Execs., Aircraft Owners and Pilots Assn., Bechtel Employees Club, Viewer Adv. Council, Alpha Chi Phi Omega. Democrat. Lutheran. Clubs: Trojans Bowling, Aeromax Flying (Oakland, Calif.). Avocations: bowling, racquetball, flying. Home: 266 Smalley Ave Suite H Hayward CA 94541

HARRIS, MARY BIERMAN, psychology educator; b. St. Louis, Feb. 9, 1943; d. Norman and Margaret (Loeb) Bierman; m. Richard Jerome Harris, June 14, 1965; children: Jennifer, Christopher, Alexander. BA, Radcliffe U., 1964; MA, Stanford U., 1965, PhD, 1968. From asst. prof. to full prof. U. New Mex., Albuquerque, 1968—; vis. assoc. prof. Ohio State U., Columbus, 1974-75; vis. prof. U. New South Wales, Australia, 1981-82; adv. bd. Nat. Inst. Edn.-N.Mex. State U. Project, Las Cruces, 1978-80; cons. NIH, Washington, 1980-81. Editor: Classroom Uses of Behavior Modification, 1972; contbr. articles to profl. jours. Bd. dirs. Rio Grande Planned Parenthood, Albuquerque, 1984—. Research grantee NIH Heart, Lung and Blood Inst., 1985-86. Mem. Am. Psychol. Assn. (div. 8 pubs. com. 1983-85), Am. Ednl. Research Assn., Phi Beta Kappa, Sigma Xi. Democrat. Avocations: jogging, reading. Home: 1719 Rita Dr NE Albuquerque NM 87106 Office: U NMex Dept Ednl Founds Albuquerque NM 87131

HARRIS, MICHAEL GENE, optometrist, educator, lawyer; b. San Francisco, Sept. 20, 1942; s. Morry and Gertrude Alice (Epstein) H.; B.S., U. Calif., 1964, M. Optometry, 1965, D. Optometry, 1966, M.S., 1968; J.D., John F. Kennedy U., 1985; m. Andrea Elaine Berman, Nov. 29, 1969; children—Matthew Benjamin, Daniel Evan. Bar: Calif., U.S. Dist. Ct. (no. dist.) Calif. Assoc. practice optometry, Oakland, Calif., 1965-66, San Francisco, 1966-68; instr., coordinator contact lens clinic Ohio State U., 1968-69; asst. clin. prof. optometry U. Calif., Berkeley, 1969-73, dir. contact lens extended care clinic, 1969-83, chief contact lens clinic, 1983—, assoc. clin. prof., 1973-76, asst. chief contact lens service, 1970-76, assoc. chief contact lens service, 1976—, lectr., 1978-80, sr. lectr., 1980—, vice chmn. faculty Sch. Optometry, 1983—, prof. clin. optometry, 1984-86; clin. prof. optometry, 1986—; John de Carle vis. prof. City U., London, 1984; pvt. practice optometry, Oakland, Calif., 1973-76; lectr., cons. in field; mem. regulation rev. com. Calif. State Bd. Optometry; cons. hypnosis Calif. Optometric Assn., Am. Optometric Assn.; cons. Nat. Bd. Examiners in Optometry, Soflens div. Bausch & Lomb, 1973—, Barnes-Hind Hydrocurve Soft Lenses, Inc., 1974—, Contact Lens Research Lab., 1976—, Wesley-Jessen Contact Lens Co., 1977—, Palo Alto VA, 1980—, Primarius Corp., Cooper Vision Optics-Alcon, 1980—; Planning commr. Town of Moraga, Calif., 1986; founding mem. Young Adults div. Jewish Welfare Fedn., 1965—, chmn. 1967-68; commr. Sunday Football League, Contra Costa County, Calif., 1974-78. Charter Mem. Jewish Community Ctr. Contra Costa County; founding mem. Jewish Community Mus. San Francisco, 1984; life mem. Bay Area Council for Soviet Jews, 1976; bd. dirs. Jewish Community Relations Council of Greater East Bay, 1979—, Campolindo Homeowners Assn., 1981—; pres. student council John F. Kennedy U. Sch. Law, 1984-85. Fellow U. Calif., 1971; Calif. Optometric Assn. Scholar 1965, George Schneider Meml. scholar, 1964. Fellow Am. Acad. Optometry (diplomate contact lens sect.; chmn. contact lens papers; mem. contact lens com. 1974—, vice chmn. contact lens sect. 1980-82, chmn. 1982-84, 84-86), Assn. Schs. and Colls. Optometry (council on acad. affairs), AAAS; mem. Assn. for Research in Vision and Ophthalmology, Am. Optometric Assn. (proctor 1969—), Calif. Optometric Assn., Assn. Optometric Contact Lens Educators, Am. Optometric Found., Mexican Soc. Contactology (hon.), Internat. Soc. Contact Lens Research, Calif. State Bd. Optometry (regulation rev. com.), Calif. Acad. Scis., U. Calif. Optometry Alumni Assn. (life), ABA, Assn. Trial Lawyers Am., Calif. Trial Lawyers Assn., Calif. Young Lawyers Assn., Contra Costa Bar Assn., Mus. Soc., Mensa. Democrat. Lodge: B'nai B'rith. Editor current comments sect. Am. Jour. Optometry, 1974-77; editor Eye Contact, 1984—; contbr. chpts. to books; author various syllabuses; contbr. articles to profl. pubs. Home: 43 Corte Royal Moraga CA 94556 Office: Univ Calif Sch Optometry Berkeley CA 94720

HARRIS, MICHAEL RAYMOND, editor; b. Pensacola, Fla., Jan. 27, 1943; s. Donald George and Alice Ruth H. B.S., So. Ill. U., 1969. Employee communications editor Unicom Systems, Rockwell Internat., Cupertino, Calif., 1973-74; service rep. Pan Am Flight Service, San Francisco, 1969-71; pub. relations writer Falstaff Brewing Corp., St. Louis, 1966; founder, editor, pub. Peninsula Mag., Palo Alto, Calif., 1975-78; editor ROLM Corp., Santa Clara, Calif., 1979-87. Named First Citizen of San Mateo County, 1976. Mem. Internat. Assn. Bus. Communicators, Pub. Relations Soc. Am., Peninsula Mktg. Assn.

HARRIS, MIKE ERVIN, optometrist; b. Mohall, N. D., Mar. 6, 1955; s. Leonard O. and Eleanor I. (Larson) H.; m. Cecilia A., Demple, Aug. 30, 1975; children—J.D., Jennifer. Student U. Wyo., 1973-75; B.S., So. Calif. Coll. Optometry, 1979, O.D., 1979. Pvt. practice optometry, Casper, Wyo., 1979—. Named Outstanding committeeman C. of C., 1982, Outstanding First Yr. Mem. Kiwanis Club Casper, 1980, Outstanding Contact Lens Student Bausch & Lomb Co., 1979, Outstanding Visual Therapy Student Bernell Corp., 1979. Mem. Am. Optometric Assn., Wyo. Optometric Assn. (pres.-elect 1986-87). Republican. Episcopalian. Lodges: Kiwanis (pres. Casper club 1985-86), Masons. Home: 1940 Kingsbury Casper WY 82609 Office: 2510 E 15th St Suite 1 Casper WY 82609

HARRIS, N. NEIL, editor; b. Lafayette, Ind., June 9, 1940; s. Cecil Worth Harris and Ardis Jane (Davis) Buis; m. Selma Ann Taul, Apr. 7, 1962 (div. May 1982); m. Jennifer S. Helzberg, Aug. 21, 1982; children: Nadine Ann, Nina Ann. Grad., Am. Sch. Photography, 1964. Asst. display mgr. May Co., Redondo Beach, Calif., 1960-61; artist, silkscreener, photographer Nortronics Aircraft Corp., El Segundo, Calif., 1961-62; sr. sci. illustrator Purdue Univ., West Lafayette, Ind., 1963-74; editor Am. Numismatic Assn., Colorado Springs, Colo., 1974—. Author: Badges and Medals of the American Numismatic Association 1908-1969, 1969; co-author, illustrator: Fundamental Techniques in Veterinary Medicine, 1975; Anatomy of the Dog, 1964; editor: Medals of the United States Mint, The First Century, 1792-1892, 1977, California Tokens, 1977, The Numismatist (recipient best writer award Numismatics Lit. Guild 1973); Designer medals, Ind. State Numismatics Assn., 1965, 72; designer, sculptor, 1973-76, 75th Anniversary medal, Med. Library Assn., 1975, Am. Numismatic Assn. Conv. medal, 1977-78, 80; co-editor: Medallic Sculpture, Am. Medallic Sculpture Assn., 1985-86; designer, sculptor: Howland Wood Meml. award medal Am. Numismatic Assn., 1980, Hall of Fame medal Colorado Springs Bowling Assn., 1985, 25th Anniv. medal Purdue U. Sch. Vet. Medicine, 1984; designer: So. Calif. Rapid Transit Dist. Olympic Transp. tokens (series of 24), 1983; exhibitor: 1st Exhibition Am. Medallic Sculpture Assn. Recipient Hall of Fame medal Colo. State Bowling Assn., 1986. Mem. Brookgreen Gardens, Am. Medallic Sculpture Assn. (trustee 1985-86), Brit. Art Medal Soc., Fedn. Internat. de la Medaille (mem. steering com. F.I.D.E.M. '87, 1986-87, editor exhibition catalog, exhibitor 21st Congress, 1987), Am. Soc. Assn. Execs., Token and Medal Soc. (bd. dirs. 1970-77, 1st v.p. 1976-77, 77-78, 2d v.p. 1978-79, 79-80, pres. 1980-82, assoc. book editor 1971-72, book editor 1972-77), Ind. Numismatic Assn. (officer 1967-72, pres. 1973-74, hon. life mem., recipient 1st ann. founder's award 1971), Lafayette Numismatic Soc. (sec., bd. dirs. 1964-68, hon. life), Am. Numismatic Assn. (recipient Burton Saxton award 1969, medal of merit award 1980). Democrat. Methodist. Clubs: Pikes Peak Pool League, High Country Pool League (Colo. Springs). Avocations: billiards, bowling, cycling, softball, swimming. Office: Am Numismatic Assn 818 N Cascade Ave Colorado Springs CO 80903

HARRIS, NORMAN ALLAN, research and development company executive; b. Los Angeles, Sept. 27, 1933; s. David Jack and Bella (Flack) H.; student (Univ. scholar) U. So. Calif., 1951; B.A. (Coll. scholar), Occidental Coll., 1955; postgrad. Vanderbilt U., 1955-56; grad. Oak Ridge Sch. Radiol. Physics, 1956; m. Sandra Gail Hill, Feb. 22, 1958; children—Todd, Tracy, Wendy. Project engr. Marquardt, Van Nuys, Calif., 1956-60; project mgr. Atomics Internat., Canoga Park, Calif., 1960-62; sr. asso. Planning Research Corp., Los Angeles, 1962-68; prin. scientist advanced sensor systems McDonnell-Douglas, Santa Monica, Calif., 1968-69; mgr. dept. environ. safety EG&G, Goleta, Calif., 1969-74; exec. v.p. Henningson, Durham & Richardson, Santa Barbara, Calif., 1974-83, dir. spl. space shuttle studies, 1974-83, dir. M-X EIS prodn. and spl. systems studies, 1976-83; pres. Motoracing News, 1978-83, Manbourne Inc., 1978-83; chmn. bd. MI Systems Applications Co. (MISA), Santa Barbara, 1983—; prin. OMI Scis., Santa Barbara, 1984—; pres., chief exec. officer Mgmt. Sci. Inc., Solvang, Calif., 1984—. Mem. com. to establish tchr. qualifications and evaluation standards, Santa Ynez, Calif. AEC fellow, 1955-56. Mem. Health Physics Soc. (charter),

Kappa Mu Epsilon, Sigma Pi Sigma. Author tech. monographs in field. Office: PO Box 1310 591 Alamo Pintado Solvane CA 93463 Office: 2432 Railway Ave Suite 1 Los Olivos CA 93441

HARRIS, RICHARD ANTHONY SIDNEY, trust company executive; b. Bklyn., Dec. 22, 1940; s. Stanley Sidney and Rose (Franquelli) H.; m. Sharon Lynne Harvey, Dec. 21, 1975; 1 child, Aaron Nathaniel Graeme. Student St. John's U., Jamaica, N.Y., 1958-61. Adminstr. Harris Trust, N.Y.C., 1972—, trustee, 1972—; adminstr. Beehive Trading Co., Provo, Utah, 1980—, Aaron Reseda Med., Calif., 1976—; pres. Reseda Mgmt., 1976—, also dir. Mem. Am. Assn. Individual Investors, Internat. Platform Assn., Heritage Found. Roman Catholic. Office: PO Box 108 Van Nuys CA 91408

HARRIS, ROBERT MCCORD, marketing, advertising executive; b. Cleve., July 16, 1946; s. John Langdon and Marilyn (Motz) H.; m. Mollie Ann Micheau, Dec. 27, 1969; children: Kimberly Ann, Robert McCord Jr. BBA, Ohio State U., 1969; M in Internat. Mgmt., Thunderbird Grad. Sch. of Internat. Mgmt., Phoenix, 1971. Account exec. Cunningham and Walsh, N.Y.C., 1973-76; account supr. William Esty Co., N.Y.C., 1976-77; account dir. J. Walter Thompson, N.Y.C. and Melbourne, Australia, 1977-84; mgmt. supr. McCann-Erickson, San Francisco, 1984-85; dir. mktg. Perchè No! Gelato, San Francisco, 1986—; pres., chief exec. officer Mariner Yacht Charters, San Francisco, 1985—. Mem. San Francisco C. of C. Served to capt. USAR, 1969-77. Mem. San Francisco Conv. and Visitors, San Francisco Advt. Club. Republican. Presbyterian. Club: Squash of San Francisco, Met. Yacht, San Francisco Tennis. Avocations: squash, skiing, yachting. Home: 120 Goodfellow Dr Moraga CA 97556 Office: Perchè No! Gelato 601 Gateway Blvd San Francisco CA 94080

HARRIS, SIGMUND PAUL, physicist; b. Buffalo, Oct. 12, 1921; s. Nathan N. and Ida (Lebovitz) H.; m. Florence Katcoff, Sept. 19, 1948; 1 child, Roslyn (Mrs. Arnold Hurwitz). BA cum laude, SUNY, Buffalo, 1941, MA, 1943; postgrad., Yale U., 1943; PhD, Ill. Inst. Tech., 1954. Physicist Metall. Lab. U. Chgo., 1943-44; jr. scientist Los Alamos (N.Mex.) Nat. Lab., 1944-46; assoc. physicist Argonne Nat. Lab., Chgo., 1946-53; sr. physicist Tracer Lab., Inc., Boston, 1954-56; sr. research engr. Atomics Internat., Canoga Park, Calif., 1956-64; head physics sect. research div. Maremont Corp., Pasadena, Calif., 1964-66; from asst. prof. to full prof. L.A. Pierce Coll., Woodland Hills, Calif., 1966-86, prof. physics emeritus, 1986—; cons. Space Scis. Inc., Monrovia, Calif., 1968—. Author: Introduction to Air Pollution, 1973. Patentee method for measuring power level of nuclear reactor, apparatus for producing neutrons. Mem. Am. Physics Soc., Am. Nuclear Soc., Am. Assn. Physics Tchrs., Phi Beta Kappa, Sigma Xi. Home: 5831 Saloma Ave Van Nuys CA 91411 Office: 6201 Winnetka Ave Woodland Hills CA 91371

HARRIS, STANLEY WARREN, wildlife orinthology educator; b. Dodson, Mont., Sept. 18, 1928; s. Michael Harold and Pearl Mary (Fry) H.; m. Lorene Johnson, June 24, 1950; children: Tonna Jean, Michael Harold. BS, Wash. State Coll., 1950, MS, 1952; PhD, U. Minn., 1957. Biologist Alaska Dept. Fish and Game, Fairbanks, 1962-63; research biologist Minn. Dept. Fish and Game, St. Paul, 1956-59; asst. prof. wildlife Humboldt State U., Arcata, Calif., 1959-64, assoc. prof. wildlife, 1964-69, chmn. dept. wildlife, 1967-71, prof. wildlife, 1969—; mem. marsh task force City of Arcata, 1977—; shorebird adv. com. Calif. Fish and Game Commn., Sacramento, 1973-75, condor adv. com., 1981-85. Contbr. articles to profl. jours. Served to 1st lt. USAF, 1954-56. Recipient Dist. Teaching award Humboldt State U., 1967. Mem. The Wildlife Soc. (pres. we. sect. 1968, v.p. 1967, past pres. 1969, named Conservationist of Yr. 1973, Educator of Yr. 1973). Avocations: birding, photography. Office: Humboldt State U Arcata CA 95521

HARRISON, CAROLE ALBERTA, museum curator, civic worker; b. Dayton, Ohio, Jan. 16, 1942; d. Chester Arthur and Mildred Irene (Focke) Shaw; student U. Dayton, 1959-60, U. Colo., 1960-61; m. Darrell Harrison, Apr. 24, 1962; children—Amelia Holmes, Ann Elizabeth, Abigail Shaw. With Council for Pub. TV, Channel 6, Inc., Denver, 1972-78, Hist. Denver, Inc., 1973—; owner Old Number One Fire House Restaurant, The Christmas Catalog; dir. devel. Sewall Rehab. Center, Denver, 1979-80; exec. v.p. Marilyn Van Derbur Motivational Inst., Inc., 1980-82. Bd. dirs. Center for Public Issues, Denver, 1979-82, Passages, 1982—, Hall of Life, 1981-83, Historic Denver, 1982-84, Denver Firefighters Mus., 1979—; bd. dirs. KRMA-TV Vols., 1970—, pres., 1973-74; founder Com. for Support of Arts, Denver, 1978-79; chmn. Graland Country Day Sch. Auction, 1979, 80, Channel 6 Auction, 1971, 72, Colo. Acad. Auction, 1980; bd. dirs. Met. Denver and Colo. Conv. and Visitors Bur. Mem. Leadership Denver Alumni Assn. (dir. 1980-82), Denver C. of C. (govt. relations com. 1983—). Club: Pinehurst Country. Home: 5303 W Oberlin Dr Denver CO 80235 Office: 1326 Tremont Pl Denver CO 80204

HARRISON, CHARLES WAGNER, JR., applied physicist; b. Farmville, Va., Sept. 15, 1913; s. Charles Wagner and Etta Earl (Smith) H.; m. Fern F. Perry, Dec. 28, 1940; children—Martha R., Charlotte J. Student, U.S. Coast Guard Acad., 1934-36; B.S. in Engring., U. Va., 1939, E.E., 1940; S.M., Harvard U., 1942, M.E., 1952, Ph.D. in Applied Physics, 1954. Registered profl. engr., N.Mex., Va., Mass. Commd. ensign U.S. Navy, 1939, advanced through grades to comdr., 1948; research staff Bur. Ships, 1939-41, asst. dir. electronics design and devel. div., 1948-50; research staff U.S. Naval Research Lab., 1944-45, dir.'s staff, 1950-51; liaison officer Evans Signal Lab., 1945-46; electronics officer Phila. Naval Shipyard, 1946-48; mem. USN Operational Devel. Force Staff, 1953-55; staff Comdg. Gen. Armed Forces Spl. Weapons project, 1955-57; ret. U.S. Navy, 1957; cons. electromagnetics Sandia Nat. Labs., Albuquerque, 1957-73; instr. U. Va., 1939-40; lectr. Harvard U., 1942-43, Princeton U., 1943-44; vis. prof. Christian Heritage Coll., El Cajon, Calif., 1976. Author: (with R.W.P. King) Antennas and Waves: A Modern Approach, 1969; contbr. numerous articles to profl. jours. Founder Fellowship Bible Ch., chmn. steering com., 1976-77, deacon, 1978-81, 83-86. Fellow IEEE (Electronics Achievement award 1966, best paper award electromagnetic compatibility group 1972); mem. Soc. Harvard Engrs. and Scientists, Internat. Union Radio Sci. (commn. B. and H), Sigma Xi. Home: 2808 Alcazar St NE Albuquerque NM 87110

HARRISON, DAVID FRANCIS, data processing executive; b. St. Louis, Aug. 1, 1936; s. Horace Earl and Lottie Ruth (Moore) H.; divorced; children: Bryon Scott, Grant David; m. Susan Jean Luttringhaus, May 13, 1979; 1 child, Clark Antony. BMusEd, St. Louis Inst. Music, 1961; MusM, U. Nebr., 1965; postgrad., U. Iowa, 1966-70. Systems analyst Control Data Corp., Arlington, Va., 1976-78; sr. systems analyst Control Data Corp., Alexandria, Va., 1978-80; cons. Control Data Corp., San Diego, 1980-84; mgr. adv. SW tech. applications Litton Systems, Inc., Woodland Hills, Calif., 1984, mgr. SW development support services, 1984—. Pres. Hollow Hills Greens Home Owners' Assn. S., Inc., 1985-86, bd. dirs., v.p. Mem. Computer Soc. of IEEE, Spl. INterest Group on Ada, Assn. Computing Machinery. Republican. Club: Litton Mgmt. Home: 2018 Covington Ave Simi Valley CA 93065 Office: Litton Systems Inc 5500 Canoga Ave B30/MS09 Woodland Hills CA 91367

HARRISON, EARLE, former county official; b. Rainsville, Ala., May 20, 1905; s. Robert Lee and Sarepta Ophelia (Hansard) H.; m. Joan Mary Jackson, Jan. 24, 1942. AB, Northwestern U., 1929, postgrad. in bus. adminstrn., 1942; LLB, Chgo.-Kent Coll. Law, 1935. With Marshall Field & Co., Chgo., 1929-68; div. operating mgr. Marshall Field & Co., 1958-60, v.p. operations, 1960-64, v.p., treas., 1964-68; bd. dirs. Credit Bur. Cook County, 1949-69, pres., 1958-69; mem. bd. suprs., chmn. planning and zoning com. Lake County, Ill., 1970—; cons. finance and adminstrn. to hosps. and health care instns. Commr. Northeastern Ill. Planning Commn., 1970—; pres. Northeastern Ill. Plan Commn., 1973, now mem. exec. com.; ret. pres., bd. dirs. Family Fin. Counseling Service Greater Chgo.; bd. dirs. Condell Meml. Hosp., Libertyville, Ill., 1971—, adminstr., 1973—, pres., 1975-78, bus. cons., 1978—. Mem. Phi Delta Phi. Episcopalian. Home: 2712 Chrysler Dr Roswell NM 88201

HARRISON, ERNEST, JR., banker; b. Whitewright, Tex., Jan. 14, 1929; s. Ernest and Ressie Dare (Booher) H.; m. Joanne Bloxom, Jan. 1, 1948 (div. Apr. 1949); m. Nancy Aleene Gore, Sept. 29, 1950; 1 child, Deborah Ann Harrison Mande. B.B.A., U. N.Mex., 1956; Am. Sch. Law, La Salle Extension U., Chgo., 1959. Spl. agt. FBI, Washington, 1947-79; sr. v.p., br. adminstr. Western Bank, Albuquerque, 1979—. Bd. dirs. Cystic Fibrosis Found., 1985—; hon. bd. dirs. Boy's Clubs Am. Served with U.S. Army, 1950-52. Mem. Am. Bankers Assn., Soc. Former FBI Agts. (chmn. Albuquerque 1979—), Ret. Chiefs of Police Assn. Republican. Club: 100 (Albuquerque). Lodges: Rotary, Elks. Home: 2703 Washington NE Albuquerque NM 87110 Office: Western Bank 505 Marquette NW Albuquerque NM 87103

HARRISON, JAMES GORDON, electronics engineer; b. Shelby, Mich., June 19, 1953; s. Robert Doak and Pauline Jean (Mathews) H. BSEE, U. Calif., Santa Barbara, 1977; MSEE, U. So. Calif., 1986. Mem. tech. staff Hughes Aircraft Co., Torrance, Calif., 1977-80; mem. tech. staff TRW Inc., Redondo Beach, Calif., 1980—, sr. staff engr., 1986—. Mem. IEEE. Libertarian. Avocations: violin, scuba diving, hiking, car restoration, herpetology. Home: 3503 Gibson Pl Redondo Beach CA 90278 Office: TRW 1 Space Park Bldg M5-1150 Redondo Beach CA 90278

HARRISON, JOHN CONWAY, state justice; b. Grand Rapids, Minn., Apr. 28, 1913; s. Francis Randall and Ethglyn (Conway) H.; widowed; children—Nina Lyn, Robert Charles, Molly M., Frank R., Virginia Lee. LL.D., George Washington U., 1940. Bar: Mont. 1947, U.S. Dist. Ct. 1947. County atty. Lewis and Clark County, Helena, Mont., 1934-60; justice Mont. Supreme Ct., Helena, 1961—. Pres. Mont. TB Assn., Helena, 1951-54; Am. Lung Assn., N.Y.C., 1972-73, local council Boy Scouts Am., Great Falls, Mont., 1976-78. Served to col. U.S. Army. Lodge: Kiwanis (pres. 1953). Home: 516 N Park St Helena MT 59601 Office: Mont Supreme Ct Justice Bldg Helena MT 59601

HARRISON, JOYCE MARIE, physical education educator, writer; b. Southgate, Calif., Jan. 21, 1943; d. Loyd M. and Gladys R. (Olsen) H. BA, Calif. State U., Long Beach, 1964, MA, 1966; EdD, Brigham Young U., 1973. Cert. tchr., Calif. Tchr. Anaheim (Calif.) Sch. Dist., 1965-66; missionary Ch. Jesus Christ Latter-day Sts., Peru, Ecuador, Columbia, 1966-68; prof. phys. edn. Brigham Young U., Provo, Utah, 1969—. Author: Fitness for Life, 1976, 3d rev. edit., 1984, Instructional Strategies, 1983, Bowling, 1986; contbr. articles to publs. Mem. AAHPERD, Daus. Utah Pioneers, Phi Kappa Phi, Phi Delta Kappa. Office: Brigham Young U 221 B Richards Bldg Provo UT 84602

HARRISON, LOU, composer, educator; b. Portland, Oreg., May 14, 1917. Student, San Francisco State U., 1934-35, Henry Cowell and Arnold Schoenberg. Prof. music Black Mountain Coll., 1947-48, San Jose State Coll., Calif., 1967-80, Mills Coll., Oakland, Calif., 1980—; Am. rep. League of Asian Composers Conf., 1975. Composer Third Symphony, 1981-82; puppet opera Young Caesar, 1970-71; Four Strict Songs (commn. from Louisville Orch.), 1955, Suite for Piano, Violin and Small Orch., 1951. Recipient grant Guggenheim, 1952; recipient grant Guggenheim, Rome, 1954, grant Rockefeller, Korea, 1962-63; Fulbright sr. scholar N.Z., 1983. Mem. Am. Acad. Arts and Letters (music mem.).

HARRISON, RICHARD ROY, financial planner, consultant; b. Chgo., Aug. 11, 1941; s. Tillman Edwin and Marguerite (White) H.; m. Violeta Ausra Druskis, Aug. 26, 1967; children: Lisa Jura, Kevin Remis. BA in History, Roosevelt U., 1969; MA in Anthropology, Idaho State U., 1972; PhD in Anthropology, Ind. U., 1985. Dir. cultural resource program Dept. Interior, Boise, Idaho, 1975-83; dir. cultural program Ctr. for Humanities, Sun Valley, Idaho, 1982-84, dir. winter lectures, 1982-83; research assoc. U. Idaho, Moscow, 1983-86; commr. Fine Arts Commn., Boise, 1976; mem. exec. council Intermountain Antiquities Computer System, Salt Lake City, 1981-83. Comtbr. articles to profl. jours. Recipient Mercury award, 1986; named Rookie of Yr., Boise div. IDS/Am. Express, 1986. Office: 6550 Emerald Suite 108 Boise ID 83705

HARRISON, SCOTT JAMES, JR., marketing executive; b. Houston, Nov. 21, 1941; s. Scott James and Grace Elizabeth (Folk) H.; m. Marianne Roberta Fasy, June 13, 1964; children—Christina, Elizabeth, James, Charles. Student Villanova, U., 1959-61; B.A., Georgetown U., 1963; postgrad. U. Chgo., 1963-68. Postgrad. Fellow, instr. U. Chgo., 1966-68; programmer Nat. Opinion Research Ctr., Chgo., 1968-75, SRI Internat., Menlo Park, Calif., 1975-78; programming mgr. Visa Internat., San Francisco, 1978-81, mktg. exec., 1981—. Mem. Ray Sch. PTA, Chgo., 1966-68. Mem. AAAS, Assn Computing Machinery, Am. Math. Assn., Smithsonian Instn. Democrat. Roman Catholic. Club: Colony (Half Moon Bay, Calif.). Home: PO Box 529 Half Moon Bay CA 94019 Office: Visa Internat PO Box 8999 San Francisco CA 94128

HARRISON, THOMAS GENE, psychotherapist; b. Montebello, Calif., Oct. 27, 1949; s. Von S. and Laura (Virginia) (Smith) H.; m. Linda Crandall, June 22, 1972; children: Lisa, Robert, Jeff, Lara, Tommy, Spencer. BS in Sociology, U. Utah, 1974, MSW, 1977. Psychiat. specialist Primary Childrens Med. Ctr., Salt Lake City, 1972-76, dir. social services dept. child psychiatry, 1977-80, coordinator child protection team, 1977-79, psychiat. social worker, coordinator child sexual assault program, 1979-84; dir., owner Psychotherapy Assocs., Salt Lake City, 1983—; chmn. Nat. Sex Edn. Com., Salt Lake City, 1977-83; cons. Utah Pornography Com., Salt Lake City, 1984—, child abuse com. Ch. Jesus Christ Latter-Day Saints; speaker in field. Author: Those Who Offend My Little Ones, 1986; also articles. News guest Sta. KSL-AM-FM-TV, Salt Lake City, 1977-79, 81, 83, 84-86; mem. Utah chpt. Nat. Com. Protection of Children Against Child Abuse, Salt Lake City, 1984-85. Recipient Connie Montenson Woolsey award U. Utah, 1976-77. Mem. Nat. Assn. Social Workers (ret., com. chmn.), Soc. Hosp. Soc. Work Dirs. (chmn. 1977-78). Avocation: vocal performance. Office: Psycho Therapy Assocs 34 S 500 East #107 Salt Lake City UT 84102

HARRISS, PETER LATHAM, criminologist, real estate investor; b. San Pedro, Calif., Sept. 2, 1932; s. George Latham and Marion (Norris) H.; m. Ute Erika Rohland, Apr. 14, 1967; 1 child, Erika Norris. Student in bus. and pub. adminstrn., U. Md., 1956-58; student in pub. adminstrn., Am. U., 1963-64; BA in Criminology, U. Calif., Berkeley, 1969; MS in Pub. Adminstrn., Calif. State U., Hayward, 1973. Commd. U.S. Army, 1951, advanced through grades to capt.; grunt 7th Cav, 2d div. U.S. Army, Republic of Korea, 1951-53; investigator CIC, CID U.S. Army, 1958-65; grunt 11th Cav U.S. Army, Viet Nam, 1965-66; resigned U.S. Army, 1966; criminologist Calif., 1969—. Mem. AAAS, U. Calif. Alum Assn., Am. Polygraph Assn. Club: Aerobats. Avocation: reproduction and redesign art nuveau, radio control model flying. Home: 518 Florence Ave Oakland CA 94618

HARROLD, ORVILLE GOODWIN, mathematics educator, retired; b. Chgo., Sept. 2, 1909; s. Orville Goodwin and Estelle (Pancake) H.; m. Gladys Estelle Buell, June 30, 1934; children: Phillip (dec.), Jeffrey. AB with gt. distinction, Stanford U., 1931, MA, 1932, PhD, 1936. Instr. math. Oreg. State Coll., Corvallis, 1937-39; NRC research fellow U. Va., 1939-40; instr. math. Nothwestern U., Evanston, Ill., 1940-42; asst. prof. math. La. State U., Baton Rouge, 1942-43, Pomona Coll., Claremont, Calif., 1943-46; lectr. math. Princeton (N.J.) U., 1946-47; prof. U. Tenn., Knoxville, 1947-64, head dept., 1961-64; prof. Fla. State U., Tallahassee, 1964-79, chmn. dept., 1964-74, prof. emeritus, 1979—; lectr. U. Mich. Conf. Math. Topology, Ann Arbor, 1940, Waseda U., Tokyo, 1971; cons. Union Carbide Corp., 1949-61. Co-author: Basic Topology, 1975; contbr. articles to profl. jours. Guggenheim fellow, 1958. Fellow AAAS; mem. Am. Math. Soc. (assoc. sec. southeastern sect. 1964-76), Math. Assn. Am., Set Theoret Topology Inst., 3-Dimensional Topology Inst., Colloquia Mathematica Societatis, Topology Conf., Woodrow Wilson Fellowship Bd (regional selectional com.), NRC (regional devel. com., research fellow 1939-40), Sigma Xi, Phi Beta Kappa. Democrat. Unitarian. Avocations: reading, studying psychology. Home: 26 Northwood Commons Chico CA 95926

HART, ALAN WALTER, petroleum geologist; b. Victoria, Tex., Feb. 3, 1951; s. Thomas Victor and Betty Anne (Berry) H.; m. Lisa Anne Woods, Aug. 21, 1976; 1 child, Sean Alan. BS in Geology, U. Tex., Arlington, 1974, MS in Geology, 1979. Photogeologist Hunt Oil Co., Dallas, 1974-78; sr. geologist Hunt Oil Co., Denver, 1978-83; staff geologist ARCO Internat. Oil and Gas Co., Los Angeles, 1983—. Vol. counselor Boy Scouts Am., Arlington, 1970-78, merit badge counselor, Denver, 1978-83. Research grantee Mobil Oil Corp., 1974. Mem. Soc. Mining Engrs. of AIME, Am. Assn. Petroleum Geologist (cert.), Geol. Soc. Am., Sigma Xi (assoc.), Phi Delta Theta (sec. 1972-74). Republican. Mem. Ch. Christian Sci. Avocations: snow skiing, hiking, swimming, volleyball, horseback riding. Office: ARCO Internat Oil & Gas Co 444 S Flower St Suite 3289 Los Angeles CA 90017

HART, ANN WEAVER, educational administration educator; b. Salt Lake City, Nov. 6, 1948; d. Ted Lionel and Sylvia (Moray) Weaver; m. Randy Bret Hart, Sept. 12, 1968; children: Kimberly, Liza, Emily, Allyson. BS in History, U. Utah, 1970, MA in History, 1981, PhD in Ednl. Adminstrn., 1983. Tchr. pub. schs. Salt Lake City, 1970-73, 80-81; jr. high sch. prin. Provo (Utah) Pub. Schs., 1983-84; asst. prof. ednl. adminstrn. U. Utah, Salt Lake City, 1984—; cons. sch. dists., Utah and Calif., 1983—, Calif. Legislature, 1985. Contbr. articles to profl. jours. Grantee U. Utah, State of Utah, U.S. Dept. Edn. Mem. Am. Ednl. Research Assn., Phi Beta Kappa, Phi Kappa Phi. Democrat. Mormon. Avocations: skiing, backpacking. Office: U Utah Dept Ednl Adminstrn 339 MBH Salt Lake City UT 84112

HART, ARCHIBALD DANIEL, seminary dean, psychology educator; b. Kimerley, South Africa, Apr. 27, 1932; came to U.S., 1973, naturalized, 1984; s. Daniel Henry and Gertrude (Smith) H.; m. Kathleen Armstrong, Dec. 4, 1954; children—Catherine, Sharon, Sylvia. M.I.C.E., Instn. Civil Engrs., London, 1955; B.Sc., U. South Africa, 1962; M.Sc., U. Natal, South Africa, 1967, Ph.D., 1969. Lic. psychologist, Calif. Civil engr. City of Pietermaritzburg, South Africa, 1959-68, clin. psychologist, 1969-73; asst. prof. psychology Grad. Sch. Psychology, Fuller Theol. Sem., Pasadena, Calif., 1974-75, assoc. prof., 1976-83, prof., dean, psychology, 1983—. Author: Feeling Free, 1979; Depression, Coping and Caring, 1981; Children and Divorce, 1982; The Success Factor, 1984; Coping with Depression in the Ministry and Helping Professions, 1984. First recipient C. Davis Weyerhauser award Fuller Theol. Sem. Bd. Trustees, 1979. Mem. Am. Psychol. Assn., Calif. State Psychol. Assn., Biofeedback Soc. Calif. (pres. 1981). Home: 1042 Cyrus Ln Arcadia CA 91006 Office: Fuller Theol Sem 177 N Madison Ave Pasadena CA 91101

HART, ARTHUR ALVIN, museum director; b. Tacoma, Feb. 13, 1921; s. Albert Arthur and Erma Lola (Maltby) H.; m. Novella D. Cochran, Feb. 26, 1944; children—Susanna, Robin, Catherine, Allison. B.A., U. Wash., Seattle, 1948, M.F.A., 1948; postgrad., Biarritz Am. U., Hans Hofmann Sch. Fine Arts, U. Calif., Berkeley; H.H.D. honoris causa, Coll. Idaho, 1985. Head art dept., chmn. div. fine arts Coll. Idaho, 1948-53; instr. art Colby Jr. Coll. Women, New London, N.H., 1953-54; head art dept., dir. adult edn. Bay Path Jr. Coll., Longmeadow, Mass., 1955-69; dir. Idaho Hist. Mus., Boise, 1969-75, Idaho Hist. Soc., 1975-86; lectr. Am. architecture Boise State U., 1970-86 ; mem. Boise Allied Arts Council, 1970-78, Idaho Historic Preservation Council, 1971-87, Boise Bicentennial Commn., 1975-76, Idaho Centennial Commn., 1985—, Idaho Humanities Council, 1985-86; mem. adv. bd. Snake River Regional Studies Center, 1969—, Boise Redevel. Agy., 1986-87, Basque Mus. and Cultural Ctr., 1985—. Author: Steam Trains in Idaho, 1971, Space, Style and Structure: Building in Northwest American, 1974, Fighting Fire on the Frontier, 1976, Historic Boise, 1979, The Boiseans: At Home, 1984, Idaho, Gem of the Mountains, 1985, Basin of Gold, 1986; also numerous articles. Served with USAAF, 1942-44; Served with AUS, 1944-46. Recipient Idaho Statesman Disting. Citizen award, 1973; Allied Arts Council award for hist. writing, 1972; Phoenix award for leadership in conservation Soc. Am. Travel Writers, 1982. Mem. AIA (hon.), AAUP, Coll. Art Assn., Soc. Archtl. Historians (pres. No. Pacific Coast chpt. 1974-76), Am. Assn. Museums (mem. council 1980-82, pres. Western regional conf. 1979-81).

HART, EDWARD B., retail drug store company executive; b. 1924; married. BS, Oreg. State U., 1948. With Pay Less Drug Stores NW, Inc., 1948—, pharmacist, then asst. store mgr., Lewiston, Idaho, then mgr. trainee, Portland, Oreg., 1951-53, store mgr., Coos Bay, Oreg., 1953-63, corp. v.p., 1963-67, pres., 1967-86, chief exec. officer, 1969—, chmn., 1980—, also bd. dirs. Served to lt. (j.g.) USN, 1943-46, USNR, 1946-56. Office: Pay Less Drug Stores NW Inc 9275 SW Peyton Ln Wilsonville OR 97070 *

HART, EDWIN JAMES, chemist; b. Port Angeles, Wash., Feb. 7, 1910; s. Fitch James and Josie Anna Elizabeth (Blater) H.; m. Rozella Patricia Clark, June 17, 1939; children: Fitch J., Ann E., John P. B.S., M.S., Wash. State U., 1931; Ph.D., Brown U., 1934; D. Degree (hon.), Technische U., Berlin, 1984. With L.I. Biol. Lab., 1934-36, U.S. Rubber Co., 1936-48; sr. chemist Argonne Nat. Lab., 1948-75, cons., 1975—; Brit. Empire Cancer Campaign fellow Mt. Vernon Hosp., Eng., 1961-62; mem. quartermaster dosimetry panel Nat. Acad. Sci., 1955-58, radiobiology com., 1958-64, food irradiation com., 1963-72; del. 2d UN Internat. Conf. on Peaceful Uses Atomic Energy, Geneva, 1958; mem. Internat. Com. on Radiol. Units, 1960-63; cons. Danish Atomic Energy Commn., 1967—; IAEA cons. to Bhabha Atomic Research Centre, Trombay, India, winter 1970; mem. sci. staff U.S. Atoms in Action Program, Tehran, Iran, 1967; vis. prof. Hebrew U., Israel, fall 1967; cons. Lawrence Berkeley Lab., 1976-79; vis. scientist Hahn-Meitner-Institut für Kernforschung, Berlin, 1984—. Author: (with M. Anbar) The Hydrated Electron, 1970. sr. U.S. scientist awardee Alexander von Humboldt Found., W. Ger., 1979-80; recipient Weiss medal Assn. for Radiation Research, Eng., 1975, citation for disting. achievement Brown U., 1983; citation for Disting. Achievement, Washington State U., 1984. Mem. Am. Chem. Soc., AAAS, Soc. Free Radical Research (hon.), Radiation Research Soc., Phi Beta Kappa, Sigma Xi, Phi Kappa Phi, Phi Lambda Upsilon. Home: 2115 Hart Rd Port Angeles WA 98362

HART, GARY, former senator, lawyer; b. Ottawa, Kans., Nov. 28, 1936; m. Lee Ludwig, 1958; children: Andrea, John. Grad., Bethany Nazarene Coll., Okla.; LL.B., Yale, 1964. Bar: Colo. 1964. Began career as atty. U.S. Dept. Justice, Washington; then spl. asst. to sec. U.S. Dept. Interior; practiced in Denver 1967-70, 72-74; nat. campaign dir. Senator George McGovern Democratic Presdl. Campaign, 1970-72; U.S. senator from Colo. 1976-84; founder, 1st chmn. Environ. Study Conf., 1975; congl. adviser Salt II Talks, 1977; adviser UN Spl. Session on Disarmament, 1978; chmn. Nat. Commn. on Air Quality, 1978-81; founder Congl. Mil. Reform Caucus, 1981. Author: Right From the Start, 1973, A New Democracy, 1983, The Double Man, 1985, America Can Win, 1986, The Strategies of Zeus, 1987. Student vol. John F. Kennedy Presdl. Campaign, 1960; vol. organizer Robert F. Kennedy Presdl. Campaign, 1968; bd. visitors U.S. Air Force Acad., 1975—, chmn., 1978-80; candidate for Democratic presdl. nomination, 1983-84. Office: SR-237 Russell Senate Office Bldg US Sen Washington DC 20510

HART, HERBERT DORLAN, chemistry educator; b. Eckert, Colo., Feb. 21, 1910; s. Alpheus Edwin and Jessie (Dorlan) H.; B.S. in Chemistry, U. Denver, 1940, M.S., 1952; m. Constance Joy Spence, Dec. 26, 1940. Sr. resident officer U.S. Fgn. Service, Augsburg, Germany, 1948-50; instr. chemistry Fort Lewis Coll., Durango, Colo., 1954-56, asst. prof., 1956-68, chmn. div. phys. sci., engring and math., 1960-68, acting pres., 1962; asso. prof. chemistry Coll. Notre Dame, Belmont, Calif., 1968-82, chmn. dept., 1968-76; instr. chemistry Canada Coll., Redwood City, Calif., 1982—; cons. on water contamination problems, ranches, fisheries; analyst vanadium and uranium ore Vanadium Corp. Am., 1956. Served to maj. AUS, 1940-48; ETO. Decorated Bronze Star. Fellow Am. Inst. Chemists (cert. profl. chemist, nat. com. for profl. tng. and edn. 1975—); mem. Am. Chem. Soc., Mil. Order World Wars (jr. vice comdr. Peninsula chpt. 1976-77, comdr. 1978-79, 83-84), Am. Watchmakers Inst., Sigma Xi, Phi Delta Epsilon, Phi Delta Phi, Phi Delta Kappa, Pi Kappa Alpha. Episcopalian. Home: 1000 Continentals Way Apt 217 Belmont CA 94002 Office: Canada Coll 4200 Farm Hill Blvd Redwood City CA 94061

HART, HOWARD ARTHUR, personnel outplacement company executive; b. Newark, Oct. 20, 1934; s. Irving J. and Helen (Franklin) H. BS, U. Pa., 1956; MBA, Fla. Atlantic U., 1973; postgrad., Golden Gate U., 1983. Mgr. mktg., cons. edn. and sales tng. IBM Corp., N.Y.C. and N.J., 1956-65; tng. chief N.J. Community Action Tng. Inst., Trenton, 1965-66; mgr. corp. manpower devel. ESB Ray-O-Vac Mgmt. Corp., Phila., 1966-82; mgr. corp. tng. and devel. Atari Inc., Sunnyvale, Calif., 1982-83; v.p. Drake Beam Morin Inc., San Francisco, 1983—; lectr., cons. in field; guest prof. Temple U., Phila., 1975-76. Served to 1st lt. Q.M.C., U.S. Army. Recipient Leadership Conf. Achievement award Am. Mgmt. Assn., Profl. Excellence award Drake Beam Morin Inc., 1985. Mem. Indsl. Relations Assn. (past v.p. Phila. chpt.), Am. Soc. Tng. and Devel., Am. Soc. Personnel Adminstrs., No. Calif. Human Resources Council, San Francisco C. of C. (arts and culture council). Office: Drake Beam Morin Inc One Embarcadero Ctr Suite 4100 San Francisco CA 94111

HART, JACK ROBERT, editor; b. Tacoma, Sept. 7, 1946; s. John Sebald and Alice Agnes (Hurlbut) H.; m. Cherie Denise Boston, Dec. 27, 1970 (div. 1978); children: Joshua John, Aaron Lee, Jesse Robert. BA in journalism, U. Wash., 1968; PhD in Mass Communications, U. Wis., 1975. Instr. Calif. State U., Northridge, 1971-74; from asst. prof. to assoc. prof. journalism U. Oreg., Eugene, 1974-82, acting dean Sch. Journalism, 1982; reporter Register-Guard, Eugene, 1980; arts and leisure editor The Oregonian, Portland, 1981-82, editor N.W. Mag., 1982—; cons. and speaker in field; vis. faculty The Poynter Inst., St. Petersburg, Fla., 1984—, Oreg. State U., Corvallis, 1985—. Author: The Information Empire, 1979; contbr. articles to profl. jours. Served to 2d lt. USAR, 1968-70. Recipient Nat. Teaching award Am. Soc. Newspaper Editors, 1981, Excellence in Newspaper Writing award Am. Assn. Schs. and Depts. Journalism. Mem. Oreg. Newspaper Pub.'s Assn. (freedom of info. com.), Oreg. Press Bar Bench Broadcasters Com. Avocations: water and snow skiing, fly fishing, tennis, racketball. Home: 2376 SW Cedar Portland OR 97205 Office: NW Mag The Oregonian 1320 SW Broadway Portland OR 97205

HART, JAMES DAVID, educator; b. San Francisco, Apr. 18, 1911; s. Julien and Helen Louise (Neustadter) H.; m. Ruth Arnstein, June 14, 1938 (dec. 1977); children: Carol Helen (Mrs. John L. Field), Peter David; m. Constance Crowley Bowles, Feb. 9, 1985. A.B., Stanford U., 1932; M.A., Harvard U., 1933, Ph.D., 1936; L.H.D., Mills Coll., 1978. Mem. faculty U. Calif.-Berkeley, 1936—, chmn. dept., 1955-57, 65-69, vice chancellor, 1957-60; acting dir. Bancroft Library, 1961-62, dir., 1969—; vis. prof. Harvard U., 1964; Phi Beta Kappa vis. scholar, 1980-81; chmn. Marshall Scholarship Com. Western U.S., 1959-63, 79-86, adv. council Brit. Ambassador, 1986—. Author: The Oxford Companion Am. Literature, 1941, rev. edits, The Popular Book, 1950, 61, America's Literature, (with C. Gohdes), 1955, American Images of Spanish California, 1960, The Private Press Ventures of Samuel Lloyd Osbourne and R.L.S, 1966, A Companion to California, 1978; New Englanders in Nova Albion, 1976, Fine Printing: The San Francisco Tradition, 1985. Editor: My First Publication, 1961, The Oregon Trail (Francis Parkman), 1963, From Scotland to Silverado (Robert Louis Stevenson), 1966, A Novelist in the Making (Frank Norris), 1970; Contbr. articles to mags., revs. Trustee Mills Coll., 1970-78, 79-86, pres. bd., 1973-76; trustee Fine Arts Mus. San Francisco, 1983—. Decorated comdr. Order Brit. Empire. Fellow Am. Antiquarian Soc., Am. Acad. Arts and Scis., Calif. Hist. Soc.; mem. Modern Lang. Assn., Philol. Assn. Pacific Coast, Book Club of Calif. (pres. 1956-60). Clubs: Bohemian (San Francisco); Grolier (N.Y.C.); Century Assn., Faculty (Berkeley). Home: 740 San Luis Rd Berkeley CA 94707

HART, JEAN MACAULAY, clinical social worker; b. Bellingham, Wash.; d. Murry Donald and Pearl N. (McLeod) Macaulay; m. Richard D. Hart, Feb. 3, 1940 (dec. Mar. 1973); children: Margaret Morrison, Pamela Horton, Patricia L. Hart; m. Lawrence Duling, Jan. 20, 1979. BA, Wash. State U., 1938; MSW, U. So. Calif., 1961. Social worker Los Angeles County, 1957-58; children's service worker Dept. Children's Services, Los Angeles, 1958-59, homemakers services cons., 1962-64; homemaker cons. Calif. State Dept., 1964-66; supr. protective services Dept. Children's Services, Los Angeles, 1966-67; dep. regional service adminstrn. Dept. Los Angeles County Children's Services, 1967-76. Mem. Portals Com., Los Angeles, 1974, Travelers Aid Bd., Long Beach, Calif. 1969. Recipient Nat. award work in community, spl. award for work with emotionally disturbed Com. for Los Angeles, 1974. Mem. AAUW, Nat. Assn. Social Workers (former delegate), Acad. Cert. Social Workers. Republican. Congregationalist. Club: Wing Point Golf and Country (Bainbridge Island, Wash.). Avocations: golf, bridge.

HART, JOAN, editor, publisher; b. London, Dec. 5, 1939; came to U.S., 1953; d. Alexander Konopla and Katie (Gordon) Konopla Vein; m. Bruce Edward Hart, Oct. 12, 1966 (div. Oct. 1981); children: John Alexander, Darren Douglas. Grad. high sch., Van Nuys, Calif., 1967. Personnel mgr. Armorlite Inc., Burbank, Calif., 1967-76; assoc. pub., editor Creative Age Pubs., Van Nuys, 1976—. Avocations: camping, reading, sewing, crafts. Home: 7740 Balboa Blvd #167 Van Nuys CA 91406 Office: Creative Age Pubs 7628 Densmore Ave Van Nuys CA 91406

HART, JOHN, artistic dir.; b. London, 1924. Student, Sch. Sadler's Wells Ballet. Dancer Sadler's Wells Royal Ballet, London, 1938-42, from 1946; created roles in ballets of Ninette de Valois, appeared in premieres of works by Frederick Ashton, including The Wanderer, 1941, Sylvia, 1952 Sadler's Wells Royal Ballet, later asst. dir., then adminstr., from 1975; artistic dir. Ballet West, Salt Lake City, 1985—; formerly artistic dir. PACT Ballet Co., S. Africa; formerly chmn. dance div. U.S. Internat. U., San Diego; formerly dance dir. San Diego Opera. Author: Ballet and Camera, The Royal Ballet. Recipient 1st Adeline Genee Gold Medal Royal Acad. Dancing, Queen Elizabeth award outstanding achievement in ballet, 1970; decorated comdr. Order Brit. Empire, 1971. Office: Ballet West 50 W 200 S Salt Lake City UT 84101 *

HART, JOSEPH H., bishop; b. Kansas City, Mo., Sept. 26, 1931. Ed., St. John Sem., Kansas City, St. Meinrad Sem., Indpls. Ordained priest Roman Catholic Ch., 1956; consecrated titular bishop of Thimida Regia and aux. bishop Cheyenne Wyo., 1976; apptd. bishop of Cheyenne 1978. Office: Bishop's Residence Box 469 Cheyenne WY 83001 *

HART, LOIS BORLAND, publisher, consultant; b. Syracuse, N.Y., May 15, 1941; d. Leslie R. and Laura S. (Styn) Borland; m. Arnold L. Hart, July 4, 1969; children: Christopher, Richard. BS, U. Rochester, 1966; MS, Syracuse U., 1972; EdD, U. Mass., 1974. Field services coordinator Program Ednl. Opportunity U. Mich., Ann Arbor, 1975-78; pres. Organizational Leadership Inc., East Lansing, Mich., 1978-80; trainer Mgmt. Devel. Ctr. of Mountain State Employers Council, Denver, 1980-81; pres. Leadership Dynamics Inc., Lyons, Colo., 1980—. Author: Are You Stuck, 1986, Survivors of Successful Sales, 1986, Taming Your Junk Jungle, 1986, Conference and Workshop Planners' Manual, 1979, Moving Up! Women and Leadership, 1980, Learning from Conflict, 1981, The Sexes at Work, 1983, Saying Hello: How to get Your Group Started, 1983, Saying Goodbye: Ending Your Group Experience, 1983. Mem. AAUW, NOW, Am. Soc. Tng. and Devel., Americans for a New Way. Home: PO Box 320 Lyons CO 80540 Office: Leadership Dynamics Inc 3775 Iris Ave Suite 3B Boulder CO 80301

HART, MARGIE RUTH, publisher, writer; b. Chesterfield, S.C., Oct. 28, 1943; d. Lonnie Carson and Carrie Jane (Hancock) Sellers; m. Ben Tucker, Mar. 9, 1963 (div. 1980); children: Chipman D., Sandra L.; m. Len Hart, Dec. 21, 1980; children: Richard W., Leonard P., Carl S., Karen J. H. Student, Greenville Tech. Sch., 1964-65. Br. mgr. Caroline Emmons Jewelry Co., western S.C., 1978-79; microwave sales specialist western N.C. and S.C., Whirlpool Corp., 1978-79; sales rep. Cleaves Office Products, 1979; asst. mgr. D & L Assocs., 1977-78; substitute tchr. Picken Jr. High Sch., Pickens, S.C., 1975-79; asst. mgr., co-pub. The Am. Patriot Mag., Barstow, Calif., 1982—. Chmn. 1st supervisorial dist., mem. cen. com. Am. Independent Party, San Bernardino County, Calif., also mem. state exec. bd. congl. dist. coordinator Freedom Counsel, San Bernardino County; chmn. first supervisoral dist. San Bernardino County Am. Ind. Party, 1983-87; mem. nat com. woman Am. Ind. Party, 1986-87; candidate for Calif. Assembly, 1986; chmn. SARB Barstow Schs., 1987; parlimentarian PTA Exec. Bd., Barstow Area, mem. area council PTA; advisor to 61st dist. assemblyman Bill Leonard, 1985-87. Recipient Good Establishment cert., Pickens, S.C., 1977; certs. of appreciation Picken PTA, 1978, Second Amendment Found., 1982. Mem. Concerned Women for Am., Moral Majority. Independent. Baptist. Home: 36832 Colby Ave Barstow CA 92311 Office: PO Box 370 Barstow CA 92311

HART, MARIANNE, medical social worker; b. Washington, Ind., Jan. 15, 1952; d. Paul Bernard Hart and Dorothy Emma (O'Brien) Acker. BS in Social Work, Ind. State U., 1974; MSW, Ariz. State U., 1982. Acting coordinator spl. services disabled student Ariz. State U., Tempe, 1980-81; social worker IV Dept. Pub. Social Services, Barstow, Calif., 1982-83; rehab. social worker Ballard Rehab. Ctr., San Bernardino, Calif., 1983-84; dir. social services St. Mary Desert Valley Hosp., Apple Valley, Calif., 1984-86; pvt. practice clin. social worker Victorville, Calif., 1986—; chmn. bd. dirs. Inland AIDS Project, Loma Linda, Calif. Vol. Hospice, Loma Linda, Calif., 1986—; active Victor Valley Infrastructure, Victorville, Calif., 1986—. Cert. Appreciation Apple Valley Lions Club, 1985, Crisis Pregnancy Ctr., 1985; named Outstanding Young Women Am., 1981. Mem. Nat. Assn. Social Work (membership chmn. 1984-85), Pilot Club of Apple Valley, Inc. (v.p. 1985-86, pres. 1986-87). Democrat. Roman Catholic. Home and Office: 14184 Ft Apache Ct Victorville CA 92392

HART, RAY LEE, educator; b. Hereford, Tex., Mar. 22, 1929; s. Albert Mann and Ruby Douglas (Bracken) H.; m. Juanita Fern Morgan, Sept. 8, 1951; children: Douglas Morgan, Stuart Bracken. B.A., U. Tex., 1949; B.D., So. Methodist U., 1953; Ph.D., Yale U., 1959. Instr., then asst. prof. Drew U. Theol. Sch., 1956-63; asso. prof. philos. and systematic theology Vanderbilt U. Div. Sch., 1963-69; prof., chmn. dept. religious studies U. Mont., 1969—; Cons. on religious studies SUNY, 1972—. Author: Unfinished Man and the Imagination, 1968; trans. into Chinese, editor: Selections from Thomas Aquinas, 1966, The Critique of Modernity, 1986, Trajectories in the Study of Religion, 1987. Mayor, Polebridge, Mont., 1969-70. Mem. Am. Acad. Religion (editor jour. 1970-80, pres. 1983-84, del. to Am. Council Learned Socs. 1980—, mem. exec. com., dir.), Metaphys. Soc. Am., Soc. Sci. Study Religion, Soc. Religion in Higher Edn., Ctr. of Study of World Religions (bd. dirs. 1986—). Home: 16 Carriage Way Missoula MT 59801

HART, ROBERT L., data processing executive; b. Yreka, Calif., July 21, 1932; s. Vicktor W. Hart. BA, U. Calif., Berkeley, 1954. Sr. programmer Calif. Farm Ins. Co., Berkeley, 1958-60; mgr. data processing City of Oakland, Calif., 1960-61, Roseburg (Oreg.) Lumber Co., 1962-77, Cascade Wood Products, White City, Oreg., 1978—. Served to lt. USN, 1955-58. Mem. Assn. Systems Mgmt. Home: 136 Upper Cleveland Rapids Rd Roseburg OR 97470

HART, ROGER M., engineer; b. Salt Lake City, Nov. 12, 1942; m. Deanna Hart, Aug. 28, 1961; children—Deenette, Troy, Tace, Thad, Nathan, Noal, Kyle, Jonathan. Ptnr. Bell Electronics, 1965-68; chief scientist, v.p. Tronac, 1968-79; chief exec. officer Hart Scientific, Provo, Utah, 1979—; dir. Calorimeter Conf., 1977-80. Co-author: Treatise of Analytical Chemistry, 1979; contbr. articles to profl. jours. Mem. The Calorimeter Conf. Address: Hart Scientific PO Box 934 Provo UT 84601

HART, THOMAS ARTHUR, education educator; b. Buenos Aires, Aug. 18, 1905; came to U.S., 1915; s. Joseph Lancaster and Tennessee Ann (Hamilton) H.; m. Catherine Royer, Sept. 26, 1976 (dec. July 1985); m. Dorothy Elvira Carlstrom, Mar. 9, 1986; children: Roger Carlstrom, R. William Carlstrom. BS, William and Mary Coll., 1930; MS, Emory U., 1933, MA, 1937; PhD, U. Chgo., 1941. Prof. biology West Ga. Coll., Carrollton, 1933-42; fgn. service officer U.S. State Dept., various nations in Latin Am., 1945-63; prof. edn. U. Pitts., 1963-76; program asst. R. William Carlstrom and Assocs., Seattle, 1987—; cons. ministries of edn., Bolivia, Ecuador, Paraguay, Venezuela, 1963-77. Author: Compendium de Biologia (2 vols.), 1962; contbr. articles to profl. jours. Served to lt. col. U.S. Army, 1943-45, PTO. Mem. Sigma Xi. Democrat. Unitarian. Avocations: travel, Spanish lang., vol. community health activities. Home: 900 University St Apt 5Q Seattle WA 98101

HART, TIMOTHY RAY, college official, lawyer; b. Portland, Jan. 5, 1942; s. Eldon V. and Wanda J. (Hillyer) H.; m. Mary F. Barlow, Aug. 31, 1964 (div. Dec. 1975); children—Mark, Matthew, Marisa, Martin; m. Annette Bryant, Aug. 8, 1981. A.A., San Jose City Coll., 1968; B.A., San Jose State U., 1970; M.A., Wash. State U., 1973; J.D., San Joaquin Coll. Law, Fresno, Calif., 1983. Bar: Calif. 1983, U.S. Dist. Ct. (ea. dist.) Calif. 1983. Police officer City of Santa Clara, Calif., 1965-71; chief of police U. Idaho, Moscow, 1971-73; crime prevention officer City of Albany, Oreg., 1973-75; instr. criminal justice Coll. of Sequoias, Visalia, Calif., 1975-81, dir. paralegal dept., 1981-83, chmn., dir. adminstrn. justice div., 1983—; sole practice, Visalia, 1983—. Served with USAF, 1960-63. Mem. ABA, Calif. Bar Assn., Assn. Trial Lawyers Am. Mennonite. Home: 2301 S Dollner Visalia CA 93277 Office: Coll of Sequoias 915 S Mooney St Visalia CA 93277 also: 310 W Murray Ave Visalia CA 93291

HART, WARD LAWRENCE, physician; b. San Francisco, Sept. 30, 1920; s. Frank Lawrence and Jessmyn Helen (Bernhard) H.; m. Frances Brunton, June 2, 1945; children—Sheron, Steven, Candace, Brad. A.B., Stanford U., 1941; M.D., St. Louis U., 1944. Diplomate Am. Bd. Internal Medicine. Intern St. Mary's Hosp., San Francisco, 1944-45, resident in internal medicine, 1947-50; chief resident Santa Clara (Calif.) County Hosp., 1949-50; practice medicine specializing in internal medicineSan Carlos, Calif., 1950-85; assoc. clin. prof. medicine Stanford U., 1974—; pres. Peninsula Med. Group, Inc., San Carlos, 1970-84; v.p. Peninsula Med. Lab., Menlo Park, Calif., 1980—; chief of medicine Sequoia Hosp., 1979-83. Served to capt. M.C., U.S. Army, 1945-47, 1953, Korea. Fellow ACP; mem. Calif. Acad. Medicine, San Mateo County Med. Soc. (pres. 1964), Calif. Med. Soc., AMA, Calif. Soc. Internal Medicine, Am. Soc. Internal Medicine. Club: Sharon Heights Golf and Country (Menlo Park). Home: 460 Sand Hill Circle Menlo Park CA 94025 Office: Peninsula Medical Group Inc 1100 Laurel St San Carlos CA 94170

HART, WAYNE DOUGLAS, energy consultant; b. Twin Falls, Idaho, Nov. 5, 1950; s. Glen Robert and Gwen Irene (Hoopes) H.; m. Nan Eleanor Hoke, Aug. 19, 1972. AB, Ind. U., 1973; MS, U. Wis., 1976. Research analyst Idaho Dept. Employment, Boise, 1977-78; dir. energy program Idaho Energy Office, Boise, 1978-79; chief new constrn. br. Bonneville Power, Portland, Oreg., 1980-85; pres. H2A, Inc., Boise, 1985—; staff chmn. Nuclear Power Com. Nat. Govs. Assn., Washington, 1978-79. Editor: Ada County Dems. newsletter, 1976-78, 86; contbr. articles to jours. Bd. dirs. Idaho Consumer Affairs, Boise, 1975-76; pres. Boise Ditch Safety Com., Boise, 1975-80; candidate Ada County Clk., Boise; 2d dist. coordinator Carter/Mondale, Pocatello, Idaho, 1976; campaign mgr. Selander for State Rep., Boise, 1976; county coordinator Kress for Congress, Boise, 1978. Avocations: computers, home maintenance, skiing, camping. Home: 2862 Parke Circle Dr Boise ID 83705 Office: H2A Inc PO Box 1513 Boise ID 83701-1513

HARTFORD, ALLEN, JR., research chemist; b. Berkeley, Calif., Sept. 7, 1945; s. Allen and Erna Hildegard (Vollkommer) H.; m. Vicki Lynn Valentine, Jan. 29, 1972. BS, U. Calif., Berkeley, 1967; PhD, U. Ill., 1971. Postdoctoral fellow U. Calif., Berkeley, 1971-73; mem. staff Lawrence Livermore (Calif.) Lab., 1973-75; staff scientist Allied Chem. Corp., Morristown, N.J., 1975-78; div. leader chem. and laser scis. div. Los Alamos (N.Mex.) Nat. Lab., 1978—; cons. Amoco, Naperville, Ill., 1985—. Mem. editorial adv. bd. Laser Focus/E-O Tech., 1982—; contbr. articles to profl. jours. Mem. AAAS, Am. Chem. Soc., Sigma Xi, Phi Beta Kappa. Avocations: numismatics, philately, photography, sail boarding. Office: Los Alamos Nat Lab CLS-DO PO Box 1663 MS J563 Los Alamos NM 87545

HARTFORD, MARGARET ELIZABETH, social work educator, gerontologist; b. Cleve., Dec. 12, 1917; d. William A. and Inez (Logan) H. BA, Ohio U., 1940; MS, U. Pitts., 1944; PhD, U. Chgo., 1962. Dir. youth service YWCA, Canton, Ohio, 1940-42; program cons. Intercultural Relations Am. Service Inst., Pitts., 1943-48, exec. dir., 1948-50; prof. social work Case Western Res. U., Cleve., 1950-75; founding dir. Sch. Gerontology U. So. Calif., Los Angeles, 1975-77, prof. gerontology, social work, 1977-83, prof. emeritus, 1983—; instr. Claremont (Calif.) Adult Sch. Dist., 1983—; instr. retirement Pasadena (Calif.) City Coll., 1983-84; cons. pre-retirement, retirement planning to corps. and ednl. systems, various cities, 1980—; cons., lectr. 1970—. Author: Groups in Social Work, 1973, (workbook) Making the Best of the Rest of Your Life, 1982, Leaders Guide to Making the Best of the Rest of Your Life, 1986; also numerous articles. Commr. Human Services, City of Claremont, 1986—. Named Outstanding Contbn. to Social Work, Alumni Assn. Schs. Social Work U. So. Calif., 1984, Outstanding Contbr. Social Group Work, Com. Advancement of Group Work, Toronto, Ont., Can., 1985, Woman or Yr., Trojan Women U. So. Calif., 1976; recipient Dart award for Inovative Teaching Assocs, U. So. Calif., 1974. Fellow Gerontol. Soc. Am.; mem. Nat. Assn. Social Workers (cert., nat. chmn. 1962-64, group work sect., chmn. Cleve. sect. 1969-72), Am. Soc. Aging (chmn. program com. 1983—, City of Claremont com. on aging), Delta Kappa Gamma, Alpha Xi Delta. Episcopalian. Avocations: bot. gardens, birdwatching, Chinese brush painting, camping, hiking. Home: 413 Willamette Ln Claremont CA 91711 Office: U So Calif Gerontology Ctr Los Angeles CA 90024

HARTLEY, FRED LLOYD, oil company executive; b. Vancouver, B.C., Can., Jan. 16, 1917; came to U.S., 1939, naturalized, 1950; s. John William and Hannah (Mitchell) H.; m. Margaret Alice Murphy, Nov. 2; children: Margaret Ann, Fred Lloyd. BS in Applied Sci., U. B.C., 1939. Engring. supr. Union Oil Co. Calif., 1939-53, mgr. comml. devel., 1953-55, gen. mgr. research dept., 1955-56, v.p. in charge research, 1956-60, sr. v.p., 1960-63, exec. v.p., 1963-64, pres., chief exec. officer, 1964-73, chmn. bd. dirs., pres., 1974-85, chmn. bd. dirs., chief exec. officer, 1985—, also mem. bd. dirs.; bd. dirs. Rockwell Internat. Corp., Union Bank. Bd. dirs. Los Angeles Philharm. Assn.; trustee Calif. Inst. Tech., Tax Found., Com. Econ. Devel.; ambassador and commr. gen. U.S. exhibition EXPO 86. Mem. Nat. Petroleum Council, Am. Petroleum Inst. (bd. dirs., former chmn. bd. dirs.), Council Fgn. Relations, Calif. C. of C. (bd. dirs.). Office: Unocal Corp PO Box 7600 Los Angeles CA 90051

HARTLEY, JOHN EDWARD, educator; b. Meadville, Pa., May 9, 1940; s. Walter and Mary Elizabeth (Lewis) H.; m. Dorothy Leone Robbins, June 7, 1961; children: Joyce, Johannah. BA, Greenville Coll., 1961; BD, Asbury Theol. Sem., 1965; MA, Brandeis U., 1968, PhD, 1969. Ordained to ministry. Pastor Free Meth. Ch., Eldorado, Ill., 1961-63; grad. asst. in greek Asbury Theol. Sem., Wilmore, Ky., 1965-66; guest prof. Asbury Theol. Sem., Wilmore, 1970; prof. Azusa (Calif.) Pacific U., 1969—; adj. prof. Fuller Theol. Sem., 1973-82. Author, editor Wesleyan Theol. Perspectives, five vols. 1981; contbr. to book Theological Wordbook of the Old Testament, 1980, International Standard Bible Encyclopedia rev. edit., 1974 82, 86. Recipient Teaching Excellence award Azusa Pacific U., 1973. Mem. Am. Sch. Oriental Research. Soc. Bib. Lit. Home: 1737 Acorn Ln Glendora CA 91740 Office: Azusa Pacific U. Alosta at Citrus Azusa CA 91702

HARTLEY-LINSE, BONNIE JEAN, college health nurse clinician, administrator, consultant; b. Chgo., July 26, 1923; d. Frank and Anna Kathleen (Koutecky) Kadlec; m. Robert William Hartley, June 23, 1949 (div. Feb. 1961); children: Robert Greig, Franklin James; m. Howard Albert Linse, June 10, 1978 (dec. Nov. 1985); stepchildren: Michael Howard, Janet Stokes. BS in Nursing, St. Xavier Coll., Chgo., 1945; cert. edn. Portland State Coll., 1965; MS in Nursing Edn., U. Oreg., 1972; cert. coll. health nurse practitioner program Brigham Young U., 1976. R.N., Oreg. Mem. faculty nursing St. Xavier Coll., 1945-47; head nurse U. Chgo. Clinics, 1947-48; nurse research newborn neurology U. Oreg. Med. Sch., Portland, summer 1961; coordinator dental assistant program, instr. biology Portland Pub. Schs., Oreg., 1965-67; health service clinician, adminstr. Clackamas Community Coll., Oregon City, Oreg., 1970-84; cons. Health Services Community Colls. of Oreg., 1972-84; pres. Coll. Health Nurses, State of Oreg., 1976-78. Mem. N.W. Oreg. Health Systems, Clackamas County Sub-Area Council, Oregon City, 1980-86. Recipient Recognition for Outstanding Service award Clackamas Community Coll., 1984; USPHS grantee, 1968. Mem. Am. Nurses Assn., Oreg. Nurses Assn. (Clackamas County unit 26), Pacific Coast Coll. Health Assn. (ann. conf. program coordinator 1980), Oreg. Coll. Health Dirs. Assn. Avocations: travel, piano, choral singing, swimming. Home: 18633 Roundtree Dr Oregon City OR 97045

HARTMAN, ASHLEY POWELL, training systems company executive; b. St. Paul, Feb. 26, 1922; s. Thomas and Mollie (Powell) H.; m. Tracy Robertson, Nov. 19, 1971; children: Timothy, Sabrina, Scott, William. B.A., U. Minn., 1948. Vice pres. Ridder Johns Co. (advt. sales), Los Angeles; v.p. Miller Freeman Pub. Co.; pub. Sea Mag., Newport Beach, Calif.; now pres. Creative Tng. Systems, El Toro, Calif.; instr. Maximize Course; lectr. on sales tng. mgmt., stress mgmt., communications, pub. speaking. Author: How to Maximize Your Life; producer: cassette album Stress Management System; Contbr. numerous travel and marine-oriented articles to profl. jours., popular mags. Served with USAAF, 1942-46. Mem. So. Calif. Marine Assn. (dir., pres. 1984-85), Am. Assn. Newspaper Reps. (pres. 1954). Republican. Mem. Reformed Ch. Am. Home: 24921 Muirlands #22 El Toro CA 92630

HARTMAN, DARIEN VERAL, business educator; b. La Grande, Oreg., Mar. 21, 1947; s. Charles Theodore Dennis and Marjorie S. (Freeman) Leonard; m. Charles R. Hartman, Oct. 14, 1972 (div. May 1978); 1 child, Dustin D. BA in Bus. Edn., Idaho State U., 1971; MA in Bus. Edn., Boise State U., 1983. Cert. secondary bus. tchr., Idaho. Sec. Idaho 1st Nat. Bank, Boise, 1971-75; instr. Link's Sch. Bus., Boise, 1975-78; prof. bus. Coll. So. Idaho, Twin Falls, 1978—, program mgr. bus. office occupations. Mem. Nat. Bus. Edn. Assn., Western Bus. Edn. Assn. (exec. bd. dirs. 1982-85), Idaho Bus. Edn. Assn. (pres. 1983-84), Am. Vocat. Assn., Idaho Vocat. Assn., Delta Kappa Gamma. Avocations: needle work, reading, cross country, downhill and water skiing. Office: Coll So Idaho 315 Falls Ave Twin Falls ID 83303-1238

HARTMAN, DAVID EUGENE, mechanical engineering educator; b. Republic of Panama, Feb. 28, 1935; s. George Fredrick and Lillian Antonnette (Hubly) H.; m. Judith Ann Sweeton, June 29, 1968; 1 child, Michael David. BA, Rice U., 1955, BS in Engring., 1956, MS, 1961, PhD, 1965. Registered profl. engr., Tex., Ariz. Sr. engr. Houston Research Inst., 1965-67, Shell Pipe Line Research and Devel., Houston, 1967-72; prin., mgr. Oceanus Enterprise, Key Largo, Fla., 1972-74; prof. mech. engring. LeTourneau Coll., Longview, Tex., 1975-85; assoc. prof. No. Ariz. U., Flagstaff, 1985—; cons. in field, 1975—. Author: Damping in Magnesium, 1965. Served with USN, 1956-59. Recipient Selby award LeTourneau Coll., 1980, Best Tchr. award, LeTourneau Coll., 1978, 80. Mem. ASME, NSPE, Am. Soc. Engring. Edn. Republican. Avocations: sailing, scuba diving. Home: 1809 N Buckskin Way Flagstaff AZ 86001 Office: No Ariz U Coll Engring and Tech Flagstaff AZ 86011

HARTMAN, HEDY ANN, fund raising company executive, consultant; b. Sept. 24, 1954; d. Alan Stuart Hartman and Joan Marcia (Lederman) Hartman Goldsmith; m. Jon Abbott Mersereau, Nov. 27, 1976 (div. June 1981); m. William Bainbridge Everett, June 2, 1984. B.A. with distinction, U. Pa., 1975; M.A., U. Wash., 1982, Ph.C., 1983. Researcher Am. Mus. Natural History, N.Y.C., 1974; curatorial asst. Univ. Mus., U. Pa., Phila., 1974-75; instr. Children's Mus., Indpls., 1976; curatorial asst. Indpls. Mus. Art, 1975-76; program adminstr. statewide services S.C. State Mus., Columbia, 1977-80; pres. Hartman Planning & Devel. Group Ltd., Bellevue, Wash., 1980—; S.C. state rep. Southeastern Mus. Conf., 1979-80. Author: Funding Sources and Technical Assistance for Museums and Historical Organizations, 1979; Fund Raising for Museums, 1985. Editor: Official Museum Guide to Products and Services, 1980. Mem. Am. Assn. Museums, Am. Assn. State and Local History (bd. dirs. 1983—), Western Museums Conf. (bd. dirs. 1980-83), Wash. Mus. Assn. (bd. dirs. 1985—; sec. 1986—). Office: Hartman Planning and Devel Group Ltd PO Box 818 Redmond WA 98073

HARTMAN, NORMAN SIDNEY, public relations executive; b. Denver, July 1, 1939; s. Samuel Charles and Marian (Finch) H.; B.A. in Radio-TV Broadcasting, Fresno State Coll., 1966; postgrad. San Francisco State Coll., 1968-69; m. Jan Claire Logan, Mar. 23, 1968; children—Jonathan Charles, Kelly Logan. Announcer KFRE AM & TV, Fresno, Calif., 1960-63, newsman, 1963-67; dir. KFRE-TV, Fresno, 1967-68; news producer KRON-TV, San Francisco, 1969-75; news dir. KOVR-TV, Sacramento, 1975-79, dir. corp. communications Pacific Bell Co., Sacramento, 1979—; lectr. Broadcast Communication Arts, San Francisco State Coll., 1970-71. Mem. Fresno County Grand Jury, 1967; mem. Nat. Ski Patrol, 1964-68; bd. dirs. United Cerebral Palsy Assn., Sacramento-Yolo Counties, 1975-77; chmn. Sacramento Citizens Crime Alert Reward Program, 1984-86; v.p. Sacramento Sci. Ctr., 1984-85; chmn. Sacramento Community Cable Found., 1986—; bd. dirs. Sacramento Symphony Assn., 1986—. Served with AUS, 1957-60. Mem. Radio-TV News Dirs. Assn. (bd. dirs. 1977-79), Fresno Jaycees. Club: Fresno Ski (pres. 1967). Home: 3334 Lynne Way Sacramento CA 95821 Office: 2700 Watt Ave Room 2343 PO Box 15038 Sacramento CA 95851

HARTMAN, ROBERT LEROY, artist, educator; b. Sharon, Pa., Dec. 17, 1926; s. George Otto and Grace Arvada (Radabaugh) H.; m. Charlotte Ann

Johnson, Dec. 30, 1951; children: Mark Allen, James Robert. B.F.A., U. Ariz., 1951, M.A., 1952; postgrad., Colo. Springs Fine Arts Center, 1947, 51, Bklyn. Mus. Art Sch., 1953-54. Instr. architecture, allied arts Tex. Tech. Coll., 1955-58; asst. prof. art U. Nev., Reno, 1958-61; mem. faculty dept. art U. Calif., Berkeley, 1961—; prof. U. Calif., 1972—, chmn. dept., 1974-76; mem. Inst. for Creative Arts, U. Calif., 1967-68. One man exhbns. include, Bertha Schafer Gallery, N.Y.C., 1966, 69, 74, Santa Barbara Mus. Art, 1973, Cin. Art Acad., 1975, Hank Baum Gallery, San Francisco, 1973, 75, 78, San Jose Mus. Art, 1983, Bluxome Gallery, San Francisco, 1984, Bluxome Gallery, San Francisco, 1984, 86, U. Art Mus., Berkeley, 1986; group exhbns. include Richmond Mus., 1966, Whitney Mus. Biennial, 1973, Oakland Mus., 1976, San Francisco Arts Commn. Gallery, 1985 (award); represented in permanent collections, Nat. Collections Fine Arts, Colorado Springs Fine Arts Center, Corcoran Gallery, San Francisco Art Inst., Roswell Mus. U. Calif. humanities research fellow, 1980. Office: Dept Art Univ of Calif Berkeley CA 94720

HARTMAN, WILLARD SAMUEL, federal agency officer; b. Barnard, Mo., Apr. 9, 1940; s. Willard Miles and Frances Powell (Thompson) H.; m. Kathleen Arvella James, July 24, 1965; children: James Frederick, Deborah Kathleen. Student, Cen. Mo. State Coll., 1957-59; BSEE, U. Wash., 1962; M in Pub. Adminstrn., Auburn U., 1976. Cert. comml. pilot. Instr. flight USAFR, Ellington AFB, Tex., 1971-75, Richards-Gabaur AFB, Mo., 1976-81; aircraft ops. officer USAFR, Kelly AFB, Tex., 1981-85, Peterson AFB, Colo., 1985—. Served to capt. USAF, 1963-70. Decorated D.F.C., Air medal, 1965-69, 79. Mem. Res. Officer's Assn. (life). Methodist. Avocations: woodworking, computer, traveling, music and art appreciation. Home: 1255 Becky Dr Colorado Springs CO 80908

HARTMANN, EDWARD CHRISTOPHER, aerospace manager; b. N.Y.C., Apr. 21, 1936; s. Wolfgang Francis and Frances Elizabeth (Larkin) H.; m. Suzanne Mary Rogell; children: Mary, Daniel, Lucy, Therese. BSEE, Manhattan Coll., 1958; MBA, U. So. Calif., 1966. Research engr. N.Am. Aviation, Anaheim, Calif., 1958-63; project staff engr. spl. test equipment N.Am. Aviation, 1963-66; radar project engr. N. Am. Rockwell, Anaheim, 1966-69; systems engr. Rockwell Internat., Anaheim, 1969-80, research mgr., 1980—; lectr. tech. writing, communications W. Coast U., Orange, Calif., 1972-74. Organizer Vietnamese Resettlement Com., Placentia, Calif., 1975-76; mem. St. Vincent De Paul Soc., Placentia, 1966-80, pres. 1969-75, trustee 1976-86. Democrat. Roman Catholic. Avocations: cycling, computers. Home: 207 Pageantry Dr Placentia CA 92670 Office: 3370 Miraloma Ave Anaheim CA 92803

HARTMANN, ELEANOR, makeup artist and designer, educator; b. N.Y.C., July 9, 1940; d. George Wilfred and Leah (Norton) Hartmann; m. John Robert von Dassow, July 19, 1967 (div. 1986); children: Sasha, Sumi, Eva, Elizabeth, George, Peter, Michaelangelo. Student, Reed Coll., 1968-60; BA, U. Wash., 1962, MA, 1964, postgrad., 1970-73. Instr. English Shoreline Coll., Seattle, 1977-85, Highline Coll., Midway, Wash., 1980—; instr. makeup Cornish Inst., Seattle, 1983—; makeup desinger Pacific Northwest Ballet Co., Seattle, 1981—, Seattle Opera, 1983—. Mem. adv. bd. Seattle Children's Theater, 1979-82, trustee, 1982-86; acitve Pacific Northwest Ballet, 1981-85; mem. adv. bd. Poncho Theater, 1979-82. Office: Highline Coll Midway WA 98032-0424 Office: Cornish Inst 710 E Roy Seattle WA 98102

HARTMANN, HUDSON THOMAS, agriculturist, educator; b. Kansas City, Kans., Dec. 6, 1914; s. Dale and Violet (Thomas) H.; m. Dorothy Henson, Sept. 23, 1940 (dec. 1977); children—Carol Robinson, Don, Marilyn, Lawrence. m. Hazel Manning, Nov. 25, 1978. B.S., U. Mo.-Columbia, 1939, M.S., 1940; Ph.D., U. Calif.-Berkeley, 1947. Asst. prof. U. Calif.-Davis, 1947-54, assoc. prof., 1954-60, prof., 1960-80, prof. emeritus agrl. research, 1980—. Author: Plant Propagation, 1959, 4th edit. 1983; Plant Science, 1981. Fulbright research grantee, 1960, 64, 69. Fellow Am. Soc. Hort. Sci.; mem. Internat. Plant Propagators Soc. (editor 1974—). Democrat. Office: Dept Pomology Univ Calif Davis CA 95616

HARTSELL, BRUCE DALE, mental health center director; b. New Orleans, Jan. 25, 1955; s. Robert Louis and Elinor (Emmons) H.; m. Cheryl Jan Hutson, Dec. 22, 1979; children: Merideth, Allison, Ethan. BS, Eastern N.Mex. U., 1978; M in Religious Edn., Social Work, So. Baptist Theol. Sem., 1980; MSW, U. Louisville, 1981. Activities dir. Brooklawn Inc., Louisville, 1980-81; dir. foster homes N.Mex. Baptist Children's Home, Portales, 1982-83; counselor Mental Health Resources, Clovis, N.Mex., 1983-84, outpatient coordinator, 1984-85, program mgr., 1985—. Pres. Eastern N.Mex. Hospice, Clovis, 1985-86. Mem. Acad. Cert. Social Workers, Nat. Assn. Social Workers. Democrat. Lodge: Kiwanis (Portales sec. 1983-84). Avocations: social justice issues. Home: 1203 Rencher Clovis NM 88101 Office: Mental Health Resources 816 W 12th Clovis NM 88101

HARTTER, MARJORIE ANN, communications executive; b. Denver, Dec. 26, 1952; d. Leon Miller and Ellen Victoria (Pearson) Corning; m. Michael James Hartter, Nov. 26, 1976; 1 child, Carl John. Student San Mateo Coll., 1971, Palo Alto Bus. Sch., 1973. With sales dept. J & M Hobby Shop, San Carlos, Calif., 1970-71; exec. sec. Randtron Systems, Menlo Park, Calif., 1972-75; mktg. asst. Marriott Corp., Santa Clara, Calif., 1975-76; coordinator edn. WEMA, 1976-77; customer liasion Moran, Lanig & Duncan Advt., Palo Alto, 1977; program and communications dir. Harman Mgmt. Corp., Los Altos, Calif. 1977—, editor monthly mag., also corp. meeting planner for Ky. Fried Chicken stores in Calif., Colo., Utah, Wash. Contbr. articles to profl. jours. Mem. Meeting Planners Internat., Nat. Restaurant Assn., Nat. Assn. Female Execs. Office: Harman Mgmt Corp 199 1st St Los Altos CA 94022

HARTWIG, RICHARD PALMER, advertising executive; b. Coalinga, Calif., July 7, 1947; s. Charles Palmer and Katherine Marie (Schamus) H.; m. Rose Marie Dolores Robles, Sept. 13, 1980. A.A. in Advt., Foothill Coll., 1968; B.A. in Advt., Mktg. and Bus., San Jose U., 1970. Prodn. and promotion mgr. The Gap Stores, San Francisco, 1975; asst. advt. mgr. Blue Cross of No. Calif., Oakland, 1975-77; advt. mgr. Roos/Atkins, San Francisco, 1977-78; account exec. retail services KTVU-TV, San Francisco, Oakland, 1978-80, retail mktg. dir., 1980—; lectr. in field. Mem. San Francisco Film/Tape Council, San Francisco Advt. Club. Contbr. articles to trade publs. Home: 1715 Clemens Rd Oakland CA 94602 Office: 2 Jack London Sq Oakland CA 94607

HARTZ, DEBORAH DILLINGHAM, social worker; b. Crane, Tex., Feb. 4, 1953; d. Mat Elmo and Joan (Cole) D.; m. Harris L. Hartz, July 23, 1977; children: Jacob, Andrew. BA, Tex. Tech U., 1974; MSW, La. State U., 1976. Juvenile justice specialist Gov.'s Council Criminal Justice Planning, Santa Fe, 1976-78; sch. social worker Albuquerque Pub. Schs., 1978—; cons. Home Study-Adoptions, Albuquerque, 1985. Mem. Nat. Assn. Social Workers (cert., bd. inquiry 1981-84, licensure com. 1984), Kappa Kappa Gamma (adv. bd. 1984-86). Republican. Baptist. Home: 1719 Lafayette NE Albuquerque NM 87106 Office: Albuquerque Pub Schs 2700 Arizona NE Albuquerque NM 87110

HARTZ, JAY DALE, editor; b. Little Rock, Oct. 8, 1940; s. Leon E. and Josephine (Steed) H. Student El Camino Coll., 1960-61, U. Md., 1963-64, U. Calif., Berkeley, 1964-65. Mem. staff U.S. Fgn. Service, 1962-69; with various newspapers and radio stas., 1969-74; news editor PPi chain, 1974-76; editor Calif. Grange News, Sacramento, 1977—; ptnr. Acting Devel. Systems, Modesto, Calif., 1976-85; tchr. journalism to grade sch. children. Served with USN, 1958-60. Recipient Meritorious Service award State Dept., 1967. Mem. Polit. action com. Calif. State Grange. Democrat. Club: Patrons of Husbandry.

HARTZELL, IRENE JANOFSKY, psychologist; b. Los Angeles, 1938; d. Leonard and Annelies Janofsky. Vor-Diplom, U. Munich, 1961; B.A., U. Calif.-Berkeley, 1963, M.A., 1965; Ph.D., U. Oreg., 1970. Lic. psychologist, Calif., Oreg., Wash. Psychologist, Lake Washington Sch. Dist., Kirkland, Wash., 1971-72; staff psychologist VA Hosp., Seattle, 1970-71, Long Beach, Calif., 1973-74; dir. parent edn. Childrens Hosp., Orange, Calif., 1975-78; clin. psychologist Kaiser Permanente, Van Nuys, Calif., 1979—; clin. instr. pediatrics dept. U. Calif. Med. Coll., Irvine, 1975-78. Author: Expert Student's Advantage, 1986, The Study Skills Advantage, 1986; contbr. articles to profl. jours. Legis. intern Oreg. Legislature, 1974-75. U. Oreg. fellow, 1969. Mem. Am. Psychol. Assn., Pi Lambda Theta. Office: Kaiser Permanente Med Group 13746 Victory Blvd Van Nuys CA 91401

HARVEY, ALAN ERIC, plant pathologist; b. Pitts., Aug. 2, 1938; s. Harold G. and Virginia (Johnson) H.; m. Sherry Crawford, Sept. 23, 1959; children: Scott, Kris, Kirk. BS, Coll. Idaho, 1960; MS, U. Idaho, 1962; PhD, Wash. State U., 1967. Plant pathologist USDA Forest Service, Moscow, Idaho, 1965—. Contbr. articles to profl. jours. Home: 1629 Damen Moscow ID 83843 Office: Forestry Scis Lab 1221 S Main Moscow ID 83843

HARVEY, BRUCE KENYON, banker; b. Port Chester, N.Y., July 6, 1946; s. Stewart Warren and Rhoda (Merritt) H.; m. Josephine Chan Go, May 24, 1982; 1 child, Anna Isabelle. BA in English, Trinity Coll., Hartford, Conn., 1968; MS in Info. Sci., Drexel U., 1972; MBA in Data Processing Mgmt., Nat. U., 1981. EDP auditor Calif. First Bank, San Diego, 1979-80; data processing standards controller U.S. Fed. Home Loan Bank, San Francisco, 1981; regional EDP auditor World Banking div. Bank of Am., Manila, 1982-84; systems mgr. EDP Bank of Am., San Francisco, 1985—; cons. EDP auditor Cen. Bank, Philippines, 1983, Thailand, 1984. Reviewer Computing Revs., 1975-78. Served with U.S. Army, 1968-70. Mem. IEEE, Inst. Cert. Computer Profls. (cert. computer data processor, computer programer), EDP Auditors Assocs. (cert. info. systems auditor). Home: F3 5425 Concord Blvd Concord CA 94521 Office: Bank Am Corp Dept 3937 PO Box 37000 San Francisco CA 94137

HARVEY, CLESSON HOPKINS, retired educator, journal editor; b. Portland, Oreg., Feb. 14, 1925; s. Frank Walter Harvey and Doris Libby (Hopkins) Mason. BS in Chemistry, U. Calif., Berkeley, 1954. Cert. sec. tchr., Calif. Sci. tchr. Easton (Calif.) High Sch., 1955-58, Berkeley High Sch., 1958-86. Author, editor The Blavatsky Theosophist jour., 1982-84, 86. Home and Office: 2630 Webster St Apt B Berkeley CA 94705

HARVEY, ELAINE LOUISE, artist, educator; b. Riverside, Calif., Mar. 1, 1936; d. Edgar Arthur and Emma Louise (Shull) Siervogel; m. Stuart Herbert Harvey, June 16, 1957; children: Kathleen Robin, Laurel Lynn, Mark Stuart. BA with highest honors, with distinction, San Diego State U., 1957. Cert. gen. elem. tchr., Calif. Tchr. Cajon Valley Schs., El Cajon, Calif., 1957, 58; free-lance artist El Cajon, 1975—; juror various art exhbns., Calif., 1983—; lectr., 1984—. Editor: Palette to Palate, 1986; contbr. The Artists Mag., 1987. Trustee San Diego Mus. Art, 1985, 86; leader El Cajon council Girl Scouts of U.S., 1968; vol. art tchr., San Diego area pub. schs., 1973-76. Recipient Merit award La. Watercolor Soc., 1984, Arches Canson Rives award Midwest Watercolor Soc./Tweed Mus., Greenbay, Wis., 1984, Winsor Newton award Midwest Watercolor Soc./Neville Mus., Duluth, Minn., 1985; awards for paintings and tapestries, McKinnon award Am. Watercolor Soc. 1985, Creative Connection award Rocky Mountain Nat. Exhibition 1986, 1st Juror's award San Diego Internat. Watercolor Exhibition 1986. Mem. Nat. Watercolor Soc. (sec. 1987—), Watercolor West (bd. dirs.), West Coast Watercolor Soc., San Diego Watercolor Soc. (pres., 1979, 80, exhbns. chmn. 1980, 81, Silver Recognition award 1986), San Diego Mus. Art Artist's Guild (pres. 1985, 86, bd. dirs. 1986-87), Western Fedn. Watercolor Socs. (del. 1983—). Club: Grossmont Garden (La Mesa, Calif.) (Elson Trophy 1977, 79). Home and Studio: 1602 Sunburst Dr El Cajon CA 92021

HARVEY, JAMES GERALD, educational consultant, counselor, researcher; b. California, Mo., July 15, 1934; s. William Walter and Exie Marie (Lindley) H. BA Amherst Coll., 1956; MAT (fellow), Harvard U., 1958, MEd, 1962. Asst. to dean grad. sch. edn. Harvard U., Cambridge, Mass., 1962-66, dir. admissions, fin. aid, 1966-69; dir. counseling service U. Calif., Irvine, 1970-72; ednl. cons., Los Angeles, 1972—. Active ACLU. Served to 1st lt. USAF, 1958-61. Amherst Mayo-Smith grantee, 1956-57; UCLA Adminstrv. fellow, 1969-70. Mem. Am. Ednl. Research Assn., Nat. Council Measurement in Edn., Am. Assn. for Counseling and Devel. Roman Catholic. Address: 1845 Glendon Ave Los Angeles CA 90025

HARVEY, JAMES ROSS, diversified service company executive; b. Los Angeles, Aug. 20, 1934; s. James Ernest and Loretta Berniece (Ross) H.; m. Charlene Coakley, July 22, 1971; children: Kjersten Ann, Kristina Ross. B.S. in Engring., Princeton U., 1956; M.B.A., U. Calif.-Berkeley, 1963. Engr. Standard Oil Co. (Calif.), San Francisco, 1956-61; acct. Touche, Ross, San Francisco, 1963-64; chmn. bd., chief exec. officer, dir. Transamerica Corp., San Francisco, 1965—; bd. dirs. Transam. Occidental Life Ins. Co., Transam. Fin. Corp., Transam. Ins. Co., Transam. Interway Inc., Transam. Title Ins. Co., Sedgwick Group, Pacific Telesis Group, McKesson Corp. Trustee West Coast Cancer Found.; bd. regents St. Mary's Coll.; bd. dirs. U. Calif. Bus. Sch., Calif. State Parks Found., Bay Area Council. Served with AUS, 1958-59. Mem. San Francisco C. of C. (dir., pres.). Clubs: Bohemian, Pacific-Union (San Francisco); Union League (N.Y.C.). Office: Transamerica Corp 600 Montgomery St San Francisco CA 94111

HARVEY, RICHARD BLAKE, political science educator; b. Los Angeles, Nov. 28, 1930; s. George Blackstone and Clara Ethel (Conway) H.; m. Patricia Jean Clougher, Aug. 29, 1965; 1 child: Timothy Harvey. BA, Occidental Coll., 1952; MA, UCLA, 1954, PhD, 1959. Prof. polit. sci. Whittier (Calif.) Coll., 1960—, acad. dean, 1970-80, chmn. polit. sci. dept., 1984—. Author: Earl Warren, Governor of California, 1970, Dynamics-California Government and Politics, 1985; contbr. articles and book revs. to profl. jours. Grantee Haynes Found., 1961, 68. Mem. Am. Polit. Sci. Assn., So. Calif. Polit. Sci. Assn., Newcomen Soc., Pi Sigma Alpha. Democrat. Presbyterian. Club: University. Avocations: reading, racquetball, avocado growing. Home: 424 Avocado Crest Rd La Habra Heights CA 90631 Office: Whittier Coll Whittier CA 90608

HARVEY, RICHARD DUDLEY, marketing consultant; b. Atlanta, Sept. 24, 1923; s. Robert Emmett and June (Dudley) H.; BA, U. Denver, 1947; postgrad. various bus. seminars Harvard U., Stanford U.; m. Donna Helen Smith, Oct. 12, 1944; 1 child, Louise Dudley. Various positions in sales, sales promotion and mktg. The Coca-Cola Co., St. Louis, Denver and Atlanta, 1948-60, v.p., brand mgr., mktg. mgr., mktg. dir., Atlanta, 1965-70, v.p. orgn. and mktg. devel., 1970-75; sr. v.p. mktg. Olympia Brewing Co., Olympia, Wash., 1975-78; with Sound Mktg. Services Inc., Seattle; dir. Lone Star Brewing Co., San Antonio. Mem. mayor's housing resources com., Atlanta, 1968-70; program chmn. United Way, Atlanta, 1969; vice chmn. Episcopal Radio-TV Found., Atlanta, 1975—; bd. dirs. Oreg. Shakespearean Festival Assn., 1982-86; chmn. mktg. com., trustee Seattle Symphony, 1983-86 . Served with USAAF, 1942-45. Mem. Am. Mktg. Assn. (pres. 1983-84), Mktg. Communications Execs. Internat. (pres. 1984-85), Inst. Mgmt. Cons., Phi Beta Kappa, Omicron Delta Kappa. Democrat. Episcopalian. Clubs: The Rainier, Seattle Tennis (Seattle). Home: 3837 E Crockett St Seattle WA 98112 Office: Sound Mktg Services Inc Grosvenor House 500 Wall St Suite 212 Seattle WA 98121-1509

HARVEY, ROBERT J., medical supplies company executive. Address: Thoratec Labs Corp 2023 8th St Berkeley CA 94710 *

HARVEY, ROBERT JOHN, air force officer; b. Lockport, N.Y., Oct. 27, 1943; s. Albert Adam and Carrie Nora (Buehring) H.; m. Dorothy Ann Scott, Dec. 16, 1970; children: Jill, Bret, Carolyn. BS in Bus. Administrn., SUNY, Buffalo, 1966; M in Logistics Mgmt., Air Force Inst. Tech., 1980. Commd. 2d lt. USAF, 1966, advanced through grades to lt. col., 1982; supply staff officer USAF 23d Air Div., Duluth, Minn., 1977-79; assigned to Hdqrs. USAF Logistics Command, Wright-Patterson AFB, Ohio, 1980-81; chief of supply, comdr. 96th Supply Squadron, Dyess AFB, Tex., 1981-83, 15th Supply Squadron, Hickam AFB, Hawaii, 1983—. Decorated Bronze Star. Mem. Air Force Assn., Air Force. Inst. Tech. Assn. Grads. (charter), Beta Gamma Sigma, Sigma Iota Epsilon. Republican. Roman Catholic. Avocations: reading, jogging. Home: 2006-B Oceana Circle Alameda CA 94501 Office: Def Subsistence Region Pacific Naval Air Sta Alameda CA 94501-5000

HARWICK, MAURICE, lawyer; b. Los Angeles, Feb. 6, 1933; m. Saowapa Butranon, July 4, 1970; children: Manasnati, Manasnapa. AA, Los Angeles City Coll., 1954; JD, Southwestern U., 1957. Bar: Calif., 1958; U.S. Supreme Ct. bar, 1962. Dep. dist. atty. County of Los Angeles, 1958-60; individual practice law, Santa Monica, Calif., 1960—; judge pro tem Municipal Ct., 1966-67, 80, 81, 85, 86. Chmn. bd. rev. Los Angeles Community Colls. and City Schs.; mem. Project Safer Calif. gov.'s com., 1974-75. Mem. ABA, Calif. Bar Assn., Los Angeles County Bar Assn., Criminal Cts. Bar Assn. (pres. 1972, bd. govs.), Assn. Trial Lawyers Am., Los Angeles County Dist. Attys. Assn. Lodge: Vikings. Office: 2001 Wilshire Blvd Suite 600 Santa Monica CA 90403

HASAK, JANET ELINORE, patent lawyer; b. Rochester, N.Y., Oct. 12, 1952; d. Charles Milton and June Charlotte (Raymond) Baird; m. James Philip Hasak, Oct. 4, 1975; children: John Clifford, Andrew Charles. BA, Hartwick Coll., 1974; MS, U. Rochester, 1976; JD, Seton Hall U., 1983. Bar: U.S. Patent Office 1977, N.J. 1983, U.S. Dist. Ct. N.J. 1983, U.S. Ct. Appeals (D.C. cir.) 1984, Calif. 1986, U.S. Dist. Ct. (no. dist.) Calif. 1986. Tutor, teaching fellow Hartwick Coll., Oneonta, N.Y., 1973-74; teaching asst., fellow U. Rochester, 1974-76; patent agt. Nat. Starch & Chem. Corp., Bridgewater, N.J., 1976-81; legal trainee Exxon Research & Engring. Co., Florham Park, N.J., 1981-83; sr. patent agt. Cetus Corp., Emeryville, Calif., 1983, sr. patent atty., 1984-86, asst. intellectual property counsel, 1986—. Mem. Seton Hall Law Rev., 1981-83. Sherman Clark fellow in chemistry U. Rochester, 1974-75. Mem. ABA, Am. Intellectual Property Law Assn., AAAS, Peninsula Intellectual Property Law Assn., Alameda Victorian Preservation Soc., San Francisco Patent and Trademark Law Assn., Alameda Swim Assn. Office: Cetus Corp 1400 53d St Emeryville CA 94608

HASAN, SYED MOHAMMAD, chemical engineering consultant; b. Fatehpur, India, Jan. 1, 1931; came to U.S., 1960; s. Siddiq and Summa (Khatoon) H.; B.Sc., U. Karachi (Pakistan); postgrad. in chemistry and chem. engring. U. So. Calif., UCLA, 1964-66; postgrad in mgmt. sci. West Coast U., Los Angeles, 1974; m. Rashida Khatoon Azim, June 6, 1956; children—Farhat, Khalid, Rafat, Nusrat, Saeeda, Tariq. Tchr. chemistry and physics Marie Colaco English Secondary Sch., Karachi, 1957-60; chemist, chief chemist Globe Elec. Co., Gardena, Calif., 1962-68; sr. mfg. engr. Burroughs Corp., Pasadena, Calif., 1968-69, now cons.; sr. chem. process engr. Lockheed Electronics Co., Los Angeles, 1969-75, cons., 1975—; tech. dir., owner Super Chem Enterprises, Los Angeles, 1975-80; pres. H & R Chems. Inc. (doing bus. as Super Chem Enterprises), Huntington Beach, Calif., 1980—. Mem. Calif. Circuit Assn., Cons. Chemists Assn., Am. Mgmt. Assn., Islamic Soc. Orange County (dir.). Developer metallizing chems. used in mfg. printed circuits and semicondrs. Home: 9852 Vicksburg St Huntington Beach CA 92646 Office: 7573 Slater St Huntington Beach CA 92647

HASENKAMP, BRUCE HENRY, association executive; b. Bklyn., May 12, 1938; s. Henry Ernst Hasenkamp and Ruth Frances (Hoyer) Savage; m. Inta Sarma Macs, May 13, 1973; 1 child, Peter Andris. AB cum laude, Dartmouth Coll., 1960; JD, Stanford U., 1963. Bar: Calif. 1964, N.Y. 1964, U.S. Dist. Ct. (no. dist.) Calif. 1964, U.S. Ct. Appeals (9th cir.) 1964, U.S. Dist. Ct. (so. dist.) N.Y. 1968, U.S. Supreme Ct. 1968. Assoc. Simpson Thacher and Bartlett, N.Y.C., 1963-68; asst. dean law sch. Stanford (Calif.) U., 1968-73; dir. Pres.'s Commn. on White House Fellowships, Washington, 1974-77; dir. pub. affairs Shaklee Corp., San Francisco, 1978-82; exec. v.p. The Hannaford Co., San Francisco, 1983-85; v.p. The Asia Found., San Francisco, 1985-86, Hosp. Council No. Calif., San Mateo, 1986—. Gov. Commonwealth Club of Calif., San Francisco, 1981-85; trustee World Affairs Council No. Calif., San Francisco, 1981—; steering com. Bay Area Council, San Francisco, 1980-82, dep. Calif. Roundtable, San Francisco, 1980-82; pres. Calif. Rep. League, 1971-73; asst. sec. Calif. Reps., 1973-74; dir. Council of Better Bus. Bur., 1980-84. Direct Selling Assn. (bd. dirs. 1981-82), Calif. State Bar Assn. (ho. dels. 1971), Sigma Phi Epsilon (nat. dir. 1973—). Mem. Anglican Ch. Avocation: Korean ceramic art. Home: 2435 Skyfarm Dr Hillsborough CA 94010 Office: Hosp Council No Calif 1825 S Grant St Suite 820 San Mateo CA 94402

HASHIMOTO, LLOYD KEN, communications executive; b. Cheyenne, Wyo., Sept. 21, 1944; s. Harry H. and Bettie M. (Kadota) H. Prin. Teltron Electronics, Laramie, Wyo., 1972—; audio visual technician U. Wyo., Laramie, 1972—; instr. workshops and seminars High Tech to a Lay Person, 1978. Contbr. articles to profl. jours. Program chmn. Snowy Range Dist. Boy Scouts Am., Laramie, 1985—. Served with U.S. Army, 1965-69. Mem. IEEE, Assn. Ednl. Communications Tech., Am. Legion. Avocations: amateur radio, electronic constrn., camping, fishing, media prodn. Home: 1932-1/2 Garfield Laramie WY 82070 Office: Teltron Electronics PO Box 1049 Laramie WY 82070

HASKELL, JOHN SINBERG, marketing executive consultant; b. Pitts., Dec. 1, 1942; s. S.K. and Ann (Sinberg) H.; m. Elisabeth Schaye, July 28, 1968; 1 son, David. AB in English Lit., Brown U., 1964; MBA in Mktg., Northwestern U., 1966. Consumer mktg. div. trainee Eastman Kodak Co., Rochester, N.Y., 1966-67; sales mgr. instnl. div. Haskell of Pitts., Inc., 1967-69; v.p. mktg. Bentson Office Furniture, 1968-70; v.p. mktg. Haskell of Pitts., Inc., 1970-71; v.p. mktg., gen. mgr. Abbey Rents Furniture, Los Angeles, 1971-73; v.p., chief operating officer Gamble Rents, Mpls., 1973-74; pres. Profl. Mktg. Group, Inc., Los Angeles, 1974-85; pvt. practice mktg. cons., 1985—. Active spl. adv. bd. Pres.'s Council on Fitness and Sports. Recipient soccer award Brown U., 1963. Mem. Sales and Mktg. Execs. Los Angeles. Republican. Jewish. Club: Riviera Golf. Author: The Twenty Minute Marketing Plan; publisher: Calif. Wine List, 1979-85; editor: Sports Retailer, 1981-85; contbr. articles to profl. jours.

HASKELL, PHYLLIS ANNE, dancer, choreographer, educator; b. Pasadena, Calif., Oct. 3, 1940; d. Eldon Hoff and Le-ora Phyllis (Archer) H.; m. John Dennis Williams, June 22, 1986. BA in Edn., U. Ariz., 1962; MFA in Dance, U. Utah, 1971. Tchr. Laguna Salada Schs., Pacifica, Calif., 1966-69; prof. dance Ariz. State U., Phoenix, 1971-75; performer Ririe-Woodbury Dance Co., Salt Lake City, 1971-79, asst. artistic dir., 1977-79; prof. dance U. Hawaii, Honolulu, 1979-83, dir. dance, 1983-87; chmn. modern dance U. Utah, Salt Lake City, 1987—; dancer Star Light Theatre, Kansas City, Mo., 1971; guest artist Bill Evans Dance Co., Washington, 1976, The Small Co., Honolulu, 1982, Tandy Beal and Co., Santa Cruz, Calif., 1982; prin. tchr.modern Hong Kong Acad. Performing Arts, 1986-87. Choreographer In Passing, 1983, Debutanz, 1984, Dreamscape, 1985, Miridae, 1986. Advisor Artist-in-the-Schs. program, Honolulu, 1979-86. Recipient Disting. Teaching award U. Hawaii, Honolulu, 1986. Mem. Council Dance Adminstrs., Nat. Assn. Schs. of Dance (div. chmn. 1985, mem. com. nominations 1986), Hawaii State Dance Council (adjudicator 1980, sec. 1981-83), Phi Kappa Phi. Office: U Utah 301 Dance Bldg Salt Lake City UT 84112

HASKINS-BARTSCH, CATHERINE ELIZABETH, clinical social worker; b. Salt Lake City, Sept. 22, 1957; d. Richard and Joan (Horsley) Haskins; m. William Robert Bartsch, Aug. 25, 1983. BS, Utah State U., 1980; MSW, U. Utah, 1982. Lic. clin. social worker. Sch. social worker Davis County Sch. Dist., Farmington, Utah, 1982-83; family therapist Valley West Social Services, West Valley, Utah, 1983-84; clin. social worker Primary Children's Med. Ctr., Salt Lake City, 1984—; pvt. practice cons., 1982—, individual and family therapy, 1985—, Salt Lake City; practicum instr. Grad. Sch. Social Work U. Utah, 1986—. Mem. Nat. Assn. Social Workers, Acad. Cert. Social Workers, Utah Soc. Clin. Hypnosis. Mormon. Avocations: photography, tennis, skiing, travel. Office: Primary Children's Med Ctr 320 12th Ave Social Services Salt Lake City UT 84103

HASLAM, GERALD PETER, publisher; b. Rotherham, England, Feb. 5, 1945; came to Can., 1952; s. Hubert Sterland and Muriel Croft (Baker) H.; m. Patricia Ann Wheatley, June 22, 1968. B.A., McGill U., Montreal, 1967. Vice pres. corp. communications MacMillan Bloedel, Vancouver, B.C., Can., 1977-79; dir. videotex services Southam Inc., Toronto, Ont., Can., 1979-82; publisher The Province, Vancouver, B.C., Can., 1982-85; v.p., publisher Pacific Press Ltd., Vancouver, B.C., Can., 1985—; also bd. dirs. Pacific Press Ltd., Vancouver, B.C.; bd. dirs. Canadian Press, Toronto, Ont., Southam Newspaper Group. Named Mktg. Exec. of Yr. Vancouver Sales & Mktg. Execs., 1987. Mem. Commonwealth Press Union, Internat. Press Inst., Can. Daily Newspaper Publishers Assn., Am. Press Inst. (chmn. Western adv. bd. 1985—). Anglican. Clubs: Royal Vancouver, Can. of Vancouver (bd. dirs.

1985—); Royal Can. Yacht (Toronto); Shaughnessy Golf and Country. Avocations: Sailing; photography. Office: Pacific Press Ltd, 2250 Granville St, Vancouver, BC Canada V6H 3G2

HASLEM, WILLIAM JOSHUA, physical scientist; b. Roosevelt, Utah, Nov. 28, 1936; s. Clair and Doris (Diamond) H.; m. Carol Boneta Freestone, Sept. 3, 1957; children: Susan Hexem, Brenda Stapp, Mark W. BS, U. Utah, 1960; MA, Cen. Mich. U., 1974. Project officer Dugway (Utah) Proving Ground, 1960-72; with ops. research Tank-Automotive Industry, Warren, Mich., 1972-75; tech. advisor Cold Regions Test Ctr., Ft. Greely, Alaska, 1975—. Contbr. articles to profl. jours. Active sch. bd., Delta, Alaska, 1976-79. Mem. Internat. Test Evaluation Assn., Assn. U.S. Army. Republican. Mormon. Avocations: outdoors, camping, fishing. Home: PO Box 624 Delta AK 99737 Office: Cold Regions Test Ctr Attn: Stecr-ta APO Seattle WA 98733

HASSELBRACK, BARBARA CAROL, nursing services administrator; b. Richlands, Va., Dec. 7, 1942; d. O.D. and Mae (Lowe) Altizer; m. Walter J. Hasselbrack, Aug. 27, 1972; 1 child, Jeni. BS, Columbia Union, 1964; MS, Loma Linda U., 1971. Staff nurse Washington Ad. Hosp., Tacoma Park, 1964-65, supr. intensive care unit, pediatrics, 1965-66; instr. sch. nursing Loma Linda (Calif.) U., 1969-71; v.p. nursing St. Helena Hosp., Deer Park, Calif., 1978—. Mem. Assn. Nurse Adminstrs., Assn. Seventh-day Adventist Nursing. Republican. Lodge: Soroptimists. Home: 1840 Crinella Dr Saint Helena CA 94574 Office: St Helena Hosp Sanitarium Rd Deer Park CA 94576

HASSETT, CHRISTOPHER MICHAEL, research scientist; b. Phila., Feb. 3, 1952; s. Maurice Martin and Mary Elizabeth (Murray) H. BA, Bridgewater Coll., 1974; MS, San Diego State U., 1979; M in Pub. Health, UCLA, 1981; PhD in Pub. Health, UCAL, 1985. Research technician Litton Bionetics Inc., Frederick, Md., 1974-76, Microbiol. Assocs., La Jolla, Calif., 1976-78, La Jolla Cancer Research Found., 1978-79; research assoc. UCLA, 1980-85; research scientist U. Wash., Seattle, 1985—; radiation safety cons. Hassett and Assocs., Los Angeles, 1979-85. UCLA Grad. Study grantee, 1982-84; HHS traineeship, Los Angeles, 1979-85. Mem. AAAS, Xi Sci. Research Soc., N.Y. Acad. Sci., UCLA Alumni Assn. (award 1985), Delta Omega. Roman Catholic. Avocations: basketball, bike riding, hiking. Home: 7312 32nd Ave NW Seattle WA 98117 Office: Univ Wash SC-34 Seattle WA 98195

HASSON, HASKIA, mathematician, consultant, educator; b. Los Angeles, May 28, 1951; s. Sam and Victoria (Coen) H.; B.A. (scholar), U. Calif., Los Angeles, 1972, postgrad., 1973-75; M.A., U. Calif., Berkeley, 1973. Asst. prof. Pepperdine U., 1975-78; lectr. Calif. State U., Long Beach, 1977-78; mathematician Hughes Aircraft Co., 1978-82; liaison officer Atenisi Inst., Nuku'alofa, Tonga, 1975—, guest lectr., 1975, adj. lectr., 1978—; adj. prof. Pepperdine U., 1978-80. Mem. AAAS, Am. Math. Soc., Math. Assn. Am., Assn. Computing Machinery, N.Y. Acad. Scis., Vols. in Tech. Assistance (vol.). Author: The Equivalence of Real Numbers Under Unimodular Transformations, 1973. Home: 308 3d St Manhattan Beach CA 90266

HASSOUNA, FRED, architect, planner, educator; b. Cairo, Mar. 26, 1918; s. Amin Sami and Dawlat (Mansour) H.; came to U.S., 1948, naturalized, 1953; diploma in architecture with honors Higher Sch. Fine Arts, Cairo, 1940; diploma in egyptology with 1st class honors U. Cairo, 1944; diploma in civic design U. Liverpool (Eng.), 1946; M.Arch., M.S. in Pub. Adminstrn., U. So. Calif., 1950; m. Verna Arlene Dotter, Mar. 9, 1950. Architect, curator Cairo Mus., Egypt, 1940-44; lectr. archeology and architecture Alexandria U., Egypt, 1944-45, 47-48; dir. planning Huyton-with-Roby Urban Dist. Council, Huyton, Eng., 1946-47; lectr. city planning U. So. Calif., 1950-55; architect Kistner, Wright and Wright, architects and engrs., Los Angeles, 1952-53; project architect Welton Becket and Assocs., architects and engrs., Los Angeles, 1954-56, Albert C. Martin and Assocs., architects and engrs., 1956-58; faculty architecture East Los Angeles Coll., 1958-75, prof. architecture, head dept. architecture; prof., head dept. architecture Saddleback Coll., 1975-83; pvt. planning cons., architect, Los Angeles, 1950-75, Laguna Niguel, 1975—. Mem. indsl. tech. adv. bd. Calif. State U. at Long Beach, 1963-83; mem. adv. bd. on environ. and interior design U. Calif., Irvine, 1976-83; pres. Calif. Council Archtl. Edn., 1977; mem. liaison com. architecture, landscape architecture, urban and regional planning in Calif. higher edn., 1976-83. Registered architect, Calif.; recipient hon. cultural doctorate World U. Roundtable, Tucson, 1983. Fellow Internat. Inst. Arts and Letters (life); mem. emeritus AIA, Am. Planning Assn. Home and Office: 31242 Flying Cloud Dr Laguna Niguel CA 92677

HASSRICK, PETER HEYL, museum director; b. Phila., Apr. 27, 1941; s. Royal Brown and E. Barbara (Morgan) H.; m. Elizabeth Drake, June 14, 1963; children: Philip Heyl, Charles Royal. Student, Harvard U., 1962; BA, U. Colo., 1963; MA, U. Denver, 1969. Tchr. Whiteman Sch., Steamboat Springs, Colo., 1963-67; also bd. dirs. Whiteman Sch., Steamboat Springs; curator of collections Amon Carter Mus., Ft. Worth, 1969-75; dir. Buffalo Bill Hist. Ctr., Cody, Wyo., 1976—. Author: Frederic Remington, 1973, The Way West, 1977, Treasures of the Old West, 1984; co-author: The Rocky Mountains, 1983. Mem. Yellowstone Assn., Cody C. of C. Office: Buffalo Bill Hist Ctr 720 Sheridan Ave Box 1000 Cody WY 82414

HASSTEDT, SANDRA JEAN, human genetics educator; b. Durango, Colo., July 26, 1949; d. Cecil Rudolph and Doris (Binder) H.; m. Peter Edmund Cartwright, May 3, 1980; children: Dustin Alexander, Allison Nicole. BS, Colo. State U., 1971; MA, U. Mich., 1975, PhD, 1976. Research asst. prof. genetics U. Utah, Salt Lake City, 1979-86, asst. prof., 1986—. Mem. AAAS, Am. Soc. Human Genetics. Office: U Utah Dept Human Genetics 50 N Medical Dr Salt Lake City UT 84132

HASTINGS, WAYNE ALEXANDER, publishing company executive; b. San Bernardino, Calif., Jan. 12, 1949; s. Ray Raymond and Catherine Edith (Stevens) H.; m. Pamela Lorraine Kucera, June 6, 1970; children: Jennifer Rebecca, Zachary Todd. BA cum laude, U. Redlands, 1971. Dept. mgr. Sears Roebuck and Co., San Bernardino, 1971-76; territory mgr. Burroughs Corp., San Bernardino, 1976-78; controller Woelke & Romero, San Bernardino, 1978-82; dir. finance Here's Life Pubs., San Bernardino, 1982-86, exec. v.p., 1986—; bd. dirs. Here's Life Found., San Bernardino. Named one of Outstanding Young Men of Am., U.S. C. of C., 1977. Mem. Am. Mgmt. Assn., Nat. Assn. Accts., Computer Users Assn. Republican. Mem. Evangelical Free Ch. Avocations: racquetball, guitar, U.S. History. Home: 249 E 34th St San Bernardino CA 92402 Office: Here's Life Pubs PO Box 1576 San Bernardino CA 92402

HASTRICH, JEROME JOSEPH, bishop; b. Milw., Nov. 13, 1914; s. George Philip and Clara (Dettlaff) H. Student, Marquette U., 1933-35; B.A., St. Francis Sem., Milw., 1940, M.A., 1941; student, Cath. U. Am., 1947. Ordained priest Roman Cath. Ch., 1941; assigned to Milw. Chancery, 1941; curate St. Ann's Ch., Milw., St. Bernard's Ch., Madison, Wis.; asst. chaplain St. Paul U. Chapel, then U. Wis.; sec. to bishop of U. Wis., Madison, 1946-52; chancellor Diocese Madison, Wis., 1952-53; apptd. vicar gen. Diocese Madison, 1953, domestic prelate, 1954, protonotary apos., 1960; aux. bishop 1963-67, titular bishop of Gurza and aux. of Madison, 1963; pastor St. Raphael Cathedral, Madison, 1967-69; bishop Gallup, N.Mex., 1969—; diocesan dir. Confraternity Christian Doctorine, 1946—, St. Martin Guild, 1946-69; aux. chaplain U.S. Air Force, 1947-67; pres. Latin Am. Mission Program; sec. Am. Bd. Cath. Missions; vice chmn. Bishop's Com. for Spanish Speaking; mem. subcom. on allocations U.S. Bishops Com. for Latin Am.; founder, episcopal moderator Queen of Americas Guild, 1979—; pres. Nat. Blue Army of Our Lady of Fatima, 1980—. Mem. Gov. Wis. Commn. Migratory Labor, 1964—. Club: K.C. (hon. life mem.). Address: PO Box 1338 Gallup NM 87301

HATCH, CALVIN SHIPLEY, retired home products executive; b. Heber City, Utah, Feb. 23, 1921; s. Edwin D. and Vernico B. (Burton) H.; m. JeNeal Nebeker, Dec. 23, 1945; children: Marcia Ann, Julie Lynne. B.S. in Fin., U. Utah, 1943. Salesman, N.Y. Life Ins. Co., Salt Lake City, 1946-47; with Procter & Gamble Co., 1947-71; sales merchandising mgr. Procter & Gamble Co., Cin., 1966-68, mgr. cen. div., 1968-71; v.p. sales Clorox Co., Oakland, Calif., 1971-73; group v.p. Clorox Co., 1973-76, exec. v.p., 1977-81, pres., chief exec. officer, 1981-82, chmn., chief exec. officer, 1982-86; dir. Interstate Bank Calif.; bd. dirs. Am. Pres. Cos. Active fund raising Salvation Army, Better Bus. Bur. Served to capt. F.A., AUS, 1942-45. Mem. Assn. Nat. Advertisers (dir. 1976-82). Home: 3853 Palo Alto Dr Lafayette CA 94549 Office: Clorox Co 1221 Broadway Oakland CA 94612

HATCH, EASTMAN NIBLEY, physics educator; b. Salt Lake City, June 14, 1927; s. Joseph Eastman and Florence (Nibley) H.; m. Anne Clawson, June 21, 1952; children: Joseph Eastman II, Richard Clawson, Anne Florence. Student, U. Utah, 1946-48, 51-52; B.S., Stanford, 1950; Ph.D., Calif. Inst. Tech., 1956. Postdoctoral fellow in physics Calif. Inst. Tech., 1956-57; research asso. physics Brookhaven Nat. Lab., Upton, N.Y., 1957-58; sci. liaison with USN in Frankfurt/Main, Germany, 1958-60; guest physicist Heidelberg U., Germany, 1960-61; assoc. prof. physics Iowa State U., 1961-66, prof. physics, 1966-69; asst. dean Grad. Coll., 1967-69; physicist Ames Lab., 1961-66, sr. physicist, 1966-69; prof. physics Utah State U., Logan, 1969—; head dept. physics Utah State U., 1972-74, dean sch. grad. studies, 1974-79; vis. prof. physics Freiburg U., W. Ger., 1979-80; vis. research assoc. Los Alamos Sci. Lab., 1971-83. Served with USNR, 1945-46. Fellow Am. Phys. Soc., Phi Beta Kappa, Sigma Xi. Home: 1795 Country Club Dr Logan UT 84321

HATCH, FRANK WHITE, science facility administrator; b. Provo, Utah, Sept. 12, 1940; s. Frank C. and Marian (White) H.; m. Linda Vernon, divorced; children: Frank V., Daniel, Brook; m. Lenny Maietta; children: Silke, Cerise. BA, Brigham Young U., 1965, MA, 1966; PhD, U. Wis., 1973. Instr. Brigham Young U., Provo, 1965-67; asst. prof. U. Wis., Steven Point, 1967-70; research fellow Social Sci. Research Council, Bahia, Brazil, 1971-72; assoc. prof. Calif. State U., Fullerton, 1972-75; dir. Ernest-Holmes Drug Clinic, Leutkirch, Republic of Germany, 1976-79; co-dir. Inst. for Kinaesthetics, Zurich, Switzerland, Hamburg, Republic of Germany, Stuttgart, Republic of Germany, 1980—; exec. dir. Inst. Cybernetic Studies, Santa Fe, 1985—; cons. instr. U. Mainz, Hamburg and Geneva, 1980—; research and theraputic cons., Pacific State Hosp., Pomona, Calif., 1975; researcher, lectr., writers in field. Producer-dir. numerous Pub. TV programs. Research fellow Social Sci. Research Council, 1971; named Prof. of Yr. U. Wis., 1970; recipient Cybernetic Research award U. Calif., Fullerton, 1974. Avocations: riding, computers, fishing, woodwork, building. Home: Rt 9 Box 86 HM Santa Fe NM 87505 Office: Verein fur Kinaesthetik, CH-5604 Hendschiken Im Buhl, Zurich Switzerland

HATCH, GAIL PETERSEN, advertising writer, administrator; b. Fertile, Minn., Oct. 7, 1940; s. Jurgen Hans and Norma Luella (Hendricks) Petersen; m. Thomas E. Hatch Jr., Apr. 24, 1976. BS in Journalism, Northwestern U., 1962. Copywriter E.H. Weiss & Co., Chgo., 1962-66; v.p., assoc. creative dir. J. Walter Thompson Co., Chgo., 1967-77, New York, 1979-83; v.p. creative devel. Arnold & Co. Advt., Boston, 1977-78; regional mktg. mgr. Phase One, Beverly Hills, Calif., 1983-84; v.p., assoc. creative dir. Evans/Weinberg Advt., Inc., Los Angeles, 1985—. Mem. Chgo. Jr. League; bd. dirs. Night Pastor Chgo., Boston Jr. League, 670 Apts. Corp, N.Y.C., Pasadena Chamber Orch.; career devel. co-chmn. N.Y. Jr. League, N.Y.C., 1982. Avocations: tennis, sailing, reading. Office: Evans/Weinberg Advt Inc 5757 Wilshire Blvd PH 1 Los Angeles CA 90036

HATCH, GEORGE CLINTON, TV executive; b. Erie, Pa., Dec. 16, 1919; s. Charles Milton and Blanche (Beecher) H.; m. Wilda Gene Glasmann, Dec. 24, 1940; children: Michael Gene Zbar Arnow, Diane Glasmann Orr, Jeffrey Beecher, Randall Clinton, Deepika Hatch Windstone. B.A., Occidental Coll., 1940; M.A., Claremont Coll., 1941. Chmn. Intermountain Network, Inc., Salt Lake City, 1941—; dir. Republic Pictures Corp., Los Angeles, 1971—, chmn., 1971-86; chmn. Kans. State Network, Wichita, 1981—; pres. Communications Investment Corp., Salt Lake City, 1945—, Sta. KUTV-TV, Inc., Salt Lake City, 1956—, Gem State Broadcasting Corp., Boise, Idaho, 1962—, Idaho Broadcasting Corp., Idaho Falls, KVEL, Inc., 1978, Sun Progress, Inc.; treas. Standard Corp., Ogden; mem. Salt Lake adv. bd. First Security Bank Utah; past chmn. Rocky Mountain Pub. Broadcasting Corp.; Past chmn. bd. govs. Am. Info. Radio Network; past bd. govs. NBC-TV Affiliates. Past pres. Salt Lake Com. on Fgn. Relations; mem., past chmn. Utah State Bd. Regents, 1964-85. Recipient Service to Journalism award U. Utah, 1966, Silver Medal award Salt Lake Advt. Club, 1969, Disting. award Utah Tech. Coll., 1984. Mem. Nat. Assn. Broadcasters (past pres. radio bd. dirs.), Utah Broadcasters Assn. (past pres., Mgmt. award 1964, Hall of Fame award 1981), Phi Beta Kappa, Phi Rho Pi (life). Office: 2185 S 3600 W Salt Lake City UT 84119

HATCH, KENNETH L., company executive; b. Vernal, Utah, Aug. 4, 1935; s. Lois and Alva Le Roy Hatch; m. Marsha Kay Rich, Dec. 7, 1974; children: Sean, Ryan, James, Michael, Elizabeth Ann. BS in Banking and Fin., U. Utah, 1957; postgrad. Stanford U., Harvard Grad. Sch. Bus. Gen. sales mgr. KSL, Salt Lake City, 1963-64; gen. sales mgr. KIRO-TV, Seattle, 1964-66, asst. gen. mgr., 1965-67, gen. mgr., 1967-71, sr. v.p., 1971-80, pres., chief exec. officer, 1980—; dir., mem. exec. com., KIRO, Inc.; sr. v.p. Bonneville Internat. Corp.; bd. dirs. Bear Creek, Inc., Wash., Olympic Bank. Bd. dirs. Seattle Conv. and Bus. Bur. Mem. Ch. of Christ. Club: Rainier of Seattle, Bellevue Athletic, Wash. Athletic, Overlake Golf and Country. Office: 3d Ave & Broad St Seattle WA 98121

HATCH, ORRIN GRANT, U.S. Senator; b. Homestead Park, Pa., Mar. 22, 1934; s. Jesse and Helen (Kamm) H.; m. Elaine Hansen, Aug. 28, 1957; children: Brent, Marcia, Scott, Kimberly, Alysa, Jesse. B.S., Brigham Young U., 1959; J.D., U. Pitts., 1962. Bar: Pa. 1962, Utah 1962. Ptnr. firm Thomson, Rhodes & Grigsby, Pitts., 1962-69, Hatch & Plumb, Salt Lake City, 1976; mem. U.S. Senate from Utah, 1977—; past chmn. labor and human resources com.; ranking minority mem. Senate Labor and Human Resources Com, mem. Senate Judiciary Com., Select Com. on Intelligence, Spl. Senate Com. Investigating Iran Arms Deal. Contbr. articles to newspapers and profl. jours. Mem. Am., Nat., Utah, Pa. bar assns., Am. Judicature Soc. Republican. Mormon. Office: 135 Russell Senate Office Bldg Washington DC 20510

HATCH, RANDALL CLINTON, journalist; b. Salt Lake City, Oct. 15, 1951; s. George Clinton and Wilda Gene (Glasmann) H.; m. Ann Darger, Apr. 11, 1975; children—Sarah, George, William, Spencer. B.A., U. Utah, 1975; M.B.A., Columbia U., 1977, M.S. in Journalism, 1976. Reporter, Salt Lake Tribune, 1977-78; ad salesman Newspaper Agy., Salt Lake City, 1978-79; promotion dir. Ogden Standard, Utah, 1979-80, mng. editor, 1980—. Dir., Communications Investment Corp., Salt Lake City, Nat. Video Clearinghouse, Syosset, N.Y., 1978—. Bd. dirs. Union Sta. Devel. Corp., 1981-83, Ogden Arts Commn., 1981-83, McKay Dee Hosp. Found., Ogden, 1981-83. Served with AUS, 1970-78. Mem. Soc. Profl. Journalists (1st v.p. 1984, bd. dirs. Utah chpt. 1984-85, pres. 1985-86). Mormon. Lodge: Rotary. Office: Ogden Standard Examiner 455 23d St Ogden UT 84401

HATCH, RICHARD, physician, obstetrician/gynecologist; b. Stockton, Calif., Jan. 28, 1948; s. Elmer Webb and Tressa (Farr) H.; m. Jennifer Stevens Adams, Mar. 13, 1981; children: Richard Elmer, Dorothy Allison, John Adams, Elizabeth Amanda. BS cum laude, Brigham Young U., 1970; MD, U. Utah, 1974. Diplomate Am. Bd. Ob-gyn, subspecialty Reproductive Endocrinology. Resident in ob-gyn U. Chgo., 1974-78, fellow in reproductive endocrinology, 1978-81, asst. prof. ob-gyn, 1981-85; practice medicine specializing in ob-gyn and reproductive endocrinology Vernal, Utah, 1985—. Contbr. articles to profl. jours. Fellow Am. Coll. Obsetricians and Gynecologists; mem. Phi Kappa Phi. Republican. Mormon. Lodge: Rotary. Home: 363 S 400 W Vernal UT 84078 Office: 175 N 100 W Vernal UT 84078

HATCH, ROBERT DUANE, business consultant educator; b. Salt Lake City, Mar. 29, 1930; s. Sisson Chase and Hazel (Coult) H.; m. Beverly Sedgwick, June 19, 1959; children: Robert, Michele. BA, Brigham Young U., 1959, MS, 1963. Mgmt. engr. USAF, Hill, Utah, 1965-70; pres. Am. Mktg. and Mfg., Bountiful, Utah, 1970-75; dept. head, indsl. engr. NRP Inc., Nehpi, Utah, 1976-84; voices coordinator Reagan-Bush 1984, Washington, 1984; debate coach Brigham Young U., Provo, 1985-86; sr. cons. Snow Coll./NRP, Ephraim, Utah, 1985-86; safety cons. Nephi Rubber Products, 1986—; mgmt. cons. Barney Inc., Spanish Fork, Utah, 1985—. Author, editor (Reagan-Bush campaign newletter) Voices for Victory, 1984. Campaign mgr. Richardson for Congress, Provo, 1978; assoc. campaign mgr. Beckman for Congress, Provo, 1982. Served to sgt. U.S. Army, 1953-55. Republican. Mormon. Avocations: writing, computer programming. Home and Office: RFD 1 Box 417 Spanish Fork UT 84660

HATCH, STEVEN GRAHAM, publishing company executive; b. Idaho Falls, Idaho, Mar. 27, 1951; s. Charles Steven and Margery Jane (Doxey) H.; B.A., Brigham Young U., 1976; postgrad. mgmt. devel. program U. Utah, 1981; m. Rhonda Kay Frasier, Feb. 13, 1982; children: Steven Graham, Kristen Leone. Founder, pres. Graham Maughan Enterprises, Provo, Utah, 1975—, Internat. Mktg. Co., 1980—; dir. Goldbrickers Internat., Inc. Sec., treas. Zions Estates, Inc., Salt Lake City, Kansas City, Mo. Eagle Scout Boy Scouts Am., 1970; trustee Villages of Quail Valley, 1984—. Recipient Duty to God Award, 1970. Mem. Provo Jaycees, Internat. Entrepreneurs Assn., Mormon Booksellers Assn., Samuel Hall Soc. (exec. v.p. 1979), U.S. C. of C., Provo C. of C. (chmn. legis. action com. 1981-82). Republican. Mormon (missionary France Mission, Paris 1970-72, pub. relations dir. 1972). Club: Rotary Internat. Office: Graham Maughan Pub Co 50 East 500 South Provo UT 84601

HATCHELL, WILLIAM O'DONALD, geologist, state government official; b. Florence, S.C., Nov. 9, 1938; s. John Lee and Mildred Colleen (Hicks) H. student Clemson U., 1957-60; B.S., U. S.C., 1964; M.S., U. N.Mex., 1967. geol. field asst. U.S. Geol. Survey, 1963-64; staff geologist AEC, Grand Junction, Colo., 1967-68; exploration geologist Kerr-McGee Corp., Salt Lake City, 1968-70; hwy. geologist State of N.Mex., Santa Fe, 1970-72; uranium geologist Phillips Petroleum Co., Albuquerque, 1972-74; research geologist Geothermal Services, Inc., San Diego, 1974-79; metals resource geologist N.Mex. Energy, Minerals and Nat. Resources Dept., Santa Fe, 1979—. Contbr. numerous articles to profl. jours. Recipient Manning award in geology U. S.C., 1963; grantee Mus. No. Ariz., 1966, NSF, 1963. Mem. Am. Inst. Profl. Geologists, Am. Assn. Petroleum Geologists, Geol. Soc. Am., N.Mex. Geol. Soc., AIME, Soc. Econ. Paleontologists and Mineralologists, Sigma Gamma Epsilon. Home: 14 Encantado Loop Santa Fe NM 87505 Office: State of N Mex Energy Minerals and Nat Resources Dept 525 Camino de los Marquez Santa Fe NM 87501

HATCHER, HERBERT JOHN, biochemist, microbiologist; b. Mpls., Dec. 18, 1926; s. Herbert Edmond and Florence Elizabeth (Larson) H.; m. Beverly J. Johnson, Mar. 28, 1953 (dec. July 1985); children: Dennis Michael, Steven Craig, Roger Dean, Mark Alan, Susan Diane, Laura Jean; m. Louise Fritsche Nelson, May 24, 1986; children: Carlos Howard Nelson, Kent Robert Nelson, Carolyn Louise Tyler. BA, U. Minn., 1953, MS, 1964, PhD, 1965. Bacteriologist VA Hosp., Wilmington, Del., 1956-57; microbiologist Smith, Kline, French, Phila., 1957-60, Clinton (Iowa) Corn Processing, 1966-67; microbiologist, biochemist Econs. Lab. Inc., St. Paul, 1967-84; biochemist EG&G Idaho Inc., Idaho Falls, 1984—; cons. Diamond-Shamrock, Morristown, N.J., 1986. Chmn. bd. edn. Cross of Christ Luth. Ch., Coon Rapids, Minn., 1974-76; pres. chpt. Aid Assn. Luths., Idaho Falls, 1986. Served with USNR, 1945-46. Mem. Henrici Soc., Am. Soc. Microbiologists, N.Y. Acad. Scis., Idaho Acad. Scis. Avocations: skiing, hiking, camping, hunting, fishing. Office: EG&G Idaho Inc Box 1625 Idaho Falls ID 83415

HATCHER, JOHN CHRISTOPHER, psychologist; b. Atlanta, Sept. 18, 1946; s. John William and Kay (Carney) H.; B.A., U. Ga., 1968, M.S., 1970, Ph.D., 1972. Psychologist, Clayton Mental Health Center, Atlanta, 1971-72; dir. intern training psychology service Beaumont Med. Center, El Paso, Tex., 1972-74; dir. family therapy program Langley Porter Inst., U. Calif., San Francisco, 1974—; adj. prof. dept. psychology U. Tex., 1972-74, dept. ednl. psychology and guidance, 1972-74; asst. clin. prof. psychology U. Calif., San Francisco, 1974-80, assoc. clin. prof., 1980-86, clin. prof., 1986—; cons. city and state govts. in U.S., Europe, Mexico, Asia, Far East; internat. cons. in hostage negotiation and terrorism chmn., Mayors Commn. on Family Violence, San Francisco; advisor arson task force San Francisco Fire Dept.; adv. bd. Nat. Firehawk Found., Kevin Collins Found. for Missing Children; advisor CBS-TV; spl. asst. to Mayor of San Francisco in charge of People's Temple Jonestown Case; mem. Calif. State Legis. Task Force on Mising Children. Mem. Am. Psychol. Assn., Calif. State Psychol. Assn. (chmn. task force on terrorism), Soc. Police and Criminal Psychology, Assn. Advancement Psychology, Am. Family Therapy Assn., Internat. Council Psychologists, Phi Kappa Phi. Author: (with Himelstein) Handbook of Gestalt Therapy, 1976; (with Brooks) Innovations in Counseling Psychology, 1977, (with Gaynor) Psychology of Child Firesetting, 1987; assoc. editor Am. Jour. Family Therapy; sr. editor Family Therapy Jour., mem. editorial bd. Family Psychology Jour. Office: U Calif Psychiatry Dept 401 Parnassus San Francisco CA 94143

HATFIELD, ELAINE CATHERINE, psychology educator; b. Detroit, Oct. 22, 1937; d. Charles E. and Eileen (Kalahar) H.; m. Richard L. Rapson, June 15, 1982. B.A., U. Mich., 1959; Ph.D., Stanford U., 1963. Asst. prof. U. Minn., Mpls., 1963-64, assoc. prof., 1964-66; asso. prof. U. Rochester, 1966-68, U. Wis., Madison, 1968-69; prof. U. Wis., 1969-81; now prof. U. Hawaii at Manoa; chmn. dept. U. Hawaii of Manoa, 1981-83. Author: Interpersonal Attraction, 1969, 2d edit., 1978, Equity: Theory and Research, 1978, A New Look at Love, 1978, Human Sexual Behavior, 1985, Mirror, Mirror: The Importance of Looks in Everyday Life, 1986. Contbr. articles to profl. jours. Fellow Am. Psychol. Assn., Am. Sociol. Assn. Home: 3334 Ano'ai Pl Honolulu HI 96822 Office: U Hawaii 2430 Campus Rd Honolulu HI 96822

HATFIELD, MARK, U.S. senator; b. Dallas, Oreg., July 12, 1922; s. Charles Dolen and Dovie (Odom) H.; m. Antoinette Kuzmanich, July 8, 1958; children: Mark, Elizabeth, Theresa, Charles. A.B., Willamette U., 1943; A.M., Stanford U., 1948. Instr. Willamette U., 1949, dean students, asso. prof. polit. sci., 1950-56; mem. Oreg. Ho. of Reps., 1951-55, Oreg. Senate, 1955-57; sec. State of Oreg., 1957-59, gov., 1959-67; U.S. senator from Oreg. 1967—, chmn. appropriations com.; mem. energy and natural resources com., rules and adminstrn. com. Author: Not Quite So Simple, 1967, Conflict and Conscience, 1971, Between A Rock and A Hard Place, 1976; co-author: Amnesty: The Unsettled Question of Vietnam, 1973, Freeze!, 1982, The Causes of World Hunger, 1982. Served to lt. j.g. USN, 1943-45. Recipient numerous hon. degrees. Republican. Baptist. Office: Room SH-711 US Senate Washington DC 20510

HATFIELD, PAUL GERHART, lawyer, judge; b. Great Falls, Mont., Apr. 29, 1928; s. Trueman LeRoy and Grace Lenore (Gerhart) H.; m. Dorothy Ann Allen, Feb. 1, 1958; children—Kathleen Helen, Susan Ann, Paul Allen. Student, Coll. of Great Falls, 1947-50; LL.B., U. Mont., 1955. Bar: Mont. bar 1955. Asso. firm Hoffman & Cure, Gt. Falls, Mont., 1955-56, Jardine, Stephenson, Blewett & Weaver, Gt. Falls, 1956-58, Hatfield & Hatfield, Gt. Falls, 1959-60; chief dep. county atty. Cascade County, Mont., 1959-60; dist. ct. judge 8th Jud. Dist., Mont., 1961-76; chief justice Supreme Ct. Mont., Helena, 1977-78; U.S. Senator from Mont., 1978-79; U.S. dist. judge for Dist. of Mont., Gt. Falls, 1979—; Vice chmn. Pres.'s Council Coll. of Great Falls. Author: standards for criminal justice, Mont. cts. Served with U.S. Army, 1951-53. Korea. Mem. Am., Mont. bar assns., Am. Judicature Soc. Roman Catholic. Office: US Dist Ct PO Box 1529 Great Falls MT 59403

HATHAWAY, FRANK GARBUTT, corporation executive; b. Los Angeles, Jan. 7, 1924; s. Charles F. and Melodile (Garbutt) H.; B.S., U. So. Calif., 1958, postgrad., 1959-64; m. Jo Ellen Robbins, July 1, 1949; children—Karen Leigh, Deborah Lynn, John King, Mary Ann, Susanna Elizabeth, Pamela Jo. With LAACO, Ltd. (formerly Los Angeles Athletic Club), 1946—, pres., chief exec. officer, 1949-76, chmn. bd., chief exec. officer, 1976—; v.p., dir. Waikikian Hotel, Honolulu, 1956-76, Calif. Yacht Club, 1966—; chmn. bd. Health Crafters, 1972—; pres. LAACO Investment Corp., Los Angeles, 1963—. Mem. bd. Los Angeles Police Commn., 1964-73, pres., 1967-68; mem. Los Angeles County Grand Jury, 1956; bd. dirs. Central City Assn. Los Angeles; trustee S.W. Mus., Cultural Heritage Found., Los Angeles. Served to 1st lt. USAAF, World War II. Recipient Durward Howes award Los Angeles Jr. C. of C., 1953. Mem. Nat. Club. Assn. (pres. 1967, dir. 1961-76), C.G. Aux. (past comdr. flotilla 42), Grand Jurors Assn. (pres. 1959-61), Nat. Rifle Assn. Clubs: Masons, Rotary. Office: 611 W 6th St Suite 3250 Los Angeles CA 90017

HATHAWAY, GARY MICHAEL, biochemist, university administrator; b. Los Angeles, Mar. 6, 1937; s. Clint Adrian and Edith Helen (Irving) H.; m. Wilhelmina Elizabeth York, Aug. 18, 1966 (div. Feb. 1982); children: John Michael, Sean Robert. BS in Chemistry, Calif. State U., Long Beach, 1964; PhD in Biochemistry, U. Calif., Davis, 1967. Asst. research biochemist Scripps Clinic and Research Found., La Jolla, Calif., 1967-71; asst. research biochemist U. Calif., Riverside, 1971-76, research assoc., 1976-85, acad. coordinator, biotech. instrumentation facility, 1985—. Contbr. revs. to profl. jours. Mem. AAAS, Am. Assn. Biol. Chemists, The Protein Soc. Avocations: skiing, Am. fur trade era artifacts. Home: 11854 Graham St Moreno Valley CA 92388 Office: U Calif Biotech Instrumentation Facility Riverside CA 92521

HATHAWAY, JOHN F., small business owner; b. Danville, Ill., Jan. 28, 1947; s. Stanley Eugene and Louise Georgina (Polt) H. AS, Danville Comunity Coll., 1972; student, So. Ill. U., 1972-74. Service mgr. Bass Tire Co., Danville, 1974-76; owner John's Tree Service, Rossville, Ill., 1976-78, GAF Music Co., Rossville, Ill., 1979-86; supr. Flomation, Inc., Colorado City, Colo., 1986—; also bd. dirs. Diversified Internat. Inc., Colorado City, Colo. Inventor in field. Active State of Ill. Solar Adv. Bd., Springfield, 1979. Served with USMC, 1966-68. Republican. Methodist. Avocations: collector and restorer of antique coin operated devices. Home: PO Box 262 Rossville IL 60963

HATHAWAY, LOLINE, zoo and botanic park curator; b. Whitter, Calif., June 27, 1937; d. Richard Franklin and F. Nadine (Applegate) H.; m. A. Roger Kundtz, Nov. 25, 1976; 1 child, Patrick Paul. BA, Reed Coll., Portland, Oreg., 1959; PhD, Washington U., St. Louis, 1969. Instr. St. Louis U., 1966-68; curator of edn. Chgo. Zool. Soc., Brookfield, Ill., 1968-71; cons. on terrestrial biology Ryckman, Edgerly, Tomlinson & Assocs., St. Louis, 1972-75; marina mgr. Lake Piru (Calif.) Recreation Area, 1976-77; curator, dir. Navajo Nation Zool. and Botanical Park, Window Rock, Ariz., 1983—. v. chmn., chmn. City of Santa Fe Springs (Calif.) Traffic Commn., 1979-83; mem. Navajo Estates Vol. fire Dept., Yah-ta-hey, N.Mex., 1984-85; treas. McKinley Co. Assn. Gifted and Talented Students, 1986—; bd. dirs. Hathaway Ranch Mus., Santa Fe Springs, 1986—. Mem. AAAS (vice chmn. Southwest-Rocky Mountain div. sci. edn. sect. 1983-84, chmn. 1984-85), Am. Assn. Zool. Parks and Aquariums, Am. Assn. Bot. Gardens and Arboretums, Assn. Living Hist. Farms and Agr. Mus., Am. Inst. Biol. Scis., Ariz. Bot. Garden Assn., Sierra Club (Ozarks chpt. founder, bd. dirs., sec. Great Lakes chpt. 1963-72). Democrat. Home: 127 LaChee PO Box 4172 Yah-ta-hey NM 87375 Office: Navajo Nat Zool & Botanical Park PO Box 308 Window Rock AZ 86515

HATTER, TERRY JULIUS, JR., judge; b. Chgo., Mar. 11, 1933. A.B., Wesleyan U., 1954; J.D., U. Chgo., 1960. Bar: Ill. 1960, Calif. 1965, U.S. Dist. Ct. 1960, U.S. Ct. Appeals 1960. Adjudicator VA, Chgo., 1960-61; asso. Harold M. Calhoun, Chgo., 1961-62; asst. public defender Cook County Chgo., 1961-62; asst. U.S. atty. No. Dist. Calif., San Francisco, 1962-66; chief counsel San Francisco Neighborhood Legal Assistance Found., 1966-67; regional legal services dir. Exec. Office Pres. OEO, San Francisco, 1967-70; exec. dir. Western Center Law and Poverty, Los Angeles, 1970-73; exec. asst. to mayor, dir. criminal justice planning City of Los Angeles, 1974-75; spl. asst. to mayor, dir. urban devel. 1975-77; judge Superior Ct. Calif., Los Angeles, 1977-80, U.S. Dist. Ct. Central Dist. Calif., Los Angeles, 1980—; asso. clin. prof. law U. So. Calif. Law Center, 1970-74; prof. law Loyola U. Sch. Law, Los Angeles, 1973-75; mem. faculty Nat. Coll. State Judiciary, Reno, 1974; lectr. Police Acad., San Francisco Police Dept., 1963-66, U. Calif., San Diego, 1970-71, Colo. Jud. Conf., 1973. Vice pres. Northbay Halfway House, 1964-65; vice chmn. Los Angeles Regional Criminal Justice Planning Bd., 1975-76; mem. Los Angeles Mayor's Cabinet Com. Econ. Devel., 1976-77, Mayor's Policy Com., 1973-77, chmn. housing econ. and community devel. com., City Los Angeles, 1975-77, chmn. housing and community devel. tech. com., 1975-77; vice chmn. Young Democrats Cook County, 1961-62; chmn. bd. Real Estate Coop; bd. dirs. Bay Area Social Planning Council, Contra Costa, Black Law Center Los Angeles, Nat. Fedn. Settlements and Neighborhood Centers, Edn. Fin. and Governance Reform Project, Mexican Am. Legal Def. and Ednl. Fund, Nat. Health Law Program, Nat. Sr. Citizens Law Center, Calif. Law Center, Los Angeles Regional Criminal Justice Planning Bd.; mem. exec. com. bd. dirs. Richmond chpt. NAACP, Constl. Rights Found.; trustee Wesleyan United Meth. Ch. Mem. Nat. Legal Aid and Defender Assn. (dir., vice chmn.), Los Angeles County Bar Assn. (exec. com.), Am. Judicature Soc., Charles Houston Law Club, Order of Coif, Phi Delta Phi. Office: US District Court US Courthouse 312 N Spring St Los Angeles CA 90012

HATTON, GAYLEN A., music educator, musician; b. Red Mountain, Calif., Oct. 4, 1928; s. Glen A. and Eva Pearl (Wolf) H.; m. Marianne Johnson, Aug. 6, 1958; children: Nannette, Keven, Heidi, David. BA, Brigham Young U., 1951, MA, 1953; PhD, U. Utah, 1962. Lectr. U. Utah, Salt Lake City, 1958-62; prof. Calif. State U., Sacramento, 1962-79, Brigham Young U., Provo, 1979—; 3d chair French horn Utah Symphony, Salt Lake City, 1954-62; 1st chair French horn Sacramento Symphony, 1967-78; prin. French horn Bedford Festival Orch., Bedford Springs, Pa., 1983-85; mem. Orpheus Winds, 1980—, Brassworks, 1982—. Composer: Music for Orch., 1958 (Rosenblatt award), Jeu de Parti, 1972 (NEA award 1972), Prelusion, 1975, Bedford Festival Overture, 1984. Named Outstanding Male Musician, Sun Valley Music Festival, 1966. Mem. Internat. Horn Soc., Phi Mu Alpha. Republican. Mormon. Home: 560 S 500 E Orem UT 84058 Office: Brigham Young U Music Dept Provo UT 84602

HAUBERG, JOHN HENRY, forestry management company executive; b. Rock Island, Ill., June 24, 1916; s. John Henry and Suzanne Christina (Denkmann) H.; m. Ann Homer Brinkley, Dec. 1, 1979; children—Fay Page, Sue B. Student Princeton U., 1939; B.S. in Forestry, U. Wash., 1949. Founder Pacific Denkmann Co., Seattle, 1948, pres., 1952—; mem. vis. com. U. Wash. Coll. Forest Resources, 1960—. Vice chmn. Republican Nat. Fin. Com., 1962-64; trustee Seattle Art Mus., 1956—, pres., 1973-78, chmn. bd. trustees, 1978-81; mem. adv. com. for Child Devel. and Mental Retardation Ctr., U. Wash.; trustee, founder, pres. Pilchuck Glass Sch., Stanwood, Wash.; trustee Bush Sch., Seattle, 1950—, pres., 1954-57; trustee Am. Fedn. Arts, 1984—, Am. Craft Council, 1979—; mem. vestry Epiphany Parish Episcopalian Ch., Seattle. Served to 2d lt. F.A. and inf. U.S. Army, 1943-46. Mem. Soc. Am. Foresters, Northwest Hardwoods Assn. (founder, trustee), Phi Beta Kappa, Phi Sigma, Xi Sigma Pi. Clubs: Seattle Tennis, Seattle Golf, Univ., Rainier, City, Bainbridge Racquet. Pub. Pilchuck Tree Farm Notes, 1981—. Office: 216 1st Ave Suite 230 Seattle WA 98104

HAUBRICH, WILLIAM SPIES, physician, gastroenterologist; b. Columbus, Ohio, July 4, 1923; s. Albert and Marie Augusta (Spies) H.; m. Eila Kaarina Kari, June 21, 1947; children: Lisa, Linda, Christina, Karen. BS, Franklin and Marshall Coll., 1943; MD, Case Western Res. U., 1947. Diplomate Am. Bd. Internal Medicine, Am. Bd. Gastroenterology. Resident Grad. Hosp., Phila., 1947-48, 51-52, City Hosp., Cleve., 1948-51; staff physician Henry Ford Hosp., Detroit, 1955-70; sr. gastroenterologist Scripps Clinic, La Jolla, Calif., 1970—; clin. prof. medicine U. Calif. San Diego, 1970—. Author: Medical Meanings, 1984; contbr. articles to profl. jours. Served to capt. M.C., USAR, 1952-55. Fellow ACP; mem. Am. Soc. Gastrointestinal Endoscopy (Rudolf Schindler award 1985, editor jour. 1971-81), Am. Gastroenterol. Assn. (Vincent Lyon award 1960), Bockus Internat. Soc. (pres. 1980-82, editor med. text 1985). Republican. Presbyterian. Avocations: oil painting, woodworking. Home: 2946 Woodford Dr La Jolla CA 92037 Office: Scripps Clinic and Research Found 10666 N Torrey Pines Rd La Jolla CA 92037

HAUENSTEIN, DONALD HERBERT, JR., aerospace manufacturing executive; b. Canton, Ohio, Dec. 29, 1942; s. Donald Herbert and Mary Alice (Andrichs) H.; m. Maria Del Socorro Moreno, June 5, 1965 (div. Apr. 1979); children: Carlos Ian, Marissa Renee. B in Indsl. Engring., Ohio State U., 1970, MS in Indsl. Engring., 1970; MBA, U. Houston, 1977; exec. mgmt. program, UCLA, Los Angeles, 1986. Indsl. engr. Schlumberger Well Services, Houston, 1970-72, supr. of methods, 1972-75; mgr. engring. services Dresser Atlas, Houston, 1975-80; mgr. mfg. engring. VETCO Offshore, Ventura, Calif., 1980-83; dir. mfg. engring. HR Textron, Valencia, Calif., 1983-87, dir. controls mfg., 1987—. Pres. St. Christopher's Sch. Bd., Houston, 1976-79, bd. dirs. Orchard Ln. Condominium Assn., Oxnard, Calif., 1986. Served with USAF, 1961-65. Mem. Inst. Indsl. Engrs. (sr.), Soc. Mfg. Engrs. (sr.), Nat. Mgmt. Assn., Tau Beta Pi, Alpha Pi Mu. Republican. Roman Catholic. Avocations: photography, philately. Home: 26105 McBean Pkwy U69 Valencia CA 91355 Office: HR Textron 25200 W Rye Canyon Rd Valencia CA 91355

HAUENSTEIN, ERIC, broadcasting executive; b. Cin., May 26, 1948; s. Henry William and Lucille (Yeatts) H.; m. Marjorie Buchanan (div.); 1 child, Garrett Buchanan. Student, St. Louis U., 1966-67, U. Cin., 1967-70, Ariz. State U., 1971-75. Pres., owner, gen. mgr. Sta. KDKB AM/FM, Mesa and Phoenix, Ariz., 1971-78; owner, exec. v.p. Natural Broadcasting Systems, Phoenix, 1974-81; owner, v.p. Sta. KEZC FM, Lake Tahoe, Calif., 1976-78; mgr. broadcast div. Sandusky Newspapers, Inc., Phoenix, 1978-81; owner, pres. TransColumbia Communications, Phoenix, 1983—. Mem. curriculum adv. bd. Phoenix Coll., 1973-76; owner, chmn. bd. dirs. Roadrunners Profl. Hockey, Phoenix, 1977-78. Mem. Nat. Radio Broadcaster Assn. (regional dir. 1976-78), Ariz. Broadcasters Assn. (bd. dirs. 1976-78), Met. Phoenix Broadcasters (pres. 1975-76). Office: TransCom Communications Co Inc 5110 N 40th St Suite 238 Phoenix AZ 85018

HAUER, ANDREAS, employee benefit consultant; b. Oslo, June 25, 1946; came to U.S., 1948, naturalized, 1958; s. Karl Andreas and Ellen Bertha (Neilsen) H.; B.S., Linfield Coll., 1967; M.B.A., Golden Gate U., 1974. Asst. brokerage mgr. Pacific Mut. Ins. Co., San Francisco, 1970-72; employee benefit cons. Johnson & Higgins, San Francisco, 1972-80; v.p. employee benefits Bayly, Martin & Fay, Oakland, Calif., 1980-81, Fireman's Fund Ins. Co., San Rafael, Calif., 1981-84; sr. benefits cons. Coopers & Lybrand, 1984—. Chmn., World Championship Domino Tournament, San Francisco; bd. dirs. Stonestown YMCA. Served with USNR, 1968-69; Vietnam. Mem. C.L.U. Soc. (dir. San Francisco chpt. 1975-76). Republican. Lutheran. Clubs: Olympic. Home: 2101 Sacramento Apt 604 San Francisco CA 94109 Office: Coopers & Lybrand 333 Market St San Francisco CA 94109

HAUG, NANCY G., marketing professional, consultant; b. Portland, Nov. 3, 1944; d. Everard O. and Doris C. (Blomberg) Johnson; m. Darrol K. Haug, May 3, 1943; 1 child, Rebecca L. Student, Linfield Coll., 1964; BS in Speech and Psychology, Portland State U., 1967. Dir. publications Mt. Hood Community Coll., Gresham, Oreg., 1971-74; mktg. rep. Cone Heiden, Seattle, 1974-77; dir. advt. and promotions Princess Tours, Seattle, 1977-81, dir. client services, 1981-83; dir. mktg. Manus Direct Mktg., Seattle, 1984—; tour escort travel groups Alaska, China, Mex., 1977-83; cons. Pacific Celebration 89, Seattle, 1986; mem. Rhodes Scholarship Com., Seattle, 1986; chair person Direct Mktg. Day, Seattle, 1986. Producer film Alaska The Great Land, 1980. Bd. dirs. Job Corp, Seattle, 1976-80; hostess Edmonds Art Festival, Wash., 1985-86. Mem. Mktg. Communications Execs. Internat. (incorporator, hostess 1979-81); Seattle Direct Mktg. Assns. (founder, sec. 1984-86), Sales Mktg. Execs. Internat., Puget Sound Advt. Fedn., Alaska Visitors Assn. Republican. Club: Skiyente (Portland) (pres.1972-73). Avocations: skiing, gardening, traveling.

HAUGER, RICHARD LYNN, research psychiatrist; b. Pitts., Feb. 1, 1949; s. Harold N. and Ruth A. (Irwin) H. BS in Math., U. Pitts., 1970, MD, 1974; MA in Lit., Am. U., 1987. Diplomate Am. Bd. Medicine, Am. Bd. Psychiatry, Am. Bd. Neurology. Pharm. research assoc., NIMH NIH, Bethesda, Md., 1980-82, staff psychiatrist, NIMH, 1982-84; intern U. Chgo., 1977-78; resident in psychiatry Columbia U., N.Y.C., 1978-80; staff psychiatrist St. John's Episc. Hosp., Bklyn., 1979; practice psychiatry specializing in mood disorders and psychopharmacology Washington, 1980-85; asst. prof. U. Calif. San Diego, La Jolla, 1985-87, assoc. prof., 1987—; research assoc. San Diego VA Med Ctr., 1985—; instr. psychiatry U. Chgo., 1977-78; clin. asst. prof. Georgetown U., Washington, 1983-84; vis. scientist NIH, 1985-87; dirs. Affective Disorders Clinic, U. Calif. San Diego. Contbr. articles to profl. jours. Served to sr. surgeon USPHS, 1980-84, with Res. 1984—. Recipient Pharmacology Research Assoc. award Nat. Insts. Health, 1980-82, Ann. Laughlin award for Merit Nat. Psychiat. Edn. Fund Fellowship, 1980, Research Assoc. award VA, Washington, 1985—, Pfizer Scholars award, Pfizer Pharmaceuticals, 1986—; postdoctoral scholar Ford Found., 1974-76, postdoctoral fellow NIH, 1976-77. Mem. AAAS, The Endocrine Soc., Soc. for Neurosci., Modern Lang. Assn., Shakespeare Assn. Am. Avocation: harpsichord. Office: U Calif San Diego Psychiatry Dept M-003 La Jolla CA 92093

HAUGHEY, BRUCE STEPHENS, pottery designer, author, educator, lecturer; b. Billings, Mont., Sept. 26, 1943; s. James McRae and Katherine (Hurd) H.; m. Marilyn Ann Golden, Jan. 15, 1967 (div. Aug. 1972); children: Tamara Ann, Patrick Glen; m. Roxanne Eileen Adams, Dec. 11, 1974. BS, Mont. State U., 1967. Staff supr. Mass. Mut. Ins. Co., Billings, 1967-70; tchr. Sch. Dist. No. 2, Billings, 1971; Arthur Stephen's Design Group, Tempe, Ariz., 1986—. One-man shows include Cody Country Art League, Cody, Wyo., 1970, Gallery '85, Billings, 1970, CR Gallery, Williston, N.D., 1973-84, Sak's Gallery, Denver, Hayden Gallery, Colorado Springs, Gallery '84, Jackson Hole, Wyo., Historic Sheridan Inn, Wyo.; exhibited in group shows Internat. Soc. Artists, London, 1975, Amarillo, Tex., 1976, Pueblo, Colo., 1983, Mont. Watercolor Soc., 1983-84, Riverside, Calif., 1983, Allied Artists Am., N.Y.C., 1984; represented in numerous pub. and pvt. collections; author: Watercolor Workbook, 1968, Dynamic Composition with Bruce Haughey, 1983; featured in various mags.; inventor blender brush, 1984. Bd. dirs. Historic Sheridan Inn, Wyo., 1980-83; mem. Billings Mayor's Council for Arts, 1970-73; leader young men's group Yellowstone County Fine Arts Ctr., Billings, 1970. Served with USMC, 1968-71. Mem. Nat. Miniature Soc. (juror 1980), Am. Artists Profl. League, N.W. Watercolor Soc., Mont. Inst. Arts (workshop instr. 1983-84), Mont. Watercolor Soc. (pres. 1981-84), Cody Country Arts League (best of show award 1973), Carbon County Arts Guild (bd. dirs. 1984—), Idaho Watercolor Soc. (juror 1980), Colo. Artists Assn. (juror 1986), Billings Art Assn. Republican. Episcopalian. Home: 1616 E Windjammer Tempe AZ 85283

HAUK, A. ANDREW, U.S. district judge; b. Denver, Dec. 29, 1912; s. A.A. and Pearl (Woods) H.; m. Jean Nicolay, Aug. 30, 1941; 1 dau., Susan. A.B. magna cum laude, Regis Coll., 1935; LL.B., Catholic U. Am., 1938; J.S.D. (Sterling fellow), Yale U., 1942. Bar: Calif. 1942, Colo. 1939, D.C. 1938, U.S. Supreme Ct. 1953. Spl. asst. to atty. gen., counsel for govt. antitrust div. U.S. Dept Justice, Los Angeles, Pacific Coast, Denver, 1939-41; asst. U.S. atty., Los Angeles, 1941-42; with firm Adams, Duque & Hazeltine, Los Angeles, 1946-52; individual practice law Los Angeles, 1952-64; asst. counsel Union Oil Co., Los Angeles, 1952-64; judge Superior Ct., Los Angeles County, 1964-66; U.S. dist. judge Central Dist. Calif., 1966—, chief judge, 1980, now sr. judge, chief judge emeritus; instr. Southwestern U. Law Sch., 1939-41; lectr. U. So. Calif. Law Sch., 1947-56; Vice chmn. Calif. Olympic Com., 1954-61; ofcl. VIII Olympic Winter Games, Squaw Valley, 1960; Gov. Calif.'s del. IX Olympic Games, Innsbruck, Austria, 1964. Bd. dirs. So. Calif. Com. for Olympic Games. Served from lt. to lt. comdr., Naval Intelligence USNR, 1942-46. Recipient scroll Los Angeles County Bd. Suprs., 1965, 66, 75; Alumnus of Yr. Regis Coll., 1967; named to Nat. Ski Hall of Fame, 1975. Mem. Los Angeles Town Hall, World Affairs Council, Los Angeles County Bar Assn. (chmn. pleading and practice com. 1963-64, chmn. Law Day com. 1965-66), State Bar Calif. (corps. com., war work com. past vice-chmn.), ABA (com. criminal law sect.), Fed. Bar Assn., Lawyers Club Los Angeles, Am. Judicature Soc., Am. Legion, Navy League, U.S. Lawn Tennis Assn., So. Calif. Tennis Assn. (dir., bd. govs. 1972—), So. Calif. Tennis Patrons Assn. (bd. govs.), Far West Ski Assn. (Nat. Sr. Giant Slalom champion 1954), Yale Law Sch. Assn. So. Calif. (dir., past pres.), Town Hall. Clubs: Yale of So. Calif. (dir. 1964-67), Newman; Valley Hunt (Pasadena); Jonathan (Los Angeles). Office: US Court House 312 N Spring St Los Angeles CA 90012

HAULENBEEK, ROBERT BOGLE, JR., government official; b. Cleve., Feb. 24, 1941; s. Robert Bogle and Priscilla Valerie (Burch) H.; B.S., Okla. State U., 1970; m. Rebecca Marie Talley, Mar. 1, 1965; children—Kimberly Kaye, Robert Bogle, III. Micro paleon. photographer Pan Am. Research Co., Tulsa, 1966-67; flight instr. Okla. State U., 1970; air traffic control specialist FAA, Albuquerque, 1970-73, Farmington, N.Mex., 1973-78, flight service specialist, Dalhart, Tex., 1978-80, Albuquerque, 1980—; staff officer CAP, Albuquerque, 1970-73, Farmington, 1974-78, advanced through grades to lt. col., 1981, dir. ops. for hdqrs., 1981-86, N.Mex. Wing, dep. commdr., 1985—; mem. faculty Nat. Staff Coll., Gunter Air Force Sta., Montgomery, Ala., 1981-82; bd. dirs. South West Region Staff Coll., Albuquerque, 1986. Served with U.S. Army, 1964-65. Recipient Meritorious Service award CAP, 1978, 81, 82, Lifesaving award, 1982. Mem. Exptl. Aircraft Assn., Nat. Assn. Air Traffic Specialists (facility rep. 1978-86), Aircraft Owners and Pilots Assn. Republican. Presbyterian. Home: 5229 Carlsbad Ct NW Albuquerque NM 87120

HAUN, CHARLES KENNETH, anatomy educator; b. Los Angeles, June 13, 1930; s. John Kenneth and Ethel Augusta (Gidlund) H.; m. Yoshi Iwase, June 23, 1956; children: Barry, Christopher, Stephanie. AB, Pomona Coll., 1952; PhD, UCLA, 1960. From instr. to asst. prof. Hahnemann Med. Coll., Phila., 1959-62; asst. prof. U. So. Calif. Sch. Medicine, Los Angeles, 1962-86, assoc. prof., 1986—; cons. Neuroscis. Inst., Los Angeles, 1976—. Served with U.S. Army, 1952-54. Mem. Am. Assn. Anatomists, Soc. Neurosci., Internat. Soc. Neuroendocrinology. Home: 1711 Tyler Dr Monterey Park CA 91754 Office: U So Calif Sch Medicine Dept Anatomy and Cell Biology 1333 San Pablo St Los Angeles CA 90033

HAUN, JOHN DANIEL, petroleum geologist, educator; b. Old Hickory, Tenn., Mar. 7, 1921; s. Charles C. and Lydia (Rhodes) H.; m. Lois Culbertson, June 30, 1942. B.A., Berea Coll., 1948; M.A., U. Wyo., 1949, Ph.D., 1953. Registered profl. engr., Colo. Geologist Stanolind, Amoco, Vernal, Utah, 1951-52; v.p. Petroleum Research Corp., Denver, 1952-57; mem. faculty dept. geology Colo. Sch. Mines, Golden, 1955-80; prof. Colo. Sch. Mines, 1963-80, part time, 1980-85, emeritus prof., 1985—; pres. Barlow & Haun, Inc., Evergreen, Colo., 1957—; cons. Potential Gas Agy., 1966-78; mem. exec. adv. com. Nat. Petroleum Council, 1968-70; mem. adv. com. Colo. Water Pollution Control Commn., 1969-70; mem. adv. council Kans. Geol. Survey, 1971-76; del. Internat. Geol. Congress, Sydney, Australia, 1976; U.S. rep. Internat. Com. on Petroleum Res. Classification UN, N.Y.C., 1976-77; mem. oil shale adv. com. Office of Tech. Assessment, Washington, 1976-79, mem. U.S. natural gas availability adv. panel, 1983; mem. Colo. Oil and Gas Conservation Commn., 1977—, vice-chmn., 1983-85, chmn. 1985—; mem. energy resources com. Interstate Oil Compact Commn., 1978—; mem. Nat. Petroleum Council, 1979—, mem. com. on unconventional gas sources, 1978-80; com. on Arctic oil and gas resources, 1980-81; mem. U.S. Nat. Com. on Geology Dept. Interior and Nat. Acad. Scis., 1982—, chmn., 1985-87; del. Internat. Geol. Congress, Paris, 1980, Moscow, 1984. Editor: The Mountain Geologist, 1963-65, Future Energy Outlook, 1969, Methods of Estimating the Volume of Undiscovered Oil and Gas Resources, 1975; asst. editor: Geologic Atlas of the Rocky Mountain Region, 1972; co-editor: Subsurface Geology in Petroleum Exploration, 1958, Symposium on Cretaceous Rocks of Colorado and Adjacent Areas, 1959, Guide to the Geology of Colorado, 1960; contbr. articles to profl. jours. Served with USCG, 1942-46. Recipient Disting. Service award Am. Assn. Petroleum Geologists, 1973, Alumnus award U. Wyo., 1986; Outstanding prof. award Colo. Sch. Mines, 1973, Halliburton award Colo. Sch. Mines, 1985. Fellow Geol. Soc. Am., AAAS; mem. Am. Assn. Petroleum Geologists (editor 1967-71, pres. 1979-80, hon. mem. 1984), Am. Inst. Profl. Geologists (v.p. 1974, pres. 1976, exec. com. 1981-82, Ben H. Parker Meml. award 1983), Am. Geol. Inst. (governing bd. 1976, 79-82, sec.-treas. 1977-78, v.p. 1980-81, pres. 1981-82), Rocky Mountain Assn. Geologists (sec. 1961, 1st v.p. 1964, pres. 1968, hon. mem. 1974—), Soc. Econ. Paleontologists and Mineralogists, Am. Petroleum Inst. (com. exploration 1971-73, 78—), Geochem. Soc., Nat. Assn. Geology Tchrs., Wyo. Geol. Assn. (hon. life), Colo. Sci. Soc., Sigma Xi, Sigma Gamma Epsilon, Phi Kappa Phi. Home: 1238 County Rd 23 Evergreen CO 80439 Office: Colo Sch of Mines Golden CO 80401

HAUS, ALAN JOSEPH, lawyer; b. N.Y.C., Apr. 21, 1954; s. Joseph Charles and Etta (McNamara) H. BA, Wesleyan U., Middletown, Conn., 1976; MBA, U. Calif., Berkeley, 1983; JD, U. Calif., San Francisco, 1983. Bar: Calif. 1983, U.S. Dist. Ct. (no. dist.) Calif. 1983, U.S. Supreme Ct. 1987. Staff counsel ComputerLand Corp., Oakland, Calif., 1983-84; sole practice Berkeley, 1984—. Mem. ABA, World Affairs Council, San Francisco Mus. Art, Santa Barbara Mus. Art, Film Arts Found., Phi Alpha Delta. Roman Catholic. Office: 2600 Tenth St Suite 508 Berkeley CA 94710

HAUSDORFER, GARY LEE, mortgage banker; b. Indpls., Mar. 26, 1946; s. Walter Edward and Virginia Lee (Bender) H.; A.A., Glendale Coll., 1966; B.S., Calif. State U.-Los Angeles, 1968; m. Debora Ann French, Dec. 17, 1966; children—Lisa Ann, Janet Lee. Research officer Security Pacific Bank, Los Angeles, 1968-73; v.p., mgr. W. Ross Campbell Co., Irvine, Calif., 1973-81; sr. v.p. Weyerhaeuser Mortgage Co., Irvine, 1982-87; exec. v.p., ptnr. L.J. Melody & Co. of Calif., 1987—. Councilman, City of San Juan Capistrano, 1978—, mayor, 1980-81, 84-85; chmn. Capistrano Valley Water Dist., 1980-81; chmn. San Juan Capistrano Redevel. Agy., 1983-84, 85—; bd. dirs. Orange County Trans. Corridor Agy. Recipient cert. of commendation Orange County Bd. Suprs., 1981, congl. commendation, 1985. Mem. Mortgage Bankers Assn. Am., Calif. Mortgage Bankers Assn., Orange County Mortgage Bankers Assn. (dir. 1979-80), Calif. League of Cities. Republican.

HAUSEL, WILLIAM DAN, economic geologist; b. Salt Lake City, July 24, 1949; s. Maynard Romain and Dorthy (Clark) H.; m. Patricia Kemp, Aug. 14, 1970; children—Jessica Siddhartha, Eric Jason. B.Sc. in Geology, U. Utah, 1972, M.Sc. in Geology, 1974. Teaching asst. U. N.Mex., Albuquerque, 1974-75; astronomy lectr., Hansen Planetarium, Salt Lake City, 1968-72; project geologist Warnock Cons., Albuquerque, 1975; geologist U.S. Geol. Survey, Casper, Wyo., 1976-77; staff geologist Geol. Survey of Wyo., Laramie, 1977-81, dep. dir., 1981—; assoc. curator mineralogy Wyo. State Mus., Cheyenne, 1983—. Author: Exploration for Diamondiferous Kimberlite, 1979; Gold Districts of Wyoming, 1980; Ore Deposits of Wyoming, 1982; Geology of Southeastern Wyoming, 1984, Minerals and Rocks of Wyoming, 1986. Served with U.S. Army, 1971-73. Grantee NASA, 1981, Office of Surface Mining, 1979, U. Wyo., 1981—. Mem. N.Mex. Geol. Soc., Wyo. Geol. Assn., Utah Geol. Assn., Am. Inst. Mining Engrs. Lutheran. Clubs: U. Utah Geology (pres. 1969-71); U. Utah Karate (Salt Lake City); Laramie Bushido Dojo Karate (pres. 1985—). Home: 4238 Grays Gables Rd Laramie WY 82070 Office: Geol Survey of Wyo Box 3008 Laramie WY 82071

HAUSER, RAY LOUIS, entrepreneur; b. Litchfield, Ill., Apr. 16, 1927; s. A. Vernon and Grace (Gregg) H.; m. Consuelo Wright Minnich, Sept. 21, 1951; children: Beth, Cynthia, Dewi, Chris. BS, U. Ill., Urbana, 1950; M in Engring., Yale U., 1952; PhD, U. Colo., 1957. Registered profl. engr., Colo.; registered safety engr., Calif. Sr. project engr. Conn. Hard Rubber Co., New Haven, 1950-52; research staff U. Colo., Boulder, 1954-57; material tech. staff Martin Co., Denver, 1957-61; pres. Tele:time Corp., Boulder, 1983—, Dental Innovations, Boulder, 1985—; owner, mgr. Hauser Labs., Boulder, 1961—; visiting lectr., U. Colo., Boulder, 1957-63; bd. dirs. Hauser Chem. Research, Boulder, 1983—. Pres. Boulder Civic Opera, 1971-72. Served as sgt. U.S. Army, 1952-54. Mem. Soc. Plastics Engrs. (bd. dirs. 1959-62), Am. Inst. Chem. Engrs., Assn. Cons. Chem. and Chem. Engrs. (bd. dirs. 1986), Am. Assn. Lab. Accreditors (bd. dirs. 1986). Lodge: Rotary (bd. dirs. 1975-77). Home: 5758 Rustic Knolls Dr Boulder CO 80301 Office: Hauser Labs 5680 Central Ave Boulder CO 80301

HAUSMAN, ARTHUR HERBERT, electronics company executive; b. Chgo., Nov. 24, 1923; s. Samuel Louis and Sarah (Elin) H.; m. Helen Mandelowitz, May 19, 1946; children: Susan Lois, Kenneth Louis, Catherine Ellen. B.S. in Elec. Engring, U. Tex., 1944; S.M., Harvard U., 1948. Electronics engr. Engring. Research Assos., St. Paul, 1946-47; supervisory electronics scientist U.S. Dept. Def., Washington, 1948-60; now advisor, v.p., dir. research Ampex Corp., Redwood City, Calif., 1960-63; v.p. operations Ampex Corp., 1963-65, group v.p., 1965-67, exec. v.p., 1967-71, exec. v.p., pres., chief exec. officer, from 1971-83, now chmn. bd.; dir. Drexler Tech. Inc., T.C.I. Inc., Synthetic Vision Systems Inc.; Chmn. tech. adv. com. computer peripherals Dept. Commerce, 1973-75; mem. Pres.'s Export Council; chmn. subcom. on Export Administrn. Trustee United Bay Area Crusade.; mem. vis. com. dept. math. MIT; Bd. dirs. Bay Area Council. Served with USNR, 1944-54. Recipient Meritorious Civilian Service award Dept. Def. Mem. IEEE, Army Ordnance Assn. (dir. chpt. 1969-71), Am. Electronics Assn. (dir.). Clubs: Commonwealth of Calif.; Cosmos. Office: 401 Broadway Redwood City CA 94063

HAUSWALD, MARK, physician, educator; b. San Francisco, May 6, 1950; s. Mathew and Pat (Grassel) H. BS, Linfield Coll., 1973; MS, U. Calif., Berkeley, 1975; MD, U. Calif., San Francisco, 1977. Diplomate Am. Bd. Emergency Medicine. Flex intern Highland Hosp., Oakland, Calif., 1977-78; resident in emergency medicine Stanford U., Palo Alto, Calif., 1978-80; chief dept. emergency medicine Indian Health Service, Gallup, N.Mex., 1980-82; asst. prof. emergency medicine U. N.Mex., Albuquerque, 1982—; med. dir. N.Mex. Emergency Med. Services Acad., Albuquerque, 1984—. Contbr. articles to profl. jours. Fellow Am. Coll. Emergency Physicians; mem. Am. Heart Assn. (bd. dirs. local chpt. 1984), Am. Coll. Emergency Physicians (pres. N.Mex. chpt.). Avocations: skiing, sail boarding, bird watching, hiking. Office: Div Emergency Med 620 Camino de Salud NE Albuquerque NM 87131

HAVAS, VALERIE CLAIRE, editor, writer; b. South Amboy, N.J., Sept. 11, 1957; d. John Milan and Stella (Flaws) H.; m. Matthew G. Schwab, Dec. 28, 1985. Student, U. Denver Pub. Inst., 1979, Mt. Holyoke Coll., 1975-76; BA in English, Middlebury Coll., 1979. Reporter, intern Addison County Ind., Middlebury, Vt., 1978; freelance writer Sumner Rider & Assocs., N.Y.C., 1977-78, 83; editorial asst. House & Garden, N.Y.C., 1980-83; fashion writer, editor Nightlight Mag., Santa Barbara, Calif., 1983; asst. editor Islands Mag., Santa Barbara, 1983-85, mng. editor, 1985—; freelance editor Olympus Press, Santa Barbara, 1985-86. Contbr. articles to profl. jours. Avocations: skiing, hiking, traveling. Office: Islands Mag 3886 State St Santa Barbara CA 93105

HAVEKOST, DANIEL JOHN, architect; b. Fremont, Nebr., May 12, 1936; s. Alvin Deidrich and Magdalen (Osterman) H.; m. Patricia Jo Haney, June 6, 1959 (div. June 1983); children: Christopher, Karen. Lic. architect, Colo., Calif., Tex., N.D.; cert. Nat. Council Archtl. Registration Bds. Designer Papachristou & Assoc., Denver, 1959-61; architect Anshen & Allen, San Francisco, 1961-62; assoc. Hornbein & White, Denver, 1962-63; ptnr. Papachristou & Havekost, Denver, 1963-64; prin. Havekost & Assocs., Denver, 1964-71; pres. HWH Assocs., Inc., Denver, 1971—; vis. lectr. U. Colo., Denver, 1969, 72, 82; sec., treas. Encore Devel. Corp., Denver, 1984—; sec. Woodmor Devel. Corp., Denver, 1983-86. Prin. works include Encore Redevel. (AIA award 1985,86), Grant Street Mansion (Colo. Soc. Architects, AIA award 1979), Reverend's Ridge (Western Mountain Region AIA award 1973, Havekost Residence Western Mountain Region AIA award 1971). Bd. dirs. Denver Community Design Ctr., 1968-72, Historic Paramount Found., Denver, 1980—, Historic Denver, 1978-82; panel mem. Gen. Services Adminstrn., Denver, 1978-79, mem. plan enforcement rev. and variation com., Denver, 1970-76. Served with USNR, 1954-62. Recipient Archtl. Excellence awards WOOD Inc., 1968-82, Honor award for Adaptive Re-use, Historic Denver, 1975, WOOD Design award Nat. Cattlemen's Hdqrs., 1982. Fellow AIA (pres. Denver chpt. 1978-81, chmn. Colo. chpt. govt. affairs com. 1984—, pres. Colo. chpt. 1981-83, officer Colo. Hist. Preservation div. 1982—, recipient excellence archtl. design award 1960), Colo. Soc. Architects (pres. 1981-83). Avocations: skiing, tennis, drawing. Office: HWH Assocs Inc 707 Washington St Suite C Denver CO 80203

HAVEN, SHARON OWEN, writer, editor consultant; b. Bell, Calif., Feb. 9, 1943; d. Guilford Achilles Owen and Virginia Hope (Molholm) O; m. Robert Matthew Dorn, Dec. 20, 1966; m. Clayton Haven, March 4, 1973; children—Matthew, Amy. B.A. magda cum laude, Pomona Coll., 1965; M.A., Columbia U., 1966. Cert. community coll. instr., Calif. Staff writer, researcher, Ctr. for Study Dem. Instns., Santa Barbara, Calif., 1966-67; instr. polit. scis., Westmont Coll., Santa Barbara, 1967-69; co-editor Zero Population Growth Monthly Jour., Palo Alto, Calif., 1972; freelance designer, cons., writer, 1973—; field editor publs., 1979—; syndicated columnist, Copley New Service, 1985. Chmn. Mid-Town Property Owner's Assn., 1981; active San Diego Symphony Assn., Mus. of Man, San Diego Zool. Soc. Cordell Hull Internat. Relations awardee, 1965; Woodrow Wilson fellow, 1966. Mem. AIA, Am. Soc. Interior Designers. Author: Room to Grow; Making Your Child's Bedroom an Exciting World, 1979. Home: 3136 Falcon St San Diego CA 92103

HAVILAND, JAMES WEST, physician; b. Glens Falls, N.Y., July 18, 1911; s. Morrison LeRoy and Mabel Eva (West) H.; m. Marion Cranston Bertram, Oct. 23, 1943; children—James Marshall, Elizabeth Bullard, Donald Sherman, Martha Adams. A.B., Union Coll., Schenectady, 1932; M.D., Johns Hopkins, 1936. Intern medicine Johns Hopkins Hosp., 1936-37, intern, asst. resident, chief outpatient dept. pediatrics, 1937-38, asst. resident medicine, 1939-40; asst. resident medicine New Haven Hosp., 1938-39; instr. medicine Yale Med. Sch., 1938-39, Johns Hopkins Sch. Medicine, 1939-40; chief services crippled children Wash. Dept. Social Security, also Dept. Health, 1940- 42; lectr. medicine U. Wash. Sch. Nursing, 1946-60; practice medicine Seattle, 1946—; clin. asst. prof., to clin. prof. U. Wash. Sch. Medicine, 1947—, asst. dean, 1949-53, 1954-59, acting dean, 1953-54, asso. dean, 1972-76. Trustee Seattle Artificial Kidney Center, Seattle Symphony Orch. Served as lt. comdr., M.C. USNR, 1942-46. Fellow Am. Geog. Soc. N.Y., Am. Heart Assn.; mem. Wash. State Med. Assn. (sec.-treas. 1948-51), Seattle Acad. Internal Medicine (pres. 1952-53), King County Med. Soc. (pres. 1962), AMA (council med. edn. 1966-76, chmn. 1974-76), Pacific Interurban Clin. Club, AAAS, Am. Fed. Med. Research, Western Soc. Clin. Research, North Pacific Soc. Internal Medicine, A.C.P. (pres. 1970), Am. Clin. and Climatol. Assn. (pres. 1981-82), Am. Assn. History Medicine, Nat. Acad. Scis. (Inst. Medicine), Phi Beta Kappa, Sigma Xi, Alpha Omega Alpha, Kappa Alpha. Home: 8208 SE 30th St Mercer Island WA 98040 Office: 1229 Madison St #8LO Seattle WA 98104

HAVLICK, SPENSER WOODWORTH, environmental design educator; b. Oak Park, Ill., June 21, 1935; s. Spenser Newton and Mildred Louise (Woodworth) H.; m. Valerie Ann Hessel, June 14, 1958; children: Scott, Jennifer, David. BA, Beloit Coll., 1957; MA, U. Colo., 1961; PhD, U. Mich., 1967. Research analyst EPA, Washington, 1967-70; asst. prof. natural resources U. Mich., Ann Arbor, 1970-73; assoc. prof. San Jose (Calif.) State U., 1973-75; prof., dir. Coll. Environ. Design U. Colo., Boulder, 1975—, from asst. dean to dean, 1985-86. Author: The Urban Organism, 1974; editor Jour. Ekistics, Athens, Greece, 1968—; producer documentary film To Kill A Dragonfly, 1963; contbr. articles to profl. jours. Mem. City Council of Boulder, 1982—; commr. Urban Renewal Authority, Boulder, 1983—; bd. dirs. artist series Thorne Trimtab Found., Los Angeles, 1985—. Recipient Dana award, U. Mich., 1968; NSF grantee, 1983, 85. Mem. AAAS, World Soc. Ekistics, Sigma Xi. Avocations: cross country skiing, bicycling, photography, gardening.

HAVRILIAK, STEPHEN JAMES, chemistry educator; b. Providence, Dec. 28, 1954; s. Stephen and Barbara Ann (Herdrickson) H.; m. Lisa Beth Caldwell, May 26, 1979; 1 child, Sarah Jane. BS, Widener Coll., 1977; PhD, SUNY, Buffalo, 1983. NRC postdoctoral fellow Nat. Acad. Scis., Washington, 1983-85; asst. prof. chemistry Grand Canyon Coll., Phoenix, 1985—. Mem. Am. Inst. Chemists, Am. Chem. Soc. Republican. Baptist. Home: 5160 N 38th Ave Phoenix AZ 85019 Office: Grand Canyon Coll 3300 W Camelback Phoenix AZ 85019

HAWE, DAVID LEE, consultant; b. Columbus, Ohio, Feb. 19, 1938; s. William Doyle and Carolyn Mary (Hassig) H.; m. Margret J. Hoover, Apr. 15, 1962; children—Darrin Lee, Kelly Lynn. Project mgr. ground antenna systems W.D.L. Labs., Philco Corp., 1960-65; credit mgr. for Western U.S., Am. Hosp. Supply Corp., Burbank, Calif., 1965-74; owner, mgr. Hoover Profl. Equipment Co., contract health equipment co., Guasti, Calif., 1974-75; pres. Baslor Care Services, owners convalescent homes, Santa Ana, Calif., 1975-80; pres. Application Assocs., 1980—; bd. dirs., chmn. of bd. Xiron, Inc., 1984—; dir. Medisco Co., Casa Pacifica, Broadway Assocs. Bd. dirs. Santa Ana Community Convalescent Hosp., 1974-79, pres., 1975-79. Served with USN, 1954-56. Lic. real estate broker, Calif. Mem. Am. Vacuum Soc. Republican. Roman Catholic. Home: 18082 Hallsworth Circle Villa Park CA 92667

HAWES, GRACE MAXCY, archival specialist, writer; b. Cumberland, Wis., Feb. 4, 1926; d. Clarence David and Mabel Hannah (Erickson) Maxcy; student U. Wis., 1944-46; B.A., San Jose State U., 1963, M.A., 1971; m. John G. Hawes, Aug. 28, 1948 (dec.); children—Elizabeth, John D., Mark, Amy. Library asst. NASA, Langley, Va., 1948-49; librarian Hoover Archives, Stanford U., 1976-80, adminstrv. asst. Office of Devel., 1980-84, Hoover Archives, 1985— . Mem. Soc. Am. Archivists, Western Assn. Women Historians, Women in Hist. Research, Calif. Archivists Assn., Inst. Hist. Study. Author: The Marshall Plan for China: Economic Cooperation Administration, 1948-1949, 1977. Home: 410 Sheridan Apt 220 Palo Alto CA 94306 Office: Stanford U Hoover Instn Archives Stanford CA 94304

HAWK, HUGH KYLE, retired government official; b. Bristol, Tenn., Mar. 24, 1921; s. Emory Quinter and Jessie Belle (Kyle) H.; m. Betty Ann Troutman, June 3, 1945; children: Ann Kyle Hawk Cronin. AB, Birmingham So. Coll., 1941; MA, U. Va., 1943, PhD, 1952. Asst. prof. Washington and Lee U., Lexington, Va., 1947-52; price officer Gen. Stores Supply Office Mil. Indsl. Supply Agy., Dept. Def., Phila., 1952-62; mgmt. analyst officer Def. Indsl. Supply Ctr., Phila., 1962-64, comptroller, 1965-85; cons. computers, econs., bus adminstrn. various cos., 1985—. Served with AUS, 1943-46. Recipient Meritorious Civilian Service award and medal Dept. Def., 1982; Outstanding Performance award Dept. Def. Mem. Fed. Mgrs. Assn. (budget officer 1982-85). Democrat. Presbyterian. Avocations: travelling, photography, gliders. Home: Apt 328 Del Prado Apts 5110 N 32d St Phoenix AZ 80518

HAWK, VIRGIL BROWN, agronomist; b. What Cheer, Iowa, Sept. 8, 1908; s. Jacob Wellington and Julia Bessie (Brown) H.; m. Marguerite Mary Backs, Apr. 18, 1936; children—Eloise Marie, John William, Lenore Janet, Kenneth Joseph. B.S., Iowa State U., 1933, Ph.D., 1948; M.S., Wash. State U., 1938. Research agt. USDA-BPI, Holgate, Ohio, 1932-33; research fellow Wash. State U., Pullman, 1934-35; agt. agronomist USDA-SCS, Pullman, 1935-45; research fellow Iowa State U., Ames, 1945-47; research agronomist Okla. State U., Stillwater, 1947-48; agronomist USDA-SCS, Ames, 1948-65, Cape May, N.J., 1965-70; cons. agronomist Condominium Chmn. Assn. of Sun City, Ariz., 1978-83, Recreation Ctrs. of Sun City, 1975-80; pres. Camelot Adv. Council, 1986—. Contbr. articles to profl. jours. Mem. Parkinsons Disease Support Group, Valley Meml. Soc., Sun City Home Owners Assn., Sun City Area Community Council. Named Conservationist of the Year, N.J. Assn. Soil Conservation Dists., 1970. Mem. Am. Soc. Agronomy, Soil Conservation Soc. Am., Sigma Xi, Alpha Zeta, Phi Kappa Phi. Democrat. Roman Catholic. Clubs: Sundial S.B., Goren Bridge (pres. 1975). Lodges: K.C., Kiwanis.

HAWKE, BERNARD RAY, planetary scientist; b. Louisville, Oct. 22, 1946; s. Arvil Abner and Elizabeth Ellen (Brown) H. B.S. in Geology, U. Ky., 1970, M.S., 1974; M.S., Brown U., 1977, Ph.D. in Planetary Geology, 1978. Geologist U.S. Geol. Survey, 1967-68; researcher U. Ky., 1972-74, Brown U., 1974-78; planetary scientist Hawaiian Inst. Geophysics, U. Hawaii, Honolulu, 1978—; dir. NASA Pacific Regional Planetary Data Ctr., 1981—; prin. investigator NASA grants. Author papers in field. Served with USAR, 1970-72. Decorated Bronze Star. Mem. Geochem. Soc., Meteoritcal Soc., Am. Geophys. Union, Sigma Xi, Sigma Gamma Epsilon, Alpha Tau Omega. Republican. Office: Hawaiian Inst Geophysics U Hawaii Honolulu HI 96822

HAWKES, EARL LEONARD, municipal county official; b. Bremerton, Wash., Mar. 18, 1947; s. Earl L. and Patria Yvonne (Fidel) H.; m. Susan E. Hawkes, Oct. 30, 1975 (div. 1983); children: Earl Leonard III, Nelson Tyler. BA, San Diego State U., 1969, M in Pub. Adminstrn., 1974. Cert. purchasing mgr. Buyer City of San Diego, 1971-76; materials mgmt. dir. City of Yuma, Ariz., 1976-78; dir. Pima County Purchasing Dept., Tucson, 1978-79, Clark County Purchasing Dept., Las Vegas, Nev., 1979-84; dir. gen. services Clark County, Las Vegas, 1985—; mem. adv. bd. BidNet Corp., Rockville, Md., 1984-86; cons. Diversified Mgmt., Amarillo, Tex., 1984-86. Served with U.S. Army, 1969-71. Mem. Nat. Purchasing Inst. (pres. 1987), Nat. Assn. Purchasing Mgmt. (chmn. govt. buyers group 1984), Nat. Inst. Govtl. Purchasing., Am. Soc. Pub. Adminstrs. Democrat. Clubs: Paradise Valley Soccer (1st v.p. 1984-85); So. Nev. Over-The-Line Players Assn. (treas. 1985—). Home: 3362 Wayne St Las Vegas NV 89121 Office: Clark County Gen Services Dept 225 Bridger Ave 10th Floor Las Vegas NV 89155

HAWKES, GLENN ROGERS, psychology educator; b. Preston, Idaho, Apr. 29, 1919; s. William and Rae (Rogers) H.; m. Yvonne Merrill, Dec. 18, 1941; children—Kristen, William Ray, Gregory Merrill, Laura. B.S. in Psychology, Utah State U., 1946, M.S. in Psychology, 1947; Ph.D. in Psychology, Cornell U., 1950. Asst. prof. to prof. child devel. and psychology Iowa State U., Ames, 1950-66, chmn. dept. child devel., 1954-66; prof. human devel., research psychologist U. Calif.-Davis, 1966—, assoc. dean applied econs. and behavioral scis., 1966-83, chmn. dept. applied behavioral scis., 1982-86, chmn. teaching div., 1970-72; prof. behavioral scis. dept. family practice Sch. Medicine U. Calif.-Davis; vis. scholar U. Hawaii, 1972-73, U. London, 1970, 80, 86; dir. Creative Playthings Inc., 1962-66. Author: (with Pease) Behavior and Development from 5 to 12, 1962; (with Frost) The Disadvantaged Child: Issues and Innovations, 1966, 2d edit., 1970; (with Schultz and Baird) Lifestyles and Consumer Behavior of Older Americans, 1979; (with Nicola and Fish) Young Marrieds: The Dual Career Approach, 1984. Contbr. numerous articles to profl. and sci. jours. Served with AUS, 1941-45. Recipient numerous research grants from pvt. founds. and govtl. bodies; recipient Iowa State U. faculty citation, 1965, Outstanding Service citation Iowa Soc. Crippled Children and adults, 1965, citation Dept. Child Devel., 1980, Coll. Agrl. and Environ. Scis., 1983; named hon. lt. gov. Okla., 1966. Home: 1114 Purdue Dr Davis CA 95616 Office: Dept Applied Behavioral Scis U Calif Davis CA 95616

HAWKES, STEPHEN JAMES., chemistry educator; b. London, May 30, 1928; came to U.S., 1963; s. Alfred J. and Maud A. (Berry) H.; m. Pamela Johnson, Jan. 21, 1965; children: Eric, Logan. BS, U. London, 1953, PhD, 1963. Analyst W.J. Bush & Co., London, 1953-63; instr. chemistry U. Utah, Salt Lake City, 1963-64; from asst. prof. to assoc. prof. Brigham Young U., Provo, Utah, 1964-68; assoc. prof. chemistry Oreg. State U., Corvallis, 1968-77, prof., 1977—. Contbr. articles to profl. jours. Mem. Am. Chem. Soc. (chmn. gen. chemistry exam com. 1987—), Soc. Coll. Sci. Tchrs. Home: 2220 Kings Blvd Corvallis OR 97330 Office: Oreg State U Dept Chemistry Corvallis OR 97331

HAWKES, WAYNE CHRISTIAN, biochemist; b. Oakland, Calif., Apr. 23, 1951; s. Wayne Clifford and Jean Elizabeth (Perkins) H.; m. Ruth L. Jackson, Aug. 31, 1985. BS in Chemistry, U. Calif., Berkeley, 1974; PhD in Biochemistry, U. Calif., Davis, 1980. Supr. prodn. Medi-Physics, Emeryville, Calif., 1972-76; research asst. U. Calif., Davis, 1976-80, research biochemist, 1980-84; prin. Hawkes Research Services, Oakland, 1982—; research chemist Western Human Nutrition Research Ctr., USDA, San Francisco, 1984—. Author, publisher (computer programs) GRAFPLOT, 1983, Picture Perfect, 1986; contbr. tech. articles on Selenium Biochemistry to profl. jours. Mem. AAAS, Am. Chem. Soc. Avocation: gardening. Office: USDA Western Human Nutrition Research Ctr PO Box 29997 San Francisco CA 94129

HAWKINS, ALBERT EDWARD, manufacturing company executive; b. El Paso, Nov. 18, 1930; s. Albert Edward and Vida Jane (Lewis) H.; B.S. in Civil Engring., U. Colo., 1952; postgrad. nuclear engring. UCLA, 1956-58; Advanced Mgmt. Program, Harvard U. Grad. Sch. Bus., 1980-81; m. Shirley Jean Henley, Dec. 16, 1951; children—Richard Albert, Sherri Kathleen. Sr. specification engr. Radioplane Co., Van Nuys, Calif., 1954-58; contract mgr. Titan I & II, Martin Marietta Corp., Denver, 1958-64, bus. mgr., 1964-70, dir. adminstrn., 1970-73, corp. dir. strategic planning, Washington, 1973-75, dep. dir. bus. mgmt., New Orleans, 1975-77, v.p. solar energy systems, Denver, 1977-84; v.p. bus. ops., Washington, 1984-85; v.p. Denver Info. and Communications Systems, 1985—. Bd. dirs. Roxbrough Found., Porter Meml. Hosp.; trustee Mile High United Way, 1979—. Served with USMC, 1952-54. Mem. Nat. Contract Mgmt. Assn. (cert.). Club: Ridge Rider's Saddle. Office: Martin Marietta Info & Communications Systems PO Box 1260 Denver CO 80201-1260

HAWKINS, AUGUSTUS FREEMAN, congressman; b. Shreveport, La., Aug. 31, 1907; s. Nyanza and Hattie H. (Freeman) H.; m. Pegga A. Smith, Aug. 28, 1945 (dec. Aug. 1966); m. Elsie Taylor, June 30, 1977. A.B. in Econs, U. Cal. at, Los Angeles, 1931. Engaged in real estate and retail bus. Los Angeles, from 1945—; mem. Calif. Assembly from, Los Angeles County, 1935-62; chmn. rules com. Calif. Assembly from, 1961-62; mem. 88th to 93d congresses from 21st dist. Calif., 94th—; chmn. House Edn. and Labor Com.; chmn. Subcom. on Elem., Secondary and Vocational Edn. Democrat. Methodist. Club: Masons. Office: 2371 Rayburn House Office Bldg Washington DC 20515

HAWKINS, KAREN LESLIE, childcare developer, educator; b. Princeton, British Columbia, Can., July 20, 1946; d. Elof Granberg and Janet McGregor (Bartholomew) Barry; m. Gary James Hawkins, May 21, 1971 (dec. Jan. 1986); 1 child, Benjamin Robert; m. Joel Henry Lanphear, May 18, 1986. BA in Social Sci., San Francisco State U., 1968, MEd, 1970. Cert. tchr., Calif. Tchr. early childhood edn. Diocese of San Francisco, 1968-71; author Pantheon Books, N.Y.C., 1972-73, 1976-77, 1982-83; tchr., tutor Ceret, France, 1973-75; program dir. Unitarian Universalist Soc., Sacramento, 1981-85; child car developer Child Action Inc., Sacramento, 1983—. Author: (with others) Bicycle Touring in Europe, 1973, Bicycle Touring in Western U.S., 1983; advisor for videotape Child Care is Everybody's Business, 1983. Employer chmn. Child Care Coalition, Sacramneto, 1983—; pub. commn. chmn. Mayor's Task Force Child Care, Sacramento, 1985; coordinator State Conf. Sick Child Care, Sacramento, 1985, State Conf. Employer Supported Child Care, Sacramento. Mem. Calif. Coalition Employer Supported Child Care, (resource chmn. 1985—), Calif. Resource and Referral Employer Com. (no. Calif. chmn. 1985—). Avocations: bicycle touring, teaching yoga. Office: Child Action Inc 2103 Stockton Blvd Sacramento CA 95817

HAWKINS, ROBERT LEE, social work administrator; b. Denver, Feb. 18, 1938; s. Isom and Bessie M. (Hugley) H.; A.A., Pueblo Jr. Coll., 1958; B.S., So. Colo. State Coll., 1965; M.S.W., U. Denver, 1967; m. Ann Sharon Hoy, Apr. 28, 1973; children—Robert, Jeanne, Julia, Rose. Psychiat. technician Colo. State Hosp., Pueblo, 1956-58, 1962-63, occupational therapist asst., 1964-65, clin. adminstr. psychiat. team, 1969-75, dir. community services, 1975—, supr. vol. services, 1975—, mem. budget com., 1975—; counselor (part-time) Family Service Agy., Pueblo, 1968-69, exec. dir., 1969-70; mem. faculty U. So. Colo., 1968-75; partner Human Resource Devel., Inc., 1970-75. Mem. Pueblo Positive Action Com., 1970; chmn. adv. bd. Pueblo Sangre de Cristo Day Care Center, 1969-72; chmn. Gov.'s So. Area Adv. Council of Employment Service, 1975-76; chmn. Pueblo's City CSC, 1976-77; mem. Colo. Juvenile Parole Bd., 1977; bd. dirs. Pueblo United Fund, 1969-74, pres., 1973; bd. dirs. Pueblo Community Orgn., 1974-76, Spanish Peaks Mental Health Center, 1976—, Neighborhood Health Center, 1977-79, Pueblo Community Corrections, 1983—, Pueblo Legal Services, 1983—. Served with U.S. Army 1958-62. Mem. Nat. Assn. Social Workers (nominating com. 1973-76), ACLU (dir. Pueblo chpt. 1980—), NAACP, Broadway Theatre Guild. Democrat. Methodist. Club: Kiwanis. Home: 520 Gaylord St Pueblo CO 81004 Office: 1600 W 24 St Pueblo CO 81003

HAWKINS, TED P., diversified computer company executive; b. Ferron, Utah, Feb. 7, 1935; s. Parker Elmer and Samuella (Rowley) H.; m. Lois Anderson, Feb. 14, 1958; children: David T., Mark D., Jeff A., James K., Cyndi, Amber. Diploma, Ch. of Jesus Christ of Latter-Day Saints Bus. Coll.; BS in Math., U. Utah, 1964. Astronomer, mathematician U.S. Naval Obs., Washington, 1964-66; sci. programmer Sperry Engring., Salt Lake City, 1966-68; system programmer Sperry UNIVAC div. Sperry Corp., Salt Lake City, 1968-70, computer support mgr., 1970-78; customer support dir. Sperry Corp., Salt Lake City, 1978—. Republican. Mormon. Office: Sperry Univac Add 322 N 2200 W Salt Lake City UT 84116

HAWKS, BILL, oil company executive; b. Tulsa, Nov. 17, 1936; s. Jeff and Mary Blanche (Scrogham) H.; m. Jan G. Heibucher, Aug. 15, 1970; children: Brents, Christopher, James, Michael. BSBA, U. Denver, 1962. Cert. landman, airplane pilot. Landman Ozark Corp., Casper, Wyo., 1957-66; pvt. practice landman Casper, 1966-71; pres. Burton-Hawks Inc., Casper, 1971—; bd. dirs. 1st Interstate Bank of Casper, 1977—. Bd. dirs. Natrona County Airport, Casper, 1980-85; mem. joint powers bd., Casper, 1984-85. Mem. Am. Assn. Petroleum Landmen, Wyo. Assn. Petroleum Landmen, Rocky Mountain Oil and Gas Assn., Aircraft Owners and Pilots Assn., Ind. Petroleum Assn. Am., Ind. Petroleum Assn. Mountain States, Petroleum Club (pres. Casper chpt. 1980-81). Clubs: Casper Country, Denver Country, PGA West (Palm Springs). Avocations: flying, fly tying and fishing, snow skiing, golf. Office: Burton-Hawks Inc PO Box 359 Casper WY 82602

HAWKS, DONNIE RAY, screenwriter, producer, actor, director; b. Hooker, Okla., Jan. 13, 1932; s. Aldon Carthell Hawks and Robinette (Yuanda) Ridgeway; m. Aneta Eva Marie Albino, Dec. 20, 1964; children: Gary Don, Cristie Marie, Carol Ann. Grad. pub. sch., Castle Rock, Colo. Actor Screen Actors Guild, Denver, 1975—; producer films Filmworks, Inc., Colorado Springs, Colo., 1978-82; lit. agt. Filmwork Prodns., 1978-82; producer Frameline Prodns., Colorado Springs, 1982—, Summernight Prodns., Colorado Springs, 1983; owner Alexander Film Co., Colorado Springs, 1984—; cons. Mediaworks, Ltd., Colorado Springs, 1981, Minshall Media Co., Salt Lake City, 1985. Producer (comml.) Pebble Creek, 1979 (Golden award), (movie) Lost, 1983; producer and dir. (movie) Beasts, 1984; exec. producer and dir. (movie) Hush Little Baby, 1985. Pres. (hon.) Boys Ranch, Amarillo, Tex., 1986—; mem. (hon.) Deaf and Blind Sch., Colorado Springs, 1986—. Recipient 3 Best Comml. awards PPAF Colo. chpt., 1978, 79, 80; Oscar award nominee, 1985. Mem. Assn. Cinema and Video Labs. Home: 4521 Winewood Village Dr Colorado Springs CO 80917 Office: Alexander Film and Video 967 Elkton Dr Colorado Springs CO 80907

HAWKS, VAL D., research educator; b. Gooding, Idaho, Apr. 2, 1955; s. Verlyn and Grace (Jorgenson) H.; m. Julie Ann Olson, Mar. 11, 1977; children: David, Douglas, Christine, Kathryn. AS, Snow Jr. Coll., 1978; BS, Brigham Young U., 1980; MS, Lehigh U., 1986. Project engr. Xerox Corp., Rochester, N.Y., 1981-84; mgr. computer-aided design Ben Franklin Ctr. Lehigh U., Bethlehem, Pa., 1984-86; asst. prof. design engring. tech. Brigham Young U., Provo, Utah, 1986—; cons. in field, Bethlehem and Provo, 1984—. Mormon. Office: Brigham Young U Dept Tech MS 435 CTB Provo UT 84602

HAWKSLEY, BARBARA JEAN, entrepreneur, educator; b. Riverside, Calif., Feb. 3, 1956; s. Robert Leonard and Virginia (Peterson) H. BA, Calif. State U., San Bernardino, 1987. Pres. BJ Hawksley Profl. Secretarial Service, Palm Springs, Calif., 1982—; instr. Coll. of the Desert, Palm Desert, Calif., 1983—. Club: Palm Springs Golf and Tennis. Home: PO Box 8182 Palm Springs CA 92264 Office: BJ Hawksley Profl Secretarial Service PO Box 8182 Palm Springs CA 92263

HAWKSWORTH, FRANK GOODE, forest pathologist; b. Fresno, Calif., Apr. 30, 1926; s. William A. and Elsie E. (Goode) Hawksworth; m. Margaret D. Rosenberger, Feb. 25, 1956; Children: David L., Mark A., William S. BS in Forestry, Idaho U., 1949; M in Forestry, Yale U., 1952, PhD, 1958. Forest pathologist U.S. Forest Service, Albuquerque, 1949-57, Ft. Collins, 1967—; also forest disease researcher 1949—. Author: Biology of Mistletoes, 1972. Served with U.S. Army, 1954. Fellow: Soc. Am. Foresters (Moore Research grantee 1984). Office: US Forest Service 240 W Prospect St Fort Collins CO 80526

HAWLEY, HAL, school administrator; b. Wenatchee, Wash., Mar. 5, 1945; s. Donald Wilmer Hawley and Bernice Alice (Richardson) Lockwood; m. Kathleen Elizabeth Woods, Apr. 2, 1966; children—Bonita Marie, Suzanne Michelle, Shari Meliesa. B.S., Wash. State U.-Pullman, 1970; M.S.T., Cornell U., 1971; Ed.D., U. Mont., 1976. Tchr. sci. and math. Elk River Pub. Schs., Idaho, 1967-69; tchr. high sch. sci. Troy and Deary Pub. Schs., Troy, Idaho, 1969-70; curriculum dir. Hardin Pub. Schs., Mont., 1972-74; elem. tchr. Missoula Pub. Schs., Mont., 1974-76; curriculum specialist Office of Pub. Instrn., Helena, Mont., 1976-83; supt. Plains Pub. Schs., Mont., 1983-84; prin. Broadus Elem. Sch., Mont., 1984—. Contbr. articles to profl. jours. Dep. registrar Lewis and Clark County, Helena, 1978-83. Mem. Am. Assn. Sch. Adminstrs., Nat. Assn. Elem. Sch. Prins., Mont. Assn. Elem. Sch. Prins., Nat. Middle Sch. Assn., Mont. Sci. Tchrs. Assn. (v.p. 1976-77), Mont. Arbitrators Assn. (v.p. 1981-82), Plains C. of C., Phi Delta Kappa. Club: Toastmasters. Lodge: Lions. Home: PO Box 58 Broadus MT 59317 Office: Broadus Elem Sch PO Box 500 Broadus MT 59317

HAWLEY, PHILIP METSCHAN, retail executive; b. Portland, Oreg., July 29, 1925; s. Willard P. and Dorothy (Metschan) H.; m. Mary Catherine Follen, May 31, 1947; children: Diane (Mrs. Robert Bruce Johnson), Willard, Philip Metschan Jr., John, Victor, Edward, Erin, George. B.S., U. Calif., Berkeley, 1946; grad., Advanced Mgmt. Program, Harvard U., 1967. With Carter Hawley Hale Stores, Inc., Los Angeles, 1958—, pres., 1972-83, chief exec. officer, 1977—, chmn., 1983—, also dir.; bd. dirs. Atlantic Richfield Co., BankAm. Corp., AT&T, The Economist. Trustee Calif. Inst. Tech., U. Notre Dame, Huntington Library and Art Gallery; bd. dirs. Assocs. Harvard U. Grad Sch. Bus. Adminstrn.; adv. council Grad. Sch. Bus. Stanford U.; vis. com. UCLA Grad. Sch. Mgmt., Bus. Council, Bus. Roundtable, Conf. Bd.; chmn. Los Angeles Energy Conservation Com. 1973-74. Decorated hon. comdr. Order Brit. Empire, knight comdr. Star Solidarity Republic Italy; recipient award of merit Los Angeles Jr. C. of C., 1974, Coro Pub. Affairs award, 1978, Medallion award Coll. William and Mary, 1983; named Calif. Industrialist of Year Calif. Mus. Sci. and Industry, 1975. Mem. Harvard Grad. Sch. Bus. Assocs. (bd. dirs.), Phi Beta Kappa, Beta Alpha Psi, Beta Gamma Sigma. Clubs: California, Los Angeles Country; Bohemian Pacific-Union (San Francisco); Newport Harbor Yacht (Newport Beach, Calif.); Multnomah (Portland); Links (N.Y.C.). Office: Carter Hawley Hale Stores Inc 550 S Flower St Los Angeles CA 90071

HAWLEY, ROBERT CROSS, lawyer; b. Douglas, Wyo., Aug. 7, 1920; s. Robert Daniel and Elsie Corienne (Cross) H.; m. Mary Elizabeth Hawley McClellan, Mar. 3, 1944; children—Robert Cross, Mary Virginia, Laurie McClellan. B.A. with honors, U. Colo., 1943; LL.B., Harvard U., 1949. Bar: Wyo. 1950, Colo. 1950, U.S. Dist. Ct. Colo. 1950, U.S. Dist. Ct. Wyo. 1954, U.S. Ct. Appeals (10th cir.) 1955, Tex. 1960, U.S. Ct. Appeals (5th cir.) 1960, U.S. Supreme Ct. 1960, U.S. Dist. Ct. (so. dist.) Tex. 1961, U.S. Ct. Appeals (D.C. cir.) 1961, U.S. Ct. Appeals (8th cir.) 1979, U.S. Ct. Appeals (11th cir.) 1981. Assoc. Barrister Weller & Friedrich, Denver, 1949-50; sr. atty. Continental Oil Co., Denver, 1952-58, counsel, Houston, 1959-62; ptnr., v.p. Ireland, Stapleton & Pryor, Denver, 1962-81; ptnr. Dechert Price & Rhoads, Denver, 1981-83, Hawley & VanderWerf, Denver, 1983—; pres. Highland Minerals, Denver; dir. Yorker Mfg., Denver, Bank of Denver, Calvin Exploration, Sante Fe. Contbr. articles to Oil & Gas Bd. dirs. Am. Cancer Soc., Denver. Recipient Alumni Recognition award U. Colo., Boulder, 1958, Meritorious Service award Monticello Coll., Godfrey, Ill., 1967; Sigma Alpha Epsilon scholar, 1941-43. Mem. Denver Assn. Oil and Gas Title Lawyers (pres. 1983-84), Denver Petroleum Club (pres. 1978-79), Harvard Law Sch. Assn. Colo. (pres. 1980-81), Associated Alumni U. Colo. (pres. and bd. dirs. 1956-57), Law Club, Denver (pres. 1958-59), ABA, Colo. Bar Assn., Denver (pres. 1958-59), Bar Assn., Tex. Bar Assn., Wyo. Bar Assn., Fed. Energy Bar Assn. (legal and lands com.), Interstate Oil Compact Commn., Rocky Mt. Oil and Gas Assn., Chevaliers du Tastevin. Republican. Episcopalian. Clubs: Denver Country, Petroleum, Gyro, Univ. (Denver); Colo. Arlberg (Winter Park). Office: Hawley & VanderWerf 730 17th St Suite 730 Denver CO 80202 Home: 4401 E 3d Ave Denver CO 80220

HAWORTH, KAYLE MERL, architect; b. Sheridan, Wyo., Aug. 28, 1947; s. Merl E. and Genvive Edna (Gross) H.; m. Cheryle Ann Keahey, Mar. 14, 1970; children: Scott Marques, Kevin Michael. BArch, Mont. State U., 1970. Registered architect, Wyo. Draftsman Adrian Malone & Assocs., Sheridan, 1970-74, architect, 1974-76; architect Gorder/South, Casper, Wyo., 1977-83, Denhert/Richardson, Lander, Wyo., 1983-84, Ira Blackwell Architects, Cheyenne, Wyo., 1985-86, Robb and Brenner, Inc. Architects/Planners, Ft. Collins, Colo., 1987—. Prin. works include Am. Bank Ctr., 1978, Animal Sci. Ctr., 1980, Northpark Elem. Sch., 1982. Mem. AIA (bd. dirs. Wyo. chpt. 1985—), Nat. Trust Hist. Preservation. Lodge: Elks. Avocations: archtl. history, art. Home: 4717 Ontario Ave Cheyenne WY 82009

HAWORTH, N. SCOTT, electrical engineer; b. Mpls., Nov. 10, 1958; s. John C. and Elsa M. (von Haeseler) H. BSEE, Cornell U., 1981; MSEE, Stanford U., 1985, postgrad. Engring. Mgmt., 1987. Assoc. engr. IBM, Boulder, Colo., 1980; head Traveling Wwave Tube Amplifier engring. Watkins-Johnson Co., San Jose, Calif., 1981—. Mem. IEEE. Mem. Soc. of Friends. Avocations: sailing, gardening, bicycling, flying. Home: 3034 Ironside Ct San Jose CA 95132 Office: Watkins-Johnson 2525 N 1st Ave San Jose CA 95131

HAWTHORNE, DAVID MADISON, advertising executive; b. San Mateo, Calif., July 20, 1946; m. Pamela Walter, Mar. 8, 1970 (div. Nov. 1978); children: Meleah, Adam; m. Eileen Mary Matzskiel, Nov. 12, 1983; 1 child, Brian Robert. Student, Coll. San Mateo, 1964-66, Union County Tech. Coll., 1971-72, U. Calif., San Diego, 1984-85. Account exec. Max Walter Advt., Inc., Newark, 1970-75; v.p., dir. advt. Mall Publs., Inc., Summit, N.J., 1975-81; dir. advt. Advt. Counseling, Madison, N.J., 1981-82; dir. mktg. Ctr. Aerospace Edn., Madison, N.J., 1982-83; dir. communications Westbridge Research Group, San Diego, 1983-84; pres., owner Hawthorne Mktg. Services, La Jolla, Calif., 1984—. Republican. Home: 8779 Gilman Ave La Jolla CA 92037

HAWTHORNE, MARION FREDERICK, chemistry educator; b. Ft. Scott, Kans., Aug. 24, 1928; s. Fred Elmer and Colleen (Webb) H.; m. Beverly Dawn Rempe, Oct. 30, 1951 (div. 1976); children: Cynthia Lee, Candace Lee; m. Diana Baker Razzaia, Aug. 14, 1977. B.A., Pomona Coll., 1949; Ph.D. (AEC fellow), U. Calif. at Los Angeles, 1953; D.Sc. (hon.), Pomona Coll., 1974. Research asso. Iowa State Coll., 1953-54; research chemist Rohm & Haas Co., Huntsville, Ala., 1954-56; group leader Rohm & Haas Co., 1956-60; lab. head Rohm & Haas Co., Phila., 1961; vis. lectr. Harvard, 1960, Queen Mary Coll., U. London, 1963; vis. prof. Harvard U., 1968; prof. chemistry U. Calif. at Riverside, 1962-68, U. Calif. at Los Angeles, 1968—; vis. prof. U. Tex., Austin, 1974; Mem. sci. adv. bd., USAF, 1980-86, NRC Bd. Army Sci. and Tech., 1986—. Editor: Inorganic Chemistry, 1969—; Editorial bd.: Progress in Solid State Chemistry, 1971—, Inorganic Syntheses, 1966—, Organometallics in Chemical Synthesis, 1969—, Synthesis in Inorganic and Metalorganic Chemistry, 1970—. Recipient Chancelors Research award, 1968; Herbert Newby McCoy award, 1972; Am. Chem. Soc. award in inorganic chemistry, 1973; Tolman Medal award, 1986; Nebr. sect. award, 1979; Sloan Found. fellow, 1963-65; named Col. Confederate Air Force, 1984. Fellow AAAS, Japan Soc. Promotion Sci.; mem. U.S. Nat. Acad. Scis., Am. Acad. Arts and Scis., Aircraft Owners and Pilots Assn., Nat. Acad. Scis., Sigma Xi, Alpha Chi Sigma, Sigma Nu. Club: Cosmos. Home: 3415 Green Vista Dr Encino CA 91316

HAWTHORNE, ROWLAND OLIVER, III, furniture executive; b. Anderson, S.C., Sept. 21, 1938; s. Rowland Oliver and Mildred Eastler (McCurdy) H.; m. Nancy Suber, July 8, 1961; children—Miles Brewton, Anna Elizabeth. A.B., Erskine Coll., Due West, S.C., 1960. Asst. to pres. Tomlinson Furniture, High Point, N.C., 1964-65, rep., Dallas, 1965-68; pres. Rowland Hawthorne & Co. Inc., Denver, 1969—. Warden, St. John's Cathedral, Denver, 1980—, sr. warden, 1984—. Served to lt. (j.g.) USN, 1960-63. Mem. Internat. Home Furnishings Reps. Assn. Clubs: University (Denver and Salt Lake City); Met. Denver Exec. (pres. 1982-83), Rotary. Home: 380 Marion St Denver CO 80218 Office: 1655 Grant St Denver CO 80203

HAY, ANDREW MACKENZIE, merchant banking and commodities company executive; b. London, Apr. 9, 1928; came to U.S., 1954, naturalized, 1959; s. Ewen Mackenzie and Bertine (Buxton) H.; M.A. in Econs., St. John's Coll., Cambridge U., 1950; m. Catherine Newman, July 30, 1977. Engaged in commodity trade, London and Ceylon, 1950-53; v.p. Calvert Vavasseur & Co. Inc., N.Y.C., 1954-61, pres., 1962-78, pres. Calvert-Peat Inc., N.Y.C., 1978—, Andrew M. Hay, Inc.; chmn. Barretto Peat Inc., N.Y.C., 1974—; Pacific NW cons. Am. Assn. Exporters and Importers, 1982—; radio and TV appearances. Mem. adv. com. on tech. innovation Nat. Acad. Scis., 1978; bd. dirs. Winston Churchill Found.; treas., trustee World Affairs Council Oreg., 1986—. Served to capt. Brit. Army, World War II. Decorated comdr. Order Brit. Empire. Mem. Am. Importer Assn. (pres. 1977-79), Pacific Northwest Internat. Trade Assn. (exec. dir. 1986—), Brit. Am. C. of C. (pres. 1966-68), Philippine Am. C. of C. (pres. 1977-79), St. George's Soc. (dir.), St. Andrew's Soc. (dir.). Episcopalian. Clubs: Recess, Downtown Assn. (N.Y.C.); University (Portland). Author: A Century of Coconuts, 1972. Home and Office: 3515 SW Council Crest Dr Portland OR 97201

HAY, BRUCE SELKIRK, accountant, consultant; b. Toledo, Mar. 21, 1945; s. Thomas Alexander and Anne (Dick) H.; m. Alyson Ruth Hatfield, Nov. 6, 1971; children—Sarah Alyson, Alexander Selkirk. B.Com., U. B.C., 1968. Chartered acct., B.C. Exec. Ford Motor Credit, Vancouver, B.C., Can., 1968-69; acct. Winspear Higgins, Vancouver, 1970-73; mgr. Coopers & Lybrand, Freeport, Bahamas, 1974-77; v.p. Wyder Properties, Vancouver, 1977-78; propr. Hay & Co. Chartered Accts., Vancouver, 1978-82; ptnr. Hay & Watson Chartered Accts., Vancouver, 1983—; cons. Provincial Govt. B.C., Vancouver, 1982-83, dir. Quadra Logic Techs., Vancouver, Genoveva Resources Inc., Vancouver; lectr. various sch. bds., assns., govts. Contbr. articles to profl. jours. Bd. dirs. Vancouver Crime Stoppers, 1984—, Kenneth Gordon Sch., Vancouver, 1982; mem. fundraising com. Vancouver YMCA, 1983. Mem. Inst. Chartered Accts. B.C., Better Bus. Bur. (bd. dirs. 1983). Office: Hay & Watson Chartered Accts, 1822 W 2d Ave, Vancouver, BC Canada V6J 1H9

HAY, JOHN LEONARD, lawyer; b. Lawrence, Mass., Oct. 6, 1940; s. Charles Cable and Henrietta Dudley (Wise) H.; m. Millicent Victoria, Dec. 16, 1967; 1 child, Ian. A.B. with distinction, Stanford U., 1961; J.D., U. Colo., 1964. Bar: Colo. 1964, Ariz. 1965, D.C. 1971. Assoc. Lewis and Roca, Phoenix, 1964-69, ptnr., 1969-82; ptnr. Fannin, Terry & Hay, 1982-87, Allen, Kimerer & LaVelle, 1987—; dir. Ariz. Life and Disability Ins. Guaranty Fund, 1983—, Ariz. Licensors and Franchisors Assn., 1985—. Mem. Democratic Precinct Com., 1966-78; Ariz. State Dem. Com., 1968-78; chmn. Dem. Legis. Dist., 1971-74; mem. Maricopa County Dem. Central Com., 1971-74; bd. dirs. ACLU, 1973-78, Community Legal Services, 1983—. Mem. ABA, Maricopa County Bar Assn. (bd. dirs. 1972-85), State Bar of Ariz., Ariz. Licensors and Franchisors Assn. (bd. dirs. 1985—), Ariz. Civil Liberties Union (recipient disting. citizen award 1979, bd. dirs. 1967-84, pres. 1973-77). Home: 201 E Hayward Ave Phoenix AZ 85020 Office: 2715 N 3d St Phoenix AZ 85004

HAY, JOHN WOODS, JR., banker; b. Rock Springs, Wyo., Apr. 23, 1905; s. John Woods and Mary Ann (Blair) H.; A.B., U. Mich., 1927; m. Frances B. Smith, Dec. 28, 1948; children—Helen Mary, John Woods III, Keith Norbert, Joseph Garrett. Pres., dir. Rock Springs Nat. Bank, 1947—, Rock Springs Grazing Assn., 1939—, Blair & Hay Land & Livestock Co., Rock Springs, 1949—. Trustee, v.p. William H. and Carrie Gottsche Found. Mem. Sigma Alpha Epsilon. Republican. Episcopalian. Clubs: Masons, Shriners, Jesters, Rotary. Home: 502 B St Rock Springs WY 82901 Office: 333 Broadway Rock Springs WY 82901

HAY, MILLICENT VICTORIA, writer; b. Long Beach, Calif., May 7, 1945; d. Glenn and Julie (DeLong) Gunnells; m. John Leonard Hay, Dec. 16, 1967; 1 child, Ian Daniel. BA, U. Ariz., 1966; MA, Ariz. State U., 1971, PhD, 1979. Instr. Ariz. State U., Tempe, 1969-73, editor Research News, 1979-82; freelance writer, Phoenix, 1982—; staff writer Phoenix Mag., 1983-84; pres. Hay Writing & Editing, Phoenix, 1984—; instr. Scottsdale (Ariz.) Community Coll., 1986—. Author: The Life of Robert Sidney, Earl of Leicester, 1984; editor: The Insomniac Reader, 1986; contbr. articles to various publs. Mem. Am. Soc. Journalists and Authors, Phi Beta Kappa, Sigma Delta Chi. Home and Office: 201 E Hayward Ave Phoenix AZ 85020

HAY, WILLIAM WINN, museum director, natural history educator; b. Dallas, Oct. 12, 1934; s. Stephen J. and Avella (Winn) H. B.S., So. Meth. U., 1955; postgrad. U. Zurich, Switzerland, 1955-56; M.S., U. Ill., 1958; Ph.D., Stanford U., 1960. Mem. faculty Rosenstiel Sch. Marine and Atmospheric Sci., U. Miami., Fla., 1968-82, chmn. div. marine geology, 1974-76, interim dean, 1976-77, dean, 1977-80; pres. Joint Oceanographic Instns., Inc., Washington, 1979-82; dir. U. Colo. Mus., Boulder, 1982—; mem. adv. panel sediment and ocean history Joint Oceanographic Instns. for Deep Earth Sampling, Washington, 1984—; mem. sci. adv. com. Ocean Drilling Program, 1979-83; mem. exec. com. div. ocean sci. NSF, 1982-85. Editor: Studies in Paleo-Oceanography, 1974. Univ. Coll. London fellow, 1972—; recipient Francis P. Shepard medal Soc. Econ. Paleontologists and Mineralogists, 1981, Best Paper award Gulf Coast sect., 1970. Fellow AAAS, Geol. Soc. Am., Geol. Soc. (London); mem. Am. Assn. Petroleum Geologists, Internat. Nannoplankton Assn. Clubs: Cosmos (Washington). Office: Univ Colo Museum 15th and Broadway Boulder CO 80309

HAYAKAWA, MARGEDANT PETERS, editor; b. Evansville, Ind., Feb. 5, 1915; d. Frederick Romer and Clara Adelaide (Margedant) Peters; m. Samuel Ichiye Hayakawa, May 29, 1937; children—Alan Romer, Mark, Wynne. B.A. with high honors, U. Wis., 1936. Assoc. editor prose dept. Poetry, A Mag. of Verse, Chgo., 1943-46; editor Co-op News, Cen. States Co-ops, Chgo., 1942-47, Fremontia pub. Calif. Native Plant Soc., 1973-83; pres. Pacific Hort. Found., 1977-86, also bd. dirs.; publ. Pacific Hort. mag., Berkeley, Calif., 1977—. Pres. Hyde Park Co-op Soc., Chgo., 1954-55; bd. dirs. Consumers Co-op of Berkeley, 1963-69. Fellow Calif. Native Plant Soc.; mem. Calif. Hort. Soc. (bd. dirs. 1971-77, pres. 1976-77). Home: PO Box 100 Mill Valley CA 94942 Office: Pacific Hort Found Box 485 Berkeley CA 94701

HAYASE, PAUL HIROMI, lawyer; b. Warren, Ohio, Mar. 20, 1955; s. Charles Koji and Michiko (Watanabe) H.; m. Aug. 12, 1978. B.A., Yale Univ., 1976; J.D., Univ. Pa., 1980. Bar: Calif. 1980, U.S. Dist. Ct. (cen. dist.) Calif. 1980, U.S. Ct. Appeals (9th cir.) 1980. Assoc. Macdonald, Halsted & Laybourne, Los Angeles, 1980-85; v.p., gen. counsel Knapp Communications Corp., Los Angeles, 1985—. Vice pres., bd. dirs. Japanese Evang. Missionary Soc., Los Angeles, 1981-85. Internat. scholar Service Employees Internat., Washington, 1973-77; Centennial scholar Japanese C. of C., Los Angeles, 1983. Mem. Japanese-Am. Bar Assn., Los Angeles County Bar Assn., Los Angeles Jr. C. of C. Democrat. Baptist. Office: Knapp Communications Corp 5900 Wilshire Blvd Los Angeles CA 90036

HAYASHI, YOSHIMI, justice state supreme court; b. Honolulu, Nov. 2, 1922; s. Shigeo and Yuki H.; m. Eleanor Hayashi, Aug. 8, 1953; 1 child, Scott K. B.A., U. Hawaii, 1950; LL.B., George Washington U., 1958. Bar: Hawaii 1958. Practice of law Lihue, Kauai, Hawaii, 1958-61; asst. U.S. atty. 1961-67, U.S. atty. for Hawaii, 1967-69; judge Hawaii Dist. Ct. 1st Circuit, 1974-80; chief judge Hawaii Intermediate Ct. Appeals, 1980-82; assoc. justice Hawaii Supreme Ct., Honolulu, 1982—. Served to sgt. U.S. Army, 1943-46. Democrat. Buddhist. Office: Hawaii Supreme Court 417 S King St Honolulu HI 96813 *

HAYCOX, STEPHEN WALTER, history educator; b. Ft. Wayne, Ind., July 19, 1940; s. Arthur and Mildred Inez (Markley) H.; m. Betty Shinabarger, June 30, 1963 (div. Aug. 1978); children: Mary, Paul, Peter; m. Carolynn Marie Nickel, Dec. 31, 1983. BA in History, Seattle U., 1966; MA in History, U. Oreg., 1967, PhD in History, 1971. Prof. history U. Alaska, Anchorage, 1970—. Editor: Alaska Bibliography: An Introductory Guide to Alaskan Historical Literature, 1977; producer (weekly radio program) Sta. KSKA, Anchorage, 1980— (Alaska Press Club award 1984, 85); contbr. articles to profl. jours. Bd. dirs. Anchorage Community Theater; mem. Alaska State Constitution Bicentennial Commn. Served with USN, 1958-62. Fellow NEH, 1980, Am. Phil. Soc., 1981, NDEA, 1967-70. Mem. Am. Hist. Assn., Orgn. Am. Historians, Alaska Hist. Soc. (bd. dirs.). Democrat. Roman Catholic. Home: 5817 E Tenth Circle Anchorage AK 99504 Office: U Alaska History Dept Anchorage AK 99508

HAYEK, CAROLYN JEAN, judge; b. Portland, Oreg., Aug. 17, 1948; d. Robert A. and Marion L. (DeKoning) H.; m. Steven M. Rosen, July 21, 1974; 1 child, Jonathan David. BA in Psychology, Carleton Coll., 1970; JD, U. Chgo., 1973. Bar: Wash. 1973. Assoc. firm Jones, Grey & Bayley, Seattle, 1973-77; sole practice law, Federal Way, Wash., 1977-82; judge Federal Way Dist. Ct., 1982—. Task force mem. Alternatives for Wash., 1973-75; mem. Wash. State Ecol. Commn., 1975-77; bd. dirs. 1st Unitarian Ch. Seattle, 1986—. Mem. ABA, Wash. Women Lawyers, Wash. State Bar Assn., AAUW (br. pres. 1978-80, chmn. state level conf. com. 1986-87), King County Dist. Ct. Judges Assn. (treas., exec. com., com. chmn.), Elected Wash. Women (dir. 1983-87), Nat. Assn. Women Judges (nat. bd. dirs., dist. bd. dirs. 1984-86), Federal Way Women's Network (bd. dirs. 1984-87, pres. 1985), Greater Federal Way C. of C. (dir. 1978-82, sec. 1980-81, v.p. 1981-82). Republican. Office: Federal Way Dist Ct 33506 10th Pl S Federal Way WA 98003

HAYES, ANNA, artist; b. Starkweather, N.D., Nov. 26, 1905; d. Axel and Carrie Anna (Hyman) Nelson; m. Clifford E. Hayes, Nov. 17, 1936; children—Robert C., Paul Richard. A.A., Long Beach City Coll., 1955; student of Robert Adams, 1960-61. Free lance artist, watercolor, India ink, Long Beach, Calif., 1954—. One man shows: Long Beach Mus. Art, 1962, Long Beach C. of C., 1965, Dana Library, Long Beach, 1972; participant exhbns. Newport Harbor Art Exhibit, 1960, Long Beach Art Assn. (Best of Show award), 1967, 73 (hon. mention), 1st Meth. Ch. 3d Ann. Lenten Art Festival, 1977 (hon. mention), Long Beach Art Assn. (best of show), 1967, 70, 73, 78, 79, 81, 85, Lakewood Artists Guild, 1973; represented in permanent collection Long Beach Mus. Art. Mem. Long Beach Art Assn. Republican. Methodist. Home: 1537 Armando Dr Long Beach CA 90807

HAYES, ARTHUR LEE, restaurant chain owner; b. Cunard, W.Va., Aug. 20, 1935; s. Brian Dutton and Marjorie Jane (Arthur) H.; m. Edith May Martin, Mar. 27, 1959; children—Dennis L., Debra L., Donald L., Darla L., Arthur L. II, Jeffrey M., Marjorie A. A.A., Orange Coast Coll., 1957. Restaurant mgr. Far Restaurant Food, Inc., Newport Beach, Calif., 1957-60; owner, operator College Restaurant, Santa Barbara, Calif., 1960-65; v.p. ops. Taco Bell, Torrance, Calif., 1965-70; asst. mgr. food and beverage Harrah's, Reno, 1970-74; exec. v.p. Dairy Queen Pacific N.W., Beaverton, Oreg., 1974-78; pres. Dairy Queen Stores Inc., Bellevue, Wash., 1978—, mem. nat. adv. council, Mpls., 1979—; chmn. Diary Queen Stores Inc., No. Calif., 1986—, N.W. Territory Inc., Bellevue, 1981—. Author: The $1,000,000 Half Hour, 1984. Fundraiser Greater Seattle Area council Boy Scouts Am., Bellevue, 1984. Republican. Home: 13918 205th NE Woodinville WA 98072 Office: Dairy Queen Stores Inc 13353 Bel-Red Road Bellevue WA 98005

HAYES, CLAUDE QUINTEN CHRISTOPHER, research scientist; b. N.Y.C., Nov. 15, 1945; s. Claude and Celestine (Stanley) H. BA in Chemistry and Geol. Sci., Columbia U., 1971, postgrad., 1972-73; postgrad., N.Y. Law Sch., 1973-75; JD, Western State Law Sch., 1978. Cert. community coll. tchr. earth scis., phys. sci., law, Calif. Tech. writer Burroughs Corp., San Diego, 1978-79; instr. phys. scis. Nat. U., San Diego, 1980-81; instr. bus. law, earch scis. Miramar Coll., 1975-82; sr. systems analyst Gen. Dynamics Convair, 1979-80, advanced mfg. technologist, sr. engr., 1980-81; pvt. practice sci. and tech. cons. Calif., 1982-86; instr. phys. sci., phys. geography San Diego Community Coll. Dist., 1976-82, 85-87; def. contractor cons., def. contractor Def. Nuclear Agy., Def. Initiative Office, Naval Ocean Systems Ctr., 1986-87; adj. asst. prof. chemistry San Diego State U., 1986; adj. prof. internat. bus. and computer mgmt. U. Redlands (Calif.) Grad. Sch., 1986—. Contbr. articles to profl. jours.; patentee in field. Mem. Am. Chem. Soc. Avocations: traveling, tech., people. Home: 7980 Linda Vista Rd #49 San Diego CA 92111

HAYES, DENIS ALLEN, lawyer, educator; b. Wisconsin Rapids, Wis., Aug. 29, 1944; s. Archibald John and Antoinette Jacqueline H.; m. Gail Boyer, June 14, 1971; 1 child, Lisa Antoinette. A.A., Clark Coll., 1964; B.A., Stanford U., 1969, J.D., 1985. Bar: Calif. 1985, U.S. Dist. Ct. (no. dist.) Calif. Founder, coordinator Earth Day, Washington, 1970; vis. scholar Smithsonian Instn., 1971-72; dir. Ill. State Energy Office, 1974-75; sr. researcher Worldwatch Inst., Washington, 1975-79; dir. Solar Energy Research Inst., Golden, Colo., 1979-81; Regents' prof. U. Calif.-Santa Cruz, 1981-82; cons. prof. civil engring. Stanford U., 1982—; atty. Cooley, Godward, Castro, Huddleston & Tatum, San Francisco, 1986—. Author: Rays of Hope, 1977. Trustee Stanford U., 1971-72; chmn. bd. Solar Lobby, 1978-79, 83—, Center for Renewable Resources, 1977-79, 85—. Recipient Jefferson medal Am. Inst. for Public Service, 1979; award for outstanding public service U.S. Dept. Energy, 1978, John Muir award Sierra Club, 1985, Cert. Outstanding achievement Am. Solar Energy Soc., 1985, Jefferson medal Am. Inst. Pub. Service, 1979. Mem. Fedn. Am. Scientists (dir.), Aspen Inst. Energy Group, Calif. Environ. Trust (dir.), Am. Solar Energy Soc. (dir.). Office: Cooley Godward Castro Huddleson & Tatum One Maritime Plaza 20th Floor San Francisco CA 94111

HAYES, DENNIS BREWSTER, science laboratory administrator, researcher; b. Mpls., Sept. 16, 1938; s. Robert William and Marian (Barling) H.; m. Janet Frances Gamble, Apr. 2, 1960; children: Denise Hayes Ebel, Douglas Lewis. BS in Physics, U. N.Mex., 1965, MS in Physics, 1968; PhD in Physics, Wash. State U., 1972. Staff mem. shock wave research Sandia Nat. Labs., Albuquerque, 1972-74, supr. detonating components, 1974-78, mgr. fluid and thermal scis., 1978-83; mgr. Solid State Devices, Albuquerque, 1983—. Republican. Avocations: guitar, backpacking, photography. Home: PO Box 591 Tijeras NM 87059 Office: Sandia Nat Labs Dept 2530 PO Box 5800 Albuquerque NM 87185

HAYES, EDWARD CARY, public administrator; b. Chgo., Dec. 28, 1937; s. Edward Bean and Helen Frances (Walker) H.; m. Rosemary Triggs, Sept. 10, 1972, (div. July 1976). BA magna cum laude, Swarthmore Coll., 1960; MA in Polit. Sci., U. Calif., Berkeley, 1962, PhD in Polit. Sci., 1968. Postdoctoral fellow U. Chgo., 1968-69; asst. prof. polit. sci. U. Wis., Milw., 1969-72, Ohio U., Athens, 1972-78; dir. econ. devel. program U.S. Cath. Conf., Columbus, 1976-78; dir. employment tng. ACCESS, San Diego, 1979-82; founder, pres. Metro Assocs., San Diego, 1982—. Author: Power Structure & Urban Politics, 1972, Public Administration on Three Continents, 1978, A Fire That Won't Go Out, 1984; editor: The Hidden Wealth of Cities, 1987. Grantee NSF, 1971, Ford Found., 1958, U.S. Office of Edn., 1970. Mem. Mensa, Am. Soc. Pub. Adminstrn., Am. Polit. Sci. Assn., Am. Edn. Research Soc., Am. Evaluation Assn. Avocations: tennis, golfing, songwriting. Home: 9157 Mesa Woods Ave San Diego CA 92126 Office: Metro Assocs San Diego PO Box 261340 San Diego CA 92126

HAYES, ERNEST M., podiatrist; b. New Orleans, Jan. 21, 1946; s. Ernest M. and Emma Hayes; B.A., Calif. State U., Sacramento, 1969; B.S., Calif. Coll. Podiatric Medicine, San Francisco, 1971, D.P.M., 1973; m. Bonnie Ruth Beigle, Oct. 16, 1970. Resident in surg. podiatry Beach Community Hosp., Buena Park, Calif., 1973-74, dir. residency program, 1974-75; practice podiatry, Anaheim, Calif., 1974-80, Yreka, Calif., 1980—; sr. clin. instr. So. Calif. Podiatric Med. Center, Los Angeles, 1975-78; vice chmn. podiatry dept. Good Samaritain Hosp., Anaheim, Calif., 1978-79; mem. med. staff Mercey Med. Ctr., Mt. Shasta, Calif. Bd. dirs. Little Bogus Ranches Home Owners Assn., 1981-83, pres., 1983—. Fellow Nat. Coll. Foot Surgeons. Baptist. Club: Kiwanis. Home: PO Box 958 Yreka CA 96097 Office: Newton Med Clinic 918 4th St Yreka CA 96097 Office: The Plaza 108 Siskiyou Ave Suites A&B Mount Shasta CA 96067

HAYES, FORREST L., counselor, consultant, lecturer; b. Tuscaloosa, Ala., Nov. 4, 1930; s. Luther L. and Aimee E. (Collins) H.; m. Moniree V. Heron, Jan. 13, 1951; children—Chris, Pamela, Marla. Student U. Alaska, 1965-69; B.A. in Sociology, U. Tampa, 1971; M.A. in Edni. Counseling, U. Alaska, 1975; Ph.D. in Human Behavior, U.S. Internat. U., 1979. Diplomate Internat. Acad. Profl. Counselors and Psychologists. Tchr., counselor Dept. Edn., U.S. Air Force, State of Alaska, 1950-72; counselor, test control officer, Anchorage and Fairbanks, Alaska, 1973-78; counselor, student services coordinator U. Alaska, Matanuska-Susitna Community Coll., Palmer, 1978—. Sec. supervisory com. Alaska U.S.A. Fed. Credit Union; deacon Anchorage Evangelical Free Ch. Recipient Outstanding Unit award, combat ready badge. Mem. Am. Psychol. Assn., Internat. Acad. Profl. Counselors and Psychotherapists, Inc., Am. Assn. Counseling and Devel. Club: Masons. Editor Mat-Su Monitor; contbr. articles to profl. jours. Home: 4711 Pavalof St Anchorage AK 99507 Office: U Alaska PO Box 2889 Palmer AK 99645

HAYES, JEFFREY CHARLES, chemistry educator; b. San Bernardino, Calif., Aug. 28, 1954; s. Donald Paul and Joy (Marjanski) H. AB, Cornell U., 1976; MA, Harvard U., 1979, PhD, 1983. NIH postdoctoral fellow U. Calif., Berkeley, 1983-85; asst. prof. U. Colo., Boulder, 1985—. Contbr. articles to profl. jours. Nat. Merit scholar, Cornell U., 1972-76; NSF hon. mention 1976; recipient Nat. Research Service award NIH, 1983-85. Mem. Am. Chem. Soc. Avocations: biking, skiing, running, squash. Office: U Colo Dept Chemistry Campus Box 215 Boulder CO 80309

HAYES, JOHN EDWARD, broadcasting executive; b. Niagara Falls, N.Y., Sept. 14, 1941; s. John H. and Margaret (Wilson) H.; m. Jean Wheeler, Jan. 1, 1964; children: John Jr., Janice. BS in Broadcasting, U. Fla., 1963. State capitol bur. chief Sta. WTVT-TV, Tallahassee, 1971-77; asst. news dir. Sta. WTVT-TV, Tampa, Fla., 1977-79; news dir. Sta. WBRC-TV, Birmingham, Ala., 1979-82, Sta. KNTV-TV, San Jose, Calif., 1982-83; v.p., gen. mgr. Sta. KLAS-TV, Las Vegas, Nev., 1983—. Recipient Nat. Headliners award

Headliners Club, 1973, Emmy award TV Acad. Arts and Sci., 1982. Presbyterian. Avocations: golf, sailing. Office: 3255 Lindell Rd Las Vegas NV 89102

HAYES, LESLIE ANN, special education educator, consultant; b. Pasadena, Calif., Jan. 6, 1951; d. W. Clark and Lois Jane (Guilbert) Graves; m. John Richard Hayes, Jr., Sept. 25, 1976; children: Lindsey Allison, Kyle Patrick. BA, U. Calif., Santa Barbara, 1973; MA, U. Mich., 1974. Cert. spl. edn. tchr., Calif.; cert. corrective therapist. Phys. edn. dir. YMCA, Palo Alto and Watsonville, Calif., 1975-78; adapted phys. edn. specialist Santa Clara County Schs., San Jose, Calif., 1978-82, Santa Cruz (Calif.) City Schs., 1982—; exec. bd. mem. Spl. Olympics San Jose, 1978-82; agy. rep. Spl. Olympics McKinnon Sch., San Jose, 1978-82; cons. Santa Cruz City Schs., 1982—. Reader Star of the Sea Cath. Ch., Santa Cruz, 1981-83; garden club mem. Recipient Outstanding Young Am. award Outstanding Young Ams., 1982. Fellow Calif. Tchrs. Assn. Democrat. Episcopalian. Club: Pogonip Swim (Santa Cruz). Avocations: horseback riding, running. Office: Santa Cruz City Schs 133 W Mission St Santa Cruz CA 95065

HAYES, MELINDA KAY, technical services librarian; b. Terre Haute, Ind., Aug. 24, 1953; d. Blair Ferguson and Julia Eva (Cesinger) H. BA, UCLA, 1980, MLS, 1982. Conservation intern Huntington Library, San Marino, Calif., 1982-83, cataloger, 1983-85; tech. services librarian Hancock Library U. So. Calif., Los Angeles, 1985—. Mem. ALA (liasion to preservation of library materials Jr. Mems. Round Table 1982-85), Am. Inst. Conservation, Western Assn. of Art Conservators. Home: 400 Monterey Rd #10 South Pasadena CA 91030 Office: U So Calif Hancock Library Los Angeles CA 90089

HAYES, NANCY VICTORIA, aerospace engineer; b. Los Angeles, Sept. 9, 1952; d. Charles and Selika Madeline (Cade) H. BS in Physics, Calif. State U., Los Angeles, 1981, postgrad. Engr. spacecraft communications Jet Propulsion Lab., Pasadena, Calif., 1981-82, engr. Voyager spacecraft team, 1983—. Contbr. articles on sci. to newspapers. Mem. AIAA, Black Profl. Engrs. (Los Angeles Council), Soc. Women Engrs., Soc. Physics Students, Mensa, Sigma Delta Epsilon. Avocations: sci. writing, sci. fiction. Home: PO Box 41454 Eagle Rock Sta Eagle Rock CA 90041-0454 Office: Jet Propulsion Lab Bldg 264 Room 519 4800 Oak Grove Dr Pasadena CA 91109

HAYES, PHILIP LOUIS, financial consulting firm executive; b. Watertown, N.Y., Sept. 30, 1934; s. Louis Neville and Lorene (Kerr) H.; B.S. cum laude, Syracuse U., 1960, M.B.A., 1962; m. Catherine M. Sears, June 5, 1955. Dist. fin. supr. Eastman Kodak Co., Rochester, N.Y., 1962-64; sr. fin. analyst Indsl. Indemnity Co., San Francisco, 1964-66, asst. mgr. fin. analysis, 1967, mgr. fin. analysis, 1968-71, asst. treas., 1971-74, asst. v.p., asst. treas., 1974-76, v.p., asst. treas., 1976-82; pres. Hayes and Assocs. Fin. Cons., 1982—; dir., nat. chmn. Excel Systems Corp. grad. alumni ann. giving campaign Syracuse U. Sch. Mgmt., 1978; bd. dirs., treas. Marin County Republican party, 1973-76. Served with USCGR, 1952-56. Mem. Ins. Acctg. and Statis. Assn., Tiburon peninsula Club (dir., treas.), Syracuse U. Alumni Assn. (nat. bd. dirs. 1976-79), Belvedere Sailing Soc., San Francisco Mus. Modern Art, M.H. de Young Meml. Mus., San Francisco Symphony Assn., Marin Symphony Assn., Beta Gamma Sigma (chpt. v.p. 1961), Phi Kappa Phi (chpt. v.p. 1960), Alpha Kappa Psi (chpt. social chmn. 1960). Clubs: Syracuse U. San Francisco Bay Area Alumni (pres. 1967-77); Tiburon Peninsula (treas., bd. dirs. 1986—); San Francisco Engrs., Commonwealth of Calif. (San Francisco); San Francisco Rotary. Home and office: 104 Sugarloaf Dr Tiburon CA 94920

HAYES, THOMAS BURKE, consulting engineer; b. Pendleton, Oreg., Aug. 25, 1912; s. Frank Burke and Galena Ann (Campbell) H.; m. Lenore Reynolds, Aug. 25, 1938; children—Gail, Thomas B. Jr., Richard R. B.S.E.E., Oreg. State U., 1938; M.S.E.E., MIT, 1940. Profl. engr. Oreg., Alaska, Wash., Idaho, Mont., Calif., Nebr., Va. Electrical engr. Jackson & Moreland, Boston, 1940-42, WR Holway & Assocs., Tulsa, 1942; ptnr. and founder CH2M, Corvallis, Oreg., 1946-66; v.p. CH2M Hill Inc., Corvallis, 1966-78, cons. engr., 1978—; dir. Agriculture Services Inc., Salem, Oreg., 1981-84, Advanced Power Structure, Boise, Idaho, 1983-85, Oreg. Hi Desert Mus., Bend, Oreg., 1980-84. Inventor Flomatcher, 1953. Dir. Action Alliance for Excellence Edn., Corvallis, 1984; pres. Oreg. State Bd. Engring. Exam., Salem, 1971-81. Served to lt. USNR, 1943-46. Fellow IEEE, ASME; mem. Profl. Engrs. Oreg., Corvallis C. of C. (pres. 1955). Republican. Presbyterian. Clubs: Corvallis Country, Bend Country. Lodge: Elks. Home: 2640 SW Whiteside Dr Corvallis OR 97333 Office: CH2M Hill Inc 2300 NW Walnut Blvd Corvallis OR 39428

HAYLER, CAROLEE, convention center manager; b. Colorado Springs, Colo., Jan. 27, 1950; d. Rodney Gould and Virginia Lee (McClung) H. Student, Fla. So. Coll., 1968-70; BS in Social Welfare, Fla. State U., 1972. Spl. services program dir. Mayport Naval Sta., Mayport, Fla., 1973-76; recreation ctr. dir. Spangdehlem (Fed. Republic Germany) Air Base, Fed. Republic Germany, 1976-80; asst. dir. tourism Jekyll Island (Ga.) Authority, 1980-83; conv. ctr. mgr. City of Juneau, Alaska, 1984—; so. region dir. resort and comml. recreation Jekyll Island, 1983, state dir. Juneau, 1984—. Mem. Internat. Assn. Auditorium Mgmt. Republican. Avocation: sports. Office: City and Borough of Juneau Juneau AK 99801

HAYNES, CALEB VANCE, geology and archaeology educator; b. Spokane, Wash., Feb. 29, 1928; m. Elizabeth Hamilton, Jan. 11, 1954; 1 child, Elizabeth Ann. Student, Johns Hopkins U., 1947-49; degree in geol. engring., Colo. Sch. Mines, 1956; PhD, U. Ariz., 1965. Mining geology cons. 1958-60; sr. project engr. Am. Inst. Research, Golden, Colo., 1956-60; sr. engr. Martin Co., Denver, 1960-62; geologist Nev. State Mus. Tule Springs Expedition, 1962-63; research asst. U. Ariz., Tucson, 1963-64, asst. prof. geology, archaeology, 1965-68, prof. geoscis., anthropology, 1974—; assoc. prof. So. Meth. U., Dallas, 1968-73, prof., 1973-74. Served with USAF, 1951-54. Guggenheim fellow 1980-81; grantee NSF, Nat. Geographic Soc., others. Fellow Geol. Soc. Am. (Archeol. award 1984); mem. AAAS, Am. Quaternary Assn. (pres. 1976-78), Soc. Am. Archaeology (Fryxell award 1978), Sigma Xi. Office: U Ariz Dept Anthropology Tucson AZ 85721

HAYNES, CATHERINE ANN, nursing educator; b. Los Angeles, May 14, 1944; d. Edgar Thomas Farnum and Irene Bertha (Haynes) Howard; m. Michael Monette LaPointe, Feb. 10, 1968 (div. Jan. 1974). BS, U. Nebr. Med. Ctr., 1973; MS, U. Calif., San Francisco, 1975; diploma in nursing, Nebr. Meth. Hosp. Sch. Nursing. Instr. critical care staff devel. Mills Meml. Hosp., San Mateo, Calif., 1975-76; assoc. program nurse and med. supr. Palo Alto (Calif.) YMCA, 1976-78; clin. coordinator cardiac therapy Loma Linda (Calif.) Med. Ctr., 1978-79; coordinator pacemaker and scanning div. Southwest Monitoring, Houston, 1980-81; asst. prof. nursing U. Ariz., Tucson, 1981-84, U. Tex. Health Scis. Ctr., San Antonio, 1984-86; clin. dir. ICU/Critical Care Unit Meml. Hosp. Natrona County, Casper, Wyo., 1986—; facilitator, cons. U. Ariz. Hosp., Tucson, 1983; mem. staff Ornish Cardiovascular Research Study, Horseshoe Bay, Tex., 1980; lectr. community and profl. orgns. various states, 1978—; expert witness Atty. Ray Speece, Tucson, 1983-85. Chmn. United Way, Tucson, 1982-83. Mem. Am. Heart Assn. (council for cardiovascular nursing 1982—), Am. Assn. Critical Care Nursing, San Antonio Nursing Research, Casper YMCA. Libertarian. Avocations: backpacking, birdwatching, cross-country skiing, gardening, running. Office: Meml Hosp Natrona County 1233 E 2d St Casper WY 82601

HAYNES, HAROLD WALTER, aircraft manufacturer; b. Snoqualmie, Wash., Jan. 23, 1923; s. Ralph and Bertha (Sewell) H.; m. Barbara J. Tatham, Oct. 11, 1943; children—Christine, Steven, Kevin. B.A., U. Wash., 1948. C.P.A., Wash. With Touche, Ross, Bailey & Smart (C.P.A.'s), Seattle, 1948-54; with Boeing Co., Seattle, 1954—, v.p. finance, 1960-70, sr. v.p. finance, 1970-75, exec. v.p., chief finance officer, 1975—, also dir.; dir. First Interstate Bank of Wash., Safeco, Itel Corp. Served as pilot USMCR, 1942-45. Mem. Financial Execs. Inst. Home: Highlands Seattle WA 98177 Office: The Boeing Co 7755 E Marginal Way S Seattle WA 98108

HAYNES, JAMES EARL, JR., association executive; b. Bakersfield, Calif., Oct. 11, 1943; s. James E. and Ruth M. (Campbell) H.; m. Norma Beth Jordan, Feb. 10, 1978; 1 child, Andrew Jordan. B.A. in Journalism, Los Angeles State Coll., 1967. Asst. mgr. West Covina C. of C., Calif., 1966-68; mgr. Monterey Park C. of C., Calif., 1968-72; gen. mgr. ops. San Francisco C. of C., 1972-76; pres. Phoenix C. of C., 1976—; mem. bd. regents Insts. for Orgn. Mgmt. U.S. C. of C. Mem. Inst. Orgn. Mgmt. (chmn. bd. regents), Am. C. of C. Execs., Ariz. C. of C. Mgrs. Assn. Office: Phoenix C of C 34 W Monroe St Phoenix AZ 85003

HAYNES, MONA LEE, marketing professional, marketing instructor; b. Nurenberg, Fed. Republic Germany, July 8, 1957; d. George Harrington and Mona LeOra (Frank) Oswald; m. Wilbur Lee Haynes, Nov. 27, 1976; 1 child, Kyle Nicholas. BA, Calif. State U., Long Beach, 1979; MBA, UCLA, 1984. Statis. analyst Gerald J. Sullivan, Los Angeles, 1980-81; market devel. mgr. Travenol Labs., Glendale, Calif., 1981-86, dir. market research, 1986—; mktg. instr. Coll. of Canyons, Valencia, Calif., 1985—. Mem. Am. Mktg. Assn., Med. Mktg. Assn. Republican. Avocations: tennis, gardening. Home: 27773 N Barrett Dr Saugus CA 91350 Office: Travenol Labs 27200 N Tourney Rd Valencia CA 91355

HAYNES, WILLIAM ERNEST, lawyer, financial consultant, educator; b. Peoria, Ill., Aug. 22, 1936; s. Clarence Ernest and Lucille Ann Haynes; m. Willette Lancia Rothschild, Dec. 2, 1972; children—Lancia Ann, Sharon Elizabeth. B.A. in Fin., Loras Coll., DuBuque, Iowa, 1959; J.D., Marquette U., Milw., 1964; M.B.A. in Bus. Econs., Loyola U., Chgo., 1969. Bar: Wis. 1964, Ill. 1965, Calif. 1970. Corp. counsel Gen. Fin. Co., Evanston, Ill., 1964-69; asst. controller internat. tax Wells Fargo Bank, San Francisco, 1969-76; tax counsel Kaiser Aluminum and Chem. Corp., Oakland, Calif., 1976-79; prin. Law Offices of William E. Haynes and Assocs., San Francisco, 1979—; pres. Gryphon Group Ltd., econ. cons., 1981—; prin. The Bus. Mart Bus. Brokers, San Francisco, 1987—; prof. taxation, adj. faculty, McLaren Coll. of Bus., U. San Francisco; lectr. on law, taxation and fin.; bd. dirs. Protective Packaging Devel. Corp., C-Case Corp., Rainbow River Foods Corp. Mem. adv. com. on edn. of bar State Bar of Calif.; bd. dirs. Meals on Wheels of San Francisco. Served with U.S. Army, 1959-61. Mem. ABA, Calif. Bar Assn., Am. Econs. Assn., San Francisco Internat. Tax Group, Internat. Assn. Fin. Planners, Calif. Hist. Soc., San Francisco Mus. Soc., World Affairs Council. Republican. Roman Catholic. Lodge: Rotary. Office: 50 California St Suite 2450 San Francisco CA 94111

HAYS, BONNIE LINN, county official; b. Silverton, Oreg., Aug. 21, 1950; d. Lacy Emmett and Ethel Marie (Hunt) Bowlsby; m. Robert Verne Hays, Mar. 21, 1972 (dec. Aug. 1976); m. Arthur J. Lewis, Aug. 22, 1981. BS, Oreg. State U., 1972; postgrad. Portland State U., 1973-74, Rocky Mt. Inst., 1982, Lewis & Clark U., Northwestern U. Sch. Law, 1985—. Cert. tchr. secondary edn., Oreg. Tchr. high sch. Astoria Sch. Dist., Oreg., 1972-75; ins. agt. Equitable Life Assurance Co., Portland, Oreg., 1975-77; br. mgr. Transamerica Title Ins. Co., Beaverton, Oreg., 1977-82; county commr. Washington County, Hillsboro, Oreg., 1980—; dir. Washington County Community Corrections, Hillsboro, 1983—, elected chmn., bd. commrs., 1987—; dir. State Job Tng. Coordinating Council, Salem, Oreg., 1985—, Multnomah-Washington Pvt. Industry Council, Portland, 1983—; project dir. Washington County Driving Under the Influence of Intoxicants Act Com., Hillsboro. Bd. dirs. Un Lugar para Niños, Hillsboro, 1984—; bd. mgmt., chmn. YMCA of Washington County, Beaverton, 1983—; corp. bd. dirs. YMCA of Columbia-Williamette, 1987—; bd. dirs. Tualatin Valley Econ. Devel. Corp., 1987—; bd. dirs. Washington County Hist. Soc., Hillsboro, 1985—, pres., 1986—; mem. Young Republicans of Oreg., Salem, 1984—; mem. Oreg. Episc. Sch. Wetlands Adv. Com., 1986. Named One of Washington County's "10 Most Influential People", Valley Times Newspaper Poll, 1985. Mem. Am. Corrections Assn., Assn. Oreg. Counties (com. pub. safety and human resources 1982—, vice chmn. 1982, chmn. 1986-87), Nat. Assn. Counties (justice and pub. safety steering com. 1987—). Republican. Roman Catholic. Club: Multnomah Athletic (Portland). Avocation: gourmet cooking. Home: 15540 SW Village Ct Beaverton OR 97007 Office: Washington County Courthouse 150 N First Ave Hillsboro OR 97124

HAYS, GEORGE WILLIAM, air force officer; b. Enterprise, Oreg., July 23, 1952; s. Marion E. and Ethel M. (Wise) H.; divorced; children: Juli Ann, Jared William. A.A.S., Community Coll. Air Force, 1981; A.A. in Bus., U. Md.-Europe, 1981, B.S. in Bus., 1982. Enlisted U.S. Air Force, 1971, commd. 2d lt., 1982, advanced through grades to capt., 1986; telecommunications specialist, Korea, Thailand, Colo., Wash., 1971-79; non-commd. officer in charge switchboard ops., Alconbury, Eng., 1979-82; program mgr. tactical air control system, Sacramento, 1983; officer in charge info.-systems maintenance br., Spokane, Wash., 1983-86, airborne parachutist, joint communications unit field ops. officer, Ft. Bragg, N.C., 1986—. Named Disting. Grad., USAF Officer Tng. Sch., 1982; Squadron NCO of Yr, 1977, 81, Officer of Yr., 1985; decorated Meritorious Service medal (2), others; Vietnam Service Medal. Mem. AF Assn., Armed Forces Communications and Electronics Assn., Phi Kappa Phi. Republican. Baptist.

HAYS, HOWARD H. (TIM), editor, publisher; b. Chgo., June 2, 1917; s. Howard H. and Margaret (Mauger) H.; m. Helen Cunningham, May 27, 1947; children—William, Thomas. B.A., Stanford U., 1939; LL.B., Harvard U., 1942. Bar: Calif. 1946. Spl. agt. FBI, 1942-45; reporter San Bernardino (Calif.) Sun, 1945-46; asst. editor Riverside (Calif.) Daily Press, 1946-49, editor, 1949-65, editor, co-pub., 1965-83, editor, pub., chief exec. officer, 1983—; Mem. Pulitzer Prize Bd., 1976-86, AP Bd., 1980—. Mem. bd. visitors John S. Knight Fellowships for Profl. Journalists at Stanford U., 1986—. Recipient Dist. award Calif. Jr. C. of C., 1951; named Pub. of Year Calif. Press Assn., 1968. Mem. Calif. Bar Assn., Am. Soc. Newspaper Editors (dir. 1969-76, pres. 1974-75), Stanford Alumni Assn. (dir. 1970-74), Internat. Press Inst. (chmn. Am. com. 1971-72, mem. exec. bd. 1977-83), Am. Press Inst. (chmn. 1978-83), Nature Conservancy Calif. (bd. dirs. 1982-86), Kappa Tau Alpha. Home: 2750 Rumsey Dr Riverside CA 92506 Office: 3512 14th St Riverside CA 92501

HAYS, JACK D.H., state supreme court justice; b. Lund, Nev., Feb. 17, 1917; s. Charles Harold and Thelma (Savage) H.; children by previous marriage—Eugene Harrington, Rory Cochrane, Bruce Harvey, Victoria Wakeling. Grad., So. Meth. U., 1941. Bar: Ariz. 1946. Since practiced in Phoenix, asst. city atty., 1949-52; U.S. atty. Dist. Ariz., 1953-60; superior ct. judge Maricopa County, 1960-69; justice Ariz. Supreme Ct., 1969—, chief justice, 1972-74; Mem. 21st Ariz. Legislature, 1952; mem. Young Republican Exec. Com., 1948-50, Rep. State Central Com., 1948-53; vice chmn. Maricopa Rep. Com., 1949-53; Ariz. chmn. Eisenhower for Pres., 1952. Mem. State Justice Planning Governing Bd., 1969-74; mem. adv. bd. Roosevelt council Boy Scouts Am.; awards juror Freedoms Found., Valley Forge, 1973; Bd. dirs. Maricopa Legal Aid Soc. Served as maj. F.A. AUS, 1941-46. Recipient Big Brother of Year award, 1966; Outstanding State Appellate Judge award Assn. Trial Lawyers Am., 1984. Mem. Am. Judicature Soc. (Herbert Lincoln Harley award 1974), Am. Law Inst., Fed. Bar Assn., ABA, Inter-Am. Bar Assn., Ariz. Judges Assn. (pres. 1965-66), Inst. Jud. Adminstrn., Ariz. Acad., Assn. Trial Lawyers Am. (Outstanding State Appellate Judge award 1984), Lambda Chi Alpha, Phi Alpha Delta. Episcopalian. Lodge: Rotary. Office: 221 West Wing State Capitol Phoenix AZ 85007

HAYS, MARVIN BRYANT, orthopaedic surgeon; b. Oklahoma City, Aug. 30, 1921; B.S., U. Okla., 1942, M.D., 1945; m. Mildred May Benjegerdes, May 28, 1952. Intern, U. Okla. Hosp., Oklahoma City, 1945-46, resident, 1949-51; practice orthopaedic surgery, Oklahoma City, 1952-56, Eureka, Calif., 1956-78; emergency med. services physician Eureka City Police; chief orthopaedic service USPHS Hosp., San Francisco, 1978-80; asst. chief orthopaedic sect. VA Med Center, Albuquerque, 1980-81, chief orthopaedic sect., 1981—; asst. prof. orthopaedic surgery U. N.Mex. Sch. Medicine, Albuquerque, 1980-84, assoc. prof., div. orthopaedic resident tng. acad. program, 1984—. Commdr. 351 Surg. Hosp. (MA), 1984-85. Mem. Calif. Gov.'s Aerospace Aviation Edn. Task Force, 1969—. Served to capt. M.C., AUS, 1946-48, Col. M.C., USAR, ret. 1985. Certified Calif. community coll. instr. Fellow ACS, Internat. Coll. Surgeons, Am. Acad. Orthopaedic Surgery; mem. Western Orthopaedic Assn., Am. Trauma Soc. (founding mem.), Flying Physicians Assn. (exec. com. state chpt., dir. nat. orgn., pres. 1972-73). Office: 2100 Ridgecrest Rd SE Albuquerque NM 87108

HAYS, PATRICK GREGORY, healthcare executive; b. Kansas City, Kans., Sept. 9, 1942; s. Vance Samuel and Mary Ellen (Crabbe) H.; m. Penelope Ann Hall, July 3, 1976; children—Julia L., Jennifer M. Meyer, Emily J. Meyer, Drew D. Meyer. B.S. in Bus. Adminstrn, U. Tulsa, 1964; M.H.A., U. Minn., 1971; postgrad., U. Mich. Grad. Sch. Bus. Adminstrn., 1977. Mfg. analyst N.Am. Rockwell Corp., Tulsa, 1964-66; asst. adminstr., adminstr. for ops. Henry Ford Hosp., Detroit, 1971-75; exec. v.p. Methodist Med. Center of Ill., Peoria, 1975-77; adminstr. Kaiser Found. Hosp., Los Angeles, 1977-80; pres. Sutter Community Hosps. and Sutter Health System, Sacramento, 1980—; trustee Central Area Teaching Hosps., Inc., Los Angeles, 1977-79; clin. preceptor U. Minn., Xavier U., Tulane U., Ariz. State U.; adj. prof. grad. program in health services adminstrn. U. So. Calif.; bd. dirs. New Center Area Council, Detroit, 1973-75, Arthritis Found. Central Ill., 1976-77; chmn. bd. Calif. Hosps. Polit. Action Com.; mem. exec. com. St. Jude Children's Research Hosp. Midwest Affilate, Peoria, 1975-77; chmn. adv. bd. grad. program in health services adminstrn. U. So. Calif.-Sacramento; chmn. Hosp. Council No. Calif., chmn. bd., 1986; chmn. bd. Option Care, Inc.; bd. dirs. Vol. Hosps. Am. Contbr. articles on health services to publs. Mem. Pvt. Industry Council, Sacramento Employment and Tng. Agy., 1984-85; bd. dirs. Consumer Credit Counselors Sacramento, United Way Sacramento Area. Served with U.S. Army, 1966-69. Decorated Army Commendation medal, cert. of appreciation Dept. Army; USPHS fellow, 1969-71; recipient Commendation resolution Calif. Senate, 1979; Recipient Whitney M. Young award Sacramento Urban League, 1983. Fellow Am. Coll. Healthcare Execs.; mem. Sacramento-Sierra Hosp. Assn. (exec. com., bd. dirs., pres. 1984), Royal Soc. Health (U.K.), Am. Mgmt. Assn. (pres.' club), Hollywood C. of C. (Hollywood revitalization com. 1979), Calif. Assn. of Hosps. & Health Systems (bd. dirs.), Assn. Western Hosps. (trustee). (bd. trustees), Sacramento C. of C. (bd. dirs. 1982-85), Kappa Sigma, Sigma Phi Epsilon. Presbyterian. Lodge: Rotary (Sacramento chpt. bd.). Office: 1111 Howe Ave Sacramento CA 95816

HAYWOOD, L. JULIAN, physician, educator; b. Reidsville, N.C., Apr. 13, 1927; s. Thomas Woodly and Louise Viola (Hayley) H.; m. Virginia Elizabeth Paige, Dec. 3, 1953; 1 son, Julian Anthony. B.S., Hampton Inst., 1948; M.D., Howard U., 1952. Intern St. Mary's Hosp., Rochester, N.Y., 1952-53; resident Los Angeles County Hosp., 1956-58; fellow cardiology White Meml. Hosp., 1959-61; traveling fellow U. Oxford, Eng., 1963; instr. medicine Loma Linda (Calif.) U., 1960-61, asst. prof., 1961-72, asso. clin. prof., 1973—; asst. prof. medicine U. So. Calif., 1963-68, asso. prof., 1968-76, prof., 1976—; dir. comprehensive sickle cell ctr. Los Angeles County-U. So. Calif. Med. Center, dir. coronary care unit; past dir. physicians tng. program (Regional Med. Programs), 1970-75; cons. Los Angeles County Coroner, Indsl. Accident Bd. Calif., Health Care Tech. Div., USPHS, Nat. Heart and Lung Inst.; past mem. cardiology adv. com. div. heart and vascular diseases. Bd. dirs., pres. Sickle Cell Disease Research Found. Contbr. articles profl. jours.; Mem. editorial bds.: Jour. Nat. Med. Assn. Served with M.C. USNR, 1954-56. Recipient award of merit Los Angeles County Heart Assn., 1968, 69, 73, 75, Disitng. Alumnus award, Howard U., 1982. Fellow Los Angeles Acad. Medicine, A.C.P., Am. Coll. Cardiology, Am. Heart Assn. (fellow council on clin. cardiology, council on atherosclerosis, exec. com. council on epidemiology; long-range planning com., dir., past sec., v.p. Greater Los Angeles affiliate, now pres.); mem. Am. Fedn. Clin. Research, AAAS, Soc. Clin. Investigation, Western Soc. Clin. Research, Assn. Advancement Med. Instrumentation, AMA, Nat. Med. Assn. (Charles Drew Med. Soc.), N.Y. Acad. Scis., Hampton Inst. Alumni Assn. (past pres. Los Angeles chpt.), Med. Faculty Assn. U. So. Calif. Sch. Medicine (past pres.), Los Angeles Soc. Internal Medicine (past pres.), Western Assn. Physicians, AAUP, Fedn. Am. Scientists, Alpha Omega Alpha. Home: 3551 Lowry Rd Los Angeles CA 90027 Office: 1200 N State St Los Angeles CA 90033

HAZARD, THOMAS WILLIAM, JR., business management consultant; b. San Jose, Calif., Nov. 13, 1925; s. Thomas William and Bernice Vernice (Butts) H.; m. Audrey Marie Knecht, July 29, 1957 (div. 1977); children—Scott Thomas, Jeanmarie Ann, Gregory Michael; m. Gloria Joan Lee, July 26, 1977. B.S., U.S. Mil. Acad., 1948; M.A., Stanford U., 1968; LL.B., LaSalle U., 1969; Ph.D., Calif. Coast U., 1977. Commd. 2d lt. U.S. Army, 1948, advanced through grades to capt. 1957; tech. engr. Gen. Electric Co., Cin., 1957-59; chief spl. publs. AEC, Washington, 1959-63; regional sci. officer AID, 1963-74; mgmt. cons., 1975-81; asst. prof. Embry-Riddle Aero. U., Prescott, Ariz., 1981-83; mem. faculty U. Phoenix, 1983—; pres. T&L Assocs., mgmt. cons., 1984—. Contbr. articles to profl. jours. Decorated Purple Heart. Mem. Inst. Indsl. Engrs., Indsl. Mgmt. Soc., Assn. for Advancement of Policy, Research and Devel., West Point Alumni Assn., Stanford U. Alumni Assn. Republican. Home: 8001 E Broadway PO Box 800 Mesa AZ 85208

HAZELKORN, IRA DAVID, lawyer; b. Chgo., May 11, 1948; s. Jules and Joyce (Kosbie) H.; M. Kathe Ann Tollefson, Apr. 4, 1974; children: Lauren, Joshua. A.B., U. Calif., Berkeley, 1970; J.D., UCLA, 1975. Bar: Ohio 1976, Calif. 1977, U.S. Dist. Ct. (no. dist.) Ohio 1978, U.S. Ct. Appeals (6th cir.) 1983, U.S. Dist. Ct. (cen. and so. dists.) Calif. 1986, U.S. Ct. Appeals (9th cir.) 1986. Sole practice, Warren, Ohio, 1976-85; Santa Ana, Calif., 1985—; mem. com. on Constitutional System, Washington, 1984—. Bd. dirs. Beth Israel Temple, Warren, 1982-85, treas., 1984-85; bd. dirs. Minority Outreach, Warren, 1984-85; environ. planner Orange County Health Planning Council, Santa Ana, Calif., 1972-73. Mem. Trumbull County Bar Assn. (chmn. pub. records com. 1980-81), Orange County Bar Assn. (fed. cts. com.), Assn. Trial Lawyers Am., Calif. Trial Lawyers Assn. Lodge: B'nai B'rith (v.p. Warren 1982-84). Office: 600 W Santa Ana Blvd Suite 802 Santa Ana CA 92701

HAZELWOOD, ROBERT NICHOLS, biophysicist; b. Milw., Jan. 22, 1928; s. Clark John Adam and Katherine (Kletzsch) H.; m. Carol Weinert, Feb. 23, 1958; children: James E., Arthur A., Daniel N. AB, Haverford Coll., 1949; MS, Marquette U., 1952; PhD, U. Calif., Berkeley, 1957. Mem. staff A.D. Little, Inc., Cambridge, Mass., 1956-63; chief scientist U.S. Strike Command, MacDill AFB, Fla., 1963-66, Litton Data Systems div. Litton Corp., Van Nuys, Calif., 1967-70; prin. Ctr. for Tech. Services, Los Angeles, 1971-74; v.p. Socio-Econ. Systems, Inc., Los Angeles, 1975-78; chief scientist Global Marine Devel., Inc., Irvine, Calif., 1978-81; dir. environ. programs Internat. Tech. Corp., Torrance, Calif., 1981—; tchr. hazardous materials mgmt. U. Calif., Irvine, 1984—; mem. adv. council So. Coast Air Quality Mgmt. Dist., 1987—. Co-author: Finite Queuing Tables, 1957; contbr. articles to profl. jours.; patentee in field. Fellow NSF, 1954-55, Nat. Heart Inst., 1955-57. Fellow AAAS; mem. Air Pollution Control Assn. (bd. dirs. local sect. 1985—), Am. Chem. Soc., Soc. Risk Analysis. Republican. Home: 18861 Via Messina Irvine CA 92715 Office: Internat Tech Corp 23456 Hawthorne Blvd Torrance CA 90505

HAZEWINKEL, VAN, corp. exec.; b. Los Angeles, Oct. 2, 1943; s. Ben J. and Betty J. (Bishop) H.; B.S., Calif. State U., Long Beach, 1967; m. Linda Bennett, Sept. 11, 1965; children—Van, Karey. With Daily Indsl. Tools Inc., Costa Mesa, Calif., 1959—, v.p., 1966-78, pres., 1978—. Founding mem. bd. dirs. Greater Irvine (Calif.) Indsl. League, 1970-73. Mem. Soc. Mfg. Engrs. Office: 3197-D Airport Loop Dr Costa Mesa CA 92626

HAZLETT, JERE M., landscape architect; b. Detroit, May 5, 1928; s. John Herbert and Mary E. (Nesbitt) H.; m. Patricia Jean Burhans, Oct. 26, 1948; children: Geri, Linda, Pam, Denise. BS, degree in land drafting, Mich. State U., 1952; degree in land drafting, UCLA, 1968. Registered landscape architect. Architect Bridgers, Troller & Hazlett, Los Angeles, 1968-76; prin. Jere M. Hazlett & Assocs., Inc., Los Angeles, 1976—; part-time instr. UCLA, 1980-84. Served with U.S. Army, 1946-48. Recipient Instnl. Landscape award Am. Assn. Nurserymen, 1968, 70, 70, Cert. Merit Am. Assn. Nurserymen, 1976, Recognition award Los Angeles County Mus. Art, 1975, Landscape Industry award Calif. Landscape Contractors Assn., 1977, Western Los Angeles Beautification award Western Los Angeles Regional C. of C., 1978, Grand award Associated Landscape Contractors Am., 1979, 81, 5th Ann. Facility award U.S. Tennis Assn., 1985. Mem. Am. Soc. Landscape Architects (sec. northwest sect. 1970, vice-chmn. 1983-85), Northridge C. of C. Republican. Avocations: hiking, camping, swimming, photography, tropical fish. Home: 7701 Lubao Ave Canoga Park CA 91306 Office: 8817 Shirley Ave Northridge CA 91324

HAZLETT, ROBERT WILKENS, aero. engr.; b. Gaskill Twp., Pa., Apr. 11, 1922; s. Robert Wilkens and Elenora (Kessler) H.; B.S. in Aero. Engring., Parks Coll., St. Louis U., 1949; M.S. in Aero.-Mech. Engring., Air Force Inst. Tech., 1955, M.S. in Aerospace Engring., 1966; m. Imogene

Roberta Elbell, Aug. 16, 1941; 1 son, Robert Wilkens. Liaison engr. Curtis Wright Aircraft, Buffalo, 1941-43, McDonnell Aircraft, St. Louis, 1948-49; B-1 test engr. Rockwell Internat., Los Angeles, 1972-78; space shuttle main engine test engr. Rocketdyne, Los Angeles, 1978-79; air-launched cruise missile fuel test engr. Boeing Co., Seattle, 1979-84, sr. test conductor, Vandenburg AFB, Calif., 1984—. Served with U.S. Army, 1943-46, USAF, 1949-70. Decorated Legion of Merit, D.F.C., Silver Star, Air medal. Republican. Clubs: Sertoma, Masons, Shriners. Home: 524 Cabo San Lucas Circle Santa Maria CA 98455 Office: Boeing Co Vandenburg AFB CA 98455

HEAD, DOUGLAS ROBERT, insurance company executive; b. Troy, Ala., Apr. 21, 1947; s. Robert Hillis and Dorothy (Albracht) H.; 1 child, Tiffany Lea. BA, Creighton U., 1969; postgrad., Am. U., Washington, 1969-71. Gen. agt. D.R. Head Assocs., Madison, Wis., 1972-80; asst. v.p. Am. Health and Life Ins. Co., Balt., 1980-81; v.p. mktg. No. Life Ins. Co., Seattle, 1981—. Mem. Seattle Life Underwriters (bd. dirs. SCA chpt. CLU, chmn. 1983—), Nat. Assn. Life Underwriters. Roman Catholic. Avocations: golfing, skiing, hunting. Home: 9910 NE 119 St #102 Kirkland WA 98034 Office: No Life Ins Co PO Box 12530 Seattle WA 98111

HEAD, LAURA DEAN, psychologist, educator; b. Los Angeles, Nov. 3, 1948; d. Marvin Laurence and Helaine Dean (Springer) H.; B.A., San Francisco State Coll., 1971; M.A., U. Mich., 1974, Ph.D., 1978. Teaching asst., asst. project dir. U. Mich., Ann Arbor, 1970-73; instr. U. Calif.-Riverside, 1973-76; project dir., research scientist Urban Inst. Human Services, San Francisco, 1978-80; sr. research scientist, project dir. Far West Lab. Ednl. Research and Devel., San Francisco, 1980-81; assoc. prof.Black Studies, San Francisco State U., 1982-85, prof. black studies, 1985-86; mem. Com. on Sch. Crime and Violence, Calif. State Dept. Edn., 1981-82. Mem. com. on sch. crime and violence Dept. Edn. Calif. State, 1982-83. Chmn. Bay Area Black Child Devel. Inst., 1978-81; chmn. bd. dirs. mem. Marin City Multi-Service Ctr. Calif. 1982—. State scholar, 1966, Nat. Cath. scholar for Negroes, 1966. Mem. NAACP, Am. Psychol. Assn. (minority fellow), Assn. Black Psychologists, Children's Def. League, Nat. Black Child Devel. Inst., Soc. Research in Child Devel., Black Women's Forum, Alpha Kappa Alpha. Home: 3614 Randolph Ave Oakland CA 94602 Office: San Francisco State U Black Studies Dept 1600 Holloway Ave San Francisco CA 94132

HEADLAND, EDWIN HARVEY, naval officer, educator; b. Litchville, N.D., Nov. 15, 1911; s. Edwin Henry and Olga (Strand) H.; m. Margaret McGinnis, Feb. 12, 1942; Student U. Chgo., 1929-31; B.S., U.S. Naval Acad., 1935; postgrad. Nat. War Coll., 1945; M.B.A., U. Puget Sound, 1963, U. Wash., 1968. Commd. ensign U.S. Navy, 1935, advanced through grades to capt., 1954; comdr. ships during World War II; ret., 1961; lectr. econs. and bus. U. Puget Sound, 1963-67, U. Md. Overseas, 1968-79, Pierce Coll., Tacoma, 1980—. Decorated for combat. Republican. Episcopalian. Mem. AAUP, Psi Upsilon. Clubs: Tacoma Country, Mil. Officers, Lions, Gyro.

HEADLEE, ROLLAND DOCKERAY, association executive; b. Los Angeles, Aug. 27, 1916; s. Jesse W. and Cleora (Dockeray) H.; m. Alzora D. Burgett, May 13, 1939; 1 dau., Linda Ann (Mrs. Walter Pohl). Student, UCLA, 1939. Asst. mgr. Par Assocs., Los Angeles, 1935-43, Finance Assocs., 1946-58; financial cons., lectr. 1958-63; account exec. Walter E. Heller & Co., Los Angeles, 1963-66; exec. dir. emeritus Town Hall Calif., Los Angeles, 1966—; dir. Am. Internat. Bank, Mfrs. Assocs., R.H. Investment Corp. Mem. adv. bd., bd. dirs., Los Angeles council Boy Scouts Am. Served to 1st lt. AUS, 1943-46. Mem. Mensa, Los Angeles World Affairs Council, Newcomen Soc. Methodist. Clubs: Commonwealth of Calif, Economic of Detroit, Los Angeles Stock Exchange. Home: 8064 El Manor Ave Los Angeles CA 90045

HEALY, DANIEL FRANCIS, engineer; b. Milw., June 26, 1954; s. Daniel Francis and Ruth (Bjornstad) H.; m. Susan Winkelman, Apr. 13, 1985. B in Chemistry and Math., U. Wis., Milw., 1977, M in Chemistry, 1986. Registered profl. chem. engr. Tchr. chemistry U. Wis., Milw., 1979-82, research asst., 1982-84; supr. quality assurance Intel Corp., Santa Clara, Calif., 1984—. Grantee U. Wis.-Milw., 1982, 83; recipient Div. award Intel Corp., 1986. Mem. Soc. Photo-optical Instrumentation Engrs. Avocation: photography. Office: Intel Corp 3065 Bowers SC3-06 Santa Clara CA 95051

HEALY, JAMES BRUCE, cooking school administrator, writer; b. Paterson, N.J., Apr. 15, 1947; s. James Burn and Margaret Mercy (Patterson) H.; m. Alice Fenvessy, May 9, 1970. BA, Williams Coll., 1968; PhD, The Rockefeller U., 1973. Mem. faculty Inst. Advanced Study, Princeton, N.J., 1973-75; J.W. Gibbs instr. physics Yale U., New Haven, Conn., 1975-77, research affiliate, 1977-80; dir. Healy-Lucullus Sch. French Cooking, New Haven, 1978-80, Boulder, Colo., 1980—; cons. Claudine's, Denver, 1985—; vis. instr. Salem (Mass.) State Coll., 1984, and various culinary schs. Author: Mastering the Art of French Pastry, 1984; contbr. articles and revs. on restaurants and cooking to mags. and profl. jours. Mem. Internat. Assn. Cooking Profls. (cert.), Confederation Nationale des Patissiers, Glaciers, et Confiseurs de France. Presbyterian. Home and Office: Healy-Lucullus Sch French Cooking 840 Cypress Dr Boulder CO 80303

HEALY, WINSTON, JR., educational administrator; b. Evanston, Ill., Oct. 20, 1937; s. Winston and Margaret (Lee) H.; m. Judith Becker, June 24, 1976; children—Nathaniel, Sarah, Jason, Elisabeth. B.A., Williams Coll., 1960; M.A., U. Hawaii, 1968; Ed.D., U. Mass., 1982. Tchr. English, Punahou Sch., Honolulu, 1960-67, chmn. dept. English, 1966-67, dean adminstrn., 1967-69, secondary sch. prin., 1969—. Chmn. bd. Early Sch.; v.p., Hawaii Pub. Radio, 1978-85; mem. Joint Econ. Council; mem. exec. bd. Honolulu Community Scholarship Program. Served with Hawaii Air N.G., 1960-71. Coe fellow; Nat. Assn. Ind. Schs. fellow, 1972-73. Mem. Nat. Assn. Secondary Sch. Prins., Assn. Supervision and Curriculum Devel., Nat. Council Tchrs. English (nat. adv. bd. achievement awards), Hawaii Council Tchrs. English (past pres.). Congregationalist. Home: 45 Piper's Pali Honolulu HI 96822 Office: 1601 Punahou St Honolulu HI 96822

HEARN, CHARLES VIRGIL, clergyman, behavioral scientist; b. Westport, Ind., Sept. 4, 1930; s. Forrest V. and Emma Florence (Marsh) H.; Ph.D., Thomas A. Edison U., 1972; D.D., Trinity Hall Coll. and Sem., 1977; diploma Palm Beach Psychotherapy Tng. Center, 1976; m. Linda Elmendorf; children by previous marriage—Debra Lynn, Charles Gregory, Martin Curtis. Ordained to ministry Methodist Ch., 1958; pastor various Meth. chs., Ind., Tex., Wyo., Calif., 1958-70; interpersonal minister St. Alban's Ch. of the Way, San Francisco, 1974—; clergyman and counselor Green Oak Ranch Boys Camp, Calif., 1969-70; dir. rehab. Mary-Lind Found., Los Angeles, 1970-71; med. asst. Fireside Hosp., Santa Monica, Calif., 1971-72; dir. alcoholism program Patrician Hosp., Santa Monica, 1972-74; propr., exec. dir. Consultation & Referral, Santa Monica, 1974—. Vice chmn. Western Los Angeles Alcoholism Coalition, 1974-78; pres. bd. dirs. Trinity Hall Coll. and Sem. Served with U.S. Army, 1951-53; Korea. Decorated Bronze Star; diplomate Am. Bd. Examiners in Psychotherapy, Bd. Examiners in Pastoral Counseling. Fellow Am. Acad. Behavioral Sci., Internat. Council Sex Edn. and Parenthood of Am. U.; mem. Am. Ministerial Assn. (pres. 1981—), Nat. Assn. Alcoholism Counselors, Calif. Assn. Alcoholism Counselors, Cons. on Alcoholism for Communities, Nat. Council Family Relations, Am. Coll. Clinic Adminstrs., Assn. Labor-Mgmt. Adminstrs. Democrat. Contbr. numerous articles on psychotherapy to profl. publs. Address: 1244 11th St Suite D Santa Monica CA 90401

HEARN, JOSEPH E(DWARD), history educator; b. Albertville, Ala., Feb. 28, 1920; s. Charles Lycurcus and Della Jane (Hubbard) H.; m. Lilya Gudrun Kristjanson, Aug. 15, 1953; children—Christian Edward, Eric Charles. B.A., U. Ala.-Tuscaloosa, 1942; M.A., U. So. Calif., 1948, Ph.D., 1956. Lectr. U. So. Calif., Los Angeles, 1951-55; instr. history Los Angeles City Coll., 1955-59, asst. prof., 1959-65; assoc. prof. history San Bernardino Valley Coll., Calif., 1965-75, prof., 1975—; vis. prof. LaVerne U., Calif., 1965-77, U. Sask., Regina, Can., 1967, U. Calif.-Riverside Extension, 1967-69; Fulbright lectr. Mongu Sch., Barotseland, Zambia, 1962-63, 81. Pres. San Bernardino County Mus. Assn., Redlands, Calif., 1976—; mem. San Bernardino County Mus. Commn., 1981—. Served with U.S. Army, 1942-46; PTO. Inducted into Tchr.'s Hall of Fame, Redlands, 1981; Fulbright scholar London Sch. Econs., 1949-51. Fellow Royal Geog. Soc. (London); mem. African Studies Assn., Zool. Soc. San Diego, Los Angeles Natural History Mus., Pi Kappa Phi. Republican. Episcopalian. Club: Fortnightly (Redlands). Home: 1542 Serpentine Dr Redlands CA 92373 Office: San Bernardino Valley Coll 701 S Mt Vernon Ave San Bernardino CA 92373

HEARN, WALTER R(USSELL), biochemist, editor; b. Shreveport, La., Feb. 20, 1926; s. Bradford and Jessie (Cheesman) H.; m. June Marie Loveless, June 22, 1947 (div. 1965); children: Christine, Russell Houston; m. Virginia Ann Krauss, Feb. 19, 1966. BA, Rice U., 1948; PhD, U. Ill., 1951. Instr. Yale U. Med. Sch., New Haven, 1951-52; asst. prof. Baylor U. Coll. Med., Houston, 1952-55; assoc. prof. Iowa State U., Ames, 1955-71; vis. biologist Am. Inst. Biol. Scis., 1961-66; vis. assoc. prof. U. Calif., Berkeley, 1972-73; adj. prof. New Coll., Berkeley, Calif., 1978—. Contbg. editor Radix mag. NIH research fellow, 1968-69. Fellow Am. Sci. Affiliation (editor newsletter 1969—, cons. editor 1969—), AAAS; mem. Am. Chem. Soc. (emeritus), Phi Beta Kappa, Sigma Xi, Phi Lambda Upsilon. Evangelical. Home and Office: 762 Arlington Ave Berkeley CA 94707

HEARST, DAVID PETER, physician; b. Oxnard, Calif., Jan. 29, 1954; s. Peter Jacob and Eva Tom (Benny) H. BS in Biochemistry with honors, U. Calif., Davis, 1974; MD, UCLA, 1979. Intern U. Colo., Boulder, 1981; resident in family practice medicine U. Calif., San Francisco, 1983; physician United Health Ctrs., Orange Cove, Calif., 1984—. Mem. Am. Acad. Family Physicians, Calif. Med. Soc., Fresno-Madera Med. Soc., Amnesty Internat., Physicians Social Responsibility, Sierra Club, Greenpeace, Phi Beta Kappa. Office: United Health Ctrs 445 11th St Orange Cove CA 93646

HEARST, JOHN EUGENE, chemistry educator, researcher, consultant; b. Vienna, Austria, July 2, 1935; came to U.S., 1938; s. Alphonse Bernard and Lily (Roger) H.; m. Jean Carolyn Bankson, Aug. 30, 1958; children—David Paul, Leslie Jean. B.E., Yale U., 1957; Ph.D., Calif. Inst. Tech., 1961. Postdoctoral researcher Dartmouth Coll., Hanover, N.H., 1961-62; prof. chemistry U. Calif.-Berkeley, 1962—; cons. HRI Assocs., Inc., Emeryville, Calif., 1978—, Advanced Genetics Research Inst., Oakland, Calif., 1980—. Author: Contemporary Chemistry, 1976. Editor: General Chemistry, 1974. Recipient NSF sci. profl. devel. award, 1977-78; John Simon Guggenheim fellow, 1968-69, Miller research prof., 1970-71, European Molecular Biology Orgn. sr. fellow, 1973-74. Mem. Am. Chem. Soc., AAAS, Biophys. Soc., Am. Soc. Biol. Chemists, N.Y. Acad. Scis. Home: 101 Southampton Ave Berkeley CA 94707 Office: Dept Chemistry U Calif 430 Latimer Hall Berkeley CA 94720

HEARST, RANDOLPH APPERSON, publishing executive; b. N.Y.C., Dec. 2, 1915; s. William Randolph and Millicent (Willson) H.; m. Catherine Campbell, Jan. 12, 1938 (div. Apr. 1982); children: Catherine, Virginia, Patricia, Anne, Victoria.; m. Maria C. Scruggs, May 2, 1982 (div. Oct. 1986). Student, Harvard U., 1933-34. Asst. to editor Atlanta Georgian, 1934-38; asst. to pub. San Francisco Call-Bull., 1940-44, exec. editor, 1947-49, pub., 1950-53; asso. pub. Oakland Post-Enquirer, 1946-47; pres., dir., chief exec. officer Hearst Consol. Publs., Inc. and Hearst Pub. Co., Inc., 1961-64; pres. San Francisco Examiner, 1972—; dir. The Hearst Corp., 1965—, chmn. exec. com., 1965-73, chmn., 1973—; Dir. Hearst Found., 1945—, pres., 1972—; dir. Wm. Randolph Hearst Found., 1950—. Served as capt., Air Transport Command USAAF, 1942-45. Roman Catholic. Clubs: Piedmont Driving (Atlanta); Burlingame Country, Pacific Union. Office: The Hearst Corp 110 5th St San Francisco CA 94103 Other Address: The Hearst Corp 959 8th Ave New York NY 10019

HEARST, WILLIAM RANDOLPH, III, newspaper publisher; b. Washington, June 18, 1949; s. William Randolph and Austine (McDonnell) H.; m. Nan Peletz, Aug. 2, 1975; children—William, Adelaide. A.B., Harvard U., 1972. Reporter, asst. city editor San Francisco Examiner, 1972-76, publisher, 1984—; editor Outside Mag., 1976-78; asst. mng. editor Los Angeles Herald Examiner, 1978-80; mgr. devel. Hearst Corp., 1980-82; v.p. Hearst Cable Communications Div., 1982-84. Office: San Francisco Examiner 110 5th St San Francisco CA 94103 *

HEASLET, MICHAEL WILLIAM, podiatrist; b. Riverside, Calif., Dec. 2, 1949. BS, U. Calif., Irvine, 1972; Dr. of Podiatric Medicine, Calif. Coll. Podiatric Medicine, 1976; Masters degree, Pepperdine U., 1978. Diplomate Am. Bd. Podiatric Surgery. Practice medicine specializing in podiatry and sports medicine Irvine, 1978—. Contbr. articles to profl. jours. Fellow Am. Acad. Podiatric Sports Medicine (pres.-elect 1987, sec. 1986, disting. service award, 1980-81), Am. Coll. Foot Surgeons. Club: Sportsrunner Orange County Track. Avocation: running. Office: 33 Creek Rd Bldg 3 #380 Irvine CA 92714

HEATH, BRENT EDWARD, educator, author, consultant; b. Redlands, Calif., Aug. 24, 1953; s. Victor Edward and Dawn Ion (Youngsma) H.; m. Carol Mae Moshier, Aug. 3, 1974; 1 son, Justin Bryant. A.A. in Social Studies, Highline Community Coll., Midway, Wash., 1973; B.A. in History and Edn., Seattle Pacific U., 1975; postgrad. San Jose State U., 1977; M.A. in Secondary Edn., Calif. State U.-Northridge, 1981. Tchr. social studies and English, Christian Center Schs., Dublin, Calif., 1975-77, Los Primeros Sch., Camarillo, Calif., 1977-79; tchr. social studies and TV prodn. Cabrillo Jr. High Sch., Ventura, Calif., 1979-80; tchr. social studies, criminal law, journalism and English De Anza Jr. High, Ontario, Calif., 1980—, also chmn. dept. social studies; cons. Calif Dept. Edn. CAP Writing com., 1986—, Golden State Exam com., 1986—. Manuscript reviewer for profl. jour. Social Edn., Nat. Council for the Social Studies, 1985—; profl. speaker at local, state and regional social studies convs. Colonial Williamsburg Found. fellow, 1985-86; Taft Inst. Govt. fellow, 1977; NEH fellow, 1985. Mem. Nat. Council for Social Studies, Calif. Council for Social Studies, So. Calif. Social Sci. Assn., Baldy-Vista Social Studies Council, Calif. Assn. for Supervision and Curriculum Devel., Calif. Humanities Assn., Gideons Internat. Republican. Author: Energizing the World History Program with Practical Novel Units. Contbr. articles to profl. jours. Home: 1298 Runningcreek Ln Upland CA 91786 Office: De Anza Jr High Sch 1450 S Sultana St Ontario CA 91761

HEATH, DIANNE GAY, audiologist; b. Albany, Oreg., June 11, 1948; d. Elwood and Evelyn (Moore) H.; m. Alejandro Dominguez, Nov. 20, 1970 (div. Apr. 1981); one child, Paloma Blanca Dominguez. Student, U. Chgo., 1966-68; BA in Communicative Disorders, San Francisco State U., 1977; MS in Speech and Hearing Scis., Portland State U., 1983. Lic. audiologist, Oreg. Intern in audiology Child Devel. Rehab. Ctr., Portland, Oreg., 1981; trainee in audiology VA Med. Ctr., Portland, 1981-82; audiologist Northwest Hearing Clin., Portland, 1982—, Kaiser Permanente Med. Ctr., Portland, 1983—, Audiology Assocs., Portland, 1983—; lectr. Portland State U., 1985, 86; supr., cons. Project ARM (Portland State U.), 1984—. Co-author: (videotape series) Fluctuating Hearing Loss and the School-Aged Child, 1981-82. Mem. Am. Speech and Hearing Assn. (cert. clin. competency), Oreg. Speech and Hearing Assn., Greenpeace. Democrat. Avocations: jogging, hiking, sailing, piano playing, skiing. Home: 3211 NE 17th Ave Portland OR 97212 Office: Northwest Hearing Clinic Derek S Lipman MD 2525 NW Lovejoy Portland OR 97210

HEATH, DONALD MALONE, computer industry executive; b. Willmar, Minn., Nov. 11, 1940; s. Drew Malone and Miranda Henrietta (Denbrook) H.; m. Judith Ann Augustson, June 7, 1958; children: Jeffrey Malone, Christopher David. B in Math., U. Minn., 1963; postgrad., U. Houston, 1979. Mgr. energy br. Sperry Corp., Houston, 1962-79; v.p. ops. Tymnet, Inc., Cupertino, Calif., 1979-82; v.p. devel. and ops. Integrated Software Systems Corp., San Diego, 1982-85; pres. XtraSoft, Inc., Santa Clara, Calif., 1985—; bd. dirs. Diversified Software Systems, Inc., San Jose, Calif. Rep. precinct capt., Silver Spring, Md., 1972 pres. Wilchester West Homeowners Assn., Houston, 1979-81; bd. dirs. San Diego Master Chorale, 1984-85, also chmn. fund-raising, 1984-85. Presbyterian. Avocations: piano, guitar, golf, chess, running. Office: XtraSoft Inc 4701 Patrick Henry Dr Bldg 21 Santa Clara CA 95054

HEATH, JIM FRANK, history educator; b. Clarendon, Tex., Apr. 9, 1931; s. James Frank and Texie Hazel (Hukel) H.; m. Carole Janice Wilson, Jan. 25, 1951 (div. June 1973); children: Nancy, Ann.; m. Judith Ann Letcher, Jan. 11, 1975. BBA, U. N.Mex., 1953, MA, 1955; PhD, Stanford U., 1967. Mgr. Heath Furniture Co., Amarillo, Tex. and Albuquerque, 1957-64, also bd. dirs.; from asst. prof. to assoc. prof. Portland (Oreg.) State U., 1967-74, prof. history, 1974—, dean undergrad. studies, 1977-81, assoc. v.p., 1983-86, dean grad. studies, 1984-86. Author: John F. Kennedy and the Business Community, 1969, Decade of Disillusionment, 1975. Treas. Santa Fe Opera Guild, 1961-63; v.p. Jaycees, Albuquerque, 1962-63; pres. Bernalillo County Young Reps., Albuquerque, 1963. Served to 1st lt. USAF, 1955-57, capt. Res., 57-68. Danforth Found. Assoc., 1970—; Am. Council Learned Socs. grantee, 1973. Mem. Orgn. Am. History, Oreg. Hist. Soc., Sigma Chi (pres. alumni chpt. 1963-64). Baptist. Avocations: tennis, running. Home: 8 Britten Ct Lake Oswego OR 97035 Office: Portland State U PO Box 751 Portland OR 97207

HEATH, WILLIAM OTTO, chemical engineer; b. Portland, Oreg., July 7, 1960; s. William Floyd and Shirley Jean (Krueger) H. BS in Chem. Engring., U. Wash., 1982. Research and devel. chem. engr. Batelle, PNC, Richland, Wash., 1982-86. Contbr. articles to profl. jours.; inventor chem. processes, equipment; copywright numerous musical compositions, 1980—. Mem. Am. Inst. Chem. Engrs. Avocations: painting, writing, sports, physical fitness. Home: 1413 Putnam Richland WA 99352 Office: Battelle 300 324 Richland WA 99352

HEATLEY, THOMAS WILLIAM, therapist, consultant, neurolinguistic programmer; b. Boston, July 31, 1954; s. Thomas Henri and Elizabeth (Webster) H. BA, Boston U., 1977; MS, Emerson Coll., 1982. Cert. speech therapist, hypnotherapist and neurolinguistic programmer. Cons. Judith Wisnia Assocs., Burlington, Mass., 1983-84; cons. Valley Hosp. Med. Ctr., Van Nuys, Calif., 1984-85, dir. communication disorders, 1985; process cons. HealthWest Found., Chatsworth, Calif., 1985-86; cons. Cedars Sinai Med. Ctr., Beverly Hills, Calif., 1986—; co-dir. Los Angeles Neurolinguistic Programming Inst., 1985—, PROSPEAK, Studio City, Calif., 1986—. Mem. Am. Speech, Lang. and Hearing Assn., Soc. Neurolinguistic Programmers. Democrat. Avocations: equestrian sports, tennis. Home: 2000 N Highland Ave #1 Los Angeles CA 90068 Office: Cedars Sinai Med Ctr 8700 Beverly Blvd Beverly Hills CA 90048

HEATON, FRITZ CHARLES, publishing executive; b. Pasadena, Calif., Aug. 24, 1954; s. Charles E. and Rose J. (Hinzo) H. BA in Journalism, San Diego State U., 1977. Promotions mgr., buyers guide editor Miller Freeman Publs., San Francisco, 1980-84; circulation, promotions mgr. The Western Jour. of Medicine, San Francisco, 1984—. Contbr. articles to profl. jours. Avocations: snow skiing, tennis, travel. Office: Western Jour Medicine PO Box 7602 San Francisco CA 94120

HEBBERT, BEVERLY JONES, retired telephone company executive; b. Ottumwa, Iowa, Aug. 31, 1930; d. Chester Earl and Chloie (Davis) Jones; m. George W. Hebbert, June 22, 1952; children—Steven Paul, Randal George. Cert. Christian Edn., Open Bible Coll., 1952. With Mountain Bell, Casper, Wyo., 1949-84, mgr., 1973-84. Mem. econ. devel. ad hoc com. City of Casper, 1983-84; bd. dirs. Boys Club Am., 1977-78, Nicolayson Art Mus., 1983—; chmn. dr. United Way, Casper, 1978; mem. County Zoning and Planning Commn. Recipient Woman and Boy award Boys Club of Am., 1978; Boss of the Year Jaycees, Casper, 1976; mem. Wyo. Federated Women's Club (dist. pres. 1981-82, legis. chmn.), C. of C. (membership dir. 1985—). Republican. Baptist. Club: Active Service (Casper) (art chmn. 1983-84). Home: 5154 Alcova Rt Box 12 Casper WY 82604

HEBERT, ALVIN JOSEPH, chemist; b. Los Angeles, Sept. 15, 1932; s. Antonio and Grace Erma (Loggie) H.; children: John Scott, Cheryl Marie. AA, El Camino Coll., 1957; BS, UCLA, 1959; PhD, U. Calif., Berkeley, 1963. Fellow Lawrence-Berkeley (Calif.) Lab., 1962-64, sr. staff scientist nuclear chemistry div., 1964-77; sr. staff scientist Altus Corp., Palo Alto, Calif., 1979-80; sr. tech. writer Kaiser Electronics, San Jose, Calif., 1981-82; pres. Am. Electrosci. Industries, Valencia, Calif., 1986—; cons. U. Calif. dept. Geology and Geophysics, Berkeley, 1977, Pres. of U.S., 1976-81. Editor Microwave Systems News, EW Communications, 1981; sr. tech. writer Kaiser Electronics, 1982; contbr. articles to profl. jours.; inventor in field. Mem. nominating com. Kaiser Elem. Sch. PTA, Oakland, Calif., 1971-72; sch. rep. to Master Plan Citizen's Com., 1972-73; mem. selection com. Master Plan Area Coordinator, Oakland Pub. Schs., 1973-74. Served with U.S. Army, 1953-54. Mem. Am. Phys. Soc., Am. Chem Soc., AAAS, Yosemite Natural History Assn., Sigma Xi. Democrat. Roman Catholic. Avocations: guitar playing, composing, bike riding, backpacking, inventing.

HEBERT, BUDD HANSEL, oil and gas operator, state senator; b. Detroit, Aug. 19, 1941; s. L. Hansel and Trudy Hebert; B.Sc. with distinction, Ariz. State U., 1963, M.A., 1964; Ph.D., Ohio State U., 1972; m. Doris Ann Brackeen, Oct. 5, 1963; children—Shirley, Julia. Asst. prof. U. Cin., 1968-71; asst. prof. urban econs. Va. Commonwealth U., 1971-74; economist, project mgr. Dames & Moore, Cin., 1974-77; landman Yates Petroleum Corp., Artesia, N.Mex., 1977-80; land mgr. Marbob Energy Corp., Artesia, 1980-81; v.p. Security Nat. Bank, Roswell, N.Mex., 1981-83; ind. oil and gas operator, 1983—; state senator Dist. 33, N.Mex., 1980—; caucus chmn. state sen. Reps., N.Mex.; mem. senate fin. com.; mem. senate conservation com.; mem. interim com. on Sci. and Tech. Oversight. Active Conquistador council Boy Scouts Am., Artesia, 1977-83. NSF grantee, 1968-69. Mem. Am. Assn. Petroleum Landmen. Republican. Mem. Ch. of Christ. Club: Kiwanis.

HEBERT, RAYMOND EARL, JR., corporation executive; b. Los Angeles; s. Raymond E. and Marcella (Bente) H.; m. Karen Beth Liner, Feb. 18, 1978; children—Shelly Lin, Stac Allen. B.S., UCLA, 1959; M.B.A., U. Calif., 1963. With sales and mktg. mgmt. Armour & Co., Los Angeles and Chgo., 1961-64; mktg. dir. Hunt Wesson div. Norton Simon, 1964-67; co-founder, exec. v.p. AMR Internat., N.Y.C., 1967-78; pres. Wilshire Mktg. Corp. div. Knapp Communications Corp. (Architectural Digest, Bon Apetit and Home mags.), Los Angeles, 1978-82; pres. Hebert & Assocs. Inc., Beverly Hills, Calif., 1982—. Active Republican Nat. Com. Served to lt. USN, 1959-61. Mem. Young Presidents Assn., Jr. C. of C. (past pres.), Sigma Alpha Epsilon. Clubs: Union League (N.Y.C.); Jonathan (Los Angeles). Home: 13080 Mindanao Way #75 Marina Del Rey CA 90292 Office: 9701 Wilshire Blvd Beverly Hills CA 90212

HEBERT, YVONNE CECILIA, psychotherapist; b. Detroit, Apr. 20, 1936; d. Philip Joseph and Ruth Veronica (Ingalls) H. B.A., Calif. State U.-Los Angeles, 1971, M.A., 1975. With J. Walter Thompson, Detroit, 1954-59; office mgr., print prodn. mgr. Lewis & Assocs., Los Angeles, 1963-69; cost acct. Comprehensive Designers, Sherman Oaks, Calif., 1969-74; free-lance writer, artist, Los Angeles, 1962-77; counselor W. Los Angeles Coll., 1978-79; pvt. practice psychotherapist, marriage, family, child and rehab. areas, Long Beach, Calif., 1976—; frequent lectr. Author: Finding Peace in Pain, 1984; editor Wright Impact, 1979, Psyche, 1981-82. Mem. Assn. Christian Therapists, Nat. Rehab. Assn., Calif. Assn. Mental Health Counselors (dir. 1981-84), Calif. Assn. Marriage and Family Therapists. Roman Catholic. Office: 4182 Viking Way Suite 108 Long Beach CA 90808

HEBNER, PAUL CHESTER, oil company executive; b. Warren, Pa., Dec. 29, 1919; s. Henry G. and Mabel (Gross) H.; m. Dorothy Farrell, Feb. 16, 1943; children—Richard P., Kathleen D., Susan M., Christine L., Elizabeth A., Jeannie M. Accountant, adminstrv. asst. Altman-Coady Co., Columbus, Ohio, 1940-41; mgr. accounting, exec. adminstr. T & T Oil Co. (and asso. cos.), Los Angeles, 1954-57; with Occidental Petroleum Corp., Los Angeles, 1957—; sec.-treas. Occidental Petroleum Corp., 1958-68, v.p., sec., 1968-80, exec. v.p., sec., 1980—, dir., 1960—; officer, dir. subs. cos.; sec.-treas., dir. The Armand Hammer United World Coll. of Am. West. Mem. Los Angeles Beautiful. Served to maj. USAAF, 1942-45. L.S.B. Leakey Found. fellow. Mem. Am. Soc. Corp. Secs., Los Angeles West C. of C. Home: 12 Amber Sky Dr Rancho Palos Verdes CA 90274 Office: 10889 Wilshire Blvd Los Angeles CA 90024

HECHABARRIA, HUBERT NATHANIAL, telecommunications executive, clinical psychologist; b. Bklyn., Dec. 3, 1937; s. Hubert I. and Helen R. (Seeley) H.; m. Mary Beth Boston, Mar. 17, 1982. B.A. in Psychology, Tokyo U., 1960, M.A. in Psychology, 1963, B.S. in Bus. Adminstrn., 1967; Ph.D. in Psychology, U. So. Calif., 1970. Lic. clin. psychologist, N.Y. Communications mgr. Skaarup Chartering Corp., Greenwich, Conn., 1967-

77; data/voice cons. Berlin Cons. Germany, 1977-81; communications supr. John Fluke Mfg. Co., Everett, Wash., 1981—. Patentee clothing protector. Cons. Democratic Party, N.Y., Calif., Wash., 1967—. Served to 2nd lt. USAF, 1955-59. Mem. Am. Records Mgmt. and Adminstrs., Word Processing Assn. Northwest, Telecommunications Assn., U.S. Postal Forum, Bd. of Profl. Psychology Europe-U.S. Democrat. Roman Catholic. Home: 2 W Northern Ave #3 Phoenix AZ 85021 Office: Am Express 2423 E Lincoln Dr Phoenix AZ 85016

HECHT, CHIC, U.S. Senator; b. Cape Giradeau, Mo., Nov. 30, 1928; m. Gail Hecht; children: Lori, Leslie. B.S., Washington U., St. Louis, 1949; postgrad., Mil. Intelligence Sch., Ft. Holibird, Mo., 1951. Mem. Nev. State Senate, 1966-74, Rep. minority leader, 1968-72; mem. U.S. Senate from Nev., 1982—, mem. Banking, Housing and Urban Affairs Com., chmn. housing and urban affairs subcom.; mem. Energy and Natural Resources Com, mem. Senate Select Com. on Intelligence. Served with U.S. Army, 1951-53. Mem. Nat. Counter Intelligence Corps. (past pres.), Nat. Mil. Intelligence Assn. Address: 302 Hart Senate Office Bldg Washington DC 20510

HECHTER, MICHAEL NORMAN, sociologist; b. Los Angeles, Nov. 15, 1943; s. Oscar Milton and Gertrude (Horowitz) H.; children: Joshua, Rachel. AB, Columbia U., 1966, PhD, 1972. From asst. prof. to prof. U. Wash., Seattle, 1970-84; prof. sociology, dir. research group for instnl. analysis U. Ariz., Tucson, 1984—; vis. prof. U. Bergen, Norway, 1984. Author: Internal Colonialism, 1975, Principles of Group Solidarity, 1987; editor: The Microfoundations of Macrosociology, 1983. Mem. Am. Sociol. Assn., Internat. Sociol. Assn. Office: U Ariz Dept Sociology Tucson AZ 85721

HECKERT, PAUL ANDREW, astrophysics educator; b. Lancaster, Pa., Sept. 20, 1953; s. Paul Charles and Sara Mae (Raezer) H.; m. Susan Carolyn Nagy, May 31, 1975; children: Jessica Mae, Carina Michelle. Student, Catawba Coll., 1970-72; BA, Frostburg (Md.) State Coll, 1974; MS, U. N.M., 1977, PhD, 1983. Instr. physics and astronomy Doane Coll., Crete, Nebr., 1980-83; asst. prof. Calif. State U., San Bernardino, 1983-86, chmn. dept. physics, 1984—, assoc. prof., 1986—. Contbr. articles to profl. jours. Mem. Am. Astron. Soc. Avocations: long distance running, bicycling, camping, backpacking. Office: Calif State U Dept Physics 5500 University Pkwy San Bernardino CA 92407

HECKLER, GEORGE EARL, educator, chemist; b. Marietta, Ohio, Dec. 20, 1920; s. Charles Davis and Georgia (Hendershott) H.; m. Hilde Unterleitner, Aug. 11, 1945; children: Mary, William, Jane, John. B.A., Marietta Coll., 1947; Ph.D., U. Wis., 1952. Research chemist E.I. duPont de Nemours & Co., 1952-56; mem. faculty Idaho State U., 1956—, prof. chemistry, 1964—, chmn. dept., 1961-83. Contbr. profl. jours. Served with USAAF, 1942-45. Decorated Air medal with 4 oak leaf clusters. Mem. Am. Chem. Soc., AAAS, ACLU, AAUP (nat. council 1967-70), Phi Beta Kappa, Sigma Xi. Home: 529 S 7th Ave Pocatello ID 83201

HECKMAN, RICHARD AINSWORTH, chemical engineer; b. Phoenix, July 15, 1929; s. Hiram and Anne (Sells) A.; BS U. Calif. at Berkeley, 1950, cert. hazardous mgmt. U. Calif., Davis, 1985; m. Olive Ann Biddle, Dec. 17, 1950; children—Mark, Bruce. With radiation lab. U. Calif. at Berkeley, 1950-51; chem. engr. Calif. Research & Devel. Co., Livermore, 1951-53; assoc. div. leader Lawrence Livermore Nat. Lab., Livermore, 1953-77, project leader, 1977-78, program leader, 1978-79, energy policy analyst, 1979-83, toxic waste group staff engr., 1984-86, waste minimization project leader, 1986—. Bd. dirs. Calif. Industries for Blind, 1977-80, Here and Now Disabled Services for Tri-Valley, Inc., 1980. Registered profl. engr., Calif. Fellow Am. Inst. Chemists; mem. AAAS, Am. Acad. Environ. Engrs. (diplomate), Am. Chemistry Soc., Am. Inst. Chem. Engrs., Soc. Profl. Engrs., Water Polution Control Assn., Air Polution Control Assn., Nat. Hist. Soc., N.Y. Acad. Scis., Am. Nuclear Soc., Internat. Oceanographic Soc. Club: Island Yacht (commodore 1971) (Alameda, Calif.), Midget Ocean Racing Club (sta. 3 commodore 1982-83), U.S. Yacht Racing Union, Midget Ocean Racing Assn. No. Calif. (commodore 1972). Co-author: Nuclear Waste Management Abstracts, 1983. Patentee in field. Home: 5683 Greenridge Rd Castro Valley CA 94552 Office: PO Box 808 Livermore CA 94550

HECOX, WALTER EDWIN, economics educator; b. Denver, Sept. 23, 1942; s. Morris Brown and Elizabeth (Rogers) H.; m. Ann Elizabeth Gourlay, Dec. 26, 1970; children: Sarah, Eric. BA in Econs., Colo. Coll., 1964; MA in Econs., Syracuse U., 1967, PhD in Econs., 1969. Research economist US Aid/Pakistan, Lahore, 1968, U.S. Mil. Acad., West Point, N.Y., 1969-70; project supr. Nat. Resources Dept. State of Colo., Denver, 1979-81; adv. trade and tariffs Minister of Fin., Nairobi, Kenya, 1982-84; from asst. prof. to assoc. prof. econs. Colo. Coll., Colorado Springs, 1970-85, prof. and chmn. dept., 1985—; sr. lect. Fulbright program, Islamabad, Pakistan, 1976-77; vis. scientist Internat. Inst. for Applied Systems Analysis, Vienna, 1981; cons. Ford Found., Islamabad, 1976-77, Kenyan Minister of Fin., Nairobi, 1982, U.S. Aid/Kenya, Nairobi, 1984, U.S. Aid/Sudan, Khartoum, 1985-86. Contbr. articles to profl. jours. Served to capt. U.S. Army, 1969-70. Fulbright scholar, 1964-65, Nat. Def. Edn. Act fellow, 1965-69. Mem. Am. Econ. Assn., Western Social Sci. Assn., assn. Environ. and Resource Economists, Soc. Internat. Devel., African Studies Assn. Office: Colo Coll Econs Dept Colorado Springs CO 80903

HEDBERG, NATALIE LANCASTER, speech pathologist, educator; b. Riverhead, N.Y., Sept. 27, 1931; d. Carlisle Norwood and Adele Blanche (Helfer) Lancaster; m. John Viking Hedberg, Apr. 12, 1954 (div.); children: Ann Marie Wyckoff, Kristen Erica, Peter Viking. BS, Syracuse U., 1952; MA, Columbia U., 1960; PhD, Northwestern U., 1971. Speech hearing therapist Children's Rehab. Ctr., Rutland, Vt., 1952-53, Cerebral Palsy Assn., Roosevelt, N.Y., 1953-55, St. Francis Hosp., Poughkeepsie, N.Y., 1956-59; asst. prof. SUNY, New Paltz, 1963-68, DePaul U., Chgo., 1970-71; prof. communicative disorders and speech sci. U. Colo., Boulder, 1971—, chmn. dept., 1987—. Contbr. articles to profl. jours. Grantee U.S. Office of Edn., 1978-80. Mem. Am. Speech-Lang.-Hearing Assn. (cert.), Colo. Speech-Lang.-Hearing Assn., Orton Dyslexia Soc. Democrat. Avocations: photography, skiing, tennis. Home: 943 Spruce St Boulder CO 80302 Office: U Colo Box 409 Boulder CO 80309

HEDDEN, KENNETH FORSYTHE, chemical engineer; b. Glendale, Calif., Aug. 13, 1941; s. Marion William and Pauline (Forsythe) H.; m. Ann Ellen Young, Jan. 26, 1963; children: Randolph, Stephen, William. BS, U. Calif., Berkeley, 1963; PhD, U. Calif., Davis, 1968; M in Pub. Adminstrn., U. Ga., 1980. Registered profl. engr., sanitarian, specialist microbiologist. Research fellow Tufts U. Med. Sch., Boston, 1968-70; research assoc. Purdue U., Lafayette, Ind., 1970-72; lab. supr. Anheuser-Busch, Inc., Lafayette, 1972-75; sanitary engr. U.S. Army Environ. Hygiene Agy., Aberdeen (Md.) Proving Ground, 1975-78, EPA, Athens, Ga., 1978-83; chem. engr. Environ. Monitoring Systems Lab. EPA, Las Vegas, Nev., 1983—. Contbr. articles to profl. jours. Mem. Air Pollution Control Assn., Conf. Fed. Environ. Engrs., Soc. Indsl. Microbiology, Sigma Xi, Alpha Chi Sigma. Republican. Baptist. Avocations: gardening, bowling, stamp collecting. Home: 1855 Quarley Pl Henderson NV 89015 Office: EPA Environ Monitoring Systems Lab PO Box 15027 Las Vegas NV 89114

HEDGCOTH, VIRGLE LELAND, electronics company executive; b. Upland, Calif., Feb. 1, 1947; s. Virgle and Jessie (Kongailis) H.; m. Susan Ann Alexander, June 26, 1982. BS, UCLA, 1969. Process engr. Northrop Corp., Hawthorne, Calif., 1969-71; staff scientist Telic Corp., Santa Monica, Calif., 1971-76; dir. research Identicator Corp., Santa Monica, 1976-78, cons., 1978—; engring. mgr. Micromask, Azusa, Calif., 1978-83; founder, v.p. ops. Cyberdisk, Anaheim, Calif., 1983—, also bd. dirs., 1983—; cons. Statek, Inc., Orange, Calif., 1985—. Patentee in field. Potlatch Forests scholar Potlatch Corp., 1964-69. Mem. Am. Phys. Soc., Am. Vacuum Soc., Am. Electronics Assn. Home: 1524 Hacienda Pl Pomona CA 91768 Office: Cyberdisk Inc 1531 S Sinclair St Anaheim CA 92806

HEDGES, CARL DEVON, inventor, mfr.; b. Rochester, Ind., Sept. 2, 1924; s. Samuel Pope and Cora Myrtle (Wood) H.; grad. King Coll., 1983; m. Margery Eileen Corliss, Aug. 15, 1953; children—Karl Eugene, Karen Eileen. Insp., trainee U.S. Border Patrol, Rochester, N.Y., 1950-53; woodworker, designer Klok Inst., Grand Rapids, Mich., 1954-57; research dir. KARLEEN Enterprises, 1964-67; research and devel. plastic mktg. mgmt., 1967-70; new product developer, corp. and patent and invention cons., 1970-74; pres., gen. mgr. World-Wide Meml., Inc., Pueblo, Colo., 1974—, maj. stockholder, new product devel. mgr. successor firm World Wide Industries, Inc., 1980—. Inventor and holder 30 patents in field. First aid instr. ARC, 1941-73, recipient 10,000 Hr. Vol. Service award, 1965; merit badge counselor Boy Scouts Am. Served with AUS, 1943-46; PTO. Recipient Internat. Gold Medal award for inventions Internat. Patent and Lic. Expn., 1967, 73. Mem. Ind. Inventors Am., Internat. Ind. Inventors, Am. Plastics and Fiberglass Research and Tech. Assn., DAV (past comdr., life mem., past Ind. state treas.), VFW (life, past comdr.). Republican. Methodist. Selected as 1st Boy Mayor in U.S., 1941. Home: 1806 E 3d St Pueblo CO 81001 Office: PO Box 322 Pueblo CO 81002

HEDIN, EDNA JENKS, musician, educator; b. Ft. Worth, Nov. 15, 1924; d. Edward Lee and Tressie (Jackson) Jenks; A.A., Central Coll. Women, Conway, Ark., 1945; B.Music, Okla. Baptist U., 1948; M.Ed., Tex. Tech. U., 1972; m. Alvin Morris Hedin, Apr. 1, 1947; children—John Alvin, Edward Morris, James Lee. Grad. asst. Central Coll. Women, Conway, 1946-47; pvt. tchr. piano, mus. dir. kindergarten Shawnee, Okla., 1948-49; dir. jr. high choir Crooked Oak Sch., Oklahoma City, 1950-51; tchr. music Norfolk Consol. Sch., Cushing, Okla., 1951-55; Artesia (N.Mex.) pub. schs., 1955—; adj. instr. N.Mex. State U., Carlsbad; organist First Bapt. Ch., 1955—; tchr. piano and organ; piano soloist and accompanist; judge pianists and ch. choirs. Mem. Nat. Guild Piano Tchrs., Nat., N.Mex., Artesia edn. assns., Internat. Reading Assn., Phi Kappa Phi, Sigma Alpha Iota, Kappa Delta Pi, Delta Kappa Gamma. Democrat. Baptist. Home: 1605 Sears St Artesia NM 88210 Office: Artesia Pub Schs 1105 W Quay St Artesia NM 88210

HEDIN, ROBERT ARNOLD, corporation executive; b. Burbank, Calif., Dec. 28, 1937; s. Ragnar Sigfred and Florence Coreene (Perry) H.; m. Ann Christine Carlsson, Nov. 3, 1968; children—Eric, Thor. B.E.E., U. So. Calif., 1960, M.E.E., 1962; Bus. Cert., UCLA, 1968. Mem. tech. staff Electronic Specialty Co., Glendale, Calif., 1962-65; mgr. systems engring. Xerox Data Systems, El Segundo, Calif., 1965-70; mgr. engring. Eaton Electronic Security, Anaheim, Calif., 1970-73; research engr. Eaton Research Ctr., Southfield, Mich., 1973-76; range ops. mgr. Dynalectron, Waimea, Kauai, Hawaii, 1977—; pres., founder Light on Industries Inc., Anaheim, 1970-73, Tropical Shirts, Kalaheo, Hawaii, 1982—; founder, mgr. Digital ID Systems, Anaheim, 1968-73; pres., dir. Electronic Message Corp., Novi, Mich., 1973-76. Patentee in field. Contbr. articles to profl. jours. Served with USNR, 1955-63. Litton Industries fellow, 1962. Mem. IEEE, UCLA Bus. Alumni Assn., Kauai Soc. Artists, Eta Kappa Nu, Sigma Nu, Tau Beta Phi. Republican. Home: PO Box 1027 Kalaheo HI 96741 Office: Dynalectron PO Box 428 Waimea HI 96796

HEDMAN, PAUL O'DELL, engineering educator; b. Murray, Utah, June 15, 1935; s. Oscar Charles and Vera Alice (Smith) H.; m. Norma Marie Godfrey, May 29, 1957; children: Zelda Ann, Carol Leigh, Damon Howard. BSME, U. Utah, 1957; PHDChemE, Brigham Young U., 1973. Registered profl. engr., Utah. Research engr. Marquardt Corp., Van Nuys, Calif., 1957-61; sr. engr. Thiokol Chem. Corp., Brigham City, Utah, 1961-67; supr. thermophysics Lockheed Propulsion Co., Redlands, Calif., 1967-69; tech. dir. energy Tetra Tech., Inc., Arlington, Va., 1973-75; sr. process design engr. Energy Research Devel. Adminstrn., Washington, 1975-77; asst. dean engring. Brigham Young U., Provo, Utah, 1977-82, prof. chem. engring., 1977—; cons. Nat. Bur. Standards, Gaithersburg, Md., Occidental Research Corp., LaVerne, Calif., Lockheed Research Corp., Palo Alto, Calif., Thiokol Chem. Corp., Brigham City, Jaycor, Inc., Del Mar, Calif., Atlantic Richfield Research Corp., Alexandria, Va., EPA Research, Triangle Park, N.C., Utah Power and Light Co., Salt Lake City. Contbr. numerous articles to profl. jours. NDEA grad. fellow Brigham Young U., 1970-73. Mem. Optical Soc. Am., Combustion Inst., Am. Flame Research Com., Sigma Xi, Phi Kappa Phi, Tau Beta Pi, Pi Tau Sigma. Republican. Mormon. Avocations: flying, photography, family and church activities. Office: Brigham Young U 350 CB Provo UT 84602

HEDRICK, BASIL CALVIN, museum director, ethnohistorian, educator; b. Lewistown, Mo., Mar. 17, 1932; s. Truman Bloice and M. LaVeta (Stice) H.; m. Anne Kehoe, Jan. 19, 1957 (div. 1979); 1 dau., Anne Lanier Hedrick Caraker; m. Susan Elizabeth Pickel, Oct. 2, 1980. A.B., Augustana Coll., Rock Island, Ill., 1956; M.A., U. Fla., 1957; Ph.D., Inter-Am. U., Saltillo, Mex., 1965; cert., U. Vienna, Strobl, Austria, 1956. Asst. prof., assoc. prof., prof. So. Ill. U., Carbondale, 1967-74, asst. dir. Univ. Mus., 1967-70, dir. Univ. Mus. and Art Galleries, 1970-77, dean internat. edn., 1972-74; asst. dir. Ill. Div. Mus., Springfield, 1977-80; prof. history U. Alaska, Fairbanks, 1980—, dir. U. Alaska Mus., 1980—, dir. inter. affairs, 1980—; Fulbright sr. lectr. Brazil, 1972; mem. nat. register adv. panel Ill., 1977-80; mem. Alaska Council on Arts, Anchorage, 1983-85; chmn. Fairbanks Hist. Preservation Commn., 1982—; mem. Alaska Land Use Council. Author: (with others) A Bibliography of Nepal, 1973, (with Carroll L. Riley) The Journey of the Vaca Party, 1974, Document Ancillary to the Vaca Journey, 1976, (with C.A. Letson) Once Was A Time, a Wery Good Time: An Inquiry into the Folklore of the Bahamas, 1975, (with J.E. Stephens) In the Days of Yesterday and in the Days of Today: An Overview of Bahamian Folkmusic, 1976, It's A Natural Fact: Obeah in the Bahamas, 1977, Contemporary Practices in Obeah in the Bahamas, 1981; compilations and collections, 1959-69; editor: (with J. Charles Kelley and Riley) The Classic Southwest: Readings in Archaeology, Ethnohistory and Ethnography, 1973, (with J. Charles Kelley and Riley) The Mesoamerican Southwest: Readings in Archaelogy, Ethnohistory and Ethnology, 1974, (with Riley) Across the Chichimec Sea, 1978, New Frontiers in the Archaeology and Ethnohistory of the Greater Southwest, 1980; Trans. of Ill. Acad. Sci., 1979-81; (with Susan Pickel-Hedrick) Ethel Washington: The Life and Times of an Eskimo Dollmaker; The Role of the Steamboat in the Founding and Development of Fairbanks, Alaska, 1986; contbr. articles to profl. jours. Chmn. Goals for Carbondale, 1972; active various local state, nat. polit. campaigns. Mem Am. Assn. Mus. (leader accreditation teams 1977—, sr. examiner); mem. Ill. Archaeol. Soc. (pres. 1973-74), Mus. Alaska, Assn. Sci. Mus. Dirs., Midwest Mus. Conf. (treas. 1977-80 merit), Phi Kappa Phi, Phi Alpha Theta, Sigma Delta Pi. Home: 1601 Central Ave Fairbanks AK 99709 Office: U Alaska Mus Fairbanks AK 99775-1200

HEDRICK, JOSEPH WATSON, JR., judge; b. Fresno, Calif., Nov. 29, 1924; s. Joseph Watson and Kathryn (Watson) H.; m. Coleena Alice Wade, June 17, 1949; children—Joseph Wade, Robert S. B.S., U. Calif.-Berkeley, 1950; LL.B., U. Calif.-San Francisco, 1952. Bar: Calif. 1953. Assoc. Rowell Lamberson & Thomas, Fresno, 1953; mcht., Fresno, 1954; atty. Fresno County Legal Services, Inc., 1967; ptnr. Lerrigo, Thuesen & Thompson, Fresno, 1971, Lerrigo, Thuesen, Walters, Nibler & Hedrick, Fresno, from 1972; judge Modesto div. Ea. Dist. Calif., U.S. Bankruptcy Ct., 1980—. Served with AUS, 1943-46. Office: PO Box 4935 Modesto CA 95352 *

HEDRICK, WALLACE EDWARD, planning and management consulting company executive; b. Malad, Idaho, Nov. 11, 1947; s. Clarence Franklin and Beth S. Hedrick; B.S., U. Nev., Reno, 1970; M.A., U. No. Colo., Greeley, 1974; m. Jerrie S. Deffenbaugh, Nov. 20, 1980; children: Ann Elizabeth, Ryan Wallace, Hallie Sue. Regional dir. No. Idaho, Idaho Planning and Community Affairs Agy., Moscow, 1970-73, assoc. chief, Boise, 1973-75; project dir. Pacific N.W. Regional Commn., Boise, 1975-76; pres. Resources N.W., Inc., Boise, 1976—, also chmn. bd. Sec.-treas. Idaho Citizens for Responsible Govt., 1978-80; trustee, chmn. Joint Sch. Dist. 2, 1985—; trustee Meridian Sch. Bd.; bd. dirs. Nat. Vandal Boosters, Inc. Served with USAR, 1971. Mem. Am. Planning Assn. Democrat. Home: 9413 Knottingham St Boise ID 83704 Office: Resources NW 537 W Bannock Suite 205 Boise ID 83702

HEDSTROM, KENNETH GERALD, insurance company executive; b. Spokane, Wash., Oct. 27, 1939; s. Elof Gerald Hedstrom and Audrey Ellen (Cox) Crawford; m. Sandra Elaine Vandersluys, Oct. 17, 1964; children: Kelli Anne, Kristina Suzanne. Grad. high sch., Spokane, 1957. Collection mgr. Pacific Fin., Spokane, 1960-63; credit mgr. Sears, Medford, Oreg., 1963-76; field underwriter Mony Fin. Services, Medford, Oreg., 1976—. Bd. dirs. Consumer Credit Counseling Service, Medford, 1984, 1st Ch. of the Nazarene, Medford, 1986, Blossom Hill Child Devel. Ctr., Medford, 1986. Served with USCG, 1958-60. Recipient Mony Top Club award Mony Fin. Services, 1986. Mem. Rogue Valley Life Underwriters (pres. 1984-86), Jackson County C. of C., Oreg. Life Underwriters (bd. dirs. 1980-86), Nat. Assn. Life Underwriters (Nat. Sales Achievement award 1978-86, Nat. Quality award 1978-86), Million Dollar Round Table (1984-87). Republican. Home: 1445 N Keeneway Dr Medford OR 97504 Office: Mony Fin Services 1175 E Main Suite 2F Medford OR 97504

HEEDE, BURCHARD HEINRICH, research hydrologist; b. Riga, Latvia, USSR, Dec. 3, 1918; came to U.S., 1952; s. Burchard F. and Irma P. (Fuhrmann) H.; m. Dorothea M. von Hollander, Mar. 4, 1944; children: Dorothea, Christine, Christopher. BS in Forestry, U. Gottingen, Fed. Republic Germany, 1947, MS in Forest Engring., 1949; PhD in Hydrology, Colo. State U., 1967. Research scientist Rocky Mountain Forest and Range Exptl. Sta., Ft. Collins, Colo., 1958-68; research hydrologist Rocky Mountain Forest and Range Exptl. Sta., Tempe, Ariz., 1970—; expert forest hydrology Food and Agrl. Orgn. of UN, Athens, Greece, 1968-70. Contbr. articles to profl. jours. Fellow Ariz.-Nev. Acad. Sci.; mem. Am. Geophys. Union, Sigma Xi. Home: 5629 S Marine Dr Tempe AZ 85283 Office: Ariz State U Forestry Scis Lab Tempe AZ 85287

HEEG, JOHN THOMAS, engineering educator, consultant; b. Queens, N.Y., Oct. 25, 1951; s. John Thomas and Margaret St. Clair (Honer) H.; m. Myra Ava Geringer, Oct. 17, 1976; 1 child, Lisa Danielle. BSEE, N.Y. Inst. Tech., 1975, MBA, 1980; cert. telecom, Golden Gate U. Field engr. Western Union Internat., N.Y.C., 1975-77; project leader Western Union Telegraph, Mahwah, N.J., 1977-79; sr. telecom officer Bankers Trust, N.Y.C., 1979-80; asst v.p. of internat. telecoms Security Pacific, Glendale, Calif., 1980-84; v.p. of Calif. ops. and support Security Pacific, Los Angeles, 1984-86; cons. Deloitte Haskins and Sells, Los Angeles, 1986—; prof. Golden Gate U., Los Angeles, 1981-87; lectr. UCLA, Westwood, Calif., 1985—, Nat. U., Los Angeles, 1987—. Mem. Tau Epsilon Phi (chpt. pres. 1971-73). Republican. Roman Catholic. Avocations: bicycling, programming, skiing, golf, softball. Home: 333 S. Grand Ave Newbury Park CA 90017 Office: Deloitte Haskins & Sells 330 Hope St Los Angeles CA 90004

HEENAN, TERENCE FREDERICK, communications company executive; b. Halifax, N.C., Can., Dec. 3, 1926; s. Joseph Gregory and Margaret Lilian (Cable) H.; children—Catherine Mary, Richard Gregory, Robert Michael, Martha Anne. B.Sc., St. Mary's U., Halifax, 1947; B.Eng. Elec., Tech. U. N.S., Can., 1949, Engring. degree (hon.), 1980; D.Sc. (hon.), St. Mary's U., Halifax, 1985. Chmn. adv. group Trans-Can. Tel & Tel., Halifax, 1965-67; v.p. staff ops. B.C. Telephone Co., Vancouver, Can., after 1967, v.p. ops. adminstrn., chief fin. officer, to 1977; pres. Trans-Can. Telephone System, Ottawa, Can., 1978-81; pres., chief exec. officer Microtel Ltd., Burnby, Can., 1982-83; pres., chief operating officer B.C. Tel. Co., Burnby, Can., 1983—. Vice chmn. St. Paul's Hosp., Vancouver, 1987—, bd. dirs. St. Paul's Hosp. Found.; bd. dirs. Vancouver Bd. of Trade; bus. gov. Vancouver Stock Exchange. Mem. Assn. Profl. Engrs. B.C., IEEE (sr.), Sr. Sun Yat-Sen Garden Soc. (bd. trustees). Clubs: Univ., Canadian of Vancouver, Shaughnessy Golf (Vancouver). Office: Brit Col Telephone Co, 3777 Kingsway, Burnaby, BC Canada V5H 3Z7 *

HEFFERIN, ELIZABETH AILEEN, nursing and health services researcher; b. Pottsville, Pa., Dec. 2, 1926; d. Cotesworth Morgan and Etta E. (Xander) Jackson; m. Mike George Hefferin, Aug. 29, 1959 (dec. May 1979). BS, Calif. State U., Los Angeles, 1965; MPH, UCLA, 1966, DPH, 1969. Assoc. ops. research specialist, systems sci. dept. Rand Corp., Santa Monica, Calif., 1969-70; lectr. health service adminstrn. UCLA Sch. Pub. Health, 1970-72; assoc. chair and clin. prof. Calif. State U., Fresno, 1972; assoc. chief nursing service research Wadsworth div. VA Med. Ctr., Los Angeles, 1972—; research cons. VA System Nursing Service, 1972—, nursing faculty and students nationwide, 1975—; assoc. clin. prof. UCLA Sch. Nursing, Los Angeles, 1975—, Calif. State U., Los Angeles, 1975—. Contbr. chpts. to books and articles to jours. Recipient Fed. Nursing Service award Assn. Mil. Surgeons U.S., 1978. Fellow Am. Acad. Nursing; mem. AAAS, Am. Nurses Assn., Nat. League Nursing, Am. Sociol. Assn., Am. Pub. Health Assn., Gerontol. Assn., Brit. Royal Soc. Health., Assn. Health Services Research. Home: 4455 Stansbury Ave Sherman Oaks CA 91423 Office: VA Adminstrn Med Ctr Wadsworth Div 691/W-118A Wilshire and Sawtelle Blvds Los Angeles CA 90073

HEFFERNAN, JAMES DANIEL, philosphy educator; b. Syracuse, N.Y., Aug. 6, 1940; s. James Daniel and Geraldine (Allen) H.; m. Maria Catherine Gulino, Feb. 4, 1967; 1 child, Daniel. BA in Chemistry, Fordham U., 1964, MA in Philosophy, 1967; PhD in Philosophy, U. Notre Dame, 1976. Systems engr. IBM, Syracuse, 1966-69; philosophy prof. U. of the Pacific, Stockton, Calif., 1972—. Contbr. articles to profl. jours. Mem. Am. Assn. Artificial Intelligence, Am. Philos. Assn., Philosophy of Sci. Assn. Democrat. Roman Catholic. Office: U of the Pacific Dept Philosophy Stockton CA 95211

HEFLEY, JOEL M., U.S. Congressman; b. Ardmore, Okla.; s. J. Maurice and Etta A. (Anderson) H.; B.A., Okla. Baptist U., 1957; M.S., Okla. State U., 1963; m. Lynn Christian, Aug. 25, 1962; children—Janna, Lori, Juli. Exec. dir. Community Planning and Research, Colorado Springs, Colo., 1966—; mem. Colo. Ho. of Reps., 1977-78; mem. Colo. Senate, 1979-87; mem. 100th Congress from Dist. 5, Colo., 1987— . Republican. Presbyterian. Clubs: Rotary, Colorado Springs Country. Office: US Ho of Reps Office of House Members Washington DC 20515

HEFNER, ROBERT ALAN, judge; b. Los Angeles, May 24, 1929; s. Earl C. and Igerna Nellie (Ferguson) H.; m. Elizabeth Sykes, Dec. 17, 1955; children—Coral E., Robert Alan. B.A., U. Calif., Los Angeles, 1955, LL.D., 1958. Bar: U.S. Dist. Ct. bar, So. Dist. Calif 1959, Calif. bar 1959, U.S. Supreme Ct. bar 1964. Practiced law Escondido, Calif., 1959-68, 71-74; asst. atty. gen. Saipan (Mariana Islands) Trust Terr., Pacific Islands, 1968-69; dep. atty. gen. Saipan (Mariana Islands) Trust Terr., 1969-70, atty. gen., 1970-71; assoc. justice High Ct. Trust Terr., Pacific Islands, Palau, Western Caroline Islands, Saipan, Mariana Isla, 1974-79; chief judge Commonwealth Ct., Saipan, 1979—; temp. judge Dist. Ct., Mariana Islands, High Ct., Trust Terr., Supreme Ct., Republic of Palau; instr. in real estate law and gen. law Palomar Jr. Coll., 1965-66. Pres. Escondido Republican Club, 1962-63; campaign mgr. Republican Congl. Candidate, N. San Diego County, 1972; chmn. Escondido Planning Commn., 1963-68. Served with USN, 1950-54, Korea. Recipient Man of Yr. award Jr. C. of C. of Escondido, 1963. Mem. Calif. Bar Assn., No. San Diego County Bar Assn. (pres. 1962-63), San Diego County Bar Assn. (v.p. 1963-64), Am. Judicature Soc., Trust Terr. Bar Assn., Escondido C. of C. (pres. 1963-64). Office: Courthouse Saipan CM 96950

HEGARTY, WILLIAM KEVIN, med. center exec.; b. Sask., Can., Feb. 14, 1926; came to U.S., 1951; s. William Alexander and Lila (Taylor) H.; m. Doreen Alice Symon, Sept. 8, 1951; children—Kelley, Kerry, Michael. B. Commerce, U. Man., 1949; M.H.A., Northwestern U., 1953. Exec. dir. Calif. Hosp., Los Angeles, 1966-69; v.p. Lutheran Hosp. Soc., Los Angeles, 1969-74; vice chmn. Huntington Meml. Hosp., Pasadena, Calif., 1974—; Bd. dirs. Blue Cross of So. Calif. Contbr. articles to profl. jours. Mem. Am. Hosp. Assn., Calif. Hosp. Assn. (pres. 1977, Outstanding Service award), Hosp. Council So. Calif. (pres. 1973), Assn. Am. Med. Colls. Congregationalist. Club: Rotary Internat. Home: 1745 Chelsea Rd San Marino CA 91108 Office: 100 Congress St Pasadena CA 91105

HEGLAR, RODGER, biological and forensic anthropologist, educator; b. Pine City, Wash., June 3, 1926; s. Benjamin Bacon and Doris Jane (Higgs) H.; m. Mary Natalie Schnall, Feb. 14, 1959; 1 child, Jennifer Dorothy. BA, U. Wash., 1950, MA, 1957; PhD, U. Mich., 1974. Instr. human anatomy U. Mich. Med. Sch., Ann Arbor, 1958-59; serologist, phys. anthropology lab. U. Mich., Ann Arbor, 1959-63, instr. anthropology, 1959-63; instr. anthropology So. Ill. U., Carbondale, 1963-66; prof. anthropology San Francisco State U., 1967—; asst. med. examiner, coroner, San Francisco, 1974—. Fellow Am. Assn. Phys. Anthropologists, Am. Acad. Forensic Scis., Human Biology Council, Calif. Homicide Investigations Assn., Am. Bd. Forensic Anthropology(v.p. 1980-82). Democrat. Avocations: art, oil painting, opera. Office: San Francisco State Univ Anthropology Dept 1600 Holloway Ave San Francisco CA 94132

HEGRENES, JACK RICHARD, educator; b. Fargo, N.D., Feb. 27, 1929; s. John and Ivy Anna (Jacobson) H.; B.S., U. Oreg., 1952, M.S., 1955; M.A., U. Chgo., 1960, Ph.D., 1970. Caseworker, Clackamas County Public Welfare Commn., Oregon City, Oreg., 1956-59, casework supr., 1960-62; instr. dept. psychiatry U. Oreg. Med. Sch., Portland, 1962-64, instr. Crippled Children's div., 1966-68, asst. prof., 1969-73, asso. prof. dept. public health and preventive medicine, and Crippled Children's div., 1973—; adj. asso. prof. social work Sch. Social Work, Portland State U., 1973—. La Verne Noyes scholar, U. Chgo., 1958-60; NIMH fellow, U. Chgo., 1964-66. Fellow Am. Orthopsychiat. Assn.; mem. Nat. Assn. Social Workers, Am. Public Health Assn., Soc. for Gen. Systems Research, Am. Assn. for Advancement of Behavior Therapy, Am. Assn. Marriage and Family Therapists. Lutheran. Contbr. articles to profl. jours. Home: 3101 McNary Pkwy 12 Lake Oswego OR 97035 Office: Oreg Health Scis U PO Box 574 Portland OR 97207

HEGSTROM, LEO THEODORE, state official; b. Sandstone, Minn., Jan. 17, 1928; s. Theodore S. and Lulu E. (Olson) H.; m. Natalie J. Shelley, Dec. 30, 1949; children—Paul S., Jon A., David B., Mark E. B.A., U. Minn., 1950. Social worker Cass County, Walker, Minn., 1950-52; adminstrv. analyst Wis. Motor Vehicle Dept., Madison, 1953-56; adminstrv. asst. traffic inst. Northwestern U., Evanston, Ill., 1956-59; dep. dir. Oreg. Motor Vehicle Dept., Salem, 1959-62; asst. adminstr. Oreg. Pub. Welfare Dept., Salem, 1962-79; dir. Oreg. Dept. Human Resources, Salem, 1979-86. Pres. State Welfare Fin. Officers, 1967-68. Recipient Disting. Service to State Govt. award Nat. Govs. Assn., 1984. Mem. Salem Senators (pres.). Republican. Club: Exchange (Salem). Office: Oreg Dept Human Resources 318 Pub Service Bldg Salem OR 97310

HEIDEL, HARRY JOHN, retail executive; b. Culver City, Calif., May 5, 1933; s. Harry Peter and Violet Alma Mae (Harris) H.; B.A., U. Calif., Los Angeles, 1955; m. Jane J. Pittman, Aug. 23, 1959. Salesman, Desmond's, Los Angeles, 1953-55; mgmt. trainee Sears, Roebuck & Co., North Hollywood, Calif., 1955, 57-59, retail dept. mgr., 1959-64, mdse. control mgr., 1964-69, mdse. mgr., 1969-85, sales mgr., 1985—. Served with USNR, 1956-57. Republican. Club: Bel-Air Bay. Home: 3501 Green Vista Dr Encino CA 91436 Office: 12121 Victory Blvd North Hollywood CA 91606

HEIDER, KATHERINE TRAPP, speech pathologist; b. Hart, Mich., Aug. 6, 1956; d. Allan LaVerne and Joyce Eilleen (Ellison) Trapp; m. Jeffrey Francis Heider, Jan. 7, 1978; 1 child, Drew Gregory. BA, Mich. State U., 1978; MA, U. Mont., 1981. Speech, lang. pathologist Missoula (Mont.) Area Spl. Edn. Corp., 1980-81; office mgr. Safer Found., Davenport, Iowa, 1981-82, Albuquerque Pub. Schs., 1982-83; pvt. practic speech, lang. pathology Kalispell and Columbia Falls, Mont., 1984—; cons. Head Start, Kalispell, 1984—, handicapped students coordinator, 1986—, health adv. com., 1986—. Coordinator Assn. Retarded Citizens Hike Bike, Columbia Falls, 1984. Mem. Am. Speech Hearing Lang. Assn. (cert. clin. competence), Mont. Speech Hearing Lang. Assn., Am. Horticulture Soc., Phi Kappa Phi. Methodist. Club: Coop. Extension Homemakers (Columbia Falls). Avocations: horticulture, ceramics, fly fishing, canoeing. Home: PO Box 2334-521 2d Ave E Columbia MT 59912 Office: Head Start 6th and Main Kalispell MT 59901

HEIDT, JOHN MURRAY, banker; b. Oceanside, N.Y., Dec. 25, 1931; s. Horace and Adaline (Sohns) H.; m. Mary Ann Kerans, June 18, 1953; children: John, Ann. A.B., Stanford U., 1954; grad., Pacific Coast Banking Sch., 1965; M.B.A., U. So. Calif., 1969. With Union Bank, Los Angeles, 1959—; exec. v.p. Union Bank, 1971-75, pres., dir., from 1975, now chmn.; dir. Union Bank, Union Venture Corp. Trustee St. John's Hosp; Bd. dirs. Greater Los Angeles Visitors and Convention Bur., Cen. City Assn. Los Angeles; bd. trustees J.B. and Emily Van Nuys Charities. Served as spl. agt. OSI USAF, 1954-57. Recipient Man of Hope award City of Hope, 1978. Mem. Calif.Bankers Assn., Am. Bankers Assn., NCCJ (bd. of govs.), Assn. Res. City Bankers, Phi Gamma Delta. Clubs: Los Angeles Country (Los Angeles), California (Los Angeles); Vintage (Palm Springs, Calif.). Office: Union Bank PO Box 3100 Term Annex Los Angeles CA 90051

HEIDT, RAYMOND JOSEPH, insurance company executive; b. Bismarck, N.D., Feb. 28, 1933; s. Stephen Ralph and Elizabeth Ann (Hirschkorn) H.; B.A., Calif. State U., San Jose, 1963, M.A., 1968; Ph.D., U. Utah, 1977; m. Joyce Ann Aston, Jan. 14, 1956; children—Ruth Marie, Elizabeth Ann, Stephen Christian, Joseph Aston. Claims supr. Allstate Ins. Co., San Jose, Calif., 1963-65; claims mgr. Gen. Accident Group, San Francisco, 1965-69; owner, mgr. Ray Heidt & Assos., Logan, Utah, 1969-76; v.p. claims Utah Home Fire Ins. Co., Salt Lake City, 1976—; with Utah State U., 1970-76; dir. Inst. for Study of Pacifism and Militarism; mem. Benton County Parks and Recreation Bd., 1987—. Active, Republican Party. Served with U.S. Army, 1952-57. Decorated Bronze Star. Mem. Utah Claims Assn. (pres. 1977-78). Mormon. Clubs: Lions, Am. Legion. Home: 126 W 21st Ave Kennewich WA 99336

HEIECK, PAUL JAY, wholesale distbg. co. exec.; b. San Francisco, Aug. 6, 1937; s. Erwin N. and Ann C. (Retchless) H.; student Golden Gate Coll., 1958; m. Kathleen Pawela, Oct. 14, 1967; children—Valerie, Yvonne, Elizabeth, Krista, Justin. Sales rep. Heieck & Moran, San Francisco, 1958-63, sec.-treas., 1963-69, Heieck Supply, San Francisco, 1969-76, pres. 1976—; pres., dir. Eureka Supply, Inc., Eureka, Calif.; 1st v.p., dir. San Francisco Bd. Trade, 1978-82. Dir., San Francisco Boys Club, 1972—. Served with U.S. Army, 1955-57. Mem. Nat. Assn. Wholesalers, Am. Supply Assn. (dir. 1984—, v.p. 1987—), No. Calif. Supplier's Assn. (pres. 81-83, dir. 1981-85). Republican. Episcopalian. Clubs: Rotary, San Mateo County Mounted Posse, Sharon Heights Country, Ingomar. Office: Heieck Supply 1111 Connecticut St San Francisco CA 94107

HEILBRON, GAIL, artistic director, choreographer, dancer; b. N.Y.C., May 8, 1951; d. Warren and Jane (Bossak) H.; m. Edgar Samuel Steinitz, Sept. 4, 1977; children: Lauren Alissa and Erica Beth (twins). BA magna cum laude, Case Western Res. U., 1973, MFA in Dance and Theatre, 1974, MA, 1975. Assoc. prof. Western Mich. U., Kalamazoo, 1976; freelance instr., dancer, choreographer various locations, 1976-78; artistic dir. Co-Motion Dance, Seattle, 1978—; instr. dance U. Wash., Seattle, 1982-85, Cornish Inst., Seattle, 1985—; artist in residence Wash. State Arts Commn., 1978—; artist in schs. NEA, Boston and Seattle, 1978-80. Choreographer (dances) On the Edge, 1979, Poem, 1982, Intersections, 1984, With the Zephyrs, 1985. Mem. Northwest Dance Coalition (bd. dirs.). Home: 3905 Burke N Seattle WA 98103 Office: Co-Motion Dance PO Box 20025 Seattle WA 98102

HEIM, WERNER G(EORGE), biology educator; b. Muhlheim Ruhr, Germany, Apr. 7, 1929; came to U.S., 1940, nturalized, 1946; s. Fred and Recha (Hirsch) H.; m. Julie I. Blumenthal, June 25, 1961; children: Susan L., David L.; m. 2d, Suzanne M. Levine, June 24, 1973; children: Elise B. Ginsburg, Lynn A. Ginsburg. B.A. in Zoology, UCLA, 1950, M.A. in Zoology, 1952, Ph.D. in Zoology, 1954. Instr. Brown U., Providence, 1956-57; asst. prof. biology Wayne State U., Detroit, 1957-63, assoc. prof. biology, 1963-67, vice chmn. biology dept., 1961-62, planning coordinator biology bldg. program, 1964-67; mem. faculty Colo. Coll., Colorado Springs, 1967—, prof. biology, 1967—, chmn. biology dept., 1971-76, 87—; prof. biophysics and genetics dept. U. Colo. Sch. Medicine, 1978, 86; cooperating geneticist regional genetic counseling program U. Colo. Health Scis. Ctr., Denver, 1978—. Del., Republican State Conv., Denver, 1982, 84, 86. USPHS-Nat. Cancer Inst. fellow, 1952-54; NIH grantee, 1958-67, NSF grantee, 1963-70, Am. Cancer Soc. grantee, 1963-65, Colo. Coll. grantee, 1979-83, Fellow AAAS; mem. Am. Soc. Zoologists, Soc. Devel. Biology, Internat. Soc. Devel. Biologists, Colo.-Wyo. Acad. Sci. (v.p. 1968-69), Nat. Soc. Genetic Counselors (assoc. mem.), Am. Soc. Human Genetics, Sigma Xi. Contbr. book revs., sci. articles to profl. publs. Office: Colo Coll Biology Dept Colorado Springs CO 80903

HEIN, ROBERT ELDOR, research institute administrator; b. Portland, Oreg., Oct. 31, 1943; s. Eldor William and Beulah Gertrude (Billeter) H.; m. Bernice Alfreda Naessens, June 19, 1965; 1 child, Trent Robert. BSEE, U. Colo., 1966. Registered profl. engr., photographer. Design engr. Woodward Gov., Ft. Collins, Colo., 1970-71; dir. design engring. Coors Container Co. div. Coors Corp., Golden, Colo., 1971-81; mgr. advanced tech. Martin Marietta Corp., Denver, 1981-85; dir. research support Solar Energy Research Inst., Golden, 1985—. Mem. adv. bd. Red Rock Community Coll., Denver, 1976-80; bd. mgrs. N.W. YMCA, Arvada, Colo., 1978-81. Served to Capt. USAF, 1966-70, Vietnam. Mem. IEEE (pres. IAS-GLASS com. 1982), Profl. Photographers Am., Denver Apple Users Group (pres. 1984-85). Lodge: Elks. Avocations: photography, microcomputers, communications, swimming. Home: 11735 W 72d Pl Arvada CO 80005-3204 Office: Solar Energy Research Inst 1617 Cole Blvd Golden CO 80401-3393

HEINDL, CLIFFORD JOSEPH, physicist; b. Chgo., Feb. 4, 1926; s. Anton Thomas and Louise (Fiala) H. B.S., Northwestern U., 1947, M.S., 1948; A.M., Columbia U., 1950, Ph.D., 1959. Sr. physicist Bendix Aviation Corp., Detroit, 1953-54; orsort student Oak Ridge Nat. Lab., 1954-55; asst. sect. chief Babcock & Wilcox Co., Lynchburg, Va., 1956-58; research group supr. Jet Propulsion Lab., Pasadena, Calif., 1959-65, mgr. research and space sci., 1965—. Served with AUS, 1944-46. Mem. AIAA, Am. Nuclear Soc., Health Physics Soc., Planetary Soc., Am. Phys. Soc. Home: 179 Mockingbird Ln South Pasadena CA 91030 Office: 4800 Oak Grove Dr Pasadena CA 91109

HEINE, HARRY OSCAR, artist; b. Edmonton, Alta., Canada; s. Bernard and Frieda (Folke) H.; m. Mary Teresa Artus, Oct. 1, 1955; children—Caren Elizabeth, Mark David, Susan Jennifer. Student pub. schs., Edmonton. Staff artist Compensation Bd., Edmonton, 1952-62; freelance archtl. and comml. artist/designer, Edmonton, 1962-65; mng. dir. Designs of Can. Ltd., Edmonton, 1965-70; freelance artist, Brentwood Bay, B.C., Can., 1970—; lectr. Fedn. Can. Artists, 1978-86, Capilano Coll., Vancouver, B.C., 1979-86, Central Community Coll., Seattle, 1981. Numerous one-man shows including Mystic Seaport Mus. Gallery, Conn., West End Gallery, Edmonton, Alta., Hollander York Gallery, Toronto, Harrison Gallery, Vancouver, B.C., Matzke Runnings Gallery, Seattle, Collectors Gallery, Kelowna, B.C., Kirsten Gallery, Seattle, others; recent group shows Royal Soc. Marine Artists, London, 1979-86, Puget Sound Exhbn., 1980-86, Mystic Invitational, Conn., 1983-86, Wash. State Capitol Mus. Exhbn., 1983-86, Can. Soc. Marine Artists Ann. Exhbn., Vancouver, 1983-86, Victoria, B.C., 1983-86; represented in permanent collections, including Capt. Cook Mus., Eng., Govt. House, Victoria, Govt. B.C., Maritime Mus., Victoria, Nat. Maritime Mus., Eng., Rainier Bank, Seattle, Royal Bank of Can., Wash. State Arts Commn., Mystic Seaport Mus.; works include (murals) facade relief mural for Royal Can. Legion, Edmonton; soft mural Syncrude Can.; murals for towns of Vegreville, and Fort Saskatchewan, Alta., Chemainus, B.C. Recipient awards including Craftsman Press award Bellevue Art Mus., Seattle, 1979, West Coast Paper Co. award Puget Sound Exhbn., Seattle, 1980, 81, 85, Purchase award Mystic Seaport Mus., 1983, 85. Mem. Royal Soc. Marine Artists, Royal Soc. Painters in Watercolor, Fedn. Can. Artists (sr., past v.p.), N.W. Watercolor Soc., Can. Soc. Marine Artists (sr., past v.p.). Home and Studio: 7059 Brentwood Dr, Brentwood Bay, BC Canada V0S 1A0

HEINEKE, JOHN MYRON, economist, educator, consultant; b. Bloomington, Ill., Aug. 21, 1938; s. Myron E. and Geraldine (Haas) H. BS in Econs., St. Ambrose Coll., 1962; PhD in Econs., U. Iowa, 1968. Asst. prof. U. Santa Clara, Calif., 1968-71, assoc. prof., 1972-79, prof. econs., 1980—; research assoc. Stanford (Calif.) U., 1977-78; prin. J.M. Heineke and Assocs., Los Gatos, Calif., 1980—; cons. Lawrence Livermore (Calif.) Nat. Lab., 1980-83, DOE, Washington, 1982-83; various high tech. firms, Silicon Valley, Calif., 1983—. Contbr. articles to profl. jours. Grantee NSF, 1968, DOE, 1980. Mem. Econometric Soc., Am. Econ. Assn. Home: 12310 Skyline Blvd Los Gatos CA 95030 Office: U Santa Clara Santa Clara CA 95053

HEINEMAN, HEINZ, chemist, scientist; b. Berlin, Aug. 21, 1913; came to U.S., 1938; s. Felix and Edith (Boehm) H.; m. Elaine Patricia Silverman, Feb. 12, 1948; children—Susan Carol, Peter Michael. Ph.D., U. Basel, Switzerland, 1938. Sect. chief Houdry Process Corp., Marcus Hook, Pa., 1948-57; dir. chem. and engring. research M. W. Kellogg Co., N.Y.C., 1958-69; research mgr. Mobil Research and Devel. Co., Princeton, N.J., 1969-78; lectr. chem. engring., staff sr. scientist Lawrence Berkeley Lab., U. Calif.-Berkeley, 1978—; cons. Mobil Research and Devel. Co., Catalytica Assocs. Editor Catalysis Revs., 1968-85; contbr. articles to profl. jours. Mem. Adult Sch. Bd., Princeton, 1968-72, Flood Control Commn., Princeton, 1970-75, Gov.'s Council for Research, N.J., 1976-78. Mem. Am. Chem. Soc. (Indsl. and Chem. Engring award 1972), Internat. Congress Catalysis (pres. 1960-64), Nat. Acad. Engring., Catalysis Soc. N.Am. (E. J. Houdry award 1974), Am. Inst. Chem. Engring. (Disting. Lectr. award), Spanish Acad. Sci. (hon.), Catalysis Club Phila. Avocations: music; photography. Home: 1588 Campus Dr Berkeley CA 94708 Office: Lawrence Berkeley Lab U Calif Berkeley CA 94720

HEINER, LAWRENCE E., mineral company executive; b. Grand Junction, Colo., Aug. 24, 1938; s. Larry R. and Lola T. (Hall) H.; m. Virginia E. Doyle, Aug. 29, 1959; children—L. Timothy, Lawrence A. B.S. in Mining Engring., U. Alaska, 1961, M.S. in Mineral Preparation Engring., 1966. Registered profl. engr., Alaska, profl. land surveyor, Alaska. Assoc. prof. U. Alaska, Fairbanks, 1964-70; v.p. Resource Assocs. Alaska, Fairbanks, 1970-79, pres., 1979—; pres. NERCO Minerals Co., Fairbanks, 1982—; v.p. NERCO, Inc., Portland, Oreg., 1982-86; pres. NERCO Oil & Gas Inc., 1986—. Contbr. articles to profl. jours. Mem. State of Alaska Bd. Engring. and Archtl. Examiners, Fairbanks, 1979, Fairbanks Council Econ. Devel., 1984. Named Outstanding Mining Grad., U. Alaska, 1961; Outstanding Alumnus U. Alaska Sch. Mining Engring., 1984; Outstanding Businessman of Yr., U. Alaska Sch. Bus., 1984. Mem. AIME, Am. Mining Congress (bd. govs. western region 1985—, chmn. western div. 1986—). Office: NERCO Minerals Co 122 First Ave Fairbanks AK 99701

HEINER, RONALD ASHER, economics educator; b. Salt Lake City, Nov. 27, 1950; s. Ralph Cash and Mona Ada (Asher) H.; m. Marilyn Davis, Dec. 27, 1974; children: Jessica, Cameron, Laura, Daniel, Michael, James B. PhD in Econs., UCLA, 1975. Asst. prof. econs. Brigham Young U., Provo, Utah, 1975-77, assoc. prof., 1977-83, prof., 1984—; vis. prof. UCLA, 1982-83; cons. Utah Energy Council, 1979—, Battelle Nat. Labs.; reviewer NSF. Referee Am. Econ. Rev., Econometrica, Jour. Econ. Theory, Econ. Inquiry, Jur. Polit. Economy, Jour. Econ. Behavior and Orgn., Quarterly Jour. Econs., Psychol. Rev.; contbr. articles to profl./scholarly jours. Recipient Elliot Jones award Western Econ. Assn., 1974. Mem. Am. Econ. Assn., Econometric Soc., Inst. Advanced Study, Phi Beta Kappa, Sigma Xi. Mormon. Avocations: golf, hiking. Home: 1054 E Dover Dr Provo UT 84604 Office: Brigham Young U Dept Econs Provo UT 84602

HEINEY, ROBERT CHARLES, social worker; b. Baraboo, Wis., Jan. 5, 1949; s. Orville Rueben and Berniece Vivian (Walker) H.; m. Kay Ann Alvey, June 3, 1972; children: Brett, Shane, Joshua. BS, U. Wis., Stevens Point, 1974; postgrad., Portland State U., 1985—. Worker youth outreach program YMCA, Portland, Oreg., 1975-76; caseworker Indochinese refugee program Children Services div. Dept. Human Resources, Portland, Oreg., 1976-77, case worker, 1978-83, family therapist, 1983—; cons. Portland Pub. Sch., 1985; cons. adv. com. S.E. Youth Service Ctr., Portland, 1978-80. Mem. Vietnam Vets. Leadership Program, Portland, 1984-85, Vietnam Vets. Am., 1985—; participant Vietnam Vets. Against the War, Wis., 1971-75. Served with USNR, 1967-73, Vietnam. Mem. Nat. Assn. Social Workers. Democrat. Avocations: skiing, scuba diving, boating, hiking, photography. Home: 3636 SE Woodward Portland OR 97202 Office: Dept Human Resources Children Services Div 815 NE Davis Portland OR 97232

HEINLEIN, OSCAR ALLEN, former air force officer; b. Butler, Mo., Nov. 17, 1911; s. Oscar A. and Katherine (Canterbury) H.; B.S., U.S. Naval Acad., 1932; M.S., Calif. Inst. Tech., 1942; M.S. in Mech. Engring., Stanford, 1949; certificate in mining U. Alaska, 1953; grad. Air War Coll., 1953; student spl. studies U. Ariz., 1956-57, Eastern Wash. U., Clark County Community Coll., U. Nice, France; D.D., Universal Sem., 1970; m. Catharine Anna Bangert, May 1, 1933 (div. Apr. 1937); 1 dau., Catharine Anna; m. 2d, Mary Josephine Fisher, Aug. 25, 1939 (dec. Dec. 1977); 1 son, Oscar Allen III; m. 3d, Suzanne Birke, Feb. 23, 1980; 1 son, Michael Andre Bertin. Marine engr. Atlantic Refining Co., Phila., 1934; civil engr. Annapolis Mineral Devel. Co., Calif., 1935-37; enlisted as pvt. U.S. Army, 1937, advanced through grades to col., 1944; comdr. Ladd AFB, Alaska, 1953-54, 11th Air Div., Fairbanks, Alaska, 1954, Air Force Logistics Command Support Group, Vandenberg AFB, Calif., 1960-65, prof. air sci. U. Ariz., Tucson, 1955-58; insp. Gen. Mobile Air Materiel Area, Ala., 1958-60; ret. 1965; now cons.; pres. O.A. Heinlein Merc. Co., Butler, Mo., 1934—; vis. prof. U. Nev., Reno; dep. dir. civil def. Boulder City, Nev., 1967; dir., sec. Boulder Dam Fed. Credit Union, 1973-79; mem. Boulder City Police Adv. Com., 1976; ordained minister Bapt. Ch., 1976. Active Boy Scouts Am. Mem. Clark County (Nev.) Republican Central Com., 1966, Exec. com., 1970; mem. Rep. Central Com., 1966; Rep. candidate Nev. Assembly, 1972; mem. Boulder City Charter Commn. Mem. community coll. adv. bd. U. Nev., 1970. Served with USN, 1928-32; to 2d lt. USMC, 1932-34. Decorated Legion of Merit, Air medal, Army, Navy and Air Force commendation medals. Mem. Inst. Aero. Scis., Am. Meteorol. Soc., Nat. Research Assn., Am. Radio Relay League, SAR, Am. Polar Soc., VFW, Daedalians, Mensa, So. Nev. Amateur Radio Club, Inst. Amateur Radio, Quarter Century Wireless Assn., Ret. Officers Assn., Air Force Assn., Nat. Rifle Assn. (life), Armed Forces Communications and Electronics Assn., USS Nevada Assn., CAP, Am. Legion, Am. Assn. Ret. Persons, West Coast Amateur Radio Service, Soc. Wireless Pioneers. Mason, Nev. Rifle and Pistol Assn. (bd. dirs.), Vet. Wireless Operator's Assn. Clubs: MM (San Diego); Intertel (Ft. Wayne, Indiana); Missile Amateur Radio (pres. 1961-65 Vandenberg AFB); Explorers (N.Y.C.); Arctic Circle Prospectors', High Jumpers (Fairbanks, Alaska); Boulder City Gem and Mineral; Stearman Alumnus; Marines Memorial (San Francisco). Author: Big Bend County, 1953. Inventor. Home: 107 Wyoming St Boulder City NV 89005

HEINRICH, AARON D., public relations executive; b. Scottsbluff, Nebr., Aug. 2, 1957; s. Arden Elwood and Elnora June (Frank) H.; m. Lisa Joan Vetter, Mar. 22, 1986. BA in Broadcast Journalism magna cum laude, Ariz. State U., 1982. Producer Sta. KTSP-TV, Phoenix, 1982; pub. relations dir. Dulaney Eye Clinic, Phoenix, 1983; communication dir. Barnet Ctr. Ophthalmology, Phoenix, 1983-85; pres. MPR Specialists in Med. Communication, Scottsdale, Ariz., 1985—; assoc. cons. HSM, Scottsdale, 1985—. Contbr. articles to profl. jours. Faculty Ariz. Cancer Soc. vol. devel., Phoenix, 1984-86; participant Phoenix Town Hall, 1984-85; reader Sun Sounds Radio for Blind, Phoenix, 1980-82. Mem. Am. Med. Writers Assn., Ariz. Soc. Hosp. Mktg. and Pub. Relations. Club: Ariz. Outdoor (Tempe, v.p. 1981); Phoenix Press. Avocations: writing, snow skiing, backpacking, golf, bicycling. Office: MPR Specialists in Med Communication PO Box 8747 Scottsdale AZ 85252

HEINRICH, JOHN WILLIAM, JR., finance company executive; b. Oakland, Calif., Oct. 19, 1943; s. John William and Ernestine (Loehwing) H.; m. Cynthia Gray, July 25, 1970; children: John William III, David Wells. BA, Antioch Coll.; MBA, Wharton Sch. Fin. Supr. diversified ops. fin. analysis Ford Motor Credit, Dearborn, Mich., 1968-69, 72-78; v.p. John Heinrich Co., Sparks, Nev., 1978-83, pres., 1983-86; pres. JCH Assocs., Reno, 1986—. Chmn. bd. mgrs. Reno YMCA, 1985—; mem. Western Indsl. Nev., Reno, 1983—. Served to comdr. USNR, 1968—. Mem. Mfrs. Agts. Nat. Assn. Republican. Avocations: car restoration, stock market investment. Home and Office: 2835 Glenwood Ct Reno NV 89509

HEINS, MARILYN, college dean, pediatrics educator; b. Boston, Sept. 7, 1930; d. Harold and Esther (Berow) H.; m. Milton P. Lipson, 1958; children: Rachel, Jonathan. A.B., Radcliffe Coll., 1951; M.D., Columbia U., 1955. Diplomate Am. Bd. Pediatrics. Intern, N.Y. Hosp., N.Y.C., 1955-56; resident in pediatrics Babies Hosp., N.Y.C., 1956-59; asst. pediatrician Children's Hosp. Mich., Detroit, 1959-78; dir. pediatrics Detroit Receiving Hosp., 1965-71; asst., assoc. dean student affairs Wayne State U. Med. Sch., Detroit, 1971-79; assoc. dean acad. affairs U. Ariz. Med. Coll., Tucson, 1979-83, vice dean, 1983—, prof. pediatrics, 1985— . Author: Parenting, forthcoming. Mem. editorial bd. Jour. AMA, 1981—. Contbr. articles to profl. jours. Bd. dirs. Planned Parenthood So. Ariz., 1983—, 2d v.p., 1985—; mem. adv. com. Tucson Assn. Child Care, Inc., 1984—; mem. adv. bd. State Hosp., Office of Gov., 1985—. Recipient Alumni Faculty Service award Wayne State U., 1972, Recognition award, 1977, Women on the Move Achievement award YWCA Tucson, 1983. Fellow Am. Orthopsychiat. Assn., Am. Acad. Pediatrics; mem. Assn. Am. Med. Colls., Am. Hosp. Assn. (chmn. com. med. edn. 1985), Ariz. Med. Assn. (com. med. service 1986—), Soc. Health and Human Values, Women in Sci. and Engring. U. Ariz. (bd. dirs. 1979—), Exec. Women's Council Tucson, Ariz. Med. Assn. (com. on med. service 1985—), Pima County Med. Soc., Pima County Pediatric Soc., Ambulatory Pediatric Assn., AAAS, Am. Pub. Health Assn., Assn. Am. Med. Colls., Med. Soc. U.S. and Mex. Soc. Health and Human Values, Western Soc. Pediatric Research. Club: Second Tuesday (co-founder). Home: 6530 Longfellow Dr Tucson AZ 85718 Office: Univ Ariz Med Coll 1501 N Campbell Ave Tucson AZ 85724

HEINTZ, CARL MARTEN, management consultant, accountant, author; b. Pasadena, Calif., May 26, 1949; s. Carl Marten and Gloria Girten (Noblitt) H.; m. Jo Ann Fister, Dec. 20, 1975; children—Matthew, Hilary. B.S. magna cum laude, U. So. Calif., 1971, M.B.A. cum laude, 1976. C.P.A., Calif. Audit supr. Ernst & Whinney, Los Angeles, 1970-75; v.p., controller Internat. Mortgage Co., Los Angeles, 1976; pvt. practice acctg., Arcadia, Calif., 1977-80; sr. v.p. Am. Mgmt. Techs., Inc., Pasadena, 1980-81; ptnr. Heintz & Assocs., Glendale, Calif., 1981-84; v.p. SFS, Inc., 1985-86; instr. acctg. U. So. Calif.; instr. C.P.A. preparation program UCLA. Trustee San Marino Community Ch. Arthur Anderson fellow, 1971. Mem. Am. Inst. C.P.A.s, Calif. Soc. C.P.A.s, Beta Gamma Sigma, Beta Alpha Psi. Republican. Presbyterian. Author: Operational Auditing Guidebook, 1975; Building A Successful Accounting Practice, 1980, Guide to Accounting Software; Guide to Inventory Software, also articles.

HEINZ, DON J, agronomist; b. Rexburg, Idaho, Oct. 29, 1931; s. William and Berniece (Steiner) H.; m. Marsha B. Hegsted, Apr. 19, 1956; children: Jacqueline, Grant, Stephanie, Karen, Ramona, Amy. BS, Utah State U., 1958, MS, 1959; PhD, Mich State U., 1961; grad., Stanford U. Exec. Program, 1982. Assoc. plant breeder Experiment Sta. Hawaiian Sugar Planters' Assn., Aiea, 1961-66, head dept. genetics and pathology, 1966-78, asst. dir., 1977-78, v.p. and dir., 1979-85, pres., dir. experiment sta., 1986—; cons. Phillippines, Egypt, Colombia, Reunion; mem. adv. com. plants Hawaii Dept. Agr., 1970—. Contbr. articles to sci. jours. on sugarcane breeding, cytogenetics, cell and tissue culture techniques. Served with USAF, 1951-54. Mem. Internat. Soc. Sugar Cane Technologists (chmn. com. germplasm and breeding 1975-86), Am. Soc. Agrl. Cons., Crop Sci. Soc. Am., AAAS, Sigma Xi. Mormon. Home: 224 Ilihau Kailua HI 96734 Office: Hawaiian Sugar Planters' Assn 99-193 Aiea Heights Dr Aiea HI 96701

HEISER, DAVID WARREN, aquatic biologist; b. Redlands, Calif., Nov. 8, 1940; s. John Edwin and Mary Frances (Ayer) H.; m. Martha Loraine Paulson, Dec. 14, 1963; children—James D., Phillip W. A.A., San Bernardino Valley Coll., 1960; B.S., Humboldt State U., 1963, M.S., 1965. Fishery biologist Alaska Fish and Game Dept., Juneau, 1962-63; aquatic biologist Idaho Fish and Game Dept., Boise, 1965-66, Wash. Dept. Fisheries, Olympia, 1966-72, Wash. Dept. Ecology, Olympia, 1972-73; environmentalist V, Wash. State Parks and Recreation Commn., Olympia, 1973—. Designer shoreline restoration Twin Harbors, 1980. Precinct committeeman Olympia. Republican Com., 1974-76. Mem. Nat. Assn. Environ. Profls., Pacific Fisheries Biologists. Republican. Mem. Covenant Ch. Home: 804 Irving St Tumwater WA 98502 Office: Wash State Parks and Recreation Commission 7150 Cleanwater Ln Olympia WA 98504

HEISLER, CHARLES RANKIN, biochemistry educator; b. Burlington, Iowa, July 1, 1924; s. Charles Francis and Margaret Estelle (Rankin) H.; m. Barbara L. Armstrong, Oct. 27, 1956; children: Charles Kevin, David Armstrong, Jonathan Drew. BS, Monmouth Coll., 1948; PhD, U. Chgo., 1957. Research fellow U. Chgo., 1953-57; asst. prof. biochemistry Oreg. State U., Corvallis, 1957-65; assoc. prof. U. Nev., Reno, 1965-72, prof., 1972—, chmn. dept. biochemistry, 1970-74; vis. prof. pathology U. Auckland, New Zealand, 1975-76. Contbr. articles to profl. jours. Served to lt. (j.g.) USN, 1943-46. Mem. Am. Chem. Soc. (chmn. local chpt. 1983-84), Sigma Xi, Gamma Sigma Delta (pres. local chpt. 1967-68). Democrat. Presbyterian. Avocations: traveling, photography, music. Office: U Nev Dept Biochemistry Reno NV 89557

HEISS, MICHAEL HARRIS, marketing executive; b. Bklyn., Sept. 26, 1949; s. Seymour and Harriette (Levy) H.; m. Leslie A. Nathan, Oct. 25, 1981; 1 child, Daniel. BS, Ithaca Coll., 1971; MS, CUNY, Bklyn., 1973. Editor, producer Barry Farber Show, WOR, N.Y.C., 1969-70; dir. field ops.

Computer TV, Inc., N.Y.C., 1973-75; gen. mgr. Home Video, Inc., N.Y.C., 1975-78; mgr. creative services NBC-TV, N.Y.C., 1978-81; dir. market devel. Bell & Howell/Columbia Pictures Video, Los Angeles, 1981—. Author: How to Select and Use Home Video, 1984, 1986 Buyers Guide to Home Video, 1985, Complete Guide to Camcorders, 1987; equipment editor: Home Video Mag., N.Y.C., 1979-81; editor-at-large Videography Mag., 1977—; technical editor Video Times Mag., 1985; contbr. articles to CompuServe, 1984-85. Mem. Soc. Broadcast Engrs., Acad. of TV Arts and Scis., Soc. Motion Picture and TV Engrs., Nat. Acad. Video Arts and Scis., Fin. and Adminstrv. Mgrs. in Entertainment. Office: Bell & Howell/Columbia Paramount Video Services 970 W 190th St Torrance CA 90502

HEISTAND, JOSEPH THOMAS, bishop; b. Danville, Pa., Mar. 3, 1924; s. John Thomas and Alta (Hertzler) H.; B.A. in Econs., Trinity Coll., Hartford, Conn., 1948, D.D. (hon.), 1978; M.Div., Va. Theol. Sem., 1952, D.D. (hon.), 1977; m. Roberta Crieger Lush, June 1, 1951; children—Hillary Heistand Long, Andrea Deferrier, Virginia Redmon. With Internat. Harvester Co., 1948-49; ordained to ministry Episcopal Ch., 1952; rector Trinity Ch., Tyrone, Pa., 1952-55; chaplain Grier Sch., Birmingham, Pa., 1952-55; asso. rector St. Paul's Ch., Richmond, Va., 1955, rector, 1955-69; rector St. Philip's in the Hill Ch., Tucson, 1969-76; bishop coadjutor Episcopal Diocese Ariz., Phoenix, 1976-79; bishop of Ariz., 1979—. Served with AUS, 1943-45. Decorated Bronze Star with oak leaf cluster, Purple Heart; Croix de Guerre (France). Office: Box 13647 Phoenix AZ 85002

HEIT, ALLYN HAROLD, chemist; b. N.Y.C., Jan. 4, 1922; s. Louis R. and Anna (Kramer) H.; m. Estelle Granofsky, Sept. 15, 1946; children: Ronna Ellen Heit Ayscue, Anne Carol. BS, Columbia U., 1949; postgrad., Bklyn. Coll., 1950-51. Research chemist Newark Coll. of Engring., 1958-59, Ionac Chem. Co., Birmingham, N.J., 1960-70; research dir. Gamlen Chem. Co., South San Francisco, Calif., 1970-75; product mgr. Garratt-Callahan Co., Millbrae, Calif., 1975—. Contbr. articles to profl. jours.; patentee in field. Committeeman Democrats, Mt. Holly, N.J., 1964-69; pres. Temple Har Zion, Mt. Holly, 1968-70. Served with USN, 1942-45. Mem. Am. Chem Soc., N.Y. Acad. Scis., Electrochem. Soc., TAPPI. Lodge: Eagles (trustee 1974-85). Avocations: playing the piano, crossword puzzles, mil. history. Home: 1414 Oak St San Mateo CA 94402 Office: Garratt-Callahan Co 111 Rollins Rd Millbrae CA 94030

HEITMAN, HUBERT, JR., animal science educator; b. Berkeley, Calif., June 2, 1917; s. Hubert and Blanche (Peart) H.; m. Helen Margaret McCaughna, Aug. 7, 1941; children: James Hubert (dec.), William Robert. B.S., U. Calif.-Davis, 1939; A.M., U. Mo., 1940, Ph.D., 1943. Asst. instr. animal husbandry U. Mo., 1939-43; mem. faculty U. Calif. at Davis, 1946—, prof. animal sci., 1961—, chmn. dept., 1963-68, 81-82, acad. asst. to vice chancellor acad. affairs, 1971-78; livestock supt. Calif. State Fair, 1948-59; v.p. at large Nat. Collegiate Athletic Assn., 1975-77; pres. Far Western Intercollegiate Athletic Conf., 1971-72, 77-78, Golden State Conf., 1979-80. Pres. Yolo County Soc. Crippled Children, 1954-56; bd. dirs. Calif. Soc. Crippled Children and Adults, 1954-56. Served to capt., San. Corps AUS, 1943-46. Mem. AAAS, Am. Soc. Animal Sci. (pres. Western sect. 1953), Animal Behavior Soc., Internat. Soc. Biometeorologists, Calif., N.Y. acads. scis., Nutrition Soc. (Gt. Britain), Brit. Soc. Animal Prodn., Sigma Xi, Alpha Zeta, Gamma Sigma Delta, Gamma Alpha, Sigma Chi. Home: 518 Miller Dr Davis CA 95616

HEIZER, IDA ANN, real estate broker; b. Oxford, Colo., Mar. 14, 1919; d. Albert Henry and Ella (Engbrook) Ordener; m. Donald Heizer, Apr. 7, 1947; children—Robert John. Diploma, Brown's Bus. Coll., 1939; student Otero Jr. Coll., 1946-47, U. So. Colo., 1962; grad. Realtors Inst., Nat. Assn. Real Estate Bds., 1972. Cert. closer real estate, cert. residential specialist. Clk., Montgomery Ward Co., LaJunta, Colo., 1935-37; bookkeeper Colo. Bank & Trust Co., LaJunta, 1937-38; cashier/bookkeeper Fox Theatre, LaJunta, 1939-40; clk. Civil Service, LaJunta, 1940-45; stenoabstractor Deaf Smith Abstract Office, Hereford, Tex., 1948-50; sec. Otero County Agt. Office, Rocky Ford, Colo., 1953-55; real estate broker Pueblo Realty & Service Co., Inc., Colo., 1958—. Mem. Pueblo Bd. Realtors, Nat. Assn. Real Estate Appraisers, Nat. Assn. Realtors, Colo. Assn. Realtors, Women's Council Realtors, Beta Sigma Phi. Lodge: Quota Internat. Home and Office: 331 Van Buren St Pueblo CO 81004

HELBACKA, DONALD WAYNE, inventor; b. Alva, Okla., June 5, 1947; s. Rayno Helbacka. Student, Dixie Coll., 1965-67, Tacoma Community Coll., Green River Comm. Coll. Researcher, inventor Priest River, Idaho, 1981—. Inventor hydro thermal power, pinch effect ion rocket motor, micro-wave boiler, liquid-vapor solar power plant. Served with USNR, 1964-70, Vietnam. Mem. AAAS, VFW, Am. Legion, Disabled Am. Vets. Avocations: designing, constructing and flying model airplanes. Home: Rt 6 PO Box 114J Priest River ID 83856

HELD, ROYER BURNELL, economics educator; b. Hinton, Iowa, Oct. 30, 1921; s. Albert Herbert and Neva Lucille (Royer) H.; m. Edith Marie Ladue, Apr. 9, 1949; children: Royer Ladue, Marcia Lee Held Poland, Eunice Lucille Held Ockerman, Karl Eliot, Karen Ann Held Hales. BS, Iowa State U., 1947, MS, 1950, PhD, 1953. Asst. prof. land and urban econs. Mich. State U., East Lansing, 1953-54; assoc. prof. Pa. State U., State College, 1954-56; natural resource economist Resources for the Future, Washington, 1956-65; div. chief Bur. Outdoor Recreation, Dept. Interior, Washington, 1965-67; prof., head dept. recreation resources and landscape architecture Colo. State U., Ft. Collins, 1967-87, prof. emeritus, 1987—. Co-Author: The Federal Lands, 1957, Land for the Future, 1960, Soil Conservation in Perspective, 1965, Rural Land Uses and Planning, 1984. Served to 1st lt. U.S. Army, 1943-46, ETO. Mem. Nat. Recreation and Parks Assn., Am. Planning Assn., Soil Conservation Soc. Am. Democrat. Unitarian. Avocations: gardening, bird watching, reading, writing. Home: 4760 Venturi Ln Fort Collins CO 80525

HELDT, JOHN JOURDAN, reliability specialist; b. Evansville, Ind., Dec. 19, 1919; s. Carl Anton and Marcella Clara (Bosse) H.; m. Marguerite Virginia Walton, May 11, 1946; children—John Jay, Nicholas W., Rebecca F., Marguerite L., Angela H., Janet M., Marcella B. B.S.E.E., U. Evansville, 1949; M.S.E.E., So. Meth. U., 1961; Ph.D., Sussex Coll. Tech. (Eng.), 1975; PhD in Reliability Engring., Columbia Pacific U., 1986. Registered profl engr. Calif., Tex., Ind. Engr. various quality and reliability cos., 1952-84; engr. Gen. Dynamics, Ft. Worth, RCA Whirlpool, Evansville, Ind., Lockheed Co., Sunnyvale, Calif., GTE Lenkurt, San Carlos, Calif., Ampex, Sunnyvale, 1975-76, Memorex, Santa Clara, Calif., Watkins Johnson Co., San Jose, Calif.; prin. engr. quality assurance Fortune Systems Corp., Belmont, Calif., 1983—; instr. De Anza Coll., Cupertino; mem. faculty U. Phoenix, No. Calif. Learning Ctr., Columbia Pacific U., San Rafael, Calif.; expert examiner for quality engring. State Bd. Registration, Calif.; coordinator Western editorial adv. bd. Quality mag. Author: a.k.a. Sam Poisson, 1985, Controlling Quality Costs, 1986. Mem. quality assurance adv. bd. De Anza Coll., U. Phoenix. Served to 2d lt. inf. AUS, World War II, ETO; to 1st lt. C.E., 1951-52, Korea. Decorated Bronze Star; Research and Innovation grantee De Anza Coll., 1978. Fellow Am. Soc. Quality Control (E.L. Grant award 1982-83). Democrat. Lutheran. Club: Westgate Cabana (San Jose, Calif.). Patentee in field; contbr. articles to profl. jours.; developer text modules and teaching aids. Home: 2205 Riordan Dr San Jose CA 95130-2063

HELFERT, ERICH ANTON, consultant, author, educator; b. Aussig/Elbe, Sudetenland, May 29, 1931; came to U.S., 1950; s. Julius and Anna Maria (Wilde) H.; B.S., U. Nev., 1954; M.B.A. with high distinction, Harvard U., 1956, D.B.A. (Ford fellow 1956), 1958; m. Anne Langley, Jan. 1, 1983; children—Claire L., Amanda L. Newspaper reporter, corr., Neuburg, W. Ger., 1948-52; research asst. Harvard U., 1956-57; asst. prof. bus. policy San Francisco State U., 1958-59; asst. prof. fin. and control Grad. Sch. Bus. Adminstrn., Harvard U., 1959-65; internal cons., then asst. to pres., dir. corp. planning Crown Zellerbach Corp., San Francisco, 1965-78, asst. to chmn., dir. corp. planning, 1978-82, v.p. corp. planning, 1982-85; pvt. practice cons., 1985—. Exchange student fellow U.S. Inst. Internat. Edn., 1950. Mem. Assn. Corp. Growth (past pres. dir. San Francisco chpt.), Corp. Planners Assn. (past pres., dir.), Phi Kappa Phi. Roman Catholic. Clubs: Commonwealth, Commercial, Harvard Bus. Sch. No. Calif. (chmn. bd., past pres., dir.). Author: Techniques of Financial Analysis, 1963, 6th edit., 1987; Valuation, 1966; co-author: Case Book, 1963; Controllership, 1965; contbr. articles to profl. jours. Home: 611 Washington St # 2306 San Francisco CA 94111 Office: 1777 Borel Pl 508 San Mateo CA 94402

HELFERT, STEPHEN CLARK, wildlife biologist; b. Ft. Brooke, San Juan, P.R., Feb. 23, 1950; s. Peter Allard and Barbara (Blair) H.; m. Rosine Marie Mills, Aug. 19, 1976; m. 2d, Jocinda Lanferman, Aug. 7, 1979; 1 dau., Erin Blair. B.S. in Fish and Wildlife Sci., Tex. A&M U., 1976; M.S. in Biology, U. Tex.-El Paso, 1978. Field asst. Chihuahuan Desert Research Inst., Alpine, Tex., 1976; grad. research asst. Lab. Environ. Biology, U. Tex., El Paso, 1977-78; environ. specialist U.S. Dept. Interior, Bur. Reclamation, Yuma Projects Office, Ariz., 1979-80; environmentalist U.S. Army, Ft. Sam Houston, Tex., 1981-82; wildlife biologist U.S. Air Force, Environ. Planning Div., Norton AFB, Calif., 1982—; Western rep. U.S. Dept. Defense com. for nat. profl. orgn. wildlife mgrs., biologists. Author script, narrator Poisonous Plants of Ft. Sam Houston, Tex., 1981. Served with U.S. Army, 1971-74. U. Tex.-El Paso grad. scholar, 1977. Mem. Wildlife Soc., Desert Tortoise Council, Chihuahuan Desert Research Inst., Beta Beta Beta, AAUP, Wildlife Biology Club. Home: PO Box 658 Forest Falls CA 92339 Office: AFRCE-BMS/DEVE Norton AFB CA 92409

HELFORD, PAUL QUINN, cable TV executive; b. Chgo., June 27, 1947; s. Norman and Eleanor (Kwin) H.; m. Leslie Gale Weinstein, July 11, 1971; children: Ross Michael, Benjamin Keith. BA, U. Ill., 1969; MA, Northeastern Ill. U., 1977. Cert. tchr., Ill., Oreg. Tchr. John Hersey High Sch., Arlington Heights, Ill., 1969-73; freelance writer Mill Valley, Calif., 1973-75; mgr., program dir. Sta. KOZY-TV, Eugene, Oreg., 1976—, mktg., sales, and program dir. Group W Cable, 1984—. Writer, producer Paul Helford's Hollywood Oldies, 1976-81, In Rev., 1981, Live from the Fair, 1981-85, Group W Cable Minutes, 1984-85, Bad Horror and Sci. Fiction, 1985 (Award for Cable Excellence 1986), KOZY movie promotional spots 1976— (Award for Cable Excellence 1984); contbr. articles to profl. publs. Recipient CLIO award 1984, 86, Cable Mktg. Grand award, 1981, 85. Mem. Nat. Assn. Cable Programmers. Avocations: jogging, camping, biking, movies. Home: 940 Madison Eugene OR 97402 Office: Group W Cable/KOZY TV 990 Garfield Eugene OR 97402

HELGERSON, ARTHUR CLARENCE, oral surgeon; b. Green Bay, Wis., Jan. 16, 1944; s. Arthur Harold and Louise (Dorschel) H.; m. Karen Jean Schouten, June 1, 1968; children: Jason, Bradley, Jena. DDS, Marquette U., 1969. Diplomate Am. Bd. Oral Surgery. Intern then resident Michael Reese Hosp., Chgo., 1969-73, mem. teaching staff, 1973-74, mem. staff, 1974—; mem. teaching staff Ill. Masonic Hosp., Chgo., 1973-74; practice dentistry specializing in oral surgery Appleton, Wis., 1974—. Contbr. articles to profl. jours. Bd. dirs. Outagamie County Bd. Am. Cancer Soc., 1985—; mem. Appleton Sch. Dist. Sch. Bd., 1982-85. Mem. ADA, Wis. State Dental Soc., Am. Assn. Oral and Maxillofacial Surgery, Outagamie County Dental Soc. (pres. 1984-85), Condominium Assn. (pres. 1985-87). Roman Catholic. Clubs: Butte Des Roets Country (Appleton); Timber Ridge Country (Minocqua, Wis.). Avocation: coaching jr. high basketball.

HELGERT, JOSEPH PETER, advertising executive; b. Kenosha, Wis., Nov. 24, 1952; s. Merrill Edward and Eugenie Patricia (Mico) H.; m. Sharon Marie Hankwitz. BA, U. Wis., Kenosha, 1974; MA, U. Iowa, 1975; M, Am. Grad. Sch. Internat. Mgmt., 1983. Cert. bus. communicator. Instr. U. Wis., Sheboygan, 1975-78; advt. mgr. A to Z Rentall, Madison, Wis., 1979-82, Motorola, Inc., Phoenix, 1984—. Copywriter Mont. Vistas brochure, 1985 (N.Y. Art Dir. award 1985). Mem. Bus./Profl. Advt. Assn. (1st v.p. 1985-86). Avocations: music, computers, genealogy. Office: Motorola Semiconductor 3102 N 56th St Phoenix AZ 85018

HELGESON, DUANE MARCELLUS, librarian; b. Rothsay, Minn., July 2, 1930; s. Oscar Herbert and Selma Olivia (Sateren) H.; B.S., U. Minn., 1952. Librarian, Chance-Vought Co., Dallas, 1956-59, System Devel. Corp., Santa Monica, Calif., 1959-62, Lockheed Aircraft, Burbank, Calif., 1962-63, C.F. Braun Co., Alhambra, Calif., 1963-74; chief librarian Ralph M. Parsons Co., Pasadena, Calif., 1974-79; pres. Mark-Allen/Brokers-in-Info., Los Angeles, 1976-80; phys. scis. librarian Calif. Inst. Tech., Pasadena, 1980-84; corp. librarian James M. Montgomery Cons. Engrs., Pasadena, 1985—; mem. adv. bd. Los Angeles Trade Tech. Coll., 1974-79, U. So. Calif. Library Sch., 1974-79. Served with USAF, 1952-54. Mem. Spl. Libraries Assn. (chmn. nominating com. 1974). Co-editor: (with Joe Ann Clifton) Computers in Library and Information Centers, 1973. Home: 2706 Ivan Hill Terr Los Angeles CA 90039 Office: James M Montgomery Cons Engrs 250 N Madison Pasadena CA 91101

HELGESON, HAROLD C., geochemistry educator, consultant; b. Mpls., Nov. 13, 1931; s. Harold Rollin and Phoebe Dorothy (Kildahl) H.; m. Velda Fay Fennell, Mar. 20, 1956 (div. Nov. 1977); children: Christopher, Kimberley; m. Suzanne Tuxen, Aug. 30, 1978 (div. June 1982); m. Frances Beth Damon, Jan. 14, 1986. BS, Mich. State U., 1953; PhD, Harvard U., 1962. Mining and exploration geologist Anglo-Am. Corp., South Africa, Southwest Africa, Zambia, 1956-59; research asst., teaching fellow Harvard U., Cambridge, 1959-62; research chemist Shell Devel., Houston, 1962-65; from asst. to assoc. prof. Northwestern U., Evanston, Ill., 1965-70; prof. U. Calif., Berkeley, 1970—; co-chmn. Gordon Research Conf. on Inorganic Geochemistry, 1977; dir., chmn. NATO Advanced Study Inst. on Chem. Transport., 1985. Contbr. articles to profl. jours. Served to 1st lt. USAF, 1954-56. Guggenheim fellow, 1977-78. Fellow Geol. Soc. Am., Mineral. Soc. Am.; mem. Internat. Assn. Geochemistry and Cosmochemistry, Geochem. Soc. (councilor 1973-76), Am. Chem. Soc., European Assn. Geochemistry (hon. mem.). Democrat. Club: Friends and Alumni of Prediction Cen. (Berkeley) (chmn. 1970—). Avocations: skiing, deep sea fishing, sailing. Office: U Calif Dept Geology Geophysics 301 ESB Berkeley CA 94720

HELICK, EILEEN JUDGE, public relations executive; b. N.Y.C., June 28, 1930; d. William Joseph and Mary A. (Kelly) Judge; m. R. Martin Helick, Feb. 14, 1954 (div.); children—Reuben Stephen, Deborah Judge. B.A. in Journalism, Calif. State U.-Fullerton, 1977. Ptnr. Regent Graphics Services, Swissvale, Pa., 1954-70; asst. to pub. relations dir. Orange County (Calif.) Unified Sch. Dist., 1971-77; pub. relations dir. Am. Cancer Soc., Newport Beach, Calif., 1977-78; pub. relations cons., Santa Ana, Calif., 1978-79; dir. corp. communications ATV Systems, Inc., Santa Ana, 1979-86; dir. mktg. communications Data Line Service Co., Covina, Calif., 1986—. Mem. Pub. Relations Soc. Am., Sigma Delta Chi. Republican. Office: Data Line Service Co 885 S Village Oaks Dr Covina CA 91724

HELIN, JAMES DENNIS, advertising agency executive; b. Carmel, Calif., Aug. 30, 1942; s. Richard James and Helen Margaret (Noonan) H.; m. Sally Katharine Pope, July 2, 1966; children—Laurie Ann, Jennifer Katharine, Holly Margaret, Christopher James, Kathleen Patricia. B.S., San Jose State U., 1964. Mktg. asst. Diamond Internat. Co., San Francisco, 1965; product mgr. Purex Corp., Lakewood, Calif., 1966-69; sr. v.p., mgmt. supr. Doyle Dane Bernbach Co., Los Angeles, 1969-81; exec. v.p., account group dir. 1981-85; Dailey & Assocs., Los Angeles, 1981-85; mng. dir., D'Arcy Masius Benton & Bowles, Los Angeles, 1985— ; instr. 4A's Inst. Advanced Advt. Studies U. So. Calif. Served with USAR, 1964-70. Recipient Alumni of Yr. award, bus. div. San Jose State U., 1979. Mem. Am. Assn. Advt. Agys. (Gov.), Western States Assn. Advt. Agys. (bd. dirs.), Beta Gamma Sigma. Republican. Roman Catholic. Office: D'Arcy Masius Benton & Bowles 6500 Wilshire Blvd Los Angeles CA 90048

HELINSKI, DONALD RAYMOND, biologist; b. Balt., July 7, 1933; s. George L. and Marie M. (Naparstek) H.; m. Patricia G. Doherty, Mar. 4, 1962; children—Matthew T., Maureen G. B.S., U. Md., 1954; Ph.D. in Biochemistry, Western Res. U., 1960; postdoctoral fellow, Stanford U., 1960-63. Asst. prof. Princeton (N.J.) U., 1963-65; mem. faculty U. Calif., San Diego, 1965—; prof. biology U. Calif., 1970—, chmn. dept., 1979-81, dir. Ctr. for Molecular Genetics, 1985—; mem. com. guidelines for recombinant DNA research NIH, 1975-78. Author papers in field. Mem. Am. Soc. Biol. Chemistry, Am. Soc. Microbiology, AAAS, Nat. Acad. Scis., Genetics Soc. Office: U Calif 4222 Bonner Hall La Jolla CA 92093

HELLEN, MARIE EVOLINE, safety engineer; b. Burbank, Calif., July 31, 1950; d. Robert Owen and Ruth Naomi (Clark) Griffin; m. Jeffrey Hearn Hellen, July 11, 1971 (div. Oct. 1984); 1 child, Scott Alexander. BS in Health and Safety, San Diego State U., 1978. Safety dir. Sharp Meml. Hosp., San Diego, 1979-83, cons., 1985; safety engr. IVAC Corp., San Diego, 1983—. Bd. dirs. Am. Lung Assn. San Diego, 1984—, San Diego Safety Council, 1985—. Mem. Am. Soc. Safety Engrs. (pres. San Diego chpt. 1984-85), Nat. Fire Protection Assn., Am. Indsl. Hygiene Assn., Internat. Health Care Safety Assn. (cert. health care safety profl.). Democrat. Office: IVAC Corp 10300 Campus Point Dr San Diego CA 92121

HELLENTHAL, LINDA BROUGHTON, psychologist; b. Seattle, May 22, 1947; d. Ray Munroe and Margret (Ryno) Broughton; m. Marc Edwin Hellenthal, June 10, 1967; children—Kristine Tara, Megan LaRue. B.A. with honors, Whitman Coll., 1969; M.A., Boston U., 1973, Ph.D., 1977. Lic. psychologist, Alaska. Lectr., Boston U., 1973-77; clin. psychologist Bear River Community Mental Health Ctr., Logan, Utah, 1978; asst. prof. U. Alaska, Anchorage, 1978-79; clin. psychologist, Anchorage, 1980—; cons. Standing Together Against Rape, Anchorage, 1980-81; treas., co-owner Hellenthal & Assocs., Anchorage, 1978—. Recipient Boston U. Grad. Scholarship award, 1971-77. Mem. Am. Psychol. Assn., Alaska Psychol. Assn. Methodist. Club: P.E.O. Home: 2220 Vanderbilt Cr Anchorage AK 99508 Office: 608 W 4th Suite 21 Anchorage AK 99501

HELLER, RONALD IAN, lawyer; b. Cleve., Sept. 4, 1956; s. Grant L. and Audrey P. (Lecht) H.; m. Shirley Ann Stringer, Mar. 23, 1986. AB with high honors, Univ Mich., 1976, MBA, 1979, JD, 1980. Bar: Hawaii 1980, U.S. Ct. Claims 1982, U.S. Tax Ct. 1981, U.S. Ct. Appeals (9th cir.) 1981; Trust Territory of Pacific Islands 1982, Republic of Marshall Islands 1982; CPA, Hawaii. Assoc. Hoddick, Reinwald, O'Connor & Marrack, Honolulu, 1980-84; ptnr. Reinwald, O'Connor & Marrack, 1984—; adj. prof. U. Hawaii Sch. Law, 1981; bd. dirs. Hawaii Women Lawyers Found., Honolulu, 1984-86, Hawaii Performing Arts Co., Honolulu, 1984—. Actor, stage mgr. Honolulu Community Theatre, 1983—, Hawaii Performing Arts Co., Honolulu, 1982—. Mem. Am. Inst. CPA's, ABA, Hawaii State Bar Assn., Hawaii Women Lawyers, Assn. Trial Lawyers Am. Office: Reinwald O'Connor & Marrack 733 Bishop St Suite 2400 Honolulu HI 96813

HELLEWELL, NEIL BOYD, utility engineer; b. Ogden, Utah, July 29, 1953; s. Dave Martin, Jr. and Luella (Thacker) H.; m. Vicki Lyn Frisby, June 1, 1977; children—Brandon Eric, Stacy Ann, Ryan Ned. A.A.S., Weber State Coll., 1977, BS, 1979, MBA, 1983. Electronic technician, instr. Deseret Industries, Ogden, 1977-78; jr. engr. Utah Power & Light Co., Salt Lake City, 1978-80, assoc. engr., 1980-82, sr. engr., 1982-84, staff engr., supr., 1984—. Mem. Nat. Assn. Radio and Telecommunication Engrs. Republican. Mormon. Home: 2263 N 1250 W Clinton UT 84015 Office: Utah Power & Light Co 1407 W North Temple Salt Lake City UT 84111

HELLICKSON, KAZUKO SATO, contract administrator; b. Tokyo, Apr. 9, 1947; d. Jun and Misao (Kobayashi) Sato; m. Howard Adrian Hellickson, Apr. 4, 1970 (dec. Oct. 1974). BA in English Lit., Macalester Coll., 1969; BS in Consumer Sci., U. Wis., 1978. Sr. engr. in contract tech. requirements, sr. contract specialist Martin Marietta Corp., Denver, 1979-82, sr. contract specialist, 1984-86, contract adminstr., 1986—; configuration engr. Gen. Telephone and Elec., Westborough, Mass., 1982-84. Bd. dirs. Congress Park Neighbors, Denver, 1979. Mem. Nat. Def. Preparedness Assn., Nat. Contract Mgmt. Assn. (sec. 1986—), Omicron Nu. Avocations: theater, arts and crafts, world travel, sports. Office: Martin Marietta Corp PO Box 179 Denver CO 80201

HELLICKSON, MARTIN LEON, agricultural engineer, educator, consultant; b. Medora, N.D., Apr. 6, 1945; s. Leon John and Gwendolyn Hellickson; m. Beverley Ann Bryant, Aug. 8, 1970; children: Amy Rebecca, Benjamin Bryant. BS in Agrl. Engring., N.D. State U., 1968; MS in Agrl. Engring., S.D. State U., 1972; PhD in Agrl. Engring., U. Minn., 1975. Registered profl. engr., Oreg. Asst. prof. Oreg. State U., Corvallis, 1975-80, assoc. prof., 1980—; cons. Lillik, McHose & Charles, Los Angeles, 1979-80, Subterra, Newburg, Oreg., 1985-86. Contbr. articles to profl. jours. Served to 1st lt. U.S. Army, 1968-70, Vietnam. Mem. Am. Soc. Agrl. Engrs. Republican. Avocations: deer and elk hunting, trout fishing, woodworking. Home: 3120 NW Greenbriar Pl Corvallis OR 97330 Office: Oreg State U Agrl Engring Dept Corvallis OR 97331

HELLMANN, MARGARET ANN, environmental health risk consultant; b. Meriden, Conn., Mar. 18, 1947; d. Reinhard K. and Ruth P. Hellmann. BS in Biology, Baldwin-Wallace U., 1969; MA in Environ. Sci., U. Colo., Denver, 1977; PhD in Environ. Health, Colo. State U., 1985. Head technician Osborn Labs., Bklyn., 1969; sec. dept. chemistry Met. State Coll., Denver, 1970-71; lab. technician State Dept. Agriculture, Denver, 1971-74, sr. agrl. chemist, 1975-82; environ. health risk cons. R.A. Cons., Aurora, CO., 1986—. Contbr. articles to profl. jours. Mem. Am. Chem. Soc., Phi Sigma. Gamma Sigma Delta. Home: 1511 S Washington St Denver CO 80210

HELLON, MICHAEL THOMAS, tax consultant; b. Camden, N.J., June 24, 1942; s. James Bernard and Dena Louise (Blackburn) H.; BS, Ariz. State U., 1972; m. Toni L. Carson; 3 children. Ins. investigator Equifax, Phoenix, 1968-69; exec. v.p. Phoenix Met. C. of C., 1969-76; ins. co. exec. Londen Ins. Group, 1976-78; pres. Hellon and Assocs., Inc., 1978—; bd. dirs. Equity Benefit Life Ins. Co., Modern Income Life Ins. Co. of Mo., First Equity Security Life Ins. Co. Mem. Ariz. Occupational Safety and Health Adv. Council, 1972-76, mem. Speaker's Select Com. Auto Emissions, 1976; Phoenix Urban League, 1972-73, Area Manpower Planning Council, 1971-72, Phoenix Civic Plaza Dedication Com., 1972, Phoenix Air Quality Maintenance Task Force, 1976. Pres. Vis. Nurse Service, 1978-79; Rep. precinct capt., 1973—; state campaign dir. Arizonans for Reagan Com., 1980; alt. del. Rep. Nat. Conv., 1980; mem. staff Reagan-Bush Nat. Conv., 1984. campaign mgr. for various candidates, 1972-82. Bd. dirs. ATMA Tng. Found., 1981-84. Served with USAF, 1964-68. Decorated Bronze Star medal, Purple Heart. Recipient George Washington Honor medal Freedom's Found., 1964; commendation Fed. Bar Assn., 1973. Mem. U.S. C. of C. (pub. affairs com. western div. 1974-76), U.S. Dept. Commerce Exec. Res., Ariz. C. of C. Mgrs. Assn. (bd. mem. 1974-76), Tucson C. of C. Club: Trunk 'N Tusk; Catalina Soccer (bd. dirs. 1984—). Home: 5775 Camono Real Tucson AZ 85718 Office: PO Box 37123 Tucson AZ 85740

HELLYER, CONSTANCE ANNE, writer, publication manager; b. Puyallup, Wash., Apr. 22, 1937; d. David Tirrell and Constance (Hopkins) H.; m. Peter Andrew Corning, Dec. 30, 1963 (div. 1977); children: Anne Arundel, Stephanie Deak; m. Don W. Conway. BA with honors, Mills Coll., 1959. Researcher Harvard U., Cambridge, Mass., 1959-60; reporter, researcher Newsweek mag., N.Y.C., 1960-63; author's asst. Theodore H. White and others, N.Y.C., 1964-69; freelance writer, editor Colo., Calif., 1969-75; writer, editor Stanford (Calif.) U. Med. Ctr., 1975-79; communications dir. No. Calif. Cancer Program, Palo Alto, 1979-82; pubs. dir. Stanford Law Sch., Palo Alto, 1982—. Founding editor (newsletter) Insight, 1978-80, Synergy, 1980-82; editor (mag.) Stanford Lawyer, 1982—; contbr. articles to profl. jours. and mags. Recipient Silver Medal award Council Advancement and Support of Edn., 1985. Mem. No. Calif. Sci. Writers Assn. (co-founder, bd. dirs. 1979—), Nat. Sci. Writers Assn. (assoc.), Phi Beta Kappa. Democrat. Avocations: singing, piano. Home: 2080 Louis Rd Palo Alto CA 94303 Office: Stanford Law Sch Stanford CA 94305

HELM, KEITH BUCHANAN, systems analyst; b. Tacoma; s. Kenneth Sumner Helm and Margaret Catherine (Harrigan) Kendall; m. Sandra Latrell Miller (div. Dec. 1974); 1 child, Michelle Andrea; m. Julie Ann Ray, Apr. 21, 1985; 1 stepchild, Robert Allan Bakkemo. Student, U. Puget Sound, Valley Coll., UCLA, Cerritos Coll. Field engr. Lockheed Calif. Co., Burbank, 1958-74; engring. writer Interstate Electronics, Anaheim, Calif., 1976-79; mem. tech. staff Rockwell Energy Systems Group, Canoga Park, Calif., 1979-82, Rockwell N.Am. Aviation, El Segundo, Calif., 1982-86; systems analyst Boeing Military Airplane Co., Seattle, 1986—. Served with USAF, 1960-64. Recipient Suggestion award RCA Radio and TV Electronics Div., 1956. Mem. Am. Philatelic Soc., Nat. Mgmt. Assn., Internat. Soc. Japanese Philately, France and Colonies Philatelic Soc., The Am. Legion, Am. Soc. Tech. Writers. Avocations: stamp collecting, swimming, camping. Home: 27015 SE 171 St Issaquah WA 98027

HELM, MARJORIE M., human service administrator, psychotherapist; b. Carmel, Calif., May 7, 1949; d. Walter Max Helm and Clara (D'Arcy) McMillan; m. Walter Wells Atkin, Dec. 29, 1983. BA in Psychology, U. Calif., Santa Cruz, 1971; MSW, San Diego State U., 1976. Lic. clin. social worker, Calif. Family therapist Oak Glen Residential Treatment Facility, San Diego, 1972-76; planner United Way, San Diego, 1976-77; coordinator Social Advocates for Youth, San Diego, 1976-80; coordinator Community Outreach, Mental Health Merced, Calif., 1980-85; adminstr. Early Childhood Spl. Edn., Merced, 1985-86; div. chief Children and Family Services Sonoma County Dept. Mental Health, Santa Rosa, Calif., 1986—; cons. Friends Can Be Good Medicine campaign, Calif., 1982-84. Treas. Friends of Supr. Ann Klinger, Merced, 1984-86; chmn. Merced Interagy. Council, 1985-86; co-chmn. I "Care" Community Team, 1985-86; trainer Spl. Edn. Resource Network, 1985-86; mem. Statewide Com. on Prevention, 1983-85; mem. edn. and research com. Calif. Elected Womens Advocacy, 1985—; mem. Calif. Mental Health Advocates for Children and Youth, 1986—. Named one of Outstanding Young Women of Am., 1985; Country Friends fellow, 1976. Mem. NOW, Soc. Clin. Social Workers, Nat. Womens Polit. Caucus, Nat. Assn. Social Workers, Infant Devel. Assn., Infant Consortium, LWV (local pres. 1983-84), Bus. and Profl. Women. Democrat. Lodge: Soroptimists. Home: 142 Winding Way Napa CA 94559 Office: 3333 Chanate Rd Santa Rosa CA 95404

HELMER, RICHARD GUY, nuclear physicist; b. Homer, Mich., Feb. 19, 1934; s. Hurshul Guy and Edith Maude (Putnam) H.; m. Mary Joan Scrivens, June 10, 1956; children: Gary Allen, Carl William. BS, U. Mich., 1956, MS, 1957, PhD, 1961. Physicist Phillips Petroleum Co., Idaho Falls, Idaho, 1961-65, Idaho Nuclear Co., Idaho Falls, 1965-70; sr. scientist Aerojet Nuclear Co., Idaho Falls, 1970-76; prin. scientist EG&G Idaho, Idaho Falls, 1976—; mem. task group on gamma-ray energies Internat. Union Pure and Applied Physics, 1972—; chmn. working group on gamma and beta-ray spectrometry Internat. Commn. on Radionuclide Metrologie, 1985—. Mem. editorial bd. Nuclear Instruments and Methods Jour., Uppsala, Sweden; contbr. articles to profl. jours. Bd. dirs. Child Devel. Ctr., Idaho Falls, 1968-74, Regional Council Christian Ministry, 1970—; trustee Sch. Dist. 91, Idaho Falls, 1979-85. Fellow Am. Phys. Soc.; mem. AAAS, Am. Nuclear Soc., N.Y. Acad. Scis. Avocations: photography, racquetball, hiking, cross-country skiing. Home: 792 Sonja Ave Idaho Falls ID 83402 Office: EG&G Idaho PO Box 1625 Idaho Falls ID 83415

HELPHREY, DAVID BRYAN, engineer; b. Spokane, Wash., Mar. 2, 1944; s. James Matson Helphrey and Elizabeth Frances (Bryan) Hartup; m. Cynthia Louise Simer, Apr. 22, 1966; children: Daniel Blaine, Caitlin Sarah. AB in Chemistry, Occidental Coll., 1966; MS in Chemistry, Purdue U., 1970. Scientist Calif. Inst. Tech., Pasadena, 1970-78; engr. Beckman Instruments, Fullerton, Calif., 1978—; cons. Durrum Instruments, Palo Alto, Calif., 1973-77. Patentee in field. Mem. AAAS. Democrat. Office: Beckman Instruments PO Box 3100 Fullerton CA 92634

HELSELL, ROBERT M., construction executive; b. Seattle, Mar. 29, 1937; s. Frank P. and Ellen (Bringloe) H.; m. Linda M. Clark, Dec. 19, 1961; children—Kristina, Ingrid, Spencer, Alexa. B.A., Dartmouth Coll., 1959, M.B.E., 1960. C.P.A., Wash. With Haskins & Sells, 1961-64; treas. Cascade Natural Gas Co., 1964-68; successively sec.-treas., exec. v.p., pres. and chief exec. officer Howard S. Wright Constrn. Co., Seattle, 1974-84; pres., chief exec. officer Wright Schuchart, Inc., 1980-84, Sprague Resources Corp., 1984—; vice chmn. bd. Schuchart & Assocs., 1980—; dir. Space Needle Corp., Rainier Nat. Bank, Rainier Bancorp. Bd. dirs. Virginia Mason Hosp., 1986—, Virginia Mason Med. Found., 1986—, Lakeside Sch., 1969-73; bd. dirs. Seattle Children's Home, 1968-77, pres., 1972-75; bd. dirs. Corp. Council for Arts, 1981—, pres., 1984, chmn., 1985; trustee Seattle Art Mus., 1973—; mem. men's adv. com. Children's Orthopedic Hosp., 1980—. Served to lt. comdr. USCG, 1961-68. Mem. Assoc. Gen. Contractors. Republican. Episcopalian. Clubs: Univ., Rainier, Seattle Tennis, Seattle Yacht, Columbia Tower, Wash. Athletic (Seattle). Office: Sprague Resources Corp PO Box 84251 Seattle WA 98124 *

HELZER, JAMES DENNIS, hospital executive; b. Fresno, Calif., Apr. 27, 1938; s. Alexander and Katherine (Scheidt) H.; m. Joan Elaine Alinder, Feb. 25, 1967; children: Amy, Rebecca. B.S., Fresno State Coll., 1960; M.Hosp. Adminstrn., U. Iowa, 1965. Adminstrv. asst. Twilight Haven, Fresno, Calif., 1960-61; asst. adminstr. U. Calif. Hosps. and Clinics, San Francisco, 1965-68; asst. adminstr. Fresno Community Hosp., 1968-71, exec. adminstr., 1971-82, pres., chief exec. officer, 1982—; pres., chief exec. officer Community Hosps. Cen. Calif., 1983—. Served with U.S. Army, 1961-63. Mem. Am., Calif. hosp. assns., Am. Coll. Hosp. Adminstrs. Presbyterian. Club: Rotary. Home: 5909 E Hamilton Fresno CA 93727 Office: PO Box 1232 Fresno CA 93715

HEM, JOHN DAVID, research chemist; b. Starkweather, N.D., May 14, 1916; s. Hans Neilius and Josephine Augusta (Larsen) H.; m. Ruth Evans, Mar. 11, 1945; children: John David Jr., Michael Edward. Student, Minot State Coll., 1932-36, N.D. State U., 1937-38, Iowa State U., 1938; BS, George Washington U., 1940. Analytical chemsit U.S. Geol. Survey, Safford, Ariz., 1940-42, 43-45; analytical chemist U.S. Geol. Survey, Roswell, N.Mex., 1942-43; dist. chemist U.S. Geol. Survey, Albuquerque, 1945-53; research chemist U.S. Geol. Survey, Denver, 1953-63, Menlo Park, Calif., 1963—; research advisor U.S. Geol. Survey, 1974-79, mem. water research adv. com., 1984—. Author: Study and Interpretation Chemistry of Natural Water, 3d rev. edit., 1985; contbr. articles to profl. publs., chpts. to books. Recipient Meritorious Service award U.S. Dept. Interior, 1976, Disting. Service award U.S. Dept. Interior, 1980, Nat. Water Well Assn. Sci. award, 1986. Mem. Am. Chem. Soc., Am. Geophys. Union, Geochem. Soc., Am. Water Works Assn., Soc. Geochemistry and Health. Democrat. Lutheran. Avocations: music, gardening. Home: 3349 Saint Michael Ct Palo Alto CA 94306 Office: US Geol Survey MS 427 345 Middlefield Menlo Park CA 94025

HEMANN, RAYMOND GLENN, aerospace company executive; b. Cleve., Jan 24, 1933; s. Walter Harold Marsha Mae (Colbert) H.; B.S., Fla. State U., 1957; postgrad. U.S. Naval Postgrad. Sch., 1963-64, U. Calif. at Los Angeles, 1960-62; M.S. in Systems Engring., Calif. State U., Fullerton, 1970, M.A. in Econs., 1972; m. Lucile Tinnin Turnage, Feb. 1, 1958; children—James Edward, Carolyn Frances; m. Leslie K. Lewis, May 23, 1980. Aero. engring. aide U.S. Navy, David Taylor Model Basin, Carderock, Md., 1956; analyst Fairchild Aerial Surveys, Tallahassee, 1957; research analyst Fla. Rd. Dept., Tallahassee, 1957-59; chief Autonetics div. N.Am. Rockwell Corp., Anaheim, Calif., 1959-69; v.p., dir. R. E. Manns Co., Wilmington, Calif., 1969-70; mgr. avionics design and analysis dept. Lockheed-Calif. Co., Burbank, 1970-72, mgr. advanced concepts div., 1976-82; gen. mgr. Western div. Arinc Research Corp., Santa Ana, 1972-76; dir. future requirements Rockwell Internat., 1982-85; dir. Threat Analysis, Corp. Offices, Rockwell Internat., 1985—; cons. various U.S. govt. agys.; mem. naval studies bd. Nat. Acad. Scis., 1985—; asst. prof. ops. analysis dept. U.S. Naval Postgrad. Sch., Monterey, Calif., 1963-64, Monterey Peninsula Coll., 1963; instr. ops. analysis Calif. State U., Fullerton, 1963, instr. quantitative methods, 1969-72; pres. Asso. Aviation, Inc., Fullerton, 1965-74; lectr. Brazilian Navy, 1980, U. Calif., Santa Barbara, 1980, Yale U., 1985, Princeton U., 1986, U.S. Naval Postgrad. Sch., 1986; cons. to various corps. and govt. agys. Troop chmn. Boy Scouts Am. Bd. dirs. Placentia-Yorba Jr. Athletic Assn. Served with AUS, 1950-53. Syde P. Deeb scholar, 1956; recipient certificate appreciation U.S. Naval Postgrad. Sch., 1963; Honor awards Nat. Assn. Remotely Piloted Vehicles, 1975, 76. Comml., glider and pvt. pilot. Fellow AAAS; mem. Ops. Research Soc. Am., IEEE, AIAA, Air Force Assn., N.Y. Acad. Scis., Soaring Soc. Am., Nat. Acad. Scis. (Naval Studies Bd. 1985—), Assn. Old Crows, Phi Kappa Tau (past pres.). Episcopalian. Contbr. articles to profl. jours. Home: 1215 Hartwood Point Dr Pasadena CA 91107 Office: 2230 E Imperial Hwy El Segundo CA 90245

HEMINGWAY, GEORGE THOMSON, marine biologist, educator, priest; b. Corvallis, Oreg., Aug. 23, 1940; s. George Danforth and Margaret Roberta Chadwick Purcell (Hardman) H.; m. Jean Ann Potym, May 25, 1968; 1 child, Gillian Christian Allison. BS, San Diego State U., 1966, MS, 1973; diploma in Theology, Episc. Sch. Theology, 1983. Ordained priest Episc. Ch., 1985. With Scripps Inst. Oceanography div. U. Calif. San Diego, La Jolla, Calif., 1966—, coord. Interamericas program, 1977—, asst. to dir. marine life research group, 1983—; prof. and chmn. biology dept. U. Autonoma de Baja Calif., Ensenada, Mex., 1973-74, adj. prof. biology, 1974—; coordinator Calif. Coop. Oceanic Fisheries Investigations, 1979-81, 1985—. Contbr. articles to profl. jours. Active Commn. Ministry, Episc. Diocese San Diego, 1980-84, chmn. Hispanic Com., 1985—; mem. citizen's adv. panel Tecolote Canyon, San Diego, 1980-83; mem. sch. closure panel San Diego Unified Sch. Dist., 1983-85. Recipient Honoris Causa award Univ. Autonoma de Baja Calif., 1974; grantee NOAA 1978-83, Tinker Found. 1982-85. Mem. Am. Zool. Soc., Western Soc. Naturalists, AAAS, Am. Inst. Biol. Scis., Hastings Inst. Soc., Ethics and Life Scis. (assoc.), Nat. Assn. Self-supporting Active Ministry, Nat. Commn. Hispanic Ministries. Republican. Avocations: horticulture, carpentry, fishing, hiking. Home: 5025 Georgetown Ave San Diego CA 92110 Office: U Calif San Diego Scripps Inst Oceanography A-027 La Jolla CA 92093

HEMINGWAY, W(ILLIAM) DAVID, banker; b. Los Angeles, Apr. 28, 1947; s. Donald William and Donna (Laws) H.; m. Gay Etta Jorgensen, Apr. 15, 1977; children: Ryan, Jonathan, Jamon. BA, Brigham Young U., 1971; MBA, U. Utah, 1973. Sr. v.p. Zions First Nat. Bank, Salt Lake City, 1982-84, exec. v.p., 1984—; pres. Internat. TV Network, 1986—, bd. dirs. Nev. State Bank, Las Vegas, Murdock Travel, Inc., Salt Lake City. Candidate Utah Legislature, Salt Lake City, 1972; mem. Electorial Coll., Salt Lake City, 1976, Utah adv. bd. to U.S. Civil Rights Commn., Salt Lake City, 1976—. Mem. Utah State Money Mgmt. Council. Republican. Mormon. Office: Zions First Nat Bank 1 S Main Salt Lake City UT 84111

HEMMATI, HAMID, research physicist; b. Tehran, Iran, Jan. 3, 1954; s. David and Ester (Delijani) H. BS in Physics, Nat. U. Iran, Tehran, 1974; MA in Physics, U. So. Calif., 1976; PhD in Physics, Colo. State U., 1981. Research asst. Colo. State U., Ft. Collins, 1977-81; research assoc. NBS, Boulder, Colo., 1981-83; sr. project engr. Allied Bendix Aerospace Corp., Columbia, Md., 1983-86; mem. tech. staff Jet Propulsion Lab., Pasadena, Calif., 1986—. Contbr. articles to profl. jours.; patentee in field. Jewish. Office: Jet Propulsion Lab 4800 Oak Grove Dr 200-122 Pasadena CA 91109

HEMMERDINGER, WILLIAM JOHN, artist; b. Burbank, Calif., July 7, 1951; s. William John Jr. and Eileen Patricia (Fitzmaurice) H.; m. Catherine Lee Cooper, Aug. 8, 1981. Student Art Ctr. Coll. Design, 1967-69, Nat. Palace Mus., Taiwan, 1973; A.A., Coll. of Desert, 1971; B.A., U. Calif.-Riverside, 1973; M.F.A., Claremont Grad. Sch., 1975, Ph.D., 1979; postgrad. Harvard U., 1977. Curator Calif. Mus. Photography, 1973-74; instr. Coll. of Desert, 1974-79, 80-84, Calif. State U., Long Beach, 1979-80, Otis Art Inst. Parsons Sch. Design, 1979-80, U. Calif., Riverside, 1981-82, co-owner William & Catherine Hemmerdinger Gallery, Palm Desert, Calif. One-man shows include: Cirrus Editions, Ltd., 1982, 84; group shows include: NAD, N.Y.C., Whitney Mus. Am. Art, N.Y.C., UNESCO Mus., Paris, Am. Watercolor Soc., N.Y.C., U. N.Mex. Art Mus., Los Angeles Visual Arts, Santa Monica City Coll., 1982, Los Angeles County Mus. Art; works in permanent collections Tate Gallery, London, UCLA, Smithsonian Instn., Washington, Mobil Oil Co., N.Y.C., Fed. Reserve Bank, San Francisco. Recipient Calif. Nat. Watercolor Soc. award, 1974, 1979; Ford Found. grantee, 1979; NEA grantee, 1979, NEH grantee, 1980. Mem. Nat. Watercolor Soc. (v.p. 1981-82, 83). Contbr. articles to profl. jours. Studio: 42-240 Green Way Suite D Palm Desert CA 92260 Office: Cirrus Editions Ltd 540 S Alameda St Los Angeles CA 90013

HEMMES, DON EVAN, biology educator; b. Hampton, Iowa, Dec. 28, 1942; s. William I. and Lydia (Pals) H.; m. Helen Ruth Van Zanten, Sept. 2, 1967; children: Kimo, David. BA, Cen. Coll., 1965; MS, U. Hawaii, 1967, PhD, 1970. Postdoctoral researcher U. Zurich, 1970-72, U. Calif., Riverside, 1972-73; prof. biology U. Hawaii, Hilo, 1973—; invited expert Nat. Cancer Inst., Bethesda, Md., 1976-77. Contbr. articles to profl. jours. Recipient Regent's Excellence in Teaching award U. Hawaii, 1976, Assoc. Student's Teaching award U. Hawaii, 1979. Mem. Mycol. Soc. Am. (W.H. Weston Jr. Teaching award 1986), Hawaiian Mycol. Soc. Democrat. Methodist. Home: 333 Kalili St Hilo HI 96720 Office: U Hawaii at Hilo Biology Dept Hilo HI 96720

HEMMINGS, PETER WILLIAM, orchestra and opera administrator; b. London, Apr. 10, 1934; s. William and Rosalind (Jones) H.; m. Jane Frances Kearnes, May 19, 1962; children—William, Lucy, Emma, Rupert, Sophie. Grad. Gonville and Caius Coll., Cambridge, 1957; LL.D. (hon.), Strathclyde U., Glasgow, 1978. Clk., Harold Holt Ltd., London, 1958-59; planning mgr. Sadlers Wells Opera, London, 1959-65; gen. adminstr. Scottish Opera, Glasgow, 1962-77; gen. mgr. Australian Opera, Sydney, 1977-79; mng. dir. London Symphony Orch., 1980-84; gen. dir. Los Angeles Music Ctr. Opera Assn., 1984—; gen. mgr. New Opera Co., London, 1956-65, now dir.; dir. Royal Acad. Music, Sadllers Wells Trust. Served to lt. Brit. Signal Corps, 1952-54; Fed. Republic Germany. Mem. Internat. Assn. Opera Dirs. Anglican. Club: Garrick (London). Home: 775 S Madison Ave Pasadena CA 91106 Office: Los Angeles Music Ctr Opera 135 N Grand Ave Los Angeles CA 90012

HEMMINGSEN, BARBARA BRUFF, microbiology educator; b. Whittier, Calif., Mar. 25, 1941; d. Stephen Cartland and Susanna Jane (Alexander) Bruff; m. Edvard Alfred Hemmingsen, Aug. 5, 1967; 1 child, Grete. BA, U. Calif., Berkeley, 1962, MA, 1964; PhD, U. Calif., San Diego, 1971. Lectr. San Diego State U., 1973-77, asst. prof., 1977-81, assoc. prof., 1981—; vis. asst. prof. Aarhus U., Denmark, 1971-72; consultant Automated Microbiology, Inc., San Diego, 1984-85. Author: (with others) Microbial Ecology, 1972; contbr. articles to profl. jours. Mem. Planned Parenthood, San Diego. Mem. Am. Soc. Microbiology, Soc. Protozoology, Soc. Gen. Microbiology, AAAS, Am. Women in Sci., Sigma Xi, Phi Beta Kappa (pres. Nu chpt. 1986-88). Democrat. Office: San Diego State U Dept Biology San Diego CA 92182-0057

HEMPHILL, ALAN POLK, management consultant; b. Montgomery, Ala., Aug. 22, 1933; s. Alan Polk and Elizabeth Evans (Orr) H.; m. Jean Tilden Baker, June 8, 1957; children—Elizabeth, Alan, Laurie. B.S.E.E., U.S. Naval Acad., 1957. Commd. ensign U.S. Navy, 1957, advanced through grades to lt. comdr., 1977; various assignments, San Diego, 1957-77; mgr. Prestige Properties, Poway Calif., 1977-80; founder Orion Bus. Systems, San Diego, 1980-82; pres., chief exec. officer Sta. KBSC-TV, Glendale, Calif., 1982-83; chmn., bd. dirs. Oak Broadcasting Systems, Glendale, 1983-84; pres. Community Bus. Cons., San Diego, 1984-85; prof. computer sci. Nat. U., Vista, Calif., 1984—; trustee Sta. KBSC-TV Stock of Oak Industries, San Diego, 1982-84; panelist TV series On Edge, 1986-87; cons. Oak Industries, San Diego, 1984; bd. dirs. Community Bus. Cons., San Diego, 1984. Contbr. articles and columns to profl. jours., chpts. to books. Gen. mgr. Remember the Pueblo, San Diego, 1969; pres., chmn. bd. Green Valley Civic Assn., Poway, 1974-75; pres., bd. dirs. N. County Bd. of Jr. Achievement, 1979. Lodge: Kiwanis. Pres., chief exec. officer, chmn. while Sta. KBSC-TV received 12 Emmys, 1982-84. Office: Ann Winton & Assoc 16476 Bernardo Cen Dr San Diego CA 92128

HEMPHILL, DELBERT DEAN, JR., horticultural consultant; b. Panama City, Fla., July 25, 1944; s. Delbert Dean and Miriam Drennen (Marshall) H.; m. Rosa Maria Hernandez, Sept. 5, 1970; children: Brian, Jeffrey, Melissa. BS, U. Notre Dame, 1966; PhD, Mich. State U., 1971. Research assoc. Cornell U., Ithaca, N.Y., 1971-73; asst. prof. U. Alaska, Fairbanks, 1973-76; asst. prof. Oreg. State U., Aurora, 1976-82, assoc. prof., 1982—. Contbr. articles to profl. jours. Mem. Prodn. and Harvest Mechanization Working Group (chmn. 1986—), Vegetable Crops Working Group (bd. dirs. 1985—), Am. Soc. Hort. Sci., Am. Soc. Plant Physiologists, AAAS, Sigma Xi, Pi Alpha Xi. Avocations: music, running, hiking. Home: 703 NW 13th Ave Canby OR 97013 Office: N Willamette Exptl Sta 15210 NE Miley Rd Aurora OR 97002

HENDERSON, CRAIG ALAN, safety consultant; b. McMinnville, Oreg., May 26, 1958; s. Thomas Dean and Helen May (Wyss) H. Student, Chemeketa Community Coll., 1982. Registered profl. property and casualty agt. Logger Gross & Son Logging Co., McMinnville, Oreg., 1976-81; safety cons. Associated Oreg. Logger, Springfield, 1983-84, 85—. Medic 1st aid instr. Mem. Am. Soc. Safety Engring., U.S. Jaycees. Democrat. Roman Catholic. Clubs: Vets. (McMinnville); Michelbook Country; Bayou Golf and Country. Lodge: Elks. Avocations: hunting, fishing, golf, reading, photography. Home: 624 Drumwood #1 McMinnville OR 97128 Office: Associated Oreg Loggers 1077 Gateway Loop Springfield OR 97477

HENDERSON, DOUGLAS JAMES, physicist; b. Calgary, Alta., Can., July 28, 1934; came to U.S., 1956; s. Donald Ross and Evelyn Louise (Scott) H.; m. Rose-Marie Steen-Nielssen, Jan. 21, 1960; children: Barbara, Dianne, Sharon. BA in Math., U. B.C., Vancouver, 1956; PhD in Physics, U. Utah, 1961. Asst. prof. physics U. Idaho, Moscow, 1961-63; assoc. prof. Ariz. State U., Tempe, 1963-64; prof. physics and math. U. Waterloo, Ont., Can., 1964-69; research scientist IBM Research div. IBM Corp., San Jose, Calif., 1969—. Author: Statistical Mechanics and Dynamics, 1964, 2d rev. edit, 1982; editor: Physical Chemistry-An Advanced Treatise, Vols. 1-15, 1966-75, Theoretical Chemistry-Advances and Perspectives, Vols. 1-5, 1975-81; assoc. editor Jour. Chem. Physics, 1974-76; mem. editorial bd. Ultitas Mathematica, 1971—, Jour. Phys. Chemistry, 1984—; mem. adv. bd. Chem. Abstracts, 1981-83; also articles. Missionary Ch. Jesus Christ Latter Day Saints, Africa, 1957-59; vol. Loma Prieta Vol. Fire Dept., Los Gatos, Calif., 1983—. Recipient Johnathan Rodgers award, 1954, Ariz. State U. Faculty award, 1963, IBM Outstanding Research Contbrn. award, 1973, 87; Univ. Gt. War scholar, 1953, Daniel Buchanan scholar, 1955; Fellow Corning Glass Found., 1959, Alfred P. Sloan Found., 1964, 66, Ian Potter Found., 1966, Commonwealth Sci. and Indsl. Research Orgn., 1966; named Manuel Sandoval Vallarta Physics lectr., Mex., 1985. Fellow Inst. Physics, Am. Phys. Soc., Am. Inst. Chemists; mem. Can. Assn. Physicists, Am. Chem. Soc. Democrat. Avocations: jogging, swimming. Office: IBM Almaden Research Ctr K33/801 650 Harry Rd San Jose CA 95120

HENDERSON, JOE LENWOOD, military educator; b. Trenton, Ky., May 12, 1938; s. Joe William and Dorothy and (Keel) H.; m. Verna L. Martin, Nov. 19, 1961; children: Elisa Adine, Elana Renee, Laura Michel. BS, U. Houston, 1964; MA, Ball State, 1977; postgrad., Copenhagen U., 1986, Claremont Grad. Sch., 1987. Cert. jr. coll. tchr., Calif.; secondary tchr., Tex. Buyer Allied Purchasing, Houston, 1959-60; with acctg./personnel D. McMillan Cos., Houston, 1960-61; mem. faculty So. Coll., Houston, 1961-84, emeritus, 1984—; from asst. to chief acctg. comptroller Crutcher Industries, Houston, 1963-64; exec. officer in charge of tng., edn. officer Sch. Sect. Fed. Civil Service, Tex., Ind., Calif., 1964—; adj. faculty, U. Redlands, Calif., 1982—, Chapman Coll., Orange, Calif., 1982—. Contbr. numerous articles to profl. jours. Mem. counsel N.E. Houston Community Council, 1969-76, mil. affairs commn. Houston C. of C., 1970-76; bd. dirs. Yucca Valley Assembly of God, 1979—. Served to lt.col. USAFR, 1968—. Mem. Western Region Assn. Colls. and Mil. Educators (founder, pres. 1985—), Calif. Assn. Colls. and Mil. Educators (pres. 1984—), Morongo Basin Coalition for Adult Literacy (bd. dirs.), Cochella Valley Industry Edn. Council, Mensa, Phi Delta Kappa. Democrat. Avocations: photography, reading, music, travelling, investments. Home: 58757 Santa Barbara Yucca Valley CA 92284

HENDERSON, MARK SCOTT, archeologist; b. Los Angeles, July 4, 1953; s. Norman B. and Vita (Legere) H.; m. Yolanda Vigil, Aug. 9, 1974. BA with distinction, U. N.Mex., 1973. Research archeologist So. Meth. U., Dallas, 1974-76; archeologist USDA Carson Nat. Forest, Taos, N.Mex., 1977; archeologist US Dept. Interior Bur. Land Mgmt., Ely, Nev., 1978-80, Socorro, N.Mex., 1980-83; archeologist US Dept. Interior Bur. Indian Affairs, Window Rock, Ariz., 1983—; sec., treas. N.Mex. Archeol. Council, Albuquerque, 1982. Author: An Archeological Inventory of Brantley Reservoir, NM, 1976. Fellow So. Meth. U., 1974-76, NSF, 1971. Mem. Soc. Am. Archeology, Plateau Scis. Soc. (pres. 1986). Democrat. Avocations: cross country skiing, hiking. Home: 743 S Patton Dr Gallup NM 87301 Office: US Dept Interior Bur Indian Affairs PO Box M Window Rock AZ 86515

HENDERSON, PATRICIA MCGOVERN, state human rights agency executive; b. Mobile, Ala., Aug. 6, 1940; d. Thomas Joseph and Babe Hope (Lowery) McGovern; children—Thomas Bain III, Patrick Sean. Student, Loretto Coll., Nerinx, Ky., 1958-61, U. So. Ala., 1965; B.A. in Psychology and Mgmt., Hawaii Pacific Coll., 1976; M.A., in Psychology and Mgmt., Antioch U., Honolulu, 1981. Cert. mgmt. Queen's Med. Ctr., 1977; cert. U. Ala. Sch. Medicine, 1979; cert. Neuropsychiat. Inst., UCLA, 1980. Dir. Mission and Youth Office for Catholic Diocese and Charities, Mobile, 1961-64; tchr. Ala. State Dept. Pub. Edn., Mobile, 1966-69; spl. edn. tchr., adminstr., social worker St. Peter Claver Sch. and Ctr., Tampa, Fla., 1970-72; chief adminstr., dir., prin., ednl. dir., social worker Salvation Army Kauluwela Corps, Kula Kokua Therapeutic Sch., Malama Makua Rehab. Ctr., 1973-77; exec. dir., chief exec. officer Protection and Advocacy Agy. of Hawaii and State Client Assistance Agy. of Hawaii, Honolulu, 1977—; cons. in field. Author, editor: A Self Advocate-You Have the Right to Speak for Yourself, 1978. Co-author, co-editor Legal Rights for Developmentally and Handicapped Citizens, 1981; The Answer Book for Parents on the Right to Education for the Handicapped Child, 1983. Bd. dirs. State Dept. Health Adv. Com., Honolulu, 1979—, Gov.'s State Planning Council on Developmental Disabilities, 1986; chmn. human rights com. State Dept. Health, 1982—; co-chmn. Mayor's City and County Transp. for Handicapped/Elderly Task Force, 1984—. Recipient Disting. Service award Salvation Army, 1977; Keen, Dedicated, Outstanding Profl., Highest Calibre award Salvation Army, 1977; Spl. Contbns. Internat. Yr. of Disabled Persons award State Hawaii and Internat. Yr. Disabled Persons Council, 1981; Promotion and Advancement of Women award Hawaiian Telephone Co., 1984; Disting. American award Am. Biog. Inst., 1985; Outstanding and Disting. Service award Gov.'s Commn. on Children and Youth, 1986. Fellow Nat. Legal Aide and Defender Assn.; mem. Nat. Tourette Syndrome Assn. (exec. dir. 1984—, NW regional dir. 1984—), Nat. Assn. Protection and Advocacy Systems (dir. 1984—), Nat. Client Assistance Orgn. (dir. 1984—). Avocations: travel; theater; music; art collecting; photography. Home: 5567 Pia St Honolulu HI 96821 Office: Protection and Advocacy Agy Hawaii 1580 Makaloa St Suite 1060 Honolulu HI 96814

HENDERSON, PAUL, III, journalist; b. Washington, Jan. 13, 1939; s. Paul and Doris Olive (Gale) H.; m. JoAnn Burnham, Sept. 10, 1964; children: Leslee, Jill, Polly Ann; m. 2d Janet Marie Horne, Jan. 22, 1982; children: Peter Paul, Brady Thomas. Student Wentworth Mil. Acad. Jr. Coll., Lexington, Mo., 1957-59, Creighton U., 1963, U. Nebr.-Omaha, 1964-67. Reporter Council Bluffs (Iowa) Nonpareil, 1962-66, Omaha World-Herald, 1966-67; investigative reporter Seattle Times, 1967-85; pvt. practice investigator, Seattle, 1985; cons. Warner Bros. Co-founder Seattle Forgotten Children's Fund, 1976. Featured investigator in Home Box Office Crime Documentary, 1986. Served with U.S. Army, 1959-62. Recipient 1st Place C.B. Blethen award, 1977, 82, Pulitzer prize for spl. local reporting, 1982, 1st Place Roy W. Howard Pub. Service award Scripps-Howard Found., 1982; named one of 50 Outstanding Achievers Am., Am. Acad. Achievement, 1982. Mem. Pacific N.W. Newspaper Guild. Methodist. Office: PO Box 70 Seattle WA 98111

HENDERSON, ROBERT LYNN, psychology consultant; b. Poplar Bluff, Mo., Oct. 21, 1923; s. Archie and Willie Elizabeth (Gladish) H.; m. Alice Louise Meyers, Aug. 10, 1949; children: Kathryn Elizabeth, Thomas William. BA, U. Mo., 1948, MA, 1950, PhD, 1953. Psychologist USAF, Mather AFB, Calif., 1953-57; tech. staff Bell Telephone Labs., Whippany, N.J., 1957-58; supr. psychologist USN, Point Mugu, Calif., 1958-61; tech. staff Space Tech. Lab., Los Angeles, 1961-62; sr. human factors scientist System Devel. Corp., Santa Monica, Calif., 1962-74; research psychologist Dept. Transp., Washington, 1974-84; human factors cons. Ventura, Calif., 1984—. Patentee radar integrating device. Served to 1st lt. USAF, 1942-46, PTO. Mem. Human Factor Soc., Sigma Xi. Democrat. Avocations: amateur radio, clock collecting, golf, tennis. Home and Office: 242 Dorothy Ave Ventura CA 93003

HENDERSON, ROGENE FAULKNER, toxicologist, researcher; b. Breckenridge, Tex., July 13, 1933; d. Philander Molden and Lenoma (Rogers) F.; m. Thomas Richard Henderson II, May 30, 1957; children: Thomas Richard III, Edith Jeanette, Laura Lee. BSBA, Tex. Christian U., 1955; PhD, U. Tex., 1960. Diplomate Am. Bd. Toxicology. Research assoc. U. Ark. Sch. Med., Little Rock, 1960-67; from scientist to sr. scientist and group supr.

chemistry and toxicology Lovelace Inhalation Toxicology Research Inst., Albuquerque, 1967—. Contbr. articles to profl. jours. Named Woman on the Move YWCA, Albuquerque, 1985; grantee NIH, 1958-60, 1960-62, 1986—. Mem. Am. Chem. Soc. (chmn. Cen. N.Mex. sect. 1981), Soc. Toxicology (pres. Mountain-West Regional chpt. 1985-86), N.Y. Acad. Scis., AAAS, Nat. Acad. Scis. (com. Toxicology 1985—, com. Epidemiology of Air Pollution 1983-85, com. Biol. Markers 1986—), NIH (toxicology study sect. 1982-86). Presbyterian. Home: 5609 Don Felipe Ct SW Albuquerque NM 87105 Office: Lovelace Inhalation Toxicology Research Inst PO Box 5890 Albuquerque NM 87185

HENDERSON, SIDNEY CHARLES, radiologist; b. Louisville, Feb. 16, 1944; s. Justus Dean and Josephine (Freeman) H.; m. Janie Henderson (div. 1983); m. Evelyn Kay Sturtz, Oct. 6, 1984. BS, Oreg. State U., 1965; MD, U. Oreg., 1969. Diplomate Am. Bd. Radiology. Intern Denver Gen. Hosp., 1969-70; resident diagnostic radiology U. Oreg. Med. Sch., Portland, 1973-76; head outpatient clinic, asst. prof. radiology U. Oreg. Health Sci. Ctr., Portland, 1976, head diagnostic ultrasound, 1977; attending physician ultrasound VA Hosp., Portland, 1977, attending physician nuclear medicine, 1978; assoc. prof. radiology U. Oreg. Health Scis. Ctr., 1981; dir. radiology Magic Valley Regional Med. Ctr., Twin Falls, Idaho, 1983—; dir. body imaging Oreg. Health Scis. Ctr., Portland, 1987—; lectr., speaker of radiology and diagnostic ultrasound at numerous orgns. and instns. 1975—. Contbr. articles to sci. jours. Served to capt. U.S. Army, 1970-72. Fellow Am. Cancer Soc. 1975-76, Oreg. Health Scis. U., 1976. Mem. AMA, Am. Coll. Radiology, Oreg. Med. Assn., Oreg. Radiol. Soc., Radiol. Soc. N.Am., Am. Inst. Ultrasound in Medicine, Multnomah County Med. Assn., Oreg. Ultrasound Soc. (pres. 1982-83), Idaho Med. Soc. Avocations: skiing, boating, racquetball, golf, flying. Home: Rt 6 Box 9120 Poleline Rd E Twin Falls ID 83301 Office: Magic Valley Regional Med Ctr Dept Radiology 650 Addison Ave W Twin Falls ID 83301

HENDERSON, THELTON EUGENE, federal judge; b. Shreveport, La., Nov. 28, 1933; s. Eugene M. and Wanzie (Roberts) H.; 1 son, Geoffrey A. B.A., U. Calif.-, Berkeley, 1956, J.D., 1962. Bar: Calif. 1962. Atty. U.S. Dept. Justice, 1962-63; assoc. firm FitzSimmons & Petris, 1964, assoc., 1964-66; directing atty. San Mateo County (Calif.) Legal Aid Soc., 1966-69; asst. dean Stanford (Calif.) U. Law Sch., 1968-76; ptnr. firm Rosen, Remcho & Henderson, San Francisco, 1977-80; judge U.S. Dist. Ct. No. Dist. Calif., San Francisco, 1980—; asso. prof. Sch. Law, Golden Gate U., San Francisco, 1978-80. Served with U.S. Army, 1956-58. Mem. Nat. Bar Assn., Charles Houston Law Assn. Office: US Dist Ct 450 Golden Gate Ave Room 19042 San Francisco CA 94102

HENDERSON, WALTER JAMES, III, ednl. adminstr.; b. Alhambra, Calif., July 31, 1945; s. Walter James and Louise (Whitener) H.; m. Carolyn Janet Epperson, Dec. 24, 1972. A.A., Monterey Peninsula Coll., 1969; B.A., U. N.Mex., 1971; M.Ed., U. Ariz., 1975, Ed.D., 1981. Tchr, Albuquerque Pub. Schs., 1971-74; tchr. Colegio Jorge Washington, Cartagena, Colombia, 1974-75; prin. Santa Cruz Valley Schs., Tumacacori, Ariz., 1977-78; asst. prin. North Pole High Sch., Fairbanks, Alaska, 1978-80; dir. tchr. edn. Sheldon Jackson Coll., Sitka, Alaska, 1981-82; prin. Wasilla (Alaska) High Sch., 1982-83; personnel dir. Mat-Su Borough Sch. Dist., Palmer, Alaska, 1983-86 ; adj. prof. U. Alaska, 1981-86 ; cons. Alaska State Dept. Edn., 1981-86; prin. Pomeroy (Wash.) Sch. Dist. #110, 1986— . Served with USN, 1966-68. Mem. Nat. Assn. Secondary Sch. Prins., Assn. Supervision and Curriculum Devel., Sigma Alpha Epsilon, Pi Lambda Theta, Kappa Delta Pi, Phi Delta Kappa. Republican. Presbyterian. Club: Rotary. Home: PO Box 528 Pomeroy WA 99347 Office: Pomeroy Sch Dist PO Box 950 Pomeroy WA 99347

HENDLER, GORDON LEE, curator; b. N.Y.C., Dec. 11, 1946; s. Jack and Charlotte (Weinstein) H. BS, Rutgers U., 1968; PhD, U. Conn., 1973. Postdoctoral fellow Woods Hole (Mass.) Oceanographic Instn., 1973-74, Smithsonian Inst., 1974-75; dir. Galeta Marine Lab., Panama, 1976-78; marine biologist Smithsonian Oceanographic Sorting Ctr., Washington, 1978-85; curator Natural History Mus., Los Angeles, 1985—. Mem. adv. bd. Jour. Diseases of Aquatic Organism, 1985—. Mem. AAAS, Am. Soc. Zoologists, Western Soc. Naturalists, Soc. Systematic Zoology, Ecol. Soc. Am. Home: 3744 S Flower St Apt 4 Los Angeles CA 90007 Office: Natural History Mus 900 Expositon Blvd Los Angeles CA 90007

HENDREN, ED WALTER, lawyer; b. Ft. Sill, Okla., May 13, 1938; s. Ed. V. and Dorthy M. (Schoggen) H.; children—Matthew F., David M., John E., Benjamin C., Ed Walter, Elizabeth Ann, William B. B.S., U.S. Mil. Acad., 1962; M.A., Am. U., 1968; J.D., Stanford U., 1976. Bar: Calif. 1976. Commd. 2d lt., U.S. Army, 1962, advanced through grades to maj., 1968, resigned, 1973; Olmsted scholar U. Freiburg, W.Ger., 1964-67; assoc. prof. sociology U.S. Mil. Acad., West Point, 1969-73; assoc. Wilson, Mosher & Sonsini, Palo Alto, Calif., 1976-78; ptnr. Mosher, Pooley, Sullivan & Hendren, Palo Alto, 1978-85; sole practice, 1985—; arbitrator/mediator small claims project Santa Clara County Bar Assn., 1980-82. Decorated Bronze Star medal, Purple Heart, Air Medal, Army Commendation medal. Named Outstanding Educator, U.S. Mil. Acad., 1972-73. Mem. ABA, San Mateo and Santa Clara County Bar Assn. Office: 525 University Ave Suite 910 Palo Alto CA 94301

HENDREN, ROBERT LEE, JR., furniture company executive, academic administrator; b. Reno, Oct. 10, 1925; s. Robert Lee and Aleen (Hill) H.; student U. Idaho, 1943-44, 46-47; BA magna cum laude Coll. Idaho; m. Merlyn Churchill, June 14, 1947; children: Robert Lee IV, Anne Aleen. Pres., Hendren's Furniture Co., Boise, Idaho; pres. Coll. Idaho, Caldwell; dir. Shore Club Lodge, Inc., 1st Interstate Bank Idaho. Trustee Boise Ind. Sch. Dist.; charter dir. Boise Valley Indsl. Found.; chmn. bd. trustees Coll. of Idaho; trustee Boise Ind. Sch. Dist.; mem. Boise Redevel. Agy. Mem. Boise Retail Mchts. (chmn.), C. of C. (pres., dir.), Am. Inst. Interior Designers, Idaho Sch. Trustees Assn., Sigma Chi. Clubs: Arid, Hillcrest, Masons, K.T., Shriner, Rotary. Home: 3504 Hillcrest Dr Boise ID 83705 Office: College of Idaho Caldwell ID 83605-9990

HENDRICKS, CHARLES DURRELL, JR., educator, physicist; b. Lewiston, Utah, Dec. 5, 1926; s. Charles Durrell and Louise (McAlister) H.; m. Leah Funk, Mar. 4, 1948; children—Katherine, Martha Jane. B.S., Utah State U., 1949; M.S., U. Wis., 1951; Ph.D., U. Utah, 1955. Research asst. U. Utah, 1953-55; staff mem. Lincoln Lab., Mass. Inst. Tech., 1955-56; faculty U. Ill. at Urbana, 1956—, prof. dept. elec. engring., 1961-79, prof. nuclear engring., 1965-79, prof. emeritus, 1979—, also dir. charged particle research lab., 1964-79; asso. program leader for fusion target fabrication U. Calif. Lawrence Livermore Nat. Lab., 1974-82, sr. scientist, 1982—; vis. prof. Mass. Inst. Tech., 1967-68; sr. research fellow U. Southampton, Eng., 1971-72; editor Blaisdell Pub. Co.; cons. indsl. firms.; vis. research fellow U. Tokyo, 1985. Fellow AAAS, Am. Phys. Soc., Am. Inst. Aeros. and Astronautics (asso.), IEEE; mem. Am. Assn. Physics Tchrs., Electrostatics Soc. Am. (exec. council 1970—), Phi Beta Kappa, Sigma Xi, Tau Beta Pi, Phi Kappa Phi, Eta Kappa Nu. Mormon. Home: 2817 Pardee Pl Livermore CA 94550

HENDRICKS, JOHN H., state agency administrator; b. Woodstock, Ill., Nov. 19, 1942. BA, Calif. State U., San Jose, 1965, MA, 1967. Adminstrv. asst. to state Senator Calif., 1970-73; field rep. to U.S. Senator Calif., 1974-76; field rep. for Dem. Nat. Com. Washington, 1976, adminstrv. asst. to U.S. Congressman, 1977-78; cons. U.S. Adv. Council on Hist. Conservation, Washington, 1978-79; congl. liaison Dept. Energy, Washington, 1979-81; staff dir. Senate Fin. Com., Sacramento, 1981-85; asst. for policy pres. pro tem of Senate, Sacramento, 1985-86; staff dir. Senate Dem. Caucus, Sacramento, 1986—. Served to lt. j.g. USNR, 1967-69. Democrat. Office: Senate Dem Caucus 1100 J St Suite 400 Sacramento CA 95814

HENDRICKS, ROBERT MICHAEL, insurance company executive; b. St. Louis, Aug. 23, 1943; s. Chester Eugene and Reba Eileen (Leake) H.; m. Yvonne Sharon McAnally, Sept. 18, 1971; 1 child, Robert Christian. B.A., U. Calif.-Berkeley, 1965. Dist. mgr. Am. Gen. Life Ins. Col., Los Angeles, 1965-70; gen. ptnr. Hendricks & Assocs., Los Angeles, 1970-75; v.p. mktg. U.S. Life Corp., Los Angeles, 1975-76; dir. agys. Bankers United Life Assurance Co., Los Angeles, 1976-77; gen. ptnr. Assurance Distbg. Co., Inc., Los Angeles, 1977-83, Diversified Ins. Mktg. Services, Santa Ana, Calif., 1983—; pres., chief exec. officer ADCO Re Life Assurance Co., Santa Ana, 1980-83, also dir.; dir. First Commerce Trust Co., Assurance Distbg. Co., Inc.; instr. C.L.U. and Life Underwriter Tng. Council programs. Recipient various awards in field. Mem. Nat. Assn. Life Underwriters, C. of C., Internat. Platform Assn. Republican. Clubs: Lincoln, Silver Circle, Balboa Bay, Santa Ana Country. Lodges: Masons, Shriners, Rotary. Home: 1611 La Loma Dr Santa Ana CA 92705 Office: 1800 E McFadden Ave Suite 260 Santa Ana CA 92705

HENDRICKSON, CARL EDWARD, manufacturing executive; b. Butte, Mont., Jan. 29, 1926; s. Albert and Tannis Sarah (Chase) H.; m. Helen Rose Hendrickson, Apr. 15, 1959 (div. Aug. 1965); children: Albert Carl, Daniel Edward, Tannis Elaine. BA in English, U. Wyo., 1972, MA in English, 1973; postgrad., Sheridan Coll., 1986—. Owner Sheridan (Wyo) Bowling Ctr., 1954-70; inventor, mfr. Hendrickson's Ject-Mix, Sheridan, 1972—. Inventor in field. Served with U.S. Army, 1944-46. Decorated Purple Heart. Republican.

HENDRICKSON, ERLAND DUANE, dentist; b. Akeley, Minn., Sept. 14, 1935; s. Nelius Bjorn and Grace Evelyn (Churchill) H.; m. Charlene Levare Specht, June 19, 1960; children—Shelly, Sandy, Scott. D.D.S., Loma Linda U., 1961. Pvt. practice family dentistry, Aztec, N.Mex., 1963—. Bd. dirs. La Vida Missions Inc., Farmington, N.Mex., 1964—, chmn. bd., 1982-83; com. mem. Rocky Mountain Conf. of 7th Day Adventists, Denver, 1972-78; chmn. bd. San Juan Adventist Sch., Farmington, 1984-85. Served to capt. Dental Corps, U.S. Army, 1961-63. Mem. ADA, N.W. Dist. Dental Soc. (charter; pres. 1982-83), N.Mex. Dental Soc. (exec. com. 1981-83), Nat. Assn. 7th Day Adventist Dentists (pres.-elect 1988, chpt. pres. 1975-82), Aztec C. of C. Republican. Office: 501 S Main St Aztec NM 87410

HENDRICKSON, GARY L(EE), fishery biologist, educator; b. Mpls., Feb. 28, 1949; s. Orville L. and Joyce (Smith) H.; m. Susan Lynn Rosacker Hendrickson, Dec. 26, 1970; children: Marne Sue, Scott Alan. BS, U. Wyo., 1972, MS, 1974; PhD, Iowa State U., 1978. Cert. fishery scientist. Fishery biologist U.S. Fish and Wildlife Service, Manchester, Iowa, 1972; grad. research asst. U. Wyo., Laramie, 1973-74; grad. teaching asst. Iowa State U., Ames, 1974-78; asst. prof. dept. fisheries Humboldt State U., Arcata, Calif., 1978-82, assoc. prof., 1982—; research assoc. U.S. Fish and Wildlife Service Fish Farming Experiment Sta., Suttgart, Ark., 1977, Iowa Lakeside Lab., Milford, 1975-76. Contbr. articles to profl. jours. Coach various youth sports, 1968-72, women's slow pitch softball team, Eureka, Calif., 1978-81. Recipient John W. and Vivian A. Scott Meml. award U. Wyo. Dept. Zoology and Physiology, 1974, George R. LaRue award 13th ann. Midwestern Conf. Parasitologists, 1978; Iowa Lakeside Lab. scholar 1975, 76; grantee U. Wyo. and Wyo. Dept. Fish and Game, 1974, Iowa State U. Grad. Sch., 1975, 76, Humboldt State U. Affirmative Action Faculty Devel. Program, 1980, Calif. Sea Grant Coll. Program, 1983, 1985—. Mem. Am. Fisheries Soc., Fish Health Sect. of Am. Fisheries Soc., Am. Inst. Fishery Research Biologists, Am. Microscopical Soc., Am. Soc. Parasitologists, Helminthological Soc. Wash., Wildlife Disease Assn., Pacific Fishery Biologists, Sigma Xi, Phi Kappa Phi. Methodist. Avocations: softball, basketball, bowling. Home: 2101 Frederick Ave Arcata CA 95521 Office: Humboldt State U Dept Fisheries Arcata CA 95521

HENDRICKSON, JEROME ORLAND, trade association executive, lawyer; b. Eau Claire, Wis., July 25, 1918; s. Harold and Clara (Halverson) H.; student Wis. State Coll., 1936-39; J.D., U. Wis., 1942; m. Helen Phoebe Harty, Dec. 27, 1948; children—Jaime Ann, Jerome Orland. Bar: Wis., 1942, U.S. Supreme Ct., 1955; sole practice, Eau Claire, 1946; sales and advt. mgr. Eau Claire Coco-Cola Bottling Co., Inc., 1947-48; exec. sec. Eau Claire Community Chest, 1948-49; in charge dist. office Am. Petroleum Inst., Kansas City, Mo., 1950-53, Chgo., 1953-55; exec. dir. Nat. Assn. Plumbing-Heating-Cooling Contractors, 1955-64; sec. Joint Apprentice Text, Inc., 1955-64; exec. v.p. Cast Iron Soil Pipe Inst., Washington, 1964-74; pres. Valve Mfrs. Assn., McLean, Va., 1975-80; exec. v.p. Plumbing and Piping Industry Council, Inc., 1981—. Treas., Wis. Community Chest, 1948-49. Treas., All-Industry Plumbing & Heating Modernization Com., 1956-57; co-sec. Joint Industry Program Com., 1958-64. Served to lt. USNR, 1943-46. Mem. ABA, Wis. Bar Assn.,, Am. Soc. Assn. Execs., Washington Soc. Assn. Execs., Wis. State Soc. Washington (pres. 1966-68), Nat. Conf. Plumbing-Heating-Cooling Industry (chmn. 1967-69), NAM, U. Wis. Alumni Assn., U. Wis. Law Sch. Alumni Assn. Washington (pres. 1970-74), C. of C. of U.S., Gamma Eta Gamma (pres. Upsilon chpt. 1941-42). Episcopalian. Mason (32 deg., Shriner). Clubs: Washington Golf and Country, Internat. (Washington). Home: 4621 N 33d St Arlington VA 22207 Office: Plumbing and Piping Industry Council 501 Shatto Pl Suite 405 Los Angeles CA 90020

HENDRIX, JOHN EDWIN, educator; b. Van Nuys, Calif., Aug. 30, 1930; s. John E. and Leona (Paul) H.; m. Joan B. Haas, Apr. 10, 1954; children: Janet L., James. A. BS, Fresno (Calif.) State U., 1956, AB, 1960; MS, Ohio State U., 1963, PhD, 1967. Orchard foreman Fresno State, 1959-60; grad. asst. Ohio State U., Columbus, 1960-65, instr., 1965-67; asst. prof. plant physiology Colo. State U., Ft. Collins, 1967-72, assoc. prof., 1972—. contbr. numerous research articles to profl. jours. Mem. AAAS, Am. Soc. Plant Physiologists. Home: 3000 Tulane Fort Collins CO 80525 Office: Colo State U Fort Collins CO 80523

HENDRY, GEORGE ORR, engineer; b. Oakland, Calif., June 23, 1937; s. George Whiting and Margaret (Munn) H. BSEE, U. Calif., Berkeley, 1960, MSEE, 1963. V.p. Cyclotron Corp., Berkeley. Contbr. articles to profl. jours.; patentee in field. Republican. Avocations: grape growing, wine making. Home: 3104 Redwood Rd Napa CA 94558 Office: Cyclotron Corp 950 Gilman St Berkeley CA 94710

HENEGHAN, GEORGE MARTIN, journalist, political science educator; b. N.Y.C., Jan. 14, 1931; s. Martin Francis and Kathleen (Brady) H.; m. Margreta La Moine Langston, Aug. 19, 1953; children: Michelle, Maura Lyle. AB in Liberal Arts, Columbia U., 1956, MS, 1957; PhD, Stanford U., 1970. Reporter, photographer San Jose (Calif.) Mercury News, 1959-62; info. mgr. Hunt Foods Corp., Fullerton, Calif., 1962-64; tng. mgr. Kaiser Med. Found., Los Angeles, 1964-66; prof. polit. sci. Calif. State U., Carson, 1967—; cons. Internat. Com., Los Angeles, 1965—. Contbr. articles to profl. jours. Cons. NEH, 1975—; chmn. State Acad. Senate, Los Angeles, 1970-72. Served with USAF, 1951-55. Recipient Disting. Teaching award Calif. State U., 1975, Merit Performance award Calif. State U., 1986, numerous fellowships, grants and scholarships, Stanford U. Mem. S.W. Polit. Sci. Assn., Stanford Alumni Assn., Danforth Found., Columbia U. Alumni Assn. Home: 3415 Dixon St Orange CA 92669 Office: Calif State U Polit Sci Dept 1000 E Victoria St Carson CA 92669

HENING, GLENN, computer information scientist, educator, infosystems specialist, consultant; b. San Antonio, Dec. 16, 1950; s. Hohn and Margo Hening; m. Alexa McKee Budero, July 27, 1980; 1 child, Helen Grace. BS, UCLA, 1972; postgrad., Calif. State U., Northridge, 1972-74. Cert. secondary tchr., Calif. Tcht. Escuela Panamericana, San Salvador, El Salvador, 1977-80; tchr. Alhambra (Calif.) City Schs., 1981-83; programmer JPL, Pasadena, Calif., 1984-86; owner, bd. dirs. Computer EASE, Los Osos and Pasadena, 1983—; founder Ind. Educators Network, Pasadena, 1983, Surfrider Found., Pasadena, 1984, also pres. Contbr. articles to Pasadena Weekly pub. Lutheran. Home: 1119 16th St Los Osos CA 93402 Office: Surfrider Found 52 N Menta Pasadena CA 91106

HENKE, RUSSELL F., computer company executive; b. Cin., Dec. 16, 1940; s. Carl A. and Luella R. (Fahey) H.; m. Susan Weichold, Aug. 10, 1962; children: Andrea Lee, J. Randall, Nathaniel R. ME with high honors, U. Cin., 1963, MS, 1965, PhD, 1968. Sr. research supr. Cin. Milacron, 1958-69; pres. SDRC, Milford, Ohio, 1969-82; exec. v.p. Applicon, Boston, 1982-84; pres. Gould Electronics Imaging and Graphics Div., Fremont, Calif., 1984-86; pres., chief exec. officer, chmn. bd. Automation Tech. Products, Campbell, Calif., 1986—; adj. asst. prof. U. Cin., 1968-82. Mem. ASME, IEEE, Soc. Mfg. Engrs., Engring. Soc. Cin., Tau Beta Pi. Office: Automation Tech Products 1671 Dell Ave Campbell CA 95008

HENLEY, ERNEST MARK, physics educator, university dean; b. Frankfurt, Germany, June 10, 1924; came to U.S., 1939, naturalized, 1944; s. Fred S. and Josy (Dreyfuss) H.; m. Elaine Dimitman, Aug. 21, 1948; children: M. Bradford, Karen M. B.E.E., CCNY, 1944; Ph.D., U. Calif. at Berkeley, 1952. Physicist Lawrence Radiation Lab., 1950-51; research asso. physics dept. Stanford U., 1951-52; lectr. physics Columbia U., 1952-54; mem. faculty U. Wash., Seattle, 1954—; prof. physics U. Wash., 1961—, chmn. dept., 1973-76, dean Coll. Arts and Scis., 1979—; bd. dirs. Pacific Sci. Ctr., 1984—, Wash. Tech. Ctr., 1983—; chmn. Nuclear Sci. Adv. Com., 1986—. Author: (with W. Thirring) Elementary Quantum Field Theory, 1962, (with H. Frauenfelder) Subatomic Physics, 1974, Nuclear and Particle Physics, 1975. Recipient sr. Alexander von Humboldt award, 1984; F.B. Jewett fellow, 1952-53; NSF sr. fellow, 1958-59; Guggenheim fellow, 1967-68; NATO sr. fellow, 1976-77. Fellow Am. Phys. Soc. (chmn. div. nuclear physics 1979-80), AAAS; mem. Nat. Acad. Scis., Sigma Xi. Research and numerous publs. on symmetries, nuclear reactions and high energy particle interactions. Office: Physics Dept FM 15 U Wash Seattle WA 98195

HENLEY, MARY ANN, psychologist; b. Altoona, Pa., Apr. 4, 1939; d. Richard Herbert and Eva Elizabeth (Crum) W.; divorced; children: Scott Alan, Chris Brian. PhD in Psychology, Ohio State U., 1970, D of Metaphys. Mind Sci., U. Metaphysics, 1973, D of Houistic Metapsychology, 1979. Pres., chief bus. ops. La Vie de CHATEAU Enterprises Inc., Palm Springs, Calif., 1974—. Mem. Inst. Applied Metaphysics (founder). Home: PO Box 662 Desert Hot Springs CA 92240 Office: La Vie de Chateau Ent Inc 250 E Palm Canyon Dr #2-E Palm Springs CA 92264

HENLEY, PRESTON VANFLEET, former banker, financial consultant; b. Fort Madison, Iowa, July 7, 1913; s. Jesse vanFleet and Ruth (Roberts) H.; m. Elizabeth Artis Watts, Mar. 31, 1940 (div. June 1956); children: Preston Edward VanFleet, Stephen Watts, John vanFleet; m. 2d, Helena Margaret Greenslade, Nov. 29, 1964; 1 adopted son, Lawrence D. Student Tulane U., 1931-34, Loyola U., New Orleans, 1935-36; A.B., Calif. State Coll. at Santa Barbara, 1939; postgrad. U. Wash., 1939-40, N.Y. U., 1943, 46. Teaching fellow U. Wash., 1939-40; sr. credit analyst, head credit dept. Chase Nat. Bank, 45th St. br. N.Y.C., 1942-49; Western sales rep. Devoe & Raynolds, Inc., N.Y.C., 1949-51; v.p., comml. loan officer, mgr. credit dept. U.S. Nat. Bank, Portland, Oreg., 1951-72; loan adminstr. Voyageur Bank Group, Eau Claire, Wis.; v.p. Kanabec State Bank, Mora, Minn., Montgomery State Bank (Minn.), Park Falls State Bank (Wis.), Montello State Bank (Wis.), 1972; v.p., mgr. main office, sr. credit officer So. Nev. region Nev. Nat. Bank, Las Vegas, 1973-75; bus. and fin. cons., 1975—; loan cons. Continental Nat. Bank, Las Vegas, 1983—; instr. Am. Inst. Banking, Portland, 1952-65, Multomah Coll., Portland, 1956-62, Portland State U., 1961-72, Mt. Hood Community Coll., 1971-72, Clark County Community Coll., 1979-83; adv. dir. Vita Plus, Inc., 1979-83; exec. dir. Nev. Minority Purchasing Council, 1979-80; dir., treas. Consumer Credit Counselling Service of Oreg. 1965-72. Treas., Ore. chpt. Leukemia Soc., 1965-66; mem. Menninger Found. 1965-67; trustee, exec. com. St. Rose delima Hosp. Found., 1982-87;dir. So. Nev. chtp. Assn. Part-Time Profls., 1985—. Served with USNR, 1943-45. Mem. Oreg. Bankers Assn., Robert Morris Assos. (pres. Oreg. chpt. 1959-60, nat. dir. 1961-64), Nat., Oreg. assns. credit mgmt., Credit Research Found., Inst. Internal Auditors, S.A.R., Am. Legion, Navy League, Beta Mu, Leaf and Scarab, Alpha Phi Omega, Portland C. of C., Oreg. Retail Council. Republican. Episcopalian. Mason (32 deg., Shriner), Elk. Club: International. Contbr. articles to profl. jours. Home and Office: 4235 Gibraltar St Las Vegas NV 89121

HENLEY, RICHARD MERLE, business executive; b. Portland, Oreg., Mar. 15, 1952; s. Roy Flanders and Grayce (Roatch) H.; m. Jan Lyn Talbert, Feb. 14, 1984. AA, Barstow (Calif.) Jr. Coll.; BA, Calif. State U., Long Beach, 1974, postgrad., 1975. Cert. highest level water treatment specialist. Adminstr., drug counselor, supr. Narconon U.S., Los Angeles, 1974-75, nat. adminstr., 1976-77; founder Northland Purewater Inc. (and predecessors), Hollywood and Los Feliz, Calif., 1975-81; exec. dir. then chief exec. officer, chmn. bd. dirs. Northland Purewater Inc. div. Northland Environ. Inc., Burbank, Calif., 1981—, founder Northland Mfg. Purewater div., 1985; chmn. nat. dealer bd. Sunland Industries, Phoenix, 1983-84. Inventor water processing system. chmn. pub. relations com. Solar Energy Industries Assn., Washington, 1984-85; mem. campaign Crusade for Religious Freedom, Hollywood, 1985—, Way to Happiness Found., 1985—, Narconon Get Am. Off Drugs, Los Angeles, 1983—. Mem. Nat. Fed. Ind. Businesses, Calif. Assn. Lic. Contractors, Concerned Businessmen Assn., Water Quality Assn., W.I.S.E. (founder), Calif. C. of C. Republican. Mem. Ch. of Scientology. Avocations: skiing, writing, lecturing, flying, video and film work, business consulting. Office: Northland Purewater Inc 1121 Chestnut Burbank CA 91506

HENLEY, WILLIAM BALLENTINE, rancher, lawyer, lectr.; b. Cin., Sept. 19, 1905; s. William Herbert and May G. (Richards) Ballentine (later assumed name of stepfather, Charles E. Henley); m. Helen McTaggart, 1942. A.B., U. So. Calif., 1928; postgrad., Sch. Religion, 1928-29, Yale, 1929-30; M.A., U. So. Calif., 1930, J.D., 1933, M.S. in P.A. 1935; LL.D., Willamette U., 1937; Sc.D., Kansas City Coll. Osteopathy and Surgery, 1949; R.Sc.D., Inst. Religious Sci. and Philosophy, 1949; L.H.D. Los Angeles Coll. Optometry, 1958; Sc.D., Pepperdine Coll., 1966. Lectr. pub. adminstrn., asst. to co-ordination officer U. So. Calif., 1928-29; dir. religious edn. First Meth. Ch., New Haven, 1929-30; lectr. in pub. adminstrn. U. So. Calif., 1930-33; exec. sec. U. So. Calif. (Women's Civic Conf.), 1930-40; acting dean U. So. Calif. (Sch. of Govt.), 1937-38; dir. U. So. Calif. (8th and 9th Inst. Govt.), 1937-38; asst. to dean U. So. Calif. (Sch. Govt., in charge in-service tng., Civic Center), 1934-36, asst. prof. pub. adminstrn., 1935-39, asso. prof., 1939-40, dir. co-ordination, 1938-40; pub. speaking instr. and debate coach Am. Inst. Banking, 1928-40; pres. Calif. Coll. Medicine, Los Angeles, 1940-66, Coll. Osteopathic Surgeons, 1940-66; provost U. Calif. at Irvine-Calif. Coll. Medicine, 1966-69; pres., chmn. bd. trustees United Ch. Religious Sci., 1969—; prof. United Ch. Religious Sci. (Sch. Ministry), 1972—; exec., speakers' panel Gen. Motors Corp., 1956-75. Author: The History of the University of Southern California, 1940, Man's Great Awakening, or Beautiful Mud, 1974, also mag. articles. Bd. dirs. Glendale Community Hosp., Glendale Adventist Med. Center, 1978-85; mem. Bd. Water and Power Commrs., Los Angeles, 1944-62, pres., 1946, v.p., 57-58; mem. Employees' Pension and Retirement Bd. Mgmt, 1946; mem. adv. bd. Los Angeles County Gen. Hosp., 1940-65; v.p. Los Angeles County Safety Council, 1971—; mem. Los Angeles Def. Council, 1941-44, War Council, 1944-45, Calif. Civil Def. Com.; guest observer UN Conf., San Francisco, 1945, A.T. Still Meml. lectr., Washington, 1958. Mem. Am., Calif., Los Angeles bar assns., NEA, Am. Pub. Health Assn., AAAS, Am. Saddle Horse Breeding Futurity Assn. (dir.), Am. Aberdeen Angus Breeders Assn., Sigma Alpha Epsilon, Phi Delta Phi, Phi Kappa Phi, Phi Sigma Gamma, Sigma Sigma Phi, Delta Sigma Rho, Phi Delta Kappa, Pi Sigma Alpha, Alpha Delta Sigma, Phi Eta Sigma, Sigma Sigma, Skull and Dagger. Republican. Clubs: Mason (32 deg.), Los Angeles Rotary (pres. 1955-56, chmn. conf. dist. 160-A, gov. dist. 528 1959-60, mem. internat. community service consultative group, chmn. host club exec. com. for 1962 internat. conv., mem. world community service com.). Home and office: Creston Circle Ranch Paso Robles CA 93446

HENNES, JOHN PETER, aerospace scientist; b. Seattle, Apr. 27, 1933; s. Albert Frank and Elma (Hawkins) H.; m. Judith Mosler, June 22, 1958 (div. July 1977); children: Scott Norman, Lisa Beth. BS in Physics, U. Wash, 1955, MS in Physics, 1957; postgrad., U. Md., 1956-59. Materials scientist Nat. Bur. Standards, Washington, 1956-57; research asst. physics dept. U. Md., College Park, 1957-59; aerospace scientist Goddard Space Flight Ctr., NASA, Greenbelt, Md., 1959-65; space scientist Boeing Aerospace Co., Seattle, 1965—. Contbr. articles to profl. sci. jours. Bd. mem. Cen. Area Sch. Council, Seattle, 1968-71; precinct com. mem. King County Dems., Seattle, 1968-72; bd. dirs. Seattle Marathon Assn., 1981-85. Mem. AAAS, Optical Soc. Am., Planetary Soc., Seattle Profl. Engring. Employees Assn. Democrat. Avocations: running, rowing, skiing. Home: 1412 N 52d St Seattle WA 98103 Office: Boeing Aerospace Co M/S 8A-24 PO Box 3999 Seattle WA 98124

HENNES, ROBERT GRAHAM, retired civil engineering educator; b. Lake Linden, Mich., July 7, 1905; s. Theodore John and Alice Mary (Graham) H.; m. Katherine Marie O'Hearn, Sept. 12, 1936; children: David Michael, Mary Elizabeth, Paul Anton, Sarah Ann. BSCE, U. Notre Dame, 1927; MS, MIT, 1928. Registered profl. engr. With city engr.'s office City of Detroit, 1928-

34; mem. faculty U. Wash., Seattle, 1934-73, prof. civil engring., 1947-71, chmn. dept., 1965-71, chmn. transp. research group, 1961-69, prof. civil engring, humanistic social studies, 1971—, prof. emeritus, 1973—; Cons. U.S. Bur. Pub. Rds., 1964-69, various agys., 1934—; guest prof. Bengal Engring. Coll., India, 1960-61, ITT, Delhi, 1966; chmn. econ. studies div. Highway Research Bd., Nat. Acad. Scis., 1959-67, Wash. State Council Highway Research, 1954-64; sec. faculty U. Wash., 1972-73; numerous other coms. Co-Author: Fundamentals of Transportation Engineering, 1955, 2d rev. edit., 1969; contbr. numerous articles to profl. jours. Mem. U. Wash. Retirement Assn. (pres. 1977-79). Home: 3811 41 Ave NE Seattle WA 98105

HENNEY, CHRISTOPHER SCOT, immunologist; b. Sutton-Coldfield, Eng., Feb. 4, 1941; s. William Scot and Rhoda Agnes (Bateman) Henney; m. Janet Barnsley, June 20, 1964; children: James Scot, Samantha Jane. BS with honors, U. Birmingham, Eng., 1962, PhD in Exptl. Pathology, 1965, DSc. in Research Immunology (hon.), 1973. Immunologist WHO, Lausanne, Switzerland; assoc. prof. medicine and microbiology Johns Hopkins U. Med. Sch., Balt., 1978; prof. microbiology and immunology U. Wash., Seattle, 1978-81; head. basic immunology Fred Hutchinson Cancer Research Ctr., Seattle, 1978-81; sci. dir., exec. v.p. Immunex Corp., Seattle, 1981—. Mem. Am. Assn. Immunology (sect. editor 1972-73), Reticuloendothelial Soc. (sect. editor 1978-79), Am. Cancer Soc. (chmn. immunology rev. com. 1982-83), NIH (mem. pathology study sect. 1978-82). Office: Immunex Corp 51 University St Seattle WA 98101

HENNING, CARL DOUGLAS, mechanical engineer; b. Cleve., Feb. 28, 1939; s. Carl and Anna Eugenia (Cherveney) H.; m. Judith Kay Buck, Dec. 26, 1962; children—Kirsten, Lisa. B.S. in Mech. Engring., Ohio U., 1961; M.S. in Mech. Engring., U. Mich., 1963; Ph.D., 1965. Project engr. Lawrence Livermore Nat. Lab., Calif., 1965-73, head mirror program office, 1978—; v.p. Intermagnetics Gen., Albany, N.Y., 1973-76; chief magnetics Dept. Energy, Washington, 1976-78. Contbr. articles to profl. jours. Recipient 1st Place award Lincoln Arc Welding Found., 1980; Outstanding Accomplishment award Am. Nuclear Soc., 1982. Mem. Cryogenics Engring. Conf. (chmn. 1982—), Am. Nuclear Soc. (conf. chmn., 1983—). Republican. Office: Lawrence Livermore Nat Lab PO Box 5511 L-644 Livermore CA 94550

HENNING, JOHN F., labor union ofcl.; b. San Francisco, Nov. 22, 1915; s. William Henry and Lulu Frances (McLane) H.; A.B., St. Mary's Coll., 1938, LL.D., 1976; LL.D., St. Anselm's Coll., 1965; D.C.S., St. Bonaventure U., 1966; m. Margueritte M. Morand, Nov. 25, 1939; children—John F., Brian H., Patrick W., Nancy R., Daniel M., Thomas R., Mary T. Research dir., adminstrv. asst. to exec. officer Calif. State Fedn. Labor, San Francisco, 1949-58; dir. Calif. Dept. Indsl. Relations, San Francisco, 1959-62; U.S. under sec. of labor, Washington, 1962-67; U.S. Ambassador to N.Z., 1967-69; exec. sec.-treas. Calif. Labor Fedn. AFL-CIO, San Francisco, 1970—. Mem. Bd. Permit Appeals, 1953-56, pres., 1955-56; mem. Pub. Welfare Commn., 1950-53; mem. Equal Employment Opportunities Commn, 1956-59 (all San Francisco); mem. bd. regents U. Calif., 1977—. Office: Calif Labor Fedn AFL-CIO 417 Montgomery St San Francisco CA 94104

HENNING, PATRICK WILLIAM, state agency administrator; b. San Francisco, June 11, 1946; s. John Francis and Margueritte Martha (Morand) H.; m. Regina Loretta McShane, Feb. 20, 1971; children: Patrick William, Robert McShane (dec.), Erin Rose, Michael Emmet. PhB, Cath. U. Am., 1969. Law clk. to justice U.S. Supreme Ct., Washington, 1968; internat. organizer, asst. nat. dir. organizing service employees Internat. Union AFL-CIO, Harrisburg, Pa. and N.Y.C., 1971-73; asst. bus. mgr., asst. dir. negotiations, internat. rep. Hotel and Restaurant Employees and Bartenders Internat. Union, AFL-CIO, Los Angeles, 1973-78; spl. rep. Internat. Union Operating Engrs., Los Angeles, 1980-81; labor commr. State of Calif., San Francisco, 1981-82; mem. agrl. labor relations bd. State of Calif., Sacramento, 1983—; exec. dir. Cath. Labor Inst. So. Calif., Los Angeles, 1975—; mem. State Commn. Status of Women, Sacramento, 1981-82, Hollywood (Calif.) Film Council, 1974-78. Co-chmn. Calif. Dem. Platform Com. Labor Plank, Los Angeles, 1981; chmn. Devel. Disabilities Bd. for Los Angeles County, 1976-82; mem. Citizens Conscience Com. for Los Angeles Apparel Industry, 1978—. Roman Catholic. Office: Agrl Labor Relations Bd 915 Capitol Mall 3d Floor Sacramento CA 95814

HENNINGSEN, RICHARD MELVIN, petroleum company management training specialist; retired air force officer; b. Oakland, Calif., July 14, 1937; s. Melvin George and Blanche Louise (Rocheau) H.; m. Barbara Jane Schmidt, Dec. 15, 1957; children—Laurie, Richard, James, Brett. A.A., A.B., U. Calif., Berkeley, 1959; postgrad. U. Laverne, 1978-80. Commd. 2d lt. U.S. Air Force, advanced through grades to lt. col., 1977; instr., navigator, 1964-70, master navigator, 1974-80, wing base plans officer, 1971-77, dir. command and control Alaskan Air Command, 1977-80; ret., 1980; tng. specialist Standard Alaska Prodn. Co., Anchorage, 1980—; founder, pres. Invesco, Inc., Anchorage, 1983—; co-founder, v.p. travel agy., Fairbanks, Alaska, 1975-77. Decorated Air medal, Meritorious Service medal, Air Force Commendation medal, Vietnamese Cross of Gallantry with palm. Mem. Air Force Assn., Am. Soc. for Tng. and Devel., Nat. Soc. for Performance and Instrn., United Vets. of Alaska. Republican. Methodist.

HENRICHS, ROY BEDDOW, quality engineer, consultant; b. Berkeley, Calif., June 25, 1953; s. LeRoy Anthony and Irene (Beddow) H.; m. Joanna Mary Ashley Larmuth, Dec. 20, 1979; 1 child, Paul Ashley LeRoy. BSCE, U. Calif., Berkeley, 1976; MBA, John F. Kennedy U., 1986. Registered profl. engr., Calif. Asst. mgr. Delta Communications and Engring., Concord, Calif., 1976-77; nuclear engr. Mare Island Naval Shipyard, Vallejo, Calif., 1977-81; quality engr. Systron Donner Inertial Div., Concord, 1981—; cons. R&J Communications, El Cerrito, Calif., 1981—. Bd, dirs. St. Moritz Ice Skating Club, Berkeley, 1974-76. Mem. ASCE, Am. Soc. Quality Control, ADC Assocs. (lic.), Am. Radio Relay League, Chi Phi. Republican. Avocations: amateur radio, figure skating, skiing. Home: 7417 Park Vista El Cerrito CA 94530 Office: Systron Donner Inertial Div 2700 Systron Dr Concord CA 94518

HENRICHS, SUSAN MARGARET, marine chemist; b. Anchorage, Nov. 23, 1952; d. John Glen and Barbara Enid (Burrier) H.; m. Luther Michael Cheek, June 7, 1985. BS in Chemistry and Chem. Oceanography, U. Wash., 1975; PhD in Chem. Oceanography, MIT, 1980. Postdoctoral research chemist Scripps Instn. Oceanography, La Jolla, Calif., 1980-81; asst. prof. Inst. Marine Sci. U. Alaska, Fairbanks, 1982—. Contbr. articles to profl. jours. Paul M. Fye fellow Woods Hole Oceanographic Instn., 1978. Mem. AAAS, Am. Soc. Limnology and Oceanography, Am. Chem. Soc., Am. Soc. Microbiology, Phi Beta Kappa. Office: U Alaska Inst Marine Sci Fairbanks AK 99775-1080

HENRICHSEN, WALTER A., foundation administrator; b. Berkeley, Calif., Feb. 20, 1934; s. Walter A. Henrichsen; m. Leette D. Dillon, June 3, 1962; children: Deborah, Jonathan, Janna Kay. AA, Modesto Jr. Coll., 1956; BA, Cen. Coll., Pella, Iowa, 1956; BD, Western Sem., 1959; postgrad. Fuller Sem., 1976. Tchr. Valley Christian High Sch., Calif., 1959-61; mem. staff The Navigators, Colorado Springs, Colo., 1961-62, area dir., 1962-66, regional dir., 1966-71, asst. to pres., 1971-73, internat. personnel coordinator, 1973-75, dep. dir., 1975-77; assoc. Leadership Found., Colorado Springs, 1977—; bd. dirs. Search Ministries, Balt., 1980—, Vision Found., Knoxville, Tenn., 1981—, Personal Devel. Found., Colorado Springs, 1984—. Author: Disciples Are Made, Not Born, 1974, A Layman's Guide to Interpreting the Bible, 1978, After the Sacrifice, 1979, How to Disciple Your Children, 1981, Layman, Look Up! God Has a Place for You, 1983. Office: Leadership Found Inc PO Box 1782 Colorado Springs CO 80901

HENRICK, CLIVE ARTHUR, chemical researcher; b. Big Bell, Australia, Jan. 13, 1941; came to U.S., 1967;; s. Gustave Bernard and Marjorie (Grey) H. BS, U. Western Australia, 1962, PhD in Organic Chemistry, 1965. Postdoctoral fellow Syntex Research, Inst. Steroid Chemistry, 1967-68; sr. chemist Syntex Research, 1968-69; chief chemist Zoecon Corp., Palo Alto, Calif., 1969-71, dir. chem. research, 1971—. Contbr. numerous articles to profl. jours.; patentee in field. Recipient Inventor Yr. award Hooker Chem. Co., 1979. Mem. AAAS, Am. Chem. Soc., The Chem. Soc. Home: 3177 Manchester Ct Palo Alto CA 94303 Office: Sandoz Crop Protection Zoecon Research Inst 975 California Ave Palo Alto CA 94304

HENRICKSEN, JOHN MAACK, dentist; b. Chehalis, Wash., Feb. 7, 1945; s. Andrew Peter and Lenora Sylvia (Maack) H.; m. Jolyn Kay Coburn, June 24, 1967; children: Erika, Andrea, Chris, Daniel. DDS, U. Wash., 1970; cert. in dental internship, Malcolm Grow Med. Ctr., Washington, 1971. Lic. dentist, Wash. Clin. instr. dept. pedodontics U. Wash. Sch. Dentistry, Seattle, 1973-76; gen. practice dentistry Chehalis, 1974—; dir. dental services Centralia (Wash.) Gen. Hosp. and St. Helen's Hosp., Chehalis, 1975—; forensic odontologist Lewis County Sheriff's Dept., Chehalis, 1983—. Pres. Wash. Dental Edn. Found., Seattle, 1979-80, Lewis County Community Concerts, Chehalis, 1975—; chmn. C.A.P.R.I. cordia rehab. program, Centralia, 1983; bishop Ch. Jesus Christ Latter-Day Sts. Served to capt. USAF, 1970-74. Mem. ADA (pres. Lewis-Pacifis soc.), Am. Soc. Dentistry for Children, Northwest Forensic Study Club, Acad. Forensic Sci. (pre-fellow). Republican. Rotary (pres. Chehalis chpt.). Office: 1292 S Marked Blvd Chehalis WA 98532

HENRIE, KIM BARTON, direct marketing professional; b. Ely, Nev., Aug. 17, 1951; s. Keith Larsen and Faye (Barton) H.; m. Linda Maree Casper, Aug. 2, 1974; children: Justin, Seth, Asher. BS, Brigham Young U., 1975, MBA, 1977. Mgr. Y-Tex Corp., Cody, Wyo., 1977-80; mktg. mgr. Reliance Co., Walnut Creek, Calif., 1980-81; pres., owner K.B. Henrie & Assocs., Inc., San Ramon, Calif., 1981—; chmn., owner Brit. Am. Collectors Soc., San Ramon, 1983—. Author: The Insiders Guide to Greater Wealth and Bargains, 1985. Club: Blackhawk (Calif.). Office: 7 Crow Canyon Ct Suite 250 San Ramon CA 94583

HENRY, ANTHONY RAY, administrator, community organizer; b. Houston, Aug. 14, 1938; s. Lawrence G. and Autry B. (Thomas) H. B.A., U. Tex.-Austin, 1960; M.Ed., Springfield Coll., 1961. Community devel. vol. Am. Friends Service Com., Tanzania, East Africa, 1961-63; dir. preadolescent enrichment program Am. Friends Service Com., Chgo., 1963-66, dir. housing program, 1966-69; dir. nationwide tenants rights program Am. Friends Service Com., Washington, 1969; dir. Nat. Tenants Orgn., Inc., Washington, 1969-71, 74-75, Nat. Tenants Info. Service, Inc., Washington, 1971-74; spl. asst. Newark Tenants Council, Inc., 1975-76; nat. rep. criminal justice programs Am. Friends Service Com., Phila., 1976-78; affirmative action sec. AFSC, Phila., 1978-81; exec. sec. AFSC No. Calif. Regional Office, San Francisco, 1981—; Mem. rent adv. bd. to Price Commn., Phase II Econ. Stblzn. Program, 1972-73; mem. community relations com. Am. Friends Service Com., 1972-76, mem. internat. affairs div. com., 1974-76; dep. nat. coordinator So. Christian Leadership Conf.'s Poor People Campaign, 1968; mem. Quaker UN Com., 1975-76; bd. dirs. Nat. Housing Conf., 1971-76, Rural Housing Coalition, 1971-73, Nonprofit Housing Center, 1972-73, Met. Washington Planning and Housing Assn., 1971-74, Tenant Resources Center, Washington, 1976-77, Nat. Coalition Against Death Penalty, 1976-78; incorporator, bd. dirs. Nat. Center for Housing Mgmt., 1972-81, vice chmn., 1974-81; bd. dirs. Tenant Action Group, Phila., 1976-81, sec., 1977-78, co-chairperson, 1978-81; bd. dirs., chmn. Low Income Housing Info. Center, Washington, 1977-82; bd. dirs. Nat. Coalition Against Grand Jury Abuse, 1977-78, Nat. Tenants Union, 1980-81. Mem. Interreligious Task Force on Criminal Justice, 1977-78; mem. Pa. Council for Sexual Minorities, 1978-81; mem. community adv. bd. Peace and Conflict studies U. Calif.-Berkeley, 1985—; mem. Lesbian/Gay adv. com. Human Rights Commn., City and County San Francisco, 1985—. Home: 1860 Turk St San Francisco CA 94115 Office: 2160 Lake St San Francisco CA 94121

HENRY, BARBARA A., newspaper editor; b. Oshkosh, Wis., July 23, 1952; d. Robert Edward and Barbara Frances (Aylesworth) H. BJ, U. Nev. Reporter Reno Newspapers, 1974-78, city editor, 1978-80, mng. editor, 1980-82; asst. nat. editor USA Today, Washington, 1982-83; exec. editor Reno Gazette-Jour., 1981-86; editor Democrat and Chronicle, also Times-Union, Rochester, N.Y., 1986—. Mem. Soc. Profl. Journalists, Associated Press Mng. Editors, Am. Soc. Newspaper Editors, Calif.-Nev. Soc. Newspaper Editors (bd. dirs.). Avocation: skiing. Home: 1395 Mount Rose St Reno NV 89509 Office: Democrat and Chronicle 55 Exchange Blvd Rochester NY 14614

HENRY, CHARLES LAVON, advertising company executive, marketing consultant, educator; b. Augusta, Ga., June 17, 1947; s. William Clark and Katie Catherine (Quinn) H.; m. Beverly Gonzalez, Aug. 2, 1972 (div.); children—Alisa, Matthew, Adam. B.A. in Communications, Brigham Young U., 1972; bus. mgmt. cert. U. Utah, 1977. Pub. relations supr. Mountain Bell, Salt Lake City, Denver, 1976-78; advt. staff mgr., Denver, 1978-79; dir. mktg. Internat. Communications Assocs., Denver, 1979; instr./lectr. pub. relations Brigham Young U., Provo, Utah, 1980-82; pub. info. officer Fed. Emergency Mgmt. Agy., Denver and Washington, 1981; v.p. mktg. Andes Mines Internat., Denver, Santiago, 1983—; dir. Quinlott Corp., Andes Mines Internat. Bus. Co., Inc.; instr. pub. relations, advt. Brigham Young U. Del., Colo. Assembly, 1980-82; capt. Jefferson County Republican party. Named Communicator of Yr., Internat. Bus. Communicators Assn., 1977; Businessman of Yr., Colo./Okla., 1983; numerous awards for journalism and photography. Mem. Pub. Relations Soc. Am., Am. Mgmt. Assn., Internat. Assn. Bus. Communicators, Sigma Delta Chi. Mormon. Author: A Guide to Fire Alarm Systems, 1973; Batteries Not Included, 1982; H.T. (the home teacher), 1982; The Missionary Companion, 1983. Home: PO Box 8555 Denver CO 80201 Office: AMI 12395 W 53d Ave Suite 208 Denver CO 80002

HENRY, CHARLES LEWIS, accountant, educator; b. Raton, N.Mex., Dec. 10, 1946; s. Virgil Oscar and Eloise (Eldridge) H.; m. Carol Ruth Gerken, Nov. 16, 1950; children: Kevin, Eric, Sarah. BBA in Acctg., U. N.Mex., 1970. CPA Surety bond underwriter USF & G, Albuquerque, 1970-71; staff acct. Lewallen & Co., Albuquerque, 1971-74; controller N.Mex. Beverage Co., Albuquerque, 1974; sr. staff acct. Neff & Co. CPA's, Albuquerque, 1974-75; ptnr. Henry, Kardas, Abeyta & Co. CPA's, Albuquerque, 1975—; tchr. acctg. U. N.Mex.; pub. speaker. Mem. Am. Inst. CPA's, N.Mex. Soc. CPA's. Democrat. Roman Catholic. Home: 6708 Loftus NE Albuquerque NM 87109 Office: Henry Kardas Abeyta & Co 1128 Pennsylvania NE Suite 200 Albuquerque NM 87110

HENRY, HOMER C., railroad company executive; b. LaFollette, Tenn., July 1, 1950; s. John David and Mabel Ann (Davis) H.; m. Julia Gallagher, Aug. 17, 1968 (div. Mar. 1986); m. Donna Lee Watson, July 19, 1986. BS in Econs., U. Calif., Riverside, 1972, MBA, 1980; Internat. Bus. Econs. deg. (hon.), U. So. Calif., Los Angeles, 1985. Lic. comml.-instrument pilot. Pilot USAF, Norton AFB, Calif., 1973-80; locomotive engr. Santa Fe Railway, San Bernadino, Calif., 1974-80; road foreman of engines Santa Fe Railway, Barstow, Calif., 1980-84; gen. road foreman of engines Santa Fe Railway, Los Angeles, 1984—. Mem. Railway Operating Officers and Fuel Assn. Republican. Avocations: aviation, hist. research, tennis, jogging, fine dining. Office: Santa Fe Railway 5200 E Sheila St Los Angeles CA 90040

HENRY, JOHN ALFRED, lawyer; b. Westbrook, Maine, Feb. 11, 1931; s. Donald M. and Josephine M. (Perry) H.; children—James Richard, Jeffrey Alan. B.A. cum laude, Bowdoin Coll., 1952, J.D. with honors, George Washington U., 1960. Bar: Va. 1960, Mass. 1961, Ariz. 1968. Tax law specialist Rulings div. Nat. Office IRS Washington 1959-61; assoc. Ropes & Gray, Boston, 1960-68, Lewis & Roca Phoenix, 1968-70; founding ptnr. Henry, Kimerer & La Velle, 1970-84; of counsel Allen, Kimerer & LaVelle, Phoenix, 1985—. Chmn. bd. Legal Profls. Credit Union; mem. exec. com. Am. Cancer Soc. Ariz. Div., Inc., 1969—, pres., 1976-77, chmn. bd., 1977-79, chmn. legacy com., 1979-83; vice chmn. ann. dinner NCCJ, 1983, 84. Served with USAF, 1952-56. Recipient Am. Cancer Soc. Annual Nat. Divisional award, 1978, 83. Mem. ABA, State Bar Va., State Bar Mass., State Bar Ariz. Republican. Clubs: Univ., Mansion, Plaza (Phoenix). Contbr. to legal jours. Home: 4936 E Arroyo Verde Dr Paradise Valley AZ 85253 Office: Allen Kimerer & LaVelle 2715 N 3d St Phoenix AZ 85004

HENRY, KAREN HAWLEY, lawyer; b. Whittier, Calif., Nov. 5, 1943; d. Ralph Hawley and Dorothy Ellen (Carr) Hawley; m. John Dunlap, 1968; m. Charles Gibbons Henry, Mar. 15, 1975; children—Scott, Alexander, Joshua. B.S. in Social Scis., So. Oreg. Coll., 1965; M.S. in Labor Econs., Iowa State U., 1967; J.D., Hastings Coll. of Law, 1976. Instr., Medford (Oreg.) Sch. Dist., 1965-66; research asst. dept. econs. Iowa State U., Ames, 1966-67; dir. research program Calif. Nurses Assn., San Francisco, 1967-72; labor relations coordinator Affiliated Hosps. of San Francisco, 1972-79; ptnr. Littler, Mendelson, Fastiff & Tichy, San Francisco, 1979-86; mng. ptnr. labor and employment law Weissburg and Aronson, Inc., San Francisco, 1986—. Mem. Calif. Soc. Healthcare Attys. (bd. dirs. 1986-87, pres.-elect), Am. Hosp. Assn. (ad hoc labor atty. com.), State Bar of Calif., San Francisco Bar Assn., Contra Costa Bar Assn., Thurston Soc., Order of Coif. Author: Health Care Supervisor's Legal Guide, 1984, Nursing Administration Law Manual, 1986.. Office: Weissburg and Aronson Inc 555 California St Suite 2400 San Francisco CA 94108

HENRY, LAWRENCE JOSEPH, automotive executive; b. Oakland, Calif., Apr. 2, 1950; s. William Lawrence and Mary Elizabeth (Wilbur) H.; m. Kathy Claire Keevan, Jan. 28, 1978. BA, Calif. State U., San Francisco, 1971. Race car driver 1971-85; owner auto test agy. Pro-Ride Co., Sacramento, 1977—. Author, publ.: (newsletter) Pro-Ride Automotive News, 1982; guest host Sta. KGO-Radio, Sta. KABC, Sta. KFBK, Sta. KGNR, 1981-86; feature columnist Sacramento Union Newspaper. Named Formula B Champion, 1972, Formula 5000 Champion, 1972, Formula Atlantic West Coast Champion, 1982, Golden West Grand Handicap Winner, 1985. Mem. Internat. Motor Sports Assn., Inc. (competition lic.), Sports Car Club of Am., Amateur Trapshooting Assn. Democrat. Roman Catholic. Avocations: bicycle racing, guitar, running, trapshooting, high country camping. Office: Pro-Ride Co PO Box 13407 Sacramento CA 95813

HENRY, MURIEL BOYD, social worker; b. Chgo., Feb. 17, 1927; d. Thomas Alexander and Muriel Alice (Engelhard) Boyd; m. Gerrit V. Henry Jr., Nov. 24, 1971; children by previous marriage: Janet Spangler, Carl Thomas Peterson, JoAnne Peterson. BA in Sociology, U. Wash., 1974, MSW, 1977. Social worker Travelers Aid Soc., Seattle, 1978-81; med. social worker Overlake Hosp., Bellevue, Wash., 1981—; mem. Evergreen Stroke Assn., Seattle, 1983-85, pres., 1984. Dir. of residential campaign United Way of King County, Seattle, 1969-73. Mem. Nat. Assn. Social Workers, Acad. Cert. Social Workers (cert.). Avocation: sailing.

HENRY, SHARLENE FAYE, medical company executive; b. North Platte, Nebr., July 24, 1951; d. John Earl and Daisy Darlene (VanWinkle) H.; m. William Glenn Schlueter, Aug. 19, 1972 (div. Sept. 1976). AA in Bus., North Platte Jr. Coll. Mgr. Motor Hotel Mgmt., Denver, 1980-83; gen. mgr. Elec. Message Ctr., Denver, 1983-84, Page Am. Communications, Denver, 1984-85; mgr. Regional Ctr. Zee Med. Service Co., Denver, 1985—; mem. adv. bd. Rocky Mountain Hosp., 1984. 1st aid trainer ARC, Denver, 1985—. Mem. U.S. Jaycees (nat. communications dir. 1980, loc. pub. relations 1984—), Denver C. of C., Profl. and Bus. Women Denver, Colo.-Wyo. Restaurant Assn., Am. Legion Aux. Democrat. Avocations: snow skiing, tennis, sports cars, gardening, travel. Home: 16202 E Flora Pl Aurora CO 80013 Office: Zee Med Service Co 14500 E 39th Ave Aurora CO 80011

HENRY, SHIRLEY ANN, press executive; b. Los Angeles, Apr. 23, 1937; d. Austin Perry Shaver and Ann (Pitrucka) Wilhelm; m. Walter Sigman Henry, July 1, 1955 (dec. Oct. 1985); children—Debbie Henry Johnson, Shelly Henry Dozier, Derek Sigman. A.A. with honors, Contra Costa Coll., San Pablo, Calif., 1969. Lic. R.N., Calif. Nurse, VA Hosp., Martinez, Calif., 1970-73; chief exec. officer Lamorinda Press, Lafayette, Calif., 1976—. Baptist. Avocations: skiing; scuba diving. Office: Lamorinda Press 3409 C Mt Diablo Blvd Lafayette CA 94549

HENRY, WALTER L., cardiologist, educator; b. Cumberland, Md., Feb. 20, 1941; s. Walter and Virginia Mae (Keller) H.; BSEE cum laude, U. Pitts., 1963; MD, Stanford U., 1969. Intern, Bronx Mcpl. Hosp., N.Y.C. and Albert Einstein Coll. Medicine, 1969-70, resident in internal medicine, 1970-71; clin. asso. Nat. Heart, Lung and Blood Inst., Bethesda, Md., 1971-73, sr. investigator, 1973-78; prof. medicine, chief div. cardiology U. Calif., Irvine, 1978—. Served with USPHS, 1971-78. Diplomate Am. Bd. Internal Medicine. Recipient Disting. Alumnus award U. Pitts. Engring. Alumni Assn, 1985, Profl. Achievement award U. Calif., Irvine, 1986. Mem. Am. Soc. Echocardiography (pres. 1981-83), N. Am. Soc. Cardiac Radiology, Am. Heart Assn., Am. Coll. Cardiography (area gov. So. Calif. 1985-88), Am. Fedn. Clin. Research, Eta Kappa Nu, Alpha Omega Alpha, Omicron Delta Kappa. Editorial bd. Am. Heart Jour. Contbr. articles to profl. jours. Office: Cardiology Div U Calif Irvine Med Center 101 City Dr S Orange CA 92717

HENSCHEL, R. PETER, municipal government officer; b. Milw., Dec. 7, 1948; s. Frederick William and Annerose (Scharlach) H.; m. Kathleen Gregory, Dec. 18, 1971. BA cum laude, Harvard U., 1971; M in Pub. Policy, U. Calif., Berkeley, 1973. Cons. Griffenhagen-Kroeger, San Francisco, 1973-75; asst. dir. program evaluation Alameda County Bd. Suprs., Oakland, Calif., 1975-78; asst. county mgr. San Mateo County, Redwood City, Calif., 1978; sr. program mgr., mayor City and County of San Francisco, 1978-83; dep. mayor mgmt. and programs Mayor's office, San Francisco, 1983—; bd. dirs. Japan Soc. No. Calif., San Francisco, 1983—, San Francisco Shanghai Com., 1980—; v.p. Friends of Photography, Carmel, Calif., 1984—. Contbr. articles to newspapers, photographs to pubs. Mem. Nat. Com. U.S.-China Relations, N.Y.C., 1982—. Mem. Am. Soc. Pub. Adminstrn., San Francisco Symphony Chorus. Democrat. Mem. Unitarian Ch. Avocations: classical music, opera, backpacking, photography, wilderness skiing. Home: 4449 23d St San Francisco CA 94114

HENZEL, WILLIAM JAMES, biochemist; b. Schenectady, N.Y., Apr. 5, 1953; s. Phillip James and Mary (De Lisa) H.; m. Bonnie Crandle, Sept 14, 1973; 1 child, Marcy Anne. BS, SUNY, Geneseo, 1976. Research asst. Boston Children's Hosp., 1976-79; research assoc. U. Mass., Boston, 1979-82, Genentech, Inc., South San Francisco, 1982—. Mem. Am. Chem. Soc. Office: Genentech Inc 460 Pt San Bruno South San Francisco CA 94404

HEPKER, WILMA MAY, sociology and social work educator; b. Sebastian, Tex., Nov. 1, 1933; d. William Jennings and Novella May (Anderson) Jones; m. Dale Bertram Hepker, June 1, 1953; children: Devin, David, Donna, Mae, Don B. BA, Union Coll., Lincoln, Nebr., 1953; MA, U. Nebr., 1966, PhD, 1976; MSW, Eastern Wash. U., 1983. Tchr. Little Rock. Jr. Acad., 1953-55, Ozark Acad., Gentry, Ark., 1955-61, Union Coll., 1961-66, Middle East Coll., Beirut, 1966-72; chmn. sociology and social work dept. Walla Walla Coll., College Place, Wash., 1974—. Grantee OMDS, 1985-86. Mem. Nat. Assn. Social Workers, Nat. Council on Family Relations, Council on Social Work Edn., Alliance for Children Youth and Families (bd. dirs. 1983—), United Way (bd. dirs. 1981-84), Phi Kappa Phi. Democrat. Adventist. Home: 504 Scenic View Dr College Place WA 99324 Office: Walla Walla Coll Dept Sociology and Social Work College Place WA 99324

HEPLER, MERLIN JUDSON, JR., real estate broker; b. Hot Springs, Va., May 13, 1929; s. Merlin Judson and Margaret Belle (Vines) H.; m. Lanova Helen Roberts, July 25, 1952; children: Nancy Andora, Douglas Stanley. BS in Bus., U. Idaho, 1977; grad., Realtors Inst., 1979. Enlisted USAF, 1947, advanced through grades to sgt., 1960, ret., 1967; service mgr. Lanier Bus. Products, Gulfport, Miss., 1967-74; sales assoc. Century 21 Singler and Assn., Troy, Idaho, 1977-79; broker B&M Realty, Troy, 1979—. Mem. Nat. Assn. Realtors, Am. Legion, U. Idaho Alumni Assn., Air Force Sgts. Assn. Republican. Lodge: Lions. Avocations: hunting, fishing. Home: Rt 1 Box 119 Troy ID 83871 Office: B&M Realty PO Box 187 102 A St Troy ID 83871

HEPPENHEIMER, THOMAS ADOLPH, science writer; b. N.Y.C., Jan. 1, 1947; s. Henry Gunther and Betty Lorraine (Amitin) H.; m. Phyllis Marcia Safdy, Dec. 9, 1967 (div. May 1977); children: Laurie, Alex, Connie; m. Angela Lee Johnson, Nov. 10, 1979. BSME, Mich. State U., 1967, MSME, 1968; PhD in Aero. Engring., U. Mich., 1972. Scientist Science Applications Inc., Schiller Park, Ill., 1972-73; tech. staff Rockwell Internat. Corp., Seal Beach, Calif., 1973-74; research fellow Calif. Inst. Tech., Pasadena, 1974-75, Max Planck Inst., Heidelberg, Federal Republic of Germany, 1976-78; pvt. practice writer Fountain Valley, Calif., 1978—; tech. v.p. FASST, Ann Arbor, Mich., 1971-73. Author: Colonies in Space, 1977 (Book of the Month club alternate 1977), Toward Distant Suns, 1979 (Book of the Month club alternate 1980), The Real Future, 1983, The Man-Made

Sun, 1984 (Sci. Book of the Month club alternate 1984); contbg. author Robotics (Marvin Minsky, editor), 1985, July 20, 2019 (Arthur C. Clarke, editor), 1986; book review editor Jour. Astron. Scis., 1979—; contbr. articles to profl. jours., popular mags. including Omni, Science Digest, Mosaic, Popular Science, High Technology, Science '86. Graduate fellow NSF, 1967; research fellow, Calif. Inst. Tech., 1974, Alexander von Humboldt Found., 1976. Fellow British Interplanetary Soc., AIAA (assoc.); mem. AAAS. Republican. Home: 11040 Blue Allium Ave Fountain Valley CA 92708

HEPPNER, CLAUS ERICH, designer; b. Wuppertal, Germany, June 13, 1930; s. Erich and Margarete (Romuender) H.; m. Margarete Elizabeth Leber; children—Diana Wiens, Deborah. B.A., Sch. Environ. Design, U. Colo., 1979. Jr. designer Am. Fixture Co., Denver; designer contract dept. Comml. Interiors, Denver, 1956-58, mgr. 1958; pres., owner Claus Heppner & Assocs., Denver, 1967—; theatrical designer. Mem. Am. Soc. Interior Designers. Republican. Clubs: Garden of the Gods (Colorado Springs); Balboa (Mazatlan, Mex.). Home: 1000 S Monaco Apt 104 Denver CO 80224 Office: 1600 Logan Denver CO 80203

HEPWORTH, CAROLYNE, soils engineering company executive; b. Augusta, Ga., Jan. 3, 1942; d. Samuel and Patricia A. (Timm) Steffen; children: Michelle Denise, Michael John, Diana Lynnette. Assoc. in Acctg., Columbia Coll., 1981; cert. in fin. mgmt. U. Denver, 1984. Sec. U.S. Army Records Ctr., St. Louis, 1960-61, Goodyear Tire & Rubber Co., St. Louis, 1963-67; bookkeeper, office mgr. Hayes C.T.S., Inc., Ironton, Mo., 1971-73; controller Chen & Assocs., Inc., Denver, 1974—. Vol. Ronald McDonald House. Mem. LWV, Am. Soc. Women Accts., Nat. Assn. Accts. (bd. dirs., mem. acquisition 1986—), Am. Assn. Accts., Acquisition 1984 (sec. 1984-85), Profl. Services Mgmt. Assn. (sec.-treas.), Network for Archtl. and Engring. Profls. (founder, exec. dir. 1985). Republican. Roman Catholic. Lodge: Zonta (membership com. Denver chpt. 1986—, corresponding sec.). Office: Chen & Assocs 96 S Zuni St Denver CO 80223

HEPWORTH, DEAN H., social work educator; b. Afton, Wyo., Nov. 15, 1928; s. Ezra James and Selma (Hanson) H.; m. Patricia Jean Brunson, Sept. 10, 1948; children: Roger Dean, Bruce E. BS, U. Utah, 1950, MSW, 1958, PhD, 1968. Caseworker Utah Dept. Pub. Welfare, Salt Lake City, 1952-55, caseworker supr., 1955-59; pvt. practice psychiatry Provo, Utah, 1959-63; prof. U. Utah, Salt Lake City, 1964—; cons., pvt. practice therapy, Salt Lake City, 1983-86; vice chmn. Salt Lake Retention Ctr. Adv. Bd., Salt Lake City, 1985-86. Co-author: Improving Therapeutic Communication, 1977, Direct Social Work Practice, 1982, 86, Bridging Ethnocultural Diversity in Social Work and Health, 1985; contbr. articles to profl. jours. Recipient of Outstanding Faculty award Graduating Students of Social Work, U. Utah, 1967, 68. Mem. Nat. Assn. Social Workers (named Social Worker of the Month 1977), Am. Assn. of Marital and Family Therapists, Council on Social Work Edn, Phi Kappa Phi. Mormon. Avocations: golf, fishing, music. Home: 4539 Wallace Ln Salt Lake City UT 84117 Office: Grad Sch Social Work University of Utah Salt Lake City UT 84112

HEPWORTH, LORNE, Canadian provincial politician; b. Assiniboia, Sask., Can., Dec. 20, 1947; s. Henry Bramall and Eileen (Malesh) H.; m. Fern Dianne Marguerite, Dec. 23, 1969; children: Graeme, Alana. Student, U. Regina, Sask., 1965-67; DVM, U. Sask., 1971. Veterinarian Hepworth, Pulfer, Weyburn, Sask., 1982; minister of agr. Provincial Govt. of Sask., Regina, 1983-85; minister of energy and mines Provincial Govt. of Sask., 1985-86, minister of edn. and minister of advanced edn. and manpower, 1986—; Mem. Province of Sask. Legis. Assembly; also minister of agr. Mem. Sask. Vet. Medicine Assn. (ex-officio), Can. Vet. Medicine Assn. Progressive Conservative. Home: 10 Dolphin Bay, Regina, SK Canada S4S 0B3 Office: Province of Sask Legis Bldg, Room 361, Regina, SK Canada S4S 0B3

HERB, EDMUND MICHAEL, optometrist; b. Zanesville, Ohio, Oct. 9, 1942; s. Edmund G. and Barbara R. (Michael) H.; divorced; children—Sara, Andrew. O.D., Ohio State U., 1966. Pvt. practice optometry, Buena Vista, Colo., 1966—; mem. faculty Ohio State U. Mem. Am. Optometric Assn., Colo. Optometric Assn. Home: Lost Creek Ranch Buena Vista CO 81211 Office: 303 N Hwy 24 Buena Vista CO 81211

HERBEL, CARLTON HOMER, range scientist; b. San Antonio, June 2, 1927; s. Carl Anton and Selma Hermina (Levin) H.; m. Carolene Cae Callahan, Oct. 4, 1952; children: Belinda Ann, Kurt Carlton. BS, Tex. U. Arts and Industries, 1949; MS, Kans. State U., 1954, PhD, 1956. Asst. agronomist Southwest Research Inst., San Antonio, 1949-50; grad. research asst. Kans. State U., Manhattan, 1953-56; agronomist Southwest Found. Research and Edn., San Antonio, 1956; range scientist Agrl. Research Service, USDA, Las Cruces, N.Mex., 1956—; adj. prof. N.Mex. State U., 1959—. Contbr. spl. reports and book chpts. in field. Served to sgt. U.S. Army, 1950-52. Recipient cert. merit Am. Forage and Grassland Council, 1974, USDA, 1982. Fellow AAAS; mem. Am. Soc. Agronomy (liaison 1973-79), Soc. Range Mgmt., (bd. dirs. 1974-76), Ecol. Soc. Am., Soil Sci. Soc. Am., Orgn. Profl. Employees Dept. Agr., Sigma Xi, Gamma Sigma Delta. Lodge: Masons. Home: 1804 Halfmoon Dr Las Cruces NM 88001 Office: Agrl Research Service USDA PO Box 3JER NMSU Las Cruces NM 88003

HERBERT, DON, electrical engineer; b. Ft. Dodge, Iowa, Feb. 15, 1928; s. Walter Joseph and Marian Josephine (DeBard) H.; m. Marie Grant, Jan. 16, 1950; children: Donna, Diane, Walter. BS, San Diego State U., 1956. Instrumentation engr. Chance Vought, Arlington, Tex., 1956-57; sect. head Gen. Dynamics, San Diego, 1957-83; sr. prin. engr. Support Systems Assocs., San Diego, 1983—; instr. electronics, servomechanisms and maths. Analope Valley Coll., Lancaster, Calif., 1957-58, Palomar Coll., San Marcos, Calif., 1960-62; pres. Noah Homes, San Diego, 1980—. Contbr. articles to profl. jours. Served to ensign USN, 1946-51. Mem. IEEE (sr., Centennial Medal 1984). Democrat. Roman Catholic. Avocation: computer software. Home: 8858 Glenhaven St San Diego CA 92123 Office: Support Systems Assocs Inc 1227 Tenth St Suite 210 Coronado CA 92118

HERBERT, PHYLLIS SYDNEY, social worker; b. Providence, Mar. 23, 1928; d. Alton Martin and Celia Marian (Robrish) T.; m. Edward Herbert, June 8, 1946; 1 child, Edward Aaron. Registered clin. social worker, Oreg. Instr. U. Oreg., Eugene, 1965-66; social worker Eugene Pub. Sch., 1966-67; social worker Child Care, Inc., Eugene, 1967-68, social worker Crippled Children div., 1968-70; trainee Boston State Hosp., Mattapan, Mass., 1970-71; pvt. practice social work Eugene and Portland, 1980—. Vol. Aslan House, Eugene, 1978-80, William Temple House, Portland, 1986—; mem. Lane County Drug Adv. Com., Eugene, 1971-72, mem. Bur. Land Mgmt. Adv. Com., Eugene, 1980-82; alt. Oreg. State Water Quality Policy Adv. Com., 1978. Mem. Nat. Assn. Social Workers (cert.), LWV, Audubon Soc. Democrat. Episcopalian. Avocations: environmentalist.

HERBST, JERRY EDWARD, service station executive, real estate developer; b. Chgo., Jan. 8, 1938; s. E. R. and Loraine G. (Lang) H.; m. Maryanna Anderson, Dec. 26, 1959; children—Ed, Tim, Troy. B.B.A., U. So. Calif., 1960. Owner, pres. Terrible Herbst Oil Co., Las Vegas, 1959—; dir. Valley Bank Nev., Frontier Savs. & Loan Assn. Mem. U. Nev.-Las Vegas Founders Club, U. So. Calif. President's Assocs., Rebels Booster Club, Las Vegas Founders Club, Gorman High Sch. Booster Club. Episcopalian. Clubs: Las Vegas Country, Hualapai, Spanish Trail. Home: 950 Rancho Circle Las Vegas NV 89107 Office: Terrible Herbst Oil Co 5195 Las Vegas Blvd S Las Vegas NV 89119

HERBST, LAWRENCE ROBERT, veterinarian, investment adviser, tax consultant, rancher, economist, promoter; b. Haverhill, Mass., Aug. 8, 1946; s. Morton and Ruth I. (Cooper) H.; student UCLA, Alexander Hamilton Bus. Inst., D.V.M., N.Am. Sch. Animal Scis.; D.D., Missionaries of New Truth, Chgo. Owner, pres. Best-way Records, Data Time Info. Records and Tapes, Larr Records; founder Future World Stores, Larry's Family Restaurant, Heavenly Waterbed Showrooms, Klarr Broadcasting Network; pres., adminstr. LH Investment Trust Fund, Inc. Larr Computer Corp., House of Robots, Larr Robots, Larry's Merchandising Data Base, Beverly Hills Music, Total Sound Records et al. Mem. Broadcast Music, Inc.; pres. Lawrence Herbst Farms; producer Spacee the Lion Cartoon. Pres., adminstr. Lawrence Herbst Found. Mem. Nat. Acad. TV Arts and Scis., Los Angeles Press Club, Internat. Platform Assn., Epsilon Delta Chi. Author: (book and movie) Legend of Tobby Kingdom, 1975; The Good, The Bad, The True Story of Lawrence Herbst; news columnist World of Investments, 1976. Designer 1st mus. electronic amplifier with plug in I.C.s; inventor Larr AM/FM satellite car radio, one-man air car. Office: PO Box 3842 Houston TX 77253-3842 Office: PO Box 1659 Beverly Hills CA 90213

HERBSTER, JAMES RICHARD, oil company executive; b. Kansas City, Mo., Oct. 16, 1941; s. Virgil Fred and Hester (Zoe) H.; m. Flora Sandra Barry, Aug. 28, 1964; children: Stacey Lee, Barry Fred, Bradley John. BBA in Indsl. Mgmt., U. Tex., 1963, MBA in Stats., 1965. Cert. data processing. Mgr. mktg. systems Exxon Co., USA, Houston, 1974-78, regulatory coordinator, 1978-79; mgr. E&P Systems, Houston, 1979-81; dir. info. systems Northwest Pipeline Corp., Salt Lake City, 1981-84, v.p. adminstrn., 1984—. Pres. Harris County Utility Dist., Houston, 1979-81, Jr. Achievement, Salt Lake City, 1986—; trustee Salt Lake City Edn. Found., 1985—; treas. Utah Health Cost Mgmt., Salt Lake City, 1985—; mem. Salt Lake United Way Com., 1984—, Utah State Compensation Commn., Salt Lake City, 1985—. Recipient Silver Leadership award Jr. Achievement, 1987. Mem. Am. Mgmt. Assns., Pacific Coast Gas Assn., Salt Lake City C. of C. Republican. Methodist. Avocations: tennis, skiing, racquetball, bicycling. Home: 1765 Ft Douglas Circle Salt Lake City UT 84103 Office: Northwest Pipeline Corp 295 Chipeta Way Salt Lake City UT 84108

HERDEG, HOWARD BRIAN, physician; b. Buffalo, Oct. 14, 1929; s. Howard Bryan and Martha Jean (Williams) H.; student Paul Smith's Coll., 1947-48, U. Buffalo, 1948-50, Canisius Coll., 1949; D.O., Phila. Coll. Osteopathic Medicine, 1954; M.D., U. Calif.-Irvine Coll. Medicine, 1962; m. Beryl Ann Fredricks, July 21, 1955; children—Howard Brian III, Erin Ann. Intern, Burbank (Calif.) Hosp., 1954-55; practice medicine specializing in family practice, Woodland Hills, Calif., 1956—; chief med. staff West Park Hosp., Canoga Park, Calif., 1971-72, trustee, 1971-73; chief family practice dept. Humana Hosp. West Hills, Canoga Park, 1982-83, mem. exec. com., 1984-85. Mem. Hidden Hills (Calif.) Pub. Safety Commn., 1978-82, chmn., 1982; bd. dirs. Hidden Hills Community Assn., 1971-73, pres., 1972; bd. dirs. Hidden Hills Homeowners Assn., 1973-75, pres., 1976-77; bd. dirs. Woodland Hills Freedom Season, 1961-67, pres., 1962; mem. Hidden Hills City Council, 1984—, mayor pro tem, 1987—. Recipient disting. service award Woodland Hills Jr C. of C., 1966. Mem. Woodland Hills C. of C. (dir. 1959-68, pres. 1967), San Fernando Valley Bus. and Profl. Assn., Theta Chi, Gamma Pi. Republican. Home: 24530 Deep Well Rd Hidden Hills CA 91302 Office: 22600 Ventura Blvd Woodland Hills CA 91364

HERDRICH, NORMAN WESLEY, editor; b. Spokane, Wash., July 17, 1942; s. Fred N. and Florice J. (Birchill) H.; m. Mary Susan Webb, Aug. 16, 1975; children: Megan Marie, Heidi Susan, Kristin Ruth. B.S., Wash. State U., 1969. Field editor Northwest Unit Farm Mags., Spokane, 1969-78; prodn. editor Western Farmer-Stockman Mags., Spokane, 1978—. Served with USNR, 1963-65. Mem. Wash. State Grange, Soc. Profl. Journalists, Nat. Rifle Assn., Spokane Editorial Soc. (sec.-treas. 1974-77, 1st v.p. 1977-78, pres. 1978-79), Wash. Wool Growers Assn., Sigma Delta Chi. Methodist. Club: Spokane Press (dir. 1978, treas. 1979). Home: E 12711 Saltese Rd Spokane WA 99216 Office: Review Tower W 999 Riverside Spokane WA 99210

HEREDY, LASZLO ALADAR, fuel scientist, cons.; b. Gödöllő, Hungary, Nov. 20, 1921; s. Kalman and Lenke (Fekete) H.; m. Ethel S. Szügyi, May 26, 1947 (dec. Jan. 1984); 1 child, Laszlo G.; m. Klara Toth, Oct. 3, 1985. MS in Chemical Engring., Tech. U., Budapest, Hungary, 1944; PhD in Phys. Chemistry, Carnegie-Mellon U., 1962. Dept. dir. Coal and Inorganic Research Inst., Veszprem, Hungary, 1950-56; sr. scientist Cons. Coal Co. Research Div., Pitts., 1957-63; mgr. phys. chemistry Rocketdyne div. Rockwell Internat., Canoga Park, Calif., 1963-84; cons. fuel sci. Irvine, Calif., 1984—; mem. Coal Mine Safety Adv. Com., Washington, 1972-75. Contbr. articles to profl. jours; patentee in field. Mem. Atomics Internat. (pres. 1971-72), Sigma Xi. Republican. Roman Catholic. Avocations: tennis, history, classical music. Home and Office: 41 Mirador Irvine CA 92715

HEREFORD, DANNY JOE, counselor, consultant, researcher, educator; b. Tekoa, Wash., Mar. 22, 1939; s. Joseph Herron and Betty Jane (Shove) H.; m. Juanita Louise Valdez, Oct. 20, 1962; children—Loretta Marie, Joseph John, Cheryl Ann, Daniel John. B.A. cum laude in Behavioral Sci., Nat. U., San Diego, 1980, M.A. in Counseling Psychology, 1981; cert. in alcohol studies U. Calif.-San Diego, 1978. Served as noncommd. officer U.S. Navy, 1957-77; various adminstrv. positions; instr. Service Schs. Command, San Diego, 1968-71; ret., 1977; screener/interviewer USN Alcohol Safety Action Program, San Diego, 1977-80; adj. instr./facilitator U. West Fla., San Diego, 1980-81, U. Arizona, San Diego, 1981-86, v.p. 1981-84; instr./facilitator U. Calif.-San Diego, 1982-86, v.p. 1982-84, Met. Area Adv. Com., San Diego, 1982-83; clin. research coordinator, program dir. alcohol detoxification and preliminary treatment program Centre City Hosp., San Diego, 1980. Decorated letter of commendation, Navy unit commendation with 3 gold stars; Gallantry Cross (Vietnam). Mem. Nat. Assn. Alcoholism Counselors, Calif. Assn. Alcoholism Counselors, Nat. Council on Alcoholism, VFW (life), Am. Legion (life), Am. Parapsychol. Assn., Nat. U. Alumni Assn. (life), Nat. Geog. Soc., Fleet Res. Assn. (life). Roman Catholic. Club: Lemon Grove (Calif.) Alano. Home and Office: 1622 Dartmoor Dr Lemon Grove CA 92045

HERGER, WALLY W., JR., congressman; b. Yuba City, Calif., May 20, 1945. Formerly mem. Calif. State Assembly; mem. 100th Congress from 2d Calif. dist., mem. agr., mcht. marine and fisheries coms.; owner Herger Gas, Inc. Office: US House of Reps Office of House Mems Washington DC 20510 *

HERING, WILLIAM MARSHALL, human resource development executive; b. Indpls., Dec. 26, 1940; s. William Marshall and Mary Agnes (Clark) H.; m. Suzanne Wolfe, Aug. 10, 1963. BS, Ind. U., 1961, MS, 1962; PhD, U. Ill., Urbana, 1973. Tchr. Indpls. pub. schs., 1962-66; asst. dir. sociol. resources project Am. Sociol. Assn., 1966-70; dir. social sci. curriculum Biomed. Interdisciplinary Project, Berkeley, Calif., 1973-76; staff assoc. Tchrs. Ctrs. Exchange, San Francisco, 1976-82; dir. research Far West Lab. Ednl. Research and Devel., San Francisco, 1979-82, sr. research assoc., 1982-85; mgr. human resource devel. Bank Am., San Francisco, 1985—; mem. Nat. Adv. Bd. Educ. Resource Info. Ctr.; cons. U.S. Dept. Edn.; pres. Social Sci. Educ. Consortium, 1981-82, bd. dirs., 1979-81; bd. dirs. Sinfonia, San Francisco, 1986—. Nat. Inst. Educ. grantee, 1979-82, 82—. Mem. Am. Soc. Tng. and Devel. (v.p. 1986), Golden Gate Soc., Nat. Audubon Soc., Phi Delta Kappa. Republican. Episcopalian. Contbr. over 100 articles on social studies edn., staff devel., ednl. research and evaluation to profl. jours. Home: 731 Duboce Ave San Francisco CA 94117 Office: PO Box 37000 Dept 3850 San Francisco CA 94137

HERMAN, ELVIN EUGENE, consulting radar engineer; b. Sigourney, Iowa, Mar. 17, 1921; s. John Lawrence and Martha Elizabeth (Conner) H.; m. Grace Winifred Eklund, Sept. 29, 1945; 1 child, Jane Ann. BSEE, U. Iowa, 1942. Staff engr. Naval Research Lab., Washington, 1942-51; sect. head Corona (Calif.) Labs., Nat. Bur. Standards, 1951-53; sr. scientist Hughes Aircraft Co., El Segundo, Calif., 1953-56, dept. mgr., 1956-58, lab. mgr., 1958-70, tech. dir. radar div., 1970-73; tech. dirs. radar systems group Hughes Aircraft Co., Pacific Palisades, Calif., 1973-83; cons. in field, Pacific Palisades, 1983—. Patentee in field. Fellow IEEE; mem. Research Soc. Am., Eta Kappa Nu. Avocations: boating, photography. Address: 1200 Lachman Ln Pacific Palisades CA 90272

HERMAN, JAMES RICHARD, union executive; b. Newark, Aug. 21, 1924; s. Milton Matthew and Larraine Catherine (Kelly) H. Student public schs., N.J. Pres. Internat. Longshoremen's and Warehousemen's Union, San Francisco, 1977—. Bd. dirs. Delancey St. Found., St. Anthony's Dining Rm., Columbia Pk. Boys Club; mem. Dem. State Central Com., Calif. Named Labor Man of Yr. Alameda County Central Labor Council, 1973. Mem. Maritime Inst. for Research and Indusl. Devel. (dir.). Democrat. Roman Catholic. Club: Concordia. Office: Internat Longshoremen's and Warehousemen's Union 1188 Franklin St San Francisco CA 94109 *

HERMAN, RICHARD BLAIR, data processing executive; b. Pomona, Calif., Aug. 5, 1955; s. Don Henry and Donna Louise (Mosley) H.;m. Loris Diane Cochran, Jan. 24, 1976; children: Jenelle Marie, Tracy Lynae. BA in Mus., Calif. Bapt. Coll., 1977; MA in Mus., U. Redlands, 1980. Pvt. practice teaching piano Riverside, Calif., 1974—; instr. piano Calif. Bapt. Coll., Riverside, 1977-81, asst. dir. data processing, 1981-82, dir. data processing, 1982—; computer cons. Christian Psychol. Services, Riverside, 1985—. Pianist Magnolia Ave Bapt. Ch., Riverside, 1978—. Mem. Mus. Tchrs. Assn. Calif., So. Bapt. Computer Users Assn. Republican. Avocations: golf, racquetball, piano, outdoor work. Office: Calif Bapt Coll 8432 Magnolia Ave Riverside CA 92504

HERMAN, WILLIAM JOSEPH, technology consulting company executive, aerospace engineer; b. Pitts., Dec. 24, 1941; s. Milton and Jane B. (Broudy) H.; m. Katherine D. White, Sept. 1, 1963; children: Michael, Stephanie, Mark. BS in Aerospace Engring., Pa. State U., 1963; MS in Aerospace Engring., Air Force Inst. Tech., 1968; MBA, U. N.Mex., 1977. Commd. 2d. lt. USAF, 1963, advanced through grades to capt., 1970; aeronautical engr., capt. USAF, Kirtland AFB, N.M., 1963-66, 68-73; resigned USAF, 1973; mem. tech. staff Sci. Applications Inc., Albuquerque, 1973-74; gen. engr. USAF Weapons Lab., Kirtland AFB, 1974-79; sr. assoc. Booz, Allen & Hamilton, Albuquerque, 1979-85, prin., 1985—. Treas. Com. to Elect Herb Hughes, 1975, Duke City Soccer League, 1979-81; founder and coach Sierra Vista Soccer Club, 1979-82; coach Sandia Peak Jr. Nordic Team, 1985-86. Mem. IEEE, AIAA, Internat. Test and Evaluation Assn., Am. Def. Preparedness Assn. Democrat. Presbyterian. Avocations: nordic skiing, running, hiking. Office: Booz Allen & Hamilton Inc 2201 Buena Vista Dr SE Albuquerque NM 87106

HERMAN, ZELEK SEYMOUR, research chemist; b. Denver, July 10, 1945; s. Ben and Mildred Irene (Tepper) H. BS in Chemistry, Case Inst. Tech., 1967; MS in Quantum Chemistry, U. Uppsala, Sweden, 1968, PhD in Quantum Chemistry, 1975. Postdoctoral assoc. U. Denver, 1977-78; postdoctoral scholar Stanford (Calif.) U., 1978-79, Rockefeller U., N.Y.C., 1979-80; postdoctoral fellow Linus Pauling Inst., Palo Alto, Calif., 1980-82, research assoc., 1982—. Translator: Johan Ludvig Runeberg, 1980; contbr. articles to profl. jours. Fellow Am. Scandinavian Found., 1967, 72; recipient Outstanding Achievement award Optimists Internat., 1962, Outstanding Work award Am. Chem. Soc., 1963; named Fulbright Disting. Prof., 1985. Mem. Internat. Soc. Quantum Biology, Rudjer Bošković Inst., Sigma Xi, Tau Beta Pi. Avocations: sports, reading, orchestral and folk music. Home: 521 Del Medio Ave #107 Mountain View CA 94040 Office: Linus Pauling Inst Sci and Medicine 440 Page Mill Rd Palo Alto CA 94306

HERMANS, COLIN OLMSTED, biology educator; b. Seattle, May 4, 1936; s. Thomas Gerald and Eslie Vida (Olmsted) H.; m. Mary Pendleton Hayden, June 16, 1958; children: Karen, Thomas, Helen. BA, Pomona Coll., 1958; MA, U. Wash., 1964, PhD, 1966. Research assoc. U. Calif., Berkeley, 1968-69; dir. electron microscope lab. Sonoma State U., Rohnert Park, Calif., 1969—, prof. biology, 1977—; vis. research prof. U. Calif., Berkeley, 1970-82, U. Osnabrück, Fed. Republic of Germany. Co-editor: Zoomorphology, Ultrastructure of Polychaetes; contbr. articles to sci. jours. Mem. Save San Francisco Bay Assn., Greenpeace, Family Service Agy. Served to capt. USAR, 1958-68. Fellow NATO, 1966-67, NIH, 1963-66, 67-68, Alexander von Humboldt Stiftung, 1975-76. Fellow AAAS; mem. ACLU, Calif. Assn. Med. Technologists, No. Calif. Soc. for Electron Microscopy (exec. com. mem. 1979-83), Electron Microscopied Soc. of Am., Am. Soc. Zoologists, Internat. Assn. Meiobenthologists, Calif. Acad. Scis., Common Cause, Western Soc. Naturalists (treas. 1980-81), Am. Mus. Natural History, Sierra Club, Audubon Soc., Nat. Geographic Soc. Democrat. Clubs: Hog Island Yacht Club, Northwestern Pacific Track Club (Santa Rosa, Calif.) (v.p. 1975—). Avocations: running, hiking, rowing, skin diving, surfing. Home: 7387 Barbi Ln Rohnert Park CA 94928 Office: Sonoma State U Biology Dept Rohnert Park CA 94928

HERN, WARREN MARTIN, physician, epidemiologist; b. Abilene, Kans., June 29, 1938; s. John Woodrow and Edna Loretta (Trivett) H.; m. Linda Gail Hodge, Sept. 27, 1981. BA, U. Colo., 1961, MD, 1965; MPH, U. N.C., 1971. Diplomate Am. Bd. Preventive Medicine. Physician Peace Corps, Brazil, 1966-68; chief program devel. and evaluation br., family planning div. Office of Econ. Opportunity, Exec. Office of Pres., Washington, 1970-72; med. dir. Boulder (Colo.) Valley Clinic, 1973-74; dir. Boulder Abortion Clinic, 1975—; med. dir. Family Planning Project Devel. Assn., Denver, 1972-74; attending physician Denver Gen. Hosp., 1972-73; cons. USAID Devel. Assn., Arlington, Va., 1972-74, ACLU, Chgo., 1985. Author: Abortion Services Handbook, 1978, Abortion Practice, 1984; co-editor Abortion in the Seventies, 1977; photographer: cover Sierra Club Wildlife Calendar, 1987. Founder, ambassador Englewood (Colo.) Community Ambassador Program, 1961, founder, chmn. Holy Cross Wilderness Def. Fund, Boulder, 1982—. Served to sr. surgeon USPHS, 1966-68. Recipient Spl. Recognition award NOW, Denver, 1974, Unsung Hero award, 1986; Wenner-Gren Found. fellow, 1964, 83. Fellow AAAS, Am. Anthrop. Assn., Soc. Applied Anthropology, Am. Coll. Preventive Med.; mem. Assn. Planned Parenthood Physicians (chmn. pub. affairs com.), Nat. Abortion Fedn. (dir. 1977-81), Sierra Club, Nat. Audubon Soc. Democrat. Avocations: hiking, skiing, guitar, piano, cooking. Office: Boulder Abortion Clinic 1130 Alpine Boulder CO 80302

HERNANDEZ, ENRIQUE, physician; b. Vega Baja, P.R., Oct. 25, 1951; s. Nathaniel and Ana Luisa (Lopez) H.; Marta Isabel Jimenez, May 29, 1971; children: David Enrique, Daniel Antonio. BS, U. P.R., Rio Pedras, 1973; MD, U. P.R., 1977. Diplomate Am. Bd. Med. Examiners, Am. Bd. Ob-Gyn, Am. Bd. Gynecol. Oncology. Resident in ob-gyn Johns Hopkins Hosp., Balt., 1977-81, fellow in gynecol. oncology, 1981-83; instr. ob-gyn Johns Hopkins U., Balt., 1981-82, asst. prof., 1982-83; commd. major U.S. Army, 1983; chief gynecol. oncology service Tripler Army Med. Ctr., Honolulu, 1983—, asst. dir. intern tng., 1984—; cons. Md. State Dept. Health, 1981-83, Hawaii Med. Assn. 1983—. Contbr. artcles to profl. jours. Recipient Bristol award P.R. Med. Assn. 1977. Mem. Am. Soc. Clin. Oncology, Am. Coll. Ob-Gyns, N.Y. Acad. Scis., Res. Officers Assn., Beta Beta Beta, Alpha Omega Alpha. Roman Catholic. Avocation: long distance running. Office: Tripler Army Med Ctr PO Box 679 Honolulu HI 96859

HERNANDEZ, ERNEST, JR., behavioral science researcher; b. San Antonio, Nov. 18, 1943; s. Ernest and Cielo (Lecea) H.; m. Carol Ann Weiser, May 23, 1965; children: James Je, Robert Re, Summer Ann. AA, El Camino Coll., 1966; BA, Calif. State U., 1968, MA, 1970; PhD, U. Calif., Riverside, 1979. Concert promoter Sta. KMET-FM, Sta. K-LOVE, 1975, Sta. KBCA-FM, 1975-76, also nat. promotion mgr. specialty records and account exec.; dep. probation officer, Los Angeles County, 1974-77; mem. faculty Calif. State U., 1974-85; ind. record promoter for mus. groups including STYX, Jose Feleciano, Shango, Richie Lecea, 1974-76; coordinator Chino Community Deliquency Prevention Project, 1972-74; behavioral scis. research analyst III, Los Angeles County, 1977—; pres. E.H.J. & Assocs., El Toro, Calif., 1979—; staff mgr. AT&T Info. Systems, Calif., 1985-86; prof. computer and info. scis. Nat. U., Vista, Calif., 1986—; computer cons., trainer; adj. instr. Nat. U., San Diego, 1986—. Author (bus. software packages) TNT-Time'n Task, C-O-N-T-A-C-T. Bd. dirs. West End Family Counseling Service San Bernardino County, 1972-73; co-chmn. Los Angeles County Research Coordinating Com., 1981-82; chmn. Los Angeles County Research Devel. and Planning Task Force com., 1980-81. Mem. Assn. Police Planning and Research Officers (1st v.p. 1983), Am. Soc. Criminology, Acad. Criminal Justice Sci., Assn. Criminal Justice Researchers Calif., Western Soc. Criminologists, Evaluation Network, Am. Acad. Polit. and Social Sci., Assn. Computing Machinery, Issues Inc., Internat. Assn. Social Sci. and Info. Service Tech. Author: Police Handbook for Applying the Systems Approach and Computer Technology, 1982; Police Chief's Guide to Using Microcomputers, 1983; contbr. articles to profl. jours. Home: 22386 Sunlight Creek St El Toro CA 92630 Office: 211 W Temple St Los Angeles CA 90012

HERNANDEZ, JOSE GILBERT, production quality executive; b. Rabinal, Guatemala, Jan. 25, 1950; came to U.S., 1965; s. Gerardo and Ulbelina (Juarez) H.; m. Darlyn H. Jacobesen, Oct. 3, 1975; children: Joslyn, Ryner G. BS in Crop Sci., Calif. Poly U., 1973; MS, U. San Francisco, 1986. Orchard mgr. Calif. Poly U., San Luis Obispo, 1971-73; supr. quality control FMC, Modesto, Calif., 1973-80; mgr. quality control Agrigenetics, Hollister,

Calif., 1980-85; mgr. prodn. quality control Ferry Morse Seed Co., Modesto, 1985—. Mem. AAAS, Weed Soc., Agronomy Soc., Alpha Zeta. Avocations: tennis, soccer, photography. Home: 3605 Dragoo Park Dr Modesto CA 95356 Office: Ferry Morse Seed Co PO Box 3948 Modesto CA 95352

HERNANDEZ, JULIE SILVA, vocational consultant, rehabilitation counselor; b. Santa Maria, Laguna, Philippines, Sept. 26, 1941; d. Catalino and Maria (Silva) H. M.S. in Sch. Counseling, U. LaVerne, 1978; M.Div., Bangor Theol. Sem., 1977. Cert. pvt. sch. tchr. and counselor, Hawaii; cert. counselor, Va.; cert. coll. counselor, Calif.; cert. rehab. provider, Hawaii. Missionary, Liebenzell Mission, Yap, Caroline Island, 1969-71; nursery assoc. tchr., Bangor, Maine, 1971-75; high sch. counselor, dept. chmn., Hilo, Hawaii, 1977-79; counselor Cosmopolitan Social Service Agy., Honolulu, 1979; vocat. cons., counselor Crawford Rehab. Services, Inc., Honolulu, 1979-84; ind. contractor with Inter-Island Rehab., 1984—; owner A-Z Rehab. Services, 1984—; coordinator Leading Quality Circle Group. Vol. Am. Cancer Soc.; active YWCA, Filipino C. of C., Women's Bd. East-West Ctr. Host Family. Recipient Profl. Employee of Yr. Crawford Rehab. Services, Inc. 1981. Mem. Am. Assn. Counseling and Devel., Hawaii Assn. Counseling and Devel. (Profl. service award 1984, treas. 1984), Am. Sch. Counselors Assn., Am. Rehab. Counselors Assn., Nat. Rehab. Assn., Rehab. Assn. Hawaii (treas. 1983-85), Am. Mental Health Counselors Assn., Am. Assn. Family Counselors and Mediators (ad hoc com. on divorce ministry Hawaii conf., cert.). Clubs: Philippine Women's Circle (pres. 1978), Hilo Women's. Office: A-Z Rehab Services Kuakini Med Plaza 321 N Kuakini St #410 Honolulu HI 96817

HERNSTADT, WILLIAM H., broadcasting company executive, former state senator; b. N.Y.C., Nov. 21, 1935; s. William L. and Alma (Cunningham) H.; m. Jerene Yap, Sept. 1985; 1 child, Hayley May; children by previous marriages—Ruth Ellen, Edward William, Liane Winifred, Stephanie Elizabeth. B.S. in Physics, Rensselaer Poly. Inst., 1957. With Globus, Inc., 1960, M.A. Lomasney & Co., 1961; staff security analyst Alleghany Corp., N.Y.C., 1962-67; asst. treas. Alleghany Corp., 1965-67; registered rep. Bruns, Nordeman, Rea & Co., N.Y.C., 1967-70; owner-mgr. Alvernie Apts., 1970-71; chmn. bd., gen. mgr. Nev. Ind. Broadcasting Corp.; operator TV sta. KVVU-TV, Henderson-Las Vegas, 1971-79; pres. Hernstadt Broadcasting Corp., WKAT, Miami, Fla., 1980-86. Rep. Town Meeting, Greenwich, Conn., 1965-69; mem. Nev. Senate, 1976-84; Bd. dirs. Clark County Apt. Owners Assn., treas., 1972, pres., 1973; bd. dirs. Nev. Apt. Assn., 1977—, Clark County chpt. Am. Cancer Soc., 1970-72; bd. dirs. Jewish Fedn. of Las Vegas, 1974-86, v.p., 1979-82, pres., 1982-83; bd. dirs. Nev. Kidney Found., 1979-84, v.p., 1980-84. Clubs: Harmonie of N.Y. Home: 3111 Bel Air Dr Apt 25G Las Vegas NV 89109

HERRERA, ALBERT ANTHONY, biology educator; b. San Francisco, Oct. 31, 1950; m. Peggy L. Alpert, June 24, 1973. BS in Zoology, U. Calif., Davis, 1972; PhD in Biology, UCLA, 1977. Postdoctoral scholar UCLA, 1977-81; asst. prof. biol. scis. U. So. Calif., Los Angeles, 1981-87, assoc. prof., 1987—. Contbr. articles to profl. jours. Recipient Research Career Devel. award NIH, 1985—; grantee NIH, 1983-85, 87—, NSF, 1986—, Muscular Dystrophy Assn., 1983—. Mem. AAAS, Soc. Neurosci. Roman Catholic. Office: U So Calif Dept Biol Scis Los Angeles CA 90089-0371

HERRERA, ROBERT BENNETT, ret. educator; b. Los Angeles, July 24, 1913; s. Royal Robert and Rachel (Mix) H.; A.A., Los Angeles City Coll., 1934; A.B., U. Calif., Los Angeles, 1937, M.A., 1939; m. Agnes Mary MacDougall, May 18, 1941; children—Leonard B., Mary Margaret, William R. Tchr. high sch., Long Beach, Calif., 1939-41; statistician U.S. Forest Survey, Berkeley, Calif., 1941-45; faculty Los Angeles City Coll., 1946-79, prof. math., 1966-79, chmn. math. dept., 1975-79, ret., 1979; lectr. math. U. Calif., Los Angeles, 1952-75; cons. Ednl. Testing Service, Princeton, 1965-68, Addison Wesley Pub. Co., 1966-68, Goodyear Pub. Co., 1970-76. Mem. Math. Assn. Am. (past sec. So. Calif. sect., past gov.), Am. Math. Soc., AAAS, Internat. Oceanic Soc., Phi Beta Kappa, Pi Mu Epsilon. Democrat. Author: (with C. Bell, C. Hammond) Fundamentals of Arithmetic for Teachers, 1962. Home: 6011 Fair Ave North Hollywood CA 91606 Office: 855 N Vermont Ave Los Angeles CA 90029

HERRICK, JOHN JEROME, naval officer; b. Warren, Minn., June 23, 1920; s. James Orval and Lillian Madelaine (Conely) H.; m. Geraldine May Kane, May 1, 1948; children—John Jerome, Patrick, Dennis, Maureen. Student, Superior State Coll., 1938-40; B.S., U.S. Naval Acad., 1943. Commd. midshipman U.S. Navy, 1940, advanced through grades to capt., 1964, commodore USN Destroyer div. 192, task group commdr. USS Maddox, 1964, then chief staff officer 9th Naval Dist., 1970-73, ret., 1973; naval sci. instr. Santa Fe (N.Mex.) High Sch. NJROTC, 1973-84. Decorated Navy Commendation medal, Combat Action ribbon. Mem. U.S. Naval Inst., U.S. Naval Acad. Alumni Assn., Ret. Officers Assn. Democrat. Roman Catholic. Clubs: Rotary, Elks.

HERRICK, TRACY GRANT, fiduciary; b. Cleve., Dec. 30, 1933; s. Stanford Avery and Elizabeth Grant (Smith) H.; B.A., Columbia U., 1956, M.A., 1958; postgrad. Yale U., 1956-57; M.A., Oxford U. (Eng.), 1960; m. Maie Kaarsoo, Oct. 12, 1963; children—Sylvi Anne, Alan Kalev. Economist, Fed. Res. Bank, Cleve., 1960-70; sr. economist Stanford Research Inst., Menlo Park, Calif., 1970-73; v.p., sr. analyst Shuman, Agnew & Co., Inc., San Francisco, 1973-75; v.p. Bank of Am., San Francisco, 1975-81; pres. Tracy G. Herrick, Inc., 1981—; lectr. Stonier Grad. Sch. Banking, Am. Bankers Assn., 1967-76; commencement speaker Memphis Banking Sch., 1974; bd. dirs. Jefferies Group, Inc., Jefferies & Co., Inc., Bank Valuation, Inc., B & H Communications Inc., Desk Top Broker, Inc., Money Analyst Inc. Fellow Fin. Analysts Fedn.; mem. Columbia Coll. Alumni Assn. (dir. 1973—), Nat. Assn. Bus. Economists, San Francisco Bus. Economists Assn., San Francisco Soc. Security Analysts. Republican. Congregationalist. Author: Bank Analysts Handbook, 1978; Timing, 1981; contbr. articles to profl. jours. Home: 1150 University Ave Palo Alto CA 94301

HERRIGEL, HOWARD RALPH, engineering company executive, chemical engineer; b. Seattle, Sept. 27, 1924; s. Walter Arthur and Violet Cleo (Keirman) H.; m. Judith Esther Robbins, Oct. 23, 1964; children: David Robbins, Nancy Ruth. BSChemE, U. Wash, 1952, postgrad., 1953-58; postgrad., U. Pitts., 1979. Research engr. The Boeing Co., Seattle, 1958-71; research engr. Resources Conservation Co., Seattle, 1971-73, chief chemist, 1973-74; process engring. mgr. Resources Conservation Co., Bellevue, Wash., 1974-80, v.p., chief scientist, 1980-84, v.p. sci. and tech., 1984—. Patentee in field. Recipient Outstanding Contbrn. award AIAA, 1978. Mem. Am. Chem. Soc., Am. Inst. Chem. Engrs., Sigma Xi, Phi Lambda Upsilon. Club: Seattle Yacht. Avocations: sailing, skiing, scuba diving, music, theater. Home: 426 36th Ave Seattle WA 98122 Office: Resources Conservation Co 3101 NE Northup Way Bellevue WA 98004

HERRIN, LEXIE ELBERT, engineering firm executive; b. Donna, Tex., May 17, 1925; s. Lexie E. and Mary Frances (Scates) H.; BSME, U. Mich., 1951, postgrad. 1951; MBA, U. So. Calif., 1964; m. Charlotte Frances Campbell, Mar. 9, 1946; children: Christopher Patrick, Timothy Michael, Bradley Terrence. Commd. 1st lt. USAF, 1951, advanced through grades to lt. col., 1967, ret., 1969; pres. KOHM Mining and Devel., 1966-69; exec. v.p. Oil Producers & Refiners, Glendale, Calif., 1969-70; gen. mgr. Broadmore Homes of Tex., Waco, 1970-72; pres. Exec. Mobile Home Service, Lighthouse Point, Fla., 1972-74; pres. L.E. Herrin Engr. Cons., Redlands, Calif., 1974-76; v.p., gen. mgr., dir. von Haenel-Herrin & Assocs., Glendale, Calif., 1977-81; pres. Herrin-Stanton & Assocs. 1981—; dir. Seagull Industries, 1966-75; chmn. sub-com. on traffic accident reporting Nat. Hwy. Safety Adv. Com.; lectr. U. Calif., Northridge; arbitrator Am. Arbitration Assn., 1978—; del. com. on transp. Calif. Commn. on the Califs. Active, Boy Scouts Am., 1951-64; co-chmn. Reagan for Pres., San Bernardino County, 1976, asst. to chmn., 1980; del. Calif. Rep. Conv., 1981—; presdl. appointee Dept. Transp. 1981-85. Decorated Air Force Commendation medal with oak leaf clusters. Mem. ASME, AIAA, Internat. Soc. Air Safety Investigators, Am. Inst. Indsl. Engrs., Soc. Automotive Engrs., Am. Assn. Automotive Medicine, Triangle, Sphinx, Michigama, Phi Sigma Kappa. Republican. Clubs: Officers, March AFB Flying, Wheeler Flying, Masons. Editor-in-chief U. Mich. Technic, 1949-51. Office: Herrin-Stanton & Assocs 302 Alabama Suite 10 Redlands CA 92373

HERRING, WILLIAM CONYERS, physicist, emeritus educator; b. Scotia, N.Y., Nov. 15, 1914; s. William Conyers and Mary (Joy) H.; m. Louise C. Preusch, Nov. 30, 1946; children—Lois Mary, Alan John, Brian Charles, Gordon Robert. A.B., U. Kans., 1933; Ph.D., Princeton, 1937. NRC fellow Mass. Inst. Tech., 1937-39; instr. Princeton, 1939-40, U. Mo., 1940-41; mem. sci. staff Div. War Research, Columbia, 1941-45; prof. applied math. U. Tex., 1946; research physicist Bell Telephone Labs., Murray Hill, N.J., 1946-78; prof. applied physics Stanford (Calif.) U., 1978-81, prof. emeritus, 1981—; mem. Inst. Advanced Study, 1952-53. Recipient Army-Navy Cert. of Appreciation, 1947; Distinguished Service citation U. Kans., 1973; J. Murray Luck award for excellence in sci. reviewing Nat. Acad. Scis., 1980; von Hippel award Materials Research Soc., 1980, Wolf prize in Physics, 1985. Fellow Am. Phys. Soc. (Oliver E. Buckley solid state physics prize 1959), Am. Acad. Arts and Scis.; mem. AAAS, Nat. Acad. Scis. Home: 3945 Nelson Dr Palo Alto CA 94306 Office: Dept Applied Physics Stanford U Stanford CA 94305

HERRINGER, FRANK CASPER, business executive; b. N.Y.C., Nov. 12, 1942; s. Casper Frank and Alice Virginia (McMullen) H.; m. Nancy Lynn Blair, Dec. 21, 1968; 1 son, William Laurence. A.B. magna cum laude, Dartmouth, 1964, M.B.A. with highest distinction, 1965. Prin. Cresap, McCormick & Paget, Inc. (mgmt. cons.), N.Y.C., 1965-71; staff asst. to Pres., Washington, 1971-73; adminstr. U.S. Urban Mass Transp. Adminstrn., Washington, 1973-75; gen. mgr., chief exec. officer San Francisco Bay Area Rapid Transit Dist., 1975-78; exec. v.p., dir. Transamerica Corp., San Francisco, 1979-86, pres., 1986—; dir. Sedgwick Group plc (London), Occidental Life Ins. Co., Transam. Ins. Co., Fred S. James Corp., Transam. Fin. Corp., Transam. Interway. Trustee Pacific Presbyn. Med. Ctr., Amos Tuck Sch. Bus. Adminstrn. Dartmouth Coll., Mills Coll. Mem. Phi Beta Kappa. Republican. Clubs: Olympic, Bankers, Commonwealth. Home: 4175 Canyon Rd Lafayette CA 94549 Office: Transamerica Corp 600 Montgomery St San Francisco CA 94111

HERRMANN, CHRISTIAN, JR., med. educator; b. Lansing, Mich., 1921; s. Christian and Agnes (Bauch) H. A.B., U. Mich., 1942, M.D., 1944. Diplomate Am. Bd. Psychiatry and Neurology. Intern Harper Hosp., Detroit, 1944-45; asst. resident medicine Henry Ford Hosp., Detroit, 1945-46; resident neurology Neurol. Inst., N.Y.C., 1948-50; research asst. neurology Neurol. Inst., 1950-51, chief resident neurology, 1951-52, asst. neurology, 1950-51, 51-52, asst. attending, 1953-54; mem. faculty U. Calif. at Los Angeles Med. Sch., 1954—, prof. neurology, 1969-86, prof. neurology emeritus, 1986—, vice chmn. dept. Neurology, 1970—. Vice chmn. Calif. chpt. Myasthenia Gravis Found., 1966—, chmn. med. adv. bd., 1968-72, pres. 1972-74, chmn. nat. med. adv. bd., 1983-85. Served as lt. (j.g.) M.C. USNR, 1946-48. USPHS research fellow neurology Columbia Coll. Phys. and Surg., 1952-54. Office: U Calif Dept Neurology Reed Neurol Research Center Los Angeles CA 90024

HERRMANN, GEORGE, educator; b. USSR, Apr. 19, 1921. Dipl. C.E., Swiss Fed. Inst. Tech., 1945, Ph.D. in Mechanics, 1949. Asst., then asso. prof. civil engring. Columbia, 1950-62; prof. civil engring. Northwestern U., 1962-69; prof. applied mechanics Stanford, 1969—; cons. SRI Internat., 1970-80. Contbr. 200 articles to profl. jours; editorial bd. numerous jours. Fellow ASME (Centennial medal 1980); mem. ASCE (Th. v. Karman medal 1981), Nat. Acad. Engring., AIAA. Address: Stanford U Div Applied Mechanics Durand Bldg Stanford CA 94305

HERRMANN, RAYMOND, geologist, hydrologist; b. Chgo., July 16, 1941; s. Raymond B. and Josephine (Rickman) H.; m. Emilie L. Juestrich, July 17, 1965; children: Stefanie M., Michelle R. BS in Geology, Columbia U., 1968; MS in Water Resources, PhD in Geology, U. Wyo., 1972. Registered profl. geologist, Ga. Hydrologist Southeast region Nat. Park Service U.S. Dept. Interior, Atlanta, 1973-74, chief nat. sci. research div. Southeast region, 1974-79; chief air and water div. Nat. Park Service U.S. Dept. Interior, Washington, 1979-81; dir. water resource field support lab. Nat. Park Service U.S. Dept. Interior, Ft. Collins, Colo., 1981-85, chief applied research br. water resource div., 1985—; adj. assoc. prof. U. Tenn., Knoxville, 1980-82, faculty assoc., 1982—; assoc. faculty Colo. State U., Ft. Collins, 1981—. Contbr. articles to profl. jours. Mem. Ft. Collins Water Bd., 1985—. Served with USMC, 1958-62. Recipient Superior Service award U.S. Dept. Interior, 1983. Fellow Geol. Soc. Am.; mem. AAAS, Am. Water Resources Assn. (mountain dist. dir. 1983-85, v.p. 1985, pres. elect 1987—), U.S. Soccer Fedn. (referee), Sigma Xi. Avocation: soccer. Office: Colo State U/Nat Park Service 339 Aylesworth Fort Collins CO 80523

HERROLD, REBECCA MUNN, music educator, writer; b. Warren, Pa., Sept. 29, 1938; d. Gordon Clifford and Edith Esther (Lind) Munn; m. Stephen Herrold, 1959. MusB, U. Miami, 1960; MA, San Jose State U., 1968; D Mus. Arts, Stanford U., 1974. Asst. prof. Youngstown (Ohio) State U., 1974-75, Oreg. State U., Corvallis, 1975-80; assoc. prof. music San Jose State U., 1980-84, prof. music, 1984—. Author: (textbook) New Approaches to Elementary Music Education, 1984. Grantee Apple Computer Co., 1981, Atari Computer Co., 1982. Mem. Calif. Council Music Tchr. Educators (sec. 1985-86). Democrat. Home: 1530 Montalban Dr San Jose CA 95120 Office: San Jose State U Dept Music San Jose CA 95192

HERRON, ELLEN PATRICIA, judge; b. Auburn, N.Y., July 30, 1927; d. David Martin and Grace Josephine (Berner) Herron; A.B. Trinity Coll., 1949; M.A., Cath. U. Am., 1954; J.D., U. Calif.-Berkeley, 1964. Asst. dean Cath. U. Am., 1952-54; instr. East High Sch., Auburn, 1955-57; asst. dean Wells Coll., Aurora, N.Y., 1957-58; instr. psychology and history Contra Costa Coll., 1958-60; dir. row Stanford, 1960-61; assoc. Knox & Kretzmer, Richmond, Calif., 1964-65; admitted to Calif. bar, 1965; ptnr. Knox & Herron, 1965-74, Knox, Herron and Masterson, 1974-77 (both Richmond, Calif.); judge Superior Ct. State of Calif., 1977-87; gen. ptnr. Real Estate Syndicates, Calif., 1967-77. Active numerous civic orgns.; bd. dirs. Rhonoh Sch., Richmond, YWCA, Econ. Devel. Council Richmond; alumnae bd. dirs. Boalt Hall, U. Calif.-Berkeley, 1980-84. Mem. ABA, Contra Costa Bar Assn. (exec. com. 1969-74), State Bar Calif., Calif. Trial Lawyers, Nat. Assn. Women Lawyers, Nat. Assn. Women Judges, Calif. Women Lawyers, Applicants Attys. Assn., Calif. Judges Assn. (ethics com. 1977-79, criminal law procedure com. 1979-80), Queen's Bench, Juvenile Ct. Judges Assn. Democrat. Home: 51 Western Dr Point Richmond CA 94801

HERSCHENSOHN, BRUCE, film director, writer; b. Milw., Sept. 10, 1932. Ed., Los Angeles. With art dept. RKO Pictures, 1953-55; dir., editor Gen. Dynamics Corp., 1955-56; dir., writer, editor Karma for Internat. Communications Found.; editor, co-dir. Friendship Seven for NASA; dir., editor Tall Man Five-Five for Gen. Dynamics Corp. and SAC; dir. motion picture and TV Service USIA, 1968-72, spl. cons. to dir., 1972—; staff asst. to Pres. U.S., 1972; dep. spl. asst. to Pres., 1973-74, mem. transition team, 1981; tchr. U. Md., 1972; spl. cons. to Rep. Nat. Conv., 1972; polit. analyst KABC-TV. Directed and wrote films for, USIA including, Bridges of the Barrios, The Five Cities of June, The President, John F. Kennedy: Years of Lightning, Day of Drums, Eulogy to 5:02; (Acad. award for Czechoslovakia 1968 as best documentary short 1969); Author: The Gods of Antenna, 1976; Contbg. editor: Conservative Digest. Bd. govs. Charles Edison Meml. Youth Fund. Served with USAF, 1951-52. Recipient Arthur S. Flemming award as 1 of 10 outstanding young mem in fed. govt., 1969; Distinguished Service medal USIA, 1972; Ann. award Council Against Communist Aggression, 1972. Office: KABC-TV 4151 Prospect Ave Los Angeles CA 90027 *

HERSCHKOWITZ, ROBERT LION, marketing executive; b. Berchem, Antwerp, Belgium, Mar. 8, 1938; came to U.S., 1966; s. Mordcha Mendel and Irène Eva (Schnabel) H.; m. Irène Marie Lichtenberg, Dec. 28, 1969; child, 1 Stephen Abraham. Student, European Coll., Brugge, Belgium, 1962, Coll. Edn., Antwerp, R.I., 1966, Naval War Coll., Newport, R.I., 1986; BSME, Higher Inst. Tech., Antwerp, 1965; MSME, U. Wash., 1970. Enlisted Belgian Navy, 1960, advanced through grades to lt., 1966, resigned, 1972; project engr. A.H. Lundgerg Engrs., Mercer Island, Wash., 1970-73; sr. research engr. Boeing Marine Systems, Seattle, 1973-76, mktg. mgr., 1976-84, prin. engr., 1984-86; product line mgr. Boeing Electronics Co., Seattle, 1986—; edn. cons. Eastside Edn. Inst., Bellevue, Wash., 1985—. Contbr. articles to profl. jours. Officer Belridge Homeowners Assn., Bellevue, 1974; mem. Bellevue Parks Dept. Adv. Bd., 1984; mem. edn. com. Temple De Hirsh Sinai. Served to comdr. USNR, 1973—. Mem. Internat. Inst. Strategic Studies (London), Mus. Flight (charter), Internat. Bonsat Assn., U.S. Navy League, U.S. Naval Inst., Assn. Old Crows. Clubs: Army, Navy and Airforces (Paris); Prince Albert (Brussels). Avocations: Bonsais, hunting, gardening, reading, mil. history. Office: Boeing Electronics Co MS 9N-36 PO Box 24969 Seattle WA 98124-6269

HERSHEY, ALLEN VINCENT, mathematical physicist; b. Kellogg, Idaho, Aug. 15, 1910; s. Oscar H. and Elizabeth C. (Allen) H.; m. Eva Jane Griffith, Mar. 19, 1949. BS, U. Calif., Berkeley, 1932, MA, 1936, PhD, 1938. Research engr. Gen. Electric, Schenectady, N.Y., 1938-39; contract employee USN, Dalhgren, Va., 1939-43; officer USNR, Dalhgren, 1943-46, research scientist, 1946-79; advanced through grades to commdr. USNR, 1970—, retired; guest faculty Naval Postgrad. Sch., Monterey, Calif., 1979—. Recipient Ed Rosse award COMTEC, 1978. Mem. AAAS, Am. Phys. Soc., Monterey Inst. for Research in Astronomy, Tau Beta Pi, Phi Beta Kappa, Sigma Xi,. Republican. Avocations: calligraphy, miniature railways, sailing. Home: 722 Redwood Ln Pacific Grove CA 93950

HERSHEY, R(UTH) CHRISTINE, graphic designer; b. Exeter, Calif., July 27, 1952; d. Richard Ivan and Dorothy Louise (James) H. Student Art Center Coll. of Design, Los Angeles, 1972-74. Graphic artist Los Angeles Times, 1972-74; graphic designer Golden State Graphics, 1974; pres., creative dir. Hershey Assocs., Los Angeles, 1977—. Active ACLU, People for the Am. Way, Common Cause. Recipient design excellence awards Communications Arts Soc., 1977, Western Art Dirs., 1981, DESI, 1982, N.Y. Art Dirs., Communication Arts, Print and Graphics. Mem. Boulevard Bus. Assn. (pres.) Internat. Assn. Bus. Communicators (bd. dirs., awards 1977, 82, 83), Printing Industries Am. (awards 1980, 81), Am. Inst. Graphic Arts, Art Dirs. Los Angeles (dir.). Democrat. Unitarian. Office: 3429 Glendale Blvd Los Angeles CA 90039

HERSKOVITZ, MARSHALL SCHREIBER, screenwriter, director, producer; b. Phila., Feb. 23, 1952; s. Alexander and Frieda (Schreiber) H.; m. Susan Amanda Shilliday, Feb. 15, 1981; 1 child, Elizabeth Gray. B.A., Brandeis U., 1973; M.F.A., Am. Film Inst., 1975. Freelance writer, dir., producer various TV shows. Writer Family, ABC-TV, 1978, also dir.; writer White Shadow, CBS-TV, 1980, 81; writer-producer Special Bulletin NBC-TV, (recipient 2 Emmys for best writing, best dramatic spl. Acad. TV Arts and Scis. 1983, Humanitas award Human Family Inst. 1983, Writers Guild Am. award 1984), 1983. Mem. Writers Guild of Am., Dirs. Guild Am. Democrat. Jewish.

HERTLEIN, BETH ANN, marketing professional; b. Urbana, Ill., July 7, 1953; d. Bernhard C. Hertlein and Elizabeth (Gable) Wichmann. Student, U. Iowa, 1974; AA in Biol. Scis. and Art, Am. River Coll., 1979. Tutor Eng., text writer Am. River coll., Sacramento; with quality control dept. FMC Corp., Davis, Calif.; cashier Safeway Stores, Inc., Davis; advt. exec. The Davis Enterprise; mgr. coop. advt. dept. The Sacramento Union, 1980-83; owner, v.p. Co-Opnet Inc., Sacramento, 1983—, also cons. Author: (with others) The Co-Op Survival Guide, 1985, Co-Op Master, 1985, Co-Op Sales Handbook, 1985; editor Writer's Workshop, 1979; contbr. articles to profl. jours. Mem. Am. Mktg. Assn. (conf. program chair 1983), Sacramento Valley Mktg. Assn. (pub. chmn.-elect 1983), Calif. Assn. Nurserymen (seminar inst. 1982-83), Photo Mktg. Assn., NACON (seminar and program mgr.). Club: Advt. (Sacramento). Avocations: scuba diving, gardening, swimming, camping, fishing. Office: Co-Opnet Inc 725 30th St #208 Sacramento CA 95816

HERTWECK, E. ROMAYNE, educator; b. Springfield, Mo., July 24, 1928; s. Garnett Perry and Nova Gladys (Chowning) H.; m. Alma Louise Street, Dec. 16, 1955; 1 child, William Scott. B.A., Augustana Coll., 1962; M.A., Pepperdine U., 1963; Ed.D., Ariz. State U., 1966; Ph.D., U.S. Internat. U., 1978. Cert. sch. psychologist, Calif. Night editor Rock Island (Ill.) Argus Newspaper, 1961; grad. asst. psychology dept. Pepperdine Coll., Los Angeles, 1962; counselor VA, Ariz. State U., Tempe, 1963; assoc. dir. Conciliation Ct., Phoenix, 1964; instr. Phoenix Coll., Phoenix, 1965; prof. Mira Costa Coll., Oceanside, Calif., 1966—, mem. senate council, 1968-70, 85-87, chmn. psychology-counseling dept., 1973-75, chmn. dept. behavioral sci., 1976-82, 87—; dept. behavioral sci., 1976-82, 87—; part-time lectr. dept. bus. adminstrn. San Diego State U., 1980-84, Sch. Human Behavior U.S. Internat. U., 1984—; prof. psychology Chapman Coll. World Campus Afloat, 1970; pres. El Camino Preschs., Inc., Oceanside, Calif., 1985—. Bd. dirs. Lifeline, 1969, Christian Counseling Center, Oceanside. Mem. Am., Western, North San Diego County (v.p. 1974-75) psychol. assns., Am. Personnel and Guidance Assn., Nat. Educators Fellowship (v.p. El Camino chpt. 1976-77), Am. Coll. Personnel Assn., Phi Delta Kappa, Kappa Delta Pi, Psi Chi. Club: Kiwanis (charter mem. Carlsbad club, dir. 1975-77). Home: 2024 Oceanview Rd Oceanside CA 92056 Office: Mira Costa Coll 1 Barnard Dr Oceanside CA 92056 Office: El Camino Preschs Inc 2002 California St Oceanside CA 92054

HERTZ, DAVID RANDALL, architect, artist, designer; b. San Francisco, Oct. 6, 1960; s. Robert Stuart and Joanne (Joseph) H. B of Architecture, So. Calif. Inst. Architecture, Santa Monica, 1983. Designer John Lautner, Arch., Hollywood, Calif., 1980-83, Frank O. Gehry, Venice, Calif., 1984; v.p. Syndesis Studio Inc., Santa Monica, 1982. Subject of numerous articles in archtl., design, and popular mags.; One-man furniture exhibitions at Schindler House, Los Angeles, 1985; exhibited in group shows at Whiteley Gallery, Los Angeles, 1985, Queens Mus., N.Y.C., 1985, Welton Becket & Assocs., Los Angeles, 1985, Pierce College Art Gallery, Los Angeles, 1985, Los Angeles Inst. Contemporary Art, 1985, Hokin/Kaufman Gallery, Chgo., 1986, Cobalt Blue/Attack Gallery, Los Angeles, 1986, A.B.C. Devel. Corp. Demostration House, Tokyo, 1986, Craft and Folk Art Mus., Los Angeles, 1986, Flow Ace Gallery, Los Angeles, 1986, Art Expo Navy Pier, Chgo., 1986, Angles Gallery, Santa Monica, Calif., Limn Gallery, San Francisco, Lyon Gallery, Redlands, Calif. Recipient Youhl Architects Competition and Forum award The Archtl. League of N.Y. Finalist in sculpture contest Art Quest, 1986. Mem. AIA (interiors award Los Angeles chpt. 1986), Am. Inst. Assoc. Architects, Internat. Sculpture Ctr., Mus. Contemporary Art, Los Angeles County Mus. Art. Office: Syndesis Studio Inc 1708 Berkeley St Santa Monica CA 90404

HERZ, CAROL LYNN, university official; b. Bklyn., Dec. 3, 1956; d. Karl Otto and Annette K. (Katz) H. Student, John Cabot Internat. Coll., Rome, 1973-74; BA in Psychology, George Washington U., 1977, MEd, 1982. Resident asst. George Washington U., Washington, 1976-78, 80-81, resident dir., 1981-82; resident asst. Am. Council on Edn., Washington, 1978-80; resident mgr. Rosslyn Garden Apts., Va., 1979-80; area dir. U. N.C., Chapel Hill, 1982-85, coordinator summer orientation, 1983-84, field instr., 1984-85; asst. dir. housing U. Calif., Santa Barbara, 1985—. Recipient Leadership Initiative award John Cabot Internat. Coll., 1974. Mem. am. Assn. Counseling and Devel., Am. Coll. Personnel Assn., N.C. Housing Officers, Omicron Delta Kappa. Avocations: songwriting, racquetball, poetry. Home: 3754 San Remo Dr #20 Santa Barbara CA 93105 Office: U Calif Office Residential Life Santa Barbara CA 93106

HERZ, MICHAEL JOSEPH, marine environmental scientist; b. Saint Paul, Aug. 12, 1936; s. Malvin E. and Josephine (Daneman) H.; m. Joan Klein Levy, Feb. 3, 1962 (div. 1982); children: David M., Daniel J., Ann K.; m. Naomi Brodie Schalit, Aug. 21, 1984. BA, Reed Coll., 1958; MA, San Francisco State U., 1962; PhD, U. So. Calif., 1966. Program coordinator postdoctoral tng. program U. Calif., San Francisco, 1969-73, asst. prof., 1969-73, assoc. prof. in residence, 1973-74; exec. dir., dir. water quality tng. program San Francisco Bay. chpt. Nat. Oceanic Soc., 1974-77; exec. v.p., codir. research and policy (Nat.) Oceanic Soc., San Francisco, 1977-84; sr. research scientist Tiburon Ctr. for Environ. Studies San Francisco State U., San Francisco, 1984—; bd. trustees Oceanic Soc., Washington; chmn. bd. govs. Tiburon Ctr. Environ. Studies, San Francisco State U., 1985—; Nat. Research Council com. mem. Effectiveness of Oil Spills Dispersants, Washington, 1985—; Calif. Dept. Health Services com. Ocean Disposal of Radwaste, Sacramento, 1985—; bd. dirs. Aquatic Habitat Inst., 1986—. Author, co-editor: Memory Consolidation, 1972, Habituation I & II, 1973, Analysis of the Puerto Rican Oil Spill, 1985; contbr. articles to profl. jours. Chmn. community adv. bd. Sta. KQED (Pub. Broadcast System affiliate), San Francisco, citizens adv. com. San Francisco Bay Conservation and Devel. Commn.; mem. tech. adv. com. San Francisco Bay Regional Water

Quality Control Bd., Oakland, Calif., 1979-82, Assn. Bay Area Govts., Oakland, 1983—; mem. bay area adv. com. Sea Grant Marine Adv. Program, San Francisco; mem. com. Bur. Land Mgmt., Pacific States Regional Tech. Working Group, 1979-83. Served with U.S. Army, 1958-64. Predoctoral fellow NIMH, U. So. Calif., 1963-64; postdoctoral fellow NIMH, UCLA Brain Research Inst, 1966-68. Mem. AAAS, Calif. Acad. Scis., San Francisco Bay and Estuarine Assn., Sigma Xi. Office: Tiburon Ctr for Environ Studies PO Box 855 Tiburon CA 94920

HERZBERG, DOROTHY CREWS, financial services administrator; b. N.Y.C., July 8, 1935; d. Floyd Houston and Julia (Lesser) Crews; A.B., Brown U., 1957; M.A., Stanford U., 1964; J.D., San Francisco Law Sch., 1976; m. Hershel Zelig Herzberg, May 22, 1962; children—Samuel Floyd, Laura Jill, Daniel Crews. Legal sec. various law firms, San Francisco, 1976-78; tchr. Mission Adult Sch., San Francisco, 1965-66; tchr. secondary and univ. levels Peace Corps, Nigeria, 1961-63; investigator Office of Dist. Atty., San Francisco, 1978-80; sr. adminstr. Dean Witter Reynolds Co., San Francisco, 1980-83; registered rep. Waddell and Reed, Oakland, Calif., 1983-84; fin. services rep. United Resources, Hayward, Calif., 1984-85, Ind. Planning Corp., San Francisco, 1985-86; alt. for supr. San Francisco Mayor's Commn. on Criminal Justice, 1978. Bd. dirs. LWV, San Francisco, 1967-69; bd. dirs. Miraloma (Calif.) Improvement Club, 1977—, pres., 1980-81; pres. Council of Co-op Nursery Schs., San Francisco, 1969-71; active LWV Speakers Bur., 1967—. Mem. Internat. Assn. Fin. Planning, San Francisco Bach Choir, San Francisco C. of C. Democrat. Unitarian. Club: West Portal Toastmistress. Editor Co-op Nursery Sch. Council newsletter, 1969-71, Miraloma Life newsletter, 1976-82, Democratic Women's Forum newsletter, 1980-81, Stanford Luncheon Club newsletter, 1984-85. Home: 238 Bella Vista Way San Francisco CA 94127 Office: 1255 Post St Suite 700 San Francisco CA 94109

HERZIG, ROBERT WILLIAM, health care company executive; b. Phila., Apr. 19, 1943; s. Richard Carl and Ruth (Hickey) H.; m. Linda Marie Kennedy, Aug. 28, 1965; children: Gregory E., R. Scott, Randy W. BS, Bloomsburg U., 1965. Regional sales mgr. IPCO Hosp. Supply, Piscataway, N.J., 1975-77; nat. sales mgr. Am. Mgmt. Services, Denver, 1978-80; v.p. mktg. sales HPI Health Care Services Inc., Los Angeles, 1980-83; pres. pharm. group Summit Health Ltd., Los Angeles, 1983—. Mem. Am. Mgmt. Assn., Am. Hosp. Assn., Am. Osteopathic Assn., Fedn. Am. Health Systems. Roman Catholic. Avocations: tennis, reading. Home: 3677 Calle La Fuego Thousand Oaks CA 91360 Office: Summit Health Ltd 1800 Ave of the Stars Los Angeles CA 90067

HERZOG, JANE, graphic designer; b. Huntington, Ind., May 31, 1927; d. Melvin C. and Margaret D. (Thompson) Kennedy; m. Max A. Herzog (dec.); children: Thomas Michael, Jerry Dane, Sandra Susan Herzog Beemer. Grad., Ft. Wayne Art Inst., 1945-47. Mgr. advt. Huntington Labs., 1966-78; advt. coordinator Quadrex, Campbell, Calif., 1980-83; mgr. art dept. Bemiss Jason Corp., Newark, Calif., 1983—. Office: Bemiss Jason Corp 37600 Central Ct Newark CA 94560

HERZOG, JOHN ORLANDO, mathematics educator, university administrator; b. Ulen, Minn., Apr. 6, 1935; s. Herman and Olga (Renslow) H.; m. Margaret Ann Tevis, Jan. 31, 1959; children: Barbara, Michael, Jane, Kathleen, Daniel. BA, Concordia Coll., Minn., 1957; MA, U. Nebr., 1959, PhD, 1963. Instr. math. U. Nebr., Lincoln, 1959-61; from asst. prof. to assoc. prof. math. Idaho State U., Pocatello, 1963-67; from assoc. prof. to prof. math. Pacific Luth. U., Tacoma, 1967—, dean natural scis., 1984—, chmn. dept. math., 1968-74, 83-84, chmn. div. scis., 1975-81; cons. NSF, India, summer 1967. Councilman Trinity Luth. Ch., Tacoma, 1969-71, 82-84. NSF fellow, U. Nebr., 1961-62; grantee NSF, Idaho State U., 1963-67, Pacific Luth. U., 1968-73; grantee Dept. Energy, Pacific Luth. U., 1976-85. Mem. Am. Math. Soc., Math Assn. Am. (treas. 1976-79), Nat. Council Tchrs. of Math., Wash. State Math Council, Sigma Xi. Avocations: hiking, gardening, running, beekeeping. Home: 505 S 132d St Tacoma WA 98444 Office: Pacific Luth U Dept Math Tacoma WA 98447

HESKIN, DARYL JAMES, architect; b. Mayville, N.D., Sept. 6, 1947; s. Norman Lester and Irene (Hanson) H.; m. Karen Elaine Kamhoot, Aug. 22, 1970; children: Kam, James, Robert. Student, U. N.D., 1965-67; BArch., Mont. State U., 1971. Registered architect, Colo. Architect, Grosz & Anderson Architects, Grand Forks, N.D., 1972-73; office mgr. Ramon F. Martinez A.I.A., Denver, 1973-75; prin. Archtl. Design Team, Lakewood, Colo., 1975-76; v.p. Cillessen Constrn. Co., Golden, Colo., 1977-81; prin. Heskin/Morgan Architects, Inc., Westminster, Colo. 1981—; chmn. archtl. control com. Valley of the Sun, Fairplay, Colo., 1984—; dir., Design Build Concepts, Inc., Denver, 1983—. Coach Arvada Soccer Assn., Colo., 1981—; active Nat. Youth Sports Coaches Assn., Denver, 1982—; bd. dirs. Denver Area Council of Campfire, 1982-86, com. mem. facilities task force 1983-86. Recipient Sebago award Denver Area council Campfire, 1983. Mem. AIA, Colo. Soc. AIA, Arvada C. of C., Sigma Alpha Epsilon. Republican. Methodist. Lodge: Elks. Office: Heskin/Morgan Architects Inc 6510 W 91st Ave Suite 106 Westminster CO 80030

HESLET, JOSEPH HARRY, broadcasting executive; b. Shreveport, La., Sept. 21, 1953; s. Harry Rueben and Lucille (Aksamit) H.; m. Linda Karen Rudloff, Oct. 29, 1983. Student, Chapman Coll., 1971-72; AA, Coll. of Sequoias, 1974; student, Calif. State U., Hayward, 1974-75, U. San Francisco, 1985. Cert. radio mktg. cons. Asst. mgr. City of Visalia (Calif.) Conv. Ctr., 1975-78; acct. exec. Stereo Broadcasting Sta. KFYE-FM, Fresno, 1978-81; gen. sales mgr. Sunbelt Communications Sta. KFYE-FM, Fresno, 1981-84; gen. sales mgr. McClatchy Broadcasting Sta. KMJ/KNAX, Fresno, 1984-85, gen. mgr., 1985-86; gen. mgr. Colo. Radio Div. Sterling Recreation Orgn. Broadcasting Sta. KHIH/KDKO, Denver, 1986—. Recipient Golden Oak awards (4) Am. Advt. Fedn., 1986. Mem. Nat. Assn. Broadcasters (master class strategist 1986), Nat. Radio Broadcasters Assn., Fresno Radio Advt. Group (past pres., v.p. 1983-86). Republican. Episcopalian. Lodge: Rotary. Avocations: golf, tennis, softball, skiing, piano. Office: Sta KHIH/KDKO Radio 7900 E Berry Pl Englewood CO 80111

HESPRICH, STEVEN FRANCIS, infosystems specialist; b. Fond Du Lac, Wis., June 7, 1951; s. Francis W. and LaVerne G. (Grusnick) H.; m. Kim Marie Lueder, Jan. 24, 1975; children: Erich Johannes, Christian. BS in Math. and Computer Sci. magna cum laude, U. Wis., River Falls, 1973; MS in Mfg. Adminstrn., Western Mich. U., 1980; MBA, U. Phoenix, 1987. Computer system designer Martin Marietta Corp., Denver, 1974-76; systems engr. Info. Industries, Inc., Kansas City, Kans., 1976-77; systems and programming specialist Upjohn Co., Kalamazoo, 1978-81; project mgr. mktg. support Philips Industries, Vienna, Austria, 1981-84; mgr. infosystems research Great-West Life Assurance Co., Englewood, Colo., 1984—; computer cons. Decision Support Adv., various locations, 1980—; teaching asst. Colo. State U., 1973. Author: Spreadsheet Analysis: An Improved Business Tool, 1983. Fellow Life Mgmt. Inst.; mem. Assn. Systems Mgmt. (pres. Western Mich. chpt. 1979-80). Avocations: running, personal computing, stamp collecting. Office: Great-West Life Assurance Co 8515 E Orchard Rd Englewood CO 80111

HESS, LAVERNE DERRYL, research laboratory executive; b. Stockton, Ill., Oct. 28, 1933; s. James and Gertrude (Posey) H.; m. Mary Daune McDermott, Jan. 20, 1954; children: Donald, Patti, Susan, Daniel, Bart, Jennifer. BA, U. Calif., Riverside, 1961, PhD, 1965. Mem. tech. staff Hughes Research Labs., Malibu, Calif., 1965-78, head tech. staff, 1978-85; asst. mgr. Chem.-Physics dept. Hughes Research Labs., Malibu, Calif., 1985, acting mgr., 1986—. Contbr. numerous articles to sci. jours. Mgr. Little League Baseball, Thousand Oaks, Calif., 1968-78. Served with U.S. Army, 1954-56. Mem. Materials Research Soc. Avocations: bridge, jogging, biking, sailing, guitar. Home: 1462 Dorset Thousand Oaks CA 91360 Office: Hughes Aircraft Co 3011 Malibu Canyon Rd Malibu CA 90265

HESS, LYNNE CRANDALL, audiovisual production company executive; b. Noblesville, Ind., June 14, 1938; d. Robert Bates and Hazel Irene (Feaster) Crandall; m. Richard Lee Stephens, July 2, 1954 (div. Dec. 1963); children: James Lee, Sue Lynne, Eric Lewis, John Andrew, Kelly Anne; m. H. Nelson vanSant, Mar. 4, 1983. Student, Butler U., 1956-58, Roosevelt U., 1960-65. Asst. dir. pub. relations Sinclair Refining Co., Chgo., 1965-67; mktg. mgr. C.H. Ellis Co., Indpls., 1967-69; prin. LCH and Assocs., Indpls., 1969-75; account supr. N.W. Ayer Inc., N.Y.C., 1975-82; prin., chief exec. officer Cerutti/Hess Prodns., N.Y.C., 1982-83; pres. Omnivision, Phoenix, 1983—. Writer/producer educational film A Promise to be Kept, 1983 (N.Y. Film Festival award, Am. Film Inst. Internat. Film Festival award). Mem. Assn. Visual Communicators (film festival judge, treas. nat. bd. dirs. 1987), Nat. Assn. Female Execs., Ariz. C. of C., Phoenix C. of C. Home: 7310 E Carol Way Scottsdale AZ 85260 Office: Omnivision 1930 W Peoria Ave Phoenix AZ 85029

HESSE, CHRISTIAN AUGUST, mining company executive; b. Chemnitz, Germany, June 20, 1925; s. William Albert and Anna Gunhilda (Baumann) H.; B.Applied Sci. with honors, U. Toronto (Ont., Can.), 1948; m. Brenda Nora Rigby, Nov. 4, 1964; children: Robin Christian, Bruce William. In various mining and constrn. positions, Can., 1944-61; jr. shift boss N.J. Zinc Co., Gilman, Colo., 1949; asst. layout engr. Internat. Nickel Co., Sudbury, Ont., 1949-52; shaft engr. Perini-Walsh Joint Venture, Niagara Falls, Ont., 1952-54; project engr. B. Perini & Sons (Can.) Ltd., Toronto, Ottawa, and New Brunswick, 1954-55; field engr. Aries Copper Mines Ltd., No. Ont., 1955-56; instr. in mining engring. U. Toronto, 1956-57; planning engr. Stanleigh Uranium Mining Corp. Ltd., Elliot Lake, Ont., 1957-58, chief engr., 1959-60; field engr. Johnson-Perini-Kiewit Joint Venture, Toronto, 1960-61; del. Commonwealth Mining Congress, Africa, 1961; with U.S. Borax & Chem. Corp., 1961—, gen. mgr. Allan Potash Mines Ltd., Allan, Sask., Can., 1974, chief engr. U.S. Borax & Chem. Corp., Los Angeles, 1974-77, v.p. engring., 1977-81, v.p. and project mgr. Quartz Hill project, 1981—; v.p. Pacific Coast Molybdenum Co., 1981-84, v.p. mining devel., 1984—, v.p. engring., 1987—. Sault Daily Star scholar, Sault Sainte Marie, Ont., Can., 1944. Mem. AIME, Can. Inst. Mining and Metallurgy (life), Assn. Profl. Engrs. Ont. Lutheran. Clubs: Los Angeles, Ambassador Tennis and Health. Office: US Borax & Chem Corp 3075 Wilshire Blvd Los Angeles CA 90010

HESSELDEN, KURT MANFRED, programmer analyst; b. Munich, Sept. 7, 1949; came to U.S., 1955; adopted s. Donald Richard and Jody (Anderson) H.; m. Vivian Jean Dench, June 11, 1968; children: Sheila, Wendy, Angie. Warehouse salesman S.W. Distbg., Albuquerque, 1969-73; mgr. Derrick Inn Inc., Farmington, N.Mex., 1973-79; programmer analyst, systems specialist City of Farmington, 1979—; instr. San Juan Coll., Farmington, 1981-85. Author (software) Police Wants/Warrants, 1982, Mcpl. Ct., 1983, Detective Intelligence, 1983, Police Records and Info., 1983. Served with U.S. Army, 1966-69, Vietnam. Republican. Roman Catholic. Avocations: computer science, ham radio. Home: 2409 Cliffside Dr Farmington NM 87401 Office: City of Farmington Box 800 Farmington NM 87499

HESSELINK, LAMBERTUS, aeronautics, astronautics and electrical engineering educator; b. Enschede, The Netherlands, Dec. 4, 1948; came to U.S., 1971; s. Lambertus and Wilhelmina (ten Tye) H.; m. Marieke van Heerde, Aug. 18, 1971. BSME, Twente Inst. Tech., Enschede, 1970, BS in Applied Physics, 1971, postgrad., 1974; MSME, Calif. Inst. Tech., 1972, PhD in Applied Mechs., Physics, 1977. Research fellow Calif. Inst. Tech., Pasadena, 1977-78, instr. applied physics, 1978-79, sr. research fellow fluid mechs., 1970-80; asst. prof. aeros. and astronautics Stanford (Calif.) U., 1980-85, assoc. prof., 1985—; asst. prof. elec. engring. Stanford U., 1980-85, assoc. prof. 1985—; cons. Hughes Aircraft Corp., Culver City, Calif., 1978-79. Patentee in field. Recipient Stheeman prize Twente Inst. Tech., 1970; Fulbright fellow 1971-74; fellow Josephine de Karman fellow, 1974-75. Mem. AIAA (Engr. of Yr. 1982), Optical Soc. Am., Soc. Photo-Optical Instrumentation Engrs. Optical Soc. Am., Am. Phys. Soc., Sigma Xi. Office: Stanford U Dept Aeors and Astronautics Durand 370 Stanford CA 94305

HESTER, GERALD LEROY, superintendent schools; b. Seattle, Aug. 6, 1928; s. Ernest Orien and Louise (Drange) H.; m. Carol Joyce Johnston, Aug. 2, 1953; children—Mark Wyn, Sue Ann. B.S., Wash. State U., 1950, B.Ed., 1953; M.Ed., Western Wash. State Coll., 1957; Ed.D., Columbia U., 1964. Prin. jr. high sch. Bellevue Sch. Dist., Wash., 1959-64, dir. guidance, 1964-65; supt. Vashon Sch. Dist., Wash., 1965-69, Auburn Sch. Dist., Wash., 1969-73, Vancouver Sch. Dist., Wash., 1973-80, Spokane Sch. Dist., Wash., 1980—; mem. Provost Commn. on Tchr. Edn., Wash. State U., Pullman, 1983-84; mem. adv. bd. U. Wash. Sch. Edn., Seattle, 1974; mem. Citizens Adv. Com. Higher Edn. Consortium, Spokane, Wash., 1984; bd. mem. Wash. Council for Econ. Edn., Seattle, 1984. Bd. dirs. Inland Empire council Boy Scouts Am., 1981—, YMCA, 1982—; trustee Holy Family Hosp.; chmn. edn. div. United Way, Spokane, 1981-82. Served to 1st lt. U.S. Army, 1951-52. Recipient Civic Fame award Rotary Club 21, Spokane, 1982; listed among Top 100 Educators, Exec. Educator Mag., 1984, 87; Alumni Achievement award Wash. State U., 1985. Mem. Am. Assn. Sch. Adminstrs. (adv. com), Suburban Sch. Supts. (pres. 1982-83), Wash. Assn. Sch. Adminstrs. (exec. bd. 1971-74), 1st Class Sch. Dist. Supts. (pres. 1984), Spokane C. of C. (bd. trustees 1983—), Phi Delta Kappa. Clubs: Royal Oaks Country (Vancouver, Wash.) (pres. 1972-73); Spokane Country, Spokane, Prosperity (Spokane, Wash.). Lodge: Rotary. Home: E 2006 24th Ave Spokane WA 99203 Office: Spokane Sch Dist Office of the Supt of Schs N 200 Bernard St Spokane WA 99201

HETH, CHARLOTTE ANNE, music educator; b. Muskogee, Okla., Oct. 29, 1937; d. Woodrow Curt and Eula Jewel (Seabolt) Wilson; m. Linton LeRoy Heth, July 5, 1966 (div. Jan. 1970). B.A., U. Tulsa, 1959, M.Mus., 1960; Ph.D., UCLA, 1975. Tchr., Jal (N.Mex.) High Sch., 1960-61, Catoosa (Okla.) High Sch., 1961-62; Peace Corps vol. Maaraga Hiwot Haile Selassie I Sch., Ambo, Ethiopia, 1962-64; tchr. A.B.C. Unified Sch. Dist. Schs., Artesia, Calif., 1965-73; asst. prof., assoc. prof. music UCLA, 1974—, dir. Am. Indian Studies Ctr., 1976—; panel mem. for folk arts Nat. Endowment for Arts, 1980-82; bd. mem. Indian Ctrs., Inc., Los Angeles, 1977-78. Editor: Selected Reports in Ethnomusicology, 1980; American Indian Culture and Research Jour., 1982; record producer Songs of Earth, Water, Fire and Sky, etc., 1976; video producer Music of the Sacred Fire, etc., 1978. Ford Found. dissertation fellow, 1973-74; So. Fellowship Fund postdoctoral fellow, 1978-79; sr. postdoctoral award Newberry Library, Chgo., 1978-79, NRC, 1984-85. Mem. Soc. Ethnomusicology (council mem. 1977-84, council chmn. 1980-82), Nat. Indian Edn. Assn., Western Social Sci. Assn., Sigma Alpha Iota. Democrat. Baptist. Office: Music Dept Schoenberg Hall UCLA Los Angeles CA 90024

HETHERINGTON, CHERYL KEIKO, lawyer; b. Honolulu, July 24, 1952; d. Sidney Ichiro and Shizuko (Murakami) Hashimoto; m. J. George Hetherington, Nov. 25, 1978. Student Whitman Coll., 1970-72; B.A. U. Wash.-Seattle, 1974; J.D., Hastings Coll. Law, San Francisco. Bar: Hawaii 1979, U.S. Dist. Ct. Hawaii 1979. Counselor Planned Parenthood of Seattle-King County, 1974-76; atty. Law Offices Sidney I Hashimoto, Honolulu, 1979-82; sole practice, Honolulu, 1982—. Mem. Hawaii State Bar Assn., Hawaii Women Lawyers, ABA (Young Lawyers div., Family Law div.), Nat. Assn. Women Lawyers, Hastings Alumni Assn., U. Wash. Alumni Assn., Mortar Board, Alpha Chi Omega Found., Alpha Kappa Delta. Democrat. Club: Kailua Racquet. Contbg. author articles in field. Office: 1001 Bishop St 480 Pauahi Tower Honolulu HI 96813

HETLAND, JOHN ROBERT, lawyer, educator; b. Mpls., Mar. 12, 1930; s. James L. and Evelyn (Lundgren) H.; m. Mildred Woodruff, Dec. 1951 (div.); children: Lynda Lee, Robert John, Debra Ann.; m. Anne Kneeland, Dec. 1972; children: Robin T. Kneeland, Elizabeth J. Kneeland. B.S.L., U. Minn., 1952, J.D., 1956. Bar: Minn. bar 1956, Calif. bar 1962. Practice law Mpls., 1956-59; asso. prof. law U. Calif., Berkeley, 1959-60; prof. law U. Calif., 1960—; practice law Berkeley, 1959—; vis. prof. law Stanford U., 1971, 80, U. Singapore, 1972. Author: Hetland, California Real Property Secured Transactions, 1970, Hetland, Commercial Real Estate Transactions, 1972, Hetland, Secured Real Estate Transactions, 1974, Maxwell, Riesenfeld, Hetland and Warren, California Cases on Security Transactions in Land, 2d edit., 1975, 3d edit., 1984, Hetland, Secured Real Estate Transactions, 1977; contbr. articles to legal, real estate and fin. jours. Served to lt. comdr. USNR, 1953-55. Mem. state bars Calif. and Minn., Am. Bar Assn., Order of Coif, Phi Delta Phi. Republican. Home: 20 Redcoach Ln Orinda CA 94563 Office: 2600 Warring St Berkeley CA 94704

HETT, JOAN MARGARET, civic administrator; b. Trail, B.C., Can., Sept. 8, 1936; s. Gordon Stanley and Violet Thora (Thors) Hett; B.Sc., U. Victoria (B.C., Can.), 1964; M.S., U. Wis., Madison, 1967, Ph.D., 1969. Ecologist, Eastern Deciduous Forest Biome, Oak Ridge Nat. Lab., 1969-72; coor. sites dir. Coniferous Forest Biome, Oreg. State U., Corvallis and U. Wash., Seattle, 1972-77; ecol. cons., Seattle, 1978-84; plant ecologist Seattle City Light, 1984-86; supr. Rights-of-Way, Seattle City Light, 1986—. Mem. Ecol. Soc. Am., Brit. Ecol. Soc., Am. Inst. Biol. Scis., AAAS, Am. Forestry Assn., Sierra Club, Sigma Xi. Contbr. articles to profl. jours.; research in plant population dynamics, land use planning, forest sucession.

HETT, ROSLIN MARTYN, finance co. exec.; b. Kamloops, B.C., Can., Nov. 22, 1931; s. Roslin Martyn and Phyllis Maude (Slater) H.; came to U.S., 1966; ed. Brentwood Coll., Victoria, B.C., 1950; m. Sophia Penelope Jane Harvey, July 10, 1953; children—Jane, Caroline, John, Jennifer, Mary. Field rep. Niagara Finance Corp., Victoria, 1953; with collections dept. Gen. Motors Acceptance Corp., Vancouver, 1953-55, from field rep. to dist. rep., 1956-60; sales mgr. Morrison Motors, Ltd., Duncan, B.C., 1955-56; with Avco Fin. Services, Inc., and predecessors, Newport Beach, Calif., 1960-79, pres., 1975-79, also dir.; pres., dir. Avco Corp., 1979-81; prin. Hett Fin. Cons., Laguna Niguel, Calif., 1981—. Episcopalian. Clubs: Balboa Bay, Masons. Home: 30882 Cypress Pl Laguna Niguel CA 92677 Office: Hett Fin Cons 30101 Town Center Dr Suite 103 Laguna Niguel CA 92677

HETTINGER, JOHN D., chemist; b. Memphis, July 27, 1938; s. Christian Dudley and Sarah Rebeccah (Grimes) H.; m. Cynthia Hartridge, May 1, 1964; children: Julie Ann, Drew Christian. BS, Rhodes Coll., 1960; PhD, U. Wis., 1966. Staff chemist Upjohn Labs., Kalamazoo, 1966-71; sr. scientist Spectra Physics, Mountain View, Calif., 1971-74; sr. applications chemist Varian Assocs., Palo Alto, Calif., 1974-76; mgr. quality assurance Dynapol, Palo Alto, 1976-79; supr. analytical chemistry Lockheed Missiles & Space Co., Sunnyvale, Calif., 1979—. Mem. Am. Chem. Soc., Soc. Advancement of Material and Process Engring. Baptist. Avocations: backpacking, sailing, music. Home: 12372 Priscilla Los Altos Hills CA 94022 Office: Lockheed Missiles and Space Co 48-92/195B PO Box 3504 Sunnyvale CA 94088-3504

HEUMAN, DONNA RENA, entrepreneur, lawyer; b. Seattle, May 27, 1949; d. Russell George and Edna Inez (Armstrong) H. BA in Psychology, UCLA, 1972; JD, U. Calif., San Francisco, 1985. Owner, Heuman & Assocs., San Francisco, 1978—. Mem. Hastings Internat. and Comparative Law Rev., 1984-85. Mem. Nat. Shorthand Reporters Assn., Women Entrepreneurs, Calif. Shorthand Reporters Assn., Calif. State Bar Assn., Nat. Mus. of Women in the Arts, ABA, San Francisco Bar Assn., Assn. Trial Lawyers of Am., Bay Area Lawyers for the Arts, Nat. Assn. Female Execs. Clubs: Commonwealth (San Francisco), World Affairs Council (San Francisco), Zonta (bd. dirs.) (San Francisco). Home: 365 Vallejo St Apt 6 San Francisco CA 94133

HEUNG, GLORIA WING, chemical engineer; b. Hong Kong, Dec. 20, 1955; came to U.S., 1973; d. Kwong Ying and So-Chun (Hung) H.; m. William Warren Rubin, May 6, 1985. AA, Yuba Coll., 1975; BS in Chemistry, U. N.Mex., 1978, MS in Chem. Engring., 1981. Research asst. U. N.Mex., Albuquerque, 1978-79; process engr. Kennecott Minerals Co., Salt Lake City, 1979-82; chem. engr. The Amalgamated Sugar Co., Twin Falls, Idaho, 1982-84; operator wholesale-import bus. Yakima, Wash., 1985-86; quality control chemist Coca Cola Bottling Co., Salt Lake City, 1986; research engr. ASARCO Inc., Salt Lake City, 1987—. Mem. Am. Soc. Sugar Beet Tech., Soc. Mining Engrs. Home: 7834A Honeycomb Rd Salt Lake City UT 84121 Office: ASARCO Inc 3422 S 700 W Salt Lake City UT 84119

HEUSCHELE, WERNER PAUL, veterinary researcher; b. Ludwigsburg, Federal Republic of Germany, Aug. 28, 1929; came to U.S., 1932, naturalized, 1951; s. Karl August and Margarete Anna (Wagner) H.; m. Mary G. Gagen, July 1, 1973 (div. Dec. 1982); m. Carolyn René Bredeson, Jan. 1, 1983; children: Erick W.K., Mark R., Jennifer M. Student, San Diego State Coll., 1947-50; BA in Zoology, U. Calif., Davis, 1952, DVM, 1956; student, NIH, Bethesda, Md., 1966; PhD in Med. Microbiology, Virology, Immunology, U. Wis., 1969. Diplomate Am. Coll. Vet. Microbiologists. Mgr. veterinary hosp. Zool. Soc. San Diego, 1956-61, head, microbiology/virology, 1981-86, dir. research and vet. medicine, 1986—; research veterinarian Plum Island Animal Disease Lab., Orient Point, N.Y., 1961-71; tng. resident in vet. pathology Armed Forces Inst. Pathology, Washington, 1965-66; assoc. prof. infectious disease Kansas State U., Manhattan, 1970-71; head, virology, research and devel. Jensen-Salsbery Labs., Kansas City, Kans., 1971-76; prof. vet. preventive medicine Ohio State U., Columbus, 1976-81; cons. Syntro Corp., San Diego, 1985—; SIBIA, San Diego, 1983—; UN-FAO-UNDP, Maracay, Venezuela, 1979, 80; grant rev. panelist USDA, Washington. Contbr. articles to profl. jours. Fellow Am. Assn. Zool. Parks and Aquariums; mem. Am. Assn. Zoo Veterinarians (pres. 1958-59, sec., treas. 1959-61, American Vet. Med. Assn., Wildlife Disease Assn. (vice-pres. 1985—), Vet. Specialist Group (species survival com.), Columbus Zoo Assn. (bd. dirs), Am. Coll. Vet. Microbiologists (bd. govs. 1984-87), U.S. Animal Health Assn. (zool. animals com. 1985—), Sigma Xi, Phi Zeta. Home: 4528 N 44th St San Diego CA 92115 Office: Zool Soc San Diego PO Box 551 San Diego CA 92112

HEVERLING, JOCK TIMOTHY, psychiatric social worker; b. Seattle, Nov. 10, 1944; s. Andrew H., Robert Alfred Magnuson (stepfather) and Doroty W. (Lade) Heverling Magnuson; m. Margaret Ann Harris, Jan 1, 1977 (div. May 1978); m. Janet Evelyn Thompson, Dec. 13, 1980. BA cum laude, U. Wash., 1967; MSW, U. N.C., 1973. Cert. social worker. Casework supr. Wash. Dept. Social and Health Services, Chehalis, 1974; job counselor Wash. Dept. Employment Security, Mt. Vernon, 1976-78; instr. Skagit Valley Community Coll., Oak Harbor, Wash., 1980-82; pvt. practice Christian counseling Oak Harbor, 1984-86, Coupeville, Wash., 1986—; media cons. pub. relations Skagitonians Concerned About Nuclear Power Plants, 1975-76, Wash. State Commn. Mex.-Am. Affairs, 1978-79. Co-writer several gospel songs including I'm Ridin' High with Jesus, 1986. Mem. Olympic Episc. Dioscean Evangelism Commn., 1986—. Served with USNR, 1969-70. Mem. LWV, Nat. Assn. Social Workers, Acad. Cert. Social Workers (cert.), ASCAP. Avocations: hiking, reading, writing poetry. Home: PO Box 551 Coupeville WA 98239 Office: PO Box 943 Coupeville WA 98239

HEVEZI, JAMES M(ICHAEL), radiological physicist, consultant; b. Gary, Ind., June 21, 1940; s. James E. and Margaret (Olah) H.; m. Suzanne Landig, Feb. 5, 1978. B.S., Ill. Benedictine Coll., 1962; Ph.D., U. Notre Dame, 1969. Diplomate Am. Bd. Radiology. Asst. prof. radiology U. Wis., Madison, 1969-71, M.D. Anderson Hosp., Houston, 1971-78; assoc. prof. S.D. Sch. Mining, Rapid City, 1978-79; asst. prof. U. Ariz., Tucson, 1979-83; v.p. Radiol. Physics Services Inc., Phoenix, 1983—; cons. in field. Contbr. articles on radiol. physics to profl. jours. Patentee imaging by point absorption radiation, 1975, electrostatic imaging method 1984. Nat. Cancer Inst. grantee, 1970, 76-77. Mem. Am. Assn. Physicists in Medicine (assoc. editor 1975-80), Am. Coll. Radiology, Am. Endocurie Therapy Soc., Radiol. Soc. N.Am., Am. Soc. Radiation Therapy and Oncology. Roman Catholic. Home: 2155 E Minton Dr Tempe AZ 85282

HEWETT, ROBERT BURCH, international education administrator; b. Detroit, Dec. 6, 1913; s. Joseph Lancaster and Lulu Marie (Burch) H.; m. Mary Joyce Morgan, Dec. 1, 1952 (dec.); children—Judith, Martha; m. Joan E. Hayes, Nov. 12, 1983. Student U. Mich., 1931-33. Reporter, Ann Arbor (Mich.) Daily News, 1933-35, Decatur (Ill.) Herald-Rev., 1935-38; capitol corr. AP, Springfield, Ill., 1939-42; AP editor, bur. chief, corr., London, Tehran, Iran, Singapore, Cairo and Beirut, Lebanon, 1946-57; corr. Cowles Publs., Beirut, Hong Kong, London, 1957-67; corp. sec., spl. asst. to pres., curator Jefferson fellowships, East-West Ctr. Honolulu, 1968—. Served to lt. col. USMCR, 1942-45. Decorated Bronze Star., Purple Heart. Recipient Nat. Headliners Club award, 1958; Overseas Press Club award, 1959. Mem. Pub. Relations Soc. Am. (accredited). Club: Army and Navy (Washington). Home: 1860 Ala Moana Blvd Apt 2001 Honolulu HI 96815 Office: East West Center 1777 East-West Rd Honolulu HI 96848

HEWITT, ARTHUR ELBERT, lawyer; b. Yuba City, Calif., Dec. 9, 1915; s. Charles Oscar and Eva Marie (Smith) H.; m. Kathryn Vera Lane, May 12, 1933 (div. 1939); 1 child, Allan A.; m. 2d Irene Flossie Heater, Jan. 15, 1943; children: Arthur Elbert, Ronald C. Bar: Calif. Sole practice law Marysville, Calif., 1938-42; dist. atty. Yuba County, Calif., 1946-47; ptnr. Gray, Hewitt, Lenhard & Sanders, Marysville, 1947-75; pres. Hewitt, Lenhard, Sanders and

Anderson, Marysville, 1975-84, Arthur E. Hewitt, Inc., Marysville, 1985—; state inheritance tax appraiser State of Calif., 1947-59, state inheritance tax referee, 1968—; mem. Yuba County Parole Bd., 1958-82, arbitration panel Sutter County Superior Ct., 1978—. Trustee Sutter County Law Library; chmn. bd. trustees Bapt. Ch. Served as lt. USNR, 1942-45. Mem. Calif. Bar. Assn., Assn. Trial Lawyers Am., Calif. Trial Lawyers Assn., Am. Arbitration Assn. (arbitrator 1962—), Yuba Sutter Bar Assn. (pres. 1956-57, mem. disciplinary com. 1965-67). Home: 1920 Sampson St Marysville CA 95901 Office: 716 D St Marysville CA 95901

HEWITT, GEORGE E., investment executive; b. N.Y.C., July 2, 1921. BME, Columbia U., 1943; cert. radar UHF techniques, MIT, 1943; postgrad., UCLA extension; student, Orange Coast Coll. Registered profl. engr., Calif.; licensed real estate agt., Calif. Mem. staff radiation lab. MIT, Boston, 1943-45; engr., project engr. Gilfillon Bros., Inc., 1946-48; founder, v.p., gen. mgr. Canoga Corp. merged with Underwood Olivetti, 1948-58; founder, pres. V-N Mfg. Co., 1949-60; founder, gen. ptnr. Airad Co., 1950-59; pvt. practice personal estate mgmt. 1970—; founder, pres., chmn. The George E. Hewitt Found. for Med. Research, 1980—; mem., trustee, U. Calif. Coll. Medicine, Irvine; bd. dirs. Ctr. Health Edn. Meml. Med. Ctr. Long Beach. Mem. World Affairs Council. Mem. Nat. Soc. Immunology, U. Calif. Med. Research and Edn. Soc., Orange County Performing Arts, Internat. Oceanographic Found., Am. Def. Preparedness Assn., Navy League, Newport Found., Newport Harbor Art Mus. Clubs: Lido Island Yacht, Balboa Bay, Hoag 552, Exchange (bd. dirs.). Home: 137 Jasmine Creek Dr Corona Del Mar CA 92626

HEWLETT, WILLIAM (REDINGTON), institutional administrator, electrical engineer; b. Ann Arbor, Mich., May 20, 1913; s. Albion Walter and Louise (Redington) H.; m. Flora Lamson, Aug. 10, 1939 (dec. 1977); children: Eleanor Hewlett Gimon, Walter B., James S., William A., Mary Hewlett Jaffe; m. Rosemary Bradford, May 24, 1978. A.B., Stanford U., 1934, E.E., 1939; M.S., MIT, 1936; LL.D., U. Calif., Berkeley, 1966, Yale U., 1976, Mills Coll., 1983; D.Sc. (hon.), Kenyon Coll., 1978, Poly Inst. N.Y., 1978; L.H.D., Johns Hopkins U., 1985; Eng.D., U. Notre Dame, 1980, Utah State U., 1980, Dartmouth Coll., 1983. Electromed. researcher 1936-39; co-founder Hewlett-Packard Co., Palo Alto, Calif., 1939, ptnr., 1939-46, exec. v.p., dir., 1947-64, pres., 1964-77, chief exec. officer, 1969-78, chmn. exec. com., 1977-83, vice chmn. bd. dirs., 1983-87, dir., emeritus dir., 1987—; dir. emeritus Hewlett-Packard Co., 1987—; mem. internat. adv. council Wells Fargo Bank, 1986—; trustee Rand Corp., 1962-72, Carnegie Inst., Washington, 1971, chmn. bd. trustees, 1980-86; bd. dirs. Nat. Acads. Corp.; dir. Overseas Devel. Council, 1969-77. Contbr. articles to profl. jours.; patentee in field. Trustee Stanford U., 1963-74, Mills Coll., Oakland, Calif., 1958-68; trustee Carnegie Instn., Washington, 1971—, chmn. bd. trustees, 1980-86; mem. Pres.'s Gen. Adv. Com. on Fgn. Assistance Programs, Washington, 1965-68, Pres.'s Sci. Adv. Com., 1966-69; mem. San Francisco regional panel Commn. on White House Fellows, 1969-70, chmn., 1970; dir. pub. policy Rand Grad. Sch., 1985; pres. bd. dirs. Palo Alto Stanford Hosp. Ctr., 1956-58, bd. dirs., 1958-62; bd. dirs. San Francisco Bay Area Council, 1969-81, Inst. Medicine, Washington, 1971-72, Univ. Corp. for Atmospheric Research Found., 1986—. Served to lt. col. AUS, 1942-45. Recipient Calif. Mfr. of Yr. Calif. Mfrs. Assn., 1969, Bus. Statesman of Yr. Harvard Bus. Sch. No. Calif., 1970, Medal of Achievement Western Electronic Mfrs. Assn., 1971, Industrialist of Yr. (with David Packard) Calif. Mus. Sci. and Industry and Calif. Mus. Found., 1973, Award with David Packard presented by Scientific Apparatus Makers Assn., 1975, Corp. Leadership award MIT, 1976, Medal of Honor City of Boeblingen, Germany, 1977, Herbert Hoover medal for disting. service Stanford U. Alumni Assn., 1977, Henry Heald award Ill. Inst. Tech., 1984, Nat. Medal of Sci. U.S. Nat. Sci. Com., 1985. Fellow IEEE (pres. 1954, Founders medal with David Packard 1973), Franklin Inst. (life, Vermilye medal with David Packard 1976), Am. Acad. Arts and Scis.; mem. Nat. Acad. Scis. (panel on advanced tech. competition 1982-83, chpt. coordinator on research in industry 5-yr. outlook report 1980-81), Nat. Acad. Engring., Instrument Soc. Am. (hon. life), Am. Philos. Soc., Calif. Acad. Sci. (hon. trustee 1969—), Assn. Quadrato della Radio, Century Assn. N.Y.C. Clubs: Bohemian, Pacific-Union (San Francisco); Menlo Country (Woodside, Calif.). Office: Hewlett-Packard Co 1501 Page Mill Rd Palo Alto CA 94304

HEWSTON, JOHN GUTHRIE, natural resources educator; b. Roy, Wash., Aug. 21, 1923; s. John G. and Jessie M. (Elder) H.; m. Audrey P. Stephenson, Aug. 27, 1949; children: Jyl A., Jody M. Hewston Wood, Joni L. BA, Pacific Luth. U., Parkland, Wash., 1950; MS, Oreg. State U., 1955; PhD, Utah State U., 1966. Fishery biologist Wash. Dept. of Fisheries, Port Angeles, 1953; fishery mgmt. biologist N.D. Dept. of Game and Fish, Dickinson, 1953-55; chief info. and edn. N.D. Dept. of Game and Fish, Bismarck, 1955-62; fishery biologist U.S. Fish and Wildlife Service, Logan, Utah, 1962-66; prof. natural resources Humboldt State U., Arcata, Calif., 1966—. Served to sgt. U.S. Army, 1943-46. Mem. Conservation Edn. Assn. (bd. dirs. 1973-76, officer 1978-87, 2d v.p. 1978-80, pres. 1981-86). Club: Audubon (Arcata) (pres.). Avocations: bird study, editing, writing. Office: Humboldt State U Coll Natural Resources Arcata CA 95521

HEY, ANGELA MARGARET, management consultant; b. Horsforth, England, July 23, 1953; s. Geoffrey Brian and Kathleen Margaret Audrey (McGill) H. MA, Cambridge U., England, 1975; M Math, U. Waterloo, Ont., Can., 1976; PhD, London U., 1980; Diploma of Membership, Imperial Coll. Sci. and Tech., U. London, 1980. Fellow Royal Geographical Soc., London, 1977; research asst. Imperial Coll., London, 1979-80; mem. tech. staff AT&T Bell Labs., Murray Hill, N.J., 1980-83; dept. chief AT&T Techs., Summit, N.J. and Palo Alto, Calif., 1983-85; product mktg. mgr. The Palantir Corp., Santa Clara, Calif., 1985-86; cons. Redwood City, Calif., 1986—; mem. adv. bd. Video Plus Techs. (formerly Magination Systems Inc.), Menlo Park, Calif., 1985—. Mem. Ops. Research Soc., Assn. Computing Machinery (sec. Princeton, N.J. br. 1981, service award 1981). Presbyterian. Club: Decathlon (Santa Clara). Avocations: windsurfing, tennis, squash, skiing, hiking. Home: 27 Pelican Ln Redwood City CA 94065

HEYCK, THEODORE DALY, lawyer; b. Houston, Apr. 17, 1941; s. Theodore Richard and Gertrude Paine (Daly) H. B.A., Brown U., 1963; J.D., N.Y. Law Sch., 1979. Bar: N.Y. 1980, Calif. 1984, U.S. Ct. Appeals (2nd cir.) 1984, U.S. Supreme Ct. 1984, U.S. Dist. Ct. (so. and ea. dists.) N.Y. 1980, U.S. Dist. Ct. (we. and no. dists.) N.Y. 1984, U.S. Dist. Ct. (ce. and so. dists.) Calif. 1984, U.S. Ct. Appeals (9th cir.) 1986. Paralegal dist. atty. Bklyn., 1975-79; asst. dist. atty. Bklyn. dist., Kings County, N.Y., 1979-85; dep. city atty., Los Angeles, 1985—; bd. dirs. Screen Actors Guild, N.Y.C., 1977-78. Mem. ABA, AFTRA, Bklyn. Bar Assn., Assn. Trial Lawyers Am., N.Y. Trial Lawyers Assn., N.Y. State Bar Assn., Calif. Bar Assn., Fed. Bar Council, Los Angeles County Bar Assn., Screen Actors Guild, Am. Fedn. TV and Radio Artists, Actors Equity Assn., Nat. Acad. TV Arts and Scis., Screen Actors Guild, Home: 11135 Calvert St North Hollywood CA 91606 also: 142 W 26th St New York NY 10001 Office: Office of City Atty City Hall East 200 N Main St Los Angeles CA 90012

HEYDMAN, ABBY MARIA, dean of college, nursing educator; b. Des Moines, June 1, 1943; d. Frederick Edward and Zeta Margaret (Harrington) Hitchcock; m. Frank J. Heydman, Dec. 20, 1967; 1 child, Amy Lee. BS, Duchesne Coll., 1967; M in Nursing, U. Wash., 1969; PhD, U. Calif., Berkeley, 1987. Registered nurse, Calif. Staff nurse Bergan Mercy Hosp., Omaha, 1964-65; student health nurse St. Joseph's Hosp., Omaha, 1965-66, instr. sch. nursing, 1966-68; staff nurse Ballard Community Hosp., Seattle, 1968-69; instr. Creighton U., Omaha, 1969-70, asst. prof., 1970-74, acting dean, 1971-72; chairperson nursing dept. St. Mary's Coll., Moraga, Calif., 1978-85; dean nursing program Samuel Merritt-Saint Mary's Coll., Oakland and Moraga, Calif., 1985—; lectr. U. Calif., San Francisco, 1974-75. Contbr. articles to profl. jours. Chmn. Newman Hall Community Council, Berkeley, 1985-87; bd. dirs. Oakland YMCA, 1981-83. Mem. Calif. Assn. Coll. of Nursing (sec. 1984-86, pres. 1986—), Am. Nurses Assn., Am. Ednl. Research Assn., Alameda County Nurses Assn. (mem. edn. com.), Calif. Nurses Found. (bd. dirs. 1986—), Sigma Theta Tau, Phi Kappa Delta. Roman Catholic. Avocations: swimming, writing, travel, reading. Home: 51 Vicente Rd Berkeley CA 94705 Office: Samuel Merritt-Saint Mary's Intercollegiate Nursing Program 370 Hawthorne Ave Oakland CA 94609

HEYING, DOUGLAS WILLIAM, computer scientist; b. Alta Vista, Iowa, May 20, 1938; s. Harold Henry and Mildred Regina (Marion) H.; m. Joyce Ann Martino, Oct. 21, 1961 (div. 1967); 1 child, Jenifer Jeanne; m. Jessie Carolyn Gutteridge, July 25, 1968; children: Heather Elizabeth, Douglas Mark. BS in Engring. Sci., U. Notre Dame, 1960; MS in Computer Sci., Carnegie Inst. Tech., 1963. Engr. Westinghouse Corp., Pitts., 1960-65; sr. engr. Sci. Data Systems, Los Angeles, 1965-69, Xerox, Los Angeles, 1969-76; cons. analyst Honeywell, Los Angeles, 1976-80, fellow, 1980-83, prin. fellow, 1983—. Contbr. articles to profl. jours. Recipient Sweatt award Honeywell Corp., 1980. Mem. IEEE, Assn. Computing Machinery, Tau Beta Pi. Republican. Avocations: bridge, skiing. Home: 1161 Embury St Pacific Palisades CA 90272 Office: 12945 Jefferson Blvd Los Angeles CA 90009

HEYL, ALLEN VAN, JR., geologist; b. Allentown, Pa., Apr. 10, 1918; s. Allen Van and Emma (Kleppinger) H.; student Muhlenberg Coll., 1936-37; B.S. in Geology, Pa. State U., 1941; Ph.D. in Geology, Princeton U., 1950; m. Maxine LaVon Hawke, July 12, 1945; children—Nancy Caroline, Allen David Van. Field asst., govt. geologist Nfld. Geol. Survey, summers 1937-40, 42; jr. geologist U.S. Geol. Survey, Wis., 1943-45, asst. geologist, 1945-47, asso. geologist, 1947-50, geologist, Washington and Beltsville, Md., 1950-67; staff geologist, Denver, 1968—; chmn. Internat. Commn. Tectonics of Ore Deposits. Fellow Instn. Mining and Metallurgy (Gt. Brit.), Geol. Soc. Am., Am. Mineral. Soc.; mem. Inst. Genesis of Ore Deposits, Soc. Econ. Geologists, Geol. Soc. Wash., Colo. Sci. Soc., Rocky Mountain Geol. Soc., Friends of Mineralogy (hon. life), Evergreen Naturalist Audubon Soc., Sigma Xi, Alpha Chi Sigma. Lutheran. Contbr. numerous articles to profl. jours., chpts. to books. Home: PO Box 1052 Evergreen CO 80439 Office: US Geol Survey Central Mineral Resources Branch MS 905 Denver Fed Branch Denver CO 80225

HEYMAN, IRA MICHAEL, university chancellor; b. N.Y.C., May 30, 1930; s. Harold Albert and Judith (Sobel) H.; m. Therese Helene Thau, Dec. 17, 1950; children—Stephen Thomas, James Nathaniel. AB in Govt., Dartmouth Coll., 1951; JD, Yale U., 1956; LLD (hon.), U. Pacific, 1981; LHD (hon.), Hebrew Union Coll., 1984; L.H.D. (hon.), U. Md., 1986. Bar: N.Y. 1956, Calif. 1961. Legis. asst. to U.S. Senator Ives, 1950-51; assoc. Carter, Ledyard & Milburn, N.Y.C., 1956-57; law clk. to presiding justice U.S. Ct. Appeals (2d cir.), New Haven, 1957-58; chief law clk. to Supreme Ct. Justice Earl Warren, 1958-59; acting assoc. prof. law U. Calif. at Berkeley, 1959-61, prof. law, 1961—, prof. city and regional planning, 1966—, vice chancellor, 1974-80, chancellor, 1980—; vis. prof. Yale Law Sch., 1963-64, Stanford Law Sch., 1971-72; bd. dirs. Pacific Gas & Electric Co., 1985—; counsel task force on demonstrations and protest Pres.'s Commn. on Violence, 1968-69; mem. Pub. Land Law Rev. Commn., 1968-70, Commn. on Isla Vista, U. Calif.-Santa Barbara, 1970; cons. various orgns. Editor Yale Law Jour.; contbr. articles to profl. jours. Sec. Calif. adv. com. U.S. Commn. Civil Rights, 1962-67; trustee Dartmouth Coll., 1982—, Lawyers' Commn. for Civil Rights Under Law, 1977—; chmn. exec. com. Nat. Assn. State Univs. and Land Grant Colls., 1986; chmn. Div. I subcom. Nat. Collegiate Athletic Assn. Pres.'s Commn., 1986—; chmn. Human Rights and Welfare Commn. City of Berkeley, 1966-68; chmn. acad. senate policy com. U. Calif., Berkeley, 1965-67, state-wide acad. assembly, 1964-66, 72-73; pres. Pres. and Chancellor group Pacific 10 Conf., 1984-85; mem. research adv. com. Oakland Inter-Agy. Project, 1964-65; bd. dirs. Am. Council on Edn., 1984-85. Served to 1st lt. USMC, 1951-53, to capt. USMCR, 1953-58. Named Chevalier de la Legion D'Honneur Govt. France, 1985. Mem. Am. Law Inst. (asst. reporter). Democrat. Home: U Calif Univ House Berkeley CA 94720

HEYMAN, STEVEN RONALD, psychologist, psychology educator; b. N.Y.C., Dec. 28, 1946; s. Leo and Faye (Gerstein) H. B.A., CCNY, 1967; M.A., Calif. State U.-Sacramento, 1970; Ph.D., La. State U., 1976. Lic. clin. psychologist, Wyo. Intern, U. Fla., Gainesville, 1974-75; vis. prof. U. Kans., Lawrence, 1976-77; asst. prof. Southwestern Okla. State U., Weatherford, 1977-81; psychologist Okla. Child Guidance Ctr., Oklahoma City, 1977-81; asst. prof. U. Wyo., Laramie, 1981-85, assoc. prof., 1985—; dir. clin. tng. U. Wyo., 1984—; mem. editorial bd. Journal of Sport Psychology, 1983—, Am. Jour. Community Psychology, 1983—; cons. editor Journal Rural Community Psychology, 1982—; reviewer Research Quarterly, 1982—. Contbr. scholarly chpts. to books, articles to profl. jours. Mem. Okla. State Mental Health Task Force (legis. apptd.), Oklahoma City, 1980-81; bd. dirs. Big Bros. Big Sisters, Laramie, 1982-85. N.Y. Regents scholar, 1963-67. Mem. No. Am. Soc. for Psychology of Sport and Physicial Activity (ethics com. 1979-81), Am. Psychol. Assn. (chmn. rural task force community psychology div. 1980-85, sec.-treas. sport psychology div. 1986—), Psi Chi, Omicron Delta Kappa, Kappa Phi Omega, Tau Kappa Epsilon.. Home: 1910 Garfield Ave Laramie WY 82070 Office: Dept Psychology Box 3415 Univ Sta Laramie WY 82071

HEYNEMAN, DONALD, parasitology educator; b. San Francisco, Feb. 18, 1925; s. Paul and Amy Josephine (KLauber) H.; m. Louise Davidson Ross, June 18, 1971; children: Amy J., Lucy A., Andrew P., Jennifer K., Claudia G. AB magna cum laude, Harvard U., 1950; MA, Rice U., 1952, PhD, 1954. Instr. zoology UCLA, 1954-56, asst. prof., 1956-60; head dept. parasitology U.S. Navy Med. Research unit, Cairo; also co-dir. U.S. Navy Med. Research unit, Malakal, Sudan, 1960-62; assoc. research parasitologist Hooper Found. U. Calif., San Francisco, 1962-64, assoc. prof., 1966-68, prof., 1968—, asst. dir. found., 1970—, acting chmn. dept. internat. health, 1976—; assoc. dean joint med. program Sch. Pub. Health Berkeley, 1987—; research coordinator U. Calif. Internat. Ctr. Med. Research and Tng., Kuala Lumpur, Malaysia, 1964-66; cons. physiol. processes sect. NSF, 1966—; environ. biology div. NIH, 1968—; mem. tropical medicine and parasitology study sect. NIAID-NIH, 1973-76; mem. adv. sci. bd. Gorgas Meml. Inst., 1967—; cons. WHO, 1967, mem. sci. tech. rev. com. on Leishmaniases, 1984; cons. UN Devel. Program, 1978—, AiD, others; panel reviewer Internat. Nomenclature of Diseases, 1984—; Am. cons. and U.S. prin. investigator U. Linkage Project, Egypt-U.S., 1984—; mem. Calif. Health Adv. Com., 1983—; chmn. joint med. program U. Calif.-Berkeley and U. Calif.-San Francisco. Author: (with R. Boolootian) An Illustrated Laboratory Text in Zoology, An Illustrated Laboratory Text in Zoology, A Brief Version, International Dictionary Medicine and Biology; contbr. articles to jours., chpts. to books.; editorial cons. Am. Jour. Tropical Medicine and Hygiene, Jour. Parasitology Exptl. Parasitology Sci., 1968—. Served with AUS, 1943-46. NIH grantee, 1966—. Mem. Am. Soc. Parasitologists (council 1970-74, pres. 1982-83), Am. Micros. Soc. (exec. com. 1971-75), Am. Soc. Tropical Medicine and Hygiene (councilor 1981-84), So. Calif. Parasitol. Soc. (pres. 1957-58), No. Calif. Parasitologists (sec., treas. 1969-72, pres. 1977-78), Phi Beta Kappa. Home: 1400 Lake St San Francisco CA 94118 Office: U Calif Health and Med Scis Program Bldg T-7 Room 106 Berkeley CA 95720

HEYSER, MARLENE KAY, human resources executive; b. Nevada, Iowa, Nov. 22, 1951; d. Charles Everette Heyser and Daisy Elizabeth (Wood) Heyser-Meyers. BSBA, U. Redlands, 1982, MA in Human Resource Mgmt., 1986. Personnel rep. CTI, Inc., Phoenix, 1972-74; paralegal adminstrv. asst. Union Bank, Los Angeles, 1974; asst. to regional mgr. Westinghouse Credit Corp., Santa Ana, Calif., 1976-78; supr. employee relations Orange County Transit Dist., Garden Grove, Calif., 1978-79, mgr. employee relations, 1979-85, dir. human resources, 1985—; lectr. Loyola Marymount U., Los Angeles, 1983—; lectr. and cons. Am. Arbitration Assn., Los Angeles, 1984—, U. Calif., Irvine, 1983—; cons. and course ldr. Am. Mgmt. Assn., N.Y.C. Author: (curriculum design) Human Resource Program for Transit Managers, 1986. Mem. Am. Soc. Tng. and Devel., Am. Compensation Assn., Am. Soc. Personnel Adminstrn., Orange County Indsl. Relations Research Assn. (v.p., bd. dirs. 1983—, service awards 1984, 85). Democrat. Mem. Religious Sci. Faith. Avocations: tennis, travel. Home: 1925 Anaheim St Costa Mesa CA 92627 Office: Orange County Transit Dist 11222 Acacia Pkwy Garden Grove CA 92642

HEYWARD, ANDY, television producer; b. N.Y.C., Feb. 19, 1949; s. Louis Mortimere and Sylvia (Block) H.; m. Evelyn Heyward, June 28, 1981; 1 child, Robert Evon. BA, UCLA, 1972. Writer, story editor Hanna-Barbera Prodns., Hollywood, Calif., 1976-80; pres. DIC Enterprises, Encino, Calif., 1981—. Producer, writer for TV cartoons Inspector Gadget, Littles, Pole Position, Rainbow Brite; producer live action shows including Hitchhiker, Zoobilee Zoo. Recipient Golden Reel award Motion Picture Sound Editors, 1984, 86. Mem. Acad. TV Arts and Scis., Writer's Guild. Office: DIC Enterprises 5445 Balboa Blvd Encino CA 91316

HEYWOOD, SANDRA SCHNOOR, volunteer services administrator; b. Mt. Kisco, N.Y., June 26, 1939; d. Richard H. and Lois G. (Brundage) Schnoor; m. John S. Heywood, July 13, 1963 (div. 1984); children—Leslie Lynne, Heidi Lynne. B.A. Middlebury Coll. 1961, M.A. U. Phoenix 1982. Cert. tchr. N.Y.; registered social worker Colo.; cert. sex counselor Am. Assn. Sex Educators, Counselors and Therapists. Tchr. French, Scarsdale (N.Y.) Pub. Sch. 1961-63, instr. adult edn. 1963-73; supr. family planning team dept. patient and family counseling Albany (N.Y.) Med. Center 1973-77; program dir. community health edn. Dept. Health and Hosps. City of Denver 1977-79; mgmt. cons. Boone, Young & Assoc., N.Y.C. 1979; dir. vol. services Tucson Med. Center 1979-86, spl. asst. to pres., 1986—; v.p. Instn. Devel. Services. Bd. dirs. Arapahoe County Mental Health Assn., Vol. Action Ctr., Unity Ch.; mem. land use com. Tucson Tomorrow; vol. Planned Parenthood. Mem. Am. Soc. Dirs. Vol. Services, Ariz. Hosp. Assn. Contbr. articles to profl. jours.

HIARING, PHILIP, publisher, wine industry consultant; b. Madison, S.D., Aug. 27, 1915; s. Philip Martin and Olene (Bergheim) H.; m. Claire Muriel Riebe, Aug. 28, 1941; children—Philip Edmund, Anne Claire Hiaring Hall. B.A., U. Idaho, 1937; diploma Air War Coll., Indsl. Coll. Armed Forces. Reporter, editor Salt Lake Tribune, Utah, 1937-39; editor, writer AP, Salt Lake City, Boise, Idaho, San Francisco, 1939-55; pub. relations staff Bank of Am., San Francisco, 1955-58; publicity chief Wine Inst., San Francisco, 1958-66; pub. relations mgr. Calif. Canners and Growers, San Francisco, 1966-69; pub., chmn. Wines & Vines Mag., San Rafael, Calif., 1969—; chmn., founder Wine Industry Tech. Symposium, San Francisco, 1973—. Past bd. dirs. Marin United Crusade, San Rafael, Marin council Boy Scouts Am. Served to col. USAF, 1942-46, 47-75. Mem. San Francisco Pub. Relations Round Table (past pres.). Sigma Nu, Sigma Delta Chi (founder/pres. U. Idaho chpt.). Clubs: San Francisco Commonwealth, San Francisco Press, Order of Mil. Wine Tasters (founder/exec. sec. 1959-65), Presidio Army Golf. Home: 95 Suffield Ave San Anselmo CA 94960 Office: Wines & Vines 1800 Lincoln Ave San Rafael CA 94901

HIATT, DOUGLAS PIERCE, interior designer; b. Oct. 8, 1946; s. Oliver Cecil and Beatrice Carolyn Hiatt. BA, Foothill Coll., 1964; BFA, Art Ctr. Coll. Design, 1969. Registered profl. interior designer. Pvt. practice interior design 1970—; pres. Hiatt Enterprises Internat., Inc., Paris, France, Beverly Hills and Palm Springs (Calif.), Wash., 1978—. Bd. dirs. H.E.Y Found., John Bosco Found. Mem. Am. Soc. Interior Designers (bd. dirs.), Nat. Home Fashions League (1st male mem., bd. dirs.), Internat. Soc. Interior Designers (internat. ambassador, pres. 1983, 85). Avocations: snorkeling, tennis. Home: 10428 Sunset Blvd Bel Air CA 90024 Office: Hiatt Enterprises Internat Inc 9701 Wilshire Blvd #850 Beverly Hills CA 90212

HIATT, DUANE EVAN, television producer and director; b. Payson, Utah, June 16, 1937; s. Ferron E. and Gladys (Wride) H.; m. Diane Robertson, Dec. 15, 1961; children: Daniel, Robert, Joseph, David, John, Matthew, Angela, Callie, Samuel, Benjamin, Kathryn, Thomas, Joshua, Lucy, Maren. BS, Brigham Young U., 1962, MA, 1982. Profl. entertainer 1959-75; chmn. communications dept. Brigham Young U., Provo, Utah, 1975-84, producer, dir. mediated prodns., 1984—. Author: Mormon Tabernacle Choir Broadcast, 1986—, scripts. Dist. commr. Boy Scouts Am., Provo, 1986—; gen. chmn. Am.'s Freedom Festival at Provo, 1981; pres. Freedom Festival Bd., Provo, 1982-85. Recipient George Washington Hon. award Freedom Found., 1981, Andy award of Merit Advt. Club. N.Y., 1975, Best in the West First award Am. Advt. Fedn., 1981, Most Profitable Program award Nat. Univ. Teleconf. Network, 1985. Mem. Phi Kappa Phi. Republican. Mormon. Home: 4320 N 650 E Provo UT 84604 Office: Brigham Young U Provo UT 84602

HIATT, PETER, library educator; b. N.Y.C., Oct. 19, 1930; s. Amos and Elizabeth Hope (Derry) H.; m. Linda Rae Smith, Aug. 16, 1968; 1 child, Holly Virginia. B.A., Colgate U., 1952; M.L.S., Rutgers U., 1957, Ph.D., 1963. Head Elmora Br. Library, Elizabeth, N.J., 1957-59; instr. Grad. Sch. Library Service Sci. Rutgers U., 1960-62; library cons. Ind. State Library, Indpls., 1963-70; asst. prof. Grad. Library Sch., Ind. U., 1963-66, assoc. prof., 1966-70; dir. Ind. Library Studies, Bloomington, 1967-70; dir. continuing edn. program for library personnel Western Interstate Commn. for Higher Edn., Boulder, Colo., 1970-74; dir. Grad. Sch. Library and Info. Sci., U. Wash., Seattle, 1974-81, prof., 1974—; prin. investigator Career Devel. and Assessment Center for Librarians, 1979-83; dir. library insts. at various colls. and univs.; adv. project U.S. Office Edn.-ALA, 1977-80. Author: (with Donald Thompson) Monroe County Public Library: Planning for the Future, 1966, The Public Library Needs of Delaware County, 1967, (with Henry Drennan) Public Library Services for the Functionally Illiterate, 1967, (with Robert E. Lee and Lawrence A. Allen) A Plan for Developing a Regional Program of Continuing Education for Library Personnel, 1969, Public Library Branch Services for Adults of Low Education, 1964; dir., gen. editor: The Indiana Library Studies, 1970; mem. editorial bd.: Coll. and Research Libraries, 1969-73; co-editor: Leads: A Continuing Newsletter for Library Trustees, 1973-75, Octavio Noda; author chpts., articles on library continuing edn. and staff devel. Mem. ALA (officer), Pacific N.W. Library Assn., Spl. Libraries Assn., Assn. Library and Info. Sci. Educators (officer, Outstanding Service award 1979), Am. Soc. Info. Sci., Adult Edn. Assn., ACLU. Home: 19324 8th Ave NW Seattle WA 98177 Office: Grad Sch Library and Info Sci U Wash Seattle WA 98195

HIATT, WILLIAM RALPH, biochemist; b. Portland, Oreg., Aug. 5, 1947; s. Lawrence Cecil and Jeanette Mae (Dye) H.; m. Beverly Jeanne Bauman, Oct. 30, 1971; children: Lisa Marie, Vanessa Lynn, Lawrence Edward. BS in Microbiology, Oreg. State U., 1969; MS in Microbiology, U. Wash., 1973, PhD, 1977. Postdoctoral fellow U. Calif., Irvine, 1977-81; prin. scientist Calgene, Inc., Davis, Calif., 1981—. Patentee in field. Served with U.S. Army, 1970-72, Vietnam. NSF fellow, U. Calif., Irvine, 1978; grantee NIH, U. Calif., Irvine, 1979. Mem. Soc. Indsl. Microbiologists. Avocations: softball, music, racquetball. Home: 2760 Blackburn Davis CA 95616 Office: Calgene Inc 1910 5th St Davis CA 95616

HIBBARD, RICHARD PAUL, industrial ventilation consultant, lecturer; lectr.; b. Defiance, Ohio, Nov. 1, 1923; s. Richard T. and Doris E. (Walkup) H.; B.S. in Mech. Indsl. Engring., U. Toledo, 1949; m. Phyllis Ann Kirchoffer, Sept. 7, 1948; children—Barbara Rae, Marcia Kae, Rebecca Ann, Patricia Jan, John Ross. Mech. engr. Oldsmobile div. Gen. Motors Corp., Lansing, Mich., 1950-56; design and sales engr. McConnell Sheet Metal, Inc., Lansing, 1956-60; chief heat and ventilation engr. Fansteel Metall. Corp., North Chicago, Ill., 1960-62; sr. facilities and ventilation engr. The Boeing Co., Seattle, 1962-63; ventilation engr. environ. health div. dept. preventive medicine U. Wash., 1964-70, lectr. dept. environ. health, 1970-82, lectr. emeritus, 1983—; prin. Indsl. Ventilation Cons.Services, 1983—; chmn. Western Indsl. Ventilation Conf., 1962; mem. com. indsl. ventilation Am. Conf. Govtl. Indsl. Hygienists, 1966—; mem. staff Indsl. Ventilation Conf., Mich. State U., 1955—. Served with USAAF, 1943-45, USAR, 1946-72. Recipient Disting. Service award Indsl. Ventilation Conf., Mich. State U., 1975. Mem. Am. Soc. Safety Engrs. (R.M. Gillmore Meml. award Puget Sound chpt.), ASHRAE, Am. Inst. Plant Engrs., Am. Indsl. Hygiene Assn. (J.M. Dallevalle award 1977), Am. Foundryman's Soc. Lodges: Elks, Masons. Contbr. articles on indsl. hygiene and ventilation to profl. jours. Home: 41 165th Ave SE Bellevue WA 98008

HIBBS, ROBERT ANDREWS, analytical chemistry educator; b. Cocoa, Fla., Sept. 9, 1923; s. Charles Harold and Virginia Hibbs; m. Pauline Johnson (div. 1950); 1 child, Sally; m. Lois Elaine Boberg, May 10, 1952; children: Bruce, Laura, Ellen, Dale, Martha, James. BSA, U. Fla., 1947, MS in Agr., 1948; PhD, Wash. State U., 1951. With quality control Darigold Farms, Spokane, Wash., 1951-54; asst. prof. dairy mfg. U. Idaho, Moscow, 1954-61; dir. Hibbs Labs., Boise, Idaho, 1961—; from asst. prof. to assoc. prof. chemistry Boise State Coll., 1965, 67; prof. analytical chemistry Boise State U., 1971—. Contbr. articles to profl. jours. Served as sgt. Infantry, 1942-45, ETO. Decorated Bronze Star. Mem. Inst. Food Technologists (profl., councilor 1977—). Republican. Episcopalian. Lodge: Masons. Avocation: hiking. Office: Hibbs Labs 2808 Cassia Boise ID 83705

HIBER, JHAN WILLIAM, broadcast consultant, writer; b. Joliet, Ill., Dec. 29, 1946; s. William M. and Marcia Jane (Slappey) H. Student U. Md., 1964-68; B.A. cum laude, Central Fla. U., 1973; M.A., Am. U., 1977. Cert. radio mktg. cons. Newsman various TV stas., 1969-73; account exec., gen. mgr. radio and TV properties, 1973-76; mgr. radio ratings div. Arbitron Ratings, 1977-78; editor/weekly columnist Radio & Records, Los Angeles, 1979-86; pres. Jhan Hiber & Assocs. Ltd., Pebble Beach, Calif., 1979—, Calif. Lit. Enterprises, Inc., 1982—. Author: Hibernetics: A Guide to Media Research, 1984. Recipient 3 Addy awards, 1972-73; Abraham Lincoln award, 1975. Mem. Internat. Radio and TV Soc., Am. Mktg. Assn., Nat. Assn. Broadcasters, Nat. Radio Broadcasters Assn., Alpha Epsilon Rho. Republican. Presbyterian. Clubs: Sports Car Am., Brit. Sch. Motor Racing. Home: 40 Shephers Knoll Pebble Beach CA 93953 Office: 8029 Kirkton Ct Sacramento CA 95828

HICK, KENNETH WILLIAM, business executive; b. New Westminster, B.C., Can., Oct. 17, 1946; came to U.S., 1950, naturalized, 1956; s. Les Walter and Mary Isabelle (Warner) H. BA in Bus., Eastern Wash. State Coll., 1971; MBA (fellow), U. Wash., 1973, PhD, 1975. Regional sales mgr., San Leandro, Calif., 1976-79; gen. sales mgr. Moore Internat., Inc., Portland, 1979-80; v.p. sales and mktg. Phillips Corp., Anaheim, Calif., 1980-81; gen. mgr. K.C. Metals, San Jose, Calif., 1981, pres., chief exec. officer, 1981-87; owner, pres., chief exec. officer Losli Internat. Inc., Portland, Oreg., 1987—; communications cons. Asso. Public Safety Communication Officers, Inc., State of Oreg., 1975-77; numerous cons. assignments, also seminars, 1976-81. Contbr. to numerous publs., 1976—. Mem. Oreg. Gov.'s Tax Bd., 1975-76; pres. Portland chpt. Oreg. Jaycees, 1976; bd. fellows U. Santa Clara, 1983—. Served with USAF, 1966-69. Decorated Commendation medal. Mem. Am. Mgmt. Assn., Am. Mktg. Assn., Assn. M.B.A. Execs., Asso. Gen. Contractors, Soc. Advancement Mgmt. Roman Catholic. Home: 3101 McNary Pkwy #6 Lake Oswego OR 97034 Office: Losli Internat 8015 SW Hunziker Rd Tigard OR 97223

HICKEY, C. TOM, retail company executive. Pres., chief exec. officer Smitty's Super Valu, Inc., Phoenix. Office: Smittys Super Valu Inc 2626 S 7th St Phoenix AZ 85034 *

HICKEY, ROSEMARY BECKER, social sciences educator; b. Miami, Ariz., July 6, 1918; d. Morris Louis and Sara (Frankel) Becker; m. Richard Charles Hickey, Dec. 19, 1959 (div. Dec. 1977); children: Morris Richard, David Richard. BA, Cen. YMCA, 1940; D in Podiatric Medicine, Ill. Coll. Podiatric Medicine, 1946; MA, Tex. Women's U., 1974; MSW, U. Houston, 1985. Cert. social worker, Tex.; lic. counselor, Tex. Pvt. practice podiatry Chgo., 1946-68; pvt. practice counseling Dallas, 1974-77; children's protective services investigator DHR Harris County Children's Protective Services, Houston, 1978-83; instr. Chgo. Coll. Chiropody, 1959. Editor/pub. Cognate mag., 1959—; contbr. articles to profl. jours. Asst. coordinator AARP Tex. 5-county area, 1984—; adv. services social worker Travelers Aid of Houston, 1985. Mem. Nat. Assn. Social Workers, Am. Soc. Foot Roentology, Am. Coll. Foot Roentgenology, Am. Coll. Foot Orthopedists (sci. chmn., v.p. midwest div. 1948-66, past nat. sec., sci. award 1957, editor jour. 1964), Fellows Pedic Research Soc. (past holder various offices), Northern Tex. Assn. Unitarian-Universalist Socs. (past pres.), Mensa, Fantasy Amateur Press Assn., Sierra Club, Kaypor Users Group. Avocations: writing, teaching, camping, music. Home: 5051 Ming Bakersfield CA 93309

HICKEY, TIMOTHY DANIEL, banker; b. Tacoma, Wash., Jan. 6, 1949; s. Maurice Burke and Geraldine Marie (Smith) H.; B.A. in Bus. Adminstrn., Seattle U., 1976. Revenue agt. IRS, Seattle, 1975-76; sr. acct. Ernst & Whinney, Seattle, 1976-80; v.p., controller First Interstate Bank of Wash., Seattle, 1980-83, sr. v.p., chief fin. officer, 1983-86, exec. v.p., chief fin. officer, 1987—; regional dir. Bank Adminstrn. Inst., Rolling Meadows, Ill., 1983-84; dir. First Interstate Ins., Seattle. Mem. Am. Inst. C.P.A.s, Wash. State Soc. C.P.A.s, Fin. Execs. Inst., Nat. Assn. Accts. Office: First Interstate Bank of Washington PO Box 160 999 3d Ave Seattle WA 98111

HICKEY, WINIFRED E(SPY), state senator, social worker; b. Rawlins, Wyo.; d. David P. and Eugenia (Blake) Espy; children—John David, Paul Joseph. B.A., Loretto Heights Coll., 1933; postgrad. U. Utah, 1934, Sch. Social Service, U. Chgo., 1936. Dir. Carbon County Welfare Dept., 1935-36; field rep. Wyo. Dept. Welfare, 1937-38; dir. Red Cross Club, Europe, 1942-45; commr. Laramie County, Wyo., 1973-80; mem. Wyo. Senate, 1980—; dir. United Savs. & Loan, Cheyenne. Pres., bd. dirs. U. Wyo. Found., 1986—; pres. Meml. Hosp. of Laramie County, 1986—; chmn. adv. council div. community programs Wyo. Dept. Health and Social Services; pres. county and state mental health assn., 1959-63; trustee, U. Wyo., 1967-71; active Nat. Council Cath. Women. Named Outstanding Alumna, Loretto Heights Coll., 1959. Democrat. Club: Altrusa (Cheyenne). Pub. Where the Deer and the Antelope Play, 1967.

HICKIE, MELVIN RUSSELL, advertising agency executive; b. Centerville, Iowa, Nov. 30, 1949; s. John Russell and Mae Leona (Bennett) H.; m. Ruth Anne Jackson, Sept. 1, 1972; 1 son, Brandon Jackson. B.A. in History, N.E. Mo. State U., 1972. Communications cons. Executone, Kansas City, Kans., 1972-73; western div. mgr. The Packer Newspaper, Los Angeles, 1973-77; pres. El Libro Verde, Inc., La Canada, Calif., 1977-80; advt. mgr. Western Growers Assn., Newport Beach, Calif., 1980-85; prin. Mel Hickie Ag Mktg. Services, Huntington Beach, Calif., 1985-87; ptnr. AG Computerized Info. Systems, 1987— . Mem. exec. bd. 1st Methodist Ch. Huntington Beach. Mem. Nat. Agri-Mktg. Assn. Calif. (v.p.), West Agrl. Mktg. Assn. (v.p., award 1983, 84, 85), Soc. Preservation Vaudevillian Arts, Calif. Seed Assn. Republican. Author: El Libro Verde Directory to Agriculture in Mexico; contbr. articles to profl. jours.

HICKIS, CHARLES FRANCIS, social services administrator, psychologist, consultant; b. Bronx, N.Y., Aug. 13, 1947; s. Charles J. and Marion S. H.; m. Judy C., Sept. 8, 1979; children—Gregory, Rebecca, Matthew. B.A., Hofstra U., 1970, M.A., 1974; Ph.D. (NIMH fellow), U. Colo., 1978; cert. postdoctoral studies UCLA, 1980. Cert. addiction specialist counselor, level III. Asst. prof. psychology Weber State Coll., 1977-79; NIMH postdoctoral trainee physiol. psychology UCLA, 1979-80; clin. dir. Chem. Dependency Ctr., West Park Hosp., Cody, Wyo., 1980-83; pvt. therapist, cons., Cody, 1983-87; vocat. rehab. counselor PRM, Inc., Olathe, Kans., 1985-87; dir. chem. dependency programs St. Mary-Corwin Hosp., Pueblo, Colo., 1987—. Contbr. profl. papers. Mem. Am. Psychol. Assn., Wyo. Psychol. Assn., Wyo. Assn. Addiction Specialists. Democrat. Mem. Reorganized Ch. of Jesus Christ of Latter-day Saints. Office: St Mary-Corwin Hosp Pueblo CO 81004

HICKMAN, CECIL RAY, safety engineer, consultant; b. Bug, Ky., Aug. 28, 1936; s. Balos Lewis and Daisy Pearl (Huddleston) H.; m. Hazel Eugena Lee, Feb. 1, 1958; children—Vickie Hickman Pankhurst, Pamela Hickman Southerland, Lisa Hickman Shyface, Eric. B.S. in Indsl. Tech., Tenn. Tech. U., 1960. Cert. safety profl., profl. safety engr. Calif. Safety supr. E.I. DuPont DeNemours, Inc., various locations in U.S., 1962-69; safety supt. Reynolds Elec. and Engring. Co., Inc., Las Vegas, Nev., 1969-73; safety engr. Stone and Webster Engring Corp., Wading River, N.Y., 1973; sr. safety rep. EBASCO, N.Y.C., 1973; chief safety programs Holmes and Narver, Inc., Las Vegas, 1974—; instr. gen. safety tech. Clark County Community Coll. Active Nev. Safety Council, 1978—. Served with USN, 1954-57. Named Safety Profl. of Yr., 1981-82; recipient past pres. award Am. Soc. Safety Engrs. (So. Nev. chpt.). Mem. Am. Soc. Safety Engrs. (nat. admission com. 1978-84). Republican. Baptist. Club: Masons. Home: 5185 Dapple Grey Las Vegas NV 89108 Office: PO Box 1 Mercury NV 89023

HICKMAN, SHARON ROSE, design consultant; b. Kansas City, Kans., May 24, 1951; d. Wilmont and Rose Marie (Cyhel) Lohoefener; m. Billy Ray Lee, July 14, 1969; m. Dan Patrick Hickman, Aug. 7, 1976; children: Jonathan Bryan, Nicole Kristen. Student pub. schs. Overland Park, Kans. Gen. mgr. Bull & Boar Restaurant, Lawrence, Kans., 1971-75, Internat. Restaurant, Lawrence, 1975-76, Sirloin Stockade, Lawrence, 1976-78, Chandler, Ariz., 1978-80; mgr. T.G.I.Friday's, Phoenix, 1980-81; pres., founder Nature's Elves, Inc., Tempe, Ariz., 1981—, Elf-O-Gram, Inc.; design cons. interior plantscape. Mem. Exec. Bus. Profl. Women's Club (v.p. Tempe chpt. 1981-82), NOW, Interior Plantscape Assn., Assn. Landscape Contractors Am. Democrat. Roman Catholic. Home and office: 13722 E Williamsfield Rd Gilbert AZ 85234

HICKS, BETHANY GRIBBEN, lawyer; b. N.Y., Sept. 8, 1951; d. Robert and DeSales Gribben; m. William A. Hicks III, May 21, 1982; children: Alexandra Elizabeth, Samantha Katherine. AB, Vassar Coll., 1973; MEd, Boston U., 1975; JD, Ariz. State U., 1984. Bar: Ariz. 1984. Sole practice Scottsdale, Ariz., 1984—. Mem. Jr. League of Phoenix, 1984—; parliamentarian Girls Club of Scottsdale, Ariz., 1985—. Mem. ABA (family law sect.), State Bar Ariz., Maricopa County Bar Assn. Democrat. Episcopalian. Club: Paradise Valley Country. Office: Suite 12 Cannes Bldg 6623 N Scottsdale Rd Scottsdale AZ 85253

HICKS, DAVID ARNELL, data processing company executive; b. San Francisco, Apr. 20, 1942; s. Louis Maurice and Lois (Alsing) H.; m. Ann Revel, Aug. 12, 1967; children—Ryan, Darren. B.A., San Jose State U., 1965; B. in Fgn. Trade, Am. Inst. Internat. Mgmt., 1967. Founder, pres. Computer Resources Group, Inc. and Programming Resources Co., San Francisco, 1969-79, David Hicks Assoc., Inc., Lafayette, Calif., 1979—. Pres. Happy Valley Estates Homeowners Assn., 1979-83. Mem. Software Services Assn. (pres.), Software Cons. Brokers Assn. Calif. (founder, pres. 1985-86). Democrat. Presbyterian. Home: 7 Toledo Dr Lafayette CA 94549 Office: David Hicks Assocs Inc 970 Dewing Ave Suite 300 Lafayette CA 94549

HICKS, GEORGE WESLEY, exploration geologist; b. St. Joseph, Mo., June 9, 1931; s. Roger L. and Frances (Connett) H.; m. Julie Cathleen Kochis, Sept. 3, 1953; children—Wesley G., David L., Timothy Roger. A.S., St. Joseph Jr. Coll., 1951; Geol. Engr., Colo. Sch. Mines, 1958. Cert. profl. geologist. Geologist Pure Oil Co., Midland, Tex. and Houston, 1958-65; area geologist Belco Petroleum Corp., N.Y. and Houston, 1965-70; chief geologist Indonesia Cities Service, Jakarta, 1970-74; sr. staff position Cities Service Internat., Houston, 1974-76, regional mgr. exploration ops. East Asia, Houston, 1981—; exploration mgr. Philippine Cities Service, Manila, 1976-81; regional mgr. Exploration Ops., East Asia, 1981-83; asst. regional mgr. Mid-East and Far East, Occidental Exploration and Prodn. Co., Bakersfield, Calif., 1983-84; exploration mgr. Occidental of Pakistan Inc., Islamabad, 1984—. Served with USAF, 1951-55. Mem. Am. Assn. Petroleum Geologists, Houston Geol. Soc., S.E. Asia Petroleum Exploration Soc., Soc. Energy Explorationists Philippines (pres. 1980-81), Tau Beta Phi, Sigma Gamma Epsilon. Republican. Roman Catholic. Office: Occidental of Pakistan Inc PO Box 11174 Bakersfield CA 93309

HICKS, SHELLY ANN, advertising executive; b. Escondido, Calif., Nov. 9, 1962; s. Noble Earl and Carol Ann (Shadburn) Craver; m. Matthew Patrick Hicks, Nov. 7, 1981; 1 child, Becki Kristine. Circulation asst. Pubs. Devel., San Diego, 1984-85, advt. asst., 1985, advt. prodn. mgr., 1985—. Republican. Roman Catholic. Avocations: rollerskating, gymnastics, drawing. Home: 1768 Summit Dr Escondido CA 92027 Office: Pubs Devel 591 Camino de la Reina #200 San Diego CA 92108

HICKS, THOMAS ARNOLD, university coach, educator; b. Long Beach, Calif., May 25, 1956; s. Joe Thompson and Joyce (Crocker) H.; m. Lori Lynn Copple, Dec. 28, 1984; 1 child, Christopher Cole. B, U. So. Calif., 1979; M, Calif State U., Long Beach, 1984. Instr., coach Azusa (Calif.) Pacific U., 1981-83; prof., coach El Camino Coll., Torrance, Calif., 1984—; v.p. U.S. Baseball Fedn., 1986-88; asst. coach USA Coll. All-Star Baseball Team, 1983. Named Coach of Yr. Nat. Assn. Intercollegiate Athletics, 1983. Mem. Amateur Athlete Counsel (U.S. Olympic Com.).

HICKS, VERONICA, publicist, advertising executive; b. San Diego, Apr. 19, 1944; d. Ben and Frances Veronica (Patrick) Bagnas; m. Lawrence Raymond Hicks, Aug. 1, 1964 (div.). Student San Diego City Coll., 1963, Mesa Coll., 1976. Pvt. practice real estate agent/broker, San Diego, 1974-76; v.p., regional mgr. Hubbert Advt. & Pub. Relations, San Diego, 1976-79; prin. Roni Hicks & Assocs., 1979—. Adv. bd. Hugh O'Brian Youth Found.; bd. dirs. The Crime Victims Fund. Recipient Sales and Mktg. Excellence awards Sales and Mktg. Council of San Diego Bldg. Industry, Assn., 1980, 1982, 83, 84, 85, 86, Silver MIRM award, 1985, 86, Nat. Gold MIRM award Nat. Assn. Home Builders, 1986. Mem. Nat. Assn. Real Estate Editors, Bldg. Industry Assn. San Diego County, San Diego Assn. Advt. Agys., Home Builders Council, Rep. Bus. and Profl. Club, San Diego Press Club, Ad Club San Diego, San Diego C. of C., Crime Victims Fund, Pub. Relations Soc. Am. Republican. Roman Catholic. Office: 3170 4th Ave Suite 200 San Diego CA 92103

HIDDLESTON, RONAL EUGENE, drilling and pump company executive; b. Bristow, Okla., Mar. 21, 1939; s. C.L. and Iona D. (Martin) H.; m. Marvelene L. Hammond, Apr. 26, 1959; children: Michael Scott, Mark Shawn, Matthew Shane. Student, Idaho State U., 1957-58. With Roper's Clothing and Bishop Redi-Mix, Rupert, Idaho, 1960-61; pres., chmn. bd., gen. mgr. Hiddleston Drilling, Rupert, 1961-66, Mountain Home, Idaho, 1966—. Mem. Mountain Home Airport Adv. Bd., 1968—; hon. mem. Idaho Search and Rescue. Mem. Nat. Water Well Assn. (cert., bd. dirs.), Idaho Water Well Assn. (dir., past pres.), Pacific N.W. Water Well Assn. (dir.), N.W. Mining Assn., Nat. Fedn. Ind. Businessmen, Aircraft Owners and Pilots Assn., Ducks Unltd. Club: Nat 210 Owners. Lodges: Optimists, Masons, Shriners. Home: 645 E 17th St N Mountain Home ID 83647 Office: Rt 1 Box 610D Mountain Home ID 83647

HIEBERT, PAUL GORDON, anthropology teacher; b. Shamshabad, India, Nov. 13, 1932; (parents Am. citizens); s. John Nicholas Christian and Anna Luetta (Jungas) H.; m. Frances Flaming, Dec. 28, 1954; children: Eloise, Barbara, John. BA, Tabor Coll., 1954; MA, Mennonite Brethern Sem., 1956, U. Minn., 1959; PhD, U. Minn., 1967. Missionary Mennonite Brethern Ch., Shamshabad, 1960-66; asst. prof. Kans. State U., Manhattan, 1966-71, assoc. prof., 1971-72; assoc. prof. U. Wash., Seattle, 1972-77; prof. anthropology Fuller Sem., Pasadena, Calif., 1977—; research cons. Mennonite Brethern Bd. of Missionary Service, Winnapeg, Man., Can., 1969—; Fulbright prof. Osmania U., Hyderabad, India, 1974-75. Author: Konduru, 1971, Cultural Anthropology, 1977, Anthropological Insights, 1985; contbr. articles to profl. jours. Named Alumnus of Yr., Tabor Coll., 1983. Fellow Am. Anthropol. Assn.; mem. Assn. Asian Studies, Soc. of S. Indian Studies, Assn. of Profs. of Missions. Democrat. Home: 1100 Leonard Ave Pasadena CA 91107 Office: Fuller Theol Sem 135 N Oakland Pasadena CA 91182

HIGBY, WILLIAM FRANK, rancher; b. Sheridan Wyo., July 26, 1940; s. William David and Edith (Drescher) H.; m. Judith Ann Taska, June 17, 1967; children—Michael James, Heather Lynn. Student Colo. State U., 1958-60. Ranch mgr., owner, Monument and Steamboat Springs, Colo., 1970—. Mayor, Monument, Colo., 1968; mem. dist. 38 Sch. Bd., 1973-79; mem. El Paso County 4-H Found. Served with USN, 1963-69. Clubs: Kiwanis (pres., 1971), Masons (Colo. consistory no. 1, 32 degrees, past master).

HIGGINBOTHAM, DONALD LEE, architect, planner; b. Tulsa, Oct. 23, 1929; s. Daniel Klieber and Anne Louise (Dittmar) H.; m. Josephine Olive Hackett, Sept. 6, 1958; children—Nelly Kathryn, Matthew Lee, Mary Jennifer. B.Archtl. Engring, Okla. State U., 1954; M.F.A., Princeton U., 1958. Registered architect, Colo., Okla., Wyo., N.Mex. Architect, mem. planning staff Architects Collaborative, Colorado Springs, Colo., 1959-60, Ternstrom & Skinner, Kaiserlautern, Fed. Republic Germany, 1960-61; prin., ptnr. Higginbotham, Nakata & Muir, Colorado Springs, 1962-72; pres. Higginbotham & Assocs., P.C., Colorado Springs, 1972—; vis. lectr. U. Colo., Boulder, 1970, Colo. Coll., 1974. Designer-planner 75 archtl. projects and 60 community master plans. Bd. dirs. Colorado Springs Fine Arts Ctr., 1972-74; mem. chancellor's adv. com. U. Colo.-Colorado Springs, 1983-84. Recipient archtl. design award Nat. YMCA, 1973, U.S. Air Force, 1962, 84. Mem. AIA, Sigma Alpha Epsilon. Presbyterian. Clubs: El Paso, Broadmoor Country, Plaza. Office: 540 N Cascade Ave Suite 300 Colorado Springs CO 80903-3392

HIGGINS, CHARLES GRAHAM, geology educator; b. Oak Park, Ill., Nov. 18, 1925; s. Charles Graham and Frances Anne (Henderson) H.; m. Rosalie Darleen Trew, Feb. 9, 1974; children: Kimberley Frances Higgins Tolley, Lesley Vivian. SB, U. Chgo., 1946, SM, 1947; PhD, U. Calif., Berkeley, 1950. Field instr. U. Mich., Jackson Hole, Wyo., 1949; instr. U. Mich., Ann Arbor, 1950-51; asst. prof. geology U. Calif., Berkeley and Davis, 1951-53; asst. prof. geology U. Calif., Davis, 1953-58, assoc. prof. geology, 1958-66, prof. geology, 1966—. Contbr. articles to profl. jours. Fellow Geol. Soc. Am.; mem. Nat. Assn. Geology Tchrs. (treas. 1954-57, vice chmn. far western sect. 1953-55), AAAS, Brit. Geomorphology Research Group, Am. Quaternary Assn., Sigma Xi, Phi Beta Kappa. Avocation: hiking. Office: U Calif Dept Geology Davis CA 95616

HIGGINS, DENNIS ROY, academic administrator; b. Spokane, Wash., Jan. 21, 1937; s. Clarence James and Vivian Grace (Rogers) H.; m. Carol Louise Land Smith, 1959 (div. 1972); m. Sandra Lee Jones Sloan, May 14, 1983. BA in Acctg., Eastern Wash. U., 1962; postgrad. in mgmt. program, U. Wash., 1980-81. Asst. chief acct. U. Wash., Seattle, 1964-73, dir. acctg., 1973—. Served to 1st lt. U.S. Army, 1962-64. Mem. Govt. Fin. Officers Assn., Assn. Govt. Accts. Republican. Methodist. Avocation: bibliophile. Home: 7741 22d NE Seattle WA 98115 Office: U Wash 3917 University Way NE Seattle WA 98105

HIGH, RICHARD GILLETTE, journalist; b. Louisville, Aug. 4, 1942; s. Richard Samuel and Laura Owsley (Gillette) H.; m. Judith Retzer, July 1, 1978; children—John Venzon, Trevor Gillette, Laura Kate Venzon. Student, Yale U., 1960-63, 64-65; M.S., Stanford Bus. Sch., Palo Alto, Calif., 1978. Reporter Times-News, Twin Falls, Idaho, 1966-67, 69, mng. editor, 1970-77; reporter The Times, Hammond, Ind., 1969-70; gen. mgr. Star Tribune, Casper, Wyo., 1978-80, editor, 1980—. Mem. Wyo. Council for Humanities. Unitarian. Avocations: economics; history; backpacking; skiing. Home: PO Box 3125 Casper WY 82602 Office: Casper Star Tribune PO Box 80 Casper WY 82602

HIGHLAND, GEORGE PAUL, science laboratory administrator; b. Denver, Oct. 11, 1928; s. Paul Harry and M. Mildred (Chater) H.; m. Eleanor June Cargile, Dec. 1, 1951; children: Paul S., David J., Patricia L., Carol A. BS, U. Calif., Berkeley, 1950. Microbiologist Ventura County (Calif.) Health Dept., 1952-54; dir. pub. health lab. Solano County (Calif.) Health Dept., Vallejo, 1954-60; co-dir. Thorpe Labs., Paso Robles, Calif., 1960-62; dir. Highland Lab., Inc., Templeton, Calif., 1962—. Councilman City of Atascadero, Calif., 1979-82. Served as cpl. U.S. Army, 1950-52. Mem. Calif. Assn. Bioanalysts (pres. 1963-64, exec. sec. 1965-71), Am. Assn. Bioanalysts (adminstrv. sec. 1972-80), AAAS, Am. Assn. Clin. Chemists, Am. Soc. Microbiology, Atascadero C. of C., Templeton C. of C. Republican. Lodge: Rotary Internat. (pres. 1974-75). Avocations: singing, fishing, rose culture, science fiction. Home: 7275 Carmelita Ave Atascadero CA 93422 Office: Highland Lab Inc 1101 Las Tablas Rd Suite J Templeton CA 93465

HIGHLANDER, RICHARD WILLIAM, communicatons executive; b. Beckley, W.Va., Feb. 17, 1940; s. Ronald William and Lucille Bernice (Bland) H.; m. Ida Mae Canterbury, June 26, 1965; one child, Alison Renee. BA, Rutgers U., 1963; MA, U. Ga., 1972. Commd. 2d lt. U.S. Army, 1963, advanced through grades to lt. col., 1979, ret., 1984; dir. communications, def. systems group FMC Corp., Santa Clara, Calif., 1984—. Contbr. articles to profl. jours., Freedom Found. award 1966, 81. Trustee San Jose Repertory Co., 1985. Decorated Legion of Merit with bronze oak leaf cluster, Bronze Star with two bronze oak leaf clusters, Purple Heart. Mem. Assn. of U.S. Army, Pub. Relations Soc. Am. (accredited), Internat. Assn. Bus. Communicators, Calif. Mfrs. Assn. (bd. dirs. 1985). Republican. Methodist. Lodge: Rotary. Avocation: racquetball. Home: 1486 Oak Canyon Dr San Jose CA 95120

HIGHT, JOHN DALE, executive search company executive; b. Dallas, Aug. 20, 1940; s. John Calvin and Mozell Ann Hight; B.S. in Bus. Adminstrn. magna cum laude, Calif. State U.-Northridge, 1975; m. Pamela Marie Ward, Oct. 6, 1961; children—Melody Ann, John Edward. From foreman to gen. mgr. Bendix Corp., Slymar, Calif., 1959-71; material control mgr./mgr. mfg. systems James B. Lansing Sound Inc., Northridge, 1975-78; mfg. mgr./dir. materials Info. Internat., Inc., Culver City, Calif., 1978-79; pres. Search Group, Redondo Beach, Calif., 1979—; dir. McAlliffe & Assocs., Inc. Pres. Sky Blue Homeowners Assn., 1966-67; v.p. Citizens Com. to Complete Coll. of Canyons, 1974-75. Mem. Am. Prodn. and Inventory Control Soc., Canyon Country C. of C. Author papers in field. Office: PO Box 7000-378 Redondo Beach CA 90277

HIGHTOWER, STEVEN KIRK, finance company executive; b. San Bernardino, Calif., Apr. 8, 1950; s. Marion and Virginia (Lewis) H.; m. Troy Kirkpatrick, Oct. 25, 1975. Student, Venture Coll., 1968-70; BSc, UCLA, 1972; postgrad., U. Sussex, Eng., 1972. Mgr. Gourmet Wines, Ltd., Los Angeles, 1971-73; gen. mgr. Curtis & Gordon, Inc., San Francisco, 1974-75; exec. v.p. Equitec, Lafayette, Calif., 1975-81; pres., chief exec. officer Westcap Fin. Group, San Francisco, 1981—. Mem. Real Estate Securities and Syndication Inst., Nat. Assn. Securities Dealers, Internat. Assn. Fin. Planners. Republican. Presbyterian. Club: Belfry (London). Avocations: tennis, squash, guitar. Office: Westcap Fin Group 999 Sutter St San Francisco CA 94109

HIKEN, ALAN DAVID, manufacturing engineer; b. Great Lakes, Ill., Apr. 26, 1962; s. Arthur Donald and Sumako (Sato) H. BSChemE, U. Mo., 1984. Cook Heritage House, St. Louis, 1976-83; research and devel. engr. Beker Industries Corp., Taft, La., 1984; mfg. tech. engr. Northrop Corp., Los Angeles, 1984—. Mem. Am. Inst. Chem. Engrs., Soc. Advancement Materials and Process Engring., Mo. Bd. Architects, Land Surveyors and Engrs. (engr. in tng.), Mizzou Alumni Assn., Tau Kappa Epsilon (fin. chair 1983). Presbyterian. Avocations: weightlifting, softball, sports, music. Home: 919 Main St #104 El Segundo CA 90245 Office: Northrop Corp Aircraft div 1 Northrop Ave 5077/96 Hawthorne CA 90250

HILBRECHT, NORMAN TY, lawyer, state legislator; b. San Diego, Feb. 11, 1933; s. Norman Titus and Elizabeth (Lair) H.; m. Mercedes L. Sharratt, Oct. 24, 1980. B.A., Northwestern U., 1956; J.D., Yale U., 1959. Bar: Nev. 1959, U.S. Supreme Ct. 1963. Atty., assoc. firm Jones, Wiener & Jones, Las Vegas, 1959-62; assoc. counsel Union Pacific R.R., Las Vegas, 1962; partner firm Hilbrecht & Jones, Las Vegas, 1962-69; pres. Hilbrecht, Jones, Schreck & Bernhard, 1969-83, Hilbrecht & Assocs, 1983—, Mobil Transport Corp., 1970-72; gen. counsel Bell United Ins. Co., 1986—; assemblyman Nev. Legislature, 1966-72, minority leader, 1971-72; mem. Nev. Senate, 1974-78; asst. lectr. bus. law U. Nev., Las Vegas. Mem. labor mgmt. com. NCCJ, 1963; mem. Clark County (Nev.) Democratic Central Com., 1959-80, 1st vice chmn., 1965-66; del. Western Regional Assembly on Ombudsman; chmn. Clark County Dem. Conv., 1966, Nev. Dem. Conv., 1966; pres. Clark County Legal Aid Soc., 1964, Nev. Legal Aid and Defender Assn., 1965-83. Served to capt. AUS, 1952-67. Named Outstanding State Legislator Eagleton Inst. Politics, Rutgers U., 1969. Mem. Am. Judicature Soc., Am. Bar Assn., Clark County Bar Assn., Am. Assn. Rev. Appraisers, Am. Acad. Polit. and Social Sci., Am. Trial Lawyers Assn., State Bar Nev., Nev. Trial Lawyers (pres. So. chpt., state v.p.), Nat. Assn. Real Estate Appraisers, Fraternal Order Police Assos. (v.p.), Phi Beta Kappa, Delta Phi Epsilon, Theta Chi, Phi Delta Phi. Lutheran. Lodge: Elks. Office: 723 S Casino Center Blvd Las Vegas NV 89101

HILCHEY, EARL WHITMAN, JR., architect; b. Chgo., Sept. 7, 1955; s. Earl Whitman Sr. and Esther Marie (Johannison) H.; m. Marcia Lee Williamson, May 1, 1982. BArch, BS in Bus., Kans. State U., 1981. Registered architect, N.Mex. Architect Charles Thompson and Assocs., Houston, 1982-83, Hoover and Assocs., Austin, Tex., 1983-84, JNR, Ptnrs., Albuquerque, 1984-85, FMBSM, Albuquerque, 1985—; intern in devel. program Nat. Council of Archtl. Registration Bds., Washington, 1982, 85. Avocations: furniture making, fishing, camping, softball, skiing.

HILD, CARL MARSHALL, health care administrator; b. Phila., July 12, 1950; s. Harry and Gladys (Dreisbach) H. BS in Biology, Pa. State U., 1972; MS in Sci. Mgmt., U. Alaska, 1987. Coordinator Children's Receiving Home North Slope Borough Health and Social Services Agy., Barrow, Alaska, 1978-83; coordinator Kona Adolescent Family Life Project, Kealakekua, Hawaii, 1984-85; affiliate scientist Pacific Gamefish Research Found., Kona, Hawaii, 1983-85. Author If and When Artic Survival Manuals, 1983; contbr. articles to profl. jours. Pres. No. Region Emergency

Med. Service Council, 1980-81, v.p., 1982; v.p. Alaska Health Edn. Consortium, 1980, pres., 1981. Recipient Alaska's Gov.'s Emergency Med. Services Provider award, 1981. Mem. AAAS, Alaska Pub. Health Assn., Alaska Soc. Pub. Health Edn., Am. Pub. Health Assn. (nat. task force for Arctic policy 1983-84), Soc. Pub. Health Edn., Am. Soc. Circumpolar Health (organizing com., session chmn. 1984, bd. dirs. 1986—), Alpha Zeta. Avocations: walking, reading, paranormal activities, thermoregulatory behavior. Home: 819 E 10th #6 Anchorage AK 99501

HILDEBRAND, DONALD CLAIR, plant pathologist; b. Astoria, Oreg., Feb. 27, 1932; s. Frank Frederick Theodore and Irma Amelia (Laumeister) H.; m. Ellen Marie Primacove, Sept., 1959 (div. Mar. 1974); children: Karin, Catherine; m. Mary Avarilla Nern, Jan. 29, 1977. Student, N. Idaho Jr. Coll., 1949; BS, Wash. State U., 1953; PhD, U. Calif., Berkeley, 1962. Plant pathologist U. Calif., Berkeley, 1962—. Assoc. editor: Annual Review of Phytopathology, 1968, 69. Contbr. research articles to profl. jours. Served to lt. (j.g.) USN, 1953-56. Recipient Research Career Devel. award NIH, 1967. Mem. Am. Phytopathol. Soc., Soc. Gen. Microbiology, Am. Soc. Microbiology, Internat. Com. Systematic Bacteriology (subcom. on pseudonmonas and related organisms). Republican. Club: Lake Merritt Joggers and Striders (Oakland). Avocations: art restoration, running. Home: 230 Glorietta Blvd Orinda CA 94563 Office: U Calif Dept Plant Pathology 147 Hilgard Hall Berkeley CA 94720

HILDEBRAND, PETER HENRY, atmospheric physicist; b. Oak Ridge, Tenn., July 9, 1945; s. Roger Henry and Jane (Beedle) H.; m. Nancy Jean Steakley; children: Vanessa, Emily, Christopher. AB, U. Chgo., 1967, MS, 1969, PhD, 1976. Weather officer U.S. Naval Cen. Weather Forcasting Office, Monterey, Calif., 1969-72; scientist Ill. State Water Survey, Champaign, 1976-78; scientist Nat. Ctr. Atmospheric Research, Boulder, Colo., 1978-82, dep. mgr. research aviation facility, 1982-85, mgr. airborne radar devel. project, 1985—; pres. Weather Analysis Assocs. Inc., Boulder, 1985—. Contbr. articles to profl. jours. Firefighter Pine Brook Fire Protection Dist., Boulder, 1979—. Mem. Am. Meterol. Soc. (1st Place Father James B. Macelwane award 1967), Sigma Xi. Home: 18 Beaver Way Boulder CO 80302 Office: Nat Ctr Atmospheric Research PO Box 3000 Boulder CO 80307

HILDEBRANDT, CLAUDIA JOAN, banker; b. Inglewood, Calif., Feb. 12, 1942; d. Charles Samual and Clara Claudia (Palumbo) H. B.B.A., U. Colo. Head teller First Colo. Bank & Trust, Denver, 1969-70; asst. cashier First Nat. Bank, Englewood, Colo., 1975-79, asst. v.p., 1979-83, v.p., 1983—; owner CJH Enterprises, Inc., Breckenridge, Colo., 1980—. Mem. Nat. Assn. Bank Women, Am. Soc. for Personnel Adminstrn., Am. Inst. Banking. Roman Catholic. Home: 6602 E Cornell Ave Denver CO 80224 Office: First Nat Bank 333 W Hampden Ave Englewood CO 80110

HILDEBRANDT, DARLENE MYERS, information scientist; b. Somerset, Pa., Dec. 18, 1944; d. Kenneth Geary and Julia (Klim) Myers; m. Byron Howard Johnson, Nov. 4, 1974 (div. 1978 ; m. Peter Anton Hildebrandt, May 26, 1983; 1 child, Robin Adaire. BA, U. Calif., Riverside, 1969; MA, U. Wash., 1970. Info. specialist U. Wash. Acad. Computer Ctr., Seattle, 1970-73, library assoc., 1974-75, mgr. computing info. services adminstr., 1976-85, 86—. Editor: (newsletter) Points Northwest, Elaine D. Kaskela award, 1973, 75, Best ASIS, 1974. Recipient Civitan award, 1963. Mem. Am. Soc. for Info. Sci. (founding mem. Pacific Northwest chpt. 1971, chairperson 1975, 76, bd. dirs. 1980, 83, chpt. award 1978). Office: U Wash Acad Computer Ctr HG-45 Seattle WA 98195

HILDERBRAND, MARTELL J., lawyer; b. Grant, Nebr., June 14, 1952; s. John A. and Verna J. (Frerichs) H.; m. Karen F. Fox, June 17, 1983; 1 child, Tyler John; 1 stepchild, William Cole Gustafson. A.D. in Engring., Okla. State U., 1972, B.S. in Engring., 1974; J.D., U. Wyo., 1981. Bar: Wyo. 1981, U.S. Dist. Ct. Wyo. 1981, U.S. Ct. Appeals (10th cir.) 1983. Dep. county atty. Campbell County, Gillette, Wyo., 1981-82, county atty., 1982—; spl. U.S. atty., Cheyenne, Wyo., 1984-85. Mem. precinct com. Republican Central Com., Campbell County, 1983—; bd. dirs. Preventing Abuse of Children Inc., Gillette, 1983—; chmn. Crisis Mgmt. Team, Gillette, 1984-85, Wyo. Child Support Commn., 1984-85. Named in Outstanding Young Men in Am., U.S. Jaycees, 1981, 83, 85. Mem. Wyo. Prosecutors Assn. (v.p. legis. com. 1982-83, co-chmn. 1984-85), ABA, Wyo. Bar Assn., Assn. Trial Lawyers Am., Wyo. Trial Lawyers Assn., Nat. Dist. Attys. Assn., Friendship Bowling League (pres. 1984-85). Lutheran. Club: Sundowner's Lions (lion tamer, tail twister 1982-84). Home: 404 Richards St Gillette WY 82716 Office: Willis Geer & Assocs PO Box 1989 Gillette WY 82716

HILDING, RONALD FREDERICK, psychiatrist; b. Toledo, Aug. 7, 1938; s. John Frederick and Viola Bessie (Pugh) H. B.S., U. Utah, 1961, M.D., 1965. Intern, Maricopa Gen. Hosp., Phoenix, 1965-66; resident in psychiatry Met. State Hosp., U. Calif.-Irvine, Norwalk, Calif., 1968-71, staff psychiatrist 1971-72; chief psychiat. inpatient service Maricopa Gen. Hosp., Phoenix, 1972-75; practice medicine specializing in psychiatry, Phoenix, 1975—; group mem., sec.-treas. Inst. Human Services, Inc.; mem. staff St. Luke's Behavioral Health Ctr., 1975—, pres. med. staff, 1982-83. Served with M.C., U.S. Army, 1966-68. Decorated Bronze Star. Mem. AMA, Am. Psychiat. Assn., Am. Soc. Adolescent Psychiatry, Maricopa County Med. Soc., Phoenix Psychiat. Council, Ariz. Soc. Adolescent Psychiatry. Office: 525 N 18th St Suite 401 Phoenix AZ 85006

HILGARD, ERNEST ROPIEQUET, psychologist; b. Belleville, Ill., July 25, 1904; s. George Engelmann and Laura (Ropiequet) H.; m. Josephine Rohrs, Sept. 19, 1931; children—Henry Rohrs, Elizabeth Ann Jecker. B.S., U. Ill., 1924; Ph.D., Yale, 1930; D.Sc., Kenyon Coll., 1964; LL.D., Centre Coll., 1974; D.Sc., Northwestern U., 1987. Asst. instr. in psychology Yale U., 1928-29, instr., 1929-33; successively asst. prof., asso. prof., prof. psychology Stanford, 1933-69, emeritus prof., 1969—, exec. head dept., 1942-50, dean grad. div., 1951-55; Bd. dirs., pres. Ann. Reviews, Inc., 1948-73; With USDA, Washington, 1942, OWI, 1942-43, Office Civilian Requirements, WPB, 1943-44; Collaborator, div. child devel. and tchr. personnel Am. Council Edn., 1940-41; nat. adv. mental health council USPHS, 1952-56; fellow (Center Advanced Study Behavioral Scis.), 1956-57; Mem. U.S. Edn. Mission to Japan, 1946. Author: several books, latest Theories of Learning, 1948, rev. edit., 1981, Introduction to Psychology, 1953, revised edit., 1987, Hypnotic Susceptibility, 1965, Hypnosis in the Relief of Pain, 1975, revised edit., 1983, Divided Consciousness, 1977, rev. edit., 1986, American Psychology in Historical Perspective, 1978, Psychology in America: A Historical Survey, 1987. Bd. curators Stephens Coll., Mo., 1953-68. Recipient Warren medal in exptl. psychology, 1940; Wilbur Cross medal Yale U., 1971; Gold medal Am. Psychol. Found., 1978. Hon. fellow Brit. Psychol. Assn.; mem. Am. Psychol. Assn. (pres. 1948-49), Am. Acad. Arts and Scis., Nat. Acad. Edn., Soc. Psychol. Study Social Issues (chmn. 1944-45), AAAS, Nat. Acad. Scis. (sci. reviewing award 1984), Am. Philos. Soc., Internat. Soc. Hypnosis (pres. 1973-76, Benjamin Franklin gold medal 1979), Sigma Xi. Home: 850 Webster Palo Alto CA 94301

HILGER, FREDERICK LEE, JR., bank executive, attorney; b. Dallas, Feb. 17, 1946; s. Frederick Lee Sr. and Maryann Taylor (Ayers) H.; m. Terri Lynn Wilson, May 13, 1984; 1 child, Matthew Charles. BA, U. Pacific, Stockton, Calif., 1967; JD, U. Calif., Berkeley, 1970. Bar: Calif. 1971. Sr. tax acct. Touche Ross and Co., San Francisco, 1971-73; atty. F. L. Hilger Prof. Corp., Eureka, Calif., 1973-75; mng. ptnr. Moses Lake (Wash.) Farms, 1975-78; sr. cons. Sites and Co. Inc., Seattle, 1978-79; v.p. ops. mgmt. U.S. Cruises, Inc., Seattle, 1980-83; pres., chief fin. officer First Nat. Bank, Chico, Calif., 1984—. Recipient Outstanding Banker award Am. Bankers Assn. First Nat. Bank, 1984, 85. Mem. ABA, Calif. Bar Assn. Republican. Presbyterian. Clubs: Butte Creek Country (Chico), Olympic (San Francisco), Riverview Golf and Country (Redding, Calif.). Office: First Nat Bank Box 40 Roseville CA 95661

HILL, ANNA MARIE, purchasing manager; b. Great Falls, Mont., Nov. 6, 1938; d. Paul Joseph and Alexina Rose (Doyon) Ghekiere. AA, Oakland Jr. Coll., 1959; student, U. Calif., Berkeley, 1960-62. Mgr. ops. OSM, Soquel, Calif., 1963-81; purchasing agt. Arrow Hiuss, Scotts Valley, Calif., 1981-82; sr. buyer Fairchild Test Systems, San Jose, Calif., 1982-83; materials mgr. Basic Test Systems, San Jose, 1983-86; purchasing mgr. Beta Tech., Santa Cruz, Calif., 1986—; cons., No. Calif., 1976—. Counselor Teens Against Drugs, San Jose, 1970, 1/2 Orgn., Santa Cruz, 1975-76. Mem. Am. Prodn. Invention Control, Nat. Assn. Female Execs., Nat. Assn. Purchasing Mgmt., Porsche Club Am., Am. Radio Relay League. Democrat. Club: Young Ladies Radio League. Avocations: amateur radio operator, music, gardening. Home: 2922 Park Ave Soquel CA 95073 Office: Beta Tech 105 Harvey W Blvd Santa Cruz CA 95064

HILL, BART BLAINE, social services administrator; b. Brigham City, Utah, Mar. 21, 1954; s. Seymour Blaine Hill and Charmane Hayward; m. Gwen McMullin, Sept. 12, 1980; children: Brooke, Nicholas, Nathan. BS in Psychology and Sociology, U. Utah, 1980, MSW, 1986. Counselor Am. Community Youth Services, Salt Lake City, 1980-82; regional dir. Intermountain Youth Care, Ogden, Utah, 1982—. Mem. Nat. Assn. Social Workers, Utah Correctional Assn. Democrat. Mormon. Avocations: gardening, skiing. Home: 1247 S 120 E Farmington UT 84025 Office: Intermountain Youth Care 533 26th St #200 Ogden UT 84401

HILL, CAROL ANN, writer, researcher; b. Detroit, Aug. 8, 1940; d. Glenn George and Evelyn Alberta (Read) Havens; m. Alan Eugene Hill, Mar. 26, 1960; children: Larry Glenn, Roy Leon. BS, U. N.Mex., 1973, MS, 1978. V.p. Plasmatronics, Albuquerque, 1978-83. Author: Cave Minerals, 1976, Cave Minerals of the World, 1986, Geology of Carlsbad Cavern, 1986; author, editor Saltpeter Symposium, 1981. Mem. AAAS, N.Mex. Geol. Soc., Union Internat. de Speleologie, Nat. Speleol. Soc. (fellow 1976, Cert. of Merit 1983), Cave Research Found., Friends of Mineralogy. Avocations: spelunking, backpacking, skiing, skating.

HILL, CAROL AUDREY, pet care center executive; b. South Gate, Calif., Apr. 19, 1934; d. Verne Thomas and Beatrice Audrey (White) Holman; m. Denton Elmer Hill, Nov. 16, 1957 (div.); m. James Arthur Pennington, Feb. 21, 1981 (div. 1983). Student Butte Coll., Calif., 1974-77. Cert. adult edn. tchr., Calif. Display advt. mgr. J.C. Penney, Chico, Calif., 1954-60; owner, operator Chico Pet Shop (now Carol's Dog-Cat Care Ctr.), 1961—; owner, instr. Dog Obedience Sch., Chico, 1963—; owner operator Designs by Carol, Chico, 1979—, Cal-A-Hi Dog Grooming Sch., 1983—. Bd. dirs., chmn. personnel com. Butte County Humane Soc., 1984-87; freelance writer, Chico, 1986-87; bd. dirs., chmn. newsletter Stansbury Preservation Soc. for Hist. Stansbury House, Chico, Calif., 1985—, sec. Recipient numerous awards in field. Mem. Greater Chico C. of C., Nat. Assn. Female Execs., Nat. Dog Groomers Assn. Am. Democrat. Author: Dog Obedience Instructors Training Manual, 1983; host TV show Care of Cats, 1964-65. Home: 282 Camino Norte Chico CA 95926 Office: 973-Q East Ave Chico CA 95926

HILL, COLIN KENNETH, radiobiologist, educator; b. London, Sept. 1, 1950; came to U.S., 1978; s. Eric Douglas and Ivy Helen (Read) H.; m. Donna Marie Williams, May 17, 1980; children: Tristan Andrew, Lauren Alice. Higher nat. diploma, Northeast London Poly., Eng., 1972; B in Tech. Applied Biology with honors, Brunel U., London, 1975, PhD in Biochemistry, 1978. Research asst. European Centre for Nuclear Research, Geneva, 1975-78; postdoctoral fellow Rush-Presbyn. St. Luke's Med. Ctr., Chgo., 1978-80; research assoc. Fermi Nat. Accelerator Lab., Batavia, Ill., 1980-81; research assoc., asst. biologist Argonne (Ill.) Nat. Lab., 1981-85; head exptl. radiotherapy U. So. Calif. Sch. Medicine, Los Angeles, 1985—; adj. lectr. Rush-Presbyn. St. Luke's Med. Ctr., 1981-85; adj. asst. prof. Colo. State U., Ft. Collins, 1984—, No. Ill. U., DeKalb, 1984—; cons. Argonne Nat. Lab., 1985—. Grantee HHS, Pub. Health Service, Nat. Cancer Inst., Argonne Nat. Lab., 1982-85, U. So. Calif. Sch. Medicine, 1985—. Mem. Chartered Inst. Biology, Radiation Research Soc., Assn. Radiation Research, AAAS. Mem. Ch. England. Avocations: soccer, skiing, hiking, gardening, stamp collecting. Home: 2384 Galbreth Rd Pasadena CA 91104 Office: Univ So Calif Hosp Med Ctr 1414 S Hope St Los Angeles CA 90015

HILL, DALE RICHARD, military officer; b. Charleston, W.Va., Dec. 20, 1939; s. Cecil Thomas Jr. and Frances Eileen (Gillespie) H.; m. Linda Lee Ergeson, Apr. 20, 1962 (dec. 1971); m. Debbie Kay Hildebrant, Feb. 19, 1972; children: Mark, Bret, Lara, Dale, Adam. BS, W.Va. State Coll., 1967; MA, Cen. Mich. U., 1977; grad., USA Command and Gen. Staff Coll., 1968. Commd. 2d lt. U.S. Army, ft. Benning, Ga., 1976; advanced through grades to lt. col. U.S. Army, 1984; aide-de-camp USA Operational Test and Evaluation Agy., Falls Church, Va., 1976-80; ops. officer Hdqrs. 3 Bde, 2 Infantry div., Camp Howze, Republic of Korea, 1980-81; emergency action officer Hdqr. Readiness Command, MacDill AFB, Fla., 1981-82; plans tng. officer Hdqrs. Multinat. Force & Observers Sinai, El Gorah, 1982-83; chief current ops. Hdqr. I Corps., Ft. Lewis, Wash., 1983-86; commdr. Yakima (Wash.) Firing Ctr., 1986—. Democrat. Avocations: gardening, individual athletics. Home: 941 Market St Prosser WA 99350 Office: Hdqr Yakima Firing Ctr Yakima WA 99350

HILL, ESTHER ANDRIOPULOS, magazine art director; b. Saugus, Mass., Feb. 23, 1956; d. Paul John and Harriet (Hamberis) Andriopulos; 1 child, Christopher Rhodes. BA, San Diego State U., 1979. Art asst. San Diego mag., 1978-79, advt. art dir., 1979-81, art dir., 1981—. Active United Cerebral Palsy, San Diego, mem. profl. services program com., parent support group. Recipient White-Silver award City and Regional Mag. Assn., U. Kans., 1986. Mem. Am. Inst. Graphic Arts, Communicating Arts Group (Merit award 1983, 84, 86). Democrat. Greek Orthodox. Avocations: biking, cooking, gardening. Home: 211 W Robinson Ave San Diego CA 92103 Office: San Diego Mag 4206 W Point Loma Blvd San Diego CA 92110

HILL, FRANK U., manufacturing company executive, engineer; b. Durham, N.C., Oct. 9, 1923; s. Frank U. and Comal (Riggs) H.; m. Teresa C. Rallis, Nov. 10, 1946; children: Stepanie Jo, Chrissa Ann, Janet Rebecca. BSME, Duke U., 1944; MSME, Case Inst. Tech., 1952. Aeroresearch scientist Nat. Adv. for Aeronautics, Cleve., 1944-52; sales mgr. solar div. Internat. Harvester Co., San Diego, 1956-71; pres. FHA, San Diego, 1971-82, Sorrento Engring. Inc., San Diego, 1982—. Patentee in field. Home: 4346 Hortensia St San Diego CA 92103 Office: Sorrento Engring Inc 2601 Hoover Ave Suite C National City CA 92050

HILL, FREDRIC WILLIAM, nutrition scientist, educator; b. Erie, Pa., Sept. 2, 1918; s. Vaino Alexander and Mary Elvira (Holmstrom) H.; m. Charlotte Henrietta Gummoe, Apr. 1, 1944; children: Linda Charlotte, James Fredric, Dana Edwin. B.S., Pa. State U., 1939, M.S., 1940; Ph.D., Cornell U., 1944. Research asst. Pa. State U., 1939-40, Cornell U., 1940-44; head nutrition div. research labs. Western Condensing Co., Appleton, Wis., 1944-48; assoc. prof., then prof. animal nutrition and poultry husbandry Cornell U., 1948-59; prof. poultry husbandry, chmn. dept. U. Calif. at Davis, 1959-65, prof. nutrition, 1965—, chmn. dept. nutrition, 1965-73, assoc. dean Coll. Agr., 1965-66, assoc. dean research, 1976-80, coordinator internat. programs, 1976-80; Mem. subcom. hormonal relationships and applications com. on Animal Nutrition, NRC, 1953, subcom. poultry nutrition, 1953-74; mem. Food and Nutrition Bd., 1975-78; commr. Calif. Poultry Improvement Commn., 1959-65; participant 8th Easter Sch. Agrl. Scis., U. Nottingham, Eng., 1961, World Conf. Animal Prodn., Rome, Italy, 1963, U.S. AID-Nat. Acad. Sci. Seminar on Protein Foods, Bangkok, 1970, USIA Asia Seminars on Food, Population and Energy, 1974-75; Japan Soc. Promotion Sci. vis. prof. Nagoya U., 1974-75; vis. scientist FDA, 1975, Nutrition Inst., USDA, 1975; cons. Institut National de Recherche Agronomique, France, 1982; plenary speaker 3d Asian-Australian Animal Sci. Congress, Seoul, Republic of Korea, 1985. Contbr. articles profl. jours.; Editorial bd.: Poultry Sci. Jour, 1960-64; editorial bd.: Jour. of Nutrition, 1964-68; editor, 1969-79. Fellow Danforth Found., 1938; recipient Nutrition Research award Am. Feed Mfrs. Assn., 1958, Newman Internat. Research award British Poultry Assn., 1959; Guggenheim Found. fellow, 1966-67; Alumni fellow Pa. State U., 1983. Fellow AAAS, Poultry Sci. Assn. (Research prize 1957, Borden award 1961), Am. Inst. Nutrition (councillor 1982-85); mem. Soc. Exptl. Biology and Medicine, Nutrition Soc. (Gt. Britain), Council Biology Editors, World's Poultry Sci. Assn., Am. Inst. Biol. Scis., Am. Soc. Animal Sci., Am. Chem. Soc., Sigma Xi, Phi Eta Sigma, Gamma Sigma Delta, Phi Kappa Phi, Delta Theta Sigma, Gamma Alpha. Clubs: Cosmos (Washington); El Macero (Calif.). Home: 643 Miller Dr Davis CA 95616 Office: U Calif Dept Nutrition Davis CA 95616

HILL, GEORGE RICHARD, educator; b. Ogden, Utah, Nov. 24, 1921; s. George Richard and Elizabeth (McKay) H.; m. Melba Parker, Aug. 25, 1941; children: George Richard IV, Margaret Hill Nielson, Robert Parker, Carolyn Hill Allen, Susan Hill Mann, Nancy Hill Bauman, David Parker. AB in Chemistry, Brigham Young U., 1942, DSc (hon.), 1980; PhD in Phys. and Inorganic Chemistry, Cornell U., 1946. Chemist Am. Smelting & Refining Co., 1937-42; asst., part-time instr. Cornell U., 1942-46; project dir. Air Force Combustion Research, 1952-57; dir. Office Coal Research, Dept. Interior, Washington, 1972-73; mem. faculty U. Utah, 1946-72, prof. chemistry, 1950-72, chmn. fuels engring., 1951-65; dean Coll. Mines and Mineral Industries, U. Utah, 1966-72; Envirotech. endowed prof. U. Utah, 1977-82, Eimco endowed prof., 1982—; dept. dir. fossil fuels Electric Power Research Inst., Palo Alto, Calif., 1973-77; dir. fossil fuel power plants dept. Electric Power Research Inst., 1976-77; project dir. Air Force Office Sci. Research, 1956-61, Equity Oil Shale Research, 1961; mem. NRC com. Mineral and Energy Resources, 1976-81; mem. fossil energy adv. com. Dept. Energy, 1977—; vice chmn. Utah Council Energy Conservation and Devel., 1978-83; chmn. Utah Task Force on Power Plant Siting, 1978; chmn. editorial com. NRC, 1977-81; com. chmn. Chemistry of Coal Utilization, 1981; mem. Nat. Coal Council, 1985—. Contbr. papers on kinetics of coal conversion, oil shale, corrosion, catalysis. Mem. exec. bd. region XII Boy Scouts Am., 1961; chmn. Explorer activities sect. 6, 1959-61; mem. Explorer com., nat. exec. bd., 1965-72, first quorum of the 70 Mormon Ch.; bd. dirs. Deseret Gymnasium, 1967. Recipient Silver Beaver, Silver Antelope awards Boy Scouts Am.; Distinguished Service award Utah Petroleum Council, 1968; Outstanding Profl. Engr. award Utah Engring. Council, 1970. Fellow Am. Inst. Chemists; mem. AAAS, AIME, Am. Chem. Soc. (Utah award Salt Lake sect. 1969, Henry H. Storch award 1971), Am. Inst. Chem. Engrs., Nat. Coal Council, Sigma Xi, Phi Kappa Phi, Sigma Pi Sigma, Alpha Phi Omega. Home: 1430 Yale Ave Salt Lake City UT 84105 Office: U Utah Dept Chem Engring 3062 Merrill Engring Bldg Salt Lake City UT 84112

HILL, GRANDVILLE ELI, social service administrator, retired U.S. Navy officer; b. Jackson, Miss., Nov. 6, 1930; s. Excell and Amendia (Byrd) H.; m. Lollie Ruth Ento, Mar. 16, 1957; children: Deidra Joyce, Lorraine, Terrance Deon. BS in Marine Engring., Tougolue Coll.; postgrad., U.S. Naval War Coll. Enlisted USN, 1951, advanced through grades to capt., ret., 1982, fighter pilot then U-2 reconnaissance pilot, 1951-82; first officer LogAir; clipper capt. on 747's PanAm; now owner, co-adminstr. Hill Family Care Home, Vallejo, Calif., 1982—; owner, operator Express Check Cashing, Vallejo. Co-adminstr. Jehovah House-Vallejo Dept Youth Authority. Decorated Bronze Star medals (3) with oak leaf cluster, Navy Cross, USN Air medal; Presdl. Unit citation (Republic of Korea). Mem. Airline Transport Pilot's Assn., Airline Passenger's Assn., VFW, U.S. Naval Inst. Profl. Soc. Home: 800 Taper Ave Vallejo CA 94589

HILL, HAMNETT PINHEY, accountant; b. Ottawa, Ont., Can., Oct. 11, 1943; s. Hamnett Pinhey and Cynthia Benson (Jaffray) Hill Eberts; m. Terry Delany, Aug. 23, 1969; children: Catherine, Hamnett, Austin, Jeremy, Darcy, Ashley, Jaffray, Morgan. BA, Carleton U., 1971. Chartered acct., 1974. Chief acct. Locweld & Forge Products Ltd., Montreal, Que., Can., 1966-69; acct. Peat Marwick Mitchell & Co., Ottawa, 1971-75; ptnr. Hudson & Co., Calgary, Alta., Can., 1975—; pres., dir. Nine Hills Resources Inc., Calgary, 1981—. Bd. dirs. Calgary French Sch., 1977-82, U. Calgary Swim Club, 1984-87. Mem. Inst. Chartered Accts. Alta., Inst. Chartered Accts. Ont., Can. Tax Found. Progressive Conservative. Mem. Ch. Jesus Christ Latter-day Saints. Office: Hudson Co, 1000-1015 4th St SW, Calgary, AB Canada T2R 1J4

HILL, HARRY DAVID, human resources executive; b. Whittier, Calif., Oct. 29, 1944; s. Harry Boreman and Winifred Nell (Purvis) Hill; m. Linda Mae Price, Nov. 8, 1969; 1 child, Jon Ryan. AA, Los Angeles Harbor Coll., Wilmington, Calif., 1964; BA in Polit. Sci., UCLA, 1966; M of Pub. Adminstrn. in Human Resources, U. So. Calif., 1972. Personnel aide City of Anaheim, Calif., 1966-67, personnel analyst, 1967-71, sr. personnel analyst, 1971-75, personnel services mgr., 1975-83, asst. human resources dir., 1983—; Surpervisory com. chmn. Anaheim Area Credit Union, 1981. Mem. So. Calif. Pub. Labor Council (treas. 1986—), Internat. Personnel Mgmt. Assn. (western region pres. 1983-84), So. Calif. Personnel Mgmt. Assn. (pres. 1978-79), Am. Soc. Tng. and Devel. Democrat. Office: City of Anaheim 200 S Anaheim Blvd 332 Anaheim CA 92805

HILL, HENRY ALLEN, educator, physicist; b. Port Arthur, Tex., Nov. 25, 1933; s. Douglas and Florence (Kilgore) H.; m. Ethel Louise Eplin, Aug. 23, 1954; children—Henry Allen, Pamela Lynne, Kimberly Renee. B.S., U. Houston, 1953; M.S., U. Minn., 1956, Ph.D., 1957; M.A. (hon.), Wesleyan U., 1966. Research asst. U. Houston, 1952-53; teaching asst. U. Minn., 1953-54, research asst., 1954-57; research assoc. Princeton U., 1957-58, instr., then asst. prof., 1958-64; assoc. prof. Wesleyan U., Middletown, Conn., 1964-66; prof. physics Wesleyan U., 1966-74, chmn. dept., 1969-71; prof. physics U. Ariz., 1966—. Contbr. articles to profl. jours. Sloan fellow, 1966-68. Fellow Am. Phys. Soc.; mem. Am. Astron. Soc., Royal Astron. Soc., Optical Soc. Am. Research on nuclear physics, relativity and astrophysics. Office: U Ariz Dept Phys Tucson AZ 85721

HILL, HERBERT HENDERSON, JR., chemical educator; b. Helena, Ark., Nov. 25, 1945; s. Herbert Henderson and Katherine (Stephens) H.; m. Jannette Riddle, Sept. 7, 1968; children: Jennifer Clare, Chandler Henderson. BS in Chemistry, Rhodes Coll., 1970; MS in Biol. Chemistry, U. Mo., 1973; PhD in Chemistry, Dalhousie U., Halifax, N.S., 1975. Postdoctoral fellow U. Waterloo, Ontario, Can., 1975-76; asst. prof. chemistry Wash. State U., Pullman, 1976-80, assoc. prof., 1980-85, mem. grad. faculty program pharmacology, toxicology, 1982—, dir. Office of Grant and Research Devel., 1985-87, prof., 1985—; guest prof. dept. chemistry Kyoto (Japan) U., 1983-84. Contbr. numerous articles to profl. jours. Served with USN, 1967-69. Fellow Japan Soc. Promotion Sci., 1983-84. Mem. Am. Chem. Soc. (chmn. Idaho-Wash. Border Regional sect. 1980-81, sec. 1978-79, mem. analytical div.), Assn. Research Profs., Am. Men and Women of Sci., Sigma Xi. Office: Chem Dept Wash State Univ Pullman WA 99163

HILL, IRVING, judge; b. Lincoln, Nebr., Feb. 6, 1915; s. Nathan and Ida (Ferder) H.; m. Maydee Taylor, June 23, 1939; children: Lawrence N., Steven C., Richard F. A.B., U. Nebr., 1936; J.D., Harvard U., 1939; L.H.D., Hebrew Union Coll., 1976. Bar: Nebr. 1939, D.C. 1942, Calif. 1946. Spl. asst. to U.S. atty. gens. Biddle and Clark, Dept. Justice, Washington, 1942-46; legal adviser U.S. del. UN Social and Econ. Council, 1946; individual practice law Beverly Hills, Calif., 1946-61; judge Calif. Superior Ct., 1961-65; U.S. dist. judge Los Angeles, 1965—; chief judge 1979-81. Pres. Jewish Fedn.-Council Greater Los Angeles, 1960-63; v.p. Council Jewish Fedns. and Welfare Funds, 1962-65; dir. gen. bd. United Way, Los Angeles County, 1963-74. Served to lt. (j.g.) USNR, 1944-46. Mem. Phi Beta Kappa. Office: US Court House 312 N Spring St Los Angeles CA 90012 *

HILL, JAMES NOAH, physician; b. Fulton, Mo., Aug. 19, 1908; s. Noah F. and Alice (Gingrich) H.; B.S., Warrensburg State Tchrs. Coll., 1933; M.S., U. Kans., 1934; M.D., Creighton U., 1938; postgrad. Johns Hopkins, 1943; m. Mabel Timken, Feb. 28, 1958. Intern, St. Mary's Hosp., Kansas City, Mo., 1938-39; pvt. practice, Hutchinson, Kans., 1940-42; staff mem. Meml. Hosp., St. Francis Hosp., Colorado Springs, Colo.; med. examiner FAA. Served as lt. col., AUS, 1942-46, 5028 Medical Unit, lt. col. Res. (Ft. Carson, Colo.), 1958—, ETO. Mem. AMA, Colo. Med. Soc., El Paso County Med. Soc., Assn. Am. Physicians and Surgeons, Aerospace Med. Assn. Home: 1212 Hermosa Way Colorado Springs CO 80906 Office: 13 S Tejon St Colorado Springs CO 80906

HILL, JOAN GAIL, rehabilitation consultant; b. Klamath Falls, Oreg., Oct. 26, 1935; d. Harold Lloyd McPherson and Ruth (Sigford) Carland; m. Richard A. Hill, July 26, 1953; children: Lois, Sharon, Russel. BA with honors, Wash. State U., 1969. Co-pres. Indsl. Counseling Service, Ashland, Oreg.; pres. Oreg. Assn. Rehab. Profl. Pvt. Sector, 1981-82, mem. legis. com., 1984—. Mem. gov.s' workers compensation claims closure com., 1981, Assn. Oreg. Industries Legis. Com., 1985-86. Office: Indsl Counseling Service PO Box 278 Ashland OR 97520

HILL, JOHN EARL, mechanical engr.; b. Ely, Nev., July 18, 1953; s. Earl M. and Florence (Lagos) H.; m. Terry Lynn Biederman, Oct. 3, 1981; 1 stepchild, Felicia Biederman. BA in Social Psychology, U. Nev., 1974, BSME, 1981. Cert. engr. in tng. Machinist B&J Machine and Tool, Sparks,

Nev., 1977-78; designer, machinist Screen Printing Systems, Sparks, Nev., 1978, Machine Services, Sparks, 1978-81; computer programmer U. Nev., Reno, 1980-81; design engr. Ford Aerospace and Communications Corp., Palo Alto, Calif., 1981-82, contract engr., 1986—; contract design engr. Westinghouse Electric Corp., Sunnyvale, Calif., 1982-83; contract project engr. Adcotech Corp., Milpitas, Calif., 1983-84; sr. engr. Domain Tech., Milpitas, 1984-85; project engr. Exclusive Design Co., San Mateo, Calif., 1985-86. Mem. Robotics Internat. of Soc. Mech. Engrs. of AIME, Tau Beta Pi, Pi Mu Epsilon, Phi Kappa Phi. Avocations: music, art, photography. Home: 147 Wildwood Ave San Carlos CA 94070 Office: Ford Aerospace & Communications Corp M/S G90 B939 Fabian Way Palo Alto CA 94303

HILL, JOHN LEE, optometrist, educator; b. Willcox, Ariz., Apr. 25, 1953; s. Austin William and Gladys Edwina Hill; A.A., Cochise Coll., 1973; student U. Ariz., 1973-74; B.S. in Visual Sci., Pacific U., 1980, O.D., 1980. Lic. optometrist, Ariz. Practice optometry, Tucson, 1980—; instr. contact lenses Pima Coll. Cochise Coll. athletic scholar, 1971. Mem. Am. Optometric Assn., Ariz. Optometric Assn., So. Ariz. Optometric Assn., Omega Epsilon Phi. Republican. Mormon. Office: 1718 W Ajo Way Tucson AZ 85713

HILL, JONEL C., gas company executive; b. Mankato, Minn., 1925. Attended, Mankato State Coll.; LLB, St. Paul Coll. of Law, 1950. Formerly editor West Publishing Co.; past public utilities commr. State of Oreg.; former atty. Am. Telephone & Telegraph Co.; exec. asst. So. Calif. Gas Co., 1968-70, asst. v.p., 1970-74, v.p. regulatory affairs, 1974-80, sr. v.p., 1980-83, exec. v.p., 1983-85; pres. So. Calif. Gas Co., Los Angeles, 1985—, also dir. Office: Southern Calif Gas Co Office of the Pres 810 S Flower St Los Angeles CA 90017 *

HILL, JUDITH DEEGAN, lawyer; b. Chgo., Dec. 13, 1940; d. William James and Ida May (Scott) Deegan; m. Dennis M. Havens, June 28, 1986; children by previous marriage: Colette M., Cristina M. BA, Western Mich. U., 1960; cert. U. Paris, Sorbonne, 1962; JD, Marquette U., 1971. Bar: Wis. 1971, Ill. 1973, Nev. 1976, D.C. 1979. Tchr., Kalamazoo (Mich.) Bd. Edn., 1960-62, Maple Heights (Ohio), 1963-64, Shorewood (Wis.) Bd. Edn., 1964-68; corp. atty. Fort Howard Paper Co., Green Bay, Wis., 1971-72; sr. trust adminstr. Continental Ill. Nat. Bank & Trust, Chgo., 1972-76; atty. Morse, Foley & Wadsworth Law Firm, Las Vegas, 1976-77; dep. dist. atty., criminal prosecutor Clark County Atty., Las Vegas, 1977-83; atty. civil and criminal law Edward S. Coleman Profl. Law Corp., Las Vegas, 1983-84; sole practice, 1984-85; atty. criminal div. Office of City Atty., City of Las Vegas, 1985—. Bd. dirs. Nev. Legal Services, Carson City, 1980-84, state chmn., 1984-87; bd. dirs. Clark County Legal Services, Las Vegas, 1980-87; mem. Star Aux. for Handicapped Children, Las Vegas, 1986. Recipient Scholarship, Auto Specialties, St. Joseph, Mich., 1957-60; St. Thomas More Scholarship, Marquette U. Law Sch., Milw., 1968-69; juvenile law internship grantee Marquette U. Law Sch., 1970. Mem. ABA, Nev. Bar Assn., Woman's Bar Assn. of Ill., So. Nev. Assn. Women Attys., Ill. Bar Assn., Washington Bar Assn. Democrat. Club: Children's Village (pres. 1980) (Las Vegas, Nev.). Home: 1110 S 5th Pl Las Vegas NV 89104 Office: City Attys Office 400 E Stewart 6th Floor Las Vegas NV 89101

HILL, KEITH J., clergyman, educator; b. Tulsa, Sept. 1, 1925; s. Javan B. and Anna Catherine (McBroom) H.; m. Jean Bond, Sept. 1, 1946 (dec. 1978); m. Joan Van Camp Woertz, June 12, 1982; children by previous marriage—Karen Jean, Deborah Sue. Grad. Central Bible Coll./Sem., 1946. Minister, Bethel Temple, Sacramento, 1946-51, Calvary Temple, Seattle, 1951-56, Calvary Temple, Denver, 1956-62, Calvary Bible Ch., Burbank, Calif., 1962-65, Bethany Bapt. Ch., Whittier, Calif., 1965-71, Grace Community Ch., Tempe, Ariz., 1971-79, First Bapt. Ch., Lakewood, Long Beach, Calif., exec. pastor, 1979-87; assoc. exec. minister Southwest Bapt. Conf. Hdqrs., West Covina, Calif., 1987—. Contbr. articles to profl. jours. Bd. trustees S.W. Bapt. Conf., 1968-71, 80-82; mem. Bd. Christian Edn., W. Covina, Calif., 1965-71, Denomination Bapt. Gen. Conf., Arlington Hts., Ill., 1965—; charter/founder Nat. Assn. Dirs. Christian Edn., 1961, Rocky Mt. Sun. Sch. Assn., 1962, others; founder So. Calif. Dirs. Christian Edn., 1962, Phoenix Area Christian Educators, Phoenix. Mem. Nat. Bd. Christian Ednl. Bapt. Gen. conf., Arlington Heights; bd. dirs. Greater Los Angeles Sunday Schs., 1965—; founder, charter mem. bd. dirs. Greater Long Beach Christian Schs., Inc., also sec. bd. dirs.; founder 1st Living/Singing Christmas Tree, Ariz., 1972, choral dir.; operating brethren Ju. and sr. high schs. in Paramount, Calif.; v.p. exec. com. Greater Los Angeles Sunday Schs. Assn. Mem. Nat. Assn. Evangelicals (So. Calif. bd.), Nat. Assn. Dirs. Christian Edn., So. Calif. Dirs. Christian Edn., Rocky Mt. Dirs. Christian Edn., Phoenix Area Dirs. Christian Edn. Office: SW Bapt Conf Office Assoc Exec Minister 925 N Sunset Ave PO Box 728 West Covina CA 91793

HILL, LOLLIE RUTH, social service administrator, check cashing service executive; b. El Dorado, Ark., July 11, 1930; d. Eddie M. and Effie (Byrd) Ento; m. Grandville Eli Hill, Mar. 16, 1957; children: Deidra J., Lorraine, Terence D. Asst. dir. Walter Brown Hosp., El Dorado; adminstr. Hill Farm Care Home, Vallejo, Calif., 1961—; v.p. Express Check Cashing Co., Vallejo, 1985—. Office: Hill Family Home Care 800 Taper Ave Vallejo CA 94590

HILL, LOPEZ HOLMES, lawyer; b. Savannah, Ga., Dec. 19, 1947; s. Raymond Alexander and Lois (Holmes) H.; m. Ann-Maria Tattersall, Jan. 21, 1973 (div. June 1979); m. Toni Maria Jimenez, Jan. 23, 1981; 1 child, Antony. BS, Howard U.; MBA, Chapman Coll., 1979; JD, Southwestern U., 1986. Cons. in logistics Washington, 1980-82; sr. systems analyst Bridgestone Tire Co., Los Angeles, 1982-83; co-owner Gaule Corp., Redondo Beach, Calif., 1983-84; mgr. fin. systems Occidental Petroleum Corp., Los Angeles, 1984-86; sole practice Los Angeles, 1986—; cons. in field, Washington, 1980-82, Los Angeles, 1980-86. Served to lt. USN, 1972-80. Mem. ABA, NAACP, Urban League, Calif. Trial Lawyers Assn. Democrat. Adventist. Lodge: Masons. Avocations: tennis, flying, martial arts.

HILL, M(ICHAEL) DENIS, publishing executive; b. Springfield, Mo., July 18, 1946; s. Kenneth R. and Mildred L. (Pering) H.; m. Reta Beeman, Feb. 14, 1970 (div. Dec. 1976); m. Pamela Zanti, Dec. 4, 1983. Student, Franklin Coll., 1966-68, Am. U., 1965-66. Publisher Stock Car Racing Mag., Alexandria, Va., 1969-73; field ops. mgr. Nat. Ctr. Health Stats., Rockville, Md., 1974-76; mktg. dir. Am. Water Works Assn., Denver, 1977-80; communications dir. Specialty Equipment Market Assn., Whittier, Calif., 1980-83; assoc. publisher Oman Publishing Inc., Mill Valley, Calif., 1984-87; editor Computers in Publishing, 1987—. Contbr. articles to profl. mags. Recipient Ambassador award Am. Water Works Assn., 1978. Mem. No. Calif. Pick Users (dir. 1985-86), Internat. Pick Users Assn. (dir. of membership 1986-87, sec. 1987). Avocations: photography, bicycling. Home: 99 Spruce Rd Fairfax CA 94930 Office: The Hill Group 412 Red Hill Ave Suite 9 San Anselmo CA 94960

HILL, ROBERT EDWIN, air force officer, fighter pilot instructor; b. Eugene, Oreg., Feb. 2, 1944; s. Hal Edwin and Ailene Leta (Elliot) H.; m. Jeaneane Lea Whitaker, June 10, 1967; children: Ty Edwin, Troy William. BSEE, U. Wash., 1967; MSEE, Air Force Inst. Tech., 1978. Commd. 2d lt. USAF, 1967, advanced through grades to lt. col., 1985; program mgr. USAF Avionics Lab., Wright-Patterson AFB, Ohio, 1975-77; chief software devel. and support equipment F-15 Program Office, Wright-Patterson AFB, 1978-81; wing inspector assigned to 81st Tactical Fighter Wing RAF, Bentwaters, Eng., 1981-84; fighter pilot instr. USAF, Holloman AFB, N.Mex., 1984—. Cubmaster Boy Scouts Am., Alamagordo, 1986—. Mem. IEEE. Avocation: computer equipment design. Home: 3107 La Cresta Alamagordo NM 88310 Office: 433d Tactical Fighter Tng Squadron USAF Holloman AFB NM 88330

HILL, STEVEN RICHARD, business executive; b. Oakland, Calif., May 17, 1947; s. Ernest Ellwood and Bettyjean (Schaegelen) H.; m. Sandra Ann Logan, Sept. 7, 1968; children: Heather Dawn, Tessa Michelle. BS in Forest Mgmt., U. Calif., Berkeley, 1969; MBA, UCLA, 1971. Planning analyst Weyerhaeuser Co., Wash. and N.C.; mgr. corp. raw material allocation Weyerhaeuser Co., Tacoma, 1974-78, dir. human resource planning, 1979-82, dir. benefits, compensation, health, 1982-86, v.p. employee relations, 1986—; staff asst. U.S. Dept. Energy, Washington, 1978-79; mem. policy com. Nat. Employee Benefits Inst., Washington, 1985—. Bd. dirs. ARC, Tacoma; trustee Multicare Med. Ctr., Tacoma, 1983; commr. Wash. State Hosp. Rate Setting Commn., Olympia, 1985—. White House fellow Pres'. Commn. on White House Fellows, Washington, 1978. Democrat. Congregationalist. Home: 5326 Hyada Blvd NE Tacoma WA 98422 Office: Weyerhaeuser Co Tacoma WA 98477

HILL, SUSAN FORBES, civic volunteer, rancher; b. Oakland, Calif.; d. Robert Parsons and Dorothy (Adams) Forbes; m. James M. Wells, Sept. 9, 1967; children—Jesse, Lilla, Elizabeth, Jason; m. Anthony Russell Hill, July 8, 1978. B.A., U. Calif.-Berkeley, 1967, M.B.A., 1985. Mem., officer bd. dirs., trustee Easter Seal Soc., Oakland, 1968-75, World Coll. West, 1977-82, Head-Royce Sch., 1977-82, Jr. League of Oakland-East Bay, Inc., 1972—, Children's Hosp. Med. Ctr., 1971—, Jr. Ctr. Arts and Sci., 1978-82; Internat. Host Com. of Calif., 1981—; pres. Children's Hosp. Found., Oakland, 1983-84, pres., 1984—; pres. Alameda County Children's Interest Commn., 1978—; mem. Piedmont Gen. Plan Com.; mem. Civil Service Commn., 1984—; vice mayor City of Piedmont, 1986—; mem. Boy Scouts Exec. Council, 1986—. Recipient Rosalie Stern award U. Calif., 1981—; service recognition award Nat. Ski Patrol System, 1981; Woman of Yr., Children's Hosp. Med. Ctr., 1973. Clubs: Claremont Country, Women's Athletic. Office: PO Box 13176 Oakland CA 94661

HILL, THOMAS LANSDALE (DANNY), advertising and public relations executive; b. Balt., Nov. 3, 1916; s. Howard Clarence and Cornelia Houston (Lansdale) H.; m. Mary Frick Bumb, June 29, 1952; children: Thomas Lansdale, Elizabeth Allen Aschenbrener, Mary Gunning, Nancy Lansdale Rasmussen. BA, St. John's Coll., 1941. Reporter Santa Barbara (Calif.) News-Press, 1946-48; assoc. prof., athletic news dir. San Jose (Calif.) State U., 1948-57; liaison officer TV com. Nat. Collegiate Athletic Assn., N.Y.C., 1954, assoc. dir. survice bur., 1957-63; ptnr. Darien, Russell, Hill & Dahl, San Jose, 1963—; exec. dir. Pacific div. Continental Football League, 1967-69, commr., 1968; commr. Calif. Football League, 1978; mem. San Jose City Sports Commn., 1965, San Francisco Bay Area Olympic Com., 1968. Co-author: Complete Handbook of Sports Scoring and Record Keeping, 1974. Pres. Santa Clara Valley Music and Arts Found.; v.p. San Jose Civic Light Opera; exec. com. Goodwill Santa Clara County, Santa Clara County Heart Assn. Served with USNR, 1942-46. Recipient Silver Medal award Am. Advt. Fedn., 1986. Mem. Santa Clara Valley Assn. Advt. Agys. (v.p.), Nat. Sports Library (bd. dirs.), Greater San Jose Advt. Golf Assn. (pres.). Episcopalian. Club: San Jose Country (dir. srs. assn.). Lodge: Rotary (bd. dirs.). Home: 5469 St Catherine Ct San Jose CA 95127 Office: Darien Russell Hill Dahl 3003 Moorpark Ave Suite 200 San Jose CA 95128

HILL, WARREN RAY, electronic engineering educator; b. Omaha, Oct. 30, 1940; s. Walter Ray and Mary Ann (Glick) H.; m. Heather Jean Fergusson, June 21, 1979; children: Erin Judith, Genny Ann. BSEE, U. Nebr., 1963; MSEE, Wayne State U., 1968; DEng, U. Detroit, 1975. Registered profl. engr., Colo., Mich. Engr. Detroit Edison, 1964-68; sr. project engr. Eaton Corp., Detroit, 1968-78; assoc. prof. Lawrence Inst. Tech., Southfield, Mich., 1978-81; prof. U. So. Colo., Pueblo, 1981—, chmn. dept. engring. techs., 1986—. Patentee in field. Mem. IEEE (sr.), Am. Soc. Engring. Educators, NSPE, Profl. Engrs. Colo. (bd. dirs. So. chpt.). Congregationalist. Lodge: Masons. Avocations: golf, tennis, reading. Home: 37 MacArthur Pueblo CO 81001 Office: Univ So Colo 2200 Bonforte Pueblo CO 81001

HILL, WILLIAM JOHN, management consultant, educator; b. Hebron, Nebr., Apr. 20, 1934; s. William J. and Ruth M. (Willmore) H.; m. Barbara Clark; children: Charles, John, Lee Ann. BA, Nebr. Wesleyan U., 1956; postgrad., U. Okla., 1959-61. Dir. alumni assn. Nebr. Wesleyan U., Lincoln, 1956-59; asst. dir. found. U. Okla., Norman, 1959-61; exec. dir. Snyder Research Found., Winfield, Kans., 1961-64; dir. devel. Wesley Med. Ctr., Wichita, Kans., 1964-69; prin. William Hill Assocs., Denver, 1970-78; prof. mgmt. Colo. Mountain Coll., Steamboat Springs, 1981—; cons. Tracon Assocs., Steamboat Springs, 1980—, Norman Losh Assocs., Denver, 1971—; trainer Nat. Grant Devel. Inst., Pocatello, Idaho, 1979-81. Author: Successful Grantsmanship, 1970; contbr. articles to profl. pubs. Chmn. Steamboat Econ. Devel. com., Steamboat Springs, 1982-86; exec. dir. and sec. Yampa Valley Found., 1978—. Mem. Am. Soc. Tng. and Devel., Club 20, Steamboat C. of C. Resort Assn. Republican. Methodist. Lodge: Rotary (bd. dirs. 1978—). Avocations: tennis, golf, skiing, trout fishing, hunting. Home: 20 Highland Dr PO Box 717 Steamboat Springs CO 80477 Office: Colo Mountain Coll 1370 Bob Adams Dr PO Box 775288 Steamboat Springs CO 80477

HILLEBRANDT, INA SILVERT, marketing consultant; b. Phila., Mar. 23, 1943; d. Abraham Silvert and Frances (Feldman) Syken; m. C. Barry Hillebrandt, Apr. 24, 1967; 1 child, Nicole Ashley. AB, U. Pa., 1964; postgrad., Tulane U. of La., 1965-67. Project dir. J. Walter Thompson, 1969-71; dir. MPI, Inc., N.Y.C., 1977-78; pres. Hillebrandt Cons., Berkeley, Calif., 1968—; cons. Visa, Internat., San Mateo, Calif., League of Am. Theatres., N.Y.C., Weight Mgrs., Berkeley. Mem. Am. Mktg. Assn., Am. Assn. Pub. Opinion, World Future Soc. (bd. dirs. 1984-85), Women in Mgmt., Women in Communications, San Anselmo C. of C. (bd. dirs., com. chmn. 1985—). NDEA fellow Tulane U.; Abbey H. Sutherland scholar, U. Pa., State Senatorial scholar, U. Pa., Phila. Avocations: travel, riding, cooking, performing arts, dancing. Home and Office: Hillebrandt Cons Inc 644 San Luis Rd Berkeley CA 94707

HILLEND, WILLIAM JACK, business consulting executive; b. Portland, Oreg., Jan. 11, 1936; s. Viljo J. and Jane E. (Wever) H.; m. Jeanette L. Potts, May 29, 1956; children: John D., James R., Jeanine L. H. Vandenberg, Julie E. H. Shannon, Jodi L., Janet E. BS in Chem. Engring., Oreg. State U., 1958; MS in Pulp and Paper Tech., Lawrence U., 1960, PhD, 1963; MBA, Portland State U., 1972. Research engr. Crown Zellerbach Corp., Camas, Wash., 1962-67; product mktg. mgr. Boise Cascade Corp., Portland, 1967-82; owner Hillend Bus. Cons., Vancouver, Wash., 1982—. Contbr. articles to profl. jours. Mem. Citizens' Com. for Good Schs., Vancouver, 1975-80; chmn. City Planning Commn., Vancouver, 1974—, cub scout pack Boy Scouts Am., 1965-70; player, agt. baseball little league, Vancouver, 1966-72. Recipient Golden Acorn award, PTA, Vancouver, 1975. Mem. Tech. Assn. of Pulp and Paper Industry, Am. Mgmt. Assn., Am. Mktg. Assn., Paper Industry Mgmt. Assn., Tau Kappa Epsilon (pres. 1955-56). Lodges: Lions, Eagles. Avocations: music, flying.

HILLENDAHL, WESLEY HARRINGTON, consulting economist, valuator; b. Palo Alto, Calif., May 27, 1921; s. John Arnold and Laura Dorothy (Russi) H.; m. A. Deanne Hendrick; children: Sandra, Gregory, Nancy, Eric; m. Marilyn Godshall, Oct. 11, 1965; children: Robin, William. BAME with distinction, Stanford U., 1942, MBA in Mktg., 1949. Sales engr., dist. engr. Linde Air Products div. Union Carbide Corp., San Francisco, 1949-54; indsl. economist SRI Internat., Menlo Park, Calif., 1954-57; dir. market research aerophysics devel. div. Curtiss Wright Corp., Santa Barbara, Calif., 1957-58; cons. economist So. Calif., 1959-66; v.p., dir. econs. div. Bank of Hawaii, 1966-81; pres. The Hillendahl Corp., Kenwood, Calif., 1981—; speaker in field; expert witness; mem. adv. bd. Nat. Bank of Redwoods, Calif. Bd. dirs. C. of C., Hawaii, 1975-78, exec. com. 1975-77; trustee Hawaii Pacific Coll., 1967-70; chmn. research com. Hawaii Vis. Bur., 1967-72, 77-78; mem. adv. bd. Salvation Army, 1982-84. Served to lt. (j.g.) USNR, World War II. Mem. Nat. Assn. Bus. Econs., Western Econ. Assn. Internat., Am. Statis. Assn., Santa Rosa C. of C., Urban Land Inst., Com. Monetary Research and Edn., Found. Econ. Edn. (trustee 1968—), Am.'s Future (trustee 1974—), Sigma Xi, Tau Beta Pi, Lambda Alpha. Lodge: Rotary. Home: 8830 Oakmont Dr Santa Rosa CA 95405 Office: The Hillendahl Corp PO Box 757 Kenwood CA 95452

HILLER, LARRY KEITH, horticulturist, researcher; b. Morning Sun, Iowa, Apr. 28, 1941; s. Keith B. and Martha R. (Blankenhorn) H.; m. Janet Hutchinson, June 9, 1963; children: Marsha Kay, David Brian. BS, Iowa State U., 1963, MS, 1964; PhD, Cornell U., 1973. Horticultural and edn. advisor Iowa State U. USAID, Uruguay, 1964-67; grad. research asst. Cornell U., Ithaca, N.Y., 1968-73; asst. prof., asst. horticulturist Wash. State U., Pullman, 1973-79, assoc. prof., assoc. horticulturist, 1979—; cons. Internat. Agrl. Devel. Service, Ecuador, 1981-85. Contbr. articles to books. Mem. Am. Soc. Hort. Sci., Internat. Soc. Hort. Sci., Am. Soc. Plant Physiologists, Potato Assn. Am., AAAS. Methodist. Lodge: Kiwanis. Office: Wash State U Dept Horticulture Pullman WA 99164-6414

HILLER, STANLEY, JR., tool company executive; b. San Francisco, Nov. 15, 1924; s. Stanley and Opal (Perkins) H.; ed. Atuzed Prep. Sch.; U. Calif., 1943; m. Carolyn Balsdon, May 25, 1946; children—Jeffrey, Stephen. Dir. Helicopter div. Kaiser Cargo, Inc., Berkeley, Cal., 1944-45; organized Hiller Aircraft Corp. (formerly United Helicopters, Inc.), Palo Alto, Calif., 1945, became pres. and gen. mgr., pres., 1950-64 (co. bought by Fairchild Stratos 1964), mem. exec. com. Fairchild Hiller Corp., 1965; chmn. bd., chief exec. officer Reed Tool Co., Houston; chmn. bd. Baker Internat. Corp., 1975; ptnr. Hiller Investment Co.; dir. Boeing Co., Lucky Stores, Inc.; chmn. bd., chief exec. officer York Internat. Recipient Fawcett award, 1944; Distinguished Service award Nat. Def. Transp. Soc., 1958; named 1 of 10 Outstanding Young Men U.S., 1952. Hon. fellow Am. Helicopter Soc.; mem. Am. Inst. Aeros. and Astronautics, Am. Soc. of Pioneers, Phi Kappa Sigma. Office: Bldg 2 Suite 260 3000 Sand Hill Rd Menlo Park CA 94025

HILLER, TOM W., advertising and publishing executive; b. Santa Monica, Calif., Aug. 8, 1956; s. Walter N. and Ann M. Hiller; m. Margo Leigh Bishop, May 29, 1979 (div. Oct. 1985); 1 child, James Ashland; m. Suanne Lee Sweeton, Feb. 14, 1987. AA in Graphic Design with honors, Santa Monica Coll., 1977. Wardrobe attendant, with art dept. Universal Studios, Universal City, Calif., 1973-78; with advt. sales dept. Hadley Newspapers, Garberville, Calif., 1979-84, gen. mgr., 1985—; prin. T.H.E. Graphic Line, Garberville, 1983—. Chmn. Garberville Redway Design Rev. Bd., Humboldt County, Calif., 1984—. Mem. Calif. Newspaper Pubs. Assn. (Best Spl. Edit. award 1985, Best Overall Display Advt. award 1985), Nat. Newspaper Assn., Garberville Redway C. of C. (v.p. 1983-85). Lodge: Rotary. Office: The Graphic Line PO Box 566 Garberville CA 95440 Office: Redwood Record PO Box 10 432 Maple Ln Garberville CA 95449

HILLIARD, CATHRYN ANN, county official, public affairs management consultant; b. Los Angeles, July 14, 1942; d. Curtis H. and Eva M. (Jessner) Sampson; children: Frederick Roy, Matthew David. AA, Los Angeles Pierce Coll., 1963; BA in Polit. Sci., Calif. State U., Hayward, 1976; cert., U. Calif., Berkeley, 1975. Sec. to congressman Ind., 1966; legis. aide to senator Ind., 1966-69; pub. adminstr., dir. pub. affairs Assn. Bay Area Govts., Oakland, 1970-76; pub. participation coordinator San Francisco Bay Region Wastewater Solids Study, Oakland, Calif., 1976-79, Orange and Los Angeles Counties Water Reuse Study, Los Angeles, 1979—; guest lectr. career devel. U. Calif., Berkeley, 1977, guest lectr. environ. mgmt. Solano Community Coll., Calif., 1979; pub. affairs mgmt. cons., 1979—; dir. pub. affairs Assn. Bay Area Govts., 1985—. Mem. pub. info. com. Am. Cancer Soc., 1976-78. Mem. Am. Soc. Pub. Adminstrn. (dir. San Francisco Sect. 1978), Calif. Water Pollution Control Assn., Nat. Assn. Govt. Communicators, Nat. Assn. County Info. Officers. Clubs: Commonwealth, Town Hall. Home: 547 Browning St Mill Valley CA 94941 Office: PO Box 2050 Oakland CA 94604

HILLIER, BEVIS, magazine editor, author; b. Redhill, Surrey, Eng., Mar. 28, 1940; came to U.S., 1984; s. Jack Ronald and Mary Louise (Palmer) H. Student, Oxford U., 1961. Reporter The Times (of London), 1963-69; dir. pub. relations British Mus., London, 1969-71; editor Connoisseur mag., London, 1973-76; freelance editor 1976-80; features editor Telegraph Sunday mag., London, 1980-82; assoc. editor Los Angeles Times mag., 1984—; guest curator Mpls. Inst. Arts, 1971. Author: Art Deco, 1968, Pottery and Porcelain, 1700-1914, 1968, John Betjeman: A Life in Pictures, 1984. Royal Soc. Arts fellow, 1967; Huntington Library Vis. fellow, 1983. Clubs: Garrick, Beefsteak (London). Avocation: piano. Office: Los Angeles Times Times Mirror Sq Los Angeles CA 90053

HILLIER, DAVID BROWN, academic communications program director; b. Hoytsville, Utah, Jan. 15, 1934; s. Robert Stephen and Minerva (Brown) H.; m. Crystal Smith; children: Debra, Brenda, Cheryl, Stephen, Eric, Dale. BA, Brigham Young U., 1958, MA, 1961. Tchr. Wasatch Sch. Dist., Heber City, Utah, 1958-59; speech pathologist Box Elder Sch. Dist., Brigham City, Utah, 1960-64, 66-68; instr. speech pathology and interpersonal communication Brigham Young U., Provo, Utah, 1965-66; prof. Ricks Coll., Rexburg, Idaho, 1968—. Mem. Am. Speech Lang. Hearing Assn. (cert. clin. competence), Idaho Speech Lang. Hearing Assn. Mormon. Avocations: music, photography, travel. Home: 575 Maple Dr Rexburg ID 83440 Office: Ricks Coll Spori 226 Rexburg ID 83440

HILLIER, GERALD EUGENE, federal agency administrator; b. Portland, Oreg., Dec. 10, 1936; s. Edward J. and Laura (Pierce) H.; m. Judith M. Griswold, Apr. 26, 1958; children: Scott G., Joanne Norman. Student, U. Calif., Davis, 1954-56; BS, Wash. State U., 1958; postgrad., George Washington U., 1966, Oreg. State U., 1969, U. Mont., 1971, U. Calif., Riverside, 1984-85. Range conservationist U.S. Bur. Land Mgmt., Susanville, Calif., 1958-61, Baker, Oreg., 1961-62; range mgr., div. chief U.S. Bur. Land Mgmt., Prineville, Oreg., 1962-64; asst. dist. mgr. U.S. Bur. Land Mgmt., Rock Springs, Wyo., 1964-66; chief soil and watershed U.S. Bur. Land Mgmt., Billings, Mont., 1967-71; dist. mgr. U.S. Bur. Land Mgmt., Salt Lake City, 1971-76; Calif. desert conservation area dist. U.S. Bur. Land Mgmt., Riverside, 1976—; asst. to dir. for liason with pres. of Commn. on Am. Outdoors of U.S. Bur. Land Mgmt., Washinton, 1986-87; mem. adv. council on agr. and natural resources U. Calif., Riverside, 1980—. Contbr. articles to profl. jours. Club: Canyon Crest Country (Riverside) (chmn. bd. govs. 1979-80). Avocations: golf, gourmet cooking, French lang., photography. Home: 801 Apache Trail Riverside CA 92507 Office: US Dept Interiro Bur Land Mgmt 1695 Spruce St Riverside CA 92507

HILLIGASS, RICHARD CHARLES, curator, writer; b. Orange, Calif., June 9, 1951; s. Frank Earl and Helen Elizabeth (Hewitt) H. BA, Brigham Young U., 1975, MA, 1983. Gallery asst. Brigham Young U., Provo, Utah, 1978-81, registrar, 1981-83, curator, 1983-86. Author: (catalogs) The American Image 1830-1940: Selections From the University Museum Collection, 1985, Daniel Baxter Estate, 1987. Avocations: reading, gardening, collecting art. Home: 275 N Main #302 Salt Lake City UT 84103

HILLMAN, ARYE LEO, economics educator; b. U.S. Zone of Occupation, Germany, Jan. 13, 1947; s. Sol and Rosa (Borenstein) H.; m. Jeannette Hillman, Mar. 12, 1967; children: Tamara, Ilana, Nachman Eliyahu, Benjamin. BA with honors, U. Newcastle, Australia, 1967; M in Econs., Macquarie U., Sydney, Australia, 1970; PhD, U. Pa., 1973. Prof. econs. Bar-Ilan U., Ramat Gan, Israel, 1980—; vis. prof. dept. econs. UCLA, 1985-87. Contbr. articles to numerous profl. jours. Mem. Am. Econ. Assn., Western Econ. Assn., Econometric Soc., Pub. Choice Soc. Office: Dept Econs UCLA Los Angeles CA 90024

HILLS, CHRISTIANA DIANE, public relations executive; b. Pasadena, Calif., Apr. 23, 1945; d. Howard Henry and Mona (Skelton) H. AA, Calif. State U., Fullerton, 1965, BA, 1966, MA, 1968. V.p., gen. mgr. Aaron Cushman & Assocs., Beverly Hills, Calif. Mem. Exec. forum (pres. West Los Angeles chpt. 1985-86), Soc. Am. Travel Writers. Office: Aaron Cushman 1801 Century Park E Suite 400 Los Angeles CA 90036

HILLS, FRANCIS ALLAN, geologist; b. Charleston, S.C., Aug. 17, 1934; s. Francis Cooper and Madelene (Steele) H.; m. Sonia Mehech, Aug. 12, 1962; children: Mark, Robert, Valerie. BS, U. N.C., 1956; PhD, Yale U., 1965. Research fellow U. Minn., Mpls.-St. Paul, 1962-65; research assoc. Yale U., New Haven, 1965-68; asst. prof. SUNY, Buffalo, 1968-75; research geologist U.S Geol. Survey, Denver, 1975—. Contbr. articles to profl. jours. Fellow Geol. Soc. Am.; mem. AAAS, Buffalo Bonsai Soc. (pres. 1974), Rocky Mountain Bonsai Soc. (pres. 1979-80), Sigma Xi. Presbyterian. Office: US Geol Survey PO Box 25046 MS 916 Denver CO 80225

HILLYARD, IRA WILLIAM, university administrator, pharmacologist; b. Richmond, Utah, Mar. 23, 1924; s. Neal Jacobsen and Lucille (Duce) H.; m. Venice Lenore Williams, July 10, 1945 (dec.); children: Christine, Kevin, Eric; m. Norma Larsen, May 1, 1970. B.S., Idaho State U., 1949; M.S., U. Nebr., 1951; Ph.D., St. Louis U., 1957. Pharmacologist Mead Johnson Co., Evansville, Ind., 1957-59; sr. pharmacologist, sect. leader Warner-Lambert Research Inst., Morris Plains, N.J., 1959-69; assoc. prof. pharmacology Idaho State U. Coll. Pharmacy, Pocatello, 1969-73, 77-79, dean, 1979-87, prof., 1979—; dir. pharmacology and toxicology ICN Pharms., Irvine, Calif., 1973-77, cons., 1977-80; cons. Pennwalt Pharm. Co., Rochester, N.Y., 1978-

83. Contbr. articles to profl. jours. Served with USN, 1945, 51-53. Decorated Purple Heart. Fellow Am. Found. Pharm. Edn.; mem. Western Pharmacology Soc., Am. Assn. Colls. Pharmacy, Am. Soc. Pharmacology and Exptl. Therapeutics, N.Y. Acad. Scis., Sigma Xi, Rho Chi, Phi Delta Chi. Lodge: Rotary. Home: 2750 Mt Borah Pl Pocatello ID 83201 Office: Idaho State U Box 8288 Pocatello ID 83209

HILLYARD, LYLE WILLIAM, lawyer; b. Logan, Utah, Sept. 25, 1940; s. Alma Lowell and Lucille (Rosenbaum) H.; m. Alice Thorpe, June 24, 1964; children: Carrie, Lisa, Holly, Todd, Matthew. BS, Utah State U., 1965; JD, U. Utah, 1967. Bar: Utah 1967. Pres. Hillyard, Low & Anderson, Logan, 1967—; senator State of Utah, Salt Lake City, 1985—. Rep. chmn. Cache County, Logan, 1970-76; Utah State Rep., 1981-84; pres. Cache County C. of C., 1977. Named Oustanding Young Man, Utah Jaycees, 1972; recipient Disting. Service award, Logan Jaycees, 1972, Merit award Cache Valley council Boy Scouts Am., 1981. Mem. ABA, Utah State Bar Assn., Cache County Bar Assn., Assn. Trial Lawyers Am., Am. Bd. Trial Advocates. Mormon. Club: Big Blue (Logan). Lodge: Kiwanis. Office: Hillyard Low Anderson 175 E First N Logan UT 84321

HILPERT, LOWELL SINCLAIR, geologist, consultant; b. Centralia, Wash., Apr. 9, 1910; s. Reinhold and Lilla Dora (Harrison) H.; m. Doris Althea Rutherford, Oct. 31, 1948; children—Renee Laraine, Michelle Denise. B.S., U. Wash., 1937. Geologist, U.S. Geol. Survey, Washington, 1941-75; geol. cons., Salt Lake City, 1975—; tech. adv. U.S. Geol. Survey Arabian Mission, Jeddah, 1974-75, Departamento Nacional da Producao Mineral, Brazil, Brasilia, 1975. Author: Uranium Resources of NW New Mexico, 1969. Editor: Environmental Geology of Wasatch Front, 1971, 1972; Red Sea research, 1970-75, 1977. Fellow Geol. Soc. Am., AAAS; mem. Soc. Econ. Geologists, Geol. Soc. Washington, Utah Geol. Assn. (pres. 1966, hon. life mem.). Home: 5230 Wander Ln Salt Lake City UT 84117

HILTON, BARRON, hotel executive; b. 1927; s. Conrad Hilton. Founder, pres. San Diego Chargers, Am. Football League, until 1966; v.p. Hilton Hotels Corp., Beverly Hills, Calif., 1954; pres., chief exec. officer Hilton Hotels Corp., Beverly Hills, 1966—, chmn., 1979—, also dir.; mem. gen. adminstrv. bd. Mfrs. Hanover Trust Co., N.Y.C. Address: care Hilton Hotels Corp 9336 Civic Center Dr Beverly Hills CA 90210

HILTON, HART DALE, commercial interiors company executive; b. Los Angeles, May 24, 1913; s. Lewis Dale and Nora Elizabeth (Hart) H.; m. Doris King, May 20, 1939; 1 dau., Margaret Pamela. B.S. in Engring., U. So. Calif., 1936; diploma Naval War Coll., 1955; M.A., Nat. Def. U., 1963. Commd. officer U.S. Navy, 1937, advanced through grades to capt., 1956, exec. asst. dep. chief. naval ops., 1958-59, commd. officer USS Mauna Kea, 1959-60, Aircraft Carrier USS Lexington, 1960-62, asst. to chief naval ops. for Joint Chiefs of Staff matters, 1963-65, ret., 1965; v.p. alumni affairs U. So. Calif., Los Angeles, 1967-81; v.p., div. mgr. Cannell & Chaffin Comml. Interiors, Inc., Los Angeles, 1981-85; pres. Hart Hilton Assocs., 1985—; pres. Hart Hilton Assocs.; guest lectr. World Geography, U. So. Calif., 1975-81. Adv. bd. Los Angeles Philanthropic Soc. Recipient Alumni Merit award U. So. Calif., 1966, Alumni Service award, 1982. Mem. Am. Arbitration Assn., Aircraft Owners and Pilots Assn., Navy League (Commodore Club), Assn. Naval Aviation, World Affairs Council, Newcomen Soc., U. So. Calif. Assocs. (life). Republican. Clubs: Rotary, Wilshire Country. Home: 1 S Orange Grove Blvd #6 Pasadena CA 91105

HILTON, JEFFREY L., marketing professional; b. Salt Lake City, May 7, 1955; s. James Waldo and Faye (Colebrook) H.; m. Karen McPhie, Sept. 7, 1978; children: Adam Jeffrey, James Wallace. BA magna cum laude, U. Utah, 1978; MS, Northwestern U., 1979; postgrad., U. So. Calif. Inst. Advanced Advt. Studies, 1981. Asst. product mgr. S.C. Johnson & Son, Racine, Wis., 1979-81; sr. account exec. Benton and Bowles, Los Angeles, 1981-83; account supr. Dentsu, Young & Rubicam, Los Angeles, 1983-84; v.p. mktg. Bonneville Internat., Salt Lake City, 1984—. Mem. Am. Assn. Advt. Agys., Am. Advt. Fedn., Utah Advt. Fedn., Phi Kappa Phi. Mormon. Avocations: music composition and performance. Home: 1213 E Cassidy Circle Bountiful UT 84010 Office: Bonneville Media Communications 179 Social Hall Ave Salt Lake City UT 84111

HILTON, JOSEPH ROY, JR., civil engineer; b. Oakland, Calif., Dec. 11, 1942; s. Joseph Roy Sr. and Wanda (Fullmer) H.; m. Anita Jeanne Bledsoe, Jan. 23, 1965; children: Kristin Ann, Jennifer Lynn, Angela Jeanne, Sarah Ruth, Elizabeth Laurel, Nicholas Joseph. BSCE, Brigham Young U., 1968. Registered profl. engr., Calif., Idaho, Utah, Wash. Engring. clk. Standard Oil Co. Calif. (name changed to Chevron), San Francisco, 1960-61; mgmt. asst. U.S. Steel, Provo, Utah, 1966-68; project engr. Kaiser Engrs., Oakland, Calif., 1968-74; staff, sr. engr. Morrison-Knudsen Co. Inc., Boise, Idaho, 1974-79, prin. engr., 1979-84; transp. engr. Morrison-Knudsen Engrs., Boise, 1984—. Author: Design Engineering Project Management, 1984. Bd. dirs. N.W. Boise Sewer Dist., 1978-80. Mem. ASCE, Brigham Young U. Mgmt. Soc. (pres. Boise chpt. 1985-86), Tau Beta Pi. Republican. Mormon. Avocations: skiing, boating. Home: 10798 Barnsdale Ct Boise ID 83704 Office: Morrison-Knudsen Engrs 720 Park Blvd Boise ID 83707

HILTON, RANDALL CRAIG, professional surveyor; b. Pueblo, Colo., May 28, 1949; s. Donald J. and Verle E. (Whitcomb) H.; m. Cindy L. Prendergast, Aug. 13, 1958; children: Brian C., Jason E. Degree in civil engring. tech. and design, U. So. Colo., 1974. Registered profl. land surveyor, Colo. Drafter Elliot and Assocs., Pueblo, 1967-70; engring. technician McIntire and Quiros, Pueblo, 1970-73; project mgr. Genge/M&Q, Pueblo, 1973-76; v.p., owner KLH Engring., Pueblo and Colorado Springs, 1976—. Mem. Surface Transp. task force, Colorado Springs, 1985—, El Paso Hwy. Adv., Colorado Springs, 1985—. Served with U.S. Army Res., 1968-74. Mem. Home Builders Assn., C. of C., Am. Congress Survey and Mapping. Republican. Methodist. Avocations: tennis, weight lifting, sports. Home: 5629 Old Farm Circle E Colorado Springs CO 80917 Office: KLH Engring Cons Inc 206 Sutton Ln Colorado Springs CO 80907

HILTON, RONALD, international studies educator; b. Torquay, Eng., July 31, 1911; came to U.S., 1937, naturalized, 1946; s. Robert and Elizabeth Alice (Taylor) H.; m. Mary Bowie, May 1, 1939; 1 dau., Mary Alice Taylor. B.A., Oxford U., Eng., 1933, M.A., 1936; student, Sorbonne, Paris, 1933-34, U. Madrid, 1934-35, U. of Perugia, Italy, 1935-36; student (Commonwealth Fund fellow), U. Calif., 1937-39. Dir. Comité Hispano-Inglés Library, Madrid, 1936; asst. prof. modern langs. U. B.C., 1939-41; assoc. prof. Romance langs. Stanford U., 1942-49, prof., 1949—; dir. Inst. Hispanic Am. and Luso-Brazilian studies; hon. prof. U. de San Marcos, Lima, Peru; vis. prof. U. Brazil, 1949; cultural dir. U. of Air, KGEI, San Francisco; founder, pres. Calif. Inst. Internat. Studies. Author: Campoamor, Spain and the World, 1940, Handbook of Hispanic Source Materials in the U.S, 1942, 2d edit., 1956, Four Studies in Franco-Spanish Relations, 1943, La América Latina de Ayer y de Hoy, 1970, The Scientific Institutions of Latin America, 1970, The Latin Americans, Their Heritage and Their Destiny, 1973; assoc. editor: Who's Who America; editor: The Life of Joaquim Nabuco, 1950, The Movement Toward Latin American Unity, 1969, World Affairs Report, 1970—. Decorated officer Cruzeiro do Sul (Brazil). Mem. Am. Assn. Tchrs. Spanish and Portuguese, Hispanic Soc. of Am., Am. Acad. Franciscan History. Home: 766 Santa Ynez St Stanford CA 94305

HIMENO, EDWARD TORAO, child psychiatrist; b. Honolulu, May 15, 1926; s. Bunzo and Irene Yoshiko (Kudo) H.; B.A., LaSierra Coll., 1950; M.D., Loma Linda U., 1958; m. Miyoko Kusuhara, June 5, 1952; children—Cheryl Aimee, Guy Randall. Intern, Los Angeles County U. So. Calif. Med. Center, 1958-59, resident gen. psychiatry, 1959-62, child psychiatry, 1963-65; practice medicine specializing in child psychiatry, Monterey Park, Calif., 1965—, Cerritos, Calif., 1983—; assoc. prof. psychiatry Loma Linda U. Sch. Medicine, 1967-77, assoc. clin. prof. psychiatry, 1977-80, dir. child psychiatry services, 1967-77; dir. child psychiatry unit Riverside (Calif.) Gen. Hosp., 1972-81; med./clin. dir. Children's Residential Care and Intensive Day Treatment Ctr., Riverside County, Calif., 1981-83; mem. child psychiatry staff Los Angeles County, U. So. Calif. Med. Center, 1962-63, 65-67; cons. Inland Adolescent Clinic, San Bernardino, Calif., 1973-83, Desert Community Mental Health Services, Indio, Calif., 1977-80; cons. child and adolescent unit mental health services San Bernardino County Gen. Hosp., 1973-75; cons. adolescent and young adult program Patton (Calif.) State Hosp., 1968-73, Boy's Republic, Chino, 1970-74, adolescent and adult unit Ingleside Mental Health Center, Rosemead, 1962-81; bd. dirs. Ingleside Mental Health Center, Rosemead, 1974-81, 2d v.p., 1975-81; chmn. med. adv. profl. symposiums, Riverside, Calif., 1979—. Mem. City of Monterey Park Human Relations Commn., 1970. Dist. chmn. Alhambra Monterey Park council Boy Scouts Am., 1969-70. Served with AUS, 1944-45. Recipient several hons. by various profl. and civic groups. Mem. Japanese Am. Med. Assn. (v.p. 1969, 81-82, sec. 1979-80, pres.-elect 1983-85, pres. 1985-86). Home: 1142 Ridgeside Dr Monterey Park CA 91754 Office: 823 S Atlantic Blvd Monterey Park CA 91754-4721 Office: 11544 South St Suite 56 Cerritos CA 90701-6612

HIMSL, MATHIAS ALFRED, state senator Mont.; b. Bethune, Sask., Can., Sept. 17, 1912; s. Victor S. and Clara C. (Engels) H.; came to U.S., 1913; B.A., St. John's U., Collegeville, Minn., 1934; M.A., U. Mont., 1940; m. Lois Louise Wohlwend, July 18, 1940; children—Allen, Marilyn Himsl Olson, Louise Himsl Robinson, Kathleen, Judith Himsl Choury. Tchr., supt. schs., Broadus, Mont., 1934-45; sec. Himsl Wohlwend Motors, Inc., Kalispell, Mont., 1945-68; pres. Skyline Broadcasters, Inc., radio sta. KGEZ, Kalispell, 1958—; part-time instr. Flathead Valley Community Coll., 1969-72; mem. Mont. Ho. of Reps. from Flathead County, 1966-72, Mont. Senate from 3d dist., 1972—. Chmn. Flathead County Republican Com., 1952-64; del. Rep. Nat. Conv., 1964; bd. govs. ARC, 1956-59. Roman Catholic. Club: Elks. Office: 4th Ave E and Center St Kalispell MT 59901

HINCH, STEPHEN WALTER, manufacturing engineer; b. Seattle, July 13, 1951; s. Harlan Delmer and Ivy Roslyn (Thrush) h.; m. Nicolette Constance Obritsch, Sept. 11, 1976; children: Gregory P., Juliana G. BS, MS in Engring., Harvey Mudd Coll., 1974. Mfg. engr. Hewlett-Packard Co., Santa Rosa, Calif., 1974-78; mfg. engring. mgr. Hewlett-Packard Co., Rohnert Park, Calif., 1978-84; corp. SMT program mgr. Hewlett-Packard Co., Palo Alto, Calif., 1984—; instr. Inst. Interconnection and Packaging of Electronic Circuits, Lincolnwood, Ill., 1985—. Contbr. chpts. to books, tech. articles to profl. jours. Mem. Surface Mount Tech. Assn. (bd. dirs.), Electronics Industry Assn. (IPC surface mount council), Internat. Soc. Hybrid Electronics. Republican. Avocations: freelance writing, photography. Office: Hewlett Packard Co 1212 Valley House Dr Rohnert Park CA 94928

HINCKLEY, GORDON B., church official. s. Bryant S. and Ada (Bitner) H.; m. Marjorie Pay, Apr. 29, 1937; children: Kathleen Hinckley Barnes, Richard G., Virginia Hinckley Pearce, Clark B. Cynthia Jane. Missionary Ch. Jesus Christ Latter Day Saints, Britain, 1933-35, mem. Sunday Sch. gen. bd., 1937-46, tchr. ch. sem. system., 1935-36, exec. sec. ch. radio publicity and mission lit. com., 1935-50, counselor East Mill Creek stake, 1946-56, pres. stake 1956-58, asst. to Council Twelve Apostles, 1958-61, mem. council from 1961, noe mem. First Presidency. Office: 1st Pres Mormon Ch 50 E N Temple St Salt Lake City UT 84150 *

HINDMAN, JOSEPH LEE, counseling administrator; b. Baker, Oreg., Dec. 24, 1933; s. Robert L. and Elsa O. (Long) Vandecar; m. Sharon McCord, Oct. 25, 1955; children: Jeffrey, Kathryn, Nancy, James. AB, Harvard U., 1956; MA, U. Oreg., 1958, PhD, 1962. Asst. prof. biology La. State U., New Orleans, 1961-63, SUNY, Buffalo, 1963-67; assoc. prof. U. Ga., Athens, 1967-70; prof., chmn. dept. biology Wash. State U., Pullman, 1970-81, dir. curriculum adv. program, 1981—. Home: NW 1350 Hall Dr Pullman WA 99163 Office: Wash State U Curriculum Adv Program Pullman WA 99164-1033

HINDS, ROBERT JAMES, chemical engineer; b. Minot, N.D., Sept. 29, 1931; s. Lonnie Robert and Mildred Louise (Monson) H. SB, MIT, 1953, SM, 1954. Registered profl. engr., Calif. Chem. engr. E.I. duPont de Nemours & Co., Penns Grove, N.J., Antioch, Calif., Louisville, 1956-62; research engr. Chevron Research Co., Richmond, Calif., 1962-65, group supr., 1965, sr. engring. assoc., 1967, mgr. computer and systems div., 1967-74, sr. environ. engr., 1975—. Contbr. articles to profl. jours.; patentee in field. Pres. Knollwood Townhouses, Inc., San Rafael, Calif., 1977-78. Served as 1st lt. chem. corps AUS, 1954-55. Mem. Am. Inst. Chem. Engrs., Aircraft Owners and Pilots Assn., Sigma Xi, Tau Beta Pi. Club: Commonwealth (San Francisco). Avocation: private pilot.

HINE, JAMES ROBERT, marriage and family relations educator; b. Lafayette, Ind., May 4, 1909; s. Frederick Robert and Nora Christina (Neighborgall) H.; m. Janet Ronald, June 24, 1938; children: Judith, Ronald, Susan. BSME, Purdue U., 1931; MDiv, McCormick Theol. Sem., 1936; DD (hon.), Hanover Coll., 1945. Minister Hanover (Ind.) Presbyn. Ch., 1936-42, McKinley Meml. Presbyn. Ch., Champaign, 1942-67; assoc. prof. marriage and family relations U. Ariz., Tucson, 1968-79, adj. prof., 1979—; pvt. practice marital therapy Tucson, 1968—. Author: What Comes After You Say I Love You, 1980, How to Have a Long, Happy, Healthy Marriage, 1985, The Springtime of Love and Marriage, 1985. Mem. Gov.'s council on Children, Youth and Families, Ariz., 1978-82; pres. Family Life Council of Greater Tucson, 1980-82. Recipient Gov.'s Service award, Ariz., 1978. Mem. Am. Assn. Marriage and Family Therapy, Ariz. Assn. Marriage and Family Therapy (pres. 1980-82), Am. Arbitration Assn. Democrat. Lodge: Kiwanis (pres. Champaign chpt. 1960). Avocations: golf, hiking, swimming. Home: 4961 N Calle Luisa Tucson AZ 85718 Office: U Ariz Sch Family and Consumer Resources Tucson AZ 85721

HINES, JAMES MONROE, mechanical engineer; b. Long Beach, Calif., Oct. 23, 1939; s. Charles Clifford and Helena Mae (Lilla) H.; m. Geraldine Janette Rucker, May 17, 1963; children—Dessa Ann, David James. B.S., Calif. State U.-Long Beach, 1971; M.Engring., UCLA, 1977. Design engr. stamping div. Norris Industries, Los Angeles, 1960-61; project engr. Apollo program Rockwell Internat. Co., Downey, Calif., 1962-70; partner auto repair bus., Bell, Calif., 1970-73; sr. project engr. space shuttle program Rockwell Internat., Downey, 1973-74; prin. mech. engr. nuclear fuel cycle Advanced Tech. div. Fluor Tech., Inc., Irvine, Calif., 1974—; partner UIT Cons.'s, 1970-73. Webelos leader Boy Scouts Am. Mem. Internat. Material Mgmt. Soc. (dir. Los Angeles chpt. 1974-76), Am. Nuclear Soc., Fluor Polit. Action Com., Nat. Rifle Assn. (life). Republican. Baptist. Club: Fluor Suprs., Toastmasters, Masons, Scottish Rite, Shriners (pres. 1983, regional bd. dirs. 1985). Home: 9412 Dewey Dr Garden Grove CA 92641 Office: 3333 Michelson Dr Irvine CA 92730

HINKINS, MARILYN MADSEN, public relations and public affairs executive; b. Manti, Utah, Nov. 11, 1934; s. Donald W. Madsen and Lula Christa (Brady) Christensen; m. Arthur Hinkins, Dec. 11, 1951 (div. June 1966); children: Arthur Lee, Ryan Tay. AA, Coll. Eastern Utah, 1965; postgrad., U. Utah, 1965-66. Pres., owner Hinkins Pub. Relations, Salt Lake City, 1969-72, Phoenix, 1980-85; accounts mgr. Western Creative Advt., Phoenix and Palo Alto, Calif., 1975-76; exec. dir. Ariz. Sign Assn., Phoenix, 1976-82; pub. affairs dir. Am. Express, Salt Lake City, 1985-86; v.p. Joanne Ralston Pub. Relations, Phoenix, 1986—. Mem. Ariz. steering com. Mountain States Legal Found., Phoenix, 1977-83; bd. dirs. Valley Forward Assn., Phoenix, 1983-85, Salt Lake Conv. Bur., 1986, Jr. Achievement of Salt Lake City, 1986; commr. Ariz. Women's Commn., Phoenix, 1977-81, Ariz. Toll Road Study Commn., Phoenix, 1983-85; pres. Utah Young Dems., Salt Lake City, 1966, nat. committeeman, 1967-73. Named One of Outstanding Young Women of Am., Gen. Federated Women's Club, Salt Lake City, 1965. Mem. Pub. Relations Soc. Am., Phoenix Press Club (bd. dirs., v.p. 1982-84), Ariz. Newspaper Assn., Ariz. Soc. Assn. Execs. (bd. dirs. 1977-81), Phoenix C. of C. (bd. dirs. 1979-85). Democrat. Mormon. Club: Soroptimists. Avocations: flying, golfing, camping, fishing, bridge. Home: 4434 N 21st Pl Phoenix AZ 85016 Office: Joanne Ralston & Assocs 3003 N Central Ave Suite 1800 Phoenix AZ 85012

HINKLE, BETTY RUTH, educational administrator; b. Atchison Kans., Mar. 18, 1930; d. Arch W. and Ruth (Baker) Hunt; m. Charles L. Hinkle, Dec. 25, 1950 (div.); children—Karl, Eric. B.A., U. Corpus Christi, 1950; M.S., Baylor U., 1956; M.A., U. North Colo., 1972, Ed.D., 1979. Cert. tchr. Tex., 1950, Mass., 1961, Colo., 1966; cert. adminstr., Colo., 1976. Mem. faculty Alice (Tex.) Independent Sch. Dist., 1950, Waco (Tex.) Ind. Sch. Dist., 1951-52, 1953-58; Hawaii Pub. Schs., Oahu, 1952-53, Newton Pub. Schs., Newtonville, Mass., 1962-63; Colorado Springs (Colo.) Pub. Schs., 1966-75; cons., exec. dir. spl. projects unit Colo. State Dept. Edn., Denver, 1975—; mem. technology com. Colorado Dept. Edn.; alt. foreman Denver Grand Jury, 1983. Recipient Dept. of Edn. Specialists award Colo. Assn. Sch. Execs., 1979, Employee Yr. award Colo. Dept. Edn., 1986. Mem. Am. Assn. School Adminstrs, Colo. Assn. Sch. Execs (coordinating council, 1976-79, v.p. dept. of edn. specialists 1974-75, pres. 1975-76), Assn. for Supervision and Curriculum Devel., Phi Delta Kappa. Republican. Home: 550 E 12th Ave Apt 903 Denver CO 80203 Office: 201 E Colfax Denver CO 80203

HINKLE, BEVERLY JEAN HARRIS, nursing educator; b. Atlanta, Nov. 15, 1948; d. Leonard Edward and Catherine Lynn (Simpson) Harris; m. Richard Paul Hinkle, Aug. 1, 1978. Diploma, Piedmont Hops. Sch. Nursing, 1969; BS in Nursing, Sonoma State U., 1980; MS, U. Calif., San Francisco, 1982. RN; cert. instr. CPR, Multimedia First Aid; cert. Pub. Health Nurse, ARC nurse; cert. advanced cardiac life support provider Am. Heart Assn. Staff nurse Cobb Gen. Hosp., Austell, Ga., 1972-73, French Hosp., San Francisco, 1974; supr. mobile units Irwin Meml. Blood Bank, San Rafael (Calif.) and San Francisco, 1974-76; charge nurse, clin. instr., then relief nursing supr. Sonoma (Calif.) Valley Hosp., 1976-82, relief staff nurse, 1982—; ADN Nursing instr. Santa Rosa (Calif.) Jr. Coll., 1982—, Napa (Calif.) Valley Coll., 1985—; instr. variety nursing courses, 1978—. Pres. Sonoma Assn. Valley Emergency Services. Served with USAF, 1970-72, with Res. 1973-77. Mem. Am. Nurses Assn., Calif. Nurses Assn., Am. Heart Assn. (scientific). Home: PO Box V Boyes Hot Springs CA 95416-1026

HINKLE, LAILA SUSAN, social worker; b. Boston, Sept. 4, 1954; d. Yunis Majid and Grace Lorraine (Hilton) Saeed; m. David Elmer Hinkle, May 11, 1980; 1 child, Jason David, Scott Majid. BA in Psychology, U. Calif., Davis, 1976; MSW, Calif. State U., Fresno, 1978. Lic. clin. social worker, Calif. Counselor San Joaquin Valley Group Homes for Youth, Fresno, 1977-78; clin. social worker Ralph K. Davies Med. Ctr., San Francisco, 1978—; pvt. practice social work First Baptist Ch. and Counseling Ctr., San Carlos, Calif., 1983—; cons. No. Calif. Cancer Program, Palo Alto, Calif., 1980—, Am. Cancer Soc., San Francisco, 1986—. Mem. Nat. Assn. Social Workers, Bay Area Social Workers in Health Care (founder, chmn. 1983—). Democrat. Avocations: tennis, weightlifting, aerobics. Home: 3510 Hillcrest Dr Belmont CA 94002 Office: Ralph K Davies Med Ctr Castro and Duboce San Francisco CA 94114

HINMAN, GEORGE WHEELER, physics educator; b. Evanston, Ill., Nov. 7, 1927; s. Norman Seymour and Bess (Bryan) H.; m. Mary Louise Cauffield, June 19, 1952; children: Norman Field, Lydia Hinman Tukey, Nancy Wheeler. BS in Physics and Math., Carnegie Mellon U., 1947, MS in Physics, 1950, DSc in Physics, 1952. Asst. prof., then assoc. prof. physics Carnegie Mellon U., Pitts., 1952-63; chmn. physics Gen. Atomic Co. subs. Gulf Oil Corp., San Diego, 1963-69; prof. physics, dir. Applied Energy Studies Wash. State U., Pullman, 1969-82, 83—; dir. N.Mex. Energy Research & Devel. Inst., Santa Fe, 1982-83; cons. Los Alamos (N.Mex.) Nat. Lab., 1976—, GAO, 1977—. Author: Dictionary of Energy, 1983; contbr. articles to profl. jours. Grantee NSF, others. Fellow Am. Phys. Soc.; mem. Am. Nuclear Soc., AAAS, Am. Soc. Engring. Edn. Democrat. Avocation: fishing. Home: SW 925 Fountain Pullman WA 99163 Office: Wash State U Room 305 Troy Hall Pullman WA 99164

HINSDALE, JERRY WALTER, physical education educator, swim coach; b. Sacramento, Oct. 17, 1936; s. Elmer George and Mona Delores (Ruhe) H.; m. Jane Martha Abbott, June 20, 1965; children: John Michael, Jill Ann. BA, U. Calif., Davis, 1959. Cert. phys. edn. tchr. Head coach swimming and water polo U. Calif., Davis, 1961—; chmn. NCAA Water Polo Rules com.; conducted nat. clinic for Union Nacional de Entrenadores de Natacion, Barquisimeto, Venezuela, 1983; supr. officials representing Venezuela 1983 Pan Am. Games, Caracas; conducted various internat. and domestic clinics, mem. Organizing com. 1984 Olympic Games, 1983 FINA Cup. Editor Nat. Collegiate Athletic Assn. Water Polo Rule Book, 1983-86. Named NCAA Swimming Coach of Yr., 1974, No. Calif. Athletic Conf. Coach of Yr. in Swimming, 12 yrs., No. Calif. Athletic Conf. Coach of Yr. in Water Polo, 16 yrs.; recipient Elite Coach certification U.S. Water Polo Assn., Highest Honor award, San Cristobal, Venezuela, 1983, Outstanding Contbn. to Swimming medal, Council of Pan Am. Games, 1983. Mem. Am. Swimming Coaches Assn., Coll. Swimming Coaches Assn. Am. (pres., Outstanding Achievement award), U.S. Internat. Olympic Com., Am. Water Polo Coaches Assn. Am. (pres.), U.S. Swimming Coaches Assn. (bd. dirs.), Internat. Swimming Hall Fame (bd. dirs.), Nat. Assn. Sport and Phys. Edn. (appointed to internat. tng. staff 1985). Republican. Achieved most victories of any coach in history of the Far Western Conf. (since 1925). Avocations: sailing, scuba diving, fishing, flying. Home: 739 Elmwood Dr Davis CA 95616 Office: U Calif Athletic Dept Davis CA 95616

HINZ, CHRISTIAN EDWARD, mental health administrator; b. Reading, Pa., Feb. 9, 1937; s. Jacob Wallace and Rhena Lavinia (Childs) H.; m. Martha Louise Potoskie, Dec. 20, 1958; children: Mark, Nadine. BA, Muhlenberg Coll., 1959; MSW, Washington U., St. Louis, 1964; M Pub. Adminstrn., U. Colo., Colorado Springs, 1982. Chief social worker Colo. State Hosp., Pueblo, 1966-69, clin. team leader, 1969-74, clin. adminstr., 1974-79, dir. geriatrics, 1979-80, dir. planning and quality assurance, 1980—; mem. Colo. Mental Health Planning Com., Denver, 1984—. Bd. dirs. Pueblo Community Health Ctr., 1984—. Mem. Nat. Assn. Social Workers (cert.), Am. Assn. Pub. Adminstrn., Mental Health Assn. Colo. Avocations: photography, jogging, scuba diving. Home: 404 Carlile Ave Pueblo CO 81005 Office: Colo State Hosp 1600 W 24th Pueblo CO 81003

HIPP, ARTHUR WILLIAM, surveyor, association administrator; b. Penfield Center, N.Y., Oct. 19, 1925; s. David William and Viola Pearl (Scofield) H.; m. Catherine Ann McGill, Feb. 12, 1944; children: James, Susan, Charles. BA in Geography, Hastings Coll., 1949; Master in Pub. Adminstrn., U. Colo., 1979. Registered land surveyor Alaska, Colo., Ga., Nebr., Wyo. Geologist, engr. Climax (Colo.) Molybdenum Co., 1950-56; surveyor U.S. Forest Service, Denver, 1957-86; sec./treas., exec. dir. Profl. Land Surveyors of Colo. Inc., Arvada, 1986—. Editor jour. Profl. Land Surveyors of Colo. Side Shots, 1975-86. Served with USMC 1942-45. Recipient Citizen Surveyor of Yr. award Profl. Land Surveyors of Colo., 1983. Fellow Nat. Soc. Profl. Surveyors of Am. Congress on Surveying and Mapping (Excellence in Profl. Journalism award 1983), VFW, DAV. Democrat. Roman Catholic. Home and Office: 9660 W 56th Pl Arvada CO 80002

HIRATA, JOSEPH MASAO, manufacturing company executive, computer engineer; b. Fuknoka, Japan, June 1, 1922; came to U.S., 1953; s. Masaichi and Setsuyo (Hirata) H.; m. Yoshie C. Hirata, June 18, 1956. BS, Mil. Acad. Japan, Tokyo, 1943; BS in Physics, Georgetown U., 1957; student, Am. U., 1952-68. Product engr. Sprague Electric Co., Rockville, Md., 1959-67; project leader Lockheed Electronic Co., Greenbelt, Md., 1967-69; aerospace technologist NASA, Goddard, SFC, 1969-72; project engr. DEA, Justice Dept., Washington, 1972-83; gen. mgr., v.p. MTI Engring. Corp., City of Industry, Calif., 1983—; v.p., bd. dirs. Micro Encoder, Inc., Seattle, 1986—. Mem. IEEE. Home: 2409 Fallen Dr Rowland Heights CA 91748 Office: MTI Engring Corp 16839 E Gale Ave Industry CA 91745

HIRATA, RHONDA GAY, advertising executive; b. Oxnard, Calif., Aug. 21, 1953; d. Willis Masato and Marlene Matsuye (Kozuki) H.; m. Donnell Wong Choy, Aug. 25, 1979. B.A., U. Calif.-Berkeley, 1975; grad., Coro Found., 1985. Account exec. McCann-Erickson, Inc., San Francisco, 1976-79, D'Arcy, MacManus & Masius, Inc., San Francisco, 1979-81; account supr. Dancer Fitzgerald Sample, Inc., Corporate Advt. Group, San Francisco, 1981—; chmn. bd. dirs. Kimochi, Inc., San Francisco, 1987. Bd. dirs. Chinatown YWCA, San Francisco, 1980; exec. com. Nihonmachi Polit. Assn., San Francisco, 1981; exec. com. Asian-Am. Dance Collective, San Francisco, 1981; mem. Bay Area Vol. Mktg. Council, Girl Scouts U.S.A., 1983. Democrat. Office: Dancer Fitzgerald Sample Inc Corp Advt Group 1010 Battery St San Francisco CA 94111

HIRD, ELLEN MARIE, food service manager; b. Madison, Wis., June 14, 1954; d. Lyle Francis and Carol Mary (Steiger) H. BS in Dietetics, Coll. St. Teresa, Winona, Minn., 1976. Registered dietitian. Dietetic intern Meth. Hosp., Indpls., 1976-77; regional dietitian Unicare Services, Mpls., 1977-79; asst. dir. food service Lutheran Med. Ctr., Wheat Ridge, Colo., 1979-82; dir. food service Nat. Jewish Hosp., Denver, 1982—; mem. adv. bd. Dietetic

Tech. Front Range Community Coll., Westminster, Colo., 1986. Recipient Bonnie Miller grad. study scholarship Am. Soc. Hosp. Food Service Administrs., 1984-86. Mem. Am. Dietetic Assn. (Young Dietitian of the Yr., 1985), Denver Dietetic Assn., Am. Soc. Hosp. Food Service Administrs. (program com. for annual meeting 1982, nat. nominating com. 1984-85, Bonnie Miller grad. study scholarship 1984-86, v.p. Colo. chpt. 1981, sec., treas. Colo. chpt. 1984-85, pres. elect Colo. chpt. 1985-86, pres. 1986—). Club: Cherry Creek Sporting (Denver). Avocations: skiing, hiking, biking, piano, reading. Home: 1180 S Clarkson St Denver CO 80210 Office: Nat Jewish Hosp 1400 Jackson St Denver CO 80210

HIRSCH, GEOFFREY ALAN, mathematics educator; b. San Francisco, Nov. 10, 1943; s. Monroe Jerome and Winifred Maud (Wilson) H.; m. Francia Marchan Villar, Apr. 21, 1970; children: Afran Abraham, Juleby Anthony. BA, U. Calif., Berkeley, 1966; MA, U. Philippines, Manila, 1975. Instr., Napa Valley Coll., Calif., 1982—, Chabot Coll., Hayward, Calif., 1983—, Vista Coll., Oakland, 1983—, Golden Gate U., San Rafael and Walnut Creek, Calif., 1984—, Coll. San Mateo, Calif., 1984—, Calif. State U., Hayward, 1985—, Ohlone Coll., Fremont, 1985—, DeAnza Coll., Sunnyvale, 1986—; pres. Rent a Prof., Berkeley, Calif., 1983—; past instr. numerous instrns. Author: One-Man Berkeley in the Philippines and Other Autobiographical Jottings, 1971, Birth Poems, 1975; reviewer textbooks. Served with Peace Corps, 1966-70. Mem. Am. Statis. Assn., Math. Assn. Am. Democrat. Home: 2605 Hilgard Ave Berkeley CA 94709

HIRSCH, HORST EBERHARD, metal company executive; b. Woelsendorf, Fed. Republic Germany, July 26, 1933; came to U.S., 1984; s. Albert and Emilie (Eberhardt) H.; m. Helga G. Gruber, May 2, 1961; children: Manon K., Fabiane M., Erin A. Diploma in chemistry, Tech. U. Karlsruhe, Fed. Republic Germany, 1959, D in Chem. Tech., 1961. Postdoctoral fellow NRC of Can., 1961-62; research and devel. engr., mgr. Cominco Ltd., Trail, B.C., Can., 1962-84; pres., chief exec. officer Cominco Electronic Materials Inc., Spokane, Wash., 1984—; bd. of mgmt. B.C. Research Council, Vancouver, 1980-84; senate U. B.C., Vancouver, 1981-85. Contbr. articles on chemistry and metallurgy to profl. publs., chpts. to books. Recipient Excellence in Innovation award Fed. Govt. Can., 1985. Mem. Soc. German Mining and Metall. Engrs., Chem. Inst. Can. Lutheran. Avocations: reading, skiing, swimming. Office: Cominco Electronic Materials Inc East 15128 Euclid Ave Spokane WA 99216

HIRSCH, JANE ELIZABETH, nurse administrator, educator; b. Bonne Terre, Mo., Dec. 26, 1948; d. John George and Rita Bernice (Gaffney) Hirsch; m. Jeffrey L. Splitgerber, Feb. 16, 1979. B.S., U. Mo.-Columbia, 1971; M.S., U. Calif.-San Francisco, 1975. R.N., Calif. Staff nurse U. Mo.-Columbia, 1971; staff nurse U. Calif.-San Francisco, 1971-72, sr. staff nurse, 1972-75, head nurse, 1975-77, staff devel. instr., 1977-79, clin. nurse V, 1979-81, asst. dir. nursing, 1981-85, assoc. dir. nursing, 1985—; asst. clin. prof., asst. dean U. Calif.-San Francisco Sch. Nursing; instr. CPR. Mem. Am. Orgn. Nurse Execs., Calif. Soc. Nursing Service Adminstrs., Sigma Theta Tau. Co-author: Clinical Nursing, 1985; editor: (with Leslie Hannock) Mosby's Manual of Clinical Nursing Procedures, 1981; contbr. articles to profl. jours.; mem. editorial bd. C.V. Mosby Co. Nursing Dictionary.

HIRSCH, JULIA CAROL, management consultant; b. Freeport, Ill., Mar. 18, 1939; d. Muriel Woessner and Lois (Peterman) Woessner Hirsch; m. Konrad Wedekind, Dec. 4, 1985. BA, Stanford U., 1960. Program dir. Stanford (Calif.) U. Alumni Assn., 1960-68; exec. asst. to pres. Calif. Inst. Arts, Valencia, 1968-72; v.p. Nat. Ctr. for Vol. Action, Washington, 1972-74; Calif. Gubernatorial campaign mgr. for Herb Hafif San Francisco, 1974; pres. J.C. Hirsch and Assocs., San Francisco, 1974-78; v.p. Boyden Assocs., Inc., San Francisco, 1978—; mem. Stanford U. Alumni exec. bd. 1973-76, trustee York Sch., 1979—. Mem. Women' Forum West, Human Relations Council, Econ. Round Table. Clubs: World Trade, St. Francis Yacht. Home: 2215 Beach St San Francisco CA 94123 Office: Boyden Internat Inc One Maritime Plaza Suite 1700 San Francisco CA 94111

HIRSCH, MARK BERTRAND, investment company executive, real estate broker; b. Wabasso, Minn., Oct. 27, 1938; s. Francis William and Gladys Elizabeth (Eichten) H.; m. Paulette Jo Ann Szable, Apr. 12, 1969 (div. Mar. 1985); 1 child, Jennifer. BA, U. Minn., 1964; JD, William Mitchell Coll. Law, 1970. Claims rep., supr. St. Paul (Minn.) Ins. Co., 1964-71; sole practice Mpls. and Lamberton, Minn., 1971-82; v.p. Hy-Yield Investments Inc., Phoenix, 1986—, bd. dirs.; ins. claims cons., Phoenix, 1982-86. Com. chmn., treas. Boy Scouts Am., Lamberton, 1976-82. Served with JAG USAF, 1956-60. Mem. ABA, Minn. Bar Assn., Nat. Bd. Realtors, Phoenix Bd. Realtors, Am. Legion (judge advocate Lamberton chpt. 1976-82), William Mitchell Coll. Law Alumni Assn. (pres. 1986). Home: 4358 E Pearce Rd Phoenix AZ 85044 Office: Hy Yield Investments Inc 1236 E Northern Ave Phoenix AZ 85051

HIRSCH, PHYLLIS SINMAN, biochemist, researcher; b. Seattle, Dec. 27; d. Hyman and Eleanor (Paster) Sinman; m. I. Don. Hirsch, July 4, 1967; children: H. Danielle, Moshe Y., Shoshana, Raquelle. BS in Chemistry, Suffolk U.; MS in Biochemistry, U. N.H.; MA in Endocrinology, U. Los Angeles, 1975. Cert. sci. tchr., Calif. Staff scientist Worcester Found. Exptl. Biology, Shrewsbury, Mass., 1967-69; supr. Tay Sachs Nat. Testing Lab., Torrance, Calif., 1975-79; instr. anatomy, physiology Southwest Coll., Inglewood, Calif., 1983—; sci. dept. cons. Bais Yaakov Sch., Los Angeles, 1979. Editor: A Little Bit of This A Little Bit of That, 1975-76; contbr. articles to profl. jours. Base commdr. Fairfax Community Patrol, Los Angeles, 1984—; pres. PTA, Los Angeles, 1980-81. Trustee scholar Suffolk U., 1962-65; U. N.H. research fellowship, 1965-67. Mem. AAAS, Am. Assn. Univ. Profs., Sigma Xi. Avocations: cooking, playing accordian, camping, sewing.

HIRSCH, WERNER ZVI, educator; b. Linz, Germany, June 10, 1920; came to U.S., 1946, naturalized, 1955; s. Waldemar and Toni (Morgenstern) H.; m. Hilde E. Zwirn, Oct. 30, 1945; children—Daniel, Joel, Ilona. B.S. with highest honors, U. Calif., 1947, Ph.D., 1949. Instr. econs. U. Calif., 1949-51; econ. affairs officer UN, 1951-52; economist Brookings Instn., Washington, 1952-53; asst. research dir. St. Louis Met. Survey, 1956-57; prof. econs. Washington U., St. Louis, 1953-63; economist Resources for Future, Inc., Washington, 1958-59; dir. Inst. Govt. and Pub. Affairs, U. Calif. at Los Angeles, also prof. econs., 1963—; scholar in residence Rockefeller Study Center, 1978; cons. Rand Corp., 1958—, U.S. Senate Com. on Pub. Works, 1972, Calif. Senate Select Com. on Structure and Adminstrn. Pub. Edn., 1973, Joint Econ. Com. of Congress, 1975-76, OECD, 1977-80, Edmund G. Brown Inst. Govt., 1981—; mem. com. to improve productivity of govt. Com. Econ. Devel., 1975-76; chmn. Los Angeles City Productivity Adv. Com., 1982—. Author: Introduction to Modern Statistics, 1957, Analysis of the Rising Costs of Education, 1959, Urban Life and Form, 1963, Elements of Regional Accounts, 1964, Regional Accounts for Public Decisions, 1966, Inventing Education for the Future, 1967, The Economics of State and Local Government, 1970, Regional Information for Government Planning, 1971, Fiscal Crisis of America's Central Cities, 1971, Program Budgeting for Primary and Secondary Public Education, 1972, Governing Urban America in the 1970s, 1973, Urban Economic Analysis, 1973, Local Government Program Budgeting: Theory and Practice, 1974, Recent Experiences with National Planning in the United Kingdom, 1977, Law and Economics: An Introductory Analysis, 1979, Higher Education of Women: Essays in Honor of Rosemary Park, 1978, Social Experimentation and Economic Policy, 1981, The Economics of Municipal Labor Markets, 1983, Urban Economics, 1984; editorial bd. Internat. Rev. Law and Econs. Bd. dirs. Calif. Council Environ. and Econ. Balance, 1973—, pres., 1974-79; bd. dirs. Calif. Found. on Economy, 1979—; bd. dirs. U. Calif. Retirement System, 1986—; mem. UCLA Bldg. Authority, 1984—; pres. Am. Friends Wilder Park, 1983-85; pres. Town Hall West of Calif., 1974-79, Friends of Graphic Arts, 1974-79, Am. Friends of Wilder Park, 1983-85; mem. UCLA Bldg. Authority, 1984—, U. Calif. Retirement System Bd., 1986—. Mem. Am., Western econ. assns., Am. Farm Econ. Assn., Western Region Sci. Assn. (dir., pres. 1978-80), Town Hall (chmn. econ. sect.), Los Angeles World Affairs Council, Phi Beta Kappa, Sigma Xi. Home: 11601 Bellagio Rd Los Angeles CA 90049

HIRSCHFIELD, ALAN J., entrepreneur. B.S., U. Okla.; M.B.A., Harvard U. V.p. Allen & Co., Inc., 1959-67; v.p. fin., dir. Warner Bros. Seven Arts, Inc., 1967-68; with Am. Diversified Enterprises, Inc., 1968-73; pres., chief exec. officer Columbia Pictures Industries, N.Y.C., 1973-78; vice chmn., chief operating officer 20th Century-Fox Film Corp., Los Angeles, 1979-81; chmn. bd., chief exec. officer 20th Century-Fox Film Corp., 1981-84; Bd. dirs. Billboard mag., Chappel Intersong, Tanglewood Music Ctr., Jackson Hole Land Trust. Vice chmn. Cancer Research Inst. Mem. Am. Film Inst. (bd. dirs.). Office: Box 871 Wilson WY 83014

HIRSCHMANN, FRANZ GOTTFRIED, aerospace executive; b. Kempten, Fed. Republic Germany, Oct. 4, 1945; came to U.S., 1973; s. Kurt Rudolf G. and Linda (Krieger) H.; m. Martha L. Ossa, Dec. 27, 1978 (div. May 1982). BS, FWG Coll., Cologne, Fed. Republic Germany, 1965; MA, U. Bonn, Fed. Republic Germany, 1973; MBA, Pepperdine U., 1981. Mktg. mgr. Western U.S. and S. Am. regions United Techs./Ambac, Los Angeles, 1978-80; mktg. mgr. Western U.S. and Pacific regions Buehler Inc., Los Angeles and N.C., 1981-83; mgr. internat. ops. Gen. Dynamics, Pomona, Calif., 1983-84, mgr. info. services, 1984—. Author: Mandaic Inscription, 1970; inventor deciphering language computer. Vol. Lincoln Club, Los Angeles, 1981. Mem. Nat. Mgmt. Assn., Pepperdine Alumni Assn., Sierra Club, Retinitis Pigmentosa Found. (co-founder). Republican. Lutheran. Avocations: photography, hiking, sailing, yoga, ancient languages, fluent in 6 langs., reads-writes 12 langs. Home: PO Box 7000-391 Palos Verdes CA 90274 Office: Gen Dynamics #303-5 PO Box 2507 Pomona CA 91769

HIRSON, ESTELLE, ret. educator; b. Bayonne, N.J.; d. Morris and Bertha (Rubinstein) Hirson; student UCLA, U. So. Calif., summers 1949-59, San Francisco, summer 1955, U. Hawaii, 1955; B.E., San Francisco State U., 1965. Tchr. High St. Homes Sch., Oakland, Calif., 1949-54, Prescott Sch., 1955-60, Ralph Bunche Sch., 1960-72; owner Puzzle-Gram Co., Los Angeles, 1946-49; pres. Major Automobile Co., 1948-60. Chpt. v.p. City of Hope, San Francisco, 1962-63; bd. dirs. Sinai-Duarte Nat. Med. Center, 1946-50, also parliamentarian, life mem. Mem. NEA, Calif., Oakland, Los Angeles tchrs. assns., Sigma Delta Tau. Democrat. Mem. Order Eastern Star; Scottish Rite Women's Assn. (v.p. Los Angeles 1982). Rights to ednl. arithmetic game Find the Answer 1948, 51. Home: 8670 Burton Way Apt 328 Los Angeles CA 90048

HIRST, WILMA ELIZABETH, consulting educational psychologist; b. Shenandoah, Iowa; d. James H. and Lena (Donahue) Ellis; m. Clyde Henry Hirst (dec. Nov. 1969); 1 dau., Donna Jean (Mrs. Alan Robert Goss). A.B. in Elementary Edn., Colo. State Coll., 1948, Ed.D. in Ednl. Psychology, 1954; M.A. in Psychology, U. Wyo., 1951. Elem. tchr., Cheyenne, Wyo., 1945-49, remedial reading instr., 1949-54; assoc. prof. edn., dir. campus sch. Nebr. State Tchrs. Coll., Kearney, 1954-56; sch. psychologist, head dept. spl. edn. Cheyenne (Wyo.) pub. schs., 1956-57, sch. psychologist, guidance coordinator, 1957-66, dir. research and spl. projects, 1966-76, also pupil personnel, 1973-84; pvt. cons., 1984—; vis. asst. prof. U. So. Calif., summer 1957, Omaha U., summer 1958, U. Okla., summers 1959, 60; vis. assoc. prof. U. Nebr., 1961, U. Wyo., summer 1962, 64, extension div., Kabul, Afghanistan, 1970, Catholic U., Goias, Brazil, 1974; investigator HEW, 1965-69; prin. investigator effectiveness of spl. edn., 1983—; participant seminar Russian Press Women and Am. Fedn. Press Women, Moscow and Leningrad, 1973. Sec.-treas. Laramie County Council Community Services, 1962; mem. speakers bur., mental health orgn.; active Little Theatre, 1936-60, Girl Scout Leaders Assn., 1943-50; mem. Adv. Council on Retardation to Gov.'s Commn.; mem., past sec. Wyo. Bd. Psychologist Examiners, vice chmn., 1965-74; chmn. Mayor's v.p. Model Cities Program, 1969; mem. Gov.'s Com. Jud. Reform, 1972; adv. council Div. Exceptional Children, Wyo. Dept. Edn., 1974; mem. transit adv. group City of Cheyenne, 1974; bd. dirs. Wyo. Children's Home Soc., treas., 1978—; bd. dirs. Goodwill Industries Wyo., chmn., 1981-83; mem. Wyo. exec. com. Partners of Americas, 1970—, ambassador to Honduras, summer 1979; chmn. bd. SE Wyo. Mental Health Center; elder 1st Presbyn. Ch., Cheyenne, 1978—; chmn. adv. assessment com. Wyo. State Office Handicapped Children, 1980, 81; mem. allocations com. United Way of Laramie County. Named Woman of Year, Cheyenne Bus. and Profl. Women, 1974. Diplomate Am. Bd. Profl. Psychology. Fellow Internat. Council Psychologists (chmn. Wyo. div. 1980—); mem. AAUP, Am. Assn. State Psychology Bds. (sec.-treas. 1970-73), Am., Wyo. (pres. 1962-63) psychol. assns., Laramie County (bd. mem., corr. sec. 1963—, pres.), Wyo. mental health assns. (bd. mem.), Internat. Platform Assn., Am. Ednl. Research Assn., Assn. Supervision and Curriculum Devel., Assn. for Gifted (Wyo. pres. 1964-65), Am. Personnel and Guidance Assn., Am. Assn. Sch. Adminstrs., NEA (life, participant seminar to China 1978), AAUW, Cheyenne Assn. Spl. Personnel and Prins. (pres. 1964-65, mem. exec. bd. 1972-76), Nat. Fedn. Press Women (dir. 1979—), DAR (vice regent Cheyenne chpt. 1975—), AARP (retirement planning specialist 1986—), Psi Chi, Kappa Delta Pi, Pi Lambda Theta, Alpha Delta Kappa (pres. Wyo. Alpha 1965-66). Presbyn. Mem. Order Eastern Star, Daus. of Nile. Clubs: Wyo. Press Women, Zonta (pres. Cheyenne 1965-66, treas. dist. 12 1974). Author: Know Your School Psychologist, 1963; Effective School Psychology for School Administrators, 1980. Home and Office: 3458 Green Valley Rd Cheyenne WY 82001

HIRT, CYRIL WILLIAM, physicist; b. Flushing, N.Y., Dec. 20, 1936; s. Cyril W. and Margret E. (Plumb) H.; m. Virginia L. Warren, June 22, 1968; children: Heather, Amber. BS, U. Mich., 1958, MS, 1959, PhD, 1963. Staff scientist Los Alamos (N.Mex.) Nat. lab., 1963-72, group leader, 1973-80; chief scientist Sci. Applications Inc., La Jolla, Calif., 1972-73; pres. Flow Sci. Inc., Los Alamos, 1980—. Contbr. numerous articles to profl. jours. Mem. AAAS. Avocations: cooking, reading, hiking, skiing. Office: Flow Sci Inc 1325 Trinity Dr Los Alamos NM 87544

HITCH, THOMAS KEMPER, economist; b. Boonville, Mo., Sept. 16, 1912; s. Arthur Martin and Bertha (Johnston) H.; m. Margaret Barnhart, June 27, 1940 (dec. Nov. 1974); children: Hilary, Leslie, Caroline, Thomas; m. Mae Okudaira. Student, Nat. U. Mexico, 1932; A.B., Stanford U., 1934; M.A., Columbia U., 1946; Ph.D., U. London, 1937. Mem. faculty Stephens Coll., Columbia, Mo., 1937-42; spl. study commodity markets Commodity Exchange Adminstrn., Dept. Agr., 1940; acting head current bus. research sect. Dept. Commerce, 1942-43; labor adviser Vets. Emergency Housing Program, 1946-47; economist labor econs. Pres.'s Council Econ. Advisers, 1947-50; dir. research Hawaii Employers Council, Honolulu, 1950-59; sr. v.p., mgr. research div. First Hawaiian Bank, 1959-82; chmn. Hawaii Gov.'s Adv. Com. on Financing, 1959-62; chmn. research com. Hawaii Vistors Bur., 1962-69; chmn. Mayor's Fin. Adv. Com., 1960-68; chmn. taxation and fin. com. Constl. Conv. Hawaii, 1968. Contbr. articles to profl. jours. Trustee Tax Found. of Hawaii, 1955-80, pres., 1968; trustee McInerny Found.; chmn. Hawaii Joint Council Econ. Edn., 1964-68. Served as lt. O.R.C., 1933-38; as lt. USNR, 1943-46. Mem. C. of C. Hawaii (chmn. bd. 1971), Nat. Assn. Bus. Economists, Am., Hawaii econs. assns., Indsl. Relations Research Assn., Am. Statis. Assn., Phi Beta Kappa, Pi Sigma Alpha, Alpha Sigma Phi. Clubs: Waialae Country (pres. 1979), Pacific. Home: 5329 Olapa St Honolulu HI 96821 Office: First Hawaiian Bank Honolulu HI 96847

HITTLE, LEROY MICHAEL, journalist, state ofcl.; b. Onawa, Iowa, June 10, 1912; s. Thomas Jefferson and Mina Abigail (Covert) H.; student Morningside Coll., Sioux City, Iowa, 1934; B.A., Drake U., 1938; m. Helen L.M. Beroen, June 29, 1941 (dec. 1954); 1 son, Leroy Bradley; m. 2d, Joan Byles David, Apr. 2, 1971. With AP, Des Moines, 1934-39, San Francisco, 1939-41, Reno, 1941-43, Olympia, Wash., 1946-67; mem. Wash. Liquor Control Bd., Olympia, 1967-82, chmn., 1981-82; pres. South Sound Pub. Co., pub. Lacey (Wash.) Leader, 1967-68. Promotion chmn., bd. dirs. Southwestern Wash. Evergreen State Coll. Com., 1965-67; chmn. Regional Civic Auditorium Com., 1968-72; pres. chpt. 2 Retired Pub. Employees Council, 1987—. Served with AUS, 1943-46. Recipient 25 Year Service award AP, 1960; Sigma Delta Chi award for outstanding coverage Wash. Legislature, 1960; Gov.'s certificate of merit for 20 years reporting activities Wash. Govt., 1966; Disting. Service award Thurston County Citizen of Yr. Program, 1968, 73. Mem. SAR, Nat. Alcoholic Beverage Control Assn. (pres. 1979-80), Capital City Press Club (past pres.), Sigma Delta Chi, Tau Kappa Epsilon. Lutheran. Clubs: Masons, Shriners, Rotary, Elks; Wash. Athletic (Seattle); Olympia (Wash.) Country and Golf. Home: 5912 Athens Beach Dr NW Olympia WA 98502

HIXSON, FLOYD MARCUS, poultry scientist; b. Holdenville, Okla., May 15, 1918; s. Ovie Faubush and Lola Mary Ann (Lee) H.; m. Martha Elizabeth Williams, Oct. 25, 1941; children: Joyce, Phillip, Mary, Myrna Loy, Thomas. BS, Okla. State U., 1941; MS, Kans. State U., 1948, PhD, 1960. Asst. prof. poultry sci. Okla. State U., Stillwater, 1949-50; prof. Calif. State U., Fresno, 1951-81, prof. emeritus, 1981. Served to 1st lt. inf. U.S. Army, 1942-46, PTO. Decorated Bronze Star. Mem. World's Poultry Sci.Assn., Poultry Sci. Assn., Pacific Egg and Poultry Assn. (exec. com. of sci. adv. com. 1978—), Ret. Pub. Employees Assn. (bd. dirs. Fresno chpt. 1985—), Tenn. Geneal. Soc., Logan County Hist. Soc., Hughes County Hist. Soc., Gideons Internat., Sigma Xi, Phi Kappa Phi. Republican. Baptist. Avocation: bowling. Home: 1712 Harvard Clovis CA 93612

HJELMSTAD, WILLIAM DAVID, lawyer; b. Casper, Wyo., Apr. 4, 1954; s. Alvin Gordon and A. Thecla (Walz) H. A.A. in Social Sci., Casper Coll., 1974; B.S. in Psychology, U. Wyo., 1976, J.D., 1979. Bar: Wyo. 1979, U.S. Dist. Ct. Wyo. 1979. Dept. county pros. atty. Hot Springs County, Thermopolis, Wyo., 1979-80; asst. pub. defender Natrona County, Casper, Wyo., 1980-82; sole practice, Casper, 1981—. Mem. ABA (family law com. 1983-84, adoption com. 1983-84), Wyo. Trial Lawyers Assn., Assn. Trial Lawyers Am., Am. Judicature Soc. Lodges: Elks, Kiwanis. Home: 2242 Thorndike Casper WY 82601

HJORTH, GEORGE EARLING, former army officer, consultant; b. Chgo., Dec. 7, 1922; s. George Louis and Dagmar Sofie (Aarsrud) H.; B.S. in Indsl. Engring., U. Ala., 1949; M.P.A. with highest honors, Western Internat. U., 1984; m. Barbara Marie Wagle, June 3, 1950; children—Debra Marie Hjorth Cluff, Janice Barbara Hjorth Swardson. Commd. 2d lt. U.S. Army, 1949, advanced through grades to col., 1970; mem. C.E., 1949-56; platoon leader, co. exec. officer 3d Engr. Combat Bn., Korea, 1950-51; engr. co. comdr., 1951-52; mem. Ordnance Corps, 1956-75; advanced weapons supply and maintenance officer, 1958-61; project officer Ordnance Bd. and Army Materiel Command Bd. staffs, 1961-64; nuclear weapons officer Hdqrs. U.S. 7th Army, Europe, 1964-66; comdg. officer Navajo Army Depot, Flagstaff, Ariz., 1967-69; project officer U.S. Army Concept Team in Vietnam, 1969-70; comdg. officer Materiel Command Surety Field Office, 1970-73; asst. chief of staff for materiel 2d Support Command VII Corps, Europe, 1973-75; ret., 1975; mgmt. cons., Scottsdale, Ariz., 1975—; mem. Interagy. Bd., U.S. Civil Service Examiners, 1967. Neighborhood commr. Boy Scouts Am., 1968, award, 1938; mem. Phoenix Paradise Valley Village Planning Commn., 1983-85. Served with Signal Corps, AUS, 1942-46; ETO. Decorated Legion of Merit, Bronze Star with oak leaf cluster, Meritorious Service medal, Army Commendation medal with oak leaf cluster (U.S.); Cross of Gallantry with palm (Vietnam); recipient Disting. Service and Commemorative badges German and Polish Labor Service, 1975. Mem. Mil. Order World Wars, Assn. U.S. Army, Am. Def. Preparedness Assn., Ret. Officers Assn. Republican. Club: Rotary. Home: 5902 E Larkspur Dr Scottsdale AZ 85254

HJORTSBERG, WILLIAM REINHOLD, author; b. N.Y.C., Feb. 23, 1941; s. Helge Reinhold and Ida Anna (Welti) H.; m. Marian Souidee Renken, June 2, 1962 (div. 1982); children—Lorca Isabel, Max William.; m. Sharon Leroy, July 21, 1982 (div. 1985). B.A., Dartmouth Coll., 1962; postgrad., Yale Drama Sch., 1962-63, Stanford U., 1967-68. Author: Alp, 1969, Gray Matters, 1971, Symbiography, 1973, Toro! Toro! Toro!, 1974, Falling Angel, 1978, Tales & Fables, 1985, films: Thunder and Lightning, 1977, Legend, 1986; co-author TV film: Georgia Peaches, 1980; contbg. editor: Rocky Mountain mag, 1979; contbr. fiction to Realist, Playboy, Cornell Rev., Penthouse, Oui, Sports Illustrated; contbr. criticism to N.Y. Times Book Rev. Wallace Stegner fellow, 1967-68; Nat. Endowment Arts grantee, 1976. Mem. Authors Guild, Writers Guild Am. Home: Main Boulder Rte McLeod MT 59052 Office: care Robert Dattila Phoenix Literary Agy Inc 315 South F St Livingston MT 59047

HLAVA, MARJORIE MAXINE KIMMEL, information scientist. Student, U. Minn., 1967; BS in Botany and Secondary Edn., U. Wis., 1970; postgrad., U. N.Mex., 1974-76. Info. scientist Tech. Application Ctr. U. N.Mex., Albuquerque, 1975-77, mgr. info., 1977-79; pres., chief ops. officer Access Innovations, Inc., Albuquerque, 1978—; bd. dirs. info. Nat. Energy Info. Ctr. affiliate U.S. Dept. Energy, U. N.Mex., Albuquerque, Documentation Assocs. Inc. Mem. editorial bd. Info. Services and Use, 1983, Database Update, 1984; tech. columnist ONline Re. 1978-81, Info. Today, 1984; contbr. articles to profl. jours. Mem. Spl. Libraries Assn. (chmn. spl. projects com. 1976, employment com. 1978-79, membership com. 1978-79, nominations com. 1983, v.p. local chpt. 1979-80, pres. 1980-81, chmn. info. techs. div. 1984-85, editor info. techs. div. pub.), S.W. Library Assn. (chmn. online bibliographic user group 1976-79), N.Mex. Library Assn. (publicity com. 1981, chmn. nominations com. 1981, chmn. online roundtable 1979, state fair com. 1981-82), Greater Albuquerque Library Assn., Western Info. Network Energy (chmn. edn. com. 1978-81, treas. 1980-84, bd. dirs. 1978-83), N.Mex. Online User Group (chmn. 1976-79), Assn. Info. and Dissemination Ctrs. (pres. 1985-86, 86-87, chmn. 1985, mem. various coms.), N.Mex. Technet Adv. Council, Am. Soc. Info. Sci. (bd. dirs. 1986-87). Office: Access Innovations PO Box 40130 Albuquerque NM 87196

HNATYSHYN, RAMON JOHN, lawyer; b. Saskatoon, Sask., Can., Mar. 16, 1934; s. John and Helen Constance (Pitts) H.; m. Gerda Andreasen; children: John, Carl. BA, U. Sask., Can., JD. Mem. Parliament, Can., 1974—; Queen's Counsel Can., 1973—; Minister Energy, Mines, Resources Govt. of Can., 1979, Minister State Sci. and Tech., chmn. Justice and Legal affairs com., opposition house leader, from 1984, govt. house leader, from 1984, pres. Queen's Privy Council, from 1985, minister regulatory affairs, 1986, minister of justice, atty. gen., 1986—; lectr. in field; pres. UN Assn. Can. Pres. Sask. Gallery and Conservatory Corp.; mem. YMCA kinsmen club; mem. United Way. Mem. Ind. Order Foresters, Saskatoon Bar Assn., Can. Bar Assn. Conservative. Office: House of Commons, Room 135 East Block, Ottawa, ON Canada K1A 0A6

HO, ADÈLE MARIA DZE-LAN, civil engineer; b. Palo Alto, Calif., May 24, 1958; s. David Kuang-Tse and Maria Johanna (De Vries) H. BSCE, Stanford U., 1979, MSCE, 1980; M Engring. in Civil Engring., U. Calif., Berkeley, 1984. Research engr. Lockheed Missiles & Space Co., Sunnyvale, Calif., 1980-82; staff engr. Dames & Moore, San Francisco, 1984—. Mem. ASCE. Democrat. Avocations: sports.

HO, DON, entertainer, singer. With Hilton Hawaiian Village, Honolulu. Office: Hilton Hawaiian Village 2005 Kalia Rd Honolulu HI 96815 *

HO, ELLICK YUE-YAT, clinical perfusionist, consultant; b. Canton, Peoples Republic of China, Aug. 23, 1948; came to U.S., 1970; s. Lai-Yun and Tin-Chee (Tse) H.; m. Polly Pau-Shuan Yang, May 1, 1970; children: Anya, Benjamin. BA, Ohio Dominican Coll., 1974; postgrad., Ohio State U., 1976. Diplomate Am. Bd. Clin. Perfusion. Chief clin. perfusionist Meml. Med. Ctr., Long Beach, 1976—; co-ordinator Perfusion Com., Long Beach, Calif., 1976—; sec. Amsect Region IX, Calif., 1984—. Fellow Am. Bd. Clin. Perfusion; mem. Am. Soc. Extracorporeal Surgery.

HO, HANSON AN-HSIN, architect; b. Nanking, China, Feb. 28, 1947; s. William Wei-Ming and Lan-Ing (Kuo) H.; m. Rachel Apostol; children: Katherine, Kristoffer, Kevin. BArch, Tunghai U., Taichung, Taiwan, 1969; grad. program in urban and regional planning, U. Iowa, 1970-72; postgrad., Harvard U. Grad Sch. Design, 1975. Registered architect, Calif. Research asst. Inst. Urban and Regional Research, Iowa City, 1970-72; planner Space Mgmt. Cons., N.Y.C., 1972-73; chief designer Deck House Inc., Acton, Mass., 1973-78; v.p. Arenco Inc. Architects/Engrs., Whittier, Calif., 1979-82; pres. Hanson Ho & Assocs., Cerritos, Calif., 1982—; pres. Royal Constrn. Corp., Cerritos, 1983—; bd. dirs. Richmark Devel. Corp., Alhambra, Calif. Recipient awards for Preliminary Design of Civic Plaza Project, NEA Am. the Beautiful Fund, Iowa City, 1971, Elderly Housing Project, Housing Authority of Commonwealth Mass., Boston, 1975. Mem. AIA, Constrn. Specification Inst. Republican. Avocations: tennis, photography. Home: 13331 Rusty Fig Circle Cerritos CA 90701 Office: 11480 South St S-209 Cerritos CA 90701

HO, IWAN, research plant pathologist; b. Souzhou, Jiangsu, China, Apr. 15, 1925; came to U.S., 1956; m. Mei-Chun Chang, Nov. 29, 1975; 1 child, Tomur M. BS, Nat. Shanghai U., 1946; MS, La. State U., 1958; PhD, Oreg. State U., 1984. Microbiologist Seattle Pub. Health Dept., 1962-66; research plant physiologist Forestry Scis. Lab., Corvallis, Oreg., 1970—; courtesy asst. prof. Coll. Forestry, Oreg. State U. Mem. Mycol. Soc. Am., Am. Soc. Plant Physiologists, Internat. Soc. Plant Molecular Biology, Sigma Xi. Democrat. Episcopalian. Avocations: painting, violin, stamp collecting. Home: 1686 Bullevard Philomath OR 97370 Office: Forestry Sci Lab Pacific Northwest Research Sta 3200 Jefferson Corvallis OR 97333

HO, PAULINE, chemist; b. Butte, Mont., Dec. 23, 1954; d. Robert Huichen and Catherine (Lu) Ho.; m. Richard James Buss, Apr. 30, 1983. BS in Chemistry, Calif. Inst. Tech., 1976; PhD in Chemistry, U. Calif., 1981. Mem. tech. staff Sandia Nat. Labs., Albuquerque, 1981—. Contbr. articles to profl. jours. Recipient Material Sci. award, Dept. Energy Basic Energy Scis., 1984. Mem. Am. Chem. Soc., Sigma Xi. Home: 13705 Pruitt Dr NE Albuquerque NM 87112 Office: Sandia Nat Labs Div 1126 PO Box 5800 Albuquerque NM 87185

HO, PHILLMAN NANCHIEN, research engineer; b. Shianghai, China, Sept. 4, 1947; came to U.S., 1973; s. Jui-Yung and Wis (King) H.; children: Sunia Y., Amelyn H. BAgr, Taiwan Prov. Coll. Marine/Oceanic Tech., 1971; MS, Ind. U., 1976; PhD, SUNY, Buffalo, 1979. Research engr. Phillips Petroleum Co., Bartlesville, Okla., 1979-81, UNOCAL, Brea, Calif., 1981—. Patentee in field. Chmn. acquisition com. Orange County Cultural Heritage Found., Project Chinese Treasures, Irvine, 1986; loaned exec. United Way, Orange County, 1986. Mem. Am. Chem. Soc., Am. Inst. Chem. Engrs., Chinese Chem. Soc., Tau Beta Pi. Buddhist. Avocations: collecting Chinese art. Home: 5960 Avenida Barcelona Yorba Linda CA 92686 Office: UNOCAL Science and Tech div 376 S Valencia Ave Brea CA 92621

HO, WEILYN (LYNN), travel agency executive; b. Honolulu, Feb. 25, 1937; d. Tai-Chun and Bernice Kwai-Jung Lum; m. Ronald Soon-Kong Ho, July 23, 1961; children: Edward (dec.), Edwyna, Ellyna, Gaylynn. Student Honolulu Bus. Coll., 1954-58. Sec. Aloha Airlines Co., 1958; asst. reservation mgr. Trans-Ocean Airlines, 1958; office mgr. Island Holidays San Francisco, 1959-60, office and sales mgr., salesman Chgo. office, 1960; island holidays groups and conv. mgr. City of Honolulu, 1961-66; with Trade-Wind Tours FIT office, Honolulu, 1966-69; owner, mgr. various gourmet shops and restaurant, Maui, Hawaii, 1969-73; mgr. Valley Island Travel, Wailuku, Maui, 1974-75, Travel Bookings, Lahaina, Hawaii, 1975-76, Maui Travel, Lahaina, 1976-78; pres., mgr., owner Travel Masters Ltd., Lahaina, 1978—; tchr. travel agys. courses. Active Roosevelt High Sch.; active, in-charge of housing Greater Lahaina Reunion 1987; bd. dirs. Salvation Army of Lahaina; vestrywoman Holy Innocents Episcopal Ch.; past dist. chmn. Youth Citizen Award, now by-laws chmn. Mem. Assn. Retail Travel Agts. (dir., past v.p., Hawaii rep. at Western Regional Conf., USSR). Club: Soroptimist (West Maui). Home: 1353 Hoapili St Lahaina Maui HI 96761 Office: Travel Masters Ltd Lahaina Shopping Ctr Office Bldg Suite 210 Lahaina Maui HI 96761

HO, ZONH-ZEN, research chemist; b. Hsin-yin, Taiwan, Republic of China, Jan. 14, 1954; came to U.S., 1976; s. Yin-han and Ching-haw (Chen) H. BS, Nat. Chung-sing U., Taiwan, 1976; MS, Ariz. State U., 1979, PhD, 1983. Research fellow Yakult Food Inc., Taipei, Taiwan, 1976; research assoc. Columbia U., N.Y.C., 1983-84; research scientist U. Ariz., Tucson, 1984—, group leader Surface Lab., 1984—; cons. Modern Tech., Taiwan, 1982—. Author: Raman Spectroscopy, 1982; contbr. articles to profl. jours. Mem. Am. Chem. Soc., Am. Optical Soc. Club: Columbia Table Tennis (N.Y.C.). Avocations: movies, dance, sports. Home: 7 Lane 7 An-ho St, Hsin-ying Republic of China 730 Office: U Ariz Dept Chemistry Tucson AZ 85721

HOAGLAND, ALBERT JOSEPH, JR., psychotherapist, minister; b. Clayton, N.J., July 2, 1939. Cert. psychiat. tech., Ancora State Hosp., 1958; BSN, Monmouth Med. Ctr., 1961; BS, Monmouth Coll., 1964; MSW, Rutgers U., 1966; M.Div., Fuller Theol. Sem., 1978; D in Ministry, Boston U., 1981. Ordained to ministry Disciples of Christ, 1978; lic. clinical social worker, Calif., marriage, family and child counselor, Calif.; cert. tchr.; cert. sch. psychologist, anger therapist. Pvt. practice counseling 1959—; psychiat. technician N.J. State Hosp., 1958-66; instr., cons. Los Angeles County Dept. Probation, 1972-75; instr. psychology Calif. Grad. Inst., 1973; instr. Chapman Coll., 1972-74; instr. psychology Calif. State U., Dominguez Hills, 1974; instr. Torrance (Calif.) Adult Sch., 1977-79, 81-85; pastor Ariz., 1984-85, Calif., 1978-79, 81-84, Mass., 1977-81; subs. tchr. Marana (Ariz.) Sch. Dist., 1985; instr. Beverly Hills Adult Sch., 1984-87; clin. dir. Personal Counseling Services, San Pedro, 1986—; religious educator various retreats, programs, summer camps, etc., 1975—. Author: Anger to Intimacy, 1987; editor Jonestown Collection, 1978, Professional Papers from the Desert, 1970; producer (film) Gestalt Therapy, 1974. Mem. Congress of Disciples Clergy, Disciples of Christ Hist. Soc., Disciples Peace Fellowship; trainer, cons. Los Angeles Council Exploring div. Boy Scouts Am., 1971-74; coach Palos Verdes (Calif.) Soccer Program, basketball Torrance City Sports Program; dir. YWCA Delinquency Prevention Program, San Pedro, 1986—. Mem. Nat. Tchrs. Assn., Nat. Assn. Social Workers, Am. Assn. Marriage and Family Therapists, Am. Sch. Counselors Assn., Psychotherapy Soc., Am. Osteo. Assn., Nat. Assn. Christians in Soc. Work, Harbor Area Police Clergy Council (pres.), Am. Guild Hypotherapists, Clowns of Am., Phi Delta Kappa. Democrat. Lodge: San Pedro Rotary (sec.). Home: 244 1/2 Sepulveda St San Pedro CA 90731 Office: Personal Counseling Services 1044 S Gaffey St #2 San Pedro CA 90731

HOAGLAND, PAMELA REDINGTON, educational consultant, administrator; b. Phoenix, June 2, 1937; d. George Appleton and Margaret Tweed (Rae) H. B.A., U. Ariz., 1959; MEd in Reading Edn., 1965, EdD in Reading and Psychology, 1973. Tchr. Tucson Unified Sch. Dist., 1959-73, asst. dir. instruction, reading, lang. arts, library services, 1980—; co-founder, co-dir. Learning Devel. Ctr., Tucson, 1970-74; curriculum specialist and supr. Pima County Spl. Edn. Coop., Tucson, 1973-76; ednl. cons. Redington Cons. Corp., Tucson, 1970—; founder, pres. Redinton Cons. Corp.; lectr. in field; bd. dirs. Behavior Assocs. Chmn. Ariz. Right to Read Council, 1978-80; bd. dirs. Tucson Westside Coalition, 1979-80, bd. dirs. Friends of Tucson Pub. Library, v.p., 1984—, pres. 1986, 87; edn. supr. Grace Episcopal Ch., 1965-67; pres. Tucson Area Reading Council, 1968; mem. alumni bd. U. Ariz. Coll. Edn., 1984—, pres. 1986-87. Mem. Nat. Council Tchrs. English, Internat. Reading Assn. (field cons.), Ariz. State Reading Council (pres. 1969), Assn. Supervision and Curriculum Devel., Alpha Delta Kappa, Pi Delta Kappa (Disting. lecture series award 1978), Pi Beta Phi Alumni Assn. Democrat. Contbr. articles to profl. publs. Office: 2025 E Winsett St Tucson AZ 85719

HOANG, DUC VAN, theoretical pathologist, educator; b. Hanoi, Vietnam, Feb. 17, 1926; came to U.S. 1975, naturalized 1981; s. Duoc Van and Nguyen Thi (Tham) H.; m. Mau-Ngo Thi Vu, Dec. 1, 1952; 1 child, Duc-An Hoang-Vu. M.D., Hanoi U. Sch. Medicine, Vietnam, 1953. Dean Sch. Medicine Army of the Republic of Vietnam, Saigon, 1959-63; dean Minh-Duc U. Sch. Medicine, Saigon, 1970-71; clin. prof. pathology U. So. Calif. Sch. Medicine, Los Angeles, 1978—. Author: Towards an Integrated Humanization of Medicine, 1957; The Man Who Weights the Soul, 1959; Eastern Medicine, A New Direction?, 1970; also short stories; translator: Pestis, introduction to the work of Albert Camus, Vietnamese translation of La Peste; editor: The East (co-founder); jour. Les Cahiers de l'Asie du Sud-Est. Founder, past pres. Movement for Fedn. Countries S.E. Asia; co-founder, past v.p. Movement for Restoration Cultures and Religions of Orient; active Vo-Vi Meditation Assn. Am. Served to lt. col. M.C., Army of Republic of Vietnam, 1952-63. Mem. AAUP, Am. Com. for Integration Eastern and Western Medicine (founder), Assn. Unitive Medicine (founder, pres.), Assn. for Unitive Medicine (founder-pres.). Republican. Roman Catholic. Clubs: U. So. Calif. Staff, U. So. Calif. Faculty Members (Los Angeles). Home: 3630 S Barry Ave Los Angeles CA 90066-3202 Office: Los Angeles County-U So Calif Med Ctr Interns-Residents Dormitory Room 132 Los Angeles CA 90033-1084

HOBART, DAVID EDWARD, research chemist; b. Middletown, Ohio, Jan. 5, 1949; s. Douglas Blake and Rosemary Therese (Henry) H.; m. Melanie Rae Howard, Aug. 23, 1986; 1 child, Michelle Anne. BA, Rollins Coll., 1971; PhD, U. Tenn., 1981. Postdoctoral research asst. Oak Ridge (Tenn.) Nat. Lab., 1981-83; mem. staff Los Alamos (N.Mex.) Nat. Lab., 1983—; prin. investigator actinides in near-neutral solutions Office Basic Energy Scis. Dept. Energy, 1985—; proposal reviewer NSF, Washington, 1982—. Mem. editorial bd. Lanthanide and Actinide Research, Reidel, The Netherlands, 1985—; contbr. articles to profl. jours. Treas. Young Dems. Club, Rollins Coll., Fla., 1970. Served as sgt. USAF, 1971-75. Mem. Am. Chem. Soc., Los Alamos Geol. Soc., Sigma Xi. Avocations: photography, stained glass, rock collecting, scuba diving. Home: 482 Aragon Ave Los Alamos NM 87544 Office: Los Alamos Nat Lab Isotope and Nuclear Chem Div MS G739 Los Alamos NM 87545

HOBBS, CHARLES H(ENRY), research laboratory administrator; b. Longmont, Colo., Oct. 4, 1942; s. Henry Charles and Kathryn (Letford) H.; m. Suzanne Louise Hayes, June 12, 1963 (div. Apr. 1981); children: Carrie A., Kathryn L. DVM, Colo. State U., 1966. Diplomate Am. Bd. Vet. Toxicology, Am. bd. Toxicology. Toxicologist Lovelace Inhalation Toxicology Research Inst., Albuquerque, 1969-75, asst. dir., 1975—. Contbr. numerous articles to profl. jours. Fellow AM. Acad. Vet. and Comparative Toxicology (sec.-treas. 1978-82); mem. Am. Vet. Med. Assn., Soc. Toxicology, N.Mex. Vet. Med. Assn., Radiation Research Soc. Home: 909 Adams NE Albuquerque NM 87110 Office: Inhalation Toxicology Research Inst PO box 5890 Albuquerque NM 87185

HOBBS, DONALD EARL, range management bureau executive; b. Jay, Okla., May 28, 1936; s. John Emery and Cordelia Elzeen (Downing) H.; m. Marian Elaine Evertz, Nov. 22, 1953 (div. 1957); children—Diane LaNette, Pixie Lynn; m. Jean Sylvia Burt, Oct. 24, 1965; 1 child, Laura Michele. B.S., U. Idaho, 1964; M.B.A., Boise State U., 1978. Agronomist, Idaho Dept Transportation, Boise, 1965-69; asst. area supr. Idaho Dept. Lands, Boise, 1969-76, chief Bur. Range Mgmt., 1976—. Author: Winter Field Key to Shrubs of Idaho, 1964. Pres., Fisher Lateral Assn., Eagle, Idaho, 1974. Mem. Internat. Platform Assn., Idaho Quarter Horse Breeders Assn. Lutheran. Lodge: Elks. Home: Route 1 Eagle ID 83616 Office: Idaho Dept Lands Statehouse Boise ID 83720

HOBBS, MILLICE FLOYD, chemical consultant; b. San Jose, Calif., Dec. 19, 1924; s. Millice Davall and Lillie May (Schneider) H.; m. Nancy Lee Duncan, Aug. 3, 1947; children: Duncan B., Roderick C., Stuart F., Victoria L., Douglas H. Student, San Jose State U., 1943-45; BA, U. Calif., Berkeley, 1948. Analytical chemist Merck & Co., South San Francisco, Calif., 1948-51; head of organic research bioferm div. IMC Corp., San Jose, Calif., 1951-65; sr. research chemist FMC Corp., Santa Clara, Calif., 1965-82; pres. M. Floyd Hobbs & Assocs., Inc., Monte Sereno, Calif., 1983—. Scoutmaster Boy Scouts Am., Santa Clara County, 1959-67, 73-79; dist. commr., 1968-72; life mem. Los Gatos (Calif.) PTA, 1968—. Recipient Silver Beaver award Santa Clara County Boy Scouts Am., 1969. Fellow Am. Inst. Chemists (chmn. Golden Gate Inst. 1986); mem. AAAS, N.Y. Acad. of Sci., Am. Chem. Soc. (chmn. Santa Clara Valley sect. 1969, A. Ottenberg award, 1976), ASCE (affiliate), Am. Soc. Enology and Viticulture (affiliate). Avocations: hiking, fishing, photography, music. Home and Office: 15604 Kavin Ln Monte Sereno CA 95030

HOBBS, NILA ALENE, mfg. co. exec.; b. Colorado Springs, Colo., Mar. 11, 1949; d. Harold Carl and Wilma Ella (French) H.; B.S. with high distinction, Colo. State U., 1971, M.B.A., 1973. Systems analyst Colo. div. Eastman Kodak Co., Windsor, 1974-80, sect. supr. systems devel., 1980-84, sr. systems analyst, 1984—. Mem. Am. Prodn. and Inventory Control Soc, Colo. State U. Alumni Assn., Phi Kappa Phi. Republican. Home: 1037 Parkview Dr Fort Collins CO 80525 Office: ISD Bldg C-42 Floor 3 Windsor CO 80551

HOBERT, LEE GORDON, educator, consultant, therapist; b. Seattle, Jan. 6, 1927; s. Harold Wesley and Emily Ingaborg (Dumert) H.; m. Laura Sherman, June 16, 1948; children—Loralie, Loren; m. 2d, Jimmie Sue Ragsdale, Feb. 18, 1977. B.Th., Northwest Christian Coll., 1950; M.Div., Phillips U., 1955; D. of Humane Letters (hon.), U. Albuquerque, 1973. Ordained to ministry Christian Ch. (Disciples of Christ), 1950; minister, Trent, Oreg., 1948-50, Wichita, Kans., 1950-52, Jefferson, Okla., 1952-55, Okmulgee, Okla., 1958-60, Mesilla Valley Christian Ch., Las Cruces, N.Mex., 1960-74; dir. The Centering Place, Las Cruces, 1975—; cons. El Paso Housing Authority, El Paso Electric, El Paso Community Coll., Tex. Nursing Home Assn., Mescallero Apache Tribe, Bent-Mescallero Elem. Sch., N.Mex. State Coll. Community and Human Services, U. N.Mex. Dept. Continuing Educ., Las Cruces C. of C., 1985-86 Mem. Gov.'s Councils on Older Am., 1965, Migrant work, 1966-67; mem. Taos Pueblo Advocate-Bluelake, 1967; chmn. Citizens Adv. Com., Las Cruces; pres. Community Services Council, 1968-72; pres. State Council Chs., 1964-68; chmn. First Ecumenical bd. dirs. Holy Cross Retreat, 1968-73; chmn. Las Cruces City Beautification Council, 1986, projects div. chmn. 1984, 85. Served with USN, 1944-46. Recipient Community Services award Community Services Council, 1972; N.Mex. Found. for Humanities grantee, 1974. Mem. Assn. Humanistic Psychology, Am. Personnel and Guidance Assn., Am. Assn. Marriage and Family Therapists, Internat. Transactional Analysis Assn., Las Cruces Jaycees (Disting. Service award 1963), N.Mex. Jaycees (Young Man of Yr. 1963). Republican. Established Hospitality House, East Las Cruces Community Center. Home and Office: 745 Baca Rd Las Cruces NM 88001

HOBSON, ROBERT LARRIE, manufacturing company executive; b. Longview, Wash., Jan. 11, 1938; s. Howard Malcolm and Mildred Francis (Mathisen) H.; m. Delois Jean Cash, Feb. 1, 1958; children: L. Scott, Shelly, Karla, Donna. BS, Va. Mil. Inst., 1959; MS, Rensselaer Poly. Inst., 1962, PhD, 1965. Registered profl. nuclear engr. Asst. prof. physics U.S. Mil. Acad., West Point, N.Y., 1965-68; various engring. and mktg. positions Gen. Electric Co., San Jose, Calif., 1968-75; various mktg. mgmt. positions Gen. Electric Co., San Jose, 1979-85, mgr. Pacific Basin Nuclear Services, 1985—; mgr. nuclear applications Gen. Electric Tech. Services Co., San Jose, 1975-78; v.p., dir. Japan Nuclear Fuel Co., Kurihama, 1978-79. Dist. pres. Ch. Jesus Christ Latter Day Saints, Tokyo, 1976-79, high council, Hollister, Calif., 1981-84, bishop, 1984—; scoutmaster San Jose troop Boy Scouts Am., 1969-70. Served to capt., U.S. Army, 1964-68. Mem. Am. Nuclear Soc. (internat. com. 1981—), Soc. of Cin. Republican. Avocations: golf, gardening, raising Christmas trees. Home: 4061 Cienega Rd Hollister CA 95023 Office: Gen Electric Co M/C 394 175 Curtner Ave San Jose CA 95125

HOCH, ORION LINDEL, corporate executive; b. Canonsburg, Pa., Dec. 21, 1928; s. Orion L.F. and Ann Marie (McNulty) H.; m. Jane Lee Ogan, June 12, 1952 (dec. 1978); children: Andrea, Brenda, John; m. Catherine Nan Richardson, Sept. 12, 1980; 1 child, Joe. B.S., Carnegie Mellon U., 1952; M.S., UCLA, 1954; Ph.D., Stanford U., 1957. With Hughes Aircraft Co., Culver City, Calif., 1952-54; with Stanford Electronics Labs., 1954-57; sr. engr., dept. mgr., div. v.p., div. pres. Litton Electron Devices div., San Carlos, Calif., 1957-68; group exec. Litton Components div., 1968-70; v.p. Litton Industries, Inc., Beverly Hills, Calif., 1970, sr. v.p., 1971-74; pres. Intersil, Inc., Cupertino, Calif., 1974-82; pres. Litton Industries, Inc., Beverly Hills, Calif., 1982—, also dir.; dir. Mesurex Corp., Maxim Integrated Products. Trustee Carnegie-Mellon U. Served with AUS, 1946-48. Mem. IEEE, Am. Electronics Assn. (bd. dirs.), Sigma Xi, Tau Beta Pi, Phi Kappa Phi. Office: Litton Industries Inc 360 N Crescent Dr Beverly Hills CA 90210

HOCHBERG, FREDERICK GEORGE, accountant; b. Los Angeles, July 4, 1913; s. Frederick Joseph and Lottie (LeGendre) H.; children: Frederick George, Ann C. Hochberg May. BA, UCLA, 1937. Chief acct., auditor Swinerton, McClure & Vinnell, Managua, Nicaragua, 1942-44; pvt. acctg. practice, Avalon, Calif., 1946-66; designer, operator Descanso Beach Club, Avalon, 1966; v.p. Air Catalina, 1967; treas. Catalina Airlines, 1967; pres. Aero Commuter, 1967; v.p., treas., dir. bus. affairs William L. Pereira & Assocs., Planners, Architects, Engrs., Los Angeles, 1967-72; v.p., gen. mgr. Mo. Hickory Corp., 1972-74; prin. Fred G. Hochberg Assocs., Mgmt. Cons., 1974—; v.p. Vicalton S.A. Mexico, 1976—; v.p., gen. mgr. Solar Engring. Co., Inc., 1977-79; pres. Solar Assocs. Internat., 1979-83. Chmn. Avalon Transp. Com., 1952, Avalon Harbor Commn., 1960, Avalon Airport Com., 1964-66, Harbor Devel. Commn., 1965-66; sec. Santa Catalina Festival of Arts, 1960, Avalon City Planning Commn., 1956-58; pres. Avalon Music Bowl Assn., 1961, Catalina Mariachi Assn., 1961-66; treas. City of Avalon, 1954-62, councilman, 1962-66, mayor, 1964-66; bd. dirs. Los Angeles Child Guidance Clinic, 1975-86, treas., 1978-79, pres., 1979-81; bd. dirs. Los Aficionados de Los Angeles, 1980-86, pres., 1980-83, 87—; pres. Nat Assn. Taurine Clubs, 1982-85. Served as ensign USNR, 1944-45. Named Catalina Island Man of Yr., 1956. Mem. Avalon Catalina Island C. of C. (past pres.), Soc. Calif. Accountants, Mensa, Am. Arbitration Assn. (panel), Catalina Island Mus. Soc. (treas. 1964), El Monte chambers commerce, Town Hall-West (vice chmn.). Lodge: Rotary (Avalon pres. 1956). Home: 6760 Hill Park Dr 505 Los Angeles CA 90068 Office: 52 E Magnolia Blvd Burbank CA 91502

HOCHBERG, HOWARD MARTIN, medical device company executive, physician; b. N.Y.C., Mar. 4, 1935; s. Philip and Jean (Lieber) H.; m. Gaye Marcia Berlfein, Dec. 24, 1957; children—Sharon, Philip, Michael, Jane. B.E., B.A., NYU, 1957; M.D., U. Buffalo, 1961. Intern, resident Montefiore Hosp., N.Y.C., 1961-64; chief med. devel. Heart Disease Control Program USPHS, Washington, 1964-69; fellow in cardiology George Washington U. Hosp., Washington, 1967; v.p. med. services Roche Med., Cranbury, N.J., 1969-81; mng. dir. Cranbury Med., 1981-82; v.p. product devel. Squibb Med., Bellevue, Wash., 1982-83; exec. v.p. med. sci. Internat. Biomedics, Bothell, Wash., 1983—; cardiologist Helene Fuld Med. Ctr., Trenton, N.J., 1972-82; asst. prof. Hahnemann Med. Coll., Phila., 1972-82; cons. Spacelabs, Bellevue, 1984—, Nuclear Pharmacy, Albuquerque, 1984—. Author and editor: Clinical Perinatal Biochemistry, 1981. Contbr. articles to profl. jours. Served to LCDR USPHS, 1964-69. Mem. Soc. Critical Care Medicine, Tau Beta Pi. Jewish. Home: 14474 156th Ave NE Woodinville WA 98072 Office: Internat Biomedics Inc 1631 220th SE Bothell WA 98021

HOCHBERGER, JOHN RICHARD, research engineer; b. Blue Island, Ill., Oct. 18, 1960; s. John Richard and Ruth Bessie (Stevo) H.; m. Marissa Lina Planta, Jan. 11, 1986. BS MetE, U. Wis., 1983. Research engr. Gen. Dynamics Corp., Pomona, Calif., 1983—. Co-inventor chip holding device, 1984. Avocations: real estate investing, hiking, skiing, gardening. Office: Gen Dynamics MZ 50-26 PO Box 2507 Pomona CA 91769

HOCHSCHILD, CARROLL SHEPHERD, company administrator, educator; b. Whittier, Calif., Mar. 31, 1935; d. Vernon Vero and Effie Corinne (Hollingsworth) Shepherd; m. Richard Hochschild, July 25, 1959; children—Christopher Paul, Stephen Shepherd. B.A. in Internat. Relations, Pomona Coll., 1956; Teaching credential U. Calif.-Berkeley, 1957; M.B.A., Pepperdine U., 1985. Cert. elem. tchr., Calif. Elem. tchr. Oakland Pub. Schs. (Calif.), 1957-58, San Lorenzo Pub. Schs. (Calif.), 1958-59, Pasadena Pub. Schs. (Calif.), 1959-60, Huntington Beach Pub. Schs. (Calif.), 1961-63, 67-68; adminstrv. asst. Microwave Instruments, Corona del Mar, Calif., 1968-74; co-owner Hoch Co., Corona del Mar, 1978—. Rep. Calif. Tchrs. Assn., Huntington Beach, 1962-63. Mem. AAUW, Bus. Women's Inst., Internat. Dance-Exercise Found., Nat. Assn. Female Execs. Republican. Presbyterian. Clubs: Toastmistress (corr. sec. 1983), Jr. Ebell (fine arts chmn. Newport Beach 1966-67).

HOCHSTEIN, PAUL, biochemist; b. N.Y.C., Feb. 7, 1926; s. Samuel and Ida (Leshan) H.; m. Gianna Smith, Mar. 9, 1956; children—Miles, Evon. BS, Rutgers U., 1950; MS, U. Md., 1952, PhD, 1954, PhD (hon.) U. Stockholm, 1986. Postdoctoral fellow Nat. Cancer Inst., 1954-57; research assoc. Columbia U., 1957-63; assoc. prof. Duke U., Durham, N.C., 1963-69; prof. toxicology and biochemistry U. So. Calif., Los Angeles, 1969—, dir. Inst. for Toxicology, 1980—, assoc. dean, 1981—. Served with AUS, 1943-46. Recipient Research Career award NIH, 1965-69. Mem. Am. Soc. Biol. Chemists, Soc. for Toxicology, Am. Soc. Pharmacology and Exptl. Therapeutics, Soc. Gen. Physiologists. Contbr. numerous articles to sci. jours. Office: 1985 Zonal Ave Los Angeles CA 90033

HOCK, RONALD FRANCIS, religion educator, historian; b. Elmhurst, Ill., June 15, 1944; s. Francis Allen and Grace Magdalen (Hiltenbrand) H.; m. Carol Elenore Erlandson, June 11, 1966; children: Jennifer Lynne, David Ronald. BA, No. Ill. U., 1966; BD, So. Meth. U., 1969; MPhil, Yale U., 1972, PhD, 1974. Asst. prof. religion U. So. Calif., Los Angeles, 1975-81, assoc. prof., 1981—; mem. steering com. Soc. Biblical Lit. Social History Early Christianity, 1983—; co-dir. Inst. Antiquity and Christianity, Asceticism in the Greco-Roman World, 1985—. Author: The Social Context of Paul's Ministry, 1980; co-author: The Chreia in Ancient Rhetoric, 1986. Mem. Soc. Biblical Lit., Inst. Antiquity and Christianity. Democrat. Congregationalist. Avocations: jogging, reading mysteries, travel. Office: U So Calif Sch ReligionTHH 328 Los Angeles CA 90089-0355

HOCKER, ROSEMARIE OLDOW, elementary school principal; b. Seattle, Dec. 28, 1935; d. Stanley and Mary (Bianchi) O.; m. Robert Warren Hocker, Aug. 19, 1959; children: David Stanley, Lynda Marie. BA in Edn., Western Wash. Coll. Edn., 1957; MA in Edn., Claremont Grad. Sch., 1975. Tchr. Bellevue (Wash.) City Schs., 1957-59, Carmel (Calif.) Schs., 1959-61; tchr. Headstart Riverside (Calif.) County Schs., 1966-67; tchr. nursery sch. Riverside, 1967-69; tchr. spl. edn. Riverside Unified Sch. Dist., 1969-74, tchr., 1975-76, elementary prin. sch., 1976—; extension instr. Univ. Calif., Riverside, 1974. Chpt. sec. ARC, Riverside; mem. Jr. League of Riverside. Mem. NAACP, LWV, Delta Kappa Gamma. Home: 2599 Field Ln Riverside CA 92501 Office: Riverside Unified Sch Dist 3380 14th St Riverside CA 92501

HOCKMAN, KARL KALEVI, transportation and management services executive; b. N.Y.C., Jan. 17, 1924; s. John Laakso and Fanny Maria (Wirtanen) H.; m. Betty Lou Heyle, June 24, 1970; children: William, James Karol, Thomas, David, Kathleen. BA, Shelton Coll., 1956; BD, Bibl. Sem., 1958; cert. in indsl. relations U. Calif.-Berkeley, 1968; cert. in personnel devel. U. Calif., Santa Barbara, 1972. V.p. Schroeder Distbg. Co. No. Calif., Oakland, 1960-66; controller Inland Cities Express, Inc., Riverside, Calif., 1967-70; data processing mgr. Moss Motors, Ltd., Goleta, Calif., 1970-73; controller LKL Industries, Fontana, Calif., 1973-82; mng. ptnr. Hockman & Hockman Assocs., Rialto, Calif., 1982—; chmn. bd. Computer Networking Specialists, Inc., 1983—; sec./treas. Moreno Valley Constrn., Inc., 1986—, also bd. dirs.; bd. dirs. Raemont & Co., Inc., MI Sueno Ranch Nursery, Inc., Quest Electronics Corp. Served with AUS, 1942-45, ETO. Mem. Assn. Computing Machinery, Data Processing Mgmt. Assn., IEEE, Nat. Def. Transp. Assn., N.Y. Acad. Scis., Bibl. Archeol. Soc. Republican. Adventist. Club: Valley Transp. Home: 1224 W Victoria Rialto CA 92376 Office: 1325 N Fitzgerald Suite E Rialto CA 92376

HODDER, EDWIN CLIFTON, investment company executive; b. Denver, July 1, 1955; s. Edwin James and Ruth Lowell (Lierd) H.; m. Susan L. Hodder, 1984. BA cum laude, U. Denver, 1977; MBA, U. Pa., 1979. Founder, pres., bd. dirs. Hodder Sinclair Enterprises, Inc., Casper, Wyo., 1980—; founder, mgr. Car Wash Supply Co., Casper, 1981—, Mountain Soft, 1982—; founder, mgr., bd. dirs. Hodco, Inc., Casper, 1982—. Inventor turn-key box system for self-service timed bus. Francis Ferris Meml. scholar; U. Pa. Wharton fellow. Mem. Omicron Delta Epsilon. Republican. Christian Scientist. Home: 1652 Begonia Casper WY 82604 Office: PO Box 407 Casper WY 82602

HODGE, BRADY JOHNSON, marketing executive; b. Los Angeles, July 8, 1951; s. Fred Johnson and Eileen Louise (Holland) H. B.S., U. Calif.-Berkeley, 1974; M.B.A., UCLA, 1976. Dir. mktg. Heavenly Valley Ski Resort, South Lake Tahoe, Calif., 1976—; pres. bd. dirs. Ski Lake Tahoe; bd. dirs., chmn. mktg. com. South Lake Tahoe Visitors Bur.; part-time instr. Lake Tahoe Community Coll. Chmn. bd. South Lake Tahoe Visitors Bur., 1984; mem. Calif. Gov.'s Tourism Mktg. Adv. Com. Mem. South Lake Tahoe C. of C. (dir.), Assn. M.B.A. Execs. Republican. Club: Lake Tahoe Rotary. Home: PO Box 13081 South Lake Tahoe CA 95702 Office: PO Box AT South Lake Tahoe CA 95705

HODGE, DAVID NASSEA, industrial designer; b. Niagara Falls, N.Y., Apr. 27, 1955; s. Nassea and Angela (McGuth) H.; m. Candace Lynn Fitzgerald, June 25, 1977 (div. Dec. 1985); children: David Justin, Menna Grace, Kirsten Fitzgerald. BArch Indsl. Design, R.I. Sch. Design, 1981. Designer Apple Comuter Inc., Cupertino, Calif., 1981-82, Frog Design, Altensteig, Fed. Republic of Germany, 1982-84; pvt. practice indsl. design Elgranada, Calif., 1984—. Prin. works include consumer appliance products for child care Hasbro Inc., cryptographic tools for NSA and Xerox Ultron Corp., patient seating for hosps. Herman Miller, competition for new office seating family Knoll Internat., side chair, exec. seating Met. Furniture, outdoor lounge furniture Cadwalader & Sangiogio, high density stacking chair Steelcase, wooden side chair Conde House, new innovative castor design Plasticglide. Mem. Indsl. Designers Soc. Am. (cert.). Home and Office: PO Box 824 El Granada CA 94018

HODGES, JAMES CYRIL, advertising agency owner; b. Sacramento, June 29, 1924; s. Cyril George and Ada (Ryals) H.; B.A., U. Pacific, 1950; m. Haroldine Dudley, Aug. 4, 1948. Sales mgr. Radio Sta. KQXR, Bakersfield, Calif., 1957-59; gen. mgr. Radio Sta. KHIQ, Sacramento, 1959-72; ops. mgr. Radio Sta. KEWT, Sacramento, 1972-73; owner Jim Hodges Advt., Sacramento, 1973—. Pres. appliance sect. Sacramento Valley Electric League, 1967-68; asst. mgr. Sacramento Conv. and Visitors Bur., 1975-79. Served with AUS, 1942-45. Recipient Go Devil award Western Oil and Gas Assn., 1953, 54. Mem. Am. Theatre Organ Soc. (chmn. Sierra chpt. 1979-80), Sacramento Traditional Jazz Soc., Sacramento Hist. Soc., Air Force Assn. Home: 5632 McAdoo Ave Sacramento CA 95819 Office: PO Box 15323 Sacramento CA 95851

HODGES, MARK ALEXANDER, safety engineer; b. Kansas City, Mo.; s. Martin Alexander and Lois (Bell) H. BS in Safety Engring., Cen. Mo. State U., 1975, MS in Indsl. Safety, 1976. Safety engr. Tex. Instruments, Dallas, 1978-82; product devel. engr. Direct Safety Co., Phoenix, 1982-84; safety engr. ASM America, Phoenix, 1984—. Bd. dirs. Colonia Del Sur I Homeowners Assn., Tempe, Ariz., 1986; troop leader Boy Scouts Am. Mem. Am. Soc. Safety Engrs. (safety com. chmn. 1984—). Avocations: sailing, hunting, motorcycling.

HODGES, MILLARD B., accountant; b. Toledo, July 31, 1907; s. William Henry and Sarah Helen (Herrington) H.; student Meadville Bus. Coll., 1927-29, bus. adminstrn. Pace Inst., 1935-37; asso. Nat. Inst. Credit, 1940-41; cert. Cades C.P.A. Sch., 1948; m. Helen Isabel Gaut, Aug. 1, 1931; children—Phyllis Marie Hodges Osler, Carol Elaine Hodges Wilson. Telegrapher, Bessemer & Lake Erie R.R., Greenville, Pa., 1927-30; acct. Am. Viscose Corp., Meadville, Pa., 1930-46, costs and budget supr., 1947-52; asst. treas. Ketchikan Pulp Co., Bellingham, Wash., 1952-62, treas., 1962-76, sec., 1964-68, v.p., 1968-76, dir., 1972-76; partner Metcalf, Hodges & Co., C.P.A.s, 1972-87, mng. partner, 1975-77; treas. Mt. Baker (Ski) Recreation Co., from 1968; dir. Savs. Bank Trust Co. N.W., Seattle; adv. bd. Bellingham br. Seattle-1st Nat. Bank; trustee Mt. Baker Mut. Savs. Bank. Instr. asso. course U.S. Army Command and Gen. Staff Coll., Ft. Leavenworth, Kan., 1959-67. Trustee, Western Wash. State Coll., 1969-71, chmn. Found., 1971-77; bd. dirs. Whatcom Med. Bur., 1980—; treas. Whatcom Museum Soc., from 1983. Served from 2d lt. to maj. AUS, 1942-46; ETO; col. Res. Decorated Bronze Star. Mem. Am. Inst. C.P.A.s, Bellingham C. of C. (trustee 1968-74). Republican. Methodist. Clubs: Masons, Rotary. Home: 2351 N Shore Rd Bellingham WA 98226 Office: 10 Prospect Mall Bellingham WA 98225

HODGINS, GRANT MILTON, Canadian cabinet minister; b. Prince Albert, Sask., Can., July 22, 1955; s. William Arnold and Betty Mildred (Finnestad) H. Diploma, Reisch Am. Sch. Auctioneering, 1973; B in Commerce, U. Sask., 1978. Pres. Hodgins Auctioneers Inc., Melfort, Sask., 1978—; instr. Mason City (Iowa) Coll. Auctioneering, 1985-86. Active Progressive Conservative Party, Melfort, 1982-86. Home: PO Box 3310, Melfort CAN SOE 1AO Office: Minister of Highways and Transp, Legis Bldg Room 315, Regina, SK Canada S4S 0B3

HODGMAN, JOAN ELIZABETH, neonatologist; b. Portland, Oreg., Sept. 7, 1923; d. Kenneth E. and Ann (Vannet) H.; m. Amos N. Schwartz, Jan. 30, 1949; children—Ann Vannet, Susan Lynn. B.A., Stanford U., 1943; M.D., U. Calif., San Francisco, 1946. Intern in pediatrics U. Calif. Hosp., San Francisco, 1946-47; resident in pediatrics Harbor Gen. Hosp., Torrance, Calif., 1947-48, Los Angeles County-U. So. Calif. Med. Center, 1948-50; practice medicine specializing in pediatrics South Pasadena, Calif., 1950-52; mem. faculty U. So. Calif. Med. Sch., 1952—, prof. pediatrics, 1969—; dir. newborn div. Los Angeles County-U. So. Calif. Med. Ctr., 1955-86; chmn. med. adv. com. Nat. Found.-March of Dimes, 1972-75; adv. com. Western sect. UNICEF, 1975; med. adv. com. Calif. Legislature, 1970; cons. Calif. Health Dept. Author articles in field, chpts. in books. Recipient cert. appreciation Am. Cancer Soc., 1964, Cameo of Commitment award B'nai B'rith, 1969, Meritorious award Nat. Found.-March of Dimes, 1969; named Woman of Year Calif. Museum Sci. and Industry, 1974, Woman of Year Los Angeles Times, 1976. Mem. Am. Pediatric Soc., Am. Acad. Pediatrics, Am. Thoracic Soc., Western Soc. Pediatric Research, Southwestern Pediatric Soc., Calif. Perinatal Assn., Calif. Med. Assn., Los Angeles County Med. Assn., Los Angeles Pediatric Soc. Home: 494 Stanford Dr Arcadia CA 91006 Office: U So Calif Med Sch 1240 Mission Rd Los Angeles CA 90033

HODGSON, JUDD LAWRENCE, electrical engineer; b. Freeport, Ill., Mar. 3, 1957; s. Sherman Francis and Marilyn June (Greene) H.; m. Linda Christine Cox, Aug. 24, 1985; children: Jason Kirkish, Jennifer Kirkish. ASEE, Highland Coll., Freeport, Ill., 1977; BSEET, LeTourneau Coll., 1980; cert. microcomputer engring., U. Calif., San Diego, 1981. Project engr. Becton & Dickinson, Holdrege, Nebr., 1980-83; elec. engr. IMED Corp., San Diego, 1983—. Mem. Digital Equipment Computer Users Soc. Republican. Mem. Assembly of God Ch. Avocations: computer programming, woodworking. Home: 7586 Windsong Rd San Diego CA 92126 Office: IMED Corp MS 9-1720 9925 Carrol Cyn Rd San Diego CA 92131-1192

HODGSON, KENNETH P., mining executive, real estate investor; b. Canon City, Colo., Sept. 20, 1945; s. Cecil L. and Jaunita J. (Murrie) H.; m. Rebecca K. Thompson, Feb. 15, 1967; 1 child, Amber K.; m. 2d, Rita J. Lewis, Apr. 22, 1979. Student Metro Coll., 1966-68. With Golden Mining Corp., Utah, 1973-79, Windfall Group Inc., Utah, 1976-77; pres. Houston Mining, Ariz., 1979-82; v.p. Silver Ridge Mining, Inc., Gold Ridge Mining Inc., Ariz., 1979-82; pres. Ken Hodgson & Co., Inc., Canon City, 1983—; gen. ptnr. Silver Venture Mines Ltd., Silverton, Colo., 1983—, Riken Resources Ltd., 1985—. Recipient numerous safety awards. Mem. AIME. Republican. Presbyterian. Lodge: Moose. Home: 2995 Jamaica Blvd S Lake Havasu City AZ 86403

HODOS, JAMES JOSEPH, natural resource company manager; b. Pitts., Oct. 21, 1946; s. Joseph Louis and Josephine Rose (Masauskas) H.; m. Ellen Frances Black, July 2, 1977; 1 child, Mark Bartholomew. BA in Geology, Columbia Coll., 1973. Project geologist Placer Service Corp., N.Y.C., 1974-79; project mgr. Placer Service Corp., Grass Valley, CA, 1979-84; pres., cons. Onstream Resource Mgrs., Inc., Carson City, Nev., 1985—. Asst. Fire Marshall, Nevada City (Calif.) Vol. Fire Dept., 1976-84; mem. mental health adv. bd. Nevada County, Calif., 1983-84. Served with U.S. Army, 1968-70, Vietnam. Mem. AIME, Geol. Soc. Am., Calif. Mining Assn., Nev. Mining Assn. Roman Catholic. Lodge: E Clampus Vitus. Avocations: cross-country skiing, karate. Home: 908 Saratoga Way Carson City NV 89701 Office: Onstream Resource Mgrs Inc PO Box 665 Carson City NV 89702

HODSON, SALLY ANN, educator; b. Yonkers, N.Y., June 1, 1950; d. Edward and Margaret (Sinnott) Liberatore; m. Robert Bruce Hodson II, June 29, 1985. BA, Ariz. State U., 1972, MA, 1975; EdD, U. Colo., 1979. Cert. tchr., Colo. Tchr. spl. edn. Gilbert (Ariz.) Sch. Dist., 1973-76; teaching asst. U. Colo., Boulder, 1977-79; dir. edn. Cleo Wallace Ctr., Broomfield, Colo., 1979—; environ. edn. cons. N.Am. Wildlife Ctr. Mem. Council Exceptional Children, Nat. Staff Devel. Council, Council Adminstrs. Spl. Edn., Council Children with Behavior Disorders. Mem. Assn. Supervision and Curriculum Devel., Collegial Assn. Devel. and Renewal of Educators, Nat. Assn. Advancement Humane Edn. Office: PO Box 345 Broomfield CO 80020

HODSON, WILLIAM MYRON, geographic systems analyst, consultant; b. Redlands, Calif., Feb. 22, 1943; s. Myron Cronk and Betty (Vanderwood) H.; m. Gene Leigh Davies, June 25, 1966; children: Theresa, Lisa, Kelli. BA in Biology, U. Redlands, 1965; MA in Botany, UCLA, 1966; PhD, U. S.C., 1971. Fulbright lectr. U. Jordan, Amman, 1974-76; environ. scientist Environ. Systems Research Inst., Redlands, Calif., 1977-82; assoc. prof. remote sensing Asian Inst. Tech., Bangkok, 1982-84; project mgr. TRW Systems, San Bernardino, Calif., 1984—; cons. environ. data base UN Econ. and Social Commn. for Asia and the Pacific Regional Remote Sensing Programme, Bangkok, 1983-84. Contbr. articles to profl. jours. Chmn. com. on nat. and world missions Redlands First Baptist Ch., 1985—. Mem. Am. Soc. Photogrammetry and Remote Sensing. Republican. Home: 835 College Ave Redlands CA 92374 Office: TRW Systems PO Box 1310 San Bernardino CA 92402

HOEKMAN, STEVEN KENT, research chemist; b. Denver, June 5, 1953; s. Steven and Jeanetta Anna (Tebben) H.; m. Sheri L. Hoekman, Aug. 17, 1973 (div. Apr. 1985) children: Matthew Philip, Brian Kent, Gregory James, Jill Marie. BS in Chem., Calvin Coll., 1975; PhD in Organic Chem., Iowa State U., 1980. Research chemist Chevron Research Co., Richmond, Calif., 1980-84, sr. research chemist, 1984—. Mem. Soc. Automotive Engrs. (Arch Colwell Merit award 1985, Horning Meml. award 1985), Am. Chem. Soc. Home: 484 East L St Benicia CA 94510 Office: Chevron Research Co 576 Standard Ave Richmond CA 94802

HOEPTNER, HERBERT WILLIAM, heating and air conditioning company executive; b. Santa Barbara, Calif., Feb. 21, 1922; s. Herbret William and Clara Mae (Ball) H.; m. Annette Avakian, June 17, 1952; children: Herbert W. III, Rahl Eric, Kurt Randall. AA in Math. and Physics, Los Angeles City Coll., 1950; BE with Aero. Sequence, U. So. Calif., 1952. Devel. engr. Marquardt Corp., Van Nuys, Calif., 1952-53; research specialist Rocketdyne Co. div. Rockwell Internat. Corp., Santa Susana, Calif., 1953-59; supr. rocket research United Tech. Ctr., Sunnyvale, Calif., 1959-67; combustion stability specialist Lockheed Air Craft Co., San Jose, Calif., 1967-68; project engr. Gen. Electric, San Jose, Calif., 1968-78; owner Weathermaker Co., Medford, Oreg., 1978—. Inventor Liquid Rocket Injector, Thrust Modulation Liquid Rocket, Liquid Injection-Hybred Rocket. Player and coach YMCA Volleyball Nats., San Jose, 1962, leader calisthenics and jogging, 1965-78; asst. scout master Boy Scouts Am., San Jose, 1965-78. Served with USAAF, 1942-46. Recipient Golden Gloves 2d Place Middle Weight Field Championship award USAAF, 1943. Mem. Am. Soc. Heating, Refrigerating and Air Conditioning Engrs. Inc., Irish Setters Club (field trial chmn. 1953-54), Weimaraner Club. Republican. Club: Oreg. Cattlemans Assn. Avocations: running, hunting, raising pure-bred cattle. Home: 2367 Brownsboro-Meridian Rd Eagle Point OR 97524 Office: Weathermaker Heating & Air 132 S Riverside Ave Medford OR 97501

HOEWING, TIMOTHY DEE, chemical company research technician; b. Taft, Calif., Jan. 6, 1942; s. Lester Dee and Audra Louise (Graves) H.; m. Sherry Kay Elsfelder, July 12, 1962; children: Noel Ann, Tamara Donice. Student, Can. Union Coll., LaCombe, Alta., 1960-61, Walla Walla Coll., 1961-62, Stanislaus State U., 1969-78. Sr. research tech. Shell Devel. div. Shell Corp., Modesto, Calif., 1964—. Contbr: articles to sci. jours. (Shell Recoginition award). Mem. Sigma Xi. Home: 2229 Senimi Circle Ceres CA 95307 Office: Shell Devel Stoddard Rd Salida CA 95368

HOFELDT, FRED DAN, physician; b. Rock Springs, Wyo., Sept. 11, 1936; s. Fred D. and Cecelia (Dolinar) H.; m. Ardyce M. Martin (div. July 1977); children: Fred D. III, Scott M.; m. Laural Hendricks, Dec. 12, 1977; children: LeAnn M., Stacey L. BS, Coll. Idaho, 1959; MD, U. Wash., 1963. Commd. capt. U.S. Army, 1963, advanced through grades to col., retired, 1984; intern, resident in internal medicine Tripler Army Med. Ctr., Honolulu, 1963-67, chief dep. hosp. clinics; fellow in endocrinology U. Calif., San Francisco, 1971; asst. chief med. cons. Office of Surgeon Gen., Washington; chief of endocrinology Fitzsimmons Army Med. Ctr., Denver, U. N.D., Fargo; chief of Endocrinology Denver Gen. Hosp.; prof. medicine U. N.D., U. Colo.; bd. dirs. Vail Diabetic Inst., Denver, dir. 1981-84. Author: Reactive Hypoglycemia; contbr. articles to profl. jours. Decorated Legion of Merit, 1984. Fellow ACP; mem. Endocrine Soc., Am. Diabetic Assn. (bd. dirs.), AAUP, Am. Soc. Clin. Nutrition. Republican. Catholic. Avocations: sports, computer electronics, photography. Home: 6680 E Mansfield Ave Denver CO 80237 Office: Denver Gen Hosp Dept Medicine PO Box 4000 777 Bannock St Denver CO 80204

HOFF, JOHN CLIFFORD, software company executive; b. Lincoln, Nebr., July 21, 1941; s. John Norman and Viola Georgina (Heyne) H.; m. Linda Diane Hoffman, Apr. 27, 1973; children: Nicholas John, Andrew Douglas, Christopher James. BA in Math., Yale U., 1963; MS in Applied Math., Purdue U., 1965, PhD in Computer Sci., 1968. Asst. prof. computer sci. U. San Francisco, 1970-75, chmn. computer sci. dept., 1971-75; v.p., software product designer and mgr. Timeware, Inc., Redwood City, Calif., 1976-86; sr. staff engr. machine vision software Optical Specialties, Inc., Fremont, Calif., 1986—; cons. in field. Author: A Practical Guide to Box-Jenkins Forecasting, 1983. Victor Wilson Fund scholar, 1959-63. Mem. Assn. for Computing Machinery, Am. Statis. Assn., Ops. Research Soc. Am., Math. Assn. Am. Republican. Presbyterian. Home: 533 Dawn Dr Sunnyvale CA 94087 Office: Optical Specialties Inc 4281 Technology Dr Fremont CA 94538

HOFFENBERG, MARVIN, political science educator, consultant; b. Buffalo, July 7, 1914; s. Harry and Jennie Pearl (Weiss) H.; m. Betty Eising Stern, July 20, 1947; children—David A., Peter H. Student, St. Bonaventure Coll., 1934-35; B.Sc., Ohio State U., 1939, M.A., 1940, postgrad., 1941. Asst. chief div. interindustry econs. Bur. Labor Statistics, Dept. Labor, 1941-52; cons. U.S. Mut. Security Agy., Europe, 1952, Statistik Sentralbyra, Govt. of Norway, Oslo, 1955; dir. research, econ. cons. dept. deVegh & Co., 1956-58; economist RAND Corp., 1952-56; staff economist Com. Econ. Devel., 1958-60; project chmn. Johns Hopkins U., 1960-63; dir. cost analysis dept. Aerospace Corp., 1963-65; research economist Inst. Govt. and Pub. Affairs, UCLA, 1965-67, prof.-in-residence polit. sci., 1967-86, prof. emeritus, 1986—; dir. M.P.A. program, co-chmn. Interdepartmental Program in Comprehensive Health Planning UCLA, 1974-76. Author: (with Kenneth J. Arrow) A Time Series Analysis of Inter-Industry Demand, 1959; editor: (with Levine, Hardt and Kaplan) Mathematics and Computers in Soviet Economics, 1967; contbr. articles to profl. jours., chpts. to books. Bd. advisers Sidney Stern Meml. Trust; bd. dirs. Vista del Mar Child Ctr., Los Angeles chpt. Am. Jewish Com., Reiss-Davis Child Study Ctr. C.C. Stillman scholar; Littauer fellow Harvard U., 1946; recipient Disting. service award Coll. Adminstrv. Scis., Ohio State U., 1971. Fellow AAAS; mem. Am. Econ. Assn., History of Sci. Soc., Acad. Polit. Sci. Jewish. Office: Dept Polit Sci U Calif Los Angeles CA 90024

HOFFMAN, ABRAHAM, history educator, researcher; b. Los Angeles, Sept. 25, 1938; s. Harry and Hilda Lya (Sofian) H.; m. Susan Frayda Levine, Nov. 11, 1973; children: Joshua, Gregory. BA, Calif. State U., Los Angeles, 1960; MA, Calif. State U., 1962; PhD, UCLA, 1970. Cert. secondary sch. tchr., Calif. Asst. prof. U. Okla., Norman, 1970-73; instr. Los Angeles Valley Coll., Van Nuys, Calif., 1974-84; tchr. Los Angeles Unified Sch. Dist., 1962-70, 1977—; cons. El Pueblo State Hist. Park, Los Angeles Pub. Library, Los Angeles Dept. Water and Power, 1984—. Author: Unwanted Mexican-Americans in the Great Depression, 1974, Vision or Villainy: Origins of the Owens Valley/Los Angeles Water Controversy, 1981; book editor Californians mag., San Francisco, 1985—; contbr. over 50 articles to profl. jours., newspapers. Postdoctoral fellow NEH; Haynes-Huntington Found. Library fellow, 1985. Mem. Am. Hist. Assn., Western History Assn., Hist. Soc. So. Calif., Orgn. Am. Historians, Los Angeles Corral Westerners (editor 1985—), Acad. Magical Arts Los Angeles. Democrat. Jewish. Office: Franklin High Sch 820 N Ave 54 Los Angeles CA 90042

HOFFMAN, ANITA L., social worker; b. St. Joseph, Mo., Feb. 2, 1960; d. Richard M. and Elaine Y. (Schneider) Hill; m. Robert W. Hoffman, May, 21, 1983. BSW, U. Mo., 1982, MSW, 1983. Lic. social worker, Md. Social worker for adult protective services Prince Georges County Dept. Social Services, Hyattsville, Md., 1983-85; counselor N. Los Angeles Regional Ctr. Devel. Disabled Persons, Panorama City, Calif., 1985—. Mem. Nat. Assn. Social Workers.

HOFFMAN, ANTHONY EARL, vocational educator; b. Detroit, Mar. 31, 1945; s. Earl Joseph and Helen Ruth (Hofland) H.; m. Kathleen Marie Styer, Feb. 14, 1976; children—Timothy, Travis. B.A. in Secondary Edn., Ariz. State U., 1970; M.A. in Indsl. Edn., No. Ariz. U., 1980. Tchr. Coolidge (Ariz.) High Sch., 1970-79; prof. automotive tech. Ariz. Western Coll., Yuma, 1979—; mechanic Garrett Motors, Coolidge, summers 1971, 72. Served with Air Force ROTC, 1965-66. Mem. Coolidge Edn. Assn. (pres. 1976-77). Roman Catholic. Club: Kiwanis (sec.-treas. 1974-76). Office: PO Box 929 Yuma AZ 85364

HOFFMAN, C. FENNO, III, architectural designer; b. Greenwich, Conn., May 28, 1958; s. Harrison Baldwin Wright and Louise Elkins (Sinkler) H.; m. Pia Christina Ossorio, Dec. 27, 1980. BA in Environ. Design, U. Pa., 1983; MArch, U. Colo., 1986. Designer Fenno Hoffman & Assocs., Boulder, Colo., 1983—; pvt. practice designer Boulder, 1985; cons. Summit Habitats, Inc., Denver, 1984—; design cons. The Denver Ptnrship, 1985, Downtown Denver, Inc., 1985. Prin. works include Ca' Venier Mus. for Venice Bienalle, 1985, Cleveland Place Connection, Denver, 1985 (1st prize 1985), hist. renovated house, Boulder, 1986, 3 Gates 3 Squares, Denver, 1986; author: Urban Transit Facility, A Monorail for Downtown Denver, 1985. Mem. AIA (assoc.), Am. Planning Assn., Constrn. Specifications Inst. Democrat. Episcopalian. Clubs: Rallysport Racquet (Boulder). Avocations: photography, motorcycling. Office: 2433 5th St Boulder CO 80302

HOFFMAN, CLIVE, public relations counsel, corporation executive, community education consultant; b. Cape Town, South Africa, July 20, 1937; s. Sydney and Hilda (Bernstein) H.; m. Carol Eunice Rischall, Dec. 18, 1962; children—Jill Lesli, Lisa Kim. B.A. in Communications, UCLA, 1959, postgrad in polit. studies, 1960-62. Prodn. asst. BBC, 1956; assoc. producer Ziv/UA Television, 1959-61; dir. So. Calif. Com. NCCJ, 1961-63; pub. relations account exec. ICPR, 1963-66; pres. Clive Hoffman Assocs. Inc., Los Angeles, 1966—; guest lectr. Calif. State U.-Northridge, U. Judaism., dept. urban Planning U. So. Calif. Mem. Youth Adv. Bd. NCCJ, 1978-83, Urban Affairs Commn. Jewish Fed. Council, Las Angeles, 1982-83, council on Jewish Life; chmn. community affairs advt. com. Los Angeles City Schs., 1971-73; press sec. Cranston for Senate, 1964; pres., sponsor Clive Hoffman Media Scholarship, Los Angeles. Mem. Nat. Assn. Real Estate Editors, Nat. Investor Relations Inst. Soc. Am. Democrat. Contbg. editorial writer on edn., integration and So. Africa, Los Angeles Times, Post Newspapers, West Los Angeles. Office: 3348 Overland Ave Los Angeles CA 90034

HOFFMAN, DARLEANE CHRISTIAN, chemistry educator; b. Terril, Iowa, Nov. 8, 1926; d. Carl Benjamin and Elverna (Kuhlman) Christian; m. Marvin Morrison Hoffman, Dec. 26, 1951; children: Maureane R., Daryl K. B.S., Iowa State U.-Ames, 1948, Ph.D., 1951. Chemist Oak Ridge Nat. Lab., 1952-53; staff mem. Los Alamos Sci. Lab., 1953-71, assoc. leader radiochemistry group, 1971-79, div. leader Chem.-Nuclear Chem. div., 1979-82, div. leader Isotope & Nuclear Chem. Div., 1982-84; prof. chemistry U. Calif., Berkeley, 1984—; faculty sr. scientist Lawrence Berkeley (Calif.) Lab., 1984—; panel leader, speaker Los Alamos Women in Sci., 1975, 79, 82; mem. subcom. on nuclear and radiochemistry Internat. Union Pure and Applied Chemistry, 1978-81, chmn. subcom. on nuclear and radiochemistry, 1982-84; mem. commn. on radiochem. and nuclear techniques Internat. Union of Pure and Applied Chem. Contbr. numerous articles in field to profl. jours. Recipient Alumni Citation of Merit Coll. Scis. and Humanities, Iowa State U., 1978, Disting. Achievement award Iowa State U., 1986; fellow NSF, 1964-65, Guggenheim Found., 1978-79. Fellow Am. Inst. Chemists, Am. Phys. Soc.; mem. Am. Chem. Soc. (chmn. nuclear chemistry and technology div. 1978-79 John Dustin Clark award Central N.Mex. sect., award for Nuclear Chemistry 1983, com. on sci. 1986-88, exec. com. div. of nuclear chem. and tech., 1987-89), N.Mex. Inst. Chemists (pres. 1976-78), Am. Phys. Soc., AAAS. Methodist. Home: 2277 Manzanita Dr Oakland CA 94611 Office: Lawrence Berkeley Lab Berkeley CA 94720

HOFFMAN, DENNIS MARK, polymer scientist; b. Huntingdon, Pa., July 22, 1947; s. Dennis Merle and Ida Gene (Lane) H.; m. Pamela Joyce Jackson, Feb. 13, 1981. BS in Chemistry, Juniata Coll., 1969; PhD in Polymer Sci., U. Mass., 1979. Polymer scientist Lawrence Livermore (Calif.) Nat. Lab., 1979—. Served as sgt. U.S. Army, 1970-72. Mem. Am. Chem. Soc., Am. Phys. Soc., AAAS, Soc. Plastics Engrs., N.Am. Thermal Analysis Soc. Republican. Baptist. Avocations: soccer, kayaking, skiing. Home: 1473 Naples Way Livermore CA 94550 Office: Lawrence Livermore Nat Lab L-338 Livermore CA 94550

HOFFMAN, GEORGE ALAN, consulting company executive; b. Albany, N.Y., May 16, 1937; s. Irving Marshall and Margaret (Coyne) H.; m. Kim Thi Nguyen, Oct. 10, 1971; children: Caroline, Christine. AB, U. Calif., Berkeley, 1980, MBA, 1982. Mgmt. analyst Am. Can Co., N.Y.C., 1966-69; cons. Vietnamese Air Force, Bien Hoa, Vietnam, 1970-74, Puslitbang, Jakarta, Indonesia, 1974-75; pres. Titan Systems, Berkeley, 1980—. Author: Indonesian Production-sharing Oil Contracts, 1982. Mem. Mensa. Club: Commonwealth (San Francisco). Avocation: mountaineering. Office: Titan Systems 2124 Kittredge Suite 65 Berkeley CA 94704

HOFFMAN, HOWARD TORRENS, multi-industry executive, management consultant; b. East St. Louis, Ill., Dec. 30, 1923; s. Edmund Howard and Beulah Esther (Hood) H.; m. Ruth Ann Gisela Koch, June 19, 1947; children: Howard Torrens, Jean Gisele, Glenn Kevin. Student, Iowa State U., 1950; MSEE, Thomas U., 1972, PhD in Mgmt. Sci., 1977. Registered profl. engr., Mo. Head engring. sect. Joy Mfg. Co., St. Louis, 1950-55; missile systems engr. McDonnell Aircraft Corp., St. Louis, 1955-57; exec. engr. IT&T Labs., Ft. Wayne, Ind., 1957-59; mgr. missile systems Litton Inds., College Park, Md., 1959-60; program mgr., chief engr., div. mgr. Teledyne Ryan Co., San Diego, 1960-69; pres. chief. exec. officer Hoffman Assocs., San Diego, 1969—; chmn. bd., exec. dir. H&R Assocs., asset mgr., mgmt. cons., San Diego, 1970—; chief exec. officer, chief fin. officer Hoffman Group, San Diego, 1987—. Patentee in field. Served with U.S. Army, 1943-46. Decorated Bronze Star; recipient Community Service award United Crusade, Univ. Industry Service award, San Diego State U., 1976-77. Mem. AIAA, IEEE, AAAS, Nat. Soc. Profl. Engrs., Am. Mgmt. Assn., Nat. Mgmt. Assn., Assn. U.S. Army, Internat. Platform Assn., Armed Forces Communications and Electronics Assn., Iowa State Alumni Assn. Home: 5545 Stresemann St San Diego CA 92122 Office: PO Box 22010 San Diego CA 92122

HOFFMAN, JACK JOSEPH, tour wholesale company executive; b. San Diego, Dec. 4, 1933; s. Melvin Carl and Betty Julia (Kennedy) H.; m. Bessie May Davis, Nov. 9, 1975; children: Michelle Marie, Kevin Carl. Student, U. Md., Munich, 1958-59, U. Calif. Bakersfield, China Lake, 1960, Brooks Inst. Photography, 1963-64. Mgr. Evergreen Travel Services, Seattle, 1960-80; pres. Evergreen Travel Services, Lynnwood, Wash., 1980—; advisor on facilities for disabled to various orgns. Contbr. articles on travel for the disabled to profl. jours. Coordinator for Wash., Idaho, Mont. Nat. Barrier Awareness Found., Richmond, Va., 1987—. Served with USN, 1953-57. Mem. Am. Soc. Travel Agts., Am. Retail Travel Agts., Eastside Writiers. Republican. Home: 24219 Crystal Lake Rd Woodinville WA 98072 Office: Evergreen Travel Services Inc 19505 44th Ave W Lynnwood WA 98036

HOFFMAN, KRIS, lawyer, shopping center development executive; b. Portland, Oreg., Jan. 5, 1941; s. Lee Hawley and Judith (Scott) H.; m. Elaine Croshier Whitaker; children—Leslie, Kristin, Eric, Carol, Adrienne. B.S., Stanford U., 1962, M.S., 1963, J.D., 1968. Bar: Calif. 1969, U.S. Dist. Ct. (no. dist.) Calif. 1969, U.S. Ct. Appeals (9th cir.) 1969. Assoc. Pettit & Martin, San Francisco, 1969-74; gen. counsel to Sutter Hill Ltd., Palo Alto, Calif., 1975; div. counsel to Kaiser Aetna, Oakland, Calif., 1976; corp. counsel, v.p. store devel. Pay Less Drug Stores, 1977-80; gen. counsel, v.p. store devel., corp. sec. Save Mart Stores, Modesto, Calif., 1980-84; ptnr. Orosco Hoffman, 1984—; lectr. in field. Trustee Meml. Hosp. Found., 1982-85. Stanford U. fellow, 1963. Mem. ABA, Calif. Bar Assn., Fresno County Bar Assn., Internat. Council Shopping Ctrs. Office: Orosco Hoffman 5380 N Fresno St Suite 101 Fresno CA 93710

HOFFMAN, MARVIN, computer company executive; b. Wauwatosa, Wis., July 27, 1933; s. Sam and Anna (Cohen) H.; m. F. Evelyn Lazar, Sept. 28, 1955; children: Loren William, Darryl Scott. BA in Math., Calif. State U., Northridge, 1962. Systems supr. N.Am. Rockwell, 1961-66; dir. software devel. Control Date Corp., 1966-69, Ampex Corp., 1969-72; mgr. software devel. F&M Systems Co., 1972-73; dir. research and devel. div. Computer Machinery Corp., 1973-76; founder, pres., chmn. bd. dirs. XXCAL, Inc., Los Angeles, 1976—; instr., mem. adv. com. Los Angeles City Coll.; past pres. Uaide & Sel Users Group, 1962-72. Served with USN, 1952-56. Mem. AMA, Data Processing Mgrs. Assn., So./Cal/Ten, West Los Angeles C. of C., Alpha Gamma Sigma. Democrat. Jewish. Avocations: skiing, golfing, jogging, bowling. Home: 2423 S Beverly Dr Los Angeles CA 90034 Office: XXCAL Inc 11500 Olympic Blvd Los Angeles CA 90025

HOFFMAN, MICHAEL GENE, electrical engineer; b. Sunnyside, Wash., Oct. 2, 1952; s. Gene Franz and Willvina Elsie (Brink) H.; m. Suzanne Carol Pickgrobe, Apr. 23, 1983. BSEE, U. Portland, 1978. Registered engr. in tng. Staff engr. Pacific Power Co., Portland, Oreg., 1978-79; project engr. Saudi Electric Co., Dhahran, Saudi Arabia, 1980-81, 1983; planner Alusuisse Services, Puerto Ordaz, Venezuela, 1981-82; project engr. Pacific Engring., Portland, 1984-86; cons. Compix, Portland, 1984. Active World Affairs Council, Portland, 1984—, Com. for Human Rights in Latin Am., 1985—. Served with U.S. Army, 1973-74. Mem. IEEE (sect. chmn. 1981, pace chmn. 1985, monthly columnist for Portland sect. 1985—, Centenial medal 1984), ACLU. Avocations: clam digging, world travel, scuba. Home: 7466 N Fiske Portland OR 97203

HOFFMAN, SARGENT GLENN, III, chemical company purchasing agent; b. Chico, Calif., May 27, 1946; s. Sargent Glenn Jr. and Marjorie Day (Nickerson) H.; m. Judith Ann Krebs, June 20, 1970; children: Stephanie, Jaime, Bonnie. BSME, U. Calif., Davis, 1972; MBA, Santa Clara U., 1985. Registered profl. engr., Calif. Research engr. Dow Chem. Co., Walnut Creek, Calif., 1973; design engr. Dow Chem. Co., Torrance, Calif., 1974-78; project engr. Raychem Corp., Menlo Park, Calif., 1979-80; sr. buyer Raychem Corp., Menlo Park, 1981—. Patentee in field. Coach Am. Youth Soccer Orgn., Cupertino, Calif., 1985—, Bobbi Sox Softball, Cupertino, 1985—. Served with USAF, 1965-68, Vietnam. Mem. Soc. Plastics Engrs. Republican. Avocation: car restoration. Home: 2315 Friars Ln Los Altos CA 94022 Office: Raychem Corp 300 Constitution Dr Menlo Park CA 94025

HOFFMAN, WAYNE MELVIN, retired airline official; b. Chgo., Mar. 9, 1923; s. Carl A. and Martha (Tamillo) H.; m. Laura Majewski, Jan. 26, 1946; children—Philip, Karen, Kristin. B.A. summa cum laude, U. Ill., 1943, J.D. with high honors, 1947. Bar: Ill. bar 1947, N.Y. bar 1958. Atty. I.C. R.R., 1948-52; with N.Y.C. R.R. Co., 1952-67, exec. asst. to pres., 1958-60, v.p. freight sales, 1960-61, v.p. sales, 1961-62, exec. v.p., 1962-67; chmn. bd. N.Y. Central Trans. Co., 1960-67, Flying Tiger Line, Inc., 1967-86, Tiger Internat., Inc., 1967-85; trustee Aerospace Corp., 1975-86; dir. Rohr Industries; dir. Kaufman & Broad, Inc.; mem. vis. com. Grad. Sch. Mgmt., U. Calif. at Los Angeles, 1972—; mem. bus. adv. com. Northwestern U. Transp. Center, 1972—. Served to capt. inf. AUS, World War II. Decorated Silver Star, Purple Heart with oak leaf cluster. Mem. Am. Bar Assn., Phi Beta Kappa. Clubs: Calif., Bel Air Country (Los Angeles), Bohemian (San Francisco). Home: Vintage CC Indian Wells CA 92210 Office: 970 Los Vallecitos Blvd Suite 224 San Marcos CA 92069

HOFFMAN, WILLIAM GEORGE, physician; b. Allentown, Pa., July 17, 1945; s. Donald B. and Margaret (Gruber) H.; m. Susan Emily Evans, Aug. 10, 1968; children—Andrea, Laura. B.S., Muhlenberg Coll., 1967; M.D., Temple U., 1971. Intern, Hunterdon Med. Center, Flemington, N.J., 1971-72, resident in family practice, 1972-74; family practice physician, adminstr. Yuba Feather Health Center, Brownsville, Calif., 1974—, health planner, 1974-80; health planning cons. Yuba Feather Rural Health Services, 1980-82; mem. Yuba-Sutter sub-area health council Golden Empire Health Systems Agy., 1976-81; chief dept. family practice Fremont Hosp., Yuba City, Calif., 1985—, exec. com. mem., 1985—; bd. dirs. Foothill Community Bank N.A. Pres. Yuba Feather Recreation Com., 1978—; co-chmn. Friends of Yuba Feather Sch., 1981—; bd. dirs. Yuba Feather Communities Services, 1981—; founder Brownsville Mountain Fair, 1975, chmn., 1975, 77. Served with USPHS, 1974-76. Recipient Community Recognition award USPHS, 1976, Seventh-day Adventist Public Service award, 1980; Yuba Feather Rural Health Systems grantee, 1977-80, Calif. Proposition II Park grantee, 1978, 81, Roberti-Z'Berg Park Fund grantee, 1979, Adolescent Stop Smoking grantee, 1979, Calif. Park Bond grantee, 1984. Mem. Am. Assn. Family Practitioners, Calif. Med. Soc., Yuba-Sutter-Colusa Med. Soc., Alpha Omega Alpha, Phi Alpha Theta. Republican. Office: Yuba Feather Health Center PO Box 609 Brownsville CA 95919

HOFFMAN, WILLIAM JAY, service executive; b. Chgo., Apr. 28, 1944; s. Charles A. and Marion F. (Johnson) H.; m. Judy M. Maxwell, July 3, 1970; children: Jennifer, Eric. BS, Western State U. Coll. Law, 1974, JD, 1976. Bar: Calif. 1976; cert. hotel adminstr., Calif.; real estate broker, Calif. Acct. supr. Chgo. & Eastern Ill. R.R., 1964-66; comml. mgr. Ill. Bell Telephone, Chgo., 1967-70; v.p. Trigild Corp., San Diego, 1971-81, pres., 1982—; bd. dirs. Calif. Lodging Industry Assn., Sacramento. Contbr. articles to mags. Mem. ABA, Calif. Bar Assn., Internat. Council Hotel-Motel Mgmt. Cos., Calif. Hotel-Motel Assn., Calif. Lodging Industry Assn., Inst. Real Estate Mgmt. Avocations: fly fishing, travel, piano. Office: Trigild Corp 12760 High Bluff Dr San Diego CA 92130

HOFFMAN-BEUKE, KATHY OTT, architectural designer; b. Allentown, Pa., July 7, 1946; s. Richard Eli and Kathryn Elizabeth (Ott) Tucker; m. Edward George Hoffman, Aug. 27, 1966 (div. June 1985); children: Edward George II, Kristina Kaye; m. Kenneth Walter Beuke, June 1, 1986. Student, Pikes Peak Community Coll., 1964-66; AAS in Med. Sci., Pa. State, 1966. Owner KH Graphics, Colorado Springs, Colo., 1979—; archtl. designer Capp Homes, Colorado Springs, Colo., 1979-82, cons., 1972-82; cons. U. Colo., Colorado Springs, 1986—; cons. various nat. publs., 1982—; drafting bd. advisor Dist. 11 Schs., Colorado Springs, 1980—. Author: Shop Math, 1981, Blueprint Reading, 1981, Engineering Fundamentals, 1982, Metrication for Engineers, 1983; illustrator: Life Safety Code Handbook, 1985. Mem. Am. Inst. Design and Drafting, U.S. Metric Assn. (nat. mem. chmn. 1981—, Spl. Citation award 1984). Club: Summit Singles (Colorado Springs) (sec. 1985—). Avocations: all crafts, model making, sight-seeing, traveling. Office: K H Graphics 3052 A Delta Dr Colorado Springs CO 80910

HOFFMANN, FRANZ JOSEF, biology educator, researcher; b. Bad Reinerz, Germany, July 15, 1945; s. Franz Josef and Marga Emilie (Voss) H.; m. Heidrun Irene Kannt; children—Marcia Anja, Carsten. Dr. rer. nat. in Plant Physiology, U. Hohenheim, Stuttgart, Fed. Republic Germany, 1974; Dr. habil. in Cell Biology and Genetics, U. Kaiserslautern, Fed. Republic Germany, 1980. Project leader Max-Planck-Inst. for Plant Genetics, Ladenburg, Fed. Republic Germany, 1974-78; group-leader Max-Planck-Inst. for Cell Biology, Ladenburg, 1978-82; lectr. U. Kaiserslautern, 1979-82; asst. prof. biology, U. Calif.-Irvine, 1982-83, assoc. prof., 1983—. Author, editor, reviewer for profl. publs. Numerous research grants, U.S.A., Japan, Fed. Republic Germany, 1978—. Mem. various sci. socs. Home: 4 Curie Ct Irvine CA 92715 Office: U Calif Devel and Cell Biology Dept Irvine CA 92717

HOFFMANN, GEORGE L., surgeon, medical administrator; b. Pitts., May 15, 1926; s. George L. and Dorothy (Hurlock) H.; m. Jewel Hunt; children—Kathryn Lee, Jon Hunt. A.B., Haverford Coll., 1949; M.D., Yale U., 1953. Diplomate Am. Bd. Surgery. Resident in surgery Phila. Gen. Hosp. and Cleve. Clinic, 1954-58; practice medicine specializing in surgery, Mesa, Ariz., 1958—; pres. Surg. Inst. of Mesa, 1958—. Served to 2d lt. U.S. Army, 1944-46. Fellow ACS (bd. regents 1975-84, exec. com. 1982-84); mem. AMA, Ariz. Med. Assn., Maricopa County Med. Assn. (pres. 1981). Episcopalian. Office: 438 W 5th Pl Mesa AZ 85201

HOFFMANN, GEZA GEORGE, manufacturing company executive; b. Budapest, Hungary, July 8, 1940; came to U.S., 1978; s. Geza Oscar and Anna (Goergenyi) H.; m. Sarolta Helen Csanyi, Apr. 2, 1976. BS in Organic Chemistry, U. Technology, Vienna, Austria, 1962, MS in ChemE, 1974. Sr. chem. engr. Sigmapharm, Vienna, 1971-75; product mgr. Merck Pharms., Vienna, 1975-78; sr. chemist ICN Pharms., Irvine, Calif., 1978-80; dir. mfg. Canon Bus. Machines Inc., Costa Mesa, Calif., 1980—. Mem. Am. Chem. Soc., N.Y. Acad. Scis., Am. Mgmt. Assn. Republican. Roman Catholic. Avocations: tennis, bridge, classical music. Home: 26 Tahoe Irvine CA 92715 Office: Canon Bus Machines Inc 3191 Red Hill Ave Costa Mesa CA 92626

HOFFMANN, JON ARNOLD, aeronautical engineering educator; b. Wausau, Wis., Jan. 13, 1942; s. Arnold D. and Rita J. (Haas) H.; m. Carol R. Frye. BSME, U. Wis., 1964, MSME, 1966. Register profl. engr., Calif. Research engr. Trane Co., 1966-68; prof. aeronautical engring. Calif. Poly. State U., San Luis Obispo, 1968—; research engr. Stanford U. NSF Program, 1970; research fellow Ames Research Ctr. Ctr. NASA/ASEE, 1974-75; tech. cons. NASA/AMES Research Ctr., 1977; design engr. Cal/ Poly ERDA contract, 1976-77; prin. investigator NASA-ARC Cooperative Agreement, 1983. Contbr. articles to profl. jours. Grantee NASA, NSF. Mem. ASME. Home: 960 Buck Ridge Ln Arroyo Grande CA 93420 Office: Calif Poly State U Aeornautical Engring Dept San Luis Opispo CA 93407

HOFFMANN, SAROLTA HELEN, veterinary medicine administrator; b. Budapest, Hungary, Mar. 16, 1943; d. Zoltan and Sarolta (Medveczky) Csanyi; m. Thomas David, June 4, 1963 (div. Feb. 1968); 1 child, Charlotte; m. Geza George Hoffmann, Apr. 2, 1976. DVM, U. Vet. Medicine, Vienna, Austria, 1974, PhD, 1977. Product mgr. Merck Sharp & Dohme, Vienna, 1978-79; sr. research assoc. Newport Pharms., Newport Beach, Calif., 1979-81; research scientist U. Calif., Irvine, 1982-83; dir. preclin. research and devel. Viratek/ICN, Covina, Calif., 1983-85; head vet. scis. NARI/ICN, Costa Mesa, Calif., 1985—. Contbr. articles to profl. jours. Mem. AAAS, Am. Assn. Lab. Animal Sci., Am. Soc. Lab. Animal Practitioners, Soc.Toxicology, Am. Vet. Med.Assn. Republican. Roman Catholic. Avocations: tennis, bridge, classical music. Home: 26 Tahoe Irvine CA 92715 Office: NARI 3300 Hyland Ave Costa Mesa CA 92626

HOFFMANN, WILLIAM FREDERICK, astronomer, educator; b. Manchester, N.H., Feb. 26, 1933; s. Maurice and Charlotte (Hibbs) H.; m. Silke Elisabeth Margaretha Schneider, June 5, 1965; children: Andrea Charlotte, Christopher James. A.B. in Physics, Bowdoin Coll., 1954; Ph.D., Princeton U., 1962. Instr. physics Princeton U., 1958-61; research asso. NASA Goddard Inst. Space Studies, N.Y.C., 1962; staff astronomer NASA Goddard Inst. Space Studies, 1965-73; instr. physics Yale U., 1963-65; adj. asso. prof. astronomy Columbia U., 1970-73; prof. astronomy U. Ariz., 1973—, astronomer Stewart Obs., 1973—, project scientist multiple mirror telescope, 1973-79, project scientist sub-millimeter telescope, 1983-84; Pres. Spuyten Duyvil Assn., N.Y.C., 1971. Editor: (with H.Y. Chiu) Gravitation and Relativity, 1964. NSF fellow, 1954; Danforth fellow, 1954-58; recipient NASA Exceptional Sci. Achievement medal, 1972. Mem. Am. Phys. Soc., Am. Astron. Soc., AAAS, Phi Beta Kappa, Sigma Xi. Club: Sierra. Home: 4225 E Kilmer St Tucson AZ 85711 Office: Steward Observatory University of Arizona Tucson AZ 85721

HOFFMEISTER, MARTIN, architect; b. Prague, Czechoslovakia, Aug. 27, 1942; came to U.S., 1966; s. Vaclav Rohlik and Milena (Hoffmeister) Klikova. BA, Yale U., 1969, MArch, 1972; postgrad., U. Chgo., 1979-84. Registered architect, Conn., Colo. Chief designer Taisei Corp., Tokyo, 1973-75; v.p., sec. Perkins & Will, Chgo., 1975-84; v.p., bd. dirs. Perez Architects, Denver, 1984—. Author: Biography of Rasilov, 1965, Hotel Design, 1975; prin. works include Place Pompidou, Paris, (2d prize 1973). Avocations: history, bicycling. Home: 2111 30th St Suite M1008 Boulder CO 80301 Office: Perez Architects 1380 Lawrence Denver CO 80204

HOFFMEYER, DOROTHY FLORENCE, consultant; b. Green Bay, Wis., Sept. 19, 1910; d. Max William and Addie (Stone) S.; B.A., U. Wis., 1932; M.P.H., Yale U., 1948; m. Ralph E. Hoffmeyer, Sept. 3, 1982. Visitor, dist. supr., dist. dir. Fla. Welfare Bd., Jacksonville, 1932-37; dir. Pub. Welfare Dept., Green Bay, Wis., 1937-42; cons. Div. Pub. Assistance, Wis. Dept. Pub. Welfare, Madison, 1942-44; counselor USPHS, 1944-45; health edn. cons. Council Social Agys., New Haven, 1946-49; heart work cons. State Com. on Tb and Pub. Health, N.Y., 1949-52; program cons., exec. asst. Am. Heart Assn., 1952-64, asst. dir. affiliate relations and services, 1964-65, asst. dir. dept. councils and internat. program, 1965-70, assoc. dir., 1970-73, assoc. dir. div. sci. affairs, chief sci. councils, 1973-75. Recipient Gold Heart Bracelet in appreciation 10 year service Staff Conf. Heart Assn., 1962. Fellow Am. Pub. Health Assn.; mem. Phi Kappa Phi, Alpha Kappa Delta. Home: 58-B Calle Cadiz Laguna Hills CA 92653 Home: 1114 11th Ave Albany GA 31707

HOFMAN, CORNELIUS ADRIANUS, economics educator; b. Rotterdam, The Netherlands, Aug. 4, 1932; came to U.S., 1937, naturalized, 1946; s. John Betting and Klazina (Kome) H.; m. Elaine Venna Davis, Dec. 14, 1956; children: Catherina Venna, John Betting, Casie Elaine, Cornelius Adrianus II. BS in Econs., U. Utah, 1957, PhD, 1964. Teaching asst. U. Utah, Salt Lake City, 1958-60; from instr. to asst. prof. econs. Idaho State U., Pocatello, 1960-65, assoc. prof., 1969-70, prof., 1970—, acting chmn. dept. econs., 1962-63, chmn., 1974—, acting assoc. dean. Coll. Liberal Arts, 1974-75; assoc. prof. Utah State U., Logan, 1965-67; assoc. prof. Middle Tenn. State U., Murfreesboro, 1967-69, chmn. dept. econs., 1967-69; cons. revenue and taxation com. Idaho State Legislature, 1963, 65; mem. market research team R.I.T.A. Project, Rio Grande del Norte, Brazil for AID, owner, developer Gen. Econ. Cons., 1970—; co-ptnr., 1976—; cons. on income taxation Gov. Idaho, 1971, cons. on property taxation, 1972, advisor implementation of one percent initiative, 1978; research reporter Joint Fin.-Appropriations Com., Idaho, 1971, 73; econ. research cons. idaho State Dept. Edn., 1977-78, Gov.'s Task Force on Taxation; invited speaker Ann. Conf., Idaho Pub. Health Assn. Editor: Rendezvous, Jour. Arts and Letters, 1970-73; contbr. articles and reports to profl. publs. Served with USAF, 1950-51. Mem. Am. Econ. Assn., Nat. Tax Assn. (standing com. 1969-72, 1977-80), Western Econ. Assn., Idaho Council on Econ. Edn., Beta Gamma Sigma. Home: 216 S 16th St Pocatello ID 83201 Office: Idaho State U Box 8053 Pocatello ID 83209

HOFMAN, HARRY TERENCE, small business owner; b. Shafter, Calif., Jan. 31, 1924; s. Ernest H. and Irene E. (Schumacher) H.; m. B. Evelyn Lewis, Mar. 12, 1950; children: Kathryn, Carol, Mary, Harry, James. AA, Bakersfield Coll., 1946; BS, San Jose State Coll., 1948. Salesman Union Oil Co. Calif., Bakersfield, 1948-58; prin. Hofman-Lewis Tire Service (now employed as agt. for Morro Bay Realty), Delano, Calif., 1958—. Councilman City of Delano, 1968-84, Mayor Pro tem, 1972, 76, Mayor, 1980-82. Served to sgt. USAF, 1943-46. Mem. Delano C. of C. (pres. 1964-66). Lodges: Kiwanis (pres. Delano chpt. 1978-80), Masons (master 1964-65). Avocations: flying, tennis, golf, traveling. Home: 2611 Laurel Ave Morro Bay CA 93442 Office: Morro Bay Realty 1203 Main St Cayucos CA 93430

HOFMANN, ELLEN SCHAEFER, humanities educator, cultural organization administrator; b. Seattle, Apr. 29, 1943; d. Roman Ferdinand and Eleanore Dagmar (Larson) Schaefer; m. William John Hofmann, Feb. 14, 1975; children: Romy, Margo. Diplome D'Etudes, Sorbonne U. de Paris, France, 1964; BA in English with honors, Wash. State U., 1966, MA in English, 1967. Cert. tchr. pub. schs., Wash. mem. bd. trustees Wash. Commn. Humanities, Olympia, 1983—, chair direct programs, Olympia, 1985—, media com., 1985—, exec. com., 1985; guest lectr. Childbirth Edn. Assn. Project dir. Wash. Commn. Humanities, 1977. World Council Internat. Trade fellow Battelle N.W. Research Ctr., 1983; grantee NEH, 1974-75, Wash. Commn. Humanities, 1977. Club: Shorewood Community. Avocations: travel, art history, theater, skiing, gourmet cooking. Home: PO Box 3200 Kent WA 98032 Office: Highline Community Coll 240th Pacific Hwy S Des Moines WA 98198-9800

HOFMANN, REVA BUTLER, engineering consulting firm executive; b. Red Bud, Ill.; d. Allen William and Bertha Elizabeth (Conway) Moore; divorced; children: Kathy, Dennis. BS in Bus., U. Mo., 1967. Exec. salesperson Butler Packaging Co., St. Louis, Mo. and Santa Ana, Calif., 1976-82; pres., owner HTS Internat., Laguna Niguel, Calif., 1982—; citizen ambassador to China, Nuclear Tech. delegation, 1985; appeared on TV program Mid Morning Los Angeles, Always on Sunday, Australia. Contbr. articles to Los Angeles Times, Orange Coast Mag., Daily Pilot. Sponsored numerous golf tournaments for Cystic Fibrosis, fund-raising drives for Muscular Dystrophy, March of Dimes. Recipient awards for innovative packaging Midwest Packaging Assn.; Man of Yr. award Sales and Mktg. Execs., 1975; 1st Lady of the Day award Sta. WORTH Radio, St. Louis, 1975. Mem. Am. Nuclear Soc. (assoc.), Am. Mgmt. Assn. (bd. dirs.), Sales and Mktg. Execs. (bd. dirs., Man of Yr. award 1975), CEO, the Exec. Com., Nat. Employment Assn. (ethics com.), Sales and Mktg. Execs. Internat. Avocations: golf, sailing. Office: HTS Internat Inc 30012 Ivy Glenn Dr Suite280 Laguna Niguel CA 92677

HOFSTADTER, ROBERT, physicist, educator; b. N.Y.C., Feb. 5, 1915; s. Louis and Henrietta (Koenigsberg) H.; m. Nancy Givan, May 9, 1942; children: Douglas Richard, Laura James, Mary Hinda. B.S. magna cum laude (Kenyon prize), Coll. City N.Y., 1935; M.A. (Procter fellow), Princeton U., 1938, Ph.D., 1938; LL.D., City U. N.Y., 1961; D.Sc., Gustavus Adolphus Coll., 1963; Laureate Honoris Causa, U. Padua, 1965; D.Sc. (hon.), Carleton U., Ottawa, Can., 1967, Seoul Nat. U., 1967; Honoris Causa, U. Clermont-Ferrand, 1967; D. Rerum Naturalium honoris causa, Julius Maximilians U., Würzburg, W. Ger., 1982, Johannes Gutenberg U. Mainz (W. Ger.), 1983; D.Sc. (hon.), Israel Inst. Tech., 1985. Coffin fellow Gen. Electric Co., 1935-36; Harrison fellow U. Pa., 1939; instr. physics Princeton U., 1940-41, CCNY, 1941-42; physicist Norden Lab. Corp., 1943-46; asst. prof. physics Princeton U., 1946-50; assoc. prof. physics Stanford U., 1950-54, prof., 1954-85, Max H. Stein prof. physics, 1971-85, prof. emeritus, 1985—, dir. high energy physics lab., 1967-74; dir. John Fluke Mfg. Co. Author: (with Robert Herman) High-Energy Electron Scattering Tables, 1960; editor: Investigations in Physics, 1958-65, Electron Scattering and Nucleon Structure, 1963; co-editor: Nucleon Structure, 1964; assoc. editor: Phys. Review, 1951-53; mem. editorial bd.: Review Sci. Instruments, 1953-55, Reviews of Modern Physics, 1958-61. Bd. govs. Technion, Israel Inst. Tech., Weizmann Inst. Sci. Calif. Scientist of Year, 1959; co-recipient of Nobel prize in physics, 1961; Townsend Harris medal Coll. City N.Y., 1961; Guggenheim fellow Geneva, Switzerland, 1958-59; Ford Found. fellow; recipient Röntgen medal, Wurzburg, Germany, 1985, U.S. Nat. Sci. medal, 1986, Prize of Cultural Found. of Fiuggi, Italy, 1986. Fellow Am. Phys. Soc., Phys. Soc. London; mem. Nat. Acad. Scis., Am. Acad. Arts and Scis., AAUP, Phi Beta Kappa, Sigma Xi. Home: 639 Mirada Ave Stanford CA 94305 Office: Stanford Univ Dept of Physics Stanford CA 94305 *

HOGAN, CLARENCE LESTER, retired electronics executive; b. Great Falls, Mont., Feb. 8, 1920; s. Clarence Lester and Bessie (Young) H.; m. Audrey Biery Peters, Oct. 13, 1946; 1 child, Cheryl Lea. BSChemE, Mont. State U., 1942, Dr. Engring. (hon.), 1967; MS in Physics, Lehigh U., 1947, PhD in Physics, 1950, D in Engring. (hon.), 1971; AM (hon.), Harvard U., 1954; D in Sci. (hon.), Worcester Poly. U., 1969. Research chem. engr. Anaconda Copper Mining Co., 1942-43; instr. physics Lehigh U., 1946-50; mem. tech. staff Bell Labs., Murray Hill, N.J., 1950-51, sub dept. head, 1951-53; assoc. prof. Harvard U., Cambridge, Mass., 1953-57, Gordon McKay prof., 1957-58; gen. mgr. semi-conductor products div. Motorola, Inc., Phoenix, 1958-60, v.p., 1960-66, exec. v.p., dir., 1966-68; pres., chief exec. officer Fairchild Inst., Mt. View, Calif., 1968-74, vice chmn. of bd. dirs., 1974-85; bd. dirs. Timeplex, Inc., Woodcliff Lake, N.J., Varian Assocs., Palo Alto, Calif., TAB Products, Palo Alto; gen. chmn. Internat. Conf. on Magnetism and Magnetic Materials, 1959, 60; mem. materials adv. bd. Dept. Def., 1957-59; mem. adv. council dept. electrical engring. Princeton U.; mem. adv. bd. sch. engring. U. Calif., Berkeley, 1974—; mem. nat. adv. bd. Desert Research Inst., 1976-80; mem. vis. com. dept. electric engring. and computer sci. MIT, 1975-85; mem. adv. council div. electrical engring. Stanford U., 1976-86; mem. scientific and ednl. adv. com. Lawrence Berkeley Lab., 1978-84; mem. Pres.'s Export Council, 1976-80; mem. adv. panel to tech. adv. bd. U.S. Congress, 1976-80. Patentee in field. Chmn. Commn. Found. Santa Clara County, Calif., 1983-85; mem. vis. com. Lehigh U., 1966-71, trustee, 1971-80; trustee Western Electronic Edn. Fund; mem. governing bd. Maricopa County Jr. Coll.; bd. regents U. Santa Clara. Served to lt. (j.g.) USNR, 1942-46. Recipient Community Service award NCCJ, 1978, Medal of Merit Am. Electronics Assn., 1978, Berkeley Citation U. Calif., 1980; named Bay Area Bus. Man of Yr. San Jose State U., 1978, One of 10 Greatest Innovators in Past 50 Yrs. Electronics Mag., 1980. Fellow IEEE (Frederick Philips Gold medal 1976, Edison Silver medal Cleve. Soc., 1978), AAAS, Inst. Electrical Engrs. (hon.); mem. Am. Phys. Soc., Nat. Acad. Engring., Sigma Xi, Tau Beta Pi, Phi Kappa Phi, Kappa Sigma. Democrat. Baptist. Club: Menlo Country (Redwood City, Calif.). Lodge: Masons. Avocations: woodworking, computer programming. Home: 36 Barry Ln Atherton CA 94025

HOGAN, CURTIS JULE, union executive, industrial relation consultant; b. Greeley, Kans., July 25, 1926; s. Charles Leo and Anna Malene (Roussello) H.; m. Lois Jean Ecord, Apr. 23, 1955; children—Christopher James, Michael Sean, Patrick Marshall, Kathleen Marie, Kerry Joseph. B.S. in Indsl. Relations, Rockhurst Coll., 1950; postgrad., Georgetown U., 1955, U. Tehran, 1955-57. With Gt. Lakes Pipeline Co., Kansas City, 1950-55; with Internat. Fedn. Petroleum and Chem. Workers, Denver, 1955-85; gen. sec. Internat. Fedn. Petroleum and Chem. Workers, 1973-85; pres. Internat. Labor Relations Services, Inc., 1976—; cons. in field; lectr. Rockhurst Coll., 1951-52. Contbr. in field. Served with U.S. Army, 1945-46. Mem. Internat. Indsl. Relations Assn., Indsl. Relations Research Assn., Oil Chem. and Atomic Workers Internat. Union. Office: PO Box 6565 Denver CO 80206

HOGAN, DONN WOODWARD, architect; b. Troy, N.Y., Sept. 2, 1946; s. Earl Duane and Vera Mae (Brownell) H.; m. Antonia Marie DeLeon, Sept. 15, 1984. BArch, Renssaeler Poly. Inst., 1969. Registered architect, Wash. Designer Lynn Harden, Architect, Beaumont, Tex., 1970-71, Edward Zdenek, Architect, Perinton, N.Y., 1971-72, Champion Turner, Everett, Wash., 1974-76; instr. Mont. State U., Bozeman, 1972-73; architect Mithun Assocs., Bellevue, Wash., 1977-78; project designer Henningson, Durham and Richardson, Seattle, 1979—. Author, designer copyrighted strategy game AXA, 1985. Recipient Home of the Month award AIA, 1980. Avocations: skiing, volleyball, swimming, running. Home: 119 NW 47th St Seattle WA 98107 Office: HDR 1100 Eastlake Ave E Seattle WA 98109

HOGAN, GREGORY DENHAM, advertising executive; b. Atlanta, Apr. 23, 1950; s. Augustus and Rubye I. (Moffett) H.; m. Joycelyn B. Walker, Dec. 25, 1980; children—Kelli, Marcus, Darryl. B.S., U. Ill., 1972; M.B.A., Northwestern U., 1974. Account exec. Foote, Cone and Belding, Chgo., 1977-80, account supr. Young and Rubicam, 1980-82; regional advt. mgr. McDonald's Corp., Los Angeles, 1982—. Office: McDonald's Corp 10960 Wilshire Blvd Suite 600 Los Angeles CA 90024

HOGAN, HERBERT WARD, history educator; b. Lien Chou, China, Sept. 6, 1921; s. Milo A.V., and Emily (Beach) Hogan; m. Janice Boadway, June 9, 1972; 1 son by previous marriage, Ronald Ward Hogan. B.A., LaVerne Coll., 1944; M.A., Claremont Grad. Sch., 1950, Ph.D., 1958. Instr. history U. LaVerne, Calif., 1946-48, asst. prof. history, 1948-51, assoc. prof. history, 1951-58, prof. history, 1958—, dean men, 1950-58, dir. summer session, 1952-62, chmn. social sci. div., 1958-64, 75—, dean coll., 1962-66, v.p., dean, 1966-72; Fulbright prof., Germany, 1965; chmn. spl. study for Ch. of the Brethren, Elgin, Ill., 1957, chmn. hist. com., 1971-83; mem. spl. study World Council Chs./Christian Council Nigeria, Geneva, Switzerland, 1960-61. Author: Christian Responsibility in Independent Nigeria, 1961. Contbr. articles to profl. jours. Coordinator Civil Def., City of LaVerne, 1948-51; mem. City of LaVerne Sch. Bd., 1953-58; mem. Bonita Unified Sch. Bd., 1958-68, chmn., 1965-68; mem. Pacific S.W. Conf. Ch. of Brethren Bd., 1966-72, chmn., 1968-72. Mem. Orgn. Am. Historians. Lodge: Kiwanis. Home: 4164 Tenango Rd Claremont CA 91711 Office: Univ LaVerne 1950 3d St LaVerne CA 91711

HOGAN, SCOTT HESS, manufacturing company executive, business consultant; b. Salt Lake City, July 2, 1947; s. Floyd H. and Catherine (Hess) H.; m. Judy Niebuhr, June 11, 1971; children: Todd, Danelle, Bradd, Timothy. BS in Econs., U. Utah, 1970, MBA, 1971. Mgr. Arthur Andersen & Co., Salt Lake City, 1971-73, 75-81; exec. v.p. interstate div. U.S. Homes Corp., North Salt Lake, Utah, 1983-84; pres. Profl. Bus. Mgmt. Assn., North Salt Lake, Utah, 1981—, Tekna Tool, Inc., North Salt Lake, 1984-86, Chain Tool Co., Inc., North Salt Lake, 1986—. Contbr. articles on fin. mgmt. to various pubs; host local bus. TV program, 1986—. Republican. Mormon. Avocations: basketball, golf. Home: 469 Heritage Dr Bountiful UT 84010 Office: Tekna Tool PO Box 216 North Salt Lake UT 84054

HOGARTH, BURNE, cartoonist, illustrator; b. Chgo., Dec. 25, 1911; s. Max and Pauline H.; m. Constance Holubar, June 27, 1953; children—Michael, Richard, Ross. Student Art Inst. Chgo., 1925-27, Chgo. Acad. Fine Arts, 1926-29, Crane Coll., 1928-30, U. Chgo., 1930-32, Northwestern U., 1931-32, Columbia U., 1956-57. Asst. cartoonist to Lyman Young, Tim Tyler's Luck, N.Y.C., 1934; cartoonist Pieces of Eight, McNaught Syndication, N.Y.C., 1935; free lance artist King Features, N.Y.C., 1935-36; staff artist Johnstone Agy., N.Y.C., 1936-37; cartoonist Sunday Color Page, Tarzan, United Feature Syndication, N.Y.C., 1937-50, Sunday page Drago, Post-Hall Syndication, N.Y.C., 1946, Miracle Jones,

United Features, N.Y.C., 1948; founder Sch. Visual Arts, N.Y.C., 1947-70, v.p., coordinator curriculum, instr., 1947-70; author Watson-Guptill, N.Y.C., 1958-85; instr. Parsons Sch., N.Y.C., 1976-79; pres. Pendragon Press Ltd., N.Y.C., 1975-79; with Art Ctr. Coll. Design, Pasadena, Calif., 1982—, Otis Art Inst., Parsons Sch. Design, Los Angeles, 1981—; numerous exhbns. worldwide; one man show Bibliotheque Municipale, 1985, Palais de Longchamps, Marseille, France, 1985; represented in permanent collections: Smithsonian Instn., Mus. Cartoon Art, U. Colo., U. Wyo., Mus. Art, Gijon, Spain, others. Author: Dynamic Anatomy, 1958, Drawing the Human Head, 1965, Dynamic Figure Drawing, 1970, Drawing Dynamic Hands, 1977; Dynamic Light and Shade, 1981; creator graphic novels Tarzan of the Apes, 1972, Jungle Tales of Tarzan, 1976, Golden Age of Tarzan, 1979; Life of King Arthur, 1984. Trustee NCS Milt Gross Fund., 1980. Named Best Illustration Cartoonist, Nat. Cartoonists Soc., 1974, 75, 76, Artist of Yr., Pavilion of Humour, 1975, Premio Emilio Freixas Silver plaque V-Muestra Internat. Conv., 1978, Pulcinella award V-Mostra Internat. del Fumetto, 1983, Caran D'Ache Silver plaque Internat. Comics Conv., 1984, Adamson Silent Sam award Comics '85 Internat. Conv., 1985. Mem. Nat. Cartoonists Soc. (pres. 1977-79), Mus. of Cartoon Art, Am. Soc. Aesthetics, Nat. Art Edn. Assn., WHO, Graphic Arts Soc., Internat. Assn. Authors of Comics and Cartoons. Address: 6026 W Lindenhurst Ave Los Angeles CA 90036

HOGG, DAVID CLARENCE, physicist; b. Vanguard, Sask., Can., Sept. 5, 1921; came to U.S., 1953, naturalized, 1964; s. Francis Sandison and Frances Katherine (Gadsby) H.; m. Jean E. MacMillan, Feb. 15, 1947; children—David Randal, Rebecca Jean. B.Sc., U. Western Ont. (Can.), London, 1949; M.Sc., McGill U., Montreal, Que., Can., 1951, Ph.D., 1953. With Bell Telephone Labs., 1953-77, head atmospheric physics research, 1966-72; head antenna and propagation research Bell Telephone Labs., Holmdel, N.J., 1972-77; chief environ. radiometry wave propagation lab. Environ. Research Lab., NOAA, Boulder, Colo., 1977-83, chief radio meteorology, 1983-86; sr. scientist Colo. Inst. Research Environ. Scis., U. Colo., Boulder, 1986—. Research, numerous publs. on microwaves, optics, satellite communications and remote sensing; patentee microwave antennas. Served with Can. Army, 1940-45. Recipient Silver medal U.S. Dept. Commerce, 1983. Fellow IEEE (Disting. Achievement award 1984); mem. AAAS, Nat. Acad. Engring., Union Radio Scientifique Internationale. Episcopalian. Office: CU Campus PO Box 449 Cires RL-2 Boulder CO 80309

HOGG, MAUREEN ELAINE, technical writer, editor; b. Boulder, Colo., May 14, 1955; d. Charles David and Eileen Mary (Autrey) H. BA, U. No. Colo., 1977. Jr. bus. adminstr., Aerospace div. Ball Corp., Boulder, 1978-80, tech. writer and editor, Advanced Programs and Pub. Relations divs., 1980-84, tech. writer and editor, Pub. Relations div., 1984—. Author numerous poems. Recipient Best Total Publ. for Printed Newsletters award Ball Corp., 1982, 83, 1st pl. Award of Distinction Soc. for Tech. Communication, 1981, Outstanding Trailblazer Alumna award U. No. Colo., 1985. Mem. Soc. Tech. Communication (judging com. Rocky Mountain chpt. 1981-83), AAAS. Avocations: running, swimming, hiking, cross-country skiing. Office: Ball Corp Aerospace Systems Div PO Box 1062 Boulder CO 80306

HOHNE, ROBERT JOSEPH, gas utility company executive; b. Olpe, Kans., Nov. 11, 1933; s. Fred Charles and Elizabeth (Voeste) H.; m. Mary L. McCarthy, Aug. 24, 1955; children: Robert, Mark, Jeffrey, Jennifer, Matthew, Laura, Richard. B.S. in Geol. Engring., Colo. Sch. Mines, 1955; M.B.A. in Bus. Econs., UCLA, 1963. With Pacific Lighting Utilities Co., Los Angeles, 1957—; v.p. Pacific Lighting Gas Supply Co., Los Angeles, 1980-83, pres., 1983-85; sr. v.p. So. Calif. Gas. Co., Los Angeles, 1983—. Served to 1st lt. C.E., U.S. Army, 1955-57. Mem. Los Angeles Energy Commn. Mem. Am. Gas Assn., Pacific Coast Gas Assn. (bd. dirs.). Republican. Roman Catholic. Clubs: Los Angeles, Jonathan. Home: 5807 Friends Ave Whittier CA 90601 Office: So Calif Gas Co 810 S Flower St Los Angeles CA 90017 *

HOILAND, ANDREW CALVIN, architect; b. Great Falls, Mont., Aug. 3, 1926; s. Andrew C. and Ida (Mohondro) H.; m. Patricia Ruth Willits, Aug. 13, 1950; children: William H., Richard C., Diana Ruth. B.S. in Architecture, Mont. State Coll., 1949. Draftsman A.V. McIver (architect), Great Falls, 1949-52; prin. A. Calvin Hoiland (architect), Great Falls, 1952-54; partner Hoiland & Lund (architects), Great Falls, 1953-63, Hoiland-Zucconi (architects), Great Falls, 1964-74, A. Calvin Hoiland (Architect), 1974—; Pres. Mont. Bd. Archtl. Examiners, 1968. Assoc. editor: Am. Architects Directory, 1969-70; editorial adv. bd. Symposia mag., 1968-78, Northwest Archtl. mag., 1983—; important works include: Great Falls swimming pools, 1963, 1967, prison facilities Mont. State Prison, 1968, Mountain View Sch., Great Falls, 1968-69, Great Falls fire stas., 1969-71, Gregson Hot Springs swimming pools, 1972, Great Falls PCA-FLBA Office, 1978, I.F.G. Leasing Bldg, Great Falls, 1980. Chmn. charity ball for Great Falls Rehab. Center, 1961-62; chmn. master plan com. Great Falls Swimming Pool, 1962-65; chmn. adv. council Great Falls chpt. DeMolay; bd. dirs. Great Falls Camp Fire Girls. Served with USAAC, World War II. Named to Legion of Honor Order DeMolay, 1956, Cross of Honor, 1976. Mem. AIA (pres. Mont. 1961-62, editor Mont. publ. 1965-71), Great Falls Soc. Architects (charter pres. 1953), Mont. Tech. Council (charter pres. 1960-61), Sigma Chi. Methodist (chmn. bd. trustees, mem. bldg. com. Wesley Center, mem. Mont. bd. missions). Lodges: Masons (master 1979), Scottish Rite (master 1980), Royal Order of Scotland, York Rite, Shriners, Kiwanis (pres. Great Falls 1964). Home and Office: 2826 3d Ave S Great Falls MT 59405

HOJ, JOAN E., personnel executive; b. Letchworth, Eng., Dec. 3, 1942; imm. came to U.S., 1965; d. Donald Albert and Isabel (Willens) Knights; m. Otto Christen, Dec. 5, 1964; children: Jens David, Norman Mark. AA, Sir Godfrey Knellers, Whitton, Eng. Sec. Brit. Fgn. Service, London, 1960-64; regional personnel and adminstrn. mgr. Comml. Union Ins. Co., San Francisco, 1968-75; personnel mgr. Richard N. Goldman, San Francisco, 1985—. Mem. Ins. Personnel Mgmt. Assn. (treas. 1978-79), Federated Employers of Bay Area, Human Resources Council. Republican. Avocation: reading. Home: 2130 Elderberry Ln San Rafael CA 94903

HOKAMA, YOSHITSUGI, immunologist; b. Kohala, Hawaii, Oct. 25, 1926; s. Royei and Kamado (Matsudo) H.; Haruko Yoshimoto, Feb. 3, 1951; children: Jon Keith Yoshimoto, Julie Lynn Rosemary Yoshimoto. Ba, UCLA, 1951, MA, 1953, PhD, 1957. Asst. researcher UCLA, 1958-66; assoc. prof. Calif. State U., Los Angeles, 1964-66, U. Hawaii, Honolulu, 1966-68; lab. dir. prof., Honolulu, 1968—, Accupath Labs., Honolulu, 1974—; cons. Courtland Lab., Los Angeles, 1964-66; cons. immunologist SKCL-Accupath Lab., Honolulu, 1974—. Coauthor: Immunology and Immunopathology, 1982; contbr. articles to profl. jours; assoc. editor Jour. Clin. Lab. Analysis, 1986—. Com. mem. Hawaii Cancer Commn., 1983—. Mem. Assn. Am. Immunologists (reticuloendothelial soc.), Assn. Am. Pathologists, Internat. Soc. Toxinology, N.Y. Acad. Sci., Am. Soc. Microbiologists, Assn. Official Analytical Chemists, Am. Assn. Cancer Research (div. medicinal chemistry), Am. Chem. Soc. Democrat. Episcopalian. Club: Japanese Am. Citizens League. Avocations: reading, tennis. Office: U Hawaii Dept Pathology 1960 EW Rd Honolulu HI 96822

HOLBROOK, ALICE MAE, nursing education administrator; b. Park City, Utah, Feb. 10, 1938; d. James Llewellyn and Alice (Lefler) Gwilliam; diploma Los Angeles County (Calif. Gen. Hosp. Sch. Nursing, 1959; B.A., U. Redlands, 1975, M.A., 1978; m. Harry Loren Holbrook, Aug. 19, 1960 (dec.); children—Jimmy Edward, William Loren, Mary Alice, Daniel Raymond. Nurse, VA Hosp., Long Beach, Calif., 1959-61; supervising nurse U. Calif., Irvine Med. Center, 1964-74; patient care coordinator Fountain Valley (Calif.) Community Hosp., 1975-78; supervising nurse Hoag Meml. Hosp., Newport Beach, Calif., 1978-79; dir. nursing service Los Banos (Calif.) Community Hosp., 1979-81, nursing edn. Rancho Arroyo Vocat. Tech. Inst., Sacramento, 1985—; dir. nurses Sonoma Valley Dist. Hosp., 1981-83; instr. North Orange County Community Coll. Dist., Merced Community Coll. Mem. Dirs. Nursing Council, AAUW. Mormon. Home: 620 Jones Way Sacramento CA 95818

HOLBROOK, BOYD LYNN, computer systems engineer; b. Ogden, Utah, Dec. 24, 1947; s. Walter Herbert and Connie (Jorgenson) H.; m. Carlene Weese, July 16, 1965; m. 2d, Margaret Vandenberg, Feb. 3, 1979; children—Sherry Lynn, Christie Sue. B.S. in Computer Sci., Weber State Coll., 1975. Computer programmer White Motor Corp., Ogden, 1975-78; computer analyst Envirotech Corp., Salt Lake City, 1978-79; computer system engr. TRW Corp., Ogden, 1979-81; data processing mgr. R.C. Willey Home Furnishings, Syracuse, Utah, 1981—; cons. Served to sgt. U.S. Army, 1968-69. Decorated Silver Star, Air Medal, Purple Heart, Vietnamese gallantry cross (2). Mem. Assn. Automated Prodn. Inventory Control Specialists, Data Processing Mgmt. Assn., Beta Theta Pi Alumni Assn. Republican. Mormon. Author: (with Arthur Anderson) MX Field Mgmt. Center Study Report, 1980; (with Allen Graves) Implementation Analysis of the Distributed Warehousing and Shipping System, 1981. Home: 1470 Cahoon St Ogden UT 84401 Office: RC Willey Home Furnishings 1693 W 2700 S Syracuse UT 84041

HOLBROOK, FREDERICK RANDALL, research entomologist; b. Warwick, Mass., Nov. 15, 1935; s. Ralph Fredelle and Barbara Thompson (Lincoln) H. BS, U. N.H., 1961; MS, U. Mass., 1964, PhD, 1967. Research entomologist USDA Agrl. Research Service, Honolulu, 1967-68, Miami, Fla., 1968-69, Orono, Maine, 1969-78, Denver, 1978-85, Laramie, Wyo., 1985—; working group mem. Office Tech. Assessment U.S. Congress, Washington, 1975-77; vet. entomol. cooperator Animal Plant Health Inspection Service USDA, 1979—; tech. advisor Coop. Extension Service, Maine, 1970-78; entomol. tech. advisor Potato Seed Bd., Maine, 1971-78. Contbr. articles to profl. jours. Served with U.S. Army, 1955-58, Korea. Mem. AAAS, Entomol. Soc. Am., Soc. Vector Ecologists, Am. Mosquito Control Assn., Soc. Invertebrate Pathology, West Cen. Mesquito and Vector Control Assn., Sigma Xi, Phi Kappa Phi, Phi Sigma. Avocations: canoeing, cross country skiing, hiking, camping, running. Office: USDA Argl Research Service PO Box 3965 University Station Laramie WY 82071

HOLBROOK, WILLIAM FRANCIS, marketing executive; b. Keene, N.H., July 10, 1944; s. Sidney Wallace and Edith (Place) H.; m. Celia Carroll Simon, Sept. 18, 1971; 1 son, William Franklin. B.A., Denison U., 1966; Cert. Inst. Modern Lang., Washington, 1968; M.B.A., Columbia U., 1971. Planning dir. Supermarkets Gen., Woodbridge, N.J., 1970-75; mktg. mgr. Pepsi-Cola Co., Purchase, N.Y., 1975-80; home market mgr. Coca Cola Co., Atlanta, 1980-82; dir. merchandising and sales promotion E & J Gallo Winery, Modesto, Calif., 1982—. Fund raiser Brunswick Sch. Parents Assn., Greenwich, Conn., 1978. Served to capt., USMC, 1966-69. Mem. Res. Officers Assn., Am. Logistics Assn. (chmn. speakers com. 1979), Mensa. Republican. Congregationalist. Clubs: Westchester Country, Oakdale Country, Oakdale Golf, Modesto Racquet, Pepsico Runners (founder, pres. 1978-79). Home: PO Box 5195 Modesto CA 95352 Home: 1250 Jones St Apt 501 San Francisco CA 94109 Office: E & J Gallo Winery 600 Yosemite Blvd Modesto CA 95353

HOLBURT, MYRON BERNARD, civil engineering executive; b. St. Louis, Jan. 27, 1925; s. Mathias and Rebecca (Russie) H.; m. Idell Gertrude Flick, June 27, 1948; children: Ernest Neil, Sharon Elaine, Jonathan Louis. Student, UCLA, 1942-43; B in Engring., U. So. Calif., 1945; postgrad., U. Calif., Berkeley, 1946-47; MSCE, U. So. Calif., 1951. Registered profl. civil engr., Calif. Jr. hydraulic engr. U.S. Bur. Reclamation, 1947; supr. Leeds Hill & Jewett Cons. Engr., Berkeley, 1951-65; asst. hydrauc engr. Colo. River Bd. Calif., Berkeley, 1947-51; chief engr. Colo. River Bd. Calif., 1965-84; asst. gen. mgr. Met. Water Dist. So. Calif., Los Angeles, 1984—. Ensign USNR, 1945-46, lt. (j.g.) USNR, 1952-54. Mem. Sigma Gamma Epsilon, Tau Beta Pi. Republican. Jewish. Office: 1111 Sunset Blvd Los Angeles CA 90054

HOLCENBERG, JOHN STANLEY, clinical pharmacologist, oncologist; b. San Francisco, Oct. 9, 1935; s. Samuel George and Miriam (Wasserman) H.; m. Esther S. Rousso, June 15, 1958; children—Rachel, David. A.B. in Chemistry, Harvard U., 1956; M.D., U. Wash., 1961. Resident internal medicine Washington U., St. Louis, 1961-63; research trainee NIH, Bethesda, Md., 1963-67; asst. prof. U. Wash., Seattle, 1967-71, assoc. prof., 1971-76; prof. Med. Coll. Wis., Milw., 1976-82; prof. pediatrics and biochemistry U. So. Calif., Los Angeles, 1982—; cons. new agts. study com. Nat. Cancer Inst., Bethesda, 1978—; mem. oncology drugs adv. com. FDA, Washington, 1982—; mem. new drugs steering com. Children's Cancer Study Group, Los Angeles, 1982—; basic research sect. head, div. hematology-oncology, Children's Hosp., Los Angeles, 1982-86 . Editor: Enzymes as Drugs, 1980. Contbr. numerous articles to profl. jours. Served as surg. USPHS, 1967-69. Grantee USPHS, 1967—; recipient award Pharm. Mfrs. Assn. Found., 1968-71, Research Career Devel. award NIH, 1971-75; Burroughs Wellcome Fund scholar, 1977-81. Mem. Am. Soc. Clin. Investigation, Am. Assn. Cancer Research, Am. Soc. Clin. Pharmacology, Am. Soc. Pharmacology (exec. com. clin. pharmacology 1978-82). Office: Div Hemat-Oncol Children's Hosp Los Angeles U So Calif PO Box 54700 Los Angeles CA 90054

HOLCOMB, GARRY ALAN, electronics engineer; b. La Junta, Colo., Feb. 7, 1956; s. Gerald Lloyd and Jeanne Francis (Berg) H. BSEE, U. Colo., 1981. Elec. engr. Space Environment Lab., NOAA, Boulder, Colo., 1977-81; elec. engr. Exlog Co., Sacramento, 1982, Lab. for Atmospheric and Space Physics, Boulder, 1983—. Designer spartan Halley spacecraft for observing Halley's comet. Mem. IEEE (local sec. 1975-76). Democrat. Avocations: golf, tennis, camping, skiing. Home: 4425 Brookfield Boulder CO 80303 Office: Lab Atmospheric and Space Physics 5525 Central Boulder CO 80301

HOLCOMBE, TROY LEON, marine geologist; b. Roxton, Tex., Mar. 8, 1940; s. Horace Cleveland and Nellie Estelle (Jenkins) H.; m. Janis Eileen O'Neal, Aug. 21, 1971; children: Leigh Harold, Virginia Luce, Terry Estelle. BA, Hardin-Simmons U., 1961; AM, U. Mo., 1964; PhD, Columbia U., 1972. Research oceanographer U.S. Naval Oceanographic Office, Chesapeake Beach, Md., 1968-75; head geology br. Naval Ocean Research and Devel. Activity, Nat. Space Tech. Labs., Miss., 1975-84; dep. chief Marine Geology and Geophysics div. Nat. Geophys. Data Ctr., NOAA, Boulder, Colo., 1984—; vis. assoc. prof. oceanography Tex. A&M U., College Station, 1980-81. Co-author: Geologic-Tectonic Map of the Caribbean Region, 1980; mem. editorial adv. bd., U.S. sci. coordinator Internat. Bathymetric Chart of the Gulf of Mex., the Caribbean and part of the Pacific Ocean off Cen. Am., 1986—; contbr. articles to profl. jours. Mem. Am. Geophys. Union, Am. Assn. Petroleum Geologists, Geol. Soc. Am. Democrat. Baptist. Home: 5071 Euclid Ave Boulder CO 80303 Office: Nat Geophys Data Ctr 325 Broadway Boulder CO 80303

HOLCROFT, JAMES WALTER, surgery educator; b. Detroit, Apr. 16, 1941; s. Walter Hendrixson and Alice May (Eastman) H.; m. Alicia Legaspi Elepano, July 31, 1965; children: Christina, Cynthia, John. BS, MIT, 1963; MD, Case Western Res. U., 1969. Cert. Am. Bd. Surgery, Am. Bd. Vascular Surgery. Intern U. Calif., San Francisco, 1969-70, resident, 1970-76, fellow in peripheral vascular surgery, 1976-77; asst. prof. surgery Wash. U. Med. Sch., St. Louis, 1977-78; asst. prof. surgery U. Calif., Davis, 1978-80, assoc. prof., 1980-83, prof., 1983—; dir. surgical intensive care unit U. Calif. Med. Ctr., Sacramento, 1978—, chief vascular surgery service, 1981—, chief staff, 1986-87. Contbr. numerous articles to profl. jours. Recipient Milton B. Schweid Meml. award, 1969. Fellow ACS; mem. Assn. Acad. Surgery (pres. 1983-84, Resident's Research award 1974), Nat. Bd. Med. Examiners, Alpha Omega Alpha. Office: U Calif Med Ctr Dept Surgery 4301 X St Room 2310 Sacramento CA 95817

HOLDCROFT, LESLIE THOMAS, clergyman, educator; b. Man., Can., Sept. 28, 1922; s. Oswald Thomas and Florence (Waterfield) H.; student Western Bible Coll., 1941-44; BA, San Francisco State Coll., 1950; MA, San Jose State Coll., 1955; postgrad. Stanford, 1960, 63, U. Cal., 1965-67; DDiv., Bethany Bible Coll., 1968; m. Ruth Sorensen, July 2, 1948; children: Cynthia Ruth, Althea Lois, Sylvia Bernice. Instr. Western Bible Coll., 1944-47; instr. Bethany Bible Coll., 1947-55, dean edn., 1955-68, v.p., 1967-68; pres. Western Pentecostal Bible Coll., 1968-87; pastor Craig Chapel, 1959-68; dir. Can. Pentecostal Corr. Coll., Clayburn, B.C., 1985—. Pres., Assn. Canadian Bible Colls., 1972-76. Author: The Historical Books, 1960, The Synoptic Gospels, 1962, The Holy Spirit, 1962, The Pentateuch, 1951, Divine Healing, 1967, The Doctrine of God, 1978. Home: 34623 Ascott Ave, Abbotsford, BC Canada V2S 5A3 Office: Box 123, Clayburn, BC Canada V0X 1E0

HOLDEN, GEORGE FREDRIC, brewing company executive, consultant; b. Lander, Wyo., Aug. 29, 1937; s. George Thiel Holden and Rita (Meyer) Zulpo; B.S. in Chem. Engring., U. Colo., 1959, M.B.A. in Mktg., 1974; m. Dorothy Carol Capper, July 5, 1959; children—Lorilyn, Sherilyn, Tamilyn. Adminstr., plastics lab. EDP, prodn., engring. and tool control supervision Hercules Inc., Parlin, N.J., Salt Lake City, Cumberland, Md., 1959-70; by-product sales, new market and new product devel., resource planning and devel. and pub. relations Adolph Coors Co., Golden, Colo., 1971-76, dir. econ. affairs corp. pub. affairs dept., 1979-84, dir. pub. affairs research, 1984-86; owner Phoenix Enterprises, Arvada, 1986—; mgr. facilities engring. Coors Container Co., 1976-79; instr. brewing, by-products utilization and waste mgmt. U. Wis.; cons., speaker in field. Del. Colo. Rep. Conv., 1976, 78, 80, 82, 84, 86; bd. dirs. Colo. Pub. Expenditures Council, 1983-86, Nat. Speakers Assn., Colo. Speakers Assn., Nat. Assn. Bus. Economists, Colo. Assn. Commerce and Industry Ednl. Found. Mem. U.S. Brewers Assn. (chmn. by-products com., Hon. Gavel, 1975), Am. Inst. Indsl. Engrs. (dir. 1974-78). Co-author: Secrets of Job Hunting, 1972; The Phoenix Phenomenon, 1984; contbr. articles to Chem. Engring. Mag., 1968-76, also over 100 published articles. Regular guest columnist La Voz, Colo. Statesman. Spkr. Heritage Found. Guide to Pub. Policy Experts, Spkrs. Bur., Commn. on the Bicentennial, U.S. Constn. Home: 6463 Owens St Arvada CO 80004 Office: Phoenix Enterprises PO Box 1900 Arvada CO 80001

HOLDEN, JOSEPH LARRY, aerospace company engineering executive; b. Tullahoma, Tenn., Jan. 2, 1935; s. Joseph Henry and Hattie Rose (Thomas) H.; m. Glenda June Browning, June 21, 1961 (div. 1980); children—Nancy, Randy, Mark; m. Jackie Lou Melvin, Sept. 2, 1982; children—Roni, Tom. BS in Engring. Mgmt., U. Fla., 1970; MS in Pub. Adminstrn., U. Ala.-Montgomery, 1976; PhD in Mgmt., Pacific U., 1987. Field service rep. Philco Corp., Fort Washington, Pa., 1959-62; project engr. Advanced Systems Office, Eglin AFB, Fla., 1962-76, system dir. Munitions Program Office, Eglin AFB, 1976-82; mgr. engring. div. Gen. Dynamics, San Diego, 1982—. Author: Decision Making For The Public Administrator, 1976; Configuration Management—How and Why, 1979. Former scoutmaster Boy Scouts Am., 20 yrs. Served to maj. USAF, 1952-59. Recipient Eagle Scout award Boy Scouts Am., 1950; named Citizen of Yr., Modern Woodmen Am., Fort Walton Beach, Fla., 1981. Mem. Nat. Mgmt. Assn. (chpt. v.p. 1982—). Lodges: Masons, Shriners. Home: 2147 Flying Hills Ln El Cajon CA 92020 Office: Convair Div Gen Dynamics Kearny Villa Rd San Diego CA 92138

HOLDEN, OTIS TYRONE, advertising executive; b. Chgo., Oct. 22, 1958; s. William Lee and Miriam Lestene (Jackson) H.; m. Betty Jean Harris, July 25, 1984; 1 chld, Tomekieo. BS in Mktg., U. Ill., Chgo. Account exec. Roberts Advt., Inc., Chgo., 1978-79; futures broker Woodstock Commodities, Chgo., 1979-80; v.p. mktg. Mini-Markets Ltd., Chgo., 1980-82; revenue officer IRS, Los Angeles, 1982-85; pres. Clay & Holden Cons., Pasadena, Calif., 1985-86; chmn. Otis T. Holden & Assocs., Pasadena, 1986—; cons. SolarAqua Farms, Inc., Success, Inc., Budget Builders, Inc.; dist. speaker IRS, Los Angeles, 1984-85; bus. tax inspector City of Pasadena, 1987—. Editor Black Events Chgo. mag., 1982. Vol. Mike Antonovichfor U.S. Senate campaign, Pasadena, 1986. Mem. Assn. MBA Execs. Republican. Avocations: herbology, bowling, fishing, walking, softball. Office: Otis T Holden & Assocs PO Box 92046 Pasadena CA 91109-2046

HOLDER, DALE DUREN, pipeline company executive; b. Tulsa, Dec. 7, 1942; s. James K. and Vida (Rupp) H.; divorced; children: Christie Ann, Kevin Charles. BSME, U. Tex., 1965; MBA, U. So. Calif., 1972; cert. in advanced mgmt. program, Harvard U., 1984. Asst. dist. supt. So. Pacific Pipelines, Tucson, 1974-75; supr. projects engring. So. Pacific Pipelines, Los Angeles, 1975-78, sr. supr. products movement and data processing, 1978-82, asst. to pres., 1982, sr. v.p., 1982-84; sr. v.p. Santa Fe Pacific Pipelines, Los Angeles, 1984—; also bd. dirs. Santa Fe Pacific Pipe Lines, Los Angeles; bd. dirs. Black Mesa Coal Slurry Pipelines, Los Angeles, Gulf Cen. Ammonia Pipeline, Los Angeles, Santa Fe Pipeline Co., Los Angeles. Served with U.S. Army, 1966-68. Mem. Assn. Oil Pipelines, Am. Petroleum Inst. Clubs: Jonathan, Athletic (Los Angeles). Avocations: skiing, running, tennis. Home: 670 N Valley Dr Westlake Village CA 91362 Office: Santa Fe Pacific Pipelines Inc 888 S Figueroa St Los Angeles CA 90017

HOLDSWORTH, JANET NOTT, registered nurse, educator; b. Evanston, Ill., Dec. 25, 1941; d. William Alfred and Elizabeth Inez (Kelly) Nott; children—James William, Kelly Elizabeth, John David. B.S. in Nursing with high distinction, U. Iowa, 1963; M.Nursing, U. Wash., 1966; postgrad. U. Colo., 1981, U. No. Colo., 1982. Registered nurse, Colo. Staff nurse U. Colo. Hosp., Denver, 1963-64, Presbyn. Hosp., Denver, 1964-65, Grand Canyon Hosp., Ariz., 1965; asst. prof. U. Colo. Sch. Nursing, Denver, 1966-71; counseling nurse Boulder PolyDrug Treatment Ctr., Boulder, 1971-77; pvt. duty nurse Nurses' Official Registry, Denver, 1973-82; cons. nurse, tchr. parenting and child devel. Teenage Parent Program, Boulder Valley Schs., Boulder, 1980—; bd. dirs., treas. Nott's Travel, Aurora, Colo., 1980—; instr., nursing coordinator ARC, Boulder, 1979—, instr., nursing tng. specialist, 1980-82. Mem. adv. bd. Boulder County LaMaz Inc., 1980—; mem. adv. com. Child Find and Parent-Family, Boulder, 1981—; del. Republican County State Congl. Convs., 1972-86, sec. 17th Dist. Senatorial Com., Boulder, 1982—; vol. chmn. Mesa Sch. Parent Tchr. Orgn., Boulder, 1982—, bd. dirs., 1982—, v.p., 1983—. Mem. Am. Nurses Assn., Colo. Nurses Assn. (bd. dirs. 1975-76, human rights com. 1981-83, dist. pres. 1974-76), Soc. Adolescent Medicine, Council High Risk Prenatal Nurses, Council Intracultural Nurses, Sigma Theta Tau. Republican. Presbyterian (elder). Home: 1550 Findlay Way Boulder CO 80303 Office: Teenage Parent Program 3740 Martin Dr Boulder CO 80303

HOLEKAMP, KAY ELLEN, zoologist; b. St. Louis, Nov. 27, 1951; d. Carl Harry and Barbara Ester (Brown) H.; m. Richard J. Berg, Dec. 6, 1982. BA, Smith Coll., 1973; PhD, U. Calif., Berkeley, 1983. Zoo keeper St. Louis Zoo, 1969-72; Amazon river guide Parador Ticuna, Leticia, Colombia, 1973-74; teaching asst. U. Calif., Berkeley, 1976-81, research asst., 1977-81; postdoctoral research fellow U. Calif., Santa Cruz, 1983-86; research on primates, rodents, dolphins, hyenas U. Calif., 1976-85. Contbr. articles to profl jours. Recipient Disting. Teaching award U. Calif., Berkeley, 1982, Nat. Research Service award NIH, 1984; grantee NSF, 1981, Charles A. Lindbergh Fund, 1982. Mem. NOW, Union Concerned Scientists, World Wildlife Fund, AAUW, Am. Behavior Soc., AAAS, Am. Soc. Zoologists, Am. Soc. Mammalogists, Nat. Assn. Underwater Instrs., Phi Beta Kappa, Sigma Xi. Democrat. Club: Sailing (Berkeley). Avocations: sailing, scuba diving, world travel. Office: U of Calif Tolman Hall Dept of Psychology Berkeley CA 94720

HOLES, JOHN EDWARD, health care administrator; b. St. Paul, Aug. 26, 1945; s. Morris John and Francis Helen (Wolf) H.; m. Mary Alice Mott, June 10, 1967; children: Paul, David. BABA, Coll. St. Thomas, 1967; MA in Procurement Mgmt., Webster Coll., 1980. Commd. USAF, 1968, advanced through grades to lt. col.; material mgr. USAF Hosp., Canon AFB, N.Mex., 1969-71, Osan, Korea, 1971-72, Hill AFB, Utah, 1972-76; procedure and plans USAF Hdqs., Washington, 1976-78; standardization staff officer USAF Office of Med. Standards, San Antonio, 1978-81; assoc. adminstr. David Grant USAF Med. Ctr., Travis AFB, Calif., 1981—. Recipient Joint Achievement award Air Force Assn., 1986. Mem. Am. Coll. Hosp. Exec., No. Calif. Young Adminstrs., Northbay Healthcare Adminstrs., Am. Soc. Mil. Surgeons. Avocations: hiking, reading, jogging, weight tng. Home: 141 Warren Dr Vacaville CA 95688 Office: David Grant USAF Med Ctr DGMC/SGC Travis AFB CA 94535

HOLGATE, GEORGE JACKSON, university president; b. Lakewood, Ohio, Feb. 19, 1933; s. George Curtis and Melba Marguerite (Klein) H.; m. Sharon Joy, Dec. 20, 1954 (div. 1961); 1 child, Leigh Meredith. Mus.B., Baldwin-Wallace Coll., 1953; Mus.M., U. So. Calif., 1954, Ed.D., 1962; Ph.D., Riverside U., 1970, LL.D., 1971. Tchr. Oxnard High Sch., Calif., 1954-56; tchr. Ventura Coll., Calif., 1956-60; exec. v.p. Sierre Found., Santa Barbara, Calif., 1960-62; campus coordinator Congo Poly. Inst., Leopoldville, 1962-64; exec. dir. Automation Inst., Sacramento, 1964; pres. Riverside Bus. Coll., Calif., 1965-67, Riverside U., Calif., 1967—. Minister music St. Paul's Methodist Ch., Oxnard, Calif., 1954-55; condr. So. Calif. Council Protestant Chs. Messiah Chorus, 1954; dir. Ventura Coll. concert Chorale, 1956-60; condr. Ojai Festivals, Calif., 1958, Ventura Bach Festival, 1960; pres. Oxnard Community Concert Assn., 1958; pres. Vineyard Estates Property Owners Assn., 1958; me. Calif. State Democratic Central Com., 1962-63; chmn. 13th Congl. Dist. Dem. Council, 1963; bd. dirs. Riverside U., 1967—, Riverside Opera Assn., 1966-71, Riverside Symphony Orch. Soc., 1966—, So. Calif. Vocal Assn., 1955-56. Flotilla comdr. USCG Aux.,

1983—, div. capt., 1986-87. Recipient Disting. Service U.S. Jaycees, 1962. Mem. NEA, Calif. Council Bus. Schs. (pres. 1970), Calif. Assn. Pvt. Edn. (treas. 1969), Music Educators Nat. Conf., Calif. Choral Condrs. Guild, Internat. Platform Assn., Phi Delta Kappa, Phi Mu Alpha Sinfonia, Sigma Phi Epsilon, Delta Epsilon. Office: Riverside U 890 N Indian Hill Blvd Pomona CA 91767

HOLLAAR, LEE ALLEN, computer science educator, company executive; b. Litchfield, Minn., Mar. 9, 1947; s. Garritt A. and Lyma Marie (Geiger) H.; m. Audrey Mack, Nov. 26, 1968. B.S.E.E., Ill. Inst. Tech., 1969; M.S. in Computer Sci., U. Ill., 1974, Ph.D. in Computer Sci., 1975. Registered profl. engr., Calif. Systems engr., coordinator engring. Datalogics Inc., Chgo., 1969-71, 72-74; design engr. Automation Tech. Inc., Champaign, Ill., 1971-72; grad. research asst. U. Ill., Champaign, 1970-75, asst. prof. aviation and computer sci., 1975-77, asst. prof. computer sci., sr. research engr., 1977-80; assoc. prof. computer sci. U. Utah, Salt Lake City, 1980-86, assoc. chmn. dept., 1983-84, 85-86, prof. computer sci., research prof. elec. engring., 1986—; pres. Contexture, Inc., 1983—; cons. in field. NASA grantee, 1978; NSF grantee, 1979, 80, 82, 83, 85; IBM Corp. grantee, 1979, 83. Sr. mem. IEEE; mem. Assn. Computing Machinery, Inst. Nav., Aircraft Owners and Pilots Assn., Balloon Fedn. Am., Sigma Xi, Phi Kappa Phi, Eta Kappa Nu. Contbr. numerous articles to profl. jours. Patentee in field. Home: 1367 E 100 S Salt Lake City UT 84102 Office: U Utah Dept Computer Science 3160 Merrill Engring Bldg Salt Lake City UT 84112

HOLLAND, GEORGE O., insurance company executive, financial planning consultant; b. Everett, Wash., Nov. 19, 1926; s. Ole J. and Gunhild (Breum) H.; m. Diana Southgate Thorp, July 18, 1953; children—George Donald, Christopher Jon, Peter Thorp. B.A., U. Wash., 1950; M.S. in Fin. Services, Am. Coll., Bryn Mawr, Pa., 1981. C.L.U.; registered health underwriter; chartered fin. cons. Asst. rep. Wash. state Nat. Found. for Infantile Paralysis, Seattle, 1951-52; rep. Western N.Y., Rochester, 1952-54; brokerage mgr. Aetna Life Ins. Co., Seattle, 1954-58; gen. agt. Union Mut. Life Ins. Co., Seattle, 1958-84; mgr. Guardian Life Ins. Co., Seattle, 1985—; bd. dirs. Continental Savings Bank. Pres. N.W. Hosp., Seattle, 1972-73, chmn. bd., 1974-75; bd. dirs. Wash. State Golf Assn., 1974—, pres. 1984-87. Served with U.S. Army, 1945-46. Mem. Nat. Assn. Estate Planning Councils (pres. Seattle council 1983-84), Am. Soc. C.L.U.s (pres. Seattle chpt. 1974-75, western regional v.p. and bd. dirs. 1983-86), Wash. Assn. Health Underwriters (pres. 1961-62), Seattle Gen. Agts. and Mgrs. Assn. (pres. 1981-82) Western Pension Conf., Nat. Assn. Health Underwriters, Sigma Alpha Epsilon. Republican. Congregationalist. Clubs: Seattle Golf, Rainier, Wash. Athletic (Seattle). Contbr. articles to profl. jours. Home: 4208 55th St NE Seattle WA 98105 Office: 2200 6th Ave Suite 1200 Seattle WA 98121

HOLLAND, H. RUSSEL, federal judge; b. 1936; m. Diane Holland; 3 children. BBA, U. Mich., 1958, LLB, 1961. With Alaska Ct. System, Anchorage, 1961, U.S. Atty.'s Office, Dept. Justice, Anchorage, 1963-65; assoc. Stevens & Savage, Anchorage, 1965-66; ptnr. Stevens, Savage, Holland, Erwin & Edwards, Anchorage, 1967-68; sole practice Anchorage, 1968-70; ptnr. Holland & Thornton, Anchorage, 1970-78, Holland, Thornton & Trefry, Anchorage, 1978, Holland & Trefry, Anchorage, 1978-84, Trefry & Brecht, Anchorage, 1984; judge U.S. Dist. Ct. Alaska, Anchorage, 1984—. Mem. ABA, Alaska Bar Assn., Anchorage Bar Assn. Office: U S District Court 701 C St Box 54 Anchorage AK 99513 *

HOLLAND, JEFFREY R., university president; b. St. George, Utah, Dec. 3, 1940; s. Frank D. and Alice (Bentley) H.; m. Patricia Terry, June 7, 1963; children: Matthew, Mary, David. B.S., Brigham Young U., 1965, M.A., 1966; M.Phil., Yale U., 1972, Ph.D., 1973. Dean religious instrn. Brigham Young U., 1974-76, pres., 1980—; commr. Latter Day Saints Ch. Ednl. System, 1976-80; dir. Deseret News Pub. Co., Comml. Security Bancorp., Salt Lake City. Bd. dirs. Polynesian Cultural Center, Laie, Hawaii. Mem. Am. Assn. Presidents of Ind. Colls. and Univs. (pres.), Nat. Assn. Ind. Colls. and Univs. (bd. dirs.), Am. Council Edn., Phi Kappa Phi. Office: D-346 ASB Brigham Young U Provo UT 84602

HOLLAND, JUDITH RAWIE, television producer; b. Long Beach, Calif., Jan. 25, 1942; d. Wilmer Ernest and Margaret Jane (Towle) Rawie; m. John Allen Holland, July 11, 1964 (div.); children: Daryn Kirsten, Dawn Malia. BBA, Marymount Coll.; BA in Visual Arts and Communication, U. Calif., San Diego, 1978;, BA in Bus. Adminstrn., Mgmt. Coll. Producer/writer PBS series Achieving (Emmy award 1982, ACE nominee), asst. dir. research and video/producer IABC, San Francisco, 1982; dir. programming Group W Cable, Westinghouse Co., 1983-85; mgr. video programming Embassy Home Entertainment, 1985—; ptnr. RH Positive Prodns. Co., 1986—; mgr. video programming Nelson/Embassy Home Entertainment, 1986—. Recipient You Can Make the Difference award S.W. Region Group W, 1983. Mem. Am. Film Inst., Women in Film, Internat. Platform Assn. Democrat. Episcopalian. Home: 2400 Palos Verdes Dr W 16 Palos Verdes Estates CA 90274 Office: Nelson/Embassy Home Entertainment 1901 Aven of the Stars Los Angeles CA 90067

HOLLAND, RAYMOND PRUNTY, JR., aeronautical engineer; b. Atchison, Kans., Nov. 7, 1910; s. Raymond Prunty and Ruth Marie (Perkins) H.; m. Astrid E. Johnson, Dec. 31, 1937; children: Nancy E., Sally Ann, Linda R. SB in Aero. Engring., MIT, 1934. Design draftsman Curtiss Aeroplane, Buffalo, 1934-39; project engr. Stinson Aircraft/Stinson Vultee, Wayne, Mich. and Nashville, 1939-41; aerodynamics research engr. Vega Airplane Co., Burbank, Calif., 1941-42; aerodynamics engr., div. engr. Lockheed Corp., Burbank, 1942-46; research assoc., registrar, dir. admissions N.Mex. Mil. Inst., Roswell, 1946-62; pres. Airplane Kite Co., Roswell, 1948—; pres., chief engr. Holland Corp., Roswell, 1976—; cons. USAF, 1952-70. Author: Jim Hunter, Sportsman, 1937; The Physical Nature of Flight, 1951; patentee in field (26). Recipient Stratton prize MIT, 1933; commendation Air Force Office Sci. Research, 1962; U.S. Dept. Energy grantee, 1979, 81. Mem. AAAS, Lambda Chi Alpha. Republican. Presbyterian. Home: 1702 W 3d St Roswell NM 88201 Office: Holland Corp 1705 W Alameda Blvd Roswell NM 88201

HOLLAND, ROBIN JEAN, employment firm executive, consultant; b. Chgo., June 22, 1942; d. Robert Benjamin and Dolores (Levy) Shaeffer; 1 child, Robert Gene. B.A. in Pub. Relations magna cum laude, U. So. Calif., 1977. Account exec., pub. relations firm, 1977-79, Mgmt. Recruiters, 1979; owner, operator Holland Exec. Search, Marina Del Rey, Calif., 1979—; pres. Bus. Communications, 1983—; cons. on outplacement to bus.; condr. seminars on exec. search; guest lectr. and instr. on exec. recruiting at community colls. Active Ahead with Horses. Recipient numerous local honors; numerous scholarships. Mem. Am. Coaster Enthusiasts, Nat. Assn. Female Execs., Mensa, Peruvian Paso Horse Owners N.Am. Home: 332 Las Casas Pacific Palisades CA 90272 Office: Holland Exec Search 4736 Admiralty Way Suite 9774 Marina del Rey CA 90295

HOLLAND, WILLIAM DAVID, electronics engineer; b. York, Pa., Sept. 3, 1955; s. Allan Lamar and Jane Frida (Anderson) H. BS., Calif. Inst. Tech., 1977; postgrad. Stanford U., 1978-82. Cons., Robert Abel Films, Hollywood, Calif., 1972-77; mem. tech. staff Hewlett-Packard, Palo Alto, Calif., 1977—. Ebell scholar, 1976. Mem. IEEE, IEEE Computer Soc., Assn. Computing Machinery, ACM Spl. Interest Group on Computer Graphics, Soc. Info. Display, Sierra Club. Home: 13331 Wildcrest Dr Los Altos Hills CA 94022 Office: Hewlett-Packard 1501 Page Mill Rd Palo Alto CA 94304

HOLLANDER, JEFFREY ARTHUR, marketing professional; b. N.Y.C., Jan. 17, 1943; s. Morris Hollander and Ruth (Feinholz) Levine; m. Marcia Lu Mercer, Jan. 1, 1965 (div. Sept. 1973); children: David James, Sabrina Michelle. BS, U. Ariz., 1965. Owner The Racquet Shop, Palm Springs, Calif., 1975-79; loan officer Directors Mortgage, Riverside, Calif., 1979-80; v.p. sales and mktg. Fed. Energy, Los Angeles, 1980-81; pres. Century Energy, Los Angeles, 1981-82; v.p. mktg. Capco Fin., Atlanta, 1983-84, Am. Pacific Securities, Pasadena, Calif., 1985-86; v.p. mktg. Intersource Ltd., Denver, 1986—, also bd. dirs., 1986—. Chmn. City of Hope, Palm Springs, 1977. Mem. Internat. Assn. Fin. Planners. Democrat. Jewish. Club: Tennis (Palm Springs). Avocations: tennis, skiing. Home: 1132 Mesquite Ave Palm Springs CA 92264 Office: Intersource Ltd 2295 S Chambers Rd Suite G-297 Aurora CO 80014

HOLLANDER, MICHAEL FREDERIC, communications executive; b. N.Y.C., Dec. 27, 1946; s. Harold Martin and Irma Jeanne (Rabinoff) H.; m. Sandra Gail Horwitz, July 3, 1983. AA, Solano Coll., 1974. Enlisted USN, 1966, resigned, 1974; instr. engring. Litton Systems, Van Nuys, Calif., 1974-79, prin. engr., 1979-84; dir. product info. William Esty Co., Los Angeles, 1984—; dir. ops. Racing Info. Systems, Santa Monica, Calif., 1976—. Author: The Complete Datsun Guide, 1979, The New Mazda Guide, 1985. Mem. Am. Auto Racing Writers and Broadcasters Assn. (gen. v.p. 1986—, western v.p. 1984-86, STP award 1975), Internat. Motor Press Assn., Am. Racing Press Assn., Datsun Owners Clubs Assn. (nat. chmn. 1977-79). Republican. Jewish. Home: 1435 26th St Unit 10 Santa Monica CA 90404-3051 Office: William Esty Co 9841 Airport Blvd Suite 700 Los Angeles CA 90045

HOLLANDER, THOMAS MICHAEL, publishing executive, newsstand consultant; b. San Diego, Apr. 23, 1952; s. Clifford Henry and Rosanna (Douglass) H.; m. Denise Ellen Dupre, Dec. 30, 1977; children: Seth Benedict, Sarah Rose. Student, Calif. State U., San Diego, 1977-79; AA, Skyline Coll., 1976; diploma in French, Def. Lang. Inst., 1973. Circulation dir. Pubs. Devel. Corp., San Diego, 1979—; distbn. mgr. Transam. and Export News Co., San Diego, 1980—. Newsstand columnist Circulation Mgmt. mag., Springfield, Oreg., 1986—. Served with U.S. Army, 1972-75, Korea. Mem. Bus. Publs. Audit Single Copy Task Force, Los Angeles, 1986—, Mensa, Tau Kappa Epsilon. Republican. Avocations: bicycling, bird watching, reading. Office: Pubs Devel Corp 591 Camino de la Reina Suite 200 San Diego CA 92108

HOLLENBACK, SYLVIA DEE, speech pathologist; b. Walla Walla, Wash., Oct. 26, 1961; d. Orlo Stevenson and Rhea (Slater) Carver; m. Gerald Delano Hollenback III, Aug. 22, 1981; children: Janae Suzanne, Drew Nickolas. BS, Brigham Young U., 1982, M in Communicative Disorders, 1983. Communication specialist Provo (Utah) Sch. Dist., 1982-83; speech pathologist Valley Med. Ctr., Renton, Wash., 1984-85; communication disorders specialist Kent (Wash.) Sch. Dist., 1984-85, Richland (Wash.) Sch. Dist., 1985-86, Kennewick (Wash.) Sch. Dist., 1987—. Mem. Richland Edn. Assn., Kennewick Edn. Assn., Wash. Speech and Hearing Assn., Am. Speech Lang. and Hearing Assn., NEA (Wash. chpt.). Republican. Mormon. Club: Lit. Reviewers (Kennewick, Wash.) (pres. 1985—). Avocations: reading, needlework, dance, creative writing. Home: 8516 W Entiat Pl Kennewick WA 99336 Office: Kennewick Sch Dist 200 S Dayton Kennewick WA 99336

HOLLENBECK, CLIFFORD ERNEST, producer, photographer, writer, columnist; b. Temple, Tex., July 26, 1943; s. Clayton (Holly) Earl and Florence May (Cariveau); H.; A.A. in Journalism, Yakima Valley Coll., 1963; B.A. in Journalism, U.S. Navy, Coronado, Calif., 1967; M.S. in Physiology, U. Australia, 1969; D.D., First Ch. of Research (Va.), 1970; postgrad. in social psychology, Tenn. Christian U., 1977; m. Nancy Eilene Davis, Sept. 23, 1971; 1 son, Craig Eric. Journalist, photographer, editor Fairbanks News Miner, Fairbanks, Alaska, 1968-69; writer, photographer bus., politics Anchorage Daily Times, Anchorage, 1970; asst. v.p. advt., pub. relations Wein Air Alaska, Anchorage, 1971; cons. pub. affairs, aviation Govt. of Can., Ottawa, Ont., 1972-73; dir. pub. affairs, advt. promotion Alaska Airlines, Seattle, 1973-74; v.p. Faces Publs., Inc., Honolulu, Seattle, 1975-76, dir., 1980-83; pres. pro tem Indsl. Promotional Toys, Seattle, 1976; prin. Cliff Hollenbeck Agy., Seattle, 1976—; producer Hot Shot Prodns., Inc., pres., chmn. bd. dirs., 1984—; dir. Pacific Advt., Inc., 1979-82; producer, dir. TV series Journeys; dir. Journeys, Inc. Mem. 7th dist. Congressional Ind. Bus. Adv. Bd., 1978-79. Author: Adverse Incident Policy, 1972, A Look into Skyjocking, 1972; columnist Seattle Post Intelligencer, 1980-81, World Traveling mag., Welcome to U.S.A., Alaskafest; contbg. editor Pacific Bus. mag., N.W. World Travel, Alaskafest, Faces mag., contbr. photographs and articles to profl. jours. Basic 35mm Photography, 1986, Intermediate 35mm Photography, 1986, People Photography, 1986; (with Nancy Hollenbeck) Travel Photography, 1986. Served with USN, 1963-68. Decorated D.F.C. (2), Air medal (4), numerous others; named Mag. Photographer of Yr., Alaska, 1978, Travel Photographer of Yr., 1982-83. Mem. Am. Soc. Mag. Photographers, Soc. Am. Travel Writers (named One of Top Ten Travel Photographers 1979, 80, 81, 84, 85, 86), Aviation-Space Writers Assn., Nat. Press Photographers Assn., Pub. Relations Soc. Am., Overseas Press Club, Internat. Divers Assn., Nat. Geog. Soc., Alaska Geog. Soc., Profl. Assn. Diving Instrs., Underwater Master Divers Internat., Plonjeurs Internat., Kappa Alpha Mu, Alpha Psi Omega. Club: Siberia-Russia Explorers..S.A., Alaskafest; contbg. editor Pacific Bus. Mag., N.W. World Travel, AlaskaFest, Faces Mag.; contbr. photographs and articles to profl. jo Address: Box 4247 Pioneer Square Seattle WA 98104

HOLLENBERG, JOHN LELAND, chemistry educator; b. LaVerne, Calif., Sept. 17, 1926; s. George Jacob and Naomi Lucille (Harshbarger) H.; m. Anna May Hoglund, June 30, 1951; children: Sandra, John, David, Stanley, James. BA, U. Redlands, 1949, BS, 1952; MS, U. Calif., Berkeley, 1952; PhD, U. So. Calif., 1962. Instr. chemistry Fullerton (Calif.) City Coll., 1954-59; staff cons. chemistry study Harvey Mudd Coll., Claremont, Calif., 1961-63; prof. chemistry U. Redlands, Calif., 1963—; owner Unilab Products, Redlands, 1956—, Rhapis Palm Growers, Redlands, 1976—. Co-Author: Miniature Palms of Japan, 1981, General Chemistry in Lab, 1987; collaborator (film) Chemical Families, 1962. Served with USN, 1944-46. Grantee NSF, 1959, 70. Mem. Am. Chem. Soc., Sigma Xi. Home: 31350 Alta Vista Dr Redlands CA 92373 Office: U Redlands 1200 E Colton Ave Redlands CA 92373-0999

HOLLENBERG, MORLEY DONALD, research physician, educator; b. Winnipeg, Man., Can., July 2, 1942; s. Jacob and Esther (Gorsey) H.; m. Joan Leslie Omson, Aug. 15, 1965; children: Elisa Michelle, Daniel Benjamin. B.Sc., U. Man., 1963, M.Sc., 1964; D.Phil. (Rhodes scholar), Oxford U., (Eng.), 1967; M.D., Johns Hopkins U., 1972. Med. intern Johns Hopkins Hosp., Balt., 1971-72; postdoctoral fellow dept. pharmacology and exptl. thereapeutics Johns Hopkins Sch. Medicine, 1972-73, asst. prof. dept. pharmacology and exptl. thereapeutics, 1973-79, instr. dept. medicine, 1974-75, asst. prof. dept. medicine, 1975-79; prof., chmn. dept.. pharmacology and therapeutics U. Calgary, Alta./Can., 1979—; investigator Howard Hughes Med. Inst., 1974-79. Contbr. articles to profl. jours. Recipient Undergrad. Research award Johns Hopkins Med. Soc., 1971; recipient Upjohn award for clin. proficiency Johns Hopkins Sch. Medicine; Med. Research Council Can. fellow, 1972-73. Mem. Am. Fedn. Clin. Research, Am. Soc. for Pharmacology and Exptl. Theapeutics, Am. Soc. Clin. Investigation, Can. Soc. Clin. Investigation, Pharmacol. Soc. Can. Office: Dept Pharmacology U Calgary, 3330 Hospital Dr, Calgary, AB Canada T2N 4N1

HOLLEY, DANIEL CHARLES, biology educator; b. San Jose, Calif., Aug. 1, 1949; married; 2 children. AS in Biology, Cabrillo Coll., 1969; BS in Biol. Scis., U. Calif., Davis, 1971, MS in Physiology, 1973, PhD in Physiology, 1976. Staff research assoc. I dept. surgery Sch. Medicine U. Calif., Davis, 1969-73, research asst. dept. animal sci., 1971-76, teaching asst. dept. animal physiology, 1973-74; instr. physiology La. State U. Med. Sch., New Orleans, 1976-78; prof. biol. scis. San Jose State U., 1978—; com. memberships at San Jose State U. include chmn. Health Physics, Safety and Animal Rooms; mem. Instl. Animal Care and Use, Instl. Rev. Bd. Human Subjects, Equipment. Contbr. numerous articles and abstracts to profl. jours. Recipient Meritorious Performance and Profl. Promise award San Jose State U., 1986; Chancellor's Grad. fellow, 1974-75, 75-76. Mem. AAUP, AAAS, Am. Physiol. Soc., Shock Soc. (charter), Aerospace Med. Assn. (aviation safety com.), Am. Inst. Biol. Scis., Sigma Xi, Phi Kappa Phi, Alpha Gamma Sigma. Office: San Jose State U Dept Biol Scis San Jose CA 95192

HOLLEY, ROBERT WILLIAM, educator, scientist; b. Urbana, Ill., Jan. 28, 1922; s. Charles E. and Viola (Wolfe) H.; m. Ann Dworkin, Mar. 3, 1945; 1 son, Frederick. A.B., U. Ill., 1942; Ph.D., Cornell U., 1947. Am. Chem. Soc. fellow State Coll. Wash., 1947-48; asst. prof., then asso. prof. organic chemistry N.Y. State Agr. Expt. Sta., Cornell U., 1948-57; research chemist plant, soil and nutrition lab. U.S. Dept. Agr., Cornell U., 1957-64; prof. biochemistry Cornell U., 1964-69, chmn. dept. biochemistry, 1965-66; resident fellow Salk Inst. Biol. Studies, La Jolla, Calif., 1968—; mem. biochemistry study sect. NIH, 1962-66; vis. fellow Salk Inst. Biol. Studies; vis. prof. Scripps Clinic and Research Found., La Jolla, 1966-67. Recipient Distinguished Service award U.S. Dept. Agr., 1965, Albert Lasker award basic med. research, 1965; U.S. Steel Found. award in molecular biology Nat. Acad. Scis., 1967; Nobel prize for medicine and physiology, 1968; Guggenheim fellow Calif. Inst. Tech., 1955-56. Fellow AAAS; mem. Am. Acad. Arts and Scis., Am. Soc. Biol. Chemists, Am. Chem. Soc., Nat. Acad. Scis., Phi Beta Kappa, Sigma Xi. Home: 7381 Rue Michael La Jolla CA 92037 Office: Salk Inst for Biolog Studies PO Box 1809 San Diego CA 92112

HOLLIDAY, GERALD JOHN, information services company executive; b. Youngstown, Ohio, Sept. 15, 1935; s. Henry John and Frances Agnes (White) H.; m. Judith L. Durig, Dec. 21, 1962; children: Jennifer L., Jeffrey J. Brokerage cons. Conn. Gen., Hartford, 1963-65; dist. mgr. Will Ross Inc., Milw., 1965-72; dir. mktg. Nilador Inc., North Canton, Ohio, 1972-74; pvt. practice mktg. cons. North Canton, 1974-81; dist. mgr. Mitchell Info. Services Inc., San Diego, Calif., 1981-86, v.p. mktg./sales, 1986—. Served with U.S. Army, 1958-60. Episcopalian. Avocations: golfing, thoroughbred horse racing, sailing. Home: 340 Donner NW North Canton OH 44720 Office: Mitchell Info Services Inc 9889 Willow Creek Rd San Diego CA 92126

HOLLINGER, LARRY GEORGE, data processor; b. Hershey, Pa., Jan. 1, 1942; s. Rufus Kautz and Anna Mary (Floyd) H.; m. Nancy Lorraine Lehman, Sept. 4, 1961 (div. 1981); children: Sharon Sue, Michael Paul; m. Karen Louise Olt, Oct. 2, 1982. Grad., Electronic Computer Programming Inst., 1968. From internal auditor to computer programmer Pa. Blue Shield, Camp Hill, 1966-69; in charge computer ops. Milton Hershey Sch., 1969-85; dir. data processing Operating Engrs. Local Union 3, San Francisco, 1985—. Served with USAF, 1961-66. Mem. Data Processing Mgmt. Assn. Home: 8 Locksley Ave Apt 7A San Francisco CA 94122 Office: Milton Hershey Sch 474 Valencia St San Francisco CA 94103

HOLLINGSHEAD, SUSAN LYNN PEARSON, dental hygienist; b. Evanston, Ill., Nov. 11, 1946; d. James Edmund and Caroline Clara (Steffens) Pearson; m. Michael G. Hollingshead, Oct. 1, 1966 (div. Aug. 1976); children: Michael Timothy, Daniel CHristopher, Kimberly Michele. AA, Marquette U., 1966; BS, U. Nev., Las Vegas, 1981; MEd., U. Nev., 1981-83. Dental hygienist William Berry, Las Vegas, 1970-71, Fae T. Ahlstrom, Las Vegas, 1972-74, J.R. Schmutz, Las Vegas, 1975-81, Ashman Dental Group., Las Vegas, 1981-87; instr. Clark County Community Coll., North Las Vegas, 1981—; also adv. bd. Clark County Community Coll., No. Las Vegas, 1980-85; keynote speaker dental hygiene graduation Clark County Community Coll., 1986. Den mother Boy Scouts Am., Las Vegas, 1977-79; oral cancer screening clinic Jaycees, Las Vegas, 1977-81; mem. space utilization com. Clark County Sch. Dist. 1983-84, health occupations skills com. 1986; dental health cons. PTA, Las Vegas, 1970-83. Mem. AAUW, Am. Dental Hygienist Assn., Nev. Dental Hygienist Assn. (treas. 1985-86), So. Nev. Dental Hygienist Assn. (treas. 1983-85), Nev. Dental Hygienist Assn. (treas. 1985-87), Fiber Arts Guild (pres. 1977-78), Rich Ms. Investment, (sec. 1985-86), Phi Kappa Phi. Democrat. Mormon. Avocations: playing the harp, weaving, spinning, cross country skiing.

HOLLIST, WILLIAM LADD, political science educator; b. Denver, May 30, 1947; s. William D and Shirley Rosina Grace (Penton) H.; m. Marleen Galvez, Apr. 15, 1970; children: Heidi, Nathan Ladd, Amy. BS, Utah State U., 1971; MA, U. Denver, 1973, PhD, 1974. Research assoc. Northwestern U., Evanston, Ill., 1974-76; asst. prof. internat. relations U. So. Calif., Los Angeles, 1976-81, dir. program internat. polit. economy, 1978-81; prof. polit. sci. Brigham Young U., Provo, Utah, 1981—; dir. grad. studies David M. Kennedy Ctr. Internat. Studies, Brigham Young U., Provo, 1985—; vis. prof. Utah State U., Logan, 1985. Contbg. editor: Exploring Comp. Arms, etc., 1978, World System Structure—Continuity and Change, 1981, An International Political Economy, 1985, Ford, State, and International Political Economy, 1986. Pres. bd. trustees Walnut (Calif.) Valley Unified Sch. Dist., 1977-81. Grantee NSF, Ford Found. Mem. Internat. Studies Assn. (conv. program chmn. 1986-87, pres. Western sect. 1986—, pres. internat. polit. economy sect. 1982-84, 86—, co-editor Internat. Polit. Economy Yearbook 1986-87). Mormon. Avocations: basketball, hiking. Home: 371 E 1140 N Orem UT 84057 Office: Brigham Young U David M Kennedy Ctr 237 HRCB Provo UT 84602

HOLLISTER, CLYDE CARROLL, health care administrator, consultant; b. Sacramento, Oct. 21, 1931; s. Richard Davis and Roxie Arizona (Oliver) H.; m. Patricia Jean Cummins, Sept. 29, 1961; 1 dau., Dana Karlene. A.A., Phoenix Coll., 1957; B.S., Ariz. State U., 1965, M.Ed., 1971. Cert. radiol. technologist, Ariz. Dir. schs. radiol. tech. St. Joseph's Hosp., Phoenix, 1962-67, Good Samaritan Hosp., Phoenix, 1967-73; adminstrv. dir. Prentice Eye Inst. St. Luke's Hosp., Phoenix, 1973-77; dir. Scottsdale (Ariz.) East Homes, Inc., 1980; cons. health care edn. and adminstrn. Scottsdale, 1977—; coordinator radiol. tech. Ariz. State U., cons. in biomed. electronics. Served with U.S. Army N.G., 1949-57. Mem. Am. Soc. Radiol. Technologists (cert. 1953), Am. Hosp. Assn., Am. Mgmt. Assn., Am. Soc. for Tng. and Devel. Developer radiol. tech. coll. degree programs. Address: 8220 E Garfield St M2 Scottsdale AZ 85257

HOLLORAN, DENNIS MICHAEL, soil scientist; b. Dayton, Ohio, Dec. 16, 1948; s. Thomas Patrick and Shirley Ann Holloran; m. Sharon Grimes, Dec. 15, 1979. B.S. in Agronomy, Ohio State U., 1974. Cert. profl. soil scientist. Soil scientist Ohio Dept. Natural Resources, 1974-77; soil scientist, soil surveyor Douglas County (Oreg.) Planning Dept. and Soil Conservation Service, 1977-81; soil scientist South Douglas Soil and Water Conservation Dist. and Soil Conservation Service, Roseburg, Oreg., 1981-83; owner Dennis Holloran Soil Cons., Idleyld Park, Oreg., 1983—; owner Northwest Soil Cons., 1984—. mem. U.S. Orienteering Fedn.; mem. U.S. team, 1978 World Orienteering Championships, Norway. Served with U.S. Army, 1969-71; Vietnam. Decorated Silver Star, DFC (5), Air medal (45). Mem. Am. Soc. Agronomy, Oreg. Soc. Soil Scientists (west-side dir.), Soil Sci. Soc. Am. Home: PO Box 699 Roseburg OR 97470 Office: PO Box 206 Idleyld Park OR 97447

HOLLOWAY, ROBERT WESTER, chemist; b. Morrilton, Ark., Jan. 3, 1945; s. Otho and Bessie Vance (Woolverton) H.; m. Mary Ella Hamel, Dec. 31, 1970; children: David, Jason. BS, Harding Coll., 1967; postgrad., U. Okla., 1968; PhD, U. Ark., 1977. Asst. prof. U. Ark., Pine Bluff, 1976-79; research chemist DuPont Corp., Aiken, S.C., 1979-81; supervisory chemist EPA, Las Vegas, 1981—. Contbr. articles to profl. jours. Served to capt. USAF, 1967-72. Mem. Am. Chem. Soc. Republican. Lodge: Optimists. Avocation: sailing. Home: 383 Tamarack Dr Henderson NV 89015 Office: EPA PO Box 15027 Las Vegas NV 89114

HOLLOWAY, WILLIAM HAROLD, physician; b. Webster City, Iowa, Feb. 27, 1924; s. Harold Earnest and Angie (Allinson) H.; student Purdue U., 1942, Akron U., 1943-44, Pa. State U., 1943; M.D., U. Pitts., 1949; postgrad. Postgrad. Center for Mental Health, 1966-68, Western Inst. Group and Family Therapy, 1971; m. June Dessie Gibson, Dec. 5, 1944 (div. Nov. 1970); children—Gayle Lynn, Joan Lorraine, Shelley Ann; m. 2d, Martha Jeffery, Jan. 1971; children—Jeff, Stephen, Timothy, Patricia. Intern, Riverside Hosp., Toledo, 1949-50; resident Ypsilanti (Mich.) State Hosp., 1954-57; dir. Summit County Mental Hygiene Clinic, Akron, Ohio, 1957-61; practice medicine specializing in psychiatry, Akron, 1958-73, Medina, Ohio, 1973-77, Aptos, Calif., 1977-78, Garden Grove, Calif., 1978-80, Hemet, Calif., 1980—; clin. chief Riverside County Dept. Mental Health (Calif.), 1984-85; psychiat. cons. Springhill Sch., Akron, 1958-61, Boys' Village, Smithville, Ohio, 1961-67; cons. group psychotherapy Summit County Receiving Hosp., 1966-69; emeritus sr. med. staff Akron City Hosp., Akron Gen. Hosp.; active med. staff Hemet Valley Hosp.; clin. asst. prof. Ohio State U., 1968-69; clin. asst. prof. psychiatry Case Western Res. U. Sch. Medicine, 1970-76; pres. Nat. Group Psychotherapy Seminars, 1969-70; tng. cons. Family and Children's Service Soc. Summit County; founder, dir. Midwest Inst. Human Understanding Inc., Akron; cons. Medina County Family Guidance Clinic, 1974-76, Brazilian Inst. Transactional Analysis, Sao Paulo, 1976-. Served with U.S. Army, 1943-46; to maj. USAF, 1949-54. Postgrad. Center for Mental Health fellow, 1966-68. Fellow Am. Psychiat. Assn., Am. Group Psychotherapy Assn. (dir. 1970-72, treas. 1974-76); mem. Ohio State Med. Assn. (del. 1969-71), Tri-State Group Psychotherapy Assn. (pres. 1968-70), Internat. Assn. Group Psychotherapy, AMA, Internat. Transactional Analysis Assn. (teaching mem., pres. 1976-78, trustee), Summit County Med. Soc. (sec. 1964-65, mem. council 1969-72), Ohio Psychiat. Assn. (pres. 1969-70, trustee edn. and research found. 1969-73), Phi Beta Pi, Alpha Omega Alpha. Author: (with Martha M. Holloway) Change Now, 1973, Collected Monographs of the Midwest Institute, 1975; Clinical Transactional Analysis, 1974; Transactional Analysis-An Integrative View in Transactional Analysis After Eric Berue, 1977. Address: 41734 Crest Dr Hemet CA 92344

HOLLOWAY, WILLIAM WELLER, patent attorney; b. Richmond, Va., June 11, 1933; s. William Weller and Mildred Adele (Siehler) H.; m. Karen Christianson; children: William Weller III, Samuel James. BA in Math., Swarthmore Coll., 1954; MSEE, Princeton U., 1956; MS, U. Ill., 1957, PhD in Physics, 1961; JD, Suffolk U., 1971; MBA, Ariz. State U., 1981. Bar: Mass. 1971, Ariz. 1978, U.S. Patent Office 1972. Assoc. corp. patent counsel Honeywell Inc., Phoenix, 1975-84; ptnr. Weiss & Holloway P.C., Scottsdale, Ariz., 1984-85; sole practice Phoenix, 1985—. Patentee in field. Mem. ABA, Ariz. Bar Assn., Mass. Bar Assn., Am. Phys. Soc., Sigma Xi. Home: 626 E Orangewood Ave Phoenix AZ 85020 Office: Parkview Ctr II Suite 102 8453 N Black Canyon Hwy Phoenix AZ 85020

HOLM, ANCHOR EARL, petroleum engineer, consultant; b. Flagstaff, Ariz., June 29, 1944; s. Charles Fenton and Lois (Bushman) H.; m. Michelle Anne Martinez, Sept. 10, 1966; children—Christopher Fenton, Michael Crawford, James Andrew, Andrea Elizabeth. B.S. in Geol. Engring., U. Ariz., 1967; postgrad. U. Tex.-El Paso, 1976-80. Registered profl. engr., Tex. Prodn. engr. Texaco Inc., Cortez, Colo., 1967-71; drilling and reservoir engr. El Paso Natural Gas Co., Farmington, N.Mex. and El Paso, 1971-78; petroleum engr. First Nat. Bank of Midland (Tex.), 1978-80; sr. reservoir engr. HNG Oil Co., Midland, 1980-82; mgr. reservoir engring. Northwest Exploration Co., Denver, 1982; mgr. petroleum engring. First Interstate Bank Denver, 1982-84; co-owner Warner-Holm Engring., Inc., Denver, 1984-86; ptnr. England, Holm and Assocs., Denver, 1987—; assoc. dir., instr. Permian Basin Grad. Ctr., Midland, 1980-82; guest lectr. Colo. Sch. Mines, Golden, 1983—. Served with U.S. Army, 1968-69; Vietnam. Decorated Bronze Star. Mem. Soc. Petroleum Engrs. (chmn. Four Corners petroleum sect. 1977-78), Am. Assn. Petroleum Geologists (assoc.), Nat. Rifle Assn., Northwest YMCA. Republican. Lutheran. Clubs: Arvada Rifle and Pistol, Arvada Soccer Assn. Home: 7878 Owens Ct Arvada CO 80005 Office: England, Holm & Assocs 1900 Grant Suite 500 Denver CO 80293

HOLM, KEVIN EUGENE, military electronics specialist; b. Tacoma, Apr. 24, 1957; s. John Victor Holm and Cecelia Margaret (Sunich) DeVaul; m. Elizabeth Paras Canlas, Feb. 22, 1980; children: Maria Theresa, Michael Canlas, Jonathan Paul. B in Tech. Edn. magna cum laude, Nat. U., 1984, MS in Computers and Edn. with distinction, 1985. Electronics technician USN, 1975—. Mem. AAAS, Friends of the Library of U. Calif. Avocation: intelligent computer assisted instruction research. Home: 8638 Larkdale Ave San Diego CA 92123 Office: USS Acadia AD-42 R4 Div FPO San Francisco CA 96647-2530

HOLM, LEROY WALLACE, oil company consultant, researcher; b. Chgo., May 19, 1923; s. Carl and Anna (Larson) H.; m. Vivian Bernice Lorenz, Nov. 3, 1945; children: Lawrence W., Carol L., Jeffrey A. BSCE, Northwestern U., 1945. Registered profl. engr., Ill. Research engr. Pure Oil Co., Northfield, Ill., 1946-51, sect. leader, Crystal Lake, Ill., 1951-65; research assoc. Union Oil Co., Brea, Calif., 1965-68, sr. research assoc., 1968-80, staff cons., 1980—; lectr. at univs., soc. meetings, Calif., Mo., Ill., Tex., 1970—. Contbr. articles to profl. publs. Numerous patents including on carbon dioxide flooding, hydrocarbon solvent flooding, high pH silicates and chelating agts. to improve micellar polymer flooding; inventor, developer micellar-polymer (Uniflood) process. Officer Crystal Lake Jr. C. of C., 1956-58; leader Boy Scouts Am., 1959-65; chmn. citizen's adv. com. elem schs. Crystal Lake, 1961-64. Served to lt. (j.g.) USN, 1943-46, PTO. Named Enhanced Oil Recovery Pioneer, Soc. Petroleum Engrs. and Dept. Energy, 1984. Mem. Am. Inst. Chem. Engrs., Soc. Petroleum Engrs. (chmn. Chgo. chpt. 1964-65, sec. Los Angeles chpt. 1971, mem. editorial rev. com., disting. lectr. 1972-73, disting. mem. 1984, John Franklin Carll award 1983, disting. mem. emeritus 1986—), AIME, Am. Chem. Soc., Nat. Acad. Engring., Sigma Xi. Republican. Presbyterian. Lodge: Kiwanis. Pioneer inventor, researcher on solvent extraction, enhanced oil recovery processes and mobility control in secondary and tertiary recovery; pioneer researcher to recognize and define relationship of crude oil composition and displacement efficiency in carbon dioxide-miscible flooding; pioneer work on use of foam in gas-driven water-flooding and gas storage. Home: 601 Elinor Dr Fullerton CA 92635 Office: Unical Sci and Tech Div 376 Valencia St Brea CA 92621

HOLM, VANJA ADELE, developmental pediatrician, educator; b. Kiruna, Sweden, Oct. 5, 1928; came to U.S. 1955.; d. C.V. Hjalmar and Elma Adele (Nystrom) H.; m. Carl Holm, June 15, 1952; children: Ingrid Adele, Erik Carl Anders. Med. Kand., Karolinska Inst., Stockholm, 1950, MD, 1955. Intern Swedish Hosp., Seattle, 1955-56; resident in pediatrics U. Wash. Sch. Medicine, Seattle, 1956, 62-64, fellow in devel. pediatrics, 1964-65, instr. pediatrics, 1965-69, asst. prof. pediatrics, 1969-81, assoc. prof. pediatrics, 1981—; attending pediatrician Children's Orthopedic Hosp., Univ. Hosp; med. dir. Boyer Children's Clinic and Presch. Editor: Early Intervention: A Team Approach, 1978 (Am. Med. writers award 1979), The Prader Willi Syndrome, 1981; contbr. 51 articles to profl. jours. Fellow Am. Acad. Pediatrics, Am. Acad. Cerebral Palsy and Devel. Medicine, Am. Assn. Mental Deficiency, Soc. Devel. Pediatrics; mem. N. Pacific Pediatric Soc., Wash. State Med. Assn. (Aesculapius award 1979). Democrat. Office: U Wash CDMRC WJ10 Seattle WA 98195

HOLMAN, GRANVILLE W., JR., heavy construction company executive; b. 1929. Student, Pa. State U. Plant engr. Phila. Coke Co., 1952-54; designer Catalytic Constrn. Co., 1954-56; with Kaiser Engrs., Inc., Oakland, Calif., 1956—, v.p., 1974-77, 1977-81, exec. v.p., 1981-85, chmn., chief exec. officer, 1985—. Office: Kaiser Engineers Inc PO Box 23210 Oakland CA 94623 *

HOLMAN, KERMIT LAYTON, chemical engineer; b. Morris, Minn., Nov. 16, 1935; s. Melvin Martinous and Jennie Ethel (Erickson) H.; m. Audrey Mae Redwing, Nov. 21, 1959; children: Erik, Jennifer, Peter. Student, St. Olaf Coll., 1953-54; B.S., U. N.D., 1957; M.S., U. Idaho, 1961; Ph.D., Iowa State U., 1964. Tape devel. engr. 3M Co., St. Paul, 1957-60; sr. chem. engr. Dow Chem. Co., Golden, Colo., 1964-65; mem. faculty dept. chem. engring. N.Mex. State U., Las Cruces, 1965-76; prof. N.Mex. State U., 1976—; prof., chmn. dept. chem. engring. U. Idaho, Moscow, 1976-81; tech. assoc. Weyerhaeuser Co., Tacoma, 1981-85; sr. engring. specialist Weyerhaeuser Co., 1985—; cons. in field. Mem. Am. Inst. Chem. Engrs., Tech. Assn. Pulp and Paper Industry, Sigma Xi, Tau Beta Pi. Republican. Lutheran. Home: 31619 37th Ave SW Federal Way WA 98023 Office: Weyerhaeuser Co Weyerhaeuser Tech Center WTC 2G22 Tacoma WA 98477

HOLMAN, PAUL DAVID, plastic surgeon; b. Waynesboro, Va., Mar. 13, 1943; s. Wallace D. and Rosalie S. Holman; m. Victoria Lynn Holman, Mar. 1, 1986. B.A., U. Va., 1965; M.D., Jefferson Med. Coll., 1968. Intern, George Washington U. Hosp., 1968-69, resident in gen. surgery, 1969-70, 72-74; resident in plastic surgery Phoenix Plastic Surgery Residency, 1974-76; practice medicine specializing in plastic surgery, Phoenix, 1977—; mem. staff Good Samaritan Hosp., Phoenix, St. Joseph's Hosp., Phoenix, Phoenix Children's Hosp. Served to lt. comdr. USNR, 1970-72. Diplomate Am. Bd. Surgery, Am. Bd. Plastic Surgery. Mem. AMA, ACS, Am. Soc. Plastic and Reconstructive Surgeons, Phi Beta Kappa. Office: 1010 E McDowell Rd 303 Phoenix AZ 85006

HOLMBERG, JAMES JOHN, III, architect; b. Council Bluffs, Iowa, June 18, 1955; s. James John and Mary Lou (Schwery) H.; m. Ann Carolyn Kluthe, May 24, 1986. AA, Platte Tech. Community Coll., 1974; BArch, U. Notre Dame, 1978; JD, Creighton U., 1981. Registered architect, Wis. Bar: Nebr. 1981, U.S. Dist. Ct. Nebr., 1981. Architect USA C.E., Omaha, 1979-85; project engr. K.M.A., San Diego, 1985-86; project architect F.A.D. Architecture and Planning, San Diego, 1986—; gen. counsel Pawnee Scout, Inc., Columbus, Nebr., 1981-85; of counsel Buller & Stansel, Omaha, 1982-83; cons. Clark/Beck & Assocs., San Diego, 1986. Prin. works include St. Vincent de Paul, San Diego, 1986. Mem. AIA (assoc.), ABA, Soc. Am. Mil. Engrs., Nebr. State Bar Assn. Democrat. Roman Catholic. Home: 2330 Grand Ave Apt 5 San Diego CA 92109 Office: FAD Architecture and Planning 1145 10th Ave Suite 2 San Diego CA 92101

HOLMBERG, SUSAN MARIE, insurance company executive; b. Orange, Calif., Mar. 19, 1958; d. Harry Charles and Anna Jean (Kavulich) H. BA in Environ. Studies, Calif. State U., Sacramento, 1980. Lic. real estate agt., Calif. Air pollution specialist Calif. Air Resources Bd., Sacramento, 1980-81; dir. pub. water supply supr. program U.S. V.I. Dept. Conservation and Cultural Affairs, Christiansted, St. Croix, 1981-82; cons. Santa Ana, Calif., 1982-84; loss control cons. Calif. Casualty Mgmt. Co., Orange, 1984-86; policyholder service rep. Citation Ins. Co., Tustin, Calif., 1986—. CPR instr. ARC, Orange County, 1984—. Mem. Air Pollution Control Assn., Am. Indsl. Hygiene Assn., Am. Soc. Safety Engrs., Sigma Delta Pi. Avocations: skiing, windsurfing, ice skating, reading.

HOLMBOE, ARTHUR HENRY, orthopedic surgeon; b. Portland, Oreg., Aug. 8, 1932; s. Arthur Franklin and Margaret Elizabeth (Schinaman) H.; m. Sally Ann Parks, Aug. 21, 1954; children: Jeffrey A., James R., Julie K. BS in Chemistry, Biology, Lewis and Clark Coll., 1954; MD, U. Oreg., 1958. Diplomate Am. Bd. Orthopedic Surgery. Commd. ensign USN, 1957; advanced through grades to comdr. USN, Vietnam, 1968; resigned USN, 1971; practice medicine specializing in orthopedic surgery Los Gatos, Calif., 1971—. Fellow ACS, Am. Acad. Orthopaedic Surgeons; mem. Am. Orthopaedic Soc. for Sports Medicine, Western Orthopaedic Assn., Soc. Mil. Orthopaedic Surgeons, Santa Clara County Med. Soc. (councilor 1978-80, treas. 1980-83), Calif. Med. Assn. (del. 1983—). Republican. Club: Orthopaedic (San Jose, Calif.). Avocations: skiing, flying, fishing, tennis. Office: Los Gatos Orthopaedic Assocs 800 Pollard Rd Los Gatos CA 95030

HOLMEN, ORRIE JEFFREY, electronics company executive; b. Denver, Mar. 17, 1953; s. Orrie Joel and Eunice May (Thompson) H.; m. Mary Jane Wenzel, Apr. 21, 1984; 1 child, Elizabeth Anne. Student, U. Colo., 1972-75. Mgr. repair La Marche Mfg. Co., Des Plaines, Ill., 1971-72; technician Motorola Corp., Schaumburg, Ill., 1972-74; salesman Mktg. Dept., Inc., Denver, 1976; pres. CBTS, Inc., Denver, 1976-78; pres., chief exec. officer U.S. Telephone, Denver and Salt Lake City, 1978—; cons. Marcom, Inc., Salt Lake City, 1983-84. Author: Operations Manual, 1986. Supporter Salt Lake City Rescue Mission, 1985-86. Mem. Full Gospel Bus. Men's Fellowship Internat. (v.p. 1983-84). Republican. Clubs: Prosperity Gold (Tulsa); Success'n' Life (Dallas). Avocations: scuba diving, skiing, tennis, programming. Office: US Telephone 230 S 500 W Salt Lake City UT 84101

HOLMES, DALLAS SCOTT, lawyer, educator; b. Los Angeles, Dec. 2, 1940; s. Donald Cherry and Hazel (Scott) H.; m. Patricia McMichael, Aug. 21, 1965; children—Mark Scott, Tobin John. A.B. cum laude, Pomona Coll., 1962; M.Sc., London Sch. Econs., 1964; J.D., U. Calif.-Berkeley, 1967. Bar: Calif. 1968. Assoc. Best, Best & Krieger, Riverside, Calif., 1968-74, ptnr., 1974—; exec. asst. to Assembly majority floor leader, Calif. State Legislature, Sacramento, 1969-70; asst. adj. prof. Grad. Sch. Mgmt., U. Calif.-Riverside, 1977—; city atty. Cities of Corona, Banning and Redlands (Calif.). Pres., Pomona Coll. Alumni Council, 1973-74, Century Club, Riverside, 1974-76, Citizens Univ. Com., 1983-85, Downtown Riverside Assn., 1987—. Named Man of Yr., Riverside Press-Enterprise, 1962, Young Man of Yr., Riverside Jr. C. of C., 1972. Mem. Riverside County Bar Assn. (pres. 1982), Calif. State Bar Assn. (exec. com. pub. law sect. 1983-86), ABA, Internat. Bar Assn. Republican. Presbyterian. Contbr. articles on mass transit, assessment of farmland in Calif., exclusionary zoning to profl. jours.; author proposed tort reform initiative for Calif. physicians. Home: 4515 6th St Riverside CA 92501 Office: 3750 University Ave PO Box 1028 Riverside CA 92502

HOLMES, JOHN THOMAS, solar energy engineer; b. Oak Park, Ill., Aug. 10, 1936; s. Glenn Thomas and Olive C. (Wolfe) H.; m. Edith M. Kramer, July 13, 1963; children: Ann E., Mark T. BSChemE, U. Wis., 1958; MSChemE, U. Calif., Berkeley, 1960. Group leader Argonne (Ill.) Nat. Lab., 1960-76; div. supr. Sandia Nat. Lab., Albuquerque, N.Mex., 1976—. Patentee in field. Recipient Indsl. Research-100 award Indsl. Research Mag., 1972. Mem. Tau Beta Pi. Democrat. Unitarian. Avocations: jogging, fishing, gardening. Home: 8225 Evangeline Ct NE Albuquerque NM 87109 Office: Sandia Nat Labs Div 6226 Albuquerque NM 87185

HOLMES, OPAL LAUREL, publisher; b. Laurens, Iowa, Oct. 14, 1913; d. Ila Laurel and Jessie Merle (Hesselgrave) Holmes; ed. pub. and pvt. schs.; m. Vardis Fisher, Apr. 16, 1940. Publisher, Opal Laurel Holmes, Pub. Co-author: Gold Rushes and Mining Camps of the Early American West. Recipient Golden Spur award, 1969. Mem. Authors Guild, Authors League Am., Nat. Soc. Lit. and Arts, Internat. Platform Assn. Office: PO Box 2535 Boise ID 83701

HOLMES, PAUL LUTHER, political scientist, educational consultant; b. Rock Island, Ill., Mar. 7, 1919; s. Bernt Gunnar and Amanda Sophia (Swenson) H.; m. Ardis Ann Grunditz, Nov. 1, 1946; children: Mary Ann, David Stephen. B.A., U. Minn., 1940; M.A., Stanford U., 1949, Ed.D., 1968; M.A., George Washington U., 1964. Career officer U.S. Navy, 1941-64, ret. as capt.; adminstr. Laney Coll., Oakland, Calif., 1965-70; dean Contra Costa Coll., San Pablo, Calif., 1970-71; pres. Coll. of Alameda (Calif.), 1971-75, prof. polit. sci., 1975-80; dir. doctoral studies program No. Calif., Nova U., 1975-80; cons. in higher edn., Gig Harbor, Wash., 1981—; regent Calif. Luth. U., 1973-76. Decorated Navy Air, Joint Service medals. Mem. AAUP, Am. Polit. Sci. Assn., Navy League, Stanford Univ. Alumni Assn., Phi Delta Kappa. Lutheran. Club: Rotary (Gig Harbor).

HOLMES, WILLIAM CHARLES, JR., engineering company executive, consultant; b. Akron, Ohio, Dec. 10, 1917; s. William Charles and Ruth Henrietta (Rockhill) H.; m. Portia Dennis Smith, Mar. 24, 1942 (div. 1965); children—Helen, William, Virginia; m. Barbara Lee White, Feb. 4, 1967. A.A., Pasadena Jr. Coll., 1938; B.S., Stanford U., 1940, M.S., 1946; postgrad. MIT, 1941. Chief design engr. Northrop, Hawthorne, Calif., 1946-57; dir. space programs Lockheed, Palo Alto, Calif., 1957-59; v.p., gen. mgr. Radiation, Inc., Mountain View, Calif., 1959-62; pres. Filt-Aire Corp., Hollister, Calif., 1963-65; mng. ptnr. The Xikon Group, Palo Alto, 1965-68; owner Holmes Engring., Palo Alto and Redding, Calif., 1969—; cons. Calif. Energy Commn., 1977—, The Xikon Group, 1965—. Author textbook: Project Management, 1976; author tech. papers in field. Dir. Econ. Devel. Corp. Shasta County, Redding; mem. Air Pollution Control Bd., Redding. Served to lt. USN, 1941-45. Assoc. fellow AIAA; mem. IEEE (sr.), Am. Inst. Bldg. Design (profl. designer, dir. 1983—), Nat. Soc. Profl. Engrs., ASHRAE. Republican. Club: Riverview Golf and Country. Lodge: Rotary (dir. Redding 1982-83). Home: 3689 Suzanne Way Redding CA 96002 Office: Holmes Engring 3689 Suzanne Way Redding CA 96002

HOLMQUIST, GERALD PETER, biology educator; b. Chgo., Feb. 22, 1942; s. Gunnar Alphonse and Elaine (Roehr) H.; divorced; 1 child, Peter Crittenden. BS in Physics, U. Chgo., 1964, MS in Botany, 1966; PhD in Cell Biology, U. Ill., 1970. Research assoc. Karolinska Inst., Stockholm, 1970-71, Harvard U. Sch. Medicine, Cambridge, Mass., 1971-73; research assoc. City of Hope Med. Ctr., Duarte, Calif., 1974-76, assoc. prof. biology, 1986—; asst. prof. Baylor U. Coll. Medicine, Houston, 1976-85. Bd. dirs. Turet's Syndrome Found., 1986. Recipient Career Devel. award NIH, 1979-85. Mem. Genetics Soc. Am., Am. Soc. Cell Biology, Tex. Genetics Soc. Republican. Home: 3764 Live Oak Pomona CA 91767 Office: City of Hope Med Ctr Dept Biology Duarte CA 91010

HOLOHAN, WILLIAM ANDREW, state justice; b. Tucson, June 1, 1928; s. Andrew S. and Dorothy L. (Bennett) H.; m. Kathryn Dewey, Dec. 12, 1953; 4 children. LL.B., U. Ariz., 1950. Bar: Ariz. 1950. Asst. U.S. atty., 1953-60; judge Superior Ct., 1963-72; justice Ariz. Supreme Ct., Phoenix, 1972—, chief justice, 1982-87. Served with U.S. Army, 1950-53. Decorated Bronze Star medal. Office: Ariz Supreme Ct 217 South-West Wing Phoenix AZ 85007

HOLSER, MARY ANN, human services agency executive; b. Detroit, May 21, 1928; d. Ray Ward and Ruth Belle (Ferguson) Harris; m. William Thomas Holser, Dec. 23, 1955; children—Thomas Dana, Alec Stuart, Margaret. B.A., U. Mich., 1950; M.S.W., Ohio State U., 1954; M. Pub. Adminstrn. Harvard U., 1985; doctoral student Community Health, U. Oreg., 1984. Young adult dir. YMCA, Amarillo, Tex., 1950-51; recreation leader Columbus Recreation Dept., Ohio, 1951-53; cottage supr. Juvenile Diagnostic Ctr., Columbus, 1955; group work specialist Spl. Service for Groups, Los Angeles, 1955-56; psychiat. social worker Met. State Hosp., Norwalk, Calif., 1958-60, League of Latin Am. Citizens, Anaheim, Calif., 1965-67, Crisis Intervention Clinic, U. Calif., Irvine Med. Ctr., 1967-70; psychiat. social work cons. Los Angeles County Health Dept., 1970; clin. dir. Alcohol Traffic Safety Program, Eugene, Oreg., 1971-76; co-dir. Drinking Decisions, Eugene, 1977-78; dir. Behanna House, Eugene, 1978-79; exec. dir. Lane County Council on Alcoholism, Eugene, 1979-83; ; mental health examiner mental hearings State of Oreg., 1973—; vis. asst. prof. U. Oreg., Eugene, 1973-76; founder Orange County Free Clinic, 1969. Contbr. articles to profl. jours. Research grantee Max Planck Inst. for Psychiatry, Munich, Fed. Republic of Germany, 1976; winner Eugene Pub. Library Poetry Contest 1st prize, 1983. Mem. rules com. Dem. Nat. Com.; orgn. chmn. Lane County Dem. Cen. Com. Mem. Nat. Assn. Social Workers, Acad. Clin. Social Workers, Oreg. Substance Abuse Assn., Lane County Affirmative Action Com. (chmn.), Oreg. Alcohol Program Mgrs. Assn. (sec.-treas.), Lane County Alcohol Program Mgrs. Assn. (sec.). Democrat. Home: 2620 Dresta de Ruta Eugene OR 97403 Office: U Oreg Sch Community Health Eugene OR 97403

HOLST, WILLIAM JAMES, data processor; b. Frederick, Md., Aug. 22, 1945; s. William Walker and Catherine M. (Loggie) H.; m. Patricia Russell, Jan. 27, 1973; children—Jennifer R., Gretchen M., William R. B.S. in Bus. Adminstrn., No. Ariz. U., 1972. Computer ops. mgr. Samaritan Health Service, Phoenix, 1972-75; material requirements mgr. Pepsi-Cola, Flagstaff, Ariz., 1975-78; dir. fiscal/info. services Flagstaff (Ariz.) Med. Center, 1978-84, mgr. data processing, 1984—. Medic Alert local rep., 1983—; mem., solicitor high tech. equipment, donations No. Ariz. Health Care Found. Served with U.S. Army, 1965-69. Mem. Data Processing Mgmt. Assn. (cert., dir.), Assn. Systems Mgmt., Health Care Fin. Mgmt. Assn., Electronic Computing Health Oriented. Roman Catholic. Home: 390 Bertrand Flagstaff AZ 86001 Office: PO Box 1268 Flagstaff AZ 86002

HOLSTE, ROBERT CLAUDE, electronics executive; b. Northbrook, Ill., Sept. 3, 1937; s. Richard Frederick and Ethelyn Phoebe (Bestor) Holste; m. Lynn Laughlin, Mar. 14, 1964; children: Richard, Kimberly, Elizabeth. BEE, U. So. Calif., 1960. Test engr. Aerojet Gen., Azusa, Calif., 1960-70; program mgr. Oceanic Products, San Diego, 1970-72; mgr. west coast facility Gould, Inc., Bremerton, Wash., 1972—. Mem. Am. Def. Preparedness Assn., Eta Kappa Nu, Tau Beta Pi. Republican. Club: Bremerton Tennis and Swim (pres. 1982-83). Home: 8708 Central Valley Rd Bremerton WA 98310 Office: Gould Inc PO Box 189 Keyport WA 98345

HOLTMAN, WILLIAM J., railroad company executive; b. 1921; married. Grad. in Metall. Engring., Colo. Sch. Mines, 1943, Met.E., 1947. With The Denver and Rio Grande Western R.R. Co., 1958—, chief mech. officer, to 1966, div. supt., 1966-68, v.p. exec. dept., 1968-69, exec. v.p., gen. mgr., 1969-76, pres., chief operating officer, 1976-78, chmn., pres., chief exec. officer, 1978—, dir.; pres., dir. Rio Grande Industries, Inc.; dir. 1st Nat. Bank of Denver. Served to 1st lt. USAAF, 1943-46. Office: Denver & RioGrande Western RR Co 1515 Araphoe St Park Central Bldg Denver CO 80202 *

HOLTON, WILLIAM CHESTER, engineer, consultant; b. Caldwell, Idaho, May 2, 1939; s. Chester Clayton and Margaret Ann (MacLaren) H.; m. Rhoberta Phaigh Romo, June 1, 1958 (div. Sept. 1976); children: William Lee, Robert Charles, Ronald Clayton. AS, Regents Coll., 1986. lic. FCC. Electronic technician Litton Industries, Los Angeles, 1963-66; applications engr. 3M Co., Camarillo, Calif., 1966-74; program analyst USN, Port Magu, Calif., 1974-75; video supr. U. Calif., Santa Barbara, 1975-77; cons. Great Am. Tech. Services, Los Angeles, 1977—; project engr. Amblin Entertainment, Universal City, Calif., 1983-84, Beijing (People's Republic of China) Film Studios, 1982. Creator first digitally controlled screening theater for sound/film/video at Universal Studios, first high speed sound-on-film editing suite in People's Republic of China. Mem. Soc. Motion Picture TV Engrs. (voting). Office: Great Am Tech Services 4219 W Olive Ave Suite 109 Burbank CA 91505

HOLTSMARK, ERIC BIRGER, architect; b. Malmköping, Sweden, July 25, 1937; came to U.S., 1945; s. Bent Erling and Birgit M. (Egerström) H.; m. Aase Kristoffersen, Sept. 5, 1976; children: Devon, Eric II, Mindi, Jenni, Nicole. BArch, U. Calif., Berkeley, 1963. Registered profl. architect, Calif., elec. installation tech., Calif.; cert. architect Nat. Council Archtl. Registration Bds. Journeyman carpenter La Jolla and Berkeley, Calif., 1954-63; owner Modell Design, Berkeley, 1960-63; field engr. Masonic Home Project, Union City, Calif., 1963-64; project coordinator Bechtel Internat., San Francisco, 1964-66; field engr. Bechtel Pacific Ltd., Tasmania, Australia, 1966-68; sr. engr. Bechtel, Inc., N.Y.C., 1968-69; architect, project mgr. Hotel Inter-Continental, Helsinki, Finland, 1969-71, London, 1971-76; mgr. Saudi Arabian projects Bechtel Corp., San Francisco, 1976-78; owner, prin. Comml. and Hotel Devels. (name changed to Holtsmark Architects 1985), San Francisco, 1978—; chmn. Mark-Bentland Properties, San Francisco, 1976—; ptnr., bd. dirs. Eurocal Hotel Devel. Co., London, 1986—. Author: "Putyshestvinik" - Russian Travels Alone, 1960. Office: Holtsmark Architects 1 Market Plaza San Francisco CA 94105

HOLTZ, DAVID, financial consultant; b. 1942; married, 1973. BS, Calif. Inst. Tech., 1964; PhD, U. Calif., Berkeley, 1968; MBA, UCLA, 1983. CPA. Mem. chemistry faculty Calif. Inst. Tech., Pasadena, 1968-71; staff officer Nat. Acad. Scis., Washington, 1971-74; asst. dir. Holcomb Research Inst., Indpls., 1975-77; pres. Glatt-Holtz, Inc., Van Nuys, Calif., 1978—; v.p. finance and chief fin. officer GNP Devel. Corp., Pasadena, Calif., 1984-86; pres. Medivest Corp., Pasadena, 1986—. Editor: Municipal Water Planning; contbr. articles to profl. jours. Mem. Am. Chem. Soc., Am. Inst. CPA's (Isaac Watt Sells award 1982), Calif. Soc. CPA's. Home: 6842 Whitaker Ave Van Nuys CA 91406

HOLTZ, SHELDON LEE, corporate communications specialist; b. Los Angeles, Aug. 6, 1954; s. David Gerald and Sally Freda (Schwimer) H.; m. Ann-Michele Samantha Refkin, Sept. 13, 1975; 1 child, Benjamin David. BA in Journalism, Calif. State U., Northridge, 1976. Staff writer Thousand Oaks (Calif.) News-Chronicle, 1974-75, Calif. Apparel News, Los Angeles, 1975-76; asst. editor Canoga Park (Calif.) Chronicle, 1976-77; employee communications rep. Atlantic Richfield Co., Los Angeles, 1977-83; employee communications editor Transam. Fin. Corp., Los Angeles, 1983-84; employee communications mgr. Mattel Toys, Hawthorne, Calif., 1984—; dir. Communications, 1986—. Editor (newspaper) In Motion, 1985— (Awards of Merit and Excellence, Internat. Assn. Bus. Communicators, 1985, 86); (mag.) Windows, 1985—. Recipient Eagle Scout award Boy Scouts Am., Canoga Park, 1969, 2 Gold Quill awards, 1987. Mem. Internat. Assn. Bus. Communicators (chpt. v.p. communications 1984-85, pres. 1986, several awards). Democrat. Jewish. Avocations: backpacking, fishing. Office: Mattel Toys 5150 Rosecrans Ave Hawthorne CA 90250

HOLTZAPFEL, PATRICIA KELLY, health facility executive; b. Madison, Wis., Jan. 29, 1948; d. Raymond Michael and Laura Margaret (Stegner) Kelly; m. Robert Adrian Bunker, Oct. 4, 1975 (div. June 1979); children: Donald, Theresa, Nicole, Douglas; m. Raymond Paul Holtzapfel, Mar. 12, 1983; children: David, Richard. RN; cert. pub. health nurse. Staff nurse Madison Gen. Hosp., 1970-72; bloodmobile staff nurse ARC, Madison, 1972-73; pub. health nurse Dane County Pub. Health Dept., Madison, 1973-75; field health nurse CIGNA Health Plan, Phoenix, 1975-84; dir. nursing Olsten Health Care, Phoenix, 1984-85; mgr. bus. Holtzapfel Phys. Therapy and Pain Control Clinic, Phoenix, 1985—. Mem. The Exec. Female Assn., Ariz. Networking Council. Avocation: target shooting. Office: Holtzapfel Phys Therapy Pain Control 4025 W Bell Rd Suite #2 Phoenix AZ 85023

HOLWAY, MICHAEL PAUL, health services facility administrator; b. Waterville, Maine, May 1, 1955; s. Paul Snowman and Helen Louise (Walker) H.; m. Stephanie Ann Sutton, Mar. 21, 1986. AS, U. Maine, 1976; BS, Thomas Coll., 1981, MBA, 1983. RN. Dir. personnel Mid-Maine Med. Ctr., Waterville, 1981-83; commd. USAF, 1983, advanced through grades to capt., 1985; assoc. hosp. adminstr. USAF, Wurtsmith AFB, Mich., 1983-86, Warren AFB, Wyo., 1986—; instr. bus. Alpena (Mich.) Community Coll., 1984-86. Supr., chmn. Wurtsmith Community Fed. Credit Union, Oscoda, Mich., 1985-86. Mem. Am. Soc. Healthcare Human Resources Adminstrn.,

Air Force Assn. Avocations: travel, camping, scuba diving. Office: USAF Hosp SGAR FE Waren AFB WY 82005

HOLWELL, BEVERLEY JEAN, nursing educator; b. Sundance, Wyo., Aug. 28, 1943; d. Jerry Merle and Katheryn Elizabeth (Roadifer) Blakeman; m. Kenneth Dean Holwell, Feb. 16, 1968; children: Stephen, Aaron, Debra. AS, Sheridan Coll., 1963; BS, U. Wyo., 1965, postgrad., 1983—. RN. Instr. nursing Sheridan (Wyo.) Coll., 1965-67, instr. nursing and dir. assoc. degree nursing program, 1982—; dir. nursing Meml. Hosp., Sheridan, 1967-76, staff RN, 1985—; charge nurse Sheridan County Pub. Health Ctr., 1976-79; staff RN, nursing supr. VA Hosp., Sheridan, 1979-82; Mem. adv. com. Sheridan County Pub. Health Dept., 1968-73. Sec., bd. dirs. Sheridan County Sr. Citizen's Council, 1974-79; bd. dirs. Meals-on-Wheels program, 1975-77, Sheridan County Health Action Team, 1972-75, Sheridan Coll. Health Sci. Found., 1973-77. Named one of Outstanding Young Women Am., 1969. Mem. Am. Nurses Assn., Wyo. Nurses Assn. (bd. dirs. 1970-74, treas. 1974-78, Spl. Service award 1978), Dist. Nurses Assn. (treas. 1968-72, 85—, bd. dirs. 1972-76, Be Involved Nurse award 1969, Hon. Nurse Yr. 1974, Nurse of Day award 1986), Wyo. Edn. Assn., NEA, Phi Kappa Phi. Republican. Lutheran. Avocations: reading, handicrafts, bicycling. Home: 1718 Big Horn Ave Sheridan WY 82801 Office: Sheridan Coll PO Box 1500 Sheridan WY 82801

HOLYER, ERNA MARIA, author, educator, artist; b. Weilheim, Bavaria, Germany, Mar. 15, 1925; d. Mathias and Anna Maria (Goldhofer) Schretter; A.A., San Jose Evening Coll., 1964; student San Mateo Coll., 1965-67, San Jose State U., 1968-69, San Jose City Coll., 1980-81; DLitt World U., 1984; m. Gene Wallace Holyer, Aug. 24, 1957. Free lance writer under pseudonym Ernie Holyer, 1960—; tchr. creative writing San Jose (Calif.) Met. Adult Edn., 1968—; mem. research bd. advisors Am. Biographical Inst., 1986; exhibited in group shows Crown Zellerbach Gallery, San Francisco, 1973, 74, 76, 77; I.B.C. Gallery, San Francisco, 1978, Los Angeles 1981. Recipient Woman of Achievement Honor cert. San Jose Mercury-News, 1973, 74, 75; Lefoli award for excellence in adult edn. instrn. Adult Edn. Senate, 1972. Mem. Calif. Writers Club. Author: Rescue at Sunrise, 1965; Steve's Night of Silence, 1966; A Cow for Hansel, 1967; At the Forest's Edge, 1969; Song of Courage, 1970; Lone Brown Gull, 1971; Shoes for Daniel, 1974; The Southern Sea Otter, 1975; Sigi's Fire Helmet, 1975; Reservoir Road Adventure, 1982; Wilderness Journey, 1985. Contbr. articles to various mags. and newspapers. Home and Office: 1314 Rimrock Dr San Jose CA 95120

HOLZAPFEL, CHRISTINA MARIE, biologist; b. Balt., Jan. 24, 1942; d. Carl Martin and Ruby (Carlson) Holzapfel; m. William Emmons Bradshaw, May 10, 1971; 1 child, Pilar Antonia Bradshaw. BA, Goucher Coll., 1964; MS, U. Mich., 1968, PhD, 1970; postdoctoral fellow, Harvard U., 1970-71. Grad. research fellow U. Mich., Ann Arbor, 1964-70, lectr., 1970; research asst. Canary Islands, Spain, 1965-66; research fellow Harvard U., Cambridge, Mass., 1970-71; research assoc. U. Oreg., Eugene, 1971—, Tall Timbers Research Sta., Tallahassee, 1977-78, Imperial Coll., Silwood Park, Ascot, U.K., 1986. Contbr. articles to profl. jours. Bd. dirs. Eugene City Planning Com., 1980-81, Eugene Youth Symphony, 1980-84. Fellow Woods Hole Marine Biol. Labs., 1963. Mem. Ecol. Soc. Am., Soc. for Study of Evolution, Sigma Xi. Lutheran. Office: U Oreg Dept Biology Eugene OR 97403

HOLZER, THOMAS LEQUEAR, geologist; b. Lafayette, Ind., June 26, 1944; s. Oswald Alois and Ruth Alice (Lequear) H.; m. Mary Elizabeth Burbach, June 13, 1968; children: Holly Christine, Elizabeth Alice. BSE, Princeton U., 1965; MS, Stanford U., 1966, PhD, 1970. Asst. prof. geology U. Conn., Starrs, 1970-75; adj. environmentalist Griswold & Fuss, Manchester, Conn., 1973-75; research geol. U.S. Geol. Survey, Menlo Park, Calif., 1975-82, research geologist, 1984—; dep. asst. dir. research U.S. Geol. Survey, Reston, Va., 1982-84. Contbr. numerous articles to profl. jours. Coach Am. Youth Soccer Orgn., Palo Alto, Calif., 1979-82. Recipient Superior Service award U.S. Geol. Survey, 1981. Fellow: Geol. Soc. Am. (editor 1983—); mem. AAAS, Am. Geophys. Union, Nat. Water Well Assn. Republican. Presbyterian. Avocation: tennis. Home: 151 Walter Hays Dr Palo Alto CA 94303 Office: US Geol Survey 345 Middlefield Rd Menlo Park CA 94025

HOLZMAN, BARBARA LAPP, social worker; b. Mpls., Apr. 20, 1942; d. Joseph H. and Teresa (Witzman) Lapp; m. Bruce R. Holzman, Sept. 4, 1966; children: Miriam, Tami. BA, U. Minn., 1963; MA, U. Chgo., 1965. Psychiat. social worker Presbyn. St. Luke's Hosp., Chgo., 1965-66, Wis. State Dept. Mental Health, Madison, 1966-67; clin. social worker Family Service Agy., Madison, 1967-70; pvt. practice clin. social work Columbia (S.C.) Pediatric Psychiat. Clinic, 1972-75; pvt. practice social work Columbia, 1975-78, Phoenix, 1978—. Chmn. Behavioral Health task force, Phoenix, 1985—; mem. ritual com. Beth El Synagogue, Phoenix, 1981—; mem Ariz. Council on Soviet Jewry; active Hadassah, Phoenix, 1978—. Recipient Elizabeth Susan Dixon award U. Chgo., 1964, Friend of Counseling award Ariz. Counselors Assn., 1984. Fellow Am. Orthopsychiat. Assn.; mem. Nat. Assn. Social Workers (cert., chmn. credentialing steering com. 1982—), Ariz. Soc. Clin. Social Work and Psychotherapy (pres. 1983-85, chmn. credentialing com. 1979—, Past Pres.'s award 1985), Internat. Conf. Advancement of Pvt. Practice Clin. Social Work (diplomate), Phi Beta Kappa. Avocations: reading, antiquing, traveling, walking. Office: 525 N 18th St #303 Phoenix AZ 85006

HOM, RICHARD YEE, research aerospace engineer; b. Phoenix, July 26, 1950; s. Tommy Look and Betty (Mah) H.; B.S. in Engring. Sci. and Aero. and Aerospace Tech., Ariz. State U., 1973; m. Kathleen Chien; 1 child, Matthew Thomas. Asst. engr. Sperry Flight System, Phoenix, 1973; sr. engr., composite tool engring. Boeing Comml. Airplane Co., Seattle, 1973-84; specialist engr. research and devel., metall. processing and advanced projects Boeing Aerospace Co., 1984—, also automation tech. Mem. Air Force Assn., Soc. Mfg. Engrs., AIAA. Home: 28704 15th Ave S Federal Way WA 98003 Office: Boeing Aerospace Co M/S 6K-43 PO Box 3999 Seattle WA 98124

HOM, STEPHEN, communications executive; b. San Francisco, Feb. 13, 1932; s. Joseph Heng and Anna (Wong Shee) Hom; m. Nellie Dolores Chew, Apr. 21, 1956; children: Christopher Shannon, Valeria Saint Elizabeth (Mrs. L. McDonald), Randolph Stevenson, Lawrence Sterling. B.S., U. San Francisco, 1980; B.A., U. Calif.-Berkeley, 1983; M.B.A., Calif. Coast U., 1984. Field engr. heavy mil. electronics div. Gen. Electric Co., Syracuse, N.Y., 1956-60; tech. dir. KRON-TV, NBC affiliate, Chronicle Broadcasting Co., San Francisco, 1960-80; del. 31st internat. conv. Internat. Brotherhood Elec. Workers Union, Atlantic City, 1978, mem. exec. bd., 1975-80, pres. Local 202, San Francisco, 1978-80; del. San Francisco Labor Council, 1978-80, Alameda Central Labor Council, Calif., 1978-80; ops. mgr. TV Broadcast Sta. KTSF, San Francisco, 1980; corp. dir. Lincoln TV, Inc., San Francisco, 1980-82; pres. Marshall Telecommunications, Inc., Oakland, Calif., 1982-83; mgmt. cons. KTSF, San Francisco, 1982-83; spl. cons. corporate pres. Radar Devices, Inc., San Leandro, Calif., 1982-83; tech., mgmt. cons. Maharlika Broadcasting System, Philippines, 1983-85; bus. cons. Shelter Metropolis, Inc., Philippines, 1983-85, Ministry Human Settlements, Devel. Communications Service Bur., Philippines, 1983-84; pres. Stevens Assocs., Cons., Oakland, Calif., 1983-85; Charlex Corp., USA, 1984-85; agt. Roblett Indsl. Constrn. Corp., Philippines, 1984—; v.p. bus. devel. Roblett Constr. (USA) Ltd., Los Angeles, 1984—; v.p. bus. devel. Engring. Traders Corp., Tokyo, 1986—; pres. The Pinnacle Group Contractors, Traders, Cons., Oakland, Calif., 1984—. Author: Managerial Supervision: A Systems Approach to Planning, Organizing and Coordinating, 1983; RF Pulse Analysis, 1983. Chmn. Oakland Civil Service Commn., Calif., 1984—. Mem. adv. com. Calif. State Welfare Dept. Social Services, Sacramento, 1986—. Served with Signal Corps, U.S. Army, 1953-55. Recipient Nat. Acad. TV Arts and Scis. award for engring. achievement, 1977-78; Dist. Leadership award, Subscription TV of Am., 1980-81; Maharlika Broadcasting System Meritorious award Philippine Ministry Pub. Info., 1983-84. Mem. Inst. Radio Engrs., Soc. Motion Picture and TV Engrs., Am. Rocket Soc., Nat. Acad. TV Arts and Scis., Assn. Cons. Mgmt. Engrs., Inst. Mgmt. Cons., Soc. Broadcast and Communications Engrs. Republican. Roman Catholic. Office: State of Calif Dept Social Services Intergovtl Affairs 744 P St Sacramento CA 95814

HOMAN, RALPH WILLIAM, finance company executive; b. Wilkes-Barre, Pa., June 7, 1951; s. Norman Ryan and Adelaide Bernice (Sandy) H.; m. Donna Marie Webb, Jan. 25, 1975. BS in Acctg., Wheeling Coll., 1977; MBA in Mktg., Nat. U., 1986. Paymaster Dravo Corp., Pitts., 1974-75; tax preparer H&R Block, Wheeling, W.Va., 1977; fin. services exec. NCR Credit Corp., Sacramento, 1977-84; leasing exec. CSB Leasing, Sacramento, 1984-85; pres. Convergent Fin. Services, Sedona, Ariz., 1985—. Co-winner Name the Plane Contest Pacific Southwest Airlines, 1984. Republican. Episcopalian. Avocations: nautilus weight lifting, camping, golf. Home and Office: Convergent Fin Services 210 Canyon Diablo Rd Sedona AZ 86336

HOMBS, KAREN KAY, financial planner; b. Denver, Aug. 3, 1942; d. Arthur Clark Eugene and Norma May (Urquhart) Ryman; grad. U. Denver/Colo. Women's Coll., 1984; m. Thomas Gibson Hombs, Apr. 12, 1978; 1 child, Timothy John. With Samsonite Corp., Denver, 1960-75, employee relations rep., supr., 1965-71, labor relations rep., 1971-75; labor relations rep. Climax Molybdenum Co. (Colo.) div. AMAX, 1975-78, prin. labor relations adminstr., 1978-83; registered rep. IDS/Am. Express, 1983—. Mem. council Lord of the Mountains Lutheran Ch., Summit County, Colo., 1979-80, founded women's chpt. Luth. Ch. Women, 1976, chpt. chmn., 1976-77, Sunday Sch. supt., 1976-81. Mem. Indsl. Relations Research Assn., Am. Mgmt. Assn., Internat. Assn. Fin. Planning. Club: Toastmasters (sec.-treas. 1984). Home: 7640 W 24th Ave Lakewood CO 80215 Office: IDS/Am Express Inc 1385 S Colorado Blvd Suite 620 Denver CO 80222

HONG, KEITH CHIEC CHAO, composite material engineer; b. Cholon, Saigon, Socialist Republic of Vietnam, Mar. 17, 1955; came to U.S., 1973; s. Yao Wan and Chou Tchen (Hoang) H. BS in Chemistry and Math. with honors, Ill. State U., 1977; MS in Chemistry, U. Wis., 1979. Research asst. Ill. State U., Normal, 1975-77; teaching and research asst. U. Wis., Madison, 1977-79; project engr. Firestone Tire & Rubber, Akron, Ohio, 1979-80; mem. tech. staff Rockwell Internat., Downey, Calif., 1980-85; sr. engr. Northrop Corp., Hawthorne, Calif., 1985—; lab. asst. Carnegie-Mellon U., Pitts., 1976. Mem. Soc. Advancement Material and Process Engring., Soc. Plastics Engrs. Avocations: collecting stamps, swimming, tennis. Home: 777 Bellflower Blvd #218 Long Beach CA 90815 Office: Northrop Corp Aircraft Div One Northrop Ave Hawthorne CA 90250

HONG, NORMAN G. Y., architect; b. Honolulu, May 5, 1947; s. Kwai Ing and Patricia Y.S. (Dye) H.; m. Lorna Sachiko Yano, Aug. 11, 1973; 1 child, Christopher. T.S.C. B.A. in Architecture, U. Hawaii, 1969. Registered architect, Hawaii. Designer, John Tatom Architect, Honolulu, 1969-71; assoc. Group 70 Inc., Honolulu, 1971-77, prin., 1977-80, ptnr., 1980-84, mng. ptnr., 1984—. Bd. dirs. Manpower Planning Agy. Honolulu, 1972; com. mem. Ann. Gov./Mayor's Prayer, Honolulu, 1984; mem. Mayor's Adv. Com. on Chinatown Gateway, 1987; mem. Haleiwa Spl. Design Adv. Com., 1986-87. Recipient C.W. Dickey award U. Hawaii, 1977, Cert. Exemplary Performance, Dept. Navy Pacific Div., 1984. Mem. Constrn. Specifications Inst., AIA, (v.p./pres.-elec. Hawaii 1987, sec. Hawaii 1984-86, chmn. state conv., 1983). Club: Plaza. Lodge: Rotary. Office: Group 70 Inc 924 Bethel St Honolulu HI 96813

HONG, STEVE, manufacturing company executive; b. Stockton, Calif., Dec. 26, 1947; s. James and Ng She Hong; m. Gladys Huey, Aug. 8, 1971; children: Roger, Russell, Aimee. BS, San Jose State U., 1970. Asst. mgr. W.T. Grant Co., San Jose, 1970-71; field underwriter N.Y. Life Ins. Co., 1971-72; asst. sales mgr. N.Y. Life Ins. Co., Palo Alto, Calif., 1972; with Paul Masson Vineyards, 1972-77, chief acct., 1975-77; asst. controller NPI Corp., 1977-79; controller Forman Industries, Hayward, Calif., 1979, controller, gen. mgr., 1979-85; sec. and treas. Alerco and Hayward Steel, Inc. (later A & H Steel, Inc.), Union City, Calif., 1985-86, v.p., 1986—. Mem. USNG, 1970-76. Republican. Methodist. Home: 1210 Shriver Ct San Jose CA 95132 Office: A & H Steel Inc 1000 Whipple Blvd Union City CA 94587

HONIG, BILL, state educational administrator; b. San Francisco, Apr. 23, 1937; s. Louis and Miriam (Anixter) H.; m. Nancy Catlin, June 2, 1973; children: Michael, Carolyn, Steven, Jonathan. BA, U. Calif., Berkeley, 1958, JD, 1963; MA, San Francisco State U., 1972. Bar: Calif. 1964; cert. tchr., Calif. Clk. Calif. Supreme Ct., 1963-64; atty. Calif. Dept. Fin., 1964-67; assoc. Pettit & Martin, San Francisco, 1967-71; tchr. San Francisco Unified Sch. Dist., 1972-76; dir. Staff Devel. Project, San Francisco, 1977-79; supt. Reed Union Elem. Sch. Dist., Tiburon, Calif., 1979-82; supt. pub. instrn. State of Calif., Sacramento, 1983—; mem. Calif. State Bd. Edn., 1975-82, past officer, pres. exec. sec. 1982; regent U. Calif., 1983—; trustee Calif. State Colls. and Univs., 1983—. Author: (with others) Handbook for Planning an Effective Reading Program, 1983; Last Chance for Our Children: How You Can Help Save Our Schools, 1985; contbr. articles to profl. jours. Mem. Carnegie Forum on Edn., PTA, YMCA; bd. dirs. Californians Preventing Violence. Served to 2d lt. U.S. Army, 1958-59. Mem. C. of C. (state edn. com.), Order of Coif. Jewish. Avocations: reading, running, swimming, piano. Office: Calif State Dept Edn 721 Capitol Mall Suite 524 San Francisco CA 95814

HONSINGER, RICHARD W., JR., physician; b. Chewelah, Wash., May 26, 1938; s. Richard W. and Della Lucille (Whitley) H.; m. Marian A. McKeirnan, June 11, 1960; children: Charles, Joyce, Richard III, Patrick, Keri. BS in Zoology with honors, Wash. State U., 1959; MD with honors, U. Wash., 1963. Diplomate Am. Bd. Internal Medicine, Am. Bd. Allergy/Immunology. Intern the resident in internal medicine U. N.C., Chapel Hill, 1963-65; resident in internal medicine U. Wash., Seattle, 1967-69; practice medicine specializing in internal medicine Los Alamos (N.Mex.) Med. Ctr., 1969—; clin. assoc. U. N.Mex., Albuquerque, 1969—; cons. Los Alamos Nat. Labs., 1987—. Co-author: Bronchial Asthma, 1978; contbr. articles to profl. jours. Mem. adv. bd. U. N.Mex., Los Alamos, 1978—. Served with USPHS, 1965-67. Meade-Johnson fellow ACP, 1967. Mem. Phi Beta Kappa, Alpha Omega Alpha. Democrat. Roman Catholic. Lodge: Kiwanis (pres. 1983). Office: Los Alamos Med Ctr Los Alamos NM 87544

HOOD, FRED H., real estate broker; b. Granite, Okla., Feb. 23, 1926; s. Fred H. and Gertrude E. (Abel) H.; B.S. in Bus. Mgmt., M.Public Adminstrn., U. No. Colo.; m. Shirley Rose Brenk, July 2, 1964. Served with USN, 1944-47, U.S. Army, 1949-52, U.S. Air Force, 1956-72, ret., 1972; indsl. engr. City of Denver, 1972-74; pres. Community Devel. Co., 1972-80; mgmt. analyst USAF, Denver, 1974-79; mayor City of Aurora (Colo.), 1975-79; guest lectr. U.S. Conf. Mayors, 1978, Colo. Mcpl. League, 1978. Mem. Denver Regional Council Govt., 1975-79, Adams County Council Govt., 1975-79, Arapahoe County Council Mayors, 1975-79; mem. transp. com. U.S. Conf. Mayors, 1976-79; mem. policy bd. Colo. Municipal League, 1976-78; pres. Wren Assn., 1980-82. Mem. Am. Inst. Indsl. Engrs., Am. Soc. Mil. Comptrollers, Western Govtl. Research Assn., Am. Mgmt. Assn., Air Force Assn., 45th Inf. Div. Assn., Aurora Hist. Soc., Internat. Platform Assn. Democrat. Clubs: Lions (state sec.-treas. 1980-84), Am. Legion (pub. service citation 1976-79), VFW, DAV, Masons, Shriners. Home: 12255 E Louisiana Ave Aurora CO 80012

HOOD, GEORGE M., chemist; b. Milo, Maine, Jan. 31, 1945; s. Ralph A. and Madeline (Cary) H. BS, U. Maine, 1970—; MS, U. Wyo., 1979. Chemist Wyo. Dept. Agr., Laramie, 1976—; bd. dirs. High Plains Liquid Chromatography, Laramie, 1984—. Served with USN, 1970-72. Mem. Am. Chem. Soc., Nat. Rifle Assn. (life), Am. Legion. Republican. Avocations: rock climbing, hunting, shooting, cross-country skiing. Office: Wyo Dept Agr 1174 Jackson Laramie WY 82070

HOOK, TODD ANTHONY, chemical engineer, consultant; b. Auburn, Calif., Sept. 28, 1959; s. Golden Duane and Judy Ann (Dahl) H.; m. Christine Lee Walsek, May 25, 1985; 1 child, Jared Dalton. Student, Sierra Coll.; BSChemE, U. Calif., Berkeley. Engring. asst. NWT Corp., San Jose, Calif., 1981-82, assoc. cons., 1982-87; cons. San Jose, 1987—. Mem. Am. Inst. Chem. Engrs., Am. Chem. Soc. Avocations: four wheeling, water and snow skiing. Home: 6997 Polvadero Dr San Jose CA 95119

HOOPER, FREDERICK RICHARD, ret. headmaster; b. San Francisco, July 31, 1908; s. John Franklin and May (Frisbee) H.; m. Grace Fletcher Read, June 24, 1937; 1 son, Robert Moore. A.B., Pomona Coll., 1933; postgrad., Claremont Grad. Sch., 1933-34. Master Webb Sch. of Calif., Claremont, 1933-62; head math. dept. Webb Sch. of Calif., 1939-1962, dir. studies, 1955-62, mem. faculty exec. com., 1957-62, headmaster, 1962-73, emeritus, 1973—. Troop committeeman Old Baldy council Boy Scouts Am., 1953-56. Mem. Calif. Assn. Ind. Schs. (head math. sect. 1958-62, treas. 1964-70), Am. Philatelic Soc., S.A.R., John More Assn., Headmasters Assn., First Century Families Calif., Cum Laude Soc., Phi Delta Kappa. Conglist. Clubs: Rotarian, Newport Beach Tennis, Bear Valley Gang Pomona Valley; California (Los Angeles). Home: PO Box 155 Corona Del Mar CA 92625

HOOPER, HENRY OLCOTT, university dean, physicist; b. Washington, Mar. 9, 1935; s. Olcott Lorin and Eleanor (Drew) H.; m. Donna Faulkingham, June 10, 1956; children: Deborah, Bruce, Katherine, Michael, Andrew. B.S. in Engring. Physics, U. Maine, 1956; M.S. in Physics, Brown U., 1959, Ph.D., 1961. Asst. prof. Brown U., Providence, 1961-64; asst. prof. physics Wayne State U., Detroit, 1964-66, assoc. prof., 1966-70, prof., 1970-73; prof., chmn. dept. physics U. Maine, Orono, 1973-76, dean Grad. Sch., 1977-80; assoc. v.p. acad. affairs, dean Grad. Coll. No. Ariz. U., Flagstaff, 1981—; con. NASA, Huntsville, Ala., 1967-68; mem. rev. panel div. ednl. programs Argonne Nat. Lab., Ill., 1982-84. Author: College Physical Science, 3d edit., 1974, Physics and the Physical Perspective, 1977, 2d rev. edit., 1980; editor: Conf. Procs. Amorphous Magnetism, 1973. Fellow Am. Phys. Soc.; mem. Am. Assn. Physics Tchrs., AAAS. Home: 3230 Meadowbrook Flagstaff AZ 86004 Office: No Ariz U PO Box 4085 Flagstaff AZ 86011

HOOPER, JOHN DOUGLAS, technical marketing executive; b. San Francisco, June 25, 1953; s. Herbert John and Ursula (Douglas) H. AS, Coll. San Mateo, 1977. Sr. engring. technician ESL, Inc. subs. TRW, Sunnyvale, Calif., 1978-80; sr. field engr. Bell & Howell, Pasadena, Calif., 1980-83; account exec. Datatape, Inc. subs. Kodak, Pasadena, Calif., 1983—. Mem. Assn. Old Crows, Armed Forces Communication Electronics Assn., Air Force Assn. Republican. Avocations: hunting, fishing, travel, tennis, sports. Office: Datatape Inc subs Kodak 599 W Mathilda Ave Suite 130 Sunnyvale CA 94086

HOOPER, JON KIRK, wildlife ecology educator; b. Oroville, Calif., Jan. 10, 1948; s. Archie Gordon and Evelyn (Overstreet) H.; m. Catherine Kent, Nov. 21, 1981; 1 child, Shawn Kent. BS, U. Calif., Davis, 1970, PhD, 1980; MS, Colo. State U., 1972. Cert. wildlife biologist. Fish culturist Colo. Div. Wildlife, Denver, 1972-73; staff research assoc. U. Calif., Davis, 1973-78; assoc. prof. Calif. State U., Chico, 1978—; owner Effective Slide Presentations, Chico, 1975—. Contbr. sci. articles to profl. publs. Named Conservation Editor of Yr., Calif. Natural Resource Fedn., 1977; recipient Meritorious Performance award Calif. State U., 1984. Mem. Wildlife Soc., Western Interpreters Assn., Conservation Edn. Assn., Loomis Mus. Assn. (bd. dirs.), Calif. Nat. Resource Fedn. (bd. dirs.). Avocations: snow skiing, sailing, backpacking, piano, gardening. Home: 1870 Vallombrosa Ave Chico CA 95926 Office: Calif State U Dept Recreation and Parks Mgmt Chico CA 95929-0560

HOOPER, ROBERT LEE, JR., safety engineer, industrial engineer; b. Milw., Apr. 8, 1956; s. Robert Lee and Martha Marion Hooper; m. Melinda Rae Kintner, Aug. 21, 1982. BS in Mfg. Indsl. Tech., Colo. State U., 1979. Cert. mfg. technologist. Assoc. indsl. engr. Motorola Govt. Electronics Div., Scottsdale, Ariz., 1979; mfg. engr. Ampex Corp., Colorado Springs, Colo., 1980-83; sr. mfg. engr. Johnson and Johnson Ultrasound, Englewood, Colo., 1983-84; sr. mfg. engr. ROLM Telecommunications div. IBM, Colorado Springs, 1984-85, safety, indsl. engr., 1986—. First aid instr. Pikes Peak chpt. ARC, Colorado Springs, 1984—. Recipient Meritorious Service award Emergency Med. Technician Assn. Colo., 1981. Mem. Inst. Indsl. Engrs., Human Factors Soc., Nat. Fire Protection Assn. Avocations: hiking, backpacking, skiing, church activies. Office: Rolm Telecommuications Div IBM 4678 Alpine Meadow Ln Colorado Springs CO 80919

HOOVER, DANIEL WAYNE, advertising executive; b. Van Nuys, Calif., Apr. 10, 1947; s. Franklin Perry and Vera Wanda (Johnson) H.; m. Joan Carol Motta, May 29, 1971; 1 son, Timothy Daniel. B.A., San Fernando Valley (Calif.) State U.-Northridge, 1969. Prodn. mailer Los Angeles Times, 1965-70; self-employed profl. entertainer Pacific states, 1968-70; regional sales mgr. N.Am. Services Inc., Orange County, Calif., 1970-71; dir., pres. Innovative Med. Systems Inc., Fullerton, Calif., 1971-72; exec. v.p. Hoover & Assocs./Hoover Communications Group Inc., Fullerton and Phoenix, 1972-74; chmn., pres. Estey-Hoover Inc., Newport Beach, Calif., 1975—; ptnr. Hoover & McKay Enterprises, 1979-80; guest lectr. colls. and civic orgns. Founding pres. Sun Valley (Calif.) Jr. Coordinating Council, 1964-65; bd. dirs. Orange County Family Service Assn., 1976-77, Orange County Arts Alliance, Hoag Hosp. 552 Club; bd. dirs. Greentree Homeowners Assn., 1980-86, pres., 1984-86; mem. communications com. Orange County United Way, 1979-81; mem. Exec. Council of Orange County; mem. govtl. affairs com. Orange County Indsl. league; mem. founding council Irvine YMCA; founder Great Irvine Campout, 1984. Named Am. Legion Young Man of Yr., Sun Valley, 1965. Mem. Am. Assn. Advt. Agys. (nat. client services com. 1979-83), Western States Advt. Agys. Assn., Am. Advt. Fedn., Orange County Advt. Fedn., Orange County Profl. Assn., Bus. Forum, Pi Kappa Alpha (pres.). Republican. Club: Newport Balboa Rotary. Feature columnist various bus. publs.

HOOVER, RICHARD DEE, professional society administrator; b. Drumright, Okla., May 4, 1941; s. John Dee and Mary Alliene (Turnbull) H.; m. Julie Ann Grever, Aug. 18, 1975; children: Erik Stefan, Kurt Uwe, Karl Dieter. BS in Engring., Utah State U., 1964. Engr. Mont. State Hwy. Dept., Helena, 1964; commd. USAF, 1965, advanced through grades to capt., resigned, 1975; v.p. Paralyzed Vets. of Am., Washington, 1983-84, pres., 1984—, also bd. dirs.; cons. 801 18th St. Assn., Washington, 1983—; mem. nat. adv. bd. on tech. and disabled HHS, Washington, 1985—; state commr. Ariz. Vets. Service Commn., Phoenix, 1984—; mem. Ariz. Whitehouse Conf. Handicapped Individuals, Phoenix, 1986; mem. vets. adv. com. on rehab. U.S. VA, Washington, 1985—; bd. dirs. PEP Corp., Wilton, N.H., 1984—, Ariz. Paralyzed Vets. Am., Phoenix, 1977—; chmn., trustee Spinal Cord Research Found., Washington, 1984—. Mem. planning com. United Way, Tucson, 1982; mem. pvt. industry council Job Tng. Ptnrship. Act, Pima County, Ariz., 1983-86; mem. planning council CETA, Pima County, 1980-83. Decorated D.F.C., Air medal with 12 oak leaf clusters; named one of Outstanding Young Men in Am., 1975. Mem. ASCE, Air Force Assn., Ret. Officers Assn., Mensa, Nat. Rifle Assn., Nat. Spinal Cord Injury Assn. (bd. dirs. 1986—). Democrat. Baptist. Lodge: Masons. Avocations: hunting, shooting. Office: 8963 E Tanque Verde Suite 251 Tucson AZ 85749

HOOVER, WILLIAM R(AY), computer service co. exec.; b. Bingham, Utah, Jan. 2, 1930; s. Edwin Daniel and Myrtle Tennessee (McConnell) H.; m. Sara Elaine Anderson, Oct. 4; children—Scott, Robert, Michael, James, Charles. B.S., M.S., U. Utah. Sect. chief Jet Propulsion Lab., Pasadena, Calif., 1954-64; v.p. Computer Scis. Corp., El Segundo, Calif., 1964-69, pres., 1969—, chmn. bd., 1972—. Office: Computer Sciences Corp 2100 E Grand Ave El Segundo CA 90245

HOPE, GERRI DANETTE, telecommunications specialist; b. North Highlands, Calif., Feb. 28, 1956; d. Albert Gerald and Beulah Rae (Bane) Hope. A.S., Sierra Coll., Calif., 1977; student Okla. State U., 1977-79. Sr. admissions clk. Bass Meml. Hosp., Enid, Okla., 1978-79; instructional asst. San Juan Sch. Dist., Carmichael, Calif., 1979-82; telecommunications supr. Calif. Dental Service, San Francisco, 1982-85; telecommunications coordinator Farmers Savs. Bank, Davis, Calif., 1985—; cons. and lectr. in field. Mem. Women in Telecommunications, Nat. Assn. Female Execs. Republican. Avocations: writing; computers; ceramics; animal behavior; traveling. Home: 3025 U St North Highlands CA 95660

HOPE, JOHN CHARLES, JR., lawyer; b. Cleve., Nov. 12, 1948; s. John Charles and Ruth Marie (Carens) H. B.A., U. Nev.-Reno, 1974; J.D., Western State U., 1977. Bar: Nev. 1978, Calif. 1977, U.S. Dist. Ct. Nev. 1979, U.S. Ct. Appeals (9th cir.) 1981, U.S. Dist. Ct. (so. dist.) Calif. 1982, U.S. Dist. Ct. (ea. dist.) Calif. 1983. Atty., Conn and Hardesty, Reno, Nev., 1979-82; sole practice, Reno, 1982—. Republican. Roman Catholic. Home: 3230 Pierremont Rd Reno NV 89503 Office: PO Box 13043 Reno NV 89507

HOPFIELD, JOHN JOSEPH, biophysicist, educator; b. Chgo., July 15, 1933; s. John Joseph and Helen (Staff) H.; m. Cornelia Fuller, June 30, 1954; children—Alison (Mrs. Charles C. Lifland), Jessica, Natalie. A.B., Swarthmore Coll., 1954; Ph.D., Cornell U., 1958. Mem. tech. staff Bell Telephone Labs., 1958-60, 73—; vis. research physicist Ecole Normale Superieure, Paris, France, 1960-61; asst. prof., then asso. prof. physics U. Calif. at Berkeley, 1961-64; prof. physics Princeton U., 1964-80, Eugene Higgins prof. physics, 1978-80; Dickinson prof. chemistry and biology Calif. Inst. Tech., Pasadena, 1980—. Trustee Battelle Meml. Inst., 1982—. Guggenheim fellow, 1969, MacArthur Prize fellow, 1983; recipient Golden Plate award Am. Acad Achievement, 1985. Fellow Am. Phys. Soc. (Oliver E. Buckley prize 1968, Biol. Physics prize 1985); mem. Nat. Acad. Scis., Am. Acad. Arts and Scis., Neuroscis. Research Program, Phi Beta Kappa, Sigma Xi. Home: 931 Canon Drive Pasadena CA 91106 Office: Calif Inst Tech 164-30 Pasadena CA 91125

HOPKINS, ANNADAWN EDWARDS, coll. pres.; b. Monroe, La., May 24, 1930; d. Robert Crawford and Annadawn (Watson) Edwards; A.B., Tift Coll., 1949; M.B.A., Loyola U., New Orleans, 1968; Ed.D., Seattle U., 1981; postgrad. New Orleans Baptist Theol. Sem., 1949-51, Va. Poly. Inst. and State U., 1969-70; m. James Wesley Hopkins, June 2, 1951 (div. Dec. 1978); children—Dawn Hopkins Warner, Lyn Hopkins Shearon. Adminstrv. sec. to pres. Reed Unit-Fans Inc., New Orleans, 1955-56; instr. sec. scis. Greenleaf Coll., Atlanta, 1958-61, asst. dir., 1959-61; adminstrv. asst. to regional mgr. petroleum supply and transp. div. Humble Oil & Refining Co., New Orleans, 1961-63; adminstrv. asst. to dean Coll. Bus. Adminstrn., Loyola U., New Orleans, 1963-66, dir. adminstrv. practices degree program, asst. prof. bus. adminstrn., 1966-68; asst. prof. bus. Radford (Va.) Coll., 1968-71; instr. Shoreline Community Coll., Seattle, 1972-74, prof. mgmt. and bus. law, 1974—, chmn. bus. adminstrn. div., 1974-83; dir. Archival Mgmt. Cons., Inc., Seattle, 1979—; pres. Everett (Wash.) Bus. Coll., 1980-84. Named Sec. of Year, Nat. Secs. Assn., 1963. Mem. Am. Mgmt. Assn., Pacific N.W. Bus. Law Assn. (pres.), Am. Bus. Law Assn., Am. Vocat. Assn., Nat. Bus. Edn. Assn., DAR, Beta Gamma Sigma, Kappa Delta Pi, Phi Chi Theta, Alpha Gamma Beta, Matrix Table. Home: 3847 NE 155th Pl Seattle WA 98155 Office: 16101 Greenwood Ave N Seattle WA 98133

HOPKINS, BARBARA PETERS, corporate communications executive, author; b. Santa Monica, Calif., Sept. 26, 1948; d. Philip Rising and Caroline Jean (Dickason) Peters; m. Philip Joseph Hopkins, May 23, 1981. AA, Santa Monica Coll., 1971; BS, San Diego State U., 1976; postgrad. UCLA, 1981-82, 84. Gen. ptnr. Signet Properties, Los Angeles, 1971-85; tech. editor C. Brewer & Co., Hilo, Hawaii, 1975-76; editor Aztec Engineer, San Diego, 1976-77; regional publicist YWCA, San Diego, 1977-78; campaign cons. Rep. Candidates, San Diego, 1978; pres. Humbird Hopkins Inc., Los Angeles, 1979—; pub. relations cons. ASCE, San Diego, 1975-76, Am. Soc. Mag. Photographers, San Diego, 1980. Author: The Layman's Guide to Raising Cane: A Guide to the Hawaiian Sugar Industry, 1976, The Student's Survival Guide, 1977, 2d edit. 1978. Council mem. Mayor's Council on Libraries, Los Angeles, 1969; mem. Wilshire Blvd. Property Owners Assn., Santa Monica, 1972-78; docent Mus. Sci. and Industry, Los Angeles, 1970; founding mem. Comml. and Indsl. Properties Assn., Santa Monica, 1982—. Recipient Acting award Santa Monica Coll., 1970. Mem. Internat. Assn. Bus. Communicators, Sales and Mktg. Execs. Assn. Club: Santa Monica Athletic. Avocations: writing, travel, opera. Office: Humbird Hopkins Inc PO Box 39 San Clemente CA 92672

HOPKINS, BRUCE WALLACE, set designer, consultant, theatre educator, administrator; b. Yakima, Wash., Dec. 22, 1945; m. Teresa Marie Reopelle, Aug. 19, 1978. BA in Polit. Sci., Cen. Wash. U., 1969; MFA in Theatre, U. Mont., 1981. Designer, consultant Missoula, Mont., 1982-83; guest lectr. U. Mont., Missoula, 1983; owner Prodn. Enterprises, Salem, Oreg., 1985—; theatre instr., adminstr. Willamette U., Salem, 1983-86, lectr. Mem. U.S. Inst. Theatre Tech. Avocations: skiing, backpacking, fly fishing. Office: Prodn Enterprises PO Box 5263 Salem OR 97304

HOPKINS, (EDWARD) CAMERON NIND, journalist, editor; b. London, Jan. 15, 1956; came to U.S., 1963; s. Alan Cripps Nind Hopkins and Margaret Cameron (Bolton) Clifton. BA, Baylor U., 1982, M in Internat. Journalism, 1984; postgrad., Rand Afrikaans U., Johannesburg, South Africa. Editor Am. Handgunner, San Diego, 1984—; advisor Gun Owners Calif., Sacramento, 1984—. Field editor GUNS mag.; contbr. articles to Safari mag. Mem. Calif. Action Shooting Assn. Republican. Avocation: big game hunting. Office: Am Handgunner 591 Camino De La Reina Suite 200 San Diego CA 92178

HOPKINS, CECILIA ANN, educator; b. Havre, Mont., Feb. 17, 1922; d. Kost L. and Mary (Manaras) Sofos; B.S., Mont. State Coll., 1944; M.A., San Francisco State Coll., 1958, M.A., 1967; postgrad. Stanford U.; Ph.D., Calif. Western U., 1977; m. Henry E. Hopkins, Sept. 7, 1944. Bus. tchr. Havre (Mont.) High Sch., Mateo, Calif., 1942-44; sec. George P. Gorham, Realtor, San Mateo, 1944-45; escrow sec. Fox & Cars 1945-50; escrow officer Calif. Pacific Title Ins. Co., 1950-57; bus. tchr. Westmoor High Sch., Daly City, Calif., 1958-59; bus. tchr. Coll. of San Mateo, 1959—, chmn. real estate-ins. dept., 1963-76, dir. div. bus., 1976—; cons. to commr. Calif. Div. Real Estate, 1963—, mem. periodic rev. exam. com.; chmn. Community Coll. Adv. Com., 1971-72, mem. com., 1975—; projector direction Calif. State Chancellor's Career Awareness Consortium, mem. endowment fund adv. com., community coll. real estate edn. com., state community coll. adv. com.; mem. No. Calif. adv. bd. to Glendale Fed. Savs. and Loan Assn.; mem. bd. advisors San Mateo County Bd. Suprs., 1981-82; mem. real estate edn. and research com. to Calif. Commr. Real Estate, 1983—; mem. edn., membership, and profl. exchange coms. Am. chpt. Internat. Real Estate Fedn., 1985—. Recipient Citizen of Day award KABL, Outstanding Contbns. award Redwood City-San Carlos-Belmont Bd. Realtors; named Woman of Achievement, San Mateo-Burlingame br. Soroptimist Internat., 1979. Mem. AAUW, Calif. Assn. Real Estate Tchrs. (state pres. 1964-65, hon. dir. 1962—, outstanding real estate educator of yr. 1978-79), Real Estate Cert. Inst. (Disting. Merit award 1982), Calif. Bus. Edn. Assn. (certificate of commendation 1979), San Francisco State Coll., Guidance and Counseling Alumni, Theta Alpha Delta, Pi Lambda Theta, Delta Pi Epsilon (nat. dir. interchpt. relations 1962-65, nat. historian 1966-67, nat. sec. 1968-69), Alpha Gamma Delta. Co-author: California Real Estate Principles; contbr. articles to profl. jours. Home: 504 Colgate Way San Mateo CA 94402

HOPKINS, DAVID STEPHEN PRINCE, university administrator; b. Pasadena, Calif., Sept. 15, 1943; s. Prynce Charles Hopkins and Fay (Cartledge) Williams; m. Rosemary Pusey, June 18, 1965; children: Michelle, Susan, Julie, David. AB, Harvard U., 1964; MS, Stanford (Calif.) U., 1967, PhD, 1969. Prin. adminstrv. analyst U. Calif., Berkeley, 1969-70; from staff assoc. to sr. staff assoc. Stanford U., 1971-78, asst. dean for adminstr. med. sch., 1978-80, dir. analysis and planning med. ctr., 1980-86, asst. v.p. for mgmt. and fin. planning, 1986—; cons. VA Hosp., San Francisco, 1984-85, U. Colo. Health Sci. Ctr., Denver, 1986—. Co-author: Planning Models for Colleges and Universities, 1980 (Lanchester prize 1981); contbr. articles to profl. jours. Vice chmn., dir. Alan Guttmacher Inst., N.Y.C., 1975—; bd. dirs. Planned Parenthood Assn. Santa Clara County, Calif., 1973-80, also several offices. Fellow IBM, 1970-71, Stanford U., 1983-84. Fellow AAAS; mem. Ops. Research Soc. Am., Inst. Mgmt. Scis. Republican. Episcopalian. Clubs: Fox (Cambridge, Mass.); Palo Alto (Calif.) Golf and Country. Home: 954 Laurel Glen Dr Palo Alto CA 94304 Office: Stanford U Office of VP for Bus and Fin Encina 105 Stanford CA 94305

HOPKINS, HENRY TYLER, art museum director; b. Idaho Falls, Idaho, Aug. 14, 1928; s. Talcott Thompson and Zoe (Erbe) H.; children—Victoria Anne, John Thomas, Christopher Tyler. B.A., Sch. of Art Inst., Chgo., 1952, M.A., 1955; postgrad., UCLA, 1957-60; Ph.D. (hon.), Calif. Coll. Arts and Crafts, 1984; PhD (hon.), San Francisco Art Inst., 1987. Curator exhbns., publs. Los Angeles County Mus. of Art, Los Angeles, 1960-68; dir. Fort Worth Art Mus., 1968-74, San Francisco Mus. of Modern Art, 1974-86, Frederick R. Weisman Collection, San Francisco, 1986—; lectr. art history, extension U. Calif. at Los Angeles, 1958-68; instr. Tex. Christian U., Fort Worth, 1968-74; dir. U.S. representation Venice (Italy) Bienniel, 1970; dir. art presentation Festival of Two Worlds, Spoleto, Italy, 1970; co-commr. U.S. representation XVI São Paulo (Brazil) Biennale, 1981; cons. Nat. Endowment for Arts, mem. mus. panel, 1979—, chmn., 1981; cons., mem. mus. panel Nat. Endowment for Humanities, 1976. Contbr. numerous articles to profl. jours., also numerous mus. publs. Served with AUS, 1952-54. Decorated knight Order Leopold II, Belgium). Mem. Assn. Art Mus. Dirs. (pres. 1985-86), Coll. Art Assn., Am. Assn. Museums, Western Assn. Art Museums (pres. 1977-78). Home: 394 Arno Way Pacific Palisades CA 90272 Office: Frederick R Weisman Collection 10350 Santa Monica Blvd Los Angeles CA 90025

HOPKINS, JEAN HUMMER, nurse; b. Cheyenne, Wyoming, Oct. 21, 1942; d. Robert O. and Elizabeth (Bixler) Hummer; m. Raymond William Hopkins, Mar. 29, 1975. (div. 1985). Student U. Wyo., 1961-63, Holy Cross Hosp. Sch. of Nursing, 1963-66; B.S.N. (cum laude), Westminster Coll., 1982. Charge nurse Holy Cross Hosp., Salt Lake City, 1966-67, staff nurse intensive care unit, 1967-68, charge nurse intensive care unit, 1968-69, clin. nursing instr. operating room, 1969-72; office nurse Dr. R.O. Hummer, M.D., 1972-74; operating room staff nurse Holy Cross Hosp., 1973-76, asst. operating room supr., 1976-79, staff nurse, 1979-83; operating room supr. Holy Cross Jordan Valley Hosp., 1983—; instr. Med. Self Help for Senior Citizens, Salt Lake City, 1976-77; CPR instr., 1982-84. Mem. Nat. Assn. Operating Room Nurses (legis. com. 1981-86), Assn. Operating Room Nurses (cert., chpt. pres.), Am. Nurses Assn., Utah Nurses Assn., Sigma Theta Tau. Contbr. articles to profl. jours. Office: Holy Cross Jordan Valley Hosp 3580 W 9000 S West Jordan UT 84084

HOPKINS, PATRICIA FUOSS, architect, planner, educator; b. Providence, May 14, 1935; d. Raymond Matthew Fuoss and Rose Elizabeth (Harrington) Spear; m. David Lawrence Hopkins, Aug. 27, 1957 (div. 1983); children—Steven Fuoss, Glenn William. B.Arch., Cornell U., 1957. Lic. architect, Colo. Project architect Gordon Sweet Architect, Colorado Springs, Colo., 1961-64, The Hopkins Architect-Planner, Aspen, 1964-82; project architect, cons. Bill Baker, Architect, Colorado Springs, 1983-84; assoc. prof., div. head solar engring. technology Colo. Tech. Coll., 1982-86; prin. Pat Hopkins Architect and Planner, Colorado Springs, 1982—; planner Higginbotham and Assocs., Colorado Springs, 1986—; cons. Robin Molny Architect, Aspen, 1981; instr., team leader Aspen Highlands Ski Sch., 1970-82. Teaching asst. Aspen pub. schs., 1969-81. Mem. Solar Energy and Conservation Assn. (charter), Nat. Assn. Home Builders, Energy Efficient Bldg. Assocs., Nat. Assn. Female Execs., Profl. Ski Instrs. Am., Alpha Alpha Gamma. Avocations: horseback riding, downhill skiing. Home: 4016 Goldenrod Dr Colorado Springs CO 80907 Office: Pat Hopkins Architect/ Planner 4016 Goldenrod Dr Colorado Springs CO 80907

HOPKINS, PATRICIA MARGARET, marketing educator; b. Ilford, Essex, Eng., June 6, 1939; came to U.S. 1958, naturalized 1964; d. Edward George and Freda Miriam (Farrant) Berg; m. McMillen Hopkins, Mar. 5, 1960 (div. 1981); children—Craig Edward, Keith Bryan. Secretarial diploma, Southwest Essex Tech. Coll., Walthamstow, Eng., 1955; A.A., Fullerton Jr. Coll., 1967; B.A., Calif. State U.-Fullerton, 1971, M.B.A., 1972; Ph.D., Claremont Grad. Sch., 1977. Sec. C.P.A., London, 1955-58; sec. Tidewater Oil, Los Angeles, 1958-63; statistician Rockwell Internat., Anaheim, Calif., 1965-69; prof. mktg. Calif. Poly. State U., Pomona, 1975—. Named Outstanding Educator Sch. Bus. Adminstrn., 1984. Mem. Acad. Mktg. Sci. (editorial bd.), Am. Mktg. Assn., Western Mktg. Educators Assn., Pi Sigma Epsilon, Phi Kappa Phi, Beta Gamma Sigma, Alpha Epsilon Omega, Mu Kappa Tau. Democrat. Home: 16326 Santa Bianca Dr Hacienda Heights CA 91745 Office: Calif State Polytech Univ 3801 Temple St Pomona CA 91768

HOPKINS, PAUL MORTIMER, mining geologist, engr.; b. Edgerton, Mo., Mar. 6, 1918; s. Walter Ashe and Vera Virginia (Denniston) H.; grad. petroleum engr., Colo. Sch. Mines, 1939, geol. engr., 1951; post grad. U. Colo., 1951-52; m. Joyce Lorraine Mundy, Nov. 16, 1946 (div. Oct. 1947); m. 2d, Marian Francis Hawk, Jan. 1, 1954 (div. Nov. 1960); m. 3d, Mary Evelyn Shurtleff Newell, Feb. 20, 1965 (div. Feb. 1977); m. 4th, Rose Marie Ashley, Oct., 1985. Employee of Socony Vacuum Oil Co., East St. Louis, Ill., 1939-41; civil engr. U.S. Air Force, Lowry Field, Denver, 1948-49; geologist Leadville Lead Corp., Park County, Colo., 1952-53; geologist engr. Silver Bell Mines, Ophir, Colo., 1952-53; jr. engr. Kennecott Copper Co., Ruth, Nev., 1953-55; cons. engr., mining geologist and engr. Colo., Utah, Nev., Wyo., S.D., N.Mex., Ariz., Idaho, Mont., Can., Alaska, Central and South Am., Africa. Served to capt. AUS, 1941-47. Registered profl. engr., Colo., B.C.; registered geologist, Calif. Mem. Colo. Mining Assn. (dir.), Am. Inst. Mining, Metall. and Petroleum Engrs., Nat. Soc. Profl. Engrs., Canadian Inst. Mining and Metallurgy. Democrat. Mem. Christian Ch. Mason (Shriner). Home: 3830 W Saratoga Denver CO 80123 Office: 2222 Arapahoe St PO Box 403 Golden CO 80401

HOPKINS, PHILIP JOSEPH, journalist, editor; b. Orange, Calif., Dec. 10, 1954; s. Philip Joseph and Marie Elizabeth (Calnan) H.; m. Barbara Humbird Peters, May 23, 1981. B.A. in Journalism, San Diego State U., 1977. Cert. tissue therapist Center for Decubitis Ulcer Research, 1981. Reporter, La Jolla Light & Journal (Calif.), 1973; editorial cons. San Diego Union, 1974; asst. producer Southwestern Cable TV, San Diego, 1974; corr. Mission Cable TV, San Diego, 1975; photojournalist United Press Internat., San Diego, 1976; co-editor The Aztec Engr. mag., San Diego, 1977; editor Rx Home Care mag., Los Angeles, 1981, Hosp. Info. Mgmt. mag., 1981; editor, assoc. pub. Arcade mag., 1982; mng. editor Personal Computer Age, Los Angeles, 1983; Bur. chief Newsbytes syndicated column, 1985-86; v.p. Humbird Hopkins Inc., Los Angeles, 1978—. Campaign cons. Rep. Congl. and Assembly candidates, 1979-80. Recipient 1st and 4th place awards Nikon, Inc., Photo Contest, 1974; 3rd prize Minolta Camera Co. Creative Photography awards, 1975; Best Feature Photo award Sigma Delta Chi Mark of Excellence contest, 1977; Advt. of Month award Communicator mag., 1980, Best Online Computer Publ. Computer Press Awards, 1986. Mem. Am. Soc. Mag. Photographers, Am. Soc. Picture Profls., Am. Soc. Mag. Editors, Am. Med. Writers Assn., Comml. and Indsl. Properties Assn. (founding mem.), Computer Press Assn. (life, hon.), Ind. Writers of So. Calif., Sigma Delta Chi. Club: Santa Monica Athletic. Co-author: The Students' Survival Guide, 1977, 78; photographs have appeared in Time and Omni mags., The Mythology of Middle Earth, Beginners Guide to the SLR, NBC-TV's Saturday Night Live; author: The Computer Press Assn. Stylebook, 1987. Office: PO Box 39 San Clemente CA 92672

HOPKINS, THAYER, JR., architect; b. San Francisco, Dec. 29, 1951; s. Thayer and Carolyn Joy (Perry) H.; m. Caroline Greer McLane, May 6, 1978; 1 child, David Greer. BFA, R.I. Sch. Design, 1974, BArch, 1975. Registered architect, Calif. Draftsman Lambert Woods Architects, San Francisco, 1975-76; designer Peter Rocchia and Assocs., San Francisco, Environetics Internat. Inc., San Francisco, 1979-81; architect Ebert, Hannum & Volz, San Francisco, 1981-85, Fee & Munson, San Francisco, 1985—. Pres. Town Sch. Alumni Council, San Francisco, 1985-86; trustee Town Sch. for Boys, San Francisco, 1985-86. Mem. San Francisco Archtl. Club (tres. 1985—). Episcopalian. Club: Calif. Tennis (San Francisco). Avocations: drawing, painting, tennis. Office: Fee & Munson 443 Sutter St San Francisco CA 94108

HOPKINSON, SHIRLEY LOIS, educator; b. Boone, Iowa, Aug 25, 1924; d. Arthur Perry and Zora (Smith) Hopkinson; student Coe Coll., 1942-43; A.B. cum laude (Phi Beta Kappa scholar 1944), U. Colo., 1945; B.L.S., U. Calif., 1949; M.A. (Honnold Honor scholar 1945-46), Claremont Grad. Sch., 1951; Ed.M., U. Okla., 1952, Ed.D., 1957 Tchr. pub. sch. Stigler, Okla., 1946-47, Palo Verde High Sch., Jr. Coll., Blythe, Calif., 1947-48; asst. librarian Modesto (Calif.) Jr. Coll., 1949-51; tchr., librarian Fresno, Calif., 1951-52, La Mesa, Cal., 1953-55; asst. prof. librarianship, instructional materials dir. Chaffey Coll., Ontario, Calif., 1955-59; asst. prof. librarian ship, San Jose (Calif.) State Coll., 1959-64; assoc. prof., 1964-69, prof., 1969—. Dir. NDEA Inst. Sch. Librarians, summer 1966; mem. Santa Clara County Civil Service Bd. Examiners. Mem. ALA, Calif. Library Assn., Audio-Visual Assn. Calif., NEA, AAUW (dir. 1957-58), Bus. Profl. Women's Club, Sch. Librarians Assn. Calif. (com. mem., treas. No. sect. 1951-52), San Diego County Sch. Librarians Assn. (sec. 1945-55), Calif. Tchrs. Assn., League Women Voters (mem. bd. dirs. 1950-51, publs. chmn.), Phi Beta Kappa, Alpha Lambda Delta, Alpha Beta Alpha, Kappa Delta Pi, Phi Kappa Phi (disting. acad. achievement award 1981), Delta Kappa Gamma. Author: Descriptive Cataloging of Library Materials; Instructional Materials for Teaching the Use of the Library. Contbr. to profl. publs. Editor: Calif. Sch. Libraries, 1963-64; asst. editor: Sch. Library Assn. of Calif. Bull., 1961-63. Office: San Jose State U Room LN-608 San Jose CA 95192

HOPP, THOMAS PATRICK, biochemist; b. Seattle, Jan. 21, 1950; s. Edwin Charles and Edith May (Warnke) H.; m. Kathryn Susan Prickett, Jan. 12, 1985. BS, U. Wash, 1972; PhD, Cornell Med. Coll., 1977. Postdoctoral fellow Rockefeller U., N.Y.C., 1977-80; research assoc. N.Y. Blood Ctr., N.Y.C., 1980-82; sr. staff scientist Immunex Corp., Seattle, 1982—, chief protein chemistry, 1983—, v.p. new research evaluation, 1986—; vis. investigator Rockefeller U., 1980-81. Contbr. numerous sci. articles to profl. jours; patentee protein hydrophilicity analysis. New Investigator grant NIH, 1982. Mem. AAAS, Nat. Space Inst., Planetary Soc. Club: Sahalie Ski (bd. dirs. 1983—). Avocations: guitar, singing, skiing. Office: Immunex Corp 51 University St Seattle WA 98101

HOPPE, CHERYL ANN, clinical social worker; b. Chgo., Sept. 22, 1956; d. Elio John and Gloria Virginia (Smolke) Da Valle; m. John H. Hoppe III, July 12, 1980. BSW, Valparaiso U., 1974-78; MSW, U. Wis., 1979. Nephrology social worker Mt. Sinai Med. Ctr., Milw., 1979-85; clin. social worker Kapiolani Women's and Children's Med. Ctr., Honolulu, 1985—; sec. Council of Nephrology Social Workers, Milw., 1980-81, pres. 1982-83. Contbg. author: Renal Problems in Critical Care, 1985. Mem. Nat. Assn. Social Workers. Avocations: scuba diving, running, pottery, knitting, basketry. Home: 626 E Kilbourn #1206 Milwaukee WI 53202 Office: Kapiolani Women's Med Ctr 1319 Punahou St Honolulu HI 96826

HOPPER, LEROY HORACE, hospital administrator, consultant; b. Nashville, Jan. 21, 1930; s. Paul Horace and Margaret Bell (Floyd) H.; m. Marlaine Carmen Stahl, Apr. 2, 1954 (div. Apr. 1976); children—Michael, Michele, Linda; m. 2d Patricia Burton, May 30, 1981. B.S., Miami U., Ohio, 1952; M.B.A., U. Dayton, 1964. Cert. hosp. adminstr. Asst. adminstr. fin. Resthaven Community Health Ctr., Los Angeles, 1969-72; adminstr. Central City Community Health Ctr., Los Angeles, 1973-74, Community Mental Health Ctr., San Fernando Valley, Calif., 1979-80; assoc. adminstr. St. Johns Hosp., Santa Monica, Calif., 1975-78; cons. First Cons. Group, Los Angeles, 1981; chief adminstrv. officer Downey Community Hosp., Calif., 1982—; dir. Downey Fed. Credit Union, Southeast Council on Alcohol and Drugs, Downey; treas. Clare Found., Venice, Calif., 1976-78; instr. Calif. State U.-Northridge, Los Angeles, 1973-75. Pres., v.p. West Los Angeles Health Adv. Council, Santa Monica, 1977-79, pres. Westwood Meth. Mental Health Clinic, Los Angeles, 1978; active Los Angeles County Mental Health Adv. Bd., 1984, United Way Budget Com. II and IV, 1978-80. Served to capt. USAF, 1953-55. Mem. Am. Coll. Hosp. Adminstrs., Assn. Mental Health Adminstrs. (pres. 1979-80), Hosp. Fin. Mgt. Assn. (advanced). Republican. Methodist. Club: Civitan (Santa Monica) (pres.). Lodge: Loyalty. Home: #28 9227 Florence Ave Downey CA 90240 Office: Downey Community Hosp 11500 Brookshire Ave Downey CA 90241

HOPPER, ROBERT DEAN, safety professional; b. Ft. Collins, Colo., Feb. 24, 1921; s. Samuel E. and Olive Irene (Chandler) H.; m. Ruth Marie Leighou, Apr. 1, 1943; children: John Robert, Ronald Dean, Marta Jane. BS, Colo. A&M Coll., 1947, postgrad., 1947-49. Cert. tchr. Kans., Colo.; safety council adminstr., 1956. Coach, tchr. Atchison (Kans.) High Sch., 1947-49, Wheat Ridge (Colo.) High Sch., 1949-50, 51-53; salesman Butler Paper Co., Kansas City, Mo., 1950-51; dep., acting dir. Colo. Hwy. Safety Council, Denver, 1953-56; regional dir. Nat. Safety Council, Denver, 1956-83; dir. occupational safety and tng. Colo. Safety Assn., Denver, 1983-86; retired 1986. Mem. Jaycees, Arvada, Colo., 1955-56; Rep. dist. capt. Jefferson County, Colo., 1982. Served to lt. USN, 1942-45, PTO. Mem. Am. Soc. Safety Engrs., Colo. Soc. Assn. Execs. Home: 6561 Saulsbury Ct Arvada CO 80003

HOPPING, RICHARD LEE, college president; b. Dayton, Ohio, July 26, 1928; s. Lavon Lee and Dorothy Marie (Anderson) H.; m. Patricia Louise Vance, June 30, 1951; children: Ronald, Debra, Jerrold. Student, Chaffey Coll., 1947-48, U. Dayton, 1948-49, Sinclair Coll., 1948-49; B.S., So. Coll. Optometry, 1952, O.D., 1952, D.O.S. (hon.), 1972. Practice optometry Dayton, Ohio, 1953-73; pres. So. Calif. Coll. Optometry, 1973—; cons. in field; chmn. adv. research council Am. Optometric Found., 1976-83; mem. Nat. Acads. of Practice, 1983—; chmn. Nat. Acad. Practice in Optometry, 1985—; mem. 13th Dist. Med. Quality Rev. Com., State of Calif. Bd. Med. Quality Assurance. Contbr. numerous articles on vision and health care to profl. publs. Vice pres. Orange County (Calif.) council Boy Scouts Am., 1977-79, mem. adv. council, 1979—; mem. Council Assocs. of Red Cross, North Orange County Service Center, 1978—; mem. adv. council YWCA, North Orange County, 1984—. Named Optimist of Yr. Dayton View Optimists, 1956, Outstanding Young Man of Yr. Dayton C. of C., 1960. Fellow Am. Acad. Optometry (chmn. sect. on primary care optometry 1973-79, chmn. awards com. 1981—), Am. Pub. Health Assn. (Vision Care Disting. Achievement award 1984); mem. Am. Optometric Assn. (pres. 1971-72, chmn. task force on practical enhancement 1982—, chmn. profl. enhancement adv. com. 1982—), Calif. Optometric Assn. (hon. life 1974—, jud. council), Assn. Ind. Calif. Colls. and Univs. (trustee 1973—), Optometric Extension Programs Found. (hon. life), Assn. Schs. and Colls. of Optometry (pres. 1985—), Ohio Optometric Assn. (pres. 1964-65, Optometrist of Yr. 1962, hon. life), Nat. Acads. Practice in Optometry (vice chmn., mem. at large 1973—), Retinitis Pigmentosa Internat. (adv. exec. com. 1984—). Club: Lincoln of Orange County (bd. dirs. 1984—). Office: 2001 Associated Rd Fullerton CA 92631

HOPPONEN, JERRY D., engineer; b. Fargo, N.D., Mar. 26, 1946; m. Pamela J. Swales, June 25, 1983. BS, N.D. State U., 1966; MS in Math., U. Ariz., 1968; PhD in Math., U. Colo., 1979. Mathemetician, applied electromagnetic sci. div., Inst. for Telecommunication Scis., U.S. Dept. Commerce, Boulder, Colo., 1972-77; instr. math. U. Colo., Boulder, 1971-76; staff engr. electronic systems engring., space systems div., Lockheed Missiles & Space Co., Sunnyvale, Calif., 1977-86, sr. staff engr. communication systems analysis, 1986—. Office: Lockheed Missiles & Space Co PO Box 504 Sunnyvale CA 94086

HORAN, CLARK JAMES, III, corporate executive; b. Syracuse, N.Y., Feb. 3, 1950; s. Clark James Horan Jr. and Joan Roumage (Kelsey) Bergin. BA, U. Waterloo, Ont., Can., 1972, LLD (hon.), 1982; STB, BTh, St. Peter's Sem., London, Ont., Can., 1976; MDiv, U. Western Ont., London, 1976. Chief exec. officer Abercombie & Waterhouse, Del., Can. Air Travellers; v.p. The Checkley Found., Can.; chmn. bd. dirs. Horan, Macmillan, Bache & Chapman, Honolulu and Ottawa, Ont., Can.; cons. Wardair Internat., Calgary, Alta., Can., 1978-82; bd. dirs. Horan-in-Trust, N.Y.C. Decorated Order of Can.; named Knight Bachelor, Queen Elizabeth II, 1978, Knight of the Holy Sepulchre, Pope John Paul II, 1982. Fellow Royal Commonwealth Soc., Can. Commonwealth Council (chancellor, editor Can. Commonwealth newsletter 1978-84), Monarchist League Can. (editor Monarchy Today mag. 1979-81). Roman Catholic. Clubs: Honolulu, Ottawa Hunt and Golf, Albany (Toronto, Can.), Empire, Confederation. Lodges: Elks, KC. Address: PO Box 38016 Honolulu HI 96837-1016

HORD, JESSE, government research executive; b. Maysville, Ky., Oct. 11, 1934; s. William Wilson and Emma Dee (Huber) H.; m. Martha Ann Oakes, Aug. 31, 1956; children—Cheryl Ann, Karen Lynne, Kevin Taylor. B.S. in Civil Engring., U. Ky., 1956; M.S. in Civil Engring., U. Colo., 1963. Test engr. N.Am. Aviation, Canoga Park, Calif., 1956-61; mech. engr. Nat. Bur. Standards, Boulder, Colo., 1961-79, chief thermophys. properties div., 1979-81, dir. Ctr. for Chem. Engring., 1981—; mem. engring. devel. council U. Colo., Boulder, 1974-83; guest lectr. UCLA, 1977—. Contbr. numerous articles to profl. jours., chpts. to books. Recipient Tech. Brief Innovations awards NASA, 1973, 76, Silver medal Dept. Commerce, 1981, Russell B. Scott Meml. award for Outstanding Engr., U.S. Cryogenic Engring. Conf., 1975. Democrat. Presbyterian. Avocations: woodwork; antique cars; skiing; hunting; camping. Office: Nat Bur of Standards 325 Broadway Boulder CO 80303

HORDESKI, MICHAEL F., computer information scientist, consultant; b. Stamford, Conn., Oct. 16, 1939; s. Michael Hordeski and Julia Marion (Ja) Zygmont; m. Delores Elaine Buell, Feb. 1, 1966. BSEE, U. Bridgeport, 1964; MSEE, U. So. Calif., 1968. Registered profl. engr., Calif. Tech. staff Rockwell Internat., Anaheim, Calif., 1964-74; cons. Siltran Digital, Atascadero, Calif., 1974—; cons. GTE, Anaheim, Calif., 1978, Gen. Motors Corp., Santa Barbara, Calif., 1979-81; lectr. Calif. Poly. State U., Pomona, 1978—, Calif. Poly. State U., San Luis Obispo, 1986—. Author: Microprocessor Cookbook, 1979, Microprocessors in Industry, 1984, The Design of Microprocessor Sensor and Control Systems, 1985, CAD/CAM Techniques, 1986, Microcomputer Design, 1986; patentee in field. Mem. Instrument Soc. Am. Office: Siltran Digital 2250 Monterey Rd Atascadero CA 93422

HORI, MARK TETSUO, biochemist; b. Los Angeles, Sept. 9, 1952; s. Haruo and Michie (Taira) H. BS, Calif. State U., Long Beach, 1978. Med. technician VA, Sepulveda, Calif., 1980-82; research asst. UCLA VA Med. Ctr., Sepulveda, 1982-84; research biochemist VA Med. Ctr., Seattle, 1984—. Contbr. articles to med. jours. Mem. AAAS. Democrat. Presbyterian. Avocations: photography, music, skiing, tennis. Office: VA Med Ctr 151 1660 S Columbian Way Seattle WA 98108

HORI, TOSH, marketing executive, consultant; b. Tacoma, Wash., Jan. 16, 1922; s. Yasujiro and Iso (Yoshida) Sakahara; m. Yoko Yamaoka, Aug. 15, 1947 (div. 1965); children—James Hirokazu (dec.), Judith Aya, Esther June; m. 2d, Fujiko Fudge Terao, Aug. 27, 1966. Student in bus. adminstrn., U. Wash., Seattle, 1940-41. Interpreter war crimes trials Judge Advocate Sec., U.S. Army, Yokohama, Japan, 1946, interpreter, asst. to prosecutor provost ct., 1946; head typing and reprodn. dept. Civil Censorship, Tokyo, 1946-48; ptnr. Hori's Ranch and Truck Garden, Whitefish, Mont., 1948-49; salesman Fujita's Produce, Fife, Wash., 1950-51; laborer King St. Sta., Seattle, 1952-54; warehouseman Capitol Records Dist., Seattle, 1953-55; buyer, salesman Disc City Record One Stop, Seattle, 1955-62; asst. mgr. Seattle Record One Stop, 1962-68; buyer Fidelity N.W., Seattle, 1968-70; head buyer Transcontinental Records, Seattle, 1970-71; founder, pres. Tosh's Record One Stop, Seattle, 1971-76; co-founder, v.p. Music Menu Retail Record, Seattle, 1973-76; co-founder, pres. World Wide Record and Tape Sales, Seattle, 1974-76; v.p. mktg. Officemporium, Seattle, 1976—; research mktg. cons. Billboard Mag., Los Angeles, 1962-76, Cashbox Mag., Hollywood, Calif., 1965-76, Record World Mag., Hollywood, 1971-76; adv. bd. cons. Music Retailer, Watertown, Mass., 1975-76. Bd. dirs. Capitol Hill C. of C., Seattle, 1981—; v.p. nat. council Nichiren Buddhist Ch. of N.Am., 1982—; treas. exec. bd. Issei Concerns, Seattle, 1979-81; adv. bd. Seattle Central Community Coll., 1983-85. Served with U.S. Army, 1944-46. Recipient Gold Record award for mktg. Scepter Records, 1968, MCA Records, 1969, Capitol Records, 1973, Mercury Records, 1975, Shelter Records, 1974, Atlantic Records, 1975. Mem. Nat. Assn. Record Merchandisers. Home: 4340 E Mercer Way Mercer Island WA 98040

HORIGAN, JAMES EUGENE, lawyer, author; b. Oklahoma City, Sept. 4, 1924; s. Joseph D. Horigan and Mary (Swirczynski) Horigan McRill; stepson Albert L. McRill; student Okla. U., 1942-44, Northwestern U., 1944; J.D., Okla. U., 1949; postgrad. So. Meth. U., 1958, Colo. U., 1966; m. Joan Murry, Mar. 8, 1945; children—Susan, Daniel James, Nancy Jean Horigan Datz. Bar: Okla. 1949, Tex. 1957, N.Y. 1959, Colo. 1961, Law Soc. Eng. (hon.), 1973. Asst. county atty. Oklahoma County, 1949-51; atty. Mobil Oil Corp., Oklahoma City, 1951-57, Beaumont, Tex., 1957, Dallas, 1958, U.S. and Can. counsel, office gen. counsel, N.Y.C., 1959-61, regional gen. atty. Denver regional office, 1961-63; gen. counsel Hamilton Bros. Oil Co. and affiliates, Denver, 1963-69; ptnr. Foliart, Shepherd, McPherson & Horigan, Oklahoma City, 1963, Horigan Thompson & Miller, Denver, 1965-69; individual practice internat. law, London, 1969-70; ptnr. Horigan & Boss, 1971; sr. resident ptnr. London office law firm Vinson, Elkins, Searls, Connally & Smith, 1971-75; of counsel Burns & Wall, 1978; ptnr. Horigan, Jumonville, Broadhurst, Brook & Miller, 1978, Holland & Hart, Denver, 1979-81; sole practice law, 1981—; bd. dirs., gen. counsel Charterhall N.Am. P.L.C., 1985—; gen. agt. Charterhall Australia Ltd. 1983-87. Trustee Town of Bow Mar (Colo.), 1976-78; mem. U.S. Congl. Adv. Bd., 1982—; mem. adv. bd. Internat. Comparative Law Ctr., Southwestern Legal Found., 1983—. Served to lt. USNR, 1943-46. Mem. ABA, Colo. Bar Assn., Okla. Bar Assn., Denver Bar Assn., Internat. Bar Assn., Am. Soc. Internat. Law, Rocky Mountain Mineral Law Found. (gen. chmn. spl. legal inst. 1975), Internat. Platform Assn., Internat. Trade Assn. Colo. (v.p. 1979-81. bd. dirs.), Phi Delta Phi, Phi Gamma Delta, Delta Sigma Rho. Roman Catholic. Clubs: American (London); Rotary; Denver Petroleum (bd. dirs. 1987—). Author: Chance or Design?, 1979; The Key to Reconcile Modern Science and Religious Thought, 1983; Petroleum Laws of the North Sea, 1975; contbg. author: The Law of Transnational Business Transactions, 1980; Foreign Participation in Domestic Oil and Gas Ventures, 1982; contbr. articles to legal jours.; charter mem. bd. editors Okla. Law Rev., 1947-49. Home: 5230 Lakeshore Dr Littleton CO 80123 Office: Denver CO

HORLER, VIRGINIA LOUISE, financial consultant to local governments; b. St. Louis, Nov. 21, 1940; d. Kenneth James and Elise Deprez (Weck) Palmer; m. Brian Leslie Horler, Sept. 4, 1965; 1 dau., Jennifer Ann. A.A. with honors, Contra Costa Coll., 1976; B.A. in Mgmt. with honors, St. Mary's Coll. of Calif., 1982, Exec. M.B.A. with honors, 1984. Bus. mgr. Heald Bus. Coll., Oakland, Calif., 1965-67; dep. treas. City of Richmond (Calif.), 1967-81, budget analyst, 1981-83; sr. cons. Rauscher Pierce Refsnes, Inc., Pub. Fin., San Francisco, 1983-86, v.p. 1987—; registered rep. N.Y. Stock Exchange; lectr. on pub. fin. at seminars, workshops; student commencement speaker St. Mary's Coll. of Calif., 1982. Mem. Pinole (Calif.) YMCA Swim Team, 1976-84, bd. dirs., 1976-84, pres., 1980; mem. Pinole Traffic Flow Com., 1980. Recipient 2d place Fine Arts award Bank of Am., Calif., 1958. Mem. Calif. Mcpl. Treas. Assn., Govt. Fin. Officers Assn. (cert. 1981, bd. dirs. 1979-83, profl. achievement recognition award 1983, 84), Calif. Soc. Mcpl. Fin. Officers, San Francisco Mcpl. Forum. Author: Guide to Public Debt Financing in California, 1982. Home: 3270 Colusa St Pinole CA 94564 Office: Rauscher Pierce Refsnes Inc One California St Suite 2630 San Francisco CA 94111

HORN, CHRISTIAN FRIEDRICH, venture capital company executive; b. Dresden, Germany, Dec. 23, 1927; came to U.S., 1954, naturalized, 1959; s. Otto Hugo and Elsa H.; m. Christa Winkler, Feb. 13, 1954; 1 child, Sabrina. M.S., Technische Hochschule, Dresden, 1951; Ph.D., Technische Hochschule, Aachen, Germany, 1958. Research scientist German Acad. Sci., Berlin, 1951-53; research scientist Farbwerke Hoechst, Germany, 1953-54; research mgr. Union Carbide, N.Y.C., 1954-65; pres. Polymer Tech. Inc., N.Y.C., 1965-74; mem. bd. mgmt. Zimmer A.G., Frankfurt, Ger., 1971-73; v.p. W.R. Grace & Co., N.Y.C., 1974-81; sr. v.p. W.R. Grace & Co., 1981—, dir., 1985—; pres. Grace Ventures Corp., Cupertino, Calif., 1983—; dir. Access Med. Systems Inc., Zoran Corp. Patentee in field. Served with German Army, 1944-45. Decorated Iron Cross. Mem. Am. Chem. Soc., German Chem. Soc. Lutheran. Club: Princeton. Home: 27827 Via Feliz Los Altos Hills CA 94022 Office: 20300 Stevens Creek Blvd Cupertino CA 95014

HORN, CLAIRE HELEN, music educator, administrator; b. Richmond, Hill, N.Y., Aug. 16, 1934; d. Albert E. and Helen (Kriger) Capitanio; m. Denis R. Horn, Sept. 5, 1955; children—Jeffrey D., Erica Jeanne, B.S. in Music Edn., Ithaca Coll., 1956; M.A., Calif. State U., 1982. Tchr. music Saddleback Valley Unified Dist., Mission Viejo, Calif., 1971-76; instrumental music tchr. Mission Viejo High Sch., 1975-80; dist. music coordinator Saddleback Valley Unified Sch. Dist., Mission Viejo, 1980—; prin. oboist Saddleback Symphony Orch.; guest lectr. Calif. State U.; guest condr. San Bernardino Honor Orch. Legis. action rep. Legis. Action Coalition for Arts Edn. Nat. Honor Soc. scholar, 1952; N.Y. Regents scholar, 1952; named Tchr. of the Month, Mission Viejo High Sch., 1978; recipient Irene Schoepfle award Orange County, 1986. Mem. Orange County Music Adminstrs. (pres.), So. Calif. Sch. Band and Orch. Assn. (sec.), Music Educators Nat. Conf., Assn. Calif. Sch. Adminstrs., Assn. Supervision and Curriculum Devel., Orange County Music Educators Assn., Calif. Music Educators Assn. (sec.), So. Sect. Calif. Music Edn. Assn. (treas.), Pi Kappa Lambda. Republican. Lutheran. Contbr. articles to profl. jours. Home: 28212 San Marcos St Mission Viejo CA 92692 Office: Saddleback Valley Unified Sch Dist 25631 Diseno Dr Mission Viejo CA 92691

HORN, DENNIS RAY, civil engineering educator; b. Independence, Mo., Sept. 28, 1942; s. Richard John and Pauline Helen (Flamme) H.; m. Sandra Watkins Hazel, June 20, 1964 (div. Mar. 1979); children: Darrin, Kevin; m. Patricia Ann Prond, Mar. 25, 1979; children: Justin, Christian, Brendan. BS in Engring., Princeton U., 1964; PhD, Johns Hopkins U., 1974. Registered profl. engr., Idaho. Sr. v.p. Anerson-Nichols & Co., Inc., Boston, 1974-84; asst. prof. civil engring. Northeastern U., Boston, 1969-74, U. Idaho, Moscow, 1984—; cons. Hittman Assocs., Columbia, 1967-68, C.E., U.S. Army, 1974, U.S. Army OASA, 1983—; assoc. Sidwell-Ross & Assocs., Inc., 1986—. Contbr. articles to profl. jours. Mem. ASCE, Army Sci. Bd. Democrat. Presbyterian. Home: 2455 W Twin Rd Moscow ID 83843 Office: U Idaho Dept Civil Engring Moscow ID 83843

HORN, PAULA LOIS, educational training consultant, technical writer; b. N.Y.C., Jan. 20, 1947; d. Herman and Sadie Florence (Spiegelburd) H. BA, Albany State U., 1969; MS, Hofstra U., 1972; MA, NYU, 1974; PhD, U. So. Calif., 1980. Reading cons. and specialist Seaford, N.Y. and Branford, Conn., 1971-74; instructional designer Systems Devel. Corp., Santa Monica, Calif., 1978-79; ednl. tng. cons. U So. Calif., Los Angeles, 1982-85; mktg. tng. cons. Xerox Corp., El Segundo, Calif., 1985-86; sr. tech. writer Ashton-Tate Corp., Torrance, Calif., 1986—; cons. in field; ednl. tng. cons. Nat. Tng. Systems, Santa Monica, 1979-80; ednl. tng. cons. Learning Systems, Encino, Calif., 1980-81; media tng. cons. Media Learning Systems, Pasadena, Calif., 1980; researcher Northridge U., Calif., 1984-85. Author: Economics Analysis for Business, 1982; (with others) RapidFile, 1987; instr., designer, editor: Consultants' Handbook, 1986. Mem. Nat. Soc. Performance and Instrn., Soc. Applied Learning Tech. (bd. dirs.), Assn. Tng. and Devel., Soc. Tech. Communication, Mensa, Phi Delta Kappa, Phi Delta Epsilon. Avocations: writing, reading, concerts, movies, theater. Home: 11023 Fruitland Dr #4 Studio City CA 91604 Office: Ashton-Tate 20101 S Hamilton Ave Torrance CA 90502-1319

HORN, (JOHN) STEPHEN, university president; b. Gilroy, Calif., May 31, 1931; s. John Stephen and Isabelle (McCaffrey) H.; m. Nini Moore, Sept. 4, 1954; children: Marcia Karen Horn Yavitz, John Stephen. AB with great distinction, Stanford, 1953, postgrad., 1953-54, 55-56, PhD in Polit. Sci, 1958; M in Pub Adminstrn., Harvard, 1955. Congl. fellow 1958-59; adminstrv. asst. to sec. labor Washington, 1959-60; legislative asst. to U.S. Senator Thomas H. Kuchel, 1960-66; sr. fellow The Brookings Instn., 1966-69; dean grad. studies and research Am. U., 1969-70; pres. Calif. State U., Long Beach, 1970—; sr. cons., host The Govt. Story on TV, The Election Game (radio series), 1967-69. Author: The Cabinet and Congress, 1960, Unused Power: The Work of the Senate Committee on Appropriations, 1970, (with Edmund Beard) Congressional Ethics: The View from the House, 1975. Mem. urban studies fellowship adv. bd. Dept. Housing and Urban Devel., 1969-70, chmn., 1969; vice-chmn. U.S. Commn. Civil Rights, 1969-80, mem., 1980-82; mem. Pres.-elect Nixon's Task Force on Orgn. Exec. Br., 1968; mem. law enforcement edn. program, adv. commn. law enforcement assistance adminstrn. Dept. Justice, 1969-71; v.p. FHP Found.; mem. Kutak Found.; co-founder Western U.S. Com. Arts and Scis. for Eisenhower, 1956; bd. dirs. Nat. Inst. Corrections, chmn., 1984-87; bd. dirs. Inst. Internat. Edn.; mem. Calif. Ednl. Facilities Authority, 1984—. Fellow John F. Kennedy Inst. Politics, Harvard U., 1966-67. Mem. Stanford Assocs., Stanford Alumni Assn. (pres. 1976-77), Am. Assn. State Coll. and Univs. (chmn. 1985-86), Nat. Acad. Pub. Adminstrn., Phi Beta Kappa, Pi Sigma Alpha. Republican. Club: El Capitan Eating (Stanford). Office: Calif State U Office of Pres 1250 Bellflower Blvd Long Beach CA 90840

HORN, TODD RICHARD WENDELL, school administrator; b. Cleve., Apr. 26, 1955; s. Richard Oscar Horn and Evelyn (Wasson) Farnum; m. C. Jane Booty, July 16, 1983; 1 child, David G. BA, Dartmouth Coll., 1977; EdM, Harvard U., 1980. Asst. dir. Mont. Outdoor Leadership Exp., West Yellowstone, 1973-75; dir. Coeur D'Alene (Idaho) Youth Conservation Corps Camp, 1979-80; acad. dean The Colorado Springs (Colo.) Sch., 1982-84, dir. upper sch., 1984—. Mem. Assn. Supervision and Curriculum Devel., Nat. Assn. Sci. Tchrs. Episcopalian. Lodge: Rotary. Avocations: flyfishing, outdoor sports.

HORNBACK, JOSEPH MICHAEL, chemistry educator; b. Middletown, Ohio, Sept. 16, 1943; s. Cletus Edward and Margaret (Long) H.; m. Margaret Ann Ruffing, July 19, 1965 (div. May 1981); children: Joseph Michael Jr., Patrick William; m. Melani Lee Poundstone, Dec. 27, 1985. BS, U. Notre Dame, 1965; PhD, Ohio State U., 1968. Research assoc. U. Wis., Madison, 1968-70; asst. prof. U. Denver, 1970-75, assoc. prof. chemistry, 1975—, acting chmn., 1984-85. Contbr. articles to profl. jours. Mem. Am. Chem. Soc. Avocations: fishing, camping. Home: 1989 Sonoma Pl Fort Collins CO 80525 Office: U Denver Chemistry Dept Denver CO 80208

HORNBEIN, THOMAS F., physician; b. St. Louis, 1930. M.D., Washington U., St. Louis, 1956. Diplomate: Am. Bd. Anesthesiology. Intern King County Hosp., Seattle, 1956-57; resident in anesthesiology Washington U. Hosp., 1957-59, research fellow in respiratory physiology, 1959-61; asst. in anesthesiology Barnes Hosp., St. Louis, 1960-61; asst. prof. anesthesiology U. Wash., 1963-67, asso. prof., 1967-70, prof. anesthesiology, 1970—, prof. physiology and biophysics, 1970—, vice chmn. dept. anesthesiology, 1972-74, chmn. dept., 1978—. Served to lt. comdr. USNR, 1961-63. Mem. Inst. Medicine. Office: U Wash Sch of Medicine RN-10 Seattle WA 98195

HORNBEIN, THOMAS FREDERIC, anesthesiologist; b. St. Louis, Nov. 6, 1930; s. Leonard and Rosalie (Bernstein) H.; m. Gene Schwartz (div. 1968); children: Lia, Lynn, Cari, Andrea, Robert; m. Kathryn Mikesell, Dec. 24, 1971; 1 child, Melissa. BA, U. Colo.; MD, Wash. U. Diplomate Am. Bd. Anesthesiology. Intern King County Hosp., Seattle; resident in anesthesiology Wash. U., St. Louis, USPHS postdoctoral residency; instr. anesthesiology div. Wash. U., 1960-61; asst. prof. U. Wash., Seattle, 1963-67, assoc. prof., 1967-70, prof., 1970—; vice chmn. Dept. Anesthesiology, U. Wash., Seattle, 1972-74, asst. chmn. research 1974-77, chmn. 1978, research affiliate Primate Ctr., 1980. Author: Everest the West Ridge, 1966. Mem. bd. trustees Little Sch., Bellevue, Wash., 1982—. Served to lt. comdr. USN, 1961-63. Recipient George Norlin award U. Colo., Denver, 1970, Alumni Centennial Symposium award 1975, Disting. Teaching award U. Wash., 1982. Mem. Soc. Critical Care Medicine, Am. Physiol. Soc. (editor 1967-73), Am. Soc. Anesthesiologists, Assn. Univ. Anesthetists (treas. 1969-72, pres. 1974-75), Soc. Acad. Anesthesia Chairmen, Inst. of Medicine, Phi Beta Kappa, Alpha Omega Alpha. Avocation: mountaineering. Office: Dept Anesthesiology RN-10 U Wash Sch of Medicine 1959 NE Pacific Seattle WA 98195

HORNBY, WILLIAM HARRY, newspaperman; b. Kalispell, Mont., July 14, 1923; s. Lloyd G. and Margaret E. (Miller) H.; children: Margaret (dec.), Megan, Melinda, John, Mary Catherine. A.B. in Humanities, Stanford U., 1944, M.A. in Journalism, 1947; postgrad., U. London, Eng., 1949-50. Reporter, copyreader San Francisco News, 1947-48; reporter A.P., San Francisco, 1949; research asst. Hoover Library, Stanford, 1949-50; info. officer ECA, Paris and The Hague, 1950-52; asst. gen. mgr. Kalispell Lumber Co., 1953-56, partner, 1955-62; reporter Great Falls (Mont.) Tribune, 1957; copy-desk chief, editorial writer Denver Post, 1957-60, mng. editor, 1960-70, exec. editor, v.p., 1970-77, editor, v.p., 1977-82, sr. editor, 1982—; v.p. Yellowstone Newspapers, Inc., Livingston, Mont. Bd. dirs. Buffalo Bill Meml. Assn., Colo. Hist. Found., Denver Found. Mem. Am. Soc. Newspaper Editors (past pres.), Sigma Delta Chi, Sigma Nu. Republican. Episcopalian. Clubs: Denver, Univ, Denver Country. Lodge: Elks. Office: Denver Post 650 15th St Denver CO 80201

HORN-DALTON, KATHY ELLEN, rehabilitation agency administrator; b. Latrobe, Pa., Apr. 12, 1952; d. William Irving and Stella Bertha (Denisiuk) Horn; m. Glenn Holbert Dalton, Aug. 4, 1973. BS in Social Work, W.Va. U., 1975, MSW, 1976; PhD in Adminstrn., Columbia Pacific U., 1983. Registered psychotherapist. Counselor Womens Info. Ctr., Morgantown, W.Va., 1973; psychiatric aid Torrance (Pa.) State Hosp., 1974; group home counselor Sommerset Bedford Mental Health Ctr., Rockwood, Pa., 1974; shop foreman Southwest Wyo. Rehab. Ctr., Rock Springs, 1975-76, exec. dir., 1976-81, pres., administr., 1981—; researcher emotionally disturbed/mentally retarded project Div. Vocat. Rehab., Cheyenne, Wyo., 1985; CD grants adminstr. Sweetwater County, Rock Springs, Wyo., 1982-83. Author: Develop and Design an Energy Efficient Sheltered Workshop, 1983, Job Placement Results of a Job Training Partnership Act Program in a Rural Sheltered Workshop, 1985; contbr. articles to profl. jours. Mem. Wyo. Devel. Disabilities Council, 1978, Wyo. Pvt. Indsl. Council, 1983, adv. bd. U. No. Colo., Greeley, 1978; state advisor U.S. Congl. Adv. Bd., Washington, 1984, YWCA. Mem. Wyo. Assn. Rehab. Facilities (legis. chmn. 1981-83), Nat. Assn. Social Workers (cert.), Exec. Females Assn., Bus. Profl. Women's Assn., Pilot Butte Sand Drag Assn., Intermountain Sand Drag Assn., Nat. Sand Co. Assn., Nat. Hot Rod Assn. Avocation: sand drag racing. Office: Southwest Wyo Rehab Ctr 2632 Foothill Blvd Suite 107 Rock Springs WY 82901

HORNE, DOROTHY HUTCH, academic administrator; b. Nutley, N.J., May 11, 1936; d. John M. and Mary Ruth (Child) H.; m. David George Horne, Mar. 16, 1966; children: Linda Rose, John David. BS, Bates Coll. Chemist Olin Mathieson Chems., New Haven, 1958-63; research chemist Dow Chem. Co., Walnut Creek, Calif., 1963-66; publs. mgr. Coll. Chemistry U. Calif., Berkeley, 1984-86, grad. adminstr., 1986—. Patentee pesticidals. Moderator 1st Congl. Ch., Oakland, Calif., 1985-87. Mem. Am. Chem. Soc., AAAS, Lace Guild, Clan Donnaichdaich Soc. Avocations: swimming, walking, needlework. Home: 166 Nova Dr Piedmont CA 94610 Office: U Calif Coll Chemistry Berkeley CA 94720

HORNE, JERRY DYER, geology educator, academic administrator, consultant; b. Bakersfield, Calif., Sept. 2, 1934; s. Floyd and Alta Beatrice (Dyer) H.; m. Margaret M. Sturm, Sept. 1, 1956 (div. 1971); children—Sheryl Kay, Mark Eugene, Dianne Margaret, Steven William; m. Judith May Woodward, June 10, 1972; 1 son, Jay Floyd. A.A., Bakersfield Coll., 1954; B.S., U. Redlands, 1956; M.S., U. Houston, 1961. Registered geologist, Calif. Geophys. interpreter Texaco, Inc., Lafayette, La., 1961-63, Bakersfield, 1963-66; asst. prof. geology San Bernardino Valley Coll., Calif., 1966-69, assoc. prof., 1969-82, prof., 1982—, head dept. geology, 1976—; pres. Geol. Systems Evaluation. Served with U.S. Army, 1957-59. Mem. Am. Assn. Petroleum Geologists, Smithsonian Inst. (assoc.), Am. Mus. Natural History (assoc.), Nat. Rifle Assn. (life), Calif. Rifle and Pistol Assn. (life), Sigma Gamma Epsilon (charter, pres. local chpt. 1960). Republican. Home: 18316 Hawthorne Bloomington CA 92316 Office: San Bernardino Valley Coll 701 S Mount Vernon Ave San Bernardino CA 92403

HORNE, WILLIAM MCHENRY, management educator; b. Shreveport, La., Mar. 17, 1921; s. William McHenry and Nora (Kalmbach) H.; m. Joan Spear, Sept. 2, 1950 (div. Oct. 1974); children: Lynellyn D., William H. III, Dee Alyson; m. Alice Hobart, Dec. 28, 1980. BA, DePauw U., 1942; JD, Harvard U., 1949. Bar: Mass. 1949, Ind. 1949, D.C. 1955, Md. 1964. Atty., advisor U.S. Tax Ct., Washington, 1949-50; staff atty. joint com. on taxation U.S. Congress, Washington, 1953-55; assoc. Warner, Stackpole, Stetson & Bradlee, Boston, 1955-57; dir. taxes Olin Mathieson Chem. Corp. (now Olin Corp.), N.Y.C., 1957-64; v.p. Comml. Credit Co., Balt., 1964-70; ptnr. Reed, Smith, Shaw & McClay, Pitts., Washington and Harrisburg (Pa.), 1970-73; sr. v.p., gen. tax counsel Citicorp and Citibank N.A., N.Y.C., 1973-80; lectr. dept. mgmt. and policy Coll. Bus. Adminstrn. U. Ariz., Tucson, 1980—; mem. adv. com. to commr. IRS, 1969-70; past mem. tax and acctg. com. N.Y. Clearing House, past chmn., taxation com. Fin. Execs. Inst.; speaker in field. Author: Proceedings of New York University Annual Institute on Federal Income Taxation: Offers in Compromise, 1958; also chpts. to books and articles to profl. jours. Served to maj. JAGC, U.S. Army, 1950-52, to lt. USAF, 1942-46, PTO. Recipient Disting. Alumni award DePauw U., Greencastle, Ind., 1976; Alfred P. Sloane fellow MIT, Cambridge, 1942. Mem. Tax Execs. Inst. (hon., pres., chmn. bd. dirs. 1968-69), Sigma Chi. Club: Harvard (N.Y.C.). Avocations: hiking, water activities, bicycling, tennis, travelling. Home: 4548 Camino de Cancun Tucson AZ 85718 Office: U Ariz Dept Mgmt and Policy Harvill Bldg Tucson AZ 85721

HORNER, ALTHEA JANE, psychologist; b. Hartford, Conn., Jan. 13, 1926; d. Louis and Celia (Newmark) Greenwald; children: Martha Horner Hartley, Anne Horner Benck, David, Kenneth. BS in Psychology, U. Chgo., 1952; PhD in Clin. Psychology, U. So. Calif., 1965. Lic. psychologist, N.Y., Calif. Tchr. Pasadena (Calif.) City Coll., 1965-67; from asst. to assoc. prof. Los Angeles Coll. Optometry, 1967-70; supr. Psychology interns Pasadena Child Guidance Clinic, 1969-70; pvt. practice specializing in psychoanalysis and psychoanalytic psychotherapy. N.Y.C., 1970-83; supervising psychologist dept. psychiatry Beth Israel Med. Ctr., N.Y.C., 1972-83, coordinator group therapy tng., 1976-82, clinician in charge Brief Adaptation-Oriented Psychotherapy Research Group, 1982-83; assoc. clin. prof. Mt. Sinai Sch. Medicine, N.Y.C., 1977—; mem. faculty Nat. Psychol. Assn. for Psychoanalysis, N.Y.C., 1982-83; sr. mem. faculty Wright Inst. Los Angeles Postgrad. Inst., 1983-85; pvt. practice specializing in psychoanalysis and psychoanalytic psychotherapy Los Angeles, 1983—; assoc. clin. prof. dept. Psychology UCLA, 1985—. Author: (with others) Treating the Oedipal Patient in Brief Psychotherapy, 1985, Object Relations and the Developing Ego in Therapy, 1979, rev. edit., 1984, Little Big Girl, 1982, Being and Loving, 1978, new ed. 1986, Psychology for Living (with G. Forehand), 4th edit., 1977; mem. editorial bd. Jour. of Humanistic Psychology, 1986—, Jour. of the Am. Acad. of Psychoanalysis; contbr. articles to profl. jours. Mem. AAAS, Am. Psychol. Assn., Calif. State Psychol. Assn., Am. Women Sci., Nat. Psychol. Assn. for Psychoanalysis, Am. Acad. Psychoanalysis (sci. assoc.). Office: 1314 Westwood Blvd Los Angeles CA 90024

HORNER, JENNIE LINN, educational administrator, nurse; b. Memphis, Tex., Feb. 27, 1932; d. Lester C. and Cecil T. (Knight) Linn; m. Billy A. Gooch, June 4, 1951 (dec.); children—Brenda Michael, Patricia Lynn, Robert Allen; m. 2d Donald M. Horner, July 26, 1975. R.N., U. Tex., 1955; B.S., No. Ariz. U., 1977, M.A., 1978, Ed.D., 1984. Cert. tchr., registered nurse, Ariz., Tex. Indsl. nurse Lipton Tea Co., Galveston, Tex., 1955-56; head nurse U. Tex. Med. Br., Galveston, 1956-58; sch. nurse Wash. Sch. Dist., Phoenix, 1970-77; tchr. middle sch., 1977-80; asst. prin. Murphy Sch. Dist., Phoenix, 1980-82; assoc. prin. middle sch. Madison Sch., Phoenix, 1982-84; lang. arts coordinator Madison Sch. Dist., Phoenix; prin. Luke Sch., Dysart Unified Sch. Dist., Phoenix, 1984—; med. cons. Medahab, Phoenix. Mem. Assn. Supervision and Curriculum Devel., Sch. Nurses Orgn. Ariz. (pres.), Am. Vocat. Assn., Nat. Assn. Sch. Nurses, Nat. Assn. Elem. Sch. Prins., Ariz. Adminstrs. Assn., Aware West, Phi Delta Kappa. Democrat. Home: 14239 N 50th Ln Glendale AZ 85306 Office: 7300 N Dysart Rd Glendale AZ 85307 Mailing Address: Route 1 Box 703 Peoria AZ 85345

HORNER, LEE, foundation executive, speaker, consultant; b. Sault Ste. Marie, Ont., Can., Mar. 18, 1944; came to U.S., 1976; d. William E. and Gladys (Boomhower) H.; m. Claude Lavallee, Jan. 21, 1960 (div. Sept. 1969); children—Kevin Lauren Lavallee/Petalos, Cindy Lee Lavallee; m. James G. Petalos, Jan. 9, 1970 (dec. Jan. 1977). Student Concordia U., Montreal, Que., Can., 1975-76, U. Nev.-Las Vegas, 1977. Pres., LHP Investments, Inc., Las Vegas, 1978—; v.p. Casa Mobile Corp., real estate, San Francisco, 1979—; founder, chmn. bd. PMS Research Found., Las Vegas, 1982—; pub. speaker premenstrual syndrome. Author: How to Chart Your Course to Freedom, 1983; Mini-Nutrition and Exercise Manual, 1983; PMS Minder, 1983; PMS Wellness Workbook, 1985, PMS Support Group Manual, 1985. Mem. Am. Soc. Fund Raising Execs., Am. Bus. Women's Assn., Nat. Speakers Assn. (pres. Las Vegas chpt. 1984-85). Club: Toastmasters (ednl. v.p. 1980, adminstrv. v.p. 1983). Home: 2754 El Toreador Las Vegas NV 89109 Office: LHP Investments Inc/ PMS Research Found PO Box 14574 Las Vegas NV 89114

HORNSBY, CHARLES AL, professional association executive; b. Tallassee, Ala., Dec. 12, 1949; s. Rogers Jackson and Amy Marie (Gordon) H.; m. Melanie Leigh Vincz, May 12, 1984; 1 stepchild, Erika Michelle Vincz. B.A., U. Ga., 1972. Photographer, Al Hornsby Photography, Atlanta, 1973-75; sales rep., instr. Dive N Surf, Inc., Redondo Beach, Calif., 1976-77; mktg. mgr. U.S. Cavalero, Irvine, Calif., 1977-78; v.p. edn. and public affairs PADI, Santa Ana, Calif., 1978—; pres. PADI (Profl. Assn. Diving Instrs.). Internat. Coll., Santa Ana, 1984—. Author: The Retail Dive Store: Management and Operations, 1979. Contbr. articles to diving mags.; editor diving mags. Recipient Tourism award Grand Cayman Islands Dept. Tourism award, 1983. Mem. Nat. Ocean Industries Assn., Diving Equipment Mfrs. Assn., Council Nat. Coop. Aquatics. Baptist. Office: PADI 1234 E Warner Ave Santa Ana CA 92705

HOROWITZ, BEN, medical center executive; b. Bklyn., Mar. 19, 1914; s. Saul and Sonia (Meringoff) H.; B.A., Bklyn. Coll., 1940; LL.B., St. Lawrence U., 1935; postgrad. New Sch. Social Research, 1942; m. Beverly Lichtman, Feb. 14, 1952; children—Zachary, Jody. Admitted to N.Y. bar, 1941, dir. N.Y. Fedn. Jewish Philanthropies, 1940-45; Eastern regional dir. City of Hope, 1945-50, nat. exec. sec., City of Hope Los Angeles, 1950-53, exec. dir.,

1953-85, gen. v.p. City of Hope, 1986—; chmn. coordinating com. City of Hope Nat. Med. Center, 1980-85, pres., bd. dirs. 1986—. Mem. Gov.'s Task Force on Flood Relief, 1969-74. Bd. dirs., v.p. Hope for Hearing Found., UCLA, 1972—. Recipient Spirit of Life award, 1970, Gallery of Achievement award, 1974, Profl. of Yr. award So. Calif. chpt. Nat. Soc. Fundraisers, 1977; Ben Horowitz chair in research established at City of Hope, 1981. Jewish (dir. temple 1964-67, 1986—). Home: 221 Conway Ave Los Angeles CA 90024 Office: City of Hope 208 W 8th St Los Angeles CA 90014

HOROWITZ, MYER, university president; s. Philip and Fanny Cotler H.; m. Barbara Rosen, 1956; 2 d.: Carol Anne, Deborah Ellen. B.A., Sir George Williams U., 1956, M. Ed., U. Alta., 1959, Ed. D., Stanford U., 1965, LL. D. (hon.), McGill U., 1979, Concordia U., 1982. Teacher, elem. and high schs., Montreal, Que., area, 1952-60; lectr. in educ., McGill U., 1960-62, asst. prof., 1963-65, assoc. prof., 1965-67, prof., 1967-69, asst. dean, 1965-69; prof., chmn. dept. elem. educ.,U. Alta., 1969-72, dean of educ., 1972-75, v.p. (acad.), 1975-79, pres., 1979—. Author articles in field. Fellow, Can. Coll. Teachers. Jewish. Office: Univ of Alta, Office of the President, Edmonton, AB Canada T6G 2J9 *

HOROWITZ, STEPHEN PAUL, lawyer; b. Los Angeles, May 23, 1943; s. Julius J. and Maxine (Rubenstein) H.; m. Nancy J. Shapiro, Apr. 4, 1971; children: Lindsey Nicole, Keri Lyn, Deborah Arielle. B.S., UCLA, 1966; J.D., 1970; M. Acctg., U. So. Calif., 1967. CPA, Calif. Bookkeeper, various law and acctg. firms, 1963-70; staff acct. Touche, Ross & Co., C.P.A.s, Los Angeles, 1968, 69; admitted to Calif. bar, 1971, U.S. Dist. Ct. bar, 1971, U.S. Ct. Appeals bar, 1972; individual practice law, Los Angeles, 1971-77; partner firm Horowitz & Horowitz, Los Angeles, 1978-79, prin. firm, 1979—; judge pro tem Los Angeles Mcpl. Ct.; classroom speaker Los Angeles County Bar Assn.; arbitrator Better Bus. Bur., Los Angeles County Bar Assn.; ombudsman VA, 1970. Bd. dirs. Vols. Am. Detoxification and Rehab. Center, Los Angeles, 1975-81, treas., 1979, vice chmn., 1980-81; legal adv. chmn., parliamentarian Temple Ramat Zion, Northridge, Calif. Served with U.S. Army, 1961-62. Mem. Calif. State Bar, Calif. Trial Lawyers Assn., Los Angeles Trial Lawyers. Jewish. Lodge: Masons. Editorial bd. UCLA-Alaska Law Rev., 1968-70, co-editor-in-chief, 1969-70. Office: 8383 Wilshire Blvd Suite 528 Beverly Hills CA 90211

HOROWITZ, SYLVIA TEICH, chemistry ecucator; b. N.Y.C., Dec. 11, 1922; d. Abraham and Gertrude (Green) T.; m. Robert Miller Horowitz, Nov. 29, 1953; children: Jonathan, David, Daniel. BA, Bklyn. Coll., 1943; PhD, Columbia U., 1949. Research assoc. Columbia U. Coll. Physicians and Surgeons, N.Y.C., 1950-53, U. Mich., Ann Arbor, 1953-55; assoc. prof. Calif. State U., Los Angeles, 1968—. Contbr. articles to profl. jours. Mem. Am. Chem. Soc., Sigma Xi. Home: 800 Fairfield Circle Pasadena CA 91106

HORRIGAN, JACK ALLEN, computer cons.; b. Des Moines, Aug. 30, 1930; s. Jack William and Earnestine Geraldine (Smith) H.; B.S., Iowa State Coll., 1955; M.A., Oreg. State Coll., 1957; D.D., Neotarian Fellowship and Coll. of Philosophy, 1967, Ph.D., 1969; m. Patricia Ann Austin, June 8, 1963; children—Marianne MiChael, Aileen Elizabeth, William George. Mathematician, tech. rep. Philco, Phila., White Sands Missile Range, N.Mex., 1959-60; with Vitro Silver Spring Lab., 1961; sr. mathematician Litton Data Systems div., Van Nuys, Calif., 1962-66; asst. dept. mgr. Wolf Western div., Sherman Oaks, Calif., 1967; staff mathematician AAI-Pacific, Northridge, Calif., 1968; staff engr. Hughes Aircraft Co., Culver City, Calif., 1969-70; chief ops. research Mental Health Research and Evaluation Team, U. Denver, 1972-76; cons. Clarett McCoy, Denver; co-owner John Paul Jones Mine, Idaho Springs, Colo., 1970-75, Translogis Corp., Denver, 1975—; cons. Westinghouse F-16 computer systems, Balt., 1976-77, ESI, Tempe, Ariz., 1978, Sperry FS, Phoenix, 1979, Lear Siegler, Grand Rapids, Airship Industries, Ramsey, Isle of Man, 1980, Am. Home Video, Denver, 1981-82, Dupont, Glasgow, Del., 1983-84, Demag Systems Techniques, Grand Rapids, 1984-86, Boeing Aerospace, Seattle, 1985-86; system designer over horizon radar Gen. Electric Co., Syracuse, N.Y. Founder Denver Libertarian Ch., 1976. Served with USCG, 1948-51. Mem. Pi Mu Epsilon. Author: Coordinate Transformations, Ship and Earth Orientated Coordinate Systems, 1962. Contbr. to Behavior Analysis and Systems Analysis: An Integrative Approach to Mental Health Programs, 1974. Contbr. articles to profl. jours. Home: PO Box 06436 Denver CO 80206

HORROCKS, RODNEY DWAIN, agronomy educator; b. Maeser, Utah, Oct. 4, 1938; s. Rodney B. and Phoebe M. (Hatch) H.; m. BarbaraJean Williams, Sept. 9, 1960; children: Rodney D., Sharilyn, Janene, Richard L., Russell D. BS, Brigham Young U., 1962; MS, Pa. State U., 1964, PhD, 1967. Cert. profl. agronomist. Asst. prof. agronomy U. Mo., Columbia, 1967-71, assoc. prof., 1971-75, prof., 1975-78; prof. Brigham Young U., Provo, Utah, 1978—, chmn. dept. agronomy, 1982—; vis. assoc. prof. dept. soil, water and engring. U. Ariz., Tucson, 1975-76; cons. U.S.A.I.D. project, West Africa, 1976. Author (lab. manual) Introduction to Crop Science, 1979; contbr. articles to profl. jours. Mem. AAAS, Am. Soc. Agronomy (assoc. editor 1983—), Crop Sci. Soc. Am., Am. Inst. Biol. Scis., Sigma Xi, Phi Kappa Phi. Home: 1616 W 1100 N Provo UT 84604 Office: Brigham Young U Dept Agronomy 275 Widtsoe Bldg Provo UT 84602

HORSELL, MARY KAY, association executive; b. Roundup, Mont., Nov. 3, 1917; d. Guy Elmer and Mary Catherine (Raridan) Smith; m. Arthur Howard Horsell, June 26, 1937; children—Barbara Horsell Koon, Mary Ann Horsell Boyette, Arthur Howard. B.S., Fresno (Calif.) State U., 1939. Owner, operator Food Merchandising Service, Oakland, Calif., 1954—; chmn. bd. Oakland Diocesan Council Cath. Women, 1962-64, program chmn., 1964-65, v.p., program chmn., 1965-66, pres., 1967-69; parliamentarian, Diocesan rep. Ch. Women United Bd., 1969-71, ways and means chmn., 1971-73; province dir. San Francisco Archdiocesan Council Cath. Women, 1973-75; pres. Nat. Council Cath. Women, Washington, 1975—; U.S. rep. from Nat. Council Cath. Women to World Union Cath. Women's Orgns., 1979—; mem. Commn. for Women in Ch., Oakland Diocese, 1978—; mem. exec. bd. Women in Community Service, Washington, 1979—; bd. dirs. World Union Cath. Women's Orgns., 1979—; Mem. central com. San Francisco Bay council Girl Scouts U.S.A., 1947-55; diocesan bd. mem., health chmn., program chmn., legis. chmn. Parent Tchrs. Groups, 1949-54; pres. East Bay Pres.'s Council, 1954-56, archdiocesan pres., 1958-60; pres. Oakland Diocese, 1962-64, St. Jarlath's Mothers Club, 1946-48, Bishop O'Dowd High Sch. Mothers Club, 1956-58; co-organizer Children's Vision Center of East Bay, 1957, pres., 1971-74; pres. East Bay Motion Picture and TV Council, 1964-66; organizer Vol. Tchr. Assistance Program for elementary schs. in Oakland Diocese, 1965; bd. dirs. Met. Horseman's Assn., 1963-75, now v.p., Past Pres.'s trophy, 1975; vol. counselor juvenile delinquents awaiting trial, 1967—; sec. Fedn. Motion Picture Councils, Inc., 1975-77. Editor: Newsreel, Fedn. Motion Picture Councils, 1973-75. Recipient Pro Ecclesia Et Pontifice, 1964, Life membership East Bay Pres.'s Council Parent Tchrs. Groups, 1964; named Oakland Mother of Year, 1970. Club: Zonta Internat. Home: 11590 Circle Way Dublin CA 94568 Office: 1312 Massachusetts Ave NW Washington DC 20005

HORSTING, WALTER JOHNSON, communications company executive; b. Chgo., Apr. 9, 1951; s. William Francis and Ruth (Johnson) H. Pres. WAH Systems Corp., Sacramento, 1971—; cons. Electro-Voice, Buchanan, Mich., 1981—, Yamaha, Japan, 1978-79, City of Roseville, Calif., 1985-86, Pac Tel, Sacramento, 1985, JBL Northridge, Calif., Gen. Parametrics, Berkeley, Calif., Zenith, Ill., Apple, Cupertino, Calif., Sony, Japan; audio engr. gubernatorial inauguration, Sacramento, 1982, presdl. speech, Sacramento, 1984, various fund raising events, Sacramento, Berkeley and throughout U.S., 1980-84. Producer, dir. (films) Hardware, 1986, Katmandu, 1986, Train to Nikko, 1986. Mem. Soc. Broadcast Engrs., Audio Engring. Soc., Nat. Assn. Broadcasters, Nat. C. of C. Club: Mac News (Sacramento) (dealer liaison 1985). Avocations: film making, golf, tennis, volleyball, sci-fi, art collecting. Office: WAH Systems Corp 915 Fee Dr Sacramento CA 95815

HORTON, BARBARA LADD, speech pathologist; b. Loveland, Colo., Jan. 4, 1931; d. James Sherman and Mildred (Gregory) Ladd; m. James R. Horton, Mar. 18, 1951; children: J. Thomas, Stephanie Louise, Gregory Wade. BA, Idaho State Coll., 1952; MA, U. Denver, 1968. Tchr. English and drama Pocatello (Idaho) High Sch., 1952-54, Englewood (Colo.) Jr. High Sch., 1955-57; tchr. English Nampa (Idaho) High Sch., 1957-59; tchr. English T.J. High Sch., Denver, 1960-67, chmn. dept. English; speech and lang. pathologist Denver Pub. Sch., 1968—, chmn. testing com., 1985—, assoc. dir. spl. project, 1986—. Mem. Colo. Speech and Hearing Assn. (pub. schs. com. 1970-80), Am. Speech Lang. and Hearing Assn., NEA, Colo. Edn. Assn., Denver Classroom Tchrs., Denver Assn. Specialized Services Personnel (pres. 1975-76). Republican. Avocation: fibre arts. Home: 1311 S Edison Way Denver CO 80222 Office: Denver Pub Schs 900 Grant St Denver CO 80222

HORTON, CRAIG LOREN, academic administrator; b. Chgo., June 10, 1953; s. Loren Burdette and Blanche Clarice (Bishop) H.; m. Sylvie Pennaforte, July 23, 1977; 1 child, Arnaud Dumont. BA, U. Iowa, 1975, MA, 1978. Recreation dir. Snowmass Resort Assn., Snowmass Village, Colo., 1977-81; a.p. clk. Snowmass Club, Snowmass Village, 1982-83; v.p. Resort Seminars, Snowmass Village, 1983—; assoc. Resort Resources, Snowmass Village, 1983-86, prin., 1987—. Active planning commn. Town of Snowmass Village, 1985—, chmn. liquor licensing authority, 1984—, election commn., 1984—. Roman Catholic. Avocations: skiing, mountaineering, golf, wine. Home: PO BOx 5214 Snowmass Village CO 81615 Office: Resort Resources PO Box 5212 Snowmass Village CO 81615

HORTON, JACK KING, utilities executive; b. Stanton, Nebr., June 27, 1916; s. Virgil L. and Edna L. (King) H.; m. Betty Lou Magee, July 15, 1937; children: Judy, Sally, Harold. A.B., Stanford U., 1936; LL.B., Oakland Coll. Law, 1941. Bar: Calif. 1941. Treasury dept. Shell Oil Co., 1937-42; pvt. law practice San Francisco, 1942-43; atty. Standard Oil Co., 1943-44; sec., legal counsel Coast Counties Gas & Electric Co., 1944-51, pres., 1951-54; v.p. Pacific Gas & Electric Co., San Francisco, 1954-59; pres. So. Calif. Edison Co., 1959-68, chief exec. officer, 1965—, chmn. bd., 1968-80, chmn. exec. com., 1980—; dir. First Interstate Bank of Calif., Pacific Mut. Life Ins., Lockheed Aircraft Corp., First Interstate Bancorp. Trustee U. So. Calif. Mem. State Bar Calif., Tax Found. (trustee), Bus. Council. Clubs: Pacific Union, Bohemian, California, Los Angeles Country, Cypress Point. Office: So Calif Edison Co 2244 Walnut Grove Ave Rosemead CA 91770

HORTON, JEROME SWEET, retired research forester; b. Stephentown, N.Y., May 17, 1910; s. Howard Francis and Chloe Cole (Sweet) H.; m. Edna E. Detwiler, Aug. 15, 1937 (dec. Oct. 1976); children: Robert F., Kenneth A. AB, U. Redlands, 1931; MS, U. Calif., Berkeley, 1940. Ecologist Calif. Forest and Range Experiment Sta. U.S. Forest Service, Glendora, 1933-54; research ctr. leader So. Forest Experiment Sta., Vicksburg, Miss., 1954-56; ecologist Rocky Mountain Forest and Range Exptl. Sta., Tempe, Ariz., 1956-72; cons. Water Resources Assocs., Phoenix, 1974—. Contbr. articles to profl. and govtl. pubs. Recipient Silver Beaver award Boy Scouts Am., Phoenix, 1963. Mem. Soil Conservation Soc. Am., Am. Forestry Assn., Wilderness Soc., Sigma Xi. Republican. Methodist. Avocations: stamp collecting, gardening, camping. Home: 444 S Higley Rd #319 Mesa AZ 85206

HORTON, LAWRENCE STANLEY, engineer, apartment developer; b. Hanston, Kans., July 25, 1926; s. Gene Leigh and Retta Florence (Abbott) H.; B.S.E.E., Oreg. State U., 1949; m. Margaret Ann Cowles, Nov. 26, 1946 (dec., 1964); children—Craig, Lawrence Stanley, Steven J.; m. 2d, Julia Ann Butler Wirrkila, Aug. 15, 1965; stepchildren—Charles Wirkkila Horton, Jerry Higginbotham Horton. Elec. engr. Mountain States Power Co., Calif. Oreg. Power Co., Calif. Pacific Power and Light Co., 1948-66; mgr. Ramic Corp., 1966-69; cons. elec. engr. Marquess and Assos., Medford, Oreg., 1969-85, sec., bd. dirs.; owner, mgr. Medford Better Housing Assn., Ashland Better Housing Assn.; partner Eastwood Living Group, Jackson St. Properties, T'Morrow Apts., Lake Empire Apts., Johnson Manor; chmn. bd. dirs. Medford State Bank; developer various apt. complexes, 1969—. Active Medford Planning Commn., Archtl. Review Commn., Housing Authority; bd. govs. State of Oreg. Citizens Utility; pres. United Fund, 1963-64. Served with USN, 1945-46. Named Rogue Valley Profl. Engr. of Yr., 1969. Mem. IEEE, Internat. Assn. Elec. Inspectors (assoc.), Nat. Soc. Profl. Engrs., Profl. Engrs. of Oreg., Elec. Safety Research Assn., So. Oreg. Apt. Owners Assn. (pres.), Rogue Valley Geneol. Soc. (pres.), Medford C. of C. (dir.). Republican. Methodist. Clubs: Rogue Valley Country Rogue Valley Yacht (commodore 1974-55, dir., local fleet capt., champion), San Juan 21 Fleet Assn. (western vice commodore, Top Ten San Juan Sailor West Coast, 1980), Jackson Toastmasters (founder 1957). Lodge: Kiwanis (life). Grad. instr. Dale Carnegie course, 1955, 56; contbr. elec. articles to profl. assns., 1956-61. Office: 1118 Spring St Medford OR 97504

HORTON, PATRICK JOHN, software and electrical engineer; b. Washington, Feb. 23, 1954; s. Kenneth Burns and Virginia Carolyn (Crever) H.; m. Julianne Marie Beyer, Mar. 3, 1984; 1 child, Craig Allen. ASEE, Lane Community Coll., 1975; BSEE, Oreg. State U., 1979; MS in Software Engring., Nat. U., 1987. Registered profl. engr., Calif. Software engr. Colo. State U., Ft. Collins, 1979-80, Hughes Aircraft Co., Fullerton, Calif., 1981-84, Rockwell Internat., Santa Ana, Calif., 1984, Grumman Corp., Irvine, Calif., 1985—. Mem. IEEE. Republican. Roman Catholic. Avocation: ham radio. Home: 5362 Stanford Ave Garden Grove CA 92645-2349 Office: RFA Assocs 25500 Hawthorne Blvd Suite 1060 Torrance CA 90505-6828

HORTON, RICHARD, medical educator; b. N.Y.C., May 3, 1932; s. Gilbert Edwin and Cecile (Weiss) H.; m. Marjy Ann Dempsay, Aug. 27, 1955; children: Dean G., Kim A. BS in Zoology, U. Wash., 1954, MD cum laude, 1958. Resident VA Hosp. and UCLA, 1959-61; med. tng. UCLA, 1959-61, mem. faculty, 1965-69; research tng. U. Calif., San Francisco, 1961-63, Worchester Found., Shrewsbury, Mass., 1963-65; mem. faculty U. So. Calif., Los Angeles, 1969—, prof. medicine, dir. endocrinology and metabolism, 1972—. Editor Jour. Clin. Endocrinology, 1978-83; contbr. articles to profl. jours. NIH Research grantee, 1965—; recipient Career Devel. award NIH, 1965-67. Mem. Am. Soc. Clin. Research, Pacific Coast Fertility Soc. (pres. 1975), Western Am. Fedn. Clin. Research (pres. 1972), Endocrine Soc. (council 1985—), Am. Assn. Physicians, Delta Upsilon. Club: Long Beach (Calif.) Yacht. Avocations: sailing, scuba diving, underwater photography, photography. Office: U So Calif Zonal Ave Los Angeles CA 90033

HORTON, ROBERT LAWRENCE, systems engineer; b. Los Angeles, Dec. 15, 1959; s. Floyd Thaddeus and Nancy Sue (Garis) H. BA in Math., BPhil, UCLA, 1980, MA in Math., 1984. Systems engr. Hughes Aircraft Co., El Segundo, Calif., 1981—. Mem. Am. Math. Soc., Math. Assn. Am., Mensa, Phi Beta Kappa, Pi Mu Epsilon. Home: 5515 Jeffrey Dr Torrance CA 90503

HORTON, THOMAS CLIFFORD, SR., farmer, rancher, water cooperative executive; b. Venus, N.Mex., Jan. 23, 1916; s. Claude C. and Ethel M. (Madole) H.; m. Rita Shook, Dec. 27, 1937; children—Rita-Loy Horton Thomas, Sharron Horton Geilenfeldt, Thomas Clifford. Grad. Menaul Sch. of United Presbyn. Ch., 1936. Farmer, rancher Santa Fe and Bernalillo Counties (N.Mex.), 1936—; farm instr. Edgewood Dist. (N.Mex.) State Coll., 1947-49; sub-contractor road constrn. Allison-Haney Co., Albuquerque, 1953-54, Northwestern Engrs., Denver, 1953-54, Floyd Hake, Santa Fe, 1953-54; gen. contractor, Albuquerque, 1954—; bldg. supr. Bd. Nat. Missions United Presbyn. Ch. U.S.A., N.Mex., Ariz., Utah, Tex., Alaska, 1954-71, asst. dir. Bd. Properties div., 1961-69; founder Entranosa Water Corp. (name changed to Entranosa Water Cooperative 1981), Santa Fe and Bernalillo Counties, 1974—, comptroller, 1982—. Sec. Edgewood Soil Conservation Dist., 1942-43; mem. adv. com. Santa Fe County Long Range Planning Program, 1948-49; organizer no. half Estancia Valley for REA com., 1949-50; pub. relations officer Central N.Mex. Elec. Coop., 1950-52. Mem. Menual Sch. Alumni Assn. Democrat. Clubs: Mason, Moriarty Rotary. Address: PO Box 150 Edgewood NM 87015

HORTON, WILLIAM RUSSELL, utility company executive; b. Toronto, Ont., Can., Aug. 25, 1931; s. Russell Burton and Freda Catherine (Middleton) H.; m. Dorothy Viva Rye, Nov. 27, 1954; children: William Russell, Robert Freeman, Douglas Lloyd, Ronald Edward. BS in Mining Engring., U. Toronto, 1955. Engr. Imperial Oil Ltd., Calgary and Camrose, Alta., Can., 1955-56; engr., mgr. Black Sivalls & Bryson Ltd., Edmonton, Alta., 1956-65; v.p. Gamma Engring. Ltd., Edmonton, 1965-68; pres. Horton Engring. Ltd., Edmonton, 1968—, also bd. dirs.; exec. v.p. utilities Can. Utilities Ltd., Edmonton, 1984—, also bd. dirs.; bd. dirs. Alta. Power Ltd., Northwestern Utilities Ltd., Can. Western Natural Gas Co. Ltd., Calgary Gas Co. Ltd., Ft. McMurray Power Co. Ltd., Northland Utilities (B.C.) Ltd., Northland Utilities (N.W.T.) Ltd., Yukon Electrical Co. Ltd., Yukon Hydro Co. Ltd., Yukon Energy Corp., CU Enterprises Inc.; mem. Centre for Study Regulated Industries McGill U.; hon. mem. Can. Assn. Members Pub. Utility Tribunals. Mem. Alta. Pub. Utilities Bd., Edmonton, 1973-76, chmn., 1976-83. Mem. Can. Gas Assn., Can. Electrical Assn., Assn. Profl. Engrs. Geologists and Geophysicists Alta., Edmonton C. of C., Calgary C. of C., Alta. C. of Resources, Northwest Electric Light and Power Assn. Clubs: Edmonton Petroleum, Edmonton, Mayfair Golf and Country (Edmonton). Avocations: sports, music, reading. Home: 11 Sunset Pl, Sherwood Park, AB Canada T8A 0X3 Office: Can Utilities Ltd, 10035-105th St, Edmonton, AB Canada T5J 2V6 *

HORVATH, STEVEN M., physiologist, biomedical engineer, educator; b. Cleve., Sept. 15, 1911; s. Steven Michael and Mary (Pinka) H.; m. Elizabeth Dill Sept. 2, 1940 (dec.); children: Aletha Mary Crowder, Steven Michael, Peter Joseph. Student, Oberlin Coll., 1930; BA in Chemistry and Phys. Edn., Miami U., Ohio, 1934, MS in Physiology, 1935; postgrad., Ohio State U., 1935-37; PhD in Physiology and Biology, Harvard U., 1942. Research asst. Woods Hole Biol. Lab., 1936; instr. Miami (Ohio) U., 1937-39; research asst. Harvard U. Fatigue Lab., Boston, 1939-42, tutor in biochem. scis., 1940-42; dir. physiol. research Met. State Hosp. for the Insane, Waltham, Mass., 1939-42; asst. prof. phys. medicine U. Pa., Phila., 1946-47, 1948-49; assoc. prof. physiology State U. Iowa, Iowa City, 1949-50, prof., 1951-58, acting dir. Inst. Gerontology, 1951-57; attendant in physiology VA Hosp., Des Moines, Iowa, 1952-58; vis. prof. U. Copenhagen, 1958-59; dept. head physiology Landenau Hosp., Phila., 1958-61; vis. prof. in physiology Jefferson Med. Coll., Phila., 1959—; prof. physiology and biomedical engring. to chmn. dept. Ergonomics and Occupational Health Scis. U. Calif., Santa Barbara, 1962—; cons. in field; com. mem. Dept. Energy Health Effects Working Group on Coal Techs., EPA, Gordon Conf. on the Chemistry of Aging (chmn.), Gov's. Com. on Aging (Iowa), Nat. Health Council (N.Y.), Nat. Inst. Occupational Safety and Health, NIH, Nat. Research Council, Nat. Social Welfare Assembly. Contbr. articles to profl. jours.; mem. editorial bd. Am. Jour. Physiology, Jour. Applied Physiology, Jour. Gerontology, Sci. and Medicine in Sports; reviewer for Am. Rev. Respiratory Disease, Climatic Change, Jour. Clin. Investigation, Jou. Neurophysiology, Jour. Occupational Medicine, Jour. of the Autonomic Nervous System Sci. Fellow AAAS, Am. Coll. Cardiology, Am. Coll. Sports Medicine, N.Y. Acad. Scis.; mem. AHA, Am. Physiol. Soc., Am. Pub. Health Assn., Gerontological Soc., Inst. Radio Engrs., Pan Am. Med. Assn., Phila. Physiol. Soc., Soc. Experimental Biology and Medicine, Undersea Med. Soc. Home: 5210 Austin Rd Santa Barbara CA 93111 Office: U Calif Inst Environ Stress Santa Barbara CA 93117

HORWIN, LEONARD, lawyer; b. Chgo., Jan. 2, 1913; s. Joseph and Jennie (Fuhrmann) H.; m. Ursula Helene Donig, Oct. 15, 1939; children—Noel Samuel, Leonora Marie. LL.D. cum laude, Yale U., 1936. Bar: Calif. 1936, U.S. Dist. Ct. (cen. dist.) Calif. 1937, U.S. Ct. Appeals (9th cir.) 1939, U.S. Supreme Ct. 1940. Assoc., Lawler, Felix & Hall, 1936-39; ptnr. Hardy & Horwin, Los Angeles, 1939-42; counsel Bd. Econ. Warfare, Washington, 1942-43; attache, legal adviser U.S. Embassy, Madrid, Spain, 1943-47; sole practice, Beverly Hills, Calif., 1948—; dir., lectr. Witkin-Horwin Rev. Course on Calif. Law, 1939-42; judge pro tempore Los Angeles Superior Ct., 1940-42; instr. labor law U. So. Calif., 1939-42. U.S. rep. Allied Control Council for Ger., 1945-47; councilman City of Beverly Hills, 1962-66, mayor, 1964-65; chmn. transp. Los Angeles Goals Council, 1968; bd. dirs. So. Calif. Rapid Transit Dist., 1964-66; chmn. Rent Stabilization Com., Beverly Hills, 1980. Fellow Am. Acad. Matrimonial Lawyers; mem. ABA, State Bar Calif., Order Coif. Clubs: Balboa Bay, Aspen Inst. Contbr. articles to profl. jours. Office: 121 S Beverly Dr Beverly Hills CA 90212

HORWITZ, DENNIS NEAL, fiber optic instrument manufacturing company executive; b. Los Angeles, Sept. 23, 1954; s. Sherwyn Irving and Edythe (Gubman) H.; m. Arlene Nancy Koster, Aug. 14, 1977. BS in Engring., UCLA, 1976, MS in Engring., Computer Sci., 1981. Research engr. UCLA, 1972-79; v.p. Photodyne Inc., Newbury Park, Calif., 1978—. Mem. IEEE, ASQC. Democrat. Home: 1623 Buena Vista St Ventura CA 93001 Office: Photodyne Inc 1175 Tourmaline Dr Newbury Park CA 91320

HOSEA, THOMAS C., hotel executive; b. Denver, Jan. 25, 1943; s. Fred T. and Theresa (Hinder) H.; m. Judith A. Epperson, Sept. 2, 1966; children: Jeffrey, Kristine, Kathlene. Student, Tarkio Coll., Colo. State U.; BA, Ft. Lewis Coll. Various positions Westin Hotels, Denver, Pitts., Winnipeg, Detroit, 1967-75; gen. mgr. Westin Hotels, San Francisco, 1975-76, Costa Mesa, Calif., 1976-79, Cin., 1979-84; gen. mgr. Westin Hotel Utah, Salt Lake City, 1984—. Named to Com. of 100, Salt Lake City C. of C., 1985-86. Mem. Utah Hotel Motel Assn. (bd. trustees 1984—, 1st v.p.), Salt Lake Convention and Visitors Bur. (bd. dirs.), Ohio Hotel and Motel Assn. (1st v.p. 1983-84), Pres.'s Club U. Utah. Methodist. Lodges: Rotary, Chaine Des Rotisseurs, SKAL. Home: Sandy UT 84092 Office: The Westin Hotel Utah Main St at South Temple Salt Lake City UT 84111

HOSICK, HOWARD LAWRENCE, cell biology educator, academic administrator; b. Champaign, Ill., Nov. 1, 1943; s. Arthur Howard and Eunice Irma (Miller) H.; m. Cynthia Ann Jacobson, June 15, 1968; children: Steven Cameron, Anna Elise, Rachel Victoria. BA, U. Colo., 1965; PhD, U. Calif., Berkeley, 1970. Postdoctoral fellow Karolinska Inst., Stockholm, 1970-72; asst. research biochemist U. Calif., Berkeley, 1972-73; asst. prof. Wash. State U., Pullman, 1973-78, assoc. prof., 1978-83, prof. cell biology, 1983—, chmn. dept. zoology, 1983—; vis. scientist U. Reading, Eng., 1978; disting. scientist Aichi Cancer Ctr. Nagoya, Japan, 1986; research com. Am. Heart Assn., 1984—. Rev. editor In Vitro Cellular and Molecular Biology, 1986—; contbr. articles to profl. jours. Recipient H.S. Boyce award, 1981, Shell Faculty Devel. award, 1984; fellow NIH, NSF, Am. Cancer Soc., 1968—; grantee NIH, NSF, Am. Cancer Soc., 1973—. Mem. Am. Soc. Cell Biology, Tissue Culture Assn., Am. Assn. Cancer Research, Internat. Assn. Breast Cancer Research. Democrat. Buddhist. Lodge: Rotary. Avocations: running, classical lit., woodworking, Italian cooking. Home: NE 1185 Lake St Pullman WA 99163 Office: Wash State U Dept Zoology Pullman WA 99164-4220

HOSIE, WILLIAM CARLTON, walnut growers company executive; b. Stockton, Calif., June 25, 1936; s. Fred A. and Janet (Russell) H.; m. Sherryl Rasmussen, Jan. 12, 1963; children: Shaen Case, Erin Frick. B.S., U. Calif.-Davis, 1960. Field rep. Flotill Inc., Stockton, Calif., 1960-61; orchardist Hosie Ranch Inc., Linden, Calif., 1961-83; chmn. bd. dirs. Diamond Walnut Growers Inc., Stockton, Calif., 1981—; advisor U. Calif. Extension-Stockton, 1975—, Calif. Farm Bur., Sacramento, 1976—, Farmer and Mchts. Bank, Linden, 1979; dir. Walnut Mktg. Bd., San Mateo, Calif., 1981—. Pres. Stockton East Water Dist., 1969-79. Served with AUS, 1958-59. Mem. Stockton C. of C. Republican. Club: Rotary Internat. Home: PO Box 226 Linden CA 95236 Office: Diamond Walnut Growers Inc 1050 S Diamond St Stockton CA 95201 *

HOSKINS, BARBARA BRUNO, speech pathologist, learning disabilities specialist; b. Havre de Grace, Md., Feb. 21, 1948; d. Onofrio Pasquale and Marjorie (Goertler) Bruno. BS magna cum laude, Syracuse U., 1970; MS, So. Ill. U., 1971; PhD, Northwestern U., 1979. Cert. clin. competence speech/lang. pathologist. Lectr. Southern Ill. U., Carbondale, 1971-72; speech, lang. specialist Los Angeles County Schs., 1973-76; dir. tng. and research Almansor Edn. Ctr., Alhambra, Calif., 1979-86; asst. prof. Whittier (Calif.) Coll., 1980-84; vis. prof. U. Redlands, Calif., 1984-86; cons. in field, Pasadena, Calif., 1985—; affiliate staff Ingleside Hosp., Alhambra, 1982—, Las Encinas Hosp., Pasadena, 1985—. Mem. Am. Speech, Lang., Hearing Assn., Internat. Neuropsychol. Soc. Home: 285 W California #3 Pasadena CA 91105 Office: 595 E Colorado Blvd #508 Pasadena CA 91101

HOSKINS, FRED HALL, food science/nutrition educator; b. Cin., May 17, 1936; s. Harold Elvin and Niota (Hall) H.; m. Mildred Ann Ball, Sept. 8, 1957; children: Michael, Darrell. BS, U. Ariz., 1958, MS, 1959; PhD, La. State U., 1963. Instr. La. State U., Baton Rouge, 1964-65, asst. prof., 1965-71, assoc. prof., 1971-76, prof. food sci., 1976-84; chmn., prof. dept. food sci. and human nutrition Wash. State U., Pullman, 1984-86, prof. food sci. and human nutrition, 1986—; cons. Ethyl Corp., Baton Rouge, 1965-67, Dairyland, Inc., St. Paul, 1977, Pillsbury Co., Mpls., 1978. Contbr. articles to profl. jours. Recipient Award of Excellence in Teaching Gamma Sigma

Delta, La. State U., Baton Rouge, 1971. Mem. Inst. Food Technologists (chmn. nutrition div. 1971), Am. Inst. Nutrition (regional assoc. editor 1969-74), Am. Home Econs. Assn., N.Y. Acad. Sci., Gamma Sigma Delta. Republican. Methodist. Office: Dept Food Sci and Human Nutrition Wash State U Pullman WA 99164

HOSMAN, CAROL MERZ, public school administrator; b. Seattle, Sept. 29, 1942; d. Herbert Ralph and Margaret Wardell (Hill) Smith; m. Martin Daniel Merz, Aug. 23, 1964; children: Sarah Katherine, Ruth Joanna; m. Gerald E. Hosman, June 28, 1986. BA, Stanford U., 1964, MA, 1965; EdD, Wash. State U., 1983. Tchr. pub. schs., Calif., 1965-68; instr. Columbia Basin Community Coll., Pasco, Wash., 1971-78; adminstr. Richland (Wash.) Sch. Dist., 1979-81; prin. Edwin Markham Elem. Sch., Pasco, 1981-84; asst. prof. Wash. State U., 1984—; dir. curriculum and staff devel. Pasco Pub. Schs., 1984-87; dean of edn. U. Puget Sound, Tacoma, 1987—; cons. in field. Loan exec. United Way, Richland, 1978; vol. Girl Scouts Am., Richland, 1977-81, chmn. service area, 1978-80. Recipient Cleveland Honors award Stanford U., 1964. Mem. Wash. State Assn. Adminstrv. Women in Edn. (pres. 1981-82), N.W. Women in Ednl. Adminstrn. (exec. bd. 1978-83), N.W. Regional Ednl. Lab. (exec. bd. 1982-84), Assn. Supervision and Curriculum Devel., Wash. Assn. Sch. Adminstrs., Assn. Wash. Sch. Prins., Kappa Delta Pi, Phi Delta Kappa. Contbr. ednl. articles to profl. publs. Office: U Puget Sound 1500 N Warner Tacoma WA 98416-0220

HOSTETTER, GENE HUBER, electrical engineering educator; b. Spokane, Wash., Sept. 14, 1939; s. John Huber and Virginia Lane (Yancey) H.; m. Donna Rae Patterson, Nov. 30, 1967; children—Colleen Rae, Kristen Lane. B.S.E.E., U. Wash., 1962, M.S., 1963; Ph.D., U. Calif.-Irvine, 1973. Dir. engring. Sta. KOL, Seattle, 1965-67; asst. prof. elec. engring. Calif. State U.-Long Beach, 1967-70, assoc. prof., 1970-75, prof., 1975-81, chmn. dept. elec. engring., 1975-81; prof. elec. engring. U. Calif.-Irvine, 1981-83, chmn. dept., 1983-85, acting dean engring., 1985-86. Author: Fundamentals of Network Analysis, 1980; Design of Feedback Control Systems, 1982; Engineering Network Analysis, 1984, Digital Control System Design, 1987. Recipient Outstanding Faculty award Calif. State U., 1975, 77, Engr. Faculty of Yr. award U. Calif.-Irvine, 1982. Fellow IEEE, Internat. Acad. Scis.; mem. AAAS, Am. Soc. Engring. Edn., Internat. Fedn. Automatic Control, Sigma Xi. Episcopalian. Home: 8811 Gallant Dr Huntington Beach CA 92646 Office: U Calif Dept Elec Engring Irvine CA 92717

HOTCHKISS, HENRY WASHINGTON, banker; b. Meshed, Iran, Oct. 31, 1937; s. Henry and Mary Bell (Clark) H. B.A., Bowdoin Coll., 1958. French tchr. Choate Sch., Wallingford, Conn., 1959-62; v.p. Chem. Bank, N.Y.C., 1962-80, v.p. Chem. Bank Internat. San Francisco, 1973-80; dir. corp. relations Crédit Suisse, San Francisco, 1980—; dir. Indonesia-U.S. Bus. Seminar, Los Angeles, 1979. Asso. bd. regents L.I. Coll. Hosp., 1969-71, pres., 1971, bd. regents, 1971-73, pres., bd. dirs. Gordonstown Am. Found, 1986—. Served to capt. U.S. Army Res., 1958-59. Mem. Explorers Club (treas. N. Calif. chpt. 1984-86), Calif. Council Internat. Trade (dir. 1976—, chmn. membership com. 1977-79, treas. 1978-79), New Eng. Soc. in City Bklyn. (v.p., dir. 1968-73). Clubs: Heights Casino (bd. govs. 1971-73) (Bklyn.); St. Francis Yacht, Golden Gate Anglers (San Francisco), Internat. Folkboat Assn. San Francisco (cruise chmn. 1976-77, pres. 1977-79, membership chmn. 1979-84, historian 1984—). Home: 1206 Leavenworth St San Francisco CA 94109 Office: 50 California St San Francisco CA 94111

HOTCHKISS, SANDRA JANE, social worker; b. Kansas City, Mo., Aug. 20, 1947; d. Robert Dismore and Marjorie Eleanor (White) H.; m. Stephen Grim Scott, Mar. 21, 1970 (div. July 1975); m. Donald Mead Hildreth, Oct. 9, 1982; 1 stepchild, Jeremy Hildreth. BA in French Lit., U. Kans., 1970; MSW, U. So. Calif., 1981. Cert. social worker, Calif. Contbr. editor Human Behavior Mag., Los Angeles, 1973-78; psychiatric social worker Los Angeles County, 1981-83; clin. social worker Glendale (Calif.) Adventist Med. Ctr., 1983-84, Huntington Meml. Hosp., Pasadena, Calif., 1984—; pvt. practice social work Los Angeles, 1984—. Supr. Los Angeles Youth Programs, 1986—; vol. Sojourn, Santa Monica, Calif., 1977, So. Calif. Counseling Ctr., Los Angeles, 1975-78, 82-84, Los Angeles Suicide Prevention Ctr., 1978-79. Mem. Soc. Clin. Social Work, Register of Clin. Soc. Workers, Acad. Cert. Social Workers, Nat. Assn. Social Workers. Democrat. Presbyterian. Office: 3111 Los Feliz Blvd #101 Los Angeles CA 90039

HOTSON, HUGH HOWISON, retired corporation executive; b. Seattle, Jan. 26, 1916; s. John William and Jennie (Doak) H.; m. Josephine Frances Richardson, Dec. 23, 1939; children—Josephine Ann, John Richardson, Hugh Howison. B.S., U. Wash., 1938, M.S., 1940; Ph.D. in Plant Pathology, U. Minn., 1950; postgrad., Cornell U., 1940-41, Harvard U., 1941, Yale U., 1949-50. Teaching fellow U. Wash., 1939-40; herbarium curator Cornell U., 1941; teaching asst. Yale U., New Haven, 1949-50; research assoc. U. Minn., 1950-51; dept. chief C. div. Dugway Proving Ground, 1951-52, asst. chief BW div., 1952-53; mgr. agrl. chem. project Minn. Mining and Mfg. Co., 1953-58, cons. bus. mgmt., 1958-62; pres. Maritime Corp., Seattle, 1961-81. Author monographs in field of botany. Pres., Pat Smith Kontum Hosp. Fund., 1965-71; treas. English Speaking Union, 1974; active Seattle council Boy Scouts Am. Served to lt. col. U.S. Army, 1941-47. Recipient Book of Yr. award Ency. Britannica, 1950. Mem. Am. Chem. Soc., AAAS, Geothermal Resource Council, N.Y. Acad. Scis., Seattle C. of C., U. Wash. Alumni Assn. (pres. Minn. chpt. 1958), Sigma Xi, Phi Kappa Psi. Clubs: Rainier, Seattle Tennis.

HOTSON, JOSEPHINE ANN, systems specialist; b. Seattle, Jan. 10, 1944; d. Hugh and Josephine (Richardson) Hotson. BA, U. Wash., 1965. With Social Security Adminstrn., 1965—, systems specialist, Seattle, 1974—; dir. Maritime Corp., Seattle; pres. chpt. 215, Nat. Treasury Employees Union, 1983-84; ptnr. Maritime Assocs., real estate mgmt., 1984—. Guardian ad litem King County Juvenile Ct., Seattle, 1982—. Mem. NW Horticultural Soc. Republican. Mem. Daus. of Confederacy, Colonial Dames. Club: Seattle Tennis.

HOTTEN, BRUCE WALTER, research chemist; b. Paris, Idaho, June 13, 1918; s. Louis T.A. and Pearl Barbara (Simpson) H.; m. Louise Cecelia Moutoux, Feb. 28, 1945; 1 child, Lenore. AB, U. Cin., 1941; PhD, Purdue U., 1945. Research fellow Purdue U., Lafayette, Ind., 1944-45; research chemist Chevron Research Co., Richmond, Calif., 1946-78, cons., 1979—. Contbr. articles to profl. jours.; patentee in field. Mem. Am. Chem. Soc. (dir. Calif. chpt. 1976-78, assoc. editor petroleum div. 1976—), Am. Soc. Lubrication Engrs. (treas. San Diego chpt. 1985—), Exchange Club, Sigma Xi, Phi Lambda Upsilon, Alpha Chi Sigma. Avocation: photography. Home and Office: 2818 Arnoldson Ave San Diego CA 92122

HOTZ, HENRY PALMER, physicist; b. Fayetteville, Ark., Oct. 17, 1925; s. Henry Gustav and Stella (Palmer) H.; m. Marie Brase, Aug. 22, 1952; children: Henry Brase, Mary Palmer, Martha Marie. B.S., U. Ark., 1948; Ph.D., Washington U., St. Louis, 1953. Asst. prof. physics Auburn U., Ala., 1953-58, Okla. State U., Stillwater, 1958-64; assoc. prof. Marietta Coll., Ohio, 1964-66; physicist, scientist-in-residence U.S. Naval Radiol. Def. Lab., San Francisco, 1966-67; assoc. prof. U. Mo., Rolla, 1967-71; physicist Qanta Metrix div. Finnigan Corp., Sunnyvale, Calif., 1971-74; sr. scientist Nuclear Equipment Corp., San Carlos, Calif., 1974-79, Envirotech Measurement Systems, Palo Alto, Calif., 1979-82, Dohrmann div. Xertex Corp., Santa Clara, Calif., 1982-86; sr. scientist Rosemont Analytical Div. Dohrmann, 1986—; cons. USAF, 1958-62; mem. lectr. selection com. for Hartman Hotz Lectrs. in law, liberal arts U. Ark. Served with USNR, 1944-46. Mem. Am. Phys. Soc., Am. Assn. Physics Tchrs., AAAS, Phi Beta Kappa, Sigma Xi, Sigma Pi Sigma, Pi Mu Epsilon, Sigma Nu. Methodist. Lodge: Masons. Home: 290 Stilt Ct Foster City CA 94404 Office: Dohrmann div Xertex Corp 3240 Scott Blvd Santa Clara CA 95054

HOU, STERLING SHANLIN, electronics company executive; b. Hunan, China, Sept. 3, 1938; came to U.S. 1962, naturalized, 1972; s. Fisher T. and Lotus H.C. (Chu) H.; m. Vivian Wang, July 4, 1965; children—Patricia, Tina. B.S. in E.E., Nat. Taiwan U., 1961; M.S. in E.E., U. Mo., 1964; postgrad. Stanford U., 1966-68. Design engr. Nat. Cash Register Co., Dayton, Ohio, 1964-65; project mgr. IBM, San Jose, Calif., 1965-70; dir. engring. Telex Corp., San Jose, 1970-72; project mgr. Hewlett Packard, Palo Alto, Calif., 1972-73; program mgr. Ampex, Sunnyvale, Calif., 1973-74; engring. mgr. Intel, Santa Clara, Calif., 1974-77; dir. devel. Nat. Semiconductor, Santa Clara, 1977-80; founder, v.p. Envision Tech. Inc., San Jose, 1981-83; pres. Tangent, Los Gatos, Calif., 1983—. Pres. Sino America Culture & Economy Assn., 1981. Served to 2d lt. Chinese Mil. Police, 1961-62. Mem. IEEE, Chinese Inst. Engrs. (dir. Bay Area chpt.).

HOUCHIN, ROBERT JAMES, dentist; b. Mpls., Mar. 22, 1947; s. Orlo Lee and Mary Eileen (Cannon) H.; m. Linda Carol Little, Dec. 9, 1971; children: Kelly Jocelyn, Elizabeth Lee. BS in Biology, Loyola U. of Los Angeles, 1973; DDS, Georgetown U., 1978. Gen. practice dentistry Covina, Calif., 1978—; instr. Georgetown U., Washington, 1979-83. Served with USN, 1966-69, Vietnam. Mem. Mensa. Lodge: Rotary (pres. local club 1986—). Avocations: flying, sailing, sports, investing. Home: 912 S Heritage Dr West Covina CA 91791 Office: 153 W College St Covina CA 91723

HOUCK, ALAN PAUL, accountant; b. Portland, Oreg., June 29, 1947; s. Albert Lyle and Pauline Roberta (Jones) H.; m. Kathleen Ruth Elwood, Aug. 15, 1969; children—Eric Alan, Mark Andrew, Brian Christopher; B.A. in Math., Seattle Pacific U., 1969; M.A. in Math., Cleve. State U., 1971, B.B.A. in Acctg., 1973. C.P.A., Oreg. Tchr. math. and computer programming Cleve. Pub. Schs., 1969-72; staff acct. Brubaker, Helfrich & Taylor, C.P.A.s, Cleve., 1972-74; staff acct. Minihan, Kernutt, Stokes & Co., Eugene, Oreg., 1974-79, ptnr. in charge data processing and mgmt. services dept., 1979—; cons. to small bus. Treas. Emerald Exec. Assn., Eugene, 1978—; bd. dirs., treas. Eugene Christian Sch., 1975—; treas. local polit. campaigns. Mem. Am. Inst. C.P.A.s, Oreg. Soc. C.P.A.s, Assn. Time-sharing Small Computer Users. Republican. Club: Kiwanis (Eugene). Office: Minihan Kernutt Stokes & Co 1170 Pearl St Eugene OR 97401

HOUCK, LAURIE GERALD, agricultural researcher; b. Tucson, Aug. 13, 1928; s. Gerald Wesley and Laura Lee (Baker) H.; m. Marlene Moore, Sept. 20, 1958 (dec. April 1970); children: Lorna Jean, Marlys Lee; m. Margaret Victoria Evers. BS, U. Ariz., 1952, MS, 1954; PhD, Oreg. State U., 1962. Research plant physiologist USDA, Phoenix, 1954-56; research plant pathologist USDA, Pomona, Calif., 1962-73, Riverside, Calif., 1973-77, Fresno, 1977—; asst. horticulturist U. Ariz., Mesa, 1956-58; research asst. Oreg. State U., Corvallis, 1958-62; lectr. Calif. State Poly. U., Pomona, 1963, 64, 66. Contbr. numerous articles to profl. jours. and publs. Served with U.S. Army, 1946-48. S.C. Johnson Wax fellow U. Ariz., 1953-54. Mem. Am. Phytopath. Soc., Am. Soc. Hort. Scis., Am. Soc. Plant Physiologists, Mycol. Soc. Am., Fla. State Hort. Soc., Council Agrl. Sci. Tech., Sigma Xi. Unitarian. Club: Toastmasters (held all club offices Fresno chpt.). Avocations: hiking, gardening, travel. Home: 1758 S Waldby Ave Fresno CA 93727 Office: USDA Agrl Research Service Hort Crops Research Lab 2021 S Peach Ave Fresno CA 93727

HOUGAN, TOM MCKAY, advertising executive; b. Colfax, Wash., June 23, 1935; s. Melvin C. and Laura (McKay) H.; m. Lois Jean McBride, Jan. 4, 1958; children—Debra, Scott, Mark. B.A., Wash. State U., 1957; postgrad., U. Kans., 1957, Portland State U., 1968. Sr. copywriter Gen. Electric Corp., Schenectady, 1960-65; pres. chief exec. officer Gerber Advt., Portland, Oreg., 1965—; dir. Assn. Oreg. Industries, Salem, 1983—; Western regional chmn. Am. Advt. Fedn., Washington, 1978-80; pres. Portland Advt. Fedn., 1975-76. Pub. relations chmn. United Way Portland, 1976. Served to 1st lt. U.S. Army, 1958-60. Recipient Advt. Pres. of Yr. Silver Medal award, Am. Advt. Fedn., 1976; named Advt. Prof. of Yr., Portland. Advt. Fedn., 1976; Mayor's Corp. Citizen award Volunteer Council, Portland, 1984. Mem. N.W. Light and Power Assn., Am. Assn. Advt. Agys. (gov. Oreg. council), Pub. Utility Communicators Assn., Ducks Unlimited, Tau Kappa Epsilon (pub. relations chmn.). Republican. Presbyterian. Home: 27212 NE Bjur Rd Ridgefield WA 98642 Office: Gerber Advt Agency 209 SW Oak Portland OR 97204

HOUGHTEN, RICHARD ALLEN, research scientist; b. Champaign, Ill., Apr. 16, 1946; m. Christy Lynn Hendrickson; children: Richard Allen III, Russell Alexander. BS, Calif. State U., Fresno, 1968; MS, U. Calif., Berkeley, 1970, PhD, 1974. Postdoctoral fellow U. Calif., San Francisco, 1975-79; asst. prof. Mt. Sinai Med. Ctr., N.Y.C., 1979-81; assoc. mem. Scripps Clinic and Research Found., La Jolla, Calif., 1981—. Contbr. numerous articles to profl. jours. Served to 1st lt. USAF, 1969-70. Mem. AAAS, Am. Chem. Soc., N.Y. Acad. Scis., Sigma Xi. Office: Scripps Clinic & Research Found 10666 N Torrey Pines Rd La Jolla CA 92037

HOUGHTON, ARTHUR VINCENT, III, mechanical engineering educator; b. Jacksonville, Ill., July 9, 1926; s. Arthur Vincent II Houghton and Georgia Charlotte (Griffths) Schance; m. Patricia Lou Ryan, June 19, 1948 (dec. Oct. 1974); children: Linda, Vincent, Jerry, Laura; m. Janet Walker, July 10, 1982. BS, U. Ill., 1948, MS, 1951; postgrad., Bradley U.; PhD, Purdue U., 1960. Registered profl. engr., Ill., N.Mex. Assoc. prof. mech. engring. U. N.Mex., Albuquerque, 1960-66, prof., 1966—, asst. dean research, 1968-71, asst. to pres., 1969-71, dir. Eric Wang Civil Engring. Research Lab., 1971-72, dir. combustion lab., 1981—; cons. USAF Office Sci. and Research, 1960-63, Sandia Corp., 1963-68, various cos. and orgns., 1960—. Inventor in field. Dem. precinct and ward chmn., Albuquerque, 1968-74. Served as petty officer USN, 1944-46, PTO. Mem. ASME. Club: Edelweiss (Albuquerque). Office: U NMex Dept Mech Engring Albuquerque NM 87131

HOUGHTON, ROBERT LEE, physicist; b. Bristol, Eng., Apr. 13, 1952; came to U.S., 1956; s. Gerald and Mildred (Sherzer) H.; m. Barbara Suzan Douds, Dec. 21, 1984. BS, Fla. State U., 1972; MS, Auburn U., 1977, PhD, 1982. Mem. tech. staff Mission Research Co., Santa Barbara, Calif., 1982-86; dir. effects dept. Gen. Research Corp., Santa Barbara, 1986—. Mem. Am. Phys. Soc., Fusion Power Assn. Home: PO Box 20101 Santa Barbara CA 93120 Office: Gen Research 5383 Hollister Ave Santa Barbara CA 93111

HOUGHTON-ALICO, DOANN, communications and information executive; b. Mt. Kisco, N.Y., Aug. 3, 1940; d. John and Stella (Houghton) Alico; m. C. Samuel Haines III, Feb. 6, 1960 (div. 1974); children: Daraya Haines Haddock, Charles Samuel Haines IV, Peter John Haines. BA, Cedar Crest Coll., 1971; postgrad., Poly. Inst., N.Y., 1986. Legis. analyst Environ. Action, Washington, 1971-73; editor, pub. Deep Creek Rev., Telluride, Colo., 1974-75; cons. Telluride and Denver, Colo., 1975-79; pres. Tech. Info. Assn., Denver, 1980—; adj. prof. Poly. Inst. N.Y., Bklyn., 1985—. Author: Creating Computer Software User Guides: From Manuals to Menus, 1985; Alcohol Fuels: Policies, Production, and Potential, 1982 (Top Hand award Colo. Authors League 1982); also articles; co-originator (film) What Can I Tell You?, 1979 (Red Ribbon award, 1979). Exec. Dialogue Centennial C. of C., Littleton, Colo., 1984-85; commr. Commn. on the Status of Women, Denver, 1976-77. Mem. Human Factors Soc. (assoc.), Assn. Computing Machinery, Soc. Tech. Communication, Data Processing Mgmt. Assn., Colo. Authors League, Colo. Masters Swim Assn. Club: Sporting, Masters Swim Team. Avocations: hiking, skiing, competitive swimming. Office: Tech Info Assocs Inc 600 S Cherry St Suite 1100 Denver CO 80222

HOUK, JULIE MARIE, lawyer; b. Evergreen Park, Ill., Apr. 14, 1957; s. Farel and Helen (Lamb) H. BA, Marquette U., 1979, MA, 1981; JD, Golden Gate U., 1984. Bar: Calif., 1984, U.S. Dist. Ct. (no. dist.) Calif., 1984, U.S. Ct. Appeals (9th cir.) 1985, Ill. 1985, U.S. Dist. Ct. (ea. dist.) Ill. 1986. Atty. Law Office of John H. Scott, San Francisco, 1984—, Law Office of Oliver Jones, Oakland, Calif., 1984-85, Law Office of James Chanin, Berkeley, Calif., 1985—; sole practice Berkeley, Calif., 1985—. Mem. ABA, San Francisco Bar Assn., Alameda County Bar Assn., Nat. Lawyers Guild, Am. Trial Lawyers Assn. Office: 3050 Shattuck Ave Berkeley CA 94705

HOUK, KENDALL NEWCOMB, chemistry educator; b. Nashville, Feb. 27, 1943; s. Charles H. and Janet (Newcomb) H.; m. Leslie Holz; 1 child, Kendall M. AB, Harvard U., 1964, MS, 1966, PhD, 1968. Asst. prof. chemistry La. State U., Baton Rouge, 1968-72, assoc. prof., 1972-75, prof., 1975-80; prof. U. Pitts., 1980-86, UCLA, 1986—. Contbr. numerous articles to profl. jours. Mem. AAAS, Am. Chem. Soc. Office: UCLA Dept Chemistry and Biochemistry Los Angeles CA 90024

HOULETTE, WILLIAM AUSTIN, association executive; b. San Bernardino, Calif., July 30, 1958; s. Walter John and Wilberta Ruth (Murray) H. BS in Bus. Mgmt., Wright State U., 1982. Firefighter, paramedic Beaver Creek Fire Dept., Ohio, 1976-82; ter. mgr. Bristol-Myers Products, Los Angeles, 1983-85; area mgr. S.C. Johnson & Sons, 1985-86; account mgr. S.B.R. Broadcast Assn., Redlands, Calif., 1986—. Mem. Am. Soc. Tng. and Devel. Republican. Methodist.

HOULIHAN, JOSEPH PATRICK, chief executive support services, consultant office systems, local networks; b. Troy, N.Y., Jan. 14, 1949; s. Charles Joseph and Carolyn Frances (Dean) H.; m. Mary Ann Sanchez, Mar. 18, 1980; children: Melody Ann, Patricia Michelle, Shara Lynn, Shannon Leigh. Assoc. in Sci., Community College of USAF, Montgomery, Ala., 1984; AA, Miss. Gulf Coast Jr. Coll., Biloxi, 1984; postgrad., Tex. Lutheran Coll., Seguin, 1981-86. Master instr. 3300 Tech. Training Wing, Keesler AFB, Miss., 1976-78; chief of office systems Hdqrs. USAF in Europe, Ramstein AFB, Germany, 1978-81, Hdqrs. Air Force Military Personnel Ctr., Randolph AFB, Tex., 1981-85; master instr. 3423 Tech. Training Squadron, Colo. Springs, Colo., 1985—. Mem. Assn. Internationale de Sci. Politique. Democrat. Mem. Assemblies of God Ch. Home: USAFA QTRS 4605J Colorado Springs CO 80840 Office: 3243 TCHTS/CCA 4040 E Bijou Colorado Springs CO 80840

HOULIHAN, PATRICK THOMAS, museum director; b. New Haven, June 22, 1942; s. John T. and Irene (Rourke) H.; m. Betsy Eliason, June 19, 1965; children: Mark T. and Michael D. (twins). BS, Georgetown U., 1964; MA, U. Minn., 1969; PhD, U. Wis., Milw., 1971. Asst. commr. N.Y. State Mus., Albany, 1980-81; dir. Heard Mus., Phoenix, 1972-80, SW Mus., Los Angeles, 1981—. Mem. Am. Assn. Mus. (council mem. 1978-81), Soc. Mus. Anthropology (bd. dirs. 1982—). Office: SW Museum 234 Museum Dr PO Box 128 Los Angeles CA 90042

HOUSDEN, KENNETH C., government auditor; b. Leavenworth, Wash., Oct. 19, 1952; s. Ernest Glen and Ruth Irene (Parton) H.; m. Colleen May Mittelstaedt, Mar. 22, 1975 (div. Dec. 1981); m. Dianne Marie Willers, June 13, 1982; children: Cameron, Morgan. AA, Wenatchee Valley Coll.; BA, Eastern Wash. State Coll.; M in Pub. Adminstrn., Eastern Wash. U. Cert. profl. fin. officer, Wash. Coordinator social services Grant County Tng., Moses Lake, Wash., 1977-78; city adminstr. City of Leavenworth, 1978-80; sale rep. The Nickel, Wenatchee, Wash., 1980-81; auditor Chelan County, Wenatchee, 1981—; teaching asst. DSHS, Spokane, 1975-77; instr. Big Bend Community Coll., Moses Lake, 1977-78, Wenatchee Valley Coll., 1984—; adj. prof. bus. and econs. Cen. Wash. Univ., Ellensburg, 1986—. Mem. Sr. Citizen Task Force, Wenatchee, 1985—; bd. dirs. YWCA, Wenatchee; com. man Rep. Precint, Leavenworth, 1980, 82, 84; bd. dirs. United Way of Chelan and Douglas Counties, Wenatchee, 1981-85; county govt. chmn. United Way, Moses Lake, 1977; co-chmn. fin. com. Chelan County Rep. Cen. Com., Wenatchee, 1981; area del. Alternative for Wash. planning conf., Wenatchee, 1974; coach Leavenworth Summer League Varsity Basketball Team; coach Leavenworth AAU Basketball team; vice chmn. State Residential Tng. Ctr., Moses Lake, 1977; pres. Wash. State Autumn Leaf Assn., Leavenworth, 1979. Recipient John Schultz Meml. award, 1972-73, Morris Merit awards, 1971-72. Mem. Land Surveyor's Assn. Wash. (Surveyor of Yr. 1986), Wash. Mcpl. Fin. Officer's Assn., Internat. Assn. Clks. Recorders and Election Ofcls., Wash. State Auditors Legis. Liaison Com. (Star of Yr. 1986), Local Govt. Adv. Com. for Rev. State Budget and Acctg. System, Washington Assn. County Auditors, Friends of Coll. (chmn. 1984), Phi Theta Kappa. Lodges: Rotary (Ways and Means chmn. Wenatchee club 1986), Masons (sr. warden Zarthan club 1986—). Home: 8040 E Bayne Rd Leavenworth WA 98826 Office: PO Box 400 Wenatchee WA 98801

HOUSE, ERNEST, SR., cultural organization administrator; b. Ignacio, Colo., Sept. 27, 1945; s. Thomas Sr. and Francis (Wall) H.; m. Brenda Gomez, July 17, 1965; children: Michelle, Jaque, Ernest. Student, Ft. Lewis Coll., 1968-69. Forester U.S. Dept. Interior, Towaoc, Colo., 1970-79; with Ute Mountain Tribe, Towaoc, 1960-65, tribal councilman, 1979-83, tribal chmn., 1983—. Bd. dirs. Colo. Commn. Indian Affairs, Denver, 1981—; mem. Colo. Centennial Commn., Cortez County Centennial. Served with U.S. Army, 1965-71. Mem. Nat. Tribal Chmn.'s Assn. (treas. 1984-85). Democrat. Mem. Assembly of God Ch. Avocations: fishing, hunting, canoeing, horseback riding, art. Office: Ute Mountain Tribal Council Towaoc CO 81344

HOUSE, NADINE LEOLA, pilot; b. Kalispell, Mont., Jan. 18, 1942; d. Roy Bertrand and Nina Frances (Jones) Grant; m. Gordon Phillip Thompson, Oct. 3, 1958 (dec. Aug. 1965); children: Craig Allen, Scott Gordon, Larry Dale; m. David Gene House, June 14, 1966. Student AG Aviation Acad., 1968. Cert. advanced ground instr., comml. pilot. Advanced ground instr. Round-Up Air Service, Pendleton, Oreg., 1969-72; claims, adjustments mgr. Shulton, Inc., Sparks, Nev., 1973-75; adminstrv. asst. Hydro-Search, Inc., Reno, 1975-79; free-lance house painter, Waldport, Oreg., 1979-83; adminstrv. asst. North Slope Borough, Barrow, Alaska, 1983—; instr. rural edn. U. Alaska, 1983—; written exam. adminstr. FAA, 1983—; advanced ground instr. various orgns., 1969—. Mem. Oreg. Pilots Assn. (sec. 1970), C.A.P. (aviation scis. instr.). Avocations: flying, fishing, bowling, horseback riding. Home: PO Box 3064 Barrow AK 99723

HOUSE-SHARP, KATHLEEN TRACEY, tax consultant, accountant; b. Indianola, Okla., Jan. 1, 1928; d. George Rolland and Cordelia Mae (Higgins) House; m. Robert S. Sharp, Jan. 23, 1947 (dec.); children—R. Steven, Rebecca Sue Sharp Stine, Karen Kay Sharp Spurlock. Student, Modesto Jr. Coll., 1959-75, Stanislaus State Coll., Turlock, Calif., 1978. Enrolled agt., U.S. Dept. Treasury, 1981. Office mgr. I.C. Refrigeration, Inc., Modesto, Calif., 1959-62; chief acct. Miller Mfg. Inc., Turlock, 1962-63; auditor, acct. U.S. Air Force, 1963-71; acct., office mgr. Winter Motor, Inc. & Winter Volvo, Inc., Sacramento, 1971-73; owner House-Sharp Bus. Service, Hughson, Calif., 1978—; pvt. practice tax preparation, acctg., 1955-83. Mem. Nat. Soc. Enrolled Agts., Calif. Assn., Enrolled Agts., Nat. Assn. Tax Cons., Nat. Soc. Pub. Accts., Internat. Platform Assn., VFW Aux. Mem. Ch. of Christ. Club: Women of Moose, Rebekah Lodge. Office: 7035 Hughson Ave Hughson CA 95326

HOUSHOLDER, KENNETH ADELBERT, architect; b. Dallas, Jan. 18, 1918; s. T. Franklin and Selma (Nicholson) H.; B.A., So. Meth. U., 1942; B.Arch., Yale, 1947; M.A., U. Calif. at Berkeley, 1965. Pvt practice architecture, Dallas 1947-50; mem. firm Marsh. Smith & Powell, Los Angeles, 1950-53; pvt. practice, San Francisco, 1953-64; exec. v.p. Donald Francis Haines, San Francisco, 1964-73; architect San Francisco Bur. Architecture, 1973—; now prof. history Golden Gate U.; lectr. history architecture, San Francisco, 1962-71. Mem. AIA, Soc. Archtl. Historians, Nat. Trust for Historic Preservation, San Francisco Symphony Soc., San Francisco Opera Guild, San Francisco Ballet Assn., Oakland Museum Soc., Nat. Wildlife Soc., Delta Chi, Alpha Rho Tau, Alpha Rho Chi. Republican. Christian Scientist. Clubs: Press (San Francisco); Oakland Athletic: S.M.U. Alumni, Rolls Royce Owners; Yale of San Francisco. Works include Oakland (Calif.) Post Office, 1965, San Mateo (Calif.) Jr. Coll., 1959. Home: 40 Lincoln Ave Piedmont CA 94611

HOUSKA, ROBERT BARON, college administrator, consultant; b. Chamberlain, S.D., Sept. 14, 1933; s. Raymond L. and Hazel E. (Potter) H.; m. Beverly Florence Ponto, Feb. 13, 1960; children—Derrick, Cerise, Carina. Student S.D. Sch. Mines, 1951-53; B.S., U. S.D., 1959; M.Ed., U. N.D., 1961; Ed.D., N. Mex. State U., 1969. Dir. guidance Junea-Douglas Schs., Juneau, Alaska, 1961-65; dormitory mgr. N. Mex. State U., 1965-69; cons. Minn. Higher Edn. Coordinating Commn., St. Paul, 1969-70; asst. acad. dean Nat. Coll. Bus., Rapid City, S.D., 1970-74; v.p. service area devel. Colo. Northwestern Community Coll., 1974-84; registered agt. Equitable Life Assurance Soc., 1984—; pub. relations coordinator Am. Sch. Counselor Assn., 1964-65. Bd. dirs. Craig (Colo.) C. of C., 1981-83; mem. Craig Planning and Zoning Commn., 1982-86; candidate for county Commr. Moffat County (Colo.), 1982. Recipient Nat. Educator of Yr. award Outstanding Educators Am., 1972; NSF scholar, 1960; NDEA scholar, 1960-61. Mem. Am. Vocat. Assn., Psi Chi, Phi Delta Kappa, Phi Kappa Phi. Republican. Mem. Ch. of Christ. Clubs: Lions, VFW, Shriners, Elks (Craig); Masons.

HOUSTON, ELIZABETH REECE MANASCO, education educator, consultant; b. Birmingham, Ala., June 19, 1935; d. Reuben Cleveland and Beulah Elizabeth (Reece) Manasco; m. Joseph Brantley Houston; 1 child, Joseph Brantley Houston III. BS, U. Tex., 1956; MEd, Boston Coll., 1969.

Cert. elem. tchr., Calif., cert. spl. edn. tchr., Calif., cert. community coll. instr., Calif. Tchr., elem. Ridgefield (Conn.) Schs., 1962-63; tchr., spl. edn. Sudbury (Mass.) Schs., 1965-68; staff intern Wayland (Mass.) High Sch., 1972; tchr., home bound Northampton (Mass.) Schs., 1972-73; program dir. Jack Douglas Ctr., San Jose, Calif., 1974-76; tchr., specialist spl. edn., coordinator classroom services, dir. Juvenile Ct. Schs. Santa Clara County Office of Edn., San Jose, Calif., 1976—; instr. San Jose State U., 1980—, U. Calif., Santa Cruz, 1982-85; cons. Houston Research Assocs., Saratoga, Calif., 1981—, Synergistic Learning, 1986. Author: (manual) Behavior Management for School Bus Drivers, 1980, Classroom Management, 1984. Bd. dirs. Ming Quong Children's Ctr., Los Gatos, Calif. Grantee Santa Clara County Office Edn. Tchr. Advisor Program U.S. Sec. Edn., 1983-84; Recipient President's award Soc. Photo-Optical Instrumentation Engrs., 1979, Classroom Mgmt. Program award School Bds. Assn., 1984. Mem. Assn. for Supervision and Curriculum Devel., Assn. Calif. Sch. Administrs., Council Exceptional Children. Home: 12150 Country Squire Ln Saratoga CA 95070 Office: Santa Clara County Office Edn 100 Skyport Dr San Jose CA 95115

HOUSTON, L.L., biochemist, researcher; b. Wichita, Kans., June 3, 1940; s. Floyd E. and Lois Lorene (DeHaven) H.; m. Teri L. DeHon, June 5, 1962; children: Leslie Ann, Scott E. BS, Kans. State U., 1962; PhD, U. Wash., 1967. Postdoctoral fellow U. Calif., Berkeley, 1967-69; asst. prof. U. Kans., Lawrence, 1969-73, assoc. prof., 1973-78, prof. biochemistry, 1978-84; sr. scientist Cetus Corp., Emeryville, Calif., 1984—; vis. lectr. U. Ill., Urbana, 1973; guest prof. U. Basel, Switzerland, 1975-76; vis. sci. Fred Hutchinson Cancer Research Ctr., Seattle, 1979-80. Recipient Research Cancer Devel. award Nat. Cancer Inst., 1975-80; fellow Swiss Nat. Sci. Found., 1975, NIH Pub. Health Service, 1964. Mem. AAAS, Am. Soc. Biol. Chemists. Office: Cetus Corp 1400 53d St Emeryville CA 94608

HOUSTON, ROBERT WADE, novelist, educator; b. Bessemer, Ala., Sept. 30, 1940; s. Claude Robinson and Bessie Vera (Brown) H.; m. Sharon Leigh Baker, July 24, 1959 (div. 1968); children: Rebecca, Jonathan; m. Patricia Gail Roth, Sept. 26, 1970; 1 child, Gregory. BA, Birmingham So. Coll., 1966; MA, Syracuse U., 1968; PhD, U. Iowa, 1973. Instr. English George Mason U., Fairfax, Va., 1968-69; asst. prof. English U. of the Ams., Puebla, Mex., 1970-72; prof. English U. Ariz., Tucson, 1973—; faculty mem. Bread Loaf Sch. of English, Middlebury, Vt., 1982-84; staff mem. Bread Loaf Writer's Conf., Middlebury, 1979—. Author: Bisbee '17, 1979, Monday, Tuesday, Wed., 1979, Ararat, 1982, The Nation Thief, 1984. Served with USAF, 1961-65. Mem. Authors Guild. Democrat. Avocation: foreign travel. Home: 1802 E Linden St Tucson AZ 85719 Office: U Ariz Dept English Tucson AZ 85721

HOUSTON, SAMUEL ROBERT, statistics educator, consultant; b. Los Angeles, May 20, 1935; s. Samuel James and Myrtle Lenore (Baker) H.; m. Judith Ann Jackson, May 20, 1963; children: Michael (dec.), Cathleen, Karen. BA cum laude, UCLA, 1957; MA, Calif. State U., Los Angeles, 1961; MS, U. Oreg., 1964; PhD, Colo. State Coll., 1967. Instr. math. Los Angeles City Schs., 1957-65; program assoc. C.F. Kettering Found., Denver, 1966-67; research specialist C.F. Kettering Found., Los Angeles, 1967-68; prof. math. and applied stats. U. No. Colo., Greeley, 1968—. Author: Judgment Analysis: Tool for Decision Makers, 1974; editor: Jour. Exptl. Edn., 1975-78; reviewer Computer Reviews, N.Y.C., 1982—; mem. editorial bd. Multiple Linear Regression Viewpoints, Akron, Ohio, 1986—; contbr. articles to profl. jours. Served with USAF, 1958-59. Fellow NSF, 1960-64, Nat. Cancer Inst., 1973-74. Mem. Am. Statis. Assn. (Colo.-Wyo. chpt.), Am. Ednl. Research Assn. (pres. spl. interest groups 1970-71), Rocky Mountain Ednl. Research Assn., Am. Inst. Cancer Research, AERA Evaluation Network, Sigma Xi, Phi Delta Kappa. Republican. Mem. Western Orthodox Cath. Ch. Home: 1841-26th Ave Pl Greeley CO 80631 Office: U No Colo Dept Math and Applied Stats Greeley CO 80639

HOUTS, MARSHALL WILSON, author, editor, lawyer; b. Chattanooga, June 28, 1919; s. Thomas Jefferson and Mary (Alexander) H.; m. Mary O. Dealy, Apr. 27, 1946; children: Virginia, Kathy, Marsha, Patty, Tom, Cindy, Tim. A.A., Brevard Jr. Coll., 1937; B.S. in Law, U. Minn., 1941, J.D., 1941. Bar: Tenn. 1940, Minn. 1946, U.S. Supreme Ct. 1967. Spl. agt. FBI, Washington, Brazil, Havana, Boston, 1941-44; partner Palmer & Houts, Pipestone, Minn., 1946-51; mcpl. judge Pipestone, 1947-51; gen. counsel Erle Stanley Gardner's Ct. of Last Resort, Los Angeles, 1951-60; prof. law UCLA, 1954, Mich. State U., East Lansing, 1955-57; adj. prof. Pepperdine U. Law Sch., 1972—; clin. prof. forensic pathology Calif. Coll. Medicine, U. Calif., Irvine, 1972—; cons. police depts. Creator, editor: TRAUMA, 1959—; Author: Houts: Lawyer's Guide to Medical Proof, 3 vols., 1967, From Gun to Gavel, 1954, From Evidence to Proof, 1956, The Rules of Evidence, 1956, From Arrest to Release, 1958, Courtroom Medicine, 1958, Courtroom Medicine: Death, 3 vols., 1964, Photographic Misrepresentation, 1965, Where Death Delights, 1967, They Asked for Death, 1970, Proving Medical Diagnosis and Prognosis, 13 vols., 1970, Cyclopedia of Sudden, Violent and Unexpained Death, 1970, King's X: Common Law and the Death of Sir Harry Oakes, 1972, Art of Advocacy: Appeals; Art of Advocacy: Cross Examination of Medical Experts; Courtroom Toxicology, 6 vols., 1981. Served with OSS, 1944-46, CBI. Decorated Bronze Arrowhead. Address: 33631 Magellan Isle Laguna Niguel CA 92677

HOWARD, BRADFORD REUEL, travel company executive; b. Honolulu, Aug. 6, 1957; s. Joseph DeSylva and Marenerite Evangeline (Barker) H.; m. Marcia Andresen, June 23, 1985. BS in Bus., U. Calif., Berkeley, 1979. Owner, operator Howard Janitorial Services, Oakland, Calif., 1970-80; prodn. mgr. Oakland Symphony Orch., 1976-80; brand mgr. The Clorox Co., Oakland, 1980-85; gen. mgr., corp. sec. Howard Tours, Inc./Howard Enterprises, Oakland, 1985—; co-owner Howard Mktg. Cons., Oakland, 1985—; cons. Marcus Foster Found., Oakland, 1984-85; pres., gen. mgr. Piedmont (Calif.) Community Theater, 1976—. Mem. U. Calif. Bus. Alumni Assn. (v.p. 1986—, pres. Bay Area Chpt. 1983-84). Club: Lake Merrit Breakfast. Lodge: Rotary (sec. 1985—, pres. 1987—). Avocations: theater, athletics, wine appreciation. Office: Howard Tours Inc 526 Grand Ave Oakland CA 94610

HOWARD, DANIEL MARTIN, mining company executive; b. New Bedford, Mass., Apr. 13, 1945; s. William and Yvonne (Poirier) H.; m. Lynne Dee Koontz, June 28, 1968; children: Brian, Jonathan, Julie. EM, Colo. Sch. Mines, 1968. Mine engr. The New Jersey Zinc Co., Ogdensburg, N.J., 1968-74; asst. mine supr. Windsor (Vt.) Minerals, 1974-80; mine supr. Thompson-Weinman, Sylacauga, Ala., 1980; project mgr. Am. Mine Services, Denver, 1981-83; ops. mgr. Western Source Inc., San Andreas, Calif., 1983—. Mem. Cavendish (Vt.) Sch. Bd., 1979; soccer coach CYSL. Mem. AIME, Calaveras County Mining Assn. (pres. 1985-87). Republican. Roman Catholic. Avocations: fishing, boating, golf. Office: Western Source Inc PO Box 280 San Andreas CA 95249

HOWARD, DAVID HAL, journalist; b. Albany, Oreg., July 21, 1944; s. Hal and Vera Louise (Bond) H.; m. Veronica Sue Kind, Sept. 4, 1966 (div. 1971); 1 child, Daniel Wayne; m. Georgetta Lavelle Cooper, Aug. 3, 1973. BA in Journalism, Whitworth Coll., 1966. Owner, operator printing shop, Spokane, Wash., 1968-69; social worker State of Wash., Spokane, 1969-70, 72-76; labor union rep. Wash. Fedn. of State Employees, Spokane, 1970-72; freelancer real estate sales Albany, 1976-82; editor, dir. info. The Grange News, Seattle, 1982—. Author: News Handbook for Granges, 1984; editor The Universal Message, 1973-77, The Grange News, 1982—. Mem. Wash. Press Assn. (3rd Pl. award 1986), Co-op. Communicators Assn., Nat. Grange (master Fairmount chpt. 1977-79, Editor of Yr. 1983). Lodges: Masons, Eastern Star (assoc. patron 1981). Avocation: cattle ranching. Home: 38281 Mountain Home Dr Lebanon OR 97355 Office: Grange News/ Wash State Grange 3104 Western Ave Seattle WA 98121

HOWARD, DAVID ROGER, university administrator; b. Olympia, Wash., July 6, 1929; s. Jared Clark and Frieda (Heisig) H.; m. Kathryn Lucille Smith, July 17, 1953; children: Ann, David Jr., Michael, Paul, Margaret, Leslie. BS in Agrl. Engring., N.Mex. A&M, 1951; BSCE, U. Ill., 1957; MSCE, U. Colo., 1961. Registered profl. engr., Tex. Commd. 2d lt. USAF, 1951, advanced through grades to col., 1971, ret., 1976; base civil engr. USAF, Thule (Greenland) Air Base, 1970-71; staff civil engr. aeronautical systems div. USAF, Wright-Patterson AFB, Ohio, 1971-73; base engr. USAF, Travis AFB, Calif., 1974-76; dir. bldgs. and grounds Oakland (Calif.) Unified Sch. Dist., 1977-81; exec. dir. facilties San Francisco State U., 1981—. Contbr. articles to profl. jours. Decorated Legion of Merit, 1973, 76. Mem. Assn. Phys. Plant Adminstrs., Nat. Assn. Coll. Univ. Bus. Officials, Air Foce Assn., Am. Inst. Plant Engrs. Methodist. Club: Presidio Riding Club (Marin County, Calif.) (stable official, 1980-82). Avocations: horsemanship, ballet, gardening, thoroughbred breeding and racing, fishing. Home: 890 Chamberlain Ct Mill Valley CA 94941 Office: San Francisco State U 19th and Holloway San Francisco CA 94132

HOWARD, DONNA MARTA, academic administrator; b. Many, La., Sept. 18, 1942; d. Walter A. and Martha V. (Tischoff) Pennino; m. Bruce Howard, July 1, 1967 (div. 1987); children: Kimberly, Matthew. BA, Pa. State U., 1965; MEd, U. Hawaii, 1975. Exec. dir. City and County of Honolulu, Kailua, Hawaii, 1973-78; v.p. Hawaii Loa Coll., Kaneohe, Hawaii, 1978-83, Mills Coll., Oakland, Calif., 1983—. Commnr. Honolulu Bd. Water Supply, 1979-84; v.p. bd. dirs. Hale Kipa, 1981-83. Mem. Council for Advancement and Support of Edn., San Francisco C. of C. Club: Lakeview. Avocations: alpine skiing, tennis. Office: Mills Coll 5000 MacArthur Blvd Oakland CA 94613

HOWARD, EDWARD IAN, plastics company executive, accountant; b. Oakmere, Cheshire, Eng., June 20, 1921; s. Edward William Vincent and Kathleen Louise (Emerson) H.; m. Marian Gertrude Moore, Apr. 3, 1944; children—Gregory Carmen, Brenton Ian. B.Commerce, U. B.C., 1947. Chartered acct., B.C. With Peat-Marwick-Mitchell, Chartered Accts., Vancouver, B.C., Can., 1947-52; founding ptnr. Dyke & Howard, Chartered Accts., Vancouver, 1952-62; pres. Columbia Plastics Ltd., Vancouver, 1962—; dir. Western Found. Advanced Indsl. Tech.; mem. adv. bd. Med. Device Devel. Ctr., Vancouver; mem. mfrs. reference group B.C. Innovation Office, Vancouver. Served to lt. comdr. Royal Can. Navy, 1941-45. Mem. Inst. Chartered Accts. of B.C., Soc. Plastics Engrs., Naval Officers Assn., Phi Kappa Sigma. Club: Royal Vancouver Yacht. Home: 8 Tamath Crescent, Vancouver, BC Canada V6N 2C9 Office: Columbia Plastics Ltd, 2155 W 10th Ave, Vancouver, BC Canada V6K 2H7

HOWARD, GARRY WILFORD, computer applications consultant; b. Murfreesboro, Ark., June 27, 1947; s. John Wilford and Ima Jean (Chaney) H.; m. Shirley Jean Campbell, May 29, 1967 (div. Aug. 1971); children—Christopher James; m. 2d, Linda Ellen Girard, Oct. 17, 1971; children—Jenny Marie, Benjamin John. Student, So. Ark. U., 1965-67. Draftsman Lone Star Ammunition Army Plant, Texarkana, Tex., 1967-69; design draftsman Tex. Instruments Inc., Dallas, 1969-70, City Dallas, 1970-72; mgr. drafting Sandwell Internat. Inc., Atlanta, 1972-82; computer applications cons. Auto-Trol Tech. Corp., Denver, 1982—. Author: (with others) CAD/CAM Management Strategies, 1984. Mem. Automated Design/ Drafting User's Assn. (treas. 1981-82), Nat. Computer Graphics Assn., Am. Inst. Design and Drafting. Home: 125 W Elm St Louisville CO 80027 Office: Auto-Trol Tech Corp 12500 N Washington St Denver CO 80233

HOWARD, HILDEGARDE (MRS. HENRY ANSON WYLDE), paleontologist; b. Washington, Apr. 3, 1901; d. Clifford and Hattie Sterling (Case) H.; m. Henry Anson Wylde, Feb. 6, 1930. A.B., U. Calif., 1924, A.M., 1926, Ph.D., 1928. Asst. in zoology UCLA, 1924-25, teaching fellow paleontology, 1925-26, research fellow zoology, 1927-28; research asst. Natural History Mus. of Los Angeles County, 1924-25, 28, avian paleontologist, 1929-38, curator avian paleontology, 1939-51, chief curator sci. div., 1951-61, research assoc., 1961-74, chief curator emeritus, 1974—; research asso. avian paleontology Santa Barbara Mus. Natural History, 1956—, Western Speleological Inst., 1958-74. Author numerous monographs in field, 1927—; editor: Los Angeles County Mus. Contbns. in Sci., 1957-61; contbr. articles to sci. jours., Ency. Paleontology. Recipient hon. Festschrift Natural History Mus. of Los Angeles County, 1980; John Simon Guggenheim Found. fellow, 1962-63. Fellow Geol. Soc. Am., Am. Ornithol. Union (Brewster Meml. award in ornithology 1953), AAAS, So. Calif. acad. sci. (pres. 1957-59), Calif. acad. sci.; mem. Cooper Ornithol. Soc. (hon. life), Soc. Vertebrate Paleontology (hon. life), Phi Beta Kappa, Sigma Xi, Phi Sigma. Club: Soroptimists. Home: 2045-Q Via Mariposa E Laguna Hills CA 92653 Office: Natural History Museum of Los Angeles Co 900 Exposition Blvd Los Angeles CA 90007

HOWARD, JAMES WEBB, investment banker, lawyer; b. Evansville, Ind., Sept. 17, 1925; s. Joseph R. and Velma (Cobb) H.; m. Phyllis Jean Brandt, Dec. 27, 1948; children: Sheila Rae, Sharon Kae. B.S. in Mech. Engring, Purdue U., 1949; postgrad., Akron (Ohio) Law Sch., 1950-51, Cleve. Marshall Law Sch., 1951-52; M.B.A., Western Res. U., 1962; J.D., Western State Coll. Law, 1976. Registered profl. engr., Ind., Ohio. Jr. project engr. Firestone Tire & Rubber Co., Akron, 1949-50; gen. foreman Cadillac Motor Car div. Gen. Motors Corp., 1950-53; mgmt. cons. M.K. Sheppard & Co., Cleve., 1953-56; plant mgr. Lewis Welding & Engring. Corp., Ohio, 1956-58; underwriter The Ohio Co., Columbus, 1959; chmn. Growth Capital, Inc., Chgo., 1960—; pres. Meister Brau, Inc., Chgo., 1965-73; others. Co-chmn. Chgo. com. Ill. Sesquicentennial Com., 1968. Served with AUS, 1943-46. Decorated Bronze Star, Parachutist badge, Combat Inf. badge. Mem. ASME, Nat. Assn. Small Bus. Investment Companies (past pres.), Am. Mgmt. Assn., ABA, State Bar Calif., Grad. Bus. Alumni Assn. Western Res. U. (past gov.), Tau Kappa Epsilon, Pi Tau Sigma, Beta Gamma Sigma. Methodist. Club: Masons.

HOWARD, JANE OSBURN, educator; b. Morris, Ill., Aug. 12, 1926; d. Everett Hooker and Bernice Otilda (Olson) Osburn; B.A., U. Ariz., 1948; M.A., U. N.Mex., 1966, Ph.D., 1969; m. Rollins Stanley Howard, June 5, 1948; children—Ellen Elizabeth, Susan (Mrs. John Karl Nuttall). Instr. U. N.Mex. Sch. Medicine, Albuquerque, 1968-70, mem. staff pediatrics, deaf blind children's program, Albuquerque, 1971-72, asst. dir. N.Mex. programs for deaf blind children, 1972—, instr. psychiatry, instr. pediatrics, coordinator deaf-blind children's program, 1972-76, edn. cons., 1976—, publicity and pub. relations cons., 1983—; Cons. Mountain-Plains Regional Ctr. for Services to Deaf-Blind Children, Denver, 1971-74, Bur. Indian Affairs, 1974. Active Cystic Fibrosis, Mother's March, Heart Fund, Easter Seal-Crippled Children. Recipient fellowships U. N.M., 1965, 66, 66-67, 67-68, U. So. Calif. John Tracy Clinic, 1973. Fellow Royal Soc. Health; mem. Council Exceptional Children, Am. Assn. Mental Deficiency, Nat. Assn. Retarded Children, AAUW, Pi Lambda Theta, Zeta Phi Eta, Alpha Epsilon Rho. Republican. Methodist. Home: 615 Valencia Dr SE Albuquerque NM 87108

HOWARD, LYNN MAUREEN, medical center director; b. Denver, June 28, 1951; d. George William and Marjorie Jean (Monckton) O'Shaughnessy; m. James William Howard, Jan. 5, 1973; 1 child, Geoffrey Randall. Student U. No. Colo., 1969-72. With Weld County Gen. Hosp., Greeley, Colo., 1972-79, coordinator staffing, 1977-78, asst. admitting officer, 1979; admitting mgr. North Colo. Med. Ctr., Greeley, 1979-82, admitting and communications mgr., 1982—. Mem. Colo. Council Hosp. Admitting Mgrs. (v.p. 1983-83, pres. 1983-85, bd. dirs. 1984-85), Nat. Assn. Hosp. Admitting Mgrs. (accredited admitting mgr., nominating com. 1982—, regional rep. 1984). Democrat. Roman Catholic Office: North Colo Med Ctr 1801 16th St Greeley CO 80631

HOWARD, MARGUERITE EVANGELINE BARKER (MRS. JOSEPH D. HOWARD), business executive, civic worker; b. Victoria, B.C., Can., July 30, 1921; d. Reuel Harold and Frances Penelope (Garnham) Barker; brought to U.S., 1924, naturalized, 1945; B.A., U. Wash., 1943; m. Joseph D. Howard, June 16, 1952; children—Wendy Doreen Frances, Bradford Reuel. Vice pres., dir. Howard Tours, Inc., Oakland, Calif., 1953—; co-owner, gen. mgr. Howard Travel Service, Oakland, 1956—, mng. dir. Howard Hall, Berkeley, Calif., 1964-75; co-owner, asst. mgr. Howard Investments, Oakland, 1960—; sec., treas. Energy Dynamics Inc. Bd. dirs. Piedmont council Campfire Girls, 1969-79, pres., 1974-79, mem. nat. council, 1972-76, zone chmn., 1974-76, 77-83, zone coordinator, 1976, nat. v.p., 1975, nat. bd. dirs., 1976-83, bd. dirs. Alameda Contra Costa council, 1984—; bd. dirs. Oakland Symphony Guild, 1969—, pres., 1972-74; mem. exec. bd. Oakland Symphony Orch. Assn., 1972-74, bd. dirs., 1972-86; 1st pres. Inner Wheel Club of East Oakland, 1983-84; bd. dirs. Piedmont Jr. High Sch. Mothers Club, 1968-69. Recipient Wohelo Order award Campfire, Inc, 1985. Mem. Oakland Mus. Assn., U. Wash. Alumni Assn., East Bay Bot. and Zool. Soc., Young Audiences, Am. Symphony Orch. League, Assn. Calif. Symphony Orchs., Chi Omega Alumni Seattle, Chi Omega East Bay Alumni Berkeley. Republican. Clubs: Womens Univ. (Seattle); Womens Athletic (Oakland) (bd. dirs. 1986—). Home: 146 Bell Ave Piedmont CA 94611 Office: 526 Grand Ave Oakland CA 94610

HOWARD, MURRAY, manufacturing, real estate, property management executive, farmer, rancher; b. Los Angeles, July 25, 1914; s. George A. J. and Mabel (Murray) H. B.S., UCLA, 1939. C.P.A., Calif. Mgr. budget control dept. Lockheed Aircraft, 1939-45; pres., chmn. bd. Stanley Foundries, Inc., 1945-59, Howard Machine Products, Inc., 1959—, Murray Howard Realty, Inc., 1959—, Murray Howard Devel., Inc., 1969—, Howard Oceanography, Inc., 1967—, Ranch Sales, Inc., 1968—, Murray Howard Investment Corp., 1961—; owner, gen. mgr. Greenhorn Ranch Co., Greenhorn Creek Guest Ranch, Spring Garden, Calif.; pres., chmn. bd. Murray Howard Cattle Co., Prineville, Oreg.; dir. Airshippers Publ. Corp., LaBrea Realty & Devel. Co., Shur-Lok Corp. Served as mem. Gov. Calif. Minority Com. Mem. Nat. Assn. Cost Accts. (dir., v.p.), NAM (dir.). Office: 1605 W Olympic Blvd Suite 404 Los Angeles CA 90015

HOWARD, RUSSELL STANLEY, organ manufacturing company executive; b. Elmhurst, Ill., July 23, 1931; s. Charles Stanley and Esther Caroline (Gray) H.; m. Lily Harris, Oct. 8, 1954; children: Peter, John, James, Philip, Andrew, Carol. Grad. high sch., Chgo. Gen. mgr. C. Howard and Sons, Lombard, Ill., 1954-66; prin. Howard Organ Co., Federal Way, Wash., 1966-77; pres. Assoc. Organ Builders, Auburn, Wash., 1977—. Served with U.S. Army, 1952-53. Mem. Nat. Assn. Music Merchants, Am. Guild of Organists (auditor 1967-68), Auburn C. of C. Home: 2414 SW 322 Pl Federal Way WA 98023 Office: Assoc Organ Builders 3419 C St NE Auburn WA 98002

HOWARD, VICTOR, management consultant; b. Montreal, Que., Can., Aug. 12, 1923; s. Thomas and Jean (Malkinson) H.; B.A., Sir George Williams U., 1947; B.Sc., 1948; Ph.D., Mich. State U., 1954; m. Dorothy Bode, Dec. 25, 1953. Mech. design engr. Canadian Vickers Ltd., Montreal, 1942-46; with Aluminum Co. Can., 1946-48, E.B. Badger Co., Boston, 1948-50; asst. prof. Mich. State U., 1952-56; social scientist Rand Corp., 1956-58; staff exec., personnel dir. System Devel. Corp., Santa Monica, Calif., 1958-66; staff cons. Rohrer, Hibler & Replogle, San Francisco, 1966-69; mng. dir. Rohrer, Hibler & Replogle Internat., London and Brussels, 1969-74, ptnr. 1974, mgr. San Francisco, 1974—, dir., 1979—. Mem. State Psychol. Examining Com., 1987. Mem. Am. Psychol. Assn., Western Psychol.Assn., Brit. Inst. Dirs., U.S. Power Squadron (comdr. Sequoia Squadron 1981, dist. comdr. 1987), Calif. State Mil. Res. (col. 1984), Sigma Xi, Clubs: Reform, Hurlingham (London); Thames Motor Yacht (Molesey, Eng.); Stockton Yacht; Univ. (San Francisco). Lodges: Masons, Shriners. Home: 1460 Cherrywood Dr San Mateo CA 94403 Office: 1601 Old Bayshore Hwy Burlingame CA 94010

HOWARD, WALTER EGNER, wildlife biology and ecology educator; b. Woodland, Calif., Apr. 9, 1917; s. Walter Lafayette and May Belle Howard; m. Elizabeth Ann Kendall; children: Thomas Kendall, Kathryn Spencer, John Casey. AB, U. Calif., Berkeley, 1939; MS, U. Mich., 1941, PhD, 1947. Fellow U. Mich., Ann Arbor, 1942, 46-47; from instr. zoology to prof. wildlife biology and vertebrate ecology U. Calif., Davis, 1947—; cons. UN, FAO and overseas assignments. Contbr. numerous articles to profl. jours.; patentee in field. Served to 2d lt. AUS, 1942-46, CBI. Fulbright scholar, Australia, New Zealand, 1957-58. Fellow AAAS; mem. Animal Behavior Soc., British Ecol. Soc., Ecol. Soc. Am., Am. Soc. Mammalogists, Wildlife Soc., Western Soc. Naturalists, Soc. Range Mgmt., Sigma Xi, Phi Kappa Phi, Phi Sigma. Lodge: Rotary. Avocations: cons. wildlife problems in developing countries, the outdoors. Home: 24 College Park Davis CA 95616 Office: U Calif Dept Wildlife Fisheries Biology Davis CA 95616

HOWATT, HELEN CLARE, library director; b. San Francisco, Apr. 5, 1927; d. Edward Bell and Helen Margaret (Kenney) H. B.A., Holy Name Coll., 1949; M.S. in Library Sci., U. So. Calif., 1972. Joined Order Sisters of the Holy Names, Roman Catholic Ch., 1945; cert. advanced studies Inst. Sch. Librarians, Our Lady of Lake U., San Antonio, 1966. Life teaching credential, life spl. services credential, Calif. Prin., St. Monica Sch., Santa Monica, Calif., 1957-60, St. Mary Sch., Los Angeles, 1960-63; tchr. jr. high sch. St. Augustine Sch., Oakland, Calif., 1964-69; tchr. jr. high math St. Monica Sch., San Francisco, 1969-71, St. Cecilia Sch., San Francisco, 1971-77; library dir. Holy Names Coll., Oakland, Calif., 1977—. Contbr. math. curriculum San Francisco Unified Sch. Dist., Cum Notis Variorum, publ. Music Library, U. Calif., Berkeley. Contbr. articles Cath. Library World, 1987, 87. NSF grantee, 1966; NDEA grantee, 1966. Mem. Cath. Library Assn. (chmn. No. Calif. elem. schs. 1971-72), Calif. Library Assn., ALA, Assn. Coll. and research Libraries. Home: 3500 Mountain Blvd Oakland CA 94619 Office: Holy Names Coll Library 3500 Mountain Blvd Oakland CA 94619

HOWE, BRUCE IVER, government official; b. Dryden, Ont., Can., May 19, 1936; s. Norman I. and Laura A. (Locking) H.; m. Elsie Evelyn Ann Ferguson, Aug. 25, 1962; children—Karen, Norman, Kristina. BSc in Chem. Engring., Queen's U., Kingston, Ont., 1958; LLD (hon.), Lakehead U., Thunder Bay, Ont., 1983. Profl. engr., B.C. Sr. paper-making engr. Que. North Shore Paper Co., 1960-63; With MacMillan Bloedel Ltd., Vancouver, B.C., Can., 1963-80; asst. to mgr. mfg. MacMillan Bloedel Ltd., 1963-65, mgr. Island Paper Mill div., 1966, asst. div. mgr. Powell River Div., 1967-70, v.p. pulp and paper group, 1971-79, exec. v.p., 1979, pres., chief exec. officer, 1980; chief exec. officer B.C. Resources Investment Corp., 1980-85, chmn., 1985-86; sec., chief sci. advisor Ministry of State for Sci. and Tech., Ottawa, Ont., Can., 1986—; chmn. bd. Westar Mining and Westar Petroleum, B.C., 1980-86; chmn. exec. com. Westar Mining, 1980-86. Contbr. numerous articles on pulp and paper to profl. jours. Mem. internat. trade adv. com. Can. Govt.; Can. chmn. Can./Korea Bus. Council, B.C., 1983-86; commr. gen. Can. Pavilion, Expo '86, B.C., 1985-86. Office: Ministry of State for Sci/Tech, 240 Sparks St 8th Floor W, Ottawa, ON Canada K1A 1A1

HOWE, DRAYTON FORD, JR., lawyer; b. Seattle, Nov. 17, 1931; s. Drayton Ford and Virginia (Wester) H.; m. Joyce Arnold, June 21, 1952; 1 son, James Drayton. A.B., U. Calif.-Berkeley, 1953; LL.B., Hastings Coll. Law, 1957. Bar: Calif. 1958, C.P.A. Calif. Atty. IRS, 1958-61; tax dept. supr. Ernst & Ernst, San Francisco, 1962-67; ptnr. Bishop, Barry, Howe & Reid, San Francisco, 1968—; lectr. on tax matters U. Calif. extension, 1966-76. Mem. Calif. Bar Assn., San Francisco Bar Assn. (chmn. client relations com. 1977), Calif. Soc. C.P.A.s.

HOWE, EDWIN HENRY, grain and cotton farmer; b. Hanford, Calif., June 7, 1926; s. Edwin Henry and Maude (Burr) H.; student public schs., Hanford; m. Larella Loraine Fincher, June 16, 1949; children—John Nelson, Rachel Loraine. With Westlake Farms, Inc., Stratford, Calif., 1946—, v.p., 1965-82, pres., 1983—; bd. dirs. Rancers Cotton Oil Co., Calif. Ammonia Co.; del. Nat. Cotton Council. Bd. dirs. Central Union Elem. Sch. Dist., 1960-76; pres. Kings River Conservation Dist., 1969; chmn. Kings County Water Commn., 1972, Kings River Water Assn., Empire Irrigation Dist., 1969, Tulare Lake Basin Water Storage Dist., 1969, Hacienda Water Dist., 1978. Served with USN, 1944-46. Recipient Carnegie medal for act of heroism, 1983. Lic. comml. pilot; amateur radio licensee. Mem. Assn. Calif. Water Agencies (dir. 1972—). Republican. Home and Office: 23311 Newton Ave Stratford CA 93266

HOWE, JOHN F., neurosurgeon, educator; b. Oakland, Calif., May 14, 1945; s. Donnell Conde and Margaret (Frantz) H.; m. Cynthia Russell, May 18, 1974; children: Beth, Emily, Nathaniel. BA, Lawrence U., 1967; MD, Case Western Res. U., 1971; degree in neurosurgery, U. Wash., 1977. Diplomate Am. Bd. Neurol. Surgeons. Instr. neurosurgery U. Wash., Seattle, asst. prof. neurosurgery, 1979-82, clin. asst. prof., 1982—; neurosurgeon Group Health, Seattle, 1982—. Contbr. articles to profl. jours. Served to maj. U.S. Army, 1977-79. Fellow Am. Bd. Neurosurgery; mem. AMA, Am. Assn. Neurosurgery, Joint Session Spinal Sect. (program com. 1986), ACLU. Democrat. Home: 6 Holly Ln Mercer Island WA 98040 Office: U Wash Sch Medicine Seattle WA 98195

HOWE, RICHARD C., state supreme court justice; b. South Cottonwood, Utah, 1924; s. Edward E. and Mildred (Cuddy) H.; m. Juanita Lyon, 1949; children—Christine Schultz, Andrea Reynolds, Bryant, Valerie Winegar, Jeffrey, Craig. B.S., U. Utah, 1945, J.D., 1948. Admitted to Utah bar, 1949; mem. Utah Ho. of Reps., 1951-58, 69-72; mem. Utah Senate, 1973-78; justice Utah Supreme Ct., Salt Lake City, 1980—. Office: State Supreme Ct State Capitol Salt Lake City UT 84114

HOWE, ROBERT LOUIS, educator, state administrator; b. San Jose, Calif., Sept. 16, 1930; s. Louis Clarence and Maud Isabel (Thorp) H.; m. Norma Claire Nadeau, Oct. 10, 1951; children: Christine, Jeanne, Robert N., Ted, Patricia, Everett. BA, San Jose State Coll., 1952, MA, 1960; EdD, U. So. Calif., 1972. cert. secondary tchr. (life), secondary adminstr. Tchr., counselor, adminstr. San Bernardino (Calif.) City Schs., 1954-62; adminstr. various programs, Info. Services-publs. and audio-visual media prodns. Calif. State Dept. Edn., Sacramento, 1962—; cons. numerous local, state and fed. orgns., agys. in edn. and mgmt. systems, 1962—. Co-author: Data Processing for Educator, 1965; contbr. articles to profl. jours. Mem. Calif. Assn. Sch. Bus. Officials, Calif. Media and Library Educators Assn. Home: 4581 Parkridge Rd Sacramento CA 95822 Office: Calif State Dept Edn PO Box 944272 Sacramento CA 94244-2720

HOWELL, ALAN PETER, lawyer, company executive, arbitrator; b. Honolulu, Aug. 1, 1927; s. Hugh and Mavis Halcyon (Shawk) H.; m. Sara Grounds, Feb. 26, 1954; children: David Wallace, Brian Cochran. BA, Yale U., 1950; LLB, Cornell U., 1953. Bar: Hawaii 1954. Law clk. to chief justice Ter. Supreme Ct. Hawaii 1953-54; asst. pub. prosecutor City and County Honolulu, 1954-58; ptnr. Hogan & Howell, 1958-71; sole practice, 1971-86; magistrate 6th dist. Dist. Ct. Honolulu, 1964-68; arbitrator Am. Arbitration Assn., 1967—. Rep. precinct pres., Hawaii, 1956-58; pres. chpt. 184 Exptl. Aircraft Assn. Served with U.S. Army, 1946-48, to 1st lt. USAFR, 1950-58. Mem. Hawaii Bar Assn. Christian Scientist. Clubs: Pacific, Outrigger Canoe. Office: 733 Bishop St Suite 2515 Honolulu HI 96813-4057

HOWELL, NANCY, media specialist, copywriter, painter; b. San Francisco, Oct. 17, 1952; d. Kenneth Warren and Frances Dee (Crawford) Howell. B.A. in Humanities, San Francisco State U., 1975. Co-pres., Rodell Co., San Francisco, 1977-79; v.p. Criswell Div., advt. and pub. relations, San Francisco, 1979-82; freelance media specialist, writer, San Francisco, 1982—. Mem. San Francisco Advt. Club, San Francisco Women in Advt.

HOWELL, RUTH MARGARET, social worker; b. San Diego, Sept. 22, 1932; s. Vernon Wilford and Grace McClellan (Davis) H.; m. James McClellan, Dec. 27, 1964 (div. July 1975) 1 child, Jason. BA, San Diego State U., 1955; MSW, U. So. Calif., 1962. Dist. dir. Girl Scouts Am., San Diego, 1955-60; group worker Avalon, Carver Community Ctr., Los Angeles, 1962-63; supr., dir. Community Vol. Program, Los Angeles, 1963-67; project dir. Los Angeles County Dept. Pub. Social Services, 1968-69; dir. child/adolescent placement project Community Services div. Calif. Dept. Social Welfare, Los Angeles, 1969-72; exec. dir. Nat. Assn. Social Workers, Los Angeles, 1972-73; community program analyst Calif. Mental Health Dept., Los Angeles, 1974-76; mgr. home services Harbor Regional Ctr., 1976-77, Community Care Licensing div. Calif. Dept. Social Services, San Diego, 1977—; cons. Control Data, Los Angeles, 1974-75. Active Los Amigos de la Humanidad, Calif. Children's Lobby, Crenshaw Neighbors. Mem. Nat. Assn. Social Workers (cert.), Assn. Study of Community Orgn. (sec., treas.), Calif. Social Workers Orgn. (pres. San Diego chpt., state bd. mem.), Nat. Conf. Social Welfare, U. So. Calif. Sch. Social Work Alumni Assn (v.p. 1963-64), Calif. Mental Health Assn., ACLU, NAACP, Nat. Assn. Edn. Young Children. Republican. Presbyterian. Home: 7303 Calle de Fuente Carlsbad CA 92009 Office: Calif Dept Social Services 8745 Aero Dr #200 San Diego CA 92123

HOWELL, TERRY LAWSON, engineer; b. Prairie City, Oreg., Apr. 28, 1936; s. Glenn Deardorf and Mary Barbara (Hale) H.; m. Barbara Jean Sokolik, June 20, 1959; children: Leigh Michele, Mary Lisa. BS, Oreg. State U., 1959; postgrad., Aviation Officers Candidate Sch., 1959, U. So. Calif., 1977, Calif. State U., Hayward, 1984-85. Commd. USN, 1959, advanced through grades to lt. comdr., 1969, ret., 1980; v.p. CAVCO Corp., San Jose, Calif., 1980-81, South Valley Mfg., Gilroy, Calif., 1982-83; dep. program mgr. VSE Corp., Oakland, Calif., 1983-86, program mgr., 1986, group mgr. Bay area, 1986—. Decorated Air medal. Mem. Ret. Officers Assn. (life), Aircraft Owners and Pilots Assn., Soc. Logistics Engrs., Red River Valley Fighter Pilots Assn. (steering com.), Phi Kappa Phi Alumni Assn., Tailhook Assn., Navy League of U.S., Western Aerospace Mus. Republican. Clubs: Moffett Field Flying, Allied Officers. Home: 5574 Ora St San Jose CA 95129 Office: VSE Corp 130 Webster St Oakland CA 94607

HOWELLS, JERRY S., paint company executive; b. Salt Lake City, Sept. 23, 1939; s. Steven D. and Margaret (Perschon) H.; m. Judy Carter Howells, June 15, 1985; children—Jerry S., Heather, Tony. B.S., U. Utah, 1963. Sales mgr. Howells Inc., Salt Lake City, 1965-75, v.p., 1965-72, pres., 1972-87; chmn. bd., chief exec. officer Kwal-Howells (formerly Howells Inc.), 1987—; dir. Summit Savs. & Loan, Park City, Utah. Mem. exec. bd. Egyptian Theatre, Park City, 1982—, Utah Opera, Salt Lake City, 1983—; active Boy Scouts Am., Salt Lake City, 1970-79. Mem. Producers Council (pres. 1972-73), Constrn. Products Mfrs. Assn. (bd. dirs. 1978-81), Nat. Decorating Assn. (bd. dirs. 1975-77), U. Utah Alumni Assn. (bd. dirs. 1983—). Club: Salt Lake City Country. Lodge: Rotary (pres. Salt Lake City 1974-75). Office: Kwal-Howells 4285 S State Salt Lake City UT 84107

HOWERTON, HERMAN HUGH, lawyer; b. Tulsa, Oct. 10, 1943; s. Albert H. and Cora M. (West) H.; m. Jane L. Axenfield, Aug. 30, 1970; children: Michael, Kimberly. BA summa cum laude, Fresno State Coll., 1965; JD cum laude, Harvard U., 1968. Assoc. McCutchen, Doyle et al, San Francisco, 1968-72; atty. Itel Corp., San Francisco, 1972-82; real estate broker Cushman & Wakefield, San Francisco, 1983-84; sr. v.p., corp. counsel Fox Group, San Mateo, Calif., 1984—; mem. dist. export council Dept. Commerce, San Francisco, 1982-83. Mem. ABA, Calif. State Bar Assn., Am. Corp. Counsel Assn. Clubs: Berkeley Tennis. Office: Fox Group 950 Tower Ln Foster City CA 94404

HOWES, MARSHALL FREDERICK, industrial and medical device company executive; b. Pittsfield, Mass., Apr. 28, 1937; s. Maurice Warren and Carrie Mae (Thomas) H.; m. Barbara Jean Thurston, May 24, 1974; children—Valerie Jean, William Thomas, Linda Michelle, Steven Mitchell, Jeffrey Scott, Charles Larry, Jane Jeanette. B.S. in Acctg., Bryant Coll., Providence, 1958. Asst. controller Phillips Petroleum Co., Idaho Falls, Idaho, 1958-66; controller, asst. treas. Aerojet Nuclear Co., Idaho Falls, 1971-76, chmn. retirement/investment com.; controller, asst. sec.-treas. Cordova Chem. Co., Sacramento, 1976-78; dir. fin. planning Aerojet Gen. Corp., El Monte, Calif., 1978-80, group controller, 1980-83; dir., chief fin. officer Nimbus, Inc., Carmichael, Calif., 1982-83, pres., dir., chief exec. officer, 1983—. Chmn. bd. trustees Idaho Nuclear Ednl. Trust Fund; chmn. co. campaign United Way of Idaho Falls; adviser Jr. Achievement. Mem. Nat. Assn. Accts., Am. Mgmt. Assn. Republican. Episcopalian. Clubs: Elks. Home: 2816 Hoffman Bluff Way Carmichael CA 95608

HOWLETT, PATRICIA ERSKINE, communications executive; b. Moscow, Maine, June 12, 1930; d. Charles Samuel and Elvina Mary (Thompson) Erskine; A.B., Colby Coll., 1952; M.A., U. San Francisco, 1979; children: Lorin Ann, Charles Erskine. English tchr. public schs., Orleans, Beverly and Brookline, Mass., 1952-57; tchr. English, Mt. Diablo Schs., Concord, Calif., 1960-67; broadcaster Radio Sta. KWUN, Concord, Calif., 1971-74; info. officer Mt. Diablo Unified Sch. Dist., Concord, 1974-79; dir. pub. relations Calif. Sch. Bds. Assn., 1980; public relations exec. Assn. Calif. Sch. Adminstrs., 1980-84, dir. communications, 1985—; also pub./editor Thrust Mag., EDCAL edn. weekly newspaper. Bd. dirs. Sch./Community Relations Found., 1979—. Mem. Internat. Assn. Bus. Communicators, San Francisco Pub. Relations Round Table, Nat. Sch. Public Relations Assn. (accredited, bd. dirs. 1985—, Gold medallion 1986), Pub. Relations Soc. Am. (accredited, Calif. coordinator 1981-83), Calif. Sch. Public Relations Assn.(pres. 1979-80), Am. Assn. Sch. Adminstrs., Ednl. Press Assn. Am., Issue Network Calif. (bd. dirs.), Am. Soc. Assn. Execs., Internat. Platform Assn., Sigma Delta Chi, Phi Delta Kappa. Clubs: Commonwealth, San Francisco Press, Ninety Nines. Author: How to Work with the Media, 1979; Single Woman, (poetry), 1983; Independent Woman, 1983. Office: Assn Calif Sch Adminstrs 1517 L St Sacramento CA 95814

HOWSDEN, ARLEY LEVERN, education educator; b. Huntley, Nebr., Oct. 17, 1926; s. Harry Ray and Hattie Kate (Donley) H.; m. Vivian May McCready, Dec. 12, 1947; children: Jo Ann, Jean, Harry, Karen, Kathie, Jan. BS, U. Nebr., 1948, MA, 1952, EdD, 1958. Tchr., coach, supt. Axtell (Nebr.) Pub. Schs., 1948-51; tchr., coach North Platt (Nebr.) Schs., 1951-53; dir. edn. Am. Samoa Schs., Pango Pango, 1953-55; supt. schs. Oxford (Nebr.) Pub. Schs., 1955-56; mem. community edn. project U. Nebr., Lincoln, 1956-58; prof. Calif. State U., Chico, 1958—, dean sch. edn., 1970-83. Elected mem. Butte County Bd. Suprs., Calif., 1965-70; elected nat. del. Calif. Dem. Conv., 1968-76; pres. Far. No. Regional Ctr., Redding Calif., 1974-76. Mem. Calif. Faculty Assn. (campus pres. 1983-85), NEA, Calif. Colls. Univ. Faculty Assn. (pres. 1974-76), Phi Delta Kappa (Outstanding Contbn. to Edn. 1985-86). Democrat. Lodge: Rotary (local pres. 1973-74). Avocation: farming. Home: 3319 Grape Way Chico CA 95926 Office: Calif State U Dept Edn Chico CA 95926

HOWSLEY, RICHARD THORNTON, lawyer, regional government administrator; b. Medford, Oreg., Jan. 31, 1948; s. Calvin Nevil and Arvilla Constance (Romine) H.; B.A., Willamette U., 1970; M.S., Va. Poly. Inst. and State U., 1974; J.D., Lewis and Clark Law Sch., 1984; m. Susan Erma Johnson, Oct. 23, 1971; children—James Denver, Kelly Ann. Tech. editor U.S. Bur. Mines, Arlington, Va., 1971-72; program mgr., sr. planner KRS Assos., Inc., Reston, Va., 1972-74; exec. dir. Rogue Valley Council Govts., Medford, 1974-78; exec. dir. Regional Planning Council of Clark County, Vancouver, Wash., 1978-84; assoc. Landeyholm, Memovich, Lansverk & Whitesides, Vancouver, 1985—; vice chmn. Oreg. Council of Govts. Dirs. Assn., 1976-77, chmn., 1977-78. Mem. regional adv. com. So. Oreg. State Coll., 1975-78; mem. Medford-Ashland Air Quality Adv. Com., 1977-78. Carpenter Found. scholar, 1966-70, Leonard B. Mayfield Meml. scholar, 1966-67, Albina Page Found. scholar, 1966-70. Mem. ABA, Oreg. State Bar Assn., Wash. State Bar Assn., Am. Planning Assn., Am. Inst. Cert. Planners, Internat. City Mgmt. Assn. (10-yr. service award), Nat. Assn. Regional Councils (10-yr. service award). Democrat. Methodist. Home: 15807 NW 27th Ct Vancouver WA 98685 Office: Landeyholm Memovich Lansverk & Whitesides 915 Broadway Vancouver WA 98666

HOXMEIER, JOHN ALLEN, software company executive; b. Holdrege, Nebr., June 14, 1955; s. John Charles and Charlene LaGay (Loar) H.; m. Cynthia Lea Hanson, May 20, 1978; 1 child, John Charles. B.S. in Bus., U. Nebr., 1977; M.S. in Info. Systems, Colo. State U., 1978. Systems analyst USDA, Ft. Collins, Colo., 1977-78; instr. Colo. State U., Fort Collins, 1977-79; product mgr. mktg. Fiscal Info., Inc., Loveland, Colo. 1979-82; v.p., owner, founder 3CI, Ft. Collins, 1980—, also dir.; nat. speaker on database mgmt. systems; cons. systems Sch. Dist. 12, Denver, 1978, Weld County Hosp., Greeley, Colo., 1979. Bd. dirs. Am. Diabetes Assn., Fort Collins, 1983. Named Outstanding Grad. Student, Coll. of Bus., Colo. State U., Ft. Collins, 1978; recipient Excellence in Teaching citation Student Body, Colo. State U., 1979. Mem. Data Processing Mgmt. Assn., Am. Mgmt. Assn., U. Nebr. Found., Colo. State U. Alumni Assn., Am. Mgmt. Assn., U. Nebr. Found., Colo. State U. Alumni Assn., Sigma Phi Epsilon, Beta Gamma Sigma. Roman Catholic. Club: Ft. Collins Triathlon. Office: 3CI 155 W Harvard Fort Collins CO 80525

HOY, MARJORIE ANN, entomology educator, researcher; b. Kansas City, Kans., May 19, 1941; d. Dayton J. and Marjorie Jean (Acker) Wolf; m. James B. Hoy; 1 child, Benjamin Lee. A.B., U. Kans., 1963; M.S., U. Calif.-Berkeley, 1966, Ph.D., 1972. Asst. entomologist Conn. Agrl. Expt. Sta., New Haven, 1973-75; research entomologist U.S. Forest Service, Hamden, Conn., 1975-76; asst. prof. entomology U. Calif.-Berkeley, 1976-80, assoc. prof. entomology, 1980-82, prof. entomology, 1982—; chairperson Calif. Gypsy Moth Sci. Adv. Panel, 1982—. Editor or co-editor: Genetics in Relation to Insect Management, 1979, Recent Advances in Knowledge of the Phytoseiidae, 1982, Biological Control of Pests by Mites, 1983, Biological Control in Agricultural IPM Systems, 1985; contbr. numerous articles to profl. jours. NSF fellow U. Calif.-Berkeley, 1963-64. Mem. Entomol. Soc. Am. (mem. Pacific br. governing bd. 1985), Am. Genetic Assn., Internat. Orgn. Biol. Control (v.p. 1984-85), AAAS, Acarological Soc. Am. (governing bd. 1980-84), Soc. for Study Evolution, Phi Beta Kappa, Sigma Xi (sec. chpt. 1979-81). Avocations: hiking; gardening; snorkeling. Home: 1004 Grizzly Peak Blvd Berkeley CA 94708 Office: U Calif Dept Entomology 201 Wellman Hall Berkeley CA 94720

HOYE, WALTER BRISCO, college administrator; b. Lena, Miss., May 19, 1930; s. William H. and LouBertha (Stewart) H.; m. Vida M. Pickens, Aug. 28, 1954; children—Walter B. II, JoAnn M. B.A., Wayne State U., 1953. Sports/auto editor Detroit Tribune, 1958-65; sports editor Mich. Chronicle, 1965-68; assoc. dir. pub. relations San Diego Chargers Football Co., 1968-76; media liason NFL, 1972-75; community services officer San Diego Coll. Dist., 1976-78; placement officer Ednl. Cultural Complex, San Diego, 1978-80, info. officer, 1980-82, placement officer, adminstrv. asst., 1982-83, placement/program support supr., 1983—; cons. in field. Bd. dirs. San Diego County ARC; active San Diego Conv. and Tourist Bur., Joint Ctr. Polit. Studies, Am. Cancer Soc., San Diego Urban League, Neighborhood Housing Assn., Public Access TV. Named San Diego County Citizen of Month, May, 1979; recipient United Way Award of Merit, 1974. Mem. Am. Personnel and Guidance Assn., San Diego Career Guidance Assn., Nat. Mgmt. Assn., Assn. Calif. Community Coll. Adminstrs., Calif. Community Coll. Placement Assn. Home: 6959 Ridge Manor Ave San Diego CA 92120 Office: 4343 Ocean View Blvd Suite 60-A San Diego CA 92113

HOYT, DAVID WALTER, scientific instrument manufacturing executive; b. Palo Alto, Calif., June 4, 1952; s. Howard Greeley and Jean (Meyn) H. BSME, Stanford U., 1975, MBA, 1979. Engr. Ralph M. Parsons Co., Pasadena, Calif., 1975-77; new product support supr. Spectra Physics, San Jose, Calif., 1979-81; ops. planning Finnigan Corp., San Jose, Calif., 1981-83, ops. controller, 1983, mgr. Pacific ops., 1983-86, mgr. strategic planning, projects, 1986—. Avocations: tennis, glider piloting. Home: 944 Rockdale Dr San Jose CA 95129 Office: Finnigan Corp 355 River Oaks Pkwy San Jose CA 95134

HOYT, JACK WALLACE, engring. educator; b. Chgo., Oct. 19, 1922; s. Claire A. and Fleta M. (Wheeler) H.; B.S., Ill. Inst. Tech., 1944; M.S., UCLA, 1952, Ph.D., 1962; m. Helen Rita Erickson, Dec. 27, 1945; children—John A., Katheryn M. (Mrs. Richard Everett), Annette M. (Mrs. Walter Butler), Denise M. (Mrs. Paul Kruesi). Research engr. gas turbines Cleve. Lab., NACA, 1944-47; mem. staff Naval Ocean Systems Center, Navy Dept., DOD, San Diego, 1948-79, asso. for sci. fleet engring. dept., 1967-79, now cons.; vis. prof. mech. engring. Rutgers U., New Brunswick, N.J., 1979-81; prof. mech. engring. San Diego State U., 1981—. Mem. ASME (Freeman scholar 1971), N.Y. Acad. Scis., Soc. Naval Architects and Marine Engrs. Author, patentee in field. Editorial bd. Internat. Shipbldg. Progress, 1965—. Spl. research propulsion and hydrodynamics. Home: 4694 Lisann St San Diego CA 92117

HOYT, LEEZA LEE, public relations/advertising firm executive; b. Cairo, Egypt, Nov. 27, 1955; (parents Am. citizens); d. Harry Grant and Lucille H. BA cum laude in Pub. Relations, U. So. Calif., 1977; MBA, Loyola U., Los Angeles, 1983. Lic. in real estate sales, Calif. Real estate salesperson Ladera Realty, Los Angeles, 1976-78; account coordinator/jr. account exec. Lewis & Assocs., Los Angeles, 1978-79; jr. account exec. Ayer Jorgensen Macdonald (now N.W. Ayer, ABH Internat.), advt. firm, Los Angeles, 1979; recruitment adminstr. Lawler, Felix & Hall, Los Angeles, 1980-81; account exec. Clive Hoffman Assocs., Los Angeles, 1981-83; sr. account exec. Rifkind, Pondel & Parsons, Los Angeles, 1983-84; founder, pres. Hoyt Orgn., Torrance, Calif., 1984—. Fund-raising chmn. for 1980 Spl. Olympics, Los Angeles Jr. C. of C. Named to Outstanding Young Women Am., U.S. Jaycees, 1980. Mem. Pub. Relations Soc. Am., Soc. Mktg. Profl. Services, Los Angeles C. of C., Torrance C. of C., U. So. Calif. South Bay Young Alumni (2d v.p. bd. dirs. 1982), Trojan Jr. Aux. (dir. 1978-80), Trojan Fourth Estate (bd. dirs.), Town and Gown Jrs., Alpha Gamma Delta Alumni (exec. council 1983-84), Los Angeles Athletic. Office: 22750 Hawthorne Blvd Torrance CA 90505

HOYT, ROSS GILBERT, architect; b. Lincoln, Nebr., July 23, 1944; s. Walter Russell and Nadine Lucille (Slife) H.; m. Janice Claire Whaley, Oct. 20, 1973. BArch, U. Nebr., 1967; postgrad., Kans. State U., 1970. Lic. architect, Colo. Draftsman Fishkin/Brin, Denver, 1970-73; design draftsman Merrick & Co., Denver, 1973-76; project architect Creative Concepts, Arvada, Colo., 1976-80; chief draftsman City of Wheatridge, Colo., 1980-81; architect Bell Engring., Denver, 1981—; cons. pvt. sector, Denver, 1976—. Designer Nebr. Builders award, 1965. Served with USN, 1967-69, Vietnam. Avocations: music, arts and crafts. Office: Bell Engring Co 500 Kalamath St Denver CO 80204

HRAHA, MARY JOSEPHINE, marketing professional; b. Des Moines, Nov. 4, 1961; d. Francis Michael and Shirley Ann (Malone) H. BJ, Iowa State U., 1984. Lic. real estate assoc., Ariz. With pub. relations dept. Story County Cen. Rep. Com., Ames, Iowa, 1982-83; asst. press sec. to presiding gov. State of Iowa, Des Moines, 1983-84; asst. mktg. dir. Des Moines Ballet Co., 1984; mktg. dir. Real Estate Mgmt. Corp., Scottsdale, Ariz., 1985—. Mem. Ariz. Multi-Housing Assn. Mem. Women in Communications. Roman Catholic. Avocations: writing, reading, jogging. Home: 6512 N 12th Way Phoenix AZ 85014 Office: Real Estate Mgmt Corp 8747 Via De Commercio Scottsdale AZ 85032

HRUBY, ŠÁRKA, immunochemist, researcher; b. Jaromer, Czechoslovakia, Jan. 17, 1920; came to U.S., 1955; d. Vlamdmir and Mila (Kalinova) Vocasek; m. Antonin Hruby, Aug. 19, 1944; children: Thomas, John. MS in Chemistry, U. Tech. Sci., Prague, Czechoslovakia, 1947. Research asst. prof. Karl's U., Prague, 1947-48; chem. technician, chief Univ. Hosp., Strasbourg, France, 1953-55, Easton (Pa.) Hosp., 1956-61; research assoc. pathology U. Wash., Seattle, 1961—. Contbr. articles to profl. jours. Avocations: skiing, swimming. Office: U Wash Sch Medicine RJ-05 Seattle WA 98105

HRUBY, VICTOR JOSEPH, chemistry educator; b. Valley City, N.D., Dec. 24, 1938; s. Victor John and Helen (Berube) H.; m. Patricia Ann McGovern, Aug. 1, 1966; children: Timothy Joseph, Stephen Michael, Patrick Andrew. BS, U. N.D., 1960, MS, 1962; PhD, Cornell U., 1965. Instr. med. coll. Cornell U., N.Y.C., 1965-67; research assoc. Cornell U., Ithaca, N.Y., 1967-68; asst. prof. chemistry U. Ariz., Tucson, 1968-72, assoc. prof., 1972-77, prof., 1977—; guest worker NIH, Bethesda, Md., 1975-76; vis. prof. Harvard U., Cambridge, Mass., 1984-85; rector's lectr. Free U. Brussels, Belgium, 1979; cons. Dow Chem. Co., Indpls., 1973—. Editor: Peptides: Structure and Function, 1983, continuing edit., 1985; The Peptides: Conformation in Biology and Drug Design, 1985; patentee in field. Served with USAR, 1955-58. Fellowships John Simon Guggenheim Found., 1984, Fulbright-Hays Found., 1979. Fellow AAAS, N.Y. Acad. Sci., Am. Inst. Chemists; mem. Am. Chem.. Soc. (pres. sas 1974), Am. Soc. Biol. Chemists, Sigma Xi. Roman Catholic. Avocations: philosophy, sociology, sports. Office: U Ariz Dept Chemistry Tucson AZ 85721

HSIA, YUKUN, microelectronics executive; b. Kunming, China, Feb. 21, 1941; came to U.S., 1956; s. Wei-Lin and Wai-Fong (Yu) H.; m. Helen Lee, Aug. 15, 1965; children: Eric C.C., Curtis C.Y. BS, U. Calif., Berkeley, 1961, MS, 1964; PhD, UCLA, 1969. Engring. supr. NCR, Hawthorne, Calif., 1961-67; mem. tech. staff Autonetics, Anaheim, Calif., 1968; prin. investigator Litton Industries, Woodland Hills, Calif., 1969-74; microelectronics br. chief MDC, Huntington, Calif., 1974-82; div. engring. mgr. Fairchild, Mountain View, Calif., 1982-87; dir. microelectronics Northrop Corp., Anaheim, Calif., 1987—; grad. faculty U. So. Calif., Los Angeles, 1979-82; grad. lectr. Santa Clara (Calif.) U., 1982—; consulting ptnr. YHL, Saratoga, Calif., 1982—; program chmn. Computer Elements Workshop, 1984; mem. program com. Internat. Solid State Circuits Conf., 1984. Author 34 scientific papers; patentee in field. Invited vis. scholar Inst. Semiconductors Academia Sinica, Beijing, 1984; recipient Product of Yr. award Electronic Products mag., 1977. Mem. IEEE (sr.), Tau Beta Pi, Phi Eta Sigma. Avocations: oil painting, bicycling, skiing. Home: 12230 Saraglen Dr Saratoga CA 95070 Office: Northrop Electro-Mech div 500 E Orangethorpe Ave Anaheim CA 92801

HSIAO, ANGELA L., corporate executive; b. Shansi, Peoples Republic of China, Jan. 1, 1943; came to U.S., 1954; d. Edward Lien and Joyce (Chen) Lai; m. Richard Fu Hsiao, June 14, 1964; children: Alexander Kai, Eric Zan. BA, Hunter Coll., 1964; MA, Calif. State U., Long Beach, 1969. Cert. tchr., Calif. Lectr. Singapore (Peoples Republic of China) Tchr. Tng. Coll., 1973-75; prin. Sather Gate Callery, Berkeley, Calif., 1978-82; pres. Marsial Corp., Richmond, Calif., 1980—. One-woman shows include Am. Artist in Singapore; exhibited in group shows at Singapore Mus. Art; art reviewer Radio Singapore Arts Circle. Mem. Mei Lan-Fang Soc. (organizer and bd. dirs.). Avocations: ballet, modern dance, piano, Chinese opera, travel.

HSIAO, FRANK S. T., economics educator; b. Kao-shiong, Taiwan, Sept. 13, 1933; s. Chi-lai and Zhao-zhi (Pan) H.; m. Mei-chu Wang, July 20, 1968; children—Edward C., Victoria C. B.A., Nat. Taiwan U., 1956, M.A., 1959; M.A., U. Rochester, 1964, Ph.D., 1967. Research asst. U. Mich., Ann Arbor, 1965-66; asst. prof., then assoc. prof. U. Colo., Boulder, 1966-75, prof. econs., 1975—; vis. scholar Hoover Instn., Stanford, Calif., summer 1983; lectr. Universidad Regiomontana, Monterrey, Mex., 1979; research assoc. East Asian Research Ctr., Harvard U., summer 1977. Author articles in field. Assn. Asian Studies grantee, 1983; Fulbright-Hays research fellow, East Asia, 1975. Mem. Am. Econs. Assn., Assn. Asian Studies, N.Am. Taiwanese Profs. Assn. Home: 5079 Holmes Pl Boulder CO 80303 Office: U Colo Campus Box 256 Boulder CO 80309

HSIAO, TING-HUAN, insect physiologist; b. Hangchow, Chekiang, People's Republic of China, Feb. 6, 1936; came to U.S., 1958, naturalized, 1972; s. Tze Yuan and Mou C. (Yang) H.; m. Catherine Tang, Mar. 21, 1961. MS in Entomology, U. Minn., 1961; PhD in Insect Physiology, U. Ill., 1966. Research assoc. dept. entomology U. Ill., Urbana, 1966-67; asst. prof. zoology Utah State U., Logan, 1967-72, prof. biology, 1979—; vis. prof. entomology Agrl. U. Wageningen, Netherlands, 1975, 77, 78, 81. Contbr. numerous articles to profl. publs. Mem. Entomol. Soc. Am., Am. Soc. Zoologists, Am. Inst. Biol. Sci., AAAS, Sigma Xi. Home: 1457 N 1640 E Logan UT 84321

HSIEH, EDWARD KUAN HSIUNG, microelectronics researcher; b. Taipei, Republic of China, Feb. 2, 1952; came to U.S., 1978; s. Fu-Shan Hsieh and Pao-Yun (Huang) Wang; m. Betty An-Ye Wu, Aug. 17, 1980; children: Bryant Philip, Christine Lois. BS, Nat. Taiwan U., 1974; MS, U. Calif., Santa Barbara, 1979; postgrad., Calif. Inst. Tech., 1979-80; PhD, Cornell U., 1983. Mem. tech. staff NASA Jet Propulsion Labs., Pasadena, Calif., 1980-81, AT&T Bell Labs., Murray Hill, N.J., 1983; mem. tech. staff, group head Hughes Research Labs., Malibu, Calif., 1984—; pres., owner Entrepreneur's Computer Systems and Softwares, Van Nuys, Calif., 1986—; pres. InfoAsia Info. Dataline, Van Nuys, 1986—; cons. 1st Assurance Fin. Group, Thousand Oaks, Calif., 1985—, Lone Eagle Investment, Inc., Encino, Calif., 1985—; session co-chmn. internat. electron device meeting, Piscataway, N.J., 1984-85. Author: Applied Probability Theory and Applications, 1978; contbr. articles to profl. jours.; patentee in field. Bd. dirs. Walnut Garden Home Owner Assn., Van Nuys, 1985-86; mem. bd. deacons 1st Evang. Ch., Glendale, Calif., 1986. Recipient Sci. Achievement award Ministry of Edn., Taiwan, 1968, Hughes Div. Invention award, 1984; Grad. fellow Rockwell Internat., 1982. Mem. IEEE, AAAS, Am. Phys. Soc., Sigma Xi. Democrat. Home: 7300 Lennox Ave J-1 Van Nuys CA 91405 Office: Hughes Research Labs 3011 Malibu Canyon Rd Malibu CA 90265

HSIEH, RUDY RU-PIN, banker; b. Taipei, Taiwan, July 6, 1950; came to U.S., 1976; s. Yu-Fu and Lan-Ying (Wu) H. B.S., Fu-Jen Catholic U., Taiwan, 1973; M.B.A., Long Island U., 1978. Credit officer Cathay Bank, Los Angeles, 1979; asst. v.p., Monterey Park, Calif., 1979-81, asst. v.p., asst. mgr., 1981-84, v.p., mgr., 1984—; fin. cons. Super Success Co., Ltd., Los Angeles, 1983—. Pres. Taiwan Benevolent Assn. of Calif., Monterey Park, 1983; bd. dirs. Taiwan Benevolent Assn. of Am., Bethesda, Md., 1982, v.p., 1983, pres., 1984. Mem. Chinese Am. Profl. Soc. Office: Cathay Bank 250 S Atlantic Blvd Monterey Park CA 91754

HSIEH, YOU-LO, textile and polymer educator, researcher; b. Taipei, Republic of China, Feb. 14, 1953; came to U.S., 1975; d. Men-Che and Sze-

Hue (Hsiao) H.; m. Arthur Bruce Playle, May 11, 1980; children: Arlo J., Alma H. BS, Fu-Jen U., Taipei, 1975; MS, Auburn U., 1977; PhD, U. Md., 1981. Asst. prof. textiles U. Calif, Davis, 1981—. Research grantee USDA. Mem. Am. Chem. Soc., The Soc. Biomaterials, Am. Assn. Textile Chemists and Colorists, Sigma Xi. Avocations: fine arts, music, pottery, travel, sports. Office: U Calif Div Textiles and Clothing Davis CA 95616

HSU, ANDREW CHIEN-YAU, research chemistry educator; b. Beijing, Oct. 13, 1934; came to U.S., 1960; s. Ju-Hsiang and Kuei-Tai (Ma) H.; m. Wan-Jean Young, Oct. 27, 1962; children: Lin C., Katharine C., Jane C., Majorie C., Andrea C. BS in Agrl. Chemistry, Taiwan Nat. Chung-hsing U., Taichung, Republic of China, 1957; MS in Biochemistry Plant Nutrition, Utah State U., 1963; PhD in Plant Physiology, U. Calif., Davis, 1969. Research biochemist Agrl. Research Service div. U.S. Dept. Agriculture, Pasadena, Calif., 1970-72; chemist Los Angeles Air Pollution Control Dist., 1972-74, Rockwell Internat/Rocketdyne, Canoga Park, Calif., 1975—; lectr. U. So. Calif., Los Angeles, 1976-84. Inventor in field. Mem. Sigma Xi. Home: 2955 Gainsborough Dr San Marino CA 91108 Office: Rockwell Internat Rocketdyne 6633 Canoga Ave SS11 Canoga Park CA 91303

HSU, CHEN-YIH, materials scientist; b. Taiwan, Republic of China, June 27, 1951; came to U.S., 1978; s. Ting-Jung and Jin-Chih Hsu; m. Shu-Cheng Chen, Jan. 1977 (dec. Mar. 1979); children: Jonathan Chun-Hung, m. Joyce Ming-Cheng Chen, Aug. 27, 1983. BSMetE, Nat. Taipei Inst. Tech., Taiwan, 1972; MS in Metallurgy, N.Mex. Inst Tech., 1980; PhD in Materials Sci. and Engring., MIT, 1983. Registered profl. metall. engr. Metall. engr. FESECO Engring. Cons., Taiwan, 1974-76; tech. asst. Taipei Inst. Tech., 1976-78; postdoctoral research assoc. MIT, Cambridge, 1984; sr. materials scientist GA Techs. Inc., San Diego, 1984—. Contbr. several articles to profl. jours. Scholar Taipei Inst. Tech., 1970-72; Grad. fellow AMAX Found., MIT, 1980-83. Mem. ASTM, Metall. Soc. of AIME, Am. Soc. Metals, Chinese Inst. Engrs USA (pres. MIT chpt. 1982-83), Simga Xi. Mem. Christian Ch. Home: 10760 Pointed Oak Ln San Diego CA 92131 Office: GA Techs Inc 10955 John J Hopkins Dr La Jolla CA 92121

HSU, CHIEH SU, engineering educator, researcher; b. Soochow, Kiangsu, China, May 27, 1922; came to U.S., 1947.; s. Chung vu and Yong Feng (Wu) H.; m. Helen Yung-Feng Tse, Mar. 28, 1953; children—Raymond Hwa-chi, Katherine Hwa-Ling. BS, Nat. Inst. Tech., Chungking, China, 1945; MS, Stanford U., 1948, Ph.D., 1950. Project engr. IBM Corp., Poughkeepsie, N.Y., 1951-55; assoc. prof. U. Toledo, 1955-58; assoc. prof. Univ Calif.-Berkeley, 1958-64, prof., 1964—, chmn. div. applied mechanics, 1969-70; mem. sci. adv. bd. Alexander von Humboldt Found. of Fed. Republic Germany, Bonn, 1985—. Author 85 tech. papers; contbg. author: Thin-Shell Structures, 1974, Advances in Applied Mechanics, vol. 17, 1977; tech. editor Jour. Applied Mechanics, N.Y.C., 1976-82; assoc. editor profl. jours. Recipient Alexander von Humboldt award Fed. Republic Germany, 1986; Guggenheim Found. fellow, 1964-65; Miller research prof., U. Calif.-Berkeley, 1973-74. Fellow ASME (Centennial award 1980), Am. Acad. Mechanics; mem. Acoustical Soc., Am. Soc. Indsl. and Applied Math., Sigma Xi. Office: Dept Mech Engring Univ Calif Berkeley CA 94720

HSU, MING-TA SUNG, chemical company executive, research chemist; b. Hopei, Republic of China, Aug. 3, 1937; came to U.S., 1960; d. Yi-Chin and Su-Jung (Wang) Sung; m. Thomas K. Hsu, Oct. 7, 1972; 1 child, Baldwin. BS, Nat. Taiwan U., Taipei, 1960; MS, N.Mex. Highlands U., 1963; PhD, Iowa State U., 1967. Postdoctoral fellow Synvar Inst., Palo Alto, Calif., 1967-68; NMR spectroscopist Stanford (Calif.) U., 1968-69; research chemist Applied Space Products, Inc., Palo Alto, 1969-70; NRC research assoc. Ames Research Ctr., div. NASA, Moffett Field, Calif., 1970-72; research chemist San Jose (Calif.) State U., 1972-82; pres., research chemist HC Chem. Research and Service Corp., San Jose, 1982—. Contbr. articles to profl. jours.; patentee in field. Mem. Am. Chem. Soc., Soc. Advancement Material and Process Engring. Republican. Roman Catholic. Office: H C Chem Research and Service Corp 3675 Skyview Dr San Jose CA 95132

HSU, SHU-DEAN, physician; b. Chiba, Japan, Feb. 21, 1943; came to U.S., 1972; s. Tetzu and Takako (Koo) Minoyama; m. San-San Hsu, Mar. 3, 1973; children: Deborah Te-Lan, Peter Jie-Te. MD, Taipei (Taiwan) Med. Coll., 1968. Diplomate Am. Bd. Internal Medicine, Am. Bd. Hematology, Am. Bd. Med. Oncology. Asst. in medicine Mt. Sinai Sch. Medicine, N.Y.C., 1975-77; asst. instr. medicine U. Tex., Galveston, 1977-78; lectr. in medicine Tex. A&M U., Temple, 1978-80; asst. prof. medicine U. Ark., Little Rock, 1980-83; practice medicine specializing in hematology-oncology Visalia (Calif.) Med. Clinic, 1983—; chief hematology and oncology VA Med. Ctr., Temple, Tex., 1978-80. Contbr. articles to profl. jours. Fellow ACP; mem. N.Y. Acad. Scis., Am. Soc. Clin. Oncology, Am. Soc. Hematology, Calif Med. Assn., Tulare County Med. Soc. Club: Visalia Racquet. Home: 3500 W Hydeway Visalia CA 93291 Office: Visalia Med Clinic 5400 W Hillsdale Visalia CA 93291

HSU, TEH-AN, chemical engineer; b. Taipei, Taiwan, Republic of China, Oct. 21, 1949; came to U.S., 1974; s. Jen-Tsi and Shung (Shen) H.; m. Yin Kwan Tung, Aug. 21, 1982. BSChemE, Nat. Taiwan U., Taipei, 1972; MSChemE, Purdue U., 1976, PhDChemE, 1979. Assoc. sugar technologist Hawaiian Sugar Planters' Assn., Aiea, 1979—. Co-inventor process for treating cellulosic materials. Mem. Am. Inst. Chem. Engrs., Am. Chem. Soc., Hawaiian Sugar Technologists, N.Am. Membrane Soc. Home: 1430 Lusitana St Apt 301 Honolulu HI 96813 Office: Hawaiian Sugar Planters Assn PO Box 1057 Aiea HI 96701

HU, JOHN CHIH-AN, chemist, research engineer; b. Nanchang, Hubei, China, July 12, 1922; came to U.S., 1954, naturalized, 1965; s. Chi-Ching and Chao-Xien (Tsen) H.; B.S. in Chemistry, Nat. Central U., Nanjing, China, 1946; M.S. in Organic Chemistry, U. So. Calif., 1957, postgrad., 1957-61; PhD (hon.) Marquis Giuseppe Scicluna Internat. Univ. Foundation, 1985; m. Betty Siao-Yung Ho, Oct. 26, 1957; children—Arthur, Benjamin, Carl, David, Eileen, Franklin, George. Dir. research dept. Plant 1, Taiwan Fertilizer Mfg. Co., Chilung, 1947-54; research assoc. chemistry dept. U. So. Calif., Los Angeles, 1957-61; research chemist Chem Seal Corp. Am., Los Angeles, 1961-62; research chemist Products Research & Chem. Corp., Glendale, Calif., 1962-66; sr. research engr., materials and tech. unit, Boeing Co., Seattle, 1966-71; specialist engr. Quality Assurance Labs., 1971—; cons. UN; lectr., China, profl. confs. Fellow Am. Inst. Chemists; mem. Am. Chem. Soc. (chmn. exec. com. Puget Sound sect. 1988), Royal Soc. Chemistry, N.Y. Acad. Sci., Phi Lambda Upsilon. Patentee Chromatopyrography; contbg. author: Analytical Approach, 1983, Advances in Chromatography, vol. 23, 1984; contbr. articles on analytical pyrolysis, gas chromatography, mass spectrometry, polymer characterization, chemistry and tech. of sealants and adhesives profl. publs. in Chinese and English; editor Puget Sound Chemist; referee profl. jours. Analytical Chemistry, Analytica Chimica Acta, Am. Chem. Soc. short courses. Home: 16212 122 SE Renton WA 98058 Office: Boeing Co M/S 2A-64 PO Box 3999 Seattle WA 98124

HU, SHIU-LOK, molecular biologist; b. Hong Kong, Nov. 10, 1949; came to U.S., 1967; s. I-Ping and Pie (Wang) H.; m. Gail Ellen Anderson, Dec. 21, 1984; children: Emily, Chu-Yuin. BA, U. Calif., Berkeley, 1971; PhD, U. Wis., Madison, 1978. Postdoctoral fellow Cold Spring Harbor (N.Y.) Lab., 1978-81; sr. scientist Molecular Genetics, Inc., Minnetonka, Minn., 1981-83, dir. molecular biology, 1983-84; dir. vaccine research ONCOGEN, Seattle, 1985—. Contbr. articles to profl. jours.; patentee in field. U.S. Dept. Def. grantee, 1981. Mem. AAAS, Am. Soc. Virology, Am. Soc. Microbiology, Phi Beta Kappa. Home: 14128 175th Ave NE Redmond WA 98052 Office: ONCOGEN 3005 1st Ave Seattle WA 98121

HU, STEVE SENG-CHIU, scientific research director, educator; b. Yangchou City, Kianksu Province, China, Mar. 16, 1922; s. Yubin and Shuchang (Lee) H.; m. Lily Li-Wan Liu, Oct. 2, 1977; children—April, Yendo, Victor. M.S., Rensselaer Poly. Inst., N.Y., 1940; Ph.D., 1957, MS postgrad. UCLA, 1964-66. Mng. tech. dir. China Aircraft/China Motor Programs, Douglas Aircraft Co., Calif., N.J., 1945-48, Kelly Engrig Co., N.Y., Ariz., 1949-54; systems engr., meteorol. sci. dir. R.C.A., Ariz., 1955-58; research specialist Aerojet Gen., Calif., 1958-60; research scientist Jet Propulsion Lab., Calif. 1960-61; dir. research analysis Northrop Corp., Calif., Ala., 1961-72; dir. Century Research, Inc., Am. Tech. Coll., and U.

Am. United Research Inst., Gardena, San Bernardino, Calif., 1973—, pres. U. Am. Found. and U. Am. Research Found., Calif. and Taiwan, Republic of China, 1981—. Dir., exec. v.p. Am. Astronautical Soc., Wash., 1963-70; cons. Hsin-Hwa Nuclear Reactor Program, Taiwan, 1954-58; prof. Auburn U., U. Ala., U. Ariz., U. So. Calif., 1957-73. Fellow Calif. Inst. Tech., 1943-44. Recipient MIT Salisbury prize and Sloane prize, 1941-42, Commission Aeronautical Affairs, Republic of China cert. of merit and cash award, 1945, Northrop Corp. cert. of merit, 1965. Mem. Am. Astronautical Soc., AIAA, Nat. Assn. Tech. Schs. Office: Century Research Bldg Office Sect 16935 S Vermont Ave Gardena CA 90247

HU, TE CHIANG, electrical engineer, computer science educator; b. Peking, Republic of China, Nov. 28, 1930; came to U.S., 1954; s. Che-Chia and Ya-Su (Yeh) H.; m. Jane Wu, Apr. 30. 1960; children: Dale, Rona, Alan. BS in Engring., Nat. Taiwan U., 1953; MS in Engring., U. Ill., 1956; PhD in Applied Math., Brown U., 1960. Research math. IBM Research Ctr., 1960-66; assoc. prof. elec. engring., computer sci. U. Wis., Madison, 1966-68, prof., 1968-74; prof. U. Calif., San Diego, 1974—; cons. RAND Corp., 1965, Office of Emergency Preparedness, 1968-72. Author: Integer Programming and Network Analysis, 1969, Combinatorial Algorithms, 1982; editor: Mathematical Programming, 1973, Theory and Concepts of Circuit Layout, 1985; contbr. chpts. to books. Mem. Assn. Computing Machinery, Soc. Indsl. Applied Math. (assoc. editor jour.), Ops. Research Soc. Am., IEEE (editor Transactions on Computers). Home: 8422 Prestwick Dr La Jolla CA 92037 Office: U Calif San Diego Dept Elec Engring and Computer Sci C-014 La Jolla CA 92093

HU, WEIBAI, mineral engineer, metallurgist, educator; b. Jiangxi, Peoples Republic of China, Nov. 26, 1922; came to U.S., 1981; BS, Chaotung U., Peoples Rep. of China, 1945; MS, U. Utah, 1949. Prof. and chmn. Cen.-South U. of Tech., Changsha, Republic of China, 1952-82; vis. prof. Colo. Sch. Mines, Golden, 1982, U. Calif., Berkeley, 1983; research prof. U. Utah, Salt Lake City, 1983—; vice-chmn. mineral processing, Chinese Soc. Metals, 1978-83; sr. adv. China Nonferrous Metal Industry Corp., 1983—; cons. ministry of Metallurgy, Peoples Republic of China, 1979—, ministry of Geology, 1976—. Author Chinese lang. univ. textbooks; editor: Ency. Sinica, Eng.-Chinese Dictionary of Mineral Technology; contbr. articles to profl. jours.; inventor and patentee in field. Mem. AIME, Chinese Soc. Metals, Chinese Soc. Non-ferrous Metals, Chinese Soc. Mineral Processing, Internat. Assn. Colloid and Surface Chemistry. Office: U Utah Dept Metallurgy 412 Mineral Sci Bldg Salt Lake City UT 84112

HUANG, CARL KUO CHANG, hotel executive; b. Chivi, Republic of China, Sept. 22, 1937; came to U.S., 1970, naturalized, 1984; s. Tien-hsi and Yen (Peng) H.; m. Show Chin, Jan. 24, 1965; children—James, Jane. M.A. in Polit. Sci., UCLA, 1971, postgrad., 1975. Instr., Taiwan Nat. Normal U., Taipei, 1968-70; owner Glendale-Manhattan Motel, Calif., 1984-86, Townhouse Motel, Van Nuys, Calif., 1978-79, Travelodge Inglewood, Calif., 1979—; Pres. AA Internat., Inc. Chmn. Taiwanese Benevolent Assn. Calif., 1984-85; bd. dirs. Taiwanese Benevolent Assn. Am. Motel. Calif. Hotel and Motel Assn., Taiwan Sister State Task Force, Chinese-Am. Soc., Inglewood C. of C. Club: Lions (dir. 1980—). Home: 1508 E Orange Ave Glendale CA 91205 Office: Travelodge Inglewood Airport 3900 W Century Blvd Inglewood CA 90303

HUANG, CHIEN CHANG, electrical engineer; b. Nanking, Peoples Republic of China, Feb. 16, 1931; came to U.S., 1957; s. Ling-Kuo Huang and Yi-Ching Liu; m. Li-May Tsai, June 2, 1962; children: Frederick G., Lewis G. BSEE, Taiwan Coll. Engring., Tainan, 1954; MSEE, U. Ill., 1959; postgrad., U. Pa., 1960-62. Engr. Burrough Corp., Paoli, Pa., 1960-64; sr. staff engr. Unisys Corp., San Diego, 1974—; sr. engr. Philco Ford Corp., Blue Bell, Pa., 1965-69; staff engr. Fairchild Semiconductor, Mountain View, Calif., 1969-71; sr. staff engr. Am. Micro Systems, Santa Clara, Calif., 1971-74. Contbr. articles to profl. jours. Regarded as one of top experts in integrated circuit design, analysis and devel. Home: 11449 Duenda Rd San Diego CA 92127 Office: Unisys Corp 10850 Via Frontera San Diego CA 92127

HUANG, FRANCIS FU-TSE, engineering educator; b. Hong Kong, Aug. 27, 1922; came to U.S., 1945, naturalized, 1960; s. Kwong Set and Chen-Ho (Yee) H.; m. Fung-Yuen Fung, Apr. 10, 1954; children: Raymond, Stanley. B.S., San Jose State Coll., 1951; M.S., Stanford U., 1952; profl. mech. engr., Columbia U., 1964. Design engr. M.W. Kellogg Co., N.Y.C., 1952-58; faculty San Jose (Calif.) State U., 1958—, assoc. prof. mech. engring., 1962-67, prof., 1967—, chmn. dept., 1973-81; hon. prof. heat power engring Taiyuan (People's Republic of China) U. Tech., 1981—. Author: Engineering Thermodynamics—Fundamentals and Applications, 1976. Served to capt. Chinese Army, 1943-45. NSF faculty fellow, 1962-64; Named Tau Beta Pi Outstanding Engring. Prof. of Year, 1967, 76, Pi Tau Sigma Prof. of Yr., 1985; recipient Calif. State Coll. System Disting. Teaching award, 1968-69. Mem. ASME, AIAA, Am. Soc. Engring. Edn., AAAS, AAUP, N.Y. Acad. Scis. Home: 1259 Sierra Mar Dr San Jose CA 95118 Office: Dept Mech Engring San Jose State U San Jose CA 95192

HUANG, JOSEPH JUIN-SHYONG, structural engr.; b. Taiwan, China, Nov. 20, 1941; came to U.S., 1966, naturalized, 1977; B.S. in Civil Engring., Nat. Taiwan U., 1965; M.S., Lehigh U., 1968, Ph.D., 1973; m. Vivian Weiwei Wang, June 20, 1970; children—Peter B., Andrew B. Post-doctoral research asso. Lehigh U., Bethlehem, Pa., 1973; sr. structural engr. Skidmore, Owings & Merrill, Chgo., 1973-75; sr. structural engring. specialist Sargent & Lundy, Chgo., 1976-81; supr. Bechtel Power Corp., San Francisco, 1981—. Recipient A.F. Davis Silver medal Am. Welding Soc., 1971; registered profl. and structural engr., Ill., Calif. Mem. ASCE, Am. Concrete Inst., Structural Engrs. Assn. Ill., Sigma Xi, Soc. structure. engring. articles to profl. jours. Home: 35682 Gleason Ln Fremont CA 94536

HUANG, NELSON SHIANG-LUNG, college administrator; b. Anxi, Fujian, China, June 9, 1941; s. Chun Sen and Chian Wan Huang. BA, Wayland Bapt. Coll., 1967; MA, Colo. State U. 1969. Instr. behavioral scis. humanities div. State Community Coll., East St. Louis, Ill., 1970-76, chmn. behavioral scis. humanities div., 1976-78, coordinator Title III project, 1978-81, coordinator planning and research, 1981-82; pres., mng. dir. Glenco Corp., Denver, 1983-86; dir. grants devel. Loretto Heights Coll., Denver, 1986—. Baptist. Office: Loretto Heights Coll 3001 S Federal Blvd Denver CO 80236

HUANG, RONG-FONG, ceramic engineer, researcher; b. Chung-Hun, Republic of China, Aug. 27, 1952; came to U.S., 1980; s. Chin-Pun and Pao-Hua (Wei) H.; n. Huiling Chen, Sept. 26, 1983; 1 child, Katherine Peiya. BS in Earth Sci., Nat. Cheng Kung U., Taiwan, Republic of China, 1976; MS in Ceramic Engring., U. Mo., Rolla, 1982, PhD in Ceramic Engineering, 1984. Staff engr. Motorola Inc., Albuquerque, 1984—. Mem. Am. Ceramic Soc., Material Research Soc. Office: Motorola Inc 4800 Alameda Ave NE Albuquerque NM 87113

HUBBARD, CHARLES RONALD, engineering executive; b. Weaver, Ala., Feb. 4, 1933; s. John Duncan Hubbard and Athy Pauline (Lusk) Thorpe; m. Betty Lou McKleroy, Dec. 29, 1951; 1 son, Charles Ronald Hubbard II. B.S. in Elec. Engring., U. Ala., 1960. Mktg. mgr. Sperry Corp., Huntsville, Ala. 1969-71, head engring. sect., 1971-74; sr. staff engr. Honeywell Inc., Clearwater, Fla., 1974-76, mgr., 1976-79, chief engr., West Covina, Calif., 1979-83, assoc. dir. engring., 1983-84, assoc. dir. advanced systems, 1984—. Served as staff sgt. USAF, 1953-57. Mem. IEEE (sect. chmn. 1972-73). Methodist. Home: 5460 Willowick Circle Anaheim CA 92807 Office: Honeywell Inc 1200 E San Bernardino Rd West Covina CA 91790

HUBBARD, DONALD, marine artist, writer; b. Bronx, N.Y., Jan. 15, 1926; s. Ernest Fortesque and Lilly Violet (Beck) H.; student Brown U., 1944-45; A.A., George Washington U., 1959, B.A., 1958; student Naval War Coll., 1965-66; m. Darlene Julia Huber, Dec. 13, 1957; children—Leslie Carol, Christopher Eric, Lauren Ivy. Commd. ensign U.S. Navy, 1944, advanced through grades to comdr., 1965; served naval aviator, ret., 1967; founder Ocean Ventures Industries, Inc., Coronado, Calif., 1969; operator, 1969-77; marine artist; author: Ships-in-Bottles, A How to Guide to a Venerable

Nautical Craft, 1971; Buddleschiffe: Wie Macht Man Sie, 1972; The Complete Book of Inflatable Boats, 1979; editor: The Bottle Shipwright; contbr. articles in field to publs. SCUBA instr.; lectr. on marine art. Decorated Air Medal. Mem. Ships-in-Bottles Assn. Ipres. N.Am. div. 1982—), Nature Printing Soc., Writers Guild, San Diego Watercolor Soc. (bd. dirs. 1981-82), La Jolla Art Assn., Marine Hist. Soc., San Diego Maritime Assn., Nautical Research Guild. Home and Office: 1022 Park Pl Coronado CA 92118

HUBBARD, EDWARD LEONARD, physicist, consultant; b. Phoenix, July 7, 1921; s. Edward Robert and Sue Virginia (Leonard) H.; m. Bonnie Eula Cushman, Oct. 4, 1952; children: Paul Edward, Glenda Kay, Ruth Susan, Alison Ann. BA in Physics, UCLA, 1943, MA in Physics, 1948, PhD in Physics, 1951. Physicist Lawrence Berkeley (Calif.) Lab., 1951-68, Fermi Nat. Accelerator Lab., Batavia, Ill., 1968-74; mgr., Doublet III engr. GA Technologies, San Diego, 1974-86; cons. San Diego, 1986—. Contbr. chpts. to books. Served with USN, 1944-45. Mem. Am. Phys. Soc., Sigma Xi. Home: 5527 Chelsea Ave La Jolla CA 92037 Office: GA TEchnologies Inc San Diego CA 92138

HUBBARD, ERNEST DEE, accounting educator; b. Wellsville, Utah, Feb. 6, 1929; s. Ernest Benjamin and Pearl (Jones) H.; m. Patricia Kaye Hurren, Aug. 27, 1959; children: Jeffrey Dee, Heidi Kaye, James Brian, Daniel Malin. BS, Utah State U., 1952; MBA, U. Utah, 1959; PhD, U. Wash., 1967. Cert. mgmt. acct. Cost acct. Ace Raymond Constrn., Logan, Utah, 1954; salesman Jones Shoes, Bountiful, Utah, 1958-59; from instr. to prof. in acctg. Brigham Young U., Provo, Utah, 1959-60, 63—; instr. U. Washington, Seattle, 1960-63; ednl. cons. U. Utah, 1967-70, IBM Corp., White Plains, N.Y. and Brussels, 1980—. Co-author: Cost and Managerial Accounting, 1985; co-contbr. articles to profl. jours. Bd. dirs., sec. Marrciest Homeowners Assn., Provo, Utah, 1982-85. Served to first lt. U.S. Army, 1952-54, Korea. Deloitee Haskins & Sells scholar, 1961. Mem. Nat. Assn. Accts. (chpt. pres. 1974), Am. Acctg. Assn. (recipient scholarship 1962, staff dir. continuing edn. 1978), Beta Alpha Psi (area counselor 1982-84). Republican. Mormon. Avocations: photography, gardening, computers. Office: Brigham Young U Sch Acctg Provo UT 84604

HUBBARD, GREGORY SCOTT, physicist; b. Lexington, Ky., Dec. 27, 1948; s. Robert Nicholas and Nancy Clay (Brown) H.; B.A., Vanderbilt U., 1970; postgrad. U. Calif., Berkeley, 1974-76; m. Susan Artimissa Ruggeri, Aug. 1, 1982. Lab. engr. physics dept. Vanderbilt U., Nashville, 1970-73; staff scientist Lawrence Berkeley Lab. Dept. Instrument Techniques, Berkeley, Calif., 1974-80; dir. research and devel. Canberra Industries, Inc., Detector Products Div., Novato, Calif., 1980-82; v.p., gen. mgr. Canberra Semicondr., Novato, Calif., 1982-85; cons., owner Hubbard Cons. Services, 1985—; cons. SRI Internat., Menlo Park, Calif., 1979—; lectr. in field. Recipient Founders Scholarship, Vanderbilt U., 1966. Mem. IEEE, Am. Soc. Psychical Research, Materials Research Soc. Office: 1719 Baker St San Francisco CA 94115

HUBBARD, HOWARD LELAND, banker; b. San Francisco, June 19, 1931; s. Albert Giles and Lorena (Watts) H.; m. Lou Juan M. Anderson, Nov. 3, 1951; children—Steven, Thomas, Richard. Student Sacramento City Coll., 1949-50; B.A., Sacramento State Coll., 1958; postgrad. U. Calif. Extension, 1958-61, Ind. U. Inst. Fin. Edn. Grad. Sch., 1974-76. Real estate salesman Watrous, McClory, Inc., Sacramento, 1957-58; loan officer Buhler Mortgage Co., Sacramento, 1959; asst. mgr. Capital Fed. Savs. & Loan Assn., Sacramento, 1959-63; exec. v.p. Senator Savs. & Loan Assn., Sacramento, 1963-71; pres. Equitable Savs. & Loan Assn., Portland, Oreg., 1971-82, also dir.; pres. Washington Fed. Savs. & Bank, Hillsboro, Oreg., 1982—, also dir.; dir. Cascade Natural Gas Corp., Oreg. Title Ins. Co. ; chmn. Oreg. Mut. Ins. Co. Bd. dirs., mem. exec. com. United Way Portland, 1977-83; bd. dirs. Oreg. Symphony Assn., 1977—, also past pres.; bd. dirs. Portland State U. Found., 1979—, pres., 1983; mem. exec. bd. N.W. Synod Luth. Ch. Am., 1973-80; regent Pacific Luth. U., 1979—. Served with USN, 1951-54. Mem. Portland C. of C. (dir. 1978-81). Republican. Clubs: Waverly Country, Arlington (Portland); Rotary (Hillsboro); Masons. Home: 5320 NW Edgebrook Pl Portland OR 97229 Office: Washington Fed Savs Bank 314 E Main St PO Box 9 Hillsboro OR 97123

HUBBARD, MARYJOANNE CHRISTINE, psychologist; b. Benton Harbor, Mich., Jan. 12, 1939; d. Harvey Howard and Vivian (Wolford) Halsey; children—Kim Rene, Craig Martin, Nicole Elizabeth. B.A., Calif. State U.-Fullerton, 1970, M.S., 1976; PhD., D.S. Internat. U., San Diego, 1981. Lic. marriage, family and child therapist, Calif.; Clin. psychologist, Calif. Counselor Orange County Juvenile System, 1967-69; psychometrist San Diego State U., 1970-71; grad assist. dept. psychology Calif. State U.-Fullerton, 1974-75; intern Olive-Vista Psychiat. Hosp., Pomona, Calif., 1975, Met. State Hosp., Norwalk, Calif., 1975-76; marriage, family and child counselor, Fullerton, 1976—; juvenile diversion psychologist Santa Ana (Calif.) Police Dept., 1976-80, police psychologist, 1980-87; dir. clin. services, 1986—; pvt. practice psychology, Batavia Woods Med. Ctr., Orange, Calif.; instr. Orange County Sheriff's Acad., 1980—. Bd. dirs. Mariposa Women's Ctr., 1981—, COPES, 1979. Mem. Acad. Criminal Justice Scis., Soc. Police and Criminal Psychology, Calif. Assn. Marriage and Family Counselors, Calif. Psychol. Assn., Am. Psychol. Assn., Calif. State Psychol. Assn., Orange County Psychol. Assn., Psi Chi. Contbr. articles to profl. jours. Office: Santa Ana Police Dept 24 Civic Center Plaza Santa Ana CA 92701 Office: Batavia Woods Med Ctr 705 W La Veta Suite 101 Orange CA 92668

HUBBARD, ROBERT LANE, research scientist; b. Portland, Oreg., Apr. 12, 1948; s. Lyle Turner and Jewel (Green) H.; m. Dianna K. Jones, Sept. 22, 1979; children: Colleen Marie, Kevin Adam. BS in Chemistry, Oreg. State U., 1970; PhD in Chemistry, Tex. A&M U., 1976. Research chemist Advanced Displays br. Ctl. Research Labs., Tex. Instruments, Inc., Dallas, 1976-78; sr. research scientist Imaging Research Lab., 1978-86; prin. scientist, mgr. Interconnect/Packaging group Solid State Research Lab., Tektronix, Inc., Beaverton, Oreg., 1986—. Author books and contbr. articles to profl. jours.; patentee in liquid crystals, displays, microelectronics, and synthetic metals. Mem. Am. Chem. Soc., Internat. Soc. Hybrid Microelectronics. Home: 14370 SW Hart Rd Beaverton OR 97005 Office: Tektronix Inc Box 500 MS 50-324 Beaverton OR 97077

HUBBARD, WILLIAM BOGEL, JR., planetary sciences educator, consultant; b. Liberty, Tex., Nov. 14, 1940; s. William Bogel and Marie (Young) H.; m. Jean North Gilliland, June 8, 1963; children: Lynne Marie, Laurie North. B.A., Rice U., Houston, 1962; Ph.D., U. Calif-Berkeley, 1967. Research fellow Calif. Inst. Tech., Pasadena, 1967-68; asst. prof. astronomy U. Tex.-Austin, 1968-72; assoc. prof. planetary scis. U. Ariz., Tucson, 1972-75, dir. Lunar and Planetary Lab., 1977-81, prof., 1975—; cons. Lawrence Livermore (Calif.) Nat. Lab., 1972-86, NASA, 1970—; exchange scientist USSR Nat. Acad. Sci., 1973, com. mem. div. for planetary scis., 1985-88. Contbr. articles to profl. jours.; assoc. editor: Icarus, 1980—. Mem. AAAS, Am. Astron. Soc., Am. Geophys. Union, Internat. Astron. Union, Sigma Xi. Democrat. Episcopalian. Home: 2618 E Devon St Tucson AZ 85716 Office: Lunar and Planetary Lab U Ariz Tucson AZ 85721

HUBER, BEVERLY J., data processing professional, social worker; b. Minot, N.D., Mar. 30, 1932; d. Fred William and Bernice Lorrayne (Cooley) Buchwitz; m. Ivan C. Huber, June 19, 1955 (div. June 1972). BS in Edn. cum laude, State Coll. Minot, 1951; B in Mus., Am. Conservatory, 1953; M of Social Welfare, U. Calif., Berkeley, 1967; cert. in programming, Computer Learning Ctr., 1981. Lic. clin. social worker, Calif. Clin. social worker Los Angeles County, 1963-72; social service mgr. St. Vincent Med. Ctr., Los Angeles, 1972-80; programmer Ferrin, Forster and Crosby, Los Angeles, 1982-84; instr., programmer Computer Learning Ctr., Los Angeles, 1983-84; instr. West Side Ctr. for Ind. Living, Los Angeles, 1984-85; sr. data processing tech. trainer Pacific Mut. Life Ins. Co., Newport Beach, Calif., 1985—. Fellow NSF, 1961, VA, 1966-67. Mem. Nat. Assn. Social Workers, Trainers Assn. of So. Calif. Roman Catholic. Club: Townhall (Los Angeles). Avocations: music, choral singing, drama, reading, walking. Office: Pacific Mut 700 Newport Ctr Dr Newport Beach CA 92660

HUBER, NEIL MOREHOUSE, bioengineering laboratory executive, researcher; b. N.Y.C., Sept. 13, 1932; s. Walter Gundlach and Margaret (Goss) H.; m. Herta Derke, July 10, 1970; children: Erik, Bruce. AB,

Columbia U., 1954; PhD, Tuebingen (Fed. Republic Germany) U., 1964. Research physiologist U. Calif., Berkeley, 1965-70; prof. biology U. Wis., Green Bay, 1970-75; pres. NW Bioengring., Inc., Bellevue, Wash., 1975-81; v.p. Biotechniques Labs., Redmond, Wash., 1982—, also bd. dirs.; sr. tech. cons. Ecova Corp., Redmond, 1986—. Inventor fermentation systems and products. Fellow Am. Anthropology Assn.; mem. Nat. Feed Ingredients Assn., Sigma Xi. Office: Biotechniques Labs Inc Biotech Rd and NE 33d Redmond WA 98052

HUBER, PAUL EDWARD, computer industry executive; b. Newark, Feb. 1, 1939; s. Joseph F. and Virginia A. (Zarn) H.; m. Estelle Reed, June 27, 1964; children: Brian, Jeffrey. BSEE, N.J. Inst. Tech., 1960; MBA, Harvard U., 1963. Mgr. product mktg. Electronic Assocs., West Long Branch, N.J., 1969-71, bus. area mgr., 1971-73; pres. Star Graphics Systems, South Hackensack, N.J., 1973-75, Mergenthaler Linotype, Melville, N.Y., 1975-78; pres., chief exec. officer Summagraphics Corp., Fairfield, Conn., 1978-83, Megatek Corp., San Diego, 1983—. Mem. U. Calif. San Diego Chancellor's Assocs. and Deans Adv. Com., 1985—, Corp. Assocs., 1985—. Mem. Nat. Computer Graphics Assocs. (v.p., bd. dirs. 1984—), Am. Electronics Assn. (bd. dirs. 1986—), San Diego C. of C., Zool. Soc., Ardvaarks and Pres.' Assocs. Avocations: model railroading, racquetball, travel. Home: PO Box 3403 Rancho Santa Fe CA 92067 Office: Megatek Corp 9645 Scranton Rd San Diego CA 92121

HUBER, VANDRA L., businesss educator, consultant; b. Salt Lake City, July 18, 1949; d. Fred L. and Twila Blanche (Jacobs) H. BS cum laude, U. Utah, 1971, MS in Econs., 1978; MBA, Ind. U., 1981, D Bus. Adminstrn. in Human Resources, 1982. Reporter, editor Salt Lake City Tribune, 1971-77; dir. communications Utah Social Services, Salt Lake City, 1977-79; instr. Ind. U., Bloomington, 1979-82, Cornell U., Ithaca, N.Y., 1982-85; prof. human resources and mgmt. U. Utah, Salt Lake City, 1985—; cons. nonprofit orgns. Rochester, Salt Lake City; mem. adv. bd. Cornell Inst. Social and Econ. Research, 1983-85. Contbr. over 20 articles to profl. jours. Treas. Community Crisis Ctr., Salt Lake City, 1978-79. Social Sci. Research Council grantee, 1982; Richard Irwin Dissertation grantee, 1982. Mem. Internat. Assn. Bus. Communicators (Intermountain Outstanding Communicator 1978), Acad. Mgmt., Am. Psychol. Assn., Am. Inst. Decision Scis. Democrat. Episcopalian. Avocations: jogging, raising pedigree Scottish Terriers. Home: 821-E 3rd Ave Salt Lake City UT 84103 Office: U Utah Sch Bus Dept Mgmt Salt Lake City UT 84112

HUCK, LARRY RALPH, manufacturers representative, sales cons.; b. Yakima, Wash., Aug. 10, 1942; s. Frank Joseph and Helen Barbara (Swalley) H.; student Wash. Tech. Inst., 1965-66, Seattle Community Coll., 1966-68, Edmonds Community Coll., 1969-70; 1 child, Larry Ralph II. Salesman, Kirby Co., Seattle, 1964-68, sales mgr., 1968-69; with Sanico Chem. Co., Seattle, 1968-69; salesman Synkoloid Co., Seattle, 1970-71; tech. sales rep. Vis Queen div. Ethyl Corp., Seattle, 1971-75; Western sales mgr. B & K Films, Inc., Belmont, Calif., 1975-77; pres. N.W. Mfrs. Assocs., Inc., Bellevue, Wash., 1977-86; pres. combined sales group, 1984 ; nat. sales mgr. Gazelle, Inc., Tomah, Wis., 1979-81; dir. sales J.M.J. Mktg. E.Z. Frame div., 1984-85; pres. Combined Sales Group, Seattle, 1984; nat. accounts mgr. Upnorth Plastics, St. Paul, 1984—. Vice pres. Bellevue Nat. Little League; basketball coordinator Cath. Youth Orgn., Sacred Heart Ch.; bd. dirs. Bellevue Baseball Assn. Served with USMC, 1959-64. Mem. Nat. Council Salesmen's Orgns., Mfrs. Agts. Nat. Assn., Am. Hardware Mfrs. Assn., Northwest Mfrs. Assn. (pres.). Hardware Affiliated Reps., Inc., Door and Hardware Inst., Internal Conf. Bldg. Officials. Roman Catholic. Office: 14925 NE 40th Redmond WA 98052

HUCK, LEONARD WILLIAM, banker; b. Sioux City, Iowa, Dec. 4, 1922; s. Jay Myles and Eula Lea (Pinkley) H.; m. Suzanne Lesher, July 26, 1947; children: Leonard William, Robert C., Wendy. B.A., DePauw U., 1944; postgrad., Southwestern Grad. Sch. Banking, 1965, Harvard U., 1944. Asst. mgr. Camelback Inn., Phoenix, 1946-50; summer resort mgr. St. Mary's Glacier Lodge, Idaho Springs, Colo., 1950; mgr. Ariz. Country Club, Phoenix, 1950-57; exec. v.p. Valley Nat. Bank, Phoenix, 1957-82; pres., chief adminstrv. officer Valley Nat. Bank, 1982—; faculty Assembly for Bank Dirs., 1968—; dir. Southwestern Grad. Sch. Banking, 1966—, dean for bankers, 1973-75; bd. dirs. Internat. MasterCard. Pres. Phoenix and Valley of the Sun Conv. and Visitors Bur., 1975, dir., 1975-77; chmn. Maricopa County Heart Assn., 1967, Desert Found., 1966-71; mem. Fiesta Bowl Com., 1983; pres. Scottsdale (Ariz.) Boys Club, 1965, St. Luke's Hosp., 1972-74; bd. dirs., mem. exec. com. Blood Systems, Inc.; trustee, sec. Phoenix Art Mus., 1971; nat. co-chmn. YWCA Fund for the Future, 1983; campaign chmn. United Way, 1985, chmn. bd. Valley of Sun United Way, 1986. Served with USN, 1942-46. Named Phoenix Man of Yr., 1978; recipient Torch of Liberty award Anti-Defamation League, 1983. Mem. Bank Mktg. Assn. (dir. 1976—, pres. 1981-82), Assn. Res. City Bankers, Phoenix C. of C. (pres. 1977, dir. 1974-79), Am. Inst. Banking, Ariz. Club Mgrs. Assn., Ariz. Hotel and Motel Assn., Ariz. Heart Assn. Episcopalian. Clubs: Valley of the Sun Kiwanis (pres. 1961), Scottsdale Dinner (pres. 1967), Paradise Valley Country (dir. 1974-77, sec. 1976), Kiva (pres. 1970, 71), Phoenix Thunderbirds (big chief 1964), Valley Field Riding and Polo (v.p. 1978-79). Home: 4854 Calle del Medio Phoenix AZ 85018 Office: Valley Nat Corp PO Box 71 Phoenix AZ 85001

HUCKEBY, KAREN MARIE, graphic arts exec.; b. San Diego, June 4, 1957; d. Floyd Riley and Georgette Laura (Wegimont) H. Student Coll. of Alameda, 1976; student 3-M dealer tng. program, St. Paul, 1975. Staff Huck's Press Service, Inc., Emeryville, Calif., 1968—, v.p., 1975—. Mem. Rep. Nat. Task Force, 1984—. Recipient service award ARC, 1977. Mem. East Bay Club of Printing House Craftsman (treas. 1977-78), N.Y. Mus. Modern Art, Nat. Trust Historic Preservation, Smithsonian Inst., San Francisco Mus. Soc., Internat. Platform Assn., Am. Film Inst. Club: Commonwealth. Home: 509 Civic Center Richmond CA 94804 Office: Staff Huck's Press Service Inc 1311A 63d St Emeryville CA 94608

HUDAK, NORMAN JOHN, chemistry professor; b. Lorain, Ohio, Jan. 24, 1933; s. John Charles and Anna Marie (Dzambik) H.; m. Mary Jo Rohland, June 22, 1963; children: Lisa, Ann, Carol. BA, DePauw U., 1954; PhD, Cornell U., 1959. Instr. chemistry Oberlin (Ohio) Coll., Ohio, 1958-60; asst. prof. Haverford (Pa.) Coll., 1960-61; assoc. prof. Willamette U., Salem, Oregon, 1961-65, prof., 1965—. Science Faculty fellowship NSF, 1971-72. Mem. Am. Chem. Soc., Am. Assn. for Advancement Sci., Royal Soc. Chem. (London), Phi Beta Kappa, Sigma Xi. Office: Dept Chemistry Willamette U 900 State St Salem OR 97301

HUDDLESTON, GREGORY LEE, computer consulting firm executive; b. Los Angeles, Nov. 20, 1956; s. Jack Lee and Helen Mae (Leach) H.; Student UCLA, 1977-79; B.S.E.E., in Computer Sci., Calif. State U., 1984. Cert. community coll. tchr., Calif. Data analyst Douglas Aircraft Co., Lakewood, Calif., 1978-81; sr. engr. Applied Radiologic Scis., South Pasadena, Calif., 1981-82; pres., chief exec. officer Bytewise Cons. Inc., South Gate, Calif., 1982—; mktg. mgr. ENRAD Corp., Paramount, Calif., 1986—; cons. Nat. Radiologic Physics, Pasadena, 1984—. Recipient Appreciation certificate ARC, 1979, Excellence award Multiple Sclorosis Soc., 1979. Mem. IEEE. Republican. Lodge: Kiwanis (appreciation award 1980, family chmn. 1978). Home: 16512 Blackbeard Ln Apt 104 Huntington Beach CA 92649 Office: Bytewise Cons Inc 4000 Tweedy Blvd Suite B South Gate CA 90280

HUDDLESTON, LAUREN BEULAH, oil company executive; b. Nashville, Nov. 19, 1933; d. John and Chattie (Rich) H.; m. Gilbert Taylor, Aug. 25, 1950 (div. July 1972); children: Jeffrey, Charles, Marianne; m. Robert W. Fisher, Apr. 5, 1976. BA, Stephens Coll., 1980; MSW, U. Denver, 1984, PhD, 1987. Clinician, psychotherapy tchr. Halcyon, Inc., Lafayette, Ind., 1972-76; biofeedback specialist New Orleans Ctr. for Psychotherapy, 1976-78; human resource developer The Anchoring System, Denver, 1972—; adminstrv. dir., v.p. Bradden Exploration, Denver, 1981-86; pres., chief exec. officer Fisher Energy Group, Denver, 1986—; developer wellness and peer counseling program Srs. Resource Ctr. Jefferson County, Denver, 1982-84. Co-organizer Citizens for Responsible Devel. of Bergen Park, Evergreen, Colo., 1983; dean search com. Grad. Sch. Social Work, Denver U. Mem. Nat. Assn. Social Workers, World Future Soc., Internat. Transactional Analysis Assn. (clin. cert.), Nat. Assn. Female Execs., Ind. Petroleum Assn. Mountain States, Am. Mgmt. Assn. Avocations: skiing, hiking, swimming. Home: 127 Sawmill Dr Evergreen CO 80439 Office: Fisher Energy Group 1020 15th St 4 L Denver CO 80202

HUDNUT, DAVID BEECHER, leasing company executive, lawyer; b. Cin., Feb. 21, 1935; s. William Herbert and Elizabeth Allen (Kilborne) H.; m. Robin Fraser, Apr. 12, 1958; children: David Beecher, Marjorie Elizabeth, Joshua Fraser, John Marshall, Benjamin Parker. A.B., Princeton U., 1957; J.D., Cornell U., 1962. Bar: N.Y. 1962, U.S. Supreme Ct. 1967. Assoc., Hughes, Hubbard & Reed, N.Y.C., 1962-67; v.p. U.S. Leasing Internat., Inc., San Francisco, 1969-76, sr. v.p., 1976—; bd. dirs. San Francisco chpt. Assn. for Corp. Growth, 1977-79, Donaldina Cameron House, 1969-76, 80—, Services for Srs., 1970—, No. Calif. Presbyn. Homes, 1971-77, chmn., 1973-76, 79-86; bd. dirs. Edgewood Children's Ctr., 1979-86, Ind. Colls. No. Calif., 1981-84, Calif. Hist. Soc., 1986—. Republican. Presbyterian. Office: US Leasing Internat Inc 733 Front St San Francisco CA 94111

HUDSON, ALVIN MAYNARD, physics educator; b. Portland, Oreg., June 28, 1922; s. Roy Randolph and Alice Mae (Phelps) H. BS in Physics, Stanford U., 1947, MS in Physics, 1950, PhD in Physics, 1957. Asst. prof. physics Occidental Coll., Los Angeles, 1956-59, assoc. prof., 1959-70, prof., 1970-87; mem. examiner com. Ednl. Testing Service advanced placement sect., 1970-78, past chmn. Co-author: University Physics, 1982; contbr. articles to profl. jours. Served as sgt. Signal Corps, U.S. Army, 1943-45. Mem. AAAS, Am. Assn. Physics Tchrs. (pres. So. Calif. sect. 1962-63, com. apparatus for ednl. instns. 1970-72), Sigma Xi. Home: 650 Crane Blvd Los Angeles CA 90065

HUDSON, DONALD J., stock exchange executive; b. Vancouver, B.C., Canada, Sept. 26, 1930; s. John Richard and Olive (McCreath) H.; m. Patricia Hockridge, Aug. 20,7 1954. B.A., U. B.C., 1952. With Shell Oil Co. of Can. Ltd., 1952-53; dir. sales devel. Can. Pacific Airlines, Vancouver, 1953-64; sr. v.p. Pacific div. T. Eaton Co., Ltd., Vancouver, 1964-81; pres. Vancouver Stock Exchange, 1982—; bd. dirs. Bird Constrn., British Pacific Properties Ltd.; bd. dirs. Internat. Fin. Centre, Vancouver; bd. govs. Vancouver Stock Exchange; mem. adv. bd. Sta. KCTS, Seattle. Mem. adv. council faculty Commerce and Bus. Adminstrn. U. B.C.; bd. dirs. Can. com. Pacific Basin Econ. Council, Vancouver Bd. Trade, Council for Can. Unity; bd. govs. Simon Fraser U.; trustee Schenley awards; mem. B.C. and Yukon Council of The Duke of Edinburgh's Award in Can.; gen. campaign chmn. Allied Crusade Against Cancer. Mem. Niagara Inst. (adv. council). Club: Can. Club of Vancouver. Office: Vancouver Stock Exchange, Stock Exchange Tower, PO Box 10333, Vancouver, BC Canada V7Y 1H1

HUDSON, DOROTHY MORGAN, civic leader, business and political consultant; b. Omaha, May 23, 1928; d. Glover and Maria Elizabeth (Agee) Morgan; student U. Colo., 1967-68, Metropolitan State Coll., 1974-75, Colo. Women's Coll., 1979-80; cert. Equal Employment Opportunity Commn. Acad., 1975; 1 dau., Ronnette Marie Marshall Davis. Owner, propr. D.M.H. Enterprises; pres. City Park Sundries, 1980-83; investigator, conciliator Colo. Equal Opportunity Commn., Denver, 1974-75, pay audit technician Air Force Finance Center, Denver, 1956-74; past owner Success Motivational INst., Inc., Waco, Tex. Motivation. Committeewoman, Democratic party; mem. New Dem. Coalition; mem. Gary's Guerrilla's (Gary Hart for Pres. group). neighborhood task force rep. Denver City Council. Recipient cert. of honor City of Denver, 1976, Colo. Centennial-Bicentennial Archivist Pin, 1976; named Colo. Outstanding Woman of Yr., 1979. Mem. NAACP, Nat. Council Negro Women, Colo. Black Women for Polit. Action, Nat. Assn. Ret. Fed. Employees, Nat. Profl. Writers Club, Nat. Fedn. Bus. and Profl. Women's Clubs, Nat. Assn. Female Execs. (rep. Nat. Ind. Bus. Assn.), Denver LWV (bd. dirs. 1977-78, editor newsletter), Colo. State League Women Voters (dir., state editor 1983), Colo. Press Assn., Adult Edn. Council Met. Denver, Am. Assn. Retired Persons, Internat. Trade Assn. Imports-Exports, Nat. Soc. Notaries, Greater Park Hill Community, Inc., Sigma Gamma Chi. Baptist. Clubs: Denver Jane Jefferson, Denver Century.

HUDSON, EDWARD GORDON, real estate development corporation executive; b. Seattle, Feb. 20, 1950; s. Edward S. and Ruth (Gordon) H.; m. Karen L. Bennett, Oct. 15, 1977 (dec. Dec. 1981). BBA, U. Wash., 1973, MBA, 1974. Project mgr. McKern Devel. Co., San Mateo, Calif., 1974-77; v.p. Demonet Industries, Los Angeles, 1977-84; pres. Hudson Devel. Co., Anaheim, Calif., 1984—; cons. Town & Country Constrn. Co., Sacramento, 1981—. Vol., Mission Rescue Ctr., Los Angeles, 1980—, Am. Cancer Soc., Los Angeles, 1981—. Home: 10505 Sandal Ln Bel Aire CA 90077

HUDSON, EDWARD VOYLE, linen supply company executive; b. Seymour, Mo., Apr. 3, 1915; s. Marion A. and Alma (Von Gonten) H.; student Bellingham (Wash.) Normal Coll., 1933-36, also U. Wash.; m. Margaret Carolyn Greely, Dec. 24, 1939; children—Edward G., Carolyn K. Asst. to mgr. Natural Hard Metal Co., Bellingham, 1935-37; partner Met. Laundry Co., Tacoma, 1938-39; propr., mgr. Peerless Laundry & Linen Supply Co., Tacoma, 1939—; propr. Independent Laundry & Everett Linen Supply Co., 1946-74, 99 Cleaners and Launderers Co., Tacoma, 1957-79; chmn. Tacoma Public Utilities, 1959-60; trustee United Mut. Savs. Bank; bd. dirs. Tacoma Better Bus. Bur., 1977—. Pres., Wash. Conf. on Unemployment Compensation, 1975-76; pres. Tacoma Boys' Club, 1970; v.p. Puget Sound USO, 1972—; elder Emmanuel Presbyn. Ch., 1974—; past campaign mgr., pres. Tacoma-Pierce County United Good Neighbors. Recipient Distinguished Citizen's cert. U.S. Air Force Mil. Airlift Com., 1977; U.S. Dept. Def. medal for outstanding public service, 1978. Mem. Tacoma Sales and Mktg. Execs. (pres. 1957-58), Pacific NW Laundry, Dry Cleaning and Linen Supply Assn. (pres. 1959, treas. 1965—), Internat. Fabricare Inst. (dir. dist. 7 treas. 1979, pres. 1982), Am. Security Council Bd., Tacoma C. of C. (pres. 1965), Air Force Assn. (pres. Tacoma chpt. 1976-77, v.p. Wash. state 1983-84, pres. 1985-86), Navy League, Puget Sound Indsl. Devel. Council (chmn. 1967), Assn. U.S. Army (Tacoma-Ft. Lewis-Olympia Army Assn. (past pres.) Republican. Clubs: Elks (vice chmn. bd. trustees 1984, chmn. 1985-86), Shriners (potentate 1979), Rotary, Masons, Scottish Rite, Tacoma, Tacoma Country and Golf, Jesters, Rotary (pres. Tacoma chpt. 1967-68), Tacoma Knife and Fork (pres. 1964). Home: 3901 N 37th St Tacoma WA 98407 Office: Peerless Laundry & Linen Supply Co 2902 S 12th St Tacoma WA 98405

HUDSON, RANDOLPH MURRAY, JR., electrical engineer; b. Richmond, Va., July 7, 1948; s. Randolph Murray Sr. and Vernelle Elizabeth (Williams) H.; m. Joyce Louise Hoyle, May 31, 1974 (div. Dec. 1984). BS in Sociology, Va. Poly. Inst. and State U., 1970, BSEE, 1977, MSEE, 1979. 1st class lic. radiotelephone. Chief engr. Blacksburg-Christianburg (Va.) Broadcasting Co., 1972-74; ptnr. Zorch Electronics, Blacksburg, 1974-77; engr. research and devel. dept. Hewlett-Packard, Loveland, Colo., 1979—; mem. adv. panel Electronics Internat. mag., N.Y.C., 1974, 75; vis. scientist Loveland Pub. Schs., 1985-86. Edn. and publicity chmn. bikeways adv. com. City of Loveland, 1986—; active Colo. Head Injury Found., Ft. Collins, 1986—. Mem. AAAS, Internat. Tesla Soc., Bicycle USA, Loveland Bicycle Club (publicity dir. 1981—). Avocations: bicycling, audio systems, home computers. Home: 620 W 2d St Loveland CO 80537 Office: Hewlett-Packard 815 14th St SW Loveland CO 80537

HUDSON, SAMUEL EUGENE, JR., chemist, researcher; b. Fresno, Calif., Dec. 30, 1946; s. Samuel Eugene and Frances Hope (Dorfmeier) H.; m. Donna Lee Harder, Sept. 9, 1967. BS, Calif. State U., Fresno, 1968, M, 1984; postgrad., U. Calif., Santa Cruz, 1986—. Assoc. engr. The Boeing Co., Seattle, 1969-70; chemist United Vintners, Madera, Calif., 1970-71; chief chemist milling div. Carnation Co., Fresno, 1971-86. Mem. Am. Chem. Soc., Assn. Analytical Chemists. Club: Fresno Airways Golf and Country. Avocation: golf. Home: 363 W Vartikian Fresno CA 93704

HUDSON, THOMAS RUSSELL, JR., advertising executive; b. Dalles, Oreg., Nov. 11, 1921; s. Thomas R. and Florence Christina (Koontz) H.; m. Pauline Gordon, Apr. 7, 1947; children—Thomas E., Heidi Hudson Baer. B.S., U. Oreg., 1943. Ins. agt. Thomas R. Hudson Ins., The Dalles, Oreg., 1947-68; newspaper pub. Blue Mountain Eagle, John Day, Oreg., 1968-69; advt. display salesman Medford Mail Tribune (Oreg.), 1969-72, advt. mgr., 1972-86. Regent Boys and Girls Aid Soc. of Oreg., 1976—; bd. dirs. Jackson County chpt. ARC, 1982-85; bd. dirs. Jacksonville Hwy. Water Dist., 1978—, Jackson County Legal Services, 1979—; mem. Oreg. Ho. of Reps., 1951-53. Served to capt. inf. U.S. Army, 1943-46. Mem. Sigma Delta Chi. Republican. Episcopalian. Clubs: Rotary, Masons, Elks. Home: 3255 Hollywood Ave Medford OR 97501 Office: Medford Mail Tribune 33 N Fir St Medford OR 97501

HUEBNER, TED RAYMOND, lawyer; b. Portage, Wis., Feb. 6, 1950; s. William Joseph and Agnes (Lytle) H.; m. Wendy Ann Lansing, May 20, 1979; children: Julie Kim, Katie Michelle, Michael Scott. BS, U. Minn., 1972; JD, UCLA, 1975. Bar: Calif. 1975. Assoc. Ansell & Ansell, Los Angeles, 1975-77, McLaughlin & Irvin, Los Angeles, 1977-79; ptnr. Lober, Clark & Huebner, Los Angeles, 1979-83, Huebner & Hirshfield, Los Angeles, 1983—. Mem. Los Angeles County Bar Assn., U. Minn. Alumni Assn., Beta Gamma Sigma, Delta Sigma Pi. Avocations: golf, flower gardening, creative writing. Office: Huebner & Hirshfield 6380 Wilshire Blvd #1115 Los Angeles CA 90048

HUEMER, RICHARD PETER, physician; b. Hollywood, Calif., June 16, 1933; s. Richard Martin and Mariette Prevosto H.; m. Gloria Wong, Dec. 17, 1964; children: Peter, Ariana, Michael, David. BA, Pomona Coll., 1954; MD, UCLA, 1958. Intern Wadsworth VA Hosp., Los Angeles, 1958-59; research fellow Calif. Inst. Tech., Pasadena, 1962-67; chief devel. biology and exptl. gerontology divs. VA Hosp., Sepulveda, Calif., 1965-71; chief profl. services Las Virgenes Med. Group, Woodland Hills, Calif., 1971-73; assoc. physician J.D. Walters, M.D., Sherman Oaks, Calif., 1974-76; practice medicine specializing in metabolic nutrition Thousand Oaks, Calif., 1976—. Author: Roots of Molecular Medicine: A Tribute to Linus Pauling, 1986; co-author The Healthy Heart Chart, 1985, Nutrition 21, 1985; mem. editorial bd. Mechanisms of Aging and Development, Jour. Applied Nutrition, 1987—; columnist health mag.; assoc. editor Jour. Internat. Acad. Preventive Medicine. Mem. Los Angeles County task force on Nutrition; former chmn. Los Angeles chpt. Com. Responsibility for War-injured Children. Served to capt. M.C. USAR, 1959-61. Recipient CARE award APFRI, 1974; Am. Cancer Inst. grantee, 1962-64. Mem. AAAS, N.Y. Acad. Scis., Am. Aging Assn., Orthomolecular Med. Soc. (pres. 1982-83), Sigma Xi. Avocation: microcomputers. Home: PO Box 7 Agoura CA 91301 Office: 99 Long Ct Thousand Oaks CA 91360

HUESTIS, LYNN GORDON, computer specialist; b. Hollywood, Calif., Jan. 4, 1942; s. Gordon Spencer and Virginina Earl (Woodbury) H.; m. Kathy O'Barr, Sept. 27, 1969 (div. Jan. 1970); m. Aida Cenia Merino, Aug. 13, 1984; children: Marvin Romero, Erick Romero. With sales, cons. Apple ComputerComputer/Apple, Santa Fe Springs, Calif., 1978-80; computer programmer, cons. Hughes Aircraft, Long Beach, Calif., 1980-86, with file transfer program, 1986—; computer cons., Buena Park, Calif., 1982-85. Vol. Brentwood Psychiat. Hosp., Westwood, Calif., 1968; vol. emergency St. Joseph Hosp., 1985-86; food distbr. La Palma (Calif.) Park, 1977. Club: T-Timers (Santa Monica, Calif.) (sec. 1963-64). Home: 1426 W Richland Ave Santa Ana CA 92703 Office: Hughes Aircraft Co 1501 Hughes Way Long Beach CA 90810

HUESTIS, STEPHEN PORTER, geology educator; b. Berkeley, Calif., Sept. 11, 1946; s. Charles Benjamin and Kathryn (Porter) H.; m. Deidra Anne Olds, July 30, 1977; 1 stepchild, Gwyneth Anne Cadenhead. BS in Physics, Harvey Mudd Coll., 1968; MS in Earth Sci., U. Calif., San Diego, 1969, PhD in Earth Sci., 1976. Lectr. engring. geosci. U. Calif., Berkeley, 1976-77; asst. research geophysicist U. Calif., San Diego, 1977; asst. prof. geology U. N.Mex., Albuquerque, 1977-83, assoc. prof., 1983—; instr. Sandia Nat. Labs., Albuquerque, 1980-86; collaborator Los Alamos (N.Mex.) Nat. Lab., 1985—. Contbr. articles to profl. jours. Served with U.S. Army, 1969-71. Fellow Royal Astron. Soc.; mem. Am. Geophys. Union, Sigma Xi. Avocations: sailboarding, banjo. Home: 444 Aliso NE Albuquerque NM 87108 Office: U N Mex Dept Geology Albuquerque NM 87131

HUEY, WILLIAM EDWARD, food products broker, career consultant, writer; b. Lakewood, Ohio, Apr. 14, 1930; s. William Edward and Virginia (Higgins) H.; B.A., Dartmouth, 1952. Sales rep. Mobil Oil Corp., Los Angeles, Tacoma, 1954-56; partner Elmer Langguth Brokearge Co., San Francisco, 1957-75; partner Forrest Randolph Co., San Francisco, 1957-75; cons. Dalgety Ltd., San Francisco and London, 1976-79; internat. sales/mktg. exec. William Sherman Co., San Rafael, Calif., 1980-85; with Hay Career Cons., San Francisco, 1986—. Adviser, Black boys clubs, San Francisco, 1959—; mem. Job Therapy Calif., Spl. Com. on Parolee Employment, San Quentin; pres. bd. dirs. Booker T. Washington Community Service Center. Served with USNR, 1952-54 (Korea), 61-62 (Vietnam). Mem. U.S. Navy League, World Affairs Council No. Calif., Kappa Sigma. Mason (32 deg., Shriner), Elk. Clubs: Dartmouth of California, Commonwealth of California (San Francisco); W. Atwood Yacht (Los Angeles). Co-editor: San Franciscan, 1960-61. Contbr. articles to Future, house organ U.S. Jr. C. of C.; editor internat. newsletter Greenline, Export Fedn. Home: 2586 Las Gallinas Ave San Rafael CA 94903 Office: Hay Career Cons 44 Montgomery St Suite 2550 San Francisco CA 94104

HUFEN, THEODORUS HENDRIKUS, educator, chemist; b. Utrecht, The Netherlands, Sept. 22, 1934; came to U.S., 1963; s. Wilhelmus Hubertus and Johanna Gertruida (Pessel) H.; m. Marion Kawaipuelani Ah Ping, July 29, 1967; 1 child, William K. BS in Chemistry, U. Hawaii, 1967, MS in Chemistry, 1969, PhD in Geoscis., 1974. Research assoc. Hawaii Inst. Geophysics, Honolulu, 1974-77; asst. researcher Water Resource Research Ctr., Honolulu, 1977-79; lectr. in chemistry Leeward Community Coll., Pearl City, Hawaii; instr. in chemistry Honolulu Community Coll., 1980—. Recipient Excellence in Teaching award U. Hawaii, 1985. Mem. Am. Chem. Soc. Avocations: classical music, gardening. Office: Honolulu Community Coll 874 Dillingham Blvd Honolulu HI 96817

HUFF, G. BRADLEY, educator; b. Endicott, N.Y., June 11, 1940; s. Willard Nettleton and Cornelia Kathryn (Bradley) H.; m. Hari Ellen Rabin, June 16, 1963; children: Amy Aileen, Jenny Kathryn. AB, Hamilton Coll., 1962; MA in Teaching, Harvard U., 1963; MS, U. Wash., 1970, PhD, 1972. Master The Pingry Sch., Elizabeth, N.J., 1963-68; asst. prof. physics Hamilton Coll., Clinton, N.Y., 1972-75, SUNY, Geneseo, 1975-78; tchr. sci. Geneseo Cen. Sch., 1978-85; tchr., specialist Fresno (Calif.) Unified Sch. Dist., 1985—; research assoc. U. Pitts., 1973-75; adj. instr. SUNY-Geneseo, 1978-85. Contbr. articles to profl. jours. Grantee SUNY awards com., Albany, 1976, 77. Mem. AAAS, Am. Assn. Physics Tchrs. (resource agt. 1985), Nat. Council Tchrs. of Math., Nat. Sci. Tchrs. Assn., Soc. Preservation and Encouragement of Barbershop Quartet Singing in Am., Calif. Sci. Teacher's Assn. (exec. bd. dirs. 1986—), Odyssey of the Mind Assn. (state dir. 1987—), Phi Delta Kappa (found. rep. 1984-85). Avocations: barbershop quartet singing. Home: 1637 W Morris Fresno CA 93711 Office: Fresno Unified Sch Dist Tulare and M Sts 3d floor Fresno CA 93721

HUFF, KENNETH O., oilfield executive, geologist; b. Daleville, Ind., Dec. 17, 1926; s. George Byron and Mary Ethel (Smith) H.; m. Donna Mae Zimmerschied, Mar. 25, 1957; children—John, Robert, Donald, Patricia. Student Purdue U., 1944-45, Ball State U., 1947-48; B.S. in Geology, Ind. U., 1956. Well logging engr. Core Labs., Inc., Williston, N.D. and Farmington, N.Mex., 1956-64, lab. mgr., sales engr. Farmington and Casper, Wyo., 1964-67, supr. Rocky Mountain dist., Casper, 1967-69, cons. geologist, 1969-72; pres. cons. geologist Adventures, Inc., Casper, 1972—; mem. dist. export council U.S. Dept Commerce, Wyo., 1977-83. Patentee in field. Served as sgt. U.S. Army, 1944-46, 50-51; Korea. Mem. Soc. Petroleum Engrs., Am. Assn. Petroleum Geologists, Wyo. Geol. Assn., Rocky Mountain Assn. Petroleum Geologists. Republican. Club: Petroleum (Casper). Home: 1106 Payne St Casper WY 82609 Office: Adventures Inc 535 N Lennox St Casper WY 82601

HUFF, KENNETH ROBERT, neurologist, neurochemist; b. Indpls., Feb. 18, 1949; s. Marvin Kenneth and Dorothy Elizabeth (Schabacker) H.; m. Myrna Lyngritt VandenEykel, Oct. 7, 1978. BA, Wabash Coll., 1970; MD, Johns Hopkins U., 1974. Diplomate Nat. Bd. Med. Examiners, Am. Bd. Pediatrics, Am. Bd. Psychiatry and Neurology. Fellow, intern, then resident in pediatrics Johns Hopkins U., Balt., 1974-76; research assoc. NIH, Bethesda, Md., 1976-79; fellow in neurology Harvard U., Boston, 1979-82, fellow in pathology, 1982-83; asst. prof. neurology U. So. Calif. Sch. Medicine, Los Angeles, 1983—; neurology cons. Rancho Los Amigos Hosp., Downey, 1984—. Contbr. articles to profl. jours. Med. missionary Presbyn. Ch., Socorro, Columbia, 1978. Served to lt. comdr. USPHS, 1976-79.

Recipient Tchr. Investigator Devel. award NIH, 1985. Mem. AAAS, Am. Acad. Neurology, Child Neurology Soc., Am. Soc. Neurochemistry, Soc. Neurosci., Computer Users Group, Phi Beta Kappa, Sigma Xi. Democrat. Avocations: sports, jogging, gardening. Home: 1946 Calafia St Glendale CA 91208 Office: Children Hosp Los Angeles Div Neurology 4650 Sunset Blvd Los Angeles CA 90027 Office: U So Calif Sch Medicine Los Angeles CA 90027

HUFF, MARY ANN, mechanical engineer; b. Portland, Maine, May 30, 1953; d. Robert Eugene and Lois Mabel (Southard) Chute; m. Dennis Michael McGee, Feb. 14, 1975 (div. Aug. 1978); m. Randall Leroy Huff, June 4, 1983; children: Anna May, Jesse Patrick. BSME, U. Maine, 1975; postgrad., Bradley U., Ill. Cen. Community Coll., U. Wash. Registered profl. mech. engr., Wash. Design engr. Caterpillar Tractor Co., Peoria, Ill., 1975-78; sales engr. Dana Corp., Toledo, 1978-80; sr. engr. Team Engring., Tacoma, 1980-81; sr. energy engr. Trans Energy Systems, Bellevue, Wash., 1981-83; sr. engr. Brown & Caldwell, Seattle, 1983-84; prin. Chute Engring., Seattle, 1983—. Patentee in field. Mem. Womens Minority Bus. Enterprise com. Seattle Pub. Schs., 1983—; v.p. Des Moines (Wash.) Parents-Students-Tchrs.-Assn., 1982-83. Named an Outstanding Younger Mem., Soc. Automotive Engrs., 1976). Mem. Soc. Women Engrs. (sr., pres. 1982-83, Disting. New Engr. 1984), ASHRAE, ASME, NSPE, AAUW, Cons. Engrs. Council Wash. (prin.). Avocations: swimming, rafting. Office: Chute Engring 3914 Midvale Ave N Seattle WA 98103

HUFF, NORMAN NELSON, educator; b. San Diego, Apr. 22, 1933; s. George Kleineberg Peabody and Norma Rose (Nelson) H.; B.S., San Diego State U., 1957; cert. UCLA, 1972; M.B.A., Golden Gate U., 1972; A.A., bus. cert., Victor Valley Coll., 1972; m. Sharon Kay Lockwood, Sept. 30, 1979. Chemist, Convair, San Diego, 1954-55, astrophysicist, 1955-56; mgmt. trainee, chem. engr. U.S. Gypsum Co., Plaster City, Calif., 1957-58; instr. data processing Victor Valley Coll., Victorville, Calif., 1967-70, chmn. data processing, 1970-81; owner High Desert Data Systems, 1972-82; mgmt. info. systems cons. Pfizer Inc., 1970-72, Mojave Water Agy. Calif., 1972-74. Served with USNR, 1950-54, to capt. USAF, 1954-67; Vietnam. Recipient Presdl. Achievement award, 1982, Presdl. Medal of Merit, 1983. Mem. Calif. Ednl. Computing Consortium, Am. Mgmt. Assn., Calif. Bus. Edn. Assn. (treas. 1967-73), Inst. Aero. Sci. (pres. 1956-57), Soaring Soc. Am. (life). Author 4 computer sci. texts. Office: 16173 Rimrock Rd Apple Valley CA 92307

HUFF, RAY VINCENT, mining industry executive, consultant; b. Centralia, Ill., Jan. 28, 1935; s. A.H. and Helen Marie (Bowlds) H.; divorced; 1 child, Tammy R. Stevens. BS, Mo. Sch. Mines, 1958; MS, Tulsa U., 1969. Registered profl. engr., Okla. Project engr. U.S. Bur. of Mines, Bartlesville, Okla., 1958-70; ops. mgr. Kennecott, Lexington, Mass., 1970-77; cons. H.K. van Poollen & Assocs., Littleton, Colo., 1977-79; project mgr. Occidental Minerals, Lakewood, Colo., 1979-82; cons. mining industry Golden, Colo., 1982—; pres., dir. ISL Ventures, Golden. Contbr. tech. articles to jours.; patentee in field. Mem. AIME. Club: La Clef D'or (Denver). Avocations: skiing, music, dancing, financial investing. Office: PO Box 1310 Golden CO 80402

HUFFMAN, JAMES CURTIS, foundation executive; b. Evansville, Ind., Nov. 23, 1941; s. Hugh Curtis and Emily Louise (Karn) H.; m. Susan Marie Coyle, Dec. 30, 1983; children: Scott Curtis, Jaime Laurine, Laura Marie. BSBA, U. Denver, 1963; M in Govt. Adminstrn., Ga. State U., 1972. Sales adminstr. Cities Service Co., Atlanta, 1969-71; account rep. Graphic Scis., Inc., Atlanta, 1971-72; eastern regional dir. Adventure Unltd., Atlanta, 1972-75; nat. devel. dir. Adventure Unltd., Denver, 1975-78; pres., exec. dir. Asher Found., Denver, 1978—; bd. dirs. Albert Baker Fund, San Francisco. Served to capt. USNR. Avocations: actor, comml. pilot, flight instructor. Office: Asher Student Found 6312 S Fiddlers Green Circle Suite 420N Englewood CO 80111

HUFFMAN, MARK PAUL, choreographer, educator; b. Bowling Green, Ohio, Nov. 9, 1959; s. Paul Richard and Sarah Jean (Bowers) H.; m. Joyette Speirs. BA in Dance Performance, Brigham Young U., 1983, MA in Choreography, 1986. Dancer Dancer's Co., Provo, Utah, 1979-84, tchr., movement edn., 1980-84; dance tchr. Brigham Young U., Provo, 1980-86, asst. dir., 1981-84; asst. choreographer World's Fair Expo '84, New Orleans, 1984; choreographer Internat. Spl. Olympics, Salt Lake City, 1985, Jackson (Wyo.) Hole Playhouse, 1986. Artistic dir., choreographer (performance) Young Ambassadors, 1984—; choreographer (performance) Lamanite Generation, 1984—. Mormon. Home: 667 S 300 W Orem UT 84058 Office: Brigham Young U 26 KMB Provo UT 84602

HUFFMAN, NONA GAY, investment retirement specialist; b. Albuquerque, June 22, 1942; d. William Abraham and Opal Irene (Leaton) Crisp; m. Donald Clyde Williams, Oct. 20, 1961; children—Debra Gaylene, James Donald. Student pub. schs. Lawndale, Calif. Lic. ins., securities dealer, N.Mex. Sec. City of Los Angeles, 1960, Los Angeles City Schs. 1960-62, Aerospace Corp., El Segundo, Calif., 1962-64, Albuquerque Pub. Schs., 1972-73, Pub. Service Co. N.Mex., Albuquerque, 1973; rep., fin. planner Waddell & Reed, Inc., Albuquerque, 1979-84; broker Rauscher Pierce Refsnes, Inc., 1984-85; rep., investment and retirement specialist Fin. Network Investment Corp., 1985—; tchr. money mgmt. seminars for sr. citizens ctr. Mem. Profl. Orgn. Women (co-chmn.), Women in Bus. (Albuquerque chpt.), Internat. Assn. Fin. Planners. Office: Fin Network Investment Corp One Exec Ctr 8500 Menaul Blvd NE Suite A-301 Albuquerque NM 87112

HUGHES, ALICE MARLENE, accounts manager; b. Peru, Nebr., Mar. 16, 1935; d. George Dewey and Lela (Gerdes Jones) H.; children: Kathleen, Louise, Steve, Judith. With Fred Meyer Inc., Portland, Oreg., 1970—, asst. buyer, 1975-80, buyer, 1980-83, buyer asst., 1983-86; sales specialist K.H. Jones and Co., Inc., Federal Way, Wash., 1986-87; accounts mgr. Matthews Candy Co., Seattle, 1987—. Lutheran. Home: 2411 SE 105 Portland OR 97216

HUGHES, ALLAN BEBOUT, chamber of commerce executive; b. Boston, June 30, 1924; s. Edwin Holt and Gladys B. (Bebout) H.; m. Margery H. Hall, Dec. 27, 1947; children: Katherine, Lee Ann, Melinda, Sally. BA, Depauw U., 1947. Commd. USMCR, 1942, advanced through grades to col., 1970; ret. USMC, 1984; sales rep. ADT Co., Los Angeles, 1954-64; sales mgr. Ernest Paper Co., Los Angeles, 1964-68; mdse. mgr. BM&T Paper Co., Los Angeles, 1968-70; pres. Hughes Paper Co., Anaheim, Calif., 1970-82, Transpark, Inc., Anaheim, 1982-84; exec. dir. C. of C., Anaheim, from 1984. Alt. Rep. Cen. Com., Orange County, Calif., 1984-85; chmn. Fullerton (Calif.) Community Hosp.; vice chmn. Indsl. Devel. Bd., Anaheim; bd. dirs. Anaheim Meml. Hosp. Home: 18661 Eunice Pl Tustin CA 92680 Office: care Anaheim C of C 100 S Anaheim Blvd Suite 300 Anaheim CA 92805

HUGHES, BRADLEY RICHARD, mktg. exec.; b. Detroit, Oct. 8, 1954; s. John Arthur and Nancy Irene (Middleton) H.; AA, Oakland Coll., 1974; BS in Bus., U. Colo., 1978, BJ, 1979; MBA in Fin. and Mktg., 1981; MS in telecommunications Nova U., 1988; m. Linda McCants, Feb. 14, 1977; children: Bradley Richard Jr., Brian Jeffrey. Cert. Office Automation Profl. Buyer, Joslins Co., Denver, 1979; mktg. adminstr. Mountain Bell, Denver, 1980-82, tech. cons. AT&T Info. Systems, mktg. exec. AT&T, 1983-86, acct. exec., 1986-87; mktg. mgr. U.S. West, 1987—. Bd. dirs. Brandychase Assn.; state del., committeeman Republican Party Colo. Mem. Assn. MBA Execs., U.S. Chess Fedn., Internat. Platform Assn., Mensa, Intertel, Assn. Telecommunications Profls., Am. Mgmt. Assn., Am. Mktg. Assn., Info. Industry Assn., Office Automation Soc. Internat., World Future Soc. Republican. Methodist. Home: 5759 S Jericho Way Aurora CO 80015 Office: AT&T 6200 S Syracuse Englewood CO 80111

HUGHES, CAROLYN SUE, business executive; b. Cin., Sept. 30, 1945; d. LeRoy Millard and Betty Jane (West) Hughes; student Secord's Bus. Coll., 1963-64. With Shilliot's, Cin., 1964-65, R.L. Polk Co., Cin., 1965, Cin. and So. Bell Telephone Co., Cin., 1965-66; buyer Sterling Electric Motors, Los Angeles, 1966-67; credit union clk. Beckman Instruments, Fullerton, Calif., 1967-68; with Federated Dept. Stores, Cin., 1968-69, Macpro, Inc., Loveland, Ohio, 1969-71, Orange Coast Advt., Inc., Santa Ana, Calif., 1971-73; pvt. acct., Orange County, Calif., 1973-75; office mgr./acct. L. Blain Co., Paramount, Calif., 1975-77; controller Relkoff Constrn., Santa Ana, Calif., 1977; controller Framing Div., Warmington Devel., Irvine, Calif., 1977, Brattain Contractors, Inc., Santa Ana, 1977-78, McQueen Electric, Inc., Riverside, Calif., 1986—; v.p., controller L. Blain Co., Paramount, 1978-82; owner C.T. Constrn., Inc., Paramount, 1977—, Jer-Jon Motors, Inc., Garden Grove, Ca., 1976-79, Fine Line Co., Romoland, Calif., 1986—; ptnr. Quality Excavation and Heavy Equipment Rental, Romoland, 1986—; agt. Preston Trucking Co., Paramount, 1982-84, Fine Line Co., San Antonio, 1984—; notary pub., Calif. Licensed gen. contractor, Calif. Mem. Nat. Assn. Women in Constrn. (treas. 1978-79, pres. chpt. 1979-81, corr. sec. 1982-83), Nat. Notary Assn., Nat. Rifle Assn., Silver Lakes Assn., Smithsonian Assn., Nat. Assn. Female Execs., Internat. Platform Assn., Household Goods Forwarders. Club: N. Am. Hunt (charter). Home and Office: PO Box 1024 Romoland CA 92380

HUGHES, CHARLES CAMPBELL, anthropology educator; b. Salmon, Idaho, Jan. 26, 1929; s. Charles Frederick and Grace (Campbell) H.; m. Jane Ellen Murphy, Feb. 6, 1951 (div. July 1962); m. Patricia Diane Devereux, Aug. 8, 1964 (div. May 1969); m. Leslie Ann Medert, Mar. 7, 1970; children: John Charles Campbell, Calisse Marie. A.B. magna cum laude, Harvard Coll., 1951; M.A., Cornell U., 1953, Ph.D., 1957. Assoc. dir., sr. research assoc. Cornell Program in Social Psychiatry Cornell U., 1957-61; asst. prof. anthropology, dept. psychiatry Cornell U. Med. Coll., 1959-61; fellow Center for Advanced Study in Behavioral Scis., Stanford, Calif., 1961-62; dir. African Studies Center, Mich. State U., 1962-70, assoc. prof., 1962-64, prof. anthropology, 1964-73, prof. anthropology and psychiatry, 1970-73; prof. anthropology, chmn. behavioral sci. div. dept. family and community Medicine U. Utah Coll. Medicine, Salt Lake City, 1973-78; dir. MSPH program dept. family and community Medicine U. Utah Coll. Medicine, 1979—; Mem. behavioral sci. test com. Nat. Bd. Med. Examiners, 1973-77. Author: An Eskimo Village in the Modern World, 1960, (with others) People of Cove and Woodlot, 1960, Psychiatric Disorder Among the Yoruba, 1963; editor: Eskimo Boyhood: An Autobiography in Psychosocial Perspective, 1974, Make Men of Them: Introductory Readings for Cultural Anthropology, 1972, The Culture-Bound Syndromes: Folk Illnesses of Psychiatric and Anthropological Interest, 1985; editor: Custom-Made: Introductory Readings for Cultural Anthropology, 1975. Fellow Am. Anthrop. Assn., Soc. Applied Anthropology (pres. 1969-70), Am. Sociol. Assn., African Studies Assn., Arctic Inst. N.Am., AAAS; mem. Am. Ethnol. Soc., Assn. for Behavioral Sci. and Med. Edn. (dir. 1975-78, pres. 1979-80), Soc. for Med. Anthropology (pres. 1981-82), Assn. Grad. Programs in Preventive Medicine (pres.-elect 1986-87), Phi Beta Kappa, Sigma Xi, Phi Kappa Phi. Home: 7453 Enchanted Hills Dr Salt Lake City UT 84121

HUGHES, DAVID ROLLAND, retired air force officer, corporate executive; b. Honolulu, June 14, 1939; s. William R. and Jessie Marion (Twine) H.; m. Lynn P. Birkland; 1 son, Steven Rolland. B.S., Mont. State Coll., 1961; M.S., Air Force Inst. Tech., 1969; disting. grad. Air Command and Staff Coll., 1971-72; disting. grad. U.S. Army War Coll., 1977. Commd. U.S. Air Force, 1961, advanced through grades to col.; squadron comdr., 1977-79, base comdr. Howard AFB, Panama, 1980-82, dep. comdr. for resource mgmt. George AFB, Calif., 1983, ret., 1984; sr. program mgr. Perkin-Elmer Corp., Garden Grove, Calif., 1983—; mgmt. cons. Pres., Panama area Boy Scouts, 1982. Decorated Air Medal, Air Force Commendation medal with 4 oak leaf clusters, Purple Heart, Legion of Merit, Meritorious service medal with 5 oak leaf clusters, Airman's medal, others; recipient Panama Canal hon. pub. service award, 1982. Mem. Combat Control Assn., Air Force Assn., Red River Valley Fighter Pilots Assn., U.S. Parachute Assn., C. of C. (dir. 1979-80), Civil Air Patrol. Congregationalist. Clubs: Rotary, Antelope Valley Soaring (pres. 1987), Internat. Cartridge Collectors Assn. Contbr. articles to profl. jours. Home: 5422 Oxford Dr Cypress CA 90630 Office: Perkin-Elmer Applied Optics Div 7421 Orangewood Ave Garden Grove CA 92642

HUGHES, DOMINIC WILFRED, physiologist; b. Berlin, N.H., Aug. 10, 1939; s. Ermond Dominic and Stella Beatrice (Halle) H.; m. Ann Elizabeth Manion, June 28, 1963; children: Michael D., Patrick T., Heather A. BS, Wayne State U., 1968; MA, PhD, Columbia Pacific U., 1983. Research assoc. Wayne State U., Detroit, 1965-70; clin. technologist U. Chgo. Med. Sch., 1970-73; asst. prof. physiology Teikyo U. Med. Sch., Tokyo, 1973-76; physiologist Portland (Oreg.) Otologic Clinic, 1977-83; pvt. practice physiology West Linn, Oreg., 1983—; bd. dirs. Med. West Tech. Inc., Portland. Contbr. articles to profl. jours. Served with USAF, 1958-62. NIH grantee 1984. Mem. AAAS, Am. Neurotology Soc., Am. Auditory Soc., Nat. Hearing Conservation Assn. Avocations: classical music, photography, back packing. Home and Office: 5525 Broadway West Linn OR 97068

HUGHES, DUNCAN F., design engineer; b. Schenectady, N.Y., July 11, 1961; s. Alan F. and Helen A. (Slayton) H. SB, MIT, 1984. CRT design engr. Tektronix Inc., Beaverton, Oreg., 1984—. Episcopalian. Avocations: outdoor sports, aerobics, jazz dancing. Office: Tektronix Inc PO Box 500 MS 46-567 Beaverton OR 97077

HUGHES, EVERETT CLARK, otolaryngology educator; b. Wadena, Minn., Nov. 22, 1904; s. Albert B. and Pearl Sylpha (Moses) H.; m. Ruth Scherer, Aug. 3, 1907; children: Mary Alice (Mrs. Donald P. Allen), Kathleen (Mrs. Frederick D. Barker III), Robert, Bruce, Randolph. B.A. in Chemistry, Carleton Coll., Northfield, Minn., 1927; Ph.D., Cornell U., 1930. Research chemist Standard Oil Co. (O.), Cleve., 1930-44; chief chem. and phys. research div. Standard Oil Co. (O.), 1944-54, mgr. research div., 1954-60, v.p., 1960-69; research dir., assoc. clin. prof. dept. otolaryngology Sch. Medicine U. So. Calif., Los Angeles, 1970—. Contbr. articles profl. jours. Fellow A.A.A.S., Am. Inst. Chemists (chem. Pioneer of 1971 award); mem. Am. Chem. Soc. (Morley award and medal 1974), Phi Beta Kappa, Sigma Xi, Alpha Chi Sigma. Patentee in field. Home: 1225 Charles St Pasadena CA 91103 Office: Sch Medicine U So Calif Room 2P70 1200 N State St Los Angeles CA 90033

HUGHES, ISABELLA ANN, nursing educator; b. N.Y.C., July 1, 1943; d. Vincent and Sylvia (Stricker) Cordoni; m. Allan Joseph Hughes, July 3, 1965; children: Lisa Ann, Christopher Allan. RN, Muhlenberg Coll., 1964; postgrad., Cabrillo Coll., 1983; Pub. Health Nurse, San Jose State U., 1984; BS in Nursing, U. Phoenix, San Jose, Calif., 1986. Cert. community coll. tchr., Calif.; RN, Pub. Health Nurse. Nurse Dominican Hosp., Santa Cruz, Calif., 1979-80; supr. County Santa Cruz, 1980-83, Samaritan Home Services, Santa Cruz, 1983-84; dir. mktg., discharge planning Casa Serena Home Health Ctr., Aptos, Calif., 1984-86; with Vis. Nurses Assn., Aptos, Calif., 1986—; instr. ARC, Santa Cruz, 1983—; clin. instr. Cabrillo coll., Aptos, 1985—. Eucharistic minister St. Joseph's Ch., Capitola, Calif., 1984—, cantor 1984. Named Community Health Nurse of Yr., Casa Serena Home Health Ctr., 1985. Mem. Am. Nurses Assn. Democrat. Roman Catholic. Club: Quota (Santa Cruz). Avocations: singing, aerobics. Office: Cabrillo Coll 5500 Soquel Dr Aptos CA 95003

HUGHES, KIMBERLEY ANN, marketing manager; b. Santa Monica, Calif., July 20, 1954; d. Arthur Testle and Harriette Ruth (Steckel) H. Student, Stephens Coll.; AA, Fashion Inst. of Design and Merchandising; BA, Pepperdine U. Account exec. Leni Inc., Los Angeles, 1977-79; supr. direct mail project Bullocks Dept. Stores, Los Angeles, 1979-80; mgr. direct mail Weinstocks, Sacramento, 1980-82; mgr. direct mail Emporium Capwell, San Francisco, 1982-85, mktg. mgr., 1985—; guest speaker San Francisco State U., U. Calif., San Jose, Golden Gate U. Mem. Nat. Assn. Exec. Females, Spinsters of San Francisco, Am. Mktg. Assn. Republican. Congregationalist. Club: San Francisco Advt. Avocations: dancing, antique collecting, theater, music, films. Home: 265 Lombard St #210 San Francisco CA 94133 Office: Emporium Capwell 835 Market St San Francisco CA 94103

HUGHES, LANCE LEROY, small business owner; b. San Bernardino, Calif., Mar. 29, 1958; s. Kenneth Ray Hughes and Carol Ann (Rehwald) Klingberg. Student, Idaho State U., 1978-79, Seattle Cen. Coll., 1980-86. Ptnr. Jim's Cafe, Seattle, 1979-80; prin. J&L Saloon, Inc., Seattle, 1980-86, Lance L. Hughes Investment Co., Seattle, 1986-87; pres. Seattle-Eagle Inc., 1987—. Contbr. Ellis Island Found., 1984. Served with USN, 1976-78. Mem. Greater Seattle Bus. Assn. (founding), Dorian Soc., Nat. Eagle Scouts Assn. Avocations: gourmet cooking, botany. Office: 314 E Pike St Seattle WA 98122

HUGHES, MARY KATHERINE, lawyer; b. Kodiak, Alaska, July 16, 1949; d. John Chamberlain and Marjorie (Anstey) H.; m. Andrew H. Eker, July 7, 1982. B.B.A. cum laude, U. Alaska, 1971; J.D., Willamette U., 1974; postgrad. Heriot-Watt U., Edinburgh, Scotland, 1971. Bar: Alaska 1975. Ptnr., Hughes, Thorsness et al, Anchorage, 1974—; trustee Alaska Bar Found., pres., 1984—; bd. visitors Willamette U. Coll. Law, Salem, Oreg., 1980—; mem. Willamette Law Fund Leadership Com., 1981-83; bd. dirs. Alaska Repertory Theatre, 1986—, pres.-elect, 1987—; mem. Coll. of Fellows U. Alaska Found., 1985—. Mem. Alaska Bar Assn. (bd. govs. 1981-84, pres. 1983-84), Anchorage Assn. Women Lawyers (pres. 1976-77), AAUW, Delta Theta Phi. Republican. Roman Catholic. Club: Soroptimists (v.p. 1981-83, pres. 1986-87). Home: 2240 Kissee Ct Anchorage AK 99517 Office: Hughes Thorsness Gantz Powell & Brundin 509 W 3d Ave Anchorage AK 99501

HUGHES, ROBERT HARRISON, former agricultural products executive; b. Puunene, Hawaii, Mar. 23, 1917; s. Robert Edwin and Alice Thayer (Walker) H.; m. Nadine Jeannette Hegler, Aug. 24, 1940 (div. 1983); children: Robert Lawrence, Linton Alice, Carole Nadine.; m. Judith R. Gething, Jan. 28, 1983. B.Sc. in Sugar Tech, U. Hawaii, 1938. With Hawaiian Comml. & Sugar Co., 1939-65, sugar mill supt., 1951-63, prodn. mgr., 1963-65; v.p. tech. services C. Brewer & Co., Ltd., Honolulu, 1965-69; sr. v.p. Hawaiian ops. C. Brewer & Co., Ltd., 1969-77, exec. v.p., 1977-80, dir. subs., 1966-80; pres. Hawaiian Sugar Planters Assn., Aiea, 1981-85; dir. Mauna Loa Resources Inc., Hilo, 1986—. Bd. regents U. Hawaii, 1961-66; trustee Hawaii Conf. Found., 1966-85, Hawaii Loa Coll., 1980—; trustee U. Hawaii Found., 1963-65, 73-78, pres., 1967-68; bd. dirs. Hawaii Multi-Cultural Center, 1979-81; chmn. adv. bd. Cancer Center of Hawaii, 1979-81; pres. Hawaii conf. United Ch. of Christ, 1962-63. Mem. Hawaiian Sugar Planters Assn. (dir. 1972-80). Home: 7148 Kukii St Honolulu HI 96825 Office: PO Box 1057 Aiea HI 96701

HUGHES, ROBERT MERRILL, engineer; b. Glendale, Calif., Sept. 11, 1936; s. Fred P. and Gertrude G. (Merrill) H.; A.A., Pasadena City Coll., 1957; 1 dau., Tammie Lynn Cobble. Engr. Aerojet Gen. Corp., Azusa, Calif., 1957-64, 66-74; pres. Automatic Electronics Corp., Sacramento, 1964-66; specialist Perkin Elmer Corp., Pomona, Calif., 1974-75; gen. mgr. Hughes Mining Inc., Covina, Calif., 1975-76; project mgr. L&A Water Treatment, City of Industry, Calif., 1976-79; dir. Hughes Industries Inc., Alta Loma, Calif., 1979—; pres. Hughes Devel. Corp., Carson City, Nev.; chmn. bd. Hughes Mining Inc., Hughes Video Corp. Registered profl. engr., Calif. Mem. AIME, Nat. Soc. Profl. Engrs., Instrument Soc. Am., Am. Inst. Plant Engrs. Republican. Patentee in field. Home: 10039 Bristol Dr Alta Loma CA 91701 Office: Box 723 Alta Loma CA 91701

HUGHES, SHIRLEY ELIZABETH, real estate appraiser, state agency official; b. Weatherford, Okla., Dec. 23, 1947; d. Harry W. and Margaret L. (Williams) H.; m. Dennis M. McCary, Sept. 19, 1969 (div. July 1972). Student, Okla. State U., 1966-68, U. Okla., 1969, U. N.Mex., 1973-77; BA, Evergreen State Coll., 1983. Clk. State of Tex., Austin, 1969-70; clk. N.Mex. Pub. Service Co., Albuquerque, 1970-72, property researcher, 1972-77, right-of-way agt., 1977; right-of-way agt. Wash. Dept. Transp., Olympia, 1978-84, staff appraiser, 1984—. Mem. Internat Fedn. Profl. and Tech. Engrs.

HUGHES, THOMAS HENRY, electronics company executive; b. Orland, Calif., May 11, 1937; s. Lionel Vernon and Anne Margaret (Heitman) H.; m. Dianne Maureen Corey, Aug. 19, 1968; children: Kimberly, Terri. AA, Diablo Valley Jr. Coll., 1972; BS, San Jose State U., 1980. Projectionist Stamm Theater, Antioch, Calif., 1960-62; draftsman Gen. Electric Corp., San Leandro, Calif., 1962-66; designer, master tech., elec. engr. Varian Corp., Palo Alto, Calif., 1966-82; sr. elec. engr. Beckman (Spinco), Palo Alto, 1982—. Served with USN, 1955-59. Democrat. Avocations: stamp collecting, camping, bowling, archery, chess. Office: Beckman Inst 1050 Page Mill Rd Palo Alto CA 94304

HUGHES, THOMAS JOSEPH, mechanical engineering educator, consultant; b. Bklyn., Aug. 3, 1943; s. Joseph Anthony and Mae (Bland) H.; m. Susan Elizabeth Weh, July 1, 1972; children: Emily Susan, Ian Thomas, Elizabeth Claire. B.M.E., Pratt Inst., Bklyn., 1965; M.M.E., Pratt Inst., 1967; M.A. in Math., U. Calif.-Berkeley, 1974, Ph.D. in Engring. Sci., 1974. Mech. design engr. Grumman Aerospace, Bethpage, N.Y., 1965-66; research and devel. engr. Gen. Dynamics, Groton, Conn., 1967-69; lectr., asst. research engr. U. Calif.-Berkeley, 1975-76; assoc. prof. structural mechanics Calif. Inst. Tech., Pasadena, 1976-80; assoc. prof. mech. engring. Stanford U., Calif., 1980-82, prof., 1983—; chmn. div. applied mechanics Stanford U., 1984—; cons. in field. Author: A Short Course in Fluid Mechanics, 1976, Mathematical Foundations of Elasticity, 1983; editor: Nonlinear Finite Element Analysis of Plate and Shells, 1981, Computational Methods in Transient Analysis, 1983; editor Jour. of Computer Methods in Applied Mechanics and Engring., 1980—; contbr. numerous articles to profl. jours. Fellow Am. Acad. Mechanics, ASME (Melville medal 1979), ASCE (Huber prize 1978); mem. AIAA, Soc. Engring. Sci., Sigma Xi, Phi Beta Kappa. Office: Stanford U Div Applied Mechanics Durand Bldg Stanford CA 94305

HUGHES, W. JAMES, optometrist, public health administrator; b. Shawnee, Okla., Oct. 15, 1944; s. Willis J. and Elizabeth Alice (Nimohoyah) H. B.A. in Anthropology, U. Okla., 1966, M.A. in Anthropology, 1972; O.D., U. Houston, 1976; M.P.H., U. Tex., 1977. Lic. Optometrist, Okla., Tex., W. Va. Physician's asst., Houston, Dallas, 1969-70; teaching asst. in clin. optics U. Houston, 1973-74, contact lens research asst., 1974; Wesley Jessen Contact Lens Rep., 1974-76; extern eye clinic Tuba City Indian Hosp., 1975; teaching fellow pub. health optometry U. Houston, 1975-76; Indian Health Service optometrist, Eagle Butte, S.D., 1976; optometrist vision care project Crockett Ind. Sch. Dist., 1977; vision care program dir. Bemidji Area Indian Health Service, 1977-78; optometrist Navajo Area Indian Health Service, Chinle Health Ctr., 1978-79; adj. prof. So. Calif. Coll. of Optometry, Los Angeles, U. Houston Coll. of Optometry, 1978—, So. Coll. Optometry, Memphis, 1980—; optometrist Shiprock USPHS Indian Hosp., 1979—, chief vision care program; Navajo area Indian Health Service rep. to optometry career devel. com. USPHS. Served with U.S. Army, 1966-69. Decorated Bronze Star, Purple Heart. Recipient House of Vision award 1974; Community Health Optometry award 1976; Better Vision scholar, 1973-76. Mem. Am. Pub. Health Assn., Am. Optometric Assn., Tex. Optometric Assn. Commd. Officers Soc., Assn. Am. Indian Physicians, Beta Sigma Kappa. Democrat. Roman Catholic. Contbr. articles to profl. jours.

HUGHES, WILLIAM JOHN, chemical engineer; b. Redmond, Wash., Nov. 24, 1951; s. William Frances and Betty Mary (Howatson) H.; m. Peggy Anne Banich, June 29, 1974; one child, Bernadette Laura. BS, Seattle U., 1975; PhD, U. Idaho, 1982. Chem. engr., environ. engr. Data I/O Corp., Redmond, Wash., 1981—. Active Environ. Affairs Com., Redmond, 1985—. Mem. Am. Chem. Soc., AAAS, Am. Electroplaters Soc., Sigma Xi. Avocations: competitive running, gemology. Home: 3206 E Samm Rd NE Redmond WA 98053 Office: Data I/O Corp PO Box 97046 Redmond WA 98073

HUGHS, MARY GERALDINE, accountant, social service adminstr.; b. Marshalltown, Iowa, Nov. 28, 1929; d. Don Harold, Sr., and Alice Dorothy (Keister) Shaw; A.A., Highline Community Coll., 1970; B.A., U. Wash., 1972; m. Charles G. Hughs, Jan. 31, 1949; children—Mark George, Deborah Kay, Juli Ann, Grant Wesley. Asst. controller Moduline Internat., Inc., Chehalis, Wash., 1972-73; controller Data Recall Corp., El Segundo, Calif., 1973-74; fin. adminstr., acct. Saturn Mfg. Corp., Torrance, Calif., 1974-77; sr. acct., adminstrv. asst. Van Camp Ins., San Pedro, Calif., 1977-78; asst. adminstr. Harbor Regional Center, Torrance, Calif., 1979-87; active bookkeeping service, 1978—; instr. math. and acctg. South Bay Bus. Coll., 1976-77. Sec. Pacific N.W. Mycol. Soc., 1966-67; treas., bd. dirs. Harbor Employees Fed. Credit Union. Recipient award Am. Mgmt. Assn., 1979. Mem. Beta Alpha. Republican. Methodist. Club: Holiday Health Spas. Author: Iowa Auto Dealers Assn. Title System, 1955; Harbor Regional Center Affirmative Action Plan, 1980; Harbor Regional Center - Financial Format,

1978—; Provider Audit System, 1979; Handling Client Funds, 1983. Home: 18405 Haas Ave Torrance CA 90504

HUGLIN, HENRY CHARLES, writer, photographer, real estate broker; b. Fairfield, Iowa, Aug. 6, 1915; s. John Albert and Clara Lenore (Porter) H.; B.S., U.S. Mil. Acad., 1938; grad. Nat. War Coll., 1957; 1 son from previous marriage—Gregory Blake. Commd. 2d lt. U.S. Army, 1938, advanced through grades to brig. gen. USAF, 1959; comdr. bomb group PTO, World War II; assigned NATO, Europe and Washington, dep. U.S. rep. NATO Mil. Com., 1959-63; ret., 1964; sr. mil. scientist TEMPO, Gen. Electric Co., Santa Barbara, Calif., 1964-72; freelance syndicated newspaper columnist, 1972-77, scenic photographer, 1976—; real estate broker, 1980—. Decorated Legion of Merit, D.F.C., Bronze Star, Air Medal. Mem. N.Y. Council Fgn. Relations, Com. Fgn. Relations Santa Barbara. Episcopalian. Club: Channel City (Santa Barbara). Home and Office: 1427 Greenworth Pl Santa Barbara CA 93108

HUIZAR, HOPE ELAINE, mycologist, researcher; b. San Antonio, May 23, 1953; d. Alfred and Hope (Hernandez) H.; m. Joe David Hernandez; 1 child, Anita Elizabeth. BS in Biology, U. Tex, El Paso, 1975, MS in Biology, 1978; PhD in Microbiology, Ariz. State U., 1983. Electron microscope technician U. Tex., El Paso, 1976-78; teaching asst. Ariz. State U., Tempe, 1978-79, research asst., 1979-82, postdoctoral assoc., 1983-84, adj. research assoc., 1985—. Contbr. articles to sci. jours. Mem. Mycol. Soc. Am., Ariz. Soc. Electron Microscopy and Microbeam Analysis, Sigma Xi. Baptist. Avocations: swimming, jogging. Home: 4614 W Commonwealth Pl Chandler AZ 85226

HULBERT, BRUCE WALKER, corporate executive, banker; b. Evanston, Ill., Feb. 5, 1937; s. Bruce Walker and Mary Alice (Utley) H.; m. Linnette Ott, June 19, 1963; children: Christina, Jennifer, William. B.S. in Bus., Northwestern U., 1961. With 1st Interstate Bank of Calif., Los Angeles and San Francisco, 1962-78; pres., chief exec. officer, dir. First Interstate Bank of Denver, 1978-84; exec. v.p. Western Capital Investment Corp., 1984—. Mem. nat. bd. trustees, regional chmn. Inst. Internat. Edn., 1979—; adv. bd. Jr. League Denver, 1980—; trustee Denver Art Mus., 1985—, Loretto Heights Coll., 1983—; bd. dirs. Denver Partnership, 1978—, Denver Civic Ventures, Inc., 1982—, chmn., 1984-86; exec. bd. Denver Area council Boy Scouts Am., 1981—, Nat. Jewish Ctr. Immunology and Respiratory Medicine, 1982—, AMC Cancer Research Ctr., 1984—; bd. dirs., chmn., bd. trustees Mile High United Way, Denver; bd. dirs., exec. com. NCCJ, 1983—. Mem. Colo. Assn. Bank Holding Cos. (exec. com., dir., 1978-84), Denver Clearing House Assn. (pres. 1982-83), Denver C. of C. Republican. Clubs: Confrerie des Chevaliers du Tastevin, Cherry Hills Country, Denver Petroleum.

HULCE, JOSH T., merchant banking principal and executive, lawyer; b. Chelsea, Mich., Apr. 2, 1942; s. Elwin Leigh and Thelma Ursel (Bahnmiller) H.; m. Carol J., Nov. 27, 1964; 1 child, Hillary Megan. B.A., Northwestern U., 1964; J.D., U. Mich., 1967. Bar: Pa. 1967, Colo. 1975. Assoc. Pepper, Hamilton & Scheetz, Phila., 1967-72; assoc. corp. counsel Manville Corp., Denver, 1972-75, asst. to chmn. bd., 1976-79, v.p. purchasing, 1979-81, div. gen. mgr., 1981-82, pres. Johns-Manville Corp., 1982-84, pres. Manville Products Corp., 1983-84, pres., 1984-86; pres. Stephenson & Hulce, Merchant Bankers, 1986—. Mem. Colo. Bar Assn., Phi Delta Theta, Phi Delta Phi. Office: JT Hulce & Assocs Merchant Bankers Suite 3400 370 17th St Denver CO 80202

HULEN, MARJORIE JANE, med. center exec.; b. Denver, Sept. 23, 1921; d. Perry E. and Garnet W. (Doty) Kellogg; student pub. schs., Redondo Beach, Calif.; m. Ray Romaine Hulen, June 10, 1950; 1 child, Lynn Robert. With A. O. Smith Corp., Los Angeles, 1948-60, exec. sec., 1956-60; exec. sec. Sterling Electric Motors, Los Angeles, 1960-61; research sec. Pasadena (Calif.) Found. for Med. Research, 1961-65; exec sec. Profl. Staff Assn., Los Angeles County/U. So. Calif. Med. Center, Los Angeles, 1965-70, office mgr., 1970-74, bus. mgr., 1974-79, exec. dir., 1979—. Instl. rep. Los Angeles Regional Family Planning, 1977-79. Nat. Pub. Relations award Nat. Assn. Accts., 1979. Mem. Am. Soc. Assn. Execs., Nat. Secs. Assn., Soc. Research Adminstrs., Nat. Assn. Accts., Nat. Council Univ. Research Adminstrs., Assn. Ind. Research Insts., Nat. Assn. Female Execs. Democrat. Home: 2311 El Paseo St Alhambra CA 91803 Office: 1739 Griffin Ave Los Angeles CA 90031

HULET, ERVIN KENNETH, nuclear chemist; b. Baker, Oreg., May 7, 1926; s. Frank E. and Marjorie (Suiter) H.; m. Betty Jo Gardner, Sept. 10, 1949; children—Carri, Randall Gardner. B.S., Stanford U., 1949; Ph.D., U. Calif. at Berkeley, 1953. AEC grad. student U. Calif. Radiation Lab., Berkeley, Calif., 1949-53; research chemist nuclear chemistry div. Lawrence Livermore Nat. Lab., Livermore, Calif., 1953-66; group leader Lawrence Livermore Radiation Lab., Livermore, Calif., 1966—. Mem. internat. editorial bd. Jour. Lanthanide and Actinide Research. Served with USNR, 1944-46. Fulbright scholar Norway. Fellow AAAS, Am. Inst. Chemists; mem. Am. Chem. Soc. (chmn.-elect div. nuclear chemistry and tech., chmn. 1987), Am. Phys. Soc. Co-discoverer Element 106. Office: U Calif Lawrence Livermore Nat Lab L-232 PO Box 808 Livermore CA 94550

HULET, MICHAEL WILLIAM, safety engineer; b. Provo, Utah, Dec. 8, 1946; s. William A. and Bettie May (Danks) H.; m. Patricia L. Tibbitts, Jan. 30, 1970; children: John, Mary, Kimberly, Holly. BA in Polit. Sci., Brigham Young U., 1971. Safety supr. Morrison-Knudsen, Carbondale, Colo., 1973-77; sr. safety engr. EG&G Idaho, Idaho Falls, 1977-79; supr. safety and security ARCO Coal Co., Gillette, Wyo., 1979-80; corp. safety supt. AMS div. CM Inc., Denver, 1980-81; mgr. safety and tng. Coors Energy Co., Golden, Colo., 1981-84; sr. system safety engr. Rockwell Internat., Golden, Colo., 1984—; supr. system safety engring. United Techs. Corp., San Jose, Calif., 1986—. Chmn. Rep. precinct, Thornton, Colo., 1983. Served with U.S. Army, 1971-72. Mem. Am. Soc. Safety Engrs. (profl. chpt. v.p. 1980). Republican. Mormon. Avocations: tennis, geneological research, soccer referee, photography. Home: 2501 E 100th Way Thornton CO 80229

HULKOWICH, GARRETT JOHN, electrical engineer; b. Chgo., Nov. 17, 1955; s. John Anton and Mary Margaret (Matras) H. BSEE, Ill. Inst. Tech., 1977. Registered profl. engr., Colo., Wash. Elec. engr. Sargent & Lundy, Chgo., 1978-81; elec. engr. Stearns Catalytic Corp., Denver, 1981-83, analyst engring. dept., 1983-84, analyst elec. engring., 1984-85, mgr. elec. systems, 1985—; cons. elec. engr. AC Cons., Chgo., 1978-83. Bd. dirs. Ill. Pegis Found., Chgo., 1979—; mem. Jr. Achievement, Chgo. Named one of Outstanding Young Men of Am., 1985, V.P. of Sales Runner Up Jr. Achievement, Chgo., 1971. Mem. IEEE, Sigma Phi Epsilon (dist. gov. 1981—, Alumnus of Yr. Ill. Beta Chpt. 1980). Roman Catholic. Home: 601 Regency Dr Charlotte NC 28211

HULL, DAVID ALVIN, librarian, writer, educator; b. Pensacola, Fla., Aug. 23, 1943; s. Ira Cornelius and Emily (Reisen) H.; m. Jean Embrey Hull, Sept. 17, 1966; children: Katherine, Steven. BA, Westmont Coll., 1965; secondary teaching credential, U. Calif., Santa Barbara, 1967; MA, San Francisco State Coll., 1971; MLS, U. Calif., Berkeley, 1972. Tchr. Villanova Prep. High Sch., Ojai, Calif., 1967-70; prin. librarian Nat. Maritime Mus., San Francisco, 1972—. Author articles on maritime history, book revs., articles on museums and libraries. Editor: Sail and Steam, 1983; The Sea Letter, 1979-83. Founder, bd. dirs. Ship Press Chapel, 1980-84, Assocs. of J. Porter Shaw Library, 1982—; founder, Maple Ave. Community, Oakland, 1983. Nat. Mus. Act grantee, 1976; CETA grantee, 1977. Democrat. Presbyterian. Club: Dolphin (San Francisco). Home: 5290 Broadway Oakland CA 94602 Office: Library Nat Maritime Mus Bldg E 3d Floor Fort Mason San Francisco CA 94123

HULL, ELEANOR HORNER, writer, editor, cons.; b. Dallas; d. Lee Meridan and Frances (Connor) Horner; student So. Meth. U.; spl. courses Columbia U.; m. Leon Gay Hull, Aug. 23, 1921 (div. July 1948); 1 dau., Carol Jean (Mrs. Jack Raymond Clark). Free-lance advt. research, 1936-40, 41-42; promoter fashion booklets, copywriter, copyreader Sterling Agy., N.Y.C., 1942-44; supr. editor govt. tng. material War Dept. Q.M. Army Corps, 1944-45; account exec. copywriter Gussow-Kahn Advt. Agy., 1945-46; advt. mgr. Kramer Bros., 1945-46; publicity dir. Henry Glass & Co., 1946-50; pres. Shoulderite, Inc., 1946-51; instr. fashion dept., extension div. CCNY, 1951-63, supr. dept., 1959-63; lectr., instr. Traphagen Sch. Fashion, 1956-67; mem. staff Fashion Digest mag., 1957-67, assoc. editor, 1962-67. Served with motor corps ARC, 1942-45. Mem. Woman's Press Club, Alpha Omicron Pi. Patentee in field. Designer Flag of States. Home: 3131 N 7th Ave Phoenix AZ 85013

HULL, MCALLISTER HOBART, JR., university administrator; b. Birmingham, Ala., Sept. 1, 1923; s. McAllister Hobart and Grace (Johnson) H.; m. Mary Muska, Mar. 23, 1946; children: John McAllister, Wendy Ann. B.S. with highest honors, Yale, 1948, Ph.D. in Physics, 1951. From instr. to asso. prof. physics Yale U., 1951-66; prof. physics, chmn. dept. Oreg. State U., 1966-69; prof. physics, chmn. dept State U. N.Y. at Buffalo, 1969-72, dean Grad. Sch., 1972-74, dean. grad. and profl. edn., 1974-77; provost U. N.Mex., 1977-85, counselor to pres., 1985—; adviser to supt. schs., Hamden, Conn., 1958-65. Author papers, books, chpts. in books, articles in encys. Bd. dirs. Western N.Y. Reactor Facility, 1970-72; trustee N.E. Radio Obs. Corp., 1971-77; pres. Western Regional Sci. Labs., 1977; chmn. tech. adv. com. N.Mex. Energy Research Inst., 1981-83, mem., 1983—; co-chmn. Nat. Task Force on Ednl. Tech., 1984-86. Served with AUS, 1943-46. Faculty fellow Yale U., 1964-65. Fellow Am. Phys. Soc.; mem. Am. Assn. Physics Tchrs. (chmn. Oreg. sect. 1967-68). Address: U New Mexico Dept Physics and Astronomy Albuquerque NM 87131

HULL, SUZANNE WHITE, administrator, educator; b. Orange, N.J., Aug. 24, 1921; d. Gordon Stowe and Lillian (Siegling) White; m. George I. Hull, Feb. 20, 1943; children: George Gordon, James Rutledge, Anne Hull Cabello. B.A. with honors, Swarthmore Coll., 1943; M.S. in L.S., U. So. Calif., 1967. Mem. staff Huntington Library, Art Gallery and Botanical Gardens, San Marino, Calif., 1969—, dir. adminstrn. and pub. services, 1972-85, dir. pub. adminstrn. and edn., 1985—. Author: Chaste, Silent and Obedient, Books for Women, 1475-1640, 1982. Editor: State of the Art in Women's Studies, 1986. Charter pres. Portola Jr. High Sch. PTA, Los Angeles, 1960-62; pres. Children's Service League, 1963-64, YWCA Los Angeles, 1967-69; mem. community adv. council Los Angeles Job Corps Center for Women, 1972-78; mem. alumni council Swarthmore Coll., 1959-62, 83—; mem. adv. bd. Hagley Mus. and Library, Wilmington, Del., 1983—; hon. life mem. Calif. Congress Parents and Tchrs.; bd. dirs. Pasadena Planned Parenthood Assn., 1978-83, mem. adv. com., 1983—; founder-chmn. Swarthmore-Los Angeles Connection, 1984-85, bd. dirs., 1985—. Mem. Monumental Brass Soc. (U.K.), Renaissance Soc., Brit. Studies Conf., Beta Phi Mu (chpt. dir. 1981-84). Home: 1465 El Mirador Dr Pasadena CA 91103 Office: 1151 Oxford Rd San Marino CA 91108

HULLAR, THEODORE LEE, university chancellor; b. Mar. 19, 1935; m. Joan J. Miller, Aug. 2, 1958; children: Theodore W., Timothy E. BS with high distinction, U. Minn., 1957, PhD in Biochemistry, 1963. Asst. prof. medicinal chemistry SUNY, Buffalo, 1964-69, assoc. prof., 1969-75, assoc. dean grad. sch., 1969-71; dep. commr. programs and research N.Y. State Dept. Environ. Conservation, 1975-79; assoc. dir. Cornell U. Agrl. Experiment Sta., 1979-81, dir., 1981-84; assoc. dir. research N.Y. State Coll. Agriculture and Life Scis., Cornell U., 1979-81, dir. research, 1981-84; prof. natural resources Cornell U., 1981-84; exec. vice chancellor U. Calif., Riverside, 1984-85, chancellor, 1985-87; chancellor U. Calif., Davis, 1987—; adj. prof. natural resoucres Cornell U., 1979-81; chmn. hazardous waste mgmt. com. So. Calif. Assn. Govs., 1986-87, chmn. air quality task force, 1985-87, mem. regional adv. council, 1985-87; chmn. com. on environment Nat. Assn. State Univs. and Land Grant Colls., 1985—, com. on biotech., 1985—, chmn. program devel. subcom., 1985—; chmn. Gov. Deukmejian's Task Force on Toxics Waste and Tech., 1985-86; lectr. various orgns. Contbr. articles to profl. jours. Commr. Environ. Quality Erie County, N.Y., 1974-75; alternate to Gov. N.Y. on Delaware and Susquehanna River Basin Commns., 1975-79; mem. N.Y. State Agrl. Resources Commn., 1974-75; first chmn. Nat. Sierra Club Wilderness Conf., 1984; mem. Arlington Heights Greenbelt Study Com., 1986-87; mem. Monday Morning Group, 1985-87; active various community orgns. NSF postdoctoral fellow SUNY Buffalo, 1963-64. Mem. Am. Chem. Soc., AAAS, Chem. Soc. London, Regional Inst. So. Calif., Greater Riverside C. of C., (bd. dirs. 1985-87), Sigma Xi. Home: 16 College Park Davis CA 95616 Office: Univ Calif Office of the Chancellor Davis CA 95616

HULLIHEN, ALICE ALVINA, safety administrator; Mellette, S.D., Aug. 5, 1932; d. Henry and Alvina Magdalena (Heinert) Reister; m. Clair Wayne Rahn, Oct. 29, 1949 (dec.); m. 2d, Robert Gene Hullihen, July 28, 1979; children—Donna Jordan, Diane Hanson, James, Jerry. Student Black Hills (S.D.) State Coll., 1968-69, Glendale (Ariz.) Community Coll., 1978-79, Ariz. State U. Cert. safety engr. Asst. to supt. Hot Springs (S.D.) Pub. Schs., 1963-71, State S.D. Dept. Pub. Instrn., 1971-72; safety and health mgr. Holsum Bakery, Phoenix, 1980-85; sr. safety engr. Motorola Inc., Mesa, Ariz., 1985—; cons. fleet safety and accident prevention. Recipient Motor Fleet Safety award Continental Ins. Co., Outstanding Safety award Argonaut Ins. Cos., Accident Prevention and Motor Fleet award Charles Laubach & Co., Outstanding Safety and Accident Prevention award Ariz. Safety Assn. Mem. Ariz. Workers Compensation Assn., Internat. TV Assn., Am. Soc. Safety Engrs., Nat. Assn. Ednl. Office Personnel (nat. membership chmn. award), Am. Soc. Pub. Adminstrn. (outstanding superior pub. service award), Bus. and Profl. Women's Assn., Assoc. Safety Engrs. of Ariz. (pres.), World Safety Orgn., S.W. Safety Congress (bd. dirs., outstanding safety and accident prevention award), Semiconductor Safety Assn. Republican. Lutheran. Office: Motorola Inc 2200 W Broadway Mesa AZ 85202

HULSE, RALPH ROBERT, business consultant, human relations trainer; b. St. Joseph, Mo., Jan. 14, 1935; s. Ralph Raymond and Eva Laduska (Hatfield) H.; m. Gwen Lea Bartosh, May 21, 1957 (div. 1959); m. Jutta-Beaujean, Jan. 14, 1961. AB, Cen. Meth. Coll., 1957; MEd, U. Mo., 1965. Continuing edn. programmer U. Mo., Columbia, 1969-71; dir. edn. tng. North Kansas City (Mo.) Meml. Hosp., 1971-74; mgmt. cons. Lawrence-Leiter, Kansas City, 1974-77; adminstr. U.S. Congress, 6th dist., Mo., 1977-78; bus. cons. Colo. Cons. Assn., Inc., Denver, 1978—; founder, bd. dirs. Opportunity Industry Inc., St. Joseph, 1965-71; pres. State Adult Edn. Assn., Mo., 1978-79; founder, pres. Colo. Cons. Assn. Inc., 1985—. Contbr. articles to profl. jours. (Nat. Pub. award 1974, 75). Served with U.S. Army, 1959-61. Republican. Methodist. Home: 11633 Steele St Thornton CO 80233 Office: Colo Cons Assn Inc 1333 W 120th Suite 110 Denver CO 80234

HULSEY, RUTH LENORA, state official; b. Athens, Ga., Nov. 28, 1927; d. Joseph Alonzo and Frances Rebecca (Bell) Johnson; student Pasadena Jr. Coll., 1938-40, San Bernardino Valley Coll., 1963-65; m. William A. Hulsey III, Mar. 28, 1958; children—William A., Stephen G., Alicia A. With State of Calif. Employment Devel. Office, 1960—, supr., San Bernardino Field Dept. Office, 1969-75, So. Region Office, Riverside, 1975-78, employment program mgr., asst. mgr. Ontario Field Office, 1979-80, employment program mgr., Fontana Field Office, 1980—; dir. Calif. State Employees Credit Union, 1972-75, mem. employer adv. council, 1978—. Mem. edn. com. Urban League, 1965, mem., 1965—; mem. Arrowhead Allied Arts Council, 1966-72; mem. Social Lites, 1963—, pres., 1964-66, 80-81, bd. dirs., 1980—, rec. sec., 1981—. Mem. Internat. Assn. Personnel in Employment Security, Calif. State Employees Assn., Bloomington C. of C., Fontana C. of C., Rialto C. of C., San Bernardino C. of C. Democrat. Methodist. Home: 1246 E Shamrock Ave San Bernardino CA 92410 Office: State of Calif Employment Devel Dept Office 17590 Foothill Blvd Fontana CA 92335

HUMAYDAN, HASIB SHAHEEN, seed company executive; b. Ain Anoub, Lebanon, Mar. 6, 1945; came to U.S., 1971; s. Shaheen Hamed and Amria M. Humaydan; m. Anna Maria DiLiegro, Mar. 8, 1980; children: Michael James, Andrew Shaheen. BS, Am. U., Beirut, 1969, MS, 1971; PhD, U. Wis., 1974. Plant pathologist and breeder Joseph Harris Co. Inc., Rochester, N.Y., 1974-82, dir. plant pathology and tissue culture, 1982-84, mgr. research and devel., 1984-85; v.p. research and devel. Harris Moran Seed Co., Salinas, Calif., 1985—. Contbr. articles to profl. jours. Mem. Am. Phytopaltol. Soc., Am. Soc. Hort. Scis., N.Y. Acad. Scis. Avocations: golf, tennis. Home: 18815 Tiburcio Ct Salinas CA 93908 Office: Harris Moran Seed Co 1155 Harkins Rd Salinas CA 93901

HUMBERGER, FRANK EDWARD, career and family counselor; b. Troy, Ohio, July 10, 1914; s. Frank Longfellow and Myrtle May (McDowell) H.; B.S., Case Inst. Tech., 1935; B.D., San Francisco Theol. Sem., 1959; Th.D., Pacific Sch. Religion, 1967; m. Jackeline H. Armstrong, Apr. 14, 1973; children by previous marriage—Sallie Marshall, Edward McDowell, Janet Lolov. Owner, mgr. Tech. Metal Processing, Inc., Cleve., 1945-57, Aerobraze Corp., 1953-57; ordained teaching elder, United Prebyterian Ch. U.S.A., 1959; pastor Presbyn. Ch., Turlock, Calif., 1960-68; dir. Logos West Tng. Ctr., Lafayette, Calif., 1968-78; pres. Interpersonal Relations, Inc., Calif. and Wash., 1964-83, Exec. Services Assocs., Bellevue, 1978-83; IPR, Inc., 1983-86; assoc. prof. mgmt. dept. San Francisco State U., 1967-70; assoc. prof. psychology John F. Kennedy U., Moraga, Calif., 1967-70; pres. Calif. Health Group, 1974-78; lectr. Sch. Edn., U. Pacific, Stockton, Calif., 1965-67. Chmn. Grower-Worker Reconciliation Task Force, United Presbyn. Ch. U.S.A., San Joaquin Valley, Calif., 1965-68; dir. coll. community relations San Francisco State U., 1970. Fellow Am. Assn. Pastoral Counselors; mem. Am. Assn. Marriage and Family Therapists (cert. supr., clin. mem.), Am. Mgmt. Assns., Blue Key, Tau Beta Pi. Republican. Clubs: St. Francis Yacht, Orcas Island Yacht, Orcas Tennis. Author: Your Personal Career, 1978, Developing Effective Communication Styles, 1979, Outplacement and Inplacement Counseling, 1984, The Executive for the 90's, 1987; contbr. articles to profl. jours. Home: PO Box 789 Eastsound WA 98245

HUMBURG, NEIL EDWARD, agronomist, consultant, researcher; b. LaCrosse, Kans., May 16, 1933; s. Harold Bernreuter and Alvene Martha (Markwart) H.; m. Renae Bygel, June 17, 1961; children: Karen, James. BS in Agr., Colo. State U., 1955, MS in Agronomy and Botany, 1965; PhD in Agronomy and Botany, U. Wis., 1970. Grad. research asst. Colo. State U., Ft. Collins, 1963-65; research asst. U. Wis., Madison, 1965-70; asst. prof. Kans. State U., Manhattan, 1970-75, U. Wyo., Laramie, 1976-83; researcher, cons. Cheyenne, Wyo., 1982—; agronomic cons. Osman-Omar Inc./Agrl. Bank Saudi Arabia, 1983; external reviewer USDA Cen. Great Plains Research Sta., Akron, Colo. 1982; mem. faculty senate U. Wyo., 1978-81, chmn. broadcast services com. 1981-82. Mem. adminstrv. bd. First United Meth. Ch., Topeka, 1972-74; mem. troop com. Boy Scouts Am., Laramie, 1981-84. Mem. Weed Sci. Soc. Am. (chmn. handbook com. 1982-86, secondary editor 1983, editor 1987, mem. publs. coordination com. 1982—, cons. weed sci. com. 1986—), Western Soc. Weed Sci. (mem. resolutions com. 1981-84, chmn. 1982-83, chmn. poster session com. 1984-85, local arrangements com. 1983), Am. Soc. Agronomy, Internat. Weed Sci. Soc., Plant Growth Regulator Soc. Am., Antique Automobile Club Am., Sigma Xi, Gamma Sigma Delta. Republican. Methodist. Lodge: Lions. Avocations: photography, antique automobiles, skiing. Home: 6615 Evers Blvd Cheyenne WY 82009

HUME, STEPHEN, writer, editor; b. Blackpool, Lancashire, Eng., Jan. 1, 1947; came to Can. 1948; s. James and Joyce (Potter) H.; m. Susan Winifred Mayse, July 29, 1970. B.A., U. Victoria, B.C., 1971. Reporter Victoria Times, B.C., Can., 1968-71; Arctic corr. Edmonton Jour., Yellowknife, NWT, Can., 1971-73; city editor Edmonton Jour., Edmonton, Alta., Can., 1975-77; weekend editor Edmonton Jour., Edmonton, Alta., 1977-78, news editor, 1978-81, editor, 1981-87, gen. mgr., 1987—. Author: (poetry) Signs Against An Empty Sky, 1980. Avocations: Fishing; rugby; basketball; writing; gardening. Office: Edmonton Jour, Box 2421, Edmonton, AB Canada T5J 2S6

HUMENICK, SHARRON SMITH, health sciences education administrator; b. Ft. Collins, Colo., Dec. 14, 1937; d. Donald Walter and Cecile Helen (Weeks) S.; m. Michael J. Humenick, June 18, 1960; children: Christine, Michael J. III. Student, Albion Coll., 1955-57; BS in Nursing, U. Mich., 1960; MPH, U. Calif., 1969; PhD, U. Tex., 1979. RN; cert. maternal child nursing, childbirth edn. Pub. health nurse Alameda County, Oakland, Calif., 1961-64, Contra Costa County, Richmond, Calif., 1964-65; sch. nurse Richmond Sch. Dist., 1966-69; asst. prof. nursing U. Tex., Austin, 1971-81; assoc. prof. nursing U. Wyo., Laramie, 1981—, asst. to dean health scis., 1985-86; cert. faculty childbirth edn. ASPO/Lamaze, Washington, 1974—, bd. dirs. 1978-79. Editor nursing text Analysis of Current Assessment, 1982 (Am. Jour. Nursing Book of Yr. award 1983); co-editor text Practice Theory and Research in Childbirth Edn., 1987; mem. editorial bd. Birth, Berkeley, Calif., 1981—; mem. rev. panel Western Jour. Nursing Research, 1984—, Maternal Child Nursing, N.Y.C., 1983—; author 10 research publs., 12 clin. publs. Bd. dirs. Campfire Girls, Richmond, 1965-68. Predoctoral fellow Dept. Health Edn. Welfare, Washington, 1978-79; research grant Dept. Health Human Services, Washington, 1984-86. Mem. Am. Nurses Assn., Wyo. Nurses Assn. (treas. dist. 12, 1985-87), Council Nurse Researchers (Wyo. legis. rep. 1982-86), Am. Pub. Health Assn., Nurses Assn. Coll. Ob-Gyn. Club: Faculty Women (Laramie), Laramie Athletic. Avocations: skiing, hiking, computers, writing. Home: 1017 Sheridan Laramie WY 82070 Office: U Wyo PO Box 3065 Laramie WY 82071

HUMMEL, FRED EDWARD, mining and metallurgical engineer, researcher; b. Los Angeles, May 8, 1906; s. Albert Edward Hummel and Minerva Louise Hardegen; m. Glenna Ruth Horton, May 10, 1926 (dec. Feb. 1955); children: Fred Ernest, Marilyn Jean Coe; m. Marianne Pence, Aug. 10, 1958. BSMetE, S.D. Sch. Mining and Tech., 1931, MS, 1938. Registered profl. engr., Calif. Chemist Holly Sugar Corp., Sheridan, Wyo., 1926-27; engr. Wyo. State Hwy. Dept., 1931; metallurgist Am. Smelting and Refining Co., Selby, Calif., 1931-35; oil, petroleum engr. Shell Oil Co., various cities, Calif., 1935-47; cons. engr. Fred E. Hummel, Ojai, Calif., 1947-86. Pres., bd. dirs. El Rabler Corp., Ojai, 1975-76, 79. Mem. Soc. Petroleum Engrs. of AIME (bd. dirs. 1960-65, Engr. of Yr. 1980), Ventura Co. Engrs. Republican. Avocations: photography, fishing, orange growing. Home: 338 Bonita Dr Ojai CA 93023 Office: Hummel & Christianson Cons Engrs 102 E Aliso St PO Box 577 Ojai CA 93023

HUMMER, DAVID GRAYBILL, astrophysicist; b. Manheim, Pa., Nov. 4, 1934; s. John Herbert and Lillian (Graybill) H.; m. Janet Wood, Mar. 25, 1961; 1 son, Julius. B.S., Carnegie Inst. Tech., 1957, M.S., 1958; Ph.D. (Fulbright scholar), Univ. Coll. London, 1963. Physicist Gen. Atomic Corp., San Diego, 1958-59; research asst. Univ. Coll. London, 1961-63, lectr., 1964-66; vis. fellow Joint Inst. for Lab. Astrophysics, Boulder, Colo., 1963-64; chmn. Joint Inst. for Lab. Astrophysics, 1973-74, 77-78; physicist Nat. Bur. of Standards and; fellow Joint Inst. for Lab. Astrophysics, 1966—; adj. prof. U. Colo., Boulder. Co-editor: Atoms in Astrophysics, 1983; Contbr. articles to profl. jours.; translator: books from Russian Planetary Nebulae (G.A. Gurzadyan), 1969, Transfer of Radiation in Spectral Lines (V.V. Ivanov), 1974, Theory of Ionization of Atoms by Electron Impact (R.K. Peterkop), 1977. Recipient cert. commendation Nat. Bur. Standards, 1969, Spl. Achievement award, 1973, 77; Arthur S. Flemming award Downtown Jaycees, Washington, 1974, U.S. Sr. Scientist award, von Humboldt Found., 1984. Fellow AAAS; mem. Am. Phys. Soc., Am. Astron. Soc., Astron. Soc. Pacific, Royal Astron. Soc., Internat. Astron. Union., Soc. Indsl. and Applied Math. Home: 313 Alder Ln Pine Brook Hills Boulder CO 80302 Office: U Colo Joint Inst Lab Astrophysics Boulder CO 80307

HUMMER-MILLER, SUSANNE, research physicist; b. Chgo., Jan. 29, 1947; d. Alfred Peter and Therese Frances (Wroblewski) Hummer m. William Michael Miller, Oct. 20, 1973; 1 child, Susanne Marie. BS, Purdue U., 1968; MS, U. Denver, 1971. Sr. engr. Martin Marietta Aerospace Co., Denver, 1968-74; planner Air Pollution Div. Colo. Dept. Health, Denver, 1975-76; research physicist U.S. Geol. Survey, Denver, 1976—. Contbr. articles to profl. jours. Mem. archtl. com. Columbine West Civic Assn., Littleton, Colo., 1985—. Mem. Soc. Exploration Geophysicists, Am. Soc. Photogammetry and Remote Sensing, Sigma Xi, Sigma Pi Sigma. Home: 6979 W Quarto Pl Littleton CO 80123 Office: US Geol Survey Box 25046 MS 964 DFC Denver CO 80225

HUMPHREY, JAYNE HULBERT, government official; b. Oakland, Calif., Apr. 1, 1947; d. Jack W. and Clare Roberta (Hittle) Hulbert; m. Donald James Humphrey, Nov. 11, 1983. Student Northwestern U., 1964-66, San Francisco State U., 1969-70. With various fed. govt. agencies, Washington, 1964-67; program asst. U.S. Dept. HUD, Washington, 1968, elderly housing program technician, San Francisco, 1969-70, housing rep., coordinator, 1970-75, dir. housing devel. div., 1975-83, dep. regional housing dir., 1983—, mgr. Honolulu office, 1986—; pres. Hulbert Humphrey, Inc., Fairfax, Calif., 1985—; instr. Calif. Mortgage Bankers Assn., Calif. Dept. Real Estate, Sacramento, 1985—; chief negotiator, mem. mgmt. contract with union

HUD, San Francisco, 1983-84; mem. rev. bd. performance standards HUD, 1986—. Named Woman of Yr., U.S. HUD, 1985, recipient outstanding performance award, 1976, 78, 80, 81, 84, 85, Disting. Service nominee, 1979, spl. achievement award, 1972, 73, 75; hon. citizen City of Alameda, Calif., 1971. Mem. Fed. Mgrs. Assn., Nat. Soc. Female Execs., Am. Soc. Pub. Adminstrn. Democrat. Presbyterian. Club: Commonwealth. Avocations: music; computers. Office: Dept HUD 450 Golden Gate Ave Box 36003 San Francisco CA 23448

HUMPHREY, JOSEPH ANTHONY CHRISTIE, mechanical engineering educator; b. London, Jan. 15, 1948; came to U.S., 1977; s. Joseph A. and Madelaine I. (Curran) H.; m. Vivienne Mooney, Aug. 24, 1970; children: Luisa, Fiona, Katie. Diploma in chem. engring., Instituto Quimico De Sarria, Barcelona, Spain, 1970; MSChemE, U. Toronto, Ont., Can., 1973; PhDME, Imperial Coll. Sci. and Tech., London, 1977. Research staff dept. mech. aerospace engring. Princeton (N.J.) U., 1977-78; asst. prof. mech. engring. U. Calif., Berkeley, 1978-83, assoc. prof., 1983—. Assoc. editor Internat. Jour. Physicochem. Hydrodynamics, 1983—; contbr. numerous articles to profl. jours. Fulbright fellow, 1984. Mem. ASME, AAAS, AAUP, Am. Phys. Soc., Instituto Quimico de Sarria, Pi Tau Sigma, Sigma Chi. Avocations: swimming, reading, classical music. Home: 1298 Oxford St Berkeley CA 94709 Office: U Calif Dept Mech Engring Berkeley CA 94720

HUMPHREY, THOMAS WARD, librarian; b. Hartford, Ky., Oct. 20, 1948; s. James William and Violet Rene (Ward) H.; m. Billie Powell Staton, May 20, 1973; children: Sybil Rene, Laura Nicole. BA, Ky. Wesleyan Coll., 1970; MLS, Peabody Coll., 1972. Cert. profl. librarian, N.Mex. Librarian Ky. Wesleyan Coll., Owensboro, 1970-79; library dir. Cen. Wyo. Coll., Riverton, 1979-83; dir. library and learning research Eastern N.Mex. U., Clovis, 1983—; library service dir. City of Clovis, 1985—. Treas. Friends of Library, Clovis, 1985—; founder, pres. Curry County Geneal. Soc., Clovis, 1985—. Mem. Am. Library Assn., N.Mex. Library Assn., Ky. Hist. Soc., Nat. Grigsby Family Assn., Humphrey Family Assn. Democrat. Methodist. Lodge: Kiwanis (bd. dirs. El Desayuno club). Avocations: genealogical research, quilting, American history. Home: 152 Crescent Dr Clovis NM 88101 Office: Eastern NMex U 417 Schepps Blvd Clovis NM 88101

HUMPHREYS, FRED C., bank executive. Chmn. bd., chief exec. officer Idaho First National Bank, Boise. Office: Idaho First Nat Bank Office of Chmn 101 S Capitol Blvd Boise ID 83733 *

HUMPHREYS, NANCY KAY, librarian, writer; b. Erie, Pa., June 24, 1946; d. Willard Charles Humphreys and Isabelle Elizabeth MacIntyre. BA, Temple U., 1969; MA, U. Wis., 1970, MS, 1971; MLS, U. S.C., 1976. Librarian U. Wis., LaCrosse, 1976-85, U. Calif., Berkeley, 1986—, Oakland (Calif.) Pub. Library, 1986—. Author: The Underground Economy, 1985; contbr. articles to profl. publs.; editor: Women Library Workers Journal. Mem. Am. Soc. Indexers, Feminist Writers Guild, Am. Library Assn., Beta Phi Mu. Avocation: creative writing. Home: 2415 12th Ave Oakland CA 94606 Office: U Calif Women's Resource Ctr T-9 Berkeley CA 94720

HUMPHREYS, ROBERT HAROLD, medical association executive; b. Los Angeles, Feb. 18, 1936; s. John Harold and Dollie (McCutcheon) H.; m. Beverly Williams Bailey, June 10, 1972; 1 stepchild, Michael Jay; 1 child, Robert Harold. Student George Washington U., 1954-58, 62-63. Congl. aide U.S. Ho. of Reps., Washington, 1954-58; planning officer Asian Cultural Exchange Found., Washington, 1960-65; exec. asst. Life Underwriter Tng. Council, Washington, 1966-69; adminstrv. asst. Gen. Agts. and Mgrs. Conf., Washington, 1969-70, exec. adminstr., 1970-73, exec. dir., 1974-76, exec. v.p., 1976-82; chief exec. officer Am. Acad. Med. Preventics, Los Angeles, 1982-86, Am. Inst. Med. Preventics, 1982-86; mng. dir. Bio-Med Health Svcs., North Hollywood, Calif., 1986—; exec. dir. Am. Acad. Esthetic Medicine, 1987—; bd. govs. Nat. Health Fedn., 1984—; cons. Oriental art Towson Coll., Balt., 1969—; chief exhibit curator Audubon Naturalistic Soc., 1968—; curator Turner Collection, Washington, 1960—. Bd. dirs. Asian Cultural Exchange Found., Lilliputian Found., Gatchell Sch., Atlanta. Served with USNR, 1958-60. Hold-Fannie B. Scheffries scholar, 1962-64. Mem. Smithsonian Assocs. Clubs: Nat. Press, Capital Yacht. Home: 32448 Saddle Mountain Dr Westlake Village CA 91361 Office: Bio-Med Health Svcs 11311 Camarillo St Suite 103 North Hollywood CA 91602

HUMPHRY, DEREK JOHN, society executive, writer; b. Bath, Somerset, U.K., Apr. 29, 1930; came to U.S., 1978; s. Royston Martin and Bettine (Duggan) H.; m. Jean Edna Crane, May 5, 1953 (dec. Mar. 1975); children—Edgar, Clive, Stephen; m. Ann Wickett Kooman, Feb. 16, 1976. Student pub. schs. Reporter, Evening News, Manchester, Eng., 1951-55, Daily Mail, London, 1955-63; editor Havering Recorder, Essex, Eng., 1963-67; sr. reporter Sunday Times, London, 1967-78; spl. writer Los Angeles Times, 1978-79; founder, exec. dir. Hemlock Soc. N.Am., Los Angeles, 1980—. Author: Because They're Black, 1971 (M.L. King award 1972), Police Power and Black People, 1972; Jean's Way, 1978, Let Me Die Before I Wake, 1982, The Right to Die, 1986. Served with Brit. Army, 1948-50. Mem. World Fedn. Right-to-Die Socs. (newsletter editor 1979-84, sec.-treas. 1983-84, pres. elect 1988-90). Office: Hemlock Soc PO Box 66218 Los Angeles CA 90066

HUMPHRY, TED (RIGGS), pediatrician; b. Denver, Dec. 2, 1944; s. Harry H. and Mary R. (Riggs) H.; m. Cindy Loomer, June 15, 1968; children: Paul, Christy, Maria, Tim, JoeBen, Nicholas, Rose. BS, Calif. Poly State U., San Luis Obispo, 1967; MD, U. So. Calif., 1971. Diplomate Am. Bd. Pediatrics. Practice medicine specializing in pediatrics Arcata, Calif., 1977—; instr. Coll. Redwoods, Eureka, Calif., 1979-83. Producer/actor (TV prodn.) Bananas, 1984-86. Chmn. Maternal, Child and Adolesant Health Bd., Eureka, 1983—. Served with USPHS, 1972-75. Fellow Am. Acad. Pediatrics. Avocations: back packing, reading, family activities. Office: 827 Bayside Rd Arcata CA 95521

HUNDAL, SARBJIT SINGH, ophthalmologist; b. Bhagoran, Punjab, India, Feb. 4, 1950; came to U.S., 1976, naturalized 1982; s. Kartar Singh and Amar Kaur (Sahota) H. M.D., Punjabi U., India, 1973. Diplomate Am. Bd. Ophthalmology. Practice medicine specializing in ophthalmology, Stockton, Calif., 1982-84, Fremont, Calif., 1984—. Fellow Am. Acad. Opthalmology, Internat. Coll. Surgeons, ACS; mem. Internat. Coll. Ocular Surgeons, AMA, Calif. Med. Assn., Alameda-Centra Costa Med. Assn., Fremont C. of C., Milpitas C. of C. Home: 43543 Puesta Del Sol Fremont CA 94538 Office: 2191 Mowry Ave Suite 600 G Fremont CA 94538

HUNDMAN-ROSS, AMIE JEANNE, publishing executive, editor; b. Bloomington, Ill., Nov. 4, 1958; d. Robert L. Hundman and Nancy J. (Watts) Cravens; m. David E. Ross, Aug. 6, 1982; children: Kimberly, Joshua. Student, Rend Lake Coll. Mgr. Jay Jacobs, Seattle, 1978-80; personnel mgr. Snelling & Snelling, Seattle, 1980-81; mng. editor Hundman Pub., Edmonds, Wash., 1981-85, v.p., 1985—; editor, design cons. Channel Watch, Seattle, 1985; design cons. Pacer Tech., Seattle, 1985. Author, editor Mainline Modeler mag., 1980—; editor, designer The Allegheny-Lima's Finest, 1985, Lima: The History, 1986. Mem. Am. Soc. Model Railroads (cons. 1985—). Republican. Mem. Ch. Religious Sci. Avocations: skiing, diving, running. Office: Hundman Pub 5115 Monticello Dr Edmonds WA 98020

HUNG, CHING-MAO, research scientist; b. Taiwan, May 28, 1941; s. Yi-shiang and Yeh (Huang) H.; m. Pei-jean Lee, Jan. 1, 1970; children—Jeffrey, Emilie, Albert. B.S.M.E., Nat. Taiwan U., 1965; M.S. in Engring., Cornell U., 1968, Ph.D., 1972. Lic. mech. engr., Calif. Research assoc. scientist Lockheed Missiles and Space Co., Huntsville, Ala., 1972-73; NRC felow NASA Ames Research Ctr., Moffett Field, Calif., 1973-75, research scientist, 1978—; cons. DCW Industries, Studio City, Calif., 1975-78. Treas. Taiwanese Alliance Interculture, 1977-80. Served to 2d lt. Taiwan A.F. Nat. Taiwan U. honor student scholar, 1963, 64, 65; Cornell U. John McMullen fellow, 1967; recipient NASA spl. achievement award, 1980. Mem. AIAA, N.Y. Acad. Scis., Sigma Xi. Contbr. articles to tech. jours. Home: 12813 La Cresta Dr Los Altos Hills CA 94022 Office: NASA Ames Center Computational Fluid Dynamics Branch Moffett Field CA 94035

HUNKIN, GEOFFREY GILBERT, cons. engr.; b. Cornwall, Eng., Aug. 2, 1923; came to U.S., 1968, naturalized, 1975; s. Edwin Gilbert and Florence Adelaide (Bunt) H.; B.S., Sch. of Mines, Cornwall, 1949; m. Margot A.E., Drinkwater, Nov. 30, 1945; children—Philip Bingham, Elinor Patricia, Geoffrey Bingham. With Mysore Gold Mining, India, 1949-52, Macalder Mines, Kenya, Africa, 1952-57, Rio Algom Mines, Can., 1957, Stanrock Mines, Can., 1958, Silvermines, Ireland, 1965-68, Anaconda Co., Utah and N.Mex., 1968-71; mgr. mining and engring. Westinghouse Electric Corp., Denver, 1971-74; cons. engr. in pvt. practice, Can., Australia, U.S., 1974; pres. Hunkin Engrs., Inc. and Ground Water Sampling, Inc., Englewood, Colo., 1976—; lectr. in field. Served to lt. Royal Navy, 1940-45. Recipient Robert Earll McConnell award AIME, 1977; named Disting. mem. Soc. Mining Engrs., 1977. Fellow Inst. of Mining and Metallurgy; mem. ASTM, Nat. Soc. Profl. Engrs., Cons. Engrs. Council Am., Soc. Mining Engrs. of AIME, Soc. Petroleum Engrs. of AIME, Can. Inst. Mining, Metall. and Petroleum Engrs. Republican. Episcopalian. Clubs: Columbine Country, Petroleum of Denver, Masons, Shriners. Patentee in field. Home: 9 Meadow Lark Ln Littleton CO 80123 Office: Hunkin Engrs Inc 4061 S Eliot Englewood CO 80110

HUNLEY, W. HELEN, Canadian provincial government official; b. Acme, Alta., Can., Sept. 6, 1920. Student pub. schs., Rocky Mountain House, Alta.; LL.D., U. Alta., 1985. Telephone operator Carstairs, Acme and Calgary, Alta.; with implement and truck dealership, ins. agy. Rocky Mountain House, 1948-57, owner, 1957-68; owner, mgr. Helen Hunley Agys. Ltd., ins. agy., Rocky Mountain House, 1968-71; town councillor Rocky Mountain House, 1960-66, mayor, 1966-71; elected mem. Legis. Assembly Province of Alta., Edmonton, 1971-79, minister without portfolio, 1971-73, solicitor-gen., 1973-75, minister social services and community Health, 1975-79, lt. gov., 1985—. Formerly active numerous community affairs and vol. agys., including Can. Red Cross, Can. Boy Scouts, Recreation Bd., Alta. Girls Parliament, Provincial Mental Health Adv. Council; hon. patron numerous assns. Served to lt. Can. Women's Army Corps, 1941-45. Office: Province of Alta, Office of Lt Gov, Legislature Bldg, Edmonton, AB Canada T5K 2BC

HUNNICUTT, ANN SPROULE, dental hygienist; b. Norfolk, Va., July 18, 1930; d. Samuel Jackson and Alfreda (Jones) Sproule; m. Glen Charles Luff, Aug. 17, 1955; children—Susan Carol, David Gerrish; m. 2d, William Howard Taake, July 18, 1981 (div.). A.A., Harcum Jr. Coll., 1950; cert. Thomas W. Evans Sch. Oral Hygien, U. Pa., 1953; B.S. with honors in Speech Pathology, Eastern N.Mex. U., 1968; postgrad. McGeorge Sch. Law, U. Pacific, 1973-77. Registered dental hygienist, Calif., Pa. Dental hygienist, 1967—; owner, operator ind. dental hygiene practice, Santa Barbara, Calif., 1977—; lectr. in field. Founder, 1st pres. Davis (Calif.) Soc. for Prevention of Cruelty to Animals, 1971. Recipient Humanitarian of Yr. award Sacramento Soc. for Prevention of Cruelty to Animals, 1974. Mem. Santa Barbara Dental Hygiene Assn. (pres. 1977, 78), Santa Barbara C. of C., Alumni U. Pa. Republican. Author: Be Your Own Boss, 1979; contbr. articles to profl. jours. Office: Dental Hygiene Office 1165 Coast Village Rd Suite J Santa Barbara CA 93108

HUNNICUTT, RICHARD PEARCE, metallurgical engineer; b. Asheville, N.C., June 15, 1926; s. James Ballard and Ida (Black) H.; B.S. in Metall. Engring., Stanford, 1951, M.S., 1952; m. Susan Haight, Apr. 9, 1954; children—Barbara, Beverly, Geoffrey, Anne. Research metallurgist Gen. Motors Research Labs., 1952-55; sr. metallurgist Aerojet-Gen. Corp., 1955-57; head materials and processes Firestone Engring. Lab., 1957-58; head phys. scis. group Dalmo Victor Co., Monterey, 1958-61, head materials lab., 1961-62; v.p. Anamet Labs., Inc., 1962-—; partner Pyrco Co. Served with AUS, 1943-46. Mem. Electrochem. Soc., AIME, Am. Soc. Metals, ASTM, Am. Welding Soc., Am. Soc. Lubrication Engrs. Research on frictional behavior of materials, devel. armored fighting vehicles; author: Pershing, A History of the Medium Tank T20 Series, 1971; Sherman, A History of the American Medium Tank, 1978; Patton, A History of the American Main Battle Tank, Vol. 1, 1984. Home: 2805 Benson Way Belmont CA 94002 Office: 3400 Investment Blvd Hayward CA 94545

HUNNICUTT, ROBERT WILLIAM, engineer; b. Pauls Valley, Okla., Aug. 12, 1954; s. James Warren Hunnicutt. BS, N.Mex. State U., 1980. Assoc. engr. IBM, Tucson, 1980—. Mem. Tucson Amateur Astronomers Assn. Republican. Avocations: photography, astronomy, martial arts, reading, philately. Home: 8421 E Stella Rd Tucson AZ 85730 Office: IBM Corp VLSI Lab 62U/304 6950 S Country Club Rd Tucson AZ 85744

HUNSAKER, DON, II, biology educator; b. Ft. Worth, Apr. 6, 1930; s. Don and Thelma (Mumford) H.; m. Barbara Hunsaker, Dec. 23, 1952; children: Robert, Don III, Holly, Russell. BA, Tex. Tech U., 1952, MS, 1957; PhD, U. Tex., 1960. Asst. prof. San Diego State U., 1960-66, prof., 1967—; assoc. research biologist Zool. Soc., San Diego, 1966—; coordinator tech. rep. U.S. Peace Corps, 1969-71; vis. prof. U. Ariz., Tucson, 1971-72. Editor: Biology of Marsupials, 1970. Bd. trustees Santee Sch. Dist., Calif., 1965-71, Grossmont High Sch., La Mesa, Calif., 1977—; pres. Calif. Sch. Bds. Assn., Sacramento, 1984. Fellow San Diego Mus. Nat. History (pres. 1970-71); mem. Am. Soc. Ichthyologists and Herpetologists, San Diego Herpetologists Soc. (pres. 1978-79), Pacific Region Nat. Sch. Bds. Assn. (pres. 1986—). Democrat. Home: 1540 Savin Dr El Cajon CA 92021 Office: San Diego State U Dept Biology San Diego CA 92182

HUNSAKER, FLOYD B., accountant; b. Collinston, Utah, Sept. 6, 1915; s. Allen G. and Mary Ann (Bowcutt) H.; grad. high sch.; m. Zella D. Hepworth, Mar. 3, 1943; children—Marcia (Mrs. Marvin Bahr), Charlene (Mrs. Abelino Ancira), Sonia (Mrs. Val Fisher), Rhonda (Mrs. Kim Veigel), Tamara. Owner, operator dairy farm, Bedford, Wyo., 1946-70; acct., Afton, Wyo., 1959—; owner Credit Bur. Star Valley, Afton, 1967—; mcpl. judge Town of Afton, 1967-77; local office claimstaker Wyo. Unemployment Compensation Dept., 1975-85. Pres., Holdaway Sch. PTA, 1960; active Boy Scouts Am., 1946-49, 58-67; bd. dirs. Star Valley Sr. Citizens, 1981-83, 84—; pres. Lower Valley 4-H council, 1961-62, leader, 1959-63; chmn. Star Valley chpt. Am. Revolution Bicentennial Adminstrn., 1975-76, Star Valley chpt. ARC, 1976—; ward pres. Sunday Sch., 1985-87. Served with Devils Brigade, 1941-45; ETO. Mem. Nat., Wyo. socs. pub. accountants, Farm Bur. (exec. sec. Lincoln County 1961-66), Nat. Platform Assn., Afton C. of C. (dir. 1973-74), VFW (dist. comdr. Wyo. 1974-75, 77-78, state dept. jr. vice comdr. 1978-79, sr. vice comdr. 1979-80, state comdr. 1980-81, dist. comdr. 1982-83, 86—). Mem. Ch. of Jesus Christ of Latter-day Saints. Home: 323 Adams St Afton WY 83110 Office: 498 Washington St Afton WY 83110

HUNSBERGER, CHARLES WESLEY, city, county library director; b. Elkhart, Ind., Sept. 25, 1929; s. Charles August and Emma Edna (Zimmerman) H.; m. Hilda Carol Showalter, July 3, 1949 (div.); children—Jonathan Wesley, Jerald Wayne, Jane Wannette. B.A., Bethel Coll., Mishawaka, Ind., 1952; M.L.S., Ind. U., 1967. Mem. Ft. Wayne (Ind.) Library Staff, 1960-62; dir. Columbia (Ind.) City Library, 1962-64, Monroe County Library, Bloomington, Ind., 1964-71, Clark County Library Dist., Las Vegas, Nev., 1971—; cons. sch., pub. libraries, 1968-70; lectr. library schs. Ind. U., 1970-71, U. Ariz., 1974, U. Nev., Reno, 1976; mem. Nev. Council on Libraries, 1973-81, chmn., 1980-81. Mem. Calif. Library Assn., ALA, Nev. Library Assn. Democrat. Club: Las Vegas-Paradise Rotary (pres. 1979-80). Home: 1544 Hialeah Dr Las Vegas NV 89119 Office: Las Vegas Clark County Library Dist 1401 E Flamingo Rd Las Vegas NV 89119

HUNSUCKER, ROBERT DUDLEY, geophysics educator, electrical engineering educator; b. Portland, Oreg., Mar. 15, 1930; s. Robert Deets and Johnnie Morris (Kuykendal) H.; m. Judith Mary Cotter, Apr. 28, 1956 (dec. Nov. 1980); children: Edith Louise, Jeanne Marie, Cynthia Lee; m. Phyllis Marie Hoover, July 25, 1981. BS in Physics, Oreg. State U., 1954, MS in Physics, 1958; PhDEE, U. Colo., 1969. Asst. prof. geophysics Geophysics Inst. U. Alaska, Fairbanks, 1958-64, assoc. prof., 1971-78, prof., 1978—; physicist nat. Bur. Standards, Boulder, Colo., 1964-67; sr. project leader ITS Office of Telecommunications Sci., Boulder, 1967-71. Contbr. articles to profl. jours. Served to lt. USNR, 1954-57. Fellow AAAS; mem. IEEE (sr.), Am. Geophys. Union, Alaska Telecommunication Assn. (pres. 1977-82), Radio Propagation Assn. (pres. 1982—). Republican. Presbyterian. Lodge: Rotary (bd. dirs. College, Alaska club 1979-81). Avocations: pvt. pilot, fishing, hunting, amateur radio operation, photography. Office: U Alaska Geophys Inst Fairbanks AK 99775-0800

HUNT, ARLON JASON, physicist, consultant; b. Iowa, Oct. 8, 1939; s. Frank and Dorothy (Tuthill) H.; m. Mary Quinby; children: Elena, Robb. BA, U. Minn., 1963; MS, U. Ariz., 1972, PhD, 1974. Physicist Stanford Research Inst., Menlo Park, Calif., 1963-65; vol. tchr. U.S. Peace Corps, Sungei Patani, Malaysia, 1965-68; research assoc. physics dept. U. Ariz., Tucson, 1968-74, postdoctoral research assoc. optical sci. ctr., 1974-76; group leader Lawrence Berkeley (Calif.) Lab., 1976—; pres. Particle Tech. Assocs., Oakland, Calif., 1979—; v.p. research and devel., bd. dirs. Quantum Optics Inc., Emeryville, Calif. Contbr. articles to profl. publs.; patentee in field. Recipient Sr. Fulbright Research award, 1985. Mem. AAAS, Am. Phys. Soc., Am. Optical Soc., Am. Meteorol. Soc., Materials Research Soc., Internat. Solar Energy Soc. Avocations: inventing. Home: 2025 Manzanita Dr Oakland CA 94611 Office: Lawrence Berkeley Lab 90-2024 Berkeley CA 94720

HUNT, ERNEST WOODROW, JR., ophthalmologist; b. Greenville, N.C., Aug. 7, 1938; s. Ernest Woodrow and Mary King (Fountain) H.; m. Coley Drohomer, June 22, 1962; children—Lisa Alexandra, Jennifer Coley, Melissa Caroline. B.S., Davidson Coll., 1960; M.D., U. N.C., 1964; grad. Navy Flight Surgeon Sch., Pensacola, Fla., 1966. Diplomate Am. Bd. Ophthalmology. Commd. officer U.S. Navy, 1964, advanced through grades to comdr.; intern Nat. Naval Med. Ctr., Bethesda, Md., 1964-65; naval flight surgeon Carrier Air Wing 15, 1966-68; resident in ophthalmology Naval Hosp., San Diego, 1968-71; staff ophthalmologist Naval Hosp., Camp Pendleton, Calif., 1971-74, resigned, 1974; pvt. practice, La Jolla, Calif., 1974—; chmn. sect. ophthalmology dept. surgery Scripps Meml. Hosp., 1979, med. dir. Mericos Eye Inst., 1984—. Served to comdr. USN, 1964-74. Decorated Air medal; Navy Achievement medal; Navy Unit Commendation with one star; Nat. Def. Service medal; Armed Forces Expeditionary medal; Vietnam Cross of Gallantry with frame and palm; Vietnam Campaign medal with 4 stars; Republic of Vietnam Campaign medal. Fellow Am. Acad. Ophthalmology, ACS; mem. AMA, Calif. Med. Assn., San Diego County Med. Soc., spl. San Diego Eye Bank, San Diego County Acad. Ophthalmology, Soc. Mil. Ophthalmologists, Calif. Assn. Ophthalmology, Am. Soc. Cataract and Refractive Surgery, Contact Lens Assn. Ophthalmologists, Ophthalmic Outpatient Surgery Soc., Soc. Office Based Surgery. Republican. Presbyterian. Office: Eye Care of La Jolla 9834 Genesee Ave Suite 200 La Jolla CA 92037

HUNT, GARY THOMAS, communications educator, consultant; b. Los Angeles, Apr. 14, 1946; s. Albert O. and Dovie L. (Church) H.; m. Marilyn Louise Deubler, Feb. 27, 1982; children—Jonathan A., Michael T. B.A., Calif. State U.-Fullerton, 1967, M.A., 1970; Ph.D., Purdue U., 1972. Asst. prof. Ohio State U., Columbus, 1972-75; prof. communications Calif. State U.-Los Angeles, 1976—; communications cons., 1972—. Author: Public Speaking, 1980, 87, interviewing, 1987; Communication skills in the Organization, 1980; Effective Communication, 1985. Contbr. articles and papers to profl. jours. Mem. adv. bd. Orange County Devel. Ctr. for Handicapped, Fullerton, 1977-78. NDEA fellow, 1971; grantee USIA, 1983, Alfred P. Sloan Found., 1974. Mem. Speech Communication Assn., Internat. Communications Assn., Western Speech Communication Assn., Calif. Speech Assn., African Council Communications Edn. Office: Dept Communication Studies Calif State Univ 5151 State University Dr Los Angeles CA 90032

HUNT, H(AROLD) KEITH, business management educator, consultant; b. Apr. 16, 1938; married; 8 children. B.S. in Mktg. and Mgmt., U. Utah, 1961, M.B.A., 1962; Ph.D. in Mktg., Northwestern U., 1972. Instr. Imperial Valley Coll., El Centro, Calif., 1962-64; teaching asst. Northwestern U., 1964-66, instr., 1966-67; asst. prof. bus. adminstrn. and journalism U. Iowa, 1967-73; cons., staff mem. Office Policy Planning and Evaluation, FTC, Washington, 1973-74; assoc. prof. bus. adminstrn. U. Wyo., Laramie, 1974-75; assoc. prof. bus. mgmt. Brigham Young U., Provo, Utah, 1975-78, prof., 1978—; speaker in field; participant, chmn. various workshops, seminars, meetings; research expert, cons., expert witness on consumer research FTC, 1974—; cons., expert witness div. drug advt. FDA, 1975—; cons., adv. on consumer research Consumer and Corp. Affairs Can., 1978—. Editor: Advances in Consumer Research, Vol. 5, 1977; co-editor: (with Frances Magrabi) procs. Interdisciplinary Consumer Research, 1980, (with Ralph Day) Consumer Satisfaction/Dissatisfaction and Complaining Behavior, conf. procs., 8 vols., 1977—; mem. editorial bd.: Jour. Advt., Jour. Consumer Affairs, Jour. Consumer Research, Jour. Pub. Policy and Mktg., Current Issues and Research in Advt.; editor: Jour. Advt., 1978-83. Elected to Orem City Council, Utah, 1986—. Recipient Maeser Research award Brigham Young U., 1981; scholar-in-residence adv. dept. U. Ill., 1979; vis. research scholar Coll. Home Econs., U. Ala., 1980; vis. research scholar dept. mktg. and transp. U. Tenn., 1981; NSF grantee, 1975-77. Mem. Assn. Consumer Research (pres. 1979, exec. sec. 1983—), Am. Acad. Advt. (pres. 1982-83, exec. sec. 1983-86), Am. Mktg. Assn., Am. Psychol. Assn., Am. Council on Consumer Interests, Beta Gamma Sigma, Kappa Tau Alpha, Omicron Delta Epsilon, Phi Kappa Phi. Home: 835 E High Country Dr Orem UT 84057 Office: Brigham Young U Grad Sch Mgmt 632 TNRB Provo UT 84602

HUNT, MARY STUART QUINBY, paleoenvironmental chemist; b. N.Y.C., Dec. 30, 1945; d. Robb and Magdalena (Vanderlyn) Quinby; m. Arlon Jason Hunt; children: Elena, Robb. BA, Wheaton Coll., Norton, Mass., 1967; PhD in History and Chemistry, U. Ariz., 1971, MA in Art History, 1974. Staff scientist Lawrence Berkeley (Calif.) Lab., 1976-85; marine chemist, marine scis. group U. Calif., Berkeley, 1985—. Author: Survey of Instrumentation for Environmental Monitoring, vol. 2, 1986; contbr. articles on environ. issues to profl. jours. Mem. Am. Chem. Soc., Am. Geophys. Union, Phi Lambda Upsilon, Alpha Chi Sigma. Avocations: photography, cello. Office: U Calif Dept Paleontology Marine Services Group 7 Earth Scis Bldg Berkeley CA 94720

HUNT, PATRICK NORMAN, university educator, archaeologist; b. San Diego, Feb. 9, 1951; s. Donald William Hunt and Patricia Grace (Rhodes) Lyon; m. Pamela Fay Sommerfeldt, June 12, 1976; children: Hilary, Allegra, Beatrix. BA, Simpson Coll., 1977; MA, Dallas Theol. Sem., 1982; postgrad., U. Calif., Berkeley, Am. Sch. Classical Studies, Athens, Greece, U. London Inst. Archaeology. Asst. prof. archaeology, chmn. Div. Humanities Simpson Coll., San Francisco, 1984—; dir. Olompali Petroglyph Project, Dept. Parks and Recreation State Calif., 1985—. Contbr. articles to profl. jours. Mem. Assn. Field Archaeology, Biblical Archaeology Soc., Archaeol. Inst. Am. (lecture sec. San Francisco chpt. 1985), Calif. Classical Assn. (v.p. No. sect. 1985-86, pres. 1986—), San Augustin Inst. Marine Archaeology (chmn. adv. bd.), Am. Schs. Oriental Research. Avocations: cartography, hiking, tennis, entomology, Renaissance minstrels. Office: Simpson Coll Humanities Div 801 Silver Ave San Francisco CA 94134

HUNT, PETER H., director, theatrical lighting designer; b. Pasadena, Calif., Dec. 16, 1938; s. George Smith and Gertrude (Ophuls) H.; m. Virginia Osborn, Jan. 19, 1965 (div. Jan. 1972); children: May, Daisy, Amy; m. Barbetti (Tweed), Feb. 6, 1972. BA, Yale U., 1961, MFA in Drama, 1963. Free-lance lighting designer N.Y.C., 1959-69, free-lance theatre dir., 1969—; free-lance motion picture dir. Los Angeles, 1972—. Dir.: (plays) "1776," 1969 (Tony award 1970), Give 'Em Hell Henry, 1975; (TV movie) Skeezer, 1981 (Peabody award 1982); (cable TV play) Bus Stop, 1982 (ACE award 1983). Recipient Christopher award, 1972, Edgar award, 1982. Avocations: flying, scuba diving, cooking, aquarium design. Office: Creative Artists Agy 1888 Century Park E Los Angeles CA 90067

HUNT, RICHARD BARRON, lawyer, anthropologist; b. Rye, N.Y., May 8, 1917; s. Richard Carley Hunt and Maria Elena Barron; m. Anne Arnold, July 26, 1941 (div. May 1959); 1 child, Catherine Carley; m. Marjorie Simmons, June 6, 1959 (div. Oct. 1981); children: Laurel Simmons, Heather Howland, Richard Simmons, Jonathan Minter. BA, Yale U., 1941, JD, 1943. Assoc. Chadbourne, Hunt, Jaeckel and Brown, N.Y.C., 1946-49; ptnr. Chadbourne, Hunt, Jaeckel and Brown (named changed to Brown, Wood Fuller, Caldwell and Ivey), N.Y.C., 1950-65, Burns and Hunt, Jackson, Wyo., 1966-68; sole practice Jackson, 1969-83; photographer, exhibitor, 1939-65; pyrotechnician, Purchase, N.Y., 1950-54, chief exec. officer West-of-the-River Fireworks Co., Jackson, 1966—; treas., asst. sec., v.p. Wenner-Gren Found. for Anthropol. Research, Inc., N.Y.C., 1952-86, bd. dirs., trustee. Co-founder Pioneer Homestead, Inc., Jackson, 1967—, Pioneer Homestead Sr. Services, Jackson, 1969-85; Served as sgt. Air Corps, U.S. Army, 1943-46. Republican. Episcopalian. Avocations: reading, computers, model railroads, fishing. Home: 1060 W Brahma Dr PO Box 1766 Jackson WY 83001 Winter Home: 113-D N Lake Dr Mid Fla Lakes Leesburg FL 32788

HUNT, ROBERT WELDON, mathematics educator, consultant; b. Portales, N.Mex., Nov. 16, 1935; s. Malcolm Garrett and Audrey Bernice (Cayton) H.; m. Kathryn Ann Akers, June 4, 1955 (div. Nov. 1963); children: Charlotte R., Shawna L, Robert M.; m. Bonnie Jean Dixon, Nov. 7, 1964; children: Tracy M., Tanya R., Michael A., Dylan A., Ashley R., Ciara J., Talisha L. BS, West Tex. State U., 1956; MS, U. Utah, 1958, PhD, 1961. Asst. prof. math. U. Ala., Huntsville, 1961-62; assoc. prof. So. Ill. U., Carbondale, 1962-68, U.S. Naval Postgrad. Sch., Monterey, Calif., 1968-70; prof., chmn. dept. math. Calif. State Coll., Bakersfield, 1970-74; vis. prof. Calif. State U., Los Angeles, 1974-75. Author: Fundamentals of Mathematics, 1965, Ordinary Differential Equations, 1973; also articles. Served to 1st lt. U.S. Army, 1961-62. Grantee NSF, 1972. Mem. Am. Math. Soc. (grantee 1963), Math. Assn. Am., Sigma Xi. Democrat. Home: 1837 Panorama Dr Arcata CA 95521 Office: Humboldt State U Dept Math Arcata CA 95521

HUNT, THOMAS PATRICK, transportation specialist, educator; b. Chgo., Oct. 24, 1943; s. Thomas P. and Mary C. (Wilkes) H. B.A., Calif. State U., Chico, 1966; M.A., U. Calif., Berkeley, 1968. High sch. tchr., Los Angeles, 1968-73; transp. analyst Calif. Pub. Utilities Commn., Los Angeles, 1973-74, assoc. transp. rep., 1976-80, transp. ops. supr., 1980-83, sr. transp. ops. supr., 1983—; instr. Diablo Valley Community Coll., Pleasant Hill, Calif., 1975-76; tchr. adult edn., Los Angeles, 1977—; mem. Paratransit Task Force of So. Calif. Assn. Govts., 1978-80. Named Tchr. of Yr., Washington Community Adult Sch., 1979; Calco award Calif. Council Adult Edn., 1981; cert. in transp. proficiency Calif. State Personnel Bd., 1976. Mem. Calif. Council Adult Edn., Adult Edn. Assn. Los Angeles. Home: 5150 Village Green Los Angeles CA 90016

HUNT, WILLIAM E., state supreme court justice. Justice Mont. Supreme Ct., Helena. Office: Mont Supreme Ct State Capitol Helena MT 59601 *

HUNTER, BYRON ALEXANDER, chemist; b. Salt Lake City, Oct. 15, 1910; s. Daniel Hunter and Mary Calderwood; m. Margaret Clark Oleson, Sept. 4, 1942; children: Shirley, James, Robert, Margaret, Wendy, Sharman, Heather, Deborah. BA, U. Utah, 1933, MA, 1937; PhD, Iowa State U., 1941. Research assoc. Uniroyal, Naugatuck, Conn., 1941-75, Brigham Young U., Provo, Utah, 1978—. Holder 60 U.S. patents of rubber chemicals, antioxidants and blowing agts. for expanded polymers. Recipient Disting. Alumni award U. Utah, 1978. Mem. Am. Chem. Soc., Sigma Xi. Republican. Mormon. Avocations: ch. activities. Home: 352 E 426 N St Alpine UT 84003 Office: Brigham Young U 320 F Engring Sci Ctr Provo UT 84602

HUNTER, CHARLES FORREST, radio broadcasting executive; b. Richfield, Utah, Aug. 19, 1919; s. Charles Rowntree and Ruth (Hall) H.; m. Dawn Andrus Hunter, Feb. 5, 1949; children—Jon, Sally, James; 1 child by previous marriage, Tamara. B.A., U. So. Calif., 1948; M.Communications, Brigham Young U., 1964. Real estate sales, Cedar City, Utah, 1945—; owner Aspen Cooler Pad Air Conditioning Co. Cedar City, 1949-58; with Park & Shop Grocery Store, Cedar City, 1955-63; pres. New Era Broadcasting, Cedar City, 1970—; also actor and entertainer; dir. Earth Space Ltd. High counselor Ch. of Jesus Christ of Latter-day Saints, Cedar City, 1976-82. Served with USN, 1942-44. Republican. Lodge: Lions.

HUNTER, DANIEL ALAN, mechanics educator; b. Lewiston, Idaho, Sept. 5, 1956; s. Rhoda Walter and Ethel Josephine (Waibel) H.; m. Rene Marie Schwartz, Sept. 23, 1978 (div. Mar. 1983); 1 child, Danyel Marie; m. Kathryn Ann Hopfner, May 17, 1986. AAS, Lewis Clark State Coll., 1978. Cert. vocat. tchr. Head mechanic, service mgr. Barnett Thompson Chevrolet, Orofino, Idaho, 1978-80; asst. prof. vocat. mechs. Lewis Clark State Coll., Lewiston, Idaho, 1980—. Roman Catholic. Avocations: hunting, fishing, remodeling. Home: 303 1st Ave Lewiston ID 83501 Office: Lewis Clark State Coll Dept Trade and Industry Lewiston ID 83501

HUNTER, DUNCAN LEE, congressman; b. Riverside, Calif., May 31, 1948; m. Lynne Layh, 1973; children: Robert Samuel, Duncan Duane. J.D., Western State U., 1976. Bar: Calif. 1976. Practiced in San Dieg; mem. 97th Congress from 42d Dist. Calif., 98th-100th Congresses from 45th Dist. Calif. Served with U.S. Army, 1969-71, Vietnam. Decorated Air medal, Bronze Star. Mem. Navy League. Republican. Baptist.

HUNTER, E. ALLAN, electric utility executive; b. Grantsville, Utah, May 27, 1914; s. James Austin and Francis (Fraser) H.; m. Helen Spindler, July 12, 1941; children: Edward Allan, James Scott. B.S. in Elec. Engring., U. Utah, 1937; postgrad., U. Mich., 1955. Registered profl. engr., Utah. With Utah Power and Light Co., Salt Lake City, 1937—; various positions including asst. to pres., comml. mgr. Utah Power and Light Co., 1937-62, v.p., 1963-68, asst. gen. mgr., dir., 1966-68, pres., chief exec. officer, 1969-79, chmn. bd., 1979—; pres., dir. Western Colo. Power Co., 1969-74; pres. WEST Assocs., 1970-72; dir. First Security Corp., ZCMI; mem. Utah Nuclear Energy Commn., 1970-73; mem. industry adv. com. Def. Electric Power Adminstrn., 1975-77; mem. electric utilities com. Fed. Energy Adminstrn., 1975-77; mem. Western Regional Council, Gov.'s Mineral Lease Fund Adv. Com.; bd. dirs. Utah Bus. Devel. Corp., Nat. Assn. Electric Cos., 1974-77. Mem. adv. council Weber State U. Sch. Bus. and Econs., 1967-71, Brigham Young U., 1969-71; mem. nat. bd. advisors U. Utah Coll. Bus., 1976—; campaign chmn., dir. Utah United Funds, 1968-69; Trustee, treas. Utah Blue Cross, 1969-74; trustee Utah Found.; bd. dirs. Ballet West, 1969-74, Utah Symphony.; Utah state chmn. Nat. Com. Employer Support of Guard and Res., 1984. Served from 1st lt to maj. AUS, 1942-46, ETO. Decorated Bronze Star, Purple Heart; named Utah Outstanding Engr. in Industry, 1968. Mem. Utah N.G. Hon. Cols. Assn., Salt Lake Area C. of C. (pres. 1971-72, bd. govs.), Edison Electric Inst. (dir. 1974-77), Nat. Soc. Profl. Engrs. (past pres. local chpt.), Utah Mfrs. Assn. (dir. 1963-70, Mfr. of Year award 1971), N.W. Electric Light and Power Assn. (past dir.), N.A.M. (former dir. Utah), Nat. Elec. Contractors Assn. (citation 1974), High Temperature Reactor Devel. Assn. (trustee 1970-73), U. Utah Alumni Assn. Emeritus Club. Mem. Ch. Jesus Christ of Latter-day Saints. Clubs: Rotarian, Alta, Timpanogos, Salt Lake Country. Home: 4234 Neptune Dr Salt Lake City UT 84117 Office: 1407 W North Temple St PO Box 899 Salt Lake City UT 84110

HUNTER, GEORGE WILLIAM, III, parasitologist, educator; b. N.Y.C., Jan. 27, 1902; s. George William and Emily Isabel (Jobbins) H.; m. Adelaide Louise White, July 11, 1941 (div.); m. Fern Emily Wood, May 15, 1972; children—Anita Anderson, Gay Culp, Mina F. Sage. Student Carleton Coll., 1919-20; B.S., Knox Coll., 1923; M.S., U. Ill., 1924, Ph.D., 1927; cert. tropical and mil. medicine, 1944. Commd. 2d lt. U.S. Army Res. 1923, advanced through grades to maj. AUS, 1943, to col. U.S. Army, 1949; asst. chief dept. parasitology Army Med. Sch., 1942-45, chief, 1946-47, staff mem. tropical and mil. medicine course, 1942-47; chief sect. med. zoology 406th Med. Gen. Lab., Tokyo, 1947-51; chief sect. parasitology-entomology 4th Army Med. Lab., 1951-55; exec. officer commn. schistosomiasis Army Epidemiol. Bd., Philippines, 1945; dep. blood adminstr. Far East Command, Korea, 1950-51; ret., 1955; interim prof. biol. sci. U. Fla., Gainesville, 1956-57, lectr. biol. scis. and tropical medicine Coll. Medicine, 1957-67, prof. microbiol. Med. Sch., 1966-67, prof. emeritus, 1967—; res. coordinator, chief sect. parasitology La. State U. Internat. Ctr. Med. Research Tng., research prof. med. parasitology, sch. medicine; mem. faculty U. Costa Rica, 1961-63; clin. prof. parasitology, div. epidemiol., dept. community medicine U. Calif. Sch. Medicine, San Diego, 1974—. Decorated Bronze Star with oak leaf cluster; Harvard U. research fellow, 1940; NIH immunology schistosomiasis grantee, 1956-64; WHO schistosomiasis grantee, 1978-80; recipient Knox Coll. Alumni Achievement award, 1954, Carlos J. Finlay award, Cuba, 1958; named hon. citizen with distinction Kurume, Japan. Fellow Royal Soc. Tropical Medicine and Hygiene, AAAS, Am. Pub. Health Assn.; mem. Entomol. Soc. Am., Japan Soc. Parasitologists, Am. Soc. Zoologists Am. Micros. Soc., Wash. Acad. Scis., Assn. Southeastern Biologists, Southeastern Soc. Parasitologists (co-founder), Royal Inst. Pub. Health and Hygiene, Am. Soc. Parasitologists (charter, emeritus), Am. Soc. Tropical Medicine and Hygiene, Union Am. Biol. Socs. (exec. com. 1941-44), So. Calif. Parasitologists, Helminthological Soc. Wash., Japanese Soc. Parasitology, Assn. Mil. Surgeons U.S., Phi Beta Kappa, Sigma Xi, Delta Sigma Rho, Phi Eta, Beta Theta Pi. Clubs: Mil. Order Boars, Mil. Order World Wars, Mil. Order Carabao; Lions. Author: (with W.W. Frye, J.C. Swartzwelder), A Manual of Tropical Medicine, 4th edit., 1966; (with J.C. Swartzwelder and David Clyde) Tropical Medicine, 5th edit., 1976; Hunter's Tropical Medicine (G.T. Strickland) 1984. Contbr. articles to med. jours. Home: 17760 Camino Murrillo San Diego CA 92128 Office: PO Box 28286 Rancho Bernardo San Diego CA 92128

HUNTER, HOWARD WILLIAM, church official, lawyer; b. Boise, Idaho, Nov. 14, 1907; s. John William and Nellie Marie (Rasmussen) H.; m. Clara May Jeffs, June 10, 1931; children: Howard William (dec.), John Jacob, Richard Allen. JD cum laude, Southwestern U., 1939. Bar: Calif. 1939; ordained apostle Ch. of Jesus Christ of Latter-day Sts., 1959, bishop, 1941-47, high councilor, 1947-50. Engaged in banking Calif., 1928-34; practiced law Los Angeles, until 1959; mem. council of 12, Ch. Jesus Christ of Latter-day Sts., 1959—; dir. Beneficial Life Ins. Co., Salt Lake City, Watson Land Co., Los Angeles, Heber J. Grant & Co., First Security Corp., 1st Security Bank of Utah, Deseret Fed. Savs. and Loan Assn., Continental Western Life Ins. C, Utah Home Fire Ins. Co. Pres. Polynesian Cultural Center, Hawaii. Mem. Calif., Utah bar assns., Geneal. Soc. Utah (dir., past pres.). Home: 2833 Sherwood Dr Salt Lake City UT 84108 Office: 47 E South Temple Salt Lake City UT 84150

HUNTER, IRENE WIBERG, credit agency executive; b. Arlington, Wash., Sept. 3, 1922; d. Frank and Anna Marie (Burns) Wiberg; m. Charles Daniel Hunter, July 18, 1942; children—Linda Hunter McCammon, Steven Jeffrey. Student U. Wash., 1940, Seattle Coll., 1940-42, Seattle Bus. Sch., 1943. Cert. credit bur. exec., collection agy. exec. With Peoples Nat. Bank, Seattle, 1943-44; with various banks Calif., Ariz., 1944-45; co owner, mgr. Washington Credit, Inc., Bellevue, 1950—; dir.-at-large Wash. Collectors Assn., 1986-87. Mem. fundraising coms. YMCA, 1976-83; leader Girl Scouts Am., 1953-55; den mother Boy Scouts Am., 1955-57; instr. water safety ARC, 1954-60; mem. coms. PTA Lake Washington Sch. Dist., 1951-65; vol. Community Services for the Blind, Seattle, 1975-77, Griffin Boys Home, 1977-78. Mem. Bellevue Credit Women Internat. (founder, past pres., named Credit Woman of Yr. 1985), Seattle Consumer Credit Assn. (speakers bur.), Washington Collections Assn. (sec., treas. 1987—), Seattle Better Bus. Bur. (arbitration com. 1972—), Credit Women Internat. (dir. dist. 10 1972-73) Internat. Fellowship Cert. Collectors. Mem. Unity Ch. Home: 1554 W Lake Sammamish Pkwy SE Bellevue WA 98008 Office: PO Box 1378 Bellevue WA 98009

HUNTER, JEFFREY CHARLES, chemist, technical company manager, educator; b. San Diego, Oct. 19, 1938; s. Theodore Lee and Dorothy (Wilson) H.; m. Doreen E. Lonergan, Nov. 26, 1983. BS, San Diego State U., 1962, MS, 1964; MA in Mgmt., U. Redlands, 1979. Cert. Calif. Community Coll. Tchr. of bus. and chemistry. Sr. chemist Avery Internat., Azusa, Calif., 1966-71, lab. supr., 1971-76, product devel. specialist research dept. Label div., 1976-79, project mgr., 1979-84, tech. mgr. Avery Consumer and Office Products div., 1984—; undergrad. and grad. bus. instr. U. Redlands, 1980—, bus. and sci. instr. Coll. Profl. Studies U. San Francisco, 1981—, state chmn. curriculum design com. Coll. Profl. Studies, 1982-84. Contbr. articles to profl. jours.; co-author curriculum handbooks; patentee in field. Co-dir. East San Gabriel-Pomona Valley Back in Control Ctr., 1985—. Mem. Assn. MBA Execs., Am. Chem. Soc., TAPPI. Republican. Episcopalian. Club: Ontario Pkwy. Lodge: Kiwanis (sec., 1980, 81, 82, Circle K Club adv. Mt. San Antonio Coll.). Avocations: numismatics, raising Shar-Pei show dogs, scuba diving. Home: 17532 Calle Del Cornal Riverside CA 92505 Office: Avery Internat Consumer Products div 777 E Foothill Blvd Azusa CA 91702

HUNTER, JOHN HARNDEN, artist; b. Westmiddlesex, Pa., Sept. 26, 1934; s. John A. and Dorothea H.; children—Gregory Andrew, Christopher John. B.A., Pomona Coll., 1956; M.F.A., Claremont Grad. Sch., 1958. prof. studio art San Jose (Calif.) State U., 1965—; adviser, critic textbooks Holt, Rinehart & Winston, N.Y.C., 1972-80; Bd. dirs. San Jose Mus. Art.; guest artist Tamarind Lithography Workshop, 1969, Lakeside Studios, Mich., 1978, 79. One-person show, Cannes Film Festival, 1966; exhibited in group shows, Basel Art Fair, Documenta VI, Kassel, Germany, Cologne Art Fair, Galerie Wolfgang Ketterer, Munich; represented in permanent collections, Nat. Gallery Art, Washington, Mus. Modern Art, N.Y.C., Norton Simon Mus. Art, Pasadena, U. Minn., Mpls., Scripps Coll., Morrison Library, U. Calif., Berkeley, Los Angeles County Mus. Art, Amon Carter Mus. Western Art, Fort Worth, Grunwald Graphic Arts Found, UCLA, others. Served with AUS, 1958-62. Fulbright fellow Florence, Italy, 1963-64, 64-65. Office: San Jose State U Dept Art San Jose CA 95192

HUNTER, KAREN ANN, public relations executive; b. Perth Amboy, N.J., Feb. 15, 1959; d. Robert Tweedy and Barbara Carol (Rauschelbach) H. BA in Communications and Sociology, U. Calif.-San Diego, La Jolla, 1981. Pub. relations asst. Sheraton Hotels, Universal City, Calif., 1981-83; pub. relations dir. Sheraton Hotels, Universal City, 1983-86; news bur. mgr. Farmers Group Inc., Los Angeles, 1983; pub. relations dir. The Pebble Beach (Calif.) Co., 1986—. Bd. dirs. Del Monte Forest Found. Mem. Pub. Relations Soc. Am., Publicity Club of San Francisco, Monterey Peninsula C. of C. Office: Pebble Beach Co 101 Dewey Ave Pacific Grove CA 93950

HUNTER, KENTON C., marketing manager; b. East Prairie, Mo., Apr. 28, 1949; s. Robert Horrell and Roberta Lee (Conn) H.; m. Susan Jane Zoller, May 1, 1971; children: Allison Claire, Emily Amanda, Emily. BA, Westminster Coll., 1971; MBA, U. Mo., 1976. Learning disability specialist New, 1971-74; corp. mktg. mgr. Petroleum Info. Corp., Denver, 1976—; cons. in field. Internat. Market Research grantee U. Mo., 1978. Mem. Am. Mktg. Assn., Internat. Exhibitors Assn., Info. Industry Assn., Rocky Mountain Direct Mktg. Assn. (founding pres.), Am. Mgmt. Assn., Petroleum Exhibitors Assn. (pres.). Avocations: skiing, hunting. Home: 6076 S Colorado Blvd Littleton CO 80121 Office: Petroleum Info Corp 4100 E Dry Creek Rd Littleton CO 80201

HUNTER, RAYMOND EUGENE, physicist, judge; b. Moultrie, Ga., Sept. 4, 1935; s. William Jesse and Ruby (Inez) H.; m. Joyce Lee Turner, June 10, 1957; children: Allan Derek, Janis Lynn Hunter Gritzo. BS magna cum laude, U. Ga., 1957, MS, 1958; PhD, Fla. State U., 1964. Staff mem. Los Alamos Nat. Lab., 1964-66, asst. div. leader, 1980-85, assoc. div. leader, 1985—; head dept. physics, dean grad. sch. Valdosta State Coll. (Ga.), 1966-72; M.S., judge County of Los Alamos, 1975—. Contbr. articles to sci. and jud. jours. Mem. Los Alamos Republican Central Com., 1972—; chmn. County Personnel Bd., Los Alamos, 1973-75, Los Alamos Credit Union Surpervisory Com., 1972-76; mem. troup and dist. com. Boy Scouts Am., 1973—. Served to capt. USAF, 1958-61. Recipient Research and Devel. award USAF, 1961, Outstanding Young Educator award U.S. Jaycees, 1969, Disting. Performance award Los Alamos Nat. Lab., 1981. Mem. Nat. Judges Assn. (sec. 1981-82, pres. 1983-84, sr. dir. 1984-85), Am. Judges Assn., N.Mex. Judges Assn. (bd. dirs. 1979-83), N.Mex. Mcpl. Judges Assn., Am. Nuclear Soc., Phi Beta Kappa, Omicron Delta Kappa. Baptist. Club: Kiwanis (Los Alamos). Home: 111 Shirlane Pl Los Alamos NM 87544 Office: Los Alamos Nat Lab PO Box 1663 Los Alamos NM 87545

HUNTER, ROBERT TWEEDY, JR., consumer products company executive; b. Mount Pleasant, Pa., June 10, 1934; s. Robert Tweedy and Dorothy Jane (Connors) H.; m. Barbara Rauschelbach, Aug. 24, 1957; children: Karen, Robert Paul, Kristen. BS in Chemistry, Westminster Coll., 1956; MS in Phys. Chemistry, Pa. State U., 1958. Research chemist, sect. head Colgate Palmolive Co., Jersey City, 1958-70; research mgr., research dir. Amway Corp., Ada, Mich., 1970-76, exec. v.p. corp. devel. and policy adminstrn., 1980-83, exec. v.p. subs. adminstrn., 1983-84; exec. v.p., chief exec officer subs. Nutrilite Products Inc., Buena Park, Calif., 1976-80, exec. v.p., chief operating officer, 1984—; also bd. dirs.; bd. dirs. Amcon Industries, Inc. Patentee in field. Chmn. sustaining membership West Mich. Shores council Boy Scouts Am. Named Jaycee of Yr., Mendham (N.J.) Jaycees, 1970. Mem. Am. Chem. Soc., Am. Oil Chemists, Soap and Detergent Assn., Cosmetic Toiletries Fragrance Assn. Lutheran. Home: 18312 Lincoln St Villa Park CA 92667 Office: Nutrilite Products Inc 5600 Beach Blvd Buena Park CA 90622

HUNTER, WILMONT LENNINGTON, computer scientist; b. Chgo., July 23, 1927; s. Howard Walter and Eve Lynn (McKinstry) H.; B.S. in Elec. Engring., U. So. Calif., 1959; m. Gloria Catherine Swanson, Feb. 20, 1961; 1 son, Brian John. Elec. engr. Hoffman Labs., Los Angeles, 1953-55, Lockheed MSD, Van Nuys, Calif., 1955-57; engring. specialist Litton Industries, Van Nuys, 1957-67; electronics engr. Interstate Electronics Corp., Anaheim, Calif., 1967-70; mem. tech. staff Rockwell Internat. Co., Los Angeles, 1971-73; sr. devel. engr. Honeywell, Inc., Seattle and West Covina, Calif., 1973-75; mem. tech. staff Tex. Instruments Inc., Dallas, 1975-78; specialist engr. Boeing Co., Seattle, 1978—. Served with USNR, 1944-46. Decorated Commendation medal. Mem. Assn. Computing Machinery, Mensa, Eta Kappa Nu. Mem. Libertarian Ch. Author, patentee in field. Home: PO Box 78038 Seattle WA 98178 Office: Boeing Co PO Box 3999 Seattle WA 98124

HUNTHAUSEN, RAYMOND GERHARDT, archbishop; b. Anaconda, Mont., Aug. 21, 1921; s. Anthony Gerhardt and Edna (Tuchacherer) H. A.B., Carroll Coll., 1943, St. Edward's Sem., 1946; M.S., Notre Dame U., 1953; LL.D., DePaul U., 1960; postgrad. summers, St. Louis U., Catholic U., Fordham U. Ordained priest Roman Cath. Ch., 1946. Instr. chemistry Carroll Coll., 1946-57, football, basketball coach, 1953-57, pres., 1957-62; bishop Helena Diocese, Mont., 1962-75; archbishop of Seattle 1975—. Recipient Martin Luther King Jr. award Fellowship of Reconciliation, 1987. Mem. Am. Chem. Soc. Office: Chancery Office 910 Marion St Seattle WA 98104 *

HUNTINGTON, ROBERT WATKINSON, pathologist, retired; b. Hartford, Conn., July 2, 1907; s. Robert W. and Constance (Alton) H.; m. Katherine Bond UpChurch, Mar. 21, 1936; children—Robert W., Ann Heldman (dec.), Edith Huntington, Deborah Ward. B.A., Yale U., 1928, M.D., 1933. Lic. physician, Conn., Calif. Instr. pediatrics Washington U., St. Louis, 1935-38, pathology Cornell Med. Ctr., N.Y.C., 1938-41; assoc. prof. pathology U. So. Calif., Los Angeles, 1946-50; pathologist, Kern Med. Ctr., Bakersfield, Calif., 1950-75, pathologist emeritus, 1975—; assoc. clin. prof. U. So. Calif., 1950-70, clin. prof. pathology, 1970, clin. prof. emeritus, 1975—. Contbr. articles to profl. jours. Served to comdr., M.C. USNR, 1941-46. Recipient citation for Outstanding Contbrns. to Study of Coccidioidomycosis, Am. Coll. Chest Physicians, 1984; for contbrn. in Neoplastic and Non-neoplastic Disease, Calif. Tumor Tissue Registry, 1986. Fellow Am. Soc. Clin. Pathologists, Coll. Am. Pathologists.; mem. Am. Soc. Microbiology, Acad. Forensic Sci. Republican. Episcopalian. Address: 470 Wellington Cambria CA 93428

HUNTINGTON, STEPHEN PATRICK, computer programmer; b. Springfield, Mass., July 14, 1948; s. Perley Douglas and Priscilla Ann (Towne). BBA in Mktg., Pace U., 1970. Computer operator IBM, White Plains, N.Y., 1967-70; systems engr. IBM, N.Y.C., 1970-71, computer programmer, 1971-73; computer programmer IBM, Palo Alto, Calif., 1974, San Jose, Calif., 1975—. Republican. Home: 4017 Ambrose Ct San Jose CA 95121 Office: IBM 5600 Cottle Rd San Jose CA 95150

HUNTLEY, ALICE MAE, mfg. exec.; b. Atoka, Okla., May 9, 1917, d. Joseph LaHay and Lula May (Stapp) Howe; B.A. U. Okla., 1939; m. Loren Clifford Huntley, Nov. 7, 1942; children—Loren Lee, Marcia Lynn. Reporter, McAlester (Okla.) News Capital, 1939-41; sec., asst. to pres. and chmn. bd. N.Am. Aviation, Los Angeles, 1941-63; v.p., co-owner Tubular Specialties Mfg., Inc., Los Angeles, 1966—. Former sec. 1st Baptist Ch. of Westchester; sec. Westchester-Del Rey Republican Women, 1959-60; asso. mem. Rep. State Central Com., 1973. Cert. profl. sec.; named Outstanding Sec. in So. Calif., So. Calif. chpt., 1954, Internat. Sec. of Year, 1955 (both Nat. Secs. Assn.). Home: 8238 Calabar Ave Playa del Rey CA 90293 Office: 13011 S Spring St Los Angeles CA 90061

HUNTLEY, ROBERT JOSEPH, management consultant; b. Rochester, N.Y., May 28, 1924; s. Carroll Thomas and Margaret (Mosier) H.; student U. Redlands, 1943-44; B.S., U. So. Calif., 1947, M.S., 1952, D. Pub. Adminstrn., 1974; m. Patricia Ann Poss, Aug. 25, 1945; children: Timothy Robert, Debra Ann, Jon Joseph. Mem. Budget Bur. City of Los Angeles, 1947-52; asst. adminstrv. officer City of Beverly Hills, Calif., 1952-56; city adminstr. City of Santa Paula, Calif., 1957-58, City of La Habra, Calif., 1959-64; exec. Alpha Beta Acme Markets, La Habra, 1964-67; city adminstr. City of Westminster, Calif., 1967-77; exec. asst. County of Orange (Calif.), 1977-80, chief, labor relations, 1980-82, chief personnel ops., 1982-84; exec. dir. Hughes Enterprises, Laguna Hills, Calif., 1984-85; lectr., U. So. Calif., 1953-58, 70-74, Ventura Coll., 1958; asst. prof. Calif. State U., Fullerton, 1964-65; lectr. Golden West Coll., Orange Coast Coll., Calif. State U. at Davis, prof. Calif. State U. at Long Beach, 1971-79. Mem. Gov.'s Policy Com. of Local Govt. Reform Task Force, 1973; active United Crusade. Served with USN, 1941-45; PTO. Mem. Am. Acad. Polit. and Social Sci., Am. Soc. Pub. Adminstrn., Western Govtl. Research Assn., Internat. City Mgmt. Assn., League Calif. Cities (exec. com. 1964-72), Blue Key, Pi Sigma Alpha, Phi Kappa Tau. Republican. Roman Catholic. Author: History of Administrative Research, 1952; Public Relations Training, 1954; The American City Manager, 1974. Home: 15172 Vermont St Westminster CA 92683 Office: Box 430 Westminster CA 92684-0430

HUNTLEY, SCOTT ALAN, architect, human resource specialist; b. Richland, Wash., Sept. 9, 1951; s. Robin Donald and Helen Mae (Houghan) H.; m. Rebecca Louise Schultz, Aug. 7, 1976; children: Nathaniel, Andrew. BS in Architecture, Wash. State U., 1973, BArch., 1977. Registered architect. Architect McCue & Assocs., Richland, 1973-74, 75-76; plans examiner City of Richland, 1974-75; architect Seracuse Lawler, Ptnrs., Denver, 1977-79; architect The Callison Partnership, Seattle, 1979—, dir. human resources dept., 1984—; bd. advisors Land Use/Transp. Plan, city of Seattle, 1981-83; mem. Nat. Trust Hist. Preservation, 1984-85. Area chmn. United Way, Seattle, 1985; mem. Leadership Tomorrow, Seattle, 1985-86. Mem. AIA, Profl. Services Mgmt. Assn. (bd. dirs. 1986—), Sigma Phi Epsilon (asst. mgr. Pullman, Wash. chpt. 1972-73). Lutheran. Club: Wash. Athletic (Seattle). Home: 5422 46th SW Seattle WA 98136 Office: The Callison Partnership Ltd 1423 3d Ave Seattle WA 98101

HUNTOON, GLENN DAVID, distribution company executive; b. Alhambra, Calif., Aug. 17, 1943; s. Glenn Russell and Irene (Severance) H.; m. Sally M. Harrison, June 24, 1967 (div. 1971); 1 child, Glenn David Jr.; m. Jane S. Nylin, July 6, 1973; children—Gregory Russell, Emily Jane. B.A., Claremont Men's Coll., 1965; M.B.A., U. So. Calif., 1967. C.P.A., Calif. Sr. acct. Cooper's & Lybrand, Los Angeles, 1966-68; exec. v.p. Federated Sales Co., Temple City, Calif., 1968-72; pres. Federated-Goodkin Corp., Industry, Calif., 1972—; chmn. bd. Allied Hardware Services, 1987—. Trustee Claremont McKenna Coll., Calif., 1981-84. Served to capt. U.S. Army, 1969-71. Mem. Am. Inst. C.P.A.s, Town Hall Calif. Republican. Office: Federated-Goodkin Corp 345 Baldwin Park Blvd City of Industry CA 91746

HUPP, HARRY L., federal judge; b. 1929. AB, Stanford U., 1953, LLB, 1955. Judge, U.S. Dist. Ct. (cen. dist.) Calif., Los Angeles.; Sole practice Beardsley, Hufstedler and Kemble, Los Angeles, 1955-72; judge Superior Ct. of Los Angeles, 1972-84; appointed fed. dist. judge U.S. Dist. Ct. (cen. dist.), Los Angeles, 1984—. Served with U.S. Army, 1950-52. Mem. State Bar Assn. Calif., Los Angeles County Bar Assn. (Trial Judge of Yr. 1983). Office: US Courthouse 312 N Spring St Los Angeles CA 90012 *

HURABIELL, JOHN PHILIP, SR., lawyer, business executive; b. San Francisco, June 2, 1947; s. Emile John and Anna Beatrice (Blumenauer) H.; m. Judith Marie Hurabiell, June 7, 1969; children—Marie Louise, Michele, Heather, John Philip Jr. J.D., San Francisco Law Sch., 1976. Bar: Calif. 1977. Sole practice, San Francisco, 1977-86; ptnr. Huppert & Hurabiell, San Francisco, 1985—; pres. San Francisco S.A.F.E., Inc.; treas. Republican election coms.; Served with U.S. Navy, Vietnam. Decorated Navy Commendation Medal. Mem. ABA, Calif. Bar Assn., San Francisco Bar Assn., Assn. Trial Lawyers Am., Calif. Trial Lawyers Assn., San Francisco Trial Lawyers Assn., Lawyers Club San Francisco, St. Thomas More Soc., Sports Lawyers Assn., Hook and Ladder Soc. Roman Catholic. Clubs: Press of San Francisco, Ferrari Owners. Lodge: Masons. Editor, primary author:

C.A.L.U. Business Practices Guidelines, rev. edit., 1980. Office: Huppert & Hurabiell 1355 Market St Suite 417 San Francisco CA 94103

HURLEY, FRANCIS T., archbishop; b. San Francisco, Jan. 12, 1927. Ed., St. Patrick Sem., Menlo Park, Calif., Catholic U. Am. Ordained priest Roman Cath. Ch., 1951; with NCWC, Washington; asst. sec. NCWC, 1958-68; asso. sec. NCCB and USCC, 1968-70; consecrated bishop 1970; titular bishop Daimlaig and aux. bishop Diocese of Juneau, Alaska, 1970-71; bishop of Juneau 1971-76, archbishop of Anchorage, 1976—. Office: Chancery Office PO Box 2239 Anchorage AK 99510 *

HURLEY, GLENN ELDRIDGE, medical technologist; b. New Orleans, Dec. 10, 1950; s. Eldrige W. and Dorothy M. (Lemons) H.; m. Monica J. Renolds, Nov. 24, 1982 (div. Feb. 1984); m. Deborah Ann Painter, Feb. 14, 1984; 1 child, Angel. AA, Compton Coll., 1970; BS, Calif. State U., Long Beach, 1977; cert., U. Calif., Irvine, 1983; MA, Calif. U. Advanced Studies, Novato, 1986. Carrier U.S. Postal Service, Gardena, Calif., 1970-74; research cons. Naples Lab., Long Beach, 1974-83; med. technologist VA Hosp., Loma Linda, Calif., 1977-79; chemist VA Hosp., Long Beach, 1979-82, supervisory med. technologist, 1982—; chmn. Long Beach Equal Employment Opportunity Adv. Com., 1980-83. Assoc. Smithsonian Instn., Nat. Geog. Soc., Am. Film Inst., Am. Soc. Microbiologists; mem. Calif. State U.-Long Beach Alumni Assn. Democrat. Methodist. Avocations: scuba diving, weightlifting, racquetball, numismatics. Home: 5350 Orangethorpe La Palma CA 90626

HURLEY, LUCILLE SHAPSON, nutritionist, educator; b. Riga, Latvia, May 8, 1922; came to U.S., 1925, naturalized, 1929; married 1945 (div. 1963); children: Barbara Hurley, Michael Hurley; m. Kenneth Thompson, 1967; stepchildren: Tamara, Marcus, Nicholas. BS in Nutrition, U. Wis., 1943; PhD in Nutrition (minors in Physiology, Biochemistry, Histology), U. Calif., Berkeley, 1950. Biochemist Child Research Council U. Colo. Sch. Medicine, Denver, 1951-52, research assoc. div Chem. Embryology, 1952-55; asst. research biochemist to asst. prof. U. Calif. Dept. Home Economics, Davis, 1955-61, assoc. prof. Nutrition, 1961-66, dept. chmn., 1963-65; prof. Nutrition dept. Nutrition U. Calif., Davis, 1966—, acting chmn. of dept., 1966-67, prof. Nutrition Sch. Medicine, 1971-77; sabbatical leave Laboratoire d'Embryologie U. Paris Med. Sch., 1962-63, Laboratoire de Biophysique, fall 1969; spl. leave Dept. Biochemistry U. Calif., Berkeley, summer 1961; vis. scientist Laboratoire des Isotopes Pasteur Inst., Paris, summers 1964, 65, Polish Acad. Sci., Nov. 1976; research collaborator Brookhaven Nat. Lab., 1966-68; vis. prof. Oreg. State U., July 1970, Wash. State U., July 1975; chercheur átranger, Inst. Nat. pour la Santeá et la Recherche Mádicale, Paris, Sept. 1974, 76; disting. lectr. Nutrition Research Inst. Oreg. State U., Feb. 1978, La. State U. Med. Ctr., Shreveport, Jan. 1980, Ga. Med. Coll., Augusta, 1981, 82, 83, 84, 85; Margaret Eppright lectr. Nutrition U. Tex., Austin, Apr. 1979; Marie Curie lectr. Sci., Tex. Women's U., 1983; York lectr. Auburn U., 1984; bd. dirs. sci. counselors Nat. Inst. Dental Research NIH, 1971-75, adv. council 1985—; mem. Nutrition study sect. NIH, 1975-79; Nat. Acad. Scis. NRC subcom. Environ. Geochemistry in Relation to Health and Disease, 1976-79, chmn. subcom. Nutrient Requirements of Mouse, 1974-78, com. on Nutrition in Med. Edn., 1984-85, com. on Diet and Health, 1986—; sci. adv. council The Nutrition Found., 1980-84. Editor: Jour. Nutrition, 1984—; mem. editorial bd. Teratology, 1967-75, Am. Jour. Clin. Nutrition, 1977-80, Jour. Inorganic Biochemistry, 1978—, Biol. Trace Element Research, 1978—, Magnesium Bull., 1980-84, Nutrition Research, 1981-84, Magnesium, 1983—, Annales de Recherches Veáterinaires, 1983—, Issues and Revs. in Teratology, 1985—. Guggenheim fellow, 1962, 69; awardee Fundamental Research in Nutrition and Exptl. Foods, Borden, 1965, Osborne and Mendel award, 1981, Lederle award, 1985; medallist IntraScience Research Found., 1978, médaille de Vermeil, Acad. Nat. de Mádecine, France, 1983; 2nd E.V. McCollum Internat. Lectr., 1980. Fellow AAAS; mem. Am. Inst. Nutrition (nominating com. 1970, membership com. 1970-72, sec. 1972-75, councillor 1979-82, pres.-elect 1982-83, pres. 1983-85), Teratology Soc. (charter mem., recorder 1968-72, pres.-elect 1974-75, pres. 1975-76), Soc. for Experimental Biology and Medicine (Nat. Membership com. 1978-81, councillor 1985—), European Teratology Soc., The Nutrition Soc., Am. Soc. Clin. Nutrition, Soc. Environ. Geochemistry and Health (pres.-elect 1973-74, pres. 1974-75, nominating com. 1979-80), Perinatal Research Soc., Sigma Xi (ann. meeting theme lectr. 1985), Iota Sigma Pi, Sigma Delta Epsilon. Office: U Calif Davis Dept Nutrition Davis CA 95616

HURLEY, MARK JOSEPH, bishop; b. San Francisco, Dec. 13, 1919; s. Mark J. and Josephine (Keohane) H. Student, St. Joseph's Coll., Mountain VIew, Calif., 1939, St. Patrick's Sem., Menlo Park, Calif., 1944; postgrad., U. Calif. at Berkeley, 1943-45; Ph.D., Cath. U. Am., 1947; J.C.B., Lateran U., Rome, 1963; LL.D., U. Portland, 1971. Ordained priest Roman Catholic Ch., 1944; asst. supt. schs. Archdiocese, San Francisco, 1944-51; tchr. Serra High Sch., San Mateo, Calif., 1944; prin. Bishop O'Dowd High Sch., Oakland, Calif., 1951-58, Marin Cath. High Sch., Marin County, Calif., 1959-61; supt. schs. Diocese, Stockton, Calif., 1962-65; chancellor, diocesan consultor Diocese, 1962-65; asst. chancellor Arcdiocese, San Francisco, 1965-67; vicar gen. Arcdiocese, 1967-69; titular bishop Thunusuda; aux. bishop Thunusuda, San Francisco, 1967-69; bishop Santa Rosa, Cal., 1969—; pastor St. Francis Assisi Ch., San Francisco, 1967—; Prof. grad. schs. Loyola U., Balt., 1946, U. San Francisco, 1948, San Francisco Coll. Women, 1949, Dominican Coll., San Rafael, Calif., 1949, Cath. U. Am., 1954; Del. Conf. Psychiatry and Religion, San Francisco, 1957; mem. bd. Calif. Com. on Study Edn., 1955-60; cons. Congregation for Cath. Edn., 1986—; del.-at-large Cal., White House Conf. on Youth, 1960; Cath. del., observer Nat. Council Chs., Columbus, Ohio, 1964; del. edn. conf. German and Am. educators, Nat. Cath. Edn. Assn., Munich, Germany, 1960; mem. commns. sems., univs. and schs. II Vatican Council, Rome, 1962-65; mem. commn. Christian formation U.S. Cath. Conf. Bishops, 1968; asst. archdiocesan coordinator Campaign on Taxation Schs. Calif., 1958, Rosary Crusade, 1961; adminstr. Cath. Sch. Purchasing Div., 1948-51, St. Eugene's Ch., Santa Rosa, Calif., 1959, St. John's Ch., San Francisco, 1961; mem. U.S. Bishops' Press Panel, Vatican Council, 1964-65, U.S. Bishops' Com. on Laity, 1964, U.S. Bishops' Com. Cath.-Jewish Relationships, 1965—, U.S. Bishops' Com. on Ecumenical and Interreligious Affairs, 1970, Conf. Maj. Superiors of Men, 1970; chmn. citizens Com. for San Francisco State Coll., 1968—; mem. adminstrn. bd. Nat. Council Cath. Bishops, 1970, mem. nominating com., 1971; mem. Internat. Secretariat for Non-Believers, Vatican, 1973; chmn. Secretariat for Human Values, Nat. Conf. Cath. Bishops, Washington, 1975. Syndicated columnist, San Francisco Monitor, Sacramento Herald, Oakland Voice, Yakima (Wash.) Our Times, Guam Diocesan Press, 1949-66, TV speaker and panelist, 1956-67; Author: Church State Relationships in Education in California, 1948, Commentary on Declaration on Christian Education in Vatican II, 1966, Report on Education in Peru, 1965, The Church and Science, 1982. Trustee N.Am. Coll., Rome, 1970, Cath. U. Am., 1978—, Cath. Relief Services, 1979. Address: PO Box 1297 Santa Rosa CA 95402

HURN, PAULA LAROSE, social worker; b. Zion, Ill., Aug. 22, 1929; d. Paul M. and Dorothy S. (Clendinen) LaRose; m. Hal Tillotson Hurn (dec. 1973); children: Steven LaRose, Julia Ann, Geoffrey Dutton. BA, Oberlin Coll., 1950; MSW, U. Pitts., 1953. Dir. social services Bensenville (Ill.) Home Soc., 1976-79; pvt. practice social work Glencoe, Ill., 1977-78; social worker Phoenix Meml. Hosp. and Phoenix Gen. Hosp., 1983-86; prin. Elder Links, Phoenix, 1986—. Founder, chmn. Ariz. Tenants Assn., Phoenix, 1979-85; mem. housing commn., City of Phoenix, 1985—, Walden Woodwind Quintet, Phoenix, 1982; bd. dirs. ACLU Cen. Chpt., Phoenix, 1985—; precinct chmn. Cavalier, Phoenix, 1984—. Recipient project grant Emma Lyman Cabot Found., Phoenix, 1983-84. Mem. Nat. Assn. Social Workers (cert.), Profl. Assn. Gerontology Edn. and Service (program chmn. 1986—). Democrat. Home and Office: 2032 E Monterey Way Phoenix AZ 85016

HURST, JAMES KENDALL, chemistry educator, consultant, researcher; b. Maquoketa, Iowa, Oct. 17, 1940; s. Ernst Paul and Mary Eleanor (Bacon) Albrecht; m. Karen Sue Elder, June 12, 1966; children: Harvey, Vincent. BA cum laude, Cornell Coll., 1962; PhD, Stanford U., 1966. Postdoctoral fellow Cornell U., Ithaca, N.Y., 1966-69; asst. prof. chemistry Oreg. Grad. Ctr., Beaverton, 1969-73, assoc. prof., 1973-79, prof., 1979—, chmn., 1979-83; vis. prof. Ecole Polytechnique Federale, Lausanne, Switzerland, 1980-81, 85-86; cons. McDonnell-Douglas, St. Louis, 1980-82. Contbr. numerous papers to profl. publs. Sec. Portland (Oreg.) Chemists Supporting the Pauling Award Com., 1982-85. Recipient Men's Senate Key, Cornell Coll., 1961; Standard Oil scholar Cornell Coll., 1962; Allied Chem. fellow Stanford U., 1965. Mem. Am. Chem. Soc., Phi Beta Kappa. Club: Somerset West Soccer (Beaverton) (pres. 1978-79). Office: Oreg Grad Ctr 19600 NW VonNeumann Dr Beaverton OR 97006-1999

HURST, TIMOTHY ALLEN, government administrator, auditor, consultant; b. Burley, Idaho, Sept. 28, 1951; s. Harold R. And Irene La Deane (Allen) H.; m. Becky A'Dora Egbert, Jan. 4, 1974; children: Kresta, Jessica, Timbri, Britany. BBA, Idaho State U., 1975. Dep. auditor Cassia County, Burley, Idaho, 1975-85, county administr., 1986—; computer cons., 1981—; cons. Idaho Sec. State, Boise, 1982—. Pres. Heyburn (Idaho) Parent Tchr. Orgn., 1985—. Mem. Govt. Fin. Officers Assn., Idaho-Oreg. IBM Users Group (founder, chmn. 1980-84). Republican. Mormon. Avocations: reading, family, woodworking, sports. Home: 825 S Boundary Heyburn ID 83336 Office: Cassia County Courthouse Burley ID 83318

HURT, CHARLIE DEUEL, III, library school director; b. Charlottesville, Va., Sept. 20, 1950; s. Charlie Deuel Jr. and Timie Oletta (Young) H.; m. Susan Edith Scudamore, May 15, 1981. BA, U. Va., 1971; MLS, U. Ky., 1975; PhD, U. Wis., 1981. Engring. librarian U. Va., Charlottesville, 1975-78, automation librarian, 1977-78; asst. prof. McGill U., Montreal, Que., Can., 1981-84, assoc. prof., 1984; assoc. prof. Simmons Coll., Boston, 1984-86; dir. lib. sch. U. Ariz., Tucson, 1986—; prin. Info. Prime, Montreal, 1984—; cons. Scudamore & Assocs. Montreal, 1984-85. Contbr. articles to profl. jours. Hollowell grantee Simmons Coll., 1984. Mem. ALA, Assn. Library and Info. Sci. Edn., History Sci. Soc., N.Y. Acad. Sci. Avocations: stats., computing. Home: 6781 E 4th St Tucson AZ 85710-2217 Office: U Ariz Grad Library Sch 1515 E First St Tucson AZ 85719

HURT, JAMES EDWARD, physicist; b. Newton, Kans., Feb. 11, 1935; s. Waldo Ernest and Pauline Belle (Vannaman) H.; B.S., Okla. State U., 1957, M.S., 1959, Ph.D., 1963. Sr. assoc. physicist IBM Corp., Poughkeepsie, N.Y., 1963-64, staff physicist, 1964-66; Boulder, Colo., 1966-68, adv. physicist, Boulder, 1968-76, San Jose, 1976-77, Boulder, 1977-78, Tucson, 1978—. Mem. AAAS, Am. Phys. Soc. Home: 9906 E Colette Tucson AZ 85748 Office: IBM Corp Gen Products Div Dept 68U Bldg 041-1 Tucson AZ 85744

HURT, NATHAN HAMPTON, JR., mechanical engineer; b. Clifton, Mo., June 7, 1921; s. Nathan Hampton Sr. and Mary Lillian (Mayo) H.; m. LuCretia Ann Cutler, Feb. 16, 1946 (dec. 1980); children: Steven Eugene, Mark Lindsay, Nikki Alexandra; m. Karin Elisabeth Tuttle, Aug. 30, 1980; stepchildren: Audrey Barbara Patt, Christine Yvonne Reed. Student in mech. engring. Mont. Sch. Mines, 1944, U. So. Calif., 1944-46; B.S. in Mech. Engring., U. Colo., 1947. Engr. Goodyear Tire and Rubber Co., Akron, Ohio, 1947-52, mgr. chem. plants engring., Brasil and Logan, Ohio, 1956-68; supt. plant engring. Goodyear Atomic Corp., Piketon, Ohio, 1952-56, mgr. plant engring., 1968-72, dep. gen. mgr., 1972-77, gen. mgr., 1977-85, pres., 1985-87; ret., 1987; mgr., Los Alamos Tech. Assocs., 1987, mgr. bus. devel., 1987—. Mem. Chief Logan council Boy Scouts Am., 1970-80; bd. dirs. Ross County Med. Ctr., Chillicothe, Ohio, 1974. Mem. Chillicothe C. of C., Waverly C. of C., Jackson C. of C., Portsmouth C. of C., AMSE (v.p. 1984—), Am. Inst. Chem. Engrs., Am. Soc. Engring. Mgmt., Atomic Indsl. Forum. Lodge: Rotary. Avocations: golf, racquetball, snow skiing. Home: 8401 Spain Rd NE Apt 36E Albuquerque NM 87111 Office: Los Alamos Tech Assocs Los Alamos NM 87544

HURTADO, CORYDON DICKS, management consultant; b. Westerly, R.I., May 18, 1937; s. Corydon Clark and Elizabeth (McInnes) H.; m. Nancy Trott, Dec. 12, 1964; children: Kevin Eric, Tracy Ellen, Sheri Michelle. BS in Mktg./Advt., U. So. Calif., 1964, postgrad., 1973-75; MBA, U. San Francisco, 1973; PhD, Calif. Coast U., 1985. Cert. mgmt. cons.; cert. in data processing. Supr. computer ops. United Calif. Bank, Los Angeles, 1960-63; asst. cashier, mgr. data processing Beverly Hills (Calif.) Nat. Bank, 1963-64; asst. cashier, asst. mgr. Northern Calif. data processing dept. United Calif. Bank, San Francisco, 1964-65; mgmt. cons. supr. Touche, Ross Bailey & Smart, San Francisco, 1965-68; mgmt. cons. supr., coordinator state and local govt. consulting Ernst & Ernst, Sacramento, 1968-70; founder, pres. Cyberserv Internat. Co., Tahoe Paradise, Calif., 1970-81; pres. Cyberserv Internat. Co., Mill Valley, Calif., 1983—; prin., dir. mgmt. adv. services div. John F. Forbes & Co., San Francisco, 1981-83. Contbr. articles to profl. jours. Mem. Inst. Mgmt. Cons., Soc. Profl. Mgmt. Cons., Am. Soc. Pub. Adminstrn., Am. Mktg. Assn., Phi Gamma Delta. Office: Cyberserv Internat Co 1091 W California Ave Mill Valley CA 94941

HURTUBISE, ROBERT JOHN, chemistry educator; b. Chgo., June 7, 1941; s. Edward John and Gretta Agnes (Ward) H.; m. Paula Francine Brokhage, Aug. 14, 1965; children: Timothy, David, Suzanne. BS in Chemistry, Xavier U., 1964, MS in Chemistry, 1966; PhD in Chemistry, Ohio U., 1969. Asst. prof. chemistry Rockhurst Coll., Kansas City, Mo., 1969-71; sect. supr. Pfizer Inc., Terre Haute, Ind., 1971-74; prof. U. Wyo., Laramie, 1974—. Author: Soild Surface Luminescence Analysis: Theory, Instrumentation, Applications, 1981; reviews; contbr. chpts. to books; articles to profl. jours. Research grantee U. Wyo., Laramie Energy Tech. Ctr., 1975-77, 1977-79, Dept. Energy, 1979-82, 80-83, 83-86, 83-86, NSF, 1975, 81, also instrumentation grantee NSF, 1981, 82, 83. Mem. AAAS, Am. Chem. Soc., Soc. Applied Spectroscopy. Avocation: shortwave radio. Office: U Wyo Chemistry Dept Laramie WY 82070

HURWITZ, LEWIS EDWARD, accountant; b. Oakland, Calif., Sept. 10, 1952; s. Lloyd Edward and Lois Jane (Unger) H.; m. Nancy Ann Brown, Sept. 16, 1972; children: Elizabeth, Michael. BS, Armstrong U., Berkeley, Calif., 1978. V.p. fin. Winfield Fin. Corp., Berkeley, 1982-84; dir. fin. Baker & McKenzie, San Francisco, 1984-85; audit mgr. Joseph B. Johnson CPA, Pleasanton, Calif., 1985-86, Andrews, Carlo & Co. CPA, Oakland, 1986—. Author: (chpt.) Current Micro-Economic Problems, 1979. Mem. Soc. Service/Human Relations bd. City of Alameda, 1984-85, city treas., 1985—. Served with USN, 1970-75. Mem. Nat. Assn. Accts., Am. Mgmt. Assn., Am. Philatelic Soc. Jewish. Home: 2841 Van Buren St Alameda CA 95401 Office: Andrews Carlo & Co CPA 460 Hegenberger Rd #730 Oakland CA 94611

HURWITZ, THEODORE PAUL, lawyer, educational administrator; b. Boston, Apr. 28, 1936; s. Irving and Rose Ida (Vigor) H.; m. Paula Mae Agranat, Nov. 10, 1963; children: Hugh James, Todd Andrew. Student, U. Iowa, 1958; JD, Boston U., 1961; LLM in Taxation, DePaul U., 1982. Bar: U.S. Dist Ct. Mass. 1964. Sole practice Boston, 1962-69; dir. estate planning Calif. Inst. Tech., Pasadena, 1969-74, v.p. inst. relations, 1985—; assoc. v.p. devel. U. Chgo., 1974-85. Served with USCG, 1961. Home: 500 S Hill Ave Pasadena CA 91106 Office: Calif Inst Tech 1201 E Calif Blvd Pasadena CA 91125

HUSHAW, JAMES S., newspaper editor; b. Bell, Calif., July 17, 1935; s. Charles Coy and Marie Katherin (Johnson) H.; m. Glenda Rose Merrick, June 14, 1958; children—Craig, Jana, Jeff. B.A., San Jose State U., 1957. Mng. editor Glendale News Press, Calif., 1959-68; asst. managing editor Riverside Press Enterprise, Calif., 1968-72; managing editor Nev. State Jour., Reno, 1972-73, Reno Evening Gazette, 1973-74, Stockton Record, Calif., 1975—. Mem. Calif. Newspaper Editors Assn. (pres. 1979), Calif. AP Editors (pres. 1978), Am. Soc. Newspaper Editors, Sigma Delta Chi (pres. Nev. chpt. 1973). Republican. Lutheran. Lodge: Rotary (bd. dirs. Stockton chpt. 1984—). Office: Stockton Newspapers Inc 530 E Market St Stockton CA 95202 *

HUSS, CHARLES MAURICE, municipal building official; b. Chgo., Nov. 11, 1946; s. Charles Maurice and June Pierce (Bailey) H.; m. Winifred Louise Traughber, Dec. 24, 1973; children—Amber Elaine, Ra Ja Lorraine, Micah Alexander, Gabriel Joe, Cameron M., Jordan Charles. A.A., Kendall Coll., 1984; student Oregon State U., Western Oreg. State Coll., U. Cinn., U. Alaska. Traffic mgr. The Harwald Co., Evanston, Ill., 1966-67, asst. v.p., 1968-69; traffic mgr. Northwestern U. Press, Evanston, 1969-71; fire chief City of Kotzebue (Alaska), 1971-76, asst. city mgr., 1973-76; dir. maintenance USPHS Hosp., Kotzebue, 1976-79; pres., gen. mgr. Action Builders, Inc., Kotzebue, 1979-82; gen. mgr. Husky Maintenance Services, 1982—; chief bldg. insp. City of Kotzebue, 1985—. Chmn., Kotzebue Planning Commn., 1978-82, Kotzebue Sch. Bd., 1974-79, 83—; founding vice chmn. Kotzebue chpt. ARC; mem. Alaska Criminal Code Revision Commn., 1976-78; mem. Alaska Fire Fighter Tng. Commn.; vol. Kotzebue Vol. Fire Dept., 1972-76, 82-86; bd. dirs, instr. Alaska Craftsman Home Program 1986—; instr. Kotzebue Regional Fire Tng. Ctr., 1982—. Pullman Found. scholar, 1964-65; Blackburn Coll. scholar, 1964-65; Ill. State scholar, 1964-66. Mem. Constrn. Specifications Inst., Soc. Fire Service Instrs., Bldg. Officials and Code Adminstrs. Internat., Alaska Firefighters Assn., Internat. Assn. Fire and Arson Investigators, ASHRAE, Western Fire Chiefs Assn., Internat. Conf. Bldg. Ofcls., Internat. Assn. Plumbing and Mech. Ofcls., Internat. Assn. Elec. Insps., Internat. Assn. Fire Chiefs, Home Builders Assn. Alaska, Nat. Fire Protection Assn., Coalition for Home Fire Safety, Kotzebue C. of C. Guest essayist: Seven Days and Sunday (Kirkpatrick), 1973. Home and Office: PO Box 277 Kotzebue AK 99752

HUSS, GLENN I., meteoriticist; b. Haswell, Colo., May 10, 1921; s. Ernest Abram and Martha Marie (Armbruster) H.; m. Margaret Ann Nininger, June 21, 1952; children: Gary Robert, Peggy Ann, Susan Marie. BA, U. Denver, 1951, MA, 1952. Mgr., preparator Am. Meteorite Mus., Sedona, Ariz., 1955-60; dir. Am. Meteorite Lab., Denver, 1960—. Served with U.S. Army, 1942-45, ETO. Mem. AAAS, Internat. Assn. Geochem. and Cosmochem., Am. Astron. Soc., Geochem. Soc., Meteoritical Soc., Ariz. Acad. Sci. Office: Am Meteorite Lab PO Box 2098 Denver CO 80201

HUSSAIN, NIHAD ABDUL LATIF, engineering educator, administrator, researcher; b. Basrah, Iraq, Jan. 9, 1941; s. Abdul Latif and Naziha (Elfrieh) H.; m. Suzanne Nancy Quillen, June 1, 1964; children—Joy, Samir, Shaun. B.Sc. with honors, Baghdad U., Iraq, 1962; M.Sc., Purdue U., 1965; Ph.D., U. Notre Dame, 1969. Asst. prof. mech. engring. San Diego State U., 1969-72, assoc. prof., 1972-75, prof., 1975-81, assoc. dean engring., 1981—; design engr. Al-Damalogy Cons. Engrs., Baghdad, Iraq, 1962-63; research asst. dept. mech. engring. U. Notre Dame, Ind., 1965-69. Contbr. articles on heat transfer and fluid mechanics to profl. jours. Com. chmn. Cub Scouts Pack 605, Boy Scouts Am., 1973-75; engring. sci. adviser Poway Sch. Bd. Edn., Calif., 1973-83. Summer faculty research fellow NASA, Lewis Research Ctr., Cleve., 1973-74, U.S. Air Force, Wright-Patterson AFB, Dayton, Ohio, 1976. Mem. ASME (chmn. K-19 environ. heat transfer com. 1987—), Am. Soc. Engring. Edn. (vice chmn. awards Pacific Southwest sect.), AAAS, Sigma Xi, Tau Beta Pi. Office: San Diego State U Coll Engring San Diego CA 92182

HUSSEY, WILLIAM BERTRAND, retired foreign service officer; b. Bellingham, Wash., Oct. 23, 1915; s. Bertrand Brokaw and Ruth (Axtell) H.; m. Fredricka Boone, Dec. 31, 1940 (div. 1957); children: Christina, Pamela, Eva, William Bertrand, Peter; m. Piyachart Bunnag, May 20, 1959. B.S., Boston U., 1938; postgrad., UCLA, 1939-40, Naval War Coll., 1953-54. Asst. housing mgmt. supr. U.S. Housing Authority, 1941-42; chmn. London (Eng.) Liaison Group, also State Dept. rep., 1948-52; spl. State Dept. rep., Rome, 1949, Paris, 1950; chmn. regional conf., Dhahran, Saudi Arabia, 1949, chief civil-mil. relations sect., Munich, Germany, 1952-53, adminstrv. officer, Frankfurt, Germany, 1953-55, attache, Rangoon, Burma, 1955-56, consul, Chiengmai, Thailand, 1957-59; acting dep. chief plans and devel. staff Bur. Ednl. and Cultural Affairs, Dept. State, 1959-60, dep. chief cultural presentations div., 1960-61; mem. del. regional confs. in, Beirut, Lebanon and Kampala, Uganda, 1960; group leader Nat. Strategy Seminar, Asilomar, Calif., 1960; counselor of embassy, Lome, Republic of Togo, 1961-65, Blantyre, Malawi, 1965-66; chargé d'affaires Am. embassy, Maseru, Lesotho, 1966-67, Port Louis, Mauritius, 1967-68; UN rep., Western Pacific, Apia, Western Samoa, 1969-74, fgn. affairs cons., 1974—; del. UN Law of Sea Conf., 1975-80; assoc. v.p. Los Angeles Olympic Organizing Com., 1982-84; dir. govt. relations Statue of Liberty Centennial, Liberty Weekend, 1986. Served with U.S. Mcht. Marine, 1930-33; served to lt. comdr. USN, 1942-48, ETO; PTO; capt. Res. Recipient Superior Service award Sec. of State, 1968. Address: 2576 Benedict Canyon Dr Beverly Hills CA 90210

HUSTON, HARRIETTE IRENE (REE) OTWELL, municipality secretary. d. Harry C. Otwell and Fannie (Mitchell) Otwell Geffert; m. Dan E. Huston, Jan. 21, 1951; children: Terry Dane, Dale Curtis, Ronald William, Randall Philip. BS, Kans. State Coll., 1951. Cert. life ins. agt., Wash.; cert. wastewater operator in tng., Wash. Tchr. Kans., Ill., 1955-68; assoc. home economist McCall's Patterns Co., N.Y.C., 1959-62; counselor, owner Dunhill of Seattle Personnel, 1968-75; enrollment officer, trainer, adminstrv. sec. Teller Tng. Insts., Seattle, 1975-76; life and health ins. agt. Lincoln Nat. Sales, Seattle, 1976-77; office mgr., adminstrv. sec. ARA Transp. Group, Seattle, 1977-78; asst. to the pres. Pryde Corp., Bellevue, Wash., 1978-80; sr. sec. Municipality of Met. Seattle, 1980—. Co-author: Homemaking textbook, 1956. Sec. exec. and gen. bd. Bellevue Christian Ch. Desciples of Christ, 1976-77, 1986—; bd. mem., sec. Surrey Downs Community Club, Bellevue, 1983-85. Recipient Clothing award check McCall's Patterns Co., N.Y.C., 1962, Cert. of Merit and $25 Metro Hdqrs., Seattle, 1983, Cert. Merit, Metro Hdqrs., 1982, 86, Cert. Merit and $25, Metro Hdqrs., 1981, Cert. Merit, Metro Hdqrs., 1981. Club: Bridge (Bellevue). Avocations: flower arranging, interior decorating. Home: 936 109th Ave SE Bellevue WA 98004 Office: Municipality of Met Seattle 821 2d Ave MS 53 Seattle WA 98104

HUSTON, JOHN RICHARD, physician; b. Columbus, Ohio, May 1, 1920; s. Harvey and Harriet Elizabeth (Schubert) H.; m. Patricia Wilkinson, Oct. 17, 1940 (dec. Oct. 1970); children: ShirleyJ., Bonnie L., Valerie E., John Richard; m. Martha Rankin, Oct. 16, 1971 (div. 1979); m. Beverly E. Gerrish, Apr. 21, 1982. BA, MD, Ohio State U., 1947. Diplomate Am. Bd. Internal Medicine. Intern US Naval Hosp., Phila., 1947-48; resident in pathology US Naval Hosp., Bethesda, Md., 1948-49; resident in internal medicine Phila. Naval Hosp., 1951-52, Ohio State U., 1953-54; resident in cardiology Ohio State U. Hosp., 1954-55; clin. instr. medicine Ohio State U., Columbus, 1953-60, clin. asst. prof., 1960-64, clin. assoc. prof., 1964-74; pvt. practice medicine specializing in internal medicine and cardiology Columbus, 1955-74; med. dir. United Comml. Travelers, Columbus, 1966-74; mem. staff dept. internal medicine VA Hosp., Phoenix, 1974-83, also dir. affiliated med. rsidency program, asst. chief of medicine; clin. dir. Maricopa County Alcohol and Substance Abuse Program, Phoenix, 1986—. Contbr. articles to med. jours. Served with USNR, 1944-46, 47-53. Mem. AMA, Ohio Med. Assn., Am. Heart Assn., Internat. Platform Assn., N.Y. Acad. Scis., Am. Med. Soc., Acad. Medicine Columbus and Franklin County (pres. 1965). Home: 2828 E Desert Cove Phoenix AZ 85028 Office: 3101 E Watkins Rd Phoenix AZ 85034

HUSTON, ROBERT EDWIN, engineering company executive; b. Windsor, Mo., Apr. 29, 1941; s. Ellis Maxwell and Pauline (Mayfield) H.; m. Malloy Ann Harvey, June 3, 1962; children: Janet Lynne, Robert E. Jr.; m. Nancy Lou Cox, Sept. 29, 1978. BSEE with honors, U. Mo., 1963; MSEE, Purdue U., 1964. Sr. engr. Gen. Motors Research Corp., Santa Barbara, Calif., 1964-67; engring. mgr. Fairchild Test Systems, San Jose, Calif., 1967-78; dir. applications Schlumberger-Sentry Corp., San Jose, 1978-80, GenRad-STI, Milpitas, Calif., 1980-83; v.p. Trillium Corp., San Jose, 1983—. Recipient spl. service award Internat. Test Conf., 1973, 74, 75, 78, 81, 83; NSF fellow. Mem. IEEE, Phi Kappa Phi, Tau Beta Pi (pres. 1962), Eta Kappa Nu, Kappa Mu Epsilom. Mormon. Home: 5819 Vargas Ct San Jose CA 95120 Office: Trillium Corp 3930 N First St San Jose CA 95134

HUSZCZA, BERT EDWARD, school district administrator; b. St. Elpidio, Italy, July 17, 1947; parents U.S. citizens; s. Stanley W. and Anna Nicola (Cipolla) H.; B.S. with spl. distinction in Bus. Adminstrn., U. So. Colo., 1976; M.B.A., U. Colo., 1977; m. Carol Jane Javernick, Dec. 13, 1969; children—Tiffany Ann, Lacey Michelle. Sales order corr. Celotex Corp., Carteret, N.J., 1970-71; warehouse/shipping foreman Celotex Corp., Charleston, Ill., 1971-73; asst. supt. Colo. State Vets. Home, Florence, 1977-84; dir. bus. services Fremont. RE-1 Sch. Dist., Canon City, Colo., 1984—. Vice pres. Fremont County Vets. Council, 1978-79. Served with U.S. Army, 1968-70. Licensed nursing home adminstr., Colo. Mem. Colo. Fiscal Mgrs., Am. Assn. Sch. Adminstrs., Assn. Sch. Bus. Ofcls., Am. Legion. Republican. Roman Catholic. Club: Elks. Home: 1360 Allison Ave Canon City CO 81212 Office: Sch Dist Fremont RE-1 1104 Royal Gorge Blvd Canon City CO 81212

HUTCHCRAFT, A. STEPHENS, JR., aluminum and chemical company executive; b. Orange, N.J., June 26, 1930; s. A. Stephens and Marguerite (Davis) H.; m. Mary Seaman, May 28, 1955; children: Pamela, Martha, A. Stephens. B.S., Yale U., 1952; postgrad. mgmt. devel., Harvard U., 1964. Registered profl. engr., Calif. Extrusion plant mgr. Kaiser Aluminum & Chem. Corp., Los Angeles, 1964-68; div. mgr. Kaiser Aluminum & Chem. Corp., Oakland, Calif., 1968-70, v.p., mgr. elec. products, 1970-75, v.p. aluminum, reduction and carbon, 1975-80, v.p., gen. mgr. aluminum div., 1980-82, pres., chief operating officer, 1982—; dir. Anglesey Aluminum, London, Valco, Ghana. Chmn. western region Nat. Amigos de Ser, Dallas, 1983; bd. dirs. Met. YMCA Alameda County, Calif., A Better Chance, Boston. Mem. Aluminum Assn. (chmn. 1982—). Republican. Presbyterian. Home: 15 Hillside Dr Danville CA 94526 Office: Kaiser Aluminum & Chem Corp 300 Lakeside Dr Oakland CA 94643

HUTCHENS, TYRA THORNTON, physician, educator; b. Newberg, Oreg., Nov. 29, 1921; s. Fred George and Bessie (Adams) H.; m. Betty Lou Gardner, June 7, 1942; children: Tyra Richard, Robert Jay, Rebecca (Mrs. Mark Pearsall). B.S., U. Oreg., 1943, M.D., 1945. Diplomate: Am. Bd. Pathology, Am. Bd. Nuclear Medicine. Intern Minn. Gen. Hosp., Mpls., 1945-46; AEC postdoctoral research fellow Reed Coll., Med. Sch. U. Oreg., 1948-50; NIH postdoctoral research fellow Med. Sch. U. Oreg., 1951-53; mem. faculty Oreg. Health Scis. U., 1953—, prof., chmn. dept. clin. pathology, 1962-87, prof. radiotherapy, 1963-71, allied health edn. coordinator, 1969-77; vis. lectr. radiobiology Reed Coll., 1955, 56. Mem. adv. bd. Oreg. Regional Med. Program, 1968-75; mem. statuatory radiation adv. com. Oreg. Bd. Health, 1957-69, chmn., 1967-69; founding trustee Am. Bd. Nuclear Medicine, 1971-77, 82-84, sec., 1973-75, 84-85 ; voting rep. Am. Bd. Med. Specialties, 1973-78, chmn. com. long range planning, 1976-78; mem. sci. adv. bd. Armed Forces Inst. Pathology, 1978-83. Served to lt. (j.g.) M.C., USNR, 1946-48. Charter mem. Acad. Clin. Lab. Physicians and Scientists, Soc. Nuclear Medicine, Am. Coll. Nuclear Physicians; mem. Oreg. Pathologists Assn. (pres. 1968), Pacific N.W. Soc. Nuclear Medicine (pres. 1958), AMA, Coll. Am. Pathologists (bd. govs. 1967-74, pres. 1977-79, chmn. commn. on internat. affairs 1979-83, chmn. planning com. for 1987 World Congress Pathology), Am. Soc. Clin. Pathologists (bd. registry med. technologists 1967-71), World Assn. of Socs. of Pathology (v.p. 1985-87, bur. of pathology 1981-87, chmn. commn. on world standards 1981-86), Assn. Am. Med. Colls., AAAS, Phi Beta Kappa, Sigma Xi, Alpha Omega Alpha. Research, publs. radioactive carbon tracer studies of lipid metabolism, clin. radioisotope techniques. Home: 7821 SW 51st St Portland OR 97219 Office: Oreg Health Scis U 3181 SW Sam Jackson Blvd Portland OR 97201

HUTCHESON, JERRY DEE, manufacturing company executive; b. Hammon, Okla., Oct. 31, 1932; s. Radford Andrew and Ethel Mae (Boulware) H.; B.S. in Physics, Eastern N. Mex. U., 1959; postgrad. Temple U., 1961-62, U. N.Mex., 1964-65; m. Lynda Lou Weber, Mar. 6, 1953; children—Gerald Dan, Lisa Marie, Vicki Lynn. Research engr. RCA, 1959-62; sect. head Motorola, 1962-63; research physicist Dikewood Corp., 1963-66; sr. mem. tech. staff Signetics Corp., 1966-69; engring. mgr. Litton Systems, Sunnyvale, Calif., 1969-70; engring. mgr. Fairchild Semiconductor, Mountain View, Calif., 1971; equipment engr., group mgr. Teledyne Semiconductor, Mountain View, 1971-74; dir. engring. DCA Reliability Labs., Sunnyvale, 1974-75; founder, prin. Tech. Ventures, San Jose, Calif., 1975—; chief exec. officer VLSI Research, Inc., 1981—. Democratic precinct committeeman, Albuquerque, 1964-66. Served with USAF, 1951-55. Registered profl. engr., Calif. Mem. Nat. Soc. Profl. Engrs., Profl. Engrs. Pvt. Practice, Calif. Soc. Profl. Engrs., Semiconductor Equipment and Materials Inst., Soc. Photo-Optical Instrumentation Engrs., Am. Soc. Test Engrs., Presbyterian. Club: Masons. Contbr. articles to profl. jours. Home: 5950 Vista Loop San Jose CA 95124 Office: VSLI Research 1754 Technology Dr Suite 117 San Jose CA 95110

HUTCHINGS, LA VERE, artist, educator; b. Lewisville, Idaho, Sept. 18, 1918; s. Marion Price and Mellie Grace (Kinghorn) H.; m. Anne Elizabeth Kirkman, Aug. 2, 1940; children—Marianne, Jeanne, Richard, Dorothy, Robert. A.A., Idaho State U., 1940; student Brigham Young U., 1940-41, Chuinard Art Inst., 1954, 55, Art Students League, summer 1970, John Pike Watercolor Sch., spring and summer 1970. Painter, art instr. Armed Forces Inst., Manila, Philippines, 1945-46, Ricks Coll., Idaho Falls, 1968-69, Hutchings Watercolor Workshops, Idaho and Calif., 1967—; painter, owner, operator Hutchings Gallery, Jamestown, Calif., 1979—; mus. collections include: Laguna Beach Mus. Fine Art, Calif., Las Vegas Mus., Nev., Merced Coll. Mus., Calif., Brigham Young U. Mus., Provo, Utah, Caldwell Library, Idaho; shows juried include: Utah Watercolor Soc., Salt Lake City, 1980, Idaho State Art Assn., Twin Falls, 1982, Wyo. State Art Assn., Pinedale, 1984; solo shows include: Brigham Young U., 1983, Merced Coll., 1982. Author: It's Fun to Paint Old Shacks and Barns, 1977; It's Fun to Paint Roads and Rivers, 1982; Make Your Watercolor Sing, 1986. Contbr. articles to newspapers and profl. jours. Pres. O.E. Bell Jr. High Sch. PTA, Idaho Falls, 1958, Toastmasters Internat., Idaho Falls, 1961, Kiwanis of E. Idaho Falls, 1968; bd. dirs. Teton Peaks Council Boy Scouts Am., Idaho Falls, 1953-60. Recipient Purchase award Inland Exhbn. VII, Elliot Block Co., 1971; Chmn.'s award and Okla. Watercolor award Okla. Watercolor Soc., 1981; 1st prize for Landscape Whiskey Painters Am., 1982. Mem. Nat. Watercolor Soc., Watercolor West (v.p. 1978-79), Soc. Western Artists (1st prize for watercolor 1984), Midwest Watercolor Soc. Mormon. Home: PO Box 249 Jamestown CA 95327 Office: Hutchings Gallery PO Box 249 Jamestown CA 95327

HUTCHINGS, LYNN SNARR, office machinery manufacturing company executive; b. Ogden, Utah, Mar. 2; s. Selar Stephan and Harriet (Snarr) H.; m. Georgia Ann Mitchell, July 5, 1963 (dec.); m. Marica Dee Cook, Apr. 18, 1975; 7 children. AAME, Weber State Coll., 1963, BS in Indsl. Engring, 1966; M. in Engring., U. Colo., 1974; student IBM Systems Research Inst., N.Y.C., 1974, IBM European Mfg. Inst., Lahulpe, Belguim, 1985. With IBM, Boulder, Colo., 1966—, mfg. supt., 1977-80, mgr. new products, 1980-81, mgr. copier support, 1981-82, site distbn. mgr., 1982-83, ops. planning mgr., 1983-84, equal opportunity and exec. resource mgr., 1984-85, mgr. prodn. facility, 1985-86, internat. procurement and distbn. mgr., 1986—. Chmn. exec. com. Boy Scouts Am. 1980-86; 1st counselor stake presidency Ch. Jesus Christ Latter-Day Saints, Boulder. Mem. Soc. Mfg. Engrs. (sr.), Am. Inst. Indsl. Engrs., Weber State Coll Alumni Assn. (pres. Rocky Mountain chpt. 1982-86). Home: 1143 Purdue Dr Longmont CO 80501 Office: IBM PO Box 1900 Boulder CO 80303

HUTCHINS, (ARTHUR) MICHAEL, therapist, consultant; b. Clinton, Mass., Oct. 13, 1943; s. Arthur Edward and Alyce Rita (Tierney) H.; m. Anne Elizabeth Boyle, June 14, 1969 (div. 1977); children: Adam Christopher, Aidan Sara. BS in Sociology, Psychology, Coll. of the Holy Cross, 1965; MA in Counseling Psychology, Assumption Coll., 1968; PhD in Counseling, U. Idaho, 1974. Counselor Cardinal Gibbons High Sch., Balt., 1968-71; dir. Ctr. for Human Organizational Research and Devel., Moscow, Idaho, 1971-74; asst. prof. Oakland U., Rochester, Mich., 1974-75, N.Mex. State U., Las Cruces, 1975-77; clin. supr. Macomb County Community Mental Health, St. Clair Shores, Mich., 1978-81; behavioral health unit mgr. Catalina Mountain Juvenile Inst., Tucson, 1981-86; exec. dir. Directions Counseling Assocs., Tucson, 1986—; cons. Creative Alternatives, Las Cruces, 1975-77, Growth Ctr., Rochester, 1978-81; therapist, cons. Catalina Counseling Assoc., Tucson, 1985-86; chmn. emotional support counselor Tucson AIDS Project, 1985—; bd. dirs. Tucson Alternative Therapies for AIDS. Pres. Canyon Del Oro High Sch. Parents, 1987—. Mem. Am. Assn. Counseling and Devel., Assn. Specialists in Group Work, Am. Correctional Assn., So. Ariz. Psychol. Assn., Old Pueblo Bus. Profl. Assn. Clubs: So. Ariz. Roadrunners, Clark Hatch Health (Tucson), El Conquistador Health. Avocations: running, bicycling, swimming, fitness, reading, writing. Home: 9960 N Placita Papalote Tucson AZ 85737 Office: Catalina Mountain Juvenile Inst Box 8988 CRB Tucson AZ 85738

HUTCHINSON, ERNEST JAMES, news wire service executive; b. San Francisco, Mar. 13, 1947; s. Ernest and Roberta Jean (Knus) H.; m. Christina Jeanne Samerjan, Mar. 25, 1972; 1 child, Theron; stepchildren: Kaisa, Annika. BSBA, So. Oreg. State Coll., 1972. Supr. 3-M Co., Medford, Oreg., 1972-74; controller Winchester Bay (Oreg.) Seafood Co., 1974-77; v.p., gen. mgr. Sta. KYNG-AM/FM, Coos Bay, Oreg., 1977-83; regional sales rep. UPI, Seattle, 1983-85; v.p., regional sales mgr. UPI, San Francisco, 1985—. Active Prefontaine Meml. Race Com., Coos Bay, 1980-83. Mem. Coos Bay Area C. of C. Democrat. Episcopalian. Avocations: photography, landscaping, writing. Home: 548 Castenada Ave San Francisco CA 94116 Office: UPI Fox Plaza 1390 Market St San Francisco CA 94101

HUTCHINSON, GORDON LEE, soil scientist, researcher; b. Yuma, Colo., Feb. 6, 1943; s. Benjamin Clyde and Margaret Christina (Olsen) H.; m. Ilene Joan Derry, June 17, 1962; children: Stuart Jay, Angela Dee, Shane Ray. BS, Colo. State U., 1965, MS, 1968; PhD, U. Ill., 1973. Technician phys. sci. Argl. Research Service, USDA, Ft. Collins, Colo., 1964-65, soil scientist, 1965-74, research soil scientist, 1974—. Mem. Am. Soc. Agronomy, Soil Sci. Soc. Am. (Emil Truog Sci. award 1973), AAAS, Am. Soc. Plant Physiologists, Council Agrl. Sci. and Tech. Home: 1025 Greenfield Ct Fort Collins CO 80524 Office: USDA Agrl Research Service PO Box E Fort Collins CO 80522

HUTCHINSON, JAMES RICHARD, engineering educator; b. San Francisco, June 1, 1932; s. George Richard and Doris Irene (James) H.; m. Patricia Ann Robinson, July 28, 1956; children: Katherine L., William D. BS, Stanford U., 1954, PhD, 1963; M in Lit., U. Pitts., 1958. Engr. Westinghouse, Pitts., 1954-58; scientist Lockheed Missiles and Space Corp., Palo Alto, Calif., 1958-64, cons., 1964-68; prof. U. Calif., Davis, 1964—; cons. Aerojet Gen., Sacrmento,, 1972-73, Lawrence Livermore (Calif.) Nat. Lab., 1985—. Contbr. articles to profl. jours. Pres. Davis Comic Opera Co., 1978, 84-86; active Davis Chorale, 1980—. ASME, Am. Acad. Mechanics, Sigma Xi. Democrat. Avocations: singing. Home: 1019 Plum Ln Davis CA 95616 Office: U Calif Civil Engring Dept Davis CA 95616

HUTCHINSON, JOSEPH CANDLER, foreign language educator; b. Hazelhurst, Ga., Jan. 10, 1920; s. George Washington and Lillie Arizona (Rowan) H.; m. June Cruce O'Shields, Aug. 12, 1950 (div. 1980); children—Junie O'Shields, Joseph Candler. B.A., Emory U., 1940, M.A., 1941; Ph.D., U. N.C., 1950; postgrad. U. Paris, summers 1951, 53. Tchr., Tech. High Sch., Atlanta, 1941-42; instr. French, German, Italian, Emory U., Atlanta, 1946-47; instr. U. N.C., Chapel Hill, 1947-50, asst. prof., 1954, assoc. prof., to 1957; asst. prof. Sweet Briar (Va.) Coll., 1950-51, 53-54; asso. prof. Tulane U., New Orleans, 1957-59; fgn. lang. specialist U.S. Office Edn., Washington, 1959-64; acad. adv. hdqrs. Def. Lang. Inst., Washington, 1964-74, Monterey, 1974-77, dir. tng. devel. Def. Lang. Inst. Fgn. Lang. Center, Monterey, Calif., 1977-82, asst. acad. dean, 1982-85; dean of policy, 1985—; vis. prof. U. Va., Charlottesville, 1966, Arlington, 1970, Georgetown U., 1968, Am. U., 1971; cons. Council of Chief State Sch. Officers, 1960, U. Del., 1966, U. Colo., 1968, U. Ill., 1968; U.S. del. Bur. Internat. Lang. Coordination, NATO, 1964-79, 81-82, 86-87. Served with U.S. Army, 1942-46, 51-53. Decorated Bronze Star. Mem. Am. Council on Edn. (task force on internat. edn. 1973), NEA (sec. dept. fgn. langs. 1961-64), Higher Edn. Assn. Monterey Peninsula, Am. Council on Teaching of Fgn. Lang., MLA, Am. Mgmt. Assn., Am. Soc. Tng. and Devel., Monterey Choral Soc., Camerata Singers. Episcopalian. Clubs: Presidio of Monterey Officers and Faculty, Washington Linguistics (v.p. 1970-72). Contbr. articles to profl. jours.; author: Using the Language Laboratory Effectively, School Executives Guide, 1964; The Language Laboratory: Equipment and Utilization in Trends in Language Teaching, 1966, others; editor Dialog on Lang. Instruction, 1986—. Office: Def Lang Inst Fgn Lang Ctr ATFL-DPL Monterey CA 93944

HUTCHINSON, WILLIAM BURKE, surgeon, research center director; b. Seattle, Sept. 6, 1909; s. Joseph Lambert and Nona Bernice (Burke) H.; m. Charlotte Rigdon, Mar. 25, 1939; children: Charlotte J. Hutchinson Reed, William B., John L., Stuart R., Mary Hutchinson Wiese. B.S., U. Wash., Seattle, 1931; M.D., McGill U., 1936; H.H.D. (hon.), U. Seattle, 1982. Diplomate: Am. Bd. Surgery. Intern Balt. City Hosp., 1936-37; resident Union Meml. Hosp., Balt., 1937-39, James Walker Meml. Hosp., Wilmington, N.C., 1939-40; surgeon Swedish Hosp. and Med. Ctr., Seattle, 1941—, Providence Hosp., Seattle, 1941—; pres., founding dir. Pacific Northwest Research Found., Seattle, 1956; founding dir. Fred Hutchinson Cancer Research Ctr., Seattle, 1972-85; dir. Surg. Cancer Cons. Service, 1982—; clin. prof. surgery emeritus U. Wash.; pres. 13th Internat. Cancer Congress, 1978-82; mem. Yarborough com. for writing Nat. Cancer Act, 1970. Contbg. editor, 13th Internat. Cancer Congress. Recipient 1st Citizen of Seattle award, 1976; recipient Alumnus Summa Laude Dignatus award U. Wash., 1983. Fellow ACS; mem. AMA, King County Med. Soc., Seattle Surg. Assn., North Pacific Surg. Assn., Pacific Coast Surg. Assn., Western Surg. Assn., Soc. Surg. Oncologists, NRC, Am. Assn. Cancer Insts., Alpha Sigma Phi. Clubs: Men's University (Seattle); Seattle Golf and Country. Home: 7126-55th Ave So Seattle WA 98118 Office: Pacific NW Research Found 1102 Columbia St Seattle WA 98104 also: Surg Oncology Cons Office Arnold Bldg Suite 901 1221 Madison Seattle WA

HUTCHISON, FANNIE MAE, educator; b. Coschocton, Ohio, Nov. 11, 1929; d. Lewis Leroy and Mary Esther (Wells) H.; B.S., Muskingum Coll., 1952; M.A., Chapman Coll., 1974; M.S., U. So. Calif., 1975; postgrad., 1976—. Tchr. elem. schs. Ventura, Calif., 1953-78, tchr. educationally handicapped, 1979-80, spl. edn. resource specialist, 1980-83, prin./program specialist, 1983-84, prin., 1984—. Mem. Ventura Unified Edn. Assn. (pres. 1972-73), Sch. Resource Network (dir. 1977-78), Orton Soc., Council Exceptional Children, EDUCARE, Assn. Supervision and Curriculum Devel., Calif. Tchrs. Assn., NEA, Phi Delta Kappa. Home: 956 Sharon Ln Ventura CA 93001 Office: 120 E Santa Clara St Ventura CA 93001

HUTCHISON, LOYAL DWAYNE, pharmacist, retail executive; b. Stockton, Calif., Jan. 3, 1933; s. Lester and Muriel (Van Nortwick) H.; m. Jean E. McColl, Jan. 26, 1961; children: Michael, Donald. BS in Pharmacy, U. Pacific, 1966. Pharmacist Fifth St. Pharmacy, Stockton, 1966-76, prin., 1976—; prin. Hutchison Pharmacies Inc., Stockton, 1976—, McKinley Pharmacy, Stockton, 1976—, Lathrop (Calif.) Pharmacy, 1976—. Served with U.S. Army, 1957-59. Fellow Am. Coll. Apothecary; mem. Calif. Pharmacists Assn. (Pac Silver Circle), Am. Pharmacists Assn. Avocations: nordic skiing, backpacking, fishing, theatre. Home: PO Box 1737 Stockton CA 95201 Office: Hutchison Pharmacies Inc 1839 S El Dorado Stockton CA 95206

HUTCHISON, ROBERT BRYCE, aerospace scientist; b. Oak Park, Ill., Jan. 2, 1941; s. Robert Alden and Hazel Pearl (Messer) H.; m. Janice Elaine Filip, Aug. 17, 1963; children: Heather Ann, Russell Thomas. BS, U. Ill., 1963; MS, Northwestern U., 1965, PhD in Astronomy, 1969. Resident research assoc. Jet Propulsion Lab., Pasadena, Calif., 1969-71; sr. staff scientist Martin Marietta Corp., Denver, 1971—; mem. Mil. Space System Tech. Panel, Air Force Space Tech. Ctr., N.Mex., 1985-86. Author: The Colchicine Factor, 1978; contbr. tech. articles to jours. Served with USAF, 1959-65. Mem. AIAA, Sigma Phi. Presbyterian. Club: Nat. Writers (Denver).

HUTCHISON, WILLIAM HENRY, III, data processing consulting company executive; b. Denver, Sept. 11, 1943; s. Carl Kenneth and Florence Jane (Mayhall) H.; tng. Burroughs Corp., 1966-67. Salesman, Caribou-Wards, Anchorage, 1965-66; field engr. trainee to sr. field engr. Burroughs Corp., Anchorage, 1966-78; owner, mgr. Alaska Systems, Anchorage, 1978-81; pres. Alaska Systems Consultants, Inc., Anchorage, 1981-82; owner, mgr. The Hutchison Co., Anchorage, 1982—; cons. in field. Served with USAF, 1961-65. Mem. Assn. Computing Machinery, Nat. Rifle Assn., U.S. Chess Fedn. Clubs: Commonwealth N., No. Bytes, Ketchikan Rod & Gun (sec.-treas. 1971-72), Anchorage Chess (v.p. 1976-77). Office: 200 W 34th Suite 799 Anchorage AK 99503

HUTNER, HERBERT LOEB, financial consultant, lawyer; b. N.Y.C., Dec. 21, 1908; s. Nathan M. and Ethel (Helhor) H.; m. Marjorie Mayer, Oct. 1, 1962 (div.); children—Jeffrey J., Lynn M. Colwell; m. 2d., Zsa Zsa Gabor, Mar. 20, 1967 (div.); m. 3d., Juli Reding, Nov. 28, 1969. B.A., Columbia U., 1928, J.D., 1931. Bar: N.Y. 1932. Ptnr., Osterman & Hutner, mem. N.Y. Stock Exchange, N.Y.C., 1945-57; successively pres. N.E. Life Insurance Co., N.Y.C.; chmn. bd. Sleight & Hellmuth Inc., N.Y.C.; chmn. bd. Pressed Metals of Am., Port Huron, Mich.; chmn. bd. Struthers Wells Corp., Warren, Pa., Plateau Mining Co. Inc., Oak Ridge; investor, cons., Los Angeles, 1963—; dir. United Artists Communications, Inc., 1965-87. Chmn., Pres.'s Adv. Com. on Arts for Kennedy Ctr., 1982—; founder Los Angeles Music Ctr.; chmn. profl. sports com. United Way. Decorated title DATO, Sultan of Johore, Malaysia, Highest Order of the Crown, 1981. Mem. ASCAP. Club: Deepdale Golf (Manhasset, N.Y.). Composer: The Super Bowl Song, Go Rams Go, others.

HUTT, LAURENCE JEFFREY, lawyer; b. N.Y.C., Dec. 15, 1950; s. George Joseph and Miriam Martha (Cohen) H.; m. Evelyn Balderman, Feb. 2, 1980; children: Marcie Arin, Ethan Lance, Amanda Rachel, Denver Allison. BA in History, U. Pa., 1972; JD, Stanford U., 1975. Bar: Calif. 1975. With Kadison, Pfaelzer, Woodard, Quinn & Rossi, Los Angeles, 1976-82, ptnr., 1982—; judge pro tem Los Angeles Mcpl. Ct. Mem. ABA, Los Angeles County Bar Del. to Calif. State Bar. Conv. (exec. com. mem. 1986—, del. 1980—), Order of Coif, Phi Beta Kappa. Club: University Club (Los Angeles). Avocation: wine tasting. Office: Quinn Kully & Morrow 612 S Flower St 5th Fl Los Angeles CA 90017

HUTTENBACK, ROBERT ARTHUR, university professor; b. Frankfurt, Germany, Mar. 8, 1928; s. Otto Henry and Dorothy (Marcuse) H.; m. Freda Braginsky, July 12, 1954; 1 dau., Madeleine Alexandra. B.A., U. Calif. at Los Angeles, 1951, Ph.D., 1959; postgrad., Sch. Oriental and African Studies, U. London, Eng., 1956-57. Mem. faculty Calif. Inst. Tech., Pasadena, 1958-78; asst. prof. Calif. Inst. Tech., 1960-63, assoc. prof., 1963-66, prof. history, 1966-78, master student houses, 1958-69, dean students, 1969-72, chmn. div. humanities and social scis., 1971-77; chancellor U. Calif., Santa Barbara, 1977-86; cons. Jet Propulsion Lab., Pasadena, 1966-68. Author: British Relations with Sind, 1799-1843, An Anatomy of Imperialism, 1962, (with Leo Rose and Margaret Fisher) Himalayan Battleground-Sino-Indian Rivalry in Ladakh, 1963, The British Imperial Experience, 1966, Gandhi in South Africa, 1971, Racism and Empire, 1976; (with Lance Davis) Mammon and the Pursuit of Empire, 1986. Served to 1st lt. U.S. Army, 1951-53. Mem. Assn. Asian Studies, Am. Hist. Assn. Office: U Calif Santa Barbara CA 93106

HUTTER, JAMES RISQUE, lawyer; b. Spokane, Wash., Mar. 20, 1924; s. James R. and Esther (Nelson) H.; m. Patricia Ruth Dunlavy, Aug. 12, 1951; children: Bruce Dunlavy, Gail Anne, Dean James, Karl Nelson. B.S., UCLA, 1947; J.D., Stanford U., 1950. Bar: Calif. 1951, U.S. Supreme Ct. 1965. Assoc. Gibson, Dunn & Crutcher, Los Angeles and Beverly Hills, Calif., 1950-58, ptnr., 1959—; dir. Fifield Manors, Los Angeles, 1955—, v.p., 1964—. Bd. dirs., chmn. fin. com. Congl. Found. for Theol. Studies, Nat. Assn. Congl. Christian Chs., 1961-68; mem. San Marino City Planning Commn., Calif., 1968—, chmn., 1976—. Served to 1st. inf. AUS, 1943-46. Decorated Purple Heart. Mem. State Bar Calif. (com. on corps. 1973-76, exec. com. bus. law sect. 1976-78), ABA, Los Angeles County Bar Assn., Beverly Hills Bar Assn. (bd. govs. 1968-70), Am. Judicature Soc., Town Hall, Phi Delta Phi, Beta Gamma Sigma, Phi Kappa Psi. Clubs: Stock Exchange of Los Angeles, Valley Hunt. Home: 1400 Circle Dr San Marino CA 91108 Office: Gibson Dunn & Crutcher 333 S Grand Ave 48th Floor Los Angeles CA 90071

HUTTON, ROBERT STANLEY, psychology educator; b. Hawthorne, Calif., Oct. 10, 1939; s. Albert Stanley and Velmador (Gregory) H.; m. Judith Ann Fuller, Oct. 29, 1960 (div. 1970); children: Robert S. Jr., Robyn Ann. BS with honors, UCLA, 1963, MS, 1964; PhD, U. So. Calif., 1969. From lectr. to asst. prof. UCLA, 1965-71; postdoctoral fellow UCLA Brain Research Inst., 1969-71; asst. prof. U. Wash., Seattle, 1971-75, assoc. prof., 1975-82, chmn. dept. kinesiology, 1978-83, prof. psychology, 1982-86, prof. psychol. psychology, 1986—; v.p. Am. Coll. Spl. Medicine, Indpls., 1983-85; guest worker NINCDS/NIH, Bethesda, Md., 1979. Editor Exercise Sport Sci. Revs., 1976-80; contbr. articles to prof. jours. Fellow Am. Acad. Phys. Edn., Am. Coll. Sports Medicine, Research Consortium AAHPERD; mem. AAAS, Soc. Neurosci. Democrat. Avocations: musician, jazz, sports. Home: 835 W Sunset Way Issaquah WA 98027 Office: U Wash Dept Psychology NI-25 Seattle WA 98195

HUZURBAZAR, VASANT SHANKAR, statistics educator, researcher; b. Kolhapur City, India, Sept. 15, 1919; came to U.S., 1979; s. Shankar Abaji and Ganga Shankar (Kanetkar) H.; m. Prabha Wasudeo Gadgil, Dec. 26, 1959; children—Snehalata, Aparna. B.A. with honors, Bombay U. (India), 1940; M.A., Banaras Hindu U. (India), 1942; Ph.D., Cambridge U. (Eng.), 1949. Sampling expert Bur. Econs. and Stats., Govt. Bombay, 1950-52; statis. reader Lucknow (India) U., 1952-53; sr. prof., head dept. math. and stats. U. Poona (India), 1953-76; Fulbright vis. prof. Iowa State U., Ames, 1962-64, U. Man. (Can.), Winnipeg, 1976-79; prof. stats. U. Denver, 1979—; researcher, cons. Recipient Chancellor's Gold medal Banaras Hindu U., 1942; Adams prize Cambridge U., 1959-60; Padma Bhushan award Pres. India, 1974; Nat. Lectr., Univ. Grants Commn. India, 1975-76. Fellow Am. Statis. Assn., Royal Statis. Soc. (London), Indian Acad. Scis., Indian Nat. Acad. Sci., Cambridge Philos. Soc., Am. Biog. Inst. Research Assn. (life); Am. Biog. Inst., Research Assn.; mem. Internat. Statis. Inst., Indian Math. Soc. (life), Indian Statis. Assn. (life, past pres.), Indian Inst. Pub. Adminstrn. (life), Indian Sci. Congress Assn. (life, past pres. stats. sect.), Inst. Math. Stats., Smithsonian Assocs. Smithsonian Inst. Author: Sufficient Statistics, 1976, contbr. articles to profl. jours. Home: 3755 E Buchtel Blvd #206 Denver CO 80210 Office: Coll Bus Adminstrn U Denver Denver CO 80208

HWANG, CORDELIA JONG, chemist; b. N.Y.C., July 14, 1942; d. Goddard and Lily (Fung) Jong; m. Warren C. Hwang, Mar. 31, 1969; 1 son, Kevin. Student Alfred U., 1960-62; B.A., Barnard Coll., 1964; M.S., SUNY-Stony Brook, 1969. Research asst. Columbia U., N.Y.C., 1964-66; analytical chemist Veritron West Inc., Chatsworth, Calif., 1969-70; asst. lab. dir., chief chemist Pomeroy, Johnston & Bailey Environ. Engrs., Pasadena, Calif., 1970-76; research chemist Met. Water Dist. So. Calif., Los Angeles, 1976—; mem. Joint Task Group on Instrumental Identification of Taste and Odor Compounds, 1983-85, instr. Citrus Coll., 1974-76. Mem. Am. Chem. Soc., Am. Water Works Assn. (cert. water quality analyst level 3, Calif.-Nev.). Office: Met Water Dist So Calif 700 N Moreno St La Verne CA 91750

HWANG, SUK R., physics educator; b. Manchuria, China, June 18, 1931; came to U.S., 1954; s. Ha-Gil and Ne-Ok (Park) H.; m. Yangsoo Lim, Jan. 27, 1968; 1 dau., Suein L. Student Seoul Nat. U. (Korea), 1952-54; B.S. in Physics, Central Mo. State U., 1956; M.S. in Physics, Ariz. State U., 1961. Instr. math. U. Tex.-El Paso, 1961-64; instr. physics U. Hawaii-Hilo, 1965-70, asst. prof., 1970-75, assoc. prof., 1975—, chmn. physics dept., 1986—; exchange prof. U. Hawaii, Honolulu, 1966-67; dir. NSF-SSTP at U. Hawaii-Hilo, 1979-81, Hawaii-SSTP, 1982—; vis. prof. U. Wash., 1987-88. NSF fellow, 1974, grantee, 1968, 79, 80, 81. Mem. Am. Assn. Physics Tchrs., Hawaiian Acad. Scis., AAUP, Sigma Pi Sigma. Club: Big Island Korean (pres. 1971-72, charter mem. 1970—) (Hilo). Home: 46 Palua Loop Hilo HI 96720 Office: U Hawaii at Hilo 523 W Lanikaula St Hilo HI 96720-4091

HYBART, FREDERICK STALLWORTH, JR., electrical engineer; b. Mobile, Ala., Oct. 16, 1956; s. Frederick Stallworth and Evelyn (Dershimer) H.; m. Patricia Helen Cole, Aug. 22, 1981; 1 child, Frederick Stallworth III. BEE, Ga. Inst. Tech., 1978; MSEE, Purdue U., 1980. Registered engr.-in-tng., Ga. Mem. tech. staff Rockwell Internat. Corp., Downey, Calif., 1981-83, TRW, Inc., Redondo Beach, Calif., 1983—. Mem. Tau Beta Pi, Eta Kappa Nu. Avocations: amateur radio, flying. Home: 1257 Rosecrans Ave Fullerton CA 92633 Office: TRW Elec Systems Group 1 Space Park M/S M4/2230 Redondo Beach CA 90278

HYBL, WILLIAM JOSEPH, lawyer, investment company executive; b. Des Moines, July 16, 1942; B.A., Colo. Coll., 1964; J.D., U. Colo., 1967. Bar: Colo. 1967. Asst. dist. atty. 4th Jud. Dist., El Paso and Teller Counties, 1970-72; pres., dir. El Pomar Investment Co., 1973-86; exec. v.p., dir. Garden City Co., 1973—; dir. Broadmoor Mgmt. Co., 1975—, Broadmoor Hotel, Inc., 1973—, also vice-chmn., 1987—; bd. dirs. 1st Nat. Bank Colorado Springs, Affiliated Bankshares of Colo., 1986—; mem. Colo. Ho. Reps., 1972-73. Pres., dir. El Pomar Found., 1973—; trustee, vice chmn. Colo. Coll., 78—; trustee Am. Council Young Polit. Leaders, 1980—; pres., trustee Air Force Acad. Found.; bd. dirs. Vail Valley Found.; sec., trustee U.S. Olympic Found., 1984—; chmn. Colo. commn. on Bicentennial com. of U.S Constitution, 1986—; spl. White House counsel, 1981; civilian aide to sec. of army for State of Colo., 1986—. Mem. U.S. C. of C. (bd. dirs., pub.

affairs com. chmn., 19856—). Home: 2 Heather Circle Colorado Springs CO 80906 Office: 10 Lake Circle Colorado Springs CO 80906

HYDE, LUCIA SOWERS, social worker; b. San Francisco, Apr. 18, 1936; d. Roy Vernon and Pauline Bridge (Seeberger) Gibberd; m. Charles Martin Hyde, Nov. 28, 1976; children: Victoria Hyde Ponvelle, William. Student, Bryn Mawr Coll., 1958, U. Denver, 1961; MSW, U. Chgo., 1962. With foster care dept. Ill. Children's Home and Aid, Chgo., 1962-64; instr. Ill. Neuropsychiat. Inst., Chgo., 1963-67; clin. social worker Albuquerque VA Hosp., 1967-69; acct. Chuch's Gunshop, Taos, N.Mex., 1972—, also bd. dir. Vol. Rape Crisis Ctr., Taos, 1976—, vol. Friends of Music, Taos, 1983-84; vestry mem. St. James Episcopal Ch., Taos, 1983-85. Fellow NIMH; mem. Nat. Assn. Social Work (cert.). Democrat. Avocations: street counseling, camping, aerobics. Home: Box 1493 Taos NM 87571

HYDE, RONALD GREGORY, educational administrator; b. Pocatello, Idaho, May 2, 1929; s. Milton D. and Mildred Yvonne (Gregory) H.; m. Mary Helen Frampton, Dec. 12, 1956; children—Kerrie Hyde Summerhays, Nathan, Paul, Catherine Hyde Boyd, Amy. B.S., U. Idaho, 1951; M.S., Brigham Young U., 1963. Field rep. Patterson Sales Clinic, Phoenix, 1957-58; alumni fund dir. Brigham Young Univ., Provo, Utah, 1958-64, exec. dir., 1964-78, spl. asst. to pres., 1981-82, asst. exec. v.p. Univ. Relations, 1982-85, asst. to pres., 1985—; pres. Eng. Birmingham Mission, 1978-81. Served with USAF, 1951-53. Recipient Dist. Tribute for Profl. Service award, 1986; Grand Gold medal, 1985; Exceptional Achievement award Council for Advancement and Support of Edn., 1982; Time/Life award Am. Alumni Council, 1974; Ernest T. Stewart award 1970; Alumni Adminstrn. award, 1969. Mem. Council for Advancement and Support of Edn. (trustee 1974-75), Pub. Relations Soc. Am., Internat. Pub. Relations Assn., Am. Alumni Council (bd. chmn. 1974), Am. Provo C. of C. (dir. 1984). Mormon. Home: 540 S Palisade Dr Orem UT 84057 Office: Brigham Young University C-366 ASB Provo UT 84602

HYMAN, JAMES MACKLIN, numerical analyst; b. Lakeland, Fla., Mar. 20, 1950; s. Samuel P. and Dorothy Ann (Jones) H.; m. Deborah Ann Herring; children: Kathryn, Jeffery. BS in Math. and Physics cum laude, Tulane U., 1972; MS in Math., Courant Inst. Math. Scis., 1974, PhD, 1976. Research staff Los Alamos (N.Mex.) Nat. Lab., 1976—, assoc. chmn. Ctr. Nonlinear Studies, 1982-83, group leader math. modeling and analysis group, 1984—. Contbr. numerous articles to profl. jours. Recipient Gendy Burke Math. medal, 1972, Best of the New Generation award Esquire Mag., 1984; Hertz fellow, 1972-76; Air Force ROTC scholar, 1969-72. Mem. Soc. Indsl. and Applied Math. (co-chmn. systems of nonlinear partial differential equations 1984, com. applied math. 1984), Nat. Acad. Scis. (com. applications of math. 1982-84). Home: 401 Connie Ave White Rock NM 87544 Office: Los Alamos Nat Lab Theoretical div Los Alamos NM 87545

HYNDS, FRANCES JANE, communications consultant; b. Martin, Tenn., Oct. 27, 1929; d. Loyd Orion and Hunter Elizabeth (Goad) H. B.S. in Journalism, McMurry Coll., 1951; M.A. in Telecommunications, U. So. Calif., 1961, Ph.D. in Communications, 1984. Dir. pub. info., instr. journalism McMurry Coll., Abilene, Tex., 1951-53; dir. pub. relations Oklahoma City U., 1953-55; acct. exec., corp. sec. Joe Leighton & Assocs. Inc., Hollywood, Calif., 1956-65; prin. Hynds Co., Los Angeles, 1965—; sr. lectr., adj. faculty, dir. pub. relations program for mgmt. U. So. Calif. Sch. Journalism Mem. Pub. Relations Soc. Am. (dir. 1975-77, nat. assembly del.), Women in Communications Inc. (dir. 1967-72; Far West region Woman of Achievement 1980, Los Angeles chpt. Freedom of Info. award, Nat. Founders award, 1982). Author (with Norma L. Bowles): Psi Search, The New Investigation of Psychic Phenomena that Separates Fact from Speculation, 1978; transl. French, 1983; contbr. articles to profl. jours.

HYNEK, FREDERICK JAMES, architect; b. Minot, N.D., May 24, 1944; s. Frederick Frank and Esther Irene (Hermanson) H.; B.Arch., N.D. State U., 1968; m. Jane Rebecca Lowitz, June 9, 1966; children: Tyler James, Scott Anthony. Intern archtl. firms in Bismarck, N.D., 1967-72; architect Gerald W. Deines, Architect, Casper and Cody, Wyo., 1972-73; v.p. Gerald Deines and Assos., 1973-77; propr. Fred J. Hynek, AIA/Architect, Cody, 1977-80; pres. Design Group, P.C., Architects/Planners, Cody, 1980-86; pres. CHD Architects, Cody and Denver, 1986—; Concept Interiors Inc., Cody, 1984—; sec.-treas. Brand-N-Board Inc., Northglenn, Colo., 1985—; mem. cert. of need rev. bd. State of Wyo., 1984—, selection com. for archtl. students for Western Interstate Commn. for Higher Edn. Profl. Student Exchange Program, U. Wyo., 1979—. Bd. dirs. Cody Stampede, Inc., 1977-82; chmn. Cody Econ. Devel. Council, 1982-84. Served with USAR, 1967-68. Mem. AIA (dir. Wyo. chpt. 1976-83, pres. 1980, 81; conf. chmn. Western Mountain region 1977, mem. awards jury 1981, treas. 1982-86; chmn. design awards jury N.D. 1981), Constrn. Specifications Inst., Cody County C. of C. (dir., pres. 1982). Republican. Presbyterian. Clubs: Cody Elks, Cody Country Ambassador. Mem. editorial adv. bd. Symposia mag., 1981-82. Home: 708 Southfork Rd Cody WY 82414 Office: 1371 Sheridan Ave Cody WY 82414

HYSLOP, RICHARD MICHAEL, biochemistry educator; b. Evansville, Ind., Feb. 7, 1949; s. Hugh Boyd and Berniece May (McKinney) H.; m. Rosann Mary Ross, June 2, 1984; children: Jennifer, Julie, Renee. BS in Chemistry, Life Scis., Ind. State U., Evansville, 1971; PhD in Biochemistry, U. Tex., 1976. Vis. instr. Purdue U., West Lafayette, Ind., 1976-79; resident fellow Mayo Clinic, Rochester, Minn., 1979-81; guest researcher Argonne Nat. Lab., Lemont, Ill., 1982-84; guest lectr. N. Cen. Coll., Naperville, Ill., 1983; assoc. prof. biochemistry Ill. Benedictine Coll., Lisle, Ill., 1981-84; asst. prof. U. No. Colo., Greeley, 1984—. Contbr. articles to profl. jours. Mem. Am. Chem. Soc. (faculty advisor Ill. Benedictine Coll. chpt. 1982-84, U. No. Colo. chpt. 1984—)), Colo.-Wyo. Acad. Sci., AAAS, Sigma Xi, Phi Lambda Upsilon, Sigma Zeta, Lambda Sigma Tau (Disting. Alumni award 1986). Avocations: backpacking, carpentry, drawing, photography. Office: U No Colo Dept Chemistry Greeley CO 80639

IACHETTI, ROSE MARIA ANNE, educator; b. Watervliet, N.Y., Sept. 22, 1931; d. Augustus and Rose Elizabeth Archer (Orciuolo) Iachetti; B.S., Coll. St. Rose, 1961; M.Ed., U. Ariz., 1969. Joined Sisters of Mercy, Albany, N.Y., 1949-66; tchr. various parochial schs. Albany (N.Y.) Diocese, 1952-66; tchr. Headstart Program, Troy, N.Y., 1966; tchr. fine arts Watervliet Jr. and Sr. High Sch., 1966-67; tchr. W.J. Meyer Sch., Tombstone, Ariz., 1968-71, Colonel Johnston Sch., Ft. Huachuca, Ariz., 1971-78; tchr. Myer Sch., Ft. Huachuca, 1978—, coordinator program for gifted and talented, 1981-85. Ann. chmn. Ariz. Children's Home Assn., Tombstone, 1973-74; trustee Tombstone Sch. Dist. #1, 1972-80; active Democratic Club; mem. Bicentennial Commn. for Ariz., 1972-76, Tombstone Centennial Commn., 1979-80, chmn. Centennial Ball, 1980; pres. Tombstone Community Health Services, 1978-80; mem. Tombstone City Council, 1982-84; governing bd. Southeast Ariz. Area Health Edn. Ctr., 1985—. Mem. Ariz. Edn. Assn. (so. regional dir. 1971-73), Ft. Huachuca Edn. Assn., Tombstone Dist. 1 Edn. Assn. (pres. 1969-71), Ariz. Sch. Bd. Assn., NEA (del. 1971-73), Ariz. Classroom Tchrs. Assn. (del. 1969-71), Internat. Platform Assn., Tombstone Bus. and Profl. Womens Club, Am. Legion Aux., Tombstone Assn. Arts, Pi Lambda Theta, Delta Kappa Gamma, (pres. 1982-84), Phi Delta Kappa (historian 1979-82, 2d v.p. 1982-83). Home: Round Up Trailer Ranch Box 725 Tombstone AZ 85638 Office: Myer School Fort Huachuca AZ 85613

IACONO, GEORGE DANTE, optometrist; b. Chgo., Oct. 21, 1922; s. Carl Umberto and Emma (Decrecchio) I.; m. Rosemary Marie Maksym, Nov. 28, 1928; children—Carl Dante, Georgeann Louise. O.D., Chgo. Coll. Optometry, 1948. Practice optometry, Tucson, 1948—; dir. Tucson Reading Inst., 1953-62; cons. Fellow Nat. Eye Research Found. (grand hons.) mem. Am. Optometric Assn., Ariz. Optometric Assn., Internat. Orthokeratology Assn., Am. Interprofl. Assn. (Living Treasure award). Office: 2553 E Broadway Tucson AZ 85716

IACONO, JAMES MICHAEL, center director; b. Chgo., Dec. 11, 1925; s. Joseph and Angelina (Cutaia) I.; children: Lynn, Joseph, Michael, Rosemary. BS, U. Ill., 1950, MS, 1952, PhD, 1954. With lipid nutrition lab. Nutrition Inst. USDA-Agrl. Research Service, Beltsville, Md., 1970-75; dep. asst. Nat. Program Staff USDA-Agrl. Research Service, Washington, 1975-77; dir. Western Human Nutriton Research Ctr. USDA-Agrl. Research Service, San Francisco, 1982—; assoc. adminstr. Office of Human Nutrition USDA, Washington, 1978-82. Served with U.S. Army, 1944-46. Recipient Research Career Devel. award NIH, 1964-70. Fellow Am. Heart Assn. (councils on arteriosclerosis, thrombosis), Am. Inst. Chemists; mem. Am. Inst. Nutrition, Am. Soc. Clin. Nutrition, Am. Oil Chemist's Soc. Office: Western Human Nutrition Research Ctr Bldg 1110 PO Box 29997 Presidio San Francisco CA 94129

IAMELE, RICHARD THOMAS, law librarian; b. Newark, Jan. 29, 1942; s. Armando Anthony and Evelyn (Coladonato) I.; m. Marilyn Ann Berutto, Aug. 21, 1965; children—Thomas, Ann Marie. B.A., Loyola U., Los Angeles, 1963; M.S.L.S., U. So. Calif., 1967; J.D., Southwestern U., Los Angeles, 1976. Bar: Calif. 1977. Cataloger U. So. Calif., Los Angeles, 1967-71; asst. cataloger Los Angeles County Law Library, 1971-77, asst. reference librarian, 1977-78, asst. librarian, 1978-80, library dir., 1980—. Mem. ABA, Am. Assn. Law Libraries, Calif. Library Assn., So. Calif. Assn. Law Libraries. Office: Los Angeles County Law Library 301 W 1st St Los Angeles CA 90012

IANNACCONE, EMIL ANTHONY, advertising agency executive; b. Bklyn., Feb. 16, 1943; s. Rudolph Joseph and Anna (Cardinale) I.; m. Serafina Benincasa, Mar. 5, 1965 (div. Dec. 1971). BA, Fordham U., 1964. Planner Dancer-Fitzgerald-Sample, N.Y.C., 1966-68; v.p., group supr. Young & Rubicam, N.Y.C., 1968-80; v.p., media dir. J. Walter Thompson, Los Angeles, 1980-81; sr. v.p., media dir. Needham Harper Worldwide(name now Rubin Postaer and Assocs.), Los Angeles, 1982—. Mem. Hollywood Radio and TV Soc., Los Angeles Ad Club, Los Angeles Media Dirs. Council. Roman Catholic. Home: 11855 Woodley Ave Granada Hills CA 91344 Office: Needham Harper Worldwide Inc 11601 Wilshire Blvd Los Angeles CA 90025

IBBETSON, EDWIN THORNTON, bus. developer; b. Los Angeles, Apr. 17, 1923; s. Robert Edwin and Ann (Thornton) I.; student Long Beach Jr. Coll., 1941-42, Calif. Inst. Tech., 1942-43; m. Harriett Alice Hudson, Dec. 28, 1947; children: Elizabeth Ann Ibbetson Hitchcock, Douglas Hudson, Gregory Bruce, Timothy Edwin, Julia Katherine Ibbetson Zilinskas, Erika Alice Ibbetson Hertzog. With Union Devel. Co., Cerritos, Calif., 1944—3 , pres., 1961—; partner Paramount Constrn., Cerritos, 1948—; v.p. Valley Properties, Inc., Imperial Valley, 1962—; chmn. bd. Dutch Village Bowling Center, Inc., Lakewood, 1965-86, partner Ibbetson-Marsh Realtors, 1975—; vice chmn. bd. Equitable Savs. and Loan Assn., 1977-85. Bd. dirs. Met. Water Dist. So. Calif., 1959—, sec., 1979-82, chmn. bd., 1983-86; chmn. Bellflower Water Devel. Com., 1965—; mem. Los Angeles County Citizens Com. Real Estate Mgmt., 1974—, now chmn.; bd. dirs. armed services YMCA, Long Beach, 1962-72. Trustee St. Mary's Hosp., Long Beach. Served with USNR, 1942-46. Named Young Man of Year, Bellflower Jaycees, 1959. Realtor of Year, Bellflower Dist. Bd. Realtors, 1962, 67, 71. Mem. Am. Soc. Real Estate Counselors (gov., pres. 1977), Calif. Assn. Realtors (treas. 1972-77, dir., hon. life pres.), Internat. Real Estate Fedn., Nat. Assn. Realtors (dir.), Nat. Inst. Real Estate Brokers (cert. comml. investment mem.), Inst. Real Estate Mgmt. (cert. property mgr.), Bellflower Dist. Bd. Realtors (pres. 1961), Central Basin Mcpl. Water Dist. (dir.), Calif. Real Estate Polit. Action Com., Internat. Council Shopping Centers, Lambda Alpha. Roman Catholic. Clubs: Elks, Kiwanis (pres. 1958); International Traders, So. Calif. Tuna (Long Beach). Office: 16550 Bloomfield Cerritos CA 90701

IBRAHIM, MOHAMED ABDALLA, banker; b. Cairo, Egypt, Aug. 16, 1938; s. Abdalla Ibrahim and Nefisa (Oaf) A.; m. Fathia Marei Ibrahim, Feb. 10, 1972; children—Yahya, Mona, Nagwa and Dalia (twins). B.Sc. in Acctg., Cairo U., 1959; M.Sc. in Banking Adminstrn., Ein-Shams U., 1964; M.Sc. in Fin., Cairo U., 1968; M.Sc. in Acctg., Calif. State U.-Northridge, 1976. Head auditing dept. Bank Misr, Cairo, 1959-70; acct. Union Bank, Los Angeles, 1971-72; sr. v.p., controller City Nat. Bank, Beverly Hills, Calif., 1973—; treas. Citinat. Devel. Trust, Beverly Hills, 1979—. Mem. Am. Acctg. Assn., Beverly Hills C. of C. Republican. Moslem. Home: 3822 Toland Ave Los Alamitos CA 90720 Office: City Nat Bank 400 N Roxbury Dr Beverly Hills CA 90210

IBSEN, KENNETH HOWARD, biochemistry educator; b. Bklyn., Feb. 4, 1931; s. Niels Christopher and Inga Sophie (Brandt) I.; m. Denise Lee Duke, June 15, 1959 (div. Oct. 1980); children: Kristine Lee, David Allen; m. Dorothy Jeanette Martin, June 30, 1984; 1 child, Kurt Martin. AA, City Coll., Los Angeles, 1951; BS, UCLA, 1955, PhD, 1959. Lab. technician Lieberman Breweries, Vernon, Calif., 1954; research biochemsit Vets. Hosp., Sepulveda, Calif., 1959-61; asst. research prof. physiol. chemistry UCLA, 1961-65, from asst. prof. to assoc. prof. biochemistry, 1964—, asst. dean Coll. Medicine, 1986—. Contbr. articles to profl. jours. Mem. AAAS, Am. Chem. Soc., Am. Soc. Biol. Chemists, Pacific Slope Biochem. Conf., Sigma Xi. Home: 15 Bascom Irvine CA 92715 Office: U Calif Dept Biol Chemistry Irvine CA 92717

ICE, RICHARD EUGENE, non-profit retirement homes company executive, clergyman; b. Ft. Lewis, Wash., Sept. 25, 1930; s. Shirley and Nellie Rebecca (Pedersen) I.; m. Pearl Lucille Daniels, July 17, 1955; children—Lorinda Susan, Diana Laurene, Julianne Adele. A.A., Centralia Coll., 1950; B.A., Linfield Coll., 1952, L.H.D. (hon.), 1978; M.A., Berkeley Bapt. Div. Sch., 1959; grad. advanced mgmt. program Harvard U., 1971. Ordained to ministry Am. Bapt. Ch., 1954; pastor Ridgecrest Community Bapt. Ch., Seattle, 1955-59; dir. ch. extension Wash. Bapt. Conv., 1959-61; dir. loans Am. Bapt. Extension Corp., Valley Forge, Pa., 1961-64; assoc. exec. minister Am. Bapt. Chs. of West, Oakland, Calif., 1964-67; dep. exec. sec., treas. Am. Bapt. Home Mission Socs., Valley Forge, 1967-72; pres. Am. Bapt. Homes of the West, Oakland, 1972—; dir. Minister's Life Ins. Co., Mpls., 1975-86, chmn. bd. dirs. 1986—; pres. Am. Bapt. Homes and Hosps. Assn., 1978-81. Rep. gen. bd. Am. Bapt. Chs. U.S.A.; bd. mgrs. Bd. Nat. Ministries; bd. dirs. Am. Bapt. Extension Corp.; Ministers and Missionaries Benefit Bd.; mem. Bapt. Joint Com. on Pub. Affairs; trustee, chmn. com. fin. affairs Linfield Coll., 1972—; trustee Calif./Nev. Methodist Homes, 1975—, Bacone Coll., 1968-77, Grad. Theol. Union, Berkeley, Calif., 1982—; trustee Am. Bapt. Sem. of West, Berkeley, 1975—, chmn. bd. dirs. 1987—. Recipient Disting. Baconian award Bacone Coll., 1977, Disting. Alumnus award Centralia Coll., 1981; Meritorious Service award Am. Assn. Homes for Aging, 1982; Merit citation Am. Bapt. Homes and Hosp. Assn., 1985. Mem. U.S. Assn. for UN, Am. Assn. Homes for Aging, Calif. Assn. Homes for Aging, Harvard Bus. Sch. Assn. No. Calif., Pi Gamma Mu. Democrat. Clubs: Harvard of San Francisco; Lakeview, Athenian Nile (Oakland). Office: 400 Roland Way Oakland CA 94621

ICENOGLE, RONALD DEAN, physical chemist, writer; b. Bismarck, N.D., May 5, 1951; s. Grover Donald and Mary Adeline (Parks) I. BS, Mich. State U., 1974; MS, Cornell U., 1977, PhD, 1981. Research chemist Shell Devel. Co., Houston, 1980-85; sci. writer Spokane, Wash., 1985—. Contbr. articles to profl. jours. Mem. Am. Chem. Soc., Phi Beta Kappa, Phi Kappa Phi. Avocations: whitewater boating, theater. Home and Office: 2931 S Howard St Spokane WA 99203-1747

ICHIKAWA, CHRISTIE OZAWA, nursing educator; b. Sacramento, Apr. 4, 1928; s. Walt Wataru and Pauline Kikuye (Tamura) Ozawa; m. Robert Setsuto Ichikawa, Oct. 22, 1950; children—Robert D., Ross A., Laura A. R.N., Los Angeles County Gen. Hosp., 1950; B.S., U. So. Calif., 1950; M.A., Calif. State U.-Dominguez Hills, 1973; MS in Nursing, Consortium of Calif. State U., 1987. Cert. women's health care nurse practitioner, Calif. Staff nurse Seaside Hosp. (now Long Beach Meml. Hosp.), Long Beach, Calif., 1950-52; office nurse Donald J. Crawford, M.D., Long Beach, 1952-54; operating room nurse Los Angeles County Harbor-UCLA Med. Ctr., Torrance, 1955-56; sch. nurse Los Angeles Unified Sch. Dist., 1956-68; prof. nursing Los Angeles Community Coll. Dist., Wilmington, 1968-79; chairperson div. nursing Los Angeles Harbor Coll., Wilmington, 1979—; chairperson Assoc. Degree Nursing Program Dirs. Los Angeles Community Coll. Dist., 1981-83. Vol. Little Tokyo Health Fair, Los Angeles, 1979-82; bd. dirs. Torrance Sister City Assn., Calif., 1982-86; vol., mem. Am. Cancer Soc., Long Beach, 1983—; bd. dirs. Torrance Sister City Assn.; pres. DeMolay Mothers Club, 1961. Recipient DeMolay Top Hat award, 1962; named South Bay Woman of Yr., Torrance YWCA, 1982. Mem. Calif. Nurses Assn., Nat. League for Nursing, Am. Fedn. Tchrs., Coll. Guild, Calif. Assn. Women Adminstrs. and Counselors, Delta Kappa Gamma (2d v.p. Eta Gamma chpt. 1976-78, pres. 1978-80, parliamentarian 1980-84, chmn. fin. and budget com. 1984—). Republican. Office: Los Angeles Harbor Coll 1111 Figueroa Pl Wilmington CA 90744

IDA, JOHN JOJI, architect; b. Honolulu, July 21, 1945; s. Lawrence and Grace Ida; m. Sandra Hatsuyo Suwa, June 29, 1968; Stephen Norio, Scott Kenji. BArch, U. Hawaii, 1969; MArch, U. Wash., 1974. Registered architect, Wash., Hawaii. Designer Edward Gamon Assocs., Bellevue, Wash., 1972-73; designer, draftsman TRA, Seattle, 1973-75; project architect Mithun Assocs., Bellevue, 1975-78; sr. assoc. Group 70 Architects, Honolulu, 1978-84; prin. Urban Works Inc., Honolulu, 1984—. Prin. works include Kvistad/Shilling Dental Bldg., (hon. 1978), Hale Pohaku Mid. Elev. Fac., (hon. 1984). Bd. dirs. Bamboo Shoots Pre-Sch., Honolulu, 1982—. Served to capt. U.S. Army, 1969-72. Recipient 1st Place award Home Builders Assn. Hawaii, Honolulu, 1968, 2d Place Louis P. Price Meml. award CCPA/AIA, Honolulu, 1968. Mem. AIA, Constrn. Specification Inst. (treas. 1984-85, bd. dirs. 1984-85), Am. soc. Profl. Estimators. Avocations: sketching, golf, tennis. Home: 6003 Haleola St Honolulu HI 96821 Office: Urban Works Inc 650 Ala Moana Blvd Suite 215 Honolulu HI 96813

IDEMAN, JAMES M., federal judge.; b. 1931; m. Gertraud Erika Ideman. BA, The Citadel, 1953; JD, U. So. Calif., 1963. Dep. atty. gen. Los Angeles County, 1964-79; judge Los Angeles County Superior Ct., 1979-84; appointed judge U.S. Dist. Ct. (Cen. Dist.) Calif., Los Angeles, 1984—. Served to 1st lt. U.S. Army, 1953-56, lt. col. JAGC Res. Office: US Courthouse 312 N Spring St Los Angeles CA 90012 *

IDSO, SHERWOOD BURTRUM, research physicist; b. Thief River Falls, Minn., June 12, 1942; s. Sherman Theodore and Gladys Elnora (Ekeberg) I.; m. Carolyn Marie Wakefield, Aug. 23, 1963; children: Wayne Stuart, Grant Alan, Keith Edward, Craig Douglas, Lance William, Jennifer Marie, Julene Marie. BS in Physics, U. Minn., 1964, MS, 1966, PhD, 1967. Research soil scientist Agrl. Research Service USDA, Phoenix, 1967-74, research physicist, 1974—; adj. prof. geography Ariz. State U., Tempe, 1980—, adj. prof. geology, 1981—, botany and microbiology, 1984—; pres. Inst. Biospheric Research, Tempe, 1981—. Author: Carbon Dioxide: Friend of Foe?, 1982; contbr. numerous articles to profl. jours. Recipient Arthur S. Flemming award Downtown Jaycees, Washington, 1977. Mem. AAAS, Am. Meteorol. Soc., Royal Meteorol. Soc. of Eng., Am. Geophys. Union, Am. Soc. Agronomy, Sigma Xi. Mormon. Home: 631 E Laguna Dr Tempe AZ 85282 Office: US Water Conservation Lab 4331 E Broadway Phoenix AZ 85040

IHARA, GRACE REIKO, speech pathologist; b. Newell, Calif., Nov. 17, 1943; d. Tamotsu and Betsy Shizue (Ito) I. BA, U. Hawaii, 1965; MS, U. Oreg., 1966. Staff speech pathologist Syracuse (N.Y.) VA Hosp., 1966; dir. adult speech and lang. program Mt. Diablo Therapy Ctr., Pleasant Hill, Calif., 1967-70; chief speech pathology Pacific Inst. Rehab. Medicine, Honolulu, 1970-72; pvt. practice as speech pathology cons. Honolulu, 1972—; bd. dirs. Spl. Edn. Ctr. of Oahu; cons. Dept. Social Services, Hawaii Ear, Nose & Throat Group, Kuakini Med. Ctr., Castle Hosp., 15 skilled nursing and intermediary care facilities; lectr. Honolulu Community Coll., 1985—; guest lectr. KMC Gerontology series; tchr. Kaimuki Adult Edn.; commr. State Bd. Speech Pathology and Audiology; faculty and guest lectr. Hawaii Stroke Seminar. Mem. stroke com. Hawaii Heart Assn., 1976—. Recipient Community Service award Hawaii Heart Assn., 1976-84; grantee Vocat. Rehab. Adminstrn. Mem. Am. Speech and Hearing Assn. (cert.), Council Exceptional Children, Hawaii Assn. Retarded Children, Phi Beta. Club: Quota (charter, pres.). Office: 1380 Lusitana St Suite 209 Honolulu HI 96813

IHRIG, JUDSON LA MOURE, chemist; b. Santa Maria, Calif., Nov. 5, 1925; s. Harry Karl and Luella (LaMoure) I.; m. Gwendolyn Adele Montz, July 22, 1950; children—Kristin, Neil Marshall. B.S., Haverford Coll., 1949; M.A., Princeton U., 1951, Ph.D., 1952. Asst. prof. chemistry U. Hawaii, 1952-58, assoc. prof., 1958-72, prof., 1972—, dir. honors program, 1958-64, 87—, dir. liberal studies program, 1973-79, chmn. chemistry dept., 1981-86; cons. chemistry local firms. Author publs. in field. Served with AUS, 1945-46. Mem. Am. Chem. Soc., AAUP, Phi Beta Kappa, Sigma Xi. Home: 386 Wailupe Circle Honolulu HI 96821 Office: U Hawaii 2545 The Mall Honolulu HI 96822

II, JACK MORITO, aerospace engineer; b. Tokyo, Japan, Mar. 20, 1926; s. Iwao and Kiku Ii; came to U.S., 1954, naturalized, 1966; B.S., Tohoku U., 1949; M.S., U. Washington, 1956; M. in Aero. Engring., Cornell U., 1959; Ph.D. in Aero. and Astronautics, U. Wash., 1964; Ph.D. in Engring., U. Tokyo, 1980; m. Aiko Nouno, Nov. 14, 1952; children—Keiko, Yoshiko, Mutsuya. Reporter, Asahi Newspaper Press, Tokyo, 1951-54; aircraft designer Fuji Heavy Industries Ltd. Co., Tokyo, Japan, 1956-58; mem. staff structures research Boeing Mil. Airplane Co., Seattle, 1962—. Mem. AIAA, Japan Shumy and Culture Soc. (pres. 1976—), Sigma Xi. Mem. Congregational Ch. Contbr. numerous articles on aerodyns. to profl. jours. Office: The Boeing Co M/S 33-04 Seattle WA 98124

IKEDA, MOSS MARCUS MASANOBU, educational administrator; b. Los Angeles, Sept. 11, 1931; s. Masao Eugene and Masako (Yamashina) I.; BE, U. Hawaii, 1960, MEd, 1962; postgrad. Stanford U., 1961-62; M in Mil. Art and Sci., U.S. Army Command and Gen. Staff Coll., 1975; grad. U.S. Army War Coll., 1976; EdD, U. Hawaii, 1986; m. Shirley Yaeko Okimoto; children—Cynthia Cecile Ikeda Tamashiro, Mark Eugene, Matthew Albert. Tchr., Farrington High Sch., Honolulu, 1962-64; vice-prin. Kailua Intermediate Sch. 1964-65; adminstrv. intern Central Intermediate Sch., Honolulu, 1965-66; vice-prin. Kaimuki High Sch., Honolulu, 1966-67; prin. Kawananakoa Intermediate Sch., Honolulu, 1967-68, Kailua High Sch., 1969-71, Kalaheo High Sch., Kailua, 1972-77; ednl. specialist Hawaii Dept. Edn., Honolulu, 1977-79; ednl. adminstr. Hawaii Dept. Edn., Honolulu, 1979—. Mem. accrediting commn. for schs. Western Assn. Schs. and Colls., bd. dirs. Served with AUS, 1951-57, 68-69, col. Res. ret. Decorated Legion of Merit, Army Commendation medal. Mem. Nat. Assn. Secondary Sch. Prins., Assn. U.S. Army, Res. Officers Assn., Army War Coll. Alumni Assn., Hawaii Govt. Employees Assn., Phi Delta Kappa, Phi Kappa Phi. Home: 47-494 Apoalewa Pl Kaneohe HI 96744 Office: Hawaii Dept Edn 2530 10th Ave Honolulu HI 96816

IKEDA, NAOMI, gemologist, gem and jewelry institute administrator; b. San Diego, May 22, 1949; d. Frank Yoshiharu and Jeanne Haruko (Masuda) I. Grad., Buena Park Beauty Sch., Calif., 1967, Gemological Inst. Am., Santa Monica, Calif., 1970. Cosmetologist, Blossom Hair Fashions, Buena Park, 1967-68, Nikko Wig Fashions, Orange, Calif., 1969-70; sales clk. Pacific Gem Cutters, Los Angeles, 1971-72; mgr. Nikko Gem & Jewelry Inst. Inc., Honolulu, 1972—, v.p., 1979—; lectr. U. Hawaii, 1980—. Mem. Gemological Inst. Am. Alumni Assn. (treas. Hawaii chpt. 1984-86, v.p. 1986, sec. 1986-87). Buddhist. Office: Nikko Gem & Jewelry Inst Inc 512 Atkinson Dr Honolulu HI 96814

IKEDA, TATSUHIKO, research cell biologist; b. Japan, May 10, 1950; came to U.S., 1985; d. Kenzo and Kimiko Ito; m. Tomiko Ikeda, Mar. 11, 1975; children: Yukiya, Leo. PhD, Tokushima (Japan) U., 1981. Asst. prof. cell biology Kobe (Japan)-Gakuin U., 1978-82, assoc. prof., 1982-85; sr. scientist ONCOGEN, Seattle, 1985—; research cons. Yamasaki Inst., Kyoto, Japan, 1985—. Author: Woman Biochemistry, 1980, Essential Cell Biology, 1982. Office: ONCOGEN 3005 First Ave Seattle WA 98121

IKEDA, TSUGUO (IKE), social services center administrator, consultant; b. Portland, Oreg., Aug. 15, 1924; s. Tom Minoru and Tomoe Ikeda; m. Sumiko Hara, Sept. 2, 1951; children: Wanda Amy, Helen Mari, Julie Ann, Patricia Kiyo. BA, Lewis & Clark Coll., 1949; MSW, U. Wash., 1951. Social group worker Neighborhood House, Seattle, 1951-53; exec. dir. Atlantic St. Ctr., Seattle, 1953-86; pres. Urban Partnerships, Seattle, 1986—; cons. Commn. on Religion and Race, Washington, 1973, North Northeast Mental Health Ctr., Portland, 1985; affirmative action cons. Nat. Assn. Social Workers, Washington, 1977. Mem. Gov.'s Select Panel for social and health services, Olympia, Wash., 1977; chairperson Asian Am. Task Force, Community Coll., Seattle dist., 1982; div. chmn. social agys. Seattle United Way campaign, 1985; vice-chairperson Wash. State Com. on Vocational Edn., Olympia, 1985-87. Served to pvt. Mil. Intelligence Lang. Sch., 1945-

46. Recipient cert. appreciation U.S. Dept. Justice, Washington, 1975-76, Am. Dream award Community Coll. Dist., Seattle, 1984, Bishop's award, PNW Conf., U. Meth. Ch., Tacoma, Wash., 1984, community service award Seattle Rotary Club, 1985, Oustanding Citizen award Mcpl. League, Seattle and King County, 1986. Mem. Nat. Conf. Social Welfare (various offices, including 3d v.p.), Nat. Assn. Social Workers (chpt. pres., Social Worker of Yr. 1971), Vol. Agy. Exec. Coalition (pres., outstanding community service award 1979), Ethnic Minority Mental Health Consortium (chmn., Outstanding Ldr. 1982), Minority Exec. Dirs. Coalition (organizer, membership chmn. 1980-86). Democrat. Methodist. Avocations: collecting mint Am. stamps and memorabilia about Japanese Am. incarceration during World War II. Office: Atlantic St Ctr 2103 S Atlantic St Seattle WA 98144

ILANIT, TAMAR, psychologist; b. Tel Aviv, Israel, May 5, 1929; d. Aharon and Ada (Berman) Pougatch; came to U.S., 1950, naturalized, 1970; grad. Levinski Tchr. Sem., 1949; Ph.D., U. So. Calif., 1959; m. Apr. 15, 1948; children—Rona, Gill. Research dir. United Cerebral Palsy Assn., Los Angeles, 1959-61; instr. Pepperdine U., Los Angeles, 1962-64; spl. cons. White Meml. Med. Center, Los Angeles; pvt. practice clin. psychology, Los Angeles, 1963—; mem. disability evaluation panel Social Security Adminstrn., 1961-85. Mem. Am. Psychol. Assn., Los Angeles County Psychol. Assn., Sigma Xi, Phi Beta Kappa, Phi Kappa Phi. Jewish. Contbr. articles to profl. jours. Office: 8610 Sepulveda#203 Los Angeles CA 90045 Office: 11665 Olympic Blvd Los Angeles CA 90064

ILETT, FRANK, JR., trucking co. exec.; b. Ontario, Oreg., June 21, 1940; s. Frank Kent and Lela Alice (Siver) I.; B.A., U. Wash., 1962; M.B.A., U. Chgo., 1969; m. Donna L. Andlovec, Apr. 3, 1971; children—James Frank, Jordan Lee. Accountant, Ernst & Ernst, Boise, Idaho, Cleve., Spokane, Wash., 1962-69, mgr., Boise, 1970-72, regional mgr., San Francisco, 1972-73; treas. Interstate Mack, Inc., Boise, 1973-81, pres., chief exec. officer, 1981-82; pres. Interstate NationaLease, Inc., Boise, 1975-81; pres. Contract Carriers, Inc., Boise, 1983—, Ilett Transp. Co., Boise, 1985—; adj. lectr. Boise State U., 1964-67; chmn. Carriers/West, Inc., Salem, Oreg., 1986—; cons. Calif. Hosp. Commn., 1973, Idaho Hosp. Assn., 1974; chmn. Mack Truck Western Region Distbr. Council, 1979-82; mem. nat. distbr. adv. com. Mack Trucks, Inc., 1980-82; dir. standards enforcement Idaho State Bd. Accountancy, 1983-84. C.P.A., Idaho, Ill., Wash. Mem. Am. Inst. C.P.A.'s, Gen. Soc. Mayflower Decendants, SAR. Episcopalian. Clubs: Hillcrest Country (Boise), Masons, Shriners. Contbr. articles in field to profl. jours. Home: 1701 Harrison Blvd Boise ID 83702 Office: 4450 Enterprise St Boise ID 83705

ILLING, HANS ALFONS, sociologist; b. Berlin, Germany, Aug. 15, 1913; s. Leopold and Alice G. (Beermann) I.; Ph.D., Friedrich Wilhelm U., 1936; B.A., U. Utah, 1944; M.S.W., Tulane U., 1948; m. Lillian E. Ulrich, Apr. 19, 1962; 1 stepson, Theodore Lloyd Baker; came to U.S., 1939, naturalized, 1944. Clin. social worker VA Outpatient Clinic, Los Angeles, 1959-60; adminstrv. asst. Calif. Home for the Aged, Reseda, 1960-62; sr. psychiat. social worker Parole Outpatient Clinic, State of Calif., Los Angeles, 1960—; staff mem. The Hacker-Clinic, Beverly Hills and Lynwood, Calif., 1962-70; charter mem. Social Work Treatment Service, 1963—, Westchester Mental Health Clinic, 1962—; pvt. practice, 1970—; mem. faculty Los Angeles Inst. for Psychoanalytic Studies, 1970—; lectr. in field; cons. M.C. Air Force workshop, 1956; speaker Nat. Conf. Social Work, 1957, Am. Psychiat. Assn., 1964; cons. Airport Marina Counseling Service, Los Angeles, 1962-75. Mem. UCLA Art Council, Goethe House, N.Y.; pres. Westport Heights Democratic Club, 1964-70. Diplomate Conf. Advancement of Pvt. Practice in Social Work. Fellow Am. Group Psychotherapy Assn., (speaker nat. conv. 1956, 58, 67, 68, 79), Am. Orthopsychiat. Assn. (life; speaker nat. conv. 1970, 78), Am. Assn. Suicidology, Soc. Clin. Social Work; mem. Nat. Assn. Social Workers (Gold Card mem.), So. Calif. Psychotherapy Assn., Internat. Soc. Study Prenatal Psychology, Assn. Rec. Sound Collections, Berlin Mus., Salzburg Mozarteum; mem. Group Psychotherapy Assn. So. Calif. (cofounder, charter mem.), Los Angeles Group Psychotherapy Soc., Los Angeles County Mus. Art, Music Library Assn., Beethoven Haus (Bonn), Mendelssohn Gesellschaft, Heinrich von Kleist Gesellschaft, Met. Opera Guild, Chamber Symphony Soc. Calif., Wilhelm Furtwängler Soc. (founder, pres.), Goethe Gesellschaft, Hugo von Hofmannsthal Gesselschaft. Contbr. numerous articles to profl. jours. and books. Cons. editor: Internat. Jour. Psychiatry, 1965—; book rev. editor: Modern Austrian Literature; contbg. editor Dynamische Psychiatrie, Berlin, Germany. Home: 6112 W 77th St Los Angeles CA 90045 Office: 656 Aerick St Inglewood CA 90301

ILLING, RAINER MILTON ERNEST, physicist; b. Berlin, Sept. 23, 1946; came to U.S., 1950; s. Milton Harry William and Ruth Hermine (Stölting) I.; m. Luanna Rae Bauman, Apr. 5, 1986. AB in Physics, Princeton U., 1968; MA, Columbia U., 1970, MPhil, 1973, PhD, 1973. Asst. astronomer U. Hawaii, Honolulu, 1974-77; research assoc. U. Colo. Lab. for Atmospheric and Space Physics, Boulder, 1977-80; scientist Nat. Ctr. Atmospheric Research High Altitude Observatory, Boulder, 1980-86; prin. mem. tech. staff mem. Ball Aerospace, Boulder, 1986—; prin. mem. technical staff, investigator Orbiting Solar Observatory 8 High Resolution Ultraviolet Spectrometer, U. Colo., 1980. Contbr. numerous research reports, articles to scientific jours. Traineeship grantee NSF, Columbia U., 1968-70; recipient Group Sci. Achievement award NASA, 1984. Mem. Am. Phys. Soc., Am. Astron. Soc. (solar physics sect.), IEEE (acoustics, speech and signal processing div.), Am. Inst. Astronautics (mem. technical com. on space scis. and astronomy), Internat. Astron. Union, Optical Soc. Am., Sigma Xi. Democrat. Lutheran. Avocations: cooking, dancing, studying history and psychology.

ILLMAN, DEBORAH LOUISE, chemist; b. Seattle, Jan. 15, 1955; s. Robert Ware and Patricia Ann (Wyman) I.; m. Michael Lloyd Brown, June 30, 1976 (div. Jan. 1983). BS in Chemistry, U. Wash., 1976; PhD in Chemistry, UNICAMP, Campinas, Brazil, 1981. High sch. tchr. Am. Sch. Campinas, 1977-79; grad. research fellow UNICAMP, 1978-81; postdoctoral lectr. chemistry U. Wash., Seattle, 1982-84, asst. dir. Ctr. Process Analytical Chemistry,, 1984—; cons. Infometrix, Inc., Seattle, 1982—. Author: (textbook) Chemometrics, 1986. Candidate for State Legislature 46th dist., Seattle, 1986. NSF travel award to attend NATO Advance Study Inst., Italy, 1983. Mem. AAAS, Chemometrics Soc., Am. Chem. Soc. (editor Puget Sound Chemist, 1983-84), Greater Univ. C. of C. (Seattle). Republican. Avocations: mountaineering, sailboat racing, bicycling, tennis, traveling. Office: U Wash CPAC Dept Chemistry BG-10 Seattle WA 98195

IMAD, AZMI PHILIP, environmental health and safety professional; b. Dhour Shweir, Lebanon, Nov. 12, 1942; came to U.S., 1976; s. Philip Khattar and Zakieh (Hanna Beshara) Emad. BS, Am. U., Beirut, 1963; MSc, U. London, 1966. Registered profl. safety engr. Dir. safety ctr. Am. U., Beirut, 1966-76; environ. protection specialist U. Md., College Park, 1976-79; dir. environ. health and safety, radiation safety officer U. Colo., Boulder, 1979—; safety cons. NIH, Bethesda, Md., 1976-77. Contbr. articles to profl. publs. Internat. Atomic Energy Agy. fellow, 1964-66. Mem. Am. Soc. Safety Engrs., Health Physics Soc., Campus Safety Assn. (cert. appreciation 1983). Avocations: skiing, swimming, body building, photography. Office: U Colo Campus Box 375 Boulder CO 80309-0375

IMAMURA, ELAINE JOY, counselor; b. Denver, Dec. 27, 1954; d. Roy S. and Priscilla Miyuki (Hamada) Hiratsuka. B.A. in Psychology, Adams State Coll., 1976, M.A. in Guidance and Counseling, 1978. Counselor, cottage parent Colo. Boys Ranch, LaJunta, 1978-79; program mgr., counselor Billings Childrens' Receiving Home, 1979-80; counselor Advance By Choice, Mont. State U., Bozeman, 1980—. Mem. Am. Personnel and Guidance Assn., Mont. Personnel and Guidance Assn., Assn. Handicapped Student Service Programs in Postsecondary Edn., Wheelchairs, Crutches and People Club. Office: Mont State U Advance By Choice Bozeman MT 59717

IMANA, JORGE GARRON, artist; b. Sucre, Bolivia, Sept. 20, 1930; s. Juan S. and Lola (Garron) I.; grad. Fine Arts Acad., U. San Francisco Xavier, 1950; cert. Nat. Sch. for Tchrs., Bolivia, 1952; came to U.S., 1964, naturalized, 1974; m. Cristina Imana; children—George, Ivan. Prof. art Nat. Sch. Tchrs., Sucre, 1954-56; prof. biology Padilla Coll., Sucre, 1956-60; head dept. art Inst. Normal Simon Bolivar, La Paz, Bolivia, 1961-62; propr., mgr. The Artists Showroom, San Diego, 1973—. Numerous one-man shows of paintings in U.S., S. Am. and Europe, 1952—, latest being: Gallery Banet, La Paz, 1965, Artists Showroom, San Diego, 1964, 66, 68, 74, 76, 77, San Diego Art Inst., 1966, 68, 72, 73, Contrast Gallery, Chula Vista, Calif., 1966, Central Public Library, San Diego, 1969, Universidad de Zulia, Maracaibo, Venezuela, 1969, Spanish Village Art Center, San Diego, 1974, 75, 76, La Jolla Art Assn. Gallery, 1969, 72, 73, 74, 75, 78, 83, Internat. Gallery, Washington, 1976, Galeria de Arte L'Atelier, La Paz, 1977; numerous group shows including: Fine Arts Gallery, San Diego, 1964, Mus. of Modern Art, Paris, 1973, exhibits in galleries of Budapest (Hungary), 1975, Moscow (USSR), 1975, Warsaw (Poland), 1976; represented in permanent collections: Museo Nacional, La Paz, Bolivia, Museo de la Universidad de Potosi, Bolivia, Muse Nacional de Bogota, Colombia, S. Am., Ministerio de Edn., Managua, Nicaragua, Bolivian embassy, Moscow, also pvt. collections in U.S., Europe and Latin Am.; executed many murals including: Colegio Padilla, Sucre, Bolivia, 1958, Colegio Junin, Sucre, Bolivia, 1959, Sindicato de Construccion Civil, Lima, Peru, 1960. Hon. consul of Bolivia, So. Calif., 1969-73. Served to lt. Bolivian Army, 1953. Recipient Mcpl. award Sucre, Bolivia, 1958. Mem. San Diego Art Inst., San Diego Watercolor Soc., Internat. Fine Arts Guild, La Jolla Art Assn. Home: 3357 Caminito Gandara La Jolla CA 92037 Office: The Artists Showroom 2168 Chatsworth Blvd San Diego CA 92107

IMBAULT, JAMES JOSEPH, electromechanical engineering executive; b. Muskegon, Mich., Oct. 31, 1944; s. Joseph Lionel and Ruth Pauline (Schutter) I.; m. Vallery Ann Rumisek, Dec. 29, 1967; children—Michelle, Allan. A.S., Muskegon Community Coll., 1965; B.S. Mech. Engring. with honors, Mich. Tech. U., 1967; postgrad. UCLA, 1972-73. Registered profl. engr., Calif. Sr. mem. tech. staff RCA, E.A.S.D., Van Nuys, Calif., 1968-74; mech. engring. mgr. Litton Italia SPA, Rome, Italy, 1974-78; electromech. engring. mgr. Incosym, Inc., Westlake Village, Calif., 1978-82, v.p., 1982—, also dir. Patentee in field. Recipient Meritorious Performance award Muskegon Community Coll., 1965; Mich. Tech. U. scholar, 1965-67. Mem. Nat. Soc. Profl. Engrs., ASME, Mich. Tech. U. Alumni Assn., Pi Tau Sigma, Tau Beta Pi, Phi Kappa Phi. Democrat. Home: 851 N Osage Circle Camarillo CA 93010 Office: Incosym Inc 780 Lakefield Rd Westlake Village CA 91361

IMBRECHT, CHARLES RICHARD, lawyer; b. Ventura, Calif., Feb. 4, 1949; s. Earl Richard and Hazel Victoria (Berg) I.; m. Alida Margit Bergseid, Sept. 23, 1979. AB, Occidental Coll.; JD, Loyola U., Los Angeles. Bar: Calif. Atty., adviser ICC, Washington, 1974-75; ptnr. Robinson, Melikan, Imbrecht & Weems, Ventura, 1975-80; assemblyman Calif. Legis., Sacramento, 1976-82; chmn. Calif. Energy Commn., Sacramento, 1983—; gov.'s energy adviser State of Calif., Sacramento, 1983—; mem. Western Interstate Energy Bd., Denver, 1983—, vice chmn., 1984-85, chmn., 1986—; state liaison Nuclear Regulatory Commn., Washington, 1983—; bd. dirs. Alternative Energy Fin. Authority, Sacramento, 1983—. Del. Commn. of the Calif.'s, San Diego, 1978—; mem. Ventura County Rep. Cen. Com., 1974—, Calif. State Rep. Cen. Com., Sacramento, 1976—. Richter fellow Occidental Coll., 1970; named one of Calif.'s Five Outstanding Young Men, Jaycees, 1981; recipient Outstanding Pub. Service award NSPE, 1984. Mem. Ventura County Bar Assn., Calif. State Bar Assn., Assn. Profl. Energy Mgrs. (bd. dirs.). Lutheran. Avocations: swimming, scuba diving, reading. Office: Calif Energy Commn 1516 9th St Sacramento CA 95814

IMHOFF, CAROL ANN, nursing administrator; b. Los Angeles, June 15, 1934; d. Neal and Frances M. (Roberts) Vogelsang; m. James C. Imhoff, Aug. 10, 1957; children: Jean, Robert, Christopher, Mary Angela. BSN, U. Utah, 1973; diploma Holy Cross Hosp. Sch. Nursing, 1955. Cert. rehab. registered nurse (CRRN). Staff nurse Holy Cross Hosp., UCLA Med. Ctr., 1955-58, staff nurse, part time supr., 1960-66, unit supr. rehab., 1977-82, rehab. clinician, 1982-83; dir. nursing Bountiful Care Convalescent Ctr., 1983—; vis. staff nurse Community Nursing Service, Salt Lake City, 1966-69; head nurse supportive care med. rehab. McKay Dee Hosp., Ogden, Utah, 1969-77. Mem. edn. com. Am. Heart Assn., 1969-81, chmn., 1972-84; bd. dirs. Utah Heart Assn., 1976-83; sec. Home Sch. Assn. Mem. Am. Nurses Assn., Assn. Rehab. Nurses (certs. for service, nat. pres. 1982-83, sec.-treas. 1979-80), Rehab. Services Adv. Council, Utah Nurses Assn. (past dist. treas., bd. dirs., 2d place Nurse of Yr.), Utah Dirs. Nurses of Long-Term Care (pres. 1983-85), Beta Sigma Phi, Sigma Theta Tau. Roman Catholic. Club: Does. Home: 4581 Taylor S Ogden UT 84403 Office: 350 S 400 E Bountiful UT 84010

IMMEL, TERRY WARREN, health center administrator; b. Enid, Okla., Apr. 6, 1942; s. Carl Theodore and Dorotha Belle (McSparrin) I.; m. Sheryl Dee Jones, Jan. 15, 1964 (div. May 1972); 1 child, Laura Nalani; m. Linda Kay Jones, Dec. 15, 1972; children: Edward James, Heath Eric. BSEd, Kans. U., 1964; MEd, Phillips U., 1966; MDiv, The Grad. Sem., 1975; MBA with distinction, U. Phoenix, Tucson, 1983. Tchr. English Hawaii Pub. Sch., Wahiawa, 1966-70, Albuquerque Pub. Schs., 1970-72; assoc. minister Christian Ch. of the Covenant, Enid, 1972-75; minister Community Christian Ch., Marana, Ariz., 1975-83; exec. dir. Marana Health Ctr., 1983—. Mem. adv. com. Child-Parent Ctrs., Tucson, 1985—; chmn. com. Christian Ch. in Ariz., Phoenix, 1975—. Mem. Nat. Assn. Community Health Ctrs., Western Assn. Theologians (discussion group 1979-86), Western Assn. Theol. Discussion, Nat. Rural Health Care Assn., Ariz. Assn. Community Health Ctrs. (sec. 1984—). Democrat. Mem. Christian Ch. Avocations: reading, continuing edn. Home: 4125 W Sandarac Tucson AZ 85741 Office: 13644 N Sandario Rd Marana AZ 85653

IMMERGLUCK, LUDWIG, psychology educator, consultant; b. Vienna, Austria, Sept. 19, 1920; came to U.S., 1938; s. Alfred and Jenny (Weiner) I.; m. Virginia Marguerite Adamson, Sept. 2, 1950; children—Paul Jacob, David Arthur, Alexander Mark. B.A., Bklyn. Coll., 1943; Ph.D., U. Iowa, 1947. Diplomate Am. Bd. Profl. Psychology. Psychologist Kings County Hosp., Bklyn., 1947-48; asst. prof. U. Calif.-Berkeley, 1948-50; mem. faculty Sarah Lawrence Coll., Bronxville, N.Y., 1950-52; supervising psychologist VA Hosp., Palo Alto, Calif., 1952-53; from asst. prof. to prof. psychology San Francisco State U., 1953—; sr. research fellow Harvard-Florence Research Project, Florence, Italy, 1963-64. Contbr. articles to sci. jour. USPHS research grantee San Francisco State U., 1967-69. Mem. Am. Psychol. Assn., AAAS. Club: Yacht (Berkeley, Calif.). Home: 2870 Buena Vista Way Berkeley CA 94708

INACKER, CHARLES JOHN, business educator, dean; b. Phila., Dec. 3, 1936; s. Charles John and Ada A. (Matthews) I. BS in Bus. Edn., Thiel Coll., 1958; EdM in Bus. Edn. and Edn1. Adminstrn., Temple U., 1960, EdD in Bus. Edn. and Econs., 1973. Tchr. bus. edn. Pitman (N.J.) High Sch., 1958-61; tchr., adminstr. Pennsauken (N.J.) High Sch., 1961-74; from assoc. prof. to prof. bus. edn. and office adminstrn. Calif. State U., Los Angeles, 1974—, acting chmn. acctg., 1984-85, chmn. dept. bus. edn. and office adminstrn., 1982-85, dean, sch. bus. and econs., 1985—; pres., bd. dirs. Aux. Services Enterprises, Inc., Los Angeles, 1985—; vis. lectr. various colls. and univs., Am. Mgmt. Assn. Ext. Inst.; mem. adv. com. Ctr. Bus. Tchr. Edn., Calif. State U., 1982-84, bus. edn. Alhambra (Calif.) High Sch., 1982-84; adv. council grad. and undergrad. programs sch. edn., Rider College, N.J., 1972-74, bus. edn. State Dept. Edn., N.J., 1972-74. Contbr. articles to profl. jours. Mem. Bus. and Econ. Devel. Council, East Los Angeles, 1985—. Served with U.S. Army, 1960-80. Mem. Acad. Mgmt., Nat. Bus. Edn. Assn., Calif. Bus. Edn. Assn. (cert. recogntionm 1983), Western Bus. Edn. Assn. (award of Merit 1958), Assn. Bus. Communications, N.J. Bus. Edn. Assn. (life), AAUP, Internat. Soc. Bus. Edn., Nat. Assn. Tchr. Educators in Bus. Edn., Western Assn. Collegiate Schs. Bus., Beta Gamma Sigma, Delta Pi Epsilon (sponsor Beta Pi chpt. 1979—, achievement award Alpha Zeta chpt. 1972), Research Found. of Delta Pi Epsilon (pres. 1984). Avocations: skiing, tennis. Home: 8015 Briar Summit Dr Los Angeles CA 90046 Office: Calif State U 5151 State University Dr Los Angeles CA 90032

INDOW, TAROW, psychology educator; b. Tokyo, Aug. 22, 1923; came to U.S., 1980; s. Sahei and Atsuko Indow; m. Minako Kawamura, Oct. 14, 1953. BA, Keio U., Tokyo, 1945, PhD, 1959. Prof. Keio U., 1961-79; research fellow Harvard U., Cambridge, Mass., 1963-66; vis. mem. Inst. for Advanced Study, Princeton, N.J., 1971-72; prof. U. Calif., Irvine, 1980—. mem. editorial bd. Mathematical Models in Psychology, 1969; contbr. articles to profl. jours. Fellow Soc. Exptl. Psychologists; mem. Assn. Internat. de la Couleur (pres. 1973-77). Office: U Calif Sch Social Scis Irvine CA 92717

INGALL, BEVERLY HELLER, botanist; b. N.Y.C., Jan. 30, 1926; d. Morris and Rose (Hollander) Heller; m. William Elfric Ingall, Jan. 18, 1951 (dec. Feb. 1976); children: Oliver Elfric, Glynnis Beth Ingall Katz, Alan Eliot, Ellery Duke. BA in Biology, Bklyn. Coll., 1947; MS in Botany, U. So. Calif., 1949; postgrad., Calif. State U., Long Beach, 1951-52, Mt. St. Mary's Coll., 1978. Instr. biology Bklyn. Coll., 1949; researcher Mistaire Lab., Millburn, N.J., 1949-51; biology tchr. Westridge Sch., Pasadena, Calif., 1978-79; researcher Los Angeles State and County Arboretum, Arcadia, Calif., 1979-82; scientist Phytogen Inc., Pasadena, 1982—. Mem. Guayule Rubber Soc. (fin. chmn. 3d Internat. Conf. 1980), AAAS, Bot. Soc. Am., Am. Inst. Biol. Scis., N.Y. Acad. Sci., Sigma Xi. Office: Phytogen Inc 101 Waverly Dr Pasadena CA 91105

INGALLS, MARGARET NICOLE, research chemical engineer; b. Washington, Dec. 6, 1956; d. Ronald Boyd and Joan Miller Ingalls; m. Terry Lance Freeland, Sept. 7, 1978 (div. Aug. 1981); m. David Alexander Lindsay, Dec. 31, 1983. BS in Engring., UCLA, 1978; MSChemE, MIT, 1983. Research engr. Unocal Corp., Brea, Calif., 1979—. Mem. Am. Inst. Chem. Engrs., Soc. Women Engrs. (UCLA student sect. pres. 1977-78), Sigma Xi, Tau Beta Pi. Democrat. Avocations: gardening, cross country skiing, backpacking. Office: Unocal Corp Sci and Tech 376 S Valencia Brea CA 92621

INGBER, LESTER, physicist, karate instructor; b. Bklyn., Mar. 26, 1941; s. Phillip and Helen (Felder) I.; m. Louise Frazer, Feb. 14, 1981. BS in Physics, Calif. Tech. U., 1962; postgrad., Niels Bohr Inst., Copenhagen, 1964; PhD in Theoretical Nuclear Physics, U. Calif. San Diego, 1966. Cert. emergency med. technician, 1978. Research asst. physics U. Calif. San Diego, La Jolla, 1962-66, asst. research physicist, Inst. for Pure and Applied Physical Scis., 1970-72, dir. Learning to Learn program, 1972-73, research assoc. music, 1972-74, research assoc., Inst. for Pure and Applied Physical Scis., 1970-72; asst. prof. physics SUNY, Stony Brook, 1969-70; pres. Phys. Studies Inst. and Ingber Physics Research, Carmel, Calif., 1970—, dir. ISA Alternative Sch., 1972-78, pres., also cons., 1984—; sr. research assoc. Naval Postgrad. Sch., Monterey, Calif., 1985-86, C3 prof. of physics, 1986—; cons. Rand Corp., Santa Monica, Calif., 1965-66; lect. adv. quantum mechanics, U. Calif., Berkeley, 1967-68; sr. research assoc. NRC, 1985—. Contbr. articles to profl. jours. Bd. dirs. Conservatory of Ballet Arts Co., 1986—. Named Kelman scholar Calif. Tech. U., 1958-62; grantee NRC, 1985-86, NSF postdoctoral fellow 1967-68, 1968-69. Mem. Am. Assn. Artificial Intelligence, Am. Coll. Sports Medicine, Am. Phys. Soc., Biophys. Soc., Fedn. Am. Scientists, Soc. Indsl. and Applied Math., Soc. Math. Biology, Soc. Neurosci., Sigma Xi, Sigma Pi Sigma. 1st Westerner to recieve instr.'s degree from Japan Karate Assn. and All-Am. Karate Fedn., 1968. Office: Naval Postgrad Sch Physics Dept Code 61IL Monterey CA 93943-5100

INGEBRITSON, JACK GORDON, real estate developer, financier; b. Berwyn, Ill., Mar. 22, 1946; s. Gordon L. and Hazel J. (Ulberg) I. B.S. in Bus. Adminstrn., Northwestern U., 1968, postgrad., 1969; postgrad. Ariz. State U., 1971. Mem. advt. dept. Chgo. Tribune, 1970; pres. Wellington Investment & Devel. Co., Inc., Phoenix, 1971-73, Ingebritson Investment Co., Inc., Phoenix, 1973—; gen. partner J.I. Assocs., Ltd., La Espanada, Ltd.; partner Residential Mktg. Systems, Crystal Technologies Ltd.; pres. Stonewood Devel. Corp., Benison Constrn. Co., Inc., Nicholas Gordon Ltd., Mistwood Devel. Co., Inc.; dir. Spear S Land & Cattle Co., Inc.; cons. maj. corps. 1st v.p. Royale Gardens II, 1977—; adv. panel Fiesta Bowl, 1978. Recipient award for Spengler Manor Complex, 1975; lic. real estate broker, Ariz. Mem. Solar Energy Inst., Urban Land Inst., Nat. Assn. Real Estate Bds., Ariz. Assn. Realtors, Nat. Inst. Real Estate Brokers, Home Builders Assn. of Central Ariz., Sales and Mktg. Council, Phoenix C. of C., Scottsdale C. of C., Friends of Channel 8, Phi Delta Theta. Republican. Lutheran. Clubs: Jockey, Metro Athletic. Adv. panel Housing Mag., 1980-81. Home: 5268 E Onyx Scottsdale AZ 85253

INGELS, HAROLD CLAYTON, video engineer; b. Annapolis, Md., Sept. 18, 1941; s. Albert Clayton and Elizabeth Francis (Philbrick) I.; m. Clairette Eveline Ingels, Jan. 28, 1967; children—Michelle, David. A.A., San Diego City Coll., 1962; student San Diego State Coll., 1962-63. With various radio stas., San Diego, 1960-65; sr. video engr. NBC Inc., Burbank, Calif., 1965—. Chmn. emergency communications Crescenta Radio Club, 1980-86. Served with U.S. Army, 1962-64. Recipient Emmy award for electronic camera work, 1982. Mem. Acad. TV Arts and Scis., Nat. Assn. Broadcast Employees and Technicians. (treas. 1977-86, regional v.p. 1983-86). Office: NBC Inc 3000 W Alameda Ave Burbank CA 91523

INGELS, MARTY, theatrical agent, TV and motion picture production executive; b. Bklyn., Mar. 9, 1936; s. Jacob and Minnie (Crown) Ingerman; m. Jean Maire Frassinelli, Aug. 3, 1960 (div. 1969); m. Shirley Jones, 1977. Ed., Erasmus High Sch., 1951-53, Forest Hills High Sch., 1953-55. Founder Ingels Inc., 1975—; formed Stoneypoint Prodns., 1981; TV and motion picture producer U.S. and abroad. Star: Dickens and Fenster series, ABC-TV, 1964; co-star: Pruitts of Southampton, 1968-69; films include Armored Command, 1962, Horizontal Lieutenant, 1965, Busy Body, 1967, Ladies Man, 1966, If It's Tuesday This Must Be Belgium, 1970, Wild and Wonderful, 1965, Guide for a Married Man, 1968; numerous TV appearances. Active various charity drives. Office: Ingels Inc 8111 Beverly Blvd Hollywood CA 90048

INGERMAN, MICHAEL LEIGH, hospital consultant; b. N.Y.C., Nov. 30, 1937; s. Charles Stryker and Ernestine (Leigh) I.; B.S., George Washington U., 1963; m. Madeleine Edison Sloane; Nov. 24, 1984; children by previous marriage—Shawn Marie, Jenifer Lyn. Health planner, Marin County, Calif., 1969-70, 70-72; regional cons. Bay Area Comprehensive Health Council, San Francisco, 1972-73; hosp. cons. Booz, Allen & Hamilton, San Francisco, 1974; health planning coordinator Peralta Hosp., Oakland, Calif., 1975-76; pres. Discern, Inc., hosp. cons., Nicasio, Calif., 1976—; instr. Golden Gate U., 1981—. Capt. Nicasio Vol. Fire Dept., 1976—; dep. coroner Marin County, 1980-83; nat. bd. dirs. Am. Friends Service Com., 1980-81, bd. dirs. Hospice of Marin, 1983—, Friends Assn. Services for the Elderly, 1984—. Mem. Marin County Civil Grand Jury, 1977-78; mem. Nicasio Design Rev. Com., 1979-83; bd. dirs. John Woolman Sch., 1980—. Mem. Am. Hosp. Assn., Calif. Hosp. Assn., Western Hosp. Assn., Healthcare Fin. Mgmt. Assn. Home: 2101 Nicasio Valley Rd Nicasio CA 94946

INGERSOLL, JOHN GREGORY, physicist, energy specialist, educator; b. Athens, Greece, July 25, 1948; came to U.S., 1971, naturalized.; s. Gregory and Catherine (Asteris) I.; m. Sally Lynn Roberts, Apr. 7, 1984. BS, Nat. Tech. U., Athens, 1970; MS, Syracuse U., 1973; PhD, U. Calif., Berkeley, 1978. Instr. physics U. Calif., Berkeley, 1974-75; research asst. Lawrence Berkeley Lab U. Calif., Berkeley, 1975-77, asst. research prof., 1978-81, assoc. research prof., 1981-82; sr. staff scientist Hughes Aircraft Co., Los Angeles, 1983—; cons. Calif. Energy Commn., Sacramento, 1981-82, U.S. Dept. Energy, Washington, 1981-83, Bldg. Industry N.Y. and Calif., 1982—; prin. investigator Energy Technology Group UCLA, 1983—. Contbr. over 50 articles on nuclear sci., renewable energy resources, indoor air quality, efficient utilization of energy in bldgs., passive solar systems and solar elec. energy to profl. jours.; contbg. author to three books on energy mgmt. in bldgs.; patentee of heat pipe devels. Mem. Rep. Presdl. Task Force, Calif., 1981-83. Served as lt. USNR, 1982—. Mem. Am. Physical Soc., N.Y. Acad. Scis., AAAS, Am. Soc. of Heating, Refrigeration and Air-conditioning Engrs (govt. and community liaison 1985—). Republican. Presbyterian. Avocations: walking, hiking, archeology ancient Greece and Egypt. Office: Hughes Aircraft Co PO Box 902 El Segundo CA 90245

INGHAM, ROBERT EDWIN, cardiologist; b. Berkeley, Calif., Dec. 30, 1944; s. Theodore Alton and Mary Lou (Bailey) I.; B.A., U. Calif.-Berkeley, 1966; M.D., Cornell U., 1970; children—William Robert, Douglas James. Intern, Cornell-N.Y. Hosp., N.Y.C., 1970-71, resident internal medicine, 1971-72; fellow in cardiology Stanford (Calif.) U., 1973-74; practice medicine specializing in cardiology Naval Regional Med. Ctr., Oakland, Calif., 1974-76; mem. staff John Muir Meml. Hosp., Walnut Creek, Calif., 1976—, sec.-treas. staff, 1981, vice-chief of staff, 1982-83, chief of staff, 1983, dir. noninvasive cardiology lab., 1979-81, dir. cardiac exercise program, 1978-85, dir. invasive cardiology lab., 1986; assoc. clin. prof. medicine U. Calif.-Davis, 1976—; bd. dirs. Omega Med. Clinic, 1985—, vice chmn., 1985—. Former bd. dirs. Danville (Calif.) Fire Protection Dist.; bd. dirs., past pres. Contra

Costa County chpt. Am. Heart Assn. Served with M.C., USNR, 1974-76. Diplomate Am. Bd. Internal Medicine; Leopold Schepp Found. scholar, 1968-69. Fellow Am. Coll. Cardiology, ACP; mem. Am. Heart Assn., Soc. Med. Friends of Wine. Contbr. articles to profl. jours. Office: 1515 Ygnacio Valley Rd Walnut Creek CA 94598

INGHAM, ROGER JOHN, speech pathology educator; b. Adelaide, Australia, Feb. 24, 1941; s. Colin Wilford and Joan Cecelia (Sjoberg) I.; m. Joan Lynn Sindel, Jan. 13, 1973 (dec. Feb. 1983); m. Janis Mahorney, Apr. 14, 1985. BS, U. New South Wales, Sydney, Australia, 1966, PhD, 1972. Research psychologist U. New South Wales, Sydney, Australia, 1966-73; head of sch. of communication disorders Cumberland College, Sydney, 1973-84; prof., chmn. dept. speech and hearing scis. U. Calif., Santa Barbara, 1984—. Author: Treatment of Stuttering in Early Childhood, 1983, Stuttering and Behavior Therapy, 1984. Recipient Australian Medal, Gov. Gen. Australia, Sydney, 1982. Fellow Am. Speech Language Hearing Assn. Avocations: squash, music, reading. Office: U Calif Dept Speech & Hearing Scis Santa Barbara CA 93106

INGHRAM, BRENT J., engineer; b. Napa, Calif., Sept. 11, 1955; s. Arland J. and June F. Inghram; m. Pamela A. Inghram, Sept. 18, 1976 (div. June 1981). BS, U. Calif., Davis, 1978; MS, U. Nev., 1981; postgrad., U. Idaho, 1979. Registered geol. engr., Nev., civil engr., Calif. Geotech. engr. Converse Cons., Pasadena, Calif., 1981-83; lectr. rock mechanics U. Nev., Reno, 1983-84; sr. engr. Leighton & Assocs., Palm Desert, Calif., 1984—; cons. in field 1983—. Contbr. tech. articles to profl. jours. Mem. ASCE, Assn. Engring. Geologists, Soc. Mining Engrs., AIA (profl. affiliate), Sigma Xi. Home: 66902 Cahuilla Ave Desert Hot Springs CA 92240

INGLEBRET, ELLA RUTH, speech pathologist; b. Grand Rapids, Minn., June 19, 1952; d. Duane Carlyle and Norma Lorraine (Tolstad) I.; m. Nick Sanyal, Mar. 28 1976; 1 child, Noel Inglebret. BA, U. Minn., Duluth, 1975; MA, U. Mont., 1985. Devel. specialist Adult/Child Devel. Ctr., Lewiston, Idaho, 1978-81, communication disorder specialist, 1983—; speech-lang. pathologist Pediatric Speech and Lang. Services, Olympia, Wash., 1981-82, Tompkins County (N.Y.) Head Start Services, Ithaca, 1982-83; affiliate prof. U. Idaho, Moscow, 1979-80. Mem. Am. Speech Lang. Hearing Assn. (cert.), Neurodevel. Treatment Assn. (cert.). Office: Adult/Child Devel Ctr PO Drawer B Lewiston ID 83501

INGLES, JOSEPH LEGRAND, utility consumer advocate, city official; b. June 15, 1939; s. Vernal Willard and Helen Josephine (Graziano) I.; m. Hazel Jeanette Palmer, Aug. 18, 1962; children—Sally, Christine, Joette, Robert, Michael. B.S., Brigham Young U., 1964; Ph.D., U. Mo., 1968. Research asst. U. Mo., Columbia, 1967-68; grant policy specialist HEW, Washington, 1970-71; asst. prof. govt. and politics U. Md., College Park, 1968-75; dir. human resources Wasatch Front Regional Council, Bountiful, Utah, 1975-77; utility consumer advocate Com. on Consumer Service Utah, 1977—; cons. Ellingson Kilpack Assocs., Salt Lake City, 1972, Bonneville Research Corp., Santa Monica, Calif., 1971, U.S. Dept. Commerce, 1970. Mem. West Bountiful City Council, 1982—. fellow NDEA, 1964-67; U. Md. grantee, 1969. Fellow Am. Soc. Pub. Adminstrn. (fellowship 1970-71); mem. Nat. Assn. Regulatory Utility Commrs., Nat. Assn. State Utility Consumer Advocates (state rep. 1979—). Mormon. Home: 1485 N 1100 W West Bountiful UT 84087 Office: Com Consumer Services 408 Heber Wells Bldg PO Box 45802 Salt Lake City UT 84145

INGLIS, STUART JOHN, retired physicist, educator; b. Van Nuys, Calif., Dec. 16, 1923; s. John Percy and Ruth (Penfield) I.; m. Elizabeth Eskildsen, Dec. 21, 1958; children: Adrienne, Jennifer. BA, U. Calif., Berkeley, 1947, MA, 1956. Tchr. U.S. Army Dependent Schs., Trieste, Italy, 1952-53, Fullerton (Calif.) High Sch. and Jr. Coll., 1954-56; instr. Contra Costa Coll., Richmond, Calif., 1956-63; assoc. prof. Sonoma State Coll., Rohnert Park, Calif., 1963-65; instr. Chabot Coll., Livermore, Calif., 1965-84; adj. prof. So. Oreg. State Coll., Ashland, 1985-87. Author: Planets, Stars and Galaxies, 1976, Physics: An Ebb and Flow of Ideas, 1970; editor: Physical Science for Nonscience Student, 1969. Bd. dirs. Livermore-Amada Symphony Assn., 1979-80, Ruch (Oreg.) Community Library, 1986. Served to 2d lt. USMCR, 1943-45. Fellow NSF, 1961-62, Westinghouse Corp, 1952. Mem. Astron. Soc. of the Pacific, Sigma Xi. Democrat. Avocations: farming, wildlife, geology.

INGRAHAM, JOHN CHARLES, plasma physicist; b. Seattle, Nov. 15, 1936; m. Karen Elizabeth Trump, June 22, 1968; children: Elizabeth, John. SB, MIT, 1958, PhD, 1963. Instr. physics MIT, Cambridge, 1963-65, asst. prof. physics, 1965-68; sci. specialist E.G.&G., Bedford, Mass., 1968-70; mem. staff Los Alamos (N.Mex.) Nat. Lab., 1970—.

INGRAM, HELEN MOYER, political science educator; b. Denver, July 12, 1937; d. Oliver Weldon and Hazel Margaret (Wickard) Hill; m. W. David Laird; children by previous marriage—Mrill, Maia, Seth. B.A., Oberlin (Ohio) Coll., 1959; Ph.D., Columbia U., N.Y.C., 1967. Lectr., asst. prof. polit. sci. U. N. Mex., 1962-69; cons. Nat. Water Commn., Washington, 1969-72; assoc. prof. polit. sci. U. Ariz., Tucson, 1972-77, prof. polit. sci., 1979—; sr. fellow Resources for the Future, Washington, 1977-79, cons., 1979—; mem. panel on climate variability and U.S. water resources AAAS, 1986—. Mem. Policy Studies Orgn., (pres. 1985), Am. Polit. Sci. Assn. (council, treas. 1985-87), Western Polit. Sci. Assn. (past pres., v.p.). Author: (with Dean Mann) Why Policies Succeed or Fail, 1980; (with Nancy Laney and John McCain) A Policy Approach to Representation: Lessons from the Four Corners States, 1980; (with Martin, Laney and Griffin) Saving Water in a Desert City, 1984, (with Brown) Water and Poverty in the Southwest: Conflict, Opportunity, and Challenge, 1987. Home: 2811 E 3d St Tucson AZ 85716 Office: Dept Polit Sci U Ariz Tucson AZ 85721

INGRAM, WILLIAM AUSTIN, federal judge; b. Jeffersonville, Ind., July 6, 1924; s. William Austin and Marion (Lane) I.; m. Barbara Brown Lender, Sept. 18, 1947; children: Mary Ingram Mac Calla, Claudia, Betsy Ingram Friebel. Student, Stanford U., 1947; LL.B., U. Louisville, 1950. Assoc., Littler, Coakley, Lauritzen & Ferdon, San Francisco, 1951-55; dep. dist. atty. Santa Clara (Calif.) County, 1955-57; mem. firm Rankin, O'Neal, Luckhardt & Center, San Jose, Calif., 1955-69; judge Mcpl. Ct., Palo Alto-Mountain View, Calif., 1969-71, Calif. Superior Ct., 1971-76, U.S. Dist. Ct. No. Dist. Calif., San Jose, 1976—. Served with USMCR, 1943-46. Fellow Am. Coll. Trial Lawyers. Republican. Episcopalian. Home: 1211 College Ave Palo Alto CA 94306 Office: US Court House Dist Judge 280 S 1st St San Jose CA 95113

INGRAM, WILLIAM ROY, JR., accountant, municipal fiscal officer; b. Norwood, Mass., Jan. 6, 1930; s. William Roy and Jessie Scott (Robinson) I.; m. Pauline Francis Burke, Jan. 19, 1951 (div.); children—Christine Stephanie, William Roy III; m. Veronica Alexandria Chipenow, Feb. 6, 1982. Student engring. Wentworth Inst., Boston, 1956-57; student bus. adminstrn. U. Hartford, 1961-63. Acct., Combustion Engring. Co., Windsor, Conn., 1958-67, F.H. McGraw Co., Hartford, Conn., 1967-69, Diesel Constrn. Co., Boston, 1969-74; chief fiscal officer Town of Payson, Ariz., 1975—; chmn. Payson San. Dist., 1981. Served to cpl. U.S. Army, 1952-53; Korea. Mem. Mcpl. Fin. Officers Assn. of U.S. and Can. (Fin. Reporting Achievement award 1977). Democrat. Home: PO Box 1962 Payson AZ 85547 Office: Town of Payson 303 N Beeline Hwy Payson AZ 85541

INGWERSEN, HENRY WILLIAM, IV, chief of police; b. San Francisco, Mar. 19, 1940; s. Henry William III and Virginia (Carson) I.; m. Carol Jean McCulloch, Aug. 1, 1958; children—Sue Ann, Henry William V. A.A., Coll. of Marin, 1972; B.A. in Adminstrn. of Justice, Golden Gate U., 1974, M.P.A., 1975. Dispatcher, police officer Police Dept., San Rafael, Calif., 1962-70, sgt., 1970-74, lt., 1974, capt., 1974-79, chief of police, 1981—; under-sheriff, Sheriff's Office, County of Marin, Calif., 1979-81; cons. assessment ctr. Office of Josephine County Sheriff, Grants Pass, Oreg., 1980; chmn. adv. com. Santa Rosa Regional Tng. Center, Santa Rosa, Calif., 1978—; cons. Peace Officer Standards and Tngs., Sacramento, Calif., 1982-83; guest lectr. Dominican Coll., San Rafael, 1975-76. Author: Crime Analysis, 1984. Chmn., bd. dirs. Marin Treatment Ctr., San Rafael, 1975—; chmn. Marin County chpt. ARC, San Rafael, 1982-87; bd. dirs. Bay Area Red Cross; mem. exec. council Marin council Boy Scouts Am., San Rafael, 1982-85; consolidation com. Citizens League Marin, Novato, Calif., 1983-85; mem. adv. bd. Marin Cath. High Sch., Kentfield, Calif., 1982-85. Served with USAF, 1958-62. Mem. Marin County Peace Officers Assn. (pres. 1974-75), Calif. Police Chiefs Assn., Calif. Peace Officers Assn. (committeeman 1982-83), Nat. Criminal Justice Assn., Internat. Assn. Chiefs of Police, Marin County Police Chief Assn. (pres. 1987—), Internat. Police Assn., Calif. Water Fowl Assn. Republican. Lodge: Lions (pres. San Rafael 1980-81); Elks (exalter ruler San Rafael 1981-82; trustee 1984—, chmn. bd. trustees 1987—). Office: City of San Rafael 1400 5th Ave San Rafael CA 94901

INJERD, WILLIAM GEORGE, chemist; b. Tucson, Aug. 2, 1951; s. Howard Wesley and Dorothy Mae (Welty) I.; m. Kathryn Diane Edleman, June 2, 1979; children: Diane Elizabeth, Kristen Johanna, Mark Timothy. BS in Chemistry, UCLA, 1973. Cert. tchr., Calif. Research assoc. Inst. Geophysics UCLA, 1971-75; tchr. Yucaipa (Calif.) High Sch., 1975-77; pres. Bi-Chem Supply, Lake Stevens, Wash., 1982-85; research and devel. engr. Boeing Comml. Airplane Co., Everett, Wash., 1978—. Inventor countersink sealant nozzle, 1978. Mem. Am. Chem. Soc., Alpha Chi Sigma. Republican. Baptist. Lodge: Sons of Norway. Office: Boeing Comml Airplane Co PO Box 3707 Org A-2020 MS OX-70 Seattle WA 98124

INKELES, ALEX, sociology educator; b. Bklyn., Mar. 4, 1920; s. Meyer and Ray (Gewer) K.; m. Bernadette Mary Kane, Jan. 31, 1942; 1 child, Ann Elizabeth. B.A., Cornell U., 1941, M.A., 1946; postgrad., Washington Sch. Psychiatry, 1943-46; Ph.D., Columbia U., 1949; student, Boston Psychoanalytic Inst., 1957-59; A.M. (hon.), Harvard U., 1957; prof. honoris causa, Faculdade Candido Mendez, Rio de Janerio, 1969. Social sci. research analyst Dept. State and OSS, 1942-46; cons. program evaluation br., internat. broadcasting div. Dept. State, 1949-51; instr. social relations Harvard U., Cambridge, Mass., 1948, lectr., 1948-57, prof. sociology, 1957-71, dir. studies social relations Russian Research Ctr., dir. studies social aspects econ. devel. Ctr. Internat. Affairs, 1963-71, research assoc., 1971—; Margaret Jacks prof. edn., prof. sociology Stanford U., Calif., 1971-78, prof. sociology, sr. fellow Hoover Instn., 1978—; mem. exec. com. behavioral sci. div. NRC, 1968-75; lectr. Nihon U., Japan, 1985. Author: Public Opinion in Soviet Russia, 1950 (Kappa Tau Alpha award 1950, Grant Squires prize Columbia 1955); (with R. Bauer, C. Kluckhohn) How the Soviet System Works, 1956; (with R. Bauer) The Soviet Citizen, 1959, Soviet Society (edited with H.K. Geiger), 1961; What Is Sociology?, 1964; Readings on Modern Sociology, 1965; Social Change in Soviet Russia, 1968; (with D.H. Smith) Becoming Modern, 1974 (Hadley Cantril award 1974); Exploring Individual Modernity, 1983. Contbr. articles to profl. jours. Editor-in-chief: Ann. Rev. Sociology, 1971-79; editorial cons. Internat. Rev. Cross Cultural Studies; editorial bd. Ethos, Jour. Soc. Psychol. Anthropology, 1978; editor Founds. Modern Sociology Series; adv. editor in sociology to Little, Brown & Co. Recipient Cooley Mead award for Disting. Contbn. in Social Psychology, 1982; fellow Ctr. Advanced Study Behavioral Sci., 1955, Founds. Fund Research Psychiatry, 1957-60, Social Scis. Research Council, 1959, Russell Sage Found., 1966, 85, Fulbright Found., 1977, Guggenheim Found., 1978, Bernard van Leer Jerusalem Found., 1979, Rockefeller Found., 1982, Eisenhower Assn., Taiwan, 1984; NAS Disting. Scholar Exchange, China, 1983;. Fellow AAAS (co-chmn. western ctr. 1984-87), Am. Philos. Soc., Am. Psychol. Assn.; mem. Nat. Acad. Scis., Am. Sociol. Soc. (council 1961-64, v.p. 1975-76), Eastern Sociol. Soc. (pres. 1961-62), World Assn. Pub. Opinion Research, Am. Assn. Pub. Opinion Research, Inter-Am. Soc. Psychology, Sociol. Research Assn. (exec. com. 1975-79, pres. 1979), Soc. for Study Social Problems. Home: 10001 Hamilton Ave Palo Alto CA 94301 Office: Hoover Instn Stanford CA 94305

INLOES, DONALD HENRY, foundation administrator; b. Lander, Wyo., Mar. 10, 1939; s. Don H. and Winifred (Estey) I.; m. Patricia Louise Weter, July 24, 1960 (dec. Aug. 1977); 1 child, David C. BA, William Jewell Coll., 1962; MDiv, Cen. Bapt. Theological Sem., 1965. Ordained to ministry Bapt. Ch., 1965. Clergyman First Bapt. Ch., Sheboygan Falls, Wis., 1965-67; social worker Kenosha (Wis.) Dept. Social Services, 1967-73; exec. dir. Kenosha County Mental Health Assn., 1973-77; dist. tng. coordinator Ariz. State U., Phoenix, 1978-79; pres. Inloes Assocs., Phoenix, 1979-81; exec. dir. H.O.W. Found., Indio, Calif., 1981—; cons. Ariz. Dept. Econ. Security, Phoenix, 1980-81, Riverside County Dept. Mental Health, Indio, 1981-84. Mem. Calif. Council Community Mental Health Contractors, Mental Health Assn. Phoenix (pres. 1982-83), Mental Health Assn. Ariz. (v.p. 1981-82), Mental Health Assn. Palm Springs (pres. 1984-86), Mental Health Assn. Calif. (regional v.p. 1986—). Democrat. Presbyterian. Club: Toastmasters (adminstrv. v.p. Indio club 1984, pres. 1985). Home: 81840 Avenida del Mar #104 Indio CA 92201 Office: The HOW Found 82 380 Miles Ave Indio CA 92201

INLOW, RUSH OSBORNE, chemist; b. Seattle, July 10, 1944; s. Edgar Burke and Marigale (Osborne) I.; B.S., U. Wash., 1966; Ph.D., Vanderbilt U., 1975; m. Gloria Elisa Duran, June 7, 1980. Chemist, sect. chief U.S. Dept. Energy, New Brunswick Lab., Argonne, Ill., 1975-78, chief nuclear safeguards br. Albuquerque ops., 1978-82, sr. program engr. Cruise missile systems, 1983-84, program mgr. Navy Strategic Systems, 1984-85, dir. weapon programs div., 1985—. Served with USN, 1966-71. Tenn. Eastman fellow, 1974-75. Mem. Am. Chem. Soc., Sigma Xi. Republican. Episcopalian. Contbr. articles to profl. jours. Home: 2024 Monte Largo NE Albuquerque NM 87112

INMAN, THURSTON HUGH, service management; b. McAllister, Okla., June 9, 1928; s. Roy Christifer and Eva Maud (Jobe) I.; children: James, Gary (dec.), Connie. Office machine technician Friden Agy., Tucson, 1945-57; supr. Friden Inc., Tucson, 1957-72; electronics technician div. Singer Corp. Friden Inc., Albuquerque, 1972-77; field service area mgr. Singer (acquisitioned by TRW-CSD), Albuquerque, 1977—. Served with U.S. Army, 1947. Democrat. Avocations: rose gardening, hunting, fishing. Home: 1401 Betts NE Albuquerque NM 87112 Office: TRW Customer Service Div 2418 San Mateo Pl NE Albuquerque NM 87110

INNES, DAVID CHARLES, minister; b. Kenosha, Wis., Feb. 6, 1940; s. Delbert Charles and Ferne Elizabeth (Shattuck) I.; m. Edith Joy Yunk, July 14, 1962; children: Delbert, David Jr., Deborah, Dorothy. BA, Bob Jones U., 1961, BD, 1964; DD (hon.), San Francisco Bapt. Theol. Sem., 1978. Ordained to ministey Bapt. Ch., 1964. Founder, pastor Tabernacle Bapt. Ch., Morganton, N.C., 1962-65; asst. pastor Cen. Bapt. Ch., Anaheim, Calif., 1965-68; pastor Calvary Bapt. Ch., Yucca Valley, Calif., 1968-76, Hamilton Sq. Bapt. Ch., San Francisco, 1977—; pres., chmn. bd. trustees San Francisco Bapt. Theol. Sem.; pres. bd. dirs. No. Calif. Fellowhip Fundamental Bapts.; mem. adv. bd. Internat. Bapt. Missions, Tempe, Ariz., 1982—; mem. exec. bd. No. Calif.-We. Nev. Assn. Christian Schs., San Francisco, 1981—; bd. dirs. Fundamental Bapt. Fellowship Am., Virginia Beach, Va. Trustee, pres., v.p. Morongo Unified Sch. Dist., San Bernardino County, Calif., 1969-77; trustee, pres. San Francisco Christian Schs., 1978-84. Office: Hamilton Sq Bapt Ch 1212 Geary St San Francisco CA 94109

INNIS, EILEEN SCHEFFLER, administrative analyst; b. Eau Claire, Wis., Oct. 15, 1929; d. Edwin Herman and Elizabeth Emma (Jaeckel) Scheffler; m. Jack Mattson Innis, Feb. 12, 1950 (div. 1967); children—Jack Scheffler, Steven Wayne, Douglas Alan. Student, Orange Coast Coll., 1959, U. Calif.-San Diego, 1979-81, Mira Costa Coll., 1983-84, 86-87. Sec. U.S. Navy, Washington, 1949-51, Kaiser Aluminum & Chem. Co., Oakland, Calif., 1952-55; office mgr. Friedkin Racing Enterprises, Escondido, Calif., 1967-68; sec. U. Calif.-La Jolla, 1968-72. adminstrv. asst., 1972-84, adminstrv. analyst, 1984—; exec. bd. mem. U. Calif.-San Diego Staff Assn., La Jolla, 1984-85. Vol. Mus. of Man, San Diego, 1979—. Mem. Archeol. Inst. Am., San Diego County Archeol. Soc., Soc. Bibl. Archaeology, Nat. History Mus., Flying Samaritans Internat. (life mem.). Republican. Episcopalian. Home: 12762 Via Donada Del Mar CA 92014 Office: U Calif San Diego Sch Medicine Dept Community Family Medicine M-028 La Jolla CA 92093

INOUYE, DANIEL KEN, U.S. senator; b. Honolulu, Sept. 7, 1924; s. Hyotaro I. and Kame Imanaga; m. Margaret Shinobu Awamura, June 12, 1949; 1 child, Daniel Ken. A.B., U. Hawaii, 1950; J.D., George Washington U., 1952. Jr. asst. pub. prosecutor Honolulu, 1953-54, practice of law, 1954—; majority leader Territorial Ho. of Reps., 1954-58, Senate, 1958-59; mem. 86th-87th U.S. congresses from, Hawaii, U.S. Senate from, Hawaii, 1963—; sec. Senate Democratic Conf.; mem. Dem. Policy Com., Dem. Steering Com., Senate Com. on Appropriations; ranking mem. subcom. fgn. ops., mem. Commerce Com.; ranking mem. subcom. mcht. marine and tourism, chmn. Select Com. on Intelligence, 1976-77, ranking mem. subcom. budget authorizations, 1979-84; mem. Select Com. Indian Affairs, Select Com. on Presdl. Campaign Activities, 1973-74; dir. Central Pacific Bank. Author: Journey to Washington. Active YMCA, Boy Scouts Am. Keynoter; temporary chmn. Dem. Nat. Conv., 1968, rules com. chmn., 1980, co-chmn. conv., 1984. Served from pvt. to capt. AUS, 1943-47. Decorated D.S.C., Bronze Star, Purple Heart with cluster; named 1 of 10 Outstanding Young Men of Yr. U.S. Jr. C. of C., 1960; recipient Alumnus of Yr. award George Washington U., 1961; Splendid Am. award Thomas A. Dooley Found., 1967; Golden Plate award Am. Acad. Achievement, 1968. Mem. D.A.V. (past comdr. Hawaii), Honolulu C. of C., Am. Legion (Nat. Comdr.'s award 1973). Methodist. Clubs: Lion. (Hawaii), 442d Veterans (Hawaii). Home: 469 Ena Rd Honolulu HI 96814 Office: 722 Hart Senate Bldg Washington DC 20510 *

INOUYE, WAYNE MICHAEL, engineering director, photographer; b. Los Angeles, Aug. 5, 1951; s. Katsumi and Toshiko (Suo) I. AS in Math., Pasadena City Coll., 1971; BSEE with honors, Calif. Poly. U., 1974, MEE, 1976. Instr. Don Bosco Tech. Inst., Rosemead, Calif., 1973-75; electronics engr. Gen. Dynamics, Pomona, Calif., 1975-78; engr. Met. Water Dist., Los Angeles, 1978-79; sr. product engr. TRW Semiconductors, Lawndale, Calif., 1979-80; mgr. project engring. Leach Control Products, Buena Park, Calif., 1980-82; dep. dir. engring. Teledyne Solid State, Hawthorne, Calif., 1982—. Contbr. articles on photography and radiation effects to profl. jours. Assoc. mem. Long Beach (Calif.) Hist. Soc., 1974—, U.S. Ski Team, Park City, Utah, 1986. Mem. Internat. Standards Orgn. (U.S. del.), Assoc. Photographers Internat., Eta Kappa Nu, Tau Beta Pi. Republican. Presbyterian. Avocations: skiing, photography, hiking, computer programming. Office: Teledyne Solid State 12525 Daphne Hawthorne CA 90250

INSEL, PAUL ANTHONY, pharmacology educator, consultant; b. N.Y.C., Nov. 22, 1945; s. Herman Herbert and Ruth Leona (Friedman) I.; m. Lola Sara Steinbaum, June 10, 1968 (div. 1970); m. Louise Rausa, Dec. 29, 1977; children: Rachel, Sarah; stepson, Jeffrey. Student, George Wash. U., 1962-64; MD, U. Mich., 1968. Diplomate Am. Bd. Med. Examiners, Am. Bd. Internal Medicine. Intern then asst. resident Boston City Hosp. Harvard Unit, 1968-70; clin. assoc., med. officer NIH, Nat. Inst. Child Health and Human Devel., Gerontol. Research Ctr., Balt., 1970-74; research fellow clin. pharmacology div. Cardiovascular Research Inst. U. Calif., San Francisco, 1974-77, resident asst. prof., 1977-78; asst. prof. medicine Pharmacology div. U. Calif. San Diego, La Jolla, 1978-81, assoc. prof., 1981-87, prof., 1987—; asst. in medicine Johns Hopkins U., 1971-74; attending physician Emergency Service San Francisco Gen. Hosp., 1974-78; cons. NIH, Am. Cancer Soc., NIMH, VA, 1978—. Mem. editorial bd. Molecular Pharmacology Jour. Cyclic Nucleotide Research, 1980—; contbr. articles to sci. jours., chpts. to books. Served with USPHS, 1970-74. Research grantee NIH, NSF, Am. Heart Assn., Am. Cancer Soc., 1977—. Fellow Council for High Blood Pressure Research; mem. Am. Heart Assn. (Katz Research prize 1976), Western Soc. Clin. Investigation (councillor 1980-83), Am. Soc. Clin. Investigation, Am. Fedn. Clin. Research, Am. Soc. Biol. Chemists, Am. Soc. Pharmacology and Exptl. Therapeutics, Am. Soc. Cell Biology, Endocrine Soc. Home: 2164 Balfour Ct Pacific Beach CA 92109 Office: U Calif San Diego Dept Medicine div Pharmacology M-036-H La Jolla CA 92093

INSELMAN-TEMKIN, BARBARA RUTH, psychologist, educator; b. Bklyn., Apr. 7, 1948; d. Alexander M. and Rae C. (Bloom) Inselman; m. Lawrence Paul Temkin, June 6, 1971; children: Joshua Michael, Deborah Ashley. AB in Psychology magna cum laude, Barnard Coll., 1968; MS, Yale U., 1972, PhD, 1973. Lic. clin. psychologist, Conn.; cert. psychologist, Ariz. Postdoctoral fellow Yale U., New Haven, Conn., 1973-74; psychologist Stamford (Conn.) Hosp., 1974-77; pvt. practice psychology Tucson, 1977—; lectr. psychiatry U. Ariz., Tucson, 1981—; assoc. staff mem. St. Mary's Hosp., Tucson, 1980—, Univ. Med. Ctr., Tucson, 1981—, Sonora Desert Hosp., Tucson, 1986—; affiliate staff mem. Palo Verde Hosp., Tucson, 1982—. Contbr. articles to profl. jours. N.Y. State Regents scholar, 1964-68, Rice Meml. Grad. fellow, 1968-69; grantee Yale U., 1971, NIMH, 1968-70, NSF, 1970-72. Mem. So. Ariz. Psychol. Assn. (treas. 1979-81, v.p. 1981-83, pres. 1983-85); Ariz. State Psychol. Assn., Am. Psychol. Assn., AAAS, Nat. Register Health Service Providers in Psychology, Sigma Xi, Phi Beta Kappa. Home and Office: 3444 N Camino Esplanade Tucson AZ 85715

INTRIERE, ANTHONY DONALD, physician; b. Greenwich, Conn., May 9, 1920; s. Rocco and Angelina (Belcastro) I.; M.D., U. Mich., 1944; m. Carol A. Yarmey, Aug. 1, 1945; children—Sherry Lynn, Michael, Nancy, Lisa. Intern, New Rochelle (N.Y.) Hosp., 1944-45; pvt. practice medicine, Greenwich, Conn., 1947-53, Olney, Ill., 1956-61, Granite City, Ill., 1961-74, San Diego, 1975—; fellow in internal medicine Cleve. Clinic, 1953-55; fellow in gastroenterology Lahey Clinic, Boston, 1955-56. Served from 1st lt. to capt. M.C., AUS, 1945-47. Fellow Am. Coll. Gastroenterology (assoc.); mem. A.C.P. (asso.), Am. Soc. Internal Medicine. Home: 9981 Caminto Chirimolla San Diego CA 92131

INTRILIGATOR, MICHAEL D., economist, educator; b. N.Y.C., Feb. 5, 1938; m. Devrie; children—Kenneth, James, William, Robert. SB in Econs., MIT, 1959; MA, Yale U., 1960; PhD, MIT, 1963. Asst. prof. econs. UCLA, 1963-66, assoc. prof., 1966-72, prof., 1972—, prof. dept. polit. sci., 1981—, dir. Ctr. Internat. and Strategic Affairs, 1982—; dir. Jacob Marschak Interdisciplinary Coll. 1977—; cons. Inst. Def. Analysis, 1974-77, ACDA, 1968, Rand Corp., 1962-65; mem. steering com. Summer Inst. for Study of Conflict Theory and Internat. Security, 1980—. Author: Mathematical Optimization and Economic Theory, 1971, also Taiwanese, Spanish and Russian edits., Econometric Models, Techniques and Applications, 1978, 83, Greek edit., 1983, (with others) A Forecasting and Policy Simulation Model of the Health Care Sector, 1979; mem. adv. editorial bd. Math. Social Scis., 1983—; assoc. editor Jour. Optimization Theory and Applications, 1979—, Jour. Bus. and Econ. Stats., 1981—, Conflict Mgmt. and Peace Sci., 1980—; co-editor: (series) Handbooks in Economics, 1980—, Advanced Textbooks in Economics, 1972—; editor: (with D.A. Kendrick) Frontiers of Quantitative Economics, vol. II, 1974, (with Kenneth Arrow) Handbook of Mathematical Economics, 3 vols., 1981-85; (with Zvi Griliches) Handbook of Econometrics, 3 vols., 1983-86, (with B. Brodie and R. Kolkowicz) National Security and International Stability, 1983, numerous others; contbr. articles to profl. jours. Woodrow Wilson fellow, 1959-60; MIT fellow, 1960-61; recipient Disting. Teaching award UCLA, 1966; Ford fellow, 1967-68; Warren C. Scoville disting. teaching award UCLA, 1976, 79, 82, 84. Fellow Econometric Soc.; mem. Internat. Inst. Strategic Studies, Council Fgn. Relations, others. Office: UCLA Dept Econs Los Angeles CA 90024

INVERSO, MARLENE JOY, optometrist; b. Los Angeles, May 10, 1942; d. Elmer Encel Wood and Sally Marie (Sample) Hirons; m. John S. Inverso, Dec. 16, 1962; 1 child, Christopher Edward. BA, Calif. State U., Northridge, 1964; MS, SUNY, Potsdam, 1975; OD, Pacific U., 1981. Cert. doctor optometry, Wash., Oreg. English tchr. Chatsworth (Calif.) High Sch., 1964-68, Nelson A. Boylen Second Sch., Toronto, Ont., Can., 1968-70, Gouverneur (N.Y.) Jr.-Sr. High Sch., 1970-74, 76-77; reading resource room tchr. Parishville (N.Y.) Hopkinton Sch., 1974-75; coordinator learning disability clinic SUNY, Potsdam, 1975-77; optometrist and vision therapist Am. Family Vision Clinics, Olympia, Wash., 1982—; mem. adv. com. Sunshine House St. Peter Hosp., Olympia, 1984-86, Pacific U. Coll. Optometry, Forest Grove, Oreg. 1986—. Contbr. articles to profl. jours. Mem. Altrusa Service Club, Olympia, 1982-86; tchr. Ch. Living Water, Olympia, 1983—. Mem. Am. Optometric Assn. (sec. 1983-84), Better Vision Inst., Assn. Children and Adults with Learning Disabilities, Optometric Extension Program, Sigma Xi, Beta Sigma Kappa. Avocations: professional speaking, training, and teaching. Home: 4204 Timberline Dr SE Lacey WA 98503 Office: Am Family Vision Clinics 406A Lilly Rd NE Olympia WA 98506 and: 1700 C-1 Cooper Point Rd Olympia WA 98502

INZANA, THOMAS JOSEPH, research and clinical microbiologist; b. Rochester, N.Y., Sept. 5, 1953; s. Anthony Edward and Josephine (Ninfo) I.; m. Ann Marie Naab, Aug. 8, 1981; 1 child, Christopher Thomas. AAS, Alfred State Coll., 1973; BS, U. Ga., 1975, MS, 1978; PhD, U. Rochester, 1982. Postdoctoral fellow Baylor Coll. Medicine, Houston, 1982-84; asst. prof. Wash. State U., Pullman, 1984—; asst. sect. head Wash. Animal Disease Diagnostic Lab., Pullman, 1984—; bacteriology/mycology cons. Regional Hosp. Labs., Pullman, 1985—; reviewer grants USDA, Washington, 1985. Contbr. articles to profl. jours.; inventor in field. Recipient NIH Research Service awards U. Rochester, 1980-82, Baylor Coll. Medicine, 1982-84; grantee USDA, others. Mem. Am. Soc. Microbiology (registered microbiologist), N.Y. Acad. Scis., AAAS, Conf. Research Workers in Animal Disease, Phi Kappa Phi. Democrat. Roman Catholic. Avocations: running, karate, skiing, music. Office: Wash State U Dept Vet Microbiology-Pathology Pullman WA 99164

INZANO, KAREN LEE, advertising agency executive; b. Cleve., July 27, 1946; d. William and Edith (Fisher) Phipps; children: Thomas, Laura, Sharon. Pres., founder AK Graphics Inc., Lakewood, Colo., 1973—; instr. advt. and small bus. Red Rocks Community Coll., Golden, Colo. Chmn. Ch. Adminstrv. Bd.; bd. dirs. Lakewood Sister Cities Internat., 1980—, Lakewood Civic Found., 1986—. Served with USN, 1975. Named State Champion of Free Enterprise for SWAP, 1985. Mem. Lakewood/South Jefferson County C. of C. (bd. dirs. 1979—, Small Bus. Person of Yr., 1982), Denver Advt. Fedn., Typographers Internat. Assn., Industries for Jefferson County, Woman Bus. Owners, Delta Epsilon Chi. Home: 778 S Alkire St Lakewood CO 80228 Office: 13185 W Green Mountain Dr Lakewood CO 80228

IONA, MARIO, retired physics educator; b. Berlin, June 17, 1917; came to U.S., 1941, naturalized, 1948; s. Mario G.V. and Dorothee (Berendes) I.; m. Nancy Mossman, Aug. 31, 1949; children: Steven, Ann. PhD, U. Vienna, Austria, 1939. Research asst., instr. U. Chgo., 1941-46; from asst. prof. to prof. physics U. Denver, 1946-85, prof. emeritus, 1985—; coordinator High Altitude Labs., Mt. Evans and Echo Lake, Colo., 1946-82; cons. Denver Schs., 1962-65, 84, Jefferson County Schs., Lakewood, Colo., 1973, Adams County Sch. Dist. 12, Northglenn, Colo., 1985; vis. prof. U. No. Colo., 1971; specialist U. Saugar, India, 1966. Assoc. editor: Physics Tchr., 1962-65, column editor, 1970—. Treas., sec., pres. Group Health Assn., Denver, 1952-66. Fellow AAAS; mem. Am. Phys. Soc., Am. Assn. Physics Tchrs. (chmn.com. on SI Units and Metric Edn., Disting. Service citation 1971, Millikan Lecture award 1986), Colo.-Wyo. Acad. Sci. (pres. 1974-75), Nat. Sci. Tchrs. Assn., AAUP. Home: 2333 S Columbine St Denver CO 80210 Office: U Denver Dept Physics Denver CO 80208-0202

IOVENITTI, JOE LINO, geologist; b. N.Y.C., Nov. 17, 1951; s. Fidio and Lydia (Taddei) I.; m. Linda L. Santorelli, June 2, 1973; children—Lisa A., Joseph, Thomas John. B.S., CCNY, 1974; M.S., N.Mex. Inst. Mining and Tech., 1977. Geologist, Chevron Resources Co., San Francisco, 1972-82; sr. geologist Diamond Shamrock Thermal Power Co., San Francisco and Santa Rosa, 1982—. Research asst. N.Mex. Bur. Mines and Mineral Resources, 1974. Mem. Calif. Acad. Scis., Geothermal Resources Council, Geol. Soc. Am., Am. Geophys. Union. Home: 2337 Panoramic Dr Concord CA 94520 Office: Diamond Shamrock Thermal Pwr Co 3333 Mendocino Ave Suite 120 Santa Rosa CA 95401

IQBAL, MOHAMMAD ZAFAR, university administrator, accounting educator; b. Jullunder, India, July 3, 1945; came to U.S., 1964; s. Mohammad Sharif and Ghulam Fatima Sharif; m. Patrice Ann Schoenen, Jan. 21, 1972. BS, U. Nev., 1969; MBA, No. Ill. U., 1972; PhD, U. Nebr., 1979. CPA; cert. cost analyst, cert. mgmt. acct., cert. internal auditor. Asst. prof. acctg. Coll. St. Thomas, St. Paul, 1976-77; instr. U. Nebr., Lincoln, 1978-79; prof. acctg. Calif. Poly. State U., San Luis Obispo, 1979, prof., 1979-83, head dept. acctg., 1981-82, assoc. dean Sch. Bus., 1983—; chmn. dept. acctg. and bus. adminstrn. Briar Cliff Coll., Sioux City, Iowa, 1974-76; cons. U.S. Small Bus. Adminstrn., Naval Ship Weapon Systems Engring. Sta. Reviewer: Successful Small Business Management, 1980. Mem. adv. bd. U. Nebr. Sch. Accountancy, Lincoln, 1985—; mem. student adv. com. Ill. Bd. Higher Edn., DeKalb, 1972, Dean's adv. coms., 1972; chmn. student adv. and search coms. for selection of univ. pres., No. Ill. U., 1972. Mem. Am. Inst. CPA's, Am. Acctg. Assn., Calif. Soc. CPA's, Beta Alpha Psi, Sigma Iota Epsilon, Phi Beta Lambda. Avocations: traveling, gardening, music, stamp and coin collecting. Home: 2164 El Dorado St Los Osos CA 93402

IRANI, RAY R., chemical company executive; b. Beirut, Lebanon, Jan. 15, 1935; came to U.S., 1953, naturalized, 1956; s. Rida and Naz I.; m. Joan D. French; children: Glenn R., Lillian M., Martin R. B.S. in Chemistry, Am. U. Beirut, 1953; Ph.D. in Phys. Chemistry, U. So. Calif., 1957. Sr. research group leader Monsanto Co., 1957-67; assoc. dir. new products, then dir. research Diamond Shamrock Corp., 1967-73; with Olin Corp., 1973-83, pres. chems. group, 1978-80; corp. pres., dir. Olin Corp., Stamford, Conn., 1980-83; exec. v.p. Occidental Petroleum Corp., Los Angeles, 1983-84, pres., chief operating officer, 1984—, also dir.; chmn., chief exec. officer subs. Occidental Chem. Corp., Norwalk, Conn., 1983—; bd. dirs. Am. Petroleum Inst. Author: Particle Size; also author papers in field; numerous patents in field. Trustee St. John's Hosp. and Health Ctr. Found., Natural History Mus. Los Angeles County. Mem. Soap and Detergent Assn., Chem. Mfrs. Assn. (bd. dirs.), Am. Inst. Chemists (hon. fellow award 1983), Am. Chem. Soc., Scientific Research Soc. Am., Indsl. Research Inst., Los Angeles C. of C. (bd. dirs.). Home: 250 Lost District Dr New Canaan CT 06840 Office: Occidental Petroleum Corp 10889 Wilshire Blvd Los Angeles CA 90024

IRANI, RAYMOND REZA, electro-mechanical company executive; b. Hamadan, Iran, Apr. 27, 1928; came to U.S., 1956, naturalized, 1959; s. Mohammad Taghi and Saheb Sultan (Ghassemi) I.; m. Nayer Ghadessi, Oct. 19, 1962; children—Sheila, Glen. B.S. in Aviation, Air Acad., Tehran, 1952; grad. in aerotech., Northrop U., 1958; B.S.E.E., Calif. State U., 1965. Lic. in aviation techn., Iran. Engr. Am. Electronics, Los Angeles, 1959-61; chief engr. IMC Magnetics, Maywood, Calif., 1961-69; co-founder, v.p. Computer devices, Santa Fe Springs, Calif., 1969-77; pres. Rapidsyn Co., Santa Fe Springs, 1977-79; pres. Astrosyn div. NMB, Chatsworth, Calif., 1979-82, Shinano Kenshi Corp., North Hollywood, Calif., 1982. Editor tech. papers, 1975; patentee. Served to capt. Iranian Air Force, 1948-56. Iranian Air Force grantee, 1956. Democrat. Moslem.

IRBY, WILLIAM OWEN, federal career administrator; b. San Antonio, Sept. 14, 1943; s. Grover and Ruby J. (Segroves) Chatman; m. Kay C. Irby, Mar. 29, 1970 (div. Jan. 1984); children: Kelly Anne, Shelly Kay. AS, Barstow Jr. Coll., 1975. Commd. USMC, Barstow, Calif., 1967, pkg. inspector, planner, 1967-71, packaging specialist, 1971-75, supr. inventory mgmt. specialist, 1975-80, quality assurance specialist, 1980-81, pres. gen. foreman, 1981-85, mgr. over packaging and maintenance sect., 1985—. Pres. Barstow Jacess, 1975; dist. gov. Calif. Jaycees, 1976. Mem. Am. Soc. Quality Control, Am. Def. Preparedness Assn. USMC Packaging Com., Fed. Mgrs. Assn. (v.p. 1984, pres. 1985—). Democrat. Lodge: Elks. Avocations: hunting, bowling, water skiing, softball, golfing. Home: 28008 Church St Barstow CA 92311 Office: Packaging and Maintenance Sect B885 Material Div Marine Corps Logistics Base Barstow CA 92311

IRELAND, ARTHUR KEITH, archeologist; b. Greenfield, Mass., Dec. 31, 1946; s. Charles Ellsworth and Dorothy (Rau) I.; m. M. Kristin Johnson, Aug. 24, 1974; children: Keith, Kaisa. BA in German, U. N.H., 1970-72; BA in Anthropology, U. Wis., Milw., 1975-77. Archeologist U. Wis., Milw., 1977, U. N.Mex., Albuquerque, 1978—; archeologist Nat. Park Service, Albuquerque, 1978-79, Albuquerque and Santa Fe, 1983—; archeologist Bur. Indian Affairs, Albuquerque, 1979-83. Co-author, editor: A Cultural Resource Management Plan for Timber Sale and Forest Development Areas on the Pueblo of Isleta, 1981, A Cultural Resource Management Plan for Timber Sale and Forest Development Areas on the Pueblo of Acoma, Volume II, 1982; A Cultural Resource Managment Plan for Timber Sale and Forest Development Areas on the Jicarilla Apache Indian Reservation, Volumes I and II, 1984, The Seedskadee Project: Remote Sensing in Non-Site Archeology, 1986. Served with U.S. Army, 1966-70. Mem. Soc. Am. Archaeology, Sigma Xi. Home: 7808 Krista Drive NE Albuquerque NM 87109 Office: USDI NPS Br Cultural Research Remote Sensing Sect PO Box 728 Santa Fe NM 87501-0728

IRELAND, DONALD RAY, materials engineer; b. St. Paul, Mar. 31, 1937; s. Raymond Norton and Mabel Claire (Loveland) I.; m. Kathleen Ann Altman; children—Scott Donald, Amy Marie. B.S., U. Minn., 1960, M.S.E., U. Mich., 1963. Metallurgist, Great Lakes Steel Corp., Detroit, 1960-62; research asst. U. Mich., Ann Arbor, 1962-63; research engr. Gen. Electric Co., Richland, Wash., 1964-66, Battelle N.W. Lab., 1966-67; sr. research engr. S.W. Research Inst., San Antonio, 1967-68; assoc. div. chief Battelle Columbus Lab., Ohio, 1968-71; mgr. Effects Tech. Inc., Dynatup, Santa Barbara, Calif., 1971-82; cons. Ireland & Assocs., Santa Barbara, 1982—. Contbr. articles to profl. jours. Named Research Man of Yr., Goleta Research and Devel. Assn., 1976. Mem. Am. Soc. Metals, ASTM, Soc. Plastics Engrs. Home: 35 W Padre St Santa Barbara CA 93101 Office: 213 W Canon Perdido St Santa Barbara CA 93101

IRETON, MERION FRANK, earth science and geology educator; b. San Mateo, Calif., Oct. 18, 1943; s. M. Frank Ireton and Arliss Laurene (Butler) Boutwell; m. Sharon Irene Larsen, July 22, 1966; 1 child, Shari Lee. BS in Earth Sci. Edn., Boise State Coll., 1973; MS in Earth Sci. Edn., Boise State U., 1977. Tchr. earth sci. Sch. Dist. 193, Mountain Home AFB, Idaho, 1973—; lectr. geology Boise (Idaho) State U., 1973—. Contbr. articles to profl. jours. Vol. Bur. Land Mgmt., 1979; recreational specialist Bur. Land Mgmt., 1980-81. Served to lt./cpl. USMCR, 1963-69. Grad. assistantship Am. Fed. Mineral Socs., Boise State U., 1972; named co-dir. of field studies NSF, 1985. Fellow Nat. Speleological Soc., mem. Idaho Sci. Tchrs. Assn. (pres. elect. 1984-85, pres. 1985-86), Idaho Acad. Sci., Gem State Grotto (life mem., chmn. 1974-78), Nat. Earth Sci. Tchrs. Assn., Nat. Sci. Tchrs. Assn., Nat. Assn. Geology Tchrs., Jaycees (bd. dirs. Mountain Home cht. 1968), Mountain Home Ednl. Assn. (del. 1975—). Lodges: Elks, Shriners, Masons, Royal Arch. Avocations: speleology, salt water boating, camping, fishing, fossil collecting. Home: PO Box 356 Mountain Home ID 83647 Office: Base Junior High 300 Main Ave Mountain Home AFB ID 83648

IRI, RICHARD TAKAO, art dealer; b. Chgo., Jan. 2, 1949; s. Carl Yoneo and Arleene Ayako (Kinoshita) I.; m. Sue Mary Paulson, Aug. 14, 1971 (div. Jan 1979); m. Monica Frances Dew, May 1, 1983. BA, U. San Diego, 1970; M in Internat. Mgmt. with honors, Am. Grad. Sch. of Internat. Mgmt., 1972. Asst. mgr. First Nat. Bank Chgo., 1972-76; pres. Farrell, Iri Inc., Dept. of Agr. The Farmers Guild, Los Angeles, 1976—, Portfolio II, Los Angeles, 1983—. Protocol mgr. Basketball Venue 1984 Olympics, Inglewood, Calif., 1983-84. Irving K. Salomon scholar U. San Diego, 1969-70. Democrat. Roman Catholic. Home: 1841 Montair Long Beach CA 90815

IRVINE, DAVID ROBERT, lawyer; b. Salt Lake City, Aug. 30, 1943; s. Robert George and Lucy (Brown) I.; m. Linda Jean Hatch, June 9, 1969; children: Scott, Cullen, Lindsay, Kristen. BS in Polit. Sci., U. Utah, 1968, JD, 1971. Bar: Utah 1981. Asst. atty. gen. State of Utah, Salt Lake City, 1971-72; ptnr. Irvine, Smith & Mabey, Salt Lake City, 1971-81; commr. Utah Pub. Service Commn., Salt Lake City, 1979-85; prin., pres. David R. Irvine, P.C., Salt Lake City, 1985—; dir. Research Assocs., Salt Lake City, 1985—. Chmn. Davis County Republican Party, Bountiful, Utah, 1969-71; mem. Utah Ho. Reps., Salt Lake City, 1973-79. Mem. Utah State Bar Assn., B.H. Roberts Soc. (bd. dirs. 1984-86). Mormon. Club: New State Duck (Woods Cross, Utah). Avocations: duck hunting, aviation, skiing, tennis. Office: 349 S 200 E Salt Lake City UT 84111

IRVINE, FRANCES GERALDENE, educator; b. Paris, Tex., Mar. 27, 1940; d. Barham W. and Lucy Elizabeth (Matthews) Simmons; m. James Richard Irvine, Nov. 8, 1959. BS, Stephen F. Austin U., 1962. Cert. elem. and secondary tchr., Colo., Tex. 1st grade tchr. Sabine Pass (Tex.) Sch. Dist., 1962-63; 2d grade tchr. Baytown (Tex.) Ind. Sch. Dist., 1963-64; 1st, 2d, 3d grade tchr. Poudre R-1 Sch. Dist., Ft. Collins, Colo., 1965-69; 4th grade tchr. Poudre R-1 Sch. Dist., Ft. Collins, 1970—; 2d grade tchr. Iowa City (Iowa) Sch. Dist., 1969-70. Grantee NDEA, 1967. Mem. Internat. Reading Assn., Alpha Delta Kappa (corresponding sec. 1984-86), Alpha Chi. Democrat. Episcopalian. Home: 1555 Miramont Dr Fort Collins CO 80524 Office: Poudre R-1 Sch Dist 2407 LaPorte Ave Fort Collins CO 80521

IRVINE, ROBERT GERALD, elec. engr., educator; b. Salt Lake City, July 27, 1931; s. Francis Gerald and Bernice (Henckel) I.; m. Joan Laura Granberg, Aug. 26, 1955; children—Gerald Andrew, John Robert. B.S.E.E., Utah State U., 1956; M.S.E.E., Calif. State U.-Los Angeles, 1975. Elec. engr. Gen. Dynamics, Ponoma, Calif., 1956-61; asst. prof. engring. Calif. State Poly. U., Ponoma, 1959-66, assoc. prof., 1976-82, prof., 1983—; sr. engr. Ling Electronics, Anaheim, Calif., 1966-70; owner, operator Stretch & Sew Fabrics, Claremont, Calif., 1971-72; sr. research and devel. engr. Safetran Systems Corp., 1972-76; mem. faculty Citrus Jr. Coll., U. LaVerne, San Bernardino Valley Coll.; cons. in field. Mem. ch. council Good Shepherd Lutheran Ch., Claremont, Calif., 1979-81; mem. exec. bd. Old Baldy council Boy Scouts Am., 1980—; mem. Los Angeles Olympic Organizing Com. Served with U.S. Army, 1949-50. Registered profl. engr., Calif. Mem. IEEE (sr.; chmn. sect. 1966-67, award of Merit 1967), Am. Soc. Engring. Edn., Precision Measurements Assn., Measurement Sci. Conf., Nat. Soc. Profl. Engrs., Tau Alpha Pi, Eta Kappa Nu. Republican. Clubs: Optimists; Masons (Salt Lake City). Author: Operational Amplifier Characteristics and Applications, 1981. Office: Calif State Poly U Dept Elec and Computer Engring 3801 W Temple Ave Pomona CA 91768

IRVINE, VERNON BRUCE, accounting educator, administrator; b. Regina, Sask., Can., May 31, 1943; s. Joseph Vern and Anna Francis (Phillip) I.; m. Marilyn Ann Craik, Apr. 29, 1967; children—Lee-Ann, Cameron, Sandra. B. Commerce, U. Sask., 1965; M.B.A., U. Chgo., 1967; Ph.D., U. Minn., 1977. Cert. mgmt. acct. Researcher, Sask. Royal Commn. on Taxation, Regina, 1964; lectr. acctg. Coll. Commerce, U. Sask., Saskatoon, 1967-69, asst. prof., 1969-74, assoc. prof., 1974-79, prof., 1979—, head dept. acctg., 1981-84; profl. program lectr. Inst. Chartered Accts., Regina, 1982-84, Soc. Mgmt. Accts., Saskatoon, 1982-84. Co-author: A Practical Approach to the Appraisal of Capital Expenditures, 1981; Intermediate Accounting: Canadian Edition, 1982, 2d edit., 1986; contbr. articles to acctg. jours. Grantee John Wiley & Sons, Ltd., 1981, 85, Soc. Mgmt. Accts. Can., 1979, Pres.'s Fund, U. Saskatchewan, 1978. Fellow Soc. Mgmt. Accts. Can. (bd. dirs. 1979-82, 85-87, chmn. Nat. Edn. Services com.); mem. Internat. Acctg. Standards Com. (Can. rep. 1984-87), Soc. of Mgmt. Accts. of Sask. (pres. 1980-81). Clubs: Sutherland Curling (treas. 1979-83), Saskatoon Golf and Country. Home: 45 Cantlon Crescent, Saskatoon, SK Canada S7J 2T2 Office: Coll Commerce U Sask, Saskatoon, SK Canada S7N 0W0

IRVING, J. LAWRENCE, federal judge; b. 1935. B.S., U. So. Calif., 1959, LL.B., 1963. Assoc. Higgs, Fletcher & Mack, San Diego, 1963-66, ptnr., 1966-69; ptnr. Jones & Irving, 1969-77, J. Lawrence Irving Inc., 1975-78, Irving & Butz Inc., 1978-82; judge U.S. Dist. Ct. (so. dist.) Calif., San Diego, 1982—. Office: US Courthouse 940 Front St San Diego CA 92189

IRVING, JACK HOWARD, planning executive; b. Cleve., Dec. 31, 1920; s. William M. and Lottie (Green) I.; m. Florence Friedman, Feb. 1, 1948; children: Paul Howard, Karen Joy, Michael William. B.S., Calif. Inst. Tech., 1942; M.A., Princeton, 1948, Ph.D. in Physics, 1965. Staff radiation lab. Mass. Inst. Tech., 1942-45; asst. physics Princeton, 1946-48; fellow chemistry Calif. Inst. Tech., 1948-49; head systems planning and analysis dept. research and devel. labs. Hughes Aircraft Co., 1949-54; head spl. devices dept. Ramo-Wooldridge Corp., 1954-55, head intelligence systems dept., 1955-56, spl. asst. to exec. v.p., 1956-57, spl. asst. to pres. space tech. labs., 1957-58; corp. staff sci. Thompson Ramo-Wooldridge, Inc., 1958-60; asst. dir. Advanced Systems Planning div. Space Tech. Labs., Inc., 1960; v.p., gen. mgr. systems research and planning div. Aerospace Corp., El Segundo, Calif., 1960-63; v.p. corp. planning Aerospace Corp., 1965-72, v.p., gen. mgr. environment and urban div., 1972-75; tech. cons. and product devel. Jack H. Irving Assocs., Los Angeles, 1976—; vice chmn. Cabintaxi Corp., 1983—; aerospace vis. fellow Princeton, 1963-65; mem. com. on interplay of engring. with biology and medicine Nat. Acad. Engring., 1967-73; chmn., dir. Med. Systems Tech. Services, Inc., 1968-80; dir. Commuter Transp. Services Inc., 1974—, mem. exec. com., 1974-79, treas., 1975-78, mem. audit com., 1979—, chmn., 1979-84. Prin. author: Fundamentals of Personal Rapid Transit, 1978; Contbr. articles to tech. publs. Asso. fellow Am. Inst. Aeros. and Astronautics; mem. Advanced Transit Assn., Am. Phys. Soc., Sigma Xi. Dir. study fire control systems, Minuteman ballistic missile, communication satellites, personal rapid transit. Home: 13202 Jonesboro Pl Los Angeles CA 90049

IRWIN, CHARLES EDWIN, JR., pediatrics educator; b. Medford, Mass., Dec. 15, 1945; s. Charles Edwin and Molly Esther (Rosenberg) I.; m. Nancie Noel Kester, Apr. 21, 1979. BS, Hobart Coll., 1967; BMS, Dartmouth Med. Sch., 1969; MD, U. Calif., 1971. Asst. prof. pediatrics U. Calif. Med. Ctr., San Francisco, 1977-84, dir. div. of adolescent med., 1977—, assoc. prof. pediatrics, 1984—. Mem. editorial bd: jour. Adolescent Health Care, 1982, Internat. jour. Adolescent Medicine, 1984, Pediatrican jour., 1984. R. W. Johnson Found. clin. scholar, 1974; W. T. Grant Found. grantee, 1985. Mem. Soc. Pediatric Research, Soc. Adolescent Med. (exec. council mem. 1985—, research award 1985), Am. Pub. Health Assn., AAAS; fellow Am. Acad. Pediatrics (exec. committeeman, 1982-85). Office: U Calif Med Ctr 400 Parnassus Ave San Francisco CA 94143

IRWIN, DIANNE E., psychology educator; b. Madison, Wis., July 22, 1946; d. Donald J. and Dorothy R. (Shaw) I. B.A., Calif. State Coll., 1972; M.A., Calif. State U., 1974; Ph.D., U.S. Internat. U., 1979. Lectr., instr. Calif. State Coll.-San Bernardino, 1974, psychometrist, 1974-78, dir. learning ctr., 1974-85; assoc. prof. psychology Glendale Coll., Calif., 1985—; lectr. Valley Coll., San Bernardino, Calif. State U., Fullerton, 1974; cons. nat. tests, psychol. corp., Harcourt Brace Jovanovich, Inc., 1985-86; mem. Calif. Statewide Legal Compliance com. instructionally related material review, 1979-84. Editor, author (with Sherman) Writing Tutor's Training Manual, 1985. Mem. Am. Psychol. Assn., Student Personnel Assn., Western Coll. Reading Assn., Western Psychol. Assn., Am. Personnel and Guidance Assn. Co-author: (with L. Sherman) Writers Tutor Training, 1986; contbr. numerous articles to profl. jours. Home: 918 W Edgemont Dr San Bernardino CA 92405 Office: Glendale Coll 1500 N Verdugo Rd Glendale CA 91208

IRWIN, R. ROBERT, lawyer; b. Denver, July 27, 1933; s. Royal Robert and Mildred Mary (Wilson) I.; m. Sue Ann Scott, Dec. 16, 1956; children—Lori, Stacy, Kristi, Amy. Student U. Colo., 1951-54, B.S.L., U. Denver, 1955, LL.B., 1957. Bar: Colo. 1957, Wyo. 1967. Asst. atty. gen. State of Colo., 1958-66; asst. div. atty. Mobil Oil Corp., Casper, Wyo. 1966-70; prin. atty. No. Natural Gas Co., Omaha 1970-72; sr. atty. Coastal Oil & Gas Corp., Denver 1972-83, asst. sec. 1972-83; ptnr. Baker & Hostetler, 1983—. Mem. ABA, Colo. Bar Assn., State Bar Wyo., Arapahoe County Bar Assn., Rocky Mountain Oil and Gas Assn. Republican. Clubs: Los Verdes Golf, Petroleum, Denver Law (Denver). Home: 9960 E Chenango Ave Englewood CO 80111 Office: Baker & Hostetler 303 E 17th Ave Suite 1100 Denver CO 80203

ISAAC, ROBERT MICHAEL, lawyer, mayor Colorado Springs; b. Colorado Springs, Colo., Jan. 27, 1928; s. Isaac Albert and Sigrid Elvira (Oksa) I.; student U. Colo., 1945-46; B.S., U.S. Mil. Acad., 1951; J.D., U. So. Calif., 1962; m. Betsy Lou McDonald, Sept. 8, 1972; children—Leslie Ann Isaac Williams, Julia Hermine, Melissa Sue, Tiffany Ann, Chance Robert. Sales engr. Trane Co., Los Angeles, 1957-62; practice law and dep. city atty. City Colorado Springs, 1962-64; asst. dist. atty. 4th Jud. Dist. Colo., 1965-66; judge Colorado Springs Mcpl. Ct., 1966-69; partner firm Trott, Kunstle, Isaac & Hughes, 1969-72, Isaac, Walsh & Johnson, 1972-74, Isaac, Johnson & Alpern, 1974—; councilman City of Colorado Springs, 1975-79, mayor, 1979—. Gen. chmn. YWCA/YMCA/USO fund dr., past pres. Pikes Peak Y/USO; past pres. El Paso County Soc. Crippled Children and Adults; past mem. Nat. USO Council; chmn. Pikes Peak Area Council Govts., 1976-78. Served as officer inf. U.S. Army, 1951-57. Mem. Am. Bar Assn., Colo. Bar Assn. Calif. Bar Assn., El Paso County Bar Assn. Episcopalian. Office: PO Box 1575 Colorado Springs CO 80901 *

ISAACS, ROBERT WOLFE, structural engr.; b. Clayton, N.Mex., Sept. 22, 1931; s. Robert Phillip and Eva Estella (Freeman) I.; student So. Meth. U., 1949-50, Amarillo Jr. Coll., Tex. Tech U.; B.S. in Civil Engring., UCLA, 1959; m. Ruth Marie Peffley, Jan. 12, 1951; children—Robert Philip, Jeannette Lucille Isaacs Darlington, Charlotte Ruth Isaacs Frye, Rebecca Grace. Structural engr. N.Am. Aviation, Rockwell Internat., Los Angeles, 1959—. Asst. scoutmaster, com. mem., fund raiser, Order of Arrow Gt. Western council Boy Scouts Am., 1964—; patron Los Angeles County Mus. Art; active Rep. Party. Served with U.S. Army, 1955. Lic. profl. engr., Tex. Recipient Pride award N.Am Aviation Orgn., 1984; named Pacemaker of Scouting, 1966. Mem. ASCE, Nat. Rifle Assn (life), Calif. Rifle and Pistol Assn. (life), Nat. Muzzleloading Rifle Assn. (endowment life, So. Calif. rep. 1976—), Western States Muzzleloading Rifle Assn. (life, charter, sportsman award 1983), Calif. Muzzleloading Rifle Assn., Colo. State Muzzleloading Rifle Assn., Bakersfield (Calif.) Muzzleloaders, Nat. Assn. Primitive Riflemen, High Desert Muzzleloaders. Clubs: Piute Mountain Men, Sante Fe Trail Gun, Rockwell Rod and Gun, Masons. Condr. research design and devel. press diffusion bonding of titanium, aircraft design and structure; underwing and overwing inflatable seals (structure liaison, final mate, asst. checkout B-18). Home: 1028 H-1 Lancaster CA 93534 Office: AF Plant 42 Site 9 Palmdale CA

ISAACSON, GERALD CURTIS, manufacturing company executive; b. Haxtun, Colo., Nov. 21, 1942; s. Curtys Burdett and Dorothy Mae (Hedstrom) I.; m. Nancy Lou Jaycox, May 5, 1963; one child, Scott Alan. BS, Colo. State U., 1974, PhD, 1977. Engr. Ion Tech Inc., Ft. Collins, Colo., 1975-78, v.p., 1978—; v.p. MOE Systems Inc., Ft. Collins, Colo., 1978—; ptnr. Tulakes Assocs., Ft. Collins, Colo., 1982—. Contbr. articles on ion beam sources and applications to profl. jours. Served with U.S. Army, 1966-69. Mem. Am. Vacuum Soc., Pi Tau Sigma. Avocations: fly fishing, fly tying, model ship building. Home: 1806 Linden Lake Rd Fort Collins CO 80524

ISABELL, MARY JOAN COLLINS, chemist; b. Birmingham, Ala., Sept. 14, 1939; d. Levi Louis and Nellie (Coar) Collins; m. Earl Miller Jones, Sept 14, 1958 (div. Nov. 1960); 1 child, Earl Miller Jones Jr. BA, Miles Coll., 1967; postgrad., Memphis State U., 1967; MS, Mont. State U., 1969; postgrad., U. Wash., Seattle, 1970-71, Ill. Inst. Tech., 1985. Research technologist U. Wash., Seattle, 1969-71; chemist U.S. FDA, Seattle, 1971—. Dir. Christian edn. Curry Temple Christian Meth. Episcopal Ch., Seattle, 1973-75, 82—, pres. lay council, 1984—; sec. Christian edn. Alaska-Pacific Conf., Portland, Oreg., 1984—; dist. chairperson Am. Cancer Soc., Seattle, 1985—. Fellow NSF, 1967. Mem. Am. Chem. Soc., Assn. Official Analytical Chemists. Avocations: reading, walking, bicycling, aerobic exercises. Home: 5526 Seward Park Ave S Seattle WA 98118 Office: US FDA 5009 Fed Office Bldg 909 First Ave Seattle WA 98174

ISAUTIER, BERNARD FRANÇOIS, investment company executive; b. St.-Symphorien, Indre et Loire, France, Sept. 19, 1942; s. Francois and Genevieve (Roy) I.; m. Charlotte Isautier, July 22, 1968; children—Anne-Caroline, Armelle, Francois. Grad., Ecole Polytechnique, Paris, 1963, Ecole des Mines, Paris, 1966, Institute d'Etudes Politiques, Paris, 1968. Head dept. mining exploration French Ministry of Industry, Paris, 1970-73, adviser to minister of industry for energy and raw materials, 1973-75; gen. mgr. SEREPT (subs. Elf-Aquitaine Group), Tunis, Tunisia, 1976-78; pres. Aquitaine Co. of Can. Ltd., Calgary, Alta., 1978-81; pres., chief exec. officer Canterra Energy Ltd., Calgary, Alta., 1981-86, Can. Devel. Corp., Toronto, Ont., 1986—; bd. dirs. Falconbridge Ltd., The Sulphur Inst., CDC Life Scis. Inc., Herald Fin. Inc., Polysar Ltd., Credit Lyonnais Can. Served to lt. Res. Army of France, 1961-64. Decorated chevalier de l'Ordre du Merite France). Club: Granite (Toronto). Office: Can Devel Corp, 444 Yonge St Suite 200, Toronto, ON Canada M5B 2H4

ISBELL, HAROLD MAX, banker; b. Maquoketa, Iowa, Sept. 20, 1936; s. H. Max and Marcella E. I.; B.A. cum laude (scholar), Loras Coll., 1959; M.A. (fellow), U. Notre Dame, 1962; grad. U. Mich. Grad. Sch. Bank Mgmt., 1982; m. Mary Carolyn Cosgriff, June 15, 1963; children—Walter Harold, Susan Elizabeth, David Harold, Alice Kathleen. Instr., U. Notre Dame, South Bend, Ind., 1963-64; assoc. prof. St. Mary's Coll., 1969-72; asst. prof. San Francisco Coll. for Women, 1964-69; with Continental Bank & Trust Co., Salt Lake City, 1972-83, v.p., 1977-83, comml. credit officer, 1978-83, also dir. Trustee Judge Meml. Cath. High Sch., Salt Lake City, 1977-84; mem. Utah Council for Handicapped and Developmentally Disabled Persons, 1980-81; bd. dirs. Ballet West, 1983—; founder Cath. Found. Utah, pres. 1984-86, trustee, 1984—; active ACLU, Common Cause. Mem. MLA, Mediaeval Acad. Am., Robert Morris Assos. Democrat. Roman Catholic. Club: Alta. Editor and translator: The Last Poets of Imperial Rome, 1971; contbr. to publs. in field of classical Latin lit. and contemporary Am. Lit.

ISELY, HENRY PHILIP, association executive, integrative engineer; b. Montezuma, Kans., Oct. 16, 1915; s. James Walter and Jessie M. (Owen) I;

m. Margaret Ann Sheesley, June 12, 1948; children—Zephyr, LaRock, Lark, Robin, Kemper, Heather Capri. Student So. Oreg. Jr. Coll., Ashland, 1934-35, Antioch Coll., 1935-37. Organizer, Action for World Fedn., 1946-50, N.Am. Council for People World Conv., 1954-58; organizer World Com. for World Constl. Conv., 1958, sec. gen., 1959-66; sec. gen. World Constn. and Parliament Assn., Lakewood, Colo., 1966—, organizer worldwide prep. confs., 1963, 66, 67, 1st session Peoples World Parliament and World Constl. Conv. in Switzerland, 1968, editor assn. bull. Across Frontiers, 1959—; co-organizer Emergency Council World Trustees, 1971, World Constituent Assembly at Innsbruck, Austria, 1977, Colombo, Sri Lanka, 1978-79, Provisional World Parliament 1st session, Brighton, Eng., 1982, 2d Session New Delhi, India, 1985, 3d Session Miami Beach, Fla., 1987; sec. Working Commn. to Draft World Constn., 1971-77; pres. World Service Trust, 1972-78; ptnr. Builders Found., Vitamin Cottages, 1955—; pres. Earth Rescue Corps, 1984—; sec.-treas. Grad. Sch. World Problems, 1984—. Author: The People Must Write the Peace, 1950; A Call to All Peoples and All National Governments of the Earth, 1961; Outline for the Debate and Drafting of a World Constitution, 1965; Strategy for Reclaiming Earth for Humanity, 1969; Call to a World Constituent Assembly, 1974; Proposal for Immediate Action by an Emergency Council of World Trustees, 1971; Call to Provisional World Parliament, 1981; People Who Want Peace Must Take Charge of World Affairs, 1982; co-author, editor: A Constitution for the Federation of Earth, 1974, rev. edit., 1977; also author several world legis. measures adopted at Provisional World Parliament. Designer prefab modular panel system of constrn., master plan for Guacamaya project in Costa Rica. Candidate, U.S. Congress, 1958. Recipient Honor award Internat. Assn. Educators for World Peace, 1975, Gandhi medal, 1977. Mem. Soc. Internat. Devel., World Union, World Federalist Assn., World Future Soc., Internat. Assn. for Hydrogen Energy, Global Edn. Assocs., Friends of Earth, Wilderness Soc., Sierra Club, SANE, Global Futures Network, Amnesty Internat., ACLU, Am. Acad. Polit. and Social Sci., Nat. Nutritional Foods Assn., Solar Lobby, Am. Humanist Assn., Audubon Soc., Worldwatch Inst., Denver Symphony Soc., Planetary Soc., Nation Assocs. Club: Mt. Vernon Country. Home: 241 Zephyr Ave Lookout Mountain Golden CO 80401 Office: 1480 Hoyt St Suite 31 Lakewood CO 80215

ISENBERG, EDWIN, real estate company executive; b. Max and Mae (Safran) I.; B.S., U. So. Calif., 1952; m. Susan Gay Ehrenberg, June 28, 1959; children: David, Daniel. V.p. Grubb & Ellis Brokerage Co., Beverly Hills, Calif., 1975-81; chmn. bd. Standard Indsl. Properties, Los Angeles, 1981—; prin. Donaty Group Corp. Real Estate, 1981. Pres. Wilshire Blvd. Temple Brotherhood, 1986-87. Mem. Town Hall of Calif., 1979-81. Served with U.S. Army, 1952-55. Mem. Los Angeles C. of C., Internat. Council Shopping Ctrs., Am. Indsl. Real Estate Assn., Real Estate Inst., Blue Key. Republican. Jewish. Clubs: Los Angeles Athletic, Masons. Office: Standard Indsl Properties 1721 S Flower Los Angeles CA 90015

ISENBERG, JON IRWIN, gastroenterogist, educator; b. Chgo., Mar. 21, 1937; s. Lucien and Roselle (Moss) I.; m. Laury Lipman, Dec. 16, 1962; children: Nancy Beth, Noah William, Rebecca Moss. BS with honors, U. Ill., 1959; MD, U. Ill., Chgo., 1963. Diplomate Am. Bd. Internal Medicine, Am. Bd. Gastroenterology. Assoc. prof. in residence UCLA, 1973-78, prof. medicine in residence, 1978-79; key investigator CURE/UCLA, 1979—; div. head U. Calif., San Diego, 1979—; vis. sci. Karolinska Hosp. and Inst., Stockholm, 1982-83; sci. com. mem. 5th Internat. Conf. on Peptic Ulcer, Boston, 1985. Author: Physicians Guide to Computers and Computing, 1985; editor: Peptic Ulcer Disease: Clinics in Gastroenterology, 1984. Served to maj. U.S. Army, 1968-70. NIH grantee, 1984-87. Fellow ACP; mem. Western Assn. Physicians (counselor 1981-85), So. Calif. Soc. Gastroenterology (pres. 1978-79), Am. Gastroenterology Assn., Am. Assn. Physicians, Am. Soc. Clin. Investigation. Democrat. Jewish. Avocation: photography. Home: 6215 Avenida Cresta La Jolla CA 92037 Office: USCD Med Ctr Div Gastroenterology 225 Dickinson St San Diego CA 92103

ISENHOUR, THOMAS LEE, chemistry educator; b. Statesville, N.C., Jan. 29, 1939; s. Harold Lee and Ruth Catherine (Peacock) I.; m. Linda Ann Adkins, June 11, 1960; children: Anastasia, Joseph Bradley. Ph.D., Cornell U., 1965. Asst. prof. chemistry U. Wash., 1965-69; assoc. prof. U. N.C., 1969-74, prof., 1974-84, chmn. dept. chemistry, 1975-80; I.M. Kolthoff sr. fellow Hebrew U., 1980; dean of sci. Utah State U., Logan, 1984; program dir. for chem. analysis NSF, 1982-83. Author numerous books; contbr. articles to profl. jours. Mem. Am. Chem. Soc., Fedn. Analytical Chemistry and Spectroscopy Soc., Phi Beta Kappa, Sigma Xi, Alpha Chi Sigma. Home: 974 N 1500 E Logan UT 84321 Office: Utah State Univ College of Science Logan UT 84322

ISHAM, DELL, independent lobbyist; b. San Rafael, Calif., Apr. 30, 1944; s. Quentin D. and Leah (Sabo) I.; student Boise State Coll., 1962-64; B.S., Weber State Coll., 1967; M.A., Colo. State U., 1969; m. Paulette Oblock, Dec. 17, 1966; children—Shane Gordon, Shaun Lane, Shannon Leah. Tchr., Siuslaw High Sch., Florence, Oreg., 1971-76; ins. agt., Isham & Sprague Ins., Lincoln City, Oreg., 1977-85; mem. Oreg. State Senate, 1977-85, majority leader, 1980-83. Mem. West Lane County Planning Commn., 1977-78; mem. Oreg. State Democratic Central Com., 1974, 76-83; del. Dem. Nat. Conv., 1980; mem. Gov.'s Small Bus. Adv. Com.; v.p. Oreg. Hwy. Users Conf.; mem. Travel Industry Council of Oreg.; mayor of Lincoln City, 1987—. Served with U.S. Army, 1969-71. Decorated Bronze Star. Mem. C. of C., Common Cause. Club: Capitol. Lodges: Lions, Rotary, Elks, Eagles. Author: Rock Springs Massacre, 1885, 1969. Office: PO Box 974 Lincoln City OR 97367

ISHIMARU, AKIRA, electrical engineering educator; b. Fukuoka, Japan, Mar. 16, 1928; came to U.S., 1952; s. Shigezo and Yumi I.; m. Yuko Kaneda, Nov. 21, 1956; children: John, Jane, James, Joyce. BSEE, U. Tokyo, 1951; PhDEE, U. Wash., 1958. Registered profl. engr., Wash. Engr. Electro-Tech. Lab, Tokyo, 1951-52; tech. staff Bell Telephone Lab, Holmdel, N.J., 1956; asst. prof. U. Wash., Seattle, 1958-61, assoc. prof., 1961-65, prof. elec. engring., 1965—; vis. assoc. prof. U. Calif., Berkeley, 1963-64; cons. Jet Propulsion Lab., Pasadena, Calif., 1964—, The Boeing Co., Seattle, 1984—. Author: Wave Propagation & Scattering in Random Media, 1978; editor: Radio Science, 1982. Fellow IEEE (mem. editorial bd., Region VI Achieveemnt award 1968, Centennial Medal 1984), Optical Soc. Am. (co-editor jour. 1983); mem. Internat. Union Radio Sci. (commn. B chmn.). Home: 2913 165th Pl NE Bellevue WA 98008 Office: U Wash Dept Elec Engring FT-10 Seattle WA 98195

ISHMAEL, WILLIAM EARL, land use planner, civil engineer; b. Mt. Sterling, Ky., Mar. 11, 1946; s. Charles William and Alice Clay (Trimble) I.; m. Valerie Ann Perkinson, June 22, 1978. BSCE, Duke U., 1968; MA in Urban Planning, U. Mich., 1975. Registered civil engr., Calif., Ky.; registered planner Am. Inst. Cert. Planners. Petroleum engr. Humble Oil (now Exxon), New Orleans, 1968-69; dep. dir. Richmond Regional Planning Commn., Richmond, Va., 1975-78; sr. planner Nolte and Assocs., Sacramento, 1978—, assoc. of the corp., 1984—; Mem. City Planning Commn., Sacramento, 1983—, vice chmn., 1985, chmn. 1986; bd. dirs. Sacramento Heritage, 1983—, chmn., 1985-86; chmn. Urban Design Task Force for Downtown Sacramento, 1986; mem. task force Govtl. Consolidation, 1986; active Big Bros., 1978-83. Served to lt. USN, 1969-72. Named Mover and Shaper Heir Apparent, Exec. Pl. Mag., 1986. Mem. Sacramento C. of C. (mem. land use com. 1983—), Am. Planning Assn. (dir. pro tem 1981-83, Disting. Service award 1983), Chi Epsilon. Office: Nolte and Assocs 1730 I St Sacramento CA 95814

ISIDORO, EDITH ANNETTE, horticulturist; b. Albuquerque, Oct. 14, 1957; d. Robert Joseph and Marion Elizabeth (Miller) I. BS in Horticulture, N.Mex. State U., 1981, MS in Horticulture, 1984. Range conservationist Soil Conservation Service, Estancia, Grants, N.Mex., 1980-82; lab. aide N.Mex. State U. Dept. Horticulture, Las Cruces, 1982, 83-84; technician N.Mex. State U. Coop. Extension Service, Las Cruces, 1983-84, county agrl. extension agt., 1985; area extension agt. U. Nev., Reno, Fallon, 1985—. Mem. AAUW, Am. Soc. Horticultural Sci., Nat. Assn. County Agr. Extension Agts., Nat. Assn. Extension 4-H AGts., Alpha Zeta, Pi Alpha Psi. Avocations: flute, ch. choir, hiking, gardening, macrame. Home: 4675 Sheckler Fallon NV 89406 Office: Churchill County Coop Extension 111 Sheckler Rd Fallon NV 89406

ISKANDER, MAGDY FAHMY, electrical engineering educator; b. Alexandria, Egypt, Aug. 6, 1946; came to U.S., 1977; s. Fahmy and Fotnah I.; m. Sonia E. Eusebio; 1 child, Elene Tiffany. B.Sc. in Elec. Engring., U. Alexandria, 1969; M.Sc. in Microwaves, U. Man. (Can.), Winnipeg, 1972, Ph.D. in Elec. Engring., 1976. Instr. U. Alexandria, 1969-71; research asst. U. Man., 1971-75, NRC of Can. postdoctoral fellow, 1975-76; research assoc. U. Utah, Salt Lake City, 1977, asst. prof., 1978-82, assoc. prof. elec. engring., 1982-85, prof., 1985—; cons. BSD Med. Corp., Salt Lake City, 1981—, Chevron Oil Field Research Co., La Habra, Calif., 1982—. Contbr. chpts. to books, papers to tech. jours., confs. and internat. symposia. Guest editor spl. issues Jour. Microwave Power, 1983. Patentee in field. Pres. David P. Gardner faculty fellow U. Utah, 1981; recipient Patent award for creative invention Coll. Engring., U. Utah, 1983, Outstanding Teaching award, 1983; Curtis W. McGraw research award Am. Soc. Engring. Edn., 1985. Sr. mem. IEEE (Engr. of Yr. Utah sect. 1984); mem. Microwave Theory and Techniques Soc. of IEEE (chmn. Utah sect. 1982—). Home: 3555 Westwood Dr Salt Lake City UT 84109 Office: U Utah Electrical Engring Dept 3053 Merrill Engring Bldg Salt Lake City UT 84112

ISLEY, ERNEST D., Canadian provincial government official; b. Vermilion, Alta., Can., June 29, 1937; m. Sheila; children—Floyd, Lori, Thea, Tracy. B.Edn. with distinction, U. Alta., 1969. Operator farm, Bonnyville, Alta., Can.; agt. ins. co.; prin. Bonnyville Centralized High Sch., 1971-78, Altario Sch., 1961-71; mem. Alta. Legis. Assembly, 1979—, mem. edn. caucus, agr. caucus coms., select com. of legislature on fisheries, select com. of legislature on surface rights, curriculum policies bd., Port Churchill Devel. Bd.; minister of manpower Province of Alta., Edmonton. Pres., Lakeland Tourist Assn., 1975; chmn. Bonnyville Sr. Citizens Project Com., 1976; dir., v.p. Bonnyville Progressive Conservative Assn., 1974-78; mem. Travel Alta. Zone Assistance Rev. Bd., 1976-78, chmn. bd., 1977-78. Minister Pub. Works, Supply and Services, 1986—. Office: Govt Alta, 131 Legislature Bldg, Edmonton, AB Canada T5K 2B6

ISMAIL, ISAMIL MAHMOUD KAMAL, research engineer; b. Alexandria, Arab Republic of Egypt, June 18, 1945; came to U.S. 1972; s. Mahmoud Kamal and Aleya A. (Elmehelemy) I.; m. Wafaa H. Elzomor, July 13, 1978. BS in Phys. Chemistry, Cairo U., 1965, MS in Phys. Chemistry, 1970; PhD in Fuel Sci., Pa. State U., 1978. Instr. chemistry Cairo U., 1965-72; research Pa. State U., University Park, 1972-78, research assoc., 1978-80; engr., scientist Allis Chalmers Co., Milw., 1980-83; research phys. scientist Air Force Astronautics Lab., Edwards AFB, Calif., 1983—. Mem. Am. Chem. Soc., Am. Carbon Soc., Sigma Xi. Home: PO Box 4455 Lancaster CA 93539 Office: AFAL/MKBN MS #24 Edwards AFB CA 93523-5000

ISOM, GERALD A., insurance company executive. Pres., chief exec. officer Transam. Ins. Co., Los Angeles. Office: Transam Ins Co 1150 S Olive St Los Angeles CA 90015 *

ISOM, LOWELL HINTON, social worker; b. Hurricane, Utah, May 23, 1938; s. Thomas Irving and Euginia (McAllister) I. MSW, U. Utah, 1963. Social worker Dept. Social Services, Office of Community Orgn., Salt Lake City, 1963-, 85-86, liaison to juvenile ct., 1973-79, supr., 1979-85. Mem. Nat. Assn. Social Workers. Democrat. Mormon. Avocations: reading, photography. Home: 2675 S 18th E Salt Lake City UT 84106

ISRAEL, ANN MARY, management consulting company executive; b. Detroit, Jan. 24, 1949; d. Barney Benjamin and Lillian Ruth (Petok) I. BA, Mich. State U., 1970; MA, U. Calif., Berkeley, 1974. Tchr. English Highland Park (Mich.) High Sch., 1970-72, Oakland (Calif.) High Sch., 1972-76; v.p., sr. ptnr. Purcell Group, Los Angeles, 1976—. Mem. United Friends of Children, Los Angeles, 1985—; founding mem. Mus. Contemporary Art, Los Angeles, 1984—. Republican. Jewish. Avocations: music, art, sports, movies, cooking. Office: Purcell Group 11845 W Olympic Blvd #880 Los Angeles CA 90064

ISRAELSEN, NED ALMA, attorney; b. Logan, Utah, Dec. 6, 1954; s. Lyle E. and Marianna (Crookston) I.; m. Cynthia Kae Saunders, Jan. 13, 1977; children: Stanford, Lisa, Kurt. BS in Chemistry magna cum laude, Utah State U., 1978; JD with high honors, George Washington U., 1981. Bar: U.S. Patent Office 1979, Utah 1981, Va. 1981, Calif. 1984. Patent agt. Schwartz, Jeffery, Schwaab, Mack, Blumenthal & Koch P.C., Alexandria, Va., 1978-81; tech. asst. U.S. Ct. Customs and Patent Appeals, Washington, 1981-82; tech. law clk. U.S. Ct. Appeals Fed. Cir., Washington, 1982-83; patent atty., ptnr. Knobbe, Martens, Olson & Bear, Newport Beach, CA, 1983—; prof. law Loyola Law Sch., Los Angeles, 1986—. Mem. law rev. George Washington U., Washington, 1979-81. Scoutmaster Boy Scouts Am., Tustin, Calif., 1985—. Mem. ABA, Am. Chem. Soc., Am. Intellectual Property Law Assn., Deseret Bus. Assn., Assn. Former Ct. Customs and Patent Appeals Law Clks. and Tech. Assts. (bd. dirs. 1985—), Phi Kappa Phi. Mormon. Lodge: Order of Coif. Avocations: backpacking, scuba diving, photography. Office: Knobbe Martens Olson & Bear 610 Newport Ctr Dr Suite 1600 Newport Beach CA 92660

ITANO, LESLIE MICHIYA, electrical engineer; b. Sacramento, Mar. 15, 1954; d. Tsuyoshi Dean and Florence (Funabiki) I.; m. W. Jerry Chang, Feb. 22, 1986. BSEE, Stanford U., 1975; MSEE, MIT, 1980, engrs. degree, 1980. Mem. tech. staff Watkins-Johnson, Palo Alto, Calif., 1975-78; research asst. MIT, Cambridge, 1978-80; mem. tech. staff Hewlett-Packard, Palo Alto, 1980-83, research and devel. engring. supr., 1983—. Active Lively Arts, Stanford, Calif., 1981—. John Stewart Low scholar Stanford U., 1974-75. Mem. IEEE, Internat. Soc. Hybrid Microelectronics, Sigma Xi. Avocations: tennis, music. Home: 3913 Bibbits Dr Palo Alto CA 94303 Office: Hewlett-Packard 1501 Page Mill Rd Palo Alto CA 94304

IVERACH, ROBERT JOHN, lawyer; b. Edmonton, Alta., Can., Dec. 13, 1947; s. David W. and Margaret L. (Ranton) I.; m. Susan Anne Long, May 6, 1977; children—Robert J., Michelle A. B.A., U. Calgary, 1969; LL.B., U. Alta., 1970; LL.M., London Sch. Econs., 1971. Bar: Alta. 1972. Student, atty., Ballem, McDill & MacInnes, Calgary, Alta., 1971-74; ptnr. Fenerty & Co., Calgary, 1974-78; founding ptnr. Bell, Felesky & Iverach, Calgary, 1978—; pres., dir. Sage Resources Ltd., Calgary, 1980—. Co-author: Canadian Income Tax Tips and Traps, 1979. Bd. dirs. Alta. Law Found., 1976-78. Viscount Bennett scholar, 1970. Mem. Law Soc. Alta., Can. Bar Assn. Progressive Conservative. Mem. United Ch. Can. Clubs: Ranchmen's, Petroleum, Professional, Glencoe (Calgary). Office: 350 7th Ave SW, Suite 3400, Calgary, AB Canada T2P 3N9

IVERIUS, PER-HENRIK, physician, educator; b. Stockholm, Sept. 26, 1942; s. Karl Gösta and Märta Christina (Engelbert) I. B in Med. Sci., U. Uppsala, Sweden, 1963, PhD in Med. Biochemistry, 1971, MD, 1975. Diplomate Am. Bd. Internal Medicine, Am. Bd. Endocrinology and Metabolism. Intern, resident Emmanuel Hosp., Portland, 1978-80; asst. prof. med. biochemistry U. Uppsala, 1972-74; sr. research fellow U. Wash., Seattle, 1980-82, acting instr. medicine, 1982-85; asst. prof. medicine U. Utah, Salt Lake City, 1985—; mem. staff VA Med. Ctr., Salt Lake City, 1985—. Contbr. articles to profl. jours. Recipient Research Career Devel. award Swedish Med. Research Council, 1971-74; fellow Arthritis Found., 1975-78. Mem. AAAS, Am. Diabetes Assn., N.Y. Acad. Scis. Office: VA Med Ctr 500 Foothill Blvd Salt Lake City UT 84148

IVEY, KEVIN JOHN, internist; b. Warwick, Queensland, Australia, Mar. 6, 1939; came to U.S., 1968; s. Albert T. and Rose Anne (Brown) I.; m. Judith G. Kelso, Dec. 31, 1964; children—Thomas, John, Catherine, Mark. M.D., U. Queensland, 1962. Diplomate Eng. Bd. Internal Medicine. Intern, U. Queensland, Brisbane, 1963, resident, 1964; sr. med. resident U. Leeds, Eng., 1965-68; fellow in gastroenterology U. Iowa, Iowa City, 1968-70; clin. lectr. U. Sydney, New South Wales, Australia, 1970-74; assoc. prof. medicine U. Mo.-Columbia, 1975-80; prof. medicine U. Calif.-Irvine, 1980—; chief gastrointestinal research Long Beach VA Med. Ctr., Calif., 1980—; chmn. research and devel. com. 1985—; mem. VA Merit Rev. Bd. Gastroenterology Research, VA Cen. Office, 1986—. Author numerous articles. Australian Nat. Health and Med. Research Council grantee, 1972-74; VA grantee, 1978-80, 79—. Fellow ACP, Royal Australian Coll. Physicians, Royal Coll. Physicians (London); mem. Am. Gastroent. Assn., Am. Fedn. Clin. Research. Clubs: Huntington Harbour Yacht; U. Calif.-Irvine Sailing. Office: U Calif Irvine CA 92717

IVY, EDWARD EVERETT, entomologist, consultant; b. Hollis, Okla., Sept. 24, 1913; s. James Thomas and Betty (Minnear) I.; m. Elizabeth Alberta Slater, Feb. 23, 1935 (dec. Mar. 1981); children: James, Betty. BS, Okla State U., 1934; PhD, Tex. A&M U., 1951. Registered profl. entomologist, all 50 states, Can., Mex. Research entomologist USDA, College Station, Tex., 1940-55; salesman pesticides Mich. Chem. Corp., St. Louis, Mich., 1955-63; research entomologist Pennwolt Corp., Phila., 1963-75; cons. in pesticide devel. 1975—. Contbr. numerous articles to profl. jours. Mem. Entomol. Soc. Am., Am. Registry Profl. Engtomologists, Sigma Xi. Presbyterian. Home and Office: 1771 Broadway Apt 217 Concord CA 95420

IVY, STEPHEN CRAIG, manufacturing company executive; b. Eugene, Oreg., May 20, 1945; s. Orley Glen and Theda June (Childs) I.; m. Connie Marie Benoit, Aug. 18, 1966 (div. Oct. 1979); children: Jeannie, Wendy; m. Charlene Ruth Minion, Oct. 22, 1982; 1 child, Christopher. Assoc. in Electronics, Oreg. Inst. Tech., 1965. Mgr. Tektronix, Inc., Beaverton, Oreg., 1965-78; gen. mgr. Output, Inc., Beaverton, 1978-79; cons., mgr. Interactive Tech., Beaverton, 1979-81; gen. mgr. Decision Dynamics, Portland, 1981; dir. Servio Logic Corp., Portland, Oreg., 1981-84; pres. Brike Internat., Portland, 1985-86; pres., chief exec. officer AirTec Internat., Portland, 1986—; pres., cons. Mgmt. Tech., Inc., Hillsboro, Oreg., 1981—. Republican. Avocations: photography, woodworking, hiking. Office: 1700 NW 167th Pl #210 Beaverton OR 97006

IWATA, RUTH YASUE, horticulturalist; b. Kealakekua, Hawaii, Apr. 21, 1937; d. Kitsuya and Grace (Fukushima) Horiuchi; m. Earl S., Sept. 23, 1967; children: Patricia, Randal, Daniel. BS, U. Hawaii, 1959, PhD, 1980; MS, St. John's U., Jamaica, N.Y., 1962. Registered nurse. Faculty mem. SUNY, Farmingdale, 1962-65; faculty mem. U. Hawaii, Honolulu, 1965-72, extension specialist, 1980—. Served to lt. (j.g.) USN, 1959-61, with Res. 1958, 62. Mem. Am. Soc. Hort. Sci., Sigma Xi. Buddhist. Home: 1739 Haleloke St Hilo HI 96720 Office: UH HITAHR CES Hawaii 875 Komohana St Hilo HI 96720

IYA, SRIDHAR KILARA, engineering administrator; b. Bangalore, India, Mar. 27, 1940; came to U.S., 1963, naturalized, 1987; s. Lakshminarasimha and Sharada (Saggere) I.; m. Malini Rao, June 17, 1970; children—Vivek, Neeta. B.Engring., U. Mysore, Bangalore, 1960; M.Engring. with distinction, Indian Inst. Sci., Bangalore, 1962; M.S., Brown U., 1965; Ph.D., Pa. State U., 1971. Research assoc. Pa. State U., University Park, 1971-72, SUNY-Binghamton, 1972-74; sr. engr. Union Carbide Corp., South Charleston, W.Va., 1974-76, cons. Tonawanda, N.Y., 1976-82, group leader, Washougal, Wash., 1982-84, program mgr. govt. research and devel. contracts 1982—, mgr. govt. programs, 1984—; mem. Combustion Inst., 1968-80. Patentee in field. Contbr. articles to profl. jours. Indian Govt. merit scholar, 1956-60. Mem. Am. Assn. Crystal Growth. Home: 2010 SE 97th Ave Vancouver WA 98664

IYER, PRADEEP SATYAMURTHY, oil company research scientist; b. Tirupattur, Tamil Nadu, India, Aug. 10, 1958; came to U.S., 1979; s. Y. and Visalakshi (Mala) Satyamurthy; m. Meenakshi Radha, Mar. 16, 1987. BS, Inst. Sci., Bombay, 1977, MS, 1979; PhD, U. So. Calif., 1984. Research assoc. Hydrocarbon Research Inst., Los Angeles, 1984-85; research scientist UNOCAL, Brea, Calif., 1986—; cons. Global Geochem. Corp, Los Angeles, 1985—, Avery Internat., Los Angeles, 1985—. Contbr. articles to profl. jours. Mem. Am. Chem. Soc., Sigma Xi, Phi Kappa Phi, Alpha Xi Sigma. Avocations: music, reading. Home: 2401 S Hacienda Blvd Apt 223 Hacienda Heights CA 91745 Office: UNOCAL Sci and Tech Div 376 S Valencia Ave Brea CA 92621

IYER, RAVI SITHARAM, mechanical engineer; b. Bombay, Nov. 3, 1945; came to U.S., 1968; s. Sitharam R. Iyer and Sharda (Kanemar) Iyer; m. Wendy Lee Penney: children: Evan Sunil, Sara Anjuli. BSEE, Poona U., India, 1967, BSME, 1968; MSME, Syracuse U., 1971; MBA, Pepperdine U., 1979. Registered profl. engr., Calif., Nebr. Project engr. State of Nebr., Omaha, 1972-74, Bechtel Corp., San Francisco, 1974-80; engring. mgr. Kaiser Internat., Lima, Peru, 1980-83; project mgr. Kaiser Engring., Oakland, Calif., 1983—. Mem. Project Mgmt. Inst. Avocations: calligraphy, gardening, tennis. Home: 210 Holton Ct Walnut Creek CA 94598 Office: Kaiser Engrs 1800 Harrison St Oakland CA 94623

IZDEBSKI, KRZYSZTOF, speech and hearing educator, voice and laryngology scientist; b. Milanowek, Poland, Mar. 6, 1945; came to U.S., 1970, naturalized, 1976; s. Julian de Pomian and Halina Heliodora (Szymanska) I.; m. Marianne I. van Zeeland, Oct. 11, 1985. Fil.Kand., U. Lund (Sweden), 1970; MA, UCLA, 1972; postgrad. U. Calif.-Santa Barbara, 1972-73; PhD, U. Calif.-San Francisco, 1976. Lic. in speech/lang. pathology, Calif., 1984; cert. clin. competence in speech/lang. pathology Am. Speech-Lang.-Hearing Assn. Asst. prof. otolaryngology U. Calif.-San Francisco, 1978-83, dir. Voice Sci. Lab., 1979-83; pvt. practice speech-lang. pathology San Francisco and Pinole, Calif., 1983—; chief speech pathologist VA Med. Ctr., Martinez, Calif., 1984—; assoc. prof. otorhinolaryngology U. Calif.-Davis/Sacramento, 1985—; assoc. staff mem. Pacific Presbyn. Med. Ctr., San Francisco, 1985—; sci. advisor BioDent Techs., Inc., San Mateo, Calif., 1986—. Author: Common Speech Disorders in Otolaryngology Practice, 1980; contbr. articles to profl. jours., chpts. to books; inventor reaction time device for measurement phonation. Earl C. Anthony grantee, 1975-76, Nat. Inst. Communicative Disorders and Stroke grantee, 1979-82, Cancer and Med. Found. grantee, 1983; VA trainee, 1973-76; recipient cert. of appreciation Am. Speech Lang. and Hearing Assn., 1982, Sci. award Am. Speech Lang. and Hearing Assn., 1982, 84. Mem. Internat. Assn. Exptl. Research in Singing (officer), Am. Assn. Phonetic Scis., Polish-Am. Congress, Sigma Xi. Democrat. Roman Catholic. Office: VA Med Ctr Martinez 150 Muir Rd Martinez CA 94553

IZENSTARK, JOSEPH LOUIS, physician, educator; b. Chgo., Mar. 29, 1919; s. Paul and Flora (Berger) I.; m. Elizabeth Kaplan, June 25, 1944; children: Susan Rebecca, John Kenneth, Florence Pauline. B.A., U. Calif., Berkeley, 1948; M.D., U. Calif., San Francisco, 1951. Diplomate: Am. Bd. Radiology, Am. Bd. Nuclear Medicine. Intern USPHS, Chgo., 1951-52; resident Kern Gen. Hosp., Bakersfield, Calif., 1952-53; resident in radiology Cedars of Lebanon Hosp., Los Angeles, 1955-56; chief radiology resident Los Angeles County Harbor Gen. Hosp., Torrance, Calif., 1957-58; practice medicine specializing in radiology Inglewood, Calif., 1953-55, Bakersfield, 1971-86; dir. radiology Imperial Hosp., Inglewood, 1959-60; asst. prof. radiology Tulane U., 1960-62, asso. prof., 1963; asso. prof. radiology Emory U., 1963-67, dir. nuclear medicine, 1963-67; prof. radiology U. So. Calif., 1969-72; prof. health scis. Bakersfield State Coll., 1973-83; chief nuclear medicine Cedars of Lebanon Hosp., 1968-71; med. dir. edn. Bakersfield Meml. Hosp., 1983—; spl. cons. radiol. health USPHS, Calif. Bur. Radiol. Health, U.S. Army; mem. La. Atomic Energy Adv. Council; dir. nuclear medicine Crawford W. Long Meml. Hosp.; mem. USPHS Commn. on Radiation Exposure Evaluation. Author: Anatomy and Physiology for X-ray Technicians, 1961; contbr. articles to profl. jours. Fellow Am. Cancer Soc., Am. Coll. Radiology; mem. Soc. Nuclear Medicine (pres. So. Calif. chpt. 1976), So. Valley Radiol. Soc. (pres. 1975), Kern County Med. Soc. (pres. 1978). Office: PO Box 1888 Bakersfield CA 93303

IZOR, PAUL HERMAN, lawyer; b. Bay Village, Ohio, July 3, 1949; s. Herman and Marilyn (Zaebst) I.; m. Judith L. Travis, June 26, 1971. B.A., Elmhurst Coll., 1971; J.D., Lincoln U., 1981. Bar: Calif. 1982, U.S. Dist. Ct. (no. dist.) Calif. 1982. Claims supr. Fireman's Fund Ins. Co., San Jose, Calif., 1977-82, claims rep., 1971-77; sole practice, San Jose, 1982—; cons. in field. Named Outstanding Grad., Lincoln U., 1981. Mem. Ins. Inst. Am., ABA, Assn. Trial Lawyers Am., Calif. Trial Lawyers Assn., Santa Clara County Trial Lawyers Assn., Central Coast Claims Assn. Club: YMCA. Office: 1999 S Bascom Ave Suite 1005 Campbell CA 95008

IZUMI, RAY MATSON, systems manager; b. Dallas, Mar. 19, 1950; s. Ernest Matson and Mary Sue (Harned) I. BA, U. Conn., 1973; postgrad., U. Utah, 1979-83. Analytical chemist UBTL, Inc., Salt Lake City, 1980-83, system mgr., 1983-86; data mgr. ECOVA Corp., Redmond, Wash., 1986—;

cons. Digicomp, Salt Lake City, 1983—. Mem. Am. Chem. Soc., Assn. Computing Machinery, Interex, Utah Classical Guitar Soc. (bd. dirs. 1986). Avocations: rock climbing, running, scuba diving. Home: 16442 NE 180th Pl Woodinville WA 98072 Office: ECOVA Corp 15555 NE 33d Redmond WA 98072

JAACKS, JOHN WILLIAM, ret. air force officer, aerospace co. exec.; b. Chgo., Sept. 3, 1928; s. Oren Ernst and Mathilda (Dritlein) J.; B.S. in Indsl. Adminstrn., U. Ill., 1949, B.S. in Indsl. Engring., 1962; M.B.A., U. So. Calif., 1970, M.L.A., 1984; m. Marilyn Joyce Walker, Sept. 24, 1952; children—John W. II, Jeffrey A., Holly S. Entered USAF, 1950, commd. 2d lt., 1952, advanced through grades to lt. col., 1968; navigator Fighter Interceptor Squadron, Alaska, 1952-55, pilot, fighter squadron ops. officer, Youngstown, Ohio, 1957-60, chief avionics and aircraft maintenance, Soesterberg, Holland, 1962-65, chief program mgmt. Space Systems div., Los Angeles, 1966-67, dir. program control space launch vehicles Missile Systems Orgn., Los Angeles, from 1967; ret., 1973; asst. program mgr. Aircraft Co., El Segundo, Calif. Chmn. Los Angeles council Boy Scouts Am., Torrance and Palos Verdes Calif. Mem. Am. Inst. Indsl. Engring., AIAA, Air Force Assn., U. Ill. Alumni Assn., U. So. Calif. Alumni Assn., Chi Gamma Iota, Phi Kappa Psi. Lutheran. Home: 3310 Seaclaire Dr Rancho Palos Verdes CA 90274 Office: Hughes Aircraft Co El Segundo CA 90009

JABARA, MICHAEL DEAN, communications company executive; b. Sioux Falls, S.D., Oct. 26, 1952; s. James M. and Jean Marie (Swiden) J.; m. Gundula Beate Dietz, Aug. 26, 1984. Student, Mich. Tech. U., 1970-72; BSBA, U. Calif., Berkeley, 1974; MBA, Pepperdine U., 1979. Internat. devel. cons. McGraw Hill Internat., London, 1982-83; dir. product mgmt. Androbot Inc., San Jose, Calif., 1983; cons. A Beeper Co., Atlanta, 1983-84; founder, chief exec. officer Friend Techs. Inc., San Francisco, 1984—. Patentee in field. Mem. Pepperdine Bus. Alumni, U. Calif. Berkeley Bus. Alumni. Club: Commonwealth (San Francisco). Avocations: travel, reading, flying. Home: 132 Goldmine Dr San Francisco CA 94131 Office: Friend Techs Inc 340 Bryant St San Francisco CA 94107

JABIN, MARVIN (MARK), real estate developer, lawyer; b. N.Y.C., Mar. 28, 1929; s. Sol and Belle Jabin; BA in Biology and Chemistry, NYU, 1952; BS in Engring., UCLA, 1954, JD, 1957; m. Lelia Honig, May 13, 1952; children: Valerie, Gregory, Anthony, Desiree. Bar: Calif. 1958, U.S. Supreme Ct. 1961; ptnr. Jabin & Jabin, Monterey Park, Calif., 1958—; v.p. CVJ Constrn. Inc., Monterey Park, 1977— ; pres. Jabin Corp., Monterey Park, 1979—; judge protem Alhambra Mcpl. Ct., Calif.; asst. prof. bus. law Calif. State U., Los Angeles, 1972-75; dir. Golden Security Thrift & Loan Assn. Adv. council Calif. State U., Los Angeles, 1971-76. Served with U.S. Army, 1946-49. Mem. Am. Arbitration Assn. (arbitrator), San Gabriel Valley Bar Assn. (pres. 1975), Los Angeles County Bar Assn. (trustee 1975-77), Monterey Park C. of C. (bd. dirs. 1982-85). Lodge: Rotary (bd. dirs. Monterey Park club 1982-83). Office: 701 S Atlantic Blvd Monterey Park CA 91754

JACK, RHONDA L., social worker; b. Medford, Oreg., June 6, 1953; d. Eldred Leroy and Joyce Lucille (Newton) Jack; m. Landon Martin Conrad, May 11, 1979; children: Grant Landon Jack, Austin Blake Jack. BS in Sociology, Oreg. State U., 1975; MSW, Portland State U., 1978. Alcohol counselor Sweathouse Lodge Inc., Corvallis, Oreg., 1978-79; clin. social worker Luth. Med. Ctr., Wheat Ridge, Colo., 1979-85; social worker geriatrics St. Lukes Regional Med. Ctr., Boise, Idaho, 1985—. Mem. Nat. Assn. Social Workers, Am. Geriatric Assn. Avocations: softball, volleyball, antiques. Home: 300 E Cresline Dr Boise ID 83702 Office: Saint Luke's Regional Ctr 190 E Bannock Boise ID 83712

JACKLICH, GAIL GRUNDMANN, educational administrator; b. Oak Park, Ill., July 1, 1941; d. Charles Richard and Emeline Pamela (Allers) Grundmann; m. John Jacklich, Apr. 19, 1964; children: John III, Christina, Steven Shore. BS in Chemistry, Mundelein Coll., 1963; postgrad., No. Ill. U., 1967; CDA, Loyola U. Dental Sch., Chgo., 11973; MBA, Pepperdine U., 1980. Research asst. Campbell Soup Co., 1963-65; tchr. chemistry pub. schs. Joliet, Ill., 1965-66; pres. Quality Porcelain Studio, 1967-72; v.p. Computer Letter Service, Joliet, 1974-76; prin., operator Continuing Edn. Ctrs. Am., Santa Cruz, Calif., 1976—; pres. Spl. Products Inc., Santa Cruz, 1978—; cons. direct mail seminars. Office: 102 Western Ct Santa Cruz CA 95060

JACKMAN, MICHELE, management consultant, educator; b. Los Angeles, Aug. 18, 1944; d. Michael and Grace (DeLeo) Pantaleo; m. Jarrell C. Jackman, Sept. 7, 1968; 1 child, Renee Grace. BA in Polit. Sci., U. Calif., Davis, 1966; MSW in Social Policy, Cath. U., Washington, 1980; MA in Human Relations Mgmt., U. Okla., 1980. Social worker Los Angeles County, 1966-70; supr., trainer Santa Barbara (Calif.) County, 1970-74; mgr. Drug/Alcohol program U.S. Army, Western Europe, 1974-78; analyst, cons. Office Dep. Chief of Staff Personnel U.S. Army, Washington, 1978-80; trainer, cons. Profit Systems, Internat., Santa Barbara, 1980—; lectr. organizational psychology U. Calif., Santa Barbara; cons. numerous agys., orgns. Co-author: Choices/Challenges Teacher's Guide, 1983; contbr. chpts. to books. Recipient Commdr.'s medal for Disting. Civilian Service U.S. Army, 1977. Mem. Am. Mgmt. Assn., Nat. Assn. Social Workers (chmn. local chpt.), Am. Soc. Tng. and Devel., Nat. Assn. Female Execs., Santa Barbara C. of C. (Bus. award Council of High Edn./Industry 1986). Club: Univ. (Santa Barbara). Lodge: Native Daus. of Golden West. Avocations: writing, sailing, stained glass, theater. Office: Profit Systems Internat 17 E Carrillo #45 Santa Barbara CA 93101

JACKSON, ALBERT SMITH, electrical engineer; b. Sylvia, Kans., Feb. 2, 1927; s. Oliff Harold and Nellie Blanche (Dewhurst) J.; m. Solace Patricia Smith, June 9, 1951; (div. Aug. 1978); children: Linda Michelle, Jill Sharon, Theresa Louise, Steven Thomas, Craig Michael; m. Elaine Sonia Spontak, Sept. 1, 1978. AA, John Muir Coll., 1948; BSEE, MSEE, Calif. Inst. Tech., 1952; PhDEE, Cornell U., 1956. From instr. to asst. prof. Cornell U., Ithaca, N.Y., 1952-59; dept. mgr. TRW Computers Co., Canoga Park, Calif., 1959-61; pres. Control Tech., Inc., Long Beach, Calif., 1961-65, 71-72; chief scientist Milgo Electronic Corp., Miami, Fla., 1965-71; pres. Opto Logic Corp., Long Beach, 1972-75; engring. mgr. Motorola, Inc., Orange, Calif., 1975—; cons. Naval Research Lab., Washington, 1964-69, Gen. Electric Corp., Ithaca, 1953-59; lectr. UCLA, 1972-77, U. Calif., Irvine, 1965—. Author: Analog Computation, 1960; contbr. articles to profl. jours.; inventor in field. Active Redevel. Agy., Seal Beach, Calif., 1972-74. Served with USN, 1945-46. Named Outstanding Mem. of Extension Faculty, U. Calif.-Irvine, 1985. Mem. IEEE (chmn. profl. group on human factors in engring. 1963-64, regional ednl. coordinator 1984-86). Republican. Avocations: skiing, photography. Office: Motorola Inc 2 City Blvd East Suite 258 Orange CA 92668

JACKSON, BEVERLEY JOY JACOBSON, columnist, lectr., photographer; b. Los Angeles, Nov. 20, 1928; d. Phillip and Dorothy Jacobson; student U. So. Calif., U. Calif. at Los Angeles; m. Robert David Jackson (div. Aug. 1964); 1 dau., Tracey Dee. Daily columnist Santa Barbara (Calif.) News Press, 1968—; nat. lectr. Santa Barbara history, hist. China recreated, also China today; free lance writer, fgn. corr. Bd. dirs. Santa Barbara br. Am. Cancer Soc., 1963—; mem. art mus. council Los Angeles Mus. Art, 1959—, mem. costume council, 1983—; docent Los Angeles Mus. Art, 1962-64; mem. exec. bd. Channel City Women's Forum, 1969—;mem. adv. bd. Santa Barbara Mus. Natural History, Council of Christmas Cheer, Women's Shelter Bldg., Direct Relief Internat., Nat. Council Drug and Alcohol Abuse. Bd., Hospice of Santa Barbara, 1981—; chmn. Santa Barbara Com. for Visit Queen Elizabeth II, 1982—. Mem. Women in Communications. Author: Dolls and Doll Houses of Spain, 1970; (with others) I'm Just Wild About Harry, 1979. Home: PO Box 5118 Santa Barbara CA 93108

JACKSON, BRUCE GEORGE, lawyer; b. Portland, Oreg., July 15, 1942; s. George William and Sally Marie (Dorner) J.; m. Jane Jackson, Sept. 8, 1972; children—Yvette, Scott. B.S. cum laude, U. Oreg., 1966; J.D., U. Calif.-Berkeley, 1970. Bar: Hawaii 1971, U.S. Dist. Ct. Hawaii 1971. Assoc. Case, Kay & Lynch, Honolulu, 1970-74; ptnr. Curtis W. Carlsmith, Honolulu, 1974-76; sole practice, Honolulu, 1977—; speaker on real property law, land trusts, estate planning, 1977—. Served with N.G., 1960-68. Mem. ABA, Hawaii Bar Assn., Sigma Phi Epsilon (life). Democrat. Clubs: Honolulu, Downtown Exchange (Honolulu). Student editor: Kragen & McNulty on Federal Income Taxation, 1970. Office: Suite 1132 Pacific Tower 1001 Bishop St Honolulu HI 96813

JACKSON, CLARKE HAWLEY, executive recruiting consultant; b. Tacoma, Jan. 10, 1935; s. Paul H. and Lucile K. (Hawley) J.; m. L. Catherine George, Dec. 13, 1958; children—Elizabeth A., Susan H., Brock W., Todd M. B.A., SUNY-Buffalo, 1959. Cert. mgmt. cons. Personnel interviewer Allstate Ins. Co., Toronto, Ont., Can., 1959-63; v.p. Western region H.V. Chapman & Assocs., Vancouver, B.C., Can., 1963-70; mgr. exec. recruitment services Price Waterhouse Assocs., Vancouver, 1970-80; mng. ptnr. The Caldwell Ptnrs. Internat., Vancouver, 1980—. Mem. Prime Minister's adv. bd. Can. Works Council; bd. dirs. West Vancouver Community Services Adv. Commn., West Vancouver Sr. Citizens Adv. Bd., 7th Step Soc. Mem. Western Inst. Mgmt. Cons. Conservative. Anglican. Home: 1390 Camridge Rd, West Vancouver, BC Canada V7S 2M8 Office: 750-999 W Hastings St, Vancouver, BC Canada V6C 2W2

JACKSON, DANIEL KELVIN, electrical engineer entrepreneur; b. Syracuse, N.Y., Apr. 23, 1950. BSEE, MSEE, MIT, 1975. Engr. data systems div. Hewlett-Packard Co., Cupertino, Calif., 1975-76; sr. engr. Intel Corp., Santa Clara, Calif. and Aloha, Oreg., 1976-80; founder Crescent Heart Software, Portland, Oreg., 1981—; lectr. Oreg. Inst. Technology, Portland, 1986. Patentee in field. Sloan Nat. Scholar.

JACKSON, DAVID WAYNE, engineering executive; b. Dayton, Ohio, Aug. 5, 1941; s. Eugene Arnold and Charlotte LaVanda (Dokken) J.; B.S. in Physics, Iowa State U., 1963; M.S. in Elec. Engring., Stanford U., 1965; m. Palma Karen Paulson, June 22, 1968; children—Christine Diane, Suzanne Annette. Research engr. laser applications Stanford U., 1963-67, program mgr., 1967-69; program mgr. Electro-optics, Stanford Research Inst., Menlo Park, Calif., 1969-76; bus. area mgr. electro-optic Probe Systems, Sunnyvale, Calif., 1976-80, dir. engring., 1980-82; sr. tech. staff ESL, Inc., Sunnyvale, 1982-87, prin. engr. 1987—. Mem. Optical Soc. Am., Soc. Photo-Optical Instrumentation Engrs., Assn. Old Crows, Sigma Xi, Phi Kappa Phi, Pi Mu Epsilon. Co-author: Acousto-Optic Signal Processing. Patentee in field.

JACKSON, DEAN ALBERT, aluminum company executive, electrical engineer; b. Clarinda, Iowa, Apr. 3, 1921; s. William Newton and Mary Adna (James) J.; m. Nadine Virginia Johnson, Apr. 15, 1948; children—Deborah Ann, Susan Atlee, Sandra Elizabeth, Jennifer Louise, Ted Bradley. B.Sc. in Edn., U. Nebr., 1946, B.Sc. in Elec. Engring., 1952. Registered engr., Wash. Coach, tchr. Superior High Sch., Wyo., 1946-48; coach Multnomah Coll., Portland, Oreg., 1948-49; electrician Commonwealth Elec. Co., Lincoln, Nebr., 1949-52; elec. engr. Reynolds Metals, McCook, Ill., 1952-57; elec. engr. Kaiser Aluminum & Chem. Corp. Spokane, Wash., 1957-65, elec. design supr., 1965—. Bd. dirs. Spokane Valley YMCA, Spokane, 1967-68, pres., 1969. Served to 1st lt. C.E., U.S. Army, 1942-46; ETO. Mem. IEEE (sr., bd. dirs. 1970-72, treas. 1972-73, sec. 1973-74, chmn. 1975-76, Spokane Elec. Engr. of Yr. 1977), Lodge: Rotary (bd. dirs. local club 1979-84, treas. 1984-85, sec. 1985-86, pres.-elect 1986—). Home: E 10716 21st Spokane WA 99206 Office: Kaiser Aluminum & Chem Corp Trentwood Works Spokane WA 99215

JACKSON, DEBORAH JEAN, physicist; b. Topeka, Sept. 23, 1952; s. Collins and Mennie Ethel Jackson. BS in Physics, MIT, 1974; MS in Physics, Stanford U., 1976, PhD in Physics, 1980. Vis. scientist IBM Corp., Yorktown Heights, N.Y., 1981-83; mem. tech. staff Hughes Research Labs., Malibu, Calif., 1983—. Contbr. articles to profl. jours.; patentee in field. Ford Found. fellow, Emory U., Atlanta, 1974-76; Bell Labs. Coop. Research fellow, 1976-80. Mem. Am. Phys. Soc., Optical Soc. Am., Los Angeles Council Black Profl. Engrs., Nat. Soc. Black Physicists, Sigma Xi. Office: Hughes Research Labs 3011 Malibu Cyn Rd Malibu CA 90265

JACKSON, DON MERRILL, JR., electronics company executive; b. Kansas City, Mo., July 31, 1934; s. Don M. and Henryette J. (Boese) J.; A.B. in Physics, William Jewell Coll., 1956; M.S. in Physics, Iowa State U., 1959; Ph.D. in Elec. Engring., Ariz. State U., 1974; m. Barbara Petre, Aug. 28, 1954; children—Susan, Paul, Kevin. Pres., ASM/America, Phoenix, 1976-84; pres., chief exec. officer Microelectronic Packaging, Inc., Scotsdale, Ariz., vice-chmn. Superwave Tech., Phoenix. Served with USNR, 1952-60. Motorola Don Noble fellow, 1972-76. Mem. Am. Electronics Assn. (nat. bd. dirs.), Assn. Corp. Growth, IEEE, Electrochem. Soc., Sigma Xi. Republican. Patentee semicondr. electronics. Home: 9756 N 90th Pl Scottsdale AZ 85258 Office: MPI 7419 E Holm Dr Scottsdale AZ 85260-2418

JACKSON, DONALD DEAN, historian; b. Glenwood, Iowa, June 10, 1919; s. Marion Dean and Eula Frances (Woods) J.; m. Mary Catherine Mayberry, Oct. 6, 1943; children: Robert Woods, Mark Richard. BS, Iowa State U., 1942; MA, U. Iowa, 1947, PhD, 1948. Editor U. Ill. Press., Urbana, 1948-68; prof. history U. Va., Charlottesville, 1969-76; cons. Colorado Springs, Colo., 1976—. Author: Archer Pilgrim, 1942, Custer's Gold, 1966, Valley Men, 1983, Voyages of Steamboat Yellow Stone, 1985; editor: Black Hawk: an Autobiography, 1955, Letters of Lewis and Clark Expedition, 1962, rev. edit., 1978, Journals of Zebulon Pike, 1966, Expeditions of John C. Fremont, 1970-73, Diaries of George Washington, 1976-79; editor (papers) Papers of George Washington, 1968-76. Served to lt. (j.g.) USNR, 1942-46. Recipient Award of Merit, Am. Assn. State and Local History, 1967. Mem. Western History Assn. (Award of Merit, 1979), Am. Antiquarian Soc., Orgn. Am. Historians. Home: 3920 Old Stage Rd Colorado Springs CO 80906

JACKSON, DONALD WILLIAM, JR., educator; b. Cleve., Jan. 7, 1944; s. Donald William and Barbara Ann (Dolsen) J.; m. Sylvia Kay Schroen, July 22, 1972; B.A., Albion Coll., 1966; M.B.A., Mich. State U., 1968, Ph.D., 1973. Mgmt. intern Eastern Airlines, N.Y.C., 1966; personnel mgr. Mich. Bell Telephone Co., Detroit, 1967; asst. prof. mktg. Ariz. State U., Tempe, 1972-75, assoc. prof., 1975-79, prof., dir. research, 1979-86; dir. MBA for Execs. Program, 1984—; cons. in mktg. to firms and trade assns. Mem. Am. Mktg. Assn., Am. Psychol. Assn., Acad. Mktg. Scis., So. Mktg. Assn., Beta Gamma Sigma (past pres.), Pi Sigma Epsilon, Alpha Kappa Psi. Republican. Methodist. Author: Marketing Profitability Analysis: An Annotated Bibliography, 1977; mem. editorial bd. Journal of Mktg., Jour. Personal Selling and Sales Mgmt.; contbr. articles to prof. jours. Office: Coll of Bus Ariz State U Tempe AZ 85287

JACKSON, EUGENE, JR., biochemist, researcher; b. Vicksburg, Miss., Aug. 21, 1957; s. Eugene Sr. and Joyce (Flood) J. BS, Millsaps Coll., 1978; MS, Jackson State U., 1980; postgrad., Meharry Med. Coll., 1982-85. Research assoc. U. Miss. Med. Ctr., Jackson, 1979-81; instr. Rust Coll., Jackson, 1981-82; research assoc. Genentech Inc., South San Francisco, 1985—; cons. Tenn. Nat. Guard, 1982-85. Contbr. articles to profl. jours. Scoutmaster Boy Scouts Am., Oakland, Calif., 1985. Recipient Nat. Disting. Service award Boy Scouts Am., 1981; fellow Soc. Neurosci., 1983. Mem. Am. Chem. Soc., AAAS, Nat. Guard Assn. U.S., Res. Officers Assn., Sigma Xi. Roman Catholic. Home: 5921 Vallejo St Emeryville CA 94608 Office: Genentech Inc 460 Point San Bruno Blvd South San Francisco CA 94080

JACKSON, FRANK CLINE, JR., management consultant; b. Seattle, Aug. 14, 1920; s. Frank C. and Bertha J. (TeRoller) J.; BS in Pre-medics, U. Wash., 1942; BS in Animal Sci., Wash. State U., 1947; postgrad. Harvard U., 1954, Columbia U., 1955, Pacific Luth. U., 1966; m. Helen Elaine Bonner, Jan. 12, 1943 (dec. 1978); children: Stanley Alan, Bruce Edward, Paul Bonner, David Brian; m. 2d, Joan Marion Hurd, Dec. 29, 1979. Vets. agrl. instr. Puyallup (Wash.) High Sch., 1947-52; vet. rep. Pfizer Labs. div. Charles Pfizer Co., Inc., 1952-53, nat. sales mgr. vet. dept., N.Y.C., 1953-57, mgr. vet. dept., 1957-61; gen. mgr. Am. Wilbert Vault Co., Inc., Puyallup, 1961-65; chmn. Pierce County Co-op Extension Service, Wash. State U., Tacoma, 1966-78; chmn. Jefferson County Coop. Extension Service div. Wash. State U., Port Townsend, 1978-79; mgmt. cons., 1979—; pres. Dolphin Reach Corp.; mng. gen. ptnr. Dolphin Reach Assocs.; founder Pacific N.W. Vet. Suppliers Assn., 1955, pres., 1955-56, dir., 1956-59; founder, dir. Wash. Meml. Soc., Seattle, 1962-64. Troop chmn. Tacoma council Boy Scouts Am., 1950-60; bd. dirs. Tacoma Rescue Mission, 1970-78; Bible tchr., lectr., 1965—. Served with U.S. Army, 1942-46; PTO. Decorated Purple Heart (4), Bronze Star; recipient Disting. Citizen award Mcpl. League Tacoma, 1978, Jefferson award Am. Inst. for Public Service, 1977. Mem. Community Devel. Soc., Nat. (Disting. Service award 1979), Wash. assns. county agrl. agts., Nat. Sales Execs. Assn. Republican. Presbyterian. Club: Elks, Tacoma Yacht. Home: 3109 SW 319th Pl Federal Way WA 98023

JACKSON, HARRY ANDREW, artist; b. Chgo., Apr. 18, 1924; s. Harry and Ellen Grace J.; m. Valentina Moya Lear, Feb. 22, 1974; children: Matthew, Molly, Jesse, Luke, Chloe. ArtsD (hon.), U. Wto., 1986. Founder pvt. foundry, Camaiore, Italy, 1964—, Wyo. Foundry Studios, Cody, 1965—; founding ptnr. Jackson-Mariani S.R.L. Fine Art Bronze Foundry, Camaiore, Italy, 1985—; founder Western Fine Arts Found., 1974—. Author: Lost Wax Bronze Casting, 1972; One man exhbns. Tibor de Nagy Gallery, N.Y.C., 1952, 53, Martha Jackson Gallery, N.Y.C., 1956, Knoedler Gallery, N.Y.C., 1960, Amon Carter Mus., Fort Worth, 1961, 68, Kennedy Gallery, N.Y., 1964, 68, 69, Smithsonian Instn., Washington, 1964, Whitney Gallery Western Art/Buffalo Bill Hist. Mus., Cody, Wyo., 1964, 80, 81, Mont. Hist. Soc., 1964, Tryon Gallery London, 1969, J. Poole Gallery, London, 1981, Southwest Mus., Los Angeles, 1979, Smith Gallery, 1981, 86, Palm Springs Desert Mus., 1981, Mpls. Inst. Art, 1982, Trailside Gallery, Scottsdale, Ariz., 1983; retrospective exhbn. Camairoe, 1985; represented in permanent collections, Am. Mus. to Gt. Britain, U.S. Dept State, Lyndon Baines Johnson Meml. Library, Nat. Cowboy Hall of Fame, Wyo. State Mus., Whitney Mus. Western Art, Buffalo Bill Hist. Center, Plains Indian Mus., Amon Carter Mus., Willaroc Mus., Mont. Hist. Soc., others; commd. works include: mural, Fort Pitts Mus., Pitts., 10-foot Sacagawea polychrome bronze monument, Cen. Wyo. Coll., 1981, 21-foot monumental equestrian bronze, The Horseman, Gt. Western Fin. Corp., Beverly Hills, Calif., 1984, 10-foot patinaed Sacagawea, Sanata Barbara, Calif., 1985, Capezzano-Pianore, Camaiore, 1985; subject of books and catalogues. Served with USMC, 1942-45. Decorated Purple Heart with gold star; recipient gold medal Nat. Acad. Design, 1968, also Presdl. citation; Best Cover Art of 1969 award for sculpture of John Wayne Am. Inst. Graphic Arts, 1969; Presdl. citation R.I. Sch. Design; Fulbright grantee, 1954; 2 bronzes presented as official gifts of state by Pres. Ronald Reagan, 1982. Fellow Nat. Acad. Western Art; mem. Nat. Sculpture Soc. Address: PO Box 2836 Cody WY 82414 *

JACKSON, HOWARD WORDELL, electronics executive, consultant; b. Glendale, Calif., Mar. 2, 1931; s. Wordell Carter and Nannie Louise (Murrell) J.; m. Dorothy Marree Taylor, Nov. 7, 1953 (div.); children—Joyce, Janice, Braden, Brent; m. 2d, Constance Lee Jarrett, Aug. 18, 1979. B.S. in Physics, UCLA, 1953; M.B.A., U. Chgo., 1961; postgrad. Am. U., 1967-70. Commd. officer U.S. Air Force, 1953, advanced through grades to lt. col.; research physicist, research and devel. mgr./program dir. U.S. Air Force, 1953-74; ret., 1974; cons. research and devel. mgmt., Glendale, Calif., 1974-78; sr. program mgr. Allegheny Internat. Corp., Santa Ana, Calif., 1978-81; mgr. applied sci. dept. EG&G, Santa Barbara, Calif., 1981—; dir. DESA, Inc.; pres. Sci. and Engring. Council Santa Barbara, Inc. Mem. AIAA (assoc. fellow), Am. Nuclear Soc. Republican. Methodist. Club: Montecito Country. Patentee in fields of photography. electronics, instrumentation and nucleonics. Home: 498 Scenic Dr Santa Barbara CA 93103 Office: 130 Robin Hill Rd Goleta CA 93117

JACKSON, JANE WELLESLEY, interior designer; b. Asheville, N.C., Aug. 5, 1944; d. James and Willie Mae (Stoner) Harris; m. Bruce G. Jackson, Sept. 8, 1972; children: Yvette, Scott. Student, Boston U., 1964; BA, Leslie Coll., 1967; postgrad., Artisan Sch. Interior Design, 1980-82. Tchr. Montessori, Brookline, Mass., 1969-72; interior designer Nettle Creek Shops, Honolulu, 1980-82, owner, 1982—. Active Mayor's Com. for Small Bus., Honolulu, 1984. Mem. Am. Soc. Interior Design Industry Found. Democrat. Club: Honolulu. Office: Nettle Creek Shops 1221 Kapiolani Blvd Honolulu HI 96814

JACKSON, JOHN THADDIUS, JR., physicist; b. Oregon City, Oreg., Apr. 11, 1948; s. John Thaddius and Rosalie Mae (Piper) J.; m. Helen Louise Gibbons, Dec. 19, 1970 (div. 1973); one child, Stephanie Marie Ann; m. Rebecca Marie Bates, Feb. 14, 1984; children: Leroy, Michael. BS in Physics, Oreg. State U., 1974. Founder Jackson Research Inc., St. Paul, Oreg., 1980—; co-founder Synektron, Tigard, Oreg., 1982—; founder, dir. research Xenophon Inc., Newberg, Oreg., 1984—; cons. Astec Ltd., Santa Clara, Calif., 1984. Patentee in field. Mem. Soc. Mfg. Engrs., Am. Soc. Metals, AAAS, Math. Assn. Am. Avocations: fishing, photography, computers. Home and Office: Xenophon Inc 1978 NW Shattock Pl Corvallis OR 97330

JACKSON, KENNETH LEE, radiobiologist, educator; b. Berkeley, Calif., Jan. 6, 1926; s. Lee Albert and Marion Mildred (Willis) J.; m. Carmen Luisa Lopez, July 12, 1948; children: Kathryn, K. Robert, Martin, Anne. Student, Doane Coll., 1944, Calif. Inst. Tech., 1944-45; AB, U. Calif., Berkeley, 1949, PhD, 1954. Sr. investigator USN Radiol. Def. Lab., San Francisco, 1954-60; head Radiobiology Group Boeing Co., Seattle, 1960-63; prof. radiol. scis. U. Wash., Seattle, 1963—. Contbr. articles to sci. jours. Served to lt. USNR, 1944-45, 51-53. Nat. Cancer Inst. tng. and research grantee; U.S. Dept. Defense research contractor. Mem. Radiation Research Soc., Health Physics Soc., Am. Physiol. Soc., AAAS, Am. Pub. Health Assn., Am. Radio Relay League, Sigma Xi. Avocations: amateur radio, computers. Office: U Wash Radiol Scis SB-75 Seattle WA 98195

JACKSON, LEROY JOHN, city manager; b. Jan. 8, 1944; s. LeRoy M. and Dorothy M. (Albert) J.; m. Constance M. Bassett, Aug. 8, 1964; children—LeRoy, Rebecca, Ramone, Rishard, Rob-Roy, Ryan. B.A. in Polit. Sci. and Pub. Adminstrn., Calif. State U.-Long Beach, 1966. Personnel analyst City of Torrance, Calif., 1966-68, sr. adminstrv. asst., 1968-70, asst. to city mgr., 1970-78, chief asst. to city mgr., 1978-81, asst. city mgr., 1981-83, city mgr., 1983—. Mem. Internat. City Mgmt. Assn., Am. Soc. Pub. Adminstrn., Am. Arbitration Assn., South Bay City Mgrs. Assn. Office: 3031 Torrance Blvd Torrance CA 90503

JACKSON, LINDA ROSE, personnel executive; b. Newark, Oct. 18, 1947; d. Emil S. and Priscilla J. (Durocher) Morelli; B.A., Caldwell Coll., 1969; M.A., Fairleigh Dickinson U., 1972; m. Riley Venning Jackson III, Aug. 22, 1981. Mktg. coordinator Airtron Div. Litton Industries, Morris Plains, N.J., 1969-70; research asst. dept. neuropsychology N.J. Neuropsychiat. Inst., Princeton, 1970-72; asst. dir./counselor S.I. (N.Y.) Rehab. Center, United Cerebral Palsy of N.Y.C., 1972-75; asst. v.p., regional human resources dir. Corroon & Black, San Francisco, 1975—. Mem. Ins. Personnel Mgrs. Assn., Calif. Unemployment Ins. Council, No. Calif. Human Resources Council, San Francisco Employers Adv. Com.

JACKSON, LOIS KATHRYN, educational institution executive; b. Flint, Mich., July 31, 1927; d. Milo N. and Edith (Kelly) Wood; m. Warren G. Jackson, Oct. 27, 1945; children—Connie L., Edith A., Christine K. B.A. cum laude, Asbury Coll., 1956; student U. Coimbra, Lisbon, Portugal, 1957-59, Scarritt Coll., Vanderbilt U., 1956-57. Treas., cost acct. Mobil Home Co., 1948-52; missionary educator Bd. Global Ministries, United Meth. Ch., Angola, Zaire, 1959-77; adminstrv. asst. to supt. Navajo United Meth. Mission Sch., Farmington, N.Mex., 1978-81; bus. mgr. Navajo Mission Acad., Farmington, 1981—. Past chmn. program Council on Ministries United Meth. Ch. Mem. Nat. Assn. Female Execs., Am. Mgmt. Assn. Office: Navajo Mission Acad 1200 W Apache St Farmington NM 87401

JACKSON, (BEATRICE) MARION, advertising agency executive; b. Chgo., May 16, 1943; d. Roscoe and Marian Beatrice (Johnson) Lansdown; divorced; children: Albert John, Randal Keith. BA, U. Colo., Denver, 1979, postgrad., 1982-83. Communications cons. Mountain Bell, Denver, 1967-77; owner Floating Art Gallery, Denver, 1975-77; mgmt. analysis GAO, Denver, 1978-82; regional sales mgr. Southwestern Bell, Denver, 1983-85; prin., chief exec. officer B. Marion & Assocs. Inc., Denver, 1985—; co-sponsor advt. seminars with SBA, Denver, 1986. Author: (manual) The Ad Kit: A Solution to Small Business Advertising, 1986. Active Colorado Springs Human Relations Commn., 1972-74; del. Colo. Rep. Conv., Denver, 1986; bd. dirs. Martin Luther King Meml. Edn. Fund, Colorado Springs, 1972-74. Mem. Denver Advt. Fedn., Pro Denver, Urban League. Avocations: traveling, art collecting, raquetball. Office: B Marion & Assocs 2075 S University Blvd Suite D-103 Denver CO 80210

JACKSON, MELBOURNE LESLIE, chemical engineering educator and administrator, consultant; b. Wisdom, Mont., Sept. 27, 1915; s. James R. and Adeline (Mallon) J.; m. Elizabeth Clara Ford, Apr. 2, 1944; children: Gary Leslie, Linda Mary, Laurie Elizabeth, Nancy Ruth. BSChemE, Mont. State U., 1941, D in Engring. (hon.), 1980; PhDChemE, U. Minn., 1948. Registered profl. engr., Wash., Idaho. Instr. chem. engring. U. Minn., Mpls., 1944-48; from asst. prof. to assoc. prof. U. Colo., Boulder, 1948-50; head process devel. U.S. Naval Ordnance Test Sta., China Lake, Calif., 1950-53; prof. U. Idaho, Moscow, 1953-65, 70-80, head dept. chem. engring., 1953-65, dean grad. sch., 1965-70, dean Coll. Engring., 1973, 78-80, 83; cons. numerous corps. including FMC Corp., Crown Zellerbach, Research Corp.; pres. U. Idaho Fed. Credit Union, Moscow, 1972-74. Patentee aeration/flotation devices, 1978, 80; contbr. articles to profl. jours. Chmn. Idaho Air Pollution Control Commn., Boise, 1959-72; chmn., trustee Moscow Sch. Dist., 1957-63. Fellow Am. Inst. Chem. Engrs; mem. Am. Chem. Soc., Am. Soc. Engring. Edn., Sigma Xi. Methodist. Avocations: boating, photography. Home: 1422 Alpowa Moscow ID 83843 Office: U Idaho Dept Chem Engring Moscow ID 83843

JACKSON, MICHAEL DEAN, engineering consultant; b. San Francisco, May 31, 1947; s. Norman William and Hazel (Shelstad) J.; m. Linda Rae Cohen, July 27, 1967; children: Jeffrey Dennis, Marc Andrew. BSME, U. Calif., Berkeley, 1969, MSME, 1971. Staff engr. Acurex Corp., Mountain View, Calif., 1972-75; section leader Acurex Corp., Mountain View, 1975-77, dept. mgr., 1977-79, project mgr., 1979—. Contbr. articles to profl. jours. Mem. AAAS, Am. Soc. Mech. Engrs., Soc. Automotive Engrs. Home: 1822 Harris Ave San Jose CA 95124 Office: Acurex Corp 485 Clyde Ave Mountain View CA 94039

JACKSON, MICHAEL LEE, academic administrator; b. Los Angeles, June 28, 1950; s. Alfred Jackson and Marilyn (Ellis) Greene; m. Patricia Saidi, Nov. 30, 1985. Ab with distinction, Stanford U., 1972; MEd, U. Mass., 1974, EdD, 1976. Staff assoc. to vice chancellor U. Mass., Amherst, 1976-78; ednl. cons. Georgetown U./George Washington U., Washington, 1978-80; asst. dir. row and fraternities Stanford (Calif.) U., 1980-82, asst. dir. overseas studies, 1982-84, asst. to v.p. and provost, 1984—. Mem. Am. Assn. Higher Edn., Council Internat. Edn. Exchange, Nat. Assn. Fgn. Study Advisors, Nat. Alliance Black Sch. Educators. Mem. Baha'i Faith. Home: PO Box 6210 Stanford CA 94305 Office: Stanford U Provost Office Bldg 10 Stanford CA 94305

JACKSON, REGINALD MARTINEZ, baseball player; b. Wyncote, Pa., May 18, 1946; s. Martinez J.; m. Juanita. Student, Ariz. State U. Outfielder with Kansas City/Oakland Athletics, 1967-75, Balt. Orioles, 1976, N.Y. Yankees, 1977-81; outfielder, designated hitter Calif. Angels, 1982—; mem. Am. League All-Star Team, 1969, 71-75, 77-82, 84. Author: (with Bill Libby) Reggie, 1975, (with Joel Cohen) Inside Hitting, 1975. Named Most Valuable Player Am. League, 1973, The Sporting News Major League Player of Year, 1973; Named to The Sporting News Am. League All-Star Team, 1969, 73, 75, 76, 80. Office: California Angels Anaheim Stadium 200 State College Blvd Anaheim CA 92806 *

JACKSON, ROBERT EVANS, construction company executive, consultant; b. Los Angeles, Aug. 29, 1928; s. Curtis and Genevee (Evans) J.; m. Jacqueline Kuemmel, June 18, 1950; children: Karen, Susanne. BSE, U. So. Calif., 1953. V.p. engring. and mfg. Challenge Cook Bros., Industry, Calif., 1968-74, sr. v.p. engring., 1974-80, v.p. internat. engring., 1980-84; cons. in field Santa Ana, Calif., 1985—. Patentee in field. Served with USN, 1946-48. Mem. ASME. Republican. Presbyterian. Club: Balboa Bay (Newport, Calif.). Avocations: gardening, tennis, skiing. Office: 2664 Newport Blvd Suite 107 Costa Mesa CA 92627

JACKSON, ROBERT HAROLD, telecommunications consultant, educator; b. Petoskey, Mich., Aug. 5, 1956; s. Harold and Peggy Ann (Willson) J.; m. Georjean Evon Livingston, July 26, 1985; 1 child, Ashley Marie. BS, USAF Acad., 1978; MS, U. So. Calif., 1983. Commd. 2d lt. USAF, Washington, 1978, resigned, 1980; mem. profl. staff Computer Scis. Corp., Falls Church, Va., 1980-81, sr. mem. profl. staff, 1981-82; computer scientist Computer Scis. Corp., Colorado Springs, Colo., 1982-83; mgr. Contel Info. Systems, Colorado Springs, 1984-85, acting v.p., 1985, dir. programs, 1985-86; telecommunications ind. cons. Secure Communication Integration Services, Colorado Springs, 1987—. Asst. scout master Boy Scouts Am., Springfield, Va., 1979; jr. asst. scoutmaster, Boyne City, Mich., 1972-74. Mem. Armed Forces Communications Electronics Assn., Air Force Assn., Assn. Old Crows. Avocation: skiing. Home: 4965 Ramblewood Dr Colorado Springs CO 80918 Office: Secure Communication Integration Services 320 N Academy Blvd #202A Colorado Springs CO 80909

JACKSON, ROBERT JOHN, industrial engineer; b. Los Angeles, Dec. 24, 1922; s. John M. and Ona Blanche (Hill) J.; m. Ethel K. Beecher, Dec. 1, 1950; children: Kathryn, Bradley, Diane, Margaret, Shirley, Kelly, Riley. AA, Pasadena Coll., 1958. Supr. assembly dept. Lockheed Aircraft Co., Burbank, Calif., 1941-51; time standards engr. Bendix Pacific Co., North Hollywood, Calif., 1951-53; indsl. engr. Walsco Electronic Co., Los Angeles, 1953-55; methods and time standards engr. Lockheed-Calif. Co., Burbank, 1955-69, dir. hours rep., 1969—. Dir. Modal Investment Co., Eagle Rock, Calif., 1955-56. Served with AUS, 1944-46; PTO. Decorated Purple Heart with oak leaf cluster, Bronze Star, Silver Star. Mem. Am. Inst. Indsl. Engrs. Lodge: Masons. Home: 415 N Plymouth Blvd Los Angeles CA 90004 Office: Lockheed-Calif Co 2555 N Hollywood Way Burbank CA 91503

JACKSON, RUTHIE FAY, government official; b. Wynne, Ark., June 2, 1948; d. Tyree and Ruth (Perry) Weaver; AAS in Secretarial Sci., Seattle Community Coll., 1968; student U. Wash., 1971; m. Charles M. Jackson, July 6, 1974; children: Vanessa Marie, Casey Nathaniel. Receptionist Mobil Oil Corp., Seattle, 1969; clk., stenographer HEW (now Dept. Health and Human Services), Seattle, 1970-74, equal opportunity specialist, 1974-78, child support specialist, 1978-80, dep. regional rep. child support office, 1980-81, regional rep. Office Child Support Enforcement, Region X, Seattle, 1981—. Mem. Wash. Statewide Steering Com. on Adolescent Pregnancy Prevention, Pregnancy and Parenting. Recipient Commendations, Dept. HHS, 1978, Cert. of Merit, Dept. HHS, 1980, Spl. Achievement Cash awards Dept. HHS, 1980, 1984, Merit award Dept. HHS, 1985, 86, Performance cash awards Dept. HHS, 1981-87. Mem. Nat. Assn. Female Execs., Am. Soc. Pub. Adminstrs., Seattle Urban League, NAACP. Mem. Church of God in Christ. Home: 12734 SE 73d St Renton WA 98056 Office: 2901 3d Ave M/S 415 Seattle WA 98121

JACKSON, WHARTON, marketing executive; b. N.Y.C., Aug. 23, 1909; s. Tatlow and Laura Estelle (Wharton) J.; m. Lois Dorothy Dyal, July 6, 1935; children—Wharton, Jr., Edmond Tatlow, Ronald. Student, Rutgers U., 1931. With Ga. Kaolin Co., Elizabeth, N.J., 1931-35, research staff, 1936-41, prodn. staff, N.J., Ga., 1942-46, sales dir., Elizabeth, N.J., 1946-53; pres. Wharton Jackson Co., Los Angeles, 1953-60; exec. v.p. Harrisons & Crosfield, San Marino, Calif., 1960-80; pres. Wharton Jackson & Sons, Inc., Laguna Beach, Calif., 1980—; pres. Western Chem. Distbrs. Council, 1977-78. Mem. Am. Chem. Soc., Am. Ceramic Soc., TAPPI, Clay Minerals Soc., Assn. International Pour l'Etude des Argiles, Soc. Mining Engrs. of AIME, Nat. Assn. Chem. Distbrs. (dir. 1977-78). Republican. Presbyterian. Address: 46 Emerald Bay Laguna Beach CA 92651

JACKSON, WILLIAM LEE, political scientist; b. Kansas City, Mo., Nov. 27, 1946; s. Harold Lee and Elizabeth Ann (Tanner) J.; m. Carleen Marie Tapfer, July 12, 1969. BS in Polit. Sci., Wash. State U., 1968, MA in Polit. Sci., 1972; BA in Orginization Devel., The Evergreen State Coll., 1978. Fuel allocator Dept. Emergency Services, Tacoma, 1972; vet. rep. on campus U.S. VA, Seattle, 1973-78; vets. coordinator Evergreen State Coll., Olympia, Wash., 1978-82; pres. Action Research Assn., Tacoma, 1976—; v.p. Video Recounters Ltd., Tacoma, 1982—; instr. St. Martin's Coll., Lacey, Wash., 1976—. Mem. Pierce County Charter Rev. Commn., 1986—; active Downtown Tacoma Assn. Served as sgt. U.S. Army, 1968-70, Vietnam. Named Eagle Scout with God and Country award Boy Scouts Am. Mem. Vet. Program Adminstrs. of Wash. (bd. dirs. 1979-82), Nat. Assn. Concerned Vets. (bd. dirs. 1980-82), Nat. Assn. Vet. Program Adminstrs. (bd. dirs. 1980-82), Tacoma Pierce County C. of C., Lakewood C. of C. Republican. Presbyterian. Office: Video Recounters Ltd PO Box 97023 Tacoma WA 98497

JACKSON-WILLIAMS, MARY IRENE, educator; b. Hugo, Okla., June 30, 1944; d. Primer and Hylar B. (Tarkington) Jackson; B.Bus. Edn., Langston U., 1967; M.S. in Bus. Edn., Emporia State U., 1973; postgrad. U. Nev., 1975-77; m. Lee A. William, Feb. 10, 1973; 1 dau., Monica Ariane. Bus. instr. Spokane (Wash.) Community Coll., 1967-69; Topeka West High Sch., 1970-71, tchr. bus. Highland Park High Sch., Topeka, Kans., 1972-73; instr. Clark County Community Coll., North Las Vegas, Nev., 1973-78, dir. bus. div., 1978—; cons. Scott Foresman Pub. Co., 1977-80; condr. seminars for Las Vegas C. of C., 1980. Recipient Educator of Yr. award, Bus. and Service award for edn. Clark County Community Coll., 1986, 87. Mem. Am. Bus. Communication Assn., Nat. Bus. Edn. Assn., Am. Assn. Women in Community and Jr. Colls., Internat. Assn. Bus. Communicators, Am. Assn. Female Execs. Office: Clark County Community Coll 3200 E Cheyenne Ave North Las Vegas NV 89030

JACOB, MARY, nutritional biochemistry educator, researcher; b. Chngannur, Kerala, India, May 28, 1933; came to U.S., 1964; d. K. Chacko and Susannah (Ittyerah) J. BS, U. Madras, 1953, MS, 1958; MS, U. London, 1963; PhD, U. Ill., 1969. Lectr. Western Australian Inst. Tech., Perth, 1976-77; asst. prof. Ariz. State U., Tempe, 1977-80; assoc. prof. Calif. State U., Long Beach, 1980—; Speaker Orange County Nutrtion Council, Santa Ana, Calif., 1986. Contbr. numerous articles to profl. jours. Mem. N.Y. Acad. Scis., Internat. Assn. Bioinorganic Scientists, Am. Coll. Nutrition, AAAS, Gerontol. Soc. Am. Office: Calif State U Dept Home Econs 1250 Bellflower Rd Long Beach CA 90840

JACOB, MARY JANE, curator; b. N.Y.C., Jan. 5, 1952; d. Elmer J. and Catherine (Marino) J.; m. Russell L. Lewis. B.F.A., U. Fla., 1973; M.A. in Art History, U. Mich., 1976. Assoc. curator modern art Detroit Inst. of Arts, Mich., 1976-80; curator Mus. of Contemporary Art, Chgo., 1980-83, chief curator, 1983-87; chief curator Mus. Contemporary Art, Los Angeles, 1987—. Author numerous exhbn. catalogues; contbg. author: A Quite Revolution: British Sculpture Since 1965, 86, Jannis Kounellis, 1986, Gordon Matta-Clark, A Retrospective, 1985, The Woven and Graphic Art of Anni Albers, 1985, In the Mind's Eye: Dad and Surrealism, 1984, The Amazing Decade: Women and Performance Art 1970-1980, 1983; Magdalena Abakanowicz, 1982, The Rouge: The Image of Industry in Art of Charles Sheeler and Diego Rivera, 1978; contbr. articles and essays to profl. jours. Office: Mus of Contemporary Art 250 S Grand Ave Los Angeles CA 90012

JACOB, NANCY LOUISE, college dean; b. Berkeley, Calif., Jan. 15, 1943; d. Irvin Carl and Ruby (Roberts) Feustel; m. George B. Fotheringham, Dec. 22, 1972; 1 child, Randy. BA magna cum laude, U. Wash., 1967; PhD in Econs. magna cum laude, U. Calif., Irvine, 1970. Econ. analyst, summer research staff Ctr. for Naval Analysis, Arlington, Va., 1969, chmn. dept. fin., bus. econs. and quantitative methods, 1978-81; with Weyerhaeuser Co. Tacoma, 1963-65; mem. faculty U. Wash., Seattle, 1970—, dean Sch. and Grad. Sch. Bus. Adminstrn., 1981—, prof. fin., 1981—; trustee Coll. Retirement Equities Fund., N.Y., 1980—; dir. Puget Sound Power and Light Co., Bellevue, Wash., 1980—, Rainier Bancorp., Seattle, 1985—. Co-author: Basic: An Intro to Computer Programming Using Basic Language, 1979, Investments, 1984; contbr. articles to profl. jours. Bd. dirs. Pacific Coast Banking Sch., Seattle, 1981—, Jr. Achievement, Seattle, 1982-84, Wash. Council on Internat. Trade, Seattle, 1981—. Recipient Wall St Jour. Achievement award U. Wash., 1967; NDEA Title IV fellow, 1968-70. Mem. Am. Econ. Assn., Am. Fin. Assn. (bd. dirs. 1975-77), Western Fin. Assn. (bd. dirs. 1976-78), Seattle Soc. Fin. Analysts, Nat. League Am. Pen Women, Fin. Mgmt. Assn. (program com. 1977), Phi Beta Kappa, Alpha Kappa Psi. Club: Rainier, Washington Athletic, Columbia Tower (Seattle). Office: Univ Washington School Grad Bus Adminstrn DJ 10 Seattle WA 98195

JACOB, PEYTON, III, research chemist, scientific consultant; b. Ann Arbor, Mich., Sept. 23, 1947; s. Peyton, Jr., and Helena Caroline (Link) J. B.S. in Chemistry, U. Calif.-Davis, 1969; Ph.D. in Organic Chemistry, Purdue U., 1975. NIH postdoctoral fellow U. Calif., San Francisco, 1975-78, research chemist, 1978—; expert witness cases involving chemistry and toxicology, 1983, 84; cons. Nat. Ctr. Toxicol. Research, 1979. Author, co-author research articles in field. Allied Chem. Corp. fellow, 1973-74. Mem. Am. Chem. Soc. Democrat. Home: 3787 Highland Rd Lafayette CA 94549 Office: Bldg 100 Room 235 Univ Calif San Francisco Gen Hosp San Francisco CA 94110

JACOBS, ARTHUR DIETRICH, health services executive, educator; b. Bklyn., Feb. 4, 1933; s. Lambert Dietrich and Paula Sophia (Knissel) J.; m. Viva Jane Sims, Mar. 24, 1952; children: Archie (dec.), David L., Dwayne C., Dianna K. BBA, Ariz. State U., 1962, MBA, 1966. Enlisted USAF, 1951, commd. 2d lt., 1962, advanced through grades to maj., 1972, ret., 1973; indsl. engr. Motorola, Phoenix, 1973-74; mgmt. cons. state of Ariz., 1974-76; mgmt. cons. Productivity Internat., Tempe, Ariz., 1976-79; faculty assoc. Coll. Bus. Adminstrn., Ariz. State U., Tempe, 1977—; productivity advisor Scottsdale (Ariz.) Meml. Health Services Co., 1979-84. Bd. dirs. United Way of Tempe, 1979-85. Mem. Ariz. State U. Alumni Assn. (bd. dirs. 1973-79, pres. 1978-79), Inst. Indsl. Engrs. (pres. Central Ariz. chpt. 1984-85), Am. Soc. for Quality Control, Ops. Research Soc. Am., Sigma Iota Epsilon, Beta Gamma Sigma, Delta Sigma Pi. Club: Optimist (life) (Tempe). Contbr. articles to profl. jours.

JACOBS, BARBARA LEEDS, interior designer; b. Chgo., Oct. 5, 1941; d. Albert Joseph and Gertrude (Klein) Leeds; AA in Interior Design, West Valley Coll., 1978; m. Melvin Jacobs, June 16, 1933 (dec.); children: Jonathan, Matthew, Alexander. Pres., Barbara Jacobs Interior Design, Saratoga, Calif., 1978—. Mem. Am. Soc. Interior Designers (chpt. sec. 1983, chpt. pres. 1985, nat. bd. dirs. 1986-87), Jr. League San Jose. Office: 12340 Saratoga-Sunnyvale Rd Suite 2-3 Saratoga CA 95070

JACOBS, CARL DAVID, management consultant; b. Phila., Apr. 14, 1944; s. Leonard and Margery (Goldberg) J.; m. Francine Berger, Dec. 24, 1972; children—Bonnie Jean, Scott Andrew. B.S., U. Calif.-Berkeley, 1965; M.A., So. Methodist U., 1967. Project specialist Eastern Airlines, Miami, Fla., 1968-70; adminstrv. tng. RCA, Princeton, N.J., 1970-71; sr. mgmt. devel. specialist Xerox Corp., Rochester, N.Y., 1971-73; sr. prin. Hay Assocs., Los Angeles, 1973-78; dir. staff orgn. devel. Anheuser Busch Co., St. Louis, 1978-79; gen. mgr. Host Internat., Los Angeles, 1979-82; sr. v.p. human resources Sambos Restaurants, Carpinteria, Calif., 1982-83; v.p. mgmt. cons. div. Alexander and Alexander, Los Angeles, 1983-87; mgr. Sibson & Co., Los Angeles, 1987—; guest lectr. NYU, UCLA, U. Mo.; cons. in human resources. Bd. dirs. So. Calif. Counselling Ctr. HEW grantee, 1972. Mem. Am. Soc. Tng. and Devel., Am. Soc. Personnel Adminstrs. Club: Kiwanis. Contbg. author: Work in America, 1972; Quality of Working Life, 1975; contbr. articles to profl. jours. Office: Sibson & Co 2029 Century Park East Los Angeles CA 90067

JACOBS, CAROL A., civic worker; b. Bemidji, Minn., Apr. 4, 1944; d. Russell W. and Marjory A. (Whitney) B.; m. James J. Jacobs, June 18, 1965; children: Teresa Jean, Dennis Scott. AA, Fergus Falls Community Coll., 1964; BS, U. Wyo., 1986. Mem. ad hoc com. Luth. Social Ministry, also other ch. activites; club leader 4-H, project leader, council mem., judge of record books, 1977-82; active Concerned Parents Action Team, 1984; counselor Crisis Pregnancy Ctr., 1985; vol. S.A.F.E. Hotline, 1984—; foster parent. Mem. Nat. Assn. Social Workers, Assn. Student Social Workers, Phi Kappa Phi. Republican. Lutheran.

JACOBS, DIANA PIETROCARLI, botanical illustrator; b. Glen Cove, N.Y., Aug. 22, 1950; d. Frank and Elizabeth (Ranaldo) Pietrocarli; m. David Jacobs, Feb. 12, 1977; children—Aaron Michael, Molly Sarah. B.A., U. Pitts., 1971. Cert. bot. and zool. illustrator, Los Angeles County Mus. Comml. artist agt. Mary Louise Flock Assn., N.Y.C., 1971-74; free lance illustrator, painter, Los Angeles, 1976—; bot. illustrator Huntington Bot. Gardens, San Marino, Calif., 1981—; instr. Otis Parsons Sch. Design, 1985-86; v.p. Roundelay Prodns., 1977—. Illustrator: Celebrating the Wild Mushroom, 1986. Bd. dirs. Los Angeles County Mus. Natural Hist. Alliance.

JACOBS, EDWIN MAX, oncologist, consultant; b. San Francisco, Sept. 9, 1925; s. Edwin Manheim and Floy (Sommer) J. BA, Reed Coll., 1950; MD, Cornell U., 1954. Intern Bellevue Hosp., N.Y.C., 1954-55, resident, 1956-57; resident Meml. Sloan-Kettering Cancer Ctr., N.Y.C., 1955-56, fellow in oncology, 1957-59; instr. medicine U. Calif., San Francisco, 1960-63, head clin. cancer research, 1960-76, asst. prof., 1963-69, assoc. clin. prof., 1969-76; assoc. chief clin. investigations br. Nat. Cancer Inst., Bethesda, Md., 1976-85; assoc. exec. officer No. Calif. Oncology Group, Palo Alto, Calif., 1985—; clin. prof. medicine Cancer Research Inst. U. Calif., San Francisco, 1987—; vis. physician Royal Marsden Hosp., London, 1970; cons. Monsanto Chem. Co., St. Louis, 1985—, G.D. Searle Co., Skokie, Ill., 1985—. Contbr. articles on testicular cancer to med. jours. Bd. dirs. San Francisco Symphony Found., 1968-76. Served with U.S. Army, 1944-46, ETO, PTO. Squibb-Olin fellow Meml. Sloan-Kettering Cancer Ctr., 1965; recipient Spl. Achievment award NIH, 1983. Fellow ACP; mem. AMA (Recognition award 1985—), Am. Soc. Hematology (neoplasia com. 1978-81), Am. Assn. Cancer Research, Am. Soc. Clin. Oncology, Soc. Surg. Oncology, Am. Radium Soc. (v.p. 1978-79), San Francisco Mus.'s Soc. Avocations: music, literature. Home: 1860 16th Ave San Francisco CA 94122 Office: No Calif Cancer Program 1301 Shoreway Rd Suite 425 Belmont CA 94002

JACOBS, HOLLIE KAE, chemistry educator; b. Dubuque, Oct. 27, 1962; d. Murray A. and Barbara K. (Warren) Kugler; m. John E., Jacobs, July 3, 1982. BS, N.Mex. State U., 1984, MS, 1986. Teaching asst. N.Mex. State U., Las Cruces, 1984-86, instr., 1986—, research asst., 1987—; summer intern NASA, Las Cruces, 1985. Recipient Justine Gentle award for Service, 1983—. Mem. Am. Chem. Soc. Avocations: sailing, camping, cooking.

JACOBS, JOSEPH JOHN, engineering company executive; b. June 13, 1916; s. Joseph and Afiffie (Forzley) J.; m. Violet Jabara, June 14, 1942; children: Margaret, Linda, Valerie. B.S. in Chem. Enging, Poly. Inst. N.Y., Bklyn., 1937, M.S., 1939, Ph.D., 1942. Registered profl. engr., N.Y., N.J., La., Calif. Chem. engr. Autoxygen, Inc., N.Y.C., 1939-42; sr. chem. engr. Merck & Co., Rahway, N.J., 1942-44; v.p., tech. dir. Chemurgic Corp., Richmond, Calif., 1944-47; pres. Jacobs Engring. Co., Pasadena, Calif., 1947-74; chmn. bd., chief exec. officer Jacobs Engring. Group, Inc., Pasadena, 1974—. Contbr. tech. articles to profl. jours. Area bd. dirs. United Way, 1978—; chmn. bd. trustees Poly. Univ. N.Y.; trustee Harvey Mudd Coll.; mem. Assocs. Calif. Inst. Tech.; bd. dirs. Genetics Inst., Inst. Contemporary Studies, Calif. Round Table. Recipient Herbert Hoover medal United Engring. Socs., 1983. Fellow Am. Inst. Chem. Engrs., Am. Inst. Chemists, Inst. for Advancement Engring.; mem. Am. Chem. Soc., AAAS, Los Angeles C. of C., Pasadena C. of C., Sigma Xi, Phi Lambda Upsilon. Clubs: Altadena Town and Country, California, Annandale Golf, Pauma Valley Country; Union League (N.Y.C.); Union League (San Francisco). Office: 251 S Lake Ave Pasadena CA 91101

JACOBS, KENT FREDERICK, physician, dermatologist; b. El Paso, Tex., Feb. 13, 1938; s. Carl Frederick and Mercedes D. (Johns) J.; m. Sallie Ritter, Apr. 13, 1971. BS, N.Mex. State U., 1960; MD, Northwestern U., 1964; postgrad., U. Colo., 1967-70. Diplomate Acad. Dermatology. Dir. service unit USPHS, Laguna, N.Mex., 1966-67; pvt. practice specializing in dematology Las Cruces, N.Mex., 1970—; cons. U.S. Army, San Francisco, 1968-70, cons. NIH, Washington, 1983, Holloman AFB, 1972-77; research assoc. VA Hosp., Denver, 1969-70; preceptor U. Tex., Galveston, 1976-77; mem. clin. staff Tex. Tech U., Lubbock, 1977—; asst. clin. prof. U. N.Mex., Albuquerque, 1972—. Contbr. articles to profl. jours. Served to lt. commdr. USCG, 1965-68. Invitational scholar Oreg. Primate Ctr., 1968; Acad. Dermatology Found. fellow, 1969; named Disting. Alumnus N.Mex. State U., 1985. Fellow Am. Acad. Dermatology, Royal Soc. Medicine, Soc. Investigative Dermatology; mem. AMA, Fedn. State Med. Bds. (bd. dirs. 1984—), N.Mex. Med. Soc., N.Mex. Bd. Med. Examiners (pres. 1983-84), N.Mex. State U. Alumni Assn. (bd. dirs. 1975—), Phi Beta Kappa, Beta Beta Beta. Republican. Presbyterian. Club: Mil Gracias (pres. 1972-74). Lodge: Rotary. Home: 3610 Southwind Rd Las Cruces NM 88005 Office: 2930 Hillrise Suite 6 Las Cruces NM 88001

JACOBS, LAURENCE WILE, marketing educator; b. Cin., May 26, 1939; s. Arthur Leonard and Josephine (Yuster) J.; m. Susan Stone, Aug. 1, 1965; children: Andrew Wile, Julie Bridget. BS, U. Pa., 1961; MBA, Ohio State U., 1963, PhD, 1966. Mgmt. trainee F&R Lazarus Co., Columbus, Ohio, 1961-62; research assoc. Mktg. Sci. Inst., Phila., 1965-66; asst. prof. mktg. U. Hawaii, Honolulu, 1966-69, assoc. prof., 1969-73, prof. mktg., 1973—. Author: Advertising and Promotion for Retailing, 1972; computer mgmt. game TIMSIM, 1967. Mem. Am. Mktg. Assn. (pres. 1970-71). Home: 1474 Kamole St Honolulu HI 96821 Office: U Hawaii 2404 Maile Way Honolulu HI 96822

JACOBS, LEO HERMAN, real estate investor; b. Des Moines, Nov. 19, 1902; s. Moses and Elizabeth Clara (Byoir) J. Student U. Iowa, 1921-24, U. Calif. So. Branch (now UCLA), 1924-25; A.B., U. So. Calif., 1926. Real estate salesman, 1926-27; pres., dir. Am. Gear and Parts Co., Ltd., San Francisco, 1928-34; owner, mgr. Advance Co., 1935—, bldg. contractor, 1935-75; pres., dir. Laurel Valley Devel. Co., Dallas, 1960-82. Worker, Pres. Birthday Ball, N.Y.C., 1935. Mem. Presidents Club, Old Gold Capital Club, U. Iowa Found., Phi Epsilon Pi. Lodges: Masons (Fifty Yr. award), Shriners.

JACOBS, RICHARD CHARLES, educator; b. Los Angeles, Jan. 26, 1934; s. Alfred Fallek and Cecelia Margaret (Schaffer) J.; m. Judith Claire Rowland, Nov. 21, 1972; children: Scott Andrew, Sean Sebastian. BS, Calif. State U., Los Angeles, 1959, MA, 1965; PhD, Claremont Grad. Sch., 1976. Art history educator Los Angeles Sch. Dist., 1960-69; art., social sci. educator Duarte (Calif.) Sch. Dist., 1969-72; multicultural coordinator La Verne (Calif.) U., 1973-76; prof. history Calif. Poly. U., Pomona, 1976—, coordinator interdisciplinary gen. edn. program, 1984—; lectr. in field. Mem. Sociol. Edn. Assn., Meilkejohn Found., Assn. Integrative Studies, Higher Edn. Found., Soc. Research in Higher Edn. Avocations: gardening. Home: 2121 E Duell St Glendora CA 91740 Office: Calif State Poly U 3801 W Temple Ave Pomona CA 91768

JACOBS, TERI GOULD, speech pathologist, educator; b. N.Y.C., Sept. 10, 1946; d. Jack and Roslyn (Menyuk) Gould; m. B. Randall Jacobs, July 4, 1976; 1 child, Jillian Gould. BS, NYU, 1968; MA in Speech Pathology, Calif. State U., Los Angeles, 1976, MA in Edn. Adminstrn., 1983; PhD, U. So. Calif., 1981. Lic. speech pathologist, Calif., 1976. Aphasia specialist Los Angeles County Supt. Schs., 1976—; speech pathologist El Rancho Unified Sch. Dist., Pico Rivera, Calif., 1976-77, Childrens Speech and Hearing Ctr., Van Nuys, Calif., 1978; pvt. practice speech pathology Santa Monica, Calif., 1978—; spl. edn. cons. 1981—; asst. prof. Calif. State U., Los Dept. Elem. Edn., 1985—; founding v.p. Los Angeles Chpt. Nat. Stuttering Project 1978. Author: A Parent's Guide to Hearing Under Public Law 94-141: The Education of All Handicapped Children Act, 1978. Bur. Edn. traineeship, 1978-80. Mem. Am. Speech Lang. Hearing Assn. (speaker San Francisco nat. conv. 1984), Council for Exceptional Children, Nat. Stuttering Project, Mensa. Home: 2309 Ocean Pk Blvd Santa Monica CA 90405-5199 Office: 2309 Ocean Park Blvd Santa Monica CA 90405-5199

JACOBSEN, KIM, publisher; b. Escanaba, Mich., Nov. 19, 1933; s. Arthur and Charlotte (Smith) J. BS, Mich. State Normal Coll., Ypsilanti, 1955. Tchr. Detroit Pub. Schs., 1957-58; tech. writer engring. firms, Mich., 1958-60; writer Hawaii Bus. Pub. Corp., Honolulu, 1960-62, editor, 1962-68, pub., 1968—. Dir. Hawaiian joint council econ. edn., 1985—; v. chmn. citizens adv. com. Oahu Transp. study; dir. Honolulu Community Theater, 1980-86. Served with U.S. Army, 1955-57. Mem. Travel and Tourism Research Assn. (v.p. Hawaiian chpt. 1984—), Japanese C. of C. (dir. 1984—), Ala Moana Jr. C. of C. (charter mem.), Assn. Area Bus. Pubs. (founder 1976—), Hawaiian Pubs. Assn. (pres. 1979-80), Hawaii Visitors Bureau, Hawaii Hotel Assn. Avocations: skiing, running. Office: Hawaii Bus Pub Corp 825 Keeaumoku St Honolulu HI 96808

JACOBSEN, LAREN, systems analyst; b. Salt Lake City, June 15, 1937; s. Joseph Smith and Marian (Thomas) J.; B.S., U. Utah, 1963; m. Audrey Bartlett, July 29, 1970 (div.); children—Andrea, Cecily, Julian. Programmer, IBM Corp., 1963-70; systems programmer Xerox Computer Services, 1970-79; sr. systems analyst Quotron Systems, Los Angeles, 1979-86; sr. systems analyst High Tech. Software Ventures, 1986—; pres. Prescient Investments

Co., 1975-82. Served with USAR, 1961. Mem. Am. Guild Organists (dean San Jose chpt. 1967), Mensa. Home: PO Box 91174 Los Angeles CA 90009 Office: 14755 Ventura Blvd Suite 1-874 Sherman Oaks CA 91403

JACOBSEN, RICHARD T., mechanical engineering educator, thermodynamics researcher; b. Pocatello, Idaho, Nov. 12, 1941; s. Thorleif and Edith Emily (Gladwin) J.; m. Vicki Belle Hopkins, July 16, 1959 (div. Mar. 1973); children: Pamela Sue, Richard T., Eric Ernest; m. Bonnie Lee Stewart, Oct. 19, 1973; 1 son, Jay Michael; 1 Stepson, Erik David Lustig. B.S.M.E., U. Idaho, 1963, M.S.M.E., 1965; Ph.D. in Engring. Sci., Wash. State U., 1972. Registered profl. engr., Idaho. Instr. U. Idaho, 1964-66, asst. prof. mech. engring., 1966-72, assoc. prof., 1972-77, prof., 1977—, chmn. dept. mech. engring., 1980-85, assoc. dean engring., 1985—, assoc. dir. Ctr. for Applied Thermodynamic Studies, 1975-86, dir., 1986—. Author: Nitrogen-International Thermodynamic Tables of the Fluid State-6, 1979; numerous reports on thermodynamic properties of fluids, 1971—; contbr. articles to profl. jours. NSF sci. faculty fellow, 1968-69; NSF research and travel grantee, 1976-83; Nat. Bur. Standards grantee, 1974-86. Mem. ASME (faculty advisor 1972-75, 78-84, chmn. region VIII dept. heads com. 1983-85, honors and awards chmn. 1985—, K-7 tech. com. thermophys. properties 1985—, chmn. 1986—), Soc. Automotive Engrs. (Ralph R. Teetor Edn. award, Detroit 1968), ASHRAE (co-recipient Best Tech. Paper award 1984), Sigma Xi, Tau Beta Pi. Mormon. Office: U Idaho Office of Dean Coll Engring Janssen Engring Bldg 125 Moscow ID 83843

JACOBSEN, ROBERT ALLEN, civil engineer; b. Cloquet, Minn., Feb. 4, 1931; s. Magnus and Gunhild Lynn (Johnson) J.; m. Darlene Joan Jacobsen, July 28, 1956; children: Richard A., Robert J., Ronald B., Julie L. BCE, U. Minn., 1964. Registered profl. civil engineer, Calif., Nev., Minn., Mich., Wis. Chief bridge instr. Minn. Hwy. Dept., St. Paul, 1959-63; structural engr. Weyerhaeuser & Co., St. Paul, 1962-63, Durox Mgmt. Co., Lake Elmo, Minn., 1963-64; civil and structural engr. Green Giant Co., Le Sueur, Minn., 1964-69; chief civil and project engr. E&J Gallo Winery, Modesto, Calif., 1969-71; ptnr., cons. engr. Morgan & Jacobsen, Modesto, 1971-77; prin., cons. engr. Robert Jacobsen & Assocs., Inc., Modesto, 1977-84; v.p., cons. engr. Morton Techs., Inc., Santa Rosa, Calif., 1984-86; prin. Robert Jacobsen & Assocs., Inc., Healdsburg, Calif., 1986—. Served as cpl. USMC, 1951-52. Mem. Am. Concrete Inst., Contrn. Specification Inst. (bd. dirs. 1986—), Structural Engrs. of No. Calif. Republican. Presbyterian. Avocations: landscaping, woodwork, tennis, golf, spectator sports. Home and Office: 919 Vista Via Dr Healdsburg CA 95448

JACOBSEN, THOMAS HAROLD, genealogist; b. Ballerup, Denmark, Aug. 12, 1918; s. Anders and Anna E. M. (Sorenson) J.; brought to U.S., 1929, naturalized by Act of Congress; student U. Utah; m. Erika Elfriede Seiter, Jan. 31, 1940; children—Carma Erika, Kathryn Irene, Connie Leah, Harold Andrew. Coordinator records div. Geneal. Soc., Salt Lake City, 1936-51, coordinator microfilm div., 1951-61, asst. treas., 1956-61; Utah State archivist, records adminstr., 1963-83. Served with AUS, 1944-48, maj. Res. ret. Fellow Assn. Info. and Image Mgmt.; mem. Nat. Rifle Assn., Utah Hist. Soc. Inventor microfilm accessories, archival table. Author: Ancestry of Carma Erika Jacobsen, 1943, 44; Genealogical Lesson Plans, 3 vols., 1954; Manual to Microfilming, 1959; Microfilming in the State of Utah, 1964; Guide to Official Records of Genealogical Value in the State of Utah, 1980. Contbr. articles on archives, geneology, law to publs. Home: 196 W 2900 S Bountiful UT 84010

JACOBSON, ALBERT HERMAN, JR., industrial and systems engineer; b. St. Paul, Oct. 27, 1917; s. Albert Herman and Gertrude (Anderson) J.; m. Elaine Virginia Swanson, June 10, 1960; children: Keith, Paul. BS, Yale U., 1939; SM, MIT, 1952; MS, U. Rochester, 1954; PhD, Stanford U., 1976. Registered profl. engr., Calif. Personnel asst. Yale U., New Haven, 1939-40; indsl. engr. Radio Corp. Am., Camden, N.J., 1940-43; chief engr. Naval Ordnance Office, Rochester, N.Y., 1946-57; staff engr. Eastman Kodak Co., Rochester, 1957-59; assoc. dean Coll. Engring. and Architecture Pa. State U., Univ. Park, 1959-61; pres. Knapic Electro-Physics Inc., Palo Alto, Calif., 1961-62; prof. sch. engring. San Jose State U., 1962—, co-founder, coordinator cybernetic systems grad. program, 1968—; cons. in field, Calif., Ariz., Ill., 1962—. Author: Military and Civilian Personnel in Naval Administration, 1952, Railroad Consolidations and Transportation Policy, 1975; editor: Design and Engineering of Production Systems, 1984. Chmn. Personnel Commn. City of Mountain View, 1958-68; scoutmaster, Stanford Area Council Boy Scouts of Am., Palo Alto, 1970-83, council mem. Served to lt. comdr. USNR, 1943-46. Fellow in exec. devel. Alfred P. Sloan, MIT, 1951-52, NSF, Stanford, 1965-66; recipient Award of Merit Stanford Council Boy Scouts, 1976. Mem. Am. Soc. Engring. Edn., Inst. Indsl. Engrs., Am. Prodn and Inventory Control Soc. (bd. dirs. 1975—), Sigma Xi, Tau Beta Pi. Lutheran. Avocations: music, swimming, tennis, skiing, photography. Home: 1864 Lime Tree Ln Mountain View CA 94040 Office: San Jose State U Sch Engring 1 Washington Sq San Jose CA 95192

JACOBSON, DONALD THOMAS, mgmt. cons.; b. Powers Lake, N.D., June 5, 1932; s. Martin I. and Gladys E. (Thronson) J.; B.A., Whitman Coll., 1954; M.B.A., Stanford U., 1956; m. Andrea Marie Moore, Aug. 14, 1954; 1 dau., Kathryn E. Hanson. Sales and mktg. mgmt. Guy F. Atkinson Co., Portland, Oreg., 1959-63; sales control mgr. Boise Cascade Corp., Portland, 1964-66; v.p. and dir. research Lund, McCutcheon, Jacobson, Inc., Portland, 1966-74; pres. Mgmt./Mktg. Assocs., Inc., Portland, 1974—; chmn. Oreg. Bus. Workshops, 1974-76; exec. com., dir. Full-Circle, Inc., 1971-77. Served to lt. U.S. Army, 1956-59. Decorated commendation ribbon; recipient Oreg. Econ. Devel. award, 1973; Cert. Mgmt. Cons. Mem. Am. Mktg. Assn. (pres. Oreg. chpt. 1972-73), Am. Mgmt. Assn., Inst. Mgmt. Consultants (cert.; founding mem., pres. Pacific N.W. chpt. 1980-81), Mktg. Research Assn., Nat. Assn. Bus. Economists, Portland C. of C. (bd. dirs. 1987—), Met. Chambers Econ. Devel. Council Portland Area (chmn. mktg. task force 1983-85, chmn. Tri-Met Task Force 1985—, chmn. transpn. com. 1987—, bd. dirs. 1987—), The Planning Forum (v.p. Oreg. chpt. 1986-87), U.S. Dept. Commerce Nat. Def. Exec. Res. (chmn. Oreg.-Idaho assn. 1969-70), Oregonians for Cost-Effective Govt. (bd. dirs. 1986—), Whitman Coll. Alumni Assn. (pres. 1975-77), Stanford U. Bus. Sch. Assn. (pres. Oreg. chpt. 1971-72), Phi Beta Kappa. Republican. Lutheran. Club: University (Portland). Contbr. articles on mgmt. and mktg. to profl. jours. Home: 2580 SW Buckingham Ave Portland OR 97201 Office: Mgmt/Mktg Assocs Inc 707 SW Washington Portland OR 97205

JACOBSON, GARY CHARLES, political science educator; b. Orange, Calif., July 7, 1944; s. Charles William and Ruth Hope (Brown) J.; m. Martha Ellen Blake, June 2, 1979. A.B. in Polit. Sci., Stanford U., 1966; M.Phil., Yale U., 1969, Ph.D. in Polit. Sci., 1972. From instr. to assoc. prof. Trinity Coll., Hartford, Conn., 1970-79; from assoc. prof. to prof. polit. sci. U. Calif.-San Diego, 1979—. Woodrow Wilson fellow, 1969; NSF grantee, 1980-82. Mem. Am. Polit. Sci. Assn. (Gladys E. Kammerer award 1981), Western Polit. Sci. Assn., Midwest Polit. Sci. Assn., So. Polit. Sci. Assn. Author: Money in Congressional Elections, 1980; (with Samuel Kernell) Strategy and Choice in Congressional Elections, 1981; The Politics of Congressional Elections, 1983. Office: Dept Polit Sci Q-060 U Calif San Diego La Jolla CA 92093

JACOBSON, JON STANLEY, history educator; b. Oxnard, Calif., Feb. 12, 1938; s. Stanley Joel and Niona Elizabeth (Lindquist) J.; m. Sybil Lease Haight, Dec. 29, 1960 (div. Mar. 1984); children: Kirsten, Margreta. BA, U. Calif., Berkeley, 1959, MA, 1960, PhD, 1965. Asst. prof. history U. Calif., Irvine, 1965-72, assoc. prof., 1972—. Author: Locarno Diplomacy, 1972; contbr. articles to profl. jours. Recipient George Louis Beer prize Am. Hist. Assn., 1972. Office: U Calif Dept History Irvine CA 92717

JACOBSON, RONALD JOEL, lawyer, artist, b. Chgo., May 17, 1948; s. Abraham and Julia E. (Lazarus) J. B.A., U. So. Calif., 1970, J.D., UCLA; postgrad. Otis Art Inst., Los Angeles, 1970-71, 76-78. Bar: Calif. 1973. Assoc. counsel Bank of Am., Los Angeles, 1974-78, Paramount Pictures Corp., Los Angeles, 1979-81; counsel Filmways, Inc., Los Angeles, 1981; sr. assoc. Stein & Kahan, Santa Monica, Calif., 1982; of counsel Katsky, Ker & Hunt, Los Angeles, 1982-83, sr. atty. Paramount Pictures Corp., Los Angeles, 1983-86; v.p. bus. affairs, 1986—. One man shows: COR Gallery, Los Angeles, 1978, Knights, Ltd., Beverly Hills, Calif., 1979, Ross Lawrence Silver Gallery, Los Angeles, 1981; group shows include: Fisher Gallery, Los Angeles, Gallery Plus, Los Angeles, 1976, Los Angeles County Mus. Sci. and Industry, 1979, Form and Function Gallery, Atlanta, 1983, Westbroadway Gallery, N.Y.C., 1984. Bd. govs. Mcpl. Elections Com. of Los Angeles. Mem. Calif. State Bar. Democrat. Jewish. Club: West Hollywood Athletic. Contbr. articles to legal jours. Office: Paramount Pictures Corp 5555 Melrose Ave Los Angeles CA 90038

JACOBSON, RONALD KEITH, mental health center executive; b. Ashland, Wis., Jan. 25, 1932; s. Albert and Madeline (Bergren) J.; m. Lorraine Gertrude Tollefson, Aug. 3, 1957; children: Steven Carl, Todd David. BA, Augsburg Coll., 1959; MSW, U. Minn., 1961. Program dir. Luth. Social Services, Wittenberg, Wis., 1961-67; interim dir. Mental Health Services, Everett, Wash., 1973-74, 1979; area dir. Luth. Social Services, Seattle, 1974-75, 1984-85; exec. dir. Luth. Child Ctr., Everett, Wash., 1967—; pres. Assn. Child Care Agy., Wash. 1971-75; chmn. Licensing task force, Wash., 1980-81; mem. council on accreditation, N.Y.C., 1982-86; v.p. coalition of execs., 1983—. Pres. Drug Abuse Council, Everett, 1969-70; chmn. Snohomish County (Wash.) Internat. Yr. Child, 1979; mem. Am. Luth. Ch. Council, Mpls., 1984-86; mem. bd. for women Evangelical Lutheran Ch. in Am., 1988—. Mem. Alliance for Children Youth and Families (bd. dirs. 1984-86). Lodge: Rotary (pres. 1980-81). Home: 13228 Marine Dr Marysville WA 98270 Office: Luth Child Ctr 4526 Federal Everett WA 98203

JACOBSON, SHELDON ALBERT, physician, pathologist; b. N.Y.C., June 25, 1903; s. Albert Edward and Rosalie Heniette (Hartogensiss) J.; m. Annette Chesin, May 4, 1939; children: Eric Sheldon, Ira Sheldon, Ruth Anne. AB, CCNY, 1922; MD, Yale U., 1928. Diplomate Am. Bd. Pathology. Resident in pathology Montefiore Hosp., N.Y.C., 1928-30; fellow Hamburg & Oresden, Republic of Germany, 1930-31; asst. pathologist Hosp. for Joint Diseases, N.Y.C., 1931-36; pathologist Crown Heights Hosp., Bklyn., 1936-40; pathologist U.S. VA Hosp., Wichita, Kans., 1946-49, Vancouver, Wash., 1949-72; clin. prof. pathology, dir. bone tumor dept. U. Oreg. Med. Sch., Portland, 1950-84. Author: Comparative Pathology of the Tumors of Bone, 1971, (novel) Fleet Surgeon to Phareoh, 1971, (novel) The Man Who Moved the World, 1980. Served to capt. USNR, 1940-46. Recipient Gold medal Am. Acad. Orthopedic Surgeons, 1934. Mem. Am. Soc. Clin. Paths (Bronze award 1969), Am. Assn. Pathologists, Coll. Am. Pathologists (Bronze award), Internat. Acad. Pathology, Pan-Am. Assn. Pathology, Pacific N.W. Soc. Orthopaedics (hon.), Alpha Omega Alpha, Sigma X. Jewish. Club: Optimists. Avocation: sailing boats. Home: 5535 E Evergreen Blvd Apt 7406 Vancouver WA 98661

JACOBSON, VICTORIA TATNALL, architect; b. Wilmington, Del., Mar. 28, 1946; d. Alan Stephen and Gertrude (Tatnall) J.; 1 child, Frances Alanna White. Student, Colo. Coll., 1963-64; BA with honors, Portland State U., 1975; MArch, U. N.Mex., 1982. Apprentice architect DMJM Philips Reister Haley Inc., Denver, 1982-83, John Gargano, Denver, 1984, Anderson Mason Dale, Denver, 1984—; mem. design rev. com. Historic Denver, 1982-83. Prin. works include book illustrations The Sunspace Primer, 1984, Starting a Passive Solar Retrofit Program, 1982, The Old House Workbook, 1980. Mem. AIA (assoc., Colo. assoc. dir. 1985-86, John Heimrich Meml. scholar Albuquerque chpt. 1981), Colo. Women in Architure(sec. 1985-86, newsletter editor 1982-83). Avocations: skiing, hiking, bicycling.

JACOBY, J. MICHAEL, architect; b. Moscow, Idaho, Dec. 19, 1937; s. Glenn J. and Dorothy (Fredrickson) J.; m. Betty Carroll Boyd, July 9, 1966; children: John Michael, Christopher James. BArch, U. Oreg., 1963. Draftsman Wheeler & Lewis Architects, Denver, 1966-69; architect Muchow Assocs. Architects, Denver, 1969-78; architect, prin. W.C. Muchow and Ptnrs. Inc., Denver, 1978—; mem. Colo. State Bd. of Exam. of Architects, Colo., 1984—, pres. 1987. Prin. works include Park Cen. Bldg., Denver (AIA Nat. Honor award 1975), Dravo Corp. bldg., Denver (Western Mountain Region Design award 1977), U. Wyo. Cen. Energy Plant (Western Mountain Region Honor award 1983), Laramie, Wyo., Eagle County Justice Ctr. (AIA Colo. Honor award 1986), Eagle, Colo. Bd. dirs. Colo. Philharm. Orch., Evergreen, 1980-83, 84-87. Served to capt. U.S. Army, 1964-72. Mem. AIA (bd. dirs. Denver chpt. 1983-84, v.p. Denver chpt. 1984-85). Republican. Club: Hiwan Golf (Evergreen). Avocations: skiing, golf, scuba diving, gardening, photography. Home: 239 Columbine Ln Evergreen CO 80439

JACOBY, JEROME JESS, mechanical engineer; b. Portland, Oreg., Apr. 30, 1940; s. John and Laberta June (Woodle) J.; m. Sarah C. Busse, Dec. 27, 1962 (dec. Oct. 1973); m. Antoinette Beauchamp, Oct. 17, 1977 (div. May 1983). BS, Oreg. State U., 1962, Oreg. State U., 1966; MS, Oreg. State U., 1968. Computational physicist, applications programmer Los Alamos Nat. Lab., N. Mex., 1968—. Sec. Santa Fe Opera Guild, 1976-78; treas. Los Alamos Concert Assn., 1984-86. Served to capt. U.S. Army, 1962-64. Mem. AAAS, Am. Nuclear Soc., ASME (affiliate). Libertarian. Club: Los Alamos Chess (bd. dirs. 1985—). Avocations: chess, gardening, reading. Home: 955 49th St Los Alamos NM 87544 Office: Los Alamos Nat Lab Group X-7 Mail Stop B257 Los Alamos NM 87545

JACOBY, LEONARD DAVID, lawyer; b. Lorain, Ohio, Mar. 27, 1942; s. Nathan and Florence (Glasser) J.; m. Barbara Rood, Jan. 24, 1966 (div.); one child, Sharre; m. Nancy Platt, Apr. 22, 1979; stepchildren: Laurie, Lindsey. Student, U. Calif., Berkeley, 1960-61; AB with honors, UCLA, 1964, JD, 1967. Bar: Calif., 1968. Sole practice Los Angeles area, 1968-70; house counsel Purex Corp., Lakewood, Calif., 1970-71; founding ptnr. Jacoby & Meyers Law Offices, N.Y.C., also Calif., 1972—; exec. v.p., chief operating officer Jamko Service Corp., Los Angeles, 1983—; founder Practical Law Courses Inc., 1974; ptnr. J&M Advt. Inc., Los Angeles, 1979—. Created systems approach to practice of law, 1972. Recipient Belding award 1981, Clio award 1981, Internat. Broadcasting Award 1981. Mem. ABA, ACLU, Los Angeles Town Hall. Democrat. Jewish. Office: Jacoby & Meyers 2285 Westwood Blvd Los Angeles CA 90064

JACOBY, ROBERT HAROLD, petroleum research consultant; b. Camden, N.J., Jan. 20, 1923; s. Harry and Rose (Leusenring) J.; m. Peggy D. Scott, June 1949; children: Bruce, Lynn, Linda. BSChemE, U. Pa., 1944; MSChemE, U. Mich., 1948. Staff research engr. Amoco Prodn. Co., Tulsa, 1948-67; research assoc. Gulf Research and Devel. Co., Pitts., 1967-77; assoc. prof. petroleum engring. Pa. State U., State College, 1977-83; prof. petroleum engring. Colo. Sch. Mines, Golden, 1983-87. Contbr. articles to profl. jours.; patentee in field. Served with USN, 1944-46. Mem. Gas Processors Assn. (chmn. K-Value Com. 1962-67, Citation for Service 1965), Am. Petroleum Inst. (mem. ECEPR com. 1968-74, refining data book com. 1973-77), Am. Chem. Soc. (assoc. mem. petroleum div. 1944-66, 74-81), Soc. Petroleum Engrs., Am. Inst. Chem. Engrs. Lutheran. Avocations: tennis, gardening, hiking. Office: Jayco Tech Products Co PO Box 261022 Lakewood CO 80226

JACOBY, SAMUEL LUDWIG, computer services company executive; b. Breslau, Fed. Republic of Germany, Feb. 3, 1932; came to U.S., 1959; s. Paul and Lotte (Segall) J.; m. Michal Rebecca Shmueli, Dec. 30, 1955; children: Karny, Hanan Gilead, David Ira. BS cum laude, Technion, Haifa, Israel, 1958; MS, U. Calif., Davis, 1960; PhD, U. Calif., Berkeley, 1962. Computer scientist The Boeing Co., Seattle, 1962-64, supr. engring. math., 1965-67, mgr. applied math., 1968-75, gen. mgr. engring. tech. applications, 1976-84, gen. mgr. computer integrated mfg. programs, 1985—; indsl. affiliate applied math. U. Wash., Seattle, 1981-84. Author: Iterative Methods for Nonlinear Optimization Problems, 1976, Mathematical Modeling with Computers, 1980. Home: 5750 S Hawthorn Rd Seattle WA 98118 Office: Boeing Computer Services Computer Integrated Mfg PO Box 24346 M/S 7R-14 Seattle WA 98124-0346

JACQUES, RONALD WESLEY, education and psychology educator; b. Pittsburg, Calif., July 30, 1947; s. Spencer Wesley and Mary LaVell (Christensen) J.; m. Brenda Loosle, Oct. 1, 1966; children: Laura, Claudine, Denise, Amy, Melissa, Brian. BS, Utah State U., 1970; MEd, Brigham Young U., 1975; EdD, Idaho State U., 1980. Tchr. Ammon Jr. High Sch., Idaho Falls, Idaho, 1970-73; counselor Bonneville Jr. High Sch., Idaho Falls, 1973-78; asst. prof. edn. and psychology N.W. Mo. State U., Maryville, 1980-85; prof. Ricks Coll., Rexburg, Idaho, 1985—; mem. adv. bd. St. Joseph (Mo.) State Hosp., 1984-85; cons. Counseling and Devel. Ctr., Vienna, Va., 1984. Author: Classroom Survival Skills, 1980; contbr. articles to profl. jours. Grantee Mo. State Dept. Vocat. Edn., 1982, N.W. Mo. State U., 1984. Mem. Am. Assn. Counseling and Devel., N.Am. Soc. Adlerian Psychology (Adlerian counseling and therapy exec. com. 1986), Assn. Mormon Counselors and Psychotherapists. Avocations: skiing, fishing, camping, furniture, refinishing. Home: 231 Harvard Rexburg ID 83440 Office: Ricks Coll Clarke 208 Rexburg ID 83440

JACQUES-CHAVEZ, PABLO ADELMO, Spanish and multicultural studies instructor; b. Durango, Colo., Feb. 24, 1939; s. Juan Pablo and Maria Adela (Chavez) J.; m. Mary Suzanne Harris, Aug. 14, 1965; children: Paul John, Gabriel Christopher, Jillinda Suzanne. MA, San Diego State U., 1968. Cert. Calif. community coll. instr. and adminstr. Designer, developer, chmn. multicultural studies dept. Palomar Coll., San Marcos, Calif., 1969-71; chmn. multicultural studies dept. Grossmont Coll., El Cajon, Calif., 1971-79, fgn. lang. tchr., 1980-85, creator and coordinator summer campus abroad Spanish lang. immersion program, chmn. elect of fgn. lan. dept., 1987—. Commr. San Diego Human Relations Commn., 1970-75; pub. relations dir. Concilio of Chicano Studies of San Diego, Imperial Valley and Baja Calif. Norte. Mem. Am. Assn. Tchrs. Spanish and Portuguese, Calif. Tchrs. Assn., La Raza Faculty Assn. Calif. Community Colls., Alpha Mu Gamma. Democrat. Roman Catholic. Avocations: painting, hiking, swimming. Office: Grossmont Coll 8800 Grossmont Coll Dr El Cajon CA 92020

JADA, SIVANANDA SIVAPPA, research chemist; b. Bellary, India, June 14, 1948; came to U.S., 1979; s. Sivappa S. and Parvatamma N. J.; m. Sushma Tammanagowda, Sept. 4, 1978; children: Nivedita, Ajit. BSc in Chemistry, Karnatak U., Dharwar, India, 1969, MSc in Organic Chemistry, 1971; PhD in Polymer Chemistry, USSR Acad. Scis., Moscow, 1977. Research assoc. U. Ala., 1979-81, Case Western Res. U., Cleve., 1981-83; sr. research assoc. Atlanta U., 1983-84; sr. research chemist Research and Devel. Ctr. Manville Corp., Denver, 1984—. Contbr. articles to profl. jours.; patentee in field. Recipient award Ministry Edn. India-USSR, 1973; scholar Govt. India. Mem. Am. Chem. Soc., Materials Research Soc., Internat. Union Pure and Applied Chemistry, N.Y. Acad. Sci. Avocations: travel, chess, reading.

JADDI, AHMED MOHIUDDIN, structural engineer; b. Hyderabad, Andhra, India, Mar. 18, 1937; came to U.S., 1959; S. Osman Ali and Sogra F. (Aziz) J.; m. Barika F. Hussain, Oct. 9, 1964; children—Adnan R., Sabica F., Rehan A., Salman. B.S. in Physics, Osmania U., Hyderabad, 1955, B.S. in Civil Engring., 1958; M.S. in Civil Engring., Columbia U., N.Y.C., 1961. Registered profl. engr., Wash. Asst., Columbia U., 1959-61; engr. Ammann & Whitney, N.Y.C., 1961-63, Severud Assocs., N.Y.C., 1963-65, Parson Jurden, N.Y.C., 1965-67, Boeing Co., Seattle, 1967-69; v.p. Arabian Am. Devel. Corp.-Wick Constrn. Co., 1969-73; ptnr. Mann Millegan Morse & Jaddi, Seattle, 1974—; pres. Millegan Jaddi, Inc., Seattle, 1974—, A&E Constrn. Co., 1986—. Mem. Am. Arbitration Assn., Am. Concrete Inst., Wash. Structural Engrs. Assn., Am. Consulting Engrs. Council. Home: 8008 W Mercer Way Mercer Island WA 98040 Office: Millegan & Jaddi Inc 1200 S Dearborn St Seattle WA 98144

JADUSZLIWER, BERNARDO, research physicist; b. Buenos Aires, Oct. 17, 1943; came to U.S., 1974; s. Jacobo Aria and Fejga (Szichman) J.; children: Ariel, David. Licenciado En Ciencias, U. Buenos Aires, 1968; MS, U. Toronto, Ont., Can., 1970, PhD, 1973. Postdoctoral fellow U. Toronto, 1973-74; assoc. research prof. NYU, 1974-84; mem. tech. staff Aerospace Corp., El Segundo, Calif., 1985—; adj. assoc. prof. U. So. Calif., Los Angeles, 1985—; tech. advisor Today Buyers Guide, Am. Inst. Physics, 1983—; Edibrid bd. Rev. Sceintific Instruments, 1987. Contbr. articles to profl. jours. Mem. AAAS, Am. Phys. Soc. Avocations: hiking, backpacking, music. Office: The Aerospace Corp PO Box 92957 M2/253 Los Angeles CA 90009

JAEGER, EDWARD JOHN, broadcast engineer, consultant; b. Chgo.; s. Edward W. and Lydia M. (Jorn) J.; m. Alma Clara Leimer, Mar. 1, 1935; children: John, James, Nancy, Carol, Dorothy, Edward C., Alma, Joan, Margaret, Michael. Student, Northwestern U., 1932-36, Grossmont Coll., 1972. Lic. engr., FCC. Sta. engr., prodn. mgr. various stas., 1935-57; pub. relations mgr. Luth. Ch. Mo. Synod/Luth. Laymen's League, La Mesa, Calif., 1957-70; newsman Sta. KECC-TV, El Centro, Calif., 1970-72; cons. engring., programming La Mesa, Calif., 1972—. Republican. Lutheran. Avocations: reading, traveling. Home and Office: 5530 Rab St La Mesa CA 92041-2028

JAFEK, BRUCE WILLIAM, otolaryngologist, educator; b. Berwyn, Ill., Mar. 4, 1941; s. Robert William and Viola Mabel (Newstrom) J.; m. Mary Bell Kirkpatrick, Sept. 1, 1962; children: Lynette A., Robert K., Timothy B., Britta C., Kayla E., Kristen E. BS, Coe Coll., 1962; postgrad., U. Omaha, 1962; MD, UCLA, 1966. Instr. dept. otology/laryngology Johns Hopkins Sch. Medicine, Balt., 1971-73; asst. prof. dept. otolaryngology U. Pa. Med. Sch., Phila., 1973-76; prof., dept. chmn. dept. otolaryngology/head and neck surgery U. Colo. Med. Sch., Denver, 1976—. Served with USPHS, 1971-73. Republican. Mormon. Office: UCHSC (B-210) 4200 E 9th Ave Denver CO 80262

JAFFE, ANNETTE BRONKESH, research scientist; b. Munich, Federal Republic of Germany, July 25, 1946; came to U.S., 1947; d. Sam and Bronia (Zimmerman) Bronkesh; m. Richard Lawrence Jaffe, June 16, 1970; children: Elizabeth, Matthew. BA, Douglass Coll., 1968; PhM, Yale U., 1970, PhD, 1972. Research scientist IBM Corp., San Jose, Calif., 1974—. Mem. (sr. 1987) Soc. Photographic Sci. and Engring. (program chmn. 1985—), Am. Chem. Soc. Office: IBM Corp Research div 650 Harry Rd San Jose CA 95120-6099

JAFFE, ROBERT DAVID, family physician; b. Chgo., July 29, 1952; s. Richard David and Evelyn Claire (Baron) J.; m. Anne Morton Rutledge, June 17, 1982; 1 child, Katharine Rebecca Rutledge. BA with honors and distinction, U. Mich., 1975; MD, Mich. State U., 1979. Intern Group Health Hosp., Seattle, 1979-80, resident in family practice, 1980-82; chief family medicine service Pacific Med. Ctr., Seattle, 1984—; clin. asst. prof. Dept. Family Medicine, U. Wash., Seattle, 1986—; med. dir. Carolyn Downs Clinic, Seattle, 1982-84, Rainier Beach Clinic, Seattle, 1984—. Producer med. films and videos. Pres., founder, bd. dirs. Wash. Doctors Ought to Care (DOC), Seattle, 1979—; bd. dirs. Wash. Physicians for Social Responsibility, Seattle, 1979-82. Fellow Am. Acad. Family Physicians; mem. King County Med. Soc., King County Acad. Family Physicians (bd. dirs.). Jewish. Avocation: collecting. Home: 1222 17th Ave E Seattle WA 98112 Office: Pacific Med Ctr 1200 12th Ave S Seattle WA 98144

JAFFE, SIGMUND, educator, chemist; b. New Haven, Mar. 1, 1921; s. Morris and Rose (Blosveren) J.; m. Elaine Leventhal, Aug. 25, 1946; children—Matthew Lee, Paul Jonathan. A.B. with high distinction in Chemistry, Wesleyan U., Middletown, Conn., 1949; Ph.D., Iowa State U., 1953. Research in rare earths Ames (Iowa) Lab., 1949-53; research in carbides, metal and high temperature inorganic reactions, research labs. Air Reduction Corp., 1953-58; prof. chemistry Calif. State U. at Los Angeles, 1958—, chmn. dept., 1958-64; vis. prof. Queen Mary Coll., U. London, 1978-79; Research solid propellant fuel systems, 1958-60; photochemistry and gas phase kinetics Jet Propulsion Lab., Calif. Inst. Tech., Pasadena, Calif., 1960-64; NIH fellow Wiezmann Inst. Sci., Israel, 1964-65, vis. prof., 1971-72. Contbr. articles to profl. jours. Served with USNR, 1942-46. Named Outstanding prof. Calif. State U. at Los Angeles, 1973-74. Mem. Am. Chem. Soc., Sigma Xi, Phi Beta Kappa, Phi Lambda Upsilon, Phi Kappa Phi. Home: 420 S Madison Ave Pasadena CA 91101 Office: Dept Chemistry Calif State U Los Angeles CA 90032

JAFFURS, LEE WARDLAW, writer, educator; b. Salina, Kans., Nov. 20, 1955; d. Joseph Patterson and Margaret Lillian (Laux) Wardlaw; m. Craig Zeisloft Jaffurs, Aug. 27, 1983. BA, Calif. Poly. State U., 1977. Cert. multiple subject tchr., Calif. Dir.'s asst. Los Ninos Head Start, Santa Barbara, Calif., 1978; head tchr. and dir. Goleta (Calif.) Head Start, 1978-79; dir. Cornelia Moore Meml. Dental Found., Santa Barbara, 1979-82, ednl. advisor, 1982—; proprietor, writer Outlaw Communications, Santa Barbara, 1982—. Author: Giggles and Grins, 1985, Corey's Fire, 1986, ME Math = Headache, 1986, Alley Cat, 1987. Troop leader Girl Scouts of Am.,

Montecito, Calif., 1977-78; vol. reading tutor Peabody Elem. Sch., Santa Barbara, 1985—; mem. library com. Office County Supt. Schs., Santa Barbara, 1986—. Recipient Recognition award for Outstanding Services to Dentistry, Santa Barbara-Ventura Dental Soc., 1981, Creative and Dedicated Service award Cornelia Moore Dental Found., 1982; Santa Barbara Found. grantee for developing ednl. program, 1985. Mem. Nat. Soc. of Children's Book Writers, Nat. and Local Chapts. Bus. Profl. Women's Club, Santa Barbara High Sch. Alumni Assn. (bd. dirs. 1986-87), Santa Barbara C. of C. Avocations: writing, reading, swimming, travel.

JAHNSEN, VILHELM JAMES, biochemist, business owner; b. Port-au-Prince, Haiti, Mar. 28, 1928; came to U.S., 1949, naturalized; s. Knud Vilhelm and Anita A. (McGuffie) J.; 1 child, Donna Maria. BS in Pharmacy, U. Haiti, Port-Au-Prince, 1949; BA in Chemistry, Evansville U., 1951; MS in Biochemistry, Purdue U., 1959, PhD in Biochemistry, 1961. Lic. pharmacist, Haiti. Postdoctoral fellow Western Regional Labs., Albany, Calif., 1960-62; dir. biochem. research Falstaff Brewing Corp., St. Louis, 1962-65; head chromatography research Biosci. Lab., Van Nuys, Calif., 1965-69; chief chemist AUDRI program JPL Caltech NASA, Pasadena, Calif., 1970-74, chief chemist CELSS program, 1977-82; v.p., tech. dir. Manhattan Inst. Co., Santa Monica, Calif., 1974-77; pres. McCausland-Jahnsen R&D, Granada Hills, Calif., 1982—; bd. dirs. W. Braun Enterprises, Haiti; cons. in field. Contbr. articles to profl. jours.; patentee in field. Served with U.S. Army, 1954-56. Recipient certs. of recognition NASA, 1975-82. Mem. Am. Chem. Soc., The Planetary Soc. Avocations: writing, painting, book collecting. Home: 11341 Stranwood Ave Granada Hills CA 91344

JAIN, PARVEEN KUMAR, nuclear engineer; b. New Delhi, India, June 18, 1953; came to U.S., 1975; Rikhi Ram and Shanti (Jain) J.; m. Neeraj Jain, Dec. 14, 1978; children: Puneet R., Muneesh R. BSc in Physics with honors, U. Delhi, India, 1972; BEE, Indian Inst. Sci., 1975; MS in Nuclear Engring., U. Cin., 1976; PhD in Nuclear Engring., U. Ill., 1981. Sr. research engr. Systems Control, Inc., Palo Alto, Calif., 1981-83; cons., project mgr. S. Levy Inc., Campbell, Calif., 1983—. Contbr. articles to profl. jours. Mem. Am. Nuclear Soc., Sigma Xi. Home: 1529 Via Cancion San Jose CA 95128 Office: S Levy Inc 3425 S Bascom Ave Campbell CA 95008

JAKINO, MICHAEL ANTHONY, oil company executive; b. Durango, Colo., May 28, 1951; s. James Charles and Lillian Lucille (Perino) J.; m. Susan R. Martin, Sept. 17, 1971 (div. Dec. 1985); children: Brandon, Summer. BA in Acctg., Ft. Lewis Coll., 1985. CPA, N.Mex. Staff acct. Mott Mcgee & Co., Farmington, N.Mex., 1976-77; asst. controller Jesco Inc., Farmington, 1977-81; v.p. Coleman Oil & Gas Inc., Farmington, 1981—. Mem. acctg. adv. bd. San Juan Coll., Farmington, 1984-86. Served with U.S. Army, 1970-76. Mem. Am. Inst. CPA's, N.Mex. Soc. CPA's. Democrat. Roman Catholic. Lodge: Kiwanis (bd. dirs. 1985-86). Avocations: tennis, golfing, skiing. Home: PO Box 635 Farmington NM 87499 Office: Coleman Oil & Gas Inc PO Box 3337 Farmington NM 87499

JAKL, EDWARD ANDREW, research and development engineer; b. Hinsdale, Ill., Dec. 12, 1960; s. Robert Allan and Elizabeth Jane (Tennant) J. BEE, Ariz. State U., 1982. Engr., scientist McDonnell Douglas, Huntington Beach, Calif., 1982-85; research and devel. engr. Ford Aerospace, Newport Beach, Calif., 1985—. Mem. Citrus Empire Model R.R. Club, Eta Kappa Nu (sec. 1980-82), Tau Beta Pi. Republican. Avocations: model railroading, marathon cycling. Home: 16222 Monterey Ln 165 Huntington Beach CA 92649 Office: Ford Aerospace Ford Rd Newport Beach CA 92660

JAKOBSEN, JAKOB KNUDSEN, mechanical engineer; b. Bording Sogn, Denmark, Aug. 7, 1912; came to U.S., 1952, naturalized, 1958; s. Laust Peder and Inger Marie (Kristensen) J.; m. Eva Koch, Nov. 19, 1941 (dec. 1983); children—Marianne Gyrithe (Mrs. Earl C. Green), Peter Laust (dec. 1969), Claus Michael, Suzanne Elizabeth (Mrs. Paul B. Marsh), Niels-Olaf Sejten, Lars Jakob. M.S. in Mech. Engring, Royal Tech. U. Denmark, 1941. Registered profl. engr., Mich., Calif. Mech. engr. Brown Boveri et Cie, Switzerland, 1941-43; project engr. Pub. Power Utilities of Copenhagen, Denmark, 1943-45; mech. engr. Burmeister & Wain, Copenhagen, 1945-52; gas turbine engr. Clark Bros. Co., Olean, N.Y., 1952-55; staff engr. automotive research Chrysler Corp., Detroit, 1955-60; sr. tech. specialist for research Rocketdyne, Canoga Park, Calif., 1960—; asst. prof. machine design Royal Tech. U. Denmark, 1941. Author: NASA monograph Rocket Engine Turbopump Inducers, 1971; Contbr. articles profl. jours. Mem. ASTM (com. for erosion by cavitation and impingement 1964—), ASME (chmn. steering com. San Fernardo Valley sect., recipient Melville Gold medal 1964), Soc. Automotive Engrs. (chmn. power plant activities), Am. Inst. Aeros. and Astronautics, Nat. Soc. Profl. Engrs., Danish Inst. Civil Engrs. Republican. Lutheran. Patentee compressor design, diesel engine turbosupercharger, pump diffusor. Home: 10531 Etiwanda Ave Northridge CA 91326 Office: Rocketdyne 6633 Canoga Ave Canoga Park CA 91304

JAKOWEC, MICHAEL WALTER, molecular geneticist; b. Brantford, Ont., Can., Aug. 30, 1960; came to U.S., 1982; s. Walter A. and Mary (Bilanski) J.; m. Giselle Petzinger, Nov. 5, 1985. BS, U. Toronto, Ont., 1982; MS, U. Calif., Davis, 1984; postgrad., U. So. Calif., 1984—. Postgrad. research fellow U. So. Calif., Los Angeles, 1984—, lectr., 1984—; seminar speaker Indsl. U., 1983—. Contbr. articles to profl. jours. Fellow Kearney Found., 1982, Nat. Sci. Engring. Research Council, 1984-86. Mem. AAAS, Am. Soc. Microbiologists, Am. Chem. Soc., Genetics Soc. Am., Nat. Geographic Soc., Can. Soc. Microbiology, Genetics Soc. Can., History of Sci. Soc., Sigma Xi. Roman Catholic. Avocations: photography, rare book collecting, hockey. Home: 971 W 30th St Apt #4 Los Angeles CA 90007 Office: U So Calif Dept Molecular Biology Los Angeles CA 90089-1481

JAKUBCZYK, JOHN JOSEPH, lawyer; b. New Britain, Conn., Dec. 21, 1953; s. Stanley Walter and Madeline Regina (Hinchliffe) J.; m. Petra Kunigunda Mead, Jan. 8, 1983; children: Kristan Marie, John Joseph II, Jamie Nicole. BA in Bus. Adminstrn. and Polit. Sci., U. San Diego, 1976; JD, U. Ariz., 1979. Bar: Ariz. 1979, U.S. Dist. Ct. Ariz. 1979. Sole practice, Phoenix, 1979—; speaker in field. Author pro-life articles; radio commentator and host. Bd. dirs., cons. Ariz. Youth for Life, Phoenix, 1979-82; chmn. polit. action com. Arizonans for Life, 1980-81; pres. Ariz. Right to Life, Phoenix, 1983-85, bd. dirs.; bd. dirs. Life Ednl. Corp., 1984—, sec.; founder, pres. Southwest Life and Law Ctr.; bd. advisers Free Speech Advs.; precinct committeeman Republican Party, Phoenix, 1982—. Recipient Pro-Life Action League Protector award, 1987. Mem. Assn. Trial Lawyers Am., Ariz. State Bar Assn. (arbitrator 1983—), Phi Delta Phi. Roman Catholic. Lodge: K.C. (pro-life chmn. 1982-83). Office: 4607 N 24th St #100 Phoenix AZ 85016

JALONEN, NANCY LEE, arts administrator; b. Hollywood, Calif., Oct. 28, 1927; d. Earle Reynolds and Hazel Lee (Griffin) MacNaught; B.A., Stanford U., 1948, M.A., 1950; m. John William Jalonen, June 26, 1955; children—Wendy Anne, Christopher Lee. Instr. drama Pasadena (Calif.) City Coll., 1950-55; instr. evening coll. Coll. of San Mateo (Calif.), 1956-78; mem. faculty Coll. Notre Dame, Belmont, Calif., 1986—; producer, moderator ednl. TV, Sta. KCSM-TV, San Mateo, 1965-78; communications cons., 1977-79; exec. dir. San Mateo County Arts Council, 1978-84. Mem. Bicentennial com. City of San Mateo. Mem. AAUW, Am. Council Arts. Republican.

JAMES, EDWIN LEE, computer consultant, computer retail executive; b. Cole Camp, Mo., Aug. 16, 1952; s. Kenneth Eugene and Gladys Opal (Webster) J.; m. Marcy Gaynel Orr, Aug. 4, 1984; 1 child, Connie. BA in Math., Ill. State U., 1975, BBA, 1975. Prin. Jamac Constrn., Boise, Idaho, 1975-81; computer cons. Computerland, Boise, 1981-83; prin. Computerland, Twin Falls, Idaho, 1983—; cons. Computerland, Twin Falls, 1983—; tchr. Computerland Learning Ctr., Twin Falls, 1983—. Republican. Baptist. Avocation: golf. Home: 368 Alturas Dr Twin Falls ID 83301 Office: Computerland 213A Eastland Dr Twin Falls ID 83301

JAMES, GEORGE BARKER, II, apparel industry executive; b. Haverhill, Mass., May 25, 1937; s. Paul Withington and Ruth (Burns) J.; m. Beverly A. Burch, Sept. 22, 1962; children: Alexander, Christopher, Geoffrey, Matthew. AB, Harvard U., 1959; MBA, Stanford U., 1962. Fiscal dir. E.G. & G. Inc., Bedford, Mass., 1963-67; fin. exec. Am. Brands Inc., N.Y.C., 1967-69; v.p. Pepsico, Inc., N.Y.C., 1969-72; sr. v.p., chief fin. officer Arcata Corp., Menlo Park, Calif., 1972-82; exec. v.p. Crown Zellerbach Corp., San Francisco, 1982-85; sr. v.p., chief fin. officer Levi Strauss & Co., San Francisco, 1985—; bd. dirs. Pacific States Industries, Inc., Sequoia Pacific Systems, Inc., Supertex, Inc. Author: Industrial Development in the Ohio Valley, 1962. Mem. Andover (Mass.) Town Com., 1965-67; mem. Select Congl. Com. on World Hunger; adv. council Calif. State Employees Pension Fund; chmn. bd. dirs. Towle Trust Fund; trustee Nat. Corp. Fund for the Dance, Cate Sch., Levi Strauss Found., Sterngrove; chmn. bd. trustees San Francisco Ballet Assn. Served with AUS, 1960-61. Mem. Newcomen Soc. N.Am., Fin. Execs. Inst. Clubs: Stock Exchange, Pacific Union, Commonwealth Calif., Family (San Francisco); Menlo Circus (Atherton, Calif.); Harvard (Boston and N.Y.C.). Home: 215 Coleridge Ave Palo Alto CA 94301 Office: Levi Strauss & Co Levi's Plaza Box 7215 San Francisco CA 94120

JAMES, HAROLD L(LOYD), geologist; b. Nanaimo, B.C., Can., June 11, 1912; s. Evan and Blodwen (Davies) J.; m. Ruth Graybeal, Feb. 13, 1936; children: David, Robert, Hugh, Herbert. Student, Western Wash. U., 1934; BS with highest honors, Wash. State U., 1938; postgrad., U. Wash., 1938-39; PhD, Princeton U., 1945. Geologist U.S. Geol. Survey, 1938—; instr. geology Princeton (N.J.) U., 1942; prof. U. Minn., Mpls., 1961-64; vis. lectr. Northwestern U., Evanston, Ill., 1953-54. Contbr. articles to profl. jours. Recipient Disting. Service award Dept. of Interior, 1966. Fellow Mineral. Soc. Am. (mem. council 1964-66), Geol. Soc. Am. (mem. council 1959-62); mem. NAS (chmn. geology sect. 1969-72), Soc. Econ. Geologists (mem. council 1962-65, pres. 1971-72, Penrose Medal 1977), Internat. Subcommn. on PreCambrian Stratigraphy (chmn. 1975-84). Avocations: fishing, golf, reading.

JAMES, HERB MARK (HERBERT GEORGE), foundation and insurance executive; b. Trail, B.C., Can., Jan. 30, 1936; s. George William and Violet Ethyl (Corbin) J.; student bus. adminstrn. Simon Fraser U., 1965-69; m. Patricia Helen Boyd, Nov. 1, 1958; 1 son, Brad Mark. Founder, pres. Internat. Sound Found., Ottawa, Can., 1967—, Blaine, Wash., 1975—; mem. bus. adv. bd. U.S. Senate, 1981—; mem. Can. Internat. Devel. Agy.; founder Better Hearing Better Life projects, Fiji, Kenya, Cayman Islands, Nepal, Costa Rica, Pakistan, Guatemala. Musician B. Pops Orch. Govt. of Can. grantee, 1973-83. Mem. Blaine C. of C. Clubs: Masons, Shriners, Demolay. Home: PO Box 95, Port Moody, BC Canada V3H 3E1 Office: USA Am Bldg PO Box 1587 Blaine WA 98230

JAMES, JAMIE GEORGE, advertising and public relations company executive; b. Healdton, Okla., Jan. 16, 1937; s. Fred Leroy and Wilma Hope (Henngar) J. BS, Lamar Tech. U., 1958; MA, U. Tex. With art dept. Dallas Morning News, 1959; art dir. Continental Advt. Co., Dallas, 1961; advt. dir. Eastwood Gen. Corp., Los Angeles, 1961-67; prin. The James Agy., Los Angeles, 1967—; founder, dir. Small Bus. Advt. and Pub. Relations Seminars, Calif., 1980—. Author: How to Do Your Own Publicity and Advertising, 1980. Arion Found. scholar, 1954. Mem. N.Y. Publicity Club. Democrat. Clubs: Greater Los Angeles Press; San Francisco Press. Avocations: weight lifting, skiing, painting. Office: 7455 Beverly Blvd Los Angeles CA 90036

JAMES, JOHN RANDOLPH, forestry consultant; b. Orange, N.J., Feb. 24, 1949; s. Edward Cecil and Elizabeth (Gillespie) J.; m. Yvonne Evans, Dec. 31, 1970 (div. May 1978); 1 child, Brain Talbot. BS in Forestry, N.C. State U., 1971; BS in Psychology, U. Oreg., 1987. V.p. Willamette Timber Systems Inc., Eugene, Oreg., 1974-79; pres. Bante Inc., Springfield, Oreg., 1980-84; prin. James Cons., Springfield, 1984—. Hon. instr. Boy Scouts Am. Mem. Am. Forest Found., Va. Forestry Assn. Republican. Methodist. Club: Court Sports II (Eugene). Avocations: racquetball, golfing, writing. Home and Office: 583 S 70th Pl Springfield OR 97478

JAMES, JONATHAN LAWRENCE, quality executive; b. Wallace, Idaho, Sept. 2, 1955; s. Lawrence Arthur and Myrtle Charlotte (Sorenson) J.; m. Janice Pasquale, Dec. 8, 1973 (div. Apr. 1982); 1 child, Jennifer Lynn; m. Sandra Louise Pretat, Aug. 28, 1982; children: Jennifer Kim, Tiffany Elizabeth. AAS in Electronic Tech., Community Coll. Spokane, 1978. Electronic tech. Keytronic Corp., Spokane, 1978-79; electronic technician programmer Keytronic Corp., Newport, Wash., 1979-81, quality supr., 1981-82, quality assurance mgr., 1982-86; quality engr. Keytronic Corp., Cheney, Wash., 1986—. CPR instr. Am. Heart Assn., Wash., 1985—; commr. mens play Am. Softball Assn., Pend Oreille Valley, Wash., 1983-84. Served with U.S. Army, 1973-75. Mem. Am. Soc. Quality Control, Soc. Mfg. Engrs. Republican. Avocations: hunting, fishing, golf. Home: E 3108 17th Ave12 Spokane WA 99223 Office: Keytronic Corp Cheney Indsl Park Cheney WA 99004

JAMES, LOUIS EARL, II, sales and marketing professional; b. Los Angeles, July 29, 1951; s. Louis Earl and Lida Faye (Snyder) J.; m. Cynthia Jean Schoenfeld, Oct. 19, 1973; children: Louis K., Kristopher, Shaun, Bonnie Jean, Rebecca. Student, El Camino Coll., 1969-70, Tulsa U., 1973, Brigham Young U., 1973-75. V.p. The Lens Man, San Diego, 1976-80; pres. Osaka Optical USA, Salt Lake City, 1981-84, Louis James and Assocs., Salt Lake City, 1984—. Missionary Mormon Ch., Okla., 1970-72. Named Eagle Scout Boy Scouts Am., Los Angeles, 1967. Avocations: water skiing, snow skiing. Office: Louis James and Assocs. 5180 S 300 W Murray UT 84107

JAMES, MICHAEL ROYSTON, materials research scientist; b. London, Sept. 11, 1950; came to U.S., 1960; s. Robert Charles and Pauline Hilda (Nuttall) J.; m. Rita Maria Riemersma, Aug. 19, 1972; children: Ryan Michael, Jeremy Scott. BSME, Tulane U., 1972; PhD in Materials Sci., Northwestern U., 1977. Research scientist in material physics U. Gronigen, The Netherlands, 1977; research scientist in materials sci. Rockwell Internat. Sci. Ctr., Thousand Oaks, Calif., 1978—. Contbr. numerous articles to profl. jours.; patentee determination of residual stress. Mem. Am. Soc. Metals, Metall. Soc. of Am. Inst. Mech. Engrs., Soc. Exptl. Mechanics (com. chmn. 1983-85), Sigma Xi, Pi Tau Beta, Tau Beta Pi. Home: 419 Thunderhead St Thousand Oaks CA 91360 Office: Rockwell Internat Sci Ctr 1049 Camino Dos Rios Thousand Oaks CA 91360

JAMES, SANDRA ELAINE, chamber of commerce administrator; b. Long Beach, Calif., Feb. 26, 1956; d. Charles and Ruth (Gould) Eien; m. Vince James, May 27, 1979. BSBA, Calif. State U., Long Beach, 1979. Visual presentation mgr. Broadway Dept. Store, Long Beach, 1977-79; from staff mem. to exec. dir. Ashland (Oreg.) C. of C. and Vis. Bur., 1979—; mem. So. Oreg. State Regional Adv. Bd., So. Oreg. Visitors Assn. Bd., Oreg. Assn. Conv. and Visitors Burs. Bd., Oreg. Chamber Execs. Bd. Mem. Oreg. Soc. Assn. Execs. Lodge: Soroptimists. Home: 1237 Ashland Mine Rd Ashland OR 97520

JAMES, THOMAS LARRY, chemistry educator; b. North Platte, Nebr., Sept. 8, 1944; s. James Jennings and Guinevere (Richards) J.; children: Marc, Tristan. BS, U. N.M., 1965; PhD, U. Wis., 1969. Research chemist Celanese Chem. Co., Corpus Christi, Tex., 1969-71; NIH post-doctorate fellow U. Pa., Phila., 1971-73; prof. chem., pharmaceutical chemistry and radiology U. Calif., San Francisco, 1973—, dir. Magnetic Resonance Lab., 1975. Author: NMR in Biochemistry, 1975; editor: Biomedical NMR, 1984; contbr. numerous articles to profl. jours. Mem. Internat. Soc. Magnetic Resonance, Am. Biophys. Soc., Am. Chem. Soc., Am. Biochem. Soc., Soc. Magnetic Resonance in Medicine, Phi Beta Kappa, Phi Kappa Phi, Kappa Mu Epsilon. Reorganized Ch. of Jesus Christ of Latter-day Saints. Avocations: skiing, Kayaking, traveling. Office: U Calif 926-S San Francisco CA 94143

JAMES, WAYNE EDWARD, electronic engineering specialist; b. Racine, Wis., Apr. 2, 1950; s. Ronald Dean James and Arlene Joyce (Mickelsen) Dawson; m. Bertie Darlene Tague, July 18, 1972; children: Terry Scott, Kevin Arthur. BS in Electronic Engring. Tech., U. So. Colo., 1976. Electronic technician Lawrence Livermore (Calif.) Nat. Lab., 1976-80; electronic technician Inmos Corp., Colorado Springs, Colo., 1980-86, assoc. computer aided design engr., 1986—. Sec.-treas. Stratmoor Hills Vol. Fire Dept., Colorado Springs, 1983, 84, lt., 1985, capt., 1986. Served with USN, 1968-72. Named Fireman of Yr., Stratmoor Hills Vol. Fire Dept., 1983. Lutheran. Office: Inmos Corp 1110 Bayfield Dr Colorado Springs CO 80906

JAMES, WILLIAM LANGFORD, aerospace engineer; b. Southampton, Va., Jan. 13, 1939; s. Leroy and Worthie (Murphy) J.; m. Elaine Cecilia Reed; children: William Jr., Terri Lynne. Student, Va. State Coll., 1956, Hampton Inst., 1958; BS, Calif. State U., Los Angeles, 1962, MS, 1964; postgrad., U. Nev., Reno, 1984-86. Research engr. non-metallic materials lab. N.Am. Aviation, Los Angeles, 1960-67; research analyst, materials scientist, mem. tech. staff The Aerospace Corp., El Segundo, Calif., 1967—. Contbr. numerous articles and reports to profl. publs.; patentee in field. Mem. Soc. Advancement Material and Process Engring. (membership com. 1980-84), AAAS. Avocations: water sports, big game fishing. Home: Box 19735 Los Angeles CA 90019 Office: Aerospace Corp M5 712 Box 92957 Los Angeles CA 90009

JAMESON, CHARLES SCOTT KENNEDY, marketing educator; b. Bonnieville, Ky., May 25, 1925; s. Charles Scott and Gillie (Addcox) J.; A.A., Ventura Coll., 1948; B.A., U. So. Calif., 1950, M.S., 1951, M.B.A., 1959, Ph.D., 1963. Asst. registrar U. So. Calif., Los Angeles, 1950-55, adminstrv. asst. to dean Sch. Bus., 1955-58, instr. bus. adminstrn., 1958-61, assoc. prof. mktg. and communications, 1963-82, prof. emeritus, 1982—; assoc. prof. Ariz. State U., Tempe, 1962-63; assoc. prof. mktg. and mgmt. Calif. State U.-Dominguez Hills, 1982—. Cons., Auto Club Soc. Calif., Long Beach Community Hosp., Calif. Dairy Council, Blue Cross Ins., others. Served with USNR, 1943-46. Mem. Am. Bus. Communication Assn., AAUP, Am. Mus. Natural History (asso.), Phi Delta Kappa, Delta Pi Epsilon, Alpha Kappa Psi, Beta Gamma Sigma, Omicron Delta Epsilon, Theta Xi. Home: 624 S Irena St Redondo Beach CA 90277 Office: Calif State U Dept Mgmt and Mktg 1000 E Victoria Carson CA 90747

JAMESON, WILLIAM JAMES, judge; b. Butte, Mont., Aug. 8, 1898; s. William J. and Annie J. (Roberts) J.; m. Mildred Lore, July 28, 1923; children: Mary Lucille (Mrs. Walker Honaker), William James, Jr. A.B., Mont. U., 1919, J.D., 1922, LL.D., 1952; LL.D., U. Man., Can., 1954, Rocky Mountain Coll., 1969; Dr. Laws, McGeorge Coll. Law, 1965. Bar: Mont. 1922. Assoc. Johnston, Coleman and Johnston, Billings, 1922-29; mem. Johnston, Coleman & Jameson, 1929-40, Coleman, Jameson & Lamey, 1940-57; judge U.S. Dist. Ct. for Mont., 1957-69, sr. judge, 1969—; judge Temporary Emergency Ct. Appeals, 1976—; Bd. dirs. Nat. Jud. Coll., 1963-64; trustee Nat. Inst. Trial Advocacy, 1971-77. Mem. Mont. Ho. of Reps., 1927-30; Sch. Bd. Trustee, Billings, 1930- 32; chmn. Yellowstone County chpt. A.R.C., 1931-45. Recipient Disting. Achievement award Law Sch., Gonzaga U., 1970. Fellow Am. Bar Found.; mem. ABA (bd. govs. 1943-46, assembly del. 1946-53, pres. 1953-54, pres. endowment 1961-63, chmn. sect. jud. adminstrn. 1963-64, chmn. spl. com. on adminstrn. criminal justice 1969-73, recipient gold medal 1973), Mont. Bar Assn. (pres. 1936- 37), Am. Law Inst. (mem. council 1956—), Am. Judicature Soc. (pres. 1956-58, Herbert Lincoln Harley award 1974), Am. Legion, Phi Delta Phi. Methodist. Lodges: Masons; Lion (dist. gov. 1941-42). Home: Westpark Village 2351 Solomon Ave #100 Billings MT 59102 Office: PO Box 2115 Fed Bldg-U S Courthouse Billings MT 59103

JAMIESON, GENE CURTIS, analytical chemist, researcher; b. Elgin, Ill., Aug. 28, 1952; s. Curtis Clayton and Mary Ruth (Morris) J.; m. Jeanne Marie Dunwoody, Sept. 4, 1973; children: Corey Scott, Lindsay Rey. BS in Chemistry, No. Ill. U. Quality control engr. GTE Corp., Genoa, Ill., 1974-76; section leader research inst. Zoecon Corp., Palo Alto, Calif., 1976—; cons. Purdue U., Lafayette, Ind., 1986—. Inventor mass spectrometry probe, 1983. Mem. AAAS, Am. Soc. Mass Spectrometry, Bay Area Mass Spectrometry, Am. Chem. Soc., Ofcl. Assn. Analytical Chemists. Avocations: mountaineering, home building, music, science. Home: 18155 China Grade Rd Boulder Creek CA 95006 Office: Zoecon Corp 975 California Ave Palo Alto CA 94304

JAMISON, DAVID W., marine scientist; b. Portland, Oreg., Apr. 23, 1939; s. Edgar W. and Nina (Ray) J.; m. Susan Elizabeth Porter, Dec. 23, 1962 (div. 1974); children—Adam, Elizabeth; m. 2d, Nancy Louise Kasper, Apr. 7, 1979; stepchildren—Kevin, Keith, Kelly. B.S., Whitman Coll., 1961; postgrad. U. Oreg., 1961-62; M.S., U. Wash., 1966, Ph.D., 1970. Remote sensing scientist Wash. Dept. Natural Resources, Olympia, 1969-70, marine scientist, 1970-74, supr. baseline studies dept. ecology, 1974-78, dir. marine research and devel., 1978-80, mgr. forestry research and devel., 1980-82, chief marine scientist, 1983—; gov.'s rep. U.S. Dept. Interior outer continental shelf research adv. com., 1974-78; cons. NOAA Interagy. Com. on Ocean Pollution Research, Devel. and Monitoring, 1981; mem. adv. com. Puget Sound Water Quality Authority, 1985-86, chmn. research com. 1987—; mem. tech. adv. com. Puget Sound Estuary Program, 1985—; mem. tech. work groups Puget Sound Dredge Disposal Analysis Study, 1985—. Bd. dirs. Boston Harbor Assn., 1980—, chmn. utilities com., 1981—; mem. Thurston County Shorelines adv. com., 1973-74, 82-83. Mem. Am. Soc. Photogrammetry, Marine Tech. Soc., Pacific Estuarine Research Soc., Sigma Xi. Contbr. articles to profl. jours. Office: State of Wash Dept Natural Resources Olympia WA 98504

JANCA, TOM STANLEY, oil company executive; b. Phoenix, Jan. 8, 1943; s. Walter T. and Sara F. (Reese) J.; m. Claudia Linne, Aug. 24, 1968 (div. 1980); children—Tom Reese, Robert Stanley, Betty Marie, David Michael, Jennifer Linne. Student, Phoenix Coll., Mesa Community Coll. Fire engr., capt. City of Mesa, Ariz., 1973-78; propr. Janca's JoJoba Oil & Seed Co., Mesa, 1973-78, pres., 1978-80, propr., 1980—. Served to 2d lt. USNG, 1961-68. Mem. Jojoba Soc. Am., Am. Oil Chemist Soc. Republican. Home: 1407 S Date Mesa AZ 85202 Office: Rt #1 Box 771 Maricopa AZ 85239

JANCAR, ROBERT E., industrial engineering executive; b. Johnstown, Pa.; m. Carol Jancar; children: Tim, Leanna. BS in Indsl. Engring., Pa. State U.; MBA, Fairleigh Dickinson U. Jr. indsl. engr. Ethicon, Inc., 1963; mgr. indsl. engr. Ethicon, Inc., Chgo.; mgr. corp. project engring. Ethicon, Inc.; supt. Needle Mfg., Suture Mfg.; plant mgr. Ethicon, Inc., Albuquerque, N.Mex., 1981—. Bd. trustees U. Albuquerque, U. N.Mex. Grad. Sch. Bus.; mem. Gov. Anaya's Businessmen's Adv. Council; bd. dirs. United Way, Albuquerque, Presbyn. Hosp. Found., Albuquerque Indsl. Devel. Service; bd. advisors Lovelace Med. Ctr. Found. Mem. Albuquerque C. of C. (bd. dirs., v.p. econ. affairs, exec. com., pres. 1986), Econ. Forum.

JANES, DONALD WALLACE, biologist, educator, academic administrator, consultant; b. Kansas City, Mo., June 12, 1929; s. H. Wallace and Leila G. (Duncan) Janes; m. Norma Marie Lee, Feb. 21, 1953 (dec. 1978); children: Todd Allan, Jeffrey Wallace, Scott Lee Duncan, Nancy Marie; m. Janina Z. Piorkowska, Nov. 14, 1981. BA, Baker U., 1951; MS, U. Kans., 1956; PhD, Kans. State U., 1962. Instr. biology Washburn U., Topeka, 1957-61; asst. prof. biology Parsons Coll., Fairfield, Iowa, 1962-63; postdoctoral research assoc. Ind. U., Bloomington, 1963, Baylor Coll. Medicine, Houston, 1964, 66, Iowa State U., Ames, 1965; assoc. prof. and dean U. So. Colo., Pueblo, 1968-78, prof. biology, 1978—; cons., examiner N. Cen. Assn. of Colls. and Schs., Chgo., 1969—; vis. prof. U. Colo., Boulder, 1978-79. Fulbright fellow U. Graz, Austria, 1956-57; Acad. Adminstrn. fellow Am. Council on Edn., Washington, 1968-69. Mem. Audubon Club, Pueblo (organizer 1968); Pueblo C. of C.1968-78; Am. Soc. Microbiology, Soc. for Indsl. Microbiology, Sigma Xi (pres.-elect 1986—). Republican. Clubs: Colo. Mountain (Pueblo) (chmn. 1973-74). Avocations: mountaineering, skiing, bicycling, music, reading. Home: 91 Ironweed Dr Pueblo CO 81001 Office: U So Colo Dept Life Scis Pueblo CO 81001

JANES, JANINA Z.P., infosystems specialist; b. Poland, May 1, 1955; came to U.S., 1966; d. Stanislaw Henryk Piorkowski and Olga (Ilnicka) Piorkowska; m. Donald Wallace Janes, Nov. 14, 1981. Student, U. Lancaster, England, 1974-75; BA, Case Western Res. U., 1976, MS, 1977; AAS, U. So. Colo., 1983. Reference librarian Alliance Coll., Cambridge Springs, Pa., 1977-80; catalog librarian U. So. Colo., Pueblo, 1980-81, serials librarian, 1981-82, automations librarian, 1982-84; med. librarian Parkview Episcopal Med. Ctr., Pueblo, 1984-85, info. mgr., 1985-86; dir. libraries Penrose Hosps., Colorado Springs, Colo., 1986—. Mem. Peaks and Valleys Med. Library Consortium (sec. 1984, v.p. 1985, pres. 1986), Colo. Council Med. Librarians. Republican. Club: Colo. Mountain (Pueblo). Avocations: birdwatching, climbing, bicycling, reading, wild flowers. Home: 91 Ironweed Dr Pueblo CO 81001 Office: Penrose Hosps PO Box 7021 Colorado Springs CO 80933

JANESKI, WILLIAM LOUIS, real estate broker; b. Pittsburg, Kans., Nov. 28, 1932; s. William Charles and Elnora Fern (Sanders) J.; m. June Elizabeth Cover, Feb. 19, 1955; children: David Scott, Stephen Gregrey, William Andrew, Nancy Elizabeth. Student, U. Kans., 1951-52, Strayer Coll. Accountancy, 1955-56, UCLA, 1985. Exec. v.p. Century 21 Real Estate Co. Va., McLean, 1972-74; founder, pres., chief exec. officer Realty World Corp., Annandale, Va., 1974-80; pres. Worldwide Organizational Systems, Los Angeles and Walnut Creek, Calif., 1980-83; v.p. Very Important Properties, Rolling Hills Estates, Calif., 1985—. Mem. Realtors Polit. Action Com., 1979—. Served with USN, 1952-54, Korea. Named to Million Dollar Club, No. Va. Bd. Realtors, 1969, 70, 71, 72, 73. Mem. Nat. Assn. Realtors. Republican. Methodist. Lodge: Optimists (local pres. 1971-72). Avocations: philately, running, swimming. Home: 2833 Via Victoria Palos Verdes Estates CA 90274 Office: Very Important Properties 609 Deep Valley Dr Rolling Hills Estates CA 90274

JANG, ALLEN WAI, school principal; b. Los Angeles, Aug. 18, 1950; s. Bock Chong and Kau Ngook (Chiang) J.; m. Loan Jang Quyen, Aug. 31, 1974; children: Timothy Bock, Julie Kau. BA, Pepperdine U., Los Angeles, 1974; MA, Pepperdine U., Malibu, 1978; PhD, Columbia Pacific U., 1984; cert. counseling, U. Calif., 1978. Cert. tchr., counselor, Calif. Adminstr. Normandie Christian Sch., Los Angeles, 1981-83; prin. Calif. Christian Sch., Sepulveda, 1983-86, Orange County Christian Sch., Cypress, Calif., 1986—; cons., security dept. enforcement instr. Pepperdine U., Malibu, Calif., 1986; faculty mentor Columbia Pacific U., San Rafael, Calif., 1985—; instr. U.S. Sch. Law Enforcement, Los Angeles, 1981—, self def. and rape prevention East Los Angeles Community Coll., 1979-80, Children's Hosp. Los Angeles, 1985. Assoc. minister Ch. of Christ, San Gabriel, Calif., 1982—. Recipient Stipend 3d Inst. for High Sch. Chemistry NSF, 1985. Mem. Am. Sci. Affiliation, Christian Martial Arts Assn. (chief instr. 1983—), Nat. Sci. Tchr. Assn., U.S. Chess Fedn. (cert. tournament dir.). Republican. Avocations: martial arts, chess, astronomy, reading. Home: 201 N Sycamore Dr San Gabriel CA 91775 Office: Orange County Christian Sch 5400 Myra Ave Cypress CA 90630

JANI, ROBERT FRANK, production company executive; b. Los Angeles, May 25, 1934; s. Ernest George and Gloria (Angona) J.; m. Joan Claire Chapman, Oct. 6, 1956; children: Joy Michelle, Jeffrey Scott. BA, U. So. Calif., 1956. V.p. entertainment Walt Disney Prodns., Anaheim, Calif., 1967-78, creative cons., 1978-84; pres., exec. producer Robert F. Jani Prodns. Inc., 1978—.

JANIS, IRVING LESTER, research psychologist, emeritus educator; b. Buffalo, May 26, 1918; s. M. Martin and Etta (Goldstein) J.; m. Marjorie Graham, Sept. 5, 1939; children: Cathy Wheeler, Charlotte. B.S., U. Chgo., 1939; Ph.D. in Psychology, Columbia U., 1948. Research asst., exptl. div. study war time communications Library of Congress, 1941; sr. social sci. analyst, spl. war policies unit Dept. Justice, 1941-43; research assoc., spl. com. Social Sci. Research Council, 1945-46, research fellow, 1946-47; mem. faculty Yale U., 1947-85, prof. psychology, 1960-85, prof. emeritus, 1985—; adj. prof. U. Calif.-Berkeley, 1985—; research cons. RAND Corp., 1948-74; mem. panel social psychol. research NSF, 1965-66; mem. com. disaster studies NRC-Nat. Acad. Scis., 1953-57; mem. Surgeon Gen.'s Sci. Adv. Com. on TV and Social Behavior, 1969-71. Author: Air War and Emotional Stress, 1951, (with Hovland and Kelley) Communication and Persuasion, 1953, Psychological Stress, 1958, (with others) Personality and Persuasibility, 1959, Stress and Frustration, 1971, Victims of Groupthink, 1972, (with L. Mann) Decision Making, 1977, (with D. Wheeler) A Practical Guide for Making Decisions, 1980, (with others) Counseling on Personal Decisions: Theory and Research on Short-term Helping Relationships, 1982, Short-term Counseling: Guidelines Based on Recent Research, 1983, Groupthink, 1983, Stress, Attitudes and Decisions: Selected Papers (Centennial Psychology Series), 1982; also articles, chpts. in books.; editor: Current Trends in Psychology: Readings from American Scientist, 1977; contbg. editor: Jour. Abnormal and Social Psychology, 1955-65; mem. editorial bd.: Jour. Exptl. Social Psychology, 1966-70, Am. Scientist, 1970-79, Jour. Behavioral Medicine, 1978—, Brit. Jour. Social Psychology, 1980—; chmn. editorial bd.: Jour. Conflict Resolution, 1972—. Served with AUS, 1943-45. Recipient Hofheimer prize Am. Psychiat. Assn., 1959; Socio-Psychol. prize AAAS, 1967; Fulbright research fellow, 1957-58; sr. faculty fellow Yale U., 1961-62, 69-70; faculty research fellow Social Sci. Research Council, 1961-62, 66-67; Guggenheim fellow, also fellow Center Advanced Study Behavioral Scis., 1973-74; research fellow Netherlands Inst. Advanced Studies, 1981-82; Kurt Lewin Meml. award for research in social psychology Soc. for Psychol. Study Social Issues, 1985. Fellow Am. Acad. Arts and Scis.; mem. Am. Psychol. Assn. (Disting. Sci. Contbn. award 1981), AAAS (judge sociol-psychol. prize 1963-64). Home: 627 Scotland Drive Santa Rosa CA 95405

JANIS, JUEL M., public health administration educator; b. Los Angeles, May 17, 1934; d. Leonard Theodore and Ida (Miller) Mendelsohn; m. Jay Janis, Sept. 7, 1954; children: Laura, Jeffrey. BA, George Washington U., 1956; MS, U. Miami, 1966; PhD, U. Md., 1971. Head Start program coordinator Dade County (Fla.) Community Action Agy., 1971-73; assoc. prof. health sci. Fla. Internat. U., Miami, 1973-75, acting chair dept., 1975; assoc. prof. pediatrics, dir. behavioral sci. U. Mass., Worchester, 1976-77; asst. to surgeon gen./asst. sec. health U.S. Dept. Health Human Services, Washington, 1977-81; asst. dean Sch. Pub. Health UCLA, 1981-85, adj. assoc. prof. health services, 1982-86; adj. asst. prof. ednl. psychology U. Miami, Coral Gables, Fla., 1970; affiliate faculty Grad. Sch. Edn. UCLA, 1984-86; cons. Abt Assocs., Boston, 1976; social sci. analyst U.S. Pres.'s Commn. Mental Health, Washington, 1977; tech. advisor Dept. Health and Human Services, Washington, 1983, child care TV com. Communiy Action Agy., Dade County, 1974-75; chair ops. com. sch. health Los Angeles County, 1984-85. Feature editor North Shore Jour., Surfside, Fla., 1956-57; mem. editorial bd. UCLA Health Insights 1980-85; reviewer Pub. Health Reports, 1983. Chairperson Dade County Model Day Care Task Force, 1973, Pub. Health Trust nominating com. Dade County Health Planning Council, 1975; mem. adv. bd. Clinica Borinquen Neighborhood Health Ctr., 1974-75; pres. bd. dirs. Fla. Internat. U. Child Care Ctr., 1975. William T. Grant fellow, 1968-69. Mem. AAAS, Assn. Advancement Psychology, Am. Pub. Health Assn. (awards com. 1984), So. Calif. Pub. Health Assn., Am. Psychol. Assn., Phi Kappa Phi.

JANIS, SALLY VEGORS, business educator; b. Sault Ste Marie, Mich., Sept. 8, 1932; d. Stanley Henry and Esther Eloise (Sharpe) Vegors; m. Thomas Patrick Janis, Apr. 8, 1961; children: Mary, Kathryn, Sally A., Paul, Elizabeth, Virginia. BA in Bus., Mich. State U., 1964; MA in Edn., U. Alaska, 1971. Instr. bus. adminstrn. Anchorage Community Coll., 1964—, clerical cluster coordinator, 1971-73, coordinator, office occupations dept., 1981-84. Mem. Bus. Edn. Assn., Anchorage Alumnae Assn. (pres. 1984—), Panhellenic Assn., Alpha Omicron Pi. Methodist. Clubs: Cotillion, P.E.O. (recording sec. 1984—) (Anchorage), Alaska Swimming (bd. dirs. 1982—, records chairperson). Avocations: swimming, reading. Home: 2400 Foxhall Dr Anchorage AK 99504 Office: Anchorage Community Coll 2533 Providence Ave Anchorage AK 99508

JANSEN, LEONARD BENJAMIN, scientific computing executive, consultant; b. Denville, N.J., July 31, 1955; s. Leonard Bernard and Bernice Carolyn (Helgeson) J.; m. Deborah Ann Datsko, June 2, 1984. BA, Sarah Lawrence Coll., 1977; MEd in Math., Pa. State U., 1985, MS in Computer Sci., 1986. Devel. cons. Nat. Systems and Research Co., Colorado Springs, Colo., 1982; programmer, analyst U.S. Olympic Com., Colorado Springs, 1982-83, systems analyst, designer, 1983-84, sci. computing dir., 1984—; cons. PRA Ltd., Colorado Springs, 1983—. Mem. Am. Math. Assn. (Faculty award Sarah Lawrence Coll. 1977, Pa. State U. 1980), Walkers Club Am. (men's devel. com. 1984-86, sports sci. sports medicine com. 1982—, tech. advisor 1985—). Club: Shore Athletic (Long Beach, N.J.). Avocations: fishing, cross country skiing, racewalking. Home: 730 N Prospect St #A-8 Colorado Springs CO 80903 Office: US Olympic Com 1750 E Boulder St Colorado Springs CO 80909

JANSEN, ROBERT BRUCE, consulting civil engineer; b. Spokane, Wash., Dec. 14, 1922; s. George Martin and Pearl Margaret (Kent) J.; m. Barbara Mae Courtney, Sept. 18, 1943. BSCE, U. Denver, 1949; MSCE, U. So. Calif., 1955. Registered profl. engr., Calif., Colo., Wash. Chief Calif. Div. Dam Safety, Sacramento, 1965-68; chief of ops. Calif. Dept. Water Resources, Sacramento, 1968-71, dep. dir., 1971-75, chief design and constrn., 1975-77; asst. commr. U.S. Bur. Reclamation, Denver, 1977-80; cons. civil engr. Spokane, 1980—; cons. bd. dirs. Tenn. Valley Authority, Knoxville, 1981—, So. Calif. Edison Co., Rosemead, 1982—, Pacific Gas and Electric, San Francisco, 1982—, Hydro-Quebec, Mon., Can., 1986—, Ala. Power Co., Birmingham, 1985—. Author: Dams and Public Safety, 1983; editor: Safety of Existing Dams, 1983. Mem. U.S. Com. on Large Dams (chmn.1979-81), ASCE, Internat. Soc. Soil Mechanics and Found. Engring., Assn. State Dam Safety Ofcls., Nat. Acad. Engring. (elected). Home and Office: E 315 High Dr Spokane WA 99203

JANTZEN, J(OHN) MARC, educator; b. Hillsboro, Kans., July 30, 1908; s. John D. and Louise (Janzen) J.; m. Ruth Patton, June 9, 1935; children: John Marc, Myron Patton, Karen Louise. A.B., Bethel Coll., Newton, Kans., 1934; A.M., U. Kans., 1937, Ph.D., 1940. Elementary sch. tchr. Marion County, Kans., 1927-30, Hillsboro, Kan., 1930-31; high sch. tchr. 1934-36; instr. sch. edn. U. Kans., 1936-40; asst. prof. Sch. Edn., U. of Pacific, Stockton, Calif., 1940-42; assoc. prof. Sch. Edn., U. of Pacific, 1942-44, prof., 1944-78, prof. emeritus, 1978—, also dean sch. edn., 1944-74, emeritus, 1974—, dir. summer sessions, 1940-72; condr. seminars; Past chmn. commn. equal opportunities in edn. Calif. Dept. Edn.; mem., chmn. Commn. Tchr. Edn. Calif. Tchrs. Assn., 1956-62; mem. Nat. Council for Accreditation Tchr. Edn., 1969-72. Bd. dirs. Ednl. Travel Inst., 1965—. Recipient Hon. Service award Calif. Congress of Parents and Tchrs., 1982; Paul Harris fellow Rotary Found., 1980. Mem. Am., Calif. edn. research assns., Calif. Council for Edn. Tchrs., Calif. Assn. of Colls. for Tchr. Edn. (sec.-treas. 1975-85), N.E.A., Phi Delta Kappa. Methodist. Lodge: Rotary. Home: 117 W Euclid Ave Stockton CA 95204

JANULAITIS, M. VICTOR, consulting company executive; b. Augsberg, Ger., Sept. 25, 1945; came to U.S., 1948, naturalized, 1953; s. Vytautas P. and Salome (Sutkatis) J.; m. Carol L. George, Nov. 23, 1968; children—Victoria C., Michael G. B.S., Loyola U., Chgo., 1967; M.B.A., U. Chgo., 1971. C.P.A., Ill.; cert. mgmt. cons.; cert. data processor. With IBM, Chgo., 1967-71, Touche Ross & Co., Chgo., 1971-78; v.p. Damon Corp., Boston, 1978-79; part-time instr. Harvard U. Grad. Sch., 1979-80, ind. cons., 1979-80; v.p. Western ops. Index Systems, Los Angeles and Boston, 1979-82; founder, chief exec. officer Positive Support Rev., Inc., Los Angeles, 1982—; chmn. UCLA Grad. Sch. Mgmt. Assocs. Program. Author: (with others) Managing the System Development Process, 1980. Treas. adv. bd. Malibu Sch., Calif., 1982, 84. Mem. Am. Inst. C.P.A.s, Ill. Soc. C.P.A.s, Am. Prodn. and Inventory Control Soc., Soc. Mgmt. Info. Systems (So. Calif. chpt.), Inst. Mgmt. Cons. (Los Angeles chpt.). Office: Positive Support Review Inc 10880 Wilshire Blvd Los Angeles CA 90024

JANURA, JAN AROL, apparel manufacturing executive; b. Chgo., May 12, 1949; s. Harold Charles and Violet Mary J.; B.S., Colo. State U., 1971; M.A., Fuller Theol. Sem., 1973. Area dir. Young Life Campaign, Seattle, 1973-76; chief exec. officer, dir. Carol Anderson, Inc., Los Angeles, 1977—; pres. Los Angeles Electric Motorcar Co., 1979-80; bd. dirs. Western Leadership Found., Starr Leadership Found.; mem Presl. Task Force, 1986; founder Janura Library, 1986. Mem. Rep. Nat. Com., 1986, Rep. Presdl. Task Force, 1984-86; trustee Janura Library, Glendale, Colo. Weyerhaeuser fellow, 1972-73; recipient Salesman of Yr. award, 1983, 84. Clubs: Snowcreek Athletic, Los Angeles Athletic, Wash. Athletic, N.Y. Athletic, Admirals (life). Office: 5770 Anderson St Vernon CA 90058

JAQUETTE, PETER BARNES, economist; b. Honolulu, Sept. 20, 1952; s. John J. and Margaret (Leaf) J.; m. Andrea Frisk, Jan. 15, 1983; 1 child, Elisabeth. A.B., Swarthmore Coll., 1974; A.M., Stanford U., 1976. Research economist UCLA Bus. Forecasting Project, 1979-81; sr. econ. analyst Atlantic Richfield Co., Los Angeles, 1981-84, planning cons., 1984-86, dir. Econ. Analysis, 1986—. Mem. Am. Econ. Assn., Nat. Assn. Bus. Economists, Internat. Assn. Energy Economists. Office: Atlantic Richfield 515 S Flower St Los Angeles CA 90071

JAQUITH, GEORGE OAKES, ophthalmologist; b. Caldwell, Idaho, July 29, 1916; s. Gail Belmont and Myrtle (Burch) J.; B.A., Coll. Idaho, 1938; M.B., Northwestern U., 1942, M.D., 1943; m. Pearl Elizabeth Taylor, Nov. 30, 1939; children—Patricia Ann Jaquith Mueller, George, Michele Eugenie Jaquith Smith. Intern, Wesley Meml. Hosp., Chgo., 1942-43; resident ophthalmology U.S. Naval Hosp., San Diego, 1946-48; pvt. practice medicine, specializing in ophthamology, Brawley, Calif., 1948—; pres. Pioneers Meml. Hosp. staff, Brawley, 1953; dir., exec. com. Calif. Med. Eye Council, 1960—; v.p. Calif. Med. Eye Found., 1976—. Sponsor Anza council Boy Scouts Am., 1966—. Gold card holder Republican Assos., Imperial County, Calif., 1967-68. Served with M.C., USN, 1943-47; PTO. Mem. Imperial County Med. Soc. (pres. 1961), Calif. Med. Assn. (del. 1961—), Nat., So. Calif. (dir. 1966—, chmn. med. adv. com. 1968-69) socs. prevention blindness, Calif. Assn. Ophthalmology (treas. 1976—), San Diego, Los Angeles ophthal. socs., Los Angeles Research Study Club, Nathan Smith Davis Soc., Coll. Idaho Assos., Am. Legion, VFW, Res. Officers Assn., Basenji Assn., Nat. Geneal. Soc., Phi Beta Pi, Lambda Chi Alpha. Presbyn. (elder). Clubs: Cuyamaca (San Diego); Elks. Office: 665 S Western Brawley CA 92227

JARAMILLO, MARI-LUCI, university official; b. Las Vegas, N.Mex., June 19, 1928. B.A., N.Mex. Highland U., 1955, M.A., 1959; Ph.D., U. N.Mex., 1970. Lang. arts cons. Las Vegas Sch. System, 1965-69; asst. dir. instructional services Minority Group Center, 1969-72; asso. prof., chmn. dept. elementary edn. U. N.Mex., 1972-75, coordinator Title VII tchr. tng., 1975-76, asso. prof. edn., 1976-77, prof., 1977, spl. asst. to pres., 1981-82, assoc. dean Coll. Edn., 1982-85, v.p. for student affairs, 1985—; ambassador to Honduras, Tegucigalpa, 1977-80; dep. asst. sec. for inter-Am. affairs Dept. State, Washington, 1980-81. Contbr. articles to jours., chpts. to books. Trustee Tomas Rivera Ctr. Mem. Nat. Assn. Bilingual Edn., Latin Am. Assn., Am. Assn. Colls. for Tchr. Edn., Nat. Council La Roza. Home: 6425 Christie Ave Emeryville CA 94608 Office: Ednl Testing Service VP and Dir Berkeley Office 6425 Christie Ave Emeryville CA 94608

JARED, DANIEL WADE, telecommunications company executive; b. Denver, Dec. 19, 1925; s. D. Wade and Lennie E. (Miller) J. BS, U. Houston, 1947; postgrad., Utah State U., 1961-62. Assoc. engr. Boeing Airplane Co., Seattle, 1959; mathematician Wasatch div. Thiokol Chem. Corp., Brigham City, Utah, 1960-63; project engr. aerospace div. Amphenol-Borg Electronics Corp., Chatsworth, Calif., 1963-64; field project engr. Bendix Field Engring Corp., Barstow, Calif., 1964; sci. programmer Air Force Rocket Propulsion Lab., Edwards AFB, Calif., 1965-68; sr. field engr. Singer-Gen. Precision, inc., Edwards AFB, Calif., 1968-69; tech. programmer Singer-Gen. Precision, Inc., Glendale, Calif., 1969-70; spl. tech. cons. System Devel. Corp., Santa Monica, Calif., 1970, spl. programming cons., 1970; sr. engring. tech. County of San Bernardino (Calif.) Pub. Works Adminstrn., 1971-74; adminstrv. analyst County of San Bernardino (Calif.) Environ. Improvement Agy., 1974-75; pres. Neptune Telecommunications, Barstow, 1975—; planner I County of El Paso, Colorado Springs, Colo., 1977-79; tech. cons. Westrans Corp., Colorado Springs, Colo., 1982. Contbr. articles to profl. jours. Mem. AAAS, Congress on Surveying and Mapping, AIAA, Am. Guild of Organists.

JARKO, MICHAEL FRANKLIN, manufacturer's representative; b. Steubenville, Ohio, May 20, 1937; s. Michael Anthony and Lillian (Wilson) J.; m. Nancy Phillips, Sept. 20, 1957; children: Michael P., Elizabeth A., Jeffrey W., Christopher S. BFA, Ohio State U., 1959; postgrad., Ariz. State U., 1962-64. V.p. Premmco Inc., Phoenix, 1961-67, also bd. dirs.; pres. Jarko Assocs. Inc., Phoenix, 1967—, also bd. dirs.; pres. Solid State Deviced Inc., Tempe, Ariz., 1968-74; bd. dirs. Continental Circuits Corp., Phoenix, Carl Gundersen Co., Tucson, Press Com. Inc., Tempe. Patentee in field. Sec. Boys Clubs of Scottsdale, Ariz., 1979. Mem. Photographic Soc. Am., Associated Photographers Internat., Scottsdale Artists League, Mesa Art League. Republican.

JARMIE, NELSON, physicist; b. Santa Monica, Calif., Mar. 24, 1928; s. Louis and Ruth (Wydman) J. B.S., Calif. Inst. Tech., 1948; Ph.D., U. Calif.-Berkeley, 1953. Staff mem. Los Alamos Sci. Lab., 1953—; vis. prof. U. Calif.-Santa Barbara, 1960; adj. prof. U. N.Mex., 1957-71; mem. adv. council Los Alamos Grad. Ctr., 1958—; participant Vis. Scientist Program, 1965-71. Contbr. numerous articles to sci. jours. and mags.; research in nuclear and particle physics and in astrophysics. Mem. Econ. Devel. Council Los Alamos County, N.Mex., 1968. Fellow Am. Phys. Soc., AAAS; mem. Am. Assn. Physics Tchrs., Sigma Xi, Tau Beta Pi. Office: Los Alamos Nat Lab Los Alamos NM 87545

JARNUTOWSKI, ROBERT JOHN, chemical company planning executive; b. Chgo., Mar. 11, 1938; s. John K. and Evelyn M (Borowinski) J.; m. Joei E. Boquist, Sept. 12, 1964; children: Paul, Wendi Eve, Daniel. PhB, Northwestern U., 1967. Product line specialist Beckman Instrument, Inc., Lincolnwood, Ill., 1961-65, applications chemist, 1965-71, mgr. applications, 1971-78; mgr. profl. devel. Beckman Instrument, Inc., Fullerton, Calif., 1978-84, mgr. strategic planning, 1984—. Mem. AAAS, Am. Chem. Soc., Am. Assn. Clin. Chemists, Am. Pharm. Assn., Soc. Cosmetic Chemists. Roman Catholic. Avocations: reading, boating, electronics and computers, square dancing. Office: Beckman Instruments Inc 2500 Harbor Blvd Fullerton CA 92634-3100

JARRETT, CHARLES EDWARD, accountant; b. Terre Haute, Ind., July 29, 1924; s. Isaac Edward and Eliza May (France) J.; m. Mary Frances Seiler, Apr. 8, 1944; children—Susan Elizabeth, Barbara Jane, Charles Edward. B.S. in Acctg., Ind. U., 1948; cert. exec. devel. program U. Mich., 1959; M.B.A. in Procurement and Contracting, George Washington U., 1971. C.P.A., Ind., Ohio, Va., Fla., Calif.; C.I.A., C.P.C.M., C.C.A. Pub. acct. Dieterle and Thompson, C.P.A.s, Bloomington, Ind., 1948-49; auditor U.S. Air Force, various locations, 1949-65; br. chief hdqrs. Def. Contract Audit Agy., Washington, 1965-67; procurement specialist Office Sec. Def., Washington, 1967-76; owner, mgr. Charles Edward Jarrett, C.P.A., Tallahassee, 1976-83; dir. Coopers & Lybrand, Govt. Contract Services Group, San Diego, 1983—; cons. on pricing and preparing proposals for govt. contracts. Served with U.S. Army, 1943-44. Fellow Nat. Contract Mgmt. Assn; mem. Am. Inst. C.P.A.s, Calif. Inst. C.P.A.s, Inst. Internal Auditors, Inst. Cost Analysts, Assn. Govt. Accts. Prin. Home: 12439 Bodega Ct San Diego CA 92128 Office: Coopers and Lybrand 401 West A St Suite 1600 San Diego CA 92101

JARRETT, JAMES WARREN, electronics executive; b. Cleve., June 25, 1944; s. Andrew Edward and Regina (Snyder) J.; m. Laurie Thornton Thompson, July 12, 1968; children: Tracey, Alison, Lindsay. BA, Kenyon Coll., 1966. Account exec. Ruder & Finn, Inc., N.Y.C., 1969-70, T.J. Ross and Assocs., N.Y.C., 1970-73; v.p. T.J. Ross and Assocs., San Francisco, 1973-79; mgr., corp. communications Intel Corp., Santa Clara, Calif., 1980-86, v.p. sales mktg., dir. corp. communications, 1987—. Chmn. adv. commn. Developmentally Disabled, Santa Clara County, 1979-81; mem. communications com. United Way, Santa Clara County, 1984—. Served with U.S. Army, 1967-69. Mem. Pub. Relations Soc. Am. (cert.), San Francisco Pub. Rlations Round Table, Bay Area Pub. Affairs Council. Republican. Episcopalian. Office: Intel Corp 3065 Bowers Ave Santa Clara CA 95051

JARRETT, (LYNN) LENTA JOYCE, computer professional, consultant; b. Owings, W.Va., Jan. 25, 1941; d. Jack Calvin and Helen Addie (Sherbs) Girod; m. Robert Henry Jarrett, Sept. 4, 1961 (div.); children: Todd and Stephanie. BBA, Nat. U., 1982, MBA, 1983. Sec. Dept. of State, Washington, 1958-59; printer Union-Tribune, San Diego, 1961-79, computer specialist, 1979-84, computer mgr., 1984—. Nat. computer columnist Digital Review mag., Boston. Leader Girl Scouts U.S., San Diego, 1975-79; bd. dirs. San Diego YWCA. Recipient Twin award YWCA, San Diego, 1985. Mem. Nat. U. Alumni Assn., Decus Computer Soc. (nat. and local rainbow chairperson 1984—), Mass 11 Users Group (chairperson), Data Processing Mgrs. Assn. Democrat. Methodist. Club: Skyliters (San Diego). Avocations: snow skiing, flying. Office: PO Box 191 350 Camino De La Reina San Diego CA 92112

JARVIK, ROBERT KOFFLER, biomedical research scientist; b. Midland, Mich., May 11, 1946; s. Norman Eugene and Edythe (Koffler) J.; B.A., Syracuse U., 1968, Dr. Sci. (hon.), 1983; M.A., NYU, 1971; M.D., U. Utah, 1976; Dr. Sci. (hon.), Hahnemann U., 1985. Research asst. Div. Artificial Organs-U. Utah, Salt Lake City, 1971-76, asst. dir. exptl. labs., 1976-82; pres. Symbion, Inc., Salt Lake City, 1981—; asst. research prof. surgery U. Utah, 1979—; mem. nat. selection panel NASA Tchr. in Space Project, Washington, 1985. Sect. editor: Internat. Jour. Artificial Organs, 1979—; inventor repeating hemostatic clip instruments and cartridges, total artificial hearts powered by electrohydraulic energy; patentee in field. Named Inventor of Yr. Intellectual Property Owners, 1983; named John W. Hyatt award Soc. Plastics Engrs., 1983, Golden Plate Am. Acad. Achievement, 1983, Gold Heart award Utah Heart Assn., 1983. Mem. Am. Soc. Artificial Internal Organs. Office: Symbion Inc 350 West 800 North Salt Lake City UT 84103 *

JARVIS, DONALD BERTRAM, judge; b. Newark, Dec. 14, 1928; s. Benjamin and Esther (Golden) J.; B.A., Rutgers U., 1949; J.D., Stanford U., 1952; m. Rosalind C. Chodorcove, June 13, 1954; children: Nancie, Brian, Joanne. Bar: Calif. 1953. Law clk. Justice John W. Shenk, Calif. Supreme Ct., 1953-54; assoc. Erskine, Erskine & Tulley, 1955; asso. Aaron N. Cohen, 1955-56; law clk. Dist. Ct. Appeal, 1956; assoc. Carl Hoppe, 1956-57; adminstrv. law judge Calif. Public Utilities Commn., San Francisco, 1957—; mem. exec. com. Nat. Conf. Adminstrv. Law Judges, 1986—; pres. Calif. Adminstrv. Law Judges Council, 1978-84; mem. faculty Nat. Jud. Coll., U. Nev., 1977, 78, 80. Chmn. pack Boy Scouts Am., 1967-69, chmn. troop, 1972; class chmn. Stanford Law Sch. Fund, 1959, mem. nat. com., 1963-65; dir. Forest Hill Assn., 1970-71. Served to col. USAF Res., 1949-79. Decorated Legion of Merit. Mem. Am. Bar Assn., State Bar Calif., Bar Assn. San Francisco, Calif. Conf. Pub. Utility Counsel (pres. 1980-81), Nat. Panel Arbitrators, Am. Arbitration Assn., Air Force Assn., Res. Officers Assn., De Young Museum Soc. and Patrons Art and Music, San Francisco Gem and Mineral Soc., Stanford Alumni Assn., Rutgers Alumni Assn., Phi Beta Kappa (pres. No. Calif. 1973-74), Tau Kappa Alpha, Phi Alpha Theta, Phi Alpha Delta. Home: 530 Dewey Blvd San Francisco CA 94116 Office: 505 Van Ness Ave San Francisco CA 94102

JARVIS, DONALD KARL, Russian language educator, university administrator; b. Ithaca, N.Y., Apr. 6, 1939; s. Karl Hamilton and Revo (Cram) J.; m. Janelle Jamison, Aug. 4, 1965; children: Tyler Jamison, Elena, Brenda Leona, Grant Jamison, Adriana Rose, Karl Jamison. BA magna cum laude, Brigham Young U., 1964; PhD, Ohio State U., 1970. Cert. secondary tchr., Utah. Prof. Russian Brigham Young U., Provo, Utah, 1970—, chmn. dept. Asian & Slavic langs., 1976-79, chmn. com. lang. teaching research, 1981-83, assoc. dean gen. edn., 1981-84, dean gen. edn., 1984-86. Author: Viewpoints, 1985; editor: Increasing Slavic Program Enrollments, 1978, Teaching, Learning, Acquiring Russian, 1984; contbr. articles to profl. jours. Chmn. City Neighborhood Com., Provo, 1974-76. NDEA fellow, 1967-70. Mem. Am. Assn. Tchrs. Slavic and Eastern European Langs. (v.p. 1976-77, pres. 1982-84, exec. com. 1982—), Am. Assn. Advancement Slavic Studies (bd. dirs. 1983-85, chmn. lang. com. 1985—), Am. Council Tchrs. Russian (bd. dirs. 1977—, v.p. 1979-83). Mormon. Avocations: gardening, reading. Home: 1256 Locust Ln Provo UT 84604 Office: Brigham Young Univ Dept Germanic & Slavic Langs Provo UT 84602

JARVIS, ROBERT BURDETTE, retired civil engineer, career naval officer; b. Weston, W.Va., July 15, 1921; s. Frank Goff and Bernice Louise (Hudkins) J.; m. Gwendolyn Jean Davis, Feb. 19, 1945; 1 child, Ellen Louise Jarvis Hoekstra. Student, Marshall Coll., 1939-41, Carnegie Inst. Tech., 1941-42, George Washington U., 1943-44; BCE and MCE, Rensselaer Poly. Inst., 1948; postgrad., U. Utah, 1964. Registered profl. engr., Calif., W.Va., Utah, Idaho. Commd. line officer USN, 1944-48, advanced through grades to lt. commdr., civil engr. corps, 1948-62, retired, 1962; structural engr. Utah Dept. Hwys., Salt Lake City, 1962-65; engr. bridge design Idaho Transp. Dept., Boise, 1965-86, retired, 1986. Prin. works include White Bird (Idaho) Canyon Bridge (named Prize Bridge, Designer Am. Inst. Steel Constrn., 1976), Sandpoint (Idaho) Bridge (Spl. Recognition award Prestressed Concrete Inst., 1983). Mem. ASCE (life), Structural Engrs. Assn. of Idaho (charter), Nat. Rifle Assn. (life), Sigma Xi (assoc.). Republican. Lutheran. Avocations: hunting, fishing, gunsmithing, poker. Home: 1801 N 29th St Boise ID 83703

JARVIS, WILLIAM TYLER, health educator; b. Takoma Park, Md., Oct. 19, 1935; s. Charles Basil Jarvis and Thelma Blanche (Archbold) Black; m. Ada Hildegard Domke, Dec. 23, 1962; children: William Tyler II, Matthew Adam. BS, U. Minn., 1961; MA, Kent State U., 1968; PhD, U. Oreg., 1973. Tchr. secondary schs., W.Va. and Ohio, 1961-68; asst. prof. physical and health edn. Loma Linda U., Riverside, Calif., 1968-71, asst. prof. dept. preventive and community dentistry, 1973-75, assoc. prof., 1975-82, prof., chmn. dept. pub. health scis., 1982-86, prof. dept. preventive medicine, 1986—; founder, pres. Nat. Council Against Health Fraud, Inc., Loma Linda, 1977—; bd. advisors Am. Council on Sci. and Health, N.Y.C., 1980—; cons. council on dental research Am. Dental Assn., Chgo., 1984; mem. Atty. Gen.'s Task Force on Health Fraud, Calif., 1985—; co-chmn. subcom. on paranormal health claims Com. for Sci. Investigation of Claims of the Paranormal; cons. com. on health care Calif. Med. Assn., 1984—; cons. Nat. Assn. Chiropractic Medicine, 1985—. Author: Food Facts and Fallacies A-Z, 1985, Quackery and You, 1983; contbr. chpts. to books; mem. editorial adv. bd. Shape Mag., 1981—, Nutrition Forum Newsletter, 1985—. Chmn. bd. dirs. Adventist Community Team Services, 1974-77; chmn. subcom. on health, physical edn. and driver edn., Gen. Conference of Seventh-day Adventists, 1966-69. NDEA fellow U. Oreg., 1971-73; recipient Meritorious Service award Calif. Dietetic Assn., 1982. Mem. Am. Cancer Soc. (com. on unproven methods of cancer mgmt. 1986-87), Am. Pub. Health Assn., Am. Alliance for Health Phys. Edn. and Recreation, Am. Sch. Health Assn., Nutrition Today Soc., So. Calif. Skeptics (bd. dirs. 1985—), Sigma Xi. Office: Loma Linda U Loma Linda CA 92350

JASINEK, GARY DONALD, newspaper executive; b. Champaign, Ill., Sept. 17, 1950; s. William Gerald and Doris Margaret (Brethorst) J.; m. Carole Riggs, Nov. 9, 1974; 1 child, Andrea Sarah. Student, San Diego State U., 1968-74. Reporter The Daily Californian, El Cajon, 1975-76, city editor, 1976-79; editor Red Oak (Iowa) Express, 1979-81; editor Los Alamos (N.Mex.) Monitor, 1981-83, editor, gen. mgr., 1983-87; asst. city editor Tacoma (Wash.) News Tribune, 1987—. Mem. N.Mex. AP Mng. Editors (bd. dirs. 1984—, pres. 1986—, 1st Pl. Column award and 2d Pl. Editorial award 1982, 2d Pl. Editorial award 1984, 1st Pl. Editorial award 1985, 86), Calif. Newspaper Pubs. (1st Pl. award 1979), Iowa Press Assn. (3d Pl. award 1981), N.Mex. Press Assn. (1st Pl. award 1982). Avocations: skiing, hiking, backpacking. Home: 6721 77th St Ct NW Gig Harbor WA 98335 Office: Tacoma New Tribune PO Box 11000 Tacoma WA 98405

JASINSKI, ANDREW JOSEPH, speech pathologist; b. Detroit, Dec. 25, 1954; s. Stanley and Jean Angeline (Napowoché) J. BS, No. Mich. U., 1979; MS, U. Wis., 1980. Adminstr. speech S.O.M.E.D., Inc., Brookfield, Wis., 1980-81; speech pathologist Rehab. Ctr., Albuquerque, 1981-82, adminstr. speech, 1982-83; pvt. practice speech pathology Albuquerque, 1983-85; speech pathologist Bur. Indian Affairs, Albuquerque, 1985—; cons. Office Indian Edn., Crownpoint, N.M., 1985-86, State of N.Mex. Office Edn., 1983-84. Author: Funding Altrenative Communication, 1982. Grantee Rehab. Service Adminstrn., 1979. Fellow Am. Speech Lang. Hearing Assn. (cert., presentor, 1986), Soc. Augmentative Communication; mem. N.Mex. Speech Lang. Hearing Assn. Avocations: backpacking, cross country skiing, phys. fitness. Home and Office: 616 Washington Ave Grants NM 87020 Office: Office Indian Edn Programs PO Box 328 Crownpoint NM 87313

JASINSKY, DAVID FRANKLIN, marketing professional; b. Kalamazoo, May 31, 1952; s. Frank and Helen Jasinsky; m. Bonnie Ann Finkle, May 24, 1980; children: Alison, Jennifer, Casey. BA, Hope Coll., 1974. With mktg. and ops. dept. Bell Pipe and Supply Co., Three Rivers, Mich., 1978-83; So. Colo. br. mgr. Fla. Tile, Sikes Corp., Colorado Springs, Colo., 1984—. Served with U.S. Army, 1975-78. Mem. Home Builders Assn. (assoc.), Constrn. Specifiers Inst. (assoc.). Democrat. Lutheran. Avocations: cross country skiing, fly fishing, hunting. Home: 19660 Four Winds Way Monument CO 80132 Office: Fla Tile Sikes Corp 3910 Sinton Rd Colorado Springs CO 80907

JASMER, DAVID LLOYD, educator; b. South Milwaukee, Wis., Oct. 17, 1942; s. Joseph Henry and Ruth Evelyn (Stevens) J.; 1 dau. by previous marriage, Sharon Kaye. BS, U. Wis., LaCrosse, 1969; MA, U. No. Colo., 1972, EdD, 1980; grad., Preacher Lewis Sch. Ministry, Albuquerque, 1983. Ordained priest Episcopal Ch., 1984. Tchr. English, speech pub. schs., DeSoto, Wis., 1969-70, Fountain (Colo.)-Ft. Carson High Sch., 1970-71; tchr. English, reading Apache Culture Globe (Ariz.) High Sch., 1974-75; tchr. English, reading Window Rock High Sch., Ft. Defiance, Ariz., 1980—, coordinator/supr. essential elements of instrn., 1984—. Served with USAF, 1960-64. Mem. Assn. Supervision and Curriculum Devel., Am. Assn. Sch. Adminstrs., Nat. Council Tchrs. English, Am. Fedn. Tchrs., Window Rock Fedn. Tchrs. Democrat. Episcopalian. Office: Window Rock High Sch PO Box 559 Fort Defiance AZ 86504

JASTREM, JOHN FRANK, auditor; b. Plains, Pa., May 28, 1955; s. Frank J. and Bernadine J.; B.S. cum laude in Commerce and Fin., Wilkes Coll., 1977. C.P.A. Jr. acct. Andrew Kovalchek, C.P.A., Wilkes-Barre, Pa., 1976; internal auditor Ingersoll-Rand Co., Woodcliff Lake, N.J., 1976; sr. audit mgr. Arthur Andersen & Co., Los Angeles, 1977-85; dir. controls evaluation and audit Wickes Cos., Inc., Santa Monica, Calif. Mem. Am. Mgmt. Assn., Nat. Assn. Accts. (pres.), Los Angeles Jaycees. Roman Catholic. Club: K.C. Home: 1913 Ripley Ave Redondo Beach CA 90278

JASTROW, WILLIAM ARTHUR, III, computer company executive; b. St. Paul, Nov. 30, 1940; s. William Arthur Jr. and Rosemary (Brown) J.; m. Gail Diane Korpi, Apr. 8, 1968; children: Nicole Ann, Douglas William. BA, U. Minn., 1963. Mgr. purchasing Sperry Corp., Roseville, Minn., 1966-74; group mgr. purchasing Sperry Corp., Santa Clara, Calif., 1974-81; dir. purchasing Amdahl Computer Co., Sunnyvale, Calif., 1981—. Republican. Roman Catholic. Home: 7032 Anjou Creek Circle San Jose CA 95120 Office: Amdahl Computer Corp 1250 E Arques Sunnyvale CA 94088

JAUHAR, PREM PRAKASH, cytogeneticist; b. West Punjab, India, Sept. 15, 1939; s. Ram Lal and Maya Devi (Bhatla) J.; m. Raj Trehan, May 15, 1965; children—Rajiv, Sandeep, Suneeta. M.Sc., Agra U., India, 1959; Ph.D., New Delhi, 1965. Mem. faculty Indian Agrl. Research Inst., New Delhi, 1963-72; sr. sci. officer U. Wales, Aberystwyth, 1972-75; research assoc. U. Ky., Lexington, 1976-78; research cytogeneticist U. Calif.-Riverside, 1978-81; research assoc. City of Hope Nat. Med. Ctr., Duarte, Calif., 1981; research dir. U.S. Agr. Labs., Research and Devel. Corp., Riverside, Calif., 1982-84; research geneticist Western Regional Research Ctr., Agrl. Research Service, USDA, Berkeley, Calif., 1985-87, Utah State U., Logan, 1987—. Area capt. Am. Heart Assn., Riverside. Recipient Chancellor's medal, United Provinces, India, 1957, Irwin Gold medal, 1957; Harcourt Butler medal United Provinces Bd. Edn., 1958; Golden Jubilee Gold medal Agra U., 1959; Genetics Soc. Am. travel award, 1978. Fellow Linnean Soc. London, Indian Soc. Genetics and Plant Breeding; mem. Tissue Culture Assn., Am.,; mem. Genetics Soc. Am., Crop Sci. Soc. Am., Am. Genetic Assn., Am. Soc. Agronomy. Author: Cytogenetics and Breeding of Pearl Millet and Related Species, 1981. Contbr. chpts. to books, articles to internat. jours. Discovered regulatory mechanism controlling chromosome pairing in polyploid species of Festuca. Home: 230 W Campus View Dr Riverside CA 92507 Office: USDA-Agrl Research Service Utah State U Logan UT 84322-6300

JAX, PETER ROBERT, data processing consultant; b. Buffalo, Sept. 14, 1946; s. William Webster and Marion Esther (Pergande) J.; m. Vicki Ann Pelusi, Apr. 15, 1973; children: Robert William, Christopher Michael. BA in Aero. and Astronautical Engring., MIT, 1968. Engr. McDonnell Douglas Corp., Long Beach, Calif., 1968-74; computer specialist McDonnell Automation Co., Long Beach, 1974-78; data processing cons. Automated Profl. Systems, Garden Grove, Calif., 1978-82, JAX Group Inc., Seal Beach, Calif., 1982—. Author (computer software) I-Create, 1983, I-Spell, 1984. Deacon Good Shepherd Presbyn. Ch., Los Alamitos, 1985—; coach Am. Youth Soccer Orgn. Soccer, Seal Beach, 1983-86. Lodge: Rotary (charter sec. Seal Beach club 1984-85, pres. 1986—). Avocations: racquetball, golf, swimming. Office: JAX Group Inc PO Box 3579 Seal Beach CA 90740

JAY, DAVID JAKUBOWICZ, management consultant; b. Danzig, Poland, Dec. 7, 1925; s. Mendel and Gladys Gitta (Zalc) Jakubowicz; came to U.S., 1938, naturalized, 1944; B.S., Wayne State U., 1948; M.S., U. Mich., 1949, postgrad., 1956-57; postgrad. U. Cin., 1951-53, Mass. Inst. Tech., 1957; m. Shirley Anne Shapiro, Sept. 7, 1947; children—Melvin Maurice, Evelyn Deborah. Supr. man-made diamonds Gen. Electric Corp., Detroit, 1951-56; instr. U. Detroit, 1948-51; asst. to v.p. engring. Ford Motor Co., Dearborn, Mich., 1956-63; project mgr. Apollo environ. control radiators N.Am. Rockwell, Downey, Calif., 1963-68; staff to v.p. corporate planning Aerospace Corp., El Segundo, Calif., 1968-70; founder, pres. PBM Systems Inc., 1970—; pres. Cal-Best Hydrofarms Coop., Los Alamitos, 1972-77, others. Pres., Community Design Corp., Los Alamitos, 1971-75. Served with USNR, 1944-46. Registered profl. engr., Calif., Mich., Ohio. Mem. Inst. Mgmt. Sci. (chmn. 1961-62), Western Greenhouse Vegetable Growers Assn. (sec.-treas. 1972-75), Tau Beta Pi. Jewish. Patentee in air supported ground vehicle, others. Home: 885 Holly Glen Dr Long Beach CA 90815

JAY, NORMA JOYCE, artist; b. Wichita, Kans., Nov. 11, 1925; d. Albert Hugh and Thelma Ree (Boyd) Braly; m. Laurence Eugene Jay, Sept. 2, 1949; children—Dana Denise, Allison Eden. Student Wichita State U., 1946-49, Art Inst. Chgo., 1955-56, Calif. State Coll., 1963. Illustrator Boeing Aircraft, Wichita, Kans., 1949-51; co-owner Back Door Gallery, Laguna Beach, Calif., 1973—. One-woman shows Milcir Gallery, Tiburon, Calif., 1978, Newport Beach City Gallery, 1981; group shows include Am. Soc. Marine Artists ann. exhbns., N.Y.C., 1978-86, Peabody Mus., Salem, Mass., 1981, Mystic Seaport Mus. Gallery, Conn., 1982-85, Mongerson Gallery Ltd., Chgo., 1984, Mariners' Mus., Newport News, Va., 1985-86; represented in permanent collections including James Irvine Found., Newport Beach, Niguel Art Assn., Laguna Niguel, Calif., Deloitte, Haskins & Sells, Costa Mesa, Calif., M.J. Brock & Sons Inc., North Hollywood, Calif., others. Recipient Best of Show award Ford Nat. Competition, 1961, First Place award Traditional Artists Exhbn., San Bernadino County Mus., 1976, Artist award Chriswood Gallery Invitational Exhbn., Rancho California, Calif., 1973. Fellow Am. Soc. Marine Artists (charter); mem. Niguel Art Assn. (first pres. 1968, hon. life mem. 1978), Artists Equity, Am. Artists Profl. League, Laguna Beach C. of C. Republican. Office: Back Door Gallery 352 N Coast Hwy Laguna Beach CA 92651

JAYARAM, SUSAN ANN, professional secretary; b. Stockton, Calif., Nov. 23, 1930; d. George Leroy and Violet Yvonne (Rushing) Potter; m. M. R. Jayaram, July 2, 1960. Student Pasadena Coll., 1951-52; Woodbury Coll., 1961; A.A., Long Beach City Coll., 1979. Cert. profl. Sec. Sec. to mgr. First Western Bank, Los Angeles, 1953-56; sec. to pres. Studio City Bank (Calif.), 1957-60; sec. to exec. vice-pres. Union Bank, Los Angeles, 1962-81; sec. to vice chmn. Imperial Bank, Los Angeles, 1981-82; personal sec. to Howard B. Keck, chmn. W.M. Keck. Found., 1982—. Sec., bd. advisors Citizens for Law Enforcement Needs, 1972-74; v.p., dir. Los Angeles/Bombay Sister City Com. Mem. DAR (Susan B. Anthony chpt.), Windsor Sq./Hancock Park Hist. Soc., Assistance League So. Calif., Freedoms Found. at Valley Forge (Los Angeles chpt.), U.S. Navy League (Beverly Hills Council) League of the Americas (1st v.p., dir.). Republican. Club: Los Angeles (dir., sec. 1967-81). Editor: Angeles Club Panorama, 1979-80; California Clarion, 1978-80. Office: HB Keck 555 S Flower St Los Angeles CA 90071

JAYE, ROBERT DONALD, architect; b. Chgo., Sept. 10, 1927; s. John Leopold and Helene (Statkiewicz) Jasinski; m. Evelyne Marie Campbell, May 20, 1958; children: Robert Donald, Scott M., Kurt W., Eric C.; m. Teruyo Kaneko, Oct. 10, 1975. BS, SUNY; MS, Pacific Western U. Registered architect, Calif. Pvt. practice architecture and planning Chgo., 1957-61, Los Angeles, 1962-85; with Western div., USN Facilities Engring. Command Archtl. Dept., San Bruno, Calif., 1985—. Author plan for Internat. Ctr. Transp. and Trade with off-shore SST airport in Santa Monica Bay, Calif., 1968; co-author plan for deep water internat. port for Chgo. and Gary, Ind., 1958; prin. works include Playboy Mag. Office Bldg., Chgo., 1957, Playboy Townhouse, 1962, Hugh M. Hefner's Brownstone Mansion swimming pool, grotto, recreation area, underwater lounge, 1961, Richard Young Residence, Malibu Colony, Calif., 1963, Tree Houses, West Mag., 1969, Curtis Sch., Los Angeles, 1983. Served with USNR, 1944-46, served to lt. col. res. Mem. Soc. Mil. Engrs., Aircraft Owners and Pilots Assn. Home and Office: 193 Crown Circle South San Francisco CA 94080

JAYME, WILLIAM NORTH, writer; b. Pitts., Nov. 15, 1925; s. Walter A. and Catherine (Ryley) J.; student Princeton, 1943-44, 47-49. With Young & Rubicam Advt., Inc., 1949, Charles W. Gamble & Assos., 1949-50; asst. circulation promotion mgr. Fortune mag., 1950-51, Life mag., 1951-53, copy dir., sales and advt. promotion CBS Radio Network, N.Y.C., 1953-55; sr. copywriter McCann-Erickson, Inc., 1955-58; established own advt. creative service, 1958-71; pres. Jayme, Ratalahti, Inc., 1971—; lectr. direct mktg. Stanford U., Radcliffe Coll., worldwide mktg. confs. Producer U.S. Army radio program Music Motorized, 1945-46; editor, producer Time, Inc. TV programs Background for Judgment, 1951, Citizen's View of '52; script editor CBS Radio-UPA motion picture Tune in Tomorrow, 1954; creator promotions for Smithsonian, New York, Bon Appetit, Food & Wine, California, American Health, Air & Space, other nat. mags.; author script adaptations for Studio One and other TV programs, articles and stories in periodicals. Served as sgt., 2d Armored Div., AUS, 1944-46. Democrat. Episcopalian. Club: Century Assn.,(N.Y.C.). Author: (with Roderick Cook) Know Your Toes and Other Things to Know, 1963; (with Helen McCully, Jacques Pepin) The Other Half of the Egg, 1967; (opera libretto, with Douglas Moore) Carry Nation. Address: 2306 Leavenworth St San Francisco CA 94133

JEBE, WALTER GEORGE, camera shop owner, photographer; b. San Francisco, Aug. 15, 1924; s. Henry Herman and Eleanore M. (Weigman) J.; m. Vivian A. Ferrera, Jan. 25, 1952; children—Vivian Ann, Walter George II. Student Pa. State Coll., 1943. Founder Jebe's Camera Shop, San Francisco, 1946, owner, 1946—; founder Jebe & Assos. Photography, San Francisco, 1960, owner, 1960—; columnist San Francisco Progress, 1963; formulator, tchr. first course photo product retailing for city and fed. govt., San Francisco Pub. Schs., 1962; lectr. San Francisco history; tch. photography classes, 1962—. Commr. Boy Scouts Am., 1965-70, scoutmaster, 1955-60; mem. Delinquency Prevention Commn., 1975; chmn. Dems. for Nixon for Gov., 1962; mem. Mayor's Com. for Africa Week, 1961, com. for Golden Gate Park Centennial, 1970, com. for Cable Car Centennial, 1973; bd. dirs. Citizens for Good Govt., 1969, Youth Devel. Center, 1967; pres. John McLaren Soc., 1969-70, 76, pres. San Francisco Pub. Library Commn., 1982, San Francisco Art Commn., 1982. Served with USAF, 1943-46, 51-52. Recipient Civic Service award, named Citizen of Week Sta. KABL, 1966; Silver Beaver award Boy Scouts Am., 1971. Mem. Master Photo Dealers and Finishers Assn. (territorial v.p. 1963; area pres. 1962), San Francisco Council Dist. Mchts. Assn. (pres. 1975). Lodge: Lions (pres. 1966). Home: 314 Pelaris Way San Francisco CA 94112 Office: 4519 Mission St San Francisco CA 94112

JEBEJIAN, VAHRAM KEVORK (JIM), architect; b. Los Angeles, Feb. 12, 1936; s. Vahram Ohaness and Anna (Harmon) J.; m. Diane Jebejian, June 28, 1963 (div. 1980); children: Mihran, Diron, Jimmy Jon, Gregory. AA in Bldg. and Constrn. Engring., Los Angeles Community Coll., 1959; BArch, U. So. Calif., 1963. Registered profl. architect. Pvt. practice architecture Glendale, Calif., 1963—. Prin. works include Holly Martyrs High Sch., 1972. Mem. Glendale Bldg. Commn., 1986; mem. archtl. rev. bd., 1986. Avocation: skiing. Home and Office: 401 W Broadway Glendale CA 91204

JEE, WEBSTER SHEW SHUN, anatomy and radiobiology educator; b. Oakland, Calif., June 25, 1925; s. Chueck Kwan Jee; m. Alice Ling Shew, Nov. 11, 1951; 1 child, Kenneth W. BA, U. Calif., Berkeley, 1949, MA, 1951; PhD, U. Utah, 1959. From instr. to assoc. prof. anatomy and radiobiology U. Utah, Salt Lake City, 1959-67, bone group leader div. radiobiology, 1959—, prof. anatomy, 1967—, acting dir. div. radiobiology, 1974-79, acting chmn. dept. anatomy, 1974-77; cons. Upjohn Co., Kalamazoo, 1980—, Monsanto Co., St. Louis, 1983—, Procter & Gamble, Cin., 1975-81, Colgate & Palmolive, Piscataway, N.J., 1975-80. Assoc. editor: Anatomical Record, 1972—; mem. editorial bd. Calcified Tissue Research Internat, 1977-82, 84—, Bone, 1978—, Bone and Mineral Research, 1987—; contbr. articles to profl. jours. Served with U.S. Army, 1943-46. Grantee Dept. Energy 1952—, NASA 1980—, NIH 1982—. Mem. Radiation Research Soc., Orthopedic Research Soc., Am. Assn. Anatomists, Internat. Assn. Dental Research, Gerontol. Soc., Am. Soc. Bone and Mineral Research, Am. Soc. Gravitational Space Biology, Sigma Xi. Home: 1948 E 5150 S Salt Lake City UT 84117 Office: U Utah Div Radiobiology Bldg 351 Salt Lake City UT 84112

JEFFERDS, MARY LEE, environmental edn. assn. exec.; b. Seattle, July 16, 1921; d. Amos Osgood and Vera Margaret (Percival) Jefferds; A.B., U. Calif. at Berkeley, 1943, gen. secondary teaching certificate, 1951; M.A., Columbia, 1947; certificate Washington and Lee U., 1945. Sec., Fair Play Com. Am. Citizens Japanese Ancestry, 1943-44; adminstrv. asst. U.C. Alumni Assn. book Students at Berkeley, 1949; dir. Student Union Monterey Jr. Coll., 1949-50; mgr. Nat. Audubon Soc. Conservation Resource Center, Berkeley, 1951-66; dir. Nat. Audubon Soc. Bay Area Ednl. Services, 1966-71; curriculum cons. Project WEY, U. Calif. Demonstration Lab. Sch., Berkeley, 1972—. Cons. Berkeley Sch. Dist., Alameda County Schs. Mem. land use com., environ. edn. com. East Bay Municipal Utility Dist., 1968—; mem. steering com. Nat. Sci. Guild, Oakland Mus., 1970-76; community adviser Jr. League of Oakland, 1972-76. Mem. Berkeley Women's Town Council, 1970—. Bd. dirs. East Bay Regional Park Dist., 1972—, pres., 1978-80; bd. dirs. Save San Francisco Bay Assn., 1969—, People for Open Space, 1977—, Calif. Natural Areas Coordinating Council, 1968—, Living History Ctr., 1982-85; mem. steering com. Bay Area Environ. Edn. Alliance, 1982-84; v.p. Friends of Bot. Garden, U. Calif., Berkeley, 1976-80, trustee, 1986. Served with USAAF, 1944-46. Recipient Merit award Calif. Conservation Council, 1953; Woman of Achievement award Camp Fire Girls, 1976; Merit award Am. Soc. Landscape Architects, 1979, Conservation award Golden Gate Audobon Soc., 1985. Mem. Prytanean Alumnae, Inc. (pres. 1969-71, chmn. adv. council 1971-73), AAUW (Calif. com. 1970-73), Nature Conservancy (chmn. no. Calif. chpt. 1970-71), LWV, Regional Parks Assn., Nat. Women's Polit. Caucus, Golden Gate Audubon Soc., Sierra Club (environ. edn. com. No. Calif. chpt. 1973-77), Urban Care, U. Calif. Art Council, U. Calif. Alumni Assn., Inst. Calif. Man in Nature, NAACP, Calif. Assn. Recreation and Park Dists. (v.p. 1978—), Calif. Elected Women for Edn. and Research, Nat. Assn. Environ. Edn., Preserve Area Ridgelands Calif. Native Plant Soc., Planning and Conservation League, Cousteau Soc., Soroptomists, Pi Lambda Theta, Mortar Board, Gavel (pres.). Democrat. Adv. com. natural history guide series U. Calif. Press, 1972—. Home: 2932 Pine Ave Berkeley CA 94705

JEFFERIES, JOHN TREVOR, observatory administrator; b. Kellerberrin, Australia, Apr. 2, 1925; came to U.S., 1956, naturalized, 1967; s. John and Vera (Healy) J.; m. Charmian Candy, Sept. 10, 1949; children: Stephen R., Helen C., Trevor R. MA, Cambridge (Eng.) U., 1949; DSc, U. We. Australia, Nedlands, 1962. Sr. research staff High Altitude Obs., Boulder, Colo., 1957-59, Sacramento Peak Obs., Sunspot, N.Mex., 1957-59; prof. adjoint U. Colo., Boulder, 1961-64; prof. physics and astronomy U. Hawaii, Honolulu, 1964—, dir., Inst. Astronomy, 1967-83; dir. Nat. Optical Astronomy Obs., Tucson, 1983—; cons. Nat. Bur. Standards, Boulder, 1960-62. Author: (monograph) Spectral Line Formation, 1968; contbr. articles to profl. jours. Guggenheim fellow, 1970-71. Fellow AAAS, Royal Astron. Soc.; mem. Internat. Astron. Union, Am. Astron. Soc., Australian Astron. Soc. Home: 6760 N Placita Manzanita Tucson AZ 85718 Office: Nat Optical Astronomy Obs PO Box 26732 Tucson AZ 85726

JEFFERS, FRANK FORREST, city official; b. Washington, Aug. 12, 1934; s. John William and Olive Elizabeth (Robertson) J.; m. Barbara Louise Kling, Dec. 12, 1951; children—Timothy, Thomas, Cheryl, Daniel. A.A., El Camino Coll., 1962; B.S., So. Bay U., 1972; grad. FBI Nat. Acad., 1976; M.Pub.Adminstrn., U. So. Calif., 1981. Cert. tchr., Calif.; profl. police certs. Calif. Commn. Peace Officers, Sgt., Manhattan Beach Police Dept., Calif., 1958-65; police advisor U.S. State Dept., Asia, 1965-69; lt. Ventura Police Dept., Calif., 1972-79; chief of police Exeter Police Dept., Calif., 1979—; cons. Calif. Commn. on Peace Officer Standards and Tng., 1974-75; chmn. Tulare County Law Enforcement Mgrs. Assn., 1981-84; mem. Tulare County Criminal Justice Com., 1982—; commr. Tulare County Juvenile Justice Commn. Com., 1983—. Author: (manuals) Police Training Program, 1974, Officer Survival, 1976. Served with USAF, 1949-51. Recipient cert. Kiwanis Club, Exeter, 1980, plaque Nat. Child Safety Council, 1982-83. Mem. FBI Nat. Acad. Assocs., Calif. Police Chiefs Assn., Internat. Assn. Chiefs of Police. Republican. Club: E. Clampus Vitus (Exeter). Office: Exeter Police Dept 115 S B St Exeter CA 93221

JEFFERSON, GEORGE THOMAS, museum assistant curator, prehistoric resources consultant; b. Huntington Park, Calif., Jan. 25, 1942; s. Thomas Allen and Catharine Martha (Parker) J.; m. Laura Louise Gallup, 1962 (div. 1971); m. Janet Elaine Helms, Apr. 9, 1979; 1 child, Jessica Morgan Helms Jefferson. BA in Geology, U. Calif., Riverside, 1965, MA in Geology, 1968. Sr. mus. scientist U. Calif., Riverside, 1964-70; curatorial asst. Los Angeles County Mus. Natural Hist., Los Angeles, 1973-80, asst. curator, 1980—, head, Rancho La Brea sect., 1982—; pvt. practice cons. prehist. resources, 1972—; research assoc. appointee Earth Sci. and Anthropology, San Bernardino County Mus., 1986. Co-author: Manix Lake and the Manix Fault, 1982; co-editor: Rancho La Brea: Treasures of the Tar Pits, 1985; contbr. sci. research and review articles to profl. jours. Care of Collections grantee, NSF, Washington, 1983-85. Mem. Am. Quarternary Assn., Paleontol. Soc., Soc. Vertebrate Paleontology (sustaining), So. Calif. Acad. Scis., Pacific Mineral. Soc. (hon. life mem. 1984), Sigma Xi. Home: 2825 Hill St Huntington Park CA 90255 Office: George C. Page Museum 5801 Wilshire Blvd Los Angeles CA 90036

JEFFERY, JAMES NELS, municipal agency official; b. Torrance, Calif., May 16, 1944; s. Daryl Fredrick and Mildred Evelyn (Sogard) J. AA, Long Beach City Coll., 1964; student, Calif. State U., Long Beach, 1964-65, Calif. State U., Sacramento, 1979-80. Capt., firefighter Los Angeles Fire Dept., 1965—; dir. Long Beach (Calif.) Search & Rescue Unit, 1968—; rep. Firescope Communications, Riverside, Calif., 1979—. Co-author emergency plans. Chmn. service com. Boy Scouts Am., Long Beach, 1979-81, tng. com., 1982—; bd. dirs. Long Beach Community Episepsy Clinic, 1971-72. Recipient Disting. Service award Long Beach Jaycees, 1977, Community Service award Long Beach Fire Dept., 1978, Silver Beaver award Boy Scouts Am., 1983, Commendation Mayor City of Los Angeles, 1985. Mem. Calif. State Firemen's Assn., Nat. Coordinating Council on Emergency Mgmt., So. Calif Assn. Foresters and Fire Wardens, Los Angeles Fire Fighters Assn. Republican. Lutheran. Lodges: Lions, Elks. Avocations: vol. work, camping, hunting. Home: 3916 Cerritos Ave Long Beach CA 90807 Office: Los Angeles City Fire Dept 200 N Main St Los Angeles CA 90012

JEFFERY, RONDO NELDEN, physics educator; b. Provo, Utah, Apr. 16, 1940; s. Rondo Nelden Jeffery and Mary Lucile (Thatcher) Jeffery Roylance; m. Janet Franson, Aug. 27, 1965; children—Ann, Laura, Sue, Ruth, Janalee, Elizabeth, Julia. BS, Brigham Young U., 1963, MS, 1965; PhD, U. Ill., 1970. Research asst. Brigham Young U., Provo, 1963-65, U. Ill., Urbana, 1965-70; research assoc. Rensselaer Poly. Inst., Troy, N.Y., 1970-73; asst. prof. Wayne State U., Detroit, 1973-80; vis. assoc. prof. Weber State Coll., Ogden, Utah, 1980-83, assoc. prof. physics, 1983-86, prof., 1986—; mem. tech. staff TRW Corp., Ogden, 1986—. Contbr. articles to sci. jours. Faculty Research grantee Wayne State U., 1974-75; Cottrell Research grantee Research Corp., 1975-78; sci. research grantee NSF, Washington, 1978-81; instructional devel. grantee Weber State Coll., 1984. Mem. Am. Phys. Soc., Am. Assn.-Physics Tchrs. (past v.p., pres.), Am. Soc. for Engring. Edn., Sigma Xi. Mormon. Office: Weber State Coll Physics Dept 3750 Harrison Blvd Ogden UT 84408

JEFFREDO, JOHN VICTOR, aerospace engineer, manufacturing company executive, inventor; b. Los Angeles, Nov. 5, 1927; s. John Edward and Pauline Matilda (Whitten) J.; m. Elma Jean Nesmith, July 1953 (div. 1958); children: Joyce Jean Jeffredo Ryder, Michael John; m. Doris Louise Hinz, Feb. 18, 1958 (div. 1980); children: John Victor, Louise Victoria Jeffredo-Warren; m. Gerda Adelheid Pillich, Nov. 29, 1980. Grad. in aero. engring. Cal-Aero Tech. Inst., 1948; AA in machine design, Pasadena City Coll., 1951; grad. electronics The Ordnance Sch. U.S. Army, 1951; AA in Am. Indian Studies, Palomar Coll., 1978; postgrad. U. So. Calif., 1955-58; MBA, La Jolla U., 1980, PhD in Human Relations, 1984. Design engr. Douglas Aircraft Co., Long Beach and Santa Monica, Calif., 1955-58; devel. engr. Honeywell Ordnance Corp., Duarte, Calif., 1958-62; cons. Honeywell devel. labs., Seattle, 1962-65; supr. mech. engr. dept. aerospace div. Control Data Corp., Pasadena, Calif., 1965-68; project engr. Cubic Corp., San Diego, 1968-70; supr. mech. engring. dept. Babcock Electronics Co., Costa Mesa,

Calif., 1970-72; owner, operator Jeffredo Gunsight Co., Fallbrook, Calif., 1971-81; chief engr. Western Designs, Inc., Fallbrook, 1972-81, exec. dir., 1981; owner, operator Western Designs, Fallbrook, 1981-87; pres. JXJ, Inc., San Marcos, Calif., exec. dir., 1981—; mgr. Jeffredo Gunsight div. JXJ, Inc., 1981—; owner, mgr. Energy Assocs., San Diego, 1982-86; pres. Jeffredo Internat., 1984—; engring. cons. Action Instruments Co., Inc., Gen. Dynamics, Alcyon Corp., Systems Exploration, Inc. (all San Diego), Hughes Aircraft Co., El Segundo, Allied-Bendix, San Marcos; bd. dirs. Indian World Corp. Contbr. articles to trade jours. and mags.; guest editorial writer Town Hall, San Diego Union; patentee agrl. frost control, vehicle off-road drive system, recoil absorbing system for firearms, telescope sight mounting system for firearms, breech mech. sporting firearm, elec. switch activating system, others. Mem. San Diego County Border Task Force on Undocumented Aliens, 1979-80, 81-82; chmn. Native Californian Coalition, 1982—. Served with U.S. Army, 1951-53. Recipient Superior Service commendation U.S. Naval Ordnance Test Sta., Pasadena, 1959. Mem. Am. Soc. for Metals, Nat. Hist. Soc., Nat. Rifle Assn. (life), San Diego Zool. Soc., Sierra Club, Nat. Wildlife Fedn., The Wilderness Soc. Republican. Home: 1629 Via Monserate Fallbrook CA 92028 Office: 133 N Pacific St Suite D San Marcos CA 92069

JEFFREY, DAVID GORDON, marketing executive; b. Pawtucket, R.I., July 31, 1946; s. David Gordon and Clara Ellen (Wilson) J.; m. Pamela J. Kunatz, Jan. 25, 1980; children: Alexandra Elizabeth, James Johnstone. BA, Furman U., 1968; MBA, Wake Forest U., 1971. With mktg. staff Hanes Corp., Winston-Salem, N.C., 1969-71, Wilson Sporting Goods Co., Chgo., 1971-73, Levi Strauss & Co., San Francisco, 1973-74; pres., mktg. dir. Caledonia Group Inc. and subs. British Am. Trading Co., Inc., Gain Activewear, Ltd., England, Jeffrey and Assocs., Inc., Jeffrey Industries, Inc., San Francisco, 1974—; expert witness Calif jud. system. Bd. dirs. San Francisco Advt. Softball League, 1978-80, commr., 1981-83. Served to 1st lt. U.S. Army, 1967-69. Republican. Episcopalian. Lodge: Rotary.

JEFFREY, RASHEL, social worker; b. Miami, Fla., Mar. 12, 1946; d. Elias and Ada (Bender) Levine; m. Daniel Balfour Jeffrey, Dec. 20, 1968; children: Erica Rose, Thomas Balfour. BA, U. Mich., 1966, MSW, 1968. Cert. social worker. Social worker Ctr. Forensic Psychiatry, Ypsilanti, Mich., 1968, Children's Service Soc., Salt Lake City, 1968-73, Mental Health Ctr., Missoula, Mont., 1985; pvt. practice Missoula, 1985—. Mem. Clark Fork Sch. Bd., Missoula, 1984-85, Citizen's Council on Air Pollution, Missoula, 1980—, Steering Com. Project Excel, Missoula, 1985—. Mem. Nat. Assn. Social Workers. Avocations: cooking, reading, aerobics, golf, family. Home: 131 Beverly Missoula MT 59801 Office: 210 Higgins Ave Missoula MT 59801

JEGHERS, SANDERSON JOHN, hospital administrator; b. Boston, May 7, 1945; s. Harold Joseph and Isabel Jean (Wile) J.; m. Kathleen Marie Guiney, Apr. 21, 1982; children—John William, James Rory. B.B.A., U. Miami, 1972; M.B.A., George Washington U., 1974. Adminstrv. intern St. Vincent Hosp., Worcester, Mass., 1969-71; adminstrv. resident St. Luke's Hosp. Med. Center, Phoenix, 1973-74, asst. adminstr., 1974-76; sr. mktg. cons. Ernst & Whinney, Los Angeles, 1977-78; asst. dir. Santa Monica (Calif.) Hosp. Med. Center, 1978-80, sr. v.p., 1980-83; pres., chief exec. officer, dir. Overlake Hosp. Med. Ctr., Bellevue, Wash., 1983—; dir. H.A.S.S., Inc., Los Angeles; guest lectr. UCLA, 1977-78, U. So. Calif., Los Angeles, 1977-78, Golden Gate U., San Francisco, 1980-83. Spl. asst. to exec. dir. Pres. Ford Com., San Diego, 1976; bd. dirs. Overlake Hosp. Found., 1983—, Overlake Health Care Assn., Inc., 1985—, Seattle Area Hosp. Council, 1985—, Overlake Preferred Provide, Inc., 1986—; area chmn. United Way, 1985. Served with USAF, 1965-69. Mem. Am. Coll. Hosp. Adminstrs., Am. Hosp. Assn., Am. Mktg. Assn., Hosp. Fin. Mgmt. Assn., George Washington U. Alumni Assn., Bellevue C. of C. Republican. Club: Rotary. Contbr. articles to profl. jours. Office: Overlake Hosp Med Ctr 1035 116th Ave NE Bellevue WA 98004

JELINEK, JOHN JOSEPH, public relations executive, consultant, columnist, editor; b. San Pedro, Calif., Sept. 3, 1955; s. Joseph Francis and Patricia Valerie (Powers) J.; m. Christl Michele Schneider, June 1986. B.A., Loyola U., 1977; M.A., Loyola-Marymount U., 1983. Assoc. editor E-Go Enterprises, Sherman Oaks, Calif., 1976-77; advt. dir. Select Promotions, Irvine, Calif., 1977-78; editor SCORE Internat., Westlake Village, Calif., 1978-79; exec. editor Petersen Pub. Co., Los Angeles, 1979-82, editor, 1982-85; pub. relations account exec. Hill and Knowlton Inc., Los Angeles, 1985-87; acct. supr. Freeman/McCue Pub. Relations, Newport Beach, Calif., 1987—. Author: (with others) Consumer's Guide to 1978 Trucks, 1978, Consumer's Guide to 1980 Trucks, 1979, Complete Guide to Used Cars, 1981, How to Buy the Best Compact Truck, 1984; columnist Guns & Ammo Mag., 1980-84, Petersen's Hunting Mag., 1986-87. Served to capt. Calif. State Mil. Res. 1982—. Recipient 1st place award Calif. Newspaper Pub. Assn., 1977. Mem. Am. Film Inst., Am. Auto Racing Writers Broadcasters Assn. (hon. mention photo 1980), Internat. Motor Press Assn., Outdoor Writers Am., Nat. Rifle Assn. (life), Los Angeles County Mus. Natural History-Automobile Collection Council, Los Angeles County Mus. Art, Am. Sportsman's Club. Republican. Roman Catholic. Avocations: travel; skiing; cooking. Office: Freeman/McCue Pub Relations 160 Newport Center Dr Suite 210 Newport Beach CA 92660 Other Address: Pickups & Mini-Trucks Petersen Publishing Co 8490 Sunset Blvd Los Angeles CA 90069

JELLINEK, L. ROBERT, sales executive; b. Ridley Park, Pa., Nov. 8, 1941; s. Leslie and Gladys Evelyn (Marquette) J.; children: Laura Renee, Sheree Lynne, Derek Anthony, Tiffni Diana. Student Rutgers U., 1969-72, Regis Coll., 1975-77; BBA and Mktg. Mgmt. magna cum laude, U. Colo., 1977; postgrad. U. Colo., 1987—. Cost acct. Johns-Manville Corp. (N.J.), 1960-64, prodn. coordinator, 1964-68, chief scheduler, 1968-70, div. indsl. engr. Finderne, N.J., 1970-72, sr. systems analyst, Denver, 1972-78, pipe div. mcpl. sales, Casper Wyo., 1978-81, territory sales mgr., 1981-84; territory sales mgr. J.M. Mfg. Co., Inc., Denver, 1984—; tour guide, lectr. Ancient Egypt Ramses II Exhbn. Denver Mus. Natural History, 1987—. Served with USCG, 1959. Mem. Am. Water Works Assn., Water Pollution Control Fedn., Wyo. Engring Assn., Wyo Water Quality Assn., S. D. Water and Wastewater Assn. Republican. Clubs: Rocky Mtn. Gun (Casper); Falcon Skeet and Trap (Denver). Home: 4 Long Spur Littleton CO 80127

JENDEN, DONALD JAMES, educator, pharmacologist; b. Horsham, Sussex, Eng., Sept. 1, 1926; came to U.S., 1950, naturalized, 1958; s. William Herbert and Kathleen Mary (Harris) J.; m. Jean Ickeringill, Nov. 18, 1950; children: Patricia Mary, Peter D., Beverly J. BSc in Physiology with 1st class honours, Kings Coll. London, 1947; MB, BS with honours (Univ. gold medal 1950), U. London, 1950; PhD Chemistry (hon.), U. Uppsala, Sweden, 1980. Demonstrator pharmacology U. London, 1948-49; lectr. pharmacology U. Calif.-San Francisco, 1950-51; postdoctoral fellow USPHS, 1951-53; asst. prof. pharmacology U. Calif.-San Francisco, 1952; mem. faculty U. Calif.-Los Angeles, 1952—; prof. pharmacology UCLA, 1960—, prof. pharmacology and biomath., 1967—, chmn. dept. pharmacology, 1968—; Wellcome vis. prof. U. Ala., Birmingham, 1984; hon. research assoc. Univ. Coll., London., 1961-62; mem. brain research inst. UCLA, 1961—. Contbr. articles in field. Served to lt. M.C., USNR, 1954-56. USPHS Postdoctoral fellow, 1951-53, NSF Sr. Postdoctoral fellow; Fulbright Short-Term Sr. Scholar award, Australia, 1983. Fellow Am. Coll. Neuropsychopharmacology; mem. Am. Soc. Pharmacology and Exptl. Therapeutics, Am. Physiol. Soc., AAAS, Physiol. Soc. (London), Soc. Neurosci., Am. Chem. Soc. (div. med. chemistry), Western Pharmacology Soc., Assn. for Med. Sch. Pharmacology, Am. Soc. Mass Spectrometry, Am. Soc. Neurochemistry, Internat. Union Pharmacology (sect. on toxicology), N.Y. Acad. Sci., Am. Soc. Med. Sch. Pharmacology, West Coast Coll. Biol. Psychology (charter fellow), Brain Research Inst. UCLA. Home: 3814 S Castlerock Rd Malibu CA 90265 Office: Dept Pharmacology Sch Medicine Center Health Scis Univ California Los Angeles CA 90024-1735

JENKINS, ANN ARNOLD, information manager; b. Columbus, Ohio, Jan. 5, 1947; d. Donald Smith and Eleanor Ann (Webster) Arnold; m. James Dean Jenkins, Nov. 13, 1970; children: Daniel Arnold, Patricia Ann. BA in Phys. Scis., U. Calif., Berkeley, 1968; MLS in Info. Systems, UCLA, 1969; MBA in Info. Systems, Calif. State U., San Diego, 1985. Tchr. D.A.V. Girls' Coll., Suva, Fiji, 1969-71; tech. librarian Systems, Sci., Software, San Diego, 1971-76; tech. librarian Kelco div. Merck & Co. Inc., San Diego, 1976-83, info. and tech. systems mgr., 1983—. Mem. Am. Chem. Soc., Am. Soc. Info. Sci. (chmn. Spl. Interest Group on Mgmt. 1986—), Prytanean Soc., Phi Beta Kappa, Upsilon Pi Epsilon. Home: 2930 Briand Ave San Diego CA 92122 Office: Kelco Div Merck & Co Inc 8355 Aero Dr San Diego CA 92123

JENKINS, BRUCE STERLING, fed. judge; b. Salt Lake City, May 27, 1927; s. Joseph and Bessie Pearl (Iverson) J.; m. Margaret Watkins, Sept. 19, 1952; children—Judith Margaret, David Bruce, Michael Glen, Carol Alice. B.A. with high honors, U. Utah, 1949, LL.B., 1952, J.D., 1952. Bar: Utah bar 1952, U.S. Dist. Ct. bar 1952, U.S. Supreme Ct. bar 1962, U.S. Circuit Ct. Appeals bar 1962. Individual practice law Salt Lake City, 1952-59; asso. firm George McMillan, 1959-65; asst. atty. gen. State of Utah, 1952; dep. county atty. Salt Lake County, 1954-58; bankruptcy judge U.S. Dist. Ct., Dist. of Utah, 1965-78, U.S. dist. judge, 1978—, chief judge, 1984—. Research, publs. in field; contbr. essays to Law jours.; bd. editors: Utah Law Rev, 1951-52. Mem. Utah Senate, 1959-65, minority leader, 1963, pres. senate, 1965, vice chmn. commn. on orgn. exec. br. of Utah Govt., 1965-66; Mem. adv. com. Utah Tech. Coll., 1967-72; mem. instl. council Utah State U., 1976. Served with USN, 1945-46. Mem. Utah State Bar Assn., Salt Lake County Bar Assn., Am. Bar Assn., Fed. Bar Assn., Order of Coif, Phi Beta Kappa, Phi Kappa Phi, Phi Eta Sigma, Phi Sigma Alpha, Tau Kappa Alpha. Democrat. Mormon. Office: Room 235 US Courthouse 350 S Main St Salt Lake City UT 84101

JENKINS, CLAUDE, academic principal; b. McComb, Miss., May 17, 1940; s. Claude and Edna (Dillon) J.; m. Lillie B. Morris, May 17, 1939; children: Claudia, Michael Claude. BA, Calif. State U., Hayward, 1972; MA, San Francisco State U., 1976; Dr. degree, Nova U., 1986. Cert. tchr., Calif. Tchr. Oakland (Calif.) Schs., 1972-81, prin., 1981—; bd. dirs. Taylor Meml. Tutoring Program, Oakland, Shattuck Ave Ch. Tutoring Program. Lay leader Taylor Meml. Ch.; mem. North Oakland Community Devel. Orgn., 1983. Served to sgt. U.S. Army, 1956-59. Mem. Phi Delta Kappa, Alpha Phi Alpha. Democrat. Lodge: Masons. Home: 11065 Golf Links Rd Oakland CA 94605 Office: Oakland Pub Schs 581 61st St Oakland CA 94621

JENKINS, DONALD JOHN, art museum administrator; b. Longview, Wash., May 3, 1931; s. John Peter and Louise Hazel (Pederson) J.; m. Mary Ella Bemis, June 29, 1956; children—Jennifer, Rebecca. B.A., U. Chgo., 1951, M.A., 1970. Mus. asst. Portland Art Mus., Oreg., 1954-56; asst. curator Portland Art Mus., 1960-69, curator, 1974-75, dir., 1975—; assoc. curator oriental art Art Inst. Chgo., 1969-74; mem. gallery adv. com. Asia House Gallery, N.Y.C., 1977—; application reviewer NEH, Washington, 1984—; lectr. various museums and art orgns., 1969—. Author: (exhbn. catalogues) Ukiyo-e Prints & Paintings, 1971, The Ledoux Heritage, 1973, Masterworks/China & Japan, 1976, Images of Changing World, 1983. Mem., chmn. Pittock Mansion Adv. Com., Portland, 1975—; chmn. NW Regional China Council, Portland, 1980—; mem. art selection com. Performing Arts Ctr., Portland, 1983—. Mem. Am. Assn. Museums, Art Mus. Assn., Am. Art Alliance, Assn. Art Mus. Dirs. (grantee 1979), Soc. Japanese Arts and Crafts. Home: 14160 NW Rock Creek Rd Portland OR 97231 Office: Portland Art Mus 1219 SW Park Ave Portland OR 97205

JENKINS, FLOYD ALBERT, biology educator, priest; b. Los Angeles, Aug. 14, 1916; s. Floyd Ernest and Irma Helena (Luer) J. AB, St. Louis U., 1940, MA, 1942, MS, 1943, PhD, 1954; ThM, Santa Clara U., 1949. Ordained priest Roman Cath. Ch., 1948. Instr. bio. Loyola U., Los Angeles, 1943-45, educator bio., 1953-86, prof. bio., 1986—. Mem. Soc. Vertebrate Paleontology, Paleontological Soc., Soc. for the Study of Evulution, Soc. Calif. Acad. Soc., Vatican Philatelic Soc., Los Angeles Philatelic Soc., Sigma Xi. Republican. Avocations: backpacking, piano, philately. Home and Office: 7101 W 80th Los Angeles CA 90045

JENKINS, JAMES ARTHUR, city government finance official; b. Hollywood, Calif., Oct. 3, 1942; s. Claude Arthur and Bobbie Irene (Foree) J.; m. Barbara Jean Lewandowski, June 19, 1965; children—Jennifer, Jill. B.S., Calif. State U.-Northridge, 1965, M.S., 1970. Acct., Texaco, Inc., Los Angeles, 1965; cost acct. Lockheed Aircraft Corp., Burbank, Calif., 1966-67, staff acct., 1967-68, sr. fin. analyst, 1969-71; asst. fin. dir. City of Scottsdale, Ariz., 1971-75, budget dir., 1975, gen. mgr. mgmt. services dept., city treas., 1976—. Pres., Found. for Blind Children, Scottsdale, 1981-83. Mem. Govtl. Fin. Officers Assn. (state rep. 1982-83, Fin. Reporting Achievement award 1977, Profl. Achievement award 1981-82), Ariz. Fin. Officers Assn. (pres. 1983), Am. Soc. for Pub. Adminstrn. (treas. 1982), Mcpl. Treas. Assn., Nat. Mgmt. Assn., Nat. Assn. Accts. Club: Toastmasters. Home: 9885 E Windrose Dr Scottsdale AZ 85260 Office: Scottsdale City Hall 3939 Civic Center Plaza Scottsdale AZ 85251

JENKINS, MYRA ELLEN, historian, archivist; b. Elizabeth, Colo., Sept. 26, 1916; d. Lewis Harlan and Minnie (Ackroyd) Jenkins; B.A. cum laude, U. Colo., 1937, M.A., 1938; Ph.D., U. N.Mex., 1953. Instr. pub. schs., Climax, Colo., 1939-41, Granada, Colo., 1941-43, Pueblo, Colo., 1943-50; fellow U. N.Mex., 1950-52, asst., 1952-53; free-lance historian and hist. cons., Albuquerque, 1953-59; archivist Hist. Soc. N.Mex., Santa Fe, 1959-60; sr. archivist N.Mex. Records Center and Archives, 1960-69, dep. for archives, 1968-70; N.Mex. state historian, 1967-80; ret., 1980; instr. St. Michael's Coll., 1962-63, Coll. of Santa Fe, 1966-74, 81-82; assoc. prof. N.Mex. State U., 1983; assoc. adj. prof. U.N. Mex., summer 1982, 84, 86. Mem. Western History Assn., Hist. Soc. N.Mex., Phi Beta Kappa, Phi Kappa Phi, Phi Alpha Theta, Kappa Delta Pi. Democrat. Episcopalian. Author: (with Albert H. Schroeder) A Brief History of New Mexico, 1974; Guides and Calendars to the Spanish, Mexican and Territorial Archives of New Mexico; contbr. articles to profl. jours. and book revs. Home: 1022 Don Cubero St Santa Fe NM 87501

JENKINS, PAUL GOODWIN, stockbroker; b. Phoenix, Dec. 1, 1927; s. Winfred Grand and Evelyn Mae (Lillie) J.; m. Mary Jane Reid, Sept. 22, 1950; children—Sherry Lee Jenkins Bolton, Stephen Grant, Reid Goodwin. B.S., U. So. Calif.-Los Angeles, 1950. Owner, date grower Jenkins Packing Co., Indio, Calif., 1951-61; broker firm Mitchum, Jones & Templeton, Indio, 1961-65; v.p., mgr. Walston & Co., Palm Desert, Calif., 1965-72, DuPont Walston, Palm Desert, 1972-74; 1st v.p., mgr. Bateman, Eichler, Hill, Richards, Inc., Palm Desert, 1974—; v.p. Eisenhower Med. Ctr., Rancho Mirage, Calif., 1969-84, Betty Ford Ctr., Rancho Mirage, 1982—. Planning commr. Riverside County, Calif., 1961-64. Served with AC USN, 1945-46. Named to Top 20 Brokers of Yr., Registered Rep. Mag., 1983. Republican. Presbyterian. Clubs: Eldorado Country (Indian Wells, Calif.); Fairbanks Ranch Country (Rancho Santa Fe, Calif.). Home: 79-830 Ryan Way Bermuda Dunes CA 92201 Office: Bateman Eichler Hill Richards Inc 45 445 Portola Ave Palm Desert CA 92260 *

JENKINS, PETER EDWIN, engineer, university administrator; b. Truro, N.S., Can., May 7, 1940; came to U.S., 1946; s. Harry P. and Jean Elizabeth (Wyse) J.; m. Lois Busche, Jan. 29, 1966 (dec. 1975); children: Diana, David; m. Kathie Winkler, Mar. 19, 1976; children—Fred, Regina, Amie, Robert. B.S.M.E., U. Kans., Lawrence, 1965; M.S.M.E., So. Meth. U., Dallas, 1970; Ph.D., Purdue U., West Lafayette, Ind., 1974; M.B.A., Pepperdine U., Malibu, Calif., 1986. Design engr. L.T.V. Vought Aerospace Co., Dallas, 1965-66; sr. research and devel. engr. Tex. Instruments, Inc., Dallas, 1966-70; research assoc. Purdue U., West Lafayette, Ind., 1970-74; asst. prof. No. Ariz. U., Flagstaff, 1974-75; prof. Tex. A&M U., College Station, 1975-84; exec. v.p. Engine Corp. Am., Long Beach, Calif., 1984-86; also dir. Engine Corp. Am.; chmn. dept. mech. engring. U. Nebr., Lincoln, 1986—. Patentee energy systems, engine technology. Active Boy Scouts Am., 1981—; pres. Bryan High Sch. Band Boosters, Tex., 1984-85. Recipient Disting. Service award Tex. A&M U. system, 1983. Fellow ASME (div. chmn. engring. bd. 1984; Outstanding Service award 1981); mem. AIAA, Soc. Automotive Engrs., ASHRAE. Baptist.

JENKINS, ROBERT RICHARD, leasing company executive; b. Chgo., June 1, 1938; s. Matthew N. and Marion (Shelby) J.; B.S., Loyola U., 1960, M.A., 1962; m. Mary Ellen Thulis, May 31, 1969; children—Tracy Jane, David Robert. Product mgr. Nat. Steel Corp., Evanston, Ill., 1965-69; sales mgr. Xerox Corp., Chgo., 1969-71; regional mgr. Gelco Corp., N.Y.C., 1971-77, v.p. mktg., Eden Prairie, Minn., 1977-80; v.p. The Van Arnem Co., Bloomfield Hills, Mich., 1980-81; exec. v.p. Republic Fin. Corp., 1981—. Mem. Planning Commn. City of Westport, Conn., 1975-77. Served to lt. USNR, 1963-65. Mem. Sales Exec. Club N.Y., Am. Equipment Leasing Assn., Western Assn. Equipment Leasors, Sales and Mktg. Exec. Mpls., Denver Area Lessors Assn. (bd. dirs.), New Eng. T Register, Colo. MG T Club, Am. Automotive Leasing Assn. Clubs: Heather Ridge Country, Denver Athletic, Colo. Racquet. Home: 16536 E Berry Pl Aurora CO 80015

JENKINS, SPEIGHT, opera director, writer; b. Dallas, Jan. 31, 1937; s. Speight and Sara (Baird) J.; m. Linda Ann Sands, Sept. 6, 1966; children: Linda Leonie, Speight. B.A., U. Tex.-Austin; LL.B., Columbia U. News and reports editor Opera News, N.Y.C., 1967-73; music critic N.Y. Post, N.Y.C., 1973-81; TV host Live form the Met, Met. Opera, N.Y.C., 1981-83; gen. dir. Seattle Opera, 1983—; classical music editor Record World, N.Y.C., 1973-81; contbg. editor Ovation Mag., N.Y.C., 1980—, Opera Quar., Los Angeles, 1982—. Served to capt. U.S. Army, 1961-66. Recipient Emmy award for Met. Opera telecase La Boheme TV Acad. Arts and Scis., 1982. Mem. Music Critics Assn., Phi Beta Kappa. Presbyterian. Home: 2125 First Ave Seattle WA 98121 Office: Seattle Opera Assn PO Box 9248 Seattle WA 98109 *

JENKINS, THOMAS MOORMAN, writer, marketing analyst, educator; b. Westfield, N.J., Apr. 25, 1927; s. Robert B. and Olive M. Jenkins; m. Hildrud Kellogg, Dec. 21, 1950; children: Jeff, Martin, Cynthia, Richard. BA, Susquehanna U., 1950; MA, U. Denver, 1967. Instr. Douglas High Sch., Castle Rock, Colo., 1962-67, Community Coll. of Denver, 1967-80; writer, editor Kellogg Corp., Littleton, Colo., 1980—; instr. various writing seminars, 1975—. Contbr. 250 articles to profl. jours. and mags. Republican. Lutheran. Office: Kellogg Corp 26 W Dry Creek Circle Littleton CO 80120

JENKINS, WILLIAM MAXWELL, banker; b. Sultan, Wash., Apr. 19, 1919; s. Warren M. and Louise (Black) J.; B.A., U. Wash., 1941; M.B.A., Harvard, 1943; m. Elisabeth Taber, Oct. 11, 1945 (div. 1976); children—Elisabeth Cordua (Mrs. John E. Nowogroski), Ann Hathaway (Mrs. George H. Rohrbacher), William Morris, Karen Louise (Mrs. Melvin A. Olanna), Peter Taber, David Maxwell, Barbara Fessenden; m. Ann Ramsay, Jan. 31, 1987. Asst. cashier, asst. v.p. Seattle-1st Nat. Bank, 1945-53, exec. v.p., mgr. Everett div., 1962, chmn., chief exec. officer, 1962-82; v.p., exec. v.p., pres. First Nat. Bank of Everett, 1953-61; chmn. Everett Trust & Savs. Bank, 1956-61, Seafirst Corp., Seattle, 1974-82; dir. United Air Lines, UAL, Inc., Scott Paper Co., SAFECO Corp. Mem. adv. com. Grad. Sch. Bus. Adminstrn., U. Wash.; chmn. men's adv. com. Children's Orthopedic Hosp.; incorporator, mem. exec. com. Fifth Avenue Theatre Assn.; Served to lt. (j.g.) USN, 1943-45. Decorated Navy Cross, Croix de Guerre with palm. Mem. Assn. Res. City Bankers (pres. 1973-74). Republican. Presbyterian. Clubs: The Reading Room, Bainbridge Racquet; Seattle Tennis, Seattle Golf; Harbor, Rainier, University (Seattle). Office: Seattle-1st Nat Bank PO Box 3586 Seattle WA 98124

JENKINSON, JUDITH ELLEN, librarian; b. Monroe, Mich., Apr. 9, 1943; d. Robert Henry Williams and Caroline (Pardee) Stephenson; m. Arnold Apsey, July 1, 1962 (div. 1977); 1 child, Amy Lou; m. Leif Jenkinson, May 21, 1977, 1 stepchild, Karl J. A.A., Alpena Community Coll., 1964; B.A., Mich. State U., 1966; Arts M.L.S., U. Mich., 1969. Elem. tchr., Lincoln, Mich., 1966-68, high sch. librarian, 1969-72; elem. librarian, Ketchikan, Alaska, 1972-75, high sch. librarian, 1975—. Mem. Ketchikan Community Coll. Council, 1980-84, pres., 1984-85; del. Alaska Democratic Conv., 1982; dir., producer, actress, mem. stage crew First City Players, 1972—. Mem. ALA, NEA, AAUW, NOW, LWV, Ketchikan Edn. Assn., NEA-Alaska, Women's Internat. League for Peace and Freedom, Alaska Library Assn. VFW Aux., Swinging Kings Square Dancers (pres. 1985-86). Lodge: Eagles. Home: Box 5342 Ketchikan AK 99901 Office: 2610 4th Ave Ketchikan AK 99901

JENKS, KARL THOMAS, computer programmer, researcher; b. Los Angeles, June 29, 1948. S. Lynn Moore and Gisela Vera (Sesse) J.; m. Barbara Jean Kennedy, May 31, 1982. BA in Maths., UCLA, 1970; postgrad., Calif. State U., Los Angeles, 1970-72; cert. in Data Processing Inst. Certification Computer Profls.; money mgmt. diplomate Coneducor Corp. Programmer/analyst City of Los Angeles Data Service Bur., 1972-85, also project leader Network Communications System; sr. systems specialist data systems div., City of Los Angeles Dept. Transp., 1985—. Vol. 1 gubernatorial, 2 presdl. campaigns Democratic Party. Recipient Commendation Data Service Bur., 1984. Mem. Engrs. and Architects Assn., Assn. Inst. Cert. Computer Profls., Am. Assn. Individual Investors, UCLA Alumni Assn., Sierra Club. Office: City of Los Angeles Dept Transp 200 N Spring St Room 1003 Los Angeles CA 90012

JENNE, RUTH MARIE, aerospace company financial executive; b. Providence, Apr. 7, 1947; d. Robert Charles and Concetta Therese (Iacovelli) J. B.A., Calif. State Coll., 1970; M.B.A., U. Phoenix, 1983. Paymaster Charlton Co., Compton, Calif., 1974-79; payroll adminstr. Northrop Corp., Hawthorne, Calif., 1979-82, fin. mgr., payroll, 1982—, membership chmn. Northrop Mgmt. Club, 1983-86; leader Northrop Integrated Fin. Systems Project, 1984-86. Recipient Performance Achievement award Northrop Corp., 1983. Mem. Nat. Assn. Female Execs., Am. Payroll Assn. Democrat. Roman Catholic.

JENNINGS, B. JOELLE, educator; b. Phila., Nov. 8, 1944; d. John Joseph and Foresta (Cianfrogna) Rodgers.; m. James T. Jennings, Sept. 25, 1971 (div. 1981). B.A., Holy Family Coll., Phila., 1966; postgrad. in edn. Immaculate Heart Coll., Los Angeles, 1977. Cert. tchr., Calif. Intake worker Mental Health Devel. Ctr., Los Angeles, 1966-69; adminstrv. asst. Los Angeles Mut. Ins. Co., 1969-70; sec. med. staff Queen of Angels Hosp., Los Angeles, 1970-76; tchr. sci. Los Angeles Unified Sch. Dist, 1977-79; sci. chmn. New Jewish High Sch., Los Angeles, 1980-83; research mgr. Heidrick & Struggles, Los Angeles, 1983—; cons. edn. pvt. psychotherapist, Woodland Hills, Calif., 1979—. Hospice vol. St. Joseph Med. Ctr., Burbank, Calif. Mem. NEA, Calif. Tchrs. Assn. Office: 445 S Figueroa St Suite 2330 Los Angeles CA 90071

JENNINGS, CALVIN HUNT, anthropology educator; b. Denver, Jan. 12, 1939; s. Clarcie Delmar and Mary Ethel (Ronson) J.; m. Dorothy Shela Stanker, Dec. 16, 1961 (div. July 1975); 1 child, Craig Arthur; m. Diane Linda France, Nov. 27, 1980. BA in Anthropology, U. Colo., 1964, MA in Anthropology, 1965, PhD in Anthropology, 1971. Fellow Mus. No. Ariz., Flagstaff, 1966-68; asst. prof. anthropology Calif. State U., Fresno, 1968-72; asst. prof. anthropology Colo. State U., Ft. Collins, 1972-75, assoc. prof., 1975—, dir. lab. pub. archaeology, 1974—, chmn. dept. anthropology, 1983—; cons. cultural resource mgmt., 1968—. Contbr. articles to profl. jours. Served with USN, 1956-60. Mem. Soc. Am. Archaeology, Sigma Xi (pres. Colo. State U. chpt. 1986). Avocation: photography. Office: Colo State U Dept Anthropology Fort Collins CO 80523

JENNINGS, GERALD MOORE, JR., lawyer; b. Santa Monica, Calif., June 10, 1945; s. Gerald Moore and Elaine Emily (Potter) J.; m. Judith Ann Prestridge, Dec. 20, 1970 (div. Mar. 1981). BA, U. Pacific, 1967; MS, U. Calif., Irvine, 1975; LLD, Southwestern U., Los Angeles, 1983. Bar: Calif. 1985. Internat. mktg. mgr. Everest & Jennings, Inc., Los Angeles, 1973-80; sole practice Woodland Hills, Calif., 1984—. Contbr. articles to profl. jours. V.p. Bird Council of Los Angeles County Mus., 1985-86; bd. dirs. Lincoln Club, San Fernando, 1978-80. Served to lt. USN, 1966-69. Mem. Am. Fed. Aviculture (founder, pres. 1974-76, 85—, First Breeding award 1978, 80, 84), ABA, Calif. State Bar Assn., San Fernando Valley Bar Assn., Phi Alpha Delta. Avocations: skiing, backpacking, photography, travel. Home: 23125 Erwin St Woodland Hills CA 91367 Office: Gilbert Law Bldg 22130 Clarendon St Woodland Hills CA 91367

JENNINGS, JOYCE CAROL, social worker; b. Mpls., Nov. 28, 1951; d. Herbert Herman and Verna Louella (Norling) J. BA, Gustavus Adolphus Coll., 1973; MSW, U. Tenn., 1981. Caseworker dept. social services Jefferson County, Lakewood, Colo., 1974-79; supr. dept. social services Arapahoe County, Littleton, Colo., 1979-80; project mgr. Nat. Conf. State Legis., Denver, 1981-84; dir. programs, pub. relations Mental Health Assn. Colo., Denver, 1984—. Editor: Mental Health: Planning and Funding Under the New Federalism, 1983, newsletter Mental Health Today, 1985—; co-producer (video) MHACS Pro Bono Project: Helping Denver's Homeless,

1987—. Dem. alt. del., Jefferson County, 1986. Mem. Nat. Assn. Social Workers (bd. dirs. Colo. chpt. 1985—), Social Workers for Peace and Social Welfare. Avocations: skiing, tennis, reading, hiking. Home: 3657 S Depew Apt 1 Denver CO 80235 Office: Mental Health Assn Colo 1391 N Speer Blvd Suite 350 Denver CO 80204

JENNINGS, JUDITH MORGAN, public relations executive, publicity director. m. Dean Jennings. With Sta. KYW-TV, Cleve., asst. publicity dir., 1963-66; talk show hostess Sta. KGO-Radio, San Francisco; prodn. coordinator Sta. KBHK, San Francisco; publicity dir. Sta. KTVU/Channel 2, Oakland, Calif., pub. relations and publicity dir. Recipient Disting. Service award No. Calif. Emmy Awards, 1985. Mem. Nat. Acad. TV Arts and Scis. (bd. govs., program chmn. 1983—), Calif. Press. Women (v.p. membership, named Woman of Achievement for No. Calif. 1984, 85), Am. Women in Radio and TV (publicity chmn.), San Francisco-Bay Area Publicity Club, Alumnae Resources, Women in Communications, The Embarcadero Ctr. Forum, Profl. Women's Network, Broadcast Promotion and Mktg. Execs. Avocations: theater, reading, travel. Office: KTVU/Channel 2 Box 22222 Oakland CA 94623

JENNINGS, ROBERT EDWARD, computer information scientist, political consultant; b. Huntington Park, Calif., Jan. 6, 1940; s. Edward Harding and Mildred Elizabeth (Walters) J.; m. Sara Alice Marshall, June 18, 1960; children: Tammy, Jeffrey, Michael. AA, Bakersfield Coll., 1960; BS, Humboldt State Coll., 1962. Range conservationist Bur. Land Mgmt., Redding, Calif., 1962-66; range staff specialist Bur. Land Mgmt., Bakersfield, Calif., 1966-70; dist. rep. office of Rep. Bob Mathias, Bakersfield, Calif., 1970-74; adminstrv. analyst Quad Cons., Visalia, Calif., 1975-78; exec. v.p. Calif. Data Mktg., Fresno, 1978—. Campaign mgr. Bill Jones for Calif. Assembly, Fresno, 1982, 84, 86; campaign dir. Trice Harvey for Calif. Assembly, Bakersfield, 1986. Republican. Avocations: fishing, hunting, gardening. Home: 15025 Ave 312 Visalia CA 93291

JENNINGS, ROBERT HAROLD, exploration geologist; b. Ft. Hood, Tex., Jan. 31, 1959; s. Robert Harold and Helen Charlotte (Walker) J. BA in Biology cum laude, Colo. Coll., 1981; MS in Geology, Tex. A&M U., 1983. Plant ecologist Western State Coll., Gunnison, Colo., 1978, 79; geotechnician Maxim Engring., Dallas, 1980; summer geologist Hunt Energy Corp., Dallas, 1981; geologist ARCO Internat. Oil and Gas Co., Los Angeles, 1983—. Contbr. articles to profl. jours. Recipient Leadership award Tex. Oil and Gas Co., 1982; Boettcher Found. scholar, 1977; grantee Geol. Soc. Am., 1981, Lechner fellow Tex. A&MU., 1981. Mem. Geol. Soc. Am., Am. Assn. Petroleum Geologists, Phi Beta Kappa, Phi Kappa Phi. Republican. Home: 1356 Kent Pl Glendale CA 91205 Office: ARCO Internat Oil and Gas Co 444 S Flower St Los Angeles CA 90017

JENNINGS, ROGER DENNIS, psychology educator, university administrator; b. Los Angeles, July 29, 1933; s. Lieuan Dennis and Lorna Margaret (Gurvine) J.; m. Jean Louise Cottrell, Aug. 9, 1957; children: Robin, Rodney. AA, City Coll. San Francisco, 1956; BA, U. Calif., Berkeley, 1959; MA, San Jose State U., 1960; PhD, U. Colo., 1963. NIMH Postdoctoral trainee U. Calif. Med. Ctr., San Francisco, 1963-65; postdoctoral psychology asst. VA Hosp., Palo Alto, Calif., 1965-66; research asst. Oceanic Inst., Waimanalo, Hawaii, 1966-67; assoc. prof. psychology Portland State U., Oreg., 1969-77, prof., 1977—, head dept. psychology, 1984—. Contbr. articles to profl. jours. Trustee Friends of Washington Park Zoo, Portland, 1985—. Served with USN, 1951-54. NIMH fellow, 1962-63. Mem. N.Y. Acad. Scis., Undersea Med. Soc., Aerospace Med. Assn., Sigma Xi. Democrat. Avocations: sailing, scuba diving, skiing, house remodeling. Home: 3151 NW Vaughn Portland OR 97210 Office: Portland State U PO Box 751 Portland OR 97207

JENNINGS, TIMOTHY ZEPH, rancher, state senator; b. Roswell, N.Mex., Sept. 4, 1950; s. James Traynor and Frances Mitchell (Schultz) J. Student N.Mex. State U., 1968-69; B.S. in Bus. Adminstrn., Creighton U., 1972. With Bill Deane Goodyear, San Jose, Calif., 1973; operator Penasco River Ranch, Roswell, 1973—; v.p. First Roswell Co.; mem. N.Mex. Senate, 1978—, mem. conservation com., edn. com. Mem. Chaves County Bd. Commrs., 1974-78; mem. N.Mex. Standards and Goals Com. for Juvenile Justice, 1974-76. Democrat. Roman Catholic. Lodge: Elks. Office: PO Box 1797 Roswell NM 88201

JENNY, JEAN MANSFIELD, psychotherapist; b. Yonkers, N.Y., Oct. 6, 1920; d. Horace J. and Ruth Paton (Nelson) Mansfield; m. Robert W. Jenny, Apr. 6, 1940; children: Robin Jenny Rothschild, Heather Jenny Chambers, Paul Douglas. Student, Russell Sage Coll., 1937-40; BA, U. Wash., 1963, MSW, 1965. Sr. social worker Family Counseling Service, Seattle, 1965-68, Children's Home Soc. Wash., Seattle; indiv. and group therapist, group therapy trainer Adult & Child Therapy Ctr. Inc., 1968-70; pvt. practice pscyhotherapy, indiv., group and family therapy Bellevue, Wash., 1969—; mem. clin. case consultation com. on sexual assault Harborview Hosp., Seattle, and Overlake Hosp. Med. Ctr., Bellevue; mem. allied health staff Fairfax Psychiatric Hosp., Kirkland, Wash. Trustee Overlake Meml. Hosp., 1958-59, Eastside Community Health Ctr., 1962-67; vol. counselor, group therapist Heads Up Youth Drop In Ctr., 1969-70; active Smithsonian Instn., ACLU, Common Cause. NIMH scholar, 1964-65; recipient Outstanding Profl. in Human Services award Am. Acad. Human Services, 1974-75. Fellow Nat. Acad. Counselors and Family Therapists Inc. (clin.); mem. Nat. Assn. Social Workers, Seattle Psychoanalytic Assn. (founding), Univ. Wash. Alumnae Assn., Adult and Child Therapy Ctr. (pres.), Nat. Alliance Family Life (supr.), Nat. Soc. Clin. Social Workers, Wash. Soc. Clin. Social Workers (founder), Am. Group Psychotherapy Assn., Acad. Cert. Social Workers, French Can. Group Psychotherapy Soc., Internat. Group Psychotherapy Soc. Mem. Unitarian Ch. Clubs: Newport Shores Yacht, Meydenbauer Bay Yacht. Home: 77 Cascade Key Bellevue WA 98006 Office: Adult & Child Therapy Ctr Inc 1310 116th St NE Bellevue WA 98004

JENSEN, ALLEN REED, lawyer; b. Tremonton, Utah, Sept. 13, 1950; s. Reed C. and Pauline (Michaelis) J.; m. Carlyn L. Phinney, June 6, 1975; children: Ashley, Kirstin, Christopher. BS in Chemistry magna cum laude, Utah State U., 1974; JD with high honors, George Washington U., 1977. Bar: Utah 1977, U.S. Ct. Appeals (Fed. cir.) 1978, U.S. Patent and Trademark Office 1976, D.C. 1980. Patent agt. Morton, Bernard, Brown, Roberts & Sutherland, Washington, 1975-77; tech. advisor, law clk. U.S. Ct. Customs and Patent Appeals, Washington, 1977-79; assoc., patent atty. Fox, Edwards & Gardiner, Salt Lake City, 1979-82, patent atty., dir., 1982-84; patent atty. Workman, Nydegger & Jensen, Salt Lake City, 1984—, also bd. dirs., 1984—; adj. prof. J. Reuben Clark Law Sch. of Brigham Young U., Provo, Utah, 1985—; bd. dirs. Nat. Inventors Hall of Fame. Mem. Utah State Bar Assn. (chmn. patent trademark and copyright sec. 1981-82), Nat. Council Patent Law Assns. (editor newsletter 1977—, councilman for Utah 1981—), Am. Intellectual Property Law Assn. (com. chmn. 1984-86), Am. Chem. Soc. Office: Workman Nydegger & Jensen 57 West 200 South 3d floor Salt Lake City UT 84101

JENSEN, ALTON DEAN, architect; b. Centerfield, Utah, May 9, 1927; s. Alton H. and Arvilla (Roylance) J.; m. Anita Heaton, Mar. 14, 1953; children: Bradly Dean (dec.), Dale Alton, Ryan Heaton. Cert. Archtl. Drafting, Utah Tech. Coll., 1950. Registered architect Utah, Nev., Ariz., Colo., Idaho, Wyo., Oreg., Calif., Nebr., Mont., N.D., S.D., Minn., Wash.; cert. architect Nat. Council Archtl. Registration Bds. Chief draftsman, office mgr. Miles E. Miller, Salt Lake City, 1950-54; chief draftsman Robert L. Spingmeyer, Salt Lake City, 1954-58; assoc. Donald H. Panushka & Assocs., Salt Lake City, 1958-62; pvt. practice architecture Salt Lake City, 1962—; chmn. graphic arts dept adv. com. Utah Tech. Coll., Salt Lake City; mem. master plan com. Salt Lake City Internat. Airport, 1979-81; mem. airport plan com. Wasatch Front Regional Council, Salt Lake City, 1979—. Mem. Utah Pilots Assn., Silver Wings, Quiet Birdmen. Republican. Mormon. Home: 268 U St Salt Lake City UT 84103 Office: 646 S 900 E Salt Lake City UT 84102

JENSEN, ANITA KRISTINA, child and family therapist, educational consultant; b. Mpls., Dec. 6, 1955; d. Bent and Inga Ruth (Eldsmark) J. BA in Psychology, Western Wash. U., 1978; MSW, U. Wash., 1985. Mgr. Westin Hotel Corp., Seattle, 1979-80; community relations coordinator Valley Gen. Hosp. Found., Renton, Wash., 1980-82; outpatient social worker in pediatrics Harborview Hosp., Seattle, 1984; ind. child and family therapist Family Counseling Ctr., Lynnwood, Wash., 1984-85, Highline West Seattle Mental Health Ctr., 1985—; mem. ethics rev. bd. U. Wash. Med. Sch., 1984-86; bd. dirs. Ctr. Human Services, Seattle. Mem. Nat. Assn. Social Workers. Office: Highline W Seattle Mental Health 1010 S 146th Seattle WA 98146

JENSEN, ARTHUR ROBERT, educator; b. San Diego, Aug. 24, 1923; s. Arthur Alfred and Linda (Schachtmayer) J.; m. Barbara Jane DeLarme, May 6, 1960; 1 dau., Roberta Ann. B.A., U. Calif. at Berkeley, 1945; Ph.D., Columbia, 1956. Asst. med. psychology U. Md., 1955-56; research fellow Inst. Psychiatry, U. London, 1956-58; prof. ednl. psychology U. Calif. at Berkeley, 1958—. Author: Genetics and Education, 1972, Educability and Group Differences, 1973, Educational Differences, 1973, Bias in Mental Testing, 1979, Straight Talk about Mental Tests, 1981; Contbr. to profl. jours., books. Guggenheim fellow, 1964-65; fellow Center Advanced Study Behavioral Scis., 1966-67. Fellow Am. Psychol. Assn., Eugenics Soc., AAAS; mem. Am. Ednl. Research Assn. (v.p. 1968-70), Psychonomic Soc., Am. Soc. Human Genetics, Soc. for Social Biology, Behavior Genetics Assn., Psychometric Soc., Sigma Xi. Office: U Calif Sch Edn Inst Learning Berkeley CA 94720

JENSEN, CRAIG CHARLES, computer software company executive; b. Springfield, Mo., Feb. 8, 1950; s. Niels Charles and Irene (Gould) J.; m. Sherry Lee McDonald, Apr. 27, 1968 (div.); 1 son, David Charles; m. Sally Ann Rosenberg, May 8, 1976; children: Laurel, Marissa. Student pub. schs. Bourne, Mass. Computer operator Western Electric, Watertown, Mass., 1968-69; computer programmer Stonemarketing, Cambridge, Mass., 1969; software engr. Brown & Sharpe Mfg. Co., N. Kingstown, R.I., 1969-70, Applied Data Research Co., Princeton, N.J., 1970-73, Data Gen. Corp., Southboro, Mass., 1973-75; ind. software devel. cons., Los Angeles, 1976-81; 'pres., sr. software engr. Exec. Software, Inc., Los Angeles, 1981—, chmn., 1982—. Author: (computer software system) EXECmail, 1983, Diskeeper, 1986; The Craft of Computer Programming, 1985. Mem. Assn. Computing Machinery, Digital Equipment Computer Users Soc. Republican. Mem. Ch. of Scientology. Home: 5132 Ocean View Blvd La Canada CA 91011-1240

JENSEN, CYNTHIA ANN, marketing professional; b. Phoenix, Sept. 24, 1953; d. Harold Emery and Jacqueline A. (Funk) Canterbury; m. Paul Eldredge Jensen, Jan. 25, 1975; children: Elizabeth Ann. Student, Ariz. State U., 1971-72; BS, U. Ariz., 1974. From exec. trainee to asst. buyer May Co. Dept. Stores, Los Angeles, 1975-77; dept. mgr. Bullocks Dept. Stores, Phoenix, 1977-78; real estate sales assoc. Jim Daniek & Assocs. Realtors, Phoenix, 1978-79; asst. buyer Broadway Southwest, Mesa, Ariz., 1979-82; mgr. Peat, Marwick, Mitchell & Co., Phoenix, 1982-87, Lewis and Roca Lawyers, 1987—; cons. Lannan & Cleverly Property Mgmt. Inc., Tempe, Ariz., 1985-86. Mem. long range planning com. Cactus Pine council Girl Scouts U.S., 1984, new dimensions foundations com. Phoenix Symphony Orch., 1983-84, religious edn. bd. Encanto Community Ch., 1980-82, 85-87, hospitality com., 1984-87. Mem. Internat. Assn. Bus. Communicators (profl. devel. com. 1984-85, v.p. profl. devel., bd. dirs. 1985-86, treas. 1986-87, Service award 1985), Pub. Relations Soc. Am., Meeting Planners Internat. (program com. 1985-86, chmn. membership com. 1986-87), Alpha Zeta. Republican. Clubs: Racquet, LaMancha Athletic (Phoenix). Avocations: gardening, needlework, interior design. Home: 306 W Virginia Phoenix AZ 85003 Office: care Lewis and Roca 1st Interstate Bank Plaza 100 W Washington Phoenix AZ 85003

JENSEN, DALLIN W., lawyer; b. Afton, Wyo., June 2, 1932; s. Louis J. and Nellie B. Jensen; m. Barbara J. Bassett, Mar. 22, 1958; children—Brad L., Julie N. B.S., Brigham Young U., 1954; J.D., U. Utah, 1960. Bar: Utah 1960, U.S. Dist. Ct. Utah 1962, U.S. Ct. Appeals (10th cir.) 1974, U.S. Ct. Appeals D.C. 1980, U.S. Supreme Ct. 1971. Asst. atty. gen. Utah Atty. Gen., Salt Lake City, 1960-83, solicitor gen., 1983—; alt. commr. Upper Colo. River Commn., 1983—; mem. Colo. River Basin Salinity Adv. Council, 1975—; spl. legal cons. Nat. Water Commn., Washington, 1971-73; mem. energy law center adv. council U. Utah Coll. Law, 1976—. Edit. bd. Rocky Mountain Mineral Law Found., 1983-85. Author: (with Wells A. Hutchins) The Utah Law of Water Rights, 1965. Contbr. articles on water law and water resource mgmt. to profl. jours. Served with U.S. Army, 1955-57. Mem. Ch. Jesus Christ Latter-day Saints. Home: 3565 S 2175 E Salt Lake City UT 84109 Office: Utah Atty Gen 1636 W N Temple #300 Salt Lake City UT 84116

JENSEN, DONALD RUSSELL, systems engineer; b. Mpls., Dec. 10, 1930; s. Otto Christ and Dora Augusta (Portz) J.; m. Hanako Morita, May 19, 1967; 1 dau., Hiroko Jensen Malatesta. B.A., U. Md., 1962. Cryptanalyst, Dept. of the Army, Far East, 1955-67; systems analyst HRB Singer Inc., State College, Pa., 1967-71; electronics engr. Lockheed Electronics Co., Tucson, 1971-74; systems analyst HRB Singer Inc., State College, 1974-77; program mgr. Motorola, Inc., Scottsdale, Ariz., 1977—. Contbr. articles to profl. jours. Mem. Rep. Nat. Com., 1974-86. Served with U.S. Army, 1952-55. Mem. Def. Preparedness Assn. Home: 8632 E Whitton Ave Scottsdale AZ 85251 Office: Motorola Inc GEG MS R4215 8220 E Roosevelt Scottsdale AZ 85252

JENSEN, DOROTHY LOU WYLIE, librarian, educator; b. Wenatchee, Wash., Feb. 27, 1933; d. Clifford Todd and Beatrice Dorothy (Masden) Wylie; m. Richard Franklin Jensen, June 15, 1952; children: Richard Todd, Susan Dorothy Jensen Purcell, Catherine Beth. BE, San Jose State U., 1966; MA in Librarianship, U. Wash., 1972. Library asst. Hoover Institution, Stanford, Calif., 1962-64; librarian Los Altos High Sch., Calif., 1966-73, 83—, Awalt High Sch., Mountain View, 1973-81; tchr. Mountain View High Sch., 1981-83. Mem. ALA, Calif. Tchrs. Assn. (treas. 1972-73, chpt. pres. 1981-83, state council rep. 1978-80), Calif. Media and Library Educators Assn., NEA, Beta Phi Mu. Republican. Lutheran. Club: Commonwealth (Calif.). Office: Los Altos High Sch 201 Almond Ave Los Altos CA 94022

JENSEN, EDMUND PAUL, bank holding company executive; b. Oakland, Calif., Apr. 13, 1937; s. Edmund and Olive E. (Kessell) J.; m. Marilyn Norris, Nov. 14, 1959; children—Juliana L., Annika M. B.A., U. Wash., 1959; postgrad., U. Santa Clara, Stanford U., 1981. Lic. real estate broker, Oreg., Calif. Mgr. fin. plan and evaluation Technicolor, Inc., Los Angeles, 1967-69; group v.p. Nat. Industries & Subs, Louisville, 1969-72; v.p. fin. Wedgewood Homes, Portland, 1972-74; various mgmt. positions U.S. Bancorp, Portland, 1974-83; pres. U.S. Bancorp, Inc., Portland, 1983—; dir. U.S. Bancorp, U.S. Nat. Bank of Oreg.; mem. Conv., Trade and Spectator Commn., 1985—. Bd. dirs. United Way, Portland, 1982—, chmn. campaign, 1986; bd. dirs. Saturday Acad., Portland, 1984—, Olympic Fundraising for Oregon Com., 1986, Providence Child Ctr. Found., Portland, 1984—, Marylhurst Coll.; mem. citizens steering com. Central City Plan, Portland, 1984-85; bd. dirs. Oreg. Ind. Coll. Found., 1983—, treas., 1986—. Mem. Portland C. of C. (bd. dirs. 1981—, chmn. 1987), Assn. Res. City Bankers. Lodge: Rotary. Office: US Bancorp Inc 111 SW 5th St Suite 3100 Portland OR 97204

JENSEN, EMRON ALFRED, zoology educator; b. Richfield, Utah, Jan. 5, 1925; s. Alfred Oscar and Julia Reina (Ogilvie) J.; m. Melva Bringhurst, Sept. 6, 1949; children: Kenneth B., Brian F., Eldon C., Paul R., Diana, Elyse, Clark E., Charlotte. BS, Utah State U., 1950, MS, 1961, PhD, 1963. Cert. tchr., Idaho, Utah. Tchr. Blackfoot (Idaho) Pub. Sch., 1950-52; technician Am. Cynamid Co., Arco, Idaho, 1952-53; tchr. Richfield (Utah) Elem. Sch., 1954-59; prof. zoology Weber State Coll., Ogden, Utah, 1963—, chmn. dept., 1967-83; mem. steering com. Utah Conf. Higher Edn., Salt Lake City, 1968-71. Author: Manual for Introductory Physiology, 1970. Rep. County delegate, Ogden, Utah, 1979-80. Served as cpl. U.S. Army, 1944-46. U. Utah scholar, 1942, Nat. Def. Edn. Act fellow, 1959-62, NIH fellow, 1962-63. Mem. AAAS, Utah Acad. Scis., Arts and Letters, Sigma Xi (pres. local chpt. 1970-71, 84-85). Republican. Mormon. Avocations: vocal music, carpentry, gardening. Office: Weber State Coll Zoology Dept 2505 Ogden UT 84408

JENSEN, ERNEST, forensic identification scientist, consultant, lecturer; b. Coulee City, Wash., July 22, 1915; Adolph Christian and Alma (Marcusen) J.; m. Helen Leponis, Dec. 2, 1939; children—Ernest Zane, Ronald Lee. Student U. Wash., 1936-40, Steilacoom Community Coll., 1974, Seattle Community Coll., 1971, FBI Acad., 1972. Cert. vocat. tchr. License examiner Wash. State Patrol, Seattle, 1940; with Seattle City Police Dept., 1941-69, supt., 1960-69; supr. Dept. Pub. Safety, Seattle, 1969-76; cons. to govt. agys. State of Wash., 1960-84; qualified expert on forensic identification fed. and state cts., 1945-84; instr. pub. safety and police acads., Seattle, 1950-76; lectr. forensic identification U.S. and Can., 1967-84; mem. Gov.'s Tech. Adv. Com., Olympia, Wash., 1972-84. Contbr. articles to profl. jours. Speaker to civic groups, Seattle, 1947—; coach Little League baseball and football, Seattle, 1954-69; dir. Western Opera Co., Seattle, 1962-64; counselor Seattle council Boy Scouts of Am., Seattle, 1962. Recipient Oustanding Community Service award Kiwanis Club, 1963. Mem. Internat. Assn. Identification (pres. 1979-80, chmn. bd. 1980-81), Wash. State Identification Assn. (pres. 1964-65). Republican. Lutheran. Clubs: Nat. Horseshoe (Seattle) (state class champion 1972), Pitcher's Assn. Office: Identification Consultant 19029 56th Ln NE Seattle WA 98155

JENSEN, GARY A., electric company executive; b. Reno, July 2, 1944; s. George L. and Velma K. Jensen; m. Diane Priess, Sept. 14, 1963; children: Christian, Elizabeth. Cert. pilot. Prin. Jensen Electric Co., Reno, 1968—, also chief exec. officer. Mem. U. Nev.-Reno Boosters. Mem. ASHRAE, Nat. Elec. Contractors Assn. (pres. 1976-80, bd. dirs. No. Nev.), Instrument Soc. Am. (sr.), Construction Specifiers Inst., Nat. Fire Protection Assn. Lodge: Elks. Home and Office: 140 Jensen St Reno NV 89502

JENSEN, GWENDOLYN MARIE, petroleum geologist; b. Los Angeles, June 24, 1944; d. Oscar Bernhard and Cora Theresa (Bergh) J.; m. Jeffrey Charles Heller, Nov. 25, 1972. B.S., UCLA, 1967. Geologist Cities Service Co., Los Angeles, 1968-72, exploration geologist, Denver, 1972-79, 81—;asst. field trip chmn. Rocky Mountain Assn. Petroleum Geologists, 1978; lectr. subsurface stratigraphy Idaho State U., Pocatello, 1981. Mem. Colo. NOW, ERA Taskforce, 1982; publicity com. Colo. Nat. Abortion Rights Action League, 1982; mem. AAUW, Jung Soc. Named Woman of Yr., Denver chpt. Assn. Women Geoscientists, 1981. Mem. Am. Assn. Petroleum Geologists, Rocky Mountain Assn. Geologists, Wyo. Geol. Assn., Soc. Econ. Paleontologists and Mineralogists, Assn. Women in Sci., Assn. Women Geoscientists (dir., publicity com. 1981, editor Denver chpt. 1981, v.p. found. 1983-84), Geol. Soc. Am., AAAS. Democrat. Office: 1600 Broadway Suite 900 Denver CO 80202

JENSEN, HELEN, musical artists mgmt. co. exec.; b. Seattle, June 30, 1919; d. Frank and Sophia (Kantosky) Leponis; student public schs., Seattle; m. Ernest Jensen, Dec. 2, 1939; children—Ernest, Ronald Lee. Co-chmn., Seattle Community Concert Assn., 1957-62; sec. family concerts Seattle Symphony Orch., 1959-61; hostess radio program Timely Topics, 1959-60; gen. mgr. Western Opera Co., Seattle, 1962-64, pres. 1963-64; v.p., dir., mgr. public relations Seattle Opera Assn., 1964—, preview artists Coordinator, 1981-84; bus. mgr. Portland (Oreg.) Opera Co., 1968, cons., 1967-69; owner, mgr. Helen Jensen Artists Mgmt., Seattle, 1970—. First v.p. Music and Art Found., 1981-84. Recipient Cert., Women in Bus in the Field of Art, 1973; award Seattle Opera Assn., 1974; Outstanding Service award Music and Art Found., 1984; award of distinction Seattle Opera Guild, 1983. Mem. Am. Guild Mus. Artists, Music and Art Found., Seattle Opera Guild (pres., award of distinction 1983), Ballard Symphony League (sec.), Seattle Civic Opera Assn. (pres. 1981-84), Portland Opera Assn., Portland Opera Guild, Seattle Civic Opera Assn. (pres. 1981-87), 200 Plus One, Aria Preview, Lyric Preview Group, Past Pres. Assembly (pres. 1977-79) North Shore Performing Arts Assn. (pres. 1981). Clubs: Helen Jensen Hiking, Kenmore Community. Home: 19029 56th Ln NE Seattle WA 98155 Office: 716 Joseph Vance Bldg Seattle WA 98101

JENSEN, JAMES LESLIE, chemistry educator, university administrator; b. Tulare, Calif., Oct. 17, 1939; s. Lester Eugene and Mabel Irene (Brown) J.; m. Nancy Ruth Peterson, Aug. 13, 1960; children: Randall Mark, Linda Suzanne. BA in Chemistry, Westmont Coll., 1961; MA in Chemistry, U. Calif., Santa Barbara, 1963; PhD in Organic Chemistry, U. Wash., 1967. Instr. chemistry Westmont Coll., Santa Barbara, Calif., 1962-64, U. Wash., Seattle, 1968; from asst. prof. to prof. Calif. State U., Long Beach, 1968—, assoc. dean Sch. Natural Scis., 1983—; vis. scientist Brandeis U.-W.P. Jencks Lab., Waltham, Mass., 1974-75; vis. prof. U. Calif. Irvine, 1981-82; chmn. Calif. State U. Long Beach com. research, found. personnel com., budget adv. com.; mem. ad hoc com., fin. com., preprofl. com., curriculum com., reappointment and advancement com., grad. com.; invited lectr. Calif. State U., Fullerton, Brandeis U., U. So. Calif., others. Reviewer NSF, Jour. Am. Chemistry Soc., Sci.; contbr. articles to profl. jours. Weyerhauser fellow, U. Wash., 1966-67; scholar Westmont Coll., 1957-58, 60-61; recipient Merit award Long Beach Heart Assn., 1970, Disting. Service award Am. Heart Assn., 1971. Mem. AAAS, Am. Sci. Affiliation, Internat. Union of Pure and Applied Chemistry, Am. Chem. Soc. (organic div.), Royal Soc. Chemistry (organic chemistry div., fast reactions groups), Sigma Xi, Phi Beta Kappa, Phi Lambda Upsilon. Republican. Office: Calif State U Sch Natural Scis Long Beach CA 90840

JENSEN, JUDY DIANNE, psychotherapist; b. Portland, Oreg., Apr. 8, 1948; d. Clarence Melvin and Charlene Augusta (Young) J.; m. Frank George Cooper, Sept 4, 1983; stepchildren: Pamela Cooper, Brian Cooper. BA in Sociology and Anthropology with honors, Oberlin Coll., 1970; MSW, U. Pitts., 1972; postgrad., U. Wis., 1977. Registered clin. social worker. Social worker Day Hosp. Western Psychiat. Inst. and Clinic, Pitts., 1972-73, South Hills Child Guidance Ctr., Pitts., 1973-74; mem. drug treatment program Umatilla County Mental Health Clinic, Pendleton, Oreg., 1975-77; social worker Children's Services Div. State of Oreg., Pendleton, 1978-80, therapist intensive family services project, 1980—, dir. intensive family services project, 1986—; pvt. practice Pendleton, 1980—. NIMH grantee, 1970-72; NDEA fellow 1977; Gen. Motors scholar Oberlin Coll., 1966-70. Mem. Am. Assn. Marriage and Family Therapists (clin.), Nat. Assn. Social Workers. Avocations: fgn. travel, backpacking, jogging, photography, personal jour. and poetry writing. Home: 325 NW Bailey Pendleton OR 97801 Office: PO Box 752 Pendleton OR 97801

JENSEN, OLE THEODOR, oral and maxillofacial surgeon; b. Salt Lake City, Aug. 22, 1949; s. Sverre Torlief and Theodora Martilda (Tonnessen) J.; m. Marty Fae Potter, Dec. 27, 1974; children—Sverre Tait, Autumn Korrine. B.S. cum laude, U. Utah, 1972; D.D.S., Northwestern U., 1976; M.S., U. Mich., 1980. Diplomate Am. Bd. Oral and Maxillofacial Surgery. Intern, resident in anesthesiology Northwestern U. Med. Sch., Chgo., 1976-77; resident in surgery U. Mich., Ann Arbor, 1977-80; pvt. practice oral surgery, Denver, 1980—; asst. clin. prof. U. Colo. Med. Ctr., Denver, 1980—; oral surgery cons. VA Med. Ctr., Denver, 1982—, researcher, 1983—; oral surgery cons. Denver U., 1981-84. Pub. The Mormon Trail. Contbr. articles to profl. jours. Served with USAR, 1968-69. Fellow Am. Soc. Oral and Maxillofacial Surgery, Am. Dental Soc. Anesthesiology, Am. Coll. Oral and Maxillofacial Surgeons; mem. Central City Opera Guild, Denver Symphony Guild, Denver Art Mus., Denver Mus. Natural History. Mormon. Office: 1633 Fillmore St Suite 5 Denver CO 80206

JENSEN, RANDY J., psychiatric nurse, researcher; b. Idaho Falls, Idaho, Jan. 5, 1949; s. Donald Wray Jensen and Lois Ethel (Corbett) Kidwell; m. Phyllis Patrice Vause, Feb. 26, 1972; 1 child, Kimberly Marie. BS in Nursing, U. Hawaii, 1979, MS in Nursing, 1987. Cert. clin. nurse specialist. Staff nurse The Queen's Med. Ctr., Honolulu, 1979-80, Straub Hosp., Honolulu, 1981-82; psychiat. nurse Tripler Army Med. Ctr., Honolulu, 1982-86, clin. nurse specialist, 1987—. Author: Grief Reactions for Families, 1979, Patient Assaults and Stress in Nursing Personnel, 1987. Served with USN, 1971-75. Mem. Am. Nurses Assn., Hawaii Nurses Assn., Am. Psychiat. Nurses Assn., Sigma Theta Tau. Roman Catholic. Avocations: stamp collecting, coin collecting, computers, writing, running. Home: 94-381-76 Kaholo St Mililani HI 96789-2537 Office: Tripler Army Med Ctr Dept Nursing Honolulu HI 96859-5000

JENSEN, ROBERT P., transportation company executive; b. Chgo., Dec. 29, 1925; s. Louis P. and Ellen (Goede) J.; m. Anne Fletcher, June 15, 1980; children—Erik P., Curtis R. BS in Mech. Engring., Iowa State Coll., Ames, 1947; postgrad., U. Mich., 1953-54; grad., advanced mgmt. program Harvard U., 1965. Salesman, br. and dist. mgr., gen. sales mgr., operations mgr. Kaiser Aluminum & Chem. Sales, Inc., 1954-61, gen. mgr. bldg. products div., 1963-66, dir. bus. planning aluminum div., 1967; exec. v.p., gen. mgr. Olin Foil Packaging Corp. (subsidiary Olin Mathieson Chem. Corp.), 1961-63; v.p. aluminum group Howmet Corp., N.Y.C., 1967-68, exec.

v.p., 1968-70, chief operating officer, dir., 1970, pres., chief exec. officer, 1971-72, also dir.; chief operating officer, pres., chief exec. officer, dir. Gen. Cable Corp. (now GK Technologies, Inc.), Greenwich, Conn., 1973-83; chmn. bd. Gen. Cable Corp. (now GK Technologies, Inc.) after 1978; chmn., chief exec. officer EF Hutton LBO Inc., 1983-85; chief exec. officer, pres., dir. Tiger Internat., Inc., 1985—, chmn., 1986—; chmn., chief exec. officer, dir. Flying Tiger Line Inc., 1985—, pres., chief operating officer, 1986—; dir. Conoco Inc., Irving Bank Corp., Irving Trust Co., Jostens, Inc., EF Hutton LBO Inc., Arrow Electronics, Aerospace Corp., Singer Co. Served to lt. (j.g.) USNR, 1944-46. Clubs: Board Room (N.Y.C.), Greenwich Country (Greenwich, Conn.), Indian Harbor Yacht (Greenwich, Conn.); Landmark (Stamford, Conn.); La Cumbre Golf and Country (Santa Barbara, Calif.); Los Angeles Country. Office: EF HUtton LBD Inc 8 E Figueroa St Santa Barbara CA 93101

JENSEN, WARREN MARTIN, materials and processes engineer; b. Olympia, Wash., Apr. 22, 1941; s. Martin H. and Roberta W. (Vanden Hoek) J.; m. Charlotte A. Anderson, Sept. 14, 1963; children—Matthew A., Jonathan A. B.S. in Chem. Engring., U. Wash., 1964. Registered profl. engr., Calif. Engr., Boeing Comml. Airplane Co., Renton, Wash., 1964-68; sr. engr. Jet Propulsion Lab., Pasadena, Calif., 1968-76; engr. specialist Litton Guidance & Control Systems, Grants Pass, Oreg., 1976-78; group leader, sr. specialist engr. Boeing Aerospace Co., Seattle, 1978-85; group leader, prin. engr. Boeing Mil. Airplane Co., Seattle, 1985—. Recipient Top 20 award of merit in materials engring., 1982. Mem. Soc. Advancement Material and Process Engring. (chmn. Seattle chpt. 1983-84, Delmonte award 1982), Inst. Interconnecting and Packaging Electronic Circuits (chmn. working group). Republican. Baptist. Patentee in field. Home: 12017 NE 68th Pl Kirkland WA 98033 Office: PO Box 3707 MS 4A-17 Seattle WA 98124

JENSEN, WILLIAM S., business educator; b. Seattle, Sept. 10, 1931; s. William Stephen and Eloise Sherman (Gibson) J.; m. Carolyn Elizabeth Moore, Nov. 23, 1958; children: Sharon, Eloise, Cynthia. AB, U. Wash., 1957; MS, Columbia U., 1959; JD, U. Calif., San Francisco, 1966; PhD, Oreg. State U., 1975. Cert. mgmt. acct. Import mgr. Washington Import-Export Corp., San Francisco, 1956-57; asst. prof. bus. Calif. State U., Hayward, 1965-67; mgr. Portland (Oreg.) Fish Co., 1967-69; prof. Lewis and Clark Coll., Portland, 1971-80, 81—, chmn. dept. bus., 1986—; exec. dir. West Coast Fisheries Found., Portland, 1980-81; advisor FTC, Seattle, 1972; cons. Office of Tech. Assessment, Washington, 1976, Wash. State Dept. Fisheries, Olympia, 1977-78; cons./advisor Pacific Fisheries Mgmt. Council, Portland, 1985-86; bd. dirs. Ingeborg Short Found., Seattle. Contbr. articles to profl. jours. Served as staff sgt. USAF, 1951-54. Standard & Poors fellow, Columbia U., 1958; Harriman scholar, Columbia U., 1958; grantee Am. Acctg. Assn., 1973. Mem. Acad. Polit. Sci., Inst. Mgmt. Acctg. Democrat. Episcopalian. Avocation: writing. Home: 17618 SW Lake Haven Dr Lake Oswego OR 97034 Office: Lewis and Clark Coll 0615 SW Palatine Hill Rd Portland OR 97219

JENSEN, WILMA, superintendent of schools; b. Choteau, Mont., Dec. 12, 1918; d. Robert and Edith Olive (Watson) van Scherpenzeel; m. John L. Jensen, Jan. 17, 1942 (div. 1967); 1 child, Dorothy Marie Backland. B.S., No. Mont. Coll., 1966; M.Ed., U. Mont., 1981. Tchr., Baker Sch. Dist., Dutton, Mont., 1939-40, Agawam Sch. Dist., Mont., 1940-45, Erickson Sch. Dist., Conrad, Mont., 1945-46, Pendroy Sch., Mont., 1949-52, 55-64, Troy Sch., Mont., 1964-67, Dutton Sch., Mont., 1967-78; county supt. schs. Teton County, Choteau, 1979—; sec. Big Sky Spl. Edn. Co-op, Conrad, 1981—. Mem. Soroptimist Internat. Choteau & vicinity, 1981—; sec. Teton County Women's Republican Club, Choteau, 1979—; mem. Teton County Rep. Central Com., Choteau, 1978—. Mem. Mont. Assn. County Sch. Supts., Sch. Adminstrs. Mont., Am. Assn. Sch. Adminstrs., Assn. Supervision and Curriculum Devel., Delta Kappa Gamma. Methodist. Home: PO Box 292 15 3d Ave SW Choteau MT 59422 Office: Teton County Supt Schs Courthouse Choteau MT 59422

JENSON, RONALD ALLEN, religious executive, educator; b. Bremerton, Wash., Apr. 15, 1948; s. Robert C. and Maxine (Mitchell) J.; m. Mary Kunz, Dec. 27, 1969; children: Matthew Robert, Mary Rachel. BA cum laude in Speech Communications, Lewis and Clark Coll., 1969; MDiv, summa cum laude, Western Conservative Bapt. Sem., 1972, DMinistry, 1974. Ordained Ch. of the Savior, 1976. Pastor, Ch. of the Saviour, Wayne, Pa., 1973-79; pres. Ch. Dynamics, San Bernardino, Calif., 1978-79, Internat. Sch. Theology, San Bernardino, 1978-86; vice chancellor Internat. Christian Grad. U., San Bernardino, 1983—; pres. Internat. Leadership Group, 1987—. Mem. nat. exec. com. Reagan's Yr. of the Bible; mem. bd. govs. Council Nat. Policy. Named Outstanding Young Man in Am., U.S. Jaycees, 1976. Mem. Am. Assn. Higher Edn. Author: How to Succeed the Biblical Way, 1981, Dynamics of Church Growth, 1981, Together We Can, 1982, Always Advancing, Always Planning, 1984, Kingdoms at War, 1986. Home: 6082 Mirada Ct Highland CA 92346 Office: Internat Leadership Group Arrowhead Springs San Bernadino CA 92414

JENTZCH, HEBER CARL, religious society administrator; b. Salt Lake City, Oct. 30, 1935; s. Carl Eugene and Pauline (Olson) J.; m. Karen Della Carriere, Sept. 9, 1978; 1 child, Alexander. Student, Weber State U., 1945-56; BFA, U. Utah, 1959; D (hon.), St. Martins Coll., 1986. Ordained to ministry Ch. of Scientology, 1975. Minister Ch. of Scientology, Los Angeles; pres. Ch. of Scientology Internat., Los Angeles. Guest on TV shows 60 Minutes, 20/20, Phil Donahue Show, Late Night America, Tom Snyder Show, various others; writer, producer Freedom Jour. TV. Mem. Citizens Commn. on Human Rights. Mem. Sea Orgn. Office: 4751 Fountain Ave Los Angeles CA 90029

JEPPESEN, M. K., university administrator; b. Logan, Utah, Dec. 31, 1935; s. Moses A. and Afton (Hillyard) J.; m. Carol Jenkins, June 10, 1955 (dec. Nov. 1963); children: Steven, Juliane, Karen, Jennifer; m. Ellen Rae Burtenshaw, July 14, 1966; children: Christine, Craig, David, Nanette. BS, Utah State U., 1957, MBA, 1971. Mgr. bus. Utah Sci. Found., 1958-60; rep. controllers Utah State U., Logan, 1960-69, dir. contracts/grants, 1972—, mem. patent com., investment adv. com., research council, 1978—, treas., trustee fedn. bd., 1987—; auditor Main Hurdman, Salt Lake City, 1969-72. Served to lt. U.S. Army, 1957-63. Fellow Nat. Contract Mgmt. Assn. (cert., chmn. program com. 1983-84); mem. Soc. Research Adminstrs. (pres. 1986—, pres. Mountain chpt. 1983-85, mem. nominating com. 1982-83), Nat. Council Univ. Research Adminstrs. (profl. devel. com. 1982-85). Republican. Mormon. Club: Logan Golf and Country. Avocations: golf, traveling, hunting, snowmobiling. Home: 1050 E 2000 N Logan UT 84321 Office: Utah State U UMC 1415 Logan UT 84322

JEPPESEN, RICHARD FERRILL, real estate developer; b. Denver, June 9, 1942; s. Elery Borge and Nadine (Liscomb) J.; m. Nancy Lynn Bell, Oct. 29, 1973; children: Randy Walker, Casey Bear, Johnny Walker, Joshua James, Kelly Lynn. Student, U. Colo., 1960, U. Ill., 1961, U. Nev., 1965; BS with honors, Ariz. State U., 1971. Capt. Northwest Airlines, Phoenix, 1965-82; pres. Continental Design, Inc., Phoenix, 1965-74, Jeppesen and Co., Chandler, Ariz., 1963—; chmn. Jeppesen Devel., Inc., Chandler, 1984—; real estate broker Jeppeson Devel. Inc., Chandler, Ariz., 1966—. Patentee in field. Bd. dirs. Winterstick Theatre, Phoenix, 1983-86. Recipient Gold medals in gymnastics AAU and Olympic trials USAF Acad., 1960, Internat. Heroism award Flight Safety Found., Inc., Arlington, Va., 1986. Mem. Airline Pilots Assn., Air Traffic Control Com. (chmn. 1970-86), Airport Standards Com. (chmn. 1968-70), Air Safety Com. (chmn. 1968-76), Helicopter Task Force (chmn. 1984—), U.S. Tennis Assn., Phoenix Dist. Tennis Assn. Republican. Club: Western Res. (Tempe, Ariz.), Ocotillo Country, Oakwood Country (Chandler), Golden Eagle, Trunk 'n Tusk. Lodge: Rotary (bd. dirs. 1986, Paul Harris fellow 1985). Home: One Oakwood Hills Dr Chandler AZ 85248 Office: Jeppesen Devel Inc One Oakwood Hills Dr Chandler AZ 85248

JEPPSON, ROBERT BAIRD, JR., bus. exec.; b. Rexburg, Idaho, Apr. 23, 1920; s. Robert Baird and Elsie (Smith) J.; B.S., U. Calif., 1942; grad. Advanced Mgmt. Program, Harvard U., 1963; m. Edith Abigail French, Jan. 9, 1947; children—Jane Elizabeth, James Robert, Virginia K. Commd. ensign U.S. Navy, 1942, advanced through ranks to capt., 1962; ret., 1969; bus. mgr. Reno Radiol. Assos. (Nev.), 1969-78; broker Alpine Realty Assos., 1971—; mgmt. cons., 1978—; gen. mgr., partner BHLS Investments. Republican. Mormon. Home: 2675 Everett Dr Reno NV 89503 Office: PO Box 7011 Reno NV 89510

JEPPSON, ROGER WAYNE, lawyer; b. San Francisco, June 26, 1936; s. Wayne O. and Maude (Josephson) J.; m. Janet Strong, Nov. 27, 1957; children—Jennifer, Jill. B.S. in Polit. Sci., Brigham Young U., 1958; J.D., Duke U., 1961. Bar: Oreg. 1961, Nev. 1961. Law clk. Justice Kenneth J. O'Connell of Oreg. Sup. Ct., 1961-62; assoc. Woodburn, Wedge, Blakey and Jeppson and predecessors, Reno, 1962-65, ptnr., 1965—. Mem. Nev. State Bar Assn. (chmn. ethics com. 1979-82, del. 9th cir. judicial conf. 1979-82), Oreg. State Bar Assn., Washoe County Bar Assn. (pres. 1974-75). Democrat. Office: 1 E 1st St Suite 1600 Reno NV 89505

JERNIGAN, JEAN ALLEN, group executive assistant; b. Brookline, Mass., May 26, 1923; d. Langdon and Dorothy (Talbot) Allen; A.A., Garland Jr. Coll., 1942; m. Roger R. Jernigan, May 31, 1943; children—Roger, Jeffrey, Bruce, Linda. Fashion and beauty editorial asst. Boston Herald Traveler, 1942-44; news editor Sun Newspapers, Contra Costa County, Calif., 1958-64; aide to county supr. Contra Costa County, 1964-66; dir. public relations Children's Hosp. Med. Center, Oakland, Calif., 1966-68; women's editor, feature writer Berkeley (Calif.) Gazette, 1968-78; dir. public relations, asst. exec. dir. Berkeley-East Bay Humane Soc., 1978-81; reporter Contra Costa Sun, Lafayette, Calif., 1979-80; adminstrv. asst. to v.p. fin. Cetus Corp., 1981-83; group exec. asst. Triad Systems Corp., 1984—. Recipient McQuade award, 1970. Mem. Women in Communication. Clubs: East Bay Press, Contra Costa Press. Republican. Office: 1252 Orleans Dr Sunnyvale CA 94088

JERREMS, ALEXANDER STAPLER, aerospace company executive; b. Kansas City, Mo., May 9, 1919; s. William G. and Anna (Stapler) J.; B.S. in Elec. Engring., Calif. Inst. Tech., 1942; postgrad. M.I.T., 1946-48; m. Eva Lion, Aug. 22, 1954; 1 son, Brian David. Mem. tech. staff radiation labs. M.I.T., 1942-45, research asso., 1946-48; sr. staff scientist Los Alamos Sci. Lab., 1945-46; tech. dir. aerospace group Hughes Aircraft Co., Culver City, Calif., 1948-70, dir. tech., 1970-82, corp. staff v.p. tech., 1982—; cons. Def. Sci. Bd., Washington, 1974—. Bd. dirs. Calif. Engring. Found., 1982—; mem. engring. dean's council UCLA, 1977—. Mem. IEEE, AAAS, Am. Soc. Engring. Edn., Sigma Xi, Tau Beta Phi. Author profl. articles. Home: 141 N Anita Los Angeles CA 90049 Office: 200 N Sepulveda Blvd El Segundo CA 90245

JESAITIS, ALGIRDAS JOSEPH, cell biologist; b. Freiburg, Fed. Rep. of Germany, Aug. 21, 1945; came to U.S., 1949; s. Kestutis Jouzas and Jadvyga (Kalinauskas) J.; m. Ellen Feeney, Mar. 31, 1979; children: Anna Marie, Christina Jadvyga, Andrew Victor. BS in Physics, NYU, 1967; PhD in Biophysics, Calif. Inst. Tech., 1973. Post doctoral fellow U. Freiburg, Fed. Rep. of Germany, 1973-75, U. Calif., San Diego, 1975-79; sr. research fellow Scripps Clinic and Research Found., La Jolla, Calif., 1979-83, asst. mem., 1983—. Contbr. articles to profl. jours. Named Established Investigator, San Diego chpt., Am. Heart Assn., 1985; NIH Individual Research grant, 1985. Mem. Am. Soc. Cell Biology, Biophysical Soc., Tau Beta Pi. Roman Catholic. Avocations: skiing, surfing. Office: Scripps Clinic & Research Found Dept Immunology IMM 12 10666 N Torrey Pines Rd La Jolla CA 92037

JESSEN, RAYMOND JAMES, business administrator, public health educator; b. San Francisco, Nov. 4, 1910; s. James Niels and Millie Marie (Ring) J.; m. Lois Barron, Dec. 24, 1940 (div. 1969); m. Charlotte Sarett, July 9, 1971; children: Tony, Marna, Van. BS, U. Calif., 1937; PhD, Iowa State U., 1943. From research assoc. to prof. stats. Iowa State Coll., Ames, 1938-57, acting dir. statis. lab., 1947-50; agrl. and math. statistician USDA, Ames, 1938-56; project dir. CEIR, Inc., Los Angeles, 1957-62; prof. mgmt. and pub. health UCLA, 1962-78, prof. emeritus, 1978—; tech. dir. allied mission observing Greek election, U.S. Dept. State, Washington and Athens, 1946. Author: Statistical Survey Techniques, 1978; co-author: Basic Statistics for Business and Economics, 1971. Fellow Am. Statis. Assn., Internat. Statis. Inst.; mem. AAAS, Sigma Xi. Home: 327 21st St Santa Monica CA 90402 Office: UCLA Grad Sch Mgmt 405 Hilgard Ave Los Angeles CA 90024

JETER, JAMES WILBUR, aerospace scientist; b. Richmond, Va., Jan. 26, 1943; s. James Wilbur Sr. and Regina (Eckert) J.; m. Carol Jean Helder, Oct. 26, 1970; children: Joanne, Amy, James III. BSCE, Va. Mil. Inst., 1964; MCE, U. Va., 1967, PhD in Applied Mechanics, 1972. Registered profl. engr., Va. Commd. 2d lt. U.S. Army, 1964, advanced through grades to capt., 1969, resigned, 1970; asst. prof. Va. Mil. Inst., Lexington, 1972-76, assoc. prof., 1976-80; sr. research engr. NMERI, Albuquerque, 1980-82, mgr. theoretical analysis div., 1982-83; sr. staff engr. Hughes Aircraft Co., Albuquerque, 1983-86, sr. scientist, 1986—; cons. N.Mex. Engring. Research Inst., Albuquerque, 1984, BDM Corp., Albuquerque, 1985—; adj. prof., U. N.Mex., Albuquerque, 1981-84. Contbr. articles to profl. jours. Decorated Bronze Star. Mem. ASCE (properties of materials com. 1982-86), N.Mex. Commodore Users Group, Sigma Xi. Republican. Roman Catholic. Avocations: photography, skiing, running, tennis, home computing. Home: 9516 Avenida de la Luna NE Albuquerque NM 87111 Office: Hughes Aircraft Co 1600 Randolph Ct SE Albuquerque NM 87106

JETER, WAYBURN STEWART, educator, microbiologist; b. Cooper, Tex., Feb. 16, 1926; s. Joseph Plato and Beulah (Stewart) J.; m. Margaret Ann McDonald, May 30, 1947; children—Randall Mark, Monette Ann, Marcus Kent. B.S., U. Okla., 1948, M.S., 1949; Ph.D., U. Wis., 1950. Diplomate: Am. Bd. Microbiology. Mem. faculty U. Iowa, 1950-63, assoc. prof., 1958-63; prof. microbiology U. Ariz., Tucson, 1963—; head dept. microbiology and med. tech. U. Ariz., 1967-83, prof. pharmacology and toxicology, 1983—; dir. lab. U. Ariz. (Cellular Immunology), 1976—, dir. med. tech. program, 1976-79; vis. prof. immunology and med. microbiology U. Fla., 1980. Contbr. articles profl. jours. Served with USNR, 1943-46. Fellow AAAS; mem. Am. Acad. Microbiology, Am. Assn. Immunologists, Ariz. Acad. Sci., Am. Soc. Microbiology (mem. council 1975-77), Soc. Exptl. Biology and Medicine, Sigma Xi. Democrat. Presbyn. Home: 2264 E Camino Rio Tucson AZ 85718

JETT, RICHARD JAMES, bank executive; b. South Gate, Calif., May 7, 1940; s. Artie Richard and Evelyn Clara (Tuksbre) J.; m. Deborrah C. Wiesman, July 14, 1975 (div. Sept. 1982); m. Michelle Diane Hall, Oct. 25, 1984; children: Sandi, Teri, Richi. Diploma in retail banking, U. Va. Collector Dial Fin., Alhambra, Calif., 1960-62; v.p. 1st Interstate Bank, Los Angeles, 1962-79; exec. v.p. Citrus State Bank, Covina, Calif., 1979-82; pres., chief exec. officer Empire Bank, N.A., Rancho Cucamonga, Calif., 1982—, also bd. dirs.; Bd. dirs. Haven Escrow Co., Inc., Covina, Calif. Mem. Am. Bankers Assn. (advisor 1979-83,), Am. Inst. Banking (bd. dirs. 1983—), Independent Bankers Assn. So. Calif. (bd. dirs. 1984—), Calif. Bankers Assn. (bd. dirs. 1985—), Covina C. of C. (pres. 1986—, named Dir. of Yr. 1984). Republican. Lutheran. Lodges: Lions, Masons. Avocation: skiing. Home: 646 Chaparro Rd Covina CA 91724 Office: Empire Bank NA PO Box 1059 Rancho Cucamonga CA 91730

JETTON, SUSAN KAREN, public information officer, state government; b. Laurens, S.C., Sept. 3, 1944; d. John Wright and Nell (Waldrep) J. BJ, U. Mo., 1966. Profl. Journalism fellow NEH, 1978-79. Democrat. Home: 2524 6th Ave Sacramento CA 95818 Office: Office Press Secy Calif Assembly Speaker Willie Brown State Capitol Rm 217 Sacramento CA 95814

JEWELL, DOROTHY ALTHEA, writer; b. Santa Barbara, Calif., Dec. 12, 1923; d. Carl and Grace Ester (Flint) Killam; m. William Eugene, Oct. 29, 1948; children: Kathleen Althea Schwab, Marianne Susan. Student, Long Beach City Coll. Staff writer Press-Telegram, Long Beach, Calif., 1947-52; freelance writer Better Homes and Gardens, Iowa, 1948-65; assoc. editor Modern Maturity, Lakewood, Calif., 1965-87; freelance writer Crestline, Calif., 1987—.

JEWELL, ERNEST C., steel company executive; b. Mesa, Ariz., Mar. 26, 1936; s. James W. and Fleeta Jewell; m. Gail Spilsbury, June 30, 1960; children: Rebecca, Michael, Christine, Marc, Linda, Sharon Larrain. BA in Indsl. Mgmt., Brigham Young U., 1961; MBA, U. Wash., Seattle, 1968. Trainee, indsl. engr. U.S. Steel, Pittsburg, Calif., 1962-66; chief indsl. engr. Davis Wire, Los Angeles, 1966-68; mgmt. cons. EMSCO, Woodland Hill, Calif., 1968-72, Ernest C. Jewell & Assocs., Fullerton, Calif., 1972-77, 80-82; v.p. mfg. Bell Helmets, Norwalk, Calif., 1977-80; gen. mgr. Selectile Calif., Los Angeles, 1982-84; bd. dirs. Cowelco, Long Beach, Calif., 1982—; lectr. mgmt. seminar U. So. Calif., 1972. Organizer ch. float Rose Bowl Parade, 1976; producer dance festival Rose Bowl, 1973, 76. Recipient Clark Tank Lines scholarship, 1960, Boeing Co. scholarship, 1961. Mem. Beta Gamma Sigma. Mormon. Avocations: tennis, jogging, reading. Home: 1542 Baronet Pl Fullerton CA 92633 Office: Cowelco 1634 W 14th St Long Beach CA 90813

JEWELL, JAMES EARL, illuminating engineer; b. Los Angeles, July 26, 1929; s. Earl Clare and Frances E. (Roe) J.; B.A., Coll. of Pacific, 1951; M.F.A., Yale Sch. Drama, 1957. Staff technician Calif. Centennials Commn., 1948, 49; lighting designer Green Mansions Theatre, 1952, 56, F. Waring, 1963; tech. dir. Smith Coll., 1952-53; designer Southwestern Sun Carnival, 1956; head engring. div. Holzmueller Corp., San Francisco, 1957-67; sr. cons. Theatre Cons. Service, Bolt, Beranek and Newman, San Francisco, 1967-68; illuminating engr. Pacific Gas & Electric Co., San Francisco, 1968-70, staff illuminating engr., 1970-76, lighting services adminstr., 1976-87; lectr. tech. theatre U. Calif. at Berkeley, 1962-66; theatre cons. Napa Coll., Gavilan College, also Scottish Rite Bodies, Cerritos Coll., Ft. Bliss Post Theatre, El Camino High Sch., Nev. Club. Mem. exec. council Episcopalian Diocese of No. Calif., 1962-64, chmn. coll. work div., 1962-64; del. Synod of Province of Pacific, 1960-65; del. Anglican Congress, 1963; dep. Episcopal Gen. Conv., 1964; pres. Canon Kip Community Center, 1970-71, bd. dirs., 1966-77; active United Way of Bay Area, chmn. allocations com. 1978-80; dist. commr. Boy Scouts Am., 1959-62, chmn. dist., 1965-67, mem. council exec. bd., 1973—, chmn. council activities com., 1974, council tng. com., 1977-80; bd. dirs. Golden Gate Neighborhood Centers Assn., 1968-69, Econ. Opportunity Council, 1969, Vol. Bur., 1969-75. Trustee St. Michael's Coll., 1963-64, 65, 66-69, sec., 1963-65, 67-69. Served with AUS, 1953-55. Recipient Silver Beaver award Boy Scouts Am., 1973, Silver Antelope award, 1980, St. George award, 1980. Mem. Am. Community Theatre Assn. (bd. govs. 1962-64) fellow Am. Ednl. Theatre Assn. (dir. 1963-65, adminstrv. v.p. 1966-68, sec. 1969-70); mem. ANTA (regional dir. 1963-65, 66-68), U.S. Inst. Theatre Tech. (dir. 1961-63, 64-66), Regional Theatre Council No. Calif. and Nev. (gov. 1958-60, 63-65, pres. 1961-62), Illuminating Engring. Soc. (dir. 1979-81, v.p. 1981-84, pres. 1984-85, chmn. office lighting com. 1978-81), Soc. Archtl. Historians, Internat. Commn. on Illumination (treas. 1984—, exec. com. U.S. Nat. Com. 1979-81), Omega Phi Alpha, Theta Alpha Phi. Republican. Club: Bohemian (San Francisco); Reform (London). Home: 749 Rhode Island St San Francisco CA 94107

JEWELL, MARK LAURENCE, plastic surgeon; b. Kansas City, Mo., Oct. 26, 1947; s. James Lemley and Martha (Bullock) J.; m. Mary Rita Lind, Nov. 30, 1975; children: Mark II, James, Hillary. BS in Zoology, U. Kans., 1969, MD, 1973; postgrad., UCLA, 1977, U. Tenn., 1979. Cert. Am. Bd. Plastic Surgery. Resident in surgery UCLA, 1973-76; burn fellow U. So. Calif., Los Angeles, 1976-77; resident in plastic surgery U. Tenn., Chattanooga, 1977-79; practice medicine specializing in plastic surgery Eugene, Oreg., 1979—. Contbr. articles to profl. jours. Served to lt. USNR, 1970-79. Recipient Research award Am. Soc. Clin. Pathologists, 1972, Research award U. Kans. Sch. Medicine, 1973. Mem. Am. Soc. Plastic Surgeons, Oreg. Med. Soc., Lane County Med. Soc., Am. Med. Joggers Soc. Episcopalian. Avocations: skiing, running, art, cooking, computers. Home: 1688 Westover Eugene OR 97403 Office: 630 E 13th Eugene OR 97401

JEWELL, WILLIAM SYLVESTER, engineering educator; b. Detroit, July 2, 1932; s. Loyd Vernon and Marion (Sylvester) J.; m. Elizabeth Gordon Wilson, July 7, 1956; children—Sarah, Thomas, Miriam, William Timothy. B.Engring. Physics, Cornell U., 1954; M.S. in Elec. Engring, MIT, 1955, Sc.D., 1958. Assoc. dir. mgmt. scis. div. Broadview Research Corp., Burlingame, Calif., 1958-60; asst. prof. dept. indsl. engring. and operations research U. Calif.-Berkeley, 1960-63, assoc. prof., 1963-67, prof., 1967—, chmn. dept., 1967-69, 76-80; dir. O.R. Ctr., U. Calif., 1985—; dir. Teknekron Industries, Inc., Incline Village, Nev., 1968-86; cons. operations research problems, 1960—; guest prof. Eidgenö ssiches Technische Hochschule, Zurich, 1980-81. Contbr. research articles to profl. jours. Recipient Halmstead prize, 1982; Fulbright research scholar France, 1965; research scholar Internat. Inst. Applied Systems Analysis, Austria, 1974-75. Mem. Ops. Research Soc. Am., Inst. Mgmt. Scis., Am. Risk and Ins. Assn., Assn. Swiss Actuaries, Internat. Actuarial Assn., Mensa, Triangle., Sigma Xi, Triangle. Home: 67 Loma Vista Orinda CA 94563 Office: U Cal Dept Indsl Engring and Operations Research Berkeley CA 94720

JEWETT, LUCILLE MCINTYRE (MRS. GEORGE FREDERICK JEWETT, JR.), civic worker; b. St. Louis, Jan. 1, 1929; d. Charles Edwin and Elizabeth (Newbery) McIntyre; student U. Puget Sound, 1950; m. George Frederick Jewett, Jr., July 11, 1953; children—Mary Elizabeth, George Frederick III. Mem. Jr. League, Tacoma. Bd. dirs. Lewiston-Clarkston YWCA, Lewiston, Idaho, 1957-65, v.p. bd. dirs., 1959-65, mem. internat. div. com. nat. bd., 1958-71, mem., world service council. 1967—; trustee emeritus San Francisco Ballet Assn.; bd. dirs. Internat. Hospitality Center, San Francisco; adv. com. China Inst. Am.; trustee U. Puget Sound, Tacoma, Nez Perce County Rep. State Committeewoman, 1962-65; pres. Nez Perce County Republican Women's Club, 1961; alt. del. Rep. Nat. Conv., 1964; nat. council Nat. Women's Rep. Club, 1964—. Mem. Order St. John of Jerusalem, Pi Beta Phi. Presbyterian. Club: Francisca. Home: 2990 Broadway San Francisco CA 94115

JEZEK, JAMES, data processing executive; b. Houston, Dec. 13, 1940; s. Marvin and Gertrude (Hutton) J.; m. Karan Lee Ridley, June 27, 1964; children: Kimberly Kay, Leigh Kristen. BA in French, U. Houston, 1963. EDP analyst The Boeing Co., Seattle, 1965-66; sr. programmer Locheed Electronics, Houston, 1966-68; sr. analyst Allied Chem., Houston, 1969-73; mgr. data processing Occidental Chem., Houston, 1973-82; cons. data processing San Francisco, 1982—; cons. bus. systems Cambridge Plan Internat. Monterey, Calif. 1982-83, fin. systems cons. Bank Am., San Francisco, 1983, Signetics, San Jose, Calif., 1984-85, communications cons. GTE Sprint, Burlingame, 1985-87. Carded ofcl. US Swimming, Stockton, Calif., 1983—; v.p. Delta Valley Aquatics, Stockton, 1983; mem. ch., deacon, dept. head Christian Mens Fellowship. Mem. Ind. Computer Cons. Assn. Republican. Mem. Christian Ch. Avocations: travel, golf, swimming,. Home: 6910 Atlanta Circle Stockton CA 95209

JHAWAR, MAKHANLAL MOHANLAL, water treatment company executive; b. Ahmednagar, India, Oct. 26, 1940; came to U.S., 1965; s. Mohanlal Harikison and Mohinibai (Binnany) J.; m. Vimla M. Daga, May 31, 1964; children: Manoj Kumar, Maya Debi. BSc in Chemistry, U. Poona, India, 1963; BSChemE, U. Mo., Rolla, 1967. Assoc. engr. Fairbanks-Morse, Beloit, Wis., 1967-69; mgr., project engr. Burns & Roe Co., Paramus, N.Y., 1969-70, 70-73; sales engr. Gulf Gen. Atomic Co., San Diego, 1973-75; sales mgr. N.Am. div. Fluid Systems div. U.O.P., San Diego, 1975-78; v.p. sales and mktg. Ultraviolet Tech., San Diego, 1978-83; pres. Ultraviolet Tech., Sacramento, 1983-86, Indsl. Water Tech., San Diego, 1986—; bd. dirs. Indsl. Water Tech., San Diego, August Techs., Inc., Solana Beach, Calif. Mem. Kohinoor (advisor 1985—). Office: Indsl Water Tech Inc PO Box 1172 Encinitas CA 92024

JILLSON, KENNETH RAYMOND, life insurance company executive; b. Los Angeles, Aug. 28, 1932; s. LeRoy Wilcox and Edith (Orr) J.; m. Pauline Elizabeth Lyman, Aug. 1, 1954; 1 son, Paul Christopher; m. Gloria del Carmen Castillo, Dec. 30, 1966; children—Teresa del Carmen, Kenneth Raymond, Deborah Edith del Carmen; 1 stepson, Rene Aristides Picota. B.A. in Econs., UCLA, 1954. C.L.U., Am. Coll.; cert. fin. planner, Coll. Fin. Planning. Served as midshipman U.S. Navy, 1950-54, advanced through grades to lt., 1961; ret., 1969; agt. field mgmt. Pacific Mut. Life Ins. Co., Los Angeles, Corona del Mar, Calif., 1961-66; regional dir. Am. Life Ins. Co., Ltd., Wilmington, Del. and Panama, 1966-69, v.p., Seguros Venezuela, Caracas, 1971-73; with Hawaiian Life Ins. Co., Ltd., Honolulu, 1974—, pres., chief exec. officer, 1980—, dir., 1979—, chmn. exec. com., 1981—; cert. Model-Netics instr., 1981—. Trustee, Chaminade U. Ednl. Found., 1978—; bd. regents Chaminade U. of Honolulu, 1980-86; bd. dirs. Hawaii Joint Council on Econ. Edn., 1981—, Catholic Youth Orgn., 1981-83. Fellow Life Mgmt. Inst.; mem. Nat. Assn. Life Underwriters, Hawaii Assn. Life Underwriters, Honolulu Assn. Life Underwriters, Am. Soc. C.L.U.s, Life Mgmt.

Soc. Hawaii, Hawaii Execs. Council. Golden Key Soc., Republican. Roman Catholic. Club: Pacific (Honolulu). Home: 211 Kawaihae St Honolulu HI 96825 Office: Hawaiian Life Ins Co Ltd PO Box 3149 Honolulu HI 96802

JOAQUIM, RICHARD RALPH, hotel executive; b. Cambridge, Mass., July 28, 1936; s. Manuel and Mary (Marrano) J.; B.F.A., Boston U., 1955, Mus. B., 1959; m. Nancy Phyllis Reis, Oct. 22, 1960; 1 dau., Vanessa Reis. Social dir., coordinator summer resort, Wolfeboro, N.H., 1957-59; concert soloist N.H. Symphony Orch., Vt. Choral Soc., Choral Arts Soc., Schenectady Chamber Orch., 1957-60; coordinator performance functions, mgr. theatre Boston U., 1959-60, asst. program dir., 1963-64, dir. univ. programs, 1964-70; gen. mgr. Harrison House of Glen Cove; dir. Conf. Service Corp., Glen Cove, N.Y., 1970-74, sr. v.p., dir. design and devel.; v.p. Arltec, also mng. dir. Sheraton Internat. Conf. Center, 1975-76; v.p., mng. dir. Scottsdale (Ariz.) Conf. Center and Resort Hotel, 1976—; pres. Internat. Conf. Resorts, Inc., 1977, chmn. bd., 1977—; mem. adv. bd. Hotel & Food Adminstrn Program, Boston U., 1986—; pres. Western Conf. Resorts; concert solist U.S. Army Field Band, Washington, 1960-62. Creative arts cons., editorial cons., concert mgr. Commr. recreation Watertown, Mass., 1967—; mem. Spl. Study Com. Watertown, 1967—; mem. Glen Cove Mayor's Urban Renewal Com. Bd. dirs. Nat. Entertainment Conf.; trustee Boston U., 1983—, Hotel and Food Adminstrn. Program Adv. Bd., Boston U., 1986—; nat. bd. dirs. Spoleto Festivals Assn., Charleston, S.C., 1984—. Served with AUS, 1960-62. Mem. Assn. Coll. and Univ. Concert Mgrs., Am. Symphonic League, Am. Fedn. Film Socs., Assn. Am. Artists, Am. Personnel and Guidance Assn., La Chaine des Rotisseurs, Knights of the Vine, Nat. Alumni Council Boston U. Club: The Lotos (N.Y.). Office: 7700 McCormick Pkwy Scottsdale AZ 85258

JOBE, ALICE, transportation executive; b. Little Rock, Nov. 24, 1935; student Long Beach City Coll., 1960-61; m. K.L. Jobe, Mar. 12, 1957; 1 dau., Cathy. With Nat. Equity Life Ins. Co., Little Rock, 1954-55, Cash Wholesale Co., Little Rock, 1956-57; with Bekins Internat., subs. Bekins Co., Wilmington, Calif., 1959-77, v.p., 1971-77; v.p. Imperial Internat., Inc., Torrance, Calif., 1977-78, exec. v.p., 1978-80, dir., 1977-81; pres. Imperial Van Lines Internat., Inc., 1980-81; industry cons., 1981-82; founder, pres. Caddo Internat., freight forwarding, Los Alamitos, Calif., 1982—. Mem. Household Goods Forwarders Assn. (exec. com. 1977-78), Nat. Def. Transp. Assn. (life), Am. Soc. Profl. Women. Republican. Office: Caddo Internat 3662 Katella Ave Suite 209 PO Box 739 Los Alamitos CA 90720

JOBS, STEVEN PAUL, computer corporation executive; b. 1955; adopted s. Paul J. and Clara J. (Jobs). Student, Reed Coll. With Hewlett-Packard, Palo Alto, Calif.; designer video games Atari Inc., 1974; co-founder Apple Computer Inc.; chmn. bd. Apple Computer Inc., Cupertino, Calif., 1975-85, former dir.; pres. NeXT, Inc., Palo Alto, Calif., 1985—. Co-designer: (with Stephan Wozniak) Apple I Computer, 1976. Office: NeXT Inc 3475 Deer Creek Rd Palo Alto CA 94304 *

JOCHUM, LESTER H., dentist; b. Chgo., Nov. 19, 1929; s. J. Harry and Hilma O. (Swanson) J.; m. Anne Elizabeth Cannon, Sept. 20, 1952 (div. Apr. 1983); 1 child, David S. Student U. Wyo., 1947-48; BS in Bus. Adminstrn. with honors, Oreg. State U., 1952; pre-dental student Portland State Coll., 1959-60; B.S. with honors in Sci., U. Oreg., 1963, D.M.D., 1964. Staff acct. Pacific Telephone and Telegraph Co., San Francisco, 1952-59; gen. practice dentistry, San Jose, Calif., 1965-83; dental cons. Delta Dental Plan of Calif., Sacramento, 1983—; ptnr. Trinity Imports. Contbr. articles Calif. Wine Press. Asst. chief Santa Clara Reserve Police Dept., Calif., 1976-83. Active No. Calif. diocese Episc. Ch. Served with U.S. Army, 1952-54. Mem. Sacramento Dist. Dental Soc., Calif. Dental Assn., ADA, Phi Kappa Phi, Psi Omega, Alpha Phi Omega, Lambda Chi Alpha (ritual chmn. 1951, soc. chmn. 1952). Republican. Office: Delta Dental Plan of Calif 7667 Folsom Blvd Sacramento CA 95826

JOE, GREGORY MARTIN, lawyer; b. San Francisco, June 2, 1949; s. Martin and Donna Joe. B.A., U. Calif.-Berkeley, 1972, Credential, 1973; J.D., U. Calif.-San Francisco, 1976. Bar: Calif. 1977, U.S. Dist. Ct. (no. dist.) Calif. 1977. Sole practice, Oakland, Calif., 1978—; legal adviser Nat. Ski Patrol System, East Bay Ski Patrol, Oakland, Calif., 1980—; legal counsel Tau Kappa Epsilon-Nu, Berkeley, Calif., 1982—. Recipient Service award Nat. Ski Patrol System, 1976, 81, 86. Mem. ABA, Calif. Young Lawyers Assn., Nat. Ski Patrol System, Soc. for Preservation Early Am. Art, Tenn. Squire Assn., Tau Kappa Epsilon (trustee 1975—), Phi Delta Kappa. Home: 21 Alta Ave Piedmont CA 94611 Office: 590 Merritt Ave Suite 4 Oakland CA 94610

JOFFRE, STEPHEN PAUL, consulting chemist; b. N.Y.C., Mar. 12, 1913. B.A. in Chemistry, NYU, 1938; postgrad., Columbia U., 1939-40; Ph.D., Poly. Inst. N.Y., 1946. Medicinal research chemist S.L. Ruskin & Assocs., 1938-40; chief chemist Loeser Lab. div. Parenteral Mfg. William S. Merrell & Co., N.Y.C., 1940-44; chief chemist devel. control labs. and mfg. Drug Products Co., Inc., L.I. and Passaic, N.J., 1944-49; dir. organic research Shulton, Inc., Clifton, N.J., 1949-63; research dir. Germaine Monteil Cosmetiques, L.I., 1964-66; mgr. exploratory research and devel. dept. Max Factor & Co., Hollywood, Calif., 1966-71; dir., owner Stephen P. Joffre & Assocs., Magalia, Calif., 1971—. Contbr. articles to profl. jours.; patentee in field. Fellow AAAS, Am. Inst. Chemists; mem. Am. Chem. Soc., Soc. Cosmetic Chemists, Intersci. Research Found. Calif., Phi Lambda Upsilon. Address: 6194 Kilgord Ct Magalia CA 95954

JOHANNSEN, NEIL CHRISTIAN, state parks official; b. Petaluma, Calif., Dec. 19, 1945; s. Harold Edward and Pauline Ann (Lassen) J.; B.S. in Park Mgmt., Calif. State U.-Sacramento, 1969; M.S. in Forestry, U. Wash., 1975. Chief planning Alaska State Parks, Anchorage, 1971-79, dir., 1983—; dep. dir. Calif. State Parks, Sacramento, 1979-83. Author: Exploring Alaska's Prince William Sound, 1975. Contbr. articles, chpt. on outdoor recreation to various publs. Mem. Calif. Heritage Preservation Commn., Sacramento, 1982. Mem. Alaska Recreation and Park Assn. (exec. mem.). Home: 1101 Cordova St Apt 418 Anchorage AK 99501 Office: Alaska State Parks Pouch 7-001 Anchorage AK 99510

JOHANOS, DONALD, orchestra conductor; b. Cedar Rapids, Iowa, Feb. 10, 1928; s. Gregory Hedges and Doris (Nelson) J.; m. Thelma Trimble, Aug. 27, 1950; children—Jennifer Claire, Thea Christine, Gregory Bruce (dec.), Andrew Mark, Eve Marie; m. Corinne Rutledge, Sept. 28, 1985. Mus.B., Eastman Sch. Music, 1950, Mus.M., 1952; D.F.A. (hon.), Coe Coll., 1962. Tchr. Pa. State U., 1953-55, So. Meth. U., 1958-62, Hockaday Sch., 1962-65. Mus. dir., Altoona (Pa.) Symphony, 1953-56, Johnstown (Pa.) Symphony, 1955-56, asso. condr., Dallas Symphony Orch., 1957-61, resident condr., 1961-62, mus. dir., 1962-70, assoc. condr., Pitts. Symphony, 1970-79, mus. dir., Honolulu Symphony Orch., 1979—, artistic dir., Hawaii Opera Theater, 1979-83, guest condr., Phila. Orch., Amsterdam Concertgebouw Orch., Pitts. Symphony, Rochester Philharmonic, New Orleans Philharmonic, Denver Symphony, Vancouver Symphony, Chgo. Symphony, San Francisco Symphony, Netherlands Radio Philharmonic, Swiss Radio Orch., Mpls. Symphony, Paris Opera, Boston Symphony, others. Advanced study grantee Am. Symphony Orch. League and Rockefeller Found., 1955-58. Mem. Am. Fedn. Musicians Internat. Congress of Strings (dir.). Office: Honolulu Symphony Orchestra 1441 Kapiolani Blvd Suite 1515 Honolulu HI 96814

JOHANSON, DONALD CARL, physical anthropologist; b. Chgo., June 28, 1943; s. Carl Torsten and Sally Eugenia (Johnson) J. B.A., U. Ill., 1966; M.A., U. Chgo., 1970, Ph.D., 1974; D.Sc. (hon.), John Carroll U., 1979, Coll. of Wooster, 1985. Mem. dept. phys. anthropology Cleve. Mus. Natural History, 1972-81, curator, 1974-81; dir. Inst. Human Origins, Berkeley, Calif., 1981—; prof. Stanford U., Calif., 1984—; prof. anthropology Stanford U., 1983—; host, narrator series Pub. Broadcasting Service, 1982. Co-author: (with M.A. Edey) Of Lucy: The Beginnings of Humankind, 1981; film producer: The First Family, 1981, Lucy in Disguise, 1982; contbr. chpts. to books, articles to profl. jours. Recipient Jared Potter Kirtland award for outstanding sci. achievement Cleve. Mus. Natural History, 1979, Am. Book award, 1982, San Francisco Exploratorium award, 1986; grantee NSF, Nat. Geog. Soc., L.S.B. Leakey Found., Cleve. Found., George Gund Found. Fellow AAAS; mem. Am. Assn. Phys. Anthropologists, Internat. Assn. Dental Research, Current Anthropology, Internat. Assn. Human Biologists, Assn. Africanist Archaeologists, Soc. Vertebrate Paleontology, Soc. Study of Human Biology, Explorers Club, Societe de l'Anthropologie de Paris. Office: Inst Human Origins 2453 Ridge Rd Berkeley CA 94709

JOHANSON, ROBERT GAIL, chemist; b. San Francisco, Aug. 26, 1936; s. Robert N. and Martha A. (Peterson) J.; m. Joan B. Lee, Sept. 25, 1964; children: Robert, Martha, Douglas, Wendy, Christopher. BA, Reed Coll., 1960; PhD, U. Vt., 1969; postdoctoral student, Case Western Res. U., 1969-70. Chemist Aerojet-Gen. Corp., Sacramento, 1960-66; mem. staff Raychem Corp., Menlo Park, Calif., 1970-72, group leader, 1972-76; sr. mem. tech. staff Signetics Corp., Sunnyvale, Calif., 1976-81; mgr. disk ops. Datapoint Corp., Mountain View, Calif., 1981-83; mgr. applications lab. Circuits Processing Apparatus, Inc., Fremont, Calif., 1984—; cons. Disk Cons., Sunnyvale, 1983-84. Contbr. articles to profl. jours. Served with U.S. Army, 1955-57. Mem. Am. Chem. Soc., Am. Vacuum Soc., Electrochem. Soc., Sigma Xi. Avocations: skiing, backpacking. Office: Circuits Processing Apparatus 47003 Mission Falls Ct Fremont CA 94539

JOHL, JUGRAJ SINGH, biomed. researcher; b. Yuba City, Calif., Aug. 7, 1952; s. Karm Singh and Swarn Klaur (Grewal) J. A.S. in Math., Yuba Coll., 1972, A.S., 1972; student U. Calif.-Davis, 1972-73; B.A. in Biology, Chico State U., 1976, B.A. in Chemistry, 1976, postgrad., 1977-80. Farm mgr. KSV Ranch, Yuba City, Calif., 1969—; biomedical researcher Stanford Research Inst. Internat., 1981—; agrl. cons. Mem. AAAS, Am. Chem. Soc., Am. Inst. Biol. Scis., Calif. Acad. Scis. Democrat.

JOHLER, JOSEPH RALPH, physicist; b. Scranton, Pa., Feb. 23, 1919; s. Joseph Jacob and Lillian (Dietzel) J.; B.A., Am. U., 1941; B.S.E., George Washington U., 1950; m. Nora Stella Callahan, Sept. 16, 1953; children—Dennis Ralph, Mark Stephen, Paul Norman, Annette Diane. Ballistic mathematician Ballistic Research Lab., Aberdeen Proving Grounds, Md., 1942-45; with Nat. Bur. Standards, Washington, 1946-51, electronic engr. Boulder Labs., 1951-65, chief electromagnetic theory sect., 1961-65; program leader, electromagnetic theory program Environmental Sci. Services Adminstrn., Inst. Telecommunication Scis. and Aeronomy, U.S. Dept. Commerce, Boulder, 1965-70, physicist, project scientist Office Telecommunications 1970-72, chief nav. and D-Region Sci. sect., 1972-76; pres. Colo. Research and Prediction Lab., Boulder, 1976-86; cons. Johler Assocs., 1986—. Served with USNR, 1944-46. Research Nat. Bur. Standards Disting. Authorship award, 1963, 66. Mem. AAAS, Am. Geophys. Union, Am. Math. Soc., Sci. Research Soc. Am., Internat. Union Radio Sci., IEEE (sr. mem., life mem.), Internat. Radio Consultative Com., Soc. Indsl. and Applied Math., Wild Goose Assn. (Gold Medal of Merit award 1982). Contbr. articles to profl. jours. Home: 16796 W 74th Pl Golden CO 80403

JOHN, KOCHUVEETTIL CHACKO, controller; b. Alleppey, India, Jan. 16, 1950; s. Kochuveettil C. and Aleyamma (John) Chacko; m. Joyce John, May 21, 1978; children: Dennis, Dessy. B in Commerce, Kerala (India) U., 1969, M in Commerce, 1971. Mgr. accounts Oman Shipping, Muscat, 1974-80; auditor Shair & Co., Muscat, 1980-82; supr. accts. Berkeley Planning Co., Oakland, Calif., 1982-83; controller City Bond and Mortgage Co., Oakland, 1983-85, Golden State Moving Co., San Jose, Calif., 1985—; cons. TEM Assocs., Oakland, 1982—. Pres. Indian Christian Congregation, Muscat, Oman, 1978-80. Mem. Heaven of Arts (founding pres. 1964-74). Mem. Indian Orthodox Christian Ch. Home: 142 Loma Verde Hayward CA 94541 Office: Golden State Moving co 557 Charcot St San Jose CA 95131

JOHN, WALTER, research physicist; b. Newkirk, Okla., Feb. 16, 1924; s. Walter and Carrie (Hollingsworth) J.; m. Carol Salin, Jan. 22, 1953; children: Kenneth, Laura, Claudia, Leslie. BS, Calif. Inst. Tech., 1950; PhD, U. Calif., Berkeley, 1955. Instr. U. Ill., Urbana, 1955-58; sr. physicist Lawrence Livermore Nat. Lab., Berkeley, 1958-71; prof. physics Calif. State Coll.-Stanislaus, Turlock, 1971-74; research scientist Calif. Dept. Health Services, Berkeley, 1974—; mem. sci. adv. com. Electric Power Research Inst., Palo Alto, Calif., 1984—; mem. peer rev. com. EPA, Research Triangle Park, N.C., 1982, 84. Contbr. articles on air pollution, aerosols, and nuclear physics to profl. jours. Served with U.S. Army, 1943-46, ETO. Fellow Am. Phys. Soc.; mem. Am. Assn. Physics Tchrs., Am. Conf. Govtl. Indsl. Hygienists (mem. air sampling procedures com. 1983—), Am. Assn. Aerosol Research, Sigma Xi, Tau Beta Pi. Avocations: photography, music, swimming. Home: 195 Grover Ln Walnut Creek CA 94596 Office: Calif Dept Health Services 2151 Berkeley Way Berkeley CA 94704

JOHNNENE, ROBERT (BOB) JOSEPH, producer, director, writer; b. Boston, Nov. 16, 1935; s. James Robert and Elizabeth Josephine (Ryan) J.; m. Francesca Ann Galante, Mar. 3, 1962 (div. Nov. 1979); children: Stephen Dominic, Roberta Francesca, Phillip Anthony. BA in English, Boston Coll., 1953; MFA in Theatre, Boston U., 1959. Regional dir. Summerthing, Boston, 1965-75; exec. dir. Smart, Plymouth, Mass., 1976-78; communication arts chmn. Don Bosco Tech, Rosmead, Calif., 1979-83; communication arts instr. Acad. Pacific, Hollywood, Calif., 1985—; exec. dir. Act One Prodns., Los Angeles, 1980—; artistic cons. Christian Herter Ctr., Boston, Mass., 1969-70; critic, commentator Sta. WBLM Radio, Plymouth, 1977-79; critic, columnist The Ledger, Quincy, Mass., 1977-79; rev. Film Adv. Bd., Hollywood, 1980—. Writer TV series Voyage to Adventure, 1985 (Award of Excellence, 1986); writer-dir. (broadway musical) Broadway Dandies, 1974, (off-broadway play) White Lies, 1971; dir. TV series Playhouse Workshop, 1968 (Best Dir. 1969). Pres. Clam Point Civic Assn., Boston, 1969-78; mem. Log Cabin Club, Los Angeles, 1986—. Served as sgt. U.S. Army, 1955-57. Named Citizen of Yr. United Neighborhood Assn., 1976. Mem. Nat. Theatre Assn., Am. Ednl. Assn., So. Calif. Theatre Assn. Avocations: swimming, boating, cooking. Office: PO Box 93607 Los Angeles CA 90093

JOHNS, ROBERT MICHAEL, advertising and merchandising company executive; b. Los Angeles, July 13, 1943; s. Bernard William and Elizabeth Jane (Sorensen) J.; m. Sharon Ruth Andersen, Sept. 9, 1965; children—Jennifer, Susan, Robert, Stephen, Sherry, Kimberly, Julie, Jamie. A.A., Pasadena City Coll., 1964; B.S., Brigham Young U., 1966. Sales and med. center rep. Hoffman-LaRoche, Inc., Los Angeles, 1966-74; So. Calif. dist. sales mgr. IVAC Corp., Los Angeles, 1974-75; fin. planner Conn. Gen. Life Ins., Los Angeles, 1975-79; pres., chief exec. officer Common Carrier Advt., Inc., Los Angeles and Salt Lake City, 1979-80; chmn. chief exec. officer AdMedia Internat., Inc., Salt Lake City, 1981—; chmn., pres. Marketcorps, Inc., 1985—. Instl. rep. Boy Scouts Am., 1969-71, explorer advisor, 1967-69, varsity scout coach, 1979-80; mem. high council of Ch. Jesus Christ Latter-day Saints, 1971-73, 77-79, 81-84, ordained bishop, 1973; soccer coach, 1978; Little League coach, 1984; basketball coach 1972-78, 79-84. Recipient Conn. Gen. Life Ins. Co. awards 1976, 77, 78; named Outstanding Young Man, U.S. Jaycees, 1979. Republican. Co-innovator and pioneer of supermarket/ convenience store advertising medium. Office: 935 S Union Blvd Midvale UT 84047

JOHNSEN, GEORGE E., audio engineer; b. Eugene, Oreg., June 28, 1953; s. Duane Ellis and Patricia Elsie (Daugherty) J.; m. Roberta L. Liebreich, July 31, 1977; 1 child, Adam. Student, U. Oreg., 1971-73. Music engr. various entertainment cos., Calif., 1975-79, film sound effects engr., 1979-81; prin., chief engr. EFX Systems, Burbank, Calif., 1981—; audio engring. cons. to artists and film studios worldwide. Spl. sound effects: Star Trek—The Movie, The Black Hole, Altered States; acoustical designer numerous studios including Falcon Video, Paramount Pictures, Panavision. Recipient Eagle Scout award Boy Scouts Am., Eugene, 1966; named Tonnmeister, Jugoton, Zagreb, Yugoslavia, 1984. Mem. Audio Engring Soc., Soc. Preservation Variety Arts (founding). Libertarian. Avocations: radio-controlled race cars, computers, music. Office: EFX Systems 919 N Victory Blvd Burbank CA 91502

JOHNSON, ABIGAIL RIDLEY, tour and travel executive; b. Vancouver, B.C., Can., Jan. 28, 1945; d. Frederic Neville and Cara Lee (Smith) Ridley; m. Ralph Maxwell Johnson, Sept. 17, 1971 (div.). B.A. in Music, Colo. Woman's Coll., 1967; postgrad. San Jose State U., summer 1967. Cert. travel counselor. Co. rep. Manhattan Festival Ballet, N.Y.C., 1967-68; asst. booking mgr. Western Opera Theatre, San Francisco, 1968-69; asst. to consul and trade commr. Can. Consulate Gen., San Francisco, 1969-71; office mgr. Whitney Properties, San Francisco, 1971-72; sales mgr. Sutter Travel Service, San Francisco, 1973-80; dir., owner Tour Arts, San Francisco, 1980—. Exec. com. Friends of Am. Conservatory Theatre; active San Francisco Opera, Symphony, Ballet; mem. task force Arts and Tourism Calif. Confedn. Arts. Mem. Am. Soc. Travel Agts., Inst. Cert. Travel Agts., English Speaking Union, Jr. League San Francisco. Episcopalian. Office: Tour Arts 231 Franklin St San Francisco CA 94102

JOHNSON, ALICE ELAINE, academic administrator; b. Janesville, Wis., Oct. 9, 1929; d. Floyd C. and Alma M. (Walthers) Chester; m. Richard C. Johnson, Sept. 25, 1948 (div. 1974); children: Randall S., Nile C., Linnea E. BA, U. Colo., 1968. Pres., administrator Pikes Peak Inst. Med. Tech., Colorado Springs, Colo., 1968—; mem. adv. com. to Colo. Commn. on Higher Edn., 1979-80, State Adv. Council on Pvt. Occupational Schs., Denver, 1978-86; mem. tech. adv. com. State Health Occupations, 1986—. Mem. Colo. Pvt. Sch. Assn. (pres. 1981-82, bd. dirs. 1976—, Outstanding Mem. 1978, 80), Phi Beta Kappa. Democrat. Unitarian. Avocations: writing, travel, reading. Office: Pikes Peak Inst Med Tech 820 Arcturus Dr Colorado Springs CO 80906

JOHNSON, ALICE LORETTA, speech pathologist; b. Escanaba, Mich.; d. Axel Malcolm and Carrie (Nelson) J. BA, No. Mich. Coll.; cert., U. Paris; postgrad., McGill U., Montreal, Que., Can.; MA, Columbia U., 1942, EdD, 1958. Cert. French tchr., N.Y., tchr. of deaf students, N.Y.; lic. speech pathologist, Calif. Tchr. Saginaw (Mich.) Schs.; tchr. French Saginaw High Sch.; cryptographer U.S. Dept. War, Washington, 1942-43; instr. English Panzer Coll., East Orange, N.J., 1950-52; speech clinician, audiologist St. Luke's Hosp., N.Y.C., 1950-58; asst. prof. English Wagner Luth. Coll., Staten Island, N.Y., 1955-58; assoc. prof. English and speech Pa. State U., East Stroudsburg, 1958-61; tchr. of lang. and hearing impared N.Y.C. Bd. Edn., 1961-72; pvt. practice speech pathology N.Y.C., 1961-72, Santa Monica, Calif., 1972—. Mem. AAUP, AAUW, Am. Speech-Lang. and Hearing Assn., Sigma Tau Delta. Avocations: hiking, reading, gardening, piano. Home: 14809 Channel Ln Santa Monica CA 90402

JOHNSON, ALLEN WILLARD, anthropology educator; b. Berkeley, Calif., Oct. 19, 1941; s. John Allen and Frances (Willard) J.; m. Esther Meyers, 1964 (div. 1970); 1 child, David; m. Orna Roth; children: Ilana, Leah, Sarah. BA, U. Calif., Berkeley, 1963; MA, Stanford U., 1965, PhD, 1968. Asst. prof. anthropology Columbia U., N.Y.C., 1968-75; assoc. prof. UCLA, 1975-80, prof., 1980—. Author: Sharecroppers of the Sertao, 1972, Quantification in Cultural Anthropology, 1978; co-author: Evolution of Human Societies, 1986. Research grantee NSF, 1972-74, 85—. Fellow AAAS, Am. Anthropol. Assn., Am. Ethnol. Soc., Soc. for Cultural Anthropology; mem. Am. Psychoanalytic Assn. (affiliate). Avocations: piano, tennis. Home: 1943 Greenfield Ave Los Angeles CA 90025 Office: U Calif Dept Anthropology Los Angeles CA 90024

JOHNSON, AMY LONG, social worker. BA, U. Ill., 1982, MSW, 1984. Sch. social work intern Alton (Ill.) Sch. Dist., 1983-84; sr. youth counselor Pioneer Human Services, Seattle, 1984; mental health cons. Greater Lakes Mental Health, Tacoma, 1984-85; sch. social worker Bethel Sch. Dist., Spanaway, Wash., 1984—. Mem. Nat. Assn. Social Workers, Wash. Assn. Sch. Social Workers (cert.), Ill. Assn. Sch. Social Workers (cert.).

JOHNSON, SISTER ANDREA, parish minister; b. Pittsburg, Kans., May 21, 1947; d. Andrew E. And Lillian Katherine (Hansen) J. BA cum laude, Kans. Newman Coll., 1972; M in Mus. Edn., Wichita State U., 1975. Parish minister St. Mark's Ch., Eugene, Oreg., 1966-68; instr. music Holy Savior Sch., Wichita, Kans., 1972, St. Mary's Ch., Derby, Kans., 1972-74, St. Patrick's Ch., Wichita, 1972-74; asst. prof. music St. Mary of the Plains Coll., Dodge City, Kans., 1975-80; parish minister of Spanish, music and youth Blessed Sacrament Ch., Hollywood, Calif., 1981—, co-dir. Spanish choir, 1981—; dir. music and liturgy St. John's Coll. Sem., Camarillo, Calif., 1982—; mem., cons. music and liturgy commn. Archdiocese of Los Angeles, 1981—; planner, dir. Archdiocesan Choir for Celebration of Our Lady of Guadalupe, 1982—; workshop conductor in liturgy and Spanish church music, 1982—. Asst. editor (Spanish songbook) La Familia De Dios Celebra, 1981; editor (Spanish songbook) Cantos for Carisma en Misiones, 1982. Mem. Nat. Assn. Pastoral Musicians, Wichita Choral Soc. (bd. dirs. 1969-75). Avocations: vocal and choral music, hiking. Home: 912 S Bronson Ave Los Angeles CA 90019 Office: Blessed Sacrament Ch 6657 Sunset Blvd Hollywood CA 90028

JOHNSON, ANTHONY RICHARDO, military officer; b. Mexia, Tex.; s. Willie Larcie and Betty Jean (Cotton) J. BS in History, USAF Acad., 1976; MBA, Columbia Pacific U., 1985. Commd. 2d lt. USAF, 1976, advanced through grades to capt., 1980; wing combat crew instr. USAF, Minot, N.D., 1980-81; airborne missile ops. commdr. USAF, Ellsworth AFB, S.D., 1981-83, Airborne Launch Control System upgrade instr., 1983-84, chief Airborne Launch Control System standardization/evaluation, 1984-86; system safety program mgr. USAF, Norton AFB, Calif., 1986—. Recipient CAP award, Rapid City, S.D., 1982. Mem. Assn. Grads. Avocations: hunting, fishing, woodworking, racquetball, cooking. Home: 2778 Irvington Ave San Bernardino CA 92407-2141 Office: BMO/AWS USAF Norton AFB CA 92409-6468

JOHNSON, ARNOLD IVAN, consulting engineer; b. Madison, Nebr., June 3, 1919; s. Casten Henry and Awilda May (Reeves) J.; B.S.C.E., U. Nebr., 1949, A.B., 1950, postgrad., 1950-54; m. Betty Lou Spencer, June 3, 1941; children—Robert Arnold, Bruce Gary, Carmen Sue Johnson Mark. With U.S. Geol. Survey, 1948-79, asst. chief Office Water Data Coordination, Washington, 1971-79; water resources cons. Woodward-Clyde Cons., Denver, 1979-84; pres. A. Ivan Johnson, Inc. Cons., Arvada, Colo., 1984—; faculty affiliate Colo. State U., 1969-70; bd. dirs. Renewable Natural Resources Found., 1971-81; pres. Internat. Commn. Ground Water, 1972-75, Internat. Commn. Remote Sensing and Data Transmission, 1980—; v.p. U.S. nat. commn. Internat. Union Geodesy and Geophysics, 1976-79. Served with USNR, 1942-44. Recipient Award of Merit Dept. Interior, 1962, Meritorious Service award, 1977; Engr. of Yr. award Profl. Engrs. in Govt., 1969; registered profl. engr., Colo., D.C. Fellow ASCE, ASTM, Am. Water Resources Assn. (pres. 1972, rep. to Nat. Acad. Sci. 1971—); mem. Am. Geophys. Union (sec., sect. on hydrology 1973-77), Assn. Engring. Geologists, Internat. Assn. Hydrological Scis. (1st v.p. 1975-79), Internat. Soc. Soil Sci., Internat. Soc. Soil Mechanics and Found. Engring., Internat. Assn. Hydrogeology, Assn. Geohydrologists Internat. Devel., NSPE (chpt. pres. 1970-71), Archaeol. Soc. Am., Bibl. Archaeol. Soc. Author, editor 90 reports and books in field.

JOHNSON, ARTHUR WILLIAM, JR., planetarium executive; b. Steubenville, Ohio, Jan. 8, 1949; s. Arthur William and Carol (Gilcrest) J.; B.Mus., U. So. Calif., 1973. Lectr., Griffith Obs. and Planetarium, 1969-73; planetarium writer, lectr. Mt. San Antonio Coll. Planetarium, Walnut, Calif., 1970-73; dir. Fleischmann Planetarium, U. Nev., Reno, 1973—. Organist, Trinity Episcopal Ch., Reno, 1980—; bd. dirs. Reno Chamber Orch. Assn., 1981-87 , 1st v.p., 1984-85. Nev. Humanities Com., Inc. grantee, 1979-83. Mem. Am. Guild Organists (dean No. Nev. chpt. 1984-85), Internat. Planetarium Soc., Cinema 360 Assn., Pacific Planetarium Assn. (pres. 1980), Rocky Mountain Planetarium Assn., Sigma Xi (treas. U. Nev. chpt. 1987—). Republican. Episcopalian. Writer, producer films: (with Donald G. Potter) Beautiful Nevada, 1978; Riches: The Story of Nevada Mining, 1984. Office: Fleischmann Planetarium U Nev Reno NV 89557

JOHNSON, BILLY DON, electrical engineering executive; b. Oklahoma City, Aug. 28, 1951; s. A.J. and Virginia Pauline (Hill) J.; m. Katie Raye Black, Dec. 23, 1971 (div. June 1976); m. Pamela Roberts Belcher, Mar. 13, 1978; children: Beverly Michelle, Lora Christine. BSEE, Oklahoma State U., 1973. Systems programmer U. Computer Ctr., Stillwater, Okla., 1970-73; systems engr. Cities Service Corp., Tulsa, Okla., 1973-77; sr. field support engr. Amdahl Corp., Sunnyvale, Calif., 1977-78; mgr. software ops. Storage Tech. Corp., Louisville, Colo., 1978-84; v.p. engring. ViaNetix, Inc., Boulder, Colo., 1984-86; dir., gen. mgr. Boulder Tech. Ctr., Western Digital Corp., 1986—. Mem. IEEE (William Bendix grantee 1975), Eta Kappa Nu. Republican. Avocations: amateur radio, racquetball, skiing, fishing, hunting. Office: Western Digital Corp 2900 Center Green Ct S Boulder CO 80301

JOHNSON, BOB, ice hockey association executive. Formerly coach Calgary Flames, N.H.L., Alta., Can.; exec. dir. Amateur Hockey Assn. of the

U.S., Colorado Springs, Colo., 1987—. Office: Amateur Hockey Assn of U S 2997 Broadmoor Valley Rd Colorado Springs CO 80906 *

JOHNSON, BRIAN LEO, computer scientist; b. Los Angeles, Nov. 13, 1949; s. Leo Richard and Elsie (Halsted) J. AA in Math., Palomar Coll., 1969; AB in Astronomy, Calif. State U., San Diego, 1973. Systems analyst Computer Sci. Corp., San Diego, 1973-76; computer scientist Systems Cons. Inc, San Diego, 1976-78; dir. engring. systems integration ops. Sci. Applications Internat. Corp., La Jolla, Calif., 1978—. Designer software systems for U.S. Dept. Def., 1981, 84, 85. Mem. Assn. Computing Machinery. Republican. Office: Sci Applications Internat Corp 10260 Campus Point Dr San Diego CA 92121

JOHNSON, BURLEY RAY, management consultant; b. Long Beach, Calif., Feb. 10, 1946; s. Burley and Bessie Beatrice (Babcock) J.; m. Dorothy Elizabeth Hahl, Mar. 11, 1978; children—Christianna Elizabeth, David Alojzy, Frederick William, Rebecca-Ann Louise. A.A., Los Angeles Harbor Jr. Coll., 1966; B.S., Calif. State U.-Long Beach, 1971; B.A., Brigham Young U., 1972; M.B.A., U. So. Calif., 1976. Cost analyst Garrett Airesearch, Los Angeles, 1974-78; v.p. Quantum Fin. Corp., Palos Verdes, Calif., 1979-80; prin. Burley Ray Johnson & Assoc., Calif., 1979—; dir. Las Vegas Mgmt. Group, Great Western Hotels Corp.; pres. Adminstrv. Bus. Cons., 1983—. Bd. dirs. Salvation Army. Mem. Nat. Assn. Accts., Am. Acctg. Assn., Am. Mgmt. Assn., Nat. Notary Assn., Am. Soc. Tng. and Devel., San Pedro C. of C. (pres.-elect.). Republican. Mem. Ch. Jesus Christ of Latter-day Saints. Lodge: Rotary. Office: 555 W 9th St San Pedro CA 90733-1484

JOHNSON, BYRON ANDREW, museum history curator; b. Greensboro, N.C., Apr. 10, 1953; s. Joseph Byron and Elizabeth (Suggs) J.; m. Sharon Peregrine, May 23, 1981. B.A., U. Ariz., 1975; M.A., Tex. Tech U., 1977. Research asst. Mus. Tex. Tech U., Lubbock, 1975-77; curatorial aide Wyo. State Mus., Cheyenne, 1976; curator history Albuquerque Mus., 1977—; lectr. U. Mex., U. Albuquerque; editor Gilded Age Press. Author: Old Town, Albuquerque, 1980; co-author: Early Albuquerque, 1981; Gilded Palaces of Shame, 1983; Wild West Bartender's Bible, 1986. Contbr. articles on history to Albuquerque Jour. Recipient award of honor Cultural Property Rev. Com., State of N.Mex., 1978; award of merit Albuquerque Conservation Assn., 1982, 84-85. Mem. Am. Assn. for State and Local History, Am. Assn. Museums, N.Mex. Mus. Assn. Office: Albuquerque Mus PO Box 1293 Albuquerque NM 87103

JOHNSON, BYRON LINDBERG, economist, educator; b. Chgo., Oct. 12, 1917; s. Theodore and Ruth Emille (Lindberg) J.; m. Catherine Elizabeth (Kay) Teter, Oct. 22, 1938; children: Steven Howard, Christine Ruth, Eric Alan. BA, U. Wis., Madison, 1938, MA, 1940, PhD, 1947. Economist, statistician State of Wisconsin, Madison, 1938-42; econ. analyst Fed. Civil Service, Washington, 1942-47; prof. econs. U. Denver, 1947-56; adm. asst. to gov. State of Colo., Denver, 1957-58; mem. U.S. Congress, Washington, 1959-60; cons. Agy. Internat. Devel. State Dept., Washington, 1961-64; prof. econs. U. Colo., Denver, 1965—; prof. econs. emeritus U. Colo., Denver; cons. economist Commn. R.R. Retirement, Washington, 1971-72, U. Colo Regent, 1970-82. Author: Need is Our Neighbor, 1966; (with Robert Ewegen) B.S.: The Bureaucratic Syndrome, 1982; contbr. articles to profl. jours. Vice-chmn. Denver Regional Transp. Dist., 1983, chmn. 1984, bd. dirs., 1983-84. Recipient Whitehead Meml. award Colo. A.C.L.U., 1960. Mem. AAAS, Nat. Tax Assn., Advanced Transit Assn. (chmn. bd. 1986-87), Soc. Internat. Devel. (exec. com. Rocky Mountain chpt. 1986). Democrat. Mem. United Ch. of Christ. Club: City (Denver). Avocation: mountaineering. Home: 2451 S Dahlia Ln Denver CO 80222

JOHNSON, CAROLYN ELIZABETH, librarian; b. Oakland, Calif., May 29, 1921; d. Ferdinand Orin and Clara Wells (Humphrey) Hassler; m. Benjamin Alfred Johnson, Feb. 12, 1943; children—Robin Rebecca, Anne Elizabeth, Delia Mary. B.A., U. Calif.-Berkeley, 1946; cert. librarian Calif. State U., Fullerton, 1960; M.L.S., Immaculate Heart Coll., 1968. Asst. children's librarian Fullerton Pub. Library, Calif., 1951-59, coordinator children's services, 1959-81, city librarian, 1981—; instr. Rio Hondo City Coll., Whittier, Calif., part time 1970-72, Calif. State U.-Fullerton, 1972-77; pres. So. Calif. Council on Lit. for Children and Young People, 1979-81; mem. 3d Pacific Rim Conf. Council, 1983-84. Mem. Library Tech. Tng. Adv. Com., Fullerton Coll., 1970; founding bd. dirs. Youth Sci. Ctr., Fullerton, 1958. Mem. ALA, Calif. Library Assn. (chmn. children's service div.), Orange County Library Assn. (v.p.), PTA (life), AAUW, LWV, Phi Beta Kappa, Theta Sigma Phi. Methodist. Home: 644 Princeton Circle E Fullerton CA 92632

JOHNSON, CATHERINE VIRGINIA, social worker; b. Baraboo, Wis., Apr. 13, 1956; d. Philip G. and Jacqueline M. (Jones) Butts; m. Thomas Reed Johnson, May 15, 1982; 1 child, Aaron Joseph. BA, U. Calif., Santa Barbara, 1978; MSW, Calif. State U., Sacramento, 1981, M Pub. Adminstrn., 1981. Psychiat. social worker Stockton (Calif.) State Hosp., 1981-82; foster care coordinator Lilliput Homes, Inc., Stockton, 1982-84; child therapist Catholic Charities, Stockton, 1984-85; child protective services practitioner II Human Services Agy. San Joaquin County, Stockton, 1985—. therapist County Sexual Abuse Treatment Program, Stockton, 1983, 85—; cons. Vis. Nurses Assn., Stockton, 1984-85; sexual child abuse lectr., Stockton, 1984—. Mem. Nat. Assn Social Workers, Kappa Kappa Gamma. Republican. Avocations: dog training and obedience competition. Home: 8260 Bennett Rd Stockton CA 95212 Office: Human Services Agy 133 E Weber Stockton CA 95202

JOHNSON, CHARLES FOREMAN, architect, architectural photographer, consultant; b. Plainfield, N.J., May 28, 1929; s. Charles E. and E. Lucile (Casner) J.; student Union Jr. Coll., 1947; B.Arch., U. So. Calif., 1958; postgrad. UCLA, 1959-60; m. Beverly Jean Hinnendale, Feb. 19, 1961 (div. 1970); children—Kevin, David. Draftsman, Wigton-Abbott, P.C., Plainfield, 1946-48; architect, cons., graphic, interior and engring. systems designer, 1952—; designer, draftsman with H.W. Underhill, Architect, Los Angeles, 1953-55; teaching asst. U. So. Calif., Los Angeles, 1954-55; designer with Carrington H. Lewis, Architect, Palos Verdes, Calif., 1955-56; grad. architect Ramo-Wooldridge Corp., Los Angeles, 1956-58; tech. dir. Atlas weapon system Space Tech. Labs., Los Angeles, 1958-60; advanced planner and systems engr. Minuteman Weapon System, TRW, Los Angeles, 1960-64, div. staff ops. dir., 1964-68; cons. N.Mex. Regional Med. Program and N.Mex. State Dept. Hosps., 1968-70; prin. Charles F. Johnson, architect, Los Angeles, 1953-68, Sante Fe, N.Mex., 1968—; free lance archtl. photographer, Sante Fe, 1971—. Major archtl. works include: residential bldgs. in Calif., 1955-66; Bashein Bldg. at Los Lunas (N.Mex.) Hosp. and Tng. Sch., 1969, various residential bldgs., Santa Fe, 1973—, Kurtz Home, Dillon, Colo., 1981, Whispering Boulders Home, Carefree, Ariz., 1981, Hedrick House, Green Valley, Ariz., 1984, Casa Largo, Santa Fe, 1983, Kole House, Santa Fe (used for film The Man Who Fell to Earth), 1974, Rubel House, Santa Fe, 1986, Smith House, Carefree, Ariz., 1987. Pres., Santa Fe Coalition for the Arts, 1977; set designer Santa Fe Fiesta Melodrama, 1969, 71, 74, 77, 78, 81. Mem. Delta Sigma Phi. Club: El Gancho Tennis. Contbr. articles on facility planning and mgmt. to profl. publs.; contbr. archtl. photographs to mags. in U.S., Eng., France, Japan and Italy, contbr. articles on facility mgmt., planning info. systems, etc. to profl. jours. Recognized for work in organic architecture. Club: El Gancho Tennis. Avocations: music, photography, collecting architecture books, Frank Lloyd Wright works. Home: 1831 Sun Mountain Dr Santa Fe NM 87501

JOHNSON, CHARLES WAYNE, mining engineer, mining executive; b. Vinita, Okla., Feb. 7, 1921; s. Charles Monroe and Willie Mae (Hudson) J.; m. Cleo Faye Wittee, 1940 (div. 1952); m. Genevieve Hobbs, 1960 (dec. Sept. 1985); m. Susan Gates Johnson, Apr. 19, 1986; 1 child, Karen Candace Limon. BE, Kensington U., 1974, ME, 1975, PhDE, 1976. Owner El Monte (Calif.) Mfg. Co., 1946-49; co-owner Anjo Pest Control, Pasadena, Calif., 1946-56, Hoover-Johnson Cons. Co., Denver, 1956-59; pres. Vanguard Chem. Co., Denver, 1957-61, Mineral Products Co., Boise, Idaho, 1957-61; owner Crown Hill Meml. Park, Dallas, 1959-61, Johnson Engring., Victorville, Calif., 1961-86; pres. Astro Minerals, Victorville, 1985-87; owner J&D Mining Co., Victorville, 1977—. Contbr. articles to profl. pubs.; patentee in field. Active Rep. VIP Club. Served with USN, 1941-45. Recipient Outstanding Achievement award East Pasadena Bus. Assn., 1948. Mem. Ch. Ancient Christianity. Avocations: prospecting, assaying, environ. pollution research. Office: Johnson Engring Astro Minerals PO Box 641 Wrightwood CA 92397

JOHNSON, CHRISTOPHER BROOKS, architect; b. Spokane, Wash., Nov. 17, 1950; s. Vern Waldo and Beryle Christine (Lundberg) J.; m. Elizabeth Lee, June 1973 (div. Nov. 1978); m. Mary Trigg, Jan. 3, 1981; 1 child, Megan Elizabeth. B Archtl. Sci., Wash. State U., 1973, BArch, 1974. Architect Burt Hill Kosar Rittellmann, Butler, Pa., 1974-78, Archtl. Alliance, Mpls., 1978-83, Dworsky Assocs., Los Angeles, 1983-85; pvt. practice architecture Los Angeles, 1985—; adj. asst. prof. UCLA, 1980-85; lectr. Wash. State U., Pullman, 1986—. Co-Author: Planning and Building the Minimum Energy Dwelling, 1977; also articles. Chmn. Santa Monica (Calif.) Landmarks Commn., 1984—. Recipient Design Research award Progressive Architecture mag., 1977, award Internat. Solar Energy Soc., 1980. Mem. AIA, Calif. Preservation Found. Home and Office: 2433 28th St Santa Monica CA 90405

JOHNSON, CLAUDE WILMER, retired geography researcher; b. Inglewood, Calif., Feb. 25, 1923; s. Charles Christiansen and Claudia Ethyl (Luckey) J.; m. Josephine Sarah Andersen, Apr. 9, 1944; children: Alice, Charles, Mary, Robert. BS, U. Ill., 1957; MS, U. Calif., Riverside, 1968. Enlisted USAF, 1943, advanced through grades to lt. col., 1963, retired, 1964; tchr. Redlands (Calif.) Unified Sch. Dist., 1964-67; research specialist U. Calif., Riverside, 1968-85, research specialist emeritus, 1985—. Contbr. chpt. to manual, articles to profl. jours. Mem. Assn. Am. Geographers, Am. Congress on Surveying and Mapping, Pacific Coast Geographers, Calif. Geography Soc., Sigma Xi. Avocation: personal computers. Home: 930 Fletcher Ave Redlands CA 92373

JOHNSON, CLAYTON ERROLD, poultry company executive; b. DeSota, Wis., Apr. 20, 1921; s. James and Louella (Goodin) J.; student U. Wis., 1940-41, Tex. A. and M. Coll., 1946; m. Betty J. Higenbotham, May 23, 1943; children—Roderick and Kenneth (twins), Richard. Pres. Flavor Fresh Brand, Inc., 1949—; Calif. gen. bldg. contractor, 1947—. Served with USAAF, 1942-45. Home: 3002 El Camino Las Vegas NV 89102 Office: 830 E Sahara Las Vegas NV 89102

JOHNSON, CONOR DEANE, mechanical engineer; b. Charlettesville, Va., Apr. 20, 1943; s. Randolph Holaday and Louise Anna (Deane) J.; m. Laura Teague Rogers, Dec. 20, 1966; children: William Drake, Catherine Teague. BS in Engring. Mechanics, Va. Poly. Inst., 1965; MS, Clemson U., 1967, PhD in Engring. Mechanics, 1969. Registered profl. engr., Calif. With Anamet Labs., Inc., 1973-82; sr. structural analyst Anamet Labs., Inc., Dayton, Ohio, 1973-75; prin. engr. Anamet Labs., Inc., San Carlos, Calif., 1975-81, v.p., 1981-82; program mgr. Aerospace Structures Info. and Analysis Ctr., 1975-82; co-founder, pres. CSA Engring., Inc., Palo Alto, 1982—. Contbr. articles to profl. jours. Pres. Crystal Springs Meth. Ch. Served to capt. USAF, 1969-73. Mem. AIAA, ASME (sec. tech. com., sound and vibration com., Structures and Materials award 1981), Sigma Xi. Methodist. Club: Gourmet Cooking. Home: 3425 Lodge Dr Belmont CA 94002 Office: CSA Engring Inc 560 San Antonio Rd Suite 101 Palo Alto CA 94306

JOHNSON, DANA KAY, state agency manager, engineering technician; b. Denver, Nov. 19, 1940; d. Ernest Christian and E. Ione (Florine) Bergmann; m. Richard G. Johnson, June 30, 1959; 1 child, Ronald G. A Arts and Scis., Arapahoe Community Coll., 1982. From clerical to jr. personnel officer, Dept. Institutions/ Ft. Logan Mental Health Ctr. State of Colo., Denver, 1965-76, adminstrv. officer, Dept. Highways, 1976-83, dist. coord. mgr., Dept. Highways, 1983—. Sec., treas. Harris Park Estates Homeowners' Assn., Bailey, Colo. Recipient Multi-Gallon Donor award Belle Bonfils Meml. Blood Ctr., Denver, 1985; named Employee of Month Colo. Dept. Highways, Denver, 1982. Mem. Colo. Assn. Pub. Employees (various offices local chpts.). Avocations: Denver Bronco football fan, handicrafts, mountain activities, bowling. Office: Colo Dept Highways 2000 S Holly St Denver CO 80222

JOHNSON, DARLA JUNE, child welfare worker; b. Steubenville, Ohio, June 15, 1936; d. John Henry Mooney and Dorothy Lucille (Mumaw) Brown; m. David Ward Johnson, Feb. 11, 1956 (div. Jan. 1979); children: Kristen, Karen, Karla, Kim; m. William Barclay Jones Jr., Jan. 29, 1983. AB, U. Md., 1960, MA, 1970; MSW, U. Calif., Berkeley, 1977, DSW, 1982. Lectr. Chabot Coll., Hayward, Calif., 1970-84; teaching assoc. U. Calif., Berkeley, 1973-79; child welfare worker Dept. Social Services, San Francisco, 1985—. Mem. library study commn. Piedmont (Calif.) City Council, 1974. Mem. Nat. Assn. Social Workers (bd. dirs. Region C 1986-87). Democrat. Home: 3738 Painted Pony Rd El Sobrante CA 94803 Office: Dept Social Services 170 Otis St San Francisco CA 94120

JOHNSON, DARRELL KURT, financial executive; b. Waukegan, Ill., Mar. 2, 1950; s. Kurt Charles and Verna Naomi (Richards) J. BA, Greenville Coll., 1972; M in Internat. Mgmt., Am. Grad. Sch. of Internat. Mgmt., 1977; MBA, So. Meth. U., 1977; BA, Baptist Christian Coll., 1984, MA, 1986. Mgmt. cons. Peace Corps, Colombia, 1973-75; fin. cons. Peace Corps, Nicaragua, 1977-78; mgmt. cons. Peace Corps, Guatemala, 1978-80; fin. and adminstrn. cons. Agrl. Coop. Devel. Internat., Bolivia, 1980-81; fin. assoc. for Asia World Vision Internat., Philippines, 1982-84; fin. exec. World Vision Internat., Monrovia, Calif., 1984—. Named one of Outstanding Young Men of Am., 1985. Mem. Soc. Internat. Devel., Evangs. for Social Action. Mem. Ch. of Nazarene. Avocations: classical guitar, tennis, biking, jogging, fgn. langs. Office: World Vision Internat 919 W Huntington Dr Monrovia CA 91016

JOHNSON, DARRYL FELTON, aerospace executive; b. Los Angeles, Mar. 25, 1948; s. Lawrence Kermit and Bertha Elizabeth (Jones) J. BA, U. Calif., Los Angeles; M in Pub. Adminstrn., Golden Gate U.; student, Northrop, Los Angeles. Commd. U.S. Army, 1970, advanced through grades to capt.; 2nd lt. med. dept. U.S. Army, Ft. Sam Houston, Tex., 1970-71; 1st lt. 7th Spl. Forces U.S. Army, Ft. Bragg, N.C., 1971-72; capt. 2nd Infantry div. U.S. Army, San Francisco, 1972-73; capt. Dentac-Meddac, Ft. Ord, Calif., 1973-78; resigned U.S. Army, 1978; adminstr. material Hughes Aircraft Co., Culver City, Calif., 1979-84; mgr. Hughes Aircraft Co., El Segudo, Calif., 1984—; maj. USAR 176th Med. Group, Los Alamitos, Calif., 1979—. Campaign adv. city councilman, Carson, Calif., 1986; mem. Youth Motivation Task Force, Los Angeles. Mem. Res. Officers Assn., Hughes Mgmt. Club., Black Officers Assn., Alpha Phi Alpha (pres. 1984, dean of pledges 1982-83, named Brother of the Yr., 1986). Democrat. Roman Catholic. Lodge: KC. Avocations: recreational activities, sports, black belt karate. Home: 19420 Eddington Dr Carson CA 90746 Office: Hughes Aircraft Co EDSG PO Box 902 El Segundo CA 90245

JOHNSON, DAVID SELLIE, civil engineer; b. Mpls., Apr. 10, 1935; s. Milton Edward and Helen M. (Sellie) J. BS, Mont. Coll. Mineral Sci. Tech., 1958. Registered profl. engr., Mont. Trainee Mont. Dept. Hwys., Helena, 1958-59, designer, 1959-66, asst. preconstrn. engr., 1966-68, regional engr., 1968-72, engring. specialities supr., 1972—, forensic engr., 1965—, traffic accident reconstructionist, 1978—. Contbr. articles on hwy. safety to profl. jours. Adv. bd. mem. Helena Vocat.-Tech. Edn., 1972-73. Mem. Nat. Acad. Forensic Engrs. (diplomate), Mont. Soc. Profl. Engrs., NSPE, Inst. Transp. Engrs., Transp. Research Bd., Wash. Assn. Tech. Accident Investigators, Corvette Club. Mem. Algeria Shrine Temple. Club: Treasure State (Helena) (pres. 1972-78). Lodges: Elks, Shriners. Avocations: photography, sports car racing. Home: 1921-6 Ave Helena MT 59601 Office: Mont Dept Hwys 2701 Prospect Helena MT 59620

JOHNSON, D'ELAINE ANN HERARD, artist; b. Puyallup, Wash., Mar. 19, 1932; d. Thomas Napoleon and Rosella Edna (Berry) Herard; m. Johnnie Laffette Johnson. B.F.A., Central Wash. U., 1954; M.F.A., U. Wash., 1956. Instr. art Seattle Pub. Schs., 1954-78, Mus. History and Industry, Seattle, 1954-56; dir. Mt. Olympus Estate, Edmonds, Wash., 1971; cons. art groups, Wash. State, 1954—. Exhibited in group shows: Fry Art Mus., Seattle, 1964, Seattle Art Mus., 1959, Henry Art Gallery, Seattle, Vancouver Maritime Mus., B.C., Can., 1981, N.S. Art Mus., Can., 1971, Whatcom Mus., Bellingham, Wash., 1975, State Capitol Mus., Olympia, Wash., 1975, Corvallis State U., Oreg., 1982, Newport Mus., Oreg., numerous others, 1950—, also Nat. Artist Equity, 1972. Recipient numerous awards. Mem. Nat. Artist Equity, Internat. Soc. Artists, Internat. Platform Assn., Kappa Delta Pi, Kappa Pi. Home and office: 16122 72d St Ave W Edmonds WA 98020

JOHNSON, DIANE KAY, solid waste systems operator, nurse; b. Coeur d'Alene, Idaho, Apr. 24, 1937; d. Raymond Francis and Irene Winifred (Nelson) Lavonture; m. Louis Bryan Granger, Aug. 10, 1958; children—Joseph, Relene; stepchildren—Richard, Kelly; m. Richard David Johnson, Aug. 16, 1969 (dec. 1979); 1 child, Rex. Diploma, Deaconess Hosp. Sch. Nursing, Spokane, Wash., 1958; B.S. in Nursing, U. Oreg., 1966. R.N., Idaho, Wash.; lic. pub. works contractor, Idaho. Head nurse surg.-psychiat. unit No. State Hosp., Sedro Wooley, Wash., 1958-59; night charge nurse surg. unit St. Mary's Hosp., Port Arthur, Tex., 1959-60; head nurse recovery room Lake City Gen. Hosp., Coeur d'Alene, 1960-62; pub. health nurse Panhandle Dist. Health Unit, Coeur d'Alene, 1962-64; staff nurse U. Oreg. Med. Sch. Out-Patient Clinic, Portland, 1966, head nurse med. unit Kootenai Meml. Hosp., Coeur d'Alene, 1967; instr. practical nursing N. Idaho Coll., Coeur d'Alene, 1967-70; owner Latah Sanitation, Inc., Moscow, Idaho, 1970—, Moscow-Pullman Recycling Ctr., 1984—, Latah Heavy Hauling, 1986—. Mem. Statewide Health Coordinating Council, 1979; bd. dirs. Gritman Meml. Hosp., Moscow, 1972—; mem. Idaho Hazardous Waste Mgmt. Planning Com., 1986—. Mem. N.Central Idaho Comprehensive Health Planning Council (sec. 1973-74), Idaho Nurses Assn. (v.p. 1973-76), Idaho Health Systems Agy., Idaho San. Service Inst., Inc. (pres. 1980-83), Moscow C. of C., Am. Nurses Assn., Nat. Solid Waste Mgmt. Assn. (Waste Haulers Council 1984-86). Presbyterian. Founder teen-age vol. program for hosp. and convalescent ctrs., Moscow, 1971. Home: PO Box 8931 Moscow ID 83843 Office: Latah Sanitation Inc PO Box 8036 Moscow ID 83843

JOHNSON, DONALD MILBY, lawyer; b. Portsmouth, Va., Oct. 14, 1944; s. Donald Milby and Harriett Eloise (Brown) J.; m. Lana Gene Kelly, June 10, 1966; children: Kelly Gene, Kara Christine. BA, U. Wyo., 1968, JD, 1971. Bar: Wyo. 1971, Alaska 1972, U.S. Dist. Ct. Alaska 1972. Asst. atty. City of Anchorage, 1971-75; asst. dist. atty. State of Alaska, Anchorage and Bethel, 1975-78; acting dist. atty. State of Alaska, Bethel, 1976; ptnr. Moderow, Walsh, Johnson & James, Anchorage, 1978-79; sole practice Anchorage, 1979-85; ptnr. Tobey & Johnson, Anchorage, 1985—. Chmn. Gov.'s Com. Revision Title 28 Alaska Statutes, 1973-77. Mem. Alaska Bar Assn. (spl. counsel 1981), Am. Judicature Soc., Assn. Trial Lawyers Am., Order of Barristers. Methodist. Avocations: flying, boating, fishing, woodworking. Home: 3440 Korovin Bay Circle Anchorage AK 99515 Office: Tobey & Johnson 880 H St Suite 200 Anchorage AK 99501

JOHNSON, EARVIN (MAGIC JOHNSON), professional basketball player; b. Lansing, Mich., Aug. 14, 1959; s. Earvin and Christine Johnson. Student, Mich. State U., 1976-78. Profl. basketball player Los Angeles Lakers, NBA, 1979—. Author: (autobiography) Magic, 1983. Named NBA Most Valuable Player, 1987; NBA player of the year, The Sporting News, 1987;. Player NBA All-Star Game, 1980, 82-87; mem. NBA championship team, 1980, 82, 85,87; most valuable player in playoffs, 1980, 82, 87; most valuable player Mich. State U. NCAA championship team, 1979. Office: care Los Angeles Lakers The Forum PO Box 10 Inglewood CA 90306 *

JOHNSON, ELSPETH ANN, librarian; b. Cambridge, Mass., Aug. 12, 1934; d. Edwin Warren and Resda Clair (Murray) Conable; m. Walter Edwin Johnson, Jan 28, 1956; children: Debora Ann Johnson Refior, Steven Forrest (dec.). BS in Edn., No. Ill. U., 1956; MA, Nat. Coll. Edn., 1969, Adminstrn. cert., 1973; Media Cert., Northeastern Ill. U., 1973. Tchr. pub. schs. Northfield (Ill.) Sch. Dist., 1962-69; librarian, learning ctr. West Pub. Sch., Glencoe, Ill., 1969-74; IMC library Kodiak (Alaska) Island Sch., 1974—. Contbr. articles to profl. jours. Mem. Council Govs.' ESEA Title IV Adv. Council, Juneau, Alaska, 1978-83; Episcopal Women; vol. Kodiak Hist. Soc., active Kodiak Reps. Mem. Alaska Library Assn. (v.p. 1976-77, pres. 1977-78), Kodiak Library Assn. (pres. 1976-77), Alaska Edn. Assn., Kodiak Edn. Assn. (media com 1979-80), AAUW (v.p. Kodiak chpt. 1982-83, pres. 1983, bd. dirs. 1984-85), Am. Orchid Soc., DAR (vice-regent Natalia Shelikof chpt. 1984-86, regent 1986—), Kodiak Pub. Procasting Assn., Kodiak Retailer's Assn., Kodiak C. of C. Office: Kodiak Island Borough Sch Dist 722 Mill Bay Rd Kodiak AK 99615

JOHNSON, ERLING MAYNARD, state official, economist, financial consultant; b. Los Angeles, Feb. 13, 1944; s. Earl and May Belle (Wood) J.; m. Penny Lynd Horne, Jan. 30, 1965 (div. Nov. 1983); children—Sandra, Eric, Grant, Heather; m. Yvonne Natalie Foster, Dec. 28, 1983; step-children—Daniel Damitio, David Cochran. A.A., El Camino Jr. Coll., 1965; B.S. in Bus. Adminstrn., Calif. State U., 1968; cert. in real estate, UCLA, 1972; M.B.A., U. So. Calif., 1975. Asst. to pres. Americana Mgmt. Co., Lomita, Calif., 1966-67; supr. officer services Teledyne Inc., Century City, Calif., 1967-68, corp. tax acct., 1968-69; sr. fin. analyst Union Bank, Los Angeles, 1969-75, profitability analyst, 1975-76; economist Wash. Dept. Revenue, Olympia, 1978—; fin. cons. Am. Advisors Group, Lacey, Wash., 1977—; co-founder Family Book & Gift Co., Lacey, 1985. Contbr. papers in field to profl. jours. Treas., St. Benedict's Episcopal Ch., Lacey, 1981—, chmn. fin. com. 1980. Mem. Forecasters of Wash. (v.p. 1981), Nat. Assn. Bus. Economists. Club: Olympia Economists. Home: 4334 Glen Terra Dr S E Lacey WA 98503 Office: Research Div Dept Revenue 711 S Capitol Way Suite 300 Olympia WA 98504

JOHNSON, F. MICHAEL, control systems engineer; b. Sacramento, Jan. 14, 1953; s. Carroll Loren and Constance (Latterell) J.; m. Donna Louise Hamilton, June 28, 1975; children: Bryan J., Cassandra L. BSChemE, U. Calif., Davis, 1975. Field engr., instrumentation Universal Oil Products, 1975-80; project engr. and leader Atkinson System Techs. Co., 1980-85; control systems project leader, system mgr. spl. project Stearns-Roger, Denver, 1985—. Recipient Top Cat award Atkinson Systems Tech. Co., 1985. Mem. Am. Chem. Soc., Instrument Soc. Am. Club: Toastmasters. Avocation: camping. Home: 8725 E Cherokee Ct Parker CO 80134 Office: Stearns-Roger PO Box 5888 Denver CO 80217

JOHNSON, FREDERICK WILLIAM, lieutenant governor Saskatchewan; b. Sedgetey, Staffordshire, Eng., Feb. 13, 1917; emigrated to Can., 1928; s. Edwin Priestley and Laura (Caddick) J.; m. Joyce Marilyn Laing, July 30, 1949; children: F. William, Royce L.C., Sheil F. B.A., U. Sask., 1947, LL.B., 1949. Justice Ct. of Queen's Bench, Saskatchewan, 1965-77, chief justice, 1977-83; lt. gov. Province of Sask., Regina, 1983—. Served to maj. Royal Can. Arty., 1941-46, Europe. Mem. Law Soc. Sask (bencher 1960-65). Mem. United Ch. of Can. Club: Assiiboia (Regina). Office: Govt House, Regina, SK Canada S4T 6N5 *

JOHNSON, GAIL DELORIES, chemist, researcher; b. Chgo., Sept. 30, 1957; d. Roger George and Delories B. (Reppert) J. BS in Chemistry, No. Ill. U., 1980. Quality control chemist Standard Pharmacal Corp., Elgin, Ill., 1980; forensic chemist Ill. Racing Bd. Lab., Elgin, 1980-82; chemist Analytical Technologies, Inc., Tempe, Ariz., 1982-84; assoc. chemist Nichols Inst., San Juan Capistrano, Calif., 1985-87; forensic chemist Reference Lab., Colton, Calif., 1987—. Mem. Am. Chem. Soc., Am. Inst. Chemists. Avocations: tennis, bicycling. Home: 33193 Friar Tuck Way Lake Elsinore CA 92330 Office: Reference Labs 952 S Mt Vernon Colton CA 92324

JOHNSON, GARDINER, lawyer; b. San Jose, Calif., Aug. 10, 1905; s. George W. and Izora (Carter) J.; A.B., U. Calif., 1926, J.D., 1928; m. Doris Louise Miller, Sept. 28, 1935; children—Jacqueline Ann, Stephen Miller. Bar: Calif. 1928; practice San Francisco, 1928—; ptnr. Johnson & Stanton, 1952-84. Mem. nat. drafting com. Council State Govts., 1944-47, chmn. Gov.'s Conf. Edn., 1955; chmn. Calif. delegation White House Conf. Edn., 1955; mem. Calif. Legislature from 18th Assembly Dist., 1935-47, speaker pro tem, 1940; mem. Republican State Central Com., 1934-46, 50—; mem. Alameda County Rep. Central Com., 1934-47, 59—; alternate del. Rep. Nat. Conv., 1940, del., 1956, 60, 64, 68, 76; pres. Calif. Rep. Assembly, 1959; mem. Rep. Nat. Com., 1964-68; mem. Citizens Legis. Adv. Commn., 1957-61; bd. dirs. U. Calif. Hosps. Aux., 1960-70, pres., 1962, 64-65; bd. dirs. Florence Crittenton Home, San Francisco, 1960-69, 76—, pres., 1967-69; bd. dirs. Florence Crittenton Assn. Am., 1969-75, v.p., 1973-75; bd. dirs. Spring Opera of San Francisco, 1963-69, Child Welfare League Am., 1976-84; bd. govs. San Francisco Heart Assn., 1963-70, chmn., 1966-69; mem. council Save-the-Redwoods League, 1970—. Fellow Am. Coll. Trial Lawyers; mem. Assn. Trial Lawyers Am., Internat. Bar Assn. (alternate del. 8th Conf.

Salzburg 1960), Inter-Am. Bar Assn., ABA (com. state legislation 1957-59, vice chmn. com. pub. contracts 1959), Presidio Soc. (dir. 1981—), Phi Beta Kappa, Phi Delta Phi, Kappa Delta Rho. Republican. Episcopalian. Clubs: Pacific-Union, Claremont Country, Lawyers (San Francisco). Home: 329 Hampton Rd Piedmont CA 94611 Office: 221 Sansome St San Francisco CA 94104

JOHNSON, GARY KENT, management education company executive; b. Provo, Utah, Apr. 16, 1936; s. Clyde LeRoy and Ruth Laie (Taylor) J.; m. Mary Joyce Crowther, Aug. 26, 1955; children—Mary Ann Johnson Harvey, Gary Kent, Brent James, Jeremy Clyde. Student Brigham Young U., 1954-55, U. Utah, 1955-58, 60-61, U. Calif.-Berkeley, 1962. Sales rep. Roche Labs., Salt Lake City, 1958-61, sales trainer, Denver, 1962, sales trainer, Oakland, Calif., 1962, div. mgr., Seattle, 1962-69; sec.-treas. Western Mgmt. Inst., Seattle, 1969-71; pres. WMI Corp., Bellevue, Wash., 1971—, Provisor Corp., 1983-86; dir. Lamson Products; speaker, cons. various nat. orgns. Bd. dirs. Big Bros.; del. King County Republican Com. Served with U.S. N.G., 1953-61. Walgreen scholar, 1955-58; Bristol scholar, 1958. Mem. Am. Soc. Tng. and Devel., Phi Sigma Epsilon. Mormon. Club: Bellevue Athletic. Author: Select the Best, 1976; Antitrust Untangled, 1977; The Utilities Management Series, 1979; Performance Appraisal, A Program for Improving Productivity, 1981. Office: WMI Corp 1309 114th Ave SE Suite 212 Bellevue WA 98004

JOHNSON, GERALD SCHOLINE, electrical engineer, industrial photographer; b. Seattle, Apr. 7, 1922; s. Russel Blaine and Myrtle Harriett (Scholine) J.; m. Mary Lou Maxine Shadinger, Oct. 22, 1948; children: Julianne, Sally, Mark, Craig. Registered profl. engr., Wash., Alaska. Elec. engr. Fischbach & Moore, Seattle, 1957-66; head elec. dept. Harmon Pray & Detrich, Seattle, 1966-74; elec. engr. Weyerhauser Corp., Tacoma, 1974-78; pres. G.S. Johnson P.S. Inc., Seattle, 1978—; pvt. practice cons. Seattle, 1978—. Served with USN, 1944-46. Mem. Nat. Assn. Profl. Engrs., Wash. State Profl. Engrs., Profl. Photographers of Am., Illuminating Engring. Soc. Republican. Methodist. Clubs: Engrs. (Seattle), Swedish (Seattle), Sand Point Country (Seattle). Lodge: Masons. Avocations: chess, philately, boating, fishing, golf. Home and Office: 4147 Sucia Dr PO Box 904 Ferndale WA 98248

JOHNSON, GERALDINE ESCH, language specialist; b. Steger, Ill., Jan. 5, 1921; d. William John Rutkowski and Estella Anna (Mannel) Pietz; m. Richard William Esch, Oct. 12, 1940 (dec. 1971); children: Janet L. Sohngen, Daryl R., Gary Michael; m. Henry Bernard Johnson, Aug. 23, 1978. BSBA, U. Denver, 1955, MA in Edn., 1958, MA in Speech Pathology, 1963. Cert. speech therapist, Colo.; cert. tchr., Colo. Tchr. music Judith St. John Sch. Music, Denver, 1946-52; tchr. West High Sch., Denver, 1955-61, chmn. bus. edn. dept., 1958-61, reading specialist, 1977-78; speech therapist, founder South Denver Speech Clinic, 1965-71; tchr. Eduducationally Handicapped Resource Rm., Denver, 1971-74, Diagnostic Ctr., The Belmont Sch., Denver, 1974-77; speech-lang. specialist elem. and jr. high schs., Denver, 1978-86; lectr. speech pathology and learning disabilities Colo. Edn. Assn., 1971-73; home lang tchr. Early Childhood Edn., Denver, 1975; mem. Ednl. TV Adv. com., Colo.; sec. Cen. Bus. Edn. Com., Colo; tchr. letter writing clinics, local bus, Denver, 1960—. Recipient Spl. Edn. award Denver Pub. Schs., 1986. Mem. Speech-Lang.-Hearing Assn. (cert.), U. Denver Sch. Bus. Alumni Bd., Beta Gamma Sigma, Kappa Delta Pi, Delta Pi Epsilon. Home: 2780 S Vance Way Denver CO 80227

JOHNSON, GLENN SCOTT, airline official; b. Redbank, N.J., Nov. 15, 1958; s. Arthur and Barbara Elizabeth (Textor) J. BBA, U. Wash., 1981. CPA, Wash. Staff acct. Arthur Andersen & Co., Seattle, 1981-83; staff auditor Alaska Airlines, Seattle, 1983, mgr. systems devel., 1984-85, mgr. passenger revenue acctg., 1985-86, dir. revenue acctg., 1986—. Mem. Am. Mgmt. Assn., Beta Alpha Psi (v.p. 1981). Roman Catholic.

JOHNSON, GORDON DUANE, management science educator; b. Nashville, Mar. 6, 1946; s. George Walter and Virginia (Anderson) J.; m. Catherine Ann Romack, Dec. 10, 1983. BBA, U. Wis., 1967, MS, 1968, PhD, 1973. Grad. coordinator sch. bus. Calif. State U., Northridge, 1979-81, chmn. mgmt. sci. dept., 1983-85, prof. mgmt. sci., 1973—; cons. Guild Mortgage Co., San Diego, 1976, Waialua (Hawaii) Sugar Co., 1982-83, Arneson Products, Corte Madera, Calif., 1982, Harmon JBL, Northridge, Calif., 1985; reviewer of texts Dryden Press, Houghton-Mifflin Pub. Co. Corp. Faculty fellow Am. Assembly Collegiate Schs. Bus., 1982. Mem. Inst. Mgmt. Sci., Ops. Research Soc. Am., Am. Risk and Ins. Assn., Beta Gamma Sigma. Office: Calif State U Dept Mgmt Sci 18111 Nordhoff St Northridge CA 91330

JOHNSON, GWENAVERE A., artist; b. Newark, S.D., Oct. 16, 1909; d. Arthur E. and Susie Ellen (King) Nelson; m. John Wendell Johnson, Dec. 17, 1937; 1 son, John Forrest. Student Mpsl. Sch. Art, 1930; B.A., U. Minn., 1937; M.A., San Jose State U., 1957. Cert. gen. elem., secondary, art tchr., Calif. Art tchr., supr. Austin (Minn.) Schs., 1937-38; art tchr. Hillbrook Sch., Los Gatos, Calif., 1947-52; art tchr., supr. Santa Clara (Calif.) Pub. Schs., 1952-55; art tchr., dept. chmn. San Jose (Calif.) Unified Schs., 1955-75; owner Tree Tops studio, San Jose, 1975—. Juried shows: Los Gatos Art Assn., 1976, 77, 78, 79, 85, 86 (1st and 2d awards), 83, 84 (Best of Show awards), Treeside gallery, Los Gatos, 1980, 81 (1st awards); Livermore Art Assn., 1977 (2d award), Los Gatos Art Mus., 1981 (1st award), 82 (2d award), Rosicrucean Mus., 1983, Centre d'Art Contemporian, Paris, 1983; creator Overfelt portrait Alexian Bros. Hosp., San Jose, Calif., 1977; exhibited in group shows Triton Art Mus., 1983, 85, 86. Recipient Golden Centaur award Acad. Italia, 1982, Golden Album of prize winning Artists, 1984, Golden Flame award Academia Italia, 1986, others. Mem. San Jose Art League, Los Gatos Art Assn., Santa Clara Art Assn. (Artist of Yr. 1983), Soc. Western Artists, Artists Equity, Nat. League Am. Penwomen (corr. sec., Merit Achiever award), Academia Italia. Home and Office: 2054 Booksin Ave San Jose CA 95125

JOHNSON, HERMAN LEONALL, research nutritionist; b. Whitehall, Wis., Apr. 1, 1935; s. Frederick E. And Jeanette (Severson) J.; m. Barbara Dale Matthews, July 3, 1960 (dec. May 1971); m. Barbara Ann Badger, Apr. 3, 1976. BA in Chemistry, North Cen. Coll., Naperville, Ill., 1959; MS in Biochemistry & Nutrition, Va. Poly. Inst. and State U., 1961, PhD in Biol. Nutrition, 1963. Research biochemist S.R. Noble Found., Ardmore, Okla., 1963-65; nutrition chemist U.S. Army Med. Research, Denver, 1965-74; nutrition physiologist Letterman Army Research, Presidio San Francisco, 1974-80, Western Human Nutrition Research Ctr. USDA, Presidio San Francisco, 1980—. Contbr. numerous articles to profl. jours. Trustee 1st Meth. Ch., San Rafael, Calif., 1985—. Served with Med. Service Corps, U.S. Army, 1954-56. Named one of Outstanding Young Men of Am., 1975; NIH traineeship Va. Poly. Inst. and State U., Blacksburg, 1961-63. Mem. AAAS, Am. Inst. Nutrition, Am. Soc. Clin. Nutritionists, Am. Coll. Nutritionists, Am. Coll. Sports Medicine, Tam Twirlers, Sigma Xi, Phi Lambda, Phi Sigma. Republican. Club: Commonwealth (San Francisco). Avocations: fishing, boating, camping, square dancing. Home: 10 Jessup St San Rafael CA 94901 Office: USDA Western Human Nutrition Research Ctr PO Box 29997 Presidio San Francisco CA 94129

JOHNSON, HOWARD WAYNE, electronic engineer; b. Kilgore, Tex., Apr. 11, 1956; s. Jim Howard and Patsy Sue (Leath) J.; m. Elisabeth Adams, Oct. 22, 1983. BSEE, Rice U., 1978, MEE, 1979, PhDEE, 1982. Mgr. advanced tech. group ROLM Corp., Santa Clara, Calif., 1979-84; cons., v.p. Spectrum Mgmt., Santa Clara, 1984-85; dir. engring. USX TeleCtrs., Sunnyvale, Calif., 1985—. Contbr. articles to profl. jours. Mem. Assn. Computing Machinery, IEEE, Sigma Xi, Tau Beta Pi. Republican. Avocations: sailing, woodworking, playing bass guitar, motorcycling, traveling. Office: USX Telectrs 595 Lawrence Expwy Sunnyvale CA 94086

JOHNSON, JAMES ARNOLD, business consultant, venture capitalist; b. Detroit, June 15, 1939; s. Waylon Z. and Elsie Jean (Peuser) J.; 1 dau., Stephanie Louise. B.A., Stanford U., 1961; M.B.A., U. Chgo., 1968. C.P.A., Hawaii, Calif. Asst. cashier internat. banking First Nat. Bank of Chgo., 1965-68; ptnr. in charge mgmt. cons. Peat, Marwick, Mitchell & Co., Honolulu, 1968-79, ptnr.-in-charge small bus. services, 1977-80; pres. Johnson Internat., Inc., Honolulu, 1980—; pres. BioEngring. Applications, Inc., Honolulu, 1981—; dir. KSH Systems, Inc., Los Angeles, 1984—, pres. Pflueger Group, Inc., 1985-87; gen. ptnr. numerous investment partnerships. Served to lt. USNR, 1962-65. Mem. Am. Inst. CPAs, Hawaii Soc. CPAs (past chmn. mgmt. adv. com.). Clubs: Waikiki Yacht, Pacific Club, Honolulu. Home: 5561 Kalanianaole Hwy Honolulu HI 96821 Office: PO Box 4680 Honolulu HI 96812

JOHNSON, JAMES BLAKESLEE, entomology educator; b. Kalamazoo, Jan. 25, 1951; s. James Leslie and Agatha (Roberts) J.; m. Janice Thornton, Aug. 31, 1974; children: Shannon Tapley, Heather Susan. BS in Zoology, U. Mich., 1973; postgrad., Mich. State U., 1973-74; PhD in Entomology, U. Calif., Berkeley, 1982. Asst. prof. entomology U. Idaho, Moscow, 1981—; vis. instr. elem. schs. and 4-H Clubs, Idaho, 1981—. Contbr. articles to profl. jours. Mem. Idaho Fair Share, Moscow, 1985-86. Mem. Internat. Soc. Neuropterists, Internat. Hymenopterists Soc., AAAS, Entomol. Soc. Am. (state membership chmn. 1985—), Sigma Xi. Office: U Idaho Dept Plant Soil and Entomol Sci Moscow ID 83843

JOHNSON, JAMES BRUCE, corporate executive; b. Los Angeles, May 31, 1951; s. James S. and Rita F. Johnson; m. Nancy Daum, Dec. 7, 1974. BSEE, U. Calif., Berkeley, 1973; MSEE, Stanford U., 1974. Design engr. Intel Corp., Santa Clara, Calif., 1974-79; engring. mgr. Intel Corp., Hillsboro, Oreg., 1977-84, gen. mgr., 1984—. Author; The Multibus Design Guidelines, 1983. Vol. Beyond War Found., Portland, Oreg., 1984—. Avocations: skiing, volleyball, white water rafting, hiking. Home: 3701 SW Beaverton Ave Portland OR 97201 Office: Intel PCEO TOD 07 5200 NE Elam Young Pkwy Hillsboro OR 97123

JOHNSON, JAMES DOW, broadcast television executive; b. Beaumont, Tex., Nov. 20, 1934; s. Walter Alonzo and Mohnike (Wheeler) J.; m. Linda Lee Rideout, Aug. 23, 1958; children: Christopher, Karen. BA in English, Tex. A&M U., 1957, MBA, 1958. Pub. relations dir., announcer Sta. WTVC-TV, Chattanooga, Tenn., 1960-66; dir. advt. promotion publicity Sta. KTVI-TV, St. Louis, 1966-68, Sta. WLWT-TV, Cin., 1968-69; dir. info. services Sta. KMOX-TV, St. Louis, 1969-71; exec. v.p., gen. mgr. NTV Network, Kearney, Nebr., 1971-80; pres., gen. mgr. Sta. KFTY-TV, Santa Rosa, Calif., 1980—. Vice-chmn. Nebr. Am. Bicentennial commn., Lincoln, 1972-78; chmn. Nebr. Ednl. TV commn., Lincoln, 1975-80; Nebr. del. to Rep. Nat. Conv., Detroit, 1980; v.p., sec. Burbank (Calif.) Ctr. for Arts, 1983—; bd. dirs. United Way of North Bay. Served with USAR, 1958-66. Recipient Disting. Service award Nebr. N.G., 1973, Service award St. Louis Advt. Club, 1968. Mem. Nat. Assn. Broadcasters, Assn. Ind. TV Stas., Nat. Assn. TV Program Execs., Nat. Broadcast Editorial Assn. (founder 1971, treas. 1972-73, v.p. 1973-74), Calif. Broadcasters Assn. (bd. dirs. 1984—), Nat. Acad. TV Arts and Scis. (pres. St. Louis chpt. 1970-71), North Bay Transp. Mgmt. (bd. dirs.), Santa Rosa C. of C. (bd. dirs.), Alpha Epsilon Rho. Club: Empire Breakfast (Santa Rosa) (pres. 1986). Lodge: Rotary. Office: Sta KFTY-TV 533 Mendocino Ave Santa Rosa CA 95401

JOHNSON, JANICE ELAINE, social worker; b. New Ulm, Minn., July 27, 1936; d. James Edward and Mathilda Marie (Nider) Honzay; m. Frank J. Johnson, Aug. 8, 1964 (div. Apr. 1982); children: Frank J. Jr., Kristin Marie. BA, St. Catherine Coll., St. Paul, 1958; postgrad., U. Minn., Mpls., 1961-63; MS in Social Adminstrn., Case Western Res. U., 1964. Caseworker Cath. Social Services, St. Paul, 1958-63; intern Kenny Rehab. Inst., Mpls., 1962-63, Cleve. Psychiat. Inst., 1963-64; social worker Family Service Assn., Cleve., 1964-66; parent facilitator San Diego City Schs., 1978; social worker San Diego County Dept. Social Services, 1984—; Mem. Foster Parent Recruitment com., San Diego, 1985—. Vol. Spl. Edn. Dept., San Diego, 1974-80, Spl. Olympics. Mem. Nat. Assn. Social Workers, AAUW, Parents of Lang. Disabled Children (treas. San Diego chpt. 1979-80), Assn. Retarded Citizens, VFW Aux. (sec. San Diego chpt. 1975-80), Phi Beta Kappa, Pi Gamma Mu. Avocations: reading, bicycling, cultural events. Office: Hillcrest Receiving Home 4307 3rd Ave San Diego CA 92103

JOHNSON, JENNY LEES, public relations director; b. Wahkon, Minn., June 10, 1944; d. Howard Edward and Frances Mildred (Wilson) Hartzie; m. Wayne Charles Johnson, Sept. 16, 1962; children: Clinton, Stacie, Kristie. Student pub. schs., Wahkon, and Oakland, Calif. Mgr. coffee shop Depot Restaurant, Reno, 1975-79; escrow sec. Title Ins. and Trust, Reno, 1980-81; with collection dept. 1st Comml. Title, Reno, 1981-82; dir. pub. relations Universal Helicopters, Reno, 1982-85; mktg./scheduling dir. High Sierra Helicopters, Reno, 1985—. Democrat. Roman Catholic. Office: High Sierra Helicopters PO Box 10768 Reno NV 89510

JOHNSON, JEROME BEN, research geophysicist; b. Ellensburg, Wash., Sept. 13, 1950; s. Ben Batchelor and Ann Carol (Bruketta) J.; m. Nancy Dean Hausle, Nov. 22, 1975; children: Nicole, Leah, Eric. BA in Physics and Math., Cen. Wash. State Coll., 1972; student, U. Alaska, 1973-74; PhD in Geophysics, U. Wash., 1978. Instr. Cen. Wash. State Coll., Ellensburg, 1978-79; sr. research engr. Oceanographic Services, Inc., Santa Barbara, Calif., 1979-80; research fellow Geophys. Inst., Fairbanks, Alaska, 1980-83; research geophysicist USA Cold Regions Research and Engring. Lab., Fairbanks, Alaska, 1983—; cons. State of Alaska, Shannon and Wilson Co., 1980-85; participant Properties of Snow Workshop, Alta, Utah, 1981; adm. assoc. prof. U. Alaska, Fairbanks, 1983—. Inventor in field; contbr. articles to profl. jours. Speaker N. Star Borough Sch. Dist., Fairbanks, 1986—. Mem. AAAS, AM. Geophys. Union, Internat. Glaciol. Soc., ASME (ice forces subcom. 1985—). Avocations: cross-country skiing, flying, exploration and mountaineering. Office: USA CRREL Bldg 4070 Fairbanks AK 99703

JOHNSON, JOHN EDLIN, aircraft design engineer; b. Bunkie, La., May 31, 1921; s. Elvy John and Euphemie (Chatelaine) J.; m. Mary Virginia Thompson, Apr. 25, 1943; children—John, Phillip, Susan, Melissa. B.C.E., La. State U., 1942. Design engr. Gen. Dynamics, Fort Worth, 1943-50, group engr., 1950-58; prin. design engr. Boeing Co., Renton, Wash., 1958-60, sr. group engr., 1960-77, sr. project engr., 1977-83; chief design engr. Boeing Comml. Airplane Co., Renton, 1983—; cons. Frye Aircraft Corp., Ft. Worth, 1957-58. Mem. Lakeworth Village City Council, Ft. Worth, 1952. Mem. Boeing Mgmt. Assn., Tau Beta Pi, Phi Kappa Phi, Phi Eta Sigma. Roman Catholic.

JOHNSON, JOHN HOWARD, data processing executive; b. Denver, Mar. 4, 1944; s. Doyle Clifford and Patricia Pauline (Hayes) J.; m. Carol Lynn Rice, Mar. 26, 1968 (div. June 1982); children: William Leslie, Stacy Heather. Student, Midland Luth. Coll., 1962-64, U. Colo., 1964-66; AA, Community Coll. Denver, 1975; BS in Acctg., Met. State Coll., 1979. Programmer 1st Fed. Savs. Bank of Colo., Lakewood, 1970-72, sr. programmer, 1972-78, supr. progamming, 1978-80, mgr. EDP, 1980, asst. v.p., mgr. EDP, 1980-82, v.p., mgr. EDP, 1982—. Vice pres. Wahkeeney Park Civic Assn., Evergreen, Colo., 1972-73, pres. 1974-75. Served with USAF, 1966-70. Mem. Am.'s Univac Users Assn., Data Processing Mgrs. Assn., Fin. Mgr. Assns. Republican. Lutheran. Club: Denver Broncos Quarterback. Lodge: Highland Park Optimists (Denver club). Avocations: soccer, hiking, coin and stamp collecting, tropical fish. Home: 7260 S Upham St Littleton CO 80123 Office: 1st Fed Savs Bank Colo 215 S Wadsworth Blvd Lakewood CO 80226

JOHNSON, JOHN MORRIS, biology educator; b. Boise, Idaho, Mar. 16, 1937; s. Carl Theodore and Fannie Margaret (King) J.; m. Margaret May, June 13, 1959; children: Mori Kay, Stephen Wade. BS, Coll. Idaho, 1959; MS, Oreg. State U., 1961, PhD, 1964; postgrad., U. Chgo., 1965-66. Asst. prof. Cen. Coll., Pella, Iowa, 1964-67, assoc. prof., 1967-69; assoc. prof. biology Western Oreg. State Coll., Monmouth, 1969-74, prof., 1974—, coordinator biology sect., 1969-72, dir. honors program, 1983-85, chmn. div. natural sci. and math., 1985—. Author: Handbook of Uncommon Plants, 1980; contbr. articles to profl. jours. Dist. chmn. Boy Scouts Am., Polk County, Oreg., 1973-77. Recipient Faculty Honors award Western Oreg. State Coll., 1980, Silver Beaver award Boy Scouts Am., 1981. Mem. Oreg. Acad. Sci. (chmn. biology sect. 1981-82), Am. Soc. Cell Biology, Bot. Soc. Am., AAAS, Phi Kappa Phi (chmn. local chpt. 1980-81).. Democrat. Methodist. Avocations: photography, camping, hiking, fishing, boating. Home: 271 Walnut Dr Monmouth OR 97361 Office: Western Oreg State Coll 345 Monmouth Ave Monmouth OR 97361

JOHNSON, JOHN PHILIP, geneticist, researcher; b. Wabash, Ind., June 6, 1949; s. Melvin Leroy and Cleo Pauline (Aldrich) J.; m. Sheryl Kay Kennedy, June 3, 1978; 1 child, Craig Eric. BS, U. Mich., 1971, MD, 1975. Diplomate Am. Bd. Pediatrics, Am. Bd. Med. Genetics. Intern, 2d-yr. resident Children's Hosp. Los Angeles, 1975-77; 3d yr. resident in pediatrics U. Utah, Salt Lake City, 1977-78, fellow in genetics, 1980-82, asst. prof. pediatrics, 1982-85; pediatrician Family Health Program, Salt Lake City, 1978-80; staff physician, geneticist Children's Hosp. Oakland, Calif., 1985—; clinic physician Utah State Tng. Sch., American Fork, 1982-85; attending and staff physician Primary Children's Med. Ctr., Salt Lake City, 1978-80. Contbr. articles to med. jours. Recipient William J. Branstrom award U. Mich., 1967. Fellow Am. Acad. Pediatrics; mem. Am. Soc. Human Genetics, Alpha Omega Alpha. Avocations: skiing, hiking, camping, piano, jazz. Home: 4451 Reinhardt Dr Oakland CA 94619 Office: Children's Hosp 747 52d St Oakland CA 94609

JOHNSON, JUDY LEE, contract bookkeeping company executive; b. Hobbs, N.Mex., Sept. 11, 1953; d. Henry Leroy Landusky and Jo (McDougal) Johnson; m. Roger Dale Johnson, Mar. 31, 1983. B.B.A. in Mktg., Tex. Tech. U., 1975. Cert. petroleum sec. Assn. Desk & Derrick Clubs. Owner, mgr. Landusky Enterprise & Assocs., Hobbs, N.Mex., 1976—. Mem. Desk & Derrick Club (recipient 3d pl. award of merit 1981). Democrat. Baptist. Home: PO Box 5692 Hobbs NM 88241 Office: 419 W Cain Hobbs NM 88240

JOHNSON, KAREN DENISE, lawyer, realtor; b. Fresno, Calif., Aug. 26, 1952; d. Leonard Leroy and Cherie Ann (Thompson) Johnson; m. Lawrence Kenneth Ho, June 6, 1976 (div. 1981). A.A., Tulsa Jr. Coll., 1973; B.S., Northeastern Okla. State U., 1975; J.D., U. Calif.-Davis, 1980; Honor Grad., USAF Law Enforcement Specialist Sch., 1973. Bar: Calif. 1980, Nev. 1981, Ariz. 1983, U.S. Dist. Ct. (ea. and cen. dists.) Calif. 1980, U.S. Dist. Ct. Nev. 1981, U.S. Dist. Ct. Ariz. 1983. Sole practice, Sparks, Nev., 1981-83, Pinetop, Ariz., 1983—; realtor Pearl Penrod Realty, Pinetop, 1984—. Bd. dirs. No. Nev. Children's Home, Reno, 1982. Served with USAF, 1973-74. Mem. Calif. State Bar Assn., Nev. State Bar Assn., Ariz. State Bar Assn., Navajo County Bar Assn., Nev. Women Lawyers Assn. Office: PO Box 213 Pinetop AZ 85935

JOHNSON, KEITH LIDDELL, chemical company executive; b. Darlington, U.K., July 22, 1939; came to U.S., 1948, naturalized, 1958; s. Arthur Henry and Beatrice (Liddell) J.; m. Margaret Elaine Meston, Aug. 29, 1959; children—Leslie Margaret, Kevin Liddell, Gregory Norman, Kathleen Elaine; 1 ward, Ann Louise Warwick. B.A., U. Mich., 1960. Chem. technician Ajem Labs., Livonia, Mich., 1956-60; research chemist labs Swift & Co., Chgo., 1960-63, project mgr., 1963-67, group leader research and devel. ctr., Oak Brook, Ill., 1967-71, adminstrv. asst. to exec. v.p., Chgo., 1971-72, quality assurance dir., 1974-78, group mgr. plant quality assurance, 1978-82; quality assurance mgr. refinery div. Swift Edible Oil Co. subs. Swift & Co., Chgo., 1972-73, corp. quality assurance mgr., 1973-74; tech. dir. Norman Fox & Co., Los Angeles, 1982-83; br. mgr., 1983—; mem. Chgo. Manpower Area Planning Com., 1971; mem. industry adv. bd. South Coast Air Quality Mgmt. Dist., Calif., 1982-84. Contbr. articles to profl. jours. Holder 17 U.S. and 25 fgn. patents. Mem. Chgo. Chemists Club, Chem. Arts Forum Chgo. (v.p. 1980, pres. 1981), Am. Chem. Soc., Soc. Cosmetic Chemists (membership chmn. Bay area chpt., 1985, chmn.-elect, 1986), Bay Area Chem. Mktg. Assn., Am. Oil Chemists Soc., Am. Soc. Quality Control, Chgo. Jr. Assn. Commerce and Industry (dir. 1968, v.p. 1969, exec. v.p. 1970, pres. 1971), U.S. Jr. C. of C. (dir. 1972), Ill. Jr. C. of C. (v.p. 1972). Episcopalian. Home: 3248 Northampton Pleasanton CA 94566 Office: PO Box 684 Pleasanton CA 94566

JOHNSON, KEITH PHILIP, archaeology educator; b. Denver, Aug. 19, 1957; s. Robert Henry and Gail Patricia (Streep) J.;. BA, UCLA, 1979, MA, 1981, postgrad., 1981—. Teaching assoc. UCLA, 1981-85; instr. Santa Monica (Calif.) Coll., 1985—; summer field archaeologist Pajarito Archeol. Research project, Santa Fe, N.Mex., 1978-80, Howe Broch project, Kirkwall Orkney Islands, Scotland, 1982, Four Resevoirs project, Bakersfield, Calif., 1984, Cahercammon project, Galway, Ireland, 1985. Mem. Sigma Xi. Democrat. Unitarian. Avocation: silversmithing. Home: 525 N Sycamore #411 Los Angeles CA 90036 Office: UCLA Dept Anthropology Los Angeles CA 90024

JOHNSON, LAWRENCE ALLAN, SR., chiropractic physician, real estate developer; b. Balt., Feb. 17, 1943; s. Harvey McMullen and Virginia Pauline (Thompson) J.; m. Sunny Lin Malone, Apr. 22, 1967; children: James, Melanie, Lawrence Jr., Jeff, Amanda, Amber, Susanne, Brittany, Courtney. BA magna cum laude, George Williams Coll., 1968; D in Chiropractic Medicine, Nat. Coll., Lombard, Ill., 1972. Pres. Chriopractic Clinics N.Mex., Los Lunas, Belen, Rio Rancho and Albuquerque, 1972—; pres. Ambulance Services N.Mex., Bernalillo and Valencia Counties, 1983-87, Lazy J Enterprises, Bernalillo and Valencia Counties, 1975—. Chmn. Rep. fin. com., Valencia County, 1983-84, 19th precinct chmn., 1985-86, vice chmn. 1980-84. Mem. N.Mex. Physicians of Chiropractic Medicine (charter, pres. 1986), N.Mex. Chiropractic Assn. (sec., treas. 1972-73, 81-82, bd. dirs. 1972-73, 79-83, editor jour. 1972-85, Nat. Excellence jour. award 1980, Outstanding Service 1972-82), Bernalillo County Chiropractic Assn. (charter, pres. 1972-74, 79-85), Nat. Coll. Alumni Assn. (field advisor 1983-86, Chiropractor of Yr. 1985, Outstanding Grad. 1982, bd. dirs. 1985—). Roman Catholic. Lodges: Lions (sec., treas. Los Lunas, N.Mex. club 1980, pres. 1981, 86, Lion of Yr. 1981), Masons, Moose. Avocations: astronomy, stamp and coin collecting, train models, golf. Home: 4203 Hwy 85 SW Los Lunas NM 87031 Office: Chiropractic Clinic NMex 4205 Hwy 85 SW Los Lunas NM 87031

JOHNSON, LAYMON, JR., budget analyst, manager; b. Jackson, Miss., Sept. 1, 1948; s. Laymon and Bertha (Yarbrough) J.; m. Charlene J. Johnson, Nov. 13, 1982. B in Tech., U. Dayton, 1970; MS in Systems Mgmt., U. So. Calif., 1978. Mem. tech. staff Rockwell Internat., Canoga Park, Calif., 1975-77; sr. dynamics engr. Gen. Dynamics, Pomona, Calif., 1978-83; sr. budget analyst , budget mgr. Northrop Corp., Pico Rivera, Calif., 1983—. Served to lt. comdr. USNR, 1970—. Mem. U.S. Naval Inst., Naval Res. Assn., Res. Officers Assn. U.S., Assn. Mil. Surgeons U.S., Assn. Systems Mgmt., Ops. Research Soc. Am., Los Angeles County Mus. Art, Smithsonian Assos., Nat. Hist. Soc., Archimedes Circle, Tau Alpha Pi. Democrat. Roman Catholic. Office: Northrop Corp Advanced Systems Div 8900 E Washington Blvd Pico Rivera CA 90660

JOHNSON, LEONARD MORRIS, pediatric surgeon; b. Gowanda, N.Y., June 11, 1931; s. Leonard Brynolf and Helen Berdena (Morris) J.; m. Ann Marie Homer, Mar. 30, 1968; children—Hilding Leif Brynolf, Nils Anders Christian. B.A., Haverford Coll., 1954; M.D., U. Pa., 1958; M.S. in Surgery, U. Minn., 1966. Intern, Colo. Gen. Hosp., 1958-59; fellow in surgery Mayo Clinic, Rochester, Minn., 1959-63; surgeon S.S. Hope, Guayaquil, Ecuador, 1964, surgeon, asst. chief of staff, Conakry, Guinea, 1965, pediatric surgeon, dir. med. edn., Corinto, Micaragua, 1965-66, pediatric surgeon, Cartegena, Colombia, 1967, Colombo, Sri Lanka, 1968; fellow in pediatric surgery Mercy Children's Hosp., Kansas City, Mo., 1964-65; vis. pediatric surgeon Univ. Hosp., Uppsala, Sweden, 1967; registrar in pediatric urology Alder Hey Children's Hosp., Liverpool, Eng., 1967-68; practice medicine specializing in pediatric surgery, Oakland, Calif., 1969—; mem. staff Children's Hosp. Med. Ctr., 1969—, chief div. gen. surgery, 1974-80, 86—, pres. med. staff, 1977-78. Decorated Orden de Ruben Dario (Nicaragua). Fellow ACS, Am. Acad. Pediatrics; mem. AMA, Calif. Med. Assn., Alameda-Contra Costa Med. Assn., Am. Trauma Soc., Am. Pediatric Surg. Assn., Brit. Assn. Pediatric Surgeons, Pacific Assn. Pediatric Surgeons, East Bay Surg. Soc., San Francisco Surg. Soc., Continental Surg. Club. Republican. Presbyterian. Club: Rotary (Oakland). Home: 7 Charles Hill Ln Orinda CA 94563 Office: 775 53d St Oakland CA 94609

JOHNSON, LINDSAY CALVIN, personnel executive; b. Fresno, Calif., June 9, 1938; s. Lindsay Calvin and Arfalura (Clark) J.; m. Carol Jean Buford, Dec. 28, 1965 (div. 1978); children: Diane Elizabeth, Debra Ann; m. Diane Suzette Spears, Oct. 17, 1981; children: Janelle Renee, E. Melvin. BA, Calif. State U., Fresno, 1965, MA, 1974. Cert. counselor, Calif.; cert. instr., Calif.; cert. supr., Calif.; cert. adminstrv. officer, Calif. Counselor Litton Industries Inc., Pleasanton, Calif., 1965-68, Calif. Dept. Edn., Fresno, 1968; intake counselor State of Calif., Fresno, 1968-69; dir. projects Model Cities

Program, Fresno, 1969-74; sr. personnel analyst State Ctr. Community Coll. Dist., Fresno, 1974-84, dir. classified personnel, 1984—; cons. Cal Johnson Assocs., Fresno, 1976—, Fresno Econ. Commn., 1985—, Family Health Ctr., Madera, Calif, 1985—. Commentator KVPR-FM. Commr. Fresno Housing Authorities, 1983; active Habitat for Humanity Inc., Fresno, 1985; counselor Victim Offender Reconciliation Program, Fresno, 1985; mem. older Americans employment and tng. program's adv. com. NAACP, 1987—; bd. dirs. Older Am. Orgn., Fresno, 1986—. Served with U.S. Army, 1956-59, Korea. Recipient commendation Phi Delta Kappa, 1976. Mem. Calif. Community Coll. Adminstrs., Calif. Black Faculty and Staff Assn., Internat. Personnel Mgmt. Assn. Democrat. Baptist. Lodges: King Solomon, Masons. Avocations: reading, golf, racquetball. Office: State Ctr Community Coll Dist 1525 E Weldon Fresno CA 93704

JOHNSON, LORNEVA, automotive interior accessories manufacturing company executive; b. Hector, Ark., Aug. 23, 1921; d. Reece Allen and Ruth (Churchill) Dixon; m. Howard S. Johnson, Oct. 19, 1953; children—Willette, Dennis, Lura, Loretta. Area supr. Hospitality Hostess Service, Inc., San Diego, 1958-70; pres. H & L Products, Inc., National City, Calif., 1970—. Named C. of C. Bus. Person of Yr., 1986; grand marshall parade National City, Calif., 1986. Mem. Automotive Parts and Accessories Assn. (com., Advocate of Merit award 1986), Calif. Small Bus. Adminstrn. (adv. com.). Republican. Presbyterian. Author: The Pearl of Potentiality. Home: 830 J Ave Coronado CA 92118 Office: 500 W 16th St National City CA 92050

JOHNSON, LOUIS RAYMOND, publishing company executive; b. Boring, Oreg., Oct. 25, 1936; s. Mathis Steven and Vera Madeline (Salmon) J.; m. Carole Ann Denham, June 11, 1960 (div.); children—Kenneth, Tammy, David, Steven; m. 2d, Patricia Ann Safra. A.A., Long Beach City Coll., 1960; B.A., Long Beach State U., 1962. With Arcata Graphics, Los Angeles, 1960-72, mgr. purchases, traffic, warehouse, 1961-72; mgr. purchasing and traffic Petersen Pub., Los Angeles, 1972-77; dir. prodn. CBS Consumer Pub., Newport Beach, Calif., 1977—. Leader, YMCA. Mem. Western Pub. Assn., Purchasing Mgmt. Assn., Traffic Club of Los Angeles, Los Angeles Litho. Roman Catholic. Home: 22232 Camino Arroya Seco Laguna Hills CA 92653

JOHNSON, LYMAN KEATING, music professor; b. Denver, Jan. 5, 1951; s. L. Preston and Susanna Johnson; m. Janet Wiita, Apr. 16, 1973. MusB, U. Pacific, 1973; MusM, U. Wis., 1974; MusD, U. So. Calif., 1986. Band dir. Boylan High Sch., Rockford, Ill., 1975-77; dir. bands Plymouth (N.H.) State Coll., 1977-79, Calif. State U., San Bernardino, 1979-83, Wash. State U., Pullman, 1983—. Recipient New Faculty Research award Wash. State U., 1985. Mem. Coll. Band Dirs. Nat. Assn. (pres.-elect NW div. 1986-87), Nat. Band Assn., Tubists Univ. Brotherhood Assn., Music Educators Nat. Conf., Pi Kappa Lambda. Club: Riverside (Calif.) Live Steamers (treas. 1982-83). Avocation: steam operated miniature locomotives. Home: NW 458 Sunset Dr Pullman WA 99163 Office: Wash State U Dept Music Pullman WA 99164-5300

JOHNSON, MAGIC See **JOHNSON, EARVIN**

JOHNSON, MARK SCOTT, computer scientist; b. Oakland, Calif., Apr. 16, 1951; s. John Harley and Marjorie (Reynolds) J. BA with high honors, U. Calif., Santa Barbara, 1973, MS, 1974; PhD, U. B.C., Vancouver, Can., 1978. Asst. prof. computer sci. San Francisco State U., 1978-80; mem. tech. staff Hewlett-Packard Labs., Palo Alto, Calif., 1980-85, engring. mgr., 1985-86; project leader Sun Microsystems, Mountain View, Calif., 1986—. Editor: (proceedings) Symposium on High-level Debugging, 1983; contbr. tech. articles to profl. jours. Grantee U. B.C., 1977-78. Mem. Assn. Computing Machinery (vice-chmn. Spl. Interest group on Programming Langs., 1984—, program chmn. symposium on high-level debugging, 1983, gen. chmn. symposium Interpreters and Interpretive Techniques, 1987, symposium Principles of Programming Languages, 1986, Recognition of Service award 1985), IEEE, Phi Beta Kappa.

JOHNSON, MARQUES KEVIN, professional basketball player; b. Nachitoches, La., Feb. 8, 1956; s. Jeff David and Baasha Violet (Kessee) J.; 1 son, Kristaan Iman. B.A., UCLA, 1977. Mem. UCLA Varsity Basketball Team, 1973-77, Milw. Bucks, Nat. Basketball Assn., 1977-84, Los Angeles Clippers, Nat. Basketball Assn., 1984—. Producer, dir., editor: film Livin' for the Weekend, 1979; producer: TV film On the Road with the Milwaukee Bucks, 1984. Recipient Bob Hope Youth award, 1979, John W. Wooden sports award, 1977, Inspiration to Youth award, 1983; named Coll. Player of Yr., 1977; named to Nat. Basketball Assn. All-Star Team, 1979, 80, 81, 83, 86, Nat. Basketball Assn. All-Pro 1st Team, 1979. Democrat. Baptist. Office: Los Angeles Clippers 3939 S Figueroa St Los Angeles CA 90037

JOHNSON, MARSHALL S., aerospace program manager; b. N.Y.C., Mar. 13, 1926; s. Joseph and Josephine (Hiesel) J.; m. Polly Copeland, Apr. 1965 (div. Mar. 1979); children: Erica W., Lara S. BA, New York U., 1955; postgrad., George Washington U., 1955-57, U. So. Calif., 1957-62. Flight dir., Ranger project Jet Probulsion Lab., Pasadena, Calif., 1961-62, devel. mgr. space flight ops. facility, 1962-64, mission ops. mgr., Mariner Mars project, 1966-69; spl. asst. to dir. Office of Sec. of Def. Advanced Research Projects Agy. Research and Devel. Ctr., Bangkok, Thailand, 1969-72; mgr. flight ops. Viking project, Martin Marietta Aerospace, Denver, 1972-74; flight ops. integration mgr. Viking project, NASA/Langley Research Ctr., Hamton, Va., 1974-77; flight dir. Pioneer Venus program, NASA/Ames Research Ctr., Mountain View, Calif., 1977-79; program mgr., numerical aerodynamic simulator NASA/Ames Research Ctr., Mountain View, Calif., 1980-82; program mgr. Space Systems div Gen. Electric Co., San Jose, Calif., 1982—; mem. Galileo project review bd. Jet Propulsion Lab., Pasadena, 1981—. Served as pfc. U.S. Army, 1944-46, ETO. Mem. AIAA, Nat. Acad. Sci. (mem. mission ops. and info. subcom. of solar systems exploration com. 1982-84). Avocations: woodworking, skiing. Office: Gen Electric Co Space Systems div 4041 N 1st St San Jose CA 95134

JOHNSON, MARTIN CLIFTON, physician; b. Santa Fe, Nov. 16, 1933; s. Henry J. and Dorothy (Clifton) J.; AB, Stanford, 1955, MD, 1959; m. Priscilla Bollam, June 13, 1959; children: Martin Clifton II, Kurt B., Kirsten L., Katharine E. Intern, Palo Alto Stanford U. Hosp., 1959-60; fellow in neurosurgery Mayo Found., Rochester, Minn., 1960-61; asst. resident gen. surgery Presbyn. Med. Ctr., San Francisco, 1963-64; asst. resident, resident, sr. resident, chief resident in neurosurgery U. Cin., 1964-68; pvt. practice medicine specializing in neurosurgery, with spl. interest in pediatric neurosurgery, Portland, Oreg., 1968—; mem. staff Emanuel Hosp., Woodland Park Hosp., Portland, Providence Hosp.; neurosurg. cons. Shriners Hosp. for Crippled Children. Served with M.C., USN, 1961-63. Diplomate Am. Bd. Neurol. Surgery. Fellow ACS; mem. Multnomah County, Oreg. med. socs., AMA, Congress Neurol. Surgeons, Am. Assn. Neurol. Surgeons (pediatric sect.), Pan Pacific Surg. Assn., Portland Surg. Soc., Soc. Critical Care Medicine, N.W. Pediatric Soc., North Pacific Soc. Neurology and Psychiatry, Oreg. Neurosurg. Soc., Internat. Soc. for Pediatric Neurol. Surgery, Portland Acad. Pediatrics, Airplane Owners and Pilots Assn., Flying Physicians Assn. Clubs: Multnomah Athletic, Columbia Aviation Country. Home: 3327 NE 126th St Portland OR 97230 Office: 2800 N Vancouver #6 Portland OR 97227

JOHNSON, MARY LOUISE, research geochemist; b. Wailuku, Hawaii, Mar. 1, 1954; d. Donald Edward Edythe Maud (Allen) J. BS, Calif. Inst. Tech., 1976; AM, Harvard U., 1978, PhD, 1982. Research asst. Calif. Inst. Tech., Pasadena, 1973-77; research and teaching asst. Harvard U., Cambridge, Mass., 1979-82; postdoctoral chemist UCLA, 1983-86; research geochemist Calif. Inst. Tech., 1986—. Contbr. articles to profl. jours. Fellow Fanny and John Hertz Found., 1975, U.S. Govt., HEW Mining and Mineral Resources, 1978-82. Mem. AAAS, Am. Geophys. Union, Mineral Soc. Am., Assn. Women in Sci., Mineral. Soc. So. Calif., Sigma Xi. Animist. Avocation: mineral collecting. Office: Calif Inst Tech 170-25 Pasadena CA 91125

JOHNSON, MATTHEW VICTOR, geothermal engineer; b. Bakersfield, Calif., June 13, 1958; s. Joseph Arch and Catherine (Campion) J.; m. Linda Lee Grippi, Mar. 9, 1985. AA, Bakersfield Jr. Coll., 1978; BSME, Calif. Poly. State U., 1981. Registered profl. engr., Calif. Geothermal prodn. engr. Unocal Geothermal, Santa Rosa, Calif., 1981-82, Indio, Calif., 1982—. Co-inventor geothermal filter. Served to sgt. USMC, 1977. Mem. Instrument Soc. Am., ASME, Aircraft Owners and Pilots Assn. Republican. Roman Catholic. Avocations: tennis, triathlon, bike racing, flying. Home: 73-147 Bursera Way Palm Desert CA 92260 Office: Unocal Geothermal 81-711 Hwy 111 Indio CA 92201

JOHNSON, MICHAEL, magazine publisher; b. Long Beach, Calif., Dec. 16, 1940; s. Norman Edwin Johnson and Anita Jane (Scharf) Warren; m. Nora Hamlin, July 14, 1961 (div. Sept. 1974); children: Michael, Michelle, Melissa; m. Kathryn Louise Sesslin, May 31, 1980; children: Jessica, Rachel. Pub. Desert Mag., Encinitas, Calif., 1978-81; pub. and founder Seacoast Mag., Encinitas, 1978-81; pub. and editor Solar Mag., Del Mar, Calif., 1981—, Wind Energy Mag., Del Mar, Calif., 1982—, Resort and Hotel Mag., Del Mar, Calif., 1985—; chmn. bd. dirs. Source Communications, Del Mar, 1981—; guest lectr. San Diego City Coll., 1982—; cons., writer Redd Foxx Corp., Hollywood, Calif., 1986—. Author: The Wizard's Magic Lessons, 1981, Talkin' Trash, 1986, The Book of Questions, 1986; editor, pub. Venture Capital Directory, 1985; contbr. articles to mags. Active Encinitas Boys Club, 1984-86. Served to capt. U.S. Army, 1957-60. Recipient Service award Ocotillo Fedn., 1985, Edn. award Ocotillo Fedn., 1985. Mem. Western Pubs. Assn. (Maggie award 1984). Avocations: anthropology, desert lore, natural history, basketball, gardening. Office: Source Communications Inc 228 S Cedros Solana Beach CA 92075

JOHNSON, MICHAEL B., financial planner; b. Portland, Oreg., Sept. 13, 1956; s. Frederick Herbert and Betty Jane Johnson. A in Mgmt., Portland Community Coll.; student, Marylhurst Coll. Prodn. assembler Tektronix, Inc., Beaverton, Oreg., 1974-77, work measurement analyst, 1977-78, indsl. engring. technician, 1978-81, indsl. engr., 1981-83; fin. planner Waddell & Reed Fin. Services, Portland, 1984—. Recipient Award for Excellence Waddell & Reed Fin. Services, 1985, $1 Million Life Ins. award Waddell & Reed Fin. Services, 1985, $1 Million Mut. Fund award Waddell & Reed Fin. Services, 1986. Republican. Nazarene. Avocations: classical music, reading, travel, photography, backpacking. Office: Waddell & Reed 8625 SW Cascade Ave Suite 290 Beaverton OR 97005

JOHNSON, MICHAEL DEAN, county official; b. Windom, Minn., Jan. 26, 1949; s. Milton and Marjean D. Johnson. BA, U. Colo., 1971, MPA, 1973. Econ. research asst. City of Boulder, Colo., 1971-73; sr. adminstrv. analyst San Mateo LAFCo, Redwood City, Calif., 1973-77; deputy county adminstrv. officer/local agy. formation exec. officer Monterey County, Calif., 1977-83; asst. county adminstrv. officer Monterey County, 1983—; lectr. on pub. adminstrn. Golden Gate U., Monterey, 1981-86; cons. econ. and govt. orgns., 1979—. Named one of Outstanding Young Men Am. Jaycees, 1984. Mem. Am. Soc. Pub. Adminstrs. (named Outstanding Pub. Adminstr. 1982), Nat. Assn. Intergovernmental Coordinators, Internat. City Mgrs. Assn. Democrat. Lutheran. Lodge: Rotary. Avocations: golf, hiking, backpacking, fishing, hunting. Home: 15249 Century Oak Rd Salinas CA 93907 Office: Monterey County PO Box 180 Salinas CA 93902

JOHNSON, NELS, accountant; b. Heppner, Oreg., Nov. 25, 1917; s. James J. and Elizabeth I. (Cox) J.; m. June C. Rose, Sept. 7, 1941; children—Carol, Terrance, Kathleen, Barbara. B.B.A., U. Oreg., 1947-50. C.P.A., Oreg. Staff acct. Harvey Michaelis, C.P.A., 1950-57; ptnr. Hunsaker & Johnson, C.P.A.s, 1957-79; sr. ptnr. Johnson & Glaze, C.P.A.s, Salem, Oreg., 1979-84; pres. Marion Devel. Co.; chmn. State Govtl. and Acctg. Com., 1967-68; pres., gen. mgr. Lucky Bar Mining Co., Golden, N.Mex; dir. Robert C. Beegle, Co., Inc. Served capt. U.S. Army, 19-. Decorated Bronze Battle Star with four oak leaf clusters. Mem. Am. Inst. C.P.A.s, Oreg. Soc. C.P.A.s. Republican. Lodges: Lions, Masons, Sons of Norway. Home: 14295 Spenner Rd Stayton OR 97383 Office: 3085 River Rd Salem OR 97303

JOHNSON, NORA ANN TONER, charter company executive, interior designer; b. Juneau, Alaska, Mar. 1, 1952; d. Felix and Mary Fredericka V. Toner; m. Paul Evert Johnson, Dec. 29, 1981. BBA, U. Portland, 1978. Village acct. Sealaska, Juneau, 1978-79; jr. acct. Alaska Div. Legis. Audit, Juneau, 1979-81; propr. Chicagof Charters, Elfin Cove, Alaska, 1981—, Elfin Gen. Supply, Elf Inn, J. & M. Fish Co., 1985—. Treas. Community of Elfin Cove Non-Profit Corp., 1984—; mem. Elfin Cove Adv. Sch. Bd., 1985—. Mem. Nat. Fedn. Ind. Businesses, Elfin Cove Hist. Soc. (sec./treas. 1986—), Elfin Cove Library Assn. (pres. 1986—). Democrat. Roman Catholic.

JOHNSON, NORDAHL KENT, mechanical engineer, wood company executive; b. Brigham City, Utah, Feb. 6, 1942; s. Chester Nordahl and Marie Townsend (Anderson) J.; m. Joyce Kay Hensley; children: Blain, Michelle, Kent, Cathryn, Kristina, Teresa. BSME, Utah State U., 1974. Product engr. Hesston Corp., Logan, Utah, 1974-76, Lockwood Corp., Gering, Nebr., 1976-79; div. project engring. mgr. incontinents products Weyerhaeuser Co., Tacoma, 1979—. Inventor diaper tape folding device, potato planter (Peno award), vibrating digger, process for applying slip elastic to diapers. Served to sgt. U.S. Army, 1960-66. Mem. ASME (assoc.), Am. Soc. Agrl. Engrs. (assoc., contbr. article Transactions (Hon. Mention 1985). Republican. Mormon. Lodge: Elks. Home: 13812 112th Ave Ct E Puyallup WA 98374 Office: Weyerhaeuser Co WTC 2C2 Tacoma WA 98477

JOHNSON, ODESSA PETERSON, college administrator; b. Greenville, S.C., Apr. 26, 1939; d. Richard and Silvere (Moore) Peterson; m. Lure J. Johnson, Oct. 20, 1973; 1 child, Sylvia Lorraine. BS, Tenn. State U., 1960; MA, Columbia U., 1962. Cert. bus. tchr., community coll. counselor, Calif. Tchr. Modesto (Calif.) City Schs., 1962-70; counselor Modesto Jr. Coll., 1960-84, community services asst., 1984-85, community services dir., 1985-87, asst. dean, 1987—. Bd. dirs. Muir Trail council Girl Scouts Am., 1983—, Modesto Symphony, 1986—;founder Women's Leadership Devel. Program, Modesto, 1985; mem. Congl. Awards Council, Merced, Calif., 1985—; mem. Foward Modesto Commn., 1987. Named one of Leaders of 80s in Community Colls., League for Innovations in Community Colls., 1984, Outstanding Woman in Stanislaus County (Calif.), Stanislaus County Commn. for Women, 1981. Mem. Stanislaus County Industry/Edn. Council, Modesto C. of C. (chair end. com. 1985-86), Black C. of C. (organizer), Western Assn. Schs. and Colls. Accrediting Commn., Delta Kappa Gamma (chpt. pres. 1984-86), Delta Sigma Theta (life). Democrat. Lodge: Soroptomists (Modesto North Soroptomist of Yr. 1986). Avocation: camping. Home: 3012 Prince Valiant Ln Modesto CA 95350 Office: Modesto Jr Coll Community Services 435 College Ave Modesto CA 95350

JOHNSON, PATRICIA GAYLE, corporate communication executive, writer; b. Conway, Ark., Oct. 23, 1947; d. Rudolph and Frances Modene (Hayes) J. Student U. Calif., Irvine, 1965-68. Advance rep. Disney on Parade, Los Angeles, 1971-75; mktg. dir./dir. field ops. Am. Freedom Train, Los Angeles, 1975-77; publ. relations mgr. Six Flags, Inc., Los Angeles, 1977-81; mgr. corp. communications Playboy Enterprises, Inc., Los Angeles, 1981-82; external relations mgr. Kal Kan Foods, Inc., Los Angeles, 1982-86; v.p. Daniel J. Edelman, Inc., 1986—; lectr. U. So. Calif., UCLA, Calif. State U., Northridge, Calif. State U., Dominguez Hills. Mem. Pub. Relations Soc. Am. (past officer), Pub. Affairs Council, Delta Soc. (advisor). Mem. Foursquare Gospel Ch. Collaborator TV scripts; contbr. articles to various consumer and profl. mags. Office: Daniel J Edelman Inc 1925 Century Park E Suite 260 Los Angeles CA 90067

JOHNSON, PATRICIA LYNN, marketing professional; b. Des Moines, July 13, 1959; d. Robert Andrew and Kathleen Noel (Heckel) J. Sec. ITT Fin., Mpls., 1979-80; mgr. office Pacific Duplicator Systems Inc., Santa Ana, Calif., 1980-81; sec., service Toshiba Am. Inc., Tustin, Calif., 1981-83, systems coordinator, 1983-85, spl. markets adminstr., 1985, product support specialist, 1986—. Avocations: bowling, sewing, needlecraft, computer programming.

JOHNSON, PAUL WILLIAM, JR., insurance broker; b. Melbourne, Fla., Apr. 13, 1935; s. Paul William and Mabel (Rose) J.; m. Lee Kriloff, Aug. 15, 1959; children: Paul W. III, Carter W., Gay W.; m. Ruth E. Kindel, July 13, 1981. BSBA, U. Fla., 1957. CPCU. Sales rep. Prudential Ins. Co. Am., San Francisco, 1960; underwriter Fireman's Fund Ins. Co., San Francisco, 1960-63; producer Pickett-Rothholz, Sacramento, Calif., 1963-68, Ferris & Butler Co., Sacramento, 1968-72; ptnr. Henderson & Dreyer, Inc., Sacramento, 1972—; bd. dirs. Ind. Ins. Agts. Assn. Sacramento, 1967-72, pres., 1970-71; bd. dirs. Calif. Ind. Ins. Agts. Assn., 1973-76. Active Sacramento Jaycees, 1963-66; pres. Sacramento Assn. for Retarded, 1971-73; past pres. Good Shepherd Luth. Home Parents Assn., Terra Bella, Calif.; mem. Sacramento County Developmentally Disabled Planning Commn. Served with USMCR, 1957-60, with Res., 1960-77. Named Agy. Adminstr. of Yr. Sacramento Ins. Agts. Assn., 1983. Mem. CPCU's Am. (pres. Sacramento Valley chpt. 1985-87). Republican. Avocations: golf, tennis, gardening, hunting, fishing. Home: 421 Sierra Ln Sacramento CA 95864

JOHNSON, PAULA GAYLE, interior designer; b. Owensboro, Ky., Nov. 2, 1947; d. Annis Paul Stogner and Jane Elizabeth (Trunnel) Stogner-Williams; m. David March Johnson, June 10, 1967; children: Branon David, Bradley Lawrence, Erica Jane. BS, Okla. State U., 1969. Interior designer Dallas Power & Light Co., 1969-71, Stateside Furniture Co., La Jolla, Calif., 1973-75, Homestead House, Denver, 1978-80; free lance interior design Colorado Springs, Colo., 1980-84; prin. Paula Johnson Interior Design, Inc., Colorado Springs, 1984—; instr. interior decorating, Zweibrucken, Fed. Republic Germany, 1973-75, Grand Forks, N.D., 1975-77, Colorado Springs, 1984—. Mem. Colorado Springs Symphony guild-En Coups, 1985—. Mem. Am. Soc. Interior Designers (assoc.), Dental Wives' Soc., Colorado Springs Jr. League, Kappa Alpha Theta Alumnae Assn. Republican. Clubs: Country of Colo. (Colorado Springs), Plaza (Colorado Springs). Home: 4110 Stepney Ct Colorado Springs CO 80906 Office: 128 E Cheyenne Rd Colorado Springs CO 80906

JOHNSON, PEARL FAY, accountant; b. Orange, Calif., Dec. 11, 1946; d. Cecil Louis and Alberta May (Jordan) J.; B.S., Whittier Coll., 1968. Cert. elem. tchr., Calif. Tchr. Los Angeles City Schs., 1970-71; clk. Alaska Dept. Commerce, Juneau, 1971-72; teller, acct. B.M. Behrends Bank, Juneau, 1972-74; acct. Alaska Dept. Transp., Juneau, 1975-80, Alaska Dept. Health and Social Services, Juneau, 1981-87. Mem. LWV, Western History Assn., Am. Assn. Individual Investors. Democrat.

JOHNSON, PETER NEILS, motion picture producer, educator; b. Caldwell, Idaho, Jan. 25, 1944; s. Clifford Lewis and Afton (Thueson) J.; m. Ann Lee Johnson, Aug. 15, 1981; children: Emily Ann, Daniel Peter. BA, Brigham Young U., 1968, MA, 1972. Dialogue dir. Quinn Martin Prodns.-NBC, San Francisco, 1974-78, Lorimar Prodns.-NBC, Los Angeles, 1979; pvt. practice producing, directing Los Angeles, 1980-83; exec. producer Motion Picture Studio Brigham Young U., Provo, Utah, 1983—. Author First Flight, 1986; dialogue dir. The Streets of San Francisco, 1974; dir. The Restoration, 1982, Man's Search for Happiness, 1986. Served as sgt. U.S. Army, 1968-70. Recipient Cine Golden Eagle U.S. Indsl. Film Festival, Washington, Gold Camera award U.S. Indsl. Film Festival, Chgo., Gold award Internat. Film and TV Festival of N.Y., N.Y.C., award Chgo. Internat. Film Festival. Mem. Dirs. Guild Am., Phi Kappa Phi. Democrat. Mormon. Skiing. Office: Brigham Young U Motion Picture Studio Provo UT 84602

JOHNSON, QULAN ADRIAN, software engr.; b. Gt. Falls, Mont., Sept. 17, 1942; s. Raymond Eugene and Bertha Marie (Nagengast) J.; m. Helen Louise Pocha, July 24, 1965; children—Brenda Marie, Douglas Paul, Scot Paul, Mathew James. B.A. in Psychology, Coll. Gt. Falls, 1964. Lead operator 1st Computer Corp., Helena, Mont., 1966-67; v.p., sec.-treas. Computer Corp. of Mt., Great Falls, 1967-76, dir., 1971-76; sr. systems analyst Mont. Dept. Revenue, Helena, 1976-78; software engr. Mont. Systems Devel. Co., Helena, 1978-80; programmer/analyst III info. systems div. Mont. Dept. Adminstrn., Helena, 1980-82; systems analyst centralized services Dept. Social and Rehab. Services State of Mont., 1982-87, systems and programming mgr. info systems, Blue Cross and Blue SHiled of Montana, Helena, 1987—. Mem. Assn. for Systems Mgmt., Mont. Data Processing Assn., Data Processing Mgmt. Assn., Mensa. Club: K.C. (rec. sec. 1975-76). Home: 2231 8th Ave Helena MT 59601 Office: Blue Cross and Blue Shield Info Systems 404 Fuller Ave Helena MT 59604-4309

JOHNSON, R. ROGER, computer company executive; b. Redwing, Minn., Aug. 18, 1949; s. Robert Kenneth and Geraldine Ann Johnson; m. Zaiga Taube, Sept. 15, 1973; children: Angela C., David C. BChemE, U. Minn., 1972, MPH, 1976. Engr. Environ. Research Corp., St. Paul, 1972-73; cons. Interpoll Inc., St. Paul, 1973-76; exec. v.p. York Research Cons., Lakewood, Colo., 1976-84; pres. Solutech Corp., Lakewood, 1984—. V.p. Luth. Ch. of the Master, Lakewood, 1986-87, pres., 1987—. Mem. Am. Pollution Control Assn. (bd. dirs. Rocky Mountain States sect. 1982-85, sec., 1986-87, treas. 1985-86, pres. 1987—), Am. Inst. Chem. Engrs., Energy Conservation Assn. (v.p., bd. dirs. 1982—). Lodge: Kiwanis (local treas. 1984-85). Office: Solutech Corp 12600 W Colfax Ave Suite C-420 Lakewood CO 80215

JOHNSON, REBECCA (REBECCA VON IFFT), public relations director; b. East Moline, Ill., June 24, 1950; d. Raymond Harold and Alberta Dean (Powell) Ifft; m. Rex T. Johnson, May 21, 1973 (div. Dec. 1980). Student, Temple Buell Women's Coll., 1968-69; BA, Colo. State U., 1972. Community relations dir. F&W Enterprises, Colorado Springs, Colo., 1975-77, Pikes Peak YMCA, Colorado Springs, Colo., 1977; pub. relations dir. Gates Land Co., Colorado Springs, Colo., 1977—. Author: Everyone's Complete Astrology and Horoscope, 1971, Astrology for Men, 1972, Astrology for Women, 1972. Bd. dirs Pikes Peak Hospice, 1980, com. mem. 1980-86; adv. bd. dirs. Colorado Springs Park and Recreation, 1979-82, The Riegel Ctr. for Alcoholism, Colorado Springs, 1985; campaign chmn. Harris for County Commr., Colorado Springs, 1980, 84. Mem. Pub. Relations Soc. Am., Pikes Peak Ad Fedn., Kappa Kappa Gamma (v.p. 1971-72). Republican. Episcopalian. Club: Jr. League (Colorado Springs). Office: Gates Land Co 155 W Lake Ave Colorado Springs CO 80906

JOHNSON, RICHARD ALLEN, telecommunications executive; b. Mobile, Ala., Oct. 23, 1943; s. Raymond Richard and Helen Louise Johnson; m. Carolyn Murphy, Oct. 23, 1965; children: Sherril, Richard M. AA, Harris Jr. Coll., 1963; BSEE, Washington U., 1965; postgrad., St. Louis U., 1966-69; MS in Engring. Mgmt., U. Mo., Rolla, 1981. Registered profl. engr., Calif., Mo. Equipment engr. Southwestern Bell Telephone Co., Kansas City, Mo., 1969-73, dir. personnel assessment, 1973-74; dist. staff mgr. Southwestern Bell Telephone Co., St. Louis, 1974-79; regional dir. GTE Corp., Stamford, Conn., 1979-81, dir. hdqrs., 1981-83; mgr. telecom Pacific Gas & Electric Co., San Francisco, 1983—. Author tng. course Equipment Engring. Mgmt., 1973; contbr. articles to profl. jours. Coach and adminstr. Youth Baseball and Basketball. Named Top-ranking grad. Nat. Bell System Ctr. Advanced Communications System Tng., 1968; recipient Service Excellence award Pacific Gas and Electric, 1984. Mem. IEEE (sr., chpt. chmn. 1985-86), Telecommunications Edn. Council (chmn., dir. 1984—). Republican. Roman Catholic. Club: Commonwealth of Calif. (San Francisco). Avocations: manual crafts, golf, oil painting, coaching. Home: 1096 Lehigh Valley Circle Danville CA 94526 Office: Pacific Gas & Electric Co 245 Market St Rm 244 San Francisco CA 94106

JOHNSON, RICHARD DAMERAU, astronautic scientist; b. Zanesville, Ohio, Oct. 28, 1934; s. Earl G. and Merlie D. J.; m. Catherine Collins, Dec. 30, 1969; children: Laurana, Karen, Eric, Gregory. BA, Oberlin Coll., 1956; MS, Carnegie-Mellon U., 1961, PhD, 1962; SM, MIT, 1982. Postdoctoral fellow UCLA, 1961-62; sr. scientist Jet Propulsion Lab., Pasadena, Calif., 1962-63; with NASA, 1963-85, chief life scis. flight expts. office, 1973-76; chief biosystems div. Ames Research Center NASA, Moffett Field, Calif., 1976-85; sr. tech. cons. Tech. and Innovation Mgmt. Ctr. SRI Internat., Menlo Park, Calif., 1985—; vis. lectr. Stanford U. Contbr. papers in field. Recipient Exceptional Service medal NASA, 1976; Alfred P. Sloan fellow M.I.T., 1981-82. Mem. Am. Chem. Soc., AAAS, AIAA. Home: 11564 Arroyo Oaks Los Altos CA 94022 Office: SRI Internat 333 Ravenswood Ave Menlo Park CA 94025

JOHNSON, (ERIC D.) RICK, advertising executive. BA in English and Psychology, U. N.Mex., 1965; postgrad., U. Wis., 1975. With mgmt. tng. program Wells Fargo Bank, San Francisco, 1965; asst. v.p., advt. mgr. Albuquerque Nat. Bank, 1967-74; v.p., acct. exec. Mellekas & Assocs. Advt., 1974-75; v.p., mktg. dir. First Nat. Bank Albuquerque, 1975-77; chmn., pres. Rick Johnson & Co., Inc., 1977. Bd. dirs. N.Mex. Symphony Orch., YMCA, Community Council, UNICEF; mem. publs. com., mem. devel. council, dir. search com. for pub. info. U. N.Mex., mem. budget com. United Way, mem. Robert O. Anderson Sch. Mgmt. Found. Mem. Am. Assn.

Advt. Agys. (vice chmn. Sun Country Council), N.Mex. Advt. Fedn., C. of C. (bd. dirs.). Office: 1200 Pennsylvania NE Albuquerque NM 87110

JOHNSON, ROBERT BETHUNE, geography educator; b. St. Louis, Dec. 4, 1920; s. James Forbes and Ora (Bethune) J.; m. June Main, Nov. 7, 1942 (dec. Aug. 1979); children: Kathryn Forbes Allison, Leslie Main Johnson-Gottesfield; m. Dorothy Ann Rogers, Mar. 28, 1980 (dec. Jan. 1985). AB, Wash. U., St. Louis, 1938; MA, Harvard U., 1947, PhD, 1960. Fellow Syracuse (N.Y.) U., 1946-47; asst. prof. geography St. Lawrence U., Canton, N.Y., 1949-50; dir. advt. research Itek Corp., Waltham, Mass., 1959; dir. programs tempo Gen. Electric Co., Santa Barbara, Calif., 1959-61; pres. Prescott (Ariz.) Schole, 1971-72; prof. geography, chmn. dept. Calif. State U. at Domenguez Hills, Carson, 1972—, prof. emeritus, acting chmn., 1986—; proprietor Johnson Research Assocs., Santa Barbara, 1961-71; lectr. U. Calif., Santa Barbara, 1960-63; cons. Santa Barbara County Sch., 1962-66. Author/editor: California Patterns on the Land, 5th edit., 1976, Projected World Patterns, 1962-70; also articles. Mem. planning adv. com. City of Los Angeles, San Pedro, Calif., 1974-82, Citizens Adv. Com. Community Plan, San Pedro, 1974-82, Rep. Cen. Com., Los Angeles, 1976-83. Served as cpl. USAAF, 1943-45, capt. U.S. Army, 1951-52. Fellow Am. Geog. Soc.; mem. Assn. Am. Geographers, Assn. Pacific Coast Geographers, Sigma Xi. Republican. Avocations: photography, travel, fishing. Home: 2534 Graysby Ave San Pedro CA 90732 Office: Calif State U Dominguez Hills Dept Geography 1000 E Victoria St Carson CA 90747

JOHNSON, ROBERT WAYNE, designer, architect; b. Warrenton, Va., Sept. 3, 1948; s. John Walden and DeNiece Trennis (Orndoff) J. BArch, Va. Polytech. Inst. and State U., 1973. Architect, planner Dept. Navy, Washington, 1973-76; freelance photographer Los Angeles, 1976-78; prin. F&R Johnson Inc., N.Y.C. and Warrenton, 1978-81, Israel-Johnson Design Studio, Santa Monica, Calif., 1982-83; look coordinator LAOOC/Jerde Partnership, Los Angeles, 1984; pres. Archisis Design Corp., Santa Monica, Calif., 1985—; vis. critic U. So. Calif., 1982-84. Look coordinator Design Quarterly Mag., 1984 Los Angeles Olympics; designed Palette Restaurant, 1984, A.P.L.A. Shelter Taskforce, 1986; participant La Jolla Mus. Archtl. Show, 1983. Founder No. Va. Regional Theatre Corp., Warrenton, 1980. Grantee Hotel and Restaurant Giant Interior Design mag., 1986; recipient Spl. Design award AIA, 1984. Fellow Washington Acad. Scis.; mem. Archtl. Found. Los Angeles (founding mem. 1986—), Constrn. Specification Inst. Office: Archisis Design Corp 1920 Main St Suite #7 Santa Monica CA 90405

JOHNSON, RODNEY DALE, policeman, photographer; b. Montebello, Calif., May 14, 1944; s. Albert Gottfreid and Maxine Elliot (Rogers) J.; m. Karen Rae Van Antwerp, May 18, 1968. A.A., Ela Community Coll., 1973; postgrad. Law Enforcement Spl., F.B.I., Acad., 1976; B.A., U. of La Verne, 1978. Cert. tchr. police sci., Calif. Dep., Los Angeles County Sheriff, 1969-75, dep. IV, 1976-78, sgt., 1978—; fire arms inst., Hacienda Heights, Calif., 1975—; photography instr., Hacienda Heights, 1983—; pres. Wheelhouse Enterprises, Inc., Whittier, 1971-86; instr. State Sheriff's Civil Procedural Sch. Los Medanos Coll., Concord, Calif., 1985—. Creator and actor, Cap'n Andy, 1973-80; song writer for Cap'n Andy theme, 1972. Served with USMC, 1965-69, Vietnam. Recipient Service award Trinity Broadcasting Network, 1979. Mem. Profl. Peace Officers Assn., Sheriff's Relief Assn., Assoc. Photographers Internat. Republican. Mem. Assembly of God. Club: Faithbuilders (pres. 1981—), (Pomona).

JOHNSON, ROGER HARRY, ophthalmologist; b. Madison, Wis., Jan. 29, 1914; s. Harry John and Louise Augusta (Nissalk) J.; m. Elizabeth Louise Hill, July 27, 1940 (div.); children—Roger H., Trygve N., Casey. B.S., U. Wis., 1937, M.D., 1939. Intern U. Oreg., Portland, 1939-40; resident Mayo Clinic, U. Minn., Rochester, 1941-45; practice medicine specializing in ophthalmology, Seattle, 1945—; clin. prof. ophthalmology U. Wash. Contbr. articles to profl. jours. Recipient Roger Johnson annual lecture award Children's Orthopedic Hosp., Seattle, 1984. Fellow Am. Acad. Ophthalmology; mem. AMA, Pacific Coast Soc. Ophthalmology, King County Med. Soc., Interocular Lens Soc. Republican. Home: 4201 NE 33rd St Seattle WA 98101 Office: Doctors Office 414 Cobb Bldg Seattle WA 98101

JOHNSON, ROGER MILES, marketing research and consulting company executive; b. Mpls., Oct. 30, 1921; s. Arthur H. and Ella M. (Mortensen) J.; m. Marian Elizabeth Scott, June 12, 1943; children—Craig W., Brian L. Student DePauw U., 1939-40; B.S., Northwestern U., 1943. Exec. asst. Ford Sammis, mktg. economist, Los Angeles, 1946-49; mktg. cons. George Fry & Assocs., Chgo., 1950-51; sr. v.p., mktg. dir. Erwin Wasey Co., Los Angeles, 1952-64, N.W. Ayer Co., 1964-68; mgr., mktg. cons. Peat, Marwick, Mitchell & Co., Los Angeles, 1968-69; pres. Roger Johnson & Assocs., Inc., Arcadia, Calif., 1969—; lectr. mktg. research Calif. State U.-Los Angeles, 1979-85, chmn. mktg. adv. bd., 1982-84. Served to lt. USN, 1943-46. Recipient Guy E. Marion award Los Angeles C. of C., 1974. Mem. Am. Mktg. Assn. (Mktg. Success Yr. award 1979, former pres. So. Calif. sect. 1969-70, v.p., nat. dir. 1975-76). Republican. Club: Rotary (Los Angeles). Editor: Dynamics of the Youth Explosion, 1967; What Makes Southern California Different, 1970. Home: 1725 N Santa Anita Ave Arcadia CA 91006 Office: Roger Johnson & Assocs 150 n Santa Anita Ave Suite 645 Arcadia CA 91006

JOHNSON, RONALD KAYE, retail company executive; b. Abilene, Tex., Feb. 26, 1939; s. Vernon Floyd and Mattye Sue (Milburn) J.; m. Sally Ann Fleet, Nov. 22, 1962 (div.); 1 dau., Sheri May. B.A. with honors in Theatre Arts, Eastern Wash. State U., 1971. Div. mgr. Nutrition Centers Fred Meyer, Inc., Portland, Oreg., 1971—, v.p. Nutrition Ctrs. div., 1979—. Actor Lake Oswego (Oreg.) Civic Theatre, 1979—. Recipient Best Supporting Actor award Spokane Civic Theatre, 1967-68; Oreg. Theat. Soc. Best Actor award, 1980-81. Breeder 1965 Nat. Grand Champion Appaloosa mare. Republican. Presbyterian. Office: Fred Meyer Inc PO Box 42121 Portland OR 97242

JOHNSON, ROYAL M., civil service administrative officer, consultant; b. Spokane, Wash., May 31, 1944; s. Ward Willis and Juanita May (Whitmore) J.; m. Anne-Marie Marshall Seale, Feb. 4, 1965 (div. Sept. 1979); children: Veronica Anne, Chad Lewis, Dale Richard; m. Virginia Laverne Pelton, June 15, 1981; stepchildren: Cynthia Conner, David Conner, Debra Conner. AA, Ventura Community Coll., 1971; BA, LaVerne U., 1972; MA, Columbia Pacific U., 1986, postgrad., 1986—. Prodn. dispatcher Naval Missile Ctr., Pt. Mugu, Calif., 1969-71, adminstrv. asst., 1971-74, mgmt. analyst, 1974-75; adminstrv. officer Shasta Lake Ranger Dist., Redding, Calif., 1975-77; program mgr. Shasta-Trinity Nat. Forest, Redding, 1977-79; adminstrv. officer Tongass Nat. Forest, Ketchikan, Alaska, 1979—; Bd. dirs. Royal Assocs., Ketchikan; pres. Opportunity Cons., Anderson, Calif., 1976-79. Author: (pamphlet) The Complete, Realistic Self-Hypnosis Program, 1982, (audio cassette) The Outside Assistance Program, 1982. Served with U.S. Army, 1961-64, Korea. Avocations: small bus. and home computer consultation, counseling, fishing. Home: PO Box 7158 Ketchikan AK 99901 Office: USDA Forest Service Fed Bldg Ketchikan AK 99901

JOHNSON, SARA JANE, audiology educator; b. Helena, Mont., May 5, 1956; d. Franklin Quentin and Ruth Ann (Sackett) J. BA, U. Mont., 1978; MA, Northwestern U., 1981. Clin. audiologist Stanford (Calif.) U. Med. Ctr., 1981-84; lectr. U. Mont., Missoula, 1985—; Vis. scholar Stanford U., 1981. Contbr. articles to profl. jours. Mem. Am. Speech Lang. Hearing Assn. (cert.), Mont. Speech Lang. Hearing Assn., Am. Auditory Soc., Mont. Healthy Mothers-Healthy Babies, Coll. and Univ. Suprs. Avocations: running, telemark skiing, weaving, kayaking. Office: U Mont Dept Communication Scis & Disorders Missoula MT 59812

JOHNSON, STANLEY OWEN, engineering company executive; b. Bismarck, N.D., Dec. 28, 1930; s. Clifford and Olga May (Steen) J.; m. Janet Ayers Chord, Aug. 3, 1957 (div. Dec. 1982); children: Kristin Marie, Eric Robert. BSEE, U. Colo., 1953; postgrad., U. Pitts., 1954-56. Registered profl. engr., Idaho. Engr. Westinghouse Electric Corp., Pitts., 1953-56, supr., 1956-61; sect. head Phillips Petroleum Co., Idaho Falls, Idaho, 1961-68; br. mgr. Phillips Petroleum Co., Idaho Falls, 1968-71, Idaho Nuclear Corp., Idaho Falls, 1971-73; pres. Intermountain Technologies, Inc., Idaho Falls, 1973—; v.p., bd. dirs. Aspen Security Advisors, Idaho Falls, 1985—, The Rockwood Growth Fund, Idaho Falls, 1985—. Contbr. articles to profl. jours.; inventor. Fellow Am. Nuclear Soc. (Exceptional Service award 1980); mem. NSPE, Idaho Soc. Profl. Engrs., Idaho Falls C. of C. Presbyterian. Avocations: flying, skiing. Office: Intermountain Technologies Inc PO Box 1604 Idaho Falls ID 83403-1604

JOHNSON, STEPHEN MICHAEL, geologist, physical scientist; b. Atlanta, Mar. 1, 1950; s. Robert Overn and Eve Lenora (Vernon) J. BA, U. Colo., 1972; MS, Colo. Sch. Mines, 1977. Project geologist Western Nuclear Inc., Denver, 1977-79; exploration geologist Tenneco Minerals Inc., Denver, 1980-83; ptnr. Roubaix Mining Venture, Golden, Colo., 1979—, Taborite Mining Co., Denver, 1985—; cons. Lithologic Research Co., Denver, 1983—. Contbr. articles to profl. jours. Western Nuclear Inc. research fellow, Golden, 1977. Mem. Am. Inst. Profl. Geologists (cert.), Geol. Soc. Am., Assn. Exploration Geochemists. Democrat. Unitarian. Avocations: inventing, technical writing. Home: 624 Ammons Way Lakewood CO 80215 Office: Lithologic Research Co PO Box 872 Golden CO 80402

JOHNSON, STEWART WILLARD, civil engineer; b. Mitchell, S.D., Aug. 17, 1933; s. James Elmer Johnson and Grace Mahala (Erwin) Johnson Parsons; m. Mary Anis Giddings, June 24, 1956; children: Janelle Chiemi, Gregory Stewart, Eric Willard. BSCE, S.D. State U., 1956; BA in Bus. Adminstrn. and Polit. Sci., U. Md., 1960; MSCE, PhD, U. Ill., 1964. Registered profl. engr., Ohio. Commd. 2d lt. USAF, 1956, advanced through grades to lt. col.; prof. mechs. and civil engring. Air Force Inst. Tech. USAF, Dayton, Ohio, 1964-75; dir. civil engring. USAF, Seoul, Republic of Korea, 1976-77; chief civil engring. research div. USAF, Kirtland AFB, N.Mex., 1977-80; ret. USAF, 1980; prin. engr. BDM Corp., Albuquerque, 1980—; cons. in space sci. and lunar basing to NASA, U. N.Mex., Los Alamos (N.Mex.) Nat. Labs., 1986—. Contbr. articles to profl. jours. Pres. ch. council Ch. of Good Shepherd United Ch. Christ, Albuquerque, 1983-85. Fellow Nat. Acad. Scis. NRC, 1970-71. Mem. AIAA, AAAS, ASCE (chmn. exec. com. aerospace div. 1979, tech. activities com. 1984, Aerospace and Tech. award 1985, Outstnding News Corr. award 1981), Am. Geophys. Union, Sigma Xi, Pi Sigma Alpha. Republican. Mem. United Ch. of Christ. Avocations: photography, swimming, running, gardening. Office: BDM Corp 1801 Randolph Rd SE Albuquerque NM 87106

JOHNSON, SYLVIA JEWELL, corrections facility administrator; b. Los Angeles, Sept. 25, 1936; d. Virgie B. Benson and Jewell L. (Franklin) Greenwood; m. Edward L. Mitchell (div. 1970); 1 child, Holly J. BA in Sociology, U. So. Calif., 1958, certs. in Mgmt. Techniques, Collective Bargaining, 1978-82; cert. in Adult and Adolescent Drug Abuse Group Counseling, Los Angeles Ctr. for Group Psychotherapy, 1971; cert. in Effective Treatment of Offenders, Adult and Adolescent, Charles Drew Postgrad. Med. Sch., 1975-76. With Los Angeles County Probation Dept., 1960-76; substance abuse counselor, program consultant Riverside County Health Dept., 1977-80; dep. supt. Calif. Instn. for Women, Chino, 1980-81; supt. Calif. Instn. for Women, 1981-84; dir. San Bernardino County (Calif.) Juvenile Hall, 1985—; tng. cons. State of Calif. Dept. of Youth Authority, Santa Barbara, Calif., USCSch. of Social Work. Recipient In Recognition of Outstanding Pub. Service and Personal Achievement, 1981, Disting. Citizen Award for Service County of Riverside, 1983, Myrtle Robinson Achievement Award Elites Club, Riverside, 1983; named Outstanding Citizen Alpha Kappa Alpha, Inc., San Bernardino, Calif., 1984. Mem. Am. Correctional Assn., Calif. Probation Parole and Correctional Assn., NAACP, Nat. Urban League, Black Women's Forum. Democrat. Avocations: reading, music, jewelry business.

JOHNSON, THOMAS EUGENE, gerontology, genetics and molecular biology educator, researcher; b. Denver, June 19, 1948; s. Albert L. Johnson and Barbara J. (Bickle) Lloyd; m. Victoria J. Simpson, Apr. 24, 1982; 1 child, Ariel Rene. BS, MIT, 1970; PhD, U. Wash., 1975. Research assoc. Cornell U., Ithaca, N.Y., 1975-77, U. Colo., Boulder, 1977-82; fellow Inst. Behavioral Genetics U. Colo., Denver, 1981-82; asst. prof. U. Calif., Irvine, 1982—; mem. com. on chem. toxicity and aging Nat. Research Council, Washington, 1986—; speaker Brookhaven (N.Y.) Symposium, 1986, Med. Biol. Theory of Aging, N.Y.C., 1986. Editor: Invert. Models in Aging Research, 1984; contbr. articles to profl. jours. Grantee USPHS, Washington, 1978, 85, NSF, Washington, 1982; USPHS fellow 1977. Fellow Gerontology Soc. of Am., Am. Fedn. for Aging Research; mem. AAAS, Soc. Devel. Biology, Genetics Soc. Am., Am. Aging Assn. Democrat. Unitarian. Avocations: tennis, backpacking. Office: U Calif Dept Molecular Biology & Biochemistry Irvine CA 92717

JOHNSON, TOM See JOHNSON, WYATT THOMAS, JR.

JOHNSON, VERNON EUGENE, corporate lawyer; b. Omaha, Feb. 11, 1930; s. Eugene Howard and Thelma Kathleen (Carter) J.; m. Martha Alvo, Dec. 18, 1953; children: Pamela Robin, Denise Gaye Johnson Holder. Student, U. Nebr., Omaha, 1948-50; JD, Pepperdine U., 1969. Bar: Calif. 1970. Lather foreman W.F. Hayward Co., Inglewood, Calif., 1956-66; claims rep. United Pacific Ins. Co., Pasadena, Calif., 1966-70; atty. United Pacific Ins. Co., Los Angeles, 1970-73; atty., dept. mgr. Western Employers Ins., Fullerton, Calif., 1973—; arbitrator, judge pro tem Orange Co. Superior Ct., Santa Ana, 1981—; arbitrator Am. Arbitration Assn., Los Angeles, 1975—. Chmn. Ways and Means com. Western High Sch. Drill Team, Anaheim, Calif., 1973; served to cpl. U.S. Army, 1951-53. Mem. Orange County Bar Assn., Calif. Bar Assn., (conf. del. 1982, 83, 86), So. Calif. Rehab. Exchange. Republican. Protestant. Home: 4480 Guava Ave Seal Beach CA 90740 Office: Metz, Johnson & Larson 1400 N Harbor Blvd Fullerton CA 92635

JOHNSON, WALTER EARL, geophysicist; b. Denver, Dec. 16, 1942; s. Earl S. and Helen F. (Llewellyn) J.; Geophys. Engr., Colo. Sch. Mines, 1966; m. Ramey Kandice Kayes, Aug. 6, 1967; children—Gretchen, Roger, Aniela. Geophysicist, Pan. Am. Petroleum Corp., 1966-73; seismic processing supr. Amoco Prodn. Co., Denver, 1973-74, marine tech. supr., 1974-76, div. processing cons., 1976-79, geophys. supr. No. Thrust Belt, 1979-80; chief geophysicist Husky Oil Co., 1981-82, exploration mgr. Rocky Mountain and Gulf Coast div., 1982-84; geophys. mgr. ANR Prodn. Co., 1985—; pres. Sch. Lateral Ditch Co.; cons. engr. Bd. dirs. Rocky Mountain Residence, nursing home. Registered profl. engr., cert. geologist, Colo. Mem. Denver Geophys. Soc., Soc. Exploration Geophysicists. Republican. Baptist. Office: 6060 S Willow Dr Englewood CO 80111

JOHNSON, WALTER WILLIAM, librarian; b. Grand Rapids, Mich., Oct. 21, 1925; s. Carl and Dewey (Vander Mass) J.; B.A., Mich. State U., 1949, M.A. in Art, 1950; M.S. in L.S., U. So. Calif., 1957; m. Marcelon Cadeaux Matteson, Apr. 9, 1948; children—Koe Johnson-Orneles, Brook, Camille, Leigh, Stacy Ferl, Chad. Tchr. art poly. High Sch., Long Beach, Calif., 1950-51, Artesia (Calif.) High Sch., 1952-53; librarian Calif. State U., Long Beach, 1956-58; dir. Huntington Beach Library, Calif., 1958—; sec. to Allied Arts Bd.; liaison to Allied Arts Assn. Former pres. Orange Coast Unitarian-Universalist Ch. Served with inf. AUS, 1944-45. Decorated Bronze Star, Purple Heart. Mem. Public Adminstrs. Orange County (past pres.), Orange County Library Assn. (past pres.), Public Library Execs. So. Calif., Calif. Library Assn., ALA. Club: Rotary. Office: Huntington Beach Library 7111 Talbert St Huntington Beach CA 92648 *

JOHNSON, WARREN ARTHUR, geography educator, writer; b. Oakland, Calif., June 12, 1937; s. Arthur Alexander and Linnea Maria (Anderson) J.; m. Martha Ann Davidson, Dec. 20, 1958 (div. Jan. 1986); children: Aaron David, Blake Eliot; m. Elizabeth Moore, Dec. 19, 1986. BCE, U. Calif., Berkeley, 1959; MS in Natural Resources, U. Mich., 1966, PhD in Natural Resources, 1969. Civ. engr. Nat. Park Service, various Western U.S. locations, 1960-67; prof. geography San Diego State U., 1969—; lectr. Fullbright Commn., Liberia, West Africa, 1983-84. Author: The Future is Not What it Used to Be, 1985, Muddling Toward Frugality, 1978, rev. edit. 1979, Public Parks on Private Lands in England and Wales, 1971; editor Economic Growth vs. the Environment, 1971. Bd. dirs. Campus YMCA San Diego State U., 1973—. Fullbright research scholar, England, 1974-75. Mem. Human Econ. Ctr. (dir. 1979-81), Sierra Club. Roman Catholic. Avocations: building, farming, hiking, photography. Office: San Diego State U Geography Dept San Diego CA 92182

JOHNSON, WAYNE HAROLD, librarian, state official; b. El Paso, Tex., May 2, 1942; s. Earl Harold and Cathryn Louise (Greeno) J.; m. Patricia Ann Froedge, June 15, 1973; 1 child, Meredith Jessica. B.S., Utah State U., 1968; M.P.A., U. Colo., 1970; M.L.S., U. Okla., 1972. Circulation librarian Utah State U., Logan, 1968, adminstrv. asst. librarian, 1969; research Okla. Mgmt. and Engring. Cons., Norman, 1972; chief adminstrv. services Wyo. State Library, Cheyenne, 1973-76, chief bus. officer library archives and hist. dept., 1976-78, state librarian, 1978—. Trustee Bibliog. Center for Research, Denver, pres., 1983, 84; Cheyenne dist. Longs Peak council Boy Scouts Am., 1982—; mem. Cheyenne Frontier Days, 1975—; v.p. Cheyenne/Laramie County Airport Bd., 1980, pres., 1981-85, 87. Served with USCG, 1960-64. Mem. ALA, Wyo. Library Assn., Aircraft Owners and Pilots Assn., Cheyenne C. of C. (chmn. transp. com. 1982, 83). Democrat. Presbyterian. Club: No. Colo. Yacht. Lodges: Masons, Kiwanis (bd. dirs. 1986, 87, Cheyenne Frontier Days 1975—). Office: Wyo State Library Cheyenne WY 82002

JOHNSON, WILLARD LYON, JR., humanities educator; b. Des Moines, May 30, 1939; s. Willard Lyon and Margerie Elta (Hackenberg) J. B.A., Oberlin Coll., 1961, postgrad., 1963-64; M.A., U. Wis., 1966, Ph.D. in Indian Langs. and Lit., 1972. Tutor English and philosophy Am. Coll. and Lady Doak Coll., Madurai, India, 1961-63; lectr. religious studies, lit., Calif. State U.-Long Beach, 1970-76, acting dir. program religious studies, 1972-73; lectr. philosophy, U. Calif.-San Diego, 1971-79; lectr. religious studies, San Diego State U., 1977—; lectr. humanities Calif. Sch. Profl. Psychology, San Diego, 1977—, U. Humanistic Studies, Del Mar, 1979—; asst. prof. religion Oberlin Coll., Ohio, 1980-81; vis. prof. religion U. Fla., Gainesville, 1983. Author: (with Robinson) The Buddhist Religion 1977, 3d rev. edit. 1983; Riding the Ox Home, 1982, 86; Glossary of Technical Terms for the Academic Study of Religion, 1982, producer cassette tape series Introduction to Eastern Religions, 1978; also articles and revs. Bd. dirs. Cuyamunque Inst., Santa Fe; Woodrow Wilson fellow, 1964-66; grantee NDEA. Home: 2248 Alta Vista Dr Vista CA 92084-7022 Office: San Diego State U Dept Religious Studies San Diego CA 92182-0304

JOHNSON, WILLARD PARKER, physician, administrator; b. Mexia, Tex., June 26, 1927; s. John Edward and Mary Anna (Blasdel) J.; m. Elaine M. Carlock, July 31, 1949 (div. 1973); children—Stephen M., Kristin A., Katherine L., Matthew L.; m. 2d, Judy M. Ismach, Mar. 15, 1975. B.A., U. Calif.-Berkeley, 1948; M.D., U. Tex.-Galveston, 1953. Diplomate Am. Bd. Internal Medicine. Resident in internal medicine USPHS Hosp., S.I., N.Y., 1956-59; research fellow in cardiology U. Wash. Med. Ctr., Seattle, 1959-61; chief of research USPHS Hosp., Seattle, 1961-68, hosp. dir., 1968-71; regional program dir. Nat. Health Service Corps, Seattle, 1971-72; from instr. to assoc. prof. medicine U. Wash., 1961-73, also assoc. dean; med. dir. Seafarers Med. Ctr., San Francisco, 1973—. Med. cons. Cardio mag., 1983; contbr. articles to profl. jours. Served with USPHS, 1953-72. NIH grantee, 1961, 62, 63, 64-68. Fellow ACP; mem. USPHS Clin. Soc. (pres. 1967-68), Am. Fedn. Clin. Research, Am. Heart Assn., Physicians for Social Responsibility. Democrat. Home: 566 Kansas St San Francisco CA 94107 Office: Seafarers Med Ctr 40 Lansing St San Francisco CA 94105

JOHNSON, WILLIAM FLOYD, hospital safety manager; b. San Bernardino, Calif., Sept. 22, 1942; s. Lloyd Johnson and Wilma Ruth Bonner; m. Sharon Ann Curley, Nov. 25, 1966; children: Candace, Sean. BS in Occupational Safety and Health, Nat. U., 1981, MBA in Indsl. Relations, 1983, MS in Occupational Safety and Health Mgmt., 1984. Enlisted USN, 1959, multiple paramed., 1959-80, retired, 1980; vector control specialist Marine Corps Base, Camp Pendelton, Calif., 1980-81; dep. safety dir. Joint Safety Ctr. MCB, Camp Pendelton, Calif., 1981-85; mgr. safety Naval Hosp., Camp Pendleton, 1985—; mem. adv. com. occupational safety and health San Diego Community Coll., 1985—; instr. Palomar Community Coll., San Marcos, Calif., 1984—. Named Outstanding Alumnus, Nat. U., San Diego, 1984. Mem. Am. Soc. Safety Engrs. (profl., cert. hazard control mgr.), Assn. Fed. Safety And Health Profls., Fed. Safety and Health Council (tech. and research com. San Diego chpt. 1981—). Home: 4124 Chasin St Oceanside CA 92056-3435 Office: Naval Hosp Safety Dept Code 02C Camp Pendleton CA 92055

JOHNSON, WILLIAM HUGH, JR., hospital administrator, consultant; b. N.Y.C., Oct. 29, 1935; s. William H. and Florence P. (Seinsoth) J.; m. Gloria C. Stube., Jan. 23, 1960; children: Karen A., William H. III. B.A., Hofstra U., 1957; M.Ed., U. Hawaii, 1969. Commd. 2d lt. U.S. Army, 1957, advanced through grades to lt. col., 1972, health adminstr., world wide, 1957-77, health adminstr., world wide, ret., 1977; chief exec. officer U. N. Mex. Hosp., Albuquerque, 1977—; asst. prof. U.S. Mil. Acad., West Point, N.Y., 1962-65; mem. clin. faculty U. Minn., Mpls., 1980-83; preceptor Ariz. State U., Tempe, 1982-83; pres. Albuquerque Area Hosp. Council, 1980. Vice pres. Vis Nurse Service, Albuquerque, 1979. Decorated Army Commendation Medal with 2 oak leaf clusters, 1979-80; decorated Meritorious Service Medal, Order of Merit, Legion of Merit. Mem. Am. Hosp. Assn. (governing bd. met. hosp. sect. 1982-86, chmn. com. AIDS), Am. Coll. Hosp. Adminstrs., Council Tchg. Hosps., N. Mex. Hosp. Assn. (bd. dirs. 1983, chmn.), Nat. Assn. Pub. Hosps., Am. Assn. Med. Colls. (exec. bd.). Roman Catholic. Club: Tanoan Country (Albuquerque). Home: 7920 Sartan Way NE Albuquerque NM 87109 Office: U N Mex Hosp 2211 Lomas Blvd NE Albuquerque NM 87106

JOHNSON, WILLIAM POTTER, newspaper publisher; b. Peoria, Ill., May 4, 1935; s. William Zweigle and Helen Marr (Potter) J.; m. Pauline Ruth Rowe, May 18, 1968; children: Darragh Elizabeth, William Potter. AB, U. Mich., 1957. Gen. mgr. Bureau County Rep., Inc., Princeton, Ill., 1961-72; pres. Johnson Newspapers, Inc., Sebastopol, Calif., 1972-75, Evergreen, Colo., 1974-86, Canyon Commons Investment, Evergreen, 1974—; pres., chmn. bd. dirs. Johnson Media, Inc., Winter Park, Colo., 1987—. Alt. del. Rep. Nat. Conv., 1968. Served to lt. USNR, 1958-61. Mem. Colo. Press Assn., Nat. Newspaper Assn., San Francisco Press Club, Beta Theta Pi, Sigma Delta Chi. Roman Catholic. Clubs: Hiwan Country (Evergreen); Oro Valley Country (Tucson); Grand Lake (Colo.) Tennis. Home: 445 W Rapa Pl Tucson AZ 85701 Office: PO Box 409 Winter Park CO 80482

JOHNSON, WYATT THOMAS, JR. (TOM JOHNSON), newspaper publisher; b. Macon, Ga., Sept. 30, 1941; s. Wyatt Thomas and Josephine Victoria (Brown) J.; m. Edwina Mac Chastain, Dec. 29, 1963; children: Wyatt Thomas III, Christa Farie. A.B. in Journalism, U. Ga., 1963; M.B.A., Harvard, 1965. Reporter, mgmt. trainee Macon Telegraph and News, 1957-65; White House fellow 1965-66; asst. press sec. to Pres. U.S., 1966, dep. press sec., 1967; spl. asst. to Pres., 1968, exec. asst., 1969-70; exec. v.p., dir. Tex. Broadcasting Corp., Sta. KTBC-AM-FM-TV, Austin, 1970-73; exec. editor, v.p., dir. Dallas Times Herald, 1973-75, publisher, 1975-77; pres. Los Angeles Times, 1977-80, publisher, 1980—, also chief exec. officer; Mem. Pres.'s Commn. on White House Fellows, 1979, Neiman Fellows Selection Com., Harvard U., 1977; Pres. adv. bd. Henry W. Grady Sch. Journalism, 1974-75. Co-author: Automating Newspaper Composition, 1965. Bd. dirs. U. Ga. Sch. Journalism, Peabody Awards, Rockefeller Found., Trilateral Commn., Reading is Fundamental; chmn. bd. Lyndon B. Johnson Found., John S. Knight/Stanford Profl. Journalism Fellows. Named Nat. Man of Year Sigma Nu, 1962, Outstanding Young Man of Ga. Jr. C. of C., 1967, One of Five Outstanding Young Texans Tex. Jaycees, 1969, One of 10 Outstanding Men of U.S., 1975. Mem. Am. Newspaper Pubs. Assn., Newspaper Advt. Bur. (dir.), Ga. Alumni Soc. (pres. 1979), Council on Fgn. Relations N.Y., Sphinx Soc., Young Pres.'s Orgn., Gridiron Soc. (Ga.), Sigma Delta Chi, Sigma Nu. Club: Harvard Business School Alumni. Office: Los Angeles Times Times Mirror Sq Los Angeles CA 90053 *

JOHNSTON, DAVID CAY BOYLE, journalist; b. San Francisco, Dec. 24, 1948; s. Leslie Jules and Gretchen Elizabeth (Taylor) J.; m. Sharon Snider, July 8, 1966 (div. Dec. 1979); children: Leslie Ann, Susan, Mark, Amy and Andy (twins), Steven; m. Mary Regina Ryan, Jan. 1, 1980 (div. Sept. 1980); m. Jennifer Leonard, May 1, 1982; 1 child, Molly Claire Leonard. Student, Foothill Coll., 1968-72, San Francisco State U., 1972, U. Chgo., 1973, Mich. State U., 1973-75. Reporter, photographer County News, Aptos, Calif., 1966-68, Valley Press, Felton, Calif., 1968; staff writer San Jose Mercury and News, Los Altos, Calif., 1968-73, Detroit Free Press, Lansing, Mich., 1973-76, Los Angeles Times, 1976—; sr. lectr. U. So. Calif., Los Angeles, 1980—;

instr. journalism UCLA, 1986. Contbg. editor Feedback, The Calif. Journalism Rev., 1976-86; contbr. articles to newspapers, mags. including The Columbia Journalism Rev., Washington Journalism Rev., others. Urban journalism fellow U. Chgo., 1973, Edward J. Meeman award Scripps Howard Found., 1974, George Polk fellow L.I. U., 1982; recipient Best Story award Detroit Press Club, 1974, Best Story award UPI Calif. News Editors, 1983. Mem. Investigative Reporters and Editors. Club: Los Angeles Athletic. Home: 659 Crane Blvd Los Angeles CA 90065 Office: Los Angeles Times Times Mirror Sq Los Angeles CA 90053

JOHNSTON, DAVID CHARLES, psychiatrist; b. Calgary, Alta., Can., Jan. 30, 1925; came to U.S., 1950, naturalized, 1956; s. Franklin Melvin and Dorothy Alma (Corneille) J.; M.D., U. Toronto, 1950; m. Lily Martha Bell, Dec. 15, 1972; children by previous marriage—Susan Johnston Amselem, David C., Kenneth D. Intern medicine and surgery Buffalo Gen. Hosp., 1950-52; resident ob-gyn Millard Fillmore Hosp., Buffalo, 1952-55; practice medicine, specializing in ob-gyn, Buffalo, 1955-60, Long Beach, Calif., 1960-62; practice medicine, specializing in psychiatry, Beverly Hills, Calif., 1962—, also Long Beach; clin. instr. U. Calif.-Irvine, 1967—; cons. U. Calif.-Long Beach, also VA Hosp., 1966—. NIMH fellow, 1963-66. Fellow Soc. Clin. and Exptl. Hypnosis, Am. Soc. Clin. Hypnosis, Acad. Psychosomatic Medicine; mem. Calif. (v.p.), So. Calif., Orange County (past pres.), Harbor socs. clin. hypnosis, Am. Psychiat. Assn., AMA, Am. Bd. Med. Hypnosis (dir., past pres., examiner), Phi Delta Theta. Clubs: Balboa Bay (Newport); Royal Canadian Yacht (Toronto); Huntington Harbour Yacht. Pioneered hypnotic childbirth; nat. precedent hypnoanalytic film as evidence Calif. Superior Ct., 1968. Home: 16078 Bonaire Circle Huntington Harbour CA 92649 Office: 4729 E Anaheim Long Beach CA 90804

JOHNSTON, DAVID FREDERICK, lawyer; b. Tiffin, Ohio, Sept. 9, 1943; s. Frederick Walter and Aleta Marguerite (Ruehle) J.; m. Ona Lee Graham, June 18, 1966; children—Matthew, Rebecca, Elisabeth, Benjamin. B.A. in Chemistry, Oreg. State U., 1965; J.D., Golden Gate U., 1971. Bar: Calif. 1972, Oreg. 1973, U.S. Ct. Mil. Appeals 1974, U.S. Supreme Ct. 1983. Commd. officer U.S. Coast Guard, 1965; sea duty U.S. Coast Guard Cutter Magnolia, 1966-67; staff atty. U.S. Coast Guard, 1971-79; dept. chief U.S. Coast Guard Marine Safety Office, Norfolk, Va., 1979-82; appeal decision supr. U.S. Coast Guard Hdqrs., Washington, 1982-85, sole practice, 1985—. Author: Suspension and Revocation of Mariner's Licenses, Certificates and Documents, 1984. Elder Presbyn. Ch., Green Acres Ch., Portsmouth, Va., 1979, Multnomah Ch., Portland, Oreg., 1986; com. chmn. Clermont Sch., Fairfax County, Va., 1983. Mem. Oreg. State Bar, Phi Kappa Phi, Phi Lamdba Upsilon. Presbyterian. Home and Office: 0550 SW Palatine Hill Rd Portland OR 97219

JOHNSTON, GAIL LIRAGIS, laboratory director; b. Atlantic City, N.J., Sept. 3, 1951; d. William and Mary Agnes (Cathcart) Liragis; m. R.C. Johnston, Jan. 14, 1984. B.A./B.S., U. Calif.-Santa Cruz, 1974, postgrad. 1978; Cert. U. Calif.-Los Angeles, 1976. Pub. info. officer Calif. State Parks, Santa Cruz, 1974-75; paralegal Berliner, Cohen & Flaherty, San Jose, 1976-78; tchr. Pajaro Unified, Watsonville, Calif., 1978-80; asst. to dir. Moss Landing Marine Labs., Calif., 1980—; adv. panel U. Santa Clara's Paralegal Program, 1976-78. Contbg. author: Central Calif. Coastal Conservation Commn.'s Coastal Land Environment, 1974; K-12 Environmental Edn. Handbook, 1979. Greek Orthodox. Address: Moss Landing Marine Labs PO Box 450 Moss Landing CA 95039

JOHNSTON, GWINAVERE ADAMS, public relations consultant; b. Casper, Wyo., Jan. 6, 1943; d. Donald Milton Adams and Gwinavere Marie (Newell) Quillen; m. H.R. Johnston, Sept. 26, 1963 (div. 1973); children: Gwinavere G., Gabrielle Suzanne; m. Donald Charles Cannalte, Apr. 4, 1981. BS in Journalism, U. Wyo., 1966; postgrad., Denver U., 1968-69. Editor, reporter Laramie (Wyo.) Daily Boomerang, 1965-66; account exec. William Kostka Assocs., Denver, 1966-71, v.p., 1971-73; exec. v.p. Slottow, McKinlay & Johnston, Denver, 1973-74; pres. The Johnston Group, Denver, 1974—; bd. dirs. The Lovelace Corp., Denver, Designers Marketplace, Denver. Bd. dirs. Leadership Denver Assn., 1975-77, 83-86. Mem. Pub. Relations Soc. Am. (pres. Colo. chpt. 1978-79, bd. dirs. 1975-80, 83-86, counselor's acad. 1974-86, profl. award), Colo. Women's Forum. Republican. Clubs: Denver Athletic, Denver Press, Com. of 200. Home: 717 Monaco Pkwy Denver CO 80220 Office: The Johnston Group 1340 Glenarm Pl #200 Denver CO 80204

JOHNSTON, HAROLD S(LEDGE), chemistry educator; b. Woodstock, Ga., Oct. 11, 1920; s. Smith L. and Florine (Dial) J.; m. Mary Ella Stay, Dec. 29, 1948; children: Shirley Louise, Linda Marie, David Finley, Barbara Dial. AB, Emory U., 1941, ScD (hon.), 1965; PhD, Calif. Inst. Tech., 1948. Instr. to assoc. prof. chemistry Stanford (Calif.) U., 1947-56; assoc. prof. Calif. Inst. Tech., Pasadena, 1956-57; prof. U. Calif., Berkeley, 1957—, dean, coll. chemistry, 1966-70; vis. prof. U. Rome, 1964; adv. com. Calif. Statewide Air Pollution Research Ctr., 1969-73, Nat. Ctr. Atmospheric Research, 1975-78, FAA High Altitude Polution Program; vis. adv. com. Brookhaven Nat. Lab., 1970-73. Author: Gas Phase Reaction Rate Theory, 1966, Gas Phase Reaction Kinetics of Neutral Oxygen Species, 1968, Reduction of Stratospheric Ozone by Nitrogen Oxide Catalysts from Supersonic Transport Exhaust, 1971; contbr. articles to profl. jours. Recipient Tyler prize Environ. Achievement, 1983, Disting. Alumni award Calif. Inst. Tech., 1985; grantee Office Naval Research, 1950-56, M.W. Kellogg Co., 1951-53, Standard Oil Calif., 1955-57, Alfred Sloan Found., 1957-59, NSF, 1959-68, 75-78, U.S. Pub. Health Service, 1963-70, EPA, 1970-72, Dept. Transp., 1972-75, Materials and Molecular Research div. Lawrence Berkeley Lab., 1966—. Fellow Am. Chem. Soc. (Gold Medal award Calif. sect. 1956, Pollution Control award 1974, award in the Chemistry of Contemporary Technol. Problems 1985), Am. Phys. Soc., AAAS; mem. Am. Geophys. Union, Nat. Acad. Scis. (adv. panel to Nat. Bur. Standards, 1965-67, com. Motor Vehicle Emissions, 1971-75), Am. Acad. Arts and Scis., Sigma Xi (nat. lectr. 1973). Home: 132 Highland Blvd Kensington CA 94708 Office: U Calif Dept Chemistry Berkeley CA 94720

JOHNSTON, JEFFREY MONROE, physician, researcher; b. Charlotte, N.C., Oct. 15, 1952; s. Joe Monroe and Camille (Newman) J.; m. Margaret B. Wheeler, Apr. 12, 1980; children: Catherine Browning, Joe Monroe. BS, Davidson Coll., 1974; MD, Duke U., 1977. Diplomate Am. Bd. Internal Medicine, Am. Bd. Infectious Diseases. Fellow in rheumatic and genetic diseases Duke U., Durham, N.C., 1978; resident in medicine Vanderbilt U., Nashville, 1978-80; epidemic intelligence service officer Ctr. for Disease Control, New Orleans, 1980-82; chief resident in medicine U. Utah, Salt Lake City, 1982-83, fellow in infectious diseases, 1983-85, asst. prof. internal medicine, 1985—; clin. asst. prof. La. State U., New Orleans, 1981-82; instr. Tulane U., New Orleans, 1980-82. Contbr. articles to profl. jours. Served with USPHS, 1980-82. Recipient Nat. Research Service awards NIH, Nat. Inst. Gen. Medicinal Scis., 1984, NIH, Nat. Inst. Allergy Infectious Diseases, 1985; Dana scholar Davidson Coll., 1971. Mem. ACP, Am. Fedn. Clin. Research, Infectious Diseases Soc. Am., Am. Soc. Microbiology, Am. Soc. Virology, Phi Beta Kappa. Democrat. Home: 509 Tenth Ave Salt Lake City UT 84103 Office: U Utah Div Infectious Diseases 50 N Medical Dr Salt Lake City UT 84132

JOHNSTON, MARJORIE DIANE, computer programming consultant; b. Fullerton, Calif., Sept. 19, 1943; d. Earl Lawrence and Ruth Junita (Long) Whipple; children—Stephen, Deborah. Grad computer programming LaSalle U., Chgo., 1973. Computer programmer Los Alamos Nat. Lab., 1972-81; contract programmer Computer Assistance, Inc., Tulsa, 1981-82; prof. services analyst Control Data Corp., Denver, 1982-84, Los Alamos, N.Mex., 1984—; cons. to Los Alamos Nat. Lab. Clubs: Rebekah, Order Eastern Star (past matron). Home: 365 Valle del Sol Los Alamos NM 87544

JOHNSTON, MURRAY VINCENT, III, chemist, educator; b. Ft. Dix, N.J., June 5, 1954; s. Murray Vincent Jr. and Judith (Brainerd) J.; m. Heather Dobbins, Nov. 27, 1982; 1 child, Andrew. BS in Chemistry, Bucknell U., 1976; PhD, U. Wis., 1980. Postdoctoral fellow Northwestern U., Evanston, Ill., 1981-82; prof., fellow Coop. Inst. Research in Environ. Scis. U. Colo., Boulder, 1982—; cons. Hewlett Packard, Palo Alto, Calif., 1984—. Contbr. articles to profl. jours. Fellow Eastman Kodak U. Wis., 1979; recipient Early Career Devel. award U. Colo., 1983; grantee NSF, 1983—, Dept. Health and Human Services, 1984—. Mem. Am. Chem. Soc., Am. Soc. Mass Spectrometry, Sigma Xi. Presbyterian. Home: 3045 25th St Boulder CO 80302 Office: U Colo Dept Chemistry Boulder CO 80309

JOHNSTON, NORMAN PAUL, nutrition educator; b. Salt Lake City, Apr. 5, 1941; s. Norman James and Olivia Harriet (Wilson) J.; m. Irene Hiller; children: Julie, Cherie Monique, Richard Paul, Clark Shane, David Erik, Jed Ryan. BA, Brigham Young U., 1966; MS, Oreg. State U., 1967, PhD, 1971; MBA, U. Utah, 1969. Prof. nutrition Brigham Young U., Provo, Utah, 1971—; nutritionist Brookfield Prod. Inc., Murray, Utah, 1971-85. Contbr. numerous articles to profl. jours. Mem. Poultry Sci. Assn., World Poultry Sci. Assn., Dairy Sci. Assn. Mormon. Avocation: genealogy. Home: 1795 S 340 E Orem UT 84058 Office: Brigham Young U 386 WIDB Provo UT 84602

JOHNSTON, RONALD VERNON, stockbroker; b. Los Angeles, Dec. 27, 1942; s. Arthur Vernon and Lillian Kristine J.; m. Patricia Joan Westerlind, Sept. 8, 1963; 1 child, Michael Arthur Roland. AA, Pasadena Coll., 1963; BA, Kensington U., 1977, MBA, 1978, PhD, 1979. Investment exec., asst. mgr., then mgr. Hornblower Weeks Hemphill Noyes, Glendale, Calif., 1968-74; v.p., resident mgr. Reynolds Securities, San Diego, 1974-78; v.p., resident mgr. Blyth Eastman Dillon/Paine Webber, San Diego, 1978-80; resident mgr., Crowell Weedon & Co., Carlsbad, Calif., 1985-87; pres. Trademark Investment Services, 1987—. Mem. Los Angeles County Dem. Cen. Com., 1966; mem. Calif. State Dem. Cen. Com., 1968. Mem. Nat. Assn. Security Dealers (bd. arbitration), San Diego Stock and Bond Club. Methodist. Office: Trademark Investment Services Inc 7777 Alvarado Rd #602 La Mesa CA 92041

JOHNSTON, VIRGINIA EVELYN, editor; b. Spokane, Wash., Apr. 26, 1933; d. Edwin and Emma Lucile (Munroe) Rowe; student Portland Community Coll., 1964, Portland State U., 1966, 78-79; m. Alan Paul Beckley, Dec. 26, 1974; children—Chris, Denise, Rex. Proofreader, The Oregonian, Portland, 1960-62, teletypesetter operator, 1962-66, operator Photon 200, 1966-68, copy editor, asst. women's editor, 1968-80, spl. sects. editor (UPDATE), 1981-83; editor FOODday, 1982—; pres. Matrix Assos., Inc., Portland, 1975—, chmn. bd., 1979—; cons. Democratic party Oreg., 1969, Portland Sch. Dist. No. 1, 1978. Mem. Women in Communications, Inc., Inst. Profl. and Managerial Women, Nat. Assn. Female Execs., Eating and Drinking Soc. Oreg. (pres.). Democrat. Editor Principles of Computer Systems for Newspaper Mgmt., 1975-76. Home: 4140 NE 137th Ave Portland OR 97230 Office: 1320 SW Broadway Portland OR 97201

JOHNSTON, WALTER WESLEY, computer information systems analyst; b. Chgo., May 20, 1946; s. Walter George and Elsie Marie (Subert) J.; m. Guadalupe Maria De Leon, Dec. 30, 1968; children: Martha, Walter. BS in Maths., No. Ill. U., 1967; postgrad., U. Ill., 1967-68; MA in Maths., Sangamon State U., 1974, MA in History, 1981. Cert. geneal. records searcher. With State of Ill., 1969-85, mgr. data procesing for health services Dept. Pub. Health, 1977-84, mgr. Info. Ctr., 1984-85; data base analyst Chevron, Inc., San Ramon, Calif., 1985—; geneal. researcher, lectr., 1975. Mem. Ill. Hist. Soc. (life), Ill. Geneal. Soc. (life, long-range planning com. 1980-84, chmn. honors and awards com. 1983-84, chmn. computer con. 1983-84), Chgo. Hist. Soc. (life), Chgo. Geneal. Soc. (life), Sangamon County Geneal. Soc. (life, 2d v.p. 1976, trustee 1978-80), Ont. Hist. Soc. (life), Ont. Geneal. Soc. (life), Soc. Genealogists London, Cornwall Family History Soc., Devon Family History Soc., Am. Assn. Artificial Intelligence, Sangamon County Hist. Soc. (life), Brown County (Minn.) Hist. Soc. (life), Holland (Mich.) Geneal. Soc., Royal Instn. Cornwall (life), Devon and Cornwall Record Soc., Cornish-Am. Heritage Soc., Assn. Profl. Genealogists, Guild of One-Name Studies, San Ramon Valley Hist. Soc. Contbr. articles to profl. jours.; editor and pub. Butson Family Newsletter, 1979—. Home: 3140 Montevideo Dr San Ramon CA 94583 Office: Chevron Inc PO Box 5032 San Ramon CA 94583-0932

JOHNSTON, WARREN EUGENE, agricultural economics educator, consultant; b. Woodland, Calif., May 27, 1933; s. Henry H. and Margaret G. Johnston; m. Donna M. Hamblet; children—Kimberly Ann, Douglas Stuart. B.S., U. Calif.-Davis, 1959; M.S., N.C. State U., 1963, Ph.D., 1964. Prof. agrl. econs. U. Calif.-Davis, 1963—; acting assoc. dean applied econs. and behavioral scis. Coll. Agrl. and Environ. Scis. U. Calif.-Davis, 1980-81, chmn. dept. agrl. econs., 1981-87. Served with U.S. Army, 1953-57. Alexander von Humboldt research scholar, W.Germany, 1969-70, Fulbright research scholar, N.Z., 1976-77. Mem. Am. Agrl. Econs. Assn., Western Agrl. Econs. Assn., Am. Soc. Farm Mgrs. and Rural Appraisers, Internat. Assn. Agrl. Economists. Office: U Calif Dept Agrl Econs Davis CA 95616

JOHNSTONE, KENNETH ERNEST, engineering executive; b. Los Angeles, Sept. 13, 1929; s. John Ernest and Lorena Hayes (Patterson) J.; m. Edna Mae Iverson, Aug. 20, 1950; children: Bruce, Kent, Anita, Christian, Daniel, Carol, Karen. BSEE, U. Wash., 1966. Registered profl. engr., Wash. Electronics technician The Boeing Co., Seattle, 1955-66, engr., 1966-75; engrng. mgr. Boeing Aerosystems Internat., Seattle, 1975-85; ptnr. North Creek Engrng., Lynnwood, Wash., 1985—; internat. lectr. in field. Mem. IEEE (sr.), Tau Beta Pi. Avocations: sailing, amateur radio, languages. Home: 927 Duchess Rd Bothell WA 98012 Office: North Creek Engrng PO Box 6608 Lynnwood WA 98036

JOHNSTONE, MARK, photographer; b. St. Louis, Aug. 20, 1953; s. John T. and Mary (Xenakes) J.; m. Robbi Cowin, Feb. 5, 1983. BA, Colo. Coll., 1975; MFA, U. So. Calif., 1982. Contbg. editor Artweek Mag., Oakland, Calif., 1980—; dir. spl. projects Seven Trees Prodn. Co., Los Angeles, 1984—; freelance writer 1977—; guest curator La Jolla (Calif.) Mus. Contemporary Art. Series content advisor PBS TV series The Photographic Vision, 1984; contbr. essays Observations-Essays on Documentary Photography, 1984; one-man and group exhibitions, U.S., Europe, Japan, 1972—. Home and Studio: PO Box 1279 Inglewood CA 90308

JOJOLA, THEODORE SYLVESTER, Native American educator and administrator; b. Isleta Pueblo, N.Mex., Nov. 19, 1951; s. Jose Levi and Juanita Bautista (Papuyo) J.; m. Adelamer Novino Alcantara, Jan. 4, 1980; 1 son, Manoa Alcantara. B.Arch., U. N.Mex., 1973; M.City Planning, MIT, 1975; Ph.D. in Polit. Sci., U. Hawaii-Manoa, 1982; cert. internat. human rights law U. Strasbourg, France, 1984. Intern planner Nat. Capital Planning Commn., Washington, 1973; legal/hist. researcher Inst. for Devel. of Indian Law, Washington, 1976; vis. research assoc. Inst. Philippine Culture, Manila, 1977-78; vis. prof. urban planning UCLA, 1984; asst. prof. planning U. N.Mex., Albuquerque, 1982—, dir. Native Am. Studies, 1980—, coordinator Ethnic/Minority Dirs.' Coalition, 1983-85; mem. chmns. adv. bd. Middle Rio Grande Conservancy Dist., 1987—; cons. Thurshun Consultants, Albuquerque, 1980—; postdoctoral fellow Am. Indian Studies, UCLA, 1984. Author: Memoirs of an American Indian House, 1976; contbr. articles to publs. Co-dir. sta. KOB-TV pub. issues prodns., Albuquerque, 1983-85; mem. U.S. organizing com. 9th Inter-Am. Indian Congress, Santa Fe, 1985; mem. adv. bd. Zuni Tribal Mus., N.Mex., 1985—, edn. affairs office Apple Computer, Inc., 1986—, Mus. Indian Culture & Arts, Mus. N. Mex., Santa Fe, 1986—; sch. bd. dirs. Isleta (N.Mex.) Isleta Elem. Sch., 1985-86; chmn. JOM/Indian Edn. Parent's Com., Isleta Pueblo, N.Mex., 1985-86; adv. bd. KIMO Cultural Arts Theatre, 1983-85; assoc. Indigenous World: El Mundo Indigena, San Francisco, 1982-84; directorate of studies on indigenous peoples Internat. Inst. Human Rights, Strasbourg, 1984. Research grantee, Lab. for Arch. and Planning, MIT, 1975, Inst. Am. Culture, UCLA, 1984; publ. grantee Atherton Trust, Honolulu, 1976; recipient Participant award, East-West Ctr., Honolulu, 1975-81. Mem. Native Am. Studies Assn. (coordinator Albuquerque 1980). Roman Catholic. Home: Rte 6 Box 578 Albuquerque NM 87105 Office: Native Am Studies Univ New Mexico Albuquerque NM 87131

JOLLEY, JERRY CLYDE, sociologist, educator; b. Murray, Utah, Feb. 9, 1945; s. Merlin Duane and Alice May (Frazier) J.; m. Carol Elaine Free, May 21, 1971; children—Darin, Jennifer. B.A., U. Utah, 1969, M.A., 1970, Ph.D., 1975. Cert. secondary tchr., Utah. Teaching asst. U. Utah, Salt Lake City, 1970, teaching fellow, 1972-75; instr. Kans. State Tchrs. Coll., Emporia, 1970-72; from asst. prof. to prof. Lewis-Clark State Coll., Lewiston, Idaho, 1975—, coordinator corrections and social services program. Mem. Am. Sociol. Assn., Acad. Criminal Justice Scis., Western and Pacific Assn. Criminal Justice Educators, Idaho Sociol. Assn. (pres. 1979-80), Idaho Correctional Assn., Criminal Justice Soc., Sigma Gamma Chi. Mormon. Contbr. articles to profl. jours. Home: 1022 Hemlock Dr Lewiston ID 83501 Office: Lewis-Clark State College Lewiston ID 83501

JOLLEY, JOHN GILBERT, scientist, chemist; b. Idaho Falls, June 28, 1954; s. John Lester and Daisy Ethel (Kershaw) J.; m. Joanne Edna Hartel, Aug. 7, 1982; children: Jodi Anne, Jane Marie. BS in Chemistry, Idaho State U., 1981; postgrad., U. Idaho, 1983—. Assoc. scientist E.G. & G. Idaho Inc., Idaho Falls, 1982-86, scientist, 1986—. Contbr. articles to profl. jours. Mem. Am. Chem. Soc. (treas. Idaho sect. 1985-87, chmn.-elect), Soc. Applied Spectroscopy. Avocations: tennis, skiing, fishing, bicycling. Office: EG & G Idaho Inc PO Box 1625 Idaho Falls ID 83415

JOLLEY, WELDON BOSEN, surgery educator, research executive; b. Gunnison, Utah, Sept. 8, 1926; s. Edward Mckinley Jolley and Rosella (Elvira) Bosen; m. Dorothy Timms, Dec. 21, 1954 (dec. Jan. 1983); children: Elizabeth Price, Kathleen Cope, Phillip Jolley; m. JoLane Laycock, Aug. 20, 1983; children: Jessica, Brian. BA, Brigham Young U., 1952; PhD, U. So. Calif., 1959; postdoctoral, UCLA, 1960. Prof. surgery, physiology and biophysics Loma Linda (Calif.) U., 1969—, assoc. dir. surg. research lab., 1969—; dir. surg. research VA Hosp., Loma Linda, 1979-85; pres. Nucleic Acid Research Inst., Costa Mesa, Calif., 1985—; bd. dirs. SPI Pharms., Inc.; sr. v.p., bd. dirs. ICN Pharms., Inc.; sci. adv. Viratek, Inc. Contbr. tech. articles to publs. Named McPherson Soc. Clin. Prof. of Yr., 1982. Home: 3825 E Woodbine Rd Orange CA 92667 Office: Nucleic Acid Research Inst 3300 Hyland Blvd Costa Mesa CA 92626

JOLLY, JAMES A., educator; b. Oceanside, Calif., Nov. 2, 1921; s. Peter Benjamine and Amelia (DeMuth) J.; B.A., U. Pacific, 1951; M.B.A., U. Santa Clara, 1963, Ph.D., 1970; m. Rose Calvina Binkley, Jan. 14, 1945; children—Mayeve O. Jolly Tate, David O., Heidi O. Jolly Wolf. Research physicist Eitel McCullough, San Bruno, Calif., 1951-54, prodn. engr., 1954-59, mgr. prodn. engrng. and indsl. engrng., 1959-60, mgr. advanced devel., 1960-64; mgr. indsl. microwave activity Varian Assos., Palo Alto, Calif., 1964-69; asso. prof. Naval Postgraduate Sch., Monterey, Calif., 1969-76; prof. Sch. Bus., Calif. State U., Sacramento, 1976—. Mem. IEEE (sr.), Internat. Microwave Power Inst. (past pres.), Acad. Mgmt. Author: (with J.W. Creighton) Technology Transfer Process Model and Annotated Selected Bibliography, 1978. Editor: (with J.W. Creighton) Technology Transfer in Research and Development, 1975; asso. editor Jour. Microwave Power, 1973-85; editor Jour. Tech. Transfer, 1976—. Home: 510 Elmhurst Circle Sacramento CA 95825

JONAS, ADRIENNE HAZEL, clothing manufacturing company executive; b. London, Feb. 9, 1935; came to U.S., 1957, naturalized, 1968; d. Henry and Sadie (Clapper) J. Gen. cert. edn., Regent St. Poly., London, 1952. Sec. to consulting engrs. and real estate cos., London, 1952-55; sec. purchasing dept. Canadian Govt., Toronto, 1955-56; sec. Lash, Lash & Pringle, Toronto, 1956-57, J.C. Penney Co., San Francisco, 1957-58; with Levi Strauss & Co., San Francisco, 1959—, sundries purchasing mgr. Jeanswear div., 1975—. Active San Francisco Big Sisters, 1972—. Mem. Nat. Purchasing Assn. No. Calif., Nat. Assn. Female Execs. Democrat. Jewish. Office: Jeanswear div Levi Strauss & Co 1155 Battery St San Francisco CA 94120

JONES, ALAN, grocery company executive; b. Portland, Oreg., May 15, 1942. B.S. in Mktg., Portland State U., 1967. Successively computer operator, buyer, dir. purchasing, then mktg. mgr. United Grocers, Inc., Portland, 1964-83, pres., 1983—. Office: United Grocers Inc Office of Pres 6433 SE Lake Rd Portland OR 97222

JONES, ALLEN LEE, marketing consultant; b. Billings, Mont., Apr. 27, 1959; s. Richard Arthur and Sonja Clara Johanna (Hartmann) J. BBA, BA in Art, Eastern Mont. Coll., 1981. Graphic designer I.D.C./E.M.C., Billings, 1981; account exec. Creative Imagery, Billings, 1982; mng. ptnr. The Mktg. Arm, Billings, 1982—, Line O'Type, Billings, 1986. Program producer Am. Legion Baseball, Billings, 1983-84, Miss E.M.C. Pageant, Billings, 1978-82, 86; print pub. relations Big Sky Hospice, Billings, 1985—; coordinator 3 Farm Aid Functions, 1986. Named one of Outstanding Young Men Am., 1980. Mem. Mont. ACLU (editor newsletter, mktg. chmn. 1986—), Billings C. of C. (mktg. com. 1986), Kappa Sigma (v.p., sec. 1978-81, asst. alumni advisor 1983—). Republican. Lutheran. Club: Billings Motorcycle (program producer 1985-86). Avocations: reading, watercolor painting, walking, learning. Office: The Mktg Arm 404 N 31st TWI Suite 213 Billings MT 59101

JONES, ANGELA MARIE DOYLE, commercial writer, periodical editor, poet, novelist; b. Compton, Calif., Nov. 23, 1949; d. Harold Edgar and Anna Giovanna (Aurelio) Doyle; m. Steven Patrick Jones, Aug. 28, 1976 (div.); children: Matthew Stephen, Leslie Therese. AA, Compton Jr. Coll., 1969; BA, Calif. State U., Los Angeles, 1977. Pres. and owner The Write Procedure, Pasadena, Calif., 1979—; proofreader, freelance writer, editor J.S. Paluch Co., Santa Fe Springs, Calif., 1986—. Contbr. articles to pubs. Recipient Writers' Forum Literary Contest award Pasadena (Calif.) City Coll., 1981; named to selection com. Touchstone mag., Cerritos Coll., Norwalk, Calif., 1980-81. Home and Office: 4306 Hendrickson Ave Ojai CA 93023

JONES, ARTHUR CURTIS, III, physician; b. Washington, Apr. 21, 1947; s. Arthur Curtis Jr. and Martha (Down) J; m. Margaret Von der Heide, June 12, 1970; children: Arthur Curtis IV, Lindsay Louise. Student, U. Mich., 1965-67; BS, Coll. Idaho, 1970; MD, Tulane U., 1973. Resident in gen. surgery Jewish Hosp., St. Louis, 1974-75; resident in otolaryngology Wash. U. affiliated hosps., St. Louis, 1975-79; pvt. practice medicine Boise, Idaho, 1979—; staff St. Luke's Hosp., Boise, 1979—, St. Alphonsus Hosp., Boise, 1979—. Fellow ACS; mem. AMA, Idaho Med. Assn., Am. Acad. Office Based Surgery, Am. Acad. Otolaryn./Head and Neck Surgery, Pacific Coast Oto-Ophthal. Soc. Lodge: Rotary. Avocations: flying, fishing, skiing, boating, trapshooting. Home: 1955 Table Rock Rd Boise ID 83712 Office: Jones Clinic 425 W Bannock Boise ID 83702

JONES, B. PAUL, banker; b. Dallas, Sept. 16, 1931; s. J. Lawrence and Pinkie (Funderburk) J.; m. Socorro Noriega, Feb. 1985. B.A., Tex. A&M U.; postgrad., So. Methodist U. Various positions Merc. Nat. Bank, Dallas, 1953-59; investment mgr. United Fidelity Life, Dallas, 1959; security analyst Valley Nat. Bank, Phoenix, 1960-61, asst. v.p., 1961-66, v.p., head trust investments, 1961-70, sr. v.p., mgr. investment div., 1970-75, sr. v.p., mgr. funds mgmt. and econ. planning, 1975-82, exec. v.p. corp. funds mgmt., 1982—. Bd. dirs. Phoenix Symphony, Theodore Roosevelt council Boy Scouts Am. Mem. Inst. Chartered Fin. Analysts, Phoenix Soc. Fin. Analysts, Phoenix Stock and Bond Club, Nat. Securities Traders Assn., Dealer Bank Assn., Asset-Liability Assn., Am. Bankers Assn., Phoenix C. of C. (bd. dirs., exec. com. mem. spending limit task force). Lodge: Rotary (local bd. dirs.). Home: 4700 E Charles Paradise Valley AZ 85253 Office: Valley Nat Bank PO Box 29514 Phoenix AZ 85038

JONES, BARBARA CHRISTINE, educator, linguist, creative arts designer; b. Augsburg, Swabia, Bavaria, Germany, Nov. 14, 1942; came to U.S., 1964, naturalized, 1971; d. Martin Richard and Margarete Katharina (Roth-Rommel) Schulz von Hammer-Parstein; m. Robert Edward Dickey, 1967 (div. 1980); m. Raymond Lee Jones, 1981. Student U. Munich, 1961, Philomatique de Bordeaux, France, 1962; BA in German, French, Speech, Calif. State U., Chico, 1969, MA in Comparative Internat. Edn., 1974. Cert. secondary tchr., community coll. instr., Calif. Fgn. lang. tchr. Gridley Union High Sch., Calif., 1970-80, home econs., decorative arts instr., cons., 1970-80, English study skills instr., 1974-80, ESL coordinator, instr. Punjabi, Mex. Ams., 1970-72, curriculum com. chmn., 1970-80; program devel. adviser Program Devel. Ctr. Supt. Schs. Butte County, Oroville, Calif., 1975-77; opportunity tchr. Esperanza High Sch., Gridley, 1980-81, Liberty High Sch., Lodi, Calif., 1981-82, resource specialist coordinator, 1981-82; Title I coordinator Bear Creek Ranch Sch., Lodi, 1981-82, instr., counselor, 1981-82; substitute tchr. Elk Grove (Calif.) Unified, 1982-84; free lance decorative arts and textiles designer, 1982—; internat. heritage and foods adv. AAUW, Chico, Calif., 1973-75; workshop dir. Creative Arts Ctr., Chico, 1972-73; workshop dir., adv. Bus. Profl. Women's Club of Gridley, 1972-74; v.p. Golden State Mobile Home League, Sacramento, Calif., 1980-82. Designer weavings-wallhangings (1st place 10 categories, Silver Dollar Fair, Chico, 1970); swimming champion Swim Club Augsburg, 1954-60. Mem. United European Am. Club, Am. Assn. German Tchrs., U.S. Army Res. Non-Commd. Officer's Assn. (ednl. adv. 1984-86), Kappa Delta Pi. Avocations: weaving, fiber designs, swimming, skiing, internat. travel and culture. Home: 8723 Cabra Ct Elk Grove CA 95624

JONES, BARRI MELISSA, editor; b. Phila., Jan. 11, 1960; s. John Wesley and Grace Barbara (Winthrop) J. BEd, Temple U., 1980. Mng. editor Petersen Pub., Los Angeles, 1981—. Avocations: hiking, reading, wine tasting. Home: 2820 Griffith Park Blvd #10 Los Feliz CA 90027 Office: Home Fitness Mag 8490 Sunset Blvd Suite 401 Los Angeles CA 90069

JONES, BARRY KENNARD, insurance brokerage executive; b. San Francisco, July 2, 1933; s. Kennard and Burnette (Grimes) J.; m. Carole Jo Cooke, June 25, 1955; children: Scott Kennard, Craig Steven, Todd Cooke. BBA, Wash. State U., 1955. CPCU. Commd. 2d lt. U.S. Army, 1955, advanced through grades to capt., 1961, resigned, 1965; v.p. Cen. Bus. Property Co., Spokane, Wash., 1957—; chmn., pres., chief exec. officer Fidelity Assocs., Inc., Spokane, 1968—; pres. Fidelity Assocs. Fin. Services, Spokane, 1982—. Chmn., treas. Spokane Dist. 83 Levy, 1984—; bd. dirs. Spokane C. of C., 1982—. Named Ins. Leader of Yr., Spokane Ins. Women, 1985, Dad of Yr., Wash. State U., 1978; fellow Paul Harris Found., 1985. Mem. Alpha Tau Omega (province dir. 1961-68, pres. house corp. 1966-82, Alumni of Yr. 1966). Republican. Episcopalian. Clubs: Spo Knife and Fork (Spokane) (exec sec. 1960-81), Knife and Fork Internat. (Topeka) (pres. 1982—, treas. 1976-81). Lodges: Rotary (pres. Spokane chpt. 1984-85), Shriners, Divan. Avocations: tennis, golf, photography, travel. Home: 1914 E 25th Ave Spokane WA 99203 Office: Fidelity Assocs Ins Brokers PO Box 3144 Spokane WA 99220

JONES, BARRY WAYNE, educator hearing impaired; b. Wichita Falls, Tex., Sept. 27, 1940; s. James Granville and Gladys Marguerite (Unsell) J.; m. Linda Susette Cartwright, June 6, 1964; 1 child, Laura Susette. BS, Eastern N.Mex. U., 1968; MS, Canisius Coll., 1972; PhD, U. Ill., 1977. Tchr. N.Y. State Sch. for the Deaf, Rome, 1973-74; vis. prof. U. Ill., Urbana, 1977-78; asst. prof. U. Miami, Coral Gables, Fla., 1978-80; assoc. prof. San Diego State U., 1980—, asst. dean, 1982—. Contbr. articles to profl. jours. Served with U.S. Army, 1961-64. Mem. Am. Speech Hearing Lang. Assn., Calif. Speech Hearing Lang. Assn., Am. Assn. Higher Edn., Conf. Am. Instrs. of Deaf, Alexander Graham Bell Assn. for the Deaf, Kappa Delta Pi, Phi Alpha Theta, Delta Phi Alpha. Club: Lions (chmn. Hearing Conservation Com., 1984—). Office: San Diego State U 5300 Campanile Dr San Diego CA 92182

JONES, BEVERLY ANN MILLER, nursing executive; b. Bklyn., July 14, 1927; d. Hayman Edward and Eleanor Virginia (Doyle) Miller. B.S.N., Adelphi U., 1949; m. Kenneth Lonzo Jones, Sept. 5, 1953; children—Steven Kenneth, Lonnie Cord. Chief nurse regional blood program ARC, N.Y.C., 1951-54; asst. dir., acting dir. nursing M.D. Anderson Hosp. and Tumor Inst., Houston, 1954-55; asst. dir. nursing Sibley Meml. Hosp., Washington, 1959-61; assoc. dir. nursing service Anne Arundel Gen. Hosp., Annapolis, Md., 1966-70; asst. adminstr. nursing Alexandria (Va.) Hosp., 1972-73; asst. adminstr. patient services Longmont (Colo.) United Hosp., 1977—; instr. ARC, 1953-57; mem. adv. bd. Boulder Valley Vo.-Tech Health Occupations Program, 1977-80; chmn. nurse enrollment com. D.C. chpt. ARC, 1959-61; del. nursing adminstrs. good will trip to Poland, Hungary, Sweden and Eng., 1980. Bd. dirs. Meals on Wheels, Longmont, Colo., 1977-80; bd. dirs. Longmont Coalition for Women in Crisis; mem. Colo. Hosp. Assn. Task Force on Nat. Commn. on Nursing, 1982; mem. utilization com. Boulder (Colo.) Hospice, 1979-83; mem. council labor relations Colo. Hopsp. Assn., 1982-87; mem.-at-large exec. com. nursing service adminstrs. Sect. Md. Nurses' Assn., 1966-69. Mem. Am. Soc. Nursing Service Adminstrs. (chmn. com. membership services and promotions), Colo. Soc. Nurse Execs. (dir. 1978-80, 84-86, pres. 1980-81, chmn. com. on nominations). Home: 8902 Quail Rd Longmont CO 80501 Office: PO Box 1659 Longmont CO 80501

JONES, BOB GORDON, bishop; b. Paragould, Ark., Aug. 22, 1932; s. F.H. and Helen Truman (Ellis) J.; m. Judith Munroe, Feb. 22, 1963; children: Robert Gordon, Timothy Andrew. B.B.A., U. Miss., 1956; M.Div., Episcopal Sem. S.W., 1959, D.D. hon., 1978. Asst. to dean Trinity Cathedral, Little Rock, 1959-62; vicar St. George-in-Arctic, Kotzebue, Alaska, 1962-67; rector St. Christopher's Ch., Anchorage, 1967-77; bishop Episcopal Diocese Wyo., Laramie, 1977—; chmn. bd. Cathedral Home Children, Laramie, 1977—; mem. exec. com. Provence N.W., Helena, Mont., 1980-83, Coalition 14, Phoenix, 1982-84. Pres. Arctic Circle C. of C., Kotzebue, 1966; mem. exec. com. Alaska C. of C., Juneau, 1967; chmn. allocations com. United Way, Anchorage, 1973-75; pres. United Way Anchorage, 1975-76. Served with USN, 1950-55, Korea. Republican. Lodges: Lions; Elks. Home: 3207 Alta Vista Dr Laramie WY 82070 Office: Episcopal Dioces Wyo 104 S 4th Laramie WY 82070

JONES, CARL FOSTER, astronautical engineer; b. Clarksburg, W.Va., Jan. 29, 1923; s. Commadore Dewey and Shirley Belle (George) J.; m. Leona Azlee Hudson, May 2, 1947; children: Allen Foster, Deborah Ann. BS in Archtl. Engring., Finlay Engring. Coll., 1948. Asst. supt. BOP Aircraft GMC, Kansas City, Kans., 1951-55; archtl., mech. and structural engr. Cent. Fedy. GMC, Defiance, Ohio, 1955-57; indsl. engr. Sylvania Elec. Co., Ottawa, Ohio, 1957-58; mfg. engr. Ford Motor Co., Lima, Ohio, 1959-63; plant engr. Ford Motor Co., Indpls., 1963-80; sr. engr. Martin Marietta Co., Vandenberg AFB, Calif., 1981-86; pressure systems mgr. Lockheed Space Ops. Co., Vandenburg AFB, Calif., 1986—. Served with USAAF, 1943-46. Mem. Am. Inst. Plant Engrs. (pres. 1978-79). Republican. Mem. Ch. Nazarene. Home: 604 E Lemon Lompoc CA 93436

JONES, CAROL LEIGH, organist, music educator; b. Covina, Calif., July 23, 1949; d. Earl Lee and Lucille Elenor (Thompson) J.; m. Robert Frank Zadel, Jan. 29, 1977. Grad. prep. Sherwood Music Conservatory, Chgo., 1964; AA, Saddleback Coll., 1986; student Bob St. John, Pomona, Calif., Bill Thomson, Woodland Hill, Calif., George Wright, Hollywood, Calif. Instr. Gould Music, Covina, 1967-72; product specialist Conn Organ Corp., Oakbrook, Ill., 1972-77; concert organist Conn Keyboards, Inc., Carol Stream, Ill., 1978-79, Yamaha Internat., Buena Park, Calif., 1979-80, Norlin Corp., Lincolnshire, Ill., 1980-81, Kimball Internat., Jasper, Ind., 1981—; dir. music edn. Organ Exchange, Inc., San Diego, 1979—; organist, instr. CLJ & Co., Mission Viejo, Calif., 1978—; judge Yamaha Electone Festival, Los Angeles, 1980; arranger Hal Leonard Artist Series, 1974. Rec. artist Have You Met Miss Jones, 1970, Conn. Organ Presents Carol Jones, 1977, Second Time Around, 1982. Sherwood Music Conservatory scholar, 1967. Mem. Keyboard World (favorite female organist 1974), Amateur Organist Assn. Internat. (industry dir. 1977-80, panelist conv. 1982-87), Am. Theatre Organ Soc., Nat. Assn. Music Mchts. Republican. Roman Catholic.

JONES, CARY DENNIS, broadcast executive; b. Los Angeles, July 20, 1950; s. Edward Douglas J. and Alice (Stanton) Serrao; m. Gail Blanchard, Nov. 22, 1980; children: Christina Peyton, Cameron Blair, Tyler Stanton. BA, Washington U., St. Louis, 1972. Account exec. TeleRep Inc., Los Angeles, 1973-75; group sales mgr. Harrington, Righter & Parsons, Los Angeles, Chgo., 1975-80; gen. sales mgr. Eastman CableRep, New York, 1980-81; sr. v.p., gen. mgr. Idaho Ind. TV Inc. and Sta. KTRV-TV, Nampa, Idaho, 1981-86; v.p. Mohawk Broadcasting Ltd., Sta. WPMT-TV, York, Pa; exec. v.p. Shoes Etc. Inc., Boise, Idaho. Mem. Assn. Ind. TV Stas., Idaho State Broadcasters Assn. Democrat. Episcopalian. Club: Crane Creek Country. Home: 797 E Braemere Rd Boise ID 83702 Office: Idaho Ind TV Inc PO Box 1212 Nampa ID 83651 Address: 4331 Fairway Nine Sun Valley ID 83353

JONES, CHARLES J., firefighter; b. Marshfield, Oreg., Jan. 29, 1940; s. Charles J. Cotter and Lois C. (Smith) Meltebeke; m. Carol S. Lund, Jan. 11, 1961 (div. 1966); children: April M., Autumn C.; m. Sharon S. Madsen, Mar. 29, 1969; children: Mary E., Judith A., Kari C. AS in Fire Sci. Tech., Portland Community Coll., 1974; BS in Fire Adminstrn., Eastern Oreg. State Coll., 1983; diploma, Nat. Fire Acad., 1983, Nat. Fire Acad., 1985. Cert. class VI fire officer, Oreg.; lic. real estate agt., Oreg. From firefighter to capt. Washington County Fire Dist., Aloha, Oreg., 1964-74, battalion chief, 1974-81, dir. research and devel., 1981-85, dir. strategic planning, 1986—; cons. Washington County Consol. Communications Agy., 1983-86, chmn. mgmt. bd., 1982-83; mem. adv. bd. Washington County Emergency Med. Services, 1981-83. Editor local newsletter Internat. Assn. Firefighters, 1970; contbr. articles on fire dept. mgmt. to jours. Active Community Planning Orgn., Washington County, 1979—. Served with USAF, 1957-59. Mem. Internat. Assn. Fire Chiefs, Oreg. Fire Chiefs Assn. (chmn. seminar com. 1982-83, co-chmn. 1981, 84, 86, 87). Republican. Congregationalist. Club: Pontiac (Portland). Avocations: photography, genealogy, antique auto restoration, traveling, writing. Office: Washington County Fire Dist 1 20665 SW Blanton Aloha OR 97007

JONES, CLARK DAVID, restaurant executive, accountant; b. Wells, Nev., May 12, 1935; s. Waldo LeRoy and Beatrice (Bollschweiler) J.; m. LaRue Morrison, Nov. 20, 1953; children—Debra, Pam, David, Diane, Christy. B.S. in Acctg., U. Nev., 1957; postgrad. U. Utah, 1964-65. C.P.A., Nev. Mgr., Al Huber, C.P.A., Elko, Nev., 1960-62; ptnr. Main Hurdman C.P.A.s, Salt Lake City, 1962-70; v.p. fin. JB's Restaurants, Inc., Salt Lake City, 1970-81, pres., 1981—. Served to 1st lt. U.S. Army, 1958-60. Mem. Utah Soc. C.P.A.s, Am. Mgmt. Assn., Am. Inst. C.P.A.s. Republican. Mormon. Club: Rotary of Sugarhouse. Home: 9717 South Ruskin Circle Sandy UT 84092 Office: JB's Restaurants Inc 1010 W 2610 S Salt Lake City UT 84119

JONES, DANIEL YOUNG, private investigation company executive; b. Los Angeles, Sept. 21, 1949; s. John Jay and Peggy (Johnson) J.; A.A., Los Angeles Valley Coll., 1976; postgrad. U. So. Calif., 1976-77; hon. degree, Van Nuys Coll. Bus.; m. Cheryl L. Blair, May 21, 1983; children: Beverly Jane, Colin Blair. Mgr. S.S. Kresge Co., 1970-74; br. rep. Transamerica, 1974-75; mgr. P & C Investigation Agy., Encino, Calif., 1975-77; partner Costello, Jones & Assos., Burbank, Calif., from 1977, sr. mng. partner, now owner; chief exec. officer D.Y. Jones & Assocs., Inc. Mem. Calif. Assn. Lic. Investigators (dir. 1979, 81, chmn. bd. dirs. 1983-84, pres. 1984-85, chmn. investigator security polit. action com. 1982-84, 86-87), Nat. Council Investigation and Security Services (bd. dirs. 1985—), Council Internat. Investigators, World Assn. Detectives. Club: Burbank Noon Lions. Office: 300 S Glendale Ave Suite 400 Glendale CA 91205

JONES, DAVID B., venture capitalist, corporation executive; b. Jamestown, N.Y., Oct. 12, 1943; s. Gustav E. and Jeane Louise (Nord) J.; m. Cornelia Corson Morris, Sept. 3, 1966; children—Caroline Vaughan, David Kristofer. A.B., Dartmouth Coll., 1965; M.B.A., U. So. Calif., 1967, J.D., 1970. Admitted to Calif. bar, 1971; assoc. firm Hufstedler, Miller, Carlson & Beardsley, Los Angeles, 1970-72; v.p. Union Venture Corp., Los Angeles, 1972-78; v.p. fin. Am. Technology, Inc., Northridge, Calif., 1978, The Tannery West Corp., San Francisco, 1978-79; pres. First Interstate Capital, Inc. and First Interstate Equities Corp., Los Angeles, 1979-85; gen. ptnr. InterVen Ptnrs., 1985—; pres. InterVen Ptnrs., Inc., 1985—; dir. The Birchter Corp., Gigabit Logic, Inc., Sensormedics Corp. Mem. Western Assn. Venture Capitalists (former v.p., dir.), So. Pacific Regional Assn. Small Bus. Investment Cos. (former pres.), Nat. Assn. Small Bus. Investment Cos. (chmn. elect 1986—, bd. govs.) (exec. com.). Club: Jonathan. Office: 333 S Grand Ave Suite 4050 Los Angeles CA 90071

JONES, DENNIS LEE, accountant; b. Sioux City, Iowa, Aug. 20, 1951; s. Loren Herbert and Harriet (Oertel) J. AA, Pasadena City Coll., 1971; BA, U. Redlands, 1973. CPA, Calif. Acct. Owl Rock Products, Arcadia, Calif., 1973-77; acct. Abahsiain-Owl, Riyadh, Saudi Arabia, 1977-78, adminstrv. mgr., 1978-80; staff acct. Lyndall Larsson, CPA, Arcadia, 1980-82; CPA R.W. Jackson, Accountancy Corp., Pasadena, Calif., 1982—. Chmn. fin. com. Pasadena Covenant Ch., 1983—. Mem. Swedish Club Los Angeles. Republican. Avocation: community theatre. Office: Richard W Jackson Accountancy Corp 1250 E Walnut Suite 210 Pasadena CA 91106

JONES, DENNY ALAN, engineering educator; b. Port Angeles, Wash., Jan. 20, 1938; s. Lloyd Leo Jones and Alice Jean (Kendrick) Vines; m. Wanda Wallace, Dec. 30, 1962; children: Regina, Gillian, Michael, Bryce. BS, U. Nev., Reno, 1960; MS, U. Ariz., 1962; PhD, Rensselaer Poly., Troy, N.Y., 1966. Research chemist Kaiser Aluminum, Spokane, Wash., 1966-68; sr. research engr. Battelle-Northwest, Richland, Wash., 1968-70; asst. prof. U. Hawaii, Honolulu, 1970-74; sr. research engr. U.S. Steel Corp., Monroeville, Pa., 1974-79; prof. engring. U. Nev., Reno, 1979—, chmn. dept. chem. and metall. engring., 1984—; cons. Electric Power research Inst., Palo Alto, Calif., 1980-85, Dept. Energy, Las Vegas, 1985-86. Contbr. articles to profl. jours. Grantee Am. Iron and Steel Inst., 1980-83, NSF, 1982-86, Electric Power Research Inst., 1985-86. Mem. Nat. Assn. Engrs. (cert. corrosion specialist), Nat. Assn. Corrosion Engrs., Am. Soc. Metals, ASTM. Republican. Mormon. Avocations: golf, camping. Home: 1705 Plymouth Way Sparks NV 89431 Office: U Nev Dept Chem and Metall Engring Reno NV 89557

JONES, DONNA RUTH, librarian; b. Denver, June 23, 1948; d. Don and Ruth Virginia (Hampton) Lusk; 1 child, Matthew Trevor. BA, Ft. Hays State U., 1969; MLS, Emporia State U., 1972. Librarian, instr. Colby (Kans.) Community Coll., 1969-76; dir. library services Pioneer Meml. Library, Colby, 1976-85; dir. Ark. Valley Regional Library Service System, Pueblo, Colo., 1985—; adj. prof. library sci. Ft. Hays State U., 1972-73, 78-80; cons. N.W. Kans. Library Systen, 1970-71, 74, humanities cons., 1979—. Researcher: (movie and brochure) Country School Legacy: Humanities on the Frontier, 1980-82. Mem., chmn. Kans. Com. for Humanities, Topeka, 1979-85; pres. Thomas County Day Care, Colby, 1983-85; chmn. state steering com. Humanities in Pub. Libraries, 1980-85; active Colo. Endowment for the Humanities, Denver, 1986—. Recipient Jr. Mems. Round Table award 3-M, 1975, Young Alumni award Ft. Hays State U., 1979. Mem. ALA, Mountain Plains Library Assn. (pres. 1984-85), Beta Sigma Phi (Sister of Yr.). Republican. Methodist. Lodge: Order of Eastern Star. Home: 2 Pedregal Ln Pueblo CO 81005 Office: Ark VAlley Regional Library Service System 205 W Abriendo Pueblo CO 81004

JONES, DOROTHY CAMERON, educator; b. Detroit, Feb. 5, 1922; d. Vinton Ernest and Beatrice Olive (Cameron) J. B.A., Wayne State U., 1943, M.A., 1944; Ph.D., U. Colo., 1965. Attendance officer Detroit Bd. Edn., 1943-44; tchr. English Denby High Sch., Detroit, 1946-56, 57-58; exchange tchr. Honolulu, 1956-57; instr., asst. prof. English Colo. Women's Coll., Denver, 1962-66; mem. faculty U. No. Colo., Greeley, 1966—; prof. English U. No. Colo., 1974—. Contbr. articles to profl. lit. Served with WAVES USNR, 1944-46. Faculty research grantee, 1970, 76. Mem. Internat. Shakespeare Assn., Central States Renaissance Soc., Patristic, Medieval and Renaissance Conf., Rocky Mountain Medieval and Renaissance Soc., Rocky Mountain MLA, Delta Kappa Gamma, Pi Lambda Theta. Home: Apt 312 1009 13th Ave Greeley CO 80631 Office: Dept English 40 Michener Library U No Colo Greeley CO 80639

JONES, DOROTHY RAVAE, psychiatric social worker; b. Kans., Nov. 24, 1938; d. William Chrisman and Georgie Ann (Truman) Wright; m. William Paul Jones, Mar. 19, 1983; children: Michael Shircliff, Steven Shircliff, Ravae Adams. BSW, U. Nev., Las Vegas, 1976. Counselor So. Nev. Drug Abuse Council, Las Vegas, 1977-78; social worker So. Nev. Mental Retardation Services, Las Vegas, 1978-81, psychiat. social worker, 1982—; psychiat. social worker Las Vegas Mental Health Ctr., Las Vegas, 1981-82; cons. Desertview Devel. Services, Las Vegas, 1982-85. Participant March for Women's Lives, Los Angeles, 1986. Mem. Nat. Assn. Social Workers, NOW, U. Nev.-Las Vegas Alumni Assn. Home: 856 N Mountridge Ct Las Vegas NV 89110 Office: So Nev Mental Retardation Services 1300 S Jones Blvd Las Vegas NV 89158

JONES, DOUGLAS CHARLES, export marketing executive; b. San Diego, May 31, 1950; s. Frank and Ruby Jones; m. Joyce Adena, Jan. 19, 1984; children: Michelle, Aaron, Desiré. AA, San Diego City Coll., 1971; student, Calif. State U., Northridge, 1971-73; BA in Fin., Nat. U., 1986. Profl. football player Buffalo, 1973-79; ops. mgr. Nuttall Styris Inc., San Diego, 1980-82; mktg. cons. Logans Mktg., San Diego, 1985—; pres., chief exec. officer Douglas Trading Co., San Diego, 1985—; world trade cons. Jadd Found., San Diego, 1985—, mktg. cons. Clark Industries, Pasadena, Calif., 1984—. Author: Finance Through Government Programs, 1985. Mem. Rep. Nat. Com., Washington, 1985. Recipient 2d 110 Meter High Hurdles award Nat. Collegiate Athletic Assn., 1972, 73. Baptist. Office: PO Box 15525 San Diego CA 92115

JONES, EARL, former college president, research specialist; b. Canton, Okla, Aug. 4, 1925; s. Hercel C. and Florence (Hill) L.; m. Eleanor Harriett Vance, July 15, 1951; children: Beverly Anne, Mark Earl, James Richard, Cindy Kay. B.S. Oreg. State U., 1949; M.S., Inter-Am. Inst. of OAS, Turrialba, Costa Rica, 1958; Ed.D., Mont. State U., 1962. Tchr. pub. schs. Ontario, Oreg., 1949-55; dir. rural programs Sta. KSRV, Ontario, 1955-56; dir. Sta. KSLM, Salem, Oreg., 1956; vocat. dir. Arcata Pub. Schs., Calif., 1956-57; instr. Inter-Am. Inst., 1957-58, asst. prof., 1960-62; assoc. prof. sociology UCLA, 1963-66; prof. sociology and edn., assoc. dean Tex. A&M U. Coll. Edn., 1967-71; pres. Incarnate Word Coll., San Antonio, 1971-73; sr. research specialist Devel. Assocs., San Francisco, 1974—; dir. research office Devel. Assocs., San Antonio, 1977—; prof. Antioch U., West San Antonio, 1977—; dir. research Caribbean Inst. Sociology and Anthropology, Caracas, Venezuela, 1963-65; chair prof. U. Chile Sch. Law, Santiago, Valparaiso, 1965-66; vis. prof. Royal Danish Acad., Copenhagen, 1955, U. P.R., Mayaguez, 1960, Cath. U., Caracas, 1963-65, U. Pacific, 1966, Calif. State Coll.-Los Angeles, Calif. State Coll.-San Francisco, 1968; prof. Antioch Coll., 1973—; cons. Mexican-Am. Cultural Ctr., San Antonio, 1973-75; mem. Gov.'s Com. on Confluence of Tex. Cultures, 1969-76, Gov's Com. to Reconstruct Tchr. Edn., 1969-72; cons. Cabinet Com. on Spanish Speaking Peoples, 1972-75. Author: Rural Youth in the Americas, 1960, Lideracao, 1961, A Study of the Costa Rican Extension Service, 1962, The Cooperative Extension Services of Jamaica, 1962, Supervision en Extension Agricola, 1963, Latin American Literature for Youth, 1968, Some Perspectives on the Americas, 1968, Self-Identification and the Americas, 1970, Social Atitudes of South Texas Primary Children, 1976, (with others) Teacher Classroom Behaviors, 1977, Case Studies in Educational Change, 1978, Client Satisfaction with Services to Limited and Non-English-Speaking Students In California, 1980, Study of Small Farmer Titling in Honduras, 1983, Supply and Demand of Professionals in Sri Lanka, 1984. Served with USMCR, 1943-46. Recipient Presdl. citation Republic of Guatemala, 1969; recipient Standard Oil Disting. Teaching Award, 1970. Mem. Am. Sociol Assn., Rural Sociol. Soc., Alpha Zeta, Phi Kappa Delta. Democrat. Roman Catholic. Lodge: Lions. Home: 2695 37th Ave San Francisco CA 94116 Office: 1475 N Broadway Suite 200 Walnut Creek CA 94596

JONES, EBON RICHARD, retailing executive; b. Oak Park, Ill., Aug. 23, 1944; s. Ebon Clark and Marilyn B. (Dow) J.; m. Sally Samuelson, Jan. 27, 1968; children: Stephanie Blythe, Heather Denise. B.A., Priceton U., 1966; M.B.A., Stanford U., 1968. Adminstrv. asst. Nat. Air Pollution Control Adminstrn., Washington, 1968-70; cons. McKinsey & Co., San Francisco and Paris, 1970-83; exec. v.p. Safeway Stores Inc., Oakland, Calif., 1983-86, group v.p., 1986—. Chmn. bd. San Francisco Zool. Soc., 1979-84, pres. 1985—; trustee San Francisco Trust; Crystal Springs Uplands Sch., 1986—. Served to lt. USPHS, 1968-70. Mem. Phi Beta Kappa. Home: 58 Chester Way San Mateo CA 94402 Office: Safeway Stores Inc 201 4th St Oakland CA 94660

JONES, EDWARD LOUIS, history educator; b. Georgetown, Tex., Jan. 15, 1922; s. Henry Horace and Elizabeth (Steen) J.; m. Dorothy M. Showers, Mar. 1, 1952 (div. Sept. 1963); children: Cynthia, Frances, Edward Lawrence; Lynne Ann McGreevy, Oct. 7, 1963; children Christopher Louis, Teresa Lynne. BA in Philosophy, U. Wash., 1952, BA in Far East, 1952, BA in Speech, 1955, postgrad., 1952-54; JD, Gonzaga U., 1967. Social worker Los Angeles Pub. Assistance, 1956-57; producer, dir. Little Theatre, Hollywood, Calif. and Seattle, 1956-60; research analyst, cons. to Office of Atty. Gen., Olympia and Seattle, Wash., 1963-66; coordinator of counseling SOIC, Seattle, 1966-68; lectr., advisor, asst. to dean U. Wash., Seattle, 1968—; instr. Gonzaga U., Spokane, Wash., 1961-62, Seattle Community Coll., 1967-68; dir. drama workshop, Driftwood Players, Edmonds, Wash., 1975-76. Author: Tutankhamon: Son of the Sun, King of Upper and Lower Egypt, 1978, Black Orators' Workbook, 1982, Black Zeus, 1972, Profiles in African Heritage, 1972; editor, pub. NACADA Jour. Nat. Acad. Advising Assn., 1981—, Afro-World Briefs newsletter, 1985—. V.p. Wash. Com. on Consumer Interests, Seattle, 1966-68. Served to 2d lt. F.A., 1940-45. Recipient Outstanding Teaching award U. Wash., 1986; Frederick Douglass scholar Nat. Council Black Studies, 1985, 86. Mem. Nat. Assn. Student Personnel Adminstrs., Smithsonian Inst. (assoc.), Am. Acad. Polit. and Social Sci., Nat. Acad. Advising Assn. (bd. dirs. 1979-82, Cert. of Appreciation 1982, editor Jour. 1981—, award for Excellence 1985). Democrat. Baptist. Avocations: travel, research, chess. Office: U Wash Seattle WA 98195

JONES, ERIC DANIEL, physicist; b. Oakland, Calif., Jan. 6, 1936; s. Howard M. and Patience K. (Falconer) J.; m. Mary Ann Hackworth, June 1, 1957; children: Jennifer, Eric Jr., Kelly, Kimberly, Suzanne. BS in Physics, Oreg. State U., 1957; MS in Physics, U. Wash., 1959, PhD in Physics, 1962. Mem. tech. staff solid state physics Bell Telephone Labs., Murray Hill, N.J., 1962-65; mem. tech. staff solid state physics Sandia Nat. Labs, Albuquerque, 1965-68, supr. laser research, 1968-83, mem. tech. staff laser research, 1983-86, mem. tech. staff solid state physics, 1986—. Contbr. articles to profl. jours. Nat. chmn. Jr. Olympics Diving, Indpls., 1980; v.p. U.S. Diving, Indpls., 1981. Fellow Am. Physics Soc.; mem. AAAS. Republican. Avocations: outdoor activities, stock market. Home: 1528 Figueroa NE Albuquerque NM 87112 Office: Sandia Nat Labs Div 1143 PO Box 5800 Albuquerque NM 87188

JONES, E.(VERETT) BRUCE, consulting civil engineer; b. Ft. Collins, Colo., Sept. 23, 1933; s. Donald Lee and Muriel Virginia (Gwynn) J.; m. M. Margie Raben, May 27, 1956; children: Elizabeth Gwynn, Janet Lee. BS, U. Wyo., 1955; MS, Pa. State U., 1959; DrPh, Colo. State U., 1964. Chief water devel. State of Wyo., Cheyenne, 1959-61; engr., hydrologist D.W. Barr and Assocs., Mpls., 1964-65; asst. dir. Inst. for Land and Water Research, Pa. State U., University. Park, 1965-68; coordinator water resources EG&G, Inc., Boulder, Colo., 1968-70; v.p., pres. M.W. Bittinger and Assocs., Ft. Collins, 1970-77; pres. Resource Cons., Inc., Ft. Collins, 1977—; v.p. Wyo. Well Service, Inc., Cody, 1965-71; v.p. research Land and Water Cons., Inc., 1972-75; pres. Aetech West, Inc., Ft. Collins, 1982-83. Contbr. articles to profl. jours. Served to 1st lt. U.S. Army, 1955-57. NDEA fellow, Colo. State U., 1961-64. Mem. ASCE, Am. Soc. Agrl. Engrs., Am. Geophys. Union, Am. Meteorol. Soc., Wyo. Engring. Soc., Cons. Engrs. Council of Colo., Sigma Xi, Phi Kappa Phi, Xi Sigma Pi, Sigma Gamma Epsilon. Republican. Presbyterian. Lodges: Masons, Rotary. Office: Resource Cons Inc 402 W Mountain Fort Collins CO 80521

JONES, G. KEVIN, lawyer; b. Salt Lake City, Dec. 11, 1951; s. Garth Nelson and Verda Marie (Clegg) J. B.S. summa cum laude, Brigham Young U., 1974, J.D. cum laude, 1977; LL.M. in Energy Law, U. Utah, 1984. Bar: Utah 1979, U.S. Dist. Ct. Utah 1979, U.S. Ct. Appeals (10th cir.) 1981. Legis. asst. to senator, Washington, 1977-78; atty. Alaska Ct. System, Kenai, 1979-80; atty., advisor U.S. Dept. Interior, Salt Lake City, 1980—; mem. adj. faculty Sch. Justice, U. Alaska, Anchorage, Brigham Young U., Utah Tech. Coll.; cons. Grad. Sch. Bus., U. Alaska, Anchorage, 1977. Contbr. articles to profl. jours. Campaign worker Republican Party, Provo, Utah, 1973-77. Mem. Utah State Bar Assn., ABA, Phi Kappa Phi. Mormon. Home: 1839 S Wasatch Dr Salt Lake City UT 84108 Office: Office Solicitor US Dept Interior 125 S State St Salt Lake City UT 84138

JONES, GARTH NELSON, educator; b. Salt Lake City, Feb. 25, 1925; s. Harry H. and Sophronia Dubois (Nelson) J.; m. Verda Marie Clegg, Sept. 29, 1950; children: Edward Hood, Garth Kevin, Drew Luke. B.S., Utah State U., 1947; M.S., U. Utah, 1948, Ph.D., 1954. Mem. faculty Brigham Young U., Provo, Utah, 1953-56; with AID, Indonesia, 1957-61, Pakistan, 1967-69; mem. faculty U. So. Calif., 1961-67; sr. scholar East-West Center, Hawaii, 1969-70; mem. faculty Colo. State U., 1970-72; with UN, N.Y.C., 1972-73; mem. faculty U. Alaska, Anchorage, 1973—; former dean Sch. Bus. and Public Adminstrn. U. Alaska; vice chmn. Alaska Council Edn.; cons. to govt. and industry, World Bank, UN Population Program, Ford Found. Rural Devel. Contbr. articles to profl. jours. Chmn. Anchorage Mayor's Ad Hoc Govtl. Rev. Commn., Anchorage Urban Obs. Fulbright-Hayes scholar, Taiwan, 1982. Mormon. Office: Univ Alaska 3221 Providence Dr Anchorage AK 99508

JONES, GERALD JOSEPH, former broadcasting exec.; b. Saginaw, Mich., May 22, 1920; s. LaVern Pierce and Yvonne Maria (Berthaud) J.; student Los Angeles Jr. Coll., 1939; m. Madelyn Fio Rito, Nov. 15, 1970; children by previous marriage—Jennifer Jones Batteau, Steven G. Account exec. Murray Dymock, 1946, West-Holliday, 1947-50, The Katz Agy., Inc., 1950-60, v.p., 1967-78, West Coast mgr., 1977-78, v.p. sta. and industry relations, 1978-80. Served to flight lt. RCAF, 1941-45. Decorated D.F.C.; col. Staff of Gov. John McKeithen, La., 1971. Mem. Pacific Pioneer Broadcasters, So Calif. Advt. Golfers Assn. Republican. Clubs: Bel Air, Woburn Golf and Country (Milton Keynes, Eng.), Milline (sec. 1963-66); Thunderbird Country. Home: 10690 Somma Way Los Angeles CA 90077

JONES, J. GILBERT, research consultant; b. San Francisco, June 1, 1922; s. Enoch Roscoe L. Sr. and Remedios (Ponce de Leon) J.; student U.S. Mcht. Marine Acad., 1942-44, San Francisco City Coll., 1942-44, 46-47; A.B., U. Calif.-Berkeley, 1949, M.A., 1952. Ins. insp. Ins. Cos. Insp. Bur., San Francisco, 1959-62; pub. relations cons., San Francisco, 1962-67; ins. insp. Am. Service Bur., San Francisco, 1967-72; propr., mgr. Dawn Universal Internat. San Francisco, 1972—, Dawn Universal Security Service, San Francisco, 1983—. Mem. Calif. Republican Assembly, 1978—. Mem. Calif. Assn. Lic. Investigators, SAR, Sons Spanish-Am. War Vets., U. Calif. Alumni Assn. Hist. research on music and revolution. Office: PO Box 4239 San Francisco CA 94101

JONES, JACK ALAN, mechanical engineer, consultant; b. Newark, Apr. 15, 1948; s. James Corbett and Mertel Mathilda (Bergbauer) J. Cert., U. Calif., Santa Barbara, 1969; BSME, Rutgers U., 1970; MSME, Rice U., 1973. Registered profl. engr., N.J. Mech. engr. Bechman Instruments, Irvine, Calif., 1973-74; sr. engr. Garrett A. Research, Torrance, Calif., 1974-79; sr. engr., mem. tech. staff Jet Propulsion Lab., Pasadena, Calif., 1979—; cons. Aerojet Electro Systems, Azusa, Calif., 1985-86. Contbr. articles to profl. jours.; patentee sorption cryogenic refrigeration. NSF fellow, 1970-73; Dirs. Discretionary grantee, 1985-86. Mem. AIAA, ASME, Sigma Xi. Democrat. Avocation: outdoor activities. Office: Jet Propulsion Lab 4800 Oak Grove Dr Pasadena CA 91109

JONES, JAMES RICHARDSON, civil engineer; b. Los Angeles, Jan. 12, 1943; s. John Richardson and Margaret Elizabeth (Hogan) J.; m. Jean Harp, Aug. 12, 1965 (div. June 1970); m. Ann Louise Engelbrecht, June 5, 1982. BSCE, Calif. State Poly. U., 1968; MSCE, Stanford U., 1972. Registered civil engr., Calif., Nev., Hawaii. Civil engr. U.S. Bur. Reclamation, Sacramento, Calif., Denver, 1968-71; sanitary engr. EPA, San Francisco, 1972-73; staff dir. Lake Tahoe Research Coordination Bd., South Lake Tahoe, Calif., 1974-77; cons. civil engr. Jones & Assocs., South Lake Tahoe, Calif., 1977—; instr. Lake Tahoe Community College, 1975-76. Contbr. tech. articles to profl. jours. Bd. dirs. South Tahoe Pub. Utility Dist., 1977—, pres., 1981-83; bd. dirs. El Dorado County Water Com., 1979-86, pres., 1983-86. Recipient Eagle Scout award Boy Scouts Am., Los Angeles, 1960. Mem. ASCE. Lodge: Kiwanis (pres. 1977-78). Avocations: skiing, sailing. Home and Office: J R Jones & Assocs Box 789 South Lake Tahoe CA 95705-0789

JONES, JAMES THOMAS, state official, lawyer; b. Twin Falls, Idaho, May 13, 1942; s. Henry C. and Eunice Irene (Martens) J.; m. Nancy June Babson, Nov. 25, 1972; 1 dau., Katherine A. Student, Idaho State U., 1960-61; B.A., U. Oreg., 1964; J.D., Northwestern U., 1967. Bar: Idaho 1967. Legis. asst. to U.S. Senator, Washington, 1970-72; law practice Jerome, Idaho, 1973-82; atty. gen. State of Idaho, Boise, 1973—. Bd. dirs. Idaho Cancer Soc. Served to capt. U.S. Army, 1967-79, Vietnam. Decorated Bronze Star; decorated Air medal with 4 oak leaf clusters, Cross of Gallantry (Vietnam), Army Commendation medal. Mem. Idaho Bar Assn., Am. Legion, Idaho Farm Bur., VFW. Republican. Lutheran. Office: Office Atty Gen Statehouse Room 210 Boise ID 83720

JONES, JERRY LYNN, educator; b. Grandfield, Okla., Mar. 28, 1933; s. Euel Taylor and Margie Leona (DeVaughan) J.; m. Gail Kathleen Jones, Aug. 8, 1954; children—Kathleen DeVaughan, Jerry Clifton, Gregory Taylor. B.A., Okla. State U., 1957; M.S. (NSF fellow 1959-60), 1960; postgrad., U. Oreg., 1957-58; Ph.D. (Am. Oil Co. fellow 1961-62), U. Ark., 1963. Asst. prof. chemistry Tex. A&M U. (College Station), 1962-68; asso. prof. chemistry Central Wash U., Ellensburg, 1968-73; prof. Central Wash U., 1973—, interim dean grad. sch. and research, 1976-77, spl. asst. to pres., 1979—. Asso. editor: sci. and tech. USA Today; contbr. articles to profl. jours. Served with AUS, 1954-56. Fellow Am. Inst. Chemists; mem. N.Y. Acad. Scis., Am. Chem. Soc., Sigma Xi, Phi Lambda Upsilon. Club: Masons. Home: 405 N Anderson St Ellensburg WA 98926

JONES, JOEL MACKEY, educational administrator; b. Millersburg, Ohio, Aug. 11, 1937; s. Theodore R. and Edna Mae (Mackey) Jones; m. Nancy Lee Magnuson, May 28, 1982; children—Carolyn Mae, Jocelyn Corinne. B.A., Yale U., 1960; M.A., Miami U., Oxford, Ohio, 1962; Ph.D., U. N.Mex., 1966. Dir. Am. studies U. Md., Balt., 1966-69; chmn. Am. studies U. N.Mex., Albuquerque, 1969-73, asst. v.p. acad. affairs, 1973-77, dean faculties, assoc. provost, prof. Am. studies, 1977-85, v.p. adminstrn., 1985—. Contbr. numerous essays, articles and chpts. to books. Founder Rio Grande Nature Preserve Soc., Albuquerque, 1974—; bd. dirs., mem. exec. com., United Way, Albuquerque, 1980-83; nat. bd. cons. NEH, 1978—. Farwell scholar Yale U., New Haven, 1960; Sr. fellow NEH, 1972; adminstrv. fellow Am. Council Edn., Washington, 1972-73. Mem. Am. Studies Assn., Popular Culture Assn., Am. Assn. Higher Edn. Home: 3109 La Mancha St NW Albuquerque NM 87104 Office: U of N Mex Scholes Hall Albuquerque NM 87131

JONES, JOHN WILLIAM, educator; b. Newark, Jan. 18, 1940; s. John Louis and Esther Virginia (Stevens) J.; m. Elsie Blanche Coogan, Oct. 17, 1964. BS, So. Utah State U., 1970; MEd, Trenton State U., 1976. Cert. tchr., N.J., Utah. Tchr. Lopatcong Elem. Sch., Phillipsburg, N.J., 1970-78, Lakeview Elem. Sch., Roy, Utah, 1978—; asst. coordinator Ogden (Utah) Community Sch., 1980—. Served with U.S. Army, 1959-62, Korea, USNR, 1980—. Mem. NEA, Am. Legion, Utah Edn. Assn., Weber County Edn. Assn. Democrat. Lodge: Elks. Avocations: classical music, skiing, swimming, reading. Home: 2939 N 975 E North Ogden UT 84404 Office: Lakeview Elem Sch 2025 W 5000 S Roy UT 84067

JONES, JOIE PIERCE, scientist, educator, writer; b. Brownwood, Tex., Mar. 4, 1941; s. Aubrey M. and Mildred K. (Pierce) J.; m. Kay Becknell, June 12, 1965. B.A. (Jr. fellow 1961-63), U. Tex., Austin, 1963, M.A., 1965; Ph.D., Brown U., 1970. Sr. scientist Bolt Beranek & Newman, Inc., Cambridge, Mass., 1970-75; asso. prof., dir. ultrasonics research lab. Case Western Res. U. Sch. Medicine, Cleve., 1975-77; prof., chief med. imaging, dir. grad. studies, dept. radiol. scis. U. Calif., Irvine, 1977—; cons. acoustics; pres. Computer Sci. Systems, 1978—; founding gen. ptnr. Of Food and Wine, 1982—, Meditherm Assocs., Ltd., 1983-85, Spar Techs., 1987—, Spar Techs., 1987—; proposal reviewer NSF and NIH, 1974—; Appointee sci. and tech. adv. com. Pres. Carter, 1977-81. Author 2 books; mem. editorial bd. Ultrasound in Medicine and Biology, 1976, IEEE Procs, 1976, Jour. Clin. Ultrasound, 1977—; contbr. 150 articles to profl. jours.; patentee in field. Active vol. local govt. Mem. Am. Inst. Ultrasound in Medicine, Acoustical Soc. Am., Am. Phys. Soc., IEEE, AAAS, Am. Assn. Physicists in Medicine, Fedn. Am. Scientists, So. Calif. Wine and Food Soc., Phi Beta Kappa. Democrat. Home: 2094 San Remo Dr Laguna Beach CA 92651 Office: Dept Radiol Sci U Calif Irvine CA 92717

JONES, JOSEPH CLARKE, gynecologist obstetrician; b. Chgo., Feb. 11, 1927; s. Joseph Oscar and Vella Ann (Clarke) J.; m. Dorene Rushforth, June 28, 1954; children: Joseph Rushforth, Mary Ann Wilson, Blaine Rushforth, Lloyd Rushforth. BA, U. Utah, 1951, MD, 1955. Resident in ob-gyn LDS Hosp., Salt Lake City, 1958-61; head ob-gyn dept Cottonwood Hosp., Murray, Utah, 1966-67, chief of staff, 1970; practice medicine specializing in ob-gyn Midvale, Utah, 1970—; med. advisor FHP State Med. Assn., Salt Lake City, 1979-82. Rank advancement chmn. Murray Boy Scouts Am., also active adult leader; mem. planning com. for expansion Cottonwood Hosp., 1975-77; mem. planning bd. Alta View Hosp., Sandy, Utah, 1977-81. Served to capt. USAF, 1956-58. Recipient Eagle Scout award. Mem. AMA, Utah State Med. Assn. (nomenclature com. 1979-85), Salt Lake County Med. Assn. Mormon.

JONES, KATHRYN NAOMI, social worker; b. Gallup, N.Mex., Mar. 1, 1921; d. James Madison and Eunice Amber (Jenkins) J. BBA, West Tex. State U., 1943; MSW, U. So. Calif., 1955. Program dir. YWCA, Wichita, Kans., 1946-49; child welfare worker State of N.Mex., Gallup, 1950-62; exec. dir. Family Consultation, Gallup, 1962-69; supr. social work Bur. Indian Affairs, Crownpoint, N.Mex., 1969-81; social work program specialist Bur. Indian Affairs, Window Rock, Ariz., 1981—. Named Woman of Yr., Bus. and Profl. Women, 1964. Mem. AAUW, Acad. Cert. Social Workers. Democrat. Methodist. Avocation: fin. planning. Home: 915 E Hill Apt 5 Gallup NM 87301 Office: Bur Indian Affairs PO Box M Window Rock AZ 86501

JONES, LARRY RICHARD, advertising executive; b. Altadena, Calif., July 31, 1947; s. Roy Herman and Helen (Gibson) J.; m. Jane Sullivan, July 22, 1971 (div. May 1980). BS in Mktg., San Diego State U., 1970; cert., Inst. Advanced Advt. Studies, 1974. Mktg. rep. IBM, Los Angeles, 1970-74; v.p., mgmt. supr. Grey Advt., Los Angeles, 1974-81; sr. v.p., group mgmt. dir. Foote, Cone & Belding, Los Angeles, 1981—, pres. mgmt., adv. bd., 1986—. Co. dir. United Way, Los Angeles, 1985. Served as sgt. U.S. Army, 1971. Mem. Advt. Club Los Angeles. Avocations: golf, racquetball. Office: Foote Cone & Belding 11601 Wilshire Blvd Los Angeles CA 90025

JONES, LEON BRUCE, research gemologist; b. Seattle, May 14, 1956; s. John Paul and Nola (DeLong) J.; divorced; children: L. Brandon, Devon Danielle. BA in Geology, Trinity U., 1978; grad., Gemmol. Inst. Am., 1978; postgrad., U. Wash., 1982-83. Pres. Pacific Gemological Services, Seattle, 1979-83; v.p., dir. of research and edn. Am. Gem Market System, Lafayette, Calif., 1984-85; sr. research gemologist Am. Gem Market System, Moraga, Calif., 1985; cons. Seattle, 1986—; gemologist Deutsche Gemolis Gesselschaft, Fed. Republic Germany, 1982. Contbr. articles to profl. jours. Fellow Gemological Assn. Gt. Britain; mem. Gemological Assn. of Australia, Mineral. Soc. of Am., Nat. Assoc. Jewelry Appraisers (sr.),Pacific N.W. Gemological Assn. (founder, past pres.). Avocations: flying, skydiving, motorcycling, boating, skiing. Home and Office: 201 E Park Dr Aisacortes WA 98221

JONES, LEWIS HAMMOND, IV, physicist; b. Cleve., Feb. 26, 1941; s. Lewis H. and Ruth R. (Iden) J. BA in Physics, Ohio Wesleyan U., 1963; MS in Physics, U. Ill., 1965, PhD in Physics, 1971. Vis. scientist CEN-SACLAY, Gif-sur-Yvette, France, 1971-72, Laboratori Nazionali di Frascati, Frascati, Italy, 1972-74; research assoc. U. Md., College Park, 1974-77; asst. research physicist U. Calif., Irvine, 1978; mem. research staff Fairchild Research and Devel., Palo Alto, Calif., 1979-83, test enging. supr., 1984—. Contbr. articles to profl. jours. Mem. AAAS, Am. Phys. Soc., Sierra Club, Phi Beta Kappa. Democrat. Avocations: skiing, backpacking, square dancing, folk dancing, flamenco guitar. Home: 693 Madrone Ave Sunnyvale CA 94086 Office: Fairchild Research and Devel 4001 Miranda Ave M/S 30-9891 Palo Alto CA 94304

JONES, LLEWELLYN HOSFORD, chemical physics researcher, consultant; b. Oberlin, Ohio, Nov. 14, 1919; s. Edward Safford and Frances Christine (Jeffery) J.; m. Eunice Jean Schuster, July 10, 1948; children: David S., Barbara B., Susan H., Cynthia L., Frances J. BS ChemE, U. Mich., 1942; MS in Phys. Chemistry, U. Buffalo, 1947; PhD in Phys. Chemistry, Calif. Inst. Tech., 1950. Instr. U. Rochester, N.Y., 1950-51; staff mem. Los Alamos (N.Mex.) Nat. Lab., 1951-83, fellow, 1983—. Author: Inorganic Vibrational Spectroscopy, 1967; author 200 jour. articles. Served to sgt. U.S. Army, 1943-46, PTO. Mem. Am. Chem. Soc. (chmn. inorganic div. 1975-76). Democrat. Avocations: backpacking, tennis, golf, snorkeling. Home: 24 Loma del Escolar Los Alamos NM 87544 Office: Los Alamos Nat Lab MS-C346 Los Alamos NM 87545

JONES, MARY LOUBRIS, librarian; b. Phila., June 29, 1934; d. Paul Edward and Mollie Frances (Cleeve) Loubris; m. William Whitfield Jones, Sept. 16, 1960 (div. 1980); children: David Cleeve, Paul Morgan. BA, Pa. State U., 1955; student, Oxford (Eng.) U., 1956-57; MA, Northwestern U., 1958; PhD, Colo. U., 1977. Rep. display advt. Boulder (Colo.) Daily Camera newspaper, 1959-63; editor Panther Pubs., Boulder, 1963-66; instr. U. N.Mex, Albuquerque, 1966-68, U. Colo., Boulder, 1968-69, 72-76; sr. editor Omega Group, Ltd., Boulder, 1977-85, librarian, 1985—. Contbr. articles to profl. jours. Active Dem. Caucus, county and state levels, Colo., 1986. Mem. MLA, Spl. Library Assn., Sigma Delta Chi. Club: Third Thursday (Boulder) (meeting com. 1986—). Avocations: reading, embroidery, gardening. Office: Omega Group Ltd PO Box 693 Boulder CO 80306

JONES, MAX DAVID, insurance agency executive, vocational education consultant; b. Bisbee, Cochise County, Ariz., Sept. 25, 1937; s. David Adam and Gladys Ornett (Barham) J.; m. Ina Lee Wilson, Jan. 30, 1959; children—Melinda Lea Jones Sherman, David Troy, Rachelle Susan. B.A., N. Mex. Western Coll., 1961; M.A., Western N. Mex. U., 1964. Cert. tchr., Ariz., N. Mex., Guam; cert. ins. agent, broker, surplus lines and life, Ariz. Tchr. indsl. arts Patagonia (Ariz.) Union High Sch., 1961-64; prin. Guam Trade and Tech. Sch., Agana, Ter. of Guam, 1964-68; dir. Micronesian Occupational Ctr., Palau, Western Caroline Islands, 1968-70; supt. adult, higher vocat. edn. Trust Ter. of Pacific Islands, 1970-72; owner, mgr. Jones-Wilson Ins. Agy., Benson, Ariz., 1972—; vocat. edn. cons. Benson Vol. Fire Dept., 1972—; leader 4-H Club, Catalina council Boy Scouts Am., 1972-79; mem. Indsl. Devel. Authority (Benson), 1983—. Served with USN, 1956-62. Decorated Ancient Order fo Chammori, Gov. Ter. Guam. Mem. Am. Indsl. Arts Assn., Am. Vocat. Assn., Ariz. Indsl. Edn. Assn., Guam Indsl. Edn. Assn. (founder), Micronesian Indsl. Edn. Assn. (founder), Ariz. Fire Chiefs Assn., Ariz. Fire Fighters Assn., Ariz. Ind. Ins. Agts. Assn., Nat. Ind. Ins. Agts. Assn., Cochise County Ind. Ins. Agts. Assn., Benson C. of C., Iota Lambda Sigma, Kappa Pi, Epsilon Pi Tau. Democrat. Clubs: Masons, Scottish Rite, Eastern Star, Eagles. Office: 700 W 4th St Benson AZ 85602

JONES, MICHAEL GEORGE, social services administrator; b. Boston, Jan. 12, 1945; s. Irving J. and Josephine (Dorler) J.; m. Gail Rianda, 1970 (div. 1974); children: Gia, Mathew; m. Toni Stoy, Mar. 5, 1983. BA in Psychology, Calif. State U., Fullerton, 1971; MA in Clin. Psychology, Lone Mountain Coll., 1973. Cert. community coll. psychology tchr., Calif.; lic. child care worker. Asst. dir. Bachmann Hill Sch., Philo, Calif., 1973-74; treatment dir. Idaho Youth Ranch, Rupert, Idaho, 1975-77; asst. dir. Idaho Youth Ranch, Rupert, 1977; v.p. Idaho Youth Ranch, Boise, Idaho, 1981—, exec. dir. Holly Acres Sch., Applegate, Calif., 1978-81. Served with USN, 1962-66. Mem. Idaho Residential Youth Ctrs. (pres. 1985—), Idaho Correctional Assn. (treas. 1983—), Nat. Assn. Homes for Children (accreditation reviewer 1982—). Democrat. Lodge: Optimists (bd. dirs. Boise club 1984—). Avocations: windsurfing, skiing. Office: Idaho Youth Ranch 1417 Main St Boise ID 83702

JONES, MICHAEL RICHARD, architect; b. Los Angeles, Nov. 14, 1944; s. Paul Jones and Charlene (Pritchard) Jennings; m. Sara Van Ammelrooy, June 10, 1972. BArch, Calif. Poly. State U., 1972; M in City Planning, San Diego State U., 1977. Registered architect, Calif., Oreg., Nev., Tex., Ariz., Hawaii. Designer Rick Enging., San Diego, 1972-73, Brian Paul, architect, San Diego, 1973-74; project architect Robert Ferris, San Diego, 1974-76; prin. Environ. Design Co., San Diego, 1976-78; pres. Michael Jones Architects, Inc., San Diego, 1978—; pres. San Diego Land Devel. Co., 1979-84. Pres. Spl. Olympics, San Diego, 1985; served as cpl. USMC, 1962-66, Vietnam. Named Vol. of Yr. Spl. Olympics, San Diego, 1983. Mem. Soc. Am. Registered Architects (pres. 1985-86, service award 1985), AIA, Nat. Council Archtl. Registration Bds. Republican. Club: Toastmasters (pres. 4 clubs, 1974, 79, 84, area gov. 1984, Toastmaster of Yr. Hard Hats chpt. 1978). Lodge: Kiwanis (pres. San Diego chpt. 1978). Avocations: traveling, racquetball, underwater photography, antique doorknobs. Home: 6045 Cirrus St San Diego CA 92110 Office: 2470 Union St San Diego CA 92101

JONES, OSCAR CALVIN, minister; b. San Antonio, Sept. 1, 1932; s. Oscar Sr. and Nonnie Lee (Cunningham) Jones Simpson; m. Peggy Ann Helm, June 12, 1967; children—Dennis Ray, Shawntelle Janora. B.Th., Am. Sch. Divinity, 1968, Th.M., 1971; Ph.D., Trinity Theol. Sem., 1981, D. Min., 1982, postgrad., 1982—. Ordained to ministry Am. Bapt. Chs., 1952. Pastor, counselor St. John Bapt. Ch., Long Beach, Calif., 1965-69; exec. dir. M.A.T.E. Inc., Los Angeles, 1969-71; area rep. ABC, N.Y.C., 1971-83; pastor, counselor Shiloh Bapt. Ch., Sacramento, 1983—; prof. Calif. State U., Sacramento, 1985; western rep. M&M benefit bd. Am. Bapt. Churches U.S.A., N.Y.C., 1986—; mem. supr. Com. Am. Bapt. Credit Union, 1986—; mem. Western Commn. on Ministry, Oakland, 1986—. Author: The Preachers Dilemma, 1978: The 10 Crowns of the Bible, 1974: The Psychological View-Point on Counseling The Black American, 1982; Motifs for Ministry, The Call to the Ministry. Exec. com. Am. Bapt. Black Chs., Valley Forge, Pa., 1969-84; exec. bd. Inter-Faith Service Bur., Sacramento, 1983-84; trustee Am. Bapt. Sem. West, Oakland, Calif., 1985—Am. Bapt. Homes of West. Pastoral clin. edn. Fellow, 1982-84. Mem. Alpha Phi Alpha, Democrat. Office: Shiloh Bapt Ch 3565 9th Ave Sacramento 95817

JONES, ROBERT CLIVE, judge; b. Las Vegas, Nev., July 21, 1947; s. Robert E. and Meryl (Dunn) J.; m. Anita Michele Bunker, Mar. 26, 1970; children: JaNae, Justin, Melissa, Kimberly. BS with honors, Brigham Young U., 1971; JD with honors, UCLA, 1975. Bar: Nev. 1976, U.S. Dist. Ct. Nev. 1976, U.S. Tax Ct. 1979; CPA, Nev. Acct. Laventhol & Horwath, Las Vegas, 1971-72, Touche Ross, Los Angeles, 1974-75, Haskins & Sells, Las Vegas, 1976; assoc. Albright & McGimsey, Las Vegas, 1976; ptnr. Jones & Holt, Las Vegas, 1977-83; chief judge U.S. Bankruptcy Ct., Dist. of Nev., Las Vegas, 1983—. Mem. Order of Coif. Office: Foley Fed Bldg 300 Las Vegas Blvd S Las Vegas NV 89101

JONES, ROBERT EDWARD, justice state supreme court; b. Portland, Oreg., July 5, 1927; s. Howard C. and Leita (Hendricks) J.; m. Pearl F. Jensen, May 29, 1948; children—Jeffrey Scott, Julie Lynn. B.A., U. Hawaii, 1949; J.D., Lewis and Clark Coll., 1953; LL.D. (hon.), City U., Seattle, 1984. Bar: Oreg. 1953. Trial atty. Portland, Oreg., 1953-63; judge Oreg. Circuit Ct., Portland, 1963-83; justice Oreg. Supreme Ct., Salem, 1983—; mem. faculty Nat. Jud. Coll., Am. Acad. Jud. Edn.; pres. Oreg. Circuit Judges Assn., 1967—, Oreg. Trial Lawyers Assn., 1959; former mem. Oreg. Evidence Revision Commn., Oreg. Ho. of Reps.; former chair Oreg. Commn. Prison Terms and Parole Standards; adj. prof. Northwestern Sch. Law, Lewis and Clark Coll. 1963—. Bd. overseers Lewis and Clark Coll. Served to capt. JAGC, USNR. Recipient merit award Multnomah Bar Assn., 1979; Citizen award NCCJ; Service to Mankind award Sertoma Club Oreg.; James Madison award Sigma Delta Chi; named Disting. Grad., Northwestern Sch. Law. Mem. State Bar Oreg. (former chmn. continuing legal edn. com.). Office: Supreme Ct Oregon 1147 State St Salem OR 97310

JONES, ROGER CLYDE, electrical engineer, educator; b. Lake Andes, S.D., Aug. 17, 1919; s. Robert Clyde and Martha (Albertson) J.; m. Katherine M. Tucker, June 7, 1952; children: Linda Lee, Vonnie Lynette. B.S., U. Nebr., 1949; M.S., U. Md., 1953; Ph.D. U. Md., 1963. With U.S. Naval Research Lab., Washington, 1949-57; staff sr. engr. to chief engr. Melpar, Inc., Falls Church, Va., 1957-58; cons. project engr. Melpar, Inc., 1958-59, sect. head physics, 1959-64, chief scientist for physics, 1964; prof. dept. elec. engring. U. Ariz., Tucson, 1964—; dir. quantum electronics lab. U. Ariz., 1968—, adj. prof. radiology, 1978-86, adj. prof. radiation-oncology, 1986—; guest prof. in exptl. oncology Inst. Cancer Research, Aarhus, Denmark, 1982-83. Served with AUS, 1942-45. Mem. Am. Phys. Soc., Optical Soc. Am., Bioelectromagnetics Soc., IEEE, AAAS, NSPE, Am. Coll. Surveying and Mapping, Eta Kappa Nu, Pi Mu Epsilon. Patentee in field. Home: 5809 E 3d St Tucson AZ 85711 Office: U Ariz Dept Elec and Computer Engring Tucson AZ 85711

JONES, RUTH ELAYNE, speech and hearing pathologist; b. Grand Rapids, Mich., July 15, 1920; d. Francis A. and Harriet E. (Madison-Wright) Housler; m. John Arthur Jones, Aug. 5, 1950; children: Jeannine, Joni. Student, Western Mich. U.; AB in Speech and Hearing, Whittier Coll., 1950; postgrad., U. Calif., U. So. Calif., U. Wis. Milwaukee, Wayne State U.; MA, U. Mich., 1960. Teacher elementary and physical edn. Royal Oak (Mich.), Des Moines, 1939-41; audiometrist Montebello (Calif.) Unified Sch. Dist., 1942-50; head cons. Hearing Impaired, Whittier, Calif., 1950-59; cons. San Juan Capistrano, San Clemente, Calif., 1966; county cons. Lake County, Lakeport, Calif., 1965-66; head of speech and hearing program Mt. Eden Hayward (Calif.) Unified Sch. Dist., 1959-67; master therapist San Jose (Calif.) State Coll., 1968; speech and hearing cons. Napa (Calif.) Unified Sch. Dist., 1972-79; speech therapist Fremont Community Clin., 1968-72; pvt. practice Fairfield, Calif. Author: For Speech Sake. Vol. convalescent homes, Carson City, Nev., 1982-85, suicide prevention; vol. RSVP program for sr. citizens hearing impaired classes, 1982-85. Recipient Spl. Hon. Award Calif. State Fedn., San Francisco, 1978, Hon. Award Napa Union Sch. Dist., 1979. Mem. Am. Speech and Hearing Assn. (cert. clin. competence); Council for Exceptional Children, Beta Sigma Phi. Club: Univ. Women's (Whittier, Calif.). Home: 31 Shady Tree Ln Carson City NV 89701

JONES, TERRY LYNN, accountant; b. Brownfield, Tex., Oct. 14, 1949; s. Edward Franklin and Leona Marie (Mangis) J.; m. Marjorie Lucille Tucker, July 25, 1969; children: Angela, Melissa, Christopher, Jonathan. BBA, Tex. Tech U., 1971. CPA, N.Mex., Tex. Jr. acct. Williams and Easterwood, Lubbock, Tex., 1971-72, Deason, Peters, Stockton & Co., Roswell, N.Mex., 1972-73, sr. acct., 1974-77; sr. acct. Alfonso Garza & Assocs., San Antonio, 1973-74; ptnr. Nulf, Jones and Co., CPA's, Ruidoso, N.Mex., 1977-86; pvt. practice acctg., Ruidoso, 1986—. Treas., Ruidoso Gymnastics Acad., 1984—. Mem. Am. Inst. CPA's, N.Mex. Soc. CPA's, Tex. Soc. CPA's Democrat. Baptist. Lodges: Rotary (v.p. internat. service Ruidoso 1983-84), Elks (treas. Ruidoso 1980-81). Home: 105 Rim Rd Ruidoso NM 88345 Office: PO Box 3210 HS Ruidoso NM 88345

JONES, THELMA LOUISA, chamber of commerce exec.; b. Price, Utah, Feb. 5, 1939; d. Levi and Luella Josephine (Heaps) Tyron; m. Vernon W. Jones, July 5, 1958; children—Brian W., Kurt A., Vicki M. Student Coll. of Eastern Utah, 1957-59. Owner/mgr. Thelma's Fabrics, 1970-76; exec. dir. Carbon County C. of C., Price, Utah, 1974—. Chmn. bd. dirs. Coll. of Eastern Utah Prehistoric Mus. Recipient Outstanding Community Service award Price Rotary Internat., 1979; Woman of Yr. award Bus. and Profl. Women of Price, 1980; Community Service award City of Price, 1981. Mem. U.S. C. of C., Utah C. of C. (dir.), Castle Country Travel Council (chmn. bd. dirs.), Bus. and Profl. Women of Price, LWV (pres. 1982-83). Democrat. Mormon. Clubs: Soroptimist Internat. (pres. 1978-80), Ladies of Elks. Home: 734 North 600 East Price UT 84501 Office: 200 E Main North Entrance Price UT 84501

JONES, THOMAS ARTHUR, chemist; b. Denver, Feb. 20, 1960; s. Robert Jay and Barbara Jane (Linder) J. BS, Colo. Sch Mines, 1982. Commd. capt. U.S. Army, Ft. Hood, Tex., 1983, chem. officer, 1983-85; lab. supr. U.S. Army, Johnston Island, 1985; project chemist U.S. Army, Dugway, Utah, 1986—, EAI Corp., Joppa, Md., 1986-87; systems analyst Boeing Corp., Seattle, 1987—. Mem. Sons Am. Revolution, Colo., 1983. Mem. Am. Chem. Soc. Republican. Lutheran. Avocations: fishing, hunting, bicycling. Home: 1591 NW Mountain View Rd Silverdale WA 98383 Office: Boeing Seattle WA 84022

JONES, THOMAS EDWARD, medical technologist; b. Los Angeles, Dec. 1, 1948; s. Leonard Martin and Ada Frances (Sprague) J. BS in Microbiology, San Diego State U., 1974. Supr. microbiology Plasma Inc., Long Beach, Calif., 1977-80, supr. microbiology and hematology, 1981-84; med. technologist San Bernardino (Calif.) County Med. Ctr., 1984-85, supervising med. technologist, 1985—. Served with U.S. Army, 1969-71. Mem. Am. Soc. Microbiology, AAAS, Am. Soc. Clin. Pathology (assoc., cert. med. technologist), Internat. Aerobatic Club, Exptl. Aircraft Assn., Mensa. Democrat. Avocations: stunt flying, photography. Home: PO Box 441 Crestline CA 92325 Office: San Bernardino County Med Ctr Clin Lab 780 E Gilbert St San Bernardino CA 92404

JONES, THOMAS ROBERT, social worker; b. Escanaba, Mich., Jan. 3, 1950; s. Gene Milton and Alica Una (Mattson) J.; m. Joy Sedlock. BA, U. Laverne, 1977; MSW, U. Hawaii, 1979. Social work assoc. Continuing Care Services, Camarillo, Calif., 1973-78; psychiat. social worker Camarillo State Hosp., 1980-84; psychotherapist Terkensha Child Treatment Ctr., Sacramento, Calif., 1984—. Mem. Nat. Assn. Social Workers, Soc. Clin. Social Work, Am. Orthopsychiat. Assn., Acad. Cert. Social Workers, Assn. for Advancement Behavior Therapy. Avocations: creative writing, photography, drawing, improvizational comedy. Home: 17 Griggs Ln Napa CA 94558 Office: Terkenska Child Treatment Ctr 9555 Kiefer Blvd Sacramento CA 95827

JONES, THOMAS VICTOR, aerospace company executive; b. Pomona, Calif., July 21, 1920; s. Victor March and Elizabeth (Brettelle) J.; m. Ruth Nagel, Aug. 10, 1946; children: Ruth Marilyn, Peter Thomas. Student, Pomona Jr. Coll., 1938-40; B.A. with gt. distinction, Stanford U., 1942; LL.D. (hon.), George Washington U., 1967. Engr. El Segundo div. Douglas Aircraft Co., 1941-47; tech. adviser Brazilian Air Ministry, 1947-51; prof., head dept. Brazilian Inst. Tech., 1947-51; staff cons. Air Staff of USAF, Rand Corp., 1951-53; asst. to chief engr. Northrop Corp., 1953, dep. chief engr., 1954-56, dir. devel. planning, 1956-57, corp. v.p., 1957, sr. v.p., 1958-59, pres., 1959-76, chief exec. officer, 1960—, chmn. bd., 1963—; dir. MCA Inc., Universal City, Calif. Author: Capabilities and Operating Costs of Possible Future Transport Airplanes, 1953. Bd. dirs. Los Angeles World Affairs Council, Calif. Nature Conservancy; trustee Inst. for Strategic Studies, London. Fellow AIAA (hon.); mem. Los Angeles C. of C., Navy League U.S. (life), Aerospace Industries Assn., U. So. Calif. Assocs., Town Hall, Nat. Acad. Engring. Clubs: California; The Beach (Santa Monica); Georgetown, California Yacht, Bohemian. Home: 1050 Moraga Dr Los Angeles CA 90049 Office: Northrop Corp 1840 Century Park E Century City Los Angeles CA 90067

JONES, THORNTON KEITH, research chemist; b. Brawley, Calif., Dec. 17, 1923; s. Alfred George and Madge Jones; m. Evalee Vestal, July 4, 1965; children: Brian Keith, Donna Eileen. BS, U. Calif., Berkeley, 1949, postgrad., 1951-52. Research chemist Griffin Chem. Co., Richmond, Calif., 1949-55; western product devel. and improvement mgr. Nopco Chem. Co., Richmond, Calif., 1955; research chemist Chevron Research Co., Richmond, 1956-65, research chemist in spl. products research and devel., 1965-1982; product quality mgr. Chevron USA, Inc., San Francisco, 1982-87, ret. Patentee in field. Vol. fireman and officer, Terra Linda, Calif., 1957-64; mem. adv. com. Terra Linda Dixie Elem. Sch. Dist., 1960-64. Served with Signal Corps, U.S. Army, 1943-46. Mem. Am. Chem. Soc., Forest Products Research Soc., Am. Wood Preservers Assn., Alpha Chi Sigma. Republican. Presbyterian. Avocations: music, gardening, wine and food.

JONES, VERNON QUENTIN, surveyor; b. Sioux City, Iowa, May 6, 1930; s. Vernon Boyd and Winnifred Rhoda (Bremmer) J.; student UCLA, 1948-50; m. Rebeca Buckovecz, Oct. 1981; children—Steven Vernon, Gregory Richard, Stanley Alan. Draftsman III Pasadena (Calif.) city engr., 1950-53; sr. civil engring. asst. Los Angeles County engr., Los Angeles, 1953-55; v.p. Treadwell Engring. Corp., Arcadia, Calif., 1955-61, pres., 1961-64; pres. Hillcrest Engring. Corp., Arcadia, 1961-64; dep. county surveyor, Ventura, Calif., 1964-78; propr. Vernon Jones Land Surveyor, Riviera, Ariz., 1978—; city engr. Needles (Calif.), 1980-87; instr. Mohave Community Coll., 1987—. Chmn. graphic tech. com. Ventura Unified Sch. Dist., 1972-78, mem. career adv. com., 1972-74; mem. engring. adv. com. Pierce Coll., 1973; pres. Mgmt. Employees of Ventura County, 1974. Vice pres. Young Republicans of Ventura County, 1965. Pres., Marina Pacifica Homeowners Assn., 1973. Mem. League Calif. Surveying Orgns. (pres. 1975), Am. Congress on Surveying and Mapping (chmn. So. Calif. sect. 1976), Am. Soc. Photogrammetry, Am. Pub. Works Assn., County Engr. Assn. Calif. Home: 913E San Juan Ct Riviera AZ 86442

JONES, WALTER EUGENE, test pilot; b. Raleigh, N.C., Feb. 23, 1946; s. Walter Riddick and Evelyn Elizabeth (Lowder) J.; m. Doris Darnell Spencer, Aug. 5, 1967; children: Amy Lynn, Tammy Jean. AA Profl. Piloting, U. Alaska, 1974; BSBA, and Econs., Alaska Meth. U., 1975; MS in Mgmt. Sci., Am. Tech. U., 1982. Cert. comml. pilot, FAA. Enlisted U.S. Army, 1963, advanced through grades to chief warrant officer 4, helicopter pilot and maintenance test pilot, 1966-83, ret., 1983; chief aviation safety McDonnell Douglas Helicopter Co. div. McDonnell Douglas Corp., Mesa, Ariz., 1983-85, helicopter test pilot, 1985—; aviation safety official and aircraft accident investigator U.S. Army, 1966-83. Decorated Purple Heart, two Bronze Stars, Air medals (23). Mem. Army Aviation Assn., Am. Helicopter Soc., Am. Soc. Safety Engrs. Republican. Baptist. Avocations: flying, computers. Home: 2703 E Fairfield Circle Mesa AZ 85203 Office: McDonnell Douglas Helicopter Co 5000 E McDowell Rd Mesa AZ 85205

JONES, WYMAN H., librarian; b. St. Louis, Dec. 17, 1929; s. Jay Hugh and Marie (Dallas) J.; m. Janet Grigsby, Jan. 17, 1953; children—Gregory Foster, Mark Jay, Manson Matthew, Ross Christopher. Student, So. Ill. U., 1945-47, Washington U., St. Louis, 1948-50; B.A., Adams State Coll., Alamosa, Colo., 1956; postgrad., U. Iowa, 1956-57; M.S. in L.S, U. Tex., 1958. Head sci. and industry div. Dallas Pub. Library, 1958-60, chief br. services, 1960-64; dir. Ft. Worth Pub. Library, 1964-70; city librarian Los Angeles Pub. Library, 1970—; cons. library bldg. and site selections, 1962—; Mem. Gov. Tex. Adv. Bd., 1969-70, Calif. Bd. Library Examiners, 1970—. Author: (with E. Castagna) The Library Reaches Out, 1964; also articles. Bd. dirs. Young Symphony Orch., Ft. Worth, 1967-69. Served with USAF, 1951-55. Mem. ALA (legis. com. 1974-78), S.W. Library Assn. (pres.-elect 1967), Tex. Library Assn. (pres. pub. library div. 1966), Calif. Library Assn. (council 1972—). Home: 1433 Via Cataluna Palos Verdes Estates CA 90274 Office: Pub Library 630 W 5th St Los Angeles CA 90017 *

JONES, YOLANDA DAWN, physical chemistry researcher; b. New Orleans, Nov. 30, 1954; d. James Paul and Lucille Ovela (Jones) J. BS cum laude, U. N.Mex., 1976, MS in Phys. Chemistry, 1980, PhD in Phys. Chemistry, 1981. Environ. scientist State of N.Mex., 1981-82; research chemist Air Force Weapons Lab., Albuquerque, 1982—. Author tech. reports on laser research. Vice-chmn N.Mex. Bd. Pharmacy, 1979-85, sec., treas. Fellow Assn. Western Univs., 1975-76. Mem. Am. Chem. Soc., Optical Soc. Am., AAAS, N.Mex. Network for Women in Sci. and Engring, Assn. Women in Sci., Mortar Bd. Alumni (pres. 1982-83), U. N.Mex. Alumni Assn. (exec. com. 1982-85, chmn. publs. 1982-84, chmn. legis. com. 1985—), Jr. League of Albuquerque (tng. core com. 1985-86, pub. affairs com., 1986, chmn. 1987). Democrat. Club: Town Sorority (Albuquerque) (pres. 1985—). Avocations: polit. campaigns, community volunteerism, skiing, arts, crafts. Office: Air Force Weapons Lab AFWL/AWYW Kirtland AFB NM 87117-6008

JONES-TWIGHT, ANGENETT, organization development company executive; b. Loma Linda, Calif., Feb. 13, 1940; d. Horace Darwin and Alice (Goen) Jones; m. Peter Alan Twight, July 3, 1958; children: Nicholas Peter, Jessica, Cedric Dixon. BS, U. Calif., Berkeley, 1971; MS in Orgn. Devel. cum laude, Pepperdine U., 1977. Orgn. devel. cons. Central Atlantic Conf., United Ch. of Christ, Silver Spring, Md., 1972-73; mgmt. cons. Corplan, Chico, Calif., 1973-74; owner, ptnr. Process for Planned Change, Richmond, Calif., 1974-86, pres., cons., Aptos, Calif., 1977-86; pres., chief operating officer Saltwater Inst., Monterey, Calif., 1986—; convenor Team Leadership Process Consortium, Santa Cruz, 1980—; mem. adj. faculty Pepperdine U. Sch. Bus. and Mgmt., 1983—. Mem. Orgn. Devel. Network, Bay Area Orgn. Devel. Network (steering com.). Republican. Presbyterian. Club: N.Am. Trail Riding Conf. Author: Proc. of 1976 New Prospectives on Recreation Mgmt. Conf.; (with William R. Daniels) Stress Reduction Strategies: A Training Curriculum For Public Contact Employees, 1975, rev. edit., 1977, Handbook: Effective Supervisory Practices Training, 1974, rev. edit., 1976. Office: 450 Pacific St Suite 340 Monterey CA 93940

JONGEWARD, GEORGE RONALD, systems analyst; b. Yakima, Wash., Aug. 9, 1934; s. George Ira and Dorothy Marie (Cronk) J.; m. Janet Jeanne Williams, July 15, 1955; children: Mary Jeanne, Dona Lee, Karen Anne. BA, Whitworth Coll., 1957; postgrad., Utah State U., 1961. Sr. systems analyst Computer Scis. Corp., Honolulu, 1969-71; cons. in field Honolulu, 1972-76; prin. The Hobby Co., Honolulu, 1977-81; sr. systems analyst Computer Systems Internat., Honolulu, 1981—; instr. EDP Hawaii Pacific Coll., Honolulu, 1982—. Mem. car show com. Easter Seal Soc., Honolulu. 1977-82; active Variety Club, Honolulu. Mem. Mensa (local pres. 1967-69). Republican. Presbyterian. Club: Triple-9. Avocations: organ, piano, community theatre, golf, sports-car rallyes. Home: 400 Hobron Ln #2611 Honolulu HI 96815 Office: Computer Systems Internat 841 Bishop St #501 Honolulu HI 96813

JONKER, PETER EMILE, gas company analyst; b. The Hague, The Netherlands, Sept. 15, 1948; came to U.S., 1966, naturalized, 1985; s. Jacob and Jurrina (Wories) J.; m. Janet Lynn Gotfredson, Sept. 6, 1974; children: Jeffrey, Annelies. BSChemE cum laude, U. So. Calif., 1971, MSChemE, 1972; JD with honors, Western State U., Fullerton, Calif., 1979. Bar: Calif. 1979. Research engr. Union Oil Co., Los Angeles, 1972-75, regulations coordinator, 1975-79, atty., 1979; mgr. govtl. and pub. affairs Western Liquified Nat. Gas, Los Angeles, 1979-81; mgr. environ. permitting Tosco Corp., Los Angeles, 1981-83; mgr. regional pub. affairs So. Calif. Gas. Co., Los Angeles, 1983-85, mgr. rate design, demand forecast and analysis, 1986—; mem. So. Coast Air Quality Mgmt. Dist. Adv. Council, Los Angeles, 1983-85. Editor Western State Law Rev., 1976-79; contbr. articles to profl. jours. Trustee, deacon San Marino (Calif.) Community Ch., 1980—; councilman U. So. Calif. Engring. Student Council, Los Angeles, 1971-72, dir. Alumni Assn., 1971-72; fgn. del. White House Conf., Washington, 1971. Mem. Air Pollution Control Assn. (v.p. West coast chpt. 1984, 85), Am. Gas Assn., Pacific Coast Gas Assn., Tau Beta Pi (pres., v.p. Calif. Delta chpt. 1970-71). Republican. Avocations: skiing, antiques, piano. Home: 2450 Melville San Marino CA 91108 Office: So Calif Gas Co 810 S Flower St Los Angeles CA 90017

JOO, GRANT KAZNO, research biologist; b. Twin Falls, Idaho, Dec. 22, 1950; s. K. and Aiko (Higaki) J.; m. Judy Eiko Okada, May 16, 1981; children: Bryan T., Derek S. BA in Biology, San Jose State U., 1974. Technician Stauffer Chem. Co., Mountain View, Calif., 1974-75, asst. biologist, 1976-78, biologist, 1979-81, assoc. research biolgist, 1982-84, research biologist, 1984—. Mem. AAAS. Buddhist. Avocation: bicycling. Office: Stauffer Chem Co 1195 W Fremont Ave Sunnyvale CA 94087

JORALEMON, BARBARA GAIL, health care administrator, minister; b. Salt Lake City, Apr. 10, 1951; d. Peter and Barbara Ann (Hayward) J.; m. Brian Kanne Hansen, Feb. 25, 1984; 1 child, David Winston Joralemon Hansen. Student, Beaver Coll., 1969-71; BA cum laude, Boston U., 1974; MDiv., Pacific Sch. Religion, 1976. Ordained to ministry United Ch. Christ, 1977. Coordinator TV monitoring project United Meth. Women, Berkeley, Calif., 1975-76; coordinator counseling Reproductive Health Services, Columbia, Mo., 1977-78; program dir., chaplain United Ecumenical Ministry, Columbia, 1977-79; coordinator service and edn. Sudden Infant Death Syndrome Project, Jefferson City, Mo., 1979-80; exec. dir. Abortion and Pregnancy Testing Clinic, Albuquerque, 1980—; bd. dirs., exec. council United Campus Ministries, Albuquerque, 1980—, v.p. bd. dirs., 1986-87; tchr. ESL, Kaohsiung, Taiwan, 1984-85. Author: Adolescents and Abortion: Choice and Loss, Adolescents and Death; co-author (booklet) Sex Role Stereotyping in Prime Time TV, 1976. State coordinator Nat. Abortion Fedn's. Policy Action Com., Washington and Albuquerque, 1982—; mem. N.Mex. Right to Choose. Mem. Religious Coalition for Abortion Rights (bd. dirs. 1980—), Profl. Orgn. Women (co-chmn., 1982—), Clergy Women Orgn. (convener 1985—). Democrat. Avocations: bicycling, camping, hiking, gardening. Office: Abortion and Pregnancy Testing Clinic 107 Girard SE Albuquerque NM 87106

JORANSON, PHILIP NATHANIEL, environment and religion educator; b. Madison, Wis., Dec. 21, 1914; s. Einar and Esther (Anderson) J.; m. Sylvia Maria Mattson, Aug. 29, 1974. Cert., U. Chgo., 1934; BS, U. Minn., 1937; MS, Iowa State Coll., 1938; PhD, U. Calif., Berkeley, 1944; postdoctoral, Union Theol. Sem., 1968-69. Asst. prof. botany Beloit (Wis.) Coll., 1946-51; research assoc. forest genetics Inst. Paper Chemistry, Appleton, Wis., 1954-61; asst. adminstr., prin. forester McIntire-Stennis Program USDA, Washington, 1962-69; lectr. nat. resources U. Conn., Torrington, 1977-78; environ. project dir. Ctr. for Ethics and Social Policy, Berkeley, 1979—; adj. faculty Pacific Sch. Religion, Berkeley, 1981—; chmn. faith-man-nature group Council Chs. Coventry, Conn., 1965-75. Sr. editor: Cry of the Environment: Rebuilding the Christian Creation Tradition, 1984; contbr. articles on ecology, forest genetics and environ. and religion to profl. jours. Mem. Dem. Town com., Andover, Conn., 1969-72; chmn. Conservation Commn., Andover, 1971-72; mem. service commn. Orinda (Calif.) Community Ch., 1981—; mem. nuclear weapons freeze initiative Contra Costa County, Calif., 1981—. Recipient Cert. Appreciation, TAPPI, 1964; Bidwell fellow U. Calif., Berkeley, 1940-41, U. Chgo. Divinity Sch. fellow, 1950; Am. Motors Corp. grantee, 1978. Mem. AAAS, Am. Acad. Religion, Am. Inst. Biol. Scis., Soc. Am. Foresters. Democrat. Avocations: hiking, swimming. Home: 3217 Golden Rain Rd #8 Walnut Creek CA 94595 Office: Grad Theol Union Ctr Ethics and Social Policy 2465 LeConte Ave Berkeley CA 94709

JORDAHL, RONALD IVAN, librarian, educator; b. Buffalo Ctr., Iowa, May 29, 1936; s. George Harry and Leota Eola (Yost) J.; m. Faye Lorraine Bixby, Aug. 29, 1964; children—Philip, Ronald, Rebekah. B.A., Luther Coll., 1958. Librarian, tchr. Prairie Bible Inst., Three Hills, Alta., Can., 1966—. Contbr. articles to profl. jours. Editor, The Christian Librarian, 1978—. Mem. ALA, Can. Library Assn., Assn. Christian Librarians (pres. 1981-82, bd. dirs. 1975—). Home: Box 4317, Three Hills, AB Canada T0M 2A0 Office: Prairie Bible Inst, Three Hills, AB Canada T0M 2A0

JORDAN, BONITA ADELE, television producer; b. Dayton, Ohio, Mar. 9, 1948; d. Theodore and Faye Annette (Fields) Sampson; divorced; 1 son, Brett Anthony. Student, Habor Jr. Coll., Wilmington, Calif., 1966-68. Assoc. producer Dick Clark Prodns., Hollywood, Calif., 1972-73, Sta. KNBC-TV, Los Angeles, Calif., 1973-75; account exec. Ameron co., Monterey Park, Calif., 1976; prodn. coordinator Movie of the Week for CBS, Paramount Studios, Hollywood, 1977-78; asst. to producer Glen Larson Prodns., Film TV Devel. and Casting, 20th Century Fox, Beverly Hills, Calif., 1978-84; prodn. coordinator Universal Studios, 1986, Rags to Riches, Len Hill Films/New World Television, 1986-87, New World TV, 1987—. Co-chmn., asst. to producer telethon United High Blood Pressure Found., 1977, mem. exec. bd., 1975-78, treas., 1977. Recipient cert. achievement City of Los Angeles and UCLA Mardi Gras, 1974. Mem. Women in Film, Nat. Assn. Media Women (corr. rec. sec. 1974-75). Home: 14215 Calvert St #4 Van Nuys CA 91401 Office: New World TV 8500 Higuera St Culver City CA 90230

JORDAN, BRUCE DIDRIK, architect; b. Concord, Mass., Mar. 3, 1951; s. Frank Edward and Gerd Rigimore (Guilibrunsen) J.; m. Deborah Kay Bertelli, Apr. 1, 1971; children: Eric, Ryan. BSArch., Calif. State Poly. U., 1978. Registered architect, Calif. Project mgr. Shamma Enterprises, Anaheim, Calif., 1972-76; architect Brion Jeannette Assocs., Newport Beach, Calif., 1976-80; pres., prin. architect Jordan Architects, Irvine, Calif., 1980—; pres. Ardevcon Inc., Irvine, 1982—, gen. ptnr. Allsize Storage, Irvine, 1982—. Served with U.S. Army, 1968-71, Vietnam. Decorated Bronze Star, Purple Heart, air medal with v device. Mem. AIA. Republican. Avocations: skiing, scuba diving, mountain climbing. Office: Jordan Architects Inc. 18218 E McDurmott Irvine CA 92714

JORDAN, CHARLES WILLIAM, JR., city official, entrepreneur; b. Pueblo, Colo., Aug. 28, 1937; s. Charles William Sr. and Gertrude Amanda (Bartels) J.; m. Carolyn Elizabeth Clifford, June 19, 1964; children—Ellen, Jenifer, Michael, Julie. B.S. in Bus. Adminstrn., Colo. State U., 1960; M.A. in Pub. Adminstrn., U. No. Colo., 1978. Cert. Purchasing mgr. Enlisted as seaman U.S. Navy, 1961, advanced through grades to lt., 1970, discharged (hon.), 1971; budget analyst Colo. Gov.'s Exec. Office, Denver, 1972; dean bus. services Lamar Community Coll., Colo., 1972-79; asst. dean fiscal services San Juan Coll., Farmington, N.Mex., 1979-83; fin. dir. City of Aztec, N.Mex., 1983-86; dir. fin. City of Cortez, Colo., 1986—; profl. devel. office staff 4 Corners Purchasing Mgmt. Assn., Farmington, 1983—. Treas., Southeast Colo. Council on Arts and Humanities, Lamar, 1975; mem. accountability com. Lamar Sch. Dist. RE-2, 1976; pres. Southeast Colo. Bd. Handicapped, Lamar, 1978-79. Mem. Colo. Assn. Community Coll. Bus. Ofcls., Phi Delta Theta (v.p. 1958-59). Lodges: Rotary (pres. 1982-83), Elks. Home: 700 N Newby Box 1894 Bloomfield NM 87413 Office: City of Cortez 210 E Main Cortez CO 81321

JORDAN, DARRYL FRANKLIN, civil engineer; b. Glenallen, Alaska, June 14, 1955; s. Franklin Jordan and Joyce Mae (Ewan) Kallander; m. Leigh Andrea Slaughter, June 30, 1979 (div. 1981); m. Cherie Jean Cottrill, Apr. 21, 1982. B.S., MIT, 1977, M.S., 1978. Staff engr. R&M Cons., Anchorage, 1979-80; sr. project engr. ARCO Oil & Gas Co., Anchorage, 1980—. Editor: Cold Region Construction, 1983. Mem. microcomputer com. Anchorage Sch. Dist., 1983, Anchorage Sch. Bd., 1986—, Anchorage Sch. Dist. Citizen Adv. Concerns Com., 1985-86, Anchorage Sch. Dist. Transp. Task Force, 1985-86, Alaska Hist. Commn., 1986—, Hugh O'Brien Youth Adv. Bd., 1986—ARCO Dependent Child Care Task Force, 1986—; bd. dirs. Anchorage Child Abuse Bd., 1986—, Musk Ox Devel. Bd., 1986—, Cook Inlet Native Assn., 1985-86. Served to 1st lt. USAR, 1977-86. Mem. ASCE, Tech. Council on Cold Region Engring., Alaska Soc. Civil Engrs. Office: ARCO Oil & Gas Co 700 G St Anchorage AK 99510

JORDAN, FRANK M., Chief of police, San Francisco. Office: Office of Chief of Police City of San Francisco 850 Bryant St San Francisco CA 94103 *

JORDAN, G. KAYE, speech pathologist; b. Albuquerque, Aug. 9, 1942; d. Davis Key and Georgia Ruth (Emond) Kelly; m. Roberto Jordan, Apr. 20, 1981 (div. Jan. 1984); children: Jolene, Kelly-Rhea Boguslawski (dec.). BS, Eastern N.Mex. U., 1964, MS, 1978. Cert. clin. speech-lang. pathologist. Speech-lang. pathologist N.Mex. Rehab. Ctr., Roswell, 1980-81, dir. speech-lang. pathology, 1984—; speech-lang. pathologist Sertoma Speech Clin., El Paso, Tex., 1981-82, Socorro Schs., El Paso, 1982-84; owner Zia Speech-Lang. Cons., El Paso, 1983-84. Co-founder, pres. Roswell Cancer Support Group, 1985—; bd. dirs., mem. adv. bd. Am. Cancer Soc., 1986—. Mem. Am. Speech-Hearing Assn., N.Mex. Speech-Hearing Assn. Avocations: caligraphy, golf, writing. Home: 403 Oakwood Roswell NM 88201 Office: N Mex Rehab Ctr D at E Eyman RIAC Roswell NM 88201

JORDAN, GARY BLAKE, electrical engineer; b. Urbana, Ill., Feb. 3, 1939; s. Robert Leslie and Lois Evelyn (Schildhammer) J.; m. Gloria Jean Heppler, Mar. 21, 1969; children: Gareth Kylae, Glynis Jerelle. BSEE, Ohio U., 1961; DEE, Pacific So. U., 1977; PhDEE (hon.), Sussex Coll. Tech., Eng., 1977. Exec. v.p. Electronic Warfare Orgn., Hermosa Beach, Calif., 1968-78; sr. program mgmt. engr. Ford Aerospace and Communications Corp., Palo Alto, Calif., 1974-79; program mgr. ESL/TRW Inc., Sunnyvale, Calif., 1979—; dir. Nat. Intelligence Agy., Sunnyvale, Calif., 1975-81. Contbr. sci., engring., tech. articles to profl. jours. and mags. Non-Resident fellow Wash. Acad. Scis. Fellow Am. Biog. Inst., Lambda Xi Pi (life); mem. Soc. Scholarly Pub. (charter), AAAS, IEEE, Am. Def. Preparedness Assn., Soc. Tech. Communication., Armed Forces Communications Electronics Assn., U.S. Naval Inst., Internat. Amateur Radio Club. Home: 1012 Olmo Ct San Jose CA 95129 Office: 495 Java Dr PO Box 3510 Sunnyvale CA 94088-3510

JORDAN, GARY LEE, oil company executive; b. San Bernardino, Calif., May 13, 1953; s. Gene Curtis and Gloria Naomi (Kropff) J.; m. Susan Carol Morris, July 15, 1977; 1 child, Paul. AA, Cosumnes River Coll., 1974; BSChemE with honors, U. Calif., Davis, 1976; postgrad., Calif. State U., Long Beach, 1982—. Registered profl. engr., Calif. Process engr. ARCO, Carson, Calif., 1976-79; sr. econ. analyst ARCO, Los Angeles, 1979-81, strategic planning coordinator, 1981-83, tech. bus. advisor, 1983-85, project devel. cons., 1985-86; dir. tech. acquisition and licensing ARCO, Anaheim, Calif., 1986—. Treas. Bethany Bible Ch., Midway City, Calif. 1985—; prodn. advisor Jr. Achievement, Carson, 1976-77. Served to sgt. USAF, 1971-72. Mem. Am. Inst. Chem. Engrs., NSPE, Am. Chem. Soc., Beta Gamma Sigma, Tau Beta Pi. Republican. Evangelical Christian. Avocation: tennis, radio controlled aircraft. Office: ARCO 1990 Crescent St Anaheim CA 92081 Mailing Address: PO Box 61004 Anaheim CA 92803-6104

JORDAN, LAWRENCE WILLIAM, manufacturing company executive; b. Lakewood, Ohio, Mar. 8, 1931; s. Lawrence William and Virginia Lee (Little) J.; m. Donna Faye Craig, June 15, 1957; children: Craig Robert, Juli Claire, Lori Elaine. BChemE, Ohio State U., 1956, MSc, 1957, PhD, 1959; JD, UCLA, 1971. Bar: Calif. 1972, U.S. Ct. Appeals (9th cir.) 1973, U.S. Supreme Ct. 1981; registered profl. engr., Ohio, Calif., Oreg. Research engr. Calif. Research, La Habra, 1959-67; research chemist Aerojet-Gen., Downey, Calif., 1967-68; assoc. Bullivant, Wright et al, Portland, Oreg., 1971-74, Norman Stoll, Portland, 1974-77; city atty. Lake Oswego, Oreg., 1977-79; asst. adminstr. Oreg. Dept. Commerce, Salem, 1979-81; pres. SITEC, Salem, 1981—. Author: Azeotropy: The Binery Systems, 1961, Continuing Legal Education Family Law, 1973 (award 1974). Mem. Orange (Calif.) City Council, 1964-72; mem. Salem Planning Commn. 1984—. Fellow Proctor & Gamble Co., 1957, Dow Chem. Corp., 1958, Ford Found., 1970; Wilson scholar UCLA, 1968. Mem. State Bar Calif., Salem C. of C. (greeter, com. chmn. 1984-85). Lodges: Rotary, Eagles, Moose. Avocations: photography, racquetball, electronics, reading, barbershop quartet singing. Home and Office: PO Box 982 Salem OR 97308-0982

JORDAN, PHILLIP LOWELL, communications executive; b. Washington, May 13, 1947; s. William Douglass and Elizabeth May (Merrick) J.; m. Judith Anne Jones, Aug. 5, 1972; 1 son, Andrew Jones. Student U.S. Air Force Acad., 1964; B.B.A., U. Wash., 1968. C.P.A., Wash. Acct. Main Lafrentz & Co., C.P.A.s, Seattle, 1968-70, Coopers & Lybrand, C.P.A.s, Seattle, N.Y.C., 1970-80; ptnr. Moss, Adams & Co., C.P.A.s, Seattle, 1980-83; exec. v.p., chief operating officer Early Winters, Ltd., Seattle, 1983; pres., chief exec. officer, chmn. Care Plus Med. Ctrs., Inc., Seattle, 1983-84; v.p. fin., chief fin. officer WFI Industries, Inc., holding co. for various corps., Seattle, 1984-87; v.p. fin. and adminstrn. Muzak Ltd. Partnership, 1987—; lectr. Sch. Bus., U. Wash.; speaker tech. bus. topics various trade, profl. orgns. Treas. United Cerebral Palsy Assn. Wash., 1979—; mem. Seattle Art Museum, Seattle Opera Assn., Seattle Symphony Assn., Pacific NW Ballet. Mem. Am. Inst. C.P.A.s, Wash. Soc. C.P.A.s (chmn. standards rev. com.), Fin. Execs. Inst., Sigma Chi Alumni Assn. Episcopalian. Clubs: Seattle Yacht, Seattle Tennis, Wash. Athletic. Office: 915 Yale Ave N Seattle WA 98109

JORDAN, RAYMOND BRUCE, health services consultant; b. Holland, Mich., Mar. 10, 1912; s. Albert Raymond and Aimee (Best) J.; m. Dorothy Caig, June 6, 1942. B.A., Sacramento State Coll., 1952; M.B.A., Stanford U., 1959. Pub. acct., Calif. Acct., auditor State Bd. Equalization, Calif. Dept. Employment, 1947-48, mgmt. analyst, 1948-52, chief analyst, 1952-59; chief mgmt. analyst Hdqrs. Office, Calif. Dept. Mental Hygiene, 1959-63; bus. adminstr. Atascadero State Hosp., 1963-68, Patton State Hosp., San Bernardino, Calif., 1968-70; mgmt. cons. hosps., Victoria, B.C., Can., 1970-72; instr. Sacramento City Coll., 1951-62; cons. Govt. Iran, faculty, U. Tehran, 1956; instr. U. Calif.-Davis, 1963, Cuesta Coll., San Luis Obispo, 1967-68, Monterey Peninsula Coll., 1974-76; adj. prof. Golden Gate U., Monterey and San Francisco Campus, 1974-84; chmn. grievance rev. bd. Monterey Peninsula Unified Sch. Dist., 1976. Pres., Monterey County Ombudsman Program, 1976-79; founder, adv. bd. mem. Monterey County Sr. Hearing Ctr., 1977-78; treas. Experience, Inc., 1973-78; bd. dirs. Monterey County Sr. Aide Program, 1976-78; mem. adv. bd. Alliance on Aging, 1976-78; founder, pres. Concerned Sr. Citizens, Monterey Peninsula Club, 1974-77; mem. adv. group Monterey Sr. Day Care Ctr., 1977-78. Recipient Bronze Achievement award Mental Hosp. Service, 1963. Served with U.S. Army, 1943-46. Club: Toastmasters. Author: Management Analysis in Health Services, 1982; Supervision—Effective Management, 1982; contbr. articles to profl. jours. Home: 33 Linda Ave Apt 1908 Oakland CA 94611

JORDAN, WILLIAM IRVING, school principal; b. Lewiston, Idaho, Jan. 16, 1947; s. Clinton Irving and Grace Marie (Ruiz) J.; children: Crystal Kay, Janelle Marie, William Christopher; m. Kathryn Jordan; children: Brian, Mike, Julie; m. Kathy Gwinn, Mar. 28, 1987. BEd, U. Idaho, 1969; MEd, Wash. State U., 1978. Tchr., Pioneer Jr. High Sch., Walla Walla, Wash., 1969-78, asst. prin., 1978-82; prin. Garrison Jr. High Sch., Walla Walla, 1982—. Chmn., NW Regional Coll. Rodeo, Walla Walla, 1984-85; dist. chief Beta Theta Pi, 1979—; mem. Guardian Ad Litum steering com., Walla Walla, 1981—. Mem. Assn. Supervision and Curriculum Devel., Yakima Valley Jr. High Middle Sch. Activities Assn. (pres.), Assn. Wash. Sch. Prins. (pres. 1979-80, legis. rep. 1983—), Yakima Valley Interscholastic Activities Assn. (exec. bd. 1984—), Nat. Assn. Secondary Sch. Prins., Greater Yakima Valley Middle Level Prins. Assn. (regional dir.), Assn. Wash. Middle Level Prins. (bd. dirs.), Phi Delta Kappa. Lodges: Elks, Exchange. Home: Rt 3

Box 287 Walla Walla WA 99362 Office: Garrison Jr High Sch 906 Chase Walla Walla WA 99362

JORGENSEN, ERIK HOLGER, lawyer; b. Copenhagen, July 18, 1916; s. Holger and Karla (Andersen) J.; children—Jette Friis, Lone Olesen, John, Jean Ann. J.D., San Francisco Law Sch., 1960. Bar: Calif. 1961. Sole practice, 1961-70; ptnr. Hersh, Hadfield, Jorgensen & Fried, San Francisco, 1970-76, Hadfield & Jorgensen, San Francisco, 1976—. Pres. Aldersly, Danish Retirement Home, San Rafael, Calif., 1974-77, Rebuild Park Soc. Bay Area chpt., 1974-77. Fellow Scandinavian Am. Found. (hon.); mem. ABA, Assn. Trial Lawyers Am., San Francisco Lawyers Club, Bar Assn. of San Francisco, Calif. Assn. Realtors (hon. life bd. dirs.). Author: Master Forms Guide for Successful Real Estate Agreements, Successful Real Estate Sales Agreements, 1982; contbr. articles on law and real estate law to profl. jours. Office: 3 Embarcadero #1685 San Francisco CA 94111

JORGENSEN, GORDON DAVID, engineering company executive; b. Chgo., Apr. 29, 1921; s. Jacob and Marie (Jensen) J.; B.S. in Elec. Engring., U. Wash., 1948, postgrad. in bus. and mgmt., 1956-59; m. Nadina Anita Peters, Dec. 17, 1948 (div. Aug. 1971); children—Karen Ann, David William, Susan Marie; m. 2d, Barbara Noel, Feb. 10, 1972 (div. July 1976). With R.W. Beck & Assos., Cons. Engrs., Phoenix, 1948—, ptnr., 1954-86; pres. Beck Internat., Phoenix, 1971—. Served to lt. (j.g.) U.S. Maritime Service, 1942-45. Recipient Outstanding Service award Phoenix Tennis Assn., 1967; Commendation, Govt. Honduras, 1970. Registered profl. engr., Alaska, Ariz., Calif., Colo., Nev., N.Mex., N.D., Utah, Wash., Wyo. Mem. IEEE (chmn. Wash.-Alaska sect. 1959-60), Nat. Soc. Profl. Engrs., Am. Soc. Appraisers (sr. mem.), Ariz. Cons. Engrs. Assn., Ariz. Soc. Profl. Engrs., Internat. Assn. Assessing Officers, Southwestern Tennis Assn. (past pres.), U.S. Tennis Assn. (pres. 1987, chmn. U.S. Open com.). Presbyterian (elder). Project mgr. for mgmt., operation studies and reorgn. study Honduras power system, 1969-70. Home: 5329 N 25th St Phoenix AZ 85020 Office: 3003 N Central St Phoenix AZ 85012

JORGENSEN, JAMES DALE, social work educator; b. Trent, S.D., Jan. 16, 1932; s. Lenius and Bertha Dorthea (Jenson) J.; m. Christine Marie Turnbull, Dec. 18, 1976; children: John, Kirsten, Catherine. BA, U. S.D., 1953; MSW, U. Denver, 1958. Child welfare worker Dept. Pub. Welfare, Pierre, S.D., 1956-61; chief social worker S.D. Tng. Sch., Plankinton, 1961-64; prof. Grad. Sch. Social Work U. Denver, 1964—; cons. Western Interstate Commn. Higher Edn., Boulder, Colo., 1969-76; mem. faculty Nat. Juvenile Justice Coll. U. Nev., Reno, 1970-71. Co-author: Solving Problems in Meetings, 1981, How You Can Make the Best Decisions in Your Life, 1978, Volunteer Training in Courts and Corrections, 1973. Mem. adv. bd. Div. Youth Services, Denver, 1985-86. Served with U.S. Army, 1953-55. Recipient Alumni of Yr. award U. Denver Grad. Sch. Social Work, 1978-79. Mem. Nat. Assn. Social Workers, Nat. Orgn. Forensic Social Workers. Democrat. Home: 2270 Albion St Denver CO 80207 Office: U Denver University Park Campus Denver CO 80210

JORGENSEN, JUDITH ANN, psychiatrist; b. Parris Island, S.C.; d. George Emil and Margaret Georgia Jorgensen; B.A., Stanford U., 1963; M.D., U. Calif., 1968; m. Ronald Francis Crown, July 11, 1970. Intern, Meml. Hosp., Long Beach, 1969-70; resident County Mental Health Services, San Diego, 1970-73; staff psychiatrist Children and Adolescent Services, San Diego, 1973-78; practice medicine specializing in psychiatry, La Jolla, Calif., 1973—; staff psychiatrist County Mental Health Services of San Diego, 1973-78; psychiat. cons. San Diego City Coll., 1973-78; asst. prof. dept. psychiatry U. Calif., 1978—; chmn. med. quality rev. com. Dist. XIV, State of Calif., 1982-83. Mem. Am. Psychiat. Assn., San Diego Soc. Psychiat. Physicians (chmn. membership com. 1976-78, v.p. 1978-80, fed. legis. rep. 1985-87), Am. Soc. Adolescent Psychiatry, San Diego Soc. Adolescent Psychiatry (pres. 1981-82), Calif. Med. Assn. (alternate del.), Soc. Sci. Study of Sex, San Diego Soc. Sex Therapy and Edn., San Diego County Med. Soc. (credentials com. 1982-84). Club: Rowing. Office: 470 Nautilus St Suite 211 La Jolla CA 92037

JORGENSEN, KAREN VIRGINIA, food toxicologist; b. Omaha, Aug. 31, 1953; d. Charles Peter and Evelyn Anna (Decker) J. BS, U. Ariz., 1980, MS, 1985. Cert. food processor. Loan processor Valley Nat. Bank, Tucson, 1973-75; supr. quality assurance Engrs. Testing Labs., Inc., Tucson, 1977-78; research asst. U. Ariz., 1980—; cons. U. Ariz. Coll. Pharmacy, Tucson, 1985—; also cons. Ariz. Cancer Research Ctr., U. Ariz., Tucson; cons. Desert Whale Jojoba, Jucson, 1981—. Contbr. articles to profl. jours. Mem. Am. Chem. Soc., Inst. Food Technologists, Ariz. Soc. Food Technologists, N.Y. Acad. Sci., Internat. Union Pure and Applied Chemists (affiliate), Gamma Sigma Delta, Iota Sigma Phi. Democrat. Roman Catholic. Avocations: sewing, tennis, fishing, camping. Home: 9016 Chickamauga St Tucson AZ 85710 Office: U Ariz 309 Shantz Bldg Tucson AZ 85721

JORGENSEN, LENNART ANDREW, electric utilities executive, entrepreneur; b. Great Falls, Mont., Apr. 17, 1947; s. Lennart Gustave and Thelma Marguerite (Loberg) J.; m. Georgielea Ann Weisgerber, July 22, 1967; children: Eric, Kristopher. Diploma, U.S. Army Air Def. Sch., El Paso, Tex., 1971, 74, U.S. Army Adjutant Gens.' Sch., Indpls., 1972. Engr. Nebr. Pub. Power Dist., Columbus, 1976-80; dir. power City of Colby, Kans., 1980-82; asst. gen. mgr. Clatskanie (Oreg.) People's Utility Dist., 1982—; v.p. and bd. dirs. Quincy Water Assn., Clatskanie, 1985—. Cubmaster Boy Scouts Am., Clatskanie, 1983; tng. mgr. USAF MARS Region 5, 1986; served as staff sgt. U.S. Army, 1966-76. Mem. Am. Pub. Power Assn. (energy services plan com. 1981-82, rates load research com. 1983—, human resources com. 1983—), N.W. Pub. Power Assn., Am. Soc. Pub. Adminstrn., Am. Radio Relay League (emergency coordinator 1976, 85, 2 Pub. Service awards, 1964, 65, phone activities mgr. 1978), VFW (life, dist. adjutant Columbus, Nebr. Post 1979-80), Am. Legion, Nat. Rifle Assn. Lodge: Kiwanis (bd. dirs. Clatskanie club 1983-84). Avocations: amateur radio, youth activities, outdoor sports. Home: PO Box 1197 Clatskanie OR 97016-1197 Office: Clatskanie People's Utility Dist PO Box 216 Clatskanie OR 97016-0216

JORGENSEN, LOU ANN BIRKBECK, social worker; b. Park City, Utah, May 14, 1931; d. Robert John and Lillian Pearl (Langford) Birkbeck; student Westminster Coll., 1949-51; B.S., U. Utah, 1953, M.S.W., 1972, D.S.W., 1979; grad. Harvard Inst. Ednl. Mgmt., 1983; m. Howard Arnold Jorgensen, June 9, 1954; children—Gregory Arnold, Blake John, Paul Clayton. Social work adminstr. nursing home demonstration project, dept. family and community medicine U. Utah Med. Center, Salt Lake City, 1972-74; mental health ednl. specialist Grad. Sch. Social Work, U. Utah, 1974-77, 77-80, asst. prof., 1974-80, assoc. prof., 1980—, dir. doctoral program, 1984—, assoc. dean, 1986—; regional mental health cons. Bd. dirs. Info. and Referral Center, 1975-82, United Way of Utah, 1976-82, Pioneer Trail Parks, 1977-83, Rowland Hall-St. Marks Sch., 1980-86; Salt Lake County housing commr., 1980-86; pres. Human Services Conf. for Utah, 1979-80. Mem. Council on Social Work Edn., Nat. Assn. Social Workers (pres. Utah chpt. 1978-79), Adminstrs. of Public Agys. Assn., Human Services Assn. Utah, Jr. League of Salt Lake City, Phi Kappa Phi. Republican. Episcopalian. Clubs: Ft. Douglas Country, Town, Eastern Star. Author: Explorations in Living, 1978; Social Work in Business and Industry, 1979; Handbook of the Social Services, 1981; contbr. articles to profl. jours. Home: 3442 East Oaks Dr Salt Lake City UT 84124 Office: U Utah Grad Sch Social Work Salt Lake City UT 84112

JORGENSEN, PAUL J., research company executive; b. Midway, Utah, Sept. 1, 1930; s. Joseph and Alice P. Jorgensen; m. Ardelle M. Bloom, Sept. 11, 1956; children: Paula, Mark, Janet, LaDell, Brett, Scott. Student, U. Utah, 1948-50, PhD, 1960; BS, Brigham Young U., 1954. Scientist Gen. Electric Co., Schenectady, N.Y., 1960-68; mgr. ceramics group Stanford Research Inst., Menlo Park, Calif., 1968-74, dir. materials research ctr., 1974-76; exec. dir. phys. sci. div. SRI Internat., Menlo Park, 1976-77, v.p. phys. and life sci. div., 1977-80, sr. v.p. scis. group, 1980—, also bd. dirs.; cons. Gen. Telephone and Electric Co., 1971-82; bd. dirs. Mirage Systems, Santa Clara, Calif.; mem. com. high temperature chemistry Nat. Acad. Sci., NRC, 1972-75, nat. materials adv. bd., 1982-85. Contbr. articles to profl. jours.; patentee in field. Served with U.S. Army, 1954-56. Recipient IR-100, Indsl. Research Mag., 1967. Fellow Am. Ceramic Soc. (chmn. basic sci. div. 1975). Republican. Mormon. Office: SRI Internat 333 Ravenswood Ave Menlo Park CA 94025

JOSEFOWITZ, NATASHA, sydicated columnist; b. Paris, Oct. 31, 1926; d. Myron T. and Tamara (Fradkin) Chapro; m. Sam Josefowitz, May 15, 1949; children: Nina, Paul. MSW, Columbia Sch. Social Work, 1965; Doctorans, Lausanne U., Switzerland, 1974; PhD, Sussex Coll., Eng., 1977. Prof. social work Lausanne U. Child Guidance Clinic, Switzerland, 1965-74; lectr., psychologist Lausanne U., Switzerland, 1972-74; prof. mgmt. U. N.H., 1974-80, Coll. Bus., San Diego State U., 1980-84; syndicated columnist Copley New Service, San Diego, 1985—. Author: Paths to Power, 1980, Is This Where I Was Going?, 1983, You're the Boss, 1985, Natasha's Words for Friends, Families, and Lovers, 1986. Mem. Organized Devel. Network, Nat. Tng. Lab. (emeritus 1985), Acad. Mgmt., Nat. Assn. Arts and Letters. Home and Office: 2235 Calle Guaymas La Jolla CA 92037

JOSELYN, JO ANN, space scientist; b. St. Francis, Kans., Oct. 5, 1943; d. James Jacob and Josephine Felzien (Firkins) Cram. BS in Applied Math., U. Colo., 1965, MS in Astro Geophysics, 1967, Ph.D. in Astro Geophysics, 1978. Research asst. NASA-Manned Space Ctr., Houston, 1966; physicist NOAA-Space Environ. Lab., Boulder, Colo., 1967-78; space scientist NOAA-Space Environ. Lab., Boulder, 1978—; U.S. del. study group 6 Consultive Com. for Ionospheric Radio, 1981, 83. Mem. U. Colo. Grad. Sch. Alumni Council, 1986—. Recipient unit citation NOAA, 1971, 80, 85, 86, group achievement award NASA, 1983, Disting. Engring. Alumnus award U. Colo., 1987. Mem. AIAA, Am. Women in Sci., Am. Geophys. Union, Union Radio Sci. Internat., Internat. Union Geodesy and Geophysics, Assn. Geomagnetism and Aeronomy, AAAS, AAUW, PEO, Sigma Xi, Tau Beta Pi, Sigma Tau. Republican. Methodist. Office: NOAA-Space Environ Lab 325 Broadway St Boulder CO 80303

JOSEPH, BABU, chemical educator; b. Trivandrum, Kerala, India, Feb. 12, 1950; came to U.S., 1971; s. Thomas and Rose; m. Ann Thomas, Jan. 22, 1977; children: Mili, Neeraj. BS, IIT, Kanpur, India, 1971; MS, Case Western Res. U., 1974, PhD, 1975. Research assoc. MIT, Cambridge, Mass., 1975-78; asst. prof. to assoc. prof. Washington U., St. Louis, 1978—; vis. prof. U. of Calif., Berkeley, 1985-86. Contbr. numerous articles to profl. jours. Named Engring. Prof. of Yr., Washington U., 1984. Mem. Am. Inst. Chem. Engrs. (continuing edn. lectr. 1984—), Am. Chem. Soc., Sigma Xi. Avocations: photography. Home: 11138 Yellowstone Saint Louis MO 63146 Office: Washington U Dept Chem Engring Saint Louis MO 63130

JOSEPH, CHARLES EDWARD, periodontist; b. Beverly Hills, Calif., Jan. 22, 1947; s. Peter C. and Mary L. (Bergen) J.; m. Jean M. Taylor, June 14, 1975. BS, Loyola U., Chgo., 1971; DDS, U. Ill., Chgo., 1975, MS, 1977, PhD, 1981. Instr. U. Ill. Med. Ctr., Chgo., 1975-81; asst. prof. U. So. Calif., Los Angeles, 1981-83, chmn. periodontal dept. Dental Sch., 1983-86; practice medicine specializing in periodotics Beverly Hills, Calif., 1985—; cons. Wadsworth Med. Ctr., attending staff mem. Cedars-Sinai Med. Ctr.; acad. cons. St. Mary's Med. Ctr. Assoc. editor Jour. Western Soc. Periodontology; contbr. articles to sci. jours. Recipient Am. Acad. Oral Pathology award, Dr. Robert Savage Meml. award; Am. Cancer Soc. fellow. Fellow Nat. Inst. Dental Research; mem. Calif. Soc. Periodontists (chmn., bd. dirs.), Am. Acad. Periodontologists, ADA. Avocation: tennis. Office: 9400 Brighton Way Suite 311 Beverly Hills CA 90210

JOSEPH, EZEKIEL (ED), manufacturing company executive; b. Rangoon, Burma, June 24, 1938; s. Joe E. Joseph and Rachel Levi; m. Sheila G. Rabinovitch, Feb. 17, 1963; children: Renah, Heather, Jerald. Mktg. mgr. Gen. Electric Corp., Waynesboro, Va., 1968-75; dir. Actron div. McDonnell Douglas Corp., Monrovia, Calif., 1975-78; pres. Joseph Machinery Inc., Huntington Beach, Calif., 1978-83; prin. Computer and Software Solutions, Huntington Beach, 1983—; pres. Tangent Inds. Inc. (now Xtalite Display Systems Inc.), Huntington Beach, 1985—; pres. Retract-a-Roof Inc., Huntington Beach. V.p. Temple Beth David, Huntington Beach, 1975—. Mem. Austin Healey Assoc. Democrat. Avocations: antique cars, sailing. Home: 16242 Typhoon Ln Huntington Beach CA 92649 Office: Xtalite Display Systems Inc 17632 Metzler Ln Huntington Beach CA 92647

JOSEPH, KARYN MARIE, speech pathologist; b. Detroit, Apr. 21, 1960; d. Ezekiel and Bobbie Dean (Jones) J. BS, Eastern Mich. U., 1983, MA, 1984. Speech lang. pathologist Lenkner, Michener and Assocs. Inc., Twin Falls, Idaho, 1984—; mem. Council Exceptional Children div. Communication Disorders div. Visually Handicapped. Mem. Am. Speech Lang. Hearing Assn. (cert.), Idaho Speech and Hearing Assn., Magic Valley Speech and Hearing Assn. Adventist. Avocations: writing, poetry, chorale, singing. Office: Lenkner Michener & Assocs 493 Eastland Dr Twin Falls ID 83301

JOSEPHSON, HAROLD ALLAN, real estate developer; b. Montreal, Que., Can., July 21, 1944; s. Joseph and Edith (Marco) J.; m. Sheila Gloria Laing, July 4, 1966 (div. July 1976); children: Daniel, Robert.; MBA with distinction, Harvard U., 1971. V.p. Marcil Mortgage Corp., Montreal, 1976-78; prin. Josephson Properties, Montreal, 1978-83, Los Angeles, 1983—. Mem. Urban Land Inst., Nat. Assn. Indsl. and Office Parks, Internat. Council Shopping Ctrs. Jewish. Club: Beverly Hills Country (Los Angeles). Avocations: skiing, tennis, flying. Office: 2029 Century Park E #1200 Los Angeles CA 90067

JOSEPHSON, JOSEPH PAUL, lawyer; b. Trenton, N.J., June 3, 1933; s. David S. and Jenny (Randelman) J.; m. Virginia McKinney; children: Peter, Andrew, Sarah, Anna. B.A., U. Chgo., 1953; J.D., Cath. U. Am., 1960. Bar: Alaska 1961. Since practiced in Anchorage; legis. asst. to territorial del. and U.S. Senator from Alaska Washington, 1957-60; mem. Alaska Ho. of Reps., Juneau, 1963-67; acting mayor Anchorage, 1968; mem. Alaska Senate, 1969-72, 83—, chmn. senate majority caucus, chmn. com. on health, edn. and social services, 1983-85; co-chmn. Joint Fed.-State Land Use Planning Commn. for Alaska, 1972-74; assemblyman Municipality of Anchorage, 1980-82; lectr. Alaska Pacific U., 1983. Editorial bd.: Cath. U. Am. Law Rev, 1959-60; columnist: Anchorage Daily News, 1976-79; contbg. editor: Alaska Bar Assn. Newspaper. Chmn. South Central Alaska ARC, 1964-65; Candidate U.S. Senate, 1970; mem., dep. chmn. Greater Anchorage Charter Commn., 1975-76. Served with AUS, 1955-57. Mem. Am., Alaska, Anchorage bar assns., Am. Arbitration Assn. (arbitrator 1977—). Democrat. Home: 1526 F St Anchorage AK 99501 Office: Alaska Senate 425 G St Anchorage AK 99501

JOSEPHSON, RONALD VICTOR, foods and nutrition educator; b. Bellefonte, Pa., May 19, 1942; s. Donald Victor and Ada Clarice (Burris) J.; m. Judith Evelyn Pinkerton, Dec. 20, 1969; children: Kirsten Elise, Erika Lyn. BS, Pa. State U., 1964; MS, U. Minn., 1966, PhD, 1970. Asst. prof. food sci. Ohio State U., Columbus, 1970-75; from assoc. prof. to prof. foods and nutrition Calif. State U., San Diego, 1978—. Contbr. articles to profl. jours. Coach basketball Boys Club Am. and Girls Club Am., Encinitas, Calif., 1980—, softball San Dieguito Bobby Sox, Encinitas, 1983-84, pres. 1985—. Mem. Inst. Food Technologists (profl., regional communicator So. Calif. area 1978-83, 86—, chmn. basic research com. 1985—), Am. Dairy Sci. Assn., Sigma Xi (sec. San Diego chpt. 1980-85, pres.-elect 1986—). Office: Calif State U Sch Family Studies & Consumer Scis San Diego CA 92182

JOSEY, PATRICK MCD., explosives expert; b. Raton, N.Mex., Mar. 22, 1956; s. Robert W. and Elizabeth A. (Berry) J.; m. Becky Lee Burton, Aug. 15, 1981; 1 child, Caitlin. BS in Chemistry, U. N.Mex., 1980. Engr. BDM Internat. Inc., Albuquerque, 1980-83; assoc. mgr. BDM Internat. Inc., Las Cruces, N.Mex., 1983-85; tech. leader BDM Internat. Inc., Albuquerque, 1986—. Active Albuquerque Leadership Program, 1986—. Mem. Am. Chem. Soc., Am. MENSA Soc., Internat. Pyrotechnics Soc., Nat. Writers Club. Roman Catholic. Avocations: hunting, fishing, woodcarving, bagpipes. Office: BDM Internat Inc 1801 Randolph St Albuquerque NM 87106

JOSHI, ARUN S., manufacturing engineering executive; b. Bombay, India, Dec. 17, 1953; came to U.S., 1978; s. Shridhar K. and Shudha S. Joshi; m. Shubha A. Joshi, Dec. 10, 1981. BE, Bombay U.; MS, Kans. State U., 1980. Supr. mfg. Godrej & Boyce Ltd., Bombay, 1976-78; sr. mfg. engr. Intel Corp., Hillsboro, Oreg., 1980-83, mfg. engring. mgr., 1983—. Contbr. tech. articles on elec. mfg. to profl. jours. Mem. Soc. Mfg. Engrs. (sr., vice-chmn. Portland chpt. 1985-86, chmn. 1986—). Home: 3251 NW 157th Pl Beaverton OR 97006 Office: Intel Corp 5200 NE Elam Young Pkwy Hillsboro OR 97123

JOSHI, CHANDRASHEKHAR JANARDAN, physics educator; b. Wai, India, July 22, 1953; came to U.S., 1981; s. Janardan Digambar and Ramabai (Kirpekar) J.; m. Asha Bhatt, Jan. 18, 1982. BS, London U., 1974; PhD, Hull U., U.K., 1978. Research assoc. Nat. Research Council, Can., 1978-81; research engr. UCLA, 1981-83, adj. assoc. prof., 1983-86, assoc. prof.-in-residence, 1986—; cons. Lawrence Livermore (Calif.) Nat. Lab., 1984, Los Alamos (N.Mex.) Nat. Lab., 1985—. Editor: Laser Acceleration of Particles, 1985; contbr. articles ot profl. jours. Grantee NSF, U.S. Dept. Energy; recipient Queen Mary Prize, Inst. Nuclear Engring., 1974. Mem. AAAS, IEEE, Am. Phys. Soc., N.Y. Acad. Scis. Avocation: traveling. Home: 2004 Pier Ave Santa Monica CA 90405 Office: UCLA 405 Hilgard Ave Los Angeles CA 90024

JOSHUA, AARON, investment company executive; b. Los Angeles, Aug. 26, 1957; s. Elmo and Pineniece Penny (Starks) J.; m. Valeri Janien. B.A. in Bus. Adminstrn., Whittier Coll., 1978, M.B.A., 1980. Life ins. agt. ITT Ins. Corp., Marina del Rey, Calif., 1977; pres., chmn. bd. Joshua's Restaurant Inc., Inglewood, Calif., 1980—; gen. ptnr. Internat. Mgmt. Assocs., fin. planning and asset mgmt., Beverly Hills, Calif., 1980—; SEC investment adviser. Mem. Am. Mgmt. Assn., Beverly Hills C. of C. (edn. com.), Inglewood C. of C., Internat. Assn. Fin. Planning. Republican. Baptist. Club: Inglewood Rotary. Office: 3216 W Manchester Blvd Inglewood CA 90302

JOSPE, MICHAEL, medical psychologist; b. Johannesburg, South Africa, Feb. 12, 1944; s. Leonhard and Gerda Jospe. B.A., U. Leeds, Eng., 1965; M.A., U. Minn., 1970, Ph.D., 1974. Chief psychologist Newington Children's Hosp., Conn., 1975-76; coordinator pediatric consultation and liaison psychiatry Kaiser-Permanente Med. Ctr., Los Angeles, 1979—, coordinator psychosocial oncology behavioral medicine, div., 1983—; asst. clin. prof. consultation and liaison psychiatry Neuropsychiat. Inst., UCLA Med. Ctr.; dir. program in clin. health psychology, Calif. Sch. Profl. psychology, Los Angeles, 1983—. Author: The Placebo Effect in Healing, 1978; Psychological Factors in Health Care: A Manual for Practitioners, 1980. Contbr. articles to profl. jours. Mem. Am. Psychol. Assn. Office: Kaiser-Permanente Med Ctr Behavioral Medicine Div 4747 Sunset Blvd Los Angeles CA 90027

JOY, CARLA MARIE, educator; b. Denver, Sept. 5, 1945; d. Carl P. and Theresa M. (Lotito) J. A.B. cum laude, Loretto Heights Coll., 1967; M.A. (Ford Found. fellow), U. Denver, 1969, postgrad., 1984—. Instr. history Community Coll. Denver; prof. history Red Rocks Community Coll., Golden, Colo., 1970—; cons. for innovative ednl. programs; reviewer fed. grants; mem. adv. panel Colo. Endowment for Humanities, 1985—. Contbr. articles to profl. pubs. Instr. vocat. edn. Mile High United Way, Jefferson County, 1975; participant Jefferson County Sch. System R-1 Dist., 1983—. Cert. in vocat. edn. Colo. State Bd. Community Colls. and Occupational Edn. Recipient cert. of appreciation Kiwanis Club, 1981; Master Tchr. award U. Tex. at Austin, 1982. Mem. Am. Hist. Assn., Nat. Council for Social Studies, Nat. Geog. Soc., Inst. Early Am. History and Culture, Colo. Council for Social Studies, Community Coll. Humanities Assn., Orgn. Am. Historians, The Colo. Hist. Soc., Am. Soc. Profl. and Exec. Women, Phi Alpha Theta. Democrat. Episcopalian. Designer adult-self-directed instructional programs for world civilization, 1972— and Am. history, 1982—. Home: 1849 S Lee St Apt D Lakewood CO 80226 Office: Red Rocks Community Coll 12600 W 6th Ave Golden CO 80401

JOY, ROBERT MCKERNON, research toxicology educator; b. Troy, N.Y., May 9, 1941; s. Edward M. and Rita Hannah (Sedgwick) J. PhD, Stanford U., 1970. Diplomate Am. Bd. Toxicology. Research assoc. Stanford Research Inst., Menlo Park, Calif., 1963-64; pharmacologist U. Calif., davis, 1969-70, asst. prof., 1970-77; assoc. prof. U. Calif., Davis, 1977-84, co-dir. health scis. neurotoxicology unit, 1981—, prof., 1984—; vis. assoc. prof. Harvard U. Med. Sch., Cambridge, Mass., 1977-78; vis. research assoc. Children's Hosp., Boston, 1977-78. Mem. AAAS, Am. Soc. Pharmacology and Exptl. Therapeutics, Soc. Toxicology, Soc. Neuroscis., Western Pharmacology Soc. Home: 3104 N El Macero Dr El Macero CA 95618 Office: U Calif Dept Pharm/Tox Davis CA 95616

JOYCE, CLAUDE CLINTON, systems analyst; b. Lordsburg, N.Mex., May 10, 1931; s. William Claude and Minnie Madline (Gibson) J.; m. Wanda Gifting, Dec. 7, 1951; children: Claude Clifton, Lani Caprice. BS in Acctg., San Diego State U., 1956. Supr. tabulator machines USN Supply Depot, San Diego, 1952-55; sales rep. Service Bur. Corp. subs. IBM, San Diego and San Francisco, 1955-59; dir. Mgmt. Adv. Services Price Waterhouse, San Francisco, 1959-68; sr. v.p. mgmt. info. systems Albertsons Inc., Boise, Idaho, 1968—. Served with USN, 1948-52. Mem. Assn. Systems Mgmt. (pres. 1972-73, Dist. Service award 1976). Republican. Lodges: Shriners (pres. 1979), Rotary, Mason. Avocations: camping, personal computers, bicycling. Home: 1400 Shoshone Boise ID 83726 Office: Albertsons Inc PO Box 20 Boise ID 83726

JOYCE, MARILYN SCHMIDT, training company executive; b. Covington, Ky., Sept. 3, 1942; d. Robert Andrew and Rita Marie (Stadtmiller) S.; m. Clayton Robert Joyce, Nov. 29, 1975; stepchildren—David Joyce, Kathryn Joyce Keehn, Robert Joyce. B.A., Thomas More Coll., 1964; M.Ed., Xavier U., 1968. Tchr., Colerain High Sch., Cin., 1964-68; tchr. N.E. High Sch., Ft. Lauderdale, Fla., 1968-69; chmn. dept. curriculum devel. Henderson High Sch., Atlanta, 1969-75; trainer, mgr. URS Corp., Seattle, 1977-80; founder, pres. Joyce Inst., Seattle, 1981—; ergonomics tng. cons. GTE, 1983—, Boeing Co., Seattle, 1981—; speaker Internat. Sci. Conf.1986, Nat. Safety Council Conf., 1986. Editor tng. courses: Dataspan, 1981, Datahealth, 1985. Co-author tng. manual: Managing Office Ergonomics, 1986, Pro-Read, 1972. Mem. Human Factors Soc. (speaker 1984), Am. Soc. Tng. and Devel., Seattle C. of C. Republican. Mem. Christian Ch. Clubs: Columbia Tower, Ranier. Home: 2220 40th Ave E Seattle WA 98112

JOYNER, THOMAS ALLEN, motion picture executive; b. Oak Park, Ill., Dec. 7, 1943; s. Major Battle and Florence Laverne (Lundgren) J.; m. Laura Diggs, July 29, 1968; children: Dawn Denise, Christopher Allen. BA, Adams State Coll. Exec. prodn. mgr. Walt Disney Pictures, Burbank, Calif., 1985—. Prodn. mgr. for films including Jaws II, 1977, Last Married Couple in Am., 1979, Blues Bros., 1979, Any Which Way You Can, 1980, Walking Tall, 1981, Seven Brides for Seven Bros., 1982, Against All Odds, 1982-83, Starman, 1983-84, Poltergeist II, 1985. Served with USMC, 1961-64. Mem. Dirs. Guild of Am. (AD/UPM council mem. 1983-85). Republican. Home: 2500 11th Ave Los Angeles CA 90018 Office: Walt Disney Pictures 500 S Buena Vista St Burbank CA 91521

JOZEFIAK, RICHARD CHESTER, aerospace engineer; b. Chgo., Aug. 4, 1960; s. Chester Joseph Jozefiak and Marilyn Ann (La Roche) Laughlin, (stepfather) Lawrence M. Laughlin; m. Karen Therese Sowers, Feb. 1, 1986. BSME, Ill. Inst. Tech., 1982. Engr. Gen. Dynamics, Space Systems and Convair Divs., San Diego, 1982-85; mem. tech. staff Satellite Systems div. Rockwell Internat., Seal Beach, Calif., 1985—. Supporting mem. Zool. Soc. San Diego, 1983—; bd. dirs. Carroll Canyon Homeowners Assn., San Diego, 1983-84. Mem. ASME (assoc., mem. Los Angeles sect., pres. student sect. 1981, cert. outstanding efforts and accomplishments 1981), Ill. Inst. Tech. Alumni Assn. (student recruiter 1986), Downey (Calif.) Symphonic Soc. Roman Catholic. Avocations: personal computers, travel, science fiction, photography. Home: 18718 Kings Row Ave Cerritos CA 90701-5235 Office: Rockwell Internat Satellite Systems Div 2600 Westminster Blvd AD35 Seal Beach CA 90740-7644

JOZWIK, FRANCIS XAVIER, agrl. bus. exec.; b. El Paso, Tex., July 4, 1940; s. Andrew and Dagmar Elizabeth (Wettermark) J.; student Casper Coll., 1958-60, U. Idaho, 1960; B.S., U. Wyo., 1962, M.S., 1963, Ph.D., 1966; postgrad. Wash. State U., 1964; m. Phyllis Ann Angevine, Dec. 28, 1974; children—Melissa, John, Monika. Asst. prof. plant physiology Wis. State U., Oshkosh, 1966-67; rangelands scientist Commonwealth Scientific & Indsl. Research Orgn., Canberra, Australia, 1967-69; owner, mgr. Johnny Appleseed, Inc., Casper, Wyo., 1969—; owner Andmar Press, Casper, Wy-

o. NSF fellow, 1963. Mem. U.S. C. of C., Sigma Xi. Roman Catholic. Author: Plants for Profit. Editor Nat. Greenhouse Industry mag. Contbr. articles in field to profl. jours. Home: 8364 W Yellowstone St Casper WY 82604 Office: 8340 W Yellowstone St Casper WY 82604

JU, FREDERICK DSUIN, mechanical engineering educator; b. Shanghai, Republic of China, Sept. 21, 1929; came to U.S., 1952; s. Pao-Hwa and Mei-Yin J.; m. Ruby K.Y. Ju, Jan. 29, 1956; children: Wilfred, Manfred, Winifred. BSME, U. Houston, 1953; MSME, U. Ill., 1956, PhD, 1958. Asst. prof. mech. engring. U. N.Mex., Albuquerque, 1958-62, assoc. prof., 1962-67, prof., 1967—, chmn. dept. mech. engring., 1973-76; vis. staff mem. Los Alamos (N.Mex.) Nat. Lab., 1962—. Pres. N.Mex. Chinese Assn., Albuquerque, 1985-86. Named to Presdl. professorship U. N.Mex., 1985—; recipient Achievement award Soc. Theoretical and Applied Mechanics, Taipei, Taiwan, Republic of China, 1986. Fellow ASME; mem. Soc. Engring. Sci., Soc. Exptl. Strees Analysis. Office: U NMex Dept Mech Engring Albuquerque NM 87131

JUAREZ, ANNA LUISA, lawyer; b. McPherson, Kans., June 18, 1958; d. Santos and Maria Luisa (Cardenas) J. AA, Kansas Newman Coll., 1979, BS, 1980; JD, Washburn U., 1983. Bar: N.Mex. 1983, U.S. Dist. Ct. N.Mex. 1984, U.S. Ct. Appeals (10th cir.) 1985. Assoc. Edward E. Triviz, P.A., Las Cruces, N.Mex., 1983-84; sole practice Las Cruces, 1984-85; staff atty. So. N.Mex. Legal Services, Las Cruces, 1985-87, mng. atty., 1986-87; spl. asst. atty. gen. Las Cruces office supr. atty. Office Gen. Counsel Human Services Dept., 1987—. Mem. Dona Ana County Bar Assn. (treas. 1985—), ABA, Assn. Trial Lawyers Am., N.Mex. Trial Lawyers Assn. Democrat. Roman Catholic. Office: Office Gen Counsel Human Services Dept PO Box 2135 Las Cruces NM 88004

JUAREZ, MARETTA LIYA CALIMPONG, social worker; b. Gilroy, Calif., Feb. 14, 1958; d. Sulpicio Magsalay and Pelagia Lagotom (Viacrusis) Calimpong; m. Henry Juarez, Mar. 24, 1984. BA, U. Calif., Berkeley, 1979; MSW, San Jose State U., 1983. Mgr. Pacific Bell, San Jose, Calif., 1983-84; revenue officer IRS, Salinas, Calif., 1984-85; social worker Santa Cruz (Calif.) County, 1985, Santa Clara County, San Jose, 1985—. Recipient award Am. Legion, 1972. Mem. NOW, Nat. Assn. Social Workers. Democrat. Roman Catholic. Avocations: snow and water skiing, tennis, reading.

JUDD, FLOYD LYMEN, physics educator; b. Jonesville, Wis., Jan. 25, 1934; s. Frank A. and Mabel (Mielke) J.; divorced; children: Gregory, Terry, Kristin. BS, Carroll Coll., 1956; MS, Iowa State U., 1958, PhD, 1967. Instr. physics N.W. La. State U., Natchitoches, 1959-63, 64-67; research CERN, Geneva, 1963-64; instr. Calif. State U., Fresno, 1967—, chmn. dept. physics, 1976-82; vis. scholar Stanford (Calif.) U., 1987. Mem. Am. Assn. Physics Tchrs. (pres. 1978-79), Sigma Xi, Sigma Pi. Home: 140 W San Jose #215 Fresno CA 93704

JUDD, KATHLEEN MARIE, human resources executive, benefit consultant; b. Los Angeles, Aug. 26, 1948; d. Joe C.J. and Betty R. (Pechacek) J.; m. John Hunter Boggs, May 18, 1974 (div. Aug. 1977). BA, UCLA, 1969. Cert. employee benefit specialist. Dept. mgr. Equity Funding, Los Angeles, 1968-74; mgr. Source Life Ins. Co., Houston, 1974-75; personnel officer Alexander & Alexander, Los Angeles, 1977-80; v.p. Imperial Industries, Burbank, Calif., 1980—; cons. UCLA, 1985; speaker, writer Self Ins. Inst. Am., Santa Ana, Calif., 1984—. Author: Walker's Constrn. Jour., 1983. Donor Guide Dogs Am., San Rafael, Calif., 1986. Mem. Soc. Profl. Benefit Adminstrs., Internat. Found. Employee Benefit Plans, Internat. Soc. Cert. Employee Benefits Specialists, Employee Benefit Planning Assn. So. Calif, Nat. Rifle Assn., Labrador Retrievers Club So. Calif. Republican. Mormon. Avocations: breeding and showing Labrador retrievers, Western riding/showing, skiing, hunting, trap shooting. Home: 1708 Terrace Ln Pomona CA 91768 Office: Imperial Industries 101 S First St Burbank CA 91502

JUDD, PATRICIA HOFFMAN, social worker; b. Pitts., June 22, 1946; d. Joseph Andrew and Irene Patricia (Bednar) Hoffman; m. Lewis Lund Judd, Jan. 26, 1974. B.A., Marquette U., 1968; M.S.W., San Diego State U., 1970; doctoral candidate Calif. Sch. Profl. Psychology, 1983—. Dir. treatment services DEFY, Health Care Agy. of San Diego County, San Diego, 1973-75; coordinator emergency psychiat. services U. Calif. Med. Ctr., San Diego, 1975-77, mem. attending staff, 1975-85; clin. coordinator crisis and brief treatment service Gifford Mental Health Clinic, U. Calif.-San Diego, 1975-79, coordinator clin. services, 1979-82, asst. dir., 1983—; clin. instr. dept. psychiatry U. Calif.-San Diego Sch. Medicine, 1976—; field instr. Sch. Social Work, San Diego State U., 1970—, lectr., 1978-80; pvt. practice psychotherapy, San Diego, 1979—. Mem. Nat. Assn. Social Workers, Acad. Cert. Social Workers, Soc. Clin. Social Workers. Office: 3427 4th Ave San Diego CA 92103

JULIAN, CAROL PATRICIA, medical center administrator; b. Portland, Oreg., Apr. 14, 1942; d. John Joseph and Alice Lucille (Riggs) J. B.S. in Nursing, U. Oreg., 1964, M.S. in Edn., 1969. Med./surg. nurse Providence Hosp., Portland, 1964-65; gerintological nurse Hassler Hosp., San Francisco, 1965-67; med. nurse St. Lukes Hosp., Denver, 1968-69, dir. edn., 1969-84, dir. patient care, 1984—. Mem. Am. Nurses Assn., Colo. Soc. Nurse Execs., Nat. Accreditation Bd. Continuing Edn. Democrat.

JULIEN, PAUL DANIEL, lawyer; b. Ypsilanti, Mich., Nov. 4, 1953; s. Daniel Joseph and Jane Abagail (Pierce) J.; m. Angela Kay Bell, May 28, 1973; children: Wendelyn Rene, Francie Jane. BS, U. Utah, 1973; MA, No. Ariz. U., 1974, Doctor in Edn., 1981; JD, U. Ariz., 1986. Cert. tchr. and adminstr., Ariz., Colo. Pulpwood cutter Southwest Forest Industries, Flagstaff, Ariz., 1977; with quality control Medussa Aggregates, Lexington, Ky., 1978; adminstr. Youth Conservation Corps, Flagstaff, 1979; mem. faculty Flagstaff Pub. Schs., 1973-80, No. Ariz. U., Flagstaff, 1980-85; law clerk, assoc. Molloy, Jones, Donahue, Tucson, 1985—; cons. Ariz., N.Mex. schs., 1980—; research technician U. Ariz., 1986—. Bd. dirs. Marshall Found., Tucson, 1985—, Am. Diabetes Assn., Tucson, 1985—, Catalina Foothills Sch. Bd, Tucson, 1985—, Ariz. Bd. Regents, 1984-85. Served with USN, 1971-72. Recipient Dist. award Merit Boy Scouts Am., 1977, Disting. Citizen award U. Ariz., 1985, Centennial award Merit, Ariz. State U., 1986. Mem. ABA, Ariz. Acad., Phi Kappa Phi, Phi Delta Kappa. Republican. Presbyterian. Avocations: beekeeping, skiing, hiking, backpacking. Home: 1730 Calle Guillermo Tucson AZ 85718 Office: Molloy Jones Donahue PC Ariz Bank Plaza Tucson AZ 85702

JUNCHEN, DAVID LAWRENCE, pipe organ manufacturing company executive; b. Rock Island, Ill., Feb. 23, 1946; s. Lawrence Ernest and Lucy Mae (Ditto) J.; B.S. in Elec. Engring. with highest honors, U. Ill., 1968. Founder, owner Junchen Pipe Organ Service, Sherrard, Ill., 1968—; co-owner Junchen-Collins Organ Corp., Woodstock, Ill., 1975-80; mng. dir. Baranger Studios, South Pasadena, Calif., 1980-81. Named Outstanding Freshman in Engring. U. Ill., 1963-64. Mem. Am. Inst. Organbuilders (bd. dirs. 1986—), Am. Theatre Organ Soc. (Tech. Excellence award 1986), Mus. Box Soc., Automatic Mus. Instrument Collectors Assn., Tau Beta Pi, Sigma Tau, Eta Kappa Nu. Author: Encyclopedia of American Theatre Organs; contbr. to Ency. Automatic Mus. Instruments; composer, arranger over 100 music rolls for self-playing mus. instruments. Office: 280 E Del Mar Suite 311 Pasadena CA 91101

JUNE, ROY ETHIEL, lawyer; b. Forsyth, Mont., Aug. 12, 1922; s. Charles E. and Elizabeth F. (Newnes) J.; m. Laura Brautigam, June 20, 1949; children—Patricia June, Richard Tyler. B.A., U. Mont., 1948, B.A. in Law, 1951, LL.B., 1952. Bar: Mont. 1952, Calif. 1961. Sole practice, Billings, Mont., 1952-57, Sanders and June, 1953-57; real estate developer, Orange County, Calif., 1957-61; ptnr. Dugan, Tobias, Tornay & June, Costa Mesa, Calif., 1961-62; city prosecutor, Costa Mesa, 1962-63, asst. city atty., 1963-67, city atty., 1967-78; sole practice, Costa Mesa, 1962—. Atty. Costa Mesa Hist. Soc., Costa Mesa Playhouse Patron's Assn., Red Barons Orange County, Costa Mesa Meml. Hosp. Aux., Harbor Key, Child Guidance Ctr. Orange County, Fairview State Hosp. Therapeutic Pool Vols., Inc.; active Eagle Scout evaluation team, Harbor Area Boy Scouts Am., YMCA; atty. United Fund/Community Chest Costa Mesa and Newport Beach; bd. dirs. Boys' Club Harbor Area, bd. dirs. Mardan Ctr. Ednl. Therapy, United Cerebral Palsy Found. Orange County. Served with USAF, World War II. Decorated Air medal with oak leaf cluster, D.F.C. Mem. Mont. Bar Assn., Calif. Bar Assn., Orange County Bar Assn., Harbor Bar Assn., Costa Mesa C. of C. (bd. dirs.). Clubs: Masons, Scottish Rite, Shriners, Santa Ana Country, Amigos Viejos, Los Fiestadores. Office: 2970 Harbor Blvd Suite 211 PO Box 3050 Costa Mesa CA 92626

JUNG, HENRY HUNG, mechanical engineer, researcher; b. Hong Kong, Aug. 3, 1957; s. Cheuk-Sun and Siu-Kuen (Ma) J.; m. Mi-Ying Miranda, Mar. 28, 1986. BS MechE, Ariz. State U., 1980; MS MechE, U. Ill., 1983. Engr. Lockheed Aircraft, Burbank, Calif., 1981-82; researcher U. Ill., Champaign-Urbana, 1982-83; engr. Pratt & Whitney Aircraft, West Palm Beach, Fla., 1983-84; research engr. Lockheed Missiles & Space Co., Sunnyvale, Calif., 1984—. Mem. ASME, AIAA, Sigma Xi, Tau Beta Pi, Pi Tau Sigma. Avocation: tennis, ballroom dancing. Home: 517 S Cashmere Terr Sunnyvale CA 94087

JUNGBLUTH, CONNIE CARLSON, investment banker; b. Cheyenne, Wyo., June 20, 1955; d. Charles Marion and Janice Yvonne (Keldsen) Carlson; m. Kirk E. Jungbluth, Feb. 5, 1977; 1 child, Tyler. BS, Colo. State U., 1976. CPA, Colo. Sr. acct. Rhode Scripter & Assoc., Boulder, Colo., 1977-81; mng. acct. Arthur Young, Denver, 1981-85; asst. v.p. Dain Bosworth, Denver, 1985—; bd. dirs. Colo. Diamond Exchange, Denver. mem. Denver Estate Planning Council, 1981-85, organizer Little People Am., Rocky Mountain Med. Clinic and Symposium, Denver, 1986; adv. bd. Children's Home Health, Denver, 1986—; fin. adv. bd. Gail Shoettler for State Treas., Denver, 1986; bd. advisors U. Denver Sch. Accountancy, 1986—; campaign chmn. Kathi Williams for Colo. State Legis., 1986. Mem. Colo. Soc. CPA's (instr. bank 1983, trustee 1984-87, pres. bd. trustees, 1986-87, bd. dirs. 1987—, strategic planning com. 1987—, Pub. Service award 1985-87, chmn. career edn. com. 1982-83), Am. Inst. CPA's, Colo. Mcpl. Bond Dealers, Venture Capital Assn. Colo., Pi Beta Phi. Club: Denver City. Avocations: gourmet cooking, art, reading. Office: Dain Bosworth Inc 1225 17th St Suite 1800 Denver CO 80202

JUNGERMANN, ERIC, chemical company executive; b. Mainz, Fed. Republic Germany, Sept. 8, 1923; came to U.S., 1946; s. Julius and Elisabeth (Hoffmann) J.; m. Eva Schlein, Dec. 28, 1951; 1 child, William. BS, CCNY, 1949; MS, N.Y. Poly. Inst., 1953, PhD, 1957. Research chemist Colgate-Palmolive, Jersey City, 1946-56; mgr. research Armour Indsl. Chem. div. Armour Corp., Chgo., 1956-59, tech. dir. Armour Grocery Products div., 1959-65; v.p. research and devel. Armour/Dial Inc., Chgo., Phoenix, 1965-75; corp. dir. new products Helene Curtis, Chgo., 1975-78; pres. Jungermann Assocs., Inc., Phoenix, 1978—; bd. dirs. Lee Pharms., South El Monte, Calif.; cons. Neutrogena, Los Angeles, 1978—. Series editor Marcel Dekker, Inc., N.Y.C., 1979—; editor: Cationics Surfantants, 1970; contbr. articles to profl. jours.; patentee in field. Mem. Am. Chem. Soc., Am. Oil Chemists Soc. (assoc. editor, Merit award 1971), Soc. Cosmetic Chemists (assoc. editor, IFF award 1974). Avocations: chess, travel. Home: 2323 N Central Phoenix AZ 85004 Office: Jungermann Assocs Inc 2323 N Central Suite 1001 Phoenix AZ 85004

JUPITER, SISTER MARY GRETA, educator, administrator; b. New Orleans, Sept. 20, 1947; d. Ulysses Pere and Emelda Mary (Oubre) J. BS, Xavier U., 1972; MEd, U. New Orleans, 1976. Joined Sisters of the Holy Family, Roman Cath. Ch. Tchr. Holy Rosary Inst., Lafayette, La., 1970-72; instr. Xavier U., New Orleans, 1972-74; tchr. St. Mary's Acad., New Orleans, 1974-80; tchr. Regina Caeli High Sch., Compton, Calif., 1980-85, vice-prin., 1985—. Mem. Nat. Sci. Tchr. Assn., Calif. Chemistry Tchrs., Calif. Edison Adv. Bd., Greater Los Angeles Sci. Tchr. Assn. Democrat. Avocations: singing, swimming. Home: 15011 S Stanford Ave Compton CA 90220 Office: Regina Caeli High Sch 823 E Compton Blvd Compton CA 90220

JUSCZYK, PETER WALTER, psychology educator; b. Providence, Jan. 31, 1948; s. Walter Frank and Eleanor Clare (Savalin) J.; m. Ann Marie Horvat, Jan. 30, 1971; children: Karla Suzanne, Thaddeus Peter. BA, Brown U., 1970; MA, U. Pa., 1971, PhD, 1975. Asst. prof. psychology Dalhousie U., Halifax, N.S., Can., 1975-80; assoc. prof. U. Oreg., Eugene, 1980-86, prof., 1986—. Editor: The Nature of Thought, 1980; mem. editorial bd. Cognition, Paris, 1979—, Perception and Psychophysics, Austin, Tex., 1983-86, Developmental Psychology, Washington, 1986—. Fellow Sloane Found. U. Pa., Phila., 1984, Fulbright Council of Internat. Exchange Schs., Lublin, Poland, 1985. Mem. Soc. Research Child Devel., Acoustical Soc. Am., Soc. Philosophy and Psychology, Sigma Xi. Democrat. Roman Catholic. Avocations: writing, running, photography, cooking. Home: 4730 Manzanita St Eugene OR 97405 Office: U Oreg Dept Psychology Eugene OR 97403

JUSTI, CHRISTIAN LEROY, financial and engineering consultant; b. Kenosha, Wis., Jan. 4, 1928; s. Harald Christian and Gertrude Emma (Schulz) J.; B.S. in Engring., Johns Hopkins U., 1950; M.S. in Fin. and Econs., N.Y. U., 1953, Ph.D., 1955; m. Rose Marie Leon, Feb. 14, 1982; children from previous marriage—Paul, Ann. Engr., Johnson Corp. (acquired by Martin Marietta Corp.), Balt., 1946-50; pro-asst. cashier fgn. dept. Bank Am., Internat., N.Y.C., 1950-55; petroleum and fin. engr. ARCO, Los Angeles, also dir. adminstrn. Vehicle Research Corp., Pasadena, Calif., 1955-60; propr. Fin. Engring. Cons., West Covina, Calif., 1960—. Mem. adv. and youth bds. Los Angeles County Dist. Atty., 1965—; pres. West Covina Beautiful, 1965-67, 81-82, Republican Assembly San Gabriel-Pomona Valley, 1971-73; advisor Nat. Commn.-Youth in Action, 1976—, Nat. Youth Commn., 1981—. Recipient numerous awards for civic contbns. Mem. Am. Inst. Econ. Research, Nat. Assn. Accountants, Nat. Registry Engrs., West Covina C. of C. (dir., Ambassador of Yr. 1980). Roman Catholic. Home: 3133 Sunset Hill Dr West Covina CA 91791 Office: 652 Sunset Suites 208-215 West Covina CA 91790

JUSTIN, JOSEPH EUGENE, military officer; b. Orange, N.J., June 3, 1945; s. James Fredrick and Elizabeth Ann (McCartney) J.; children: James Kenneth, Joseph Patrick. BS, USAF Acad., 1969; MS, Ohio State U., 1973; MA, U. So. Calif., 1980. Commd. 2d lt. USAF, 1969, advanced through grades to maj., 1980; lead project engr. USAF Avionics Lab. USAF, Wright-Patterson AFB, Ohio, 1970-74; exchange officer USAF Systems Commd. USAF, F.E. Warren AFB, Cheyenne, Wyo., 1974; mgr. guidance improvement program USAF Ballistic Missiles Office, Norton AFB, Calif., 1975-77, chief flight test integration div., 1985—; asst. prof. astronautics USAF Acad., Colorado Springs, Colo., 1977-81; research fellow USAF Hdqrs.-Rand Corp., Santa Monica, Calif., 1981-82; dir. space system studies Hdqrs. USAF, Washington, 1982-85. Mem. AIAA (sr.), Air Force Assn. (life), USAF Acad. Assn. Grads. (life), Ohio State U. Alumni Assn. (life), USAF Research Assocs. Assn. Office: USAF Ballistic Missile Office Norton AFB CA 92409

JUVET, RICHARD SPALDING, JR., scientist, chemistry educator; b. Los Angeles, Aug. 8, 1930; s. Richard Spalding and Marion Elizabeth (Dalton) J.; m. Martha Joy Myers, Jan. 29, 1955 (div. Nov. 1978); children: Victoria, David, Stephen, Richard P.; m. Evelyn Raeburn Elthon, July 1, 1984. B.S., UCLA, 1952, Ph.D., 1955. Research chemist Dupont, 1955; instr. U. Ill., 1955-57, asst. prof., 1957-61, assoc. prof., 1961-70; prof. analytical chemistry Ariz. State U., Tempe, 1970—; vis. prof. UCLA, 1960, U. Cambridge, Eng., 1964-65, Nat. Taiwan U., 1968, Ecole Polytechnique, France, 1976-77; Mem. air pollution chemistry and physics adv. com. EPA, HEW, 1969-72; cons. R.J. Reynolds Industries, 1966-72; mem. adv. panel on advanced chem. alarm tech., devel. and engring. directorate Def. Systems div. Edgewood Arsenal, 1975. Author: Gas-Liquid Chromatography, Theory and Practice, 1962; Editorial advisor to: Jour. Chromatographic Sci., 1969-85, Jour. Gas Chromatography, 1963-68, Analytica Chimica Acta, 1972-74, Analytical Chemistry, 1974-77, biennial reviewer in, 1962-76. NSF sr. postdoctoral fellow, 1964-65; Sci. Exchange Agreement awardee Czechoslovakia, Hungary, Romania and Yugoslavia, 1977. Fellow Am. Inst. Chemists; mem. Am. Chem. Soc. (nat. chmn. div. analytical chemistry 1972-73, nat. sec.-treas. div. analytical chemistry 1969-71, councilor 1978—, council com. analytical reagts. 1985—, chmn. U. Ill. sect. 1968-69, sec. 1962-63, co-author Reagent Chems. 7th edit., 1986, directorate div. officers' caucus 1987—), AAAS, Internat. Platform Assn., Internat. Union of Pure and Applied Chemistry, Am. Radio Relay League, Sigma Xi, Phi Lambda Upsilon, Alpha Chi Sigma. Presbyn. (deacon 1960— , ruling elder 1972— , commr. Grand Canyon Presbytery 1974-76). Research on gas and liquid chromatography, instrumental analysis, computer interfacing. Home: 4821 E Calle Tuberia Phoenix AZ 85018 Office: Dept Chemistry Arizona State Univ Tempe AZ 85287

KACHOUEI, MAHMOUD H., mechanical and nuclear engineer; b. Isfahan, Iran; came to U.S., 1974; s. Abbas Ali; m. Parvin M. Mohammad Sadeghi, 1985. BS in Physics, U. Isfahan, 1971; BS in Nuclear Engring., U. Okla., 1977; MS in Mech. Engring., Calif. State U., Los Angeles, 1980; cert. control systems, UCLA, 1981, cert. advanced microprocessor, 1983. Sr. mech. engr. Wed Enterprises, Glendale, Calif., 1980-83, Holmes & Narver Inc., Orange, Calif., 1984; sr. control systems engr., mech. engr. Bechtel Power co., Norwalk, Calif., 1984—. Address: PO Box 3171 Glendale CA 91201

KACKLEY, EVAN MORGAN, physician; b. Soda Springs, Idaho, Mar. 30, 1906; s. Ellis and Ida (Sarver) K.; B.S. with distinction, Stanford, 1927; M.D., Harvard, 1930; m. Lois Louise Lynch, Oct. 2, 1940; children—Ellis N., Alvin E. Intern Los Angeles County Hosp., 1930-31; preceptorship in urology Washington U. Med. Sch., St. Louis, 1933-35; practice medicine specializing in urology, Soda Springs, 1933-41, supt. Caribou County Hosp., Soda Springs, 1935-37. Dir. Phillip-Daucker Mfg. Co., Astoria, Oreg., Caribou Water Devel. Co., Soda Springs. Mem. Idaho Bd. Med. Examiners, 1937-39. Mem. Idaho Senate, Bear River Interstate Compact Commn., 1965-67, Idaho Water Resource Bd., 1967-69. Served to comdr. USNR, 1942-45. Mem. Phi Beta Kappa. Club: Arid (Boise, Idaho). Contbr. articles to profl. jours. Research in carcinoma of the prostate. Developer Caulk-Kackley transurethral resectoscope, 1934; originator of new concept in establishment of nat. wildlife refuges; established wildlife refuge Grays Lake, Idaho. Home: 1323 Ellis Ave Boise ID 83702

KACZYNSKI, VICTOR WALTER, environmental scientist; b. Niagara Falls, N.Y., Dec. 7, 1938; s. Walter V. and Adolpha (Jacks) K.; m. Marianne Donnelly, June 27, 1964; children: Peter, Elizabeth, Greg. BS, SUNY, Buffalo, 1964; MS, Cornell U., 1967, PhD, 1970. Asst. prof. oceanography U. Wash., Seatle, 1969-72; environ. tech. dir. Tex. Instruments, Dallas, 1972-74; pres. Beak Cons., Inc., Portland, Oreg., 1974-77; dir. environ. scis. CH2M-Hill, Portland, 1977—; curriculum advisor Duchess Community Coll., Poughkeepsie, N.Y., 1973-74, Mt. Hood Community Coll., Gresham, Oreg., 1984-85. Contbr. articles to profl. jours. Mem. bicentennial com. Oreg. State U., Corvallis, 1985-86; found. trustee Portland Community Coll., 1985—. Served with USAF, 1956-60. Mem. Am. Fisheries Soc. (cert., sec./treas. bioengineering sect. 1984-86, membership com. 1984-85, resolutions com., 1984-85), Am. Soc. Limnology and Oceanography, Ecol. Soc. Am., N.Y. Acad. Sci., Sigma Xi, Kappa Delta Pi. Republican. Roman Catholic. Office: CH2M-Hill 2020 SW 4th Ave Portland OR 97201

KADASH, KENNETH WARREN, publishing executive; b. Joliet, Ill., Dec. 23, 1945; s. Warren I.F. and Joan J. (Wagner) Kiedaisch; m. Kathleen A. Sharp, July 13, 1968 (div. 1984); 1 child, Kristine. BSBA, Roosevelt U., 1971; MBA, Seattle U., 1981. Acct. Woodmoor (Colo.) Corp., 1972-73; chief acct. Golden Cycle Corp., Colorado Springs, Colo., 1973-77; controller Loomis Moving Co., Seattle, 1977-80, Cardiff Communications, Denver, 1980-83; pub. Cardiff Publ., Denver, 1983—. Served with USN, 1967-71. Mem. Healthcare Info. Systems Sharing Group (bd. dirs.), Colo. Assn. Hosp. Info. Systems (sec., treas. 1986-88). Methodist. Club: Dillon (Colo.) Yacht. Avocations: sailing, skiing, reading, writing, teaching. Office: Cardiff Publ Co 6530 S Yosemite St Englewood CO 80111

KADEN, BARBARA ANN, educator; b. Milw., May 2, 1934; d. David Charles and Esther Elizabeth (Schroth) Schilke; m. Harold R. Kaden, July 21, 1956; children—Kristin Sue, Laurie Ann. B.S., Concordia Tchrs. Coll., 1955; M.A., U. San Francisco, 1975; postgrad. Calif. State U.-Sacramento, 1964-70. Tchr., Immanuel Luth. Sch., Albuquerque, 1955-56, St. Paulus Luth. Sch., San Francisco, 1956-57, Town and Country Luth. Sch., Sacramento, 1958-71, Legette Sch., Fair Oaks, Calif., 1972-82, Sch. for Gifted Children, Orangevale, Calif., 1982-85, Mary A. Deterding Elem. Sch., Carmichael, Calif., 1985—. Pres., pub. relations dir. Luth. Women's Missionary League, 1974-80; pres. Theatre Ballet Assn., 1981-82. Mem. Calif. Assn. Gifted, Sacramento Area Gifted Assn. Lutheran. Club: River City Chorale. Author: Opening Wider Doors: An Approach to Gifted Education, 1975. Home: 2740 Tioga Way Sacramento CA 95821 Office: Mary A Deterding Elem Sch 6000 Stanley Ave Carmichael CA 95608

KADEY, FREDERIC LIONEL, JR., geological consultant; b. Toronto, Ont., Can., June 21, 1918; came to U.S., 1925; s. Frederic Lionel and Catherine Amelia (Davies) K.; m. Brenda Boocook, Oct. 7, 1950; children—Brenda Catherine Kadey King. Frederick Lionel III. B.Sc., Rutgers U., 1941; M.A., Harvard U., 1947. Cert. profl. geologist. Teaching fellow Harvard U., 1946-47; field geol. asst. Sinclair Oil Co., Casper, Wyo.; petrographer, research/devel. dept. U.S. Steel Corp., Pitts., 1947-51; mineralogist Manville Corp., N.J., 1951-66, sect. chief fillers, 1966-71, exploration mgr., Denver, 1972-83; cons. indsl. minerals, Englewood, Colo., 1983—; nat. def. exec. reservist, metals and minerals br. U.S. Dept. Interior, Washington, 1972—. Contbr. chpt. to book, numerous articles in field to profl. jours. Patentee indirect perlite expander. Pres., Chester Twp. Taxpayers Assn., N.J., 1957-61, Chester Twp. Bd. Edn., 1961-68. Served with AUS, 1941-45. Decorated Croix de Guerre (France). Recipient Hal Williams Hardinge award, 1986. Fellow AAAS; mem. Mineral Soc. Am., AIME (Disting. mem. 1981 Soc. Mining Engrs., soc. program chmn. 1981, soc. pres. 1984), Am. Inst. Profl. Geologists (charter, pres. N.Y. State sect. 1967-68), Sigma Xi, Alpha Sigma Phi. Republican. Episcopalian. Address: 7653 S Rosemary Circle Englewood CO 80112

KADKO, DAVID CHARLES, oceanographer, researcher; b. Bronx, N.Y., Oct. 2, 1951; s. Meyer and Edna (Weiss) K. BS in Chemistry cum laude, Bklyn. Coll., 1973; MA in Oceanography, Columbia U., 1974, PhM in Oceanography, 1975, PhD in Oceanography, 1981. Research asst. Columbia U., N.Y.C., 1974-81; postdoctoral appointment U.S. Geol. Survey, Menlo Park, Calif., 1981—; research assoc. Oreg. State U., Corvallis, 1983—; cons. Oreg. Dept. Geology and Mining Industries, Portland, 1985—. Contbr. numerous articles to profl. jours. Grantee NSF, 1973, 86—, NOAA; Nat. Research Council fellow, 1981. Mem. Am. Geophys. Union, Sigma Xi. Avocations: flute playing, fly fishing, soccer, running, volleyball. Office: Oreg State U Coll Oceanography Corvallis OR 97330

KADLEC, GREGORY JOHN, physician, allergist; b. Dickinson, N.D., Sept. 25, 1936; s. George Conrad and Lenore L. (Larin) K.; m. Judy Annette Miesen, June 19, 1965; children: Andrea, Melissa, David. BS, U.S. Mil. Acad., 1958; MD, U. Nebr., 1968. Diplomate Am. Bd. Allergy and Immunology, Nat. Bd. Med. Examiners. Commd. 2d lt. U.S. Army, 1959, advanced through grades to capt.; aviator U.S. Army, Hawaii and Thailand, 1959-64; resigned U.S. Army, 1965; practice medicine specializing in asthma, allergies and immunology Twin Falls, Idaho, 1969-75; pediatrics intern U. La., 1975-77, fellow in allergy, immunology, 1977-78; resident in pediatrics U. Louisville, 1975-77; pres. Allergy and Asthma of Idaho, P.A., Twin Falls, 1978—; Adv. bd. mem. NIH, Bethesda, Md., 1984—; speakers bur. Mead Johsnon, Key Pharms., 1978—; asst. prof. pediatrics, U. Wash., 1982—. Contbr. articles to profl. jours. Active Orgn. Com. Citizens of Idaho for Bush for Idaho, 1980, Twin Falls Airport Bd., 1986—; mem. steering com., Citizens for Progressive Idaho. Fellow Am. Acad. Allergy/Immunology, Am. Coll. Allergists, Am. Thoracic Soc., Am. Coll. Chest Physicians; mem. U.S. Mil. Acad. Assn. Grads. (trustee). Republican. Roman Catholic. Lodge: K.C. Avocations: Am. presidency and Am. polit. history. Home: 1961 Falls Ave East Twin Falls ID 83301 Office: Asthma and Allergy of Idaho PA 526 B Shoup Ave W Twin Falls ID 83301

KADNER, CARL GEORGE, biology educator emeritus; b. Oakland, Calif., May 23, 1911; s. Adolph L. and Otilia (Pecht) K.; m. Mary Elizabeth Moran, June 24, 1939; children: Robert, Grace Wickersham, Carl L. BS, U. San Francisco, 1933; MS, U. Calif., Berkeley, 1936, PhD, 1941. Prof. biology Loyola Marymount U., Los Angeles, 1936-78, prof. emeritus, 1978—; trustee Loyola U., Los Angeles, 1970-73. Served to maj. U.S. Army, 1943-46. Mem. Entomol. Soc. Am. (emeritus), Sigma Xi, Alpha Sigma Nu.

Republican. Roman Catholic. Avocation: insect photography. Home: 8100 Loyola Blvd Los Angeles CA 90045

KAELLIS, JOSEPH, chemical engineer; b. Phila., July 6, 1925; s. Alexander and Esther (Wilenchik) K. BSChemE, CCNY, 1949; MSChemE, U. Mo., 1950; PhD, Ill. Inst. Tech., 1970. Registered profl. engr., Ill. Asst. engr. Griscom Russel Co., Massillon, Ohio, 1950-55; assoc. engr. Argonne (Ill.) Nat. Lab., 1955-77, Advanced Reactors div. Westinghouse Electric Corp., Madison, Pa., 1972-74, C.F. Braun and Co., Murray Hill, N.J., 1974-76, TRW Inc., Redondo Beach, Calif., 1977-80; sr. engr. Basic Tech., Manhattan Beach, Calif., 1980-81; cons. in field. Torrance, Calif., 1981—. Editor Advances in Enhanced Heat Transfer, 1979; contbr. articles to profl. jours. Served with USN, 1943-44. Mem. Am. Nuclear Soc. (Silver Cert., 1985), Am. Inst. Chem. Engrs., Sigma Xi, Phi Lambda Upsilon. Jewish. Home and Office: 20939 Anza Ave Apt 369 Torrance CA 90503

KAES, ANTON, language educator; b. Eggenfelden, Fed. Republic Germany, Feb. 4, 1945; came to U.S., 1970; s. Anton and Maria (Kotter) K.; m. Christine Mueller, Sept. 5, 1971; children: Bettina, Peter. MA, Munich U., 1970; PhD, Stanford U., 1973. Asst. prof. U. Calif., Irvine, 1973-81; assoc. prof. German U. Calif., Berkeley, 1981—. Author: Expressionism in America, 1975, Kino-DeBatte, 1978, Weimar Republic, 1981. Rockefeller Found. fellow, 1978, 79; grantee Humboldt Found., 1984, 85. Mem. MLA, Assn. Tchrs. of German, Brecht Soc. Home: 1741 Madera St Berkeley CA 94707 Office: U Calif Dept German Berkeley CA 94720

KAGAN, BENJAMIN M., pediatrician; b. Washington, Pa., July 18, 1913; m. Katherine Hamburger, June 2, 1940; children: Christopher, Robert. AB, Washington & Jefferson Coll., 1933; MD, Johns Hopkins U., 1937. Diplomate Am. Bd. Pediatrics (examiner, chmn. written examination com., mem. exec. com. 1967-83), Am. Bd. Nutrition. Intern Sinai Hosp., Balt.; resident Willard Parker Hosp. Infectious Diseases, N.Y.C.; fellow in pediatrics Presbyn. Hosp., N.Y.C., 1938-40; instr. Med. Coll. Va., 1941; from assoc. prof. to clin. prof. pediatrics U. Ill., Chgo., 1945-48; prof. Northwestern U., Chgo., 1948-55; dir., chmn. dept. pediatrics Michael Reese Hosp., Chgo., 1945-55; from. clin. prof. to prof., vice-chmn. dept. pediatrics UCLA, 1955-84; dir., chmn. dept. pediatrics Cedars-Sinai Med. Ctr., Los Angeles, 1955-84, sr. cons. pediatrics, dir. pediatric infectious disease unit, 1984—; dir. Cystic Fibrosis Ctr., Los Angeles, 1955—. Author, editor numerous books in field; contbr. articles to profl. jours. Served to maj. M.C., U.S. Army, 1942-46, MTO. Fellow Am. Acad. Pediatrics, ACP, Am. Coll. Chest Physicians, Infectious Diseases Soc. Am.; mem. Am. Pediatric Soc., Soc. Pediatric Research, Western Soc. Pediatric Research (award), Western Soc. Physicians, Western Soc. Clin. Research, Am. Pub. Health Assn., Am. Soc. Microbiology, Southwestern Pediatric Soc., Los Angeles Pediatric Soc., Los Angeles Acad. Medicine, Phi Beta Kappa, Sigma Xi, Alpha Omega Alpha. Home: 5005 Finley Ave Los Angeles CA 90027 Office: Cedars-Sinai Med Ctr 8700 Beverly Blvd Los Angeles CA 90027

KAGAN, ROBERT MICHAEL, real estate executive; b. Oakland, Calif., Apr. 15, 1943; s. Harry and Irene (Manuck) K.; A.B., U. Calif., Berkeley 1965, M.B.A., 1969. Pres., Kagan-Bennett, Inc., Oakland 1971-81, Beach St. Properties, Oakland 1981-82; v.p. for No. Calif., Cal Fed Enterprises, San Francisco 1982—; adj. prof. Grad Sch. Bus. Golden Gate U. Calif. Real Estate Assn. scholar 1969. Address: 575 Throckmorton Mill Valley CA 94941

KAHLE, LYNN RICHARD, business and social psychology educator; b. Hillsboro, Oreg., Dec. 6, 1950; s. Walter Raymond and Dorothea Elizabeth (Schaus) K.; m. Debra Claire Eisert, Aug. 19, 1978; 1 child, Kevin. AA, Concordia Coll., Portland, Oreg., 1971; BA, Concordia Coll., Ft. Wayne, Ind., 1973; MA, Pacific Luth. U., 1974; PhD, U. Nebr., 1977. Asst. prof. U. Nebr., Lincoln, 1977-78; postdoctoral fellow U. Mich., Ann Arbor, 1978-80; asst. prof. U. N.C., Chapel Hill, 1980-83; from asst. prof. to assoc. prof. consumer behavior U. Oreg., Eugene, 1983—. Author: Attitudes and Social Adaptation, 1984; author, editor Social Values and Social Change, 1983; editor: Methods for Studying Person-Situation Interactions, 1979; assoc. editor Psychology and Marketing, 1983—; also articles. Recipient Nat. Research Service award U. Mich., 1978. Fellow Am. Psychol. Assn.; mem. Am. Mktg. Assn., Assn. For Consumer Research, Western Psychol. Assn. Democrat. Lutheran. Home: 2362 Stansby Way Eugene OR 97405-1330 Office: U Oreg Coll Bus Adminstrn 388 Gilbert Hall Eugene OR 97403-1208

KAHLENBERG, MARY HUNT, art dealer, curator; b. Wallingford, Conn., Oct. 19, 1940; d. Joel Paddock and Emma-Louise (Warner) Barnes; m. Robert T. Coffland, Sept. 25, 1982. BA in Art History, Boston U., 1962; postgrad., The Berlin Acad. Fine Arts, 1963-64, Master Sch. of Craft, Berlin, 1964-65, The Art Inst. of Chgo., 1965-66. Curator The Textile Mus., Washington, 1966-68, Los Angeles County Mus., 1968-78; pres. Textile Arts Inc., Los Angeles, 1978—. Author: A Book About Grass, 1981 (with Anthony Berlant) Walk in Beauty, 1977, The Navajo Blanket Catalogue, 1972. Bd. dirs. Calif. Creative Awards, 1977. Mem. Costume Soc. Am. (bd. dirs.), Am. Assn. Mus. (bd. dirs. Western regional conf.), Costume Council Los Angeles County Mus. Art, Am. Assn. Mus., Art Table. Home: 1571 Canyon Rd Sante Fe NM 87501

KAHLER, BRUCE HEATH, electrical enginner; b. Rahway, N.J., Sept. 15, 1939; s. George Joseph and Alice Rose (Heath) K.; m. Mary Annette Pileski, Apr. 28, 1962; children: Suzanne Marie, Bruce Scott, Andrew Joseph. B-Tech, Nat. U., San Diego, 1972; MA, Webster U., 1982; MS, U. So. Calif., 1985. Enlisted USN, 1958; mgr. Nat. Security Agy., Ft. Meade, Md., 1974-78; ret. Nat. Security Agy., 1978; mgr. Felec Services ITT, Colorado Springs, Colo., 1978-79, Ampex Corp., Colorado Springs, 1979-83; pres., chief exec. officer Cyber Techs., Colorado Springs, 1982—; mgr. Contel Info. Systems, Colorado Springs, 1984—. Author: EMC/Tempest Control, 1985, Security Test and Evaluation, 1985, Automatic Data Processing Manual, 1985, Tempest Data Package, 1986. Recipient Letter of Appreciation, Nat. Security Agy., 1978. Mem. IEEE, Soc. Motion Picture and TV Engrs., Data Processing Mgmt. Assn. Republican. Avocations: reading, sailing, computers. Home: 4631 Bella Dr Colorado Springs CO 80918 Office: Contel Info Systems 5725 N Mark Dabling Blvd Colorado Springs CO 80919-2216

KAHN, EARL LESTER, market research executive; b. Kansas City, Mo., May 30, 1919; s. Samuel and Sarah (Kaufman) K. BA, Harvard U., 1940; MA, U. Chgo., 1947. Pres. Social Research, Inc., Chgo., 1946-74; chmn. bd. KPR Assocs., Inc., Scottsdale, Ariz., 1974—. Contbr. articles to profl. jour. Served to capt. USAF, 1942-46. Mem. Am. Mktg. Assn, Am. Sociol. Assn. Home: 5608 N Scottsdale Rd Scottsdale AZ 85253 Office: KPR Assocs Inc 7321 E Shoeman Ln Scottsdale AZ 85251

KAHN, EPHRAIM, public health physician; b. N.Y.C., Sept. 19, 1915; s. Max and Ray Gertrude (Wattman) K.; m. Barbara Bliss Allen, June 30, 1940; children: Kathleen, Georgia, Michael. BA, Harvard U., 1936; MD, NYU, 1940; MPH, U. Calif., Berkeley, 1972. Cert. Am. Bd. Internal Medicine. Chief of medicine Kaiser Found. Hosp., Vallejo, Calif., 1949-51; chief bur. occupational health Calif. Dept. Health, Berkeley, 1973-75, chief epidemiol. studies sect., 1975-81; cons. Calif. Dept. Health, Berkeley, 1981—. Served to maj. U.S. Army, 1942-46, PTO. Fellow ACP. Clubs: Harvard (San Francisco); NYU (N.Y.C.).

KAHN, IRWIN WILLIAM, industrial engineer; b. N.Y.C., Feb. 3, 1923; s. Milton and Clara (Clark) K.; B.S., U. Calif.-Berkeley, 1949; student Cath. U., 1943-44; m. Mildred Cross, May 14, 1946 (dec. May 1966); children: Steven Edward, Michael William, Evelyn Ruth, Joanne Susan; m. 2d, Marajayne Smith, Oct. 9, 1979. Chief indsl. engr. Malsbary Mfg. Co., Oakland, Calif., 1953-57, Yale & Towne Mfg. Co., San Leandro, Calif., 1957-60; sr. indsl. engr. Eitel McCulloch, San Carlos, Calif., 1961-62, Lockheed, Sunnyvale, Calif., 1962-69; v.p. Performance Investors, Inc., Palo Alto, 1969-74; with Kaiser-Permanente Services, Oakland, 1974-76; nat. mgr. material handling Cutter Labs., Berkeley, Calif., 1976-83; sr. mgmt. engr. Children's Hosp. Med. Ctr., Oakland, 1983; sr. indsl. engr. Naval Air Rework Facility, Alameda, Calif., 1983—; vis. lectr. U. Calif., Berkeley, 1986; tchr. indsl. engring. Laney Coll., Oakland, 1967—, Chabot Coll., Hayward, Calif. Chmn. Alameda County Library Adv. Commn., 1965—. Served with AUS, 1943-46. Registered profl. engr., Calif. Mem. Am. Inst. Indsl. Engrs. (chpt. pres. 1963-64, chmn. conf. 1967 nat. publ. dir. aerospace div. 1968-69), Calif. Soc. Profl. Engrs. (pres. chpt.). Club: Toastmasters (dist. gov. 1960-61). Home: 4966 Elrod Dr Castro Valley CA 94546 Office: Naval Air Rework Facility Alameda CA 94501

KAHN, LINDA MCCLURE, maritime industry executive; b. Jacksonville, Fla.; d. George Calvin and Myrtice Louise (Boggs) McClure; m. Paul Markham Kahn, May 20, 1968. B.S. with high honors, U. Fla.; M.S., U. Mich., 1964. Actuarial trainee N.Y. Life Ins. Co., N.Y.C., 1964-66, actuarial asst., 1966-69, asst. actuary, 1969-71; v.p., actuary US Life Ins., Pasadena, Calif., 1972-74; mgr. Coopers & Lybrand, Los Angeles, 1974-76, sr. cons., San Francisco, 1976-82; dir. program mgmt. Pacific Maritime Assn., San Francisco, 1982—. Sec.-Bd. dirs. Pacific Heights Residents Assn., sec.-treas., 1981; trustee ILWU-PMA Welfare Plan, SIU-PD-PMA Pension and Supplemental Benefits Plans, Seafarers Med. Ctr., others. Fellow Soc. Actuaries, Conf. Actuaries in Pub. Practice; mem. Internat. Actuarial Assn., Internat. Assn. Cons. Actuaries, Actuarial Studies Non-Life Ins., Am. Acad. Actuaries, Western Pension Conf. (newsletter editor 1983-85, sec. 1985—), Actuarial Club Pacific States, San Francisco Actuarial Club (pres. 1981). Clubs: Metropolitan Soroptimist (v.p. 1973-74), Commonwealth. Home: 2430 Pacific Ave San Francisco CA 94115 Office: Pacific Maritime Assn 635 Sacramento St San Francisco CA 94111

KAHN, NANCY TURPPA, speech pathologist, university administrator; b. Waukegan, Ill., June 12, 1931; d. William E. and Rauha (Salina) T.; m. Irwin Horwitz, June 6, 1953 (dec. Oct. 1959); married, Mar. 12, 1960 (div. June 1980); 1 child, Alia Ann Kahn. BS, U. Ill., 1953; MA, Calif. State U., Los Angeles, 1966; PhD, UCLA-Calif. State U., Los Angeles, 1978. Lic. speech pathologist, Calif. Speech-lang. specialist Los Angeles Unified Sch. Dist., 1953-72, adminstr., 1972—; pvt. practice, Newport Beach, Calif., 1980—; adj. prof. Pepperdine U., Irvine, Calif., 1982, U. Calif.-San Diego, La Jolla, 1986—; asst. prof. Calif. State U., Long Beach, 1986—. Mem. Calif. Speech Lang. Hearing Assn. (commr. edn. 1983-85, Outstanding Achievement award 1986), Am. Speech Lang. Hearing Assn. (cert. clin. competence in speech/lang. pathology), Council for Exceptional Children, Sierra Club, Phi Delta Kappa. Democrat. Avocations: biking, reading, cultural events. Home: 21382 Fleet Ln Huntington Beach CA 92646 Office: Los Angeles Unified Sch Dist 1555 Norfolk St Los Angeles CA 90033

KAHN, PAUL MARKHAM, actuary; b. San Francisco, May 8, 1935; s. Sigmund Max and Alexandrina K. (Strauch) K.; B.S., Stanford U., 1956; M.A., U. Mich., 1957, Ph.D., 1961; m. Linda P. McClure, May 20, 1968. Asst. actuary Equitable Life Assurance Soc., N.Y.C., 1961-71; v.p., life actuary Beneficial Standard Life, Los Angeles, 1971-75; v.p., actuary Am. Express Life Ins. Co., San Rafael, Calif., 1975-77, P.M. Kahn & Assos., 1977—. Fellow Soc. Actuaries (Triennial prize 1961-64), Canadian Inst. Actuaries, Conf. Actuaries in Pub. Practice; mem. Am. Acad. Actuaries, Internat. Actuarial Assn., Inst. Actuaries (Eng.), Spanish, Swiss, German, Italian actuarial assns. Clubs: Zamorano (Los Angeles); Roxburghe; Concordia-Argonaut, Commercial (San Francisco); Pacific, Waikiki Yacht (Honolulu). Editor: Dictionary of Actuarial and Life Insurance Terms, 1972, 2d edit., 1983; Credibility: Theory and Practice, 1975; Computational Probability, 1980. Address: 2430 Pacific Ave San Francisco CA 94115

KAHN, ROBERT IRA, physician, urologist; b. Goshen, N.Y., Jan. 1, 1950; s. Lester Bertram and Jeanne (Eisenberg) K.; m. Rebecca Anne Shelley, July 15, 1973 (div. Aug. 1979); m. Geraldine Suzanne Holl, June 21, 1981; children: Jeremy, Meredith. Student, SUNY, Stonybrook, 1967-69; BS, Cornell U., 1971; MD, Duke U., 1975. Diplomate Am. Bd. Urology. Intern in surgery U. Calif. Sch. Medicine, San Francisco, 1975-76, resident in surgery and urology, 1976-81; fellow in urology Johannes Gutenberg U., Mainz, Fed. Republic Germany, 1979-80; asst. prof. urology U. Calif., San Francisco, 1981-85; practice medicine specializing in urology Sharlip/Kahn Med. Group, Inc., San Francisco, 1985—; med. dir. No. Calif. Urolithiasis Ctr., San Francisco, 1985—. Contbr. articles to jours. and chpts. to books. Mem. AMA, ACS (candidate), Am. Urologic Assn. (western sect.), Calif. Med. Assn., San Francisco Med. Soc., No. Calif. Urologic Soc., Endourology Soc. Avocations: golf, backpacking, rafting, carpentry, cooking. Office: Sharlip/Kahn Med Group Inc 3838 California St #408 San Francisco CA 94118

KAHN, ROBERT IRVING, management consultant; b. Oakland, Calif., May 17, 1918; s. Irving Herman and Francesca (Lowenthal) K.; m. Patricia E. Glenn, Feb. 14, 1946; children: Christopher, Roberta Anne. B.A. cum laude, Stanford U., 1938; M.B.A., Harvard U., 1940; LL.D. (hon.), Franklin Pierce Coll., 1977. Exec. researcher R.H. Macy's, Inc., N.Y.C., 1940-41; controller Smith's, Oakland, 1946-51; v.p., treas. Sherwood Swan & Co., Oakland, 1952-56; prin. Robert Kahn & Assocs. (mgmt. cons.), Lafayette, Calif., 1956—; pres. Kahn and Harris Inc., fin. cons., San Francisco, 1971—; v.p. Hambrecht & Quist (investment bankers), San Francisco, 1977-80; prin. Pacific Area Corp. Exchange, 1986—; cons. to comdr. gen. U.S. Army and USAF, 1987—; dir. Wal-Mart Stores, Inc., Marc Paul, Inc., Piedmont Grocery Co., Components Corp. Am., Lipps, Inc., Berkeley Enterprises Inc., Coast Med. Corp.; cons. to commdg. gen. Army and Air Force Exchange Service. Publisher: newsletter Retailing Today, 1965—; author: weekly newspaper column Pro and Kahn, 1963-77, 86—. Past bd. dirs. Oakland council Boy Scouts Am.; past bd. dirs. Oakland Area ARC; bd. dirs., officer, mem. exec. com. Unitd Way Bay Area, 1946-81, chmn. allocations, membership, fin., by-laws, and personnel coms.; trustee Kahn Found.; past sec. League to Save Lake Tahoe; mem. adv. com. Retail Mgmt. Inst. U. Santa Clara, 1983—. Served with USAAF, 1941-46; with USAF, 1951-52; lt. col. Res. ret. Recipient Mortimer Fleishhacker award as outstanding vol. United Way Bay Area, 1980; founding mem. Baker Scholar Harvard U. Mem. Assn. Mgmt. Consultants (pres. 1977), Inst. Mgmt. Consultants (a founder), Nat. Retail Mchts. Assn. (asso. cons. mem.), Mensa, Phi Beta Kappa. Home: 3684 Happy Valley Rd Lafayette CA 94549 Office: PO Box 249 Lafayette CA 94549

KAHNE, STEPHEN JAMES, systems engineer, educator, administrator; b. N.Y.C., Apr. 5, 1937; s. Arnold W. and Janet (Weatherlow) K.; m. Irena Nowacka, Dec. 11, 1970; children: Christopher, Katarzyna. B.E.E., Cornell U., 1960; M.S., U. Ill., 1961, Ph.D., 1963. Asst. prof. elec. engring. U. Minn., Mpls., 1966-69; assoc. prof. U. Minn., 1969-76; dir. Hybrid Computer Lab., 1968-76; founder, dir., cons. InterDesign Inc., Mpls., 1968-76; prof. dept. systems engring. Case Western Res. U., Cleve., 1976-83; chmn. dept. Case Western Res. U., 1976-80; dir. div. elec., computer and systems engring. NSF, Washington, 1980-81; prof. Poly Inst. N.Y., 1983-85, dean engring., 1983-84; prof. Oreg. Grad. Ctr., Beaverton, 1985—, pres., 1985-86, prof. dept. applied physics and elec. engring., 1985—; cons. in field; exchange scientist Nat. Acad. Scis., 1968, 75. Editor: IEEE Transactions on Automatic Control, 1975-79; hon. editor: Internat. Fedn. of Automatic Control, 1975-81; editorial bd.: IEEE Spectrum, 1979-82; dep. chmn. editorial bd.: Automatica, 1976-82; dep. chmn. mng. bd.: Internat. Fedn. Automatic Control Publs, 1976—; contbr. articles to sci. jours. Active Mpls. Citizens League, 1968-75; regent L.I. Coll. Hosp., Bklyn., 1984-85; chmn. Beaverton Sister Cities Found., 1986-87. Served with USAF, 1963-66. Recipient Amicus Poloniae award POLAND Mag., 1975, John A. Curtis award Am. Soc. Engring. Edn.; Case Centennial scholar, 1980. Fellow IEEE (pres. Control Systems Soc. 1981, bd. dirs. 1982-84, v.p. tech. activities 1984-85, Centennial medal 1984), AAAS. Office: Oreg Grad Ctr 19600 NW Von Neumann Dr Beaverton OR 97006

KAISER, JOHN MICHAEL, mail marketing executive; b. Mpls., May 22, 1956; s. Carl Koch and Florence Mary (Jacoby) K.; m. Joan Marie Wedell, June 12, 1981. Student, Colo. State U., 1974—. With advt. and customer service dept. McDonald's Restaurants, Ft. Collins, Colo., 1975-78; owner, local distbr. Val-Pak of Colo., Ft. Collins, 1979-84, dir. mktg., 1984—. Mem. Dir. Mktg. Assn. Avocations: skiing, softball, tennis, soccer.

KAISER, MARY KISTER, research psychologist; b. St. Charles, Mo., Oct. 25, 1956; d. Robert Paul and Mary Virginia (Jost) Kister; m. Franz Nicholas Kaiser, June 21, 1980. BA, U. Va., 1977, MA, 1980, PhD, 1982. NIMH postdoctoral fellow U. Mich., Ann Arbor, 1982-84; research psychologist NASA Ames Research Ctr., Moffett Field, Calif., 1985—. Contbr. articles to profl. jours. Fellow NSF, 1979-82. Mem. Am. Statis. Assn., Psychonomics Soc., Western Psychol. Assn., Internat. Soc. Ecol. Psychology, N.Y. Acad. Scis. Avocations: skiing, hiking, photography. Home: 11691 Par Ave Los Altos CA 94022 Office: NASA Ames Research Ctr Mail Stop 239-3 Moffett Field CA 94035

KAISER, THOMAS BURTON, physicist; b. St. Louis, May 11, 1940; s. Edward Thomas and Bernice Aurelia (Burton) K.; m. Phyllis D. Holmstrum, July 8, 1967; 1 child, Jonathan Thomas. BS maxima cum laude, St. Edward's U., 1962; MS, U. Md., 1971, PhD, 1973. Sr. analyst programming LTV Aerospace Corp., Cambridge, Mass., 1966-68; research assoc. Goddard Space Flight Ctr., Greenbelt, Md., 1973-75; physicist magnetic fusion div. Lawrence Livermore (Calif.) Lab., 1976—. Contbr. articles to profl. jours. Mem. Am. Phys. Soc., AAAS, Fedn. Am. Scientists, Sigma Xi. Home: 17507 Holiday Dr Morgan Hill CA 95037 Office: Lawrence Livermore Nat Lab PO Box 5511 Livermore CA 94550

KAISER, THOMAS GRIFFETH, insurance executive; b. Schenectady, N.Y., Feb. 11, 1947; s. Ofrville H. and Norma (Griffeth) K.; m. Diane L. Hanna, Nov. 22, 1970. A of Arts and Scis., SUNY, Alfred, 1967; BS, SUNY, Albany, 1970; MS, SUNY, Plattsburgh, 1975. CPCU; assoc. Risk Mgmt. Account rep. Arkwright-Boston Ins. Co., Greenwich, Conn., 1975-77; mgr. field sales Arkwright-Boston Ins. Co., N.Y.C., 1977-79; mgr. regional sales Arkwright-Boston Ins. Co., Greenwich, 1979-83; regional mgr. Arkwright-Boston Ins. Co., San Mateo, Calif., 1983—; instr. Ins. Edn. Assn., 1984—. Served to capt. USAF, 1970-75. Mem. No. Calif. Assn. CPCU's, San Francisco C. of C. Club: Banker (San Francisco). Avocations: walking, reading. Office: Arkwright-Boston Ins Co 875 S Grant St San Mateo CA 94403

KAISER, WALTER EDWARD, law enforcement official; b. Albany, N.Y., Sept. 29, 1947; s. Rudy and Esther Elizabeth (Bergman) K.; m. Judy Lee Holderegger, Mar. 24, 1952; children—Jason Thomas, William Erich. Student, San Jose City Coll., 1974; B.A., U. San Francisco, 1976. Patrolman, then detective, Mountain View (Calif.) Police Dept., 1971-79, spl. agt. Bur. Narcotic Enforcement, Calif. Dept. Justice, San Jose, 1979—, tchr. Advanced Tng. Ctr., Sacramento, 1980-83. Served with U.S. Army, 1967-70. Mem. Motorcycle Safety Found., Calif. Narcotic Officers Assn. (officer). Republican. Club: Blue Knight Law Enforcement Motorcycle (Sunnyvale, Calif.). Lodge: Elks. Office: Calif Dept Justice 2025 Gateway Pl Suite 474 San Jose CA 95110

KAITSCHUK, ROBERT CHARLES, psychologist, travel agency exec.; b. Oak Park, Ill., Sept. 28, 1934; s. Oscar C. and Victoria Marguerite (Schmaus) K.; B.A., Wittenberg U., 1956; M.A., Pepperdine U., 1967. Tchr., Henry Ford II Sch., Chicago Ridge, Ill., 1961-64; counselor, psychologist, div. vocat. edn. West Covina (Calif.) Unified Sch. Dist., 1966-70; prin. Renaissance High Sch., Santa Paula, Calif., 1970-72; personnel mgmt. specialist Ventura County Personnel Dept., Ventura, Calif., 1972-73; vocat. psychologist Calif. Dept. Rehab., Bakersfield dist., 1974-76; psychologist, account exec. Dean Witter & Co., Inc., 1976-77; owner, pres. Elegant Travel, Inc., Mission Viejo, Calif., 1977—; mem. pres. adv. bd. Mission Viejo Nat. Bank, 1982—; mem. Saddleback Community Hosp. Assocs., Laguna Hills, Calif., 1986—. Bd. convocators Calif. Luth. Coll., Thousand Oaks, 1969-77; bd. dirs. Santa Paula Boys Club, 1971-74, Kern County Campfire Girls, 1976-77; v.p. Orange County Assn. for Retarded Citizens, 1978-79. HEW grantee, 1970. Mem. Am. Psychol. Assn., Western Psychol. Assn., Calif. Psychol. Assn., Assn. Retail Travel Agts., Am. Soc. Travel Agts., Soc. Advancement Travel Handicapped. Assn. Calif. Sch. Adminstrs., Benjamin Prince Soc. Wittenberg U. (life), Phi Kappa Psi, Theta Alpha Phi. Republican. Lutheran. Clubs: Rotary (sec. 1978-79, v.p. 1979-80, pres. 1980-81) (Mission Viejo); Mission Viejo Country; Town Hall of Calif. Home: 25751 Knotty Pine Laguna Hills CA 92653 Office: Gateway Ctr 24000 Alicia Pkwy Suite 16 Mission Viejo CA 92691

KAKUDA, DICK TAMOTSU, art educator; b. Orange, Calif., Jan. 5, 1947; s. George Y. and Michico (Nishikawa) K.; m. Sand Lyn Alter, Dec. 23, 1968; children: Wendy Alter, Tyler Robin. AA, Orange Coast Coll., 1967; BA, San Jose State U., 1969, MA, 1971. Instr. art Shasta Coll., Redding, Calif., 1971-81; asst. prof. of art U. of the Pacific, Stockton, Calif., 1983-86, assoc. prof., 1986—. One-man shows include Redding Museum and Art Ctr., 1972, 78, Hank Baum Gallery, San Francisco, 1978, 83, Shasta Coll. Art Dept. Gallery, Redding, 1983; exhibited in group shows at No. Calif. Artist Exhibition Calif. Expo Ctr., 1974, Mono Gallery, Chgo., 1977, Contemporary Artisans Gallery, San Francisco, 1981, Shasta Coll. Art Dept. Gallery Art Faculty Exhibition, 1981, Student Ctr. Gallery U. Pacific, 1983. Home: 1830 N Edison St Stockton CA 95204 Office: U of the Pacific Pacific Ave Stockton CA 95211

KALAHAR, PAT ANN, marketing and communications executive; b. Fort Collins, Colo., Aug. 1, 1951; d. James N. and Florence B. Kalahar; m. James A. Jamison, Apr. 28, 1977 (div.). B.A. in Tech. Journalism, Colo. State U., Fort Collins, 1974. Info. specialist, tech. writer Tri-State Generation and Transmission Assn., Denver, 1977-79; tech. editor, dir. communications Willard Owens Assocs., Inc., Denver, 1979; self-employed, Golden, Colo., 1980; project mgr. U. Colo. Health Scis. Ctr., Denver, 1981; dir. mktg., tech. editor Muller Engring. Co., Inc., Lakewood, Colo., 1981-82; v.p. bus. devel. BHCD Engrs., Inc., Denver, 1982-84; founder, owner Mktg. Adv. Assocs., Denver, 1984—; cons. in field. Recipient Best Staffer award Rocky Mountain News, 1969. Mem. Soc. Mktg. Profl. Services (cert. excellence 1983). Contbr. articles to mags. Home: 442 S Eliot Denver CO 80219

KALB, BENJAMIN STUART, television producer, director; b. Los Angeles, Mar. 17, 1948; s. Marcus and Charlotte K.; B.S. in Journalism, U. Oreg., 1969. Sportswriter, Honolulu Advertiser, 1971-76; traveled with tennis profl. Ilie Nastase, contbr. articles N.Y. Times, Sport Mag. and Tennis U.S.A., 1976; editor Racquetball Illustrated, 1978-82; segment producer PM Mag. and Hollywood Close-Up, 1983-86; exec. producer Delicious Prodns., 1986—; instr. sports in soc. U. Hawaii, 1974-75. Served with Hawaii Army N.G., 1970-75. Named Outstanding Male Grad. in Journalism, U. Oreg., 1969. Mem. Sigma Delta Chi (chpt. pres. 1968). Democrat. Jewish. Contbr. articles to mags. and newspapers. Home: 605 San Vicente Blvd Apt 104 Santa Monica CA 90402

KALBACH, JOHN FREDERICK, electrical engineer, consultant; b. Seattle, Jan. 2, 1914; s. Taylor Patterson and Pauline (Stopplemann) K.; m. Bettina Truesdale Cook, Dec. 28, 1939; children: David Patterson, Jean Louise Kalbach Dent, Paul Douglas. BSEE magna cum laude, U. Wash., 1937. Registered profl. engr., Calif. Rec. equipment designer Seattle Rec. Studios, 1935-37; elec. equipment designer Gen. Electric Co., Ft. Wayne Ind., Schenectady, N.Y. and Lynn, Mass., 1937-47; staff scientist Van de Graff Accelerator, Los Alamos, N.Mex., 1947-51; analog computer designer, engring. mgr. Miller Instruments, Pasadena, Calif., 1951-55; various design mgmt. positions ElectoData and Burroughs Co., Pasadena, 1955-79; cons., owner Kalbach Engring. Assocs., Altadena, Calif., 1979—; lectr. engring. U. Calif., Berkeley, 1947-48. Contbr. articles to profl. jours.; patentee in field. Fellow IEEE, Inst. Advancement Engring.; mem. Am. Soc. Computing Machinery, Electrostatic Soc. Am. Republican. Club: Electronic. Home and Office: Kalbach Engring Assocs 920 Alta Pine Dr Altadena CA 91001

KALBERER, WILLIAM DAVID, psychology educator, small business owner; b. Lafayette, Ind., Sept. 27, 1933; s. Rudolph William and Grace Louise (Oswalt) K.; children: Julie Kathryn, William Christopher. BS, Purdue U., 1959, MS, 1962, PhD, 1969. Resident lectr. psychology Ind. U., Kokomo, 1964-65; from asst. prof. to prof. psychology Calif. State U., Chico, 1965—; owner The Homebrewshop, Chico, 1979—. Contbr. articles to profl. jours. Served with USAF, 1952-56. Recipient numerous ribbons in amateur beer and wine competitions. Mem. Western Psychol. Assn., Animal Behavior Soc., Am. Homebrewing Assn. (stats. research com. 1985—), Home Wine and Beer Trade Assn. (design cons. 1986—, columnist 1986—), Psi Chi (faculty adv. Calif. State U. Chico chpt. 1976—), Sigma Xi. Avocations: photography, fishing, home fermentation wines and beers. Home: 908 W 11th Ave Chico CA 95926 Office: Calif State U Psychology Dept Chico CA 95926

KALEJS, KARLIS, aerospace engineer; b. Tukums, Latvia, June 23, 1926; came to U.S., 1949, naturalized 1955; s. Janis and Olga (Smits) K.; m. Klitija Pilmanis, Apr. 5, 1953; children—Lija, Nora, Valdis. A.A., Los Angeles City Coll., 1952; B.S., U. So. Calif., 1962, M.S., 1965. Registered profl. mech. engr., Calif. Design engr. Weber Aircraft Co., Burbank, Calif., 1955-59; design engr. Marquardt Aircraft Corp., Van Nuys, Calif., 1959, N.Am. Aviation, Canoga Park, Calif., 1959-61; sr. design engr. Rocketdyne div. N.Am. Rockwell, 1961-65; mem. tech. staff Rocketdyne div. Rockwell Internat., 1965—. Pres. Peace Luth. Ch. of Los Angeles, 1969-72; v.p. Latvian Welfare Assn. So. Calif., 1970—; chmn. bd. Latvian Community Ctr. So. Calif., 1978—; bd. dirs. Baltic Am. Freedom League, 1981—. Served with USAF, 1948-49. Recipient Apollo Achievement award NASA, 1969; cert. of appreciation of contbn. to Apollo II, NASA and Rocketdyne, 1969; tech. utilization cert. George Marshall Space Ctr., 1972. Mem. AIAA, Latvian Engrs. Assn., Soc. Profl. Indsl. Engrs., Deutsche Gesellschaft fur Luft- und Raumfahrt. Club: Latvian Community. Home: 3822 Markridge Road La Crescenta CA 91214 Office: 6633 Canoga Ave Apt FA 30 Canoga Park CA 91304

KALENSCHER, ALAN JAY, physician and surgeon; b. Bklyn., July 9, 1926; s. Abraham and Julia (Horwitz) K.; B.S., Union Coll., Schenectady, 1945; M.D., N.Y. U., 1949; m. Hannah Blaufox, June 18, 1949; children—Judith Lynne, Mark Robert. Intern Morrisania City Hosp., N.Y.C., 1949-50; surg. resident Maimonides Med. Center, Bklyn., 1950-51, 54; asst., then chief resident Bronx Mcpl. Hosp. Center, 1954-56; mem. faculty surgery dept. Albert Einstein Coll. Medicine, 1956-59; practice medicine specializing in surgery, Sacramento, 1959-84; chief med. cons. Disability Evaluation div. Calif. State Dept. Soc. Services, 1984—; attending surgeon Sacramento Med. Center; clin. faculty dept. surgery U. Calif. Coll. Medicine, Davis, 1970-75; sr. staff Sutter Community Hosps., Sacramento . Served with USNR, 1943-45, 51-53; ETO, Korea. Recipient citation N.Y.C. Cancer Com., 1959. Diplomate Am. Bd. Surgery, Nat. Bd. Med. Examiners (examiner 1957-59). Fellow Am. Soc. Contemporary Medicine and Surgery; mem. AAAS, Calif. Med. Assn., Sacramento County Med. Soc., Am. Diabetes Assn., Am. Mensa Ltd.

KALER, ERIC WILLIAM, chemical engineering educator; b. Burlington, Vt., Sept. 23, 1956; s. Ronald Maurice and Mary Elizabeth (Kindred) K.; m. Karen Fults, Dec. 30, 1979. BS, Calif. Inst. Tech., 1978; PhD, U. Minn., 1982. Asst. prof. chem. engring. U. Wash., Seattle, 1982-87, assoc. prof., 1987—; Cons. Shell Devel. Co., 1983—, 3M Corp., 1983—. Conbr. numerous articles to profl. jours. Elder Andrew Riverside Presbyn. Ch., Mpls., 1980-82, Northminster Presbyn. Ch., Seattle, 1984—. Named Presdl. Young Investigator NSF, Washington D.C., 1984; Presdl. Scholar Dept. Edn., Washington, 1978. Mem. Am. Chem. Soc., Am. Inst. Chem. Engring., Am. Crystallographic Assn. Republican. Lodge: Masons. Home: 13333 11th Ave NE Seattle WA 98125 Office: U of Wash Dept of Chem Engring BF 10 Seattle WA 98195

KALFUSS, HELENE AARONSON, speech pathologist; b. Phila., Feb. 28, 1941; d. Norman Ralph and Lillian Rose (White) Aaronson; m. Leonard M. Kalfuss, Aug. 29, 1965; children: Lenore, Ronald, Barry. BS, MEd, Wayne State U., 1963, PhD, 1968. Speech pathologist in chief VA Hosp., Allen Park, Mich., 1963-70; assoc. prof. Wayne State U. Med. Sch., Detroit, 1968-70; dir. speech and hearing div. Camarillo (Calif.) State Hosp., 1970-71; pvt. practice speech pathology Palm Springs, Calif., 1971—; cons. AV Crippled Childrens Fund, Palm Springs, Calif., 1973—; bd. dirs. Palm Valley Sch., Palm Springs, 1974—; past pres., bd. dirs., treas. Angel View Crippled Children's Found., Desert Hot Springs, 1974-87; adv. bd. mem. Stroke Activity Ctr., Palm Springs, 1986—. Contbr. articles to profl. jours. Commr. Human Relations Commn. City of Palm Springs, 1976-78; past. v.p. Palm Valley Sch., Palm Springs, 1974—, sec., bd. dirs.; past pres. Sisterhood of Temple Isaiah, Palm Springs, 1973-74, pres. 1986—. Recipient Founders award Angel View Crippled Children's Found, 1980. Mem. Internat. Assn. Logopedics and Phoniatrics, Alexander Graham Bell Assn. for the Deaf, Calif. Speech and Hearing Assn., Am. Acad. Pvt. Practice in Speech Pathology and Audiology (sec. 1982-84, mem. nat. bd. dirs. 1982—, editor nat. jour. 1984—), Am. Speech-Lang. Hearing Assn. (cert.). Republican. Jewish. Avocations: swimming, tennis, piano, organ. Office: 225 S Civic Dr Suite 1-1 Palm Springs CA 92262

KALINOSKI, HENRY THOMAS, research chemist; b. Phila., Dec. 26, 1957; s. Henry Francis and Vivian Marie (Sullivan) K.; m. Margaret Ann Cistone, Mar. 26, 1984; one child, Adrielle Arienne. BS, Phila. Coll. Textiles and Sci., 1979; MS, Lehigh U., 1981, PhD, 1984. Post-doctoral fellow U. Wash., Richland, 1984-85; Hanford research fellow Pacific Northwest Labs., Richland, 1985-86; research scientist Battelle Meml. Inst., Pacific N.W. Labs., Richland, 1986—. Contbr. articles on applications of analytical mass spectrometry to profl jours. Mem. Am. Chem. Soc., Am. Soc. Mass Spectrometry. Home: 4490 Hampton St West Richland WA 99352 Office: Battelle-Pacific NW Labs PO Box 999 Richland WA 99352

KALIS, MURRAY, writer, advertising agency executive, writer; s. Bernard and Bernis Kalis. B.S. in Communications, U. Ill.; postgrad. Drake U., U. Iowa. Former chmn. art dept. Midwestern Coll., Denison, Iowa; creative dir., v.p. Leo Burnett Advt., Chgo., 1970-81; exec. creative dir., sr. v.p. Marsteller Advt., Los Angeles, 1982—, HCM Advt., Los Angeles, 1985—. Served to 1st lt. U.S. Army. Recipient cert. of merit N.Y. Art Dirs. One Show; Bronze Lion, Cannes Festival; gold medal Chgo. Film Festival; Clio award; Best in West; intaglio art in permanent collection Phila. Mus. Art. Author: Candida by Amy Voltaire, 1979; Love in Paris, 1980; Are You Experienced? The Jimi Hendrix Story, 1984. Clubs: Creative, Los Angeles Advt.

KALISCH, GERHARD KARL, mathematics educator; b. Breslau, (formerly) Republic of Germany, Dec. 21, 1914; came to U.S., 1937; s. Hans and Margarete (Freund) K.; m. Leonora Liph, Nov. 28, 1942; children: John M., Peggy J. BA, U. Iowa, 1937, MS, 1938; PhD, U. Chgo., 1942. Asst. mem. Inst. for Advanced Study, Princton, N.J., 1941-41, 55-56; instr. math. U. Kans., Lawrence, 1942-44, Cornell U., Ithaca, N.Y., 1944-46; prof. math. U. Minn., Mpls., 1946-65, U. Calif., Irvine, 1965—. Contbr. articles to profl. jours. Fellow AAAS; mem. Am. Math. Soc., Math. Assn. Am., Sigma Xi. Home: 4530 Roxbury Rd Corona del Mar CA 92625 Office: U Calif Dept Math Irvine CA 92717

KALISH, DONALD, philosophy educator; b. Chgo., Dec. 4, 1919; s. Lionel and Mildred K.; m. Ann Graham, 1982. A.B., U. Calif. at Berkeley, 1943, M.A. in Psychology, 1945, Ph.D. in Philosophy, 1949. Instr. Swarthmore Coll., 1946-47, U. Calif. at Berkeley, 1947-48; mem. faculty UCLA, 1949—, prof. philosophy, 1964—, chmn. dept., 1964-70, treas. concerned faculty, 1980—. Author: (with Richard Montague and Gary Mar) Logic Techniques of Formal Reasoning, 2d edit, 1980; also articles. Co-chmn. Nat. Mblzn. Com. to End War in Vietnam, 1967-68, mem. steering com. Resist, 1967-70; mem. exec. com. So. Calif. Interfaith Task force on Central Am., 1985—. Mem. AAUP, Am. Philos. Assn., Assn. Symbolic Logic. Address: U Calif Dept of Philosophy 405 Hilgard Ave Los Angeles CA 90024

KALKWARF, DONALD RILEY, research chemist; b. Portland, Oreg., Aug. 17, 1924; s. Harro Onnen and Irene (Joslin) K.; m. Carol Louise Rider, Aug. 28, 1949; children: Kristi Ann, Timothy Onnen, Heidi Johanna, Trina Louise. BA, Reed Coll., 1947; PhD, Northwestern U., 1951. Chemist Hanford Labs. div. Gen. Electric Co., Richland, Wash., 1951-64; sect. mgr. Battelle Pacific N.W. Labs., Richland, 1965-70, staff scientist, 1970—. Contbr. articles to profl. jours. Served with U.S. Army, 1943-45, ETO. Mem. ASTM, Am. Chem. Soc., Royal Soc. Chemistry, Internat. Union of Pure and Applied Chemistry (assoc.), Sigma Xi. Democrat. Methodist. Avocations: photography, mountain climbing. Home: 1201 Birch Ave Richland WA 99352 Office: Battelle Pacific NW Labs 329 Bldg Area 300 Richland WA 99352

KALLAHER, MICHAEL JOSEPH, mathematics educator; b. Cin., Sept. 4, 1940; s. Martin Henry and Lou Will (Huff) K.; m. Donalyn May Laraway, Aug. 17, 1963; children: Jay, Michael, Christopher, Daniel, Raymond. BS, Xavier U., 1961; MS, Syracuse U., 1963, PhD, 1967. Postdoctoral fellow U. Man., Winnipeg, Can., 1967-69; from asst. prof. prof. math. Wash. State U., Pullman, 1969—, assoc. dean scis., 1979-84, acting dean scis., 1982, chmn. math dept., 1984—. Author: Affine Planes with Transitive Collineation Groups; contbg. editor Finite Geometries, 1982; contbr. articles to profl. jours. Grantee NSF; Fulbright Research scholar, Kaiserslautern, Fed. Republic Germany, 1975-76. Mem. Am. Math. Soc., Math. Assn. Am., N.Y. Acad. of Scis., Assn. of Research Profs. (pres. 1986—), Sigma Xi. Home: NW 235 Joe St Pullman WA 99163 Office: Wash State U Dept of Math Pullman WA 99163

KALLAY, MICHAEL FRANK, II, medical devices company official; b. Painesville, Ohio, Aug. 24, 1944; s. Michael Frank and Marie Francis (Sage) K.; B.B.A., Ohio U., 1967; m. Irma Yolanda Corona, Aug. 30, 1975; 1 son, William Albert. Salesman, Howmedica, Inc., Rutherford, N.J., 1972-75, Biochem. Procedures/Metpath, North Hollywood, Calif., 1975-76; surg. specialist USCI div. C. R. Bard, Inc., Billerica, Mass., 1976-78; western and central regional mgr. ARCO Med. Products Co., Phila., 1978-80; Midwest regional mgr. Intermedics, Inc., Freeport, Tex., 1980-82; Western U.S. mgr. Renal Systems, Inc., Mpls., 1982—; pres. Kall-Med, Inc., Anaheim Hills, Calif. Mem. Am. Mgmt. Assn., Phi Kappa Sigma. Home and Office: 6515 Marengo Dr Anaheim Hills CA 92807

KALLEM, DONALD EDWARD, academic administrator, educator; b. Des Moines, July 7, 1934; s. Curtis M. and Grace M. (Seibert) K.; m. Patricia A. Barker, Apr. 15, 1967 (div. Aug. 1967); children: Joann Kallem Spaulding, Daniel L. Kallem, Stephanie Kallem Hobbs; m. Marjory A. Lakewold, Aug. 5, 1968; 1 child, Khristopher. BS, U. Iowa, 1958; MS, N. Ill. U., 1961; EdD, U. Mont., 1972; postdoctoral studies, Oreg. State Tchg. Research Data, 1984. Tchr., coach Cen. High Sch., Burlington, Ill., 1958-61; grad. teaching asst. U. Iowa, Iowa City, 1961-63; program dir., coach Drake U., Des Moines, 1963-64; tchr., coach, program dir. Eastern Wash. U., Cheney, 1964—, dir. adapted Phys. Edn., 1982—, dir. grad. programs in Phys. Edn., 1983—; instr. Project Active Workshop, 1986. Editor: Nat. Assn. Intercollegiate Athlectics Mag., 1977; contbr. articles to profl. jours. Bd. dirs. Junction Teen Ctr., Spokane, Wash., 1985-86; chmn. subcom. edn. Bicentennial Constitutional Observance Com. Grantee U. Iowa, 1968. Mem. Am. Alliance for Health, Phys. Edn., Recreation and Dance (bd. dirs. NW dist. 1985—), Nat. Assn. Phys. Edn. in Higher Edn., Nat. Consortium on Phys. Ednl. Recreation for Handicapped, Wash. Alliance Health, Phys. Edn., Recreation and Dance, Nat. Assn. Intercollegiate Athletics Golf Coaches Assn. (pres. 1977, Disting. Service award 1978). Lutheran. Lodges: Kiwanis (bd. dirs. Cheney club), Masons (Master 1982-83). Home: 515 Irene Pl Cheney WA 99004 Office: Eastern Wash U Dept Phys Edn PECB 248 Cheney WA 99004

KALLENBACH, W(ILLIAM) WARREN, educator, consultant; b. Palo Alto, Calif., July 16, 1926; s. Frederick Valentine and Marcia Alma (Thompson) K.; m. Patricia Lauraine Adams, Apr. 6, 1947; children: Ann Thalia, Sallee Renee, Sue Alison. AB, Drury Coll., 1949; MA, Stanford U., 1953, EdD, 1960. Tchr. Red Bluff (Calif.) Schs., 1949-52, Los Altos (Calif.) Schs., 1952-56; project dir. Far West Ednl. Research, Berkeley, Calif., 1966-69; assoc. dean research San Jose (Calif.) State U., 1978-82, prof., 1957—; dir. Kallenbach Assn., Palo Alto, Calif., 1962—, Project Interchange, San Jose, 1975-76, Individually Guided Edn., San Jose, 1970-75; cons., chief Calif. Tchr. Devel. Project, Fremont, 1969-71. Editor: Education & Society, 1963; contbr. numerous articles to profl. jours. Pres. Forum for Edn., Palo Alto, 1973, Council for Arts, Palo Alto, 1977, Friends of Children's Theatre, Palo Alto, 1970; chmn. Citizens' Com. on Sch. Fin., Palo Alto, 1965. Served with USNR, 1944-46, PTO. Recipient Innovative Devel. Teaching award Calif. Tchrs. Assn., 1971. Mem. Am. Edn. Research Assn., Calif. Research Assn. (exec. bd.), Calif. State U. Research Adminstrs. (chmn. 1981-82), Nat. Commn. Univ. Research Adminstrs., Phi Delta Kappa (service award 1959). Democrat. Unitarian. Home: 1232 Harriet St Palo Alto CA 94301 Office: San Jose State U Sch Edn 1 Washington Sq San Jose CA 95192

KALLENBERG, JOHN KENNETH, librarian; b. Anderson, Ind., June 10, 1942; s. Herbert A. and Helen S. K.; m. Ruth Barrett, Aug. 19, 1965; children—Jennifer Anne, Gregory John. A.B., Ind. U., 1964, M.L.S., 1969. With Fresno County Library, Fresno, Calif., 1965-70, dir., 1976—; librarian Fig Garden Pub. Library br., 1968-70; asst. dir. Santa Barbara (Calif.) Pub. Library, 1970-76. Mem. Calif. Library Assn. (councilor 1976-77, v.p., pres.-elect 1986, pres. 1987), Calif. County Librarians Assn. (pres. 1977), Calif. Library Authority for Systems and Services (chmn. authority adv. council 1978-80). Presbyterian. Club: Kiwanis (pres. Fresno 1981-82). Office: Fresno County Library 2420 Mariposa St Fresno CA 93721

KALLGREN, JOYCE KISLITZIN, political science educator; b. San Francisco, Apr. 17, 1930; d. Alexander and Dorothea (Willett) K.; m. Edward E. Kallgren, Feb. 8, 1953; children: Virginia, Charles. BA, U. Calif., Berkeley, 1953, MA, 1955; PhD, Harvard U., 1968. Jr. researcher to asst. researcher Ctr. Chinese Studies U. Calif., Berkeley, 1961-65, research assoc., 1965—, chair, 1983—; from lectr. to prof. polit. sci. U. Calif., Davis, 1965—; cons. in field. Contbg. editor: China After Thirty Years, 1979; editor, Jour. Asian Studies, 1980-83; mem. editorial bd. Polit. Sci. Quar., Asian Survey, World Affairs; contbr. articles to profl. jours., chpts. to books. Ford Found. awardee, 1978-79. Mem. Am. Polit. Sci. Assn., Assn. Asian Studies, China Council, Nat. Com. U.S./China Relations. Home: 28 Hillcrest Rd Berkeley CA 94705 Office: Ctr Chinese Studies U Calif Berkeley CA 94720

KALLMAN, BURTON JAY, foods association director; b. N.Y.C., Nov. 1, 1927; s. Leo Melville and Muriel Kallman; m. Ellis Katherine Hachikian, Dec. 12, 1958; children: Lisa, David. BS, Bethany Coll., 1947; MS, U. So. Calif., 1951, PhD, 1958. Research biochemist U.S. Govt., Denver, Los Angeles, 1959-67; mem. profl. staff TRW Systems, Redondo Beach, Calif., 1967-76; sr. scientist Sci. Applications Inc., La Jolla, Calif., 1976-80; prin. Interdisciplinary Sci. Assocs., Torrance, Calif., 1980-82; lab. dir. Applied Biol. Scis., Glendale, Calif., 1982-85; dir. sci. and tech. Nat. Nutritional Foods Assn., Costa Mesa, Calif., 1985—; cons. Children's Asthma Research Inst., Denver, 1961-63, Behavioral Health Services, Redondo Beach, 1973-77, Centinela Child Guidance, Inglewood, Calif., 1984-86. Contbr. articles to profl. jours.; reviewer sci. books and films, 1978—. Recipient Merit award NASA, 1976. Mem. AAAS, Am. Chem. Soc., Inst. Food Technologists, N.Y. Acad. Sci., Sigma Xi. Democrat. Jewish. Home: 23214 Robert Rd Torrance CA 90505 Office: Nat Nutritional Foods Assn 125 Baker St #230 Costa Mesa CA 92626

KALMAN, ANN ELIZABETH, marketing, advertising executive; b. Champaign, Ill., Nov. 27, 1941; d. George Hampton and Freida Irene (Harshbarger) Hyde; m. Jerry Lee Kalman, Aug. 19, 1961; children: Wendy, David. BS, U. Ill., 1963; postgrad., Ariz. State U., 1974-76. Assoc. media dir. McCann-Erickson Advt. Agy., Los Angeles, 1964-70; asst. advt. mgr. Haggarty's, Los Angeles, 1964; account exec. Max Goldberg Advt. Agy., Denver, 1963-64; teaching asst. Ariz. State U., Tempe, 1974-76; advt. and pub. relaitons dir. Ariz. Biltmore, Phoenix, 1977-78; media supr. Foote, Cone and Belding Advt. Agy., Los Angeles, 1978—; account supr. Dalla Femine and Travisano Advt. Agy., Los Angeles, 1978-81; v.p. media services CBS Entertainment div., Los Angeles, 1981—. Mem. Broadcast Mktg. Promotion Execs., Los Angeles Advt. Club. Avocations: running, racquetball, sailing, camping, sewing.

KALMBACH, JOHN HENRY, oil company executive; b. Drexel Pa., Oct. 17, 1952; s. Charles Frederic and Elizabeth (Uhl) K.; BSE with high honors, Princeton U., 1973; AM with distinction, Harvard U., 1975; m. Cecilia Elizabeth Rice, June 22, 1974; children: Hilary Elizabeth, Whitney Alison, Eliot Ramsay. Cons. geologist, Boston, 1976-78; geologist, credit exec. First Nat. Bank Boston, 1978-80; asst. to pres., corp. officer Pauley Petroleum, Inc., Los Angeles, 1980-87; v.p. KTA Ltd., Frazer, Pennsylvania, 1987—. Author: Notes on the Upper Crataceous Invertebrate Fauna of Haddonfield, 1969. NSF grad. fellow, 1973-76. Mem. Am. Inst. Mining Engrs., Am. Assn. Petroleum Geologists, Sigma Xi, Tau Beta Pi. Clubs: Jonathan, Petroleum (Los Angeles); Princeton Ivy; Harvard of Boston.

KALOIAN, RACHEL DIANE, telecommunications executive; b. Los Angeles, June 21, 1958; d. Paul J. and Connie (Bojorquez) Robles; m. Michael S. Kaloian, May 17, 1980. Ops. mgr. API Telephone Systems, Los Angeles, 1981-82; systems design coordinator Universal Communications Systems, Fullerton, Calif., 1982-83; sales mgr. Phoneby, Inc., Newport Beach, Calif., 1983-84; pres. Calif. Mgmt. Services, Huntington Beach, 1984-87; project adminstr. No. Telecom, Redondo Beach, Calif., 1987-89. Mem. Women in Mgmt. (sec. 1984), Internat. Orgn. of Women in Telecommunications (sec. 1984, v.p. 1985, pres. 1986), Nat. Assn. Women Bus. Owners (bd. dirs. advisor 1984—). Republican.

KALT, HOWARD MICHAEL, public relations executive; b. Racine, Wis., June 11, 1943; s. Nat and Fay (Schwartz) K.; m. Barbara Lee Schowalter, Feb. 2, 1963; children—Jennifer, Jeffrey. B.S. in Journalism, U. Wis., 1964. Writer, Wis. State Jour., Madison, 1963-64; v.p. Gardner, Jones & Co., Chgo., 1964-74, v.p. communications Fred S. James & Co., Chgo., 1974-75; dir. communications The Marmon Group, Chgo., 1975-76, v.p. Ruder & Finn, San Francisco, 1976-77, Hoefer Amidei Assocs., San Francisco, 1977-79; v.p. communications ISU Cos., Inc., San Francisco, 1979-82; ptnr., co-owner Kalt & Hamlin Pub. Relations, San Francisco, 1982-84; owner Kalt & Assocs., Pub. Relations, San Francisco, 1984—. Life mem. Community Renewal Soc. Chgo; dir. Am. Lung Assn., San Francisco. Mem. Pub. Relations Soc. Am. (accredited, mem. pub. affairs task force, best pub. relations program No. Calif. chpt. 1980, dir., past pres. San Francisco chpt., assembly del.), San Francisco Pub. Relations Round Table. Jewish. Club: The Family. Office: Kalt & Assocs Pub Relations 100 Bush St Suite 1100 San Francisco CA 94104

KALTENBACH, CARL COLIN, agriculturist, educator; b. Buffalo, Mar. 22, 1939; s. Carl H. and Mary Colleen (McKeag) K.; m. Ruth Helene Johnson, Aug. 22, 1964; children: James Earl, John Edward. BS, U. Wyo., 1961; MS, U. Nebr., 1963; PhD, U. Ill., 1967. Prof. animal sci. U. Wyo., Laramie, 1969—, head dept. animal sci., 1978-80, assoc. dir. coll. agr., 1980-84, assoc. dean and dir., 1984—; chmn. Exptl. Sta. Com. on Orgn. and Policy, 1986—. Contbr. articles to profl. jours. Recipient Young Scientist award West Sect. Am. Soc. Animal Sci., 1976, Faculty award merit Gamma Sigma Delta, 1980. Mem. AAAS, Soc. Study Reproduction (treas. 1980-83), Am. Soc. Animal Sci., Soc. for Study of Fertility. Home: 1858 N 15th St Laramie WY 82070 Office: U Wyoming PO Box 3354 Laramie WY 82071

KAMEMOTO, HARUYUKI, horticulture educator; b. Honolulu, Jan. 19, 1922; s. Shuichi and Matsu (Murase) K.; m. Ethel Hideko Kono, June 7, 1952; children—David Yukio, Mark Toshio, Claire Naomi. B.S., U. Hawaii, 1944, M.S., 1947; Ph.D., Cornell U., 1950. Asst. in horticulture U. Hawaii, Honolulu, 1944-47; asst. prof. horticulture U. Hawaii, 1950-54, assoc. prof., 1954-58, prof., 1958—, chmn. dept., 1969-75; horticulture adviser Kasetsart U., Bangkok, Thailand, U. Hawaii AID contract, 1962-65; UNFAO hort. cons. to, India, 1971, 80. Author: (with R. Sagarik) Beautiful Thai Orchid Species, 1975; contbr. articles to profl. jours. Fulbright research fellow Kyoto U., Japan, 1956-57; recipient Gold medal Malayan Orchid Soc., 1964; Norman Jay Coleman award Am. Assn. Nurserymen, 1977. Fellow AAAS, Am. Soc. Hort. Sci.; hon. mem. Am. Orchid Soc., Japan Orchid Soc., Orchid Soc. Thailand (award of honor 1978), Orchid Soc. S.E. Asia; mem. Am. Genetic Assn., Am. Hort. Soc., Bot. Soc. Am., Internat. Soc. Hort., Internat. Assn. Plant Taxonomy, Soc. Advancement Breeding Research in Asia and Oceania, Phi Kappa Phi. Home: 3246 Lower Rd Honolulu HI 96822 Office: 3190 Maile Way Honolulu HI 96822

KAMIMOTO, DAVID ROSS, college admissions counselor; b. Gilroy, Calif., Jan. 5, 1956; s. Kay K. and Yoshiko (Tamura) K. B.A. in Psychology and Social Welfare, U. Calif.-Berkeley, 1978; M.S. in Counseling, San Francisco State U., 1980. Program coordinator Cogswell Poly. Coll., 1979-80; admissions counselor, U. Calif.-Santa Cruz, 1980-84; assoc. to dir. admissions, U. Calif.-Santa Cruz, 1984—. Mem. Japanese Am. Citizens League, Nat. Assn. Coll. Admissions Counselors, Western Assn. Coll. Admissions Counselors, Nat. Eagle Scout Assn., Phi Lambda Theta. Clubs: Calif. Alumni Assn., Calif. Alumni Band, Am. Field Services. Home: 115 Felix St Apt 8 Santa Cruz CA 95060 Office: U Calif Office of Admissions Cook House Santa Cruz CA 95064

KAMINE, BERNARD SAMUEL, lawyer; b. Oklahoma City, Dec. 5, 1943; s. Martin and Mildred Esther K.; m. Marcia Phyllis Haber, Sept. 9, 1982; children: Jorge Hershel, Benjamin Haber, Tovy Haber. BA, U. Denver, 1965; JD, Harvard U., 1968. Bar: Calif. 1969, Colo. 1969, U.S. Supreme Ct. 1973. Dep. atty. gen. Calif. Dept. Justice, Los Angeles, 1969-72; asst. atty. gen. Colo. Dept. Law, Denver, 1972-74; ptnr. Kamine, Steiner & Unger (and Predecessor firms), Los Angeles, Calif., 1976—; instr. Glendale (Calif.) U. Coll. Law, 1971-72; judge pro tem Beverly Hills Mcpl. Ct., 1974-77, Los Angeles Mcpl. Ct., 1977—; panel of arbitrators Am. Arbitration Assn., 1976—; mem. adv. com. legal forms Calif. Jud. Council, 1978-82; lectr. Calif. Continuing Edn. of the Bar Programs, 1979—. Mem. Los Angeles County Dem. Cen. Com., 1982-85. Served to maj., inf. USAR, 1969—. Mem. ABA, Calif. State Bar Assn. (conf. dels. Calif. coordinating com. 1987—), Los Angeles County Bar Assn. (chmn. Superior Cts. com. 1977-79, del. to state bar conf. dels., 1978-87, chmn. constrn. law subsect. of real property sect. 1981-83) Engring. Contractors' Assn. (bd. dirs. 1985—), Res. Officers Assn. (pres. chpt. 1977-78), Assoc. Gen. Contractors (legal adv. com. 1982—) . Contbr. articles to profl. jours. Office: Kamine Steiner & Ungerer 350 S Figueroa St Suite 250 Los Angeles CA 90071

KAMINS, MICHAEL ABRAHAM, marketing educator; b. N.Y.C., Nov. 22, 1952; s. Samuel and Anita Ruth (Freed) K.; m. Yolande Julie Zerbib, Jan. 24, 1975. BBus., Bernard M. Baruch Coll., 1974, MBus., 1977; PhD, NYU, 1984. Lab. technician Bernard M. Baruch Coll., N.Y.C., 1975-79, sr. lab. technician, 1979-80; instr. mktg. NYU, N.Y.C., 1980-83, asst. prof., 1983-84; asst. prof. U. So. Calif., Los Angeles, 1984—. Contbr. articles to profl. jours. Mem. Am. Mktg. Assn. (contbr. articles to educators conf. 1985-86), Am. Statis. Assn., Assn. Consumer Research. Democrat. Jewish. Avocations: coin collecting, world travel. Home: 950 N Kings Rd #331 West Hollywood CA 90069 Office: U So Calif Sch Acctg Dept Mktg Los Angeles CA 90089

KAMINSKI-DA ROZA, VICTORIA CECILIA, human resource administrator; b. East Orange, N.J., Aug. 30, 1945; d. Victor and Cynthia Helen (Krupa) Hawkins; m. Thomas Howard Kaminski, Aug. 28, 1971 (div. 1977); 1 child, Sarah Hawkins; m. Robert Anthony da Roza, Nov. 25, 1983. BA, U. Mich., 1967; MA, U. Mo., 1968. Contract compliance mgr. City of San Diego, 1972-75; v.p. personnel Bank of Calif., San Francisco, 1975-77; with human resources Lawrence Livermore (Calif.) Nat. Lab., 1978-86; pvt. cons. Victoria Kaminiski-da Roza & Assocs., 1986—; lectr. in field; videotape workshop program on mid-career planning used by IEEE. Contbr. numerous articles to profl. jours. Mem. social policy com. City of Livermore, 1982. Mem. Am. Soc. Tng. and Devel., Western Gerontol. Soc. (planning com. Older Worker Track 1983), Gerontol. Soc. Am. Home and Office: 385 Borica Dr Danville CA 94526

KAMINSKY, EDWARD SCOTT, endodontist, researcher; b. Bklyn., June 25, 1957; s. Stanley and Anne (Orlofsky) K.; m. Marilee Gail Elliott, Feb. 6, 1978; children: Aaron Scott, Allison Renée. MS in Dentistry, Ind. U., 1986; DDS, Creighton U., 1982. Gen. practice dentistry Albuquerque, 1982-84; resident in endodontics VA Med. Ctr., Indpls., 1984-86; endodontist USPHS, Denver, 1986—; edodontic cons. VA Med. Ctr., Denver, 1986—. Mem. ADA, Am. Assn. Endodontists (Meml. and Endowment Fund grantee 1986), N.Mex. Dental Assn. Jewish. Avocations: scuba diving, skiing, hiking. Home: 10729 Albion St Denver CO 80233 Office: Eastside Health Ctr 501 E 28th St Denver CO 80205

KAMINSKY, HARRY, health science facility administrator; b. N.Y.C., Nov. 29, 1952; s. David and Dolores Pauline (Glass) K.; m. Hillary Barbara Resnick, May 3, 1981; 1 child, David. BA, CUNY, Queens, 1974, MEd, 1978; MSW, Ariz. State U., 1983. Tchr. Bd. Edn., N.Y.C., 1974-79; family therapist Phoenix S. Mental Health Ctr., 1980-83, dir. family dimensions, 1983-86, dir. div. adjustment project, 1984—, v.p. div. services ctr., 1985—; dir. div. adjustment project, cons. Ariz. State U., Phoenix, 1984—; dir. community mediation program N. Community Behavioral Health Ctr., Phoenix, 1986—; cons., trainer various child care orgns. Phoenix, 1983—. Mem. Ariz. State Foster Care Review Bd., Phoenix, 1984—. Div. Adjustment Project grantee NIMH, 1984, Medication Program grantee City of Phoenix, 1986. Mem. Nat. Assn. Social Workers (cert.), Acad. Family Mediators, Assn. Family Conciliation Cts. Democrat. Jewish. Avocations: songwriting, guitar playing, singing, racquetball. Home: 4519 N 11th Ave Phoenix AZ 85013 Office: N Community Behavioral Health Ctr 8841 N 8th St Phoenix AZ 85020

KAMINSKY, RAY, consulting analytical chemist; b. N.Y.C., Dec. 20, 1950; s. Paul William and Esther Brina (Finklestein) K.; m. Katherine Lynne Hansen, June 17, 1979; children: Sarah Muriel, Peter Bernard. BA, UCLA, 1973; MA, U. Calif., Santa Barbara, 1975, PhD, 1980; postdoctoral, Ind. U., 1983. Cert. jr. coll. tchr., Calif. Chemist Acurex Corp., Mountain View, Calif., 1983-84, Emcon Assocs., San Jose, Calif., 1984—. Contbr. articles to profl. jours. Mem. AAAS, Am. Soc. Mass Spectrometrists, Ecol. Soc. Am. Democrat. Avocations: astronomy, carpentry. Home: 3136 Drywood Ave San Jose CA 95132

KAMLIN, DAVID ALLEN, data processing company executive; b. Cody, Wyo., Dec. 21, 1938; s. Robert Charles and Marie Louise (Berry) K.; m. Lisa Marie Colton, June 2, 1963 (dec. Sept. 1975); m. Judith Ann Fleming, July 15, 1981; children: Lori, Lesley, James. LLB, U. Wyo., 1962; M in Journalism, U. Mo., 1964. Commd. 2d lt. USMCR, 1961, advanced through grades to major, resigned, 1975; field supr. Burke-Waite Corp., Kansas City, Mo., 1975-78; prodn. executive Rupert-Shaun Corp., Glendale, Calif., 1978-80; chief exec. officer Jada Techs., Torrance, Calif., 1980—; cons. USN and govtl. agys., 1983—. Author: The TLC Connection, 1985. Decorated Medal of Honor, DFC, Purple Heart, Bronze Star, Silver Star. Mem. So. Calif. Typesetter's Assn. (pres. 1983—). Republican. Mormon. Lodge: Kiwanis (editor newsletter 1984). Avocations: computer programming, writing, golf, flying. Office: JADA Techs Inc 3547 Voyager St #103 Torrance CA 90503

KAMMANN, ANA TERESA, social service administrator, minister; b. Hyannis, Mass., July 27, 1947; d. Durand and Ruth Patricia (Smith) Echeverria; m. Gregory Alan Kammann, Apr. 29, 1969; children: Gabriel Soren, Shin Ja Elizabeth, Sean Matthew. BA, Brown U., 1971; MA, M Div., Pacific Sch. Religion, 1976; postgrad., Portland State U., 1986—. Ordained to ministry United Ch. Christ, 1976. Co-pastor 2d United Ch. Christ (Congl.), Portland, Oreg., 1976-79; program dir. Luth. Family Services, Portland, 1979—. Mem. mediation team Irvington Sch., Portland, 1984-85. Mem. Nat. Assn. Social Workers (student). Democrat. Avocations: soccer, cross-country skiing. Home: 3003 NE 18th Portland OR 97212 Office: Luth Family Services 605 SE 39th Portland OR 97214

KAMMER, DANIEL CHARLES, consulting engineer; b. New Castle, Pa., Aug. 9, 1953; s. Roger Allen and Rosemarie (Forney) K.; m. Catherine Anne Cram, Oct. 1, 1983. BS, U. Wis., MS, PhD. Dynamics engr. Convair div. Gen. Dynamics Corp., San Diego, 1978-79; sr. project engr. Structural Dynamics Research Corp., San Diego, 1983—. Engring. Research fellow U. Wis., Madison, 1982-83. Mem. AIAA, ASME, Soc. Indsl. and Applied Math., Am. Acad. Mechanics, W Club, sigma Xi. Episcopalian. Avocations: golf, biking, hiking, astronomy, sports cars. Office: Structural Dynamics Research Corp 11055 Roselle St San Diego CA 92121

KAMPHOEFNER, FRED J(OHN), research institute director; b. San Francisco, Mar. 23, 1921; s. Fred J. and Alice (Martin) K.; m. Jean Henderson, July 23, 1960. BSEE, U. Calif., Berkeley, 1943; MAEE, Stanford U., 1946, PhDEE, 1949. Registered profl. engr., Calif. Research asst. U. Calif., Berkeley, 1942-43; research assoc. Harvard U., Cambridge, Mass., 1943-45; teaching asst., research assoc. Stanford (Calif.) U., 1945-49; dep. dir. advanced techs. div. SRI Internat., Menlo Park, Calif., 1949—. Contbr. tech. papers to profl. publs.; patentee in field. Mem. IEEE (sr.), Sigma Xi, Tau Beta Pi, Eta Kappa Nu. Avocations: music, painting. Home: 175 Ravenswood Ave Atherton CA 94025 Office: SRI Internat 333 Ravenswood Ave Menlo Park CA 94025

KAMSKY, EARL CHARLES, human resource development specialist, educator, consultant; b. Chgo., Sept. 3, 1946; s. William and Anne Frieda (Gerstein) K.; student U. Granada, 1965-66; BA, Beloit Coll., 1969; postgrad. San Francisco Theol. Sem., 1969-70; MS, U. Oreg., 1976; JD, Northwestern U., 1987. Faculty mem. Wallace Sch. Community Service, Pub. Affairs, U. Oreg., Eugene, 1976-81; acad. dir. Sch. Internat. Tng., Ahmedabad, India, 1979; tng. devel. officer, City of Portland (Oreg.), 1981-83; human resource devel. mgr. Portland Gen. Elec., 1983—; orgn. devel. cons., 1976—. Mem. Head Start adv. bd., 1977 Oreg. State Career Devel. Com., 1973. HEW grantee. Mem. Am. Soc. Tng. and Devel., Am. Pub. Works Assn., U.S.-China People's Friendship Assn. Democrat. Toured China in 1978. Office: 121 SW Salmon St TB 14 Portland OR 97204

KAN, JOSEPH RUCE, physicist, educator; b. Shanghai, China, Feb. 10, 1938; s. John H. S. and Mary A. (Chen) K.; m. Rosalind J. Chen; children—Christina, Deborah, Steven. Ph.D., U. Calif.-San Diego, 1969. Asst. prof. U. Alaska, Fairbanks, 1972-76, assoc. prof., 1976-81, prof. geophysics, 1981—. Grantee NSF, NASA, Air Force Geophysics Lab., 1974—. Mem. Am. Geophys. Union, Am. Phys. Soc., AAAS. Contbr. papers to profl. publs. including: Jour. Geophysical Research, Jour. Plasma Physics, Solar Physics, Planetary and Space Sci., Geophysical Research Letters, Rev. of Space Physics. Office: Geophysical Inst Univ Alaska Fairbanks AK 99701

KANAGAWA, ROBERT KIYOSHI, citrus co. exec.; b. Sanger, Calif., Sept. 10, 1917; s. Yasoichi T. and Jitsuyo (Sumii) K.; B.B.A., Central Calif. Comml. Coll., 1939; m. Yukiye Nakamura, Feb. 12, 1944; children—Rodney M., Floyd A., Dallas W. Vice pres., treas. Kanagawa Citrus Co., Sanger, 1939-65, pres., 1965—; charter dir. Sequoia Community Bank, 1980—, chmn. bd., 1981—;bd. chmn. Agrl Export Calif., Inc., 1985—. Chmn. Agrl. Exhibit, Fresno Dist. Fair, 1953-58, Nations Christmas Tree Festival, Sanger, 1959, Sanger Grape Bowl Festival, 1964-74; bd. dirs. Valley Children's Hosp., 1968-72; bd. trustees St. Agnes Hosp., 1972-86, v.p., 1979, 81-86; bd. trustees Fairmont Elem. Sch., 1954-58, Sanger Union High Sch., 1958-65, Sanger Unified Sch. Dist., 1965-69, Sanger Parks and Recreation Commn., 1963-73, Sanger Sr. Citizens Commn., 1975-79; mem. Republican. State Central Com., 1972-76; bd. dirs. 21st Dist. Agrl. Assn., 1970-79, pres., 1977; exec. bd. Sequoia council Boy Scouts Am., 1971-84 , v.p., 1979; mem. Calif. Council Humanities in Public Policy, 1977-82; campaign chmn. Am. Heart Assn., 1981-82, v.p. Central Valley chpt., 1984-85, pres., 1985-86; bd. dirs., treas. Calif. Agrl. Mus., 1980-85 . Named Man of Yr., Sanger Dist. C. of C., 1968; recipient Golden Apple award Fresno County Sch. Adminstrs., 1976. Mem. Sanger Citrus Assn. (dir. 1961-72, pres. 1972), Orange Cove-Sanger Citrus Assn. (dir., v.p. 1973—), Sanger Japanese Am. Citizens League (charter, charter pres., dist. gov. 1977-78). Republican. Methodist. Club: Rotary of Sanger (pres. 1970-71, dist. gov. internat. 1974-75). Home: 16156 E McKinley Ave Sanger CA 93657 Office: 2720 Jensen Ave Sanger CA 93657

KANAMORI, KEIKO, chemist; b. Tokyo, Nov. 20, 1939; came to U.S., 1972; d. Takashi and Hatsue (Kajiyama) Ihara; m. Hiroo Kanamori, Apr. 21, 1964; children: Atty, Teddy. BA, Tokyo U., 1962; BS in Biochemistry, Calif. State U., Los Angeles, 1976; PhD in Chemistry, Calif. Inst. Tech., 1981. Postdoctoral research fellow Calif. Inst. Tech., Pasadena, 1981-82; research chemist UCLA, 1982—. Home: 4424 Coldwater Canyon Ave #4 Studio City CA 91604 Office: UCLA 405 Hilgard Ave Los Angeles CA 90024

KANDELL, HOWARD NOEL, pediatrician; b. Bklyn., Dec. 25, 1934; s. Allan J. and Ruth (Adelman) K.; m. Trudy Ann Lippert, June 8, 1958; children—David, Debra, Lauren, Lisa. B.S., U. Miami, 1956; M.D., Tulane U., 1959. Diplomate Am. Bd. Pediatrics. Intern Phila. Gen. Hosp., 1959-60; resident N.Y. Hosp. Cornell Med. Ctr., N.Y.C., 1960-62; practice medicine specializing in pediatrics, Phoenix, 1965—; bd. dirs. Health Maintenances Assocs., Ltd., Phoenix, 1975-82, chief pediatrics, 1977-82; assoc. chmn. dept. pediatrics Maricopa County Hosp., Phoenix, 1965-71, service chief dept. pediatrics, 1972-77; assoc. in pediatrics U. Ariz. Coll. Medicine, 1970-82, clin. instr. 1982-83; asst. prof., 1983—; chmn. pediatric dept. Cigna Health Plan of Ariz., Phoenix, 1984—; adj. faculty mem. Ariz. State U. Coll. Nursing, 1986—; faculty Phoenix Hosps. Affiliated Pediatric Program, 1965—; med. dir. INA Health Plan (CIGNA) South Fla., 1982-83. Served to capt., USAF, 1962-64. Recipient Tchr. of Yr. award dept. pediatrics Maricopa County Gen. Hosp., 1972. Fellow Am. Acad. Pediatrics; mem. Ambulatory Pediatric Assn., Am. Acad. Med. Dirs., Ariz. Pediatric Soc. (treas., exec. com. 1970-76), Maricopa County Pediatric Soc. (v.p. 1970-72). Office: 12635 N 42d St Phoenix AZ 85032 Home: 7257 E Echo Ln Scottsdale AZ 85258

KANDELL, MARSHALL JAY, public relations counselor; b. Bklyn., Dec. 5, 1937; s. Harry and Mollie Rebecca (Remstein) K.; m. Judith Ann Zeve, May 28, 1961; children: Paul Bryon, Robin Pilar. AA in Journalism, Los Angeles City Coll., 1958; student Calif. State U., Los Angeles, 1963-65. Cert. tchr. community colls., Calif. Pub. relations staff City of Hope (Calif.) Nat. Med. Ctr., 1966-68; v.p. Roger Beck Pub. Relations, Sherman Oaks, Calif., 1968-71; account supr. Laurence Laurie & Assoc., Los Angeles, 1971-72; community relations dir. St. Mary Med. Ctr., Long Beach, Calif., 1972-75; dir. pub. relations Cedars-Sinai Med. Ctr., Los Angeles, 1975; founder Marshall Jay Kandell Pub. Relations, Huntington Beach, Calif., 1976—; vis. faculty mem. Calif. State U., Long Beach; mem. founding faculty Coastline Community Coll. Pres. Encino Jaycees, 1970-71; pres. Community Vol. Office, Long Beach, 1975-76; bd. dirs. Long Beach chpt. ARC, 1974-75, Civic Ctr. Barrio Housing Corp., Santa Ana, Calif.; mem. Citizen's Adv. Commn. 1984 Olympic Games, adv. panel Jewish Family Service of Orange County, Calif.; v.p. Irvine Jewish Community, 1973; founding mem., v.p. Congregation B'nai Tzedek, Fountain Valley, Calif., 1976. Served in USAF, 1958-63. Recipient Disting. Service award Encino Jaycees, 1972; MacEachern award Acad. Hosp. Pub. Relations, 1973-74; Best written story award Press Club Greater Los Angeles, 1965. Mem. Pub. Relations Soc. Am. Democrat. Jewish. Home: 18882 Deodar St Fountain Valley CA 92708 Office: 18700 Beach Blvd Huntington Beach CA 92648

KANDLER, JOSEPH RUDOLPH, financial executive; b. Vienna, Austria, Dec. 13, 1921; came to Can., 1952; s. Franz and Maria Franziska (Stanzel) K.; m. Lubomyra-Melitta Melnechuk, June 15, 1963. D.Rerum Commercialium, Sch. Econs., Vienna, 1949; Chartered Acct., Inst. Chartered Accts. Alta., 1965. Sales exec. Philips, Vienna, 1951; acct. Brown & Root, Ltd. Edmonton, Alta., Can., 1952-54, 56, chief acct., 1957-64; v.p. fin. Healy Ford Ctr. and Assoc. Cos., Edmonton, 1964—; pres. Sentha Investments, Ltd., Edmonton, 1978—. Bd. dirs. Edmonton Symphony, 1969-72, Alta. Cultural Heritage Council, 1973-81, Edmonton Opera, 1982-84, Tri-Bach Festival, 1982-84; founder Johann Strauss Found., Alta., bd. dirs. 1975-84, pres. 1975-78, founder B.C. chpt., 1985—; bd. govs. U. Alta., 1982-86, mem. senate, 1973-79, 82-86; mem. adv. com. on cultural and convention ctr. City of Edmonton, 1974-78, vice chmn. 1976-78. Recipient Achievement award for service to community Govt. Alta., 1975. Mem. Inst. Chartered Accts. Alta., Adminstrv. Mgmt. Soc. (pres. 1967-68), Mensa, Edmonton C. of C. (council 1971-75). Roman Catholic. Address: Healy Ford Ctr and Assocs, 10620 Jasper Ave, Edmonton, AB Canada T5J 2A4

KANDO, THOMAS MATHEW, sociology educator, author; b. Budapest, Hungary, Apr. 8, 1941; came to U.S., 1965; s. Jules and Ata Edith (Gorog) K.; m. Anita Chris Costa, June 30, 1973; children—Danielle, Leah. Student Union Coll., 1960-61; B.S., U. Amsterdam (Netherlands), 1965; M.A., U. Minn., 1967, Ph.D., 1969. Asst. prof. sociology U. Wis.-Stout, Menomonie, 1968-69; cons. Calif. Dept. Parks and Recreation, Sacramento, 1969-70; asst. prof. Calif. State U.-Sacramento, 1969-72, U. Calif.-Riverside, 1972-73; assoc. prof. Calif. State U.-Sacramento, 1973-77; assoc. prof. recreation and parks Pa. State U., 1978-79; prof. sociology and criminal justice Calif. State U.-Sacramento, 1979—. U. Amsterdam fellow, 1962-65; U. Minn. fellow, 1967; Fulbright fellow, 1960-61. Mem. AAUP (pres. local chpt. 1974—, pres. statewide 1976-78), Am. Sociol Assn., Internat. Sociol. Assn., Internat. Com. Leisure Research, Nat. Recreation and Parks Assn., Pacific Sociol. Assn., Popular Culture Assn., Internat. Com. on Sports Sociology, Athletic Congress, Phi Sigma Kappa. Republican. Author: Sex Change: The Achievement of Gender Identity Among Feminized Transsexuals, 1973; Leisure and Popular Culture in Transition, 1975, 80; Social Interaction, 1977; Sexual Behavior and Family Life in Transition, 1978; assoc. editor Pacific Sociol. Rev., 1973-78; Contemporary Sociology, 1975-79; contbr. numerous articles to profl. jours., popular mags. Home: 8267 Caribbean Way Sacramento CA 95826 Office: Dept Sociology Calif State U 6000 Jay St Sacramento CA 95819

KANE, BARTHOLOMEW ALOYSIUS, state librarian; b. Pitts., Nov. 2, 1945; s. Bartholomew A. and Ruth M. (Loerlein) K.; m. Kathleen Osborne, Aug. 7, 1967; 1 dau., Leah. B.A. in Journalism, Pa. State U., 1967; M.L.S., U. Pitts., 1971. Dir. Bradford Meml. Library, El Dorado, Kans., 1972-74; researcher Hawaii Dept. Planning and Econ. Devel., Honolulu, 1974-75, state librarian, 1982—; librarian Hawaii State Library System, Lanai City, 1975-79, Honolulu, 1979-82. Founder Lanai Community Services Council, 1976-79; founder Hawaii Visual Arts Consortium Inc., Honolulu, 1976-81; mem. Hawaii Literacy Inc., 1982—; mem. Hawaii Commn. for Humanities, 1984—. Hazel McCoy fellow Friends of Library of Hawaii, 1971. Mem. ALA, Hawaii Library Assn., Librarians Assn. Hawaii (v.p. 1982), Hawaii Commn. for Humanities. Democrat. Home: 60 N Kuakini St #2H Honolulu HI 96817 Office: Hawaii State Pub Library System 465 S King St Honolulu HI 96813

KANE, CHARLES, neurologist; b. Boston, Oct. 2, 1917; s. Meyer Charles and Alice Louise (Richardson) K.; m. Rita Margaret Abbott, Nov. 10, 1966; children: Charles A. Jr., Priscilla E., Richard J., Catherine, Andrew, Marc, Tim. AB, Harvard U., 1939, MD, 1943. Diplomate Am. Bd. Neurology and Psychiatry. Intern Boston City Hosp., 1943-44; resident Goldwater Meml. Hosp., N.Y.C., 1944; resident in neurology Bronx VA Hosp., 1947-50; instr. neurology Cornell Med. Sch., N.Y.C., 1946-51; from asst. prof. to assoc. prof. Boston U. Med. Sch., 1951-66; instr. Harvard U. Med. Sch., Boston, 1951-66; chief dept. neurology Permanente Med. Group, Hayward, Calif., 1966-83; mem. research com. Kaiser H.P./TPMG, Inc., Oakland, Calif., 1967—, instnl. rev. bd. Kaiser H.P./TPMG, Inc., 1980—. Contbr. chpts. to books and articles to profl. jours. Recipient Presdl. Unit Citation for Malaria Research U.S. Govt., 1946. Mem. San Francisco Neurol. Soc. (pres. 1984—), Am. Acad. Neurology, No. Calif. Med. Golf Assn. (tournament com.), Sigma Xi, Alpha Omega Alpha. Democrat. Roman Catholic. Clubs: Las Positas Golf (Livermore, Calif.); Harvard (San Francisco). Avocations: golf, music, traveling, history. Home: 614 Thornhill Rd Danville CA 94526 Office: The Permanente Med Group Inc 27400 Hesperian Blvd Hayward CA 94545

KANE, CHARLES A., academic administrator. BS, Pepperdine U.; MS, U. So. Calif., EdD. Pres., supt. Riverside (Calif.) Community Coll. Dist., 1978—; coach basketball, student activities dir. Dominguez High Sch., Compton, Calif., 1957-64. Mem. Inland Empire Higher Edn. Council; bd. dirs. Community Health Corp., Riverside Community Hosp. Served with U.S. Army, 1954-56. Presented with Key to City, Long Beach, Calif. Mem. Calif. Assn. Community Colls. (chmn. commn. on athletics), Assn. Calif. Community Coll. Adminstrs., Calif. Community Coll. Chief Exec. Officers Assn., So. Calif. Interscholastic Basketball Coaches Assn. (life), Riverside City Coll. Alumni Assn. Avocations: sports, music, the arts. Office: Riverside Community Coll 4800 Magnolia Ave Riverside CA 92506

KANE, DANIEL EDWIN, chemical engineer; b. Iowa Park, Tex., Aug. 12, 1923; s. Daniel James and Ruth (Davis) K.; m. Inga Maria Brolin, Aug. 7, 1953; children: Jeffrey, Daniel. BS, Iowa State Coll., 1947; MS, Lawrence Coll., 1950, PhD, 1953. Planning engr. Phillips Petroleum Co., Bartlesville, Okla., 1947-48; sr. chem. engr. Fibreboard Corp., Antioch, Calif., 1953-59; tech. dir. NVF Co., Yorklyn, Del., 1959-70; pilot prodn. mgr. Bus. Equipment div. SCM, Palo Alto, Calif., 1970-75; sterilization engr. mgr. Miles Labs., Berkeley, Calif., 1976—. Patentee corrugating medium treatment and paper coating method. Served as master sgt. U.S. Army, 1942-46, ETO. Mem. Am. Chem. Soc., TAPPI. Home: 5815 Amapola Dr San Jose CA 95129 Office: Miles Labs 4th & Parker Sts Berkeley CA 94710

KANE, ELIZABETH GLEASON, history and computer science educator; b. Yakima, Wash., May 8, 1921; d. Claude Franz and Olive Wanda (Hibarger) Gleason; m. Harold Walter Kane, July 10, 1942 (dec.); children—Robert Vaness (dec.), Kathryn Ann Kane Huckaby. B.A. in Music Edn., U. Wyo., 1942. Tchr. Guernsey Sch. Dist., Wyo., 1943-45; sec. Robert Donner, Colorado Springs, Colo., 1946-52; exec. sec. Calif. Credit Union League, Oakland, 1953-57; mgr. Lawrence Livermore Nat. Lab. Credit Union, Livermore, Calif., 1957-59; tchr. history and computer sci. Livermore Sch. Dist., 1959—, dist. curriculum coordinator, 1975-81, dept. chmn. 1976—; task force coordinator Calif. Sch. Improvement Program, Livermore, 1979-81; workshop coordinator Law In A Free Soc., Livermore, 1978. Author: (tchr.'s manual) Youth and Justice, 1979; A Proud Nation, 1983. Sponsoring educator Project Bus., Livermore, 1981-87; foster home parent Alameda County Welfare Dept., 1974-79. Named Tchr. of Yr. Livermore Mgmt. Assn., Assn. Calif. Sch. Adminstrs., 1982. Mem. Calif. Tchrs. Assn., NEA, Calif. and Nat. Council for Social Studies, Nat. Hist. Soc., Am. Hist. Soc., Kappa Kappa Gamma, Sigma Alpha Iota, Kappa Delta Pi. Episcopal. Club: Soroptimist. Home: 590 North P St Livermore CA 94550 Office: Junction Sch 298 Junction Ave Livermore CA 94550

KANE, MARY ELIZABETH, audiologist; b. Seattle, Aug. 15, 1959; d. Robert Thomas and Martha Louise (Fast) K. BS, U. Wash., 1981, MS, 1984. Cast tech. Hugh Sobottka, Seattle, 1983-84; research asst. U. of Wash. Exptl. Edn. Unit, Seattle, 1983—; outreach audiologist Northwest Hosp., Seattle, 1984—; audiologist Herbert C. Thomas, MD, Seattle, 1986—, Childrens Orthopedic Hosp., Seattle, 1986—. V.p. Children's Orthopedic Hosp. Guild, Seattle, 1986—. Mem. Am. Speech Lang. Hearing Assn. (cert.), Wash. Soc. Audiology, Am. Auditory Soc. Republican. Presbyterian. Avocation: tennis. Home: 531 Bellevue Ave E #204 Seattle WA 98102 Office: Herbert C Thomas MD 4540 Sandpoint Way NE Suite 320 Seattle WA 98105

KANE, ROBERT EDWARD, biologist, educator; b. Erie, Pa., Mar. 22, 1931; s. Edward Thomas and Dorothy Marie (Lavery) K.; m. Nancy Kay Lind, Apr. 11, 1970 (div. June 1976). BS, MIT, 1953; PhD, Johns Hopkins U., 1957. Asst. prof. biochemistry Brandeis U., Waltham, Mass., 1958-61; asst. prof. Dartmouth Med. Sch., Hanover, N.H., 1961-66; assoc. prof. U. Hawaii, Honolulu, 1966-69, prof., 1969—; mem. panel Nat. Inst. Health, Bethesda, Md., 1983-85. Contbr. articles to profl. jours. Recipient Career Devel. award NSF, 1963-66; research grantee NSF, 1958-61, Nat. Inst. Health, 1961—; predoctoral fellow NSF, 1955-57. Mem. AAAS, Am. Soc. for Cell Biology, Internat. Soc. of Devel. Biologists, Sigma Xi. Office: Pacific Biomed Research Ctr 41 Ahui St Honolulu HI 96313

KANEKO, RYOJI LLOYD, training and management development consultant; b. Los Angeles, Apr. 11, 1951; s. Hayao and Yoshiko (Kawaguchi) K.; m. Marie Antoinette Bawany, June 29, 1985, 1 child, Laura Shigemi. BA in English, Calif. State U., Long Beach, 1974. Marching instr. Third Generation Drum and Bugle Corps, Los Angeles, 1973-75; trainer, supr. Teledyne-Geotronics, Long Beach, 1975-79; tng. coordinator, supr. tng. and procedures, tng. adminstr. Hughes Aircraft Co., El Segundo, Calif., 1980—; guest lectr., speaker, cons. in field. Elder, mem. chancel choir, mem. Cornerstone Vocal Ensemble Bellflower (Calif.) First Christian Ch. Recipient Profl. Designation award UCLA. Mem. Am. Soc. Tng. and Devel. (cert. outstanding service 1982, editor Los Angeles Interchange newsletter), So. Calif. Judges Assn., Assn. Disciple Musicians, All-Am. Judges Assn., Western States Judges Assn., Calif. State U., Long Beach Alumni Assn. Club: Nanka Hiroshima Kenjinkai. Columnist Drum Corps News, contbr. articles to various gen. interest publs. Home: 11139 Loch Avon Dr Whittier CA 90606 Office: 2000 E El Segundo Blvd El Segundo CA 90245

KANENWISHER, GARY LOUIS, financial executive; b. Spokane, Wash., Aug. 10, 1941; s. Ben Kanenwisher and Verna Marie (Graham) Kanenwisher Young; m. Gloria Louisa Lotz, Feb., 1985; children—Glen, Janice, Patricia. B.A., Cen. Wash. State Coll., 1969. C.P.A. Staff accountant Arthur Young and Co., Seattle, 1969-72; exec. asst. Pacific Trail, Inc., Seattle, 1972-78, v.p. fin., 1978—. Served with U.S. Army, 1961-64, Korea. Republican. Office: Pacific Trail Inc 1310 Mercer St Box C19023 Seattle WA 98109

KANG, HEE CHOL, research chemist; b. Yangju, Republic of Korea, Aug. 15, 1948; came to U.S., 1978; s. Youngkun Kang and Kumdan Kim; m. Kwang Yee Kim, Jan. 14, 1976; 1 child: Dae-Wha. BS, Seoul (Republic of Korea) Nat. U., 1972; PhD, U. Oreg., 1982. Researcher Song-Won Ind. Co., Ltd., Pusan, Republic of Korea, 1976-78; teaching and research asst. U. Oreg., Eugene, 1978-82, research assoc., 1982-86, instr., 1985-86; research chemist Molecular Probes, Inc., Eugene, 1986—. Contbr. articles to profl. jours. Served to lt. Republic of Korea Air Force, 1972-76. Mem. Am. Chem. Soc., Korean Scientists and Engrs. Assn. Am., Inc. Avocations: swimming, tennis, hiking. Home: 485 Kingswood Eugene OR 97405 Office: Molecular Probes Inc 4849 Pitchford Ave Eugene OR 97402

KANGAS, MARTTI Y.O., textile engineer; b. Kajaani, Finland, Oct. 31, 1945; came to U.S., 1978; s. Yrjö and Meimi L. (Nikupeteri) K.; m. Marjatta Fanny Toivonen, June 19, 1970; children: Miikka Matias, Marcus Kristian. MSc, Helsinki (Finland) Tech. U., Otaniemi, 1971. Registered profl. engr., Wash. Supt. Veitsiluoto (Finland) Oy, 1970-73, Myllykoski (Finland) Oy, 1973-74; project mgr. Paperinkeräys Oy, Helsinki, Finland, 1974-75, tech. dir. Keräyskuitu Oy, Karhula, Finland, 1975-78; sr. project engr. Ekono, Inc., Bellevue, Wash., 1978-86; prin. Info Cons., Bellevue, 1986—. Patentee in field. Chmn. constitution com. Finnish Bethel Luth. Ch., Seattle, 1985. Mem. AAAS, NSPE, Engring. Soc. Finland, Tech. Assn. Pulp and Paper Industry, Finnish Paper Engrs. Assn. Avocations: outdoor activities, computers.

KANIECKI, DONALD ALAN, accountant; b. Buffalo, Oct. 30, 1952; s. Thaddeus A. and Lorraine V. (Piotrowski) K. B.S., Canisius Coll., 1974; M.B.A., SUNY, 1977. C.P.A., N.Y., Colo. Staff and sr. acct. Seidman & Seidman, Buffalo, 1974-77; policy and control analyst Anaconda Co., Denver, 1978-79; pres., owner Donald A. Kaniecki, PC, Boulder, Colo., 1979—; dir. Diverse Investments Inc., Denver. Treas. Rocky Mountain Inventors Congress, Denver, 1984. Mem. Am. Inst. C.P.A.s, Colo. Soc. C.P.A.s, Boulder C. of C. Club: Optimist (pres. 1983, dir. 1982—) (Boulder). Office: Donald A Kaniecki PC 2355 Canyon Blvd Boulder CO 80302

KANIECKI, MICHAEL JOSEPH, S.J., bishop; b. Detroit, Apr. 13, 1935; s. Stanley Joseph and Julia Marie (Konjora) K. BA, Gonzaga U., 1958, MA in Philosophy, 1960; MA in Theology, St. Mary's, Halifax, Can., 1966. Ordained priest, 1965; consecrated bishop, 1984. Missionary Alaska, 1960-83; coadjutor bishop Diocese of Fairbanks, Alaska, 1984-85, bishop, 1985—. Address: 1316 Peger Rd Fairbanks AK 99709

KANNA, ART ALLAN, educator; b. Vormsi, Estonia, Mar. 31, 1939; s. Edward Johannes and Svea Linnea (Ekebom) K.; m. Helene Patricia Del Valle, Aug. 15, 1958 (div. Oct. 1961); 1 child, Arvo; m. Donna Elaine Edsell, Ap. 7, 1963; 1 child, Jeanette Elaine. BS in Chemistry, So. Missionary Coll., 1969; postgrad., Loma Linda U. Lithographer Pacific Press Pub. Assn., Mountain View, Calif., 1960-63; sci. tchr. Jacksonville (Fla.) Jr. Acad., 1969-71; head sci. dept. San Gabriel (Calif.) Acad., 1971-78, Hawaiian Mission Acad., 1979—. Served with U.S. Army, 1963-65. Recipient Cert. of Achievement Dept. of the Army, 1965, Cert. of Merit, Am. Assn. of Tchrs. of German, 1967, Outstanding Secondary Educator award Outstanding Secondary Educators of Am., 1973. Mem. Am. Chem. Soc., Nat. Sci. Tchrs. Assn. Seventh Day Adventist. Avocations: backpacking, photography, mechanics. Home: 1502 Pensacola St Honolulu HI 96822 Office: Hawaiian Mission Acad 1438 Pensacola St Honolulu HI 96822

KANNBERG, LANDIS DEE, research engineer; b. Spokane, Wash., Feb. 6, 1950; s. Walter Arthur Kannberg and Ethel Grace (Tweden) Nelson; m. Margaret Ann Monson, June 14, 1975; children: Kerrie Beth, Peter Kenneth. BSME, Gonzaga U., 1972; PhDME, Oreg. State U., 1976. Research engr. Battelle N.W. Labs., Richland, Wash., 1976—, mgr. undergound storage, 1982—. Contbr. articles to sci. jours. Mem. ASME (assoc., tech. com. chmn. 1985-86, div. exec. com. 1987—). Democrat. Lutheran. Avocations: sailing, golf, tennis, woodworking. Home: 1720 Widgeon Ct West Richland WA 99352 Office: Battelle Pacific NW Labs Battelle Blvd Richland WA 99352

KANSA, EDWARD JOHN, computational physicist; b. Youngstown, Ohio, Sept. 27, 1942; s. John and Ann (Cipa) K.; m. Kristine A. Masic, June 22, 1968; 1 child: Eric C. BS, U. Detroit, 1964; PhD, Vanderbilt U., 1972. Physicist U.S. Bur. of Mines, Pitts., 1971-80; computer physicist Lawrence Livermore (Calif.) Nat. Lab., 1980—. Contbr. articles to profl. jours.; mem. internat. adv. bd. Advances in Hyperbolic Equations Jour. Cub scout master Boy Scouts Am., Livermore, 1981-82; pres. Livermore Gifted and Talented Students, 1981-83. Fellow NDEA, 1964-67; grantee NATO, 1967. Mem. Livermore Valley Coin Club, Am. Phys. Soc., Soc. Indsl. and Applied Math., Sigma Xi. Democrat. Roman Catholic. Avocations: coin collecting, reading, swimming, biking. Home: 5218 Theresa Way Livermore CA 94550

KANTER, JAY, film company executive; b. 1927. Began career with MCA, Inc.; then pres. First Artists Prodn. Co., Ltd.; v.p. prodn. 20th Century-Fox, 1975-76, sr. v.p. worldwide prodns., 1976-79; v.p. The Ladd Co., 1979-84; pres. worldwide prodns. motion picture div. MGM-United Artists Entertainment Co., 1984-85; pres. worldwide prodns. United Artists Corp., from 1985; now pres. MGM Film Co. Office: Metro-Goldwyn-Mayer Film Co Office of the Pres 10000 Washington Blvd Culver City CA 90232 *

KANTZ, MELVIN ROY, research chemist; b. Phila., Sept. 26, 1940; s. Philip and Mildred (Garnick) K.; children: Scott, Matthew , Barnett, Eric; m. Kathleen Eleanor Fulcher, Jan. 17, 1981. AB in Chemistry, Temple U., 1963; MS in Chemistry, U. Dayton, 1968; PhD in Materials Engring., Drexel U., 1975. Research chemist Shell Devel. Co., Woodbury, N.J., 1966-75; mgr. materials engring. Solar Industries Inc., Manasquan, N.J., 1979-82; supr. research Congoleum Corp., Trenton, N.J., 1982-83; dir. research and devel. Composites div. Ferro Corp., Culver City, Calif., 1983—; cons. in field, Cherry Hill, N.J., 1975-79. Contbr. articles to profl. jours.; inventor tangent fitter. Crisis intervention counselor, dir. tng., bd. dirs. CONTACT 609, Cherry Hill, 1977-81. Fellow Am. Inst. Chemists; mem. Am. Chem. Soc., Soc. Plastics Engrs., Soc. Advancement Materials and Process Engring., Suppliers Advanced Composite Materials Assn. (chmn. tech. com. 1985—). Republican. Jewish. Avocations: piano, bridge, travelling. Home: 6911 Septimo St Long Beach CA 90815 Office: Ferro Corp Composites Div 5915 Rodeo Rd Los Angeles CA 90016

KANURY, ANJANEYA MURTY, mechanical engineering educator; b. Kavutaram, India, Aug. 28, 1940; came to U.S., 1961; s. Seshayya and Punnamma (Vellanki) K.; M. Kathleen Ann Marie Scheurer, Oct. 11, 1969; children: Sesh Marshall and Perry Ananth. BE with honors, Andhra U., Waltair, A.P., India, 1961; MS, U. Minn., 1963, PhD, 1968. Sr. research scientist F.M. Research Corp., Norwood, Mass., 1969-73; sr. mech. engr. Stanford Research Inst., Menlo Park, Calif., 1973-75; assoc. prof. U. Notre Dame, Ind., 1975-84; prof. Oreg. State U., Corvallis, 1985—; cons. various orgns., 1973—. Author: Introduction to Combustion, 1975; me. editorial bd. Jour. Fire Safety, 1979—; contbr. numerous tech. articles in combustion and heat transfer to profl. jours. Recipient Western Electric Fund award, 1982, Outstanding Tchr. award Notre Dame Coll. Engring., 1980, Faculty award Notre Dame dept. aerospace and mech. engring, 1983, numerous research grants. Mem. Combustion Inst., Am. Soc. Mech. Engrs. (K-19 com. on environ. heat transfer 1981-84), Am. Soc. Engring. Educators, Sigma Xi, Pi Tau Sigma. Avocations: nature, woodworking, writing. Office: Oreg State U Dept Mech Engring Corvallis OR 97331

KAO, CHENG CHI, electronics executive; b. Taipei, Taiwan, Republic of China, Aug. 3, 1941; s. Chin Wu and Su Chin (Wu) K.; m. Susan Lin, July 4, 1970; children: Antonia Hueilan, Albert Chengwei, Helen Siaolan. BS, Taiwan U., 1963; AM, Harvard U., 1965, PhD, 1969. Research fellow Harvard U., Cambridge, Mass., 1969-70; scientist Xerox Corp., Webster, N.Y., 1970-75; mgr. Internat. Materials Research, Inc., Santa Clara, Calif., 1976-78; exec. v.p. President Enterprises Corp., Tainan, Taiwan, 1979-85; pres. Kolyn Enterprises Corp., Los Altos, Calif., 1979—. Contbr. articles to profl. jours. Bd. dirs. Taipei Am. Sch., 1980-82. Mem. IEEE, Chinese Inst. Elec. Engring. (bd. dirs. 1982-85), Sigma Xi. Club: Am. in China (Taipei), Palo Alto Hills Golf and Country. Avocations: jogging, golf. Office: Kolyn Enterprises Corp 4962 El Camino Real Suite 119 Los Altos CA 94022

KAO, FA TEN, education researcher; b. Hankow, Peoples Republic of China, Apr. 20, 1934; came to U.S., 1956; s. Ling-mai and Hang-seng (Feng) K.; m. Betty Chia-mai Tang, Dec. 17, 1960; 1 child, Alan. PhD, U. Minn., 1964. Instr. U. Colo. Med. Ctr., Denver, 1965-67, asst. prof., 1967-70, assoc. prof., 1970-81; prof. Health Scis. Ctr, Denver, 1981—; sr. fellow Eleanor Roosevelt Inst. for Cancer Research, Denver, 1965—; vis. scientist, Oxford U., Eng., 1973-74; research scientist European Molecular Biology Lab., Heidelberg, Fed. Repubic of Germany, 1985. Contbr. articles to profl. jours. Mem. Genetics Soc. Am., Am. Soc. Human Genetics, Am. Soc. Cell Biology, Am. Assn. Cancer Research, Tissue Culture Assn., AAAS. Home: 305 Leyden St Denver CO 80220 Office: Eleanor Roosevelt Inst Cancer Research 1899 Gaylord St Denver CO 80206

KAO, RICHARD HSIUNG-FEI, marketing educator; b. Hupei, Republic of China, June 1, 1941; s. Yuh H. and Yin (Wu) K.; m. Nancy Wen-Bih, Sept. 6, 1969; 1 child, Yuh-Ting. B.B.A., Nat. Chengchi U., 1964; M.B.A., Mich. State U., 1971; Ph.D. in Bus. Adminstrn., U. Mich., 1978. Assoc. dir. Metal Indsl. Research Labs., Taipei, Taiwan, 1971-75; prof. Nat. Chengchi U., Taipei, Taiwan, 1978-80; from assoc. prof. to prof. mktg. Calif. State U.-Los Angeles, 1981—. Author: Dynamic Marketing, 1985. Mem. Am. Mktg. Assn., Acad. Internat. Bus., Acad. Mktg. Sci., Chinese Inst. Mgmt. Sci., Beta Gamma Sigma (hon.). Office: 5151 State University Dr Los Angeles CA 90032

KAPLAN, GARY, executive recruiter; b. Phila., Aug. 14, 1939; s. Morris and Minnie (Leve) K.; m. Linda Ann Wilson, May 30, 1968; children: Michael Warren, Marc Jonathan, Jeffrey Russell. B.A. in Polit. Sci., Pa. State U., 1961. Tchr. biology N.E. High Sch., Phila., 1962-63; coll. employment rep. Bell Telephone Labs., Murray Hill, N.J., 1966-67; supr. recruitment and placement Univac, Blue Bell, Pa., 1967-69; pres. Electronic Systems Personnel, Phila., 1969-70; staff selection rep. Booz, Allen & Hamilton, N.Y.C., 1970-72; mgr. exec. recruitment M&T Chems., Rahway, N.J., 1972-74; dir. exec. recruitment IU Internat. Mgmt. Corp., Phila., 1974-78; v.p. personnel Crocker Bank, Los Angeles, 1978-79; mng. v.p. ptnr. western region Korn-Ferry Internat., Los Angeles, 1979-85; pres. Gary Kaplan & Assocs., Pasadena, Calif., 1985—. Mgmt. columnist, Radio and Records newspaper. Chmn. bd. dirs. Vis. Nurse Assn., Los Angeles. Served to capt. Adj. Gen. Corps., U.S. Army, 1963-66. Mem. Hollywood Radio and TV Soc. Home: 5150 Solliden Ln La Canada CA 91011 Office: Gary Kaplan & Assocs 201 S Lake Ave Pasadena CA 91101

KAPLAN, HESH J., botanist, agricultural consultant; b. Bklyn., Feb. 16, 1933; s. Samuel Ray and Estelle Beatrice (Schuman) K.; m. Meredith McGovney, Oct. 14, 1962; children: Sarah, Esther, Sharon, Rachel. Student, Cornell U., 1950-52; BA in Indsl. Engring., Ga. Inst. Tech., 1954; MA in Bus. Econs., Claremont Grad. Sch., 1966; PhD, Oreg. State U., 1977. Indsl. engr. Westinghouse Electric, Lester, Pa., 1954-55; methods engr. Mergenthaler Linotype, Bklyn., 1955-57; reliability engr. Gen. Dynamics Corp., Pomona, Calif., 1959-61; product assurance mgr. Aerojet Gen. Corp., Tacoma, Wash., 1961-72; instr. Oreg. State U., Corvallis, 1973-77; ops. mgr. Pennwalt Corp., Monrovia, Calif., 1978-85; cons. FAO, Rome, 1986—; bd. dirs. Calif. Citrus Quality Council, Claremont, 1980-85. Author: (book chpt.) Improving Saleability, 1986; patentee in field; contbr. articles to profl. jours. Congl. candidate Peace and Freedom Party, Claremont, 1970; mem. planning com. Benton County, Kings Valley, Oreg., 1975-76; leader Oregon 4H Club, Corvallis, 1973-78, supr. Benton County 4H, Corvallis, 1974-78. Served with U.S. Army, 1957-59. Recipient Tech. Excellence award Pennwalt Corp., 1985, Pres. award Fla. State Hort. Soc., 1979. Mem. AAAS, Am. Phytopath. Soc., Am. Soc. Hort. Sci., Groupement Internationl des Association Nationales de Fabricants de Produits Agrochimiques (del. 1984-85). Jewish. Avocations: camping, gardening, racquetball. Home and Office: 725 Santa Barbara Dr Claremont CA 91711

KAPLAN, IRVING EUGENE, human ecologist, psychologist; b. Phila., May 1, 1926; s. Abraham and Bertha (Posner) K.; married Harriet Bromberg, Sept. 29, 1951; children: Addie Eve, Meryl Denise. BS, L.I. U., 1950; MA, New Sch. Social Research, 1953; PhD, U.S. Internat. U., 1971. Lic. psychologist, Calif. Depth interviewer Dr. Ernest Dichter, N.Y.C., 1950-52; employment interviewer N.Y. State Employment Service, N.Y.C., 1952-56; research, program dir. U.S. Naval Personnel Research Activity, San Diego, 1957-66; cons. psychologist San Diego, 1957—, human ecologist, designer, 1962—; cons., writer Ctr. for Study Democracy, Santa Barbara, Calif., 1964-78, UN Law of Sea, N.Y.C. and Jamaica, N.Y., 1970—, Found. Reshaping the Internat. Order, Rotterdam, The Netherlands, 1980-82, UN Commn. Peaceful Uses of Outer Space, N.Y.C. and Vienna, Austria, 1982, Sri Lanka Inst. Advanced Study, 1982. Contbr. articles to profl. jours. Served with USN, 1944-46. Mem. AAAS, Am. Geophys. Union, Am. Psychol. Assn. Home: 3121 Beech St San Diego CA 92102 Office: New Life Med Group Div Biomed Inc 3023 Bunker Hill St San Diego CA 92109

KAPLAN, JOSEPH HAROLD, urologist; b. Chgo., Jan. 23, 1912; m. Shirley Busch; children: Lynda Kaplan Estrin, Ohad E., Marcia Kaplan Koch. BS, U. Ill., 1935, MD, 1938; MS in Urology, U. Minn., 1950. Cert. Am. Bd. Urology. Intern Cook County Gen. Hosp., Chgo., 1938-39; fellow in urology May Found., Rochester, Minn., 1947-50, asstistantship, 1950; assoc. clin. prof. U. So. Calif., Los Angeles, 1950-87, clin. prof. emeritus, 1987—; appointment. to hosp. staffs include Los Angeles County-U. So. Calif. Med. Ctr., Cedars Sinai Med. Ctr., Los Angeles, chief of staff, 1977-78, bd. trustees, 1977-83; pres. Univ. Urologic Forum, 1975; mem. acad. adv. council Consortium for Continuing Med. Edn. and Research. Contbr. numerous articles to profl. jours.; films. Mem. AMA, ACS, Calif. Med. Assn., Los Angeles County Med. Assn., Los Angeles Urol. Soc., Am. Urol. Assn., Soc. Urologie Internat., Priestly Soc., Mayo Clinic Urologic Alumni Assn. (pres. 1975), Sigma Xi. Home: 8635 W 3d St Suite 1060W Los Angeles CA 90048

KAPLAN, JOSEPH M., association executive; b. Cleve., May 29, 1914; s. Edward Kaplan and Mamie Krislove; m. Henzi Lurie, Mar. 30, 1941; children: Paul, Drew. AB, UCLA, 1935; MA in Traffic Engring., Harvard U., 1938. Cert. assn. exec., hazard control mgr. With Greater Los Angeles chpt. Nat. Safety Council, 1939—, pres., 1979—; cons. White House Conf. on Traffic Safety. Recipient award of honor Assn. Safety Council Execs., 1973; named Assn. Exec. of Yr., So. Calif. Soc. Assn. Execs., 1979. Mem. Am. Soc. Assn. Execs. (Key award 1974), Am. Soc. Safety Engrs., Inst. Traffic Engrs. Lodge: Rotary. Avocations: swimming, reading. Office: Los Angeles Nat Safety Council 616 S Westmoreland Ave Los Angeles CA 90005

KAPLAN, MAX, ophthalmologist; b. Winslow, Ind., Mar. 31, 1911; s. David Louis and Kate (Wolf) K.; m. Ethel Fishman, Jan. 28, 1940; children: David William, Catherine Ellen Levinson. AB, U. Rochester, 1933; MD, U. Ill., Chgo., 1937; postgrad., U. Ill., 1950. Diplomate Am. Bd. Pediatrics. Intern St. Anthony De Padua Hosp., Chgo., 1937; intern Michael Reese Hosp., Chgo., 1938-39, asst. resident in pediatrics, 1939-40; resident in pediatrics Children's div. Cook County Hosp., Chgo., 1940; resident Ill. Eye-Ear Infirmary, Chgo., 1950-52; asst. med. supt. children's div. Cook County Hosp., Chgo., 1941-42; pvt. practice medicine specializing in pediatrics Denver, 1946-50, pvt. practice medicine specializing in ophthalmology, 1952—; assoc. clin. prof. U. Colo. Dept. Pediatrics, 1946—, Dept. Ophthalmology, 1952—; acting med. dir. Childrens Hosp., Denver, 1978-79. Contbr. articles to profl. jours.; contbr. chpts. to books. Served to lt. col. Med. Corps, U.S. Army, 1942-46. Fellow Am. Acad. Pediatrics; mem. Am. Acad. Ophthalmology, AMA, Colo. Ophthal. Soc., Common Cause, Physicians for Social Responsibility, ACLU. Democrat. Jewish. Avocations: tennis, photography. Home: 3066 S St Paul St Denver CO 80210

KAPLAN, ROBERT B., linguistics educator, consultant, researcher; b. N.Y.C., Sept. 20, 1929; s. Emanuel B. and Natalie K.; m. Audrey A. Lien, Apr. 21, 1951; children—Robin Ann Kaplan Gibson, Lisa Kaplan Morris, Robert Allen. Student, Champlain Coll., 1947-48, Syracuse U., 1948-49; B.A., Willamette U., 1952; M.A., U. So. Calif., 1957, Ph.D., 1962. Teaching asst. U. So. Calif., Los Angeles, 1955-57, instr. coordinator, asst. prof. English communication program for fgn. students, 1965-72, assoc. prof., dir. English communication program for fgn. students, 1972-76, assoc. dean continuing edn., prof. applied linguistics, 1976—, dir. Am. Lang. Inst., 1986—; instr. U. Oreg., 1957-60; cons. field service program Nat. Assn. Fgn. Student Affairs, 1964—. Author: Reading and Rhetoric: A Reader, 1963; (with V. Tufte, P. Cook and J. Aurbach) Transformational Grammar: A Guide for Teachers, 1968; (with R.D. Schoesler) Learning English Through Typewriting, 1969; The Anatomy of Rhetoric: Prolegomena to a Functional Theory of Rhetoric, 1971; On the Scope of Applied Linguistics, 1980; The Language Needs of Migrant Workers, 1980; (with P. Shaw) Exploring Academic English, 1984; (with U. Connor) Writing Across Languages: Analysis of L2 Text, 1987; contbr. articles to profl. jours., U.S. Australia, Brazil, Can., Germany, Holland, Japan, Mexico, N.Z., Philippines and Singapore; contbr. notes, revs. to profl. jours. U.S. and abroad. Editor-in-chief Ann. Rev. Applied Linguistics, 1980—. Served with inf. U.S. Army, Korea. Fulbright sr. scholar, Australia, 1978, Hong Kong, 1986. Mem. Am. Anthrop. Assn., AAAS, Am. Assn. Applied Linguistics, AAUP, Assn. Internationale de Linguistique Applique, Assn. Internationale Pour La Researche et La Diffusion Des Methodes Audio-Visuelles et Structuro-Globales, Assn. Tchrs. English as Second Lang., Calif. Assn. Tchrs. English to Speakers Other Langs., Can. Council Tchrs. English, Nat. Assn. Fgn. Student Affairs (nat. pres. 1983-84), Linguistics Soc. Am. Office: Dept Linguistics U So Calif Los Angeles CA 90089-1693

KAPLAN, ROBERT MALCOLM, psychology educator; b. San Diego, Oct. 26, 1947; s. Oscar Joel and Rose (Zankan) K.; m. Catherine J. Atkins; children—Cameron Maxwell, Seth William. A.B. in Psychology, San Diego State U., 1969; M.A., U. Calif.-Riverside, 1970, Ph.D., 1972. Lic. psychologist, Calif. Teaching asst. U. Calif.-Riverside, 1969-72, vis. assoc. prof. psychology, 1977-78; sr. research assoc. Am. Inst. for Research, Palo Alto, Calif., 1972-73; asst. prof. in residence U. Calif.-San Diego, 1973, asst. research psychologist and cons. dept. community medicine div. health policy, assoc. adj. prof., 1980-86, prof., 1986—; from asst. prof. to prof. psychology San Diego State U., 1974—; dir. Ctr. for Behavioral Medicine, San Diego State U.; acting chief div. health care springs, Sch. Medicine, U. Calif., San. Diego, 1987—; dir. NATO Advanced Research Workshop on Behavioral Epidemiology and Disease Prevention; mem. health services research study sect. Nat. Ctr. Health Services Research 1981-85; cons., lectr. in field. Author: (with H. Harari) Social Psychology: Basic and applied, 1982; (with D.P. Saccuzzo) Psychological Testing: Principles, Applications and Issues, 1982, Clinical Psychology, 1984; (with M.H. Criqui) Behavioral Epidemiology and Disease Prevention, 1985; Basic Statistics for the Behavioral Sciences, 1987; also numerous articles, chpts. in books; editor: (with others) Aggression in Children and Youth, 1984. Bd. dirs. Am. Lung Assn., Am. Diabetes Assn. Faculty fellow San Diego State U., 1977; epidemiology fellow Am. Heart Assn., 1983; recipient Career Devel. award NIH, 1981-82, Alumni and Assocs. Disting. Faculty award San Diego State U., 1982, citation San Diego City Council, 1982, Exceptional Merit service award San Diego State U., 1984. Fellow Am. Psychol. Assn.; mem. Am. Pub. Health Assn., Soc. for Personality and Social Psychology, Western Psychol. Assn., AAAS (exec. com. 1978-82), Soc. for Psychol. Study Social Issues, Assn. for Advancement Behavior Therapy, Soc. for Exptl. Social Psychology. Office: San Diego State U Ctr for Behavioral Medicine San Diego CA 92182 also: U Calif-San Diego Dept Community Medicine M-022 Sch of Medicine La Jolla CA 92093

KAPLANSKY, IRVING, educator, mathematician, research institute director; b. Toronto, Ont., Can., Mar. 22, 1917; came to U.S., 1940, naturalized, 1955; s. Samuel and Anna (Zuckerman) K.; m. Rachelle Brenner, Mar. 16, 1951; children—Steven, Daniel, Lucille. B.A., U. Toronto, 1938, M.A., 1939; Ph.D., Harvard, 1941; LL.D. (hon.), Queen's U., 1969. Instr. math. Harvard, 1941-44; mem. faculty U. Chgo., 1945-84, prof. math., 1956-84, chmn. dept., 1962-67, George Herbert Mead Distinguished Service prof. math., 1969-84; dir. Math. Scis. Research Inst., Berkeley, Calif., 1984—; Mem. exec. com. div. math. NRC, 1959-62. Author books, tech. papers. Mem. Nat. Acad. Scis., Am. Math. Soc. (pres. 1985-86). Office: Math Scis Research Inst 1000 Centennial Dr Berkeley CA 94720

KAPPAS, JOHN G., hypnotist, institute director; b. Chgo., Sept. 11, 1925; s. George John and Frances (Anton) K. B.A. in Psychology, Antioch Coll., 1976; M.A., Lindenwood Coll., 1978; Ph.D., Internat. Coll., 1979. Lic. marriage counselor; hypnosis cert. Counselor, instr., dir. Hypnosis Soc. Am., Los Angeles, 1963-67, Self-Improvement Soc., Los Angeles, 1967-68; counselor, instr., dir. Hypnosis Motivation Inst., Van Nuys, Calif., 1968—. Served with USN, 1941-45. Mem. Am. Psychol. Assn., Can. Psychol. Assn., Marital Therapists Union (charter), Hypnotists Union (founder Local 472, past pres., now tech. advisor), Hypnotists Exam. Council Calif. (past v.p., tech. advisor), Counselors on Alcholism and Related Dependencies (cert. addictions counselor), Am. Hypnosis Assn. (founder, past pres., now tech. advisor), Am. Assn. Sex Educators, Counselors and Therapists. Author: Your Sexual Personality, 1975; The Professional Hypnotism Manual, 1975; Success Is Not an Accident, The Mental Bank Concept, 1982; Improve Your Sex Life through Self-Hypnosis, 1984. Office: Hypnosis Motivation Inst 14640 Victory Blvd Suite 210 Van Nuys CA 91401

KARABEL, JEROME BERNARD, sociologist, educator; b. Phila., May 20, 1950; s. Henry Leon and Dorothy (Forstein) K. BA, Harvard U., 1972, PhD, 1977; postgrad., Nuffield Coll., Oxford, Eng., 1972-73, Ecole Pratique des Hautes Etudes, Paris, 1974-75. Sr. research assoc. Huron Inst., Cambridge, Mass., 1977-84; asst. prof. sociology U. Calif., Berkeley, 1984-86, assoc. prof., 1986—; cons. Nat. Inst. Edn., Washington, 1976-80. Author and co-editor: Power and Ideology in Education, 1977; editorial cons. Oxford U. Press, N.Y.C., 1977—; sr. editor: Theory and Society, 1978—; assoc. editor: Sociology of Edn., 1982-85; contbr. articles to profl. jours. Grantee Nat. Inst. Edn., 1977-81, NSF, 1972-75, 81-87, Ford Found., 1981-83. Mem. Am. Sociol. Assn. (council mem. soc. edn. sect. 1984—), Soc. Study Social Problems, Phi Beta Kappa. Home: 2314 1/2 Blake St Berkeley CA 94704 Office: U Calif Dept Sociology Berkeley CA 94720

KARAKEY, SHERRY JOANNE, aerospace manufacturing company executive; b. Wendall, Idaho, Apr. 16, 1942; d. John Donald and Vera Ella (Frost) Kingery; m. James Joseph Dalgleish, Oct. 6, 1973 (div. 1980); children: Artist Roxanne, Buddy (George II), Kami JoAnne, Launi JoElla. Student, Ariz. State U., 1960. Corp. sec., treas. Karbel Metals Co., Phoenix, 1963-67; sec. to pub. Scottsdale (Ariz.) Daily Progress, 1969-72; with D-Velco Mfg. of Ariz., Phoenix, 1959-62, dir., exec. v.p., sec., treas., 1972—. Mem. Nat. Rep. Com. Mem. Nat. Tool and Die Assn. Office: D-Velco Mfg Ariz 401 S 36th St Phoenix AZ 85034

KARBY, MICHAEL EDWARD, architectural designer, planner; b. San Francisco, June 20, 1956; s. Warren Edward and Marie Etoyal (Stoddart) K.; m. Beverly Marie Tharp, Feb. 28, 1981; 1 child: Evelyn Amelia. AA, Fresno City Coll., 1978; student, Calif. Poly. Inst., Pomona, 1978; BA in Indsl. Arts, Architecture, Calif. State U., Fresno, 1980, MCRP in City and Regional Planning, 1983. Draftsman L. Gene Zellmer AIA, Fresno, 1977-80; designer Armen Dervishian AIA, Fresno, 1981-84; prin. Meka Design/Planning, Fresno, 1984—; design cons. Walter Deissler AIA, Visalia, Calif., 1984—, Stan Stanovich AIA, Orinda, Calif., 1985, Richard Marshall FAIA, San Francisco, 1985. Prin. works include Prototypical Community, Los Cielo, Calif., New Millerton, Calif., China Bay, Calif. Mem. AIA, Am. Mensa Ltd., Am. Planning Assn., Architects, Designers, Planners for Social Responsibility. Avocations: swimming, astronomy, going to the desert. Home and Office: 1445 E Bulldog Ln #201 Fresno CA 93710

KARE, JORDIN T., physicist; b. Ithaca, N.Y., Oct. 24, 1956; s. Morley Richard and Carol (Abramson) K. BS in Physics, MIT, 1978, BSEE, 1978; PhD in Astrophysics, U. Calif., 1984. Research assoc. U. Calif. Space Sci. Lab., Berkeley, 1984-85; physicist Lawrence Livermore Labs., Livermore, Calif., 1985—. Fellow F. & J. Hertz Found. Avocations: reading science fiction. Home: 16264 Saratoga St San Leandro CA 94578 Office: L-278 Lawrence Livermore Nat Labs PO Box 808 Livermore CA 94550

KARIN, SIDNEY, data processing executive; b. Balt., July 8, 1943. BSME, CCNY, 1966; MS in Nuclear Engring., U. Mich., 1967, PhD in Nuclear Engring., 1973. Registered profl. engr., Mich. Computer programmer, nuclear engr. ESZ Assocs., Inc., Ann Arbor, Mich., 1968-72; sr. engr., sect. leader GA Techs., Inc., San Diego, 1973-75; mgr. fusion div. Computer Ctr. GA Techs., Inc., 1975-82, dir. info. systems div., 1982-85; dir. San Diego Supercomputer Ctr. div. GA Techs., Inc., 1985—; NRC panel mem. at Nat. Bur. Standards; tech. adv. panel Sci. Computer Systems, Inc., 1986—; adj. prof. elec. engring. U. Calif., San Diego. Contbr. articles to profl. jours. NDEA fellow, AEC fellow. Mem. AAAS, Assn. for Computing Machinery, IEEE Computer Soc. Avocations: flying, technical rock climbing, motorcycle riding, alpine skiing, reading. Home: 817 Appleridge Encinitas CA 92024 Office: San Diego Supercomputer Ctr GA Technologies Inc PO Box 85608 San Diego CA 92138

KARINEN, ARTHUR ELI, educator; b. Comptche, Cal., Feb. 25, 1919; s. Eli and Anna (Koskelo) K.; m. Florence Irene Wickstrom, Apr. 12, 1946; children—Sandra Jean, Nancy Ruth (Mrs. Ronald Wallace Magnus), Patricia Anna (Mrs. Alan Stanley Hightman), Judith Riika (Mrs. William Arvid Lane). A.B., U. Cal. at Berkeley, 1944, M.A. in Geography, 1948; Ph.D. in Geography, U. Md., 1958. Cartographer OSS, 1942-43; instr. Ohio State U., 1946-47; asst. prof. geography U. Md., 1948-59; prof. geography Calif. State U. at Chico, 1959-86, chmn. dept., 1967-72, prof. emeritus, 1987—; Fulbright lectr. U. Oulu, Finland, 1970; vis. prof. Helsinki (Finland) Sch. Econs., 1979-80. Author: (with others) California: Land of Contrast, rev. 3d edit, 1981. Mem. Assn. Am. Geographers, Am. Congress Surveying and Mapping, Calif. Geog. Soc., Cal. Council Geog. Edn. (pres. 1965-66), Finnish Geog. Soc. (corr.). Presbyn. Home: 834 Arbutus Ave Chico CA 95926 Office: Calif State U Dept Geography Chico CA 95926

KARINEN, JOHN FRANKLIN, oceanographer; b. Lead, S.D., May 2, 1933; s. Albert Matthew and Hilda Gustava (Matson) K.; B.S., Black Hills State Coll., 1957, B.S. in Edn., 1958; M.S., Oreg. State U., 1965; m. Joan Arlene Blanck, Dec. 21, 1966; 1 son, James Albert. Fishery biologist S.D. Dept. Fish and Game, Spearfish, 1958; USPHS trainee fellow Oreg. State U., Corvallis, 1962-65, research project leader, 1965-68; project/program leader NOAA/Nat. Marine Fisheries Service, Auke Bay (Alaska) Lab., 1968-72, program mgr., 1972—; guest lectr. U. Alaska, 1978-79; cons. Nat. Marine Fisheries Service, Alaska Legislature, Atty. Gen. Office; adviser Internat. North Pacific Fisheries Commn., 1969-72, Alaska Council on Sci. and Tech., 1979-80. Served with U.S. Army, 1958-60. Recipient unit citation award NOAA/Nat. Marine Fisheries Service, 1979. Mem. Am. Inst. Fisheries Research Biologists (citizen ambassador for People to People Fisheries Research Del. to East Asia 1985), AAAS, Am. Fisheries Soc., Nat. Shellfisheries Assn., Am. Soc. Limnology and Oceanography, Cousteau Soc., Western Soc. Naturalists, Sigma Xi (asso.). Home: PO Box 210304 Auke Bay AK 99821 Office: Nat Marine Fisheries Service Auke Bay Lab PO Box 210155 Auke Bay AK 99821

KARL, GEORGE, professional basketball coach; b. Penn Hills, Pa., May 12, 1951; m. Cathy Karl; children—Kelci Ryanne, Coby Joseph. Grad., U. N.C., 1973. Guard San Antonio Spurs, NBA, 1973-78, asst. coach, head scout, 1978-80; coach Mont. Golden Nuggets, Continental Basketball Assn., 1980-83; dir. player acquisition Cleve. Cavaliers, 1983-84, coach, 1984-86; head coach Golden State Warriors, Oakland, Calif., 1986—. Named Coach of Yr., Continental Basketball Assn., 1981, 83. Office: care Golden State Warriors Oakland Coliseum Arena Oakland CA 94621 *

KARLEN, CYNTHIA ANN, advertising executive; b. Tucson, Feb. 21, 1959; d. William John and Loretta Delores (Cronin) Grossmiller; m. Paul Andrew Karlen, July 9, 1983. BS in Journalism, Calif. Poly. State U., San Luis Obispo, 1981. Advt. mgr. Trail Blazer Publs., Paso Robles, Calif., 1978-81; account adminstr. J. Walter Thompson, San Francisco, 1981-82; prin. Karlen Design, San Luis Obispo, 1982—. Author various promotional publs.; editor Easy Research Methods, 1980. Office: Karlen Design PO Box 12238 San Luis Obispo CA 93406

KARLESKINT, BARRY MICHAEL, retail store executive; b. Santa Maria, Calif., May 25, 1941; s. John Peter and Mary Alward (Fitzgerald) K.; student Calif. State Poly. U., 1959-62; m. Brenda Signorelli, July 20, 1963; children: Kenneth Brian, Robert Jasen, Ann Marie. Foreman, Landscape Dept., Karleskint's Florist & Nursery, San Luis Obispo, 1962-67; gen. mgr. Landscape Dept., Karleskint-Crum, Inc., San Luis Obispo, Calif., 1969, v.p., 1969, 85—, v.p., retail gen. mgr., 1975, pres., 1980-85, dir., 1967—; pres., dir. Canyon Leasing Co., 1984—; pres. KC Stores Inc., San Luis Obispo, 1985—, also bd. dirs.; instr. San Luis Coastal Sch. Dist. Adult Sch., 1977-78; gen. ptnr. Suburban Assocs.; cons. in field. Mem. organizing com. Obispo Beautiful Assn., 1970; mem. San Luis Obispo City Joint Use Adv. Com., 1985—; pres. Mission-Nativity Parents Assn., 1974-76, mem. sch. bd., 1974-76; pres. Nativity of Our Lady Cath. Ch. Council, 1977; mem. San Luis Obispo City Parks and Recreation Commn., 1981—; com. chmn. 1987—; mem. San Luis Obispo City Tree Com., 1981-84. Served with U.S. Army, 1962, USAR, 1962-66, USNG, 1966-68. Cert. nurseryman, Calif. Mem. Calif. Assn. Nurserymen (chpt. dir. 1978-80), Calif. Landscape Contractor's Assn. (chpt. dir. 1964-66), Calif. Assn. Park and Recreation Commrs. and Bd. Mems., Calif. State Sheriff's Assn., Exec. Assn. San Luis Obispo, Controller's Roundtable San Luis Obispo, Alpha-Micro Users Soc., Roman Catholic. Clubs: San Luis Obispo Swim (pres. 1977-78); KC, Old Mission

Sch. Booster (sec. 1961-63) Home: 623 Jeffrey Dr San Luis Obispo CA 93401 Office: 225 Suburban Rd San Luis Obispo CA 93401

KARLIN, SAMUEL, mathematics educator, researcher; b. Yonova, Poland, June 8, 1924; s. Morris K.; m. Elsie (div.); children—Kenneth, Manuel, Anna. B.S. in Math., Ill. Inst. Tech., 1944; Ph.D. in Math., Princeton U., 1947; D.Sc. (hon.), Technion-Israel Inst. Tech., Haifa, 1985. Instr. math. Calif. Inst. Tech., Pasadena, 1948-49; asst. prof. Calif. Inst. Tech., 1949-52, assoc. prof., 1952-55, prof., 1955-56; vis. asst. prof. Princeton U., N.J., 1950-51; prof. Stanford U., Calif., 1956—; Andrew D. White prof.-at-large Cornell U., 1975-81; Wilks lectr. Princeton U., 1977; pres. Inst. Math. Stats., 1978-79; Commonwealth lectr. U. Mass., 1980; 1st Mahalanobis Meml. Lectr., Indian Statis. Inst., 1983; prin. invited speaker XII Internat. Biometics Meeting, Japan; prin. lectr. Quebec Math. Soc., 1984; adv. dean math. dept. Weizmann Inst. Sci., Israel, 1970-77. Author: Mathematical Methods and Theory in Games, Programming, Economics, Vol. I: Matrix Games, Programming and Mathematical Economics, 1959, Mathematical Methods and Theory in Games, Programming, Economics, Vol. II: The Theory of Infinite Games, 1959, A First Course in Stochastic Processes, 1966, Total Positivity Vol. I, 1968; (with K. Arrow and H. Scarf) Studies in the Mathematical Theory of Inventory and Production, 1958; (with W.J. Sudden) Tchebycheff Systems: With Applications in Analysis and Statistics, 1966; (with H. Taylor) A First Course in Stochastic Processes, 2d edit., 1975, A Second Course in Stochastic Processes, 1980, An Introduction to Stochastic Modeling, 1984; (with C.A. Micchelli, A. Pinkus, I.I. Schoenberg) Studies in Spline Functions and Approximation Theory, 1976; editor: (with E. Nevo) Population Genetics and Ecology, 1976; (with T. Amemiya and L.A. Goodman) Studies in Econometric, Time Series, and Multivariate Statistics, 1983; (with K. Arrow and P. Suppes) Contributions to Mathematical Methods in the Social Sciences, 1960; (with K. Arrow and H. Scarf) Studies in Applied Probability and Management Sciences, 1962; (with S. Lessard) Theoretical Studies on Sex Ratio Evolution, 1986; editor: (with E. Nevo) Evolutionary Processes and Theory, 1986; sr. editor Theoretical Population Biology, Jour. D'Analyse; assoc. editor Jour. Math. Analysis, Lecture Notes in Biomath., Jour. Applied Probability, Jour. Multivariate Analysis, Jour. Approximation Theory, SIAM Jour. Math. Analysis, Jour. Linear Algebra, Computers and Math. with Applications, Ency. of Math. and Its Applications, Advanced in Applied Math.; contbr. articles to profl. jours. Recipient Lester R. Ford award Am. Math. Monthly, 1973, Robert Grimmett Chair Math., Stanford U., 1978, The John Von Neumann Theory prize, 1987; Proctor fellow, 1945, Bateman Research fellow, 1947-48; fellow Guggenheim Found., 1959-60, NSF, 1960-61; Wald lectr., 1957. Fellow Internat. Statis. Inst., Inst. Math. Stats., AAAS; mem. Am. Math. Soc., Am. Acad. Arts and Scis., Nat. Acad. Scis. (award in applied math. 1973), Am. Soc. Human Genetics, Genetic Soc. Am., Am. Naturalist Soc. Office: Stanford Univ Bldg 380 Stanford CA 94305

KARLTON, LAWRENCE K., federal judge; b. Bklyn., May 28, 1935; s. Aaron Katz and Sylvia (Meltzer) K.; m. Mychelle Stiebel, Sept. 7, 1958. Student, Washington Sq. Coll.; LL.B., Columbia U., 1958. Bar: Fla. 1958, Calif. 1962. Acting legal officer Sacramento Army Depot, Dept. Army, Sacramento, 1959-60; civilian legal officer Sacramento Army Depot, Dept. Army, 1960-62; individual practice law Sacramento, 1962-64; mem. firm Abbott, Karlton & White, 1964, Karlton & Blease, until 1971, Karlton, Blease & Vanderlaan, 1971-76; judge Calif. Superior Ct. for Sacramento County, 1976-79; judge U.S. Dist. Ct., Sacramento, 1979—, now chief judge. Co-chmn. Central Calif. council B'nai B'rith Anit-Defamation League Commn., 1964-65; treas. Sacramento Jewish Community Relations Council, chmn., 1967-68. Mem. Am. Bar Assn., Sacramento County Bar Assn. Club: B'nai B'rith (past pres.). Office: 2012 US Courthouse 650 Capitol Mall Sacramento CA 95814

KARO, ARNOLD MITCHELL, physicist; b. Wayne, Nebr., May 14, 1928; s. Henry Arnold and Ethel Leila (Mitchell) Maynard; m. Daniella Thea Cassvan, July 1, 1966; children: Barbara Melissa, Stephen Arnold. BS in Chemistry, Stanford U., 1949, BS in Physics, 1949; PhD in Chem. Physics, MIT, 1953. Teaching fellow MIT, Cambridge, 1949-51; staff physicist Lincoln Lab., Lexington, Mass., 1952; teaching assoc. dept. chemistry U. Utah, Salt Lake City, 1953-54; research assoc. Solid State and Molecular Theory Group, MIT, Cambridge, 1955-58; vis. research scientist European Ctr. Atomic and Molecular Theory U. Paris, Orsay, France, 1975; sr. scientist U. Calif. Lawrence Livermore Nat. Lab., 1958—; cons. in field. Author: (with others) The Lattice Dynamics and Statics of Alkali Halide Crystals, 1979. Contbr. articles to profl. jours. Mem. rev. com. City Pleasanton, Calif., 1973-74. Served with Chem. Corps AUS, 1953-55. Nat. Coffin fellow Gen. Electric Co., 1951-52. Fellow Am. Phys. Soc., AAAS, Am. Inst. Chemistry, N.Y. Acad. Scis.; mem. Calif. Inst. Chemists, (charter), Calif. Acad. Scis., Am. Chem. Soc., Phi Theta Kappa, Phi Lambda Upsilon, Sigma Xi. Presbyterian.

KARP, CHERYL L., psychologist; b. San Francisco, July 19, 1946; d. Vernon Arthur and Kathleen Marian (Taylor) Davison; B.A., U. Ariz., 1968, M.Ed., 1972, Ph.D., 1978; m. Leonard Irwin Karp, June 10, 1967; children—Alan, David (dec.), Scott. With Catalina Psychologists, Tucson, 1980—;lectr. developmental psychology and psychology of learning U. Ariz., Tucson, 1979-80; pvt. practice psychology, Tucson, 1980—; police psychologist Dept. Pub. Safety, Tucson, 1981—; research cons. U. Ariz., Tucson, 1978-80; trainer behavior cons. Dept. Econ. Security, 1978-80; speaker Am. Periodontics Assn. Nat. Conv., 1986, Ariz. Assn. of Family and Conciliation Court Fall Inst., 1986, Family Law Inst., Vail, Colo., 1986. Mem. Young Jewish Leadership Council, 1970-72; div. co-chmn. Combined Jewish Appeal, 1974; bd. dirs. Brewster Home Aux., 1973-75, Brandeis U. Nat. Women's Com., 1970-74; sec. Pima County Bar Aux., 1971-72. Mem. Am. Psychol. Assn., Am. Soc. Clin. Hypnosis, Internat. Soc. Hypnosis, Assn. Advancement of Behavior Therapy, Ariz. State Psychol. Assn. (membership/pub. info. chmn. 1981-82, sec. 1982-84, treas. 1984-86, Meritorious Achievement award 1981), COPE (bd. dirs.), So. Ariz. Psychol. Assn., Ariz. Council Attys. for Children, Inc., So. Ariz. Roadrunners Club. Democrat. Jewish. Clubs: Skyline Country, Ventana Canyon Country. Office: 5190 E Farness St Bldg 1000 Suite 1006 Tucson AZ 85712

KARP, KEVIN RUSSELL, lawyer; b. Cleve., Sept. 1, 1954; s. Kenneth and Sandra Louise (Orloff) K.; m. Kathryn Ann Weber, Dec. 11, 1982; 1 child, Sean Benjamin. B.A. in Interpersonal Communications, Cleve. State U., 1975; J.D., Whittier Sch. Law, 1978. Bar: Nev. 1979, U.S. Dist. Ct. (no. dist.) Nev. 1979, U.S. Ct. Appeals (9th cir.) 1984. Sole practice, Reno, Nev., 1979—. Bd. dirs. Space Theatre, Inc., Reno, 1983-84. Mem. Assn. Trial Lawyers Am., Nat. Assn. Criminal Def. Lawyers, ACLU (bd. dirs.). Democrat. Jewish. Office: Karp Kevin R Esq 995 Forest St Reno NV 89509

KARPAN, KATHLEEN MARIE, lawyer, journalist, state official; b. Rock Springs, Wyo., Sept. 1, 1942; d. Thomas Michael and Pauline Ann (Taucher) K. B.S. in Journalism, U. Wyo., 1964, M.A. in Am. Studies, 1975; J.D., U. Oreg., 1978. Bar: D.C. 1979, Wyo. 1983, U.S. Dist. Ct. Wyo., U.S. Ct. Appeals (D.C. cir.). Editor Cody Enterprise, Wyo., 1964; press asst. to U.S. Congressman Teno Roncalio U.S. Ho. of Reps., Washington, 1965-67, 71-72, adminstrv. asst., 1973-74; asst. news editor Wyo. Eagle, Cheyenne, 1967; free-lance writer 1968; teaching asst. dept. history U. Wyo., 1969-70; desk editor Canberra Times, Australia, 1970; dep. dir. Office Congl. Relations, Econ. Devel. Adminstrn. U.S. Dept. Commerce, Washington, 1979-80, atty. advisor Office of Chief Counsel, Econ. Devel. Adminstrn., 1980-81; campaign mgr. Rodger McDaniel for U.S. Senator, Wyo., 1981-82; asst. atty. gen. State of Wyo., Cheyenne, 1983-84, dir. Dept. Health and Social Services, 1984-86, sec.of state, 1987—. Del. Democratic Nat. Conv., San Francisco, 1984; del., chmn. platform com. Dem. State Conv., Douglas, Wyo., 1984. W.R. Coe fellow, 1969. Mem. D.C. Bar Assn., Wyo. Bar Assn., Wyo. Trial Lawyers Assn., Bus. and Profl. Women, Women Execs. in State Govt., Am. Pub. Welfare Assn., Nat. Assn. Lt. Govs., Nat. Assn. Secs. of State. Roman Catholic. Home: 2919 Carey Ave Cheyenne WY 82001 Office: Secretary of State State Capitol Bldg Cheyenne WY 82002

KARPENKO, VICTOR NICHOLAS, mech. engr.; b. Harbin, China, Jan. 23, 1922; s. Nicholas Stephan and Sophia Andrea (Kootas) K.; came to U.S., 1941, naturalized, 1943; student San Francisco State Coll., 1941-42, Oreg. State Coll., 1943; B.S. in Mech. Engring., U. Calif., Berkeley, 1948; m. Lydia Kamotsky, June 23, 1950; children—Victor, Mark, Alexandra. Staff engr. Atomic Products Equipment div. Gen. Electric Co., San Jose, Calif., 1956-57; project engr. nuclear explosives engring. Lawrence Livermore (Calif.) Lab., 1957-65, sect. leader nuclear explosives engring., 1965-66, div. leader Nuclear Test Engring. div., 1966-76, project mgr. Mirror Fusion Test Facility, 1976-85; div. head Magnet System Superconducting Super Collider, Univ. Research Assn., Berkeley, Calif., 1986—; mem. fusion reactor safety com. Dept. Energy; mem. Containment Evaluation Panel, ERDA; cons. undergrounding of nuclear reactors. Dist. chmn. U. Calif. Alumni Scholarship Program, 1976—; com. mem. U. Calif. Alumni Scholarship Program, 1972-76; com. mem. San Ramon High Sch. Boosters, 1969; pres. San Ramon AAU Swim Club, 1964. Served with AUS, 1943-46. Registered profl. mech. and nuclear engr., Calif. Mem. Am. Nuclear Soc., Calif. Alumni Assn. Republican. Greek Orthodox. Home: 613 Bradford Pl Danville CA 94526 Office: Univ Research Assn Cyclotron Rd Berkeley CA 94720

KARPILOW, CRAIG, physician; b. San Francisco, Oct. 23, 1947; s. David and Babette (David) K.; B.Sc., U. Alta. (Can.), 1967; M.A., U. So. Calif., 1970; M.D., Dalhousie U., 1973. Intern, Dalhousie U., Halifax, N.S., Can., 1974-75; resident in family practice medicine Meml. U. Nfld. Hosp., St. John's, 1975-77; practice medicine specializing in family medicine with subspecialty dermatology and occupational medicine, 1978-81; practice occupational medicine, Snohomish, Wash., 1981-83; med. health officer Storey County, Nev., 1978-80; med. dir. Med. Center, Dayton, 1978-81; pres. Internat. Profl. Assos. Ltd., 1979—; med. dir./clin. N.W. Occupational Health Ctrs., Seattle, 1983-84; ptnr. physician, co-dir. CHEC Med. Ctr., Seattle, 1984-85; head dept. occupational and diagnostic medicine St. Cabrini Hosp., Seattle, 1984-86; med. dir. N.W. Indsl. Services, 1985-86, Queen Anne Med. Ctr., Seattle, 1985—; bd. dirs. Travelers Med. and Immunization Clinic of Seattle, 1986—. Diplomate Am. Bd. Family Practice; licenciate Med. Coll. Can. Fellow Am. Acad. Family Practice; mem. AMA, Am. Soc. Tropical Medicine and Hygiene, Wash. State Med. Assn. King County Med. Soc., Wash. Acad. Family Physicians (research collaborative, dir. Commn. on Research), Coll. Can. Med. Assn., Am. Occupational Med. Assn., N.W. Occupational Med. Assn. (bd. dirs. 1985—), Marimed Found. Pacific N.W. (adv. bd.) Seattle Swiss Soc., Finnish Soc., Kappa Sigma. Clubs: Corinthian Yacht, Mountaineers, Nature Conservancy. Lodge: Rotary. Office: 525 1st Ave W Seattle WA 98119

KARR, THOMAS JOHN, research physicist; b. Chgo., Mar. 11, 1950; s. Joseph and Valeria (Lewandowski) K.; m. Karen Landis, Nov. 14, 1982. AB, Princeton U., 1971; postgrad., U. Calif., Berkeley, 1971-72; PhD, U. Md., 1976. Research fellow U. Pierre et Marie Curie, Paris, 1977-78, Ctr. Theoretical Studies-U. Miami, 1978-79; staff scientist Lockheed Research Lab., Palo Alto, Calif., 1979-84; physicist Lawrence Livermore (Calif.) Nat. Lab., 1984—, assoc. leader free electron laser program, 1986—; cons. Titan Systems, Kaman Aerospace, Dove Electronics, Leading Techs.; research faculty Universite Pierre et Marie Curie, Paris, 1977-78; assoc. program leader of Free Electron Laser program Lawrence Livermore Nat. Lab., 1986—. Contbr. articles to profl. jours.; patentee in field. Joliot-Curie fellow Commissariat a l'Energie Atomique, Paris, 1977-78. Mem. IEEE, Am. Phys. Soc., Optical Soc. Am. (del. to China 1983). Avocations: skiing, flying, scuba diving, exploring. Home: 212 Austin Ln PO Box 295 Alamo CA 94507 Office: Lawrence Livermore Nat Lab L495 PO Box 808 Livermore CA 94550

KARRAS, DONALD GEORGE, tax analyst; b. Sioux City, Iowa, Dec. 23, 1953; s. George D. and Mary T. (Kyriakos) K.; m. Donna Lynn Ciripompa, Mar. 6, 1982; 1 child, Dane Anthony. BA, Augustana Coll., 1977; MBA, U. S.D., 1980, JD, 1981. CPA, S.D. Bar: S.D. 1981. Legal intern Strange & Strange, Sioux Falls, S.D., 1980; instr. U. S.D. Sch. Bus., Vermillion, 1980-81; tax sr. acct. Deloitte Haskins & Sells, Denver, 1981-84; tax supr. The Anschutz Corp., Denver, 1984—. Advisor Denver Area Jr. Achievement, 1982; coach YMCA Tri-Y Basketball, Denver, 1984-85; mem. Vermillion Area Jaycees, 1977; mem. Evergreen (Colo.) Ctr. for Arts. Mem. S.D. Bar Assn., ABA, SMITES Users Group, Inc. (rep.), Am. Hellenic Ednl. Progressive Assn. Republican. Greek Orthodox. Avocations: golf, softball, guitar, choir. Home: 28505 Little Big Horn Dr Evergreen CO 80439 Office: The Anschutz Corp 2400 Anaconda Tower 555 17th St Denver CO 80202

KARRELS, KENNETH VERNON, organizational psychologist, administrator; b. Chgo., July 31, 1941; s. Vern F. and Irene G. (Sylvester) K.; B.S. in Psychology, Bradley U., 1963, M.A. in Clin. Psychology, 1964; M.A. in Mgmt., U. Phoenix, 1983; m. Mary K. Flory, Nov. 14, 1970; children—Kathryn Rose, Kenneth Karsten. Psychology intern Elgin (Ill.) State Hosp., 1964, dir. transitional care program, 1965-68, dir. community services, 1968-73; devel. disabilities adminstr. Dept. Mental Health and Retardation, Elgin, 1973-75; assoc. exec. dir. Ray Graham Assn., Oak Brook, Ill., 1975-77, project mgr. Dist. II State of Ariz., Ariz. Tng. Program at Tucson, 1977—; cons. Nat. Found. for The Handicapped, Oak Brook, Ill.; cons. career counseling, indsl. psychology, human resource mgmt.; lectr. time mgmt., staff tng. and devel. Bd. dirs. Mental Health Assn. Greater Tucson, So. Ariz. Health Facility Council, Pima County Assn. for Retarded Citizens, So. Ariz. Health Facilities Council, Tanque Verde Homeowners' Assn.; mem. Sch. Bd. Planning Com. Tax Reform Com. Recipient Gerty award Gov. of Ill., 1967; registered psychologist, Ariz.; cert. alcoholism counselor. Mem. Am. Psychol. Assn., Am. Soc. Personnel Adminstrn., Am. Soc. Tng. and Devel., Nat. Registry Health Service Providers in Psychology. So. Ariz. Soc. Model Engrs. Unitarian. Contbr. articles to profl. confs. Home: 3930 N Smokey Topaz Tucson AZ 85749 Office: PO Box 13178 Tucson AZ 85732

KARREN, KENNETH WILLIAM, civil engineering consultant; b. Vernal, Utah, May 20, 1932; s. William Horton Karren and Ethelwynne (Stringham) White; m. Anne Louise Henderson, Nov. 21, 1953; children: Kenneth Jr., Elizabeth, Phillip, Scott, Laura, Thomas, Catherine. BS, U. Utah, 1953, MS, 1951; PhD, Cornell U., 1965. Project devel. engr. Phillips Petroleum, Bartlesville, Okla., 1955-56; chief engr. Buehner concrete, Murray, Utah, 1956-61; prof. civil engring. Brigham Young U., Provo, Utah, 1961-78; sr. research engr. Hercules, Inc., Magna, Utah, 1970-71; owner Karren & Assocs., Salt Lake City, 1978—. Contbr. tech. papers to profl. jours. Mem. Bd. Appeals, Provo, 1980-85. Served to lt. USN, 1953-56. Fellow ASCE (pres. Utah sect. 1974-75); mem. Structural Engrs. Assn. Utah (bd. dirs. 1984—, pres. elect 1986). Republican. Mormon. Home: 424 E 4750 N Provo UT 84604 Office: Karren & Assocs 524 S 600 E Salt Lake City UT 84102

KASAMEYER, PAUL WILLIAM, geophysicist; b. Detroit, Sept. 9, 1943; s. Alfred Louis and Frances Loreen (Eagleson) K.; m. Ann Marie Dombrosk, Sept. 18, 1965; children: Karen, Amy, Alan. BS in Physics, MIT, 1965, MS in Physics, 1966, PhD in Earth Scis., 1974. Geophysicist Lawrence Livermore (Calif.) Nat. Lab., 1974-78, group leader, 1978-82, sect. leader geophysics sect., 1982-83, leader geothermal project, 1983—. Contbr. articles to profl. jours. Bd dirs. Livermore-Amador Symphony Assn., Livermore, 1978—. Mem. Am. Geophys. Union, Soc. Exploration Geophysicists, Sigma Xi. Avocations: piano performance, hiking. Office: Lawrence Livermore Nat Lab PO Box 808 Livermore CA 94550

KASARI, LEONARD SAMUEL, quality control professional; b. Los Angeles, Sept. 22, 1924; s. Kustaa Adolph and Impi (Sikio) K.; m. Elizabeth P. Keplinger, Aug. 25, 1956; children: Lorraine Carol, Lance Eric. Student, Compton Coll., 1942-43, UCLA, 1964-70. Registered profl. engr., Calif. Gen. construction Los Angeles, 1946-61; supr. inspection service Osborne Labs., Los Angeles, 1961-64; mgr. customer service Lightweight Processing, Los Angeles, 1965-77; dir. tech. service Crestlite Aggregates, San Clemente, Calif., 1977-78; quality control mgr. Standard Concrete, Santa Ana, Calif., 1978—. Camp dir. Torrance YMCA, High Sierras, Calif., 1969-80, mem. bd. mgrs., 1970—. Served with USN, 1943-46. Named Hon. Life Mem. Calif. PTA, 1983. Mem. Am. Concrete Inst., So. Calif. Structural Engrs. Assn. Democrat. Lutheran. Avocations: skiing, hunting, fishing, backpacking. Home: 2450 W 233 St Torrance CA 90501 Office: Standard Concrete Products 117 W 4th St Santa Ana CA 92701

KASDAN, HARVEY LEE, computer scientist, consultant; b. Bklyn., July 31, 1940; s. Selig David and Reba (Lesches) K.; m. Judith Sperman, Sept. 2, 1962; 1 child, Sheldon David. BSEE, MIT, 1963, MSEE, 1963; PhD in Engring., UCLA, 1971. Mem. tech. staff Hughes Aircraft Co., Los Angeles, 1963-67; sr. engring. specialist Litton Industries, Van Nuys, Calif., 1967-1971; v.p. Recognition Systems Inc., Van Nuys, 1971-82; dir. research and devel. Internat. Remote Imaging Systems, Chatsworth, Calif., 1982—; cons. photo research div. Kollmorgen Corp., Burbank, Calif., 1982-83, 1985. Contbr. articles to profl. jours; patentee in field. Mem. IEEE, Optical Soc. Am., Soc. Photo-Optical Instrumentation Engrs. (editor conf. proceedings 1979-80), Sigma Xi, Tau Beta Pi, Eta Kappa Nu. Democrat. Jewish. Home: 5414 Sunnyslope Ave Van Nuys CA 91401 Office: Internat Remote Imaging Systems 9825 DeSoto Ave Chatsworth CA 91311

KASEL, JANE MARIE, publishing company executive; b. Bay City, Mich., June 19, 1947; d. Vincent A. and Jenotte Marie (Lipan) Emeott Curtis; B.A., U. Calif., Santa Barbara, 1970; postgrad. Calif. State U., Fullerton, 1972-73; m. Richard S. Kasel, Jr., Dec. 12, 1981. Salesperson bookkeeper Heth Hardware, Baldwin Park, Calif., 1962-66; mgrs. asst. univ. approved housing U. Calif., Santa Barbara, 1968-70; exec. sec. contracts div. Aerojet Gen., Azusa, Calif., 1966-71; tchr. English, yearbook adv., adv. council Walnut (Calif.) High Sch., 1971-77; yearbook specialist Taylor Pub. Co., Dallas, 1977—, mem. pres. adv. council, 1980-82, mem. sales adv. council, 1981-82. Graphics cons. Christian Edn. Today mag. Mem., guide for communication seminars House of White Shell Woman; mem. Eastside Christian Ch., Fullerton, 1977—, pub. dir. PPFF Capital Funds Program; adult Bible Sch. tchr. Named Woman of Yr., Bank Am., 1967; recipient Mktg. awards Taylor Pub. Co., 1979, Pacesetter award, 1979, also named Rookie of Yr. Mem. Journalism Educators Assn., So. Calif. Journalism Educators Assn., Nat. Assn. Female Execs., AAUW, Taylor Pub. Co. Half Million Dollar Club, Christian Leaders and Speakers, Alpha Gamma Sigma. Office: 562 Laguna Canyon Way Brea CA 92621

KASSAKHIAN, GARABET HAROUTIOUN, environmental scientist; b. Jerusalem, Aug. 15, 1944; came to U.S., 1968; s. Haroutioun Garabet and Arsine (Arsenian) K.; m. Loussik Antonian, July 20, 1969; 3 children. MSc, Yerevan (Armenia) State U., USSR, 1968; AM, Harvard U., 1970, PhD, 1975. Sr. teaching fellow Harvard U., Cambridge, Mass., 1968-75; asst. prof. U. Mass., Boston, 1975-76; project mgr. Environ. Health Ctr., Ottawa, Ont., Can., 1977-78; head environ. research and devel. sect. Eldorado Nuclear Ltd., Ottawa, 1978-80; spl. projects mgr. Amerada Hess Corp., Woodbridge, N.J., 1980-82; cons. various internat. corps. and govtl. agys., 1982-85; project mgr. Lockman & Assocs., Monterey Park, Calif., 1985-87; v.p. H.V. Lawmaster & Co., Stanton, Calif., 1987—; vis. prof. chemistry U. LaVerne, Calif., 1985—. Contbr. articles to profl. jours., tech. reports to Can. govt. Mem. AAUP, Chem Inst. Can., Am. Chem. Soc., Water Pollution Control Fedn. (Willem Rudolfs award 1982). Avocations: hiking, history, writing. Home: 221 N Cedar A-39 Glendale CA 91206-4442 Office: H V Lawmaster & Co 7940 Main St Stanton CA 90680

KASSNER, MICHAEL ERNEST, materials science researcher, educator; b. Osaka, Japan, Nov. 22, 1950; (parents Am. citizens); s. Ernest and Clara (Christa) K.; m. Marcia J. Wright, Aug. 19, 1972 (div. Dec. 1976). BS, Northwestern U., 1972; MS, Stanford U., 1979, PhD, 1981. Metallurgist Lawrence Livermore (Calif.) Nat. Lab., 1981—; prof. Naval Postgrad. Sch., Monterey, Calif., 1984—. Assoc. editor Materials Letters; contbg. editor Internat. Program for Alloy Phase Diagrams. Served to lt. USN, 1972-76. Fulbright scholar Council for Internat. Exchange of scholars, Netherlands, 1983-84. Mem. Am. Soc. Metals, Materials Research Soc., Sigma Xi. Roman Catholic. Home: 311 Cedar Pacific Grove CA 93950

KASTEN, GERALD ALLEN, computer marketing executive, consultant; b. N.Y.C., July 24, 1945; s. Alexander and Etta (Karlikow) K.; m. Hermine Rochelle Gottlieb, Jan. 10, 1971; children: Mallary Jill, Ainsley Brooke, Lauren. BS in Mktg., NYU, 1965; MBA in Mgmt., CCNY, 1969. Advt. mgr. Ideal Toy Corp., N.Y., 1968-70; dir. mktg. The Perl-Mack Cos., Denver, 1970-75; dir. corp. communications Info. Handling Service, Denver, 1975-80; prin. and cons. G.A. Kasten & Assocs., Denver, 1980-82; dir. mktg. Precision Visuals, Boulder, 1982-84; dir. mktg. and sales Ana Tech. Corp., Littleton, Colo., 1985—; cons. SBA, 1974-79. Served to sgt. U.S. Army, 1966-68. Recipient Alfie awards Denver Advt. Fedn., 1973, 74, 75. Mem. Denver Advt. Fedn. (bd. dirs. 1975-77), Am. Mktg. Assn., Prof. Mktg. Aurora Community Coll. Avocations: skiing, sailing. Home: 4620 E Oxford Ave Englewood CO 80110

KASZNIAK, ALFRED WAYNE, neuropsychologist; b. Chgo., June 2, 1949; s. Alfred H. and Ann Virginia (Simonsen) K.; B.S. with honors, U. Ill., 1970, M.A., 1973, Ph.D., 1976; m. Mary Ellen Beaurain, Aug. 26, 1973; children—Jesse Beaurain, Elizabeth Beaurain. Instr. dept. psychology Rush Med. Coll., Chgo., 1974-76, asst. prof. dept. psychology, 1976-79; from asst. prof. to assoc. prof. dept. psychiatry U. Ariz. Coll. Medicine, Tucson, 1979-82, assoc. prof. dept. psychology and psychiatry, 1982—; staff psychologist Presbyn.-St. Luke's Hosp., Chgo., 1976-79; mem. human devel. and aging study sect. div. research grants NIH, 1981-86. Trustee So. Ariz. chpt. Nat. Multiple Sclerosis Soc., 1980-82; mem. med. and sci. adv. bd. Nat. Alzheimer's Disease and Related Disorders Assn., 1981-84; mem. med. adv. bd. Fan Kane Fund for Brain-Injured Children, Tucson, 1980—. Grantee Nat. Inst. Aging, 1978-83, NIMH, 1984—, Robert Wood Johnson Found., 1986—. Mem. Am. Psychol. Assn. (Disting. Contbr. award div. 20 1978), Internat. Neuropsychol. Soc., Soc. for Neurosci., Gerontol. Soc. (research fellow 1980), AAAS, Editorial cons. Jour. Gerontology, 1979—; mem. editorial bd. Psychology and Aging, 1984-87; The Clin. Neuropsychologist, 1986—; contbr. articles to profl. jours. Home: 2327 E Hawthorne St Tucson AZ 85719 Office: Univ Ariz Dept Psychology Tucson AZ 85721

KATAGUE, DAVID BALLEZA, analytical chemist, consultant; b. Iloilo City, Philippines, Dec. 20, 1934; came to U.S., 1959, naturalized, 1971; s. David J. Katague Sr. and Paz (Barrido) Balleza; m. Macrine Nieva Jambalos, May 8, 1957; children: Diosdado Dodie, Dinah E., David E., Ditas M. BS in Chemistry, U. Philippines, 1955; MS in Chemistry, U. Ill., Chgo., 1962, PhD in Chemistry, 1964. Instr. chemistry U. Philippines, 1955-59; instr. chemistry U. Ill., Chgo., 1962-64, teaching asst., 1959-62; chemist Mobay Chems., Kansas City, Mo., 1964-69; prin. research chemist Stauffer Chem. Co., Richmond, Calif., 1974-85; research chemist Shell Devel. Co., Modesto, Calif., 1969-74, Chevron Chem. Co., Richmond, 1986—; cons. United Nations Tokten Project, Diliman, U.P., Philippines, 1985—. Fellow Am. Inst. Chemists; mem. Am. Chem. Soc., Philippine Am. Acad. Sci. and Engring. (founding mem.). Avocations: tennis, duplicate bridge, rose growing. Home: 3256 Ramona St Pinole CA 94564 Office: Chevron Chem Co 15049 San Pablo Ave Richmond CA 94804

KATHER, GERHARD, air force base administrator; b. Allenstein, Germany, Jan. 30, 1939; came to U.S., 1952, naturalized, 1959; s. Ernst and Maria (Kempa) K.; m. Carol Anne Knutsen, Aug. 18, 1962; children—Scott T., Cynthia M., T. Stephen, Chris A.; m. Mary Elsie Frank, Oct. 25, 1980. B.A. in Govt., U. Ariz., 1964; M.P.A., U. So. Calif., 1971. Tchr. social studies, Covina, Calif., 1965-67; tng. officer Civil Personnel, Ft. MacArthur, Calif., 1967-70; chief employee tng. and devel. Corps Engrs., Los Angeles, 1970-72; chief employee tng. and devel. Frankfurt Area Army Personnel Office, 1972-73; chief employee relations and tng. brs. Corps Engrs., Los Angeles, 1973-74; chief employee devel. and tng. Kirtland AFB, N.Mex., 1974-87; labor relations officer, Kirtland AFB and detachments in 13 U.S. cities, 1987—. Mem. adv. com. Albuquerque Tech.-Vocat. Inst., 1982—, U. N.Mex. Valencia Campus, 1985—. Served with USAF, 1958-64. Named Prominent Tng. and Devel. Profl., H. Whitney McMillan Co., 1984; Outstanding Handicapped Fed. Employee of Yr., all fed. agys., 1984. Mem. Am. Soc. Tng. and Devel. (pres. chpt. 1984-85), Paralyzed Vets. Am. (bd. dirs. 1986—, pres. local chpt. 1986—), Toastmasters Internat. (chpt. treas., v.p., pres. 1967-70), Phi Delta Kappa. Democrat. Roman Catholic. Office: 1606 ABW/DPCEL Kirtland AFB NM 87117

KATSOULEAS, THOMAS CHRISTOS, physicist; b. Tucson, Apr. 24, 1958; s. Soterios Christos and Carole Lee (Engelhardt) K. BS, UCLA, 1979, MS, 1981, PhD in Physics, 1984. Research physicist, engr. UCLA, 1984—. Editor: (with others) Laser Acceleration of Particles, 1985; contbr. articles to profl. jours. Mem. AAAS, Am. Phys. Soc., IEEE (program com. 1986-87, guest editor 1987), Phi Beta Kappa. Republican. Avocations: sailing, diving, ocean lifeguard. Office: UCLA Physics Dept Los Angeles CA 90024

KATZ, HELEN ELAINE, association executive; b. Indpls., May 23, 1946; d. Henry Elsworth and Pearl Elaine (Richardson) Mears; m. Vernie Leroy Katz, Jan. 30, 1965; children—Lea Renee, Vernie Leroy. Student pub. schs.,

Indpls. Typist, United Christian Missionary Soc., Indpls., 1964-65; sec. Met. Planning Dept., Indpls., 1965-66; mgr. Eagles Roost Apts., Indpls., 1973-79; adminstrv. asst. Georgetown Soc., Inc., Georgetown, Colo., 1980—. Bd. dirs. Georgetown Fasching, 1983-85, Fasching Princess, 1984; officer, Georgetown Police Reserves, 1983-86. Club: Internat. Order Job's Daus. (honored queen 1963-64), Order Eastern Star (worthy matron 1978-79, 86-87). Home: PO Box 125 Georgetown CO 80444 Office: Georgetown Soc Inc PO Box 667 Georgetown CO 80444

KATZ, JERRY BENJAMIN, insurance executive; b. Louisville, Jan. 8, 1947; s. David Frederick and Carolyn (Flumbaum) K.; m. Kathleen Brown, Mar. 29, 1969; children: Kristen Carole, Damon Michael, Danielle Laura. Student, Bradley U., 1964-65; BA, U. Louisville, 1968. Sr. systems analyst Indsl. Indemnity, San Francisco, 1974-76, mgr. premium data entry, 1976-78; home office mgr. premium audit and collections Fremont Compensation Ins. Co., Los Angeles, 1978-79, asst. v.p. premium audit and collections, 1978-81, asst. v.p. underwriting, 1981-84, v.p. planning, 1984—. Nat. chief YMCA Young Indian Guides, Anaheim, Calif., 1984-85, asst. nat. chief, 1983-84; asst. coach Am. Youth Soccer Orgn., Cypress, Calif., 1985-86; coach Little League baseball, Cypress, Calif., 1987; bd. dirs. Cypress Fed. Little League Bd., 1987. Served with USCG, 1968-72. Club: Los Angeles Athletic. Home: 5408 Vista Fortuna Cypress CA 90630 Office: Fremont Compensatin Ins Co 1709 W 8th St Los Angeles CA 90017

KATZ, JOHN W., lawyer, state official; b. Balt., June 3, 1943; s. Leonard Wallach and Jean W. (Kane) K.; m. Joan Katz, June 11, 1969 (div. 1982); 1 child, Kimberly Erin. B.A., Johns Hopkins U., 1965; J.D., U. Calif.-Berkeley, 1969. Bar: Alaska, Pa., U.S. Dist. Ct. D.C. 1971, U.S. Ct. Appeals (D.C. cir.), U.S. Tax Ct., U.S. Ct. Claims, U.S. Ct. Mil. Justice, U.S. Supreme Ct. Legis. and adminstrv. asst. to Congressman Howard W. Pollock of Alaska, Washington, 1969-70; legis. asst. to U.S. Senator Ted Stevens of Alaska, Washington, 1971; assoc. McGrath and Flint, Anchorage, 1972; gen. counsel Joint Fed. State Land Use Planning Commn. for Alaska, Anchorage, 1972-79; spl. counsel to Gov. Jay S. Hammond of Alaska, Anchorage and Washington, 1979-81; commr. Alaska Dept. Natural Resources, Juneau, 1981-83; dir. state fed. relations and spl. counsel to Gov. Bill Sheffield of Alaska, Washington and Juneau, 1983-86; dir. state-fed. relations, spl. counsel to Gov. Alaska, Washington, 1986—; mem. Alaska Power Survey Exec. Adv. Com. of FPC, Anchorage, 1972-74; mem. spl. com. hard rock minerals Govs. Council of Sci. and Tech., Anchorage, 1979-80; guest lectr. on natural resources U. Alaska, U. Denver. Contbr. articles to profl. jours. Acad. supr. Alaska Externship Program, U. Denver Coll. Law, 1976-79; mem. Reagan-Bush transition team for U.S. Dept. Justice, 1980. Recipient Superior Sustained Performance award Joint Fed. State Land Use Planning Commn. for Alaska, 1978. Republican. Office: State of Alaska Office of Gov 444 N Capitol St NW #518 Washington DC 20001

KATZ, JOSEPH, electrical engineer, researcher; b. Tel Aviv, June 6, 1952; came to U.S., 1978; s. David and Dvora (Quint) K.; m. Yael Schapira, Aug. 12, 1974; children: Yariv C., Tamir B., Hila E. BSEE with honors, Technion, Israel Inst. Tech., Haifa, 1973; MSEE with honors, Tel Aviv U., 1976; PhD, Calif. Inst. Tech., 1981. Project engr. Ministry of Def., Tel Aviv, 1974-78; sr. engr. Jet Propulsion Lab., Pasadena, Calif., 1979-81, mem. tech. staff, 1981-84, tech. group leader, 1984-86, group supr., 1986—; lectr. Calif. State U., Los Angeles, 1982—; cons. Gen. Electric Co., Syracuse, N.Y., 1984-86. Contbr. articles to profl. jours.; patentee in field. Recipient Cert. Recognition, NASA, 1982—; Northrop Corp. fellow, 1979; U.S.-Israel Ednl. Found. scholar, 1978. Mem. IEEE. Home: 2176 Lambert Dr Pasadena CA 91107 Office: Jet Propulsion Lab Mail Stop 512-103 Pasadena CA 91109

KATZ, PHYLLIS ALBERTS, social services administrator. married; 2 children. AB in Psychology summa cum laude, Syracuse U., 1957; PhD in Devel. Clin. Psychology, Yale U., 1961. Clin. intern West Haven (Conn.) VA Hosp., 1959-60; clin. trainee Clifford Beers Child Guidance Clinic, New Haven, Conn., 1960-61; instr. psychology So. Conn. State Coll., 1960-61, Queens Coll., N.Y.C., 1962-63; asst. prof. psychology, cons. dept. edn. NYU, 1963-67, assoc. prof., 1967-69; assoc. prof. CUNY, 1969-72, chairperson devel. psychology sect. PhD program in edn., 1969-75, acting exec. officer PhD program in edn., 1974-75, prof., 1973-76; vis. research assoc., research cons. Behavioral Research Inst. U. Colo., Boulder, 1975-76; dir. Inst. Research on Social Problems, Boulder, 1975—; mem. ad hoc research adv. com. Office Child Devel., HEW, 1970-71; mem. program com. Am. Ednl. Research Assn., 1974. Editor: Sex Roles: A Jour. of Research, 1976—; cons. editor Devel. Psychology, Jour. Exptl. Child Psychology, Rev. Ednl. Research, Psychol. Bull., Am. Psychologist; mem. editorial bd. Child Devel., 1975-77, Archives of Sexual Behavior, 1975—; contbr. numerous articles to profl. jours. Trustee Colo. Music Festival, 1982-84, pres. bd. trustees, 1984-85; mem. City of Boulder planning com. Cultural Arts Ctr.; bd. dirs. Women's Found. Colo., 1986—. USPHS trainee Yale U., 1956-59; grantee NYU Arts and Sci. Research, 1963-66, CUNY Faculty Research, 1973, Nat. Inst. Child Health Human Devel., 1966-68, 68-72, 79-81, 81-83, Office of Child Devel., 1972-75, Nat. Inst. Mental Health, 1977-79, 84-86, NSF, 1984—. Mem. Am. Psychol. Assn. (jour. editor 1974-77, chairperson child advocacy com. 1973, exec. com. 1980—, head affirmative action com. 1981—, council rep. 1983-86, div. pres. 1986-87), Southeastern Psychol. Assn., Soc. Research in Child Devel., Assn. Women in Sci., Sigma Xi. Home: 1035 Pearl St 5th Floor Boulder CO 80302

KATZ, RONALD LEWIS, physician, educator; b. Bklyn., Apr. 22, 1932; s. Joseph and Belle (Charnis) K.; children: Richard Ian, Laura Susan, Margaret Karen. B.A., U. Wis.-Madison, 1952; M.D., Boston U., 1956; postgrad. in Pharmacology (NIH fellow), Coll. Physicians and Surgeons, Columbia U., 1959-60; postgrad. (John Simon Guggenheim fellow), Royal Postgrad. Med. Sch., U. London, 1968-69. Intern USPHS Hosp., S.I., 1956-57; resident Columbia-Presbyn. Med. Center, 1957-60; asst. prof. anesthesiology Coll. Physicians and Surgeons, Columbia U., 1960-66, assoc. prof., 1966-70, prof., 1970-73; prof., chmn. dept. anesthesiology UCLA, 1973—, chief staff Med. Ctr., 1984-86; Cons. NIH, FDA, numerous state agys. Author, editor: Muscle Relaxants, 1975; Contbr. numerous articles to profl. jours.; Mem. editorial bd.: Handbook of Anesthesiology, 1972—, Progress in Anesthesiology, 1973—; editor in chief Seminars in Anesthesia, 1982—. Mem. Am. Soc. Anesthesiologists, Am. Physiol. Soc., Am. Soc. Pharmacology and Exptl. Therapeutics, N.Y. Acad. Medicine; Faculty Anaesthetists of Royal Coll. Surgeons of Eng. Inventor peripheral nerve stimulator. Home: 2910 Neilson Way #407 Santa Monica CA 90405 Office: UCLA Dept Anesthesiology Los Angeles CA 90024

KATZ, VERA, college administrator, state legislator; b. Dusseldorf, Germany, Aug. 3, 1933; came to U.S., 1940; d. Lazar Pistrak and Raissa Goodman; m. Mel Katz (div. 1985); 1 child, Jesse. BA, Bklyn. Coll., 1955, postgrad., 1955-57. Market research analyst TIMEX, B.T. Babbitt, N.Y.C., 1957-62; citizen's lobbyist United Farm Workers, Kennedy Action Corp., Portland, 1962-72; lectr. Portland State U., Oreg., 1976; mem. Oreg. Ho. of Reps., Salem, 1973—, speaker of house, 1985—; dir. devel. Portland Community Coll., 1982—; mem. Gov.'s Council on Alcohol and Drug Abuse Programs, Oreg. Legis., Salem, 1985—; mem. adv. com. Gov.'s Council on Health, Fitness and Sports, Oreg. Legis., 1985—; mem. Carnegie task Force on Teaching as Profession, Washington, 1985—; vice-chair assembly Nat. Conf. State Legis., Denver, 1986—. Bd. dirs. Keith Martin Ballet, Portland, 1985—; hon. bd. dirs. Victims Offender Reconciliation Program, Portland, 1985—. Recipient Abigail Scott Duniway award Women in Communications, Inc., Portland, 1985, Jeanette Rankin First Woman award Oreg. Women's Polit. Caucus, Portland, 1985, Leadership award The Neighborhood newspaper Portland, 1985, Woman of Achievement award Commn. for Women, 1985, Outstanding Legis. Advocacy award Oreg. Primary Care Assn., 1985, Service to Portland Pub. Sch. Children award Portland Pub. Schs., 1985. Fellow Am. Leadership Forum (Oreg. chpt.); mem. Dem. Legis. Leaders Assn. Democrat. Jewish. Avocations: camping, jogging, dancing. Office: Office of the Speaker H 269 State Capitol Bldg Salem OR 97310

KATZIN, LEONARD ISAAC, chemist, consultant; b. Eau Claire, Wis., Jan. 18, 1915; s. Morris and Ida Golda (Stein) K.; m. Alice Ginsburg, Sept. 2, 1938 (dec. Sept. 1984); children: Ruth N., Martha R., Lisbeth E., Judith H. AB, UCLA, 1935; PhD, U. Calif., Berkeley, 1938. Asst. aquatic biologist USPHS, Washington, 1940-42; fellow in radiology U. Rochester, N.Y., 1942-43; asst. sect. chief Manhattan Project U. Chgo., 1943-46; sr. scientist, group leader Argonne (Ill.) Nat. Lab., 1946-78; pres. Cons. Services, Port Hueneme, Calif., 1978—; vis. prof. U. Chgo., 1956-57, Hebrew U., Jerusalem, 1969-70, U. Tel Aviv, 1969-70; extension lectr. U. Ill., Chgo., 1961. Author/editor: Production and Separation of U233, 1951; contbr. articles to profl. jours.; patentee in field. Mem. AAAS, Am. Chem. Soc. (councillor 1962-64, Chemist of Yr. 1964), Am. Phys. Soc. Avocations: golf, photography, fishing. Home and Office: 428 Hudson Ln Port Hueneme CA 93041

KAUCHICH, JOHN STEVEN, oil and gas company executive; b. Rock Springs, Wyo., Feb. 1, 1943; s. Steve and Pauline (Martelok) K.; m. Georgia Rae Malicoat, Aug. 24, 1968; children: Bryan, Paul, Janet. BSEE, U. Wyo., 1965, MS in Indsl. Mgmt., Stats., 1967. Registered profl. engr., Wyo., Utah, Colo. Measurement and control engr. supr. Mountain Fuel Supply, Rock Springs, 1972-73, measurement and communication engr. supr., 1973-76, tech. services mgr., 1976, asst. gen. mgr. transmission, 1976-83, gen. mgr. transmission, 1983-84; gen. mgr. ops. Mountain Fuel Resources, Rock Springs, 1984—; bd. dirs. Am. Nat. Bank, Rock Springs, 1982—. Mem. operating com. S.W. Wyo. Indsl. Assn., Rock Springs. Mem. Wyo. Engrng. Soc., Pacific Coast Gas Assn., U. Wyo. Alumni Assn. (life), Petroleum Assn. Wyo. Lodge: Elks. Home: 605 Rhode Island Ave Rock Springs WY 82901 Office: Mountain Fuel Resources 1005 D St Rock Springs WY 82901

KAUFFMAN, DAVID, educator, chemical and nuclear engineering consultant; b. Glenside, Pa., Aug. 18, 1940; s. Martin Luther and Jane Anne (Pratt) K.; m. Stephanie Elizabeth Hingston, Sept. 1, 1962; 1 child, Dorothy. BS in Chem. Engrng., Calif. Inst. Tech., 1962, MS in Chem. Engrng., 1963; PhD in Chem. Engrng., U. Colo., 1970. Process engr. Shell Devel. Co., Emeryville, Calif., 1970-72; research engr. Shell Devel. Co., Houston, 1972-77; assoc. prof. U. N.Mex., Albuquerque, 1977—; assoc. dean Coll. Engrng. U. N. Mex., 1986—; cons. in field, Albuquerque, 1978—. Contbr. articles to profl. jours.; patentee in field. Faculty Senate pres. U. N.Mex., 1984-85. Served to 1st lt. USAF, 1962-66. Mem. Am. Inst. Chem. Engrs., Am. Chem. Soc., Am. Soc. Engrng. Edn., Sigma Xi, Tau Beta Pi. Episcopalian. Avocations: choral singing, skiing. Home: 752 Tramway Ln NE Albuquerque NM 87122 Office: U N Mex Dept Chem Nuclear Engrng Albuquerque NM 87131

KAUFFMAN, DONALD GOODWIN, food broker; b. Hillsboro, Wis., Jan. 13, 1918; s. Jesse and Grace (Goodwin) K.; m. Ethelynn Helen Bays, Feb. 22, 1942; children—Camille Taylor, Donald G., Patrick Taylor, Thomas W.; m. 2d, Marilyn Jean Miller Taylor, Dec. 2, 1960; Ph.B., U. Wis., 1940. Salesman, food brokerage co., Portland, Oreg., 1946-47; owner D.G. Kauffman Co., 1947-48; pres., gen. mgr. Stater-Kauffman Co., Portland, Oreg., 1948-61, Edwards/Kauffman Co., Portland, 1961-79; pres. Erlandson-Kauffman, Seattle, 1965-80; sr. v.p. charge corp. devel. Bromar, Inc., Newport Beach, Calif., 1979—, dir., 1980—. Dir. ops. and tng. Oreg. Air N.G., 1946-50; past chmn. food div. Multonomah County ARC, United Fund Drive; bd. deacons St. Andrews United Presbyn. Ch., 1959-62; v.p. USO for Oreg., 1977-80, bd. dirs., 1978-80. Served to maj. USAAF, 1941-45. Mem. Portland Food Brokers Assn. (past pres.), Nat. Food Brokers Assn. (regional dir. 1965-66), Republican. Presbyterian. Clubs: Multnomah Athletic, Waverley Country, Eldorado Country, Rotary (pres. 1975-76). Home: 4014 SW 36th Pl Portland OR 97221 Office: 1900 SE Milport Rd Portland OR 97222

KAUFFMAN, ERLE GALEN, geologist, educator; b. Washington, Feb. 9, 1933; s. Erle Benton and Paula Virginia (Graff) K.; m. Carolyn Stinebower, Aug. 25, 1956; children: Donald Erle, Robin Lyn, Erica Jean. BS, U. Mich., 1955, MS, 1956, PhD, 1961. Teaching fellow U. Mich., Ann Arbor, 1956-60; from asst. to full curator Mus. Natural History Smithsonian Inst., Washington, 1960-80; prof. geology, chmn. U. Colo., Boulder, 1980-86; adj. prof. geology George Washington U., Washington, 1962-80; cons. geologist, Boulder, 1980—. Author/editor: Cretaceous Facies, Faunas and Paleoenvironments Across the Cretaceous Western Interior Basin, 1977; contbg. editor: Concepts and Methods of Biostratigraphy, 1977, Fine-grained Deposits and Biofacies of the Cretaceous Western Seaway, 1985, High-Resolution Event Stratigraphy, 1987; contbr. articles to profl. jours. Recipient U.S. Govt. Spl. Service award, 1969, NSF Best Tchr. award, U. Colo., 1985; named Disting. Lectr. Am. Geol. Inst., 1963-64, Am. Assn. Petroleum Geologist, 1984, 85; Fullbright fellow, 1986. Fellow Geol. Soc. Am., AAAS; mem. Paleontol. Soc. (councilor under 40, pres. elect 1981, pres. 1982, 83, chmn. 5 coms., rep. and mem. NRC, Palaeontol. Assn., Internat. Paleontol. Assn. (v.p. 1982—), Paleontol. Research Instn., Internat. Malacological Union, Malacological Soc. London, Soc. Econ. Paleontologists and Mineralogists (com. mem.) (Spl. Service award 1985, Best Paper award 1985), Rocky Mountain Assn. Geologists (project chief) (Scientist of Yr. 1977), Paleontol. Soc. Wash. (pres., sec., treas.), Geol. Soc. Wash. (councilor), Colo.-Wyo. Paleontol. Soc., Four Corners Geol. Soc., Saskatchewan Geol. Soc., Md. Acad. Scis. (hon. Paleontology sect.), Sigma Xi, Phi Kappa Phi, Sigma Gamma Epsilon. Democrat. Avocations: folk music, fishing, climbing, photography. Home: Flagstaff Star Rt Boulder CO 80302 Office: U Colo Dept Geol Scis Campus Box 250 Boulder CO 80309

KAUFFMAN, GEORGE BERNARD, chemistry educator; b. Phila., Sept. 4, 1930; s. Philip Joseph and Laura (Fisher) K.; m. Ingeborg Salomon, June 5, 1952 (div. Dec. 1969); children: Ruth Deborah, Judith Miriam; m. Laurie Marks Papazian, Dec. 21, 1969; stepchildren: Stanley Robert Papazian, Teresa Lynn Papazian Baron. B.A. with honors, U. Pa., 1951; Ph.D., U. Fla., 1956. Grad. asst. U. Fla., 1951-55; research participant Oak Ridge Nat. Lab., 1955; instr. U. Tex., Austin, 1955-56; research chemist Humble Oil & Refining Co., Baytown, Tex., 1956; Gen. Electric Co. Humble Oil & Refining Co., Cin., 1957, 59; asst. prof. chemistry Calif. State U., Fresno, 1956-61; assoc. prof. Calif. State U., 1961-66, prof., 1966—; guest lectr. coop. lecture tours Am. Chem. Soc., 1971; vis. scholar U. Calif., Berkeley, 1976, U. Puget Sound, 1978; dir. undergrad. research participation program NSF, 1972. Author: Alfred Werner—Founder of Coordination Chemistry, 1966, Classics in Coordination Chemistry, Part I, 1968, Part II, 1976, Part III, 1978, Werner Centennial, 1967, Teaching the History of Chemistry, 1971, Coordination Chemistry: Its History through the Time of Werner, 1977, Inorganic Coordination Compounds, 1981, The Central Science: Essays on the Uses of Chemistry, 1984, Frederick Soddy (1877-1956): Early Pioneer in Radiochemistry, 1986, Aleksandr Porfirevich Borodin, 1987; contbr. numerous articles to profl. publs.; contbg. editor: Jour. Coll. Sci. Teaching, 1973—, The Hexagon, 1980—, Polyhedron, 1983-85, Jour. Chem. Edn., 1987—; editor tape lecture series: Am. Chem. Soc, 1975-81. Named Outstanding Prof. Calif. State U. and Colls. System, 1973, recipient Exceptional Merit Service award, 1984; recipient Coll. Chemistry Tchr. Excellence award Mfg. Chemists Assn., 1976; Dexter award in History of Chemistry, 1978; Research Corp. grantee, 1956-57, 57-59, 59-61; Am. Chem. Soc. Petroleum Research Fund grantee, 1962-64, 65-69; Am. Philos. Soc. grantee, 1963-64, 69-70; NSF grantee, 1960-61, 63-64, 67-69, 76-77; John Simon Guggenheim Meml. Found. fellow, 1972-73; grantee, 1975; NEH grantee, 1982-83; Strindberg fellow Swedish Inst., Stockholm, 1983. Mem. AAAS, AAUP, Assn. Univ. Pa. Chemists, History Sci. Soc., Soc. History Alchemy and Chemistry, Am. Chem. Soc. (chmn. div. history of chemistry 1969, exec. com. 1970, councilor 1976-78), Mensa, USSR Acad. Sci. (award 1976), Sigma Xi, Phi Lambda Upsilon, Phi Kappa Phi, Alpha Chi Sigma, Gamma Sigma Epsilon. Home: 3881 Pico Ave Fresno CA 93726 Office: Calif State U Dept of Chemistry Fresno CA 93740

KAUFMAN, ANNA, social worker, consultant; b. N.Y.C., Nov. 16, 1925; d. William and Ida (Paul) Strizhak; m. Clarence Kaufman, Nov. 24, 1949; children: Ellen, Terry, Betty, Norma. BA, Bklyn. Coll., 1945; MA, U. Chgo., 1947. Lic. social worker, Calif. Psychiat. caseworker Family Services Bur. United Charities, Chgo., 1947-52, Jewish Family and Community Service, Chgo., 1952-53; casework supr. Juvenile Protective Assn., Chgo., 1954-56; cons. Social Work Cons. Inc., Huntington Beach, Calif., 1967—; pvt. practice counseling Anaheim, Calif., 1976—; instr. No. Orange Community Coll., Anaheim and Fullerton, 1974—, Calif. Community Coll., Nurse educators, Huntington Beach, 1976—. Pres. Stoddard PTA, Anaheim, 1968-70; charter mem. Orange County Council of Aging, 1972—, mem. adv. com. Long Term Ombudsman Program, Orange County, 1979-83; mem. ednl. longterm care adv. com. Vis. Nurse Assn. of Orange County, 1984-86. Recipient Hon. Service award Calif. Congress Parents and Tchrs., 1974. Mem. Nat. Assn. Social Workers, Acad. Social Workers, Calif. Nat. Assn. Social Workers (sec. long term care council 1976-79), s. Continuity Care Assn. of Orange County (v.p. 1979, 80), Am. Assn. Aging, Calif. Assn. Med. Dirs. Jewish. Avocations: reading, cooking, baking. Home: 1902 Gail Ln Anaheim CA 92802 Office: Social Work Cons Inc 4952 Warner Ave Suite 217 Huntington Beach CA 92649

KAUFMAN, CAROL LORENE YIP, environmental consultant; b. Los Angeles, Oct. 1, 1958; d. Sinclair and Mary Dora (Quon) Yip; m. Anthony Keith Kaufman, Feb. 14, 1981. BS in Biochemistry, Calif. State U., Los Angeles. Analytical chemist Truesdail Labs., Los Angeles, 1979-80, Jacobs Labs., Pasadena, Calif., 1980-81; environ. and regulatory rep. Ferro Corp., Santa Fe Springs, Calif., 1981-85; regulatory mgr. Ferro Corp. PMC Spltys. Group, Inc. div. PMC, Inc., Santa Fe Springs, Calif., 1985—; cons. Biota, Inc., Los Angeles, Calif., 1985—. Mem. Am. Chem. Soc., Am. Indsl. Hygiene Assoc., Asian Am. Pacific Artists Assn., Calif. Scholar. Fedn. (life). Avocations: piano, music appreciation, atheletics, electronics, photography. Office: PMC Specialties Group Inc div PMC Inc 10051 Romandel Ave Santa Fe Springs CA 90670

KAUFMAN, ELLEN LINDA, psychiatric social worker; b. Chgo., Feb. 12, 1954; d. Clarence and Anna (Strizhak) K. BA, U. Chgo., 1975, MA, 1976. Dir. childrens' services Hyde Park Jewish Community Ctr., Chgo., 1976-78; psychiat. social worker Aroostook Mental Health Ctr., Houlton, Maine, 1978-81; coordinator Jewish Family Service, Orange County, Calif., 1981-86; asst. prof. clin. social work U. So. Calif., Los Angeles, 1986—; instr. Unity Coll., Houlton, 1979-81, Hebrew Union Coll., Los Angeles, 1982-86, U. So. Calif., 1982-86. Mem. Nat. Assn. Social Work, Acad. Cert. Social Workers, So. Calif. Conf. Jewish Communal Services, Nat. Assn. Jewish Family Childrens and Health Profls. Democrat. Jewish. Avocations: music, theatre. Office: U So Calif Sch Social Work 12181 Buaro St Suite F Garden Grove CA 92640

KAUFMAN, KAREN LYNN, construction company executive; b. Akron, Ohio, Mar. 19, 1948; d. William B. and Edith (Gruber) Rogovy; div.; children—Amanda, Jonathan. Student U. Akron, 1966-68, Tex. Tech U., 1968-69, U. Calif.-Riverside, 1977-80; B.S., U. San Francisco, 1981. Lic. contractor, Calif. Project mgr. Bilsan Corp., Riverside, 1977-79; housing specialist County of Riverside, 1979-80; project mgr. Lewis Homes of Calif., 1980-81; cons. Williams & Burrows, Belmont, Calif., 1982-83; scheduling cons. LAX Terminal 1, Sheraton Grandé Hotel, Los Angeles; project mgr. Hyperion Energy Recovery System Site Utilities, Los Angeles, Morley Constrn. Co., 1983-86; owner, mgr. Amajon, Upland, Calif., 1982—. Mem. Bldg. Industry Assn., Nat. Assn. Home Builders, Community Assns. Inst., Comml. Indsl. Council. Democrat. Jewish. Club: Aero Club of So. Calif.

KAUFMAN, ROBERT DAVID, anesthesiologist; b. Los Angeles, June 17, 1947; s. Edwin Nathanial and Sylvia (Kopelman) K.; m. Neerad Varshney, Apr. 10, 1983. BS in Physics, UCLA, 1969; MD, U. Cin., 1973. Diplomate Am. Bd. Anesthesiology, Nat. Bd. Med. Examiners, Am. Coll. Anesthesiology. Asst. prof. dept. anethesia UCLA, 1977-84, adj. assoc. prof., 1984—. Contbr. articles to profl. jours. Mem. AAAS, Am. Soc. Anesthesiologists, Calif. Soc. Anesthesiologists. Avocations: flying, autocross, camping. Office: UCLA Dept Anesthesiology Ctr Health Scis Los Angeles CA 90024

KAUFMAN, SUSAN JANE, bank executive; b. Denver, Nov. 13, 1942; d. William Douglas and Catherine Sue (Orrison) Morrison; m. Jerry Allen Kaufman, Mar. 10, 1962; children: Eric Douglas, Carrie Annette. BA, U. Colo., 1968; MA, U. Denver, 1972; MBA, John F. Kennedy U., Orinda, Calif., 1981. Cert. fin. planner. Librarian, Littleton (Colo.) Pub. Library, 1972-74, Kent Denver Country Day Sch., 1974-76; exec. dir. Colo. Library Assn., Denver, 1974-76; customer service rep. bus. office Pacific Telephone Co., Berkeley, Calif., 1977-80; br. mgr., asst. v.p. Citicorp Savs., Orinda, 1981—. Mem. Contra Costa County M-11 Commn. (Calif.), 1983—; Children's Hosp. of Oakland, Alexander Lindsay Jr. Mus. Mem. Jr. League Oakland/East Bay, Orinda C. of C. (pres.), Orinda Hist. Soc., Bus. Vol. for the Arts, 1987—. Mem. Internat. Council Fin. Planners, Inst. Cert. Fin. Planners, Delta Gamma. Republican. Club: Soroptimists (treas.). Home: 6 Lavenida Orinda CA 94563 Office: 77 Moraga Way Orinda CA 94563

KAUFMANN, MERRILL RAY, plant physiologist; b. Paxton, Ill., June 17, 1941; s. Leo A. and Lorine (Weerts) K. BS, U. Ill., 1963; MF, Duke U., 1965, PhD, 1967. Asst. prof. plant physiology U. Calif., Riverside, 1967-73, assoc. prof., 1973-77; prin. plant physiologist USDA Forest Service, Ft. Collins, Colo., 1977—. Co-editor: Coupling of Carbon, Water and Nutrient Interactions in Woody Plant Soil Systems, 1986; contbr. numerous articles to profl. jours. Mem. AAAS, Am. Soc. Plant Physiologists (editorial bd.). Home: 3737 Landings Dr Unit E-19 Fort Collins CO 80525 Office: USDA Forest Service 240 W Prospect Rd Fort Collins CO 80526

KAUFMANN, THOMAS DAVID, educator; b. Rye, N.Y., July 23, 1922; s. Fritz and Irma (Heiden) K.; B.A., Oberlin Coll., 1943; M.P.A., Harvard U., 1947, M.A., 1947, Ph.D., 1949; m. Maureen Liebl, June 4, 1983; children—Peter F., David T. Economist, U.S. del. NATO and OEEC, Paris, 1949-56; dir. new bus. Amax, Inc., N.Y.C., 1956-67; v.p. Alumax, Inc., Greenwich, Conn., 1967-69; dir. bus. planning Hunter-Douglas, London, 1969-75; trader Asoma, N.Y.C., 1975-77; cons. Daniel K. Ludwig, N.Y.C., 1977-82; Philip Bros. prof. mineral econs. Colo. Sch. Mines, Golden, 1982—. Contbr. articles to profl. jours. Served with U.S. Army, 1943-46. Mem. Am. Econ. Assn., Phi Beta Kappa. Jewish. Home: 1966 Mount Zion Dr Golden CO 80401 Office: Colo Sch Mines Golden CO 80401

KAUNE, JAMES EDWARD, ship repair co. exec., former naval officer; b. Santa Fe, N.Mex., Mar. 4, 1927; s. Henry Eugene and Lucile (Carter) K.; B.S., U.S. Naval Acad., 1950; Naval Engr. degree Mass. Inst. Tech., 1955; B.S. in Metallurgy, Carnegie-Mellon U., 1960; m. Pauline Stamatos, June 24, 1956; children—Bradford Scott, Audrey Lynn, Jason Douglas. Commd. ensign U.S. Navy, 1950, advanced through grades to capt., 1970; asst. gunnery officer U.S.S. Floyd B. Parks, 1950-52; project officer U.S.S. Gyatt, Boston Naval Shipyard, 1955-57; main propulsion officer U.S.S. Tarawa, 1957-58; asst. planning officer Her Majesty's Canadian Dockyard, Halifax, N.S., Can., 1960-62; repair officer U.S.S. Cadmus, 1962-64; fleet maintenance officer Naval Boiler and Turbine Lab., 1964-68; various shipyard assignments, 1968-70, material staff officer U.S. Naval Air Forces Atlantic Fleet, 1971-74; production officer Phila. Naval Shipyard, 1974-79; comdr. Long Beach Naval Shipyard, Calif.; exec. v.p. Am. Metal Bearing Co., Garden Grove, Calif., from 1979; gen. mgr. San Francisco div. Topp Shipyards, Alameda, Calif., v.p. engrng. Point Richmond Shipyard (Calif.); v.p. engrng., mktg. Service Engrng. Corp, San Francisco. Mem. Am. Soc. Naval Engrs., Am. Soc. Quality Control, Soc. Naval Architects and Marine Engrs., U.S. Naval Inst., Am. Soc. Metals. Episcopalian. Club: Masons. Contbr. articles to profl. jours. Home: 403 Camino Sobrante Orinda CA 94563 Office: Service Engring Corp Pier 38 San Francisco CA 94107

KAUS, OTTO MICHAEL, lawyer; b. Vienna, Austria, Jan. 7, 1920; came to U.S., 1939, naturalized, 1942; s. Otto F. and Gina (Wiener) K.; m. Peggy A. Huttenback, Jan. 12, 1943; children: Stephen D., Robert M. B.A., UCLA, 1942; LL.B., Loyola U., Los Angeles, 1949. Bar: Calif. 1949. Pvt. practice Los Angeles, 1949-61; judge Superior Ct. Calif., 1961-64; assoc. justice Calif. Ct. Appeal (2d appellate dist., div. 3), Los Angeles, 1965-66; presiding justice Calif. Ct. Appeal (div. 5), 1966-81; assoc. justice Supreme Ct. Calif., San Francisco, 1981-85; ptnr. Hufstedler, Miller, Carlson & Beardsley, Los Angeles, 1986—; mem. faculty Loyola U. Law Sch., 1950-75, U. So. Calif., 1974-76. Served with U.S. Army, 1942-45. Mem. Am. Law Inst., Phi Beta Kappa, Order of Coif. Office: 700 S Flower St 16th Floor Los Angeles CA 90017

KAVANDI, JANET LYNN, aerospace power engineer; b. Springfield, Mo., July 17, 1959; d. William Winfred and Wanda Ruth (Garner) Sellers; m. Farhad John Kavandi, June 5, 1982. BS magna cum laude, Mo. So. State Coll., 1980; MS, U. Mo., Rolla, 1982. Project engr. Eagle-Picher Industries, Joplin, Mo., 1982-84; engr. electrical power div. Boeing Aerospace Co., Seattle, 1984—. Mem. Electrochem. Soc., AIAA, Am. Chem. Soc. Republican. Avocations: snow skiing, horseback riding, windsurfing, sailing, camping. Home: 25246 106th Ave SE # A215 Kent WA 98031 Office: Boeing Aerospace Co PO Box 3999 M/S 8K-25 Seattle WA 98124

KAWABE, FRANK HIROSHI, business executive; b. Japan, May 5, 1934; came to U.S., 1960; s. Satoru and Masako (Maki) K.; m. Akiyo Nakamura, Oct. 10, 1959; children—Carl, Carolyn. B.A., Keio U., Tokyo, 1957. Acct. Nippon Rubber, Tokyo, 1957-60; div. mgr. Kanematsu-Gosho, Los Angeles, 1962-65; founder, pres. Universal Bus. Interiors, Los Angeles, 1965—; gen. ptnr. Kawabe Enterprises, Los Angeles, 1979—; pres. Nippon Rubber U.S.A., Los Angeles, 1973—, San Angeles Devel., Los Angeles, 1983—, Peana Protein USA, Los Angeles, 1986—; chmn. bd. U.S.-Japan Travel, Los Angeles, 1983—; dir. Bus. News, Los Angeles, 1975—; mem. Pres.'s Council, Washington, 1978. Chmn. Japanese Pres. Club, Los Angeles. Recipient Life Saving award Japan Police Dept., 1956, award of appreciation White House, 1980. Mem. So. Calif. Japanese C. of C. (vice chmn. 1980-84). Club: Riviera Country (Los Angeles). Office: 219 S San Pedro Los Angeles CA 90012

KAY, ALAN STEVEN, newpaper editor; b. Bklyn., Feb. 15, 1945; s. Joseph J. and Gertrude (Feinman) K. BA cum laude, Bklyn Coll., 1965; postgrad., Princeton U., 1966; MPhil, Yale U., 1971. Pres. GMN, Inc., New Haven, 1974-75; master photographer New Haven Sch. System, New Haven, 1975-76; city editor New Haven Adv., 1976-79; city editor San Francisco Bay Guardian, 1980, mng. editor, 1980-86, exec. editor, 1986—; TV interview show host Viacom-Cable 6, San Francisco, 1982—; bd. dirs. Inst. Alternative Journalism, Seattle, 1983—. Contbr. articles to profl. publs. Mem. Calif. Soc. Newspaper Editors (founder). Jewish. Avocations: motorcycles, pipe collecting, politics. Home: 53 White St San Francisco CA 94109 Office: San Francisco Bay Guardian 2700 19th St San Francisco CA 94110

KAY, DANA W., therapist, educator; b. Newport News, Va., Apr. 23, 1941; d. Daniel J. and Isabelle K. (Barnes) Whealton; m. John Alfred Kay Jr., June 21, 1963; children: John A. III, Daniel E., Karen M. BA, Profl. Inst. of Coll. William and Mary, Richmond, Va., 1963; MSW, U. Md., 1974. Therapist, administrator Eastern Shore Hosp., Cambridge, Md., 1965-75; therapist, coordinator crisis service Whitman County Mental Hosp., Pullman, Wash., 1975-77; therapist Cen. Wash. Comprehensive Mental Health, Yakima, 1980-82; pvt. practice therapy Yakima, 1981—; social worker Yakima Valley Home Health, 1982—; educator alcoholism studies Yakima Valley Community Coll., 1982—; cons. Sunny Haven Institution for Mentally Retarded, Sunnyside, Wash., 1982-86, Omni Clinic, Yakima, 1985—. Mem. Valley Alcohol Council, Toppenish, Wash., 1985—, Family Violence Resource Ctr., Sunnyside, 1980-83, Lower Valley Hospice, Sunnyside, 1980-83. Mem. Nat. Assn. Social Workers, Acad. Cert. Social Workers, Alcoholism Profl. Staff Soc. Avocations: painting, bridge, swimming, reading. Mailing Address: 412 S 12th Ave Yakima WA 98402

KAY, DOUGLAS HAROLD, optometrist, optometry educator; b. Oakland, Calif., Oct. 7, 1949; s. Marvin Jack and Lois Natalie (Bernstein) K. A.B., U. Calif., 1971, B.S. in Optometry, 1973, O.D., 1975. Registered optometrist, Calif. Assoc. Woodland Clin. Med. Group (Calif.), 1975-78; cons. Calif. Vision Service Plan, Sacramento, 1977-82; pvt. practice optometry, Davis, Calif., 1978—; indsl. vision cons. Hunt-Wesson Foods, 1980—; asst. clin. prof. Sch. Optometry, U. Calif., Berkeley, 1983—; chmnsupervisory com. Calif. Optometric Credit Union. Bd. dirs. Valley Artist Prodns., Library Assocs., U. Calif.-Davis, Salvation Army, Davis, Econ. Devel. Council of Davis, 1985—; mem. Davis Comic Opera Co.; chmn. South Davis Traffic Study Com., 1984, Davis 2000 Study Com., 1985. Named Young Optometrist of Yr., Sacramento Valley Optometric Soc., 1981. Mem. Am. Optometric Assn., Calif. Optometric Assn., Sacramento Valley Optometric Soc. (pres. 1985-86), Vision Conservation Inst., C. of C. (dir. membership Davis Area). Democrat. Jewish. Lodge: Rotary (Davis) (sec. 1981—). Office: 1111 Kennedy Pl Suite 6 Davis CA 95616

KAY, ELIZABETH ALISON, zoology educator; b. Kauai, Hawaii, Sept. 27, 1928; d. Robert Buttercase and Jessie Dowie (McConnachie) K. BA, Mills Coll., 1950, Cambridge U., Eng., 1952; MA, Cambridge U., Eng., 1956; PhD, U. Hawaii, 1957. From asst. prof. to prof. zoology U. Hawaii, Honolulu, 1957-62, assoc. prof., 1962-67, prof., 1967—; research assoc. Bishop Mus., Honolulu, 1968—. Author: Hawaiian Marine Mollusks, 1979; editor: A Natural History of The Hawaiian Islands, 1972. Chmn. Animal Species Adv. Commn., Honolulu, 1983—; v.p. Save Diamond Head Assn., Honolulu, 1968—; trustee B.P. Bishop Mus., Honolulu, 1983—. Fellow Linnean Soc., AAAS; mem. Marine Biol. Assn. (Eng.), Australian Malacol. Soc. Episcopalian. Office: U Hawaii Manoa Dept Zoology 2538 The Mall Honolulu HI 96822

KAY, FENTON RAY, wildlife biologist; b. Pacolma, Calif., Oct. 10, 1942; s. Lyle E. Kay and Donna F. (Estill) Allan; m. Carol Ann Rolph, June 13, 1971 (div. Jan. 1985); children: Aelene B., Jennifer M. BS in Biology, U. Nev., 1967, MS in Zoology, 1969; PhD in Biology, N.Mex. State U., 1974, postgrad., 1982-83. Sr. ecologist H.D.R. Scis. Div., Santa Barbara, Calif., 1978-79; sr. subject matter specialist OAO Kenton Internat., White Sands Missile Range, N.Mex., 1979-82; ops. mgr. OAO Corp., White Sands Missile Range, N.Mex., 1982-83; treas. CEI Corp., Las Cruces, N.Mex., 1979-82; habitat staff specialist Nev. Dept. Wildlife, Reno, 1984—; mem. faculty Truckee Meadows Community Coll., Reno, 1984—; cons. Nev. State Mus., Carson City, 1983-84; cons. in field, 1984—; vis. scientist Tall Timbers Research Sta., Tallahassee, 1977. Author: (computer program) Butler-Adventure, 1983, Keno-Game, 1984; contbr. articles to profl. jours. Active Citizen's Adv. Com. on Endangered Species, Las Vegas, 1968. Postdoctoral trainee NIH, 1974-76. Mem. AAAS, Am. Soc. Mammalogists, Ecol. Soc. Am., Herpetologists' League, So. Nev. Herpetol. Soc. (founder 1967), Sigma Xi (grantee 1973). Democrat. Avocations: running, photography, gardening. Office: Nev Dept Wildlife 1100 Valley Rd Reno NV 89520

KAY, MICHAEL AARON, researcher and developer of safe cleaning agents and hazardous material controls; b. San Francisco; May 7, 1943; s. Abraham and Lillian Yetta (Sokol) K.; m. Judith Toby Greenbach, June 9, 1963 (div. Oct. 1974); children—Andrew Roger, Daniel Saul; m. Rachel Ann Foley, July 3, 1976. B.S., U. Calif.-Berkeley, 1965; Sc.D., MIT, 1970. Radiochemist, U.S. Naval Radiol. Def. Lab., San Francisco, 1964-65; sr. research chemist U. Mo., Columbia, 1970-78; sr. scientist Rockwell Hanford Ops., Richland, Wash., 1978-80; dir. Reed Reactor Facility Reed Coll., Portland, Oreg., 1980-86, assoc. prof. chemistry, 1980-86; mgr. chemistry research and devel. Hanna Internat., Milwaukie, 1986—; forensic cons. Radiation Systems Assocs., Milwaukie, Oreg., 1981—. Contbr. articles to profl. jours. NIH grantee, 1978. Mem. Am. Chem. Soc., Am. Nuclear Soc., Health Physics Soc., AAAS. Jewish. Office: Hanna Internat 2000 Hanna Dr PO Box 22266 Portland OR 97222

KAY, RICHARD STANLEY, finance executive; b. Milw., Apr. 24, 1942; s. Stanley Joseph and Louise Amanda (Kowalski) K.; m. Sandra Ruth Standiford, Nov. 15, 1969; 1 child, Tracy Marie. BBA, U. Wis., Milw., 1965. CPA. Sr. auditor Price Waterhouse & Co., Milw., 1967-72; acct. Miller Shockey & Co., La Jolla, Calif., 1972-74; v.p. fin. Continuous Curve Contact Lenses Inc., San Diego, 1974-82, Urgent Care Ctrs. Am., San Diego, 1982-83; sr. v.p. fin. Energy Factors Inc., San Diego, 1983—. Served to capt. U.S. Army, 1965-67, Korea. Mem. Fin. Execs. Inst. (pres. San Diego chpt. 1985-86), San Diego Corp. Fin. Council, Am. Inst. CPA's, Calif. Soc. CPA's, Wis. Soc. CPA's. Republican. Clubs: La Jolla Country (mem. greens com.); Century (San Diego). Avocation: golf. Home: 4217 Caminito Terviso San Diego CA 92122 Office: Energy Factors Inc 401 B St Suite 1000 San Diego CA 92101-4219

KAYA, LAWTON NOBUO, structural, civil and computer engineer, consultant; b. Hilo, Hawaii, July 2, 1956; s. Chikara and Toshie (Nakayama) K.; m. Jill Chie Tanaka, June 12, 1982; 1 son, Laren Shunichi. B.S., U. Hawaii, 1978, J.D., 1981, postgrad. in bus. adminstrn., 1983—; M.S., U. Ill., 1979. Registered profl. engr., Hawaii. Structural and computer engr. Metcalf & Eddy-Pacific, Inc., Honolulu, 1977-81; engring. systems mgr. Navy Pub. Works Ctr., Pearl Harbor, Hawaii, 1981—; computer cons., Honolulu, 1981—; with Navy Pub. Works Mgmt. Devel. Program, 1985-86. Author research paper. Active campaigns Democratic Party, Honolulu, 1975-81. Grad. fellow U. Ill., 1979; Nat. Soc. Profl. Engrs. fellow for engrs. in mgmt., 1985. Mem.NSPE, Structural Engrs. Assn., Mortar Bd., Phi Kappa Phi, Phi Eta Sigma, Chi Epsilon, Beta Gamma Sigma. Buddhist. Office: Navy Pub Works Ctr Code 425 Pearl Harbor HI 96860-5470

KAYA, ROBERT MASAYOSHI, contractor; b. Waialua, Oahu, Hawaii, Feb. 3, 1914; s. Jinhichi and Aki (Tanimoto) K.; student pub. schs.; m. Florence Shinayo Okinaka, Mar. 15, 1939; children—Kathleen Tatsue, Merle Nobue, Virginia Sachie, Winifred Fumie. Carpenter, Hawaiian Contracting Co., 1935, carpenter, foreman D. Orita, contractor, 1936-37; owner contracting bus., Honolulu, 1937—; dir. City Bank Honolulu. Active YMCA; bd. dirs. Kuakini Med. Ctr. Mem. Gen. Contractors Assn. Hawaii, Oahu Contractors Assn. (pres. 1954-55), Building Industry Assn. Hawaii (pres. 1956), Honolulu C. of C., Honolulu Japanese C. of C. (pres. 1974-75), Nat. Assn. Home Builders (life dir. 1976—), Nat. Fedn. Ind. Bus., Japan Am. Soc. Honolulu, Bishop Museum Assn., U.S. Army Museum, U. Hawaii Found. Buddhist (pres. Zen sect. Soto Mission 1973-74). Clubs: Lions (dist. gov. Hawaii 1964-65, pres. 1955-56; life mem.), 200 (Honolulu). Home: 2380 Beckwith St Honolulu HI 96822 Office: 525 Korea St #B3 Honolulu HI 96817

KAYE, ALAN STEWART, linguistics educator; b. Los Angeles, Mar. 2, 1941; s. Sam and Ray Kaye; m. Susan Marianne Mazur, Aug. 27, 1972; children: Jennifer Danielle, Jeremy Daniel. Teaching assoc. U. Calif., Berkeley, 1967-69; asst. prof. linguistics U. Colo., Boulder, 1969-71; asst. prof. Calif. State U., Fullerton, Calif., 1971-74; dir. phonetics lab. Calif. State U., Fullerton, 1971—, assoc. prof., 1974-78, prof., 1978—. Author: Chadian and Sudanese Arabic, 1976 (UCI Library award 1977), A Dictionary of Nigerian Arabic, 1982 (UCI Library award 1983), Nigerian Arabic-English Dictionary, 1986 (UCI Library award 1986); contbr. articles to profl. jours. Bd. trustees Yorba Linda (Calif.) Library Dist., 1979; bd. trustees N. Orange Coutny Community Coll. Dist., Fullerton, 1979-83. Grantee NSF, 1969-70, NEH, 1973-74, Am. Phil. Soc., 1973-74, 75-76, Fulbright, 1978-79, Werner-Gren Found., 1985-86,. Mem. Linguistic Soc. Am., Am. Oriental Soc. (bd. dirs.), Can. Linguistics Assn., Middle East Studies Assn. of N.Am. Republican. Roman Catholic. Avocations: chess, bridge, athletics. Office: Calif State U Dept Linguistics Fullerton CA 92634

KAYE, DAVID NORMAN, public relations executive; b. N.Y.C., Feb. 25, 1942; s. Samuel H. and Helen (Hantman) K.; m. Bea Soltz, June 10, 1962; children: Roni Sue, Ari Anne. BSEE, Carnegie Mellon U., 1962; MSEE, Poly. Inst. N.Y. (now Poly. U. N.Y.), 1966. Mem. tech. staff AIL div. Eaton Corp., Melville, N.Y., 1962-66; sr. project mgr. Micromega, Venice, Calif., 1966-68; sr. Western editor Electronic Design mag., Los Angeles, 1968-76; pres. KPR Inc., Granada Hills, Calif., 1976—; bd. dirs. JALA, Van Nuys, Calif. Contbr. articles to profl. jours. Bd. dirs. VBS Day Sch., Encino, Calif., 1978-80. Recipient Jesse Neal award Am. Bus. Press, 1971. Mem. IEEE, Aviation/Space Writers Assn. Club: Publicity of Los Angeles. Home: 12740 Deon Pl Granada Hills CA 91344 Office: KPR Inc 17057 Chatsworth St Granada Hills CA 91344

KAYE, RONALD LEE, physician, educator; b. Toledo, Apr. 15, 1932; s. Philip and Gertrude (Berman) K.; m. Tobye Davidson, June 19, 1955; children: Brian, Todd, Douglas, Jeffrey. BA, U. Mich., 1953, MD, 1957. Diplomate Am. Bd. Rheumatology, Am. Bd. Internal Medicine. Intern Sinai Hosp., Detroit, 1957-58; fellow and staff mem. Mayo Clinic, Rochester, Minn., 1959-63; chmn. dept. rheumatology Palo Alto (Calif.) Med. Clinic, 1963—; prof. medicine Stanford U., Palo Alto, 1963—. Contbr. articles to profl. jours. Bd. dirs. Am. Mogan David Adom., N.Y.C., 1967—, U.S.-China Ednl. Inst., San Francisco, 1975—, Sino-Judaic Inst., Palo Alto, 1985—. Served to capt. USAF, 1959-61. Fellow ACP; mem. AMA, Am. Soc. Clin. Rheumatology (pres. 1975-80), Arthritis Found. (bd. dirs., Disting. Service award 1974). Jewish. Avocations: philately, minerals, numismatics, travel, jazz. Office: Palo Alto Med Clinic 300 Homer Ave Palo Alto CA 94301

KAYFETZ, VICTOR JOEL, journalist, editor, translator; b. N.Y.C., July 20, 1945; s. Daniel Osler and Selma Harriet (Walowitz) K.; B.A., Columbia U., 1966; postgrad. U. Stockholm (Sweden), 1966-67; M.A. in History, U. Calif.-Berkeley, 1969. Teaching asst. in Swedish, U. Calif., Berkeley, 1969-70; tchr., adminstr. Dalaro Folk Coll., Sweden, 1970-71, Visingso Folk Coll., Sweden, 1972-73; head tchr. English, Studieframjandet Adult Sch., Stockholm, 1973-74, sec. head, 1974-75; corr. Reuters, Stockholm, 1975-78; sub-editor Reuters World Ser., London, 1978; corr. London Fin. Times, Stockholm, 1979-80; copy editor, translator Scandinavian Bus. World, 1981-82; free lance translator Swedish, Danish, Norwegian, 1967—; free lance journalist, editor Swedish and Am. mags., Stockholm, 1979-80, San Francisco, 1980—. Henry Evans traveling fellow, 1966-67; Nat. Def. Fgn. Lang. fellow, 1967-69; Thord Gray fellow Am.-Scandinavian Found., 1970. Mem. Media Alliance, Swedish Am. C. of C., Swedish Bus. and Soc. Research Inst., Soc. Advancement Scandinavian Studies, World Affairs Council No. Calif., Sierra Club, Phi Beta Kappa. Author: Sweden in Brief, 1974, 2d edit., 1977; Invest in Sweden, 1984, Skanska, the First Century, 1987; editor, translator numerous books and articles Swedish Inst., 1971—; editor, translator Fed. Swedish Industries, 1977—, Swedish Industry Faces the 80s, 1981; translator ann. reports Swedish indsl. corps., banks, 1977—; others. Office: Scan Edit World Trade Center Room 268 San Francisco CA 94111

KAYLAN, HOWARD LAWRENCE, musical entertainer, composer; b. N.Y.C., June 22, 1947; s. Sidney and Sally Joyce (Berlin) K.; m. Mary Melita Pepper, June 10, 1967 (div. Sept. 1971); 1 child, Emily Anne; m. Susan Karen Olsen, Apr. 18, 1982. Grad. high sch., Los Angeles. Lead singer, rock group The Turtles, Los Angeles, 1965-70, Mothers of Invention, Los Angeles, 1970-72; radio, TV, recording entertainer various broadcast organizations, Los Angeles, 1972—; screenwriter Larry Gelbart, Carl Gotleib prodns., Los Angeles, 1979-85; producer children's records Kidstuff Records, Hollywood, Fla., 1980—; singer, producer Flo and Eddie and the Turtles, Los Angeles, 1980—; actor, TV and film Screen Actors Guild, Los Angeles, 1983—; v.p. Flo and Eddie, Inc., Los Angeles, 1972—; background vocalist for Bruce Springsteen, T. Rex, Blondie, Andy Taylor, Psychedelic Furs, John Lennon. Contbr. articles to Creem Magazine, Los Angeles Free Press, Rockit Magazine, Phonograph Record; screenwriter motion picture Death Masque, 1985; actor motion picture Get Crazy, 1985; performed in the White House, 1970. Recipient 6 gold and platinum LP album awards while lead singer, 1965—, cert. achievement State of Calif., 1982, Fine Arts award Bank of Am., Los Angeles, 1965. Mem. AFTRA, Screen Actors Guild, Am. Fedn. Musicians, AGVA. Democrat. Avocations: collector rare, ltd. edit. books, video movies, rare rock recordings.

KAYS, DOUGLAS BRUCE, lawyer; b. Eugene, Oreg., Mar. 14, 1954; s. James W. and Marilyn (Griffith) K.; m. Jean Marie McEvoy, Aug. 14, 1982; children: Megan Marie, Tara Jean. B.S., Willamette U., 1976; J.D., Southwestern U., 1979. Bar: Calif. 1980. Gen. counsel McMahan's Furniture Co., Santa Monica, Calif., 1980—; sole practice law, Santa Monica, 1980—; staff counsel Nat. Home Furnishings Assn.-West, 1982—; staff council, treas. Calif. Home Furnishings Council; mem. consumer fin. services com. Calif. State Bar; pres. Greater Los Angeles Consumer Credit Assn., 1984-85; lectr. in field. Bd. dirs. Greater Los Angeles Consumer Credit Assn., 1982-83. Named Future First Citizen, Eugene, 1972; Am. Legion award, 1969. Mem. ABA, Calif. Bar Assn., Los Angeles County Bar Assn. Republican. Methodist. Lodge: Lions. Club: Santa Monica Y's Men's (pres. 1983-84). Home: 859 Harvard St Santa Monica CA 90403 Office: 2121 Wilshire Blvd Santa Monica CA 90403

KAYS, JAMES WILLIAM, investment executive; b. Princeton, Ind., Aug. 19, 1924; s. James Oscar and Mildred June (Hedge) K.; m. Marilyn Griffith, June 13, 1948; children—J. Alan, Nancy Lynn Kays Read, Douglas B., David W., Scott T., Holly J., John P. B.S. in Bus. Adminstrn., U. Oreg., 1948. Gen. mgr. Eugene (Oreg.) Country Club, 1948-53; supr. Standard Ins. Co., 1953-58; with Adams, Hess, Moore & Co., Eugene, and predecessor E.M. Adams & Co., 1958—, chmn. bd., 1982—; bd. dirs. R.A. Chambers & Assocs., UOA Embarcadero Resort, Yaquina Rental Agy.; pres. Eugene Open, Inc. Mem. Eugene Civic Ctr. Comm.; fin. chmn. Oreg. Bach Festival; chmn. 1st United Methodist Ch. Found.; bd. dirs. Sr. Masters Golf Assn.; trustee Eugene Symphony Endowment Fund. Served with AUS, 1943-45; ETO. Named Eugene Jr. 1st Citizen, 1954; Boss of Yr., Nat. Secs. Assn., 1972. Mem. Roundtable (pres. 1984-85), Nat. Assn. Corp. Dirs., Nat. Register of Health Service Providers in Psychology. Republican. Clubs: Eugene Country (past pres.), Arlington, Lions (past pres.), Town (dir.) (Eugene). Home: 2280 Charnelton Eugene OR 97405 Office: Adams Hess Moore & Co 975 Oak St Suite 1080 Eugene OR 97405

KAZDA, LOUIS FRANK, electrical and computer engineering educator, consultant, researcher; b. Dayton, Ohio, Sept. 21, 1916; s. Ludwig Augustus and Elizabeth Theresa (Novak) K.; m. Jane Elizabeth Glover, Aug. 24, 1940; children—Judith Ann Kazda Burd, Sally Louise Kazda Stites, Joan Elizabeth. E.E., U. Cin., 1940, M.S.E., 1943; Ph.D., Syracuse U., 1962. Research engr. Bendix Corp., Teterboro, N.J., 1943-45; mem. elec. and computer engring. faculty U. Mich., Ann Arbor, 1946—; prof., dir. power systems lab. U. Mich., 1979-84, prof. emeritus, 1984—; prof. N.Mex. State U., Las Cruces, 1987; cons. Willow Run Labs., U. Mich., Ypsilanti, 1953-72; cons. summer study Nat. Acad. Sci., Falmouth, Mass., 1973; co-chmn. NSF Workshop, Ann Arbor, 1972; chmn. Joint Automatic Control Conf., Ann Arbor, 1968. Author: (with others) Optimal and Self Optimizing Control, 1966; contbr. articles to profl. jours. Recipient Prize Paper award Am. Inst. Elec. Engrs., N.Y.C., 1960; named Disting. Alumnus U. Cin., 1981. Fellow IEEE (Centennial medal 1984; disting. mem. Control System Soc.); mem. U. Cin. Alumni Assn., Syracuse U. Alumni Assn., U. Mich. Alumni Assn., Sigma Xi, Eta Kappa Nu. Republican. Presbyterian. Avocations: swimming; horseback riding. Home: 3013 Ronna Dr Las Cruces NM 88001 Office: NMex State Univ Elec and Computer Engring Dept Box 30 Las Cruces NM 88003

KAZOR, WALTER ROBERT, mechanical engineer; b. Avonmore, Pa., Apr. 16, 1922; s. Steven Stanley and Josephine (Lestic) K.; B.S. in Mech. Engring., Pa. State U., 1943; M.S., U. Pitts., 1953, M.Letters in Econs. and Indsl. Mgmt., 1957; m. Gloria Rosalind Roma, Aug. 10, 1946; children—Steven Edward, Christopher Paul, Kathleen Mary Jo. Research engr. Gulf Oil Corp., Pitts., 1946-57; with Westinghouse Electric Corp., 1957-84, quality assurance mgr. breeder reactor components project, Tampa, Fla., 1977-81, mgr. nuclear service center, Tampa, 1981-84; pres. Integrated Quality Systems Corp., Mgmt. Quality Assurance Cons., St. Petersburg, Fla., 1984-86; quality assurance specialist in nuclear waste mgmt. Sci. Applications Internat. Corp., Las Vegas, 1986—; cons., guest lectr. in field. Bd. dirs. New Kensington (Pa.) council Boy Scouts Am., 1958-62. Served with USNR, 1944-46. Registered profl. engr., Pa. Mem. ASME, Am. Soc. Quality Control. Republican. Roman Catholic. Club: Lions (past pres. clubs). Author, patentee in field. Home: 1120 88th Ave N Saint Petersburg FL 33702 Office: 101 Convention Ctr Dr Las Vegas NV 89103

KEALA, FRANCIS AHLOY, security executive; b. Honolulu, June 1, 1930; s. Samuel Louis and Rose (Ahloy) K.; m. Betty Ann Lyman, Nov. 28, 1952; children—Frances Ann, John Richard, Robert Mark. B.A. in Sociology, U. Hawaii, 1953. Patrolman Honolulu Police Dept., 1956-62, detective, 1962-65, lt., 1965-68, capt., 1968-69, chief of police, 1969-83; dir. security Hawaiian Telephone Co., 1983—; mem. civilian adv. group U.S. Army. Bd. dirs. YMCA, Aloha council Boy Scouts Am., Palama Settlement, 200 Club, Sex Abuse Treatment Center, AAA of Hawaii, Hawaii Meml. Park Assn.; trustee St. Louis High Sch.; bd. govs. Boys and Girls Clubs of Honolulu; advisor Hawaii Meml. Park; mem. Civilian Adv. Group U.S. Army; Girl Scouts U.S. Council of the Pacific, Honolulu C. of C. Served with U.S. Army, 1953-55. Mem. Internat. Assn. Chiefs of Police, Hawaii State Law Enforcement Ofcls. Assn., C. of C. of Honolulu, FBI Nat. Acad. Assocs. Clubs: Oahu Country, Pacific. Lodge: Rotary (Honolulu). Office: 1177 Bishop St Honolulu HI 96813

KEAMMERER, WARREN ROY, ecological scientist, consultant, infosystems specialist; b. Gary, Ind., Nov. 25, 1946; s. Norman P. and Laura E. (Nicholson) K.; m. Deborah Anne Barton, Aug. 29, 1970; children: Linnaea, Holly. BS, Capital U., 1968; PhD, N.D. State U., 1971. Lectr. biology Capital U., Columbus, Ohio, 1971-72; postdoctoral fellow U. Colo., Boulder, 1972-73; pres., research ecologist Keammerer Ecol. Cons., Boulder, 1973—; active High Altitude Revegetation com., Colo., 1974—. Contbr. articles to profl. jours. NDEA fellow, 1968-71. Mem. Ecol. Soc. Am., British Ecol. Soc., Soc. Range Mgmt., Sigma Xi. Republican. Avocations: photography, hiking, golf. Home and Office: 5858 Woodbourne Hollow Rd Boulder CO 80301

KEANE, WILLIAM FRANCIS, photographer; b. La Habra, Calif., June 8, 1948; s. William Edward and Joan Francis Keane; children: Cameron Patrick, Chelsea Shannon. BA, Claremont Men's Coll.; Craftsman Photographer Profl. Photographers Am., 1980. Owner, Bill Keane Photography, Claremont, Calif., 1968-71; apprentice Charis Studios, Pasadena, Calif., 1971; chief photographer Fotomat Corp., La Jolla, Calif., 1972-75; owner Keane Studios, Santa Ana, Calif., 1982-84, San Diego, 1976-86; owner Keane Prodns, San Diego, 1986—; The Bridal Bazaar, San Diego, 1975-84; lectr. in field. Columnist Profl. Photographer, 1978-81, Rangefinder, 1981-82. Mem. Profl. Photographers Am., Profl. Photographers Calif., Am. Soc. Photographers. Republican.

KEANE, WILLIAM PATRICK, stockbroker; b. Santa Monica, Calif., July 15, 1936; s. William Patrick and Martha (Tuttle) K.; m. Sally Stocking (div.); children—William Patrick, Stacy Ann; m. 2d, Susan Raiford Wilson, Oct. 21, 1977. Vice pres. Calif. Co., Los Angeles, 1958-71; first v.p. Bateman, Eichler, Hill, Richards, Los Angeles, 1971-84, Drexel, Burnham, Lambert, Beverly Hills, Calif., 1984—; fin. reporter KWHY-Channel 22, Los Angeles, 1978—. Pres. Westwood Sertoma Club, West Los Angeles, 1983. Mem. Bond Club Los Angeles, AMEX Club Los Angeles, Stockbrokers Soc. Los Angeles. Republican. Presbyterian. Clubs: Jonathon (Commodore 1980-82), Calif. Yacht. Home: 29th Ave #4 Venice CA 90291 Office: Drexel Burnham Lambert 9560 Wilshire Blvd Beverly Hills CA 90212

KEAR, FRED WINSTON, manufacturing company executive; b. Clayton, N.Mex., Nov. 11, 1930; s. James Clifford and Lillie Mae (Ogle) K.; student Union Coll. (Nebr.), 1950-51; m. Fonda Anita Scott, Jan. 11, 1953; children—Steven Scott, Stephanie Kay, Pamela Mae. Dir. research and devel. lab. Lytle Corp., Albuquerque, 1960-64; chief mfg. engr. Sparton S.W., Inc., Albuquerque, 1964-72, 77—; sr. quality assurance engr. Singer Bus. Machines, Albuquerque, 1972-75; mgr. mfg. MRL S.W., Albuquerque, 1975-76; engr. supr. GTE Lenkurt, Albuquerque, 1977-86; mgr. engring. Siemens Transmission Systems, 1986—. Served with USN, 1950-54. Mem. Soc. Mfg. Engrs. Democrat. Seventh-Day Adventist. Author: The Design and Manufacture of Printed Circuits, 1971; Production Engineering, 1973; Printed Circuit Assembly Manufacturing, 1987; contbr. articles to profl. jours.; chief contbr. to Handbook of Electronic Circuits, 1969, others. Home: 1729 Shirley St Albuquerque NM 87112

KEARNEY, CHERYAL ANN, set decorator, interior designer; b. Los Angeles; d. Donald and Henrietta (Robinson) K. BS in Interior Design, Woodbury U., Los Angeles, 1964; student Parson Sch. Musée des Arts Decoratifs, 1979. Set decorator for TV shows including Cannon, 1971, Harry-O, 1973, 74, Spiderman, 1978, Tucker's Witch, 1981, L.A. Law, Moonlighting, Love Lives On, A letter to 3 Wines, News at 11:00, Christmas Eve, Gangin the Savage (emmy award); set decorator films including Sounder II, 1975, Bad News Bears, 1975, Mother, Jugs and Speed, 1975, A Hero Ain't Nothin' But a Sandwich, 1976, Semi-Tough, 1977, The Promise, 1978, Lazarus Syndrome, 1979, Under the Rainbow, 1980, Poltergeist, 1981, Two of a Kind, 1982, Captain E.O. Active NAACP, Los Angeles. Mem. Am. Soc. Interior Designers, Acad. Motion Picture Arts and Scis., Acad. TV Arts and Scis. (Emmy 1980). Office: Unique Design Experience 4506 Valdina Pl Los Angeles CA 90043

KEARNS, DAVID RICHARD, chemistry educator; b. Urbana, Ill., Mar. 20, 1935; s. Clyde W. and Camille V. (French) K.; m. Alice Chen, July 5, 1958; children: Jennifer, Michael. BS in Chem. Engring., U. Ill., 1956; PhD., U. Calif., Berkeley, 1960. USAF doctoral fellow U. Chgo., 1960-61, MIT, Cambridge, 1961-62; asst. prof. chemistry U. Calif., Riverside, 1962-63, assoc. prof., 1964-67, prof., 1968-75; prof. U. Calif., San Diego, 1975—. Assoc. editor Molecular Photochemistry, 1969-75, Photochemistry and Photobiology, 1971-75, Chem. Revs., 1974; assoc. editor Biopolymers, 1975-78, editorial bd., 1978—. Sloan Found. fellow, 1965-67; Guggenheim fellow, 1969-70. Mem. Am. Chem. Soc. (Calif. sect. award 1973), Am. Phys. Soc.,

Am. Soc. Photobiology. Home: 8422 Sugarman Dr La Jolla CA 92037 Office: U Calif San Diego Dept Chemistry La Jolla CA 92093

KEATHLEY, JACKSON PHILLIP, agricultural scientist; b. Dustin, Okla., Mar. 22, 1942; s. Luster Lovic and Stella Mae (Liles) K.; m. Florence Ann Paulsen, Sept. 2, 1967; children: Laura Beth, Craig Phillip. BA, Okla. State U., 1965, MS, 1966; PhD, U. Ga., 1972. Sr. research biologist Dow Chem. Co. USA, Walnut Creek, Calif., 1972-74; field research and devel. rep. Gulf Oil Chem. Co., Concord, Calif., 1974-80; devel. rep. DuPont & Co., Menlo Park, Calif., 1980-82; pres. J. Phillip Keathley, Inc., Ripon, Calif., 1982—. Little League mgr. Jr. Optimists Baseball, Concord, Calif, 1982-84; coach Babe Ruth Baseball, Ripon, Calif, 1986; dir. Royal Ambassadors, Ripon, 1985—. Served to lt. comdr. USNR, 1966-78. Mem. Entomol. Soc. Am., Weed Sci. Soc. Am., Am. Phytopath. Soc., No. Calif. Entomol. Club, Ripon C. of C., Sigma Xi, Gamma Sigma Delta. Democrat. Baptist. Avocations: softball, basketball, choir, music soloist, fishing. Home and Office: 25330 S Ruess Rd Ripon CA 95366

KEATING, CHARLES H., JR., construction company executive; b. 1923. J.D., U. Cin., 1948. Formerly with firm, partner Keating Muething & Klekamp; now chmn., chief exec. officer Am. Continental Corp., Phoenix, Ariz. Office: Am Continental Corp 2735 E Camelback Rd Phoenix AZ 80516 *

KEATING, JOE FRANCIS, science educator; b. Glens Falls, N.Y., Jan. 5, 1947; s. Joseph Francis and Irene Susan (Power) K.; m. Josephine Susan Melenchek, June 14, 1969; children: Rachel Irene, Sean Anthony. BS in Biology, SUNY, Albany, 1968; MS in Biology, Union Coll., 1972; postgrad., U. N.Mex. Cert. tchr. math., sci., N.Y., N.Mex. Prefect LaSalle Sch. for Boys, Albany, 1964-68; instr. sci. Pascal Sherman Indian Sch., Omak, Wash., 1968-71; research asst. Lake George (N.Y.) Research Ctr., 1968; instr., chmn. dept. sci. Thoreau (N.Mex.) High Sch., 1971—; instr., dir. Navajo Community Coll., Thoreau, 1978—; task force rep. Gallup (N.Mex.) McKinley Schs., 1981—, chmn. sci. com., 1985—; lectr. N.Mex. State Sci. Council, 1983. Chmn. Cystic Fibrosis Fundraiser, Thoreau, 1977-79; campaign mgr. Dist. III McKinley County Magistrate, Gallup, 1978; co-dir. Olympics of the Mind, 1984-86. Grantee NSF, 1981, Native Am. Sci. Educators N.Mex. State U., 1982; Alfred Husteo fellow, 1987; named 4-State Tchr. of Yr., Arco, Tsaile, Ariz., 1982-83; recipient N.Mex. Research Council Teaching award, 1986. Mem. Nat. Sci. Tchrs. Assn. (Sci. Screen award 1986), Not Man Apart, N.Mex. Environ. Edn. Assn. Democrat. Roman Catholic. Avocations: cross-country skiing, long distance running, coaching runners, reading. Home: Box 448 Thoreau NM 87323 Office: Thoreau High Sch Box 96 Thoreau NM 87323

KEATING, LARRY GRANT, electrical engineer, educator; b. Omaha, Jan. 15, 1944; s. Grant Morris and Dorothy Ann (Kauffold) K.; m. Barbara Jean Merley, Dec. 21, 1968. LLB, Blackstone Sch. Law, 1968; BS, U. Nebr., 1969; BS summa cum laude, Met. State Coll., 1971; MS, U. Colo., Denver, 1978. Chief engr. broadcast electronics 3 radio stas., 1965-69; coordinator engrng. reliability Cobe Labs., Lakewood, Colo., 1972-74; quality engr. Statitrol Corp., Lakewood, Colo., 1974-76; instr. electrical engring. U. Colo., Denver, 1976-78; assoc. prof. Met. State Coll., Denver, 1978-84, chmn. dept., 1984—; cons. Transplan Assocs., Boulder, Colo., 1983-84. Co-author: (book) South Santa Fe Corridor, 1985. Served to 1st lt. U.S. Army, 1962-70. Recipient Outstanding Faculty award U. Colo., Denver, 1980, Outstanding Alumnus award Met. State Coll., 1985. Mem. IEEE (sr.), Instrument Soc. Am. (sr.), Robotics Internat. (sr.), Am. Soc. Engring. Edn., Nat. Assn. Radio and Telecommunications Engrs. (cert. 1st class)., Eta Kappa Nu, Tau Alpha Pi, Chi Epsilon. Avocations: skiing, astronomy. Home: 6455 E Bates Ave 4-108 Denver CO 80222 Office: Met State Coll 1006 11th St Campus Box 29 Denver CO 80204

KEATING, THOMAS FRANCIS, state senator; b. Langdon, N.D., Nov. 26, 1928; s. Thomas Delbert and Olive Mary (Bear) K.; student Eastern Mont. Coll., 1951; B.A. in Bus. Adminstrn., U. Portland, 1953; m. Anna Louise Walsh, Aug. 22, 1953; children—Thomas J., Patrick, Michael, Kathryn, Terence. Landman, Mobil Oil Corp., Billings, Mont., 1954-61, Oklahoma City, 1961-66, Burlington No. R.R., Billings, 1966-67; Mont., landman, Billings, 1967-81; mem. Mont. Senate, 1981—. Served with USAF, 1946-49. Mem. Mont. Assn. Petroleum Landmen (pres. 1969), Am. Assn. Petroleum Landmen (dir. 1971-73), Ind. Petroleum Assn., Billings C. of C. Republican. Roman Catholic. Office: PO Box 20522 Billings MT 59104

KEATING, WALTER JAMES, finance executive; b. Atlantic City, May 23, 1947; s. John J. and Alice (Mercer) K.; B.B.A., U. Okla., 1970; m. Aug. 6, 1969; children—Jennifer Lynn, Jared Alan. Loan officer Security Pacific Bank, Westwood Village, Calif., 1970-72; account exec. Merrill Lynch, Long Beach, Calif., 1972-75; with E.F. Hutton, Long Beach, 1975-78; with Paine Webber, City of Industry, Calif., 1981-82, nat. trust and devel. officer, 1979-80, br. mgr., Walnut Creek, Calif. 1980-81, City of Industry, 1982, sales mgr./asso. mgr. Los Angeles regional hdqrs., 1982-85, mem. dir.'s council 1987; mem. faculty, UCLA, retirement counceling officer, 1984—; cons. in retirement planning to many corps. Trustee, Mt. Diablo Health Care Found., 1981-83; chmn. community adv. com. Torrance Meml. Hosp., 1975-76. Mem. City of Industry C. of C. Republican. Mem. Ch. Assemblies of God. Office: Paine Webber 700 S Flower St Los Angeles CA 90017

KECK, BARBARA ANNE, management consulting company executive; b. Goshen, Ind., Aug. 10, 1946; d. Howard and Mary Elizabeth (Taylor) Brumbaugh; m. Gerald Nadel, June, 1966 (div. 1972); Chad Whitney Keck, May 16, 1976; children: Martin Whitney, Matthew James Howard. BA cum laude, Rutgers U., 1968; MBA, Harvard U., 1976. Communications specialist U.S. Dept. Agrl., New Brunswick, N.Y., 1968-71; asst. dir. pub. relations dept. Hill & Holliday, Boston, 1971-73; dir. advt. and pub. relations Paperback Booksmith, Boston, 1973-74; mktg. mgr. food packaging Continental Can Co. Hdqrs., Stamford, Conn., 1976-79; chmn., chief exec. officer Keck & Co. Bus. Cons. Inc., N.Y.C., 1979-85; pres. Keck & Co. Bus. Cons., Atherton, Calif., 1985—. Sec. N.J. Tenants Assn., 1969-70; bd. dirs. Puppetry Guild Greater N.Y., N.Y.C., 1981-84. Mem. Assn. Mgmt. Cons., Women in Mgmt. (founder 1978, pres. 1979-80). Episcopalian. Club: Harvard Bus. Sch. (San Francisco). Avocation: puppetry. Home and Office: 410 Walsh Rd Atherton CA 94025

KECK, HENRY CHAPMAN, product engineering executive; b. N.Y.C., Feb. 10, 1921; s. Maxfield H. and Estella E. (Marcellus) K. B.A. in Engring. and Bus., Dartmouth Coll., 1943; Profl. Degree in Indsl. Design, Calif. Inst. Tech., 1947. Engr., Lockheed Aircraft Corp., 1943-45, Corning Glass Works, 1947-48; asst. mgr. West Coast office Raymond Loewy Assocs., 1948-49; founder, ptnr. Keck-Craig Assocs., cons. product engrs., South Pasadena, Calif., 1949—. Pres. Econ. Round Table Los Angeles, 1981-82. Served with U.S. Navy, 1944-46. Mem. Calif. Inst. Tech. Alumni Assn., Calif. Inst. Tech. Assocs. Republican. Congregationalist. Clubs: Athenaeum. Office: Keck-Craig Assocs 245 Fair Oaks Ave South Pasadena CA 91030

KEEFE, DENIS, physicist; b. Dublin, Ireland, Feb. 28, 1930; came to U.S., 1959; s. Joseph Francis and Eileen (Riordan) K.; m. Joan Trodden; children: Patrick, Eileen, Rory. BS, Nat. U. Ireland, Dublin, 1951, MS, 1953; PhD, Bristol (Eng.) U., 1955. Lectr. U. Coll. Dublin, 1951-59; sr. scientist Lawrence Berkeley Lab., Berkeley, Calif., 1959—. Editor: Particle Accelerators; contbr. articles to profl. jours. Recipient 2-yr. traveling student scholarship Nat. U. Ireland, 1953-55. Fellow Am. Phys. Soc.; mem. Royal Irish Acad., Scientists for Sakharov, Orlov and Shcharansky (exec. com. 1978-87). Roman Catholic. Club: Royal Dublin Soc. Avocations: reading, arts, travel, outdoors. Office: Lawrence Berkeley Lab Bldg 47 Berkeley CA 94720

KEEFER, DAVID KNIGHT, geologist; b. Laramie, Wyo., June 24, 1949; s. William Richard and Eleanor Audrey (Knight) K.; m. Karen Sue Harrison, Sept. 18, 1970; children: Bryan Richard, Alan Harrison. BS and MS in Geology, Stanford U., 1971; MSCE, U. Ill., 1973; PhD in Applied Earth Scis., Stanford U., 1977. Geotech. engr. Harza Engring. Co., Chgo., 1973; geologist U.S. Geol. Survey, Menlo Park, Calif., 1974—, research group leader, 1986—; cons. geology Govt. Argentina, 1978-79, Govt. Japan, 1978, 84, U. Ind. archeol. excavation Great Bedwyn, Eng., 1983, 85. Contbr. articles to profl. jours. Recipient Spl. Achievement award U.S. Geol. Survey, 1985. Mem. AAAS, ASCE, Geol. Soc. Am., Internat. Assn. Engring. Geology. Avocations: history, archaeology, swimming, hiking, folk dancing. Office: US Geol Survey 345 Middlefield Rd MS 998 Menlo Park CA 94025

KEEFFE, EMMET BRITTON, medicine educator; b. San Francisco, Apr. 12, 1942; s. Emmet Britton and Corinne M. (Walsh) K.; m. Melenie M. Laskey, June 18, 1966; children: Emmet III, Brian, Meghan. BS, U. San Francisco, 1964, secondary teaching credential, 1965; MD, Creighton U., 1969. Intern straight medicine Oreg. Health Sci. U., Portland, 1969-70, resident, 1970-73, fellow gastroenterology, 1973-74, assoc. prof. medicine, 1979—; fellow gastroenterology U. Calif., San Francisco, 1977-79. Author: Flexible Sigmoidoscopy, 1985; contbr. 40 articles to profl. jours. Served to lt. comdr. USN, 1974-77. Fellow ACP; mem. AAAS, Am. Gastroenterologic Assn., Am. Assn. Study Liver Diseases, Am. Soc. Gastrointestinal Endoscopy, Am. Fedn. Clin. Research. Home: 2753 SW Rutland Terr Portland OR 97201 Office: Oreg Health Sci U Div Gastroenterology 3181 SW Sam Jackson Park Rd Portland OR 97201

KEEHN, NEIL FRANCIS, aerospace executive; b. Massillon, Ohio, Oct. 24, 1948; s. Russell Earl and Mary (Danner) K.; B.S. in Math., Ariz. State U., Tempe, 1970, postgrad. in elec. engring., 1970. Mem. tech. staff Tech. Service Corp., Santa Monica, Calif., 1972-74, Hughes Aircraft, El Segundo, Calif., 1974-77; program mgr. TRW Inc., Redondo Beach, Calif., 1977-79; mgr. advanced concepts Mil. Space Systems div. Sci. Applications Inc., El Segundo, 1979-80; pres. Strategic Systems Scis., Santa Monica, 1980—. Mem. IEEE (vice chmn. aerospace def. systems panel 1972-76, chmn. 1976-79), AIAA, U.S. Strategic Inst., Internat. Inst. for Strategic Studies (chmn. mil. space strategy and doctrine com.) Contbr. articles to profl. jours.; patentee in digital signal processing.

KEELAND, DELPHA FLORINE, librarian; b. Glendive, Mont., June 3, 1925; d. Fred Peter and Anna (Buller) Deckert; m. Charles William Keeland, July 25, 1943; children—Charles, Richard James, Norma Lynn, Princess Ann, Ramona Joy, Dixie Lee, Dana Scott. Student pub. schs., Richey, Mont. Nurses aide McCone County Hosp., Circle, Mont., 1962-66, 74-76; owner Trail's End Cafe, Olympia, Wash., 1967-71; librarian Richey Pub. Library, Mont., 1980—. Mem. V.F.W. Aux., Am. Legion Aux. Methodist. Office: Richey Pub Library Richey MT 59259

KEELER, EMMETT BROWN, research mathematician; b. West Point, N.Y., Sept. 28, 1941; s. George Eldridge and Miriam (Brown) K.; m. Shan Cretin, Sept. 26, 1976; children: Lauren, Alexis. BA, Oberlin Coll., 1962; PhD, Harvard U., 1969. Research fellow Harvard U., Cambridge, Mass., 1969, 75, 82; mathematician Rand Corp., Santa Monica, Calif., 1968—. Author: Cholesterol Children and Heart Disease, 1980, Geriatrics in the United States, 1981; contbr. articles to profl. jours. NSF fellow, 1962-65. Mem. Math. Assn. Am., Assn. Pub. Policy and Mgmt., Sigma Xi, Phi Beta Kappa. Office: The Rand Corp 1700 Main St Santa Monica CA 90406

KEELEY, JON EDWARD, biological sciences educator; b. Chula Vista, Calif., Aug. 11, 1949; m. Sterling (Carter) Keeley. BS in Biology, San Diego State U., 1971, MS in Biology, 1973; PhD in Botany, U. Ga., 1977. Asst. prof. Occidental Coll., Los Angeles, 1977-82, assoc. prof., 1982—, chmn. dept. biology, 1983—; research assoc. Los Angeles County Nat. History Mus., 1978—; Please spell out middle name and give field of teaching. Please also verify office address and phone number, and give home address (not for publication). Your biographical data form and curriculum vitae were separated in the mail. Contbr. numerous articles to profl. jours. Recipient Graham Sterling Meml. award, 1985; Guggenheim Found. fellow, 1985-86; grantee NSF, 1980, 81, 82-84, 83, 84-86, Am. Philos. Soc., 1979, 80, UNESCO, 1980, Am. Assn. Plant Physiologists, 1983, MEDECOS Conf., 1984, Brit. Ecol. Soc., 1985, Nat. Geog. Soc., 1985-86. Mem. Soc. Study Evolution, Ecol. Soc. Am. Calif. Botan. Soc., Societas Intern. de Planatarium Demographia, Botan. Soc. Am., UN East West Ctr., Am. Assn. Plant Physiologists, Am. Soc. Naturalists, So. Calif. Acad. Scis. (editor bulletin 1984—), AAAS. Office: Occidental Coll Dept Biology 1600 Campus Rd Los Angeles CA 90041

KEELING, GERALDINE ANN, musicologist, educator; b. Mason City, Iowa, Aug. 10, 1946; s. John Odell and Marie Christine (Birkedal) F.; m. Steven R. Keeling, Aug. 17, 1974. BA cum laude, St. Olaf Coll., 1968; MMus. with high distinction, Ind. U., 1973; postgrad., UCLA, 1983. Assoc. instr. music Ind. U., Bloomington, 1968-70; asst. prof. music Valley City (N.D.) State Coll., 1970-78; teaching fellow UCLA, 1980-83; pvt. piano tchr. San Gabriel, Calif., 1980—; ch. organist Trinity United Meth. Ch., Pomona, Calif., 1981—; instr. music. Calif. State U., Fullerton, 1985—. Contbr. articles to profl. jours. Fellow NEH, 1977; grantee Internat. Edn. Program Alpha Delta Kappa, 1982; recipient John Lennon award, 1982, Atwater Kent award in Musicology, UCLA, 1980. Mem. Music Tchrs. Assn. Calif. (Cert. Merit chmn. 1985—), Am. Musicol. Soc., Am. Liszt Soc., The Liszt Soc., Am. Guild Organists, Pi Kappa Lambda. Home: 6318 N Muscatel Ave San Gabriel CA 91775

KEEN, DERL WALTER, child development educator; b. Leonard, Tex., July 18, 1932; s. Willard Francis and Ora Edda (Martin) K.; m. Shirley Marie Smith, Nov. 14, 1954; children—Deborha, Gregory, Karen, Cynthia. B.S., U. Calif.-Davis, 1954; M.A., Calif. State U.-Fresno, 1973; Ed.D., U. So. Calif., 1978. Cotton gin mgr. Anderson Clayton & Co., Tulare, Calif., 1956-60, farm mgr., Mendota, Calif., 1960-69; owner, operator Liquor Market Country Store, Chatsworth, Calif., 1969-70; owner, operator Keen's Day Sch., Fresno, Calif., 1970-75; instr. child devel., Fresno City Coll., 1975—; mem. Agr. Adv. Council, U. Calif., Berkeley, 1968-72, West Side Field Sta. Adv. Council, U. Calif., Five Points, 1962-72; dir. Calif. Tomato Growers Assn., Stockton, 1964-70; mem. Calif. State Articulation Council Early Childhood Edn., 1975-85, chmn., 1984-85. Served to 1st lt. U.S. Army, 1955-56.Mem. Calif. Assn. for Edn. Young Children (scholarship chmn. 1981-83), World Orgn. for Edn. Young Children. Republican. Methodist. Office: Fresno City Coll 1101 E University Ave Fresno CA 93741

KEEN, PHILIP EARL, physician, laboratory administrator, pathologist; b. Berryville, Ill., Dec. 11, 1942; d. Budd and Ruby Virginia (Doty) K.; m. Lois Marie Anderson, June 6, 1966; children: MariLynn, Sharilynn, Harvey, April. BS in Chemistry, U. N.Mex., 1965, MD, 1969. Diplomate Am. Bd. Pathology. Fellow in forensic pathology Med. Examiner's Office, Oklahoma City, 1973-74; cons. pathologist Western Pathologists, Phoenix, 1974-75; lab. dir. Yavapai Regional Med. Ctr., Prescott, Ariz., 1975—, chief of staff, 1984-85; med. examiner Yavapai (Ariz.) County, 1975—. Lay minister Ch. of Christ. Fellow Coll. Am. Pathologists, Am. soc. Clin. Pathologists; mem. AMA, Ariz. Med. Assn., Yavapai County Med. Soc. (del. to Ariz. Med. Assn.). Republican. Avocatoins: playing music for stringed instruments, singing. Home: 2193 Richard St Prescott AZ 86301 Office: Yavapai Regional Med Ctr 1003 Willow Creek Rd Prescott AZ 86301

KEENAN, EDWARD JOSEPH, management consultant; b. N.Y.C., Oct. 3, 1932; s. Edward Joseph and Leona (Tansey) K.; married; 2 children. B.A., U. Minn., 1967; M.A. in Edn., Chapman Coll., 1977; M.B.A., Pepperdine U., 1984. Served with U.S. Air Force, 1951-71; ptnr. Edman-Keenan & Assocs., San Bernardino, Calif., 1971-73; adminstr. for pvt. law firms, Los Angeles and Beverly Hills, Calif., 1973-78; cons. to law firms and hosps., 1978—; instr. law office mgmt. U. So. Calif., U. West Los Angeles, Calif. State U., Long Beach; cons. in field. Mem. Am. Inst. Indsl. Engrs., Assn. Legal Adminstrs. (charter; pres. Beverly Hills chpt. 1977-78), Internat. Platform Assn., Hosp. Mgmt. Systems Soc. Republican. Lodges: Elks, Moose, K.C. Office: 1334 Park View Ave Manhattan Beach CA 90266

KEENE, DAVID CLAY, lawyer; b. Denver, May 14, 1949; s. Clay Keene and Diana (Phipps) Braden; m. Ellin Oliver, Dec. 18, 1983. BA, Vanderbilt U., 1971; MA, Peabody Coll., 1973; JD, Southwestern U., Los Angeles, 1976. Bar: Colo. 1977, Calif. 1977. Assoc. Treece, Zbar and Webb, Littleton, Colo., 1979-81; ptnr. Corporon, Keene & Hoehn, Englewood, Colo., 1981—. Mem. Colo. Bar Assn., Douglas County Bar Assn. (pres. 1983-84). Republican. Episcopalian. Office: Corporon Keene & Hoehn 12835 E Arapahoe Rd Englewood CO 80112

KEENE, MICHAEL ANDREW, molecular biologist; b. Abington, Pa., Aug. 23, 1956; s. Robert Clinton and Flora Mildred (Etherington) K.; m. Mary Jane Pennington, Apr. 27, 1985. BA in Biochemistry, Princeton U., 1977; PhD in Biochemistry and Molecular Biology, Harvard U., 1983. Postdoctoral fellow Fred Hutchinson Cancer Research Ctr., Seattle, 1984-86; research assoc. Howard Hughes Med. Research Unit, U. Utah, Salt Lake City, 1986—. Contbr. numerous articles to profl. sci. jours. Recipient Nat. Research Service award Nat. Inst. Health, 1983-86. Mem. AAAS, Am. Soc. Cell Biology (legis. alert com. 1985—), Genetics Soc. Am., Photog. Soc. Am. (bd. dirs. 1985-86), Seattle Photog. Soc. (bd. dirs., competition chmn. 1985-86), Am. Philatelic Soc., Sigma Xi. Avocations: photography, philately, hiking. Home: 2615 S Melbourne St Salt Lake City UT 84106 Office: U Utah Dept Biology Salt Lake City UT 84112

KEENEY, KRISTOPHER K., financial service company executive, consultant; b. Portland, Oreg., Jan. 26, 1952; s. Kenneth K. and Eleanor M. (Fossum) K.; m. Teresa A. Lisac, Aug. 29, 1975. Exec. v.p. Global Trade Enterprises, Clackamas, Oreg., 1974-79; pres. Sinclair Internat. Co., Portland, 1979—. Author: Inflation: It's a Crime, 1977, hon. mention award, 1978. Served with USMC, 1970-73, Vietnam. Mem. Am. Mgmt. Assn., Pres. Assn. div. Am. Mgmt. Assn. Republican. Avocations: sports. Office: Sinclair Internat Co PO Box 06526 Portland OR 97206

KEEP, JUDITH N., federal judge; b. 1944. B.A., Scripps Coll., 1966; J.D., U. San Diego, 1970. With Defenders Inc., 1971-73; sole practice 1973-76; asst. U.S. atty. Calif., 1976; judge Mcpl. Ct., San Diego, 1976-80, U.S. Dist. Ct. (so. dist.) Calif., San Diego, 1980—. Office: US District Court 940 Front St San Diego CA 92189

KEEPORTS, DAVID DALE, physical science educator; b. York, Pa., June 15, 1951; s. Dale and Madeline (Mitzel) K. BS in Chemistry, U. Del., 1973; MS in Chemistry, Yale U., 1974; PhD in Phys. Chemistry, U. Wash., 1982. Lectr. in physics, chemistry and math. Quinnipiac Coll., Hamden, Conn., 1975-79; lectr. in math. So. Conn. State Coll., New Haven, 1976-79; lectr. in physics and math. U. New Haven, 1976-79; asst. prof. phys. scis. Mills Coll., Oakland, Calif., 1982—. Contbr. articles to sci. jours. Mem. Am. Chem. Soc., Am. Assn. Physics Tchrs., Mensa, Sigma Xi. Avocations: music, reading, running. Home: PO Box 9144 Oakland CA 94613 Office: Mills Coll Dept Phys Scis Oakland CA 94613

KEETON, SHARON ANNE, schoolteacher, consultant; b. Oakland, Calif., Aug. 20, 1944; d. William Henry Follmer and Anne Harrison (Curtiss) Baughman; m. Thomas Henry Hayden, Jan. 29, 1966 (div. 1974); 1 child, Geoffrey Matthew; m. James Winston Keeton, June 6, 1976; children: Michael Andrew, Elizabeth Erin. BA, U. Colo., 1966; MA, U. No. Colo., 1977; credential, Calif. State U., Hayward, 1985. Cert. secondary tchr., Colo. Tchr. lab. sch. U. No. Colo., Greeley, 1972-73, instr. summer program, 1982-83; tchr., dept. chmn. Windsor (Colo.) High Sch., 1973-80; owner, mgr. Day Care Ctr., Greeley, 1980-84; pres. Corp. Day Care Mgmt., Walnut Creek, Calif., 1984-85; tchr. Pine Valley Intermediate Sch., San Ramon, Calif., 1985—; tour guide Intercultural Student Experiences, Excelsior, Minn., 1980-81. Rep. precinct committeewoman, Greeley, 1969-70. Named an Outstanding Young Woman of Colo., 1970. Mem. Calif. Tchrs. Assn., San Ramon Valley Edn. Assn., P.E.O. Sisterhood, Delta Delta Delta (alumni chpt. pres. 1984), Scroll and Fan (chpt. pres. 1983-84), Nat. Polit. Sci. Hon. Soc. Episcopalian. Avocations: skiing, reading, aerobics, running. Home: 1705 Liahona Ln Danville CA 94526 Office: Pine Valley Intermediate 3000 Pine Valley Rd San Ramon CA 94526

KEGEBEIN, JAMES ALBERT, industrial hygienist; b. LaPorte, Ind., Feb. 17, 1951; s. Robert Royal and Jeanette (Howard) K.; m. Valerie Janeen Nygra, Feb. 13, 1981; 1 dau. Kimberly Ann. B.S., Ind. State U., 1973; M.S. in Indsl. Hygiene, Central Mo. State U., 1983. Registered pub. sanitarian, Ind.; cert. indsl. hygienist in tng. Sanitarian Elkhart (Ind.) County Health Dept., 1974; sr. environ. health tech. Bethlehem Steel Corp., Burns Harbor, Ind., 1974-79; field indsl. hygienist Bechtel Power Corp., Midland, Mich. and Port Gibson, Miss., 1979-81, indsl. hygienist, San Francisco, 1981—. Adv. com. safety program Cogswell Coll., San Francisco. Mem. Am. Indsl. Hygiene Assn., Am. Soc. Safety Engrs. Home: 1244 S Mary Sunnyvale CA 94087 Office: Visucom Prodn 1255 Veteran Blvd Redwood City CA 94063

KEGLEY, JACQUELYN ANN, philosophy educator; b. Conneaut, Ohio, July 18, 1938; d. Steven Paul and Gertrude Ethel (Frank) Kovacevic; m. Charles William Kegley, Aug. 12, 1964; children: Jacquelyn Ann, Stephen Lincoln Luther. BA cum laude, Allegheny Coll., 1960; MA summa cum laude, Rice U., 1964; PhD, Columbia U., 1971. Asst. prof. philosophy Calif. State U., Bakersfield, 1973-77, assoc. prof., 1977-81, prof., 1981—; vis. prof. U. Philippines, Quezon City, 1966-68; grant project dir. Claif. Council Humanities, 1977, project dir. 1980, 82. Author: Introduction to Logic, 1978; editor: The Humanistic Delivery, 1982; contbr. articles to profl. jours. Mem. Soc. Advancement Am. Phil. soc. (chmn. Pacific div. 1979-83, nat. exec. com. 1974-79), Philosophy Soc., Soc. Interdisciplinary Study of Mind, Soc. Philosophy and Psychology, Dorian Soc., Phi Beta Kappa. Democrat. Lutheran. Avocations: music, tennis. Home: 7312 Kroll Way Bakersfield CA 93309 Office: Calif State U Dept Philosophy and Religious Studies Bakersfield CA 93309

KEHE, ROBERT NELSON, engineer; b. Eden, N.Y., Feb. 8, 1938; s. Alwin William and Evelyn Grace (Omphalius) K.; m. H. Barbara Arndt, Dec. 22, 1962; children: Brian David, Bruce Darren. BSME, U. Buffalo, 1961; MBA in Indsl. Mgmt., U. So. Calif., 1964. Sales engr. Worthington Corp., Buffalo, 1960-61; sales rep. Worthington Corp., Los Angeles, 1964-66; devel. officer space systems div. USAF, Los Angeles, 1961-64; program engr. Douglas Aircraft Co., Long Beach, Calif., 1966-79, br. mgr., 1981—; project mgr. Fed. Express Corp., Memphis, 1979-81. Contbr. articles on air cargo to profl. jours. Fund-raising capt. YMCA, Torrance, Calif., 1975-76; asst. coach Swifts team Am. Youth Soccer Orgn., Torrance, 1976-77; sec. Eastport Village Condominium Assn., Canyon Lake, Calif., 1977-79; chmn. awards com. Boy Scouts Am., Torrance, 1979; chmn. fin. com. Germantown (Tenn.) Thunderbirds team U.S. Youth Soccer Assn., 1980-81. Served to 1st lt. USAF, 1961-64. Recipient N.Y. Bd. Regents Scholarship, Engring. Soc. Buffalo Scholarship, 1956-60. Mem. AIAA (session chmn. Internat. Air Transport Conf. 1985), Los Angeles Air Cargo Assn. (recognized for outstanding contbn. to air transport industry 1985), Theta Chi (sgt.-at-arms U. Buffalo chpt. 1958, house mgr. 1960, Outstanding Mem. award 1960), Beta Gamma Sigma. Republican. Avocations: landscaping, rose gardening, music, supporting boys' sports and music.

KEHLMANN, ROBERT, artist, critic; b. Bklyn., Mar. 9, 1942. B.A., Antioch Coll., 1963; M.A., U. Calif.-Berkeley, 1966. One-man shows include: Richmond Art Ctr. (Calif.), 1976, William Sawyer Gallery, San Francisco, 1978, 82, 86, Galerie M, Kassel, W.Ger., 1985; group shows include: Am. Craft Mus., N.Y.C., 1978, 86, Corning (N.Y.) Mus. Glass, 1979, Tucson Mus. of Art, 1983, Kulturhuset, Stockholm, Sweden, 1985; represented in permanent collections at Corning Mus. Glass, Leigh Yawkey Woodson Art Mus., Hessisches Landes Mus., W.Ger., Bank of Am. World Hdqrs., San Francisco, Hokkaido Mus. Modern Art, Sapporo, Japan, Huntington Galleries (W.Va.), Am. Craft Mus., N.Y.C., Musée des Arts Décoratifs, Lausanne, Switzerland; instr. glass design Calif. Coll. Arts and Crafts, Oakland, 1978-80; instr. glass design Pilchuck Glass Ctr., Stanwood, Wash., 1978-80; contbg. editor Glass Art Mag., Oakland, Calif., 1975-76, editor Glass Art Soc. Jour., Berkeley, Calif., 1981-84. Nat. Endowment Arts grantee, 1977, 78. Advisor Glass Art Soc. (dir. 1980-84). Office: William Sawyer Gallery 3045 Clay St San Francisco CA 94115

KEHOE, VINCENT JEFFRÉ-ROUX, photographer, author, cosmetic company executive; b. Bklyn., N.Y., Sept. 12, 1921; s. John James and Bertha Florence (Roux) K.; student M.I.T., 1940-41, Lowell Technol. Inst., 1941-42, Boston U., 1942; B.F.A. in Motion Picture and TV Production, Columbia U., 1957; m. Gena Irene Marino, Nov. 2, 1966. Dir. make-up dept. CBS-TV, N.Y.C., 1948-49, NBC Hallmark Hall of Fame series, 1951-53; make-up artist in charge of make-up for numerous film, TV and stage prodns., 1942—; dir. make-up Turner Hall Corp., 1959-61, Internat. Beauty Show, 1962-66; pres., dir. research Research Council of Make-up Artists, Inc., Los Angeles, 1963—; chief press officer at Spanish Pavilion, N.Y. World's Fair, 1965; free-lance photographer, 1956—; contbr. photographs to numerous mags. including Time, Life, Sports Illustrated, Argosy, Popular Photography. Author books including: The Technique of Film and Television Make-up for Color, 1970; The Make-up Artist in the Beauty Salon, 1969; We Were There-April 19, 1775, 1975; The Military Guide, 1975; The Technique of the Professional Makeup Artist; 1985; author-photographer bullfighting books: Aficionado! (N.Y. Art Dirs. Club award 1960); Wine, Women and Toros (N.Y. Art Dirs. award 1962). Served with inf. U.S. Army, World War II; ETO. Decorated Purple Heart, Bronze Star; recipient Torch award Council of 13 Original States, 1979. Fellow Co. Mil. Historians; mem. Soc. for Preservation of Colonial Culture (curator), Tenth Foot Royal Lincolnshire Regimental Assn. (life, named hon. col. 1968), Soc. Motion Picture and TV Engrs., Acad. TV Arts and Scis. Soc. for Army Hist. Research (Gt. Britain) (life), Brit. Officers Club New England (life). 10th Mountain Div. Assn., DAV (life), Nat. Rifle Assn. (life). Producer documentary color film: Matador de Toros, 1959. Address: 3547 Mountain View Ave Los Angeles CA 90066

KEIL, KLAUS, geology educator, consultant; b. Hamburg, Ger., Nov. 15, 1934; s. Walter and Elsbeth K.; m. Rosemarie, Mar. 30, 1961; children: Kathrin R., Mark K.; m. Linde, Jan. 28, 1984. M.S., Schiller U., Jena, Ger., 1958; Ph.D., Gutenberg U., Mainz, W.Ger., 1961. Research assoc. Mineral. Inst., Jena, 1958-60, Max Planck-Inst. Chemistry, Mainz, 1961, U. Calif.-San Diego, 1961-63; research scientist Ames Research Center NASA, Moffett Field, Calif., 1964-68; prof. geology, dir. Inst. Meteoritics, U. N.Mex., Albuquerque, 1968—; pres. prof. U. N.Mex., 1985—; chmn. dept. of geology U. N.Mex., Albuquerque, 1986—; cons. Sandia Labs., others. Contbr. over 400 articles to sci. jours. Recipient Apollo Achievement award NASA, 1970; recipient George P. Merrill medal Nat. Acad. Scis., 1970, Exceptional Sci. Achievement medal NASA, 1977, Regents Meritorious Service medal U. N.Mex., 1983, numerous others. Fellow Meteoritical Soc., AAAS, Mineral. Soc. Am.; mem. Am. Geophys. Union, German Mineral. Soc., others. Office: U N Mex Dept Geology Albuquerque NM 87131

KEIL, ROBERT ALVIN, operations research analyst; b. Chgo., Sept. 9, 1919; s. Walter Alvin and Della Sophia (Danielson) K.; B.S. in Bus. (fellowship), U. Richmond, 1941; M.A., U. Hawaii, 1963; m. Betsy Tingle Breece, Feb. 21, 1945 (dec.); m. 2d, Louise Victoria Wigchert, Apr. 25, 1981. Exec. trainee C & P Telephone Co. of Va., 1941-42; assoc. Planning research Corp., Honolulu, San Diego, 1964-67; ops. research analyst Naval Ocean Systems Ctr., San Diego, 1967-80, scientist, 1980-85, emeritus, 1985—. Pres., Coronado Residential Assn., 1968-71; chmn. Coronado Planning Commn., 1975, 77, 78, commr., 1972-78. Served with USN, 1942-64. Mem. U.S. Naval Inst., Phi Beta Kappa, Omicron Delta Kappa, Phi Kappa Sigma. Episcopalian. Club: Rotary. Contbr. tech. research papers. Home: 110 Carob Way Coronado CA 92118

KEILIN, BERTRAM, psychotherapist, educator; b. N.Y.C., Oct. 18, 1922; s. Albert and Cecelia (Baron) K.; m. Carol Baum, Oct. 23, 1954 (div. Apr. 1979); children: William Gregory, Anita Marie, Robert Edward. BA, NYU, 1942; MS, Calif. Inst. Tech., 1945, PhD, 1950; MA, Pepperdine U., 1981. Cert. hypnotherapist, Calif., jr. coll. tchr., Calif. Chemist Paragon Dyestuff Corp., Paterson, N.J., 1943-44, Douglas Aircraft, Santa Monica, Calif., 1949-50; instr., research assoc. U. So. Calif., Los Angeles, 1950-52; research chemist Olin-Mathieson Chem. Corp., Pasadena, Calif., 1953-56; research chemist Aerojet-Gen. Corp., Azusa, Calif., 1956-66; v.p. Amicon Corp., Lexington, Mass., 1966-70; exec. dir. Pacific Water Quality Assn., Irvine, Calif., 1971-81; pres. EnviroMgmt. Services, Irvine, 1981—; ptnr. Newport Therapy Group, Calif., 1982—; adj. prof. Pepperdine U., 1986—; bd. dirs. Calif. Assn. Marriage and Family Therapists, Orange County, 1984—; allied health practitioner staff St. Joseph Hosp., Orange, Calif; mem. med. staff Orange County Med. Ctr., Costa Mesa, Calif., Brea (Calif.) Neuropsychiat. Hosp. Author: Encyclopedia of Chemical Technology, 1968; contbr. articles to profl. jours.; patentee in field. Bd. dirs. Fountain Valley C. of C., 1979; pres. Fountain Valley Exchange Club, 1978-79, Unitarian Universal Ch., Costa Mesa, Calif., 1979-81. Served as radar technologist, U.S. Signal Corps, 1942-43. Fellow Calif. Inst. Tech., 1949. Avocations: tennis, piano, bike riding, stamp collecting, reading. Home: 18 Springwater Irvine CA 92714 Office: Newport Therapy Group 2043 Westcliff Dr 203 Newport Beach CA 92660

KEILTY, MICHAEL JOSEPH, engineer, system specialist; b. Evergreen Park, Ill., Aug. 15, 1952; s. James Joseph and Therese Catherine (Martin) K.; m. Susan Marie Sanchez, May 28, 1978 (div. Nov. 1985); children: Alison Rebecca, Colleen Nicole. AS in Engring., Wright Jr. Coll., 1980; BS in Engring., U. Ill., Chgo., 1982. Chemist Revere Sugar Co., Chgo., 1972-78; technician Cole-Palmer Instrument Co., Chgo., 1980-83; field service engr. Micro Motion, Inc., Boulder, Colo., 1983—. Active Big Bros./Big Sisters Am., Boulder, 1985—. Avocations: folk guitar, bowling, rollerskating, softball. Office: MicroMotion Inc 7070 Winchester Circle Boulder CO 80301

KEIM, PAUL FERDINAND, civil engineer, educator; b. Falls City, Nebr., Apr. 22, 1902; s. Will Seward and Fernande Rose (Godfirnon) K.; m. Marjorie Little, Dec. 31, 1927 (dec. Dec. 1982); children: Seward Russell (dec.), Charles Bruce. BSc, U. Calif., Berkeley, 1925; MSc in C.E., U. Nebr., 1932. Registered profl. engr., Calif., Oreg., Wash. Engr. contracting co., Los Angeles, 1925-26; instr. civil engring. U. Nebr., 1926-32; cons. Platte Valley Pub. Power and Irrigation Dist. Nebr., 1933-36, Calif. Hwy. div., Marysville, 1936-37; hydraulic engr. Los Angeles County Flood Control Dist., 1937-39; prin. engr. FPC, Washington, 1939-41, 46; pub. works officer, damage control officer Midway Islands, 1942; pub. works and constrn. officer Whidbey Island Naval Air Sta., 1943; staff civil engring. officer 13th Naval dist. Naval Air Command, 1944-46; mem. res. 1946—; cons. transp. and water supply U.S. Dept. State Econ. Mission to Liberia, 1947-48; assoc. Tippets, Abbett, McCarthy, Stratton, Engrs., N.Y.C., 1948-52; ops. Greece, Turkey, Alaksa, throughout U.S., 1948-52; prof. civil engring. U. Calif., Berkeley, 1952-69, prof. emeritus, 1970—; on leave cons. ports Taiwan, 1957; adv. to dir. U.S. Ops. Mission Egypt, tchr. U. Cairo Grad. Sch., 1959-61; cons. Calif. Joint Senate-House com. Water Resources, various times, 1952-59; chief staff civil engr. Ralph M. Parsons Co., Pasadena, Calif., Peru, Greece, Argentina, Mex., Tunisia, Morocco, 1968-71; cons. Internat. Exec. Service Corps, N.Y.C.; port cons., Taiwan, 1975; OAS cons., Brazil, 1971; FMC cons., Rumania, 1972. Contbr. articles to profl. jours. Recipient citation for disting. profl. conduct during Battle of Midway, 1942. Mem. ASCE (permanent del. to Los Angeles Council Engring. and Sci., mem. profl. practice com. 1984-87, continuing cons. and expert witness Los Angeles cts., 1984-87), Los Angeles Council Engrs. and Scientists (pres. 1979-81), Inst. Advancement Engring. (pres.-elect 1981, emeritus dir. 1983-84, award of merit 1982), Am. Soc. Engring. Edn., Nat. Reclamation Assn., Am. Geophys. Union, Soc. Mil. Engrs., Chi Epsilon, Tau Beta Pi. Clubs: Town Hall of Calif., Los Angeles Breakfast. Lodge: Lions. Address: 4552 Fountain Ave Apt 2 Los Angeles CA 90029

KEITH, BRUCE EDGAR, political analyst, genealogist; b. Curtis, Nebr., Feb. 17, 1918; s. Edgar L. and Corinne E. (Marsteller) K.; m. Evelyn E. Johnston, Oct. 29, 1944; children—Mona Louise, Kent Marsteller, Melanie Ann. A.B. with high distinction, Nebr. Wesleyan U., 1940; M.A., Stanford U., 1952; grad. Command and Staff, Marine Corps Schs., 1958, Sr. Resident Sch., Naval War Coll., 1962; Ph.D., U. Calif.-Berkeley, 1982. Commd. 2d lt. U.S. Marine Corps, 1942, advanced through grades to col., 1962, ret., 1971, comdg. officer 3d Bn., 11th Marines, 1958-59, ops. officer, Pres. Dwight D. Eisenhower visit to Okinawa, 1960, G-3 ops. officer Fleet Marine Force, Pacific, Cuban Missile Crisis, 1962, mem. U.S. del. SEATO, Planning Conf., Bangkok, Thailand, 1964, G-3, Fleet Marine Force, Pacific, 1964-65, head Strategic Planning Study Dept., Naval War Coll., 1966-68, genealogist, 1967—, exec. officer Hdqrs. Marine Corps programs, Washington, 1968-71; election analyst Inst. Govtl. Studies, U. Calif.-Berkeley, 1974—; teaching asst. U. Calif.-Berkeley, 1973-74. Bd. dirs., Bay Area Funeral Soc., 1980-83, v.p., 1981-83. Decorated Bronze Star, Navy Commendation medal, Presdl. Unit citation with 3 bronze stars. Recipient Phi Kappa Phi Silver medal Nebr. Wesleyan U., 1940, Alumni award, 1964. Mem. Am. Polit. Sci. Assn., Acad. Polit. Sci., Am. Acad. Polit. and Social Sci., Marine Corps Assn., Ret. Officers Assn. Phi Kappa Phi, Pi Gamma Mu. Republican. Unitarian. Clubs: Commonwealth of Calif. (San Francisco), Marines' Meml. (San Francisco). Lodge: Masons. Contbg. author: The Descendants of Daniel and Elizabeth (Disbrow) Keith, 1979-81; History of Curtis, Nebraska-The First Hundred Years, 1984; author: A Comparison of the House Armed Services Coms. in the 91st and 94th Congresses: How They Differed and Why, 1982; The Johnstons of Morning Sun, 1979; The Marstellers of Arrellton, 1978; The Morris Family of Brookville, 1977; Japan-the Key to America's Future in the Far East, 1962; A United States General Staff: A Must or a Monster?, 1950; co-author: California Votes, 1960-72, 1974; The Myth of the Independent Voter, 1977; Further Evidence on the Partisan Affinities of Independent " Leaners" , 1983. Address: PO Box 156 El Cerrito CA 94530

KEITH, DAVID, symphony orchestra conductor; b. Tacoma, Oct. 9, 1930; s. David and Barbara (Ferry) K.; m. Ginni Paynton, July 5, 1972. Student, San Francisco Conservatory of Music, 1948-50; studied with, Dr. Stanley Chapple, U. Wash., 1968-72. Assoc. conductor Bellevue (Wash.) Philharm. Orch., 1968-70; conductor, music dir. Seattle Concert Orch., 1970-73; founder, conductor, dir. Los Angeles Mozart Orch., 1974—, also trustee, 1974—. Mem. Musicians' Union. Avocation: aviculture.

KEITH, GORDON, publisher; b. Kent, Wash., Aug. 27, 1913; s. John Albert and Grace (Calkins) K.; student San Jose State Coll., 1938-39, U. Calif. at Oakland, 1940; m. Barbara Louise Henson, Sept. 4, 1953 (div. Apr. 1979); 1 dau., Michelle Louise. Operator several small chain dance schs. No. Calif., 1933-42; free lance writer, 1945-50; pub., editor Dance Digest, 1951-62; pub., printer Personnel Improvement Booklets, also specialized greeting cards, note paper, San Jose, Calif., 1962—; feature writer Island Sounder newspaper, San Juan, 1971—; mng. editor Pub. Forum of San Juan County, 1983—. Served with AUS, 1942-45. Mem. Dance Masters Am. (past pres. Calif., dir.). Lion (sec. 1972). Author: (booklets) A Special 48-State Survey on Examining and Licensing of Dance Teachers in America, 1958; Why You Should Belong to an Accredited Dance Teachers' Organization, 1958; Private Dance Schools vs. Recreation Departments, 1960; (books) (with Roderic Marble Olzendam) Liberty's Grandson, An Unconventional Autobiography, 1977, It Came to Pass in the San Juan Islands, 1978; Green Gold for America, 1981; Voices from the Islands, 1982. compiler, editor The James Francis Tulloch Diary 1875-1910, 1978. Home and Office: PO Box 280 Eastsound Orcas Island WA 98245

KEITH, KENT MARSTELLER, business executive, state official, lawyer; b. N.Y.C., May 22, 1948; s. Bruce Edgar and Evelyn E. (Johnston) K.; m. Elizabeth Misao Carlson, Aug. 22, 1976. BA in Govt., Harvard U., 1970; BA in Politics and Philosophy, Oxford U., Eng., 1972, MA, 1977; JD, U. Hawaii, 1977. Bar: Hawaii 1977, D.C. 1979. Assoc. Cades, Schutte, Fleming & Wright, Honolulu, 1977-79; coordinator Hawaii Dept. Planning and Econ. Devel., Honolulu, 1979-81, dep. dir., 1981-83, dir., 1983-86; energy resources coordinator State of Hawaii, Honolulu, 1983-86, chmn. State Policy Council, 1983-86; chmn. Aloha Tower Devel. Corp., Honolulu, 1983-86; project mgr. Mililani Tech. Park Oceanic Properties, Inc., 1986—. Contbr. articles on ocean law to law jours. Pres. Manoa Valley Ch., Honolulu, 1976-78; mem. platform com., Hawaii Dem. Conv., 1982, 84, 86. Rhodes scholar, 1970; named one of 10 Outstanding Young Men of Am., U.S. Jaycees, 1984. Mem. Am. Assn. Rhodes Scholars, Internat. House of Japan, Nature Conservancy. Clubs: Plaza, Harvard of Hawaii (Honolulu) (bd. dirs. 1974-78, sec. 1974-76). Home: 2626 Hillside Ave Honolulu HI 96822 Office: Oceanic Properties PO Box 2780 Honolulu HI 96803

KEITH, NORMAN THOMAS, engineering company administrator, management specialist; b. Antioch, Calif., Jan. 12, 1936; s. Dean Theodore and Edna Margaret (Doty) K.; m. Marla Mildred Osten, Sept. 9, 1962. B of Tech., Tex. State Tech. Inst. Cert. profl. mgr. Field service engr. Gen. Dynamics Corp., San Diego, 1955-66, supr. Data Ctr., 1966-76, chief data systems, 1976-81, chief property adminstrn., 1981-83, motivational mgr., 1983-86, program adminstr., 1986—. Contbr. articles to profl. jours. Mem. mil. adv. bd. congressman Ron Packard, 1983-86; sgt. Res. Dep. Sheriff's Office, San Diego County; bd. dirs. San Dieguito Boys/Girls Clubs, Encinitas, 1966-69; loaned exec. United Way, San Diego, 1980-81. Mem. Nat. Mgmt. Assn. (bd. dirs., pres.), Nat. U. Alumni Assn. (life), Woodbury Coll. Alumni Assn., San Diego State U. Alumni Assn., Hon. Dep. Sheriff's Assn. (bd. dirs.). Republican. Lutheran. Lodges: Lions (sec. 1962-63), Elks. Home: 620 E St Encinitas CA 92024 Office: Gen Dynamics Convair div 5001 Kearny Villa Rd San Diego CA 92138

KELAHAN, J(OSEPH) RICHARD, transportation company executive; b. Granite City, Ill., Nov. 6, 1919; s. Joseph Richard Sr. and Concordia (Scheveling) K.; m. Frances Louise Bour, July 10, 1943; children: Mary Frances, BettyAnn, Kathleen Marie, Timothy Paul. Degree in marine engring. and ocean transpn., U.S. Merchant Marine Acad., 1942. Exec. and educator Regrigerating Engrs. and Technicians Assn., Chgo., 1952-60; chief engr. Atlantic Co., Atlanta, 1960-65; regional mgr. Frick Co. div. Utilities Internat. Corp., Atlanta, 1965-71; mgr. refrigeration engring. Spitzley Corp. div. Utilities Internat. Corp., Detroit, 1971-74; utilities engr. Armour & Co. div. Greyhound Corp., Phoenix, 1974-79; dir. loss prevention Greyhound Corp., Phoenix, 1979—; dist. instr. U.S. Maritime Commn., San Francisco, 1946-47; marine engr. Corinco, div. Vesty's Ltd., San Francisco, 1947-52. Editor Ice & Refrigeration mag., 1952-54, Indsl. Refrigeration mag., 1954-60, (book) NAPRE Data Book, 1954-60; contbng. editor Loss Prevention by Design, 1979—. Vol. coach and official youth soccer, Ga., Mich., and Ariz., 1969-85. Served to lt. USNR, 1941-46, PTO. Mem. ASHRAE (chmn. Chgo. chpt. 1958-59), Refrigerating Engrs. and Technicians Assn. Democrat. Roman Catholic. Lodge: KC, Moose. Home: 3009 W Desert Cove Phoenix AZ 85029 Office: Greyhound Corp 0455 Greyhound Tower Phoenix AZ 85077

KELEN, JOYCE ARLENE, social worker; b. N.Y.C., Dec. 5, 1949; d. Samuel and Rebecca (Rochman) Green; m. Leslie George Kelen, Jan. 31, 1971; children: David, Jonathan. BA, Lehman Coll., 1970; MSW, Univ. Utah, 1974, DSW, 1980. Recreation dir. N.Y.C. Housing Authority, Bronx, 1970-72; cottage supr. Kennedy Home, Bronx, 1974; sch. social worker Davis County Sch. Dist., Farmington, Utah, 1976-86; clin. asst. prof. U. Utah., Salt Lake City, 1976—; sch. social worker Salt Lake City Sch. Dist., 1986—; cons. in field, Salt Lake City, 1981—. Editor: To Whom Are We Beautiful As We Go?, 1979; contbr. articles to profl. jours. Utah Coll. of Nursing grantee, 1985. Mem. Nat. Assn. Social Workers (chairperson Gerontology Council, 1983-84, Utah Sch. Social Worker of Yr., 1977), NEA, Utah Edn. Assn., Davis Edn. Assn. Democrat. Jewish. Avocations: tennis, camping, guitar. Home: 128 M St Salt Lake City UT 84103 Office: Franklin Elem Sch 1100 W 400 S Salt Lake City UT 84104

KELL, ERNEST EUGENE, JR., mayor, contractor; b. N.D., July 5, 1928; s. Ernest Eugene and Katherine (Moynier) K.; m. Jacqueline; children—Julie, Brian. Owner, operator Western Detailing Service, Inc., Anaheim, Calif., 1955-71; gen. contractor Long Beach, Calif., 1971—; councilman 5th dist. City Long Beach, Calif., 1975—, mayor, 1984—. Commr. Los Angeles County Transp. Commn., 1982-84; trustee Mosquito Abatement Dist., Los Angeles County, 1977—; chmn. Californians for Consumers No-Fault. Mem. Calif. Steel Detailers Assn. (pres.). League of Calif. Cities. Democrat. Lodge: Lions. Home: 3471 Marna Ave Long Beach CA 90808 Office: City of Long Beach 333 W Ocean Blvd Long Beach CA 90802 *

KELLEHER, DIANA LEE, strategic marketing consultant; b. Phila., July 9, 1947; d. Lee Roy and Margaret Hopkins (Hey) McKean; m. Gregory Kelleher, Feb. 9, 1968 (div.). B.S. in Fin., Drexel U., 1969; M.B.A., U. Chgo., 1975. With McKinsey & Co., Inc., Chgo., 1970-75; mgr. merchandise group fqrecasts and tech. service Sears Roebuck & Co., Chgo., 1975-77; assoc. dir. mktg. planning, mktg. mgr. Kitchens of Sara Lee, Consolidated Foods Co., Chgo., 1977-80; mktg. mgr. E & J Gallo Winery, Modesto, Calif., 1980-82; dir. mktg. Pharmavite Corp., Arleta, Calif., 1982, v.p. mktg., 1982-85; prin. Kelleher and Assocs., Sherman Oaks, Calif., 1985—; pres. The Saturn Group, 1985-86. Tchr. Jr. Achievement classroom course, 1983, mktg. com. So. Cal. office, 1986. Mem. AAUW. Office: Kelleher & Associates 14755 Ventura Blvd #1-416 Sherman Oaks CA 91403

KELLEHER, ROBERT NEAL, chemist, chemical engineer; b. Teaneck, N.J., June 26, 1943; s. Vincent J. and Gladys A. (Storms) K.; m. Sandra A. Martin, Dec. 27, 1969 (div. Jan. 1986); children: Scott V., Kristen A. Student, Grove City Coll., 1961-62, Fairleigh Dickenson U., 1962-64; BSChemE, U. Eastern Fla., 1965; cert. pharmacist, USAF Med. Coll., 1966; cert. bus. mgmt., Rutgers U., 1971-72; cert. indsl. safety and hygeine, U. N.C., 1976. Chief control chemist Washine-Intex Chem., Lodi, N.J., 1962-64; asst. city chemist City of Ft. Lauderdale, Fla., 1965; asst. research and devel. chemist Amerace-Esna Corp., Tenafly, N.J., 1965-66, 67-68, terminal supr., 1968-69; ops. coordinator Jefferson Chem. Co., N.Y.C., 1969-71; gen. mgr. Ajax Chem. div. Biscayne Chem. Corp., Miami, Fla., 1971-79; mgr. ops. Trojan Chem., Newbury Park, Calif., 1979-81; mgr. ops. west coast ops. Cyclo Chem., Los Angeles, 1981-84; plant mgr. Chemron Corp., Paso Robles, Calif., 1984-85; pres., chief exec. officer Clean-Agrl. Fruit Chemicals, Inc. div. R7D Enterprises, Tulare, Calif., 1985—; chem. and engring. cons. R&D Enterprises, Lindsay, 1984—. Patentee in field. Bd. youth advisor Melrose Park Meth. Ch., Ft. Lauderdale, 1965; pres. coll. youth fellowship Good Shepard Meth. Ch., Bergenfield, N.J., 1964-65; co-chmn. PTO Valle Lindo Sch. Camarillo, Calif., 1980-82; div. dir. Am. Youth Soccer, Camarillo, 1982-84. Served with USAF, 1966-67. Mem. Pa. Soc. Profl. Engrs., Am. Chem. Soc., AAAS, Am. Inst. Plant Engrs., Chem. Week Adv. Panel. Republican. Avocations: traveling, camping, outdoor sports, photography, archtl. designing. Home: PO Box 2011 Tulare CA 93275-2011 Office: Clean Agrl Fruit Chemicals 3645 S K St Tulare CA 93274

KELLER, ALICE SMITH, magazine editor; b. New Haven, Mar. 6, 1948; s. Stephen Raymond and Jane Elizabeth (Burroughs) S.; m. Peter Charles Keller, May 20, 1972; children: Elizabeth Austin, Bret Charles. BA, Cornell U., 1969; MA, Georgetown U., 1973. Asst. editor Jour. Mktg., U. Tex., Austin, 1972-76; mgr. profl. periodicals med. div. Houghton Mifflin Co., Pacific Palisades, Calif., 1977-79; editor Gems & Gemology, Gemological Inst. Am., Santa Monica, Calif., 1980—; mng. editor Muscle & Nerve, Head & Neck Surgery, Jour. Microsurgery, 1977-80, Harry Winston: The Ultimate Jeweler, 1984, 86. Episcopalian. Office: Gemological Inst Am 1660 Stewart St Santa Monica CA 90404

KELLER, ANDREW DAVID, human factors engineer; b. Faribault, Minn., Apr. 20, 1942; s. Andrew Harold and Marjorie Ann (Kroenke) K.; m. Anne Gore Innes Moore, Aug. 8, 1970. BA in Psychology, Mankato State U., 1965; MA in Human Factors Psychology, U. S.D., 1972. Tech. asst., sales asst. Folsom TV-Radio Co., Faribault, 1965-67; human factors engr. IBM Corp., Endicott, N.Y., 1968-72, East Fishkill, N.Y., 1972-77; human factors engr. IBM Corp., Boulder, Colo., 1977-84, ergonomics coordinator, 1984-85; pvt. practice human factors engr. Longmont, Colo., 1985—. Inventor toner cartridge packaging system. Bd. dirs. Longmont Symphony Orchestra, 1984—, Longmont Mus., 1984—, Birthright, Longmont, 1977-86. Served with U.S. Army, 1966-68. Mem. Human Factors Soc. (chpt. treas. 1985-86), Inst. Indsl. Engrs. (sr.), Robotics Internat., Soc. Mfg. Engrs. (sr.). Republican. Roman Catholic. Avocations: vintage sports car racing, music, photography, fine arts, community activities. Home and Office: 1455 Twin Sisters Dr Longmont CO 80501

KELLER, DIANE CECELIA, religious organization administrator; b. Queens, N.Y., Sept. 23, 1955; d. John G. Sr. and Cecelia M. (Welsh) Wall. BA in Human Relations, Marian Coll., 1978; MSW, U. Denver, 1982. Cert. drug and alcohol counselor, Colo. Family therapist Ctr. Creative Living, Denver, 1983; dir. br. office Crossroads Counseling, Denver, 1983-84; mktg. dir. Raleigh Hills Hosp., Denver, 1984-85; parish administr. Christ the King Ch., Denver, 1985—. Served with U.S. Army, 1974. Mem. Nat. Assn. Social Workers, Nat. Assn. Ch. Bus. Adminstrn. (com. chairperson for Nat. 1988 Conv.). Democrat. Roman Catholic. Avocations: tennis, cross country skiing, downhill skiing, running, racquetball. Office: Christ The King Cath Ch 845 Fairfax St Denver CO 80220

KELLER, GEORGE HENRIK, marine geologist; b. Hartford, Conn., Sept. 9, 1931; s. George and Eva (Damschneider) K.; m. Suzanne Bray, Sept. 10, 1955; children: Mark, Lauri. AB, U. Conn., 1954; MS, U. Utah, 1956; PhD, U. Ill., 1966. Marine geologist USN, Washington, 1959-64; dir. marine G&G Lab. NOAA-AOML, Miami, Fla., 1966-75; assoc. dean oceanography Oreg. State U., Corvallis, 1975-82; rep. Oreg. State U. Univ. Corp. Atmospheric Research, Boulder, Colo., 1966-75; acting dean oceanography Oreg. State U., Corvallis, 1978, acting dean research, 1981-82, v.p. research and grad. studies, 1983—, v.p. internat. programs, 1987—; bd. dirs. Nat. Assoc. State Univs. and Land Grant Colls. Marine div., Washington, 1984—, Oreg. Resource and Tech. Devel. Corp., 1986—; council mem. Ctr. for Research Libraries, Chgo., 1984—. Editorial bd. mem. Marine Geotechnology Mag., 1974—; contbr. articles to profl. jours. Recipient C.A. Hogentolger award ASCE. Fellow Geol. Soc. Am.; mem. AAAS, Am. Geophys. Union, Internat. Sedimentol. Soc., Soc. Sigma Xi. Home: 3360 NW Witham Hill Dr Corvallis OR 97330 Office: Oreg State U Research Office Corvallis OR 97331

KELLER, GEORGE MATTHEW, oil executive; b. Kansas City, Mo., Dec. 3, 1923; s. George Matthew and Edna Louise (Mathews) K.; m. Adelaide McCague, Dec. 27, 1946; children: William G., Robert A., Barry R. BS in Chem. Engring., MIT, 1948. Mem. engring. dept. Standard Oil Calif., now Chevron Corp., San Francisco, 1948-63, fgn. ops. staff, 1963-67, asst. v.p., asst. to pres., 1967-69, v.p., 1969-74, dir., 1970—, vice-chmn., 1974-81, chmn., chief exec. officer, 1981—; bd. dirs. First Interstate Bancorp., First Interstate Bank Calif., Boeing Co.; SRI Internat. Trustee Notre Dame Coll., Belmont, Calif., Am. Enterprise Inst., Com. for Econ. Devel. Served to 1st lt. USAAF, 1943-46. Mem. Bus. Council, Bus. Roundtable, Trilateral Commn., Council Fgn. Relations, Nat. Petroleum Council. Home: San Mateo CA 94402 Office: Chevron Corp 225 Bush St San Francisco CA 94104 *

KELLER, HAROLD KEFAUVER, retired major league baseball executive; b. Middletown, Md., July 7, 1927; s. Charles Ernest and Naomi Sheffer (Kefauver) K.; m. Marietta Catherine McKee, Aug. 2, 1946 (div. Mar. 1965); children: Harold Kefauver, Jo Ann Lee, John David, Patricia Lu, Jan McKee; m. Dorothy Carol Mims, Mar. 27, 1965; 1 son, William Nevin. B.S., U. Md., 1953. Baseball player 1948-54; tchr. Frederick (Md.) High Sch., 1954-59; asst. farm dir. Washington Senators (later Minn. Twins), 1959-60; farm dir. Wash. Senators-Tex. Rangers, 1961-62, 64-78; Eastern scouting supr. Minn. Twins, 1963-64; dir. player devel. Seattle Mariners, 1979-83, v.p., gen. mgr., 1983-85. Served with AUS, 1947-49. Mem. Assn. Profl. Baseball Players of Am. Republican. Club: Am. Contract Bridge League (pres. Ft. Western unit 1977-78). Home: 2018 245th Ave SE Issaquah WA 98027 Office: PO Box 4100 Seattle WA 98104

KELLER, MILLETT FREDRICK, data processing management consultant; b. Great Falls, Mont., Jan. 7, 1940; s. Millett Fredrick and Mary Antoinette (Robischon) K.; m. Patricia Ann Quilty, June 15, 1963; children: Lisa Marie, Jeffrey Francis. BS in Geophysics, Stanford U., 1962, MS in Geophysics, 1963. Geophysicist Texaco Inc., Anchorage, 1963-64; data processing rep. IBM Corp., Anchorage, 1964-68; pres. SCS Data Processing Inc., Anchorage, 1968-76; v.p. Alaska Pacific Bank, Anchorage, 1979-81; data processing mgmt. cons. Anchorage, 1977—. Columnist Anchorage Daily News, 1985—. Bd. dirs. Humana Hosp. Alaska, Anchorage, 1982-84; elected rep. Anchorage Sch. Bd., 1975-81; mem. Mcpl. Bd. Ethics, Anchorage, 1982-84; pres. Anchorage Community UMCA, 1979. Named Outstanding Mem., Anchorage C. of C., 1982; recipient Outstanding Achievement award Stanford (Calif.) Assocs., 1982. Mem. Am. Geophys. Union, Data Processing Mgmt. Assn. Republican. Roman Catholic. Club: Commonwealth North (Anchorage) (v.p.). Lodge: Lions (pres. Anchorage club 1975). Avocations: running, hiking. Home: 1667 Crescent Dr Anchorage AK 99508 Office: Millett Keller Co 921 W 6th Ave Anchorage AK 99501

KELLER, RICHARD BROWNSON, entrepreneur; b. Evanston, Ill., Feb. 17, 1929; s. Ira C. and Lauretta (Taylor) K.; m. Ruth Elinor Olson, Mar. 30, 1957; children—Richard, Elizabeth Anne, Charles. B.S., U.S. Mil. Acad., 1950; M.B.A., Harvard U., 1952. Asst. to vice chmn. Ga. Pacific, Olympia, Wash., 1952-53; engring. and staff Western Kraft Corp., Portland, Oreg., 1954-75, sr. v.p., 1970-75; pres. western sales Keller Enterprises, Portland, 1975—; dir. N.W. Natural Gas, Portland, 1983—. Bd. dirs. Multnomah County Library, 1983—, Oreg. Grad. Ctr., 1984—; life trustee Lewis & Clark Coll. Served with U.S. Army, 1946-50. Republican. Clubs: Waverly, Arlington. Home: 4700 SW Northwood Ave Portland OR 97201 Office: Keller Enterprises Inc 1001 SW 5th Ave Portland OR 97204

KELLER, SHARON PILLSBURY, speech pathologist; b. Los Angeles, Sept. 28, 1935; d. Edward Gardner and Iris Noriene (Hager) Pillsbury; m. Clarence Stanley Keller (dec. 1982); children: Jann Kathleen, Jennifer Beth, Lauren Elaine. AA, Chaffey Community Coll., Alta Loma, Calif., 1971; BA, U. La Verne, 1978, MS, 1983. Lic. speech pathologist, Calif.; lic. sch. audiologist, Calif.; life service credential - clin. and rehabilitative, Calif. Lang. speech and hearing specialist Chino (Calif.) Unified Schs., 1978-86, Rim of the World Sch. Dist., Lake Arrowhead, Calif., 1986—. Mem. AAUW, Am. Speech-Lang. Hearing Assn. (cert. clin. competence speech-lang. pathologist), Calif. Speech and Hearing Assn., Calif. Tchrs. Assn. Republican. Presbyterian. Avocation: interior design. Home: 24414 Bernard Dr PO Box 1745 Crestline CA 92325 Office: Lake Arrowhead Elem Sch PO Box 430 Lake Arrowhead CA 92352

KELLERMEYER, ROBERT ALLISON, data processing executive; b. Los Angeles, Mar. 18, 1941; s. William Fredrick and Jane (Allison) K.; m. Terri Lee Smallwood (div.); children: Morgan, Tania; m. Virginia Dale Rogers, Dec. 17, 1970; 1 child, Eric. BS in Math., Calif. Poly Inst., San Luis Obispo, 1963. With First Interstate Services Co., Los Angeles, 1964-80; sr. v.p. First Interstate Services Co., Reno, 1980—. Served with USAR, 1966-72. Mem. Am. Nat. Standards Com. for Banking, 1982-84, Am. Contract Bridge League (life master). Home: 1725 Davis Ln Reno NV 89511

KELLEY, CYNTHIA C., social worker; b. Worcester, Mass., Feb. 8, 1940; d. Temple Chapman and Helen Laura (Crafts) Patton; m. Rory James Kelley, Apr. 24, 1977; children: Simone Leland, Lindsay. BA, Ariz. State U., 1961, MSW, 1974. Mgr. social work dept. Scottsdale (Ariz.) Meml. Hosp., 1974-85; pvt. practice specializing in social work Scottsdale, 1985—; bd. dirs. Inter-faith Counseling Service, Scottsdale. Mem. Nat. Assn. Social Workers, (cert.). Democrat. Lutheran. Avocations: tennis, bridge, gardening. Home and Office: 2625 North 58th St Scottsdale AZ 85257

KELLEY, FENTON C., biology educator; b. Chgo., Aug. 24, 1926; s. Will Ghost and Frances (Fenton) Kelley. BS in Biology, U. N.Mex., 1951, MS in Biology, 1954; PhD in Physiology, U. Calif., Berkeley, 1967. Fisheries biologist Dept. Fish and Game, Fresno, Calif., 1954-57; teaching asst. U. Calif., Berkeley, 1959-63, research asst., 1960-66; postdoctoral research fellow U. Calif., Santa Barbara, 1967-68, lectr. biology, 1968-69; assoc. prof. Boise (Idaho) State U., 1969—; aquatic cons. C.E., U.S. Army, Walla Walla, Wash., 1975-79, Sterns-Rogers, Denver, 1974-76, Morrison-Knudsen, Boise, 1977-78, Morrison-Knudsen Engring., Boise, 1985—; environ. cons. parks dept. City of Boise, 1970—, Boise. State U., 1970—; fishery cons. Boise Valley Fly Fisherman, 1978—, Ada County Planning and Zoning, Boise, 1978-84. Mem. legis. com. Idaho Legislature, Boise, 1973. Served as pvt. U.S. Army, 1945. U. Calif. scholar, Berkeley, 1957-58; research grantee Boise State U., 1973, 1978-84. Mem. Idaho Acad. Scis., Boise Valley Fly Fishermen (bd. dirs. 1982-85), Sigma Xi. Club: Metallic Silhouette Shooters (Boise). Avocations: hunting, fishing, photography. Home: 2260 Berkeley St Boise ID 83705 Office: Boise State U 1910 University Dr Boise ID 83725

KELLEY, JACQUELYN FRANCES, gerontologist; b. Palo Alto, Calif., Oct. 28, 1945; d. John Monroe and Glendora Drusilla (Sampson) Larson; m. Stephen Earl Kelley, Dec. 24, 1963; children: Kristina Leona Jane, Stephenie Victoria. AA, Coll. San Mateo, 1974; BS summa cum laude, Coll. Notre Dame, Belmont, Calif., 1980; postgrad., San Francisco State U., 1980—. ESL aide Cabrillo Unified Sch. Dist., Half Moon Bay, Calif., 1975-76; community services specialist Ret. Sr. Vol. Program, Menlo Park, Calif., 1980-82, dir., 1982-83; dir. vol. services Vis. Nurse Assn. San Francisco, 1983-85; gerontology specialist San Jose (Calif.) Office on Aging, 1986—; cons. mgmt. and retirement, 1981—. Founder Ocean Shore Resident's Assn., Half Moon Bay, 1976; founder Friends of RSVP Inc., Redwood City, Calif., 1983. Mem. Internat. Soc. Preretirement Planners (chpt. pres., bd. dirs. 1985—), Nat. Council Aging, Am. Soc. on Aging (com. chmn. 1984—), Assn. Profl. Vol. Mgrs. (founder, chmn. 1984—), ACTION Volunteerism Council, Human Resources Council, Alpha Gamma Sigma, Delta Epsilon Sigma, Kappa Gamma Pi. Republican. Lutheran. Avocations: reading, hiking, swimming, cross-country skiing. Home: 339 Grand Blvd Half Moon Bay CA 94019

KELLEY, KEVIN PATRICK, security, safety administrator; b. Indpls., Apr. 21, 1954; s. Everett Lee and Emily Louise (Bottoms) K.; m. Kathie Jo Fluegeman, Oct. 13, 1984. BS, Calif. State U., Long Beach, 1984; cert. mgmt. supervision, UCLA, 1984. Mgmt. asst. FBI, Los Angeles, 1973-79; security supr. UCLA, 1979-82; security, safety adminstr. Micom Systems, Inc., Chatsworth, Calif., 1982-83; loss prevention, safety auditor Joseph Magnin, Inc., San Francisco, 1983-84; loss prevention, safety adminstr. Wherehouse Entertainment, Inc., Gardena, Calif., 1984-86; risk control cons. Indsl. Indemnity Co., Los Angeles, 1986—; commr. pub. safety City of Norwalk, Calif., 1984-86. Mem. security com. Los Angeles Olympic Organizing Com., 1984. Mem. Am. Soc. Indsl. Security (cert., Peter Updike Meml. scholar 1985), Am. Soc. Safety Engrs., Chief Spl. Agts. Assn., Risk Ins. Mgmt. Soc., Nat. Safety Mgmt. Soc. (sec. 1985-86), Am. Heart Assn. (governing bd. chmn. 1986-88), Ins. Inst. Am. (cert.). Republican. Roman Catholic. Lodges: Rotary, Kiwanis. Avocations: tennis, swimming, reading, movies, skiing. Home: 5930 Via Santana Yorba Linda CA 92686 Office: Indsl Indemnity Co 505 S Virgil Ave Los Angeles CA 90020

KELLEY, NEIL DAVIS, applied meteorologist; b. Clayton, Mo., Jan. 8, 1942; s. Davis Franklin and Louise Minnie (Zager) K.; divorced; B.S. in Meteorology, St. Louis U., 1963; M.S., Pa. State U., 1968. Mem. staff Meteorology Research Inc. Altadena, Calif., 1963-66; field supr. Exxon Research and Engring., Linden, N.J., 1967; instr. meteorology Pa. State U., 1969-71; chief of capability devel. Research Aviation Facility, Nat. Ctr. for Atmospheric Research, Boulder, Colo., 1972-77; prin. scientist Solar Energy Research Inst., Golden, Colo., 1977—. Recipient spl. award Nat. Ctr. Atmospheric Research, 1974; outstanding award Solar Energy Research Inst., 1982. Mem. Instrument Soc. Am., Am. Meteorol. Soc., AAAS, AIAA, Am. Theater Organ Soc., Sigma Xi. Club: Elks Today. Contbr. articles to profl. jours. Office: Solar Energy Research Inst 1617 Cole Blvd Golden CO 80401

KELLEY, NILES ELMER, graphics designer; b. Ft. Dodge, Iowa, June 15, 1916; s. Niles E. and Mabel (Severson) K.; m. Joyce Ordell Gjerde, mar. 13, 1941; children: Amanda O., Martha Anne, Robert N., Ellen N. Student, U. Wash., 1934-38, Cornish Art Sch., 1940-43. Illustrator Boeing Co., Seattle, 1943-45; free lances artist Niles Kelley, Inc., Seattle, 1945-50, free lance art dir., 1956-58; creative visual dir. Cole & Weber, Inc., Seattle, 1950-56; chmn. bd. dirs. Western Graphics, Inc., Seattle, 1958—; cons. art dir. Sta. KOMO-TV, Seattle, 1952-75, McCann-Erickson, Seattle, 1956-57, Fiberbd. Products, Seattle, 1946-50; instr. U. Wash., 1952-55; portrait artists, lanscape artists. Mem. Puget Sound Group of NW Painters (life), Soc. Profl. Graphic Artists. Club: Seattle Tennis, Swedish. Home: 3849-42 NE Seattle WA 98105

KELLEY, RAYMOND JOHN, free lance musician; b. Hollywood, Calif., Feb. 26, 1938; s. Richard Frederick and Anna (Overstreet) Kelley; m. Jan Ellen Reinhart Kelley, May 8, 1962; children: Daniel Patrick, Joyce Ann. Studies with Gregor Piatigorsky, U. So. Calif., 1963-65. Cellist Spade Cooley's Band, Hollywood, 1956, Salt Lake Symphony, 1956-57, Dallas Symphony, 1957-63, Los Angeles Philharm., 1963-68; freelance cellist Los Angeles, 1964—; 1st cellist on movie Back to the Future; 1st cellist for Neil Diamond, Barbra Streisand, other performers; also cellist various T.V. shows. Served with N.G. and USAF, 1961-67. Mem. Recording Musicians of Am. (pub. relations dir. 1983—), Nat. Acad. Recording Arts and Scis. (mem. bd. govs. 1982-86, Most Valuable Player 1981-83, Most Valuable Player Emeritus, 1985). Republican. Presbyterian. Avocations: cooking, traveling, tennis, gardening. Home and Office: 3700 Wrightwood Dr Studio City CA 91604

KELLEY, ROBERT PAUL, JR., management consultant; b. Mansfield, Ohio, Mar. 27, 1942; s. Robert Paul and Rachel Marie Kelley; B.B.A., Notre Dame U., 1964; M.B.A., Harvard U., 1969; m. Mimi Grant, June 15, 1975; children—Robert, Laura, Elizabeth. Mktg. cons., supr. Laventhol & Horwath, Los Angeles, 1972-73; dir. mktg., entertainment and mdsg. Knott's Berry Farm, Buena Park, Calif., 1974-76; sr. v.p. mktg. Am. Warranty Corp., Los Angeles, 1978-80; chief exec. officer Strategy Network Corp. Dirs., Inc., 1976—; exec. program dir. So. Calif. Tech. Execs. Network, 1984—; dir. Orange County sect. So. Calif. Tech. Exec.'s Network, 1984-85, pres., chief exec. officer, 1985—. Author: The Board of Directors and its Role in Growing Companies, 1984. Served with USNR, 1964-67. Home: 13992 Malena Dr Tustin CA 92680 Office: 4600 Campus Dr Suite 200 Newport Beach CA 92660

KELLEY, WILLIAM J., urban planning educator; b. Silsbee, Tex., July 25, 1945; s. William Joseph and Zelda (Kimball) K.; m. Teresa Rene Stueckle, Feb. 14, 1981; 1 child, Tamsin Rayne. BA with honors, Pan Am. U., 1973; M in Urban Planning, Tex. A&M U., 1978; postgrad., U. Wash., 1982—. Research assoc. Tex. Transp. Inst. Tex. A&M U., College Station, 1977-78, Transp. Ctr. U. Wash., Seattle, 1981-82; research prof. Program in Environ. Sci. Wash. State U., Pullman, 1982-84; assoc. prof. urban planning Eastern Wash. U., Cheney, 1978—, chmn. dept. urbal planning, 1986—, dir. transp. research services ctr., 1978—, dir. grad. program dept. planning, 1982—. Mem. Neighborhood Design task force, Spokane, 1983—, Spokant Transit Commn., 1980-81, Spokane Regional Transp. Adv. com., 1980-84; del. Wash. State Dem. Conv., Tacoma, 1984. Mem. Am. Soc. Pub. Adminstrn., Am. Planning Assn., Community Devel Soc. (exec. bd. dirs. Wash. chpt. 1980—), Assn. Mgmt., Phi Kappa Phi. Democrat. Office: Eastern Wash U Dept Urban and Regional Planning Isle Hall 206 Cheney WA 99004

KELLEY-CRESCI, MARILYN V., bookkeeping service owner; b. Tucson, Jan. 13, 1937; d. Marion and Lovetta (Merchant) Adkins; children: Russell D., Wanda L. (dec.), James H.; m. Frank V. Cresci, Sept. 13, 1986. Student Heald Bus. Sch., 1977, Regional Occupational Ctr., 1981. Bookkeeper Barbary Coast, San Jose, Calif., 1980-82, Argon Steel, San Jose, 1982-83, Indsl. Chimney, Hayward, Calif., 1984-85; owner Marilyn's Bookkeeping Service, Union City, Calif., 1983—; corp. sec.-treas. Rod's Trucking, Inc., Newark, Calif., 1985—; corp. v.p., sec. Newark Wreckers, 1987—. Fellow Nat. Assn. Female Execs. Republican. Episcopalian. Lodge: Order of Demolay (pres. mother's club 1979-80). Avocations: fishing; camping. Address: 118 Madrone Way Union City CA 94587

KELLIHER, MICHAEL MORTIMER, criminologist, educator; b. Spokane, June 13, 1934; s. Michael M. and Helen E. Kelliher B.Ph., Gonzaga U., 1960; B.Th., U. Santa Clara, 1968; M.Criminology, U. Calif.-Berkeley, 1969, D.Criminology, 1972. Tchr., Loyola High Sch., Missoula, Mont. 1961-64; aux. chaplain 682d Radar Squadron, New Almaden, Calif., 1966-67; assoc. prof. Criminal Justice, Seattle U., 1972—; mem. law enforcement tng. bd. State of Wash., 1974-78, mem. corrections tng. bd., 1982-86; dir. Criminal Justice Program, 1987—. Mem. Acad. Criminal Justice Scis., Am. Soc. Criminology, Am. Correctional Assn., Am. Judicature Soc., Nat. Council Crime and Delinquency, Wash. Assn. Criminal Justice Educators, Am. Polygraph Assn., N.W. Polygraph Examiners Assn. (v.p. 1983—).

KELLING, HANS-WILHELM, foreign language educator; b. Schwerin, Mecklenburg, Fed. Republic of Germany, Aug. 15, 1932; came to U.S., 1952; s. Wilhelm and Emma (Hinkfoth) K.; m. Joyce Kay Coy, June 10, 1958; children: Sven, Kareen, Kirsten, Kerryl Anna. BA, Brigham Young U., 1958; MA, Stanford U., 1960, PhD, 1966. Asst. prof. German classical lit. and cultural history Brigham Young U., Provo, Utah, 1962-67, assoc. prof., 1967-72, prof., 1972—, chmn. dept. German and Slavic Langs., 1977-83, dir. fgn. lang. housing, 1985—; dir. fgn. residence programs Brigham Young U., Salzburg, Vienna, 1963, 68, 69, 85; pres. Mission of the Ch. of Latter-day Saints, Munich, 1973-77. Recipient Disting. Teaching award Brigham Young U., Provo, 1971, 80, 85, 86; grantee Woodrow Wilson Found., Stanford, Calif., 1958, 82; DADD fellow German Govt., 1964. Mem. Rocky Mountain Modern Lang. Assn. (sect. chair 1964), Assn. German Studies, Am. Assn. Tchrs. German (various assignments). Republican. Office: Brigham Young U 4096 JKHB Provo UT 84602

KELLNER, DAVID HERMAN, communications company executive; b. Coeur d'Alene, Idaho, Dec. 9, 1941; s. Theador Henry and Dorthy Marie (Secour) K.; m. Joan Hagadone, June 12, 1966. A.A., North Idaho Coll., 1963; B.S.E.E., U. Idaho, 1970; M.B.A., U. Ohio, 1981. Systems engr. B.P.A., Moses Lake, Wash., 1974-78; product mgr. NCR, Cambridge, Ohio, 1978-81; dir. mgmt. info. systems Hagadone Corp., Coeur d'Alene, 1981—. Mem. city planning commn., Moses Lake, 1978. Served to lt. USN, 1966-74. Mem. IEEE. Lodges: Masons, Rotary (dir. 1983—). Office: Hagadone Corp care Hagadone Bldg on the Lake Coeur d'Alene ID 83814

KELLNER, RICHARD GEORGE, computer scientist; b. Cleve., July 10, 1943; s. George Ernest and Wanda Julia (Lapinski) K.; BS, Case Inst. Tech., 1965; MS, Stanford U., 1968, PhD, 1969; m. Charlene Ann Zajc, June 26, 1965; children: Michael Richard, David George. Staff mem. Los Alamos (N.M.) Scientific Lab., 1969-79, Los Alamos Nat. Lab., 1983—; co-owner, dir. software devel. KMP Computer Systems, Inc., Los Alamos, 1979-84; mgr. spl. projects KMP Computer Systems div. 1st Data Resources Inc., Los Alamos, 1984—; owner CompuSpeed, 1986—; co-owner Computer-Aided Communications, 1982-84; cons., 1979—. Mem. AAAS, IEEE, Assn. Computing Machinery, Math. Assn. Am., Soc. Indsl. and Applied Math. Home: 4496 Ridgeway Dr Los Alamos NM 87544 Office: KMP Computer Systems 2075 Trinity Dr Los Alamos NM 87544

KELLOGG, BERTRAM CECIL, safety consultant; b. Port Angeles, Wash., Sept. 16, 1924; s. Bertram Fredrick and Lorette Louise (Woods) K.; student UCLA, 1961, U. Wash., 1966, U. So. Calif., 1956-57, U. Minn., 1967, Anchorage Community Coll., 1956, Calif. State U., Sacramento, 1968; children—Bertram Scott, Mary Alice, Deborah Jo Ellen Kellog Douglas, Dennis Bertram. Mgr. engring. Fireman's Fund Am., Seattle, 1965-69; dir. indsl. relations Feather River Lumber Co., Loyalton, Calif., 1960-62; v.p., gen. mgr. Kelor Corp., Anchorage, 1969-76; mgr. loss control div. Aetna Cravens Dargar & Co., Sacramento, 1978-81; safety cons. Callosha Cons. Service, Sacramento, 1981—; cons. City of Pasadena. Dir. safety services and disasters ARC, Pasadena, 1957-60. Served with U.S. Mcht. Marine, 1944-47. Mem. Am. Soc. Safety Engrs. (profl.), Nat. Fire Protection Assn., U.S. Power Squadron, Vets. of Safety, Engring. Council Sacramento Valley. Republican. Episcopalian. Clubs: Lions, Toastmasters, Elks. Contbr. articles to profl. jours. Home: 161 Magnolia Ave Sacramento CA 95828 Office: Callosha Cons Service 2424 Arden Way Sacramento CA 95825

KELLOGG, BRUCE MICHAEL, real estate investor, agent; b. Buffalo, Jan. 3, 1947; s. Harlan Wood and Hilma Moore (Yarrington) K.; m. Diane Linda Mancuso, Dec. 25, 1979; children—Jeremy, Catherine, Michael, Elizabeth, David, Allison. B.S.E.E., Rutgers U., 1969; M.B.A., Golden Gate U., 1976, Securities investor, Wilmington, N.C., 1970-73; real estate investor, San Jose, Calif., 1973—; assoc Gt. Am. Realty, San Jose, 1982—. Mem. Tri-County Apt. Assn., Calif. Apt. Assn. Nat. Apt. Assn., San Jose Bd. Realtors, Calif. Assn. Realtors, Nat. Assn. Realtors, Nat. Multihousing Council. Republican. Roman Catholic. Contbr. articles to profl. jours. Office: 2845 Moorpark Ave Suite 209 San Jose CA 95128

KELLOGG, FREDERICK, historian; b. Boston, Dec. 9, 1929; s. Frederick Floyd and Stella Harriet (Plummer) K.; A.B., Stanford U., 1952; M.A., U. So. Calif., 1958; Ph.D., Ind. U., 1969; m. Patricia Kay Hanbery, Aug. 21, 1954, (dec., 1975); 1 dau., Kristine Marie Calvert; m. 2d, Rebecca Anne Boone, July 11, 1979. Instr., Boise State U., 1962-64, asst. prof., 1964-65; vis. asst. prof. U. Idaho, 1965; asso. prof. Boise State U., 1966-67; instr. history U. Ariz., 1967-68, asst. prof., 1968-71, asso. prof., 1971—. Founder, chmn. Idaho Hist. Conf., 1964. U.S.-Romania Cultural Exchange Research scholar, 1960-61; Sr. Fulbright-Hays Research scholar, Romania, 1969-70. Recipient Am. Council Learned Socs. Research grant, 1970-71; Internat. Research and Exchanges Bd. Sr. Research grant, 1973-74. Mem. Am. Hist. Assn., Am. Assn. Advancement Slavic Studies, Am. Assn. Southeast European Studies. Mng. editor Southeastern Europe, 1974—; contbr. articles to scholarly publs. Office: Dept History U Ariz Tucson AZ 85721

KELLOGG, GARY LEE, physicist; b. Cambridge Springs, Pa., Jan. 16, 1950; s. Richard and Elizabeth Noreen (Collen) K.; m. Susan Jean Lechefsky, June 26, 1971; children: Brian Richard, Justin Mark. BS, Pa. State U., 1971, PhD, 1976. Staff physicist Sandia Nat. Labs., Albuquerque, 1976—. Contbr. numerous publs. to sci. jours. Mem. Am. Phys. Soc., Am. Chem. Soc., Am. Vacuum Soc. (chmn. N.Mex. chpt. 1982-83). Avocations: country and western dancing, golfing. Home: 917 LaCharles Dr NE Albuquerque NM 87112 Office: Sandia Nat Labs Div 1134 Albuquerque NM 87185

KELLOGG, MEG ANNE, health care administrator; b. Chgo., Oct. 24, 1948; d. Harry E. and Kathleen M. (Cahill) K. B.A. in French, U. Calif.-Berkeley, 1970, M.S. in Community Health and Phys. Therapy, Stanford U., 1972. Pub. health analyst Med. Services Adminstrn. HEW, Washington, 1972-73, br. chief Systems Devel. Bur. of Quality Assurance div. HEW (now Health and Human Services), Rockville, Md., 1973-75; coordinator accreditation and regulation Kaiser-Permanente Med. Care Program, Oakland, Calif., 1975-80; dir. corp. planning Pacific Med. Ctr., Inc., San Francisco, 1980-83; health care investment analyst, co-editor med. tech. stock letter Venture Capital Mgmt., 1984-85, dir. policy and strategic planning hdqrs. Kaiser Found. Health Plan, Oakland, Calif., 1985—; lectr. in field. Bd. dirs. San Francisco Opera Guild. Recipient HEW Outstanding Service Merit award, 1975. Mem. Health Care Execs. No. Calif., Soc. Hosp. Planning, N.Am. Soc. Corporate Planning, Phi Beta Kappa. Roman Catholic. Club: Claremont Resort.

KELLOGG, WILLIAM WELCH, meteorologist; b. New York Mills, N.Y., Feb. 14, 1917; s. Frederick S. and Elizabeth (Walcott) K.; m. Elizabeth Thorson, Feb. 14, 1942; children: Karl S., Judith K. Liebert, Joseph W., Jane K. Holien, Thomas W. B.A., Yale U., 1939; M.A., UCLA, 1942, Ph.D., 1949. With Inst. Geophysics, U. Calif., Los Angeles, 1946-52, asst. prof., 1950-52; scientist Rand Corp., Santa Monica, Calif., 1947-59, head planetary scis. dept., 1959-64; assoc. dir. Nat. Ctr. Atmospheric Research, Boulder, Colo., also dir. lab. atmospheric scis., 1964-73, sr. scientist, 1973—; Mem. earth satellite panel IGY, 1956-59; mem. space sci. bd. Nat. Acad. Scis., 1959-68, mem. com. meteorol. aspects of effects of atomic radiation, 1956-58, mem. com. atmospheric scis., 1966-72, mem. polar research bd., 1972-77; mem. Rocket and Satellite Research Panel, 1957-62; mem. adv. group supporting tech. for operational meteorol. satellites NASA-NOAA, 1964-72; rapporteur meteorology of high atmosphere, commn. aerology World Meteorol. Orgn., 1965-71; chmn. internat. commn. meteorology upper atmosphere Internat. Union Geodesy and Geophysics, 1960-67, mem., 1967-75; mem. internat. com. climate Internat. Assn. Meteorology and Atmospheric Physics, 1978—; mem. sci. adv. bd. USAF, 1956-65; chmn. meteorol. satellite com. Advanced Research Projects Agy., 1958-59; mem. panel on environment President's Sci. Adv. Com., 1968-72; mem. space program adv. council NASA, 1976-77; chmn. meteorol. adv. com. EPA, 1970-74, mem. nat. air quality criteria adv. com., 1975-76, air pollution transport and transformation adv. com., 1976-78; mem. council on carbon dioxide environ. assessment Dept. Energy, 1976-78; adv. to sec. gen. on World Climate Program, World Meteorol. Orgn., 1978-79; dir. research Naval Environ. Prediction Research Facility, Monterey, Calif., 1983-84; chmn. adv. com. Div. Polar Programs NSF, 1983-86. Served as pilot-weather officer USAAF, 1941-46. Co-recipient spl. award pioneering work in planning meteorol. satellite Am. Meteorol. Soc., 1961; recipient Risseca award contbn. human relations in scis. Jewish War Vets. U.S.A., 1962-63; Exceptional Civilian Service award Dept. Air Force, 1966; Spl. award for pioneering meteorol. satellites Dept. Energy, 1985. Fellow Am. Geophys. Union (pres. meteorol. sect. 1972-74), Am. Meteorol. Soc. (council 1960-63, pres. 1973-74), AAAS (chmn. atmospheric and hydrospheric sect. 1984); mem. Internat. Acad. Astronautics, Sigma Xi. Club: Cosmos (Washington). Research on meteorology, dynamics and turbulence of upper atmosphere, use rockets and satellites for atmospheric research; prediction radioactive fallout and dispersal; applications of infrared techniques; atmospheres of Mars and Venus; theory of climate and causes of climate change. Home: 445 College Ave Boulder CO 80302 Office: Nat Ctr Atmospheric Research Boulder CO 80307

KELLY, BRIAN MATTHEW, industrial hygienist; b. Ogdensburg, N.Y., June 16, 1956; s. Lauris F. and Catherine M. (McEvoy) K. BA, SUNY, Oswego, 1978; BS, Clarkson U., 1981. Cert. indsl. toxicologist. Maintenance engr. Kelly Sales Corp., Madrid, N.Y., 1978-80, carpenter, 1981-82; hygienist indsl. hygiene and toxicology div. Sandia Nat. Labs., Albuquerque, 1983—. Mem. Am. Chem. Soc. (div. chem. health and safety), Am. Inst. Chemists, Am. Indsl. Hygienists Assn., Am. Welding Soc., Gamma Sigma Epsilon, Phi Kappa Phi. Republican. Roman Catholic. Avocations: cycling, fishing, carpentry. Home: 1570 W Bosque Loop Bosque Farms NM 87068 Office: Sandia Nat Labs Div Indsl Hygiene & Toxicology PO Box 5800 Org 3311 Albuquerque NM 87185

KELLY, CONNIE DIANE, real estate development company executive; b. Reno, July 22, 1951; d. Angelo Bernard and Florence Irene (Powell) Landa. Student U. Nev., Truckee Meadows Community Coll. Lic. real estate broker, Nev.; loan officer, asst. v.p. Family Savs. and Loan Assn., Reno, 1976-78; br. mgr. Lomas & Nettleton Co., Reno, 1978-81; ptnr. Homes & Land Mag., Reno, 1980-81; project adminstr. R.J.B. Devel. Co., Reno, 1981-82, mng. loan fee underwriter, 1982-85; mgr. loan ctr. AVP Pacific 1st Mortgage, San Diego, Calif., 1985—; counselor Am. Inst. Fgn. Studies. Mem. Nat. Assn. Female Execs., Winners Circle. Clubs: Sierra Yacht, Multihull Racing Assn., Prindle Fleet 8. Home: 2774 Levante St Carlsbad CA 92009 Office: 11939 Rancho Bernardo Rd San Diego CA 92128

KELLY, DAVID RICHARD, accountant; b. Oakland, Calif., June 9, 1940; s. David Philip and Annetta Marie K.; m. Margo Ann Lourdeaux, May 9, 1964; children: Brian D., Timothy A. BS in Econs., Bus. Adminstrn., St. Mary's Coll., Moraga, Calif., 1962; MBA, U. Calif., Berkeley, 1971. CPA, Calif. Staff acct. Price Waterhouse, San Francisco, 1962-65, Victor Equipment Co., San Francisco, 1965-66; staff acct., mgr. taxes Hood & Strong, San Francisco, 1966-69; pvt. practice acctg. Walnut Creek, Calif., 1970-74; officer Kelly Tama & Shiffman Accountancy Corp., Walnut Creek, 1974—. Chmn. CPA com. Children's Hosp. Med. Ctr. Found., 1981-82; bd. dirs. (hon.) Contra Costa County Dist. Council Soc. St. Vincent de Paul; Bd. Regents, trustee St. Mary's Coll., 1979-80, treas. St. Mary's East Bay Scholarship Fund, Inc.; mem. budget and fin. coms. Mt. Diablo Family YMCA, 1982-84; past treas. Easter Seal Soc. Contra Costa County; past bd. dirs. Diablo Valley Estate Planning Council. Mem. Am. Inst. CPA's, Calif. Soc. CPA's (statewide dir. 1977-80, pres. East Bay chpt. 1978-79, task force for community service, 1982, task force CPA requirements 1985), St. Mary's Coll. Nat. Alumni Assn. (bd. dirs. 1972—, pres. 1979-80). Democrat. Roman Catholic. Avocations: fishing, hiking, tennis, Calif. and Civil War histories. Office: Kelly Tama & Shiffman Acctg Corp 1990 N California Blvd Suite 902 Walnut Creek CA 94596

KELLY, DENNIS RAY, sales executive; b. Olympia, Wash., Aug. 20, 1948; s. William E. and Irene (Lewis) K.; m. Pamela Jo Kresevich, Mar. 16, 1974. BA, Cen. Wash. U., 1972; postgrad., U. Wash., 1977-78. Sales rep. Bumble Bee Sea Foods, Seattle, 1972-74; retail sales mgr. Pacific Pearl Sea Foods, Seattle, 1974-76; regional sales mgr. Castle & Cooke Foods, Seattle, Phila., and N.Y.C., 1976-80; v.p. sales mktg. Frances Andrew Ltd., Seattle, 1980-82; regional sales mgr. Tenneco West, Seattle, 1982-85; sales and mktg. mgr. for western U.S. David Oppenheimer, Seattle, 1985—. Alumni advisor Cen. Wash. U., Ellensburg, 1979-87, alumni bd. dirs., 1986—, mem. sch. community group bd. Republican. Avocations: hiking, backpacking, skiing. Home: 7234 237 Ave NE Redmond WA 98053

KELLY, ERIC DAMIAN, lawyer, city planner; b. Pueblo, Colo., Mar. 16, 1947; s. William Bret and Patricia Ruth (Ducy) K.; m. Viana Eileen Rockel, 1980; children: Damian Charles, Eliza Jane, Valissitie Christina Heeren, Douglas Ray Heeren. B.A., Williams Coll., 1969; J.D., U. Pa., 1975, M.City Planning, 1975. Bar: Colo. 1975, U.S. Dist. Ct. 1976, U.S. Tax Ct. 1976, U.S. Ct. Appeals (10th cir.) 1986. Chief citizens' participation unit EPA, Region III, Phila., 1971-72; project planner Beckett New Town, N.J., 1972-73; v.p., project mgr. Rahenkamp Sachs Wells & Assocs., Inc., Denver and Phila., 1973-76; sole practice law, Pueblo, 1976-83; pres. Kelly & Potter, P.C., Pueblo, Albuquerque and Santa Fe, 1983—; adj. asst. prof. U. Colo. Coll. Planning and Design, 1976—, land use seminars Fed. Publs., Inc., 1976-84; instr. grad. sch. bus. U. So. Colo., 1986—; spl. counsel City of Westminster, Colo., 1976—; pres. Color Radio, Ltd., 1979—; sec., dir. Lodging Service Corp., 1980—; dir. Mar Tec Broadcasting Corp., Pueblo Growth Corp., Wildflower, Inc.; cons. Colo. Land Use Commn., 1976-77, Wyo. Land Use Adminstrn., 1977-78, City of Santa Fe, 1981-83, City of Reno, 1984-86, City of Albuquerque, 1985-86. Author: Land Use Controls, 1976-80, 82; editor, prin. author: The Roadtripper, 1969. Contbr. articles to profl. planning and legal jours. Bd. dirs. Broadway Theatre League, Pueblo, 1976-77, Pueblo Beautiful Assn., 1978-82; trustee Sangre de Cristo Arts and Conf. Ctr., 1981—, chmn. 1986, Christ Congl. Ch., 1982-83. Served with U.S. Army, 1969-71. Named outstanding student Am. Inst. Planners, 1976. Mem. Am. Inst. Cert. Planners (charter), Am. Planning Assn., Urban Land Inst., ABA, Colo. Bar Assn., Denver Bar Assn., Pueblo County Bar Assn., Williams Coll. Alumni Assn. (class sec. 1969-74, regional sec. 1980-82, class agt. 1985—). Democrat. Club: Pueblo Country. Lodge: Rotary. Office: 200 E Abriendo Ave Pueblo CO 81004

KELLY, FLOYD WESLEY, chemistry educator; b. Greeley, Colo., Dec. 30, 1941; s. Floyd W. and Edith (Burton) K.; m. Heather Dee Pepple, June 21, 1965; children: Bradley, Brenda. AS, Ft. Lewis Coll., 1961; BS, Colo. State U., 1963; MS, U. Oreg., 1965; PhD, U. Idaho, 1968. Postdoctoral fellow Utah State U., Logan, 1968-69; instr. chemistry Casper (Wyo.) Coll., 1969—; cons. Grade Sch. Enrichment Program, Casper, 1985-86. Author: Study Guide for Chemistry for Health Sciences, 1982; manuscript reviewer, 1970—. Mem. Am. chem. Soc., Sigma Xi. Avocations: fishing, hunting, backpacking, running, cross-country skiing. Office: Casper Coll Chemistry Dept Casper WY 82601

KELLY, JACK, city mayor; b. Astoria, N.Y.; m. Jo Kelly; 1 dau., Nichole. Student, UCLA, 1945, 47. Mem. city council City of Huntington Beach, 1980-83, 84—, mayor, 1983, 87; owner, real estate investor August 2 Investment Firm, Huntington Beach. Appeared as youth five Broadway plays, 300 radio dramas, numerous 2-reel motion pictures, later in films Young Mr. Lincoln, Alexander Graham Bell; as young adult appeared in Suspense, Studio One, Playhouse Ninety, Ripley's Believe It or Not, Pond's Theatre, others; co-star TV series Maverick; appeared in musicals including Guys and Dolls, Music Man, The Pajama Game; on Broadway shows include Night Life, Family Way; guest star many TV series including B.J. and the Bear, Rockford Files, Vegas; emcee game show Sale of the Century; appeared in Get Christie Love, 1976, The Hardy Boys; currently voice many TV commls. including Lowenbrau Beer, General Tires, Aurora Toys, others. Served with USAF, 1945-46. Office: Office of Mayor 2000 Main St Huntington Beach CA 92648

KELLY, JAMES FRANCIS, department store executive; b. Mt. Vernon, N.Y., Nov. 7, 1906; s. Hugh and Elizabeth (Dunne) K.; m. Ruth Wellington Dee, Oct. 19, 1935; children—Barbara (Mrs. John G. Ryden), Hampton Merrill (stepson). LL.B., St. John's U., 1930. Bar: N.Y. bar 1940. With Assoc. Dry Goods Corp., 1934-72, sec., 1956-71, also v.p., dir. Club: Dunes Golf (Myrtle Beach, S.C.). Home: 310 73d Ave #3A Myrtle Beach SC 29577

KELLY, JAMES PATRICK, JR., engineering and construction executive; b. Bklyn., July 19, 1933; s. James Patrick and Marion Rita (Gleason) K.; m. Nancy Karen Sather, June 10, 1967; children: Kathryn, Mark, Lisa Angelique, Trevor, Lisa, James. B.S. in Engring, U.S. Naval Acad., 1955; postgrad., U. Houston. Registered profl. engr., Calif. Asst. site mgr. Pathfinder; reactor Allis Chalmers Mfg. Co., Sioux Falls, S.D., 1963-67; nuclear project mgr. Brown & Root, Houston, 1967-69; constrn. project mgr., then asst. v.p. Gibbs & Hill, Omaha and N.Y.C., 1969-75; pres. Dravo Lime Co., Pitts., 1975-77; group v.p. natural resources Dravo Corp., Pitts., 1976-81; sr. v.p. engring. and constrn., domestic and internat. Dravo Corp., 1982-84; pres., dir. C.F. Braun & Co. (name now Santa Fe Braun Inc.), Alhambra, Calif., 1984-86; pres. Ultra Systems Power & Environ. Group, Irvine, Calif., 1986—; dir. So. Industries, Inc. Bd. dirs. S.D. Mental Health Assn., 1966-67, Western Pa. Sch. Blind Children, 1978-84; mem. Sioux Falls Bd. Edn., 1965-66, Assn. Retarded Citizens Pitts., 1970—; vice chmn. United Way, Region II, Los Angeles; pres. found. bd. Calif. State U., Los Angeles. Served as officer USN, 1955-63. Mem. Nat. Soc. Profl. Engrs., Am. Nuclear Soc., Mensa, Sierra Club. Home: 12122 Sky Ln Santa Ana CA 92705 Office: Ultra Systems Power & Environ Group 16845 Von Karmon Ave Irvine CA 92714

KELLY, JOHN MILAN, mayor; b. Parnell, Iowa, June 5, 1926; m. Rosemary Easter Malloy, Dec. 30, 1947 (dec. May 1964); children: John, Michael, Kathleen, Theresa; m. Helen Frances Schwartz, Feb. 12, 1965; children: stepchildren: Susan, Pitt, Tom Covert. BA, U. Iowa, 1951; MEd, U. Wyo., 1961. Cert. tchr., Wyo. Prin. Carbon County Sch. Dist., Clear Creek, Utah, 1948-49; dist. scout exec. Boy Scouts Am., Omaha, 1951-55, Casper, Wyo., 1955-59; elem. prin. Natrona County Sch. Dist., Casper, 1959-84; councilman City of Casper, 1985-86, mayor, 1987—. Served with USN, 1944-46, PTO. Democrat. Roman Catholic. Avocations: photography, railroading, traveling. Home: 736 S Beech Casper WY 82601 Office: Office of Mayor 200 N David St Casper WY 82601

KELLY, JOSEPH JAMES, oil company executive; b. El Paso, Tex., Jan. 22, 1941; s. John M. and Esther (Ladenburg) K.; m. Barbara Harter, Nov. 25, 1967; children: Christine, David, Peter, Mark, Brian, Suzanne. BSC, U. Santa Clara, 1964; MBA, Am. U., Washington, 1966. Dir. Glover Inc., Roswell, N.Mex., 1979-80; assoc. dir. Security Nat. Bank, Roswell, 1979-81; mem. Tech. Adv. Commn. N.Mex., Socorro, 1981-83; dir. St. Mary's Hosp., Roswell, 1985—, Oil Field Tng. Sch., Roswell, 1986—; pres. Elk Oil Co., Roswell, 1972—. Served to cpt. U.S. Army, 1966-69. Mem. Ind. Petroleum Assn. Am. (v.p. 1983-86), Ind. Petroleum Assn. N.Mex. (sec.-treas. 1979—), Am. Assn. Petroleum Landmen, N.Mex. Oil and Gas Assn., N.Mex. Landmen's Assn. (pres. 1975). Democrat. Roman Catholic. Lodge: Rotary. Office: Elk Oil Co Box 310 Roswell NM 88201

KELLY, LEONTINE T.C., bishop; b. Washington; d. David D. and Ila M. Turpeau; m. Gloster Current (div.); children—Angela, Gloster Jr.; m. James David Kelly (dec.); children—John David, Pamela. Student W.Va. State Coll.; grad. Va. Union U., 1960; M.Div., Union Theol. Sem., Richmond, Va., 1969. Formerly sch. tchr.; former pastor Galilee United Methodist Ch., Edwardsville, Va.; later mem. staff Va. Conf. Council on Ministries; pastor Asbury United Meth. Ch., Richmond, 1976-83; mem. nat. staff United Meth. Ch., Nashville, 1983-84; bishop Calif.-Nev. Conf., San Francisco, 1984—. Office: United Meth Ch PO Box 467 San Francisco CA 94101 *

KELLY, ROBERT JOSEPH, clinical psychologist; b. Sayville, N.Y., Dec. 21, 1957; s. Richard Joseph and Anna Elizabeth (Diehl) K. BS, U. Scranton, 1979; MA, SUNY, Buffalo, 1981, PhD, 1984. Lic. clin. psychologist. Intern U. So. Calif. Med. Ctr., Los Angeles, 1983-84; postdoctoral fellow UCLA Dept. Psychology, 1984-86, asst. research psychologist, 1986—; clin. asst. prof. Fuller Theol. Sem. Grad. Sch. Psychology, Pasadena, Calif., 1985-86; clin. psychologist UCLA Psychology Clinic, 1985—; co-prin. investigator Nat. Ctr. Child Abuse and Neglect, Washington, 1985—. NIMH fellow, 1984-86. Mem. AAAS, Am. Psychol. Assn., Internat. Soc. Prevention of Child Abuse and Neglect, Western Psychol. Assn. Avocations: racquet sports. Home: 15231 Magnolia Blvd #214 Sherman Oaks CA 91403 Office: UCLA Psychology Dept 2172 Franz Hall Los Angeles CA 90024

KELLY, SHANNON LYNN, stockbroker; b. Monterey, Calif., Sept. 10, 1956; d. Leonard Howard and Joni Dorothy (Twitchell) Higginbotham; m. Brian Andrew Kelly, Sept. 12, 1982. A.A., U. South Fla., 1974-76; B.A., U. Hawaii, 1979. Outer islands mgr. Gatliff Corp., Honolulu, 1979-81; stockbroker Paine Webber Jackson & Curtis, Honolulu, 1981—, also dir.; bd. dirs. Honolulu Bd. Realtors, 1983—; freelance writer. Mem. Investment Soc. Hawaii (bd. dirs.). Republican.

KELLY, SHARON YVONNE, insurance company executive; b. Martinez, Calif., May 18, 1937; d. John Edgar and Doyle B. (Keeling) Heyne; m. James Lowell Kelly, May 18, 1954 (dec.); children—Lowell Zane, Patrick Shaun. Assoc. in Liberal Arts Sci., North Idaho Coll., 1974; B.S. in Psychology, Western Oreg. Coll., 1979. Lic. real estate broker, Oreg. Sales agt. Bankers Life & Casualty, Spokane, Wash. and Salem, Oreg., 1974-76, Floyd McNall Real Estate, Salem, 1976-80; mktg. cons. Saif Corp., Salem, 1980-84, Updegraff-Gardiner Ins., 1984—; sales agt. Prudential Ins. Co. Am., 1986. Precinct com. woman Rep. Party, Kootenai; bd. dirs. Willamette Valley Hospice, 1984. Recipient numerous awards in field. Mem. Am. Bus. Women, Nat. Assn. Female Execs., Salem Bd. Realtors, Salem C. of C., Detroit Lake Bus. Assn., Nat. Life Underwriters Assn. Baptist. Club: Toastmasters (Salem). Home: 1766 Icabod Ct NE Salem OR 97305 Office: 10220 SW Greenburg Rd Suite 310 Portland OR 97223

KELLY, THOMAS EUGENE, consulting geologist; b. San Diego, Oct. 15, 1931; s. Thomas E. Kelly and Fay (Renfro) Kelly Halbouty; m. Mary Jane Moore, June 15, 1956; children—Mark, Brooke, Adrienne, Isla. B.S., Tex. A&M U., 1953, M.S., 1955. Cert. profl. geologist. Geologist, Conoco Inc., Durango, Colo., 1956-58; exec. v.p. Halbouty Alaska Oil Co., Anchorage, 1958-67; commr. Dept. Natural Resources, State of Alaska, Juneau, 1967-70; cons., geologist, Anchorage, 1970-83, Seattle, 1984—. Contbr. articles to profl. jours. Pres., Anchorage Sch. Bd., 1972-76. Served as 1st. lt. USAF, 1954-56. Mem. Am. Assn. Petroleum Geologists, Am. Inst. Mining, Matallurgy Engrs., Soc. Exploration Geophysicists, Alaska Geol. Soc., Alaska Landmens Assn. Republican. Roman Catholic. Clubs: Houston Country; Seattle Golf. Home: The Highlands Seattle WA 98177 Office: 500 Maynard Bldg 119 1st Ave S Suite 470 Seattle WA 98104

KELLY, TIM, state senator; b. Sacramento, Aug. 15, 1944. Formerly legis. aide to Calif. and Nev. Legislatures; mortgage banker; mem. Alaska Ho. of Reps., 1976-78, Alaska Senate, 1978—. Active youth sports. Served with USMC, Alaska Air NG. Office: Pouch V Juneau AK 99811

KELLY, TIMOTHY MICHAEL, newspaper editor; b. Ashland, Ky., Nov. 28, 1947; s. Robert John and Pauline Elizabeth (Henneman) K.; m. Carol Ann Knight, Aug. 2, 1969; children—Kimberly, Kevin. B.A., U. Miami, Fla., 1970. Sports copy editor, writer The Courier-Jour., Louisville, 1970-71; exec. sports editor The Phila. Inquirer, 1971-75; dep. mng. editor Dallas Times Herald, 1975-81; mng. editor The Denver Post, 1981-84; exec. editor Dallas Times Herald, 1984; editor Daily News, Los Angeles, 1984—. Mem. Am. Soc. Newspaper Editors, AP Mng. Editors, Sigma Delta Chi. Roman Catholic. Office: Daily News 14539 Sylvan St Van Nuys CA 91411

KELLY, VIANA EILEEN, marketing and public relations professional; b. Pueblo, Colo., Feb. 10, 1953; d. Duane Albert and Mary Vinta (Ames) Rockel; m. Douglas Ray Heeren, July 22, 1972 (dec.); children: Douglas Ray, Valissitie Christina; m. Eric Damian Kelly, May 31, 1980; children: Damian Charles, Eliza Jane. V.p. bd. dirs. Color Radio, Ltd., Leadville, Colo., 1980-83; mktg. cons. U. Park Mchts. Assn., Pueblo, 1985; mktg. specialist Pueblo Community Coll., 1985—; advt. cons. Seal Pharmacy, Pueblo, 1984-85. Bd. dirs. Pueblo Girls Club, 1986—; active Jr. League of Pueblo, 1982-85; vol. tng. Channel 8 Auction, Pueblo, 1980—. Mem. AAUW (bd. dirs.), State Bd. Community Colls. (rep., mem. mktg. com. 1985—), Alpha Chi. Avocations: art, hydroponics, geoponics, reading, hiking. Home: 11 Fireweed Ct Pueblo CO 81001 Office: Pueblo Community Coll 900 West Orman Ave Pueblo CO 81004

KELLY, WILLIAM BRET, insurance executive; b. Rocky Ford, Colo., Sept. 28, 1922; s. William Andrew and Florence Gail (Yant) K.; B.A. cum laude, U. Colo., 1947; m. Patricia Ruth Ducy, Mar. 25, 1944; children—Eric Damian, Kathryn Gail Kelly Schweitzer. With Steel City Agencies, Inc., and predecessor, Pueblo, Colo., 1946—, pres., 1961-76, chmn. bd., 1977—; dir. United Bank Pueblo, 1963—, chmn. bd., 1983—; dir. Pub. Expenditure Council, 1984—; v.p. Colo. Ins. Edn. Found., 1981, pres., 1982. Mem. Pueblo Area Council Govts., 1971-73; Colo. Forum 1985—, trustee Pueblo Bd. Water Works, 1966-80, pres., 1970-71; pres. Pueblo Single Fund Plan, 1960-61, Pueblo Heart Council, 1962, Family Service Soc. Pueblo, 1963; mem. 10th Jud. Dist. Nominating Com., 1967-71; trustee U. So. Colo. Found., 1967—, Jackson Found., 1972—, Farley Found., 1979—, Roselawn Cemetery Assn., 1982—; Kelly-Ducy Found., 1983—. Served with inf. AUS, 1943-45. Decorated Silver Star, Bronze Star with oak leaf cluster, Purple Heart with oak leaf cluster; C.P.C.U. Mem. Soc. C.P.C.U.'s, Pueblo C. of C. (past pres.), Phi Beta Kappa. Democrat. Clubs: Pueblo Kiwanis (past pres.), Pueblo Country (treas. 1964-66). Home: 264 Sifford Ct Pueblo West CO 81007 Office: 1414 W 4th St Pueblo CO 81004

KELSAY, JERI DIANE, educational administrator; b. Marion, Ind., Aug. 18, 1931; d. Hugo L. and Honey (Roepke) Kuester; children—Kathi Dawn, Bruce David. B.S., Western N. Mex. U., 1952; M.S., No. Ill. U., 1974, Ed.D., 1978. English and speech tchr. Flowing Wells Pub. Schs., Tucson, 1960-62; English tchr. Deming Pub. Schs., N.Mex., 1962-66; dir./tchr. retarded class Santa Fe Assn. Retarded, 1967-68; tchr. social maladjusted class Sch. Dist. 45, Villa Park, Ill., 1969; dir. children's services Ray Graham Assocs., Addison, Ill., 1970-76; extension instr. spl. edn. No. Ill. U., DeKalb, 1975; vis. instr. U. Ill.-Chgo., 1975; instr. spl. edn. No. Ill. U., 1976-77, Ill. State U., 1981; spl. edn. specialist Ill. Office Edn., Springfield, 1977-78, asst. mgr., 1978-82; dir. Central Assn. Spl. Edn., Decatur, Ill., 1982-84; exec. dir. spl. edn. Denver Sch. Dist. 1, 1984—; mem. task force severely and profoundly handicapped, 1976-77. Chmn. adv. bd. human services div. Coll. of DuPage, 1975-76; chmn. adv. bd. Madden Zone Pavilion 11, 1976. Music Edn. Nat. Conf. scholar, 1948-49; Alpha Psi Omega scholar, 1948-49; Nat. Inst. Edn. fellow, 1978-79. Mem. Ill. Assn. Retarded Citizens, Am. Assn. Mental Deficiency, Ind. Program Dirs. Assn. (sec. 1975-76), Nat. Assn. Retarded Citizens, Assn. Spl. Edn. Tech., Am. Assn. Edn. of Severely/Profoundly Handicapped, Council Exceptional Children, Assn. Sch. Adminstrs. (assoc. supervision and curriculum devel.), Pi Lambda Theta, Phi Delta Kappa, Delta Kappa Gamma. Lutheran. Contbr. articles to profl. jours. Home: 3350 S Albion St Denver CO 80222 Office: Denver Sch Dist 1 900 Grant St Denver CO 80203

KELSEY, EDITH JEANINE, psychotherapist, consultant; b. Freeport, Ill., Oct. 15, 1937; d. John Melvin and Florence Lucille (Ewald) Anderson; m. Craig Ken Kelsey, Dec. 12, 1960; children: Steven Craig, Kevin John. Student, Pasadena Coll., 1955-58; BA in Psychology, Calif. State U., San Jose, 1980; MA in Counseling Psychology, Santa Clara U., 1984. Lic. marriage, family and child counselor. Counselor, cons. Omega Assocs. Santa Clara (Calif.) U., 1981-85, dir. research, 1982-84; intern in counseling Sr. Residential Services, San Jose, 1983-84; psychotherapist Process Therapy Inst., Los Gatos, Calif., 1983-86, Sexual Abuse Treatment Ctr., San Jose, 1984—; cons. in field, Santa Clara Valley, 1982—. Contbr. articles to profl. jours. Vol. Parental Stress Hotline, Palo Alto, Calif., 1980-85. Mem. Am. Assn. Counseling and Devel., Calif. Assn. Marriage and Family Therapists (clin.), Sierra Club, Phi Kappa Phi. Republican. Presbyterian. Avocations: skiing, windsurfing, music. Home: 4250 El Camino Real C328 Palo Alto CA 94306 Office: 4250 El Camino Real D224 Palo Alto CA 94306

KELSEY, FLOYD LAMAR, JR., architect; b. Colorado Springs, Colo., Jan. 2, 1925; s. Floyd Lamar and Myrtice (Graves) K.; m. Ruth Ann Witty, June 22, 1946; children—Patricia Ann, Carol Susan. Student, Colo. Coll., 1942-44; B.S. in Architecture with honors, U. Ill., 1947. Partner Bunts & Kelsey (architects), Colorado Springs, 1952-66; prin. Lamar Kelsey Assos.; pres. The LKA Ptnrs. Inc., 1986—; cons. design rev. bd. U. Colo., 1969-70, 86—; adv. panel, region 8 Gen. Services Adminstrn., 1969-70; vis. lectr. U. Colo., 1960, U. Denver, 1958. Author: Schools for America, 1967, Open Space Schools, 1971; Contbr. to profl. jours. Recipient design awards AIA, design awards Am. Inst. Steel Constrn., design awards Am. Assn. Sch. Adminstrs., design awards Nation's Schs. mag. Fellow AIA (former mem. nat. coms. on ednl. facilities, edn., architecture for arts and recreation); mem. Colorado Springs C. of C. (past dir.), Gargoyle Archtl. Hon. Soc., Phi Delta Theta. Methodist. Clubs: El Paso, Winter Night (pres. 1976), Broadmoor Golf (Colorado Springs). Home: 10 Briarcrest Pl Colorado Springs CO 80906 Office: 430 N Tejon St Colorado Springs CO 80903

KELSEY, JOHN PAUL, naval officer; b. Kewanna, Ind., Nov. 14, 1942; s. Lawrence E. and Catherine L. (Cooney) K.; m. Vera M. Vlcek, July 9, 1966; children: Lara Jo, John L., Ramona L., Patricia M. BS, U. S. Naval Acad., 1964; Ocean E. in Naval Engring. and SMEE, MIT, 1972. Commd. ensign USN, 1964, advanced through grades to comdr., 1978; service in USN, Europe, Western Pacific, Indian Ocean; officer-in-charge USN Office, Singapore. Mem. IEEE, Am. Soc. Naval Engrs., Am. Soc. Quality Control, Am. Radio Relay League, Sons of Norway, Singapore Microcomputer Soc., Sigma Xi. Home: 118 Coronation Rd, Singapore 1026, Singapore Office: US Navy Office Singapore FPO San Francisco CA 96699-2100

KEMLER, KATHERINE PENELOPE, instrumental music educator, soloist; b. Washington, D.C., July 31, 1951; d. Edgar Jerome and Estelle Rachel (Wyner) K.; 1 child, Jonathan Henry Boyce. BA, Oberlin Coll., 1973; MusM, SUNY, Stony Brook, 1975, MusD, 1986. Instr. flute Prince Georges Community Coll., Largo, Md., 1975-76; instr. flute U. Wyo., Laramie, 1976-77, asst. prof. music, 1977-82, assoc. prof., 1982—. Soloist with British Chamber Orch., London, 1984, BBC Radio, Birmingham, Eng., 1983; featured soloist Wigmore Hall, London, 1983; prin. flutist Oxford (Eng.) Orch., 1982-83; performed for Nat. Flute Assn., Denver, 1985; contbr. articles on flute to profl. jours. Named Semi-Finalist Concert Artist Guild Competition, N.Y.C., 1984, Finalist Oxford Music Festival Competition, 1983; Tanglewood Music Festival fellow, 1976. Mem. Nat. Flute Assn., Rocky Mountain Flute Assn., Music Tchrs. Nat. Assn., Delta Omicron (faculty adv. Alpha Pi chpt. 1983—). Democrat. Episcopalian. Avocation: aerobic dancing. Home: 709 Lewis St Laramie WY 82070 Office: U Wyo Music Dept Laramie WY 82071

KEMP, BARBARA ELLEN, librarian; b. Toledo, June 6, 1944; d. Charles Donald and Blanche Gertrude (Gruber) K. BA, Northwestern U., 1966; MLS, U. Mich., 1968. Reference librarian U. Mich., Ann Arbor, 1968-71, asst. head undergraduate library, 1971-83; head humanities and social scis. pub. services Wash. State U., Pullman, 1983—. Contbr. to book Twentieth Century Romance and Gothic Writers, 1982; contbr. articles to profl. jours. Mem. ALA (Library Instruction Round Table), Assn. Coll. and Research Libraries (chmn. ad hoc subcom. microcomputer issues in edn. libraries), Library Adminstrn. and Mgmt. Assn. Home: PO Box 2756 CS Pullman WA 99165 Office: Holland Library Wash State Univ Pullman WA 99164-5610

KEMPER, WILLIAM ALEXANDER, educator, physics consultant; b. Balt., Jan. 1, 1911; s. Julius and Carrie (Alexander) K.; m. Genevieve Haile, May 26, 1956 (div. Apr. 1973); m. Marcia Jeannette Berndt, Apr. 21, 1973. PhD, Johns Hopkins U., 1934. Chemist Gas and Electric Co., Balt., 1934-43; physicist Navy Surface Weapons Ctr., Dahlgren, Va., 1947-75; physics instr. Met. State Coll. and U. Colo., Denver, 1976—; chmn. USN Aeroballistic Adv. Com., 1966-68; gunnery advisor USN Adv. Mission, Korea, 1968; sci. advisor Commander, Cruisers, Destroyers, Atlantic Fleet, Newport, R.I., 1972-73; U.S. del. The Tech. Cooperation Panel on Ballistics. Reviewer Sci. Books and Films mag. Scoutmaster Boy Scouts Am., Dahlgren, 1954-64. Served to lt. comdr., USN, 1943-46, capt. Res., 1954. Mem. AAAS, Am. Phys. Soc., Naval Inst., Am. Def. Preparedness Assn. (treas. Wyo. chpt. 1984—). Jewish. Club: Balt. Ski (pres. 1939-42). Avocations: skiing, bicycling, mountain walking. Home: 7363 W 26th Pl Denver CO 80215

KEMPER, WILLIAM LINDSAY, computers marketing executive; b. Pitts., May 22, 1949; s. William Judson and Gertrude Fralich (Lindsay) K.; m. Marc Slaughter, Aug. 28, 1971; children—Keska, Daniel Nathan. B.S. in Physics with honors, Denison U., Granville, Ohio, 1972; M.S. in Computer Sci., U. Colo., 1974. Programmer, Hewlett-Packard Co., Loveland, Colo. 1974-77, application engr. Corvallis Div., Hewlett-Packard, Oreg., 1977-81, application devel. mgr., 1981-82, software product mgr., 1982, portable computer product mgr. Portable Computer Div., 1982-84, data communications product mgr., 1984, custom ROM program mgr., 1985-86, office program product mgr., 1987—. English Speaking Union fellow, 1967; Physics Dept. Alumni scholar Denison U., 1985. Mem. Sigma Pi Sigma. Republican. Methodist. Home: 3730 NW Harrison Corvallis OR 97330 Office: Hewlett-Packard 1000 NE Circle Blvd Corvallis OR 97330

KEMPNER, LEON, JR., structural engineer; b. Jamaica, N.Y., Sept. 30, 1946; married Oct. 21, 1979; children: Jessica, Justen, Jayme. BSCE, U. Nebr., 1972; MSCE, Oreg. State U., 1974. Registered profl. engr., Wash. Structural engr. Bonneville Power Adminstrn., Portland, Oreg., 1973—; engring. instr. Portland State U., 1975-84. Contbr. articles on transmission towers to profl. jours. Mem. community adv. com. Adolescent Chem. Health Program, Portland, 1986. Served to sgt. USAF, 1963-67. Recipient Exceptional Service award Dept. Energy and Bonneville Power Adminstrn., Portland, 1985. Mem. ASCE (student contact mem. 1986, elec. transmission structures com., 1986), Structural Engrs. Assn. of Oreg. (assoc.), Sigma Xi. Avocations: reading, family. Home: 3314 NE 22nd Ave Portland OR 97212 Office: Bonneville Power Adminstrn PO Box 3621 Portland OR 97208

KEMPTHORNE, DIRK ARTHUR, mayor; b. San Diego, Oct. 29, 1951; s. James Henry and Maxine Jesse (Gustason) K.; m. Patricia Jean Merrill, Sept. 18, 1979; children: Heather Patricia, Jeffrey Dirk. BS in Polit. Sci., U. Idaho, 1975. Exec. asst. to dir. Idaho Dept. Lands, Boise, 1975-78; exec. v.p. Idaho Home Builders Assn., Boise, 1978-80; campaign mgr. Batt for Gov., Boise, 1980-82; lic. securities rep. Swanson Investments, Boise, 1983; Idaho pub. affairs mgr. FMC Corp., Boise, 1983-86; mayor Boise, 1986—. Pres. Assn. Students U. Idaho, Moscow, 1975; chmn. bd. dirs. Wesleyan Presch., Boise, 1982-85; mem. magistrate commn. 4th Jud. Dist., Boise, 1986—. Republican. Methodist. Home: 2211 Cornhusk Ct Boise ID 83706 Office: Office of the Mayor PO Box 500 Boise ID 83701

KEMPTON, MARVIN LAMAR, mechanical engineer; b. Safford, Ariz., Sept. 5, 1920; s. Nathan Thomas and Martha Jane (Stewart) K.; m. Leva Gene Stewart, July 13, 1940; children: Stuart Lamar, Pamela Gene, Brent Stanley, Wesley Warren. BS, U. Ariz., 1942, M in Engring., 1958. Registered profl. engr. Leader process control group Goodyear Aircraft Corp., Phoenix, 1942-45; head dept. phys. testing Prosthetic Research Lab., Washington, 1946; dir. of Tera, contract ordnance research N.Mex. Inst. of Mining and Tech., Socorro, 1986—. Recipient Disting. Service award USN, 1957. Avocations: hunting, fishing, golf, tennis. Home: 1201 Apache NW Socorro NM 87801 Office: N Mex Inst Mining and Tech Campus Station Socorro NM 87801

KENAGY, JOHN WARNER, surgeon; b. Lincoln, Nebr., May 28, 1945; s. Wyman Black and Sylvia (Adams) K.; m. Barbara Penterman, Feb. 1968 (div. 1975); 1 child, Jennifer; m. Jonell Day, Apr. 21, 1978; children: Susanne, Emma. BS, U. Nebr., 1967, MD, U. Nebr., Omaha, 1971. Diplomate Am. Bd. Surgery; splty. cert. in gen. vascular surgery. Intern, Hosps. of U. Wash., Seattle, 1971-72, resident in surgery, 1971-76; surgeon Longview Gen. & Thoracic Surgery, Longview, Wash., 1976—; clin. instr. surgery U. Wash., Seattle, 1979-82, clin. asst. prof. surgery, 1982—; dir. peripheral vascular services St. Johns Hosp., Longview, 1979—; editor current concepts in vascular diagnosis St. Johns Vascular Lab., Longview, 1982—. Contbr. articles to profl. jours. Chmn. bd. dirs. Cowlitz Med. Service, Longview, 1985-86. Regents scholar U. Nebr., Lincoln, 1963-67. Fellow ACS, Henry Harkins Surg. Soc. (trustee 1983-84), Seattle Surg. Soc.; mem. Internat. Cardiovascular Soc., Pacific N.W. Vascular Soc. (pres.-elect 1986-87), Alpha Omega Alpha, Theta Nu, Phi Gamma Delta. Republican. Office: Longview Gen and Thoracic Surgery 900 Fir St Suite 1-J Longview WA 98632

KENDALL, JANE ELIZABETH, psychotherapist, consultant; b. Jersey City, Oct. 22, 1947; d. Max and Tem (Fagelman) Finkelstein, m. Ross Samuel Kendall, May 30, 1968; children: Joshua Ryan, Seth Leigh. AB, U. Rochester, 1969; MSW, SUNY, Buffalo, 1972. Social worker Buffalo State Hosp., 1969-72; sr. social worker Children's Heart Hosp., Phila., 1972-75, Children's Bur. Los Angeles, Van Nuys, Calif., 1979-80; pvt. practice specializing in family therapy Tacoma, 1980—; cons. Mary Bridge Children's Health Ctr., Tacoma, 1981—; co-chmn. Cert. Bd. Child Abuse and Neglect Profl., Tacoma. vol. investigator Yokota AFB Program for Prevention of Child Abuse, Japan; mem. vol. Civic Arts Com., Tacoma, 1981-86. Mem. Nat. Assn. Social Workers (registry 1982—), Acad. Cert. Social Workers, Am. Assn. Marriage and Family Therapists (clin.). Democrat. Jewish. Clubs: City (founding mem. 1984-86), Allied Arts. Avocations: skiing, swimming, painting.

KENDALL, REBECCA KAY, social work administrator; b. Des Moines, Nov. 25, 1955; d. R. Kenneth and Lorraine (Jenkins) K. BA, U. Iowa, 1978, MSW, 1983; cert. activity coordinating, Kirkwood Community Coll., 1980. Field experience student Beverly Manor, Iowa City, Iowa, 1977; social worker, activity asst. Beverly Manor, Iowa City, 1977-79, social worker, activity dir., 1979-82; field experience student Univ. Hosp., Iowa City, 1978; intern Beverly Found., Pasadena, Calif., 1982-83, project adminstr., 1983—; fellow U. So. Calif./UCLA Long-Term Care Gerontology Ctr. Author: Choice, Challenge and Companionship: Establishing Shared Living Programs for Older Adults, 1986; co-author: (with Lois E. Krauss) The Time and

Teamwork Manager: the Activity Director in Long-term Care, 1987. Chmn. adv. com. Share-A-Home of Pasadena, 1983-85; chmn. steering com. Consortium of Agys. Serving the Elderly, Pasadena, 1985-86; mem. United Way Task Force on Aging, Arcadia, Calif., 1984—; mem. foster family and computer coms. Jr. League of Pasadena, 1984—; council mem. Salem Luth. Ch., Glendale, Calif., 1986—; chmn. young adults com., 1985—; mem. Los Angeles City and County AAA Community Task Force on Long-Term Care, 1986—. Mem. Nat. Assn. Social Workers (cert.), Am. Soc. Aging, Nat. Council Aging., U. Iowa Alumni Assn. Republican. Club: Toastmasters. Avocations: music, needlework, aerobic dancing, nutrition. Office: Beverly Found PO Box 90667 Pasadena CA 91109

KENDALL, THOMAS LEE, engineering manager; b. Long Beach, Calif., Aug. 23, 1946; s. Albert Russell and Constance Mary (Thady) K.; m. Kathryn Ann Delperdang, Jan. 29, 1966; children: Shalimar Anne, Scott Alexander. AA, Pasadena City Coll., 1967; Bachelors, Calif. State U., Los Angeles, 1973; postgrad. in Bus. Adminstrn., Nat. U., Vista, Calif., 1986—. Engr. The Digitran Co., Pasadena, Calif., 1968-73; mgr. electronics The Toro Co., Riverside, Calif., 1973-79; mgr. engring. Electro-Static Sound Systems, Sacramento, 1979-81; supr. design services Gen. Electric Med. Systems, Sacramento, 1981-84; mgr. mfg. material control Dynatech Fluid Tech. Corp., Sacramento, 1984-85; mgr. engring. Advanced Structures, San Marcos, Calif., 1985—; mem. Modern Plastics Mgmt. Adv. Council, 1981-82. Contbr. articles to profl. jours.; patentee in field. Res. dep. San Bernardino County Sheriff's Office, Big Bear Lake, 1974-79, comdr. res. unit, 1976-78. Recipient Letter of Commendation San Bernardino County Sheriff's Office. Mem. ASME, Soc. Mfg. Engrs., Am. Soc. Metals, Am. Production and Inventory Countrol Soc., Nat. Mgmt. Assn. Republican. Methodist. Avocations: bibliophile, firearms, golf, fishing, crewel. Home and Office: 1019 Partridge Ct San Marcos CA 92069

KENDIG, FLORENCE GEERTZ (BOBBI), social worker; b. Aurora, Ill., Feb. 7, 1936; d. Eric and Florence Elizabeth (Hard) Geertz; m. Edwin Walton Kendig, June 13, 1964; children: David Eric, Susan Louise, Lisa Jean. BA, Northwestern U., 1957; MSW, U. So. Calif., 1965. Lic. clin. social worker. Social caseworker Bur. Pub. Assistance, Long Beach, Calif., 1957-59, 1962-63; contract counselor Family Services, Long Beach, 1972-75; co-founder, dir. Children's program Cedar House, Long Beach, 1974-82, Sarah Ctr., Long Beach, 1984—; cons. Interagy. Council Child Abuse and Neglect, ICAN Assocs., Long Beach YWCA; educator filial therapy Long Beach Unified Sch. Dist., 1973-74. Chmn. bd. dirs. New Directions Sch., Long Beach, 1974-75. Recipient Cert. Appreciation Interagy. Council Child Abuse and Neglect, Los Angeles, 1985, Resolution and Key to City City of Long Beach, 1979. Mem. Nat. Assn. Social Workers, Long Beach Area Child Trauma Council (vice chmn. 1984, chmn. 1985). Democrat. Unitarian. Avocations: piano music, camping, hiking. Office: Sarah Ctr 2026 Cherry Ave Long Beach CA 90806

KENDRICK, HUGH, high technology company executive; b. Ewell, Eng., Jan. 25, 1940; came to U.S., 1963; s. John Bebbington Bernard and Amelia Ruth (Kendall) K.; m. Diana Wendy Adams, Feb. 23, 1963; children: Stuart, Amanda Karen. BS Engring., City & Guilds Coll., 1961; MS, Calif. Inst. Tech., 1962; PhD, U. Mich., 1968. Registered profl. engr., Calif. Sr. engr. Sci. Applications Inc., McLean, Va., 1972-74, div. mgr., 1974-77; sr. analyst Office of Nuclear Energy, Dept. Energy, Washington, 1977-79, acting dir. plans and analysis, 1979-81; v.p. mktg. Sci. Applications Internat. Corp., McLean, 1981-85; dep. chief operating officer Sci. Applications Internat. Corp., La Jolla, Calif., 1985—; cons. Arms Control Disarmament Agy., Washington, 1985-86, Nat. Research Council, Washington, 1986—. Contbr. articles to profl. jours. Served with RAFVR, 1958-61. NATO fellow, London, 1963, Phoenix Meml. fellow, U. Mich.-Ann Arbor, 1963-67, Rackham fellow, U. Mich.-Ann Arbor, 1967-68; Henrici medal for math., U. London, 1959. Mem. Am. Phys. Soc., Am. Nuclear Soc., Sigma Xi. Republican. Episcopalian. Clubs: Fell & Rock Climbing (Eng.); San Diego Track. Avocation: running. Home: 13062 Caminito Pointe Del Mar Del Mar CA 92014 Office: Sci Applications Internat Corp 1200 Prospect St La Jolla CA 92037

KENDRICKS, JAMES WILLIAMS, financial services company executive; b. Van Lear, Ky., Feb. 28, 1938; s. Roy Johnson and Clara Eugena (Newland) K.; m. Christine Johnson, Dec. 26, 1962 (div. Mar. 1965); 1 dau., Angel R.; m. 2d, Earsey Marie Pryor, Apr. 6, 1968; children—Jacquelyn Endeara, Jeanine Marie. Student, Hillsdale Coll., 1961-63, Pepperdine Coll., 1965; B.A., Calif. State U.-Los Angeles, 1967; J.D., UCLA, 1971. Systems analyst Arco, 1967-71; legal fellow Regionald Heber-Smith, 1971-73; hearing officer Los Angeles Police Commn., 1972-73; dep. dir. Los Angeles Urban Coalition, 1973-75; founder, exec. dir. Afro-Am. Cultural Edn. Center, 1974-80; v.p. Social Engring. Tech., Los Angeles, 1978-81; organizer, cons. GHS Enterprises, Los Angeles, 1981—; pres. Kendricks Internat. Co., Culver City, Calif., 1970—, Kendricks Internat. Co., Culver City, Calif.; spl. cons. to sr. policy analyst The White House, 1983-84, 84—; sec., asst. treas. Black PAC, Culver City; editorial bd. Mainstream mag., Los Angeles, 1984-85. Campaign mgr. David L. Pierson to Calif. Legislature, 1972; spl. cons. econ. devel. and bus. Govt. Nigeria, Liberia, Kenya, Tanzania, and Indonesia, 1978—. Served with USAF, 1957-61. Mem. NAACP, Fellowship Falcons, Tau Kappa Epsilon. Republican.

KENNA, BERNARD THOMAS, chemistry educator, environmentalist; b. Hays, Kans., Jan. 4, 1935; s. LeRoy Austin and Sara Elisabeth (Shoup) K.; m. Laura-Donna Ashley, June 4, 1960; children: Woodrow Austin, Randall Roy. BS, No. Ariz. U., 1956; MS, U. Mo., 1958; PhD, U. Ark., 1961. Mem. tech. staff Sandia Nat. Lab., Albuquerque, 1961—; lectr. Albuquerque Pub. Schs., 1965-84; prof. chemistry U. N.Mex., Albuquerque, 1966-70. Contbr. articles to profl. jours. Mem. Am. Chem. Soc. Republican. Office: Sandia Nat Lab Div 5248 Albuquerque NM 87185

KENNEDY, ART RALPH, governmental affairs cons.; b. Cumberland, Md., Oct. 18, 1935; s. Arthur Martin and Jessie (Beck) K; m. Maryann Cowgill (div.); children: Lisa, Carol, Scott; m. Kathleen Ohrt; children: Jerod, Bronwyn. Student, William Jewell Coll., 1958-60, Oreg. State U., 1960-61; BS in Forestry, U. Wash., 1962, MS in Forestry, 1963. With NSF, 1960-61; dir., pub. infor. officer, forester USDA, 1961-70; asst. to state dir. U.S. Dept. Interior, Bur. Land Mgmt., Alaska, 1970-76; spl. asst. for Alaska U.S. Sec. Interior, Washington, 1976-77; chief of staff, adminstrv. asst. to U.S. Congressman Don Young, Alaska, 1977-79; pres., chmn. bd. dirs. Alaska Resource Analysts, Inc., Anchorage, 1979—. Eagle Scout Boy Scouts Am. Mem. Anchorage C. of C. Avocations: antique clock repair and collection, photgraphy, golf, scuba diving. Home: 2431 Autumn Cir PO Box 200576 Anchorage AK 99504 Office: Alaska Resource Analysts Inc Box 200571 Anchorage AK 99520

KENNEDY, CAROLYN ARVANITES, writer; b. Austin, Tex., Aug. 19, 1943; d. Thomas Arthur Arvanites and Evelyn Lucy Morse; m. W. Keith Kennedy, June 19, 1965; children: Matthew Keith, Mark David. BS, Cornell U., 1965, MA in Teaching, 1966. Tchr. Ithaca (N.Y.) City Elem. Schs., 1966-68; freelance stringer and columnist Meredith Newspapers, Cupertino, Calif., 1981-85. Contbr. articles to newspapers, humor columns, 1981—. Vol. Cupertino High Sch., 1982-86; presenter folk music programs local libraries and schs., Cupertino and San Jose, Calif., 1977-79. Mem. Nat. Soc. Newspaper Columnists, Women In Communications Inc., Writers Connection. Democrat. Episcopalian. Club: Folk Music (San Carlos, Calif.) (editor newsletter 1977-79). Avocations: piano, guitar, singing, photography. Home: 10165 McLaren Pl Cupertino CA 95014

KENNEDY, DAVID KITTLE, educational administrator, clergyman; b. Alamosa, Colo., Oct. 29, 1932; s. Harry Sherbourne and Katharine Jane (Kittle) K.; m. Anna Marie Hemberger, Nov. 1, 1956; children—Chris W., Paul K., Karl S., Eric D. B.A., Trinity Coll., 1954; M.Div., Ch. Div. Sch. of the Pacific, 1963. Ordained priest Episcopalian Ch., 1964; vicar St. Barnabas' Ch., Ewa Beach, Hawaii, 1968-73; rector St. Peter's Ch., Honolulu, Ch. of the Ascension, Kwajalein Atoll, Marshall Islands, 1968-73, St. Timothy's Ch., Aiea, Hawaii, 1973-81; headmaster St. Andrew's Priory Sch., Honolulu, 1981—. Mem. Gov.'s Commn. Jud. Qualifications, 1970-76, Hawaii State Health Coordinating Council, 1977-82, State Health Cert. of Need Com., 1978-83, Neighborhood Bd., City and County of Honolulu, 1984-87. Served with USAF, 1954-60, USAFR, 1969—. Recipient Diocesan Disting. Service Cross, 1969. Mem. Nat. Assn. Ind. Schs., Nat. Assn. Secondary Sch. Prins., Nat. Assn. Prins. Schs. for Girls. Democrat. Clubs: Pacific, Plaza, Rotary (Honolulu). Home: 491 Opihikao Pl Honolulu HI 96825 Office: Saint Andrews Priory Sch 224 Queen Emma Square Honolulu HI 96813

KENNEDY, DEBRA JOYCE, marketing professional; b. Covina, Calif., July 9, 1955; d. John Nathan and Drea Hannah (Lancaster) Ward; m. John William Kennedy, Sept. 3, 1977 (div.). B.S. in Communications, Calif. State Poly. U., 1977. Pub. relations coordinator Whittier (Calif.) Hosp., 1978-79, pub. relations mgr., 1980; pub. relations dir. San Clemente (Calif.) Hosp., 1979-80; dir. pub. relations Garfield Med. Ctr., Monterey Park, Calif., 1980-82; dir. mktg. and community relations Charter Oak Hosp., Covina, 1983-85; mktg. dir. CPC Horizon Hosp., Pomona, 1985—. Mem. Am. Soc. Hosp. Pub. Relations, So. Calif. Soc. Hosp. Pub. Relations, Covina and Covina West C. of C., West Covina Jaycees. Republican. Methodist. Club: Soroptimists (coord. council Pomona chpt.). Contbr. articles to profl. jours.

KENNEDY, DONALD, university president; b. N.Y.C., Aug. 18, 1931; s. William Dorsey and Barbara (Bean) K.; m. Jeanne Dewey, June 11, 1953; children: Laura Page, Julia Hale. AB, Harvard U., 1952, AM, 1954, PhD, 1956; DSc (hon.), Columbia U., Williams Coll., U. Mich., U. Ariz., U. Rochester, Reed Coll. Mem. faculty Syracuse U., 1956-60; mem. faculty Stanford U., 1960-77, prof. biol. scis., 1965-77, chmn. dept., 1965-72; sr. cons. Office Sci. and Tech. Policy, Exec. Office of Pres., 1976; commr. FDA, 1977-79; v.p., provost Stanford U., 1979-80, pres., 1980—; bd. overseers Harvard U., 1970-76; bd. dirs. Health Effects Inst., Clean Sites Inc., Calif. Nature Conservancy. Author: (with W. H. Telfer) The Biology of Organisms, 1965; also articles.; editor: The Living Cell, 1966, From Cell to Organism, 1967; editorial bd. Jour. Exptl. Zoology, 1965-71, Jour. Comparative Physiology, 1965-76, Jour. Neurophysiology, 1969-75, Science, 1973-77. Fellow Am. Acad. Arts and Scis., AAAS; mem. Nat. Acad. Scis., Am. Physiol. Soc. Office: Office of President Stanford U Stanford CA 94305

KENNEDY, ELDWIN EUGENE, environmentalist; b. Glendale, Calif., July 23, 1951; s. Ellsworth Edgar and Sylvia Harriet (Carpenter) K.; m. Janet Kay Lindvall, Jan 20, 1973; children: Eric Eugene, Tara Janel. BA in Religion, So. Calif. Coll., 1972. Lic. to ministry, 1973. Minister Assemblies of God, various locations, Calif., 1974-82; maintainer of pools Mr. Poolman, Anaheim, Calif., 1973-75; carpenter Los Angeles Unified Sch. Dist., 1975-82, asbestos coordinator, 1982-83; pres., owner Cons. Internat., Los Angeles, 1983-85; v.p. ops. Hall-Kimbrell Environ. Services, Los Angeles, 1985—; Bd. dirs. Miss Brea (Calif) Fullerton Pageant, 1986. Mem. Hazardous Waste Assoc. (bd. dirs. 1983—). Republican. Office: Hall Kimbrell Environ Services 10926 E Rush St Suite 3 South El Monte CA 91733

KENNEDY, GERALDINE ANN, urban planner; b. McKeesport, Pa., Sept. 1, 1940; d. Joseph and Mary Markos; B.A., Pa. State U., 1962; M.A., UCLA, 1980; m. James W. Kennedy, 1965; 3 children. Tchr., U.S. Peace Corps, Liberia, 1962-64; archtl. designer Geraldine Kennedy Design, Santa Monica, Calif., 1975-78; analyst Urban Projects Inc., Los Angeles, 1979; researcher Urban Innovations Group, Los Angeles, 1980; asso. Econs. Research Assos., Los Angeles, 1980-82; cons. Environ. Mgmt. Inst., U. So. Calif., 1977-80; strategic planner Investors Mortgage Service Co., 1982—; environ. planner JH&A, Marina del Rey, Calif., 1986-87. Mem. Santa Monica Planning Commn., 1977-81; founder/dir. Community Planning Coalition, Santa Monica, 1976—; bd. dirs., v.p. Santa Monica YWCA, 1971-73; bd. dirs. Santa Monica LWV, 1977-79, Los Angeles Community Design Center, 1982-83. Mem. Am. Inst. Cert. Planners, Am. Planning Assn. Author: MGM, A Handbook for Parents of Gifted Children, 1976, Harmattan, A Peace Corps Remembrance, 1987; editor: Liberia One, 1962-1982, A Peace Corps 20th Anniversary Album, 1982; editorial bd. West Plan, 1983.

KENNEDY, J. DANIEL, publishing executive; b. Bklyn., May 7, 1946; s. Joseph Daniel and Gloria Elizabeth (Knapp) K.; m. Diane Ellen Tymorek, July 25, 1970; children: John, Brian, Jane. BA in Lit., Boston U., 1969; MA in Lit., U. Toronto, Ont., Can., 1970. Mng. editor Times-Crescent, La Plata, Md., 1975-79; dir. mktg. ops. Census Bur., Washington, 1979-80; dir. info. services U.S. SBA, Washington, 1980-83, dist. dir., 1983-85; pres. Sacramento Bus. Jour., 1985—; vis. prof. U. Calif., Davis, 1986; cons., instr. in field. Contbr. articles to profl. jours. Bd. dirs. United Way, Sacramento, 1986, Make-a-Wish Found., Sacramento, 1986, Greater Sacramento Cert. Devel. Corp., Sacramento, 1986. Recipient Silver Anvil award Pub. Relations Soc. Am., 1980, Silver Bell award The Advt. Council, 1980. Roman Catholic. Avocations: fiction writing, golf, tennis. Office: Sacramento Bus Jour 2030 J St Sacramento CA 95814

KENNEDY, JAMES STEWART, JR., real estate investor; b. Balt., Dec. 16, 1922; s. James Stewart Sr. and Maude (Buie) K.; m. Arlene Overton, Nov. 10, 1945 (div. June 1976); 1 child, James Stewart III; m. Susan Wilson, Dec. 21, 1976; children—Cynthia, Thomas, James. Student The Citadel, 1944; M.B.A., Harvard U., 1947. Pres., Am. Health Facilities, Evanston, Ill., 1970-72; corp. v.p. C. R. Bard, Murray Hill, N.J., 1972-77, also dir.; sr. v.p., Damon Corp., Newton, Mass., 1977-81, also dir.; pres. Wilken Investment Co., Phoenix, Ariz., 1981-83, also dir.; pres. Vega Biotechnologies, Inc., Tucson, 1983-86, also dir.; sr. assoc. J. S. Kennedy Assocs., Phoenix, 1981-83; dir. Criticare Systems, Inc., Milw. Trustee Phoenix Meml. Hosp., 1982-85. Served to capt. USMC, 1943-46, PTO. Republican. Congregationalist. Club: Registry, Plaza, Skokie Country. Home and Office: 8826 N 47th Pl Phoenix AZ 85028

KENNEDY, JANET LEE, tapestry weaver, artist; b. San Francisco, Jan. 26, 1951; d. John Clarence and Annette Claire (Driscoll) K. AA, City Coll. San Francisco, 1971; BA, U. Calif., Berkeley, 1973. Apprentice Helena Hernmarck Tapestries, Ridgefield, Conn., 1976-78, asst., 1980-81; owner, artist Kennedy Tapestries, San Francisco, 1981—. Group shows include Rosa Esman Gallery, N.Y.C., 1983, Inc. Gallery, N.Y.C., 1981, Friends Soc. Benefit for Cambodian Relief, San Francisco, 1979; tapestry commissions include IDA Ireland, N.Y.C., 1985, Olympia & York, N.Y.C., 1985, Harvard U. Grad. Sch. Bus., Cambridge, Mass., 1985, 1st State Bank of Abilene, Tex., 1984, Daon Corp., Washington, 1984, Honeywell, Inc. Computer Ctr., Mpls., 1983, IBM, Greencastle, Ind., 1983, Prudential Ins. Co., Norwalk, Conn., 1983, Eastman-Arnold Co., Phila., 1982, Gloria F. Ross Tapestries, N.Y.C., 1982, Chekiang First Bank, San Francisco, 1980, Hughes Aircraft, Santa Monica, Calif., 1985, Fla. Nat. Bank, Jacksonville, 1986, Deloitte, Haskins and Sells, Boston, 1986. Home and Office: 41 Newburg St San Francisco CA 94131

KENNEDY, JEANNE DEWEY, hospital administrator; b. Worcester, Mass., Jan. 4, 1933; d. Charles Nichols and Barbara Plum (Bruske) Dewey; m. Donald Kennedy, June 11, 1953; children: Laura Page, Julia Hale. BA, Smith Coll., 1954. Fin. mgr. William Kaufmann Inc., Los Altos, Calif., 1972-74; indexer Stanford U. Press, 1961-76; assoc. dir. med. devel., assoc. gen. sec. Stanford U., 1976-77; dir. resources devel., spl. asst. to pres. Inst. Medicine Nat. Acad. Scis., Washington, 1977-79; dir. community relations Stanford U. Hosp., 1979-84, dir. community and patient relations, 1984—. Mem. com. art Stanford U., 1961—, treas., 1966-68, chmn., 1968-70, advisor, 1979—; bd. dirs. Children's Health Council, 1980—, v.p., 1984—. Mem. Soc. Patient Reps., Am. Hosp. Assn., Calif. Soc. Patient Reps. Club: Stanford Faculty. Office: Stanford Univ Hosp P3018 Stanford CA 94305

KENNEDY, JOHN HARVEY, chemistry educator; b. Oak Park, Ill., Apr. 24, 1933; s. John Harvey and Margaret Helen (Drenthe) K.; m. Joan Corinne Hipsky, June 9, 1956 (div. Mar. 1969); children: Bruce Laurence, Bryan Donald, Brent Peter, Jill Amy.; m. Victoria Jane Matthew, July 2, 1970; 1 child, Karen Anne. BS, UCLA, 1954; AM, Harvard U., 1956, PhD, 1957. Sr. research chemist E.I. du Pont de Nemours, Wilmington, Del., 1957-61; asst. prof. chemistry U. Calif., Santa Barbara, 1961-63, prof., 1967—, chmn. dept., 1982-85; assoc. prof. Boston Coll., Chestnut Hill, 1963-64; head inorganic chemistry Gen. Motors, Santa Barbara, 1964-67; cons. Union Carbide Corp., Cleve., 1983—; bd. dirs. Astro Industries, Santa Barbara; vis. professor U. N.C., Chapel Hill, 1980-81, Japan Soc. Promotion of Sci., Nagoya, 1984-85. Author: Analytical Chemistry, Principles, 1984, Analytical Chemistry, Practice, 1984; contbr. articles to profl. jours; patentee in field. Mus. dir. Christ the King Episcopal Ch., Santa Barbara, 1982—. Mem. Am. Chem. Soc., Electrochem. Soc. Democrat. Avocation: music. Home: 5357 Agana Dr Santa Barbara CA 93111 Office: U Calif Dept Chemistry Santa Barbara CA 93106

KENNEDY, JOHN WILLIAM, lawyer; b. Toronto, Ont., Can., Apr. 26, 1926; s. John and Mary (Strong) K.; m. Mary Alice Millar, Aug. 12, 1952; children—Sandra Kennedy Forster, William I., Mary Lee Kennedy de Vales, Elizabeth. B.A., U. Alta., Can., 1950, LL.B., 1951. Bar: Alta. 1952, Queen's counsel 1969. Student and assoc. Smith Clement Partee & Whittaker, Edmonton, Alta., 1951-53; ptnr. Cornie Kennedy, Edmonton, 1953—; chmn. bd. Churchill Devel. Corp., Edmonton, 1980-84. Bd. govs. U. Alta., 1981-85; treas. Edmonton South Progressive Conservative Assn., 1965-84; mem. fin. com. Alta. Progressive Conservative Assn., 1972-84. Served to lt. Royal Can. Navy, 1948-53. Mem. Internat. Bar Assn. (treas. 1982-86, council 1980—), Edmonton Bar Assn., Law Soc. Alta., Can. Bar Assn. (past chmn. comparative law com.). Clubs: Edmonton, Mayfair Golf and Country (Edmonton); Centre. Office: 1900 Scotia Pl, 10060 Jasper Ave, Edmonton, AB Canada T5J 3V4

KENNEDY, L. THOMAS, restaurateur and developer; b. Metropolis, Ill., Oct. 5, 1934; s. Nellis Lowell and Dora Esther (Womack) K.; m. Binni Jo Lewis, June 10, 1955; children: Lori Ann, Scott Thomas. Owner Kennedy's Kwik Inn, Colorado Springs, Colo., 1956—, A&W Drive-In, Security, Colo., 1959-77; developer Security (Colo.) Shoppette, 1983-84, Ivywild Plaza, Colorado Springs, 1986—. Treas. Ch. Christ, Security, 1965-77; cons. Widefield High Sch. Adv. Council, Security, 1974-76. Mem. Colo. A&W Operators Assn. (bd. dirs., v.p. 1970-75, pres. 1974-75), Security Businessmen's Assn. (pres. 1969-70). Republican. Clubs: Broadmoor Figure Skating (bd. dirs. 1968-72); Adaman (Colorado Springs) (named Mem. of Year 1979). Avocations: skiing, boating, mountain climbing, traveling, hunting. Home: 2607 Leo Dr Colorado Springs CO 80906 Office: Kwik Inn 385 Main St Colorado Springs CO 80911

KENNEDY, MARY BERNADETTE, neurobiology educator; b. Pontiac, Mich., July 4, 1947; s. Thomas Stuart and Rosemary Cecile (Lalonde) K. BS in Chemistry, St. Mary's Coll., Notre Dame, Ind., 1969; PhD in Biochemistry, Johns Hopkins U., 1975. Postdoctoral fellow Harvard Med. Sch., Boston, 1975-78, Yale Med. Sch., New Haven, 1978-81; asst. prof. neurobiology Calif. Inst. Tech., Pasadena, 1981-83, assoc. prof., 1983—. Mem. Hereditary Disease Found., Santa Monica, Calif., 1984—, chmn. sci. adv. bd., 1986. Recipient Neurosci. Devel. award McKnight Found., 1984; grantee NIH, 1981—, Epilepsy Found., 1986. Mem. Soc. Neurosci. (assoc. editor 1986). Office: Calif Inst Tech Div Biology 216-76 Pasadena CA 91125

KENNEDY, ORIN, film company executive; b. N.Y.C., May 24, 1939; s. Solomon Fuchs and Gertrude Krex. BFA, N.Y. Sch. Interior Design, 1963. Prodn. assoc. Fries Entertainment, Los Angeles, 1976-84; exec. location mgr. Metro-Goldwyn-Mayer subs. United Artists Entertainment, Culver City, Calif., 1984-85; exec. location mgr. The Twilight Zone TV series CBS Entertainment, Los Angeles, 1985-86; exec. location mgr. LA Law TV series 20th Century Fox Film Corp., Los Angeles, 1986—.

KENNEDY, RAYMOND MCCORMICK, JR., interior designer; b. Glendale, Calif., Sept. 19, 1930; s. Raymond McCormick and June (Sparks) K.; adopted son Myrtle Abrahamson Kennedy. B.A. in Architecture, U. Calif.-Berkeley, 1956. Draftsman, Bechtel Corp., San Francisco, 1956-58; draftsman/designer Maher & Martens, Architects, San Francisco, 1956; free lance designer, San Francisco, 1966-67; designer Bernard J. Block, Architect, San Francisco, 1967-69; v.p. Rodgers Assocs., San Francisco, 1969-77; pres. RMK Design, Inc., San Francisco, 1977-83; pres. Kennedy-Bowen Assocs., Inc., San Francisco, 1983—; mem. faculty Acad. of Art Coll., San Francisco, 1982-86. Bd. dirs. San Francisco Easter Seals Soc., 1974-79; bd. dirs., pres. Design Found., Inc., 1986—. Served with U.S. Army, 1952-54. Mem. Golden Gate U. Assocs., Am. Soc. Interior Designers (dir., v.p. No. Calif. chpt. 1983, sec. bd. 1984, pres. 1987), Nat. Trust for Hist. Preservation, Assocs. for San Francisco's Archtl. Heritage. Presbyterian. Clubs: Commonwealth, Press (San Francisco). Office: Kennedy-Bowen Assocs Inc 930 Lombard St San Francisco CA 94133

KENNEDY, ROBINN RODGERS, speech pathologist; b. Hampton, Iowa, Sept. 25, 1955; d. Kenneth Rodgers and Kathryn (Stackhouse) Laipple; m. Kenneth Douglas Kennedy, May 26, 1979; children: Beau Douglas, Bryson Joseph. BA, U. No. Iowa, 1977; MS, U. Wyo., 1979. Cert. clin. competence. Speech, lang. pathologist Carbon County Child Devel. Ctr., Rawlins, Wyo., 1980-83, Carbon County Sch. Dist., Hanna, Wyo., 1983. Am. Speech & Hearing Assn., Wyo. Speech and Hearing Assn. Republican. Methodist. Home: Box 168 Elk Mountain WY 82324 Office: Hanna Elementary Sch Box 1000 Hanna WY 82324

KENNEDY, SHEILA GRACE, medical social worker; b. San Jose, Calif., May 17, 1949; d. Irwin Thomas and Martha Ruth (Markey) O'Connell; m. Timothy Anthony Kennedy, Apr. 4, 1975; children: Maureen, Timmy, Patrick. BA in Social Work, Coll. Notre Dame, 1971; MA in Counseling Psychology, U. Santa Clara, 1977. Elem. sch. tchr. St. Louise de Marrillac Sch., Covina, Calif., 1971-72; dir. social services and hospice Sequoia Hosp., Redwood City, Calif., 1972—. Mem. adv. bd. peer counseling for srs. San Carlos (Calif.) Sr. Ctr., 1986—; bd. dirs. San Mateo (Calif.) County com. on child abuse, 1981-83, Parish bd. edn., Nativity Ch., 1984—; v.p. bd. dirs. Am. Cancer Soc., San Mateo County, Burlingame, Calif., 1983-85, pres. bd. dirs., 1985-86. Mem. Nat. Assn. Social Workers, Am. Hosp. Assn., Hosp. Social Work Dirs., Nat. Hospice Orgn. Democrat. Roman Catholic. Avocations: guitar, swimming, softball, basketball. Home: 67 Lorelei Ln Menlo Park CA 94025 Office: Sequoia Hosp Whipple and Alameda Redwood City CA 94062

KENNEL, JOHN MAURICE, physicist, aerospace engineer; b. Sioux City, Iowa, Oct. 7, 1927; s. Elmer M. and Blanche (Augsburger) K.; A.B., Miami U. (Ohio), 1948; Ph.D., U. Tex., 1955; m. Clara Jane Whaley, Dec. 28, 1952; children—Susan, Sandra, John, William. Physicist, Naval Ordnance Lab., 1949-51; engr. Aerophysics Lab., N.Am. Aviation, 1951-52; teaching fellow U. Tex., 1952-55; successively engr., engring. supr., project engr., engring. program mgr. Inertial Navigation Autonetics div. N.Am. Aviation, 1955-67; program mgr. research and devel. Microelectronics div. Rockwell Internat., 1967-71, mgr. liquid crystal devel., 1971-75, engr. ICBM guidance, 1975-85; mgr. inertial navigation system design Northrop Electronics div., 1985—. Mem. Am. Phys. Soc., AAAS, AIAA, Soc. Automotive Engrs., Town Hall Calif. Home: 11591 Suburnas Way Santa Ana CA 92705 Office: 2301 W 120th St Hawthorne CA 90250

KENNEY, CAROLYN TERRY, surgical products company sales executive; b. Aberdeen, S.D., Apr. 5, 1950; d. Raymond Joseph and Esther M. (Mullally) Reis; m. Raymond Nelson Kenney, June 17, 1972 (dec.). B.A. in Drama and Sociology, U. Wash., 1973. Profl. sales rep. Bristol Labs., Seattle, 1974-77; sales rep. med. ctr. Roche Labs., Seattle, 1977-80; heart valve specialist Shiley Labs., Seattle, 1980-82; surg. specialist Bard Cardiosurgery div. C.R. Bard, Seattle, 1982—. Bd. dirs. Benefactor for Issaquah Village Theatre; active Young Widows United Way group. Recipient Rookie of Yr. award Shiley, Inc., 1981; Pres.'s Club award C.R. Bard, 1984; named Young Career Woman of Yr., Seattle Bus. and Profl. Womens Assn., 1978. Mem. Nat. Assn. Female Execs., Bus. Profl. Women's Assn. Democrat. Roman Catholic. Clubs: Pres.'s U. Wash., Bellevue Athletic.

KENNEY, JOHN WILLIAM, III, chemistry educator; b. Long Beach, Calif., Aug. 15, 1950; s. John William Jr. and Janice (Kendrick) K.; m. M. Inga Samuelsen, Sept. 11, 1982. BS in Chemistry, U. Nev., 1972; PhD in Chemistry, U. Utah, 1979. Postdoctoral assoc. in chem. physics Wash. State U., Pullman, 1979-81; asst. prof. chemistry Eastern N.Mex. U., Portales, 1982—. Contbr. articles to profl. jours. Troop leader Sangre de Cristo council Girl Scouts U.S., 1985—. Named one of Outstanding Young Men of Am., 1982-84. Mem. AAAS, Am. Vaccum Soc. (research award 1986), Am. Chem. Soc. (research award 1984), Am. Phys. Soc., Sigma Xi (research award 1986), Phi Kappa Phi. Democrat. Lutheran. Avocations: skiing, running, bicycling, fishing, backpacking, antique automobiles. Home: 1112 Leo Dr Portales NM 88130

KENNEY, WILLIAM CLARK, research scientist; b. Grand Forks, N.D., Feb. 25, 1940; s. James Clement and Dorothy (Clark) K. BA with honors, Carleton Coll., 1962; PhD, U. Calif., Berkeley, 1967. Asst. research biochemist U. Calif., San Francisco, 1970-72, assoc. research biochemist, 1973-79, assoc. prof. bio-chemistry, 1979-84; research chemist VA Med. Ctr., San Francisco, 1979-84, cons., 1971-76; research scientist AMGen, Thousand Oaks, Calif., 1984—. Contbr. articles to profl. jours. Fellow Am. Cancer Soc., 1969-70; recipient Alcoholism Research award VA, 1979. Mem. AAAS, Am. Chem. Soc., Am. Soc. Biol. Chemists, N.Y. Acad. Sci., Research Soc. Alcoholism, Sigma Xi, Alpha Chi Sigma. Avocation: outdoor activities. Home: 2654 Castillo Circle Thousand Oaks CA 91360 Office: AMGen 1900 Oak Terrace Ln Thousand Oaks CA 91320

KENNEY, WILLIAM FITZGERALD, lawyer; b. San Francisco, Nov. 4, 1935; s. Lionel Fitzgerald and Ethel Constance (Brennan) K.; m. Susan Elizabeth Langfitt, May 5, 1962; children—Anne, Carol, James. B.A., U. Calif.-Berkeley, 1957; J.D., Hastings Coll. Law, 1960. Bar: Calif. 1961. Assoc. firm Miller, Osborne Miller & Bartlett, San Mateo, Calif., 1962-64; ptnr. Tormey, Kenney & Cotchett, San Mateo, 1965-67; pres. William F. Kenney, Inc., San Mateo, 1968—, Kennetex, Inc., Dallas, 1981—; com. mem. State Bar of Calif. taxation com., 1973-76. Trustee San Mateo City Sch. Dist., 1971-79, pres., 1972-74; pres. March of Dimes, 1972-73; bd. dirs. Boys Club of San Mateo, 1973—. Served with U.S. Army, 1960-62. Mem. State Bar of Calif., San Mateo County Bar Assn. (dir. 1973-75), Calif. Assn. Realtors (legal affairs com. 1978—), San Mateo C. of C. (bd. dirs. 1983—). Republican. Roman Catholic. Club: Rotary (pres. 1978-79). Lodge: Elks (exalted ruler 1974-75). Home: 221 Clark Dr San Mateo CA 94402 Office: William F Kenney Inc 120 N El Camino Real San Mateo CA 94401

KENNON, TOM LEE, social worker; b. Bosier, La., Mar. 31, 1952; s. Robert Lee Kennon and Flavy Anita (Harper) Ector; m. Andrea Owens, July 16, 1978; children: Raquel Deborah, Taja Li. AA, Monterey Peninsula Coll., 1972; BA, UCLA, 1974, MSW, 1977; M in Pub. Adminstrn., U. So. Calif., 1985, postgrad., 1985—. Drug rehab. counselor Venice (Calif.) Drug Coalition, 1974-75; clin. social work trainee UCLA Neuropsychiat. Inst., 1975-76, psychiat. social worker, 1977—; clin. social work trainee St. John's Hosp., Santa Monica, Calif., 1976-77; psychiat. social worker Hillview Mental Health Ctr., Pacoima, Calif., 1977—; founder, exec. dir. Inner Strength, Inc., Westwood, Calif., 1984—; cons. Author song Mystical Lover (Hon. Mention, Am. Song Festival 1978). Fellow Bank Am., 1970, Ford Found., 1972-74. Mem. NAACP, Am. Coll. Health Care Execs. (Albert W. Dent fellow 1983), Am. Group Psychotherapy Assn., Am. Soc. Polit. Scientists, Am. Soc. Pub. Adminstrs., Nat. Assn. Social Workers, Nat. Assn. Black Social Workers. Club: Triple Crown (West Los Angeles) (chmn. 1974—). Avocations: jogging, guitar, singing, magic, writing songs.

KENNY, MARY LOMBARDI, program administrator; b. Cleve., Oct. 20, 1950; d. Angelo and Anne (DeFazio) Lombardi; m. Richard Patrick Kenny, June 23, 1979. Diploma in graphic design, Cooper Sch. Art, Cleve., 1968-70; BSBA, U. Phoenix, Salt Lake City, 1987; student, Baldwin Wallace Coll., 1976-79; BSBA, Eastern Mich. U., 1981. Account rep. Xerox Corp., Houston, 1981-82; advt. account rep. Big Spring (Tex.) Herald, 1982-83; co-founder, dir., crisis counselor Rape Crisis Services, Big Spring, 1984-85; adminstrv. asst. Family Support Ctr., Salt Lake City, 1986-87; program adminstr. Children's Mus. Utah, Salt Lake City, 1987—; instr. prevention program child abuse and neglect Family Support Ctr., Salt Lake City, 1985—. Co-founder Blue Blazers div. Big Spring C. of C., 1983-85. Named one of Outstanding Young Women of Am., 1981. Mem. Nat. Com. for Prevention Child Abuse. Mem. Christian Ch. Club: Newcomers. Avocations: snow skiing, tennis, reading, travel, theater. Home: 9628 Kelly Brook Dr Sandy UT 84092

KENNY, MICHAEL H., bishop; b. Hollywood, Calif., June 26, 1937. Ed., St. Joseph Coll., Mountain View, Calif., St. Patrick's Sem., Menlo Park, Calif., Cath. U. Am. Ordained priest Roman Cath. Ch., 1963; ordained bishop of Juneau, Alaska, 1979—. Office: Diocese of Juneau 419 6th St Juneau AK 99801 *

KENT, ALLISON BROWNLEE, public affairs executive; b. Birmingham, Ala., Dec. 10, 1958; d. Sidney Paige and Lanie (Hogan) K. BA, U. Ala., 1981, M in Communications, 1983. Staff writer Ala. Power Co., Birmingham, 1983-84; dir. pub. affairs Wash. Credit Union League, Seattle, 1985—. Mem. Wash. Press. Assn., Fin. Mktg. Assn., Internat. Assn. Bus. Communicators (Award of Excellence, Award of Merit, Birmingham 1984). Office: Wash Credit Union League 15440 Bellevue-Redmond Rd Redmond WA 98052-5509

KENT, DONALD MARTIN, geology educational administrator, consultant; b. Medicine Hat, Alta., Can., Jan. 25, 1933; s. George Wyman and Alice Marie (Choiniere) K.; m. Alvina Dolores Deverou, Mar. 10, 1962 (dec. 1984); children—Mark Joseph, Christopher Donald, Paul Edward, Teresa Marie, Carmel Jane. B.S. in Geol. Engring., U. Sask. (Can.), 1957, M.S., 1959; Ph.D., U. Alta., Edmonton, 1968. Registered profl. engr., Sask. Research geologist Dept. Mineral Resource, Regina, Sask., 1958-71; assoc. prof. U. Regina, 1971-78, prof. geology, 1978—, head dept. geology, 1981—; geol. cons. Can. Occidental Oil Co., Toronto, Ont., 1976-80; tech. advisor Union Oil Co. Ltd., Calgary, Alta., 1978-79; pres. D.M. Kent Cons. Geologist Ltd., Regina, 1981—. Author numerous tech. reports; contbr. articles to profl. jours.; co-editor symposium vol.; Lloydminster and Beyond, 1980; co-editor: Williston Basin: Anatomy of a Cratonic Oil Province, 1987. Vice pres. Sask. Amateur Football Inc., Regina, 1984; pres. Sask. Amateur Football Ofcls. Assn., Regina, 1987 bd. dirs. Regina Football Ofcls. Assn., 1984. Pan Am. Oil Co. fellow, 1960; Nat. Sci. and Engring. Research Council grantee, 1972. Mem. Sask. Geol. Soc. (pres. 1965, 69, 78), Am. Assn. Petroleum Geologists (dist. rep. 1978-81), Soc. Econ. Paleontologists and Mineralogists (chmn. research com. 1986-87), Geol. Assn. Can. (fellow), Can. Soc. Petroleum Geologists (assoc. editor 1985). Liberal. Roman Catholic. Home: 2800 Lacon St, Regina, SK Canada S4N 2A8 Office: Dept Geology U Regina, Regina, SK Canada S4S OA2

KENT, HARRY CHRISTISON, geologist, educator; b. Los Angeles, May 20, 1930; s. Harry and Florence (Christison) K.; m. Sheila Marie Kelly, Aug. 18, 1956; children—Colleen Marie, Bruce Kelly. Geol. Engr., Colo. Sch. Mines, 1952; M.S., Stanford, 1953; Ph.D., U. Colo., 1965. Geologist The California Co., Fla. and La., 1953-56; mem. faculty Colo. Sch. Mines, Golden, 1956—, asso. prof., 1967-69, prof., 1969—, head geology dept., 1969-75; dir. Inst. Energy Resource Studies, 1976—. Bd. mgrs. Jeffco br., N.W. br. YMCA, Denver. Fellow Geol. Soc. Am.; mem. Am. Assn. Petroleum Geologists, Soc. Econ. Paleontologists and Mineralogists, Soc. Petroleum Engrs., Sigma Xi. Democrat. Home: 5131 Jellison Ct Arvada CO 80002 Office: Colo Sch Mines Inst Energy Resource Studies Golden CO 80401

KENT, LORI MARIAN, public relations manager; b. Los Angeles, June 18, 1957; d. Irving and Estelle (Weiss) Allen; m. Carl Reed Kent, July 14, 1985. BS in Bus., Calif. State U., Northridge, 1979. Mktg. analyst Joy Mfg. Co., Los Angeles, 1980-81; assoc. editor Am. Savings, Beverly Hills, 1982-84; pub. relations mgr. Ericsson, Garden Grove, Calif., 1984-86; free lance writer North Hollywood, 1986—. Editor numerous articles to profl. jours. Mem. Pub. Relations Soc. Am.

KENT, PAULA, public relations, marketing and management consultant, lecturer; b. N.Y.C.; d. John and Estelle (Frye) Smith; BS, State Tchrs. Coll., Worcester, Mass., 1939; MBA, Boston U., 1941; m. Stanley J. Lloyd, Jan. 23, 1943; children: Diane Adrienne Noel, Robin Michele Cheri, Kevin Christopher Kent, Gisele Nicolette Jolie. Methods engr. Internat. Bus. Machines, 1941-42; personnel dir. Daily Jour., San Diego, also radio sta. KSDJ, 1946-48; fashion editor The San Diego Union, 1949; promotion dir. The San Diego Union and the Evening Tribune, 1948-70, also UCLA Extension Div. Faculty, 1961-63; pub. relations, mktg. and mgmt. cons., 1970—; v.p. La Jolla Clin. Labs., 1970—. Lectr. mktg. workshop tour, Brussels, London, Paris, Madrid, 1972; speaker nat. and regional confs. in maj. U.S. cities; del. Nat. Fedn. Press. Women Touring Russia, 1973. Formerly active ARC, Am. Cancer Soc., Med. Aux. San Diego. Recipient over 158 awards 1950—, including: 39 nat., 18 western states, over 100 Calif. state awards, 1 local award, resulting from ann. competitions sponsored by Los Angeles Advt. Women's Club, Nat. Newspaper Publs. Assn., Calif. Press Women, Los Angeles Sales Promotion Execs. Assn., Nat. Fedn. Press Women, Editor and Pub. Mag.; recipient Outstanding Service award Boy Scouts Am., 1962, 65; civic awards City of San Diego, Distinguished Service award Investment Edn. Inst., Detroit, 1969, Golden Spear award Twin Cities Sales Promotion Execs. Assn., Mpls., 1965; Outstanding Service thru Annual Investment Clinics N.Y. Stock Exchange, 1964; named Woman of Achievement, 1958, 59, 64, Woman of Valor, 1958, Woman of Year, San Diego, 1965, Woman of Achievement, Nat. Fedn. Bus. and Profl. Women's Clubs, 1966, Advt. Man of Distinction, San Diego, 1970, Don award, Legion of Portola, 1968. Mem. Advt. and Sales Club San Diego (former dir.), Sales Execs. Club San Diego (pres. 1970-71), Personnel Mgmt. Assn. (hon. mem.), Sales and Mktg. Execs. Internat. (dir. at large 1971-73), Sales Promotion Execs. Assn. Los Angeles (Man of Year 1965), Am. Advt. Fedn. (western region chmn. edn. com., mem. nat. edn. com. 1971-72) Nat. Newspaper Promotion Assn. (pres. Western region 1964, dir. 1968-70), Calif. Assn. Press Women, Nat. Fedn. Press Women, Internat. Newspaper Promotion Assn. (bd. dirs.), Am. Mgmt. Assn. Roman Catholic. Editor: Monthly Bull., Personnel Mgmt. Assn., 1955-59, monthly bull., Sales Execs. Club. Chmn. San Diego's Ann. Giant Sales Rally, 1953-55, 70-71, co-chmn., 1964, 65; chmn. Advt. Recognition Week Campaign, 1953-54, Nat. Unltd. Hydroplane Races, San Diego, 1953-54; pub. relations advisor, dir. Nat. Mrs. Am. Pageant, honored London Press Club Members Luncheon, 1970, San Diego 200th Anniversary celebration; producer, emcee ann. Holiday for Housewives, San Diego, 1955-60; producer, co-ordinator U. Calif., Today's World, San Diego, 1962; exec. dir., producer San Diego Ann. Golden Gloves Boxing Tournament, 1961-68; San Diego Ann. Metrotennis Championships, 1952-70; dir. Ann Power Boat Regatta, 1950-62; exec. dir. Ann Jr. Golf Championships; dir. Ann. Hole-in-One Tournament, 1951-70; master ceremonies, producer, emcee Distinction Awards, 1967, 68, 69; producer/dir. San Diego Advt. Salesrama, 1971; producer, dir. master ceremonies San Diego Ann. Woman of Yr. Awards, 1967, 68, 69; producer/designer 34 exhibits for convs. and fairs. Del. Nat. Fedn Press Women touring Russia. Commd. ensign, Women's Reserve, USNR, 1942, transferred USCG, served from ensign to lt., 1943-46. Avocation: world travel. Home: 515 Bon Air St La Jolla CA 92037 Office: PO Box 2243 La Jolla CA 92038

KENT, STEPHEN BRIAN HENRY, research scientist; b. Wellington, New Zealand, Dec. 12, 1945; came to U.S., 1970; s. John Basset and Doreen (Kalaugher) K.; m. (Cheryl) Joy Sullivan, Aug. 23, 1969; children: Julia Elizabeth, Geoffrey John. BS, Victoria U., Wellington, 1968; MS, Massey U., Palmerston North, New Zealand, 1970; PhD, U. Calif., Berkeley, 1975. Research assoc. The Rockefeller U., N.Y.C., 1974-77, asst. prof., 1977-81; dir. protein chemistry Molecular Genetics, Inc., Minn., 1981-82; sr. research assoc. Calif. Inst. Tech., Pasadena, 1983—; cons. Applied Biosystems, Inc., Foster City, Calif., 1982-85, Applied Molecular Genetics, Inc., Allied Corp. Research. Contbr. articles to sci. jours., patentee automated protein synthesis, novel hepatitis B vaccines. Victoria U. scholar, 1968. Mem. AAAS, Am. Chem. Soc., N.Y. Acad. Scis., The Harvey Soc. Home: 615 W California Blvd Pasadena CA 91105 Office: Calif Inst Tech Biology Div 147-75 Pasadena CA 91125

KENT, THEODORE CHARLES, psychologist; m. Shirley, June 7, 1948; children: Donald, Susan, Steven. PhD, U. So. Calif., 1951; Dr. Rerum Naturalium, Johannes Gutenberg U., Mainz, Germany, 1960. Diplomate in clin. psychology. Head dept. behavioral sci. U. So. Colo., Pueblo, 1965-78, emeritus, 1978—; staff psychologist Yuma Behavioral Health, Ariz., 1978-82, chief profl. services, 1982-83; dir. psychol. services Rio Colo. Health Systems, Yuma, 1983-85; clin psychologist, dir. mental health Ft. Yuma (Calif.) Indian Health Service, USPHS, 1985—; exec. dir. Human Sci. Ctr., Yuma, 1982—. Columnist Yuma Daily Sun, 1982-86. Author (tests) non-verbal test of suffering, 1982; (books) Skills in Living Together, 1983, Conflict Resolution, 1986, A Psychologist Answers Your Questions, 1987. Served to col. USAF, 1951-65. Named Outstanding prof. U. So. Colo., 1977. Fellow Am. Psychol. Assn. (disting. visitor undergrad. edn. program). Office: Ft Yuma Indian Health Service PO Box 1368 Yuma AZ 85364

KENTON, BERNARD, physicist; b. N.Y.C., July 9, 1929; s. Charles and Sadie (Rosenberg) Kletsky; m. Barbara Heyman, Nov. 8, 1953; children: Richard H., Lori R., Daniel L. BS, UCLA, 1962, MS, 1964, PhD, 1967. Cert. acupuncturist. Postdoctoral fellow UCLA Brain Research Inst., 1967-69; research anatomist UCLA, 1969-71; sr. neurophysiologist City of Hope Med. Ctr., Duarte, Calif., 1971-80, New Hope Pain Ctr., Alhambra, Calif., 1980-84; systems engr. Hughes Aircraft Co., El Segundo, Calif., 1984—; assoc. prof. U. So. Calif., Los Angeles, 1980; media and pub. research specialist Scientists Inst. for Pub. Info., 1978. Editor: Best Evidence, 1980; contbr. articles to profl. jours. V.p. Acupuncture Polit. Action Com., Los Angeles, 1981. Mem. Am. Phys. Soc., AAAS, Internat. Assn. for Study of Pain, Am. Pain Soc., N.Y. Acad. Scis. Democrat. Jewish. Avocation: violinist. Home: 2943 Kelton Ave Los Angeles CA 90064 Office: Hughes Aircraft Co Bldg R8/2660 PO Box 92426 Los Angeles CA 90009

KENTON, FRANK JOSEPH, geology firm executive; b. Uniontown, Pa., June 22, 1950; s. Frank Joseph and Jean (Centofanti) K.; m. Maureen Evelyn Rooker, Aug. 16, 1980; children—Frank Joseph, Gabriel William. B.A, Whittier Coll., 1972. Registered geologist, Oreg., Calif., cert. engring. geologist, Calif., Oreg. Staff geologist Leighton & Assocs., La Habra, Calif., 1972-74, Irvine, Calif., 1977-79, sr. geologist, 1979-80, project geologist, 1980-86, chief engring. geologist, 1986—; ranch mgr. Windfield Mannor, Fargo, N.D., 1976-77; v.p. Silver Queen Mining and Refining, Inc., Mojave, Calif., 1980-81; breeder quality Appaloosa show, race horses, 1980—. Mem. Assn. for Engring. Geologists, Am. Inst. Profl. Geologists (cert.), Appaloosa Horse Club of Moscow (Idaho). Home: 4911 Leeds St Simi Valley CA 93063 Office: Leighton & Assocs 790 Hampshire Rd Suite H Westlake Village CA 91361

KENTULA, MARY ELIZABETH, project scientist; b. Windber, Pa., June 7, 1949; d. Andrew Peter and Mary Elizabeth (Racosky) K.; m. Donald James Armstrong, Aug. 3, 1984. BS, St. Francis Coll., 1971; MS, Oreg. State U., 1973, PhD, 1983. Instr. Oreg. State U., Corvallis, 1981-82, asst. prof., 1982-84; lectr. San Diego State U., 1984-85; project scientist Northrop Services, Corvallis, 1986—; cons. Northwest Timber Assn., Eugene, Oreg., 1980, Danil Hancock, Corvallis, 1984; ind. cons. EPA, Corvallis, 1985. Mem. Soc. Wetland Scientists, Ecol. Soc. Am., Estuarine Research Fedn., Am. Soc. Limnologists and Oceanographers, Sigma Xi, Delta Epsilon Sigma, Gamma Sigma Delta. Office: Northrop Services Inc 200 SW 35th St Corvallis OR 97333

KENYON, DAVID V., federal judge; b. 1930; m. Mary Cramer; children: George Cramer, John Clark. B.A., U. Calif.-Berkeley, 1952; J.D., U. So. Calif., 1957. Law clk. to presiding justice U.S. Dist. Ct. (ce. dist.) Calif., 1957-58; house counsel Metro-Goldwyn-Mayer, 1959-60, Nat. Theatres and TV Inc., 1960-61; sole practice law 1961-71; judge Mcpl. Ct. Los Angeles, 1971-72, Los Angeles Superior Ct., 1972-80, U.S. Dist. Ct. (cen. dist.) Calif.,, Los Angeles, 1980—. Office: US Courthouse 312 N Spring St Los Angeles CA 90012

KENYON, KENNETH JAMES, research librarian; b. Phila., Oct. 30, 1930; s. H. Edison and Astrid (Sorensen) K.; m. Mary Ann Strong, Mar. 28, 1959; children—Kenneth, Jr., Norman. A.A., Los Angeles City Coll., 1961; student Santa Ana Coll., 1963, UCLA, 1964. Record librarian ABC, Hollywood, Calif., 1953-55; with camera dept. Walt Disney Prodns., 1955-56; research librarian 20th Century Fox Film Corp., Beverly Hills, Calif., 1957-70, head research dept., 1970—. Served with USMC, 1948-52. Mem. Spl. Libraries Assn., Acad. Motion Picture Arts and Scis., TV Acad. Arts and Scis., Am. Film Inst., Am. Legion, USMC Combat Corrs. Assn. Lodges: Masons, VASA. Office: 20th Century Fox Research Library PO Box 900 Beverly Hills CA 90213

KENYON, ROGER ALAN, private law judge; b. Wagner, S.D., Mar. 15, 1953; s. Robert Lee and Virginia Marie (Homcho) K.; m. Patricia Maureen Sullivan, May 30, 1981. BA, Gonzaga U., 1975; PhD, U. Ottawa, Ont., Can., 1981; JCD, St. Paul U., Ottawa, 1983. Assoc. dir. Tribunal Cath. Archdiocese of Seattle, 1977-86, judge, jud. programs coordinator, canonical cons., 1985—. Author: Existential Structures, 1976; contbr. articles to profl. jours. Mem. AAAS, Canon Law Soc. Am., Can. Canon Law Soc. Avocation: studying epiphenomenology.

KEOCHEKIAN, CAROL, public relations and marketing executive; b. Glendale, Calif., Dec. 8, 1938; d. John and Roxie (Poochigian) Shahinian; m. Sarkis Keochekian, July 5, 1958; children: Annette, Kathryn, Christine, Armen. AA, East Los Angeles Coll., 1958; BA, Calif. Luth. U., 1981. Women's editor East Los Angeles Tribune, 1958-60; coordinator fund devel. Girl Scouts U.S., Ventura, Calif., 1977-78; dir. pub. info. Conejo Future Found., Thousand Oaks, Calif., 1978-79; dir. women's program Calif. Luth. U., Thousand Oaks, 1979-82, dir. adult edn., 1982-84; mgr. community services Pleasant Valley Hosp., Camarillo, Calif., 1984-86; dir. mktg. communications Golden Health System, Camarillo, 1986—. Script cons., editor Atlantis Prodns., Thousand Oaks, 1970—; script editor: (films) The Forgotten Genocide, 1976 (Emmy nominee 1976, Chris award Columbus Film Festival 1976), Strangers in a Promise Land, 1984 (CINE award 1984). Chmn. Ventura County Parks and Harbor Commn., 1984-86; co-chmn. Conejo Valley Bicentennial Com., Thousand Oaks, 1974-77; mem. Ventura County Commn. for Women, 1983, Ventura County Cultural Heritage Bd., 1976. Named Woman of Yr., Conejo Valley C. of C., 1986, Dona Triunfo, Conejo Valley Hist. Soc., 1978; recipient Commendation for Com. Service, Ventura County Bd. Suprs., 1984, Appreciation award City of Thousand Oaks, 1978. Mem. Hosp. Mktg. Pub. Relations Assn., Pub. Info. Communications Assn., Conejo Future Found. (trustee 1982-84), Conejo Valley Hist. Soc. (pres. 1974-75). Home: 2318 Sirius St Thousand Oaks CA 91360 Office: Golden Health System 3801 Las Posas Rd Camarillo CA 93010

KEOUGH, JAMES GORDON, editor, publisher; b. Rahway, N.J., Feb. 15, 1946; s. James Creamer and Kathleen (Van Gordon) K.; m. Linda Sparrowe, Sept. 1, 1977; children: Sarah Forbes, Megan Elizabeth. BS, U. Colo., 1968; MA, U. Chgo., 1970, PhD, 1976. Editor Hosp. Forum, San Francisco, 1978; mng. editor Home Mag., N.Y.C., 1979-82, contbg. editor, 1984—; manuscript editor Sierra Mag., San Francisco, 1977, mng. editor, 1982-84, editor, pub., 1984—. Mem. Mag. Pubs. Assn., Western Publs. Assn. Office: Sierra 730 Polk St San Francisco CA 94109

KEOWN, LAURISTON LIVINGSTON, JR., industrial psychologist, consultant; b. Balt., Feb. 24, 1942; s. Lauriston Livingston and Gladys May (Dykes) K.; m. Patje Alexandra Susemihl, Aug. 7, 1962 (div. 1977); children: Christina, Cassandra, Lauriston, Clayton; m. Nancy Ann Hastie, Mar. 18, 1978. BA cum laude, U. Balt., 1965; MS, U. Alta., 1970, PhD, 1977. Cert. psychologist, Alta. Lectr. Nippissing Coll., Laurentian U., North Bay, Ont., Can., 1968-69; chief systems analyst Dept. Youth, Edmonton, Alta., Can., 1969-71, research dir., 1971-72; dir. planning and research Dept. Culture, Youth and Recreation, Alta., 1972-74; dir. planning and devel. Dept. Recreation, Parks and Wildlife, Alta., Edmonton, 1974-75; asst. dir. Transp. Safety Alta. Transp. Dept., 1975—; cons. R. Dehaas Assocs., Edmonton, 1979-80, Draherin Group, Edmonton, 1980-82. Author: (with others) Evaluation of Traffic Safety Programs, 1980; contbr. articles to profl. jours. Mem. Alta. Planning Bd., 1974-82, bd. dirs. Alta. Royal Can. Mounted Police Hist. Celebrations Commn., 1974-75; exec. bd. Traffic Records Commn., Nat. Safety Council, 1978—. Indsl. psychology scholar Lamond Dewhurst & Assocs., U. Alta., 1966. Mem. Am. Assn. Motor Vehicle Adminstr., Can. Conf. Motor Transp. Adminstrs., Alta. Psychologists Assn. (chartered psychologist province of Alba.). Episcopalian. Home: PO Box 148, Bon Accord, AB Canada T0A 0K0 Office: AB Transp, Twin Atria Bldg, 4999-98 Ave, Edmonton, AB Canada T6B X3

KEPLER, RAYMOND GLEN, physicist; b. Long Beach, Calif., Sept. 10, 1928; s. Glen Raymond and Erma Martina (Larsen) K.; m. Carol Flint, Apr. 19, 1953; children: Julianne, Linda, Russell B., David L. B.S., Stanford U., 1950; M.S., U. Calif.-Berkeley, 1955, Ph.D., 1957. Mem. tech. staff central research dept. E.I. duPont de Nemours & Co., 1957-64; div. supr. Sandia Nat. Labs., Albuquerque, 1964-69, dept. mgr., 1969—; vice chmn. panel materials Sci. and Engring. Study Commn., NRC, 1985-88; mem. solid State scis. panel Nat. Acad. Sci., 1977-82; mem. evaluation panel for materials sci. Nat. Bur. Standards, 1982-87. Fellow Am. Phys. Soc. (chmn. edn. com. 1979-80); mem. AAAS, Sierra Club. Office: Sandia Nat Labs Albuquerque NM 87185

KEPNER, RICHARD EDWIN, chemistry educator; b. Los Angeles, July 27, 1916; s. Louis Gilbert and Gertrude (Kennedy) K.; m. Beverly Brewster, Nov. 27, 1946; children: Elizabeth Jeanne, Douglas James. BS, U. Calif., Berkeley, 1938; MS, UCLA, 1942, PhD, 1946. Instr. chemistry U. Calif., Davis, 1946-48, asst. prof., 1946-54, assoc. prof., 1954-60, prof., 1960-86, prof. emeritus, 1986—. Mem. Am. Chem. Soc., Am. Soc. Viticulture and Enology, Sigma Xi. Home: 736 Elmwood Dr Davis CA 95616 Office: U Calif Dept Chemistry Davis CA 95616

KERBER, GEORGE ALEXANDER, city official; b. Fresno, Calif., Sept. 4, 1925; s. George and Leona (Flohr) K.; m. Esther Louise Williams, Oct. 12, 1928; children—George Lawrence, Gary William. B.A., Fresno State Coll., 1950, cert. in pub. adminstrn., 1957. City planner City of Fresno, 1947-57, asst. dir. planning, 1958-72, dir. planning, 1972-82, dir. devel., 1982—; planning cons. Mangor Assocs., Fresno, 1957-59; mem. People to People Found., Seattle, 1982—. Mem. Fresno County Hist. Soc., 1970, Fresno Art Ctr., 1975. Served with USN, 1944-46. Recipient Disting. Pub. Service award San Joaquin chpt. AIA, 1983. Mem. Am. Inst. Cert. Planners (chpt. pres. 1959), Am. Soc. Pub. Adminstrn. (chpt. pres. 1965). Republican. Lutheran. Home: 4030 N Angus St Fresno CA 93726 Office: City of Fresno Devel Dept 2326 Fresno St Fresno CA 93721

KERBY, STEWART LAWRENCE, oilfield equipment manufacturing company executive; b. Winnipeg, Man., Can., Mar. 7, 1936; s. John Brant and Muriel Eliza (Ireland) K.; m. Gwen Anne Aylesworth, Aug. 20, 1958 (div. 1969); 1 child, Stewart John; m. Marsha Lynn Stewart, Nov. 21, 1971; 1 child, Scott Kerr. B.M.E., McGill U., 1957. Registered profl. engr., Alta., Ont. Design engr. Toronto Iron Works Co., Ont., Can., 1957-59, sales engr., 1959-62, mgr. engring., 1962-66; v.p., asst. gen. mgr. TIW Industries Ltd., 1966-72, sr. v.p., gen. mgr., 1972-79; pres., gen. mgr. TIW Western Div., Can., Erectors Ltd., Calgary, Alta., 1979—. Mem. Can. Inst. Steel Constrn. (bd. dirs., exec. com. Toronto 1966-86), Boilermaker Contractors Assn. (vice chmn., dir. 1969-81), Am. Petroleum Inst. (sub-com. mem. 1962-72). Home: 2344 Palisade Dr SW, Calgary, AB Canada T2V 3V1 Office: Can Erectors Ltd, 7770 44th SE, Calgary, AB Canada T2C 2L5

KERCHER, CONRAD JOHN, animal nutrition educator; b. Yakima, Wash., June 17, 1926; s. George John and Anna Sophia (Kretchman) K.; m. Lydia Sophia Zier, Sept. 7, 1946; children: Kathryn Ann, Nina Louise, Jane Marie, Kise Sabina. BS, Mont. State U., 1950; MS, Cornell U., 1952, PhD, 1954. Asst. prof. animal sci. dept. U. Wyo., Laramie, 1954-58, assoc. prof., 1958-62, prof., 1962—, acting v.p. acad. affairs, 1975-76; cons. U.S. AID, Kabul, Afghanistan, 1971. Contbr. articles to profl. jours. Served with USN, 1945-46. Teaching award Amoco Found., 1973. Fellow AAAS, Am. Soc. Am. Sci. (sec., treas., pres. elect, pres. 1974-80); mem. Am. Dairy Sci. Assn., Am. Registry Profl. Animal Scientists (bd. dirs. 1985—), Am. Forage and Grassland Council, Laramie C. of C. (chmn. Univ. Relations com. 1978), Luth. Layman's League (dist. sec. 1959-63, bd. govs. 1965-69), Omicron Delta Kappa (Teaching award 1961), Alpha Zeta (Teaching award 1962). Avocations: bldg. home and yard work. Home: Box 3251 Laramie WY 82071 Office: U Wyo Animal Sci Dept Box 3354 Laramie WY 82071

KERCHEVAL, ROBERT GILKIE, utility company executive; b. Des Moines, May 6, 1931; m. Janet Kercheval; 1 child. Student, Peirce Jr. Coll., Valley Jr. Coll., UCLA. Various So. Calif. Gas Co., Riverside, 1950-1961; appliance and dealer supr. So. Calif. Gas Co., Los Angeles, 1961-62, new bus. supr., 1962-63, supt. staff, dealer promotion, 1963-64, supr. new bus. staff, 1964-65, mgr. div. sales, 1965-67, mgr. mktg., residental new constrn., 1968-70, mgr. sales promotion and advt., 1970-72, mgr. market services staff, 1972-75, mgr. ops. support, 1975-76, div. mgr., 1976-80, mgr. pub. affairs planning, 1980-81, div. mgr., 1981—. Pres. Corral 15 Equestrian Trails, Whiting Woods Home Owners Assn.; new mem. leader Glendale (Calif.) First Meth. Ch.; chmn. Riverside Bus. Educational Round Table, Western Riverside United Way Campaign, 1986-87; bd. dirs., chmn. devel. com. Riverside Downtown Assn; mem. Mission Inn Ad Hoc Study Com., sec. mng. group, Community Hosp. Found., Frank Miller Found., Mayor's

Econ. Devel. Council, mem. Mission Inn Found. Bd.; mem. exec. bd. Arlington Health Services; mem. steering com., exec. com. Keep Riverside Ahead; treas. Inland World Affairs Council; mem. 1985 Mayor's Charter Rev. Com. Mem. Am. Gas Assn. (nat. advt. com., chmn. nat. mktg. com.), Pacific Coast Gas Assn., Bldg. Contractors Assn., Am. Soc. Trainers and Developers, Young Home Builders Council, Assn. Nat. Advertisers, Gas Co. Rod and Gun Club, Norwalk C. of C. (pres.), South Bay C. of C. (pres.), Air Force Assn. (pres. Riverside chpt.), Greater Riverside C. of C. (past pres.), Monday Morning Group, Automobile Club So. Calif. (bd. dirs.). Avocations: horseback riding, swimming, boating, skiing, tennis. Home: 17265 Ridge Canyon Riverside CA 92506 Office: So Calif Gas Co Div Mgr Eastern Div 3700 Central Riverside CA 92506

KERFOOT, HENRY BARTLETT, environmental chemist; b. Southington, Conn., Oct. 14, 1952; s. Bartlett and Rosemary Katherine (Cushing) K. BA, Johns Hopkins U., 1975; MS, Fla. State U., 1977. Asst. prof. Charles County Community Coll., La Plata, Md., 1978-82; research chemist Naval Surface Weapons Ctr., Indian Head, Md., 1980-82; prin. scientist Lockheed Engring. and Mgmt. Services Co., Las Vegas, Nev., 1981—; cons. Earth Tech., Long Beach, Calif., 1985—. Mem. ASTM, Am. Chem. Soc. (exec. council 1983-85), Assn. Official Analytical Chemists, Air Pollution Control Assn. Clubs: Las Vegas Track, LEMSCo Running (pres.). Home: 3057 Hebard Dr Las Vegas NV 89121 Office: Lockheed Engring & Mgmt Services Co 1050 E Flamingo Rd Las Vegas NV 89119

KERKVLIET, NANCY ISAACSON, immunotoxicology researcher; b. Eau Claire, Wis., June 24, 1947; d. LeRoy Isaacson and Beverly Jane (Eldridge) Wittig; m. Paul Edmund Kerkvliet, Aug. 22, 1970; children: Kelly Christine, Breanne Nicolle. BS, Wis. State U., Eau Claire, 1970; MS, Oreg. State U., 1973, PhD, 1976. Asst. prof. Oreg. State U. Sch. Vet. Medicine and Environ. Health Scis. Ctr., Corvallis, 1979-85, assoc. prof., 1985—; cons. John Lowe, Atty., Oregon City, Oreg., 1984—, Hanft, Fride, Obrien, Harries, Duluth, Minn., 1985—. Contbr. articles to profl. jours. Fellow NSF; grantee NIH, EPA. Mem. Soc. Toxicology (sec., treas. 1985—, immunotoxicology splty. sect. 1985-87), AAAS, Assn. Women in Sci., Council for Agrl. Sci. and Tech. Republican. Lodge: Zonta. Office: Oreg State U Coll Vet Medicine Corvallis OR 97331

KERMAN, BARRY MARTIN, ophthalmologist, educator; b. Chgo., Mar. 31, 1945; s. Harvey Nathan and Evelyn (Bialis) K.; B.S., U. Ill., 1967, M.D. with high honors, 1970; m. Pamela Renee Berliant, Aug. 18, 1968; children—Gregory Jason, Jeremy Adam. Intern in medicine Harbor Gen. Hosp., Torrance, Calif., 1970-71; resident in ophthalmology Wadsworth VA Hosp., Los Angeles, 1971-74; fellow in diseases of the retina, vitreous and choroid Jules Stein Eye Inst. UCLA, 1974-75; fellow in ophthalmic ultrasonography Edward S. Harkness Eye Inst., Columbia U., N.Y.C. and U. Iowa Hosps., Iowa City, 1975; asst. prof. ophthalmology UCLA, 1976-78, Harbor Gen. Hosp., 1976-78; asst. clin. prof. ophthalmology UCLA, 1978-83, assoc. clin. prof., 1983—, dir. ophthalmic ultrasonography lab., 1976—; cons. ophthalmologist, Los Angeles, 1976—. Served with USAFR, 1971-77. Diplomate Am. Bd. Ophthalmology. Fellow Am. Acad. Ophthalmology; mem. Calif. Med. Assn., Los Angeles County Med. Assn., Los Angeles Soc. Ophthalmology, Am. Inst. Ultrasound in Medicine, Am. Soc. Ophthalmic Ultrasound, Am. Registry of Diagnostic Med. Sonographers (exec. bd.). Contbr. articles to profl. jours. Office: 2080 Century Park E Suite 800 Los Angeles CA 90067

KERN, CLIFFORD DALTON, meteorologist; b. Oakland, Calif., Jan. 6, 1928; s. Arthur William and Blanche Naomi (Brown) K.; A.B., U. Calif., Berkeley, 1952; certificate in Meterology, UCLA, 1953, M.A., 1958; Ph.D., U. Wash., 1965; m. C. Joyce Durant, Feb. 21, 1951; children—Michael Richard, Janice Rae, Michelle Ann. Commd. 2d lt. USAF, 1952, advanced through grades to lt. col., 1972; staff meteorologist Air Force Systems Command, McClelland AFB, Calif., 1953-55, Hanscom Field, Mass., 1955-56, 58-61, Vietnam, 1964-65, Air Force Satellite Control Facility, Sunnyvale, Calif., 1965-67, Air Force Global Weather Central Offutt AFB, 1969-71, Los Angeles Air Force Sta., 1971-72; ret., 1972; asst. prof. St. Louis U., 1972; vis. scientist Nat. Center Atmospheric Research, Boulder, Colo., 1972-73; with Atomic Energy div. E.I. duPont de Nemours & Co., Savannah River Lab., Aiken, S.C., 1973-78; with Space Systems div. Lockheed Missiles & Space Co., Sunnyvale, Calif., 1978—. Served with AUS, 1946-48. Decorated Bronze Star medal, Air medal with one oak leaf cluster. Mem. Am. Meteorol. Soc., Am. Geophys. Union, Sigma Xi. Mason. Home: 556 Hacienda Dr Scotts Valley CA 95066 Office: PO Box 504 Sunnyvale CA 94086

KERN, HAL COLEMAN, III, security management executive; b. Long Beach, Calif., Oct. 8, 1949; s. Hal C. and Robyn (Adair) K.; m. Phyllis Grable, Dec. 16, 1967 (div.); children—Keri Mari, Kasey Elizabeth. B.S. in Criminal Justice, Calif. State U., 1967; M.A. in Edn., Pepperdine U., 1971. With U.S. Secret Service, 1976-77; sr. security specialist Fluor Corp., Irvine, Calif., 1977-80; v.p. Shield Security, Orange, Calif., 1980-82; mgr. security and safety Air Cal, Newport Beach, Calif., 1981-82; loss prevention dir. Sav-on Drugs Inc., Anaheim, Calif., 1982-83; dir. security management Hughes Aircraft Co., Culver City, Calif., 1983—. Served to lt. col. USMCR. Mem. Am. Soc. Indsl. Security, Am. Soc. Safety Engrs., Am. Mgmt. Assn. Republican. Presbyterian.

KERN, JOE VAUGHN, public relations executive; b. Hannibal, Mo., Dec. 26, 1925; s. Paul Dean and Jeannette (Vaughn) K.; m. Gerry Slutes; children: Ruth Anne Kern Bush, Nancy Jane Kern Fruitman, Donna Jo. BBA, U. Tex., El Paso, 1949. Tchr. Carlsbad (N.Mex.) City Schs., 1949-50; asst. to research mgr. U.S. Potash Co., Carlsbad, 1950-68; mgr. personnel U.S. Borax Co., Boron, Calif., 1968-69; dir. pub. relations U.S. Borax Co., Los Angeles, 1969—. Author: You and U.S. Potash, 1984. Ruling elder Presbyn. Ch. Served as cpl. USMC, 1943-46, PTO. Mem. Am. Mining Congress (communications com.), Calif. Mining Assn. (chmn. communications com. 1980), Calif. Mfrs. Assn., Death Valley Natural History Assn. (bd. dirs. 1984—). Republican. Avocation: stamp collecting. Home: 25198 Avenida Ignacio Valencia CA 91355 Office: US Borax 3075 Wilshire Blvd Los Angeles CA 90010

KERN, PAUL ALFRED, advertising executive; b. Hackensack, N.J., Mar. 17, 1958; s. Paul Julian and Edith Helen (Colten) K. BS in Commerce, U. Va., 1980; MBA, U. So. Calif., 1983. Sales rep. Procter and Gamble, Cin., 1980-81; research services mgr. Opinion Research, Long Beach, Calif., 1984; consumer planning supr. Dentsu, Young and Rubican, Los Angeles, 1984-85; research executive DJMC Advt., Inc., Los Angeles, 1986—; bd. dirs. Applicon, Inc., Hillsdale, N.J., Kernakopia, Hillsdale; cons. Venture Six Enterprises, Encino, Calif., 1985—, DFS/Dorland, Torrance, Calif., 1986. Coach, supr. Little League Football, Alexandria, Va., 1981. Recipient Most Calls Per Day award Procter and Gamble, 1980. Mem. Profl. Research Assn., Am. Mktg. Assn., Am. Film Inst., U.S. Tennis Assn. (Michelob Light 4.5 Team Championship 1982), U. Va. Alumni Assn. Club: Alta Vista Racquet. Avocations: tennis, chess, softball, skiing, reading. Home: 516 S Irena Redondo Beach CA 90277

KERNAN, JOHN T., education systems company executive; b. Balt., Feb. 17, 1946; m. Dianne M. Kernan, May 11, 1973; 1 child, Amy B. BS, Loyola Coll., Balt., 1969. Dir. info. systems McCormick & Co., Balt., 1969-77, Borden Inc., Columbus, Ohio, 1977-79; v.p. product devel. Deltak Inc., Chgo., 1979-82; v.p., gen. mgr. Gill Mgmt. Services, San Jose, Calif., 1983-85; pres. Edn. Systems Tech. Corp., San Diego, 1985—. Served to capt. U.S. Army, 1965-73. Home: 310 Colima Ct La Jolla CA 92037 Office: Edn Systems Corp 6170 Cornerstone Ct E San Diego CA 92121

KERNELL, JOHN LAURI, marketing communications consultant; b. White Plains, N.Y., Oct. 2, 1933; s. Alfred B. and Dorothy V. (Small) K.; m. Sandra L. Horn, Apr. 12, 1966 (div. Sept. 1974); 1 child, Liam A. B.A., Cornell U., 1955; M.A., Antioch Coll., 1977. Asst. editor McGraw Hill, N.Y.C., 1958-59; news dir. Sta. KGU, Honolulu, 1960-62, Sta. KONA-TV, Honolulu, 1962-64; radio-TV dir. W.S. Myers & Assocs., Honolulu, 1964-68; dir. info. City and County Honolulu, 1968-70; v.p. community affairs Heftel Broadcasting, Honolulu, 1970-74; v.p. spl. projects Cole & Weber, Seattle, 1974-85; pres. John Kernell Mktg. Communications, Seattle, 1985—. Served to lt. USN, 1955-58. Mem. Pub. Relations Soc. Am. (past v.p.), Mktg. Communications Execs. Internat. Home and Office: 2300 E Mercer St Seattle WA 98112

KERNER, JEREMIAH WADSWORTH, radiologist; b. N.Y.C., Sept. 8, 1910; s. Sigmund S. and Rose S. (Seligman) K.; student U. Ga., 1934; B.S., Duke U., 1934, M.D., 1937; m. Jeannette Victoria Herman, Jan. 20, 1939; children—Jeffrey S., Jordan R. Intern, Los Angeles County Hosp., 1937-39, resident, 1940-43, attending radiologist, 1946-71; radiologist, chief staff West Covina (Calif.) Hosp., 1960-83; assoc. clin. prof. U. So. Calif. Med. Sch., Los Angeles, 1937-65. Bd. dirs. Am. Cancer Soc., San Gabriel Valley br.; mem. com. admissions Duke U. Med. Sch., 1950-76. Served to lt. col., M.C., AUS, 1943-46. Fellow Am. Coll. Radiology; Mem. AMA, Am. Bd. Radiology, Radiol. Soc. N.Am., Calif. Med. Assn., Los Angeles County Med. Assn., Calif. Radiol. Soc., Phi Delta Epsilon. Clubs: So. Hills Country, Industry Hills Country. Office: 725 S Orange Ave West Covina CA 91790

KERNODLE, UNA MAE, educator; b. Jackson, Tenn., Mar. 4, 1947; d. James G. and Mary E. (McLemore) Sikes. B.S. in Home Econs., U. Tenn., 1969; M.Edn., U. Alaska, 1974. Tchr., head dept. vocat. edn. and electives Chugiak High Sch., Anchorage; instr. Anchorage Community Coll.; edn. cons. State of Alaska, Anchorage Talent Bank; presenter Gov.'s Conf. on Child Abuse, Alaska Vocat. Edn. Assn. Conf. Active Women's Resource Ctr.; state officer Alaska Home Econs. Mem. Am. Home Econs. Assn., Anchorage Assn. Edn. Young Children, NEA, Am. Vocat. Assn. Democrat. Baptist. Office: Chugiak High School PO Box 218 Eagle River AK 99577

KERR, BAINE PERKINS, JR., lawyer, writer; b. Houston, June 23, 1946; s. Baine Perkins and Mildred Pickett (Caldwell) K.; m. Cynthia Anne Carlisle; children—Dara, Baine. B.A., Stanford U., 1968; M.A., U. Denver, 1976, J.D., 1979. Bar: Colo. 1979, U.S. Dist. Ct. (Colo.) 1979, U.S. Ct. Appeals 1979. Editor-in-chief Place Mag., Palo Alto, Calif. 1971-74; ptnr. Hutchinson, Black, Hill & Cook, Boulder, 1979—; fiction writer. Active Nat. Wildlife Fedn., Sierra Club. Nat. Endowment Arts fellow 1983; work appeared in Houghton Mifflin Co. Best American Short Stories of 1977. Mem. ABA, Colo. Bar Assn., Boulder County Bar Assn. (co-chmn. civil litigation com. 1983). Democrat. Author: Jumping Off Place, 1981; contbr. numerous short stories and articles to periodicals and literary jours.; contbr. legal articles to law reviews. Home: 411 Spruce Boulder CO 80302

KERR, CHARLES GIESE, mechanical engineer; b. Oct. 26, 1956; s. Charles Hodges and Margareta (Giese) K. AS in Engring., Mesa Coll., 1978; BSME, U. Wyo., 1981. Sr. draftsman Adolph Coors Corp., Golden, Colo., 1978-79; engr., architect Stearns-Roger Engring., Denver, 1981-83; mech. engr. Sinclair (Wyo.) Oil Corp., 1983-85; project engr. Amoco Oil Corp., Casper, Wyo., 1985—. Local chmn. Muscular Dystrophy Assn. Telethon, Carbon County, Wyo., 1984, Amoco Fire Brigade. Mem. ASME, Instrument Soc. Am., Jaycees (local sec. 1984-86, v.p. 1986—, pres. 1987—), Am. Heart Assn., Alumni Assn. U. Wyo. Republican. Lutheran. Club: Casper Social. Avocations: racquetball, skiing, weightlifting, reading, photography. Home: 4500 S Poplar #202 Casper WY 82601 Office: Amoco Oil Corp PO Box 160 Casper WY 82602

KERR, EMILY SUSAN, clinical social worker; b. Eng., July 3, 1957; came to U.S., 1959; d. Jerry and Shirley Forsch; m. Steven James Kerr, Mar. 16, 1980. Student, U. Calif.-San Diego, La Jolla; BSW, San Diego State U., 1979; MSW, Calif. State U., Sacramento, 1982. Lic. clin. social worker, Calif. Therapist Sacramento Child Sexual Abuse Treament Ctr., 1982-84; med. social worker Nursing Services Inst., Sacramento, 1983-84; psychiat. social worker Stanford Home for Children, Sacramento, 1983-84; clin. social worker Orange County (Calif.) Mental Health Assn., Mission Viejo, 1984—; also private practice Auburn, 1984—; clin. program dir. Equinox Ctr., Auburn, Calif., 1983-84. Active Orange County Sexual Assault Network, Orange, 1985—, So. Orange County Task Force for Child Abuse Prevention, El Toro, 1986—. Mem. Nat. Assn. Social Workers, AAUW, Alpha Phi Alumni Assn. Avocations: sports, crafts, reading. Office: 26302 E La Paz #215 Mission Viejo CA 92691

KERR, JAMES WILFRID, artist; b. N.Y.C., Aug. 7, 1897; s. James Fairbairn and Leah M. (Galer) K.; grad. Poppenhusen Inst., 1914, N.Y. Sch. Fine and Applied Arts, 1923; m. Rose R. Netzorg, June 24, 1922; children: Andra Gail (dec.), Paul F. (adopted); m. 2d, Mary N. Wenzel, Aug. 27, 1980. Dir., Art Summer Sch., Detroit, 1923-24; artist, lectr., art adminstr., 1923—; painter in oils, tchr.; one-man and group shows include: Galeria Del Sol, Allied Artists Am., NAD, Am. Vets. Soc., N.J. Painters and Sculptors Soc., Carnegie Inst. Pitts., 1949 (by invitation), Conn. Acad. Fine Arts, Davenport (Iowa) Mus., Houston Mus., Irvington (N.J.) Mus., Norfolk Mus. Arts and Scis., Dialists Exhibit, N.J. Artists, Newark Mus., Ridgewood, N.J., Salmagundi Club, N.Y.C., Delgado Mus., New Orleans, Art U.S.A., Madison Sq. Garden, N.Y.C., 1958, Richmond Mus., Artists Equity Assn. show Botts Meml. Hall, Albuquerque, 48th-50th Fiesta shows at Mus. Fine Arts, Santa Fe, Springville, Utah, 1962-63, 1st Air Force Acad. Exhbn., 1962-63, Juried Arts Nat. Exhbn., Tyler, Tex., 1963, Western Mich. U., Kalamazoo, 1983; represented in permanent collections: Mus. City N.Y., Joslyn Art Mus., Omaha, Newark Mus., Mus. Albuquerque, Fla. So. Coll., Lakeland, N.Mex. State Fair, Fergusson Library, Albuquerque, Waldwick (N.J.) Elem. Sch., Western Mich. U. Trustee, Mus. Albuquerque. Recipient awards, prizes N.J. State Exhibit, Montclair, 1943 (hon. award); NAD, 1945 (1st Altman prize); Plainfield (N.J.) Art Assn. (hon. award), 1946; prize Oil, Morristown (N.J.) Art Assn.; Irvington Art and Mus. Assn., 1st prize in Oil, 1948, 49; Ridgewood (N.J.) Art Assn., 1st prize Oil, 1948; Art Council N.J., 2d Oil prize, 1948; Am. Vets. Soc. Artists purchase award, 1951; Ridgewood (N.J.) Art Assn. (hon. award), 1952; citation Fla. So. Coll., Lakeland, 1952; 1st prize 50th Fiesta Show, Mus. N.Mex., 1963; purchase prize N.Mex. State Fair, 1963, grand award, 1964; silver medal Am. Vets. Soc. Artists, 1963; prizes Ouray County Ann. Exhbn., 1964, State Fair, 1966; The Rose M. Kerr and James W. Kerr Found. named in his honor at Western Mich. U. Served with USN, World War I. Mem. Allied Artists Am. (treas. 1952, mem. jury awards oil painting 1958, dir. 1955, chmn. membership com. 1955), Internat. Assn. Plastic Arts (Joint com. for Am. participation), Assn. Artists N.J. (dir.), Artists Equity Assn. (chmn. nat. mus. com., co-chmn. nat. artists-museums com. 1958, nat. treas. 1959), Dialists (N.J.), Grand Central Galleries (artist-mem.), Irvington (N.J.) Art and Mus. Assn. (artist mem.), N.J. Soc. Painters and Sculptors, New Mexican Art League (dir. 1966), Ridgewood Art Center (past pres.), Salmagundi Club (artist mem.), Art Assn. New Orleans, Artists Equity Assn. (nat. treas. 1952-55), Am. Vets. Soc. Artists (pres. 1958-60), Albuquerque Mus. Assn. (pres. 1967-68, dir.), Smithsonian Instn. Archives Am. Art, Pres.'s Club Western Mich. U. Co-artist, author: Historic Design for Modern Use; also articles on art for School Arts mag. and Everyday Art mag. Lectr. women's clubs, high schs., colls., univs., art clubs and assns. on painting, graphic arts, modern movements in arts, and psychology related to art, radio and TV. Address: 7017 Bellrose Ave NE Albuquerque NM 87110

KERR, KLEON HARDING, educator, state senator; b. Plain City, Utah, Apr. 26, 1911; s. William A. and Rosemond (Harding) K.; Asso. Sci., Weber Coll., 1936; B.A., George Washington U., 1939; M.S., Utah State U., Logan, 1946; m. Katherine Abbott, Mar. 15, 1941; children—Kathleen, William A., Rebecca Rae. Tchr., Bear River High Sch., Tremonton, Utah, 1940-56, prin. jr. high sch., 1956-60, prin. Bear River High Sch., 1960-71; city justice Tremonton, 1941-46; sec. to Senator Arthur V. Watkins, 1947. Mayor, Tremonton City, 1948-53; mem. Utah Local Govt. Survey Commn., 1954-55; mem. Utah Ho. of Reps., 1953-56; mem. Utah State Senate, 1957-64, chmn. appropriation com., 1959—, majority leader, 1963; mem. Utah Legis. Council. Dist. dir. vocat. edn. Box Elder Sch. Dist. Recipient Alpha Delta Kappa award for outstanding contbn. to edn., 1982, award for outstanding contbrs. to edn. and govt. Theta Chpt. Alpha Beta Kappa, 1982, Excellence Achieved in Promotion of Tourism award; named Tourism Ambassador of Month, 1986. Mem. NEA, Utah, Box Elder edn. assns., Nat., Utah secondary schs. prins. assns., Bear River Valley. C. of C. (sec., mgr. 1955-58), Phi Delta Kappa. Mem. Ch. of Jesus Christ of Latter-day Saints. Lion, Kiwanian. Author: (poetry) Open My Eyes 1983, Trouble In the Amen Corner, 1985; We Remember, 1983; (history) Those Who Served Box Elder County, 1984, Those Who Served Tremonton City, 1985. Home: Box 246 Tremonton UT 84337

KERRI, KENNETH DONALD, civil engineering educator; b. Napa, Calif., Apr. 25, 1934; s. Kenneth R. and Eunice E. (Beck) K.; m. Judith Reeves, Aug. 22, 1958; children: Christopher, Kathleen. BSCE, Oreg. State U., 1956, PhDCE, 1965; MS in Sanitary Engring., U. Calif., Berkeley, 1959. Registered profl. engr., Calif.; diplomate Am. Acad. Environ. Engring. Asst. sanitary engr. USPHS, San Francisco, 1956-58; asst. prof. Sacramento State U., 1959-63; assoc. prof. Calif. State U., Sacramento, 1963-68, project dir., 1965—, prof., 1968—; cons. in field, Sacramento, 1960—. Author: Operation of Waste Water Treatment Plants, 1980, Water Treatment Plant Operation, 1983, Water Supply System Operation, 1983. Fellow ASCE; mem. Nat. Environ. Tng. Assn. (pres. 1979-80, Trainer of Yr., 1982), Assn. Bds. Cert. (pres. 1983), Calif. Water Pollution Control Assn. (pres. 1983-84), Water Pollution Control Fedn. (hon.). Office: Calif State U 6000 J St Sacramento CA 95819

KERSEY, TERRY L(EE), astronautical engineer; b. San Francisco, June 9, 1947; s. Ida Helen (Schmeichel) K. Houseman, orderly Mills Meml. Hosp., San Mateo, Calif., 1965-68; security guard Lawrence Security, San Francisco, 1973-74; electronic engr. technician McCulloch Corp., Los Angeles, 1977; warehouseman C.C.H. Computax Co., Redondo Beach, Calif., 1977-78; material expeditor/planner Airesearch Mfg. Co., Torrance, Calif., 1978—. Participant 9th Space Simulation conf., Los Angeles, 1977, 31st Internat. Astronautical Fedn. Congress., Tokyo, 1980, Unispace 1982 for the U.N., Vienna.Served as sgt. USAF, 1968-72, Vietnam. Mem. AIAA (mem. space systems tech. com. 1981—, mem. aerodynamics com. 1980—, Wright Flyer Project Aerodynamics com. 1980—), Nat. Space Inst., Am. Astronautical Soc., The Planetary Soc., Internat. L5 Soc., Ind. Space Research Group. Zen Buddhist. Avocations: computers, sports, astronomy.

KERSTEN, TIMOTHY WAYNE, economics educator, consultant; b. Algona, Iowa, Nov. 18, 1944; s. Harold Arthur and Marcella (Heger) K.; m. Carol Ann Oliver, Dec. 22, 1967; one child, Jeffrey Alexander. BA, Calif. State U., Sacramento, 1967; MA, U. Oreg., 1971, PhD, 1973. Asst. prof. econs. Calif. Poly. State U., San Luis Obispo, 1971-75, assoc. prof., 1976-80, prof., 1981—; chmn. Calif. State U. Acad. Senate, San Luis Obispo, 1980-82; mem. Calif. State U. state-wide Acad. Senate, 1983—, chmn. faculty affairs com., 1984—. Author: Instructors Guide to Accompany Contemporary Economics, 1975. Mem. citizens adv. com. San Luis Obispo City Council, 1976-77. Fellow U.S. Govt., 1969-71. Mem. Am. Econ. Assn., Western Econ. Assn., Omicron Delta Epsilon, Phi Mu Alpha Sinfonia. Avocations: reading, concert going, skiing. Office: Calif State Poly U Dept Econs San Luis Obispo CA 93407

KERSTETTER, JAMES DAVID, energy resource specialist; b. Darby, Pa., Dec. 27, 1941; s. Guy Raymond and Elizabeth Lois (Simister) K.; m. Judy Louise Dunnuck, Feb. 26, 1977; children: Michael, Laresa. BS, Drexel U., 1964; MS, Yale U., 1968, MPhil, 1969, PhD, 1970. Mass spectroscopist U. Wash., Seattle, 1974-77; program mgr. Nat. Ctr. Appropriate Tech., Butte, Mont., 1977-80, Calif. Energy Commn., Sacramento, 1980-83, Wash. State Energy Office, Olympia, 1983—; mem. policy rev. com. Dept. Energy, Washington, 1978; cons. Calif. Energy Commn., Sacramento, 1979-84. Mem. Am. Chem. Soc., Phi Kappa Phi. Avocations: hiking, camping, beach combing. Home: 5113 Brenner Rd Olympia WA 98502 Office: Wash State Energy Office 809 Legion Way SE Olympia WA 98504

KERSTING, IRENE HELEN, museum administrator; b. Pueblo, Colo., Jan. 8, 1942; d. Henry M. and Lela (Atencio) Sanchez; m. James Edward Kersting, May 28, 1961 (widowed Mar. 1978); children: Lloyd A., Elena L.; m. Albert V. Chavez, Oct. 18, 1986; 1 stepchild, Alejandra V. Chavez. Student, Western Bus. Coll., 1960-61. Asst. dir. Albuquerque Mus., 1983—. Mem. N.Mex. Assn. Museums, Mountain-Plains Mus. Conf., Bus. and Profl. Womens Club (legis. chmn. 1984). Democrat. Roman Catholic. Avocations: jazzworks, Spanish dancing, reading, activities with children. Home: 1449 Saunders Rd SW Albuquerque NM 87105 Office: Albuquerque Mus 2000 Mountain Rd NW Albuquerque NM 87104

KERZIE, TED L., JR., fine arts educator; b. Tacoma, May 10, 1943; s. Ted L. Sr. and Frances (Chesky) K.; m. Diane Vines; children: Kristin, Jennifer, Michael. BA, Wash. State U., 1966; MFA with honors, Claremont Grad. Sch., 1972. Asst. prof. fine arts Claremont (Calif.) Grad. Sch., 1973-76; assoc. prof. Calif. State U., Bakersfield, 1976-86, prof., 1986—; artist Cirrus Gallery, Los Angeles, 1980—; pres. Info-Sell, Los Angeles, 1986—. Served to capt. USAF, 1966-70;. Home: 2606 Purdue Los Angeles CA 90064

KESKINEN, S. KAY, computer systems analyst; b. Wadena, Minn., Oct. 8, 1948; d. Ervin John and Lila Marie (Lindstrom) K. BA, U. Minn., 1970; postgrad., Mankato State U., 1970-71, U. Idaho, 1971-73. Computer programmer U. Idaho, Moscow, 1973-77, programmer, analyst, 1977-79, systems analyst, 1979—; lectr. U. Idaho, 1980, 83, 86; bd. dirs. Coll. Univ. Machine Records Conf., 1983—, v.p., 1986—. Mem. City Police Chief Search com., Moscow, 1981, Moscow City Sch. Dist. Facilities Planning Coms., 1983-85; chairperson HUD Grant Citizens Adv. Bd., Moscow, 1985—; regional co-dir. Idaho Commn. Women's Programs, Boise, Idaho, 1979-85; vice chairperson Latah County Dem. Cen. Com., Moscow, 1985—. Named the Idaho Outstanding Young Women of Am., 1981. Mem. Coll. Univ. Machine Records Conf. (bd. dirs. 1983—, v.p. 1986—), Friends of the Library (pres. 1975-78). Lutheran. Avocations: photography, reading, horseshoe pitching. Office: U Idaho Computer Services Moscow ID 83843

KESSARIS, ELIZABETH JOLLEY, social worker; b. Mexico, Mo., Dec. 9, 1916; James Frank and Florence Leola (York) Jolley; m. Constatine Kessaris, May 18, 1961. AB, Lindenwood Coll., 1938; MSW, Smith Coll., 1947. Psychiat. social worker VA Hosp., Topeka, Kans., 1947-49; caseworker family service bur. Salvation Army, Bklyn., 1949-51; sr. caseworker Youth Consultation Service, Newark, 1951-52; supr. student unit Office of Commnr. of Welfare, Hartford, Conn., 1952-54; dist. rep., child welfare worker Alaska Dept. Pub. Welfare, Juneau, 1954-57; supr. social work Beth El Hosp., Bklyn., 1957; sr. psychiat. social worker N.Y. State Dept. Mental Hygiene, 1957-63, Calif. State Dept. Mental Hygiene, Oakland, 1963-64; asst. dir. Contra Costa County Social Services, Concord, Calif., 1966-76; child welfare specialist Eastern Nev. Tribal Social Service, Elko, 1976-78; child welfare worker Jewish Family and Children's Services, Pheonix, 1979; social worker Bur. Indian Affairs, Carson City, Nev., 1979—. Mem. ACLU. Club: Am. Duplicate Bridge (Elko). Avocations: knitting, reading, gambling. Home: 330 W Nye Ln #40 Carson City NV 89701 Office: Bur Indian Affairs 1300 S Curry St Carson City NV 89701

KESSELRING, JOHN PAUL, mechanical engineering executive; b. Detroit, Mar. 26, 1940; s. Paul Herbert and Gwendolyn (Currie) K.; m. Jane Edwards, July 23, 1966; children: Joan Paula, Thomas Max. BS in Aero. Engring., U. Mich., 1961; MS in Aero. and Astronautics, Stanford U., 1962, PhD in Aero. and Astronautics, 1968. Registered profl. mech. engr., Calif., Tenn. Staff engr. Rocketdyne div. N. Am. Aviation, Canoga Park, Calif., 1962-63, mem. tech. staff, 1967-69; asst. prof. mech. and aerospace engring. U. Tenn., Knoxville, 1969-74; project mgr. Acurex Corp., Mountain View, Calif., 1974-82; v.p. Alzeta Corp., Santa Clara, Calif., 1982-86; sr. project mgr. Electric Power Research Inst., Palo Alto, Calif., 1986—; cons. U.S. Army Research Office, Durham, N.C., 1972-73; lectr. Stanford (Calif.) U., 1977. Patentee in field; contbr. articles to profl. jours. Treas. Mountain View Little League, 1982-84, Mountain View Youth Baseball, 1985—. Fellow N. Am. Aviation, 1963-67; named Outstanding Young Tchr. U. Tenn. Coll. Engring., 1971. Mem. ASME, AIAA, Combustion Inst. (exec. com. 1985—). Methodist. Club: Camera of Los Altos (pres. 1983-84). Avocations: photography, hiking, travel. Home: 279 Apricot Ln Mountain View CA 94040 Office: Electric Power Research Inst 3412 Hillview Ave Palo Alto CA 94303

KESSLER, A. D., property development company executive, financial consultant; b. N.Y.C., May 1, 1923; s. Morris William and Belle Miriam (Pastor) K.; m. Ruth Schwartz, Nov. 20, 1944; children: Brian Lloyd, Judd Stuart, Earl Vaughn. Student U. Newark, 1940-41, Rutgers U., 1941-42, 46, Albright Coll., 1942, Newark Coll. Engring., 1946; MBA, Kensington U., 1976, PhD in Mgmt. and Behavioral Psychology, 1977. Sr. cert. rev. appraiser; cert. exchangor. Pvt. practice real estate, ins. and bus. brokerage, N.J., Pa., Fla., N.Y., Nev., Calif., Hong Kong, 1946; pres. Armor Corp. , 1947-68; pres. Folding Carton Corp., Am., N.Y.C., 1958-68; exec. v.p. Henry

Schindall Assocs., N.Y.C., 1966-67; tax rep. Calif. State Bd. Equalization, 1968-69; aviation cons. transp. div. Calif., Dept. Aeros., also pub. info. officer; 1969-71; FAA Gen. Aviation Safety Counselor; broker, mgr. La Costa (Calif.) Sales Corp., 1971-75; chmn. bd. Profl. Ednl. Found., 1975—, Timeshare Resorts Internat., 1975—, Interex, Leucadia, Calif., 1975-82, The Kessler Orgn., Rancho Santa Fe, Calif., 1975—, The Kessler Fin. Group, Fin. Ind. Inst., 1977—; pres. Ednl. Video Inst., 1978—, Fin. Planning Inst., 1975—; treas., exec. bd. dirs. Nat. Challenge Com. on Disability, 1983—; dir. Practice Mgmt. Cons. Abacus Data Systems, 1984—; publisher, editor in chief Creative Real Estate Mag., 1975—; publisher Creative Real Estate Mag. of Australia and New Zealand; chmn. bd. The Brain Trust, Rancho Santa Fe, Calif., 1977—; cons. and lectr. in field. Scoutmaster Orange Mountain council Boy Scouts Am., 1955-62; harbor master N.J. Marine Patrol, 1958-67; dep. sheriff, Essex County, N.J., 1951-65. Served with USAF, 1942-45. Decorated D.F.C., Air medal, Purple Heart; named to French Legion of Honor, Order of Lafayette. Mem. Am. Soc. Editors and Publishers, Author's Guild, Internat. Platform Assn., Nat. Speakers Assn., Nat. Press Photographers Assn., Guild Assn. Airport Execs., Aviation and Space Writers Assn., Internat. Exchangors Assn. (founder), Nat. Press Club, Overseas Press Club. Clubs: La Costa Country, Cuyamaca, Rancho Santa Fe Country. Lodges: Masons, Shriners. Author: A Fortune At Your Feet, 1981, How You Can Get Rich, Stay Rich and Enjoy Being Rich, 1981, Financial Independence, 1987, The Profit, 1987; editor: The Real Estate News Observer, 1975—; fin. editor API, 1978—; fin. columnist Money Matters, 1986—; producer (movies) The Flight of the Cobra, Rena, We Have Your Daughters, Music Row; speaker for radio and TV as The Real Estate Answerman, 1975—; host (radio and TV show) Ask Mr. Money. Home: Box 1144 Rancho Santa Fe CA 92067

KESSLER, JOHN OTTO, physicist, educator; b. Vienna, Austria, Nov. 26, 1928; came to U.S., 1940, naturalized, 1946; s. Jacques and Alice Blanca (Neuhut) K.; m. Eva M. Bondy, Sept. 9, 1950; children: Helen J., Steven J. A.B., Columbia U., 1949, Ph.D., 1953. With RCA Corp., Princeton, N.J., 1952-66; sr. mem. tech. staff RCA Corp., 1960-66, mgr. grad. recruiting, 1964-66; prof. physics U. Ariz., Tucson, 1966—; Vis. research asso. Princeton, 1962-64; sr. vis. fellow, vis. prof. physics U. Leeds, Eng., 1972-73; vis. prof. Technische Hogeschool Delft, Netherlands, spring 1979; Fulbright fellow dept. applied math. and theoretical physics Cambridge U., Eng., 1983-84. Contbr. articles to tech. jours.; patentee in field. Fellow AAAS; mem. Phycological Soc. Am., Am. Phys. Soc., Phi Beta Kappa. Home: 2740 E Camino La Zorrela Tucson AZ 85718 Office: U Ariz Physics Dept Bldg 81 Tucson AZ 85721

KESSLER, MARCIA SUE, consultant, trainer, private therapist; b. Cleve., Sept. 30, 1947; d. Max and Guta (Small) K. B.S., U. Cin., 1970; M.S., U. Oreg., 1981. Tchr., Shaker Heights (Ohio) City Schs., 1971-72; with juvenile delinquency prevention project-youth devel. program Case Western-Res. U., Cleve., 1973-75; with Women's Growth Coop., Cleve., 1976-79; guest lectr. Gestalt Inst. Cleve., 1978-79; dir. crisis services Free Med. Clinic, Cleve., 1971-79; co-leader Eugene (Oreg.) Cancer Support Group, 1980-81; dir. scheduling Ross Anthony for Congress, Eugene, 1981; coordinator/trainer vols. Womenspace-Battered Women's Shelter, Eugene, 1982-86 ; therapist Hospice of Lane County, 1980-82; cons. child abuse, Domestic Violence Helpline, 1983-86 ; presenter Oreg. Coalition Against Sexual and Domestic Violence Conf., 1982, Oreg. Crisis Prevention Workshop, 1985, numerous other workshops. Trustee Community Health and Edn. Clinic, 1979-81; cons. Community Sharing Helpline, Cottage Grove, Oreg., 1984-85, Vol. Action Ctr., Eugene, 1986—; specialist in vol. systems Crisis Intervention Suicide Prevention, 1986—; active Students for a Democratic Soc., 1966-73. Mem. Am. Personnel and Guidance Assn., Assn. Humanistic Psychology, Phi Sigma Sigma. Democrat. Home: 991 W 12th St Eugene OR 97402 Office: 1163 Willamette #7 Eugene OR 97401

KESSNER, LYNN SHERRELL, lawyer, educator; b. Rochester, N.Y., Nov. 2, 1940; d. Leo P. and Elsie Beeman (Trickey) Sherrell; m. Arthur B. Kessner, Apr. 17, 1962 (div. Dec. 1974); 1 child, Gawain. BA, U. Calif., Berkeley, 1963; MA, San Francisco State U., 1978; JD, Golden Gate U., 1983. Bar: Calif. 1983, U.S. Dist. Ct. (no. dist.) Calif. 1983, U.S. Ct. Appeals (9th cir.) 1984. Tchr. Berkeley Unified Sch. Dist., 1966-77; assoc. Law Offices J.J. Duryea, San Francisco, 1983-86; adj. prof. Golden Gate U., San Francisco, 1983—; assoc. Law Offices Weltin, Van Dam & Flores, San Francisco, Calif., 1986—; instr. Russian Berkeley Adult Sch., 1975-78. Editor (poetry) The Laurentian, 1960-61; writer numerous poems. Mem. Calif. Trial Lawyers Assn., Lawyers Alliance for Nuclear Arms Control, Queens Bench, Phi Delta Epsilon. Club: Olympic Circle Sailing. Home: 2141 Emerson St Berkeley CA 94705 Office: 444 Market St Suite 930 San Francisco CA 94111

KESTER, RANDY STUART, lawyer; b. Payson, Utah, Dec. 18, 1953; s. Everett Solomon and Ruth Janet (Bowers) K.; m. Connie Rae Spencer, Mar. 31, 1976; children: James Ryan, Lindsey. AAS, Utah Tech. Coll., 1978; BA, Brigham Young U., 1980, JD, 1984. Bar: Utah 1984. Paralegal Howard, Lewis and Petersen, Provo, Utah, 1978-81, assoc., 1984—; adj. instr. Utah Tech. Coll., Orem, 1981-82, 85-86. Lt. gov. Utah Intercollegiate Assembly, 1978-79. Served with U.S. Army, 1972-75, Korea. Named one of Outstanding Young Men of Am., U.S. Jaycees, 1982, 85. Mem. ABA, Assn. Trial Lawyers Am., Utah Bar Assn. (vol. lawyers project 1985—), Utah Trial Lawyers Assn. Lodge: Lions. Avocation: collecting baseball cards. Office: Young & Kester 101 East 200 S Springville UT 84663

KESTER, WILLIAM DAVIS, drama educator; b. Spokane, Wash., May 23, 1939; s. Herbert Gordon and Dorothy Alice (Brown) K. BA, San Francisco State U., 1963, MA, 1966. Instr. drama Yakima (Wash.) Valley Coll., 1965-67; instr. drama San Jose (Calif.) City Coll., 1967—, asst. dean humanities, 1986—; actor various cos., N.Y.C. and San Jose, 1978—. Pres. faculty senate San Jose City Coll., 1974-75. Mem. Am. Theater Assn., AFTRA. Office: San Jose City Coll 2100 Moorpark Ave San Jose CA 95128

KETCHERSID, WAYNE LESTER, JR., hospital laboratory administrator, chemist, consultant; b. Seattle, Oct. 16, 1946; s. Wayne Lester and Hazel May (Greene) K.; m. Wilette LaVerne Mautz, Oct. 6, 1972; 1 son, William Les. Staff technologist Tacoma Gen. Hosp., 1978-79, chemistry supr., 1979-81, head chemistry, 1981-83; head chemistry Multicare Med. Ctr., 1984-86, mgr., 1986—. Mem. Nat. Republican Com. Served with U.S. Army, 1966-68. William E. Slaughter Found. scholar, 1975-76. Mem. Am. Assn. Clin. Chemistry, Am. Hosp. Assn., Am. Soc. Med. Tech. (cert.; Region IX adminstrn. chmn. 1984—), Wash. State Soc. Med. Tech. (chmn. biochemistry sect. 1983-86 dist. pres. 1986—, cert. merit 1983, 84, 86), N.W. Med. lab. Symposium (chmn. 1986). Lutheran. Contbr. articles to profl. jours. Office: Multicare Med Ctr 315 S K St Tacoma WA 98405

KETCHUM, DANA EDGAR, JR., electronic manufacturing company executive; b. Pasadena, Calif., Mar. 27, 1939; s. Dana Edgar and Margaret I. Ketchum; m. Laura J. Spivey, Apr. 8, 1978. B.A., Colo. Coll., 1963; M.B.A., U. So. Calif., 1976. Contract adminstr. Lockheed Calif., Burbank, 1966-69; mgr. contracts Lockheed Internat., Los Angeles, 1969-73, project dir., 1973-76; mktg. assoc. Dart Industries, Los Angeles, 1976-80; corp. mktg. mgr. Abbott Transistor Lab Inc., Burbank, Calif., 1980—. Served to 1st lt., arty. U.S. Army, 1963-65. Mem. Am. Mktg. Assn., U. So. Calif. Alumni Assn., U. So. Calif. M.B.A.s, Past Officers and Dirs. Assn., Los Angeles Jaycees, (advisor 1970—, bd. dirs. 1973), Power Sources Mfrs. Assn. (steering com.), Beta Gamma Sigma. Office: Abbott Transistor Lab Inc 639 S Glenwood Pl Burbank CA 91506

KETCHUM, MILO SMITH, civil engineer; b. Denver, Mar. 8, 1910; s. Milo Smith and Esther (Beatty) K.; m. Gretchen Allenbach, Feb. 28, 1944; children: David Milo, Marcia Anne, Matthew Phillip, Mark Allen. B.S., U. Ill., 1931, M.S., 1932; D.Sc. (hon.), U. Colo., 1976. Asst. prof. Case Sch. Applied Sci., Cleve., 1937-44; engr. F.G. Browne, Marion, Ohio, 1944-45; owner, operator Milo S. Ketchum, Cons. Engrs., Denver, 1945-52; partner, prin. Ketchum, Konkel, Barrett, Nickel & Austin, Cons. Engrs. and predecessor firm, Denver, 1952—; prof. civil engring. U. Conn., Storrs, 1967-78; emeritus U. Conn., 1978—; mem. Progressive Architecture Design Awards Jury, 1958, Am. Inst. Steel Constrn. Design Awards Jury, 1975, James F. Lincoln Arc Welding Found. Design Awards Jury, 1977; Stanton Walker lectr. U. Md., 1966. Author: Handbook of Standard Structural Details for Buildings, 1956; editor-in-chief Structural Engineering Practice, 1981-84; contbr. engring. articles to tech. mags. and jours. Recipient Disting. Alumnus award U. Ill., 1979. Fellow Am. Concrete Inst. (hon. mem.; dir., Turner medal 1966), ASCE (pres. Colo. sect., hon.), Instn. Structural Engrs. (London), Am. Cons. Engrs. Council; mem. Nat. Acad. Engring., Am. Soc. Engring. Edn., Internat. Assn. Shell and Space Structures, Structural Engrs. Assn. Colo. (pres.), Cons. Engrs. Council Colo. (pres.), Old Saybrook (Conn.) Hist. Soc., Sigma Xi, Tau Beta Pi, Chi Epsilon, Phi Kappa Phi, Alpha Delta Phi. Club: North Cove Yacht. Home: 165 Estes St Denver CO 80226

KETTEL, EDWARD JOSEPH, oil co. ofcl.; b. N.Y.C., Sept. 13, 1925; s. Harold J. and Evelyn M. (Melbourne) K.; student St. John's U., 1943; B.A., St. Francis Coll., 1949; M.A., Columbia U., 1953; m. Janet M. Johnson, Nov. 27, 1952; children—Dorothy A., David A. Ins. mgr. Arabian Am. Oil Co., 1950-56, Ethyl Corp., 1956-65; asst. treas. Atlantic Richfield Co., Los Angeles, 1965-85, asst. treas., Chevron Corp., San Francisco, 1985—; chmn. bd. Oil Ins., Ltd.; pres. Greater Pacific, Ltd.; dir. Am. S.S. Owners Mut. Protection and Indemnity Assn., Inc., Internat. Tanker Indemnity Assn., Ltd. Served with inf. AUS, 1943-46. Decorated Bronze Star, Purple Heart with oak leaf cluster. Mem. Am. Petroleum Inst., Mfrs. Chem. Assn., Nat. Fire Protection Assn., Risk and Ins. Mgmt. Soc. Clubs: N.Y. Athletic, Los Angeles Athletic, Palos Verdes Country, Jonathan (Los Angeles), Commercial (San Francisco), Colony Golf (Half Moon Bay, Calif.). Office: 225 Bush St San Francisco CA 94104

KETTENHOFEN, BILL WYATT, accounting firm executive; b. Evanston, Ill., June 11, 1932; s. Leonard James and Gwendolyn Nancy (Wyatt) K.; m. Janet Seward, Aug. 20, 1957; children—Colleen, Alison. B.S. in Bus. Adminstrn., UCLA, 1954; M.S. in Mgmt., Calif. State U.-Long Beach, 1970. Sales rep. Mobil Oil Corp., Portland, Oreg., 1956-62; mgr. adminstrn., McDonnell Douglas, Huntington Beach, Calif., 1962-70, Conn. Gen. Life Ins., Los Angeles, 1974-75, Hill, Farrer & Burrill, Los Angeles, 1976-79; v.p. Am. Investment Counseling Co., Los Angeles, 1970-74; dir. adminstrn. Price Waterhouse, Los Angeles, 1979—; treas., dir. Am. Investment Counseling Fund, Los Angeles, 1970-74. Treas., mem. exec. com. Calif. Mus. Sci. and Industry Adv. Bd., Los Angeles, 1984; precinct capt. Young Republicans, Los Angeles, 1964. Mem. AIM, Phi Kappa Phi. Club: San Marino City. Home: 1317 Oxford Rd San Marino CA 91108

KEVANE, RAYMOND A., career consultant, management consultant; b. Rembrandt, Iowa, Dec. 18, 1928; s. Michael and Sarah A. (Distel) K.; m. Lillian A. Schiltz, July 26, 1972; children—Karen, Mark, Mary. B.A., Loras Coll., Dubuque, Iowa, 1950; S.T.L., Gregorian U., Rome, 1954; Doctorate, Lateran U., Rome, 1957. Adminstr. social programs and assistance to disadvantaged projects, 1957-71; chief cons., assoc. dir. J. Frederick Marcy & Assocs., Portland, Oreg., 1972-78; pres., chief cons. R.A. Kevane & Assocs., Inc., Portland, 1978—. Served to capt. Army N.G., 1959-61. Mem. Am. Assn. for Counseling and Devel., Portland C. of C., Nat. Career Devel. Assn., Oreg. Assn. Personnel Cons. Club: City (Portland). Author: Career Development Manual, 1979; Business Procedure Manual, 1982. Office: 111 SW Columbia Suite 1350 Portland OR 97201

KEVERKAMP, HARRY GEORGE, data processing executive, consultant; b. New Westminster, B.C., Can., Oct. 8, 1954; came to U.S., 1967; s. John Henry and Elisabeth Mary (Heins) K.; m. Pamela Alta McElhaney, Aug. 16, 1975; children: Vanessa Noelle, Amanda Alta, Emma Faye. AA in Applied Sci., Highline Community Coll., 1974. Computer programmer Howard S. Wright Constrn. Co., Seattle, 1974-76; programmer Burlington No. R.R., Seattle, 1976-77, systems analyst, 1977-78; supr. data processing Burlington No. Timberlands, Seattle, 1978-83; personal computer mgr. Plum Creek Timber Co., Seattle, 1983-84; mgr. data processing World Wide Distbrs., Kent, Wash., 1984—; data processing adv. bd. Highline (Wash.) Community Coll., 1986—. vol. firefighter King County Fire Dist. #40, Renton, Wash., 1978-80; advisor Jr. Achievement, Bellevue, Wash., 1978-79; coach girls softball Cascade Vista Athletic Club, Renton, 1980-81. Roman Catholic. Avocations: golf, bicycle riding, chess, tennis. Home: 12905 SE 158th Pl Renton WA 98058 Office: World Wide Distbrs 8211 S 194th Kent WA 98032

KEVLES, DANIEL JEROME, history educator, writer; b. Phila., Mar. 2, 1939; s. David and Anne (Rothstein) K.; m. Bettyann Holtzmann, May 18, 1961; children: Beth Carolyn, Jonathan David. BA in Physics, Princeton U., 1960; postgrad., Oxford U., 1960-61; PhD in History, Princeton U., 1964. From asst. to full prof. of history Calif. Inst. Tech., Pasadena, 1964-86, Koepfli prof. humanities, 1986—; vis. research fellow U. Sussex, Brighton, Eng., 1976; vis. prof. U. Pa., Phila., 1979. Author: The Physicists, 1978 (Nat. Hist. Soc. prize 1979), In the Name of Eugenics, 1985; (mag. series) Annals of Eugenics (Page One award 1985); contbr. articles to The New Yroker, other mags. Charles Warren fellow Harvard U., 1981-82, Ctr. for Advanced Study Behavorial Scis. fellow, 1986-87, Nat. Endowment for Humanities sr. fellow, 1981-82, Guggenheim fellow, 1983. Mem. PEN, Author's Guild, History of Sci. Soc. (council 1980-82, publ. com. 1984—), Orgn. Am. Historians, Am. Hist. Assn., AAAS (chmn. sect. L 1983-85, lectr. 1985), British Soc. History of Sci., Phi Beta Kappa. Democrat. Office: Calif Inst Tech 1201 E California Blvd Pasadena CA 91125

KEY, MARY RITCHIE (MRS. AUDLEY E. PATTON), linguist, author, educator; b. San Diego, Mar. 19, 1924; d. George Lawrence and Iris (Lyons) Ritchie; children: Mary Helen Key Ellis, Harold Hayden Key, Thomas George Key. Student, U. Chgo., summer 1954, U. Mich., 1959; M.A., U. Tex., 1960, Ph.D., 1963; postgrad., UCLA, 1966. Asst. prof. linguistics Chapman Coll., Orange, Calif., 1963-66; asst. prof. linguistics U. Calif., Irvine, 1966-71; assoc. prof. U. Calif., 1971-78, prof., 1978—, chmn. program linguistics, 1969-71, 75-77, 87—; cons. Am. Indian langs., Spanish, in Mexico, 1946-55, S.Am., 1955-62, English dialects, 1968-74, Easter Island, 1975, Calif. Dept. Edn., 1966, 70-75, Center Applied Linguistics, Washington, 1967, 69; lectr. in field. Author: numerous books including Comparative Tacanan Phonology, 1968; Male/Female Language, 1975, Paralanguage and Kinesics, 1975, Nonverbal Communication, 1977, The Grouping of South American Indian Languages, 1979, The Relationship of Verbal and Nonverbal Communication, 1980, Catherine the Great's Linguistic Contribution, 1980, Polynesian and American Linguistic Connections, 1984; founder, editor: newsletter Nonverbal Components of Communication, 1972-76; mem. editorial bd.: Forum Linguisticum, 1976—, Lang. Scis., 1978—, La Linguistique, 1979—; contbr. articles to profl. jours. Recipient Friends of Library Book award, 1976; U. Calif. Regent's grantee, 1974; Fulbright-Hays grantee, 1975; Faculty Research fellow, 1984-85. Mem. Linguistic Soc. Am., Am. Dialect Soc. (exec. council; regional sec. 1974-83), Internat. Reading Assn. (dir. 1968-72), Delta Kappa Gamma (local pres. 1974-76). Office: Program in Linguistics U Calif Irvine CA 92717

KEY, RAMONA THORNTON, health facility administrator; b. Little Rock, Ark., Dec. 13, 1939; s. J.P. and H. Belle (Jones) T.; m. Charles E. Winters, Jan. 21, 1961 (dec. Dec. 1965); children: Lesa Ingram, Kellie Winters, Dale Winters; m. George Trujillo, May 24, 1970 (div. July 1977); 1 child, Melinda Trujillo; m. Dennis Russell Key, May 15, 1982. BS in Psychology, Southwestern Coll., 1963; cert. coronary intensive care, U. Tenn., 1973; postgrad., Memphis State U., 1979-81. Nurse various hosps., 1961-72; dir. personal adjustment ctr. Mental Health and Retardation Ctr., Oxford, Miss., 1972-75; cons. Interagy. Commn.'s Devel. Disabilities Tng. program State of Miss., 1974-75; coordinator for adult acute psychiat. services, liaison with local mental health ctr. Boulder (Colo.) Psychiat. Inst., 1975-77; head nurse behavior modification VA Hosp., Memphis, 1978-81; hosp. supr. Vista Sandia Psychiat. Hosp., Albuquerque, 1981-85, dir. nursing services, 1985—; leader health workshops, Miss., 1974; bd. dirs. Nurse Profl. Standards Bd., VA Med. Ctr., Memphis, 1979-81; mem. faculty U. N.Mex. Coll. Nursing, 1986—. Mem. Am. Nurses Assn., N.Mex. Nurses Assn. (CEU com. 1986—), N.Mex. Orgn. Nurse Execs. (program chmn. 1986). Democrat. Methodist. Home: 6205 La Joya NW Albuquerque NM 87120 Office: Vista Sandia Hosp 501 Alameda Blvd NE Albuquerque NM 87113

KEYES, JAMES BONDURANT, business consultant; b. Des Moines, May 22, 1927; s. Arthur Hyde and Dorothy (Bondurant) K.; B.S., Iowa State U., 1950; M.B.A., Northwestern U., 1951; m. Mary Jane McAfee, July 26, 1957; children—Edward, Jason. Asst. cashier Bank of Am., Los Angeles, 1952-57; profl. bus. cons. Dental Bus. Adminstrn., Laguna Beach, Calif., 1957—. Pres. Laguna Beach Community Chest, 1961-62; treas. Orange County (Calif.) United Way, 1972-74. Treas. Orange County Republican Central Com., 1960-62; pres. Young Reps., 1960-61. Served with AUS, 1945-46. Mem. Acad. Prof. Bus. Cons.'s (pres. 1974-75, 85-87), Soc. Profl. Bus. Cons.'s (pres. 1974-75), Inst. Cert. Profl. Bus. Cons.'s, Inst. Cert. Fin. Planners, Internat. Assn. Fin. Planning, Ankylosing Spondylitis Assn. (v.p. 1986), Delta Upsilon. Episcopalian. Editorial cons. Dental Mgmt. Mag., 1972-80, Dental Econ. Mag., 1980-83. Address: 1125 Emerald Bay Laguna Beach CA 92651

KEYES, WAYNE PORTER, aerospace company executive; b. Oakland, Calif., Sept. 2, 1927; s. William Reed and Ruth Adalaide (Bigelow) K.; m. Helen Jean Padua; children: Leilani, David; children from previous marriage: Nancy Lee, Robert Wayne, Graham Lee, Wanda Claire; stepchildren: Phillip Lawrence Camero, Michael Allen Camero. BS, Coll. Notre Dame, Belmont, Calif., 1971; MS, U. So. Calif., 1974; MS, Stanford U., 1977, PhD, 1982. Enlisted USN, 1945; commd. ensign USN, 1957, advanced through grades to lt., 1961; ret., 1967; with Lockheed Missiles & Space Co., Sunnyvale, Calif., 1967-79, support engr., sr. logistics specialist, 1975-79; mgr. field order adminstrn. Amdahl Corp., Sunnyvale, 1979-81; mgr. development planning STC Computer Research Corp., Santa Clara, Calif., 1981-83; project mgr. Trident II Integrated Logistics Support, Westinghouse Marine div., Sunnyvale, Calif., 1983-85; project mgr. Peacekeeper Integrated Logistics Support, Northrop Electronics div., Hawthorne, Calif., 1985-86, chief systems engr. Acurex Corp., Aerotherm div., Mountain View, Calif., 1986—; nat. def. exec. reserve U.S. Dept. Transp., 1981—; lectr. systems mgmt. U. So. Calif., Los Angeles and Sunnyvale, 1978—. Active Boy Scouts Am. Named an Eagle Scout Boy Scouts Am., 1944; recipient Silver Beaver award Boy Scouts Am., 1986. Registered profl. engr., Calif.; cert. community coll. instr., Calif. Mem. NSPE, Calif. Soc. Profl. Engrs., Inst. Indsl. Engrs., Soc. Logistics Engrs. (Cert. Profl. Logistician award), Soc. Advancement Mgmt., Ret. Officers Assn., Nat. Assn. Uniformed Services, Nat. Eagle Scout Assn., V.F.W., Nat. Rifle Assn., Calif. Rifle and Pistol Assn., Am. Philatelic Soc., Am. Radio Relay League. Republican. Club: Toastmasters (Disting. Toastmaster award). Home: 1024 Oaktree Dr San Jose CA 95129 Office: Acurex Corp 555 Clyde Ave PO Box 7040 Mountain View CA 94039

KEYSER, RICHARD LEE, hospital executive; b. Gary, Ind., Nov. 4, 1941; s. Edward Arnold and Mildred Lee (Hernly) K.; m. Joan Carolyn Whitson, Apr. 2, 1967; children: Brian Lester, Lauren Elizabeth. B.Acctg., U. Ill, 1963, M.Acctg., 1964. Mgr. Arthur Andersen & Co., San Francisco, 1965-71; health services coordinator Sisters of Mercy, Burlingame, Calif., 1971-76; v.p. ops. Health Care Devel., Newport Beach, Calif., 1976-77; sr. v.p. Amherst Assocs., Walnut Creek, Calif., 1977-83; pres. Mercy Hosp. and Med. Ctr., San Diego, 1983—; bd. dirs. Community Care Network, San Diego, 1984—. Mem. budget panel United Bay Area Crusade, San Francisco, 1972-73. Mem. Am. Coll. Hosp. Adminstrs., Am. Hosp. Assn., Calif. Hosp. Assn., Calif. Assn. Cath. Hosps. (bd. dirs. 1984—), Hosp. Council San Diego/Imperial Counties (trustee 1985—). Republican. Presbyterian. Lodge: Rotary. Avocations: golf; skiing. Office: Mercy Hosp and Med Ctr 4077 5th Ave San Diego CA 92103-2180

KEYSTON, STEPHANI ANN, businesswoman; b. Baytown, Tex., Aug. 6, 1955; d. Herbert Howard and Janice Faye (Stowe) C.; m. George Keyston III, Oct. 8, 1983. AA with honors, Merced Coll., Merced, Calif., 1975; BA in Journalism with distinction, San Jose State U., 1976. Reporter, Fresno (Calif.) Bee, 1974-75; reporter, photographer Merced (Calif.) Sun-Star, 1974-77; pub. info. officer Fresno City Coll. (Calif.), 1977-80; dir. communications Aerojet Tactical Systems Co., Sacramento, 1980-83; co-owner, v.p. Keyco Landscape Contractor, Inc., Redwood City, Calif., 1984—. Co.-coordinator Aerojet United Way Campaign, 1981; Aerojet Tactical Systems Co. coordinator West Coast Nat. Derby Rallies, 1981-83. Mem. Internat. Assn. Bus. Communicators (dir. Sacramento chpt. 1983), Citrus Heights C. of C. (v.p. 1983). Republican. Home: Redwood City CA 94064 Office: PO Box 3461 Redwood City CA 94064

KHALIL, MOHAMMAD ASLAM KHAN, atmospheric science educator; b. Jahnsi, India, Jan. 7, 1950; came to U.S., 1963; s. Mohammad Ahsan Khan and Aleem-Un (Nisa) K.; m. Giti Ara Eshraghi, June 17, 1973. B Physics, BA in Math. and Psychology, U. Minn., 1970; MS in Physics, Va. Poly. Inst. and State U., 1972; PhD in Physics, U. Tex., 1976; MS, PhD in Environ. Sci., Oreg. Grad. Ctr., 1979. Faculty Oreg. Grad. Ctr., Beaverton, 1979—, sr. research assoc., 1979-80, asst. prof. environ. sci., 1980-82, assoc. prof., 1982-84, prof., 1984—; instr. physics Pacific U., Forest Grove, Oreg., 1978. contbr. numerous articles to profl. jours. Mem. Am. Phys. Soc., Am. Chem. Soc., Am. Geophys. Union, AAAS, Air Pollution Control Assn., Sigma Pi Sigma. Avocations: writing, computer programming. Home: 9961 NW Kaiser Rd Portland OR 97231 Office: Oreg Grad Ctr 19600 NW Von Neumann Dr Beaverton OR 97231

KHAN, AHSANUL KARIM, pediatric physician, medical educator; b. Dhaka, Bangladesh, Aug. 28, 1946; came to U.S., 1977, naturalized 1983; s. Alauddin Khan and Sherina Khanum; m. Talat T. Kahn, Nov. 29, 1967; children: Talat A.K., Anwarul K. Degree in Sci., Notre Dame Coll., Dhaka, 1964; MB, Dhaka Med. Coll., 1970. Diplomate Am. Bd. Pediatrics. Intern Dhaka Med. Coll., 1970-71; asst. prof. human nutrition Dhaka U., 1973-74; resident in pediatrics Youngstown (Ohio) Hosp Assn., 1978-80; pediatric house physician St. Elizabeth Hosp., Youngstown, 1981-82; pediatrician Boardman Medictr., Ohio, 1982-83; physician specialist dept. pediatrics and anesthesiology Martin Luther King Jr.-Charles R. Drew Med. Ctr., Los Angeles, 1985—; instr. pediatrics NE Ohio U. Coll. Medicine, Youngstown, 1983-85; asst. prof. Charles R. Drew Postgrad. Med. Sch., Los Angeles, 1985—. Fellow Am. Acad. Pediatrics. Avocations: gardening, traveling.

KHAN, M. AZAM, surgeon; b. Hafizabad, Pakistan, Apr. 11, 1948; s. Mahboob Alam and Khursid (Begum) K.; M.D., King Edward Med. Coll., Lahore, Pakistan, 1970; m. Naghma Khan, Feb. 5, 1977; children—Uzma, Aqsa, Azam. Intern, Knickerbocker Hosp., N.Y.C., 1971-72; resident in surgery Misericordia Hosp., Bronx, N.Y., 1972-76; attending physician Pelham Bay Gen. Hosp. and Lincoln Hosp., Bronx, 1976-77, Kingman Regional Hosp. (Ariz.), 1977—; practice medicine specializing in gen. and vascular surgery, Kingman, 1977—; pres. med. staff Mohave Gen. Hosp., Kingman, 1983—; med. dir. Dynamic Health Services, Kingman; pres. M. Azam Khan, M.D., P.C. Diplomate Am. Bd. Surgery. Fellow Internat. Coll. Surgeons, Am. Soc. Abdominal Surgeons; mem. AMA, Ariz. Med. Assn., Mohave County Med. Soc. Republican. Condr. research pancreatic and biliary diseases. Home: 3783 Castle Dr Kingman AZ 86401 Office: 1330 Sycamore Ave Suite 4 Kingman AZ 86401

KHAN, MAZHAR IQBAL, pathologist; b. Quetta, Pakistan, Nov. 12, 1947; came to U.S., 1975; s. Faiz-ullah and Sofia Khan; children: Mubashir, Mudasar, Sarah. BVSc (A.H.), U. Panjab, Lahore, Pakistan, 1970; MPVM, U. Calif., Davis, 1982, PhD, 1987. Cert. veterinarian. Vet. surgeon Ministry of Agr., Quetta, Pakistan, 1970-72; tech. advisor Lever Bros. Ltd., Lahore, 1972-75; vet. asst. U. Calif., Davis, 1982-85, postgrad. researcher, 1985—. Contbr. articles to profl. jours. Recipient Distinction in Vet. Parasitology award U. Panjab, 1968. Mem. Assn. Avian Pathologists, Internat. Orgn. Mycoplasmologists, Am. Vet. Med. Assn. Republican. Avocations: tennis, swimming, traveling. Home: 410 Russell Park #8 Davis CA 95616 Office: U Calif Dept Epidemiology and Preventive Medicine Davis CA 95616

KHAN, MOHAMMAD ALI, health care administrator; b. Ghazipur, India, Feb. 15, 1936; came to U.S., 1968; s. Ali Gauhar and Anwari Begum; m. Zaheda Khanem, June 18, 1960; children: Arshad Iqbal, Rukhsana B., Zeba M. BS in Sci., A.M. U., Aligarh, India, 1955, MS in Phys. Chemistry, 1957; PhD in Phys. Chemistry, U. Del., 1972. Lectr. chemistry G.F. Coll., Shahjahanpur, India, 1957-61, Regional Engring. Coll., Srinagar, India, 1961-68; postdoctoral research assoc. U. Pa., Phila., 1971-77; specialist product and materials evaluation Parke-Davis/Warner-Lambert Co., Greenwood, S.C., 1977-81; mgr. Deseret Med./Warner-Lambert Co. (now Becton Dickinson Co.), Sandy, Utah, 1981—; researcher dept. research and devel. Warner-Lambert Co., Morris Plains, N.J., 1977-86. Contbr. articles to profl. jours. Smith, Kline and French fellow, Phila., 1968-71, fellow NIH, Nat. Cystic Fibrosis Research Found. (now Cystic Fibrosis Found.). Mem.

Am. Chem. Soc. Muslim. Avocations: reading, music. Home: 10005 S Falcon Hurst Dr Sandy UT 84092 Office: Deseret Med Inc 9450 S State St Sandy UT 84070

KHAN, MUHIB MOWLA, research materials engineer; b. Chittagong, Bangladesh, July 15, 1952; came to U.S., 1977; s. Aslam M. and Noorjahan Kahn. BS, U. Dacca, Bangladesh, 1976; PhD, So. Ill. U., 1982. Postdoctoral fellow U. Calif., Berkeley, 1983-84; mem. tech. staff Advanced Micro Devices, Sunnyvale, Calif., 1984—; guest cons. Lawrence Berkeley (Calif.) Lab., 1983-86. Contbr. articles to Jour. Catalysis. Mem. Am. Chem. Soc., Am. Inst. Physics, Am. Vacuum Soc., Am. Inst. Chemists, Phi Kappa Phi. Avocations: photography, fitness, racquetball, camping. Home: 471 Acalanes Dr Apt 46 Sunnyvale CA 94086 Office: Advanced Micro Devices 901 Thompson Pl MS 58 Sunnyvale CA 94088

KHAN, WAJID ALI, science administrator; b. Aurangabad, India, Dec. 16, 1930; came to U.S., 1963; s. Sadiq Ali and Shahzadi Begum Khan; m. Laique Sultana Shahmohammad, Aug. 5, 1963; children: Zarina, Tehmina, Usman. BSc, Osmania U., Hyderabad, India, 1952, MSc, 1954, PhD, 1960. Instr. U. Utah, Salt Lake City, 1972-74; vis. sci. Syva Research Inst., Palo Alto, Calif., 1974-76; supr. Syva Co., Palo Alto, Calif., 1976-78; mgr. Syva Co., Cupertino, Calif., 1978—; prin. Islamic Sch., San Jose, Calif., 1985—. Contbr. articles to profl. jours. Mem. Am. Chem. Soc., Chem. Soc. of London, Sigma Xi. Home: 440 Greenwood Dr. Santa Clara CA 95054 Office: Syva Co 20400 Mariani Ave Cupertino CA 95014

KHANNA, PYARE LAL, research scientist; b. Lahore, India, Mar. 28, 1945; s. Chaman Lal and Satya Wati (Malhotra) K.; m. Swatanter Kapoor; children: Sonia, Pavan. MSc, Delhi (India) U., 1967, PhD, 1970; postgrad., Columbia U., 1974-76. Asst. prof. Delhi U., 1971-74; from research chemist to asst. dir. research Syva/Syntex, Palo Alto, Calif., 1977-86; v.p. research and devel. Microgenics Corp., Concord, Calif., 1986—. Contbr. articles to profl. jours.; patentee in field. Mem. AAAS, Am. Chem. Soc., N.Y. Acad. Scis., Am. Assn. Clin. Chemistry. Home: 864 Gregory Ct Fremont CA 94539 Office: Microgenics Corp 2380 A Bisso Ln Concord CA 94520

KHASIGIAN, AMOS, economist, educator, farmer; b. Fresno, Calif., Nov. 21, 1918; m. Anna Rose Machoian, June 27, 1930; children—Paul A., Mary E. B.A., UCLA, 1950; M.A., U. So. Calif., 1958, Ph.D., 1971. Farmer, Fowler, Calif., 1961—; prof. econs. Los Angeles Pierce Coll., 1970—. Active Los Angeles council Boy Scouts Am. Served with Signal Corps, AUS, 1941-49; PTO. Mem. Am. Econ. Assn., Am. Hist. Assn., Orgn. Am. Historians, Am. Acad. Polit. and Social Sci., History of Econs. Soc., Econ. History Assn. Mem. Armenian Apostolic Ch. Club: Knights of Vartan. Home: 7479 S Peach Fowler CA 93625 Office: Los Angeles Pierce Coll 6201 Winnetka Ave Room 4F02 Woodland Hills CA 91371

KHEIFETS, SEMYON (SAM) ABRAHAM, physicist; b. Minsk, USSR, Apr. 17, 1928; came to U.S., 1977; s. Abraham Hilel and Emma (Pinhas) K.; m. Julia Entin, July 10, 1952; 1 child, Leeka. M in Physics, Moscow U., 1952; PhD, Inst. Theoretical and Exptl. Physics, Moscow, 1961. Physicist Yerevan (USSR) Phys. Inst., 1952-75, Deutsches Electric Synchrotron, Hamburg, Fed. Republic Germany, 1975-77, Stanford U., Palo Alto, Calif., 1978—. Author: Electron Synchrotron, 1963; contbr. articles to jours. Mem. Am. Phys. Soc. Republican. Home: 2131 Ashton Ave Menlo Park CA 94025 Office: Stanford U 2575 Sand Hill Rd SLAC Bin 26 Menlo Park CA 94025

KHERA, ASHOK KUMAR, professional engineer; b. Chakwal, India, Dec. 10, 1944; came to U.S., 1969; s. Tilak Raj and Rattan K. (Khatri) K.; m. Sushila Bedi, Apr. 18, 1965; children: Ritu, Susan. BE with honors, U. Jabalpur, India, 1965; ME, U. Roorkee, India, 1969; MS, U. Cin., 1970. Registered profl. engr., N.Y., Ohio, Ind., N.Mex. Environ. lab. supr. Monsanto Enviro-Chem., Dayton, Ohio, 1970-73; project engr. Malcom Pinnie Inc., Columbus, Ohio, 1973-74, Union Carbide Corp., Buffalo, N.Y., 1974-78; capital projects mgr. City of Albuquerque, 1979-83; project mgr. CH2MHILL, Albuquerque, 1983-85; v.p. Precision Engring., Albuquerque, 1985—; pres. Gardner, Mason & Assoc., Inc., Albuquerque, 1986—. Contbr. articles to tech. jours. Recipient Gold Medal U. Roorkee, India, 1969. Mem. Water Pollution Control Fedn., Am. Water Works Assn., Rocky Mountain Water Pollution, Control and Water Works Assn. Hindu. Avocations: camping, music. Office: Gardner Mason & Assoc Inc 2127 Menaul Blvd NE Albuquerque NM 87107

KHILNANI, GUL M., chemical engineer; b. Karachi, Pakistan, Dec. 7, 1937; s. Motiram T. and Lachmi M. (Bhambhani) K.; m. Margaret L. Khilnani, Oct. 6, 1962 (div. Aug. 1978); children: Sheela K., Jeena L. BS, U. Bombay, 1959. Chemist Union Assay Office, Salt Lake City, 1963-68; mem. tech. staff Friden Research, Palo Alto, Calif., 1968-70; sr. technician Bacharach Intruments, Mt. View, Calif., 1970-74; chemist Dictaphone Corp., Mt. View, Calif., 1974-77; sr. engr. Rexnord Inc., Sunnyvale, Calif., 1978—. Patentee in field. Mem. Am. Chem. Soc. Avocations: camping, music, sports, dancing. Home: 39663 Leslie St #295 Fremont CA 94538 Office: Rexnord Gas Detection Products 207 E Java Dr Sunnyvale CA 94086

KHINOO, EVELYN MILDRED, human resources executive; b. Washington, May 2, 1945; d. Albert Ephrum and Mildred Consuelo (Adams) K. AA in Bus., Modesto Jr. Coll., 1965; student, San Jose State U. Asst. to dir. SRI Internat., Menlo Park, Calif., 1967-76; asst. to sr. v.p. Arcata Corp., Menlo Park, 1976-82; asst. to pres. Catalytica, Mountain View, Calif., 1982-84, dir. personnel, 1984—. Mem. Am. Mgmt. Assn., Santa Clara Valley Personnel Assn. Home: 1008 Almanor Ave Menlo Park CA 94025 Office: Catalytica 430 Ferguson Dr Bldg 3 Mountain View CA 94043

KHOO, KEIKO INADA, audiology educator; b. Japan, Mar. 17, 1946; came to U.S., 1970; d. Inagiro and Yuri (Kato) Inada; m. David Khoo, Aug. 12, 1971; children: Kenneth, Kathleen. BS in English, Philippine Union Coll., Manila, 1968; postgrad., UCLA, 1970; MS in Audiology, Loma Linda U., 1979. Lic. audiologist Calif. Clin. audiologist Loma Linda U., Riverside, Calif., 1977-80, asst. prof. audiology, 1980—. Mem. Am. Speech-Lang.-Hearing Assn. (cert. clim. competence, com. aural rehab. 1985-86). Adventist. Home: 11470 LaVerne Riverside CA 92505 Office: Loma Linda U Loma Linda CA 92354

KHOSLA, VED MITTER, oral and maxillo-facial surgeon, educator; b. Nairobi, Kenya, Jan. 13, 1926; s. Jagdish Rai and Tara V. K.; m. Santosh Ved Chabra, Oct. 11, 1952; children: Ashok M., Siddarth M. Student, U. Cambridge, 1945; L.D.S., Edinburgh Dental Hosp. and Sch., 1950, Coll. Dental Surgeons, Sask., Can., 1962. Prof. oral surgery, dir. postdoctoral studies in oral surgery U. Calif. Sch. Dentistry, San Francisco, 1968—; chief oral surgery San Francisco Gen. Hosp.; lectr. oral surgery U. of Pacific, VA Hosp.; vis. cons. Fresno County Hosp. Dental Clinic.; Mem. planning com., exec. med. com. San Francisco Gen. Hosp. Contbr. articles to profl. jours. Examiner in photography and gardening Boy Scouts Am., 1971-73, Guatemala Clinic, 1972. Granted personal coat of arms by H.M. Queen Elizabeth II, 1959. Fellow Royal Coll. Surgeons (Edinburgh), Internat. Assn. Oral Surgeons, Internat. Coll. Applied Nutrition, Internat. Coll. Dentists, Royal Soc. Health, AAAS, Am. Coll. Dentists; mem. Brit. Assn. Oral Surgeons, Am. Soc. Oral Surgeons, Am. Dental Soc. Anesthesiology, Am. Acad. Dental Radiology, Omicron Kappa Upsilon. Club: Masons. Home: 1525 Lakeview Dr Hillsborough CA 94010 Office: U Calif Sch Dentistry Oral Surgery Div 3d and Parnassus Aves San Francisco CA 94122

KIANG, JOSEPH K.Y., polymer engineer; b. Peking, Republic of China, Feb. 12, 1948. BS, Chung Yuan U., Republic of China, 1970; MS, U. Lowell, 1973; MBA, U. Santa Clara, 1981; PhD, U. Mass., 1979. Sr. engr. Raychem Corp., Menlo Park, Calif., 1978—. Contbr. articles to jours.; patentee in field. Mem. Am. Chem. Soc., Soc. Plastic Engrs. Avocation: outdoors. Office: Raychem Corp 300 Constitution Dr Menlo Park CA 94025

KIANG, JULIANN DZE-UEN GONG, research pharmacologist, toxicologist; b. Hsin-Zu, Republic of China, Dec. 3, 1952; came to U.S., 1975; d. See Chung and Mei Ching (Hong) Gong; m. Peter Ming-Kin Kiang, July 13, 1977; children: Sharon C., Andrew Gene. BS, Fu-Jen Cath. U., 1975; MA, U. Nebr., 1977; PhD, U. Calif., Berkeley, 1983. Teaching asst. U. Nebr., Omaha, 1975-77; research technologist Creighton U. Hosp., Omaha, 1977-78; teaching asst. U. Calif., Berkeley, 1979-82, research scientist, 1984—. Asst. editor Cheng-Show mag., 1981-83; article reviewer Internat. Sci. Jours., 1984—; contbr. articles to Chinese newspapers, 1980—, articles to profl. jours.; patentee in field. Scholar Wong's Soc., Taiwan, Republic of China, 1973, Fu-Kin People's Soc., Taiwan, 1971-75, predoctoral scholar Nat. Inst. Health, 1978-79; Environ. Health Scis. Tngship., 1980-82. Mem. AAAS, Internat. Narcotic Research Conf. (speaker, Traveling awards 1983—), Assn. Chinese Biologists in Am. Democrat. Roman Catholic. Office: U Calif Dept Pharmacy Berkeley CA 94720

KIANG-ULRICH, MARILYN KUO SHUEI, research physiologist; b. Beijing, July 18, 1915; came to U.S., 1949; d. Hua-Peng and Yuen (Sheng) K.; m. George John Ulrich, Mar. 25, 1949 (dec. July 1975); children: Patricia, Lisa. Student, Osaka (Japan) Women's Med. Coll., 1934-37, U. Calif., San Francisco, 1950-51; MA, U. Calif., Santa Barbara, 1973, PhD, 1977. Cert. med. technologist, clin. lab. scientist. Med. technologist Harriman Jones Hosp., Long Beach, Calif., 1951-53; supervising lab. technologist Valley Clin. Lab., Santa Barbara, 1953-73; research physiologist Inst. Environ. Stress, U. Calif., Santa Barbara, 1977—. Contbr. articles to profl. jours. Mem. Am. Assn. for Advancement Sci., Am. Soc. Med. Tech., Calif. Assn. Med. Lab. Tech., Gerontol. Soc. Am., N.Y. Acad. Scis. Office: Inst Environ Stress U Calif Santa Barbara CA 93108

KIBBY, CHARLES LEONARD, chemist; b. Wenatchee, Wash., Jan. 2, 1938; s. Leonard L. and Evy K. (McAuley) K.; m. Diana Lynn Morrison, Nov. 27, 1970; 1 child, Kenneth Charles. BA, Reed Coll., 1959; PhD, Purdue U., 1964. Fellow Harvard U., Cambridge, Mass., 1963-65; research assoc. Brookhaven Nat. Lab., Upton, N.Y., 1965-67; fellow Mellon Inst., Pitts., 1967-69; research chemist Gulf Research and Devel. Co., Pitts., 1970-75, sr. research chemist, 1977-81, research assoc., 1981-85; research chemist Pitts. Energy Tech. Ctr., 1976-77; sr. research assoc. Chevron Research Co., Richmond, Calif., 1985—. Contbr. articles to profl. jours.; patentee in field. NSF fellow, 1961-62. Mem. AAAS, Pitts.-Cleve. Catalysis Soc. (pres.-elect 1984-85, sec. 1983-84), Am. Chem. Soc. (bd. dirs. Pitts. sect. 1977-80), Phi Lambda Upsilon. Avocations: gardening, golf, bowling. Home: 846 Clifton Ct Benicia CA 94510 Office: Chevron Research Co 1627 Standard Ave Richmond CA 94802

KIBLER, RUTHANN, immunology educator; b. Mansfield, Ohio, Dec. 1, 1942; d. Orville David and Elizabeth June (Hale) K. BS, Marietta Coll., 1964; MS, Purdue U., 1967; PhD, U. Calif., Berkeley, 1973. Postdoctoral researcher U. Wurzburg, Fed. Republic Germany, 1973-76; research assoc. U. Ariz., Tucson, 1976-79, asst. prof. immunology, 1980—; postdoctoral reseacher Calif. State Dept. Health Services, Berkeley, 1979-80; dir. research Southwestern Clinic and Research Inst., Tucson, 1982—. Contbr. articles to profl. jours. Mem. Am. Assn. Immunologists, Am. Soc. Microbiology, Am. Rheumatism Assn. Home: 429 1/2 S 5th Ave Tucson AZ 85701 Office: U Ariz Dept Microbiology/Immunology Health Scis Ctr Tucson AZ 85724

KIDD, DAVID EUGENE, biology educator, university administrator; b. Evanston, Ill., Apr. 13, 1930; s. Albert Eugene and Elizabeth (Ayres) K.; m. DoloresEtta Dichtenmiller, Aug. 26, 1955; children: David Edward, Dennis Eugene, Deborah Elizabeth. BS in Biology, No. Ariz. U., 1951; MS in Biology, Northwestern U., 1952; MS in Chemistry Edn., U. N.H., 1960; PhD in Phycology/Limnology, Mich. State U., 1963. Tchr. gen. sci., biology Ajo (Ariz.) High Sch., 1954-55, tchr. chemistry, physics, biology, 1956-60; tchr. botany, zoology, gen. and organic chemistry Lindsey Wilson Jr. Coll., Columbia, Ky., 1955-56; instr. natural sci. Mich. State U., East Lansing, 1960-64, asst. prof. natural sci., 1964-67, assoc. prof., 1967; assoc. prof. biology U. N.Mex., Albuquerque, 1967-72, prof., 1973—, coordinator, asst. dean acad. affairs Gen. Coll., 1984—, chmn. faculty senate curricula com., 1983-85; dir. Albuquerque Sci. Fair, 1985—; proposal reviewer U.S. Geol. Survey, 1984—; lectr. NSF-AAAS short courses, U. Tex., Stanford U., Harvey Mudd Coll., Syracuse U., Clark Coll., Hampshire Coll., U. Md., U. Wis., others; undergrad. advisor Mich. State U., 1960-67; undergrad., grad. advisor U.N.Mex., 1967-74, spl. freshman advisor, 1975-79; mem. search com. Dean Gen. Coll., U.N.Mex., 1983-84, freshman instrnl. support com., 1984-85, acad. freedom and tenure com., 1984—, pres.'s Gen. Coll. transition task force, 1986—; cons. Nat. Park Service, Environ. Improvement Agy., Los Alamos environ. group, No. Ariz. Council Govts., others. Author: A Notebook for University Skills Students, 1986; contbr. articles to profl. jours. Active local Little League, local high sch. baseball team. Recipient numerous research grants, 1961—. Mem. AAAS, Nat. Assn. Biology Tchrs. (dir. awards program 1968-86), Nat. Sci. Tchrs. Assn. (mem. regional meeting steering com. 1983-84), Am. Chem. Soc., Am. Microscopical Soc., No. Ariz. Soc. Arts and Scis., N.Mex. Acad. Sci. (Outstanding Univ. Level Tchr. 1982), Am. Legion, Sigma Xi. Avocations: bicycling, art, music, history, baseball. Home: 8213 Harwood NE Albuquerque NM 87110 Office: U NMex Gen Coll Onate Hall 107 Albuquerque NM 87131

KIDD, DAVID THOMAS, lawyer, corporate officer; b. Laramie, Wyo., Feb. 1, 1934; s. David T. and Sarah Lucille (Love) K.; m. Sally Noble, Sept. 1, 1956; children—Lynden Louise, David Thomas II. Student, Dartmouth Coll., 1952-55; B.A., U. Wyo., 1957, J.D., 1960. Bar: Wyo. 1960, U.S. Dist. Ct. Wyo. 1960, U.S. Ct. Appeals (10th cir.) 1978, U.S. Supreme Ct. 1974. Assoc. Brown, Healy, Drew, Apostolos & Barton, Casper, Wyo., 1960-62; mem. firm McCrary, Schwartz, Bon & Kidd, Casper, 1962-74; western counsel for natural resources Union Pacific Corp., 1974—; counsel subs. Union Pacific Corp., Champlin Petroleum Co., Rocky Mountain Energy and Upland Industries. Bd. dirs. litigation Mountain States Legal Found., 1977—, vice chmn., 1984—; judge Municipal Ct., Casper, 1963-68; mem. Wyo. Ho. of Reps., 1963-67; mayor, Casper, 1971. Mem. State of Wyo. Commn. on Edn., 1983-84, chmn. educator subcom. Mem. ABA, Wyo. Bar Assn., Am. Judicature Soc., Rocky Mountain Mineral Law Found., Rocky Mountain Oil and Gas Assn. (chmn. legal com. 1982-86, v.p. Wyo. 1985-87, pres. Petroleum Assn. Wyo. subs. 1985-87), Wyo. Mining Assn., Dartmouth Lawyers Assn. Clubs: Casper Petroleum, Casper Country. Contbr. articles to profl. jours. Home: 2076 Willow Creek Rd Casper WY 82604 Office: Union Pacific Corp 104 S Wolcott Suite 600 Casper WY 82601

KIDD, REUBEN PROCTOR, management engineer; b. Bedford, Va., Feb. 18, 1913; s. Oscar Kibbler and Estelle (Johnson) K.; B.S., Va. Poly. Inst., 1936; m. Margaret Jerome, June 23, 1952. Pres., Frito Corp. of Roanoke (Va.), 1947-49; indsl. engr. USAF, Sacramento, 1956-73; chmn. bd. USDR, Inc., Sacramento, 1961-69, MEN Internat., Inc., Mpls., 1977—; owner The Kidd Cos., operator Precision Tune-Up, Sacramento, 1974—. Served to capt. U.S. Army, 1942-46, to maj., 1949-51. Decorated Silver Star; registered profl. engr., Calif. Republican. Presbyterian. Home: 5809 Northgrove Way Citrus Heights CA 95610 Office: Precision Tune-Up 6241 Spruce Ave Sacramento CA 95841

KIDD, RICHARD WAYNE, chemist; b. Westminster, Md., June 16, 1947; s. Russell I. and Emma Louise (Zile) K.; m. Millie M. Hamilton, Aug. 16, 1969; 1 child, Adam J. BA cum laude, Western Md. Coll., 1969; MS, PhD, U. Ill., 1975. Sr. research scientist Battelle's Columbus (Ohio) Labs., 1977-85; assoc. tech. dir. San Fernando Labs., Pacoima, Calif., 1985-87; sr. tech. mgr. Sci. Applications Internat. Corp., Pacoima, 1987—. Contbr. articles to profl. jours. Served to maj. USAR, 1969—. Mem. Am. Chem. Soc., Reserve Officer Assn. of U.S., Sigma Xi. Avocations: coin collecting, gardening. Office: Sci Applications Internat Corp 10258 Norris Ave Pacoima CA 91331

KIEFFER, WILLIAM ANTHONY, air force officer, social worker; b. St. Louis, Aug. 26, 1948; s. Alphonse Frank and Ova Marie (Karleskint) K.; m. Cody Sue Strader, Nov. 24, 1972; children: Matthew William, Katherine Anne. BA, Cardinal Glennon Coll., 1970; MSW, St. Louis U., 1974, PhD, 1985. Therapist Family and Children's Services, St. Louis, 1974-82; personnel analyst City of St. Louis, 1982-83; commd. 1st lt. USAF, 1983, advanced through grades to capt., 1984; chief of social work services USAF Hosp., Malmstrom, Mont., 1983—; bd. dirs. Cascade County Mental Health Assn., Mont. Chpt. Prevention of Child Abuse; mem. Cascade County Sexual Abuse Task Force, Great Falls, 1985—. Mem. Nat. Assn. Social Workers, Acad. Cert. Social Workers, Am. Assn. Marriage and Family Therapy (clin. cert.). Roman Catholic. Avocations: hiking, golf, fishing, travel. Home: 4933 B Locust Great Falls MT 59405 Office: USAF Hosp Malmstrom Great Falls MT 59405

KIEHNE, ANNA MARIE, accountant, educator, systems analyst; b. Preston, Minn., Dec. 15, 1947; d. Alvin H. and Anna M. (Goldsmith) K. B.B.A., Winona State U.; postgrad. Calif. State U.-Los Angeles, 1974-78; cert. in systems analysis UCLA, 1984. Acct. Murray Howard Realty, Los Angeles, 1974-78; staff acct. Bowest Corp., La Jolla, Calif., 1978-79; acctg. supr. Majestic Investment, Denver, 1979-81; adminstrv. acct. ECA/Intercomp. systems analyst Home Savs., 1983—; tchr. adult edn. Election judge, Denver; del. to primary, county, state Democratic convs., 1980, 82. Mem. Nat. Assn. Accts. (cert. in flexible budgeting and performance reporting), Internat. Platform Assn., Nat. Assn. Female Execs.; Nat. Women's Polit. Caucus. Lutheran. Home: 2445 E Del Mar Pasadena CA 91107

KIELHORN, RICHARD WERNER, chemist; b. Berlin, Germany, June 17, 1931; s. Richard H. and Auguste (Lammek) K.; m. Anneliese Heinrich, Aug. 9, 1952; children: Anita, Margit. BS, Chem. Tech. Sch., Berlin, 1953. Lab. tech. Zoellner Werke, Berlin, 1950-57, Montrose Chem. Corp., Henderson, Nev., 1957-78; chief chemist Stauffer Chem. Corp., Henderson, 1978—; tax cons. H&R Block, Las Vegas, Nev., 1972—, instr, 1978—. Mem. Am. Chem. Soc., ASTM, Am. Mgmt. Assn., Nev. Soc. Tax Cons. (v.p.). Home: 1047 Westminster Ave Las Vegas NV 89119 Office: Stauffer Chem Co Lake Mead Dr Henderson NV 89015

KIELMEYER, WILLIAM HENRY, research engineer; b. Columbus, Ohio, Jan. 6, 1943; s. Peter Henry and Dorothy Ruth (Potts) K.; B.S. in Ceramic Engring., Ohio State U., 1966, M.S., 1973; m. Marjorie E. Kaufman, Oct. 5, 1968; children—Cheryl A., Thomas W. Project engr. Owens-Corning Fiberglas Corp., Granville, Ohio, 1968-72; research engr. Johns-Manville Sales Corp., Littleton, Colo., 1973-78, sr. research engr., 1978—. Mem. Am. Ceramic Soc., Mineral Insulation Mfrs. Assn. Republican. Lutheran. Copatentee process for making high-purity silica fiber for use in space shuttle reusable surface insulation; loose-fill residential insulation, comml. insulation materials and systems. Home: 3374 W Chenango Ave Englewood CO 80110 Office: 10100 W Ute Ave Littleton CO 80127

KIELSMEIER, CATHERINE JANE, sch. adminstr.; b. San Jose, Calif; d. Frank Delos and Catherine Doris (Sellar) MacGowan; M.S., U. So. Calif., 1964, Ph.D., 1971; m. Milton Kielsmeier; children—Catherine Louise, Barry Delos. Tchr. pub. schs. Maricopa, Calif.; sch. psychologist Campbell (Calif.) Union Sch Dist., 1961-66; asst. prof. edn. and psychology Western Oreg. State Coll., Monmouth, 1966-67, 70; asst. research prof. Oreg. System Higher Edn., Monmouth, 1967-70; dir. spl. services Pub. Schs., Santa Rosa, Calif., 1972—. Mem. Sonoma County Council Community Services, 1976—, Sonoma County Orgn. for Retarded/Becoming Independent, 1978—. Mem. Council for Exceptional Children. Club: Commonwealth of Calif. Home: 7495 Poplar Dr Forestville CA 95436 Office: 211 Ridgeway Ave Santa Rosa CA 95402

KIENHOLZ, LYN SHEARER, arts projects coordinator; b. Chgo.; d. Mitchell W. and Lucille M. (Hock) Shearer; student Sullins Coll., Md. Coll. Women. Assoc. producer Kurt Simon Prodns., Beverly Hills, Calif., 1963-65; owner, mgr. Vuokko Boutique, Beverly Hills, 1969-75; bd. dirs. Los Angeles Inst. Contemporary Art, 1976-79, Fellows of Contemporary Art, 1977-79, Internat. Network for Arts, 1979—, Los Angeles Contemporary Exhbns., 1980-82; exec. sec., bd. dirs. Beaubourg Found. (now George Pompidou Art and Culture Found.), 1977-81; visual arts adv. Performing Arts Council, Los Angeles Music Center, 1980—; bd. govs. Calif. Inst. Tech. Baxter Art Gallery, 1980-85; mem. adv. bd. dirs. Fine Arts Communications, pub. Images & Issues mag., 1981-85; founder, pres. bd. dirs. Calif./Internat. Arts Found., 1981—; bd. dirs., western chmn. ArtTable 1983—; exec. bd. Sovereign Fund, 1981—; exec. bd. dirs. Scandinavia Today, 1982-83; mem. adv. bd. Otis/Parsons Sch. Design, 1983-85, U. So. Calif. dept. fine arts, 1983-85; bd. dirs. UK/LA Festival of Britain, 1986, L'Ensemble des Deux Mondes, 1986—; mem. Comité International pour les Musées d'Art Moderne, 1985—. Co-host radio program ARTS/L.A., 1987—; contbg. editor Calif. mag., 1984—. Address: 2737 Outpost Dr Los Angeles CA 90068

KIER, JAMES FREDERIC, architect; b. Seattle, May 23, 1951; s. Robert Dan and Evelyn Claudia (Cliche) K.; m. Julie Finn, Dec. 4, 1970; children: Amber, Rachel, Ryan. BS in Psychology cum laude, U. Utah, 1974, MArch, 1977. Registered architect, Utah. Architect Scott Louie & Browning, Salt Lake City, 1977-80, 82, FFKR Architects, Salt Lake City, 1981, CDSR Architects, Salt Lake City, 1983; project mgr. Gensler & Assocs. Architects, Salt Lake City, 1984; projects dir. Gengler & Assocs., Salt Lake City, 1985, office dir., 1986; bd. dirs. Musicale Promotion, Inc., Salt Lake City. Fund-raiser Utah Symphony Orch., Salt Lake City, 1986. Served with USNG, 1970-76. Mem. Salt Lake area C. of C. (grad. Leadership Utah program, 1985). Lutheran. Home: 2272 Lonsdale Dr Salt Lake City UT 84121 Office: Gensler & Assocs Architects 48 Post Office Pl Suite 250 Salt Lake City UT 84101

KIERNAN, ELAINE RUTH, investment manager, brokerage house executive; b. Portland, Oreg., Feb. 27, 1947; d. Merle and Margaret (Nielsen) Schevenius; m. Walter R. Kiernan Jr.; children: Walter, Michael, Patty, Lexie. BS in Human Relations, U. San Francisco, 1984. Registered investment advisor. Account exec. P.H.H., Balt., 1970-80; nat. account mgr. Diasonics, Milpitas, Calif., 1980-82; pvt. practice fin. planning San Jose, Calif., 1982-85; v.p., regional mgr. N.Am. Securities, Mountain View, Calif., 1986—. Editor: newsletter The Financial Informer. Active pub. affairs com. Fremont City Council. Mem. Internat. Order Fin. Planners, Palo Alto Fin. Planning Forum, Am. Bus. Women's Assn. Republican. Lutheran. Home: 44959 Washo Ct Fremont CA 94539 Office: 43255 Mission Blvd Fremont CA 94539

KIERSCH, GEORGE ALFRED, geological consultant, emeritus educator; b. Lodi, Calif., Apr. 15, 1918; s. Adolph Theodore and Viola Elizabeth (Bahmeier) K.; m. Jane J. Keith, Nov. 29, 1942; children—Dana Elizabeth Kiersch Haycock, Mary Annan, George Keith, Nancy McCandless Kiersch Bohnett. Student, Modesto Jr. Coll., 1936-37; B.S. in Geol. Engring., Colo. Sch. Mines, 1942; Ph.D. in Geology, U. Ariz., 1947. Geologist 79 Mining Co., Ariz., 1946-47; geologist underground explosion tests and Folsom Dam-Reservoir Project U.S. C.E., Calif., 1948-50; supervising geologist Internat. Boundary and Water Commn., U.S.-Mex., 1950-51; asst. prof. geology U. Ariz., Tucson, 1951-55; dir. Mineral Resources Survey Navajo-Hopi Indian Reservations, 1952-55; exploration mgr. resources survey So. Pacific Co., San Francisco, 1955-60; assoc. prof. geol. sci. Cornell U., Ithaca, N.Y., 1960-63, prof., 1963-78, prof. emeritus, 1978—, chmn. dept. geol. scis., 1965-71; geol. cons., Ithaca, 1960-78, Tucson, 1978—; chmn. coordinating com. on environment and natural hazards, Internat. Lithosphere Program, 1986-1991. Author: Engineering Geology, 1955; Mineral Resources of Navajo-Hopi Indian Reservations, 3 vols., 1955; Geothermal Steam-A World Wide Assessment, 1964. Editor: Case Histories in Engineering Geology, 4 vols., 1963-69. Mem. editorial bd. Engring. Geology/Amsterdam. Mem. adv. council to bd. trustees Colo. Sch. Mines, 1962-71; mem. coms. Nat. Acad. Engring./Nat. Acad. Scis., 1966—; chmn. coordinating com. 1 CC1 Nat. Hazards U.S. GeoDynamics Com., 1985—. Served to capt. C.E., U.S. Army, 1942-45. Recipient award for best articles Indsl. Mktg. Mag., 1964; NSF sr. postdoctoral fellow Tech. U. Vienna, 1963-64. Fellow Geol. Soc. Am. (chmn. div. engring. geology 1960-61, cert. of appreciation 1980, Disting. Practice award 1986, mem. U.S. nat. com. on rock mechanics 1980-86), ASCE; mem. Soc. Econ. Geologists, U.S. Com. on Large Dams, Internat. Soc. Rock Mechanics, Internat. Assn. Engring. Geologists (U.S. com. 1980-86, chmn. com. 1983-86, v.p. N.Am. 1986—), Assn. Engring. Geologists (1st recipient Claire P. Holdredge award 1965, hon. mem. 1985, Presdl. Cert. of Appreciation, 1986). Republican. Episcopalian. Clubs: Cornell (N.Y.C.); Statler, Tower (Ithaca); Mining of Southwest (Tucson). Home and Office: 4750 N Camino Luz Tucson AZ 85718

KIESLING, ROY ADOLPH, JR., consumer affairs consultant, writer, land developer; b. Houston, Mar. 11, 1934; s. Roy Adolph and Ninon (Collins) K.; B.A., Yale U., 1955; J.D., U. Tex., 1959; B.A., San Jose State Coll., 1966; m. Nancy Lou Hunt, Dec. 22, 1955 (div. 1975); children—Eugenia Collins, John Brady, Stephen Howard, Roy Adolph; m. Ann Adrian, Aug. 7, 1980 (div. 1984). Research contract adminstr. Lockheed Missiles & Space

Co., Sunnyvale, Calif., 1960-62, systems test engr., 1966-69; staff mem. Zero Population Growth, Los Altos, Calif., 1969-70; cons. environ. and consumer affairs, Palo Alto, Calif., 1970—. Past pres. Consumer Fedn. Calif., Consumers Co-op Palo Alto; adv. bd. Calif. Bur. Automotive Repair, chmn., 1978-84. Lic. real estate broker, Calif. Mem. Tex. Bar Assn. Address: 502 Woodhaven Ct Aptos CA 95003

KIESS, DEAN WILLIAM, military officer; b. Williamsport, Pa., Feb. 21, 1940; s. Clyde Davis and Harriet (Ritter) K.; m. Carolyn Andrea Coates, Feb. 9, 1963; children: Michael, Jennifer, John. BSME, Pa. State U., 1962; MSME, Naval Postgrad. Sch., 1967-69. Commd. USN, 1962, advanced through grades to capt.; dep. dir. integrated logistics Trident Ship Aquisition USN, Washington, 1977-79, dir. integrated logistics Trident Ship Acquisition, 1983-85, submarine elec. inspector and surveyor, 1979-81; repair officer USN, Mare Island Naval Shipyard, Valleto, Calif., 1981-83; comding. officer Strategic Weapons Facility, Pacific, Bremerton, Wash., 1985—. Councilman Boy Scouts Am., Alexandria, Va., 1977-81. Mem. Naval Submarine League, Naval Inst., Cen. Kitsap C. of C. (bd. dirs. 1985—), Sigma Xi. Republican. Episcopalian. Avocations: golf, jogging, woodworking, skiing. Office: Strategic Weapons Facility Pacific Bremerton WA 98315

KIGER, RONALD LEE, price analyst; b. Pasadena, Calif., Dec. 30, 1940; s. Wallace Lee and Ilo Marie (Smith) K.; m. Carole Ann Bates, Apr. 10, 1965 (div. Dec. 1978); children: Darren Lee, Lorene Elizabeth. Student, U. Calif., Berkeley, 1958-62; BBA, Armstrong Coll., 1964. Auditor GAO, San Francisco, 1964-66; sr. auditor Def. Contract Audit Agy., San Francisco, 1966-84; material price analyst Lockheed Missiles and Spcae Co., Sunnyvale, Calif., 1984—. State dir. U.S. Jaycees, Castro Valley, Calif., 1968, pres., 1969, dist. lt. gov., Alameda County, Calif., 1970, state credentials chmn., Calif., 1970. Mem. Assn. Govt. Accts. (sec. 1968, spl. activities dir. 1982-83, pres. 1983-84, newsletter editor 1984-85, nat. chpt. recognition com. 1985—). Democrat. Mem. Christian Ch. Avocations: golf, softball, tennis. Home: 1975-U Barrymore Common Fremont CA 94538

KIHLSTROM, KENNETH EDWARD, physics educator; b. Buffalo, May 11, 1954; s. Ernest H. and Victorine A. (Salvage) K.; m. Kim Potter, Sept. 10, 1978; children: Katherine Joy, Karen Janelle. BS in Physics, Stanford U., 1976, MS in Physics, 1979, PhD, 1982. Research assoc. Nat. Research Council Naval Research Lab., Washington, 1982-84; asst. prof. physics Westmont Coll., Santa Barbara, Calif., 1984—; bd. dirs. Sci. and Engring. Council of Santa Barbara; speaker in field. Contbr. articles to profl. jours.; patentee in field. Recipient David S. Levine award Stanford U., 1975. Mem. Am. Phys. Soc. Democrat. Evangelical. Avocation: astronomy. Home: 684 Circle Dr Santa Barbara CA 93108 Office: Westmont Coll Dept Physics 955 La Paz Rd Santa Barbara CA 93108

KIKER, EDWARD BRUCE, lunar mining geologist, educator; b. London, Aug. 1, 1947; (parents Am. citizens); s. Wellborn Clark and Evelyn (Williams) K. AB, Harvard U., 1970. Natural resources specialist U.S. Army, Ft. Greely, Alaska, 1975-83; dir. High Frontier, Delta, Alaska, 1985-87; mil. analyst space ops. U.S. Army Space Inst, Ft. Leavenworth, Kans., 1987—; cons. hist. affairs, Delta, 1985—; bd. dirs. Outer Space Indsl. Resources Investigations Systems. Contbr. articles on space to profl. jours. Asst. dist. commnr. Boy Scouts Am., Delta, 1975—, scoutmaster; space lobbyist L-5 Soc., Delta, 1975—. Served to capt. U.S. Army, 1971-75. Recipient Silver Beaver award Boy Scouts Am., 1986, Merit award Boy Scouts Am., 1981, 83; named Eagle Scout Boy Scouts Am., 1962; grantee Sigma Xi, 1969;. Fellow Brit. Interplanetary Soc.; mem. Nat. Space Council, Alaska Acad. Scis. (bd. dirs. 1983—), Am. Legion, Am. Acad. Scis., Soc. Am. Foresters, Am. Forestry Assn., NRA, AAAS, Am. Space Assn., Air Force Assn., Planetary Soc., Space Studies Inst., U.S. Def. Com., Nat. Space Soc. Avocations: model bldg., taxidermy, sculpture, painting, camping.

KIKUCHI, RYOICHI, physics educator; b. Osaka, Japan, Dec. 25, 1919; came to U.S., 1950; m. Toshiko Sono; children: John M., Ann K. Snyder. BS, Tokyo U., 1942, PhD, 1951. Research assoc. MIT, Cambridge, 1951-53; asst. prof. U. Chgo., 1953-55; research physicist Armour Research Found., Chgo., 1955-56; assoc. prof. Wayne State U., Detroit, 1956-58; sr. scientist Hughes Research Labs., Malibu, Calif., 1958-85; research prof. U. Wash., Seattle, 1985—; vis. prof. Purdue U., West Lafayette, Ind., 1977—, Tohoku U., Sendai, Japan, 1982, Technische Hugeschool, Delft, The Netherlands, 1980, 81; adj. prof. UCLA, 1975-86. Contbr. articles to profl. jours. Recipient A. Von Humboldt Sr. U.S. Scientist award, Bonn, Fed. Republic of Germany, 1985. Mem. Am. Phys. Soc. Office: U Wash Dept Materials Sci FB-10 Seattle WA 98195

KILBOURN, JOAN PRISCILLA, microbiologist; b. Portland, Oreg.; d. Jesse W. and Iris M. (Chenoweth) Payne; m. Lee Ferris Kilbourn, June 11, 1961; children: Laurie Jane, Ellen Mae. BS in Gen. Sci., U. Oreg., 1958, MS in Microbiology, 1960; PhD in Microbiology, Oreg. State U., 1963. Grad. research asst. microbiology dept. Oreg. State U., Corvallis, 1961-63; instr. biology dept. U. Oreg., Eugene, 1963-66; research assoc. pediatrics dept. U. Oreg., 1966-68; tutor sci. and math., GED program Portland Community Coll. Adult Literacy Project, 1968-80; med. technologist and environ. surveillance officer VA Hosp., Portland, 1971-74; assoc. dir. biology services ICN Med. Labs., Inc., 1974-76; instr. div. continuing edn. Portland State U., 1977, Clackamas Community Coll., 1978, Physicians Med. Lab., 1979, 81; dir. vaccine research Willamette Lab., 1980-82; lab. dir. Miracle Med. Lab., 1979-84; lab. dir., owner Cons. Clin. and Microbiol. Lab., Inc., Portland, 1984—; instr. clin. pathology U. Oreg. Med. Sch., 1973-74; research cons., 1976—; adv. Nat. Com. for Clin. Lab. Standards, also observer; cons. CHOICE; microbiology time study vol. Coll. Am. Pathologists. Reviewer Current Microiology jour., Sci. Software Quarterly jour., other sci. books and films; vol. editorial bd. Dictionary of Microbiology; contbr. numerous articles to profl. jours.; patentee in field. Chmn. Mary Dimond Scholarship Fund, Lewis and Clark Coll. Recipient 2 Recognition awards Am. Soc. Clin. Pathologists for Continuing Med. Lab. Edn.; grantee Portland VA Hosp., Flow Labs., Inc., Wampole Labs. div. Carter-Wallace, Inc., Hoffmann-LaRoche, Inc., Gen. Diagnostics. Mem. Am. Soc. Microbiology, Nat. Registry Microbiologists, Am. Soc. Clin. Pathologists, Assn. Advancement Med. Instrumentation, AAAS, N.Y. Acad. Sci., Assn. Women in Sci., Sigma Xi, Iota Sigma Pi. Democrat. Episcopalian. Home: 3178 SW Fairmount Blvd Portland OR 97201 Office: Cons Clin and Microbiol Lab Inc 1033 SW Yamhill St Suite 101 Profl Bldg Portland OR 97205

KILBY, DAVE, chamber of commerce executive. Exec. v.p. Modesto C. of C., Modesto, Calif. Office: Modesto C of C PO Box 844 Modesto CA 95353 *

KILCOYNE, RAY F., radiologist; b. Springfield, Ohio, May 14, 1937; s. Ray Leo and Marie Gertrude (Brown) K.; m. Claire Marie Nickeson, July 7, 1977; Paula, Patrick, Martin. BS, U. Dayton, 1960; MD, Marquette U., 1964. Lic. med. diplomate, Wash., Calif., Wis. Chief resident radiology Med. Coll. Wis., Milw., 1970, asst. prof., 1970-75; radiologist Milw. Med. Clin., 1975-80, also bd. dirs; radiologist Allenmore Hosp., Tacoma, 1980; asst. prof. U. Wash., Seattle, 1981-83, assoc. prof. radiology, 1983—; dir. radiology U. Hosp., Seattle, 1983—. Co-author: Handbook of Orthopaedic Radiologic Terminology, 1986; contbr. articles to profl. jours. Served to capt. U.S. Army, 1965-67. Mem. Am. Coll. Radiology (alternate del. 1985—), Radiol. Soc. N. Am., Am. Roentgen Ray Soc. (fellow Armed Forces Inst. Pathology 1969), Internat. Skeletal Soc. (mem. planning com. 1985—). Avocations: computers, photography, scale models, electronics, harpsichord playing. Office: VA Med Ctr Dept Radiology 7400 Merton Minter Blvd San Antonio TX 78284 Office: U Wash Dept Radiology Seattle WA 98105

KILDAY, JAMES MICHAEL, real estate development executive; b. Dixon, Ill., Dec. 23, 1942; s. John Edward and Virginia Arlene (Garber) K.; m. Judith Ann Bott, Feb. 23, 1963; children: Kathleen Anne, Kevin John. MS, Stanford U., 1976. CPA, Ill., Ariz. Pub. acct. 1965-69; with Coopers & Lybrand, Rockford, Ill. and Milw., 1969-73; v.p. fin., treas. Eaton Internat., Phoenix, 1973-77; pres., chief exec. officer Markland Properties Inc., Phoenix, 1977—. Bd. dirs. Scottsdale (Ariz.) Meml. Health Systems Inc., 1985-86, v.p. bd. dirs. 1986-87; chmn. Scottsdale Meml. Hosp. Emergency Dept. Fund Raising Campaign, 1985-86; vice chmn. Scottsdale C. of C. Econ. Devel. Fund Raising Campaign, 1986; bd. dirs. Scottsdale Arts Ctr. Assn., 1986-87, Founders Bank of Ariz., 1986—. Alfred P. Sloan fellow Stanford U. Grad. Sch. Bus., 1975-76. Mem. Am. Inst. CPA's, Ariz. Soc. CPA's, Stanford U. Alumni Assn., Nat. Realty Com. Democrat. Roman Catholic. Office: Markland Properties Inc 5251 N 16th St #900 Phoenix AZ 85016

KILEY, SUSAN JOAN, social worker; b. Montreal, Que., Can., May 8, 1946; d. Thomas Fleming and Lexie Johnson (Ward) W.; m. John Edward Kiley, Aug. 10, 1968; children: Christopher John, Jessica Susan. BA, Cornell U., 1968; MSW, Portland State U., 1975; MBA, Portland U., 1987. Social worker Stark County Child Welfare Services, Canton, Ohio, 1969-70, DISRS, Lawton, Okla., 1970-72; social worker Oreg. Health Scis. U., Portland, 1975-85, acting dir. social work dept., 1986—. Mem. Nat. Assn. Social Workers (cert., mem Oreg. Com. on Inquiry), Nat. Assn. Perinatal Social Workers, Oreg. Assn. Hosp. Social Work Dirs. Home: 2734 NE Bryce St Portland OR 97212 Office: Oreg Health Scis U Social Work Dept 3181 SW Sam Jackson Park Rd Portland OR 97201

KILGORE, MARGARET ADELAIDE, public relations consultant; b. Ravenna, Ohio, Mar. 1, 1935; d. Alfred David Kilgore and Donna Page (Voorhees) Hall. AA, Stephens Coll., 1955; BA, Syracuse U., 1957; MBA, Pepperdine U., 1982. Journalist UPI, Washington, 1957-73, Los Angeles Times, 1973-79; asst. v.p. pub. relations Caesars World, Inc., Los Angeles, 1979-82; dir. corp. pub. relations Ernst & Whinney, Los Angeles, 1982-84; pub. relations cons. Kilgore and Assocs., Los Angeles, 1984—. Ford Found. fellow, 1976; named Outstanding Alumna, Stephens Coll. 1976. Mem. Pub. Relations Soc. Am., Washington Ind. Writers, YWCA (bd. dirs. 1972-75), Sigma Delta Chi. Club: Women's Nat. Press (pres. 1968-69). Avocations: swimming, golf. Home and Office: 2800 Neilson Way Santa Monica CA 90405

KILKENNY, WILLIAM H., materials handling company executive; b. Portland, Oreg., Jan. 29, 1919; s. Earl Robert and Ella (Edmondson) K.; m. Doris Pauline Dunbar, Oct. 13, 1941; 1 child, Robert Earl. B.A., Willamette U., 1941; postgrad., Harvard U., MIT. With Hyster Co., Los Angeles, 1946-59, sales mgr.; sales mgr. Hyster Co., Danville, Ill.; exec. v.p., dir. Hyster S.A. Tessanderlo, Nijemgen, Belgium, 1965-66; dir. Hyster Can. Ltd., Toronto, Ont., 1968-71; pres. Hyster Co., Portland, Oreg., 1971-75; chief exec. officer Hyster Co., Portland, 1975—, chmn., 1976—, also dir.; dir. Esco Corp., Portland, BanCal-Bank Calif., San Francisco,. Mem. exec. bd. Columbia Pacific council Boy Scouts Am.; chmn. Com. to Reform Double Taxation; trustee, Portland Art Assn.; trustee, past chmn. fin. and bus. affairs Willamette U., Salem, Oreg. Recipient Cert. of Distinction, Fin. World Mag., 1984; Silver award Wall St. Transcript, 1984. Mem. Indsl. Truck Assn. (pres. 1968), Oreg. Bus. Council (bd. dirs. 1985). Republican. Presbyterian Clubs: Waverly Country, Arlington, Multnomah Athletic (Portland). Avocations: tennis; golf. Office: Hyster Co PO Box 2902 Portland OR 97208 *

KILLMASTER, JOHN HENRY, III, artist, educator; b. Allegan, Mich., Dec. 2, 1934; s. John H. and Ora Mae (Backus) K.; m. Linda Aileen Olson, Mar. 27, 1965; m. Jeanette Esther Hendricks, May 15, 1971; m. Laverne Horting, 1986; children—Dana, Karen, John Henry IV. B.A. cum laude, Hope Coll., Holland, Mich., 1968; M.F.A., Cranbrook Acad. Art, Bloomfield Hills, Mich., 1969. Artist, designer Ambrose Assocs., 1953-56, LaDriere Inc., Detroit, 1957-62; asst. prof. art Ferris State Coll., Big Rapids, Mich., 1966-67, 69-70; prof. art Boise State U., 1970—; important works include: exterior mural Boise Gallery of Art, 1974; sculpture City of Portland, 1977; lobby mural Morrison Knudsen Corp., Boise, 1982; wall sculpture Idaho First Nat. Bank, 1980; wall relief mural Morrison Performing Arts Ctr., 1984. Recipient Gov.'s award for excellence in the arts State of Idaho, 1978; Western States Art Found. grantee, 1975. Mem. Nat. Enamelist Guild, Idaho Art Assn., N.W. Designers and Craftsmen. Home: 2611 Davis Boise ID 83702 Office: 1910 University Dr Boise ID 83725

KILMER, JOYCE CARL, real estate company executive; b. Malmo, Minn., Aug. 29, 1924; s. Carl William and Anna Christine (Ostermann) K.; m. Ione Bernice Hust, Jan. 3, 1953; children—Jeffrey K., Jana Lee Kilmer Wallace. Student, U. Minn., 1944-45, Colo. U., 1967-68; cert. in real estate sales Regis Coll., 1981. Lineman Mountain Bell Telephone Co., Denver, 1947-50, recordman, 1950-53, right-of-way engr., Denver, 1953-55, right-of-way agent, 1955-83; field supr. U.S. Telecommunications, Kansas City, Kans., 1985-86; project supt. acquisitions, Williams Telecommunications Co., Tulsa, 1986—; real estate cons., Livingston, Mont., 1983-84, GTE-Sprint, Orlando, Fla., 1984—, Mountain Bell Telephone Co., Grand Junction, Colo., 1984—, City of Grand Junction, 1984—, Butler Service Group, Durango, Colo. and Orlando, Fla., 1983-84; right-of-way cons. U.S. Telecom, Inc., 1985-86, Wiltel, Inc., 1986; cons. and supr. United Telephone Co. of Ohio, 1986. Active Boy Scouts Am., Denver, 1954, 61-78; vice commdr. USCG Aux., Grand Junction, 1975-76, flotilla commdr., 1976-78. Served with U.S. Army, 1943-43. Sr. mem. Internat. Right-of-Way Assn. (pres. Colo. West chpt. 70, 1978, dir. Rocky Mountain region 1982, Profl. of Yr. 1982, 83, Frank C. Balfour award finalist, 1983, 85); mem. Nat. Assn. Ind. Appraisers, Am. Legion. Republican. Methodist.

KILPATRICK, BEVERLY AVIS, advertising/public relations executives; b. Sacramento, Mar. 1, 1936; d. Frank and Irene J. (Avis) Bernardo; m. Joseph W. Kilpatrick, June 7, 1958; 1 son: Joseph Warren. Ed. Sacramento State Coll. Tchr., Lakeland Sch. Dist., Goldwater, Mich., 1960-61; copywriter Sta. WTVB Radio, Angola, Ind., 1961; dep. Unemployment Dept., State of Ind., Ft. Wayne, 1961-63; copywriter/prodn. Sta. KXRQ Radio, Sacramento, 1963-65; media dir. Dannenfelser, Runyan & Craig, Inc., 1965-73; v.p.,treas. Boyle/Kilpatrick & Assocs., Modesto, Calif., 1973—; dir. Stanislaus Media and Advt. Club, 1976-78. Vice chmn. Modesto Selective Service Bd., 1982—; v.p. bd. dirs. Stanislaus County YMCA, 1976-79; sec. bd. dirs. Bldg. Industry Assn. Central Calif., 1979-82; bd. dirs. Stanislaus County United Way, 1982—, Scenic Gen. Hosp. Found., 1982—; exec. bd. Valley Video Network for Community TV, 1979-81; pres. Muir Trail council Girl Scouts U.S., 1985—; dir. adv. bd. Women's Ctr., 1982—, others. Recipient YMCA Appreciation for Service to Youth plaque, 1978; Bldg. Industry Assn. of Central Calif. Assoc. of Yr., 1980. Mem. Network, Nat. Assn. Female Execs. Clubs: Cabrillo Civic, Modesto Trade (exec. bd. dirs.), Soroptimist (past pres. Modesto). Home: 1315 Sycamore Modesto CA 95350 Office: 1226 11th St Suite C Modesto CA 95354

KILPATRICK, FRANK STANTON, investment banker, management consultant; b. San Jose, Calif., Dec. 2, 1950; s. Frank George and Marian (Polk) K.; AB in Polit. Sci., U. Calif., Berkeley, 1975, postgrad., 1976; student U. Wis., 1968-71, Stanford U. Grad. Sch. Bus., 1981. Successively writer, advt. sales rep., Midwest regional mgr., Western mktg. mgr. 13-30 Corp., pub. Esquire mag., 1970-74; with Grey Advt., 1977; mktg. mgr. East/West Network, 1978-79; mktg. dir. Calif. Bus. mag., Los Angeles, 1979-81; v.p. mktg. Laufer Co. div. Harlequin Enterprises, 1981; gen. mgr. new venture devel. Knapp Communications Corp. (pub. Archtl. Digest, Bon Appétit, GEO and Home mags.), 1981-84; gen. ptnr. Pacific Cellular, 1982-86; gen. ptnr. Calif. Coast Communications, 1981-84; dir. Pasadena Media Inc., 1984-85, pres. 1984-85; mgmt. cons. Frank S. Kilpatrick & Assocs., Los Angeles, 1984—; lectr. entrepreneur program U. So. Calif. Sch. Bus. Adminstrn., 1984-85; guest lectr. grad. sch. mgmt. UCLA, 1985—; pres. Capital Equity Group, 1986—. Mem. Los Angeles Advt. Club (Belding award 1980), Direct Mktg. Club So. Calif., Western Publs. Assn., Town Hall Calif., U. Calif. Alumni Assn., Stanford Grad. Sch. Bus. Alumni Assn. (sec. 1985-86, v.p. events 1986-87), Los Angeles Venture Assn. (charter mem. 1985—). Home: 3890 Rambla Orienta Malibu CA 90265 Office: 1800 Century Park E Suite 400 Los Angeles CA 90067

KILTS, CLAIR THEODORE, educator; b. Ogden, Utah, Sept. 13, 1930; s. William Theodore and Alice Elnora (Simpson) K.; m. Liliane Lucie Burgat, Apr. 29, 1954; children: Jeffery, Timothy, Mark, Rebecca, Matthew. AS, Weber State Coll., 1950; BA, Brigham Young U., 1957, MA, 1959. Cert. secondary tchr., Utah. Tchr. Ogden City Schs., 1959—; instr. night sch. Weber State Coll., Ogden, 1960-63, Brigham Young U., Ogden, 1964-68. Author: Utah Territorial Court Conflict 1850-1874, 1959. Trustee Hooper (Utah) Water Improvement Dist., 1968—; mem. council advancement com. Lake Bonneville Council Boy Scouts Am., 1980-82. Served with M.I. Corps, U.S. Army, 1954-56. Recipient Award of merit Boy Scouts Am., 1967, Silver Beaver award Boy Scouts Am., 1969, Outstanding Tchr. award Utah State Hist. Soc., 1978, Liberty Bell award Utah State Bar Assn., 1980. Mem. NEA, Utah Edn. Assn., Ogden Edn. Assn. (pres. 1974, 80, 85, Award of Honor, 1980), Phi Delta Kappa, Phi Alpha Theta. Democrat. Mormon. Avocations: fishing, hunting, gardening, travelling. Home: 6008 W 5500 S Hooper UT 84315 Office: Mt Ogden Middle Sch 3260 Harrison Blvd Ogden UT 84403

KILZER, HOWARD JAMES, electrical engineer; b. Richardton, N.D., Sept. 13, 1958; s. Bernard Anton and Eva (Stroh) K. A in Applied Sci., N.D. State Sch. Sci., 1979; BS, N.D. State U., 1985. Engr. in tng. Engring. technician Finley Engring. Co., Bismarck, N.D., 1980-83; elec. engr. Goodyear Aerospace Co., Litchfield Park, Ariz., 1985—. Roman Catholic. Lodge: KC. Avocations: running, electronic repair, hiking, fishing. Home: 7077 W McDowell #223 Phoenix AZ 85035 Office: Goodyear Aerospace Corp PO Box 85 MS 1312 Litchfield Park AZ 85340

KIM, DEWEY HONGWOO, public service consultant; b. Washington, July 4, 1928; s. Henry Cu and Edith (Ahn) K.; B.A. with honors, U. Hawaii, 1950; M.P.A. with highest distinction (Hugh D. Ingersol Outstanding Grad. award), Maxwell Sch., Syracuse (N.Y.) U., 1961; LL.D. (hon.), Myong Ji U., Seoul, Korea, 1981; m. Lila Lee, Mar. 10, 1951; children—Melissa, Dewey Hongwoo, Michael. Personnel officer 14th Coast Guard Dist., 1953-54; with IRS, 1956-68, dir. mgmt. tng., 1966-68; assoc. dean Coll. Continuing Edn., U. Hawaii, 1968-70, asst. v.p. acad. affairs, 1970-78, vice-chancellor for community colls., 1978-80, chancellor community colls., 1980-83, chancellor emeritus, 1983—; dir. Pacific and Asian affairs Pub. Adminstrn. Service, 1983—; mgmt. cons., 1960—; dir. 1st Fed. Savs. & Loan Assn., Firstfed of Am., Inc.; v.p. Friends of the Ctr. for Korean Studies U. Hawaii, 1986—. Exec. asst. Honolulu Fed. Exec. Bd., 1967; chmn. Hawaii Task Force Police and Pub. Protection, 1970-74; commr. Accrediting Commn. Jr. and Community Colls. Trustee U. Hawaii Found., 1972-82; co-sponsor Dewey and Lila Kim fellowship for univ. faculty in English from Korea to study in U.S.; chmn. adv. council Kapiolani Community Coll., 1985—. Recipient awards IRS, 1958, 59, 67, 68; William E. Mosher fellow, 1960-61. Mem. Am. Soc. Pub. Adminstrn. (pres. Honolulu 1959), Honolulu Fed. Businessmen's Assn., Western Assn. Schs. and Colls. (chmn. and pres. 1981-83), Soc. Fellow Syracuse U. (founding mem. 1986), Phi Kappa Phi.

KIM, DONALD CHANG WON, consulting engineering company executive; b. Seoul, Republic of Korea, Dec. 14, 1928; s. Yu Ho and Sook Kyung (Lee) K.; m. Iris Kyong Ok Yoo, Dec. 29, 1962; children: Rex Kee Chul, Dean Sang Kee. Student, Seoul Nat. U., 1949-52; BS, U. Hawaii, 1953-58. Design engr. R.M. Towill Corp., Honolulu, 1958-65, project engr., 1965-69, mgr. engring. dept., 1969-72, v.p., 1971-72, exec. v.p., 1972-78, pres., chmn. bd. dirs., 1978—; pres., bd. dirs. Kilohana Corp., Honolulu; bd. dirs. Genex Inc., Honolulu; chmn. bd. dirs. Amkor A&E, Inc., Seoul. Editor: Korean Pacific Weekly, 1956-70. Chmn. Korean Community Council of Hawaii, Honolulu, 1967-69; trustee of funds Inha Inst. Tech., Inchun, Korea, 1967-70. Named Engr. of Distinction, Engring. Joint Council of USA, 1973, Leader of Hawaii Star Bull., 1972; recipient Disting. Alumni award U. Hawaii, 1982. Mem. Hawaii Council Engring. Socs. (chmn. 1971-72), NSPE (nat. bd. dir. 1974-78), Hawaii Soc. Profl. Engrs. (pres. 1972-73), Soc. Am. Mil. Engrs. (bd. dir. 1977-78), Am. Assn. Engring. Socs., Air Pollution Control Assn., Bldg. Industry Assn. of Hawaii, ASCE, ASTM, Am. Water Works Assn., Water Pollution Control Fedn. Mem. United Ch. Christ. Clubs: Internat. Country., President's (U. Hawaii), Korean U. (Honolulu pres. 1967, 85), Dongji Hoi (pres. 1987). Lodge: Rotary. Home: 1833 Laukahi St Honolulu HI 96821 Office: R M Towill Corp 677 Ala Moana Blvd Suite 1016 Honolulu HI 96813

KIM, EDWARD WILLIAM, ophthalmic surgeon; b. Seoul, Korea, Nov. 25, 1949; came to U.S., 1957; s. Shoon Kul and Pok Chu (Kim) K.; m. Carole Sachi Takemoto, July 24, 1976; children—Brian, Ashley. B.A., Occidental Coll., Los Angeles, 1971; postgrad. Calif. Inst. Tech., 1971; M.D., U. Calif.-San Francisco, 1975; M.P.H., U. Calif.-Berkley, 1975. Diplomate Nat. Bd. Med. Examiners, Am. Bd. Ophthalmology. Intern, San Francisco Gen. Hosp., 1975-76; resident in ophthalmology Harvard U.-Mass. Eye and Ear Infirmary, Boston, 1977-79; clin. fellow in ophthalmology Harvard U., 1977-79; clin. fellow in retina Harvard, 1980; practice medicine in ophthalmic surgery, South Laguna and San Clemente, Calif., 1980—; vol. ophthalmologist Eye Care Inc., Ecole St. Vincent's, Haiti, 1980; core investigator Staar Surg., Monrovia, Calif., 1984—; chief of staff-elect South Coast Med. Ctr., 1986-87. Founding mem. Orange County Ctr. for Performing Arts, Calif., 1982; pres. Laguna Beach Summer Music Festival, Calif., 1984. Reinhart scholar U. Calif.-San Francisco, 1972-73; R. Taussig scholar, 1974-75. Fellow ACS, Am. Acad. Ophthalmology, Internat. Coll. Surgeons; mem. Calif. Med. Assn., Keratorefractive Soc., Orange County Med. Assn., Mensa, Expts. in Art and Tech. Office: Ophthalmic Assocs 31872 Coast Hwy Suite 203 South Laguna CA 92677

KIM, HARRY HYUNKIL, urban geographer; b. Seoul, Korea, Jan. 17, 1938; came to U.S., 1964, naturalized, 1971; s. Yoon Ha and Saeng Kun (Chong) K.; M.A., U. Wash., Seattle, 1967, Ph.D., 1972; m. Jiyon Kim, May 9, 1970; children—Peter H., Hanna H. Urban planner II, King County Planning Commn., Seattle, 1972-74; prof. U. South Fla., Tampa, 1974-79; specialist U.S. Dept. HUD, Seattle, 1979—; Fulbright scholar, India, 1978; cons. in Asian devel., housing devel. and mgmt., urban environment, water/solid waste; lectr. urban geography, housing mgmt. to profl. and civic groups. Bd. dirs. program agy. Presbyn. Ch. U.S.A.; mem. nat. com. of Self-Devel. of People. Served with Korean Army, 1960-62. Fla. State Energy Office grantee, 1976. Mem. Assn. Am. Geographers, Nat. Geog. Soc., Am. Geog. Soc., Presbyn. Housing Assn. (pres.), Presbyn. Ministry Inc. (bd. dirs.), Seattle-Wash. Korean Assn. (chmn. bd. dirs. 1982), Tampa Korean Assn. in Fla. (pres. 1976). Republican. Presbyterian (staff personnel com. Synod of Alaska-N.W., mem. strategy com. dept. mission and evangelism Presbytery of Seattle). Contbr. articles to profl. jours. Home: 4239 NE 74th St Seattle WA 98115 Office: HUD 1321 2d Ave Seattle WA 98101

KIM, HEE-JIN, religious studies educator, administrator; b. Masan, Korea, Apr. 8, 1927; came to U.S., 1952; s. Young-Ho and Um-Chon Kim; m. Kyue-In Lee, June 4, 1957 (dec. Aug. 1963); children—Sun-Chul, Hae-Sil; m. Jung-Sun, Feb. 7, 1965; 1 child, Yeong-Jue. B.A., U. Calif.-Berkeley, 1957, M.A., 1958; Ph.D., Claremont Grad. Sch., Calif., 1966. Asst. prof. philosophy and religion U. Vt., Burlington, 1965-67; asst. prof. religion Wright State U., Dayton, Ohio, 1967-70; vis. asst. prof. religion Claremont Grad. Sch. Sch. Theology, Calif., 1970-72; prof. religious studies U. Oreg., Eugene, 1973—. Author: Dogen Kigen—Mystical Realist, 1975, rev. edit., 1987, Flowers of Emptiness: Selections from Dogen's Shobogenzo, 1985; contbr. articles to profl. jours. Recipient Faculty Research award U. Oreg. Grad. Sch., 1976-77; Blaisdell Inst. for Advanced Study in World Cultures and Religions research fellow, 1970-72. Mem. Assn. for Asian Studies, Soc. for Asian and Comparative Philosophy, Am. Acad. Religion, Internat. Assn. Buddhist Studies, Tibet Soc. Democrat. Home: 570 Ful Vue Dr Eugene OR 97405 Office: U Oreg Dept Religious Studies Eugene OR 97403

KIM, KWANG SIK, pediatrician, researcher; b. Seoul, Korea, June 9, 1947; came to U.S., 1974; s. Taejong and Kyung Ja (Cho) K.; m. Aeran Yoon, June 30, 1983; children: Melissa Yongsun, Brian Yongjin. BS, Seoul Nat. U. Korea, 1967, MD, 1971. Intern Ellis Hosp., Schenectady, N.Y., 1974-75; resident La. State U. Med. Ctr., New Orleans, 1975-78; fellow Harbor UCLA Med. Ctr., Torrance, 1978-80; asst. prof. pediatrics UCLA Sch. Medicine, 1980-86; assoc. prof. Children's Hosp. Los Angeles, 1986—. Recipient Basil O'Connor award March of Dimes, 1982; NIH grantee, 1984. Mem. Western Soc. Pediatric Research, Soc. Pediatric Research, Am. Soc. Microbiology, Infectious Diseases Soc. Am., Am. Fedn. Clin. Research, Am. Heart Assn. (sr. investigator 1983). Office: Children's Hosp Los Angeles 4650 Sunset Blvd Los Angeles CA 90027

KIM, SOON SAM, research chemist; b. Seoul, Republic of Korea, Jan. 3, 1945; came to U.S., 1969; s. Chul and Young Ae (Jin) K.; m. Inho Park, Feb. 27, 1970. BS, Seoul Nat. U., 1967; PhD, U. Chgo., 1974. Postdoctoral fellow Washington U., St. Louis, 1975-79; research scientist Occidental Research Corp., Irvine, Calif., 1979-82; mem. tech. staff Jet Propulsion Lab., Pasadena, Calif., 1982—. Contbr. articles to profl. jours. Served to 2d lt. with Republic of Korea Army, 1967-69. Mem. Am. Chem. Soc., Am. Phys.

Soc. Methodist. Home: 3666 S Mall Irvine CA 92714 Office: Jet Propulsion Lab MS 67-201 4800 Oak Grove Dr Pasadena CA 91109

KIMBALL, BRUCE ARNOLD, soil scientist; b. Aitkin, Minn., Sept. 27, 1941; s. Robert Clinton and Rica (Barneveld) K.; m. Laurel Sue Hanway, Aug. 20, 1966; children: Britt, Rica, Megan. BS, U. Minn., 1963; MS, Iowa State U., 1965; PhD, Cornell U., 1970. Soil scientist USDA-Agrl. Research Service U.S. Water Conservation Lab., Phoenix, 1969—. Co-editor: CO2 Enrichment of Green House Crops, 1986; contbr. articles to profl. jours. Mem. AAAS, Am. Soc. Agronomy, Soil Sci. Soc. Am. (assoc. editor 1977-83), Am. Soc. Agrl. Engring. (assoc. editor 1984—), Internat. Solar Energy Soc. Avocations: computer programming, woodworking, jogging. Office: US Water Conservation Lab 4331 E Broadway Phoenix AZ 85040

KIMBALL, CHARLES DUNLAP, physician; b. Watertown, N.Y., Oct. 14, 1908; s. Charles Campbell and Elizabeth (Dunlap) K.; m. Helen Stryker; 1 child, Nöel. MD, SUNY, Buffalo, 1934. Diplomate Am. Bd. Ob-Gyn. Intern Virginia Mason Hosp., Seattle, 1934-35, resident in surgery, 1936-37; resident in ob-gyn U. Chgo. Lying-In Hosp., 1938-39; fellow in ob-gyn Mayo Found., 1940-41; clin. assoc. prof. ob-gyn W. Wash., Seattle, 1953-58, 60-62; research assoc. U. Chgo., 1958-60; practice medicine specializing in ob-gyn Seattle, 1947-57, 1961-84; endorphin research Virginia Mason Rsearch Ctr., Seattle, 1978—. Patentee in field. Served to lt. col. USAAF, 1943-46. Fellow ACS, Am. Coll. Ob-Gyn (founder, chmn. 8th dist. 1951-53, asst. sec. 1953-55), Pacific Coast Ob-Gyn Soc. (pres. 1985-86). Episcopalian. Avocations: skiing, golf. Home: 900 University St #1-Y Seattle WA 98101

KIMBALL, DAN ANDERSON, chemist; b. Malad, Idaho, Feb. 26, 1951; s. Eldon Clifford and Esther Louise (Anderson) K.; m. Pamela Gail Ingoldsby, Dec. 29, 1973; children: Benjamin Alan, Bridget Aleen, Clinton Dan, Trudy Rochelle. Degree in polish linguistics, Def. Lang. Inst., 1974; BS in Chemistry, Brigham Young U., 1978; MS in Chemistry, San Diego State U., 1980. Dir. quality control, research and devel. Calif. Citrus Products, Inc., Lindsay, Calif., 1980—; Cert. community coll. tchr., Calif. Contbr. articles to profl. jours. Chmn. Calif. Citrus Symposium, Lindsay, 1985; dist. leader Mt. Whitney Council Boy Scouts Am., Visalia, Calif., 1985—. Served with U.S. Army, 1972-76. Mem. AAAS, Fla. State Hort. Soc. (Pres. Industry award 1984), Citrus Products Tech. Com., Inst. Food Technologists, Am. Chem. Soc., SUC, Lindsay Jaycees (chmn. 1985-86, pres. 1984-85), Calif. Jaycees (exec. com dist. gov. 1986-87). Republican. Mormon. Home: 483 Garden Ave Lindsay CA 93247

KIMBALL, DICK (CHARLES RICHARD ROBATOR), organist, educator; b. Essex, Mass., June 19, 1937; s. Lionel William and Viola May (Kimball) R.; A.A., Seattle Community Coll., 1981; div.; children—Julie Marie, Carson Leonard, Lisa. Organist, cocktail lounges, Helena, Mont., 1959-61, Everett and Seattle, 1961-69; organ instr. Holiday Music Co., Seattle, 1971-78, Evans Music Co., Seattle, 1980-82, Sherman-Clay Co., San Francisco, 1982—; organist Seattle Totems Hockey Club, 1973-75, Seattle Supersonics basketball, 1974-75, Seattle Sounders Soccer Club, 1976-78, Seattle Mariners Baseball Club, 1977-82; musician Walter Hawkins' Love Ctr. Ch., Oakland, Calif. Mem. Am. Fedn. Musicians, Am. Theatre Organ Soc. Record album: A Natural Man; (organist) Walter Hawkins Love Alive III. Home: 22 Gardenside Dr #14 San Francisco CA 94131

KIMBALL, ROGER STANLEY, physician; b. Portland, Oreg., May 18, 1935; s. Stanley M. and Sylvia M. (Seymour) K.; B.A., Stanford U., 1957; M.A., U. Calif., Berkeley, 1958; M.D., Albany Med. Coll., 1962; m. Patricia M. Wadsworth, Apr. 11, 1970; children—Keri Ann, Dyana Jean. Intern, Highland Hosp., Oakland, Calif., 1962-63; resident U. Calif. Med. Center, San Francisco, 1963-67; practice medicine specializing in internal medicine, San Francisco, 1969—; mem. staffs U. Calif. Hosps., Ralph K. Davies Med. Center Hosp.; fellow in cardiology, dept. medicine Stanford U., 1965; asso. clin. prof. medicine Sch. Medicine, U. Calif., San Francisco. Mem. AMA, Am. Soc. Internal Medicine, Calif. Med. Soc. Presbyterian. Home: 183 Los Robles Dr Burlingame CA 94010 Office: 350 Parnassus Ave San Francisco CA 94117

KIMBELL, JEFF CRAIG, sr. industrial engineer; b. Everett, Wash., July 16, 1959; s. Gordon Craig and Arlene Anne (Gannon) K.; m. Kimberly Jane Johnson, Mar. 20, 1982. BS in Indsl. Engring., U. Wash., 1981. Lic. profl. engr., Wash. Assoc. engr. Snohomish County Pub. Utilities Dist., Everett, 1979-80; indsl. engr. Bethlehem Steel Corp., Seattle, 1981-83; sr. indsl. engr. Teltone Corp., Kirkland, Wash., 1983—. conf. staff Jr. Achievement, 1978-80, advisor, judge, 1981-86. Mem. Inst. Indsl. Engrs. (bd. dirs. Puget Sound chpt. 1984—; Oustanding Indsl. Engr. award 1985), Puget Sound Engring. Council, Tau Beta Pi. Republican. Baptist. Club: Mountaineers (Seattle). Avocations: climbing, hiking, bicycling, photography.

KIMBELL, MARION JOEL, systems engring. cons.; b. McDonough, Ga., Sept. 7, 1923; s. Charles Marvin and Mary (McMillian) K.; B.S. in Civil Engring., U. Houston, 1949, M.Chem. Engring., 1953; m. Judy Weidner, Dec. 18, 1946; children—Nancy, Susan, Candice. Civil engr. U.S. Dept. Interior, Lemmon, S.D., 1954; chief piping engr. M.W. Kellog Co., Paducah, Ky., 1955; nuclear engr. Westinghouse Atomic Power Div., Pitts., 1956-59; control systems prin. engr. Kaiser Engrs., Oakland, Calif., 1959-80; control systems supervising engr. Bechtel Inc., San Francisco, 1980—; control systems tchr. Laney Coll. cons. engr. NASA, Gen. Atomic Co.; advisory bd. Chabot Collage on radiation tech. Served as sgt. U.S. Army, 1943-46. Registered profl. nuclear engr., Calif.; control systems engr., Calif. Mem. Instrument Soc. of Am. (sr. mem. exec. com.). Clubs: Moose. Contbr. articles to profl. jours. Home: 22324 Ralston Ct Hayward CA 94541 Office: Bechtel Inc 50 Beal St PO Box 3965 San Francisco CA 94119

KIMBLE, CAROL, marketing professional; b. Seattle; d. James M. and Grace (Dolan) Cain. Student, U. Wash., 1962; BA, U. Ariz., 1964. Project sales mgr. Mike McCormack Realtors, Honolulu, 1974-76, project account mgr., 1976-78, projects mktg. dir., 1978-81; mktg. cons. Kimble and Assocs., Honolulu, 1981-84; project sales mgr. Gentry Realty Ltd., Honolulu, 1984-85; mktg. dir. Gentry Cos., Honolulu, 1985—. Contbr. articles to profl. jours. Recipient awards Parade of Homes, 1976-80, 83, 85-86. Mem. Local and Nat. Assn. Realtors, Bldg. Industry Assn., Nat. Sales and Mktg. Council, MIRM. Avocation: long distance swimming. Home: 554 Ahina St Honolulu HI 96816 Office: Gentry Cos. 94-539 Puahi St Honolulu HI 96797

KIMBLE, DANIEL PORTER, psychology educator; b. Chgo., Nov. 18, 1934; s. Ralph Archibald and Ruth (Hazen) K.; m. Reeva Jacobson; children: Matthew, Evan, Sara. BA, Knox Coll., 1956; PhD, U. Mich., 1961. Asst. prof. U. Oreg., Eugene, 1963-66, assoc. prof., 1966-69, prof. psychology, 1969—. Author: Physiological Psychology: A Unit for Introductory Psychology, 1963, Psychology as a Biological Science, 2d rev. edit. 1977; editor: The Anatomy of Memory, 1965, The Organization of Recall, 1967, Experience and Capacity, 1968, Readiness to Remember, 1970, Contrast and Controversy in Modern Psychology, 1977, Biological Psychology, 1987; contbr. articles to profl. jours. Fellow Woodrow Wilson, 1956-57, Horace Rackham, 1958-59, NIH, 1961-63, NSF, 1969-70. Mem. Am. Assn. Sci., Neurosci. Soc. Avocations: philately, sports. Office: U Oreg Inst Neuroscience Dept Psychology Eugene OR 97403

KIMBRELL, GRADY NED, author, educator; b. Tallant, Okla., Apr. 6, 1933; s. Virgil Leroy Kimbrell and La Veria Dee Underwood; m. Marilyn Louise King, May 30, 1953 (div.); m. Mary Ellen Cunningham, Apr. 11, 1973; children: Mark Leroy, Lisa Christine, Joni Lynne. BA, Southwestern Coll., Winfield, Kans., 1956; MA, Colo. State Coll., 1958. Cert. tchr. (life), Calif., Colo.; cert. adminstr., Calif. Bus. tchr. Peabody (Kans.) High Sch., 1956-58; bus. tchr. Santa Barbara (Calif.) High Sch., 1958-60, coordinator work edn., 1965-75, dir. research and evaluation, 1975—; cons., textbook researcher and author. Author: Introduction to Business and Office Careers, 1974, The World of Work Career Interest Survey, 1986, The Testmaker for Succeeding in the World of Work, 1986; co-author: Succeeding in the World of Work, 1970, 4th rev. edit., 1986, Entering the World of Work, 1978, 3d edit., 1987, Independent Study for the World of Work, 1974, 3d edit., 1984, The Savvy Consumer Activities, 1984. Served as cpl. U.S. Army, 1953-55. Mem. NEA, Calif. Assn. Work Experience Educators (life, v.p. 1968-70), Nat. Work Experience Edn. Assn., Calif. Tchrs. Assn., Coop. Work Experience Assn. Republican. Lodge: Kiwanis (sec. local chpt. 1968-70). Avocations: breeding and racing quarter horses and thoroughbreds. Office: Santa Barbara Sch Dists 723 E Cota Santa Barbara CA 93103

KIMENYI, ALEXANDRE, linguistics educator; b. Butare, Rwanda, Aug. 15, 1948; s. Dionizi Muterahejuru and Laurentia Nyirabagenzi; m. Mathilde Mukantabana, Dec. 27, 1980; children: Saro Kanyambo, Gitego Shema, Ndahiro Bazimya. BA, Institut Pedagogique National, Butare, 1971; MA in English, UCLA, 1973, MA in Linguistics, 1974, PhD in Linguistics, 1976. Prof. linguistics Calif. State U.-Davis, Sacramento, 1976—. Author: Studies in Kinyarwanda and Bantu Phonology, 1979, A Relational Grammar of Kinyarwanda, 1980; editor Impuruza Jour., 1983—. NEH grantee, Los Angeles, 1979, Austin, Tex., 1982. Mem. Linguistics Soc. Am., Semiotics Soc. Am., African Studies Assn., N.Y. Acad. Scis. Home: 7400 Flores Way Sacramento CA 95819 Office: Calif State U Dept Linguistics 6000 J St Sacramento CA 95819

KIMME, ERNEST GODFREY, research communications engr.; b. Long Beach, Calif., June 7, 1929; s. Ernest Godfrey and Lura Elizabeth (Dake) K.; B.A. magna cum laude, Pomona Coll., 1952; M.A., U. Minn., 1954, Ph.D., 1955; m. Margaret Jeanne Bolen, Dec. 10, 1978; children by previous marriage—Ernest G., Elizabeth E., Karl Frederick. Mem. grad. faculty Oreg. State U., Corvallis, 1955-57; mem. tech. staff Bell Telephone Labs., Murray Hill, N.J., 1957-65, supr. mobile radio research lab., 1962-65; head applied sci. dept. Collins Radio Co., Newport Beach, Calif., 1965-72; research engr. Northrop Electronics, Hawthorne, Calif., 1972-74; sr. staff engr. Interstate Electronics Corp., Anaheim, Calif., 1974-79; dir. advanced systems, dir. advanced communications systems, tech. dir. spl. communications programs Gould Navcomm Systems, El Monte, Calif., 1979-82; pres. Cobit, Inc, 1982-84; tech. staff Gen. Research Corp., Santa Barbara, 1984-87; dir. communications engring. Starfind, Inc., Laguna Niguel, Calif., 1987—; prin. assoc. Ameta Cons. Technologists. Mem. AAAS, IEEE, Soc. Indsl. and Applied Math., Aircraft Owners and Pilots Assn., Phi Beta Kappa, Sigma Xi. Contbr. articles to profl. jours. Home: 301 Starfire St Anaheim CA 92807 Office: 160A N Fairview Suite 107 Goleta CA 93117

KIMMEL, CARY ALLEN, electronics executive; b. N.Y.C., Sept. 21, 1943; s. Sam and Helen (Siegal) K.; m. Rita Terese Kinsella, Nov. 24, 1967; children: David Larkin, Robert Lowell, Sarah Catherine. BA, Queens Coll., 1964; postgrad., Air Force Inst. Tech., 1967. Fgn. service res. officer U.S. Dept. State, N.Y.C., 1964; planning analyst U.S. Dept. Navy, Washington, 1964-67; sr. parametric analyst Grumman Aircraft Co., Bethpage, N.Y., 1967-69; fin. mgmt. positions Xerox Corp, Rochester, N.Y., 1969-84; program mgr. Xerox Corp., El Segundo, Calif., 1984—. Mem. Assn. Info. Processing, Am. Mgmt. Assn. (lectr. 1986). Office: Xerox Corp 701 S Aviation Blvd El Segundo CA 90245

KIMMEL, MARK, venture capital co. exec.; b. Denver, Feb. 15, 1940; s. Earl Henry and Gerry Claire Kimmel; B.S. in Elec. Engring., U. Colo., 1963, B.S. in Mktg., 1963; M.B.A. in Fin., U. So. Calif., 1966; m. Gloria J. Danielewicz, Jan. 29, 1966 (div.), children—Kenton, Kristopher. Sales engr., market research analyst 3M Co., Calif. and Minn., 1963-70; mktg. mgr. Am. Computer and Communications, Calif., 1970-71; mgr. new bus. devel. Motorola, Inc., Schaumburg, Ill., 1971-76; v.p. corp. devel. Nat. City Lines, Denver, 1976-77; pres. Enervest, Inc., Denver, 1977-84; now gen. ptnr. Columbine Venture Fund Ltd.; pres. Columbine Venture Mgmt. Inc.; bd. dirs. MAXIM Fund, Am. Internat. Communications, Athens Inc., Stolar Corp., Krysalis Corp., Innovus Inc. Mem. Nat. Assn. Small Bus. Investment Cos. (past bd. govs.), Venture Capital Assn. Colo. (chmn.). Republican. Home: 7500 E Dartmouth Ave Apt 20 Denver CO 80231 Office: 5613 DTC Pkwy Suite 510 Englewood CO 80111

KIMMERLE, GERALD WILLIAM, insurance company executive; b. Seattle, Dec. 11, 1928; s. John William and Elsie Evelyn (Gustafson) K.; m. Joan Beverly Hinxman, Sept. 11, 1953; 1 child, Susan D. Foltz. BA in Econs., U. Wash., 1951; postgrad., Stanford U., 1978. Broker Wash. Union Group, Seattle, 1956-59; group field rep. Pacific Mut. Life Ins. Co., Seattle, 1955-56, pension specialist, 1959-60, mgr., 1960-62; regional dir. Pacific Mut. Life Ins. Co., Los Angeles, 1962-71, asst. v.p., 1971-72; from v.p. to exec. v.p. Pacific Mut. Life Ins. Co., Fountain Valley, Calif., 1972—; bd. dirs. Life Ins. Mktg. Research Assn., Farmington, Conn., CaPP Care, Inc. ; chmn. bd. dirs. Imperial Industries, Pacific Fin. HMO Holding Co.; chmn. bd. dirs., chief exec. officer Group Holding Co., Pacific Fin. Life Ins. Co. Bd. dirs. Pacific Mut. Polit. Action Com., Newport Beach, 1985. Mem. Life Ins. Mktg. Research Assn. (bd. dirs.), Health Ins. Assn. Am. (corr. officer). Republican. Lutheran. Avocation: golf. Office: Pacific Mut Life Ins Co 17360 Brookhurst St Fountain Valley CA 92708

KIMSEY, LYNN SIRI, entomologist; b. Oakland, Calif., Feb. 1, 1953; d. William E. and Jean B. (Brandenburg) Siri; m. Robert B. Kimsey, Oct. 13, 1976; children: Benjamin, Erin. BS, U. Calif., Davis, 1975, PhD, 1979. Freelance sci. illustrator Davis, 1972-85; postdoctoral research assoc. U. Calif., Davis, 1979-80, 82—, lectr., 1982; postdoctoral research assoc. Smithsonian Tropical Research Inst., Balboa, Republic of Panama, 1981; cons. Calif. Dept. Food and Agrl., Sacramento, 1984. Contbr. articles to profl. jours. AAUW fellow, 1982; grantee Can. Coll. Research, Can. Nat. Collection, Ottawa, Ont., 1983, NSF, 1984—. Fellow Sigma Xi; mem. AAAS, Pacific Coast Entomol. Soc., Kans. Entomol. Soc., Hymenopterists Soc. Democrat. Avocations: raising orchids, drawing. Office: U Calif Dept Entomology Davis CA 95616

KIMURA, FELICIA SOY KEE, health administrator, official; b. Honolulu, Dec. 11, 1955; d. Alfred Dai Cheong and Wai Quen (Chang) Goo; m. Brian Takao Kimura, July 1, 1978; children—Sharmaine L.M.T., Evan K.M.T. Student Creighton U., 1973-74, 76, U. Nebr.-Omaha, 1977-78; B.A. in Psychology, Chaminade U., 1982. Audiometric technician Dept. Health, State Hawaii Sch. Health Support Services Br., Kona, Hawaii, 1982-84, casework mgr. Kona Krafts Dept. Mental Health, Kealakekua, 1986—; sales, mgr. H. Kimura, Inc., Kealakekua, 1978—; silk screener Felicia's Tees, Kealakekua, 1982—; sales cons. Liberty House of Hawaii, Kailua-Kona, 1985-86. Mem. Nat. Assn. Female Execs., Kainaliu Bus. and Profl. Assn., Kainaliu Bus. and Profl. Assn. (sec. 1986-87). Roman Catholic. Home: PO Box 557 Kealakekua HI 96750 Office: Dept Mental Health PO Box 228 Kealakekua HI 96750

KIMURA, WAYNE DELL, research scientist; b. Seattle, Apr. 22, 1954; s. Dick and Connie Kaneko (Katayama) Kawahara. BSEE, U. Wash., 1976; MSEE, Stanford U., 1977, PhD, 1981. Cert. engr. in tng., Wash. Research engr. U. Wash., Seattle, 1976; research assoc. Stanford U., Calif., 1981; prin. research scientist Spectra Tech. Inc., Bellevue, Wash., 1982—; cons. Los Alamos (N.Mex.) Nat. Lab., 1984—. Contbr. articles to profl. jours.; patentee in field. George Porter Baldwin scholar Stanford U., 1976-77. Mem. IEEE, Am. Phys. Soc., Optical Soc. Am., Sigma Xi. Avocations: skiing, bicycling, hiking. Home: 2417 S Hanford St Seattle WA 98144 Office: Spectra Tech Inc 2755 Northup Way Bellevue WA 98004

KINCAID, PATRICK JAMES, computer systems consultant; b. Newberry, Mich., June 28, 1947; s. James Wilson and Shirley Ann (Wilson) K. BA in Fgn. Affairs, U. Cin., 1971. Tech. rep. Dialog Computing, Cin., 1969-71; tech. rep. Nat. CSS Inc., San Francisco, 1971-75, database cons., 1975-77; computer systems cons. Kindcaid Cons., Mill Valley, Calif., 1977—. Author: A Visual Guide to Telecommunications, 1985; inventor: Telepath computer communications program. Mem. Ind. Computer Cons. Assn., Small Computer Users of Marin, Marin Sonoma PC Users Group, Planetary Soc. (charter), Bay Area Nomad Group. Avocations: hiking, photography, swimming, reading. Home and Office: Kincaid Cons 618 Douglas Dr Mill Valley CA 94941

KINCHELOE, LAWRENCE RAY, state official; b. Twin Falls, Idaho, Jan. 1, 1941; s. Kenneth Kincheloe and Wilma Gladys (Barnett) Routt; m. Sharon Kathleen Moseley, July 14, 1964; children—Gerry, Corey, Michelle, Lawrence, Jeffrey. BA, Mont. State U., 1963; MA, Pacific Luth. U., 1978. Assoc. supt. Dept. Corrections, Wash. State Penitentiary, Walla Walla, 1978-82, warden, 1982—. Served to maj. U.S. Army, 1963-78. Decorated Silver Star, Bronze Star with oak leaf cluster, Legion of Merit, Air medal with oak leaf cluster, Army Commendation medal (2); Vietnamese Cross of Gallantry (3). Mem. Am. Corrections Assn., N.Am. Assn. Wardens. Home: Rt 5 Box 354 Walla Walla WA 99362 Office: Wash State Pentientiary N 13th St PO Box 520 Walla Walla WA 99362

KINCZEWSKI, KATHRYN, French educator; b. LaSalle, Ill., Nov. 9, 1951; d. Joseph C. and Dorothy M. (Urban) K. BA in Language and Linguistics, U. Ill., 1973; MA in French, Yale U., 1974, MPhil., 1977, PhD in French, 1981. Teaching fellow Yale U., New Haven, 1976-79; vis. asst. prof. Miami (Ohio) U., 1979-80; asst. prof. St. John's Coll., Collegeville, Minn., 1981, La. State U., Shreveport, 1981-82, U. Denver, 1982—; vis. asst. prof. French U. Colo., Boulder, 1986; organizer Interdisciplinary Coll. Colloquium, Denver, 1984; cons. Yale-Wellesley Annenberg Grant, New Haven, 1981-86, Heinle & Heinle Publishing, Boston, 1986—; guest lectr. Le Club Sévigné, Denver, 1984,86. Contbr. articles to profl. jours. Bd. dirs. Sartre's Huis Clos, Denver, 1985, Tricentennial of La Salle, La. State U., 1982. Mem. MLA (adv., nominating com.), Internat. Assn. Philosophy and Lit., Soc. Critical Exchange, Rocky Mountain Modern Lang. Assn., Pacific Northwest Council on Fgn. Langs. Home: 2708 Stout St Apt A Denver CO 80205-2943 Office: U Denver Dept Fgn Langs and Lit Denver CO 80208-0293

KIND, KENNETH WAYNE, lawyer, real estate broker; b. Missoula, Mont., Apr. 1, 1948; s. Joseph Bruce and Elinor Joy (Smith) K.; m. Diane Lucille Jozaitis, Aug. 28, 1971. B.A., Calif. State U.-Northridge, 1973; J.D., Calif. Western U., 1976. Bar: Calif. 1976, U.S. Dist. Ct. (ea. dist.) Calif. 1976. Mem. celebrity security staff Brownstone Am., Beverly Hills, Calif., 1970-76; tchr. Army and Navy Acad., Carlsbad, Calif., 1975-76; real estate broker, Bakersfield, Calif., 1978—; sole practice, Bakersfield, 1976—; lectr. mechanic's lien laws, Calif., 1983—. Staff writer Calif. Western Law Jour., 1975. Served as sgt. U.S. Army, 1967-70. Mem. ABA, VFW, Nat. Order Barristers. Libertarian. Office: 1715 Chester Ave Suite 300 Bakersfield CA 93301

KINDER, JAMES ALLEN, professional services firm executive; b. Cin., Nov. 3, 1946; s. Paul Edwin and Elvira Mary (Hartman) K.; m. Jean Y. Mori, Feb. 27, 1970; children—James Allen, Erica, John H. Underwriter, Pacific Indemnity, Los Angeles, 1964-68; mgr. Alexander & Alexander, Los Angeles, 1968-72; sr. v.p., dir. Assn. Adminstrs. and Cons., Inc., Irvine, Calif., 1972-78; pres., chief exec. officer Kinder & Assocs. Inc., Santa Ana, Calif., 1978—; cons. Inst. Assn. Mgmt. Cos., Los Angeles, 1983. Mgr., dir. Tustin Nat. Little League, Calif., 1983-84; coach Am. Youth Soccer Orgn., Tustin, 1978-84. Mem. Profl. Services Mgmt. Assn. (life, mgr. 1978-84), Inst. Assn. Mgmt. Cos., Meeting Planners, Internat., Nat. Assn. Expn. Mgrs., Am. Soc. Assn. Execs., So. Calif. Assn. Execs. Club: So. Calif. Kart (dir., promoter). Office: Kinder & Assocs Inc 1700 E Dyer Rd Suite 165 Santa Ana CA 92705

KINDER, SHARON MARIE, real estate division education manager; b. Spokane, Wash., May 13, 1939; d. Merle L. and Anna Marie (Petersen) Kinder. B.S. in Phys. Edn. and Edn., Wash. State U., 1961; postgrad. Eastern Wash. State Coll., 1962, Wash. State U., 1963, 64, U. Idaho, 1964. Cert. tchr., Wash. Phys. edn. instr. Sch. Dist. 140, Walla Walla, Wash., 1961-64; dir. vols. State Hosp. N., Orofino, Idaho, 1964-67, coordinator activity therapy, 1967-70; coordinator and pub. info. specialist State Hosp. S., Blackfoot, Idaho, 1970-74; ind. contractor real estate assoc. broker, Spokane, Wash., 1974-80; edn. mgr. Real Estate Div., Olympia, Wash., 1981-86; bd. dirs. Northwest Danish Home, Seattle, 1976—. Editor Interagy. Council Service Directory, 1968, Wash. Real Estate News, 1981-86. Mem. Interagy. Council, Orofino, 1968; pres. Clearwater County Comprehensive Health Plan Agy., Orofino, 1968; precinct worker Spokane Election Bd., 1976; sec. Health Systems Agy., Spokane, 1976. Mem. AAUW, Real Estate Educators Assn. (pres. Northwest chpt. 1985), Orofino C. of C. (v.p. 1970). Democrat. Lutheran (ch. council, v.p., pres.). Club: Internat. Toastmistress (regional supr. 1974, internat. chmn. speech contest 1975). Lodges: Danish Brotherhood (v.p. 1983, chmn. Nat. law com. 1987), Pacific NW Dist. Danish Brotherhood (pres. 1986—). Home: 1206 D Boone St SE Olympia WA 98503 Office: Real Estate Div Dept Licensing PO Box 247 Olympia WA 98503

KINDLER, HERBERT S., management educator; b. N.Y.C., Feb. 16, 1928; s. Samuel and Alice (Yankowitz) K.; m. Phyllis Pitegoff, May 15, 1952 (div. 1975); m. Marilyn Jacobs, Nov. 3, 1979; children: Alex, David, Peggy. BS, MIT, 1948; MPub. Adminstrn., U. Pitts., 1974; PhD, UCLA, 1978. Design engr. Honeywell Co., Phila., 1948-52; project engr. Catalytic Construction Co., Phila., 1948-52; chief engr. Black, Sivalls & Bryson, Oklahoma City, 1954-56; exec. dir. Instrument Soc. Am., Pitts., 1956-74; asst. prof. mgmt. Loyola Marymount U., Los Angeles, 1978-80, assoc. prof., 1980-85, prof., 1985—; bd. dirs. Ctr. Mgmt. Effectiveness Inc., Pacific Palisades, 1979—. Contbr. articles to profl. jours.; patentee. Home: 427 Beirut Ave Pacific Palisades CA 90272 Office: Ctr Mgmt Effectiveness Inc PO Box 1202 Pacific Palisades CA 90272

KINDLER, JUDITH MARIE, textile designer, owner interior design showroom; b. Buffalo, N.Y., Feb. 14, 1949; d. Donald Sidney and Janet Francis (Harbeck) Cornell; m. George Levinton, Aug. 20, 1971 (div. July 1979); m. Christian G. Kindler, July 31, 1979; 1 child, Radha. Student, Kent State U., Villa Maria Coll., U. Calif., Berkeley, Can. Coll., Redwood, Calif. Interior designer Judith Kindler and Assocs., San Francisco, 1982-85; owner Judith Kindler Textiles, San Francisco, 1980—; ptnr., co-owner Kavalaris-Kindler, San Francisco, 1985—; free lance designer, cons., San Francisco, 1974—; lectr. interior design, The De Young Mus., Can. Coll., Pacific Basin Sch. Textile Design, U. Calif.-Berkeley, 1982—; organizer 1st Calif. textile show, San Francisco, 1984. Designer (fabric line) Kavalaris Collection, 1980 (Roscoe award 1985); represented in residences and bus. including Saudi Arabian Palace, Bell Telephone Exec. Offices, Sitmar Ocean Liners. Mem. Nat. Home Furnishings League, Am. Soc. Interior Designer Industry Found. Club: San Francisco Bay. Avocations: skiing, racquetball. Office: Judith Kindler Textiles 208 Utah St San Francisco CA 94103

KINDRED, SHARON ROSS, interior designer; b. Balt., June 23, 1944; d. Paul Edward and Eileen Mary (Cole) R.; m. William Watkins Kindred, June 15, 1968 (dec. Aug. 1973); 1 child, Justin Watkins. BA, Agnes Scott Coll., 1966; BVA, Ga. State U., 1972; student, U. Utah. Interior designer Jon McGowan, Salt Lake City, 1974-75; developer Salt Lake City, 1976-77; space planner Clark Leaming, Salt Lake City, 1977-79; design, project mgr. Huntsman Christensen, Salt Lake City, 1979-85; sr. designer Conant Assoc., Salt Lake City, 1985-86; ind. designer 1986—. Active Heritage Soc., Salt Lake City, 1985; sec. East Liberty Park Community Orgn., Salt Lake City, 1980—. Avocations: gardening, renovating old bldgs., training and showing dogs. Home: 1105 South 8th East Salt Lake City UT 84105 Office: 1105 S 8th E Salt Lake City UT 84105

KING, ALAN ODELL, state transportation official, civil engineer; b. Omak, Wash., Nov. 23, 1947; s. Charles T. and Virginia L. (Byers) K.; m. Linda R. Thompson, Sept. 19, 1969; children: Troy A., Charles H. B.S.C.E., U. Wash., 1970. Registered profl. engr., Wash., Alaska, Calif. Hwy. engr. I. Wash. State Dept. Transp., Spokane, 1970-73; asst. civil engr. Engring. Corp. Am., Coeur D'Alene, Idaho, 1973-74; civil engr. Victor O. Gray & Co., Seattle, 1974-77; dir. pub. works Okanogan County, Okanogan, Wash., 1977-86, engr. local traffic services Wash. State Dept. Transp., Olympia, 1987—; prin. AOK Engring. & Design, Olympia, 1972—; mem. T2 com. Wash. State Dept. Transp., 1983-86. Mem. Okanogan Planning Commn., 1979-86; mem. Okanogan Sch. bd., 1980-86, chmn. 1985. Mem. Nat. Assn. County Engrs. (dir. research 1986), Wash. State Assn. County Engrs. (pres. central dist. 1980, chmn. research com. 1983-86, chmn. design com. 1983-86), ASCE, Am. Pub. Works Assn., Am. Rd. and Transp. Builders Assn., Wash. State Rifle and Pistol Assn., Aircraft Owners and Pilots Assn., Nat. Rifle Assn. Lodges: Elks, Masons, Kiwanis. Home: 5140 88 Yelm Hwy Olympia WA 98503 Office: Wash State Dept Transp State Aid Transp Bldg KF-01 Olympia WA 98504

KING, ALLAN PALMER, JR., foodservice consultant; b. Healdsburg, Calif., July 30, 1941; s. Allan Palmer and Janie Elizabeth (Newton) K.; m. Karen Louise Gott (div. Aug. 1972); children: Gregory, Jeffrey, Lorrie; m. Wendy Loo, Aug. 24, 1980. BS, Oreg. State U., 1962. Contract sales rep. Sardell's, Oakland, Calif., 1962-66, Herbert's Refrigeration, Reno, 1966-71, Toledo Mfg., Oakland, 1971-73, Dohrmann Co., Reno, 1973-78, East Bay

Restaurant Supply, Sparks, Nev., 1978-79; prin. Allan King & Friends, Reno, 1979—. Dep. Washoe County Sherriff's Mounted Posse, Reno, 1978-82. Recipient Excellence in Kitchen Design award Restaurant Hospitality mag., 1985. Mem. Foodservice Cons.' Soc. Internat. (profl., cert.), Internat. Foodservice Execs. Assn. (assoc.), Reno Horsemen's Assn. (bd. dirs. 1975-76). Republican. Avocation: fishing. Office: 1475 B Terminal Way Reno NV 89502

KING, ANTHONY GABRIEL, historical association executive; b. Needham, Mass., June 13, 1953; s. Henry Brazell and Ottilie Rosena (Sandrock) K.; m. Debra Harte, Oct. 3, 1981; children: Courtney, Michael. B.S., Springfield Coll., Mass., 1976; M.A., NYU, 1978. Curatorial asst. Mus. of Am. Indian, NYC, 1975-76; asst. dir. Bronx County Hist. Soc., NYC, 1976-79; exec. dir. Berkshire County Hist. Soc., Pittsfield, Mass., 1979-83; dir. Wash. Hist. Soc., Tacoma, 1983-86, Onondaga Hist. Assn., Syracuse, N.Y., 1986—. Mem. preservation adv. bd. State of Wash., Olympia, 1984-86, mem. hist. records adv. bd., 1984-86; pres. Tacoma Centennial Com., 1983-84; chmn. Pittsfield Hist. Commn., 1981-83, Pittsfield Civic Ctr. Commn., 1982-82; mem. Steering com. Mass. Arts Advocacy Com., Boston, 1979-83. Mem. Am. Assn. State and Local History, Am. Assn. of Museums, Wash. Mus. Assn. Democrat. Roman Catholic. Lodge: Rotary. Avocation: rugby football. Office: Onondaga Hist Assn 311 Montgomery St Syracuse NY 13202-2098

KING, CAROL SOUCEK, editor, journalist, b. Los Angeles, Sept. 8, 1943; d. Romus and Anne (Merrill) Soucek; m. Richard Carlton King, Jan. 31, 1976. B.A. in English Lit., U. So. Calif., 1966, Ph.D., 1976; M.F.A., Yale U., 1966. Lectr. contemporary theater U. So. Calif., Los Angeles, 1969; drama critic Santa Monica (Calif.) Evening Outlook, 1972-73; staff writer Los Angeles Herald Examiner, 1973-77, editor Lifestyle sect., 1977; editor in chief, Designers West Mag., Los Angeles, 1978—. Mem. Am. Soc. Interior Designers, Internat. Soc. Interior Designers, Nat. Home Fashions League, Women in Bus.

KING, CARY JUDSON, III, chemical engineer, educator, university dean; b. Ft. Monmouth, N.J., Sept. 27, 1934; s. Cary Judson and Mary Margaret (Forbes) K., Jr.; m. Jeanne Antoinette Yorke, June 22, 1957; children: Mary Elizabeth, Cary Judson IV, Catherine Jeanne. B. Engring., Yale, 1956; S.M., Mass. Inst. Tech., 1958, Sc.D., 1960. Asst. prof. chem. engring. Mass. Inst. Tech., Cambridge, 1959-63; dir. Bayway Sta. Sch. Chem. Engring. Practice, Linden, N.J., 1959-61; asst. prof. chem. engring. U. Calif. at Berkeley, 1963-66, asso. prof., 1966-69, prof., 1969—, vice chmn. dept. chem. engring., 1967-72, chmn., 1972-81, dean Coll. Chemistry, 1981—; cons. Procter & Gamble Co., 1969—, CPC Internat., 1982—. Author: Separation Processes, 1971, 80, Freeze Drying of Foods, 1971; Contbr. numerous articles to profl. jours. Active Boy Scouts Am., 1947—; pres. Kensington Community Council, 1972-73, dir., 1970-73. Fellow Am. Inst. Chem. Engrs. (Inst. lectr. 1973, Food, Pharm. and Bioengring. Div. award, 1975, William H. Walker award, 1976); mem. Nat. Acad. Engring., Am. Soc. Engring. Edn. (George Westinghouse award 1978), Am. Chem. Soc., AAAS. Patentee in field. Home: 7 Kensington Ct Kensington CA 94707 Office: Coll Chemistry U Calif Berkeley CA 94720

KING, CHAROLETTE ELAINE, navy division director; b. Baker, Oreg., Apr. 10, 1945; d. Melvin Howard and Rella Maxine (Gwilliam) Wright; m. Craig Seldon King, April 14, 1965; children: Andrea Karen, Diana Susan. Clerical positions various firms, Idaho, Va., Conn., 1964-71; nursing sec. VA, San Diego, 1974-77; sec. USN, Agana, Guam, 1972-73; procurement clk. USN, Bremerton, Wash., 1977-80; procurement clk. USN, San Diego, 1980, support services supr., 1980-83, div. dir., 1983—. Recipient Model Agy. cup USN, San Diego, 1986. Republican. Avocations: reading, camping, sewing, writing, quilting. Office: USN Pub Works Ctr Code 129 Box 113 Naval Station San Diego CA 92136

KING, CLARENCE HILYER, JR., management consultant; b. San Diego, Sept. 24, 1915; s. Clarence H. and Lucille (Brown) K.; m. Betty Lou Pennell, Nov. 11, 1944. B.Sc., U. So. Calif., Shipping supt. Ratner Mfg. Co., San Diego, 1940-42; cost acct. Consol. Vultee Aircraft, San Diego, 1942-44; mgr. data processing Golden State Mut. Life Ins. Co., Los Angeles, 1946-62; project adminstr. Rockwell Internat., Los Angeles, 1962-81; ind. mgmt. cons., Los Angeles, 1981—. Served with U.S. Army, 1944-45. Mem. Assn. for Systems Mgmt. (past internat. pres., disting. service award, 1981), Data Processing Mgmt. Assn., Quarter Century Wireless Assn., Amateur Radio Relay League. Club: Masons. Home and office: 3951 Carmona Ave Los Angeles CA 90008

KING, DAVID THOMAS, entrepreneur; b. Perth, Ont., Can., June 22, 1946; s. Albert Edward and Ethel (Dickson) K.; m. Clare Elaine Ann Piven, Oct. 19, 1968; children: Troy Oliver Albert, Jason Darren Tod. Student U. Victoria, 1964-65; BA in Polit. Sci., U. Alta. Mem. Legis. Assembly Alta. (Can.), Edmonton, 1971-86, minister of edn. Alta., 1979-86, minister tech., research and telecommunications, 1986; bd. dirs. various pub. and pvt. corps. and orgns., 1986—. Progressive Conservative. Mem. United Ch. Canada. Office: 2301 Royal Trust Tower, Edmonton Centre, Edmonton, AB Canada T5J 2Z2

KING, FRANK, oil company executive; b. Redcliff, Alta., Can.; married; 4 children. BS in Chem. Engring., U. Alta., 1958. Pres. Amerigo Internat.; also bd. dirs. other cos., Can. Chmn., chief exec. officer XV Olympic Winter Games Organizing Com.; bd. dirs. Calgary Olympic Devel. Assn.; mem. Calgary Econ. Devel. Authority; bd. govs. Olympic Trust; mem. adv. bd. Nat. CPASUS; mem. Calgary Booster Club; active many community/sports programs. Recipient Air Can. Amateur Sports award, Premier's Award of Excellence, 1981. Mem. Assn. Profl. Engrs., Geologists and Geophysicists of Alta., Calgary C. of C. (bd. dirs.), Young Pres.' Orgn. Club: Men's Can. (hon. life). Lodge: Lions (hon. life). Office: Olympic Winter Games Com, PO Box 1988, Station C, Calgary, AB Canada T2T 5R4

KING, FRANK WILLIAM, writer; b. Port Huron, Mich., Oct. 1, 1922; s. William Ernest and Catherine Theresa (Smith) K.; student U. Utah, 1963-65, Santa Monica City Coll., 1941, 48-49; B.A., Marylhurst Coll., 1979; M.A., U. Portland, 1982; m. Carma Morrison Sellers, Sept. 16, 1961; children—Rosanne, Jeanine Nell, Melanie, Lisa June; one stepson, Michael Sellers. Air traffic controller FAA, Salt Lake City, Albuquerque and Boise, Idaho; 1949-65, info. officer Western Region, Los Angeles, 1965-68; pub. affairs officer Los Angeles Dist. C.E., U.S. Army, 1968-69, Walla Walla (Wash.), 1969-77, N. Pacific div., Portland, Oreg., 1977-79; dir. pub. relations U. Portland, 1979-80; adj. asst. prof. communications U. Portland, 1982-83; instr. Portland Community Coll., 1980—; freelance writer, 1980—. Exec. asst. Los Angeles Fed. Exec. Bd., 1965-67; chmn. Walla Walla County Alcoholism Adminstrv. Bd., 1974-75; vice-chmn. Walla Walla County Human Services Adminstrv. Bd., 1976-78, chmn., 1977-78. Served with USMCR, 1942-45. Decorated Air medal; William Randolph Hearst scholar, 1965. Mem. Soc. Profl. Journalists, Pub. Relations Soc. Am. (accredited), Kappa Tau Alpha. Democrat. Roman Catholic. Home and Office: 1570 SE Schooner Crk Rd #B Lincoln City OR 97367

KING, FREDERIC, health services management executive, educator; b. N.Y.C., N.Y., May 9, 1937; s. Benjamin and Jeanne (Fritz) K.; m. Linda Ann Udell, Mar. 17, 1976; children by previous marriage—Coby Allen, Allison Beth, Lisa Robyn, Daniel Seth. B.B.A. cum laude, Bernard M. Baruch Sch. Bus. and Public Adminstrn., CUNY, 1958. Dir. adminstrn. Albert Einstein Coll. Medicine, Bronx, N.Y., 1970-72; assoc. v.p. health affairs Tulane Med. Ctr., New Orleans, 1972-77; dir. fin. Mt. Sinai Med. Ctr., N.Y.C., 1977-78; v.p. fin. Cedars-Sinai Med. Ctr., Los Angeles, 1978-82; pres. Vascular Diagnostic Services, Inc., Woodland Hills, Calif., 1982-84; exec. dir. South Bay Ind. Physicians Med. Group Inc., Torrance, Calif., 1984—; ptnr. Health Ventures, San Rafael, Calif., 1984—; assoc. adj. prof. Tulane U. Sch. Pub. Health; asst. prof. Mt. Sinai Med. Ctr.; instr. Pierce Coll., Los Angeles. Served with U.S. Army, 1959-62. Mem. Hosp. Fin. Mgmt. Assn., Am. Pub. Health Assn. Republican. Jewish. Home: 1116 Rose Ave Venice CA 90291 Office: 23505 Crenshaw Blvd Suite 132 Torrance CA 90505

KING, GEOFFREY ROBERT, management educator; b. Hull, Eng., Feb. 10, 1918; s. William Ralph and Agnes (Morgan) K.; m. Mary Elsie Wheeler, July 27, 1940; children—Robert William, Gillian. B.S., Calif. State U.-Los Angeles, 1964, M.S., 1966; M.A., U. So. Calif., 1968, Ph.D. in Econs., 1972. Registered profl. engr. Ont., Can. Contracts mgr. Aerojet Gen., Downey, Calif., 1960-66; mgr. contract adminstrn. Interstate Electronics, Anaheim, Calif., 1966-72; prof. mgmt. Calif. State U.-Fullerton, 1973—, chmn. dept. mgmt., 1975-79. mem. Laguna Greenbelt, Laguna Beach Homeowners Assn., LWV. Mem. Assn. Profl. Engrs. Ont., Omicron Delta Epsilon, Beta Gamma Sigma. Contbr. articles to profl. jours. Office: Calif State U Dept Mgmt Fullerton CA 92634

KING, HWA-KOU, anesthesiologist; b. Shanghai, China, Aug. 20, 1928; came to U.S., 1963, naturalized, 1982; m. Alice Lu-ping, Oct. 18, 1958; 5 children. M.D., Nat. Def. Med. Ctr. Sch. Medicine, Taipei, Taiwan, 1953. Diplomate Am. Bd. Anesthesiology. Resident in surgery Army First Gen. Hosp., Taipei, 1953-55, resident in anesthesiology, 1955-60; resident in anesthesiology Meml. Cancer Ctr., N.Y.C., 1963-65; fellow in anesthesiology, Mt. Sinai Med. Ctr., N.Y.C., 1965-67; attending staff anesthesiology Army First Gen. Hosp. and VA Gen. Hosp., Taipei, 1960-63; chief intensive care unit Triservice Gen. Hosp., Taipei, 1967-78, attending staff anesthesiology, 1967-78, chief accupuncture, 1973-78, chief out-patient dept., 1976-78; chief anesthesiology VA Gen Hosp., Taipei, 1978-81, Taiwan Adventist Hosp., Taipei, 1981-82; attending staff anesthesiology Harbor-UCLA Med. Ctr., Los Angeles, 1982-83, VA Med. Ctr., West Los Angeles, 1984—; clin. prof. Nat. Def. Med. Ctr. and Taipei Med. Coll., 1968-70; prof. China Med. Coll., Taichung, 1971-72; prof. Nat. Def. Med. Ctr., 1970-81; prof., chmn. anesthesiology Nat. Yang Ming Med. Coll., Taipei, 1978-81. Author: Clinical Anesthesiology (in Chinese), 1971, 4th edit., 1981; Introduction to Anesthesiology (in Chinese), 1982. Contbr. sci. papers to topical publs. Editor-in-chief Anesthesiologica Sinica; editor: Med. Research, Chinese Med. Jour., Clin. Medicine. Fellow Am. Coll. Anesthesiologists, Internat. Coll. Surgeons; mem. Soc. Anesthesiology Republic of China (pres. 1976-80), Chinese Bd. Anesthesiology (examiner 1981—), Chinese Med. Assn., Formosa Med. Assn., Surg. Assn. Republic of China, Assn. Surgeons S.E. Asia, West Pacific Intensive Care Medicine, Am. Soc. Anesthesiology. Home: 30452 Via Rivera Rancho Palos Verdes CA 90274 Office: West Los Angeles VA Med Ctr Wilshire and Sawtelle Blvd Los Angeles CA 90073

KING, JAMES BRUCE, newspaper consultant; b. Enterprise, Oreg., Oct. 30, 1922; s. Oscar Lawrence and Julia Etta (Bruce) K.; m. Betty Ruth Berkley, June 27, 1944; 1 child, James Bruce. Student, Lower Columbia Community Coll., 1941-43, Whitman Coll., 1943-44; B.A. in Journalism, U. Wash., 1948. With Seattle Times, 1948-86, began as reporter, successively copy editor, asst. news editor, news editor, asst. mng. editor, 1948-75, mng. editor, 1975-77, exec. editor, 1977-86, v.p. news and editorial, 1980-85, exec. editor, sr. v.p., 1985-86; vis. com. U. Wash. Sch. Communications, 1971-77, 84—; western dir. Am. Press Inst., 1985-86. Former mem. Community Devel. Round Table Seattle; former cons. self-improvement group McNeil Island Fed. Penitentiary. Served to lt. comdr. USNR, 1943-46, PTO. Recipient Disting. Alumnus award Sch. Communications, U. Wash., 1984. Mem. AP Mng. Editors (dir. 1977-83, regent 1985—), Am. Soc. Newspaper Editors (bd. dirs. 1982-86), U. Wash. Alumni Assn., Soc. Profl. Journalists, Sigma Delta Chi (Disting. Service award 1986), Beta Theta Pi. Episcopalian. Club: Blue Ridge Community. Home: 10003 Vinton Ct NW Seattle WA 98177

KING, JAMES LAWRENCE, JR., mathematics educator; b. Detroit, Mar. 20, 1935; s. James Lawrence and Olive Lenore (Vibbard) K.; m. Gloria Herrera; 1 child, Gloria Lynn. BS in Physics, Wayne State U., 1960, BS in Math., 1962, MA in Math. Stats., 1965, postgrad. First aid medic Great Lakes Steel, Ecorse, Mich., 1956-65; instr. Wayne State U., Detroit, 1960-62, 65; sci., math. tchr. Yeshivath Beth Yehudah Schs., 1960-65; sr. mathematician Gen. Motors Corp., Warren, Mich., 1965-67; tchr. math., sci. Los Angeles Unified Schs., 1967-68; prof. math., student advisor Los Angeles S.W. Coll., 1968—; numismatist, 1974—. Bass-baritone concert choir Wayne State U., 1956-64. Served with USN, 1952-56, USNR, 1956-64. Grantee NSF, 1969. Mem. Am. Numismatic Assn. (cert.), Nat. Geographic Soc. Republican. Club: Interval Internat. Time Share. Avocations: opera singing, investing, coins, gems, stamps. Office: Los Angeles SW Coll 1600 W Imperial Hwy Los Angeles CA 90047

KING, JAMES MING, computer company consultant; b. Nanking, Republic of China, Aug. 15, 1948; came to U.S., 1971; s. Jason Sung and Ka Zou (Chan) K.; m. Marsha Li-yuan Lee, Nov. 7, 1979; 1 child, Deborah. BS in Indsl. Engring., Tunghai U., Taiwan, Republic of China, 1970; MS in Indsl. Engring., Miss. State U., 1973. Indsl. engr. ROPER Corp., LaFayette, Ga., 1973-74; sr. indsl. engr. AMSCO, Erie, Pa., 1974-76; sr. project engr. Volks Wagon of Am., Westmoreland, Pa., 1976-78; project mgr. Fed. Mogul, Los Angeles, 1979-81; application specialist Hewlett Packard, Fullerton, Calif., 1981-84; mfg. support mgr. Far East region Hewlett Packard, Palo Alto, Calif., 1984—; far east mfg. cons. 1984—. Mem. Am. Prodn. and Inventory Soc. (cert.), Inst. Indsl. Engrs., Overseas Am. Club, Alpha Pi Mu. Home: 17924 Vierra Ave Cerritos CA 90701 Office: Hewlett Packard Intercontinental 3495 Deer Creek Rd Palo Alto CA 94304

KING, JOHN DOUGLAS, systems scientist; b. Beckenham, Kent, Eng., June 1, 1934; s. Douglas Stanley and Mary (Carpenter) K.; m. Shirley Anne Spencer; children—Linda, Alan, Douglas, Pamela, Lynn Angela, Gary. B.S., Oglethorpe U., 1956; M. Aerospace Ops. Mgmt., U. So. Calif., 1969; D Bus. Adminstrn., U.S. Internat. U., 1980. Commd. officer, U.S. Navy, 1956, advanced through grades to lt. comdr., 1965, ret., 1977; mem. faculty Troy State U., Kolsaas, Norway, 1976; with Davlyn Enterprises, San Diego, 1977, Northrop Services, Inc., San Diego, 1977-78, Intercon Corp., Camp Pendleton, Calif., 1978-79; tech. staff P.E. Systems, Inc., San Diego, 1979-83; sr. systems scientist Computer Scis. Corp., San Diego, 1983-85 ; research asst. U.S. Internat. U., San Diego, 1981-84; mem. adj. faculty Nat. U., San Diego, 1983—; dir. bus. programs, La Jolla Univ., 1986—; cons. The Cons. Group, 1985-86; ptnr. The Corp. Cons. Group. 1986—. Bd. dirs. Scripps Ranch Community Theatre, 1979-80, 83-86. Decorated Navy Commendation medal. Lowry Meml. scholar, 1956. Mem. Am. Mgmt. Assn., Am. Soc. Tng. and Devel., Nat. Speakers Assn., Assn. Old Crows, Am. Assn. Profl. Cons. Mem. Anglican Ch. Home: 10287 Grayfox Dr San Diego CA 92131 Office: 111 Russell Senate Office Bldg San Diego CA 92131

KING, JOHN W., biologist, program administrator, statistics educator; b. East Ely, Nev., May 18, 1942; s. Harry Cameron and Lois Nancy (Bally) K.; m. Mary Ervene Williams, Nov. 23, 1962; children: John Cameron, Robert (dec.). BS with high distinction, U. Nev., 1977, MS in Biology, 1982. Cert. wildlife biologist. Asst. mech. supt. Elko (Nev.) Daily Free Press, 1970-73; biology teaching fellow U. Nev., Reno, 1977-78; fisheries biologist Nev. Dept. Wildlife, Verdi, 1978-80; hunter edn. coordinator Nev. Dept. Wildlife, Reno, 1980—; stats. tchr. Chapman Coll., Reno, 1983—. Chmn. planning commn., City of Elko, 1971-73; nature merit badge counselor Boy Scouts Am., Reno, 1976—. Recipient award for Outstanding Contribution to Hunter Safety, Nev. Wildlife Fedn., 1982. Mem. The Wildlife Soc., Am. Fisheries Soc., N.Am. Assn. Hunter Safety Coordinators (dir. Region I 1985—), Western Assn. of Hunter Edn., Sigma Xi. Presbyterian. Lodge: Masons. Avocations: hunting, fishing, photography, camping. Home: 735 F St PO Box 1516 Fernley NV 89408 Office: Nev Dept Wildlife 1100 Valley Rd PO Box 10678 Reno NV 89520

KING, JOSEPH JERONE, assn. exec.; b. Spokane, Wash., Sept. 27, 1910; s. Joseph Jerone and Alice (Halferty) K.; B.A. with gt. distinction, Stanford U., 1935; M.A., Duke U., 1937; m. Irma Kathleen Martin, Aug. 22, 1937; children—Sally Jo (Mrs. John S. Thompson), Nikki Sue (Mrs. Dennis Ring), Cindy Lou (Mrs. Richard Mullen). Instr. econs. Black Mountain Coll., 1937-38; numerous adminstrv. positions Farm Security Adminstrn., U.S. Dept. Agriculture, Portland, 1939-51; Oreg. state dir. Christian Rural Overseas Program, 1950-51; sr. civilian for indsl. relations Puget Sound Naval Shipyard, 1951-58; public affairs dir. Assn. Wash. Industries, Olympia, 1958-78, exec. cons., 1978—; Western mgr. Inst. Applied Econs., 1981—. Mem. President's Assos., Central Wash. U., mem. Gov.'s Council for Reorg. Wash. State Govt.; mem. adv. council Coll. Edn. Washington State U.; dir. manpower Statewide Public Edn. Mgmt. Survey; mem. Gov.'s Commn. on Employment of Physically Handicapped; mem. adv. council, dept. econs. and bus. adminstrn. Central Wash. U., 1973—, Coll. of Edn., mem. exec. com. Rural Edn. Ctr.; mem. profl. edn. adv. council Wash. State Dept. Public Instrn., 1977—, chmn. community edn. adv. council, 1981—; chmn. adv. com. for Anderson Landing Wildlife Project, Kitsap County (Wash.) Bd. Commrs.; bd. dirs. State-Wide Project Bus. Liaison with Edn.; mem. Spokane Bd. Scholastic Excellence; bd. dirs. Paul Linder Found. for Edn. in Cen. Kitsap. Served with USAAF, 1944. Recipient Outstanding Service awards DAV, Assn. Wash. Bus., Golden Bell award Washington Assn. Sch. Adminstrs.; named hon. citizen City of Vancouver (Wash.), hon. Wash. adm., hon. Wash. gen. Mem. Am. Soc. Pub. Adminstrn., Am. Legion (hon. life mem.), Phi Beta Kappa, Pi Gamma Mu. Clubs: Washington Athletic, Kitsap Country, Elks, Masons (Shriner). Author: Winning, Printings, 1961. Home: Ioka Beach-Hood Canal 11655 Ioka Way NW Silverdale WA 98383

KING, JOY KERLER, classics educator; b. Glencoe, Ill., Mar. 6, 1926; d. William J. and June (Bennett) K.; m. Edward Louis King, Dec. 20, 1952; children—Paul Gregory, Marcia (dec.). B.A. in Classical Langs., Knox Coll., 1947; M.A. in Latin, U. Wis., 1952; Ph.D. in Classics, U. Colo., 1969. Assoc. prof. classics U. Colo., Boulder, 1968—, chmn. dept., 1982-85. Editor Colo. Classics: A Newsletter, 1979—. Author articles on Latin poetry. Recipient Student-Alumni award U. Colo., 1974. Mem. Am. Philol. Assn., Classical Assn. Middle West and South (promotion of Latin com. 1982-85), Women's Classical Caucus (co-chair 1983-84), Phi Beta Kappa. Office: U Colo Box 248 Boulder CO 80309

KING, KENNETH WILLIAM, JR., optometrist; b. Kearney, Nebr., Dec. 9, 1942; s. Kenneth William and Dorothy Evelyn (Kapple) K.; m. Alona Marie Marean, Aug. 25, 1966; children—Darren Michael, Holly Michelle. Student Boise Jr. Coll., 1961-63, U. Oreg., 1963-64; B.S., Pacific U., Forest Grove, Oreg., 1967, O.D., 1968. Cert. optometrist, Idaho, Oreg. Pvt. practice optometry, Idaho Falls, Idaho, 1971-76; optometrist, pres. Intermountain Optometric Ctr., Idaho Falls, 1976—; cons. optometry U.S. Naval Dispensary, Idaho Falls, 1978—; clin. investigator FlexLens Inc., Rio Rancho, N.Mex., 1980—, Optacryl, Inc., Englewood, Colo., 1982—, Precision Cosmet, Minnetonka, Minn., 1984—, N&N Menicon, Lynnwood, Wash., 1979-82, Paragon Optical, Inc., Mesa, Ariz., 1982—, Polymer Tech. Corp., Wilmington, Mass., 1983—; adj. faculty health div. Ea. Idaho Vocat.-Tech. Sch., 1979-82, Coll. Optometry Pacific U., 1978—. Scout chmn. Eagle Rock Dist., Teton Peaks council Boy Scouts Am., 1984—. Served to capt. U.S. Army, 1968-71. Fellow Am. Acad. Optometry; mem. Idaho Optometric Assn. (bd. dirs. 1973-75), Am. Optometric Assn. (Optometric Recognition award 1980, 81, 84), S.E. Idaho Optometric Soc. (pres. 1972-75), Optometric Extension Program (clin. assoc.), Armed Forces Optometric Soc. (assoc.), Republican. Methodist. Club: Civitan (pres. Idaho Falls chpt. 1977-78, intermountain dist. gov. 1980-82, Disting. Gov. 1981, 82). Mem. 1st optometry delegation to Peoples Republic China. Home: 1854 Coronado Idaho Falls ID 83403 Office: 884 S Holmes Ave Idaho Falls ID 83403

KING, KEVIN DANIEL, data processing executive; b. Los Angeles, Mar. 6, 1963; s. Daniel D. and Doris M. (Lange) K. BA in Computer Info. Systems, Chadron State Coll., 1984. Programmer Chadron (Nebr.) State Coll., 1982-84; dir. computer services Sheridan (Wyo.) Coll., 1984—. Writer, performer (recorded music) Time Away, 1984, Lonely Boy, 1985, Someone Like Me, 1985. Stage dir. Miss Wyo. USA Pageant, Sheridan, 1986. Lutheran. Avocations: writing and performing music. Home: 389 Johnson Ln #B Sheridan WY 82801 Office: Sheridan Coll Box 1500 Sheridan WY 82801

KING, KEVIN KENT, engineer; b. Quincy, Ill., July 4, 1958; s. LeRoy Norbert and Dorcas E. (Allen) K.; m. Lori Sue Witte, Oct. 23, 1982. BS in Indsl. Engring., Bradley U., 1980; MBA, San Diego State U., 1985. Registered profl. engr., Calif. Assoc. numerical control engr. Gen. Dynamics/Convair, San Diego, 1980-81, numerical control engr., 1981-83, sr. numerical control engr., 1983-84; sr. qualtiy assurance engr. Gen. Electric Calma Co., San Diego, 1984-86; software quality assurance and product mgr. Talaris Systems Inc., San Diego, 1986—. Mem. IEEE (sr.), NSPE, Calif. Soc. Profl. Engrs., Soc. Mfg. Engrs. (sr.), Sigma Chi. Avocations: golfing, tennis, softball, bowling, baseball. Office: Talaris Systems Inc 6059 Cornerstone Ct W San Diego CA 92121

KING, MANUELA ANNE, landscape architect, horticulturist; b. Butler, Pa., May 16, 1956; d. Bartolome B. and Eugenia (Zavacky) K.; m. Wes Lee Romine, Apr. 5, 1986. BS, Pa. State U., 1978; B in Landscape Architecture, U. Oreg., 1985, postgrad., 1983—. Horticulturist Berkeley (Calif.) Horticulture, 1980-83; teaching fellow U. Oreg., Eugene, 1983-85; landscape architect SWA Group, Sausalito, Calif., 1984, Royston, Hanamoto, Alley & Abey, Mill Valley, Calif., 1985—; cons. Ortho Info. Services. Mem. Am. Soc. Landscape Architects, Nat. Trust Hist. Preservation, Mensa. Office: Royston Hanamoto Alley & Abey 225 Miller Ave Mill Valley CA 94109

KING, MARCIA, library director; b. Lewiston, Maine, Aug. 4, 1940; d. Daniel Alden and Clarice Evelyn (Curtis) Barrell; m. Howard P. Lowell, Feb. 15, 1969 (div. 1980); m. Richard G. King, Jr., Aug. 1980. B.S., U. Maine, 1965; M.S.L.S., Simmons Coll., 1967. Reference, field advisory and bookmobile librarian Maine State Library, Augusta, 1965-69; dir. Lithgow Pub. Library, Augusta, 1969-72; exec. sec. Maine Library Adv. Com., Maine State Library, 1972-73; dir. Wayland (Mass.) Free Pub. Library, 1973-76; state librarian State of Oreg., Salem, 1976-82; dir. Tucson Pub. Library, 1982—. Bd. dirs., sec. Tucson United Way; mem. adv. bd. com. Sta. KUAT (PBS-TV and Radio). Mem. ALA, Pub. Library Assn., Ariz. State Library Assn., AAUW, Assn. Specialized and Coop. Library Agys., Exec. Women's Council So. Ariz., Tucson C. of C. Unitarian. Office: Tucson Pub Library 111 E Pennington PO Box 27470 Tucson AZ 85726

KING, ROBERT FRANCIS, software engineer, educator; b. Rockville Centre, N.Y., Sept. 11, 1947; s. Francis Michael and Catherine Rose (Bahr) K.; m. Loretta Margaret Radosta, June 14, 1969; children: Robert Francis II, James William, Loretta Marie, Christopher John Phillip, Timothy Stephen. MS in Systems Mgmt., U. So. Calif., 1977; BA in Psychology, Marist Coll., 1969. Commd. 2d lt. USAF, 1969, advanced through grades to capt., 1972; electronic warfare officer USAF, Mather AFB, Calif., 1969-79; resigned USAF, 1979; system analyst System Integrators, Inc., Sacramento, 1979-80; sr. software engr. Gen. Dynamics Corp., Sacramento, 1980-85; programmer analyst GTE Sprint, Rancho Cordova, Calif., 1985-86; software engr. Allnet Communication Services, Sacramento, 1986—; core faculty mem. Nat. U., 1983—. Author: (software) Regional Surveillance System, 1986. Team mem. Worldwide Marriage Encounter, Sacramento, 1979—, zone coordinator, 1982-83; lectr. Holy Family Parish, Citrus Heights, Calif., 1982. Decorated D.F.C. Mem. Nat. Model Railroading Assn., Sacramento PC User's Group. Roman Catholic. Club: Nat. Model Railroading Assn., Canton, Ohio, 1975—. Lodge: KC. Avocations: personal computing, model railroading. Office: Allnet Communication Services Inc 1303 J St Suite 700 Sacramento CA 95814

KING, ROY EDWARD, safety engineer; b. San Francisco, Apr. 2, 1921; s. Walter John Hartman and Ella Anna (Kauck) K.; m. Marilyn Audrey Happ, Sept. 22, 1946; 1 child, Brian Edward. Degree in engring., U.S. Mcht. Marine Acad., 1943; postgrad., Oakland City Coll., 1957, U. Calif., Berkeley, 1959. Registered profl. safety engr., Calif. Personnel and safety dir. Am. Manganese Steel Co., Oakland, Calif., 1952-58; safety engr. Crum and Forester, Reliance Ins. Co., Pacific Employers Ins. Co., San Francisco, 1958-66; mgr. safety Sacramento br. Transam. Ins. Co., 1966-86; safety cons. cities of Sacramento, Lodi and Rio Vista, Calif. Dir. pub. speaking Sacramento Learning Exchange. Served with USN, 1943-46. Mem. Am. Soc. Safety Engrs. (profl., exec. com., legis. affairs com.), No. Calif. Indsl. Safety Soc., U. Calif. Alumni Club. Republican. Roman Catholic. Clubs: Engrs. (Sacramento), 20-30 (Oakland) (past pres.). Lodge: Toastmasters (local pres.).

KING, SHARON DENISE, legal secretary, poet; b. Dallas, Dec. 6, 1949; d. John Charles and Patsy Marie (Carter) K. Student Glendale Community Coll., 1968-72. Legal sec. Filler, Paytas, Shannon, Fleming and Stephenson, Phoenix, 1968-75, Kenneth K. Miller, 1976-79, F. Reid Nathan, Ltd., 1979-81, Gillenwater and Meyers, P.C., 1981, Warner, Angle, Roper and Hallam, 1981—. Democrat. Baptist. Author: (pen name Sharon Walters) Cast a Ray of Light, 1978.

KING, SHELDON SELIG, medical center administrator, educator; b. N.Y.C., Aug. 28, 1931; s. Benjamin and Jeanne (Fritz) K.; m. Ruth Arden Zeller, June 26, 1955 (div. 1987); children: Tracy Elizabeth, Meredith Ellen, Adam Bradley. A.B., NYU, 1952; M.S., Yale U., 1957. Adminstrv. intern Montefiore Hosp., N.Y.C., 1952, 55; adminstrv. asst. Mt. Sinai Hosp., N.Y.C., 1957-60; asst. dir. Mt. Sinai Hosp., 1960-66, dir. planning, 1966-68; exec. dir. Albert Einstein Coll. Medicine-Bronx Municipal Hosp. Center, Bronx, N.Y., 1968-72; asst. prof. Albert Einstein Coll. Medicine, N.Y.C., 1968-72; dir. hosps. and clinics Univ. Hosp., assoc. clin. prof. U. Calif., San Diego, 1972-81; acting head div. health care scis., dept. community medicine U. Calif. (Sch. Medicine), 1978-81; pres. Stanford Univ. Hosp., 1986—; assoc. v.p. Stanford U. Med. Center, 1981-85; clin. assoc. prof. dept. community, family and preventive medicine Stanford U.; mem. adminstrv. bd. Council Teaching Hosps., 1981-86, chmn. adminstrv. bd., 1985; preceptor George Washington U., Ithaca Coll., Yale, U. Mo., CUNY; chmn. health care com. San Diego County Immigration Council, 1974-77; adv. council Calif. Health Facilities Commn., 1977-82; chmn. ad hoc bd. advs. Am. Bd. Internal medicine, 1985—, chmn. adv. bd., 1986—. Mem. editorial adv. bd.: Who's Who in Health Care, 1977; mem. editorial bd. Jour. Med. Edn, 1979-84. Bd. dirs. Hosp. Council San Diego and Imperial Counties, 1974-77, treas., 1976—, pres., 1977—; bd. dirs. United Way San Diego, 1975-80, Brith Milah Bd.; active Accreditation Council for Grad. Med. Edn., 1987—, Prospective Payment Assessment Commn., 1987—. Served with AUS, 1952-55. Fellow Am. Coll. Hosp. Adminstrs., Am. Pub. Health Assn., Royal Soc. Health; mem. Am. Hosp. Assn. (gov. council Met. sect. 1983—, council on fin. 1987&, house of dels. 1987—), Calif. Hosp. Assn. (trustee 1978-81), Am. Podiatric Med. Assn.(Project Council 2000 1985-86), Hosp. Research and Devel. Inst. Home: 716 University Dr Menlo Park CA 94025 Office: Stanford Univ Hosp C-204 Stanford CA 94305

KING, THOMAS LAWSON, industrial manufacturing executive; b. Washington, Mar. 10, 1935; s. Paul Leonard and Ethel Mae (Ramsey) K.; m. Carol Anne Plumhoff, June 13, 1959; children: Jeffrey Scott, Deborah Lynn, Matthew Todd. BS, U. Md., 1958. Engr. Martin-Marietta Corp., Balt., 1958-62, Westinghouse Electric Corp., Balt. and Pitts., 1962-64; engr., mgr. Gen. Electric Co., Valley Forge, Pa., Phoenix, Ontario, Calif. and Bridgeport, Conn., 1964-78; dir. Bourns, Inc., Riverside, Calif., 1978-81; corp. dir. Palco Industries, Inc., San Francisco, 1981—; bd. dirs. Travel Commdr. Inc., Santa Ana, Calif., 1982-83; cons. Walnut Creek, Calif., 1983—. Scoutmaster Boy Scouts Am., Conn., Calif., 1971-85; CPR instr. Am. Heart Assn., 1972—, CPR chmn., Bridgeport, 1978; first aid instr. ARC, Pa., Calif., Conn., 1966-80; co-chmn. United Fund-Gen. Electric Co., Conn., 1975; patroller Nat. Ski Patrol System, Inc., Pa., Calif., Conn., 1965—, first aid advisor, Calif., Conn., 1972-73, 75-76, 80, new candidate advisor, Calif., 1980-81; emergency med. technician Trumbull Conn. Emergency Med. System, 1976-78, emergency med. technician instr., 1976-78. Recipient Order of Arrow, Boy Scouts Am., 1975, Scouter's Knot award Boy Scouts Am., 1979, Dist. award of Merit, Boy Scouts Am., 1980, Woodbadge, Boy Scouts Am., 1981, Honor Community Service award Town of Trumbull, Conn., 1978, Outstanding Service award Nat. Ski Patrol System, Inc., 1974, Nat. Appointment, #5722 Nat. Ski Patrol System, Inc., 1980. Mem. Am. Soc. Quality Control, System Safety Soc., Human Factors Soc., Am. Welding Soc. Republican. Lutheran. Club: Valley Forge Ski Club (pres. 1967-68). Avocations: downhill skiing, sailing, weight training, running, racketball. Home: 532 Allegheny Dr Walnut Creek CA 94598 Office: Palco Industries Inc 500 Washington St San Francisco CA 94120

KING, WILLIAM RICHARD, dentist; b. Inglewood, Calif., May 15, 1930; s. William Dunn and Ruth A. (Bell) K.; m. Mary Joan Ergenbright, Dec. 19, 1951; children: William Eric, Jon C., Kristin S. A.A., Los Angeles City Coll., 1951; D.D.S., U. So. Calif., 1957. Pvt. practice dentistry, Fullerton, Calif., 1959—. Founding bd. dirs. Mariners Ch., Newport Beach, Calif., 1964-80; founder, pres. Orange County Freedom Found., Costa Mesa, Calif., 1960-62. Served to capt. U.S. Army, 1957-59. Fellow Am. Coll. Dentists, Acad. Internat. Dental Studies, Am. Endodontic Soc.; mem. ADA, Am. Prosthodontic Soc., Pierre Fouchard Acad., Calif. Dental Assn. (jud. council 1971—, chmn. 1972-76, 86—), Orange County Dental Soc. (chmn. ins. com., chmn. dental care com., chmn. profl. assistance com. 1982, mem. ethics com. 1982), Fedn. Internat. Dentaire, U. So. Calif. Alumni Assn. (life), Alpha Tau Epsilon. Office;: 2651 E Chapman Suite 208 Fullerton CA 92631

KING, WILLIAM TRAVIS, radiologist; b. Vicksburg, Miss., June 11, 1947; s. Travis Menton and Mary Cecile (Dornbusch) K. BS in Pharmacy, U. Miss., 1970; MD, U. Miss., Jackson, 1974. Pharmacy research asst. U. Miss., University, 1965-70; resident in radiology U. Tenn., Memphis, 1975-78; pharmacist Doctors Hosp., Jackson, 1970-74; staff physician U. Ariz., Tucson, 1978-79, radiology fellow, 1978-79; radiologist Phoenix Radiology Assts. Ltd., 1980—; dir. CAT scanning, ultrasound and thermography St. Luke's Hosp., Phoenix, 1983—. Contbr. articles to profl. jours. Mem. AMA, Ariz. Med. Assn., Phoenix Radiol. Soc., Am. Pharm. Assn., Multiple Sclerosis Soc., Sigma Xi, Omicron Delta Kappa, Rho Chi, Alpha Tau Omega, Kappa Psi (pres. 1968-69). Democrat. Methodist. Home: 1602 E Weahtervane Tempe AZ 85283 Office: St Luke's Hosp 1800 E Van Buren Phoenix AZ 85006

KINGETT, KATHIE LEE, athletic educator; b. Freeport, N.Y., June 13, 1946; d. William Frederick Kingett and Ottilie Adele (Hamann) Henderson. BE, SUNY, Cortland, 1968; MA, Calif. State U., Northridge, 1977. Cert. athletic trainer. Instr. West Babylon (N.Y.) High Sch., 1970-73; program coordinator Girls Club of Santa Barbara, Calif., 1973-74; instr. Lowell High Sch., LaHabra, Calif., 1975, Garfield High Sch., East Los Angeles, Calif., 1975-76; assoc. prof. East Los Angeles Coll., Calif., 1976—; fitness cons. R.J. Assocs., Arcadia, Calif., 1986—. Vol. firefighter/rescue squad, City of LaHabra Heights, Calif., 1985—. Mem. ACLU, NOW, LWV, Nat. Athletic Trainers Assn. Democrat. Avocations: marathon running, weight training, gardening, theater. Home: 807 West Rd La Habra Heights CA 90631 Office: East Los Angeles Coll 1301 Brooklyn Ave Monterey Park CA 91754

KINGMAN, ELIZABETH YELM, anthropology researcher; b. Lafayette, Ind., Oct. 15, 1911; d. Charles Walter and Mary Irene (Weakley) Yelm; B.A., U. Denver, 1933, M.A., 1935; m. Eugene Kingman, June 10, 1939; children—Mixie Kingman Eddy, Elizabeth Anne Kingman. Asst. in anthropology U. Denver, 1932-34; mus. asst. Ranger Naturalist Force, Mesa Verde Nat. Park, Colo., 1934-38; asst. to husband in curatorial work, Indian art exhibits Philbrook Art Center, Tulsa, 1939-42, Joslyn Art Mus., Omaha, 1947-69; tutor humanities dept. U. Omaha, 1947-50; asst. to husband in exhibit design mus. of Tex. Tech. U., 1970-75, bibliographer Internat. Center Arid and Semi-Arid Land Studies, 1974-75; librarian Sch. Am. Research, Santa Fe, 1978-86; research assoc., 1986—; v.p. Santa Fe Corral of the Westerners, 1985-86. Mem. Archeol. Inst. Am. (v.p. Santa Fe chpt. 1981-83), N.Mex. Library Assn., LWV, Santa Fe Hist. Soc. (sec. 1981-83), Council Internat. Relations. Presbyterian. Home: 604 Sunset St Santa Fe NM 87501 Office: Sch Am Research 660 Garcia St Santa Fe NM 87501-1118

KINGSBURY, CAROLYN ANN, aerospace engineer.; b. Newark, Ohio, Aug. 4, 1938; d. Cecil C. Layman and Orpha Edith (Hisey) Layman Dick; m. James Kingsbury, Apr. 25, 1959; children—Donald Lynn, Kenneth James. B.S. in Math., B.S. in Info. and Computer Scis., U. Calif.-Irvine, 1979; postgrad. West Coast U., 1982-84. Integrated test engr. Rockwell Internat., Downey, Calif., 1979-82, system engr., analyst, 1982-84; software test engr. Northrop Corp., Pico Rivera, Calif., 1984—. Pres., PTA, Manhattan Beach, Calif., 1971-73; Cub Scout den mother Boy Scouts Am., Manhattan Beach, 1972-73. Recipient Service award Calif. Congress Parents and Tchrs., 1973, Leadership Achievement award YWCA, Los Angeles, 1980, 84, NASA Achievement awards, 1983. Mem. Nat. Assn. Female Execs., Nat. Mgmt. Assn., AAUW. Republican. Club: Newtowners (pres. 1962). Home: 11392 Stonecress Ave Fountain Valley CA 92708 Office: Northrop Corp 8900 E Washington Blvd Pico Rivera CA 90660

KINGSBURY, KENNETH EARL, JR., publisher, producer, disc jockey, business executive; b. Black Rock, Ark., Sept. 30, 1945; s. Kenneth Earl and Dora (Bell) K.; AA in Bus. Mgmt., El Camino Coll., Torrance, Calif., 1977. Freelance film dir., N.Y.C., 1968-71; ednl. cons. Programmed Systems Co., Los Angeles, 1972-77; credit cons. Computer Credit Co., 1977-78; credit mgr. Windsor Publs. Co., Woodland Hills, Calif., 1978-80; pres. Black Stallion Country, Inc.; sec.-treas. King-Bart Group, Inc., Culver City, Calif., 1980—. Editor, pub. Kingsbury's Who's Who In Country and Western Music, 1981; producer, co-host Kenn 'n' Harry Show Sta. KCSN (nat. pub. radio), 1984—. Trustee Billy Barty Found., 1984—, personal mgr. entertainer Billy Barty, 1985—. Served with USAR, 1963-68. Mem. Variety Entertainers Guild Am. (sec.-treas. 1975-77), Country Music Assn., Acad. Country Music, Country Music Found. (assoc.), Salvation Army. Republican. Club: Green Hat (pres. wildlife waystation 1985—, v.p. 1987) (San Fernando, Calif.). Office: PO Box 2250 Culver City CA 90230

KINGSLEY, SHERWOOD CLARK, accountant; b. Los Angeles, July 5, 1939; s. William Jackson and Eleanor Nevin (Veale) K.; m. Rona Toby Fretter, Nov. 8, 1980; 1 son, Aron Sherwood. Staff acct. Arthur Young & Co., Los Angeles, 1965-66; supr. accounts payable Interpace Co., Los Angeles, 1966-67; controller Illig Constrn. Co., Los Angeles, 1967-73; supr. John F. Forbes Co., Los Angeles, 1974; practice public acctg., Los Angeles, 1975—. Organizer alumni fund raising orgn. Webb Sch. C.P.A., Calif. Mem. Am. Inst. C.P.A.s, Calif. Soc. C.P.A.s, SAR. Republican. Congregationalist. Clubs: Lions (pres. 1981-82), Masons (master 1976). Home: 4159 Keystone Ave Culver City CA 90232

KINION, EDWARD FRANKLIN, law enforcement administrator; b. Casper, Wyo., June 4, 1933; s. Ernest Lemial and Jessie Irene (Phillipsen) K.; m. Doris Marlene Hahn, Aug. 5, 1956; children—Kimberly Irene, Karen Louise. A.A. in Law Enforcement, Casper Coll., 1959, A.S., 1967. Cert. profl. peace officer, Wyo. With Casper (Wyo.) Police Dept., 1959—, sgt. in charge of traffic div., 1969-73, master lt. in charge of traffic div., 1973-76, comdr. patrol div., 1976-80, chief of police, 1980—; instr. driver tng. Casper Coll., 1969-76; cert. assessor Police Assessment Center for Hirings and Promotions; mem. Peace Officers Standards and Tng. Commn. Served with M.P., U.S. Army, 1955. Named Peace Officer of Yr., Casper Exchange Club, 1967; recipient Frank Morgan award Explorer Scouting, 1977. Mem. Internat. Assn. Chiefs of Police, Nat. Assn. Chiefs of Police, Wyo. Assn. Chiefs of Police (past pres.), Wyo. Peace Officers Assn. (1st v.p., past pres.). Republican. Lodges: Kiwanis, Masons. Founder Community Service Patrol, Casper, 1976, hit and run accident investigative unit, 1980, crime prevention programs, 1980, Crime Watch Program, 1982; co-founder Explorer Post, 1974. Office: City of Casper Police Dept 200 N David St Casper WY 82601

KINKADE, KATE, publishing executive, magazine editor, insurance executive; b. N.Y.C., Jan. 22, 1951; d. Joel M. and Peeta S. (Sherman) Sandleman; m. Patrick Ramsey, June 27, 1981; children: Jamaa Ramsey, Kikanza Ramsey. BS in Speech, Emerson Coll., Boston, 1972; postgrad., Am. Coll., Bryn Mawr, Pa. CLU. Agt. Equitable Life Ins., Los Angeles, 1973-75, mgr., 1975-77; v.p. Lincoln Nat. Life Ins., Tarzana, Calif., 1977-80; pres. TIME Ins., Encino, Calif., 1980—; mng. editor McGee Pub., Burbank, Calif., 1983—; exec. v.p. Life Underwriters Assn., Encino, 1978-81. Contbr. articles to profl. jours. Mem. steering com. nat. office Beyond War, Palo Alto, Calif., also Los Angeles regional fin. support and chairperson local chpt., Burbank, Calif., 1984—. Recipient Asst. Prodn. awards Equitable Life, 1973, 77, Lincoln Nat. Life, 1978, 80, Pacific Mut. Life, 1983. Mem. Assn. CLU's. Democrat. Jewish. Avocations: model trains, whitewater rafting, running. Office: Ramkade Inc 15760 Ventura #1734 Encino CA 91436

KINKADE, RICHARD PAISLEY, university administrator; b. Los Angeles, Jan. 7, 1939; s. Joseph Marion and Mary Elizabeth (Paisley) K.; m. Raquel Liebes, June 2, 1962 (div. 1977); children: Kathleen, Richard Jr., Scott; m. Kiki J. Gekas, Aug. 27, 1986. BA, Yale U., 1960, PhD, 1965. From asst. to assoc. prof. U. Ariz., Tucson, 1965-71, prof. Spanish, dean of humanities, 1982—; prof., dept. head Emory U., Atlanta, 1971-77, U. Conn., Storrs, 1977-82; cons. NEH, Washington, 1976-77, 84-86. Co-author: Iconography in Medieval Spanish Literature, 1984, Studies in Honor of Gustavo Correa, 1986; editor Critical Edition of Lucidarios Espanoles, 1968; mem. editoral bd. Ky. Romance Quartley, 1978-84, Revista de Estudios Hispanicos, 1977-84, Scripta Humanistica, 1982-86; mng. editor La Coronica, 1973-76; contbr. articles to profl. jours. Trustee Green Fields Country Day Sch., Tucson, 1983—. NEH research fellow, 1978-79. Mem. Medieval Acad. Am., MLA (chmn. Spanish I 1974, 77), Chi Psi. Republican. Clubs: Graduate, Elizabethan. Lodge: Rotary. Home: 1200 Paseo Pavon Tucson AZ 85718 Office: U Ariz Coll Arts and Scis Tucson AZ 85721

KINMAN, R. DEWAYNE, data processing professional; b. Gunnison, Colo., Oct. 30, 1936; s. J. Howard and I. Roine (Wright) K.; m. Sharon F. Hutka, July 25, 1964; children: Kathryn A., Beverly J., Jonathan E. BA, Western State Coll., 1958. Programmer Martin Co., Denver, 1958-60, Lawrence Radiation Lab., Livermore, Calif., 1960-65, Sperry Univac, Hanover, N.J., 1966-67; mgr. engring. program Stearns-Roger, Denver, 1967-74; supr. data processing Stone & Webster Engring., Denver, 1974—; mem. computer-aided drafting com. Arapahoe Community Coll., Littleton, Colo., 1983—; chmn. drafting adv. com. Denver Community Coll., 1984—. Mem., tchr. Evang. Free Ch. Am., Littleton. Mem. Data Processing Mgmt. Assn. Republican. Avocations: camping, fishing. Home: 7116 S Elm Ct Littleton CO 80122 Office: Stone & Webster Engring PO Box 5406 Denver CO 80217-5406

KINNEBREW, JOSEPH E., IV, designer, artist; b. Tacoma, Wash., Oct. 12, 1942; s. Joseph E. Kinnebrew III and Elaine (Montgomery) Dexter; m. Ellen Carol McKittrick, June 28, 1970; children: Alexis, Heather, Peter Jospeh Tobias. BA, Syracuse U., 1964; MFA, Mich. State U., 1970; postgrad., Inst. Study Instructional Devel. and Tech., 1969-70. Prin. The Kinnebrew Design Collaborative, Clinton, Wash., 1976—; with Oberon Group, Lowell, Mich., 1977—; mng. dir. Jacquot Ltd., St. Lucia, West Indies, 1981—; dir. The Black Dahlia Ltd., Langley, Wash., 1987—; artist in residence NEA, Mich. State U. Sch. Packaging, Sch. of Human Ecology; cons. Mich. Joint Legis. Com. Arts, Mich. Council for Arts, McMillan, Palmer, Fritz & Assocs., WBDC Inc. Architects, Wayne State U. Sch. Edn., others. Represented in permanent collections Nat. Collection Fine Arts, The Art Inst. Chgo., Walker Art Ctr., Mpls., The Guggenheim Mus., The Met. Mus. Art, Mus. Modern Art, Library of Congress, Bkln. Mus., The Montreal Mus. Fine Arts, Detroit Inst. Art, Phila. Mus. Art, Atkins Mus. Fine Arts, Kansas City, The Houghton Library, Harvard U., New Orleans Mus. Art, The Mpls. Inst. Arts, Honolulu Acad. Arts, Flint Inst. Arts, others; works pub. in various mags. including Fortune mag., Art Forum, Saturday Rev., AIA Jour., Sports Illustrated, Esquire, Accent mag., Interior Design, numerous others; patentee in field. Recipient Mich. Product of Yr. award, 1979, Nat. Design award Indsl. Design Soc. Am., 1980, First Honor award Mich. Soc. Landscape Architecture, 1983; grantee NEA, Mich. Council Arts, Mich. State U. Communications Inst., Assoc. Truck Lines Found., Wis. State Arts Council, Thomas Erler Seidman Found., Dexter Charitable Trust. Home: 7595 Swede Hill Rd Clinton WA 98236 Office: The Black Dahlia Ltd PO Box 430 Langley WA 98260

KINNEY, FOSTER TODD, investment realtor; b. Wakefield, R.I., Mar. 4, 1934; s. Lorenzo Foster and Elizabeth (Todd) K.; m. Sharon Lee Heaton, Dec. 16, 1961; children—Karin Elizabeth, Linda Irene, Eileen Ruth. B.A., Cornell U., 1956; M.B.A., Stanford U., 1958. Mktg. research mgr. Packaging div. Mobil Chem., Macedon, N.Y., 1962-65, Ameron Protective Coatings div., Brea, Calif., 1965-70; new products mgr. Skyclimber div. Western Gear, Gardena, Calif., 1970-71; investment realtor Investment div. Colwell Properties, Orange, Calif., 1972-75, Cambio Realty & Investments, Fullerton, Calif., 1976-82, Westline Investments Ltd., 1982-86, investment div. Merrill Lynch Realty, 1987—; lectr. on income property ownership. Dir., treas. N.Orange County Edn., Found.; mem. Orange County Transit Dist. citizens adv. com., chmn., 1982-83, Fullerton Transp. Commn., chmn. 1980; bd. dirs. Friends of the Univ.; Calif. State U.-Fullerton Mem. Orange County Apt. Assn., Orange County Assn. Real Estate Investment Brokers (pres. 1980, 81), Realty Investment Assn. Calif. (dir. 1986—), North Orange County Bd. Realtors (investment chmn. 1977), Fullerton C. of C. (bd. dirs. 1975-77; educator of yr. 1982), Phi Sigma Kappa. Presbyterian. Home: 1017 Richman Knoll Fullerton CA 92635 Office: Merrill Lynch Realty 1021 W Bastanchury Suite 110 Fullerton CA 92633

KINNEY, HARRY EDWIN, mechanical engineer, business development executive, building contractor; b. Trinidad, Colo., June 7, 1924; s. Oliver Earl and Opal (Sanger) K.; m. Carol N. Roberts, Aug. 30, 1970; children: Charlotte Jean, Donald Bruce. B.S. in Mech. Engring., U. N.Mex., 1945; hon. degree in pub. adminstrn., U. Albuquerque, 1985. Staff mem. Sandia Labs., 1956-73; commr. City of Albuquerque, 1966-73, vice chmn. City Commn., 1970-71, chmn., 1971-73, mayor, 1974-77, 81-85; gen. contractor, residential constrn. 1977-81; bldg. contractor, dir. bus. devel. Jacobs Engrng. Group, Inc., Albuquerque, 1981—; commr. Bernalillo County, N.Mex., 1956-58, 61-65; mem. adv. panel on infrastructure to U.S. Senate budget com., 1985-86; mem. mgmt. adv. group for constrn. grants EPA, 1982-86. Chmn. Middle Rio Grande Council Govts. of N.Mex., 1970-72; mem. U.S. Adv. Commn. on Intergovtl. Relations, 1975-77; mem. adv. bd. U.S. Conf. Mayors, 1975-77, 82-85, chmn., 1977; Pres. Albuquerque-Bernalillo County Econ. Opportunity Bd., 1964-66; pres. N.Mex. Council Social Welfare, 1965-67; chmn. City-County Joint Alcoholism Bd., 1969-72; pres. Ams. for Rational Energy Alternatives, 1980-84, 85—; v.p. Chapparal council Girl Scouts U.S.A., 1978-81; bd. dirs. Met. YMCA, 1977-81; bd. dirs. Lovelace Med. Ctr. Health Plan, 1985—; spl. asst. to U.S. senator, 1973-74. Served with USNR, 1943-46, 50-52. Mem. ASME (Pub. Service award Region VIII, 1977, 84), Naval Res. Assn., Kappa Sigma. Episcopalian. Address: 3006 Vista Grande NW Albuquerque NM 87120

KINNEY, JEREMY FOWLER, oil company executive; b. N.Y.C., July 20, 1945; s. Francis Sherwood and Mary Dalton (Fowler) K. B.A., Yale U., 1968; M.B.A., Harvard U., 1973. Assoc. Eastdil Realty, Inc., N.Y.C., 1973-78, v.p., 1978-79; prin. Kinney Myers Interests, Dallas, 1979-81; pres. Kinney Oil Co., Denver, 1982—. Co-chmn. Opera Colo., Denver, 1985—. Served to 1st lt. USMCR, 1968-71. Mem. Ind. Petroleum Assn. of Mountain States (pub. lands com. 1982—). Republican. Roman Catholic. Clubs: Racquet and Tennis (N.Y.C.); Denver; Nat. Golf Links Am. (Southampton, N.Y.), Shinnecock Hills Golf (Southampton). Office: Kinney Oil Co 1331 17th St Suite 710 Denver CO 80202

KINNEY, LISA FRANCES, state senator; b. Laramie, Wyo., Mar. 13, 1951; d. Irvin Wayne and Phyllis (Poe) K.; m. Rodney Philip Lang, Feb. 5, 1971; 1 child, Cambria Helen. BA, U. Wyo., 1973, JD, 1986; MLS, U. Oreg., 1975. Reference librarian U. Wyo. Sci. Library, Laramie, 1975-76; outreach dir. Albany County Library, Laramie, 1975-76, dir., 1977-83; mem. Wyo. State Senate, Laramie, 1985—. Author: (with Rodney Lang) Civil Rights of the Developmentally Disabled, 1986; contbr. articles to profl. jours; editor, compiler pub. relations directory for ALA, 1982. Bd. dirs. Big Bros./Big Sisters, Laramie, 1980-83. Recipient Beginning Young Profl. award Mt. Plains Library Assn., 1980; named Outstanding Wyo. Librarian Wyo. Library Assn., 1977, Outstanding Young Woman State of Wyo., 1980. Mem. ABA , Nat. Confs. of State Legislatures (fiscal affairs and budget com.), LWV, Am. Bus. Women's Assn., Laramie C. of C. Democrat. Club: Snowy Range Internat. Folk Dance (pres. 1980—). Lodges: Zonta Internat., Gem City Lioness. Avocations: photography, dance, reading, travel, languages. Home: 603 Spring Creek Laramie WY 82070

KINNEY, MARJORIE SHARON, finance and marketing executive; b. Gary, Ind., Jan. 11, 1940; d. David H. and Florence C. Dunning; student El Camino Coll., 1957, 58; LHD (hon.), West Coast U., 1982; m. Daniel D. Kinney, Dec. 31, 1958 (div. 1973); children: Steven Daniel, Michael Alan, Gregory Lincoln, Bradford David; m. Bradley Morris Thomas, Nov. 9, 1985 (div. Mar. 1987). Ptnr., Kinney Advt. Inc., Inglewood, Calif., 1958-68; pres. Greeters of Am., 1967-69; chmn. Person to Person Inc., Cleve., 1969-72; pres. Kinney Mktg. Corp., Encino, Calif., 1972-80; sr. v.p. Beverly Hills (Calif.) Savs. & Loan Assn., 1980-84; chmn., pres. Kinney Corp., Dana Point, Calif., 1985—; dir. Safeway Stores, Inc., Chubb/Pacific Indemnity Co.; lectr. Bd. dirs. ARC, 1976-81, United Way, 1979-81; trustee West Coast U.; adv. bd. U.S. Human Resources, Womens Legal Edn. Fund; briefing del. to Pentagon Fed. Res. Dept. and White House, 1986; pres. Santa Fe Rep. Women, 1987—. Presbyterian.

KINNEY, WILLIAM JAMES APOLO, quality assurance engineer; b. Honolulu, June 28, 1948; s. James Everett Apolo and Frances (Korneszcuk) K.; m. Martha Lynn Spring, Apr. 28, 1973; children: Louis Andrew Larson, Nathan William Apolo, Rachel Lynn Ann. AA in Liberal Arts, AS in Quality Tech., Allan Hancock Coll., 1982; BS in Bus. Mgmt., U. Laverne, 1986. Quality assurance specialist Air Force Plant Rep. Office Hughes Aircraft Co., Culver City, Calif., 1972-77; mgr. quality assurance Western Space and Missile Ctr., Vanderberg AFB, Calif., 1977-85, coordinator quality circles, 1982-85, chief plans and requirements div., 1985-86; rep. Dept. Def. for F-16 Multinat. Fighter Program Fabrique Nationale, Liege, Belgium, 1986—. Trustee Ch. Nazarene, Santa Maria, Calif., 1982-84; vol. Combined Fed. Campaign, 1973-83. Served as staff sgt. USAF, 1966-72, Vietnam. Named one of Outstanding Young Men of Am., Jaycees, 1984. Mem. Am. Soc. Quality Control (cert., chmn. sect. 0601 1982-83), Soc. Logistics Engrs., Santa Maria C. of C. Avocations: mineralogy, stamp collecting, motorcycles, surfing. Home: 576 Lupin Ln Santa Maria CA 93455 Office: F-16 Contract Adminstrn Services Europe, Brussels Belgium also: Det 33 AFCMC CASEUR APO New York NY 09667-6027

KINNISON, ROBERT WHEELOCK, certified public accountant; b. Des Moines, Sept. 17, 1914; s. Virgil R. and Sopha J. (Jackson) K.; m. Randi Hjelle, Oct. 28, 1971; children—Paul F., Hazel Jo Huff. B.S. in Acctg., U. Wyo., 1940. C.P.A., Wyo., Colo. Ptnr. 24 hour auto service, Laramie, Wyo., 1945-59; pvt. practice acctg., Laramie, Wyo., 1963-71, Las Vegas, Nev., 1972-74, Westminster, Colo., 1974-76, Ft. Collins, Colo., 1976—. Served with U.S. Army, 1941-45; PTO. Mem. Am. Soc. C.P.A.s, Wyo. Soc. C.P.A.s, Am. Legion (past comdr.), Laramie Soc. C.P.A.s (pres. 1966), VFW. Clubs: Laramie Optimist (pres. 1950), Sertoma. Home: PO Box 168 Fort Collins CO 80522 Office: 2050 Airway Ave Fort Collins CO 80524

KINRADE, KERRY FRANCIS, insurance executive; b. Los Angeles, Oct. 1, 1936; s. John T. and Claire (Bovee) K.; B.A., UCLA, 1959; M.P.A., U. So. Calif., 1969; m. Linda C. Wolf, May 31, 1969. With State Compensation Ins. Fund, San Francisco, 1960—, supervising mgmt. analyst, 1979-83, claims mgr., 1983—. Bd. dirs. Salem Luth. Home, Oakland, Calif. Mem. Am. Soc. Pub. Adminstrn. Office: 1275 Market St San Francisco CA 94103

KINSALA, SCOTT DOUGLAS, biological researcher; b. Santa Monica, Calif., June 13, 1955; s. Douglas Quill and Donna Jean (Tannehill) K.; m. Edel-Linde Webster, Feb. 1983; 1 child, Elizabeth Louise. AA, Orange Coast Coll., 1978; BS in Biology, Calif. Polytech. U., Pomona, 1982. Vet. asst. Balboa Animal Hosp., Newport Beach, Calif., 1977-82; expeditor Linear Instrument Corp., Reno, 1982-83; chemist Sunrise Industries, Sparks, Nev., 1983-85; research assoc. Eagle-Picher Industries Inc., Reno, 1985—. Home: 1901 3d St Sparks NV 89431 Office: Eagle-Picher Industries Inc PO Box 10480 Reno NV 89510

KINSELL, JEFFREY CLIFT, banking executive; b. Santa Barbara, Calif., Sept. 13, 1951; s. Clift Seybert and Shirlee Grace (Burwash) K.; divorced. BS in Biology, Tulane U., 1973; MBA in Fin., UCLA, 1976. Trader First Boston Corp., N.Y.C., 1976-77; investment banker First Boston Corp., San Francisco, 1978—. Mem. San Francisco Mcpl. Bond Club, Beta Beta Beta. Republican. Episcopalian. Avocations: sailing, skiing, travel, running. Home: 1599 Huston Rd Lafayette CA 94549 Office: First Boston Corp 101 Calif St Suite 4300 San Francisco CA 94111

KINSKY, IVAN, electronics engineer; b. Temesvar, Romania, Apr. 24, 1947; came to Israel, 1962, U.S., 1984.; s. Stefan and Margareta (Reiter) K.; m. Yael Grynberg, Aug. 12, 1970; children: Danna, Gilly. BSEE, Technion, Israel, 1969, MSEE, 1973. Project mgr. Tamam Israel Aircraft Industries, Tel Aviv, 1975-81, program mgr., 1981-82; dep. div. mgr. Elco Ltd., Tel Aviv, 1982-83, div. mgr., 1983-84; prin. Quad Inc., Canoga Park, Calif., 1985—; cons. Elco Ltd., 1984-85, FMC, San Jose, Calif., 1985—, Condor Pacific, Canoga Park, 1984—. Served to capt. Israel Army, 1979. Mem. Inst. Navigation, Royal Inst. Navigation (Eng.). Home and Office: Quad Inc 23601 Draco Canoga Park CA 91307

KINSLER, BRUCE WHITNEY, air traffic controller; b. Ukiah, Calif., Jan. 11, 1947; s. John Arthur and Mary Helen (Hudson) K.; m. Mickey Kinsler, Apr. 1, 1969 (div. Nov. 1976); 1 child, Arthur Todd; m. Segundina L. Pangilinan, May 27, 1978; 1 stepchild, Stephanie Camalig. AA, El Camino Coll., 1979; BA, Calif. State U., Long Beach, 1984. Air traffic controller FAA, various locations, 1971-81; cen. sta. mgr. Times Mirror Security

Communications, Irvine, Calif., 1982-84; supr. office services Law Offices Paul, Hastings, Janofsky & Walker, Los Angeles, 1984-85; air traffic control cons. to Hughes Aircraft Corp. Fullerton, Calif., 1985—; with Datatec, Torrance, Calif.; pres. NAS Services, Inc., Fullerton, 1986—; mem. citizens adv. com. Calif. Dept. Transp., Sacramento, 1982—. Author air traffic control tng. manuals. Mem. Air Traffic Control Assn., Aircraft Owners and Pilots Assn., Fullerton C. of C., U.S. Naval Res., Am. Legion. Democrat. Club: Corvettes of So. Calif. (Anaheim). Avocations: flying, sports cars. Home: 640 Buckboard Ct Brea CA 92621

KINZIE, JEANNIE JONES, radiation oncologist; b. Great Falls, Mont., Mar. 14, 1940; d. James Wayne and Lillian Alice (Young) Jones; m. Joseph Lee Kinzie, Mar. 26, 1965 (div. Sept. 1982); 1 child, Daniel Joseph. Student, Oreg. State U., 1960; BS, Mont. State U., 1961; MD, Washington U., St. Louis, 1965. Diplomate Am. Bd. Radiology. Intern. in surgery U. N.C., Chapel Hill, 1965-66; resident in therapeutic radiology Washington U., St. Louis, 1968-71, instr. in radiology, 1971-73; asst. prof. in radiology Med. Coll. of Wis., Milw., 1973-75; asst. prof. in radiology U. Chgo., 1975-78, assoc. prof. in radiology, 1978-80; assoc. prof. of radiation oncology Wayne State U., Detroit, 1980-85; prof. radiology U. Colo., Denver, 1985—; dir. radiation oncology U. Hosp., Denver, 1985—; cons. Denver Vets. Hosp., Denver Gen. Hosp., Rose Med. Ctr., FDA Ctr. for Devices and Radiologic Health; sci. adv. bd. Cancer League of Colo.; examiner Am. Bd. Radiology; cons. Food and Drug Adminstrn., 1987—. Assoc. editor Internat. Jour. Radiation Oncology Biology and Physics; contbr. articles to profl. jours.; chpts. to books. Bd. dirs. Denver unit Am. Cancer Soc., 1986—. NIH grantee, 1973-75; Am. Coll. Radiology fellow, 1984. Mem. Denver Med. Soc., Colo. Med. Soc., Colo. Radiol. Soc., Rocky Mountain Oncology Soc., Am. Coll Radiology, Soc. Head and Neck Surgeons, AMA, Am. Radium Soc., Am. Soc. Therapeutic Radiologists, Am. Cancer Soc. (bd. dirs. Denver unit). Republican. Lutheran. Avocations: stamp collecting, cross country skiing, gardening, rug latching. Home: 3221 Interlocken Dr Evergreen CO 80439 Office: Radiation Oncology Box A031 4200 E 9th Ave Denver CO 80262

KIPP, THOMAS EUGENE, JR., engineer; b. Hawkinsville, Ga., Sept. 20, 1948; s. Thomas Eugene and Jane (Ray) K.; m. Glenna Roper, June 26, 1971; 1 child, Christopher Lee. AS, Middle Ga. Coll., 1968; B in Aero. Engring., Ga. Inst. Tech., 1970; MS in Aero. Engring., Ga. Tech. U., 1975. Engr.- scientist McDonnell Douglas A.C., Huntington Beach, Calif., 1975—; engring. assoc. PDA Engring., Santa Ana, Calif., 1978—. Served to sgt. USAF, 1971-75. Avocations: music, skiing, tennis. Office: PDA Engring 1560 Brookhollow Dr Santa Ana CA 92705

KIPP, WILLIAM PAUL, educational administrator,consultant; b. Wilkensburg, Pa., Jan. 22, 1932; s. William Paul and Eldene Patsy Emerson, May 27, 1954; children—William Paul III, Kathryn Susan, Jeffrey Alan, Michael Alvin. B.A., Northeastern Okla. U., 1955; M.A., Calif. State U., 1962; Ed.D., U. So. Calif., 1973. Cert. elem. and secondary tchr., gen. sch. administr. Tchr., Rowland Union Schs., La Puente, Calif., 1957-61, sch. prin., 1961-63, asst. supt. schs., Rowland Heights, Calif., 1963-73; supt. schs. Sulphur Springs Schs., Canyon Country, Calif., 1973-77, Redondo Beach City Schs. (Calif.), 1977-82, Redding Sch. Dist. (Calif.), 1982—; cons. various sch. dists., 1975—. Commr., Parks and Recreation Commn., Redondo Beach, 1979-82; elder Presbyterian Ch., Redding, 1984—. Served to cpl. USMC, 1949-51; Korea. Named Outstanding Young Man of Am., Jr. C. of C., Placentia, Calif., 1965; recipient Civic award City of Redondo Beach, 1982. Mem. Am. Assn. Sch. Adminstrs., Assn. Calif. Sch. Adminstrs. (charter, liaison adminstr. 1970-84, Disting. Achievement award 1977, 78, Keeper of Dream award 1985), Assn. Curriculum Devel. and Supervision, Shasta County Sch. Adminstrs. (dir.), Phi Delta Kappa (pres. 1969-70). Republican. Lodges: Kiwanis (pres. 1968-69), Rotary (bd. dirs. 1982-83). Home: 6136 Riverside Dr Redding CA 96001 Office: Redding Sch Dist 1855 Sequoia St Redding CA 96099

KIPROV, DOBRI DOBREV, immunology researcher; b. Sofia, Bulgaria, May 1, 1949; came to U.S., 1977; s. Dobri and Zvetana Kiprov; 1 child, Dobri Kiprov, Jr. MD, Med. Acad., Sofia, 1974. Resident in pathology Sackler Sch. Medicine, Tel Aviv, 1974-77, instr. pathology, 1975-77; resident in pathology Mt. Sinai Hosp., Cleve., 1977-79; clin. and research fellow Mass. Gen. Hosp., Boston, 1979-81; fellow in immunology and plasmapheresis Children's Hosp., San Francisco, 1981-82, dir. plasmapheresis unit, research immunologist, 1982—, cons. immunopathology, 1982—; instr. U. Calif., San Francisco, 1984—. Contbr. articles to profl. jours. Research grantee Myasthenia Gravis Found., 1982, 83, 84, Cobe Labs. Inc., 1982-83; recipient Tng. and Research award NIH, 1979-81. Mem. AAAS, AMA, Am. Soc. Clin. Pathologists, Am. Soc. Apheresis, Coll. of Am. Pathologists, World Med. Assn., Nat. Inst. Allergy and Infectious Diseases (spl. rev. com. 1985). Avocations: snow and water skiing, windsurfing. Office: Childrens Hosp San Francisco 3700 Calif St OPR 623 San Francisco CA 94118

KIPUST, RAYMOND, electrical engineer, consultant; b. N.Y.C., Jan. 20, 1934; s. Max and Fannie (Toffel) K.; m. Ann Rubinson, Jan. 30, 1955 (div. July 1983); children: Sharon L. Rosenhaus, Rochelle F. Schapiro, Alan S., Joanne S. AAS, N.Y.C. Community Coll., 1955; BS, Bklyn. Coll., 1960, postgrad., 1960-61. Registered profl. engr. N.J., N.Y., Calif. Ptnr., chief engr. A.L. Spaet, N.Y.C., 1968-72; chief engr. Economides & Goldberg, N.Y.C., 1972-73; mgr. Monroe (N.Y.) Devel. Co., 1973-76; chief engr. Segner & Dalton, Valhalla, N.Y., 1978-79; asst. chief engr. A.C. Martin, Los Angeles, 1979—; lectr. N.Y.C. Community Coll., Bklyn., 1960-79; cons. engr., Los Angeles, 1980—. Home: 12931 Hilton St Van Nuys CA 91401 Office: Albert C Martin and Assocs 811 W 7 St Los Angeles CA 90017

KIRBY, KEVIN ARTHUR, podiatrist, educator; b. Danville, Va., Jan. 30, 1957; s. James Clyde and Dorothy Annette (Skeen) K.; m. Pamela Joy Pearce, May 31, 1980; 1 child, Keegan James. BS, U. Calif., Davis, 1979; D, Calif. Coll. Podiatric Medicine, 1983, MS, 1985. Resident in podiatry VA Med. Ctr., Palo Alto, Calif., 1983-84; fellow in podiatry Calif. Coll. Podiatric Medicine, San Francisco, 1984-85, asst. prof. dept. biomechanics, 1985—; podiatrist Pacific Health Ctr., Sacramento, 1985—; dir. clin. biomechanics Precision Intricast Co., Lodi, Calif., 1985—, Kaiser Hosp., Sacramento, 1985—; tchr. Internat. Biomechanics Found., Auburn, Calif., 1985—. Contbr. articles to jours. Mem. Am. Podiatric Med. Assn., Calif. Podiatric Med. Assn., Am. Coll. Foot Surgeons, Am. Acad. Podiatric Sports Medicine. Democrat. Baptist. Avocations: windsurfing, running, photography, computers, teaching. Office: Pacific Health Ctr 1675 Alhambra Blvd Sacramento CA 95816

KIRCH, PATRICK VINTON, museum director; b. Honolulu, July 7, 1950; s. Harold William and Barbara Ver (MacGarvin) K.; m. Debra Connelly, Mar. 3, 1979. BA, U. Pa., 1971; MPhil, Yale U., 1974, PhD, 1975. Assoc. anthropologist Bishop Mus., Honolulu, 1975-76, anthropologist, 1976-82, head archaeology div., 1982-84, asst. chmn. anthropology, 1983-84; dir., assoc. prof. Burke Mus. U. Wash., Seattle, 1984—; adj. faculty U. Hawaii, Honolulu, 1979-84; mem. lasting legacy com. Wash. State Centennial Commn., 1986—; pres. Soc. Hawaiian Archaeology, 1980-81. Author: Feathered Gods and Fishhooks, 1985, Evolution of the Polynesian Chiefdoms, 1984; editor: Island Societies, 1986; contbr. articles to profl. pubis. Grantee NSF, 1974, 76, 77, 82, 87, NEA, 1985, Hawaii Com. for Humanities, 1981. Fellow Am. Anthropol. Assn.; mem. Assn. Sci. Mus. Dirs., Assn. Field Archaeology, Polynesian Soc. (New Zealand), Seattle C. of C., Sigma Xi. Democrat. Avocation: cross country skiing. Office: U Wash Thomas Burke Meml Mus DB-10 Seattle WA 98195

KIRCHER, CARL CONVERSE, research chemist; b. El Paso, Tex., Jan. 9, 1956; s. Carl Converse and Harriet Marie (Riebe) K. BS, U. Ariz., 1978; PhD, Mich. State U., 1982. Research assoc. Jet Propulsion Lab., NRC, Pasadena, Calif., 1982-84; chemist J.M. Montgomery Engrs., Pasadena, 1984; research chemist Unocal Sci. and Tech. Div., Brea, Calif., 1984-87; quality assurance, quality control oil shale environ. program Unocal Sci. and Tech. Div., Brea, 1987—. Contbr. articles to profl. jours. Judge Calif. State Sci. Fair, Los Angeles, 1986; mem., leader Boy Scouts Am., Yuma, Ariz., 1969-74; tenor All Saints' Canterbury Choir, Pasadena, 1985-86; trombonist Calif. Inst. Tech. Music Ensembles, Pasadena, 1984-86. Cy Rubel scholar U. Ariz., Tucson, 1974-78, L.L. Quill fellow Mich. State U., 1978-82. Mem. Am. Chem. Soc. Republican. Episcopalian. Clubs: JPL Hiking, JPL Skiing (Pasadena). Avocations: astronomy, space scis., camping, music, dancing. Home: 285 N Garfield Ave #10B Pasadena CA 91101 Office: Unocal Sci and Tech Div 376 S Valencia Ave Brea CA 92621

KIRCHER, LORENCE TOBIAS, III, pathologist, epidemiologist, consultant; b. Denver, Nov. 2, 1950; s. Lorence Tobias Jr. and Shirley Ann (Evans) K.; m. Patricia Albertina Anderson, Oct. 4, 1975; children: Thomas Alexander Szczech, Sara Elizabeth Szczech, Ashley Anderson. BA cum laude, Harvard U., 1972, MD, 1976. Resident in family practice U.Colo. Med. Ctr., Denver, 1976-77; resident in pathology Penrose Hosp., Colorado Springs, Colo., 1977-81, pathologist, 1983—. Contbr. articles to profl. jours. Dem. committeeman, Colorado Springs, 1984—. Served with USPHS, 1981-83. Tng. grantee NIH, Haiti, 1976. Fellow Coll. Am. Pathologists; mem. Colo. Soc. Clin. Pathologists, Physicians for Social Responsibility (bd. dirs. 1985—). Episcopalian. Avocations: carpentry, gardening, pottery, guitar, singing. Home: 2840 N Chelton Rd Colorado Springs CO 80909 Office: Penrose Hosp Dept Pathology 2215 N Cascade Ave Colorado Springs CO 80907

KIRCOS, CHRISTINE THEODORE, special education educator; b. Chgo., July 16, 1937; d. Gus and Kaliope Theodore; m. Spiro B. Kircos, Nov. 19, 1961; children: Suzanne, William. B, Chgo. Tchrs. Coll., 1959; M, Nat. Coll. Edn., 1983. Elem. tchr. Niles (Ill.) Pub. Schs., 1959-60; elem. tchr. Chgo. Pub. Schs., 1960-65, spl. edn. tchr., 1979-86; spl. edn. tchr. Scottsdale, Ariz., 1986—. Art and ceramic exhbns. include Cultural Ctr., Hist. Mus., Mus. Sci. and Industry, Chgo., 1986. Mem. Council for Exceptional Children.

KIRDAR, EDIB E., civil engineer; b. Izmir, Turkey, Dec. 25, 1931; s. Emin and Nuzhet K.; came to U.S., 1959, naturalized, 1977; B.S. in Civil Engring., Robert Coll., Istanbul, Turkey, 1955; postgrad. Ariz. State U., 1959-68; m. Zeynep Keymen, Jan. 28, 1961; children—Leyla, Murad. Mgr. Office Internat. Affairs, Salt River Project, Phoenix, 1959—; mem. Am. Spl. Study Program, Dept. State visit Middle East, 1977; mem. U.S. Delegation to UN Conf. Hungary, 1985; U.S. Agy. Internat. Devel. cons. to Pakistan, 1985. Pres., Scottsdale Community Players, 1973; bd. dirs. Ariz. Teen Talent Search Inc. Recipient cert. of service Salt River project Employees Recreational Assn., 1969, 72. Mem. ASCE, Am. Water Resources Assn., Am. Public Works Assn., Western Snow Conf., Ariz. Water Resources Com., World Affairs Council Phoenix (v.p. 1985-86), Phoenix Com. on Fgn. Relations. Republican. Moslem. Lodges: Lions (pres. Tempe), Moose (dir. 1978, Rookie of Yr. award 1979); Papago Toastmasters (pres. 1969, 75, Able Toastmasters cert. and speech awards). Contbr. tech. articles on hydrology, runoff forecast, reservoir ops., computer modeling to profl. jours. Office: Salt River Project PO Box 1980 Phoenix AZ 85001

KIREMIDJIAN, ANNE AGHAVNY, civil engineering educator; b. Sofia, Bulgaria, Aug. 11, 1949; came to U.S., 1965; d. Hrant Aram and Tzvetanka Petrova Setian; m. Garo K. Kiremidjian, July 17, 1972; 1 child, Seta N. BA, Queens Coll., 1972; BS, Columbia U., 1972; MS, Stanford U., 1973, PhD, 1977. Postdoctoral research affiliate Stanford (Calif.) U., 1976-78, asst. prof. civil engring., 1978-85, assoc. prof., 1985—; vis. lectr. Stanford U., 1976-77. Contbr. numerous articles to profl. jours. Mem. ASCE (mem. various coms.), Earthquake Engring. Research Inst. (mem. various coms.), Structural Engrs. Assn. Calif., Sigma Xi, Tau Beta Pi. Republican. Christian Orthodox. Avocations: piano, music, swimming, traveling, gourmet cooking. Office: Stanford U Dept Civil Engring Terman 238 Stanford CA 94305

KIRK, CASSIUS LAMB, JR., lawyer, investor; b. Bozeman, Mont., June 8, 1929; s. Cassius Lamb and Gertrude Violet (McCarthy) K.; A.B., Stanford U., 1951; J.D., U. Calif., Berkeley, 1954. Bar: Calif. 1955. Assoc. firm Cooley, Godward, Castro, Huddleson & Tatum, San Francisco, 1956-60; staff counsel for bus. affairs Stanford U., 1960-78; chief bus. officer, staff counsel Menlo Sch. and Coll., Redwood City, Calif., 1978-81; pres. Eberli-Kirk Properties, Inc., Menlo Park, 1981—; mem. faculty Coll. Bus. Adminstrn. U. Calif., Santa Barbara, 1967-73; bd. dirs. Just Closets, Inc., San Rafael, Calif.; bd. dirs. San Francisco Pocket Opera. Served with U.S. Army, 1954-56. Lic. real estate broker. Mem. Calif. Bar Assn., Stanford Assocs., Order of Coif, Phi Alpha Delta. Republican. Clubs: Stanford Faculty. Home: 1330 University Dr Apt 52 Menlo Park CA 94025 Office: 3520-B Haven Ave Redwood City CA 94063

KIRK, DUDLEY, sociologist, educator; b. Rochester, N.Y., Oct. 6, 1913; s. William and Margaret Louise (Dudley) K.; m. Ruth Louise Avelar, Nov. 21, 1947; children: Margaret Louise, John Dudley, Deborah Avelar. A.B., Pomona Coll., 1934; M.A., Fletcher Sch. Law and Diplomacy, Tufts U., 1935, Harvard U., 1938; Ph.D., Harvard U., 1946; student, U. Mexico, 1930, London Sch. Econ. and Polit. Sci., 1936. Tutor sociology Harvard U., 1937-39; research asst., later research asso. Office Population Research, Princeton U., 1939-47, asst. prof. sociology at univ., 1945-47; demographer Office Intelligence Research, State Dept., 1947-51; chief div. research Office Intelligence Research, State Dept., Near East, South Asia and Africa, 1952; chief planning staff for research and intelligence Office Intelligence Research, State Dept., 1952-54; staff mem. Pres.'s Com. Immigration and Naturalization, 1951; demographic dir. Population Council, N.Y.C., 1954-67; prof. demography Food Research Inst. and dept. sociology Stanford U., 1967—, Morrison prof. population studies, 1971—, chmn. dept. sociology, 1975-76; vis. sr. research demographer Princeton U., 1978; coordinator Courses by Newspaper, NEH, 1981-82; mem. U.S. Nat. Com. on Health and Vital Stats., 1961-65; mem. research adv. com. AID, 1968-72. Author: (with others) The Future Population of Europe and the Soviet Union, 1944, Europe's Population in the Interwar Years, 1946, The Principles of Political Geography, 1957, (with Ellen K. Eliason) Food and People, 1982. Fellow Center Advanced Study in the Behavioral Scis., 1964-65. Fellow AAAS, Am. Sociol. Assn., Am. Statis. Assn., Inter-Am. Statis. Inst., Am. Pub. Health Assn.; mem. Am. Soc. Study Social Biology (dir., chmn. editorial bd. Social Biology, pres. 1969-72), Am. Acad. Polit. and Social Sci., Internat. Union Sci. Study Population, Population Assn. Am. (pres. 1959-60), Sociol. Research Assn. Home: 53 Peter Coutts Circle Stanford CA 94305

KIRK, JOHN G(ALLATIN), astronomer; b. Wilmington, Ohio, Oct. 21, 1938; s. Charles Roger and Dorothy Evelyn (Mason) K. AB, Amherst Coll., 1960; AM, U. Mich., 1962, PhD, 1966. Jr. astronomer Kitt Peak Nat. Obs., Tucson, 1966-69; asst. prof. astronomy U. Toledo, Ohio, 1969-74; systems analyst Computer Scis. Corp., Silver Spring, Md., 1974-79; systems analyst electronics div. Gen. Dynamics Corp., Vandenberg AFB, Calif., 1979-80; mem. profl. staff Geodynamics Corp., Santa Barbara, Calif., 1980—. Recipient NASA Tech. Innovation award 1981. Mem. Am. Astron. Soc., Am. Geophys. Union, Sigma Xi. Home: 325 Palisades Dr Santa Barbara CA 93109 Office: Geodynamics Corp 5520 Ekwill St Suite A Santa Barbara CA 93111

KIRK, REA HELENE (GLAZER), social services administrator, educator; b. N.Y.C., Nov. 17, 1944; d. Benjamin and Lillian (Kellis) Glazer; 3 stepdaughters. B.A., UCLA, 1966; M.A., Eastern Mont. Coll., 1981. Life cert. spl. edn. tchr., Calif., Mont. Spl. edn. tchr., Los Angeles, 1966-73; clin. sec. speech and lang. clinic, Missoula, Mont., 1973-75; spl. edn. tchr., Missoula and Gt. Falls, Mont., 1975-82; dir. Woman's Resource Ctr., Gt. Falls, Mont., 1981-82; dir. Battered Woman's Shelter, Rock Springs, Wyo., 1982-84; dir. Battered Victims Program Sweetwater County, Wyo., 1984—; mem. Wyo. Commn. on Aging, Rock Springs. Pres. bd. dirs. battered woman's shelter, Gt. Falls, Woman's Resource Ctr., Gt. Falls; founder, advisor Rape Action Line, Gt. Falls; founder Jewish religious services, Missoula; 4-H leader; hostess Friendship Force; Friendship Force ambassador from Wyo. to W. Germany; mem. YMCA Mont. and Wyo. Recipient honors Missoula 4-H; recognized as significant Wyo. woman as social justice reformer and peace activist Sweetwater County, Wyo.; nominated Wyo. Woman of the Yr. Mem. Council for Exceptional Children (v.p. Gt. Falls 1981-82), Assn. for Children with Learning Disabilities, Delta Kappa Gamma, Psi Chi. Democrat. Jewish.

KIRKENDOLL, ROY NATHAN, JR., real estate broker, educator; b. Joplin, Mo., June 22, 1950; s. Roy Nathan Sr. and Ruth Mae (King) K.; m. Diana Lucille Brown, Aug. 7, 1971 (div. Apr. 1975); 1 child, Christopher Michael. BA in English, U. Kans., 1972. Salesman Mayer-Rossberg Realtors, Overland Park, Kans., 1972-74; mgr. Kroh Bros. Realty, Kansas City, Mo., 1974-75; salesman Coldwell Banker, La Jolla, Calif., 1975-81; pres. Kirkendoll Co., Malibu, Calif., 1981—; broker, gen. mgr. Better Homes Realty, Dublin, Calif., 1985—; sponsor Dept. Real Estate, Sacramento, 1981—. Author: California Escrow Guide, 1985, Keys to Success, 1986, Negotiationg, The Power of Effective Listening; various ednl. video tapes. Recipient Outstanding Sales Achievement award Coldwell Banker, 1975-80. Mem. Phi Beta Kappa, Delta Chi. Avocations: classical piano, bodybuilding, skiing. Address: 245 Upper Terrace San Francisco CA 94117

KIRKHAM, LINDSAY JACK, physician; b. Kansas City, Mo., Sept. 11, 1923; s. Lindsay Jack and Abigail Lenore (Lillis) K.; m. Mary Ann Reynolds, July 15, 1952; children—Clifford John, Richard Ladd, William Reynolds, Maura Ann, Jeffrey Scott, Christine Marie, Douglas Joseph. Student Va. Mil. Inst., 1940-41, U. Kans., 1941-43; M.D., Washington U., St. Louis, 1946; M.P.H., U. Hawaii, 1981; postgrad U. No. Iowa, 1975-77. Intern, 1946; resident in internal medicine Harper Hosp., Harper Hosp., Detroit, 1946-47; resident in internal medicine Harper Hosp., Detroit, 1949-52, also VA Hosp.; practice medicine specializing in internal medicine, Mason City, Iowa, 1952-75; part-time examining physician, HEW; med. cons. Iowa Found. Med. Care, Iowa Dept. Public Instrn., 1977-80; chief hosp. and med facility br. Hawaii Dept. Health, Honolulu, 1982-86, chief office of research and stats., 1986—; founder, pres. adv. com. Sch. Nursing N. Iowa Community Coll., 1965. Founder, pres. Mason City Coordinating Com. for Treatment Alcoholism, 1970, Mason City Sr. Citizen Assn., 1960; Iowa del. White House Conf. on Aging, 1960; mem. Major's Commn. on the Handicapped, Honolulu. Pres. med. staff St. Josephs Mercy Hosp., chmn. med. sect. Served as officer, M.C., USNR, 1947-49. Mem. Cerro Gordo County Med. Soc. (pres.). AMA, A.C.P., Hawaii Med. Soc., Am. Soc. Internal Medicine, Hosp. Fin. Mgmt. Assn., Hawaii Pub. Health Assn., Am. Coll. Health Assn., Am. Public Health Assn., Nat. Assn. Health Facility Licensure and Certification Dirs. Office: Dept Health Hawaii 1250 Punchbowl St Honolulu HI 96813

KIRKHAM, ROGER LESLIE, management consultant, engineering and management educator; b. Salt Lake City, Apr. 23, 1944; s. Ralph N. and Mary (Barkdull) K.; m. Judy Ann Gowans, July 9, 1967; children—Nathan, Heather, Ryan, Darin, Kellie. B.S. in Indsl. Engring., U. Utah, 1969, M.Engring. Adminstrn., 1971. Registered profl. engr., Utah. Project engr. Inst. Biomed. Engring., 1968-73, asst. adminstr., 1973-76; instr. indsl. engring. U. Utah, 1976-78, research instr. surgery, 1971—, adj. asst. prof. indsl. engring., 1974—; pres. Am. Tng. Alliance, Salt Lake City, 1978—; mgmt. trainer and cons. to corps. and govt. agencies. Mem. Salt Lake Area C. of C., Am. Soc. Tng. and Devel., Inst. Indsl. Engrs. (sr.), Sigma Xi. Republican. Mormon. Club: Evergreen Swim and Tennis. Contbr. articles to profl. jours. Office: PO Box 8193 Salt Lake City UT 84108

KIRKLAND, BERTHA THERESA (MRS. THORNTON CROWNS KIRKLAND, JR.), engineer; b. San Francisco, May 16, 1916; d. Lawrence and Theresa (Kanzler) Schmelzer; m. Thornton Crowns Kirkland, Jr., Dec. 27, 1937 (dec. July 1971); children: Kathryn Elizabeth, Francis Charles. Supr. hosp. ops. Am. Potash & Chem. Corp., Trona, Calif., 1953-54; office mgr., T.C. Kirkland, elec. contractor, 1954-56; sec.-treas., bd. dirs. T.C. Kirkland, Inc., San Bernardino, Calif., 1958-74; design-install estimator Add-M Electric, Inc., 1972-82, v.p., 1974-82; estimator, engr. Corona Indsl. Electric, Inc. (Calif.), 1982-83; asst. project engr. Fischbach and Moore, Inc., Los Angeles, 1984—. Episcopalian. Club: Arrowhead Country (San Bernardino). Home: 526 E Sonora St San Bernardino CA 92404 Office: Fischbach and Moore Inc 4690 Worth St Los Angeles CA 90063

KIRKLAND, VIRGIL WAYNE, electrical engineer; b. Carthage, Tex., July 29, 1939; s. J. B. and Evelyn Virginia K.; B.S. in Elec. Engring., Lamar State U., 1962; 1 dau., Olga Lynn. With Hughes Aircraft Co., Fullerton, Calif., 1962—, mgr. tech. staff, 1979—, asst. program mgr., 1980—. Mem. Air Force Assn. Republican. Baptist. Office: PO Box 3310 Fullerton CA 92634

KIRKMAN, MICHAEL JAMES, chemical engineer; b. Honolulu, Aug. 28, 1941; s. Lewis William and Helen (Smith) K.; m. Pamela Kay Hamblin, Feb. 7, 1976; children: Stacie Nicole, Angela Kristin, Molly Elizabeth. B-SChemE, U. Utah, 1965. Registered profl. engr., Wash. Chem. engr. Atlantic-Richfield Co., Richland, Wash., 1965-71, Exxon Corp., Richland, 1971-86, Advanced Nuclear Fuel Corp., Richland, 1986—. Pres. Rancette Estates Homeowners Assn., Kennewick, Wash., 1978; reader Holy Spirit Ch., Kennewick, 1980—; soccer referee Tri-city chpt. Wash. State Soccer Refree Assn., 1985. Mem. Am. Inst. Chem. Engrs. Clubs: Ranchette Estates Swim & Racquet (Kennewick) (pres. 1980). Office: Advanced Nuclear Fuels Corp 2101 Horn Rapids Rd Richland WA 99352

KIRKORIAN, DONALD GEORGE, college official, management consultant; b. San Mateo, Calif., Nov. 30, 1938; s. George and Alice (Sergius) K. BA, San Jose State U., 1961, MA, 1966, postgrad., 1968; postgrad., Stanford U., 1961, U. So. Calif., 1966; PhD, Northwestern U., 1972. Tchr. Los Angeles City Schs., 1963; instrnl. TV coordinator Fremont Union High Sch. Dist., Sunnyvale, Calif., 1963-73; assoc. dean instrn learning resources Solano Community Coll., Suisun City, Calif., 1973-85, dean instrnl. services, 1985—; owner, pres. Kirkorian and Assocs., Suisun City; field cons. Nat. Assn. Edn. Broadcasters, 1966-68; extension faculty San Jose State U., 1968-69, U. Calif. Santa Cruz, 1970-73, U. Calif. Davis, 1973-76; chmn. Bay Area TV Consortium, 1976-77, 86-87; mem. adv. panel Speech Communication Assn./Am. Theater Assn. tchr. preparation in speech, communication, theater and media, N.Y.C., 1973-77. Editor: Media Memo, 1973—, Intercom: The Newsletter for Calif. Community Coll. Librarians, 1974-75, Exploring the Benicia State Recreation Area, 1977, California History Resource Materials, 1977, Time Management, 1980; contbr. articles to profl. jours. chmn. Solano County Media Adv. Com., 1974-76; bd. dirs. Napa-Solano United Way, 1980-82; mem. adv. bd. Calif. Youth Authority, 1986—. Mem. Nat. Assn. Ednl. Broadcasters, Assn. for Edn. Communications and Tech., Broadcast Edn. Assn., CAlif. Assn. Ednl. Media and Tech. (treas.), Western Ednl. Soc. for Telecommunications (bd. dirs. Calif. chpt. 1973-75, pres. 1976-77), Learning Resources Assn. Calif. Community Colls. (exec. dir. 1976—, sec.-treas.), Assn. Calif. Community Coll. Adminstrs. (bd. dirs. 1985—), Phi Delta Kappa. Home: 1655 Rockville Rd Suisun CA 94585 Office: Solano Community Coll 4000 Suisun Valley Rd Suisun City CA 94585

KIRKPATRICK, CHARLES HARVEY, physician, immunology researcher; b. Topeka, Nov. 5, 1931; s. Hazen Leon and Clarice Opal (Privott) K.; m. Janice Faye Fosha, July 11, 1959; children: Heather, Michael, Brian. BA, U. Kans., 1954; MD, U. Kans., Kansas City, 1958. Diplomate Am. Bd. Internal Medicine, Am. Bd. Allergy and Immunology. Asst. prof. U. Kans., Kansas City, 1965-68; sr. investigator Nat. Inst. Allergy and Infectious Diseases, NIH, Bethesda, Md., 1968-79; dir. allergy and clin. immunology Nat. Jewish Ctr., Denver, 1979—; active NIH study sects., Bethesda. Contbr. numerous articles to profl. jours. NIH research grantee, 1981-86. Fellow Am. Acad. Allergy and Immunology; mem. Am. Soc. Clin. Investigation. Episcopalian. Avocations: enology, antique corkscrews, antique automobiles. Home: 295 Leyden Denver CO 80220 Office: Nat Jewish Ctr Immunology Dept Medicine 1400 Jackson St Denver CO 80206

KIRKPATRICK, PETER FORDYCE, publishing executive; b. Princeton, N.J., May 9, 1946; s. Roger Bertine and Nancy Fordyce (Goldsmith) K.; m. Vera Gehlert, Sept. 21, 1975; children: Peter Paxton, Carter Fordyce. BA, Middlebury Coll., 1968; MA, U. No. Colo., 1974. Tchr., coach Colo. Acad., Englewood, 1971-75; dir. mktg. Worldwide Ski Corp., Aspen, Colo., 1975-81; dir. advt. Ski Mag., N.Y.C., 1981-83; dir. mktg. McCaw Cablevision, Medford, Oreg., 1983-84; pres. P.K. Co., Ashland, Oreg., 1984—. Bd. dirs. So. Oreg. Leaders, Medford, 1983. Served to 1st lt. U.S. Army, 1969-71. Recipient award for Excellence, Times Mirror Mags., 1982. Republican. Episcopalian. Avocations: skiing, tennis, golf. Home: 10950 Corp Ranch Rd Ashland OR 97520 Office: PK Co 236 East Main St Ashland OR 97520

KIRKPATRICK, RICHARD ALAN, internist; b. Rochester, Minn., Jan. 17, 1947; s. Neal R. and Ethel C. (Hull) K.: B.A. in Chemistry with honors, U. Wash., 1968, B.S. in Psychology, 1968, M.D., 1972; children—James N., Ronald S., David B., Mary J. Intern, resident in internal medicine Mayo Grad. Sch., Rochester, 1972-76, spl. resident in biomed. communications, 1974-75; practice medicine specializing in internal medicine, Longview, Wash., 1976—; sr. ptnr. Kirkpatrick Richards Thorson Zeilenga Gee Gorton Peterson Internal Medicine Clinic; mem. clin. faculty U. Wash.; dir. cardiac rehab. program St. John's Hosp. Mem. City Council, Longview; bd. dirs. SW Washington Symphony; pres., bd. dirs. Sta. KLTV. Diplomate Am. Bd. Internal Medicine. Fellow ACP; mem. Wash. State Soc. Internal Medicine (trustee, past pres.), Am. Geriatrics Soc., Am. Soc. Echocardiography, Am. Soc. Internal Medicine, Wash. Med. Assn. (council med. service), Am. Cancer Soc. (local bd. dirs.), Am. Soc. Clin. Oncology, AMA, Am. Med. Writers Assn. Editor: Drug Therapy Abstracts, Wash. Internists; mem. editorial adv. bd. Your Patient and Cancer, Primary Care and Cancer; weekly med. talk show host; contbr. articles to med. jours. Office: PO Box 578 748 14th Ave Longview WA 98632

KIRKPATRICK, RONALD LEE, food company executive; b. Rapid City, S.D., June 2, 1950; s. Archibald Thomas and Genevieve (Mae) K.; m. Linda Lee Steinmetz, Sept. 20, 1981; 1 child, Grant Michael. BA in Journalism, Calif. State U., Fullerton. Staff writer Register newspaper, Santa Ana, Calif., 1977-78; pub. info. officer Santa Ana Coll., 1978-79; account supr. Bob Thomas and Assocs., Redondo Beach, Calif., 1979-82; area pub. relations mgr. Adolph Coors Co., Lakewood, Calif., 1982-84; community relations regional mgr. Adolph Coors Co., Cerritos, Calif., 1984—; planner Adolph Coors Black Fair Share Agreement, Los Angeles and Golden, Colo., 1984. Recipient Lulu award, Los Angeles Ad Club, 1981. Mem. Pub. Relations Soc. Am., Publicity Club of Los Angeles, Orange County Press Club (v.p. 1977, bd. dirs. 1978, Best Story on Fire Prevention, 1975, 76). Avocations: racquetball, walking, golf. Office: Coors Community Relations 10900 183rd St #390 Cerritos CA 90701

KIRKWOOD, CALLA SUSAN, architect; b. Spokane, Wash., May 18, 1954; d. Gerald Nelson and Lois Virginia (James) K. BArch, Wash. State U., 1980. Registered architect, Wash., Idaho. Draftsman Walter Parr, A.R.A., Lewiston, Idaho, 1972-74; assoc. R.F. Broyles and Assocs., Lewiston, 1980-83; project architect Lombard and Conrad Architects, Boise, Idaho, 1983-84; prin. Kirkwood Architects & Assocs., Spokane, 1984—; mem. Sullivan Group City of Spokane and Architects, 1985-86. Recipient Project Design award City of Lewiston Chamber Regency Plaza Retirement Community, 1985. Mem. AIA (social chmn. N.W. region 1985—, conf. 1987), Nat. Assn. Women in Constn., Nat. Trust for Hist. Preservation, Wash. State Women Owned Bus. Enterprise (cert.), Spokane Art Sch. Club: Network (Lewiston). Avocations: ballet, running, sailboarding, weightlifting. Office: Kirkwood Architects & Assocs W 905 Riverside Suite 316 Spokane WA 99201

KIRONDE-KIGOZI, SAMS SENDAWULA, data processing executive; b. Mityana, Uganda, Oct. 17, 1943; s. Samson Kironde and Solome (Nalukwago) Birabwa; m. Alice Norah, Jan. 18, 1970 (dec. June 1975); 1 child, Solome Nampala; m. Flavia Nakawombe, Feb. 25, 1984; children: Andrew Joseph Sempala, Isaac Philip Kisitu. Cert. edn., Makerere U., Kampala, Uganda; Dip. TH candidate, Trinity Coll., Bristol, Eng.; MABS, Covenant Sem., St. Louis, 1980; DTh candidate, Internat. Bible Inst. and Seminary, Orlando, Fla., 1985—. Tchr. Namutamba Sch., Kampala, Uganda, 1966; depot mgr. Brooke Bond Ltd., Kamuli, Uganda, 1966-71; ter. mgr. Wrigley Co. E.A., Kampala, 1971-72; asst. pastor Redeemed Ch., Kampala, 1971-73; computer operator Sauer Computers, St. Louis, 1977-79; data processing mgr. Anheuser-Busch, Inc., Sylmar, Calif., 1980—. Exec. sec. Com. on Uganda, Inc., Van Nuys, Calif. 1978—; sec. Uganda Human Rights League, Washington, 1982-83; chmn. Ugandan Com. Dem. Assn., Los Angeles, 1982-84. Avocations: soccer refereeing, tennis. Home: 6541 Kester Ave Van Nuys CA 91411 Office: Anheuser Busch 15420 Cobalt Sylmar CA 91342

KIRSCH, DANIEL LAWRENCE, medical device company executive, medical device designer and consultant; b. Bklyn., Nov. 20, 1954; s. Robert J. and May (Vichengrad) K. Student CUNY-Queens Coll., 1972-74, Los Angeles City Coll., 1975-76; BS, Los Angeles Coll. Chiropractic, 1976-79; PhD in Neurobiology, City U. Los Angeles, 1980-81. Assoc. dir. Nat. Acad. Acupuncture, N.Y.C., 1973-75; exec. dir. Nat. Electro-Acutherapy Found., Glendale, Calif., 1976-79; clin. dir. Electro-Acuptherapy Med. Ctr., Laguna Beach, Calif., 1979-80, Electro-Acuptherapy Pain Ctr., Palm Springs, Calif., 1980-81; chmn., chief exec. officer Electromed. Products, Inc., Hawthorne, Calif., 1981—; dean, grad. sch. electromedical scis. City U. Los Angeles, 1985—; vis. clin. dir. Ctr. for Pain and Stress, Columbia Univ., N.Y., 1985; Author: The Complete Clinical Guide to Electro-Acutherapy, 1978; editor Am. Jour. Electromedicine, 1984—; contbr. articles to profl. jours. Patentee Alpha-Stim. Mem. Los Angeles Better Bus. Bur., 1982—, Sell Overseas Am., Woodland Hills, Calif., 1982—. Mem. Health Industry Mfrs. Assn., AAAS, Internat. Electromedicine Inst. (chmn. adv. bd. 1982-83), Nat. Inst. Electromed. Info. (chmn. adv. bd. 1983-84), N.Y. Acad. Scis., AAUP Republican. Jewish. Home: PO Box 2486 Malibu CA 90265 Office: Electromedical Products Inc 12591 Crenshaw Blvd Hawthorne CA 90250

KIRSCH, RALPH M., oil company executive; b. Burton, Nebr., Nov. 15, 1928; s. George J. Kirsch and Gladys Hudson; m. Delores M. Birkel, Feb. 3, 1952; children: Michael, Alan. BS in Edn., U. Nebr.-Lincoln, 1953; JD, U. Wyo., 1956. Bar: Wyo. 1956, Utah 1961. Spl. asst. to atty. gen. State of Wyo., Cheyenne, 1957-59; legal dept. Mountain Fuel Supply, Salt Lake City, 1959-74, mgr. contracts, lands, 1974-79; exec. v.p. Wexpro Co., Salt Lake City, 1977-80, pres., chief exec. officer, 1980—; pres., chief exec. officer Celsius Energy Co., Salt Lake City, 1982—, also dir., 1982—; dir. Entrada Industries, Inc., Salt Lake City, 1982—, Wexpro Co., 1976—. Served with USN, 1945-47, 50-51, PTO. Mem. Ind. Petroleum Assn. Am., Rocky Mountain Oil and Gas Assn., Rocky Mountain Mineral Law Found., Utah Petroleum Assn., Domestic Petroleum Council, Utah State Bar Assn., Wyo. State Bar Assn. Office: Celsius Energy Co 79 St State St Salt Lake City UT 84147

KIRSCH, THOMAS BASIL, psychoanalyst; b. London, June 14, 1936; came to U.S., 1940, naturalized, 1945; s. James Issac and Hilde Clara (Kirschstein) K.; m. Marguerite Odette Stein, June 10, 1960 (div. Mar. 1968); 1 child, David Adam; m. Jean P. Cover, May 26, 1968; 1 child, Susannah Renee. BA, Reed Coll., 1953-57; MD, Yale U., 1958-61. Diplomate in counseling, C.G. Jung Inst. of San Francisco, 1968. Intern Tufts U., Boston, 1961-62; resident in psychiatry Stanford U., Palo Alto, 1962-65; psychiatrist NIMH, San Francisco, 1965-67; practice medicine specializing in psychoanalysis Palo Alto, 1967—; assoc. clin. prof. psychiatry Stanford U., 1968—; cons. Agnews State Hosp., Agnews, Calif., 1968-73. Fellow Acad. Psychoanalysis; mem. Internat. Assn. Analytical Psychology (v.p. 1977—), Jung Inst. San Francisco (pres. 1976-78), Jung Found. Democrat. Jewish. Avocations: music, stamp collecting. Office: 945 Middlefield Rd Palo Alto CA 94301

KIRSCHBAUM, JAMES LOUIS, mortgage banker; b. Missoula, Mont., Oct. 19, 1940; s. Louis Elsworth and Margaret Marie (Lloyd) K.; m. Marilyn Jean McCann, Sept. 5, 1964; children—Kristyn Marie, Heidi Maureen. Student Eastern Wash. U., 1958-61, Whitworth Coll., 1963-65. Vice pres. Far West Securities, Spokane, 1963-73; v.p. Columbia Mortgage, Spokane and Portland, Oreg., 1973-75; regional v.p. Sherwood & Roberts, Spokane, 1975-80; pres., chief exec. officer Bancshares Mortgage, Spokane, 1980-86; exec. v.p. Seafirst Mortgage Co., Seattle, 1986—; chmn. Housing Fin. Commn. State of Wash., Seattle, 1983—. Mem. exec. Eastern Wash. U. Found., Cheney, 1982—; chmn. Leadership Spokane, 1983; pres. United Way, Spokane County, 1984. Served to 1st lt. USAR, 1961-63. Mem. Wash. Mortgage Bankers (pres. 1982-83), Nat. Assn. Rev. Appraisers and Mortgage Underwriters. Republican. Lutheran. Club: Broadmoor Golf. Home: 3233 24th Ave W Seattle WA 98199 Office: Columbia Seafirst Ctr-15 701 5th Ave Seattle WA 98104

KIRSCHBAUM, JOEL BRUCE, molecular geneticist; b. Palo Alto, Calif., Aug. 29, 1945; s. Howard William and Wilhelmina (Jensen) K.; m. Felicity Russell, Sept. 14, 1974. B.A. in Chemistry, Pomona Coll., 1967; Ph.D., Harvard U., 1972. Chargé de recherche U. Geneve (Switzerland), 1975-77; research assoc. in neurosci. Children's Hosp. Med. Ctr., Boston, 1977-81; instr. neuropathology Harvard Med. Sch., Boston, 1977-81; supr. molecular biology sect. Stauffer Chem. Co., Richmond, Calif., 1981-85; dir. research and devel. CODON Corp., Brisbane, Calif., 1985—; asst. instr. Cold Spring Harbor bacterial genetics course, 1971; course instr. European Molecular Biology Orgn., 1976. Contbr. articles to profl. and scholarly jours. Woodrow Wilson fellow, 1967-68, Helen Hay Whitney fellow, 1973-75; Med. Found. Boston, Inc. fellow, 1978-80; prin. investigator Am. Cancer Soc. research grant, 1979-81. Mem. AAAS. Office: CODON Corp 430 Valley Dr Brisbane CA 94005

KIRSCHMAN, JEANNETTE ROSALIND, financial services company executive, consultant; b. Everson, Wash., Nov. 2, 1940; d. William and Amelia (Rommel) K. Student, Western Washington U., 1958-61, U. Wash., 1965; cert., LaSalle Extension U., 1966. CPA, Wash. Div. acct. Wash. State Dept. Highways, Seattle, 1961-65; sr. acct. Knight, Vale & Gregory, Tacoma, 1965-69; from asst. v.p. to v.p. Frank Russell Co., Tacoma, 1969-81, sr. v.p., 1981—. Bd. dirs. Jr. Achievement, Tacoma, 1985-86. Mem. Am. Inst. CPA's, Wash. Soc. CPA's, Am. Womens Soc. CPA's, Am. Soc. Women Accts., MENSA. Office: Frank Russell Co 1100 First Interstate Plaza Tacoma WA 98402

KIRSHBAUM, HOWARD M., judge; b. Oberlin, Ohio, Sept. 19, 1938; s. Joseph and Gertrude (Morris) K.; m. Priscilla Joy Parmakian, Aug. 15, 1964; children—Audra Lee, Andrew William. B.A., Yale U., 1960; A.B., Cambridge U., 1962, M.A., 1966; LL.B., Harvard U., 1965. Ptnr. Zarlengo and Kirshbaum, Denver, 1969-75; judge Denver Dist. Ct., Denver, 1975-80, Colo. Ct. Appeals, Denver, 1980-83; justice Colo. Supreme Ct., Denver, 1983—; adj. prof. law U. Denver, 1972—; dir. Colo. Jud. Inst., Denver, Am. Law Inst. Phila., Am. Judicature Soc., Chgo., 1983-85; pres. Colo. Legal Care Soc., Denver, 1974-75. Bd. dirs. Young Artists Orch., Denver, 1976-85; pres. Community Arts Symphony, Englewood, Colo., 1972-74; dir. Denver Opportunity, Inc., Denver, 1972-74; vice-chmn. Denver Council on Arts and Humanities, 1969. Mem. ABA, Denver Bar Assn. (trustee 1981-83), Colo. Bar Assn., Colo. Bar Found., Am. Judicature Soc. Avocations: music performance; tennis. Office: Colo Supreme Ct Two E 14th Ave Denver CO 80203

KIRSHEN, EDWARD JEROME, obstetrician and gynecologist; b. Syracuse, N.Y., Oct. 30, 1944; s. Gerald Bernard and Corrine (Markson) K.; B.A., Syracuse U., 1962-65; M.D., SUNY, Syracuse, 1969. Intern, then resident in ob-gyn U. Calif. Med. Center, San Diego, 1969-73; fellow in reproductive endocrinology Boston Hosp. Women, also instr. Harvard U. Med. Sch., 1973-74; practice medicine specializing in ob-gyn, San Diego, 1974-86; dir. Ob-Gyn Emergency Services Sharp Meml. Hosp., 1986—; mem. staff Donald Sharp Hosp., Mission Bay Hosp.; mem. exec. med. bd. Sharp Meml. Hosp., 1980—, chief ob-gyn, 1983—; clin. instr. U. Calif. Med. Sch., San Diego. Mem. Am. Coll. Ob-Gyn, Am. Fertility Soc., Am. Assn. Gynecol. Laparoscopy, Pacific Coast Fertility Soc., Calif. Med. Assn., San Diego County Med. Soc. Office: 7901 Frost St San Diego CA 92123

KIRST, WILLIAM JAMES, JR., geophysicist; b. Kenmore, N.Y., June 3, 1923; s. William James and Barbara Louise (Wagner) K.; B.S., Yale U., 1947; postgrad. Casper (Wyo.) Jr. Coll., 1954, Santa Barbara Jr. Coll., 1955, U. Alta., 1960, 67, U. Calgary, 1966, So. Alta. Inst. Tech., 1977, Mt. Royal Coll., Calgary, 1979; m. Frances Patricia Borders, Nov. 19, 1948; children—Dubhe, Heidi, William James, Joshua, Forest, Tracy, Alexander, Whitehorn. Party mgr., party chief, computer Western Geophys. Co., Wyo., Utah, Colo., N.D., Mont., Calif., 1948-55, Alta., B.C., N.W.T., Can., Arctic, 1955-66; No. dist. physicist Canadian Pacific Oil and Gas Co. Ltd., Calgary, Alta., Can., 1966-67; geophys. cons. Kirst Exploration, Calgary, 1967—, Voyager Energy Co., 1985-86, Virago Energy Corp., 1986—; pres., chmn. bd. Marazan Petroleums Ltd., Marazan Petroleums Inc., Lochfayne Resources Inc., 1983—; dir. cable TV show; photographer, owner Kirst Photographers studio; photographer Calgary Real Estate Bd.; pres. 267313 Atla. Ltd.; dir. Take 5 Graphic Arts Ltd. Vol. resource person, bd. dirs. Calgary Drug Info. Centre, 1970-81; pres. Southwood Community Assn., 1962, 63; pres. Calgary Boys and Girls Band and Baton Corps, 1966-67; chmn. bd. dirs. Calgary Distress Centre/Drug Centre, 1980-81. Served with USMC, 1943-46. Registered profl. engr., Alta.; profl. geophysicist, Alta.; geophysicist, Calif.; pvt. pilot. Mem. Can. Soc. Exploration Geophysicists, Yale Football Y Assn., Yale Sci. and Engring. Assn., Calgary Flying Club, Can. Owners and Pilots Assn., Am. Yankee Assn., St. Elmo Soc., Soc. Exploration Geophysicists, Alta. Aviation Council, Can. C. of C. Attempted circumnavigation of Banks Island, Arctic Ocean, in kayak with son, 1971. Home: 3809 Elbow Dr SW, Calgary, AB Canada T2S 2J9

KISER, ELLIS EUGENE, police chief; b. North Platte, Nebr., Feb. 22, 1936; s. Coy D. and Dorthy M. (Todd) K.; m. LuElla M. Faught, June 7, 1958; 1 son, Tim E. Student Eastern Mont. Coll., 1955-59. With Billings (Mont.) Police Dept., 1961—, chief of police, 1977—. Bd. dirs. Mont. Bd. Crime Control, 1981—. Mem. Internat. Assn. Chiefs of Police, Mont. Police Chiefs Assn. Baptist. Club: Exchange. Office: Billings Police Dept PO Box 1554 Billings MT 59101 *

KISER, KENNETH WALKER, electrical engineer, laboratory administrator; b. San Francisco, Nov. 29, 1927; s. Kenny Keller and Cora D. (Farney) K.; m. Beverly Vanbergen Bennett, Aug. 11, 1955 (div. 1974); m. Lisa Togonon, May 1985; children: Steven, Debbie, Gary, Karen, Danny. BSEE, U. Calif., Berkeley, 1949, MSEE, 1950. Mgr. Delta Mission checkout McDonnell Douglas Astronautics, Huntington Beach, Calif., 1950-84; chief exec. Kiser Labs., Overton, Nev., 1984—. Contbr. articles to profl. jours. Served with USN, 1946-48. Mem. Sigma Xi. Avocations: flying, boating, skiing, jazz. Home: 901 Old Simplot Rd Overton NV 89040 Office: Kiser Labs PO Box 238 Overton NV 89040

KISER, NAGIKO SATO, librarian; b. Taipei, Republic of China, Aug. 7, 1923; came to U.S., 1950; d. Takeich and Kinue (Sooma) Sato; m. Virgil Kiser, Dec. 4, 1979 (dec. Mar. 1981). Secondary teaching credential, Tsuda Coll., Tokyo, 1945; BA in Journalism, Trinity U., 1953; BFA, Ohio State U., 1956, MA in Art History, 1959; MLS, cert. in library media, SUNY, Albany, 1974. Cert. community coll. librarian, Calif., cert. jr. coll. tchr., Calif., cert. secondary edn. tchr., Calif., cert. tchr. library media specialist and art, N.Y. Pub. relations reporter The Mainichi Newspapers, Osaka, Japan, 1945-50; contract interpreter U.S. Dept. State, Washington, 1956-58, 66-67; resource specialist Richmond (Calif.) Unified Sch. Dist., 1968-69; editing supr. CTB/McGraw-Hill, Monterey, Calif., 1969-71; multi-media specialist Monterey Peninsula Unified Sch. Dist., 1975-77; librarian Nishimachi Internat. Sch., Tokyo, 1979-80, Sacramento City Unified Sch. Dist., 1977-79, 81-85; sr. librarian Camarillo (Calif.) State Hosp., 1985—. Editor: Short Form Test of Academic Aptitude, 1970, Prescriptive Mathematics Inventory, 1970, Tests of Basic Experience, 1970. Mem. Calif. State Supt.'s Regional Council on Asian Pacific Affairs, Sacramento, 1984—. Library Media Specialist Tng. Program scholar U.S. Office Edn., 1974. Mem. ALA, AAUW, Calif. Library Assn., Calif. Media and Library Educators Assn., Asunaro Shoogai Kyooiku Kondankai Lifetime Edn. Promoting Assn. (Japan), The Mus. Soc., Internat. House of Japan, Matsuyama Sacramento Sister City Corp., Japanese Am. Citizens League, UN Assn. U.S., Ikenoboo Ikebana Soc. Am. Democrat. Mem. Christian Science Ch. Avocations: flower arranging, ballroom dance, classical music. Home: 1101 Mission Verde Dr Camarillo CA 93010 Office: Camarillo State Hosp Profl Library 1878 S Lewis Rd Camarillo CA 93011

KISER, ROBERTA KATHERINE, daycare administrator; b. Alton, Ill., Aug. 13, 1938; d. Stephen Robert and Virginia Elizabeth (Lasher) Golden; m. James Robert Crisman, sept. 6, 1958 (div. May 1971); 1 child, Robert Glenn; m. James Earl Kiser, Dec. 19, 1971; 1 child, James Jacob. BEd, So. Ill. U., 1960. Cert. tchr., Ill., Calif. Librarian Oaklawn (Ill.) Elem. Sch., 1960-62, Alsip (Ill.) Elem. Sch., 1966-69; tchr. Desert Sands Unified Sch. Dist., Indio, Calif., 1969-79; prin. Mothercare Infant Sch., Rancho Mirage, Calif., 1980—. V.p. Palm Desert (Calif.) Community Ch. Montessori Sch. Bd., 1982-85. Republican. Presbyterian. Avocation: handbell ensemble musician. Home and Office: Mothercare Infant Sch 39-575 Keenan Dr Rancho Mirage CA 92270

KISH, LESLIE PAUL, entomologist, educator; b. Johnstown, Pa., Nov. 28, 1944; s. Joseph August and Evelyn Celeste (Tomasel) K.; student U. Mass., 1963; B.S., U. Fla., 1970, M.S., 1971, Ph.D., 1975; 1 dau., Heather Kathleen. Research assoc. U. Fla., Gainesville, 1973-75, asst. research scientist, 1975-78; assoc. prof. entomology U. Idaho, Moscow, 1978-86; prof., 1986—; cons. Fla. Dept. Nat. Resources, 1973-77; Multi-state research coordinator Chalkbrood Program, Wash., Oreg., Nev., Idaho and Utah, 1978-83; cons. Interam. Inst. Agrl. Scis., 1979-80. Served with USAF, 1962-66. Idaho Alfalfa Seed Com. grantee, 1978-83, Wash. Alfalfa Seed Com. grantee, 1978-82; Nev. Seed Council grantee, 1978-82; Malheur County (Oreg.) Seed Growers grantee, 1978-82; NSF travel grantee, 1979; Idaho Research Council grantee, 1980; USDA grantee, 1979-84, 86-87. Mem. Entomol. Soc. Am., Mycol. Soc. Am., Soc. for Invertebrate Pathology, Gamma Sigma Delta, Sigma Xi. Roman Catholic. Club: Lions. Contbr. articles to profl. jours. Home: 723 East F St Moscow ID 83843 Office: U Idaho Dept Plant Soil and Entomological Scis Moscow ID 83843

KISHEL, GREGORY FRANCIS, management consultant; b. Wilkes-Barre, Pa., Aug. 18, 1946; s. Joseph John and Josephine (Krzywicki) K.; m. Patricia Charlotte Gunter, July 1, 1977. B.S., San Jose U., 1973; M.S. in Bus. Adminstrn., Calif. State U.-Long Beach, 1977. Cert. Calif. Community Coll. instr., Calif, real estate broker. Asst. nat. bank examiner Office Comptroller of Currency, Los Angeles, 1973-78; partner K & K Enterprises, Marina del Rey, Calif., 1978—. Served to sgt. USAF, 1964-68. Mem. Authors Guild. Author: The Student Survival Guide, 1979; How to Start, Run and Stay in Business, 1981; Your Business is a Success; Now What?, 1983; Dollars on your Doorstep, 1984, Cashing In On the Consulting Boom, 1985; contbr. articles to bus. mags. and newspapers. Home and Office: 22311 Caminito Tecate Laguna Hills CA 92653

KISSLING, CHARLOTTE ELAINE, real estate broker; b. Jacksonville, Fla.; d. Albert Jacob and Viola Gertrude (Olive) K. B.A. magna cum laude, Carleton Coll.; M.A.T. in History, Harvard/Radcliffe Sch. Edn., 1961. Real estate broker, Calif.; cert. tchr., Calif. Guide, World's Fair, Brussels, Belgium, 1958; tchr. history, French and English, Newton (N.J.) High Sch., 1960-61, Montclair (N.J.) High Sch., 1961-62; adminstrv. officer Inst. Internat. Edn., San Francisco, 1962-69; publications officer, editor adult edn. UNESCO, Paris, 1969-72; broker, agent Hill Co. Real Estate, San Francisco, 1972—. Bd. dirs. YWCA, Bay Area, 1982-86, 1st v.p., 1986. Mem. Phi Beta Kappa (past pres. No. Calif. 1979-80). Democrat. Presbyterian. Clubs: Harbor Point Tennis, Radcliffe, Commonwealth. Contbr. articles to profl. jours. Home: 450 Strawberry Dr #12 Mill Valley CA 94941

KISSLINGER, CARL, educator, geophysicist; b. St. Louis, Aug. 30, 1926; s. Fred and Emma (Tobias) K.; m. Millicent Ann Thorson, Mar. 27, 1948; children: Susan, Karen, Ellen, Pamela, Jerome. B.S., St. Louis U., 1947, M.S., 1949, Ph.D., 1952. Faculty St. Louis U., 1949-72, prof. geophysics, geophys. engring., 1961-72, chmn. dept. earth and atmostpheric scis., 1963-72, prof. geophysics, 1972—; dir. Coop. Inst. Research in Environ. Scis., U. Colo., Boulder, 1972-79, Systems, Sci. and Software, Inc., LaJolla, Calif., 1976-78; UNESCO expert in seismology, chief tech. adviser Internat. Inst. Seismology and Earthquake Engring., Tokyo, 1966-67; chmn. com. seismology NRC-Nat. Acad. Scis., 1970-72; mem. U.S. Geodynamics Com., 1975-78; U.S. nat. corr. Internat. Assn. Seismology and Physics of Earth's Interior, 1970-72; mem. U.S. nat. com. for Internat. Union Geodesy and Geophysics, 1974—, bur., 1975-83, v.p., 1983-87; mem. Gov.'s Sci. Adv. Council, State of Colo., 1973-77, com. on scholarly communication with People's Republic of China, Nat. Acad. Scis., 1977-81, NRC/Nat. Acad. Scis. adv. com. to U.S. Geol. Survey, 1983—. Recipient Alumni Merit award St. Louis U., 1976; Alexander von Humboldt Found. Sr. U.S. Scientist award, 1979; Commemorative medal USSR Acad. Scis., 1985. Fellow Am. Geophys. Union (bd. dirs. sect. seismology 1970-72, fgn. sec. 1974-84), Geol. Soc. Am., Assn. Exploration Geophysics (India), AAAS; mem. Soc. Exploration Geophysicists, Seismol. Soc. Am. (dir. 1968-74, pres. 1972-73), Austrian Acad. Sci. (corr.), Phi Beta Kappa, Sigma Xi. Club: Cosmos. Home: 4165 Caddo Pkwy Boulder CO 80303

KISTER, BENJAMIN JOSEPH, optometrist; b. Worland, Wyo., May 11, 1951; s. Victor and Millie (Lehman) K.; m. Dorthy Ellen Baker, Dec. 27, 1972; children: Stephanie Suzanne, Tyson John, Megan Marie. Student U. Wyo., 1969-72; B.S. with honors, Pacific U., Forest Grove, Oreg., 1974, O.D. with distinction, 1976. Pvt. practice optometry, Riverton, Wyo., 1978—; state dir. Optometric Extension Program, Oreg. Served to lt. (s.g.) U.S. Navy, 1976-78. Mem. Am. Optometric Assn., Wyo. Optometric Assn. (treas. 1981-84, v.p. 1984—, pres. 1985-86), C. of C., Alpha Omega Epsilon, Beta Sigma Kappa. Republican. Mem. Ch. of Christ. Club: Rotary (chmn. youth exchange 1981-85).

KISTLER, MILTON JAY, banker; b. Allentown, Pa., Feb. 24, 1933; s. Robert J. and Mabel Ruth (Arndt) K.; m. Katherine Swope, Nov. 3, 1962; children: William MacKay, N. Hugh MacKay. Student, S.D. State Coll., U. N.Mex., U. Colo. Asst. cashier Albuquerque Nat. Bank, 1962-69; v.p. Diner's Club, N.Y.C., 1969-74; dir. collections Pan Am. World Airways, N.Y.C., 1974-78; v.p. San Diego Trust and Savs. Bank, 1979—. Mem. Am. Arbitration Assn., So. Calif. Credit Card Group. Lodge: Kiwanis. Avocations: golf, music. Home: 16110-10 Avenida Venusto San Diego CA 92128 Office: San Diego Trust and Savs Bank 7333 Convoy Ct San Diego CA 92111

KITADA, SHINICHI, biochemist; b. Osaka, Japan, Dec. 9, 1948; came to U.S., 1975; s. Koichi and Asako Kitada; M.D., Kyoto U., 1973; M.S. in Biol. Chemistry (Japan Soc. Promotion Sci. fellow 1975-76), UCLA, 1977, Ph.D., 1979. Intern, Kyoto U. Hosp., 1973-74, resident physician Chest Disease Research Inst., 1974-75; research scholar lab. nuclear medicine and radiation biology UCLA, 1979—. Mem. Am. Oil Chemists Soc., N.Y. Acad. Scis., Sigma Xi. Author papers in field. Home: 478 Landfair Ave Apt 5 Los Angeles CA 90024 Office: 900 Veteran Ave Los Angeles CA 90024

KITCHELL, SAMUEL FARRAND, construction company executive; b. Hingham, Mass., Nov. 6, 1921; s. Francis R. and Jeanette (Abbott) K.; m. Betty Heimark, June 17, 1943; children: Kaaren, Jane Kitchell LaPrade, Jonathan Abbott, Ann Kitchell Kenk, Susan Kitchell Edwards. B.A., Amherst Coll., 1943, LL.D., 1983. Field engr. Anchorage Homes, Inc., Westfield, Mass., 1946-48; chief insp., specification writer E.L. Varney Assocs., Phoenix, 1948-49; estimator J.R. Porter Constrn. Co., Phoenix, 1949-50; ptnr. Kitchell-Phillips Constrn. Co., Phoenix, 1950-54; chmn. Kitchell Corp., Phoenix, 1954—; dir. Ariz. Bank, Phoenix, Ariz. Employers Council, Phoenix; guest speaker constrn. mgmt. seminars. Active Phoenix Art Mus., Phoenix Symphony Assn., Internat. Heart Found.; founding pres., bd. dirs. Ariz. Kidney Found., Phoenix, 1963-69; trustee, past pres. St. Luke's Hosp. Med. Ctr., Phoenix, 1962-77; bd. dirs. Heard Mus. Anthropology, Phoenix, 1975—, pres. 1985-87; trustee, pres. Scottsdale Sch. Bd., Ariz., 1966-71; bd. dirs. Ariz. Acad.; trustee Amherst Coll., Mass., 1983—. Served to lt. (j.g.) USN, 1943-46, ATO, PTO. Mem. Assoc. Gen. Contractors Am. (past pres., past bd. dirs. Ariz. bldg. chpt.), Phoenix C. of C. (past bd. dirs. and officer). Republican. Club: Thunderbirds (Phoenix). Home: 30 Colonia Miramonte Scottsdale AZ 85253 Office: Kitchell Corp 1006 S 24th St Phoenix AZ 85034

KITCHEN, LAWRENCE OSCAR, aircraft/aerospace corporation executive; b. Ft. Mill, S.C., June 8, 1923; s. Samuel Sumpter and Ruby Azalee (Grigg) K.; m. Brenda Lenhart, Nov. 25, 1978; children by previous marriage: Brenda, Alan, Janet. Ed., Foothill Coll. Aero. engr. U.S. Navy Bur. Aeronautics, Washington, 1946-58; staff asst. to asst. chief bur. U.S. Navy Bur. Aeronautics, 1958; with Lockheed Missiles & Space Co., Sunnyvale, Calif., 1958-70; mgr. product support logistics Lockheed Missiles & Space Co., 1964-68, dir. fin. controls, 1968-70; v.p.-fin. Lockheed-Ga. Co., Marietta, 1970-71; pres. Lockheed-Ga. Co., 1971-75; pres. Lockheed Corp., Burbank, Calif., 1975-76, pres., chief operating officer, 1976-85, chmn. bd. dirs., chief exec. officer, 1986—; bd. dirs. Security Pacific Nat. Bank, Security Pacific Corp. Mem. nominating com. Aviation Hall of Fame. Served with USMC, 1942-46. Mem. Nat. Def. Transp. Assn., AIAA, Nat. Assn. Accountants, Navy League, Am. Def. Preparedness Assn., Soc. Logistics Engrs., Air Force Assn., Assn. U.S. Army. Clubs: Burning Tree, North Ranch, Lakeside Golf, Wings. Office: Lockheed Corp 4500 Park Granada Blvd Calabasas CA 91399

KITCHENER, RICHARD FRANK, philosophy educator; b. Covina, Calif., May 28, 1941; s. Frank Leonard and Gussie Ellen (Farmer) K.; m. Karen Gay Strohm, Aug. 21, 1965; children: Gregory, Brian. BA, Calif. State U., Los Angeles, 1963, MA, 1967; PhD, U. Minn., 1970. Asst. prof. philosophy Colo. State U., Ft. Collins, 1970, assoc. prof., 1975, prof., 1981. Author: Piaget's Theory of Knowledge, 1986; editor: New Ideas in Psychology Jour. Democrat. Home: 1419 Ash Dr Fort Collins CO 80521 Office: Colo State U Dept Philosophy Fort Collins CO 80523

KITE, CYNTHIA EAMES DAY, publishing executive; b. Denver, June 10, 1955; d. Horace Eames and Jane (Stevenson) Day; m. Ralph Beverly Kite, Feb. 4, 1978. BA in Spanish and French, U. Colo., 1976. Asst. editor Omega Group, Ltd., Boulder, Colo., 1979-80, assoc. editor, photographer, 1980-83, prodn. mgr., 1983-85, prodn. dir., 1985—. Author: Spanish Country Inns and Paradors, 1985, Portuguese Country Inns and Pousadas, 1986. Mem. Graphic Arts and Prodn. Club Denver, Western Publs. Assn. Avocations: travel, reading, writing, running, theatre. Office: Omega Group Ltd 5735 E Arapahoe Ave Boulder CO 80303

KITTEL, PETER, research scientist; b. Mt. Vernon, Va., Mar. 23, 1945; s. Charles and Muriel (Lister) K.; m. Mary Ellen Murchio, Aug. 12, 1972; 1 child, Katherine. BS, U. Calif., Berkeley, 1967; MS, U. Calif., San Diego, 1969; PhD, Oxford U., England, 1974. Research asst. Clarendon Lab., Oxford, Eng., 1969-74; research assoc., adj. asst. prof. U. Oreg., Eugene, 1974-78; research assoc. Stanford (Calif.) U., 1978, Nat. Research Council, Moffett Field, Calif., 1978-80; research scientist NASA, Moffett Field, Calif., 1980—. Contbr. over 60 articles to profl. jours. Mem. Am. Phys. Soc., AAAS, Cryogenic Engring. Conf. (bd. dirs. 1983—, adv. editor to Cryogenics 1987—). Home: 3132 Morris Dr Palo Alto CA 94303 Office: NASA-Ames Research Ctr M/S 244-10 Moffett Field CA 94035

KITTELSON, DAVID JAMES, archivist; b. Grand Rapids, Minn., Jan. 28, 1931; s. Ole and Alice Matilda (Pedersen) K.; m. Marion Louise Ortiz, Aug. 24, 1957; children: Anne Katherine Dorsey, Karen Swaba. Student, Itasca Jr. Coll., 1949-50; BA in History, U. Hawaii, 1957, MA in History, 1966; MA in Librarianship, U. Minn., 1958. Librarian I, U. Hawaii, Honolulu, 1958-62, Hawaiian curator, 1971-82, univ archivist, 1982—, mem. grad. faculty pacific islands studies, 1972—; head librarian Hilo (Hawaii) Coll., 1962-71; cons. Peace Corps, Hilo, 1967-68; bd. dirs. U. Hawaii Bd. Publs., Honolulu, 1985—. Author: The Hawaiians: an annotated bibliography, 1985, (column) Yesteryear in Ka Leo O Hawaii, 1984; editor (jour.) Edn. Perspectives, 1981; contbr. articles profl. jours. Trustee Hawaii Found. for History and Humanities, Honolulu, 1974-76. Served with USN, 1950-54. Microfilming grantee Hawaiian Studies Program, 1978. Mem. Hawaii Library Assn., Puerto Rican Heritage Soc. Hawaii. Democrat. Roman Catholic. Avocations: cooking, reading, basketball. Home: 421 Mamaki St Honolulu HI 96821 Office: U Hawaii Manoa Dept Librarian Spl Collections Honolulu HI 96822

KITTLEMAN, LAURENCE ROY, JR., geologist; b. Colorado Springs, Colo., Mar. 31, 1931; s. Laurence Roy and Jessie Marguerite (Shelden) K. BS, Colo. Coll., 1953; MS, U. Colo., 1956; PhD, U. Oreg., 1962. Registered profl. geologist, Oreg. Engring. aide U.S. Bur. Reclamation, Denver, 1952; geologist U.S. AEC, Grand Junction, Colo., 1955-57; instr. U. Oreg., Eugene, 1959-60, curator of geology Mus. Natural History, 1962-77, dir. Mus. Natural History, 1973-77; pvt. practice geology Eugene, 1977—. Author: Canyons Beyond the Sky, 1985. Mem. AAAS.

KITTO, FRANKLIN CURTIS, computer systems specialist; b. Salt Lake City, Nov. 18, 1954; s. Curtis Eugene and Margaret (Ipson) K.; m. Collette Madsen, Sept. 16, 1982; 1 child, Melissa Erin. BA, Brigham Young U., 1978, MA, 1980. Tv sta. operator Sta. KBYU-TV, Provo, Utah, 1973-78; cable TV system operator Instructional Media U. Utah, Salt Lake City, 1980-82, data processing mgr., 1982-83, media supr., 1983-85, bus. mgr., 1985-87; dir. computer systems tng. MegaWest Systems, Inc., Salt Lake City, 1987—. Recipient Kiwanis Freedom Leadership award, Salt Lake City, 1970, Golden Microphone award Brigham Young U., 1978. Mem. Assn. Ednl. Communications and Tech., Utah Pick Users Group (sec. 1983—87, pres. 1987—), Am. Soc. Tng. and Devel., Phi Eta Sigma, Kappa Tau Alpha. Mormon. Home: 8892 Flatiron Dr Sandy UT 84092 Office: MegaWest Systems Inc 345 Bearcat Dr Salt Lake City UT 84115

KITTREDGE, NANCY, artist; b. Ellsworth, Maine, Nov. 12, 1938; d. Milton Donald and Beatrice (Ingalls) K.; m. Robert Kaye Jellison, Apr. 7, 1979. B.A. in Theatre Arts, U. Maine, 1961; M.A., U. Miami, Fla., 1963; student U. N.H., 1957-59. One woman shows Triad Gallery, San Diego, 1976, Designbank, San Diego, 1978, Challis Gallery, Laguna Beach, 1980, San Diego Mus. Art, 1981, John Douglas Cline Gallery, Phoenix, 1982, Suzanne Brown Gallery, Scottsdale, Ariz., 1983, Joy Horwich Gallery, Chgo., 1984, San Francisco Art Exchange, 1986; group shows include U. Maine, Orono, 1961, U. Miami, Fla., 1963, La Jolla Mus. Art, 1975, Laguna Beach Mus. Art, 1976, San Diego Artists Guild, 1976, San Diego-Yokohama Invitational, Japan, 1979, Gallery, One, San Francisco, 1981, Riggs Gallery, San Diego, 1981, John Douglas Cline Gallery, Phoenix, 1981, Ankrum Gallery, Los Angeles, 1982, Maple Creek Gallery, San Diego, 1982, Deicas Art Gallery, La Jolla, 1983, Alexandria (La.) Mus. Art Internat. Exhibition, 1986, Riverside (Calif.) Mus. Art., 1987, J.J. Brookings and Co. Gallery, San Jose, Calif., 1987; represented in permanent collections at Household Corp., Chgo., Morton Foods, Dalas., Capital Intermediaries, Des Moines, others. Mem. San Diego Artists Guild (bd. dirs. 1975-76, 80-81), Artists Equity Assn., Phi Kappa Phi. Episcopalian. Address: care J.J. Brookings & Co Gallery PO Box 1237 San Jose CA 95108

KITTSON, AUGUSTAN, building materials company executive, land developer; b. St. Louis, Oregon, Aug. 15, 1913; s. Nazaire (Ned) and Virginia Elizabeth (Brouillard) K.; m. Myrna Ann Nickisch, Dec. 3, 1947; children—Janet Grace Kittson Hartman, Cynthia Jane Kittson Peterson, Nicki Jean Kittson Keohohou, Lori Lee Kittson Turping, Constance Kittson Rogers, Augustan Daniel. Student U. Alaska, 1946. Constrn. engr. many Alaskan firms, 1946-48; gen. foreman electricians Atkinson-Jones, Richland, Wash., 1948-53; gen. foreman electrician Foothill Electric, Richland, 1953-55; owner/pres. Kennewick (Wash.) Indsl. and Elec. Supply, Inc., 1955—. Served with C.E. U.S. Army Air Corps, 1943-46. Recipient Internat. Boss of Yr. award Tri-Cities Credit Women, 1981; Cert. of Recognition, Nat. Rep. Congl. Com., 1982; Presdl. Achievement award Pres. Ronald Reagan. Republican. Club: Riverside Investment. Club: Elks. Home: 407 W 29th Ave Kennewick WA 99336 Office: 113 E Columbia Dr Kenniwick WA 99336

KITZHABER, JOHN ALBERT, physician, state senator; b. Colfax, Wash., Mar. 5, 1947; s. Albert Raymond and Annabel Reed (Wetzel) K. BA, Dartmouth Coll., 1969; MD, U. Oreg., 1973. Intern Gen. Rose Meml. Hosp., Denver, 1976-77; Emergency physician Mercy Hosp., Roseburg, Oreg., 1974-75; mem. Oreg. Ho. of Reps., 1978-80; mem. Oreg. Senate, 1980—, pres., 1985—; assoc. prof. Oreg. Health Sci. U., 1986—. Mem. Am. Coll. Emergency Physicians, Douglas County Med. Soc., Physicians for Social Responsibility, Am. Council Young Polit. Leaders, Oreg. Trout. Democrat. Home: 1033 W Brown Roseburg OR 97470 Office: Oreg Senate State Capital Salem OR 97310

KIVELSON, MARGARET GALLAND, physicist; b. N.Y.C., Oct. 21, 1928; d. Walter Isaac and Madeleine (Weiner) Galland; m. Daniel Kivelson, Aug. 15, 1949; children: Steven Allan, Valerie Ann. AB, Radcliffe Coll., 1950, AM, 1951, PhD, 1957. Cons. Rand Corp., Santa Monica, Calif., 1956-69; asst. geophysicist UCLA, 1967-83, prof., 1983—, also chmn. dept. earth and space scis.; prin. investigator of magnetometer, Galileo Mission, Jet Propulsion Lab., Pasadena, Calif., 1977-83; overseer Harvard Coll., 1977-83; mem. adv. coms. NASA, Dept. of Energy, Com. Solar and Space Physics, 1977—. Editor: The Solar System: Observations and Interpretations, 1986; assoc. editor Jour. Geophys. Research; contbr. articles to profl. jours. Named Woman of Yr., Los Angeles Mus. Sci. and Industry, 1979, Woman of Sci., UCLA, 1984; recipient Grad. Soc. medal Radcliffe Coll., 1983, 350th Anniversary Alumni medal Harvard U. Mem. Am. Geophysics Union, Am. Phys. Soc., AAAS. Office: Dept Earth & Space Sci UCLA 3806 Geology Bldg Los Angeles CA 90024

KJELDGAARD, EDWIN ANDREAS, chemist; b. Brush, Colo., Sept. 14, 1939; s. Daniel H. and Ena I. (Jensen) K.; m. Linda Lane, Aug. 14, 1965; children: Todd, Kristin. BA summa cum laude, St. Olaf Coll., 1961; PhD, U. Colo., 1966. Mem. tech. staff Sandia Nat. Labs., Albuquerque, 1966-69, 84—, supr., 1969-84; mem. assessment panel Nat. Bur. Standards, Gaithersburg, Md., 1984—. Mem. Am. Chem. Soc., Phi Beta Kappa. Republican. Lutheran. Avocations: woodworking, tennis. Home: 2532 Harold Pl NE Albuquerque NM 87106 Office: Sandia Nat Labs Div 6321 Box 5800 Albuquerque NM 87185

KJELLAND, JAMES MARTIN, musician, music educator; b. Monroe, Wis., Sept. 26, 1948; s. George Robert and Lois Bryson (Kratz) K. BA in Music Edn., U. Wis., 1970, MusM, 1977; PhD in Music Edn., U. Tex., 1985. Music tchr. elem. and high sch. Middleton, Wis., 1971-74; condr. Wis. Youth Symphony Orch., Madison, 1974-76; prof. music edn. U. So. Calif., Los Angeles, 1977—; dir. string orchs. Community Sch. Performing Arts, Los Angeles, 1984—; cons. string devel., Calif., 1977—. Contbr. articles to profl. jours. U. Tex. grad. research grantee, 1983, 84. Mem. Music Educators Nat. Conf., Calif. Music Educators Assn., Am. String Tchrs. Assn. (pres. elect Calif. chpt. 1986-88), So. Calif. Sch. Band and Orch. Assn., Mothers Against Drunk Drivers, Sierra Club, Phi Kappa Phi, Pi Kappa Lambda. Democrat. Avocations: chamber music, folk music, reading, hiking. Home: 3770 S Flower St #2 Los Angeles CA 90007 Office: U So Calif Sch Music MUS 412 Los Angeles CA 90089

KLAINER, STANLEY MELVIN, chemical research company executive; b. Chelsea, Mass., Apr. 11, 1930; s. Ruben Hyman and Ida (Saslavsky) K.; m. Hovey Zarlow, Aug. 17, 1952; children: Rose, Mark, Elizabeth, Steven, Kim, Stanley. BA in Chemistry, Clark U., 1952, MA in Phys. Chem., 1955, PhD in Phys. Chem., 1959. Chemist Bendix Corp., Detroit, 1959-60; sr. chemist Nat. Research Corp., Cambridge, Mass., 1960-61; div. mgr. Tracerlab., Waltham, Mass., 1961-67, Block Engring., Cambridge, Mass., 1967-78; group mgr. Lawrence Berkeley (Calif.) Lab., 1978-82; pres. ST&E, Inc., Livermore, Calif., 1983—; cons. U.S. Govt. and various companies, 1966—. Editor: (assoc.) Optical Engring. Mag., 1983-84; contbr. numerous articles to profl. jours. Mem. AAAS, Am. Chem. Soc., The Internat. Soc. Optical Engring., Soc. Environ. Toxicology and Chemistry, Soc. Applied Spectroscopy. Unitarian. Avocations: restoring old cars, bldg. muscle cars. Home: 20 Belinda Ct San Ramon CA 94583

KLAKEG, CLAYTON HAROLD, physician; b. Big Woods, Minn., Mar. 31, 1920; s. Knute O. and Agnes (Folvik) K.; student Concordia Coll., Moorhead, Minn., 1938-40; B.S., N.D. State U., 1942; B.S. in Medicine, N.D. U., 1943; M.D., Temple U., 1945; M.S. in Medicine and Physiology, U. Minn.-Mayo Found., 1954; children—Julie Ann, Robert Clayton, Richard Scott. Intern, Med. Center, Jersey City, 1945-46; mem. staff VA Hosp., Fargo, N.D., 1948-51; fellow in medicine and cardiology Mayo Found., Rochester, Minn., 1951-55; internist, cardiologist Sansum Med. Clinic Inc., Santa Barbara, Calif., 1955—; mem. staff Cottage Hosp., St. Francis Hosp. Bd. dirs. Sansum Med. Research Found. Served to capt. M.C., USAF, 1946-48. Diplomate Am. Bd. Internal Medicine. Fellow ACP, Am. Coll. Cardiology, Am. Coll. Chest Physicians, Am. Heart Assn. (mem. council on clin. cardiology); mem. Calif. Heart Assn. (pres. 1971-72, Meritorious Service award 1968, Disting. Service award 1972, Disting. Achievement award 1975), Santa Barbara County Heart Assn. (pres. 1959-60, Disting. Service award 1958, Disting. Achievement award 1971), Calif. Med. Assn., Los Angeles Acad. Medicine, Santa Barbara County Med. Assn., Mayo Clinic Alumni Assn., Santa Barbara Soc. Internal Medicine (pres. 1963), Sigma Xi, Phi Beta Pi. Republican. Lutheran. Club: Channel City. Contbr. articles to profl. jours. Home: 4772 Calle Camarada Santa Barbara CA 93110 Office: Sansum Med Clinic Inc 317 W Pueblo St Santa Barbara CA 93102

KLAMMER, JOSEPH FRANCIS, management consultant; b. Omaha, Mar. 25, 1925; s. Aloys Arcadius and Sophie (Nadolny) K.; B.S., Creighton U., 1948; M.B.A., Stanford, 1950; cert. in polit. econs. Grad. Inst. Internat. Studies, U. Geneva, 1951. Adminstrv. analyst Chevron Corp. (formerly Standard Oil Co. Calif.), San Francisco, 1952-53; staff asst. Enron Corp. (formerly Internorth, Inc.), Omaha, 1953-57; mgmt. cons. Cresap, McCormick and Paget, Inc., San Francisco, 1957-75, v.p., mgr. San Francisco office; mgmt. cons., prin. J.F. Klammer Assocs., San Francisco, 1975—. Served to 1st lt. USAAF, 1943-46; lt. col. USAFR (ret.). Rotary Found. fellow, 1950-51. Republican. Roman Catholic. Clubs: Univ. Home: 1998 Broadway San Francisco CA 94109 Office: 1 Market Plaza San Francisco CA 94105

KLANDERUD, HELEN KALIN, social worker; b. Kansas City, Mo., June 9, 1937; d. Leander Meinrad and Julana (Byrnes) K.; children: Kurt Thomas, Erik Stephen, Soren Michael, Kaela Louise. BA cum laude, St. Mary's Coll., 1959; MSW, U. Nebr., 1961. Med. social worker San Diego County Gen. Hosp., 1961-62; staff social worker Fort Logan Mental Health Ctr., Denver, 1964-71; sch. social worker Aspen (Colo.) Sch. Dist., 1971-73; clinic dir. Touchstone Mental Health Clinic, Aspen, 1972-76; pvt. practice clin. social work Aspen, 1976—; adv. bd. Aspen Mental Health Clinic, 1985—, Mental Health Colo. Dept. Insts., Denver, 1972-76; mem. Colo. Commn. on Children and Their Families, Denver, 1979-81, Pitkin County Human Resources Council, Aspen, 1974-76. Contbr. articles to profl. jours. Commr. Pitkin County, Aspen, 1980-86; bd. dirs. Roaring Fork Transit Agy., Aspen, 1983-86; chmn. Ruedi Reservoir Water and Power Authority, Basalt, Colo., 1981-85; mem. Aspen Women's Forum. Mem. Acad. Cert. Social Workers, Nat. Assn. Social Workers, LWV. Democrat. Roman Catholic. Home and Office: Box 1558 Aspen CO 81612

KLASSEN, PETER JAMES, academic administrator, history educator; b. Crowfoot, Alta., Can., Dec. 18, 1930; came to U.S., 1955; s. John C. and Elizabeth (Martens) K.; m. Nancy Jo Cooprider, Aug. 1, 1959; children: Kenton, Kevin, Bryan. BA, also cert., U. B.C., Can., 1955; MA, U. So. Calif., 1958, PhD, 1962. Cert. secondary tchr. Lectr. U. So. Calif., Los Angeles, 1957-62; prof. history Fresno (Calif.) Pacific Coll., 1962-66; prof. history Calif. State U., Fresno, 1966—, dean sch. social scis., 1979—. Author: The Economics of Anabaptism, 1964, Europe in the Reformation, 1979, Reformation: Change and Stability, 1980; contbr. articles to jours. Pres. West Fresno Home Improvement Assn. 1966—. Research grantee Deutscher Akademischer Austauschdienst, 1975. Mem. Am. Hist. Assn., Am. Soc. Ch. History, Fresno City and County Hist. Soc. (pres. 1983-85), Soc. Reformation Research, German Studies Assn., Assn. Advancement Slavic Studies, Phi Alpha Theta, Phi Kappa Phi. Home: 1838 S Bundy Dr Fresno CA 93727 Office: Calif State U Sch Social Scis Fresno CA 93740

KLAUM, ARTHUR DAMIAN, photomask engineer; b. N.Y.C., July 4, 1961; s. Arthur Henry and Katherine Loretta (Curran) K.; m. Geraldine Mary O'Keefe, Nov. 19, 1983; 1 child, Maureen. BSChemE, Manhattan Coll. Photomask engr. Gen. Instrument, Chandler, Ariz., 1983—; now mfg. engr. Control Data Corp., Mpls. Mem. Bay Area Chrome Users Soc. Roman Catholic.

KLAYMAN, JOSEPH JASON, electrical engineer; b. Boston, July 11, 1925; s. Louis and Sarah (Broder) K.; m. Dina Souchot, Mar. 2, 1952; children: Valerie Sharon, Karen Lee. BSEE, Northeastern U., 1946. Engr. Research Assocs. Inc., Woodland Hills, Calif. Mem. IEEE. Republican. Jewish. Club: Dorchester-Roxbury Mattapan, (Los Angeles) (treas. 1981—). Home: 5030 Canoga Ave Woodland Hills CA 91364

KLEEMAN, ALAN LEROY, chemist; b. Huntingburg, Ind., Aug. 7, 1949; s. Leroy and Dorita (Altman) K.; m. Barbara Eakley, July 30, 1983. BS in Chemistry, Ind. U., 1971; MS in Mgmt., Lesley Coll., 1985. Chemist Texaco, Inc., Lawrenceville, Ill., 1971-75, sr. chemist, 1975-78; chief chemist Plateau Inc., Bloomfield, N.Mex., 1978-84, Bloomfield Refining Co., 1984-85, ASAMERA Oil, Inc., Commerce City, Colo., 1985—. Coach Amateur Girls Softball Assn., Farmington, N.Mex., 1980-83. Mem. Am. Chem. Soc. Republican. Roman Catholic. Lodge: Elks. Avocations: sailing, skiing, outdoor events. Home: 11588 Harlan St Broomfield NM 80020 Office: ASAMERA Oil Inc 5800 Brighton Blvd Commerce City CO 80022

KLEHS, HENRY JOHN WILHELM, ret. civil engr.; b. Dornbusch bez Stade, Germany, Dec. 7, 1910; s. Frederick and Anna (Mahler) K.; B.S., U. Calif., 1935; m. Clodell Peters, July 17, 1948; came to U.S., 1920, naturalized through father, 1922. Engr. So. Pacific Transp. Co., 1936-75, supr. hazardous materials control, until 1975; ret., 1975. Mem. Calif. Fire Chiefs Assn., Internat. Assn. Fire Chiefs, Steuben Soc. Am., Am. Ry. Engring. Assn., ASCE. Home: 604 Glenwood Isle Alameda CA 94501

KLEIMAN, JOSEPH, consultant, retired life sciences company executive; b. Grand Rapids, Mich., Oct. 1, 1919; s. Jacob and Bessie (Targowitch) K.; m. Shirley Ruth Present, Aug. 30, 1942; children: Richard Neil, Robert, William. B.S. in Engring, U. Mich., 1941, M.S., 1942. Engr. Reeves Instrument Corp., N.Y.C., 1946-51; v.p., gen. mgr. Belock Instrument Corp., College Point, N.Y., 1951-58, Whittaker Gyro (div. Telecomputing Corp.), Los Angeles, 1958-59; exec. v.p. corp. Whittaker Gyro (div. Telecomputing Corp.), 1959-64; v.p. corp. devel. Whittaker Corp., 1964-67, sr. v.p., 1967-84, dir., 1958-84; dir. Yardney Elec. Corp., 1983-85, Diagnostic Products Corp., Syncor, Inc., 1979—, Syncor, Inc., 1985—. Vice pres. Am. Soc. for Technion-Israel Inst. Tech.; officer Union Am. Hebrew Congregations, 1975—. Mem. Nat. Soc. Profl. Engrs., Calif. Soc. Profl. Engrs., Sigma Xi, Phi Lambda Upsilon, Iota Alpha. Jewish. Home: 11240 Chalon Rd Los Angeles CA 90049

KLEIN, CORNELIS, geology educator; b. Haarlem, The Netherlands, Sept. 4, 1937; came to U.S., 1960; s. Cornelis and Wilhelmina (van'tHoen) K.; m. Angela M. Nobbs, Sept. 14, 1960; children: Marc Alexander, Stephanie Wilhelmina. BS in Geology with honors, McGill U., Montreal, Que., Can., 1958, MS in Geology, 1960; PhD in Geology, Harvard U., 1965. Lectr. in mineralogy Harvard U., Cambridge, Mass., 1965-69, assoc. prof., 1969-72, asst. dean, 1966-70; prof. mineralogy Ind. U., Bloomington, 1972-84; prof. geology U. N.Mex., Albuquerque, 1984—. Author: (with C.S. Hurlbut) Manual of Mineralogy, 20th edit., 1985; contbr. articles to profl. jours. Fellow Parker, Harvard U., 1962-63, Guggenheim, 1978. Fellow Mineral. Soc. Am., Geol. Soc. Am., AAAS; mem. Soc. Econ. Geologists, Mineral. Assn. Can. Home: 736 Val Verde SE Albuquerque NM 87108 Office: U NMex Dept Geology 200 Yale Ave NE Albuquerque NM 87131

KLEIN, (MARY) ELEANOR, retired clinical social worker; b. Luzon, Philippines, Dec. 13, 1919; came to U.S., 1921; (parents Am. citizens); d. Roy Edgar and Edith Lillian (Dransfield) Hay; m. Edward George Klein, June 24, 1955. BA, Pacific Union Coll., 1946; MSW, U. So. Calif., 1953. Lic. clin. social worker. Social worker White Meml. Hosp., Los Angeles, 1948-56; clin. social worker UCLA Hosp. Clinics, 1956-65, supr. social worker, 1965-67, assoc. dir., 1967-73, dir., 1973-82; mem. vol. bd. Calif. div., 1964—, Am. Cancer Soc., del., nat. dir., 1984—, chmn. Residential Crusade for Orange County (Calif.) Unit, 1985-86. Bd. dirs., treas. Los Amigos de la Humanidad, U. So. Calif. Sch. Social Work. Recipient Disting. Alumni award Los Amigos de la Humanidad, 1984, Outstanding Performance award UCLA Hosp., 1968, various service awards Am. Cancer Soc., 1972-85. Fellow Soc. Clin. Social Work; mem. Nat. Assn. Soc. Workers (charter), Am. Hosp. Assn., Soc. Hosp. Social Work Dirs. of Am. Hosp. Assn. (life; pres. 1981, bd. dirs. 1978-82), Am. Pub. Health Assn. Democrat. Adventist. Avocations: travel, gardening. Home: 1661 Texas Circle Costa Mesa CA 92626

KLEIN, FREDERICK DEWEY, telecommunication executive, marketing professional; b. Morristown, N.J., Dec. 27, 1944; s. Edwin and Irene (Burgess) K.; m. Gail Crisman, Apr. 5, 1969; 1 child, Christopher. AA, Manatee Jr. Coll., 1965; student, Fla. State U., 1968; BS in Bus. Mgmt., Fairleigh Dickinson U., 1972. Gen. mgr. Nat. Telephone Directory Corp., Rochelle Park, N.J., 1969-76; sr. v.p. Tele-Pages Inc., Parsippany, N.J., 1976-85; pres. Telephone Mktg. Programs West Inc., North Hollywood, Calif., 1985—. Served to sgt. U.S. Army, 1965-67. Recipient Directory Product Excellence awards Assn. N.Am. Directory Pubs., 1977-85. Republican. Roman Catholic. Avocations: golf, tennis, chess, pvt. flying. Home: 3009 Parkview Dr Thousand Oaks CA 91362 Office: TMP West Inc 12800 Riverside Dr North Hollywood CA 91607

KLEIN, HAROLD PAUL, microbiologist; b. N.Y.C., Apr. 1, 1921; Alexander and and Lillyan (Pal) K.; m. Gloria Nancy Dolgov, Nov. 14, 1942; children—Susan Ann, Judith Ellen. B.A., Bklyn. Coll., 1942; Ph.D., U. Calif., Berkeley, 1950. Am. Cancer Soc. fellow Mass. Gen. Hosp., Boston, 1950-51; instr. microbiology U. Wash., Seattle, 1951-54; asst. prof. U. Wash., 1954-55; asst. prof. biology Brandeis U., Waltham, Mass., 1955-56; assoc. prof. Brandeis U., 1956-60, prof., 1960-63, chmn. dept. biology, 1956-63; vis. prof. bacteriology U. Calif., Berkeley, 1960-61; div. chief exobiology, dir. life scis. Ames Research Center, NASA, Mountain View, Calif., 1963-84; scientist-in-residence Santa Clara U., Calif., 1984—; mem. U.S.-USSR Working Group in Space Biology and Medicine, 1971-84; leader biology team Viking Mars Mission, 1976; mem. space sci. bd. Nat. Acad. Scis., 1984—. Mem. editorial bd. Origins of Life, 1970—. Served with U.S. Army, 1943-46. NSF Sr. Postdoctoral fellow, 1963; grantee NIH, 1955-63; NSF, 1957-63. Mem. Am. Soc. for Microbiology, Am. Soc. Biol. Chemists, Internat. Astronautical Fedn., Am. Chem. Soc., AAAS, Phi Beta Kappa. Home: 1022 N California Ave Palo Alto CA 94303 Office: Santa Clara U Dept Biology Santa Clara CA 95053

KLEIN, JAMES CRAIG, computer room peripheral company executive; b. Oklahoma City, Sept. 14, 1949; s. William Henry and Audrey Nell (Cronkhite) K.; m. Nancy Jean Tuthill, Sept. 25, 1970; children—Robert Mathew, Michael David. B.S., U. N.Mex., 1978. Vice pres. Klein Enterprises, Inc., Albuquerque, 1975-82, pres., 1982—; dir. Data Processing Mgmt. Assn., Albuquerque, 1979-81. Served with USN, 1969-73; Vietnam. Mem. Am. Subcontractors Assn. (dir. 1985-87), Execs. Assn. Greater Albuquerque (bd. dirs. 1985). Republican. Presbyterian. Office: Klein Enterprises Inc 4420 Prospect St NE Albuquerque NM 87110

KLEIN, JAMES MIKEL, music educator; b. Greenville, S.C., Aug. 27, 1953; s. Rubin Harry Klein and Billie (Mikel) Newton. BM, U. Tex., 1975, MM, 1977; MusD, U. Cincinnati, 1981. Prin. trombone player Austin (Tex.) Symphony Orch., 1973-77; conducting asst. U. Tex., Austin, 1975-77, U. Cin., 1977-78; dir. instrumental music Valparaiso (Ind.) U., 1978-84; prof. music Calif. State U. Stanislaus, Turlock, 1984—; mem. faculty Nat. Luth. Music Camp, Lincoln, Nebr., 1985—; guest conductor, clinician, adjudicator various states, 1978—; trombone player Modesto (Calif.) Symphony Orch., 1984—; conductor Stanislaus Youth Symphony, Modesto, 1985, Modesto Symphony Youth Orchestra, 1986—; site adminstr. Nat. Honors Orch., Anaheim, Calif., 1986. pres. Turlock Arts Fund for Youth, 1986. Mem. Music Educators Nat. Assn., Nat. Sch. Orch. Assn., Am. Fedn. Musicians local 1, Coll. Band Dirs. Nat. Assn., Am. Symphony Orch. League. Avocations: sailing, racquetball, reading. Home: 430 E Linwood Ave Turlock CA 95380 Office: Calif State U. Music Dept 801 W Monte Vista Ave Turlock CA 95380

KLEIN, JEFFREY BRUCE, health care administrator; b. N.Y.C., May 8, 1948; s. Herbert and Rose (Ginsberg) K.; B.A., Alfred U., 1970; M.B.A., Temple U., 1972; m. Barbara Cynthia Greenstein, May 12, 1973. Adminstrv. extern L.I. Jewish Med. Center, New Hyde Park, N.Y., 1968; pub. health asst. Nassau County Dept. Health, Mineola, N.Y., 1970; adminstrv. resident Frankford Hosp., Phila., 1971-72; assoc. dir. community medicine Brookhaven Meml. Hosp., Patchogue, N.Y., 1972-73; adminstrv. asst. Moss Rehab. Hosp., Phila., 1973-74, asst. adminstr., 1974-78; assoc. adminstr. Daniel Freeman Hosp., Inglewood, Calif., 1978-80, v.p. rehab. services, 1980-84; corp. v.p. mgmt. and cons. services Freeman Health Services, 1984-85; exec. dir. Freeman Health Ventures, 1984-85, Carondelet Rehab. Ctrs. Am., 1984-85, pres., 1985—. Mem. council on aging Fedn. Jewish Agys., Phila., 1974—; co-chmn. U.S. Orgn. and Adminstrn. Com. Rehab. Internat. Orgn. and Adminstrn. Commn. Recipient Appreciation award Commn. Accreditation of Rehab. Facilities, 1982. Fellow Am. Acad. Med. Adminstrs.; mem. Am. Hosp. Assn., Am. Coll. Hosp. Adminstrs., Assn. Rehab. Med. Dirs. and Coordinators (profl. achievement award 1984), Calif. Assn. Physically Handicapped, Calif. Assn. Rehab. Facilities (Appreciation and Recognition of Exceptional Leadership award 1980), Nat. Assn. Rehab. Facilities, Soc. Advancement Traveling for Handicapped, Am. Pub. Health Assn., Nat. Fire Protection Assn., Royal Soc. Health (London), Beta Gamma Sigma. Office: 6053 Bristol Pkwy Culver City CA 90230

KLEIN, JOSEPH DAVID, audio video producer; b. Chgo., July 2, 1953; s. Morey and Florence (DuBow) K. Grad. high sch. Tech. engring. asst. Ryder Sound Service, Hollywood, Calif., 1969-70; disc jockey, prodn. man Sta. KAFY, Bakersfield, Calif., 1971; engr., producer, ptnr. Hollywood Spectrum, Inc., Los Angeles, 1972-77; producer, pres. L.A. Trax, Inc., Los Angeles, 1977—; music and comml. cons. Recipient Clio awards 1982, 84, 85, 87, Internat. Broadcasting awards 1982, 83, others. Mem. SAG, AFTRA, Nat. Assn. Recording Arts and Scis. Democrat. Office: LA Trax Inc 8033 Sunset Blvd Suite 1010 Los Angeles CA 90046

KLEIN, MILTON, utilities executive, researcher, energy consultant; b. St. Louis, Jan. 13, 1924; s. Isador and Ilona (Tichler) K.; m. Frances Annette Motto, Dec. 28, 1947; children: Richard I., Barbara A., Janet. BSChemE, Wash. U., 1944; MBA, Harvard U., 1950. Chem. engr. Argonne (Ill.) Nat. Lab., 1946-48; dir., asst. mgr. AEC of Chgo., Argonne, Ill., 1950-60; dir. NASA and AEC, Washington, 1961-71; asst. gen. mgr. AEC, Washington, 1974-75; dir. Internat. Energy Agy., Paris, 1976-80; group v.p. Electric Power Research Inst., Palo Alto, Calif., 1980—; chmn. adv. com. Internat. Energy Agy., Paris, 1982-83, cons., advisor, 1983—; mem. Atlantic Council of the U.S., Washington, 1979—, adv. bd. panel Dept. Energy, 1984-85; cons. Taiwan Power Co., Taipei, 1986. Author: A Group Strategy for Energy Research and Development, 1980, (pamphlet) U.S.-Japan Energy Relationship, 1981; contbr. articles to profl. jours. Served with USN, 1944-46. Recipient Outstanding Alumnus citation Wash. U., 1972, Engring. Alumni Achievement award Wash. U., 1984, Exemplary Leadership medal NASA, Washington, 1971. Mem. AAAS, AIAA, Am. Nuclear Soc. (div. chmn. 1984—), Sigma Xi, Tau Beta Pi. Club: Cosmos (Washington). Avocations: tennis, reading, hiking. Home: 48 Politzer Dr Menlo Park CA 94025 Office: Electric Power Research Inst 3412 Hillview Ave Palo Alto CA 94303

KLEIN, NIEL K., advertising executive; b. Chgo., Sept. 7, 1938; s. Louis C. and Edith K.; m. Kaye M., June 18, 1960 (div. 1975); children: Jeffrey, Tracy; m. Valerie A., May 31, 1975; children: Hilerie, Tyler. BA in Creative Writing, Stanford U., 1960; MA in Music, UCLA, 1964. Asst. product mgr. Proctor and Gamble, Cin., 1964-67; account exec. Doyle Dane and Bernbach Advt., Los Angeles, 1967-72; account supr. Keye Donna Perlstein Advt., Los Angeles, 1972-73; dir. export Viviane Woodward Cosmetics, Panorama City, Calif., 1973-74; ptnr. Hale Hanson and Co., Pasadena, Calif., 1974-75; pres., creative dir. Klein/Richardson, Inc., Beverly Hills, Calif., 1975—; instr. Advt. Ctr., Los Angeles. 1982—; judge Clio, Sunny and other award competitions, 1983—. bd. dirs. Montessori Sch. of West Los Angeles, 1982-86. Served to lt. USNR, 1960-62. Recipient Belding Cup, Lulu award, "Best in West" award, Sunny award, all in 1986. Mem. Western Assn. Advt. Agys., Los Angeles Advt. Club, Los Angeles Creative Club. Republican. Club: Stanford (Los Angeles). Avocations: tennis, skiing, music, woodworking, creative writing. Office: Klein/Richardson Inc 8665 Wilshire Blvd Suite 409 Beverly Hills CA 90211

KLEIN, OTTO GUSTAV, ophthalmologist, physician; b. Helena, Mont., Aug. 2, 1938; s. Otto Gustav and Mary Alshire K.; m. Susan Vincent, Jan. 5, 1980; 1 child, Kent Michael. BA, Stanford U., 1960; MD, Cornell U., 1964. Cert. Am. Bd. Ophthalmology. Intern King County Hosp., Seattle, 1964-65; resident then chief resident NYU-Bellevue, N.Y.C., 1967-71; ptnr. Mason Clinic, Seattle, 1971-79, Rocky Mountain Eye Ctr., Missoula, Mont., 1979—; assoc. clin. prof. U. Wash. Med. Sch., Seattle, 1971-79; bd. trustees Missoula Youth Home, 1984—; v.p. Mont. Eye Research Found., Missoula, 1981-85; active staff mem. Missoula Gen. Hosp., St. Patrick's Hosp., Missoula Community Hosp.; bd. dirs. Western Savs. and Laon, 1987—. Contbr. chpt. to book, articles to profl. jours. Served to capt. U.S. Army, 1965-67, Vietnam. Decorated Bronze Star. Fellow ACS; mem. Am. Acad. Ophthalmology, Mont. State Acad. Ophthalmology, AMA, Pacific Coast Oto-Ophthalmological Soc., Am. Intraocular Lens Implant Soc., West Coast Retinal Study Club, Alpha Omega Alpha. Republican. Home: 3 Elk Ridge Ct Missoula MT 59802 Office: Rocky Mountain Eye Ctr 700 W Kent Missoula MT 59801

KLEIN, RALPH, city official; mayor, city of Calgary, Alta., Can. Office: Office of Mayor City of Calgary, PO Box 2100 Sta M, Calgary, AB Canada T2P 2M5 *

KLEIN, RAYMOND MARTIN, periodontist; b. N.Y.C., Jan. 4, 1947; s. Max Ludwig and Suzette Martina (Perls) K. BS, CCNY, 1968; DMD, U. Pa., 1972. Lic. periodontist Calif., Ga., N.Y. Resident in peridontics Ga. Retardation Ctr., 1975-76; practice dentistry specializing in peridontics Fairfield, Calif., 1976—, San Jose, Calif., 1976-77, Dixon, Calif., 1980-83, Vallejo, Calif., 1981—; cons. dental research Nutran Inc., Atlanta, 1974-86. Author weekly newspaper column Daily Republic, Fairfield, 1983—; contbr. articles to profl. jours. Pres. Downtown Homeowners Assn. Fairfield, 1977—; active Fairfield City Ctr. Redevel. Project, 1981—. Served with USAF, 1972-74, to capt. Res., 1985—. Grantee NIH, 1971. Fellow Acad. Gen. Dentistry; mem. Am. Acad. Periodontology, ADA, Bay Area Dentists Study Club, Calif. Dental Assn., Calif. Soc. Periodontists, Napa Solano Dentist Soc. (chmn. pub. relations com. 1983-84, chmn. continuing edn. com. 1985—, bd. dirs.), Western Soc. Periodontology, Travis Hist. Soc. (chmn. audio-visual dept. Travis Air Force Mus.). Home: 745 Jackson St Fairfield CA 94533 Office: 1225 Travis Blvd Fairfield CA 94533

KLEIN, SNIRA L(UBOVSKY), Hebrew Language and literature educator. came to U.S., 1959, naturalized, 1974; d. Avraham and Devora (Unger) Lubovsky; m. Earl H. Klein, Dec. 25, 1975. Tchr. cert., Tchrs. Seminar, Netanya, Israel, 1956; B. Rel. Edn., U. Judaism, 1961, M in Hebrew Lit., 1963; BA, Calif. State U., Northridge, 1966; MA, UCLA, 1971, PhD, 1983. Teaching asst. UCLA, 1969-71, vis. lectr., 1985—; instr., continuing edn. U. Judaism, Los Angeles, 1971-76, instr., 1975—. Mem. Assn. for Jewish Studies, Nat. Assn. of Profs. of Hebrew, World Union of Jewish Studies. Jewish. Avocations: gardening, music. Office: U Judaism 15600 Mulholland Dr Los Angeles CA 90077

KLEINBERG, MARVIN H., patent lawyer; b. N.Y.C., Aug. 17, 1927; s. Herman and Lillian (Grossman) K.; m. Irene Aertker, July 7, 1962; children—Sarah Elizabeth, Ethan Chaim, Joel Victor. B.A. in Physics, UCLA, 1949; J.D., U. Calif. at Berkeley, 1953. Bar: Calif. 1954, also U.S. Patent Office, U.S. Supreme Ct. 1954. Dep. pub. defender Los Angeles County, 1954; patent atty. RCA, Camden, N.J., 1955-57, Litton Industries, Inc., Beverly Hills, Calif., 1957-61; patent counsel Modal Systems Inc., La Jolla, Calif., 1961-63; mem. firm Golove & Kleinberg, Los Angeles, 1963-70, Golove, Kleinberg & Morganstern, Los Angeles, 1970-72, Kleinberg, Morganstern & Scholnick, Los Angeles, 1973-76, Kleinberg, Morganstern, Scholnick & Mann, Beverly Hills, 1976-79; sole practice Marvin H. Kleinberg, Inc., Beverly Hills, 1979-84; ptnr. Arant, Kleinberg & Lerner, 1985—; adj. lectr. patent law, mem. Innovation Clinic Adv. Council Franklin Pierce Law Center, Concord, N.H., 1975—; adv. council PTC Research Found., 1981-85; dir., sec. Digem, Inc., Los Angeles. Active YMCA Indian Guides, 1974-79; pres. Opportunity Houses Inc., Riverside, Calif., 1973-76, UCLA Class of '49, 1979-84; co-chairperson Sholem Ednl. Inst., Los Angeles, 1974-75; chief referee Region 58, Am. Youth Soccer Orgn., 1976-84. Served to sgt. AUS, 1946-47. Mem. ABA, Am. Inst. Patent Lawyers, Los Angeles Patent Law Assn., Los Angeles County Bar Assn., Am. Intellectual Property Law Assn., Zeta Beta Tau. Home: 3901 Cody Rd Sherman Oaks CA 91403 Office: Arant Kleinberg & Lerner 2049 Century Park E Suite 880 Los Angeles CA 90067

KLEINHOFS, ANDRIS, genetics educator, department director, agronomist; b. Dobele, Latvia, Dec. 25, 1937; came to U.S., 1950; s. Arturs and Ida (Zusters) K.; m. Jolanta Vita Smeils, June 4, 1965; children: Laura, Anita. BS, U. Nebr., 1958, MS, 1964, PhD, 1967. Instr. U. Nebr., Lincoln, 1965-67; asst. prof. genetics Wash. State U., Pullman, 1967-72, assoc. prof., 1972-77, prof., 1977—, chmn. program genetics and cell biology, 1983—; cons. Native Plants, Inc., Salt Lake City, 1982—. Editor: Genetic Engineering in Eukaryotes, 1983; contbr. articles to sci. jours. Served to capt. U.S. Army, 1958-62. Research grantee NSF, USDA, U.S. Dept. Energy. Mem. AAAS, Sigma Xi. Lutheran. Club: Clearwater Flycasters (Pullman) (pres. 1983-84). Avocation: fishing. Office: Wash State U Program Genetics and Cell Biology Pullman WA 99164-6419

KLEINROCK, LEONARD, computer scientist; b. N.Y.C., June 13, 1934; s. Bernard and Anne (Schoenfeld) K.; m. Stella Schuler, Dec. 1, 1967; children—Nancy S., Martin C. BEE, CCNY, 1957; M.S., MIT, 1959, Ph.D., 1963. Asst. elec. engr. Photobell Co. Inc., 1951-57; research engr. Lincoln Labs., M.I.T., 1957-63; mem. faculty UCLA, 1963—, prof. computer sci., 1970—; pres. Linkabit Corp., 1968-69, Tech. Transfer Inst., 1976—; cons. in field, prin. investigator govt. contracts. Author: Queueing Systems, Vol. I, 1975, Vol. II, 1976, Communication Nets: Stochastic Message Flow and Delay, 1964, Solutions Manual for Queueing Systems, Vol. I, 1982, Vol. II, 1986; also articles. Recipient Paper award ICC, 1978, Leonard G. Abraham paper award Communications Soc., 1975, Outstanding Faculty Mem. award UCLA Engring. Grad. Students Assn., 1966, Townsend Harris medal CCNY, 1982, L.M. Ericsson Prize Sweden, 1982, 12th Marconi award, 1986; Guggenheim fellow, 1971-72. Fellow IEEE (disting. lectr. 1973, 76); mem. Nat. Acad. Engring., Ops. Research Soc. Am. (Lanchester prize 1976), Assn. Computing Machinery, Internat. Fedn. Info. Processes Systems, Amateur Athletic Union. Jewish. Avocations: karate, hiking, jogging. Home: 801 N Kenter Ave Los Angeles CA 90049 Office: UCLA Computer Sci Dept 405 Hilgard Ave Boelter Hall Los Angeles CA 90024

KLEINSCHMIDT, ERIC WALKER, chemical engineer, consultant; b. Indpls., Aug. 10, 1955; s. Walter J. and Martha (Walker) K.; m. Sally Marshall, Jan. 25, 1986. BChemE, Purdue U., 1978. Chem. engr. Avery Internat., Schererville, Ind., 1978-80; process engr. Rogers Corp., BPD, Chandler, Ariz., 1980-82; materials engr. Rogers Corp., CMD, Mesa, Ariz., 1982-85; sales engr. Gila River Products, Chandler, 1985-86, mgr. sales, mktg. electronic products, 1986—. Mem. Am. Inst. Chem. Engrs., Soc. Advancement Material and Process Engrs., Internat. Electronics Packaging Soc., Am. Chem. Soc., N.Y. Acad. Sci. Avocations: camping, fishing, golf, tennis. Home: 856 W Kiva Ave Mesa AZ 85202 Office: Gila River Products 6615 W Boston St Chandler AZ 85226

KLEINSMITH, GENE, artist; b. Madison, Wis., Feb. 22, 1942; B.A., Augustana Coll., Sioux Falls, S.D., 1963; M.A., U. No. Ariz., Flagstaff, 1969; children—Jon Darin, Paul, Christin. Tchr. art high schs. in S.D., Colo., Minn. and Calif., 1963-71; mem. faculty San Bernardino Valley Coll., eves. 1967-71; instr. ceramics Victor Valley Coll., Victorville, Calif., 1971—, chmn. art dept., also coordinator artist-in-residence programs; lectr., condr. workshops in field; Keynote presenter Clay ... U.S.A., 1984, Nat. Council on Edn. Ceramic Arts, Boston, 1984; presenter Nat. Council on Edn. for Ceramic Arts, Atlanta, 1983. One-man shows include U. Minn., Mankato, 1967, U. Calif., Riverside, 1969, U. S.D., 1976, No. Ariz. U., 1980, Olive Tree Gallery, Ft. Collins, Colo., 1966, Yavapai Coll., Prescott, Ariz., 1976, Apple Valley, Calif., 1977, Hi-Desert Symphony, Victor Valley, 1979, The Gallery in Flagstaff, Ariz., 1986; group and invitational exhbns. include Gallery II, Charlottesville, Va., 1983, Gallery II, St. George, Utah, 1984, Nat. Council on Edn. for Ceramic Arts, Atlanta, 1983; represented in permanent collections Mpls. Art Inst., Valparaiso (Ind.) U., Gustavus Adolphus Coll., St. Peter, Minn., No. Ariz. U., Ariz. Western Coll., Yuma, U. S.D., U. Minn., Mankato, Miami-Dade Community Coll., Gallery II, Charlottesville, Va., Rodell Gallery, Los Angeles, Pompidou Ctr., Paris, Tupkapi Palace, Istanbul, Turkey; also pvt. collections; presenter workshops; internat. lectr. Faculty fellow Victor Valley Coll., 1973. Mem. Nat. Council Art Adminstrs., Nat. Council Edn. for Ceramic Arts (mem. exhbns.), Am. Crafts Council, Calif. Art Italy), Paris, Inst. Ceramic History, Athens, Greece. Art Mus., Phi Delta Kappa, Kappa Delta Pi. Author: Earth, Fire, Air and Water, 1974, Clay's The Way, 3d edit., 1986; writer Ceramics monthly mag.; contbg. writer TV series Search; contbr. articles to profl. jours. Address: 13925 Kiowa Apple Valley CA 92307

KLEKAR, STEVEN GARY, aeronautical engineer; b. St. Louis, July 28, 1959; s. Henry Leon and Amelia Josephene (Kratochville) K.; m. Susan Marie Shaikewitz, Nov. 10, 1984. BS in Aircraft Maintenance Engring., Parks Coll. Aero. Tech., 1979. Lic. airframe and powerplant mechanic. Logistics engr. McDonnell Aircraft Co. subs. McDonnell-Douglas Corp., St. Louis, 1979-85; sr. maintainability engr. Martin Marietta-Denver Aerospace Corp., 1985—. Mem. AIAA, ASME, Soc. Automotive Engrs. Republican. Roman Catholic. Avocations: photography, scuba diving, touring, hunting. Office: Martin Marietta-Denver Aerospace PO Box 179 Denver CO 80201

KLEPINGER, JOHN WILLIAM, trailer manufacturing company executive; b. Lafayette, Ind., Feb. 7, 1945; s. John Franklin and R. Wanda (North) K.; m. Mary Patricia Duffy, May 1, 1976; 1 child, Nicholas Patrick. BS, Ball State U., 1967, MA, 1968. Sales engr. CTS Corp., Elkhart, Ind., 1969-70; exec. v.p. Woodlawn Products Corp., Elkhart, 1970-78; v.p. Period Ind., Henderson, Ky., 1976-78, Sotebeer Constrn. Co., Inc., Elkhart, 1978-81; gen. mgr. Wells Industries Inc., Ogden, Utah, 1981—; regional dir. Zion's First Nat. Bank, Ogden, 1986—. Bd. dirs. St. Benedict's Hosp., Ogden, 1986, chmn. 1987. Named Ogden Bus. Man of Yr., Weber County Sch. Dist., 1984. Mem. Weber County Prodn. Mgrs. Assn. (pres. 1984-85), Weber County Indsl. Devel. Corp. (exec. officer 1984—), Weber/Morgan Pvt. Industry Council, Nat. Assn. Pvt. Industry Councils (pres., bd. dirs. 1986), Nat. Job Tng. Ptnrship Inc. (bd. dirs. 1986—), Ogden Area C. of C. (bd. dirs., treas. 1986—). Roman Catholic. Club: Exchange (Ogden) (bd. dirs. 1984-86). Avocations: finance, community service, leadership, sports, travel. Home: 5181 Aztec Dr Ogden UT 84403 Office: Wells Industries Inc PO Box 1619 Ogden UT 84402

KLEPPER, ELIZABETH LEE, physiologist; b. Memphis, Mar. 8, 1936; d. George Madden and Margaret Elizabeth (Lee) K. BA, Vanderbilt U., 1958; MA, Duke U., 1963, PhD, 1966. Research scientist Commonwealth Sci. and Indsl. Research Orgn., Griffith, Australia, 1966-68, Battelle Northwest Lab., Richland, Wash., 1972-76; asst. prof. Auburn (Ala.) U., 1968-72; Plant physiologist USDA Agrl. Research Service, Pendleton, Oreg., 1976-85, research leader, 1985—. Assoc. editor Crop Sci., 1977-80; mem. editorial bd. Plant Physiology, 1977—; mem. editorial adv. bd. Field Crops Research, 1983—; contbr. chpts. to books and articles to jours. Marshall scholar British Govt., 1958-59; NSF fellow, 1964-66. Mem. AAAS, Am. Soc. Plant Physiologists, Crop Sci. Soc. Am., Soil Sci. Soc. Am., Am. Soc. Agronomy (monograph com. 1983-86), Sigma Xi. Home: 1454 SW 45th Pendleton OR 98701 Office: USDA Argl Research Service PO Box 370 Pendleton OR 98701

KLEPSA, RADMILA VITA, financial executive, business manager; b. Pisek, Czechoslovakia, June 6, 1946; came to U.S., 1970; naturalized, 1978; d. Jaroslav and Marie (Volfova) Vita; m. Eric Mirek Klepsa, July 22, 1967. M.B.A. with honors, Karl's U., Prague, 1968; postgrad. UCLA, 1978. Bus. sec., acct. Mary Pickford Co., Beverly Hills, Calif., 1974-76; controller Wakeford/Orloff, Los Angeles, 1976-77; dir., controller Dreyfus Agy., Los Angeles, 1978-80; v.p. fin., treas. BBDO/West, Inc., Los Angeles, 1980-84; controller United Vacations Inc., Marina Del Rey, Calif., 1984—; dir., treas. Advt. Industries Emergency Fund. Mem. Nat. Assn. Accts., Motion Picture and TV Controllers Assn. Republican. Roman Catholic. Office: United Vacations Inc 4505 Glencoe Ave Marina del Rey CA 90292

KLETTKE, DWIGHT RONALD, physician; b. Kalamazoo, Oct. 10, 1952; s. Walter G. and Esther E. (Schroeder) K.; m. Patricia Ann Heindel, Dec. 21, 1974; 1 child, Jennifer Ann. MD, U. Mich., 1977. Resident Deaconess Hosp. Family Practice Program, Evansville, Ind., 1977-80; pvt. practice medicine Granger Med. Clinic, West Valley City, Utah, 1980—. Fellow Am. Acad. Family Practice; mem. Utah State Med. Assn., Salt Lake County Med. Soc. Avocations: photography, computer programming, camping, hiking. Home: 630 Parkview Dr Summit Park UT 84060 Office: Granger Med Clinic 3280 W 3500 S West Valley City UT 84119

KLIEN, WOLFGANG JOSEF, architect; b. Hollabrunn, Austria, Sept. 29, 1942; s. Josef and Maria (Kainz) K.; Dipl. Ing., Vienna Tech. U., 1967; m. Charlotte Olga Kutscherer, Aug. 14, 1968; children—Christina Olga, Angelika Maria. Designer, E. Donau, Architect, Vienna, 1968; with C. Nitschke & Assos., Architects, Columbus, Ohio, 1968-71; project architect GSAS Architects, Phoenix, 1971-75, 77-78; prodn. architect Harry Glueck, Vienna, 1976-77; v.p. architecture Am. Indian Engring. Inc., Phoenix, 1978-81; pres. S.W. Estate Group, Inc., real estate devel., San Diego, 1980-82; pres., tech. dir., branch mgr. Ariz. br. office SEG-S.W. Estate Group, Inc., Phoenix, 1982-86; prin. Klien & Assoc., Architecture, Planning, Devel. Cons., Phoenix, 1986—, Atlantic-Pacific Trading Corp., Internat. Trade, Phoenix, 1986—. Mem. AIA, Austro-Am. Council West, Austrian Soc. Ariz. (founder 1985, v.p. 1985-86, pres. 1987). Roman Catholic. Home: 214 E Griswold Rd Phoenix AZ 85020 Office: 4501 N 22nd Street Phoenix AZ 85016

KLINE, DAVID TWERY, furniture and lighting designer; b. Chgo., May 31, 1932; s. Sol Twery and Lottie (Yankelowitz) Kline; m. Marsha Jean Sagorsky, Mar. 3, 1957; children: Mark Allen, Daniel Steven, Jeneé Helene (dec.). BS in Indsl. Design, U. So. Calif., 1955. Designer Melvin Best Assocs., Pasadena, Calif., 1955, Sunset Lamp Corp., Los Angeles, 1957-58; designer Kline Assocs., Los Angeles and Sherman Oaks, Calif., 1958-85, North Hollywood, Calif., 1985—. Served with U.S. Army, 1955-57. Mem. Calif. Furniture Designers Assn. (pres. 1960—), U. So. Calif. Indsl. Design Alumni Assn. (pres. 1959—), West Valley Camera Club (pres. 1984-85). Democrat. Jewish. Avocations: photography, sculpture, woodworking. Office: Kline Assocs 12501 Chandler #207 North Hollywood CA 91607

KLINE, EDWARD, biology and chemistry teacher; b. Peru, Ind., June 25, 1947; s. Adrian Dale and Mary Patricia (Walsh) K.; m. Cheryl Ann Dragoun, May 30, 1970; children: Eric, Jason. BS, Ball State U., 1969; MA, N.M. State U., 1985. Tchr. Los Angeles Unified Sch. Dist., 1970-73, Alamogordo (N.M.) Pub. Sch., 1973-87; head tchr. Weed (N.M.) Pub. Sch., 1983-86. Chief, Sacramento Vol. Fire Dept., 1982-85; emergency med. tech. Sacramento Fire/Rescue, 1982—. Mem. Nat. Assn. Secondary Sch. Prins., Assn. for Supervision and Curriculum Devel., Nat. Sci. Tchrs. Assn., Am. Chem. Soc. Roman Catholic. Avocations: golf, tennis, softball, Notre Dame football. Home: Star Rt Weed NM 88354 Office: Weed Pub Sch PO Box 548 Weed NM 88354

KLINE, ELLIOT HOWARD, university dean, business educator; b. Denver, July 16, 1940; s. Morris and Sadie (Uswalk) K.; m. Linda Sue Newman, May 18, 1964; children: James, Edward. B.A., U. Colo., 1963, M.P.A., 1966, Ph.D., 1971. Instr. Tex. A&M U., College Station, 1966-67; lectr. U. Colo., Colorado Springs, 1968-69; asst. prof. U. Denver, 1968-70; dir., asso. prof. Inst. Public Affairs and Adminstrn. Drake U., Des Moines, 1970-77; dean, prof. Sch. Bus. and Pub. Adminstrn. U. Pacific, Stockton, Calif., 1977—; planning cons. State Savs. and Loan Assn., Stockton, 1979; dir. adminstrv. analysis Office City Clk., Indianola, Iowa, 1975; lectr. Brookings Instn., 1982, 83; vis. lectr. Washington Sem. Program, Am. U., 1982; cons. various orgns., 1973—. Guest editor: The Stockton Record, 1980—; contbr. articles to various publs. Served with USCGR, 1960-65. Recipient Grad. Sch. Research grants Drake Univ., 1972, 74. Mem. C. of C., Acad. Mgmt., Am. Assn. Higher Edn., Am. Mgmt. Assn., Am. Soc. Public Adminstrn. (mem. nat. council 1976-79), Calif. Assn. Public Adminstrn., Edn., Internat. Personnel Mgmt. Assn., No. Calif. Polit. Sci. Assn. (mem. exec. bd. 1981—), Western Govtl. Research Assn. (exec. com. 1981—), Western Assn. Collegiate Schs. Bus. (exec. bd. 1981—, pres. 1985-86). Office: Sch Bus and Pub Adminstrn Univ of Pacific Stockton CA 95211

KLINE, ERIC HART, antiquarian bookseller; b. Los Angeles, May 20, 1951; s. Preston Jerome and Gertrude (Hartfield) K. BA, Wilmington Coll., 1974; MA, Brandeis U., 1981. Cert. tchr. Researcher Brandeis U./Hamburg U., Fed. Republic Germany, 1982-83; dir. tech. seminars ANCO Engrs. Inc., Culver City, Calif., 1983-85, mgr. robotics, 1985-86; owner Morrison & Kline Books, Santa Monica, Calif., 1986—; cons. library collection div. Univ. Research Libraries, 1984—. Author: Judaica Volume One Fall, 1985. Mem. Robotics Industries Assn. (edn. chmn. 1984-86), Assn. Jewish Librarians, Assn. for Jewish Studies, Soc. Mfg. Engrs. Avocations: writer, movie critic. Office: Morrison & Kline Books 309 Arizona Ave Santa Monica CA 90401

KLINE, FRED WALTER, communications corporation executive; b. Oakland, Calif., May 17, 1918; s. Walter E. and Jean M. Kline; m. Verna Marie Taylor, Dec. 27, 1952; children—Kathleen, Nora, Fred Walter. B.A. in Calif. History, U. Calif.-Berkeley, 1940. With Walter E. Kline & Assocs. and successor Fred Kline Agy., Inc., from 1937; chmn. bd., pres. Kline Communications Corp., Los Angeles, 1956—; pres. Capitol News Service. Commr. Los Angeles County Fire Services Commn., Calif. Motion Picture Devel. Council; former fed. civil def. liaison; developer state-wide paramedic rescue program; Calif. chmn. Office of Asst. Sec. Def.; mem. Calif. Com. for Employer Support of Guard and Res. Served with USAAF, World War II; brig. gen. Calif. Mil. Dept. Recipient Inter-Racial award City of Los Angeles, 1963, named Man of Yr., 1964. Mem. Acad. Motion Picture Arts and Scis., Radio and TV News Assn. So. Calif., Pub. Relations Soc. Am., Calif. Newspaper Pubs. Assn., Cath. Press Council (founding mem.), Pacific Pioneer Broadcasters, Footprinters Internat., Am. Mil. Govt. Assn. (past pres.), Navy League, Calif. State Police Officers Assn., Internat. Assn. Profl. Firefighters (hon. life), Peace Officers Assn. Los Angeles County (life), Internat. Assn. Chiefs of Police, Internat. Assn. Fire Chiefs, Calif. Fire Chiefs Assn., Fire Marshals Assn. N.Am., Nat. Fire Protection Assn., Nat. Fin. Writers Assn., Hollywood C. of C., Nat. Fire Sci. Acad., Calif. State Mil. Forces, Calif. Pubs. Assn., So. Calif. Cable Club. Sigma Delta Chi. Clubs: Greater Los Angeles Press, Media (Los Angeles), Sacramento Press. Columnist Calif. newspapers. Office: 6340 Bryn Mawr Dr Los Angeles CA 90068

KLINE, JAMES SANBORN, physician; b. Mpls., Feb. 23, 1947; s. James DeWitt and Mary Elizabeth (Ryder) K.; m. Grace Ann Lueck, June 22, 1985. AB, Brown U., 1967; MS, Cornell U., 1970; MD, Dartmouth Coll., 1975. Med. dir. Indian Health Service, Browning, Mont., 1976-78; emergency physician Multicare Med. Ctr., Tacoma, Wash., 1983—. Contbr. articles to profl. jours. Fellow Am. Coll. Emergency Physicians (bd. dirs. 1983—); mem. King County Med. Assn., Phi Beta Kappa, Sigma Xi. Club: Mountaineers (Seattle). Office: Tacoma Gen Hosp 311 South K St Tacoma WA 98405

KLINE, LOIS TWOMBLEY, communications educator; b. Belle Fourche, S.D., May 28, 1949; d. Marvin Wayne and Agnes Ruth (Roetman) Twombley; m. David Randall Kline, Aug. 2, 1971; 1 child, Alex Marvin. BS, No. State Coll., 1970; MA, U. No. Colo., 1971; PhD, U. Denver. Instr. speech communication, English Alpena (Mich.) Community Coll., 1971-73; instr., grant adminstr. Whittemore (Mich.)/Prescott Sch., 1973-74; tchr. Widefield High Sch., Security, Colo., 1974-76; instr. Communications Pikes Peak Community Coll., Colorado Springs, Colo., 1976—. Co-author: A Basic Report Writer's guide, 1983. Judge Toastmistress Regional Contest, Colorado Springs, 1983; speaker Colorado Springs council Girl Scouts U.S., 1985. Mem. NEA, Colo. Edn. Assn., Pikes Peak Community Coll. Faculty Assn. (pub. relations com. 1976-77), Speech Communication Assn., Western Speech Communication Assn. (chmn. community coll. interest group 1985-86) Credit Women Internat. (speaker, trainer Colo. chpt. 1981-83), Colorado Springs C. of C. (trainer 1986). Avocations: skiing, hunting, camping, water skiing, volleyball. Home: 6450 Hawkeye Circle Colorado Springs CO 80919 Office: Pikes Peak Community Coll 5675 S Academy Blvd Colorado Springs CO 80906

KLINE, RICHARD STEPHEN, public relations executive; b. Brookline, Mass., June 20, 1948; s. Paul and Helen (Chartoff) K.; m. Carroll Potter, (dec. Apr. 1984); m. Sharon Tate, June 16, 1985; stepchildren: Allison, Kevin. BA, U. Mass., Amherst, 1970. Reporter Worcester (Mass.) Telegram & Gazette, 1970-71; account exec. Wenger-Michael Advt., Los Angeles, 1971; asst. v.p., dir. promotions Gt. Western Savs. and Loan, Beverly Hills, Calif., 1972-75; v.p., dir. mktg. Union Fed. Savs. and Loan, Los Angeles, 1975-78; chmn. bd. dirs. Berkhemer & Kline Inc., Los Angeles, 1978—; former instr. Am. Savs. and Loan Inst. Pres., mem. exec. com. Big Bros. Los Angeles; v.p. Crittenton Ctr., Los Angeles; bd. dirs. Am. Cancer Soc., Los Angeles; pub. info. chmn. United Way of Los Angeles; mem. Los Angeles Philharm. Men's Com., Town Hall Forum, Los Angeles, Hollywoodland Improvement Assn.; pub. relations dir. Oakland (Calif.) Symphony Orch., 1972; commr. Parks and Recreation, City of Oakland, 1973-74. Mem. Internat. Assn. Bus. Communicators, Pub. Relations Soc. Am., Publicity Club Los Angeles, The Pub. Relations Exchange (mktg. chmn.). Clubs: Wilshire Country, Jonathan (Los Angeles). Avocation: horseback riding, fishing. Office: Berkhemer & Kline 261 S Figueroa Suite 250 Los Angeles CA 90012

KLING, LYNN WILLIAM, technical writer; b. Lewiston, Idaho, Nov. 7, 1944; s. William Lee and Delia Emma (Faler) K.; m. Alice Patricia Keyes, July 1, 1984; 1 child, Molly O'Neill. Student, Menlo Coll., 1963-64; BA, Stanford U., 1967. Tech. writer Grid Systems, Mt. View, Calif., 1981-83, Bill Kling, Carmel, Calif., 1983—; cons. VisiCorp, Sunnyvale, Calif., 1982-83, Apple Computer, Cupertino, Calif., 1985—. Author: The ABC's of Lotus 123, 1984, Framework: A Developr's Handbook, 1985. Home: 363 Hannon Ave Monterey CA 93940 Office: Bill Kling 5th and Lincoln Carmel CA 93921

KLING, MADELINE TERRY, lawyer; b. Boston, May 3, 1930; s. Norbert P. and Viola M. (Alward) K.; m. Aubrey A. Dykes, Apr. 10, 1948 (dec. Mar. 1973). AA cum laude, Saddleback Coll., 1980; BL, JD, Western State

U., 1982. Bar: Calif. 1983, U.S. Dist. Ct. (cen. dist.) Calif. 1983. Pvt. investigator Stein Investigations, Los Angeles, 1961-71, Los Angeles, 1971-78; sole practice Tustin, Calif., 1983—. Author: A Time to Kill, 1985; contbr. articles to Western State U. Law Rev., 1981—. Served with USAR, 1961-71, USNR, 1971-76. Recipient Presdl. Achievement award Rep. Nat. Com., 1980. Mem. Orange County Bar Assn., Calif. Trial Lawyers Assn., ABA, Am. Trial Lawyers Assn., Orange County Women Lawyers. Avocations: music writing, photography, golf. Home: 320 Crescent Bay Dr Laguna Beach CA 92651 Office: 17862 E 17th St #101 Tustin CA 92680

KLINGEL, JOAN ELIZABETH, English educator; b. N.Y.C., Dec. 8, 1950; d. Frank Raymond and Jean Elizabeth (Pottebaum) K. B.A., SUNY-Stony Brook, 1972; A.M., Brown U., 1973, Ph.D. in English, 1977. Asst. prof. English, U. Colo., Colorado Springs, 1978-84, assoc. prof., 1984—, chmn. Enlish dept., 1980-83, asst. dean Coll. Letters, Arts, Scis., 1983-85, assoc. dean. 1985-86, interim vice chancellor for acad. affairs, UCCS, 1986—; oriented campus, 1983-86 interim vice chancellor for acad. affairs, 1986—; panelist div. edn. and research NEH, project dir. Humanities Enrichment at a Technically Oriented Campus, 1983-86; cons., evaluator NCA, 1987—. Assoc. editor: Letters of Hester Piozzi, 1987. Contbr. articles to profl. jours. Lector Grace Episcopal Ch., Colorado Springs. Brown U. fellow, 1972-73, Am. Council Learned Socs. grantee-in-aid, N.Y.C., 1979, U. Colo. Grad. Sch. research grantee, 1978, 79; recipient Chancellor's award U. Colo., Colorado Springs, 1983. Mem. MLA. Democrat. Office: U Colo PO Box 7150 Colorado Springs CO 80933

KLINGENSMITH, ARTHUR PAUL, state agency administrator; b. Los Angeles, May 23, 1949; s. Paul Arthur and Hermine Elinore (Wacek) K.; m. Donna J. Bellucci, Apr. 26, 1976 (div. Jan. 1981). AA in Social Sci., Indian Valley Jr. Coll., 1976; BA in Indsl. Psychology, San Francisco State U., 1979; MA in Indsl. Psychology, Columbia Pacific U., 1980. Enlisted USAF, 1968, advanced through grades to staff sgt. USAF; instr. radio ops. Biloxi, Miss.; advanced through grades to staff sgt. USAF; instr. radio ops. USAF, Biloxi, 1968-72; air traffic control operator USAF, Hamilton AFB Novato, Calif., 1972-74; resigned USAF, 1974; elec. technician Calif. Dept. Transp., Oakland, 1975-78; right of way agt. Calif. Dept. Transp., San Francisco, 1978-85; sr. right of way agt. Calif. Dept. Transp., Sacramento, 1985—, computer researcher, 1985—. Mem. Internat. Right of Way Assn. (instr. 1982—), Am. Arbitration Assn., Marin County Bd. Realtors, Assn. Humanistic Psychology, Nat. Assn. Housing and Redevel. Officials. Republican. Avocations: automobile restoration, painting, writing, study of light. Office: APK Enterprises PO Box 574 Sausalito CA 94966

KLINGER, BARNEY, consulting engineering executive; b. Chgo., Nov. 14, 1928; s. Max and Eva Klinger; children: Karen, Deborah, Cynthia, Annette. Grad., Utility Engring. Inst., 1950; MBA, Pepperdine U., 1976. Lic. contractor, Calif.; registered steam and turbine engr., City Los Angeles. V.p. engring. Kissell Refrigeration, Los Angeles, 1956-58; chmn., chief exec. officer The Applied Cos., San Fernando, Calif., 1958—; ptnr. Cogeneration, San Fernando, 1983—. Trustee U. Calif., Santa Barbara; mem. Found. Pepperdine U., Malibu; bd. dirs. Am. Cancer Soc., Santa Barbara, U.S Marshall Found. Recipient Alumni of Yr. award Pepperdine U., 1985. Mem. Am. Welding Soc. Republican. Lodges: Shriners, Masons. Avocations: politics, gardening, collecting antique clocks, fundraisings.

KLINGNER, JOHN ROGER, communications executive; b. South St. Paul, Minn., June 30, 1950; s. Carl Edward and Lorraine Marion (Rauchwarter) K.; m. Sharon Lee Bigleman, May, 19, 1970; children: Jacob Reed, Samuel Miles, John Casey. Student, Glendale (Ariz.) Community Coll., 1968-69, Phoenix Coll., 1970-75. Supr. printing prodn. U-Haul Internat., Phoenix, 1975-77; mgr. printing services 1st Farwest Ins. Cos., Portland, Oreg., 1977-80; div. mgr. communications 1st Farwest Ins. Cos., Portland, 1980—; instr. graphic arts, Mt. Hood Community Coll., Gresham, Oreg, 1979-83, mem. adv. bd., 1979-87, chmn. adv. bd. 1980-81. Mem. Adminstrv. Mgmt. Soc. (treas. 1983-84), Adminstrv. Records Mgrs. Assn. Republican. Roman Catholic. Office: 1st Farwest Ins Cos 400 SW 6th St Portland OR 97204

KLINKHAMER, FRANS RICHARD, research physicist; b. Utrecht, The Netherlands, Sept. 9, 1956; came to U.S., 1983; s. Johannes and Jeannine (Barrière) K. Doctoraal, U. Utrecht, 1980; PhD, U. Leiden, 1983. Research physicist U. Leiden, 1980-83, U. Calif., Santa Barbara, 1983-84, Lawrence Berkeley (Calif.) Lab., 1984—. Contbr. articles on cosmology and physics of elem. particles to profl. jours. Office: Lawrence Berkeley Lab Mailstop 70A-3307 Berkeley CA 94720

KLINNER, ALVIN RICHARD, accountant, information systems professional; b. Glen Ullin, N.D., Jan. 28, 1930; s. Herman Joseph and Elizabeth Magdelan (Hoerner) K.; m. Chestine Wanda Smith, Dec. 31, 1956 (div. May 1976); children: Devnee, Bobbi, Steven; m. Patricia Ann Krueger, July 22, 1978. Assoc. of Arts and Scis., Yakima Valley Jr. Coll., 1955; BBA, U. Wash., 1957, MBA, 1971. Cert. systems profl. Mgr. gen. and cost acctg. Gen. Electric Co., Richland, Wash., 1957-64; mgr. adminstrn. Battelle-N.W., Richland, 1965-81; mgr. fin. services Wash. Pub. Power Supply System, Richland, 1981—. Treas. Gesa Fed. Credit Union, Richland, 1968-74, pres., 1975; bd. dirs. Mid Columbia Mental Health and Psychiat. Hosp., Richland, 1975-85. Served with U.S. Army, 1950-53, Korea. Mem. Assn. Systems Mgmt. (div. dir. 1983-85, div. 20 chmn. 1984-85, Columbia chpt. pres. 1985-86). Avocation: orchardist. Office: WPPSS MD 065 PO Box 968 Richland WA 99352

KLIORE, ARVYDAS JOSEPH, radio scientist; b. Kaunas, Lithuania, Aug. 5, 1935; came to U.S., 1949, naturalized, 1955; s. Bronius Joseph and Antonia (Valaitis) K.; B.S., U. Ill., 1956; M.S., U. Mich., 1957; Ph.D., Mich. State U., 1962; m. Birute Anna Ulenas, Sept. 3, 1960; children—Saule Andrea, Rima Birute. Research engr. Armour Research Found., Chgo., 1956-58, sr. scientist, 1962-65; mem. tech. staff, research scientist Jet Propulsion Lab., Calif. Inst. Tech., Pasadena, 1965—; lectr. UCLA, 1963-64. Recipient NASA medal, 1972, also several Group Achievement awards. Mem. Internat. Com. for Space Research, Am. Astron. Soc. (a founder div. for planetary scis.), Am. Geophys. Union, AAAS, Planetary Soc., Am. Lithuanian Commn. (council), Sigma Xi. Roman Catholic. Club: Backa Athletic. Contbr. radio sci. articles to profl. jours. Office: Calif Inst Tech Jet Propulsion Lab 4800 Oak Grove Dr Pasadena CA 91109

KLIPSCH, LEONA KATHERINE, former newspaper publisher-editor; b. Vancouver, Wash., Feb. 24, 1914; d. Louis John and Marie Rosetta (Debitt) Hinkel; A.B., Smith Coll., 1935; student Sorbonne, Paris, 1934, Columbia U. Grad. Sch. Library Service, summers 1942-44; m. Robert Darius Klipsch, Nov. 25, 1937; children—Phyllis Marie Klipsch Smith, Katharine Klipsch Abbott, Marjorie Klipsch McCracken. Tchr. French and library sci. Marshall U., Huntington, W.Va., 1949-54; br. librarian Albuquerque Public Library, 1955-56; high sch. librarian, Gallup, N.Mex., 1963-65; co-owner, editor Defensor Chieftain, Socorro, N.Mex., 1965-82, pub., 1980-82. Bd. dirs. Socorro Gen. Hosp. Mem. AAUW, PEO, Sigma Delta Chi. Republican. Presbyterian. Author: Treasure Your Love (Librarian prize for jr. novel 1958); (as Jean Kirby) A Very Special Girl, 1963. Home: 1304 Kitt Pl Socorro NM 87801

KLOBE, TOM, art gallery director; b. Mpls., Nov. 26, 1940; s. Charles S. and Lorna (Effertz) K.; m. Delmarie Pauline Motta, June 21, 1975. BFA, U. Hawaii, 1964, MFA, 1968; postgrad., UCLA, 1972-73. Vol. peace corps Alang, Iran, 1964-66; tchr. Calif. State U., Fullerton, 1969-72, Santa Ana (Calif.) Coll., 1972-77, Orange Coast Coll., Costa Mesa, Calif., 1974-77, Golden West Coll., Huntington Beach, Calif., 1976-77; art gallery dir. U. Hawaii, Honolulu, 1977—; acting dir. Downey (Calif.) Mus. Art, 1976; cons. Judiciary Mus., Honolulu, 1982—, Visual and Performing Arts Ctr., Maui, Hawaii, 1984—; exhibit designer Inst. for Astronomy, Honolulu, 1983-86. Recipient Best in Exhbn. Design award Print Casebooks, 1984, 86, Vol. Service award City of Downey, 1977; Exhbn. grantee NEA, 1979—, State Found. Culture and the Arts, 1977—. Mem. Hawaii Mus. Assn., Art Mus. Assn. Roman Catholic. Office: Univ Hawaii Art Gallery 2535 The Mall Honolulu HI 96822

KLOBUCHER, JOHN MARCELLUS, judge; b. Spokane, Wash., July 12, 1932; m. Virginia Rose Nilles; children—Marcella Marie, John Marcellus, Christopher. Student Wash. State U., 1952; student Gonzaga U., 1954-57, J.D., 1960. Bar: Wash. 1960, U.S. Dist. Ct. (ea. dist.) Wash. 1961, U.S. Ct. Appeals (9th cir.) 1972. Law clk. to judge U.S. Dist. Ct. (ea. dist.) Wash., 1960-61; dep. pros. atty. criminal div. Spokane County Pros. Atty.'s Office, 1961-63; ptnr. Ennis & Klobucher, Spokane, 1963-78, Murphy, Bantz, Jansen, Klobucher, Clemons & Bury, Spokane, 1981; U.S. bankruptcy judge Eastern Dist. Wash., Spokane, 1981—. Served with U.S. Army, 1953-54. Mem. Wash. State Bar Assn., Spokane County Bar Assn., Am. Trial Lawyers Assn. Club: Inland Empire Fly Fishing. Home: E 11320 17th Spokane WA 99206 Office: 304 US Post Office Bldg W 904 Riverside Ave Spokane WA 99210 *

KLOHS, MURLE WILLIAM, consulting chemist; b. Aberdeen, S.D., Dec. 24, 1920; s. William Henry and Lowell (Lewis) K.; student Westmar Coll., 1938-40; B.Sc., U. Notre Dame, 1947; Riker fellow, Harvard U., 1950; m. Dolores Catherine Borm, June 16, 1946; children—Wendy C., Linda L. Jr. chemist Harrower Lab., Glendale, Calif., 1947, Rexall Drug Co., Los Angeles, 1947-49; sr. chemist Riker Labs., Inc., Los Angeles, 1949-57, dir. medicinal chemistry, Northridge, Calif., 1957-69, mgr. chem. research dept., 1969-72, mgr. pharm. devel. dept., 1972-73, mgr. tech. liaison and comml. devel., 1973-82; cons. chemist, 1982—. Served to lt. USNR, 1943-46. Mem. Am. Chem. Soc., N.Y. Acad. Scis., Am. Pharm. Assn., Soc. Econ. Botany, Am. Pharmacognosy Soc. Club: Adventures (Los Angeles). Contbr. articles to profl. jours. Home and office: 19831 Echo Blue Dr Lake Wildwood Penn Valley CA 95946

KLOPFER, JEAN MCQUARY, interior design educator; b. Lexington, Ky., Sept. 30, 1922; d. Rodney L. and Helen Maurine (Longman) McQuary; m. Florenz Dudley Klopfer, June 26, 1945 (div. Dec. 1982); children: Richard Dean, Linda Maurine. BA summa cum laude, U. Minn., 1944; MA, Wash. State U., 1950. Instr. Wash. State U., Pullman, 1950-62, assoc. prof. interior design, 1968—, acting chmn. dept. clothing, interior design and textiles, 1980, 82-85. Research reviewer Jour. Interior Design Edn. Research, 1978—. Mem. AAUW, Environ. Design Research Assn., Interior Design Educators Council (circulation mgr. 1978-85, placement 1978-83), Am. Home Econs. Assn., Am. Assn. Housing Educators, Women Investing Now, Phi Kappa Phi, Omicron Nu. Democrat. Avocations: sewing, swimming. Home: NW 1420 Orion Dr Pullman WA 99163 Office: Wash State U White Hall Clothing Interior Design Textiles Pullman WA 99164-2020

KLOPPEL, THOMAS MATHEW, research biologist; b. Denver, Oct. 27, 1950; s. Keith M. and Betty A. (Mathews) K.; m. Carol Greve, June 6, 1972 (div. Sept. 1974); m. Myra Sue Nugent, June 26, 1976; children: Erika L., Seth M. BS, Colo. State U., 1972, MS, 1974; PhD, Purdue U., 1979. Research biologist VA Med. Ctr., Denver, 1982—; asst. prof. U. Colo. Sch. Medicine, Denver, 1982—. Contbr. articles to profl. jours. Am. Cancer Soc. postdoctoral fellow, 1981. Mem. Am. Soc. Cell Biology, Am. Fedn. Clin. Research, Am. Assn. Study Liver Disease. Avocations: handball, hunting, fishing. Home: 16932 E Eastman Pl Aurora CO 80013 Office: VA Med Ctr Box 151 1055 Clermont St Denver CO 80220

KLOSTERMAN, DONALD FRANCIS, executive recruiter, educator; b. Elkton, S.D., June 1, 1939; s. Myles Francis and Frances Marie K.; m. Veralyn Joyce, June 8, 1939; children—Philip, Kara, Scott. M.P.A., Lewis and Clark Coll., 1982; Ph.D. (Univ. Bd. Regents fellow), U. Nebr., 1973. Project cons. Lincoln (Nebr.) Hosp. and Health Council, 1971; prin. investigator research project Edutek, Inc., Lincoln, 1972; dist. dir. and coordinator community mental health/social sci. services Human Relations Services, Biddeford, Maine, 1972-75; dir. psychology Fairview Tng. Center, Salem, Oreg., 1975-81, asst. supt., 1981-83; asst. pub. health adminstr. Marion County Dept. Health, Salem, 1983-84; exec. recruiter, 1985—; instr. Linfield Coll., 1981-83. Democratic precinct committeeman, Salem, 1976—; mem. allocations panel United Way, Salem, 1979-84. Served with U.S. Army, 1958-60. Mem. Am. Psychol. Assn., Oreg. Soc. Tng. Dirs. Presbyterian.

KLOTZ, MEL PAUL, superintendent schools; b. Macklin, Sask., Can., Mar. 3, 1939; s. Joseph Henry and Helen (Leibel) K.; m. Norma Marie Waltemath, Apr. 28, 1962; children—Jeffrey David, Jacqueline Ann. B.Ed., U. Alta. (Can.), Edmonton, 1964; M.Ed., U. Oreg., 1966, Ph.D., 1974. Tchr. Warman Sch. Dist., Sask., 1958-59; prin., tchr. Edmonton Pre-Employment Sch., 1959-64; asst. prin., coordinator spl. edn. St. Joseph Composite High Sch., Edmonton, 1964-68; prin. O'Leary Composite High Sch., Edmonton, 1968-73; dir. high schs. Edmonton Cath. Schs., 1973-75, area supt., 1975—; group leader, presenter Can. Leadership Inst., Banff, Alta., 1978, 82, 83; mem. senate Newman Theol. Coll., Edmonton, 1973-75; mem. edn. adminstrn. adv. com. U. Alta., 1980-83. Contbr. papers to profl. lit. Mem., rep. Edmonton Annexation Com., 1982-83; campaign chmn. Alta. Progressive Conservative Party, 1983. Grantee Alta. Tchrs. Assn., 1970, Edmonton Separate Sch. Dist., 1966, 68, 72; IDEA fellow Kellogg Found., Calif., 1975. Mem. Can. Edn. Assn. (bd. dirs.), Greater Edmonton Tchrs. Conv. Assn. (bd. dirs.), Edmonton Regional Council of Adminstrs. (bd. dirs. 1973—), Can. Legion, Am. Power Squadron, Phi Delta Kappa. Roman Catholic. Lodge: K.C. Home: 16112-88 A Ave, Edmonton, AB Canada T5R 4N6 Office: Edmonton Catholic Schs, 9807 106th St, Edmonton, AB Canada T5K 1

KLOTZ, STEPHEN PAUL, engineer, consultant; b. Rochester, N.Y., Jan. 11, 1947; s. Harold Edward and Lois Virginia (Kober) K. BS in Nuclear and Aerospace Engring., U. Mich., 1970; MS in Aeronautics and Astronautics Engring., Stanford U., 1976, PhD in Aeronautics and Astronautics Engring., 1982. Sr. research assoc. Stanford (Calif.) U., 1981—; cons. IBM, Palo Alto, Calif., 1984-85, Lawrence Livermore (Calif.) Nat. Lab., 1985—. Served to lt., (j.g.) USN, 1970-74. Mem. AIAA, Sigma Xi. Avocations: sailing. Home: 3379 Brittan Ave #10 San Carlos CA 94070 Office: Stanford U Dept Civil Engring Stanford CA 94305

KLUCK, CLARENCE JOSEPH, physician; b. Stevens Point, Wis., June 20, 1929; s. Joseph Bernard and Mildred Lorraine (Helminiak) K.; m. Joan Catherine Larkin, May 26, 1955; children: Paul Bernard, Annette Louise Kluck Winston, David John, Maureen Ellen. BS in Med. Sci., U. Wis., 1951, MD, 1954. Resident San Joaquin Hosp., French Camp, Calif., 1955-56; asst. instr. medicine Ohio State U., Columbus, 1958-60; physician, chief of medicine Redford Med. Ctr., Detroit, 1960-69; practice medicine specializing in internal medicine Denver, 1969-83; med. dir. Atlantic Richfield Co., Denver, 1983-85; corp. med. dir. Cyprus Minerals Co., Englewood, Colo., 1985—; bd. dirs. Climbo Catering, Detroit, 1967-69, Met. Labs., Denver, 1970-81; pres., bd. dirs. Pack Investments, Inc., Denver, 1985—. Contbr. articles to profl. jours. Served to capt. U.S. Army, 1956-58. Recipient Century Club award Boy Scouts Am., 1972. Mem. Am. Occupational Med. Assn., Rocky Mountain Acad. Occupational Medicine (bd. dirs. 1985-88), Denver Med. Soc. (bd. dirs. 1973-74, council mem. 1981—), Colo. Med. Soc. (del. 1973-74, 81—), Am. Mining Congress Health Commn., Am. Soc. Internal Medicine, Colo. Soc. Internal Medicine. Roman Catholic. Clubs: Flatirons (Boulder, Colo.). Avocations: fishing, hiking, skiing, flying, golf. Home: 5245 E Oxford Ave Englewood CO 80110 Office: Cyprus Minerals Co 7200 S Alton Way Englewood CO 80112

KLUGMAN, ROBERT, brewery executive; b. Phila., Sept. 20, 1947; s. Jack and Marian (Eveloff) K.; m. Kathleen Burke Martin, Apr. 28, 1979; children: Maura Martin, Terence Burke. B.A., Amherst Coll., 1969; M.B.A., Harvard U., 1973. With Leo Burnett USA, Chgo., 1973-79, v.p., 1978-79; v.p. mktg. Adolph Coors Co., Golden, Colo., 1979—. Club: Olde Boys Rugby Assn. (Denver). Home: 773 Williams St Denver CO 80218 Office: Adolph Coors Co Golden CO 80401

KLUTE, PETER PEARSALL, public relations executive; b. Detroit, Sept. 12, 1941; s. Anthony Francis and Mary Gertrude (Pearsall) K.; m. Patricia Ann Kahler, May 8, 1965; children: Kathleen, Peter, Paul, Michelle, Jennifer. BA in Communication-Arts, Loyola U., 1964; postgrad., Boston U., 1966, Am. U., 1968, Pepperdine U., 1973. Supr. of news bur. So. Calif. Gas Co., Los Angeles, 1963-74; radio-tv pub. info. officer Air Force Systems Command, Washington, 1964-68; news bur. editor Flying Tiger Line, Los Angeles, 1974-75; tech. programs devel. Detroit Edison Co., 1975-78; mgr. pub. and employee info. Ariz. Pub. Service Co., Phoenix, 1978-84; owner Klute Communications, Scottsdale, Ariz., 1984—. V.p. Community Info. and Referral Services, Phoenix, 1981-87, pres., 1987—; pub. relations com. Valley of the Sun United Way, Phoenix, 1985—; com. mem. Fiesta Bowl, Phoenix, 1986—, chmn. publicity com., 1987. Served to capt. USAF, 1964-68. Mem. Pub. Relations Soc. of Am. (pres. Phoenix chpt. 1981-82, South Pacific dist. chmn. 1985, nat. assembly del. at large 1986, counselors acad. mem. 1984—, bd. dirs. 1987-88, PERCY award 1984, Pres.' Citations, 1984, 85), Scottsdale C. of C. (govtl. affairs com. 1985—, chmn. local affairs com. 1986-87). Republican. Roman Catholic. Club: Phoenix City (mem. programs com. 1985—, chmn. pub. relations com. 1986, bd. dirs. 1986—). Lodge: Rotary. Avocations: music, electronics, golfing, gardening, photography. Home: 6625 E North Ln Scottsdale AZ 85253 Office: Klute Communications 7500 E Butherus Dr Suite K Scottsdale AZ 85260

KNAEBEL, MICHAEL LEE, naval officer, electronics technician; b. New Albany, Ind., July 29, 1946; s. Vincent Joseph, Jr. and Anna Lee (Milligan) K.; children—Nicole Marie, Michael Lee. B.S.E.S.C., Purdue U., 1975, M.S.E. (Sec. Navy scholar), 1976. Cert. electronics technician Internat. Soc. Cert. Electronics Technicians; lic. real estate salesperson, Calif. Commd. ensign U.S. Navy, 1975, advanced through grades to lt. comdr., 1984; electronics technician, 1967-75; main propulsion asst USS. Blandy, 1976-79; head missile systems br. engring. div. Naval Plant Rep. Office, Strategic Systems Project Office, Sunnyvale, Calif., 1979-84; aast. head guidance sect. Fire Control and Guidance br. Strategic Systems Program, Washington, 1984-86; head engring. div. Naval Plant Rep. Office, Sunnyvale, Calif., 1986—; lectr. design of missile systems. Recipient award of merit Purdue U.-Gen. Dynamics Corp., 1975. Mem. AIAA, Am. Soc. Naval Engrs., U.S. Naval Inst. Planetary Soc., Order of the Engr., Am. Legion, Purdue Alumni Assn. Phi Beta Kappa, Tau Beta Pi, Phi Kappa Phi, Sigma Pi Sigma. Roman Catholic. Home: 1295 Ayala Dr #2 Sunnyvale CA 94086

KNAKE, BARRY EDWARD, management consulting executive, industrial psychologist; b. Chgo., Oct. 1, 1946; s. Louis Edward and Betty Agnus (Ryden) K.; m. Rita Kaye Watson, Feb. 7, 1967; children: Sean, Ryan, Julene. BA, Eastern Wash. U., 1969, MS, 1971. Grad. teaching fellow Eastern Wash. U., Cheney, 1969-70; personnel analyst City of Seattle, 1972-74; psychology instr. So. Seattle Community Coll., 1974; personnel psychologist U.S. Office Personnel Mgmt., Seattle, 1974-81; pres. KMB Assocs., Seattle, 1981—. Contbr. articles on personnel mgmt., testing, job analysis, affirmative action, job element testing. Mem. Seattle Urban League Employment Com., Seattle, 1983-86; mem. Gov.'s Com. on Employment of Handicapped, Olympia, 1980-86. Mem. AAAS, Am. Psychol. Assn. (assoc.). Avocations: science, bowling, hiking, swimming, astronomy. Home and Office: 6730 13th Ave SW Seattle WA 98106

KNAPP, CLEON T., publisher; b. Los Angeles, Apr. 28, 1937; s. Cleon T. and Sally (Brasfield) K.; m. Elizabeth Ann Wood, Mar. 17, 1979; children: Jeffrey James, Brian Patrick, Aaron Bradley, Laura Ann. Student, UCLA, 1955-58. With John C. Brasfield Pub. Corp. (purchased co. in 1965, changed name to Knapp Communications Corp. 1977); now pub. Bon Appetit mag., Archtl. Digest, Home mag., Los Angeles, 1958—; chief exec. officer Bon Appetit mag., Archtl. Digest, Home mag., 1965—, chmn. bd.; chmn. Knapp Press, Rosebud Press; owner Wilshire Mktg. Corp., Wood Knapp Home Video; organizer, dir. Wilshire Bancorp. Trustee UCLA Found.; bd. dirs. Damon Runyon-Walter Winchell Cancer Fund. Mem. Mag. Pubs. Assn. (bd. dirs.). Office: Knapp Communications Corp 5900 Wilshire Blvd Los Angeles CA 90036

KNAPP, EBER GUY, accountant; b. Seattle, Sept. 18, 1916; s. Eber G. and Ernestine C. (Verner) K.; student Wilson's Bus. Coll., 1938-39, U. So. Calif., 1946-47; m. M. Lorraine Knapp, July 2, 1947; children—Candyce Lorraine, Ardyce Christine, Carol Lynn. Cert. acct. Owner, Knapp's Tax & Bus. Service, Westminster, Calif., 1959—; overall coordinator Orange County (Calif.) Am. Assn. Ret. Persons Tax-Aide Program. Mem. Vice chmn. Mobile Home Commn., Westminster, Calif. Served with U.S. Army, 1941-45. Mem. Inland Soc. Tax Cons., Assn. Bus. and Tax Cons. Orange County (v.p.), Am. Legion, Calif. Assn. Ind. Accts. (charter), Nat. Assn. Pub. Accts., VFW. Republican. Mem. Christian Ch. Author: Groom's Survival Handbook, or How to Teach Your Bride to Cook, 1982. Home: 7152 Santee Ave PO Box 1 Westminster CA 92684

KNAPP, JOHN KIRKPATRICK, science educator; b. Salem, Oreg., Sept. 3, 1946; s. Charles Rowland Knapp and Frances L. (Weatherford) Knapp Hammer; m. Deborah Diane Sept, Apr. 9, 1976; children: Nicole F., Jonathan R. BS in Chemistry and Phys. Sci., Oreg. Coll. Edn., 1968; BS in Agrl. Food Tech., Oreg. State U., 1971; MS in Earth Sci. Edn., Boise State U., 1978. Cert. tchr., Idaho; FDA Food Processing cert. Prodn. asst. Green Giant Co., Waitsburg, Wash., 1974-76; prodn. mgr. Clarmont West Inc., Hillsboro, Oreg., 1976-77; grad. asst. Boise (Idaho) State U., 1977-78; instr. sci. Castleford (Idaho) Sch. Dist., 1978-80, Gem County Sch. Dist., Emmett, Idaho, 1980—. Served with Oreg. N.G., 1970—. Mem. AAAS, Idaho Sci. Tchrs. Assn. (dist. rep. 1985—), Gem County Edn. Assn., Idaho Edn. Assn., NEA, N.G. Assn. Republican. Presbyterian. Avocations: photography, outdoor activities. Home: 611 S DeClark Emmett ID 83617 Office: Emmett High Sch 304 E 4th St Emmett ID 83617

KNAPP, THOMAS EDWIN, sculptor, painter; b. Gillette, Wyo., Sept. 28, 1925; s. Chester M. and Georgia Mabel (Blankenship) K.; m. Dorothy Wellborn; children: Gordon, Kathy, Dan, Kent, Keith. Student, Santa Rosa Jr. Coll., 1952-53; A.A., Calif. Coll. Arts and Crafts, 1953-54; student, Art Ctr. Sch., Los Angeles, 1954-55. Animation artist Walt Disney Studios, Burbank, Calif., 1954-56, Portrait & Hobby Camera Shops, WyoFoto Studios, Cody, Wyo., 1956-64; owner Rocky Mountain Land Devel. Corp., Cody, Wyo., 1965-66; comml. artist Mountain States Telephone Co., Albuquerque, 1966-69; lectr. at art seminars. Exhibited one-man shows, Cody County Art League, 1968, Jamison Gallery, Santa Fe, 1969, Mesilla Gallery, 1971, Inn of Mountain Gods, Mescalero Apache Reservations, N.Mex., 1978, Mountain Oyster Club, Tucson, 1978, Dos Pajaros Gallery, El Paso, 1978, (with Dorothy Wellborn) joint shows, Rosquist Gallery, Tucson, 1975, 77, Colony House, Roswell, N.Mex., 1974, 75, (with Michael Coleman), Zantman Gallery, Palm Desert Calif., 1977, group shows, Saddleback Inn, Santa Ana, Calif., 1968-77, Zantman Gallery, Carmel, Calif., 1975, 76, 77, Borglum Meml. Sculpture Exhbn. Nat. Cowboy Hall of Fame, Oklahoma City, 1975-76, Maxwell Gallery, San Francisco, 1975; represented permanent collections, Whitney Gallery Western Art, Cody, Senator Quinn Meml. Auditorium, Spencer, Mass., Heritage Mus., Anchorage, Indpls. Mus. Art, Mescalero Tribe, N.Mex.; works include Dance of the Mountain Spirits (Blue Ribbon award 1976), Laguna Eagle dancer (spl. award 1974, Blue Ribbon los Angeles Indian Art Show, 1975-76), Santa Clara Buffalo dancer (Spl. award San Antonio Indian Nat. show 1974, Spl. award Los Angeles Indian show 1976), Mandan chieftan (Spl. award San Diego Indian show 1974, Spl. award Los Angeles Indian show 1976); commd. to sculpt bronze statue of Tex. ranger Capt. Bill McMurrey, now in Tex. Ranger Mus., San Antonio, bronze Giant Galapagos Tortoise now in pvt. collection. Active Boy Scouts Am., 1947-68. Served with USN, World War II, Korea. Decorated Air medal; recipient Order Arrow award Boy Scout Am., 1968. Mem. Am. Foundrymen's Soc., N.Mex. Amigos, Mensa. Club: Safari Internat. Homeand Office: PO Box 510 Ruidoso Downs NM 88346

KNAUSS, FREDERICK ERWIN, insurance company executive; b. San Francisco, Aug. 17, 1947; s. Fred Gottlieb and Olga (Frank) K.; m. Barbara Santana, Apr. 3, 1971 (div.). BA, U. San Francisco, 1969, JD, 1971. Bar: Calif. 1972, U.S. Dist. Ct. (no. dist.) Calif. 1972, U.S. Ct. Appeals (9th cir.) 1972. Atty. Hansen & Sharum, Los Altos, Calif., 1973-1974; assoc. counsel, asst. sec. Pacific Standard Life Ins. Co., Davis, Calif., 1974-1978; v.p. Johnson & Higgins, San Francisco, 1978-86; exec. v.p. Calif. Accts. Mut. Ins. Co., Palo Alto, 1986—. Active Assn. for Calif. Tort Reform, SPUR. Served to capt. U.S. Army, 1972-78. Mem. Bar Assn. San Francisco, Calif. Bar Assn. Republican. Avocations: gardening, flying, skiing. Home: 17523 High Rd Sonoma CA 95476

KNECHT, RONALD LEE, economist; b. Belleville, Ill., May 4, 1949; s. Wayne Alfred and Lela Kathryn (Berlin) K. BA in Math., U. Ill., 1971, postgrad., 1977. Registered profl. mech. engr., Calif. Asst. city engr. City of Urbana, Ill., 1972-73; research engr. U. Ill., Urbana, 1973-77; cons. Calif. Energy Commn., Sacramento, 1977-78, adv., economist, 1978-79; project mgr. supr. Calif. Pub. Utility Commn., San Francisco, 1979-86; sr. economist Dames & Moore, San Francisco, 1986; prin. QED Research, Inc., Palo Alto, Calif., 1986—; cons., expert witness States of Ill., 1975-76, Mich., 1980, City of Phila., 1985, State Consumer Agys., Ga., Minn., Pa., Ill., 1979-84, various utility cos., 1977-86. Contbr. articles to profl. jours. Sec. City Zoning Bd. Appeals, Urbana, 1975-77. Mem. AAAS, NSPE, Nat. Assn. Bus. Economists. Avocations: sports, film, symphony, ballet. Home: 1995 Chestnut #304 San Francisco CA 94123 Office: QED Research Inc 125 California Ave Suite 200 Palo Alto CA 94306

KNECHTLI, RONALD CHARLES, retired research scientist; b. Geneva, Aug. 14, 1927; s. Alfred Charles and Edith (Beran) K.; m. Diane Frances Weisul, Nov. 7, 1953; children: Alain, Bernard, Daniel. Diploma, Swiss Fed. Inst. Tech., 1950, PhD, 1955. Research engr. Brown Boveri & Co., Switzerland, 1950-51, 52-53; research asst. MIT, Cambridge, 1951-52; sr. scientist Hughes Research Labs. div. Hughes Aircraft Co., Malibu, Calif., 1958-86. Contbr. articles profl. jours.; patentee in field. Recipient Outstanding Research award RCA Labs., 1957, L.A. Hyland Patent award, 1974. Mem. Am. Phys. Soc., IEEE, AIAA, Sigma Xi. Republican. Presbyterian. Home: 22929 Ardwick St Woodland Hills CA 91364

KNEPP, GERALD EVERETT, hospital administrator; b. La Harpe, Kans., Jan. 21, 1934; s. Alvin Lester, Wilma Manetta (Johnson) K.; m. Tona Louise Shanks, Sept. 1, 1961 (div. May 1982); children—Kristopher Karsten, Karla Kristin (dec.); 1 stepchild, Steven Lynn York. B.S.B.A., U. Kans., 1956; M.P.A., U. Mo., 1971. Asst. controller St. Lukes Hosp., Kansas City, Mo., 1961-62; assoc. adminstr. North Kansas City Mem. Hosp., 1962-74; sr. cons. Peat-Marwick-Mitchell, 1974-75; adminstr. Panorama Community Hosp., Calif., 1975-80, Western Park Hosp., Los Angeles, 1980, Redding Med. Ctr., Calif., 1980—; preceptor masters program U. So. Calif., Los Angeles, 1970-80; bd. dirs. Downtown Hosp., Kansas City, 1974-76. Contbr. articles to profl. jours. Exec. sec. County Indigent Med. Fund, Clay County, Mo., 1965-75; mem. Gov.'s Adv. Council on Drug and Alcoholism, Planning Council Adv. Com., Shasta County Mental Health Adv. Com. Served to capt. USAF, 1956-59. Recipient Disting. Service award Mo. Jaycees, 1968, Outstanding Young Man award 1968, Outstanding Young Man Am. award, 1970, Circle of Excellence award Nat. Med. Enterprises, Inc., 1985. Mem. Hosp. Council No. Calif. (Blue Cross adv. com. 1982—, fin. and econ. com. 1982—), Healthcare Fin. Mgmt. Assn. (pres. 1968-69) (Follmer award 1968, Reeves award 1972, Muncie award 1978), Hosp. Council So. Calif. (bd. 1979-80), Am. Hosp. Assn., SAR. Republican. Methodist. Lodges: Rotary, Elks, Masons, Shriners. Home: 562 Rafael St Redding CA 96002 Office: Redding Med Center 1450 Liberty St Redding CA 96001

KNIERIM, K. PHILLIP, lawyer; b. Tacoma, Nov. 18, 1945; s. Oscar Fitzpatrick and Dorothy Margaret (King) K.; m. Pamela Gail Waller. B.S. in Sociology, U. Wash., Seattle, 1968; J.D. (Harlan Fiske Stone scholar 1971-72, James Kent scholar 1972-74), Columbia U., 1974. Dir. human resources planning N.Y. Telephone Co., 1969-71; assoc. Pillsbury, Madison & Sutro, San Francisco, 1974-76, Fulop, Polston, Burns & McKittrick, Beverly Hills, Calif., 1976-81, Gordon, Weinberg & Zipser, Los Angeles, 1982-84, Wood, Lucksinger & Epstein, Los Angeles, 1984-85; sole practice Los Angeles, 1985—; judge pro tem Beverly Hills Mcpl. Ct., 1979—, Los Angeles Mcpl. Ct., 1985—; guest lectr. Pepperdine U. Law Sch., Los Angeles, 1981; mem. Los Angeles City Atty.'s Regulatory Reform Task Force, 1982—; mem. U.S. Army War Coll. Nat. Security Seminar, 1984. Chmn. pub. affairs Planned Parenthood N.Y.C., 1971-74; gen. counsel Los Angeles Ballet, 1979-80; chmn. bd. Bethune Ballet, 1981-82, pres., 1982-83. Served with RNSC, 1957-63; with USNR, 1969. Decorated Nat. Def. Service medal; Order Hosp. St. John Jerusalem. Mem. ABA (vice chmn. young lawyers div. com. jud. tenure, selection and performance 1980-81), Calif. State Bar (del. 1980—), Los Angeles County Bar Assn. (arbitrator 1979—), Beverly Hills Bar Assn. (chmn. environ. law com. 1979-82, vice chmn. resolutions com. 1983-85), Beverly Hills Barristers (gov. 1979-81), U.S. Combined Tng. Assn., English Speaking Union. Anglican. Clubs: West Hills Hunt; Brit. United Services. Home: 11700 Iowa Ave Apt 304 Los Angeles CA 90025 Office: 1900 Ave of Stars Suite 2200 Los Angeles CA 90067

KNIERIM, ROBERT VALENTINE, electrical engineer, consultant; b. Oakland, Calif., Sept. 27, 1916; s. Otto Valentine and Edith May (Bell) K.; m. Esther Perry Bateman, July 10, 1954; children: Kathleen Dianne, David Lyell, Daniel Goddard. BS, U. Calif., Berkeley, 1941; postgrad., U. Pitts., 1942, U. Colo., 1944-45, Raytheon Field Engring Sch, 1945. Registered profl. elec. engr., Calif. Marine elec. engr. U.S. Maritime Commn., Oakland, 1943-44; elec. engr. U.S. Bur. Reclamation, Denver, 1944-45, Sacramento, 1945-48; field engr. Raytheon Corp., Waltham, Mass., 1945; electronics engr. Sacramento Signal Depot, 1948-49; assoc. elec. engr. Calif. Office Architecture and Constrn., 1949-57, sr. elec. engr., 1957-76; cons. engring. 1976. Mem. Century Club of Golden Empire Council Boy Scouts Am., 1969—, instnl. rep., 1948-54, dist. chmn. camping and activities com., 1951-54. Mem. Sacramento Engrs. Club (charter), IEEE (sr., life), Nat. Rifle Assn. (life), Sierra Club (life, chpt. treas. 1962-65), Nat. Assn. Corrosion Engrs. (life), Calif. Alumni Assn. (life), Eta Kappa Nu, Alpha Phi Omega (life). Republican. Congregationalist. Lodge: Masons. Home and Office: Cons Elec Engring 10325 SW Ashton Circle Wilsonville OR 97070

KNIGHT, CHARLES ALFRED, atmospheric scientist; b. Chgo., Mar. 28, 1936; s. Frank Hyneman and Ethel Eunice (Verry) K.; m. Nancy Elizabeth Chase, Jan. 13, 1962. MS, U. Chgo., 1957, PhD, 1959. Research assoc. U. Wash., Seattle, 1959-61; geologist U.S. Geol. Survey, Denver, 1962; scientist Nat. Ctr. Atmospheric Research, Boulder, Colo., 1962—. Author: Freezing of Supercooled Liquids, 1967; editor: Hail, 1976, The National Hail Research Experiment, 1981; contbr. articles to profl. jours. Mem. Am. Meteorol. Soc., Am. Geophys. Union, Glaciol. Soc., Soc. for Cryobiology. Avocations: mountaineering. Home: 1313 7th St Boulder CO 80302 Office: Nat Ctr Atmospheric Research PO Box 3000 Boulder CO 80307

KNIGHT, DAVID EDWARDS, marketing professional; b. St. Louis, June 10, 1951; s. Harold Edwards and Nancy Jane (Coffman) K.; m. Nancy Anne Casey, Apr. 18, 1982; children: Casey Jane, Graham Edwards. Student, U. Colo., 1969-71; BJ, U. Mo., 1974. With pub. relations, promotions dept. Six Flags Over Mid-Am., Eureka, Mo., 1971-74, State Fair of Tex., Dallas, 1974; mgr. spl. events R.J. Reynolds Tobacco Co., Winston-Salem, N.C., 1974-81; mgr. sports promotions The Southland Corp., Dallas, 1981; TV producer Casey/Knight Prodns., Salt Lake City, 1982; dir. mktg. Pro Rodeo Cowboys Assn. Properties, Inc., Colorado Springs, Colo., 1982-86; exec. v.p. Pro Rodeo Cowboys Assn., Colorado Springs, Colo., 1986—; v.p. TRX, Inc., Colorado Springs, 1985—. Contbr. sports articles to local newspapers. Avocations: tennis, sailing, cycling. Home: 590 Crosstrail Dr Colorado Springs CO 80906 Office: Pro Rodeo Cowboys Assn Properties Inc 101 Pro Rodeo Dr Colorado Springs CO 80919

KNIGHT, DOUGLAS WAYNE, computer science educator; b. Batavia, N.Y., Oct. 7, 1938; s. Harold Stanley and Marjory Ruth (Bryde) K.; m. Rose Marie Heywood, June 8, 1961; children: Christian, Jennifer, Eric. Student, MIT, 1956-57; BS, Ariz. State U., 1961, MS, 1971, PhD, 1975. Geophysicist Shell Oil Co., Houston, 1961-67; supr. data processing Dynalectron, Pueblo, Colo., 1974-79; program mgr. Kentron Hawaii, Dallas, 1979; head computer sci. dept., acting head engring. dept. U. So. Colo., Pueblo, 1980—; cons. N.Mex. Highlands, Las Vegas, 1985; faculty assoc. Ariz. State U., Tempe, 1971-73; prin. Computerland of Colorado Springs, Colo., 1979-81. Contbr. articles to numerous govt. publs. Mem. Assn. Computing Machinery (pres. Ariz. State U. chpt. 1971), Pueblo Geneol. Soc. Republican. Episcopalian. Avocations: fishing, gaming, collecting. Office: U So Colo 2200 Bonforte Pueblo CO 81001

KNIGHT, GEORGE PRESTON, psychology educator; b. Denver, Nov. 21, 1950; s. George P. and Doris (Scott) K.; Janet C. Anderson, Sept. 1, 1974; children: Christopher John, Kathryn Michelle. BA, Macalester Coll., 1972; MA, U. Calif., Riverside, 1976, PhD, 1980. Teaching asst. U. Calif., Riverside, 1975-80; cons. Vet. Hosp., Loma Linda, Calif., 1979-80; mem. faculty U. Ariz., Tucson, 1980-86; assoc. prof. psychology Ariz. State U., Tempe, 1986—. Contbr. articles to profl. jours. Mem. Soc. Research in Child Devel., Southwestern Soc. Research in Human Devel. Office: Ariz State U Dept Psychology Tempe AZ 85287

KNIGHT, JACK LARRY, management consultant; b. Guin, Ala., Oct. 30, 1939; s. Hillman T. and Robbie M. (Sandlin) K.; m. Wynelle Turner, Oct. 12, 1958; children: Eric Alan, Keith Edward. PharmB, Samford U., 1961; MS in Health and Hosp. Adminstrn., U. Ala., Birmingham, 1972, MPH, 1973; MHRD, U. Ariz., 1987. Registered profl. pharmacist. Chief pharmacist USPHS, N.C., Okla., Ariz., 1961-68; health adminstr. USPHS, 1968-74; health adminstr., cons., educator USPHS, Tucson, 1974-78; dir. Indian Health Service Mgmt. Support Ctr., Tucson, 1978-86; pres. The Roundtable Assocs., Tucson, 1986—; adj. asst. prof. U. Als., Birmingham, 1973-75; assoc. faculty Pima Community Coll., Tucson, 1976, U. Wis., Stevens Point, 1978; mgr. Indian Health Service Info. Systems, Rockville, Md., 1979-80. Rexall Drug Co. scholar, U. Ala., 1957-61; fellow USPHS, U. Ala., 1970-72; recipient spl. assignment award USPHS, Washington, 1980. Mem. Assn. Univ. Programs in Health Adminstrn., Am. Pub. Health Assn., Am. Hosp. Assn., Nat. Eagle Scout Assn., Ariz. Med. Assn. (rural and migrant health com. 1974-76). Democrat. Episcopalian. Avocations: skiing, reading, hiking, photography. Office: Roundtable Assocs PO Box 37166 Tucson AZ 85740-7166

KNIGHT, PHILIP H(AMPSON), shoe manufacturing company executive; b. Portland, Oreg., Feb. 24, 1938; s. William W. and Lota (Hatfield) K.; m. Penelope Parks, Sept. 13, 1968; children: Matthew, Travis. B.B.A., U. Oreg.; M.B.A., Stanford U. C.P.A., Oreg. Pres., chmn., chief exec. officer Nike, Inc., Beaverton, Oreg., 1967—; dir. Metheus Corp. Trustee Reed Coll., Portland; mem. adv. council Stanford U. Grad. Sch.; bd. dirs. U.S.-Asian Bus. Council, Washington. Served to 1st lt. AUS, 1959-60. Named Oreg. Businessman of Yr., 1982. Mem. Am. Inst. C.P.A.s. Republican. Episcopalian. Office: Nike Inc 3900 SW Murray Blvd Beaverton OR 97005

KNIGHT, VICK (RALPH), JR., educational administrator; b. Lakewood, Ohio, Apr. 6, 1928; s. Vick Ralph and Janice (Higgins) K.; B.S., U. So. Calif., 1952; M.A., Los Angeles State Coll., 1956; postgrad. Whittier Coll., 1959-61, Long Beach State Coll., 1960-61, Calif. State Coll.-Fullerton, 1961-64, Claremont Grad. Sch., 1963-65; Ed.D., Calif. Coast U., 1985; m. Beverly Joyce McKeighan, Apr. 14, 1949 (div. 1973); children—Stephen Foster, Mary Ann; m. 2d, Carolyn Schlee, June 6, 1981. Producer-dir. Here Comes Tom Harmon radio series ABC, Hollywood, Calif., 1947-50; tchr., vice-prin. Ranchito Sch. Dist., Pico Rivera, Calif., 1952-59; prin. Kraemer Intermediate Sch., Placentia, Calif., 1959-64; dir. instructional services Placentia Unified Sch. Dist., 1964-65, asst. supt., 1965-71; program dir. World Vista Travel Service, 1970-72; dir. grad. extension La Verne Coll., 1971-73; v.p. Nat. Gen. West Investments, 1971-74; dir. community relations and devel. Childrens Hosp. of Orange County (Calif.), 1974-84; sr. dir. curriculum and edn. services Elsinore Union High Sch. Dist., Lake Elsinore, Calif., 1985—; pres. Aristan Assocs.; dir. Key Records, Hollywood. Dist. chmn. Valencia council Boy Scouts Am.; chmn. Cancer Soc. Partners of Ams., also chmn. Sister City Com.; chmn. of Community Chest Drives; chmn. adv. com. Esperenza Hosp.; mem. Educare; hon. life mem. Calif. PTA. Bd. dirs. U. Calif.-Irvine Friends of Library, pres., 1975-77; bd. dirs. Muckenthaler Cultural Groups Found.; chmn. bd. William Claude Fields Found. Served with USN, 1946-48. Named One of Five Outstanding Young Men, Calif. Jr. C. of C., 1959; recipient Distinguished Citizen award Whittier Coll., 1960; Educator of Yr. award Orange County Press Club, 1971; Author and Book award U. Calif., 1973; Children's Lit. award Calif. State U.-Fullerton, 1979; Bronze Pelican award Boy Scouts Am. Mem. Nat. Sch. Pub. Relations Assn. (regional v.p.), U.S. (dir.), Calif. (state v.p.), Pico Rivera (pres.) jr. chambers commerce, Audubon Soc., Western Soc. Naturalists, Calif. Tchrs. Assn., NEA, Internat. Platform Assn., ASCAP, Soc. Children's Book Writers, Authors Guild, Authors League Am., Anti-Slubberdegullion Soc., Bank Dicks, Assn. Hosp. Devel., Art Experience, Good Bears of World, Los Compadres con Libros, Blue Key, Skull and Dagger, Les Amis du Vin, Phi Sigma Kappa, Alpha Delta Sigma, E Clampus Vitus, Theta Nu Epsilon. Kiwanian (pres.), Mason. Club: West Atwood Yacht (commodore). Writer weekly Nature Notebook newspaper columns, 1957—; fine arts editor Placentia Courier. Editor curriculum guides: New Math., Lang. Arts, Social Scis., Pub. Relations, Biol. Sci. Substitute Tchrs. Author: (ecology textbooks) It's Our World; It's Our Future; It's Our Choice; Snakes of Hawaii; Earle the Squirrel; Night the Crayons Talked; My Word!; Send for Haym Salomon!; Joby and the Wishing Well; Twilight of the Animal Kingdom; A Tale of Twos; Who's Zoo; A Navel Salute; Friend or Enema?; also math. instrn. units; contbr. articles to various jours. Home: PO Box 4664 Canyon Lake CA 92380 Office: Elsinore Union High Sch Dist 1201 W Graham Lake Elsinore CA 92330

KNIGHT, VIRGINIA LUCINDA, interior designer; b. Cleve., Dec. 10, 1931; d. Vick Ralph and Janice (Higgins) Knight. Student Los Angeles City Coll., 1951, UCLA, 1975—. Designer Albert Van Luit Wallpaper Co., Los Angeles, 1955; interior designer W. & J. Sloane Co., Beverly Hills, Calif., 1955-62, Barnett Bros., Beverly Hills, 1962-69; sr. designer for Cannell & Chaffin, 1969-82; free lance designer, 1982—; instr. UCLA Extension, 1981—. Mem. bldg. and sites com. Los Angeles Epilepsy Soc.; bd. dirs. Los Angeles Community Design Center, 1974—. Mem. Am. Inst. Interior Designers (corp. mem. bd. govs., v.p. 1971-76, chmn. community affairs com.), Am. Soc. Interior Designers (corp. mem. 1975—), Archtl. Guild U. So. Calif. Republican. Club: Altrusa (charter; South West Los Angeles, pres. 1967-69, dir. 1969-72). Home: 1601 Sunset Plaza Dr Los Angeles CA 90069 Office: 1601 Sunset Plaza Dr Los Angeles CA 90069

KNIGHTON, ROBERT SYRON, neurosurgeon, educator; b. Vallejo, Calif., Aug. 17, 1914; s. David William and Mae Virginia (Clauson) K.; m. Cora Louise Taylor, Sept. 9, 1939; children—Robert W., George L., James E., Joan L., Thomas D. B.S., Pacific Union Coll., 1939; M.D., Loma Linda U., 1942. Diplomate Am. Bd. Neurol. Surgery. Intern Los Angeles County Hosp., 1942-43; resident in neurosurgery White Meml. Hosp., Los Angeles, 1943-44, 46-47; NRC fellow Montreal Neurol. Inst., Que., Can., 1947-48; chief div. neurosurgery Henry Ford Hosp., Detroit, 1952-71, chmn. dept. neurology and neurosurgery, 1971-79, emeritus chmn. dept. neurology and neurosurgery, cons., 1979—; prof. neurosurgery, chmn. div. neurosurgery Loma Linda U., Calif., 1981—; chief neurosurgeon Jerry L. Pettis VA Hosp., Loma Linda, Calif., 1982—; clin. prof. surgery U. Mich., Ann Arbor, 1971-79. Editor: Reticular Formations of Brain, 1957, Pain, 1966; contbr. papers to profl. publs. Served to capt. U.S. Army, 1944-46; ETO. Fellow ACS; mem. Soc. Neurol. Surgeons, Am. Assn. Neurol. Surgeons, Am. Acad. Neurol. Surgeons (v.p. 1977), Neurosurg. Soc. Am. (pres. 1975), Calif. Med. Assn., San Bernardino County Med. Soc. Home: 9388 Avenida San Timoteo Cherry Valley CA 92223 Office: Loma Linda U Div Neurol Surgery 11234 Anderson Loma Linda CA 92354

KNIPE, WILLIAM BERNARD, JR., real estate broker, consultant; b. Emmett, Idaho, July 27, 1923; s. William Bernard and Frances Kathryn (Jones) K.; student U. Idaho, 1941-42, 46, Boise State U., 1946-47, U. Ariz., 1947-49; B.S., Calif. Western U., 1978, M.B.A., 1979; Ph.D., Calif. Coast U., 1983; m. Diane Adele Shaw, Nov. 25, 1960; children—Bradford T., Quentin M., John P., William Bernard III, Curtis A., Karen, Kathleen, Kellett. Staff adjuster Motor Ins. Corp., Gen. Motors Corp., Boise, Idaho, 1949-51; gen. mgr. The Sawtooth Co., Boise, 1952-62; cattle rancher, Horseshoe Bend, Idaho, 1963-69; pres. Robison Realty, Inc., Boise, 1974—, Knipe Land & Livestock Co., Boise, 1976—, William Knipe & Assocs., Boise, 1970—; cons. to farms and ranches, 1967—. Mem. adv. bd. Am. Security Council, 1968—, Security and Intelligence Fund, 1969—, Nat. Com. for Employer Support of the Guard and Res., 1973—. Served with USAAF, 1943-46; ATO. Cert. residential specialist. Mem. Jerusalem Cattle Assn. (pres. 1966-68), Farm and Land Inst. (accredited), Nat. Assn. Realtors, Nat. Mktg. Inst., Nat. Cattlemen's Assn., Am. Soc. Farm Mgrs. and Rural Appraisers, Nat. Pilots Assn., Nat. Assn. Rev. Appraisers (cert. rev. appraiser), Assn. M.B.A. Execs., Am. Soc. Agrl. Consultants (cert.). Phi Delta Theta. Republican. Roman Catholic. Club: Elks. Contbr. articles to profl. jours. Office: 1120 Lewis St Boise ID 83712 Address: PO Box 986 Boise ID 83701

KNITTER, KEITH WAYNE, utility rate/financial analyst, consultant; b. Chgo., June 10, 1949; s. Gerald Howard and Dorothy Jane (Dorge) K.; m. Stephanie Alane Thompson, July 2, 1983. B.A. in Math., Wilamette U., 1971, M. Adminstrn., 1976; student in stats. U. Wash., 1971-72. Indsl. engr. Boeing Airplane Co., Seattle, 1972-74; research analyst Puget Sound Power & Light Co., Bellevue, Wash., 1976-77; prin. analyst R. W. Beck and Assocs., Seattle, 1977-87, Econ. and Engring. Services, Inc., 1987—; chmn. load forecasting workshop NW Pub. Power Assn., 1981. Contbr. papers to various symposiums. Republican. Congregationalist. Clubs: Fleet 14 Catalina 27 (sec./treas. 1980-81, vice capt. 1981-82, measurer 1986), East Lake Wash. Audubon. Home: 10104 117th Pl NE Kirkland WA 98033 Office: Econ and Engring Services Inc 12301 NE 10th Place PO Box 4046 Bellevue WA 98009

KNIZE, MARK GARRETT, biomedical scientist; b. Chgo., Feb. 23, 1953; s. Duane Joseph and Florence Helen (Wiesneiwski) K.; m. Gayle Sanders, Nov. 22, 1975; children: Megan, Sarah. BA, Calif. State Coll. Stanislaus, 1975. Biomed. scientist Lawrence Livermore (Calif.) Nat. Lab., 1976—. Contbr. articles to profl. jours. Mem. Genetic and Environ. Toxicology Assn. (charter). Avocation: beekeeping. Home: 28263 S Chrisman Rd Tracy CA 95376 Office: Lawrence Livermore Nat Lab 8000 E Ave Livermore CA 94550

KNODELL, CLAYTON WILLIAM, business executive; b. Enterprise, Oreg., Mar. 19, 1927; s. Clayton Leroy Knodell and Isel Ruby (Hunter) Knodell Hug; m. Donna Mae Paulson, Sept. 16, 1950; children—Steven William, Brad Clayton, Kathy Diane, Susan Gail. B.S.B.A., Oreg. State U., 1951; postgrad. in acctg. and law, U. Oreg., 1952. C.P.A., Oreg. Sr. acct. Peat, Marwick, Mitchell & Co., Portland, Oreg., 1952-56; divisional controller Textron, Inc., Coquille, Oreg., 1956-59; fin. v.p. Western Kraft Corp., Portland, Oreg., 1959-71; exec. v.p., chief fin. officer, sec. and treas. Willamette Industries, Inc., Portland, Oreg., 1971—; dir. Pacific Am. Liquid Assets Inc., N.Y.C. Mem. exec. com. Columbia Pacific council Boy Scouts Am., 1964—; pres. bd. trustees Good Samartian Hosp. and Med. Ctr., Portland, Oreg., 1970—; trustee Oreg. State U. Found., Corvallis, 1980—. Mem. Fin. Execs. Inst. (chpt. pres. 1965, nat. bd. dirs. 1967), Am. Inst. C.P.A.s, Oreg. State Soc. C.P.A.s, Tax Execs. Inst., Am. Legion. Republican. Clubs: Arlington, University (Portland). Lodge: Elks. Office: Willamette Industries Inc 3800 First Interstate Tower Portland OR 97201

KNOEBEL, BETTY LOU, food service company executive; b. Hobart, Ind., July 12, 1931; d. Frank O. and Louise C. (Sohn) Burnett; m. F.C. Knoebel, Apr. 27, 1974. Grad., Sch. X-Ray, Methodist Hosp., Gary, Ind., 1950; student, Ind. U., 1952-53. X-ray technician, then various secretarial positions; X-ray technician, asst. adminstr. Melissa Meml. Hosp., Holyoke, Colo.; dir. Nobel/Sysco, Inc., Denver, 1982—; now corp. sec., dir. Capitol Warehouse Co.; v.p., sec. B&K Motor Sports, Inc., Englewood, Colo.; dir. Gen. Mgmt. Corp. Grantee Am. Cancer Soc., 1949-50. Mem. Profl. Women's Assn., Am. Soc. X-Ray Technicians, Colo.-Wyo. Restaurant Assn. (pres. ladies aux. 1978-79). Republican. Office: 5030 S Broadway Englewood CO 80110

KNOERNSCHILD, KURT WESLEY, educational administrator, consultant; b. Waterbury, Conn., July 11, 1950; s. Kenneth George and Maryellen (Earle) K.; m. Sally Claire Nogg, Apr. 11, 1981. B.A., U. Conn., 1973; M.A., U. N.Mex., 1981. Tchr. Rough Rock (Ariz.) Demonstration Sch., 1973-76; dir. Black Mesa Community Sch., Chinle, Ariz., 1976-80; spl. asst. N.Mex. Research and Study Council, Albuquerque, 1980-84, sec. grad. students in ednl. adminstrn., 1980-83, pres. 1983-84 mem. U. N.Mex. Senate Library Com., 1981-82; supt. Vaughn Municipal Schs., 1984—; mem. N.Mex. State Adv. Commn. for Edn. Consolidation and Improvement Act, 1986—; sec., mem. exec. com. Coop. Edn. Services/JPA, 1986—. Recipient Outstanding Service award N.Mex. Research Study Council, 1981, 82, Academic Excellence award Phi Kappa Phi, 1981, Navajo Nation award for Outstanding Service, 1985. Mem. Am. Assn. Sch. Adminstrs., N.Mex. Sch. Adminstrs. Assn. (co-chair commn. on mgmt. tng. 1985—), Phi Beta Kappa. Democrat. Home: PO Box 297 Vaughn NM 88353 Office: PO Box 158 Vaughn NM 88353

KNOLLMAN, GIL CARL, research physicist; b. Cleve., Mar. 14, 1928; s. Paul Carl and Louise Catherine (Heidebrink) K.; m. Tommie Lorraine Gordon, Mar. 14, 1959; children: Kristi Jean, Katrina Paulet, Tom Jenkins, Scott Jenkins. BS, Ga. Inst. Tech., 1949, MS, 1950, PhD, 1961; postdoctoral student, Stanford U., 1965-66, Foothill Coll., 1974. Research physicist Ga. Research Inst., Atlanta, 1950-62; prof. math. Ga. Inst. Tech., Atlanta, 1954-62; head fluid physics Lockheed Research Lab., Palo Alto, Calif., 1962-67, sr. staff scientist, 1964—, sr. mem. research, 1966—, dir. acoustics lab., 1967-74, mem. research dir.'s staff, 1974-76, head advanced ultrasonics lab., 1976—; cons. Saratoga Systems Inc., Cupertino, Calif., 1971-76, USN, Washington, 1968-70, Lockheed Calif. Co., Burbank, 1964-67, NRC of Can., 1986. Author: Meson Mass Determination, 1950, Quantum Mechanical Model, 1961; contbr. articles to profl. jours.; inventor acoustic beam focuser, acoustic bond evaluation; orbital particle velocimeter, hydroacoustic lens, DC circuit breaker; patentee adhesive bond integrity. Mem. Carter Campaign Com., San Francisco, 1976, Carter Re-election Com., San Francisco, 1980, Reagan Campaign Com., Sunnyvale, Calif., 1984. Served as spl. agt. Counter Intelligence Corps., 1946-47, ETO. Ericson Found. scholar, 1944-45; NSF grantee, 1961. Fellow AAAS, Am. Phys. Soc., N.Y. Acad. Sci., Acoustical Soc. Am.; mem. Am. Inst. Physics, Am. Assn. Physics Tchrs., Sigma Xi, Sigma Pi Sigma. Republican. Home: 705 Charleston Ct Palo Alto CA 94303 Office: Lockheed Research Lab 3251 Hanover St Palo Alto CA 94304

KNOP, SHEILA ANN, public relations company executive; b. Rugby, N.D., Nov. 26, 1947; d. Alfred Fritjof and Jeanette Bernice (Molden) Frydenlund; m. Edward C. Knop, July 21, 1977. BS, N.D. State U., 1968; MEd, Colo. State U., 1973; PhD, Tex. A&M U., 1977. Extension agent Coop. Extension Service, Ft. Collins, Colo., 1968-71; instr. Colo. State U., Ft. Collins, 1971-75, 1975-77; research assoc. Tex. A&M, College Station, 1975-77; edn. cons. Cairo, 1978-80; project dir. Colo. Commn. on Higher Edn., Denver, 1980-86; exec. officer Pub. Perceptions Corp., Ft. Collins, 1982—. Contbr. articles to profl. jours.; editor: K-Byte, 1984-85, PACE, 1983-86. Mem. Planning Com. Expatriate Community Orgn., Heliopolis, Cairo, Egypt, 1979-80. Mem. High Plains Soc. Applied Anthropology (election com. 1985-87), KUAFC Computer User's Group (sec. 1984-85), Rural Sociol. Soc., Western Social Sci. Assn. Avocations: travel, gardening. Home and Office: 2608 Avocet Rd Fort Collins CO 80526

KNOPOFF, LEON, educator; b. Los Angeles, July 1, 1925; s. Max and Ray (Singer) K.; m. Joanne Van Cleef, Apr. 9, 1961; children—Katherine Alexandra, Rachel Anne, Michael Van Cleef. Student, Los Angeles City Coll., 1941-42; B.S. in Elec Engring, Calif. Inst. Tech., 1944, M.S. in Physics, 1946, Ph.D. in Physics, 1949. Asst., then assoc. prof. physics Miami U., Oxford, Ohio, 1948-50; mem. faculty U. Calif. at Los Angeles, 1950—, prof. physics, 1961—, prof. geophysics, 1959—, research musicologist, 1963—; assoc. dir. Inst. Geophysics and Planetary Physics, 1972—; prof. geophysics Calif. Inst. Tech., 1962-63, research assoc. seismology, 1963-64; vis. prof. Technische Hochschule, Karlsruhe, Germany, 1966, Harvard, 1972, U. Chile, Santiago, 1973; Chmn. U.S. Nat. Upper Mantle Com., 1963-71; sec. Internat. Upper Mantle Com., 1963-71; chmn. com. math. geophysics Internat. Union Geodesy and Geophysics, 1971-75; mem. Internat. Union Geodesy and Geophysics (U.S. nat. com.), 1973-75. Recipient Wiechert medal German Geophys. Soc., 1978; Gold medal Royal Astron. Soc., 1979; NSF sr. postdoctoral fellow Cambridge (Eng.) U., 1960-61; Guggenheim Found. fellow, 1976-77. Fellow Am. Acad. Arts and Scis.; mem. Nat. Acad. Scis., Am. Phys. Soc., Am. Geophys. Union, Seismol. Soc., Royal Astron. Soc. (Jeffreys lectr. 1976), AAAS. Office: U Calif Dept Physics Los Angeles CA 90024

KNORR, DONNA DANIEL, advertising executive; b. Topeka, Kans., Aug. 9, 1932; d. Eddie Dean and Lorene (Donnelley) Glosup; m. Theodore H. Knorr, Nov. 7, 1971; children: Shellee Richardson, Deborah Richardson, Karen, Jeff Scales. BBS, Woodbury Coll., 1952; cert. in Advanced Advt. Studies, U. So. Calif., 1979. Clk., St. Luke Hosp., Altadena, Calif., 1963-64; sec. Stacoswitch, Costa Mesa, Calif., 1965-70; with Casa Advt., Orange, Calif., 1970—, pres., 1976—; account exec. Hunter Barth Advt., 1983-84, Brassett Co., Inc., 1984—, Keeler Advt. Inc., Anaheim, Calif., 1985—; guest lectr. various colls. Mem. Orange County Advt. Fedn., Western States Advt. Agys. Execs., Internat. Soc. Gen. Semantics, NOW, Nat. Assn. Female Execs. Clubs: Patrons, Costa Mesa Playhouse. Home: 293 Bowling Green Dr Costa Mesa CA 92626 Office: 250 N Manchester Ave Anaheim CA 92801

KNOTT, ALBERT WILLIAM, forensic engineer; b. Hebron, Nebr., Apr. 26, 1931; s. Albert William and Irma Llewelyn (Emely) K.; m. Roberta Aline Ray, Sept. 4, 1951; children: Susan Knott Burks, Tom Frederick, Lawrence Albert. BS in Archtl. Engring., U. Colo., 1955; MSCE, U. Calif., Berkeley, 1959; PhDCE, Stanford U., 1968. Registered profl. engr., Colo.,

Wyo., Kans., Nebr., Pa. Asst. prof. civil engring. U. Colo., Boulder, 1958-61; asst. prof. archtl. engring. Pa. State U., State Coll., 1961-65; sci. fellow NSF, Palo Alto, 1965-68; assoc. prof. archtl. and civil engring. U. Okla., Norman, 1968-69; v.p., tech. dir. Testing Cons., Inc., Denver, 1969-74; pres. Albert Knott & Assocs., Denver, 1974-81, Knott Lab., Denver, 1981—. Author 14 tech. pubs. Pres. Colo. Sci. Ctr., Denver, 1978-79. Rosenblume scholar, 1955, Weibel scholar, 1967. Mem. NSPE (S.W. regional v.p. profl. engrs. in pvt. practice 1984), Profl. Engrs. Colo. (pres. 1974-75, Engr. of Yr. 1978), Am. Concrete Inst. (com. mem.), ASCE, Soc. Exptl. Stress Analysis. Republican. Episcopalian. Avocation: model-building. Home: 7500 E Dartmouth #27 Denver CO 80231 Office: Knott Lab Inc 2727 W 2d Ave Denver CO 80219

KNOTT, HERBERT FREDERICK JOHN CHARLES, architect; b. Johannesburg, South Africa, Dec. 29, 1942; came to U.S., 1962; s. Robert Charles and Mary Lilian (Buroughs) K.; m. Diantha Lurline Dorfman, July 5, 1968. B.Arch., U. Oreg., 1968. Registered architect, Oreg., Zambia. Architect Nat. Housing Authority, Lusaka, Zambia, 1969-72, Pringle Zambia Ltd., Lusaka, 1972-76, Zimmer Gunsul Frasca, Portland, Oreg., 1976-78; architect cons. Ivars Lazdins AIA, Portland, 1978-82; prin. cons. H.F.J.C. Knott, AIA, West Linn, Oreg., 1982—; cons., ptnr. Diantha Knott & Assocs., Portland, 1982—. Govt. Zambia scholar, 1961; African scholar, 1962-68; U. Oreg. tuition scholar, 1962-68. Mem. AIA (urban design rev. com.), Constrn. Specifications Inst., Zambia Inst. Architects. Office: H F J C Knott AIA 101 SW Main St Portland OR 97204

KNOTT, WILLIAM ALAN, library director, library management and building consultant; b. Muscatine, Iowa, Oct. 4, 1942; s. Edward Marlan and Dorothy Mae (Holzhauer) K.; m. Mary Farrell, Aug. 23, 1969; children—Andrew Jerome, Sarah Louise. B.A. in English, U. Iowa, 1967, M.A. in L.S., 1968. Asst. dir. Ottumwa (Iowa) Pub. Library, 1968-69; library cons. Iowa State Library, Des Moines, 1968-69; dir. Hutchinson (Kans.) Pub. Library and S. Central Kans. Library System, Hutchinson, 1969-71; dir. Jefferson County Pub. Library, Lakewood, Colo., 1971—. Served with U.S. Army, 1965-67. Mem. Colo. Library Assn. Author: Books by Mail: A Guide, 1973; co-author: A Phased Approach to Library Automation, 1969; editor: Conservation Catalog, 1982. Office: Jefferson County Pub Library 10200 W 20th Ave Lakewood CO 80215

KNOWLES, TONY, mayor; b. Tulsa, Jan. 1, 1943; m. Susan Knowles; children: Devon, Lucas. BA in Econs., Yale U., 1968. Owner, mgr. The Works, Anchorage, 1968—, Downtown Deli, Anchorage, 1978—; mayor Municipality of Anchorage, 1981—. Mem. citizen's com. to develop comprehensive plan for growth and devel., Anchorage, 1972; mem. Borough Assembly, Anchorage, 1975-79; bd. dirs. Fairview Community Ctr., March of Dimes, Pub. TV Sta. KAKM, numerous sports facilities coms. Served with U.S. Army, Vietnam. Mem. Anchorage C. of C. (bd. dirs.). Office: Municipality of Anchorage PO Box 6650 Anchorage AK 99502

KNOX, CHARLES ROBERT, football coach; b. Sewickley, Pa., Apr. 27, 1932; s. Charles McMeehan and Helen (Keith) K.; m. Shirley Ann, Aug. 2, 1952; children: Christeen, Kathy, Colleen, Chuck. B.A., Juniata Coll., 1954; postgrad., Pa. State U., 1955. Asst. football coach Wake Forest Coll., 1959-60, U. Ky., 1961-62, N.Y. Jets, 1963-66, Detroit Lions, 1967-72; head football coach Los Angeles Rams, 1973-78; head football coach, v.p. football ops. Buffalo Bills, 1978-82; head football coach Seattle Seahawks, 1983—. Named NFL Coach of Yr., Sporting News, 1973, 80. Lutheran. Club: Big Canyon Country. Address: care Seattle Seahawks 5305 Lake Washington Blvd Kirkland WA 98033 *

KNOX, JOHN THERYLL, lawyer, former state legislator; b. Reno, Sept. 30, 1924; s. Ernest B. and Jean (Monat) K.; A.B., Occidental Coll., 1949; J.D., Hastings Coll. Law, 1952; m. Jean Henderson, Dec. 27, 1949; children—John Henderson, Charlotte, Mary. Admitted to Calif. bar, 1953, in pvt. practice at Richmond; mem. Calif. Assembly from Richmond, from 1960, speaker pro tem, from 1976, mem. Ways and Means com.; now ptnr. Nossaman, Guthner, Knox & Elliott, San Francisco. Mem. Contra Costa County Dem. central com., 1955-60; trustee Occidental Coll., Hastings Coll. Law. Served with USAAF, 1943-45. Mem. ABA, Contra Costa County Bar Assn., Sigma Alpha Epsilon, Phi Delta Phi. Moose, Lion. Home: 229 Bishop Ave Richmond CA 94801 Office: 100 The Embarcadero San Francisco CA 94105

KNUBIS, JESS ELLIS, advertising executive; b. Gastonia, N.C., Aug. 11, 1952; s. Voldemars and Irmgard (Müeller) K.; m. Gabriela Brigette Ulrich, Aug. 15, 1970; 1 child, Vhea Brigette. Student, U. Wis., Milw., Wis. Coll. Conservatory. Freelance writer, musician Los Angeles, 1972-83; advt. dir. The Barnyard Agy., Carmel, Calif., 1983—; cons. JE Knubis Advt., Pacific Grove, Calif., 1983—. Author: Brainworks: Music and the Mind, 1982; contbr. articles to profl. jours. Mem. Advt. Club Monterey Peninsula (bd. dirs. 1985-86, award of Excellence 1986). Avocations: tennis, walking, kayaking. Home: 243 Granite St Pacific Grove CA 93950 Office: The Barnyard Agy PO Box 22830 Carmel CA 93922

KNUDSEN, HELEN EWING ZOLLARS, librarian; b. Kittery, Maine, Apr. 5, 1939; d. Allen Marshall and Marian (Himes) Zollars; m. Arnold Christian Knudsen, June 22, 1958 (div. 1974); children: Karen Christianne, Christina Louise, Lois Kathrine. AB, Principia Coll., 1958; BA, Calif. State U., Los Angeles, 1970; MSLS, U. So. Calif., 1973. Librarian Calif. Inst. Tech., Pasadena, 1973—; lit. search specialist, IPAC, Pasadena, 1985—, Space Telescope, Pasadena, 1987—; dir. Olivetree Assocs., Sierra Madre, Calif., 1975—. Editor/pub. Astronomy and Astrophysics Monthly Index, 1975—. Mem. Spl. Libraries Assn. (pres. elect 1971—). Avocations: backpacking, photography. Home: PO Box 236 Sierra Madre CA 91024-0457 Office: Calif Inst Tech Astrophysics Library 1201 E California Blvd Pasadena CA 91125

KNUDSEN, LARRY STEPHEN, fund raising executive; b. Fort Madison, Iowa, May 11, 1936; s. Orlando Stephen and Zora (White) K.; B.A., U. So. Calif., 1958; postgrad Inst. for Ednl. Mgmt. Harvard, 1974; m. Patricia Jean McCallum, Jan. 27, 1967; children—Thomas Howard, Lauren Jean. Dir. support orgns. U. So. Calif., 1961-64, dir. ann. giving, 1964-66; dir. spl. gifts program Calif. Inst. Tech., 1966-68; devel. officer Rand Corp., Santa Monica, Calif., 1968-69; exec. v.p. Ind. Colls. of So. Calif., Los Angeles, 1969-86; presiding officer Ind. Coll. Funds of Am., 1984-86, trustee, 1969-86; chmn., pres. Knudsen Assocs., Inc., La Canada, Calif., 1986—; fund raising cons. Mem. governing bd. La Canada Unified Sch. Dist., 1983—. Served to lt. (j.g.) USN, 1958-61. Recipient direct mail awards Alumni Council Am., 1966-67, 1st prize IBM incentive award Ind. Coll. Funds of Am., 1970, 2d prize, 1976, 80, Levi Straus Found. incentive award, 1983. Clubs: Jonathan, Los Angeles Rotary. Home: 4937 Oakwood Ave La Canada CA 91011

KNUDSEN, WALTER IRVING, JR., engineer; b. Newton, Mass., Dec. 27, 1933; s. Walter I. and Threasa E. (Anderson) K.; m. Linda C. Cheney, Nov. 26, 1966; children: Peter N., Kathryn E. Degree, Colo. Sch. Mines, 1960. Registered profl. engr., Colo. Engr. Los Angeles County Flood Control Dist., 1960, Lockheed Missiles and Space Co., Lompoc, Calif., 1960-63; sr. engr. Martin Marietta Corp., Denver, 1963-70; asst. engr. Colo. Div. Water Resources, Denver, 1970—. Served with USAF, 1952-56. Mem. NSPE, Profl. Engrs. Colo. (pres. 1974-75), Am. Water Resources Assn., Rocky Mountain Assn. Geologists. Republican. Episcopalian. Club: Toastmasters (Littleton, Colo.) (pres. 1970). Lodge: Masons. Avocations: hiking, skiing, camping, shooting, photography. Home: 12290 W Ohio Pl Lakewood CO 80228 Office: Div Water Resources 1313 Sherman St Denver CO 80203

KNUDSON, MELVIN ROBERT, management consultant, business executive; b. Libby, Mont., Oct. 27, 1917; s. John and Serina (Bakken) K.; B.S. in Wood Chemistry, Oreg. State U., 1942; m. Melba Irene Joice, Mar. 5, 1946; children—Mark Bradley, Kevin Marie, Kari Lynne. Mgr. quality control J. Neils Lumber Co., Libby, Mont., 1946-55; mgr. research and devel. St. Regis Paper Co., Libby, 1955-65, div. dir. tech. devel., Tacoma, Wash., 1965-69, div. dir. short and long-range planning, 1969-70; exec. v.p. Property Holding and Devel. Co., Tacoma, 1970-75; exec. v.p. and gen. mgr. U.S. Computers, Inc., Tacoma, 1975-79; corp. mgmt., orgn., univ. governance and adminstrn. cons., 1979—; owner Knudson Travel, Tacoma, 1981—; dir. Property Holding and Devel. Co., U.S. Computers; adv. bd. Coll. Engring., Wash. State U., 1967—, chmn., 1971-73. Trustee 1st Luth. Ch., Libby, 1948-56, chmn., 1954-56; trustee Sch. Dist. #4, Libby, 1964-65; trustee Christ Luth. Ch., Tacoma, 1966-71, com. chmn.; trustee Greater Lakes Mental Health Clinic, 1969-73, com. chmn., 1970-73; bd. regents Pacific Luth. U., Tacoma, 1969—, chmn., 1976-81; mem. Steilacoom Improvement Com., 1971-73; chmn. Pacific Luth. U. Pres. Search Com., 1974-75; dir. Wauna Dance Club, 1976-79; dir. Pacific Luth. Univ. ' ' Q" Club, 1976—; bd. dirs. Tenzler Library, Tacoma, 1980-83, Crime Stoppers, 1981-84. Served to lt. col. F.A., Paratroops, U.S. Army, 1941-46. Recipient Disting. Service award Pacific Luth. U., 1986. Mem. Wash. Realtors Assn., Wash. Securities Sales, Am. Governing Bds., Center for Study of Democratic Institutions. Republican. Clubs: Tacoma Country and Golf, Normana Male Chorus (Norwegian Singers Assn. Am.). Patentee high-temperature wood-drying process; developer domestic natural gum. Home: 6928 100th St SW Tacoma WA 98499 Office: 1103 A St Suite 200 Tacoma WA 98402

KNUE, JAMES LEROY, athletic trainer; b. Denver, Oct. 20, 1953; s. Joseph Edward and Edythe Marie (McCracken) K.; m. Nancy Lee Stroud, July 9, 1983. BA, U. Colo., 1975; MA, U. No. Colo., 1977. Asst. trainer U. No. Colo., Greeley, 1975-77; athletic trainer El Camino Coll., Torrance, Calif., 1977—. Named Outstanding Young Man in Am. Kiwanis, 1980, 82, 84, 86. Mem. Nat. Athletic Trainers Assn. (cert.), Am. Coll. Sports Medicine, Far West Athletic Trainers Assn. (cert., Calif. rep. to mng. bd. 1983—), Calif. Athletic Trainers Assn. (cert., pres. 1982-86). Avocations: fishing, hiking, gardening. Office: El Camino Coll 16007 Crenshaw Blvd Torrance CA 90506

KNUTESON, KNUT JEFFERY, computer engineer; b. Spanish Fork, Utah, Nov. 1, 1949; s. Harold and Donna Fay (Gardner) K.; m. Kirsti Krogvik, Aug. 25, 1971; children: Kathrine, Knut-Sigurd, Joshua, Kristian, Harold, Marie Elizabeth. Student, Brigham Young U., 1967-72; A in Electronics Tech., Utah Tech. Coll., 1979. Electronics monitor Amund Clausen A/S, Porsgrunn, Norway, 1972-73; electronics technician, librarian Orem (Utah) City Pub. Library, 1977-79; electronics test and lab. technician Gen. Products div. IBM Corp., Tucson, 1979-82; computer systems technician and asst. programmer OmniSoft Corp., Salt Lake City, 1982-83; computer systems technician and cons. World Industries Cons., Inc., Tacoma, 1983-84; engr.-in-charge customer engring. KET Services, Inc., Tooele, Utah and Minnetonka, Minn., 1984—; cons. engr. Collier's Pub., 1980—. Author religious booklets; compiler indices to Mormon scholarly books. Active neighborhood Crime Watch Pima County Sheriff's Dept., Tucson, 1980-82. Mem. Second Amendment Found. (nat. bd. advisors 1986—), Citizen's Com. for the Right to Keep and Bear Arms (nat. adv. council 1987—, Citizen of Yr. award 1982, 83, 84, 86). Libertarian. Mormon. Avocations: metaphysics, etymology, lit., music, sci. Office: KET Services PO Box 2695 Salt Lake City UT 84110

KNUTH, ELDON LUVERNE, engineering educator; b. Luana, Iowa, May 10, 1925; s. Alvin W. and Amanda M. (Becker) K.; m. Marie O. Parrat, Sept. 10, 1954 (div. 1973); children: Stephen B., Dale L., Margot O., Lynette M.; m. Margaret I. Nicholson, Dec. 30, 1973. B.S., Purdue U., 1949, M.S., 1950; Ph.D. (Guggenheim fellow), Calif. Inst. Tech., 1953. Aerothermodynamics group leader Aerophysics Devel. Corp., 1953-56; asso. research engr. dept. engring. UCLA, 1956-59, asso. prof. engring., 1960-65, prof. engring. and applied sci., 1965—, head chem., nuclear thermal div. dept. engring., 1963-65, chmn. energy kinetics dept., 1969-75, head molecular-beam lab., 1961—; Gen. chmn. Heat Transfer and Fluid Mechanics Inst., 1959; vis. scientist, von Humboldt fellow Max-Planck Inst. fü r Strö mungsforschung, Gö ttingen, West Germany, 1975-76. Author: Introduction to Statistical Thermodynamics, 1966; also numerous articles. Served with AUS, 1943-45. Mem. AIAA, Am. Soc. Engring. Edn., Am. Inst. Chem. Engrs., Combustion Inst., Soc. Engring. Sci., AAAS, Am. Phys. Soc., Am. Vacuum Soc., Sigma Xi, Tau Beta Pi, Gamma Alpha Rho, Pi Tau Sigma, Sigma Delta Chi, Pi Kappa Phi. Club: Gimlet (Lafayette, Ind.). Patentee radial-flow molecular pump. Home: 18085 Boris Dr Encino CA 91316 Office: Sch Engring and Applied Sci U Calif 405 Hilgard Ave Los Angeles CA 90024

KNYCHA, JOSEF ROBERT, journalist; b. Summerside, P.E.I., Can., Apr. 19, 1953; s. Michael Stanley and Marjorie Mary (Gallant) K. Student pub. schs., Auburn, N.S., Can. Reporter Halifax Herald Ltd., N.S., 1971-81; editor The Mirror, Cameron Publs., Kentville, N.S., 1981-82, editor The Register, 1982-84; bus./markets reporter Star-Phoenix, Saskatoon, Sask., Can., 1984—. Southam fellow U. Toronto. Mem. Sask. Farm Writers' Assn. (bd. dirs.), Can. Farm Writers' Fedn. Home: 702 425 3d Ave N, Saskatoon, SK Canada S7K 5C4 Office: The Star-Phoenix, 204 5th Ave N, Saskatoon, SK Canada S7K 2P1

KOBAYASHI, CHARLOTTE CHIYO, import food company executive; b. Olaa, Hawaii, Sept. 2, 1942; d. Ginzo and Yukie (Horike) K.; B.A., U. Hawaii; M. Early Childhood Edn., Loyola U., Chgo., 1970; 1 dau., Marissa Rikka. Vice pres., mgr. Soken Trading Inc., Mill Valley, Calif., also. dir.; pres., mgr. Bon Parti, Mill Valley, Calif. Contbr. articles to jours., mags. Mem. Nat. Assn. Edn. of Young, Internat. Platform Assn.

KOBAYASHI, CHRIS, TV producer-writer; b. Tokyo, Nov. 18, 1949 (parents Am. citizens); d. Kan and Sadae (Suehiro) Tagami. Producer, writer, host Sta. KTVU, San Francisco, 1974-81; exec. dir. Minorities and Women's Telecommunications Network, 1980-83; nat. coordinator Nat. Regional Pub. Telecommunications Consortium, 1981-82; propr. Joint Prodns. Inc., 1980—; instr. Laney Commuity Coll., 1984-86; coordinator Third World Apprenticeship Program in Film, 1974; grants coordinator Calif. TV Found., 1986—; video editor for Ishmael Reed, 1983-84; founding bd. dirs. Bay Area Video Coalition, Japantown Art and Media Workship, Asian Am. TV Services; freelance videographer; cons. in field. Grantee Calif. Arts Council, 1979. Contbr. poetry to anthologies. Mem. Anthrology Japanese-Am. Poetry Writers. Address: 25 Eugenia Ave San Francisco CA 94110

KOBAYASHI, LESLIE EMI, lawyer; b. Mt. Holly, N.J., Oct. 9, 1957; s. Herbert Makoto and Ruth Hideko (Takakura) K. BA, Wellesley Coll., 1979; JD, Boston Coll., 1983; JD (hon.), U. Hawaii, 1983. Bar: Hawaii 1983, U.S. Dist. Ct. Hawaii 1983. Dep. prosecutor Office of Prosecuting Atty., Honolulu, 1983-84; assoc. Fujiyama, Duffy & Fujuyama, Honolulu, 1984—. Mem. Hawaii Bar Assn., Assn. Trial Lawyers Am. Office: Fujiyama Duffy and Fujiyama 2650 Pacific Tower 1001 Bishop St Honolulu HI 96813

KOBAYASHI, RONALD MASAO, physician, neurologist; b. Los Angeles, Apr. 3, 1940; s. Arthur E. and Mae M. (Ozawa) K.; m. Naomi Mori, July 26, 1964; children: Anne, Caroline. BA, UCLA, 1961; MD, U. So. Calif., 1965. Resident in medicine Cornell Med. Ctr., N.Y.C., 1966-67; resident in neurology Harvard U. Med. Ctr., Boston, 1969-72; fellow MIT, Boston, 1971-72; fellow in neuropharmacology NIH, Bethesda, Md., 1972-74; clin. investigator VA Hosp., San Diego, 1975-77; pvt. practice specializing in neurology San Diego, 1978—; asst. prof. U. Calif.-San Diego, La Jolla, 1974-78, assoc. clin. prof., 1979—; clin. dirs. Neurodiagnostic Lab. Sharp Meml. Hosp., San Diego, 1982—; med. dir. Parkinson's Disease Clinic, Sharp Hosp., San Diego, 1982—; med. dir. Parkinson's Disease Clinic, Sharp Meml. Hosp., 1983—. Served to capt. U.S. Army, 1967-69. NIH reseach grantee, 1974-77. Fellow Am. Acad. Neurology (S. Weir Mitchell award 1974); mem. AMA, Calif. Med. Assn. (chmn. neurol. sect. 1986-87), Fedn. Western Socs. Neurol. Sci. (pres. 1986-87), San Diego Neurol. Soc. (chmn. 1983-85), Alpha Omega Alpha. Avocations: tennis, skiing, fly fishing. Office: 3444 Kearny Villa Rd #303 San Diego CA 92123

KOBE, LAN HWA, medical physicist; b. Semarang, Indonesia; naturalized; d. O.G. and L.N. (The) Kobe. B.S. in Physics, IKIP U., Bandung, Indonesia, 1964, M.S. in Physics, 1967; M.S. in Med. Physics and Biophysics, U. Calif.-Berkeley, 1975. Physics instr. Sch. Engring., Tarumanegara U., Jakarta, Indonesia, 1968-72; research fellow dept. radiation oncology U. Calif.-San Francisco, 1975-77; clin. physicist in residence dept. radiation oncology UCLA, 1977-78, asst. hosp. radiation physicist, 1978-80, hosp. radiation physicist, 1980—; instr. radiation oncology physics to resident physicians and med. physics graduate students. Contbr. sci. papers to profl. publs. and Newhouse grantee U. Calif.-Berkeley, 1974-75, grantee dean grad. div. U. Calif.-Berkeley, 1975; recipient Pres. Work Study award U. Calif., Berkeley, 1974-75, Employee of Month award UCLA, 1983, Outstanding Service award UCLA, 1986. Mem. Am. Assn. Physicists in Medicine (nat. and So. Calif. chpts.), Am. Assn. Individual Investors (life). Lodge: Rosicrucian Order. Office: UCLA Hosp and Clinics Dept Radiation Oncology Los Angeles CA 90024

KOBER, CARL LEOPOLD, exploration company executive; b. Vienna, Austria, Nov. 22, 1913; s. Leopold and Maria Gertrud (Cremer) K.; m. Christiana Futschig, Mar. 26, 1942; children: Wolfgang, Peter Christian. PhD in Physics, U. Vienna, Austria, 1935; PhD in Electronics, Tech. U., 1939. Dir. GEMA G.M.B.H., Berlin, Germany, 1940-45; cons. armament lab. USAF, Wright Patterson AFB, 1949-55; v.p. electronics div. AVCO Corp., Cin., 1958-61; dir. Martin Marietta, Denver, 1961-74; pres. DEMEX Mineral Exploration Co., Denver, 1974—; prof. Colo. State U., Ft. Collins, 1968-79. Patentee in field. Fellow IEEE (life), AAAS, Explorer Club. Club: Columbine Country (Littleton). Home: 605 Front Range Rd Littleton CO 80120 Office: DEMEX Denver Mineral Exploration Co PO Box 4206 Highlands Ranch CO 80126

KOBLASA, GEORG JAN, film director, cinematographer; b. Prague, Czechoslovakia, June 15, 1933; came to U.S., 1959; s. Jan Matěj Koblasa and Anežka (Patakova) Koblasova; m. Kathleen Karole Kondall, Aug. 23, 1975; 1 child, G. Tyler. Grad., Charles U. Film Inst., Prague, 1954-58. Cinematographer Petersen Co., Hollywood, Calif., 1962-70, dir., cameraman, 1970-77; dir., cameraman EUE/Screen Gems Prodns., Hollywood, 1977-79, Coast Prodns., Hollywood, 1979-85, Bluebird, Inc., Hollywood, 1986—; pres. Icarus Enterprises, Ltd., 1977—. Dir., cinematographer (film) The Challenger; dir. photography (films) Wako and Rhinehart, The Richest Cat in the World, My Town, Case Busters, 2 1/2 Dads, The Last Electric Knight, Run, Don't Walk, Fisher of Men; dir., cameraman over 3,300 TV commls.for major corporations. Served as sgt. Czechoslovakian Army, 1953-55. Recipient 2 Cleo Finalist awards, 4 Andy awards The Am. Advt. Club, Lion D'Or award The Venice Film Festival, Diplome The Cannes Film Fest., many other awards. Mem. Dirs. Guild Am. (bd. dirs. 1970—), Internat. Photogrphers Guild (dir. photography 1966—), Acad. TV Arts and Scis. Lodge: Lions. Avocations: classical music, photography, arts. Office: Icarus Enterprises Ltd PO Box 55157 Sherman Oaks CA 91403

KOBLIN, RONALD LEE, business management, real estate development consultant; b. Santa Monica, Calif., Nov. 28, 1946; s. Bernard Lewis and Sadie Irene K.; student U. Oreg., 1965, U. Ariz., 1967; B.A., Calif. State U., Northridge, 1969, postgrad., 1970-71; postgrad. U. So. Calif., 1971. Field advt. rep. Procter & Gamble, 1969; urban planner cities of Compton and Simi Valley, Calif., 1970-72; dir. planning and constrn. Nat. Med. Enterprises, Beverly Hills, Calif., 1972-74; dir. planning and devel. So. Counties Mgmt. Co., Beverly Hills, 1974-75, v.p./cons. planning and devel., 1978-79; mgmt. cons. Gottfried Cons., Inc., Los Angeles, 1975-76; exec. v.p. David D. Brill, Inc., Los Angeles, 1976-78, vice chmn. bd. dirs., 1978-82; founder, pres., vice chmn. bd. dirs. Art Showcases, Inc., Glendale, Calif., 1976-82; founder, owner Firstworld Travel of Century City, Inc., 1982—; gen. ptnr. various Calif. real estate ltd. ptnrships.;cons. in mgmt. and sales, founder, pres. The Concept Implementation Co., 1982—; Notary public County of Los Angeles, 1977-84. Recipient Outstanding Service award City of Simi Valley, 1972. Mem. Am. Planners Assn., Am. Mgmt. Assn., Urban Land Inst. Office: PO Box 115 La Canada-Flintridge CA 91011

KOBOSA-MUNRO, LYN ANN, mental health clinic administrator; b. Pitts., Sept. 29, 1938; d. John Joseph and Madeleine (Hillgrove) Munro; m. Daniel Frank Sedey, Feb. 26, 1960 (div. 1974); children: Allison, Erika; m. David Nick Kobosa, May 31, 1975. BA magna cum laude, U. Pitts., 1960; postgrad, U. Mich., 1963-65; MSW, U. So. Calif., 1973. Psychotherapist Family Service, Ypsilanti, Mich., 1965; counselor Planned Parenthood, Los Angeles, 1972-73; psychotherapist, adminstr. Hathaway Home for Children, Los Angeles, 1973—; cons. Valley Village for the Retarded, Los Angeles, 1978-81, Los Angeles Community Colls., 1986—. Mem. Nat. Assn. Social Workers (cert.), Hope Mental Health Profl. Adv. Bd., Los Angeles Conservancy, So. Calif. Archtl. Historians, Los Angeles Dance Alliance, Mortar Bd., Phi Beta Kappa. Democrat. Unitarian. Avocations: clogging. Home: 16750 Parthenia St Apt 232 Sepulveda CA 91343 Office: Hathaway Home for Children 11500 Eldridge Ave #204 Lake View Terrace CA 91342

KOBZA, DENNIS JEROME, architect; b. Ullysses, Nebr., Sept. 30, 1933; s. Jerry Frank and Agnes Elizabeth (Lavicky) K.; B.S., Healds Archtl. Engring., 1959; m. Doris Mae Riemann, Dec. 26, 1953; children—Dennis Jerome, Diana Jill, David John. Draftsman, designer B.L. Schroder, Palo Alto, Calif., 1959-60; sr. draftsman, designer Ned Abrams, Architect, Sunnyvale, Calif., 1960-61, Kenneth Elvin, Architect, Los Altos, Calif., 1961-62; partner B.L. Schroder, Architect, Palo Alto, 1962-66; pvt. practice architecture, Mountain View, Calif., 1966—. Served with USAF, 1952-56. Recipient Solar PAL award, Palo Alto, 1983, Mountain View Mayoral award, 1979. Mem. C. of C. (dir. 1977-79, Archtl. Excellence award Hayward chpt. 1985, Outstanding Indsl. Devel. award Sacramento chpt., 1980) , AIA (chpt. dir. 1973), Constrn. Specifications Inst. (dir. 1967-68), Am. Inst. Plant Engrs., Nat. Fedn. Ind. Bus. Orgn. Club: Rotary (dir. 1978-79, pres. 1986-87). Home: 3840 May Ct Palo Alto CA 94303 Office: 2083 Old Middlefield Way Mountain View CA 94043

KOBZINA, JOHN WILLIAM, chemical research executive; b. Chgo., Oct. 22, 1942; s. John Owen and Dorthy Beth (Diederich) K.; m. Norma Alva Gallins, June 18, 1967; 1 child, David Mark. BS, U. Fla., 1963, MS, 1964; PhD, Cornell U., 1969. Research chemist Chevron Chem. Co., Richmond, Calif., 1969-78, supr., 1979-82; dept. mgr. Stauffer Chem. Co., Richmond, 1983—. Patentee in field. Ford Found. fellow, 1964, NIH Predoctoral fellow, 1967-69, NSF Predoctoral fellow, 1965-67. Mem. Am. Chem. Soc., Phi Eta Sigma. Avocations: gardening, woodworking. Home: 505 Wimbledon Rd Walnut Creek CA 94598 Office: Stauffer Chem Co 1200 S 47th St Richmond CA 94804

KOCH, ALWIN GEORGE, engineering consultant; b. Wisconsin Rapids, Wis., Mar. 7, 1919; s. Alwin G. and Elizabeth (Lusk) K.; B.S., U. Wash., 1949; m. Virginia Murrell, July 11, 1943; children—Mary Elizabeth, Robert James. Sales engr., field rep. Dorr Co., Seattle, 1949-51; dist. engr. Wash. State Dept. Health, Seattle, 1951-72; sr. engr. tech. services unit Wash. Dept. Social and Health Services, 1972-74, dist. engr. for King County, 1974-79; ret., 1979; engring. cons. Chaves & Kearny, Bogata, Colombia, 1968-69, Chaves & Assos., engrs., Bogata, 1974-80; sr. civil and san. engr. Hernando Chaves & Assos., Seattle, 1979-80; cons. engr., Seattle, 1980—. Served to capt. AUS, 1940-46. Registered profl. engr., Wash. Fellow ASCE (life mem.); mem. Am. Mensa. Home and Office: 6845 32d Ave NE Seattle WA 98115

KOCH, CHARLES ARTHUR CHRYSLER, chemist; b. Newark, Nov. 7, 1952; s. Otto Carl and Gertrude (Carr) K.; m. Stacie Sara Canan, May 21, 1983. BA, U. Mass., 1977; MS, Rutgers U., 1979; PhD, Pa. State U., 1983. Postdoctoral fellow U. Calif., Riverside, 1984-85; lab. dir. Associated Labs., Orange, Calif., 1985-86; tech. asst. Hewlett Packard Corp., Fullerton, Calif., 1986—. Mem. Am. Chem. Soc., Am. Soc. Mass Spectrometry, So. Calif. Environ. Chemists Soc., Phi Kappa Phi. Republican. Roman Catholic. Home: 4514 Verano Pl Irvine CA 92715 Office: Hewlett Packard Corp 1421 S Manhattan Fullerton CA 92631

KOCH, GEORGE BYRON, software company executive; b. Chgo., Nov. 5, 1946; s. George Oscar and Patricia LaVay (McCormick) K.; B.A. in Physics, Elmhurst (Ill.) Coll., 1968; m. Victoria Lynn Cole, May 3, 1979; children: George August, Isaiah James. Asst. chief engr. Aaron-Stevens Corp., Chgo., 1968-69; v.p. Tomorrow, Inc., Los Angeles, 1969-70; pres. Koch Research and Devel. corp., San Francisco, 1970—; chmn. Koch Systems Corp., 1983—; dir. Guidance Industries Corp. cons. Bank of Am., FHLB, Mem. Am. Phys. Soc., AAAS, Prometheus Soc., Four Sigma Soc. Republican. Club: Commonwealth Club of Calif. Former editor. Jour. of Episcopalian. Four Sigma Soc.; contbr. articles on sci. and philosophy to mags. and anthologies; patentee edn. devices, furniture, computer peripherals, med. equipment. Office: PO Box 2510 San Francisco CA 94126

KOCH, JAMES VERCH, economist; b. Springfield, Ill., Oct. 7, 1942; s. Elmer O. and Wilma L. K.; m. Donna L. Stickling, Aug. 20, 1967; children:

Elizabeth, Mark. B.A., Ill. State U., 1964; Ph.D., Northwestern U., 1968. Research economist Harris Trust Bank, Chgo., 1966; from asst. prof. to prof. econs. Ill. State U., 1967-78, chmn. dept., 1972-78; dean Faculty Arts and Scis., R.I. Coll., Providence, 1978-80; prof. econs., provost, v.p. acad. affairs Ball State U., Muncie, Ind., 1980-86; pres. U. Mont., Missoula, 1986—. Author: Industrialization Organization and Prices, 2d edit, 1980, Microeconomic Theory and Applications, 1976, The Economics of Affirmative Action, 1976, Introduction to Mathematical Economics, 1979. Mem. Am. Econ. Assn., Econometric Soc., Am. Assn. Higher Edn., AAUP. Lutheran. Home: 1325 Gerald Ave Missoula MT 59801 Office: U Montana Office of the Pres Missoula MT 59812

KOCH, ROY WILLIAM, hydrologist, water resource engineer, educator; b. Bellevue, Ohio, Apr. 17, 1950; s. Orville E. and Jacqueline J. (Richards) K.; children: Nathan, Constance. BSCE, Ohio State U., 1972, MSCE, 1973; PhDCE, Colo. State U., 1982. Registered profl. engr., Oreg., Mont. Hydrologist State of Mont., Helena, 1974-77, HKM Assocs., Billings, Mont., 1977-78, U.S. Geol. Survey, Lakewood, Colo., 1980-82; asst. prof. civil engring. Portland State U., 1982-85, assoc. prof., 1985—. Contbr. articles to profl. jours. Mem. Am. Geophys. Union, ASCE, Am. Water Resources Assn., Am. Meteorol. Soc. Home: 13360 SW Carr St Beaverton OR 97005 Office: Portland State U PO Box 751 Portland OR 97207

KOCH, SHARON LEE, sales executive; b. C.Z., Sept. 9, 1947; d. Daniel William and Dorine Evelyn (Weaver) K. B.A. in Internat. Relations, U. So. Calif., 1969. Exec. sec. Mitsubishi Internat. Corp., Los Angeles, 1970-73; order clk. sales aviation systems div. RCA, Van Nuys, Calif., 1973-74; internat. sales adminstr. Del Mar Avionics, Irvine, Calif., 1974—. Cert. internat. exec. export mgmt. Mem. AAUW, Internat. Mktg. Assn. Orange County. Home and Office: 4200 Park Newport #410 Newport Beach CA 92660

KOCH, WALTER KARL, lawyer; b. Denver, Nov. 8, 1901; s. Karl and Wanda Otellia (Tischler) K.; m. Lillian E. Lind, Sept. 23, 1925 (dec. July 1940); children: Wanda Elizabeth Wilson, Ellen Janet Buchholz; m. Ruth Brooks Reid, Aug. 11, 1945. AB, U. Colo., 1923; JD, U. Denver, 1925, postgrad., 1929-31; D in Engring. (hon.), Colo. Sch. Mines, 1958; LLD (hon.), Colo. Coll., 1962. Dist. traffic supt. Mountain States Tel & Tel Co., Pueblo, Colo., 1925-28; traffic chief Mountain States Tel & Tel Co., Denver, 1928-30, Utah comml. supr., 1930-33, Colo. comml. supr., 1935-39, gen. comml. supr., 1939-45, gen. comml. mgr., 1945-49, v.p., 1949-52, dir., 1949-70, pres., 1952-66; bd. dirs. Colo. Safety Assn., Nat. Western Stock Show, Am. Growth Fund, AF Acad. Found., Colo. Gov.'s Ethics Com. Trustee Boettcher Found.; bd. dirs. Denver Mus. Natural History, Luth. Community Health Services, Nat. Commn. Hosp. Governing Bds., Luth. Med. Bldg. Corp., Inst. Health Care, Luth. Med. Ctr.; former bd. dirs. Colo. Assn. Commerce and Industry, Colo. Council on Econ. Edn., Denver Symphony Soc., also former trustee, YMCA, Radio Free Europe, Colo. Gov.'s Sci. Devel. Com., Seven State Bus. Devel. Commn., Colo. Outdoors Devel. Assn., Colo. Mil. Affairs Com., Mountain States Employers Council. Recipient Brotherhood award NCCJ, 1963, Silver Beaver award Boy Scouts Am., 1965, U.S. Savs. Bond Patriots medal 1965, Liberty Bell award Luth. Brotherhood, 1966, Disting. Service to Safety award Nat. Safety Council, 1966, Pub. Service award Colo. Assn. Commerce and Industry, 1977, Children's Hosp. Disting. Service award, 1979; named Exec. of Yr., Am. Coll. Hosp. Adminstrs., 1972. Mem. Telphone Pioneers Am. (past pres.), Denver C. of C. (past pres.), Res. Officers Assn. U.S. (hon. life), Colo. Assn. Ind. Colls. and Univs. (past pres., bd. dirs.), ABA, Colo. Bar Assn., Denver Bar Assn., U.S. Sr. Golfers Assn., Colo. Sr. Golfers Assn., Alpha Kappa Psi (hon.), Delta Sigma Rho, Phi Alpha Delta, Pi Kappa Alpha, Beta Gamma Sigma. Clubs: Cherry Hills Country, Denver Athletic, Denver Country, Denver Execs., Denver Press, Mile High, Rocky Mountain Wine and Food, Tower, University. Lodge: Rotary. Home: 33 Sunset Dr Englewood CO 80110 Office: 1700 Broadway Denver CO 80290

KODIS, MARY CAROLINE, retail and restaurant consultant; b. Chgo., Dec. 17, 1927; d. Anthony John and Callis Ferebee (Old) K.; student San Diego State Coll., 1945-47, Latin Am. Inst., 1948. Controller, div. adminstrv. mgr. Fed. Mart Stores, 1957-65; controller, adminstrv. mgr. Gulf Mart Stores, 1965-67; budget dir., adminstrv. mgr. Diana Stores, 1967-68; founder, treas., controller Handy Dan Stores, 1968-72; founder, v.p., treas. Handy City Stores, 1972-76; sr. v.p., treas. Handy City div. W.R. Grace & Co., Atlanta, 1976-79; founder, pres. Hal's Hardware and Lumber Stores, 1982-84; retail and restaurant cons., 1979—. Treas., bd. dirs. YWCA Watsonville, 1981-84, 85—; mem. Santa Cruz County Grand Jury, 1984-85. Recipient 1st Tribute to Women in Internat. Industry, 1978; named Woman of the Yr., 1986. Republican. Home and Office: 302 Wheelock Rd Watsonville CA 95076

KODMAN, DENNIS PAUL, aerospace engineer; b. Hamilton, Ont., Can., May 25, 1946; came to U.S., 1965; s. Stephen Julius and Juliana Margaret (Andrews) K.; m. Pauline Vivian Lefebvre, Sept. 4, 1971; 1 child, Jeffrey Allan. AS in Mfg. Tech., Rio Salado Community Coll., 1983; BBA, U. Phoenix, 1986. Cert. computer graphics operator, Ariz., 1984. Prodn. engr. Garrett Turbine Engine Co., Phoenix, 1979-84; repair, devel. engr. Garrett Gen. Aviation Services Co., Phoenix, 1984, rework tech. engr., 1985—. Author/editor (procedures manual) Rework Engring. Procedures Manual, 1986; editor Prodn. Engring. Handbook, 1983. Served as sgt. U.S. Army, 1967-70. Mem. Smithsonian Inst. Nat. Air and Space Mus. Avocation: motorcycle touring and off-roading. Office: Garrett Gen Aviation Services Co 2401 E Magnolia St 1001-A Phoenix AZ 85038

KODRES, UNO ROBERT, computer science educator; b. Tartu, Estonia, May 21, 1931; came to U.S., 1948; s. Johannes and Susanne (Rosenbladt) K.; m. Elaine Francis Kratosky, Jan. 24, 1959 (div. Apr. 1984); children: Laura, Gregory; m. Irmgard Ida Muensch, June 24, 1984; stepchildren: Martin, Stephan, Vera, Thomas. BA, Wartburg Coll., 1954; MS, Iowa State U., 1956, PhD, 1958. Staff mathematician IBM, Poughkeepsie, N.Y., 1958-63; cons. IBM, Menlo Park, Calif., 1967-69, San Jose, Calif., 1984-85; prof. Naval Postgrad. Sch., Monterey, Calif., 1963—; cons. Collins Radio, Cedar Rapids, Iowa, 1969-70. Co-author Design Automation, 1972; contbr. articles to profl. jours. Mem. Soc. Indsl. and Applied Math., Assn. Computing Machinery, Math. Assn. Am., Sigma Xi (chpt. pres. 1977). Democrat. Club: Carmel Ski (pres. 1964-65). Avocations: skiing, hiking. Home: 22920 Guidotti Dr Salinas CA 93908 Office: Naval Postgrad Sch Computer Sci Dept Monterey CA 93943

KOEHLER, FRED EUGENE, soils educator; b. Naylor, Mo., Jan. 25, 1923; s. Walter Carl and Maude Inez (Miller) K.; m. Helen Hansen, Apr. 19, 1947; children: Carolyn, Mary Ruth Schaumberg, Jane E., Kristin. BS in Agriculture, U. Mo., 1943, MS in Soils, 1950, PhD in Soils, 1951. Agt. county agrl. extension Coop. Extension Service, New Madrid, Mo., 1946-47; soil scientist USDA and U. Nebr., Lincoln, 1951-57; assoc. prof. soil sci. Wash. State U., Pullman, 1958-65, prof. and soil scientist, 1965—. Contbr. articles to profl. jours. Served to capt. U.S. Army, 1943-46. Mem. Am. Soc. Agronomy, Soil Sci. Soc. Am., Internat. Soil Sci. Soc., Sigma Xi, Gamma Sigma Delta. Home: SE 1140 Spring St Pullman WA 99163 Office: Wash State U Dept Agronomy and Soils Pullman WA 99164

KOELLING, RICHARD WILLIAM, financial planner; b. New Haven, Mar. 1, 1935; s. William Norman and Elsie Agnes (Bruns) K.; m. Betty Louise Hemler, June 13, 1961; children—Karyn S., Richard William, Steven M., Christopher S. B.S., Syracuse U., 1956; postgrad. Air U., 1963, 72, Indsl. Coll. Armed Forces, 1973-74. Commd. 2d lt. U.S. Air Force, 1956, advanced through grades to lt. col.; air ops. staff officer Hdqrs. 22AF, Travis AFB, Calif., 1969-73, chief MAC Command Post U-Tapao Thailand, 1973-74, chief Hdqrs. 22AF CP, Travis AFB, 1974-75, sr. maintenance officer 60 FLD Mx Sqdn., 1975-77, chief combat support 60 MIL. ALFT. Wing, 1977-80; ret., 1980; ind. account exec. Dick Keefling Fin. Services, Vacaville, Calif. Pres., Towne Point Civic Assn., Dover, Del., 1965-66, Vacaville Community Players. Decorated Air Force Commendation medal, Meritorious Service medal. Mem. Vacaville C. of C., Vacaville Softball Players Assn. Democrat. Lodges: Lions (pres. Vacaville Alamo chpt. 1984-85, zone chmn. dist. 4-C7 1985-86), Masons. Home: 1942 Forest Ln Vacaville CA 95688 Office: 419 Mason St Suite 210 Vacaville CA 95688

KOELSCH, M. OLIVER, federal judge; b. Boise, Idaho, Mar. 5, 1912; m. Virginia Lee Daley, Oct. 30, 1937; children—Katherine, John, Jane (Mrs. Dennis P. Houghton). B.A., U. Wash., LL.B., 1935. Judge U.S. Ct. Appeals, San Francisco; now sr. judge 9th Circuit, Seattle. Office: US Ct Appeals US Courthouse Seattle WA 98104

KOELZER, WILLIAM, marketing consultant; b. Lansing, Mich., May 25, 1942; s. Charles Robert and Lois Audrey K.; m. Kathi Winter; children—Jacqueline, Shelley. A.A., Orange Coast Coll., 1965; B.A., San Jose State U., 1968. Editor, Mich.-Out-of-Doors, Lansing, 1968, Otsego County Herald Times, Gaylord, Mich., 1968-69, Mich. North, 1968-69; v.p. Cochrane, Chase, Livingston & Co., Inc., 1969-75; pres. Golf Rush Advt., Eureka, Calif., 1977-78; owner, operator Gold Rush Ice Cream Co., Arcata, Calif., 1977-78; v.p. Basso & Assocs., Newport Beach, Calif., 1979-80; pres. Koelzer & Assocs., Fountain Valley, Calif., 1980—; exec. v.p., co-owner Travel Reps., Inc., Huntington Beach, Calif., 1983—; account exec. Lenac, Warford, Stone, Inc., Newport Beach, Calif., 1986-87; pres. China Commerce Co., Ltd., Huntington Beach, 1985-87; pres. Yak Hats Import Co., 1986—; U.S. del. to First China Internat. Tourism Conf., 1983. Campaign mgr. Hank Appleton for County Supr., Eureka, 1976; media chmn. Orange County Holiday Project, 1981-82. Served with USN, 1961-63. Mem. Pub. Relations Soc. Am. (accredited mem.; 2 Prism awards 1982), Accredited Pub. Relations Soc. Am. Democrat. Club: Orangr County Advt. Author: Scuba Diving: How to Get Started, 1965; sr. editor Marketing Problem Solver, 1973. Home: 9168 El Azul Circle Fountain Valley CA 92708 Office: 4701 Teller Ave Newport Beach CA 92660

KOENEMAN, JAMES BRYANT, biomechanical engineer; b. Graceville, Minn., Nov. 24, 1936; s. Egmund Alfred and Luverne Althea (Bryant) K.; m. Mary Ann Endecavageh, Apr. 11, 1964; children: Edward, Paul, Brian. BSME, U. Minn., 1959; MS, Case Western Res. U., 1966, PhD, 1970. Reactor engr. Argonne Nat. Lab., Idaho Falls, Idaho, 1959-60, U.S. Army Corps of Engrs., Argonne, Ill., 1960-64; mem. tech. staff Bell Telephone Labs., Columbus, Ohio, 1970-74; mgr. bioengring. dept. Lord Corp., Erie, Pa., 1974-81; pres. Paulson Med. Devel., Erie, 1981-84; head bioengring. Harrington Arthritis Research Ctr., Phoenix, 1984—; dir. research Shrine Hosp., Erie, 1978-81. Contbr. articles to tech. jours.; patentee in field. Leader, Indian Guides, Erie, 1975-78; com. mem. Boy Scouts Am., Erie, 1981-84. Mem. Am. Soc. Mech. Engrs. (sect. chmn. 1978-79, Mem. Yr. 1982), Am. Soc. Biomaterials (nat. program chair, 1987), Orthopaedic Research Soc., Am. Soc. Testing, and Materials. Club: Toastmasters (Erie) (pres. 1979-80). Home: 1760 E Hale Mesa AZ 85203 Office: Harrington Arthritis Research Ctr 1800 E Van Buren Phoenix AZ 85006

KOENIG, JOAN FOSTER, real estate broker; b. Harrisburg, Ill., Feb. 15, 1930; d. William Jennings and Adria May Foster; B.S., Miami U., 1951; M.A., Ariz. State U., 1967; m. Alan Eastman Disbrow, June 26, 1978; children—William R., Theodore J. Airline stewardess Am. Airlines, Inc., 1951-52; research investigator Procter & Gamble Co., Cin., 1952-53; co-owner, v.p. Koenig Aviation, Inc., Casa Grande, Ariz., 1953-69; real estate sales assoc. Ed Post Realty, Scottsdale, Ariz., 1978-79; real estate broker Koenig Real Estate, Casa Grande, 1980—. Bd. govs. Casa Grande Town Hall, 1972-75; bd. dirs. Hoemako Hosp. Aux.; vice-chmn. Pinal County Democratic Com., 1972-76, dist. 6 chmn., 1972-76, mem. state exec. com., 1972-76; pres. West Pinal County Dem. Women's Club, 1975, 84. Recipient Women's Flight Achievement award Internat. Flying Farmers, 1964. Mem. AAUW (pres. Casa Grande br. 1986-88), Women's Council Realtors, Ariz. Fedn. Democratic Women's Clubs (3d v.p.), Casa Grande Valley Cotton Wives, Casa Grande Hist. Soc., Casa Grande Panhellenic (pres. 1970), Mortar Board, Kappa Kappa Gamma. Democrat. Episcopalian. Club: Woman's of Casa Grande (bd. dirs. 1985-87), Desert Woman's. Home: Route 1 Box 469 Casa Grande AZ 85222 Office: PO Box 432 Casa Grande AZ 85222

KOEPPEL, GARY MERLE, writer, publisher, art gallery owner; b. Albany, Oreg., Jan 20, 1938; s. Carl Melvin and Barbara Emma (Adams) K. B.A., Portland State U., 1961; M.F.A., State U. Iowa, 1963. Writing instr. State U. Iowa, Iowa City, 1963-64; guest prof. English, U. P.R. San Juan, 1954-65; assoc. prof. creative writing Portland (Oreg.) State U., 1965-68; owner, operator Coast Gallery, Big Sur and Pebble Beach, Calif., Maui, Hawaii, 1971—; owner Koeppel Pub. Co.; editor, pub. Big Sur Gazette, 1978-81; producer, sponsor Maui Marine Art Expo., Monterey Marine Art Expo. Author: Sculptured Sandcast Candles, 1974. Founder Big Sur Vol. Fire Brigade, 1975; chmn. coordinating com. Big Sur Area Planning, 1972-75; chmn. Big Sur Citizens Adv. Com., 1975-78. Mem. Big Sur C. of C. (pres. 1974-75, 82-84), Big Sur Grange, Audubon Soc., Cousteau Soc., Phi Gamma Delta, Alpha Delta Sigma. Address: Coast Gallery Hwy One Big Sur CA 93920

KOESTEL, ALFRED, mechanical engineer; b. Bruchsal, Baden, Fed. Republic of Germany, Jan. 18, 1921; came to U.S., 1924; s. William and Anna Magdelana (Holfelder) K.; m. Lucille Irma Koestel, Mar. 31, 1945 (dec. 1983); children, Mark Alfred; m. Ursula Helena Koestel, Jan. 19, 1985. BSME, Cleve. State U., 1943; diploma, Yale U., 1944; MSME, Case Western Res. U., 1949. Registered profl. engr., Ohio. Assoc. prof. mech. engring. Case We. Res. U., Cleve., 1946-59; staff engr. TRW, Cleve., 1959-69; cons. engr. Los Alamos (N.Mex.) Nat. Lab., 1970—, collaborator, 1972—. Contbr. articles to profl. jours. Mem. Sigma Xi. Home and Office: Buena Vista Ranch Rural Rt 2 Box 4 Nogales AZ 85621

KOESTER, BERTHOLD KARL, lawyer; honorary consul Federal Republic of Germany; b. Aachen, Germany, June 30, 1931; s. Wilhelm P. and Margarethe A. (Witteler) K.; m. Hildegard Maria Buettner, June 30, 1961; children: Georg W., Wolfgang J., Reinhard B. JD, U. Muenster, Fed. Republic Germany, 1957. Cert. Real Estate Agt., Ariz. Asst. prof. civil and internat. law U. Muenster, 1957-60; atty. Cts. of Duesseldorf, Fed. Republic Germany, 1960-82; v.p. Bank J.H. Vogeler & Co., Duesseldorf, 1960-64; pres. Bremer Tank-u. Kuehlschifahrts Gesellschaft, Bremen, Fed. Republic Germany, 1969-72; atty., trustee internat. corps., Duesseldorf and Phoenix, 1973-82, Phoenix, 1983—; of counsel Tancer Law Offices, Phoenix, 1978-86; prof. internat. bus. law Am. Grad. Sch. Internat. Mgmt., Glendale, Ariz., 1978-81; with Applewhite, Laflin & Lewis, Real Estate Investments, Phoenix, 1981-86, ptnr., 1982-86, Beucler Real Estate Investments, 1986—, Scottsdale, Ariz.; hon. consul Fed. Republic of Germany for Ariz., 1982—; pres. Arimpex Ariz. Import Export Trading Agy., Phoenix, 1981—. Contbr. articles to profl. jours. Pres. Parents Assn. Humboldt Gymnasium, Duesseldorf, 1971-78; active German Red Cross, from 1977. Mem. Duesseldorf Chamber of Lawyers, Bochum (Fed. Republic Germany) Assn. Tax Lawyers, Bonn German-Saudi Arabian Assn. (pres. 1976-79), Bonn German-Korean Assn., Assn. for German-Korean Econ. Devel. (pres. 1974-78), Ariz. Consular Corps, German-Am. C. of C., Phoenix Met. C. of C. Club: Rotary (Scottsdale, Ariz.). Home: 6201 E Cactus Rd Scottsdale AZ 85254 Office: 4250 E Camelback Rd Suite 120 K Phoenix AZ 85018

KOETSCH, PHILIP WAYNE, electronics executive; b. Vanceburg, Ky., Nov. 25, 1935; s. Clarence Robert and Ethel Louise (Phillips) K.; m. Joyce Moore, May 30, 1957; children: Karen, Tanya, Sharon, Christopher. BSEE, U S C., 1959, MSEE, 1960. Engr. Westinghouse Corp., Pitts., 1960-63; sr. engr. Lockheed Aircraft Corp., Marietta, Ga., 1963-66; cons. Rockford, Ill., 1966-70; design supr. Honeywell, San Diego, 1970-71; test systems mgr. NCR, San Diego, 1971-76; chief engr. ACDC Electronics, Oceanside, Calif., 1976-80; v.p. engring. Powertec Inc., Chatsworth, Calif., 1980—. Contbr. tech. papers to profl. publs.; patentee in field. Mem. IEEE, Am. Elec. Assn., Tau Beta Pi, Sigma Pi Sigma, Pi Mu Epsilon, Omicron Delta Kappa. Avocations: skin diving, chess. Office: Powertec Inc 20550 Nordhoff Chatsworth CA 91311

KOFF, THEODORE H., researcher, educator; b. Phila., July 9, 1928; s. Harry and Yetta (Bernstein) K.; m. Nancy Koff; children: Louis, Susan, David. BS in Psychology, CCNY, 1950; MSW, Columbia U., 1953; EdD in Rehab. Adminstrn., U. Ariz., 1971. Program asst. Jewish Community Ctr., Houston, 1953-56; program dir. Jewish Community Ctr., Dallas, 1956-60; asst. exec. dir. Dallas Home for Jewish Aged, 1960-62; exec. dir. Handmaker Jewish Nursing Home for the Aged, 1962-73, exec. dir. Community Mental Health Services Adult Day Health Program, 1962-73; prof. mgmt. and policy Coll. Bus. and Pub. Adminstrn. U. Ariz., Tucson, 1973—, dir. Ariz. Long Term Care Gerontology Ctr., 1973—, dir. pub. sector programs, 1986—. Contbr. articles to profl. jours. Recipient Research award, Am. Coll. Health Care Adminstrs., 1986, Outstanding Gerontologist award, Western Gerontol. Soc., 1984, Outstanding Gerontol. Educator, Weber State Coll., 1982, Outstanding Leadership and Dedicated Service award, Tucson Community Council, 1972, Outstanding Citizen of Tucson award, 1972, Profl. Service award, Tucson Jewish Community Council, 1967. Fellow Gerontol. Soc. (chmn. edn. com.); mem. Nat. Assn. Long Term Care Gerontology Ctrs. (pres. 1986—), Ariz. License Bd. for Nursing Home Adminstrs., Am. Soc. Aging, Tex. Assn. Homes for the Ages, Pima Council on Aging, Am. Hosp. Assn. Council on Long Term Care (Assembly on Long Term Care), Sr. Now Generation (treas.), Am. Assn. Homes for the Aged. Am. Pub. Health Assn. (bd. govs. Gerontol. Health sect.), Am. Coll. Nursing Home Adminstrs., Nat. Hospice Orgn., Am. Soc. Pub. Adminstrs., Nat. Assn. Social Workers, Acad. Cert. Social Workers. Home: 5209 E Woodspring Dr Tucson AZ 85712 Office: Ariz Long Term Care Gerontology Ctr 1807 E Elm Tucson AZ 85719

KOFFLER, HENRY, university president; b. Vienna, Austria, Sept. 17, 1922; naturalized U.S. citizen.; B.S., U. Ariz., 1943; M.S., U. Wis., 1944, Ph.D., 1947. Asst. to assoc. prof. bacteriology Purdue U., West Lafayette, Ind., 1947-52, coodinator research, 1949-59, prof. biology, 1952-74, asst. to dean Grad. Sch., 1957-59, asst. dean, 1959-60, head dept. biol. sci., 1959-75, F. L. Hovde Disting. prof., 1974-75; prof. biochemistry and microbiology, v.p. acad. affairs U. Minn., Mpls., 1975-82; pres. U. Ariz., Tucson, 1982—; mem. Commn. Undergrad. Edn. in Biol. Sci., 1966-69, vice chmn., 1966-67, chmn., 1967-69; mem. Purdue Research Found., 1967—; cons., examiner North Central Assn. Colls., 1967—; mem. 2d-7th Internat. Congress Biochemistry, Paris, Brussels, Vienna, Moscow, Tokyo; mem. 6th-8th, 10th Internat. Congress Microbiology, Rome, Stockholm, Montreal, Mexico City; mem. 9th, 11th Internat. Bot. Congress, Montreal, Seattle; mem. 1st-3d Internat. Biophys. Congress, Stockholm, Vienna, Boston; mem. 5th Internat. Congress Electron Microscopes, Phila., 16th Internat. Zool. Congress, Washington, 4th Internat. Congress Chemother, Washington; 24th Internat. Congress Physiol. Sci., 1st Internat. Congress Bacteriology, Jerusalem, 1st Internat. Congress Internat. Assn. Microbiology Soc., Tokyo. Guggenheim fellow Sch. Medicine, Case Western Res. U., 1953-54. Fellow Am. Acad. Microbiology; mem. Am. Soc. Biol. Chemists, Biophys. Soc., Am. Soc. Microbiology, Am. Soc. Cell Biologists. Office: U Ariz Office of Pres Tucson AZ 85721 *

KOGA, ROKUTARO, astrophysicist; b. Nagoya, Japan, Aug. 18, 1942; came to U.S., 1961, naturalized, 1966; s. Toyoki and Emiko (Shinra) K.; m. Cordula Rosow, May 5, 1981; 1 son, Evan A. B.A., U. Calif.-Berkeley, 1966; Ph.D., U. Calif.-Riverside, 1974. Research fellow U. Calif.-Riverside, 1974-75; research physicist Case Western Res U., Cleve., 1975-79, asst. prof., 1979-81; physicist Aerospace Corp., Los Angeles, 1981—. Mem. Am. Phys. Soc., Am. Geophys. Union, IEEE, N.Y. Acad. Scis., Sigma Xi. Contbr. articles to profl. confs.; research on gamma-ray astronomy, solar neutron observation, space scis., charged particles in space and the effect of cosmic rays on microcircuits in space. Home: 8005 Stewart Ave Los Angeles CA 90045 Office: Aerospace Corp Space Scis Labs PO Box 92957 Los Angeles CA 90009

KOGAN, VLADIMIR ALEKSANDROVICH, physicist; b. Tbilisi, Georgia, USSR, June 2, 1937; came to U.S., 1980; s. Alexander D. and Helena R. (Haikevich) K.; m. Tatiana E. Berezhinskaya, Feb. 14, 1960; children: Irene, Victoria. BS, State U., Tbilisi, 1959; MS, Agrophys. Inst., Leningrad, USSR, 1966, PhD, 1968. Research assoc. Inst. of Cibernetics, Tbilisi, 1959-62; sr. scientist Agrophys. Inst., 1966-80; research scientist Gen. Monitors, Inc., Costa Mesa, Calif., 1981—; tchr. physics Coll. Mining Engrs., Leningrad, 1966-80; cons. Nat. Patent Com., Moscow, 1975-80. Co-author: Humidity Measurements, 1977; contbr. numerous articles to publs.; patentee in field. Recipient Honorary medal Supreme Counsel, Moscow, 1970, Achievement medals USSR Expn. Com., Moscow, 1971-79, Achievement certs. Internat. Expns., Montreal, Canada, Leipzig, German Democratic Republic. Mem. Am. Chem. Soc., Catalysis Soc. Home: 10172 Gregory St Cypress CA 90630 Office: Gen Monitors Inc 3037 Enterprise St Costa Mesa CA 92626

KOHL, HAROLD WILLIS, JR., physician; b. Tucson, Jan. 16, 1935; s. Harold Willis Sr. and Ann Kathleen (O'Flaherty) K.; m. Rose Ann Michelli, Dec. 27, 1958; children: Harold Willis III, Elizabeth Ann, John Thomas. AB, U. Ariz., 1956; MD, St. Louis U., 1960. Pvt. practice medicine Tucson, 1962—; chief of staff St. Mary's Hosp. and Health Ctr., Tucson, 1975-77; bd. dirs. Carondelet Health Service, Tucson; chief exec. officer Profl. Directory Services, Inc., Tucson, 1987—. Recipient Physician Recognition award, AMA, Chgo., 1973, 76, 79, 82, 85. Mem. AMA, Am. Coll. Cardiology, Am. Geriatrics Soc., Am. Soc. Internal Medicine,Phi Rho Sigma, Phi Kappa Theta. Republican. Roman Catholic. Lodge: Elks. Avocations: backpacking, racquetball, philately, photography. Office: Country Club Med Assocs PC 1002 N Country Club Rd Tucson AZ 85718

KOHL, JOHN PRESTON, management educator; b. Allentown, Pa., Dec. 26, 1942; s. Claude Evan and Edna Lenoir (Woodland) K.; m. Nancy Ann Christensen, Mar. 11, 1967; children—John P. Jr., Mark C. B.A., Moravian Coll., 1964; M.Div., Yale U., 1967; M.S. in Mgmt., Am. Tech. U., 1974. M.S. in Counseling, 1976; Ph.D. in Bus. Adminstrn., Pa. State U., 1982. Ordained to ministry United Ch. of Christ, 1967. Minister, Christ Congl. Ch., New Smyrna Beach, Fla., 1968-71, First Congl. Ch., Hutchinson, Minn., 1971-73; instr. Pa. State U., University Park, 1978-82; asst. prof. mgmt. U. Tex., El Paso, 1982-85; assoc. prof. mgmt. San Jose State U., Calif., 1985—; cons. in field. Co-author: (text) Personnel Management, 1986. Served to capt. U.S. Army, 1973-78; to maj. USAR, 1978—. Decorated Nat. Def. Service medal, Meritorious Service medal, Army Commendation medal. Mem. Acad. Mgmt. Contbr. articles to profl. publs. Home: 855 DeLeon Dr El Paso TX 79912 Office: San Jose State U Sch Bus San Jose CA 95192

KOHLER, BRYAN EARL, research chemistry educator; b. Heber City, Utah, June 9, 1940; s. Earl J. and Dawna Marie (Fraughton) K.; m. Susan Whitaker, Dec. 22, 1960; children: Bernard, Dylan, Brynja. BA, U. Utah, 1962; PhD, U. Chgo., 1967; postdoctoral student, Calif. Inst. Tech., 1968. Asst. prof. Harvard U., Cambridge, Mass., 1969-75; asst. prof. Wesleyan U., Middletown, Conn., 1975-77, prof., 1977-85, Beach prof. chemistry, 1982; prof. U. Calif., Riverside, 1985—; guest prof. Kamerlingh Onnes Lab. U. Leiden, The Netherlands, 1973, Physikalische Inst. U., Bayreuth, Fed. Republic of Germany, 1984-85; mem. biophysics and biophys. chemistry study sect. NIH. Contbr. articles to profl. jours. Grantee NIH, 1976—, NSF, 1967—. Mem. Acad. Sci., Conn. Acad. Arts and Scis., Am. Phys. Soc., Biophys. Soc., inst. Gonzo Spectroscopy (chmn. bd. dirs. 1975—), Sigma Xi. Office: U Calif Dept Chemistry 900 University Ave Riverside CA 92521

KOHLER, ERIC DAVE, history educator; b. Cin., Oct. 24, 1943; s. Walter Joseph and Irmgard (Marx) K.; m. Kathryn D. K. Kohler, June 22, 1968. AB, Brown U., 1965; MA, Stanford U., 1967, PhD, 1971. Vis. asst. prof. history Calif. State U., Humboldt, 1970-71; asst. prof. U. Wyo., Laramie, 1971-78, assoc. prof., 1978—. Recipient Deutcher Akademischer Austauchdienst award, 1968, U. Wyo. Faculty Devel. award, 1972. Mem. Am. Cath. Hist. Assn., Am. Hist. Assn., German Studies Assn. Club: Laramie Country. Avocations: golf, elec. wiring, computers. Office: U Wyo Dept History PO Box 3198 Laramie WY 82071

KOHLER, GEORGE OSCAR, research chemist, consultant; b. Milw., Apr. 9, 1913; s. Oscar Charles and Thora (Zachariasen) K.; m. Christine Gilchrist, Oct. 5, 1940; children—Cynthia Ann Castner, Sylvia Luftig, William Mark Kohler. B.S., U. Wis., 1934, M.S., 1936, Ph.D., 1938. Postdoctoral research fellow U. Wis., Madison, 1938-39; lab. dir., v.p. research Cerophyl Labs., Inc., Kansas City, Mo., 1939-55, owner, pres., 1955-56; lab. chief Western Regional Research Ctr., Dept. Agr., Albany, Calif., 1956-81; pres., cons. G. O. Kohler & Assocs., Inverness, Calif., 1981—; cons. France Luzerne, Chalons-Sur-Marne, France, 1972—, Gen. Electric Co., Valley Forge, Pa., 1981-82, NASA, Moffet Field, Calif., 1983, Hokuto Koki Enging. Co., Sapporo, Japan, 1980-82; U.S. del. OECD, Paris, 1979-81, UN-FAO Working Group, Rome, 1976, Brazil Conf. on Leaf Protein-Nat. Acad. Sci., 1978; mem. U.S.-Japan Coop. Program on Natural Resources, Tokyo, 1979-

81; charter mem. Sr. Exec. Service, U.S. Dept. Agr., 1979-81. Contbr. articles to tech. jours., chpts. to books on forages, oilseeds and agrl. processing. Patentee processing of agrl. commodities. Recipient Superior Service award Dept. Agr., 1962, award of merit, 1970; award of merit Am. Dehydrators Assn., 1962. Mem. Am. Chem. Soc., Am. Assn. Cereal Chemists, Am. Poultry Sci. Assn., Am. Inst. Nutrition, Inst. Food Tech., Am. Soc. Animal Sci., Sigma Xi, Phi Beta Kappa, Phi Lambda Upsilon, Gamma Alpha. Lutheran. Lodge: Masons. Home and Office: 12700 Sir Francis Drake Blvd PO Box 454 Inverness CA 94937

KOHLER, MARTHA HANSEN, engineering and construction company executive; b. Milw., Oct. 29, 1947; d. Ellis A. and Helen (Anderson) Hansen; m. Andrew S. Kohler, Dec. 18, 1971; children: Petra, Lara. BS in Geology, U. Wis., 1969, MS in Water Resource Mgmt., 1970, PhD in Oceanography and Limnology, 1973; MBA, Golden Gate U., 1981. Research asst. Marine Research Lab., Madison, Wis., 1970-73; environ. project mgr. Bechtel Nat., Inc., San Francisco, 1973-78, project devel. specialist, 1978-81, environ. services dept. mgr., 1981-84, bus. dept. mgr., 1984—; mem. rev. bd. U. Chgo. for Argonne Nat. Lab., Chgo., 1983—; mem. Marine Bd. Nat. Research Council, Washington, 1977-80. Mem. Soc. Econ. Paleontologists and Mineralogists, Marine Tech. Soc., Soc. Women Engrs., Sigma Xi, Phi Kappa Phi. Club: Commonwealth (San Francisco) (Engrs. Club). Office: Bechtel Nat Inc 45 Fremont San Francisco CA 94119

KOHLER, ROYDEN RAMON, speech pathology educator; b. Midway, Utah, July 24, 1931; s. Reed Karl and Elda (Olsen) K.; m. Sally Aleen Braithwaite, Aug. 24, 1956; children: Janice Oliver, Bradley, Catherine Hurst, Stephen, Amy Ann, Lisa Beth, Robert Karl. BS, Brigham Young U., 1958, MS, 1961; PhD, U. Utah, 1967. Lic. speech pathologist, Wyo. Speech pathologist Mont. Soc. Crippled Children, Kalispell, 1959; tchr. Idaho Falls (Idaho) Schs., 1960-62; speech pathologist Daggett, Hinckley and Newberry Schs., Calif., 1962-65; chmn. dept. speech pathology Salt Lake City Schs., 1966-68; prof. speech pathology U. Wyo., Laramie, 1962—, chmn. dept. speech pathology, 1968-82; cons./mem. Wyo. Cleft Palate Team, Cheyenne, 1968—. Served as sgt. U.S. Army, 1953-54. Mem. Am. Speech Lang. Hearing Assn. (cert.), Am. Cleft Palate Assn., Ptnr.'s of Ams. Home: 1084 Colina Dr Laramie WY 82070 Office: U Wyo Dept Speech Pathology Audiology PO Box 3311 University Sta Laramie WY 82071

KOHLER, SUSAN, speech pathologist; b. Lakewood, Ohio, Apr. 16, 1955; d. Richard Theodore and Patricia Ann (Vore) K.; m. C. Brady Wilson, Apr. 20, 1980 (div. June 1984). BS, Ariz. State U., 1977, MS, 1979. Speech-lang. pathologist Phoenix Day Sch. for the Deaf, 1979-80, Kyrene (Ariz.) Sch. Dist., 1980-82; pvt. pracitce speech pathology Scottsdale, Tempe, Ariz., 1982-85, Los Angeles, 1985—; instr. voice improvement seminars, Phoenix, 1984-85; guest speaker on speech and lang. improvement problems, Phoenix, 1984-85; cons. Langs. Devel. Program Pub. Schs., Tempe, 1980-82; instr. creative dramatics activities seminars, Phoenix, 1980-82. Named one of Outstanding Young Women of Am., 1979. Mem. Am. Speech Lang. and Hearing Assn., Screen Actors Guild, Actors Equity Assn., Am. Fedn. TV and Radio Artists, Alpha Pi (pres. 1974), Curiosity Corps (pres. 1981-84). Avocations: theatre, film, TV, singing, dancing.

KOHLER, TED RANEY, physician, vascular surgeon; b. Columbus, Ohio, May 16, 1950; s. Paul Whisler and Geraldine (Raney) K.; m. Hope Lynn Druckman, Dec. 17, 1978; children: Andrew Samuel, Laura Ann. BS summa cum laude, Harvard U., 1972; MD, Harvard Med. Sch., 1976. Diplomate Am. Bd. Surgery. Surg. resident Brigham and Women's Hosp., Boston, 1976-82, vascular fellow, 1982-83; asst. prof. U. Wash., Seattle, 1983—; bd. dirs. Vascular Lab., Harborview Med. Ctr., Seattle, 1985—; chief vascular surgery Harborview Med. Ctr., 1983—. Author numerous publications and articles. Fellow ACS; mem. Western Vascular Soc. (founding), Northwest Vascular Soc. (founding), Assn. Acad. Surgery, Puget Sound Vascular Soc. (co-chmn. 1985—), U. Wash. Henry Harkins Surg. Soc., King County Med. Soc., Wash. State Med. Assn. Home: 602 36th Ave Seattle WA 98122 Office: Harborview Med Ctr ZA-16 325 9th Ave Seattle WA 98104

KOHLMANN, HENRY GEORGE, corporation executive, lawyer; b. Lincoln, Nebr., Oct. 20, 1939; s. John Henry Kohlman and Lottie Louise (Marzok) Kohlman Linch; m. Ramona Marie Turinia, Aug. 17, 1968; children: Henry George, Elizabeth Eileen. AA, Coll. San Mateo, 1965; BSEE, San Jose State Coll., 1971; JD, Hastings Sch. Law, U. Calif., 1974. Bar: U.S. Patent Office 1972, Calif. 1974. Engring. asst. Lockheed Missles and Space, Sunnyvale, Calif., 1966-69; computer procedures analyst Varian Assocs., Palo Alto, Calif., 1969-70; computer cons. Lockheed Missles and Space, Sunnyvale, 1973; sole practice, San Mateo, Calif., 1974-77; patent counsel McDonnell Douglas Corp., Long Beach, Calif., 1977-79; chief counsel Microdata Corp., Newport Beach, Calif., 1979-86; corp. v.p., gen. counsel Cipher Data Products Inc., San Diego, 1986—. Served with USNR, 1958-60. Mem. Calif. Bar Assn., Orange County Bar Assn., San Francisco Bar Assn., IEEE, Eta Kappa Nu, Tau Beta Pi. Republican. Developer patentability of computer software, technical idea exchange.

KOHL MAXWELL, LOIS, marketing professional; b. Balt., Mar. 28, 1952; d. Morton Barnard and Gwen (Caplan) Cole; m. Michael Kim Maxwell, July 11, 1980. BA, U. Colo., 1975. V.p. Mill Valley (Calif.) Film Festival, 1977-80; prin. Lois Cole Designs, Fairfax, Calif., 1978-82; asst. v.p. advt. Fireman's Fund Ins., Novato, Calif., 1982-86; mgr. mktg., design Hornblower Yachts, Inc., San Francisco, 1986—; cons., designer San Francisco, Oakland, Calif., 1985—. Author Innkeeper Newsletter advt. column, 1984. Mem. Direct Mktg. Creative Guild. Democrat. Avocations: ballet, aviation, writing. Home: 500 Pinewood Dr San Rafael CA 94903

KOHN, GERHARD, psychologist, educator; b. Neisse, Germany, Nov. 18, 1921; s. Erich and Marie (Prager) K.; m. Irene M. Billinger, Feb. 9, 1947; children—Mary, Eric. B.S., Northwestern U., 1948, M.A., 1949, Ph.D., 1952; postgrad. U. So. Calif., 1960. Instr., Northwestern U., 1947-49; instr., counselor, dir. pub. relations Kendall Coll., Evanston, Ill., 1947-51; psychologist, counselor Jewish Vocat. Services, Los Angeles, 1951-53, Long Beach Unified Sch. Dist., Calif., 1953-61; instr. Long Beach City Coll., 1955-61; asst. prof. psychology Long Beach State U., 1955-56; counselor, instr. Santa Ana Coll., Calif., 1961-65; prof. Calif. State U., Fullerton, 1971-72; lectr. Orange Coast Coll., 1972-75; asst. clin. prof. psychiatry U. Calif.-Irvine; dir. Reading Devel. Ctr., Long Beach, 1958—, Gerhard Kohn Sch. Ednl. Therapy, 1967—; exec. dir. Young Horizons; pvt. practice psychology, 1958—; cons. HEW, Bur. Hearing and Appeals, Social Security Adminstrn., Long Beach/Orange County B'nai B'rith Career and Counseling Services (cons. to Long Beach Council), Long Beach Council of Parent Coop. Nursery Sch., Orange County Headstart, Orange County Coop. Pre-Schs. Served with AUS, 1942-47. Mem. Am. Personnel and Guidance Assn., Nat. Vocat. Guidance Assn., Am. Psychol. Assn., Calif. Psychol. Assn. (dir. 1976-79, sec. 1980-81), Orange County Psychol. Assn. (dir., pres. 1974), Long Beach Psychol. Assn. (pres. 1985, 86), Los Angeles County Psychol. Assn. (treas., sec.), NEA, Calif. Assn. Sch. Psychologists, Phi Delta Kappa, Psi Chi. Lodge: Elks. Office: 5479 Abbeyfield St Long Beach CA 90815

KOHN, ROBERT SAMUEL, JR., real estate consultant; b. Denver, Jan. 7, 1949; s. Robert Samuel and Miriam Lackner (Neusteter) K.; B.S., U. Ariz., 1971; 1 son, Randall Stanton; m. 2d, Eleanor B. Kohn; children: Joseph Robert, Andrea Rene. Asst. buyer Robinson's Dept. Store, Los Angeles, 1971; agt. Neusteter Realty Co., Denver, 1972-73, exec. v.p., 1973-76; pres. Project Devel. Services, Denver, 1976-78, pres., chief exec. officer, 1978-83; pres. Kohn and Assos., Inc., 1979-83, The Burke Co., Inc., Irvine, Calif., 1983-84, ptnr. 1984—. Mem. Bldg. Owners and Mgrs. Assn. (pres. 1977-78, dir. 1972-78, dir. S.W. Conf. Bd. 1977-78), Denver Art Mus., Denver U. Library Assn., Central City Opera House Assn., Inst. Real Estate Mgmt. Republican. Jewish. Club: Newport Beach Tennis. Home: 10 Skysail Dr Corona DelMar CA 92625 Office: The Burke Co Inc 2111 Bus Center Dr Irvine CA 92715

KOJIAN, VARUJAN HAIG, conductor; b. Beirut, Mar. 12, 1935; came to U.S., 1956, naturalized, 1965; s. Haig Awak and Anouche (Der-Parseghian) K. Student (1st prize), Paris Nat. Conservatory, 1947-50; diploma, Curtis Inst. Music, 1959; student, U. So. Calif., 1964. Asst. concertmaster and asst. condr. Los Angeles Philharm., 1965-71; assoc. condr. Seattle Symphony, 1972-75; prin. guest condr. Royal Opera, Stockholm, 1973-80; music dir. Utah Symphony, Salt Lake City, 1980-83, Chautauqua (N.Y.) Symphony, 1981-84, Ballet West, Salt Lake City, 1984—, Santa Barbara (Calif.) Symphony, 1985—; faculty dept. music U. Utah, Salt Lake City, 1980-83, U. Calif., Santa Barbara., 1985—; music dir. Santa Barbara Sympnony, 1985—. Recipient 1st prize Internat. Conducting Competition, Sorrento, Italy, 1972; decorated Order of Lion Finland, 1975, Order of Lion also by govts. Greece, 1956, Iran, 1955, Lebanon, 1956. Home: 1650 La Coronilla Dr Santa Barbara CA 93109 Office: 1650 La Coronilla Dr Santa Barbara CA 93109 Office: Santa Barbara Symphony 214 East Victoria Santa Barbara CA 93101

KOKKINOS ASHLEY, SOPHIA, research mechanical engineer; b. Athens, Greece, Jan. 15, 1943; came to U.S., 1961; d. John Spyro and Efthimia (Panagiotithou) Kokkinos; m. Joseph Lavon Ashley III, May 15, 1965; 1 child, Natalia. BS in Physics, N.E. La. U., 1965, MS in Physics, 1968; MS in Engring., Old Dominion U., 1978; postgrad., U. La Verne. Registered profl. engr., Calif. Tchr. several states, 1968-77; mech. engr. Navy Atlantic Div., Norfolk, Va., 1978-79, Naval Civil Engring. Lab., Port Hueneme, Calif., 1979—; cons. in field, Camarillo, Calif., 1983—. Contbr. articles to profl. jours. Tchr. Greek, Greek Orthodox Ch., 1982-83. Named Engr. of Yr., Naval Civil Engring. Lab. 1985, Engr. of Yr. Naval Facilities Engring. Comand, 1986, Engr. of Yr. Engring. Council San Fernando Valley, Calif., 1986, Engr. of Yr. Engring. Council Ventura, Calif., 1986; recipient Fed. Engr. of Yr. award NSPE, 1986. Mem. Soc. Women Engrs. (pres. 1985-86, v.p. 1983-85), Soc. Mil. Engrs., Daus. Penelopy (Grand Marshall 1984-85), Sigma Xi. Avocations: oil painting, golf, reading. Home: 1461 Brookhaven Ave Camarillo CA 93010

KOKOT, DAVID FRANK, engineer; b. Encino, Calif., Sept. 20, 1959; s. Frank and Marilyn Ruth (Parker) K.; m. Robyn Joyce Bechtold, Aug. 28, 1982; 1 child, Gillian Robyn. AS, North Idaho Coll., 1979; BSME, U. Idaho, 1981. Energy technician Thomas Gerard and Assocs., Spokane, Wash., 1982-83, project engr., dir. computer ops., 1983-86; design engr. Bovay N.W., Spokane, 1986—. Mem. ASME, N.W. Computer Aided Drafting/Computer Aided Mfg. Assn. Avocations: model railroading, computers, hiking, camping. Home: N 7633 Wiscomb St Spokane WA 99208 Office: Bovay NW E 808 Sprague Ave Spokane WA 99202

KOLANOSKI, THOMAS EDWIN, financial company executive; b. San Francisco, Mar. 1, 1937; s. Theodore Thaddeus and Mary J. (Luczynski) K.; m. Sheila O'Brien, Dec. 26, 1960; children: Kenneth John, Thomas Patrick, Michael Sean. BS, U. San Francisco, 1959, MA, 1965. Secondary sch. tchr. San Francisco Unified Sch. Dist., 1960-64; adminstr. Huntington Beach (Calif.) Union, 1969-79, counselor, 1965-69; v.p. fin. services Waddell & Reed, Inc., Ariz., Nev., Utah, 1969—. Fellow NDEA, 1965. Mem. Nat. Assn. Secondary Sch. Prins., Internat. Assn. of Fin. Planners, Nat. Assn. Securities Dealers. Republican. Roman Catholic. Lodge: Kiwanis. Avocation: racketball. Home: 1783 Panay Circle Costa Mesa CA 92626 also: 10218 N Central Phoenix AZ 85021

KOLAR, OSCAR CLINTON, physicist; b. South Gate, Calif., Sept. 26, 1928; s. Oscar Clinton and Elizabeth (Deeds) K.; m. Rose Marilyn Markley, Jan. 31, 1953 (div. 1971); children: Elizabeth Louise, John Clinton, Walter Markley; m. Ingeborg Anna Bräutigam, Feb. 2, 1982. BA, UCLA, 1949; PhD, U. Calif., Berkeley, 1955. Registered profl. engr., Calif. Research asst. Lawrence Berkeley Nat. Lab., 1950-55; group leader Lawrence Livermore (Calif.) Nat. Lab., 1955—; v.p. Atomic Labs. Inc., Berkeley, 1953-60; pres. MCI, Inc., Livermore, 1960-68. Contbr. articles to profl. jours. Mem. Am. Phys. Soc., Am. Nuclear Soc. (exec. com. 1983—), AAAS, Am. Assn. Physics Tchrs., Sigma Xi. Avocations: reading, travelling. Home: 620 Zircon Way Livermore CA 94550 Office: Lawrence Livermore Nat Lab PO Box 808 Livermore CA 94550

KOLAZ, THOMAS MICHAEL, public relations executive; b. Springfield, Ill., Apr. 12, 1955; s. Kenneth Michael and Mary Joyce (Lamie) K. BA, U. Ariz., 1977, MEd, 1982. Draftsman Sangamon State U., Springfield, 1978-80; asst. supr. pub. program Ariz. State Mus., Tucson, 1982-83, exhibits preparator, 1983-84; dir. pub. programs Inst. for Am. Research, Tucson, 1984—. Co-author: Archaeology in the Urban Setting: The Hohokam Village of Las Colinas, Phoenix, Arizonia, 1986. Vol. Tucson Festival Soc., 1982—. Mem. Am. Assn. Mus., Am. Assn. State and Local History, Ariz. Mus. Assn., Mus. Studies Assn. Avocations: attending Yaqui Indian fiestas, visiting museums, hiking, running, swimming. Home: 3819 E 3d St #15 Tucson AZ 85716 Office: Inst Am Research 245 S Plumer #14 Tucson AZ 85719

KOLBE, JAMES THOMAS, congressman; b. Evanston, Ill., June 28, 1942; s. Walter William and Helen (Reed) K.; m. Sarah Marjorie Dinham, Apr. 16, 1977. B.A. in Polit. Sci., Northwestern U., 1965; M.B.A. in Econs., Stanford U., 1967. Asst. to coordinating architect Ill. Bldg. Authority, Chgo., 1970-72; spl. asst. to Gov. Richard Ogilvie Chgo., 1972-73; v.p. Wood Canyon Corp., Tucson, 1973—; mem. Ariz. Senate, 1977-83, majority whip, 1979-81; cons. Tucson, 1983-85; mem. 99th and 100th Congresses, 1985—; mem. appropriations com. 1985—. Trustee Embry-Riddle Aero. U., Daytona Beach, Fla.; bd. dirs. Community Food Bank, Tucson, Casa de los Niños Crisis Nursery, Tucson; Republican precinct committeeman, Tucson, 1974—. Served as lt. USNR, 1977-79, Vietnam. Mem. Am. Legion, VFW. Republican. Methodist. Office: 5th Dist Congl Office 4444 E Grant Rd Suite 125 Tucson AZ 85712

KOLENDER, WILLIAM BARNETT, police chief; b. Chgo., May 23, 1935; s. David Solomon and Esther (Dickman) K.; children—Michael, Myrna, Joy, Randie, Dennis. Student, San Diego City Coll., 1963; B.A. in Pub. Adminstrn, San Diego State U., 1964. With San Diego Police Dept., 1956—, chief of police, 1976—; tchr. U. Calif., San Diego, 1971—, San Diego State U., 1972—; mem. Commn. on Peace Officers Standards and Tng. Calif. Vice pres. San Diego County council Boy Scouts Am.; mem. Mayor's Crime Control Commn.; pres. Boys' Clubs San Diego. Served with USN, 1953-55. Named Alumnus of Year San Diego State U., 1973, Outstanding Young Man of Year San Diego, 1970; recipient Mayor's Award for Human Relations and Civil Rights City of San Diego, 1972, Human Relations Award Am. Jewish Com., 1975; Diogenes award San Diego chpt. Public Relations Soc. Am., 1978; Man of Yr. award Irish Congress So. Calif., 1981; Histadrut award Am. Trade Union Council, 1981; Equal Opportunity award San Diego Urban League, 1981; Man of Yr. award Charter 100 Profl. Women's Club, 1981. Mem. Calif. Police Chiefs Assn., Calif. Police Officers Assn., Internat. Assn. Chiefs Police, Police Exec. Research Forum (dir.). Republican. Jewish. Club: San Diego Rotary. Home: 4035 Tambor Rd San Diego CA 92123 Office: City of San Diego Police Dept 801 W Market St San Diego CA 92101 *

KOLKER, HAL, entertainment arena executive, sports marketing executive; b. Buffalo, Oct. 4, 1949; s. Benjamin and Rose (Lippes) K.; student U. So. Caliif., 1969-72. Exec. asst. Neil Diamond, Los Angeles, 1972-74; cons. Norman Lear Tandem Prodns., Los Angeles, 1974-76; pres. Century City Sound, Los Angeles, 1976-77; pres. Budget Rent-A-Car, San Diego, 1976-78; v.p. San Diego Clippers NBA Basketball Club, Inc., 1978-80; v.p. San Diego Entertainment Inc., operator San Diego Sports Arena, 1980—; pres. Spectator Mktg. Corp., San Diego, 1983—, Edwin Schlossberg Prodns., 1987—; cons. Paramount Pictures Corp.; Bob Speck Sports Prodns.; exec. producer Bill Walton Show, 1979-80. Campaign chmn. George C. Hardie for 46th Dist. Assembly Calif., 1976. Mem. Am. Mgmt. Assn., Am. Mktg. Assn. Office: 1133 Columbia St Suite 101 San Diego CA 92101

KOLKEY, DANIEL MILES, lawyer; b. Chgo., Apr. 21, 1952; s. Eugene Louis and Gilda Penelope (Cowan) K.; m. Donna Lynn Christie, May 15, 1982; children: Eugene, William. B.A., Stanford U., 1974; J.D., Harvard U., 1977. Bar: Calif. 1977, U.S. Dist. Ct. (cen., no., ea. dists.) Calif., U.S. Ct. Appeals (9th cir.) 1979, U.S. Supreme Ct., 1983. Law clk. U.S. Dist. Ct. judge, N.Y.C., 1977-78; ptnr. Gibson Dunn & Crutcher, Los Angeles, 1978—. Contbr. articles to profl. publs. Vice chmn. and sec. internat. relations sect. Town Hall of Calif., Los Angeles, 1981—; chmn. internat. trade legis. subcom., internat. commerce steering com. Los Angeles Area C. of C., 1983—; mem. adv. council Asia Pacific Ctr. for Resolution of Internat. Bus. Disputes; bd. dirs., sec., treas. Los Angeles Ctr. for Internat. Comml. Arbitration, 1986—; assoc. mem. central com. Calif. Rep. Party, 1983—; mem. Los Angeles Com. on Fgn. Relations, 1983—; mem. Los Angeles World Affairs Council, Rep. Assocs. Mem. ABA, Internat. Bar Assn., Los Angeles County Bar Assn. Chartered Inst. Arbitrators, London (assoc.), Wilton Park Alumni of So. Calif. (chmn. exec. com.). Jewish. Office: Gibson Dunn & Crutcher 333 S Grand Ave Los Angeles CA 90071

KOLKOWICZ, ROMAN, political science educator, academic administrator, consultant; b. Poland, Nov. 15, 1929; came to U.S., 1949, naturalized, 1955; s. William and Edwarda (Goldberg) K.; children—Susan, Lisa, Gabriella. B.A., U. Buffalo, 1954; M.A., U. Chgo., 1958, Ph.D., 1964. Sr. staff mem. Rand Corp., Santa Monica, Calif., 1961-66, Inst. Def. analysis, Washington, 1966-70; prof. polit. sci. UCLA, 1970—, dir. Ctr. Internat. Strategic Affairs, 1974-82; co-dir. Project on Arms Control, 1983-85; dir. Project on Politics and War, 1985—; cons. to govt., others. Chmn. fgn. policy platform Calif. Dem. Party, 1972, 76. Served with U.S. Army, 1954-56. Ford Found. grantee, 1975-83; Rockefeller Found. grantee, 1975-77. Mem. Am. Polit. Sci. Assn., Internat. Sociol. Assn., Internat. Polit. Sci. Assn. Author: Soviet Military-Communist Party, 1967; Soldiers, Peasants, Bureaucrats, 1982; National Security and International Stability, 1983; Arms Control and International Security, 1983; Soviet Calculus of War, 1983, Logic of Nuclear Terror, 1987, Dilemmas of Nuclear Deterrence, 1987. Home: 21310 Bellini Dr Topanga CA 90290 Office: Dept Polit Sci UCLA Los Angeles CA 90024

KOLLER, HERBERT, mathematics educator, computer consultant; b. Vienna, Austria, Sept. 22, 1924; s. Franz and Hilde (Horak) K.; m. Kimlaing Connie Koller; children: Jonie Koller Fedor, Larraine Koller Hood, Martin, Monique. BSChemE, U. Nacional de Ingenieria, Peru, 1946; MS in Math., N.Y.U., 1964; PhD in Math., Yeshiva U., 1974. Sales engr. Cosmana, Lima, Peru, 1948-54; process devel. engr. A.M.F., Springdale, Conn., 1955-60; process design engr. Crawford and Russell Inc., Stamford, Conn., 1960-64; chmn. math. dept. U. Bridgeport, Conn., 1960-81; sr. lectr. Hong Kong Poly., 1978-79; vis. prof. U. P.R., 1981-84; lectr. computer sci. San Francisco State U., 1984—; cons. Resource Ctr. Sci. and Engring., U. P.R.; free-lance computer programmer and cons; participating guest Lawrence Livermore (Calif.) Nat. Lab. Contbr. articles to profl. jours. Active Darien (Conn.) Dem. Town Com., 1976-78; moderator Electoral Dist., Darien. Recipient J.F. Kennedy Library award, 1974. Mem. AAUP, Am. Math. Soc., Math. Assn. Am., Assn. Computing Machinery, Oesterr. Math. Gesellschaft, Sigma Xi. Home and Office: 326 Delano Ave San Francisco CA 94112-2526

KOLLER, HERBERT RICHARD, information scientist; b. Cleve., Sept. 5, 1921; s. Daniel D. and Frieda A. (Wiener) K.; m. Shirley Ann Leavitt, Mar. 7, 1943; children: Donald Lee, Susan Lizbeth (Mrs. Willard C. VanHorne), Laura Frances. B.S. in Chemistry, Case-Western Res. U., 1942; J.D., Am. U., 1952. Chemist Indsl. Rayon Co., 1942-43; patent examiner, information systems research and devel. U.S. Patent Office, 1943-66; dir. client services EBS Mgmt. Cons., Washington, 1966-68; prin. info. scientist Leasco Systems & Research Corp., Bethesda, Md., 1968-69; exec. dir. Am. Soc. Information Sci., Washington, 1969-73; prin. asso. Moshman Assos., Inc., Bethesda, 1973-74; legal editor Bur. Nat. Affairs, Washington, 1975-76; with chem. documentation group U.S. Patent and Trademark Office, 1977—; Research asso. Patent, Trademark and Copyright Research Inst., George Washington U., 1968-72; cons., lectr. in field. Contbr. articles to profl. jours. Sci. and tech. fellow Dept. Commerce, 1964-65. Fellow AAAS; Mem. Am. Chem. Soc., Assn. Computing Machinery, Am. Soc. Information Sci., Zeta Beta Tau. Home: 2700 Virginia Ave NW Washington DC 20037

KOLLIN, YONA, psychotherapist, administrator; b. Bklyn., Sept. 17, 1941; d. Benjamin and Betty (Gamzon) Rosen; m. Gilbert Kollin, June 18, 1961; children: Dalia Anne, Daniel, Jonathan. Student, Stern Coll. for Women, 1959-61, U. Mich., 1973-75; BA summa cum laude, William Patterson Coll., 1976; MSW, Yeshiva U., 1980. Lic. clin. social worker, Calif. Dir. synagogue youth Fairlawn (N.J.) Jewish Ctr., 1977-80; clin. social worker Jewish Family Service of Los Angeles, so. region, 1980-83; pvt. practice counseling Los Angeles and South Bay, Calif., 1983—; regional dir. Jewish Family Service of Los Angeles, Torrence, Calif., 1984—; adv. bd. Casa Colina Day Hosp. and Rehab. Ctr.; bd. dirs. Harbor Interfaith Ctr., Inc. Mem. Nat. Assn. Social Workers, Nat. Assn. Jewish Communal Services, Soc. Clin. Social Workers. Avocations: horseback riding, singing. Home: 1344 N Genesee Los Angeles CA 90046 Office: Jewish Family Services 22410 Palos Verdes Blvd Torrance CA 90505

KOLMAN, DAVID ABRAHAM, magazine editor; b. Balt., Dec. 4, 1951; s. Lawrence H. and Irene S. (Lansman) K. BJ, U. Md., 1973. Freelance writer, photographer Balt., 1973-76; announcer, reporter various radio stas., Md., 1976-78; reporter Times Leader newspaper, Wilkes-Barre, Pa., 1978-80; editor Overdrive mag., Los Angeles, 1981-83, Heavy Truck Salesman mag., Santa Ana, Calif., 1983—; sr. editor Heavy Duty Trucking mag., 1983—. Co-recipient Jesse H. Neal Editorial Achievement award Heavy Duty Trucking mag., 1983, 85. Mem. Freight Haulers Am., Investigative Repoters and Editors, Sigma Delta Chi. Avocations: truck and bus driving, wrestling, basketball, reading. Home: 1101 W Stevens Ave Apt 221 Santa Ana CA 92707 Office: Heavy Truck Salesman Mag 1800 E Deere Ave Santa Ana CA 92705-5721

KOLODIN, STEVEN J., food industry marketing executive; b. Santa Monica, Calif., Sept. 1, 1955; s. William Kenneth Kolodin and Joan Lorraine (Herman) Tancredi; m. Graciela Casas, Aug. 16, 1981. BA in History, UCLA, 1978; MBA, Harvard U., 1982. Controller UCLA Cen. Ticket Office, 1978-80; asst. buyer Bullock's Dept. Store, Los Angeles, 1982-83; product mgr. Carnation Co., Los Angeles, 1983—. Adv. Jr. Achievement Los Angeles, 1982-86. Fellow Harvard Bus. Sch. Alumni of So. Calif.; mem. UCLA Alumni Assn., Sierra Club, Friends of Coro. Home: 11858 Goshen Ave #204 Los Angeles CA 90049 Office: Carnation Co 5045 Wilshire Blvd Los Angeles CA 90036

KOLONEL, LAURENCE NORMAN, epidemiologist, public health educator; b. Corner Brook, Can., Apr. 29, 1942; came to U.S., 1958; s. Arthur and Reta (Marshall) K. BA magna cum laude, Williams Coll., 1964; MD, Harvard U., 1968; MPH, U. Calif., Berkeley, 1970, PhD, 1972. Lic. physician, Calif.; diplomate Am. Bd. Gen. Preventive Medicine. Assoc. epidemiologist Cancer Research Ctr. U. Hawaii, Honolulu, 1974-76, dir. epidemiology program Cancer Research Ctr., 1977—, acting exec. dir., 1984-85, assoc. prof. epidemiology Sch. Pub. Health, 1976-81, prof. Sch. Pub. Health, 1981—; vis. prof. Stanford (Calif.) U. Med. Ctr., 1986. Assoc. editor Jour. Nutrition and Cancer; contbr. articles to profl. jours. Served to maj. USAF, 1972-74. Grantee Nat. Cancer Inst., 1977—. Mem. AAAS, Nat. Cancer Inst. (bd. sci. counselors 1982-86), NAS (diet, nutrition and cancer com. 1980-83), Am. Pub. Health Assn., Soc. Epidemiol. Research, Am. Assn. Cancer Research, Phi Beta Kappa, Delta Omega. Democrat. Office: U Hawaii Cancer Research Ctr 1236 Lauhala St Honolulu HI 96813

KOLSRUD, HENRY GERALD, dentist; b. Minnewaukan, N.D., Aug. 12, 1923; s. Henry G. and Anna Naomi (Moen) K.; m. Loretta Dorothy Cooper, Sept. 3, 1945; children—Gerald Roger, Charles Cooper. Student Concordia Coll., 1941-44; D.D.S., U. Minn., 1947. Gen. practice dentistry, Spokane, Wash., 1953—. Bd. dirs. Spokane County Republican Party, United Crusade, Spokane. Served to capt. USAF, 1950-52. Mem. ADA, Wash. State Dental Assn., Spokane Dist. Dental Soc. Lutheran. Clubs: Spokane Country, Spokane. Lodges: Masons, Shriners. Home: 2107 Waikiki Rd Spokane WA 99218 Office: 3718 N Monroe St Spokane WA 99218

KOLTAI, LESLIE, college administrator; b. Hungary, Apr. 6, 1931; came to U.S., 1956; s. Nicholas and Maria (Deutch) K.; BA, U. Budapest, 1954; MA, UCLA, 1960, EdD, 1967; LLD, Pepperdine U., 1975; DHL, U. Judaism, 1978; m. Katherine Koltai, May 10, 1953; children—Steve, Marian, Robert. Asst. prof. U. Budapest, 1954-56; instr. Los Angeles City Schs., 1958-60; assoc. prof., chmn. dept. Pasadena City Coll., 1960-67, dean institutional research 1967-68; chancellor Met. Community Coll., Kansas City, Mo., 1968-72; chancellor Los Angeles Community Coll. Dist., 1972—; adj. prof., U. So. Calif.; vis. prof. UCLA; v.p. Ctr. for Study of Community Colls., Los Angeles; pres. Nat. Ctr. for Devel. Edn., Calif.; mem. NSF adv. com. Directorate of Sci. and Engring Edn., Washington; mem. Los Angeles County Bus. Labor Council; mem. Medici Found., Princeton (N.J.) U.; trustee Ednl. Resources Info. Ctr., UCLA. Mem. Am. Council on Edn.

(commn. on internat. edn., adv. council Ednl. Record), Assn. Governing Bds., Internat. Assn. Univ. and Coll. Presidents (mem. N.Am. council), League for Innovation in the Community Coll. (bd. dirs.), Am. Assn. Community and Jr. Colls. (urban Community Colls. Commn.), council), Am. Council on Edn. (nat. panel for indentification and advancement of women in higher edn. adminstrn., labor/higher edn. council AFL-CIO), Los Angeles C. of C. (mem. exec. com. on edn.). Office: 617 W 7th St Los Angeles CA 90017

KOLTAI, STEPHEN MIKLOS, consulting engineer; b. Ujpest, Hungary, Nov. 5, 1922; came to U.S., 1963; s. Maximilian and Elisabeth (Rado) K.; m. Franciska Gabor, Sept. 14, 1948; children: Eva, Susy. MS in Mech. Engring., U. Budapest, Hungary, 1948, MS in Econs., MS, BA, 1955. Engr. Hungarian Govt., 1943-49; cons. engr. and diplomatic service various European countries, 1950-62; cons. engr. Pan Bus. Cons. Corp., Switzerland and U.S., 1963-77, Palm Springs, Calif., 1977—. Patentee in field. Charter mem. Rep. Presdl. task force, Washington, 1984—. Avocations: tennis, golf.

KOMAI, RALPH YUTAKA, utility company administrator; b. Los Angeles, May 20, 1942; s. Khan and Kiyoko Kay (Moritani) K.; m. M. Trinidad Lara, Mar.3, 1979. AB, Whittier Coll., 1964; MSc, Calif. Inst. Tech., 1967; PhD, U. Calif., Riverside, 1971. Chemistry Kodansha Sci., Tokyo, 1971-73; engr. So. Calif. Edison Co., Rosemead, 1973-79; project mgr. Elec. Power Research Inst., Palo Alto, Calif., 1979-86; adminstr. environ. affairs So. Calif. Gas Co., Los Angeles, 1986—. Mem. Am. Chem. Soc., Air Pollution Control Assn. Club: Kusamura Bonsai (Palo Alto). Avocations: trivia, bonsai gardening, piano, guitar. Office: So Calif Gas Co 720 W 8th St #110K Los Angeles CA 90017

KOMAR, KATHLEEN LENORE, literature educator; b. Joliet, Ill., Oct. 11, 1949; d. Joseph Andrew and Sophie (Boldego) K. BA in English, U. Chgo., 1971; MA in Comparative Lit., Princeton U., 1975, PhD in Comparative Lit., German, 1977. Asst. prof. UCLA, 1977-84, assoc. prof. Germanic lang., lit., 1984—, chair comparative lit., 1986—. Author: Pattern & Chaos: Multilinear Novels by Dos Passos, Faulkner, Döblin, and Koeppen, 1983; contbr. articles to profl. jours. Grantee Am. Council Learned Socs. 1978, 86, UCLA, 1979, 81; Deutsche Akademische Austauschdienst fellow, 1971-72, Kent fellow Danforth Found., 1974-77. Mem. MLA, Am. Comparative Lit. Assn., Soc. Values in Higher Edn., Am. Assn. Tchrs. German, Philol. Assn. Pacific Coast. Office: UCLA Royce Hall 334 Program Comparative Lit Hilgard Ave Los Angeles CA 90024

KOMDAT, JOHN RAYMOND, data processing consultant; b. Brownsville, Tex., Apr. 29, 1943; s. John William and Sara Grace (Williams) K.; m. Linda Jean Garrette, Aug. 26, 1965 (div.); m. Barbara Milroy O'Cain, Sept. 27, 1986. Student U. Tex., 1961-65. Sr. systems analyst Mass. Blue Cross, Boston, 1970-74; pvt. practice data processing cons., San Francisco, 1974-80, Denver, 1981—; sr. systems analyst mgmt. info. servcies div. Dept. of Revenue, State of Colo., 1986—; mem. CODASYL End User Facilities Com., 1974-76. Served with U.S. Army, 1966-70. Mem. AAAS, Assn. Computing Machinery, Denver Downtown Dem. Forum (mem. exec. com.), Mus. Modern Art, Denver Art Mus., Friend of Pub. Radio, Friend of Denver Pub. Library. Democrat. Office: PO Box 10666 Denver CO 80261

KOMERSKA, SALLY ARLENE, microbiologist; b. Mpls., Dec. 16, 1930; d. Helmer William and Esther Ingeborg (Reinertsen) Kestila; student Pa. State U., 1949-51, U. Pitts., 1951-52, Montefiore Hosp. Sch. Med. Tech., Pitts., 1952-53; B.S., U. Ariz., 1970, M.S., 1979; m. Robert James Komerska, Aug. 19, 1955; 1 son, Steven. Med. technologist Sch. Public Health, U. Pitts., 1953-54, Pima County Hosp., 1954-55, Thomas-Davis Clinic, 1955-60; freelance med. technologist St. Joseph's Hosp., Tucson, 1962-63; weekend supr., microbiologist St. Joseph's Hosp., Tucson, 1962-63; med. technologist Thomas-Davis Clinic, Tucson, 1966-68, head microbiologist, 1970—, lab. supr., 1974—; bd. dirs., sec. St. Joseph's Hosp. Credit Union, 1977-78. Den mother Cub Scouts, 1971-73; mem. Altar Guild, Our Savior's Luth. Ch., 1975-78; active Heard Mus., Phoenix, Mus. No. Ariz., Flagstaff. Mem. Am. Soc. Clin. Pathologists (asso.), Am. Soc. Med. Tech. (pres., merit award 1972), Am. Soc. Microbiology, Assn. M.B.A. Execs., Nat. Assn. Female Execs., Ariz. Med. Lab. Assn. (pres. Tucson chpt.). Republican. Lutheran. Mem. profl. adv. panel Med. Lab. Observer mag., 1980—. Home: 3804 E Calle DeSoto Tucson AZ 85716 Office: Alvernon at 5th St Tucson AZ 85726

KOMOTO, SHIRLEY A., marketing and corporate strategist; b. Tokyo, July 21, 1950 (parents Am. citizens); d. Yasuro and Irene (Fujimoto) K.; B.A., Calif. State U., Long Beach, 1973; MPA, 1976; MBA, U. So. Calif., 1986; Mgmt. cons. various cos., Los Angeles County, 1970-; program coordinator Orange County/Long Beach Health Consortium, Inc., Irvine, Calif., 1975-76; program analyst dept. ob-gyn Charles R. Drew Postgrad. Med. Sch. Los Angeles, 1976-79; sr. project planner WED Enterprises div. Walt Disney Prodns., Glendale, Calif., 1979-80, sr. bus. adminstr., 1980-82, sr. bus. devel. analyst, 1983-. Mem. Los Angeles Olympic Organizing Com., Cultural and Fine Arts Commn., also treas. 1985, v.p. 1986, pres. 1987; Travel and Tourism Research Assn.;bd. dirs. T.H.E. Clinic for Women, 1982-, chmn., pres., 1984-; treas. Asian/Pacific Women's Network, 1983-85; vice chmn. Asian Pacific Family Outreach, 1979-80; mem. Long Beach Pioneer Project, 1970-, chmn., 1972-73; mem. Long Beach Commn. on Econ. Opportunities, 1972, So. Calif. Assn. Govts. Regional Adv. Council, 1986-. Mem. N.Am. Soc. Corp. Planners, Am. Mktg. Assn., So. Calif. Assn. Corp. Planners, Planners, Travel and Tourism Research Assn. (bd. dirs. 1985-), Urban Land Inst., Nat. Restaurant Assn. Co- author: Source Book on Perinatal and Other Health Initiatives, 1978; contbr. articles on edn. study and plans to profl. publs., papers to confs. Office: WED Enterprises div Walt Disney Prodns 1401 Flower St Glendale CA 91201

KON, CHUCKRIT SOLOMON, dentist; b. Bangkok, Thailand, Jan. 24, 1950; came to U.S, 1970; s. Vui Leong and Sui Len (Hee) K.; m. Wendy Sugiono, June 12, 1977; children: Ryan Christopher, Christina Alexis. B.A. in Chemistry, Loma Linda U., 1973, D.D.S., 1980. Med. technologist Loma Linda (Calif.) Community Hosp., 1975-77; pvt. practice dentistry Kon & Sugiono Profl. Dental Corp., Alta Loma and Colton, Calif., 1980—; lectr. in field. Recipient Loma Linda U. Oral Surgery award, 1980. Fellow Acad. Gen. Dentistry; mem. Tri-County Dental Assn., ADA, Calif. Dental Assn. Seventh-day Adventist. Home: 2314 N Euclid Ave Upland CA 91786 Office: 9482 Baseline Rd Alta Loma CA 91701

KONDRAT, RICHARD WALTER, staff spectroscopist; b. Chgo., Dec. 6, 1951; s. Walter and Bernice (Koszulinski) K. BS, De Paul U., 1973; PhD, Purdue U., 1978. Research chemist Shell Devel. Co., Houston, 1978-83; staff spectroscopist U. Calif., Riverside, 1983—. Contbr. articles to profl. jours. Mem. Am. Chem. Soc., Am. Soc. Mass Spectrometry. Roman Catholic. Avocations: photography, hiking, camping. Office: U Calif Dept Chemistry Riverside CA 92521

KONG, ERIC SIU-WAI, research scientist; b. Hong Kong, Jan. 14, 1953; s. Woon-Man and Chau-Mui K.; m. Susanna May-Man Lee, June 24, 1974; 1 child, Myron Hok-Ben. AB in Biochemistry, U. Calif., Berkeley, 1974; MSc in Chemistry, Rensselaer Poly. Inst., 1976, PhD in Chemistry, 1978. Research fellow Va. Poly. Inst., Blacksburg, 1978-79; research scientist NASA-Ames/Stanford U. Joint Inst., Moffett-Field, Calif., 1979-83; mem. tech. staff Sandia Nat. Labs., Livermore, Calif., 1983-84, Hewlett-Packard Labs., Palo Alto, Calif., 1984—. Contbr. articles to profl. jours. Fellow N.Y. Acad. Scis., Am. Inst. Chemists; mem. Materials Research Soc., Soc. Polymer Sci. of Japan, Soc. Plastics Engrs. (chmn. Golden Gate Plastics Analysis div. 1983-84). Home: 936 Bluebonnet Dr Sunnyvale CA 94086 Office: Hewlett Packard Labs 3500 Deer Creek Rd Palo Alto CA 94304

KONNICK, RONALD JOHN, data processing executive, consultant; b. East Chicago, Ind., May 18, 1943; s. Michael and Sophie (Kostrubala) K.; m. Marie Anne Kwiecien, Dec. 9, 1972; children: Eric, Bryan. BSEE, Carnegie-Mellon U., 1966; MS in Indsl. Engring., Wayne State U., 1972; MBA, Calif. Poly. State U., 1974. Indsl. engr. Carrier Corp., LaPuente, Calif., 1973-76; sr. indsl. engr. Harris Corp., Quincy, Ill., 1976-78; dir. mgmt. info. service IML Freight, Salt Lake City, 1978-84; site mgr. data ctr. Sun Carriers, Salt Lake City, 1985—; instr. data processing, U. Phoenix, Salt Lake City, 1974—. Chmn. 4th of July com. City of Sandy, Utah, 1980-81. Mem. Data Processing Mgmt. Assn. (bd. dirs. 1974—), Inst. Cert. Computer Profls. (cert., award for excellence 1979). Roman Catholic. Avocations: jogging, camping, biking. Home: 9513 Buttonwood Dr Sandy UT 84092 Office: Sun Carriers Systems Inc 275 W 2755 S Salt Lake City UT 84115

KONNYU, ERNEST L., congressman; b. Tamasi, Hungary, May 17, 1937; s. Leslie and Elizabeth Konnyu; m. Lillian Konnyu, 1959; children: Carol, Renata, Lisa, Victoria. BS in Acctg., Ohio State U., 1965. Mem. Calif. Assembly, Sacramento, 1980-86, 100th Congress from 12th Calif. dist., 1987—. Served to maj. USAF, 1959-69. Mem. Sci. Space and Tech. Com., Govt. Ops. Com. Republican. Roman Catholic. Lodge: Elks. Avocations: politics, golf, fishing.

KONRATH, EILEEN MARIE, speech-language pathologist; b. Rochester, N.Y., Apr. 18, 1960; d. John Richard and Mary Elizabeth (Frisch) Finucane; m. Paul Steven Konrath, Apr. 27, 1985. BS, Nazareth Coll., 1981; MA, U. Colo., 1984. Speech and lang. pathologist Mapleton Pub. Schs., Thornton, Colo., 1984—; cons. Lakewood, Colo., 1985—. Grantee U. Colo., Boulder, 1983-84. Mem. Am. Speech-Lang.-Hearing Assn. (cert. clin. competence), Colo. Speech-Lang.-Hearing Assn. (mem. profl. relations com. 1986—), Mapleton Edn. Assn. Republican. Roman Catholic. Avocations: skiing, camping, hiking, photography. Home: 12097 W Jewell Dr Lakewood CO 80228 Office: Meadow Elem Sch 602 E 64th Ave Thornton CO 80229

KOOGLER, RUSSELL LEWIS, security specialist; b. Zanesville, Ohio, Sept. 12, 1938; s. Emerson L. and Betty J. (DeSantel) King; student Sacramento Jr. Coll., 1972-74; B.Police Sci. and Bus., Fullerton Coll., 1975; m. Sue Ann Hicks, Dec. 10, 1982; 1 child, Malissa Sue; 1 child by previous marriage, Patricia Louise. Fed. police officer U.S. Postal Inspectors, Los Angeles, 1967-77; owner Koogler & Assoc., Pvt. Investigators, Phoenix, 1979—; loss prevention dist. mgr. K-Mart Corp., Covina, Calif.; spl. agt. Internat. Police Congress, Washington. Tchr., instr. CPR and first aid and disaster courses ARC, Santa Ana, Calif., 1971-78, disaster chmn., 1976-78. Served with Signal Corps, U.S. Army, 1961-64. Recipient awards, ARC 1973, 74, 75, Freedom Train award, 1976. Mem. Internat. Assn. Credit Card Investigators, Ariz. Retail Investigators Assn., Credit Data of Am., Internat. Consumer Credit Assn., Am. Soc. Indsl. Security Internat., Alpha Gamma Sigma, Calif. State Assn. EMT's. Lodge: Elks. Contbr. articles to profl. jours. Address: 7202 LaLuna Ct Citrus Heights CA 95621 Address: PO Box 684 Citrus Heights CA 95611-0684

KOOKEN, JOHN FREDERICK, bank holding company executive; b. Denver, Nov. 1, 1931; s. Duff A. and Frances C. K.; m. Emily Howe, Sept. 18, 1954; children: Diane, Carolyn. M.S., Stanford U., 1954, Ph.D., 1961. With Security Pacific Nat. Bank-Security Pacific Corp., Los Angeles, 1960—; exec. v.p. Security Pacific Corp., Los Angeles, 1981-87, chief fin. officer, 1984—, vice chmn., 1987—; bd. dirs. U.S. Facilities Corp.; lectr. Grad. Sch. Bus., U. So. Calif., 1962-67. Pres. bd. dirs. Children's Bur. Los Angeles, 1981-84; bd. dirs. United Way Los Angeles, 1982—, Huntington Meml. Hosp., Pasadena, 1985—. Served to lt. (j.g.) USNR, 1954-57. Mem. Fin. Execs. Inst. (pres. Los Angeles chpt. 1979-80, dir. 1981-84). Office: Security Pacific Corp 333 S Hope St Los Angeles CA 90071

KOOS, BRIAN JOHN, physiology educator, physician; b. Los Angeles, Mar. 23, 1949. PhD, Oxford (Eng.) U., 1982. Diplomate Am. Bd. Ob-gyn., Am. Bd. Maternal-Fetal Medicine. Intern Brigham & Women's Hosp., Boston, 1975-76, resident in ob-gyn, 1976-79; fellow Women's Hosp., Los Angeles, 1982-83; asst. prof. physiology, ob-gyn Loma Linda (Calif.) U., 1983—. USPHS grantee Inst. Child Health and Human Devel., Bethesda, Md., 1985; Basil O'Connor scholar March of Dimes, 1985. Mem. Am. Physiol. Soc., N.Y. Acad. Scis., Am. Fedn. Clin. Research, Perinatal Research Soc. Home: 22950 DeBerry St Grand Terrace CA 92324 Office: Loma Linda U Dept Perinatal Biology Loma Linda CA 92354

KOOYMAN, GERALD LEE, physiology researcher; b. Salt Lake City, June 16, 1934; s. Albert John and Virginia L. (Monson) K.; m. Melba Mae Bingham, July 6, 1962; children: Carsten, Tory. AB, UCLA, 1957; PhD, U. Ariz., 1966. Postdoctoral fellow NSF, London, 1966-67; asst. research physiologist to research physiologist U. Calif.-San Diego, La Jolla, 1967—. Author: Weddell Seal, Consummate Diver, 1981; editor: Fur Seals, 1986. Recipient Antarctic medal NSF. Fellow AAAS, London Zool. Soc., Explorers Club; mem. Am. Physiol. Soc. Office: U Calif at San Diego PRL/A004 La Jolla CA 92093

KOPANIA, ANDREW ALVIN, geologist; b. Oak Park, Ill., Apr. 10, 1958; s. Alvin Andrew and Patricia Jean (Crowl) K. BS in Geology summa cum laude, UCLA, 1981; MS in Geology, U. Mich., 1984. Geologist Amoco Prodn. Co., Denver, 1981, Mobil Oil Co., Denver, 1982, Champlin Petroleum Co., Englewood, Colo., 1983—. Contbr. articles to profl. jours. Grantee NSF, 1982, Mobil Oil, 1982. Mem. Am. Soc. Petroleum Geologists, Geol. Soc. Am., Am. Geophys. Union, Soc. Econ. Paleontologists and Mineralogists, Phi Beta Kappa. Republican. Office: Champlin Petroleum Co PO Box 1257 Englewood CO 80150

KOPCYCH, TONY, data processing executive; b. Bridgewater, Mass., Mar. 23, 1941; s. Anthony and Bertha (Smith) K.; m. Shirley Anne Lawton, June 12, 1971; children: Karissa, Anthony III. BBA, U. Hawaii, 1969. Mgr. data prcessing Ampex Corp, Redwood City, Calif., 1971-75; dir. mgmt. infosystem Nat. Semiconductor, Santa Clara, Calif., 1976-81, Velo-Bind, Sunnyvale, Calif., 1982-83; dir. mgmt. infosystems Altos Computer Systems, San Jose, Calif., 1983—; owner Valley Software, Cupertino, Calif., 1984—. Author: The Evolution of the MIS Function. Active De-anza Cupertino Acquatics, 1986. Served with USN, 1962-66. Named Eagle Scout Boy Scouts Am., 1958. Mem. No. Calif. Pick Users Group. Republican. Home: 1028 Tuscany Pl Cupertino CA 95014 Office: Altos Computer Systems 2641 Orchard Pkwy San Jose CA 95134

KOPEC, DANNY, computer science educator, chess master; b. Kfar-Saba, Israel, Feb. 28, 1954; came to U.S., 1957; s. Vladimir and Magdalena (Hoff) K.; m. Sylvia Antos, Dec. 18, 1985; 1 child, Oliver. BA in Psychology and Math., Dartmouth Coll., 1975; PhD in Machine Intelligence, U. Edinburgh, Scotland, 1982. Prof. computer sci. San Diego State U., 1982—. Co-author: Best Games of the Young Grand Masters, 1981, Master Chess: A Course in 21 Lessons, 1986; contbr. articles to profl. jours. Mem. Edinburgh Chess Masters (bd. dirs. 1981-82), Assn. Computing Machinery, Can. Chess Fedn., U.S. Chess Fedn. U.S. Nat. Chess Master, Newburgh, N.Y., 1971, Scottish Chess Master, Edinburgh, 1978, Que. (Can.) Chess Master, Montreal, 1983, Fedn. Internat. des Echecs Master, Montreal, Calif., 1983, Internat. Chess Master, San Diego, 1986. Avocations: classical music, tennis, baseball. Office: San Diego State U Coll Scis Dept Math Sci San Diego CA 92182-0314

KOPELOVE, ALAN BRIAN, research chemist; b. Norfolk, Va., Feb. 22, 1954; s. Morris and Ethel (Chernack) K.; m. Merry Gutzler, Aug. 16, 1975. BS in Chemistry, Va. Poly. Inst. and State U., 1976; MS in Inorganic Chemistry, Colo. State U., 1981, postgrad., 1981—. Grad. research asst. Colo. State U., Ft. Collins, 1976-78; instr. CUNY, 1979-81; staff chemist Hach Co., Loveland, Colo., 1981-83; sr. chemist Corp. Research, 1983-85; chemist Electrometric Sensors, 1985—. Recipient Excellence in Teaching award Colo. State U. Mem. Am. Chem. Soc., Sigma Xi. Avocations: mountaineering, skiing, piano. Office: Hach Co PO Box 389 Loveland CO 80539

KOPELS, DANIEL MARC, video company executive, graphic designer; b. N.Y.C., Dec. 12, 1945; s. Samuel Lee and Ethel C. (Binder) K.; m. Marva Hanaan, Oct. 6, 1974; 1 son, Samuel Lee. B.S. in Advt., U. Fla., 1968. Promotion mgr. Sta. WFTV-TV, Orlando, Fla., 1968-69; v.p., co-founder Vatican II Advt. Co., Los Angeles, 1969-71; ptnr., creative dir. Bue/Kopels Advt., Los Angeles, 1971-73; v.p., dir. Markham Products, Inc., Los Angeles, 1973-84; v.p. mktg. advt. Continental Video, Inc. div. Cinema Group, Los Angeles, 1984—; pres., prin. Danny Kopels Advt., Los Angeles, 1973-84. Recipient numerous awards in field. Club: South Bay Yacht Racing (Venice, Calif.). Office: Continental Video 2320 Cotner Ave Los Angeles CA 90064

KOPENHAVER, JOSEPHINE YOUNG, painter, educator; b. Seattle, June 9, 1908; d. George Samuel and Blanche Cecilia (Castle) Young; A.B., U. Calif., 1928; M.F.A. (scholar 1936-37), U. So. Calif., 1937; spl. student Claremont Grad. Sch., 1951, 67, Chouinard Art Inst., 1946-47, Otis Art Inst., 1954-55; m. Ralph Witmer Kopenhaver, Apr. 11, 1931. Prof. art Chaffee Jr. Coll., Ontario, Calif., 1946-47, Los Angeles City Coll., 1948-73, Woodbury U., Los Angeles, 1973-76, summer sessions Calif. State U., Los Angeles, 1950, Pasadena City Coll., 1949, Otis Art Inst., Los Angeles, 1959, Pasadena Art Inst., 1948; profl. painter, exhibiting artist, 1933—; work included in exhibits mus. and pvt. galleries U.S. and Mex., 1933—, including Hatfield Galleries, Los Angeles; art juror. Winner first award in oil Los Angeles Art Festival, 1936, various art awards. Mem. Los Angeles Art Assn. (trustee), Nat. Watercolor Soc. (sec.), Audubon Artists, Artists for Econ. Action, Calif. Tchrs. Assn. Clubs: Los Angeles Athletic, Zeta Tau Alpha. Office: PO Box 10666 Glendale CA 91209 Office: PO Box 10666 Glendale CA 91209

KOPFF, E(DWARD) CHRISTIAN, classical philology educator; b. Bklyn., Nov. 22, 1946; s. Frederick Louis and Willie Maude (Compton) K. BA summa cum laude, Haverford Coll., 1968; PhD in Classics, U. N.C., 1974. Asst. instr. Intercollegiate Ctr., Rome, 1972-73; asst. prof. dept. classics U. Colo., Boulder, 1973-77, assoc. prof., 1977—. Book rev. editor The Classical Jour., 1977—; arts editor The Southerner, 1983—; Am. editor Quaderni di Storia, Bari, Italy, 1982—; editor critical edit. Euripides' Bacchae, 1982. Contbr. articles and book revs. to Classics. Pres., Friends of Library, Boulder, 1984-86. Prix de Rome fellow Am. Acad. in Rome, 1978; U. Colo. faculty fellow, 1978, 86. Mem. Am. Philol. Assn., Classical Assn. Middle West and South, Assn. Ancient Historians. Republican. Lutheran. Home: 3800 Carlock Dr Boulder CO 80303 Office: Dept Classics U Colo Campus Box 248 Boulder CO 80309

KOPP, CLAIRE JOAN BERNSTEIN, psychologist, educator; b. N.Y.C., July 8, 1931; d. Gerson Jerome and Martha Jane (Stavisky) Bernstein; m. Eugene Howard Kopp, Aug. 31, 1950; children: Carolyn, Michael, Paul. BS, NYU, 1951; MS, U. So. Calif., 1961; PhD, Claremont Grad. Sch., 1970. Cert. psychologist, Calif. Teaching staff UCLA, 1970-77, faculty, 1977—. Fellow Am. Psychol. Assn. (sec., treas. div. 7 1985—), Am. Occupational Therapy Assn.; mem. Soc. Research in Child Devel., AAAS, Internat. Orgn. Ninety-Nines (chmn. San Gabriel Valley Chpt. 1985-86). Avocations: pilot, tennis. Office: UCLA Psychology Dept Los Angeles CA 90024

KOPP, RICHARD ALLEN, geologist; b. Eau Claire, Wis., Dec. 25, 1951; s. Richard Edward and Deloris Annabelle (Miller) K.; m. Jacqueline Kay Cole, May 25, 1975; children—Richard Elverne, Carrie Lynn, Brenda Alice. B.Sc., U. Wis.-Eau Claire, 1975; M.S., U. Tex., 1977. Geologist, Mobil Oil Exploration-Producing, Houston, 1977-79, Mobil Oil Corp. Denver, 1979-80, Superior Oil Co., Denver, 1980-81; sr. geologist Tricentrol U.S. Inc., Englewood, Colo., 1981-84, Wintershall and Oil and Gas Co., Englewood, Colo., 1984—. Contbr. Tri-State Field Conf. Guidebook, 1974, (with others) West Texas Geol. Soc. Guidebook, 1981, Oil and Gas Fields - Four Corners Guidebook, 1984. Mem. Am. Assn. Petroleum Geologists, Geol. Soc. Am., Soc. Exploration Geophysicists, Rocky Mountain Assn. Geologists, Wyo. Geol. Assn. Home: 9272 N LaCross Ln Parker CO 80134 Office: Wintershall Oil and Gas 5675 DTC Blvd Englewood CO 80111

KOPPERUD, DAVID MATTHEWS, English language professional, educator; b. Chgo., Aug. 8, 1954; s. Andrew Kopperud and Barbara (Bugbee) Foley; m. Mary Kathryn Henley, June 26, 1981; children: James Andrew, Sarah Elizabeth. BA, Claremont McKenna Coll., 1976; MA, U. San Francisco, 1985. Asst. to magnet schs. San Diego City Unified Sch. Dist., 1979-80; English tchr. Brawley (Calif.) Union High Sch., 1980—, adminstrv. intern, 1984-85, English dept. chmn., 1985—; secondary program reviewer Office of Sch. Improvement, Brawley, 1986—; coach Tennis Team, Brawley, 1980-83; participant Tchr. Expectation-Student Achievement, Brawley, 1984—; adv. Am. Field Service Club, Brawley, 1985—. Spl. Minister of Eucharist, Diocesan Office of San Diego, 1984; bd. dirs. Sacred Heart Sch., 1987. Named Eagle Scout, Boy Scouts Am., 1970. Fellow San Diego Area Writing Project; mem. NEA, Assn. Calif. Sch. Adminstrs, Nat. Council of Tchrs. of English, Calif Tchrs. Assn. Republican. Roman Catholic. Avocations: tennis, jogging, poetry. Home: 259 I St Brawley CA 92227 Office: Brawley Union High Sch 480 N Imperial Ave Brawley CA 92227

KORAL, ROD LEE, instruments manufacturing company executive; b. Los Angeles, Nov. 8, 1949; s. Ben B. and Mabel M. (Miller) K.; m. Pat A. Gomez, Aug. 11, 1973; children—Jeffrey, Jennifer, Gregory. A.A. in Liberal Arts, Santa Ana Coll., 1970; B.A. in Bus. Adminstrn., Chapman Coll., 1972. Gen. mgr. Advanced Telecommunications, Santa Ana, Calif., 1974-76; communications cons. City of Anaheim (Calif.), 1976-78; mem. staff corp. employee relations Beckman Instruments, Inc., Fullerton, Calif., 1978—. Active March of Dimes, Boy Scouts Am., Nat. Search and Rescue Assn.; bd. dirs. ARC; founder Saddleback Search and Rescue Team; cons. Fed. Emergency Mgmt. Agy., U.S. Olympic Com.; bd. dirs. Rescue Coordination Ctr. Recipient Disting. Service award Jaycees, 1972; cert. of appreciation Orange County Sheriffs Dept., 1976. Mem. Am. Soc. Safety Engrs. Republican. Club: Lions. Contbr. articles to profl. jours.

KORALEK, LESLIE JAMES, psychologist, consultant; b. Newark, Sept. 5, 1949; s. Adolph Hugo and Anita Sonja (Popper) K.; M.A. in Clin. Psychology, Psychol. Studies Inst., Palo Alto, Calif., 1979, Ph.D. in Clin. Psychology, 1983. Alcohol counselor Starting Point, Hayward, Calif., 1979-80, asst. dir., Santa Clara, Calif., 1981; pvt. practice psychology, Cupertino, Calif., 1981-82; counselor Ctr. for Alcohol Treatment, Medford, Oreg., 1982-83; alcohol therapist Care Unit, Medford, 1983-84, dir. Care Unit, 1984-85, dir. Program 180, 1985—; cons. alcoholism to FAA. Jewish.

KORB, LAWRENCE JOHN, metallurgist; b. Warren, Pa., Apr. 28, 1930; s. Stanley Curtis and Dagna (Pedersen) K.; B.Chem.Engring., Rensselaer Poly. Inst., Troy, N.Y., 1952; m. Janet Davis, Mar. 30, 1957; children—James, William, Jeanine. Sales engr. Alcoa, Buffalo, 1955-59; metall. engr. N. Am. Rockwell Co., Downey, Calif., 1959-62; engring. supr. metallurgy Apollo program Rockwell Internat. Co., Downey, 1962-66, engring. supr. advanced materials, 1966-72, engring. supr. metals and ceramics space shuttle program, 1972-86; mem. tech. adv. com. metallurgy Cerritos Coll., 1969-74. Served with USNR, 1952-55. Registered profl. engr., Calif. Mem. Am. Soc. Metals (chmn. aerospace activity com. 1971-76; judge materials application competition 1969, handbook com. 1978-83, chmn. handbook com. 1983, chmn. publs. council 1984). Republican. Author articles, chpts. in books. Home: 251 Violet Ln Orange CA 92669 Office: 12214 Lakewood Blvd Downey CA 90241

KORMAN, (EPHRAIM) FRANK, retired biochemist, researcher; b. North Wildwood, N.J., Mar. 14, 1929; s. Benjamin (Shimon) and Eva (Benjamin) K.; m. Katherine Elizabeth Moore, Jan. 19, 1969; children: Jonathan Benjamin, Adam Richard. BS in Chemistry, UCLA, 1956, PhD in Chemistry, 1962. Postdoctoral fellow Inst. for Enzyme Research, U. Wis., Madison, 1965-67, research asst. prof., 1967-72; asst. prof. Ill. State U., Charleston, 1972-73; research biochemist Charles R. Drew Postgrad. Med. Sch., Los Angeles, 1974; research biochemist in nuclear medicine, radiation biology UCLA, 1974-78, research biochemist, biology dept., 1978-80; vol. lectr. chemistry, U.S. Peace Corps, U. of Ife, Ibadan, Nigeria. 1963-65; overseas tech. rep. Calbiochem, Lucerne, Switzerland, 1962-63; organic chemist Calbiochem, Los Angeles, 1956-59. Contbr. research articles to profl. jours. Served as cpl. U.S. Army Med. Service Corps, 1950-52, Korea. Recipient Teaching Excellence award chemistry dept. UCLA, 1959, Jonsson Cancer Research Ctr. award UCLA 1980; spl. postdoctoral fellow U. Wis., 1973-74. Mem. Am. Soc. Biol. Chemists, Biophys. Soc., Am. Chem. Soc., AAAS. Democrat. Jewish. Avocations: swimming, ice skating, watercolor painting, studying history of sci. Home: 11104 Orville St Culver City CA 90230

KORMAN, NATHANIEL IRVING, research and development company executive; b. Providence, Feb. 23, 1916; s. William and Tillie (Jacobs) K.; m. Ruth C. Kaplan, Apr. 6, 1941; children—Michael, Robert. B.S. summa cum laude, Worcester Poly. Inst., 1937; M.S. (Coffin fellow), M.I.T., 1938; Ph.D., U. Pa., 1958. Dir. advance mil. systems RCA Corp., 1958-67; pres., chief exec. officer Ventures Research and Devel. Group, Albuquerque, 1968—; chmn. radar panel U.S. Research and Devel. Bd., 1948-56; lectr. U. Pa. Evening Grad. Sch., 1967-68; cons. in field Color Sci. Mem. Citizens Com. for Better Schs., Moorestown, N.J., 1958. Recipient Award of Merit RCA, 1951. Fellow IEEE; mem. Sigma Xi. Patentee in field. Home and Office: 108 Yucca Ln Placitas NM 87043

KORMONDY, EDWARD JOHN, university official, biology educator; b. Beacon, N.Y., June 10, 1926; s. Anthony and Frances (Glover) K.; m. Peggy Virginia Hedrick, June 5, 1950; children: Lynn Ellen, Eric Paul, Mark Hedrick. B.S. in Biology summa cum laude, Tusculum Coll., 1950; M.S. in Zoology, U. Mich., 1951, Ph.D. in Zoology, 1955. Teaching fellow U. Mich., 1952-55; instr. zoology, curator insects Mus. Zoology, 1955-57; asst. prof. Oberlin (Ohio) Coll., 1957-63, assoc. prof., 1963-67, prof., 1967-69, acting assoc. dean, 1966-67; dir. Commn. Undergrad. Edn. in Biol. Scis., Washington, 1968-72; dir. Office Biol. Edn., Am. Inst. Biol. Scis., Washington, 1968-71; mem. faculty Evergreen State Coll., Olympia, Wash., 1971-79, interim acting dean, 1972-73, v.p., provost, 1973-78; sr. profl. assoc., directorate sci. edn. NSF, 1979; provost, prof. biology U. So. Maine, Portland, 1979-82; v.p. acad. affairs, prof. biology Calif. State U., Los Angeles, 1982-86; chancellor U. Hawaii at Hilo and West Oahu Coll., 1986—, prof. biology. Author: Concepts of Ecology, 1969, 76, 83, General Biology: The Integrity and Natural History of Organisms, 1977, Handbook of Contemporary World Developments in Ecology, 1981; high school textbook Biology, 1984, 88; contbr. articles to profl. jours. Served with USN, 1944-46. U. Ga. postdoctoral fellow radiation ecology, 1963-64; vis. research fellow Center for Bioethics, Georgetown U., 1978-79; research grantee Nat. Acad. Scis., Am. Philos. Soc., NSF, Sigma Xi. Mem. AAAS, Ecol. Soc. Am. (sec. 1976-78), Nat. Assn. Biology Tchrs. (pres. 1981), Nat. Sci. Tchrs. Assn., So. Calif. Acad. Scis. (bd. dirs. 1985-86), Sigma Xi. Home: 61 Halaulani Pl Hilo HI 96720 Office: Univ Hawaii-Hilo Office Chancellor Hilo HI 96720

KORN, ERROL RICHARD, gastroenterologist; b. Phila., Apr. 3, 1940; s. Joseph and Mildred (Bogutz) K.; m. Judith, 1963 (div. 1982); children: Meredith, Darren; m. Nancy Carol Schadewald, May 27, 1983. AB, Temple U., 1962; MD, Hahnemann U., 1966. Diplomate Am. Bd. Gastroenterology, Am. Bd. Internal Medicine. Commd. 1st lt. USN, 1965, advanced through grades to lt. comdr., 1968, served in U.S., Vietnam, resigned, 1974; intern Naval Hosp., Camp Pendleton, Calif., 1966-67; resident Naval Hosp., San Diego, 1967-69; fellowship in gastroenterology Scripps Clinic, La Jolla, Calif., 1972-74; pvt. practice specializing in gastroenterology Chula Vista, Calif., 1974—; clin. faculty mem., U. Calif. San Diego Sch. Medicine, 1974—; speaker. cons.; pres. Pratt, Korn and Assocs., La Jolla, Calif., 1984—; v.p. Seaport Village Travel, Inc., San Diego, 1983—; bd. dirs. Optimax, Inc., Chula Vista, 1985—. Author: Visualization, 1983, Hyper-Performance, 1987. Fellow Am. Coll. Physicians, Am. Soc. Clin. Hypnosis, Am. Coll. Gastroenterology. Avocations: flying, scuba diving, skiing, composing music, sailing. Office: 450 4th Ave Suite 400 Chula Vista CA 92010

KORN, WALTER, writer; b. Prague, Czechoslovakia, May 22, 1908; came to U.S., 1950, naturalized, 1956; s. Bernard and Clara (Deutsch) K.; m. Herta Klemperer, Dec. 24, 1933. Dr.Comm., Charles U., Prague, 1938; postgrad. London Sch. Econs., 1949-50; cert. systems and procedures Wayne State U., 1957. Dir. mktg. Kosmos Works, Prague, 1934-39; contract mgr. Cantie Switches, Chester, Eng., 1941-44; dir. UNRRA, U.S. Zone Occupation, Germany, 1945-47; country dir. Orgn. for Rehab. and Vocational Tng., Geneva, 1948; contract mgr. Royal Metal Mfg. Co., N.Y.C., 1951-55; bus. mgr. J. Community Ctr., Detroit, 1956-59; dir. adminstrn. joint distbn. com. United Jewish Appeal, Tel Aviv, 1960-64; exec. asst. Self Help/United Help, N.Y.C., 1965-69; housing mgmt. cons. Exec. Dept. Div. Housing and Community Renewal, State N.Y., N.Y.C., 1970-76; lectr. housing for aged and housing fin., 1958-74; lectr. Brit. Allied Council, Liverpool, Eng., 1942-44. Nat. field rep. United Jewish Appeal, 1968—; mem. Vols. for Internat. Tech. Assistance, 1968-71. Served to capt. Czechoslovakian Army, 1938. Mem. Acad. Polit. Sci., Acad. Polit and Social Sci., Am. Judicature Soc., Internat. Platform Assn., Amnesty Internat. Clubs: Princeton of N.Y.; Commonwealth of Calif.; Press (San Francisco); Sierra, Masons. Author: On Hobbies, 1936; Earn as You Learn, 1948; The Brilliant Touch, 1950; Modern Chess Openings, 12th edit., 1982; American Chess Art, 1975; America's Chess Heritage, 1978; Moderne Schach Eroeffnungen I and II, 1968, 75; contbr. to Ency. Brit.

KORNBERG, ARTHUR, biochemist; b. N.Y.C., Mar. 3, 1918; s. Joseph and Lena (Katz) K.; m. Sylvy R. Levy, Nov. 21, 1943; children: Roger, Thomas Bill, Kenneth Andrew. B.S. (N.Y. State scholar), CCNY, 1937, LL.D., 1960; M.D. (Buswell scholar), U. Rochester, 1941, D.Sc., 1962; L.H.D., Yeshiva U., 1963; D.Sc., U. Pa., U. Notre Dame, 1965, Washington U., 1968, Princeton U., 1970, Colby Coll., 1970; M.D. (h.c.), U. Barcelona, Italy, 1970. Intern in medicine Strong Meml. Hosp., Rochester, N.Y., 1941-42; commd. officer USPHS, 1942, advanced through grades to med. dir., 1951; mem. staff NIH, Bethesda, Md., 1942-52; nutrition sect., div. physiology NIH, 1942-45; chief sect. enzymes and metabolism Nat. Inst. Arthritis and Metabolic Diseases, 1947-52; guest research worker depts. chemistry and pharmacology coll. medicine N.Y. U., 1946; dept. biol. chemistry med. sch. Washington U., 1947; dept. plant biochemistry U. Calif., 1951; prof., head dept. microbiology, med. sch. Washington U., St. Louis, 1953-59; prof., biochemistry Stanford U. Sch. Medicine, 1959—, chmn. dept., 1959-69; Mem. sci. adv. bd. Mass. Gen. Hosp., 1964-67; bd. govs. Weizmann Inst., Israel. Contbr. sci. articles to profl. jours. Served lt. (j.g.), med. officer USCGR, 1942. Recipient Paul-Lewis award in enzyme chemistry, 1951; co-recipient of Nobel prize in medicine, 1959; Max Berg award prolonging human life, 1968; Sci. Achievement award AMA, 1968; Lucy Wortham James award James Ewing Soc., 1968; Borden award Am. Assn. Med. Colls., 1968. Mem. Am. Soc. Biol. Chemists (pres. 1965), Am. Chem. Soc., Harvey Soc., Am. Acad. Arts and Scis., Royal Soc., Nat. Acad. Scis. (mem. council 1963-66), Am. Philos. Soc., Phi Beta Kappa, Sigma Xi, Alpha Omega Alpha. Office: Dept of Biochemistry Stanford U Medical Ctr Stanford CA 94305 *

KORNBERG, JAMES PHILLIP, physician; b. St. Louis, May 4, 1947; s. Sanford and Elinor K.; m. Sally E. Weissman, June 11, 1969; children: Mariah, Jamie, Terra. BS in Aero. and Astronautical Engring., MIT, 1969, MS, 1970; ScD in Environ. Health Sci. and Engring., Harvard U., 1974; MD, Dartmouth Coll., 1976. Diplomate Am. Bd. Preventive Medicine. Engr. McDonnell Douglas Corp., St. Louis, 1967; cons. environ. engring. and air pollution control 1972-77; intern Mary Imogene Bassett Hosp., Cooperstown, N.Y., 1976-77; resident in occupational medicine Harvard Sch. Pub. Health, 1978; sr. staff cons. occupational medicine and environ. health Arthur D. Little, Inc., Cambridge, Mass., 1977-78; pres. COHBI Corp., Leominster, Mass., 1978-79, Boulder, Colo., 1980—; med. adviser Colo. Mining Assn.; cons., med. dir. to numerous cos. in Rocky Mountain area; expert witness occupational medicine and toxicology, fed. and state judiciary system; sr. aviation med. examiner FAA. Contbr. articles to profl. jours. Gen. Electric fellow, 1974. Mem. AMA (Physicians Recognition award 1979, 82), Am. Occupational Med. Assn., Boulder County Med. Soc., Colo. Med. Soc., Mass. Pub. Health Assn., Rocky Mountain Acad. Occupational Medicine (dir. 1981-84), Sigma Xi, Phi Eta Sigma, Sigma Gamma Tau. Home: 506 Skytrail Rd Jamestown Star Rt Boulder CO 80302 Office: COHBI Corp 1777 Conestoga St #A Boulder CO 80301

KORP, PATRICIA ANNE, communications/public info. specialist; b. Lincoln, Nebr., Nov. 15, 1942; d. Theodore R. and Elizabeth Anne (Olson) Munn; BS in Journalism, U. Wyo., 1967, M.A., 1974; m. Vince L. Korp, Jan. 15, 1965 (div. 1986); children—Kathleen Anne, Karen Lee. Women's editor Sheridan (Wyo.) Press, 1964-66; public info. and research asst. Wyo. Dept. Edn., 1967-69; dir. public relations and communications Wyo. Edn. Assn., 1969-71; coordinator info. services Mountain Plains Program, Glasgow, Mont., 1972-73; freelance public relations, Laramie, Wyo., 1973-74; public info. specialist Bur. Land Mgmt., Rawlins, Wyo., 1975-76, Cheyenne, Wyo., 1976-81, chief Office Pub. Affairs, 1981-85, Washington hdqts. office, 1985—; communications specialist Wyo. Spl. Olympics, 1978-79. Mem. Wyo. Council Children and Youth, 1976-77. Recipient All-Am. award Ednl. Press Assn. Am., 1st place award Nat. Fedn. Press Women, 1980. Mem. Nat. Fedn. Press Women, Federally Employed Women, Wyo. Press Women (sec.), Seton Cath. High Sch. Athletic Assn. (sec. 1981-83, pres. 1984), Sigma Delta Chi. Democrat. Roman Catholic. Editor: Wyo. Edn. News, 1969-71; asst. editor Wyo. Horizons, 1976-80, editor, 1980-85. Home: 409 Maple Ct Herndon VA 22070 Office: 18th and C Sts NW Room 5600 Washington DC 20240

KORPI, GLEN KAY, manufacturing executive; b. Detroit, Mar. 6, 1934; s. Roy P. and Elva A. (Campbell) K.; m. Regina Hein, Oct. 3, 1980; 1 stepchild, Stefan. AA, Pasadena City Coll., 1956; BS in Metallurgy, Mich. Tech. U., 1958; MS in Mineral Engring., MIT, 1960; PhD in Phys. Chemistry, Stanford U., 1965. Lic. chemist. Sr. research scientist Internat. Mining and Chem. Co., Libertyville, Ill., 1965-67; surface phenomena mgr. Continental Can Corp., Chgo., 1967-72; tech. dir. Mobil Chem. Corp., Pitts., 1972-74; mgr. long range research Desoto Inc., Des Plaines, Ill., 1974-79; group mfg. dir. Bostik Corp., Oberursel, Fed. Republic Germany, 1979-82; product planning mgr. Ameron Corp., Brea, Calif., 1982—. Sec. Highland Park (Ill.) Harbor Commn., 1977-79. Fellow Am. Inst. Chemists (cert.); mem. Am. Chem. Soc., Fedn. of Coating Socs. Libertarian. Avocations: sailing, photography, political philosophy. Home: 680 Driftwood Ave Brea CA 92621 Office: Ameron Corp 201 N Berry St Brea CA 92621

KORPMAN, RALPH ANDREW, physician executive, educator, researcher; b. N.Y.C., Aug. 9, 1952; s. Ralf and Vera Henriette (Terry) K. B.A., Loma Linda U., 1971, M.D., 1974; cert. in exec. mgmt., Claremont Grad. Sch., 1979. Diplomate Am. Bd. Pathology, Nat. Bd. Med. examiners, Am. Coll. Physician Execs. Intern in pathology Loma Linda U. Sch. Medicine, Calif., 1974-75, resident in anatomic pathology and clin. pathology, 1975-78, fellow in hematology, 1978; lead systems designer acad. records Loma Linda U., 1969-74, dir. systems, dept. pathology and lab. medicine, 1974—, asst. prof. Sch. Med., 1979-84, assoc. prof., 1984—; cons., dir. Med. Data Corp., San Bernardino, Calif., 1976-81; chief sci. adv. to pres. and chmn. of bd. HBO & Co., 1981-83; dir. labs. Faculty Med. Lab., Loma Linda, 1979—; pres., chmn. Health Data Scis. Corp., 1983—; dir. various med. corps.; cons. in field; lectr. various confs. Mem. editorial bd. Jour. Clin. Lab. Automation, 1980-85, Software in Healthcare, 1984—, Informatics in Pathology, 1985—. Contbr. articles to profl. jours. Fellow Am. Soc. Clin. Pathologists (Sheard-Sanford award 1975), Assn. Clin. Sci., Coll. Am. Pathologists; mem. Am. Mgmt. Assn., AMA, Am. Soc. Hematology, Assn. Computing Machinery, Calif. Med. Assn., Am. Coll. Physician Execs., Data Processing Mgmt. Assn., IEEE, MUMPS User Group, N.Y. Acad. Scis., San Bernardino County Med. Soc., Sigma Xi, Alpha Omega Alpha. Home: PO Box 548 Loma Linda CA 92354 Office: Health Data Scis Corp 348 W Hospitality Ln San Bernardino CA 92408

KORTSCH, WILLIAM JOSEPH, architect, landscape executive; b. Butte, Mont., June 21, 1954; s. William Elmo and Florence (Brenner) K.; m. Joan Lynn Dadmun, Aug. 23, 1980. BArch, U. Notre Dame, 1977. Registered architect. Calif., Wis. Architect Flad and Assocs., Milw., 1977-80, Wexler/Urrutia, Rancho Mirage, Calif., 1980-82; architect, fin. mgr. Urrutia Architects, Palm Desert, Calif., 1982-84; v.p. Ronald Gregory Assocs., Palm Desert, 1984—. Mem. AIA (dir. Calif. desert chpt. 1985-86, treas. 1986—). Avocations: painting, bicycle racing, swimming. Office: Ronald Gregory Assocs Inc 73960 Hwy 111 Suite 2 Palm Desert CA 92260

KOSAI, KENNETH, electrical engineer; b. Spokane, Wash., July 27, 1944; s. Kiso and Mary (Mukai) K.; m. Carol Marie Fuller, Sept. 14, 1962; 1 child, Kim Marie. BS with honors, Calif. Inst. Tech., 1966; MSEE, U. So. Calif., 1968, PhDEE, 1973. Research asst. U. So. Calif., Los Angeles, 1966-73; mem. tech. staff Philips Labs., Briarcliff Manor, N.Y., 1973-81, Santa Barbara Research Ctr., Goleta, Calif., 1981—; Vis. scientist Swedish Natural Scis. Council, U. Lund, Sweden, 1979. Co-author Semiconductors and Semimetals, 1983; contbr. articles to profl. jours. Fellow NDEA, 1966-69. Mem. IEEE, Am. Phys. Soc., Sigma Xi. Avocations: bridge, hiking, photography. Home: 234 Old Ranch Dr Goleta CA 93117 Office: Santa Barbara Research Ctr 75 Coromar Dr Bldg B2 MS-8 Goleta CA 93117

KOSHLAND, DANIEL EDWARD, JR., educator, biochemist; b. N.Y.C., Mar. 30, 1920; s. Daniel Edward and Eleanor (Haas) K.; m. Marian Elliott, May 25, 1945; children: Ellen, Phyllis, James, Gail, Douglas. BS, U. Calif., Berkeley, 1941; PhD, U. Chgo., 1949; PhD (hon.), Weizmann Inst. Sci., 1984; ScD (hon.), Carnegie Mellon U., 1985; LLD (hon.), Simon Fraser U., 1986. Chemist Shell Chem. Co., Martinez, 1941-42; research asso. Manhattan Dist. U. Chgo., 1942-44; group leader Oak Ridge Nat. Labs., 1944-46; postdoctoral fellow Harvard, 1949-51; staff Brookhaven Nat. Lab., Upton, N.Y., 1951-65; affiliate Rockefeller Inst., N.Y.C., 1958-65; prof. biochemistry U. Calif. at Berkeley, 1965—, chmn. dept., 1973-78; Harvey lectr., 1969; fellow All Souls, Oxford U., 1972; Phi Beta Kappa lectr., 1976; John Edsall lectr. Harvard U., 1980; William H. Stein lectr., Rockefeller U., 1985; Robert Woodward vis. prof. Harvard U., 1986. Author: Bacterial Chemotaxis as A Model Behavioral System, 1980; mem. editorial bds.: jour. Accounts Chem. Research; editor: jour. Procs. Nat. Acad. Scis, 1980-85; editor Sci. mag., 1985—. Recipient T. Duckett Jones award Helen Hay Whitney Found., 1977; Guggenheim fellow, 1972; delivered Rudin Lectures, Columbia U., 1985. Mem. Nat. Acad. Scis., Am. Chem. Soc. (Edgar Fahs Smith award 1979, Pauling award 1979, Rosenstiel award 1984, Waterford prize 1984), Am. Soc. Biol. Chemists (pres.), Am. Acad. Arts and Scis. (council), Academy Forum (chmn.), Japanese Biochem. Soc. (hon.), Royal Swedish Acad. Scis. (hon.). Home: 3991 Happy Valley Rd Lafayette CA 94549 Office: Biochemistry Dept U Calif Berkeley CA 94720

KOSHLAND, MARIAN ELLIOTT, immunologist, educator; b. New Haven, Oct. 25, 1921; d. Waller Watkins and Margaret Ann (Smith) Elliott; m. Daniel Edward Koshland, Jr., May 25, 1945; children—Ellen R., Phyllis A., James M., Gail F., Douglas E. B.A., Vassar Coll., 1942, M.S., 1943; Ph.D., U. Chgo., 1949. Research asst. Manhattan Dist. Atomic Bomb Project, 1945-46; fellow dept. bacteriology Harvard Med. Sch., 1949-51; asso. bacteriologist biology dept. Brookhaven Nat. Lab., 1952-62, bacteriologist, 1963-65; asso. research immunologist virus lab. U. Calif., Berkeley, 1965-69; lectr. dept. molecular biology U. Calif., 1966-70, prof. dept. microbiology and immunology, 1970—, chmn. dept., 1982—; mem. Nat. Sci. Bd., 1976-82; mem. adv. com. to dir. NIH, 1972-75. Contbr. articles to profl. jours. Mem. Nat. Acad. Scis., Am. Acad. Microbiology, Am. Assn. Immunologists (pres. 1982-1983), Am. Soc. Biol. Chemists, Phi Beta Kappa, Sigma Xi. Office: Dept Microbiology and Immunology U Calif Berkeley CA 94720 *

KOSIK, NANCY MAY, organization executive; b. Cicero, Ill., Apr. 17, 1945; d. Peter J. and Cecelia (Longawa) Nega; m. Fred J. Kosik, July 26, 1969. Adminstrv. asst. Am. Coll. Testing Program, 1970-71; instr. dept. journalism, dept. secretarial adminstrn. N.Mex. State U., 1977-80; co-owner F.J. Kreative Advt. Agy., Las Cruces, N.Mex., 1976-80; part-time instr. U. Nev., Reno, 1980; with conv. sales dept. Harrah's Hotels, Reno, 1980-81; tng. mgr. Tropicana Hotel and Country Club, Las Vegas, 1981-84; state exec. dir. Nev. Easter Seal Soc., 1984—. Judge, State of Nev. Spelling Contest. Mem. Am. Soc. Tng. and Devel. Author office procedures manuals. Office: Nev Easter Seal Soc 1455 E Tropicana Suite 660 Las Vegas NV 89119

KOSKI, ELSA LAVERNE, educator, nurse, adolescent pregnancy consultant; b. Red Lodge, Mont., Feb. 23, 1929; d. Edgar Max and Elma Matilda (Prinkki) Gruel; m. Walfred Conrad Koski; children—Mark, Maureen. Nursing diploma, Carroll Coll., 1950; B.S. cum laude in Gen. Studies, So. Oreg. State Coll., 1976. Pediatric supr. St. James Hosp., Butte, Mont., 1951; night supr. Barrett Hosp., Dillon, Mont., 1951; asst. hosp. adminstr. Stillwater Meml. Hosp., 1952; pvt. duty nurse Josephine Meml. Hosp., Grants Pass, Oreg., 1952-53; clinic staff nurse ob-gyn Grants Pass Clinic, 1953-65; health tchr. Grants Pass High Sch., 1967—; adv. Future Med. Workers Club; adolescent pregnancy cons.; dir. Model H.H.E.Y. Project, Am. Heart Assn., 1983-86; guest lectr. local confs., 1975—. Task force mem. health edn., home econs. edn. Seaside Health Team, Heart Health Edn.; bd. dirs. Josephine County March of Dimes, Am. Cancer Soc.; project dir. Oreg. affiliate Josephine County unit Am. Heart Assn., 1984—; vital signs nurse instr. ARC; elder Bethany Presbyterian Ch. Recipient Conf. Coordinator Regional award March of Dimes, 1971, Health Educator Oreg., 1985. Assn., Oreg. Edn. Assn., NEA, Phi Delta Kappa, Delta Kappa Gamma. Democrat. Lodge: P.E.O., Daughters of the Nile. Office: Grants Pass High Sch 522 NE Olive St Grants Pass OR 97526

KOSKI, RAYMOND ALLEN, molecular biologist; b. Corvallis, Oreg., Aug. 21, 1951; s. William Arthur and Lucille Marie (Yungen) K.; m. Barbara Petzoldt, Mar. 24, 1979; 1 child, Benjamin. BS, Stanford U., 1973; MPhil., Yale U., 1976, PhD, 1978. Postdoctoral fellow U. Zurich, Switzerland, 1978, U. Geneva, 1978-80, U. Wash., Seattle, 1980-81; research scientist Amgen, Thousand Oaks, Calif., 1981—. Office: Amgen 1900 Oak Terrace Ln Thousand Oaks CA 91320

KOSKINEN, SULO MATIAS, electronics company executive b. Vaasa, Finland, Sept 15, 1922; s. William and Emma (Ollus) K.; student Kansan Valistus Seura Inst., 1941-45, Cleve. Inst. Radio Electronics, 1949-51; m. Anna Miriam Linnakallio, Aug. 4, 1946; children—Jarmo, Pirjo, Ellen; came to Can., 1951, naturalized, 1956. Product mgr. Chisholm Industries, 1952-56; dir. engring. Anaconda Electronics Ltd. (formerly Tele Signal Electronics), Vancouver, B.C., Can., 1956-75, also dir.; pres. Koskinen Electronic Lab., Ltd. Pres., Finnish Can. Rest Home Assn., 1964—, Finnish Kalevava Bros., Vancouver, 1964—; treas. Loyal Finns in Can., 1962-75. Served with Finnish Air Force, 1941-44. Mem. IEEE, Soc. Cable TV Engrs., Internat. Soc. Hybrid Microelectronics. Club: Finlandia (pres. 1978-79) (Vancouver). Contbr. articles to tech. jours. Patentee in field (3). Home: 5390 Frances St, Burnaby, BC Canada V5B 1T5

KOST, GERALD JOSEPH, physician, cardiovascular researcher, scientist; b. Sacramento, July 12, 1945; s. Edward William and Ora Imogene (Casey) K.; m. Angela Louise Baldo, Sept. 9, 1972; children: Christopher Murray, Laurie Elizabeth. BS in Engring., Stanford U., 1968, MS in Engring., 1969; PhD in Bioengring., U. Calif., San Diego, 1977; MD, U. Calif., San Francisco, 1978. Diplomate Nat. Bd. Med. Examiners, Am. Bd. Pathology. Resident dept. medicine UCLA, 1978-79, resident dept. neurology, 1979-80; resident dept. lab. medicine U. Wash., Seattle, 1980-81, chief resident dept. lab. medicine, 1981-82, cardiopulmonary-bioengring. and clin. chemistry researcher, 1982-83; asst. prof. pathology, dir. clin. chemistry, faculty biomed. engring., Sch. Medicine U. Calif., Davis, 1983—; sci. cons. numerous cos., nat. and internat. speaker, invited lectr. Author: Medial Gastrocnemius and Soleus Muscle in vivo Responses to Arterial Ischemia, Hemorrhagic Shock, and Catecholamine Infusions: Muscle Surface pH, Membrane Potential, and Histochemistry Studies, 1977; also author monographs; contbr. numerous articles to profl. and sci. jours.; various video productions. Recipient over 25 awards and research grants including Bank Am. Fine Arts award 1963, Millberry Art award, 1970, Nat. Research Service award Nat. Heart, Lung and Blood Inst., U. Calif. San Diego, 1972-77, Young Investigator award Acad. Clin. Lab. Physicians and Scientists, 1982, 83, Nuclear Magnetic Resonance award U. Calif., Davis, 1984, 85, 86; S.A. Pepper Collegiate scholar, 1963; Fellow Stanford U., 1967-68, Internat. scholar MOP, Venezuela, 1967, NIH, 1970, Highest Honor Calif. Scholarship Fedn.; grantee Am. Heart Assn./U. Calif., Davis, 1983—, others. Mem. AAAS, Am. Assn. Clin. Chemistry, Acad. Clin. Lab. Physicians and Scientists, Am. Heart Assn., Biomed. Engring. Soc., Am. Soc. Testing Materials (hon.), Soc. Mfg. Research Medicine, Sigma Xi, Phi Kappa Phi. Avocations: trumpet soloist, photography, art, outdoor sports.

KOST, RICHARD STEPHEN, SR., aviation foundation executive; b. San Diego, Oct. 18, 1947; s. Ned Franklin and Helen Lucille (Mahaffey) K.; m. Jennifer Edna Smith, Aug. 12, 1975 (div. Sept. 1979); children: Jaylene Elaine, Richard Stephen Jr. Student, U. Wyo., 1965-66, 67-68, NW Community Coll., 1967. V.p. Slyko Laramie, Wyo., 1969-70; pres. Unico, Laramie, 1970-71; editor Berthoud (Colo.) Bull. Newspapers, 1971-72; v.p. Aviation Maintenance Pubs., Basin, Wyo., 1973-78, pres. Aviation Maintenance Found., 1972-82; exec. v.p. Aviation Maintenance Pubs., Riverton, Wyo., 1982-84; pres. Bus. Computer Network, Riverton, 1983-85, Aviation Maintenance Found., Redmond, Wash., 1985—; founder, chmn. Space Tng., Applications & Research Corp., Redmond, 1986—; cons. Midway Airlines, Chgo., 1981, Frontier Services Co., Denver, 1982, Ethiopian Airlines, Addis Ababa, 1983; exec. bd. dirs., cons. Aviation Maintenance Ednl. Fund, Redmond, 1974—; gen. ptnr. Factory Showroom, Basin, 1981-82; chmn. and chief exec. officer Space Tng. Applications and Research Corp., Redmond, Wash., 1986—. Contbr. articles to profl. jours. Treas. Big Horn County (Wyo.) Rep. Cen. Com., 1976, chmn., 1978-82; bd. dirs. Wyo. State Rep. Cen. Com., 1976-82. Recipient Achievement award Aviation Technician Edn. Com., 1982. Lodge: Elks. Avocation: travel. Office: Aviation Maintenance Found Inc PO Box 2826 Redmond WA 98073

KOSTEK, PAUL JOHN, electrical engineer; b. Fall River, Mass., May 29, 1957; s. John Michael and Doris Claudette (Levesque) K. ASEE, Bristol Community Coll., 1977; BSEE, Southeastern Mass. U., 1979. Design engr. Grumman Aerospace Corp., Bethpage, N.Y., 1979-81, Boeing Co., Seattle, 1981—; pres., cons. Personal Systems Inc., Seattle, 1984—. Vol. Seattle Pub. Library, 1982—; vol. coordinator Spl. Olympics, Wash., 1983—. Mem. IEEE (chmn. profl. activities com. for engrs. 1984-86), Seattle Profl. Engring. Employees Assn. (sec. 1984—). Democrat. Roman Catholic. Avocations: golf, tennis, cross-country skiing, biking, travel. Home: 13517 Empire Way S #406H Seattle WA 98178 Office: Boeing Aerospace Co PO Box 3999 M/S 8 K-32 Seattle WA 98124

KOSTER, JEAN NICOLAS, mechanical engineer, educator; b. Luxembourg, Sept. 28, 1948; s. Dominique and Marcelle (Weyrich) K.; m. Irene J. Koster, June 29, 1973; children: Dennis, Natalie. D Engring., U. Karlsruhe, Fed. Republic Germany, 1980. Instr. U. Utah, Salt Lake City, 1980-82; research scientist Kernforschungszentrum, Karlsruhe, 1982-84; asst. prof. U. Colo., Boulder, 1984—; assoc. dir. Ctr. Low Gravity Fluid Mechanics and Transport Phenomena, U. Colo., 1986—. Contbr. articles to profl. jours. Mem. Verein Deutscher Ingenieure, N.Y. Acad. Scis., AIAA, Nat. Space Soc., Sigma Xi. Home: Aegean Dr Lafayette CO 80026 Office: U Colo Aerospace Dept Box 429 Boulder CO 80309

KOSTKA, WILLIAM JAMES, JR., public relations exec.; b. Mpls., Oct. 17, 1934; s. William James and Dorothy (Parmenter) K.; B.A. in Journalism, U. Colo., 1956; m. Cynthia Gleason, Apr. 6, 1974; children—Cheryl Elizabeth, Wendy Dorelle, Jennifer Anna, William James. Chmn., pres. William Kostka & Assos., Denver, 1964—; nat. news bur. chief Martin Marietta Corp., Balt., 1961-64; reporter Rocky Mountain News, Denver, 1958-61; faculty U. Colo., Boulder, 1975—. Served with U.S. Army, 1956-58. Named Outstanding Grad. in Journalism, U. Colo., 1977. Mem. Public Relations Soc. Am., Denver Advt. Fedn., Colo. Press Assn. Clubs: Denver Press, Denver Country, Univ., Mt. Vernon Country. Home: 13955 E Hamilton Dr Aurora CO 80014 Office: 1407 Larimer Sq Denver CO 80202

KOSTOULAS, IOANNIS GEORGIOU, physicist, aerospace engineer; b. Petra, Pierias, Greece, Sept. 12, 1936; came to U.S., 1965, naturalized, 1984; s. Georgios Ioannou and Panagiota (Zarogiannis) K.; m. Katina Sioras Kay, June 23, 1979; 1 child, Alexandra. Diploma in Physics U. Thessoloniki, Greece, 1963; M.A., U. Rochester, 1969, Ph.D., 1972; M.S., U. Ala., 1977, Instr. U. Thessaloniki, 1963-65; teaching asst. U. Ala., 1966-67, U. Rochester, 1967-68; guest jr. research assoc. Brookhaven Nat. Lab., Upton, N.Y., 1968-72; research physicist, lectr. UCLA, U. Calif.-San Diego, 1972-76; sr. research assoc. Mich. State U., East Lansing, 1976-78, Fermi Nat. Accelerator Lab., Betavia, Ill., 1976-78; research staff mem. MIT, Cambridge, 1978-80; sr. system engr., physicist Hughes Aircraft Co., El Segundo, Calif., 1980-86; sr. physicist electro-optics and space sensors Rockwell Internat. Corp., Seal Beach and Anaheim, Calif., 1986—. Contbr. articles to profl. jours. Served with Greek Army, 1961-63. Research grantee U. Rochester, 1968-72. Mem. Am. Phys. Soc., Los Alamos Sci. Lab. Exptl. Users Group, Fermi Nat. Accelerator Lab. Users Group, High Energy Discussion Group of Brookhaven Nat. Lab., Pan Macedonian Assn., Save Cyprus Council Los Angeles, Sigma Pi Sigma. Club: Hellenic U. Lodge: Ahepa. Home: 2016 Vanderbilt Ln Apt 7 Redondo Beach CA 90278 Office: Rockwell Internat Co MC OB34 3370 Miraloma Ave PO Box 4192 Anaheim CA 92803

KOTHARI, SAMIR PRABODHCHANDRA, systems engineering manager; b. Ahmedabad, Gujarat, India, Dec. 3, 1954; came to U.S., 1976; s. Prabodh M. and Kunjbala P. Kothari; m. Sadhana S. Shah, Jan. 19, 1980; 1 chil, Neel. Diploma in German, M.S. U., Baroda, India, 1975, BS in Engring., 1976, MSChemE, U. Cin., 1978. Registered profl. engr., Fla. Project engr. Pedco Environ. Inc., Cin., 1978-80; design engr. Henningson, Durham & Richardson, Pensacola, Fla., 1980-81; engring. supr., design engr.

Hoffman-La Roche, Nutley, N.J, 1981-84; systems engr. Procter and Gamble, Sacramento, 1984—; tchr. lang. Berlitz Inst., Cin., 1979. Contbr. articles to profl. jours. Mem. Am. Inst. Chem. Engrs. (Cert. Profl. Devel. Recognition, 1981). Club: Toastmasters (Cin.) (v.p. 1979-80). Office: Procter and Gamble 8201 Fruitridge Rd Sacramento CA 95825

KOTHS, KIRSTON EDWARD, biochemist; b. La Fayette, Ind., Dec. 24, 1948; s. Jay Sanford and Margaret Louise (Edwards) K.; m. Catherine Elizabeth Lutes, Aug. 24, 1985. BS, Amherst Coll., 1971; PhD, Harvard U., 1979. Scientist Cetus Corp., Emeryville, Calif., 1979-82, dir. protein chemistry, 1982—, sr. scientist, 1984—. Patentee in field. Avocations: gold prospecting, photography, teaching dance. Office: Cetus Corp 1400 Fifty Third St Emeryville CA 94608

KOTSUR, LEONARD STEPHEN, police chief; b. Hazleton, Pa., Sept. 21, 1938; s. John and Elizabeth (Grula) K.; m. JoDee Louise True, Nov. 26, 1961; children—Kevin, Brian, Troy, Brent. A.A. with high distinction, Mesa Community Coll., 1969; B.A. with high distinction, Ariz. State U., 1973. Patrolman, Mesa Police Dept., Ariz., 1961-69, sergeant, 1969-73, lt., 1973-77, capt., 1977-78, maj., 1978-80, asst. chief, 1980-82, chief, 1982—; mem. Ariz. Criminal Justice Info. Systems Bd., 1980-82; pres. elect FBI Nat. Acad. Assocs., 1985—. Bd. dirs. YMCA, 1980-82, treas., 1983. Served with USAF, 1956-60. Mem. Ariz. Assn. Chiefs Police. Democrat. Roman Catholic. Lodges: Rotary, Fraternal Order Police. Office: Mesa Police Dept 130 N Robson St Mesa AZ 85201 *

KOTTKE, FREDERICK EDWARD, economics educator; b. Menominee, Mich., Sept. 6, 1926; s. Edward Frederick and M. Marie (Braun) K.; B.S., Pepperdine U., 1950; postgrad. U. Wis., 1950-52; M.A., U. So. Calif., 1957, Ph.D., 1960; m. Lillian Dorathy Larson, Aug. 27, 1950; children—Karin Lee, Kurt Edward. Lectr., Pepperdine U., 1952-53; asst. prof. U. So. Calif., 1956-63; assoc. prof. econs., chmn. dept., speaker of gen. faculty Stanislaus State Coll., Turlock, Calif., 1963-68, prof., also chmn. div. arts and scis., 1968—; pres. KK Economic Consultants, Inc.; independent tax adviser, managerial adviser, 1960—. Chmn., Stanislaus County United Crusade, 1964-65; pres., Stanislaus State Coll. Found., 1972; trustee Emanuel Med. Center, 1974—; v.p. Good Shepherd Lutheran Ch. Served with USNR. 1943-46. Recipient Pologrammatic award Pepperdine Coll., 1952. Haynes Found. Postgrad. Research award U. So. Calif., 1959. Mem. Am., Western econ. assns., Nat. Tax Assn., Am. Finance Assn., C. of C., Omicron Delta Epsilon. Lodge: Kiwanis. Author: An Economic Analysis of Toll-Highway Finance, 1956, An Economic Analysis of Financing an Interstate Highway System, 1959. Home: 1890 N Denair Ave Turlock CA 95380 Office: Calif State Coll Stanislaus 801 W Monte Vista Ave Turlock CA 95380

KOTTLOWSKI, FRANK EDWARD, geologist; b. Indpls., Apr. 11, 1921; s. Frank Charles and Adella (Markworth) K.; m. Florence Jean Chriscoe, Sept. 15, 1945; children: Karen, Janet, Diane. Student, Butler U., 1939-42; A.B., Ind. U., 1947, M.A., 1949, Ph.D., 1951. Party chief Ind. Geology Survey, Bloomington, summers 1948-50; fellow Ind. U., 1947-51, instr. geology, 1950; adj. prof. N.Mex. Inst. Mining and Tech., Socorro, 1970—; econ. geologist N.Mex. Bur. Mines and Mineral Resources, 1951-66, asst. dir., 1966-68, 70-74, acting dir., 1968-70, dir., 1974—; geologic cons. Sandia Corp., 1966-72. Contbr. articles on mineral resources, stratigraphy and areal geology to tech. jours. Mem. Planning Commn. Socorro, 1960-68, 71-78, chmn. 86—; mem. N.Mex. Energy Resources Bd.; chmn. N.Mex. Coal Surface Mining Commn.; sec. Socorro County Democratic party, 1964-68. Served to 1st lt. USAAF, 1942-45. Decorated D.F.C.; decorated Air medal; recipient Richard Owen Disting. Alumni award in Govt. and Industry U. Ind., 1987. Fellow Geol. Soc. Am. (councilor 1980-82, exec. com. 1981-82); mem. Am. Assn. Petroleum Geologists (dist. rep. 1965-68 Disting. Service award, hon.; editor 1971-75), Assn. Am. State Geologists (pres. 1985-86), Soc. Econ. Geologists, AAAS, AIME, Am. Inst. Profl. Geologists (Pub. Service award 1986), Am. Commn. Stratigraphic Nomenclature (sec. 1964-68, chmn. 1968-70), Sigma Xi. Home: 703 Sunset Dr Socorro NM 87801 Office: NMex Bur Mines NMex Tech Socorro NM 87801

KOUTZ, KENNETH HUNT, safety and occupational health executive; b. Berkeley, Calif., Aug. 26, 1945; s. Ernest Henry Koutz and Loya Genevieve (Hunt) Mott; m. Jean L. Loux, Sept. 6, 1969. BS, Calif. State U., Hayward, 1969; MS, U. So. Calif., 1981. Cert. safety profl. Head sci. dept. Larkspur (Calif.) Sch. Dist., 1970-79; safety specialist Naval Supply Ctr., Oakland, Calif., 1979-84; safety mgr. Naval Sta. Treasure Island, San Francisco, 1984; safety and occupational health mgr. Navy Pub. Works Ctr., Oakland, 1984—. Mem. Am. Soc. Safety Engrs., Am. Indsl. Hygiene Assn., NEA, Assn. Fed. Safety Profls. Democrat. Roman Catholic. Avocations: swimming, hiking, reading. Office: Navy Pub Works Ctr PO Box 24003 Code 20A Oakland CA 94623

KOUYMJIAN, DICKRAN, art historian, educator; b. Tulcea, Romania, June 6, 1934; came to U.S. (parents Am. citizens), 1939; s. Toros S. and Zabelle I. (Calusdian) K.; m. Angèle Kapoïan, Sept. 16, 1967. BS in European Cultural History, U. Wis., 1957; MA in Arab Studies, Am. U., Beirut, 1961; PhD in Near East Lang. and Culture, Columbia U., 1969. Instr. English Columbia U., N.Y.C., 1961-64; dir. Am. Authors, Inc., N.Y.C., 1965-67; asst. prof. and asst. dir. Ctr. for Arabic Studies Am. U., Cairo, 1967-71; assoc. prof. history Am. U. Beirut, 1971-75; prof. art history Am. Coll., Paris, 1976-77; prof. history and art, dir. Armenian Studies program Calif. State U., Fresno, 1977—; cons. archaeology UNESCO, Paris, 1976. Author: Index of Armenian Art, part I, 1977, part II, 1979, The Armenian History of Ghazar P'arpetzi, 1986; co-author: (with A. Kapoïan) The Splendor of Egypt, 1975; author and editor: William Saroyan: An Armenian Trilogy, 1986; editor: (books) Near Eastern Numismatics, Iconography, Epigraphy and History, 1974, Essays in Armenian Numismatics in Honor of C. Sibilian, 1981, Armenian Studies: In Memoriam Haïg Berbérian, 1986; editorial bd. Armenian Rev., 1974—, Ararat Lit. mag., 1975—, Revue des Etudes Arméniennes, 1978—, NAASR Jour. Armenian Studies; contbr. articles to profl. jours. Served with U.S. Army, 1957. Recipient Outstanding Prof. award Am. U., Cairo, 1968-69, 69-70, Outstanding Prof. of Yr. faculty award Calif. State U., 1985-86; Fulbright fellow, 1986—; grantee NEH, Paris, 1980-81. Mem. Am. Oriental Soc., Am. Numismatic Soc., Middle East Studies Assn. (charter), Coll. Arts Assn., Soc. Armenian Studies (charter, pres. 1985-86), Armenian Assembly (exec. council Calif. chpt. 1979-81), Société Asiatique, Medieval Acad., other orgns. Avocations: music, theater, bibliophile. Home: 30 rue Chevert, 75007 Paris France Office: Calif State U Armenian Studies Program Fresno CA 93740

KOVALEVSKY, LEONID, structural engineer, educator; b. Kiev, Russia, Apr. 16, 1916; s. George Paul and Sophia (Doroginski) K.; C.E. in Structural Engring., U. Belgrad (Yugoslavia), 1935-42; Dr.-Ing. in Structural Engring., Technische Hochschule, Munich, Germany, 1950; m. Danica Kosutich, Nov. 6, 1952 (dec. 1976). Came to U.S., 1950, naturalized, 1955. Design engr., Germany, 1942-50, Corbett & Tinghir, Inc., N.Y.C., 1950-53; sr. engr. Erdman & Hosley, Syracuse, N.Y., 1953-56, Daniel, Man, Johnson & Mendenhall & Assos., Los Angeles, 1958-60; structures research specialist space and info. div. Space div. Rockwell Internat. (co. formerly N.Am. Rockwell) Downey, Calif., 1957-58, 61-71, mem. tech. staff B1 div., Los Angeles, 1971-81, N.Am. Aircraft div., 1971-81, now ret.; prof. World Open U. Mem. ASCE. Nat. Mgmt. Assn., Author: (with others) Shell Analysis Manual, 1966, Analysis of Webs of Partial-Tension-Field Beams Subjected to Lateral Pressure Loadings, 1966; Structural Analysis of Shells, 1972, 2d edit., 1981; contbr. articles on stability, inflatable structures, statistics to tech. publs. Home: 1024 Via Nogales Palos Verdes Estates CA 90274

KOVNER, JOEL WYATT, banker; b. N.Y.C., May 19, 1941; s. Sidney J. and Natalie (Lieberman) K.; B.A., Cornell U., 1963; M.P.H., UCLA, 1964, Ph.D., 1968; postgrad. Harvard U., 1975-79; m. Virginia Samuels, June 17, 1965; children—Chloe, Emily, Noah, Jacob. Mem. faculty UCLA, 1968; economist Kaiser Found. Health Plan, Los Angeles, 1969-72, dir. med. econs., 1972-79, v.p., 1979-81; mgr. planning and support services Kaiser-Permanente Med. Care Program, Los Angeles, 1979-81; now chmn., chief exec. officer First Profl. Bank, N.A., Los Angeles; cons. in field. Mem. Am. Public Health Assn. (chmn. med. care 1980-81), Health Info. Soc. (pres. 1971-72), Ops. Research Soc. Jewish. Contbr. articles to profl. jours. Home: 15912 Alcima Ave Pacific Palisades CA 90272 Office: 606 Broadway Santa Monica CA 90401

KOWALSKI, KENNETH R., Canadian government official; b. Bonnyville, Alta., Can., Sept. 27, 1945; m. Jeannine Kowalski; children: Lori Anne, Michael Paul. BA in History, U. Alta., 1966, MA in East Asian History, 1970. Tchr. social studies Lorne Jenken High Sch., Alta., 1969-74; dir. decentralization program Alta. Transp., 1977-79; exec. asst. to dep. premier Minister of Agr., Alta., 1975-77; chmn. regional transp. services 1977-79, MLA Barrhead, Alta., 1979-86; MLA, chmn. Legis.'s Heritage Savs. Trust Fund Select com. Minister Environment, Alta. Pub. Safety Services, 1982-86; Minister of Environment Minister Alta. Pub. Safety Services, 1986—. Office: Office Minister of Environment, Alta Pub Safety Services, 132 Legislature Bldg, Edmonton, AB Canada T5K 2B6

KOWEL, STEPHEN THOMAS, electrical engineering educator; b. Phila., Nov. 20, 1942; s. Abraham and Anna (Forman) K.; m. Janis Zoltan, June 7, 1970; children: Ann, Eugene, Rose. B.S. in Elec. Engring., U. Pa., 1964; Ph.D in Elec. Engring., 1968; M.S. in Elec. Engring., Poly. Inst. Bklyn., 1966. Research assoc. U. Pa., Phila., 1968-69; asst. prof. elec. and computer engring. Syracuse U., N.Y., 1969-74, assoc. prof., 1974-79, prof., 1979-84; prof. U. Calif., Davis, 1984—, vice-chair dept., 1986—; vis. prof. Cornell U., Ithaca, N.Y., 1982-83; cons. in field. Contbr. articles to profl. jours.; patenteein field. Grantee NASA; grantee U.S. Air Force, U.S. Army, NSF. Mem. IEEE (sr.), AAAS, AAUP, Sigma Xi. Home: 2301 Poppy Lane Davis CA 95616 Office: U Calif Dept Elec and Computer Engring Davis CA 95616

KOZIAK, JULIAN G.J., former Canadian provincial minister; b. Edmonton, Alta., Can., Sept. 16, 1940; s. John H. and Maria (Woytkiw) K.; m. Barbara Lee Melnychuk, Aug. 19, 1961; children—Leanne M., Donald I., Deborah, Susan, Julian P.N. B.A., U. Alta., 1962, LL.B., 1963. Called to Alta. bar; created Queen's Counsel. Ptnr. firm Kosowan & Wachowich, Edmonton, 1964-75; mem. Legis. Assembly, Edmonton-Strathcona, 1971-86; minister of edn. Govt. of Alta., 1975-79, minister consumer and corp. affairs, 1979-82, minister mcpl. affairs, 1982-86. Mem. Law Soc. Alta. Mem. Progressive Conservative Assn. Ukranian Catholic. Office: 224 Legislature Bldg, Edmonton, AB Canada T5K 2B6

KOZIOL, BRIAN JOSEPH, nutrition educator; b. Gardner, Mass., Aug. 24, 1951; s. Joseph Walter and Irene Theresa (Kosakowski) K. BS in Physiology, U. Mass., 1973; MS Kinesiology, U. Calif., 1977, PhD in Nutrition, 1984. Lab. dir. UCLA Sch. Pub. Health, 1978—, assoc. research, 1984—; asst. prof. UCLA Sch. Medicine, 1984—, lab. dir., 1984—; lectr. chemistry and biochemistry UCLA Chem. and Biochem. depts., 1984—; assoc. prof. U. Bridgeport, Conn., 1984-87; asst prof. chemistry and biochemistry U. Bridgeport, 1987—; cons., lectr. Northrop Aircraft, Hawthorne, Calif., 1982—; cons. Calif. Mus. Sci. and Industry, Los Angeles, 1983—, Walt Disney Studios, Burbank, Calif., 1982—, cons. Brooks Film Inst., Santa Barbara, Calif., 1979-81. Contbr. articles and revs. to profl. jours. Instr. Am. Heart Assn., Los Angeles, 1980—, lectr.; vol. Los Angeles Philharm. Orch., 1977-83; vol. Skid Row Hospitality Kitchen, Los Angeles, 1978-83; mentor UCLA Mentor Program, 1979-82. NIH scholar, 1981. Mem. AAAS, Am. Council Sci. and Health, Am. Soc. Clin. Nutrition, Am. Inst. Nutrition (travel award, lectr. 1985), Jonsson Comprehensive Cancer Ctr., Sigma Xi, Delta Omega Soc. Democrat. Roman Catholic. Avocations: recreational sports, running, swimming, cycling. Home: 11640 Mayfield Ave #8 Los Angeles CA 90049 Office: U Calif CHS 61-297 Sch Pub Health Los Angeles CA 90024

KOZLOFF, EUGENE NICHOLAS, zoologist, educator, author; b. Tehran, Iran, Sept. 26, 1920; came to U.S., 1921; s. Nicholas Emilianovich and Eugenie Afanasievna (Kuznetsova) K.; m. Anne Solomon, Oct. 20, 1944; 1 child, Rae Annette. AB in Zoology, U. Calif., Berkeley, 1942, MA in Zoology, 1946, PhD in Zoology, 1950. Lectr. U. Calif., Berkeley, 1945; from instr. to prof. Lewis and Clark Coll., Portland, Oreg., 1945-66; prof. zoology U. Wash., Seattle, 1966—; assoc. dir. Friday Harbor (Wash.) Labs., 1966-73, acting dir., 1979-81. Author: Essentials of Practical Microtechnique, 1964, 71; Seashore Life of Puget Sound, 1973, Keys to the Marine Invertebrates of Puget Sound, 1974, Plants and Animals of the Pacific Northwest, 1976, Seashore Life of the Northern Pacific Coast, 1983. Guggenheim fellow, 1953-54. Mem. Am. Microscopical Soc. (editorial bd.), Soc. Protozoologists, Marine Biol.Assn., Western Soc. Naturalists (pres. 1962). Democrat. Home: 40 Hillcrest Pl S Friday Harbor WA 98250 Office: U Wash Dept Zoology Seattle WA 98195

KOZLOFF, JUDITH BONNIE, lawyer; b. St. Louis, Mar. 4, 1926; d. Isador and Ruth (Gould) Friedman; B.S., Northwestern U., 1947; J.D., U. Denver, 1968; m. Lloyd M. Kozloff, June 16, 1947; children—James S., Daniel I., Joseph H., Sarah R. Law clk. Mr. Justice Day, Colo. Supreme Ct., Denver, 1969-70; admitted to Colo. bar, 1969, Calif. bar, 1981; asso. Holland & Hart, Denver, 1970-73; sec., gen. counsel Affiliated Bankshares Colo., Boulder, 1973-78; atty. Mountain States Tel. & Tel. Co., Denver, 1979-80, Pacific Bell, San Francisco, 1981-87 . Recipient award Pacific Telephone Employees for Women's Affirmative Action, 1981. Mem. Colo. Bar, Calif. Bar Assn., San Francisco Bar Assn.

KOZLOFF, LLOYD M., university dean educator; b. Chgo., Oct. 15, 1923; s. Joseph and Rose (Hollobow) K.; m. Judith Bonnie Friedman, June 16, 1947; children—James, Daniel, Joseph, Sarah. B.S., U. Chgo., 1943, Ph.D., 1948. Asst., then assoc. prof. biochemistry U. Chgo., 1949-61, prof., 1961-64; prof. microbiology U. Colo., Denver, 1964-80, chmn. dept. microbiology, 1966-76, assoc. dean, prof., 1976-80; dean, prof. U. Calif.-San Francisco, 1981—; career investigator USPHS, U. Chgo., 1962. Editor Jour. Virology, 1966-76. Contbr. articles to profl. jours., chpts. to books. Chmn. bd. govs. Proctor Found., San Francisco, 1982—; bd. overseers U. Calif.-San Francisco Found., 1981—. Served with USN, 1944-46. Commonwealth Fund fellow, 1953, Lederle Found. fellow, 1954. Fellow AAAS; mem. Am. Soc. Biol. Chemistry, Am. Soc. Microbiology (head virology sect. 1974-76), Am. Chem. Soc., N.Y. Acad. Sci. Home: 2026 Green St San Francisco CA 94123 Office: U Calif Grad Div S-140 San Francisco CA 94143-0404

KRACHMALNICK, SAMUEL J., music conductor, educator; b. St. Louis; s. Abe and Jennie Krachmalnick. Diploma, Juilliard Sch. Music, 1950. Assoc. music dir. Met. Opera Nat. Co., 1965-67; prof., dir. symphony and opera U. Wash., Seattle, 1971-76; dir. symphony and opera UCLA, 1976—; music dir. Harkness Found., 1970-76. First conductor Zurich Stadtheater, 1961-63. Office: UCLA Dept Music 405 Hilgard Ave Los Angeles CA 90024

KRAEGER-ROVEY, CATHERINE EILEEN, engineering consultant; b. Ft. Collins, Colo., May 16, 1948; d. Leonard George and Vera eileen (Stairs) Kraeger; m. Edward William Rovey, Mar. 31, 1973. BS, Colo. State U., 1970, MS, 1972, PhD, 1974. Registered profl. engr., Colo., Mont. Prof. engring. Oreg. State U., Corvallis, 1974-76; project engr. CH2M-Hill, Inc., St. Louis, 1976-77; sr. engr. Wright Water Engring., Denver, 1977-80; regional mgr. Ott Water Engrs., Denver, 1980-81, sr. geohydrologist, 1980-82; v.p. Terra Therma, Inc., Denver, 1983—; pvt. practice cons. Denver, 1982—; bd. dirs. Terra Therma, Inc., Denver. Contbr. articles to profl. jours. Corp. pres., dir. fin. N. Presbyn. Ch., Denver, 1985-86. NDEA fellow, 1970; recipient Ralph A. Parshall award Colo. State U., 1970. Mem. Am. Water Resources Assn. (legis. com. Colo. sect. 1986), Am. Cons. Engrs. Council (bur. reclamation, liaison com., 1984—), Colo. Ground Water Assn. (legis. com. 1984—, treas. 1986-87), Cons. Engrs. Council Colo. (bd. dirs., chmn. pub. relations com. 1985-86). Avocations: backpacking, hiking, skiing, needlework, piano. Home: 2927 W 36th Ave Denver CO 80211 Office: Terra Therma Inc 8341 S Sangre de Cristo Denver CO 80211

KRAFT, LISBETH MARTHA, veterinarian, scientist; b. Vienna, Austria, May 16, 1920; came to U.S., 1923, naturalized, 1929; d. Rudolph and Marie F. (Mikota) K. B.S., N.Y. State Coll. of Agr., Cornell U., 1942; D.V.M., N.Y. State Coll. Vet. Medicine, Cornell U., 1945. Diplomate: Am. Coll. of Lab. Animal Medicine (pres. 1966, dir. 1965-67). Research asst. dept. parasitology N.Y. State Vet. Coll., Ithaca, 1945-46, N.Y. State Vet. Coll. (div. of nutrition), Harvard Med. Sch., Boston, 1946; bacteriologist N.Y. State Dept. Health, Albany, 1947-49; research asst. Yale Med. Sch. New Haven, 1949-50, instr. preventive medicine, 1950-52, asst. prof. dept. microbiology, 1952-55, research assoc. dept. of pathology, 1957-61; veterinarian Yale Med. Sch. New Haven (Med. Center), 1960-61; asst. dir. N.Y.C. Dept. of Health (Bur. of Labs.), 1961-65; assoc. mem. dept. lab. diagnosis Pub. Health Research Inst., N.Y.C., 1961-65; assoc. prof. microbiology Sch. Vet. Medicine, U. Pa., Phila., 1965; cons. to Bioquest, div. of Becton Dickinson & Co., Hackensack, N.J., 1965-66; research veterinarian, cons. med. div. of Oak Ridge Asso. Univs., Oak Ridge, Tenn., 1966-67; founder L.M. Kraft Assos. (consultants in lab. animal sci.), Goshen, N.Y., 1968-72; dir. research and devel. Carworth div. of Becton Dickinson & Co., New City, N.Y., 1972-73; also mgr. spl. services Carworth div. of Becton Dickinson & Co., 1972-73; asso. scientist dept. physics U. San Francisco, 1974-77; research scientist, NASA-Ames Research Center, Moffett Field, Calif.; Cons. to Sloan Kettering Ins., Walker Labs., Rye, N.Y., 1958-59, WHO, Azul, Argentina, S. Am., 1965, NASA (Ames Research Center), Moffett Field, Calif., 1972—. Contbr. articles on immunology and diseases of lab. animals and space flight effects to profl. jours. Mem. Am. Assn. for Lab. Animal Sci. (dir. 1960-67, chmn. awards com. 1967, editorial bd. 1964-65, assoc. editor 1966—, Griffin award 1972), AVMA (Charles River prize 1981), Assn. for Applied Gnotobiology, Am. Soc. Microbiology, Am. Soc. Lab. Animal Practitioners, AAAS, Nat. Research Council (adv. council Inst. Lab. Animal Resources 1966-67), N.Y. Acad. Scis., Sigma Xi. Address: PO Box 28 Moffett Field CA 94035

KRAGULAC, OLGA GOLUBOVICH, interior designer; b. St. Louis, Nov. 27, 1937; d. Jovica Todor and Milka (Slijepcevich) Golubovich; A.A., U. Mo., 1958; cert. interior design UCLA, 1979. Interior designer William L. Pereira Assocs., Los Angeles, 1977-80; assoc. Reel/Grobman Assocs., Los Angeles, 1980-81; project mgr. Kaneko/Laff Assocs., Los Angeles, 1982; project mgr. Stuart Laff Assocs., Los Angeles, 1983-85; restaurateur The Edge, St. Louis, 1983-84; pvt. practice comml. interior design, Los Angeles, 1981—. Mem. invitation and ticket com. Calif. Chamber Symphony Soc., 1980-81; vol. Westside Rep. Council, Proposition 1, 1971; asst. inaugural presentation Mus. of Childhood, Los Angeles, 1985. Recipient Carole Eichen design award U. Calif., 1979. Mem. Am. Soc. Interior Designers, Inst. Bus. Designers, Phi Chi Theta, Beta Sigma Phi. Republican. Serbian Orthodox. Office and Home: 700 Levering No 4 Los Angeles CA 90024

KRAHN, OWEN LA MARR, municipal housing authority executive; b. Gooding, Idaho, Dec. 6, 1943; s. Fred Rovert Herman Krahn and Hazel (Prince) Debban; m. Selina Rae Harris, June 24, 1982; children: Justin B., Timothy M., Selina M. BA, Boise State U., 1973, MBA, 1976. Cert. pub. housing mgr. Dir. St. Luke's Hosp., Boise, Idaho, 1977-78; sales mgr. Payless Drug Stores, Boise, 1979-81; trainee U.S. Postal Service, Boise, 1981-82; exec. dir. Ada County Housing Authority, Boise, 1983—, Boise Housing Authority, 1983—; sec. treas. Shoreline Plaza, Boise, 1983—, Boise Housing Authority, 1983—, Ada County Housing Authority, 1983—. Trustee ch., Boise, 1984—; campaign coordinator Glenn Wegner, Idaho, 1972; campaign mgr. Kidwell for Idaho Atty. Gen., 1975-76; legis. dist. chmn. Rep. Party, Boise, 1967-68, precinct committeeman, 1972-84. Served with USN, 1961-64. Mem. Assn. Idaho Housing Authorities (v.p. 1984—), Idaho Assn. Nat. Housing and Redevel. Officials (pres. 1983—), Human Resources Assn. of Treasure Valley. Club: Toastmasters. lodges: Kiwanis, Elks. Avocations: skiing, white water rafting. Home: 11849 Combes Park Boise ID 83704 Office: Boise ADA County Housing Authority 680 Cunningham Pl Boise ID 83704

KRAJACICH, THOMAS JOHN, psychologist; b. Gt. Falls, Mont., Jan. 15, 1952; s. Nick and Rose (Bruschella) K.; m. Linda Hitch, Apr. 24, 1976; children—Danielle Marie, Jeffrey Thomas. B.S., Mont. State U., 1974; M.A., Pepperdine U., 1976; Ph.D., Calif. Sch. Profl. Psychology, 1982. Lic. clin. psychologist, Mont. Ins. underwriter Home Insurance, Gt. Falls, 1974-75; Urban 4H agent, counselor Coop. Extension, Great Falls, 1975-76; sch. psychologist Sch. Dist. 1, Gt. Falls, 1976-79; clin. psychologist trainee Kern County Mental Health Ctr., Bakersfield, Calif., 1979-80; intern Des Moines Child Guidance Ctr., 1981-82; ptnr., clin. psychologist Rushworth & Krajacich Psychol. Affiliates, Gt. Falls, 1982—; cons. psychologist Dept. Instns., Gt. Falls, 1982—; mem. aux. med. staff Mont. Deaconess Med. Ctr., Gt. Falls, 1983—, Columbus Hosp., Gt. Falls, 1983—; chmn. Child Sexual Abuse Task Force, Gt. Falls, 1984—. Mem., v.p. Rape Action Line, 1983. Scholar Mont. State U., 1973-74. Mem. Mont. Assn. Sch. Psychologists (cert.; regional dir. 1978), Am. Psychol. Assn., Mont. Psychol. Assn. Democrat. Roman Catholic. Lodge: Kiwanis (youth services dir. 1979). Office: Rushworth & Krajacich Psychol Affiliates Coll Park Med Ctr 2300 12th Ave S Suite 117 Great Falls MT 59405

KRAJEWSKI, JEFFREY JAMES, accountant; b. East Chicago, Ind., Apr. 30, 1957; s. Raymond Joseph and Marie Helen (Almason) K.; m. Cynthia Jean White, Feb. 6, 1982; 1 child, Heather Nicole. BS in Acctg., Calumet Coll., 1979. Controller Rand McNally & Co., Hammond, Ind., 1977-82; acct. Roy M. Charles & Assocs., P.A., Scottsdale, Ariz., 1982-85; pvt. practice acctg., Scottsdale, 1986—. Mem. Ariz. Soc. CPA's. Lodge: KC. Office: 7432 E Camelback Rd Scottsdale AZ 85251

KRALL, NICHOLAS ANTHONY, physicist, technological company executive; b. Kansas City, Kans., Feb. 16, 1932; s. Nicholas Joseph and Catherine Elizabeth (Carr) K.; m. Teresa J. Sloan, June 12, 1954 (div. Mar. 1985); children—Carolyn, Laura, Nicholas, Jonathan, Teresa, Elizabeth; m. Diane C. Miller, July 4, 1985. B.S. in Physics, U. Notre Dame, 1954; Ph.D. in Theoretical Physics, Cornell U., 1959. Staff scientist Gen. Atomic Co., San Diego, 1959-64, mgr. fusion theory, 1965-67; prof. physics U. Md., College Park, 1967-73; vis. prof. U. Calif.-San Diego, 1973-74; v.p. fusion Sci. Applications, Inc., 1974-78; exec. v.p. and chief scientist Jaycor, Inc., 1978—; dir. joint program for plasma physics Naval Research Lab., U. Md., 1970-73; NSF lectr. Internat. Sch. Physics, Varenna, Italy, 1962; adj. prof. U. Calif.-San Diego, 1982—. Author: (research monograph) Shock Waves in Collisionless Plasma, 1971; (grad. textbook) Principles of Plasma Physics, 1973. Contbr. articles to profl. jours. Chmn., Dept. of Energy Sci. Ct. on Alt. Fusion Concepts, 1977; panelist or chmn. Magnetic Fusion Adv. Com. Subpanels, 1983—. Guggenheim fellow, 1973. Fellow Am. Phys. Soc. (chmn. div. plasma physics 1981-82, additional offices), Sigma Xi; mem. AAAS, Fusion Power Assn. (co-founder, bd. dirs. 1979—, chmn. bd. 1983). Clubs: U.S. Chess Fedn., Am. Contract Bridge League. Avocations: ocean racing, tennis, skiing, music. Home: 1070 America Way Del Mar CA 92014 Office: Jaycor Inc PO Box 85154 San Diego CA 92138

KRAMER, ANNE PEARCE, writer, communications executive, educator, film company executive; B.A. magna cum laude, U. So. Calif., M.A., 1965, Ph.D., 1972; m. Stanley Kramer (div.); children—Larry David, Casey Lise. Gen. exec. asst. to producer/dir. Stanley Kramer Prodns., prodn. exec., story editor, casting dir., dialogue dir.; sr. lectr. cinema, comparative lit. U. So. Calif., Los Angeles; acting asst. prof. comparative lit. and film Calif. State U.-Long Beach; pres. Cathexis 3, Los Angeles; story editor, v.p. creative affairs Castle Hill Prodns., Inc., Los Angeles, 1978-80; story analyst Columbia Pictures, 1980-81, story editor, 1981-83, exec. story editor, 1983—; creative collaborator Clifton Fadiman, Ency. Brit. Films; communications cons. KPFK Radio, govt., other orgns. Bd. dirs. Model UN; expert witness on censorship for Los Angeles Dist. Atty.; nurses aide ARC, Children's Hosp.; former pres. Recovery Found. for Disturbed Children; former edni. cons., instr. Camarillo State Mental Hosp.; mem. Psychoanalytic Ctr. Calif. Mem. MLA, AAUP, Women in Film, Delta Kappa Alpha, Phi Kappa Phi, Pi Beta Phi. Author: Neo-Metamorphoses - A Cyclical Study, Comparative Transformations in Ovidian Myth and Modern Literature, 1972; Interview with Elia Kazan, 1974; Focus on Film and Theatre; co-author: Directors at Work, 1970.

KRAMER, BARRY ALAN, psychiatrist; b. Phila., Sept. 9, 1948; s. Morris and Harriet (Greenberg) K.; m. Paulie Hoffman, June 9, 1974; children—Daniel Mark, Steven Philip. B.A. in Chemistry, NYU, 1970; M.D., Hahnemann Med. Coll., 1974. Resident in psychiatry Montefiore Hosp. and Med. Ctr., Bronx, N.Y., 1974-77; practice medicine specializing in psychiatry, N.Y.C., 1977-82; staff psychiatrist L.I. Jewish-Hillside Med. Ctr., Glen Oaks, N.Y., 1977-82; asst. prof. SUNY, Stony Brook, 1978-82; practice medicine specializing in psychiatry, Los Angeles, 1982—; asst. prof. psychiatry U. So. Calif., 1982—; ward chief Los Angeles County/U. So. Calif. Med. Ctr., 1982—; mem. med. staff Brotman Hosp., Cedars Sinai Hosp.; cons. Little Neck Nursing Home (N.Y.), 1979-82, L.I. Nursing Home, 1980-82. Reviewer, Am. Jour. Psychiatry, Convulsive Therapy Jour. Contbr. articles to profl. jours., papers to sci. meetings. NIMH grantee, 1979-80; fellow UCLA/U. So. Calif. Long-Term Gerontology Ctr., 1985-86. Mem. AMA,

Am. Psychiat. Assn., AAAS, Internat. Soc. Chronobiology, Internat. Psychiat. Assn. for Advancement of Electrotherapy, Soc. Biol. Psychiatry, Calif. Med. Assn., Los Angeles Med. Assn., Am. Assn. Geriatric Psychiatry, Gerontol. Soc. Am. Jewish. Office: Los Angeles County/Univ So Calif Med Ctr 1934 Hospital Pl Los Angeles CA 90033 Office: PO Box 2681 Beverly Hills CA 90213

KRAMER, GEORGE CALVERT, physiologist, educator; b. Phoenix, Nov. 8, 1945; s. Julius George and Lillian Gloria (Osterwald) K.; m. Lilaine Consten, Dec. 1977 (div. May 1985); 1 child Beliza Cleia. BS in Physics, USAF Acad., 1968; BA in Meteorology, San Jose State U., 1969; MS in Bioengring., U. Calif., San Diego, 1975; PhD in Physiology, U. Tex., 1979. Commd. 2d lt. USAF, 1968, advanced through grades to capt., resigned, 1972, airborne weather officer, 1969-72; asst. prof. U. Calif., Davis, 1982—. Contbr. articles to profl. jours. Fellow Parker Francis Pulmonary Medicine, 1983-85, NIH, 1979-82. Mem. Am. Physiol. Soc., Microcirculatory Soc., Am. Burn Soc., Shock Soc. Office: U Calif Dept Human Physiology Davis CA 95616

KRAMER, GORDON, mechanical engineer; b. Bklyn., Aug. 1937; s. Joseph and Etta (Grossberg) K.; B.S., Cooper Union, 1959; M.S., Calif. Inst. Tech., 1960; m. Ruth Ellen Harter, Mar. 5, 1967 (div. June 1986); children—Samuel Maurice, Leah Marie. With Hughes Aircraft Co., Malibu, Calif., 1959-63; sr. scientist Avco Corp., Norman, Okla., 1963-64; asst. div. head Batelle Meml. Inst., Columbus, Ohio, 1964-67; sr. scientist Aerojet Electrosystems, Azusa, Calif., 1967-75; chief engr. Beckman Instrument Co., Fullerton, Calif., 1975-82; prin. scientist McDonnell Douglas Microelectronics Co., 1982-83, Kramer and Assocs., 1983-85; project mgr. Hughes Aircraft Co., 1985—; cons. Korea Inst. Tech. NSF fellow, 1959-60. Mem. IEEE. Democrat. Jewish. Home: 16141 Malaga Ln Huntington Beach CA 92647 Office: 16141 Malaga Ln Huntington Beach CA 92647

KRAMER, GORDON EDWARD, mfg. co. exec.; b. San Mateo, Calif., June 22, 1946; s. Roy Charles and Bernice Jeanne (Rones) K.; B.S. in Aero. Engring., San Jose State Coll., 1970; m. Christina Hodges, Feb. 14, 1970; children—Roy Charles, Charlena. Purchasing agent Am. Racing Equipment, Brisbane, Calif., 1970-71, asst. to v.p. mktg., 1971-72; founder, pres. Safety Direct Inc., hearing protection equipment, Sparks, Nev., 1972—; dir. Hodges Transp., Condor Inc. Named Nev. Small Businessperson of the Year, Nev. Small Bus. Adminstrn. Mem. Am. Soc. Safety Engrs., Safety Equipment Distributors Assn., Indsl. Safety Equipment Assn., Nat. Assn. Sporting Goods Wholesalers, Nat. Sporting Goods Assn., Nev. State Amature Trapshooting Assn. (dir. 1978-79), Pacific Internat. Trapshooting Assn. (Nev. pres. 1979-80, 80-81), Advanced Soccer Club (pres.1985-86). Republican. Methodist. Club: Rotary. Office: Safety Direct Inc 23 Snider Way Sparks NV 89431

KRAMER, MARVIN LEWIS, corporation executive, communications and computers consultant; b. Cleve., Jan. 16, 1931; s. Edward Aaron and Alma Zoe (Gaskill) K.; m. Edith Mae Nash, Nov. 25, 1949; children: Stuart C., Gregory B., Mark H. BS in Chemistry, George Washington U., 1951, postgrad., 1951-52; MEE, U. Ill., 1963. Lic. comml. balloon pilot, FAA. Commd. lt. U.S. Air Force, 1952; advanced through grades to col., 1972; dep. dir. communications SAC, Offutt AFB, Nebr., 1973-75; vice comdr. Strategic Communication Area, Offutt AFB, 1975-77; dir. communications NORAD, Peterson AFB, Colo., 1977-79, dep. comdr. for strategic def. forces, 1979-80; ret., 1980; pvt. practice communication, computer, command and control cons., Colorado Springs, Colo., 1980—; v.p. Orion Scis., Inc.; pres. M.E.K., Ltd. Decorated Bronze Star, Meritorious Service medal, Legion of Merit with oak leaf cluster. Mem. IEEE, Armed Forces Comm. Elec. Assn., Assn. Computing Machinery, Eta Kappa Nu, Alpha Chi Sigma. Jewish. Lodge: Elks. Home and Office: 1030 Doyle Pl Colorado Springs CO 80915

KRAMER, PHILIP EARL, industrial consultant; b. Hammond, Ind., Apr. 9, 1940; s. Ralph George and Helen (Curtis) K. BA, U. Houston, 1965; BS, U. Ky., 1972; MA, U. Colo., 1978. Prin., cons. Intra World Enterprises, Lakewood, Colo.; author Bell Books Inc., Boulder, Colo., 1972—; profl. advisor Beyond Divorce, Denver, 1975-79; adminstrv. dir. Denver Opportunity, 1981-83; prin. cons. Kramers Enterprises, Lakewood, 1977—; recruiter Red Rocks Community Coll., Golden, Colo., 1983—; indsl. cons. Denver Opportunity Inc., 1979-83, McGees Restaurant, Hammond, 1977-79; psychologist aide Saugus Rehab. Ctr., Calif., 1964-70; psychologist intern Litton Industries, Woodland Hills, Calif., 1959-64. Author Jour. Red Rocks, 1984. Fellow Am. Mgmt. Assn., Am. Psychol. Assn. Roman Catholic. Clubs: Optimists, Toastmasters. Lodge: KC.

KRAMER, RICHARD ALAN, social work consultant; b. Monticello, N.Y., Jan. 12, 1949; s. Harry Leon and Sylvia (Novick) K.; m. Dora Gutman, Sept. 2, 1979; 1 child, Rachel Jean. AA, Miami-Dade Jr. Coll., 1969; BSW, Fla. Internat. U., 1974; MSW, U. Denver, 1977. Cert. level III addiction counselor, level II social worker, Colo. Pvt. practice social work Denver, 1984—. Author: The Me Nobody Knows: Common Traits of Well-Functioning Adolescents and What They Tell Us, 1986. Mem. Nat. Assn. Social Workers (cert.), Colo. Addictions Counselors. Democrat. Avocations: reading, theater, symphony, movies, baseball. Office: 7150 E Hampden Ave Suite #307 Denver CO 80224

KRAMMER, KATHERINE HEDWIG, speech language pathologist, nurse; b. Chgo., Aug. 27, 1949; d. Robert and Ruth (Loeser) K.; m. Robert Dodes, June 22, 1969 (div. Aug. 1977). AS, Suffolk Coll., 1973; BS, U. Hawaii, 1977, MS, 1980. RN, Hawaii; lic. speech lang. pathologist, Hawaii, Oreg. Nurse ICU Kuakini Hosp., Honolulu, 1973-75; nurse emergency room Kauikeolani Children's Hosp., Honolulu, 1975-78; neurol. nurse team leader Straub Hosp., Honolulu, 1978-81; speech-lang. pathologist Hawaii Dept. Edn., Honolulu, 1980; chief speech-lang pathologist St. Francis Hosp. Home Care Services, Honolulu, 1980—; mem. stroke protocol devel. team St. Francis Hosp., 1981—, leader rehab. rounds, 1984-86; speech lang. pathologist grad. student practicum supr. U. Hawaii, Honolulu, 1983—; mem. augmentative communication ad hoc com. State of Hawaii, Honolulu, 1985—. Contbr. chpts. to books, articles to profl. jours.; co-inventor glossectomy feeding device. Profl. advisor Am. Cancer Soc., Honolulu, 1981—, Hawaii Heart Assn., 1982—. Mem. AAAS, Hawaii Speech-Lang. and Hearing Assn. (pres. 1985-86, dir. ednl. affairs 1984-85, chmn. ethics com. 1983-84), Am. Speech-Lang. and Hearing Assn. (cert., Clin. Achievement award 1984), N.Y. Acad. Scis., Hawaii Heart Assn. (speaker, Cert. Appreciation, 1982, 83). Club: Toastmasters (adminstrv. v.p., Toastmaster of the Yr. 1986). Avocations: swimming, singing, public speaking. Home: 19819 NW Rock Creek Blvd Portland OR 97229

KRANDA, MICHAEL LOUIS, biotechnology company executive, political and policy adviser; b. Seattle, Nov. 18, 1953; s. Louis H. and Shirley W. (Adams) K.; m. Joyce L. Capri, Aug. 27, 1983. BA, U. Wash., 1976, MBA, 1984. Budget dir. King County Prosecutor, Seattle, 1977-78, chief of staff, 1979-83, spl. asst. to prosecutor, 1983-85; dir. corp. devel. Immunex Corp., Seattle, 1985-86; gen. mgr. Immunology Ventures, 1986—; campaign mgr. Maleng for Prosecutor, 1978, Pritchard for Congress, Seattle, 1980. Alt. Wash. state del. Nat. Rep. Conv., Seattle, 1980; bd. dirs. Mental Health North, Seattle, 1982—; mem. Reagan-Bush Fin. Com. Wash., 1984, Fund for Am.'s Future, 1985—. Office: Immunex Corp 51 University St Seattle WA 98101

KRANE, MARY COLLEEN, social services administrator; b. Langley Field, Va., Mar. 6, 1945; d. Brainard Clarence and Evelyn Charlotte (Calhoun) Shay; m. John Frances Garcia Jr., Mar. 10, 1984. BA, Parsons Coll., 1967; MSW, U. Denver, 1971. Lic. social worker, Colo. Social worker Dept. Social Services, Denver, 1967-71, supr. adult services, 1971-79, tng. dir., 1979-82, supr. child neglect, 1982-83, supr. sex abuse team, 1983, mgr., 1983—; mem. Mayor's Cabinet, Denver, 1983—; cons. Adult Care Mgmt., Inc., Denver, 1985—. bd. dirs. Griffith Youth Services, Denver, 1985—; Information Exchange, Young Adult Patients, N.Y.C., 1984—. Recipient Outstanding Citizen award Sertoma Club, 1979; named Direct Service Worker of Yr., Colo. Mental Health Assn., 1983. Mem. Nat. Assn. Social Workers, Acad. Cert. Social Workers, Colorado Alliance for the Mentally Ill (pres., bd. dirs. 1981—), Denver Alliance for Mentally Ill (founder, bd. dirs. 1979—).

KRANICH, DARRYL DUANE, aerospace company executive; b. Carson, N.D., Nov. 28, 1937; s. Antone A. and Ella Melita (Henke) Eichenlaub; m. Willa Lea Schupbach; children: Monty, Paul, Steve, Mark. BS in Bus. Mgmt., U. La Verne, 1974. Engr. Martin Marietta Corp., Denver, 1956-60; various engring. mgmt. positions, including Titan missile programs, Peacekeeper missile flight test program Martin Marietta Corp., Vandenberg AFB, Calif., 1960-82, mgr., 1982—. Recipient Gold Medalion award Martin Marietta Corp., 1979, Excellence award Martin Marietta Corp., 1984. Mem. Nat. Mgmt. Assn., Nat. Contract Mgmt. Assn., Nat. Property Mgmt. Assn. Republican. Presbyterian. Avocations: photography, travel, tennis. Office: Martin Marietta Corp PO Box 1681 Vandenberg AFB CA 93437

KRANZDORF, JEFFREY PAUL, lawyer, advertising, marketing and recording company executive, TV producer; b. Phila., Jan. 28, 1955; s. Charles David and Hilda (Eisenberg-Nahama) K.; m. Perri Scott Lovell, Sept. 16, 1979; 1 child, Charles David. A.B., U. So. Calif., 1976; J.D., Southwestern U., Los Angeles, 1979. Bar: Calif. 1979, U.S. Dist. Ct. (cen. dist.) Calif. 1979. Assoc., Davis & Cox, Los Angeles, 1980-81; dir. bus. affairs Am. Variety Internat. Inc., Los Angeles, 1981-82, gen. counsel, mng. dir., 1982-85; v.p., gen. mgr. LaBuick & Assocs. Media, Inc., 1985—; sec., dir. Ernie's Record Mart, Nashville, 1981-85. Producer Ricky Nelson and Fats Domino Live at the Universal Amphitheatre, Blueberry Hill, A Tribute to Ricky Nelson; producer, dir.: Roy Orbison Live. Office: LaBuick & Assocs Media Inc 444 Via Las Palmas Palm Springs CA 92262

KRASNER, OSCAR JAY, educator; b. St. Louis, Dec. 3, 1922; s. Benjamin and Rose (Persov) K.; B.S. in Public Adminstrn., Washington U., St. Louis, 1943; M.A. in Mgmt. with honors, U. Chgo., 1950; M.S. in Quantitative Bus. Analysis, U. So. Calif., 1965, D.B.A. in Mgmt., 1969; m. Bonnie Kidder, June 4, 1944; children—Bruce Howard, Glenn Evan, Scott Allan, Steve Leland, Michael Shawn, Bettina Jeanine. Mem. staff Exec. Office of Sec., U.S. Dept. Navy, 1944-56; supervising cons. Bus. Research Corp., Chgo., 1956-57; mem. staff flight propulsion div. Gen. Electric Co., Cin., 1957-61, mgr. VTOL project planning, 1959-61; exec. adviser long range planning space div. N.Am. Rockwell Corp., Downey, Calif., 1962-64, dir. tech. resources analysis exec. offices, 1964-70; pres. Solid State Tech. Corp. Calif., 1968-70; prof. mgmt. Pepperdine U., Los Angeles, 1970—; pres. Rensark Assos., 1976—; dir. U.S. Innovative Products Corp.; founder XCI Corp., 1984; cons. Active community orgns.; mem. nat. adv. bd. Nat. Congress Inventor Orgns., 1983-84; bd. dirs. Long Beach (Calif.) JCC, 1969-70. Served with Anti-Aircraft, AUS, 1942-44. Mem. Am. Acad. Mgmt., M.B.A. Internat. (chmn. 1976-77), AIAA, AAAS, World Future Soc., Beta Gamma Sigma. Home: 4709 Autry Ave Long Beach CA 90808 Office: 3415 Sepulveda Blvd Los Angeles CA 90034

KRATZER, REINHOLD HERMANN, chemist; b. Kaaden, Czechoslovakia, Nov. 14, 1928; s. Reinhold Richard and Johanna Maria (Maehner) K. BS, Ludwig-Maximilian U., Munich, 1955, MS, 1958, DSc., 1960. Postdoctoral fellow U. So. Calif., Los Angeles, 1960-61; research chemist U.S. Naval Ordnance Lab., Corona, Calif., 1961-64; sr. scientist MHD Research Inc., Newport Beach, Calif., 1964-66; mgr. chem. research Marquardt Corp., Newport Beach, 1966-70; mgr. chemistry dept. Dynamic Sci., Irvine, Calif., 1970-72, Ultrasystems, Inc., Irvine, Calif., 1972—. Contbr. articles to profl. jours.; patentee in field. Mem. AAAS, N.Y. Acad. Scis., Am. Chem. Soc., Chem. Soc. of London, German Chem. Soc., Water Pollution Control Fedn. Home: 17 SHooting Star Irvine CA 92714 Office: Ultrasystems Inc 16845 Von Karman Ave Irvine CA 92714

KRAUS, ERIC BRADSHAW, oceanographer; b. Reichenberg, Czechoslovakia, Mar. 22, 1912; came to U.S., 1960; s. Paul and Bertha Kraus; m. Heather Bradshaw Johnson, Jan. 5, 1942; children: Nigel, Sibella, Deborah. PhD, Charles Univ., Prague. Research officer CSIRO, Sydney, Australia, 1946-50; exec. scientist Snowy Mountains Auth., Cooma, Australia, 1951-60; sr. scientist Woods Hole Oceanographic Inst., Falmouth, Mass., 1961-66; prof., dir. CIMAS U. Miami, Fla., 1966-81, prof. emeritus, 1981—; sr. research assoc. U. Colo., CIRES, Boulder, 1981—; chief U.N. Tech. Asst. Mission, Nairobi, Kenya, Africa, 1954-55; adj. prof. Yale U., New Haven, 1961-64; vis. prof. Monash U., Melbourne, Australia, 1984, U. Liège, Belgium, 1986-87; dir. NATO Advanced Study Insts., Urbino, Italy, 1975, Bonas, France, 1981. Author: Atmosphere-Ocean Interaction, 1972; editor: Modelling of Upper Ocean, 1977; contbr. numerous articles to profl. jours. Served with Royal Air Force, 1940-46. Decorated Air Force Cross (Eng.), Medal of Bravery (Czechoslavakia); Rossby Fellow, Woods Hole Oceanographic Inst., 1960. Fellow: AAAS, Royal Meteorol. Soc. (Weath. Meml. Prize), Am. Meteorol. Soc.; mem. Am. Geophys. Union, Sigma Chi. Avocations: skiing, tennis, music, gardening. Home: 1820 Lehigh Boulder CO 80303

KRAUS, PANSY DAEGLING, gemology consultant; b. Santa Paula, Calif., Sept. 21, 1916; d. Arthur David and Elsie (Pardee) Daegling; m. Charles Frederick Kraus, Mar. 1, 1941 (div. Nov. 1961). AA, San Bernardino Valley Jr. Coll., 1938; student Longmeyer's Bus. Coll., 1940; grad. gemologist diploma Gemological Assn. Gt. Britain, 1960, Gemological Inst. Am., 1966. Clk. Convair, San Diego, 1943-48; clk. San Diego County Schs. Publs., 1948-57; mgr. Rogers and Boblet Art-Craft, San Diego, 1958-64; part-time editorial asst. Lapidary Jour., San Diego, 1963-64, assoc. editor, 1964-69, editor, 1970—, sr. editor, 1984-85; pvt. practice cons., San Diego, 1985—; lectr. gems, gemology local gem, mineral groups; gem & mineral club bull. editor groups. Mem. San Diego Mineral & Gem Soc., Gemol. Soc. San Diego, Gemol. Assn. Great Britain, Mineral. Soc. Am., Epsilon Sigma Alpha. Editor, layout dir.: Gem. Cutting Shop Helps, 1964, The Fundamentals of Gemstone Carving, 1967, Appalachian Mineral and Gem Trails, 1968, Practical Gem Knowledge for the Amateur, 1969, Southwest Mineral and Gem Trails, 1972, revision editor Gemcraft (Quick and Leiper), 1977; contbr. articles to Lapidary jour., Keystone Mktg. catalog. Home and Office: 6127 Mohler St San Diego CA 92120

KRAUS, SAMUEL, aerospace engineer; b. Irvington, N.J., Mar. 15, 1925; s. Otto Edward and Betty Rose (Braelow) K.; m. Joan Davida Bramson, Nov. 21, 1954; children: Barbara Diane, Edward Otto, Russell Alan. Student, N.Y.U., 1941-43; B. in Aero. Engring., Rensselaer Poly. Inst., 1943-44, M. in Aero. Engring., 1947-49; postgrad., Stanford U., 1949-55, West Coast U., 1983-84. Jr. engr. Curtiss Propeller div. Curtiss Wright Corp., Caldwell, N.J., 1946-47; aerospace scientist Ames Research Ctr. div. NASA, Moffett Field, Calif., 1949-62; aerospace engr. Rockwell Internat., Downey, Calif., 1962—. Contbr. NASA reports to pubs. Served to lt. USNR, 1943-46, PTO. Recipient Apollo Multiple Shuttle Group awards NASA, 1969—. Fellow AIAA (assoc.); mem. Nat. Mgmt. Assn., Sigma Xi. Democrat. Jewish. Lodge: Masons. Home: 6108 Monero Dr Rancho Palos Verdes CA 90274 Office: Rockwell Internat Space Transp Systems Div 12214 Lakewood Blvd Downey CA 90241

KRAUS, THAYNE LEE, chemical company executive; b. Garnett, Kans., Apr. 11, 1933; s. Harvey and Alberta Martha (Offutt) K.; m. Leona Ruth Kaiser, Aug. 31, 1952; children: Ronell Kraus Berttucci, Curt. BSME, Kans. State U., 1956; postgrad., St. Louis U., 1963, Stamford (Conn.) U., 1979. With Union Carbide Corp., St. Louis, Kansas City (Kans.), Boston and Cleve., 1959-61, 62-81; pres. Cardox Corp. subs. Liquid Air Corp., Chgo. and San Francisco, 1981—; bd. dirs. Duramex, Cleve. Served to capt. USAF, 1956-59, 61-62. Mem. Compressed Gas Assn. (bd. dirs. 1981—), Calif. C. of C., Walnut Creek C. of C. Republican. Lutheran. Club: Diablo Country (Danville, Calif.). Avocations: golf, singing, tennis, gardening. Home: 391 Bryan Dr Danville CA 94526 Office: Cardox Corp 2121 N California Walnut Creek CA 94596

KRAUSE, LAWRENCE ALLEN, financial adviser, financial planner; b. Chgo., Oct. 28, 1939; s. Leo and Sylvia Harriet (Bergman) K.; m. Donna Lee Ferkel, Aug. 14, 1971; children—Danielle, Alexis. B.A., State U. Iowa, 1961. Cert. fin. planner. Exec. v.p. Jobs, Inc., Waukegan, Ill., 1961-62; pres. Inventory and Bus. Controls, Waukegan, 1963-66; broker real estate Shoen Realtors, Rockford, Ill., 1967-69; registered rep. Reynolds & Co., San Francisco, 1970-75; dir. fin. planning Sutro & Co., Inc., San Francisco, 1975-79; chmn., pres. Lawrence A. Krause & Assocs., Inc., San Francisco, 1979—; pres. KW Securities Corp., San Francisco, 1979—; adj. prof. fin. planning San Francisco State U., 1982-86; mem. adv. com. on fin. planning Golden Gate U., San Francisco, 1982—; mem. faculty U. So. Calif., Los Angeles, 1984; mem. adv. bd. Stanger Register, 1986—. Author: The Money-Go-Round, Sleep-Tight Money; (with others) Marketing Your Financial Planning Practice; contbr. chpts. to books, articles to profl. jours.; columnist Los Angeles Times, ABA Jour., Calif. Bus. mag. Bd. dirs. Am. Cancer Soc., San Francisco, 1980—; bd. govs., bd. dirs. NTL Ctr. Fin. Edn., San Francisco, 1982—. Recipient Fin. Writer's award Fin. Planner mag., 1981; named Nation's Outstanding Fin. Planner for 1980's. Mem. Registry Fin. Planning Practitioners, Internat. Assn. Fin. Planners (San Francisco Fin. Planner of Yr. award 1982, pres. 1980-82, chmn. 1982-83), Inst. Cert. Fin. Planners. Republican. Jewish. Club: Concordia-Argonaut (San Francisco). Office: Lawrence A Krause & Assocs Inc 500 Washington St Suite 750 San Francisco CA 94111

KRAUSHAAR, JACK JOURDAN, physics educator, nuclear physicist; b. Newark, Sept. 6, 1923; s. Lester Adam and Helen (Osterhoudt) K.; m. Nancy Whiting Curtis, Apr. 7, 1951; children: Jeffrey Curtis, Steven Lester, Matthew Jourdan. BS in Physics, Lafayette Coll., 1945; MS in Physics, Syracuse U., 1948, PhD, 1952. Research asst. Brookhaven Nat. Lab., Upton, N.Y., 1949-51, research assoc., 1951-53; instr. Stanford (Calif.) U., 1953-56; asst. prof. physics U. Colo., Boulder, 1956-59, assoc. prof., 1959-63, prof., 1963—, co-dir. nuclear physics lab., 1956-70. Author: (with R. Ristinen) Energy and Problems of a Technical Society, 1984; contbr. numerous articles to profl. jours. Served to lt. (j.g.) USNR, 1943-46. Recipient Fulbright award U.S. Govt., 1967-68; U. Colo. Faculty fellow, 1977-78. Fellow Am. Phys. Soc.; mem. AAAS, Fedn. Am. Scientists. Democrat. Mem. Soc. of Friends. Home: 530 Aurora Ave Boulder CO 80302 Office: U Colo Dept Physics Campus Box 390 Boulder CO 80309

KRAUSS, GEORGE, metallurgist; b. Phila., May 14, 1933; s. George and Berta (Reichelt) K.; m. Ruth A. Oeste, Sept. 10, 1960; children: Matthew, Jonathan, Benjamin, Thomas. B.S. in Metall. Engring., Lehigh U., 1955; M.S., MIT, 1958, Sc.D., 1961. Registered profl. engr., Colo., Pa. Devel. metallurgist Superior Tube Co., Collegeville, Pa., 1955-56; prof. Lehigh U., Bethlehem, Pa., 1963-75, Colo. Sch. Mines, Golden, 1975—; dir. Advanced Steel Processing and Products Research Ctr., 1984—; cons. Colo. Sch. Mines, Golden, 1964—; Amax Found. prof. 1975—; dir. Univ.-Industry Steel Research Ctr., 1984—. Author: Principles of Heat Treatment of Steel, 1980; editor: Deformation Processing and Structure, 1984, Jour. Heat Treating, 1978-82; co-editor Fundamentals of Microalloying Forging Steels, 1987; contbr. articles profl. jours. NSF fellow Max Planck Inst. fur Eisenforschung, 1962-63. Fellow Am. Soc. Metals; mem. AIME, Am. Soc. Metals Internat., Electron Microscope Soc. Am., Sigma Xi. Home: 3807 S Ridge Rd Evergreen CO 80439 Office: Dept Metall Engineering Colorado Sch Mines Golden CO 80401

KRAUSS, HOWARD R., neuro-ophthalmologist, educator; b. Bronx, N.Y., Apr. 15, 1950; s. Randolph and Rose (Weiss) K.; m. Cheryl Ellen Gelman, May 25, 1974; children: Joshua, Stephanie, Lauren. BE, Cooper Union, 1971; SM, MIT, 1972; MD, N.Y. Med. Coll., 1977. Diplomate Am. Bd. Ophthalmology. Intern Harbor Gen. Hosp., Torrance, Calif., 1977-78; resident Jules Stein Eye Inst., Los Angeles, 1978-81, asst. clin. prof. ophthalmology, 1984—; fellow U. Pitts., 1981-82; asst. prof. U. Tex., Dallas, 1982-84; practice medicine specializing in ophthalmology Santa Monica, Calif., 1984—; engr. Hughes Aircraft Co., El Segundo, Calif., 1972-74. Contbr. articles to profl. jours. Fellow Am. Acad. Ophthalmology; mem. AMA, Calif. Assn. Ophthalmology, Sigma Xi, Tau Beta Pi, Eta Kappa Nu. Office: 2021 Santa Monica Blvd Suite 337E Santa Monica CA 90404

KRAUSS, MICHAEL EDWARD, linguist; b. Cleve., Aug. 15, 1934; s. Lester William and Ethel (Sklarsky) K.; m. Jane Lowell, Feb. 16, 1962; children: Marcus Feder, Stephen Feder, Ethan, Alexandra, Isaac. Bacc. Phil. Islandicae, U. Iceland; B.A., U. Chgo., 1953, Western Res. U., 1954; M.A., Columbia U., 1955; Cert. d'études supérieures, U. Paris, 1956; Ph.D., Harvard U., 1959. Postdoctoral fellow U. Iceland, Reykjavik, 1958-60; research fellow Dublin Inst. Advanced Studies, Ireland, 1956-57; vis. prof. MIT, Cambridge, 1969-70; prof. linguistics Alaska Native Lang. Ctr., U. Alaska, Fairbanks, 1960—, dir., 1972—, head Alaska native lang. program, 1972—; panel mem. linguistics NSF. Author: Eyak Dictionary, 1970, Eyak Texts, 1970, Alaska Native Languages: Past, Present and Future, 1980; editor: In Honor of Eyak: The Art of Anna Nelson Harry, 1982, Yupik Eskimo Prosodic Systems, 1985; mem. editorial bd.: Internat. Jour. Am. Linguistics; editor: dictionaries and books in Alaska Eskimo and Indian Langs. Halldór Kiljan Laxness fellow Scandinavian-Am. Found. Iceland, 1958-60; Fulbright study grantee Iceland, 1958-60; grantee NEH and NSF, 1978—; recipient Humanist of Yr. award Alaska Humanities Forum, 1981, Athabaskan and Eyak research award NSF, 1961—. Mem. Linguistics Soc. Am., Am. Anthropol. Assn. Jewish. Office: Alaska Native Lang Ctr U Alaska PO Box 111 Fairbanks AK 99775-0120

KRAUT, EDGAR ALVIN, physicist; b. Cleve., May 4, 1934; s. Joseph J. and Stella C. (Friedman) K.; m. Renee Sperling, July 1, 1962 (div. Apr. 1980); children: Ted William, Teri Elizabeth; m. Jefna K. Purcell, Apr. 20, 1980. AB, UCLA, 1956, MA, 1956, PhD in Theoretical Physics, 1962. Asst. prof. UCLA, 1964-66; mem. tech. staff Rockwell Internat. Sci. Ctr., Thousand Oaks, Calif., 1966—. Contbr. articles on physics and mathematics to profl. jours. Mem. IEEE, Am. Phys. Soc., Assn. Computing Machinery, Soc. Indsl. Applied Math., Phi Beta Kappa. Home: 2890 Parkview Dr Thousand Oaks CA 91362 Office: Rockwell Internat Box 1085 Thousand Oaks CA 91360

KRAUTBLATT, CHARLES JOHN, electrical engineer; b. College Point, N.Y., Sept. 28, 1950; s. Jack Charles and Catherine (DiDio) K.; m. Ann Florczak, Oct. 12, 1974; 1 child, Kristina Ann. BSEE, DeVry Inst. Tech., Phoenix, 1979. Mem. tech. staff TRW Def. and Space Corp., Los Angeles, 1979-81; dept. mgr. Kyocera Internat., San Diego, 1981-82; pres., tech. dir. EVS Engring., San Diego, 1982-84; cons. San Diego, 1983—. Served as cpl. with USMC, 1967-71. Mem. IEEE, Armed Forces Communications and Electronics Assn., Internat. Computer Cons. of Am. (nominating com. 1986), Calif. Chpt. Internat. Computer Cons. of Am., Scripps SR Club, Scripps Civic Assn. Home: 11826 Semillon Blvd San Diego CA 92131 Office: 9842 Hbert St Suite 256 San Diego CA 92131

KRAVITZ, ELLEN KING, musicologist, educator; b. Fords, N.J., May 25, 1929; d. Walter J. and Frances M. (Prybylowski) Kokowicz; m. Hilard L. Kravitz, Jan. 9, 1972; 1 child, Julie Frances; stepchildren—Kent, Kerry, Jay. B.A., Georgian Ct. Coll., 1964; M.M., U. So. Calif., 1966, Ph.D., 1970. Tchr. 7th and 8th grade music Mt. St. Mary Acad., North Plainfield, N.J., 1949-50; cloistered nun Carmelite Monastery, Lafayette, La., 1950-61; instr. Loyola U., Los Angeles, 1967; asst. prof. music Calif. State U., Los Angeles, 1967-71; asso. prof. 1971-74, prof., 1974—; founder Friends of Music, 1976. Editorial bd.: Jour. Arnold Schoenberg Inst, Los Angeles; jour. editor Vol. I, No. 3, 1977, Vol. II, No. 3, 1978; author: (with others) Catalog of Schoenberg's Paintings, Drawings and Sketches. Mem. Schoenberg Centennial Com., 1974, guest lectr., 1969—. Recipient award for masters thesis U. So. Calif., 1966. Mem. Am. Musicol. Soc., Los Angeles County Mus. Art, Mu Phi Epsilon, Phi Kappa Lambda. Home: 402 Doheny Rd Beverly Hills CA 90210 Office: California State University 5151 State University Dr Los Angeles CA 90032

KRAVITZ, HILARD L(EONARD), physician, consultant; b. Dayton, Ohio, June 26, 1917; s. Philip and Elizabeth (Charek) K.; divorced; children: Kent C., Kerry, Jay; m. Ellen King, Jan. 9, 1972; 1 child, Julie Frances. BA, U. Cin., 1939, MD, 1943. Lic. physician, Calif., Ohio. Resident in internal medicine Miami Valley Hosp., VA Hosp., Dayton, 1946-49; practice medicine specializing in internal medicine Dayton, 1950-54, Beverly Hills and Los Angeles, Calif., 1955—; practice medicine specializing in internal medicine and cardiology Los Angeles, 1955—; attending physician Cedars-Sinai Med. Ctr., 1955—; cons., med. dir. Adolph's Ltd., Los Angeles, 1955-74; mem. exec. com. Reiss-Davis Clinic, Los Angeles, 1966-70; chmn. pharmacy and therapeutic com. Cent City Hosp., Los Angeles, 1974-79; mem. pain commn. service Dept. Health and Human Services, Washington, 1985-86. Patentee sugar substitute, 1959, mineral-based salt, 1978. V.p. Friends of Music Calif. State U., Los Angeles, 1979-81. Served to capt. U.S. Army, 1944-46, ETO. Decorated Bronze Star with oak leaf cluster; Fourragere (France). Mem. AMA, Calif. Med. Assn., Los Angeles County Med.

Assn., Am. Soc. Internal Medicine, Calif. Soc. Internal Medicine (del. 1974). Jewish. Office: 2080 Century Park E Los Angeles CA 90067

KRAW, GEORGE MARTIN, lawyer; b. Oakland, Calif., June 17, 1949; s. George and Pauline Dorothy (Herceg) K.; m. Sarah Lee Kenyon, Sept. 3, 1983. B.A., U. Calif.-Santa Cruz, 1971; postgrad., Lenin Inst., Moscow, 1971; M.A., U. Calif.-Berkeley, 1974, J.D., 1976. Bar: Calif. 1976, U.S. Dist. Ct. (no. dist.) Calif. 1976, U.S. Supreme Ct. 1980. Assoc. Bacon, Skillicorn, Watsonville, Calif., 1976-79, Trepel & Clark, San Jose, Calif., 1979-81; ptnr. Mount, Kraw & Stoelker, San Jose, 1981—; asst. sec. Sysgen, Inc., Fremont, Calif., 1982—. Mem. ABA, Inter-Am. Bar Assn. Clubs: Metropolitan, University (San Jose). Office: Mount Kraw Stoelker 333 W San Carlos 10th Floor River Park Tower San Jose CA 95112

KREBS, ROGER DONAVON, architect; b. Waverly, Iowa, Nov. 22, 1949; s. Martin Andrew and Ruby Lilas (Homan) K.; m. Deborah Lynn Homerstad; children: Gretchen Marie, Emma Louise. BA, Rice U., 1973, BArch, 1974. Registered architect, Wyo. Archtl. designer John F. Houchins, Houston, 1974-77; archtl. designer Gorder South Group, Casper, Wyo., 1977-78, project architect, 1978-83; architect VA Med. Ctr., Salt Lake City, 1984-85, supervisory architect, 1985—. Prin. works include Wyo. Womens Ctr., Casper Events Ctr.

KREBS, WILLIAM NELSON, geologist; b. Santa Monica, Calif., Sept. 4, 1948; s. Adolph and Jeanne D. (Nelson) K.; m. Candace Moore, Dec. 30, 1983; 1 child, Timothy George. Student Santa Monica City Coll., 1966-67; B.S. in Geology, UCLA, 1970; Ph.D., U. Calif., Davis, 1977. Research asst. U. Calif., Davis, 1971-73, teaching asst. gen. and hist. geology, 1974-77; micropaleontologist Amoco Prodn. Co. Denver, 1978—. Recipient Antarctic Service medal, 1979. Mem. Paleontol. Soc. Am., Soc. of Econ. Paleontologists and Mineralogists, L'Alliance Française, Hist. Denver, Friends of Mozart, Sigma Xi. Republican. Contbr. articles on Antarctic marine diatom ecology, micropaleontology, lacustrine diatom micropaleontology to sci. jours. Home: 719 S Vine St Denver CO 80209 Office: Amoco Prodn Co Amoco Bldg Denver CO 80202

KREDITOR, ALAN, urban, regional planner, educator; b. N.Y.C., May 2, 1936; s. Maurice and Rachel (Baron) K.; B.Arch., Pratt Inst., 1959; M. City Planning, U. Pa., 1961; diploma in Engring. (hon.), U. Mex., 1973; m. Marcia Francine Green, June 14, 1959; children—Juliet Tamar, Eoin Lyle, Garrett Paul, Claudia Marya. Chief project planner Boston Redevel. Authority, 1961-63; pres. African Area Affiliates and Am. Assistance Group, Boston, 1962-64; dir. planning Worcester (Mass.) Redevel. Authority, 1963-64; UN adv. to rep. of Ireland and vis. lectr. U. Coll. Dublin, 1964-66; mem. faculty Sch. Urban and Regional Planning, U. So. Calif., Los Angeles, 1966—, dir., 1970-76, asso. dean Center Public Affairs, 1974-76, dir. environ. lab. Gerentology Center, 1974-76, coordinator coastal zone mgmt. U. So. Calif. Sea Grant Program, 1976—, dean Sch. Urban and Regional Planning, 1982—; cons., adv. Irvine Co., TRW, Westinghouse Corp., State of Mex., Emirate of Bahrain. Research grantee HEW, HUD, U.S. Dept. Transp., State of Calif., Ford Found., Nat. Endowment for the Arts. Mem. Am. Planning Assn. (nat. edn. devel. com. 1978—), Am. Inst. Certified Planners (gov. 1975-78), Regional Sci. Assn., Internat. Assn. Urban and Regional Research and Edn., AAUP. Democrat. Episcopalian. Contbr. articles, monographs, reports to profl. jours. Home: 888 Winston Ave San Marino CA 91108 Office: U So Calif VKC 351 U Park Los Angeles CA 90089

KREEGER, ROMA, children's center administrator; b. Logan, Utah, May 25, 1929; s. Leonard Clarence and Vivian John Mathews; m. Lawrence Eugene Kreeger, Nov. 15, 1947; children—Stephen Eugene, Michael Lawrence, Carolyn Suzette. A.A., Long Beach City Coll., 1964; student U. Long Beach, 1965-67, Calif. State U.-Los Angeles, 1968. Instr. Pioneer Sch., Bellflower, Calif., 1959-60; tchr. music Exceptional Children's Found., Long Beach, 1960-62; dir. head start program Lakewood, Calif., 1968-69; devel. cons. Orange Glen High Sch., Escondido, Calif., 1971-72; counsel, Wonderday Sch., Escondido, 1969—. Tchr. adult and children Ch. Jesus Christ Latter-day Saints, 1958-69; mem. Voting Bd. Mcpl. Elections, Lakewood, Calif., 1961. Mem. Pre-School Assn. (treas. 1972-75), Escondido C. of C. (exec.). Republican.

KREGER, MELVIN JOSEPH, lawyer; b. Buffalo, Feb. 21, 1937; s. Philip and Bernice (Gerstman) K.; m. Patricia Anderson, July 1, 1955 (div. 1963), children: Beth Barbour, Arlene Roux; m. Renate Hochleitner, Aug. 15, 1975. JD, Mid-valley Coll. Law, 1978; diploma in taxation, U. San Diego, 1985, postgrad., 1985—. Bar: Calif. 1978, U.S. Dist. Ct. (cen. dist.) Calif. 1979, U.S. Tax Ct. 1979. Life underwriter Met. Life Ins. Co., Buffalo, 1958-63; bus. mgr. M. Kreger Bus. Mgmt., Sherman Oaks, Calif., 1963-78, enrolled agt., 1971-78; sole practice North Hollywood, Calif., 1978—. Mem. Nat. Assn. Enrolled Agts. (pres. Los Angeles chpt. 1980-81, chmn. legal com. 1983-86), San Fernando Valley Estate Planning Council, State Bar of Calif., Los Angeles Bar Assn., San Fernando Valley Bar Assn. (probate sect.), Lawyers Club, Calif. Soc. Enrolled Agts. Jewish. Avocations: computers, travel. Office: 11424 Burbank Blvd North Hollywood CA 91601

KREIG, RAYMOND ARTHUR, terrain analysis consulting firm executive; b. Chgo., May 19, 1946; s. Albert Arthur and Margaret Thresa (Baltzell) K. BS, Cornell U., 1968, MS, 1970. Registered profl. engr., Alaska; cert. profl. geologist, Alaska. Sr. engring. geologist R&M Cons., Fairbanks, Alaska, 1970-75; pres. RA Kreig & Assocs., Inc., Anchorage, 1975—; mem. com. on permafrost Polar Research Bd., NRC, Washington, 1984—, U.S. Permafrost Del. to People's Republic of China, 1984; air-photo analyst L.F. soil properties Trans Alaska Pipeline System, 1982. Author: (with others) Guidebook to Permafrost and Related Features-Elliott and Dalton Highways, 1983. Mem. Anchorage Library Adv. Bd., 1980, vice chmn., 1980-83. Mem. Am. Inst. Profl. Geologists, Am. Soc. Photogrammetry, ASCE, Arctic Inst. N.Am., Alaska Geol. Soc. Home: 3818 Clay Products Dr Anchorage AK 99517 Office: RA Kreig & Assocs Inc 1503 W 33 Ave Anchorage AK 99503

KREINDEL, STEVEN ROBERT, marketing professional, communications executive; b. Los Angeles, Apr. 9, 1953; s. Abraham and Ada (Levy) K.; m. Joanne M. Ehrhart, June 24, 1979; children: Russell, Monica. AA, Cypress Coll., 1973; BA, Long Beach State U., 1976; student, Chapman Coll. Asst. mgr. Storer Broadcasting, Hermosa Beach, Calif., 1977-79; sales, affiliate ops. mgr. SelecTV, Marina Del Rey, Calif., 1979-80; mktg. rep. Premiere Pay TV, Los Angeles, 1980-81; western regional mgr. USA Network, Los Angeles, 1981-82; regional mgr. Home Box Office, Los Angeles, 1982—. Exhibited photographs in group show Los Angeles County Exhbn., 1973 (Hon. Mention, 1974); one-man pvt. show Our Calif. Coast, 1974. Grantee Chapman Coll., 1974. Mem. Ariz. Cable TV Assn. (bd. dirs. 1985—), So. Calif. Cable Assn. (com. chmn. 1981—), Women in Cable. Democrat. Avocations: tennis, photography, basketball, child raising. Office: Home Box Office 2049 Century Park E #4250 Los Angeles CA 90067

KREISEL, HENRY, university administrator; b. Vienna, Austria, June 5, 1922; s. David Leo and Helene (Schreier) K.; m. Esther Lazerson, June 22, 1947; 1 child, Philip. B.A., U. Toronto, 1946, M.A., 1947; Ph.D., U. London, 1954. With dept. English U. Alta., 1947—, prof., 1959—, head dept., 1961-67, asso. dean Grad. studies, 1967-69, acting dean grad. studies, 1969-70, acad. v.p., 1970-75, Univ. prof., 1975—, chmn. Can. studies program, 1979-82; vis. fellow Wolfson Coll., Cambridge U., 1975-76; Chmn. English lit. Can. Council Fellowship Com., 1963-65, Gov.-Gen.'s Jury for Lit., 1966-69; v.p. Edmonton Art Gallery, 1969-70. Author: The Rich Man, 1948, The Betrayal, 1964, The Almost Meeting, 1981, Another Country, 1985. Contbr.: numerous short stories, anthologies to mags., books, including Best American Short Stories, 1966, A Book of Canadian Stories, 1962. Author: plays for radio and TV, including Bob Hope Theatre, 1965. Bd. govs. U. Alta., 1966-69; v.p. Edmonton Chamber Music Soc., 1978-80, pres., 1980-83. . Recipient U. Western Ont. President's medal, 1960; J. I. Segal Found. award lit., 1983; Rutherford award for excellence in teaching U. Alba., 1986, Sir Frederick Haultain prize Govt. Alta., 1986; Reuben Wells Leonard fellow U. Toronto, 1946-47; Royal Soc. Can. Travelling fellow, 1953-54. Fellow Royal Soc. Arts (London), Internat. Inst. Arts and Letters (Geneva); mem. Assn. Can. U. Tchrs. English (pres. 1962-63). Home: 12516 66th Ave, Edmonton, AB Canada

KREITZBERG, FRED CHARLES, engineering management company executive; b. Paterson, N.J., June 1, 1934; s. William and Ella (Bohen) K.; m. Barbara Kreitzberg, June 9, 1957; children: Kim, Caroline, Allison, Bruce, Catherine. BSCE, Norwich U., 1957. Registered profl. engr., Alaska, Ariz., Calif., Colo., Conn., D.C., Ill., Ind., Md., Mass., Nev., N.J., N.Mex., N.Y., Ohio, Oreg., Pa., Va., Wash. Asst. supt. Turner Constrn. Co., N.Y.C., 1957; project mgr. Project Mercury RCA, N.J., 1958-62; schedule, cost mgr. Catalytic Constrn. Co., Pa., 1963-65, 65—; owner, pres. O'Brien-Kreitzberg and Assocs. Inc., San Francisco, also bd. dirs.; lectr. Stanford (Calif.) U., U. Calif., Berkeley. Contbg. author Crit. Path Method Scheduling for Contractor's Mgmt. Handbook, 1971; contbr. articles to profl. jours. bd. dirs. Norwich U.; mem. Marin Charitable Assn., Council Internat. Visitors. Served to 1st lt. C.E., U.S. Army, 1957-58. Fellow ASCE (Constrn. Mgr. of Yr., 1982); mem. Am. Arbitration Assn., Constrn. Mgmt. Assn. Am. (founding, bd. dirs.), Soc. Am. Value Engrs., Alden Partridge Soc., Community Field Assn. (Marin County bd. dirs.), Ross Hist. Soc. Clubs: San Francisco Tennis; Palm Springs (Calif.) Tennis; Marin Tennis. Avocations: running, bicycling, tennis, scuba, tropical fish. Home: 19 Spring Rd PO Box 1200 Ross CA 94957 Office: O'Brien-Kreitzberg & Assocs Inc 188 The Embarcadero San Francisco CA 94111

KREJCI, ROBERT HENRY, aerospace engineer; b. Shenandoah, Iowa, Nov. 15, 1943; s. Henry and Marie Josephine (Kubicek) K.; m. Carolyn R. Meyer, Aug. 21, 1967; children—Christopher S., Ryan D. B.S. with honors in Aerospace Engring., Iowa State U., Ames, 1967, M.Aerospace Engring., 1971. Commd. 2d lt. U.S. Air Force, 1968, advanced through grades to capt., 1978; served with systems command Space Launch Vehicles Systems Program Office, Advanced ICBM program officer; research asso. U.S. Dept. Energy Lawrence Livermore lab.; dept. mgr. advanced tech. programs ops. Wasatch div. Thiokol Corp., 1978-84, mgr. space programs, 1984-85, mgr. Navy strategic programs, 1986—. Decorated A.F. commendation medal, Nat. Def. Service medal. Mem. AIAA. Home: 885 N 300 E Brigham City UT 84302 Office: Thiokol Corp PO Box 524 Brigham City UT 84302

KREMER, RUSSELL EUGENE, physicist; b. Milford, Nebr., May 10, 1954; s. Lorne William and Hazel Aileen (King) K.; m. Debra Lee Staggs, Aug. 25, 1984. BA, Goshen Coll., 1976; MS, Purdue U., 1978, PhD, 1983. Asst. prof. physics Oreg. Grad. Ctr., Beaverton, 1983-86, assoc. prof., 1986—; cons. United Epitaxial Tech., Beaverton, 1986—. Contbr. articles to profl. jours. Mem. Am. Phys. Soc., Electrochem. Soc. (councilor 1984-86, sec., treas. 1986—), Sigma Xi. Mennonite. Avocations: cross-country skiing, hiking, photography, travel. Home: 2920 SW 196th Ave Aloha OR 97006 Office: Oreg Grad Ctr 19600 NW Von Neumann Dr Beaverton OR 97006

KREMPEL, ROGER ERNEST, city ofcl.; b. Waukesha, Wis., Oct. 8, 1926; s. Henry and Clara K.; m. Shirley Ann Gray, June 16, 1948; children—John, Sara, Peter. Student Ripon Coll., 1944, Stanford U., 1945; BCE, U. Wis.-Madison, 1950. Registered profl. engr., Wis., Colo.; diplomate Am. Acad. Environ. Engrs. Asst. city engr., Manitowoc, Wis., 1950-51; city engr. dir. pub. works, Janesville, Wis., 1951-75; dir. water utilities, pub. works Ft. Collins, Colo., 1975-84, dir. natural resources, streets and stormwater utilities, Ft. Collins, 1984-87; lectr. various univ., coll. Contbr. articles to profl. pubs. Served with U.S. Army, 1944-46. Recipient numerous awards. Fellow ASCE; mem. Water Pollution Control Fedn., Am. Water Works Assn., Am. Pub. Works Assn. (past pres. Colo. and Wis. chpts.), Hist. Soc. of Am. Pub. Works Assn. (bd. dirs., trustee), Research Found. of Am. Pub. Works Assn. Nat. Soc. Profl. Engrs., Wis. Soc. Profl. Engrs. (past pres.), Am. Acad. Environ. Engrs. (diplomate). Office: 300 LaPorte Ave PO Box 580 Fort Collins CO 80522

KRENKEL, PETER ASHTON, engineer, educator, university dean; b. San Francisco, Jan. 3, 1930; s. Harry Nichols and Daisy Genevieve (Ashton) K.; m. Jessica Ann Jones. A.A., Coll. City San Francisco, 1952; B.S., U. Calif.-Berkeley, 1956, M.S., 1958, Ph.D., 1960. Registered profl. engr., Ga., Tenn., Nev., N.C. Instr. U. Calif. at Berkeley, 1958-60; founder Associated Water & Air Resources Engrs., Inc., Nashville, 1968—; chmn., prof. dept. environ. and water resources engring. Vanderbilt U., Nashville, 1960-73; dir. div. environ. planning TVA, 1974-78; exec. dir. Water Resources Center U. Nev., Reno, 1978-82, dean Coll. Engring., 1982—; disting. lectr. Am. Inst. Chem. Engrs.; cons. WHO, Internat. Joint Commn. on Great Lakes Water Quality, U.S. EPA, U.S. Dept. Energy, Roy F. Weston, Inc. Stauffer Chem. Co., Gen. Motors, Monsanto, Korean Advanced Inst. Sci. and Tech., Seoul, 1985, others; chmn. thermal pollution panel Nat. Water Commn., Washington, 1970—, Tenn. Air Conservation Commn., 1971—; eminent overseas speaker Inst. Engrs., Australia, 1986. Author: (with V. Novotny) Water Quality Management, 1980; editor: (with F.L. Parker) Thermal Pollution, Biological Aspects, 1970, Thermal Pollution, Engineering Aspects, 1970, Water Quality Monitoring in Europe, 1972, Heavy Metals in the Aquatic Environment, 1974; Contbr. numerous articles on environmental control to profl. jours. Pres. Tenn. Lung Assn., 1974-75. Served with AUS, 1953-55. Fellow USPHS, 1963; recipient award outstanding research san. engring. ASCE, 1963, Skill, Integrity, Responsibility award Am. Gen. Contractors, 1984. Mem. Am. Water Works Assn., Water Pollution Control Fedn. (bd. control), Air Pollution Control Assn., Am. Public Health Assn., Am. Inst. Chem. Engrs., ASCE, Internat. Assn. Water Pollution Research (governing bd.), Am. Acad. Environ. Engring. (diplomate), Sigma Xi, Tau Beta Pi, Chi Epsilon. Home: 3500 Cashill Blvd Reno NV 89509

KRENZER, ROBERT WAYNE, scientific company executive; b. Springfield, Ill., Aug. 17, 1940; s. John Frank and Edna Iola (Rigsby) K.; Profl. Engr., Colo. Sch. Mines, 1962; M.S., U. Denver, 1966, Ph.D., 1968, M.S.B.A., 1980; m. Patricia Ann Gant, June 24, 1961; children—Deborah Ann, Kurt Wayne. Metallurgist U.S. Steel Corp., Gary, Ind., 1962-63; engr. Hercules Inc., Magna, Utah, and Rocky Hill, N.J., 1963-64; staff Sandia Labs., Livermore, Calif., 1968-72; research specialist, research mgr. Rockwell Internat. Co., Golden, Colo., 1972-84, mgr. spl. projects, 1984-86, program mgr. productivity, 1986—, mem. Rockwell Speakers Bur., 1981—; cons. lasers. Commr. dist. Boy Scouts Am., 1971-72, 76-82, fund drive chmn., 1981, Explorer post adv., 1980-83, exec. com. Outdoor Program, 1986—, mem.-at-large Denver council, 1987—; v.p. Livermore (Calif.) Republican Assembly, 1972; participant Leadership Denver, 1979-80; tour guide Ramses II Egyptian Exhibit, Denver Mus. Nat. History. Joint Honor scholar, 1958; NSF fellow, 1964; ASTM student awardee, 1966. Named Rockwell Engr. of Yr., 1976, Rocky Flats Engr. of Yr., 1976. Fellow Am. Soc. Metals (chmn. chpt. 1978, organizer extractive metallurgy chpt. 1980, mem. fellow selection com. 1982-85, council for profl. interests 1983-87); mem. AIME, Nat. Mgmt. Assn., Nat. Eagle Scout Assn., Colo. Mountain Club, Denver C. of C. (energy, transp. and environ. com. 1980-81), Egypt Exploration Soc., Colo. Hist. Soc., Tahosa Alumni Assn. (bd. dirs. 1981—), Sigma Xi, Sigma Phi Epsilon (alumni bd. 1977), Alpha Sigma Mu, Sigma Gamma Epsilon. Club: Elks. Contbg. author book, contbr. articles to profl. publs. Patentee in field. Home: 8426 Quay Dr Arvada CO 80003 Office: PO Box 464 Golden CO 80401

KRESA, KENT, aerospace executive; b. N.Y.C., Mar. 24, 1938; s. Helmy and Marjorie (Boutelle) K.; m. Joyce Anne McBride, Nov. 4, 1961; 1 child, Kiren. B.S.A.A., MIT, 1959, M.S.A.A., 1961, E.A.A., 1966. Sr. scientist research and advanced devel. div. AVCO, Wilmington, Mass., 1959-61; staff mem. MIT Lincoln Lab., Lexington, Mass., 1961-68; dep. dir. strategic tech. office Def. Advanced Research Projects Agy., Washington, 1968-73; dir. tactical tech. office Def. Advanced Research Project Agy., Washington, 1973-75; v.p., mgr. Research & Tech. Ctr. Northrop Corp., Hawthorne, Calif., 1975-76; v.p., gen. mgr. Ventura div. Northrop Corp., Newbury Park, Calif., 1976-82; group v.p. Aircraft Group Northrop Corp., Los Angeles, 1982-86, sr. v.p. tech. devel. and planning, 1986-87, pres., chief operating officer, 1987—; mem. Chief of Naval Ops. exec. panel Washington, sci. adv. bd. U.S. Air Force, Washington, Def. Sci. Bd., Washington, DNA New Alternatives Working Group, Los Angeles, Dept. Aeronautics and Astronautics Corporating Vis. Com. MIT. mem. editorial bd. Jour. of Def. Research, Washington. Recipient Henry Webb Salsbury award MIT, 1959, Arthur D. Flemming award, 1975; Sec. of Def. Meritorious Civilian Service medal, 1975, U.S. Navy Meritorious Pub. Service citation, 1975. Fellow AIAA (assoc.); mem. Naval Aviation Mus. Found., Navy League U.S., Soc. Flight Test Engrs., Assn. of U.S. Army, Nat. Space Club, Am. Def. Preparedness Assn. (bd. dirs. Los Angeles chpt.). Club: Mountaingate Country. Office: Northrop Corp 1840 Century Park E Los Angeles CA 90067

KRESTA, ELMER JOHN, systems specialist, communications specialist; b. El Campo, Tex., Aug. 25, 1946; s. Elmer Edward and Agnes Ann (Mares) K.; m. Harlie Jean Yakel, Nov. 7, 1969 (div. Aug. 1971); m. Rhonda Lea Hampton, July 7, 1972; children—Carie Michelle, Christina Marie. A.A., Grossmont Coll., 1972; B.A. in Bus. Adminstrn., Calif. State U.-Fullerton, 1981; M.B.A., Pepperdine U., 1982. Customer engr. Sperry Univac, San Diego, 1970-76; hardware engr. EMI Med., Northbrook, Ill., 1976-77; regional product specialist Varian Med., Palo Alto, Calif., 1977-79; software engr. Norden Systems, Santa Ana, Calif., 1979-80; systems engr. Hughes Aircraft GSG, Fullerton, Calif., 1980-83; systems specialist Xerox Systems Mktg., Santa Ana, 1983—; systems engr. De La Rue Printrak Systems, Anaheim, Calif., 1985, NBI Corp., Tustin, Calif., 1985—; pres. Small Systems Cons. , Corona, Calif., 1986—; exec. v.p. BTE Systems Ltd., Irvine, Calif., 1982-83. Served with USN, 1966-70. Club: Unlimited Dive (San Diego) (pres. 1974). Home: 1581 Mariposa Dr Corona CA 91719 Office: Xerox Systems Mktg 2200 E McFadden Santa Ana CA 92705

KRESTOFF, ROBERT NICKOLAS, manufacturing executive; b. Sacramento, Apr. 24, 1937; s. Nickolas Fredrick Krestoff and Vera (Cassella) Morris; m. Joanne McDonald, June 24, 1957 (dec. Sept. 1961); children: Cheri, Susan, Robert Jr.; m. Esther Neoma Sisk, Feb. 1, 1964; children: Jason, Nickolas. BS, U. San Francisco, 1978. Instrmentation tech. Douglas Aircraft, Rancho Cordova, Calif., 1963-67; field engr. Applied Tech., Sunnyvale, Calif., 1967-70, program mgr., 1970-76, dir. programs, 1979-84; dir. mfg. M. B. Assocs., San Ramon, Calif., 1976-79; v.p., plant mgr. Narda Microwave Western Ops., Rancho Cordova, Calif., 1984—. Served as sgt. USAF, 1954-62. Mem. Am. Electronic Assn., Assn. Old Crows, , Rancho Cordova C. of C., Soc. Wild Weasels. Republican. Roman Catholic. Club: Sheepherders Golf (Rancho Cordova). Avocations: golf, power boating, bowling, auto racing. Office: Narda Microwave Western Ops 11101 Trade Center Dr Rancho Cordova CA 95670

KRETCHMAN, ALLAN MICHAEL, sales and marketing executive; b. Phila., July 29, 1942; s. Sidney and Frances (Hirsch) K.; m. Elaine Rita Tolchin, Feb. 20, 1966; children: Courtney, Jolie. BS, Calif. State U., Northridge, 1965. Product mgr. Bristol Myers Corp., N.Y.C., 1965-76; v.p., gen. mgr. Neutrogena Corp., Los Angeles, 1976-86; v.p. sales and mktg. Western Trimming Corp., Chatsworth, Calif., 1986—. Chmn. fund raising Jr. C. of C., Los Angeles, 1984. Served to sgt. USAR, 1965-71. Democrat. Jewish. Avocations: skiing, basketball, running. Home: 4764 Nomad Dr Woodland Hills CA 91364 Office: Western Trimming Corp 9667 Canoga Ave Chatsworth CA 91311

KRETZMANN, JOHN ALBERT, civil engineer, consultant; b. Baguio City, Philippines, May 2, 1951; came to U.S., 1969; s. Herbert Robert Emil and Dorothy Ruth (Meier) K.; m. Esther May Powell, Sept. 16, 1973; children: Erica Ruth, Eliza Anne, Martin Emil. BSCE, Valparaiso (Ind.) U., 1973. Registered profl. engr., N.Mex. Asst. engr. Gordan & Assocs., Santa Fe, 1975, design engr., 1979-80; design engr. Turney, Sayre & Turney, Santa Fe, 1975-79; project engr. Scanlon & Assocs., Santa Fe, 1980—. Designer various water supply and wastewater projects, 1975—. Avocations: gardening, tai chi chu'an. Office: Scanlon & Assocs 1570 Pacheco St Suite A-7 Santa Fe NM 87501

KREVANS, JULIUS RICHARD, university chancellor, physician; b. N.Y.C., May 1, 1924; s. Sol and Anita (Makovetsky) K.; m. Patricia N. Abrams, May 28, 1950; children: Nita, Julius R., Rachel, Sarah, Nora Kate. B.S. Arts and Scis, N.Y. U., 1943, M.D., 1946. Diplomate: Am. Bd. Internal Med. Intern, then resident Johns Hopkins Med. Sch. Hosp., mem. faculty, until 1970, dean acad. affairs, 1969-70; physician in chief Balt. City Hosp., 1963-69; prof. medicine U. Calif. at San Francisco, 1970—, dean Sch. Medicine, 1971-82, chancellor. Contbr. articles on hematology, internal med. profl. jours. Served with M.C. AUS, 1948-50. Mem. A.C.P., Assn. Am. Physicians. Office: U Calif Chancellor's Office San Francisco CA 94143

KRIBS, PATRICIA MCKEEVER, computer systems professional; b. N.Y.C., Dec. 14, 1933; d. Cornelius John and Marianne (Fenauer) McKeever; m. Charles Augustus Kribs Jr., Apr. 28, 1962. BA, Coll. New Rochelle, 1955; MA, NYU, 1957. Programmer trainee IBM Corp., N.Y.C., 1957-58; programmer System Devel. Corp., Santa Monica, Calif., 1959-61, computer systems specialist, 1963-72; sr. systems programmer Xerox Corp., Los Angeles, 1972-75, 77—. Mem. AAAS, MENSA Soc. Democrat. Roman Catholic.

KRIEGER, ERIC WESTON, military officer; b. Miami, Fla., Mar. 24, 1941; s. Eric Weston Krieger VIII and Cuba Lee (Sadler) Ambrosius; m. Lynda Ann McGinnis, Aug. 21, 1965; children: Melissa Mari, Eric James. BS, U.S. Naval Acad. Cert. nuclear powered warship operator and commander. Commd. ensign USN, 1959, advanced through grades to capt., 1985, various offices communications and engring. divs., 1959-79, exec. officer USS Sam Rayburn, 1979-83, comdg. officer USS Andrew Jackson, 1980-83; chief staff officer submarine squadron 14 USN, Holy Loch, Scotland, 1983-85; chmn. nuclear weapons safety group, head surface/subsurface and amphibious weapons dept. Naval Weapons Evaluation Facility, Albuquerque, 1985—. Republican. Roman Catholic. Lodge: KC. Avocations: computers, sailing, fishing. Home: 3424 Pickard Ave NE Albuquerque NM 87110-2226 Office: Kirtland AFB Naval Weapons Evaluation Facility Albuquerque NM 87117-5000

KRIEGER, GARY ROBERT, environmental medical physician; b. Valdese, N.C., May 10, 1951; s. Marvin and Jean Sylvia (Elder) K.; m. Jeanne Faye Arrington, May. 6, 1978; children: Lauren, Taylor. AB, U. N.C., 1973, MD, 1978; MPH, Johns Hopkins, 1982. Diplomate Am. Bd. Internal Medicine, Am. Bd. Preventive Medicine. Resident in medicine Mayo Clinic, Rochester, Minn., 1978-81; med. dir. Exxon Chem., Houston, 1982-83; dir. occupational, environ. medicine Boulder (Colo.) Med. Ctr., 1984—; cons. Circadian Physiology Lab. Harvard Med. Sch., Boston, 1983-84; research fellow French Red Cross, Paris, 1975-76; expert witness U.S. House Com. on Sci. Tech., Washington, 1983, Nuclear Regulatory Com. Task Force, Washington, 1984; med. dir. Ball Aerospace div., Boulder, 1985—; cons. in. field., Boulder, 1984—; adj. asst. prof. toxicology U. Colo., Boulder, 1986—. Advisor emergency preparedness Boulder Valley (Colo.) Sch. Dist., 1985. Mem. AAAS, ACP (assoc.), Rocky Mountain Acad. Occupational Medicine (bd. dirs. 1986—), N.Y. Acad. Scis., Am. Acad. Clin. Toxicology, Semi-Conductor Safety Assn., Am. Acad. Occupational Medicine, Phi Beta Kappa. Avocations: tennis, skiing, music. Home: 4842 Tanglewood Ct Boulder CO 80301 Office: Boulder Med Ctr 2750 Broadway Boulder CO 80302

KRIEGER, JOHN NEWTON, urology educator; b. Phila., May 3, 1948; s. Rivan and Leah (Moses) K.; m. Monica Schoelch, July 22, 1972. AB, Princeton U., 1970; MD, Cornell U., 1974. Diplomate Am. Bd. Urology. Resident in surgery N.Y. Hosp., N.Y.C., 1974-76, resident in urology, 1976-80; fellow in urology U. Va., Charlottesville, 1980-82; asst. prof. urology U. Wash., Seattle, 1982-86, assoc. prof., 1986—. Contbr. articles to profl. jours. Mem. Am. Urol. Assn. (F.C. Valentine prize, N.Y.C. sect. 1977, Scholar award, Balt. 1980), ACS, Am. Soc. Microbiology, Am. Venereal Disease Assn., Infectious Disease Soc. Am. Avocation: competitive long distance running. Office: U Wash Dept Urology RL-10 Pacific St NE Seattle WA 98195

KRIEGER, MARTIN H., planning and design educator; b. Bklyn., Mar. 10, 1944; s. Louis and Shirley Krieger. BA, Columbia U., 1964, MA, 1965, PhD, 1969. Lectr., researcher U. Calif., Berkeley, 1968-73; asst. prof. U. Minn., Mpls., 1974-80; lectr., researcher MIT, Cambridge, 1980-84; assoc. prof. planning and design U. So. Calif., Los Angeles, 1984—. Author: Advice and Planning, 1981; contbr. articles to profl. jours. Fellow: Am. Council Learned Societies, Ctr. for Advanced Study in Behavioral Scis., Nat. Humanities Ctr.; mem. Am. Phys. Soc. Office: U So Calif Sch Urban and Regional Planning Los Angeles CA 90089-0042

KRIEGER, WILLIAM CARL, English educator; b. Seattle, Mar. 21, 1946; s. Robert Irving Krieger and Mary (McKibben) Durfee; m. Patricia Kathleen

Callow, Aug. 20, 1966; children: Richard William, Robert Irving III, Kathleen Elizabeth. BA in English, Pacific Luth. U., 1968, MA in Humanities, 1973; PhD in Am. Studies, Wash. State U., 1986. Instr. Pierce Coll., Tacoma, 1969—; adj. prof. hist. and English Cen. Wash. State U., 1980; vis. prof. hist. and English So. Ill. U., Carbondale, 1981-84, Pacific Luth. U., Tacoma, 1981-84; Chmn. English dept. Pierce Coll., Tacoma, 1973-75, 76-79, 81-84, humanities div. chair, 1979-81; bd. dirs. Thoreau Cabin Project, Tacoma, 1979—; project dir. Campus Wash. Centennial Project, Tacoma, 1984—; spl. cons. Clover Park Sch. Dist., Tacoma, 1985. Mem. Thoreau Soc. (life), Community Coll. Humanities Assn. (standing com. 1982-83), Am. Studies Assn., Wash. Community Coll. Humanities Assn. (bd. dirs. 1982-84, grantee, 1984), Western Wash. Ofcls. Assn. Avocations: officiating high sch. and coll. football, hiking, powerlifting, poetry. Home: 4415 68th St Ct NW Gig Harbor WA 98335 Office: Pierce Coll 9401 Farwest Dr SW Tacoma WA 98498

KRIEGER, ZBIGNIEW TADEUSZ, chemical engineer; b. Strzelin, Poland, Nov. 5, 1951; came to U.S., 1984; s. Leopold and Jozefa (Zygmunt) K.; m. Grazyna Stanislawa Buk, Aug. 11, 1973; children: Ewelina Maria, Marcin Marek. MS in Chemistry, Tech. U. of Wroclaw, Poland, 1974, PhD in Chem. Engring., 1979. Asst. prof. chem. engring. Tech. U. of Rzeszow, Poland, 1979-81; chem. engr. Exo-Sensors Inc., Anaheim, Calif., 1984—. Mem. Am. Inst. Chem. Engrs., Am. Chem. Soc., Am. Inst. Chemists. Avocations: amber jewelry and fossils. Home: 226 Turf Dr Placentia CA 92670 Office: Exo Sensors Inc 1220-B Simon Circle Anaheim CA 92806

KRIENKE, CAROL BELLE MANIKOWSKE (MRS. OLIVER KENNETH KRIENKE), realtor; b. Oakland, Calif., June 19, 1917; d. George and Ethel (Purdon) Manikowske; student U. Mo., 1937; B.S., U. Minn., 1940; postgrad. UCLA, 1949; m. Oliver Kenneth Krienke, June 4, 1941; children—Diane (Mrs. Robert Denny), Judith (Mrs. Kenneth A. Giss), Debra Louise (Mrs. Ed Paul Davalos). Demonstrator, Gen. Foods Corp., Mpls., 1940; youth leadership State of Minn. Congl. Conf., U. Minn., Mpls. 1940-41; war prodn. worker Airesearch Mfg. Co., Los Angeles, 1944; tchr. Los Angeles City Schs., 1945-49; realtor DBA Ethel Purdon, Manhattan Beach, Calif., 1949; buyer Purdon Furniture & Appliances, Manhattan Beach, 1950-58; realtor O.K. Krienke Realty, Manhattan Beach, 1958—. Manhattan Beach bd. rep. Community Chest for Girl Scouts U.S., 1957; bd. dirs. South Bay council Girl Scouts U.S.A., 1957-62, mem. Manhattan Beach Coordinating Council, 1956-68; mem. Long Beach Area Childrens Home Soc. (v.p., 1967-68, pres. 1979; charter mem. Beach Pixies, 1957—, pres. 1967; chmn. United Way, 1967); sponsor Beach Cities Symphony, 1953—. Mem. DAR (life, citizenship chmn. 1972-73, v.p. 1979, 83—), Colonial Dames XVII Century (charter mem. Jared Eliot chpt. 1977, v.p., pres. 1979-81, 83-84), Friends of Library, Torrance Lomita Bd. of Realtors, South Bay Bd. Realtors, Nat. Soc. New England Women (life, Calif. Poppy Colony), Internat. Platform Assn., Soc. Descs. of Founders of Hartford (life), Friends of Banning Mus., Manhattan Beach Hist. Soc., Manhattan Beach C. of C. (Rose and Scroll award 1985), U. Minn. Alumni. Republican. Mem. Community Ch. (pres. Women's Fellowship 1970-71). Home: 924 Highview St Manhattan Beach CA 90266 Office: O K Krienke Realty 1716 Manhattan Beach Blvd Manhattan Beach CA 90266

KRIKOS, GEORGE ALEXANDER, pathologist, educator; b. Old Phaleron, Greece, Sept. 17, 1922; came to U.S., 1946; s. Alexios and Helen (Spyropoulou) K.; m. Aspasia Manoni, June 22, 1949; children: Helen, Alexandra, Alexios. D.D.S., U. Pa., 1949; Ph.D., U. Rochester, 1959; Ph.D. hon. doctorate, U. Athens, Greece, 1981. Asst. prof. pathology U. Pa. Sch. Dentistry, 1958-61, asso. prof., 1961-67, prof., 1967-68, chmn. dept., 1964-68; asso. prof. oral pathology U. Pa. Grad. Sch., 1962-68, prof. oral pathology, 1968; prof. pathobiology Sch. Dentistry, U. Colo., Denver, 1968-75, chmn. dept. pathobiology, 1968-73, prof. oral biology, 1975-86, clin. prof. oral biology, 1986—, chmn. dept., 1976-77; asst. dean basic sci. affairs Sch. Dentistry, U. Colo., 1973-75, asso. dean oral biology affairs, 1975-76; vis. prof. Sch. Dentistry, U. Athens, 1980-81; mem. dental study sect. NIH, 1966-70; mem. cancer com. Colo.-Wyo. Regional Med. Program, 1970-72; cons. oral pathology Denver VA Hosp., 1970-72. Served with AUS, 1949-54. Mem. Am. Assn. Pathologists, Internat. Assn. Dental Research, Sigma Xi. Research in connective tissue, wound healing, cytodifferentiation. Home: 350 Ivy St Denver CO 80220 Office: U Colo Sch Dentistry 4200 E 9th Ave Denver CO 80262

KRILL, MARY ALICE, association executive; b. Longmont, Colo., Mar. 21, 1924; d. James Blaine and Agnes Elsie (Brown) Hitt; m. Arhtur Melvin Krill, July 6, 1944; children: Susan Krill Smith, Juli Lapin, Arthur M. Jr. BA in Chemistry, U. Colo., 1941-44; MA, U. Denver, 1969-71, PhD, 1971-73. Asst. project dir. Ctr. for Research in Ambulatory Health Care Adminstrn., Denver, 1974-76, proj. dir., 1977-79, dir. research, 1979-85, adminstrv. dir., 1985—; assoc. dir. parent orgn. Med. Group Mgmt. Assn., Denver, 1986—; cons. Rand Corp., Los Angeles, 1985—, Honolulu Med. Group Research and Edn. Found. Honolulu, 1985—, Applied Mgmt. Scis., Silver Spring, Md., 1983-84. Contbr. articles to profl. jours. Active Welcome Colo., Denver. Mem. Assn. Health Services Research, Nat. Ctr. Health Edn., Assn. Univ. Programs in Health Adminstrn., Sigma Xi, Phi Beta Kappa, Kappa Kappa Gamma. Republican. Episcopalian. Avocations: jogging, music. Home: 450 Westwood Dr Denver CO 80206 Office: Ctr Research Ambulatory Health 1355 S Colorado Blvd Denver CO 80222

KRIM, ARTHUR B., motion picture executive, lawyer; b. N.Y.C., Apr. 4, 1910; s. Morris and Rose (Ocko) K.; m. Mathilde Galland, Dec. 7, 1958; 1 child, Daphna. B.A., Columbia U., N.Y.C., 1930, J.D., 1932, LL.D. (hon.), 1982. Bar: N.Y. 1933. With Phillips, Nizer, Benjamin, Krim & Ballon, N.Y.C., 1932—, sr. ptnr., 1935-78, of counsel, 1978—; pres. Eagle Lion Films, N.Y.C., 1946-49; chmn. United Artists Corp., N.Y.C., 1951-78, Orion Pictures Corp., N.Y.C., 1978—; dir. Occidental Petroleum Corp., Los Angeles, Cities Service Corp., Tulsa, Iowa Beef Corp., Iowa City. Editor in chief Columbia Law Rev., 1931-32. Spl. cons. to Pres. U.S., 1968-69; mem. Pres.'s Gen. Adv. Com. Arms Control, 1977-80; chmn. Democratic Nat. Fin. Com., 1966-68, Dem. Adv. Council Elected Ofcls., 1973-76; bd. dirs. Weizmann Inst. Sci., 1948—, UN Assn., 1961—, Lyndon Baines Johnson Found., 1969—, John F. Kennedy Library Found., 1964—, Arms Control Assn., 1985—; chmn. bd. trustee Columbia U., 1977-82, chmn. emeritus, 1982—. Served to lt. col. U.S. Army, 1942-45. Decorated Cavaliere Ufficiale Della award Republic of Italy, Chevalier dans l'Ordre Nat. de la legion d'Honneur (France); recipient Jean Hersholt Humanitarian award Acad. Motion Picture Arts and Scis., 1975.

KRIPPNER, STANLEY CURTIS, psychologist; b. Edgerton, Wis., Oct. 4, 1932; s. Carroll Porter and Ruth Genevieve (Volenberg) K.; m. Lelia Anne Harris, June 25, 1966; stepchildren—Caron, Robert. B.S., U. Wis., 1954; M.A., Northwestern U., 1957, Ph.D., 1961; Ph.D. (hon.), Univ. Humanistic Studies, San Diego, 1982. Speech therapist Warren Pub. Schs. (Ill.), 1954-55, Richmond Pub. Schs. (Va.), 1955-56; dir. Child Study Ctr. Kent State U. (Ohio), 1961-64; dir. dream lab. Maimonides Med. Ctr., Bklyn., 1964-73; dir. Ctr. Consciousness Studies Saybrook Inst., San Francisco, 1973—; vis. prof. U. P.R., 1972, Sonoma State U., 1972-73, Univ. Life Scis., Bogotá, Colombia, 1974, Inst. for Psychodrama and Humanistic Psychology, Caracas, Venezuela, 1975, West Ga. Coll., 1976, John F. Kennedy U., 1980-82; lectr. Acad. Pedagogical Scis., Moscow, 1971, Acad. Scis., Beijing, China, 1981. Author: (with Montague Ullman) Dream Telepathy, 1973, Song of the Siren: A Parapsychological Odyssey, 1975; (with Alberto Villoldo) The Realms of Healing, 1976, Human Possibilities, 1980; (with Alberto Villoldo) Healing States, 1987; (with Jerry Solfvin) La Science et les Pouvoirs Psychiques de l'Homme, 1986; editor: Advances in Parapsychological Research, Vol. 1, 1977, Vol. 2, 1978, Vol. 4, 1984, Vol. 5, 1987, Psychoenergetic Systems, 1979; co-editor: Galaxies of Life, 1973, The Kirlian Aura, 1974, The Energies of Consciousness, 1975, Future Science, 1977; mem. editorial bd.: Gifted Child Quar., Internat. Jour. Paraphysics, Jour. Humanistic Psychology, Jour. Transpersonal Psychology, Revision Jour., Jour. Theoretical Parapsychology, Jour. Indian Psychology, Psi Research, Metanoia, Dream Network Bulletin, Humanistic Psychologist, Internat. Jour. Psychosomatics, Jour. Creative Children and Adults, InterAm. U. Press; contbr. 500 articles to profl. jours. Mem. adv. bd. A.R.E. Clinic; bd. dirs. Acad. Religion and Psychical Research, Survival Research Found., Aesculapian Inst. for Healing Arts, Hartley Film Found., Inst. for Multilevel Learning, Internat. Horizon Ednl. Audio Recordings, John E. Fetzer Energy Medicine Research Inst., Forest Inst. Profl. Psychology, Humanistic Psychology Ctr. N.Y., Ctr. Transcendence and Transintegration, Ky. Ctr. Psychosynthesis. Recipient Service to Youth award YMCA, 1959; recipient citation of merit Nat. Assn. Gifted Children, 1972, citation of merit Nat. Assn. Creative Children and Adults, 1975, cert of recognition Office of Gifted and Talented, U.S. Office Edn., 1976, Volker Medal South Africa Soc. Psychical Research, 1980. Fellow Am. Soc. Clin. Hypnosis, Am. Psychol. Assn., Soc. Sci. Study Sex; mem. Am. Soc. Psychical Research, N.Y. Soc. Clin. Psychologists (assoc.), Am. Acad. Social and Polit. Sci., AAAS, Am. Ednl. Research Assn., Am. Assn. of Counseling and Devel., Internat. Council Psychologists, Assn. for Study of Dreams, Assn. Anthrop. Study of Consciousness, Assn. Transpersonal Anthropology Internat., Internat. Kirlian Research Assn., Com. for Study Anomalistic Research, Inter-Am. Psychol. Assn., Assn. Humanistic Psychology (pres. 1974-75), Assn. Transpersonal Psychology, Internat. Psychomatics Inst., Internat. Soc. Hypnosis, Internat. Soc. for Study Multiple Personality and Dissociative States, Nat. Assn. for Gifted Children, Sleep Research Soc., Soc. Sci. Exploration, Biofeedback Soc. Am., Council Exceptional Children, Soc. Accelerative Learning and Teaching, Soc. Gen. Systems Research, Swedish Soc. Clin. and Exptl. Hypnosis, Western Psychol. Assn., World Council for Gifted and Talented Children, Internat. Soc. Gen. Semantics, Menninger Found., Nat. Soc. Study of Edn., Parapsychol. Assn. (pres. 1983), Soc. Clin. and Exptl. Hypnosis, Soc. for Sci. Study of Religion, World Future Soc. Home: 79 Woodland Rd Fairfax CA 94930 Office: Saybrook Inst 1772 Vallejo St San Francisco CA 94123

KRISHNAN, MAHADEVAN, physicist; b. Madras, India, July 31, 1950; came to U.S., 1971; s. T. Viswanathan and Parvathy (Iyer) Mahadevan; m. Martine Carbonie, Oct. 26, 1974; children: Nathalie Maya, Corinne Geeta. BS (hon.), U. London, 1971; MA, Princeton U., 1973, PhD in Aerospace and Mech. Scis., 1976. Scientist research staff Yale U., New Haven, Conn., 1976-78, lectr., 1977-78, asst. prof. engring. and applied sci., 1978-82, assoc. prof. applied physics, 1982-85; staff physicist Physics Internat. Co., San Leandro, Calif., 1985—, also cons., 1984—, now mgr. plasma physics and electromagnetics dept.; cons. Lawrence Livermore Nat. Labs, Livermore, Calif., 1985—. Editor: Princeton Conference on Partially Ionized Plasmas and Uranium Plasmas, 1976; contbr. over 30 articles to profl. jours.; patentee apparatus for separation of isotopes. Rolls-Royce scholar, 1967-71; Jr. Faculty fellow Yale U., 1980-81. Mem. Am. Physical Soc., Optical Soc. Am. Avocations: soccer, tennis, squash, wine tasting, gourmet cooking. Home: 6250 Bullard Dr Oakland CA 94611

KRISTENSEN, CHARLES PAUL, venomist, chemist; b. Ames, Iowa, Nov. 5, 1950; s. Paul Albert Kristensen and Gail Marie (Heppner) Busha; m. Barbara Jean Younk, Aug. 23, 1975 (div. 1983); m. Diana Stirling Straayer, May 2, 1986 (div. 1986); 1 child, Jasmine. Student, St. John's U., 1970, U. Minn., 1973; BS in Chemistry, Calif. State U., Long Beach, 1980. Research and devel. chemist Rochelle Corp., Huntington Beach, Calif., 1978, McGean Chem. Co., Downey, Calif., 1978-82; pres. Bio Actives Inc dba Spider Pharm, Black Canyon City, Ariz., 1981-86; cons. U. Utah, Salt Lake City, 1984—, U. Calif. San Francisco, 1984—, Zoecon, Palo Alto, Calif., 1984—, U. Calif., Riverside, 1986—. Inventor in field. Home and Office: Bioactives Inc dba Spider Pharm PO Box 339 Black Canyon City AZ 85324

KRISTENSEN, SCOTT DENNIS, electrical engineering educator; b. Poulsbo, Wash., Feb. 2, 1958; s. Karl Johan and Bernice Sophia (Kvinsland) K.; m. Anne Elisa Kipfer, Aug. 17, 1985. BABA, Pacific Luth. U., 1981; BSEE, Seattle U., 1984. Mgr. reliability program Honeywell, Everett, Wash., 1985-86; lead engr. ELDEC Corp., Bothel, Wash., 1986—; instr. electronics N. Seattle Community Coll., 1986—. Home: 14341 Burke Ave N Seattle WA 98133

KRISTIAN, JEROME, astronomer; b. Milw., June 5, 1933; s. Michael and Alma (Wasilewski) K.; 1 child, John Michael. AB, Shimer Coll., 1953; MS, U. Chgo., 1956, PhD, 1962. Research assoc. ctr. for relativity theory U. Tex., Austin, 1962-64; asst. prof. astronomy U. Wis., Madison, 1964-67; astronomer Mt. Wilson and Las Campanas Obs., Pasadena, Calif., 1967—. Editor: Galaxies and the Universe, 1978; contbr. sci. articles to profl. jours. Mem. Am. Astron. Soc., Internat. Astron. Union, Astron. Soc. of Pacific. Office: Mt Wilson and Las Campanas Obs 813 Santa Barbara St Pasadena CA 91101

KRISTJANSON, LEO FRIMAN, ednl. adminstr., economist; b. Gimli, Man., Can., Feb. 28, 1932; s. Hannes and Elin Thordis (Magnusdottir) K.; m. Jean Evelyn Cameron, June 29, 1957; children—Terri, Darryl, Brenda, Johanne. B.A., U. Man., 1954, M.A., 1959; Ph.D., U. Wis., 1963; LL.D., U. Winnipeg, 1980. Instr. history United Coll., Winnipeg, Man., 1956-57; research economist Centre for Community Studies, Saskatoon, Sask., 1959-64; prof. econs., head, dept. U. Sask., Saskatoon, 1964-75; v.p. U. Sask., 1975-80, pres., 1980—; cons. agrl. marketing Govt. Sask., 1972—. Author 2 booklets in field. Mem. Am. Econ. Assn., Canadian Econ. Assn. (exec. mem.), Canadian Assn. U. Tchrs. (treas., exec. mem. 1970-72), Am. Farm Econs. Assn., Canadian Agrl. Econs. Soc. Office: U Saskatchewan, Saskatoon, SK Canada S7N 0W0 *

KRISTOF, JANE, art history educator; b. Chgo., May 25, 1932; d. Donald Saxon and Mary (Shakespeare) McWilliams; m. Ladis K.D. Kristof, Dec. 29, 1956; 1 child, Nicholas D. BA, U. Chgo., 1950, MA, 1956; PhD, Columbia U., 1972; postgrad., U. Edinburgh, Scotland, 1951-52. Instr. art history City Colls. Chgo., 1957-59, U. Waterloo, Ont., Can., 1970-71; assoc. prof. Portland (Oreg.) State U., 1973—; vis. prof. Linfield Coll., McMinnville, Oreg., 1985—. Author: Steal Away Home, 1969. Treas. Yamhill County (Oreg.) Dem. Cen. Com., 1972-73;. Mem. Coll. Instrs. Art History, Coll. Art Assn., Northwest Renaissance Soc., 16th Century Studies Council, Amnesty Internat. (local group coordinator 1978-79), Curly Coated Retriever Club Am. (northwest coordinator 1983-85). Presbyterian. Avocations: dog breeding, showing, obedience tng. Home: 23050 NW Roosevelt Dr Yamhill OR 97148 Office: Portland State U Dept Art PO Box 751 Portland OR 97207

KRISTOF, LADIS KRIS DONABED, political scientist, author; b. Cernauti, Rumania, Nov. 26, 1918; came to U.S., 1952, naturalized, 1957; s. Witold and Maria (Zawadzki) Krzysztofowicz; m. Jane McWilliams, Dec. 29, 1956; 1 son, Nicholas. Student, U. Poznan, Poland, 1937-39; B.A., Reed Coll., Portland, Ore., 1955; M.A., U. Chgo., 1956, Ph.D., 1969. Regional exec. dir. Sovromlemn, Rumania, 1948; mgr. Centre du Livre Suisse, Paris, France, 1951-52; lectr. U. Chgo., 1958-59; asso. dir. Inter-Univ. Project History Menshevism, N.Y.C., 1959-62; mem. faculty dept. polit. sci. Temple U., 1962-64; research fellow Hoover Instn., Stanford U., 1964-67; faculty polit. sci. U. Santa Clara, 1967-68; asso. Studies Communist System, Stanford, 1968-69; mem. faculty polit. sci. U. Waterloo, Ont., Can., 1969-71; prof. polit. sci. Portland (Oreg.) State U., 1971—. Author: The Nature of Frontiers and Boundaries, 1959, The Origins and Evolution of Geopolitics, 1960, The Russian Image of Russia, 1967; also articles in Romania; co-author, co-editor: Revolution and Politics in Russia, 1972. Active Internat. YMCA Center, Paris, 1950-52, NAACP, Chgo., 1957-59, Amnesty Internat., Portland, 1975—. Served with Corps Engrs. Romanian Army, 1940-43. Fulbright scholar Romania, 1971, 84. Mem. Am. Polit. Sci. Assn., Assn. Am. Geographers, AAAS, Internat. Polit. Sci. Assn., Western Slavic Assn. (v.p., pres. elect 1986—). Home: 23050 NW Roosevelt Dr Yamhill OR 97148 Office: Portland State Univ Portland OR 97207

KROGSTAD, REUBEN STANLEY, physics educator; b. Sletten, Minn., Sept. 7, 1923; s. Jens and Julia (S—nstelie) K.; m. Elise Elliott, Apr. 19, 1953; children: Heidi, Eirik Jens, Roald Erling, Marta R—mo, Finn Tryggve Olav, Christian Dag. BS, U. Minn., 1948; PhD, Wash. State U., 1955. Research scientist Gen. Electric, Richland, Wash., 1952-53; instr. Wash. State U., Pullman, Wash., 1954-55; research scientist Lockheed Aircraft Corp., Palo Alto, Calif., 1955-59, Boeing Research Labs., Seattle, 1959-70; instr. physics Seattle Community Coll., 1971—; cons. U. Utah Research Inst., Salt Lake City, 1975-80. Inventor in field; contbr. articles to profl. jours. Recipient Faculty Achievement award Burlington No. Found., 1986. Avocation: sailing. Home: 2632 SW 120th St Seattle WA 98146 Office: Seattle Community Coll Dept Sci 6000 16th Ave SW Seattle WA 98106

KROHN, KENNETH ALBERT, radiology educator; b. Stevens Point, Wis., June 19, 1945; s. Albert William and Erme Belle (Cornwell) K.; m. Marijane Alberta Wideman, July 14, 1968; 1 child, Galen. BA in Chemistry, Andrews U., 1966; PhD in Chemistry, U. Calif., 1971. Acting assoc. prof. U. Wash., Seattle, 1981-84, assoc. prof. radiology, 1984—, prof. radiology, 1986—, adj. prof. chemistry, 1986—; guest scientist Donner Lab. Lawrence Berkeley (Calif.) Lab., 1980-81; radiochemist, VA Med. Ctr., Seattle, 1982—. Contbr. numerous articles to profl. jours.; patentee in field. NDEA fellow. Mem. AAAS, Am. Chem. Soc., Radiation Research Soc., Soc. Nuclear Medicine, Acad. Council, Sigma Xi. Home: 11322 23d Ave NE Seattle WA 98125 Office: U Wash Div Nuclear Medicine RC-70 Seattle WA 98195

KROKEE, JAMES OLIVER, II, architect; b. San Francisco, Dec. 29, 1945; s. James Oliver and Clara (Thibodo) K.; m. Marianne Banke, June 21, 1971 (div. Oct. 1974); 1 child, James Oliver III; m. Harriet Lenor Brasch, Feb. 12, 1978; children—John Lee, Michael Patrick Martin. City Planning Study, U. Copenhagen, Denmark, 1971; B. Arch., Calif. Poly. State U., 1972; postgrad., 1973. Registered architect, Calif. Architect, San Mateo, Calif., 1975—, City Mountain View, Calif., 1977, City Palo Alto, Calif., 1978-82, Coast Guard, Alameda, Calif., 1983, Navy Pub. Works, San Diego, 1984—; housing program mgr. City Palo Alto, 1979-82; cons. Palo Alto Housing Corp., 1979-82, Sr. & Low Income Housing Corp., Palo Alto, 1979-82; grant writer Calif. State Low Income Housing Corp., 1981. Chmn. Mayor Blue Ribbon Bd. Condo Conversion, San Mateo, 1981; commr. Human Resources Com., San Mateo, 1981, council candidate San Mateo Council, 1981; team mgr. San Mateo Little League, 1982-83. Served to pfc U.S. Army, 1963-64. Recipient Spl. Achievement award U.S. Coast Guard Vice Admiral, 1984, Appreciation Service award San Mateo City Council, 1984. Mem. AIA (editor 1982-83). Democrat. Baptist. Club: Cobra Owners U.S.A. (pres. 1967). Home: 1253 Opal Pacific Beach CA 92109

KROKENBERGER, LINDA ROSE, chemist, environmental analyst; b. Ridley Park, Pa., July 17, 1954; d. Roy Frank and Rose Marie (Kraffert) K. BS in Chemistry, Syracuse U., 1976. Radiopharm. chemist Upstate Med. Ctr., SUNY, Syracuse, 1976-78; chemist IT Corp. (formerly West Coast Tech. Services), Cerritos, Calif., 1978-80, analytical chemist, 1980-81, sr. chemist, 1981-84, asst. lab mgr., 1984-85, environ. protection agency project mgr., 1985-86—; mgr. data control Enseco-Cal Lab., West Sacramento, Calif., 1987—. Recipient Citizenship award DAR, 1972. Mem. Am. Chem. Soc., ASTM, Assn. Official Analytical Chemists, Soc. Environ. Toxicology and Chemistry. Republican. Methodist. Home: 1230 Pebblewood Dr Sacramento CA 95833 Office: Enseco-Cal Lab 2544 Industrial Blvd West Sacramento CA 95691

KRONES, DUANE FRANCIS, communications executive; b. Gilman, Ill., Oct. 10, 1938; s. Patrick Donald and Ethel Rosanna (LaBounty) K.; m. Delorace Ann Emmons, Aug. 8, 1964; children: Patrick Sean, Monique Ann, Michelle Renée, Michael Francis. BS in Bus., U. Nebr., 1972; MS in Systems Mgmt., U. So. Calif., 1976. Commd. USAF, 1961, advanced through grades to capt., 1977, ret., 1983; mgmt. cons. CACI, Inc.-Fed., Arlington, Va., 1983-85; sr. assoc. 1983—; communications maintenance mgr., integrated logistics tech. Air Force Consolidated Space Ops. Ctr. CACI Internat., Inc. (formerly CACI, Inc.-Fed.), Colorado Springs, Colo., 1985—. Recipient Outstanding Community Service award Ohio Ho. of Reps., 1979. Mem. Soc. Logistics Engrs., Ret. Officer Assn., Air Force Assn., Armed Forces Communication and Electronics Assn., U.S. Space Found. Roman Catholic. Lodge: KC. Avocations: golf, collecting comics, auto rebuilding, football, skiing. Office: CACI Inc Fed 980 Technology Ct Colorado Springs CO 80915

KRONINGER, LUTHER HENDRICKS, JR., medical computerization executive; b. Allentown, Pa., May 13, 1930; s. Luther Hendricks and Bea (Brobst) K.; m. Mary Esther Kunkel, June 21, 1952; children: Luther III, Amy Louise, Catharine Rhoads. BS, Cornell U., 1951; postgrad., George Washington U., 1952-53. Product mgr. Mead Johnson & Co., Evansville, Ind., 1969-70; mktg. dir. Bristol Myers Inc., N.Y.C., 1970-72; exec. v.p. Biochem. Procedures Inc., North Hollywood, Calif., 1972-74; pres. MD Systems Inc., Encino, Calif., 1974-78, chmn., chief exec. officer, 1978—. Inventor animal shaped chewable vitamin tablets. Served to 1st lt. U.S. Army, 1952-55. Recipient Pres.'s award Mead Johnson Co., 1965. Mem. Am. Mgmt. Assn., Newport Fleet. Avocations: sailing, skiing, photography. Home: 5244 Armida Dr Woodland Hills CA 91364 Office: MD Systems Inc 16133 Ventura Blvd Encino CA 91436

KRONOWITZ, ELLEN LINDA, educator; b. N.Y.C., July 15, 1945; d. Maurice H. and Beatrice K.; B.A. magna cum laude, Queens Coll., City U. N.Y., 1966; M.A., Columbia U., 1969, Ed.M., 1974, Ed.D., 1976. Tchr. elem. schs., N.Y.C., 1966-70, Agnes Russell Sch. of Tchrs. Coll., Columbia U., 1970-73; instr. Preservice Tchr. Edn. Program, Columbia U., 1973-74; instr. early childhood div. Bklyn. Coll., City U. N.Y., 1974-76; program devel. specialist Tchr. Corps Project, N.Y. U., 1976-78; assoc. prof. elem. edn. Calif. State U., San Bernardino, 1978, coordinator elem. edn. program, 1978—; cons. Rialto (Calif.) Unified Sch. Dist., 1980, Tchr. Corps Projects, Fordham U., Bank St. Coll. Edn., N.Y. Bd. Edn. Bilingual Tchr. Corps Project, 1973-74; condr. workshops. Author: Right Foot Forward, 1986. Fulbright awardee, 1982, Japan Inst. Social and Econ. Affairs fellow, 1986. Mem. Assn. Supervision and Curriculum Devel., Nat. Council Social Studies, Calif. Assn. Profs. Elem. Edn., Calif. Council Edn. of Tchrs., Calif. Assn. Colls. for Tchr. Edn., Foothill Reading Council, Fulbright Alumni Assn., Calif. Council Social Studies, Phi Beta Kappa, Kappa Delta Pi. Contbr. articles to profl. jours. Home: 200 E 30th St San Bernardino CA 92404 Office: Calif State U Dept Elem Edn San Bernardino CA 92407

KRONSTAD, WARREN ERVIND, educator, researcher; b. Bellingham, Wash., Mar. 3, 1932; s. Ervind Raymond and Valintine (Ayers) K.; m. Mary Kathleen Holt, Sept. 19, 1952; children: Robin Kathleen, James Warren, Brian David, Nancy Ann. BS, Wash. State U., 1957, MS, 1959; PhD, Oreg. State U., 1963. Research asst. Wash. State U., Pullman, 1957-59; instr. Oreg. State U., Corvallis, 1959-63, asst. prof., 1963-69, assoc. prof., 1969-72, prof. plant breeding and genetics, 1972—; cons. in field, 1967—. Served with USNR, 1952-54. Recipient Alexander Von Humboldt award, 1981; Nixon Disting. Prof., 1980; named Oreg. State U. Alumni Disting. Prof. Fellow Am. Soc. Agronomy, Crop Sci. Soc. Am. (Crop Sci. award 1983); mem. Nat. Assn. Fgn. Student Affairs, Sigma Xi, Gamma Sigma Delta, Phi Kappa Phi, Phi Sigma. Office: Oreg State U Coll Agriculture Corvallis OR 97331

KROPOTOFF, GEORGE ALEX, engineer; b. Sofia, Bulgaria, Dec. 6, 1921; s. Alex S. and Anna A. (Kurat) K.; came to Brazil, 1948, to U.S., 1952, naturalized, 1958; B.S. in Civil Engring., Inst. Tech., Sofia, 1941; postgrad. in computer sci. U. Calif., 1968; m. Helen P., July 23, 1972. Tech. asst. Standard Eletrica S.A., Rio de Janeiro, 1948-52; structural designer Pacific Car & Foundry Co., Seattle, 1952-64; structural draftsman T.G. Atkinson Assocs., Structural Engrs., San Diego, 1960-62; structural engr. Tucker, Sadler & Bennett A-E, San Diego, 1964-74; research engr. Gen. Dynamics-Astronautics, San Diego, 1967-68; structural engr. Engring. Sci., Inc., Arcadia, Calif., 1975-76; cons. Incomtel, Rio de Janeiro, Brazil, 1976; assoc. Bennett Engrs., structural cons., San Diego, 1976-82; project structural engr. Hope Cons. Group, San Diego and Saudi Arabia, 1982-84; cons. structural engr. Registered profl. engr., Calif. Mem. ASCE, Structural Engrs. Assn. San Diego, Soc. Am. Mil. Engrs., Soc. Profl. Engrs. Brazil. Republican. Orthodox. Home: 742 Brockton St El Cajon CA 92020

KROPP, WILLIAM RUDOLPH, physicist; b. Chgo., Nov. 10, 1936; s. William R. Sr. and Nora J. (King) K.; divorced; children: Marianne, Kathryn. BS, DePaul U., 1958; PhD, Case Inst. Tech., 1964. Postdoctoral fellow Case Inst. Tech., Cleve., 1964-66; postdoctoral fellow U. Calif., Irvine, 1966-68, asst. prof. physics, 1968-74, research physicist, 1974—. Mem. AAAS, Am. Phys. Soc. Home: 17 Newton Ct Irvine CA 92715 Office: U Calif Dept Physics Irvine CA 92717

KROSCHE, ERIC RUDOLF, semiconductor process engineer; b. Akron, Ohio, May 31, 1957; s. Rudy and Donna Ann (Forster) K.; m. Katherine Louise vanGoidtsnoven, July 11, 1981. AS in Engring. Sci., Middlesex County Coll., 1978; BS in Math., BSMetE, N.Mex. Inst. Mining, 1980, MS in Metallurgy, 1985. Implant process engr. Intel Corp., Rio Rancho, N.Mex., 1984-85, sputter and implant process engr., 1985—. Mineral Inst. Research fellow U.S. Dept. Interior, 1981; Kennecott Copper Co. scholar, 1981. Mem. Am. Soc. Metals, The Metall. Soc., Order of Engr., Tau Beta Pi (charter), Phi Theta Kappa, Alpha Sigma Mu. Avocations: sailing, audiophile, home improvements. Home: 628 Littler Dr Rio Rancho NM 87124 Office: Intel Corp 4100 Sara Rd Rio Rancho NM 87124

KROTKI, KAROL JOZEF, economist, demographer; b. Cieszyn, Poland, May 12, 1922; emigrated to Can., 1964; s. Karol Stanislaw and Anna Elzbieta (Skrzywanek) K.; m. Joanna Patkowski, July 12, 1947; children—Karol Peter, Jan Jozef, Filip Karol. B.A. (hons.), Cambridge (Eng.) U., 1948, M.A., 1952; M.A., Princeton U., 1959, Ph.D., 1960. Civil ser. Eng., 1948-49; dep. dir. stats. Sudan, 1949-58; vis. fellow Princeton U., 1958-60; research adviser Pakistan Inst. Devel. Econs., 1960-64; asst. dir. census research Dominion Bur. Stats., Can., 1964-68; prof. sociology U. Alta., 1968-83, Univ. Prof., 1983—; vis. prof. U. Calif., Berkeley, 1967, U. N.C., 1970-73, U. Mich., 1975; coordinator program socio-econ. research Province Alta., 1969-71; cons. in field. Author 10 books and monographs; contbr. numerous articles to profl. jours. Served with Polish, French and Brit. Armed Forces, 1939-46. Recipient achievement award Province of Alta., 1970; grantee in field. Fellow Am. Statis. Assn., Royal Soc. Can. (v.p. 1986-88), Acad. Humanities and Social Scis. (v.p. 1984-86, pres. 1986-88); mem. Fedn. Can. Demographers (v.p. 1977-82, pres. 1982-84), Can. Population Soc., Association des Demographes du Quebec, Cen. and E. European Studies Soc. (pres. 1986-88), Population Assn. Am., Internat. Union Sci. Study Population, Internal Statis. Inst. Roman Catholic. Home: 10137 Clifton Pl, Edmonton, AB Canada T5N 3H9 Office: Dept Sociology, U Alta, Edmonton, AB Canada T6G 2H4

KROUSE, DIANE MURRAY, advertising company executive; b. Far Rockaway, N.Y., May 24, 1954; d. Jan and Kathleen (Mann) Murray; m. David Allan Krouse, Oct. 10, 1982; 1 child, Sarah Elizabeth. BA, Stanford U., 1977. Promotion coordinator Beetleboards Internat., Los Angeles, 1977-78; account exec. RAP Communications, Los Angeles, 1978-79; v.p., mgmt. supr. D'Arcy, Masius, Benton and Bowles, N.Y.C., 1979-85, Los Angeles, 1985—. Mem. Phi Beta Kappa. Avocations: music, films, theatre. Home: 2256 Linnington Ave Los Angeles CA 90064 Office: D'Arcy Masius Benton and Bowles 6500 Wilshire Blvd Los Angeles CA 90048

KROUSE, STAN SAMUEL, pastor; b. Mena, Ark., Apr. 10, 1947; s. Samuel Krouse and Wanda Lee (Rhodes) Clark; m. Ann Caroline Bowden, June 20, 1965; children: Dena Annette, Jenica Rebecca. AA in Social Sci., Yuba Coll., 1967; BA in Philosophy, Calif. State U., Chico, 1969; MDiv., Golden Gate Bapt. Seminary, 1975, D in Ministry, 1979. Ordained to ministry Bapt. Ch., 1974. Assoc. pastor 1st Bapt. Ch., Colusa, Calif., 1972-75; pastor 1st Bapt. Ch., Ripon, Calif., 1975-79, Calvary Bapt. Ch., Merced, Calif., 1980-81; founding pastor Grace Christian Fellowship, Lincoln, Calif., 1982—; bd. dirs. Solo Ministries, Campbell, Calif. Author: Discipleship/Evangelism in the Local Church, 1979. Mem. High Sch. Curriculum Com., Lincoln, 1984-87. Served with U.S. Army, 1969-71. Mem. Ripon Ministerial Assn. (pres. 1976-78), Cen. Valley Assn. (moderator 1978-79), Lincoln Ministerial Assn. Republican. Lodge: Rotary. Avocations: water and snow skiing, bicycling, swimming, volleyball, basketball. Home: 1600 Shamrock Ct Lincoln CA 95648 Office: Grace Christian Fellowship 1530 Third St Suite 207 Lincoln CA 95648

KRUCHEK, THOMAS FRANCIS, psychiatrist; b. Montgomery, Minn., Aug. 15, 1922; s. Joseph and Nettie (Washa) K.; B.S., Coll. St. Thomas, 1944; M.D., Creighton U., 1946; m. Esther Kelly, Feb. 17, 1950; 1 son, Joseph. Intern, St. Mary's Hosp., Mpls., 1946-49; resident VA Hosp., Ft. Lyon, Colo., 1948-49, Norristown (Pa.) State Hosp., 1949-50, U. Pitts., 1953-54; practice medicine specializing in psychiatry, Chgo., 1954-62, Phoenix, 1962—; mem. staff St. Joseph's Hosp., chmn. dept. psychiatry, 1973-76; mem. staff Camelback Hosp., chief staff 1965-66; mem. staff Good Samaritan, St. Luke's, Dr.'s hosps., Phoenix, Scottsdale (Ariz.) Community/Hosps.; clin. instr. psychiatry Stritch Sch. Medicine, Chgo., 1955-62; prof. psychology St. Procopius Coll., Lisle, Ill., 1954-62; pres. Thomas F. Kruchek, M.D., Ltd. Served to capt. M.C., AUS, 1951-53. Diplomate Am. Bd. Psychiatry and Neurology. Fellow Am. Psychiat. Assn. (life), Royal Soc. Health; mem. AMA, Am. Psychotherapy Assn., Maricopa County Med. Soc., Ariz. Psychiat. Soc. (treas. 1968-69, pres. 1970-71), Phoenix Psychiat. Council, Chgo. Neurol. Soc., Am. Group Psychotherapy Assn., Acad. Psychosomatic Medicine, Ariz. Med. Assn. Home: 4921 Prickly Pear Ln Paradise Valley AZ 85253 Office: 350 W Thomas Rd Phoenix AZ 85013

KRUEGER, JAMES, lawyer; b. N.Y.C., Oct. 27, 1938; s. Carl and Ida (Levey) K.; m. Merry Michael Hill, July 5, 1967; children—Melissa Carlton, James Michael. B.A., UCLA, 1960; LL.B., Loyola U., Los Angeles, 1965. Bar: Hawaii 1966, U.S. Dist. Ct. Hawaii 1966, U.S. Ct. Appeals (9th cir.) 1967, U.S. Tax Ct. 1974, U.S. Supreme Ct. 1982. Assoc. firm Padgett, Greeley, Marumoto & Akinaka, Honolulu, 1967-72; pres. James Krueger Law Corp., Wailuku, Maui, Hawaii, 1972—; speaker, lectr. profl. orgn. convs.; spl. counsel County of Maui, 1974; spl. agt. Internat. Police Congress, Washington. Contbr. articles to profl. jours. Fellow Internat. Soc. Barristers, Internat. Acad. Trial Lawyers; mem. Assn. Trial Lawyers Am. (gov. 1976-82, state committeeman 1975-76, constl. revisions com. 1977-78, nat. exec. com. 1981-82, amicus curiae com. 1979-80, fed. liaison com. 1980-81, nat. vice chmn. profl. research and devel. com. 1980-81, nat. vice-chmn. publs. dept. 1982-83, nat. vice chmn. edn. policy bd. 1983-84), Hawaii Bar Assn., Fed. Bar Assn., Maui County Bar Assn. (pres. 1975), Melvin M. Belli Soc., Hawaii Acad. Plaintiffs Attys., Am. Coll. Legal Medicine, Am. Soc. Hosp. Attys., Phi Alpha Delta. Democrat. Jewish. Clubs: Outrigger Canoe (Honolulu); Transpacific Yacht (Los Angeles); Maui Country. Avocations: swimming, running, cycling, skiing. Office: 2065 Main St PO Box T Wailuku HI 96793

KRUEGER, PHYLLIS ANITA, insurance agency executive; b. Twin Falls, Idaho, Nov. 13, 1944; d. Herman Hyrum Huff and Maxine Helen (Snodgrass) Risbon; m. Gerald Arch Parmenter, Oct. 20, 1962 (div. Oct. 1965); 1 child, Teri; m. Ronald Eldon Krueger, July 12, 1975. Cert. in Gen. Ins., Ins. Inst. Am. Office mgr. Appaloosa Horse Club, Inc., Moscow, Idaho, 1962-70; personal lines CSR Am. Ins. Agy., Lewiston, Idaho, 1970-75, Martin Lipps Ins., Lewiston, Idaho, 1975-77; office mgr. Martin Ins. Inc., Lewiston, Idaho, 1977-80, adminstrv. mgr., 1982—; agt., part owner Krueger Ins. Specialists Inc., Clarkston, Wash., 1980-82. Mem. Ind. Ins. Agts. Am., Ind. Ins. Agts. Idaho, Lewiston Assn. Ind. Ins. Agts., Lewiston Clarkston Ins. Women (pres. 1985—), Nat. Assn. Ins. Women Internat. (co-chmn. state meeting 1979, 82), Valley Assn. Ins. Women (pres. 1972-74). Lodge: Daus. of Nile (Lady in Waiting 1983-85, Marshall 1985—). Avocations: camping, boating, skiing, tennis, travel. Home: 800A Lapwai Rd Lewiston ID 83501 Office: Martin Ins Inc 1122 Idaho St Lewiston ID 83501

KRUEGER, ROBERT BLAIR, lawyer; b. Minot, N.D., Dec. 9, 1928; s. Paul Otto and Lila (Morse) K.; m. Virginia Ruth Carmichael, June 3, 1956; children: Lisa Carmichael, Paula Leah, Robert Blair. A.B., U. Kans., 1949; J.D., U. Mich., 1952; postgrad., U. So. Calif., 1960-65. Bar: Kans. 1952, Calif. 1955, D.C. 1978. Practiced in Los Angeles, 1955—; assoc. O'Melveny & Myers, 1955-59; ptnr. Nossaman, Krueger & Marsh and predecessor firms, 1961-83, Finley, Kumble, Wagner, Heine, Underberg, Manley, Myerson & Casey, 1983—; chmn. Nat. Practice Group on Energy and Natural Resources; adj. prof. natural resource law U. So. Calif. Law Ctr., 1973—; Mem. Gov.'s Adv. Commn. on Ocean Resources, 1966-68, Calif. Adv. Commn. on Marine and Coastal Resources, 1968-73, chmn., 1970-73; mem. adv. council Inst. on Marine Resources, U. Calif., 1966-74, Commn. on California, 1977—; mem. Nat. Security Council Adv. Com. on Law of Sea, 1972-82, chmn. internat. law and relations subcom., 1972-82; U.S. del. to UN Seabeds Com., 1973, 3d UN Law of Sea Conf., 1974-82; cons. petroleum policy to UN, fgn. govts. U.S. Centre on Transnat. Corps.; mem. exec. bd. Law of Sea Inst., U. Hawaii, 1977-83; mem. Nat. Adv. Com. on Oceans and Atmosphere, 1986—; fellow U. So. Calif. Inst. on Marine and Coastal Studies., 1977—. Author: Study of Outer Continental Shelf Lands of the United States, 1968, The United States and International Oil, 1975, World Petroleum Policies Report, 1981; also articles on energy and natural resources.; Asst. editor: Mich. Law Rev., 1951-52; editor: Los Angeles Bar Bull., 1961-63; bd. editors: Calif. Bar Jour., 1962-68. Mem. com. visitors U. Mich. Law Sch.; founder Mus. Contemporary Art. Served to 1st lt. USMCR, 1952-54. Fellow Am. Bar Found.; mem. ABA (chmn. spl. com. on energy law 1979-83, chmn. coordinating group on energy law 1983-86), Los Angeles County Bar Assn., Internat. Bar Assn., Am. Soc. Internat. Law., Fellows Contemporary Art, Barristers, Tau Kappa Epsilon, Phi Alpha Delta. Republican. Clubs: Calif, University, Chancery; Metropolitan (Washington); Valley Hunt (Pasadena); Princeton (N.Y.C.). Home: 9828 La Jolla Farms Rd La Jolla CA 92037 Office: Finley Kumble Wagner Heine et al 707 Wilshire Blvd 44th Floor Los Angeles CA 90017

KRUEGER, ROLAND FREDERICK, oil company executive; b. Fond du Lac, Wis., Oct. 18, 1918; s. William Frederick and Amelia (Kloeden) K.; m. Elaine Kenyon, Oct. 1943 (div. 1952); 1 child, Kerry R.; m. Lucille Rowland, Apr. 16, 1955; children: Robert R., Francisca M. BA in Math. and Physics, Ripon Coll., 1939; MA in Math. and Physics, U. Ill., 1941. Physicist Tenn. Eastman Corp., Kingsport, 1941-42, Holston Ordnance Works, Kingsport, 1942-43; radiation lab. physicist Manhattan Project, Berkeley, Calif., 1943; tech. supr. Manhattan Project, Oak Ridge, Tenn., 1943-44, asst. dept. supt., 1944-46; research physicist Douglas Aircraft Co., Santa Monica, Calif., 1946-48, Union Oil Co. of Calif., Wilmington, 1948-51; sect. leader Union Oil Co. of Calif., Brea, 1951-62, research supr., 1962-81, research mgr., 1981-85, cons. to pres. sci. and tech. div., 1985—; lectr. Stanford (Calif.) U., U. So. Calif., 1975—. Contbr. articles to profl. jours. Pres. Peralta Hills Improvement Assn., Anaheim, Calif., 1965-70, also bd. dirs.; gen. mgr., pres. Peralta Hills (mut.) Water Co., Anaheim, 1965—, also bd. dirs.; active several citizens adv. coms. Fellow Inst. Advancement Engrng.; mem. AAAS, Soc. Petroleum Engrs. (past chmn. several tech. coms., sr. tech. editor 1979-82, bd. dirs. 1983—, Disting. Lectr. 1975-76, Disting. Service 1982, Disting. Mem. 1983, Disting. Author 1986), Am. Petroleum Inst. (subcom. chmn. 1977—), Pi Epsilon Tau (Diploma of Honor 1983). Republican. Lutheran. Avocations: orchards, golf. Home: 561 Peralta Hills Dr Anaheim CA 92807 Office: UNOCAL Sci & Tech Div 376 Valencia Brea CA 92621

KRUGER, LAWRENCE, neuroscientist; b. New Brunswick, N.J., Aug. 15, 1929; s. Jacob C. and Kate M. (Newman) K.; m. Virginia Findlay, Sept. 30, 1960; children: Erika, Paula. PhD, Yale U., 1954. Postdoctoral fellow Johns Hopkins U., Balt., 1955-58, Coll. de France, Paris, 1958, Oxford (Eng.) U., 1958-59; asst. prof. anatomy UCLA, 1960-62, assoc. prof., 1962-65, prof., 1966—; Wellcome vis. prof., Albany (N.Y.) Med. Coll., 1981. Recipient Lederle Med. Faculty award, 1964-67, Javits Neurosci. Investigator award, 1984; Fogarty Sr. Internat. Scholar, St. Mary's Hosp. Med. Sch., London, 1977. Mem. Internat. Brain Research Orgn. of UNESCO, Internat. Assn. Study of Pain, Am. Assn. Anatomists, Am. Physiol. Soc., Am. Assn. Anatomists, Soc. Neurosci. Office: Univ of Calif Los Angeles Dept of Anatomy Los Angeles CA 90024

KRUGMEIER, PAULA JEAN, architect; b. Los Angeles, May 8, 1954; d. Charles William and Joanne (Sienko) K. AB in Architecture with highest honors, U. Calif., Berkeley, 1975; MArch, MIT, 1980. Registered architect, Mass., Calif. Job capt. Fisher Friedman Assocs., San Francisco, 1976, proj. architect designer, 1985—; draftsperson, designer William Remick, Architects, AIA, Piedmont, Calif., 1976-77; assoc., project mgr. Arrowstreet Inc., Cambridge, Mass., 1980-85. Mem. design/research team under N. John Habraken for publ. The Grunfeld Variations, MIT, 1980. Mem. AIA. Democrat. Avocations: traveling, sports, art. Office: Fisher Friedman Assocs 242 California St San Francisco CA 94111

KRUMM, JOHN MCGILL, bishop; b. South Bend, Ind., Mar. 15, 1913; s. William F. and Harriett Vincent (McGill) K. A.A., Pasadena Jr. Coll., 1933; A.B., U. Calif., 1935; B.D., Va. Theol. Sem., 1938, D.D. (hon.), 1974; Ph.D., Yale U., 1948; S.T.D. (hon.), Kenyon Coll., Gambier, Ohio, 1962; D.D. (hon.), Berkeley Div. Sch., Gen. Theol. Sem., 1975; L.H.D. (hon.), Hebrew Union Coll., Cin. Ordained to ministry Episcopal Ch., 1938; vicar Episc. chs., Compton, Lynwood and Hawthorne, Calif., 1938-41; asst. rector St. Paul's Ch., New Haven, 1941-43; rector Ch. of St. Matthew, San Mateo, Calif., 1943-48; dean St. Paul's Cathedral, Los Angeles, 1948-52; chaplain Columbia U., 1952-65; rector Ch. of Ascension, N.Y.C., 1965-71; bishop of So. Ohio, Episc. Ch., 1971-80; suffragan bishop in Europe Paris, 1980-83; assisting bishop Los Angeles, 1983—, St. Paul's Ch., Tustin, Calif., 1983—; vis. lectr. N.T. Berkeley Div. Sch., New Haven, 1942-43; ch. history Va. Theol. Sem., Alexandria, 1942; instr. Prospect Hill Sch., New Haven, 1942-43; instr. religion U. So. Calif., 1950-52; chmn. clergy div. U. Religious Conf., Los Angeles; pres. San Mateo-Burlingame (Calif.) Council Chs., 1947-48, Ch. Fedn. Los Angeles, 1951-52; chmn. nat. council Panel of Ams., 1953-61. Author: (with J.A. Pike) Roadblocks to Faith, 1953, Modern Heresies, 1961, The Art of Being a Sinner, 1967, Why Choose the Episcopal Church, 1974, (with others) Denver Crossroads, 1979. Trustee Mt. Holyoke Coll., 1962-72, Bexley Hall of Colgate-Rochester, Kenyon Coll., Children's Hosp., Cin., 1971-80; chmn. Canterbury Irvine Found., U. Calif.-Irvine. Mem. Ch. Soc. for Coll. Work (bd. dirs.). Democrat. Clubs: Century Assn. (N.Y.C.); University (Cin.). Office: St Paul's Ch 1221 Wass Ave Tustin CA 92680

KRUMM, VICTOR CARL, district attorney; b. St. Paul, Mar. 1, 1947; s. Carl J. and Evelyn M. Krumm; m. Jean M. Ellsberg, May 23, 1969; children: Alexander, Andrew, Marissa. BA, Macalester Coll., 1969; JD, U. Minn., 1974. Ptnr. Christianson & Krumm, Sitka, Alaska, 1974-76; dist. atty. State of Alaska, Bethel, 1976-79, Ketchikan, 1979-81; asst. atty. gen. State of Alaska, Juneau, 1981-82; dist. atty. State of Alaska, Anchorage, 1982—. Served with U.S. Army, 1970-72. Office: Anchorage Dist Atty 1031 W 4th Ave Suite 520 Anchorage AK 99501

KRUPA, JOSEPH FRANK, process development scientist; b. Dec. 1, 1946; s. Frank John and Lucinda (Manning) K.; m. Susan Petrofsky, June 21, 1969; children: Katherine Anne, Nathan John, Alicia Rose. BSc in Chemistry, USAF Acad., 1968; MSc in Chemistry, U. Calif., Berkeley, 1969; MEChemE, U. Idaho, 1984. Nuclear research officer USAF, 1970-74; analytical engr. fuel cell devel., power systems, United Technologies, Inc., 1974-77; sr. chemist Allied Chem. Idaho Ops., 1977-79, Exxon Nuclear Lab., Idaho, 1979-83; sr. scientist Winco, Idaho Falls, Idaho, 1983-86, process devel. scientist, 1986—. Co-inventor purifying bidentate organophosphorous compounds, 1981. Fellow AEC, 1968. Mem. Am. Chem. Soc. Republican. Roman Catholic. Avocations: fishing, art. Home: 2649 Newman Dr Idaho Falls ID 83402 Office: Winco PO Box 4000 Idaho Falls ID 83403

KRUPKA, MILTON CLIFFORD, systems analyst; b. N.Y.C., Jan. 1, 1924; s. Nathan and Sadie (Perler) K.; m. Emilia Theresa Clara, Apr. 10, 1954; children: Denise Leah, John Lawrence, Nilda Elizabeth. BS, CUNY, 1944; MS, U. N.Mex., 1958, PhD, 1962. Jr. chemist Columbia U., N.Y.C., 1944-45; staff mem., supr. Los Alamos (N.Mex.) Nat. Lab., 1945-60, research chemist, asst. mgr., 1960-78, staff mem., prin. investigator, 1978—. Contbr. articles to profl. jours; patentee in field. Recipient 40 Yrs. service award Los Alamos Nat. Lab., 1986. Fellow: Am. Inst. Chemists; mem. Am. Chem. Soc., Soc. Sigma Xi. Democrat. Lodge: Elks. Avocations: athletics, stamps, travel. Home: 1337 Sage Loop Los Alamos NM 87544 Office: Los Alamos Nat Lab Los Alamos NM 87544

KRUPP, EDWIN CHARLES, astronomer; b. Chgo., Nov. 18, 1944; s. Edwin Frederick and Florence Ann (Olander) K.; m. Robin Suzanne Rector, Dec. 31, 1968; 1 son, Ethan Hembree. B.A., Pomona Coll., 1966; M.A., UCLA, 1968, Ph.D. (NDEA fellow, 1970-71), 1972. Astronomer Griffith Obs., Los Angeles Dept. Recreation and Parks, 1972—, dir., 1976—; mem. faculty El Camino Coll., U. So. Calif., extension divs. U. Calif.; cons. in ednl. TV Community Colls. Consortium; host teleseries Project: Universe. Author: The Comet and You, 1986 (Best Sci. Writing award Am. Inst. Physics 1986), Echoes of the Ancient Skies; editor/co-author: In Search of Ancient Astronomies, 1978 (Am. Inst. Physics-U.S. Steel Found. award for Best Sci. Writing 1978), Archaeoastronomy and the Roots of Science; Editor-in-chief: Griffith Obs., 1974—. Mem. Am. Astron. Soc. (past chmn. hist. astronomy div.), Astron. Soc. Pacific (dir.), Explorers Club, Sigma Xi. Office: Griffith Obs 2800 E Observatory Rd Los Angeles CA 90027

KRUPP, JONATHAN MAURICE, botanical researcher, facility coordinator; b. Oakland, Calif., Oct. 3, 1948; s. Robert Fabin and Rose (Helmers) K.; m. Delia Katherine Schalansky, Oct. 11, 1980; 1 child, Alexis. BS in Biol. Scis., U. Calif., Davis, 1970, PhD in Botany, 1983; MA, BA in Botany, Humboldt State U., 1976. Lectr. U. Calif., Davis, 1983-85, research assoc., 1984-85; electron microscope facility coordinator U. Calif., Santa Cruz, 1985—. Mem. AAAS, Electron Microscope Soc. Am., Bot. Soc. Am., Phycological Soc. Am., Sigma Xi. Democrat. Avocations: gardening, bird watching. Office: U Calif Div Natural Scis Santa Cruz CA 95064

KRUPP, MARCUS ABRAHAM, physician; b. El Paso, Tex., Feb. 12, 1913; s. Maurice and Esther (Siegel) K.; m. Muriel McClure, Aug. 9, 1941 (dec. Oct. 1954); children: Michael, David (dec.), Peter, Sara; m. Donna Goodheart Millen, Feb. 28, 1958. A.B., Stanford U., 1934, M.D., 1939. Diplomate: Am. Bd. Internal Medicine. Intern Stanford U. Hosp., Calif., 1938-39; resident in internal medicine Stanford U. Hosp., 1939-42; chief clin. pathology VA Hosp., San Francisco, 1946-50; dir. Palo Alto Med. Research Found., Calif., 1950-86; dir. labs. Palo Alto Med. Clinic, 1950-80; asst. clin. prof. medicine Stanford U., 1946-56, asso. clin. prof., 1956-65, clin. prof., 1965—; mem. med. tech. adv. com. Public Employees Retirement System Calif., 1972—. Editor: (with Milton Chatton) Current Medical Diagnosis and Treatment, ann., 1971-87, (with others) Physicians Handbook, 7th-21st edits., 1985. Vice pres. bd. dirs. Calif. Heart Assn., 1974-75; pres. bd. trustees Channing House, Palo Alto. Served to capt. U.S. Army, 1942-46. Recipient Albion Walter Hewlett award Stanford U. Med. Sch., 1987. Fellow ACP; mem. Western Soc. Clin. Research, Calif. Acad. Medicine (pres. 1966), Pacific Interurban Clin. Club (pres. 1977), AAAS, AMA, N.Y. Acad. Scis., Assn. Ind. Research Insts. (pres. 1966-67), Phi Beta Kappa, Alpha Omega Alpha. Home: 195 Ramoso Rd Portola Valley CA 94025 Office: 860 Bryant St Palo Alto CA 94301

KRUSZENSKI, DONALD MICHAEL, management consultant; b. Kingston, N.Y., May 30, 1942; s. Michael S. and Helen T. (Wendryhowski) K.; m. Louise R. Venditti, June 20, 1964; children: Sandra, Kevin, David. BEE, Rensselaer Poly. Inst., 1963; student, MIT, 1964-65; MSEE, Northeastern U., 1968; MBA, Boston U., 1972. Sr. systems engr. Sanders Assocs., Bedford, Mass., 1966-68; mktg. mgr. Honeywell, Inc., Waltham, Mass., 1968-72; prin. A.T. Kearney, Inc., Cleve., 1972-79, Los Angeles, 1984—; dir. strategic planning Rockwell Internat., Pitts., 1979-81; v.p. bus. devel. Rockwell Internat., Canoga Park, Calif., 1981-84. Pres. Ridgeview Estates Assn., Westlake Village, Calif., 1982. Republican. Roman Catholic. Avocations: tennis, computers. Office: AT Kearney Inc One Wilshire Bldg Suite 2501 Los Angeles CA 90017

KU, JERRY CHIH, mechanical engineering educator; b. Tainan, Taiwan, Apr. 4, 1953; s. Po-Fen and Chian-Min (Chen) K.; m. Janet Chien-Hisia Hsu, Oct. 10, 1977; 1 child, Lawrence Chunhao. BS, Tatung Inst. Tech., Taiwan, 1975; MS, SUNY, Buffalo, 1982, PhD, 1985. Research and devel. engr. Tanung Co., Taipei, Taiwan, 1977-79; lectr. SUNY, Buffalo, 1983-84; asst. prof. N.Mex. State U., Las Cruces, 1985—. Contbr. articles to profl. jours. Served to 2d lt. Taiwan Mil. Police, 1975-77. Sandia U. Research Program grantee Sandia Nat. Labs., 1985-86; grantee Los Alamos (N.Mex.) Nat. Lab., U.S. Army Atmospheric Sci. Lab. Mem. AIAA, ASME (sect. vice chmn., 1986, mem. K-11 com.), Internat. Soc. Optical Engring., Am. Assn. Aerosol Research, Combustion Inst. Avocation: sports. Office: N Mex State U Dept Mech Engring Las Cruces NM 88003

KUBAS, GREGORY JOSEPH, research chemist; b. Cleve., Mar. 12, 1945; s. Joseph Arthur and Esther (Polcyn) K.; m. Jeanne Henry, Dec. 22, 1973; children: Kelly Richmond, Sherry Richmond. BS, Case Inst. Tech., 1966; PhD, Northwestern U., 1970. Postdoctoral fellow Princeton (N.J.) U., 1971-72; postdoctoral fellow Los Alamos (N.Mex.) Nat. Lab., 1972-74, mem. staff, 1974—. Contbr. articles to profl. jours. Mem. Am. Chem. Soc. Clubs: Los Alamos Tennis (pres. 1983-84), Los Alamos Duplicate Bridge. Avocations: tennis, bridge, basketball, softball, hiking. Home: 190 Manhattan Loop Los Alamos NM 87544 Office: Los Alamos Nat Lab MS-C346 Los Alamos NM 87545

KUBELKA, RICHARD PRESTON, mathematician, educator; b. Burbank, Calif., Mar. 5, 1952; s. Joseph D. and B. Eunice Kubelka. Student, Georg-August U., Goettingen, Fed. Republic Germany, 1972-73; AB, U. Calif., Berkeley, 1974; MS in Math., Stanford U., 1976, PhD in Math., 1980. Vis. asst. prof. dept. math. U. Okla., Norman, 1980-83; asst. prof. San Jose State U., Calif., 1983—. Contbr. articles to profl. jours. Mem. Am. Math. Soc., Math. Assn. Am., Phi Beta Kappa. Office: San Jose State U Dept Math and Computer Sci San Jose CA 95192

KUBIDA, WILLIAM JOSEPH, patent lawyer; b. Newark, Apr. 3, 1949; s. William and Catherine (Gilchrist) K.; m. Mary Jane Hamilton, Feb. 4, 1984. B.S.E.E., U.S. Air Force Acad., 1971; J.D., Wake Forest U., 1979. Bar: N.C. 1979, U.S. Patent Office 1979, Ind. 1980, U.S. Dist. Ct. (no. dist.) Ind. 1980, U.S. Dist. Ct. (so. dist.) Ind. 1980, U.S. Ct. Appeals (7th cir.) 1981, U.S. Dist. Ct. (Ariz.) 1982, U.S. Ct. Appeals (9th cirs. and fed.) 1982, Ariz. 1982. Patent and trademark lawyer Lundy and Assocs., Ft. Wayne, Ind., 1979-81; patent atty. Motorola, Inc., Phoenix, 1981-85; Intellectual Property Counsel Nippon Motorola, Ltd., Tokyo, 1985—. Served to 1st lt. USAF, 1971-76. Mem. ABA (patent/trademark/copyright sect., litigation sect.), Am. Intellectual Property Law Assn., Am. C. of C. (patents, trademarks and lic. sect., Japan), Mensa. Republican. Presbyterian. Club: Tokyo Am. Home: 8110 N 18th Pl Phoenix AZ 85020 Office: Nippon Motorola, Ltd 5-2-32 Minami-Azabu, Minato-ku, Tokyo 106 Japan

KUBOKAWA, CHARLES CHIHARU, research scientist; b. San Francisco, Dec. 2, 1929; s. Yoshitomo and Makiyo (Hashimoto) K.; m. Beth Yasuko Nekoda, June 23, 1956; children: Lori Kay, Lisa Kim, Keri Leigh. Student, U. Calif., Berkeley, 1948-51; postgrad., U. Calif., 1957-58; BA, UCLA, 1957; postgrad., U. Mich., 1963, 65. Tng. analyst Rand Corp., Systems Devel. Corp., Santa Monica, Calif., 1956-57; sr. engr. Philco-Ford, Palo Alto, Calif., 1958-63; head Human Factors Group NASA Ames Research Ctr., Moffett Field, Calif., 1963-75, chief tech. utilization office, 1975-81, asst. to dir. of adminstrn. for community relations, 1981—, dir. for ind. research and devel., 1985—; cons. Santa Clara County Dept. Transp.; guest lectr. colls. and univs.; chmn. space sci. adv. bd. Foothill Coll.,1973-76. Author: Databook for Human Factors Engineers, 1970; editorial bd. Jour. Tech. Transfer, 1977-79; inventor aircraft safety equipment. Pres. Sequoia chpt. Japanese Am. Citizens League, 1972, gov. No. Calif. Western Nev. Dist. Council, 1977-79, nat. v.p. for pub. affairs, 1982-84; bd. dirs. Santa Clara United Way, 1980-84, Alto Area ARC, 1983—; regional v.p. Mountain View United Way, 1984, bd. dirs. 1979—. Served with USAF, 1951-55. Recipient Superior Performance award NASA, 1966, 86, Apollo Achievement award, 1970; Japanese Govt. Sci. and Tech. Research fellow, 1972; recipient Letter of Appreciation, Sec. Interior, 1973, Silver medal Nat. Nisei of Biennium, 1972, Japan Diving Assn. award, 1974. Mem. U.S.-Japan Natural Resources Panel, Fed. Lab. Consortium Tech. Transfer, Human Factors Soc., Peninsula Home Enologist Workship (founder), Pan Am. Nikkei Assn. (founder, treas.), Japanese-Am. Citizens League (life), U. Calif. Nikkei Alumni Assn. (life). Democrat. Methodist. Was first man to spend one month on ocean floor as part of Project Tektite II, NASA, 1972. Home: 3365 Stockton Pl Palo Alto CA 94303 Office: NASA Ames Research Ctr Moffett Field CA 94035

KUBOTA, SCOTT EDWARD YUKIO, lawyer; b. Honolulu, Dec. 5, 1958; s. Ernest Hisao and Florence Sachiko (Matsuoka) K.; m. Denise Emi Omoto, Nov. 30, 1985; 1 child, Reyn Hisao. BA, U. Wash., 1980; JD, U. Hawaii, 1983. Law clk. 1st Cir. Ct., Honolulu, 1983-84; atty. Shim, Tam, Kirimitsu & Naito, Honolulu, 1984—. Mem. ABA, Assn. Trial Lawyers Am., Honolulu Jaycees. Democrat. Buddist. Avocations: golf, softball, basketball, volleyball, tennis. Office: Shim Tam Kirimitsu & Naito 333 Queen St Suite 900 Honolulu HI 96813

KUCERA, JEFFEREY WILSON, corporate controller; b. Mpls., May 16, 1951; s. William John and Elizabeth Wilcox (Jones) K. BA in Theatre, U. Denver, 1973; MBA, Pepperdine U., 1983. Controller Elsboy Inc., Los Angeles, 1982-85, Heritage Entertainment, Los Angeles, 1983-85, LTM Corp. Am., Hollywood, Calif., 1985—. Avocations: collecting 1st edit. books, antiques, swimming, history. Home: 13345 Debby St Van Nuys CA 91401 Office: LTM Corp Am 1160 N Las Palmas Ave Hollywood CA 90038

KUCERA GIENGER, JANE, research chemical engineer; b. Chgo., June 2, 1959; d. Oldrich and Margaret (Eser) Kucera; m. Jeffery A. Gienger, Oct. 2, 1982. BA in Chemistry summa cum laude, Linfield Coll., 1981; MSChemE, UCLA, 1984. Research chemical engineer Bend (Oreg.) Research, Inc.,

1984—. Mem. Am. Inst. Chem. Engr., Am. Chem. Soc., Am. Physics Soc., European Soc. Membrane Sci. and Tech., N.Am. Membrane Soc., Sigma Pi Sigma. Avocations: traveling, photography, skiing, tennis. Office: Bend Research Inc 64550 Reserch Rd Bend OR 97701

KUCIJ, TIMOTHY MICHAEL, engineer, pianist, composer; b. Whittier, Calif., Sept. 2, 1954. BA in Music, Calif. State Poly. U., Pomona, 1978; ThM cum laude, Christian Bible Coll., 1983; studies with, Frank Sanucci, Edward D. Berryman and Ronald R. Gearman, 1965-73; student, Sherwood Music Sch. of Chgo., 1965-68. Tech. writer Honeywell Inc., 1979-84; hydromech. reliability engr. Advanced Systems div. Northrop Corp., Pico Rivera, Calif., 1984-86; sr. engr. quality and reliability Swedlow, Inc., Garden Grove, Calif., 1986—; cons. Lockman Found. Performer Wiltern Theater, Los Angeles, 1966-68, Busch-Reisinger Mus., Harvard U., Cambridge, Mass., 1972, 73, 74; composer over 35 piano compositions. Asst. to pastors local Baptist Chs. in Tex., Ga., Wis., Minn. and Calif.; pastor Victory Baptist Ch., Pine City, Minn., 1982-83, Lexington Ave. Bible Baptist Ch., Shoreview, Minn., 1983-84. Named one of Outstanding Young Men in Am., U.S. Jaycees, 1980. Mem. Soc. Logistics Engring., Minn. Composer's Forum, Am. Symphony Orch. League, Fundamental Baptist Fellowship Am., Dean Burgon Soc., Bible-Sci. Assn. Republican. Home: 26920 Peach St Meadowbrook CA 92370 Office: Swedlow Inc 12122 Western Ave Garden Grove CA 92641

KUCKERTZ, THOMAS HARRY, electrical engineer, researcher; b. Chgo., May 27, 1945; s. Thomas Harold and Rita (Maurus) K.; m. Suzanne Judith Meegan, July 5, 1969; children: Patrick, Carolyn. BSEE, U. Ill., 1968; MSEE, U. Idaho, 1969, PhD, 1974. Registered profl. engr., N.Mex., Ill. Engr. Westinghouse Airbrake Co., Chgo., 1967, Ill. Bell Telephone Co., Chgo., 1969; group leader Los Alamos (N.Mex.) Nat. Lab., 1974—; adj. prof. U. N.Mex., Los Alamos, 1978—. Contbr. articles to profl. jours. Served to 1st lt., U.S. Army, 1969-71. Mem. IEEE (sr.), Assn. Computing Machinery, Sigma Xi. Avocation: skiing. Office: Los Alamos Nat Lab Box 1663 Los Alamos NM 87545

KUDENOV, JERRY DAVID, zoology educator; b. Lynwood, Calif., Dec. 19, 1946; s. William and Marion Kudenov; m. Kathryn Anne Brown, May 30, 1969; children: Peter Alexander, Michael William. BA, U. Calif., San Diego, 1968; MS, U. Pacific, 1970; PhD, U. Ariz., 1974. Research scientist Ministry for Conservation, Melbourne, Australia, 1974-79; asst. prof. zoology U. Alaska, Anchorage, 1980-82, assoc. prof., 1982—; vis. asst. prof. U. So. Calif., Los Angeles, 1979-80. Mem. AAAS, Am. Soc. Zoologists, Sci. Research Soc. N. Am., So. Calif. Acad. Scis. (bd. dirs. 1980). Avocation: fishing. Home: 3930 Alitak Bay Circle Anchorage AK 99515 Office: U Alaska Dept Biol Scis 3211 Providence Dr Anchorage AK 99508

KUDO, EMIKO IWASHITA, former county official Hawaii; b. Kona, Hawaii, June 5, 1923; s. Tetsuzo and Kuma (Koga) Iwashita; B.S., U. Hawaii, 1944; M.S. in Vocational Edn., Pa. State U., 1950; postgrad. U. Hawaii, U. Ore., others; m. Thomas Mitsugi Kudo, Aug. 21, 1951; children—Guy J.T., Scott K., Candace F. Tchr. jr. and sr. high sch., Hawaii, 1945-51; instr. home econs. edn. U. Hawaii Tchrs. Coll., Honolulu, 1948-51, Pa. State U., State College, 1949-50; with Hawaii Dept. Edn., Honolulu, 1951-82, supr. sch. lunch service, 1951-64, home econ. edn., 1951-64, dir. home econ. edn., 1964-68, adminstr. vocat.-tech. edn., 1968-76, asst. supt. instructional services, 1976-78, dep. supt. State Dept. Edn., 1978-82; cons. Am. Samoa vocat. edn. state plan devel., 1970-71, vocat. edn. U. Hawaii, 1986, internat. secondary program devel. Ashiya Ednl. System, Japan, 1986; state coordinator industry-labor-edn., 1972-76; mem. nat. task force edn. and tng. for minority bus. enterprise, 1972-73; steering com. Career Info. Ctr. Project, 1973-78; co-dir. Hawaii Career Devel. Continuum project, 1971-74; mem. Nat Accreditation and Instl. Eligibility Adv. Council, 1974-77, cons., 1977-78; mem. panel Internat. Conf. Vocat. Guidance, 1978, 80, 82, 86; dir. Dept. Parks and Recreation, City and County of Honolulu, 1982-84. Exec. bd. Aloha council Boy Scouts Am., 1978—. Japan Found. Cultural grantee, 1977; Pa. State U. Alumni fellow, 1982. Mem. Western Assn. Schs. and Colls. (accreditation team mem. Ch. Coll. of Hawaii 1972-73), Am. Vocat. Assn., Hawaii Practical Arts and Vocat. Assn., NEA, Hawaii Edn. Assn., Hawaii State Ednl. Officers Assn., Am., Hawaii home econ. assn., Nat., Hawaii assns. for supervision and curriculum devel., Am. Tech. Edn. Assn., 1 Omicron Nu, Pi Lambda Theta, Phi Delta Kappa, Delta Kappa Gamma. Author handbooks and pamphlets in field. Home and Office: 217 Nenue St Honolulu HI 96821

KUEHL, LEROY ROBERT, educator, biochemist; b. Ketchikan, Alaska, Aug. 15, 1931; s. Eric O. and Marie Anne (Rowald) K.; m. Barbara Rose Eschmann, Mar. 21, 1959; children: Eric, Laurel, Brian. BS, Iowa State U., 1953; MS, Oreg. State U., 1955; PhD, U. Calif., Berkeley, 1961. Instr. biochemistry U. Utah, Salt Lake City, 1965-67, asst. prof. biochemistry, 1967-71, assoc. prof. biochemistry, 1971-80, prof. biochemistry, 1980—. Served with U.S. Army, 1955-57. Fulbright fellow, 1986—. Mem. AAAS, Am. Chem. Soc. (lectr. 1983—), Am. Soc. Biol. Chemists. Home: 1934 Michigan Ave Salt Lake City UT 84108 Office: U Utah Dept Biochem 410 Chipeta Way Salt Lake City UT 84108

KUEHN, GLENN DEAN, biochemistry educator researcher; b. Terry, Mont., Apr. 13, 1942; s. Gust and Freida Georgia (Scheid) K.; m. Donna Faye Reuther, June 12, 1965; children: Tara Lynn. BA in Math. and Chemistry, Concordia Coll., 1964; PhD in Biochemistry, Wash. State U., 1968. Postdoctoral fellow NIH UCLA, 1968-70; asst. prof. chemistry N.Mex. State U., Las Cruces, 1970-75, assoc. prof. chemistry, 1975-80, MBRS program dir., 1976—, prof. chemistry, 1980—. Contbr. articles to profl. jours. Grantee NIH, 1970-86, NSF, 1973-80, Am. Cancer Soc., 1970-76, 81-83, USDA, 1986-87; Roche Found. fellow, 1978. Mem. AAAS, Am. Soc. Biol. Chemists, Am. Chem. Soc., Sigma Xi, Alpha Xi Sigma. Lutheran. Home: 2032 Crescent Dr Las Cruces NM 88005 Office: NMex State U Box 3C Chemistry Dept Las Cruces NM 88003

KUEHN, JUDSON SPORRY, electrical engineer; b. Appleton, Wis., Jan. 19, 1957; m. Dianne Grimes, Apr. 30, 1983. BSEE, U. Colo., 1979. Data communications engr. Standard Oil Co. Calif., San Francisco, 1979-82; electrical engr. Chevron Corp., San Ramon, Calif., 1982—; mem. editorial adv. bd. Subnotes Mag., Spring Valley, Calif. 1986. Patentee in field. Mem. IEEE. Office: Chevron Corp PO Box 5045 San Ramon CA 94583

KUEHN, KLAUS KARL ALBERT, physician, ophthalmologist; b. Breslau, Germany, Apr. 1, 1938; came to U.S., 1956, naturalized, 1971; s. Max and Anneliese (Hecht) K.; m. Eileen L. Nordgaard, June 22, 1961 (div. 1972); children—Stephen Eric, Kristina Annette; m. Lynda O. Hubbs, Oct. 2, 1974. Student, St. Olaf Coll., 1956-57; B.A., B.S., U. Minn., 1961; M.D., 1963. Diplomate Am. Bd. Ophthalmology. Resident in ophthalmology UCLA Affiliated Hosps., 1968-71; practice medicine specializing in ophthalmology, San Bernardino, Calif., 1971—; chief ophthalmology dept. San Bernardino County Med. Ctr., 1979-80; assoc. clin. prof. ophthalmology Jules Stein Eye Inst. and UCLA Med. Ctr., 1978-81. Served to capt. U.S. Army, 1963-64. Fellow Am. Acad. Ophthalmology; mem. AMA, Calif. Med. Assn., Calif. Assn. Ophthalmology (bd. dirs.). Office: 1920 N Waterman Ave San Bernardino CA 92404

KUEHN, RICHARD LEE, obstetrician gynecologist; b. Cherokee, Iowa, Jan. 29, 1949; s. Carroll Howard and Irene Mary (Oswald) K. BA, U. Iowa, 1971, MD, 1975. Diplomate Am. Bd. Ob-Gyn. Resident ob-gyn Valley Med. Ctr., Fresno, Calif., 1975-79; staff physician Kaiser Permanente, South San Francisco, Calif., 1979-82; staff physician Kaiser Permanente, Hayward, Calif., 1982-86, asst. chief dept. ob-gyn, 1983—. Mem. Bay Area Physicians for Human Rights, San Francisco, 1980—. Mem. Am. Coll. Ob-Gyn, Consumers Union, Greenpeace USA. Democrat. Avocations: cross country skiing, videotaping, stamp collecting. Home: 2701 Sequoia Way Belmont CA 94002-1451 Office: Kaiser-Permanente 27400 Hesperian Blvd Hayward CA 94545

KUGELMASS, JOEL NATHANIEL, telecommunications consultant; b. N.Y.C., Oct. 11, 1946; s. J. Alvin and Elizabeth A. (Ambramchik) K.; m. Lois Johnson, June 21, 1972; one child, Joseph. BA, Stanford U., 1967; MA, Brandeis U., 1971. Asst. program mgr. Mass. Dept. Pub. Health, Boston, 1974-76; exec. dir. Pacifica Found., Los Angeles, 1977-80, Calif. Pub. Broadcasting Commn., 1980-84; telecommunications cons. Mendocino, Calif., 1984—. Contbr. articles to profl. jours. and newspapers. Office: PO Box 914 Mendocino CA 95460

KUH, DAVID MICHAEL, banker; b. Los Angeles, May 16, 1944; s. Michael Edward and Eileen Claire (Egerer) K.; children—Anne Marie, Tina Eileen. B.B.A., U. Hawaii-Manoa, 1967. With Central Pacific Bank, Honolulu, 1969—, asst. br. mgr., 1971-78, asst. v.p. mktg. dept., 1979-86; v.p. CPB Properties, Inc., 1987—. Pres., Ewa Estates Community Assn., 1971-72; treas. Central/Leeward unit Am. Cancer Soc., 1982-83; mem. dept. edn. Speakers Bur., 1978-86; asst. v.p. CPB Properties, 1986—; mgr. Cen. Bus. Club Honolulu, 1987—. Served with USNR, 1962-69. Named Citizen of Day, Sta. KGU, July 7, 1973. Mem. Ewa Beach Jaycees (pres. 1977-78; Gold Key award 1974-77), Honolulu Jaycees (v.p. 1974-75; Silver and Bronze Key awards 1974-77), Honolulu Press Club, C. of C. Hawaii, Honolulu Advt. Fedn. (treas.), Am. Inst. Banking, Hawaii Bankers Assn. (pub. relations and edn. com.), Moiliili Bus. and Profl. Assn. (dir. 1973-79), U. Hawaii Alumni (life), Alpha Phi Omega (life). Lodge: Elks (orgnl. com.). Office: Central Pacific Plaza 220 S King St Suite 2200 Honolulu HI 96813

KUHAR, MARTIN JOSEPH, medical equipment manufacturing company executive; b. South Bend, Ind., Mar. 8, 1946; s. Joseph S. and Gladys Kuhar; m. Darlene M. Stachowski, Nov. 7, 1970 (div. Oct. 1977). BBA in Acctg., St. Edward's U., Austin, Tex., 1968; MSBA, Ind. U., Ft. Wayne, 1976. Budget dir. Zimmer Inc., Warsaw, Ind., 1973-74, fin. reporting dir., 1974-76, plant acctg. dir., 1976-77; controller Aspen Labs. Inc., Englewood, Colo., 1977-80, v.p. fin., adminstrn., 1980—. Served with U.S. Army, 1968-70. Republican. Roman Catholic. Avocations: skiing, tennis, golf. Home: 7488 E Windlawn Way Parker CO 80134

KUHL, ANNA FAYE, educator, forensic consultant; b. Seattle, Sept. 1, 1941; d. John and Marie Anna (Phillips) Belcher; m. Albert F. Lyle, Jr., Dec. 9, 1960 (div. 1964); children: Robert David, Donna Marie, John Michael; m. Wesley Clarence Kuhl, June 10, 1977. BA in Psychology, Ft. Wright Coll., 1977, MA in Psychology, 1978; PhD in Psychology, Wash. State U., 1981. Therapist Spokane Mental Health Ctr., Wash., 1968-71, 77-80; dir. Domestic Violence Research Bank, Wash. State U., Pullman, 1979-81; lectr. depts. sociology and edn., 1979-81; assoc. prof., chmn. adminstrn. justice San Jose State U., Calif., 1981—; owner Anna F. Kuhl & Assocs., San Jose, 1981—; bd. dirs. Mid.-Peninsula Support Network, San Jose, 1981-84; bd. commrs. Delinquency Prevention Commn., San Jose, 1981-84; bd. dirs. Juvenile justice Commn., 1986—; chmn., bd. dirs. Women and their Children Housing, 1986—. Co-author: Research Methods, Damned If She Does; contbr. articles to profl. jours. Mem. NOW, 1977—, W.A.T.C.H. (bd. dirs. 1986—), Nat. Coalition Against Domestic Violence, 1977—. Mem. Am. Soc. Criminology (sect. Women's div. 1982-84), Am. Psychol. Assn., Inst. Criminal Justice Ethics, Soc. for Study of Social Problems, Law and Soc. Assn., Phi Kappa Phi, Phi Delta Kappa. Democrat. Mem. Unity Ch. Office: San Jose State U Adminstrn of Justice Dept One Washington Sq San Jose CA 95192

KUHL, PATRICIA K., science educator; b. Mitchell, S.D., Nov. 5, 1946; d. Joseph John and Susan Mary (Schaeffer) K.; m. Andrew N. Meltzoff. BA, St. Cloud (Minn.) State U., 1967; MA, U. Minn., 1971, PhD, 1973. Postdoctoral research assoc. Cen. Inst. for Deaf, St. Louis, 1973-76; research assoc. U. Wash., Seattle, 1976-77, asst. prof., 1977-79, assoc. prof., 1979-82, prof. speech, language, hearing, 1982—. Recipient Women in Research citation Kennedy Council, 1978. Mem. NRC (com. on hearing, 1977—), Nat. Inst. Child Health and Human Devel. (ten-year planning com. 1978—), Acoustical Soc. (speech communication tech. com. 1980—). Office: U Wash CDMRC WJ-10 Seattle WA 98195

KUHL, PAUL BEACH, lawyer; b. Elizabeth, N.J., July 15, 1935; s. Paul Edmund and Charlotte (Hetche) K.; m. Janey Mae Stadheim, June 24, 1967; children: Alison Lyn, Todd Beach. BA, Cornell U., 1957; LLB, Stanford U., 1960. Atty. Law Offices of Walter C. Kohn, San Francisco, 1961-63, Sedgwick, Detert, Moran & Arnold, San Francisco, 1963—. Served to lt. USCG, 1961. Mem. Am. Bd. Trial Advisors, ABA, Def. Research Inst., No. Calif. Assn. Def., Tahoe Tavern Property Owners Assn. (sec. 1979-81, pres. 1981-83).), San Francisco Trial Lawyers Assn., Am. Arbitration Assn. (mem. arbitration panel). Club: Canon Tennis (Fairfax, Calif.). Avocations: tennis, reading. Home: PO Box 574 Ross CA 94957 Office: Sedgwick Detert Moran & Arnold One Embarcadero Ctr 16th Floor San Francisco CA 94111-3765

KUHLMAN, JOSIE-LEE, social work administrator; b. Malakoff, Tex., Aug. 23, 1917; d. Marvin Ernest and Dora Elizabeth (Andress) Humphrey; m. Harold Herman Kuhlman, Aug. 8, 1938; 1 child, Janice Elizabeth. AB, U. Redlands, 1943; MA, Am. Bapt. Sem., 1944, postgrad., 1977-79; postgrad., Hartford Sem., 1945-46; MSW, U. Denver, 1958; postgrad., NYU, 1961-65. Cert. profl. fund raiser, cert. community coll. instr. (life), Calif.; ordained to ministry Bapt. Ch. Missionary Am. Bapt. Ch., Roxas City, Philippines, 1946-51; exec. dir. Girl Scouts U.S., Benton Harbor, Mich., 1958-61; dir. orgn. commn. Office Mayor of N.Y.C., 1961-65; exec. dir. Camp Fire Girls, San Francisco, 1967-72; program mgr. Childrens Home Soc., Sacramento, 1979-85; exec. dir. Chrysalis Ho., Fresno, Calif., 1985—. Co-chmn. Mayors Status of Women com., San Francisco, 1969-73, forum coordinator, 1973; candidate for mayor City of San Francisco, 1975; mem. mayors community devel. com., San Francisco, 1975-79. Recipient Women Helping Women award Soroptimists, San Francisco, 1979. Mem. Am. Bapt. Ministers Council, Calif. Assn. Adoption Agys. (chmn. no. sect. 1984-86, pres. 1986—), Pvt. Adoption Agy. Coalition, Reach, State and Nat. Rehab. Assn. (pres. 1977-78), Caledonians Clan Donald Scottish. Republicans. Lodges: Zonta (pres. San Francisco chpt. 1972-73, area dir. 1973-74, v.p. Fresno chpt. 1986—). Avocation: fgn. travel. Home and Office: Chrysalis House Inc 2134 W Alluvial Fresno CA 93711

KUHN, FRANKLIN HOWARD, advertising agency executive; b. Escondido, Calif., Nov. 28, 1947; s. Franklin Kinset and Margaret Ellen (Johnson) K.; AA, No. Va. Community Coll., 1975; BFA, La Salle Inst., 1971. Pres. founder Studio 3 & Assocs., Escondido, Calif., 1980—; founder Franklin Group/West Advt. Agy., Escondido, 1986—. Served to sgt. U.S. Army, 1967-73. Republican. Lutheran. Designed typeface used in major polit. campaign, 1968; author major funding proposal for U.S. Olympic Amateur Cycling Team. Office: Franklin Group/West Advt Agy 362 W Misson Ave Suite 200 Escondido CA 92025

KUHN, IRVIN NELSON, hematologist, oncologist; b. Winnipeg, Man., Can., Aug. 8, 1928; m. Doreen Mary L. Elvedahl, July 3, 1956; children: Jill A., Erin R., Jay N. BA, Loma Linda U., Riverside, Calif., 1950, MD, 1955. Diplomate Nat. Bd. Med. Examiners, Am. Bd. Internal Medicine; cert. Thai Med. Bd., Clin. Hematology, Med. Oncology; lic. physician, Calif. Rotating intern then resident gen. internal medicine White Meml. Med. Ctr., Los Angeles, 1955-59; resident gen. pathology U. B.C. at Vancouver Gen. Hosp., 1959-60; instr. medicine Loma Linda (Calif.) U., 1961-65, asst. prof., 1965-72, assoc. prof., 1972-78, prof., 1978—, cons. in clin. hematology and oncology, 1966—, dir. Adult Hemophilia Treatment Ctr., 1974-85; chief med. service Jerry L. Pettis Meml. VA Hosp., Loma Linda, 1977-80, assoc. chief staff of edn., 1980—, active staff, 1977—; independent investigator Nat. Cancer Inst. Leukemia and Chemotherapy, 1970-85; assoc. investigator Western Cancer Study Group, subcom. Lymphoma and Leukemia, 1972-76; mem. Loma Linda Med. Oncology research team Coop. Group Outreach program/Puget Sound Oncology Consortium of Southwest Oncology Group, 1985—; com. grad. med. edn. Loma Linda U. Sch. Medicine, 1980—, health adv. com. 1980-83, chmn. research funding adv. com. 1982-86, acad. com. 1977—, resident tng. com. 1979—, adv. com. Med. Record adminstrn. 1976-78, quality assurance com. 1972-76, transfusion com. 1972-80, risk mgmt. com. 1973-75; mem. clin. exec. council Jerry L. Pettis Meml. VA Hosp, 1979—, radiosotope and nuclear medicine com. 1977—, clin. exec. bd. 1977—, pharmacy and therapeutics com. 1977-80, research devel. com. 1977-84, dean's com. 1980—, chmn. hosp. edn. com. 1980—, chmn. travel and tuition funds con. 1980-84, joint conf. council, 1982-85, chmn. Case Mix Mgmt. steering com. 1984—; presenter numerous symposia, seminars and confs. to various agys., schs. and health orgns., 1970—; cons. in field. Contbr. articles to profl. jours. Fellow Blood Coagulation Research Lab. Churchill Hosp., Oxford, Eng., 1964, Laboratorie d' Hemostase, St. Louis Hosp., Paris, 1964; clin. and research fellow U. Wash., Seattle, 1965-66. Fellow ACP (gov.'s adv. com. 1980—), Royal Coll. Physicians and Surgeons of Can.; mem. AAAS, Walter E. MacPherson Soc. (charter), AMA, Calif. Med. Assn. (legis. com. 1983—, dist. II del. 1983—, alt. del. 1974-83, comprehensive health planning commn. 1974-76), San Bernardino County Med. Assn., Loma Linda U. Sch. Medicine Alumni Assn. (life, med. evangelism council 1975-76, conv. governing bd. dirs. 1983—), Am. Soc. Internal Medicine, Calif. Soc. Internal Medicine, Inland Soc. Internal Medicine, Am. Soc. Hematology, N.Y. Acad. Scis., Am. Soc. Clin. Oncology, Los Angeles Acad. Medicine, Nat. Assn. VA Physicians, San Bernardino County Med. Soc. (numerous offices and com. memberships found. med. care 1970—), Loma Linda Physicians Med. Group, Inc. (bd. dirs. 1969-73), Sigma Xi (life), Alpha Omega Alpha. Home: 36333 Panorama Dr Yucaipa CA 92399 Office: Loma Linda U Med Ctr Room 1531 Loma Linda CA 92354 Office: Jerry L Pettis Meml VA Hosp Office Assoc Chief Staff Edn 11201 Benton St Loma Linda CA 92357

KUHN, PETER MOUAT, atmospheric physicist; b. Janesville, Wis., Feb. 2, 1920; s. Peter V. and Marjorie F. (Mouat) K.; m. Beth Ione Larson, Nov. 21, 1941; 1 child, Lori Lee Kuhn Arnold. BS, U. Wis., 1951, MS, 1952, PhD, 1962. Sr. research meteorologist NOAA, Boulder, Colo., 1952-80; sr. research scientist Northrop Services Inc., Boulder, 1981—; cons. in field, 1984—. Contbr. numerous articles on atmospheric physics to profl. jours.; patentee in field. Served to 2d lt. U.S. Army 1942-46, maj. USAFR ret. Recipient Disting. Authorship award NOAA, 1979, Inventors award U.S. Dept. Commerce, 1983. Fellow Optical Soc. Am., Explorers Club; mem. AIAA, Phi Beta Kappa, Sigma Xi. Republican. Roman Catholic. Avocations: mountaineering, boating, celestial mechanics. Home and Office: 315 Bellevue Dr Boulder CO 80302

KUHN, WAYNE EDWARD, retired oil company executive; b. Oct. 25, 1903; married; 1 son. BA, Reed Coll., 1925; PhD, Cornell U., 1929; AMP, Harvard U., 1956. Chemist Texaco Inc., Bayonne, N.J., 1929; chem. engr. Texaco Inc., Port Arthur, Tex., 1929-32, dept. head, 1932-35, asst. chief research and devel., 1935-37; asst. to tech. div. Texaco Inc., N.Y.C., 1937-38, asst. mgr. research and tech., 1938-39, mgr. research and tech., 1939-54, gen. mgr. dept., 1954-65; bd. dirs. Omark Industries, Inc., Kentrox, Inc., Northwest Research and Devel., ATL Inc., Tex. Devel. Corp. Fellow AIAA, Soc. Automotive Engrs., Am. Inst. Chemists (Honor Scroll, Gold Medal), Am. Inst. Chem. Engrs., Am. Comml. Devel. Assn. (Nat. Honor award), Am. Inst. Chem Engrs., Am. Petroleum Inst. (2 awards). Home and Office: 1840 W Ramsey Dr Portland OR 97229

KUHNER, DAVID ARNOLD, librarian, archivist; b. Columbus, Ohio, Mar. 20, 1921; s. Walter James and Effie Leota (Ranck) K. B.Sc., Ohio State U., 1943; M.Ed., U. Miami, 1951; M.L.S., U. Calif.-Berkeley, 1962. Feature writer Fla. State News Bur., Tallahassee, 1955-61; librarian Stanford U., Calif., 1962-66, John Crerar Library, Chgo., 1966-69; asst. dir. libraries Claremont Colls., Calif., 1970-85, cons. 1985—. Co-editor: Bibliotheca De Re Metallica, 1980. Editor Map of Fla. Industry and Sci., 1961. Contbr. articles to profl. jours. and newspapers. Served to lt. USAF, 1943-46. Mem. ALA (book reviewer 1966-73), Bibliog. Soc. Am., Soc. Am. Archivists. Club: Westerners (Los Angeles). Home: 152 E La Verne Ave Pomona CA 91767 Office: Honnold Library Claremont Colls Claremont CA 91711

KUKLIN, JEFFREY PETER, lawyer, talent agency executive; b. N.Y.C., Dec. 13, 1935; s. Norman Bennett and Deane (Cable) K.; m. Jensina Olson, Nov. 18, 1960; 1 son, Andrew Bennett; m. 2d, Ronia Levene, June 22, 1969; children—Adam Blake, Jensena Lynne, Jeremy Brett. A.B., Columbia U., 1957, J.D., 1960. Bar: N.Y. 1962, U.S. Supreme Ct. 1965, Calif. 1973. Atty., TV sales adminstrn. NBC-TV, N.Y.C., 1966-67; asst. to dir. bus. affairs CBS News, N.Y.C., 1967-69; atty., assoc. dir. contracts ABC-TV, N.Y.C. and Los Angeles, 1969-73; v.p. bus. affairs and law Tomorrow Entertainment, Inc., Los Angeles, 1973-75; v.p. legal and bus. affairs Billy Jack Enterprises, Inc., Los Angeles, 1975-76; atty., bus. affairs exec. William Morris Agy., Inc., Beverly Hills, Calif., 1976-79, head TV bus. affairs, 1979-81, v.p., head TV bus. affairs, 1981—. Mem. ABA, Acad. TV Arts and Scis., Los Angeles Copyright Soc. Address: 151 El Camino Dr Beverly Hills CA 90212

KULACKI, FRANCIS ALFRED, engineering educator; b. Balt., May 21, 1942; s. Frank Alfred and Ida (Jarowski) K.; m. Jane H. Davidson, Nov. 29, 1985; children: Sarah, Nancy. BSME, Ill. Inst. Tech., 1963, MS in Gas Engring., 1966; PhD, U. Minn., 1971. From asst. prof. to assoc. prof. mech. engring. Ohio State U., Columbus, 1971-79; prof., chmn. dept. mech. and aerospace engring. U. Del., Newark, 1980-85; dean engring. Colo. State U., Ft. Collins, 1986—; cons. in field. Contbr. numerous articles to profl. jours. V.p. Columbus Tech. Council, 1979; pres. Arbour Park Civic Assn., Newark, 1985. Mem. ASME (exec. com. heat transfer div., pres. Columbus sect. 1978), Am. Assn. Higher Edn., Am. Soc. Engring. Edn., Internat. Assn. Advancement Hydrogen Energy, Sigma Xi, Phi Kappa Sigma, Tau Beta Pi, Pi Tau Sigma. Lodge: Rotary Internat. Home: 1612 Linden Lake Rd Fort Collins CO 80524 Office: Colo State U Coll Engring Fort Collins CO 80523

KULBIN, VELLO, publisher, writer; b. Valga, Karula, Estonia, May 8, 1937; came to U.S., 1949, naturalized, 1956; s. Jaan and Emilie (Sona) K.; m. Juta Meius, 1967; children: Kalev Mark, Lembit Jaan. Student U. Ill., 1956-59, Ambassador Coll., 1969-70, Valley Coll., 1976—. Pres. Western Mktg. Assn., Pasadena, Calif., 1972-78, Penny Stocks Newsletter, Redlands, Calif., 1978—; pub. Vello Kulbin's Investments Newsletter, 1981—, Vello Kulbin's Commentary, 1984—. Author: Your Resume and Job Campaign, 1973. Mem. Alpha Delta Phi. Mem. Worldwide Ch. of God. Club: Spokesman (past pres.) (Yucaipa, Calif.). Office: Penny Stocks Newsletter 31731 Outer Hwy 10 Redlands CA 92373

KULKOSKY, PAUL JOSEPH, psychology educator, researcher; b. Newark, N.J., Mar. 3, 1949; s. Peter Francis and Rose Mary (Leonetti) K.; m. Tanya Marie Weightman, Sept. 16, 1978. BA, Columbia U., N.Y.C., 1971, MA, 1972; PhC, U. Wash., 1974, PhD, 1975. Research assoc. Cornell U., White Plains, N.Y., 1980-81, instr. psychiatry, 1981-82; asst. prof. psychology U. So. Colo., Pueblo, 1982-86, assoc. prof., 1986—; bd. dirs. Pueblo Zool. Soc. Contbr. chpts. to books, articles to profl. jours.; referee psychol. jours. Named Hon. Affiliate Prof. Am. U., Washington, 1977-80; research grantee NIH, 1984—; staff fellow Nat. Inst. Alcohol Abuse and Alcoholism, 1976-80. Mem. AAAS, N.Y. Acad. Scis., Internat. Soc. Biomed. Research on Alcoholism (charter), Psychonomic Soc., Soc. Study Ingestive Behavior (charter), U. So. Colo. Club Sigma Xi (treas. 1986—, Outstanding Faculty Research award 1985-87). Home: 417 Tyler St Pueblo CO 81004 Office: U So Colo 2200 N Bonforte Blvd Pueblo CO 81001-4901

KULLAS, MICHAEL GLADUE, pharmacist; b. Balt., July 5, 1943; s. Albert John and Joyce (Gladue) K.; m. Barbara Kay, May 17, 1969. Student, Worcester Poly. Tech., 1961-62, U. Colo., 1962-64; BS in Pharmacy, U. N.Mex., 1972. Registered pharmacist, Colo., N.Mex. Pharmacist Windsor Gardens Drug, Denver, 1972-73, Presbyn. Denver Hosp., 1973-76; dir. pharmacy Presbyn. Aurora (Colo.) Hosp., 1976-86; pharmacist Swedish Med. Ctr., Englewood, Colo., 1986—; mem. faculty U. Colo. Coll. Pharmacy, Denver, 1980—; mem. adv. bd. Home Med. Support Services, Denver, 1983-86, Caremark, Denver, 1983-85; preceptor Bd. Pharmacy of Colo., 1975—. Served with U.S. Army, 1968-70, Korea. Mem. Colo. Pharmacal Assn. (exec. com. 1986—), Colo. Soc. Hosp. Pharacists (bd. dirs., treas. 1981-83), Denver Area Pharmacy Assn., N.Mex. Pharm. Assn., Am. Soc. Hosp. Pharmacists. Clubs: Petroleum (Denver); Heather Ridge Country (Aurora). Avocations: jogging, photography, stained glass fabrication. Home: 2596 S Eagle Circle Aurora CO 80014-2428 Office: Swedish Med Ctr 501 E Hampden Ave Dept 7311 Englewood CO 80110-2796

KULSTAD, GUY CHARLES, public works official; b. Bend, Oreg., Feb. 28, 1930; s. John Marlyn and Annie Mildred (Boyd) Kulstad Ibison; B.S. in Civil Engring., U. Calif.-Berkeley, 1958; Registered profl. engr., Calif., Oreg., Wash.; registered traffic engr., Calif.; registered land surveyor, Oreg.; cert. community coll. instr., Calif. m. Bonnie Jane Sherman, Aug. 28, 1955; children—Anne Marie Kulstad Hurst, Mark, Alice Kulstad Krause. Engring. aide county rd. dept., Los Angeles, 1951, asst. civil engr., 1953-58; dir. pub. works, Benicia, Calif., 1958-59; dep. dir. pub. works, Solano County, Calif., 1959-65; dir. pub. works, Humboldt County, Calif., 1965—; gen. mgr. gen. Humboldt Bay Wastewater Authority 1975, 82—. Mem. joint liaison com.

Mcpl. Pub. Works Officers and Calif. Council of Civil Engrs. and Land Surveyors. Served with AUS, 1951-53. Recipient Outstanding Service award North Bay chpt. Calif. Soc. Profl. Engrs., 1964, Boss of the Year award Arcata Jaycees, Recognition award Humboldt Toastmasters. Fellow ASCE; mem. Nat. Soc. County Engrs. (joint liaison com.), Nat. Soc. Profl. Engrs., Am. Congress Surveying and Mapping, Am. Mgmt. Assn., Calif. Land Surveyors Assn. (surveyor award Humbolt chpt.), Calif. County Engrs. Assn. (chmn.). Clubs: Commonwealth of Calif., Sons of Norway, Toastmasters Internat. Author profl. dissertations. Office: 1106 2d St Eureka CA 95501

KUMAR, ARUN, metallurgist; b. Jaunpur, India, Feb. 12, 1948; came to U.S., 1969.; s. Kripa Shankar and Malti (Srivastava) Lal; m. Shalini Kumar, Sept. 3, 1976; children: Anjuli, Sumita. BS, U. Lucknow, India, 1965; B in Engring., U. Roorkee, India, 1969; MS, UCLA, 1971, PhD, 1974. Mem. tech. staff Rockwell Internat., El Segundo, Calif., 1976-78; group head failure analysis Hughes Aircraft Co., Culver City, Calif., 1978-80; mgr. metallurgy and materials sci. Scanning Electron Analysis Labs., Inc., Los Angeles, 1980—. Editor: Fracture and Failure, 1981; patentee in field. Mem. Am. Soc. Metals (sec. 1970—), AIME (metall. soc.), Internat. Soc. Testing and Failure Analysis, Internat. Soc. Hybrid Microelectronics. Republican. Hindu. Avocations: travel, photography, reading. Office: Scanning Electron Analysis Labs 5301 Beethoven St Los Angeles CA 90066

KUMAR, RAJESH NARAYAN, pediatrician; b. Dehra Dun, India, Feb. 2, 1950; came to U.S.; 1975; s. Brijlal and Subhadra (Gurwara) K.; m. Vinita Nath, June 24, 1979; children: Aditya, Abhishek. MBBS, Armed Forces Med. Coll., Poona, India, 1973. Diplomate Am. Bd. Pediatrics. Intern No. Railway Cen. Hosp., New Delhi, India, 1974, Ellis Hosp., Schenectady, N.Y., 1975-76; resident in pediatrics Luth. Gen. Hosp., Park Ridge, Ill., 1976-78; attending physician Guadalupe Med. Ctr., Carlsbad, N.Mex., 1978—; pres. Kumar, Dara MD, FAAP, PA, Carlsbad, 1978—. Fellow: Am. Acad. Pediatrics. Republican. Hindu. Avocations: traveling, stamps. Home: 1607 Live Oak Pl Carlsbad NM 88220 Office: 2402 W Pierce #6G Carlsbad NM 88220

KUMMER, GLENN F., mobile home company executive; b. Park City, Utah, 1933; married. B.S., U. Utah, 1961. Sr. acct. Ernst & Ernst, 1961-65; trainee Fleetwood Enterprises Inc., Riverside, Calif., 1965-67, purchasing mgr., 1967-68, plant mgr., 1968-70, gen. mgr. recreational vehicle div., 1970-71, asst. v.p. ops. to v.p. ops., 1971-72, sr. v.p. ops., 1972-77, exec. v.p. ops., 1977-82, pres., chief exec. officer, 1982—, dir. Office: Fleetwood Enterprises Inc 3125 Myers St Box 7638 Riverside CA 92523

KUMPFER, KAROL LINDA, research psychologist; b. Neptune, N.J., July 30, 1943; d. Beverly Donald and Mary Belle (Campbell) K.; m. Henry Overton Whiteside, Mar. 6, 1978; 1 child, Jane H. BA, Colo. Women's Coll., 1966; MA, U. Utah, 1970, PhD, 1972; postdoctoral, U. Minn., 1975. Lic. psychologist, Utah. Asst. prof. psychology Oberlin (Ohio) Coll., 1971-73; research assoc. Inst. Child Devel. U. Minn., Mpls., 1975-76; asst. prof. Colo. Women's Coll., Denver, 1976-78; psychologist Salt Lake County Mental Health Dept., 1979-80; dep. dir. State Div. Alcoholism and Drugs, Salt Lake City, 1980-84; vis. assoc. prof. Grad. Sch. Social Work U. Utah, Salt Lake City, 1984—. Editor/author: Childhood and Chemical Abuse: Prevention and Intervention, 1986, Social Facts: Utah in Perspective, 1986. Bd. dirs. Repetory Dance Theatre, Salt Lake City, 1983—, Western Assn. Concerned Adoptive Parents, Salt Lake City, 1985—, Utah Alliance for Mentally Ill, Salt Lake City, 1979-80; pres. U. Utah. Faculty Women's Club, 1974-75. Grantee Utah Dept. Social Services, Salt Lake City, 1984—. Mem. Utah Psychologists in Pvt. Practice Assn. (pres. 1985—), Am. Psychol. Assn., Am. Pub. Health Assn., AAAS, Nat. Council Social Work Edn., Utah Psychol. Assn. (bd. dirs. 1985—), Am. Acad. Child Psychiatry (spl. task force 1986—), Nat. Inst. Drug Abuse (spl. task force 1985—, grantee 1982-86), Nat. Inst. Alcoholism and Alcohol Abuse (spl. task force 1985—, grantee 1980), Council on Social Work Edn., Evaluation Research Soc., Utah Mental Health Assn., Sigma Xi. Democrat. Unitarian. Avocations: skiing, sailing, travelling. Office: Social Research Inst Grad Sch Social Work Salt Lake City UT 84112

KUNIN, RICHARD ALLEN, physician, psychiatrist; b. Mpls., Oct. 22, 1932; s. Maxim and Jeannette (Simons) K.; m. Matilda Lucretia Manning, Feb. 16, 1961; 1 child, Gregory M. BS, U. Minn., 1953, MD, 1955. Diplomate Am. Bd. Neurology and Psychiatry. Asst. resident in psychiatry N.Y. Hosp., N.Y.C., 1956-59; staff psychiatrist VA Hosp., Mpls., 1961-62; postdoctoral fellow Stanford U., Palo Alto, Calif., 1962-63; practice medicine specializing in psychiatry San Francisco, 1963—; cons. dept. psychology Stanford U., 1963-64; lectr. dept. psychiatry U. Calif. San Francisco Med. Ctr., 1969-71; clin. prof. psychiatry Coll. Osteo. Medicine of Pacific, 1985—. Author: Meganutrition, 1980, Meganutrition for Women, 1983. Served to capt. M.C., U.S. Army, 1959-61. Fellow Acad. Orthomolecular Psychiatry; mem. AMA, Orthomolecular Med. Soc. (pres. 1979-81), San Francisco Women's Found. (pres. 1969), San Francisco Acad. Hypnosis (pres. 1970). Republican. Clubs: Olympic, Presidio (San Francisco). Avocations: golf, piano. Home and Office: 2698 Pacific Ave San Francisco CA 94115

KUNKEE, RALPH EDWARD, viticulture and enology educator; b. San Fernando, Calif., July 30, 1927; s. Azor Frederick and Edith Electa (Engle) K. AB, U. Calif., Berkeley, 1950, PhD, 1955. Research biochemist E.I. Du Pont De Nemours, Wilmington, Del., 1955-60; prof. enology U. Calif., Davis, 1963—; cons. UNFAO, Bangalore, India, 1986. Co-author: Technology of Winemaking, 1971. Fulbright fellow, Mainz, Fed. Republic Germany, 1970-71, France fellow, Montpellier, France, 1977-78. Mem. Am. Chem. Soc., Am. Soc. Microbiology, Am. Soc. Enology and Viticulture (sec./treas. 1983-85). Home: 820 Radcliffe Dr Davis CA 95616 Office: U Calif Dept Viticulture and Enology Davis CA 95616

KUNKEL, GLENN EVERETT, educator; b. Heavener, Okla., June 25, 1927; s. John Burl and Annie Mary (Graham) K.; m. Jacqueline Louise Lemm, Dec. 20, 1952; children—Glenda Suzanne, Sharon Lynn, John Timothy. B.S., Western Bapt. Coll., 1967; M.A., Holy Names Coll., 1969; D.A., Cath. U. Am., 19—. Cert. community coll. instr., Calif. Instr. English, Acad. Christian Edn., Oakland, Calif., 1953-64, chmn. dept., 1955-64; prof. English, Patten Coll., Oakland, 1964—, chmn. div. gen. studies, 1977—. Editor: Give Me Back My Soul, 1973; manuscript editor The Trumpet Call., 1958-72. Contbr. articles to jours. Mem. Fruitvale Community Devel. Dist. Council, 1980. Served with USN, 1945-46. Recipient Heart award Patten Coll., 1967, Alumni Service award, 1981, Pres.'s award, 1984. Mem. Nat. Council Tchrs. English, Calif. Assn. Tchrs. English, Philol. Assn. Pacific Coast. Christian Evangel. Home: 3257 Galindo St Oakland CA 94601 Office: Patten Coll 2433 Coolidge Ave Oakland CA 94601

KUNTZ, RICHARD POWELL, manufacturing and metal processing executive; b. Peru, Ind., Mar. 19, 1951; s. George William and Carolyn Lee (Blake) K.; m. Cynthia Rene, July 2, 1976; children: Ashley Nicole, Blake Armstrong. BA, Purdue U., 1973; MBA, City U., Bellevue, Wash., 1985. Mfg. mgr. S.W. Steel Rolling Mills, Los Angeles, 1973-76; gen. mgr. Calif. Steel Works, Inc., Livermore, 1976-80; v.p., gen. mgr. Cascade Steel Rolling Mills Inc., McMinnville, Oreg., 1980—. Mem. Soc. Mfg. Engrs., Assn. Iron and Steel Engrs. (bd. dirs.). Republican. Methodist. Avocations: reading, swimming, tennis, golf. Office: Cascade Steel Rolling Mills Inc Main Office 3299 N Hwy 99 W McMinnville OR 97128

KUO, PING-CHIA, historian, educator; b. Yangshe, Kiangsu, China, Nov. 27, 1908; s. Chu-sen and Hsiao-kuan (Hsu) K.; m. Anita H. Bradley, Aug. 8, 1946. A.M., Harvard U., 1930, Ph.D., 1933. Prof. modern history and Far Eastern internat. relations Nat. Wuhan U., Wuchang, China, 1933-38; editor China Forum, Hankow and Chungking, 1938-40; counsellor Nat. Mil. Council, Chungking, China, 1940-46, Ministry Fgn. Affairs, 1943-46; participated in Cairo Conf. as spl. polit. asst. to Generalissimo Chiang Kai-shek 1943; during war yrs. in Chungking, also served Chinese Govt. concurrently in following capacities: mem. fgn. affairs com. Nat. Supreme Def. Council, 1939-46; chief, editorial and pubs. dept. Ministry Information, 1940-42, mem. central planning bd., 1941-45; tech. expert to Chinese delegation San Francisco Conf., 1945; chief trusteeship sect. secretariat UN, London; (exec. com. prep. commn. and gen. assembly), 1945-46; top-ranking dir. Dept. Security Council Affairs, UN, 1946-48; vis. prof. Chinese history San Francisco State Coll., summers 1954, 58; assoc. prof. history So. Ill. U., 1959-63, prof. history, 1963-72, chmn. dept. history, 1967-71, prof. emeritus, 1972—; sr. fellow Nat. Endowment for Humanities, 1973-74; Pres. Midwest Conf. Asian Studies, 1964. Author: A Critical Study of the First Anglo-Chinese War, with Documents, 1935, Modern Far Eastern Diplomatic History (in Chinese), 1937, China: New Age and New Outlook, 1960, China, in the Modern World Series, 1970; Contbr. to Am. hist. pubs. and various mags. in China and Ency. Brit. Decorated Kwang Hua medal A-1 grade Nat. Mil. Council, Chungking, 1941; Auspicious Star medal Nat. Govt., Chungking, 1944; Victory medal, 1945. Mem. Am. Hist. Assn., Assn. Asian Studies. Club: Commonwealth (San Francisco). Home: 8661 Don Carol Dr El Cerrito CA 94530

KUO, YUE, semiconductor engineer, researcher; b. Taipei, Republic of China, Jan. 2, 1953; came to U.S., 1976; m. T.C. Chang, Nov. 22, 1980. BS, Nat. Taiwan U., Taipei, 1974; MS, Columbia U., 1978, DEngSci, 1980. Pilot lab. supr. Mobay Chem. Corp., Charleston, S.C., 1980-82; vis. research engr. U. Calif., Berkeley, 1982-84; prin. process engr. Data Gen. Corp., Sunnyvale, Calif., 1984—. Contbr. articles to profl. jours.; patentee in field. Mem. Am. Chem. Soc., Am. Inst. Chem. Engrs., Materials Research Soc., IEEE. Office: Data Gen Corp 433 N Mathilda Ave Sunnyvale CA 94086

KUPEC, ROBERT F., corporate lawyer; b. N.Y.C., May 9, 1940; s. Frank J. and Mary L. (Krulis) K.; m. Patricia Boyd Appel, Feb. 3, 1962; children: Susan P., Katherine A. BA in Psychology, Lehigh U., 1962; JD, Seton Hall U., 1968. Bar: N.J. 1968, Calif. 1985, Ariz. 1986. Staff asst. Pub. Service Electric & Gas, Newark, 1962-69; asst. dir. legal affairs Gen. Instrument Corp., N.Y.C., 1969-73; sr. atty. The N.J. Zinc Co., Bethlehem, Pa., 1973-75; real estate mgr. Famous Players, Toronto, Ont., Can., 1975-77; v.p. Sega Enterprises, Los Angeles, 1977-85; sr. counsel MeraBank, Phoenix, 1985—. Mem. Roseland (N.J.) Bd. Edn., 1971-73, Hanover Twp. (Pa.) Planning Commn., 1974-75. Mem. Ariz., Calif. Bar Assns. Republican. Avocations: golf, tennis. Home: 8538 E San Jacinto Dr Scottsdale AZ 85258 Office: MeraBank 3003 N Central Ave Phoenix AZ 85012

KUPER, DANIELA F., advertising executive; b. Chgo., June 18, 1950; d. Harry W. and Anne F. (Fisher) K.; children—Judah E., Sahra J. B.A., So. Ill. U., 1971. Account exec., copywriter, creative dir. Griff Advt., Boulder, Colo., 1978-82; pres., creative dir. Kuper-Finlon Advt., Boulder, 1982—; speaker in field. Vol. creative writing with children Foothill Sch., Boulder, 1985. Recipient Alfie award Denver Ad Fedn., 1983, 84, 85, 86, Addie award, 1984, 85, 86, Peak award 1985, 86, BPAA award 1984, 85, 86. Mem. Denver Ad Fedn., Boulder C. of C., Art Dirs. Club Denver (award 1985, 86). Office: Kuper-Finlon Advt 2060 Broadway Suite 400 Boulder CO 80302

KUPERMAN, ROBERT IAN, advertising agency executive; b. Bklyn., Dec. 31, 1941; s. Morris and Gertrude Kuperman; m. Ellen Rose, June 6, 1973; children—Jason, Molly. B.F.A., Pratt Inst., 1963. Vice pres., sr. art dir. Doyle Dane Bernbach, N.Y.C., 1963-71; v.p., creative dir. Della Femina Travisano & Ptnrs., N.Y.C., 1971-72; sr. v.p., creative dir. Wells, Rich & Greene, N.Y.C. and Los Angeles, 1972-80, BBDO/West, Los Angeles, 1980-82; exec. v.p., exec. creative dir. Doyle Dane Bernbach/West, Los Angeles, 1982—; instr. Sch. Visual Arts, N.Y.C., 1968-74, Pratt Inst., Bklyn., 1966-68, Art Ctr., Los Angeles, 1975-79. Art dir. TV comml. 1949 Auto Show, 1970 (Clio Hall of Fame award 1979), Volkswagen advertisements, 1979 (now in Smithsonian Mus. Art), other TV commls. Recipient Gold medals N.Y. Art Dirs. Show, 1969, 71, Andy award Advt. Club N.Y., 1970, Clio awards for excellence in worldwide advt., 1970, 72, 74, 78, 83. Mem. Los Angeles Creative Club (co-founder, chmn. bd. dirs.), Los Angeles Advt. Club (bd. dirs. 1979). Office: Doyle Dane Bernbach Needham Worldwide 5900 Wilshire Blvd Los Angeles CA 90036

KUPPENBENDER, CLAIR LAWRENCE, executive; b. Portland, Oreg., Nov. 25, 1930; s. Lawrence E. and Opal M. (Brown) K.; m. Patricia F. Imel, Sept. 17, 1955; children: Kim M. Tschoppe, Keith B., Gary J., Gene A., Patsy K. Student, Multnomah Coll., Clackamas Community Coll., Portland Community Coll. Purchasing agt. Arcoa, Inc., Portland, 1957-67; systems analyst Hosp. Computer Ctr., Portland, 1967-71; pres. Autorent, Inc., Portland, 1971-75; mgmt. cons. Milwaukie, Oreg., 1975-78; pres. Patsy's Artistry in Thread, Milwaukie, 1978—; v.p. I&I Enterprises Inc., Portland, 1978—; purchasing agt. North Clackamas Sch. Dist., Milwaukie, 1979—. Mem. Milwaukie Neighborhood Council, 1976-78, Milw. Civil Service Com.; bd. dirs. Milwaukie Traffic Safety Commn.; local troop leader Boy Scouts Am. Mem. Adminstrv. Mgmt. Soc., Oreg. Pub. Purchasing Assn., Purchasing Mgmt. Assn. Oreg., Nat. Inst. Govt. Purchasing, Systems and Procedures Assn., Am. Mgmt. Assn., Assn. Bus. Writers Am., Oreg. Assn. Sch. Bus. Ofcls., Nat. Purchasing Inst., Pacific N.W. Pub. Purchasing Assn. Republican. Roman Catholic. Club: Toastmasters. Lodge: Elks. Home: 10753 SE 29th Ave Milwaukie OR 97222 Office: North Clackamas Sch Dist #12 4444 SE Lake Rd Milwaukie OR 97222

KURAN, TIMUR, economics educator; b. N.Y.C., Mar. 19, 1954; s. Aptullah E. and Sylvia (Stockdale) K.; m. Wendy Weisend, Sept. 6, 1980; 1 child, Kenter W. BA, Princeton U., 1977; MA, Stanford U., 1979, PhD, 1982. Asst. prof. econs. U. So. Calif., Los Angeles, 1982—. Mng. assoc. editor: Jour. Econ. Behavior and Orgn., 1983—; contbr. articles to profl. jours. Trustee Am.-Turkish Assn. So. Calif., Irvine, 1986—. Grantee NSF, 1985. Mem. Am. Econ. Assn., Royal Econ. Soc., Middle East Studies Assn. N.Am., Western Econ. Assn., Pub. Choice Soc. Avocations: philately, jazz, travel, Turkish lit. Home: 11810 Mayfield Ave #305 Los Angeles CA 90049 Office: U So Calif Dept Econs Los Angeles CA 90089-0035

KURANO, HIROO, architect; b. Tokyo, Feb. 7, 1938; came to U.S., 1969; s. Atsushi and Sumi (Kuma) K.; m. Judith A. Rainville, Aug. 3, 1975; 1 child, Junko. BArch, Yokohama (Japan) U., 1964, MArch, 1966; MArch, MIT, 1971. Architect T. Yanashita Architects and Engrs., Tokyo, 1966-67; architect Nihon Architects, Engrs. and Cons., Inc., Tokyo, 1967-69, 73-77, advisor, 1977—; architect Johnson-Hotvedt and Assocs., Inc., Boston, 1970, Sasaki, Dawson, DeMay Assocs., Watertown, Mass., 1971-73, Al Whittle Assocs., Inc., Canoga Park, Calif., 1977-79; pres., ptnr. Forme Internat., San Diego, 1979-82; pres. Kurano Assocs., Inc., San Diego, 1982—; lectr. Tokyo U. Sci., 1974, Calif. State Poly. U., Pomona, 1975. Contbr. articles to profl. jours. Trustee Japanese Christian Ch., San Diego, 1986, bd. deacons, 1984-86; mem. adv. bd. Japanese Friendship Garden, San Diego, 1986, bd. dirs., 1984-86. Recipient Honor award House of Japan, San Diego, 1986; MIT scholar, 1971, Yokohama U. scholar, 1966; Japan Soc. grantee, N.Y. Mem. AIA (San Diego chpt.), Archtl. Inst. Japan. Home: 3104 Hataca Carlsbad CA 92008 Office: Kurano Assocs Inc 5703 Oberlin Dr Suite 307 San Diego CA 92121

KURCH, WILLIAM DAVID, union exec.; b. Honolulu, Aug. 2, 1944; s. Michael and Joan Elizabith (O'Leary) K.; m. Colleen Christina, Dec. 1, 1969; children: Derek, Leah, Colleen Christina, William David; m. 2d, Fay Dora Roxenberg, Oct. 25, 1981. Student U. So. Calif., 1963-66; DD, Hebrew Union Sem., 1966. Profl. entertainer, 1960—; union agt., organizer local 5 Hotel Workers Union, Honolulu, 1971-79; with local 555 Culinary and Service Employees Union, Honolulu, 1979—, pres., exec. officer, 1981—; chmn. Hawaii Entertainment Trades Council; exec. officer Hawaii Entertainers and Profls. Union. Active Mental Health Assn. Hawaii, Cystic Fibrosis Found., Aloha United Way; mem. exec. bd. Variety Club Tent, Hawaii Spl. Olympics; cantor Emanuel Temple, Honolulu. Mem. Hotel Workers Union, Teamsters Union, Am. Guild Variety Artists (Hawaii rep.), Musicians Union of Am. Fedn. Musicians. Democrat. Club: Press (Honolulu).

KURIGER, RONALD JOE, military career officer, electrical engineer; b. Dayton, Ohio, July 9, 1958; s. Jerrald Lee and Beyrl Ruth (Davis) K.; m. Janie Louise Foreit, Dec. 23, 1985. BSEE, Ohio U., 1980. Avionics intern USAF, Wright-Patterson AFB, Dayton, 1975-76; electronic technician United Systems Corp., Dayton, 1978; electrician Dayton, 1977-80; avionics intern Ohio U., Athens, 1979-80; sr. engr. Motorola Gen. Electronics Group, Scottsdale, Ariz., 1980-83; commd. USAF, 1983, advanced through grades to capt., 1986; pilot tactical air command USAF, George AFB, 1983—. Mem. IEEE, Officer's Club, Aircraft Owner's and Pilot's Assn. Republican. Avocations: hiking, hunting, fishing, skiing, golfing. Home: 672 Mountain View Wrightwood CA 92397 Office: 27 TASS/DO George AFB CA 92394

KUROVSKY, RICHARD EDWARD, editor; b. Milw., Oct. 4, 1953; s. Edward and Helga (Winkler) K. BA, U. Wis, 1975. Reporter Milw. Jour., 1975-78; dir. news, publs. Macalester Coll., St. Paul, 1978-82; editor Stanford (Calif.) Grad. Sch. Bus. Mag., 1982—. Recipient Excellence award Communication Arts mag., 1979, Council for Advancement Support Edn. awardee, 1978-86. Office: Stanford U Grad Sch Bus Stanford CA 94305

KURSCHNER, RICHARD CARL, computer software engineer; b. Denver, Apr. 4, 1958; s. Adam Carl and Edith LaVon (Harkin) K. BS in Elec. Engring. and Computer Sci., U. Colo., 1980; MS in Elec. Engring. and Computer Sci., Oreg. State U., 1985. Elec. engr. Tektronix Inc., Beaverton, Oreg., 1980-82, software engr., 1982—. Mem. Assn. Computing Machinery, Mensa, Planetary Soc. Republican. Avocations: bridge, fantasy role playing games. Home: 14095 SW Walker Rd Apt 7 Beaverton OR 97005 Office: Tektronix Inc PO Box 500 19-075 Beaverton OR 97077

KURSEWICZ, LEE Z., marketing consultant; b. Chgo., Oct. 26, 1916; s. Antoni and Henryka (Sulkowska) K.; ed. Chgo. and Bata ind. schs.; m. Ruth Elizabeth Venzke, Jan. 31, 1940; 1 son, Dennis. With Bata Shoe Co., Inc., 1936-78, plant mgr., Salem, Ind., 1963-65, v.p., mng. dir., Batawa, Ont., Can., 1965-71; v.p., dir. Bata Industries, Batawa, 1965-71, plant mgr., Salem, 1971-76; pres. Bata Shoe Co., Inc., Belcamp, Md., 1976-77, sr. v.p., dir., 1977-79; gen. mgr. Harford Insulated Panel Systems div. Hazleton Industries, 1981-82. City mgr. City of Batawa, 1965-71; vice chmn. Trenton (Ont.) Meml. Hosp., 1970-71; pres. Priestford Hills Community Assn., 1979-80; chmn. adv. bd. Phoenix Festival Theatre, Hartford County Community Coll., 81; vice chmn. Harford County chpt. ARC, 1980-81, chmn., 1982-83; chmn. Harford County Econ. Devel. Adv. Bd., 1983-85; mem. Susquehanna Region Pvt. Industry Council, 1983-85. Mem. Am. Mgmt. Assn. Clubs: Rotary, Bush River Yacht (commodore 1956), Bush River Power Squadron (comdr. 1957), Western Hills Country of Salem (pres. 1975), Trenton Country (pres. 1968-69), Md. Country. Home and Office: 29707A Niguel Rd Laguna Niguel CA 92677

KURTZ, KENNETH JOHN, physician, educator; b. Pitts., Feb. 20, 1944; s. John Edmund and Elizabeth (Weimer) K.; m. Patricia Mae Albright, Dec. 17, 1972; 1 child, Roger. BA in Biology with honors, Williams Coll., 1966; MD, Cornell U., 1970; postgrad., Naval Aerospace Med. Inst., 1972. Diplomate Am. Bd. Internal Medicine, Nat. Bd. Med. Examiners. Fellow in Endocrinology U. Wash., Seattle, 1970-71; intern U. Calif., San Diego, 1971-72; resident II, III in internal medicine U. Calif., San Francisco, 1976-78; asst. prof. internal medicine and family and community medicine U. Nev., Reno, 1978-79, asst. prof. internal medicine, 1979-83, chief, div. gen. internal medicine, 1981—, coordinator Washoe Med. Ctr. student and residency programs, 1982—, assoc. prof., 1983—, physician coordinator, Wahoe Med. Ctr. and County Med. Service, 1985—; active staff VA Med. Ctr., Reno, 1978—, St. Mary's Hosp., Reno, 1984—. Contbr. chpts. to books, articles to med. jours. Served as flight surgeon USN, 1973-76. Recipient Dwight Botanical Prize, 1966, Seligman award, 1970, citation for Outstanding Support, Advocacy and Teaching U. Nev. Med. Sch., 1982. Fellow ACP; mem. Am. Fedn. Clin. Research, Soc. Research and Edn. in Primary Care Internal Medicine, Nev. State Med. Assn., Washoe County Med. Soc. Avocations: jogging, skiing. Home: 3235 Markridge Dr Reno NV 89509-3837 Office: Nev Med Group Internal Med div 781 Mill St Reno NV 89502

KURTZ, MAXINE, personnel services executive, lawyer; b. Mpls., Oct. 17, 1921; d. Jack Isadore and Beatrice (Cohen) K. BA, U. Minn., 1942; BS in Govt. Mgmt., U. Denver, 1945, JD, 1962; postdoctoral student U. Calif., San Diego, 1978. Bar: Colo. Planning analyst Tri-County Regional Planning, Denver, 1945-47; chief, research and spl. projects, Planning Office, City and County of Denver, 1947-66, tech. dir., evaluation dir. Model Cities Program, 1966-71; personnel research officer, Denver Career Service Authority, 1972-86, dir. personnel services, 1986—; expert witness, nat. com. on urban problems U.S. Ho. of Reps., U.S. Senate. Author: Law of Planning and Land Use Regulations in Colorado, 1966; co-author: Care and Feeding of Witnesses, Expert and Otherwise, 1974; bd. editors: Pub. Adminstrn. Rev., Washington, 1980-83; prin. investigator book: Employment: An American Enigma, 1979. Active Women's Forum of Colo., LWV, Denver, Democratic Party, Denver; chmn. Colo. adv. com. to U.S. Civil Rights Commn., 1985—. Sloan fellow, U. Denver, 1944-45; recipient Outstanding Achievement award U. Minn., 1971. Mem. Am. Inst. Planners (sec. treas. 1968-70, bd. govs. 1972-75), Am. Soc. Pub. Adminstrn. (nat. council 1978-81; Donald Stone award), ABA, Colo. Bar Assn., Denver Bar Assn., Order St. Ives, Pi Alpha Alpha. Jewish. Home: 2361 Monaco Pkwy Denver CO 80207 Office: Denver Career Service Authority 414 14th St Denver CO 80202

KUSTER, ROBERT KENNETH, scientist; b. Los Angeles, July 11, 1932; s. Arthur Rollo Kuster and Ermine Rosebud (Prittchett) Woodward. AS, Gavilan Coll., 1974, AA in Humanities, 1981; student, San Jose State U., 1955, 1974-76, UCLA, 1977. Installer Western Electric Co., Inc., Corpus Christi, Tex., 1951-52, 1955, San Jose, Calif., 1957-58, 1960-83; ptnr., scientist, cons. WE-Woodward's Enterprises, Morgan Hill, Calif., 1975—; technician AT&T Tech., Inc., San Jose, 1983-85; scientist pvt. practice, Gilroy, 1978—. Served to sgt. U.S. Army Corps Engrs., 1952-54. Mem. AAAS, Astron. Soc. Pacific, Calif. Acad. Scis., N.Y. Acad. Scis., Am. Legion, VFW. Baptist. Lodge: Elks. Avocations: photography, golf, camping, hiking, music. Home: 420 W Ninth St PO Box 1113 Gilroy CA 95021 Office: Woodward's Enterprises 179 Bender Dr Morgan Hill CA 95037

KUSWA, WEBSTER STIELOW, freelance commercial writer; b. West Bend, Wis., Aug. 25, 1907; s. Max Robert and Wilhelmina (Stielow) K.; m. Elvira Lucy Lipman, June 29, 1929; 1 child, Glenn. Student, Marquette U., U. Wis. Sr. v.p., creative dir. Paulson-Gerlach & Assocs., Inc., Milw., 1950-57; exec. v.p. Morrison Advt., Inc., Milw., 1957-60; pres. Kuswa-Greene & Assoc., Inc., Milw., 1960-61, Kuswa-Hoover Advt., Milw., 1961-65; pub. relations dir. Mathisson & Assocs., Milw., 1965-69, McCann-Erickson, Milw., 1969-72; freelance writer Kuswa Creative Service, Albuquerque, 1972—; bd. dirs. Sr. Arts. Author: Sell Copy, 1979, Big Paybacks from Small-Budget Advertising, 1982, Sales Rep's Letter Book, 1984; freelance editor Podium Rev.; contbr. short fiction to nat. mags. Named Man of Yr., Sales Promotion Exec.'s Assn., 1970. Mem. First Friday Club. Republican. Mem. Unitarian Ch. Club: Raconteurs. Avocations: swimming, chess, reading, woodworking. Home and Office: 9620 Lona Ln NE Albuquerque NM 87111

KUTNER, S. JEROME, psychologist; b. N.Y.C., Mar. 7, 1938; s. Abraham Lewis and Frances (Gorelick) K.; m. Kathleen Ann Kutner. BS, NYU, 1960; MA, New Sch. Social Research, 1964, PhD, 1966. Asst. prof. SUNY, New Paltz, 1965, Fredonia, 1965-66; asst. prof. Ft. Hays State U., Hays, Kans., 1966-67; research psychologist Kaiser Found Research Inst., Oakland, Calif., 1967-72, U. Calif., San Francisco, 1972-75; pvt. practice psychology San Jose, Calif., 1975-86; psychologist Agnews Devel. Ctr., San Jose, 1987—; asst. to dean Calif. Sch. Profl. Psychology, San Francisco, 1969; forensic evaluator panel criminal div. Superior Ct. Santa Clara County, Calif., 1981; cons., researcher VA Hosp., Palo Alto, Calif., 1974-75, Woodside Women's Hosp., Redwood City, Calif., 1986; instr. Inst. Transpersonal Psychology, Menlo Park, 1985-86. Contbr. articles to profl. jours. Active community service in substance abuse Pathway Soc., San Jose, 1978. Fellow Soc. Personality Assessment, Internat. Neuropsychol. Soc.; mem. AAAS, Nat. Acad. Neuropsychologists (cert.), Am. Psychol. Assn. (div. Clin. Neuropsychology), Soc. Psychologists in Addictive Behaviors, N.Y. Acad. Scis. Home: 166 Middlefield Rd Palo Alto CA 94301 Office: 166 Middlefield Rd Palo Alto CA 94301

KUTSKO, JACQUELYN PATTI, educator, writer; b. Akron, Ohio, Mar. 27, 1945; d. Pete and Carolyn (Naglic) Patti; B.A., U. Akron, 1967; M.Ed., Colo. State U., 1983; m. James Andrew Kutsko, June 10, 1967; 1 son, James Andrew. Tchr. bus. N.E. High Sch., Pasadena, Md., 1967, Athens-Draughon Bus. Coll., Athens, Ga., 1967, McAuley High Sch., Cin., 1971-72; tchr. bus., coordinator Scarlet Oaks Joint Vocat. Sch., Cin., 1972-73; instr. bus. Barnes Bus. Coll., Denver, 1974-76; pres., owner Finishing Touches, Englewood, Colo., 1976-78; bus. and med. office cons., 1976-78; tchr. bus. Smoky Hill High Sch., Aurora, Colo., 1976—; lectr. profl. groups. Mem. Med. Office Asst.'s Adv. Bd., Community Coll. Denver, 1976; pres. bus. adv. com. Cherry Creek Schs., 1983-84; mem. Superintendent's Com. in Excellence, 1983-84; mem. Subcom. to Study the Content of the Curricular Program,

1983-84; mem. Secondary Computer Edn. Council, 1983-84; co-chmn. Smoky Hill Computer Edn. Com., 1983-84; mem. com. to Plan Needs/ Design of District's Fourth High Sch., 1983-84; chmn. Life Skills/Concepts task force, mem. staff devel. com. Mem. NEA, Nat. Bus. Edn. Assn., Mountain Plains Bus. Edn. Assn., Colo. Vocat. Assn., Colo. Educators For and About Bus., Nat. Speaker's Assn., Colo. Speaker's Assn., Cherry Creek Tchrs. Assn., Am. Vocat. Assn., U.S. Figure Skating Assn., Delta Pi Epsilon, Phi Delta Kappa. Club: Denver Figure Skating. Author: Broncos: From Striped Socks to Super Bowl and Beyond, 1980; Houghton-Mifflin Typewriting-Keyboard Mastery and Applications, 1st and 2d yr. texts, 1984, Houghton-Mifflin Keyboarding and Applications, 1986; contbr. articles in field. Home: 8378 E Jamison Circle S Englewood CO 80112 Office: Smoky Hill High Sch 16100 E Smoky Hill Rd Aurora CO 80015

KUVSHINOFF, BERTHA HORNE, painter, sculptor; b. Dungeness, Wash., Aug. 29, 1915; d. Mellon Tobias and Mariamagdalena (Volnagel) Horne; m. Nikolai V. Kuvshinoff. Represented in numerous mus., pvt. and pub. collections, including Evansville (Ind.) Art Mus., Miami (Fla.) Mus. Modern Art, Seattle Art Mus., World's Fair, Seattle, 1962-63. Recipient Diploma of Merit of Univ. of Arts, Univ. Delle Arti, Rome, Italy. Studio: 121 1/2 Yale Ave N Seattle WA 98109

KUVSHINOFF, NICOLAI VASILY, painter, sculptor. m. Bertha Horne. Exhibited in group shows at Cimaise de Paris Galerie, 1956, 57, La Galerie Norval, Paris, 1957, Smith Tower Gallery, Seattle, 1960, World's Fair, Seattle, 1962, 63, Wash. Capitol Mus., Olympia, 1965, Cath. Ctr. Art Gallery, Balt., 1967, Kupsick Art Gallery, 1969 and numerous others; represented in permanent collections Seattle Art Mus., Phoenix Art Mus., Santa Fe Art Mus., Tacoma Art Mus., Miami (Fla.) Art Mus. and many others; represented in numerous pub. and pvt. collections in France, Brazil, India, Can., Alaska, Japan, Tangier and U.S.; author: (books) Art Book, 1959, Drawings, 1966. Studio: 121 1/2 Yale Ave N Seattle WA 98109

KUWABARA, DENNIS MATSUICHI, optometrist; b. Honolulu, July 20, 1945; s. Robert Tokuichi and Toshiko (Nakashima) K.; m. Judith Naomi Tokumaru, June 28, 1970; children: Jennifer Tomiko, Susan Kazuko. BS, So. Calif. Coll. Optometry, 1968, OD cum laude, 1970. Pvt. practice optometry Waipahu, Hawaii, 1972—; Pres. 1st Study Club for Optometrists, Honolulu, 1982-83; chmn. bd. examiners in Optometry, Honolulu, 1982—; state dir. Optometric Extension Found., Honolulu, 1980—. Served to lt. Med. Service Corps, USN, 1970-72. Named Outstanding Young Person of Hawaii, Hawaii State Jaycees, 1979. Fellow Am. Acad. Optometry; mem. Hawaii Optometric Assn. (pres. 1979-80, Man of Yr. award 1976, Optometrist of Yr. 1983), Am. Optometric Assn., Armed Forces Optometric Soc. Home: 94-447 Holaniku St Mililani Town HI 96789 Office: 94-748 Hikimoe St Waipahu HI 96797

KUWAHARA, STEVEN SADAO, biochemist; b. Lahaina, Hawaii, July 20, 1940; s. Toshio and Hideko (Sasaki) K.; m. Rene Mikie Miyajima, June 24, 1972; children: Daniel T., Sara S. BS, Cornell U., 1962; MS, U. Wis., 1965, PhD, 1967. Research assoc. U. Wash., Seattle, 1966-67; asst. prof. biochemistry Calif. State U., Long Beach, 1967-71; asst. research biologist U. Calif., Irvine, 1971-73; unit chief Mich. Dept. Pub. Health, Lansing, 1973-76, sect. chief, 1976-82; mgr. test tech. Hyland Therapeutics, Los Angeles, 1982—; adj. research assoc. Mich. State U., East Lansing, 1980-82. Contbr. articles to profl. jours. Asst. cubmaster Boy Scouts Am., Claremont, Calif., 1984-85, com. mem., 1985—; bd. dirs. West Covina (Calif.) Buddhist Ch., 1985—, treas., 1986. Recipient Award of Merit, Long Beach Heart Assn., 1969; NIH spl. research fellow, 1971-73. Mem. AAAS, Am. Chem. Soc., Soc. Exptl. Biol. Medicine, Am. Fedn. Clin. Research., Am. Soc. Microbiology, N.Y. Acad. Scis., So. Calif. Hemophilia Found. Club: Torch (Lansing) (v.p. 1981-81). Avocations: stamp collecting, gardening. Home: 975 W Amador St Claremont CA 91711 Office: Hyland Therapeutics 4501 Colorado Blvd Los Angeles CA 90039

KUZIRIAN, DONALD LEE, retail executive; b. Fresno, Calif., May 22, 1945; s. Andrew and Mary (Proodian) K. AS, Fresno City Coll. Salesman Leon's Mens Wear, Fresno, 1960-66; ptnr. Gentry Ltd., Fresno, 1966-73; prin. Pants 'n' Stuff, Fresno, 1973-74; ptnr. Exterior Concepts, Sherman Oaks, Calif., 1974-75; mgr. E. Gottschalk's & Co., Fresno, 1975—; chief exec. officer Cen. Calif. Men's Apparel Shows, Fresno, 1980—. Chmn. Citizens Redevel. Com., Fresno, 1982. Mem. Downtown Assn. Fresno (bd. dirs., pres. 1980-81, Dir.'s award 1983), Fresno C. of C., Vols. of Older Am.s (charter, pres.). Republican. Apostolic. Avocations: travelling, art, racquetball. Home: 6377 N Millbrook Ave Fresno CA 93710 Office: E Gottschalk's & Co PO Box 1872 Fresno CA 93718

KVITASH, VADIM I(SSAY), allergist-immunologist, scientist; b. Odessa, USSR, Mar. 19, 1936; came to U.S. 1974; m. Ivetta Kopilovsky, Apr. 2, 1961; children: Zoya, Sofia. MD, Odessa Med. Sch., 1961; PhD, Mechnikov's Sci. Research Inst. of Virology and Epidemiology, Odessa, 1969. Chief pediatrics Novo-Ivanovsk (USSR) Hosp., 1961-64; postdoctoral researcher Moscow Cen. Inst. Med. Specialization, 1965; postdoctoral researcher exptl., clin., indsl. virology and immunology Mechnikov's Sci. Research Inst. of Virology and Epidemiology, Odessa, 1965-69, research immunologist, 1969-70, chmn. bd. Young Scientists, 1969-74, mem. sci. council, sci. cons., 1970-74; sci., med. cons. systemology lab. Odessa U., 1970-74; med. dir. pediatric depts. Odessa Med. Sch. Hosp., 1970-74; asst. prof. pediatrics Odessa Med. Sch., 1970-74; orderly Mt. Zion Hosp. and Med. Ctr., San Francisco, 1975, research assoc., 1980-82, prin. investigator, 1980-84, resident dept. pathology and lab. medicine, 1981-82; research asst. IMMUNOPATHWAYS LAB., San Francisco, 1976-77, research assoc., 1980-81; sci. dir., founder Balascopy Inst., San Francisco, 1981-82; pvt. practice specializing in allergy-immunology San Francisco, 1982—; affiliate sr. scientist Med. Research Inst. of San Francisco, Pacific Presbyn. Med. Ctr., 1985—. Contbr. articles to profl. jours; patentee in field. Named Laureate Best Research Work of Young Scientists, All-Soviet Union Competition, 1968, laureate Best Med. Student Research Work, Ukrainian Soviet Socialist Rep. Competition, 1960; recipient Mechnikov Sci. award, 1966-67, Best Med. Student Research Work award Odessa Med. Sch., 1958-61; Mt. Zion Hosp. and Med. Ctr. research grantee. Fellow Am. Coll. Allergists; mem. AMA, AAAS, Calif. Med. Assn., San Francisco Med. Soc., San Francisco Soc. Internal Medicine, Am. Acad. Allergy and Immunology, Am. Assn. Clin. Immunology and Allergy, Joint Council Allergy and Immunology, European Acad. Allergology and Clin. Immunology, Pan Am. Allergy Soc., Internat. Corr. Soc. Allergists, Bay Area Huff and Puff Club, Bay Area History Medicine Club, Am. Heart Assn., Am. Assn. Med. Systems and Informatics, Soc. Med. Decision Making, Am. Assn. Artificial Intelligence, Soc. Gen. Systems Research, Am. Soc. Cybernetics, Assn. Automated Reasoning, Cognitive Sci. Soc., Assn. Integrative Studies, N.Y. Acad. Sci. Avocations: fencing, art, philosophy. Home: 1775 17th Ave San Francisco CA 94122 Office: 2352 Post St San Francisco CA 94115

KWIRAM, ALVIN L., physical chemist, educator; b. Riverhills, Man., Can., Apr. 28, 1937; came to U.S., 1954; s. Rudolf and Wilhelmina A. (Bilske) K.; m. Verla Rae Michel, Aug. 9, 1964; children: Andrew Brandt, Sidney Marguerite. B.S. in Chemistry; B.A. in Physics, Walla Walla (Wash.) Coll., 1958; Ph.D. in Chemistry, Calif. Inst. Tech., 1963. Alfred A. Noyes instr. Calif. Inst. Tech., Pasadena, 1962-63; research asso. physics dept. Stanford (Calif.) U., 1963-64; instr. chemistry Harvard U., Cambridge, Mass., 1964-67; lectr. Harvard U., 1967-70; asso. prof. chemistry U. Wash., Seattle, 1970-75; prof. U. Wash., 1975—, chmn. dept. chemistry, 1977-87, vice provost, 1987—. Contbr. numerous articles to sci. jours. Co-founder, 1st pres. Assn. Adventist Forums, 1967-72; chmn. bd. editors, co-editor quar. jour. Spectrum, 1975-77. Recipient Eastman-Kodak Sci. award, 1962, Indsl. Realtions award Council for Chem. Research, 1986; Woodrow Wilson fellow, 1958; Alfred P. Sloan fellow, 1968-70; Guggenheim Meml. Found. fellow, 1977-78. Fellow AAAS; mem. Am. Phys. Soc., Am. Chem. Soc., Council Chem. Research (dir. 1980-84, chmn. 1982-83), Sigma Xi. Office: U Wash Office of the Provost Seattle WA 98195

KWOH, THEODORE JESSE, research molecular biologist; b. N.Y.C., June 6, 1951; s. Theodore Huan-tzing and Emily Tze-ing (Lu) K.; m. Deborah Yantis, Nov. 9, 1974; children: Theodore Carl, Katherine Christine. BS, Cornell U., 1973; MS, U. Tex. Dallas, Richardson, 1975, PhD, 1978. Postdoctoral fellow Cold Spring Harbor (N.Y.) Lab., 1978-82; asst. prof. veterinary microbiology U. Sask., Saskatoon, Can., 1982-84; scientist La Jolla Biol. Labs., San Diego, 1985—. Mem. AAAS, Am. Soc. Microbiology. Home: 2404 Jacaranda Ave Carlsbad CA 92008 Office: La Jolla Biol Labs 505 Coast Blvd S La Jolla CA 92037

KWOK, YEN MEE, chemist; b. Canton, China, Oct. 24, 1947; came to U.S., 1964; d. Yui Keung and Shui Yin (Won) Wong; m. Joseph Man Kwok, Dec. 22, 1973; children: Elaine, Albert. AA, City Coll. San Francisco, 1970; BS, U. Calif., Berkeley, 1972; MS, San Jose State U., 1979. Analytical chemist Lawrence Livermore Nat. Lab., Livermore, Calif., 1972-80; sr. chemist, tech. supr. Ampex Corp., Redwood City, Calif., 1980-86. Mem. Calif. Cir. Assn., Am. Chem. Soc. Avocations: swimming, tennis, skiing, dancing, gardening. Office: Ampex Corp 401 Broadway Redwood City CA 94063

KWON, JOONG GUN, orthodontist; b. An Dong, Kyungbuk, Korea, Jan. 4, 1948; came to U.S., 1975; s. Chi Ryun and Tak Bok (Kim) K.; m. Hyun Sook Choi, Mar. 15, 1978; children—Joyce, Donald, Gerald. A.A., Seoul Nat. U., 1967, D.D.S., 1971; D.D.S., U. So. Calif., 1978, orthodontic cert., 1980. Pvt. practice orthodontics, Los Angeles, 1980—. Served to capt. Korean Army, 1971-74. Mem. Korean Dental Assn. U.S.A. (sec. gen. 1983-84). Office: 3053 W Olympic Blvd Suite 311 Los Angeles CA 90006

KWON, PETER HISANG, chaplain, marriage counselor; b. Seoul, Aug. 11, 1921; s. Tharm Kwon and Chong Ai Joe; 1 child, Peter H. Kwon Jr. BA, Yonsei U., Seoul, 1944; MDiv., San Francisco Theol. Sem., 1951; MA, Hartford S Minary Found., 1953. Lic. marriage, family and child counselor; cert. profl. mental health clergy. Sr. pastor Wahiawa (Oahu) Ch., Hawaii, 1953-59, Korean United Presbyn. Ch., Los Angeles, 1959-68; head chaplain John Wesley County Hosp., Los Angeles, 1968—; area chaplain Los Angeles County-U. So. Calif. Med. Ctr., Los Angeles, 1968—. Contbr. articles to profl. jours. Pres. Asian Pacific Counseling and Treatment Ctr., 1986—; pres. Asian Presbyn. Council, Los Angeles and Hawaii; vice chmn. Los Angeles County Com. on Aging. Recognized for Outstanding Services for Elderly Los Angeles City Mayor, Outstanding Block Club Mem. Los Angeles City Councilmen. Fellow: Coll. Chaplains; mem. Nat. Assn. Social Workers (cert.), State Assn. of the Counselor, Marriage, Family and Children, Nat. Council of Chs. (bd. dirs.). Democrat. Home: 1517 4th Ave Los Angeles CA 90019 Office: 1200 N State St Los Angeles CA 90033

KYL, JON LLEWELLYN, congressman; b. Oakland, Nebr., Apr. 25, 1942; s. John and Arlene (Griffith) K.; m. Caryll Louise Collins, June 5, 1964; children: Kristine Elizabeth, John Jeffry. BA, U. Ariz., 1964, LLB, 1966. Atty. Jennings, Strouss & Salmon, Phoenix, 1966-86; mem. 100th Congress from 4th Ariz. dist., 1987—. Del. Nat. Rep. Conv., 1972; Rep. gen. counsel State of Ariz., 1972-75; bd. dirs. Crime Victim Found., Phoenix, Ariz. Acad., Phoenix. Mem. Ariz. State U. Coll. Bus. Dean's Council of 100, Ariz. State Bar. Presbyterian. Home: 1600 S Eads Arlington VA 22202 Office: US House of Reps 313 Cannon Bldg Washington DC 20515

KYONO, STEVEN MASATOSHI, civil engineer; b. Tokyo, Dec. 30, 1953; came to U.S., 1954; s. Hisao and Jean Shizuko (Miwa) K.; m. Kathryn Anne McLarn, Dec. 30, 1984. BSCE, Purdue U., 1975. Registered profl. engr., Hawaii. Civil engr. Dept. Transp., State of Hawaii, Lihue, 1975-84; project engr. Sam O. Hirota, Inc., Honolulu, 1984-86; county engr. County of Kauai, Lihue, 1986—. Mem. ASCE, NSPE (com. mem. 1985-86), Hawaii Soc. Profl. Engrs. Democrat. Home: PO Box 1886 Lihne HI 96766-5886 Office: County of Kauai Dept Pub Works 4396 Rice St Lihue HI 96766

KYRALA, GEORGE AMINE, physicist; b. Bhamdoun, Lebanon, Apr. 20, 1946; came to U.S., 1967; s. Amine Asaad and Moura (Saliby) Khayrallah; m. Trish Mylet, Nov. 18, 1973; children: Michaelene, Kamaal George. BS, Am. U. Beirut, 1967; MPhil, Yale U., 1969, PhD, 1974. Postdoctoral fellow Joint Inst. Lab. Astrophysics, Boulder, Colo., 1974-76; lectr. physics U. Colo., Boulder, 1975-76; research fellow physics and optical sci. ctr. U. Ariz., Tucson, 1976-78; mem. staff Los Alamos (N.Mex.) Nat. Lab., 1978—; faculty cons. Al-Hazen Research Ctr., Baghdad, Iraq, 1979. Contbr. articles to profl. jours. Recipient Michael Chiha prize Lebanese Govt., 1964; Rockefeller fellow Am. U. Beirut, 1967, Gibbs fellow Yale U., 1967-68. Mem. Am. Phys. Soc., Arab Phys. Soc., Internat. Soc. Optical Engring. Home: 382 Catherine Los Alamos NM 87544 Office: Los Alamos Nat Lab MS E526 Los Alamos NM 87545

KYTHE, ASCIAN See MEADER, JONATHAN GRANT

LAABS, WALTER WILLIAM, traffic engineer, consultant; b. San Francisco, July 24, 1938; s. Walter William and Clara Christine (Moe) L.; m. Kathleen Ann Sullivan, Feb. 26, 1977; children: Donald, David. BS, U. Calif., Berkeley, 1962, MS, 1970. Registered profl. engr., Va., Calif. Sr. traffic engr. Gruen Assocs., Los Angeles, 1970-73; county traffic engr. Sonoma County, Santa Rosa, Calif., 1973-77; sr. traffic engr. Aramco, Dhahran, Saudi Arabia, 1978-80; prin. Laabs Traffic Engring., Santa Rosa, 1980-85; pres. Laabs, Tilton & Assocs., Santa Rosa, 1985—. Served to lt. USNR, 1962-69. Mem. Soc. Mil. Engrs., Transp. Research Bd., Inst. Transp. Engrs., North Bay Forum Traffic Engrs. (chmn. 1976-77). Democrat. Roman Catholic. Home: 5494 Kay Dr Windsor CA 95492 Office: Laabs Tilton & Assocs 3404 Mendocino Ave Santa Rosa CA 95401

LAALY, HESHMAT OLLAH, research chemist; b. Kermanshah, Iran, June 23, 1927; came to Germany, 1951, Can., 1967, U.S., 1984; s. Jacob and Saltanat (Afshani) L.; m. Parvaneh Modarai, Oct. 7, 1963 (div. 1971); children: Ramesh, Edmond S.; m. Parivash M. Farahmand, Feb. 7, 1982. BS in Chemistry, U. Stuttgart, Republic of Germany, 1955, MS in Chemistry, 1958, PhD in Chemistry, 1962. Chief chemist Kress Sohne, Krefeld, Republic of Germany, 1963-67; analytical chemist Gulf Oil Research Ctr., Montreal, Que., Can., 1967-70; material scientist Bell-Northern Research, Ottawa, Ont., Can., 1970-71; research officer NRC of Can., Ottawa, 1972-84; pres. Roofing Materials Sci. and Tech., Los Angeles, 1984—; scientist, bd. dirs. Non Smokers Assn. Ottawa, 1982; lectr. profl. assns., U.N. Devel. Programs worldwide. Mem. Chem. Inst. Can., Inst. Roofing and Waterproofing Cons., Single-Ply Roofing Inst., Assn. Profl. Engrs. Ontario, AAAS (Can.), Am. Chem. Soc., ASTM, Internat. Union of Testing and Research Labs. for Material and Structures (tech. com. 1975), UN Indsl. Devels. Orgns., Internat. Conf. Bldg. Ofcls., Can. Standard Assn., Can. Gen. Standards Bd. Home and Office: 9037 Monte Mar Dr Los Angeles CA 90035

LABADIE, JOHN WOODSON, civil engineering educator; b. Los Angeles, Nov. 29, 1942; s. George Sherman and Jeanne Elizabeth (Woodson) L.; m. Susan Wyss Rowe, Aug. 11, 1973; children: Joy Cherise, Ethan Charles. BS in Engring., UCLA, 1966, MS in Engring., 1968; PhD in Ops. Research, U. Calif., Berkeley, 1972. Registered profl. engr., Colo. Asst. prof. civil engring. Colo. State U., Ft. Collins, 1972-77, assoc. prof., 1977-82, prof., 1982—; vis. scientist U.S. Army C.E., Cin., 1981-82; cons. Waterways Exptl. Sta., Vicksburg, Miss., World Bank, Nicosia, Cyprus, 1982-83, Steffen Robertson Kirsten, Denver, 1984-85, U.S. Agy. for Internat. Devel., Dhaka, Bangladesh, 1986, UN Devel. Project/World Bank Egypt Water Master Plan, 1979; invited instr. K.U. Leuven, Belgium, 1986. Contbr. numerous articles to profl. jours. cons. City Ft. Collins Water Dept., 1984. Co-recipient paper award Am. Soc. Agrl. Engrs., 1978; Grantee NSF, USDA, U.S. Army C.E., U.S. Bur. Reclamation, U.S. Dept. Energy. Mem. ASCE (publs. com., sec. control group, ops. mgmt. com.), Am. Geophys. Union, Ops. Research Soc. Am., Sigma Xi. Avocations: church related activites, music, guitar, travel, tennis. Office: Colo State U Dept Civil Engring Fort Collins CO 80523

LABAUVE, RAPHAEL JOSEPH, III, industrial hygienist, state agency official; b. Shreveport, La., June 20, 1947; s. Rapahel Joseph Jr. and Patricia Marston (Pardue) LaB.; m. Anna Moore, Dec. 23, 1972; children: Elisa Marie, Claire Therese, Annette Estelle. BS in Biology, U. N.Mex., 1971; MS in Radiol. Health, U. Ark., 1975; PhD in Environ. Health, Purdue U., 1979. Research asst. Lovelace Inhalation Toxicology Research Inst., Albuquerque, 1975-79; inhalation toxicologist Stauffer Chem. Co., Farmington, Conn., 1979-83; indsl. hygienist EID State of N.Mex., Santa Fe, 1983, writer regulations EID Air Quality Bur., 1986—, compliance officer Occupational Health and Safety Bur., 1983-86, environ. specialist Air Quality Bur., 1986—. Contbr. articles to profl. jours.; inventor in field. Mem. Health Physics Soc., Indsl. Hygiene Assn. Rio Grande chpt., Sigma Xi. Democrat. Episcopalian. Avocation: mechanics. Home: 2343 Camino Carlos Rey Santa Fe NM 87505 Office: N Mex Air Quality Bur PO Box 0968 Santa Fe NM 87505

LABDON, KENNETH CHARLES, lawyer; b. Syracuse, N.Y., Dec. 10, 1949; s. Kenneth Brown Jr. and Janet (Manley) L.; m. Diane Freeman, Dec. 28, 1974 (div. 1978); m. Catherine Conner, May 15, 1982; 1 child, Charles Atwood. B.S., St. Lawrence U., 1972; J.D., Ariz. State U., 1980. Bar: Ariz. 1980, U.S. Dist. Ct. Ariz. 1981, U.S. Ct. Appeals (9th cir.) 1983. Assoc. F. Creasy, Phoenix, 1980-81; ptnr. Tidwell & Labdon, Apache Junction, Ariz., 1981-82; sole practice, Scottsdale, Ariz., 1982-85; ptnr. Labdon & Morgan, P.A., 1986—; judge pro tem. Tempe Mcpl. Ct., 1986; contract pub. defender Scottsdale Mcpl. Ct., 1983—; mem. Scottsdale Criminal Justice Com., 1983-85; mem. misdemeanor subcom. com. on representation of indigents Ariz. Supreme Ct., 1985, mem. Auto Negligence Group, Ariz. State Bar CLE Mini Task force, 1985—. Mem. Assn. Trial Lawyers Am., Ariz. Trial Lawyers Assn., ABA, Ariz. Bar Assn., Scottsdale Bar Assn., Phi Delta Phi (v.p. 1979-80).

LABELLE, DONALD JOSEPH, public administrator; b. Kansas City, Mo., Sept. 8, 1942; s. James and Grace Hilland (Smith) LaB.; m. Sharon Kay Popp, Sept. 5, 1965; children: Todd Alan, Renee Kathleen. BA in Personnel Adminstrn., U. Kans., 1966, M in Pub. Adminstrn., 1973. Sr. budget analyst City of Ft. Worth, 1972-73, asst. pub. works dir., 1973-79; pub. works dir. Lane County, Eugene, Oreg., 1979-82, King County, Seattle, 1982—; bd. dirs. Wash. State Pub. Works Bd. Project coordinator clean community program City of Ft. Worth, 1978-79; coach Eugene Sports program, 1980-82; co-founder and mem. Issaquah (Wash.) High Band Assn., 1985—. Served to capt. USAF, 1966-71. Mem. Am. Pub. Works Assn. (named one of Top Ten Pub. Works Leaders 1987), Nat. Assn. County Engrs., Wash. Assn. County Engrs. (co-chmn. mgmt. principles, 1983-85), Internat. City Mgmt. Assn. Presbyterian. Club: Toastmasters (Ft. Worth). Lodge: Elks. Avocations: weather observation, athletics coaching. Home: 4528 169th Ave SE Issaquah WA 98027 Office: King County Pub Works 900 King County Adminstrn Bldg Seattle WA 98104

LA BELLE, JENIJOY, literature educator, writer; b. Olympia, Wash., Nov. 5, 1943; d. Joy and Carlye April (Vieth) LaB. BA cum laude, U. Wash., 1965; PhD in English and Am. Lit., U. Calif., 1969. Asst. prof. lit. Calif. Inst. Tech., Pasadena, 1969-76, assoc. prof., 1976—. Author: The Echoing Wood, 1976, Night Thoughts, 1975, Flaxman's Illustrations to Homer, 1977; contbr. articles to profl. publs. Recipient Graves award Am. Council Learned Socs., 1983; grantee Ford Found., 1964; Woodrow Wilson fellow, 1965-66, 68-69. Mem. MLA, Philol. Assn. Pacific Coast. Home: 1379 La Solana Altadena CA 91001 Office: Calif Inst Tech Humanities Social Scis Pasadena CA 91125

LABER, MARIAN ROBERTA OPPENHEIM, real estate broker; b. Hanford, Calif., Jan. 18, 1918; d. Leon and Isabelle (Estrada) Oppenheim; student San Francisco City Coll., 1966, Golden Gate Coll., 1969; m. Lawrence E. Laber, Feb. 22, 1941 (dec. 1980); children—Lawrence E., Pamela, Deborah Laber McDermott, James Harrison. Telephone operator Pacific Tel.&Tel. Co., 1936-39, instr., 1940-42; mgr. office Press Wireless, Washington, 1942-43; owner Marian Lawrence, children's shop, San Francisco, 1945-48; owner, mgr. San Bruno 5-10, San Francisco, 1947-50; with Lampley Realty, San Francisco, 1968-72, owner, real estate broker Century 21 Lampley Realty, 1972-84,, Marian Laber Real Estate, 1983-86; owner HMP Investment Co., San Francisco, 1986—. Active Boy Scouts Am., Girl Scouts U.S.A., Camp fire Girls, ARC; pres. local PTA, 1954-55; trustee Drew Coll. Prep. Sch., chmn. bd., 1975-76, 81-83. Mem. Am. Cancer Soc., San Francisco Real Estate Bd., Calif. Real Estate Assn. Roman Catholic (pres. ch. group 1950-51). Lodge: Rotary (1st woman San Francisco club 1987). Home: 2235 Laguna St Apt 405 San Francisco CA 94115 Office: HMP Investment Co 1255 Port St #405 San Francisco CA 94115

LABINGER, JAY ALAN, chemistry researcher; b. Los Angeles, July 6, 1947; s. Harry and Dorothy (Fryer) L.; m. Andrea Graubart, May 31, 1970; one child, Barbara. BS, Harvey Mudd Coll., 1968; PhD, Harvard U., 1974. Instr. chemistry Princeton (N.J.) U., 1973-75; asst. prof. U. Notre Dame, Ind., 1975-81; sr. research chemist Occidental Research Co., Irvine, Calif., 1981-83; sr. research scientist Atlantic Richfield Co., Chatsworth, Calif., 1983-84, prin. research scientist, 1984-85, research advisor, 1985-86; mem. profl. staff Calif. Inst. Tech., Pasadena, 1986—; lectr. Royal Soc. Chemistry, Coventry, Eng., 1986. Editor: Dictionary of Organometallic Compunds, 1982; contbr. articles to profl. jours. Recipient Spl. Achievement award Occidental Research Co., 1983. Mem. Am. Chem. Soc. (assoc. editor jour. 1979-81). Avocations: music, reading, tennis. Home: 2204 Villa Maria Rd Claremont CA 91711 Office: Calif Inst Tech 127-72 Pasadena CA 91125

LA BOUNTY, HUGH ORVICE, university administrator; b. Chgo., Sept. 22, 1927; s. Hugh Orvice and Dorothy (Cooper) La B.; m. Gwen Evans, Sept. 5, 1950; children—Brian, Mark, Kim, Paul, Eric. B.A., U. Redlands, 1950, M.A., 1951; Ed.D., UCLA, 1961. Mem. faculty Citrus Coll., Azusa, Calif., 1950-53; mem. faculty dept. social scis. and history Calif. State Poly. U., Pomona, 1953—; v.p. acad. affairs Calif. State Poly. U., 1967-77, pres., 1977—; cons., Tanzania, Greece, United Arab Emirates. Author: Government of California, 1957. Served with USNR, 1945-46. Mem. Inland Valley World Affairs Council (dir.), Pomona C. of C. (dir.). Office: Calif State Polytechnic Univ 3801 W Temple Ave Pomona CA 91768 *

LA BRUE, TERRY J., advertising executive; b. Fresno, Calif., Feb. 25, 1949; s. John Lawrence and Zepha Ruth (Frankum) La B.; m. Noel Elna Bodie, Sept. 8, 1979. BA in Journalism and Fine Arts, Calif. State U., Fresno, 1972. Art dir. San Francisco Progress Newspaper, 1973-74, Carter Hawley Hale, Oakland, Calif., 1974-75, Nordstrom, Inc., Seattle, 1975-77; art dir., writer Meyers, Wolfe, Kilgore& Sutter, Seattle, 1977-79; creative dir., v.p. Fisher, Brady & La Brue, Seattle, 1979—; mktg. cons., Wash., 1976—. Editor: Great British Breakfasts, 1982, British Recipes from Country Inns, 1983. Active Rep. campaigns for elected Wash. offices, 1980—. Recipient MAME Grand award Seattle Master Builders, 1985. Mem. Pub. Relations Soc. Am. (citation of excellence 1985, Totem award 1985, 86, 87), Am. Advt. Fedn. (awards com. 1984), Northwest Culinary Alliance (bd. dirs., dir. communications 1984-86), Wash. Athletic Club, Seattle Art Dirs. and Copywriters Club. Episcopalian. Clubs: Seattle Ad (Silver award 1982, 83, 84, 85), Portland Ad (Best of Show award 1982). Avocations: photography, gourmet cooking. Home: 8020 SE 34th Pl Mercer Island WA 98040 Office: Fisher Brady & La Brue Inc 2033 6th Ave Suite 717 Seattle WA 98121

LA CENTRA, BRUCE FRANK, advertising agency executive; b. Fresno, Calif., May 16, 1932; s. Anthony James and Anna (Bruce) La Centra; m. Antonia Thérèse, Nov. 22, 1961; children: Michelle, Thomas, Noelle. AB, St. Mary's Coll., Moraga, Calif., 1954. Dir. advt. Friden/Singer, San Leandro, Calif., 1960-70; dir. communications Iomec Inc., Santa Clara, Calif., 1970-71; dir. communications Rockwell Internat., Sunnyvale, Calif., 1971-73, v.p., 1973-74; pres. La Centra Advt. Inc., Palo Alto, Calif., 1974—. Served with U.S. Army, 1954-56. Democrat. Home: 35560 Blackburn Dr Newark CA 94560 Office: La Centra Advt Inc 1101 Embarcadero Palo Alto CA 94303

LACHAPELLE, CAROLE, executive secretary; b. Los Angeles, May 16, 1941; d. Clay David Key and Jean Lee (Waldie) Key Zuetel; m. Rogers E. Crane, Dec. 17, 1960; m. Frank J. LaChapelle, Oct. 11, 1975; children—Steven Scott, Shawn Marie. A.A., Santa Monica Coll., 1975. Cert. profl. sec., Calif. With Systems Devel. Corp., A. Burroughs Co., Camarillo, Calif., 1960-84, exec. sec. II Office of Chmn. and Pres., 1975-84; exec. sec. to pres., chief operating officer Angeles Corp., Los Angeles, 1984-85; staff asst. to pres. Intersci. Computer Services, Inc., 1985—; notary pub. State of Calif. Recipient Outstanding Sec. of So. Calif. award Inst. Profl. Secs. Internat., 1982. Mem. Profl. Secs. Internat. (v.p. 1982-83), Nat. Notary Assn. Republican. Methodist. Office: 5171 Clareton Dr Agoura Hills CA 91301

LACHMAN, MARY ELIZABETH, patent agent; b. Balt., Nov. 17, 1942; d. Harry and Emma Mary (Richelderfer) L. A.B. summa cum laude,

Goucher Coll., 1962. Research asst. Johns Hopkins U., Balt., 1962-63; tech. asst. AEC, Brookhaven Nat. Lab., Upton, N.Y., 1963-64, analytical chemist Nat. Reactor Testing Sta., Idaho Falls, Idaho, 1964-65; tech. info. asst. Lawrence Radiation Lab Inorganic Materials Research, Berkeley, Calif., 1965; patent asst. Shell Devel. Co., Emeryville, Calif., 1965-68; mem. tech. staff Hughes Aircraft Co., Culver City, Calif., 1969-73, project engr., 1973-77, patent agt., 1977-81, sr. patent agt., El Segundo, 1981—. Mem. Los Angeles Patent Law Assn., Hughes Aircraft Co. Mgmt. Club, Phi Beta Kappa. Office: Hughes Aircraft Corp Patents/Licensing Bldg E12 Mail Sta A161 PO Box 902 El Segundo CA 90245

LACK, FRED SEVIER, III, motorcycle and jet ski accessory manufacturer; b. Los Angeles, Oct. 4, 1947; s. Fred S. and Ruth Munro (Reynolds) L.; m. Barbara Ann Bell, June 19, 1971 (div.); 1 child, Kelly Suzanne. BS in Mktg., U. So. Calif., 1970. Account mgr. Mattel, Inc., Hawthorne, Calif., 1971-72; owner Fredmark Distbg. Co., Inglewood, Calif., 1972-76; nat. sales mgr. Filter Dynamics, Inc., Santa Ana, Calif., 1976-78; account mgr. Flecto Co., Oakland, Calif., 1978-80; owner Fred S. Lack III and Assocs., Culver City, Calif., 1981—, Atlantis Enterprises. Mem. Internat. Jet Ski Boating Assn., Sigma Alpha Epsilon. Republican. Presbyterian. Office: Fred S Lack and Assocs 5900 Canterbury Dr Suite A107 Culver City CA 90230

LACY, CAROL ANGELA, insurance executive; b. Watford, Eng., July 15, 1943; came to U.S., 1967, naturalized, 1976; d. Thomas and Winifred Joan (Stromberg) Carney; m. Floyd Raymond Lacy, May 25, 1968; children—Susan, Timothy. Claims adjuster Central Mut. Ins. Co., Toronto, Can., 1964-68; exec. sec. TransFresh Corp., Salinas, Calif., 1968-70; claims examiner Monterey Bay Found., Salinas, 1972-78; pres., account mgr. ABC Med. Claims Services, Salinas, 1978—; chmn. bd. dirs. Monterey County Spl. Health Care Authority, Salinas, 1982-85. mem. adv. bd. Natividad Hosp., Salinas, 1979-82, North Monterey County Bd. Edn., Salinas, 1977-83; treas. Monterey County Bds. Assn., Salinas, 1981-83; mem. Monterey County Grand Jury, Salinas, 1984-85; pres. Prunedale PTA, Salinas, 1976. Recipient Honorary Service award Prunedale PTA, 1982. Mem. Monterey Bay Life Underwriters Assn. Republican. Baptist. Avocations: stamp collecting; fishing; gardening.

LACY, LEE MARVA LOU, educator; b. Longview, Tex., Dec. 28, 1942; d. Louis and Grace Tecumseh (Davis) Armstrong; BS in Math., Prairie View (Tex.) A&M U., 1965; MA in Secondary Math. Edn. (grantee Roosevelt Sch. Dist. 1977-78), Ariz. State U., 1978; m. Troy Lee Lacy, June 20, 1965; children: Corwyn Enrico, Aimee Siubhan, Gardenia Catriona. Tchr. math. schs. in Tex., Nebr., Md. and Ariz., 1965-68, 69-77; sr. gen. edn. instr., counselor Washington Jobs Corps, 1968; tchr. math., spl. tchr. for gifted C.O. Greenfield Jr. High Sch., Phoenix, 1978-82; math and gifted resource tchr. T.B. Barr Sch., Phoenix, 1982-85; instr. math. South Mountain Community Coll. at Ariz. State U., Tempe, 1985—; faculty assoc. Prairie View A&M U., 1981-83; vis. math. tchr. South Mountain Community Coll., Phoenix, 1982-85; workshop leader, cons. in field. Vol., Arthritis Found., Leukemia Soc.; v.p., trustee sanctuary choir First Instl. Bapt. Ch., Phoenix. Mem. Nat. Council Tchrs. Math., NEA, Assn. Supervision and Curriculum Devel., Ariz. Edn. Assn., Ariz. Assn. Tchrs. Math., Roosevelt Classroom Tchrs. Assn., Ariz. State U. Alumni Assn., Delta Sigma Theta Alumnae. Baptist. Home: 416 E Greenway Dr Tempe AZ 85282 Office: Ariz State U PSA 444 Tempe AZ 85287

LAD, PRAMOD MADHUSUDAN, research scientist; b. Bombay, Dec. 25, 1948; came to U.S., 1970; s. Madhusudan Mangesh and Lila Madhusudan (Nadkarni) L.; m. Urmila Waman Desai, Mar. 31, 1978; 1 child, Shivanand. BS with honors, King's Coll., London, 1970; MS, Cornell U., 1972, PhD, 1974. Research fellow NIH, Bethesda, Md., 1975-77, sr. staff scientist, 1977-80; dir. Regional Research Lab., Los Angeles, 1981—; cons. Amicon Corp., Boston, 1975-76. Contbr. articles to profl. jours. Recipient Am. Heart Assn. prize, 1984; NIH grantee, 1981, Am. Heart Assn. grantee 1986—. Mem. Endocrine Soc., Am. Soc. Pharmacology (symposia chmn. 1985-86), Biophys. Soc., Am. Acad. Allergy and Immunology, Am. Chem. Soc., Sigma Xi. Club: Cornell. Avocations: cinema, poetry, hiking. Home: 520 N San Marino Ave North San Gabriel CA 91775 Office: Regional Research Lab Kaiser Found Hosps 4953 Sunset Blvd Los Angeles CA 90027

LADANYI, BRANKA MARIA, chemist, educator; b. Zagreb, Yugoslavia, Sept. 7, 1947; came to U.S., 1969; d. Branko and Nevenka (Zilic) L.; m. Marshall Fixman, Dec. 7, 1974. BSc, McGill U., Montreal, Can., 1969; M in Philosophy, Yale U., 1971, PhD, 1973. Vis. prof. of chemistry U. Ill., 1974; postdoctoral research assoc. Yale U., 1974-77, research assoc., 1977-79; asst. prof. chemistry Colo. State U., Ft. Collins, 1979-84, assoc. prof. chemistry, 1985-87, prof. chemistry, 1987—. Referee and contbr. articles to profl. jours. Fellow Sloan Found., 1982-84, Dreyfus Found., 1983-87; NSF grantee. Mem. AAAS, Am. Chem. Soc. (PRF grantee 1979-82), Am. Phys. Soc., NOW, Sigma Xi. Home: 1100 E Pitkin St Fort Collins CO 80524 Office: Colo State U Dept Chemistry Fort Collins CO 80523

LADD, ALAN WALBRIDGE, JR., motion picture executive; b. Los Angeles, Oct. 22, 1937; s. Alan Walbridge and Marjorie Jane (Harrold) L.; m. Patricia Ann Beazley, Aug. 30, 1959 (div. 1983); children: Kelliann, Tracy Elizabeth, Amanda Sue; m. Cindra Kay, July 13, 1985. Motion picture agt. Creative Mgmt., Los Angeles, 1963-69; v.p. prodn. 20th Century Fox Film Corp., Los Angeles, 1973-74; sr. v.p. 20th Century Fox Film Corp. (Worldwide Prodns. div.), Beverly Hills, Calif., 1974-76; pres. Twentieth Century-Fox Pictures, 1976-79, Ladd Co., Burbank, Calif., 1979-83; pres., chief operating officer MGM/UA Entertainment Co., 1983-86, chief exec. officer, from 1986, also chmn. bd. dirs.; now chmn., chief exec. officer Metro-Goldwyn-Meyer Pictures, Inc., Culver City, Calif. Producer: films Walking Stick, 1969, A Severed Head, 1969, TamLin, 1970, Villian Zee and Co, 1971; exec. producer: films Nightcomers, 1971; producer: films Fear is the Key, 1973. Served with USAF, 1961-63. Office: MGM Pictures Inc 10000 Washington Blvd Culver City CA 90232 *

LADD, DONALD MC KINLEY, JR., lawyer; b. Huntington Park, Calif., Oct. 24, 1923; s. Donald McKinley and Rose (Roberts) L.; B.A., Denison U., 1945; J.D., Stanford U., 1950; m. Eleanor June Martin, June 29, 1951; children—Donald, Richard, Cameron. Admitted to Calif. bar, 1950; asso. firm Anderson McPharlin & Conners, Los Angeles, 1951; legal staff Union Pacific RR, Los Angeles, 1953-56; sr. dep. prosecutor City of Pasadena (Calif.), 1956-58; with Office of Dist. Atty., Santa Clara County, Calif., 1958—, asst. dist. atty., 1971—. Served to capt. USMCR, 1943-46, 51-52. Certified criminal law specialist Calif. Mem. Bay Area Prosecutors Assn., Calif. State Bar, Calif. Dist. Attys Assn., Stanford Law Alumni Assn., Blue Key, Omicron Delta Kappa, Phi Alpha Delta. Clubs: Marines Meml., Am. Commons. Home: 1034 Golden Way Los Altos CA 94022 Office: Office of Dist Atty Santa Clara County 70 W Hedding St San Jose CA 95110

LADD, RICHARD CORRIN, state official; b. Kalispell, Mont., May 2, 1939; s. John Corrin and Betty Jean (Demory) L.; m. Marda Lu Pinkerton, Apr. 22, 1960; children—Laura, Michael. B.A., Oreg. State U., 1976, M.Ed., 1977. With pvt. industry, Oreg., 1961-76; researcher cons. pub. agys., Salem, Oreg., 1976-77; chief researcher Oreg. Dept. Human Research, Salem, 1977-79, mgr. FIG-Waiver Project, 1979-80, dir. spl. projects, 1980-81; adminstr. Oreg. Sr. Services Div., Salem, 1981—. Served with USN, 1957-61; PTO. Mem. Am. Acad. Polit. and Social Sci., Acad. Polit. Sci., Am. Soc. on Aging, Nat. Council of State Human Resource Adminstrs., Nat. Assn. State Units on Aging, Oreg. Gerontol. Assn., State Medicaid Dirs. Assn., Phi Kappa Phi. Democrat. Home: 1003 Madrona S Salem OR 97302 Office: Sr Services Div 313 Pub Service Bldg Salem OR 97310

LADISCH, STEPHAN, medical researcher, pediatrician, educator; b. Garmisch-Partenkirchen, Fed. Republic Germany, July 18, 1947; came to U.S., 1948, naturalized, 1959; s. Rolf Karl and Brigitte (Gareis) L.; m. Brigitte Bidault, May 22, 1974; children: Gwenola, Virginie. BS in Chemistry, U. Pa., 1969, MD, 1973. Diplomate Am. Bd. Pediatrics; subcert. in pediatric hematology/oncology. Intern Children's Hosp. Med. Ctr., Boston, 1973-74, resident, 1974-75; clin. assoc. pediatric oncology br. Nat. Cancer Inst., Bethesda, Md., 1975-77, investigator, 1977-78; asst. prof. pediatrics, sr. mem. human immunobiology group UCLA Sch. Medicine, 1978-82, assoc. prof., 1982-86, prof., 1986—. Contbr. articles to profl. jours. Recipient Research Career Devel. award, 1982; Grantee NSF, 1968-69, NIH, 1980—, Am. Cancer Soc., 1985—; Von L. Meyer travel fellow, 1975; Leukemia Soc. Am. scholar, 1982—. Mem. AAAS, Am. Assn. Immunologists, Am. Soc. Hematology, Western Soc. For Pediatric Research, Am. Fedn. for Clin. Research, Soc. for Pediatric Research, Soc. Complex Carbohydrates, Phi Beta Kappa, Alpha Chi Sigma, Phi Lambda Upsilon. Home: 650 Via de la Paz Pacific Palisades CA 90272 Office: UCLA Sch Medicine Dept Pediatrics Los Angeles CA 90024

LADMAN, JERRY R., economist, educator; b. Sioux City, Iowa, Dec. 30, 1935; s. Harry L. and Amy I. (Swearingen) L.; m. Mary E. Ladman, June 4, 1960; children—Jeffrey, James, Michael. B.S., Iowa State U., 1958, Ph.D., 1968. Placement officer Coll. Agr., Iowa State U., Ames, 1963-65, research asst., 1965-67; asst. prof. Ariz. State U., 1967-72, assoc. prof., 1972-78, prof. econs., 1979—, dir. Ctr. for Latin Am. Studies, 1976—; program asst. Ford Found., Mexico City, 1971-72; vis. prof. Nat. Sch. Agr., Chapingo, Mex., 1965-67, 71-72, Ohio State U., 1979; vis. scholar Stanford U., 1975; hon. prof. Cath. U. Bolivia, 1986; participant U.S.-U.S.S.R. Cultural Exchange, 1986. Author: The Development of Mexicali Regional Economy, 1975, United States-Mexican Energy Relationships: Realities and Prospects, 1981, Modern Day Bolivia: The Legacy of the Revolution and Prospects for the Future, 1982, Mexico: A Country in Crisis, 1987; contbr. articles to profl. jours., chpts. to books. Chmn. troop com. Boy Scouts Am., Tempe, Ariz., 1976-84; bd. dirs. Friends of Mexican Art, 1977-86. Served to capt. USAR, 1958-65. Fulbright lectr., Ecuador, 1974. Mem. Am. Econ. Assn., Am. Agrl. Econ. Assn., Latin Am. Studies Assn., Pacific Coast Council Latin Am. Studies (treas. 1977—, v.p. 1986, pres. 1987), Rocky Mountain Council Latin Am. Studies (bd. dirs. 1976—), Phoenix Com. Fgn. Relations, Ariz.-Mex. Commn. (bd. dirs. 1982—), Assn. Borderlands Scholars (pres. 1983-85), PROFMEX (bd. dirs. 1983—). Home: 1201 E Loyola Dr Tempe AZ 85282 Office: Ctr Latin Am Studies Ariz State U Tempe AZ 85287

LAFAVOR, JUDITH ANN, sales executive; b. Cushing, Okla., Aug. 1, 1943; d. Forrest W. Faith and Virginia L. (Whiteside) Baker; m. John Michael Gibson, Aug. 3, 1973 (div. Oct. 1975); children: Faith Ann, Charles Forrest; m. Larry Leroy Lafavor, Oct. 31, 1984. AA, Mira Costa Jr. Coll., 1963; student, Calif. State U., San Diego, 1968-69, Calif. State U., Long Beach, 1980-81. Credit mgr. Sears Roebuck & Co., Vista, Calif., 1963-65; supr. bus. office Pacific Telephone, Vista, San Diego, 1965-73; credit mgr. Data Pathing, Sunnyvale, Calif., 1975-79; sr. sect. supr. McAuto, Cypress, Calif., 1979-82; supr. sales Anchorage Telephone Utility Services, 1982-86, chmn. product research and devel., 1985-86, supr. billing and collection, 1986—; cons. State of Alaska Telecom Commn., Juneau, 1983-85. Mem. Nat. Assn. Female Execs., Alaska Telecommunications Profl. Assn., Beta Sigma Phi (Woman of Yr., 1977, 80). Democrat. Episcopalian. Avocations: bowling, reading, arts and crafts, building own home, boating. Home: SRC Box 8096 Palmer AK 99645 Office: Anchorage Telephone Utility Service Telephone Ave Anchorage AK 99503

LAFFERTY, LAVEDI ROBERTA CAROL, non-profit corporate executive, consultant; b. Cin., Dec. 30, 1936; d. Robert Baird and Ruth Faye (Cone) L.; m. Ray Nicholas Wiebe, June 5, 1955 (div. 1962); m. Stanley Thomas Bulstrode, Oct. 30, 1962 (div. 1964); m. Steven Preston Pipella, May 22, 1973 (div. Oct. 1974); 1 child, Roblyn Lafferty Bulstrode. Student U. of the Americas, Mexico City, 1967-68, U. Alaska, 1972-83. Ordained to ministry Collegiate Ch., 1977. Exec. dir. The Alaskan Ctr. for Ind. Living, Inc., Fairbanks, 1979-82; trustee Collegians Internat. Ch., Fairbanks, 1977—; pres., founder The Philos. Heritage Inst. Inc., 1978—, Library Esoteric Studies, Fairbanks, 1971-84, The Vortex Inst., Inc., Fairbanks, 1971-77, Aquarian Cons., Inc., Fairbanks, 1982-85; instr. Tanana Valley Community Coll., Fairbanks, 1976-77, World U., Ojai, Calif., 1972-79. Author: Reincarnation: Explained, 1977; The Past-Life Memory Program, 1977; The Eternal Dance, 1983, Spiritual Synthesis, 1987. Editor The Vortex Voice, 1972-74. Exec. planning legis. cons. Gov.'s Council for Handicapped and Gifted, State of Alaska, 1980-83. Recipient Vol. Recognition award Arctic Alliance for People, Fairbanks, Alaska, 1983, Cert. of Appreciation, Gov.'s Council for Handicapped and Gifted, State of Alaska, 1983. Mem. Theosophical Soc., Assn. Humanistic Psychology, Assn. Transpersonal Psychology, Unity-in-Diversity Council, Planetary Citizens, Ctr. Tibetan Buddhist Studies and Culture, Northstar Wholistic Network (co-founder), Assn. for Past-Life Research and Therapy, Assn. for Research and Enlightenment. Democrat. Lodge: Order Eastern Star. Office: PO Box 929 Fairbanks AK 99707

LA FLASH, GEORGE WINTHROP, physician; b. Worcester, Mass., June 3, 1920; s. George Robert and Elizabeth B. (Worden) La F.; B.S., Wesleyan U., 1947; M.D., Columbia U., 1951; m. Kasandra Edin, Aug. 15, 1964; 1 child, Joanell. Intern, St. Luke's Hosp., N.Y.C., 1951-52, resident in medicine, 1952-53; practice medicine, specializing in family medicine, Long Beach, Calif., 1953-68, occupational and indsl. medicine, 1968—; chief physician McDonnell Douglas Space Systems Center, Huntington Beach, Calif., 1968-73; med. dir. and partner occupational and indsl. medicine Avenue Med. Group, Santa Fe Springs, Calif., 1973—; co-owner med. ptnr. Stadium East Med. Group, Orange, Calif., 1979—; sr. med. aviation examiner FAA; mem. sci. adv. bd. Nat. Acad. Child Devel. Author: Mysteries, Miracles and Molecules of New Age Medicine; New Age Medicine in the Workplace, Masters of Our Molecules, Stop Dying and Start Living, How to Listen to the Human Heart. Served with M.C., USAAF, 1941-46. Diplomate Nat. Bd. Med. Examiners. Fellow Am. Soc. Contemporary Medicine and Surgery; mem. Am. Occupational Med. Assn., Am. Coll. Preventive Medicine, AMA (Physicians Recognition award 1979, 80), Calif. Med. Assn., Orange County Med. Assn., Internat. Coll. Applied Nutrition, Aerospace Med. Assn., Orthomolecular Med. Soc., Nat. Seminar Team, Nat. Platform Assn. Home: 738 Elizabeth Dr Orange CA 92667 Office: 1215 W Katella Ave Orange CA 92667

LAFLASH, JEANNETTE RAYMOND, aerospace and marketing executive; b. Moosup, Conn., Sept. 15, 1924; d. Arthur Raymond and Alice Gauthier; m. Judson LaFlash; children: Mark Steven, Christopher Raymond. BS, U. Mass., 1950. RN St. Vincent's Hosp., Worcester, Mass., Ankara and Izmir, Turkey and Athens, Greece, 1951-55; dir. Long Beach (Calif.) Med. Ctr., 1956-63; v.p. ops. Govt. Mktg., Inc., Woodland Hills, Calif., 1975-82, chief ops. officer, 1982—; seminar dir. Govt. Mktg., Inc.; exec. v.p. Govt. Mktg. Pub., Santa Fe. Editor aerospace and def. reports, proposals, etc. Office: Govt Mktg Inc 2305 Catalina Ave Vista CA 92084

LAFLASH, JUDSON CLINTON, defense/aerospace marketing exec.; b. Mashpee, Mass., May 19, 1924; s. George Robert and Elizabeth Bancker (Worden) LaF.; BA Syracuse (N.Y.) U., 1949, postgrad., 1949-51; postgrad. Fgn. Service Inst., 1951, Northrop U., 1975; m. Jeannette Raymond, Jan. 17, 1951; children: Mark Steven, Christopher Raymond. Journalist, Syracuse Herald-Jour., 1949-51; fgn. service officer, press officer, pub. affairs officer U.S. Fgn. Service, Dept. State, Turkey, Greece, Washington, 1951-55; pub. info. officer Ramo-Wooldridge Corp., Los Angeles, 1955-58; mktg. writer, pub. info. officer TRW and Aerospace Corp.; lectr. in field; head advanced tech. mktg. Hughes Aircraft Co., El Segundo, Calif., and Canoga Park, Calif., 1962-73; sr. marketing mgr. fgn. mil. and NATO sales planning Rockwell Internat., Anaheim, Calif., 1973-74; mktg. mgr. Systems Devel. Corp., Santa Monica, 1974-77; pres., chmn. bd. Govt. Mktg. Inc., Woodland Hills, Calif., 1977—; mktg. cons. Gen. Electric, Northrop, Honeywell, Textron, Westinghouse, McDonnell Douglas, IBM, Rockwell Internat., Electronic Data Systems, numerous others; pres., chief operating officer Govt. Mktg. Pub., Santa Fe; cons. USN; prof. mktg. Grad. Sch., Northrop U.; mem. faculty UCLA Extension. Served with AUS, 1943-46; ETO. Mem. AIAA (sr.), Nat. Contracts Mgmt. Assn., Am. Astron. Soc., Nat. Space Club, Aviation/Space Writers Assn., Phi Kappa Tau. Author: An Assessment of International Markets and Priorities; The Proposal: Document of Decision; How the U.S. Government Conducts Source Selection; mem. editorial adv. bd. Defense Electronics mag.; publisher Proposal/Mktg. World, ScienTech Newservice. Home and office: 23113 Dolorosa St Woodland Hills CA 91367

LA FLEUR, HELENE, electronic company executive; b. Paris, France, Apr. 17, 1926; came to U.S., 1950; m. James K. La Fleur, May 4, 1964. Certificat Secondaire Coll. de Jeunes Filles, Pau, France. Lang. prof., translator, 1950-57; internat. pub. relations interpreter Douglas Aircraft Co., Santa Monica, Calif., 1957-58, J. Walter Thompson Indsl. Div., Los Angeles, 1958-60; pres., owner Kaylane Co., Los Angeles, 1959-66; v.p. Indsl. Cryogenics, Toluca Lake, Calif., 1966—. Kaylane Advt., Toluca Lake, 1980—; sec. Am. Graves Registration Services, U.S. Army, Paris, 1944-46, Radiodiffusion Francaise, Paris, France, 1948-50, Office Fgn. Liquidation in Europe, Paris, 1946-48. Republican. Clubs: University, Duquesnes (Pitts.); New York Yacht (N.Y.C.); Royal Cork Yacht (Crosshaven, Ireland); Lakeside Golf (Toluca Lake); Assocs. Caltech (Pasadena, Calif.). Home: 4337 Talofa Ave Toluca Lake CA 91602

LAFLEUR, LAWRENCE EUGENE, research chemist; b. Everett, Wash., Sept. 18, 1951; s. Eugene Harvey and Marie Margarett (Longberg) LaF. B.S. summa cum laude, U. Puget Sound, 1975; M.S., U. Oreg., 1977. Cert. profl. chemist. Lab. technician U.S. Oil & Refining Co., Tacoma, 1972-75; research asst. U. Oreg., Eugene, 1975-77; research chemist Nat. Council Paper Industry for Air and Stream Improvement, Corvallis, Oreg., 1977-83, organic analytical program mgr., 1983—; environ. cons. forest products industry, 1979—. Recipient Student Affiliate award Am. Chem. Soc., 1975; La Pore award U. Puget Sound, 1974. Fellow Am. Chem. Soc.; mem. Am. Soc. Mass Spectrometry, AAAS, Assn. Ofcl. Analytical Chemists, Standard Methods Com. (chmn. joint task group), Phi Kappa Phi. Home: 27060 Forest Springs Lane Corvallis OR 97330 Office: NCASI 720 SW 4th St PO Box 458 Corvallis OR 97339

LA FORTUNE, GAIL C., educator; b. Oakland, Calif., June 19, 1930; d. Horace Radley and Celia Leona (Marchus) LaF. B.A., Pomona Coll., 1952; M.A., Calif. State U.-Sacramento, 1972; postgrad. Tchr., choir dir. Bret Harte Sch., Sacramento, 1953-66; tchr., choir dir. Sutterville Sch., Sacramento, 1966-87, vice prin., 1981-84, tchr. gifted and talented edn., 1982-87; dir. elem. honor choir Sacramento City Schs., 1980; dir. youth choir Westminster Ch., Sacramento, 1977-80. Recipient honor service award PTA, 1962, 71. Mem. Music Educators Nat. Conf., NEA, Internat. Soc. Music Educators, Sierra Club, Phi Delta Kappa (pres.-elect Sacramento chpt. 1986—), Delta Kappa Gamma (state music chmn. 1983-85, state ceremonials chmn. 1985—), Alpha Delta Kappa (state music chmn. 1982-84, S.W. region music chmn. 1985—), Pi Lambda Theta (pres. Sacramento area 1986—). Republican. Presbyterian. Office: 4967 Monterey Way Sacramento CA 95822

LAFRENZ, MARY ADELE, home economics consultant, journalist; b. Princeton, Ill., Jan. 18, 1943; d. Conrad Walter and Hildagard Catherine (Montavon) Knuth; m. Wayne Augustine Lafrenz, June 24, 1967; children—Michelle Felice, Renée Marie. Student Rosary Coll., 1961-62; B.S. in Home Econs., U. Dayton, 1965; M.A. in Consumer Econs., San Francisco State U., 1974. Staff asst. Westinghouse Electric Corp., sales office, San Francisco, 1965-67; home economist consumer services Del Monte Corp., world hdqrs., San Francisco, 1967-76; home econs. cons., journalist Waydel Enterprises, San Francisco, 1976—. Editor San Francisco State U. Home Econs. Alumni News, 1983—. Mem. Home Economists in Bus. (sec. 1973-74, nominations com. 1981-82), Internat. Fedn. Home Econs., Am. Home Econs. Assn., Calif. Home Econs. Assn.

LAGASSE, BRUCE KENNETH, structural engineer; b. Bklyn., Feb. 1, 1940; s. Joseph F. Lagasse and Dora Gould. BSME, U. Calif., Berkeley, 1964. Structures engr. Rockwell Internat., Canoga Park, Calif., 1964-69; mem. tech. staff Hughes Aircraft Co., Los Angeles, 1969-70; sr. staff engr. Hughes Aircraft Co., El Segundo, Calif., 1972—; sr. engr. Litton Ship Systems, Los Angeles, 1971-72; lectr. Hughes Aircraft Co., El Segundo, 1980—; cons. in field, Van Nuys, Calif., 1979—. Libertarian state chmn., Los Angeles, 1977-79, nat. committeeman, Washington, 1979-81. Mem. ASME. Avocations: reading, jogging, hiking, symphonic music, photography. Home: 14607 Erwin St #311 Van Nuys CA 91411

LAGINESS, DUANE AUGUST, furniture manager; b. Rockwood, Mich., Feb. 25, 1934; s. Legrand Jerome and Lucile Marie (Goniea) L. Grad. high sch., Trenton, Mich. Mgr., designer Design Imports, Pasadena, Calif., 1964-72, Mel Brown Furniture, Los Angeles, 1972—. Mem. Rep. Task Force. Roman Catholic. Avocations: water color and charcoal portraits, horseback riding. Home: 4621 Allott Ave Sherman Oaks CA 91423

LAGOMARSINO, ROBERT JOHN, congressman; b. Ventura, Calif., Sept. 4, 1926; s. Emilio J. and Marjorie (Gates) L.; m. Norma Jean Mabrey, Nov. 10, 1960; children: Dexter, Karen, Dana. B.A., U. Calif., Santa Barbara, 1950; J.D., U. Santa Clara, Calif., 1954. Bar: Calif. 1954. Individual practice law Ventura, 1954; mem. Ojai (Calif.) City Council, 1958-61, mayor, 1958-61; mem. Calif. Senate, 1961-74, 93d-100th Congresses from 19th Calif. Dist., 1974—; mem. fgn. affairs com., house interior and insular affairs com.; sec. Rep. Conf. Served with USNR, 1944-46. Recipient Pearl Chase Conservation Edn. award, 1970; recipient Legislator Conservationist of Year award Calif. Wildlife Fedn., 1965, Honor award Calif. Conservation Council, 1967, Peace Officers Research Assn. award, 1966. Mem. Calif. Bar Assn., Ventura County Bar Assn., D.C. Bar Assn. Republican. Roman Catholic. Clubs: Elks, Moose, Eagles, Rotary. Office: 2332 Rayburn House Office Bldg Washington DC 20515

LAGRAVE, LOUIS JOSEPH, JR., corporate professional counselor; b. Pasadena, Calif., Jan. 13, 1942; s. Louis Joseph Sr. and Ruth Estelle (Neuman) L.; m. R. Jean Higgins, Aug. 24, 1960 (div. Jan. 1981); children: Dean Kenneth, Don Louis; m. Cheryl Dockstader, Aug. 22, 1981; 1 child, Sean Jay. BA, Claremont Men's Coll. (now Claremont McKenna Coll.), 1965. Various retail positions Goodyear Tire and Rubber Co., So. Calif., 1965-73; store mgr. Goodyear Tire and Rubber Co., San Diego, 1973-74; asst. dist. mgr. retail div. Goodyear Tire and Rubber Co., Portland, Oreg., 1974-76; mgr. dealer devel. Goodyear Tire and Rubber Co., Salt Lake City, 1976-78, dist. mgr., 1978-85; counselor dealer devel. Goodyear Tire and Rubber Co., Phoenix, 1985-87; dist. sales mgr. Goodyear Tire and Rubber Co., Los Angeles, 1987—. Coach various youth sports teams in Calif., Oreg. and Utah, 1960-80. Recipient Goodyear Spirit award P.W. Litchfield Found., 1979, Affiliate award Claremont McKenna Coll., 1982. Democrat. Avocations: fly fishing, dog tng., collecting Indian pottery, guitar playing, tennis. Office: Goodyear Tire and Rubber Co 6666 E Washington Los Angeles CA 90051

LAI, MICHAEL MING-CHIAO, microbiology educator; b. Tainan, Taiwan, Republic of China, Sept. 8, 1942; came to U.S., 1969; s. Tsai-Sen and Tsan-Hwa (Shih) L.; m. Cathy Hwei-ying Wung, Jan. 1, 1971; children: Cindy, Jennifer. MD, Nat. Taiwan U., Taipei, 1968; PhD, U. Calif., Berkeley, 1973. Asst. prof. U. So. Calif., Los Angeles, 1973-78, assoc. prof., 1978-83, prof. microbiology, 1983—. Mem. NIH (exptl. virology study sect.), Am. Soc. Microbiology, Am. Soc. Virology, Am. Soc. Biol. Chemists. Home: 1215 Wabash St Pasadena CA 91103 Office: U So Calif Sch Medicine Dept Microbiology 2011 Zonal Ave Los Angeles CA 90033

LAI, SHIH-TSE JASON, chemistry researcher; b. Chia-yi, Republic of China, Oct. 29, 1951; came to U.S., 1977, naturalized, 1985; s. Chi-Kuei and Yu-Lien (Kao) L.; m. Wei Bamboo Lee, June 25, 1980; 1 child, Shin-Hwa Jeffrey Lee. BS, Nat. Chung-Hsing U., Taichung, Republic of China, 1974; PhD, CUNY, 1983. Adminstrn. asst. Tunghai U., Taichung, 1976-77; adjunct lectr. CUNY, Bklyn., 1977-78; research fellow CUNY, Flushing, 1978-83; sr. chemist Rockwell Internat., Newport Beach, Calif., 1983-85; head mass spectrometry lab. Tech. & Ventures div. Baxter Travenol, Irvine, Calif., 1985—. Contbr. numerous articles to profl. jours. Coach Tunghai U. Rugby Team, 1976-77; patron Laguna Moulton Playhouse, Laguna Beach, Calif., 1986—. University fellow, CUNY, 1977; recipient Fellow A scholarship CUNY, 1978-83. Fellow Am. Inst. Chemists; mem. AAAS, N.Y. Acad. Scis., Am. Chem. Soc. (mem. program com. Orange County chpt. 1985-87), Chinese Culture Assn. (pres. CUNY chpt. 1978-80), Am. Soc. Mass Spectrometry, Sigma Xi.

LAI, WAIHANG, educator; b. Hong Kong, Jan. 7, 1939; s. Sing and Yu-ching (Wong) L.; came to U.S., 1964; B.A., Chinese U. Hong Kong, 1964; M.A., Claremont Grad. Sch., 1967; m. Celia Cheung, Aug. 13, 1966. Asst. prof. art Maunaolu Coll., Maui, Hawaii, 1968-70; instr. art Kauai (Hawaii) Community Coll., 1970—. Vis. prof. art Ariz. State U., Tempe, summer 1967. Mem. Am., Kauai (pres. 1974—) watercolor socs., Phila. Watercolor Club, Kauai Oriental Art Soc. (pres. 1981—). Author: The Chinese Landscape Paintings of Waihang Lai, 1966; The Watercolors of Waihang Lai,

1967. Home: PO Box 363 Lihue HI 96766 Office: Kauai Community Coll Lihue HI 96766

LAIDLAW, HARRY HYDE, JR., entomology educator; b. Houston, Apr. 12, 1907; s. Harry Hyde and Elizabeth Louisa (Quinn) L.; B.S., La. State U., 1933, M.S., 1934; Ph.D. (Univ. fellow, Genetics fellow, Wis. Dormitory fellow, Wis. Alumni Research Found. fellow), U. Wis., 1939; m. Ruth Grant Collins, Oct. 26, 1946; 1 dau., Barbara Scott Laidlaw Murphy. Teaching asst. La. State U., 1933-34, research asst., 1934-35; prof. biol. sci. Oakland City (Ind.) Coll., 1939-41; state apiarist Ala. Dept. Agr. and Industries, Montgomery, 1941-42; entomologist First Army, N.Y.C., 1946-47; asst. prof. entomology, asst. apiculturist U. Calif.-Davis, 1947-53, asso. prof. entomology, asso. apiculturist, 1953-60, prof. entomology, apiculturist, 1960-74, asso. dean Coll. Agr., 1960-64, prof. entomology emeritus, apiculturist emeritus, 1974—; coordinator U. Calif.-Egypt Agrl. Devel. Program, AID, 1979-83. Rockefeller Found. grantee, Brazil, 1954-55, Sudan, 1967. Trustee, Yolo County (Calif.) Med. Soc. Scholarship Com., 1965-83. Served to capt. AUS, 1942-46. Recipient Cert. of Merit, Am. Bee Jour., 1957; Spl. Merit award U. Calif.-Davis, 1959; Merit award, Calif. Central Valley Bee Club, 1974; Merit award Western Apicultural Soc., 1980, Gold Merit award Internat. Fedn. Beekeepers' Assns., 1986; NIH grantee, 1963-66; NSF grantee, 1966-74. Fellow AAAS; mem. Am. Genetics Assn., Am. Inst. Biol. Scis., Am. Soc. Naturalists, Am. Soc. Zoologists, Entomol. Soc. Am. (C.W. Woodworth award Pacific br. 1981), Genetics Soc. Am., Internat. Bee Research Assn., Nat. Assn. Uniformed Services, Ret. Officers Assn., Scabbard and Blade, Sigma Xi (treas. Davis chpt. 1959-60, v.p. chpt. 1966-67), Alpha Gamma Rho (pres. La. chpt. 1933-34, counsellor Western Province 1960-66). Democrat. Presbyterian. Club: Commonwealth (San Francisco). Author books, the most recent being: Instrumental Insemination of Honey Bee Queens, 1977; Contemporary Queen Rearing, 1979; author slide set: Instrumental Insemination of Queen Honey Bees, 1976. Home: 761 Sycamore Ln Davis CA 95616 Office: Davis CA 95616

LAIRD, PAMELA SUE, entrepreneur; b. Conneaut, Ohio, Aug. 6, 1955; d. Howard Duane and Joan Elaine (Walrath) L.; m. Paul Lyman Bixby, June 14, 1979 (div. June 1983); m. Mark Peter Jacobsen, May 30, 1987. BSJ, Northwestern U., 1978, M in Mgmt., 1979. Asst. brand mgr. Procter & Gamble, Cin., 1979-81; brand mgr. Clorox Co., Oakland, Calif., 1981-84; product mgr. DHL Worldwide Express, Redwood City, Calif., 1984-86; founder Valet Express, 1987. Bd. dirs. Advs. for Women, San Francisco, 1983-86. Home: 1128 Chestnut San Francisco CA 94109

LAJCZOK, MARTIN RALPH, aerospace engineer; b. Bradford, Eng., Nov. 19, 1950; came to U.S., 1951; s. Leon and Eugenia (Badetko) L.; m. Elizabeth Perkin Parker, Dec. 15, 1975 (dec. Aug. 1981); m. Carol Susan Thompson, Jan. 3, 1982; children: Nicholas, China. BSME, N.C. State U., 1972, MSME, 1975, PhDME, 1980. Stress analyst Rockwell Internat., Raleigh, N.C., 1978-81; staff engr. Martin Marietta, Denver, 1981—. Mem. Tau Beta Pi, Pi Tau Sigma, Pi Mu Epsilon, Phi Kappa Phi, Sigma Pi. Avocations: bowling, bridge, tennis, chess, sailing. Home: 2338 La Mesa Dr Boulder CO 80303 Office: Martin Marietta Mail Stop D-6072 Denver CO 80201

LAKE, BRUCE MENO, applied physicist; b. Los Angeles, Nov. 22, 1941; s. Meno Truman and Jean Ivy (Hancock) L. B.S.E., Princeton U., 1963; M.S., Calif. Inst. Tech., 1965, Ph.D., 1969. Mem. tech. staff advanced instrumentation dept. TRW Corp., Redondo Beach, Calif., 1969-73, head exptl. hydrodynamics sect., 1973-81, asst. mgr. fluid mechanics dept., 1977-81, mgr. fluid mechanics dept., 1981—; v.p. Site-Mixed Concrete Corp., Fontana, Calif., 1978—. Ford Found. fellow, 1964-65. Mem. Am. Phys. Soc., AIAA, Democrat. Contbr. articles to profl. jours. Office: One Space Park Redondo Beach CA 90278

LAKE, JAMES A., molecular biology educator; b. Kearney, Nebr., Aug. 10, 1947; m. Lauri M. Lake, June 4, 1967; children: Caroline, Jeremy. BA, U. Colo., 1963; PhD, U. Wis., 1967. Postdoctoral fellow MIT, Cambridge, 1967-68; research fellow Harvard U. Sch. Medicine, Boston, 1968-70; asst. prof. molecular biology Rockefeller U., N.Y.C., 1970-73; assoc. prof. NYU Sch. Medicine, 1973-76; prof. UCLA, 1976—. Contbr. articles to profl. jours. Recipient Burton award Am. Soc. Electron Microscopy, 1975; Overseas fellow Churchill Coll. Cambridge (Eng.) U., 1983. Mem. Cell Biology Soc. of U.S., Biophys. Soc. of U.S., Biochem Soc. of U.S.

LAKE, KEVIN BRUCE, physician; b. Seattle, Jan. 25, 1937; s. Winston Richard and Vera Emma (Davis) L.; B.S., Portland State U., 1960; M.D., U. Oreg., 1964; m. Suzanne Roto, Oct. 25, 1986; children from previous marriage: Laura, Kendrick, Wesley. Intern, Marion County Gen. Hosp. and Ind. Med. Center, Indpls., 1964-65; resident U. Oreg. Hosps. and Clinics, 1968-70; fellow in infectious and pulmonary diseases, 1970-71; fellow in pulmonary diseases U. So. Calif., 1971-72, instr. medicine, 1972-75, asst. clin. prof., 1975-79, assoc. clin. prof., 1979-84, clin. prof., 1986—; dir. med. edn. and research La Vina Hosp., 1972-75; dir. respiratory therapy Methodist Hosp., Arcadia, Calif., 1975—; mem. staff Los Angeles County/U. So. Calif. Med. Center, Santa Teresita Hosp., Duarte, Calif., Huntington Meml. Hosp., Pasadena, Calif.; attending physician, mem. med. adv. bd. Foothill Free Clinic, Pasadena. Mem. exec. com. Profl. Staff Assn. U. So. Calif. Sch. Medicine; 2d v.p. bd. mgmt. Palm St. br. YMCA, Pasadena, 1974, 1st v.p., 1975, chmn., 1976-78, met. bd. dirs., 1976—; bd. dirs. Mendenhall Ministries, La Vie Holistic Ministries, Hastings Found. co-pres. PTA, Allendale Grade Sch., Pasadena, 1975-76; deacon Pasadena Covenant Ch., 1976-79. Served to lt. U.S. Navy, 1965-68. NIH grantee, 1971-72. Fellow A.C.P., Am. Coll. Chest Physicians; mem. Am. Thoracic Soc., Calif. Thoracic Soc., Oreg. Thoracic Soc., Trudeau Soc., Am. Soc. Microbiology, N.Y. Acad. Scis., Calif. Med. Assn., Los Angeles County Med. Assn. Democrat. Contbr. articles to profl. jours. Home: 875 S Madison St Pasadena CA 91106 Office: 50 Alessandro Suite 330 Pasadena CA 91105

LAKE, WALTER BENJAMIN, broadcasting exec.; b. Lincoln, Nebr., Oct. 4, 1918; s. Walter Benjamin and Zelma Elizabeth L.; m. Dorothy Elsie Brabec, Dec. 24, 1947. Student, U. Nebr., 1937-39; B.A., San Diego State U., 1948; postgrad., Pasadena Inst. for Radio, 1949-50. Sales mgr. Inland Broadcasting Co., Weiser, Idaho, 1950-52; regional mgr. San Diego Broadcasting, Inc., Los Angeles, 1953-56; gen. mgr. McGavren-Quinn, Los Angeles, 1957-60; exec. v.p. McGavren-Guild, Los Angeles, 1961-70; pres. North Sacramento Valley Broadcasting Co., Red Bluff, Calif., 1962-68; partner KSLY Broadcasting Co., San Luis Obispo, Calif., 1962-68; pres. KFRE Broadcasting Inc. (Stas.-KFRE-AM-FM), Fresno, Calif., 1971—; also dir.; pres. Lake Enterprises, Inc., Fresno, 1975-77; also dir. Lake Enterprises, Inc.; dir. Cali-Block, Inc.; advisor Continental Nat. Bank. Trustee Sierra Hosp. Found., 1980—. Served to maj. USAAF, 1942-46, NATOUSA. Mem. Nat. Assn. Broadcasters, Calif. Broadcasters Assn. (dir. 1979-80), San Joaquin Valley Broadcasters Assn. (dir. 1973-74), Broadcast Fin. Mgmt. Assn., Am. Legion, VFW, Sigma Chi. Republican. Methodist. Clubs: Lions, Elks, Masons, Shriners, Sunnyside Country, San Joaquin Country. Home: 5205 N Pleasant Ave Fresno CA 93711 Office: 999 N Van Ness Ave Fresno CA 93728

LAKIN, ALLAN WILLIAM, aerospace company executive; b. Kansas City, Mo., Sept. 23, 1952; s. Paul and Elizabeth Marian (Angell) L.; m. Sandra Fisher, Aug. 24, 1974; children: Paul, Andrew. SB in Chemistry, MIT, 1974, SM, 1975; JD, Loyola U., Los Angeles, 1982. Bar: Calif. Materials engr. Rockwell Internat., Canoga Park, Calif., 1975-83; supr. engring. HITCO/Owens Corning, Gardena, Calif., 1983—. Inventor in field. Bd. dirs. referees Am. Youth Soccer Orgn., San Fernando Valley, Calif., 1978-80. Fellow Am. Inst. Chemists; mem. Am. Chem. Soc., Soc. Mfg. Engrs., Sigma Xi. Republican. Mormon. Office: HITCO Fabricated Composites Div 1600 W 135th St Gardena CA 90249

LAKOFF, SANFORD, political scientist, educator; b. Bayonne, N.J., May 12, 1931; s. Herman and Gertrude (Robins) L.; m. Evelyn Schleifer, June 4, 1961. BA, Brandeis U., 1953; MA, Harvard U., 1955, PhD, 1959. Instr. to asst. prof. govt. Harvard U., Cambridge, Mass., 1958-65; assoc. prof. to prof. polit. sci. SUNY, Stony Brook, 1965-67; prof. polit. sci. U. Toronto, Ont., Can., 1967-74, U. Calif., San Diego, 1974—; cons. Commn. on MIT edn., Cambridge, 1970-71, NSF, Washington, 1979, Calif. Humanities Council, San Francisco, 1983—. Author: Equality in Political Philosophy, 1964; co-author Science and the Nation, 1962, Energy and American Values, 1982; editor Knowledge and Power, 1966; co-editor Strategic Defense and the Western Alliance, 1987. V.p. World Affairs Council of San Diego, 1985-86. Recipient Bowdoin Prize, Harvard U., 1955, Outstanding Community Service award U. Calif. San Diego, 1985; research grantee Carnegie Corp. N.Y, 1984; fellow Nat. Humanities Ctr., 1980-82. Mem. Am. Polit. Sci. Assn. (council 1977-79), AAAS. Democrat. Jewish. Home: 3510 Dove Ct San Diego CA 92103 Office: Univ Calif San Diego Dept Polit Sci Q-060 La Jolla CA 92093

LAKS, MICHAEL MILTON, medical educator, cardiovascular researcher; b. Cleve., July 25, 1928; s. Alexander and Helen (Klein) L.; m. Sandra Beller, June 13, 1959; children: Helaina Sharon, Alexander Paul. BA, UCLA, 1951; MD, U. So. Calif., 1956. Diplomate Am. Bd. Internal Medicine, Am. Bd. Cardiovascular Diseases. Asst. dir., dept medicine Cedars-Sinai Med. Ctr., Los Angeles, 1961-64, dir. dept. medicine, 1964-65, physician in charge cardiovascular research lab., 1965-71, sr. research scientist, 1969—; dir. cardiovascular research Harbor-UCLA Med. Ctr., Torrance, Calif., 1971—, dir. heart sta., 1971—; assoc. chief cardiology Harbor UCLA Med. Ctr., Torrance, Calif., 1975—; cons. cardiovascular care VA Hosp., Los Angeles, 1971—; ECG research cons. Hewlett-Packard Co., McMinnville, Oreg., 1973—. Author: Vectorial Approach to Electrocardiography, 1986; contbr. over 300 papers, abstracts and reviews to profl. jours. Am. Chem. Soc. scholar, 1947. Fellow Am. Coll. Cardiology, Royal Soc. Medicine, ACP (research paper award 1961), Am. Coll. Chest Physicians, Council Clin. Cardiology, Am. Geriatrics Soc. (founder); mem. Internat. Soc. Computerized Electrocardiography (pres., chmn. 1984—), Phi Beta Kappa, Alpha Omega Alpha, Phi Kappa Phi. Avocations: swimming, photography. Home: 1939 N Edgemont St Los Angeles CA 90027 Office: Harbor UCLA Med Ctr 1000 W Carson St F-9 Torrance CA 90509

LAL, DEVENDRA, nuclear geophysics educator; b. Varanasi, India, Feb. 14, 1929; s. Radhe Krishna and Sita Devi (Gupta) L.; m. Aruna Damany, May 17, 1955. BS, Banaras Hindu U., Varanasi, 1947, MS, 1949, DSc, 1984; PhD, Bombay U., 1958. Research student Tata Inst. of Fundamental Research, Bombay, 1949-50, research fellow, assoc. prof., 1950-63, prof., 1963-70, sr. prof., 1970-72; dir. Phys. Research Lab., Ahmedabad, India, 1972-83; sr. prof. Phys. Research Lab., Ahmedabad, 1983—, vis. prof., 1965-66, 83-84; prof. Scripps Instn. Oceanography, La Jolla, Calif., 1967—. Editor: Early Solar System Processes and the Present Solar System, 1980. Recipient K.S. Krishnan Gold Medal Indian Geophys. Union, 1965, S.S. Bhatnaga award for Physics Govt. India, 1967, Padma Shri award GOvt. India, 1971, award for Excellence in Sci. and Tech. Fedn. of Indian Chamber Com., 1974. Fellow Royal Soc.; mem. Nat. Acad. Scis. (fgn. assoc.), Third World Acad. Scis. (founding mem.), Royal Astron. Soc. (assoc.) Internat. Acad. Aeronautics, Internat. Union of Geodesy and Geophysics (pres. 1980-84), Internat. Assn. Phys. Scis. of the Ocean (pres. 1980-84). Hindu. Avocations: chess, photography, painting, math. puzzles. Office: Univ of Calif-San Diego Scripps Inst of Oceanography A-020 La Jolla CA 92093

LAM, ANNIE SIU-HING, librarian; b. Hong Kong, Jan. 10, 1950; came to U.S., 1972; d. Cham-Yan and Sai-Ying (Kwong) L. BBA, Pepperdine U., 1976, MBA, 1978. Asst. dir. continuing edn. Pepperdine U., Los Angeles, 1978-79; research assoc. Nat. Econ. Research Assn., Los Angeles, 1979-82, librarian/research assoc., 1982—. Office: Nat Econ Research Assn 555 S Flower St Los Angeles CA 90071

LAM, TONY WAI-MAN, petroleum engineer; b. Kowloon, Hong Kong, Feb. 11, 1960; came to U.S., 1979; s. Paul Tak-Yam Lam and Helen Chen-Yee Chow. BS, U. So. Calif. Petroleum engr. Mobil Oil Corp., Los Angeles, 1983—. Mem. Trojan Commuter Alliance, Los Angeles, 1983. Recipient Howard O. Welty award Welty Found., 1981, Powell Found. award, 1983. Meme. AAAS, Soc. Petroleum Engrs., Am. Chem. Soc., Chinese Engrs. and Scientists Assn. So. Calif., Phi Kappa Phi. Adventist. Club: Chinese. Office: Mobil Oil Corp PO Box 2145 Los Angeles CA 90051

LAMANNO, DANIEL DEVENISH, realty developer, contractor; b. Bremerton, Wash., Oct. 4, 1944; s. Daniel Fredric LaManno and Joan Adlade (Muller) Hanecak; m. Jill Ann Cash, 1965 (div. 1973); m. Florence Marie Leon Guerrero Perez, Apr. 21, 1974; children: Kathleen, Angela, Penelopy, David. BSME, L.I. U. Registered profl. engr.; lic. real estate broker; lic. gen. contractor. Enlisted USN, 1964, supr. nuclear power plant, 1968-73, resigned, 1973; quality engr. Byron Jackson Pump Co., Los Angeles, 1973-75; supr. water system Byron Jackson Pump Co., Fresno, Calif., 1975-77; pres. DFD Enterprises Inc., Oxnard, Calif., 1977—; mktg. cons. Alpha VII, Camarillo, Calif., 1984—. Author: The 10 Minute Cook, 1986; screen play Sasha, 1985; TV sitcom Maria, 1985; TV adventure series The Wrong Hostage, 1986. Bd. dirs. election campaigns for local candidates, Oxnard; vol. Ann. Strawberry Festival, Oxnard, 1986; fund raiser Police Dog Fund, Oxnard, 1982—. Mem. Ventura County Contractors Assn., Painting and Decorating Assn., Am. Soc. Quality Control, Associated Builders and Contractors, Oxnard C. of C., Nat. C. of C. Republican. Roman Catholic. Lodges: Masons, KC. Avocations: reading, writing, water sports, sailing, bird hunting. Home: 3473 Canoga Pl Camarillo CA 93010

LAMAR, LAURA, art director, educator; b. Pasadena, Calif., Oct. 27, 1951; d. Richard S. and Jeanne E. (Weide) L.; m. Max W. Seabaugh, May 20, 1979. BA magna cum laude, UCLA, 1973. Graphic artist C.R. Crockett & Assocs., Irvine, Calif., 1969-73; illustrator Figg Jewelry, Claremont, Calif., 1974; graphic artist Lifestyle mag., Sacramento, 1975, The Graphic Ctr., Sacramento, 1975; sr. designer Communications Design, Sacramento, 1975-81; art dir. San Francisco Focus mag. KQED Inc., 1981-86; ptnr. MAX, San Francisco, 1986—; lectr. in typographic design Calif. Coll. Arts and Crafts, Oakland, 1984—. Editor and art dir. (newsletter) Etcetera, 1978-81; art dir. Our Town mag., 1978-79, San Francisco Ballet mag., 1985—. Recipient 3 Design awards San Francisco Art Dirs. Club, 1981, 6 Merit Design and Art Direction awards Western Art Dirs. Club, 1981, 7 Merit Art Direction awards Los Angeles Soc. Illustrators, 1981-83, Excellence of Design award Western Pubs. Assn., 1983-85, Cert. of Merit for Art Direction N.Y. Soc. Illustrators, 1985, 2 Excellence of Art Direction awards Communication Art mag., 1985, White Award for Design, William Allen White Sch. of Journalism, U. Kans., 1985-86, 4 Design awards William Allen White Sch. of Journalism, U. Kans., 1986, 2 Silver awards for black and white and 4-color William Allen White Sch. of Journalism, U. Kans., 1986, 2 Commendations City and Regional Mag. Assn., 1986. Mem. Am. Inst. Graphic Artists (steering com. 1986—), Soc. Pub. Designers, Soc. Typographic Arts. Presbyterian. Office: MAX 149 New Montgomery Suite 405 San Francisco CA 94105

LAMB, GARY BERNARD, safety director; b. LaMesa, Calif., Feb. 29, 1956; s. Bernard Perry and Betty Jean (Webb) L.; m. Tammi Lynn Mayfield, Apr. 19, 1980; children: Michele Elizabeth, Tania Nicole. BS in Health, Oreg. State U., 1979. Cert. assoc. safety profl. Bd. Cert. Safety Profls. Salesman Les and Bob's Sporting Goods, Corvallis, Oreg., 1976-78; asst. safety and personnel mgr. Morse Bros. Inc., Tangent, Oreg., 1979-82, human resources mgr., 1982-84; safety, security dir. Bear Creek Corp., Medford, Oreg., 1984—. Bd. dirs. Oregon Bus. Health Care Coalition, Salem, 1983-85. Mem. Am. Soc. Safety Engrs, Whipski Investments Club (pres. 1985). Democrat. Avocations: boat building, aviation, law, outdoor sports. Home: 5277 S Pacific Hwy Phoenix OR 97535 Office: Bear Creek Corp 2518 S Pacific Hwy Medford OR 97501

LAMB, JOHN DAVID, chemistry educator, research administrator; b. Brockville, Ont., Can., Oct. 10, 1949; came to U.S., 1967; s. David and Mildred (Hill) L.; m. Betty Villella, Dec. 16, 1976; children: Michael, Jeremy, Joshua, Zachary, Matthew. BS, Brigham Young U., 1971, PhD, 1978. Research assoc. Thermochem. Inst., Provo, Utah, 1978-81, asst. research scientist, 1981-82, assoc. research scientist, 1982; program mgr. Dept. of Energy, Washington, 1982-84; assoc. prof. chemistry Brigham Young U., Provo, 1984—, dir. research, 1985—; bd. dirs. Associated Western Univs., Salt Lake City; mem. Utah State Sci. Adv. Council. Mem. Am. Chem. Soc. (awards chmn., sec., treas. 1979-82), Utah Acad. Scis. Arts and Letters, Utah Ion Chromatography Users Group, Soc. Research Adminstrs. Mormon. Avocations: classical music, gourmet food, painting, racquetball, computers. Home: 1540 N 200 W Orem UT 84057 Office: Brigham Young U Dept Chemistry C-37 ASB Provo UT 84602

LAMB, MICHAEL ERNEST, psychology researcher; b. Lusaka, Zambia, Oct. 22, 1953; came to U.S., 1973; s. Francis B. and Michelle M. (de Lestang) L.; m. Jamie E. Lewis, Dec. 11, 1973; children: Damon G., Darryn N. BA, U. Natal, Durban, Republic of S. Africa, 1972; MA, Johns Hopkins U., 1974; MS, MPhil, Yale U., 1975, PhD, 1976. Asst. prof. psychology U. Wis., Madison, 1976-78; asst. prof. U. Mich., Ann Arbor, 1978-80; prof. U. Utah, Salt Lake City, 1980—; vis. prof. U. Haifa, Israel, 1980, Hokkaido U., Sapporo, Japan, 1985. Editor: The Role of the Father in Child Development, 1976, rev. edit., 1981; co-author: Development in Infancy, 1982, rev. edit., 1987, Infant-Mother Attachment, 1985, Child Psychology Today, 1986, and others. Recipient Young Psychologist award Am. Psychol. Assn., 1976, Boyd McCandless award Am. Psychol. Assn., 1978, Superior Research award U. Utah, 1985, Disting. Research award U. Utah, 1986. Mem. Soc. Research in Child Devel., Soc. Pediatric Research, Internat. Soc. for Study of Behavioral Devel., Sci. Research Soc. N.Am. Office: U Utah Dept Psychology Salt Lake City UT 84112

LAMB, WILLIS EUGENE, JR., physicist, educator; b. Los Angeles, July 12, 1913; s. Willis Eugene and Marie Helen (Metcalf) L.; m. Ursula Schaefer, June 5, 1939. B.S., U. Calif., 1934, Ph.D., 1938; D.Sc., U. Pa., 1953, Gustavus Adolphus Coll., 1975; M.A., Oxford (Eng.) U., 1956, Yale, 1961; L.H.D., Yeshiva U., 1965. Mem. faculty Columbia, 1938-52, prof. physics, 1948-52; prof. physics Stanford, 1951-56; Wykeham prof. physics and fellow New Coll., Oxford U., 1956-62; Henry Ford 2d prof. physics Yale, 1962-72, J. Willard Gibbs prof. physics, 1972-74; prof. physics and optical scis. U. Ariz., Tucson, 1974—; Morris Loeb lectr. Harvard, 1953-54; cons. Philips Labs., Bell Telephone Labs., Perkin-Elmer, NASA.; Vis. com. Brookhaven Nat. Lab. Recipient (with Dr. Polycarp Kusch) Nobel prize in physics, 1955; Rumford premium Am. Acad. Arts and Scis., 1953; Research Corp. award, 1955; Guggenheim fellow, 1960-61; recipient Yeshiva award, 1962. Fellow Am. Phys. Soc., N.Y. Acad. Scis.; hon. fellow Inst. Physics and Phys. Soc. (Guthrie lectr. 1958), Royal Soc. Edinburgh (fgn. mem.); mem. Nat. Acad. Scis., Phi Beta Kappa, Sigma Xi. Office: Dept of Physics U Ariz Tucson AZ 85721 *

LAMBERT, DAVID ARMSTRONG, speech-language pathologist; b. Salt Lake City, July 26, 1959; s. Calvin Arnold and Ruth Jane (Armstrong) L. BS, U. Utah, 1983, MS, 1985. Salesman Zion's Coop. Merc. Instn., Salt Lake City, 1975-82; phys. edn. specialist Salt Lake City Sch. Dist., 1980-85; communication disorder specialist Davis County Sch. Dist., Syracuse, Utah, 1985-86; speech-language pathologist Mountain Bell Outreach Program U. Utah, Salt Lake City, 1986—; faculty rep. Communication Disorder Specialists, Farmington, Utah, 1985—. Exec. bd. dir. Davis Edn. Assn., Farmington, 1986; mem. activities com. Big Bros. and Big Sisters, Salt Lake City, 1980—; league dir. Foothill Western Boys Baseball Assn., Salt Lake City, 1980—. Mem. NEA, Am. Speech-Lang.-Hearing Assn. (congl. contact mem. Rockville, Md., 1985-86), Utah Speech-Language-Hearing Assn., Utah Edn. Assn. Republican. Mormon. Avocations: Little League, researching family history. Home: 2681 Roxbury Circle Salt Lake City UT 84108 Office: U Utah 1201 Behavioral Sci Bldg Salt Lake City UT 84112

LAMBERT, GLEN RAY, social worker, consultant; b. Lethbridge, Alta., Can., Mar. 1, 1946; s. Theron M. and Verl (Johnansen) L.; m. Marijane Johnson, Jan. 29, 1973; children: Michael, Melissa. BS, Brigham Young U., 1970; MSW, U. Utah, 1972. Lic. clin. social worker. Counselor Neighborhood House, Salt Lake City, 1972; clin. dir. Youth Devel. Ctr., Ogden, Utah, 1977; exec. dir. Odyssey House, Inc., Salt Lake City, 1977—; pvt. practice social work Salt Lake City, 1977—; cons., lectr. throughout U.S., Australia and Asia, 1976—; asst. clin. prof. U. Utah, Salt Lake City, 1983—; lectr. New Eng. Sch. on Alcoholism Studies, Boston. Mem. subcom. on Alternatives for Troubled Youth, Salt Lake City, 1977-84, mem. State Adv. Bd. Child Abuse and Neglect, Salt Lake City, 1980-86, State COmmn. on Criminal and Juvenile Justice; chmn. Dem. voting dist., Salt Lake City, 1982-84, N.I.D.A. Providers Group, Salt Lake City; trustee Sunstone Found. Served to capt. U.S. Army, 1972-77. Named one of Outstanding Young Men of Am. Mem. Nat. Assn. Social Workers, Youth Providers Assn. (Salt Lake County chpt.), Utah Assn. Drug and Alcohol Program Dirs. Assn. (rep.). Mormon. Avocations: travel, skiing, tennis, golf, reading. Home: 1361 Rebecca Circle Salt Lake City UT 84112 Office: Odyssey House 68 S 600 E Salt Lake City UT 84117

LAMBERT, JEFF LEE, environmental engineer; b. Urbana, Ill., Aug. 13, 1953; s. Ted L. and Edith E. (Wittka) L.; 1 child, Rachel Vera Paris. BA in Environ. Sci., Rice U., 1976, M in Environ. Sci., 1980. Registered profl. engr., Wash. Research scientist Rice U., Houston, 1977-80; design engr. Bovay Engrs. Inc., Houston, 1980-81; prin. engr. Bovay N.W. inc., Spokane, Wash., 1982—. Dem. precinct committeeman. Mem. ASCE (assoc., bd. dirs. inland empire sect. 1985—), Wash. Soc. Profl. Engrs. (bd. dirs. scholarship found. 1984—, pres.-elect Spokane chpt.), Am. Pub. Works Assn., Nat. Computer Graphics Assn., Automatic Mapping Facilities Mgmt. Assn. Clubs: Spokane Mountaineers, Spokane Tennis. Home: E 12114 Cataldo #19 Spokane WA 99206 Office: Bovay NW Inc E 808 Sprague Spokane WA 99202

LAMBERT, NADINE MURPHY, educator; b. Ephraim, Utah; m. Robert E. Lambert, 1956; children—Laura Allan, Jeffrey. Ph.D. in Psychology, U. So. Calif., 1965. Sch. psychologist Los Nietos Sch. Dist., Whittier, Calif., 1952-53, Bellflower (Calif.) Unified Sch. Dist., 1953-58; research cons. Calif. Dept. Edn., Los Angeles, 1958-64; dir. sch. psychology tng. program U. Calif., Berkeley, 1964—; asst. prof. edn. U. Calif., 1964-70, asso. prof., 1970-76, prof., 1976—; mem. Joint Com. Mental Health of Children, 1967-68; cons. state depts. edn., Calif., Ga., Fla.; cons. Calif. Dept. Justice.; Mem. panel on testing handicapped people Nat. Acad. Scis., 1978-81. Author: (with Windmiller and Cole) School Version of the AAMD Adaptive Behavior Scale, 2d edit, 1981; (with Wilcox and Gleason) Educationally retarded child: Comprehensive assessment and planning for the EMR and slow-learning child, 1974; (with Hartsough and Bower) Process for Assessment of Effective Functioning, 1981; (with Windmiller and Turiel) Moral Development and Socialization—Three Perspectives, 1979; assoc. editor Am. Jour. Orthopsychiatry, 1975—, Am. Jour. Mental Deficiency, 1977—; cons. editor to jours. NIMH grantee, 1965—; Calif. State Dept. Edn. grantee, 1971-72, 76-78. Fellow Am. Psychol. Assn. (council reps. div. sch. psychologists, bd. dirs. 1983-86, bd. profl. affairs 1981-83, Disting. Service award 1980, award for Disting. Profl. Contributions 1986), Am. Orthopsychiat. Assn.; mem. Calif. Assn. Sch. Psychologists and Psychometrists (pres. 1962-63, Sandra Goff award 1985), Am. Ednl. Research Assn., NEA, Am. Bd. Profl. Psychology (diplomate in sch. psychology). Office: Dept Edn U Calif Berkeley CA 94720

LAMBERTI, N. A., operations management consultant; b. Ankeny, Iowa, Aug. 25, 1920; s. Frank and Caroline (Vignaroli) L.; m. Joan Schneider, Sept. 13, 1952; children—Catherine Marie, Linda Carol, Michael Joseph. B.S. in Indsl. Engring, Iowa State U., 1943; M.B.A., U. So. Calif., 1950, M.S. in Indsl. Engring, 1960, D.Bus. Adminstrn., 1961. Registered profl. engr., Calif. Mech. engr. Northrop Aircraft Corp., 1947-49; chief indsl. engr., dir. materials, asst. v.p. mfg. McCulloch Motors, Los Angeles, 1950-54; v.p., gen. mgr., dir. Ryder-Elliott, Inc., Los Angeles, 1954-58; cons. Lamberti & Assos., 1958-61; asso. prof. U. So. Calif., 1961-64; v.p. ops., exec. asst. to pres. Studebaker Corp., South Bend, Ind., 1964-69; sr. v.p., dir. ops. Universal Am. Corp.; pres. Lamberti & Assos. (mgmt. cons.), 1970—; chmn. bd. Lamberti Industries, 1976—; dir. Franklin Electric Corp., Bluffton, Ind. Bd. dirs. San Gabriel Valley council Boy Scouts Am.; bd. councilors engring. sch. Calif. State Poly. U., Pomona; trustee Mayfield Sch., Pasadena, Calif.; bd. regents La Salle Sch., Pasadena. Served to lt. (j.g.) USNR, 1944-46. Mem. Soc. Advancement Mgmt., Am. Inst. Indsl. Engrs. Republican. Clubs: Annandale Country (Pasadena); Jonathan (Los Angeles); Lake Arrowhead Country. Home: Morgan Ranch 2211 Meadowbrook Ln Glen Dora CA 91740 also: 26671 Thunderbird Dr Lake Arrowhead CA 92352

LAMBETH, DEBORAH HAYES, interior designer; b. Thomasville, N.C., July 14, 1956; d. Wilburn Roy and Doris (Welborn) Hayes; m. William Roderick Lambeth, Nov. 11, 1978. AA, Davidson County Community Coll., 1976; BS in Econs. and Bus. Adminstrn., U. N.C., Greensboro, 1977. Adminstrv. design asst. Lambeth Ltd., Thomasville, 1979-80, cons., 1978—; interior designer Furniture Galleries Inc., Denver, 1983-84; interior design adminstr. Aircoa, Denver, 1984-85, design dir., 1985—; cons. L.J. Best Inc., Thomasville, 1986—; bd. dirs. D.L. Designs Inc., Littleton, Colo.; mem. nat. adv. council Allied Fibers. Active Jr. Symphony Guild, Denver, 1980-82, Denver Alliance, 1985—. Profl. mem. Am. Soc. Interior Designers, Inst. Bus. Designers. Republican. Baptist. Club: Lone Tree Country (Littleton). Avocations: traveling, water skiing, boating, golf. Office: AIRCOA 4600 S Ulster St Suite 1200 Denver CO 80237

LAMBORN, JANICE BOND, nurse; b. San Francisco, Nov. 25, 1952; d. Willis L. and Betty J. (Anderson) Bond; m. Lee Reuel Lamborn, June 10, 1977; children: David Reuel, Katie Marie. BSN magna cum laude, U. Utah, 1976. Staff nurse, pediatrics U. Utah Med. Ctr., Salt Lake City, 1976-77; community health nurse Bear River Health Dept, Logan, Utah, 1977; staff and charge nurse Logan Hosp., 1977-80; clin. instr. nursing Weber State Coll., Ogden, Utah, 1981-85; staff nurse Primary Children's Med. Ctr., Salt Lake City, 1985—. Mem. primary bd. West Jordan 30th Ward, Ch. Jesus Christ Latter-day Saints, 1985. Mem. Alpha Lambda Delta, Phi Kappa Phi. Home: 9291 S Brown Ave West Jordan UT 84088 Office: Primary Chilcren's Med Ctr Infant Spl Care Unit 320 12th Ave Salt Lake City UT 84103

LAMBOU, VICTOR WILLIAM, aquatic biologist, educator; b. New Orleans, Apr. 28, 1929; s. Victor T. and Regina H. (Byrnes) L.; m. Lorraine Rita Lambou; children: Denita, Geralyn, Vickie. BS, La. State U., 1951, MS, 1952. Research biologist La. Wildlife and Fisheries Commn., Baton Rouge, 1953-63; dir. fishery research lab. U. Okla., Norman, 1963-66; aquatic biologist EPA, Las Vegas, Nev., 1966—; adj. prof. biology U. Nev., Las Vegas, 1976—. Author books and articles to profl. jours. Mem. Ecol. Soc., Am. Fisheries Soc. (cert.), Am. Soc. Limnology and Oceanography, Am. Water Resources Assn., N.Am. Lake Mgmt. Soc. (bd. dirs.), Soc. Wetland Scientists. Home: 5320 W Eugene Ave Las Vegas NV 89108 Office: EPA PO Box 15027 Las Vegas NV 89114-5027

LAMBUTH, ALAN LETCHER, forest products company executive; b. Seattle, Jan. 5, 1923; s. Benjamin Letcher and Olive Serena (Schram) L.; m. Susan Jane De Melt; children: Wendy, Peter, John, Douglas. BS in Chemistry, U. Wash., 1947; student, Yale U., 1942-43, Santa clara U., 1943-44. Research chemist Monsanto Co., Seattle, 1947-57, research group leader, 1958-69; asst. mgr. mfg. tech. services Boise Cascade Corp., Boise, Idaho, 1969-70, mgr. product devel., 1971-76, mgr. research and devel., 1971-81, mgr. product and process devel., 1981—; guest lectr. Wash. State U., U. Idaho; reviewer research proposals and tech. publications NSF, U. Calif. Forest Products Lab., U. Idaho Dept. Forest Products, Wash. State U. Wood Tech. Dept., USDA Forest Products Lab., Forest Products Research Soc. Contbr. articles to profl. jours; patentee in field. V.p. Meadows Owners Assn., Boise, 1982-83, pres., 1976-77. Recipient Monsanto award for Innovative Chem. Research, 1969. Mem. Am. Chem. Soc., Am. Inst. for Timber Constrn. (past chmn. tech. adv. com., mem. adhesive task com.), Am. Plywood Assn. (past chmn. tech. services com., chmn. industry standards/products com.), ASTM (coms. and subcoms.), Forest Products Research Soc. (northwest regional mem., bd. dirs. 1979-80, v.p. 1980-81, pres. 1982-83 Borden award for Outstanding Contbns. to Forest Products Adhesives, 1984), Internat. Union Forestry Research Orgns. (U.S. working party on wood bonding and adhesives), Nat. Forest Products Assn. (com. on research evaluation, chmn. adhesives subcom., mem. coatings subcom., joint wood and coatings industries steering com.), Nat. Paint and Coatings Assn. (tech. mem.), Western Wood Products Assn. (mem. tech. com., chmn. glued products com.), USA/Can. Light Frame Structures Program (mem. liaison com.). Republican. Congregationalist. Club: Hillcrest Country (Boise). Home: 7240 Cascade Dr Boise ID 83704 Office: Boise Cascade Corp 220 S 3d St Boise ID 83702

LAMEIRO, GERARD FRANCIS, product manager; b. Paterson, N.J., Oct. 3, 1949; s. Frank Raymond and Beatrice Cecilia (Donley) L.; BS, Colo. State U., 1971, MS, 1973, PhD, 1977. Sr. scientist Solar Energy Research Inst., Golden, Colo., 1977-78; asst. prof. mgmt. sci. and info. systems Colo. State U., Fort Collins, 1978-82, lectr. dept. computer sci., 1983, lectr. dept. mgmt., 1983; pres. Successful Automated Office Systems, Inc., Fort Collins, 1982-84; product mgr. Hewlett Packard, 1984—. Mem. Presdl. Electoral Coll., 1980. Recipient nat. disting. Service award Assn. Energy Engrs., 1981. Colo. Energy Research Inst. fellow 1976; NSF fellow 1978. Mem. AAAS, Assn. for Computing Machinery. Roman Catholic. Contbr. articles in mgmt. and tech. areas to profl. jours. Home: PO Box 9580 Fort Collins CO 80525 Address: 3313 Downing Ct Fort Collins CO 80526 Office: Hewlett Packard Co 3404 E Harmony Rd Fort Collins CO 80525

LAMEMAN, TULLY, association executive; b. Home-Red Mesa, Utah, Feb. 15, 1939; s. Jack and Elsie (Adakaitso) L.; m. Nancy Tina Tsosie, Aug. 15, 1969; children—Stanford, Christina, Virginia Anne, Tully. B.S., Ariz. State U., 1969. Agr. coordinator San Juan Resource Devel. Council, Blanding, Utah, 1969-71; extension agt. Utah State U., Montezuma Creek, 1971-72; agr. dir. Utah Navajo Devel. Council, Blanding, 1972-75, adminstrn. asst., 1975-77, exec. dir., 1977—; program coordinator, extension agt. Utah State U., 1971-72; farm tng. coordinator, tchr. animal sci. Navajo Community Coll., 1975. Mem. sch. bd., vice chmn. San Juan Sch. Dist., 1970-72; chmn. bd. Utah Navajo Devel. Council Credit Union, 1978-83; bd. dirs. mem. Utah Housing Coalition, 1982-86; monitoring contracts officer UNDC; mem. Br. Coll. Adv. Council; vice chmn. Navajo Health Systems Agy., 1981—; bd. dirs. Southeastern Utah Econ. Devel. Dist., 1986—, mem. exec. bd.; mem. exec. bd. Southeast Utah Assn. Local Govts. 1983—; mem. Southeast Utah Pvt. Industry Council for Job Tng. Partnership Act. Mem. Nat. Indian Edn. Assn. Republican. Mem. Ch. Jesus Christ of Latter-day Saints. Home: 290 East 400 South 94-9 Blanding UT 84511 Office: PO Box 908 Blanding UT 84511

LAMIE, EDWARD LOUIS, computer science educator; b. Kingsley, Mich., Aug. 27, 1941; s. Louis Edward Lamie and Pauline Theresa (Harrand) La Bonte; m. Mary Ellen Bronson, Sept. 9, 1960; children: William, David, Marla, Melissa. AB, San Diego State U., 1969; MS, U. So. Calif., 1971; PhD, Mich. State U., 1974. Drafter Security Title Ins. Co., San Diego, 1962-64; engring. aide City of San Diego, 1964-69; mem. tech. staff Rockwell Internat., Downey, Calif., 1969-71; prof. computer sci. Cen. Mich. U., Mount Pleasant, Mich., 1971-82; chmn. dept. Cen. Mich. U. Mount Pleasant, 1972-82; prof., chmn. dept. Calif. State U. Stanislaus, Turlock, 1982—. Author: PL/1 Programming, 1982, Pascal Programming, 1987; contbr. articles to profl. jours. Served with USN, 1959-62. Recipient Meritorious Service award Calif. State U. Stanislaus, 1984. Mem. Assn. Computing Machinery, IBM Computer Club. Republican. Roman Catholic. Avocations: personal computers, genealogy. Home: PO Box 2637 Turlock CA 95381 Office: Calif State U Stanislaus Computer Sci Dept 801 W Monte Vista Ave Turlock CA 95380

LAMM, FRANKLIN CHARLES, bus. exec.; b. Reading, Pa., Jan. 9, 1945; s. John Herman and Helen Rosa (Stamm) L.; student Shattuck Sch., Faribault, Minn., 1961-64, Chulalongkorn U., Bangkok, 1967-68, La Escuela de Agricultura y Cria, Venezuela, 1968; B.A., St. Olaf Coll., 1968; M.A., U. No. Colo., 1973; m. Marion Isabella Banks, Sept. 24, 1968; children—Tammy Michelle, Shattuck Franklin, Robin Julie. Child care worker Northwood Treatment Ctr. for Emotionally Disturbed Children, Duluth, Minn., 1965-66; vol. Peace Corps, Campiarito, Venezuela, 1968-71; assoc. headmaster Vershire Sch. (Vt.), 1971-72; learning disabilities specialist Sch. Dist. #51, Grand Junction, Colo., 1973-78; investment property locator Mesa Properties Ltd., Grand Junction, 1978-79; pres., proprietor, dir. Energy Belt Enterprises, Grand Junction, Colo., 1980-86; pres. Energy Belt Property Mgmt., Energy Belt Farm and Ranch, Energy Belt Devel., Inc., Energy Belt Investments, Inc.; learning disabilities specialist, Whitemountain Apache Indian Reservation, Whiteriver, Ariz., 1986—. Chmn. N.W. Citizens Task Force, Mesa County, Colo., 1979-82; scoutmaster Boy Scouts Am., 1980-82. Mem. Kappa Delta Pi. Republican. Mem. Ch. Jesus Christ Latter-Day Saints. Address: Box 697 Grand Junction CO 81502

LAMM, RICHARD DOUGLAS, former governor of Colorado; b. Madison, Wis., Aug. 3, 1935; s. Arnold E. and Mary (Townsend) L.; m. Dorothy Vennard, May 11, 1963; children: Scott Hunter, Heather Susan. B.B.A., U. Wis., 1957; LL.B., U. Calif., Berkeley, 1961. Bar: Colo. 1962; C.P.A., Colo. Accountant Salt Lake City, 1958; tax clk. Calif. Franchise Tax Bd., San Francisco, summer 1959; law clk. firm Michael, Best & Friedrich, San Francisco, summer 1960; accountant Ernst & Ernst, Denver, 1961-62; atty. Colo. Anti-Discrimination Commn., Denver, 1962-63, Jones, Meiklejohn, Kilroy, Kehl & Lyons, Denver, 1963-65; individual practice law 1965-74; mem. Colo. Ho. of Reps., 1966-74, asst. minority leader, 1971-74; gov. Colo., 1975-87; asso. prof. law U. Denver, from 1969; chmn. natural resource and environ. mgmt. com. Nat. Gov.'s Assn., 1978-79, mem., from 1979, also mem. exec. com. and environment com., and chmn. task force on synthetic fuels. Pres. Denver Young Democrats, 1963; v.p. Colo. Young Democrats, 1964; mem. Conservation Found., Denver Center Performing Arts Center for Growth Alternatives, Central City Opera House Assn. Served as 1st lt. U.S. Army, 1957-58. *

LAMME, DENNIS WAYNE, advertising executive; b. Trenton, Mo., Mar. 19, 1955; s. John Robert and Earlene Marie (Trump) L.; m. Cindy Kay Wright, July 30, 1977; children: Kelly Marie, Jacob Fremont, Kristen Kay, Kaylie Elizabeth. B.S., Northwest Mo. State U., 1976. Account exec. Sta. KKJO, St. Joseph, Mo., 1976-77; gen. mgr. Sta. KVMT-FM, Vail, Colo., 1977-78; sta. mgr. Sta. KYEZ-FM, Salina, Kans., 1978; account exec. Sta. WRMN, Elgin, Ill., 1978-79; v.p., corp. sales Brewer Broadcasting Co. (Stas. KUAD, KSGR, KKBG) Windsor, Colo. and Hilo, Hawaii, 1979-84; advt. exec. Jefferson-Pilot Communications, Stas. KIMN and KYGO, Denver, 1984-86; gen. mgr., Surrey Broadcasting, Stas. KATR and KYOU, Denver, 1986—; mem. research bd. advisors Am. Biographical Inst. Inc. Chmn. bd. dirs. Thompson Valley Preschool, 1982-84. Mem.Nat. Assn. of Broadcasters, Colo. Broadcasters Assn., Mktg. Advt. and Communications Assn. (v.p.), Am. Advt. Fedn., Denver Advt. Fedn., Am. Mgmt. Assn., Am. Film Inst., Alpha Epsilon Rho. Republican. Presbyterian. Home: 3829 Logan Ave Loveland CO 80538 Office: PO Box 1607 Greeley CO 80632

LAMONA, THOMAS ADRIAN, engineering, marketing company executive, consultant; b. Los Angeles, Aug. 19, 1925; s. Thomas Adrian and Joy A. (Kirkman) L.; m. Jeanne Muse, May 21, 1953 (div. 1958); m. Joyce Maurer, Dec. 12, 1971. Student San Fernando Valley Jr. Coll., 1945-46, UCLA, 1948, U. So. Calif., 1955. Various positions 1943-54; sales engr. Everlube Corp., North Hollywood, Calif., 1954-57; cons. engring., Newport Beach, Calif., 1957-67, 1973—; sales engr. Lubeco, Compton, Calif., 1963-73; v.p., bd. dirs. Coating Tech. Corp., Glen Ellyn, Ill., 1986—. Served with U.S. Army, 1951. Recipient Special Service citation Soc. Mfg. Engrs., region VII, 1979. Mem. Standards Engring. Soc. (Los Angeles sect., mem. chmn. 1975-77, program dir. 1977-78, treas. 1978-81, chmn. 1981-82, Spl. Service citatation 1978, cert. in standards engring. 1979, Outstanding Sect. Mem. 1984), Porsche Owner's Club, Calif. Sports Car Club Am. (Los Angeles) (press relations com. 1955-63). Home: PO Box 2195 Newport Beach CA 92663 Office: Thomas A Lamona and Assocs Inc PO Box 2195 Newport Beach CA 92663 Office: Coating Tech Corp PO Box 2126 Glen Ellyn IL 60137

LAMONDS, HAROLD AUGUSTUS, energy company executive; b. Greensboro, N.C., Aug. 22, 1924; s. Alexander and Lurah Victoria (Bonkemeyer) L.; m. Dorothy Veronica Richards, Mar. 17, 1945 (div. Feb. 1969); children: Lori Michelle La Borde, Mark Christopher; m. Dorothy Ileana Bough, May 15, 1976. BS, N.C. State U., 1953, MS, 1954, PhD, 1958. Dept. head N.C. State U., Raleigh, 1960-63, Aerojet Gen. Corp., Azusa, Calif., 1963-64; program mgr. EG&G, Inc., Santa Barbara, Calif., 1964-74; pres. Orion Scientific Corp., San Diego, 1974-76; prin. scientist IRT Corp., San Diego, 1976-77; v.p. EG&G Energy Measurements, Inc., Las Vegas, Nev., 1977—. Author: Nuclear Reactor Laboratory Manual, 1961; contbr. articles to profl. jours. Mem. Am. Legion, Phi Kappa Phi. Republican. Lodge: Elks. Avocations: golf, sailing. Office: EG&G Energy Measurements Inc PO Box 1912 Las Vegas NV 89125

LAMONICA, JOHN, food executive; b. Bklyn., Apr. 26, 1954; s. Lou and Alda (Merola) L.; married Nancy Lamonica. B.S. in Acctg., Bklyn. Coll., 1977. With N.S.L. Enterprises, 1982—; with Aniellos Pizza, 1979—, Lamonicas N.Y. Pizza, 1980—; restaurant cons. Developer in field. Republican. Clubs: Beverly Hills Gun, Shelby Am. Office: 1066 Gayley Ave Los Angeles CA 90024

LAMONT, JOHN WILLIAM, research electrical engineer; b. Cape Girardeau, Mo., Mar. 7, 1942; s. William Eugene and Thelma Neal (Smarr) L.; m. Kathryn Ann Mitchell, June 1, 1968; children: William Eugene, Kathryn Michelle. BSEE, U. Mo., Rolla, 1964; MSEE, U. Mo., Columbia, 1966, PhD, 1970. Registered profl. engr., Calif., Tex., Mo. Research asst. U. Mo., Columbia, 1964-68, inst. elec. engr., 1968-70; asst. prof. elec. engr. U. So. Calif., Los Angeles, 1970-73, U. Tex., Austin, 1973-78; research project mgr. Electric Power Research Inst., Palo Alto, Calif., 1978—; cons. Los Angeles Dept. Water and Power, 1968-73, Southwestern Pub. Service, Amarillo, Tex., 1975-78. Mem. Power Soc. IEEE (sr.), Sigma Xi. Home: 1463 James Town Dr Cupertino CA 95014 Office: Electric Power Research Inst 3412 Hillview Dr Palo Alto CA 94304

LAMOREAUX, RICHARD DALE, geophysicist; b. Cedar City, Utah, June 6, 1951; s. Donald Clarence and Lola (Prestwich) L. BS in Physics, U. Utah, 1975, MS in Physics, 1978; PhD in Geophysics, U. Alta., Edmonton, Can., 1982. Processing geophysicist Chevron Geoscis., Houston, 1982-83; supr. exploration and producing services Chevron Geoscis., San Francisco, 1984-86; mem. exploration applications staff Chevron Can. Resources Ltd., Calgary, Alta., 1986—. Contbr. articles to profl. jours. Mem. Soc. Exploration Geophysicists, Bay Area Geophys. Soc. Mormon. Avocations: rock climbing, mountaineering, backpacking, skiing, horseback riding. Home: 808-80 Point McKay Ctr NW, Calgary, AB Canada T3B 4w4 Office: Chevron Can Resources Ltd, 500 5th Ave SW, Calgary, AB Canada T2P 0L7

LA MORTE, ANDREW WILLIAM, technical writer; b. Mt. Kisco, N.Y., Sept. 19, 1955; s. Richard Peter and Anne Louise (DeVan) La M. BSCE cum laude, U. Mass., 1979, MSME, 1981. Project engr. BEETO div. Bendix Corp., Englewood, Colo., 1981-83; mgr. engring. Maxaxam Corp., South Portland, Maine, 1983-84; engring. tech. writer Ball Aeorspace Systems, Boulder, 1984-85, Stanley Aviation Corp., Denver, 1986-87; bd. dirs. Mandala Enterprises, Denver; tech. cons. Mandala Enterprises, Denver, 1985-86, mgr. bus., 1986—, also bd. dirs. Mem. ASME. Club: BMW Motorcycle of Colo. (Littleton) (sec./treas. 1986, tech. editor Rocky Mountain chpt. 1986—). Avocations: motorcycling, bicycling, hiking, sailing, homebrewing.

L'AMOUR, LOUIS DEARBORN, author; b. Jamestown, N.D., 1908; s. Louis Charles and Emily (Dearborn) LaMoore; m. Katherine Elizabeth Adams, Feb. 19, 1956; children: Beau Dearborn, Angelique Gabrielle. Self ed.; LLD (hon.), Jamestown Coll., 1972, Pepperdine U., 1984. Appearances on: Great Tchrs. TV program; Author: poems Smoke From This Altar, 1939, Hondo, 1953, The Burning Hills, 1956, Sitka, 1957, The Daybreakers, 1960, Kid Rodelo, Mustang Man, Kilrone, 1966, The Sky-Liners, 1967, The Broken Gun; Matagorda, 1967, Brionne, 1968, Chancy, 1968, Down the Long Hills, 1968 (Golden Spur awards Western Writers Assn.), The Empty Land, 1969, The Lonely Men, 1969, Conagher, 1969, A Man Called Noon, 1970, Reilly's Luck, 1970, Galloway, 1970, North to the Rails, 1971, Under the Sweet-Water Rim, 1971, Tucker, 1971, Callaghen, 1972, Ride the Dark Trail, 1972, Treasure Mountain, 1972, The Ferguson Rifle, 1973, The Man from Skibbereen, 1973, The Quick and the Dead, 1973, The Californios, 1974, Sackett's Land, 1974, War Party, 1975, Rivers West, 1975, Over on the Dry Side, 1975, Rider of Lost Creek, 1976, Where the Long Grass Blows, 1976, To the Far Blue Mountains, 1976, Borden Chantry, 1977, Fair Blows the Wind, 1978, Showdown at Yellow Butte, 1978, The Mountain Valley War, 1978, Bendigo Shafter, 1979, The Proving Trail, 1979, The Iron Marshal, 1979 (Golden Plate award), Shalako, 1980, The Strong Shall Live, 1980, Yondering, 1980, The Warrior's Path, 1980, The Comstock Lode, 1981, Buckskin Run, 1981, The Shadow Riders, 1982, The Lonesome Gods, 1983, The Walking Drum, 1984, Son of a Wanted Man, 1984, Louis L'Amour's Frontier, 1984, Jubal Sackett, 1985, Passin' Through, 1985, Last of the Breed, 1986. Served to 1st lt. AUS, 1942-46. Named Theodore Roosevelt Rough Rider by N.D., 1972; recipient Congl. Medal of Honor, 1983, Presdl. Medal of Freedom, 1984; Am. Book award, 1980, Buffalo Bill award, 1981, Disting. Newsboy award, 1981, Nat. Geneal. Soc. award, 1981. Mem. Acad. Motion Picture Arts and Scis., Calif. Acad. Scis. Address: care Bantam Books 666 Fifth Ave New York NY 10019 *

LAMOURE, BRIAN THOMAS, auditor; b. Helena, Mont., Apr. 1, 1954; s. Edward T. and Louise C. (Stanich) LaM. BA in Fin., Carroll Coll., 1977, BA in Bus., 1978, AA in Acctg., 1979. Taxpayer service rep. IRS, Helena, 1976-79; adminstrv. asst. City of Helena, 1978-79; contract monitor Mont. Community Services, Helena, 1980-81; auditor, investigator Bd. Realty Regulation, Helena, 1981-82; auditor IV Mont. Medicaid, Helena, 1982—. Ski patrolman Belmont, Helena, 1970-84, Big Sky (Mont.), 1984—; bd. dirs., treas. Leadership Helena, 1986; bd. dirs. Leadership Helena Alumni, 1986—. Democrat. Roman Catholic. Clubs: Green Meadow Country, Prickley Pear Sportsman. Lodge: Elks, Moose. Avocations: archery, rafting, sailing, scuba diving, mountain climbing. Home: 1427 Highland Helena MT 59601 Office: State of Mont Dept Social Services 111 Sanders Helena MT 59601

LAMOUREUX, GLORIA KATHLEEN, military nursing administrator; b. Billings, Mont., Nov. 2, 1947; d. Laurits Bungaard and Florence Esther (Nielsen) Nielsen; m. Kenneth Earl Lamoureux, Aug. 31, 1973 (div. Feb. 1979). BS, U. Wyo., 1970; MS, U. Md., 1984. Enrolled USAF, 1970, advanced through grades to lt. col.; staff nurse ob-gyn dept. 57th Tactical Hosp., Nellis AFB, Nev., 1970-71, USAF Hosp., Clark AB, Republic Philipines, 1971-73; charge nurse ob-gyn dept. USAF Rgn. Hosp., Sheppard AFB, Tex., 1973-75; staff nurse ob-gyn dept. USAF Rgn. Hosp., MacDill AFB, Fla., 1976-79; charge nurse ob-gyn dept. USAF Med. Ctr., Andrews AFB, Md., 1979-80, MCH coordinator, 1980-82; chief nurse USAF Clinic, Eielson AFB, Alaska, 1984-86, USAF Hosp., Edwards AFB, Calif., 1986—. Named one of Outstanding Women Am., 1983. Mem. Nurses Assn. of Am. Coll. Obstetricians and Gynecologists (sec.-treas. armed forces dist. 1986—), Am. Nurses Assn., Assn. Mil. Surgeons U.S., Bus. and Profl. Women's Assn., Sigma Theta Tau. Republican. Lutheran. Avocations: reading, needlework, piano, photography. Home: 4500 W Rosamond Blvd Space 5 Rosamond CA 93560 Office: USAF Hosp Edwards/SGHN Edwards AFB CA 93523-5300

LAMPE, MATTHEW MARK, municipal building official; b. Ann Arbor, Mich., Apr. 30, 1951; s. Isadore and Rae Ethel (White) L.; m. Janet McIntosh, Oct. 22, 1975 (div. Sept. 1979); m. Karen Marie Bean, July 21, 1983. BA, U. Mich., 1973, M in Pub. Adminstrn., 1976. Dir. community ctr. Ann Arbor Community Coalition, 1971-73; assoc. substance abuse coordinator Washtenaw County CMHC, Ann Arbor, 1971-75, coordinator emergency services, 1974-77; dir. services to mentally ill Dept. Mental Health, Lansing, Mich., 1977-80; assoc. dir. Ypsilanti (Mich.) Regional Psychiat. Hosp., 1980-83; fin. mgr. constrn. and land use dept. City of Seattle, 1983-85, dir. constrn. inspection, 1985—; cons. Gov's. Office, Lansing, 1976, Am. Pharm. Assn., Washington, 1972-73. Author: Drugs: Information for Crisis Treatment, 1972; contbg. author: Management of Adolescent Drug Use, 1973, Impressions of Imagination, 1986. Bd. dirs., treas. Wash. Trust for Historic Preservation, Olympia, 1984—; mem. Allied Arts, Seattle, 1984—; founder Drug Help Inc., Ann Arbor, 1970-75, Free Peoples Clinic Inc., Ann Arbor, 1970-73. Mem. Am. Soc. Pub. Adminstrn. Democrat. Jewish. Home: 7330 Keen Way W Seattle WA 98103 Office: Dept Constrn and Land Use Room 400 Mcpl Bldg Seattle WA 98104

LAMPERT, CARL MATTHEW, research materials scientist; b. Portland, Oreg., Feb. 20, 1952; s. Gailard Carl and Gwen (Enersen) L.; m. Harue Yasuda Howard, July 10, 1975. AS, Contra Costa Coll., 1972; BS in Elec. Engring. and Materials Sci., U. Calif., Berkeley, 1974, MS in Materials Sci., 1977, PhD in Materials Sci., 1979. Electronics technician Contra Costa Coll., San Pablo, Calif., 1970-72; computer programmer U.S. Forestry Service, Berkeley, 1972-74; research asst. Lawrence Berkeley (Calif.) Lab., 1974-79, staff scientist, 1979—; cons. UN Devel. Program, N.Y.C., 1985—, Lyon & Lyon, Los Angeles, 1985, Deposition Tech., San Diego, 1984-86; project leader Internat. Energy Agy., Paris, 1984—. Gen. editor Solar Energy Materials Jour., 1982—; contbr. articles to profl. jours. Fulbright scholar, 1983; recipient Achievement award Bank of Am., San Francisco, 1970. Fellow Internat. Soc. Optical Engring.; mem. IEEE (br. chmn. 1974-75, Outstanding Leadership award 1975), Am. Soc. Metals, Am. Ceramic Soc., Am. Vacuum Soc. (planning bd. 1982-84), Internat. Solar Energy Soc. (session chmn. 1973), Am. Inst. Metall. Engrs., Sigma Xi, Tau Beta Pi, Eta Kappa Nu. Democrat. Club: Twin Pines Stamp (San Pablo). Avocations: fishing, camping, traveling. Office: Lawrence Berkeley Lab 1 Cyclotron Rd Bldg 62-203 Berkeley CA 94720

LAMPERT, ELEANOR VERNA, employment development specialist; b. Porterville, Calif., Mar. 23; d. Ernest Samuel and Violet Edna (Watkins) Wilson; student in bus., fin. Porterville Jr. Coll., 1977-78; grad. Anthony Real Estate Sch., 1971; student Laguna Sch. of Art, 1972, U. Calif.-Santa Cruz, 1981; m. Robert Mathew Lampert, Aug. 21, 1935; children—Sally Lu Winton, Lary Lampert, Carol R. John. Bookkeeper, Porterville (Calif.) Hosp., 1956-71; real estate sales staff Ray Realty, Porterville, 1973; sec. Employment Devel. Dept., State of Calif., Porterville, 1973-83, orientation and tng. specialist CETA employees, 1976-80. Author: Black Bloomers and Han-Ga-Ber, 1986. Sec., Employer Adv. Group, 1973-80; mem. U.S. Senatorial Bus. Adv. Bd., 1981-84; charter mem. Presdl. Republican Task Force, 1981-86; mem. Rep. Nat. Congl. Com., 1982-86; vol. Calif. Hosp. Assn., 1983-86. Recipient Merit Cert., Gov. Pat Brown, State of Calif., 1968. Mem. Lindsay Olive Growers, Sunkist Orange Growers, Am. Kennel Club, Internat. Assn. Personnel in Employment Security, Calif. State Employees Assn. (emeritus Nat. Wildlife Fedn., Nat. Rifle Assn., Friends of Porterville Library, Heritage Found. Clubs: Porterville Women's, Internat. Sporting and Leisure. Author: Black Bloomers and Han-Ga-Ber.

LAMPERT, SEYMOUR, mechanical engineering educator, consultant; b. Bklyn., Mar. 5, 1920; s. Max and Esther (Bakst) L.; m. Shirley Ruth Axelrod; children: Rachel B., David A., Martin D., Benjamin A. BS, Ga. Inst. Tech., 1943; MS, Calif. Inst. Tech., 1947, AE, 1948, PhD, 1954. Instr. Ga. Inst. Tech., Atlanta, 1943-44; aero. research scientist NACA, Moffet Field Air Base, Calif., 1944-51; research engr. JPL, Pasadena, Calif., 1951-54; also cons. JPL, Pasadena, 1967-69; mgr. aero. mechanics Aeronutronic, Newport Beach, Calif., 1956-62; dir. advanced systems research N.Am., Downey, Calif., 1962-67; v.p. Systems Assocs. Inc., Long Beach, Calif., 1967-71; dir. solar research U. So. Calif., Los Angeles, 1971—; sci. advisor Dept. of Def., Washington, 1968-70; v.p., bd. dirs. Davato Corp., Placentia, Calif., 1979—. Co-author: Solar Curriculum, 1981; editor: Jour. Solar Sci., 1982; contbr. articles to profl. jours.; co-patentee light gas cartridge. Served with USNR, 1944-46, PTO. Avocations: art, track and field. Home: 5722 Oakley Terr Irvine CA 92715 Office: U So Calif Dept Mech Engring Los Angeles CA 90089-1453

LANCASTER, HAZEL MARGRITH UTZ, investigator, retired lawyer; b. Goldfield, Nev., Jan. 31, 1907; d. Frank J. and Rose Elise (Boenzli) Utz; m. William Lancaster, Dec. 10, 1944 (dec.). Student, U. Calif., Berkeley, 1924-26; JD, U. Calif., San Francisco, 1929. Sec. to statistician, sec. of bd. dirs. Bank of Italy, San Francisco, 1926; sec. Brobeck, Phleger & Harrison, San Francisco, 1928, Pilsbury, Madison & Sutro, San Francisco, 1929; reporter Bd. Freeholders, San Francisco, 1931; ct. apptd. appraiser Bankruptcy Ct., San Francisco, 1934-35; sole practice San Francisco, 1929-42, Los Angeles, 1954—. Office: 5670 Wilshire Blvd Suite 1320 Los Angeles CA 90036

LANCASTER, JACK REYNOLDS, biochemist, educator; b. Memphis, Aug. 27, 1948; s. Jack R. and Shirley (Gade) L.; children: Madeline Alden, Tanya Marie. BS in Chemistry, U. Tenn., 1967-70; PhD in Biochemistry, U. Tenn. Ctr. for Health Scis., 1974. Research assoc. Cornell U., Ithaca, N.Y., 1974-76, Duke U., Durham, N.C., 1976-80; asst. prof. Utah State U., Logan, 1980-83, assoc. prof., 1983—. Recipient Established Investigatorship award Am. Heart Assn., 1983-88. Mem. AAAS, Am. Chem. Soc., Am. Soc. Biol. Chemists, Biophys. Soc. Office: Utah State U Dept Chemistry and Biochemistry Logan UT 84322

LANDA, ESTHER ROSENBLATT, civic worker; b. Salt Lake City, Dec. 25, 1912; d. Simon and Sylvia Gertrude (Liberman) Rosenblatt; B.A., Mills Coll., 1933, M.A., 1937, H.H.D. (hon.), 1980; LL.D. (hon.), U. Utah, 1978; H.L.D. (hon.), Westminster Coll., 1982; m. Jerome Joseph Landa, Sept. 26, 1943; children—Carol Leslie, Howard Simon, Terry Ellen. Public relations Mills Coll. (Clif.), 1934-39, Bennington (Vt.) Coll., 1941; account exec. Constance Hope Assos., N.Y.C., 1941-42; info. specialist various agys. U.S. Govt., 1942-43; cons. burs. Community Devel. and Indian Services, U. Utah, 1962-65; dir. women's programs U. Utah, 1965-71; nat. pres. Nat. Council

Jewish Women, 1975-79; mem. Pres.'s Adv. Com. Women, 1978-80, Pres.'s Commn. for Nat. Agenda for 80's, 1979-80; mem. Salt Lake City Bd. Edn., 1958-70, Utah State Bd. Edn., 1970-74; sec.-treas. Nat. Assn. State Bds. Edn., 1973-74; pres. Salt Lake County Community Action Program, 1968-70; pres. LWV Salt Lake City, 1956-58; chairperson task force on equal opportunity for women Nat. Jewish Community Relations Adv. Council, 1977-83; bd. dirs. Council of Jewish Fedns. N.Am., Planned Parenthood Assn. of Utah; mem. planning com. White House Conf. on Children, 1970; Utah del. White House Conf. on Families, 1980; U.S. del. World Conf. UN Decade for Women, Copenhagen, 1980; mem. adv. council Grad. Sch. Social work U. Utah, mem. Utahns United Versus Nuclear Arms Race; pub. mem. Commn. on Accreditation, Council on Social Work Edn., 1984-86. Named to Salt Lake Council of Women Hall of Fame, 1958; hon. life mem. PTA, 1963; recipient Libety Bell award Utah Bar Assn., 1963; Utah Woman of Year, AAUW, 1965; Woman of Year, B'nai B'rith, 1965; Man of Year in Utah Edn., Phi Delta Kappa, 1967; Civil Rights Worker of Year award NAACP, 1968; Disting. Service award Utah Sch. Bds. Assn., 1969, 72; U. Utah Alumni Merit award, 1976; Disting. Woman award U. Utah, 1978; Susa Young Gates award Nat. Women's Polit. Caucus, 1979; U. Utah Disting. Alumnae award, 1984; Citation Utah chpt. NCCJ, 1980. Mem. Nat. Council Jewish Women, LWV, NOW, Nt. Women's Polit. Caucus, ACLU, Phi Beta Kappa, Delta Kappa Gamma. Democrat. Jewish. Clubs: Hadassah, B'nai B'rith Women, ORT. Author Pres.'s column Nat. Council Jewish Women Jour., 1975-79; contbg. editor for UN end of decade women's conf. Good Housekeeping mag., 1985, Nairobi, Kenya. Home: 5006 S 1034 E Salt Lake City UT 84117 Office: 1130 Kennecott Bldg Salt Lake City UT 84133

LANDE, JAMES AVRA, lawyer, engineering and construction company executive; b. Chgo., Oct. 2, 1930; s. S. Theodore and Helen C. (Hamburger) L.; m. Ann Mari Gustavsson, Feb. 21, 1959; children—Rebecca Susanne, Sylvia D. B.A., Swarthmore Coll., 1952; J.D., Columbia U., 1955; Bar: N.Y. 1958, Calif. 1967. Assoc. Rein, Mound & Cotton, N.Y.C., 1957-59; atty. VA, Seattle, 1959-61, Weyerhaeuser Co., Tacoma, 1961-63, Lande Assoc., San Francisco, 1963-67; with NASA, Ames Research Center, Moffett Field, Calif., 1967-70; house counsel Syntex Corp., Palo Alto, Calif., 1970-73; dir. contracts dept. Electric Pwer Research Inst., Palo Alto, Calif., 1973-81; corp. atty., dir contracts Lurgi Corp., Belmont, Calif., 1981-82; contracts mgr. Bechtel Nat., Inc., San Francisco, 1982—; adj. prof. U. San Francisco Sch. Law, 1972-73; lectr. law U. Santa Clara Sch. Law, 1968—. Pres. Syntex Fed. Credit Union, 1971-72. Served with U.S. Army, 1955-57. Mem. Calif. Bar Assn., ABA. Clubs: Commonwealth of Calif., Lawyers of San Francisco.

LANDEL, ROBERT FRANKLIN, physical chemist; b. Pendleton, N.Y., Oct. 10, 1925; s. Carlisle Oscar and Grace Elisabeth (McEachren) L.; m. Aurora Mamauag, Aug. 1, 1953; children: Carlisle P., Grace P., Hans F., Robert F. Jr., Kevin L., Matthew N. BA, U. Buffalo, 1949, MA, 1950; PhD, U. Wis., 1954. Research assoc. U. Wis., Madison, 1954-55; sr. research engr. Jet Propulsion Lab., Pasadena, Calif., 1955-59, sect. mgr., 1959-85, sr. research scientist, 1984—; vis. prof. Ecole Poly. Fed., Lausanne, Switzerland, 1984; cons. Sandia Nat. Labs, Albuquerque, 1983; cons. in field; mem. U.S./U.K. Working Group on Antimisting Aircraft Fuels, 1978-82. Mem. editorial bd. various polymers jours.; contbr. articles to profl. jours.; patentee in field. Mem., officer YMCA Indian Guides, Altadena, Calif., 1960-74. Served as pvt. inf. U.S. Army, 1943-46, PTO. French Govt. fellow Strasbourg, 1972, Sr. Fulbright fellow, 1971-72; recipient Exceptional Sci. Achievement award NASA, 1976. Fellow Am. Phys. Soc. (exec. com. high polymer physics div.); mem. Soc. Rheology (v.p. 1985, pres. 1987), Am. Chem. Soc., Council Sci. Soc. Pres's., Mgmt. Club. Avocations: skiing, backpacking, camping, photography, hiking. Office: Jet Propulsion Lab Calif Inst Tech 4800 Oak Grove Dr Pasadena CA 91109

LANDERS, VERNETTE TROSPER, educator, author; b. Lawton, Okla., May 3, 1912; d. Fred Gilbert and LaVerne Hamilton (Stevens) Trosper; A.B. with honors, U. Calif. at Los Angeles, 1933, M.A., 1935, Ed.D., 1953; Cultural doctorate (hon.), Lit. World U., Tucson, 1985; m. Paul Albert Lum, Aug. 29, 1952 (dec. May 1955); 1 child, William Tappan; m. 2d, Newlin Landers, May 2, 1959; children: Lawrence, Marlin. Tchr. secondary schs., Montebello, Calif., 1935-45, 48-50, 51-59; prof. Long Beach City Coll., 1946-47; asst. prof. Los Angeles State Coll., 1950; dean girls Twenty Nine Palms (Calif.) High Sch., 1960-65; dist. counselor Morongo (Calif.) Unified Sch. Dist., 1965-72, coordinator adult edn., 1965-67, guidance project dir., 1967; clk.-in-charge Landers (Calif.) Post Office, 1962-82; ret., 1982 Vice-pres., sec. Landers Assn., 1965—; sec. Landers Vol. Fire Dept., 1972—; life mem. Hi-Desert Playhouse Guild, Hi-Desert Meml. Hosp. Guild. Bd. dirs., sec. Desert Emergency Radio Service. Recipient internat. diploma of honor for community service, 1973; Creativity award Internat. Personnel Research Assn., 1972; cert. of merit for disting. service to edn., 1973; Order of Rose, Alpha Xi Delta, 1978; named Soroptimist of Year, 29 Palms Soroptimist Club, 1969; poet laureate Center of Internat. Studies and Exchanges, 1981; diploma of merit in letters U. Arts, Parma, Italy, 1982; Golden Yr. Bruin UCLA, 1983; World Culture prize Nat. Ctr. for Studies and Research, Italian Acad., 1984; Golden Palm Diploma of Honor in poetry Leonardo Da Vinci Acad., 1984; Diploma of Merit and titular mem. internat. com. Internat. Ctr. Studies and Exchanges, Rome, 1984; Recognition award San Gorgonio council Girl Scouts U.S., 1984, 85; Cert. of appreciation Morongo Unified Sch. Dist., 1984; plaque for contribution to postal service and community U.S. Postal Service, 1984; Biographee of Yr. award for outstanding achievement in the field of edn. and service to community Hist. Preservations of Am.; named Princess of Poetry of Internat. Ctr. Cultural Studies and Exchange, Italy, 1985; community dinner held in her honor for achievement and service to Community, 1984; Star of Contemporary Poetry Masters of Contemporary Poetry, Internat. Ctr. Cultural Studies and Exchanges, Italy, 1984, other awards and certs. Life fellow Internat. Acad. Poets, World Lit. Acad.; mem. Am. Personnel and Guidance Assn., Internat. Platform Assn., Nat. Ret. Tchrs. Assn., Calif. Assn. for Counseling and Devel., Nat. Assn. Women Deans and Adminstrs., Montebello Bus. and Profl. Women's Club (pres.), Nat. League Am. Pen Women (sec. 1985-86), Leonardo Da Vinci Acad. Internat. Winged Glory diploma of honor in letters 1982), Landers Area C. of C. (sec. 1985-86, Presdl. award for outstanding service), Desert Nature Mus., Phi Beta Kappa. Clubs: Soroptimist (sec. Twenty Nine Palms 1962, life mem.); Whitter (Calif.) Toastmistress (pres. 1957); Homestead Valley Women's (Landers). Author: Impy, 1974, Talkie, 1975; Impy's Children, 1975; Nineteen O Four, 1976, Little Brown Bat, 1976; Slo-Go, 1977; Owls Who and Who Who, 1978; Sandy, The Coydog, 1979; The Kit Fox and the Walking Stick, 1980; contbr. articles to profl. jours., poems to anthologies. Home: 632 Landers Ln PO Box 3839 Landers CA 92285

LANDHOLM, HARVEY DEAN, information scientist; b. Osmond, Nebr., May 23, 1950; s. Chester Roland and Lois Geraldean (Erickson) L.; m. Sherry Lee Freeouf, Aug. 19, 1972 (div. June 1983); children: Michelle Renee, Scott Dean; m. Angi Elisabeth Crockett, Apr. 25, 1987. BS in Computer Sci., U. Nebr., 1972. Programmer, analyst Bankers Life of Nebr., Lincoln, 1972-74, Cen. Corp., Lincoln, 1974-76; systems coordinator K-N Energy, Lakewood, Colo., 1976-81; mgr. info. systems Ensource, Inc., Englewood, Colo., 1981-87; adminstr. data processing Total Petroleum, Inc., Denver, 1987—. Mem. Data Processing Mgmt. Assn. Lutheran. Club: Colo. Mountain (Denver). Home: 10310 E Jewell Ave #51 Denver CO 80231 Office: Ensource Inc 5575 DTC Pkwy Suite 200 Englewood CO 80111

LANDHOLM, WALLACE MARVEN, ophthalmologist; b. N. Platte, Nebr., Sept. 8, 1933; s. Marven K. and Alma L. (Phillips) L.; B.A., U. Nebr., 1956, M.D., 1959; m. Marcia Greenlee, 1955; children—James, Ceryl. Intern, San Bernardino (Calif.) County Hosp., 1959-60; resident in ophthalmology State U. Iowa Hosp., 1963-65; practice medicine specializing in ophthalmology, Newport Beach, Calif., since 1967; mem. staff Hoag Meml. Hosp.; asst. clin. prof. U. Calif. Med. Sch., Irvine; fellow intraocular lens implants Pacific Hosp., Long Beach, Calif., 1976. Served to capt. M.C., USAF, 1960-63. Decorated Air medal; diplomate Am. Bd. Ophthalmology. Mem. AMA, Soc. Eye Surgeons, Am. Acad. Ophthalmology, Am. Intraocular Implant Soc., Newport Beach C. of C., Alpha Omega Alpha. Lutheran. Club: Balboa Bay (Newport Beach). Office: 320 Superior Ave Newport Beach CA 92663

LANDMAN, DAVID, chemistry consultant; b. Landsberg, Fed. Republic Germany, June 19, 1948; came to U.S., 1974; s. Zacharya and Lucy (Biber) L.; m. Lenore June Buck. BS, U. Sydney, Australia, 1966, PhD, 1973. Postdoctoral fellow U. Tex., Austin, 1974-76; vis. asst. prof. Va. Poly. Inst. and State U., Blacksburg, 1976-77; devel. chemist Milliken & Co., Spartanburg, S.C., 1977-80; assoc. scientist Hysol div. Dexter Corp., Pittsburg, Calif., 1980-85; cons. Monterey, Calif., 1985—. Contbr. articles on theoretical chemistry and composite materials to profl. jours. Recipient Coffin award Dexter Corp., 1984. Mem. Am. Chem. Soc., Soc. Advancement of Material and Process Engring. Avocations: stamp collecting, golf. Home and Office: 5 Montsalas Dr Monterey CA 93940

LANDOLPH, JOSEPH RICHARD, JR., microbiology educator; b. Upper Darby, Pa., Nov. 9, 1948; s. Joseph Richard Sr. and Ada Nolia (Welch) L.; m. Alice Lee Kaufmann, Jan. 19, 1980; children: Joseph Richard III, Louis Samuel. BS in Chemistry, Drexel U., 1971; PhD in Chemistry, U. Calif., Berkeley, 1976. Jr. technician Smith, Kline & French, Upper Marion, Pa., 1969-70; research asst. U. Calif., Berkeley, 1971-76; postdoctoral fellow cancer ctr. U. So. Calif., Los Angeles, 1977-80; asst. prof. research pathology U. So. Calif. Sch. Medicine, 1980-82, asst. prof. microbiology and pathology, 1982—; cons. Am. Petroleum Inst., Washington, 1983-85. Assoc. editor profl. microbiology, carcinogenesis, mutagenesis, genetic toxicology jours.; ad hoc reviewer NIEHS, Research Triangle Park, N.C., 1985-86; grant reviewer EPA, Washington, 1985—; contbr. articles to profl. jours. Served to capt. U.S. Army, 1976-77. Research grantee Am. Cancer Soc., 1982-84, NIH, Research Triangle Park, 1983—, Nat. Cancer Inst., Bethesda, Md., 1986—. Mem. Am. Assn. for Cancer Research, Am. Soc. Biol. Chemists, Am. Soc. Cell Biologists, Am. Assn. Cancer Research, Am. Chem. Soc., Soc. Toxicologists, Environ. Mutagen Soc. Republican. Unitarian. Avocations: jogging, photography. Home: 1009 E Mendocino St Altadena CA 91001 Office: U So Calif Med Ctr Noris Cancer Hosp & Research Inst 1441 Eastlake Ave Los Angeles CA 90033

LANDRETH, GERALD KEITH, archaeologist; b. Ware Shoals, S.C., Sept. 13, 1955; s. Leck and Caroline Landreth; m. Melinda Russell, Feb. 14, 1986. BA, Lander Coll., 1978; MA, U. Idaho, 1986. Various field and lab. positions numerous archeol. excavations, throughout U.S., 1977-84; archeologist Archeol. and Hist. Services Eastern Wash. U., Cheney, 1984-85; staff archeologist R. Christopher Goodwin and Assocs., New Orleans, 1985; assoc. dir. Agy. for Conservation Archaeology-Eastern N.Mex. U., Portales, 1985—; project co-dir. site LA 49405, near Maljamar, N.Mex., 1985—; field dir. sites LA 21177, LA 27676, near Carlsbad, N.Mex., 1985-86; chmn. Hist. Archaeology symposium 37th Ann. Northwest Anthrop. Conf., Spokane, Wash., 1984. Contbr. articles to profl. jours. Home: Rte 3 PO Box 57 Portales NM 88130 Office: Eastern NMex U ACA Sta 9 Portales NM 88130

LANDRUM, JERRY HARLAND, chemist; b. Littlefield, Tex., Feb. 21, 1939; s. Kenneth Harland and Gladys Pearl (Boyles) L.; m. Velma Corene Gunter, June 7, 1959; children: Stephen, Vaughan, David. BS in Chemistry, N.Mex. State U., 1961. Analytical chemist Los Alamos (N.Mex.) Sci. Lab., 1962-66; research radiochemist Lawrence Livermore (Calif.) Nat. Lab., 1966-84, mgr. nuclear facility, 1984—; dirs. office rev. com. Lawrence Livermore Nat. Lab., 1986—. Contbr. articles to profl. jours. Recipient Recognition of Excellence award Def. Systems Program Lawrence Livermore Nat. Lab., 1986. Mem. Am. Chem. Soc. (nuclear chemistry and tech. div.), AAAS, Calif. Youth Soccer Assn. (referee adminstr. 1977-79, Referee of Yr. 1979). Democrat. Lodge: Elks. Home: 475 Malibu Ct Livermore CA 94550 Office: Lawrence Livermore Nat Lab PO Box 808 L-378 Livermore CA 94550

LANDRUM, LARRY JAMES, computer engineer; b. Santa Rita, N.Mex., May 29, 1943; s. Floyd Joseph and Jewel Helen (Andreska) L.; m. Ann Marie Hartman, Aug. 25, 1963 (div.); children—Larry James, David Wayne, Andrei Mikhail, Donal Wymore; m. 2d, Mary Kathleen Turner, July 27, 1980. Student N.Mex. Inst. Mining and Tech., 1961-62, N. Mex. State U., 1963-65; A.A. in Data Processing, Eastern Ariz. Coll., 1971; B.A. in Computer Sci., U. Tex., 1978. Tech. service rep. Nat. Cash Register, 1966-73; with ASC super-computer project Tex. Instruments, Austin, 1973-80, computer technician, 1973-75, tech. instr., 1975-76, product engr., 1976-78, operating system programmer, 1978-80; computer engr. Ariz. Pub. Service, Phoenix, 1980-84, sr. computer engr., 1984-87, sr. lead computer engr., 1987—; instr. computer fundamentals Eastern Ariz. Coll., 1972-73, Rio Salado Community Coll., Phoenix, 1985-86. Mem. Assn. Computing Machinery, Mensa, Phi Kappa Phi. Methodist. Home: 6025 W Medlock Dr Glendale AZ 85301 Office: Ariz Nuclear Power Project PO Box 52034 Phoenix AZ 85072-2034

LANDRY, ALAN EDWARD, marketing consultant; b. Escondido, Calif., May 14, 1953; s. Allen Edward and Madeline May (Gibson) L.; m. Lisa Ann Edgerley, May 30, 1981. B.A. in English, Chico State U., 1976, B.A. in Mass Communications, 1977. Cert. real estate agt., Calif. Editor Rancher Publs., Vista, Calif., 1977-84; v.p. mktg. Calif. Avocado Commn., Irvine, 1979-84; pres. Landry Assocs., Inc., 1984—; cons. sales, mktg., real estate devel. Vice-pres. Lake Forest Oaks Homeowners, 1977. Mem. Alpha Sigma Phi. Republican. Founder Avocado Grower Mag. Home: 26582 Sotelo Mission Viejo CA 92692 Office: 23052 Lake Forest Dr Suite A2 Laguna Hills CA 92653

LANDRY, CALISTE JOHN, JR., engineer, educator; b. Glendale, Calif., Aug. 28, 1941; s. Caliste John and Evangeline Priscilla (Wright) L.; m. Cathy Marie Peterson, May 5, 1983. BS, U. Calif., Santa Barbara, 1966, PhD, 1972. Lectr. U. Calif., Santa Barbara, 1972-76, head mechano-optics research Ctr. Robotic Systems, 1985—; engr. Gen. Research Corp., Santa Barbara, 1976-80; research specialist Lockheed Research, Palo Alto, Calif., 1980-82; project engr. Santa Barbara Research Ctr., 1982-84; pres. Electro-Optics Cons., Santa Barbara, 1983—; mem. faculty Brooks Inst. Photography, Santa Barbara, 1978—; co-founder and exec. dir. Sci. Discovery Ctr., Santa Barbara, 1984—. Contbr. numerous tech. publs.; patentee in field. Bd. dirs. Santa Barbara Sci. Fair Council, 1975—; mem. Sci. and Engring. Council., Santa Barbara, 1983—. Mem. AAAS, IEEE (Outstanding Tech. Paper, 1966), Seismol. Soc. Am., Optical Soc. Am., Aircraft Owner's and Pilots Assn., Santa Barbara C. of C., Santa Barbara Flying Club (bd. dirs. 1985), Sigma Xi. Democrat. Lutheran. Avocations: sailing, flying, photography, amateur radio. Home: 663 Wakefield Rd Goleta CA 93117 Office: U Calif Ctr for Robotic Systems 6740 Cortona Dr Goleta CA 93106

LANDRY, DONNA, English educator; b. Balt., Apr. 23, 1954; d. Barney McCoy and Muriel Hattie (Marketto) L.; m. Gerald Martin MacLean, June 9, 1981. BA summa cum laude, Duke U., 1976; MA, U. Va., 1979, PhD, 1983. Asst. prof. English Princeton (N.J.) U., 1982-83, U. So. Calif., Los Angeles, 1985—; vis. asst. prof. U. Mich., Ann Arbor, 1983-85. Contbr. articles to scholarly jours. Am. Council Learned Socs. fellow, 1985. Avocations: traveling, riding. Home: 7608 Lexington Ave West Hollywood CA 90046 Office: U So Calif Dept Englist THH 420 University Park Los Angeles CA 90089

LANDRY, GARY STEPHEN, priest; b. Maywood, Calif., Nov. 30, 1946; s. Steven Joseph and Lois Marie (Dufour) L. BA, St. Mary's Sem., Perryville, Mo., 1969; MDiv, DeAndreis Sem., 1984; MA, U. San Francisco, 1984. Ordained priest Congregation of the Mission, Province of the West, 1973. Asst. dean students St. Vincent's Sem., Lemont, Ill., 1973, tchr. sci. and math., 1973-76, dean students, 1973-75, vocation dir., 1976; asst. dean students St. Vincent's Sem., Montebello, Calif., 1976-77, tchr. sci. and math., 1976-85, dean students, 1977-80, rector, prin., 1980-86; cath mission vocation commn. Vincentian Community, Los Angeles, 1980-83, governing bd., 1980-82, corp. bd., 1983—. Recipient Good Sheperd award Friends of St. Vincent, 1984. Mem. Nat. Assn. Secondary Sch. Prins., Nat. Cath. Endl. Assn., Nat. Council Tchrs. Math., Nat. Sci. Tchrs. Assn., Calif. Assn. Chemistry Tchrs. Democrat. Avocations: art, woodworking, racquetball, volleyball. Home and Office: 1105 Bluff Rd Montebello CA 90640-6198

LANDRY, JAMES MICHAEL, chemistry educator; b. Toledo, July 26, 1956; s. Frank E. and Ann M. (Pietrykowski) L.; m. M. Kiene Hayes, Sept. 22, 1979; children: Kevin R., J. Seamus. BS in Chem. Sci., Xavier U., Cin., 1978, MS in Chemistry, 1983; PhD in Chemistry, Miami U., Oxford, Ohio, 1984. Instr. Miami U., Hamilton, Ohio, 1984; asst. prof. chemistry Loyola Marymount U., Los Angeles, 1984—. Contbr. articles to profl. jours. Mem. Am. Chem. Soc., Soc. Applied Spectroscopy, Coblentz Soc., Sigma Xi. Democrat. Roman Catholic. Avocations: family, tennis, golf, hockey, camping. Office: Loyola Marymount U Dept Chemistry Loyola Blvd at W 80th St Los Angeles CA 90045

LAND-WEBER, ELLEN, photography educator; b. Rochester, N.Y., Mar. 16, 1943; s. David and Florence (Miller) Epstein. B.A., U. Iowa, 1965, M.F.A., 1968. Faculty mem. UCLA Extension, 1970-74, U. Nebr., Lindoln, 1974; asst. prof. photography Humboldt State U., Arcata, Calif., 1974-79, assoc. prof., 1979-83, prof., 1983—; photographer Seagram's Bicentennial Courthouse Project, 1976-77, Nat. Trust for Hist. Preservation/Soc. Photographic Edn., 1987. Author: The Passionate Collector, 1980; contbr. sects. to books. Fellow Nat. Endowment for Arts, 1974, 79, 82; recipient artists's support grant Unicolor Corp., 1982. Mem. Soc. for Photog. Edn. (exec. bd. 1979-82, treas. 1979-81, sec. 1981-83). Office: Humboldt State U Art Dept Arcata CA 95521

LANE, DON VELENSION, photographer; b. Newport News, Va., May 24, 1953; s. Paul and Louise Lane. AA, City Coll. San Francisco, 1973; BA, San Francisco State U., 1977, MA, 1983. Freelance photographer San Francisco, 1973—, ind. film maker, 1983—; lectr. San Francisco State U. Dept. Film, 1979-80; prin. Don Lane Photographs, San Francisco, 1981—. Mem. Profl. Photographrs Am., Profl. Photographers San Francisco, Film Arts Found., Internat. Platform Assn., Western Sect. Independent Feature Project Assn. Avocations: swimming, bowling. Home and Office: 2429 Diamond St San Francisco CA 94131

LANE, HOWARD RAYMOND, architect; b. Chgo., Oct. 13, 1922; s. Mose and Libbie (Sax) L.; m. Shirley Robbins, June 14, 1947; children: Rod, Laura, Barbara. Student, Carnegie Inst. Tech., 1943-44, Archtl. Assn. Sch., London, 1946; B.S. in Architecture, Ill. Inst. Tech., 1947. Assoc. Skidmore, Owings & Merrill, Chgo., 1947, Allison & Rible (Architects), Los Angeles, 1948, A.C. Martin & Assocs., 1949, Robert Alexander, 1949, Pereira & Luckman, 1950-53; pvt. practice architecture Encino, Calif., 1953-79, Woodland Hills, Calif., 1979—; pres. Lane Archtl. Group, 1953—. Prin. works include Beverly Med. Bldg., West Hollywood, Calif., Solar Dining Facility, Camp Pendleton, Calif. (Coalition Engery Profls. 1st award 1981), PermaByte Magnetics, Inc. bldg., Chatsworth, Calif. (excellence awards AIA 1985), Fleet Computer Programming Operation Bldg., San Diego, Core Instrumentation Facility, Ft. Irwin, Calif. (Corps Engrs. Design award 1985), Faculty Office Bldg., Northridge, Calif., Bus. Edn. Bldg., Woodland Hills, Calif., Flight Simulator Bldg., El Toro, Calif. (excellence awards AIA 1986). Founder, co-chmn. Valley Round Table Council, 1968-69; chmn. San Fernando Valley Conv. Center Com., 1968-69; patron Los Angeles County Mus. Art; mem. Greater Los Angeles Zoo Assn. Served with U.S. Army, 1943-47. Recipient Pub. Service award Los Angeles County, 1970. Fellow AIA (pres. Calif. council 1977, pres. Los Angeles chpt. 1974, vice-chmn. nat. energy com. 1979, chmn. nat. energy com. 1980-81, chmn. Calif. council ins. trustees 1982, chmn. architecture for edn. com. Los Angeles chpt. 1985); mem. Nat. Council Archtl. Registration Bds., Encino C. of C. (past pres.), Soc. Am. Mil. Engrs. (sustaining), Associated Chambers of Commerce (pres. 1968), Tau Epsilon Phi. Office: 5950 Canoga Ave Suite 260 Woodland Hills CA 91367

LANE, ROBERT CASEY, corporate lawyer; b. 1932. JD, Loyola U., 1960. Atty. U.S. Dept. Justice, Washington, 1960-61; assoc. Lewis, Overbeck & Furman, 1962-69; atty. Weyerhaeuser Co., Tacoma, 1969-71, adminstrv. asst. to sr. v.p., 1971-77, asst. gen. counsel, 1977-80, v.p., gen. counsel, 1980—. Office: Weyerhaeuser Co Tacoma WA 98477 *

LANER, MARY RIEGE, sociology educator; b. Chgo., Dec. 9, 1927; d. Frederick J. Granicher and Mary (Holasek) Vognsen. AB, U. Chgo., 1966; MA, U. N.Mex., 1969; PhD, Va. Poly. Inst. and State U., 1976. Instr. No. Ariz. U., Flagstaff, 1969-73; asst. prof. Ariz. State U., Tempe, 1976-80, assoc. prof., 1980—. Author: (with others) Confronting Social Problems, 1984; editor: The Pairing Process, 1978, Courtship, Marriage, & Divorce, 1983, Coupling and Uncoupling, 1986; assoc. editor Family Relations, 1986, Deviant Behavior: An Interdisciplinary Jour., 1979—; cons. editor Jour. Homosexuality, 1978; contbr. articles to profl. jours. Recipient certs. of teaching excellence Acad. of Teaching Excellence, Va. Poly. Inst. and St. Univ., 1974-75 and 1975-76; named departmental nominee Acad. of Teaching Excellence, 1973-74; grantee Ariz. St. U., 1978, 1979. Mem. Am. Sociol. Assn., Nat. Council on Family Relations, Pacific Sociol. Assn. (sec.-treas. 1978-81, 85-87). Office: Ariz State U Sociology Dept Tempe AZ 85287

LANG, JEROME PETER, physician; b. Chgo., Nov. 6, 1952; s. John Joseph and Frances Elizabeth (Kirke) L.; m. Joann Elizabeth Young, May 24, 1986. BS in Chemistry, Case Western Reserve U., 1974, MD, 1982. Clin. dir. Indian Health Service, Harlem, Mont., 1983-84; gen. med. officer Indian Health Service, Mescalero, N.Mex., 1984-86. Served to lt. USPH, 1983-86. Mem. Am. Acad. Family Physicians, AMA, Alpha Omega Alpha. Mem. Soc. of Friends. Avocations: backpacking, sailing, comet-watching. Office: 3915 Talbot Rd S #300 Renton WA 98055

LANG, KATHERINE ANNE, counseling psychologist; b. Benson, Minn., Jan. 22, 1947; d. Howard James and Barbara Anne (Bennett) L. B.A. in Art History, Smith Coll., Northampton, Mass., 1969; M.A., Bethel Theol. Sem., St. Paul, 1973; M.Ed., U. Mo.-Columbia, 1978, Ph.D., 1982. Lic. psychologist, Calif. Tchr., Am. Sch., Barcelona, Spain, 1970-71; campus ministry Univ. Reformed Ch., East Lansing, Mich., 1973-76; counselor Univ. Counseling Ctr., U. Mo., Rolla, 1978-79; coordinator Ctr. for Student Vols. Action, 1979-81; counseling psychologist U. Calif., Davis, 1982—; pvt. practice counseling psychologist, Sacramento, Calif., 1986—; cons. in field. Mem. Am. Psychol. Assn., Christina Assn. Psychol. Studies. Avocations: workshops on prayer; skiing; tennis; racquetball; writing. Office: Counseling Ctr Univ Calif Davis CA 95864

LANG, MARGO TERZIAN, artist; b. Fresno, Calif.; d. Nishan and Araxie (Kazarosian) Terzian; m. Nov. 29, 1942; children: Sandra J. (Mrs. Ronald L. Carr), Roger Mark, Timothy Scott. Student, Fresno State U., 1939-42, Stanford U., 1948-50, Prado Mus., Madrid, 1957-59, Ariz. State U., 1960-61; workshops with, Dong Kingman, Ed Whitney, Rex Brandt, Millard Sheets, George Post. Maj. exhbns. include, Guadalajara, Mex., Brussels, N.Y.C., San Francisco, Chgo., Phoenix, Corcoran Gallery Art, Washington, internat. watercolor exhbn., Los Angeles, Bicentennial shows, Hammer Galleries, N.Y.C., spl. exhbn. aboard, S.S. France, others, over 50 paintings in various Am. embassies throughout world; represented in permanent collections, Nat. Collection Fine Arts Mus., Smithsonian Instn.; lectr., juror art shows; condr. workshops.; interviews and broadcasts on Radio Liberty, Voice of Am. Bd. dirs. Phoenix Symphony Assn., 1965-69, Phoenix Musical Theater, 1965-69. Recipient award for spl. achievements Symphony Assn., 1966, 67, 68, 72, spl. awards State of Ariz., silver medal of excellence Internat. Platform Assn., 1971. Mem. Internat. Platform Assn., Ariz. Watercolor Assn., Nat. Soc. Arts and Letters (nat. dir. 1971-72, nat. art chmn. 1974-76), Nat. Soc. Lit. and Arts, Phoenix Art Mus., Friends of Mexican Art, Am. Artists Profl. League, English-Speaking Union, Musical Theater Guild, Ariz. Costume Inst., Phoenix Art Mus., Scottsdale Art Center. Home: 6127 Calle del Paisano Scottsdale AZ 85251

LANG, NEVALON B., business college adminstrator; b. Seattle, Nov. 29, 1933; d. Arthur Roy and Beaulah Etta (Dasher) Thompson; m. Alfred Wayne Lang, Feb. 19, 1965; children: Linda Kay Boyle, Janice Rae Blaine. BS, Lewis Clark State Coll., Lewiston, Idaho, 1970; postgrad. Ariz. State U., Calif. State U., Los Angeles. Cert. vocat. edn., Calif. Bookkeeper, Idaho 1st Nat. Bank, Lewiston, 1952-53; sec. Boeing Aircraft, Seattle, 1953-56, State of Alaska, Soldatna, 1960-62; note teller Rainier Bank, Clarkston, Wash., 1962-65; dir., owner Valley Bus. Coll., Lewiston, 1970—; owner, tour guide Vacations Unltd., Lewiston; owner, mgr. several apts., Lewiston. Mem. Pacific N.W. Bus. Schs. Assn. (sec.-treas.), Wash. Bus. Edn. Assn., Western Bus. Edn. Assn., Nat. Bus. Edn. Assn., Idaho Bus. Edn. Assn., Am. Bus. Edn. Assn., Wash. Vocat. Assn., Am. Vocat. Assn., Lewiston C. of C. (pres.). Methodist. Club: Jet Set Travel (Seattle). Office: Valley Bus Coll 508 Thain Lewiston ID 85301

LANG, RICHARD WENZEL, anthropologist, educator; b. Pitts., Oct. 21, 1943; s. Wenzel Paul and Alice (Logue) L.; m. Rebecca Lee Collignon, Jan.

1969 (div. 1979); 1 child, Matthew C.; m. Mary Ann Moser, June 2, 1984; stepchildren—Jenny Boone, Deborah Boone, Amy Boone. Student, Ivy Sch. Profl. Art, Pitts., 1961-62, U. Pitts., Pitts., 1964-66, U. N.Mex., 1966-68, Coll. Santa Fe, N.Mex., 1979-80. Field and lab. asst. sect. of man Carnegie Mus. Natural History, Pitts., 1962-65, field archaeologist, 1966-67; research asst. Maxwell Mus. Anthropology, U. N.Mex., Albuquerque, 1966-68; curator, asst. to dir. Mus. Navaho Ceremonial Art Inc., Santa Fe, N.Mex., 1968-71; sr. staff archaeologist Sch. Am. Research, Santa Fe, 1971-82; acting dir. Wheelwright Mus. Am. Indian, Santa Fe, 1982-83, dir., 1983-85; tchr. Little Earth Sch., Santa Fe, 1985—; cons. archaeologist Richard W. Lang Archaeol. Cons., Santa Fe, 1985—; cons., lectr. in field. Sr. author: The Faunal Remains from Arroyo Hondo Pueblo, New Mexico: A Study in Short-term Subsistence Change. Contbr. articles to profl. jours.; curator ethnol., contemporary art, archaeol. exhibits in numerous museums. Incorporator, West Santa Fe Assn., 1976—; trustee Olive Rush Meml. Studio, Sante Fe, 1979-83, Wheelwright Mus. Am. Indians, 1979-82, Little Earth Sch., 1983—. Grantee, N.Mex. Div. Hist. Preservation, 1979, Sch. Am. Research, Santa Fe, 1982, Witter Bynner Found. for Poetry, 1983, Gannett Found., 1984-85. Mem. Am. Assn. Museums, N.Mex. Assn. Museums. Democrat. Mem. Society of Friends. Avocations: painting and illustration; poetry; environmental action; nature studies; outdoor activities. Home: 520 Jose St Santa Fe NM 87501

LANG, ROSLYNNE ELIZABETH, comptroller; b. St. Paul, Aug. 19, 1943; d. William Albrecht and Ruth (Hamerman) Indecks; divorced. Student, Calif. State U., Los Angeles, 1978—. Office mgr. James A. Knowles & Assocs., Los Angeles, 1970-77, Levine/Seegel Assocs., Los Angeles, 1977-80; comptroller Levine/Seegel Assocs., Santa Monica, Calif., 1980—. Mem. Nat. Assn. Women in Constrn. (edn. chmn. 1985-86, chmn. nat. occupation research and referral ad hoc com. 1985-86, nat. com. mem. redistricting 1985-86, region 12 dir. 1984-85, pres. Los Angeles chpt. 1982-83, treas. nat. edn. found. 1986—), Women Constrn. Owners and Execs. USA (charter mem., treas. So. Calif. chpt. 1985-86), Women in Mgmt. (bylaws chmn. and parliamentarian, 1982-86), Profl. Services Mgmt. Assn. Republican. Avocations: travel, reading, walking, swimming. Home: 401 Palm Dr Apt D Glendale CA 91202 Office: Levine/Seegel Assocs 2601 Ocean Park Blvd Santa Monica CA 90405-5271

LANG, SUSAN REBECCA, water quality chemistry educator; b. Milw., June 3, 1955; d. Robert George and Dolores May (Mikuleky) L. BS in Water Sci., No. Mich. U., 1985. Instr. chemistry U. Alaska, Anchorage, 1986; water quality technician II Municipality of Anchorage, 1986—; tutor, career counselor Alaska Native Health Careers Program, Anchorage, 1985—. Mem. Am. Chem. Soc., Sigma Xi. Home: PO Box 92055 Anchorage AK 99509 Office: Municipality of Anchorage Point Woronzof Lab 3000 Arctic Blvd Anchorage AK 99502

LANG, THOMPSON HUGHES, publishing company executive; b. Albuquerque, Dec. 12, 1946; s. Cornelius Thompson and Margaret Miller (Hughes) L.; m. Kimberley M., Mar. 1980. Student, U. N.Mex., 1965-68, U. Americas, Mexico City, 1968-69. Advt. salesman Albuquerque Pub. Co., 1969-70, pres., treas., gen. mgr., dir., 1971—; pub., pres., treas., dir. Jour. Pub. Co., 1971—; pres., dir. Masthead, Internat., 1971—; pres. Magnum Systems, Inc., 1973—; pres., treas., dir. Jour. Ctr. Corp., 1979—; chmn. bd., dir. Starline Printing, Inc., 1985—; v.p., dir. Rio Tech, 1985—; dir. Sun West Bank of Albuquerque; chmn. bd. dirs. Corp. Security and Investigation, Inc., 1986—; pres., bd. dirs. Eagle Systems, Inc., 1986—. Mem. H.O.W. Orgn. Home: 1615 Park St SW Albuquerque NM 87104 Office: 7777 Jefferson NE Albuquerque NM 87109

LANGE, LINDA S., infosystems specialist; b. Greensburg, Ind., July 29, 1949; d. C. Dale E. and Evelyn M. (Tatem) L. BA in Sociology cum laude, Wittenberg U., 1971; MS in Communications, U. Pitts., 1976; MBA in Fin., U. Denver, 1982. Teaching asst. U. Pitts., 1971-72; promotion asst. Sta. KWGN-TV 2, Denver, 1972-76; acct. exec. Sta. KFML-AM, Denver, and Sta. KBVL-FM, Boulder, Colo., 1976-77; adminstrv. mgr. devel. U. Denver, 1977-80, mgr. adminstrv. computer services, 1980-83; bus. mgr., treas. U. Graphics, Englewood, Colo., 1983-87; adminstrv. mgr. Nat. Guardian Security Services, Inc., Littleton, 1987—; owner, pres. Consolidated Systems, Inc., Denver, 1982—; v.p. fin. B&L Office Systems Corp., Denver, 1979—; instr. continuing edn. U. Denver, 1982-83. Editor: (newsletter) The Prompt Line, 1983-85 (first pl. 1984); columnist The Prompt Line, 1986-87. Polls judge Dem. Precinct, Denver, 1979-81; treas. Epiphany Luth. Ch., Denver, 1980-85, com. chmn.; bd. dirs. Washington Park Community Ctr., Denver, 1979-85. Mem. Assn. Info. Systems Profls. (bd. dirs. 1983-85, 86-87, pres. 1987-88), Assn. Records Mgrs. and Adminstrs., Soc. Satellite Profls., League of Women Voters. Avocations: gardening, camping, hiking, reading mysteries, natural history essays.

LANGEL, CHARLES ALFRED, manufacturing engineer; b. Vandalia, Ill., Apr. 2, 1940; s. David Alfred and Minnie Gwendollyn (Morgan) L.; m. Sally Edith Schumacher, Sept. 21, 1968; 1 dau., Karen Edith. B.S. in Natural Sci., Greenville Coll., 1963. Research technician Chevron Research Co., Richmond, Calif., 1968-69; electronic technician Recortec Inc., Mountain View, Calif., 1969-71; test engr. Western Elec. Co., Dublin, Calif., 1971-74; sr. electronic technician Searle Cardio-Pulmonary, Hayward, Calif., 1974-77; mfg. engr. Varian Assocs., Palo Alto, Calif., 1977—. Served with USN, 1964-68. Mem. IEEE, Soc. Mfg. Engrs. Club: Masons (San Leandro, Calif.); Scottish Rite (32 deg.). Home: 563 McKinley Ct San Leandro CA 94577 Office: Varian Assocs 611 Hansen Way D-177 Palo Alto CA 94303

LANGENHEIM, JEAN HARMON, biology educator; b. Homer, La., Sept. 5, 1925; d. Vergil Wilson and Jean (Smith) H.; m. Ralph Louis Langenheim, Dec. 1946 (div. Mar. 1961). BS, U. Tulsa, 1946; MS, U. Minn., 1949, PhD, 1953. Research assoc. botany U. Calif., Berkeley, 1954-59; research fellow biology Harvard U., Cambridge, Mass., 1962-66; asst. prof. biology U. Calif., Santa Cruz, 1966-68, assoc. prof. biology, 1968-73, prof. biology, 1973—; academic v.p. Orgn. Tropical Studies, San Jose, Costa Rica, 1975-78; mem. sci.adv. bd. EPA, Washington, 1977-81; chmn. com. on humid tropics U.S. Nat. Acad. Nat. Research Council, 1957-77; mem. com. floral inventory Amazon NSF, Washington, 1975—. Contbr. articles to profl. jours. Grantee NSF, 1966-86; recipient Disting. Alumni award U. Tulsa, 1979. Fellow AAUW, Calif. Acad. Scis.; mem. Botanical Soc. Am., Internat. Soc. Chem. Ecology (v.p. 1985-86), Ecol. Soc. Am. (pres.-elect 1985-86), Assn. Tropical Biology (pres. 1985-86). Home: 191 Palo Verde Terrace Santa Cruz CA 95060 Office: U Calif Thimann Labs Santa Cruz CA 95064

LANGENWALTER, PAUL EDWARD, II, archaeologist; b. Whittier, Calif., Aug. 5, 1948; s. Paul Edward and Audrey Virginia (Tierney) L.; m. Rebecca Elizabeth Baker, June 27, 1976; children: Elizabeth Anne, Paul Edward III. AB, Calif. State U., Long Beach, 1974; MA, U. Calif., Riverside, 1980. Curatorial asst. Los Angeles County Mus., 1972-76, research assoc., 1976—, collaborator Rancho La Brea Project, 1973-76; dir. Heritage Resource Cons., La Mirada, Calif., 1974—; collaborator Mission San Antonio Archeol. project Calif. Poly. State U., San Luis Obispo, 1979—. Contbr. articles to profl. jours. Mem. Am. Soc. Mammalogists (life), Soc. Am. Archaeology, Soc. Hist. Archaeology, Southwestern Anthropol. Assn., Phi Kappa Phi. Republican. Avocations: reading, collecting books, walking. Office: Heritage Resource Cons 14318 La Fonda Dr La Mirada CA 90638

LANGER, EVA MARIE, marketing executive; b. Oceanside, Calif., Sept. 23, 1958; d. William Frank and Clotilde (Gonzalo) L. B.S., San Diego State U., 1980. Audio engr. Peters Prodns., San Diego, 1980-83; news writer Sta. KSDO, San Diego, 1981-82; audio prodn. engr. Tuesday Prodns., San Diego, 1983-85; video technician Voice & Video, San Diego, 1983-84, ednl. sales staff, 1984-85, govt. and ednl. mktg. saleswoman, 1985-86, corp. and comml. mktg. saleswoman, 1986—; ind. radio producer, San Diego, 1984—, ind. music searcher, 1984-85. Producer Persons with AIDS Project, 1987. Camera operator Mothers Embracing Nuclear Disarmament, San Diego, 1985. Mem. Am. Women in Radio and TV (dir.-at-large 1985, 1st v.p. 1986, editor newsletter 1985-86), Nat. Assn. Female Execs., Am. Film Inst., Internat. Interactive Communications Soc. Democrat. Home: 4025 Jackdaw St San Diego CA 92103 Office: Voice & Video Inc 5038 Ruffner St San Diego CA 92111

LANGER, JAMES STEPHEN, physicist, educator; b. Pitts., Sept. 21, 1934; s. Bernard F. and Liviette (Roth) L.; m. Elinor Goldmark Aaron, Dec. 21, 1958; children: Ruth, Stephen, David. B.S., Carnegie Inst. Tech., 1955; Ph.D., U. Birmingham, Eng., 1958. Prof. physics Carnegie-Mellon U., Pitts., 1958-82, assoc. dean, 1971-74; prof. physics U. Calif-Santa Barbara, 1982—; mem. solid state scis. com. NRC. Contbr. articles to profl. jours. Vice pres. physics Com. Concerned Scientists, 1979—. Guggenheim fellow, 1974-75; Marshall scholar, 1955-57. Fellow Am. Phys. Soc., Am. Acad. Arts and Scis.; mem. AAAS, Nat. Acad. Scis., N.Y. Acad. Scis. Democrat. Jewish. Home: 1130 Las Canoas Ln Santa Barbara CA 93105 Office: U Calif Inst Theoretical Physics Santa Barbara CA 93106

LANGER, WILLIAM RICHARD, financial services executive, investment consultant; b. South Bend, Wash., Feb. 18, 1940; s. Otto Frank and Josephine (Randal) L.; m. Karren Lynn Nov. 7, 1964; children—Shelby Lynn, Brett Richard. A.D. in Acctg., Oreg. Inst. Tech., 1963; B.S. in Fin., Ariz. State U., 1977. Internal audit mgr. Arcoa Internat., Phoenix, 1963-67, controller, 1967-73, pres., 1973-77; office mgr. Wilhelm Trucking Co., Portland, 1977-81; dist. mgr. Waddell & Reed, Inc., Portland, 1981-85; div. mgr., Portland, 1985— . Bd. dirs. Williamette Tariff Bur., Portland, 1978-80; treas. U-Haul Fed. Credit Union, Phoenix, 1963-68, pres., 1968-73. Mem. Am. Assn. Individual Investors, Inst. Internal Auditors, Am. Mgmt. Assn. Democrat. Home: 285 NW 87th Ave Portland OR 97229 Office: Waddell & Reed Inc 8625 SW Cascade Ave Suite 290 Braverton OR 97005

LANGEREIS-BACA, MARIA, speech-language pathologist; b. Hoorn, Netherlands, Dec. 16, 1930; came to U.S., 1956; d. Jan and Ditje (Schollée) Langereis; m. Stanely H. Skigen (dec.); 1 child, Michelle Arlene; m. Wilhelm Voebel (div.); children: George L., Helene Patimah; m. Gregorio Baca. BS, N.Mex. State U., 1982, MS in Speech, MS in Ednl. Mgmt. Devel., 1985. Cert. clin. social worker State Office of Edn., N.Mex. Asst. personnel mgr. D.M. Read Inc., Bridgeport, Conn., 1960-62; order librarian U. Bridgeport (Conn.), 1962-65; dir. community house Nichols Improvement Assn., Trumbull, Conn., 1960-65; speech-lang. pathologist Las Cruces (N.Mex.) Pub. Schs., 1984—, Hatch (N.Mex.) Pub. Schs., 1985—; cons. Hospice Inc., Las Cruces, 1985—, Associated Health Service, Las Cruces, 1986—. Leader Girl Scouts Am., Las Cruces, 1976-77; leader 4H Club, Las Cruces, 1978-80; vol. Las Cruces Pub. Schs., 1978-79. Mem. Am. Speech Hearing and Lang. Assn., N.Mex. Speech Hearing and Lang. Assn. Republican. Roman Catholic. Club: Singles Scene (bd. dirs. 1985—). Avocations: Sierra Club hikes, big band era dances, needlecrafts. Home: 465 Milton Ave Las Cruces NM 88005

LANGERMAN, NEAL RICHARD, chemist, waste consultant; b. Phila., Mar. 11, 1943; s. Albert and Minnie (Sherman) L.; married June, 1965 (div. 1974); children: Fawn, Sheri; m. Heidi Fickinger, Dec. 30, 1985. AB, Franklin and Marshall Coll.; PhD, Northwestern U., 1969; postdoctrate studies, Yale U., 1969-70. NIH postdoctoral fellow Yale U.; asst. prof. Tufts U. Sch. Med., Boston, 1970-75; asst. prof. Utah State U., 1975-77, assoc. prof., 1977-83; pres., cons. Chem. Safety Assocs., San Diego, 1982—. Contbr. articles to profl. jours. Research grantee NSF, 1980, Utah State U., 1979-80, 80-81. Mem. Am. Chem. Soc., Am. Soc. Safety Engrs. Avocation: scuba diving. Office: Chem Safety Assocs Inc 8388 Vickers St Suite 216 San Diego CA 92111

LANGFELD, MARILYN IRENE, creative art company director; b. St. Louis, Apr. 28, 1951; d. Norman Max and Celeste (Brown) L. Student, Vanderbilt U., 1968-70; B.A. cum laude, Sonoma State U., 1978-80. Printer, Sojourner Truth Press, Altanta, 1971-73; carpenter apprentice Housebuilders Union, Atlanta, 1973-74; self employed housebuilder, Perry, Me., 1974-75; graphic artist Cuthberts Printing, San Rafael, Calif., 1976-77; graphic Designer Community Type & Design, Fairfax, Calif., 1977-80; owner, creative dir. Langfeld Assocs., San Francisco, 1980—. Recipient Am. Corp. Identity award, 1986, Type Dirs. Club award, 1987, Desi award, 1987. Mem. People Speaking Adv. Bd., 1979-84. Sonoma State scholar, Bank of Sonoma County, 1979-80; Vanderbilt U. scholar, 1968-69, 69-70. Mem. San Francisco C. of C., Am. Inst. Graphic Artists, San Francisco Art Dirs. Club, Western Art Dirs. Club. Art Dirs. and Artists of Sacramento, San Francisco Better Bus. Bur. Club: San Francisco Advt. Democrat. Jewish. Office: 381 Clementina St San Francisco CA 94103

LANGFORD, BILL D., chemist; b. Hanford, Calif., Aug. 12, 1944; s. McDonald Langford and Dorotha Loree (Stafford) McDarment; m. Trudy Bethel Allen, June 19, 1965; 1 child, Atha Dee. AA, Coll. of Sequoias, 1965; BS, Oreg. State U., 1982. Supervisory chemist Teledyne Wah Chang, Albany, Oreg., 1969—. Pres. Linn County (Oreg.) 4-H Horse Leaders Assn., 1979-82, mem. exec. council, 1981-83. Served as sgt. U.S. Army, 1966-69. Mem. Am. Chem. Soc. Democrat. Club: Linn County Kennel (v.p. 1977-78). Lodge: Elks. Avocations: horses, hunting, fishing, billiards. Home: 37603 KGAL Dr Lebanon OR 97355 Office: Teledyne Wah Chang 1600 Old Salem Hwy Albany OR 97321

LANGFORD, ROLAND EVERETT, army officer, environmental scientist; b. Owensboro, Ky., Apr. 11, 1945; s. John Roland and Mary Helen (Cockriel) L.; m. Son-Hee Shin, Dec. 18, 1971; children: John Everett, Lee Shin. AA, Armstrong State Coll., 1965; BS, Ga. So. Coll., 1967; MS, U. Ga., 1971, PhD, 1974; grad., U.S. Army Command and Gen. Staff Coll., 1985. Registered sanitarian, Ariz. Instr. Savannah (Ga.) Sci. Mus., 1971-72, Bainbridge (Ga.) Jr. Coll., 1973-74; asst. prof. chemistry Ga. Mil. Coll., Milledgeville, 1975-77; asst. prof. Ga. So. Coll., Statesboro, 1977-78; commd. capt. U.S. Army, 1978, advanced through grades to major, 1986; chief chemistry sect. U.S. Army Acad. Health Scis., Ft. Sam Houston, Tex., 1978-79; sanitary engr. U.S. Army Environ. Hygiene Agy., Aberdeen Proving Ground, Md., 1979-81; comdr. environ. sanitation detachment Taegu, Republic of Korea, 1981-83; environ. sci. officer Ft. Huachuca, Ariz., 1984—; panel mem. Comprehensive Assistance to Undergrad. Sci. Edn., NSF, 1975-77; judge Internat. Sci. Fair, San Antonio, Tex., 1979; mem. sci. rev. panel NIH, 1986—. Contbr. articles to profl. jours. Active Boy Scouts Am., Ft. Sam Houston, 1978-79; mem. parish council, lay minister Holy Family Parish, Ft. Huachuca, 1985—; advisor Med. Explorer Post, Ft. Huachuca, 1986—. Mem. Am. Acad. Indsl. Hygiene (cert.), Am. Chem. Soc., Nat. Environ. Health Assn., Korean Chem. Soc., Royal Asiatic Soc. (bd. dirs. 1982-83), Assn. Mil. Surgeons U.S., Am. Acad. Sanitarians (cert.). Republican. Roman Catholic. Avocations: ham radio, oriental studies, photography. Home: 111 Luke St NBU-28M Fort Huachuca AZ 85613 Office: U S Army Med Dept Activity Preventive Medicine Service Fort Huachuca AZ 85613-7040

LANGLEY, TODD HYATT, banker; b. Mineola, N.Y., June 15, 1934; s. Burr Todd and Ethel Louise (Sanborn) L.; m. Frances Adra Stephens, June 23, 1956; chilren: Sharon, Stuart, Scott. B.S. in Bus. Adminstrn., U. Ariz., 1956; grad. Pacific Coast Banking Sch., U. Wash. Vice chmn., chief adminstrv. officer Ariz. Bank, Phoenix, 1960—. Bd. dirs. ARC, Phoenix, 1967-83, Jr. Achievement, Phoenix, 1977-84, Scottsdale Art Ctr. Assn., 1984—; bd. govs. ARC, Washington, 1985—. Served with U.S. Army, 1956-58. Named Dir. of Yr., Jr. Achievement, 1983; Humanitarian of Yr., Phoenix O.I.C., 1983. Mem. Am. Inst. Banking, Human Resource Commn., Bank Adminstrn. Inst. Republican. Episcopalian. Club: Ariz. Country. Office: Ariz Bank 101 N 1st Ave Phoenix AZ 85003

LANGONI, RICHARD ALLEN, civil engineer; b. Trinidad, Colo., Aug. 7, 1945; s. Domenic and Josephine (Maria) L.; A.Applied Sci., Trinidad State Jr. Coll., 1966; BSCE Colo. State U., 1968; M.A., U. No. Colo., 1978; m. Pamela Jill Stansberry, Aug. 19, 1972; children—Kristi, Kerri. Civil engr. Dow Chem. Co., Golden, Colo., 1968-71; city engr., dir. public works City of Trinidad, 1971-74; civil engr. Clement Bros. Constrn. Co., 1974-75; instr. Trinidad State Jr. Coll., 1975-78; dir. public works City of Durango (Colo.), 1978-82; asst. dist. design engr. Colo. Dept. Hwys., Durango, 1982—. Recipient Meritorious Service award City of Durango; registered profl. engr. Colo., N.Mex. Mem. Nat. Soc. Profl. Engrs., ASCE, Am. Public Works Assn., Water Pollution Control Fedn., Profl. Engrs. Colo., Nat. Ski Patrol, Durango C. of C., Phi Theta Kappa, Chi Epsilon. Club: Purgatory, Wolf Creek, Hesperus. Home: 2911 Holly Ave Durango CO 81301

LANGPAAP, ELEANOR MADELINE, hospital administrator; b. San Francisco, Apr. 9, 1922; d. Otto Bismarck and Emilie Marie Louise (Euvrard) Langpaap; A.B., U. Calif., Berkeley, 1943, M.P.H., 1962. Statistician Oakland (Calif.) City Health Dept., 1943-45; x-ray technologist Drs. Garland, Hill & Mottram, San Francisco, 1946-48; research asst. Pack Med. Group, N.Y.C., 1948-49; pub. health analyst, bus. mgr. Santa Barbara County (Calif.) Health Dept., 1949-54, dept. asst., 1954-60; with Santa Clara County Health Dept., 1954-60; adminstrv. asst. building and construction program Childrens Hosp. of Los Angeles, 1963-65, adminstrv. asst. physician in chief, 1965-67, asso. adminstr., 1967-68; project adminstr. Calif. Regional Med. Program, U. Calif., Davis, 1968-71, asst. to dean, 1971-73, spl. asst. to chancellor, 1972-73; asso. dir. hosps. and clinics Sacramento Med. Center of U. Calif., 1973-74, exec. asso. dir., 1974-75; adminstr. Eskaton Am. River Hosp., Carmichael, Calif., 1975-86; with St. John's Hosp., Santa Monica, Calif., 1986—. Bd. dirs. Commn. Profl. and Hosp. Activities, 1986—. Mem. Am. Coll. Hosp. Adminstrs., Am., Calif. Hosp. assns., Hosp. Council No. Calif., U. Calif. Berkeley Alumni Assn., Sacramento Sierra Hosp. Assn. (dir. 1973—), Assn. Western Hosps. (dir.). Republican. Episcopalian. Office: St John's Hosp 1328 22nd St Santa Monica CA 90404

LANGSTON, MICHAEL ALLEN, computer science researcher; b. Glen Rose, Tex., Apr. 21, 1950; s. Allen Deliphus and Wanda Hepsi (Gray) L.; m. Ina Marie Stedham, May 18, 1975; children: Glen, Katie, Keith. BS, Tex. A&M U., 1972, PhD, 1981; MS, Syracuse U., 1975. Instr. computer sci. Overseas div. U. Md., 1976-78; lectr. Tex. A&M U., College Station, 1978-81; asst. prof. Wash. STate U., Pullman, 1981-86, assoc. prof., 1986—. Contbr. articles to profl. jours. Served to capt. U.S. Army, 1972-78. Recipient Outstanding Teaching award Tex. A&M U., 1981; NSF grantee, 1982, 84, 86. Mem. AAAS, IEEE, Assn. Computing Machinery, Soc. Indsl. and Applied Math., Am. Math. Soc. Office: Wash State U Dept Computer Sci Pullman WA 99164

LANGWORTHY, WILLIAM CLAYTON, college official; b. Watertown, N.Y., Sept. 3, 1936; s. Harold Greene and Carolyn (Peach) L.; m. Margaret Joan Amos, Sept. 6, 1958; children: Kenneth, Jennifer. B.S. magna cum laude, Tufts U., 1958; Ph.D., U. Calif.-Berkeley, 1962. Asst. prof. Alaska Meth. U., Anchorage, 1962-65; asst. prof. chemistry Calif. State U.-Fullerton, 1965-67, assoc. prof., 1967-72, prof., 1972-73, assoc. dean Sch. Letters Arts and Scis., 1970-73; prof. chemistry Calif. Poly. State U., San Luis Obispo, 1973-76, head dept. chemistry, 1973-76; dean Sch. Sci. and Math Calif. Poly State U., San Luis Obispo, 1976-83; v.p. acad. affairs Ft. Lewis Coll., Durango, Colo., 1983—. Author: monograph Environmental Education, 1971; contbr. articles to profl. jours. Treas. Council Concerned Citizens, Inc., Arroyo Grande, Calif., 1976-83; mem. Clean Air Coalition, San Luis Obispo, 1978-83; active Mozart Festival, 1981-82; bd. dirs. Durango Choral Soc., 1984—. Mem. Am. Chem. Soc., AAAS, Council Colls. Arts and Scis. (bd. dirs. 1982), Sierra Club, Phi Beta Kappa, Sigma Xi.

LANKFORD, ANDREW JAMES, physicist; b. Pitts., Aug. 28, 1950; s. William T. and Gretchen (Goldsmith) L.; m. Sharron Dripps, Dec. 5, 1981; 1 child, Christopher Andrew. BS, Yale U., 1972, MA, 1974, PhD, 1978. Physicist Lawrence Berkeley Lab., Berkeley, Calif., 1978; staff scientist Lawrence Berkeley Lab., Berkeley, 1978-81; exptl. physicist Stanford (Calif.) Linear Accelerator Ctr., 1981—. Contbr. articles to profl. jours. Mem. Am. Phys. Soc. Home: 1124 Royal Ln San Carlos CA 94070 Office: Stanford Linear Accelerator Ctr PO Box 4349 Stanford CA 94305

LANO, CHARLES JACK, management auditor; b. Port Clinton, Ohio, Apr. 17, 1922; s. Charles Herbin and Antoinette (Schmitt) L.; m. Beatrice Irene Spees, June 16, 1946; children—Douglas Cloyd, Charles Lewis. B.S. in Bus. Adminstrn. summa cum laude, Ohio State U., 1949. C.P.A., Okla. With U.S. Gypsum Co., 1941-46, Ottawa Paper Stock Co., 1946-47; accountant Arthur Young & Co. (C.P.A.'s), Tulsa, 1949-51; controller Lima div. Ex-Cell-O Corp., 1951-59, electronics div. AVCO Corp., 1959-61, Servomation Corp., 1961; asst. comptroller Scovill Mfg. Co., Waterbury, Conn., 1961-62; comptroller Scovill Mfg. Co., 1962-67; controller CF&I Steel Corp., Denver, 1967-69; v.p., controller CF&I Steel Corp., 1969-70; controller Pacific Lighting Corp., 1970-76; exec. v.p. Arts-Way Mfg. Co., Armstrong, Iowa, 1976-85; mgmt. auditor City of Anaheim, Calif, 1985—. Served with USMCR, 1942-45. Mem. Am. Inst. C.P.A.'s, Calif. Soc. C.P.A.'s, Financial Execs. Inst., Nat. Assn. Accountants, Iowa Soc. C.P.A.'s. Home: 6274 E Calle Jaime Anaheim CA 92807 Office: Civic Ctr 2005 Anaheim Blvd Anaheim CA 92805

LANS, CARL GUSTAV, architect, economist; b. Gothenburg, Sweden, Oct. 19, 1907; came to U.S., 1916; s. Carl and Ida Carolina (Schon) L.; m. Gwynne Iris Meyer, Dec. 21, 1935; children: Douglas C., C. Randolph. Student, CCNY, 1925-26, Sch. Architecture, Columbia U., 1926-30. Registered architect, Calif. Architect with Harry T. Lindeberg N.Y.C., 1930-32; architect Borgia Bros. Ecclesiastical Marble, N.Y.C., 1932-34; with architects Paist & Stewart, Miami, Fla., 1934-35; chief engr. insp. Dept. Agr., 1936-38; asst. tech. dir. FHA, 1938-48; tech. dir. Nat. Assn. Home Builders, Washington, 1948-52; with Earl W. Smith Orgn., Berkeley, Calif., 1952-56; architect, economist Huntington Beach, Calif., 1956—; ptnr. John Hans Graham & Assocs. Architects, Washington, 1947-55; spl. adviser Pres. Rhee, Republic of Korea, 1955-56; guest lectr. various univs., 1949-52. Author: Earthquake Construction, 1954. Chmn. bd. edn. adv. com., Arlington, Va., 1948. Recipient Outstanding and Meritorious Services citation Republic of Korea, 1956. Mem. AIA (citation), Nat. Acad. Scis. (bldg. research adv. bd. dirs.), S.W. Research Inst., Seismol. Soc. Am., Prestressed Concrete Inst., Urban Land Inst. Club: Nat. Press (Washington). Home and Office: 21821 Fairlane Circle Huntington Beach CA 92646

LANSDOWNE, KAREN MYRTLE, retired English language and literature educator; b. Twin Falls, Idaho, Aug. 11, 1926; d. George and Effie Myrtle (Ayotte) Martin; B.A. in English with honors, U. Oreg., 1948, M.Ed., 1958, M.A. with honors, 1960; m. Paul L. Lansdowne, Sept. 12, 1948; chilren—Michele Lynn, Larry Alan. Tchr., Newfield (N.Y.) High Sch., 1948-50, S. Eugene (Oreg.) High Sch., 1952; mem. faculty U. Oreg., Eugene, 1958-65; asst. prof. English, Lane Community Coll., Eugene, 1965-82, ret., 1982; cons. Oreg. Curriculum Study Center. Rep., Cal Young Neighborhood Assn., 1978—; mem. scholarship com. First Congl. Ch., 1950-70. Mem. MLA, Pacific N.W. Regional Conf. Community Colls., Nat. Council Tchrs. English, U. Oreg. Women, AAUW (sec.), Jaycettes, Pi Lambda Theta (pres.), Phi Beta Patronesses (pres.), Delta Kappa Gamma. Co-author: The Oregon Curriculum: Language/Rhetoric, I, II, III and IV, 1970. Home: 15757 Rim Rd LaPine OR 97739

LANSING, JOHN STEPHEN, anthropologist, educator; b. Ann Arbor, Mich., May 19, 1950; s. John Belcher and Marjorie (Tillis) L.; m. Therese de Vet, June 27, 1982; children: John, Lorena. BA with highest honors, Wesleyan U., 1972; PhD, U. Mich., 1977. Research asst. The Inst. for Advanced Study, Princeton, N.J., 1976-77; asst. prof. U. So. Calif., Los Angeles, 1977-83, assoc. prof. anthropology, 1983—, chmn. dept. anthropology, 1987—. Author: (books) Evil in the Morning of the World, 1974, The Three Worlds of Bali, 1983, (films) Three Worlds of Bali, 1981 (Cine Golden Eagle award 1982), The Temple of the Crater Lake, 1986. Social Sci. Research Council fellow, 1974-76, Fulbright fellow, 1986. Mem. Am. Anthropol. Assn., Koninklijk Instituut vour Taal, Land en Volkenkunde. Office: U So Calif Dept Anthropology University Park Los Angeles CA 90089-0661

LANTOS, THOMAS PETER, congressman; b. Budapest, Hungary, Feb. 1, 1928; m. Annette Tillemann; children: Annette, Katrina. B.A., U. Washington, 1949, M.A., 1950; Ph.D., U. Calif.-Berkeley, 1953. Mem. faculty U. Wash., San Francisco State U., 1950-83; TV news analyst, commentato, sr. econ. and fgn. policy adviser to several U.S. senators; mem. Presdl. Task Force on Def. and Fgn. Policy, 97th-100th Congresses from 11th Dist. Calif. (ranking mem. Middle East subcom. of fgn. affairs com.); founder study abroad program Calif. State U. and Coll. System.; Mem. Millbrae Bd. Edn., 1950-66. Democrat. Office: 1707 Longworth House Office Bldg Washington DC 20515 *

LANTZ, KENNETH EUGENE, consulting firm executive; b. Altoona, Pa., Mar. 9, 1934; s. William Martin and Alice Lucretia (Glass) L.; m. D. Arlene Yocum, Nov. 28, 1959; children—Antonia Marie, Theresa Antoinette. B.S. cum laude, Fordham U., 1956. Spl. rep. IBM, Los Angeles, 1962-67; dir. info. services Loyola-Marymount U., Los Angeles, 1967-70; pres. CBIS, Los Angeles, 1970-72, Kenneth Lantz Assocs., Los Angeles, 1977-82; mgr. fin.

systems Occidental Life Ins. Los Angeles, 1973-77; dir. systems Sayre & Toso, Los Angeles, 1982-83; prin. Atwater, Lantz, Hunter & Co., Los Angeles, 1983—. Author: The Prototyping Methodology, 1984. Contbr. articles to profl. jours. Served to 1st lt. USAF, 1957-60. Mem. Future of Automation Roundtable (dir. 1983—), Ins. Acctg. and Systems Assn. (Nat. Merit award 1984), Woodland Hills C. of C. Republican. Roman Catholic. Club: First Friday Friars. Office: Atwater Lantz Hunter & Co 22458 Ventura Blvd Woodland Hills CA 91364

LANYI, JANOS KAROLY, biochemist, educator; b. Budapest, Hungary, June 5, 1937; came to U.S., 1957, naturalized, 1962; s. Istvan and Klara (Rosthy) L.; m. Carol Ann Giblin, Sept. 15, 1962 (div. Dec. , 1984); children: Clara Aileen, Sean Renton, Gabriella. Student, Eotvos Lorand U. Scis., Budapest, 1955-56; B.S., Stanford U., 1959; M.A., Harvard U., 1961, Ph.D., 1963. Postdoctoral fellow Stanford U. Sch. Medicine, 1963-65; Nat. Acad. Scis. resident assoc. NASA-Ames Research Ctr., 1965-66; sr. scientist NASA-Ames Research Ctr., Moffett Field, Calif., 1966-80; prof. physiology and biophysics U. Calif.-Irvine, 1980—; vis. fellow Cornell U., 1976. Recipient NASA medal for exceptional sci. achievement, 1977; recipient H. Julian Allen award for best sci. paper Ames Research Ctr., 1978, Alexander von Humboldt award for sr. U.S. Scientists W.Ger., 1979-80. Mem. Am. Soc. Biol. Chemists, Biophys. Soc., Am. Soc. Microbiology, Phi Beta Kappa, Sigma Xi. Office: Dept Physiology and Biophysics U Calif Irvine CA 92717

LANZER, WILLIAM LINWOOD, orthopedic surgeon; b. Passaic, N.J., Nov. 10, 1946; s. William Scheer and Matilda Patricia (Ferrara) L.; m. Lynda Gale Farmer, June 15, 1968 (div. June 1979); m. Mary Jo Fangmeyer, July 18, 1981; children: Stephanie Jean, William Patrick. BA, UCLA, 1968; MEd, N.C. State U., 1971; M Med. Sci., Rutgers State U., Piscataway, N.J., 1975; MD, Washington U., St. Louis, 1977. Intern surgery U. Calif., San Diego, 1977-78, resident, 1978-83; commd. 2d lt. USAF, 1969, advanced through grades to major, 1986; clin. assoc. Nat. Cancer Inst. NIH, Bethesda, Md., 1979-81; fellow Mayo Clinic, Rochester, Minn., 1983-84; asst. prof. U. Wash., Seattle, 1984—. Mem. Gov.'s Commn. on Handicapped, Wash., 1986—. Recipient Zimmer Award Orthopedic Research and Edn. Found., Chgo., 1985. Mem. Orthopedic Research Soc., AMA, Psi Chi. Club: Wings Aloft (Seattle). Avocations: flying, clarinet, piano. Home: 4680 174th Ave SE Issaquah WA 98027

LAPETER, JAMES MICHAEL, real estate executive; b. Troy, N.Y., May 10, 1953; s. Alfred Paul and Grace Martha (Alvarez) L.; m. Susan Marie Brickner, May 31, 1986. BA in Econs. with honors, UCLA, 1975. Sales rep. 3M Co., Los Angeles, 1975-76; pres. Americana Realtors, Bellflower, Calif., 1976—; real estate instr. Cerritos Coll., Norwalk, Calif., 1980—; guest lectr. Calif. State U., 1981. Bd. dirs. Cerritos Coll. Real Estate Adv. Bd., Norwalk, 1981—; mem. Calif. Com. Real Estate Continuing Edn., 1983—. Named Realtor of Yr. Rancho Los Cerritos Bd. Realtors, 1981; Chancellor's Marshal UCLA, 1975; recipient Calif. State Resolution award Calif. Senate and Assembly, 1982. Mem. Calif. C. of C., Calif. Assn. Realtors. (dir. 1978—, exec. com.), Nat. Assn. Realtors, Rancho Los Cerritos Bd. Realtors (pres. 1982, regional v.p.), Blue Key, Lambda Chi Alpha (pres. 1974-75). Republican. Roman Catholic. Home: 3210 Abbey Ln Orange CA 92667 Office: Americana Realtors 9944 Flower St Bellflower CA 90706

LAPIERRE, MARYLOU, management training consultant; b. Seattle, May 22, 1934; d. Albert Louis and Aida Mary (Little) LaP.; children: Stephen, Monica, Paul, Roger, Sara, Marc. BA, U. Wash., 1973; MA, Antioch U., 1983. Asst. dir. admissions U. Wash., Seattle, 1973-76, asst. registrar, 1976-78, adminstr., 1978-83; mgmt. tng. cons. Karen Johnston & Assocs., Edmonds, Wash., 1983-86; prin. LaPierre Assocs., Edmonds. Contbr. articles to profl. jours. Pres. YMCA Br. Bd. Mgmt., Edmonds, 1983-86; bd. dirs. ACT Theatre, Seattle, 1984-86; mem. Econ. Devel. Council, Snohomish City, Wash., 1986. Mem. Am. Soc. Tng. and Devel. (v.p. fin. 1982-83). Avocations: tennis, racquetball, theatre, travel. Office: LaPierre Assocs 628 Bell St SW #C Edmonds WA 98020

LAPIERRE, PHILIP RICHARD, electronics company executive; b. Inglewood, Calif., Oct. 11, 1939; s. Louis Junior and Clara Helen (Wilson) LaP.; m. Joanne Elizabeth LaMore, Aug. 26, 1972 (div. Dec. 1976); m. Karen Sue Berkoff, Apr. 16, 1983. AA, Mt. San. Antonio Coll., 1960; student, Calif. State Poly U., Pomona, 1963; MBA, U. Redlands, 1987. Recreation leader City of Pomona, 1957-66, recreation supr., 1969-78; sr. recreation leader City of Claremont, Calif., 1966-69; sr. project mgr. Gen. Dynamics Electronics Div., San Diego, 1978-82, ops. mgr., 1982—. Chmn. youth soccer, 1975-76; mgr. Little League Baseball, Pomona, 1957-66; coach Pomona Pop Warner Football, 1963-66, Pomona Post 30 Am. Legion Baseball, 1969-74; asst. football coach Claremont High Sch., 1966-69. Mem. Am Prodn. Control Inventory Soc., Nat. Mgmt. Assn., Data Processing Mgmt. Assn., So. Calif. Golf Assn. Republican. Lodge: Elks (sec. Pomona club 1976-77). Avocations: reading, swimming, gardening, camping. Home: 1751-346 W Citracado Pkwy Escondido CA 92025 Office: Gen Dynamics Electronics PO Box 85227 San Diego CA 92138

LA PIERRE, SHARON DALE, artist, art educator; b. San Francisco, Mar. 1, 1945; d. George L. La Pierre and Maybelle F. (Swanson) L. B.A., Calif. State U.-San Jose, 1966; M.A. in Woven Textiles, Calif. State U.-San Diego, 1970. Cert. jr. coll. tchr., Calif. Owner, designer Basket Studio, Denver, 1970—; instr. fiber dept. Arapahoe Community Coll., Littleton, Colo., 1971-76; instr. weaving and design, U. Colo., Boulder, 1972, 1980; dir. fiber and design dept. Community Coll. Denver, Red Rocks, 1975-82, dir. gallery, 1982—; pres. Genre Communications Ltd.; artist-in-residence fibers design U. No. Colo., Greeley, 1978; instr. arts Colo. Women's Coll., Denver, 1981; lectr.; dir. workshops; exhbns. include Denver Art Mus., 1972; art ctrs. in Colo., N.Y., Nebr. Active NOW, San Diego, 1971. Recipient 1st place award Midwest Weavers Conf., 1973; Colo. Council Arts and Humanities grantee, 1978. Mem. Am. Soc. Interior Design, Handweavers Guild Am., Am. Crafts Council. Republican. Christian Scientist. Author: Design and Creativity; Drawing Out the Creative Potential by Understanding Design, 1979; You Can Design: An Adventure in Creating, 1983; contbr. articles in field. to publs. Home: 5697 Xenon Ct Arvada CO 80002 Office: Community Coll Denver Red Rocks Campus Dept Human Resource 6th Ave Golden CO 80401

LAPIN, CHARLES ALLAN, toxicologist; b. Ridgecrest, Calif., Feb. 21, 1950; s. Leo and Naomi Emma (Allen) L. BA in Math., U. Calif., Santa Cruz, 1972; MS in Toxicology, U. Ariz., 1975, PhD in Toxicology, 1978. Diplomate Am. Bd. Toxicology. Sr. toxicologist DuPont Corp., Newark, Del., 1978-81, Atlantic Richfield Co., Los Angeles, 1981—. Contbr. articles to profl. jours. Mem. Soc. Toxicology, Am. Coll. Toxicology. Office: Atlantic Richfield Co 515 S Flower St Los Angeles CA 90071

LA POLL, FRANCIS ALBERT, lawyer; b. West Hartford, Conn., Dec. 20, 1958; s. Albert Francis and Wilhemina Elvadora (Garrison) L.P. BA, U. Va., 1981; JD, Stanford U., 1984. Bar: Calif. 1984, U.S. Dist. Ct. (no. dist.) Calif. 1984, U.S. Tax Ct. 1986, U.S. Ct. Appeals (9th cir.) 1985. Law clk. U.S. Ct. Appeals 9th Cir., 1984-85; assoc. Fenwick, Davis and West, Palo Alto, Calif., 1985—. Editor-in-chief Stanford Jour. Internat. Law, 1983-84. Mem. Raven Soc., Jefferson Soc. (sec. 1980, treas. 1980-81). Avocations: running, skiing. Office: Fenwick Davis and West Two Palo Alto Sq Suite 800 Palo Alto CA 94306

LAPORTA, ROBERT LOUIS, SR., oceanarium executive; b. Scranton, Pa., Apr. 4, 1941; s. James and Julia (Maiolatesi) L.; m. Esther Marie Bottone, May 25, 1963; children—Carolyn, Robert Louis Jr., Richard. B.F.A., Carnegie Mellon U., 1966. Producer, dir. Westinghouse Broadcasting Sta. KDKA-TV, Pitts., 1966-67; assoc. producer Mike Douglas Show, Sta. KYW-TV, Phila., 1967-72; head entertainment, v.p. Sea World, Inc., San Diego, 1972—; dir. San Diego Holiday Bowl; dir., producer Whatisit Youth Theatre, 1979—; pres., dir. producer Chancery Ln. Players, Pitts., 1964-66. Author plays including: Makin' Movies, 1982, Homefront, 1983, Step Right Up, 1984, Dreams 'n Things, 1986. Recipient Mgmt. Tng. Program award Westinghouse Broadcasting, 1966. Mem. Nat. Assn. TV Programing Execs., West Coast Drama Clan. Roman Catholic. Office: Sea World Inc 1720 S Shores Rd San Diego CA 92109

LA PORTE, WILLIAM BRUCE, educational administrator, consultant; b. Los Angeles, July 13, 1925; s. William Ralph and Lura Estella (Adams) L.; m. Virginia Lee Andrew, June 4, 1949; children—Dean Bruce, Diane Lee, Dan Andrew. Student U. So. Calif., 1943-51; B.A., U. Calif.-Santa Barbara, 1953; M.S., Calif. State U.-Fullerton, 1965. Tchr. auto, machine, metal, welding El Rancho High Sch., 1953-57; coordinator indsl. edn. Whittier Union High Sch. Dist., 1957-59, coordinator adult vocat. edn., 1957-61, coordinator career edn., 1967-74; tchr. auto, drafting Pioneer High Sch., 1959-67, chmn. indsl. arts dept., 1959-61, 63-67, curriculum coordinator, 1960-63; instr. Rio Hondo Coll., 1963-64; prof. Calif. State U.-Los Angeles, 1973, 75-77; dir., sec. to bd. dirs. Tri-Cities Regional Occupational Program Dist., Whittier, Calif., 1974-84; mem. Calif. State Vocat. Edn. Sch. Dist. Rev. Team, 1974, chmn., 1975-76; cons. in field. Bd. dirs. East Whittier YMCA, 1978-84; pres. North Hills Home Owners Assn., 1979-80, 81-82, v.p., 80-81; bd. dirs. San Gabriel Valley Area Health Edn. Ctr. Served with USAAF, 1944-45. Named Hon. Plymouth Trouble Shooter Chrysler Corp., 1978. Mem. Am. Indsl. Arts Assn., Am. Vocat. Assn. (legis. com. for Calif., 1975-77), Assn. Calif. Sch. Adminstrs., Calif. Assn. Regional Occupational Ctrs. and Programs (v.p. 1976-77, pres. 1978-79, chmn. membership com., bd. dirs., legis. com. 1979-84), Calif. Assn. Vocat. Edn., Calif. Assn. Work Experience Educators, Calif. Council Indsl. Arts Suprs. (pres. 1970-71), Calif. Indsl. Edn. Assn. (pres. 73-74, legis. com. 74-77), Cal Adminstr. Vocat. Edn. and Practical Arts (pres. 72-73), Los Angeles County Indsl. Edn. Assn. (pres. 68-69), Pico Rivera C. of C. (legis. com.), Santa Fe Springs C. of C. Indsl. League (v.p. 73-74, bd. dirs. 73-76), Whittier Area C. of C. (edn. com.), Alpha Phi Omega (pres. 1952-53), Epsilon Pi Tau. Methodist. Club: East Whittier Lions. Home: 882 Elkridge St Brea CA 92621 Office: Tri-Cities Regional Occupational Program Dist 9401 S Painter Ave Whittier CA 90605

LARAMEE, JAMES ANDRE, analytical chemist; b. Los Angeles, Mar. 23, 1954. BS in ACS, Sonoma State U., 1976; MS, PhD, Purdue U., 1980. Research chemist Exxon Research Co., Baytown, Tex., 1980-81; postdoctoral fellow Warwick (Eng.) U., 1981-84; with Dept. Agrl. Chemistry Oreg. State U., Corvallis, 1984—. Contbr. articles to chem. jours. Mem. Am. Soc. Mass Spectrometry, Sigma Xi, Phi Lambda Upsilon.

LARGENT, STEVE, professional football player; m. Terry Largent; children: Kyle, Kelly, Kramer, Casie. Grad. in Biology, U. Tulsa. Wide receiver Seattle Seahawks, NFL, Kirkland, Wash., 1976—; player Pro Bowl, 1979, 80, 82, 85, 86; holds NFL record for passes caught in consecutive games. Office: Seattle Seahawks 11220 NE 53d St Kirkland WA 98033 *

LARIMORE-ALBRECHT, DOTTI DENISE, social work consultant, musician; b. Auburn, Calif., Apr. 20, 1954; d. Woodrow Franklin and Shirley Arvada (Houge) Larimore; m. Milton Joseph Albrecht, Apr. 11, 1985; stepchildren: Shawna Penelope (dec.), Racheal Constance, Joshua Clayton. Student, U. Nev., 1971-72, Sierra Coll., 1973; BA in Anthropology, U. Calif., Berkeley, 1975; MSW, Calif. State U., Sacramento, 1984. Social work cons. Auburn, Calif., 1984—; bookkeeper Milt's Machine Shop, Auburn, 1986—; med. social worker Auburn Faith Community Hosp., 1987—. Active vol. work. Auburn Faith Hospice, 1981-85; group facilitator Am. Cancer Soc., Auburn, 1984, vol. 1987; dir. music Bethlehem Luth. Ch., Auburn, 1977-83; active various local political campaigns, Placer County, Calif., 1976—; bd. dirs. Auburn Community Concert Assn., 1976—, Sierra Coll. Disabled Students Adv. Com., Rocklin, Calif., 1978-81. Mem. Nat. Assn. Social Workers, Smithsonian Instn., Elisabeth Kubler-Ross Ctr., . Calif.-Berkeley Alumni Assn., Calif. State U.-Sacramento Alumni Assn., Greenpeace. Democrat. Avocations: water sports, camping, photography, music, calligraphy. Home: 177 Valley View Dr Auburn CA 95603

LARIZADEH, MOHAMMED REZA, business educator; b. Tehran, Iran, Apr. 14, 1947; came to U.S., 1966; s. Hassan and Nosrat (Saremi) L.; m. Dianne Ellen Pincus, Mar. 25, 1973; children: Dariush, Darya Anna. BA in Econs., Bus., UCLA, 1972, cert. in acctg., 1974. Cert. colls. teaching credential, Calif. (life); lic. real estate agent, Calif. Auditor Peat, Marwick & Mitchell, Los Angeles, 1972-74; controller Petromain Constrn. Co., Tehran, 1975-77; v.p. fin. Pilary Marine Shipping Co., Tehran, 1977-79; prof. Iranian Inst. Banking, Tehran, 1975-78; pres. Audicount Acctg. and Auditing Group, Los Angeles, 1984—; prof. bus. and acctg. East Los Angeles Coll., 1980-87, vice-chmn. dept. bus. and acctg., 1987—; mgmt. cons. L.P. Assocs. Mfg. Co., Los Angeles, 1981—; mng. dir. Barrington Enterprises, Los Angeles. Author/translator: Accounting/Auditing, 1975. Mem. NEA, Am. Fedn. Tchrs., Calif. Tchrs. Assn., Am. Entrepreneur Assn., Nat. Assn. Realtors, Calif. Assn. Realtors, Iranian Student Assn. (pres. 1969-70), Iran-Am. C. of C., Nat. Trust for Hist. Preservation, Smithsonian Assocs., Alpha Kappa Psi.

LARK, DONALD HUGH, energy company executive, consultant; b. Bostwich, Nebr., Jan. 1, 1920; s. George William and Elizabeth Bessie (Parsons) L.; m. Virginia Mae Valant, May 21, 1920 (div. 1962); children—Donna Rae, Dennis Michael, Richard Wayne; m. Kathryn Marion Peak, Aug. 31, 1965. B.S. in Mech. Engring., Columbia Coll. (now Loras Coll.), Dubuque, Iowa, 1940; postgrad. in metallurgy UCLA, 1957; postgrad. in petroleum refining El Camino Coll., Lawndale, Calif., 1957. Cert. energy mgr. Engr. Standard Oil Co., El Segundo, Calif., 1945-59; pres. Plan-It Assocs. Inc., Hawthorne, Calif., 1959-64; v.p. Globe Chem. Internat., Los Angeles, 1959-64, Louriers & Lark, Hawthorne, 1959-64; mgr. engring. Kelco div. Merck Co., San Diego, 1966-83; pres. Energetics Systems, San Diego, 1983—; dir. Western Resource Group of Cos.; dir. engring. Tektra Enterprises Corp., Los Angeles; dir., adjunct prof. Energy Engring. Inst. of San Diego State U.; cons. DMJM/TMSI, Los Angeles. Co-author: Industrial Cogeneration Applications; contbr. articles to profl. jours. Mem. emergency mgmt. com. City of San Diego, 1983—; precinct capt. San Diego Republican Com., 1984; mem. policy com. Calif. Assemblyman Larry Stirling, 1984; dir. So. Calif. Energy Council; dir. Alt. Energy Coll., San Diego Poly. Inst. Served with USN, 1942-52, Korea. Mem. Am. Inst. Plant Engrs. (pres. San Diego 1974-75, Engr. of Yr. award 1974), Am. Assn. Corrosion Engrs. (pres. Los Angeles 1955-56), Am. Soc. Energy Engrs. (pres. San Diego 1983-84), Cogeneration Soc. (chmn. 1983—). Methodist. Home and Office: 7871 Compass Lake Dr San Diego CA 92119

LARK, RAYMOND, artist; b. Phila., June 16, 1939; s. Thomas and Bertha (Lark) Crawford. Student, Phila. Mus. Sch. Art, 1948-51, Los Angeles Trade Tech. Coll., 1961-62; B.S., Temple U., 1961; L.H.D., U. Colo., 1985. Ednl. dir. Victor Bus. Sch., Los Angeles, 1969-71; public relations exec. Western States Service Co., Los Angeles, 1968-70; owner, mgr. Raymond Lark's House of Fine Foods, Los Angeles, 1962-67; exec. sec. to v.p. Physicians Drug and Supply Co., Phila., 1957-61; lectr. Los Angeles Trade Tech. Coll., 1973, Compton (Calif.) Coll., 1972, Nat. Secs. Assn., Hollywood, Calif., UCLA, numerous others. One-man shows include, Dalzell Hatfield Galleries, Los Angeles, 1970-80, Arthur's Gallery Masterpieces and Jewels, Beverly Hills, Calif., 1971, Dorothy Chandler Pavillion Music Center, Los Angeles, 1974, Honolulu Acad. Arts, 1975, UCLA, 1983, U. Colo. Mus., 1984; group exhbns. include, Smithsonian Instn., 1971, N.J. State Mus., Trenton, 1971, Guggenheim Mus., N.Y.C., 1975, Met. Mus. Art, 1976, La Galerie Mauffe, Paris, 1977, Portsmouth (Va.) Mus., 1979, Ava Dorog Galleries, Munich, W. Ger., 1979, Accademia Italia, Parma, 1980, Ames Art Galleries and Auctioneers, Beverly Hills, 1980, Le Salon des Nations at Centre International d'Art Contemporain, Paris, 1983; represented in permanent collections, Library of Congress, Ont. Coll. Art, Toronto, Mus. African and African Am. Art and Antiquities, Buffalo, Carnegie Inst., numerous others. Recipient Gold medal Accademia Italia, 1980, also numerous other gold medals and best of show awards, and 3 presdl. proclamations; Nat. Endowment Arts grantee; ARCO Found. grantee; Colo. Humanities Program grantee; Adolph Coors Beer Found. grantee. Mem. Art West Assn. (pres. 1968-70). Address: PO Box 8990 Los Angeles CA 90008

LARKIN, DONALD JAMES, electrical engineer; b. Miles City, Mont., May 29, 1933; s. Harold and Marion (Huelster) L.; m. Phyllis Elaine Buckingham, Aug. 31, 1955; children: Donnie, Eddie, Rodney, Tresa, Timothy, Kevin, Keith, Cheryl, Kristina, Amanda, Joyce. BA in Physics, Nebr. Wesleyan U., 1956. Radar scientist U.S. Dept. Def., White Sands Missle Range, N.Mex., 1956-60, supervising elec. engr., 1960-64, quality assurance phys. scientist, 1964-81, supervising metrology engr., 1981—. Scoutmaster Boy Scouts Am., Las Cruces, N.Mex., 1963-85. Republican. Roman Catholic. Club: Las Cruces Sport (officer 1979-81). Lodge: Elks (local treas. 1963-70). Avocations: backpacking, fishing, hunting. Home: 3119 Fairway Las Cruces NM 88001 Office: AMXTM-CW-WS White Sands Missile Range NM 88002

LARKIN, GLENN RALPH, electronics technologist; b. Los Angeles, Dec. 31, 1955; s. Ralph Winfield L. and Donna (Read) Baker; m. Barbara Anne Hunter, Dec. 30, 1978 (div. June 1981); 1 child, Jon Richard. BSEET, DeVry Inst. Tech., Phoenix, 1981. Vacuum technician Beckman Instruments, Tempe, Ariz., 1979-80; elec. technician Honeywell PMSD, Phoenix, 1980-81; sr. elec. technologist Lawrence Livermore (Calif.) Nat. Lab., 1981—; pvt. practice audio-video recording 1980—. Mem. Calif. Scholastic Fedn. (life). Avocations: racquetball, audio-video recording, skiing. Office: Lawrence Livermore Nat Lab East Ave L-124 Livermore CA 94550

LARKS, LEONARD, optical engr.; b. Chgo., Apr. 29, 1937; s. Saul David and Golda (Gezuk) L.; B.A., U. Calif. at Los Angeles, 1957; O.D., Los Angeles Coll. Optometry, 1961; m. Eleanor Judith Glukes, June 14, 1959; children—Caryn, Deena. Practice optometry Glendale, Calif., 1961-64, Los Angeles, 1962-64; bio./med., optical engr./scientist Hycon Mfg. Co. Monrovia, Calif., 1964-69; optical-lens designer engr. design, devel. interplanetary telescopes Jet Propulsion Lab., Calif. Inst. Tech. at Pasadena, 1969-78; cons. in optical design, interplanetary optical design, 1978—; optometrist So. Calif. Permanente Med. Group, West Covina, 1978—. Chief data processing observer Los Angeles County Dem. Party, 1967-75, mem. County Dem. Central Com., 1968-72, committeeman, chmn. 49th assembly dist. Delegation, 1968-70. Recipient Younger Lens award Los Angeles Coll. Optometry, 1961, NASA Group Achievement award for Mariner Venus/Mercury 1973 project TV Subsystem Devel. Team, 1974, for Viking Mars 1976 project Orbiter Design and Devel. Team, 1977, for Voyager Sci. Instrument Devel., Imaging Instrument 1981. Mem. Am. Inst. Physics, Optical Soc. Am., Optical Soc. So. Calif. Contbr. articles profl. jours. Patentee in field. Home: 1028 Blue Dr West Covina CA 91790 Office: So Calif Permanente Med Group 1249 Sunset West Covina CA 91720

LARMORE, LEWIS, physics educator; b. Anderson, Ind., July 29, 1915; s. Forest and Lettie (Lowman) L.; m. Mary Elizabeth Russell, June 8, 1939; children—Thomas Russell, Marilou Larmore Morris. A.B., Ind. U., Bloomington, 1937, M.A., 1938, M.A., 1939; Ph.D., UCLA, 1952. Asst. prof. physics Ariz. State U., Tempe, 1947-49; physicist Rand Corp., Santa Monica, Calif., 1952-57; corp. research adviser Lockheed Aircraft Corp., Burbank, Calif., 1957-59; chief scientist Lockheed Calif. Co., Burbank, 1959-64; v.p., dir. advanced research lab. McDonnell Douglas Corp., Huntington Beach, Calif., 1964-72; physicist Office Naval Research, Pasadena, Calif., 1972-86. Chmn. trustees West Coast U., Los Angeles, 1981—. Patentee roll rate measuring device. Author: Photographic Principles, 1958; Applications of Infrared, 1954; contbr. articles to profl. jours. Bd. dirs. Easter Seal Soc., 1965-72. Served to lt. USN, 1943-46. Lowell Obs. fellow, Flagstaff, 1938. Fellow Am. Acad. Arts and Scis., Optical Soc. Am., AAAS, Am. Astronautical Soc. (pres. 1966-68); mem. Soc. Photo-Optical Instrumention Engrs. (pres. 1985), Internat. Acad. Astronautics. Republican. Methodist. Lodges: Rotary, Masons. Home: 1245 Calle Estrella San Dimas CA 91773 Office: Office Naval Research 1030 E Green St Pasadena CA 91106

LARNER, JACQUELINE LEE, clinical social worker; b. Aberdeen, Wash., Mar. 23, 1952; d. Frank Harris and Verlee Louise Larner; married, Sept. 23, 1978; children: Jonathan Robert, Jacey Brooke. BA, Colo. Women's Coll., 1974; MA, U. Colo., 1980; MSW, U. Denver, 1984. Instr. women's history and studies Colo. Women's Coll., Denver, 1980-83; instr. women's studies Loretto Heights Coll., Denver, 1984-86; pvt. practice psychotherapist Denver, 1986—; psychotherapist Mi Casa Resource Ctr. for Women, Denver, 1984—; cons. women's studies Loretto Heights Coll., 1986. Grantee Loretto Heights Coll., 1986, Colo. Council Arts and Humanities, Denver, 1980. Mem. NOW, Nat. Assn. Social Workers, Colo. Soc. Clin. Social Workers. Avocations: writing, skiing, scuba diving. Office: Mi Casa Resource Ctr for Women 571 Galapago St Denver CO 80204 Office: 5600 Greenwood Plaza Suite 208 Greenwood Village Denver CO 80111

LAROCK, TERRANCE EDMOND, planning executive; b. Detroit, Aug. 29, 1952; s. Wendell and Donna Jean (Elliott) LaR.; m. Bonnie Jo Campbell, July 21, 1979. A.A., Ohlone Jr. Coll., 1972; postgrad. Calif. State U.-Hawyard, 1976, U. N.Y., 1984; B. Polit. Sci., San Jose State U., 1974. Project planner Gould Inc., Santa Clara, Calif., 1977-79; materials mgr. Stanford Assocs., Menlo Park, Calif., 1979, Delta Assocs., Milpitas, Calif., 1979-81, Masstor Systems, Sunnyvale, Calif., 1981-84; purchasing/planning mgr. Fairchild ATS, San Jose, Calif., 1984—; v.p. ops. REDIFAB, San Jose, 1984— ; mgr. Tandy Corp., San Jose, 1976-78; city mgr. Thrifty Rent-A-Car, San Francisco, 1975-76. Author: Manufacturing Terms and Definition, 1978. Recipient Region 7 & 10 Excellent award, Am. Prodn. & Inventory Control, 1983, Edn. award, 1980, Membership award, 1979. Mem. Am. Prodn. and Inventory Control Soc. (region 10 edn., pres. 1980-81, v.p. bd. dirs. 1986-87), Purchasing Mgmt. Assn. Republican. Lutheran. Address: 2088 W Hedding St San Jose CA 95128

LA ROCQUE, MARILYN ROSS ONDERDONK, communications executive; b. Weehawken, N.J., Oct. 14, 1934; d. Chester Douglas and Marion (Ross) Onderdonk; B.A. cum laude, Mt. Holyoke Coll., 1956; postgrad. N.Y. U., 1956-57; M. Journalism, U. Calif. at Berkeley, 1965; m. Bernard Dean Benz, Oct. 5, 1957 (div. Sept. 1971); children: Mark Douglas, Dean Griffith; m. 2d, Rodney C. LaRocque, Feb. 10, 1973. Jr. exec. Bonwit Teller, N.Y.C., 1956; personnel asst. Warner-Lambert Pharm. Co., Morris Plains, N.J., 1957; editorial asst. Silver Burdett Co., Morristown, 1958; self-employed as pub. relations cons., Moraga, Calif., 1963-71, 73-77; pub. relations mgr. Shaklee Corp., Hayward, 1971-73; pub. relations dir. Fidelity Savs., 1977-78; exec. dir. No. Calif. chpt. Nat. Multiple Sclerosis Soc., 1978-80; v.p. public relations Cambridge Plan Internat., Monterey, Calif., 1980-81; sr. account exec. Hoefer-Amidei Assocs., San Francisco, 1981-82; dir. corp. communications, dir. spl. projects, asst. to chmn. Cambridge Plan Internat., Monterey, Calif., 1982-84; dir. communications Buena Vista Winery, Sonoma, Calif., 1984-86, asst. v.p. communications and market support, 1986-87; dir. communications Rutherford Hill Winery, St. Helena, Calif., 1987—; bd. dirs. Carneros Quality Alliance; instr. pub. relations U. Calif. Extension, San Francisco, 1977-79. Mem. exec. bd., rep-at-large Oakland (Calif.) Symphony Guild, 1968-69; co-chmn. pub. relations com. Oakland Museum Assn., 1974-75; cabinet mem. Lincoln Child Center, Oakland, 1967-71, pres. membership cabinet, 1970-71, 2d v.p. bd. dirs., 1970-71. Bd. dirs. Calif. Spring Garden and Home Show, 1971-77, Dunsmuir House and Gardens, 1976-77, San Francisco Symphony Assn., 1984—; mem. Calif. State Republican Central Com., 1964-66; v.p. Piedmont council Boy Scouts Am., 1977. Mem. D.A.R. (chpt. regent 1960-61, 66-68), U. Calif. Alumni Assn., Public Relations Soc. Am. (chpt. dir. 1980-82; accredited), Sonoma Valley Vintners Assn. (dir. 1984-87), Calif. Hist. Soc., San Francisco Mus. Soc., Nat. Trust for Historic Preservation, Smithsonian Assocs., Sonoma Valley C. of C. (bd. dirs. 1984-87), Am. Inst. Wine and Food, Sonoma County Press Club, Knights of the Vine (master lady 1985—). Clubs: Commonwealth of Calif.; Mount Holyoke Coll. Alumnae. Author: Maestro Baton and His Musical Friends, 1968; Happiness is Breathing Better, 1976. Address: 99 Dominican Dr San Rafael CA 94901

LARRABEE, RICHARD BRIAN, organic chemist; b. Sacramento, Apr. 29, 1940; s. Charles E. and Sigme (Porsche) L.; divorced; children: Craig, Susan. BS, U. Santa Clara, 1962; MS, U. Chgo., 1965, PhD, 1967. Staff scientist IBM Corp., Yorktown, N.Y., 1967-71, San Jose, Calif., 1971—. Contbr. articles to profl. jours.; author patent pubs. Fellow NSF, NASA, NIH. Mem. AAAS, Am. Chem. Soc., Calif. Native Plant Soc. Office: IBM Corp GPD 5600 Cottle Rd San Jose CA 95120

LARRICK, JAMES WILLIAM, science administrator; b. Englewood, Colo., Jan. 4, 1950; s. William Franklin and Louise (Gottschalk) L.; m. Kathy Louise Burck, Apr. 1, 1985. BA in Chemistry magna cum laude, Colo. Coll., 1972; MD, PhD, Duke U., 1980. Research fellow Marie Stauffer Sigall Found., Stanford U., Palo Alto, Calif., 1981-82; staff physician Kaiser Permanente Hosp., Santa Clara, Calif., 1982—; sci. project leader Human Monoclonal Antibodies Cetus Immune Research Labs, Palo Alto, Calif., 1982—; research scientist Cetus Immune Research Labs., Palo Alto, Calif., 1982-85, sr. research scientist, 1985, dir. research, 1985—. Contbr.

numerous articles to profl. jours.; chpts. to books. Staff Young Lords Free Health Clinic, Chgo., 1972-73; staff Edgemont Health Clinic, Durham, N.C., 1975-76; mem. curriculum com. Duke U. Sch. Medicine, 1974-75; active Bay Area Physicians for Socia Responsibility, 1982—; vol. physician Haight-Ashbury Free Health Clinic, San Francisco, 1983—; bd. dirs. Emergency Relief Fund Internat., San Francisco, 1985—. Mem. AAAS, Am. Fedn. Clin. Research, Am. Assn. Immunologists, Am. Assn. Phys. Anthropology, Calif. Acad. Scis., N.Y. Acad. Scis., Phi Beta Kappa. Avocations: cross country skiing, bicycling, scuba diving, mountaineering, sailing. Home: Star Rt Box 48 Woodside CA 94062 Office: Cetus Immune Research Labs 3400 West Bayshore Rd Palo Alto CA 94303

LARSEN, HAROLD EDWARD, artist; b. Gowen, Mich., Oct. 3, 1934; s. Henry Rosevelt and Olive Catherine (Sommers) L.; m. Frances Ann Terwilliger, Oct. 10, 1959; children: Kristin Ann, Edwin Terwilliger. BA, Mich. State U., 1959. Asst. mgr. Stouffer's Restaurants, Detroit, 1959-60; asst. mgr. Black River Orchids, South Haven, Mich., 1960-62, mgr., 1962-68, corp. pres., 1968-76; free lance artist South Haven, 1976-79; prin., artist H&F Larsen Studios, Santa Fe, 1980—; sole juror Sterling (Kans.) Coll. Prairie Ann. Art Exhibition, 1985, Gold Coast Watercolor Soc., Ft. Lauderdale, Fla., 1987; demonstrator Spring Arts N.Mex., Santa Fe, summer 1986. Graphics pub. and Romm-Lande Internat. Arts pub., 1984-86; works appear Southwest Art mag., Painting the Spirit of Nature (book), 1984, The Santa Fean mag., 1984, Art Gallery Internat. mag., 1985. Zoning dir. City South Haven, 1971; del. Van Buren County (Mich.) Rep. Conv., 1972. Served with U.S. Army, 1953-55. Mem. Nat. Watercolor Soc., Ky. Watercolor Soc., N.Mex. Watercolor Soc., Soc. Layerists in Multi-Media, N. Coast Collage Soc., Am. Orchid Soc. (judge 1970-80), Mich. Orchid Soc. (regional v.p. 1972-76), Old Santa Fe Assn. Republican. Roman Catholic. Lodge: Rotary (pres. South Haven club 1969). Avocation: traveling. Home and Office: 109 1/2 Victoria Santa Fe NM 87501

LARSEN, JAMES WARNER, vitamin manufacturing company executive; b. Mpls., Sept. 7, 1926; s. Alvin and Stella Helen (Villesvik) L.; m. Shirley May Rolin, Jan. 3, 1951; children—Terry Jane, Sydney Lee, Kristi Anne. B.S., U. Minn., 1948. Athletic coach Los Banos High Sch., (Calif.), 1948-51; salesman McKesson Drug Co., Mpls., 1951-63, v.p. sales, San Francisco, 1963-75; pres. Gen. Mdse. Distbrs., Dallas, 1975-81; v.p. ops. Vita-Fresh Vitamin Co., Garden Grove, Calif., 1981-86, exec. v.p. ops. and chief exec. officer, 1986—. Served with USN, 1944-46. Republican. Clubs: El Niguel Country (Laguna Niguel, Calif.); Lakes Country (Palm Desert, Calif.). Lodges: Masons, Shriners. Home: 29911 Running Deer Ln Laguna Niguel CA 92677 Office: Vita-Fresh Vitamin Co 7366 Orangewood Garden Grove CA 92642

LARSEN, JEAN MAYCOCK, educator; b. Provo, Utah, Feb. 23, 1931; d. Lawrence S. and Lorna (Booth) Maycock; B.S., Brigham Young U., Provo, 1953, M.S., 1960; Ph.D., U. Utah, 1972; m. A. Dean Larsen, Feb. 14, 1958; children—David Lawrence, Paul Joseph, Ann, Charlotte. Tchr. schs. in Oreg. and Utah, 1953-55, 57-58; mem. faculty Brigham Young U., 1960—, prof. family scis., 1976—, coordinator early childhood edn. program, 1980—. Mem. Nat. Assn. Edn. Young Children, Assn. Childhood Edn. Internat., Utah Assn. Edn. Young Children (past pres., chmn. adv. bd.), Am. Ednl. Research Assn., Soc. Research Child Devel., Phi Kappa Phi. Republican. Mormon. Author curriculum materials in field; also research. Home: 2678 North 880 East Provo UT 84604 Office: Brigham Young U 1319-A SFLC Provo UT 84602

LARSEN, JEANETTE LENORE, insurance safety consultant; b. Fresno, Calif., Mar. 3, 1955; d. William Hans and Barbara Jean (Busch) L.; m. David Wagenleitner, Nov. 8, 1980. BA, Calif. State U., Fresno, 1977. Cert. safety profl., 1987. Health planner City of San Joaquin, Calif., 1977-78; safety cons. Fireman's Fund Ins. Co., Fresno, 1978—; bd. dirs. San Joaquin Health, 1978—. Mem. Am. Soc. Safety Engrs., Cen. Calif. Safety Soc. (pres. 1980-81), Phi Mu Alumnae (scholarship chmn.). Republican. Club: Toastmasters (chpt. pres. 1985-86). Avocations: backpacking, skiing. Home: 3098 W Indianapolis Fresno CA 93722 Office: Fireman's Fund Ins Co 2490 W Shaw Fresno CA 93705

LARSEN, KEITH G., health care executive; b. Inglewood, Calif., June 26, 1951; s. Grant B. and Gladys Marie (Klobucar) L.; m. Vicki Adams, Sept. 10, 1974 (div. Sept. 1976); 1 child, Michael Seth; m. Jan C. McGary, Nov. 24, 1978; children: Zachary Aaron, Whitney Ann. BS in Pharmacy magna cum laude, U. Utah, 1976. Lic. pharmacist, Utah, Calif. Clin. pharmacist Latter Day Sts. Hosp., Salt Lake City, 1976-78, computer application developer, 1978-82, dir. computer services, 1983-85, dir. computer applications devel., 1986; dir. clin. applications devel. Intermountain Health Care, Salt Lake City, 1986—; cons. Control Data, 1978-85, GTE, 1981. Contbr. articles to profl. jours. Mem. Rho Chi. Avocations: backpacking, swimming, art. Home: 1199 N Winston Kaysville UT 84037 Office: Intermountain Health Care 36 S State Salt Lake City UT 84111

LARSEN, KIM ANN, business and marketing consultant; b. N.J., May 17, 1956; d. Joseph Richard and Letitia (Merola) L. B.A. in Econs., Northwestern U., 1977, M. Mgmt., 1979. Assoc. product mgr. Libby, McNeill & Libby, Inc., Chgo., 1979-80, product mgr., 1980-81; mktg. mgr. Shasta Beverages Inc., Hayward, Calif., 1982-83, INMAC, San Mateo, Calif., 1983-85; bus., mktg. cons., MIssion Viejo, Calif., 1985—; lectr., guest speaker. Docent San Francisco Zoo. Northwestern U. scholar, 1974-75. Mem. Internat. Fund Animal Welfare, Union Concerned Scientists, Am. Fedn. TV and Radio Artists, Alpha Lambda Delta.

LARSEN, TIMOTHY GORDON, health care executive; b. Susquehanna, Pa., Aug. 20, 1944; s. Norman James and Margarete Anne (Wunsch) L.; children—Erik Cristopher, Heather Louise. B.A. summa cum laude, Fla. Atlantic U., 1965; M.A. (NDEA fellow), Vanderbilt U., 1968; M.B.A., Pepperdine U., 1978, Doctor honoris causa, 1981; cert. hosp. adminstrn. U. So. Calif., 1980; Ph.D., Bedford U., 1981. Commd. 2d lt. USAF, 1968, advanced through grades to capt., 1971; aircraft comdr. March AFB, Calif., 1972-75; assoc. prof. aerospace studies Loyola Marymount U., Los Angeles, 1975-76, U. So. Calif., Los Angeles, 1976-78; admissions counselor Air Force Acad., USAF Res., 1978-82 ; asst. mgr. Lincoln Pacific Mktg. Corp., Long Beach, Calif., 1978-79; dep. dir. Social Rehab. Agy., Los Angeles, 1979-81; adminstr. Colima Internal Medicine, Whittier, Calif., 1981-82; exec. dir. Diamond Bar (Calif.) Med. Center, 1982-84; asst. clin. prof. health service adminstrn. U. So. Calif., 1981-84; exec. v.p., prin. D'Argent Investment Network, Inc., 1984-85; exec. dir. COMPNET, Coll. of Osteopathic Medicine of the Pacific, 1985—; pres. Diamond Bar Improvement Assn., 1984-86; v.p. Diamond Bar C. of C., 1984; bd. dirs. YMCA Diamond Bar, 1982-83. Maj. USAF Res. Decorated D.F.C., Air medal (3); Commendation medal (2), Republic Vietnam Campaign medal, Republic Vietnam Cross of Gallantry with palm. Mem. Am. Acad. Polit. and Social Sci., Med. Group Mgmt. Assn., Hosp. Fin. Mgmt. Assn., Assn. Western Hosps., Internat. Police Assn., Assn. Mental Health Adminstrs., Am. Mgmt. Assn., Diamond Bar Improvement Assn. (pres. 1984-86), Diamond Bar C. of C. (v.p. 1984), Air Force Assn., Soaring Soc. Am., Calif. Wildlife Fedn. Home: 21155 Running Branch Rd Diamond Bar CA 91765

LARSON, ARTHUR STANLEY, marine surveyor; b. N.Y.C., Sept. 1, 1925; s. Louis and Hilma (Finn) L.; m. Joan Murray, Oct. 10, 1962 (div. Mar. 1965). Student Dickinson Coll., 1943. Owner, gen. mgr. Cruising Enterprises, Balboa, Calif., 1946—; pres. Newport Export, Inc., Calif., 1958-66; free-lance master marine surveyor, Balboa, Calif., 1969—. Inventor simplified automatic weapons ejection system, also rotary engine design, 1943, halyard silencer for sailboats, 1971; designer canvas sailing hat, 1961. Served as sgt. USAAF, 1943-46, PTO. Republican. Clubs: Trans Pacific Yacht, Pacific Yacht and Balloon. Lodge: Elks. Home: 2114 W Ocean Front St Apt 208 Newport Beach CA 92663 Office: Cruising Enterprises Box 621 Balboa CA 92661

LARSON, BRENT THEODORE, broadcasting executive; b. Ogden, Utah, Sept. 23, 1942; s. George Theodore and Doris (Peterson) L.; m. Tracy Ann Taylor; children: Michelle, Brent Todd. Student, pub. schs., Los Angeles; diploma in radio operational engring., Burbank, Calif., 1962. Owner, mgr. Sta. KAIN, Boise, Idaho, 1969-77; owner, operator radio Sta. KXA, Seattle, 1975-83, radio Sta. KYYX, Seattle, 1980-83, radio Sta. KCKO, Spokane, Wash., 1978-84, radio Sta. KUUZ, Boise, 1976-82, radio Sta. KOOS, North Bend, Oreg., 1980-81, radio Sta. KODL, The Dalles, Oreg., 1974-80, radio Sta. KKWZ, Richfield, Utah, 1980—, Sta KSVC Radio, Richfield, Utah, 1980—, Sta. KSOS-FM, Sta. KNKK-Am, Salt Lake City, 1984—; v.p. Casey Larson Fast Food Co., Oreg. and Idaho, 1976—, Imperial Broadcasting Corp., Idaho, 1970—, Sta. KSOS-FM and KFRZ-AM, 1983—; pres. First Nat. Broadcasting Corp., 1970—; v.p. Larson-Wynn Corp., 1974—, Brentwood Properties, Ogden, 1977—; pres. Gt. Am. Radio Corp., Wash., 1977—, Gold Coast Communications Corp., Oreg., 1980-81, Sevier Valley Broadcasting Co., Inc., Utah, 1980—, Brent Larson Group Stas., Western U.S., 1969—; v.p. mktg. Internat. Foods Corp., Boise, 1983—; ptnr. Larson Tours and Travel, Burley, Idaho, 1977—; dir. Casey-Larson Foods Co., La Grande, Oreg. Bd. dirs. Met. Sch., 1981—. Served with U.S. Army, 1962-63. Mem. Am. Advt. Fedn., Nat. Assn. Broadcasters, Nat. Radio Broadcasters Assn., Wash. Broadcasters Assn., Oreg. Broadcasters Assn., Idaho Broadcasters Assn., Utah Broadcasters Assn., Citizens for Responsible Broadcasting (bd. dirs.). Republican. Mormon. Home: 4014 Beus Dr Ogden UT 84403 Office: care First Nat Broadcasting Corp PO Box 2129 Salt Lake City UT 84110-2129

LARSON, CHARLES LESTER, television writer-producer, author; b. Portland, Oreg., Oct. 23, 1922; s. Charles Oscar and Ina May (Couture) L.; m. Alice Mae Dovey, Aug. 25, 1966; 1 stepson, Wyn Donavan Malotte. Student, U. Oreg., 1940. Contract writer MGM Studios, Culver City, Calif., 1943-46; freelance mag. writer 1941-51. Assoc. producer: TV program Twelve O'Clock High, 1964; producer: TV program The FBI, 1965-68, The Interns, 1970-71, Cades County, 1971-72; exec. producer: TV program Nakia, 1974; producer: TV movie Crime Club, 1973; co-creator: TV series Hagen, 1979-80; author: The Chinese Game, 1969, Someone's Death, 1973, Matthew's Hand, 1974, Muir's Blood, 1976, The Portland Murders, 1983. Mem. Writers Guild Am. West, Producers Guild, Mystery Writers Am. (spl. award 1974), Authors League Am. Democrat. Home: 2422 SW Broadway Dr Portland OR 97201

LARSON, DAYL ANDREW, architect; b. Denver, Aug. 13, 1930; s. Andrew and Esther (Freiberg) L.; m. Kay W. Larson; children: Linda, Lesli, Lucy. BS in Architecture, BSBA, U. Colo., 1953. Pres. Haller & Larson Architects, Denver, 1962—. Served to capt. C.E., U.S. Army, 1953-55. Mem. AIA (pres. Denver chpt. 1978, pres.-elect state sect. 1986-87, pres. Colo. sect. 1987—). Home: 2153 S Beeler Way Denver CO 80231 Office: Haller & Larson 1725 S Blake St Denver CO 80202

LARSON, DENNIS LUVERNE, agricultural engineering educator, researcher; b. Mason City, Iowa, Feb. 3, 1940; s. Vernon C. and Adelaide L. (Wamstad) L.; m. Cheryl A. Davisson, June 1, 1963; children: Scott A., Kristine A., Steven A., Kathryn A. BS, Iowa State U., 1963; MS, U. Ill., 1964; PhD, Purdue U., 1971. Registered profl. engr., Ariz., Calif. Design engr. John Deere, Moline, Ill., 1966-68; internat. tech. advisor U. Nebr., Colombia, 1970-72; extension engr. Mich. State U., East Lansing, 1973; asst. prof. agrl. engring. U. Ariz., Tucson, 1973-79, assoc. prof., 1979—; dir., solar power plant evaluation, 1979-83;. Served to 1st lt. U.S. Army, 1964-66. Vis. scholar Melbourne U., Australia, 1983-84. Mem. Am. Soc. Agrl. Engrs., Am. Soc. Engring. Edn., Am. Solar Energy Soc. Avocations: woodworking, jogging, choral singing. Home: 1310 W Roller Coaster Rd Tucson AZ 85704 Office: U Ariz 507 Shantz Bldg Tucson AZ 85721

LARSON, DOUGLAS W., limnologist; b. Moline, Ill., June 22, 1937; s. Gunnard and Berniece Olive (Gaare) L.; m. Judith Kay Jones, Dec. 26, 1962 (div. Aug. 1976); 1 child, Angie Lyn. BS, Jamestown (N.D) Coll., 1963; MS, U. N.D., 1965; PhD, Oreg. State U., 1970. Wildlife aide U.S. Fish and Wildlife Service No. Prairie Research Ctr., Jamestown, N.D., 1965; aquatic biologist Oreg. Dept. Environ. Quality, Portland, 1971-74; limnologist U.S. Army Corps Engrs., Portland, 1974—; lectr. Portland State U., 1972-78; mem. Water Adv. Commn., Portland, 1978-80; cons. Nat. Park Service, Crater Lake, Oreg., 1982-84; cons. in field. Contbr. articles to profl. jours. Assoc. advisor Boy Scouts Am., Jamestown, 1961-62, scoutmaster, Corvallis, Oreg, 1968-69. Served as sgt. USMC, 1955-59. Research grantee Office Water Resources, 1966-70, Mazama Research Com.; Recipient Eagle Scout award Boy Scouts Am., 1962. Mem. Am. Soc. Limnology and Oceanography, Northwest Sci. Assn., Internat. Assn. Theoretical and Applied Limnology, N.Am. Lake Mgmt. Soc. (bd. dirs. 1985—), Sigma Xi, Phi Kappa Phi, Mensa. Democrat. Lutheran. Avocations: sailplaning, hiking, outdoor photography, writing, stamp collecting. Home: 5300 Parkview Dr #2044 Lake Oswego OR 97034 Office: US Army Corps Engrs Hydraulics-Hydrology 319 SW Pine St Portland OR 97204

LARSON, EDWARD WILLIAM, civil engineering educator, aerospace engineer; b. New Haven, Apr. 17, 1923; s. Edward W. and Clara (Garlick) L; m. Lila Mae Adkinson, Apr. 26, 1952; children: John Edward, Susan Diane. BSCE, Ind. Tech. Coll., 1943; MSCE, Northwestern U., 1948, PhD, 1953. Mgr. turbomachinery Rocketdyne div. Rockwell Internat., Canoga Park, Calif., 1966-68, mgr. engring., 1968-78, assoc. chief engring., 1978-79, dir. design tech., 1979-84, assoc. program mgr., 1984-86; lectr. in engring. Calif. State U., Northridge, 1986—. Served with USAAF, 1946-47. Mem. AIAA, Nat. Mgmt. Assn. (Silver Knight award 1984), Inst. Cert. Profl. Mgrs. (chmn. bd. regents 1975-77), Soc. Exptl. Mechanics, Sigma Xi. Home: 18621 Ringling St Tarzana CA 91356

LARSON, FREDERIC ROGER, research forester; b. Los Angeles, Mar. 26, 1942; s. Kenneth Frederic and Helen Cathcart (Stiles) L.; m. Kathleen Bennett, Oct. 13, 1962 (div. Feb. 1973); m. Angela Marie DiSandro, June 24, 1974; 1 child, Eva Marie. BS in Forestry, No. Ariz. U., 1966, MS, 1968; PhD, Colo. State U., 1975. Logger-sawmill operator Fred Donaldson, Lake Arrowhead, Calif., 1958-65; forester Kaibab Nat. Forest, Williams, Ariz., 1965-66, Nez Perce Nat. Forest, Kooskia, Idaho, 1966-67; research forester Rocky Mountian Exptl. Sta., Flagstaff, Ariz., 1967-78, Pacific N.W. Exptl. Sta., Anchorage, 1978—; instr. No. Ariz. U., 1971-72, adj. prof., 1975-78; cons. Peter F. Ffolliott, Tucson, 1976-77. Contbr. articles to profl. jours. No. Ariz. U. scholar, 1967-68. Mem. Soc. Am. Foresters (chmn. local chpt. 1976), Soc. Range Mgmt., The Wildlife Soc., Am Soc. Photogrammetry and Remote Sensing, Sigma Xi. Lodge: Masons. Avocation: native art. Office: Forestry Scis Lab 201 E 9th Ave Suite 303 Anchorage AK 99501

LARSON, HAROLD OLAF, chemistry educator; b. Port Wing, Wis., May 27, 1921; s. Melvin C. and Frieda T. (Christenson) L. BS, U. Wis., 1943; MS, Purdue U., 1947; PhD, Harvard U., 1950. Jr. chemist Shell Devel. Co., Emeryville, Calif., 1943-44; navigator Pan Am. Airways, San Francisco, 1944-45; chemist Hercules Powder Co., Wilmington, Del., 1950-54; research fellow Harvard U., Cambridge, Mass., 1954-55; asst. prof. U. W.Va., Morgantown, 1955-57; asst. prof. U. Hawaii, Honolulu, 1958-72, prof., 1972—. Contbr. articles to profl. jours. Mem. Am. Chem. Soc., Sigma Xi. Office: U Hawaii Dept Chemistry 2545 The Mall Honolulu HI 96822

LARSON, JAMES ALAN, investment executive; b. Vermillion, S.D., Aug. 21, 1948; s. Melville Ashley and Betty E. (Johnson) L.; m. Karen Kay Dagerman, Apr. 13, 1985; children: Nicole, Cassie. BA in Maths., U. S.D., 1970, MBA, 1971. Investment asst. Nat. Bank Commerce, Lincoln, Nebr., 1971-73; credit analyst Luth. Brotherhood Ins., Mpls., 1973-76; bond portfolio mgr. Sears Investment Mgmt. Co., Chgo., 1976-79; asst. v.p., bond portfolio mgr. Valley Nat. Bank, Phoenix, 1979-82; asst. v.p. bond trader Ariz. Bank, Phoenix, 1982-84; v.p., bond portfolio mgr. Anchor Nat. Life Ins., Phoenix, 1984-86; v.p. investments United Bank of Ariz., Phoenix, 1986—. Mem. Inst. Chartered Fin. Analysts, Stock and Bond Club (bd. dirs. 1984—), Fin. Analysts Soc. of Phoenix (ethics dir. 1986—). Republican. Lutheran. Lodge: Elks. Avocations: football, golf, tennis.

LARSON, MARY KATHLEEN, publishing executive; b. Ft. Dodge, Iowa, May 2, 1954; d. John Joseph and Mary Alice (McCarville) Coleman; m. Ronald Robert Larson, Nov. 22, 1978. BA, Creighton U., 1976. Tchr. Diocese of Omaha, 1976-78; advt. prodn. asst. Bus. News Pub. Co., Troy, Mich., 1978-79, advt. mgr., 1979-82, with advt. sales, 1980-83; gen. mgr. Reeves Jour., Laguna Hills, Calif., 1983-84, pub., 1984—; bd. dirs. Plumbing Heating Cooling Info. Bur., Chgo. Mem. Western Publs. Assn. Republican. Roman Catholic. Avocations: travel, lit., film. Office: Bus News Pub Co/ Reeves Jour 23187 La Cadena Laguna Hills CA 92653

LARSON, MILTON B., educator; b. Portland, Ore., July 3, 1927; s. Oscar Gilbert and Martha (Opedal) L.; m. Wilma Eloise Lawrence, Sept. 9, 1950; children—Steven Leroy, Gregory Lawrence, Arnold William, Linda Louise. B.S. in Mech. Engring, Ore. State U., 1950, M.S. in Physics, 1955; M. Engring., Yale, 1951; Ph.D., Stanford, 1961. Design engr. J. Donald Kroeker, Portland, Ore., 1950; research engr. Boeing Airplane Co., Seattle, 1951-52; from instr. to asso. prof. Ore. State U., Corvallis, 1952-64; prof. mech. engring. Ore. State U., 1969—; dean Sch. Engring. U. N.D., 1964-68; Ford Found. resident plastics dept. DuPont, Parkersburg, W.Va., 1968-69; summer indsl. positions, 1953-63, cons. to govt. Served in AUS, 1945-46. Recipient Lloyd Carter award outstanding and inspirational teaching Ore. State U., 1956; NSF sci. faculty fellow, 1957-59. Mem. Am. Soc. Engring. Edn., Am. Soc. M.E.'s, Tau Beta Pi, Pi Tau Sigma, Sigma Tau. Republican. Lutheran. Address: 206 N W 30 Corvallis OR 97330

LARSON, ORLA PATRICIA, distribution company executive; b. Glenwood, Minn., June 9, 1942; s. Roy Odin Ingvald and Sigri (Nerbo) Christianson; divorced; children: Andrea Renee and Angela Rhea (twins). BS with honors, U. Minn., 1965. Cert. secondary tchr., Minn., Ariz. Tchr. English, Theatre Arts Osseo (Minn.) Jr. High Sch., 1965-69; tchr. Lake Havasu (Ariz.) High Sch., 1970-74; adminstrv. asst. Scottsdale (Ariz.) Arts Ctr., 1975-78; exec. dir. Combined Phoenix Arts and Scis., 1978-80, Scottsdale Arts Ctr. Assn., 1980-82; pres. Internat. Marble Distbrs. Inc., Phoenix, 1983—. Bd. dirs. Roosevelt Action Assn., Phoenix, 1983; com. mem. Ariz. Women's Ptnrship., Phoenix, 1985; fundraiser Goddard for Mayor Campaign, Phoenix, 1983, 85; mem. Cen. Ave Deck Park Citizen Adv. Com., Phoenix, 1986; bd. dirs. Urban Coalition West. Mem. Marble Inst. Am., Am. Hotel and Motel Assn. (affiliate), Screen Actors Guild Am. Democrat. Club: Phoenix City (chmn. arts action com. 1985). Avocation: theatre. Home: 74 West Culver Phoenix AZ 85003 Office: Internat Marble Distbrs Inc 421 N 19 Ave Phoenix AZ 85009

LARSON, SHERRI LYNN, speech pathologist; b. Chgo., Nov. 2, 1960; d. Daniel George and Gayle Arlene (Schroeder) L. BA in Communicative Disorders, U. Redlands, 1982, MS in Communicative Disorders, 1984. Speech pathologist Riley's Speech Lang. Inst., Santa Ana, Calif., 1984-85, Parker Hearing Speech Inst., Torrance, Calif., 1985-86, Craig and Ford Inc., Anaheim, Calif., 1986—. Mem. Am. Speech Lang. Hearing Assn. (cert.), United Stroke Found. (recording sec. 1985—), Delta Kappa Psi. Republican. Baptist. Avocations: aerobics, swimming. Home: 16341 Woodruff St Westminster CA 92683 Office: Craig and Ford Inc 1535 E Orangewood Suite 113 Anaheim CA 92805

LARSON, WILLIAM RAYMOND, sociologist, educator; b. Spokane, Wash., Feb. 14, 1930; s. Einar Gustav and Elma Teresia (Johannson) L.; m. Aili Evelyn Hupila, Feb. 14, 1953 (div. Jan. 1982); children: Marina Teresia, Peter Gustav; m. Kristen Karen Ann Norris, Mar. 19, 1983. BA, U. Wash., 1955, MA, 1958, PhD, 1965; postgrad., Indsl. Coll. of the Armed Forces, 1967, U.S. Army Command and Gen. Staff Coll., 1973, U.S. Army War Coll., 1976. Sr. research assoc. Youth Studies Ctr. U. So. Calif., Los Angeles, 1960-65; assoc. prof. pub. adminstrn. U. So. Calif., 1960-69; prof. behavioral sci. Calif. State Polytech. U., Pomona, 1969—; chmn. behavioral scis. dept. Calif. State Poly. U., Pomona, 1969-75, coordinator Gerontology Cert. Program, 1982; mem. sr. cons. faculty mem. Command and Gen. Staff Coll., Leavenworth, Kans., 1973-84; research advisor Command Coll., Calif. Dept. Justice, Sacramento, 1985—. Contbr. articles to profl. jours. Mem. Gov's Task Force on Earthquake Preparedness, Calif., 1983—. Served to col. USAR, 1951-85. Decorated Army Commendation medal with two oak leaf clusters, Meritorious Service medal with two oak leaf clusters, Legion of Merit award, 1985; recipient George Washington Honor Medal award Freedoms Found., 1969, Meritorious Performance and Profl. Promise award Calif. State Polytech. U., 1986. Mem. Calif. Council Gerontology and Geriatrics, Res. Officer's Assn. (life; chpt. pres. 1983-84). Republican. Episcopalian. Club: Redondo Beach Yacht (commd. 1973-74). Avocations: sailing, navigation. Home: 255 Portofino Way Redondo Beach CA 90277 Office: Calif State Polytech U Pomona CA 91768

LARTER, PATRICK CLAUDE, reliability engineer; b. Salt Lake City, July 1, 1942; s. Clark Claude and Helen (Huber) L.; m. Winifred McAfee, July 11, 1970 (div. Nov. 1981); children: Wendy Patrice, Kristy Lynette; m. Linda Gail McAdam, Mar. 13, 1982; 1 child, Jennifer Karen. BS in Pysics, U. Utah, 1968; MS in Systems Engring., U. So. Calif., 1975; PhD in Mgmt., Calif. Coast U., 1985. Cert. community coll. instr., Calif. Electronic engr. Naval Ship Weapons Systems Engring. Sta., Port Huememe, Calif., 1968-81; reliability engr. Sacramento Air Logistics Ctr. Engring. Div./MME, McClellan AFB, Calif., 1981—; instr. Ventura Community Coll., 1978-80. commr. Boy Scouts Am., Thousand Oaks, Calif., 1970-80. Mem. Inst. Environ. Scis., Soc. Reliability Engrs. (pres. 1985—). Republican. Mormon. Avocations: farming, gardening. Home: 6256 Pinecreek Way Citrus Heights CA 95621 Office: SM-ALC/MMEA McClellan AFB CA 95652

LARUSSA, ANTHONY, JR., baseball manager; b. Tampa, Fla., Oct. 4, 1944; m. Elaine Coker, Dec. 31, 1973; 2 daughters: Bianca, Devon. Student, U. Tampa; B.A., U. So. Fla., 1969; LL.B., Fla. State U., 1978. Player numerous major league and minor league baseball team; mgr. Knoxville, So. League, 1978, Iowa, Am. Assn., 1979, Chgo. White Sox (Am. League), 1979-86, Oakland A's (Am. League), Oakland, Calif., 1986—. Office: Oakland A's Oakland-Alameda County Coliseum Oakland CA 94621 *

LA RUSSA, PHILIP JOHN, data processing executive, consultant; b. Bklyn., June 26, 1947; s. Pat and Rosaria (Misita) La R.; m. Marilyn Ann Purdoski, Sept. 5, 1970; 1 child, Aimee Lynn. Student, Hofstra U., 1965-66; AAS, Nassau Community Coll., Garden City, N.Y., 1970. Project leader Eastern States Bankcard Assn., New Hyde Park, N.Y., 1969-75; sr. programmer St. John's Hosp., Smithtown, N.Y., 1975-76; sr. program analyst Periphonics, Bohemia, N.Y., 1976-77; system analyst 1st Fed. Savs. and Loan, Phoenix, 1977-78; project mgr. Internat. Micor, Phoenix, 1978-84; I.S. mgr. The Pointe Resorts, Phoenix, 1984—; bd. dirs. Micor User Group, Orlando, Fla.; cons. Galler Hospitality Systems, Phoenix, 1983-84. Designed several computer systems. Served with USMC, 1966-68. Republican. Roman Catholic. Club: Ariz. Outdoor and Travel (Scottsdale). Avocation: radio-controlled model planes. Home: 2629 W Wood Dr Phoenix AZ 85029 Office: The Pointe Resorts Inc 7500 N Dreamy Draw Dr Phoenix AZ 85020

LASAROW, WILLIAM JULIUS, chief bankruptcy judge; b. Jacksonville, Fla., June 30, 1922; s. David Herman and Mary (Hollins) L.; m. Marilyn Doris Powell, Feb. 4, 1951; children: Richard M., Elisabeth H. B.A., U. Fla., 1943; J.D., Stanford U., 1950. Bar: Calif. 1951. Counsel judiciary com. Calif. Assembly, Sacramento, 1951-52; dep. dist. atty. Stanislaus County, Modesto, Calif., 1952-53; pvt. practice Los Angeles, 1953-73; bankruptcy judge U.S. Cts., Los Angeles, 1973—; chief judge U.S. Bankruptcy Ct., Central dist., Calif., 1978—; judge Bankruptcy Appellate Panel 9th Fed. Cir., 1980-82; faculty Fed. Jud. Ctr. Bankruptcy Seminars, Washington, 1977-82. Contbg. author, editor legal publs.; staff: Stanford U. Law Review, 1949. Mem. ABA, Los Angeles County Bar Assn., Wilshire Bar Assn., Blue Key, Phi Beta Kappa, Phi Kappa Phi. Democrat. Jewish. Lodge: Masons. Home: 11623 Canton Place Studio City CA 91604 Office: US Bankruptcy Ct 930 US Courthouse 312 N Spring St Los Angeles CA 90012

LASATER, ERIC MARTIN, neurobiologist; b. Stuttgart, Fed. Republic Germany, Jan. 6, 1953; (parents Am. Citizens); s. Gene Martin and Naomi Ruth (Krahn) L.; m. Jill Ann Smith, Aug. 6, 1977; 1 child, Brandon. BS, Colo. State U., 1975; MS, U. Calif., Davis, 1977; PhD, U. Tex. Med. Branch, Galveston, 1980. Postdoctoral fellow Harvard U., Cambridge, Mass., 1980-83, research assoc., 1983-84, biology lectr., 1984-85; asst. prof. U. Utah Med. Sch., Salt Lake City, 1985—. Contbr. articles to jours. Mem. AAAS, Assn. for Research Vision Ophthalmology, Neurosci. Soc., Sigma Xi (excellence in research award 1980). Office: U Utah Dept Physiology 410 Chipeta Way Salt Lake City UT 84108

LASITER, JACK BRINKLEY, utility holding co. exec.; b. Ft. Smith, Ark., July 20, 1930; s. Brinkley Cyrus and Ruth Leona (Wear) L.; B.S., Pepperdine U., Los Angeles, 1954, M.B.A., 1975; m. Julia Clara Simmons, June 16, 1957; 1 son, Paul Brinkley. With Aerophysics Devel. Corp., Santa Barbara, Calif., 1956-57, Kibbee, Peterson & Co., C.P.A.'s, Hollywood, Calif., 1957-58; with So. Calif. Gas Co., Los Angeles, 1958—, audit coordinator, 1978—;

audit support supr. Pacific Lighting Corp., Los Angeles, 1980—. Served with U.S. Army, 1954-56. Cert. internal auditor. Mem. Inst. Internal Auditor (chmn. scholarship com. Los Angeles chpt. 1980-81), Town Hall Calif. Republican. Mem. Ch. of Christ. Home: 1330 N Valley Home Ave La Habra CA 90631 Office: 810 S Flower St Los Angeles CA 90017

LASKA, MARK SROL, dentist; b. Pitts., Apr. 26, 1945; s. Sol and Lena Irene (Berman) L.; m. Joan Margaret Dunlap, Dec. 16, 1973; children—Shawn Renee, Sheila Marie, Shaye Michael. Student UCLA, 1966; D.D.S., U. So. Calif., 1970. Cert. dentist, Calif. With Group Dental Service, Los Angeles, 1970-81, head dentist, 1973-81, dental dir., 1980-81; dental assoc. S. Jay Welborn, D.D.S., Pasadena, Calif., 1981-82; pvt. practice dentistry, Los Angeles, 1981—. Bd. dirs. Laughlin Park Homeowners Assn., 1980—, pres., 1981, 84, 86, 87, treas., 1983, v.p., 1985—; bd. dirs. Hollywood Los Feliz Jewish Community Ctr., 1979-85, Los Feliz Improvement Assn., 1986—; mem. citizens adv. com., also dental commn. Los Angeles 1984 Olympic Games, staff dentist for games U. So. Calif. Polyclinic Los Angeles Olympic Med./Dental Com. Mem. ADA (com. on dental care), Los Angeles Dental Soc., Calif. Dental Assn., Acad. Gen. Dentistry, Alpha Omega, Zeta Beta Tau. Office: 3460 Wilshire Blvd Suite 104 Los Angeles CA 90010

LASKO, ALLEN HOWARD, pharmacist; b. Chgo., Oct. 27, 1941; s. Sidney P. and Sara (Hoffman) L.; B.S. (James scholar), U. Ill., 1964; m. Janice Marilynn Chess, Dec. 24, 1968; children—Stephanie Paige, Michael Benjamin. Staff pharmacist Michael Reese Hosp. and Med. Center, Chgo., 1964-68; clin. pharmacist City of Hope Med. Center, Duarte, Calif., 1968-73; chief pharmacist Monrovia (Calif.) Community Hosp., 1973-74, Santa Fe Meml. Hosp., Los Angeles, 1974-77; pvt. investor, 1977—. Recipient Roche Hosp. Pharmacy Research award, 1972-73. Mem. Magic Castle, Flying Samaritans, Mensa, Rho Pi Phi. Jewish. Author books: Diabetes Study Guide, 1972; A Clinical Approach to Lipid Abnormalities Study Guide, 1973; Jet Injection Tested As An Aid in Physiologic Delivery of Insulin, 1973. Home: 376 N Hill St Monrovia CA 91016

LASORDA, TOM CHARLES, professional baseball team manager; b. Norristown, Pa., Sept. 22, 1927; s. Sam and Carmella (Covatto) L.; m. Joan Miller, Apr. 14, 1950; children—Laura, Tom Charles. Student pub. schs., Norristown. Pitcher with Bklyn. Dodgers, 1954-55, Kansas City A's, 1956; with Los Angeles Dodger Orgn., 1956—; mgr. minor league clubs Pocatello (Idaho), Ogden (Utah), Spokane, Albuquerque, 1965-73; mgr. Los Angeles Dodgers, 1973-76, 1976—. Served with U.S. Army, 1945-47. Los Angeles Dodgers winner Nat. League pennant, 1977, 78, winner World Championship, 1981; 2d Nat. League mgr. to win pennant first two yrs. as mgr.; named Mgr. of Yr. (3). Mem. Profl. Baseball Players Am. Roman Catholic. Club: Variety of Calif. (v.p.). Office: care Los Angeles Dodgers 1000 Elysian Park Ave Los Angeles CA 90012 *

LASOTA, PETER DOUGLAS, lawyer; b. Sacramento, Oct. 23, 1957; s. Peter Eugene and Helen Jane (Beyers) LaS.; div.; 1 child, Christopher Douglas. B.S. summa cum laude, Our Lady of Lake U., 1977; Cert., Inst. on Comparative Polit. and Econ. Systems, Georgetown U., 1976; J.D., Ariz. State U., 1980. Bar: Ariz. 1980, U.S. Dist. Ct. Ariz. 1980, U.S. Ct. Appeals (9th cir.) 1980. Prosecutor intern Maricopa County, Phoenix, 1979; asst. city prosecutor City of Phoenix, 1980-81, pub. defender, 1981-82; assoc. Thomas A. Thinnes P.A., Phoenix, 1981-82; pub. defender City of Mesa, Ariz., 1982-83; dep. pub. defender Maricopa County, Phoenix, 1983-85; sr. ptnr. Rice & LaSota, Phoenix, 1985—; cons. horse law, Phoenix, 1980—. Sen. Barry M. Goldwater scholar, 1976. Mem. ABA, Ariz. Bar Assn., Ariz. Buckskin Horse Assn. (bd. dirs.), Appaloosa Horse Club, Am. Quarter Horse Assn. Republican. Roman Catholic. Home: 5021 E Pershing St Scottsdale AZ 85254 Office: Rice & LaSota 5060 N 19th Ave #112 Phoenix AZ 85015

LASSER, DAVID, retired labor executive, writer; b. Balt., Mar. 20, 1902; s. Leonard and Lena (Jaffe) L.; m. Florence Glassberg, Aug. 26, 1927 (div. Sept. 1937); children: Daniel Joseph, Helen Gerber; m. Amelia Tolbert, Dec. 23, 1963. Engr. Rossendale-Reddaway Co., Newark, 1924; mgr. prodn. Halperin Mills, Bklyn., 1925-26; mng. editor Gernsback Pubs., N.Y.C., 1927-34; pres. Workers Alliance Am., Washington, 1935-40, Am. Security Union, Washington, 1940-41; asst. dir. plant productivity div. War Prodn. Bd., Washington, 1942, dir. office Labor Adv. Coms., 1944-47, spl. labor advisor, sec. commerce, 1947-48; asst. to pres. AFL-CIO, Washington, 1950-69; cons. Dept. State, various countries, 1968-72. Author: Conquest of Space, 1931, Private Monopoly: The Enemy at Home, 1945; contbr. articles to profl. jours. V.p. Ctr. Continuing Edn. San Diego State U., 1979-82. Served as sgt. U.S. Army, 1918-19. Fellow AIAA (Founder award 1981); mem. AAAS, DAV. Home: 12539 Plaza Centrada San Diego CA 92128

LASTER, LEONARD, physician; b. N.Y.C., Aug. 24, 1928; s. Isaac and Mary (Ehrenreich) L.; m. Ruth Ann Leventhal, Dec. 16, 1956; children: Judith Eve, Susan Beth, Stephen Jay. A.B., Harvard U., 1949, M.D., 1950. Diplomate: Nat. Bd. Med. Examiners, Am. Bd. Internal Medicine (gastroenterology). From intern to resident in medicine Mass. Gen. Hosp., Boston, 1950-53; fellow gastroenterology Mass. Meml. Hosp., 1958-59; vis. investigator Pub. Health Research Inst., N.Y.C., 1953-54; commd. lt. USPHS, 1954, advanced through grades to asst. surgeon gen. (rear adm.), 1971; mem. staff Nat. Inst. Arthritis, Metabolic and Digestive Diseases, NIH, Bethesda, Md., 1954-73; chief digestive and hereditary diseases br. Nat. Inst. Arthritis, Metabolic and Digestive Diseases, NIH, 1969-73; spl. asst., then asst. dir. human resources President's Office Sci. and Tech., 1969-73; exec. dir. Assembly Life Scis.; also div. med. scis. Nat. Acad. Scis.-NRC, 1973-74; resigned USPHS, 1973; v.p. acad. affairs and clin. affairs Med. Center, also dean Coll. Medicine, prof. medicine Downstate Med. Center, State U. N.Y., Bklyn., 1974-78; pres. Oreg. Health Scis. U., Portland, 1978—; prof. medicine Oreg. Health Scis. U., 1978—; dir. Tektronix Inc., Standard Ins. Author articles on gastrointestinal disease, inborn errors metabolism, devel. biology.; Editorial bds. med. jours. Bd. dirs. Found. Advanced Edn. Scis., Bethesda, 1965-69, Bedford Stuyvesant Family Health Center, Bklyn., 1976-78, Med. Research Found. Oreg., 1978—, Oreg. Symphony, 1979-85, Oreg. Contemporary Theatre, 1981-83; pres. Burning Tree Elementary Sch. PTA, Bethesda, 1972-73. Fellow ACP; mem. Am. Assn. Study Liver Diseases, Am. Fedn. Clin. Research, Am. Gastroenterol. Assn., Am. Soc. Biol. Chemists, Am. Soc. Clin. Investigation, Assn. Am. Med. Colls. (council deans 1974-78), Multnomah County Med. Soc. (trustee), Marine Biol. Lab. Corp., Portland C. of C. (dir. 1980-84), Phi Beta Kappa, Sigma Xi, Alpha Omega Alpha. Clubs: Cosmos (Washington); Harvard (N.Y.C.); University, City, Arlington (Portland). Lodge: Downtown Rotary (Portland). Home: 1863 SW Montgomery Dr Portland OR 97201 Office: Oregon Health Scis U 3181 SW Sam Jackson Park Rd Portland OR 97201

LATHROP, KAYE DON, nuclear scientist, educator; b. Bryan, Ohio, Oct. 8, 1932; s. Arthur Quay and Helen Venita (Hoos) L.; m. Judith Marie Green, June 11, 1957; children: Braxton Landess, Scottfield Michael. B.S., U.S. Mil. Acad., 1955; M.S., Calif. Inst. Tech., 1959, Ph.D., 1962. Staff mem. Los Alamos Sci. Lab., 1962-67; group leader methods devel. Gen. Atomic Co., San Diego, 1967-68; with Los Alamos Sci. Lab., 1968-84, asso. div. leader reactor safeguards and reactor safety and tech. div., 1975-77, alt. div. leader energy div., 1977-78, div. leader computer sci. and services div., 1978-79, asso. dir. for engring. scis., 1979-84; assoc. lab dir., prof. applied research Stanford Linear Accelerator Ctr. Stanford U., Calif., 1984—; vis. prof. U. N.Mex., 1964-65, adj. prof., 1966-67; guest lectr. IAEA, 1969; mem. adv. com. reactor physics ERDA, 1973-77; mem. reactor physics vis. com. Argonne Nat. Lab., 1978-83; mem. mgmt. adv. com. y-12 div. Union Carbide Corp., 1979-82; mem. engring. nat. adv. com. U. Mich., 1983—; mem. steering com. Joint MIT-Idaho Nat. Engring. Lab. Research Program, 1985—; cons. in field. Author reports, papers, chpts. to books; mem. editorial adv. bd. Progress in Nuclear Energy, 1983-85. Served to 1st lt. C.E. U.S. Army, 1955-58. Spl. fellow AEC, 1958-61; R.C. Baker Found. fellow, 1961-62; recipient E.O. Lawrence Meml. award ERDA, 1976; Disting. Service award Los Alamos Nat. Lab., 1984. Fellow Am. Nuclear Soc. (chmn. math. and computation div. 1970-71, nat. dir. 1973-76, 79-82, treas. 1977-79, Outstanding Performance award 1980); mem. Am. Phys. Soc., Nat. Acad. Engring. Republican. Episcopalian. Home: 672 Junipero Serra Blvd Stanford CA 94305 Office: BIN 07 SLAC PO Box 4349 Stanford CA 94305

LATHROP, MITCHELL LEE, lawyer; b. Los Angeles, Dec. 15, 1937; s. Alfred Lee and Barbara (Mitchell) L.; children—Christin Lorraine, Alexander Mitchell, Timothy Trewin Mitchell. B.Sc., U.S. Naval Acad., 1959; J.D., U. So. Calif., 1966. Bar: D.C., Calif. 1966, U.S. Supreme Ct. 1969, N.Y. 1981. Dep. counsel Los Angeles County, Calif., 1966-68; with firm Brill, Hunt, DeBuys and Burby, Los Angeles, 1968-71; ptnr. firm Macdonald, Halsted & Laybourne, Los Angeles and San Diego, 1971-80; sr. ptnr. Rogers & Wells, N.Y.C., San Diego, 1980-86, Adams, Duque & Hazeltine, Los Angeles, N.Y.C. and San Diego, 1986—; presiding referee Calif. Bar Ct., 1984-86, mem. exec. com., 1981—; lectr. law Advanced Mgmt. Research Inc., Practicing Law Inst. N.Y., Continuing Edn. of Bar, State Bar Calif., ABA. Western Regional chmn. Met. Opera Nat. Council, 1971-81, v.p. and mem. exec. com., 1971—, now chmn.; trustee Honnold Library at Claremont Colls., 1972-80; bd. dirs. Music Ctr. Opera Assn., Los Angeles, sec., 1974-80; bd. dirs. San Diego Opera Assn., 1980—, v.p., 1985—; bd. dirs. Met. Opera Assn., N.Y.C. Served to capt. JAGC, USNR. Mem. ABA, N.Y. Bar Assn., Fed. Bar Assn., Fed. Bar Council, Calif. Bar Assn., D.C. Bar Assn., San Diego County Bar Assn. (chmn. ethics com. 1980-82, bd. dirs. 1982-85, v.p. 1985), Assn. Bus. Trial Lawyers, Assn. So. Calif. Def. Counsel, Los Angeles Opera Assos. (pres. 1970-72), Soc. Colonial Wars in Calif. (gov. 1970-72), Order St. Lazarus of Jerusalem, Friends of Claremont Coll. (dir. 1975-81, pres. 1978-79), Friends of Huntington Library, Am. Bd. Trial Advocates, Judge Advocates Assn. (dir. Los Angeles chpt. 1974-80, pres. So. Calif. chpt. 1977-78), Internat. Assn. Def. Counsel, Brit. United Services Club (dir. Los Angeles 1973-75), Mensa Internat., Calif. Soc., S.R. (pres. 1977-79), Phi Delta Phi. Republican. Clubs: California (Los Angeles); Valley Hunt (Pasadena, Calif.); Metropolitan (N.Y.C.). Home: 706 Stafford Pl San Diego CA 92107 Office: 401 W A St 23d Floor San Diego CA 92101 Office: 440 Madison Ave 22d Floor New York NY 10022

LATHROP, NINA, psychotherapist; b. USSR, Sept. 8, 1911; came to U.S., 1922; d. Eli and Sonya (Khutoretzkaya) B.; m. Welland Lathrop, Feb. 6, 1960 (dec. Feb. 1981); children: Mark Cummings, Conrad Cummings. BA, U. Calif., Berkeley, 1937, MSW, 1953. Cert. marriage, family and child counselor; cert. clin. social worker. Psychiat. social worker San Francisco Gen. Hosp., 1940-42; research assoc. U. Calif., Berkeley, 1942-44; pvt. practice psychotherapy San Francisco, 1945—; lectr. Contra Costa Jr. Coll., San Pablo, Calif., 1953-54; cons. East Bay and San Francisco Coop. Nursery schs., 1949—. Commonwealth fellow, 1945. Home and Office: 1526 Masonic Ave San Francisco CA 94117

LATIMER, DOUGLAS ALAN, environmental engineer; b. Buffalo, Jan. 19, 1948; s. Robert Edmond and Doris (Palmquist) L.; m. Victoria Anne Evan, Feb. 14, 1982. BSME, Ga. Inst. Tech., 1969; MS, U. Calif., Irvine, 1975. Registered profl. engr., Calif. Sr. engr. Bechtel Power Corp., Los Angeles, 1969-77; prin. engr. Systems Applications, Inc., San Rafael, Calif., 1977—. Mem. Air Pollution Control Assn. (chmn. visibility com. 1984—).

LATTA, ANGELA TRAUTMAN, rehabilitation institute executive; b. N.Y.C., June 27, 1944; d. Franz Josef and Pauline (Hernandez) Trautman; m. William Anthony Latta, May 18, 1973. BA, CUNY, Queens, 1970; Masters, Calif. State U., Los Angeles, 1975. Cert. clin. competence in speech and lang. pathology. Pvt. practice in speech pathology Calif., 1970—; tech. cons. St. Mary's Med. Ctr., Long Beach, Calif., 1976-81; asst. adminstr., pres. Out Patient Rehab. Inst. Inc., Corvallis, Oreg., 1983—, also bd. dirs., 1983—. Mem. Am. Speech, Lang., Hearing Assn., Oreg. Speech and Hearing Assn., Calif. Speech Pathologists and Audiologists in Pvt. Practice. Avocations: reading, dancing, gardening, landscapeing, architectural design. Office: Outpatient Rehab Inst 999 NW Circle Blvd Corvallis OR 97330

LATTANZIO, STEPHEN PAUL, astronomy educator; b. Yonkers, N.Y., June 29, 1949; s. Anthony Raymond and Anella Lattanzio; m. Barbara Regina Knisely, Aug. 14, 1976. BA in Astronomy, U. Calif., Berkeley, 1971; MA in Astronomy, UCLA, 1973, postgrad., 1973-75. Planetarium lectr. Griffith Obs., Los Angeles, 1973-75; instr. astronomy El Camino Coll., Torrance, Calif., 1974-75; planetarium lectr. Valley Coll., Los Angeles, 1975; prof. astronomy Orange Coast Coll., Costa Mesa, Calif., 1975—, planetarium dir., 1975—; regional resource person Nat. Air & Space Mus., Washington, 1982-84. Co-author: Study Guide for Project: Universe, 1978, 2d rev. edition 1981; textbook reviewer, 1978—. Mem. Astron. Soc. Pacific, Nat. Space Soc., The Planetary Soc., Internat. Planetarium Soc., Sigma Xi (assoc.), Phi Beta Kappa. Avocation: astronautics. Office: Orange Coast Coll 2701 Fairview Rd Costa Mesa CA 92628

LAU, EDWARD PAK-TUNG, biochemist; b. Hong Kong, Nov. 17, 1949; s. Stephen H. and Lai-Kiu (Chan) L.; m. Claudia Wong, July 18, 1976; children: Erica, Austin. BA, Cen. Wash. U., 1970, MSc, 1972; PhD, U. Wyo., 1977. Research assoc. U. Colo., Boulder, 1977-81; research scientist Amgen, Boulder, Colo., 1981—. Contbr. articles to profl. jours. Mem. N.Y. Acad. Sci., Sigma Xi. Home: 1685 Quince Ave Boulder CO 80302 Office: Amgen 2045 32d St Boulder CO 80301

LAU, ELIZABETH KWOK-WAH, clinical social worker; b. Hong Kong, Jan. 7, 1940; m. Edmond Y. Lau, June 5, 1965; children: Melissa, Ernest. BA, Brigham Young U., 1963; MSW, U. Kans., 1965. Supr. N.E. Community Mental Health Ctr., San Francisco, 1968-73; clin. dir. Chinatown Child Devel. Ctr., San Francisco, 1973-75; program specialist Kai Ming Head Start Program, San Francisco, 1975-77; clin. social worker VA Hosp., Palo Alto, Calif., 1977—; host, interviewer Sta. KTSF-TV, San Francisco, 1982—; bd. dirs. Kai Ming Head Start Program. Author: Innovative Parenting, 1980, How to Love Your Children, 1983, How to Raise a Successful Child, 1984, How to Train a Bright Child, 1985. V.p. Parents-Tchrs. League Zion Luth. Sch., San Francisco, 1981-83. Recipient Performance award VA Med. Ctr., Palo Alto, 1979, 83, Social Wokr Research award VA Med. Ctr., Palo Alto, 1985. Mem. Nat. Assn. Social Workers (cert.). Home: 470 Ortega St San Francisco CA 94122 Office: VA Adminstrn Med Ctr 3801 Miranda Ave Palo Alto CA 94304

LAU, IRENE OI LIN, banker, import company executive; b. Canton, China, Mar. 24, 1950; d. Kin Hon and Wai Ching (Lee) Yee; m. Danny Lau, Mar. 14, 1971 (div.); Student San Francisco City Coll., 1977—. Asst. mgr. Violet's Fashions, Hong Kong, 1967-68; teller Bank of Am., San Francisco, 1969-78, unit supr., 1978-80, shift supr., 1980-81, asst. v.p., 1981—; v.p. merchandising Silky Way, Inc. of Calif., 1979-81, pres., 1981—. Bilingual election officer Election Bd., San Francisco, 1981-82. Mem. Nat. Assn. Female Execs., Nat. Retail Mcht. Assn. Democrat. Club: Postal Commemorative Soc. Columnist for Chinese Community newspaper.

LAU, JOHN HON SHING, mechanical engineer; b. China, June 17, 1946; came to U.S., 1973; s. Shui Hong and Mary Au L.; m. Teresa Yu, Sept. 2, 1972; 1 child, Judy M. B.S. in Civil Engring., Nat. Taiwan U., 1970, M.A.Sc. in Structural Engring., U. B.C., 1973; M.S. in Engring. Mechanics, U. Wis., 1974; Ph.D. in Theoretical and Applied Mechanics, U. Ill., 1977; M.S. in Mgmt., Fairleigh Dickinson U., 1981. Registered profl. engr., N.Y., Calif. Research engr. Exxon Prodn. and Research Co., Houston, 1977; structural specialist Control Data Corp., Sunnyvale, Calif., 1977-78; research assoc. Internat. Paper Co., Tuxedo Park, N.Y., 1978-79; sr. engr. Ebasco Services Inc., N.Y.C., 1979-81; sr. engr. Bechtel Power Corp., San Francisco, 1981-83; MTS, Sandia Nat. Lab., N.Mex., 1983-84, Hewlett-Packard Labs., 1984—. Contbr. articles to profl. jours. U. Wis. Madison Engring. Exptl. Sta. fellow, 1973-74. Fellow Chinese Engrs. Assn.; mem. AAAS, N.Y. Acad. Scis., Sigma Xi. Roman Catholic. Home: 961 Newell Road Palo Alto CA 94303 Office: Hewlett Packard Labs 1501 Page Mill Rd Palo Alto CA 94304

LAU, KIN-HING WILLIAM, biochemistry educator; b. Hong Kong, Hong Kong, July 4, 1953; came to U.S., 1973; s. Chat Kee an Fung Lin (Wan) L.; m. Marjory Jean Doyle, Nov. 26, 1983. BA, SUNY, Plattsburgh, 1976; PhD, Iowa State U., 1982. Research asst. Iowa State U., Ames, 1976-82; research instr. Loma Linda (Calif.) U., 1982-84, asst. prof. biochemistry and medicine, 1984—. Cons. reviewer Annals of Internal Medicine, 1985—; contbr. articles to profl. jours. NSF fellow, 1975; recipient Premium Acad. Excellence award Iowa State U., 1976. Mem. AAAS, Am. Chem. Soc., Am. Soc. Cell Biology, N.Y. Acad. Scis., Am. Fedn. Clin. Research, Am. Soc. Bone and Mineral Research, Soc. Calif. Bone Club. Avocations: fishing, sports, reading, music, traveling. Office: Jerry L Pettis Meml Vets Hosp 11201 Benton St Loma Linda CA 92357

LAU, LAWRENCE JUEN-YEE, economics educator, consultant; b. Guizhou, China, Dec. 12, 1944; came to U.S., 1961, naturalized, 1974; s. Shai-Tat and Chi-Hing (Yu) Liu; m. Tamara K. Jablonski, June 23, 1984. B.S. with gt. distinction, Stanford U., 1964; M.A., U. Calif.-Berkeley, 1966, Ph.D., 1969. Acting asst. prof. econs. Stanford U., Calif., 1966-67, asst. prof., 1967-73, assoc. prof., 1973-76, prof., 1976—; cons. The World Bank, Washington, 1976—; vice chmn. Bank of Canton of Calif. Bldg. Corp. 1981-85; dir. Bank of Canton of Calif., San Francisco, 1979-85; dir. Property Resources Equity Trust, Los Gatos, 1987—; vice-chmn. Complete Computer Co. Far East Ltd., Hong Kong, 1981—; bd. dirs. Property Casulaty Resources Equity Trust. Author: (with D.T. Jamison) Farmer Education and Farm Efficiency, 1982, Models of development: A Comparative Study of Economic Growth in South Korea and Taiwan, 1986; contbr. articles in field to profl. jours. Mem. adv. bd. Self-Help for the Elderly, San Francisco, 1982. John Simon Guggenheim Meml. fellow, 1973; fellow Ctr. for Advanced Study in Behavioral Scis., 1982; Overseas fellow Churchill Coll., Cambridge U., Eng., 1984. Fellow Econometric Soc.; mem. Academia Sinica, Conf. Research in Income and Wealth. Republican. Episcopalian. Office: Stanford U Dept Econs 405 Encina Hall West Wing Stanford CA 94305

LAUB, RICHARD JAMES, chemist, educator; b. San Francisco, Aug. 4, 1945; s. Samuel Harold and Marie Eloise (Roumasette) L. BS in Chemistry, Regis Coll., 1967; MS in Chemistry, UCLA, 1971; PhD in Chemistry, U. Hawaii, 1974. Sci. research council fellow, chemistry dept. U. Swansea, Wales, 1974-78; asst. prof. chemistry Ohio State U., Columbus, 1978-82; prof. San Diego State U., 1982—; cons. analytical chemistry, various orgns. Contbr. articles to profl. jours. Served with USMC, 1967-69, Vietnam. Alcoa Found. fellow, 1983-85. Mem. Am. Chem. Soc., Royal Soc. Chemistry, Royal Inst. Chemistry (charter), Sigma Xi. Office: San Diego State U Dept Chemistry San Diego CA 92182

LAUB, WILLIAM MURRAY, utility executive; b. Ft. Mills, Corregidor, Philippines, July 20, 1924; s. Harold Goodspeed and Marjorie M. (Murray) L.; m. Mary McDonald, July 26, 1947; children: William, Andrew, Mary, David, John. B.S. in Bus. Adminstrn, U. Calif. at Berkeley, 1947, LL.B., 1950. Bar: Calif. 1951. Practice law Los Angeles, 1951-55; with Southwest Gas Corp., Las Vegas, Nev., 1958—; v.p., gen. counsel Southwest Gas Corp., 1958-60, exec. v.p., 1960-64, pres., chief exec. officer, 1964-82, chmn., chief exec. officer, 1982—, pres., 1984—; also dir. Pres. Boulder Dam Area council Boy Scouts Am., 1967-69, So. Nev. Indsl. Found., 1967-68, So. Nev. Meth. Found., 1967-74; chmn. Nev. Equal Rights Commn., 1966-68; Chmn. Clark County Republican Central Com., 1964-66; nat. committeeman Nev. Rep. Com., 1968-80; trustee Sch. Theology at Claremont, Calif., 1977—; trustee Inst. Gas Tech., 1983; nat. bd. advisors, coll. bus. and pub. adminstrn. The U. Ariz., 1985—; bd. dirs. Alliance for Acid Ranin Control, 1985—. Served to lt. (j.g.) USNR, 1941-45. Mem. ABA, Am. Gas Assn. (chmn. 1986-87), Pacific Coast Gas Assn. (chmn. 1983,), Calif. Bar Assn., Nat. Coal Council. Methodist (trustee). Clubs: Jonathan (Los Angeles); Pauma Valley (Calif.) Country; Spanish Trail Golf & Country (Nev.), Las Vegas Country. Office: Southwest Gas Corp 5241 Spring Mountain Rd Las Vegas NV 89102 *

LAUBE, ROGER GUSTAV, financial consultant; b. Chgo., Aug. 11, 1921; s. William C. and Elsie (Drews) L.; m. Irene Mary Chadbourne, Mar. 30, 1946; children: David Roger, Philip Russell, Steven Richard. BA, Roosevelt U., 1942; student, John Marshall Law Sch., 1942, 48-50; LLB, Nat. Trust Sch., Northwestern U., 1960; cert., Trust Div., Pacific Coast Grad. Sch. Banking, U. Wash., 1962-64. Cert. fin. cons., registered rep. With Chgo. Title & Trust Co., Chgo., 1938-42, 48-50, Nat. Bank Alaska, Anchorage, 1950-72; mgr. mortgage dept. Nat. Bank Alaska, 1950-56, v.p., trust officer, mgr. trust dept., 1956-72; v.p., trust officer, mktg. dir., mgr. estate and fin. planning div. Bishop Trust Co., Ltd., Honolulu, 1972-82; instr. estate planning U. Hawaii, Honolulu, 1978-82; exec. v.p. Design Capital Planning Group, Inc., Tucson, 1982-83; pres., chief exec. officer Advanced Capital Devel., Inc. of Ariz., Tucson, 1983-85, Prescott, 1985—; registered investment advisor, mng. exec. Integrated Resources Equity Corp., 1983—; pres. Anchorage Estate Planning Council, 1960-62, charter mem., 1960-72; charter mem. Hawaii Estate Planning Council, 1972-82, v.p., 1979, pres., 1980, bd. dirs., 1981-82; mem. Prescott Estate Planning Council, 1986—. Pres. Anchorage Community Chorus, 1946-72, pres., 1950-72; mem. Anchorage camp Gideons Internat., 1946-72, Honolulu camp, 1972-82, mem. Central camp, Tucson, 1982-85, Prescott, 1985—; mem. adv. bd. Faith Hosp., Glennallen, Alaska, 1960—, Central Alaska Mission of Far Eastern Gospel Crusade, 1960—; sec.-treas. Alaska Bapt. Found., 1955-72; bd. dirs. Bapt. Found. of Ariz., 1985—, mem. investment com.; pres. Sabinovista Townhouse Assn., 1983-85; bd. dirs. Alaska Festival Music, 1960-72, Anchorage Symphony, 1965-72; bd. advisers Salvation Army, Alaska, 1961-72, chmn., Anchorage, 1969-72, bd. advisers, Honolulu, 1972-82, chmn. bd. advisers, 1976-78. Served to 1st lt., JAGD U.S. Army, 1942-48; asst. staff judge adv. Alaskan Command, 1946-48. Recipient Others award Salvation Army, 1972. Mem. Am. Inst. Banking (instr. trust div. 1961-72), Am. Bankers Assn. (legis. council trust div. 1960-72), Nat. Assn. Life Underwriters (nat. com. for No. Ariz.), Ariz. Assn. Life Underwriters, Anchorage C. of C. (mem. awards com. 1969-71), Internat. Assn. Fin. Planners (cert. investment advisor, Anchorage chpt. 1969-72, treas., exec. com. Honolulu chpt. 1972-82, Ariz. chpt. 1982—, del. to world congress Australia and New Zealand 1987), Million Dollar Round Table. Baptist (exec. com. Alaska conv. 1959-61, dir. music Alaska 1950-72, Hawaii 1972-82, Tucson 1982-85, Prescott Valley Ch. 1985—, chmn. bd. trustees Hawaii 1972-81, Prescott Valley 1986—, worship leader Waikiki Ch. 1979-82). Home: 649 Filaree Dr Prescott AZ 86301 Office: Sun Pine Exec Ctr 915 E Gurley Suite 303 Prescott AZ 86301

LAUBER, MIGNON DIANE, food processing company executive; b. Detroit, Dec. 21; d. Charles Edmond and Maud Lillian (Foster) Donaker; student Kelsey Jenny U., 1958, Brigham Young U., 1959; m. Richard Brian Lauber, Sept. 13, 1963; 1 dau., Leslie Viane (dec.). Owner, operator Alaska World Travel, Ketchikan, 1964-67; founder, owner, pres. Oosick Soup Co., Juneau, Alaska, 1969—. Treas., Pioneer Alaska Lobbyists Soc., Juneau, 1977—. Mem. Bus. and Profl. Women, Alaska C. of C. Libertarian. Club: Washington Athletic. Author: Down at the Water Works with Jesus, 1982; Failure Through Prayer, 1983. Home: 321 Highland Dr Juneau AK 99801 Office: PO Box 1625 Juneau AK 99802

LAUDA, DONALD PAUL, university dean; b. Leigh, Nebr., Aug. 7, 1937; s. Joe and Libbie L.; m. Sheila H. Henderson, Dec. 28, 1966; children: Daren M., Tanya R. B.S., Wayne State Coll., 1963, M.S., 1964; Ph.D., Iowa State U., 1966. Assoc. dir. Communications Center U. Hawaii, 1966-67; assoc. prof. indsl. arts St. Cloud (Minn.) State Coll., 1967-69; asst. dean Ind. State U., 1970-73; chmn. tech. edn. W.Va. U., 1973-75; dean Sch. Tech., Eastern Ill. U., Charleston, 1975-83, Calif. State U., Long Beach, 1983—; cons. in field. Author: Advancing Technology: Its Impact on Society, 1971, Technology, Change and Society, 1978, 2d edit., 1985; contbr. articles to profl. jours. Pres. Council on Tech. Tchr. Edn.; dir. Charleston 2000 Futures Project, 1978-81. Served with USAR, 1957-59. EPDA research fellow, 1969-70; Eastern Ill. U. faculty research grantee, 1971. Mem. Future Soc. Internat. Tech. Edn. Assn., Council Tech Tchr. Educators (Tchr. of Yr. award 1978, pres.), World Future Soc., Internat. Tech. Edn. Assn., Am. Vocat. Assn., Phi Delta Kappa, Epsilon Pi Tau. (Laureate citation 1982). Office: Calif State U Applied Arts and Scis Long Beach CA 90840

LAUDENSLAGER, WANDA LEE, speech pathologist; b. San Jose, Calif., July 22, 1929; d. Victor Vierra and Florence Lorene (Houck) Silveira; A.A., Coll. San Mateo, 1960; B.A., San Jose State U., 1962, M.A., 1965; m. Leonard E. Laudenslager, Apr. 26, 1952; children—Leonard E. II, Dawn Marie. Speech pathologist Newark (Calif.) Unified Sch. Dist., 1962-65, dist. coordinator speech, hearing and lang. dept., 1965—; trainer student tchrs. Certified in supervision, teaching, speech, standard designated services, Calif.; lic. real estate broker, gen. bldg. contractor, audiometrist, speech pathologist, Calif.; lic. speech pathologist, Calif.; cert. clin. competence in speech pathology Am. Speech, Lang. and Hearing Assn. recipient Crown Zellerbach Found. award, 1961; hon. life mem. Calif. Congress Parents and Tchrs., Inc.

Mem. Phi Kappa Phi, Alpha Gamma Sigma, Pi Lambda Theta, Kappa Delta Pi. Home: 37733 Logan Dr Fremont CA 94536 Office: Newark Unified Sch Dist 5715 Musick Ave Newark CA 94560

LAUDENSLAYER, WILLIAM FRANKLIN, JR., wildlife ecologist; b. Reading, Pa., May 23, 1948; s. William Franklin and Isabel (Tewkesbury) L.; m. Donna Louise Slocum, Aug. 28, 1971; children: Amanda Lynn, Sara Eileen. AB in Biology, Eastern Bapt. Coll., 1970; MS in Biology, No. Ariz. U., 1973; PhD in Zoology, Ariz. State U., 1981. Cert. wildlife biologist, cert. ecologist. Wildlife biologist Bur. Land Mgmt. U.S. Dept. Interior, Riverside, Calif., 1977-80; regional wildlife ecologist Forest Service USDA, San Francisco, 1981—. Editor: Guide to Wildlife Habitats of California, 1987. Recipient Spl. Achievement award U.S. Bur. Land Mgmt., 1981. Mem. Am. Soc. Naturalists, Am. Ornithologists Union, Cooper Ornithol. Soc., Wilson Ornithol. Soc., Am. Soc. Mammalogists, Cactus and Succulent Soc., Calif. Native Plant Soc., Ecol. Soc. Am., Western Field Ornithologists, Herpetologists League, Wildlife Soc. (editor Transactions 1985-86, Western sect. newsletter 1982-83), Sigma Xi. Home: 105 Names Dr Grass Valley CA 95949 Office: Tahoe Nat Forest R-5 Hwy 49 and Coyote St Nevada City CA 95959

LAUDERDALE, WALTER JOHN, air force officer, research chemist; b. Pasadena, Calif., Oct. 5, 1962; s. Robert Val and Sylvia Ann (Krakowka) L. BS in Chemistry, USAF Acad., 1984. Commd. 2d lt. USAF, 1984, advanced through grades to lt., 1986; research chemist USAF Astronautics Lab., Edwards AFB, Calif., 1984—. Mem. Am. Chem. Soc. Republican. Roman Catholic. Avocations: jazz music, snow skiing, science fiction, fantasy books, outdoors. Home: 43310 7th St E Lancaster CA 93535 Office: Air Force Astronautics Lab AFAL/CX Edwards AFB CA 93523

LAUER, GEORGE, environmental consultant; b. Vienna, Austria, Feb. 18, 1936; came to U.S., 1943; s. Otto and Alice (Denton) L.; m. Sandra Joy Comp, Oct. 1, 1983; children by previous marriage—Julie Anne, Robert L. B.S., UCLA, 1961; Ph.D., Calif. Inst. Tech., 1967. Mem. tech. staff N.Am. Aviation, Canoga Park, Calif., 1966-69; mgr. Rockwell Internat., Thousand Oaks, Calif., 1969-75; div. mgr. ERT, Inc., Westlake Village, Calif., 1975-78; dir. Rockwell Internat., Newbury Park, Calif., 1978-85; dir. Tetra-Tech Inc., Pasadena, Calif., 1985-86; pres. Environ. Monitoring and Services, Inc., 1986—. Contbr. articles to profl. jours. Patentee in field. Served with U.S. Army, 1957-59. Fellow Assn. for Computing Machinery; mem. Am. Chem. Soc., Air Pollution Control Assn. Republican. Jewish. Home: 6009 Maury Ave Woodland Hills CA 91367 Office: Environ Monitoring Services Inc 4765 Calle Quetzal Camarillo CA 93010

LAUFENBERG, FRANCIS, school system administrator; b. Rock Island, Ill., Aug. 5, 1921; s. August J. and Jane (Higgins) L.; m. Frances Lee Windsor, Oct. 22, 1944; children: Lawrence Windsor, Linda Lea. Student, St. Ambrose Coll., 1940-41; BS, U. Calif., Santa Barbara, 1948; EdM, U. So. Calif., 1950, EdD, 1958. Tchr. Los Angeles pub. schs., 1948-50, adminstr., 1950-58; asst. supt. Oxnard (Calif.) City Schs., 1958-60; asst. supt., assoc. supt., dep. supt. Long Beach (Calif.) Unifed Sch. Dist., 1960-78, supt., 1978-85; v.p. Calif. State Bd. Edn., 1985—; lectr. U. So. Calif., Calif. State Coll., Long Beach. Served to maj. USMCR, 1942-46. Mem. Assn. Calif. Sch. Administrs., Delta Tau Delta, Phi Delta Kappa. Episcopalian. Lodge: Kiwanis. Office: Long Beach School Dist Office Supt Schs 701 Locust Ave Long Beach CA 90813

LAUGHLIN, LOUIS GENE, economic analyst, consultant; b. Santa Barbara, Calif., Sept. 20, 1937; s. Eston A. and Cornelia Helen (Snively) L.; student Pomona Coll., 1955-58; B.A., U. Calif.-Santa Barbara, 1960; postgrad. Claremont Grad. Sch., 1966-70, 85—, Sch. Bank Mktg., U. Colo., 1974-75, Grad. Sch. Mgmt., U. Calif.-Irvine, 1983. Mgr., Wheeldex-Los Angeles Co., 1961-62; v.p. Warner/Walker Assos., Inc., Los Angeles, 1962; cons. Spectra-Sound Corp., Los Angeles, 1964-65; rep. A.C. Nielsen Co., Chgo., 1962-64; research analyst Security Pacific Nat. Bank, Los Angeles, 1964-67, asst. research mgr., 1967-68, asst. v.p., 1968-72, v.p., mgr. market info. and research div., 1972-76, v.p. research adminstrn., pub. affairs/research dept., 1976-82, v.p. govt. relations dept., 1982-85; dir. research and devel. Applied Mgmt. Systems, South Pasadena, Calif., 1986—; mem. Nat. Conf. on Fin. Services, 1982-84, mem. policy council, 1983-84; mem. policy council Nat. Conf. on Competition in Banking, 1978-79, 81. Sec. econs. Town Hall of Calif., 1966. Mem. Am., Western econ. assns., Nat. Assn. Bus. Economists, Am. Mgmt. Assn., Los Angeles Pub. Affairs Officers Assn., Los Angeles C. of C. (food and agr. adv. com. 1981), Packard Automobile Classics, Packard Internat., Corvair Soc. Am. Office: PO Box 1504 South Pasadena CA 91030

LAUGHLIN, WINSTON MEANS, soil scientist; b. Fountain, Minn., May 2, 1917; s. Laurence Losson and Stella Valeria (Means) L.; m. Dorothy Florence Fuleihan, June 7, 1947; children: Ellen, Laurence, Keith, Brian. BS, U. Minn., 1941; MS, Mich. State U., 1947, PhD, 1949. Soil surveyor U. Minn., Glencoe, 1940; soil scientist Agrl. Research Service, USDA, Palmer, Alaska, 1949-85. Served with U.S. Army, 1942-46, ETO, PTO. Mem. AAAS, Am. Soc. Agronomy (cert.), Soil Sci. Soc. Am. (cert.), Internat. Soc. Soil Scientists, Am. Inst. Biol. Sci. Presbyterian. Home: Star Rt D Box 9965 Palmer AK 99645 Office: 533 E Firewood Palmer AK 99645

LAUNER, ROBERT DAVID, data processing executive; b. N.Y.C., May 10, 1951; s. Arthur and Eileen Ilona (Steingeisser) L.; m. Kris Vilma Launer, Sept. 27, 1985. BSEE., UCLA, 1973. Computer lab. instr. U. So. Calif., 1969-70; computer programmer I, Sch. Engring., UCLA, 1972-75; computer systems engr. Electronic Data Systems Corp., San Francisco, 1975-80; dir. data processing Summit Workshops, Inc., Redwood City, Calif., 1980-85; chief information officer Tash, Inc., Emeryville, Calif., 1983—; tchr. computer programming Los Angeles Sch. Dist., 1970-71. Los Angeles Council of Engrs. and Scientists scholar, 1970-71, 71-72; recipient Men of Achievement award, Cambridge, Eng., 1982. Inst. for Advancement of Engring. scholar, 1970-71. Mem. IEEE, Am. Soc. Engrs. and Architects, Engring. Soc. of UCLA, Data Processing Mgrs. Assn., Nat. Speakers Assn. Contbr. articles to profl. jours. Office: Tash Inc 1719 64th St Emeryville CA 94608

LAURIE, EDWARD JAMES, marketing educator; b. Sparks, Nev., Nov. 21, 1925; s. Albert Edward and Margaret Mary (Fraser) L.; B.S., UCLA, at Los Angeles, 1946, M.B.A., 1950, Ed.D., 1959; m. Patricia Jean Johnson, Mar. 31, 1962; children—Katherine Louise, Margaret Dee, Elizabeth Ann. Prof. San Jose (Calif.) State U., 1956—, past chmn. dept. mktg., past assoc. dean Sch. of Bus. IBM Nat. Faculty fellow, 1962. Mem. AAUP, Am. Mktg. Assn., Am. Acad. Polit. and Social Scis., Newcomen Soc., Beta Gamma Sigma, Phi Kappa Phi, Phi Delta Phi, Pi Omega Pi, Delta Pi Epsilon. Author: Applications of Domestic Digital Computing Systems in Business and Schools of Business in U.S., 1960; Computers and How They Work, 1963; Computers and Computer Languages, 1966; Modern Computer Concepts, 1970; Computers, Automation, and Society, 1979; contbr. articles to profl. jours. Home: 1287 Pampas Dr San Jose CA 95120

LAURITZEN, PETER OWEN, electrical engineering educator; b. Valparaiso, Ind., Feb. 14, 1935; s. Carl W. and Edna B. (Seebach) L.; m. Helen M. Janzen, Apr. 6, 1963; children: Beth K., Margo S. B.S., Calif. Inst. Tech., 1956; M.S., Stanford U., 1958, Ph.D., 1961. Asso. evaluation engr. Honeywell Aero. Div., Mpls., 1956-57; mem. tech. staff Fairchild Semiconductor Div., Palo Alto, Calif., 1961-65; asst. prof. elec. engring. U. Wash., Seattle, 1965-68; asso. prof. U. Wash., 1968-73, prof., 1973—, adj. prof. social mgmt. of tech., 1977-83; engring. mgr. Avtech Corp., Seattle, 1979-80; cons. x-ray div. Chgo. Bridge & Iron Works, 1967-71, 78, Eldec Corp., 1982, Energy Internat., 1986—. Pres. Coalition for Safe Energy, Wash. Citizens Group, 1975-76. Danforth asso., 1966-78; NASA-Am. Soc. Engring. Edn. summer faculty fellow, 1974. Mem. IEEE, Am. Soc. Engring. Edn., AAAS. Home: 7328 58th Ave Seattle WA 98115 Office: Elec Engring Dept U Wash Seattle WA 98195

LAURSEN, GARY ALLEN, mycology educator; b. Seattle, Aug. 13, 1942; s. Richard Frank Laursen and Harriette Jean (Gray) Lamb; m. Mary Elizabeth Dierken, Aug. 31, 1963; children: Shawna Lea, Heather Frances. BA in Sci. and Edn., Western Wash. State U., 1965; MS, U. Mont., 1970; PhD, Va. Poly. Inst. and State U., 1975, postgrad., 1975-76. Cert. secondary tchr., Wash., Alaska. Biology instr., pub. schs. Toppenish, Wash., 1965-71; graduate research asst. Va. Poly. Inst. and State U., Blacksburg, 1971-75; graduate research assoc. Va. Poly. Inst. and State U., 1975-76; asst. dir. sci. Naval Arctic Research Lab., Barrow, Alaska, 1976-80, interim dir., 1976-77; project officer Office of Naval Research, Arlington, Va., 1980-82; assoc. prof. mycology U. Alaska, Fairbanks, 1986—; vis. asst. prof. U. Alaska, Fairbanks, 1982. Editor: Arctic and Alpine Mycology I, 1982, II, 1987, Human Performance in Cold, 1986. Pres. Christ Luth. Ch. Council, Fairbanks, 1984-86. Research grantee Dept. of Energy, 1984-86, Andrew Mellon Found., 1984, Nat. Acad. Sci., 1985-86, USDA Forest Service, 1984—. Mem. NEA (life), N.Am. Mycology Assn., Arctic Inst. N.Am., Mycol. Soc. Am. Lodges: Lions (editor 1969-70), Kiwanis (sponsor, faculty advisor Key Club div.). Avocations: fungi, photography, skiing. Home: 4830 Villanova Fairbanks AK 99709

LAUT, MARVIN EUGENE, JR., publishing executive; b. Pueblo, Colo., Sept. 9, 1956; s. Marvin Eugene and Virginia (Maggard) L.; m. Judith A Zakrasick, Aug. 14, 1982. BSBA in Acctg., U. So. Colo., 1981. CPA. Auditor Arthur Andersen & Co., Denver, 1981-84; mgr. fin. reporting Emcor Petroleum Co., Denver, 1984-85; treas. Cardiff Pub. Co., Inc., Denver, 1985—. Mem. Am. Inst. CPA's, Colo. Soc. CPA's. Republican. Club: Pinehurst Country (Denver). Avocations: golf, tennis, photography. Office: Cardiff Pub Co Inc 6300 S Syracuse Suite 650 Englewood CO 80111

LAUTER, JAMES DONALD, stock broker; b. Los Angeles, Sept. 3, 1931; s. Richard Leo and Helen M. (Stern) L.; B.S., U. Calif. at Los Angeles, 1956; m. Neima Zwieli, Feb. 24, 1973; 1 son, Walter James (dec.); 1 stepson, Gary Myerberg. Market research mgr. Germain's Inc., Los Angeles, 61; 1st v.p., mgr. Dean Witter & Co. Inc., Pasadena, Calif., 1961—. Served with Armed Forces, 1954-56. Recipient Sammy award Los Angeles Sales Execs. Club, 1961. Home: 17237 Sunburst St Northridge CA 91325 Office: Dean Witter & Co Inc 751 Cordova St Pasadena CA 91109

LAUTER, JUDITH LARUE, speech and hearing scientist; b. Austin, Tex., Apr. 30, 1944; d. Lloyd Kendrick and Mary Laura (Herrmann) Snider; m. Kenneth Allen, Oct. 17, 1966. BA in English, U. Mich., 1966; MA in English, U. Ariz., 1968; MA in Linguistics, Washington U., St. Louis, 1974, PhD in Communication Scis., 1979. Research assoc. Cen. Inst. for the Deaf, St. Louis, 1979-85; assoc. research scientist U. Ariz., Tucson, 1985—; cons. McDonnell Ctr. for Study of Higher Brain Functions, St. Louis, 1982-85. Editor: Planning and Production of Speech, 1985, contbr. articles to profl. jours. Mem. Acoustical Soc. Am., Internat. Soc. Phonetic Scis., Sigma Xi, Phi Kappa Phi. Avocations: poetry, literary criticism. Office: U Ariz Dept Speech and Hearing Scis Tucson AZ 85721

LAUTH, ROBERT EDWARD, geologist; b. St. Paul, Feb. 6, 1927; s. Joseph Louis and Gertrude (Stapleton) L.; student St. Thomas Coll., 1944; B.A. in Geology, U. Minn., 1952; m. Suzanne Janice Holmes, Apr. 21, 1947; children—Barbara Jo, Robert Edward II, Elizabeth Suzanne, Leslie Marie. Wellsite geologist Columbia Carbon Co., Houston, 1951-52; dist. geologist Witco Oil & Gas Corp., Amarillo, Tex., 1952-55; field geologist Reynolds Mining Co., Houston, 1955; cons. geologist, Durango, Colo., 1955—. Served with USNR, 1944-45. Mem. N.Mex., Four Corners (treas., v.p., pres., symposium com.) geol. socs., Rocky Mountain Assn. Geologists, Am. Inst. Profl. Geologists, Am. Inst. Mining, Metall. and Petroleum Engrs., Am. Assn. Petroleum Geologists, Helium Soc., N.Y. Acad. Sci. Am. Assn. Petroleum Landman, Soc. Econ. Paleontologists and Mineralogists, The Explorers Club. Republican. Roman Catholic. K.C. Clubs: Durango Petroleum (dir.), Denver Petroleum, Elks. Author: Desert Creek Field, 1958; (with Silas C. Brown) Oil and Gas Potentialities of Northern Arizona, 1958, Northern Arizona Has Good Oil, Gas Prospects, 1960, Northeastern Arizona; Its Oil, Gas and Helium Prospects, 1961; contbr. papers on oil and gas fields to profl. symposia. Home: 2020 Crestview St PO Box 776 Durango CO 81302 Office: 555 S Camino del Rio Durango CO 81301

LAUTZ, JAMES ERNEST, production company executive; b. San Bernardino, Calif., Mar. 14, 1950; s. Carl Ernest and Carole Mae (Lindsay) L.; m. Diane Claire Duart, Feb. 14, 1976; children: Eric, Grant. AA in Telecommunications, San Bernardino Valley Coll., 1970; BA in Cinema Prodns., U. So. Calif., 1974. Ops. asst. instruction TV U. So. Calif., Los Angeles, 1972-74; asst. ops. mgr. Sta. KHJ-TV, Los Angeles, 1974-75; nat. sales coordinator Sta. KRON-TV, San Francisco, 1975-76, account exec., 1976-81; ptnr. Positive Video, Orinda, Calif., 1981—; bd. dirs. Film/Tape Council, San Francisco, 1984—. Mem. Internat. TV Assn., Film Arts Found., Assn. Internationale du Film D'Animation, U. So. Calif. Cinema Alumni Assn. (pres. 1986—), U. So. Calif. Commerce Assn. (pres. 1981-82), U. So. Calif. Pres.'s Circle (pres. 1980-81), Nat. Acad. TV Arts and Scis. (pres. San Francisco chpt. 1986—), Internat. Teleprodn. Soc. (bd. dirs. 1987—). Republican. Clubs: Olympic (San Francisco), Moraga (Calif.) Country. Avocations: skiing, flying, scuba diving, golf. Home: 24 Oakwood Rd Orinda CA 94563 Office: Positive Video 15 Altarinda Rd Orinda CA 94563

LAVALLEE, ROBERT LEON, communications executive; b. Halifax, Can., Apr. 24, 1940; m. Frederick Alphonse and Florence Elsie (Wilson) L.; m. Linda Beth Neal, May 7, 1986. BBA, U. Redlands, 1980. Communications technician Gen. Telephone of Can. Ltd. div. Gen. Telephone and Electronics Corp., Lenkurt, 1976-78, Gen. Telephone Co. Internat. div. Gen. Telephone and Electronics Corp., Saudi Arabia, 1978-79; mgr. enhanced real estate Gen. Telephone of Calif. div. Gen. Telephone and Electronics Corp., 1985—. Archtl. design works include Gen. Telephone and Electronics Smart Park, 1985, also enhanced residential prewire, 1985. Home: 12416 Willow Forest Moorpark CA 93021 Office: Gen Telephone Calif 3500 Willow Ln Thousand Oaks CA 91362

LAVE, CHARLES ARTHUR, economics educator; b. Phila., May 18, 1938; s. Israel and Esther (Axlerod) L.; 1 child, Rebecca. BA, Reed Coll., 1960; PhD, Stanford U., 1968. Mem. faculty U. Calif., Irvine, 1966—, prof. econs., chmn. dept. econs., 1978-86; vis. prof., vis. scholar Hampshire Coll., 1972, Stanford U., 1974, MIT, 1982, Harvard U., 1982. Author: (with James March) An Introduction to Models in the Social Sciences, 1975; Energy and Auto Type Choice, 1981; Education and Cognitive Development, 1979; Urban Transit, 1985, others. Trustee Reed Coll., Portland, Oreg., 1978-82; chmn. bd. Irvine Campus Housing Authority, 1982—. Served with USAF, 1957. Dept. Energy grantee, 1975-83; Dept. Transp. grantee, 1977-81. Fellow Soc. Applied Anthropology; mem. Am. Econ. Assn., AAAS, Transp. Research Bd. Office: U Calif Dept Econs Irvine CA 92717

LAVI, RAHIM, aerospace executive; b. Tehran, Iran, May 13, 1934; came to U.S., 1953; s. Moosa and Soltan (Elga) L.; m. Nadine Pruyan, Sept. 15, 1957; children: Loren David, Donald Lee, Dale Lewis. BSME, U. Wash., 1956, MSME, 1957; MBA, Pepperdine U., 1971. Engr. Boeing Corp., Renton, Wash., 1957-62; sr. engr. N.Am. Rockwell, Downey, Calif., 1962—; v.p. mktg. programs Northrop Corp., Los Angeles, 1962-85; pres. Lavi Tech. Services, Inc., Newbury Park, Calif., 1985—. Contbr. articles to profl. jours.; patentee in field. Assoc. fellow AIAA (pres. Pacific region 1975); mem. Assn. Unmanned Vehicle Systems (pres. Los Angeles sect. 1985-86), Am. Def. Preparedness Assn. (chmn. Los Angeles sci. chpt. 1978), Old Crow Assn., Navy League, Assn. U.S. Army. Avocations: tennis, photography. Home: 11490 Presilla Rd Camarillo CA 93010 Office: Lavi Tech Services Inc 1323 Newbury Rd Suite 112 Newbury Park CA 91320

LAVIDGE, WILLIAM ROBERT, advertising agency executive; b. Chgo., Dec. 10, 1955; s. Robert James and Margaret Mary (Zwigard) L.; m. Julie Becker, May 24, 1981; 1 child, Nicholas William. BS in Gen. Bus., Ariz. State U., MBA in Mktg. Research asst. Foote, Cone & Belding, Chgo., 1976-77, media planner, 1977, account exec., 1978-79; account exec. Bozell & Jacobs, Phoenix, Dallas, 1981-83; v.p. Hutelmyer Agy., 1983; sr. v.p. Hutelmyer & Lavidge, Phoenix, 1984—; mem. advt. council Ariz. Office Econ. Planning and Devel., Phoenix, 1982-84; teaching faculty assoc. Ariz. State U., Tempe, 1984-85. Contbr. articles to profl. jours. Mem. advt. council Phoenix Symphony Orch., 1985, Compas 8 Fundraiser, Phoenix, 1982; mem. Men's Art Council, Phoenix, 1985—. Recipient Bronze award United Way, Phoenix; named one of Ten Outstanding Young Phoenicians, Phoenix Jaycees, 1986. Mem. Phoenix Advt. Club (bd. dirs. 1986—), Phoenix C. of C. (advt. council). Club: Scottsdale Country (Ariz.). Avocation: sports. Home: 4302 E Onyx Ave Phoenix AZ 85028 Office: Hutelmyer & Lavidge Inc 4747 N 7th St Suite 400 Phoenix AZ 85014

LAVINE, MARY ANN, educational consultant; b. Austin, Minn., June 15, 1935; d. Leslie Ted and Alice Seneva (Erie) Young; m. Lyndon B. Petersen, Aug. 22, 1954 (dec.); children—Elizabeth Hilton (dec.), Penny; m. 2d, Maurice Charles Lavine, Aug. 21, 1969 (dec. 1984); 1 dau., JoAnne. B.A. in Edn., Ariz. State U.-Tempe, 1973, M.A., 1979. Program developer, instructional team leader Washington Elementary Dist. 6, Phoenix, 1973-81; cons. home health care personnel Referral Services, Inc., Phoenix, 1982-83; owner Kids Are Spl., 1983—. Active Glendale Community Council, pres. Beth Hilton Found., 1986—. Mem. Disabled Am. Vets. Aux. (past dept. commdr.), Am. Soc. Tng. and Devel., Nat. Council Social Studies, Midtowners Bus. and Profl. Women's Club, Glendale C. of C., Nat. Assn. Homebased Bus., Am. Soc. Curriculum and Devel., Nat. Assn. Women Bus. Owners, Nat. Assn. Female Execs., Kappa Delta Pi, Pi Lambda Theta. Presbyterian. Office: PO Box 1696 Glendale AZ 85311-1696

LAW, HELEN MARGARET, educational association administrator; b. Cambridge, N.Y., June 16, 1936; d. Curtis Wehler and Esther Martha (Phillips) Lau. Student, U. Mex., 1956; BA, U. Redlands, 1957; MA, Stanford U., 1958; postgrad., U. So. Calif., 1963, UCLA, 1964, U. Calif., Irvine, 1964-66, Pepperdine U., 1965, 74, Syracuse U., 1967, Immaculate Heart Coll., 1969, Calif. Poly. State U., San Luis Obispo, 1969, U. Wash., 1970, Calif. State U., Fullerton, 1980, San Diego State U., 1983. Dept. coordinator Oroville (Calif.) Joint Sch. Dist., 1961-63; resource, master tchr., dept. chairperson Garden Grove (Calif.) Unified Sch. Dist., 1963-78; faculty fellow Orange Coast Coll., Costa Mesa, Calif., 1964-78; supr. curriculum devel. Anaheim (Calif.) Unified High Sch. Dist., 1978-80; adj. prof. composition, Spanish San Bernardino (Calif.) Valley Coll., 1981-82; translator Econ. Text Found. Econ. Edn., 1981-82; dir., tng. and evaluating advisor Law & Lau Assocs., Redlands, Calif., 1982—; nat. bd. dirs. Univ. Profs. Acad. Order; founder Profl. Educators Group; faculty advisor Intercollegiate Studies Inst., 1971—; translator Austrian econs. text; advisor, dir. tng. and evaluation, local sch. bd. Cons. editor Free Enterprise Edn. mag., 1981, Dart Ind.; contbr. articles to profl. jours. Mem. Sister City com.; coach acad. decathlon teams, Garden Grove; advisor fgn. lang. camps, Orange County; elected to governing bd. San Bernardino County (Calif.) Schs., 1983—. Fellow Hillsdale Coll. Polit. Econs. Inst., Found. Econ. Edn., Northwood Inst. Mem. Assn. Calif. Sch. Adminstrs., Assn. Supervision Curriculum Devel., Am. Soc. Tng. Devel., Am. Assn. Tchrs. Spanish and Portuguese, Am. Council Teaching Fgn. Langs., Nat. Assn. Profl. Educators, Profl. Educators' Group, DAR (Willard, Mont. chpt.), Stanford Profl. Women's Club, Stanford Alumni Assn., Stanford New Founders League, Heritage Found. Acad. Bank, Am. Assn. Sch. Adminstrs., Phila. Soc., Gem and Mineral Soc. (pres.), Calif. Art Edn. Assn., Sci. Supervisors So. Calif., Bus. Profl. Women's Club. Lodges: Order Eastern Star, Order White Shrine Jerusalem.

LAWER, BETSY, banker; b. Anchorage, July 27, 1949; d. Daniel Hon and Betty Jane (Puckett) Cuddy; m. David A. Lawer, June 9, 1972; 1 dau., Sarah Anne. B.A. in Econs., Duke U., 1971; postgrad. Calif. State U., Sacramento, 1974-75. With First Nat. Bank of Anchorage, 1974—, now v.p. mktg. div., also bd. dirs; owner PlayCare Pre-Sch. Active Alaska State Troopers Safety Bear Program, Commonwealth N.; sec., past dir. Neighborhood Watch; bd. dirs., treas., investment chmn. Providence Health Care Found. and Law Bd.; dir. Alaska Jr. Theatre; past bd. dirs. ARC, Anchorage Library Found.; keyperson fundraising campaign United Way, 1984. Names one of Outstanding Young Women Am., 1982. Mem. Am. Inst. Banking, Alaska Council Econ. Edn. (past bd. dirs, past treas., mem. exec. com.), Advt. Fedn. Alaska, Pub. Relations Soc. Am., Alaska C. of C. Club: Anchorage Woman's Office: First Nat Bank of Anchorage PO Box 720 Anchorage AK 99510

LAWLER, JAMES HENRY LAWRENCE, chemical engineer; b. Detroit, Jan. 31, 1936; s. James Lawrence and Mary S. (Savely) L.; m. Ruth Ann Borger (div. 1962); 1 child, Donald Lawrence; m. Mary Iris Gates, Oct. 9, 1964; children: M. Jeannette, Mary F., Duncan M., James L., Thomas H., Bruce D., Heather M., Meaghan A. BSChemE, U. Louisville, 1959, BME, 1972; MS, Brigham Young U., 1966; PhD, U. Utah, 1968, MEd, 1969. Engr. Boeing Co., Huntsville (Ala.) and Seattle, 1962-65; asst. prof. chemistry Dixie Coll., St. George, Utah, 1969-72; chmn. dept. chem. engring., nuclear engr. Trident Tech. Coll., Charleston, S.C., 1972-77; chmn. depts. chemistry and bioengring., environ. engring. technician U. Dayton, Ohio, 1977-80; staff engr. Rockwell Hanford Ops., Richland, Wash., 1980-86; engring. specialist Gen. Dynamics Co., 1986—. Author: Patterns for Prediction, 1977, Socio Math and Cyclic History, 1969; contbr. articles to profl. jours. Kaiser fellow Brigham Young U., 1966, NSF fellow U. Utah, 1966-69; recipient Pres.'s scholarship U. Louisville, 1954. Mem. Am. Chem. Soc., Am. Inst. Chem. Engrs., Am. Nuclear Soc., Soc. for Creative Anachronism (sci. 1983-85). Mormon. Home: 4068 Ironton Dr West Richland WA 99352

LAWLER, JUDY ANN, data processor; b. West Bend, Wis., Aug. 4, 1944; d. Alexander John and Elsie Frieda (Zumach) Boettcher; m. Michael Francis Lawler, Jan. 28, 1968 (div.); children—Timothy Shane, Alisandra Michelle. B.S., U. Ariz. Tucson, 1966, M. Ed., 1967. Systems engr. IBM Co., Phoenix, 1967-71; systems mgr. Kaibab Industries, Phoenix, 1972-78; pres. System/3 Assocs. S.W. Inc., Scottsdale, Ariz., 1975-79; dir. mgmt. info. systems Marathon Steel, Phoenix, 1978-82; dir. mgmt. info. systems Ariz. Mail Order, Inc., Tucson, 1982—; instr. N. Am. Coll. of Data Processing, Phoenix, 1980-81. Sec. bd. dirs. COMMON (Nat. IBM Small Systems Users Group), Border Ariz. System 38 User's Group (chmn. and founder). Lutheran. Contbg. editor Small Systems World, 1979-81. Office: Ariz Mail Order Inc 3740 E 34th St Tucson AZ 85713

LAWRANCE, CHARLES HOLWAY, consulting engineer; b. Augusta, Maine, Dec. 25, 1920; s. Charles William and Lois Lyford (Holway) L.; m. Mary Jane Hungerford, Nov. 22, 1947; children—Kenneth Arthur, Lois Ruth, Robert Jefferson. B.S., MIT, 1942; M.P.H., Yale U., 1952. Registered profl. engr., Calif.; diplomate Am. Acad. Environ. Engrs. Sr. san. engr. Conn. Dept. Health, Hartford, 1946-53; assoc. san. engr. Calif. Dept. Pub. Health, Los Angeles, 1953-55; chief san. engr. Koebig & Koebig Inc., Los Angeles, 1955-75; engr., mgr. Santa Barbara County Water Agy., Calif., 1975-79; prin. engr. James M. Montgomery, Pasadena, Calif., 1979-83; v.p. Lawrance, Fisk & McFarland, Santa Barbara, 1983—; propr. Charles H. Lawrance, Cons. Engr., Santa Barbara, 1983—. Author: The Death of The Dam, 1971. Contbr. articles to profl. jours. Dir., Pacific Unitarian Ch., Palos Verdes Peninsula, Calif., 1957-61; chmn. bd. dirs., 1959-60. Served to 1st lt. USMCR, 1942-46. Mem. ASCE (life, Norman medal 1966), Am. Water Works Assn. (life), Water Pollution Control Fedn., Am. Pub. Works Assn., Calif. Water Pollution Control Assn. Republican. Unitarian. Home: 1340 Kenwood Rd Santa Barbara CA 93109 Office: Lawrance Fisk & McFarland Inc 314 E Carrillo St Santa Barbara CA 93101

LAWRENCE, ARLENE HART WHITE, bishop, author; b. Zarephath, N.J., Nov. 11, 1916; d. Arthur Kent and Kathleen (Staats) White; m. E. Jerry Lawrence, Sept. 10, 1941 (dec. 1983); children—Arthur Evan, Verona Kathleen Lawrence Friedly. A.A., Belleview Coll., 1936; B.A., Alma White Coll., 1941; M.A. Columbia U., 1963. Vice pres. Pillar of Fire Ch. Soc., Inc., Bklyn., 1969, London, 1971, Cin., 1969, Denver, 1969, Zarephath, 1972, bishop, 1974—, pres., gen. supt., 1978—; violinist, vocalist and interviewer radio stas., pres. Pillar of Fire Christian Network. Author: Come Along, 1956, Lady Blue Bell's Forest Banquet, 1973. Editor mags. Pillar of Fire, Pillar of Fire Jr., London Pillar of Fire. Mem. Washington Campground Assn., Juvenile Diabetic Assn., Am. Diabetes Assn., Nat. Trust for Hist. Preservation, Internat. Platform Assn., Nat. Religious Broadcasting Assn., N.J. Hist. Soc., Am. Diabetic Assn.

LAWRENCE, DAVID ANTHONY, educator; b. Saginaw, Mich., Aug. 1, 1951; s. Cecil Anthony and Bernadine Bernice (Symkowiak) L. A.A. in Architecture, Orange Coast Coll., 1971; B.A. in Indsl. Arts, Calif. State U.-Long Beach, 1973; M.A. in Secondary Curriculum, U. San Francisco, 1978. Standard secondary teaching credential, community coll. supervision credential, adminstrv. services credential, Calif. Tchr. indsl. arts Villa Park (Calif.) High Sch., 1975—; dist. dept. chmn. indsl. arts Orange (Calif.) Unified Sch. Dist., 1981—; tech. instr., architecture and engring. Santa Ana (Calif.) Coll.,

1976—; cons. archtl./engring. drawing to Calif. Dept. Edn. Recipient Hats Off award Orange Unified Sch. Dist., 1982; Epsilon Pi Tau scholar, 1971-75. Mem. Am. Vocat. Assn. (Calif. chmn. indsl. arts div. 1981—, Western regional chmn. indsl. arts div. 1984—), NEA, Calif. Indsl. Edn. Assn., Calif. Assn. Vocat. Educators, Epsilon Pi Tau (sec. 1973—). Roman Catholic. Home: 768 N Grand Ave Orange CA 92667 Office: 18042 E Taft Ave Villa Park CA 92667

LAWRENCE, DEAN GRAYSON, lawyer; b. Oakland, Calif.; d. Henry C. and Myrtle (Grayson) Schmidt; A.B., U. Calif.-Berkeley, 1934, J.D., 1939. Admitted to Calif. bar, 1943, U.S. Dist. Ct., 1944, U.S. Ct. Appeals, 1944, Tax Ct. U.S., 1945, U.S. Treasury Dept., 1945, U.S. Supreme Ct., 1967; asso. Pillsbury, Madison & Sutro, San Francisco, 1944, 45; gen. practice Oakland, 1946-50, San Jose, 1952-60, Grass Valley, 1960-63, 66—; county counsel Nevada County, 1964-65. Nevada County Bd. Suprs., 1969-73, chmn., 1971. Sec. Nev. County Humane Animal Shelter Bd., 1966-86; state humane officer, 1966-82; pres. Nev. County Humane Soc., 1974-86, mem. Humane Soc. U.S., Fund for Animals; bd. dirs. Nevada County Health Planning Council, Golden Empire Areawide Health Planning Council, 1974, 75. Mem. Bus. and Profl. Women's Club, AAUW, State Bar Calif., Animal Protection Inst. Am. (Humanitarian of Yr. 1986), Golden Empire Human Soc. Phi Beta Kappa, Sigma Xi, Kappa Beta Pi, Pi Mu Epsilon, Pi Lambda Theta. Episcopalian. Office: PO Box 66 Grass Valley CA 95945

LAWRENCE, ERNEST S., psychologist and psychoanalyst; b. N.Y.C., Apr. 12, 1920; m. Gerda Lawrence, Aug. 31, 1947; children—David, Annette; m. 2d, Anne Lawrence Nov. 4, 1974; 1 son, James F. Ph.D., U. So. Calif., 1953. Lic. psychologist, Calif.; diplomate Am. Bd. Profl. Psychology. Pvt. practice psychotherapy and psychoanalysis, Los Angeles, 1955—; dir. tng. psychoanalysis Los Angeles Inst. Psychoanalytic Studies, 1977-83, supr., tng. analyst 1970—; cons. Didi Hirsch Community Mental Health Ctr., 1970—, Wright Inst., 1975—. Served with U.S. Army, 1941-45. Elected to Nat. Acads. Practice, 1982. Mem. Am. Psychol. Assn. (pres. div. psychoanalysis 1982, pres. sect. psychologist/psychoanalyst practitioners div. psychoanalysis 1986-87), Am. Bd. Psychologists in Psychoanalysis (chmn. bd. dirs. 1986—), Calif. Psychol. Assn. (pres. 1970-71). Office: Suite 923 1100 Glendon Ave Los Angeles CA 90024

LAWRENCE, GARY BRENT, building company executive; b. Ft. Belvoir, Va., Nov. 20, 1948; s. Ray Goodman and Bertha A. (Urbanczyk) L.; m. Jackie Caleen Clyne, June 9, 1978; children: Brenna Lee, Ryan Ray. BS, N.Mex. State U., 1971, MS, 1973. Prin. B&R Welding Co., Albuquerque, 1972-75; pres. Albuquerque Casting, 1975-84, S.W. Jewelry Mart, Albuquerque, 1979-83, Action Canopy, Albuquerque, 1983—; pres., chief exec. officer Build-It Corp., Albuquerque, 1984—. Vol. Carruthers of Gov., Albuquerque, 1986. Mem. S.W. Mfg. Jewelers Assn. (v.p. 1981-82), Home Builders Assn., Rio Grande Kennel Club. Republican. Roman Catholic. Avocations: photography, skiing. Home: 2408 Broadway NE Albuquerque NM 87102 Office: Build It Corp PO Box 1630 Bernalillo NM 87004

LAWRENCE, JACOB, educator, painter; b. Atlantic City, Sept. 7, 1917; s. Jacob and Rosealee (Armstead) L.; m. Gwendolyn Knight, July 24, 1941. Student, Harlem Art Workshop, N.Y.C., 1932-39; scholar, Am. Artists Sch., N.Y.C., 1938-39; AFD, Denison U., 1970; DFA (hon.), Pratt Inst., 1970, Colby Coll., 1976, Md. Inst. Coll. Art, 1979, Carnegie-Mellon U., 1981, Yale U., 1986. Artist Yaddo Found., Saratoga, 1954-55; instr. Pratt Inst. Art Sch., N.Y.C., 1958-65, Art Students League, N.Y.C., 1967-69, New Sch. Social Research, N.Y.C., 1966-71; artist in residence Brandeis U., 1965—; coordinator of the arts Pratt Inst., 1970—, prof. art, 1970; prof. art U. Wash., Seattle, 1970-83, prof. emeritus, 1983—; Disting. Faculty lectr. U. Wash., 1978; mem. Nat. Council Arts, 1979—. Exhibited: John Brown Series, under auspices Am. Fedn. Art, 1947, 30 paintings on history U.S., Alan Gallery, 1957; one-man shows include Migration Series, Mus. Modern Art, 1944, Downtown Gallery, N.Y.C., 1941, 43, 45, 47, 50, 53, M'Bari Artists and Writers Club, Nigeria, 1962, Terry Dintenfass Gallery, N.Y.C., 1963, Francine Sedona Gallery, Seattle, 1985; works included Johnson Wax Co. World tour group exhbn., 1963, U.S. State Dept. group exhbn. in, Pakistan, 1963, retrospective exhbn., Whitney Mus. Am. Art, 1974, traveling retrospective Exhbn., Seattle Art Mus., 1986; commd. for graphic impressions 1977 Inauguration, Washington, mural commd., Kingdome Stadium, Seattle, 1979, Mural Howard U., 1980, 85, U. Wash., 1985, others; represented in, Met. Mus. Art, Mus. Modern Art, Whitney Mus., Phillips Meml. Gallery, Wash., Portland (Oreg.) Mus., Worcester (Mass.) Mus., Balt. Mus. Art, Wichita Art Mus., Albright Art Gallery, Buffalo, AAAL, N.Y.C., Mus. Modern Art, Sao Paulo, Brazil, R.I. Sch. Design, Va. Mus. Fine Arts, Bklyn. Mus., IBM Corp., Container Corp. Am., various univs.; Author: Harriet and the Promised Land, 1968; illustrator: Aesop's Fables, 1970; (book catalogue for retrospective exhbn.: Jacob Lawrence-American Painter, 1986. Bd. govs. Skowhegan Sch. Painting and Sculpture; mem. Fulbright Art Com., 1966-67, Wash. State Arts Commn., 1976—; elector Hall of Fame for Gt. Americans, 1976—; mem. Nat. Endowment for Arts, 1978—. Rosenwald fellow, 1940, 41, 42; recipient purchase prize Artists for Victory, 1942, purchase prize Atlanta U., 1948; Guggenheim fellow, 1945; Opportunity mag. award, 1948; Norman Wait Harris medal Art Inst. Chgo., 1948; Acad. Arts and Letters grantee, 1953; Chapelbrook Found. grantee, 1955; 1st prize in mural competition for UN Bldg. Nat. Council U.S. Art, Inc., 1955; recipient Retrospective Exhbn. with Definitive Catalogue Ford Found., 1960, Retrospective Exhbn. with Definitive Catalogue Whitney Mus. Modern Art, 1974; works selected as part of exchange exhibit with Soviet Union, 1959; Spingarn medal N.A.A.C.P., 1970; ann. citation Nat. Assn. Schs. Art, 1973. Mem. Artist Equity Assn. (past sec., pres. N.Y. chpt. 1957), Nat. Inst. Arts and Letters. Address: 4316 37th Ave NE Seattle WA 98105 *

LAWRENCE, JEROME, playwright, director, educator; b. Cleve., July 14, 1915; s. Samuel and Sarah (Rogen) Schwartz. B.A., Ohio State U., 1937, L.H.D. (hon.), 1963; D.Litt., Fairleigh Dickinson U., 1968; Dr. Fine Arts (hon.), Villanova U., 1969; Dr. Letters hon., Coll. Wooster, 1983. Reporter, telegraph editor Wilmington (O.) News Jour., 1937; editor Lexington Daily News, Ohio, 1937; continuity editor radio sta. KMPC, 1937-39; staff writer CBS, 1939-41; vis. prof. Ohio State U., 1969, Salzburg Seminarin Am. Studies, 1972, Baylor U., 1978; prof. playwriting U. So. Calif. Grad. Sch., 1984—. Scenario writer Paramount Studios, 1941; free lance writer-dir. as Lawrence and Lee, 1942—, master playwright, N.Y. U. Inst. Performing Arts, 1967-69; author-dir. for: radio and television UN Broadcasts; Army-Navy programs D-Day, VE-Day, VJ-Day; author: Railroad Hour; author Hallmark Playhouse, Columbia Workshop; author biography, book made into PBS-TV spl.; actor: Life and Times of Paul Muni, 1978; co-author, dir.: album One God; author (play) Live Spelled Backwards, 1969, Off Mike; co-author (all with Robert E. Lee) musicals Look, Ma, I'm Dancin', 1948, Shangri-La, 1956, Mame, 1966, Dear World, 1969; plays Inherit the Wind (translated and performed in 32 langs.) (named best fgn. play of year London Critics Poll 1960), Auntie Mame, 1956, The Gang's All Here, 1959, Only in America, 1959, A Call on Kuprin (now called Checkmate), 1961, Diamond Orchid (revised as Sparks Fly Upward, 1966), 1965, The Incomparable Max, 1969, The Crocodile Smile, 1970, The Night Thoreau Spent in Jail, 1970; play and screenplay First Monday in October, 1978; screenplay The Night Thoreau Spent in Jail, 1971; play written for opening of Thurber Theatre: Columbus, Jabberwock, 1974; play written with Norman Cousins and Robert E. Lee: Whisper in the Mind, 1986; Decca Dramatic Albums, Musi-Plays.; contbg. editor Dramatics mag.; Lawrence and Lee collections at Library and Mus. of the Performing Arts, Lincoln Ctr., N.Y., Harvard's Widener Library, Cambridge, Mass., Jerome Lawrence & Robert E. Lee Theatre Research Inst. at Ohio State U., Columbus, est. 1986. A founder, overseas corr. Armed Forces Radio Service; founder, trustee Am. Playwrights Theatre, pres., 1968—; co-founder, judge Margo Jones award; mem. Am. Theatre Planning Bd.; bd. dirs. Nat. Repertory Theatre, Am. Conservatory Theatre; mem. adv. bd. USDAN Center for Creative and Performing Arts, East-West Players, Performing Arts Theatre of Handicapped., Inst. Outdoor Drama; mem. State Dept. Cultural Exchange Drama Panel, 1961-69; del. Chinese-Am. Writers Conf., 1982, 86, Soviet-Am. Writers Conf., 1984, 85; Am. Writers rep. to Hiroshima 40th Anniversary Commemorative, Japan, 1985; mem. U.S. Cultural Exchange visit to theatre communities of Beijing and Shanghai, 1985. Recipient N.Y. Press Club award, 1942; CCNY award, 1948; Radio-TV Life award, 1948, Mirror awards, 52, 53; Peabody award, 1949, 52; Variety Showmanship award 1954; Variety Critics poll 1955; Outer- Circle Critics award 1955; Donaldson award, 1955; Ohioana award, 1955; spl. citation War Dept.; Ohio Press Club award, 1959; Brit. Drama Critics award, 1960; Moss Hart Meml. award, 1967; State Dept. medal, 1968; Pegasus award, 1970; Lifetime Achievement award Am. Theatre Assn., 1979; Nat. Thespian Soc. award, 1980; Pioneer Broadcasters award, 1981; Ohioana Library career medal; Master of Arts award Rocky Mountain Writers Guild, 1982; named playwright of year Baldwin-Wallace Coll., 1960; Centennial Award medal Ohio State U., 1970; William Inge award and lectureship Independence Community Coll., 1983, 86, 87. Mem. Acad. Motion Picture Arts and Scis., Acad. TV Arts and Scis., Authors League (council), ANTA (dir., v.p.), Ohio State U. Assn. (dir.), Radio Writers' Guild (a founder, pres.), Writers Guild Am. (dir., founding mem. Valentine Davies award), Dramatists Guild (council), A.S.C.A.P., Phi Beta Kappa, Sigma Delta Chi, Zeta Beta Tau. Club: Players (N.Y.C.).

LAWRENCE, LU, educator, photographer; b. Massillon, Ohio; d. Carl Wynn and Ruth Wynetta (Moser) L.; m. Altus Leon Simpson, Dec. 20, 1970; children: Candace, Susan. BA, MA, Calif. State U., Fullerton, 1968. Tng. cons. Host Internat., Los Angeles, 1961-77, Western Airlines, Los Angeles, 1961-67; prof. Cypress (Calif.) Coll., 1967-84; adj. faculty U. Puget Sound, Tacoma, 1984—; cons. Ross Loos Med., Los Angeles, 1964-65, Santiago Bank, Tustin, Calif., 1971-74. Author: Airline and Travel Career, 1979; contbr. articles to mags., jours.; patentee in field. Republican. Club: Women's Univ. Home: PO Box 11435 Bainbridge Island WA 98110

LAWRENCE, MARC, actor, director; b. N.Y.C., Feb. 17, 1913; s. Israel Simon Goldsmith, Minerva Norma (Sugarman) G.; m. Fanya Foss, Oct. 7, 1942; children—Michael, Antoinette. Student CCNY, 1928-30. Appeared in films including: Dr. Socrates, 1935, I Am the Law, 1939, Johnny Appollo, 1940, The Great Profile, 1940, The Ox-Bow Incident, 1940, Cloak and Dagger, 1946, I Walk Alone, 1947, Key Largo, 1948, Asphalt Jungle, 1950, White Slavery, 1951, Man with Golden Gun, 1976, Marathon Man, 1977; director television programs, 1959-61; writer, producer, dir., star film Daddy's Girl, 1973; cons. Ursus Prodn. Co., Marina del Rey, Calif., 1972—. Columnist The Dream Makers, 1977. Recipient award Hollywood Achievement Soc., 1982. Mem. AFTRA, Screen Actors Guild, Dir.'s Guild Am., Acad. Motion Picture Arts and Scis. Address: 14016 Bora Bora Way #119 Marina del Rey CA 90291-6810

LAWRENCE, MARK G., real estate developer; b. St. Louis, May 26, 1949; m. Carol Lee Sherman, July 18, 1976; children: Megan Elizabeth, Courtney Sara. BA, U. Denver, 1971. Cert. real estate broker, Colo. V.p. Solar Cell Corp., Denver, 1977-79; sr. v.p. Richmond Homes, Denver, 1979-85; v.p. 1st Capitol Corp., Denver, 1985—; sec., bd. dirs. Windscreens West, Denver, 1985—; v.p. Wright Farms Met. Dist., Denver, 1986—; chmn. bd. dirs. Oxford Fin. Inc., Denver, 1986—. Founder, bd. dirs. Builder Realtor Council, Denver, 1984. Recipient Disting. Sales award Sales and Mktg. Execs. Denver, 1981, Named Echo-Direct Mktg. Leader, 1983. Mem. Home Builders Assn. Met. Denver, Nat. Sales Mktg. Council (named Mktg. Dir. of Yr. 1984), Sales and Mktg. Council Denver (named Mktg. Dir of Yr. 1985), Nat. Assn. Builders (recipient Gold Million Dollar Circle award 1983, 84, 85), Aurora Bd. Realtors. Office: 1st Capitol Corp PO Box 22631 Denver CO 80222

LAWRENCE, MARY CAROLE, art retailer; b. Oregon City, Oreg., Mar. 18, 1944; d. Richard Franklin and Mary Virginia (Poljnar) Pitts; m. Gary D. Lawrence, June 13, 1971; children—Brad, Brent, Angela. B.S. in Home Econs., Oreg. State U., 1966. High sch. home econs. tchr. West Linn, Oreg., 1966-70; co-owner (with husband), mgr. Lawrence Galleries, Portland, Sheridan and Salishan, Oreg., 1977—; sec. bd. dirs. Art Focus Inc., Lawrence/Lawrence Inc. Mem. Omicron Nu, Phi Kappa Phi. Republican. Episcopalian. Office: PO Box 187 Sheridan OR 97378

LAWRENCE, MICHAEL DAVID, electrical engineer; b. Tucson, Aug. 30, 1960; s. David Burton and Charlene Diane (James) L. BSEE, U. Ariz., 1982. Test engr. Burr Brown Research Corp., Tucson, 1983—. Contbr. articles to profl. jours. Mem. IEEE, Catalina Commodore Computer Club, Tau Beta Pi, Phi Kappa Phi. Avocations: computer programming, juggling.

LAWRENCE, SANFORD HULL, physician, writer; b. Kokomo, Ind., July 10, 1919; s. Walter Scott and Florence Elizabeth (Hull) L. AB, Ind. U., 1941, MD, 1944. Intern Rochester (N.Y.) Gen. Hosp., 1944-45; resident Halloran Hosp., N.Y., 1946-49; dir. biochemistry research Lab. San Fernando (Calif.) VA Hosp.; asst. prof. UCLA, 1950—; cons. U.S. Govt., Los Angeles County; lectr. Faculte de Medicine, Paris, various colls. Eng., France, Belgium, Sweden, USSR, India, Japan. Author: Zymogram in Clinical Medicine, 1965; contbr. articles to sic. jours. Mem. Whitley Heights Civic Assn., 1952—; pres. Halloran Hosp. Employees Assn., 1947-48. Served to maj. U.S. Army, 1945-46. Recipient Research award TB and Health Assn., 1955-58, Los Angeles County Heart Assn., 1957-59, Pres.' award, Queen's Blue Bookaward, Am. Men of Sci. award; named one of 2000 Men of Achievement, Leaders of Am. Sci. Mem. AAAS, AMA, N.Y. Acad. Scis., Am. Fedn. Clin. Research, Am. Assn. Clin. Investigation, Am. Assn. Clin. Pathology, Am. Assn. Clin. Chemistry, Los Angeles County Med. Assn. Republican. Methodist. Avocations: bridge, comml. pilot, pianist, organist. Home: 2014 Whitley Ave Hollywood CA 90068 Home: 160 rue St Martin, Paris France

LAWRENCE, SUSAN PATRICIA, sales executive; b. St. Louis, July 4, 1942; d. George Oscar and Ethel May (Gwen) Bland; m. Edmond Peter FitzWilliam III, Dec. 27, 1962 (div. June 1978); 1 son, Patrick Brian; m. 2d Thomas Lee Lawrence, Sept. 2, 1982. A.A., William Woods Coll., 1962. Lic. ins. broker, Mo. Adminstr. asst. Sherwood Industries div. Brunswick, St. Louis County, Mo., 1962-66; assoc. First Capitol Savs. & Loan Assn., St. Charles, Mo., 1967-77; client retention services James E. Frick Inc., St. Louis, 1977-79; sales rep. Reed, Roberts Assocs., Los Angeles, 1979-82; regional mgr. Hamilton Taft & Co., Los Angeles, 1982-83; dist. mgr. sales CPC, 1984-85; bus. devel. officer Pacific Bus. Bank, Carson, Calif., 1985-86; bus. banking officer Wells Fargo Bank, Long Beach, Calif., 1986—. Mem. Nat. Assn. Profl. Saleswomen, Nat. Assn. Female Execs. Inc. Republican. Episcopalian. Clubs: Toastmasters, Scottish Terrier of Calif., Nat. Breed, Welsh Terrier. Home: PO Box 3111 Culver City CA 90231 Office: Wells Fargo Bank 180 E Ocean Blvd Suite 840 Long Beach CA 90802

LAWRENCE, VIRGINIA WALKER, computer software executive; b. New Bedford, Mass., Sept. 12, 1943; d. Frederick and Mildred Irene (Hibbits) Walker; m. John Keeler Lawrence, Oct. 14, 1967 (div.); 1 child, Francis; m. John William Paige, Dec. 27, 1986. B.S., Merrimack Coll., 1965; B.A., U. Windsor, 1972; M.A., U. So. Calif., 1977, Ph.D., 1979. Computer software exec. Human Systems Dynamics, Northridge, Calif., 1980—. Mem. So. Calif. Tech. Execs. Network, Am. Stat. Assn. Office: Human Systems Dynamics 9010 Reseda Blvd Suite 222 Northridge CA 91324

LAWSON, BRUCE GILBERT, human resources consultant; b. Phoenix, Feb. 5, 1945; s. Bernard and Jewel (Ecker) L; married. BA, Calif. State U., San Francisco, 1966; MPA, Calif. State U., Fullerton, 1971; postgrad., Golden Gate U., 1975-81. City mgr. Los Altos Hills, Calif., 1973-74, Belvedere, Calif., 1974-76; county assessor, tax collector Multnomah County, Portland, Oreg., 1976-79, dir. county mgmt., 1979-81; mgr. Arthur Young & Co., Los Angeles, 1981-84; prin. Arthur Young & Co., Phoenix, 1984—; sr. assoc. McDonald & Assocs., San Francisco, 1971-74; instr. Cañada Coll., Redwood City, Calif., 1971-72; adj. prof. U. Oreg, Eugene, 1981-84. Author: Program Budgeting, 1974. Served as sgt. USAF, 1967-73. Mem. Am. Compensation Assn., Internat. City Mgmt. Assn., Am. Soc. Pub. Adminstrn. Democrat. Jewish. Avocations: snow and water skiing, traveling. Office: Arthur Young & Co 1700 Valley Bank Ctr Phoenix AZ 85073

LAWSON, JAMES RICHARD, devel. engr.; b. Salamanca, N.Y., Nov. 27, 1934; s. Arthur Edward and Velma (Helby) L.; A.S., SUNY, 1955; m. Joyce Rebecca Kame, Apr. 24, 1954; children—Jerry Richard, Jamie Robert. Lab. asst. Westinghouse Co. Scholarship Program, Bath, N.Y., 1952-53; shop asst. A.S. Wickstrom Co., 1954-55; application and market engr. Clark Bros. Co., Olean, N.Y., 1957-66; with Solar Turbines Internat., San Diego, 1966—, now sr. devel. engr. Mem. 44th Dist. Congl. Adv. Com. Served with U.S. Army, 1955-57. Republican. Presbyterian. Home: 6283 Lake Lomond San Diego CA 92119 Office: Solar Turbines Internat 2200 Harbor Dr San Diego CA 92138

LAWSON, JOEL SMITH, JR., military consultant; b. N.Y.C., July 3, 1924; s. Joel Smith and Garetta (Reboul) L.; m. Grace Rumbough, Jan. 5, 1956; children: Joel, Grace L. Hutchinson, William H., David R. BA, Williams U., 1947; MS, U. Ill., 1949, PhD, 1953. Spl. asst. electronics Office of Sec. Navy, Washington, 1965-67; sci. advisor Commander in Chief of Pacific, Honolulu, 1967-68; dir. Navy labs. USN, Washington, 1968-74; tech. dir. Naval Electronic Systems Command, Washington, 1974-81, tech. dir. C2, 1981-84, cons., 1985—. Contbr. articles to profl. jours. Recipient Disting. Civilian Service award USN, 1968, Meritorious Civilian Service award USN, 1984. Fellow AAAS; mem. IEEE, Am. Phys. Soc., Marine Tech. Soc., Sigma Xi. Club: Cosmos (Washington). Home: 4773-C Kahala Ave Honolulu HI 96816

LAWSON, KELLY LEE, medical and business consultant; b. Winchester, Ky., Mar. 27, 1938; s. John Floyd and Leona Elizabeth (Jones) L.; m. Barbara Gene Burton, June 23, 1957. BA summa cum laude, St. Leo Coll., 1978; A in Health Care Scis., USAF Community Coll., Maxwell AFB, Alabama, 1979. Enlisted USAF, 1960; chief adminstrv. and personnel services USAF, various locations, 1960-84; ret. USAF, 1984; supt. constrn. Jim Swails Constrn. Co., Mountain Home, Idaho, 1985-86; med. and bus. cons. Mountain Home, Idaho, 1986—; computer cons., Oklahoma City, 1985. Deacon Emmanuel Bapt. Ch. Mem. Air Force Assn., Bapt. Brotherhood. Avocations: woodworking, fishing, golfing, swimming, racquetball. Home and Office: 3955 N 3d E PO Box 233 Mountain Home ID 83647

LAWSON, NEIL HENRY, oil company executive; b. Springfield, Mass., Nov. 21, 1934; s. Henry Way and Cecelia (Choinere) L.; m. Priscilla F. Conover, July 1, 1960 (div. June 1985). BSME, U. Vt., 1958. Registered profl. engr., N.Y., S.C., Ga., Tex. Constrn. and maintenance supr. Shell Oil Co., Syracuse, N.Y., 1958-62, dist. engr., 1962-63; sales rep. asphalt sales Shell Oil Co., Savannah, Ga., 1963-68; sales rep. asphalt sales Shell Oil Co., N.Y.C., 1968-69, head office rep. systems devel., 1969-72; dist. mgr. comml. sales Shell Oil Co., San Francisco, 1972-80, dist. account rep. fuels sales, 1980—; instr. leadership skills workshop Shell Oil Co., Houston, 1975, 77, 80. Pres. boosters club Contra Costa Christian High Sch., Walnut Creek, Calif., 1981-83, mem. sch. bd., 1984—; trustee Walnut Creek Presbyn. Ch., 1982-85, fin. cons., 1984—. Recipient Oustanding Service award Contra Costa Christian High Sch., 1983. Mem. Sales and Mktg. Execs. Bay Area. Republican. Clubs: Commonwealth (San Francisco) Diablo Hills Men's Golf (Walnut Creek) (sec., v.p.). Avocations: golf, singing, stamp collecting. Home: 1912 Apollo Ct Walnut Creek CA 94598 Office: Shell Oil Co. PO Box 7004 Lafayette CA 94549

LAWSON, ROSANNE TAUBER, psychotherapist; b. Allentown, Pa., Dec. 19, 1946; d. Herbert J. and Sylvia (Annoni) Tauber; m. Alphonzo S. Lawson, Jan. 15, 1971 (div. 1979); 1 child, Gregory Michael. BA, Notre Dame Coll., Cleve., 1968; MSW, Rutgers U., 1971. Psychotherapist Bonnie Brae Residential Treatment Ctr., N.J., 1971-73, Somerset County (N.J.) Family Counseling Service, Bound Brook, 1973-76; social worker Walnut Creek (Calif.) Hosp., 1980-81; pvt. practice psychotherapy Flanders, N.J., 1976-80, San Francisco, 1980—. Editor book revs. Women and Therapy, N.Y.C., 1983-86. Mem. Internat. Transactional Analysis Assn. (trustee 1982-85, program chmn. 1981-84). Democrat. Avocations: skiing, aerobics, travel. Office: 2309 Van Ness Suite 206 San Francisco CA 94109

LAWSON, SANDRA SUE, personnel executive; b. Chester, Pa., Jan. 26, 1945; d. George William and Kathleen (Burnettee) Lawson; m. Frank Pratt Newton, Jr., Feb. 8, 1969 (div. June 1980). BS, U. Tenn., 1966, postgrad., 1973-75; postgrad U. Va., 1967-68. Personnel asst. U. Tenn., Knoxville, 1973-75; benefits mgr. M.D. Anderson Hosp., Houston, 1975-76; asst. personnel dir. Jefferson Davis Hosp., Houston, 1976-77; co-owner, mgr. 3d St. Souvenir Mart, Las Vegas, 1977-80; owner mgr. T Shirts by Sandra, Las Vegas, 1980-86; employment mgr. EG&G/EM, Las Vegas, 1984—. Bd. dirs. Family Planning, Las Vegas, 1985, Child Find/Nev. Assn. Missing Children, 1984-85; supporting mem. Opportunity Village for Retarded Citizens. Mem. So. Nev. Personnel Assn. (sec. 1985-86), Rocky Mountain Personnel Assn. (conv. com. Las Vegas chpt. 1987), So. Nev. Indsl. Employers, Nat. Asn. Exec. Females. Republican. Club: Soroptimists (pres. 1983-85, Blanch Edgar award 1985). Avocations: travel, collect clowns and wind chimes, reading, golfing. Home: 4634 Michillinda St Las Vegas NV 89121 Office: EG&G/EM PO Box 1912 Las Vegas NV 89125

LAWSON, TERRY MEREDITH, law firm administrator; b. Frederic, Wis., Apr. 14, 1943; s. Meredith C. and Edna V. (Johansen) L.; m. Faye E. Nelson, May 21, 1966 (div. 1971); m. Barbara J. Harper, Sept. 1, 1972. B.B.A., U. Wis.-Madison, 1965; M.Pub. Affairs, U. Colo., Denver, 1976. Dir. mgmt. systems U. Colo. Health Sci. Ctr., Denver, 1975-78, controller, 1978, asst. vice chancellor, 1978-81, vice chancellor, 1981-84; v.p. Denver Consortium Group, Evergreen, Colo., 1982—; sec.-treas., dir. Health Data Analysis, Inc., Littleton, Colo., 1983—; exec. dir. law firm Gorsuch, Kirgis, Campbell, Walker and Grover, Denver, 1984—; pres. Terry M. Lawson & Assocs., 1986—; chmn. exec. com. group on faculty productivity and acad. decision-making model Assn. Acad. Health Ctrs., Inc., 1983-84. Mem. Assn. Legal Adminstrs. (bd. dirs. Mile High chpt., editor Mile High Newsletter), ABA (assoc.). Republican. Lutheran. Home: 6591 Hwy 73 Evergreen CO 80439 Office: Gorsuch Kirgis Campbell et al 1401 17th St Suite 1100 Denver CO 80217

LAWSON, THOMAS CHENEY, security, information and credit bureau company executive; b. Pasadena, Calif., Sept. 21, 1955; s. William McDonald and Joan Bell (Jaffee) L.; m. Cathy Lee Taylor. Student Calif. State U., Sacramento, 1973-77. Pres., Tomatron Co., Pasadena, 1970—, Tom's Tune Up & Detail, Pasadena, 1971—, Tom's Pool Service, Sacramento, 1975—, Tom Supply Co., 1975—; mgmt. trainee Permoid Process Co., Los Angeles, 1970-75; regional sales cons. Hoover Co., Burlingame, 1974-76; mktg. exec. River City Prodns., Sacramento, 1977-78; prof. automechanics Calif. State U., Sacramento, 1973-75; territorial rep. Globe div. Burlington House Furniture Co., 1978; So. Calif. territorial rep. Marge Carson Furniture, Inc., 1978-80; pres. Ted L. Gunderson & Assos., Inc., Westwood, Calif., 1980-81; pres., chief exec. officer Apscreen, Newport Beach, Calif., 1981—; pres., chief exec. officer Creditbase Co., Newport Beach, 1982—; pres. Worldata Corp., Newport Beach, 1985—. Calif. Rehab. scholar, 1974-77; exec. v.p. Trademark Services, Inc., Culver City, Calif. Mem. Christian Businessmen's Com. Internat. Am. Soc. Indsl. Security. Office: 1701 Westcliff Dr Suite A Newport Beach CA 92660

LAWTON, EMIL ABRAHAM, chemist; b. Detroit, Oct. 12, 1922; s. Irvin A. and Jennie (Belkin) L.; m. Renee Berk, Dec. 7, 1966 (dec. Feb. 1969); m. Cynthia Ann Block, Mar. 12, 1976; children: Gil M., Ron D., Leora E. AB, Wayne State U., 1946; PhD, Purdue U., 1952. Program mgr. Rocketdyne Corp., Canoga Park, Calif., 1957-72; sect. head Thiokol, Wasatch div. Corp., Brigham City, Utah, 1972-75; project mgr. NEUS, Santa Monica, Calif., 1975-77; mgr. adv. programs Shock Hydrodynamics, North Hollywood, Calif., 1977-82; mem. tech. staff Jet Propulsion Lab., Pasadena, Calif., 1983—. Contbr. articles to profl. jours.; patentee in field. Served to lt. (j.g.) USNR, 1943-46, PTO. Recipient of Cert. of Patriotic Civilian Service U.S. Army Missile Command, Huntsville, Ala., 1985. Mem. AAAS, Am. Chem. Soc. Avocations: hiking, backpacking, cross country skiing. Office: Jet Propulsion Lab 4800 Oak Grove Dr Pasadena CA 91109

LAWTON, MICHAEL JAMES, entomologist, exterminator; b. Balt., Aug. 6, 1953; s. James Walter and Mary Eileene (O'Conner) L.; m. Barbara Ann Byron, Dec. 19, 1983. BS, U. Md., 1975. Registered profl. entomologist. Technician, tech. dir. Atlas Exterminating Co., Towson, Md., 1975-78; asst. tech. dir. Western Exterminator Co., Irvine, Calif., 1978-83, tng. and tech. dir., 1984—. Republican. Office: Western Exterminator Co 1732 Kaiser Ave Irvine CA 92714

LAWYER, DAVID NORMAN, JR., educator, real estate consultant; b. N.Y.C., May 18, 1946; s. David N. Lawyer Sr. and Jean Ward Smith; m. Mary H. County, June 29, 1968 (div. Mar. 1984); children: David N. III, Kerry, Tracye. AB, Princeton U., 1968; MA cum laude, U. Calif., Santa

Barbara, 1971, postgrad., 1974. Tchr. Thacher Sch., Ojai, Calif., 1968-69; lectr. U. Calif., Santa Barbara, 1969-76; prof. Santa Barbara City Coll., 1969—; agt. Merill-Lynch Realty, Santa Barbara, 1978-82; supervisory com. Santa Barbara Tchrs. Fed. Credit Union, 1980-83. Bd. dirs. Santa Barbara chpt. NAACP, 1972-76. Recipient Service award, Santa Barbara City Coll., 1974. Democrat. Office: Santa Barbara City Coll 721 Cliff Dr Santa Barbara CA 93109

LAWYER, THOMAS CARLTON, mechanical service company executive; b. Huntington, Mass., Aug. 18, 1940; s. Denzil T. and Charlotte (Wills) L.; m. Bonnie Clappier, June 10, 1965; children—Anne, Sara, B.S.M.E., Purdue U., 1962; M.B.A., U. Nev., 1971. Registered profl. engr., Nev., Tenn. Sales engr. The Trane Co., Memphis, 1962-69, dist. mgr., Las Vegas, 1969—; sec., treas. Nevada Supply, Inc., Las Vegas, 1976—; pres. Lawyer Mech. Service, Las Vegas, 1969—; lectr. econs. dept. U. Nev., Las Vegas, 1979—, instr. continuing edn., 1980—. Mem. steering com. Nev. State Energy Forum, Reno, 1982-84; mem. Com. to Write Nev. Energy Standards for New Constrn., 1982; v.p. Nat. Kidney Found. Nev., Las Vegas, 1984. Recipient Nev. Energy award, Gov. State of Nev., 1982. Mem. ASHRAE (pres. 1976-77). Republican. Methodist. Club: Executive Association (pres. 1978-79) (Las Vegas). Office: The Trane Co 3040 S Valley View Blvd Las Vegas NV 89102

LAXALT, PAUL, U.S. Senator; b. Reno, Aug. 2, 1922; s. Dominique and Theresa (Alpetche) L.; m. Jackalyn Ross, June 23, 1946 (div.); children: Gail, Sheila, John, Michelle, Kevin, Kathleen; m. Carol Wilson, Jan. 2, 1976. Student, Santa Clara U., 1940-43; B.S., LL.B., Denver U., 1949. Bar: Nev. bar 1949. Practice in Carson City; partner firm Laxalt, Ross & Laxalt, 1954-62; dist. atty. Ormsby County, 1951-54; city atty. Carson City, 1954-55; lt. gov. Nev., 1962-66, gov., 1966-70; sr. partner Laxalt, Berry & Allison, Carson City, 1970-74; U.S. senator 1974-86; mem. law firm Finley, Kumble Wagner, Heine, Underberg, Manley, Myerson & Casey, Washington, DC, 1987—; gen. chmn. Rep. Party, 1983—; pres., gen. mgr. Ormsby House Hotel and Casino, Carson City, 1972—. Gen. chmn. Nat. Republican Party, 1983—. Mem. Am. Bar Assn., Am. Legion, VFW. Club: Eagles. Office: Finley Kumble Wagner Heine et al 1120 Connecticut Ave NW Washington DC 20036

LAY, KENNETH LEE, diversified company executive; b. Tyrone, Mo., Apr. 15, 1942; s. Omer and Ruth E. (Reese) L.; m. Judith Diane Ayers, June 10, 1966; children: Mark Kenneth, Elizabeth Ayers. B.A., U. Mo., 1964, M.A., 1965; Ph.D., U. Houston, 1970. Corp. economist Exxon Corp., Houston, 1965-68; assoc. prof. and lectr. in econs. George Washington U., 1969-73; tech. asst. to commr. FPC, 1971-72; dep. undersec. for energy Dept. Interior, 1972-74; v.p. Fla. Gas Co. (now Continental Resources Co.), Winter Park, Fla., 1974-79; pres. 1979-81, Fla. Gas Transmission Co., Winter Park, 1976-79; pres., chief operating officer Transco Cos. Inc., Houston, 1981-84, Transcontinental Gas Pipe Line Corp., 1981-84; chmn., pres., chief exec officer Houston Natural Gas Corp., 1984-85; pres., chief exec. officer, chief operating officer Enron Corp. (formerly Internorth), Omaha, 1985; chmn. Enron Corp. (formerly Internorth), Houston, 1986—; chmn. bd. dirs. Slurry Transport Assn., 1979-81; dir. Nat. Energy Found., Gas Research Inst., Baker Internat., Sun Banks, Fla. Bd. dirs. John Young Museum, Orlando, Fla., 1974-76, Winter Park Library, 1977-78, Central Fla. Funds Drive; mem. U. Central Fla. Found. Served with USN, 1968-71. Decorated Navy Commendation award; N.A.M. fellow; State Farm fellow; Guggenheim fellow. Mem. Am. Econ. Assn., Interstate Natural Gas Assn. Am. (dir.), Young Presidents Orgn., U.S. C. of C. (natural resource com.). Republican. Methodist. Clubs: Winter Park Racquet, Citrus. Office: Enron Corp 2223 Dodge St Omaha NE 68102 also: Enron Corp 1200 Travis St Houston TX 77002

LAYCRAFT, JAMES HERBERT, judge; b. Veteran, Alta., Can., Jan. 5, 1924; s. George Edward and Hattie (Cogswell) L.; m. Helen Elizabeth Bradley, May 1, 1948; children: James B., Anne L. BA, U. Alta., Edmonton, 1950; LLB, U. Alta., 1951; LLD (hon.), U. Calgary, Alta., 1986. Bars: Alta. Barrister Nolan Chambers & Co., Calgary, 1952-75; justice trial div. Supreme Ct. of Alta., Calgary, 1975-79; justice Ct. of Appeal of Alta., Calgary, 1979-85; chief justice of Alta. Calgary, 1985—. Contbr. articles to law jours. Served to lt. Royal Can. Arty., 1941-46, PTO. Mem. United Ch. of Can. Avocations: hiking, skiing, fishing. Office: Court of Appeal Bldg, 530 7th Ave SW, Calgary, AB Canada T2P 0Y3

LAYDEN, DAVID ARTHUR, accountant; b. Providence, Oct. 17, 1945; s. Thomas Addin and Mary Elizabeth (Hoey) L. B.B.A., Sacred Heart U., 1967. Acct., Dictaphone Corp., Bridgeport, Conn., 1967-69, City of Bridgeport, 1969-80; fin. dir. City of Gillette (Wyo.), 1980—. Mem. Am. Mgmt. Assn., Nat. Assn. Accts., Mcpl. Fin. Officers Assn., Mcpl. Treas. Assn., Wyo. Assn. Mcpl. Clks. and Treas. Roman Catholic. Lodge: Moose, K.C. (treas. 1981—), Kiwanis. Office: City of Gillette 301 S Gillette Ave Gillette WY 82716

LAYDEN, FRANCIS PATRICK, professional basketball coach; b. Bklyn., Jan. 5, 1932; m. Barbara Layden; children: Scott, Michael, Katie. Student, Niagara U. High sch. basketball coach L.I., N.Y.; head coach, athletic dir. Adelphi-Suffolk Coll. (now Dowling Coll.); head basketball coach, athletic dir. Niagara U., Niagara Falls, N.Y., 1968-76; asst. coach Atlanta Hawks, 1976-79; gen. mgr., now v.p. basketball ops. Utah Jazz, Salt Lake City, 1979—, head coach, 1981—. Bd. dirs. Utah Soc. Prevention Blindness; bd. dirs. Utah chpt. Multiple Sclerosis Soc., Utah Spl. Olympics. Served to 1st lt. Signal Corps, AUS. Office: Utah Jazz Exec Offices 5 Triad Ctr Suite 500 Salt Lake City UT 84180 *

LAYE, JOHN E(DWARD), emergency management and disaster recovery consulting firm executive, consultant; b. Santa Monica, Calif., May 26, 1933; s. Theodore Martin and Evelyn Rosalie (Young) L.; m. Jeanne Tutt Curry, Dec. 23, 1955; children—John Russell, Linda Helen. A.A., Los Angeles Community Coll., 1952; B.A., Naval Postgrad. Sch., 1967; M.S., U. So. Calif., 1975. Enlisted U.S. Navy, 1951, advanced through grades to lt. comdr., 1965; naval aviator, electronics mgr., worldwide, 1955-75; ret., 1975; emergency services exec. Marin County, Calif., 1975-76, Salano County, Calif., 1976-82; cons., pres. Applied Protection Systems, Walnut Creek, Calif., 1982—; cons. disaster med. com. Calif. Gov.'s Earthquake Task Force, 1981—; mem. faculty Emergency Mgmt. Inst., Nat. Emergency Tng. Ctr., Emmitsburg, Md., 1982—; pres. cen. chpt. Calif. Emergency Services Assn., 1984-86, sec.-treas., 1986—; lectr. emergency mgmt. and disaster recovery, 1976—. Decorated Air medal, Navy Commendation medal, Navy Achievement award. Mem. Internat. Assn. Profl. Security cons. (bd. dirs. 1984—), Nat. Coordinating Council Emergency Mgmt. (chmn. bus. and industry com. 1984—), Am. Soc. Profl. Emergency Planners. Presbyterian. Club: Greater Contra Costa U. So. Calif. Alumni (bd. dirs. 1980—, pres. 1984). Office: Applied Protection Systems 346 Rheem Blvd Suite 100 Moraga CA 94556

LAYMON, KENNETH HOWARD, water quality analyst; b. Los Angeles, July 10, 1947; s. Leslie Carl and Doris Eileen (Prater) L.; m. Debbe Lynn Flack, July 10, 1971. Student, Cerritos Coll., 1965-67; AS, Rio Hondo Jr. Coll., 1967; student, Fresno State Coll., 1967-69, Indiana U., 1985—. Chem. technician electronics div. Nat. Cash Register Co., Hawthorne, Calif., 1969-70; lab. asst. Aerochem Inc., Orange, Calif., 1970-73; lab. technician Los Angeles County Sanitations Dists., Whittier, Pomona, Calif., 1973-81; lab. technician, lab. technologist Met. Water Dist. So. Calif., Winchester, 1981—. Author, pub.: The Laymon Family: A Record of the Laymon, Prater and Related Families, 1981. Mem. Am. Chem. Soc., Alpha Gamma Sigma. Democrat. Methodist. Avocations: geneal. research, woodworking. Home: 24342 Bostwick Dr Moreno Valley CA 92388 Office: Met Water Dist So Calif 33740 Borel Rd Winchester CA 92396

LAYNE, KAREN SUMMERS, police administrator; b. Summerville, S.C., Oct. 9, 1947; d. George Washington and Constance Kathryn (Crow) Layne. BA, Westhampton Coll., U. Richmond, Va., 1969; MA, George Washington U., Washington, 1971. Research analyst Va. Dept. Welfare and Instn., Richmond, Va., 1970-71; county planner Henrico County Planning Office, Richmond, 1971-74; housing planner Arlington County Dept. Environ. Affairs, Arlington, Va., 1974-75; planner Henrico County Div. Police, Richmond, 1975-82; planning mgr. Las Vegas Met. Police Dept. Planning Bur., 1982—; instr. Richmond Regional Tng. Ctr., 1978-82. Co-author: Incar Mobile Terminals-The 10 Year Experience of Las Vegas Mcpl. Police Dept., 1986. Precinct committeewoman Henrico County Dem. Com., Richmond, 1969; counsellor Rape Crises Outreach, YWCA, Richmond, 1981-82; mem. Richmond Regional Coordinating Council Housing Com., 1972-74. Served with Va. Air N.G., 1980-82; with USAFR, 1982—. Recipient Cert. of Appreciation, Richmond Regional Criminal Justice Tng. Ctr., 1982; Commendation, Las Vegas Metro Police Dept., 1983. Mem. Nat. Assn. Criminal Justice Planners (exec. bd. 1982—), Am. Planning Assn., Am. Soc. Pub. Adminstrn., Assn. Police Planning and Research Officers, Assn. Pub. Safety Communications Officers, Inc. Club: Allied Arts Council (Las Vegas).

LAYTON, DONALD MERRILL, aeronautics educator; b. Cuyahoga Falls, Ohio, Sept. 23, 1922; s. Clifton Merrill and Flossie Belle (Payne) L.; m. Kathleen Gingras, Sept. 3, 1948; children: Mary, Patricia, Jane, Susan, Carol, James, Robert (dec.). BS in Sci., U.S. Naval Acad., 1945; MS in Aeros., Princeton U., 1954; MS in Mgmt., Naval Postgrad. Sch., 1968. Registered profl. safety engr., Calif. Commd. ensign USN, 1945, advanced through grades to comdr., 1960, ret., 1968; from mem. facultyto prof. and assoc. chmn. dept. Naval Postgrad. Sch., Monterey, Calif., 1968—; pres. Per Safe, Salinas, Calif., 1985—. Author Helicopter Performance, 1984, Aircraft Performance, 1986. Fellow AIAA (assoc., chpt. pres. 1976-78, mem. tech. com. 1975—); mem. Am. Soc. Safety Engrs., System Safety Soc. (sr., bd. dirs. 1974-77, Safety Educator of Yr. 1985), Navy League of U.S. (bd. dirs. 1978—, past pres.), Sigma Xi. Democrat. Episcopalian. Lodge: Masons. Avocation: world travel. Home: 44 Seca Pl Salinas CA 93908 Office: Naval Postgrad Sch Code 67-Ln Monterey CA 93943

LAYTON, HARRY CHRISTOPHER, artist, lecturer; b. Safford, Ariz., Nov. 17, 1938; s. Christopher E. and Eurilda (Welker) L.; LHD, Sussex Coll., Eng., 1967; DFA (hon.), London Inst. Applied Research, 1972; DD (hon.), St. Matthew U., Ohio, 1970, PhD (hon.), 1970; m. Karol Barbara Kendall, July 11, 1964; children: Deborah, Christopher, Joseph, Elisabeth, Faith, Aaron, Gretchen, Benjamin, Justin, Matthew, Peter. Lectr. ancient art Serra Cath. High Sch., 1963-64, Los Angeles Dept. Parks and Recreation, summer 1962, 63, 64; interior decorator Cities of Hawthorne, Lawndale, Compton, Gardena and Torrance (Calif.), 1960-68; one-man shows paintings; Nahas Dept. Stores, 1962, 64; group shows include: Gt. Western Savs. & Loan, Lawndale, Calif., 1962, Gardena (Calif.) Adult Sch., 1965, Serra Cath. High Sch., Gardena, 1963, Salon de Nations Paris, 1983; represented in permanent collections: Sussex Coll., Eng., Gardena Masonic Lodge, Culver City-Foshey Masonic Lodge, Gt. Western Savs. & Loan; paintings include: The Fairy Princess, 1975, Nocturnal Covenant, 1963, Blindas Name, 1962, Creation, 1962. Elder Ch. of Jesus Christ of Latter-day Saints, Santa Monica, Calif., 1963—. Mem. Am. Hypnotherapy Assn., Gardena Valley Art Assn., Centinell.a Valley Art Assn., Internat. Soc. Artists, Internat. Platform Assn., Am. Security Council, Soc. for Early Historic Archaeology, Am. Councilor's Soc. of Psychol. Counselors, Am. Legion, Alpha Psi Omega. Republican. Clubs: Masons (32 deg.), Shriners, K.T. Home: 3932 McLaughlin Ave Los Angeles CA 90066 Office: Layton Studios Los Angeles CA 90066

LAYTON, JANICE MARY, nursing educator; b. Ludington, Mich., Aug. 31, 1937; d. Ray and Carmen (Sauers) L. BS in Nursing, Wayne State U., 1962, MS in Nursing, 1964; PhD, Mich. State U., 1978. Instr. Mercy Sch. Nursing, Detroit, 1967-69; asst prof. coll. of nursing U. Ill., Chgo., 1969-75; asst. dean for curriculum Case Western Res. U., Cleve., 1978-81, assoc. prof., 1978-85; prof., chairperson dept. nursing Calif. State U., San Bernardino, 1985—; curriculum cons. Cleve. State U., 1980-81, 84, Cuyahoga Community Coll., Cleve., 1979-81, Edinboro (Pa.) U., 1983, 85; editorial adv. bd. Nurse Educator, Nashua, N.H., 1985—. Author: (with others) Mental Health Nursing, 1977; contbr. articles to profl. jours. Recipient, Nat. Research Service award, USPHS, 1978; Book of Yr. award, Am. Jour. Nursing, 1978, Janice Marston Meml. Scholarship, Mich. State U., 1978; Ohio Dept. Mental Health research grantee, 1983-84. Mem. Am. Nurses Assn., Am. Ednl. Research Assn., Sigma Theta Tau, Phi Kappa Phi. Office: Dept Nursing Calif State U 5500 Univ Pkwy San Bernardino CA 92407

LAYTON, MARILYN SMITH, English language educator; b. Des Moines, Nov. 29, 1941; d. Sam Solomon and Mollie (Leiserowitz) Hockenberg; m. Charles Kent Smith, July 1, 1962 (div. Nov. 1974); children: Laurence Joseph, Eleanor Gwen; m. Richard Howard Layton, Dec. 14, 1975. BA, Northwestern U., 1963; MA, U. Mich., 1964; postgrad., U. Wash., 1972-74. Instr. N. Seattle Community Coll., 1969-74, tenured instr., 1975—; lectr. on pedagogy. Author: (with others) Let Me Hear Your Voice, 1983 (Gov's Writers' award 1984); mem. editorial bd. Jour. Basic Writing, 1986—; contbr. articles to profl. jours. Mem. Conf. on Coll. Composition and Communication (mem. exec. com. 1983—, editorial bd. 1987—), Nat. Council Tchrs. English (chmn. nat. two-yr. coll. council 1985-86), Pacific Northwest Conf. on English in the Two-Year Coll. (chmn. 1982-83), Soc. Internat. Tng., Edn., Research, Wash. Community Coll. Humanities Assn. Avocations: traveling, people, hiking, reading. Office: N Seattle Community College 9600 Coll Way N Humanities Div Seattle WA 98105

LAYTON, RICHARD GARY, physics educator, researcher; b. Salt Lake City, Dec. 24, 1935; s. Lynn Cornell and Leone (Gedge) L.; m. Susan Emily Brinkman, Dec. 27, 1963; children: Catherine Louise, Paul Richard, Spencer Lee. BA, U. Utah, 1960, MA, 1962; PhD, Utah State U., 1965. Assoc. research physicist Electro-Dynamic Labs., Utah State U., Logan, 1962-65; from asst. prof. to assoc. prof. SUNY, Fredonia, 1965-69; from assoc. prof. to prof. physics No. Ariz. U., Flagstaff, 1969-82, prof., 1982—, chmn. physics dept., 1986—; research assoc. Lowell Obs., Flastaff, 1970-71; interim chmn. 1985-86. Contbr. articles to profl. jours.; patentee in field. Mem. Am. Assn. Physics Tchrs. (1st prize apparatus), Am. Phys. Soc., Am. Meteorol. Soc., Internat. Soc. of Surface and Colloid Scientists, Sigma Xi. Republican. Mormon. Office: No Ariz U Dept Physics NAU Box 6010 Flagstaff AZ 86011

LAZAR, JERALD HOWARD, magazine editor; b. Phila., July 11, 1954; s. Leonard M. and Shirley (Greenburg) L. B.A., U. Mass., 1975; M.S., Columbia U. Grad. Sch. Journalism, 1976. Chief of research Esquire Mag., N.Y.C., 1976-78; assoc. editor Feature Mag., N.Y.C., 1978-79, Look Mag., N.Y.C., 1979; sr. editor Houston City Mag., 1979-80; editor East/West Network, Los Angeles, 1983—; contbg. editor Calif. Mag., 1984—. Contbr. articles to mags. Democrat. Jewish. Avocations: photography, music.

LAZAROF, HENRI, composer; b. Sofia, Bulgaria, Apr. 12, 1932. Private study with Paul Ben Haim, Israel; student, New Conservatory of Music, Jerusalem, Santa Cecilia Musical Acad., Rome, 1955-57; MFA, Brandeis U., 1959. Teacher French lang., lit. UCLA, 1959-62; instructor UCLA Dept. of Music, from 1962, now prof.; artist-in-residence Berlin, Fed. Republic of Germany, 1970-71; Organizer, Festival of Comtemporary Music, 1963; artistic dir., Contemporary Music Festival, UCLA, 1973-75; conductor various orchs. Composer concerti, other works for orch., chamber ensembles, piano, organ, chorus; recipient first Internat. Prize of Milan for Structures Sonores, 1966; compositions include Cadence I-Cadence VI, Volo, Canti, ballet work Mirrors, Mirrors, Intonazione et Variazioni. Office: UCLA Dept of Music Los Angeles CA 90024 *

LAZARUS, RICHARD MICHAEL, research manager; b. Bklyn., Apr. 2, 1945; s. Julian Edmond and Adele (Nadler) L.; m. Eileen Sandra Ponier, Dec. 25, 1966; children: Randy Todd, Scott Brandon. BA, C.W. Post Coll., 1966; PhD in Organic Photochemistry, Syracuse U., 1971. Postdoctoral researcher U. Rochester (N.Y.), 1971-72; chemist Printing Devel. Inc., Racine, Wis., 1972-76; sr. chemist, research mgr. Keuffel & Esser Co., Morristown, N.J., 1976-84; research mgr. Dynachem, Tustin, Calif., 1984—. Patentee in field. Treas. Community Concerts, Racine, 1973, v.p., 1974. Syracuse U. fellow, 1966-71. Mem. Am. Chem. Soc. Avocations: wood working, auto mechanics, fishing, golf. Office: Dynachem 2631 Michelle Dr Tustin CA 92680

LAZARUS, STEVEN S., management consultant, marketing consultant; b. Rochester, N.Y., June 16, 1943; s. Alfred and Ceal H. Lazarus; m. Elissa C. Lazarus, June 19, 1966; children: Michael, Stuart, Jean. BS, Cornell U., 1966; MS, Poly. U. N.Y., 1967; PhD, U. Rochester, 1974. Pres. Mgmt. Systems Analysis Corp., Denver, 1977—; dir. Sci. Application Intern Corp., Englewood, Colo., 1979-84; assoc. prof. Metro State Coll., Denver, 1983-84; sr. v.p. Pal Assocs. Inc., Denver, 1984-85; with strategic planning and mktg. McDonnell Douglas, Denver, 1985-86; pres. Mgmt. Systems Analysis Corp., Denver, 1986—; spl. cons. State of Colo., Denver, 1976-81; mktg. cons. Clin. Reference Systems, Denver, 1986—, IMX, Louisville, Ky., 1986—; speaker Am. Hosp. Assn., Chgo., 1983—; speaker Med. Group Mgmt. Assn., 1975—. Author chpts. to books; patentee med. quality assurance. NDEA fellow U. Rochester, 1968-71. Mem. Inst. Indsl. Engring. (sr.), Med. Group Mgmt. Assn., Operations Research Soc. Am., Assn. MBA Execs. Lodge: Optimists (program chmn. Denver club 1976-78). Home: 7023 E Eastman Ave Denver CO 80224 Office: Mgmt Systems Analysis Corp 3801 E Florida Ave Suite 400 Denver CO 80210-2543

LAZORIK, WAYNE RODERIC, art educator, university administrator; b. Mpls., May 8, 1939; s. Peter Paul and Fern (Thompson) L.; m. Carol Nieman, Mar. 16, 1966 (div. Jan. 1971); m. Karen Svendsen, Oct. 19, 1973 (div. Jan. 1980); 1 child, Pablo Anwar de Armijo. BS, U. Minn., 1967, MFA, 1971. Dir. Westbank Gallery, Mpls., 1962-65; mem. faculty U. N.Mex., Albuquerque, 1966—, chmn. dept. art, 1978-80, assoc. chmn. depts. art, art history, 1986—; designer, film maker Minnamath NSF Project, Mpls., 1964-66; vis. faculty U. Minn. studio arts dept., Mpls., 1984-85. Dem. state del., 1968. Fellow NEA, 1976, 80, Bookcliff Petroleum Corp., 1982—. Mem. Soc. Photographic Edn. (bd.dirs., treas. 1973-77). Home: 2933 Monte Vista NE Albuquerque NM 87106 Office: U NMex Dept Art and Art History Albuquerque NM 87131

LAZZARA, CRAIG JOSEPH, investment executive; b. Balt., Nov. 5, 1953; s. Joseph Louis and Marjorie Hope (Euler) L.; m. Sally Ann Spencer, June 5, 1976; children—Virginia Jackson, Christian Spencer. A.B., Princeton U., 1975; M.B.A., Harvard U., 1977. Chartered fin. analyst. Cons. Boston Cons. Group, 1977-78; investment counselor T. Rowe. Price Assoc., Balt., 1978-81, v.p., 1981-82; v.p. Mellon Bank, N.A., Pitts., 1982-86; mng. dir. TSA Capital Mgmt., Los Angeles, 1986—. Fellow Fin. Analysts Fedn.; mem. Inst. Chartered Fin. Analysts, Princeton Alumni Assn. So. Calif. treas. Class of 1975, 81—). Republican. Presbyterian. Clubs: Princeton; La Canada Flentridge Country; Edgeworth (Sewickley, Pa.). Office: TSA Capital Mgmt 700 Wilshire Blvd Los Angeles CA 90017

LEACH, JAMES DONALD, civil and structural engineer; b. Evanston, Ill., Sept. 9, 1930; s. Donald Lloyd and Lavon (Duke) L.; m. Geraldine Janet Fowler, Mar. 22, 1952; children—Gregory, Jeffrey, Fred. Student Stanford U., 1947-48; B.S., Fresno State U., 1951; postgrad. U. Calif.-Berkeley, 1956. Registered profl. engr., Calif., Hawaii, Tenn., N.Mex., Calif., Iowa, Tex., Nev. Engr., Pacific Gas & Electric Co., Oakland, Calif., 1951-52; asst. engr. City of Berkeley, 1955-57; chief structural engr. Garretson & Elmendorf, San Francisco, 1957-80; project mgr. Brown and Caldwell, Walnut Creek, Calif., 1981—; v.p., dir. Sterling Salmon, Inc., Tanana, Alaska, 1979—; owner, pres. L.L. Leasing Ltd., Lafayette, Calif., 1979—; owner, dir. Nutrient Inc., Lafayette, 1978-83; expdn. leader Arctic Research, 1953; lectr., tchr. Creative Initiative Found., Palo Alto, Calif., 1970-83. Mem. ASCE, Am. Concrete Inst., Structural Engrs. Assn., Geothermal Resources Council, Internat. Cogeneration Soc., Engring. Soc. for Minority Manpower Tng. (founder). Republican. Methodist. Lodge: Masons. Home: 3252 Hillview Ln Lafayette CA 94549 Office: Brown and Cladwell 3480 Buskirk Ave Pleasant Hill CA 94523

LEACH, LARRY MELVIN, lawyer; b. East Chicago, Ind., July 20, 1945; s. Lawrence Melvin and Frances (Stewart) L.; m. Anastasia Johnson, Sept. 15, 1984; 1 child, Lawrence Dakota. BS, Ind. U., 1970; JD, U. Denver, 1973. Bar: Colo. 1973, U.S. Dist. Ct. Colo. 1973. Intern EPA, Washington, Denver, 1971-73; dir. family law ctr. Denver Legal Aid Soc., 1973-75; sr. ptnr. Hughes, Pelz, Leach & Cliteman, Denver, 1976—. Chmn. Dem. precinct, Denver, 1974; campaign aid Richard Lamm for Gov., Denver, 1974; vol. Big Bros. Corp., Bloomington, Ind., 1969. Served as cpl. USMC, 1965-67, Vietnam. Mem. ABA, Colo. Bar ASsn., Denver Bar Assn. Democrat. Methodist. Club: TMFC (Denver) (pres. 1981-86). Avocations: basketball, skiing, softball, camping, fishing. Home: 441 Pearl St Denver CO 80203 Office: Hughes Pelz Leach and Clikeman 4155 E Jewell #500 Denver CO 80222

LEACH, LOIS ELLEN, public relations executive; b. Kingston, Pa., Jan. 12, 1943; d. Fabian and Edna A. (Spray) Bogdan; m. Willis Roy Leach Jr., Nov. 21, 1969; children: Bradley Thomas, Ryan Roy. Student, Long Beach (Calif.) City Coll., 1965-68. Pub. relations rep. Long Beach Promotions, 1965-67; adminstrv. asst. United Foam Corp., Compton, Calif., 1967-69; outside sales rep. Control Data Corp., La Mirada, Calif., 1969-72; sales mgr. Embassy Suites Hotel, Downey, Calif., 1985; pres., owner L.E. Leach Pub. Relations, Downey, 1984—. Mem. task force and mktg. com. Downey Family YMCA, 1985, chmn.'s roundtable, 1986; exec. com. Downey Community Hosp., 1985-86, bd. trustees, 1985-86, steering com. charter ball, 1985-86, 12:15 club, 1985—, Million Dollar club, 1985, 86, 87; active Assistance League of Downey; pub. relations rep. Downey Rose Float Assn., 1984-85. Mem. Downey C. of C. (bd. dirs. 1985-87, Appreciation of Service award 1985), WomanCare, (adv. bd. 1986—), Am. Bus. Women's Assn. (chmn. publicity, fashion show1987), Profl. Secs. Internat. (program chmn. 1980-82), Pub. Relations Soc. Am., Publicity Club of Los Angeles, Greater Los Angeles Press Club. Republican. Baptist. Lodge: P.E.O. Sisterhood (program chmn. 1985-86). Avocations: reading, research, traveling. Home: 7823 4th Pl Downey CA 90241 Office: 11002 Downey Ave Downey CA 90241

LEACH, NORMAN EDWARD, minister; b. Farmingdale, N.Y., May 17, 1940; s. George Alexander and Irene Alice (Bowen) L. AB, U. Mo., 1962; postgrad., Mo. U. Sch. Social Work, 1962-63; MDiv, San Francisco Theol. Sem., 1970, D in Ministry, 1973. Ordained to ministry Presbyn. Ch., 1971. Mgr. Third Rail Coffee House First Presbyn Ch., San Anselmo, Calif., 1968-70; adj. staff cons. Golden Gate Mission Area Ch. and World Com. United Presbyn. Ch. USA, San Francisco, 1970-72; dir. San Francisco Bay Area Healing Community Program, 1975—; program adminstr. San Francisco Council Chs., 1976-82, interim acting exec. dir., 1982-84, acting exec. dir., 1984, exec. dir., 1984—; chmn. Presbytery Program Coordinating Council; mem. Presbytery Gen. Council, Presbytery Long-Range Planning Com., Presbytery Nominations Com., Presbytery Permanent Jud. Commn., Interfaith BiCentennial Com., San Francisco, 1975-76, No. Calif. Ecumenical Council, 1975-78, World Council Chs., Vancouver, B.C., Can., 1983; founding mem., pres. Presbyn. Disabilities Concerns Caucus 1981; bd. dirs. World Conf. on Religion and Peace West, 1975-77; founding mem., task force on disabilities Archdiocese of San Francisco, 1975-80. Editor, pub.: Heritage and Hope, 1978, (newspaper) To Free Mankind; mem. editorial bd. Caring Congregation Mag.; contbr. columns to mags., chpts. to books. Mem. Congress on Racial Equality, U. Mo., Columbia, 1958-63, Coalition on Nat. Priorities and Mil. Policy, Washington, 1967-71; bd. dirs. Cambodian-Am. Benevolent Assn., 1975-78, Ind. Living Expn., San Francisco, 1983—, Am.-Israel Friendship League 1984—, assoc. United Way Execs., San Francisco, 1982—; founding mem. San Francisco Intergroup Clearinghouse, 1982—; founder, pres. San Francisco Mayor's Council on Disabilities Concerns, 1982—. Recipient Vigil Honor award Boy Scouts Am., 1974, Nat. Council Chs. award, 1977. Mem. Am. Acad. Polit. and Social Scis., Alpha Sigma Phi, Alpha Phi Omega, Pi Omicron Sigma. Home: 1471 B 46th Ave San Francisco CA 94122 Office: San Francisco Council Chs 942 Market St Suite 408 San Francisco CA 94102

LEACH, RICHARD MAXWELL (MAX), JR., consultant; b. Chillicothe, Tex., June 14, 1934; s. Richard Maxwell and Lelia Booth (Page) L.; m. Wanda Gail Groves, Feb. 4, 1956; children: Richard Clifton, John Christopher, Sandra Gail, Kathy Lynn. BS in Acctg. magna cum laude, Abilene Christian U., 1955. Registered Fin. Planner., CLU. Asst. dir. agys. Am. Founders Ins. Co., Austin, Tex., 1960-62; owner A.F. Ins. Planning Assocs., Temple, Tex., 1962-65; v.p. sales Christian Fidelity Life Ins. Co., Waxahachie, Tex., 1966-67; exec. v.p. Acad. Computer Tech., Inc., Dallas, 1968-69; pres., chief exec. officer Inta-Search Internat., Inc., Dallas, 1969-71; prin., chief exec. officer, fin. cons. Leach and Assocs., Albuquerque, 1971—; chmn. bd. Hosanna Inc., Albuquerque; real estate broker; commodity futures broker; exec. dir., bd. dirs. New Heart, Inc., Albuquerque, 1975-85; owner Insta-Copy, Albuquerque, 1973-76, Radio Sta. KYLE-FM, Temple, 1963-64. Editor, author Hosanna newspaper, 1973-74. Gen. dir. Here's Life, New Mexico, Albuquerque, 1976; exec. dir. Christians for Cambodia, Albuquerque, 1979-80. Served with U.S. Army, 1955-57. Mem. Nat. Futures Assn. Ranked 2d in 50's div. Southwest Tennis Assn., 1985. Home: 3308 June NE Albuquerque NM 87111 Office: Leach and Assocs 10200 Menaul NE #204 Albuquerque NM 87112

LEADER, ELAINE, psychotherapist; b. London, Oct. 15, 1927; came to U.S., 1965; d. Joseph and Leah (Cassenbaum) Lipert; m. Joseph Leader, Aug. 29, 1948 (div. Dec. 1972); children: Denise, Malcolm, Brian Frank, Corinne Netta. Diploma in Social Studies with distinction, U. London, 1964; BA, UCLA, 1968, MSW, 1970; PhD, Calif. Inst. Clin. Social Work, 1981. Lic. clin. social worker. Caseworker Invalid Children's Aid Assn., London, 1964-65; psychiat. social worker Council Jewish Women, Los Angeles, 1970-71; co-founder, program coordinator Ctr. Study Young People in Groups Cedars-Sinai Med. Ctr., Los Angeles, 1972—. Fellow Soc. Clin. Social Work (edn. com. 1985—); mem. Am. Group Psychotherapy Assn., Am. Orthopsychiatry Assn., Los Angeles Group Psychotherapy Assn. (program com. 1984—), Internat. Assn. Group Psychotherapy, Nat. Assn. Social Workers.

LEAGUE, VINCENTE CONRAD, management company executive; b. Indpls., June 28, 1947; s. Jonah Bemouth and Thelma Ruth (Pride) L.; student Butler U., 1965-68; B.A. in Pub. Adminstrn., Chgo. State U., 1976. Dir. in charge outreach Soul Ark Youth ministry, Indpls., 1970-71; project dir. Community Orgn. Program, Eastside Indpls., 1971-72; asst. dir. Region 5 Alcohol & Drug Abuse Tng. Center, Chgo., 1972-78; project dir. Western Tng. and Devel. Center, Oakland, 1978—; pres. A.H. Tng. & Devel. Systems, Inc., Oakland, Calif., 1981—; prin. Calif. Wine Country, Napa, Calif., 1981-83; dir. A.H. Tng. & Devel., 1983—; cons. numerous orgns. Bd. dirs. Person Edn.-Devel. Edn., Mpls., 1981—; chmn. bd. dirs. Grantsmanship Center, Los Angeles, 1974-81. Mem. Am. Soc. Tng. and Devel., Nat. Mgmt. Assn. (bd. dirs. 1983-84), Nat. Assn. Prevention Profls. (pres., co-founder Eugene Oreg., co-conv. coordinator 3d ann. conv. 1980). Co-editor Prevention Action Manual, 1986; author: Developing Successful Programs, 1978, rev. edit., 1983; Funding Handbook, 1981; Management: A Guide for Prevention Programs, 1982; Inside Napa Valley, 1982. Home: 151 Lakeside St Apt 302 Oakland CA 94612 Office: 100 Webster Suite 104 Oakland CA 94607

LEAHY, DEAN MILTON, psychotherapist, consultant; b. St. Johns, Nfld., Can., Oct. 13, 1947; came to U.S., 1952; s. Carroll Mancel and Ellen Francis (Lindahl) L.; m. Dorothy Ann Garcia, Nov. 1, 1969 (div. May 1981); 1 child, Edward Dean; m. Christina Evangeline Newhill, Aug. 15, 1981. BA in Psychology, Calif. State U., Sacramento, 1969; grad. (hon.), U.S. Army Leadership Acad., Ft. Ord, Calif., 1970; MSW, Calif. State U., Sacramento, 1976. Lic. marriage, family and child couselor, Calif. Clin. psychology specialist U.S. Army Med. Corps, Ft. Carson, Colo., 1970-74; group therapist City-County Health Dept., Colorado Springs, 1973-74; intern in psychiatry U. Calif. Med. Sch., Davis, 1975-76; clin. social worker San Joaquin County Mental Health Ctr., Stockton, Calif., 1976—; pvt. practice psychology Stockton, 1979—; profl. examiner Bd. Behavioral Sci. Examiners, Sacramento, 1979—; exec. bd. dirs. Profl. Counseling Assocs., Stockton, 1979—; adj. prof. Calif. State U., Sacramento, 1985—; personnel specialist standard oil Co., Calif., 1969; sta. mgr. Standard Stations, Inc., Napa, Calif., 1970. Fellow Nat. Assn. Social Workers (diplomate in clin. social work); mem. Acad. Cert. Social Workers (cert.), Nat. Registry Clin. Social Workers (cert.), Am. Assn. Marriage and Family Therapists (clin.), NOW, Stockton Women's Ctr., Sierra Club. Democrat. Roman Catholic. Office: Profl Counseling Assocs 2626 N Calif St Stockton Med Ctr E Stockton CA 95204

LEAKE, DONALD LEWIS, oral and maxillofacial surgeon; b. Cleveland, Okla., Nov. 6, 1931; s. Walter Wilson and Martha Lee (Crow) L.; m. Rosemary Dobson, Aug. 20, 1964; children: John Andrew Dobson, Elizabeth, Catherine. A.B., U. So. Calif., 1953, M.A., 1957; D.M.D., Harvard U., 1962; M.D., Stanford U., 1969. Intern Mass. Gen. Hosp., Boston, 1962-63; resident Mass. Gen. Hosp., 1963-64; postdoctoral fellow Harvard U., 1964-66; practice medicine specializing in oral and maxillofacial surgery; asso. prof. oral and maxillofacial surgery Harbor-UCLA Med. Center, Torrance, 1970-74; dental dir., chief oral and maxillofacial surgery Harbor-UCLA Med. Center, 1970—, prof., 1974—; asso. dir. UCLA Dental Research Inst., 1979-82, dir., 1982-86; cons. to hosps.; dental dir. coastal health services region, Los Angeles County, 1974-81. Contbr. articles to med. jours. Recipient 1st prize with greatest distinction for oboe and chamber music Brussels Royal Conservatory Music Belgium, 1956. Fellow ACS; mem. Internat. Assn. Dental Research, So. Calif. Soc. Oral and Maxillofacial Surgeons, Internat. Assn. Oral Surgeons, AAAS, Soc. for Biomaterials, Los Angeles County Med. Assn., N.Y. Acad. Sci., Los Angeles Acad. Medicine, ASTM, European Assn. Maxillofacial Surgeons, Brit. Assn. Oral and Maxillofacial Surgeons, Internationale Gesellschaft fur Kiefer-Gesichts-Chirurgie, Phi Beta Kappa, Phi Kappa Phi. Clubs: Harvard (Boston and N.Y.C.). Home: 2 Crest Rd W Rolling Hills CA 90274 Office: Harbor-UCLA Med Center 1000 W Carson St Torrance CA 90509 also: 701 E 28th St Suite 415 Long Beach CA 90806

LEANEY, JOHN ANDREW, university athletic coach; b. London, Nov. 18, 1948; s. George and Lilian (Bolton) L. Diploma in teaching, Manchester (Eng.) U. Asst. dept. phys. edn. Salford (Eng.) Grammar Sch., 1971-73; head dept. phys. edn. Broughton High Sch., Salford, 1973-81, sr. counsellor, 1981-83; head coach Mission Bay Soccer Club, San Diego, 1983—, N.W. Soccer Club, Mpls., 1985—; head coach women's soccer team U. Calif., San Diego, 1984-87; advisor World Cup Soccer, soccer tours, travel It's a Small World Travel Agy., San Diego, 1985-86. Home: 3730 Southview Dr #418 San Diego CA 92117 Office: John Leaney Soccer Camps PO Box 9952 San Diego CA 92109

LEAR, JOE BENNETT, economics and management educator; b. Sweet springs, Mo., May 1, 1933; s. Oscar Finley and Ethel Margaret (Bennett) L.; m. Donna Marie Lybarger, Feb. 9, 1957; children: Diane R., Judith M. AA, Santa Maria Jr. Coll., 1953; BCE, U. Omaha, 1964; MS, U. N.D., 1969; PhD, U. Calif., Santa Barbara, 1985. Commd. USAF, 1955, advanced through grades to lt. col., 1982, ret., 1980; instr. econs., mgmt. Cuesta Coll. Calif. Poly. State U., San Luis Obispo, 1980—. Decorated DFC. Mem. Ret. Officers Assn. (pres. Cen. Calif. Coast chpt. 1986—).

LEAR, NORMAN MILTON, writer, producer, director television and films; b. New Haven, July 27, 1922; s. Herman and Jeanette (Seicol) L.; children: Ellen Lear Reiss, Kate B. Lear LaPook, Maggie B. Student, Emerson Coll., 1940-42, H.H.D., 1968. Engaged in pub. relations 1945-49. Comedy writer for TV, 1950-54; writer, dir. for TV and films, 1954-59, writer, dir., producer for, 1959—; writer, producer: films Come Blow Your Horn, 1963, Divorce American Style, 1967, The Night They Raided Minsky's, 1968; writer, producer, dir.: film Cold Turkey, 1971; creator, producer: TV shows TV Guide Awards Show, 1962, Henry Fonda and the Family, 1963, Andy Williams Spl., also, Andy Williams Series, 1965, Robert Young and the Family, 1970; developer: TV shows All in the Family, 1971; creator: TV show Maude, 1972; co-developer: TV show Sanford and Son, 1972; developer: TV show Good Times, 1974, The Jeffersons, 1975, Hot L Baltimore, 1975, Mary Hartman, Mary Hartman, 1976, One Day At a Time, 1975, All's Fair, 1976, A Year at the Top, 1977; co-creator: TV show All That Glitters, 1977; creator: TV show Fernwood 2 Night, 1977; developer: TV show The Baxters, 1979, Palmerstown, 1980; creator, developer TV show I Love Liberty, 1982; creator a.k.a. Pablo, 1984; exec. producer Heartsounds, 1984. Pres. Am. Civil Liberties Found. So. Calif., 1973—; trustee Mus. Broadcasting; bd. dirs. People for the American Way, mem. adv. bd. Nat. Women's Polit. Caucus. Served with USAAF, 1942-45. Decorated Air medal with 4 oak leaf clusters; named One of Top Ten Motion Picture Producers Motion Picture Exhibitors, 1963, 67, 68; Showman of Yr. Publicists Guild, 1971-77, Assn. Bus. Mgrs., 1972; Broadcaster of Yr. Internat. Radio and TV Soc., 1973; Man of Yr. Hollywood chpt. Nat. Acad. Television Arts and Scis., 1973; recipient Emmy awards for All in the Family 1970-73, Peabody award for All in the Family 1977; Humanitarian award NCCJ, 1976; Mark Twain award Internat. Platform Assn., 1977; William O. Douglas award Pub. Counsel, 1981; 1st Amendment Lectr. Ford Hall Forum, 1981; Gold medal Internat. Radio and TV Soc., 1981; Disting. Am. award, 1984; inducted into TV Acad. Hall of Fame, 1984; recipient Mass Media award Am. Jewish Com. Inst. of Human Relations, 1986, Internat. award of Yr., Nat. Assn. TV Program Execs., 1987. Mem. Writers Guild Am. (Valentine Davies award 1977), Dirs. Guild Am., AFTRA, Caucus Producers, Writers, and Dirs. Office: Act III Communications 1800 Century Park E Los Angeles CA 90067

LEARS, MARYON PATRICIA, retail executive; b. Portland, Oreg., Oct. 8, 1919; d. Benjamin Franklin and Iris Florentine Lears. Student, U. So. Calif., 1936-37. Buyer J.W. Robinson, Los Angeles, 1940-44; buyer Silverwoods, Los Angeles, 1944-49, mdse. mgr., 1949-72, v.p., 1972-85, exec. v.p., chief exec. officer, 1985—; bd. dirs. Wilshire Regent, Los Angeles, 1974—. Exhibited oil paintings at Beverly Hills Gallery, 1972. Active Los Angeles County Mus.; bd. dirs. Better Bus. Bur., Los Angeles, 1985—. Recipient Angel award Cen. City Assn., 1973. Mem. Fashion Group, Advt. Club Los Angeles. Republican. Roman Catholic. Avocations: painting, travel. Home: 10501 Wilshire Blvd Los Angeles CA 90024 Office: Silverwoods 2410 E 38th St Los Angeles CA 90058

LEASE, JANE ETTA, librarian; b. Kansas City, Kans., Apr. 10, 1924; d. Joy Alva and Emma (Jaggard) Omer; B.S. in Home Econs., U. Ariz., 1957; M.S. in Edn., Ind. U., 1962; M.S. in L.S., U. Denver, 1967; m. Richard J. Lease, Jan. 16, 1960; children—Janet (Mrs. Jacky B. Radifera), Joyce (Mrs. Robert J. Carson), Julia (Mrs. Earle D. Marvin), Cathy (Mrs. Edward F. Warren); stepchildren—Richard Jay II, William Harley. Newspaper reporter Ariz. Daily Star, Tucson, 1937-39; asst. home agt. Dept. Agr., 1957; homemaking tchr., Ft. Huachuca, Ariz., 1957-60; head tchr. Stonebelt Council Retarded Children, Bloomington, Ind., 1960-61; reference clk. Ariz. State U. Library, 1964-66; edn. and psychology librarian N.Mex. State U., 1967-71; Amway distbr., 1973—; cons. solid wastes, distressed land problems reference remedies, 1967; ecology lit. research and cons., 1966—. Ind. observer 1st World Conf. Human Environment, 1972; mem. Las Cruces Community Devel. Priorities Adv. Bd. Mem. ALA, Regional Environ. Edn. Research Info. Orgn., Nat. Assn. Female Execs., P.E.O., D.A.R., Internat. Platform Assn., Las Cruces Antique Car Club, Las Cruces Story League, N.Mex. Library Assn. Methodist (lay leader). Address: 2145 Boise Dr Las Cruces NM 88001

LEASE, RICHARD JAY, former police officer, educator, consultant; b. Cherokee, Ohio, Dec. 10, 1914; s. Harold and Mabelle (Fullerton) L.; m. Marjorie Faye Stoughton, Sept. 2, 1939 (div. Apr. 1957); children: Richard Jay II, William Harley; m. Jane Etta Omer, Jan. 16, 1960; stepchildren: Janet Radifera, Joyce Garson, Julia Marvin, Catherine Warren. Student, Wittenberg U., 1932-33; BA, U. Ariz., 1937, MA, 1961; postgrad., Ind. U., 1950, 60, Ariz. State U., 1956, 63-65, 67—; grad., U. Louisville So. Police Inst., 1955. Grad. asst. U. Ariz., Tucson, 1937-38; with Tucson Police Dept., from 1938; advanced from patrolman to sgt., also served as safety officer Pima County Sheriff's Dept., Tucson, 1953, patrol supr., 1953-55, investigator, 1955-56; tchr. sci. pub. schs. Tucson, 1957-59; lectr. dept. police adminstrn. Ind. U., Bloomington, 1960-65; asst. prof. dept. police sci. N.Mex. State U., Las Cruces, 1965—; cons. law enforcement problems HEW, 1960, Indpls. Police Dept., 1962, Harrisburg Community Coll. Police Sci. Dept., 1967, Phoenix Police Dept., 1968—; advisor police tng. programs several small city police depts., Ind., 1960-63, Indpls., 1962; mem. oral bd. for selection chief in Bateville, Ind., 1962, oral bd. for selection sgts. and lts., Las Cruces Police Dept., 1966—. Author: (with Robert F. Borkenstein) Alcohol and Road Traffic: Problems of Enforcement and Prosecution, 1963; cons. editor Police, various research publs. on chem. intoxication tests, psychol. errors of witnesses, reading disabilities and delinquency. Participant numerous FBI seminars; active youth work, philanthropy, among Am. Indians in Southwest; founder awards outstanding ROTC cadets N.Mex. State U., 1967—; founder Wiltberger ann. awards Nat. Police Combat Pistol Matches; scoutmaster Yucca council Boy Scouts Am., 1966—. Served to 1st lt. USMCR, 1942-45, PTO. Fellow Am. Acad. Forensic Scis. (sec. gen. sect.); mem. Internat. Assn. Chiefs of Police, Internat. Assn. Police Profs., Brit. Acad. Forensic Scis., Can. Soc. Forensic Sci., Am. Soc. Criminology, Ret. Officers Assn., Assn. U.S. Army (2d v.p. 1969—), NEA, N.Mex. Edn. Assn., N.Mex. Police and Sheriffs Assn., Internat. Crossroads, NRA (benefactor mem.), Sigma Chi. Lodges: Masons, Elks. Home and Office: 2145 Boise Dr Las Cruces NM 88001

LEAVITT, DANA GIBSON, management consultant; b. Framingham, Mass., Dec. 4, 1925; s. Luther C. and Margaret (Gibson) L.; m. Frances Smith, Apr. 12, 1952; children: Margaret Gibson, Jonathan. B.A., Brown U., 1948; postgrad., Harvard U. Bus. Sch., 1954-55. Home office rep. Aetna Life Ins. Co., Boston, also Long Beach, Calif., 1949-54; v.p., sec.-treas., exec. v.p. N. Am. Title Ins. Co., Oakland, Calif., 1955-64; pres. Transam. Title Ins. Co., Oakland, 1964-72; v.p. Transam. Corp., 1969-71, group v.p., 1971-77, exec. v.p., 1977-81; bd. dirs. Syntex Corp., Napa Valley Bank, Chgo. Title and Trust Co., Chgo. Title Ins. Co. Bd. dirs. Children's Hosp. Med. Center and Found., 1969-72; trustee Lewis and Clark Coll., Portland, Oreg., 1972-75; trustee Brown U., Providence, 1973-78, trustee emeritus, 1978—. Served with USMCR, World War II. Mem. World Bus. Council (bd. dirs. 1986), Delta Kappa Epsilon. Republican. Clubs: Brown U. of No. Calif, Harvard Bus. Sch. of No. Calif, Napa Valley Country; Bohemian (San Francisco), Pacific Union (San Francisco). Office: 1100 Union St San Francisco CA 94109

LEAVITT, LOIS HUTCHEON, consumer and homemaker educator; b. Whiterocks, Utah, Nov. 6, 1920; d. Arthur James and Ada E. (Peterson) Hutcheon; m. Jack William Leavitt, June 19, 1943; children—VaLoy, Joyce, LaJean. B.S., Brigham Young U., 1943, postgrad. 1955-83. Cert. vocat. home econs., secondary edn. tchr. Utah. Tchr. consumer and homemaking edn. Spanish Fork (Utah) High Sch., 1943-45, Roosevelt (Utah) High Sch., 1945-47, Union High Sch., Roosevelt, 1954-83; chpt. advisor Future Homemakers Am. Named Outstanding Utah Home Econs. Tchr., Utah Cowbells of Utah Cattlemen's Assn.; Adviser of Yr., Utah chpt. Future Homemakers Am. 1983. Mem. Am. Home Econs. Assn., Utah Home Econs. Assn. (Home Econs. Tchr. of Yr. 1982), Nat. Assn. Vocat. Home Econs. Tchrs. Vocat. Assn., Utah Assn. Vocat. Home Econs. Tchrs. Vocat. Assn., Am. Vocat. Assn., Utah Vocat. Assn., Bus. and Profl. Women (pres., sec.). Mormon. Home: Box 235 Neola UT 84053 Office: Union High School PO Box 400 Roosevelt UT 84066

LEBARON, RUTHANN HAYES, biology educator, solar consultant; b. Denver, Nov. 8, 1925; d. John Edward and Anna Elizabeth (Hansen) Hayes; m. Marshall John LeBaron, Aug. 7, 1948 (div. Feb. 1980); children: Anne, Michael Roy. BA cum laude, U. Colo., 1946; MA in Zoology, Mt. Holyoke Coll., 1948; postgrad., U. Idaho, 1948-70. Histology instr. U. Idaho, Moscow, 1948-49; assoc. to asst. prof. Coll. So. Idaho, Twin Falls, 1965-70, prof. biology, 1970-76, chmn. dept. sci., 1965-73; prof. biology Linfield Coll., McMinnville, Oreg., 1983-84, Linn-Benton Coll., Newport, Oreg., 1986—. Contbr. articles to profl. jours. Bd. dirs. Regional Studies Ctr., Caldwell, Idaho, 1972-77. NSF grantee 1966, 1967, 1973. Mem. Am. Inst. Biol. Scis., AAAS, Idaho Environ. Council, Idaho Fedn. Music Clubs (pres. 1963-65), Idaho Art Assn., Phi Beta Kappa, Sigma Xi, Delta Delta Delta. Republican. Episcopalian. Avocations: underwater photography, watercolor painting, solar architecture design. Home: 1713 Sandpiper Dr Waldport OR 97394

LEBEDEFF, NICHOLAS BORIS, consulting executive; b. Hollywood, Calif., Apr. 16, 1944; s. Boris Paul and Alexandra Esidorovna (Koshell) L.; m. Judith Leah Moffett, Nov. 22, 1969 (div. Aug. 1985); children: Christina, Christopher. BBA, Loyola U., Los Angeles, 1967; MBA, U. So. Calif., 1970. Budget and adminstrv. analyst City of Los Angeles, 1967-73; mgr. budget and fiscal ops. Van de Kamp's Holland Dutch Bakers div. Gen. Host Corp., Los Angeles, 1973-74; mgr. fin. planning and analysis dept. U.S. Borax and Chem. Co., Los Angeles, 1974-75; pres. NBL Assocs., Los Angeles, 1976—, Micro-Software, Inc., Los Angeles, 1977—, Planning Systems Group, Los Angeles, 1982—, Forecasting and Fin. Planning Group, 1982—. Bd. dirs. Friends of Ft. Ross, Am. Med. and Ednl. Services in Africa; mem. Calif. State Citizen's Adv. Com. on Ft. Ross, 1975—. Mem. So. Calif. Corp. Planners, Planning Execs. Inst., Am. Mgmt. Assn., British Interplanetary Soc., U. So. Calif. Alumni Assn., Commerce Assos. Republican. Mem. Orthodox Ch. Am. Home: 11774 Monte Leon Way North Ridge CA 91326

LEBLANC, MAURICE ARTHUR, JR., rehabilitation engr.; b. Long Beach, Calif., Oct. 10, 1938; s. Maurice Arthur and Irene Amy (Palladine) LeB.; m. Ingrid Thea Uhlig, Dec. 23, 1967; 1 child, Branden. BSME, Stanford U., 1960, MSME, 1961. Staff specialist UCLA Med. Ctr., Los Angeles, 1965-69; staff engr. Nat. Acad. Sci., Washington, 1969-74; dir. research Children's Hosp. Stanford, Palo Alto, Calif., 1974—; lectr. Stanford U., Palo Alto, 1975—; cons. VA Med. Ctr., Palo Alto, 1975—. Contbr. articles to profl. publs. Served to lt. USN, 1962-65. Recipient Achievement in Tech. award United Cerebral Palsy Assn., 1984. Mem. ASME, Assn. Advancement Rehab. Tech., Am. Acad Orthotists and Prosthetists, Internat. Soc. Prosthetics and Orthotics. Avocations: tennis, golf. Home: 29 Woodhill Dr Redwood City CA 94061 Office: Children's Hosp Stanford 520 Sand Hill Rd Palo Alto CA 94304

LECINSKI, ALICE R., scientist; b. Boulder, Colo., Mar. 9, 1956. BS ChemE, U. Colo., 1980, BA in Physics, 1980. Support scientist I Nat. Ctr. Atmospheric Research, Boulder, Colo., 1980-82; support scientist II Nat. Ctr. Atmospheric Research, Boulder, 1982-86, assoc. scientist III, 1986—; tutor, Boulder, 1980—. Contbr. articles profl. jours. Mem. Am. Chem. Soc., Am. Inst. Chem. Engrs. Avocation: spelunking. Office: Nat Ctr Atmospheric Research 1850 Table Mesa Dr Boulder CO 80307

LEDBETTER, CARL SCOTIUS, counselor, educator; b. Pyatt, Ark., Aug. 19, 1910; s. James Oliver and Lillie Belle (Wall) L.; student Phillips U., Enid, Okla., 1930-32; A.B., Ky. Christian Coll., 1937; A.B., Butler U., 1939, M.A., 1940; M.A., U. Redlands, 1967; postgrad. Claremont Grad. Sch., 1961-64, Mankato (Minn.) State Coll., 1970-73, Calif. State Coll., 1974-76; m. Ruth Slocum Weymouth, June 20, 1948; children—Carla Sue Ledbetter Holte, Carl Scotius, Charles Stephen, Craig Slocum, Candace Sybil Ledbetter Heidelberger, Christa Sharyn Ledbetter Sanders. Ordained to ministry Christian Ch., 1933; student pastor, Huntington, W.Va., 1935-36, Russell, Ky., 1936-39, Atlanta, Ind., 1939-40; mem. editorial staff Standard Pub. Co., Cin., 1940-41; commd. 1st lt. U.S. Army, 1941; advanced through grades to col., 1961; command chaplain Augsburg (W. Ger.) area, 1950-53; div. chaplain 3d Inf. Div., 1953-55; dep. army chaplain 6th U.S. Army, 1955-58; command chaplain 5th Region Army Air Def. Command, 1959-61; ret., 1961; dean men U. Redlands, 1961-69; dir. counseling, v.p. acad. affairs Lea (Minn.) Coll., 1969-74; rehab. counselor J.O.B. Work Activities Ctr., Hesperia, Calif., 1976-80, dir., 1980-85, dir. emeritus, 1985—; adj. prof. psychology and religion Chapman Coll., 1976-85. Recipient award of merit Boy Scouts Am., 1967, Silver Beaver award, 1969. Mem. Am. Personnel and Guidance Assn., Nat. Vocat. Guidance Assn., Am. Rehab. Counselors Assn., Alpha Phi Gamma, Phi Delta Kappa, Pi Ch, Pi Gamma Mu, Alpha Phi Omega. Democrat. Club: Masons. Home: 611 Juniper Ct Redlands CA 92374

LEDBETTER, DONALD HENRY, corporate executive; b. St. Louis, Aug. 27, 1948; s. Henry Patrick and Mary Willetta (Blaise) L.; B.A. in Indsl. Psychology, St. Louis U., 1971; M.B.A. in Personnel and Indsl. Relations, Central Mo. State U., 1977; postgrad. U. Mo. Law Sch., Kansas City, 1978; m. Helen Briggs, Sept. 15, 1973; children: Jamie Kristin, Lauren Michelle. Indsl. relations rep. Consol. Aluminum Corp., Madison, Ill. 1972-73; mgr. manpower planning Whitaker Cable Corp., North Kansas City, Mo., 1973-78; personnel dir. Nordson Corp., Amherst, Ohio, 1978-81, Megatek Corp., San Diego, 1981-84, Oak Ind., San Diego, 1984-85, ptnr. Mgmt. and Fin. Ptnrs., 1985—; dir. human resources Starnet Internat. Inc., San Diego, 1985—; speaker lectr. on EEO/AAP to mfrs. and personnel groups, 1975—. Accredited sr. profl. in human resources Personnel Accreditation Inst. Mem. Am. Soc. for Personnel Adminstrn., Am. Soc. for Tng. and Devel., Personnel Mgmt. Assn. Greater Kansas City (v.p. fin., treas. 1978), Personnel Mgmt. Assoc., San Diego, Am. Mensa Ltd. Author: (booklets) The Employment Application Explanation, 1978, The Engineering Professional/Technical Classification Plan, 1981, Rational Quantitative Technique of Workforce Evaluation, 1986, Model to Estimate Time to Implement Landamatics, 1986; radio program Minding Your Business-Megafitness-An Innovative Wellness Program at Work (published in Am. Airlines Inflight mag. 1984). Avocation: reading. Office: 10951 Sorrento Valley Rd Suite 2J San Diego CA 92121

LEDBETTER, DONALD LEE, civil engineer; b. Sulphur, Okla., May 18, 1926; s. Lloyd Webb and Ella Louise (Wilson) L.; m. Nelda Beth Belding, May 17, 1946 (dec. Oct. 1983); children: Karen Louise, Kathy Lynn Carrol, Donald Ray.; m. Pauline Gorder, Feb. 11, 1984. BSCE, U. Okla., 1946; MBA, Golden Gate U., 1975. Registered profl. engr. Okla., Kans., N.Mex., Calif. Engr. City of Oklahoma City, 1948, Argonne Nat. Labs., 1949-51; engring. supr. Nat. Gypsum Co., 1953-54; sr. engr. Bettis Atomic Power Lab., Pitts., 1955-59; project mgr. Honeywell Corp., Duarte, Calif., 1959-63, NSPE, Washington, 1971-72; mgr. nuclear engring. Aerojet Nuclear Systems, Sacramento, 1963-71; project mgr. Bechtel, San Francisco, 1972-80, 84-86, mgr. bus. devel., 1981-83; dir. bus. devel. Kaiser Engrs., Oakland, Calif., 1986—; asst. prof. Am. U., Beirut, 1953. Contbr. articles to profl. publs. Served to comdr. C.E., USN, 1943-47. Mem. NSPE (chmn. industry div. 1971-73, chmn. employment commn. 1983-84), Soc. Am. Mil. Engrs. Republican. Lutheran. Club: Engineers (San Francisco). Lodge: Masons. Avocations: photography, swimming, career counseling. Home: 1775 Manzanita Dr Oakland CA 94611 Office: Kaiser Engrs 1800 Harrison St Oakland CA 94623

LEDBETTER, EDWARD WARREN, clothing executive; b. Memphis, Apr. 29, 1916; s. Hugh and Landon (Elliott) L.; m. Martha Jane Clifton; 1 child, Patricia Ann Ledbetter Cole. Graduated, Wylies Bus. Sch., 1937. Clk. mail orders Sears Roebuck & Co., Memphis, 1939-40; sales rep. Swift & Co. Refinery, Memphis, 1941-43; cons. retail sales Simmon's Store, New Albany, Miss., 1945-46; ptnr. Ledbetter's Inc., Phoenix, 1947—, pres. and chief exec. officer, 1970—. Served with USAF, 1943-45. Mem. Nat. Assn. Textile and Apparel Distbrs. (pres. 1969-70), Nat. Assn. Wholesalers, Salvation Army (life, chmn. adv. bd. 1979). Republican. Baptist. Lodge: Rotary. Avocations: stamp collecting, archaeology. Office: Ledbetter's Inc 2702 E Washington PO Box 3635 Phoenix AZ 85030

LEDERER, JOHN MARTIN, aeronautical engineer; b. Solomon, Kans., May 12, 1930; s. George Martin and Angie Bell (Faubion) L.; m. Joan Elizabeth Patrick, June 15, 1963; children: Jeffrey Mark, Carol Elizabeth. BS in Aero. Engring., Kans. State U., 1953; MSEE, Air Force Inst. Tech., 1955; postgrad., U. N.Mex., 1962-63. Registered profl. aero. engr., Ohio. Chief project engring.div. Air Force Spl. Weapons Ctr., Albuquerque, 1963-67, chief electromagnetics div., 1967-70; tech. adviser Air Force Weapons Lab., Albuquerque, 1970-73, 76—; tech. dir. 4900th test group, Albuquerque, 1973-76; chmn. DOD Design Rev. and Acceptance Group, Albuquerque, 1979—. Co-inventor digital distance measuring instrument. Founder One of Ten Young Am. Football League, Albuquerque, 1964. Served to 1st lt. USAFR, 1953-58. Recipient Outstanding Performance award Dept. Air Force, Albuquerque, 1965, 66, 68, 73, 74, 79, Sustained Superior Performance award Dept. Air Force, Albuquerque, 1961, 81, 83, 84, 85, 86. Mem. NSPE, Inst. Aerospace Scis. Republican. Episcopalian. Avocations: archery, flying. Home: 3012 El Marta Ct NE Albuquerque NM 87111-5618 Office: Air Force Weapons Lab NTS Kirtland AFB NM 87117-6008

LEDERER, MARION IRVINE, cultural administrator; b. Brampton, Ont., Can., Feb. 10, 1920; d. Oliver Bateman and Eva Jane (MacMurdo) L.; m. Francis Lederer, July 10, 1941. Student, U. Toronto, 1938, UCLA, 1942-45. Owner Canoga Mission Gallery, Canoga Park, Calif., 1967—; cultural heritage monument Canoga Mission Gallery, 1974—; Vice pres. Screen Smart Set women's aux. Motion Picture and TV Fund, 1973—; founder sister city program Canoga Park-Taxco, Mexico, 1963; Mem. mayor's cultural task force San Fernando Valley, 1973—; mem. Los Angeles Cultural Affairs Commn., 1980-85; bd. dirs. Muses (Mus. Sci. and Industry Los Angeles). Mem. Los Angeles Cultural Affairs Commn., 1980-85. Recipient numerous pub. service awards from mayor, city council, C. of C. Mem. Canoga Park C. of C. (cultural chmn. 1973-75, dir. 1973-75). Presbyn. Home: PO Box 32 Canoga Park CA 91305 Office: Canoga Mission Gallery 23130 Sherman Way Canoga Park CA 91307

LEDIG, F. THOMAS, population geneticist, research administrator; b. Dover, N.J., Aug. 13, 1938; s. Charles Jacob and Rita Elizabeth (Fitzgerald) L.; m. Florence Margaret Stanton, Aug. 25, 1956 (div. 1976); children: Colleen Bernadette, Sean Cormac, Brendan Owen; m. Linda Marie Lux, Sept. 27, 1986. BS cum laude, Rutgers U., 1962; MS, N.C. State U., 1965, PhD, 1967. Instr. N.C. State U., 1963-65; from lectr. to full prof. Yale U.,

1966-81; dir. Inst. Forest Genetics, Berkeley and Placerville, Calif., 1979—; research geneticist Inst. Tropical Forestry, Rio Piedras, P.R., 1978. Editor: Toward The Future Forest, 1974; co-editor: Proceeding Workshop on Eucalyptus in Calif, 1983, and others; contbr. articles to profl. jours. Recipient Disting. Publ. award Pacific Southwest Forest and Range Experiment Sta., Berkeley, 1983; NSF fellow, 1965-66; Ford Found. grantee. Mem. AAAS, Soc. Am. Foresters, Internat. Soc. Tropical Foresters, N.Am. Quantitative Forest Genetics Group (chmn. 1974-75), Wilderness Soc., N.Am. Forestry Commn. (chmn. taxonomy working group 1984—), Sierra Club. Avocations: scuba diving, back packing. Home: 5325 Lawton Ave Oakland CA 94618 Office: Inst Forest Genetics US Forest Service 1960 Addison St Berkeley CA 94704

LEDIN, GEORGE, JR., computer science educator; b. Seekirchen, Austria, Jan. 28, 1946; came to U.S., 1962; naturalized, 1967; s. George Sr. and Helen (Folwarkow) L.; m. Suzánne Marie Fisher Smith Scudder, June 15, 1968; children: Kathryn E., Alexander M. BS in Math., U. Calif., Berkeley, 1967; JD, U. San Francisco, 1982. Sec., co-founder Scind Reserch and Devel. Co., Inc., San Francisco, 1966-69; info. scis. dir. Automated Health Systems, Inc., Burlingame, Calif., 1969-71; exec. v.p. More of Calif., Inc., San Francisco, 1971-73, also chmn. bd. dirs.; lectr. computer sci. and math. dept. U. San Francisco, 1968-75, chmn. dept. computer sci., 1976-83, project dir., sr. research assoc. Inst. Chem. Biology, 1973-75, asst. prof. computer sci., 1975-80, assoc. prof. computer sci., 1980-84, prof. computer sci., 1984—; legal cons., 1973-84; prof. computer sci. Sonoma State U., Rohnert Park, Calif., 1984—; chmn. bd. dirs., Micromental, Inc., Santa Rosa, Calif., 1985—. Author books; contbr. articles to profl. jours. Avocations: light athletics, ping pong, baseball, tennis, golf. Office: Sonoma State U Darwin Hall 124 Rohnert Park CA 94928

LEE, ALBERT YIN-PO, economist; b. China, Sept. 1, 1930; s. Lan Ken and Weis Wee; m. Linda Shief-mei, Feb. 23, 1962; children—Min-wei, Angel, Finny. Ph.D. in Econs., So. Ill. U., Carbondale, 1970. Asst. prof. econs. Calif. State U.-Stanislaus, Turlock, 1970-73, assoc. prof., 1973-77, prof. 1977—; assoc. prof. U. Pacific, Stockton, Calif., 1977; prof. Golden Gate U., San Franicsco, 1980—. Mem. Am. Econs. Assn., Western Econs. Assn. Contbr. articles to profl. jours. Home: 1225 Estate Dr Turlock CA 95380 Office: Calif State U-Stanislaus Dept Econs 800 Monte Vista Turlock CA 95380

LEE, ALDORA G., social psychologist; b. Schenectady, N.Y.; d. Alois W. and M. Dorothy (Swigert) Graf. AB, Ind. U.; MA, Stanford U.; PhD, U. Colo. Dir. women studies Wash. State U., Pullman, 1976-78, dir. unit on aging, 1976-81; cons. in market research Syva, Palo Alto, Calif., 1982; market research analyst Allstate Research and Planning Ctr., Menlo Park, Calif., 1983—; rep. Wash. Assn. Gerontol. Edn., N.W. region rep. Nat. Women's Studies Assn., 1978-81. Contbr. articles to profl. jours. Chairperson Menlo Park Library Commn., 1985—; instr. Resource Ctr. for Women, Palo Alto, 1984—. Mem. Am. Mktg. Assn., Am. Sociol. Assn., Western Psychol. Assn., Phi Beta Kappa, Sigma Xi.

LEE, BRIAN DALVIN, pediatric dentist; b. Berkeley, Calif., Dec. 23, 1942; s. David Alan and May (Hum) L.; m. Dorlene Sandria Yee, Aug. 13, 1966; children: Lisa Ann, Jonathon Everett. Student, U. Calif., Berkeley, 1960-62; DDS, U. Calif., San Francisco, 1966; MSD, Ind. U., 1970. Diplomate Am. Bd. Pedodontics. Practice pediatric dentistry Foster City, Calif., 1972—; guest lectr. U. Calif. Sch. Dentistry; clin. instr. Ind. U. Sch. Dentistry; dental examiner Calif. Bd. Dental Examiners. Contbr. articles to profl. jours. Served as capt. Dental Corps, U.S. Army, 1966-68. Decorated Army Commendation medal with oak leaf cluster; Crippled Children's fellow, 1968-70. Fellow Am. Acad. Pedodontics, Am. Coll. Dentists; mem. Am. Bd. Pedodontics (examiner), Am. Soc. Dentistry for Children, Calif. Soc. Dentistry for Children, Calif. Soc. Pediatric Dentists, ADA, Calif. Dental Assn., Golden Gate Pedodontic Study Club, Am. Bd. Pediatric Dentistry (chmn. 1986—), Foster City C. of C. Lodge: Lions. Home: 198 Flying Mist Isle Foster City CA 94404 Office: 1289 Hillsdale Blvd Foster City CA 94404

LEE, CHI-HANG, bio-organic chemist; b. Vinh Long, Vietnam, Jan. 1, 1939; came to U.S., 1955; s. Shao-Bin and Yun-Fang (Yeh) L.; m. Mee-Han Chan, Sept. 19, 1964; children: Maurice, Irving. BA, So. Ill. U., 1960; PhD, Rutgers U., 1966. Sr. chemist, sr. research specialist Gen. Foods Corp., Tarrytown, N.Y., 1967-78; sr. research scientist R. J. Reynolds Foods, Winston-Salem, N.C., 1978-80; mgr. food biochemistry Del Monte Corp., Walnut Creek, Calif., 1980-85, dir. chemistry, 1985—; vis. prof. King's Coll., 1973-77. Editor Ambassadors mag., 1962-63, 76-80; patentee in field. Rutgers U. research fellow, 1962-66. Mem. Am. Sci. Affiliation (mem. exec. council 1979-83, pres. 1982), Am. Chem. Soc. Office: Del Monte Research Ctr 205 N Wiget Ln Walnut Creek CA 94598

LEE, CHI-HO, pharmacologist, researcher; b. Taitung, Republic of China (Taiwan), July 2, 1941; came to U.S., 1972; s. Ching and Shih (Chen) L.; 1 child, Roger. BS, Kaohsiung Med. Coll., Taiwan, Republic of China, 1967; MS, U. Tokyo, Japan, 1972; PhD, Cornell U., 1976. Predoctoral fellow Roche Inst. Molecular Biology, Nutley, N.J., 1972-76; postdoctoral fellow Cornell U., N.Y.C., 1976-78; postdoctoral fellow Syntex Research, Palo Alto, Calif., 1978-79, staff researcher I, 1979-81, staff researcher II, 1981—. Pres. Taiwanese Alliance for Interculture, San Jose, Calif., 1985. Mem. Western Pharmacology Soc., Am. Soc. Hypertension. Presbyterian. Home: 3758 La Donna Palo Alto CA 94306 Office: Syntex Research Dept Cardiovascular Pharmacology 3401 Hillview Ave Palo Alto CA 94304

LEE, CHUN PING, research scientist; b. Hong Kong, Dec. 12, 1948; came to U.S., 1969; s. Cheuk Yin and Yuk Wah (Shiu) L.; m. Jean Chuan Wang, Dec. 26, 1979; 1 child, Angela Jean. BA, Calif. State U., Hayward, 1972; MS, U. Hawaii, 1974; PhD, UCLA, 1981. Research scientist Jet Propulsion Lab., Pasadena, Calif., 1981—; engr. Poseidon Research, Santa Monica, Calif., 1980-81. Mem. Am. Inst. Physics, Acoustical Soc. Am., Sigma Xi. Republican. Office: Jet Propulsion Lab 4800 Oak Grove Dr Pasadena CA 91103

LEE, CLARENCE EDGAR, computational physicist; b. San Jose, Calif., Aug. 18, 1931; s. Jack and Jean (Stüssy) L.; m. Marth Owings, Feb. 29, 1976; children: Marlene, Marcello, Chris, Katherine, Marietta, David, Margo. BA in Physics, U. Calif., Berkeley, 1953; MA in Physics, Cornell U., 1963; PhD in Physics, U. Colo., 1973. Staff mem. Los Alamos (N.Mex.) Nat. Lab., 1953-78; prof. nuclear sci. Tex. A&M U., College Station, 1978-85; sr. project engr. Technadyne Enging. Cons., Albuquerque, 1985-86; computational physicist JTA, Sandia Park, N.M., 1986—. Contbr. articles to profl. jours. Mem. Am. Phys. Soc., Am. Nuclear Soc. (admissions chmn. 1983-86). Avocations: tennis, racquetball, skiing. Home: 12805 Arroyo de Vista NE Albuquerque NE 87111 Office: JTA PO Box 549 Sandia Park NM 87047

LEE, CONNIE LOUISE, teacher; b. Roswell, N.Mex., Dec. 2, 1948; d. William Jackson and Zilpha Miranda (Taylor) Graham; m. Bill D. Lee, Aug. 6, 1977. BS, N.Mex. State U., 1969, MAT, 1972. Cert. elem. prin., elem. profl., social sci. and lang. arts tchr., N.Mex. Tchr. Las Cruces (N.Mex.) Schs., 1969-77; head bookeeper Hobbs (N.Mex.) Gas Co., 1977-79; mortgage loan servicer First Interstate Bank, Hobbs, 1979-80; tchr. Hobbs Sch., 1980-84; mortgage loan servicer Portales (N.Mex.) Schs., 1984—; chmn. lang. arts curriculum com. Hobbs Mcpl. Schs., 1984; mem. textbook selection com. for Math, Reading and Computers, Portales, Hobbs and Las Cruces; appointed mem. Profl. Standards Commn. N.Mex. Sch. Bd., 1986—. Pres. Las Cruces Edn. Assn., 1976-77, bd. dirs., 1974-77, fin. services com., 1975-77, conv. delegate, 1975, 76, council delegate, 1975-77. Home: 2108 W Aspen PO Box 605 Portales NM 88130 Office: RM James Elem Sch 701 W 18th Portales NM 88130

LEE, CURTIS HOWARD, consulting engineer; b. San Francisco, June 7, 1928; s. Lum Quong and Kum Ho (Lee) L.; B.S. with honor, Calif. State Poly. Coll., 1952; postgrad. McGeorge Coll. Law, 1964-67; m. Mildred Lee; children—Melinda, Roberta, Lorie, Sabrina, Kristina. Mech. engr. Buonaccorsi & Assos., cons. engrs., San Francisco, 1953-57, Eagleson Engrs., cons. engrs., San Francisco, 1957-59; 60-63; chief engr. C.S. Hardeman, San Francisco, 1959-60; spl. project engr. A.E. D'Ambly, cons. engrs., Phila., 1963-64; self-employed as cons. engr., Sacramento, 1964-67; chief engr. George W. Dunn & Assos., cons. engrs. San Diego, 1967-69; prin. Dunn-Lee-Smith-Klein & Assocs., San Diego, 1969-87, Curtis H. Lee Cons. Group, Chula Vista, 1987—. Mem. Accrediting Commn. of Assn. of Ind. Colls. and Schs., 1970-76; mem. adv. panel Calif. State Bldg. Standards Commn., 1971-76; mem. San Diego City Bd. Bldg. Appeals, 1974-79; mem. Chula Vista City Bd. Appeals, 1980—. Served with AUS, 1947-48. Registered profl. engr., Ariz., Calif., Colo., Fla., Ga., Wash., Nev., N.Mex., Ohio, Oreg., Pa., Tex. Fellow ASHRAE; mem. Am. Arbitration Assn. (mem. nat. panel 1969—, regional adv. bd. 1977—), Am. Acad. Forensic Scis., Am. Cons. Engrs. Council (mem. Calif. mech.-elec. cons. engrs. com. 1972-80), Nat. Soc. Profl. Engrs. (pres. San Diego chpt. 1972-73, state dir. 1973-74, nat. dir. 1974-76), ASME, Am. Soc. Plumbing Engrs. (charter pres. San Diego chpt. 1970, nat. 3d v.p. 1970-72), Constrn. Specifications Inst. (dir. San Diego chpt. 1974-75, pres. 1976-77, Inst. com. 1978—, named fellow 1983), Am. Soc. Profl. Estimators, Am. Soc. Quality Control, Archeol. Inst. Am., Instrument Soc. Am., Internat. Solar Energy Soc., Internat. Assn. Plumbing and Mech. Ofcls., Nat. Fire Protection Assn. Office: 492 3d Ave 101 Chula Vista CA 92010-4614

LEE, DAI-LIH, dietitian; b. Taipei, Taiwan, Republic of China, May 27, 1954; came to U.S., 1977; d. Tzer-Hong and Fu-Sue (Tien) L.; m. Owen F. Cargol, Apr. 20, 1979; 1 child, Austin Lee Owen Spencer. BS, Nat. Taiwan U., 1976; MS, Oreg. State U., 1979; AS, North Idaho Coll., 1982; BS, U. Idaho, 1984. Registered dietitian. Researcher Pa. State U., Univ. Park, 1980-81; clin. dietitian Sacred Heart Med. Ctr., Spokane, Wash., 1984—. Mem. Am. Dietetic Assn., Idaho Dietetic Assn., Greater Spokane Dietetic Assn., Inst. Food Tech. Home and Office: 722 Empire Ave Coeur d'Alene ID 83814

LEE, DAVID MALLIN, physicist; b. Bklyn., Jan. 18, 1944; s. George Francis Lee and Winifred Rita (Jones) Wyatt; m. Judith Carol Silliman, Aug. 20, 1966; children: David, Timothy, Karen, Jeffrey, Rebecca. BS, Manhattan Coll., 1966; PhD, U. Va., 1971. Vis. mem. staff Los Alamos (N.Mex) Nat. Lab., 1971-74, mem. staff, 1974-80, 81—; U.S. tech. expert IAEA, Vienna, Austria, 1980-81. Patentee in field. Mem. Am. Phys. Soc., AAAS, Sigma Xi. Democrat. Roman Catholic. Home: 126 Piedra Loop Los Alamos NM 87544 Office: Los Alamos Nat Lab MS H838 MP-13 Los Alamos NM 87545

LEE, DAVID ROBERT, information management educator; b. San Francisco, Dec. 22, 1940; s. Robert Reid and Gwen (Jones) L. BA in Internat. Conflict, U. Calif., Berkeley, 1966; MEd in Adminstrn., Columbia U., 1972, DEd in Adminstrn., 1976. Asst. to asst. commr. of edn. N.J., 1971-72; mgr., release program supr. N.Y. Supreme Ct., N.Y.C., 1973-74; asst. dean undergrad. bus., pub. and police adminstrn. John F. Kennedy, Orinda, Calif., 1975-85; assoc. prof. info. resource mgmt. San Jose (Calif.) State U., 1985—. Ednl. Leadership fellow Ford Found., 1972. Mem. Internat. Assn. Chiefs of Police (assoc.), Assn. Systems Mgmt. (pres. Santa Clara chpt., pres.), Data Processing Mgmt. Assn. (edn. chmn.). Home: 1046 S Winchester Blvd Apt 9 San Jose CA 95128 Office: San Jose State U Mktg Dept Info Resource Mgmt Program San Jose CA 95152

LEE, DOUGLAS CRAIG, beverage distribution executive; b. San Francisco, June 28, 1945; s. Joseph Stanley and Janet (Chan) L.; m. Kay Hatamiya, Sept. 14, 1974. B.A., U. Calif.-Berkeley, 1966, M.B.A., 1969. Account exec. Benton and Bowles Advt., N.Y.C., 1970-72; sr. mktg. mgr. E & J Gallo Winery, Modesto, Calif., 1972-77; v.p., gen. mgr. RC Cola Co., Sacramento, 1977-81; pres. Affiliated Beverages, Inc., Salinas, Calif., 1981—; mem. nat. distbr. adv. council Miller Brewing Co.; instr. various Calif. colls.; cons. in field. Mem. Am. Mktg. Assn., Salinas C. of C. Office: Affiliated Beverages Inc 881 Vertin Ave Salinas CA 93901

LEE, FRANK F., sociologist, anthropologist; b. N.Y.C., Mar. 19, 1920; s. Burton James and Louise (Freeman) L.; m. Margaret Gallaher, June 5, 1945 (div. Sept. 1974); children: Margaret Parks, Burton Hoyt, Susan Freeman; m. Ruth Balch, May 3, 1975. BA, Yale U., 1943, MA, 1947, PhD, 1953. Asst. prof. sociology Northeastern U., Boston, 1952-54, prof., 1964-83, chmn. dept., 1964-68; asst. prof. sociology U. Calif., Riverside, 1954-60; assoc. prof. and chmn. dept. Adelphi U., Garden City, N.Y., 1960-63, Oakland U., Rochester, Minn., 1963-64; cons. Sociology Assocs., Santa Fe, 1983—; dir. publicity Fisk U., Nashville, 1948-50; cons. San Bernadino (Calif.) Com. Coll., 1955-60; dir. summer workshop in ethnic problems and intergroup relations, U. Vt., Burlington, 1960, 61, 62. Contbr. articles on racial relations to profl. jours. Mem. Riverside County Bd. Edn., 1956-58; bd. dirs. Community Settlement Assn., Riverside, 1956-60. Served to lt. USNR, 1942-46. Grantee HEW, 1969-73, NIMH div. NIH, 1967-70, Ford Found., 1963-64, 65. Fellow Am. Anthropol. Assn., Soc. Applied Anthropology; mem. Soc. Study Social Problems (treas. and bus. mgr. 1961-65, v.p. 1965-66), Santa Fe Squash Racquets Assn. (pres. 1985—), Red Hot Chiles Dixieland Jazz Band. Republican. Episcopalian. Lodge: Rotary (pres. 1986-87). Avocations: hiking, squash, reading. Home and Office: Sociology Assocs 1410 Don Gaspar Ave Santa Fe NM 82501

LEE, GRACE SOU-HUEI CHEN, chemist, researcher; b. Tainan, Republic of China, Dec. 16, 1946; came to U.S., 1979; d. Lai Sou and Heng (Wang) Chen; m. Argon Nai-Kang Lee, Jan. 12, 1979. BSc, Cheng Kung U., Tainan, 1969; PhD, U. New Brunswick, Can., 1978. Postdoctoral research assoc. NASA Ames Research Ctr., Moffett Field, Calif., 1979-80; research assoc. SRI Internat., Menlo Park, Calif., 1981-83; research assoc. Syntex Research, Palo Alto, Calif., 1983-85, sr. chemist, 1985—. Mem. Am. Chem. Soc. Home: 830 Bay St Mountain View CA 94041 Office: Syntex Research 3401 Hillview Ave Palo Alto CA 94304

LEE, HARRY REES, civil engineer; b. Des Moines, July 21, 1929; s. Harry Rees and Evelyn Marie (Croxen) L.; B.S. in Civil Engring., U. Wash., 1953, M.S. in Civil Engring., 1954; m. Mary Ann Penty, Nov. 12, 1955; children—Mark, Marica, Michael. Materials engr. Naval Civil Engring. and Research Lab., Port Hueneme, Calif., 1954-56; pres. Alaska Testlab, Anchorage, 1956-78; partner Dowl Engrs., Anchorage, 1973-78; pres. H4M Corp., Anchorage, 1979—; chmn. bd. Denali Drilling Co. Chmn. sch. budget advisory com. Municipality of Anchorage, 1979-84, mem. geotech. com., 1977-83, chmn. geotech. com., 1977, chmn. mcpl. budget com., 1966-77, chmn. economic devel. com., 1972-75. Served with USNR, 1950-51. Decorated Air medal. Fellow ASCE; mem. Nat. Soc. Profl. Engrs., Alaska Soc. Profl. Engrs. (pres. 1963), ASTM, AAAS. Home: 1915 Stanford Dr Anchorage AK 99508 Office: H4M Corp 810 Whitney Rd Anchorage AK 99501

LEE, HI YOUNG, physician, acupuncturist; b. Seoul, Korea, Oct. 18, 1941; came to U.S., 1965, naturalized, 1976; s. Jung S. and Hwa J. (Kim) L.; m. Sun M. Lee, June 4, 1965; children—Sandra, Grace, David. M.D., Yon Sei U., Seoul, 1965. Diplomate Am. Bd. Family Practice. Intern Grasslands Hosp., Valhalla, N.Y., 1965-66; resident VA Hosp., Dayton, Ohio, 1966-70; mem. staff Eastern State Hosp., Medical Lake, Wash., 1970-74; practice family medicine, acupuncturist Empire Med. Office, Spokane, Wash., 1974—; active staff St. Lukes Meml. Hosp., Spokane, 1974—, bd. trustees St. Georges Prep Sch., Wash., 1986— ; courtesy staff Deaconess Med. Center, Spokane, 1974—, Sacred Heart Med. Ctr., Spokane, 1974—. Author: Von Recklinghousen's Disease, 1970 (McDermit award). Elder First Presbyterian Church, Spokane, 1975. Fellow Am. Acad. Family Practice; mem. ctr. for Chinese Medicine, Spokane County Med. Soc., Nat. Acupuncture Research Soc., Christian Med. Soc. Home: 2006 W Liberty Ave Spokane WA 99205 Office: Empire Med Office E 17 Empire Ave Spokane WA 99207

LEE, HO JOHN, electrical engineer; b. Boston, Nov. 4, 1962; s. Kwan Young and Kum Hwa (Yoo) L. BSEE, MSEE, MIT, 1985. Mem. tech. staff HP Labs., Palo Alto, Calif., 1983—; mem. faculty dept. elec. engring. Northwestern Poly. U., 1985—. Avocations: classical piano, electric guitar. Office: HP Labs 1501 Page Mill Rd Palo Alto CA 94304

LEE, HOWARD MING, biotechnologist, chemist; b. Tainan, Republic of China, Jan. 19, 1948; came to U.S., 1971; s. John Chen and Yee (Guao) L.; m. May Chu Wu, Aug. 28, 1971; children: Eugene Howard, Amy Mae. BS, Nat. Tsing Hua U., Taiwan, Republic of China, 1970; MA, Boston U., 1974, PhD, 1976; postdoctoral, Harvard Med. Sch., 1977. Assoc. Peter Bent Brigham Hosp. Harvard Med. Sch., Boston, 1975-77; instr. Mt. Sinai Sch. Medicine, N.Y.C., 1977-78; sr. chemist Am. Cyanamid Co., Cliffton, N.J., 1978-79; sr. pharm. scientist Richardson-Vick Inc. (merger Proctor & Gambel), Mt. Vernon, N.Y., 1979-81; dir. immunotherapy Med. Research Inst. Pacific Med. Ctr., San Francisco, 1981-85; v.p., dir. product devel. and protein chemistry Xoma Corp., Berkeley, Calif., 1983-87; dir. research Thornstar Ltd., Inc., Petaluma, Calif., 1987—; chief exec. officer Internat. Pharmacosmetic Mfrs., San Francisco, 1987—; cons. in field. Contbr. articles to profl. jours. Xoma Corp. grantee, 1981-85, biotech. patent grantee Nat. Cancer Inst., 1985. Mem. Am. Chem. Soc., Soc. Chinese Bioscientists N.Am. Avocations: real estate investment, stamp and coin collecting, lic. cosmetic and health care products cons. Home: 163 14th Ave San Francisco CA 94118 Office: Thornstar Ltd 163 14th Ave San Francisco CA 94118

LEE, HYUNG JAI, material scientist; b. Seoul, Republic of Korea, Jan. 7, 1950; s. Yong Suk and Il Soon (Oh) L.; m. Sun Ok Whang Lee, Aug. 17, 1982; 1 child, Benjamin Jonghoon Lee. BS, Seoul Nat. U., 1972; MS, N.C. State U., 1978; PhD, U. Calif., Berkeley, 1982. Engr. IS Steel Co., Seoul, 1974-76; research asst. Engring. Research Div., Raleigh, N.C., 1977-78; research asst. Lawrence Berkeley Lab., Berkeley, Calif., 1978-82, post doctoral fellow, 1982-83; sr. scientist Memorex Corp., Santa Clara, Calif., 1983—; cons. Lawrence Berkeley Lab., 1981-82; lectr. Northwestern Poly. U., Fremont, Calif., 1986. Contbr. articles on materials properties and structures; 2 patents in field. Recipient Achievement award for Excellence, Burroughs Corp., Santa Clara, 1985, Invention award Burroughs Corp., 1986. Mem. IEEE, Magnetic Soc. of IEEE. Home: 5249 War Wagon Ct San Jose CA 95136 Office: Unisys Corp San Tomas at Central Expressway Santa Clara CA 95052

LEE, IVY, JR., public relations consultant; b. N.Y.C., July 31, 1909; s. Ivy and Cornelia (Bartlett) L.; m. Mary T. Meese, Mar. 16, 1986; children: Peter Ivy III (dec.), Jean Downey. BA, Princeton U., 1931; MBA, Harvard U., 1933. Ptnr. Ivy Lee & T.J. Ross, N.Y.C., 1933-45; with Pan Am. World Airways, Miami, Fla. and San Francisco, 1940-45; adminstrv. asst. to prin. Bechtel Group, Inc., San Francisco, 1950-54; pres. Ivy Lee Jr. & Assocs., San Francisco, 1945-55; pres., cons. Ivy Lee Jr. & Assocs., Inc., San Francisco, 1955—. Trustee Princeton (N.J.) U., 1965-69; bd. dirs. San Francisco TB Assn., Bay Area Red Cross, San Francisco, Edgewood Childrens Ctr. Mem. Pub. Relations Soc. Am., Internat. Pub. Relations Assn. (pres. 1966-67). Republican. Presbyterian. Clubs: Bohemian, San Francisco Golf, Pacific Union. Home: 1940 Broadway San Francisco CA 94109 Office: 210 Post St San Francisco CA 94108

LEE, JAMES KING, technology corporation executive; b. Nashville, July 31, 1940; s. James Fitzhugh Lee and Lucille (Charlton) McGivney; m. Victoria Marie Marani, Sept. 4, 1971; children—Gina Victoria, Patrick Fitzhugh. B.S., Calif. State U.-Pomona, 1963; M.B.A., U. So. Calif., 1966. Enging. adminstr. Douglas MSSD, Santa Monica, Calif., 1965-67; mgr. mgmt. systems TRW Systems, Redondo Beach, Calif., 1967-68; v.p. corp. devel. DataStation Corp., Los Angeles, 1968-69; v.p., gen. mgr. Aved Systems Group, Los Angeles, 1969-70; mng. ptnr. Corp. Growth Cons., Los Angeles, 1970-81; chmn., pres. chief exec. officer Fail-Safe Tech. Corp., Los Angeles, 1981—. Author industry studies, 1973-79. Mem. Los Angeles Mayor's Community Adv. Com., 1962-72; asst. adminstr. SBA, Washington, 1974; vice chmn. Traffic Commn., Rancho Palos Verdes, Calif., 1975-78; chmn. Citizens for Property Tax Relief, Palos Verdes, 1976-80; mem. Town Hall Calif. Recipient Golden Scissors award Calif. Taxpayers' Congress, 1978. Mem. So. Calif. Tech. Execs. Network, Am. Electronics Assn. (vice chmn.), Nat. Security Industries Assn., Nat. Def. Exec. Res. Republican. Baptist. Home: 28874 Crestridge Rd Rancho Palos Verdes CA 90274-5063 Office: Fail-Safe Tech Corp 5757 W Century Blvd Suite 645 Los Angeles CA 90045-6407

LEE, JAMES MOON, chemical engineering educator; b. Seoul, Republic of Korea, Nov. 3, 1946; came to U.S., 1976; s. Joo-Ho and Chung-Ja (Choi) L.; m. Inn-Soo Sohn, Oct. 6, 1972; 1 child, Jenny. BS in Chem. Engring., Yon-Sei U., Seoul, 1970, MS in Chem. Engring., 1972; PhD in Chem. Engring., U. Ky., 1978. Lectr. Yon-Sei U., Seoul, 1972-73, Korea Mil. Acad., Seoul, 1973-76; asst. prof. Cleve. State U., 1978-82, assoc. prof., 1982-83; assoc. prof. Wash. State U., Pullman, 1983—. Contbr. articles to profl. jours. Research grantee NSF, 1980-82, 85-87. Mem. Am. Inst. Chem. Engrs., Am. Chem. Soc. Home: SE 1005 Glen Echo Rd Pullman WA 99163 Office: Wash State U Chem Engring Dept Pullman WA 99164-2710

LEE, JESSE BISHOP, aerospace engineer; b. Ansted, W.Va., July 24, 1933; s. Raymond Archer and Monad (Bishop) L.; m. Laura Ann Covington, Aug. 26, 1956; children: Elizabeth Ann, James Bruce, Laura Anne. BSME, Ohio U., 1955, MSME, 1965; M in Automotive Engring., Chrysler Inst., 1957. Registered profl. engr., Ohio. Engr. Chrysler Corp., Highland Park, Mich., 1955-59; design engr. Convair Astronautics, San Diego, 1959-62; acting instr. Ohio U., Athens, 1963-64; from assoc. engr. to devel. specialist Garrett Turbine Engine Co., Phoenix, 1964—. Instl. rep. Boy Scouts Am., Scottsdale, Ariz., 1969-70, commr., 1969-72, scoutmaster 1972-75; asst. leader Girl Scouts U.S., Scottsdale, 1976-77. Recipient Scouters Key, Boy Scouts Am., 1973, Scoutmasters Key, Boy Scouts Am., 1976, Woodbadge, Boy Scouts Am., 1975. Republican. Lodge: Masons. Avocations: backpacking, hiking.

LEE, JOHN JIN, lawyer; b. Chgo., Oct. 20, 1948; s. Jim Soon and Fay Yown (Young) L.; m. Jamie Pearl Eng, Apr. 30, 1983. BA magna cum laude, Rice U., 1971; JD, Stanford U., 1975; MBA, 1975. Bar: Calif. 1976. Assoc. atty. Manatt Phelps & Rothenberg, Los Angeles, 1976-77; asst. counsel Wells Fargo Bank N.A., San Francisco, 1977-79, counsel, 1979-80, v.p., sr. counsel, 1980, v.p., mng. sr. counsel, 1981—. Bd. dirs. Asian Bus. League of San Francisco, 1981—, gen. counsel, 1981. Mem. ABA (chmn. subcom. on housing fin., com. on consumer fin. services, sect. of corp., banking and bus. law 1983—), Consumer Bankers Assn. (lawyers com.), Asian Am. Bar Assn. of Greater Bay Area, Soc. Physics Students. Democrat. Baptist. Office: Wells Fargo Bank NA Legal Dept 111 Sutter St San Francisco CA 94163

LEE, JONG HYUK, accountant; b. Seoul, Korea, May 6, 1941; came to U.S., 1969, naturalized, 1975; s. Jung Bo and Wol Sun Lee; B.A., Sonoma State U., Rohnert Park, Calif., 1971; M.B.A. in Taxation, Golden Gate U., San Francisco, 1976; m. Esther Kim, Jan. 24, 1970. Cost acct., internal auditor Foremost-McKesson Co., San Francisco, 1971-74; sr. acct. Clark, Wong, Foulkes & Barbieri, C.P.A.s, Oakland, Calif., 1974-77; pres. J.H. Lee Accountancy Corp., Oakland, 1977—; instr. Armstrong Coll., Berkeley, Calif., 1977-78. Bd. dirs. Korean Residents Assn., 1974, Multi-service Center for Koreans, 1979, Better Bus. Bur., 1984—; chmn. caucus Calif.-Nev. ann. conf. United Methodist Ch., 1977; commr. Calif. State Office Econ. Opportunity, 1982-86; pres. Korean-Am. Democratic Network; mem. Dem. Nat. Fin. Council. Served with Korean Marine Corps, 1961-64; 1st lt. Calif. State Mil. Res. C.P.A., Calif. Mem. Am. Inst. C.P.A.s, Nat. Assn. Asian Am. C.P.A.s (dir.), Am. Acctg. Assn., Nat. Assn. Accountants, Internat. Found. Employee Benefit Plans, Calif. Soc. C.P.A.s, Oakland C. of C., Korean Am. C. of C., Democrat. Club: Rotary. Author tax and bus. column Korea Times, 1980. Home: 180 Firestone Dr Walnut Creek CA 94598 Office: 369 13th St Oakland CA 94612

LEE, JUDITH C., publishing executive; b. Myrtle Point, Oreg.; d. Ralph F. and Lola M. (Greene) Milne; m. Myron E. Lee, 1967. BA, U. Oreg., 1959; MLS, San Jose State U., 1981. Tech. writer GTE Sylvania, Mountain View, Calif., 1962-66, sr. tech. writer, 1968-73; sr. tech. writer Microelectronics div. Philco-Ford, Santa Clara, Calif., 1966-67; sr. publs. writer Lockheed Corp., Sunnyvale, Calif., 1974; mgr. tech. communications Catalytica Assocs., Santa Clara, 1977-80; mgr. info. resources Hydro Research Sci., Santa Clara, 1982-83; staff editor Bus. Software Mag., Redwood City, Calif., 1984-85, mng. editor, 1986-87; mng. editor SandCastles, Inc., Mountain View, 1986-87; mem. steering com. Silicon Valley Tech. Communications Conf., 1985. Recipient Award of Merit No. Calif. Tech. Communication Competition, 1979. Mem. IEEE, AAUW (com. chmn. 1970), Soc. Tech. Communication (sec. Silicon Valley chpt. 1968), Assn. Tchrs. Tech. Writing, Spl. Libraries Assn., Sigma Delta Pi, Alpha Lambda Delta, Beta Phi Mu. Home and Office: 3322 St Michael Dr Palo Alto CA 94306

LEE, KATHRYN EILEEN, social worker; b. Grand Forks, N.D., Sept. 2, 1942; d. Robert Eugene and Bette Mae (Hewitt) L.; m. Thomas E. Zinkle, July 16, 1983. BA, U. Minn., 1964; MSW, Ariz. State U., 1972. Lic. clin. social worker, Calif. Social service practitioner Child Welfare Service, San Bernardino, Calif., 1972-74; clin. social worker Alcohol Counsel Ctr., Pensacola, Fla., 1974-78; mental health clinician San Bernardino Mental Health Agy., 1978-83; psychiat. social worker Knollwood Ctr., Riverside, Calif., 1983-86, Kaiser Permanente Med. Group, Fontana, Calif., 1986—; organizer workshops Women and Alcohol, 1975-77, How to Help Your Alcholic Before He/She Hits Bottom, 1976; cons. social worker Northwest Fla. Home Health, Pensacola, 1976-77, Med. Ctr. Dialysis, Pensacola, 1976-77, Desert Alcohol Coalition, Palm Springs, Fla., 1977-78. Mem. Nat. Assn. Social Workers (cert.). Democrat. Home: 1227 Mira Monte Dr Redlands CA 92373 Office: Kaiser Permanente Med Group 9961 Sierra Ave Fontana CA 92335

LEE, KEITH ALAN, project engineer; b. Denver, June 22, 1957; s. Ainsworth Culbert and Paulette (Geodert) L. BS, Colo. Sch. Mines, 1981. Engr. technician Ortloff Minerals, Golden, Colo., 1978-81; plant engr. Enserch Explorations, Anchorage, 1982-83, project engr., 1986—; project mgr. 'Laska Environ. Control Services, McGrath, 1984-86; owner, pres. Alaska Environ. Engring. Co., Anchorage, 1985—. Home: PO Box 1042 Willow AK 99688 Office: Enserch Explorations 7750 King St Anchorage AK 99502

LEE, KENNETH, physicist; b. San Francisco, July 3, 1937; s. Kai Ming and Ah See Lee; A.B. with honors in Physics, U. Calif., Berkeley, 1959. Ph.D., 1963; m. Cynthia Ann Chu, June 28, 1959; children—Marcus Scott, Stephanie Denise. Research physicist Varian Assocs., Palo Alto, Calif., 1963-68; mem. research staff, mgr. IBM, San Jose, Calif., 1968-83; dir. memory techs. Southwall Techs., Palo Alto, Calif., 1983-84; sr. v.p. product devel. Domain Tech., Milpitas, Calif., 1984—. Fellow Am. Phys. Soc.; sr. mem. IEEE; mem. Phi Beta Kappa, Sigma Xi. Contbr. articles to profl. jours.; patentee in field. Home: 20587 Debbie Ln Saratoga CA 95070 Office: Domain Technology 304 Turquoise St Milpitas CA 95035

LEE, KIMUN, investment banker; b. Stockton, Calif., June 17, 1946; s. Don Y. and Lily (Fong) L. B.A. in Econs., U. Pacific, 1968; M.B.A., U. Nev., 1974. Instr. U. Pacific, Stockton, Calif., 1970-72; asst. to chmn. Y.H. Kwong China Engrs. Ltd., Hong Kong, 1972-75; mng. corp. planner Castle and Cooke, Singapore, 1975-77, asst. to treas., San Francisco, 1977-79; mng. ptnr. Resources Consol., San Francisco, 1980—; lectr. Am. Inst. of Banking; guest lectr. MBA Program Lingnan Inst. Bus., Chinese U., Hong Kong. Bd. dirs. Film Arts Found., San Francisco, 1980-82, adv. dir., 1983-86; mem. host com. San Francisco Ballet, 1981-82, trustee 1987—. Faculty fellow Calif. Bankers Assn., U. Wash., 1970, Am. Iron and Steel Inst., U. Chgo., 1972; Ford Motor Co. grantee, 1971-72. Mem. San Francisco Security Analysts Soc., Hong Kong Security Analysts Soc. Clubs: San Francisco Tennis, San Francisco Press; American (Hong Kong); Singapore Cricket. Office: Resources Consol 220 Montgomerey St Suite 688 San Francisco CA 94104

LEE, MARGARET ANNE, psychotherapist; b. Scribner, Nebr., Nov. 23, 1930; d. William Christian and Caroline Bertha (Benner) Joens; m. Robert Kelly Lee, May 21, 1950 (div. 1971); children: Lawrence Robert, James Kelly, Daniel Richard. AA, Napa Coll., 1949; student, U. Calif., Berkeley, 1949-50; BA, Calif. State Coll., Sonoma, 1975; MSW, Calif. State U., Sacramento, 1977. Lic. clin. social worker, marriage and family counselor, Calif. Columnist/stringer Napa (Calif.) Register, 1946-50; eligibility worker, supr. Napa County Dept. Social Services, 1968-75; instr. Napa Valley Community Coll., 1978-83; practice psychotherapy Napa, 1977—. Trustee Napa Valley Community Coll., 1983—, v.p. bd. trustees, 1984-85, pres. bd. trustees, 1985-86; bd. dirs. Napa County Council Econ. Opportunity, 1984-85, Napa Chpt. March of Dimes, 1957-71. Recipient Fresh Start award Self mag., 1983. Mem. Nat. Assn. Social Workers (bd. dirs. 1982-85), Mental Health Assn. Napa County, Calif. Assn. Physically and Handicapped, Women's Polit. Caucus. Democrat. Lutheran. Lodge: Soroptimists. Home: 15 Camilla Dr Napa CA 94558 Office: Napa Valley Ctr 1100 Trancas PO Box 2099 Napa CA 94558

LEE, MARTIN LAURENCE, pharmaceutical company executive; b. London, June 8, 1953; came to U.S., 1957, naturalized, 1962; s. Victor and Edie (Lefcovitch) L.; m. Marilyn Ina Arbetman, Dec. 12, 1976; children—Elliot, Daniel. B.A., UCLA, 1974, M.S. in Biostats., 1976, Ph.D. in Biostats., 1979. Statistician dept. epidemiology UCLA, 1975; sr. statistician dept. gastroenterology Sch. Medicine, UCLA, 1976-79; research biostatistician Hollywood Presbyn. Med. Ctr., Los Angeles, 1978-79; sr. biostatistician Hyland Therapeutics div. Travenol Labs., Inc., Los Angeles, 1979-81, mgr. clin. devel., 1984-86, assoc. dir. med. affairs, 1986—; pres. Internat. Quantitative Cons., 1986—; lectr. stats. Calif. State U.-Los Angeles, Calif. State U.-Northridge, 1976-79; vis. lectr. biostats. UCLA, 1979—. Recipient Disting. alumni award UCLA Sch. Pub. Health Alumni Assn., 1979. Regents' fellow, 1977-79; USPHS trainee, 1976-77. Fellow Royal Statis. Soc.; mem. Am. Statis. Assn., Biometric Soc., Soc. for Clin. Trials, Am. Heart Assn., Math. assn. Am., Am. Pub. Health Assn., Internat. Soc. for Clin. Biostats., Phi Beta Kappa. Democrat. Jewish. Home: 5525 Bellaire Ave North Hollywood CA 91607 Office: 444 W Glenoaks Blvd Glendale CA 91202

LEE, MAYA, clinical psychologist, educator; b. Chgo., Sept. 30, 1937; d. Philip Bruno and Renee (Roll) Dispensa; children—Barbara Pauline, Elizabeth Renee, Renee Marie Foss, Kelly Anne. B.A., Gov.'s State U., 1974, M.A., 1975; Ph.D., U.S. Internat. U., 1978. Lic. psychologist, Calif. Intern, San Bernardino County Mental Health (Calif.), 1977-78, psychologist, 1978-80; pvt. practice psychology, San Bernardino, 1980—. Gov.'s State U. grantee, 1973, 74. Mem. Am. Psychol. Assn., Inland Empire Psychol. Assn., NOW. Democrat. Jewish. Home: 1797 N Arrowhead San Bernardino CA 92405

LEE, MICHAEL DAVID, television and motion picture producer; b. San Francisco, Dec. 30, 1950; s. John Git and Ruth Marian (Chow) Wong. B.A. in Broadcast Communications, San Francisco State U., 1973; M.B.A. in Mgmt., Golden Gate U., 1983. Lic. real estate broker, Calif.; lic. life and disability agt., Calif. Producer ABC-TV, San Francisco, 1975-77; pres. Media Inc., San Francisco, 1977—; pres. On-Air Auctions Inc., San Francisco, 1981—; owner Red Carpet House Realty, San Bruno, Calif., 1986—; pres. Ind. Video News Inc., San Francisco, 1981—; gen. mgr. Cable TV Channel 8, Pacifica, Calif.; producer, dir., host Sta. KVCR-TV, San Bernardino, Calif., 1983-84; tchr. TV dept. Coll. of San Mateo (Calif.); prof. Golden Gate U., San Francisco, Los Altos and Los Angeles; mem. adv. bd. Gateway Savs. and Loan Assn. Bd. dirs. Asian Bus. League. Mem. Screen Actors Guild, AFTRA, Nat. Acad. TV Arts and Scis. Clubs: Mensa, Commonwealth (Calif.). Author: Success-A Guide to Creating Your Own, 1982; movie producer The Kill Squad, 1981; movie co-producer The Clonus Horror, 1979. Office: Red Carpet House Realty 297 El Camino Real San Bruno CA 94066

LEE, PAMELA ANNE, Corporate accounting manager; b. San Francisco, May 30, 1960; d. Larry D. and Alice Mary (Reece) L. B.A. in Bus., San Francisco State U., 1981. CPA, Calif. Typist, bookkeeper, tax acct. James G. Woo, CPA, San Francisco, 1979-85; tutor bus. math. and statistics San Francisco State U., 1979-80; teller to ops. officer Gibraltar Savs. and Loan, San Francisco, 1978-81; sr. acct. Price Waterhouse, San Francisco, 1981-86; corp. acctg. mgr. First Nationwide Bank, Daly City, Calif., 1986—; acctg. cons. New Performance Gallery, San Francisco, 1985, San Francisco Chamber Orch., 1986. Mem. Am. Inst. CPA's, Calif. Soc. CPA's, Nat. Assn. Female Execs., Nat. Assn. Asian-Am. CPA's (bd. dirs. 1986, news editor 1987). Republican. Avocations: Reading; music; travel. Office: First Nationwide Bank 455 Hickey Blvd Daly City CA 94015

LEE, PHILLIP DUKEAL KWAIYUEN, pediatric endocrinologist, researcher; b. Honolulu, May 29, 1956; s. Dukeal and Evelyn (Pang) L. BS in Medicine, Northwestern U., 1978, MD, 1980. Diplomate Am. Bd. Pediatrics. Intern U. Tex. Med. Br., Galveston, 1980-81; resident in pediatric Children's Meml. Hosp., Northwestern U., Chgo., 1981-83; postdoctoral fellow Stanford (Calif.) U., 1983-86; pediatric endocrinologist The Children's Hosp., Denver, 1986—; mem. staff Barbara Davis Ctr. for Childhood Diabetes, Denver, 1986—; asst. prof. pediatrics U. Colo. Health Scis. Ctr., 1986—. Juvenile Diabetes Found. fellow, 1985-86. Mem. AMA, The Endocrine Soc., Am. Diabetes Assn., Am. Fedn. Clin. Research, Tissue Culture Assn. Home: 3125 E 6th Ave Denver CO 80206 Office: The Children's Hosp 1056 E. 19th Ave Denver CO 80218-1088

LEE, POLLY JAE STEAD (PALI KEALOHALANI KI LOA LEE), librarian, writer; b. Toledo, Nov. 26, 1929; d. Jonathan Everett Wheeler and Ona Katherine (Grunder) Stead; m. Richard H.W. Lee, Apr. 7, 1945 (div. 1978); children: Lani Kay Lee, Karin Lee Robinson, Ona Lee Yee, Laurie Lee Lam, Robin Louise Lee Halbert. Catologuer and processor U.S. Army Air Force, 1945-46; with U.S. Weather Bur. Film Library, New Orleans, 1948-50, FBI, Wright-Patterson AFB, Dayton, Ohio, 1952, Ohio Wholesale Winedealers, Columbus, Ohio, 1956-58, Coll. Engring., Ohio State U., Columbus, 1959; writer tech. manual Annie Whittenmeyer Home, Davenport, Iowa, 1960; with Grand Rapids (Mich.) Pub. Library, 1961-62; dir. Waterford (Mich.) Twp. Libraries, 1962-64; acquisition librarian Pontiac (Mich.) Pub. Libraries, 1965-71, dir. East Side br., 1971-73; librarian Bishop Mus., Honolulu, 1975—. Author: Mary Dyer, Child of Light, 1973; Giant: Pictorial History of the Human Colossus, 1973; History of the Kaneohe Bay Area, 1976; Na Po Makole--Tales of the Night Rainbow, 1981, 2d edit., 86, Mo'olelo O Na Pohu Kaina, 1983; contbr. articles to Aloha and Honolulu mags., other pubs. Chmn. Oakland County br. Multiple Sclerosis Soc., 1972-73, co-chmn. Pontiac com. of Mich. area bd., 1972-73; sec. Ohana o Kokua, 1979-83, Paia-Willis Ohana, 1982—; bd. dirs. Detroit Multiple Sclerosis Soc., 1971; mem. Mich. area bd. Am. Friends Service com., 1961-69. Recipient Mother of Yr. award Quad City Bus. Men, Davenport, Iowa, and Moline, Ill., 1960. Mem. Internat. Platform Assn. Office: Atherton Halau Bishop Mus PO Box 19000-A Honolulu HI 96819

LEE, QWIHEE PARK, plant physiologist; b. Republic of Korea, Mar. 1, 1941; d. Yong-sik and Soon-duk (Paik) Park; m. Ick-whan Lee, May 20, 1965; children: Tina, Amy, Benjamin. MS, Seoul Nat. U., Republic of Korea, 1965; PhD, U. Minn., 1973. Head dept. plant physiology Korea Ginseng and Tobacco Inst., Seoul, 1980-82; instr. Sogang U., Seoul, 1981, Seoul Women's U., 1981; research assoc. U. Wash., Seattle, 1975-79, 86—. Exec. dir. Korean Community Couseling Ctr., Seattle, 1983-86. Named one of 20 Prominent Asian Women in Wash. State, Chinese Post Seattle, 1986. Mem. AAAS. Buddhist. Home: 10723 Bartlett Ave NE Seattle WA 98125 Office: U Wash Ctr Bioengring RJ-30 1959 Northeast Pacific Seattle WA 98195

LEE, RANDALL BRUCE, association executive; b. Berwyn, Ill., Oct. 30, 1946; s. Oswen Grelly and Kathryn Jeannette (Rietema) L.; student U. Ga., 1964-65, Community Coll. Denver, 1970-71; m. Mary Catherine Otte Myers, Oct. 25, 1980; children—Christy Lynn, Rhett Brian. With engring. support services dept. Western Electric Co., Aurora, Colo., 1966-71; mng. editor Communications, also TV Communications, Englewood, Colo., 1971-73; asst. exec. dir. Am. Soc. Bariatric Physicians, Englewood, 1973-76, exec. dir., 1976-84; mng. editor Obesity and Bariatric Medicine, 1973-84; adminstr. Obesity Found., 1980-84; exec. v.p. Internat. Acad. Bariatric Medicine, Inc., 1985—. Del., Colo. Republican Conv., 1976; Rep. precinct committeeman, 1976-80. Served with USAR, 1966-68; Vietnam. Recipient Presdl. citation Am. Soc. Bariatric Physicians, 1979. Mem. Am. Soc. Assn. Execs., Colo. Soc. Assn. Execs. (dir. 1981, sec.-treas. 1982-83, v.p. 1983-84), Nat. Model R.R. Assn. (Vol. award 1980; conv. chmn. 1977), Denver HO Model R.R. Club (dir. 1982—, sec. 1983—), Am. Assn. Med. Soc. Execs. Office: PO Box 2888 Littleton CO 80161

LEE, ROBERT ANDREW, librarian; b. Washington, Dec. 7, 1923; s. Frederic Edward and Edna (Stewart) L. BA in English, Oberlin Coll., 1947; MLS, U. So. Calif., 1966. Jr. cataloger Columbia U. Law Library, 1950-51; reference librarian N.Y. Daily Mirror, 1952-54; researcher for Dore Schary MGM, Culver City, Calif., 1955; with Universal City Studios, Calif., 1955—, research librarian, 1960-69, head research dept., 1969—. Contbr. articles to profl. jours. Served with AUS, 1943-46. Decorated Bronze Star with oak leaf cluster. Mem. Acad. Motion Picture Arts and Scis. (gov. 1973-75), Acad. TV Arts and Scis., Am. Film Inst., Los Angeles Internat. Film Exposition, Spl. Libraries Assn. Home: 2212 Cahuenga Blvd Apt 104 Los Angeles CA 90068 Office: Universal City Studios 100 Universal City Plaza Universal City CA 91608

LEE, ROBERT DEEMER, political science educator; b. Colorado Springs, Colo., June 4, 1941; s. Deemer and Everyld (Anderson) L; m. Susan A. Ashley, Sept. 9, 1967; children: William, Matthew. BA, Carleton Coll., 1963; MS, Columbia U., 1965, MA, 1968, PhD, 1972. Reporter Mpls. Tribune, 1963-65; free-lance journalist Africa, 1965-66; asst. prof. polit. sci. Colo. Coll., Colo. Springs, 1971-79, assoc. prof., 1979—. Pulitzer Traveling fellow Columbia Sch. Journalism, 1965; William P. Gray fellow Fgn. Correspondence Overseas Press Club N.Y., 1965-66. Mem. Am. Polit. Sci. Assn., Middle East Studies Assn., Middle East Inst., Phi Beta Kappa. Democrat. Home: 1425 N Tejon St Colorado Springs CO 80907 Office: Colorado College Dept Polit Sci Colorado Springs CO 80903

LEE, SHAW MING, mechanical engineer; b. Taichung, Republic of China, Feb. 22, 1951; came to U.S., 1974; s. Ti-chiang and Li (Kao) L.; m. Diane Tsou-ming Liu, July 20, 1974; children: Pamela Lee. BS, Nat. Taiwan U., Taipei, Republic of China, 1972; MS, Yale U., 1975; PhD, MIT, 1978. Mem. tech. staff Bell Telephone Labs., North Andover, Mass., 1978-79; staff scientist Ciba-Geigy Corp., Ardsley, N.Y., 1979-83; sr. staff scientist Ciba-Geigy Corp., Fountain Valley, Calif., 1983—. Contbr. articles to profl. jours. Served to 2d lt. Chinese Army, 1972-74. Fellow Yale U., 1974-75, Monsanto Co. MIT, 1975-77, Rohmand Haas Co. MIT, 1977, Johnson and Johnson Co. MIT, 1978. Mem. ASME (assoc.), Am. Soc. Metals, Soc. Advancement Material and Process Engring. Republican. Avocations: hiking, camping, photography. Office: Ciba-Geigy Corp 10910 Talbert Ave Fountain Valley CA 92708

LEE, STANLEY TAK, dentist; b. Chungshan, Canton, China, Mar. 1, 1946; s. Man Hoy and Bo Yuk (Lau) L.; m. Rita Sook Chin, July 3, 1976; children—Winnie Sita, Jennie Wanda. A.S., City Coll. San Francisco, 1971; B.S., U. Calif.-Berkeley, 1973; D.D.S., Loma Linda U., 1977. Gen. practice dentistry, San Jose, Calif., 1978—. Mem. ADA, Calif. Dental Assn., Santa Clara County Dental Soc. (dental care com. 1983-84), Am. Endodontic Soc., Chungshan Benevolence Assn., Chinese Cultural Assn., Alpha Gamma Sigma, Beta Gamma Sigma. Office: Lee Dental Ctr 1832 Tully San Jose CA 95136 Office: 3 Star Dental Center 2139 Tully Rd San Jose CA 95122

LEE, STUART MILTON, materials scientist, consultant; b. N.Y.C., Apr. 14, 1920; s. Herman and Bertha (Horowitz) L.; m. Miriam Drucker, Apr. 28, 1948; children: Gary, Scott, Randy. BS, L.I. U., 1941; MS, U. Nev., 1947; PhD, Fla. State U., 1953. Research chemist Aerojet-Gen., Azusa, Calif., 1959-61; mgr., chem. research and devel. Electro-optical systems, Pasadena, Calif., 1961-64; sr. tech. specialist Rockwell Internat., Anaheim, Calif., 1964-71; sr. staff scientist Ford Aerospace and Communications, Palo Alto, Calif., 1971-85; cons. Palo Alto, 1985—. Editor-in-chief: Technomic Pub. Co. jour., Lancaster, Pa., 1985—, VCH Publishers, 1987; cons. Material and Design jour., London, 1981—; contbr. author or editor 13 books; contbr. articles to profl. jours.; patentee in field. Reasearch corp. fellow Fla. State U., 1950-52. Fellow Soc. Adv. Material and Process Engring. (editor jour. 1979—, meritorious bronze award, 1982); mem. Am. Chem. Soc. (sr.). Home and Office: 3718 Cass Way Palo Alto CA 94306

LEE, THOMAS WAY, obstetrician, gynecologist; b. Bhamo, Burma, Dec. 20, 1943; s. Way Ywan and Kim Ho (Kyang) L.; came to U.S., 1968, naturalized, 1973; I.Sc., U. Rangoon (Burma), 1962; M.B., B.S., Inst. of Medicine, Rangoon, 1967; m. Rita Chan, May 10, 1968; children—Patrician, Jefferey. Cert. Am. Bd. Ob-Gyn. Intern, Rangoon Gen. Hosp., 1967-68, St. Mary's Hosp., Phila., 1968-69; resident in ob-gyn Milard Fillmore Hosp., Buffalo, 1969-72; practice medicine specializing in ob-gyn, Easton, Pa., 1972-73, Upland, Calif., 1973—; mem. staffs San Antonio, Drs., Ontario (Calif.) Community hosps., Covina Valley Hosp., West Covina, Calif.; asst. clin. instr. SUNY, Buffalo, 1970-72; teaching staff dept. ob-gyn San Bernardino County (Calif.) Med. Center, 1976—. Fellow Am. Coll. Obstetricians and Gynecologists, ACS, Internat. Coll. Surgeons; mem. AMA, Am. Fertility Soc., Am. Assn. Gynecologic Laparoscopists, Calif. Med. Assn., San Bernardino County Med. Soc. (pres. 1984-85), Burma Med. Soc. (pres. 1985-86), San Bernardino-Riverside Obstetrics and Gynecology Soc. Contbr. articles to Jour. Reproductive Medicine. Office: 7388 Carmelian St Suite B Rancho Cucamonga CA 91730

LEE, TIEN CHANG, geophysicist; b. Nantou, Republic of China, July 1, 1943; came to U.S., 1967; s. Chen-Chou and Kuan (Shih) L.; m. Zora M. Lee, Dec. 22, 1969; children: Cin-Ty, Cin-Young. BS in Geology, Nat. Taiwan U., Taipei, Republic of China, 1965; MS in Geology, U. Idaho, 1969; PhD in Geol. Sci., U. So. Calif., Los Angeles, 1973. Registered profl. geophysicist, geologist. Postdoctoral fellow Woods Hole (Mass.) Oceanog. Inst., 1973-74; assoc. prof. geophysics U. Calif., Riverside, 1974—. Contbr. articles to profl. jours. Mem. Am. Geophys. Union, Soc. Exploration Geophysicists, Seismol. Soc. Am. Republican. Office: U Calif Dept Earth Sci University Ave Riverside CA 92521

LEE, VIN JANG THOMAS, financial company executive, physicist; b. Honan Province, China, Feb. 14, 1937; came to U.S., 1958; s. Tsin-Yin and Hwa-Neu (Mar) L.; m. Y.T. Margaret Nee, Dec. 29, 1963; 1 child, Maxwell. Diploma in ChemE, Ordnance Engring. Coll., Taipei, Taiwan, 1955; MSChemE, U. Notre Dame, 1959; PhD, U. Mich., 1963. Assoc. prof. chem. engring. U. Mo., Columbia, 1965-74; pres. Econo Trading Co., Santa Monica, Calif., 1975-80, Cyberdyne Inc., Santa Monica, 1980—; vis. prof. catalysis and physical chemistry UCLA, 1972-73. Contbr. numerous articles to sci. jours. Mem. Sigma Xi. Lodge: Masons. Avocations: physics, natural philosophy. Office: Cyberdyne Inc 1045 Ocean Ave Suite 2 Santa Monica CA 90403

LEE, WANDA ANN, personel administrator; b. Phila., May 15, 1941; d. Harry Eugene Carlsson and Anna Pearl (Hulse) Seidler; m. E.T. Megules, Dec. 12, 1959 (div. Feb. 1967); m. William D. Lee, Dec. 28, 1973; children: Penny Lee, Dawn M. BS in Orgnl. Behavior, U. San Francisco, 1984, postgrad., 1986—. Purchasing agt. Tri-Metals Co., Santa Fe Springs, Calif., 1966-69; employee relations adminstr. Super-Temp Co., Santa Fe Springs, 1969-74; personnel adminstrn. mgr. Winchell's Donuts, La Mirada, Calif., 1974-77; v.p. human resources and adminstrv. services Proficient Food Co., Irvine, Calif., 1977—; Bd. dirs. Personnel Accreditation Inst., Washington. Mem. Personnel and Indsl. Relations Assn. (pres. 1985-86), Am. Soc. Personnel Adminstrn. (nat. com. 1983-86, regional v.p. 1986, area v.p. 1987), Merchants and Mfrs. (legis. task force 1986—, bd. dirs. 1986). Republican. Avocations: golf, gardening. Office: Proficient Food Co 17872 Cartwright Rd Irvine CA 92714

LEE, WILLIAM WEI, organic chemist, researcher; b. San Francisco, May 17, 1923; s. Jun Wong and Chung-Ngan (Fong) L.; m. Pauline Lin Lee, June 29, 1947; children: Peter Hong, Kerwin Jong, Roderick Mun. BS, U. Calif., 1947; PhD, U. Minn., 1952. Jr. chemist Shell Devel. Co., Emeryville, Calif., 1947-48; teaching asst. U. Minn., Mpls., 1948-51; organic chemist, researcher Monsanto Chem. Co., Dayton, Ohio, 1952-54; organic chemist SRI Internat., Menlo Park, Calif., 1954-77, dir. synthetic cancer drugs program, 1977—. Co-author sci. pubs.; patentee in field. Cub master, asst. scoutmaster, com. man Boy Scouts Am., Palo Alto, 1958-64. Served to sgt. C.E., U.S. Army, 1943-46, ETO. DuPont fellow U. Minn., 1951-52. Mem. Am. Chem. Soc., N.Y. Acad. Scis., Radiation Research Soc. Am., Sigma Xi. Republican. Methodist. Home: 991 California Ave Palo Alto CA 94303 Office: SRI Internat 333 Ravenswood Ave Menlo Park CA 94025

LEE, YONG TSUN, lawyer; b. Shanghai, China, June 12, 1952; s. Kwong Cheong and Ching So (Lee) L.; came to U.S., 1970, naturalized, 1973; student Orange Coast Coll., 1971-72, So. Calif. Coll., 1970-71; J.D. and B.S. in Law, Am. Coll. Law, 1978; m. Josephine Suen; children—Mia, Erin, Jennifer, Christin, Candice, Robin. Lab. instr. math. Orange Coast Coll., Costa Mesa, Calif., 1971; mgr. Shanghai Pine Garden, Balboa Island, 1973-78; admitted to Calif. bar, 1978; practice law, Costa Mesa, 1979—. Mem. Am. Bar Assn., Orange County Bar Assn. Democrat. Roman Catholic. Office: 628 W 19 St Costa Mesa CA 92627

LEE, YOSUP, business administration educator; b. Seoul, Republic of Korea, May 4, 1948; came to U.S., 1976; s. Kyoung Jai and Moonchae (Noh) L.; m. Okhee Lee, Aug. 15, 1976; children: Grace, Joseph. BA, Seoul Nat. U., 1971; MBA, U. Santa Clara, 1976; PhD, Claremont Grad. Sch., 1982. Prof. Azusa (Calif.) Pacific U., 1981—. Home: 819 W Pepperdine Ln Claremont CA 91711 Office: Azusa Pacific U Alosta and Citrus Azusa CA 91702

LEE, YUAN T(SEH), chemistry educator, consultant; b. Hsinchu, Taiwan, China, Nov. 29, 1936; came to U.S., 1962, naturalized, 1974; s. Tsefan and Pei (Tasi) L.; m. Bernice Wu, June 28, 1963; children: Ted, Sidney, Charlotte. BS, Nat. Taiwan U., 1959; MS, Nat. Tsinghua U., Taiwan, 1961; PhD, U. Calif., Berkeley, 1965. From asst. prof. to prof. chemistry U. Chgo., 1968-74; prof. U. Calif., Berkeley, 1974—, also prin. investigator Lawrence Berkeley Lab. Contbr. numerous articles on chem. physics to profl. jours. Recipient Nobel Prize in Chemistry, 1986, Ernest O. Lawrence award Dept. Energy, 1981, Nat. Medal of Sci., 1986, Peter Debye award for Phys. Chemistry, 1986; fellow Alfred P. Sloan, 1969-71, John Simon Guggenheim, 1976-77; Camille and Henry Dreyfus Found. Tchr. scholar, 1971-74. Fellow Am. Phys. Soc.; mem. Am. Acad. Arts and Scis., Am. Chem. Soc., AAAS, Nat. Acad. Scis. Office: U Calif Dept Chemistry Berkeley CA 94720

LEEB, CHARLES SAMUEL, clinical psychologist, consultant; b. San Francisco, July 18, 1945; s. Sidney Herbert and Dorothy Barbara (Fishstrom) L.; m. Storme Lynn Gilkey, Apr. 28, 1984; 1 child, Morgan Evan. BA in Psychology, U. Calif.-Davis, 1967; M.S. in Counseling and Guidance, San Diego State U., 1970; Ph.D. in Edn. and Psychology, Claremont Grad. Sch., 1973. Counselor Mayor's Com. on Unemployment, San Diego, 1969-70, VA, San Diego State Coll., 1969-70, Claremont Coll. Counseling Ctr., 1971-72; assoc. Steven Fahrion, Claremont, Calif., 1973-75; assoc. So. Regional Dir. Mental Retardation Ctr., Las Vegas, Nev., 1976-77; pvt. practice, Las Vegas, 1978-79;dir. biofeedback and athletics Menninger Found., Topeka, 1979-82, dir. children's div. biofeedback and psychophysiology ctr. The Menninger Found., 1979-82; dir. of psychol. services Harlem Hosp., 1986—; chief psychologist Raleigh Hills Hosp., San Gabriel, Calif., 1982-83; pvt. practice, Claremont, Calif., 1982—; lectr. in field. Contbr. articles to profl. jours. Mem. AAAS, Biofeedback Soc. Am., Nev. Psychol. Assn. Office: 250 W 1st St Claremont CA 91711

LEECING, WALDEN ALBERT, educator; b. Glendale, Calif., Sept. 6, 1932; s. Horace Walden and Leona Belle (Dudek) L.; m. Elizabeth Joan Miller, Aug. 16, 1958; children: Jeffrey Scott, Brian Walden. BA, U. Redlands, 1954; MA, Stanford U., 1956, postgrad., 1973—. Tchr. El Rancho High Sch., Whittier, Calif., 1957-59, Santa Ana (Calif.) High Sch., 1959-66; from instr. to assoc. prof. lang. arts Chabot Coll., Hayward, Calif., 1967-86, prof., 1986—; chmn. speech dept. Author: The Santa Ana Community Players: 1920-27, 1956, (with James Armstrong) The Curious Eye, 1970, Viva la Causa! a Historiographic Survey of Chicano Studies Programs at Five Bay Area Colleges and Universities. V.p. Santa Ana Community Players, 1964-66; asst. organist San Ramon Valley Ch., 1968—. Mem. Nat. Council English Tchrs., AAUP, No. Calif. Forensics Assn., Am. Guild Organists, Stanford Alumni Assn. (life). KRON-NBC Viewer Adv. Council. Republican. Congregationalist. Home: 697 Paradise Valley Ct S Crow Canyon Country Club Danville CA 94526 Office: Chabot Coll 25555 Hesperian Blvd Hayward CA 94545

LEED, ROGER MELVIN, lawyer; b. Green Bay, Wis., July 15, 1939; s. Melvin John and Veronica Sarah (Flaherty) L.; m. Jean Ann Burg, Mar. 1967; children: Craig, Maren, Jennifer. AB, Harvard U., 1961; JD cum laude, U. Mich., 1967. Bar: Wash. 1967, U.S. Dist. Ct. (we. dist.) Wash. 1968, U.S. Ct. Appeals (9th cir.) 1969, U.S. Supreme Ct. 1973. Law clk. Wash. Supreme Ct., Olympia, 1967-68; assoc. Perkins, Coie et al, Seattle, 1968-70; ptnr. Schroeter, Goldmark et al, Seattle, 1970-77; sole practice Seattle, 1977—; adj. prof. law U. Puget Sound, Tacoma, 1974-77. Editor Shorelines Mgmt., the Wash. Experience, 1972. Pres. Cen. Seattle Community Council Fedn., 1972, Wash. Environ. Council, 1980-82; bd. dirs. Allied Arts, Seattle, 1971-72, Downtown Human Services Council, Seattle, 1985—. Mem. Wash. State Bar Assn., Seattle-King County Bar Assn., Assn.

Trial Lawyers Am. Clubs: Met. Dem., Washington Athletic, Corinithian Yacht. Office: 1411 4th Ave Suite 520 Seattle WA 98101

LEEDS-HORWITZ, SUSAN BETH, speech-language pathology educator; b. Los Angeles, Mar. 14, 1950; d. Henry Herbert and Lee (Weiss) Leeds; m. Stanley Martin Horwitz, Nov. 28, 1975; 1 child, Brian David. BA, Calif. State U., Northridge, 1971; MEd, U. S.C., 1973; adminstrv. credential, U. LaVerne, 1984. Itinerant speech pathologist Los Angeles City Schs., 1973-74; sever lang. disorders tchr. Los Angeles County Bd. Edn., Downey, Calif., 1974—; tchr. on spl. assignment Santa Clarita Valley Spl. Edn. Local Plan Area, Newhall, Calif., 1986—. Active Santa Clarita Valley Spl. Edn. PTA, Newhall, 1984—. Mem. Am. Speech-Lang.-Hearing Assn. (cert.), Down Syndrome Congress, San Fernando Valley Panhellenic (rep. 1976—), Delta Kappa Gamma, Alpha Xi Delta (Delta Rho chpt. dir. 1978—, Edna Epperson Brinkman award, 1985). Office: Santa Clarita Valley SELPA Valley View Annex 19420 W Sierra Estates Dr Newhall CA 91321

LEEPER, RAMON JOE, physicist; b. Princeton, Mo., Apr. 1, 1948; s. Joe Edd and Jeanne (Gaul) L.; m. Sumiko Yasuda, Dec. 21, 1976; 1 son, Joe Eric. B.S., MIT, 1970; Ph.D., Iowa State U., 1975. Research assoc. Ames Lab., U.S. Dept. Energy, Iowa, 1975-76; supr. diagnostics div. Sandia Nat. Labs., Albuquerque, 1976—; guest scientist Argonne Nat. Lab., Ill., 1971-76; invited lectr. NATO Advanced Study Inst., Italy, summer 1983. Contbr. articles to profl. jours. Recipient Outstanding Teaching award Iowa State U., 1973; NDEA fellow, 1971-73. Mem. Am. Phys. Soc., IEEE (session chmn. 1984), Sigma Xi. Republican. Home: 6905 Rosewood Rd NE Albuquerque NM 87111 Office: Sandia Nat Labs Diagnostics Div 1234 Albuquerque NM 87185

LEESE, DAVID, business educator, lawyer; b. Detroit, Jan. 5, 1944; s. Sydney Elmer and Marcella (Taylor) L.; m. Judith Anne Parker, June 7, 1969; children: Bradley, Cynthia. BA in Philosophy, Amherst Coll., 1965; JD, Northwestern U., 1968; MA in English and Am. Lit., Brandeis U., 1972, PhD in English and Am. Lit., 1975; MBA, Calif. State U., Northridge, 1985. Instr. Brandeis U., Waltham, Mass., 1972-74; asst. prof. bus. Ariz. State U., Tempe, 1974-75; prof. Mt. St. Mary's Coll., Los Angeles, 1975—; pres. Realcorps Investment Group, Agoura, Calif., 1979—. Elder Christian Ch. of Hills, Agoura, 1976—. Fellow Brandeis U., 1970; named Prof. of Yr. Mt. St. Mary's Coll., 1980. Mem. AAUP, Western Assn. Collegiate Schs. of Bus., Calif. Bar Assn., Calif. Bd. Realtors. Home: 30403 Passageway Pl Agoura CA 91301 Office: Mt St Marys Coll 12001 Chalon Rd Los Angeles CA 90049

LEFEBVRE, PEGGY ANDERSON, advertising executive; b. Springfield, Mo., Dec. 2, 1951; d. Paul William and Norma Jean (Turk) Anderson; m. Donald E. Lefebvre, July 25, 1980. BFA, U. Ill., 1974. Art. dir. Bell & Howell, Salt Lake City, 1977-80; owner, creative dir. Lefebvre Advt., Anaheim, Calif., 1980—. One woman shows Ward Gallery, Chgo., 1974, Atrium Gallery, Salt Lake City, 1976. Republican. Office: Lefebvre Advt 1092 N Tustin Anaheim CA 92807

LEFEBVRE D'ARGENCÉ, RENÉ-YVON MARIE MARC, museum director emeritus; b. Plouescat, France, Aug. 21, 1928; came to U.S., 1962; s. Marc and Andrée (Thierry) L. d'A.; m. Ritva Pelanne, Nov. 2, 1955; children—Chantal, Yann, Luc. Licencié-ès-Lettres, Sorbonne, Paris, 1952; Breveté, de l'Ecole Nationale des Langues Orientales Vivantes, Paris; Breveté de Chinese, 1950, Breveté de Japanese, 1951, Breveté de Finnish, 1952; Ph.D. (hon.), Chinese Acad., Taiwan, 1969. Curator Musée Cernuschi, Paris, 1953, Blanchard de la Brosse Mus., Saigon, 1954-58, Louis Finot Mus., Hanoi, N. Vietnam, 1954-58; prof. art history U. Calif., Berkeley, 1962-65; curator Asiatic collections M.H. de Young Meml. Mus., San Francisco, 1964; dir. Avery Brundage Found., San Francisco, 1965-68; dir., chief curator Asian Art Mus., San Francisco, 1969-85; writer, cataloguer Avery Brundage Collection, 1985—; Pres. French-Am. Internat. Sch., San Francisco, 1975-79; founder, bd. dirs. Ecole Française, San Francisco, 1967—; bd. dirs. Alliance Française, San Francisco, 1974-77, Asian Art Found., San Francisco, 1978-85, Inst. Sino-Am. Studies, 1981—. Author: Chinese Jades in the Avery Brundage Collection, 1972, Chang Dai-chien, 1972, The Hans Popper Collection, 1973, Avery Brundage Collection: Chinese, Korean, and Japanese Sculpture, 1974, A Decade of Collecting, 1976, Bronze Vessels of Ancient China in the Avery Brundage Collection, 1977; gen. editor: Asian Art Museum and University Collections in the San Francisco Bay Area, 1977, 5, 000 Years of Korean Art, 1979, Treasures from the Shanghai Museum—6, 000 Years of Chinese Art, 1983, Japanese Art in the Avery Brundage Collection, 1987. Bd. dirs. Osaka-San Francisco, Seoul-San Francisco and Shanghai-San Francisco sister city coms. Decorated Order Cultural Merit (Korea); chevalier de l'Etoile du Nord Sweden; chevalier Legion of Honor, chevalier de l'Ordre National du Mérite, Médaille de la Reconnaissance Française, Croix du Combattant Volontaire de la Résistance (France); recipient Order of Merit, Avery Brundage Found., 1968; Quai d'Orsay grantee Taiwan and Japan, 1959-61. Mem. Sociedad Asiatica de la Argentina, Soc. Asian Art (adv. com. 1972—). Home and Office: 16 Midhill Dr Mill Valley CA 94941

LEFEVRE, GEORGE, JR., biology educator; b. Columbia, Mo., Sept. 13, 1917; s. George and Julia (Faris) L.; m. Elsbeth Victoria Wahlin, June 11, 1943 (dec.); children—George W., Julia L. Phelps, Kathryn E. Mudgett; m. Dora Elizabeth Tincher, Dec. 16, 1972. A.B., U. Mo., 1937, M.A., 1939, Ph.D., 1949. Biologist Oak Ridge Nat. Lab., 1946-47; asst. prof. U. Utah, Salt Lake City, 1949-54; asso. prof. U. Utah, 1954-56; program dir. genetic biology NSF, Washington, 1956-59; dir. biol. labs. Harvard, 1959-65; prof. San Fernando Valley State Coll. (now Calif. State U.), Northridge, 1965-84; emeritus prof. San Fernando Valley State Coll. (now Calif. State U.), 1984—, chmn. dept. biology, 1965-79; mem. genetics study sect. NIH, 1962-66, 79-83. Editor: Genetics, 1976-81. Served with C.E., AUS, 1942-46. Mem. Genetics Soc. Am. (treas. 1972-75), Phi Beta Kappa, Sigma Xi, Beta Theta Pi. Home: 10132 Eton Ave Chatsworth CA 91311 Office: Biology Dept Calif State U Northridge CA 91330

LEFEVRE, GREG (LOUIS), news correspondent; b. Los Angeles, Jan. 28, 1947; s. Robert Bazille and Anna Marie (Violé) L.; m. Mary Deborah Bottoms, July 10, 1971. AA, Valley Coll., 1970; BS, San Diego State U., 1972, postgrad. Asst. news dir. Sta. KDEO-TV, San Diego, 1971-73; reporter Sta. KFMB-TV, San Diego, 1973-76; sr. reporter Sta. KDFW-TV, Dallas, 1976-81; news dir. Sta. KSEE-TV, Fresno, Calif., 1981-83; corr. Cable News Network, San Francisco, 1983—. Mem. AP Broadcasters (bd. dirs. 1981—), Soc. Profl. Journalists (pres. 1979-81), Radio and TV News Dirs. Assn. Club: Dallas Press (v.p. 1978-81). Office: Cable News Network 50 California St Suite 835 San Francisco CA 94044

LEFEVRE, MAURICE EDWARD, electrical engineer; b. Spry, Utah, Feb. 7, 1934; s. Peter and Jean (Wood) LeF.; m. Sharon Laree Parkinson, Dec. 22, 1961; children: Verda Jean, Wendy Kaye, Clayton Maurice, Shane Edward, Carla Sue. BSEE, Utah State U., 1964. Elec. engr. The Boeing Co., Seattle, 1964—. Scoutmaster Boy Scouts Am., Seattle, 1978-83, com. chmn., 1983—; br. clk. Mormon Ch., Seattle, 1986—. Served with USAF, 1955-58. Mem. Seattle Profl. Engrs. and Employees Assn. (rep. 1970-85, recruiting award 1971). Republican. Avocations: watch and intricate equipment repair, auto mechanics. Home: 14004 33d Ave S Seattle WA 98168 Office: Boeing Aerospace Co 20403 68th Ave S Kent WA 98032

LEFF, BARRY JOSEPH, electronics company executive; b. Heidelberg, Fed. Republic Germany, Oct. 28, 1955; s. Michael Irwin Leff and Maria (Karl) Leff Holder; m. Christine Elizabeth Thompson, Nov. 26, 1974 (div. May 1978); m. Cheryl Lynn Fluty, June 17, 1978; one child, Kiri Elise. AA in Liberal Arts, SUNY, Albany, 1974, BS in Psychology, 1976; MBA, Golden Gate U., 1980, postgrad. Cert. comml. pilot. Gen. mgr. Taco Bell Inc., Denver, 1975-76; tech. instr. GTE Sylvania, Mountain View, Calif., and Tehran, Iran, 1977-79; internat. sales mgr. EG&G Geometrics, Sunnyvale, Calif., 1980-82; product planner GTE Lenkurt, San Carlos, Calif., 1982-83; pres. Peninsula Engring. Group, San Carlos, 1983—; lectr. Golden Gate U., San Francisco, 1980-82. Contbr. articles to profl. jours. Served with U.S. Army, 1972-75. Mem. Am. Electronics Assn., Aircraft Owners and Pilots Assn., Assn. Former Intelligence Officers, Mensa. Avocations: flying, scuba diving (divemaster), karate (1st dan black belt), skiing, music. Home: 2760 Belmont Canyon Rd Belmont CA 94002 Office: Peninsula Engring Group Inc 1091 Industrial Rd San Carlos CA 94070

LEFFLER, FRED ROSS, electrical engineering educator; b. Denver, Jan. 30, 1929; s. John and Dora (Pooley) L.; m. Carol Ann Christian, Dec. 22, 1962; children: Colin, Russell. BSEE, U. Denver, 1951; postgrad., Purdue U., 1951-52; MSc, Oreg. State U., 1969, PhD, 1970. Registered profl. engr., Colo. Assoc. A.F. Weers & Co., Denver, 1952-57; prin. F.R. Leffler, Engrs., Colorado Springs, Colo., 1957-65; asst. prof. elec. engring. U. Akron, Ohio, 1970-75; assoc. prof. Colo. Sch. of Mines, Golden, 1975-83, prof., 1983—; cons. NSF, Washington, law firms, Denver, Chgo., 1980—; chair Mining Industry Tech. Conf., 1985. Contbr. articles to tech. jours. Troop com. mem. Wheat Ridge (Colo.) council Boy Scouts Am., 1983—. Recipient Merit award Illumination Engring. Soc., 1954; grantee Ohio Edison Co., Akron, 1970, U.S. Bur. Mines, 1984. Mem. IEEE (sr., Merit award 1969). Avocations: camping, fishing, automotive repair.

LEFOHN, ALLEN SEYMOUR, research scientist; b. Los Angeles, Apr. 21, 1944; s. Sam Martin and Rosamond (Steinberg) L.; m. Phyllis Ellen Adler, Sept. 3, 1967; children: Kevin Ari, Aaron Eliot. BS, UCLA, 1966; PhD, U. Calif., Berkeley, 1969. Vis. research scientist NASA Manned Spacecraft Ctr., Houston, 1969-71; research chemist EPA, Research Triangle Park, N.C., 1971, Washington, 1971-73; research adminstr. EPA, Corvallis, Oreg., 1973-76, Helena, Mont., 1976-79; researcher, pres., cons. A.S.L. & Assoc., Helena, Mont., 1981—; cons. Flow Gen., Helena, 1979-81. Contbg. columnist various newspapers and profl jours.; contbr. numerous peer revs. and articles in field. Chmn. Oreg. Land Use Goal Com., Corvallis, 1973-75. Mem. AAAS, Air Pollution Control Assn., N.Y. Acad. Scis., Mont. Acad. Scis., Sigma Xi. Club: Capital City Amateur Radio (Helena)(pres. 1983-84). Avocations: photography, skiing, writing, computing. Office: ASL & Assocs 111 N Last Chance Gulch Helena MT 59601

LEFOND, ANNE MAY, real estate broker; b. Ashland, Wis., Apr. 26, 1917; d. Charles and Anna (Erickson) Newman; B.A. cum laude, Northland Coll., Ashland, 1939; M.L.S., U. Wis., 1940; m. Stanley J. Lefond, Dec. 26, 1946 (dec. Nov. 1985); children—Dennis C., Robert E.; m. George V. VonVihl, 1986. Reference librarian Colgate U., Hamilton, N.Y., 1945-46, U. Mich., Ann Arbor, 1949-52; librarian Euclid (Ohio) Public Schs., 1953-66; sales assoc. Lloyd C. Helgager Co., Woodland Hills, Calif., 1967-70; broker New Eng. Realty Co., Westport, Conn., 1970-72; broker-mgr. Crown Realty Co., Evergreen, Colo., 1972-75; broker-assoc. Junction Realty Co., Evergreen, 1976-84, Remax-Evergreen, 1984—; v.p. Indsl. Minerals, Inc., Evergreen, 1976-85. Mem. Evergreen Bd. Realtors (dir.), Colo. Assn. Realtors, Nat. Assn. Real Estate Brokers, Nat. Inst. Real Estate Brokers. C. of C. Lutheran. Clubs: Hiwan Country, Swedish of Denver. Home: 29983 Canterbury Circle Evergreen CO 80439

LEGARE, HENRI FRANCIS, archbishop; b. Willow-Bunch, Sask., Can., Feb. 20, 1918; s. Phillippe and Amanda (Douville) L. B.A., U. Ottawa, 1940; theol. student, Lebret, Sask., 1940-44; M.A., Laval U., 1946; Dr. Social Sci., Cath. U. Lille, France, 1950; LL.D. (hon.), Carleton U., Ottawa, 1959, Windsor (Ont.) U., 1960, Queens U., Kingston, Ont., 1961, U. Sask., 1963, Waterloo (Ont.) Luth. U., 1965, U. Ottawa, Can., 1984; Doctor of Univ., U. of Ottawa. Ordained priest Roman Cath. Ch., 1943; prof. sociology Laval U., 1947, U. Ottawa, 1951; exec. dir. Cath. Hosp. Assn. Can., 1952-57; dean faculty social scis. U. Ottawa, 1954-58, pres., 1958-64; provincial Oblate Fathers, Winnipeg, Man., 1966-67; bishop of Labrador, 1967-72; archbishop Grouard-McLennan, Alta., 1972—. Contbr. articles to profl. jours. Chmn. Canadian Univs. Found., 1960- 62. Decorated grand cross merit Order Malta, 1964; order merit French Lang. Assn. Ont., 1965. Mem. Assn. Canadian Univs. (pres. 1960-62), Can. Conf. Cath. Bishops (pres. 1981-83), Internat. Assn. Polit. Sci. Address: Archbishop's House, CP 388, McLennan, AB Canada T0H 2L0

LEGEND, MOLLY, artist; b. Chgo., Apr. 30, 1927; d. Jack and Bessie (Yedwalsky) Schulman; m. Albert Sol Singer, July 23, 1945 (dec.); m. 2d, Mark Legend, Mar. 13, 1975. Student Chgo. Art Inst., 1940-44, Chouinard Art Sch., 1950-53, UCLA, 1955-76. Artist in oils and acrylics, 1952—, specialist in custom made Egyptian paintings and hieroglyphics, Los Angeles, 1978—; one-woman shows: All-State Savs. & Loan, Prudential Savs. & Loan, 1980-81, Los Angeles; group shows in Westwood, Beverly Hills, San Francisco, San Jose, Walnut Creek, Palm Springs and Palm Desert, Calif.; represented in numerous pvt. collections U.S. and abroad. Mem. Orange Art Assn., Cerritos Art Assn., South Bay Art Assn., Am. Nat. Theatre Assn., Artist Equity Assn. Office: PO Box 24446 Los Angeles CA 90024

LEGRAND, SHAWN PIERRE, computer systems programmer; b. San Diego, Nov. 27, 1960; s. Roger and Violet Louise (Howe) L. Grad. high sch., El Cajon, Calif. Computer operator Grossmont CCD, El Cajon, 1978-79; computer systems programmer ICW, San Diego, 1979—. Recipient Math. Achievement award Bank of Am., 1978. Mem. IEEE, Assn. Computing Machinery. Republican. Office: ICW 10140 Campus Point Dr San Diego CA 92121

LEHMAN, EDGAR RUSSELL, financial services executive; b. Los Angeles, Aug. 15, 1933; s. Phillips D. and Louise (Bachelor) L.; m. Sonja Jean Park, Aug. 12, 1961; children—David, Mary. B.A., U. So. Calif., 1955; diploma magna cum laude Biola U., 1957. With Pacific Fin. Cos., Newport Beach, Calif., 1956—, asst. v.p., 1971, 2d v.p., 1972-82, v.p., 1982—. Trustee Biola U., 1966—, chmn., 1982—. Mem. Life Office Mgmt. Assn. (former dir. and chmn. human resources council). Republican. Contbr. articles to mgmt. jour. Office: Pacific Mut Life Ins Co 700 Newport Center Dr Newport Beach CA 92660

LEHMAN, RICHARD HENRY, congressman; b. Sanger, Calif., July 20, 1948; m. Patricia Ann Kandarian, Aug. 9, 1971. AA, Fresno City Coll., 1968; BA, Calif. State U.-Fresno, 1969. Adminstrv. aide to Calif. State Assemblyman George N. Zenovich, Sacramento, 1969-76; mem. Calif. State Assembly, Sacramento, 1976-82, 98th-100th Congresses from 18th Dist. Calif., 1983—; regional whip 99th and 100th Congresses; mem. Calif. State Assembly, 1976-82, asst. majority leader, 1980-82. Served with Calif. NG, 1970-76. Democrat. Office: 1319 Longworth House Office Bldg Washington DC 20515 *

LEHMER, DERRICK HENRY, math educator; b. Berkeley, Calif., Feb. 23, 1905; s. Derrick Norman and Eunice (Mitchell) L.; m. Emma Trotskaia, Apr. 20, 1928; children: Laura, Donald. AB, U. Calif., Berkeley, 1927; MS, Brown U., 1929, PhD, 1930. Instr. Lehigh U., Bethelem, Pa., 1934-36, asst. prof., 1937-39; asst. prof. U. Calif., Berkeley, 1940-42, assoc. prof., 1943-50, prof. math., 1951—. Home: 1180 Miller Ave Berkeley CA 94708 Office: U Calif Dept Math Berkeley CA 94720

LEHRER, HARRIS IRVING, biochemist; b. Boston, May 28, 1939. BA, Brandeis U., 1960, PhD, 1965; MBA, Calif. State U., Long Beach, 1984. Sr. biochemist Monsanto Corp., Everett, Mass., 1968-69; group leader Ortho diagnostics, Raritan, N.J., 1969-78; asst. to v.p., research and devel. ICL Sci. Co., Fountain Valley, Calif., 1978-84; v.p. tech. services Spectrum Chem. Co., Gardena, Calif., 1985—; cons. to various firms, Bklyn., 1977-78. Contbr. articles to profl. jours.; patentee in field. Grantee NIH, 1965-67, NSF, 1967-68. Mem. AAAS, Am. Chem. Soc., Am. Soc. Quality Control. Home: 127 Corona Ave Long Beach CA 90803 Office: Spectrum Chem Co 14422 S San Pedro St Gardena CA 90284

LEIBERT, RICHARD WILLIAM, producer of public spectacles; b. N.Y.C., Nov. 11, 1948; s. Richard William and Rosemarie Martha (Bruns) L. BS, Boston U., 1966-70; student, Northwestern U., 1971. Producer Sta. WBZ AM/FM, Boston, 1968-70; prodn. dir. Sta. WMMR-FM, Phila., 1970; exec. producer Sta. WIND-AM, Chgo., 1970-72; program dir. Sta. KGB AM-FM, San Diego, 1972-80; pres. Rick Leibert Prodns., Los Angeles, 1980—; dir. Nat. Fireworks Ensemble, Los Angeles, Calif., 1985—. Creator (mascot, publicity stunts) Sta. KGB Chicken, 1974; creator, producer (radio fireworks show) Sta. KGB Sky Show, 1976; writer, producer (network radio show) New Music News, 1983; creator, dir. (touring co.) Nat. Fireworks Ensemble, 1985. Recipient Emmy award, 1978; named Program Dir. of Yr. Billboard Mag., 1976, Radio Program of Yr. Billboard Mag., 1976. Avocations: sailing, baseball. Office: Rick Leibert Prodns PO Box 65694 Los Angeles CA 90065

LEIBSON, NORMAN HOWARD, information technology executive; b. Pitts., Mar. 20, 1945; s. Phillip Adam and Freda (Bronstein) L.; m. Jeri Elyse Amber, Dec. 24, 1969; children: Daniel, Katherine. BS, Calif. State U., Northridge, 1968, MS, 1969. 1st v.p. Security Pacific Nat. Bank, Los Angeles, 1969-83; v.p. Carter Hawley Hale Stores, Inc., Los Angeles, 1983—; bd. dirs. Assn. for Retail Mgmt. Info. Systems, Los Angeles, 1985—; mem. adv. com. Golden Gate U., San Francisco, 1982—. Mem. The Guilds of the Orange County Performing Arts Ctr., Costa Mesa, Calif. Served with USAR, 1969. Republican. Jewish. Home: 27522 Cenajo Mission Viejo CA 92691 Office: Carter Hawley Hale Stores Inc 1600 N Kraemer Anaheim CA 92806

LEIBSON, STEVEN HOWARD, magazine editor, consultant; b. Louisville, Sept. 11, 1953; s. Charles Morris Leibson and Helene Ruth (Brownstein) Judah; m. Patricia Elaine Cochran, Oct. 6, 1979; 1 child, Shaina Pearl. BSEE, Case Western Res. U., 1975. Devel. engr. Hewlett-Packard, Loveland, Colo., 1975-78; project mgr. Hewlett-Packard, Ft. Collins, Colo., 1978-79; devel. engr. Auto-Trol Tech., Thornton, Colo., 1980-82, Cadnetix Corp., Boulder, Colo., 1982-85; regional editor EDN Mag., Newton, Mass., 1985—; cons. in field 1980—. Author: Handbook of Microcomputer Intfc, 1982; contbr. numerous articles to profl. jours. Mem. IEEE (pres. local chpt. computer soc. 1979-80). Club: Personal Computer Users' Group of Colo. (Boulder) (founder, pres. 1982-83). Avocations: writing, skiing, racquetball, reading. Home and Office: EDN Mag 4040 Greenbriar Blvd Boulder CO 80303

LEICHTLING, BEN HERSCH, biochemist, researcher; b. N.Y.C., Oct. 29, 1939; s. Stanley A. and Roslyn P. (Fuhr) L.; m. Mary P. Holliday (div.); children: Adam B., Gillian J.; m. Donna S. Piper; 1 child, Robyn J.; stepchildren: Karen E. Pond, Jeffrey G. Pond, Jonathan A. Pond. BS in Chemistry, Clarkson Coll., 1961; PhD in Biochemistry, Northwestern U., 1966. Asst. prof. SUNY, Stony Brook, 1968-72; research assoc. U. Colo. Health Sci. Ctr., Denver, 1972-79; staff scientist Nat. Jewish Ctr., Denver, 1979—. Contbr. articles to profl. jours. Mem. Am. Soc. Cell Biology, AAAS, Am. Assn. Counseling and Devel. Home: 7822 W 17th Ave Lakewood CO 80215 Office: Nat Jewish Ctr 1400 Jackson St Denver CO 80206

LEIFER, LARRY JOHN, mechanical engineering design educator, health science facility administrator; b. Ely, Nev., July 2, 1940; s. Lewis Carl and Nelle Nadine (Evasovic) L.; m. Aimee Dorr, Sept. 20, 1963 (div. Oct. 1973); 1 child, Simeon Kel; m. Ines Jenal, Aug. 26, 1976; children: Tjarko Zuri, Sascha Bjorn, Kalani Kai. BS, Stanford U., 1962, MS, 1963, PhD, 1969. Staff scientist, human machine integration NASA Ames Research Ctr., Calif., 1969-73; scientist, man-vehicle lab MIT, Cambridge, 1972-73; asst. prof. Inst. Biomed. Systems Analysis Swiss Fed. Inst. Tech., Zurich, Switzerland, 1973-76, prof., 1976—; assoc. prof. mech. engring. Stanford (Calif.) U., 1978—; dir. rehab. research and devel. ctr. VA Med. Ctr., Palo Alto, Calif., 1978—; dir. Smart Product Design Lab., Stanford U., 1977—, Ctr. for Design Research, Stanford U., 1984—. Editor: Distribute Nerve Conduction Velocity, 1981; contbr. articles to profl. jours. NASA, VA, NSF, IBM grantee. Mem. AAAS, ASME, IEEE, Biomed. Engring. Soc., Assn. Computer Machinery, Artificial Intelligence Soc., Rehab. Engring. Soc. N.Am. Avocations: design theory and methodology, interactive robotics, rehab. engring. Office: Stanford U Dept Mech Engring Stanford CA 94305

LEIFSON, JUNE, nursing science educator, university administrator; b. Spanish Fork, Utah, June 27, 1933; d. J. Victor and Mary A. (Bradford) L. BS, Brigham Young U., 1957, PhD, 1979; MS, Wayne State U., 1964. Instr. nursing U. Utah, Salt Lake City, 1965-67; asst. prof. U. Utah/Brigham Young U., Salt Lake City, 1967-75; assoc. prof. Brigham Young U., Provo, Utah, 1975-82, prof., 1982—, dir. grad. program, 1980—, asst. dean, 1982-86, dean, 1986—. Mem. Am. Pub. Health Assn. (governing council 1986—), Utah Pub. Health Assn. (bd. dirs. 1980-82, Beatly award 1982), Utah Nurses Assn., Nat. Council on Family Relations, Brigham Young U. Alumni Assn. (Disting. Service award 1976), Sigma Theta Tau, Phi Kappa Phi. Mormon. Avocations: gardening, reading. Home: 925 E 1050 N Orem UT 84057

LEIGA, ALGIRD GEORGE, diversified electronics company executive; b. N.Y.C., Mar. 25, 1933; s. George and Mary (Strepeikis) L.; m. Ann L. Dumig, Sept. 3, 1955; children: Gerard, Susan, Kathryn, Steven. AB, NYU, 1955, MS, 1960, PhD, 1963. Research fellow NYU, 1963-64; research scientist Xerox Corp., Webster, N.Y., 1964-73; materials tech. mgr. Xerox Med. Systems div. Xerox Corp., Pasadena, Calif., 1973-77, 1981—; materials sci. mgr. Xerox Corp., Palo Alto, Calif., 1977-81. Contbr. articles to profl. jours.; patentee in field. Mem. Am. Chem. Soc., Am. Phys. Soc., Soc. Photog. Scientists and Engrs. Republican. Roman Catholic. Avocation: foreign car restoration. Office: Xerox Med Systems 125 N Vinedo Ave Pasadena CA 91107

LEIGHNINGER, DAVID SCOTT, retired cardiovascular surgeon; b. Youngstown, Ohio, Jan. 16, 1920; s. Jesse Harrison and Marjorie (Lightner) L.; m. Margaret Jane Malony, May 24, 1942; children—David Allan, Jenny. B.A., Oberlin Coll., 1942; M.D., Case Western Res. U., 1945. Intern Univ. Hosps. of Cleve., 1945-46, resident, 1949-51, asst. surgeon, 1951-68; research fellow in cardiovascular surgery research lab. Case Western Res. U. Sch. Medicine, Cleve., 1948-49, 51-55, 57-67, instr. surgery, 1951-55, sr. instr., 1957-64, asst. prof., 1964-68, asst. clin. prof., 1968-70; resident Cin. Gen. Hosp., 1955-57; practice medicine specializing in cardiovascular surgery, Cleve., 1957-70; pvt. practice medicine specializing in cardiovascular and gen. surgery Edgewater Hosp., Chgo., 1970-82, staff surgeon, also dir. emergency surg. services, 1970-82; staff surgeon, also dir. emergency surg. services Mazel Med. Ctr., Chgo., 1970-82; emergency physician Miner's Hosp., Raton, N.Mex., 1982-83, 84-85, No. Colfax County Hosp., Raton, 1983-84, Mt. San Rafael Hosp., Trinidad, Colo., 1984-85; assoc., courtesy, or cons. staff Marymount Hosp., Cleve., Mt. Sinai Hosp., Cleve., Geauga Community Hosp., Chardon, Ohio, Bedford Community Hosp (Ohio), 1957-70. Tchr. tng. courses in CPR for med. personnel, police, fire and vol. rescue workers, numerous cities, 1950-70. Served to capt., M.C., AUS, 1946-48. Recipient Chris award Columbus Internat. Film Festival, 1964, numerous other award for sci. exhibits from various nat. and state med. socs., 1953-70; USPHS grantee, 1949-68. Fellow Am. Coll. Cardiology, Am. Coll. Chest Physicians; mem. AMA, N.Mex. Med. Assn., Colfax County Med. Assn., Ill. Med. Assn., Chgo. Med. Assn., U. Cin. Grad. Sch. Surg. Soc. Contbr. numerous articles to med. jours., chpts. to med. texts; spl. pioneer research (with Claude S. Beck) in physiopathology of coronary artery disease and CPR; developed surg. treatment of coronary artery disease; achieved 1st successful defibrillation of human heart, 1st successful reversal of fatal heart attack; provided 1st intensive care of coronary patients. Home: HCR 68 BX77 Fort Garland CO 81133

LEIGHT, BETSY LEVY, data processing executive, consultant; b. N.Y.C., July 22, 1946; d. Maurice and Elaine (Lind) Levy; m. Gary Allan Leight, Aug. 17, 1975; children: Debbie, David. BS, Carnegie Inst. Tech., 1966. Programmer, instr. IBM Can., Toronto, Ont., 1966-72; systems engr. World Trade Corp div IBM, Poughkeepsie, N.Y., 1972-73, HP Palo Alto, Palo Alto, 1973-76; exec. v.p., owner Ops. Control Systems, Palo Alto, 1976—, also bd. dirs. Leader local troop Girl Scouts U.S., Los Altos, 1984—. Named one of 1985 Women of Achievement in Bus., Santa Clara County (Calif.) Commn. on Status of Women, 1986. Mem. Am. Assn. Artificial Intelligence, EDP Auditors Assn., AAUW, Data Processing Mgmt. Assn. Jewish. Home: 14200 Sholes Ct Los Altos Hills CA 94022 Office: Ops Control Systems 560 San Antonio Rd Palo Alto CA 94022

LEIGHTON, DAVID KELLER, SR., retired bishop; b. Edgewood, Pa., June 22, 1922; s. Frank Kingsley and Irene (Keller) L.; m. Carolyn Ruth Smith, Jan. 18, 1945; children—Charlotte, David Keller, Nancy Elizabeth (Mrs. Harold Otto Koenig). B.S., Northwestern U., 1947; D.D., Va. Theol. Sem., 1969. Personnel interviewer Ohio Rubber Co., Willoughby, 1947-50; asst. supr. employment Fisher Body div. Gen. Motors Corp. (Pitts. plant), 1950-54; ordained priest Episcopal Ch., 1955; curate Calvary Episcopal Ch.,

Pitts., 1955-56; rector St. Andrews Episcopal Ch., Pitts., 1956-59, Ch. of Holy Nativity, Balt., 1959-63; tchr. sacred studies St. Paul Schs., Brooklandville, Md., 1960-63; archdeacon Episcopal Diocese Md., Balt., 1964-68; bishop coadjutor Episcopal Diocese Md., 1968-72, bishop, 1972-85; Vice pres. Diocesan Council Md., 1964-72, pres., 1972-85; v.p. Cathedral chpt. Md., 1968-71. Chmn. bd. Hannah More Acad., Reisterstown, Md., 1968-74; bd. dirs. Md. Council Chs., St. Timothy's Sch., Stevenson, Md., Ch. Mission of Help, Balt.; bd. dirs. Ch. Home and Hosp., Balt., v.p., 1969-85; bd. mem. U. Balt. Served with USAAF, 1942-45, ETO. Mem. Engring. Soc. Balt., Cum Laude Soc. Balt., St. Andrews Soc. Club: Army-Navy. Home: PO Box 310 Greenwood VA 22943

LEIGHTON, DAVID STRUAN ROBERTSON, businessman, author; b. Regina, Sask., Can., Feb. 20, 1928; s. Gordon Ernest and Mary Haskins (Robertson) L.; m. Margaret Helen House, Aug. 25, 1951; children: Douglas, Bruce, Katharine, Jennifer, Andrew. B.A., Queen's U., Kingston, Ont., 1950; M.B.A., Harvard U., 1953, D.B.A., 1956; LL.D., U. Windsor, 1972. Editor Canadian Press, 1950-51; research assoc. Harvard U., 1953-55, vis. prof., 1974; from asst. prof. to prof. U. Western Ont., 1955-70; pres. Banff (Alta.) Centre, 1970-82; chmn. Nabisco Brands Ltd., Toronto, Ont., Can.; dir. Scott's Hospitality, Inc., Gulf Can. Ltd., GSW Ltd., CAMCO, Inc., Acres Internat. Ltd., Rio Algom Ltd., Lornex Mines, John Wiley & Sons Ltd., Montreal Trustco, Telemedia, Inc., Cambridge Shopping Ctrs., Nat. Centre for Mgmt. Research and Devel.; mem. Conf. Bd. Can. Author: (with McNair, Brown and England) Problems in Marketing, 1957, (with E.J. Fox) Marketing in Canada, 1958, (with Donald H. Thain) Canadian Problems in Marketing, 1959, 66, 72, (with Donald H. Thain and C.B. Johnston) How Industry Buys, 1959 (Media-Scope award as best indsl. market research of 1960), (with Wilding and Wilson) The Distribution of Packaged Consumer Goods: An Annotated Bibliography, 1963, International Marketing: Text and Cases, 1965, (with Donald Thompson) Canadian Marketing: Problems and Prospects, 1973, (with Kenneth Simmonds) Case Problems in Marketing, 1973, (with Peggy Leighton) Artists, Builders and Dreamers, 1982; editor-in-chief: Business Quarterly, 1958-61. Chmn. Canadian Consumer Council, 1968-70; bd. govs. Toronto Symphony, Can. Ctr. for Philanthropy, Queen's U. George F. Baker scholar Harvard U.; recipient Alta. Achievement award, 1978, Alta. Order of Excellence, 1985. Mem. Am. Mktg. Assn. (past pres.). Home: 110 Elk St, Harvie Heights, PO Box 1260, Canmore, AB Canada T0L 0M0 Office: Nabisco Brands Ltd, 1 Dundas St W, Toronto, ON Canada M5G ZA9

LEIGHTON, HENRY ALEXANDER, physician; b. Manila, Philippines, Nov. 12, 1949; (parents U.S. citizens).; s. Raymond Harry and Theola Marie (Alexander) L.; m. Helga Maria Hell, Jan. 17, 1970; children: Alan Raymond, Henry Alexander, Michael Ballinger, John, Marni, Tammy Ballinger. BA in History, U. Calif., Berkeley, 1952, MPH, 1971; MD, U. Calif., San Francisco, 1956. Diplomate Am. Bd. Preventive Medicine. Intern So. Pacific Gen. Hosp., San Francisco, 1956-57; resident in surgery Brooke Gen. Hosp., Ft. Sam Houston, Tex., 1960-62; commd. 2d. lt. U.S. Army, 1957, advanced through grades to col., 1971; div. surgeon 8th Inf. div. U.S. Army, Germany, 1964-66; comdr. 15th Med. Bn. U.S. Army, Vietnam, 1966-67; instr.Med. Field Service Sch. U.S. Army, San Antonio, 1968-70; resident preventive medicine U.S. Army, Ft. Ord, Calif., 1971-72, chief preventive medicine, 1973-76; chief preventive medicine U.S. Army-Europe, 1976-79, ret., 1979; chief occupational health MEDDAC U.S. Army-Europe, Ft. Ord, 1981—; cons. preventive medicine U.S. Army Res., Europe. Neighborhood commr. Boy Scouts Am., 1964-66; bd. dirs. Am. Lung Assn. of Calif., 1982-84, and of affiliate, 1980-86; pres. The Bluffs Homeowners Assn., 1986. Decorated Air medal with oak leaf cluster, Bronze Star, Legion of Merit, Meritorious Service medal. Fellow Am. Coll. Preventive Medicine; mem. Am. Pub. Health Assn., Am. Occupational Med. Assn., Assn. Mil. Surgeons, Ret. Officers Assn., Assn. U.S. Army, Theta Xi. Lodges: Masons, Shriners. Office: US MEDDAC Occupational Health Fort Ord CA 93941

LEIGHTON, JOHN CRICHTON, engineering company executive; b. Elgin, Scotland, Aug. 30, 1925; s. William and Davidson L.; m. Carmen Miranda Vasquez, May 26, 1962; children: Lorna, Carla. Grad., Indian Mil Acad., 1944; B.S., U. Aberdeen, Scotland, 1950. Project mgr. aluminum plant expansion Kaiser Engrs., India, 1964-67; resident mgr. Kaiser Engrs., Holyhead, Wales, 1968-69; project mgr. Kaiser Engrs., Australia and New Zealand, 1969-71; project mgr. iron ore devel. Kaiser Engrs., Australia, 1971-72; group v.p. Kaiser Engrs., Oakland, Calif., 1979-82, now pres.; exec. v.p. Raymond Kaiser Engrs., Oakland, 1973-79, Milder-Kaiser Engenharia, Brazil, 1973-79; v.p. Latin Am. ops. Kaiser Engrs., 1973-79. Seved to capt. Indian Army, 1944-47. Mem. ASCE. Home: 627 Miner Rd Orinda CA 94563 Office: Kaiser Engrs 300 Lakeside Dr PO Box 23210 Oakland CA 94623 *

LEINBERGER, CHRISTOPHER BROWN, urban development consultant, writer; b. Charleston, W.Va., Jan. 2, 1951; s. Fredrick Arthur and Helen (Brown) L.; m. Madeleine LeMoyne McDougal, Aug. 25, 1973; children: Christopher Jr., Rebecca. BA in Urban Sociology, Swarthmore Coll., 1972; MBA, Harvard U., 1976. Asst. to pres. ARA Food Services, Inc., Phila., 1973-74, 76-77; dir. concept devel. Saga Corp., Menlo Park, Calif., 1977-79; exec. v.p. Robert Charles Lesser & Co., Beverly Hills, Calif., 1979-82, mng. ptnr., co-owner, 1982—. Contbr. articles to profl. jours. and nat. print media including The Wall Street Jour. and The Atlantic Monthly. Vice chmn. Swarthmore (Pa.) Coll. Capital Funds Dr., 1986. Fellow NSF, 1971, NCAA, 1972, Coro Found., 1972-73. Mem. Urban Land Inst. (council mem. 1984—). Democrat. Clubs: Zamarono (Los Angeles); Flintridge Riding (Pasadena, Calif.). Home: 407 Norwood Dr Pasadena CA 91105 Office: Robert Charles Lesser & Co 8484 Wilshire Blvd #340 Beverly Hills CA 90211

LEININGER, WAYNE CARL, environmental science educator; b. Lewistown, Mont., Dec. 31, 1949; s. Woodrow Clemens and Marilynn (Buckentin) L.; m. Dana Lynn Hardin, Oct. 19, 1975; children: Erin Lynn, Will Clemens. BS, Mont. State U., 1972, MS, 1974; PhD, Oreg. State U., 1983. Research assoc. Mont. State U., Bozeman, 1974-80; grad. research asst. Oreg. State U., Corvallis, 1980-83; asst. prof. Colo. State U., Ft. Collins, 1984—; cons. Woodward & Clyde, Denver, 1976, Uniscale, Ft. Collins, 1986. Contbr. articles to profl. jours. Treas. Peace With Christ Pre-Sch., Ft. Collins, 1985—. Named Outstanding Range Sci. Prof., Colo. State U., 1985—. Mem. Soc. Range Mgmt., Ecol. Soc. Am., Soil Cons. Soc. Am. Republican. Lutheran. Club: Range (Bozeman) (v.p. 1971-72). Avocations: photography, backpacking. Home: 1030 Wagonwheel Dr Fort Collins CO 80526 Office: Colo State U Range Sci Dept Fort Collins CO 80523

LEINO, DEANNA ROSE, educator; b. Leadville, Colo., Dec. 15, 1937; d. Arvo Ensio Leino and Edith Mary (Bonan) Leino Malenck. B.S. in Bus. Adminstrn., U. Denver, 1959, M.S. in Bus. Adminstrn., 1967; postgrad. Community Coll. Denver, U. No. Colo., Colo. State U., U. Colo., Met. State Coll. Cert. tchr., vocat. tchr., Colo. Tchr. Jefferson County Adult Edn., Lakewood, Colo., 1963-67; tchr. bus., coordinator coop. office edn., Jefferson High Sch., Edgewater, Colo., 1959—; instr. Community Coll. Denver, Red Rocks, 1967-81, U. Colo. Denver, 1976-79, Parks Coll. Bus., 1983—; dist. adviser Future Bus. Leaders Am. Active City of Edgewater Sister City Project Student Exchange Com.; pres. Career Women's Symphony Guild; treas. Phantoms of Opera, 1982—; active Opera Colo. Assocs., I Pagliacci; ex-officio trustee Denver Symphony Assn., 1980-82. Recipient disting. service award Jefferson County Sch. Bd. 1980; Jefferson High Sch. Wall of Fame 1981. Mem. NEA (life), Colo. Edn. Assn., Jefferson County Edn. Assn., Colo. Vocat. Assn., Am. Vocat. Assn., Colo. Educators for and about Bus., Profl. Secs. Internat., Career Women's Symphony Guild, Profl. Panhellenic Assn., Colo. Congress Fgn. Lang. Tchrs., Wheat Ridge C. of C. (edn. com.), Delta Pi Epsilon, Phi Chi Theta, Beta Gamma Sigma, Alpha Lambda Delta. Republican. Roman Catholic. Club: Tyrolean Soc. Denver.

LEIPOLD, WAYNE H., electrical engineer; b. Buffalo, Jan. 19, 1938; s. Hugo C. and Pearl L. (Fisher) L.; m. Barbara J. Wilson, Dec. 17, 1960; children—Mark, Karen. B.S, U. Buffalo, 1958, M.S., 1962. Registered profl. engr., N.Y., Ariz. With Cornell Aero. Lab., Buffalo, 1958-67, research electronics engr., 1965-67; sr. electronics design engr. Delevan Electronics div. Am. Precision Ind., East Aurora, N.Y., 1967-71; with Airco Speer Electronics, Nogales, Ariz., and Airco de Mexico Nogales, Mexico, 1971-72; prodn. engr. West Cap div. San Fernando Electric, Tucson, 1973, Rogers Corp., Chandler, Ariz., 1973-74; with Phelps Dodge Corp., Douglas (Ariz.) Reduction Wks., 1974-87, tech. services dept. head, 1979-87; environ. engr. Chino Mines, Hurley, N.Mex., 1987—; instr. U. Buffalo, 1962-65, Cochise Coll., Douglas, 1979-86. Mem. Rep. Com., Pirtleville, Ariz., 1982. Mem. IEEE, AIME, Nat. Soc. Profl. Engrs., Air Pollution Control Assn. Presbyterian. Office: PO Box 7 Hurley NM 88043

LEISEY, DONALD EUGENE, learning systems company executive; b. Pa., Sept. 23, 1937; s. Alvin L. and E. Marie L.; BS in Edn., West Chester (Pa.) State U., 1959; MA in Adminstrn., Villanova (Pa.) U., 1962; EdD in Adminstrn., U. So. Calif., 1973; m. Patricia M. Leisey; children: Kristen, Kendra. Tchr., Coatesville, Pa., 1959-62; prin., Downingtown, Pa., 1962-64; prin. Dept. Def. Dependent Schs., Tachikawa, Japan, 1964-67; asst. supt. Lennox Schs., Inglewood, Calif., 1967-71; dir. adminstrv. services San Rafael (Calif.) City Sch. Dist., 1971-73, supt. schs., 1973-79; v.p., regional mgr. Am. Learning Corp., Huntington Beach, Calif., 1979-80; v.p., treas. Kittredge Sch. Corp., San Francisco, 1980-83; pres., chmn. bd. Merryhill Schs. Inc., Sacramento, 1980—; gen. ptnr. L&L Investments Ltd., 1980—. Appointed to Gov.'s Child Care Task Force, Calif., 1984, Gov.'s Child Devel. Programs Adv. Com., Calif., 1985—. Recipient Disting. Alumnus award West Chester State U., 1983, Disting. Service award Los Angeles County Sheriff, 1969, Hon. Service award PTA, 1970. Mem. Nat. Assn. Child Care Mgmt., Nat. Ind. Pvt. Schs. Assn. (bd. dirs.), Nat. Assn. Edn. Young Children, Am. Assn. Sch. Adminstrs., Assn. Calif. Sch. Adminstrs., Delta Epsilon, Phi Delta Kappa. Certifications: gen. adminstrv., gen. secondary, gen. elementary, Calif. Home: 10 Oak Mountain Ct San Rafael CA 94903 Office: Merryhill Schs Inc 2730 Eastern Ave Sacramento CA 95821

LEISY, JAMES FRANKLIN, publisher; b. Normal, Ill., Mar. 21, 1927; s. Ernest Erwin and Elva (Krehbiel) L.; m. Emily Ruth McQueen, June 8, 1949; children: James Franklin, Scot, Rebecca. BBA, So. Meth. U., 1949. Field rep., then editor Prentice-Hall, Inc., N.Y.C., 1949-54; editor Allyn & Bacon, Inc., Boston, 1954-56; founder, exec. editor Wadsworth Pub. Co., Inc., San Francisco, 1956-59, v.p., 1959-60, pres., 1960-77, chmn., chief exec. officer, 1977-85; dep. chmn. Internat. Thomson Orgn., Inc., 1978-85; founder, chmn. Sci. Books Internat., Inc., 1981-83; founder, chmn. Linguistics Internat., Inc., 1983-85; bd. dirs. Baron Data Systems, Inc., San Francisco Mag., Inc., 1979-81, Van Nostrand Reinhold, Inc., 1982-84, Anaheim Pub. Co., Inc., 1981-84, Lange Med. Publs., Inc., 1981-84, Thomas Nelson Internat., Ltd., 1982-84, Mayfield Pub. Co., Inc., Franklin, Beedle and Assocs. Author: Abingdon Song Kit, 1957, Let's All Sing, 1958, Songs for Swinging Housemothers, 1960, Songs for Singin', 1961, Songs for Pickin' and Singin', 1962, Beer Bust Song Book, 1963, Hootenanny Tonight, 1964, Folk Song Fest, 1964, Folk Song Abecedary, 1966, Alpha Kappa Psi Sings, 1967, The Good Times Songbook, 1974, Scrooge, The Christmas Musical, 1978, Alice, A Musical Comedy, 1980, Pinocchio, A Musical Play, 1981, Tiny Tim's Christmas Carol, A Musical Play, 1981, The Pied Piper, 1982, The Nutcracker and Princess Pirlipat, 1982, A Visit from St. Nicholas, 1983, Pandora, 1984, Talkin' 'bout America, 1986, Mouse Country, 1987, The Dingaling Circus Holiday, 1987; composer: songs including Keep a Little Christmas In Your Heart, A Little Old Lady in Tennis Shoes, A Personal Friend of Mine, Please Tell Me Why, An Old Beer Bottle. Bd. dirs. Bethel Coll., Ctr. Entrepreneurial Devel., U. Calif.-Santa Cruz; bd. dirs., mem. exec. com. Calif. Council for Econ. Edn., 1968-71; mem. deans council Sch. Bus. Calif. State U., San Jose; mem. Nat. UN Day Com., 1978. Served with USNR, 1945-46. Named to Career Hall of Fame So. Meth. U., 1968. Mem. Young Pres.'s Orgn. (bd. dirs. 1970-73), Assn. Am. Pubs. (bd. dirs. 1982-85), ASCAP, So. Meth. U. Alumni Assn. (bd. dirs. 1965-70), Chief Execs. Forum, World Business Council, Phi Eta Sigma, Alpha Phi Omega, Alpha Kappa Psi (nat. chmn. song com. 1963-71), Kappa Alpha. Club: Bohemian. Office: 10 Davis Dr Belmont CA 94002

LEISZ, G. W., aerospace industry executive; b. 1923; married. BSEE, U. Calif., Berkeley, 1947. Exec. v.p. N. Am. Rockwell Corp., 1952-70; v.p., group gen. mgr. Fairchild Camera and Instrument Corp., 1970; with Aerojet Gen. Corp., 1970—, corp. group v.p., from 1975, exec. v.p., from 1981, now pres., also bd. dirs. Office: Aerojet-Gen Corp 10300 N Torrey Pines Rd La Jolla CA 92037 *

LEITCH, CLARENCE MERVIN, barrister; b. Creelman, Sask., Can., Jan. 13, 1926; s. Peter Harold and Martha Ann (Walker) L.; m. Ardine Catherine Brissette, Feb. 23, 1980; children: Hugh Campbell, Margaret Jan, Catherine Anne, James Harold. BA, U. Alta., 1951, LLB, 1952. Called to Alta. bar, 1953, created queen's counsel, 1968; mem. firm Macleod Dixon, Calgary, Alta., Can., 1952-71, 1983—; atty. gen. Province of Alta., 1971-75, provincial treas., 1975-79, minister energy and natural resources, 1979-82; dir. Can. Pacific Ltd., Alta. Energy Co. Ltd., Alta. Govt. Telephones Commn., Bank Montreal, Can. Utilities Ltd., Chieftain Devel. Co. Ltd. Served with Royal Can. Navy, 1943-45. Mem. Can. Inst. Resources Law (bd. dirs.). Conservative. Clubs: Calgary Golf and Country, Mission Hills Country. Office: Macleod Dixon, 324 8 Ave SW, Suite 1500, Calgary, AB Canada T2P 2Z2

LEITCH, JOHN ANDREW, dentist, conservationist; b. Cleve., Aug. 22, 1940; s. John Davie and Jessie Irene (Pollard) L.; m. Jo Ellen Eklund, June 20, 1964; children—Kimberly Ann, Heather Elizabeth. B.A., Albion Coll., 1962; D.D.S., Northwestern U., 1965. Gen. practice dentistry, Las Vegas, 1967—. Pres. Nev. Wildlife Fedn., 1982-85. Served to capt. USAF, 1965-67. Recipient Cert. of Recognition, Air Def. Command, Mem. Clark County Dental Soc. (sec. (1979-80, v.p. 1980-81, pres. 1981-82), Omicron Kappa Epsilon. Democrat. Office: 820 E Sahara Ave Las Vegas NV 89104

LEITE, RICHARD JOSEPH, aeronautical engineer; b. Fremont, Ohio, Mar. 8, 1923; s. Carl Albert and Marie Margaret (Dolweck) L.; m. Barbara Marie Higgins, Nov. 19, 1955; children: Mark Richard, Jeffrey Howard, Mary Elizabeth. B in Naval Sci. magna cum laude, U. Notre Dame, 1945, BS in Aero. Engring. cum laude, 1947; MS in Aero. Engring., U. Mich., 1948, PhD in Aero. Engring., 1956. Research assoc. U. Mich., Ann Arbor, 1948-56, research engr., 1958-71; sr. engr. Booz-Allen Applied Research Inc., Dayton, Ohio, 1956-58; sr. staff engr. Bendix Aerospace Corp., Ann Arbor, 1971-72, research cons., 1968-71; sr. scientist KMS Fusion, Inc., Ann Arbor, 1972-77; staff mgr. Engring. and Test div. TRW, Inc., Redondo Beach, Calif., 1977—. Patentee pyrochem. process, 1982. Mem. Scio Twp. (Mich.) Planning Comm., 1970-76, vice chmn., 1976-77. Mem. Am. Vacuum Soc., Sigma Xi, Phi Kappa Phi. Roman Catholic. Avocations: fishing, hunting, gardening. Office: TRW Inc 1 Space Park 135/3869 Redondo Beach CA 90278

LELAND, CHARLES JAMES, accountant; b. Santa Monica, Calif., Nov. 11, 1938; s. Charles H. and Rulana A. (Glover) L.; m. Doreen T. Young, Apr. 24, 1965; 1 child, Jonathan Tray. B.A.A., U. Hawaii, 1968. C.P.A., Hawaii. Acct., Coopers & Lybrand, 1968-69; chief acct. Foreign Trade Zone 9, 1970-74; pvt. practice acctg., Honolulu, 1974-78; ptnr. Leland-Maynard & Co., 1979-83; pres. Leland-Maynard, Inc., Honolulu, 1983—; commr. Hawaii State Bd. of Tax Rev., 1980—; instr. acctg. Hawaii Pacific Coll., 1984—. Author: Incorporation Trap, 1984. Treas., Chong for Hawaii Senator, 1969, 73. Served with USCG, 1958-62. Mem. Hawaii Soc. C.P.A.s (com. chmn. 1974—), Hawaii Assn. Pub. Accts., Am. Inst. C.P.A.s, C. of C., Small Bus. Council. Democrat. Lutheran. Club: Hawaii Yacht. Lodge: Elks. Home: 269 Mahimahi Pl Honolulu HI 96813 Office: Leland Maynard Inc 50 S Beretania St Honolulu HI 96813

LEM, RICHARD DOUGLAS, painter; b. Los Angeles, Nov. 24, 1933; s. Walter Wing and Betty (Wong) L.; B.A., UCLA, 1958; M.A., Calif. State U.-Los Angeles, 1963; m. Patricia Ann Soohoo, May 10, 1958; 1 son, Stephen Vincent. Exhibited in one-man shows at Gallery 818, Los Angeles, 1965; group shows at Lynn Kottler Galleries, N.Y.C., 1973, Palos Verdes Art Gallery, 1968, Galerie Mouffe, Paris, France, 1976, Le Salon des Nations, Paris, 1984, numerous others; represented in permanent collections; writer, illustrator; Mile's Journey, 1983. Served with AUS, 1958-60. Mem. UCLA Alumni Assn. Address: 1861 Webster Ave Los Angeles CA 90026

LEMAY, BARRY WILLIAM, financial planner; b. Berkeley, Calif., Apr. 23, 1945; s. Remi Bernard and Barbara Evelyn (LeM.); m. Charlotte Ellen Butler, Nov. 1, 1969; 1 dau., Monique Francoise. Cert. fin. planner, Coll. Fin. Planning. With Investors Diversified Services, San Jose, Calif., 1969-74; fin. planner Belmont Reid & Co., San Jose, 1974-76; owner Ambar Fin Group, Campbell, Calif., 1976—. Past pres. St. Lucy's PTA, 1982-83. Mem. Internat. Assn. Fin. Planning, Inst. Cert. Fin. Planners. Republican. Roman Catholic. Club: Kiwanis (past pres. South San Jose 1976). Home: 1852 Dry Creek Rd San Jose CA 95124 Office: Ambar Fin Group 340 E Hamilton Ave Campbell CA 95008

LEMAY, HAROLD EUGENE, JR., chemistry educator; b. Tacoma, May 28, 1940; s. Harold Eugene LeMay and Alberta Olga (Sieverson) Shandrow; m. Carla Aline Hansen, June 6, 1964; children: John Charles, David Eugene. BS, Pacific Luth. U., 1962; MS, U. Ill., 1964, PhD, 1966. Asst. prof. chemistry U. Nev., Reno, 1966-70, assoc. prof., 1970-79, prof., 1979—, vice-chmn. dept. chemistry, 1974-76, chmn., 1984-85, assoc. chmn., 1985—; vis. prof. U. N.C., Chapel Hill, 1977-78, U. Coll. Wales, Alberystwyth, 1978. Author: Chemistry: The Central Science; contbr. articles to profl. jours. Recipient Alan Bible Teaching Excellence award U. Nev., 1985. Mem. Am. Chem. Soc. Republican. Mem. 4-square Ch. Avocation: photography. Home: 1780 Aquila Ave Reno NV 89509 Office: U Nev Dept Chemistry Reno NV 89557

LEMBERSKY, MARK RAPHAEL, engineered products executive; b. Pitts., Sept. 30, 1945; s. Herman K. and Alice Lillian (Berger) L.; m. Barbara Jean Diemond, June 6, 1965; 1 child, Carol Sharon. BS, MIT, 1967; MS, Stanford U., 1968, PhD, 1971, postdoctoral, 1983. Prof. Oreg. State U., Corvallis, 1971-76; mgr. merchandising and allocation Weyerhaeuser Co., Tacoma, 1977-79, dir. raw materials research and devel. div., 1979-81, dir. forestry and timber products research and devel. div., 1981-83, dir. fin. and group systems, 1984-85, gen. mgr. Engineered Products div., 1985—; cons. forest products cos., western U.S., 1972-76. Patentee in field; contbr. articles to profl. jours. Mem. MIT Edn. Council, 1983—, Wash. Council for Tech. Advancement, chmn. subcom. edn., 1984—; bd. dirs. Sci. Affiliates U. Wash., 1983-86; trustee Somerset Community Assn., Bellevue, Wash., 1977-79. Recipient Carter award Oreg. State U., 1975. Mem. Inst. Mgmt. Sci. (Franz Edelman Internat. prize 1985), Computer and Automated Systems Assn. (sr.), Ops. Research Soc. Am. (edn. com. 1976-77, assoc. editor jour. 1984—), Mgmt. Sci. Roundtable (exec. bd. dirs. 1985—). Avocations: photography, carpentry. Office: Weyerhaeuser Co Div Engineered Products PC2-2 Tacoma WA 98477

LEMERT, JAMES BOLTON, journalist, educator; b. Sangerfield, N.Y., Nov. 5, 1935; s. Jesse Raymond and Caroline Elizabeth (Brown) L.; m. Rosalie Martha Bassett, Mar. 23, 1972. A.B., U. Calif.-Berkeley, 1957, M.J., 1959; Ph.D., Mich. State U., 1964. Newspaper reporter Chico Enterprise-Record, Calif., 1957, 58-60; asst. prof. journalism So. Ill. U., Carbondale, 1964-67, U. Oreg., Eugene, 1967-69; assoc. prof. U. Oreg., 1969-76, prof., 1976—, dir. div. communication research, 1967—, dir. grad. program Sch. Journalism, 1983-86; chair U. Oreg. Task Force to Revise Faculty Governance, 1983-84; Mem. senate, U. Oreg., 1981-83, 86—; chmn. intercollegiate athletics com., U. Oreg., 1986—. Producer, on-air host: Old Grooves show, KWAX-FM, 1977-80, 82-84; author: Does Mass Communication Change Public Opinion After All? A New Approach to Effects Analysis, 1981, Criticizing the Media: Empirical Approaches; editor: Daily Californian, 1957; contbr. articles profl. jours. Mem. Oreg. Alcohol and Drug Edn. Adv. Com., 1968-69; pres. South Hills Neighborhood Assn., 1976-77, bd. dirs., 1982-84, 86—; bd. dirs. Traditional Jazz Soc. Oreg., 1981-83, 87; v.p. Met. Cable Access Corp., 1983-84. Recipient Outstanding Journalist award Sigma Delta Chi, 1957; NSF fellow, 1963-64; Calif. Newspaper Pubs. fellow, 1957; Butte County Alumni scholar, 1953-54. Mem. AAUP (exec. bd. 1975-76), Assn. Edn. Journalism, Am. Assn. Public Opinion Research, Internat. Communication Assn., Assn. Oreg. Faculties (head chpt., mem. state exec. com. 1981-83, 85—, U. Oreg. del. to Oreg. Faculties Polit. Action Com., 1986—), Phi Beta Kappa (membership chmn. 1985-86), Sigma Delta Chi. Home: 10 E 40th Ave Eugene OR 97405

LEMERY, EUGENE FRANKLIN, social worker; b. Lockwood, Mo., Sept. 17, 1927; s. John Nelson and Ann (Black) L.; m. Noreen Mary Paulson, Aug. 12, 1961; children—Mary Christine, Mark Eugene. B.A, U. Calif.-Berkeley, 1952; M.S.W., U. Utah, 1963. With Alaska Div. Pub. Welfare, 1959-63, dist. rep., Fairbanks, 1963-65; commd. corps officer Indian Hosp., USPHS, Pine Ridge, S.D., 1965-66; cons. Nev. Dept. Pub. Welfare, Carson City, 1966; psychiat. social worker Mo. Div. Mental Health, Springfield, 1967-75; social worker VA Med. Ctr. Hosp., Hot Springs, S.D., 1975-82, chmn. Internat. Yr. of Disabled Persons com., 1981; social worker Community Counseling Ctr., Ft. Richardson, Alaska, 1982—; social work field supr. U. Alaska, Anchorage, 1986-87. Hot Springs mayor's rep. for Internat. Yr. of Child, 1979. Served with AUS, 1946-47. Recipient letter of commendation Gov. of Alaska, 1979. Mem. Acad. Cert. Social Workers, Nat. Assn. Social Workers, Commd. Officers Assn. USPHS. Lutheran. Lodges: Kiwanis (v.p. 1978-79), Elks (Hot Springs); Masons. Home: 11639 Loveland Circle Eagle River AK 99577 Office: Community Counseling Ctr 6th Infantry Div L Fort Richardson AK 99505

LEMIRE, DAVID STEPHEN, school counselor; b. Roswell, N.Mex., May 23, 1949; s. Joseph Armon and Jeanne (Longwill) L.; B.A., Linfield Coll., 1972, M.Ed., 1974; Ed.S., Idaho State U., 1978; postgrad. in counselor edn. U. Wyo., Laramie. Sch. counselor, psychol. technician Goshen County Sch. Dist. 1, Torrington, Wyo. Cert. sch. counselor, student personnel worker, psychology instr., Calif.; coordinator research and devel. Lifelong Learning Ctr. Uinta County Sch. Dist., Evanston, Wyo., 1986—; pres. David Lemire Software Enterprises, Evanston; dir. Inst. for Advanced Study of Thinkology. Mem. Assn. Poetry Therapy, Nat. Council for Creative Therapies, Am. Assn. for Counseling and Devel. Editor WACD Jour.; cons. editor WCRLA Jour.; contbr. articles to profl. jours. Address: PO Box 2326 Evanston WY 82930 Address: U Wyo Box 4285 Laramie WY 82071

LEMME, MARGARET LEE, speech and language pathologist; b. West Point, N.Y., May 31, 1943; d. William Philip and Eileen (Randle) L. BS, U. Okla., 1965; MA, Okla. Health Scis. Ctr., 1967; PhD, U. Colo., 1974. Instr. Gallaudet Coll., Washington, 1968-70; trainee VA Hosp., Denver, 1970-72; instr. Health Scis. Ctr., Denver, 1972-74; from asst. to assoc. prof. speech-lang. pathology U. Denver, 1974—; profl. adv. bd. Rehab. Ctr., Denver, 1976-79; research cons. VA Hosp., Mpls., 1976-77; cons. Children's Hosp., Denver, 1976—, Child Devel. Ctr., Denver, 1977-78. Editor: Neurology of Speech, Language and Hearing, 1987. Hew grantee Social Rehab Services. Fellow Am. Speech-Lang. and Hearing Assn. (cert., legis. councilor 1977-84); mem. Colo. Speech-Lang. and Hearing Assn. (v.p. comprehensive planning 1985), Clin. Aphasiology Soc. (treas. 1978—). Democratic. Episcopalian. Home: 7321 S Columbine Way Littleton CO 80122 Office: U Denver Columbine Hall W Denver CO 80208

LEMON, OLA TESS GOODRICH, nurse; b. Tridell, Utah, May 9, 1932; d. Forrest Odra and Ethel (McConkie) Goodrich; m. Boyd R. Lemon, June 20, 1951; children: John, Edna, James, Charles, Ethel, Kathie, Susan, Rick. Student in nursing, U. Utah, 1949-51, 67-68, U. Philippines, Manila, 1965-66, U. Nebr., 1969-71; AS in Nursing, Weber State Coll., 1973, student. R.N., Utah. Dir. nursing Snyders Convalescence Villa, Roosevelt, Utah, 1973-76; night supr. Duchesne County Hosp., Roosevelt, 1976-80, 85—, supr. labor/delivery, 1982-85; dir. nursing Stewart's Nursing Home, Roosevelt, 1981-82. Mem. PTA, March of Dimes, Cancer Drive, Blood Drive. Recipient Appreciation award ARC, 1964-71. Mem. Utah Nursing Assn., Am. Nursing Assn., No. Utah Basin Dist. Nursing Assn. Republican. Mormon. Avocations: books, music, handwork.

LEMONDS, KATHRYN JOYCE, technical executive; b. Oroville, Calif., June 9, 1948; d. Homer Bertus Daily and Betty Louise (Owens) Daily Owens; m. Thomas Andrew Lemonds, Apr. 1, 1967 (div. Aug. 1972); 1 child, Laura Marie. Student Wash. State U., 1966-67; A.A., Diablo Valley Coll., 1985; student J.F. Kennedy U., 1985—. Engring. asst. Pacific Gas & Electric Co. Research Lab., San Ramon, Calif., 1972-82, sr. tech. specialist, 1982—; chief software designer LeMonde Designer Software, San Ramon, 1986—. Supr. host com. Democratic Nat. Conv., San Francisco, 1984. Mem. Software Entrepreneurs Forum, NOW, Summit Orgn. Club: Lafayette Orinda Presbyterian Ch. Singleship (Calif.). Avocations: studying ballet, tap and jazz dancing, skiing, traveling, reading. Home: 2604 Shadow Mountain Dr San Ramon CA 94583

LEMP, JOHN, JR., telecommunications engineer; b. Trenton, N.J., Dec. 10, 1936; s. John and Helena M. (Braddock) L.; B.S. in Elec. Engring., Princeton U., 1959; M.S. in Elec. Engring., Poly. Inst. Bklyn., 1968; M.B.A., Colo. State U., 1973; grad. Air Command and Staff Coll., 1974; grad. Indsl. Coll. Armed Forces, 1981; m. Susan N. Rose, 1955; children—John, Thomas K., Carl A., Adam F.H. Project engr. Gen. Devices, Inc., Princeton, N.J., 1959-60; with Bell Telephone Labs., N.J. and Colo., 1962-74; mgr. bus. planning Aeronutronic Ford Corp., Willow Grove, Pa., 1974-76; mgr. research and devel. ITT, Corinth, Miss., 1976-78; lectr. Sch. Bus., Temple U., Phila., 1976, Sch. Bus., U. Colo., 1982—; project leader Nat. Telecommunication and Info. Adminstrn., U.S. Dept. Commerce, Boulder, Colo., 1978-82; dir. Info. Access Systems, Inc., 1981-84. Lemp Devel. Co., Inc., 1975—. Mem. CAP, 1970—; pres. Carolyn Heights Civic Assn., 1972-73; treas. Frazier Woods Civic Assn., 1975-76. Served with USAF, 1960-63; served to col. USAFR, 1973-74, 80-81. Decorated Air Force Commendation medal, Meritorious Service medal; named Outstanding Elec. Engr., Armed Forces Communications & Electronics Assn., 1959; cert. instrument flight instr., FAA. Mem. IEEE (sr.), Armed Forces Communications and Electronics Assn., Assn. Computing Machinery, Inst. Mgmt. Sci., Air Force Assn. Patentee in field; contbr. articles to profl. jours. Home: 3745 23d St Boulder CO 80302 Office: U Colo PO Box 419 Boulder CO 80309

LEMUS, GEORGE, educator; b. Del Rio, Tex., Apr. 14, 1928; s. Leopoldo and Ines (Suarez) L.; student U. Nacional Autónoma de México, 1946-48; B.A., U. Tex., 1952, M.A., 1956, Ph.D., 1963; m. Carmen Garcia, Aug. 6, 1957; children—Agnes Marie, Sarita Ann, Henry Edward, Robert Leopold, William Anthony. Tchr. pub. high sch., Aberdeen, Idaho, 1953-54; teaching fellow U. Tex., Austin, 1955-57; instr. USAF Lang. Sch., Lackland AFB, Tex., 1957-58, Loyola U., Los Angeles, 1958-60; asst. prof. Spanish, San Diego State U., 1960-64, assoc. prof., 1965-68, prof., 1968—, dir. summer program, 1964, 65, chmn. Latin Am. Studies Com., 1963-66, grad. adv. Latin Am. Studies Program, 1966-70; vis. prof. U. Colo., summer 1968. Sec.-treas. Pacific Coast Council Latin Am. Studies, 1964, mem. governing bd., 1967-69. Direccion General de Relaciones Culturales fellow, Madrid, 1957; Del Amo Found. fellow, 1970. Mem. Am. Assn. Tchrs. Spanish and Portuguese, Assn. Latin Am. Studies, Real Sociedad Bascongada de los Amigos del País, Sigma Delta Pi, Alpha Mu Gamma. Democrat. Roman Catholic. Author: Francisco Bulnes: su vida y sus obras, 1965. Contbr. articles to profl. jours. Home: 5730 Lance St San Diego CA 92120

LENARZ, WILLIAM HENRY, fishery biologist; b. Sacramento, Sept. 18, 1940; s. Raymond J. and Catharine I. (Langston) L.; m. Kara Koffron, Oct. 7, 1970 (div. Feb. 1978); m. Paget Leh, Oct. 27, 1985. AA, Sacramento City Coll., 1961; BS, Calif. State U.-Humboldt, Arcata, 1963; MS, U. Wash., 1965, PhD, 1969. Fishery biologist Nat. Marine Fisheries Service, La Jolla, Calif., 1968-76, Tiburon, Calif., 1976—; dir. Point Rayes Bird Obs., Stinson Beach, Calif., 1983—. Contbr. articles to profl. jours. Mem. AAAS, Am. Statis. Assn., Biometric Soc., Am. Inst. Fishery Research Biologists, Marin County Audubon Soc. (bd. dirs. 1983—, pres. 1985). Avocations: skiing, hiking, birdwatching. Office: Nat Marine Fisheries Service 3150 Paradise Dr Tiburon CA 94920

LENDVAY, GLENDA LOUISE FITE, personnel adminstrator; b. Henryetta, Okla., Oct. 14, 1946; d. Elvin Glenn and Bettie Louise (Carlton) F.; B.S. in Elem. Edn., Okla. State U., 1968. Sec. to v.p. Bank & Trust Co., Tulsa, 1968-71; adminstrv. asst. to new accounts supr. Cities Service Oil Co., Tulsa, 1971-73, sec. to credit card center asst. mgr., legis. coordinator, systems and programming coordinator, 1973-74; sec. to pres. and owner, bookkeeer, receptionist WRP Lumber Corp., Sedro Woolley, Wash., 1974-75; personnel asst. Homequity, 1975-76, personnel adminstr., Wilton, Conn., 1976-77, regional mgr., mgr. adminstr., San Mateo, Calif., 1977-82.

LENGACHER, EDWARD VICTOR, engineering executive, consultant; b. Portland, Oreg., Apr. 14, 1942; s. Victor Howard and Lucille M. (Lown) L.; m. Joan Marie Lindow, Jan. 29, 1966; children—Michael Edward, Laura Ann. Student Portland State U., 1960-62; B.S.C.E., Oreg. State U., 1965. Registered profl. engr. Structural engr. Swan Wooster Cons. Engrs., Portland, 1965-69, Kramer & Assocs., Vancouver, Wash., 1972-74; mgr. engring. dept. Microflect Co., Salem, Oreg., 1969-72; owner, pres., structural engr. E.L. Engring. Inc., Vancouver, 1974—. Mem. Structural Engrs. Oreg., Cons. Engrs. Oreg. Republican. Lutheran. Lodge: Elks. Office: E L Engring Inc 9013-O Northeast Hwy 99 Vancouver WA 98665

LENHART, BOB GENE, grain company engineer; b. Wren, Ohio, Aug. 7, 1932; s. Orval M. and Rose N. (Elzey) L.; student Purdue U., 1956-62; m. Deloris M. Werling, June 21, 1953; children—Deborah, Kristi, Kim, Nancy. Engr., Central Soya Co., Inc., Ft. Wayne, Ind., 1956-66, maintenance engr., Gibson City, Ill., 1966-67, Ft. Worth, 1967-69; chief engr. Hayes & Stolz Co., Ft. Worth, 1969-70; engr. Continental Grain Co., Chgo., 1970-74, regional engr. Pacific Coast Region. Tacoma, 1974-81, regional ops. engring. mgr. Pacific Coast region, Portland, Oreg., 1981—. Served with U.S. Army, 1953-55. Mem. IEEE Grain Elevator and Processing Soc. Lutheran. Home: 19900 Roan Circle West Linn OR 97068 Office: Continental Grain Co 200 Market Bldg Suite 1050 Portland OR 97201

LENHOFF, HOWARD MAER, educator; b. North Adams, Mass., Jan. 27, 1929; s. Charles and Goldy Sarah (Rubin) L.; m. Sylvia Grossman, June 20, 1954; children: Gloria, Bernard. B.A., Coe Coll., 1950, D.Sc. (hon.), 1976; Ph.D., Johns Hopkins U., 1955. USPHS fellow Loomis Lab., Greenwich, Conn., 1954-56; vis. lectr. Howard U., Washington, 1957-58; postdoctoral fellow Carnegie Instn., Washington, 1958; investigator Howard Hughes Med. Inst., Miami, 1958-63; prof. biology, dir. Lab. for Quantitative Biology U. Miami, Coral Gables, 1963-69; prof. biol. scis. U. Calif.-Irvine, 1969—, prof. polit. sci., 1986—, dir. marine biology program, 1969-73, assoc. dean biol. scis., 1969-71, dean grad. div., 1971-73, asst. to vice chancellor of student affairs for grant devel. and faculty relations, 1986—; vis. scientist, Louis Lipsky fellow Weizmann Inst. Sci., Rehovot, Israel, 1968-69; vis. prof. chem. engring., Rothschild fellow Israel Inst. Tech., 1973-74; vis. prof. Hebrew U., Jerusalem, spring 1970, fall 1971, 77-78; Hubert Humphrey Inst. fellow Ben Gurion U., Beersheva, Israel, 1981; dir. Nelson Research & Devel. Co., Irvine, 1971-73; chmn. bd. dirs. BioProbe Internat., Inc., Tustin, Calif., 1983—. Editor: Biology of Hydra, 1961, Hydra, 1969, Experimental Coelenterate Biology, 1972, Coelenterate Biology—Review and Perspectives, 1974, Hydra: Research Methods, 1983, Enzyme Immunoassay, 1985, From Trembley's Polyps to New Directions in Research on Hydra, 1985, Hydra and the Birth of Experimental Biology, 1986; mem. editorial bd.: Jour. Solid Phase Biochemistry, 1976-80. Mem. sci. adv. bd. Orange Empire council Boy Scouts Am., 1971-73; vice chmn. So. Calif. div. Am. Assn. Profs. for Peace in Middle East, 1972—; v.p. bd. dirs. Am. Assn. for Ethiopian Jews, 1973-78, 82—, pres., 1978-82; bd. govs. Israel Bonds Orange County, Calif., 1974-80, Dade County Heart Assn., Miami, 1958-61, So. Calif. Technion Soc.,1976; pres. Hillel Council of Orange County, 1976-78; nat. chmn. faculty div. State of Israel Bonds, 1976; mem. sci. adv. bd. Am. Friends of Weizmann Inst. Sci., 1980-84; bd. dirs. Hi Hopes Identity Discovery Found., Anaheim, Calif., 1982—, pres. bd. govs., 1983-85. Served to 1st lt. USAF, 1956-58. Recipient Career Development award USPHS, 1965-69, Alumni award for community service U. Calif., Irvine, 1977; Louis Lipsky fellow, 1968-69; Disting. fellow Iowa Acad. Sci., 1986. Fellow AAAS, Iowa Acad. Sci. (disting.); mem. Am. Chem. Soc., Am. Biophys. Soc., History of Sci. Soc., Am. Soc. Cell Biologists, Am. Soc. Biol. Chemists, Biophysics Soc., Soc. Gen. Physiologists, Soc. Growth and Devel., Phi Beta Kappa, Sigma Xi, Phi Kappa Phi. Home: 304 Robin Hood Ln Costa Mesa CA 92627 Office: U Calif Sch Biol Scis Irvine CA 92717

LENKER, JAY ALAN, aeronautical engineer; b. Harrisburg, Pa., Dec. 31, 1949; s. William Archibald and Alethia Winifred (Snell) L.; m. Karen Janice Grosser, June 9, 1978; 1 child, Jennifer Elisabeth. BS in Aerospace Engring., Pa. State U., 1971, MS in Aerospace Engring., 1974, PhD in Aerospace Engring., 1978. Sect. mgr. Baxter-Travenol Lab., Round Lake, Ill., 1977-79; sr. project engr. Shiley, Inc., Irvine, Calif., 1979-82, engring. group mgr., 1982-87; dir. research and devel. Advanced Surgical Intervention, Inc., Laguna Hills, Calif., 1987—. Contbr. articles to profl. jours.; patentee tissue heart valves. Mem. Sigma Xi, Tau Beta Pi, Sigma Gamma Tau. Democrat. Lutheran. Avocations: sailing, swimming, running. Office: Advanced Surgical Intervention Inc 25241 Paseo De Alicia Suite 120 Laguna Hills CA 92653

LENNARTSSON, OLAF WALTER, research scientist; b. Laxsjö, Sweden, Oct. 27, 1943; came to U.S., 1978.; s. Nils Lennart and Märta Kristina (Olsson) Nilsson; m. Nancy Karllee Harris, June 10, 1978. Master in Theoretical Physics, Royal Inst. Tech., 1969, PhD in Plasma Physics, 1974, docent, 1977. Engr. Swedish Air Force, Stockholm, 1969-70; tching. asst. Royal Inst. Tech., Stockholm, 1969-74, research assoc., 1976-78; NAS/NRC research assoc. NASA Marshall Space Flight Ctr., Huntsville, Ala., 1974-76; cons. scientist Lockheed Missiles and Space Co., Inc., Palo Alto, Calif., 1978-79, research scientist, 1979—. Contbr. articles to profl. jours. Served to lt. Swedish Air Force, 1969-70, Stockholm. Mem. Am. Geophysical Union, Swedish Grad. Engrs. Union, Tech. Physicists Assn. Democrat. Avocations: painting, flying, scuba diving, horseback riding, photography. Home: 415 Distel Dr Los Altos CA 94022 Office: Lockheed Missiles and Space D/91-20 B/255 3251 Hanover St Palo Alto CA 94304

LENNETTE, EDWIN HERMAN, virologist; b. Pitts., Sept. 11, 1908; s. John and Natalie Frances (LeManek) L.; m. Elizabeth Hubenthal, Sept. 2, 1930 (dec. Apr. 1981); children: Edwin Paul, David Alan. BS, U. Chgo., 1931, PhD, 1935, MD, 1936. Diplomate Am. Bd. Preventive Medicine, Am. Bd. Med. Microbiology. Instr. pathology Wash. U. Med. Sch., St. Louis, 1938-39; staff mem. internat. health div. Rockefeller Found., N.Y.C., 1939-47; dir. virus lab. Calif. Dept Health Services, Berkeley, 1947-78; cons. WHO, Geneva, 1952-78, Dept. of Army, Washington, 1948-78, NIH, 1948-75; pres. Armed Forces Epidemiol. Bd., Dept. of Army, 1973-76, Virion (U.S.), Inc., 1985—. Contbr. numerous articles to sci. and med. jours. Pres. Calif. Pub. Health Found., Berkeley, 1980—; bd. dirs. Rush Med. Coll., Chgo., 1970-74, Peralta Cancer Research Inst., Oakland, Calif., 1978—, pres., 1985—. Recipient Bronfman award Am. Pub. Health Assn., 1969, Profl. Achievement award U. Chgo., 1981. Mem. Am. Assn. Immunologists (pres. 1961), Fedn. Am. Socs. Exptl. Biology (pres. 1968-69), Tissue Culture Assn. (pres. 1976-78), Am. Soc. Microbiology (pres. 1978, Wyeth award 1976, Wellcome Diagnostics award 1986). Republican. Home: 6605 Ascot Dr Oakland CA 94611 Office: Calif Dept Health Serivices 2151 Berkeley Way Berkeley CA 94611

LENNOX, SHIRLEY ANN, artist, educator, consultant; b. San Francisco, Nov. 8, 1931; d. James Joseph and Mildred Mae (Hall) Amos; m. Arthur James Lennox, Jan. 6, 1951; children: Sharron Kay, Kathleen Melanie, Bonnie Marie, Colleen Leta. Student pub. schs., South Glens Falls, N.Y. Window display artist Fowlers' Inc., Glens Falls, 1948-51; owner, operator Discovery House Gallery, Palo Alto, Calif., 1969-71; owner, operator, tchr. porcelain painting Lennox Art Sutdio, Santa Maria, Calif., 1972—; cons. art, Santa Maria, 1985—; owner, operator Gallerie 272, Morton, N.Y., 1979-81; resident artist, gallery mgr. Options Gallery, Shell Beach, Calif., 1985. Exhibited paintings in one-woman shows: Village Gallery, Hilton, N.Y., Lake George Inst. History and Art, N.Y., 1974, Swan Gallery, Albion, N.Y., 1979, Options Gallery, Shell Beach, Calif., 1984, Morro Bay Mus. Natural History, 1985; group shows include: The Calif. Scene (with Ansel Adams and others), Foothill Coll., Los Altos, Calif., 1970, Suburban Rochester Art Group shows, N.Y., 1976-80, Santa Ynez Art Shows, Calif., 1983-84, Los Padres Artists Guild Shows, 1983-86, Faulkner Gallery, 1985, Gallery 113, Santa Barbara, 1987; represented in permanent collections: Old Courthouse Mus., Lake George, N.Y., Shelter Cove Lodge, Pismo Beach, Calif; represented by Valley Art Gallery, Los Olivos, Calif., The Sandpiper, Pismo Beach, Calif. Bd. dirs. Santa Maria Arts Council, 1983-85. Mem. Internat. Porcelain Arts Tchrs., Internat. Soc. Marine Painters Inc. (juried profl. mem.), Nat. Soc. Painters in Casein and Acrylic (assoc.), Santa Maria Women's Network, Santa Barbara Art Assn. (juried), Cen. Coast Watercolor Soc., San Luis Obispo Art Assn., Artists Guild of Santa Ynez Valley, Porcelain Portrait Soc. Republican. Avocations: photography, camping.

LENT, BERKELEY, state supreme court justice; b. Los Angeles, Sept. 22, 1921; s. Oscar Paul and Patricia Lucile (Berkeley) L.; m. Joan Kay Burnett, Dec. 27, 1968; children: Patricia Brandt, Deirdre, Eric, Terry Ling. Student, Reed Coll., 1941, 46-47, Occidental Coll., Los Angeles, 1944-45; J.D., Willamette U., 1950. Bar: Oreg. 1950. Asso. editor Bancroft-Whitney Law Pub. Co., San Francisco, 1950; with Office Gen. Counsel, Bonneville Power Adminstrn., Portland, Oreg., 1950-51, 52-53; individual practice law Coos Bay, Oreg., 1951-52; asso. firm Peterson & Pozzi, Portland, 1952-53; partner firm Lent, York, Paulson & Bullock (and predecessor firms), Portland, 1953-70; individual practice law Portland, 1970-71; judge Circuit Ct., Multnomah County, 1971-77; assoc. Oreg. Supreme Ct., Salem, 1977-82, 83—, chief justice, 1982-83. Mem. Oreg. Ho. of Reps., 1957-65, minority whip, 1965; mem. Oreg. Senate, 1967-71, majority leader, 1971. Served with USNR, 1942-45. Mem. VFW, Am. Legion. Democrat. Club: Elks. Office: Oreg Supreme Ct 1147 State St Salem OR 97310

LENTES, DAVID EUGENE, corporate executive; b. Spokane, Dec. 14, 1951; s. William Eugene and Ellen Elsie L.; m. Debra Kay White, May 19, 1973 (div. 1984); children: Janette Adele, Damon Arthur. AA, Spokane Falls Community Coll., 1972; BBA, Gonzaga U., 1975. V.p. Dellen Wood Products, Inc., Spokane, 1972—, also bd. dirs.; v.p. Custom Computer Services, Inc., Spokane, 1980—, also bd. dirs.; mng. ptnr. Com-Lease, 1980—, Len-Lease, 1980—; v.p., bd. dirs. DWP Trucking, Inc., 1982-85, Sentel Corp., 1983—, BDR Investment Corp., 1983—; pres., bd. dirs. ASA Mgmt. Corp., 1984—, also Link Internat., Inc., 1985. Treas. Dishman Hills Natural Area Assn., 1970—; elder Bethany Presbyn. Ch., 1980-83; active Spokane Econ. Devel. Council. Mem. Assn. Wash. Bus., Nat. Fedn. Ind. Businessmen, Am. Fedn. Bus., Better Bus. Bur. (Spokane chpt.), U.S. C. of C., Spokane C. of C., Timber Products Mfrs., Hoo-Hoo Internat. Republican. Office: N 3014 Flora Rd Spokane WA 99216

LENZ, PHILIP JOSEPH, municipal administrator; b. Monterey Park, Calif., Sept. 15, 1940; s. Philip George and Irene Mary (Bowers) L.; m. Mary Lou Antista, July 16, 1966; children: Brian Joseph, Jonathan Thomas. BA, Calif. State U., Los Angeles, 1966; MS, Pepperdine U., 1974. Dir. West Valley div. San Bernardino County (Calif.) Probation Dept., 1977-79, dir. juvenile div., 1979-82, dir. adminstrv. services, 1982—. Sec. bd. trustees Upland (Calif.) Sch. Dist., 1985—; mgr., coach Upland Am. Little League, 1981—, bd. dirs. 1982—; pres. Fontana (Calif.) Family Service Agy., 1972-74; mem. adv. com. corrections Chaffey Coll., Alta Loma, Calif., 1977—; mem. City of Upland Parks and Recreation com., 1986—. Recipient Tim Fitzharris award Chief Probation Officers of Calif., 1987. Mem. Calif. Probation, Parole and Correctional Assn. (regional v.p. 1981-83, 2d v.p. 1985-86, 1st v.p. 1986—, pres. 1987—), Probation Bus. Mgr.'s Assn. (regional chmn. 1984-86, v.p. 1987), Western Correctional Assn., Calif. Probation Parole and Correctional Assn. (liaison). Democrat. Roman Catholic. Avocations: baseball, bicycle riding, hiking. Home: 1375 N Stanford Ave Upland CA 91786 Office: San Bernardino County Dept Probation 175 W 5th St San Bernardino CA 92415

LEO, GENE EDWARD, JR., zoo and aquarium administrator; b. Portland, Oreg., Dec. 13, 1949; s. Gene Edward and Ann (Reynolds) L.; m. Gaila Margaret Constant, June 19, 1971; children: Jay Robert, Benjamin Constant. B.S., Portland State U., 1975; M.S., U. Wis., 1978; postgrad. profl. mgmt. sch., U. N.C., 1980. Cert. profl. adminstr., Wis., Wash. With Washington Park Zoo, Portland, 1967-72, dir., 1985—; asst. dir. Henry Vilas Park Zoo, Madison, Wis., 1972-81; dir. Point Defiance Zoo and Aquarium, Tacoma, 1981-85. Chmn. spl. events mktg. com. South Sound Regional Tourism Devel., Wash. Dept. Econ. Devel., 1982-83; chmn. South Sound Regional Tourism Devel, Wash. Dept. Econ. Devel., 1983-84; bd. dirs. Greater Portland Conv. and Visitors Assn., 1985—, chmn. tourism com., 1985—; bd. dirs., mem. exec. com. Washington County Visitors Assn.; bd. dirs. Portland Civic Theater, Portland Rose Fest. Assn. Fellow Am. Assn. Zool. Parks and Aquarium (vice chmn. membership bylaw com. 1981-82); mem. Nat. Recreation and Park Assn., Wash. Park and Recreation Assn., Wis. Park and Recreation Assn., Wis. Zoo Assocs. Lodge: Rotary. Office: Washington Park Zoo 4001 SW Canyon Rd Portland OR 97221

LEO, MARY GAYE, theatre director; b. Colorado Springs, Colo., Oct. 19, 1951; d. Bernard Johnston and Mary Ellen (Hardy) Lamar; m. Dominick Louis Leo; 1 child, Dominick Christopher. B.A., U. Colo., 1973, M.A., 1978; PhD in Ednl. Adminstrn. Denver U., 1985. Communications, group dynamics instr., Denver area, 1972-73; with Denver Public Sch. System, 1973—, arts mgmt./theatre dir., 1973—. Vol., Colo. Arts and Humanities Council as lectr., workshop coordinator, 1974-75. Cert. bicultural/bilingual instr. Mem. Am. Theatre Assn., Women in Theatre, Nat. Council Tchrs. English, Nat. Assn. Female Execs., Colo. Assn. Sch. Execs. Author: Celebration (rock musical), 1979; Bob, The Magical Unicorn (children's fantasy), 1981; The Raven and I-E Locus of Control as Measures of High Ability; dir., designer, producer profl. and ednl. theatrical prodns. including Godspell, 1974, Guys and Dolls, 1975, My Fair Lady, 1976, Carousel, 1977, Music Man, 1978, Celebration!, 1979, Annie Get Your Gun, 1980, Jesus Christ Superstar, 1982, Grease, 1982, Camelot, 1983, Guys and Dolls, 1987. Home: 11224 E Harvard Dr Aurora CO 80014 Office: Denver Pub Sch System 2960 N Speer Blvd Denver CO 80211

LEO, ROBERT JOSEPH, association executive, consultant; b. Paterson, N.J., Nov. 24, 1939; s. Dewey J. and Jean (Bianco) L.; m. Margaret Elena Ingafu, Aug. 5, 1962; children—Christopher, Nicholas. B.A. in Speech, Temple U., 1960, M.A., 1962; Ph.D., U. Wash., 1968. Instr. Monmouth Coll., West Long Branch, N.J., 1962-64; spl. asst. to chancellor Dallas County (Tex.) Community Coll. Dist., 1968-71, dir. spl. services and gov. relations, 1971-76; assoc. exec. dir. League for Innovation in the Community Coll., Los Angeles, 1976-80, exec. dir., Dallas, 1980-82; exec. dir. Los Angeles Jr. C. of C., 1982—; founding pres. Nat. Council Resource Devel., adj. assoc. prof. East Tex. State U., 1975-76; chmn. Tex. Health Planning Council. Recipient Disting. Service award Oak Cliff Jaycees, 1973; Spl. Recognition award Nat. Council Resource Devel., 1981; named Significant Contbr. to Fair Housing, Greater Dallas Housing Opportunity Ctr., 1973. Mem. Am. Soc. Tng. and Devel., Am. Soc. Assn. Execs., Nat. Council Resource Devel., Am. Youth Soccer Orgn. Roman Catholic. Clubs: Rotary, Los Angeles Athletic, Univ. Author articles in field. Home: 12055 Woodley Ave Granada Hills CA 91344 Office: Jr Chamber of Commerce 404 S Bixel St Los Angeles CA 90017

LEONARD, BARBARA ANN, magazine editor, writer, photographer; b. Phila., Mar. 11, 1940; d. Curtis Allen Emerson and Dolores Erminia (Veneziale) Tiedje; children: Bruce, Brett, Brigette. Student, Notre Dame Acad., Los Angeles, 1957; AA, Santa Monica City Coll., 1959; BA, UCLA, 1966; postgrad., Calif. Luth. Coll., 1980. Cert. secondary tchr., Calif. Librarian Douglas Aircraft Co., Santa Monica, Calif., 1959-64, Planning Research Corp., Westwood, Calif., 1966-67; tchr.'s aide Mentaly Gifted Students' program Malibu Park Jr. High Sch., Calif., 1967-78; tchr. Poindexter Grammar Sch., Moorepark, Calif., 1978-80; editorial dir. TL Enterprises, Inc., Agoura, Calif., 1980—. Contbr. travel articles to pubs. Democrat. Roman Catholic. Avocations: skiing, camping, tennis, cooking. Office: TL Enterprises Inc 29901 Agoura Rd Agoura CA 91301

LEONARD, LEO DONALD, educational sociologist; b. Salt Lake City, Nov. 23, 1938; s. Leo Bradford and Florence (Robbins) L.; B.S., U. Utah, 1961, student U. Wash., 1961-62, 64-65; M.S., Utah State U., 1967, Ed.D., 1969; m. Marilynn Rae Hoyt, Jan. 2, 1962; 1 son, Richard Corey. Acting head King County Dept. Mental Health and Adoptions, Seattle, 1962; dir. programs and youth Snoline YMCA, Seattle, 1962-64; instr. Shorecrest High Sch., 1967-68, Roy (Utah) High Sch., 1966-67; instr. ednl. methods Utah State U., 1968-69; prof. edn. U. Toledo, 1969-80; dean Sch. Edn., U. Portland (Oreg.), 1979—; univ. coordinator Catholic Diocese of Toledo Curriculum Devel. Project, 1970-75; coll. dir. Canadian Dissemination Project, 1971-74; bd. dirs. Internat. Tchrs. Edn. Council, 1970—; mem. Nat. Task Force on Tchr. Edn., 1984-86. Bd. dirs. Toledo Symphony Orch., 1970-79; trustee, v.p. Choral Arts Soc. Portland, 1983-85; trustee Tucker Maxon Sch., Open Meadows Learning Ctr. Fellow Internat. Tchr. Edn. Council, 1971—; Fulbright scholar, Africa, 1967; grantee U.S. Office Edn-Tchr. Corps, 1970, many others. Mem. Am. Assn. Individual Guided Edn., Am. Edn. Research Soc., Comparative Edn. Soc. U.S., Comparative Edn. Soc. Can., Am. Assn. Colls. of Tchr. Edn. (pres. state council deans of edn. 1983-85), Marine Corps League (commandant Portland detachment 1983-84), Phi Kappa Phi, Phi Alpha Theta, Phi Delta Kappa. Author: (with Robert T. Utz) The Building Skills for Competency Based Teaching, 1974, The Foundations of Competency Based Education, 1975, A Competency Based Curriculum, 1971, La Enseñanza como Desarrollo de Competencias, 1979; (with others) 7 instructors guides for individually guided edn.; contbr. chpts. to books and articles to profl. jours. Office: Sch Edn U Portland 5000 N Willamette Blvd Portland OR 97203

LEONARDS, KENNETH STANLEY, educator, researcher; b. Detroit, July 19, 1950; s. Stanley M. and Emily (Lukasik) L.; m. Royce Marie Hazard, June 2, 1980; 1 child, Amelia Royce. BA, Kalamazoo Coll., 1972; MS, Mich. State U., 1975, PhD, 1980. Assoc., postdoctoral fellow SUNY Med. Sch., Buffalo, 1980-82; NIH postdoctoral trainee U. Va. Med. Sch., Charlottesville, 1982-83, Am. Heart Assn. postdoctoral fellow, 1983-84; asst. prof. UCLA Med. Sch., 1984—. Mem. editorial bd. Molecular and Cellular Biochemistry, 1987—; contbr. articles to profl. jours. Recipient New Investigator award NIH, 1985—; fellow Dept. Energy, 1975-80; grantee NSF, 1971-72, Am. Heart Assn., 1986—. Mem. AAAS, Am. Chem. Soc., Am. Physiol. Soc., Biophys. Soc. Avocations: hiking, fly fishing, chess, classical music. Office: UCLA Med Sch Cardiovascular Lab A3-381 CHS 10833 LeConte Ave Los Angeles CA 90024-1760

LEONE HAMM, DONNA M., criminal justice administrator; b. Woonsocket, R.I., Mar. 3, 1947; d. Thomas Dominic and Julia Evelyn (Sullivan) L.; divorced; 1 child, Angela; m. James J. Hamm, Mar. 20, 1987. BA, Miami U., Oxford, Ohio, 1968; postgrad., Ariz. State U., 1983; cert., Nat. Jud. Coll. U. Nev., 1981. Prin. Lance Aire, Inc., Dayton, Ohio, 1974-79; justice of peace Coconino County, Flagstaff, Ariz., 1980-82; exec. dir. Ariz. Council Child Care Agys., Phoenix, 1983-84, Florence Crittenton, Phoenix, 1984-86, Ariz. Attys. for Criminal Justice, Phoenix, 1986—; founder, pres. Middle Ground, Tempe, Ariz., 1980—. Bd. dirs. United Way No. Ariz., Flagstaff, 1981; pres. bd. dirs. Northland Crisis Nursery, Flagstaff, 1981-82. Mem. Ariz. Found. Children, Child Welfare League Am., Am. Correctional Assn., Ariz. Probation Parole and Corrections Assn. Democrat. Avocations: piloting, hiking, reading, scuba diving (cert.). Home: 139 E Encanto Dr Tempe AZ 85281 Office: Hamm & Assocs 139 E Encanto Dr Tempe AZ 85281

LEONHARD, GREGORY FORREST, infosystems specialist, consultant; b. Downey, Calif., Oct. 20, 1951; s. George Ludwig and Rubye Hanna (Holmes) L.; m. Linda Kay Sharp, Sept. 9, 1979. BA summa cum laude, Whitman Coll., 1973; MS, U. Colo., 1979. Mgmt. info. systems dir. Aspen Leaf Co., Denver, 1977-78; EDP mgr. Sinclair Paint Co., Los Angeles, 1978-79; EDP planning and programs coordinator ARAMCO, Dhahran, Saudi Arabia, 1979-85; pres. Pinecliffe Internat., Coal Creek Canyon, Colo., 1985—; instr. U. Colo., Boulder, 1976-77; cons. Western Interstate Commn. Higher Edn./Nat. Ctr. Higher Edn. Mgmt. Systems, Boulder, 1977. Author: How to Win the College Game, 1986. Active Coal Creek Canyon (Colo.) Improvement Assn., 1985—. Mem. Assn. Computing Machinery, Nat. Writers Club, Data Processing Mgmt. Assn. (chpt. sec. 1979), Am. Philatelic Soc., E. African Wildlife Soc., Phi Beta Kappa, Pi Kappa Delta. Avocations: photography, travel. Office: Pinecliffe Internat Box 7168 Crescent Lake Br Golden CO 80403

LEONHARD, WILLIAM E., construction and engineering company executive. Chmn., chief exec. officer Parsons Corp, Pasadena Calif. Office: Parsons Corp 100 W Walnut Pasadena CA 92124 *

LEONTOS, CAROLYN JONES, dietitian, nutritionist; b. Detroit, Dec. 20, 1937; d. Charles Louis and Mary Elizabeth (Kane) Jones; m. Arthur Harry Leontos, Apr. 4, 1979. BS, Mercy Coll. of Detroit, 1968; MS, Case Western Res. U., 1970. Dietitian Meml. Sloan Kettering Cancer Ctr., N.Y.C., 1971-77; mgr. hotel services Delta Queen Steamboat, New Orleans, 1977-78; dietitian Victoria Hosp., Miami, Fla., 1979, Montelepre Hosp., New Orleans, 1980; diabetes outpatient dietitian Humana Hosp. Sunrise, Las Vegas, Nev., 1981-85; area extension specialist-foods and nutrition Nev. Coop. Extension, Las Vegas, 1985—. Contbr. articles on nutrition to mags. and newspapers. Mem. Am. Dietetic Assn., Nev. Dietetic Assn. (pres. 1986-87), Am. Assn. Diabetes Educators, Am. Home Econs. Assn., Nat. Assn. Extension Home Economists, Am. Diabetes Assn. (bd. dirs. Nev. div. 1984—), Am. Heart Assn. (bd. dirs. Nev. div. 1985—), Juvenile Diabetes Found. (bd. dirs. Las Vegas chpt. 1983-86). Democrat. Roman Catholic. Home: 365 Santali Ct Henderson NV 89015 Office: Nev Coop Extension 953 E Sahara ST&P Bldg 207 Las Vegas NV 89104

LEOPOLD, IRVING HENRY, physician, medical educator; b. Phila., Apr. 19, 1915; s. Abraham and Dora (Schlow) L.; m. Eunice Robinson, June 24, 1937; children—Ellen Robinson, John. Student, Pa. State U., 1934; M.D., U. Pa., 1938, D.Sc., 1943. Diplomate: Am. Bd. Ophthalmology (chmn. bd. 1971-72, chmn. visual scis. study sect. 1968-70, subcom. impaired vision and blindness 1967-69, task force on ocular pharmacology, 1967-69, cons. 1975-79, asso. examiner 1974-81). Intern Hosp. U. Pa., 1938-40; fellow, instr. ophthalmology Hosp. U. Pa., also U. Pa. Med. Sch., 1940-45, assoc., 1945-54; research investigator chem. warfare OSRD, 1941-45; mem. faculty U. Pa. Grad. Sch. Medicine, 1946-64, successively assoc., asst. prof., assoc. prof., 1946-55, prof., head dept. ophthalmology, 1955-64; chief dept. ophthalmology Grad. Hosp., 1955-61; dir. research Wills Eye Hosp., 1949-64, attending surgeon, 1952-64, med. dir., 1961-64, cons. surgeon, 1965—; chmn. sci. adv. com. Allergan Pharms., 1974, exec. v.p., 1975; prof., chmn. dept. ophthalmology Mt. Sinai Sch. Medicine, 1965—; dir. dept. ophthalmology Mt. Sinai Hosp., N.Y.C., 1964-75; prof., chmn. dept. ophthalmology U. Calif. at Irvine, 1975—, prof. pharmacology, 1982—, prof. emeritus ophthalmology, 1985—; clin. prof. ophthalmolgy Coll. Physicians and Surgeons, Columbia, 1964-66; cons. ophthalmologist St. Joseph's Hosp., 1959—, Albert Einstein Med. Center, 1959—; Proctor lectr. U. Calif., 1962; Gifford Meml. lectr., Chgo., 1967; Edwin B. Dunphy lectr. Harvard, 1968; Walter Wright lectr. U. Toronto, 1969; Richardson Cross lectr. Royal Soc. Medicine, 1970; Doyne Meml. lectr. Ophthal. Soc. U.K., 1971; DeSchweinitz Meml. lectr., Phila., 1972; Jules Stein lectr. UCLA, 1974; Bedell lectr., Phila., 1975; Edwin B. Dunphy lectr. Harvard, 1975; Francis H. Adler lectr., Phila., 1980, Dwight Towne lectr., Ky., 1979, C.S. O'Brien lectr., New Orleans, 1979; Disting. vis. lectr. Jefferson Med. Coll., 1980, Moorfields Hosp., Eng., 1980, U. Helsinki, Finland, 1980, Third Francis Heed Adler lectr., 1980, 2d ann. Tullos O. Coston lectr., 1981, Sir Stewart Duke-Elder lectr., 1982, Everett R. Viers lectr., Scott and White Clinic and Tex. A&M U. Coll. Medicine, Temple, Tex., 1982, U. Phillipines 1st lectr. Eye Resident Soc., Eye Referral Ctr., 1982, Royal Soc. Medicine lectr., London, 1985; lectr. Internat. Congress Ophthalmology, Japan, 1978, Phillipine Bd. Opthamology; cons. Chem. Warfare Service, U.S. Army, 1948-52, 81; surgeon gen. USPHS, 1953—, FDA, HEW, 1963; mem. med. adv. com. Orange County chpt. Multiple Sclerosis Soc., 1979-81; chmn. ophthalmology panel U.S. Pharmacopeia, 1960-70, mem. revision panel, 1970—; chmn. panel drug efficacy in ophthalmology Nat. Acad. Scis.-NRC, 1966-67, 80—; mem. tng. grants com. USPHS, 1952-58, mem. spl. sensory study sect. research record diseases and blindness, 1954-58; mem. field investigating com. Nat. Inst. Neurol. Diseases and Blindness, 1959-61, mem. neurol. project com., 1961-63, chmn. vision research tng. com., 1967-68; mem. adv. bd. Am. Behcet's Found., Inc., 1980, 81; expert agree to Ministry of Health, France, 1981—; curator ophthalmic pharmaceuticals Found. Am. Acad. Ophthalmology, 1983—; mem. nat. adv. eye council panel on cataract sect. Nat. Eye Inst. and HEW, 1981-85; mem. med. research and devel. command-chemical welfare U.S. Army, 1981-85; Everett R. Veins lectr. Scott and White Clinic, Tex. A&M U. Coll. Medicine, Temple, 1982; 1st Irving H. Leopold lectr. Wills Eye Hosp., 1987. Editor-in-chief: Survey of Ophthalmology, 1958-62; cons. editor, 1962—; editorial bd.: Am. Jour. Diabetes, 1956-73, Investigative Ophthalmology, 1961-74; assoc. editor: Am. Jour. Ophthalmology, 1974-81, now mem. editorial bd.; assoc. editor Archives of Ophthalmology, 1974-81; cons. Jour. AMA, 1974-81; editorial cons. Jour. Ocular Pharmacology, 1985—; editor: Ocular Inflammation and Therapeutics, 1981. Trustee Seeing Eye Guide. Recipient Zentmayer award, 1945, 49; honor award Am. Acad. Ophthalmology, 1955, subscriber award, 1984; Edward Lorenzo Holmes citation and award, 1957; Friedenwald medal Assn. Research Ophthalmology, 1960; Disting. Research award U. Calif., Irvine, Calif., 1980; Disting. Research award U. Calif. Alumni Assn., 1980; Physician's award Pa. Acad. Ophthalmology and Otolaryngology, 1981; Sir Steward Duke-Elder award, Lederle Medal and Prize for Research in Glaucoma Internat. Glaucoma Congress VI and Am. Soc. Contemporary Opthamology, 17th ann. sci. assembly, Orlando, Fla., 1982. Mem. N.Y. Acad. Medicine, Am. Ophthal. Soc. (Verhoeff Meml. lectr. 1973, Lucien Howe medal 1974), N.Y. Ophthal. Soc., Am. Acad. Ophthalmology and Otolaryngology (chmn. drug com. ophthalmology 1963-74, Edward Jackson Meml. lectr. 1965, honor guest 1971, 75), Am. Soc. Contemporary Ophthalmology (chief cons. editorial bd. 1981), Assn. Research Ophthalmology (trustee, chmn.), Nat. Soc. Prevention Blindness (dir. 1974-81, v.p., exec. com., hon. bd. dirs.), A.C.S., AAAS, Art Alliance Phila., John Morgan Soc., Coll. Physicians Phila., Am. Diabetes Assn., AMA (chmn. residency rev. com. ophthalmology 1970-72, Physician's Recognition award 1980, 81, 82, 83, 84, 85, 86), N.Y. Acad. Sci., Pan Am. Assn. Ophthalmology, Pan Pacific Surg. Assn., Royal Soc. Medicine (London), N.Y. State, N.Y. County, Philadelphia County med. socs., Calif., Orange County med. assns., Orange County Soc. Ophthalmology, Am. Med. Student Assn., Los Angeles Research Study Club (dir. 1979-81), Nat. Soc. to Prevent Blindness (hon. bd. dirs. 1986—), Sigma Xi, Alpha Omega Alpha. Clubs: Medical Biochemist, Vesper (Phila.); Newport Beach Tennis, Big Canyon Country, Balboa Bay (Newport Beach, Calif.); Century Country, Princeton (N.Y.C.). Home: 1484 Galaxy Dr Newport Beach CA 92660 Office: Dept Ophthalmology Calif Coll Medicine U Cal Irvine CA 92717

LEOPOLD, JOAN SILVERBERG, educational administrator, educator; b. N.Y.C., Mar. 18, 1947; d. Al and Shirley (Zimmerman) Silverberg; m. John William Leopold, June 22, 1969; 1 dau., Ellen. B.A. summa cum laude, Vassar Coll., 1967; cert. in Victorian Studies, U. London, Eng., 1967; M.A., Harvard U., 1968, Ph.D., 1975; postgrad. Oxford U., Eng., 1970-77. Mellon fellow U. Pa., Phila., 1979-80; research assoc. U. Calif.-Berkeley, 1979-82; adminstrv. service officer Calif. Spanish Lang. Data Base, Hayward, 1981-82; asst. prof. Chapman Coll., Alameda and Mare Island, Calif., 1981-82; dean Coll. Arts and Scis. Internat. Coll., Los Angeles, 1982-83; vis. scholar UCLA, 1982-85, dir. Volney Prize Essay Project, 1982—; instr. Rutgers U., Camden, N.J., 1970. Author: Culture in Comparative and Evolutionary Perspective, 1980; The Letter Liveth: The Life, Work and Library of A.F. Pott, 1983. Contbr. articles, revs. to hist. publs. Rhodes fellow, Oxford U., 1972-74, Humboldt fellow, 1976-78, Volkswagen fellow, 1979, Danforth fellow, 1967-75, Woodrow Wilson Found. Fellow, 1967-68; grantee Am. Council Learned Socs., 1981; recipient Univs. Essay Prize Royal Asiatic Soc., 1971. Mem. Grad. History Assn. (founder, Oxford 1970), Intellectual History Seminar (founder, Oxford 1971), Internat. Assn. Ind. Scholars (founder, pres. 1984-85), Am. Hist. Assn., Assn. Univ. Adminstrs., AAUW (hon. fellowship, Germany 1976-77). Office: PO Box 24250 Los Angeles CA 90024

LEPAK, REVA LORENE, sales executive; b. Denver, Jan. 5, 1942; d. Kenneth Charles and Frances Thelma (Voorhees) Burt; B.S., U. Colo., 1967; children—Renza Gayle, Regina Liesl. Tchr. spl. edn. Boulder Valley (Colo.) Sch. System, 1967-74; adminstrv. asst. to v.p. mktg. Central Bank for Coops., 1974-76; market mgr. Residential Products Mktg. Div., Johns-Manville Sales Corp., Denver, 1976-82; pres. Christy Metals & Mfg., Inc.; dir. Fortune Wall Systems, Inc., 1982-83; dist. sales mgr. Calif. Lifetile Inc., 1985-86; acct. exec. N.W. states Devel. Dimensions Internat., 1986—. Recipient Merit award Johns Manville Corp., 1978. Mem. Am. Bus. Women's Assn., LWV, Friends of Library. Republican. Office: 6033 W Century Blvd Suite 340 Los Angeles CA 90045-6412

LEPERA, LEONARD J., real estate corr.; b. Gilroy, Calif., Feb. 16, 1941; s. Louis and Louisa (Carpignano) L.; B.S., U. Calif., Berkeley, 1966, M.B.A. (fellow), 1967; m. Meriel Mura, Feb. 3, 1973. Rep. Pacific Mut. Life Ins. Co., Los Angeles, 1969-70, supr., 1970-71, mgr., 1971-73, dir., 1973-74, asst. v.p., 1974-76, 2d. v.p., 1976-77, v.p., 1977-80; partner Property Corrs., Newport Beach, Calif., 1980—. Mem. Alpha Kappa Psi (life). Home: 3592 South Mall Irvine CA 92714 Office: 840 Newport Center Dr Suite 670 Newport Beach CA 92660

LEPLEY, ARTHUR RAY, chemical consultant; b. Peoria, Ill., Nov. 1, 1933; s. Ray and Maud (Meyers) L.; m. Jean E. Zener, Nov. 28, 1957 (div Sept. 1982); children: Margaret, Elizabeth, Jennifer, Richard; m. Dorothy Gambill, Aug. 25, 1985. AB with honors, Bradley U., 1954; MS, U. Chgo., 1956, PhD, 1958. Postdoctoral fellow NSF, Munich, 1958, NIH, Chgo., 1960; jr. chemist Argonne Cancer Research, Chgo., 1956-57; asst. prof. SUNY, Stony Brook, 1960-65; assoc. prof. Marshall U., Huntington, W.Va., 1965-68, prof., 1968-85; cons. Resources Conservation, Bellevue, Wash., 1986—; visiting prof. U. Utah Salt Lake City, 1969-71; guest worker NIH Bethesda, Md., 1975-76; owner-operator A Research Lab., Huntington, 1981-83. Contbr. articles to profl. jours. Fellow Standard Oil, Chgo., 1956-57, Carbide and Carbon, Chgo., 1955-56. Mem. AAAS, Royal Soc. Chemistry, Am. Chem. Soc. (cert.), Am. Inst. Chemists, W.Va. Acad. Sci., N.Y. Acad. Sci., Sigma Xi. Avocations: reading, dancing, skiing, hiking. Office: Resources Convention Bellevue WA 98007

LEPOFF, WAYNE ALBERT, business executive, accountant; b. Santa Monica, Calif., July 12, 1951; s. Samuel O. and Rebecca (Auerbach) L.; m. Deborah M. Baldwin, May 5, 1954; children—Talia Claire, Karissa Anne. B.B.S. with honors, U. Calif.-Berkeley, 1973; postgrad. in acctg. UCLA, 1974-76. C.P.A., Calif. Sr. acct. Berglund & Assocs., Los Angeles, 1977-79; v.p. fin. Western Security Systems & Services, Torrance, Calif., 1979-80, exec. v.p., 1980-81, pres., 1981-84; pres. Wayne A. Lepoff & Co., 1984-85; pres. Genesis Entertainment, 1985—; tech. adviser Palos Verdes Estates Police. Recipient J. Edgar Hoover award Nat. Assn. Chiefs of Police, 1982. Mem. Amer. Inst. C.P.A.s, Calif. Soc. C.P.A.s, Am. Soc. Indsl. Security, Nat. Assn. Chiefs of Police. Democrat. Home: PO Box 8361 Van Nuys CA 91409 Office: 5743 Corsa Ave Suite 216 Westlake Village CA 91362

LEPOME, PENELOPE MARIE, rehabilitation counselor, educator; b. Buffalo, Dec. 17, 1945; d. Raymond Arthur and Mildred Evelyn (Johnson) Kramer; m. Robert Charles LePome, May 26, 1966 (div. Jan. 1982); children: Lisa Anne, Kathryn Jane, Robert Charles II. BA in Biology, SUNY, Buffalo, 1967; MS in Vocat. Rehab., U. Nev., Las Vegas, 1984. Cert. rehab. counselor; cert. tchr., Nev. Co-owner, salesman Flamingo Realty, Las Vegas, Nev., 1974-76; tchr. Clark County Sch. Dist., Las Vegas, 1969-74, 1982-84; adj. faculty Clark County Coll., Las Vegas, 1984-86, Truckee Meadows Community Coll., Reno, 1987; bus. and industry field specialist, Tng. Inst. Clark County Community Coll., 1985-86; probation officer on call Clark County Juvenile Services, Las Vegas, 1984; counselor Nike House, Las Vegas, 1984; mental health technician III, State of Nev., 1984-86 ; rehab. coordinator I, Nev. Bur. Vocat. Rehab., Reno, 1986—; pvt. practice rehab. counseling, 1984—. Active Nev. Womens Polit. Caucus, Las Vegas, 1983-85 ; carnival chmn. Rex Bell PTA, Las Vegas, 1974-75, treas., 1975-76; leader Frontier Area Girl Scouts, Las Vegas, 1975-76, cookie sale chmn., 1980; treas., bd. dirs. Young Audiences, Las Vegas, 1979-80. N.Y. State Regents scholar, 1963. Mem. Am. Assn. Counseling & Devel., AAUW (div. officer Nev. 1983-85, pres. 1982-83, v.p. programming 1981-82, v.p. membership 1980-81, life mem.), Assn. Part-time Profls. (bd. dirs.), Reno C. of C. Republican. Lodge: Toastmasters. Office: 1050 Matley Ln Reno NV 89502

LEPORACE, LOUIS ANTHONY, physicist; b. Pitts., Nov. 23, 1958; s. Louis and Martha Dorothy (Walko) L. BS in Physics, U. Pitts., 1981; postgrad., U. Houston, 1983-84. Field engr. Schlumberger Co., La Porte, Tex., 1981-82; payload systems engr. Ford Aerospace Corp., Houston, 1982-84; sr. engr. Martin Marietta, Sunnyvale, Calif., 1984—; cons. Houston, Sunnyvale and San Jose, Calif. Grantee U. Pitts., 1981. Mem. IEEE, Exploratorium. Avocations: music, woodworking, skiing, skydiving, scubadiving.

LEPORE, JOSEPH VERNON, physicist; b. Detroit, Oct. 9, 1922; s. Joseph and Agda Viola (Monstrom) L. B.S., Allegheny Coll., 1943; postgrad., Princeton U., 1943-44; Ph.D., Harvard U., 1948; postgrad., Inst. for Advanced Study, 1948-50. Instr. Princeton U., N.J., 1943-44; physicist Manhattan Dist., Oak Ridge, Tenn., 1944-46; asst. prof. Ind. U., Bloomington, 1950-51; staff sr. scientist Lawrence Berkeley Lab. U. Calif., 1951-81; lectr. U. Calif., Berkeley, 1952-65; cons. in field, 1977—. Contbr. articles to profl. jours. AEC fellow, 1948-50. Mem. Am. Phys. Soc., Assn. Mems. Inst. for Advanced Study, Sigma Xi. Republican. Clubs: Harvard, Princeton. Lodge: Rotary. Home: 712 Moraga Rd Moraga CA 94556 Office: Lawrence Berkeley Lab Univ of Calif 1 Cyclotron Rd Berkeley CA 94720

LEPPER, MARK ROGER, psychology educator; b. Washington, Dec. 5, 1944; s. Mark H. and Joyce M. (Sullivan) L.; m. Jeanne E. Wallace, Dec. 22, 1966; 1 child, Geoffrey William. BA, Stanford U., 1966; PhD, Yale U., 1970. Asst. prof. psychology Stanford (Calif.) U., 1971-76, assoc. prof., 1976-82, prof., 1982—; fellow Ctr. Advanced Study in Behavioral Scis., 1979-80; chmn. mental health behavioral scis. research rev. com. NIMH, 1982-84, mem. basic sociocultural research rev. com., 1980-82. Co-editor: The Hidden Costs of Reward, 1978; cons. editor Jour. Personality and Social Psychology, 1977-85, Child Devel., 1977-86, Jour. Ednl. Computing Research, 1983—, Social Cognition, 1981-84; contbr. articles to profl. jours. Woodrow Wilson fellow, 1966-67; NSF fellow, 1966-69; Sterling fellow, 1969-70; Mellon fellow, 1975; grantee NSF, 1978-82, NIMH, 1978—, NICHD, 1975—, U.S. Office Edn., 1972-73. Fellow Am. Psychol. Assn.; mem. Soc. Exptl. Social Psychology, Am. Ednl. Research Assn., Soc. Personality and Social Psychology, Soc. Research in Child Devel., Soc. Psychol. Study of Social Issues. Home: 1544 Dana Ave Palo Alto CA 94303 Office: Stanford U Stanford CA 94305

LE PROHN, NICOLE SUZANNE, child welfare researcher; b. Oakland, Calif., Oct. 12, 1958; d. Robert Charles Le Prohn and Frances Adele (Morrison) Burnette. BA, Wellesley coll., 1980; MSW, U. Calif., Berkeley, 1985. Mileau counselor Kennedy Meml. Hosp., Brighton, Mass., 1980-82; research assoc. Family Welfare Research Group U. Calif., Berkeley, 1985—. Mem. Nat. Assn. Social Workers, Social Welfare Alumni Assn. (treas. 1985—).

LERAAEN, ALLEN KIETH, arbitrageur, trader; b. Mason City, Iowa, Dec. 4, 1951; s. Myron O. and Clarice A. (Handeland) L.; m. Mary Elena Partheymuller, Apr. 14, 1978. BBA in Data Processing and Acctg., No. Ariz. U., 1975. Data processing supr. Stephenson & Co., Denver, 1978-81, controller, 1981-85, arbitrageur, trader, 1985—, v.p., 1986—; asst. sec. Satellink Corp., Denver, 1984—; v.p. Isis Entertainment Inc., Denver, 1985—; v.p., sec., bd. dirs. Circle Corp., Denver, 1985—. Avocation: flying. Home: 5692 S Robb St Littleton CO 80127 Office: Stephenson & Co 100 Garfield St 4th Floor Denver CO 80206

LERCH, ROBERT DONALD, educational administrator; b. Wooster, Ohio, May 23, 1934; s. John Walter and Clara Ellen (Meyer) L.; m. Annabelle Lee Stuckey, June 22, 1959; children: Robbin Lynn Lerch O'Leary, Laura Jane Lerch Horst, Robert Allen, Barbara Ellen. BS, Goshen Coll., 1956; MEd, Bowling Green State U., 1962; EdD, N.Mex. State U., 1971. Basic research Am. Vicose Corp., Marcus Hook, Pa., 1958-59; tchr. Fremont (Ohio) Sch. Dist., 1959-61; secondary tchr. Wooster Sch. Dist., 1961-69; grad. asst. N.Mex. State U., Las Cruces, 1969-71; prof., chmn. dept. of edn. Idaho State U., Pocatello, 1971—. Contbr. articles to profl. jours. Mem. City Council Wooster City Govt., 1968-69. Grantee NSF, 1979, 80. Mem. Assn. Supervision and Curriculum Devel., Am. Assn. Physics Tchrs., Phi Delta Kappa. Democrat. Presbyterian. Home: 40 Fordham St Pocatello ID 83201 Office: Box 8059 Dept Edn Idaho State U Pocatello ID 83209-0009

LERMA, MALVINA KAY, reservoir engineer; b. Fairfield, Calif., Mar. 1, 1960; d. Dante Salvador Caravaggio and Frieda Kay (Kluck) Garrison; m. Robert Raymond Lerma, May 15, 1982. BS in Petroleum Engring., U. So. Calif., 1982; MA in Bus., Calif. Luth. Coll., 1986. Drilling rep., rig foreman Chevron USA, Inc., La Habra and Ventura, Calif., 1982-84; drilling engr. Chevron USA, Inc., Ventura, 1984-86, reservoir engr., 1986—; held summer positions with Mobil Oil Corp., San Ardo, Calif., 1979, Sun Oil Corp., Taft, Calif., 1980, Newhall, Calif., 1981, part-time position with Amin Oil, Huntington Beach, Calif., 1981-82. Recipient Outstanding Service award U. So. Calif. Engring. Alumni Assn., 1981, 82. Mem. Soc. Women Engrs. (v.p. 1980-81, scholar 1981), Soc. Petroleum Engrs. (registered 1987, chmn. publicity com. 1985-86, sec. membership com. 1985—, dep. gen. chmn. 1986), Tau Beta Pi, Pi Epsilon Tau. Avocations: music, dancing, gardening. Office: Chevron USA 646 County Square Dr PO Box 6917 Ventura CA 93003

LERMAN, EILEEN R., lawyer; b. N.Y.C., May 6, 1947; d. Alex and Beatrice (Kline) L.; B.A., Syracuse U., 1969; J.D., Rutgers U., 1972; M.B.A., U. Denver, 1983. Admitted to N.Y. State bar, 1973, Colo. bar, 1976; atty. FTC, N.Y.C., 1972-74; corp. atty. RCA, N.Y.C., 1974-76; corp. atty. Samsonite Corp. and consumer products div. Beatrice Foods Co., Denver, 1976-78, assoc. gen. counsel, 1978—, asst. sec., 1979-85; ptnr. Davis and Lerman, Denver, 1985—; dir. Legal Aid Soc. of Met. Denver, 1979-80. Bd. dirs., vice chmn. Colo. Postsecondary Ednl. Facilities Authority, 1981—, HMO Colo.; bd. dirs., treas. Am. Jewish Com., also v.p.; mem. Leadership Denver, 1983. Mem. Colo. Women's Bar Assn. (dir. 1980-81), ABA, Colo. Bar Assn., Denver Bar Assn., N.Y. State Bar Assn., Rutgers U. Alumni Assn. Club: Soroptimist. Home: 1018 Fillmore St Denver CO 80206 Office: Davis and Lerman 50 S Steele St Suite 420 Denver CO 80209

LERNER, LAWRENCE, corporate executive; b. N.Y.C., Sept. 21, 1923; s. Abraham Lerner and May Epstein; m. Leslie Karpen, June 1, 1950; 1 child, Erik. BA in Design, Bklyn. Coll., 1948. Designer Michael Saphier Assocs., Calif., 1948-58; pres. Saphier, Lerner, Schindler, 1958-67; pres. environetics div. Litton Industries, 1967-72; pres., chmn., chief exec. officer Environetics Internat., 1972-83; pres. Megeterg Inc., 1983—. Space planner, interior designer Sears Tower, Chgo., 1969-73; contbr. articles to profl. jours. and mags. Bd. governors Cedars Sinai Med. Ctr., Los Angeles, 1986—. Served to 2d lt. inf. U.S. Army, 1942. Recipient Hall of Fame award Interior Design mag., 1985. Club: Brentwood (Los Angeles). Office: Mega-Erg Inc 9328 Santa Monica Blvd Beverly Hills CA 90210

LERNER, LAWRENCE S., physicist, historian, educator; b. N.Y.C., Mar. 10, 1934; s. Isidor and Manya (Shraga) L.; m. Narcinda Reynolds, Dec. 11, 1959. AB, U. Chgo., 1953, MS, 1955, PhD, 1962. Group leader Inst. Systems Research, Chgo., 1958-60; instr. U. Chgo., 1960-61; mem. tech. staff Hughes Research Labs., Malibu, Calif., 1962-65; research physicist Hewlett-Packard Labs., Palo Alto, Calif., 1965-67, Lockheed Research Labs., Palo Alto, 1967-69; prof. physics Calif. State U., Long Beach, 1969—; mem. Nat. Faculty of Humanities, Arts and Scis., Atlanta, 1977—; cons. in field. Editor, translator: Giordano Bruno, The Ash Wednesday Supper, 1977; author: Physics: Foundations and Applications, 1981; editorial cons. various textbook pubs.; contbr. articles to profl. jours; patentee in field. Pres. Newfoundland Club Am., 1976-79; founder Newfoundland Club No. Calif., San Francisco, 1971—. Mem. AAAS, Am. Phys. Soc., Am. Assn. Physics Tchrs., History Sci. Soc., Centre Pour l'Histoire des Idées dans le Monde Anglo-Américain, Ctr. for Theology and the Natural Scis. Grad. Theol. Union, Phi Beta Kappa, Sigma Xi. Home: 10 Stadler Dr Woodside CA 94062 Office: Calif State U Dept Physics and Astronomy Long Beach CA 90840

LERNER, SHELDON, plastic surgeon; b. N.Y.C., Mar. 3, 1939; s. Louis and Lillian L.; A.B. with honors, Drew U., Madison, N.J., 1961; M.D., U. Louisville, 1965. Intern, resident Albert Einstein Coll. Medicine, Bronx-Mcpl. Hosp. Center, 1965-73; practice medicine, specializing in plastic surgery Plastic Cosmetic and Reconstructive Surgery Center, San Diego, 1973—. Served with USPHS, 1968-70. Mem. AMA, Am. Soc. Plastic and Reconstructive Surgeons, Calif. Med. Soc., San Diego County Med. Soc., San Diego Internat. Plastic Surgery Assn. Clubs: Masons, Shriners. Office: 3399 1st Ave San Diego CA 92103

LEROY, DAVID HENRY, lawyer, state official; b. Seattle, Aug. 16, 1947; s. Harold David and Lela Fay (Palmer) L.; m. Helen LaVonne Transue, Aug. 5, 1972; 2 children. B.S., U. Idaho, 1969, J.D., 1971; LL.M., NYU, 1972. Bar: Idaho 1971, N.Y. State 1973, U.S. Supreme Ct. 1976. Law clk. Idaho 4th Dist. Ct., Boise, 1969; legal asst. Boise Cascade Corp., 1970; assoc. firm Rothblatt, Rothblatt, Seijas & Peskin, N.Y.C., 1971-73; dep. prosecutor Ada County Prosecutor's Office, Boise, 1973-74; pros. atty. Ada County Prosecutor's Office, 1974-78; atty. gen. State of Idaho, Boise, 1978-82, lt. gov., 1983-87; ptnr. Runft, Leroy and Harrop; candidate for Gov. of Idaho, 1986; polit. cons. Leading Edge, Inc., Boise and Washington. Mem. State Task Force on Child Abuse, 1975; mem. Ada County Council on Alcoholism, 1976; del. Republican Nat. Conv., 1976, 80; chmn. Nat. Rep. Lt. Gov.'s Caucus, from 1983; bd. dirs. United Fund, 1975-81; del. Am. Council Young Polit. Leaders, USSR, 1979, Am. Council for Free Asia, Taiwan, 1980, U.S./Taiwan Investment Forum, 1983; del. leader Friendship Force Tour USSR, 1984; legal counsel Young Republicans, 1974-81. Mem. Nat. Dist. Attys. Assn., Idaho Prosecutors Assn., Am. Trial Lawyers Assn., Idaho Trial Lawyers Assn., Nat. Assn. Attys. Gen. (chmn. energy subcom., exec. com., del to China 1981), Western Attys. Gen. Assn. (vice chmn. 1980-83, chmn. 1981), Nat. Lt. Govs. Assn. (exec. bd. 1983), Idaho Bar Assn., Sigma Alpha Epsilon. Presbyterian. Office: Statehouse Room 225 Boise ID 83720 *

LERUDE, WARREN LESLIE, journalism educator; b. Reno, Oct. 29, 1937; s. Leslie Raymond and Ione (Lundy) L.; m. Janet Lagomarsino, Aug. 24, 1961; children: Eric Warren, Christopher Mario Leslie, Leslie Ann. BA in Journalism, U. Nev., 1961. Reporter, editor, correspondent The AP, Las Vegas, Reno, Nev., 1960-63; reporter, editor, pub., pres. Reno Evening Gazette, Nev. State Jour., 1963-81; prof. journalism U. Nev., Reno, 1981—; bd. dirs. Oakland (Calif.) Tribune; lectr. Am. Press Inst.; cons. ABA, Nat. Broadcasting Co., Nat. Jud. Coll. Co-author: American Commander in Spain, Robert Hale Merriman and the Abraham Lincoln Brigade, 1986; mem. editorial bd. USA Today, 1982—. Trustee U. Nev.-Reno Found., Sta. KNPB-TV, Reno; mem. legis. com. Greater Reno C. of C. Served with USNR, 1957-59. Co-recipient Pulitzer prize, 1977. Mem. Nev. State Press Assn. (past pres.), Calif.-Nev. News Execs. Council of the AP, Calif. Newspaper Pub. Assn. (editors conf.), Sigma Delta Chi. Club: Rotary. Avocations: skiing, sailing, traveling, reading. Home: 3825 N Folsom Dr Reno NV 89509 Office: U Nev Reynolds Sch Journalism Reno NV 89557

LESATZ, STEPHEN, JR., lawyer; b. Greeley, Colo., Aug. 5, 1937; s. Stephen J. and Rose (Scholz) LeS.; m. LaDonna M. Distel, June 10, 1961; 1 son, Eric S. B.S. in Bus. Adminstrn., U. Denver, 1959, LL.B., 1961. Bar: Colo. 1962, Minn. 1968, Mich. 1969. Assoc. Haskell, Helmick, Carpenter & Evans, Denver, 1962-68, Arthur E. Anderson, LeSueur, Minn., 1968-69; atty. Whirlpool Corp., Benton Harbor, Mich., 1969-74; assoc. gen. counsel Rocky Mountain Energy Co., Denver, 1974—. Mem. Denver Art Mus., Denver Mus. Natural History, U. Denver Chancellor's Soc. Mem. ABA, Colo. Bar Assn., Denver Bar Assn. Republican. Congregationalist. Office: PO Box 2000 Broomfield CO 80020

LESH, NANCY LOU, librarian; b. Anchorage, May 25, 1944; d. Keith Myron and Enid Mabel (King) L. BA in English, Willamette U., 1966; MLS, Simmons Coll., 1967. Librarian Anchorage Community Coll., 1968-72; asst. dir. Library Tech. Services, U. Alaska, Anchorage, 1972-80, assoc. dir., 1980—; chairperson Alaska WLN Users Group, 1980-84. Co-editor: Alaska is a Library, 1984. Mem. Hist. Landmarks Preservation Commn., Anchorage, 1983-84. Mem. Alaska Library Assn. (v.p., 1971-72, pres. 1972-73, exec. bd. dirs. 1970-81, co-editor Sourdough jour., 1977-79), Pacific N.W. Library Assn. (rep. 1974-76), Am. Library Assn. (councilor 1977-81, Citation for Excellence in newsletter pub. 1978). Avocations: reading, walking, writing, travel, cooking. Office: Library Tech Services U Alaska Anchorage AK 99508

LESHER, MARGARET LISCO, newspaper publishing executive, songwriter; b. San Antonio, Tex., May 4, 1932; d. Lloyd Elmo Lisco and Dovie Deona (Maynard) Lisco Welch; m. William Jarvis Ryan (dec.); children: Patricia D., Wendi L. Ryan Alves, Jill A. Ryan Heidt, Roxanne F. Ryan; m. Dean Stanley Lesher, Sr., Apr. 4, 1972; children: Dean S. II, Melinda K., Cynthia A. Student Coalinga (Calif.) Jr. Coll., 1957-59. Dir. sales Chatmar, Inc., Concord, Calif., 1970-73; dir. community services Contra Costa Times Newspaper, Walnut Creek, Calif., 1973—; 1st v.p. corp. bus. Lesher Communications, Inc., Walnut Creek, 1974—, Calif. Delta Newspapers, Inc., Antioch, 1975—, No. Calif. Newspapers, Inc. Composer, lyricist gospel song Margaret Lesher Album, 1976 (So. Calif. Motion Picture Council Bronze Halo award 1982); author 14 published poems. Regent Holy Names Coll., Oakland, Calif., 1979-86; chief of protocol Contra Costa County, 1980—; dir. Bay Area Sports Hall of Fame, San Francisco, 1982—; bd. overseers U. Calif., San Francisco, 1983—; mem. San Francisco Host Com., 1983—, Internat. Visitors Ctr., San Francisco, 1983-85, Internat. Host Com. of Calif., 1983-86; commr. Port of Richmond, Calif., 1983-86; chmn. adv. bd. Crisis Nursery of Bay Area, Concord, 1983-86; adv. bd. Oakland A's Baseball Team, 1984-85, Battered Women, 1983—; pres. bd. dirs. Mt. Diablo Hosp. Found., 1980-81; bd. dirs. Contra Costa Council, 1984—; mem. adv. bd. Las Trampas Sch. Mentally Retarded, chmn., 1984—; trustee Oakland Symphony Orch., 1985-86. Recipient Spl. Merit award State of Calif., 1982. Mem. Gospel Music Assn., ASCAP. Republican. Christian. Clubs: Blackhawk Country. Office: care Contra Costa Times Lesher Communications Inc 2640 Shadelands Dr Walnut Creek CA 94598

LESIEUR, HELEN ELAINE, public relations consultant; b. Coffeyville, Kans., Feb. 16, 1920; d. Frank R. and Grace (Koon) LeS. B.S. in Edn., S.E.

Mo. State Coll., 1943; student in art Washington U., St. Louis, 1943-44; student in bus. adminstrn. Northwestern U., 1945-46. Dir. Mcpl. Concerts Bur., Houston, 1950-52; free-lance theatrical publicist, Chgo., 1952-54; pub. relations account exec. Aaron D. Cushman & Assocs., Chgo., 1954-60; pub. relations dir. Ill. chpt. Arthritis Found., 1960-61, pub. relations dir., v.p. pub. relations So. Calif. chpt., Los Angeles, 1961-84; pub. relations cons., 1984—. Mem. Pub. Relations Soc. Am. (sec. Los Angeles Area Chpt. 1971-73), Soc. Fund Raisers, Publicity Club (pres. 1966-67), Women's Ad Club, Internat. Assn. Bus. Communicators, Los Angeles Soc. Pub. Relations Counselors. Home: 5709 Fallsgrove St Los Angeles CA 90016

LESLIE, ALISTAIR CHARLES DAY, atmospheric chemist; b. Belfast, Northern Ireland, July 4, 1943; came to U.S., 1974; s. George William and Elizabeth Alison (Holmes) L.; m. Virginia Anne Dwyer, Nov. 24, 1983. BA, U. Keele, United Kingdom, 1966; PhD, Glasgow (Scotland) U., 1975. Research asst. Glasgow U., 1966-74, Brandeis U., Waltham, Mass., 1974-75; NIH fellow Fla. State U., Tallahassee, 1975-77, research assoc., 1977-83; sr. research scientist Battelle Pacific N.W. Labs., Richland, Wash., 1983—; pres. Environex Inc., Tallahassee, 1980-83. Contbr. articles to profl. jours. Research grantee NSF, Tallahassee, 1980, EPA, 1980-83, others, 1979-83. Mem. AAAS, Am. Chem. Soc., Am. Geol. Union, Air Pollution Control Assn. Avocations: travelling, flying, cooking, music. Home: 1814 S Yost Pl Kennewick WA 99337 Office: Battelle Pacific NW Labs 2400 Stevens PO Box 999 Richland WA 99352

LESLIE, EMILY A., social services administrator; b. Charleston, W.Va., May 25, 1951; d. George and Gladys (Lockhart) L. BA, Wittenberg U., 1973; MSW, U. Wash., 1975. Planning cons. United Way of King County, Seattle, 1975-80, sr. planning cons., 1980—. com. mem. YMCA of Greater Seattle, 1979—, Municipality of Met. Seattle, 1978-80; chmn. med. ctr. council Group Health Coop., Seattle, 1983—; mem. Leadership Tomorrow, 1986-87. Mem. Nat. Assn. Social Workers. Democrat. Avocations: skiing, hiking, whitewater rafting, music, travel. Home: 119 N 50th St Seattle WA 98103 Office: United Way King County 107 Cherry St Seattle WA 98104

LESLIE, JACQUES ROBERT, JR., journalist; b. Los Angeles, Mar. 12, 1947; s. Jacques Robert and Aleen (Wetstein) L.; m. Leslie Wernick, June 21, 1980; 1 child, Sarah Alexandra. B.A., Yale U., 1968. Tchr. New Asia Coll., Chinese U., Hong Kong, 1968-70; free-lance journalist Washington, 1970-71; fgn. corr. Los Angeles Times, Saigon, 1972-73, Phnom-Penh, 1973, Washington, 1974; chief New Delhi (India) bur. Los Angeles Times, 1974-75, Madrid, 1975-76; chief Hong Kong bur. Los Angeles Times, 1976-77; free-lance journalist 1977—. Recipient Best Fgn. Corr. award Sigma Delta Chi, 1973, citation reporting Overseas Press Club, 1973. Home: 124 Reed St Mill Valley CA 94941

LESLIE, JEANNE CLAIRE, chemist; b. Long Beach, Calif., June 11, 1954; d. Kenneth Vincent and Genevieve Clara (Lambertson) L. BA, U. Calif., Irvine, 1977, MS, 1979, PhD, 1984. Chem. and nuclear engr. So. Calif. Edison, Rosemead, 1983—. Contbr. articles to profl. jours. Mem. Am. Nuclear Soc., Am. Chem. Soc. Republican. Avocations: travelling, church activities. Office: So Calif Edison GO-1 Room 415 2244 Walnut Grove Ave Rosemead CA 92714

LESLIE, ROBERT LORNE, lawyer; b. Adak, Alaska, Feb. 24, 1947; s. J. Lornie and L. Jean (Conelly) L.; children—Lorna Jean, Elizabeth Allen. B.S., U.S. Mil. Acad., 1969; J.D., Hastings Coll. Law, U. Calif.-San Francisco, 1974. Bar: Calif. 1974, D.C. 1979, U.S. Dist. Ct. (no. dist.) Calif. 1974, U.S. Ct. Claims 1975, U.S. Tax Ct. 1975, U.S. Ct. Appeals (9th and D.C. cirs.), U.S. Ct. Mil. Appeals 1980, U.S. Supreme Ct. 1980. Commd. 2d lt. U.S. Army, 1969, advanced through grades to maj., 1980; govt. trial atty. West Coast Field Office, Contract Appeals, Litigation Div. and Regulatory Law Div., Office JAG, Dept. Army, San Francisco, 1974-77; sr. trial atty. and team chief Office of Chief Trial Atty., Dept. Army, Washington, 1977-80; ret., 1980; ptnr. McInerney & Dillon, Oakland, Calif., 1980—; lectr. on govt. contracts CSC, Continuing Legal Edn. Program; lectr. in govt. procurement U.S. Army Materiel Command. Decorated Silver Star, Purple Heart, Meritorious Service medal. Mem. ABA, Fed. Bar Assn. Club: Commonwealth (San Francisco). Home: 4144 Greenwood Ave Oakland CA 94602 Office: Ordway Bldg Suite 1850 Oakland CA 94612

LESSARD, GEORGE MERIDITH, biochemistry educator; b. San Jose, Calif., Sept. 27, 1939; s. Roy Beverly and Dorita Esther (Thomann) L.; m. Cheryl Phyllis (Neilsen) Lessard, June 12, 1963; children: Elise, Margot. BA, Pacific Union Coll., 1962, MA, 1964; PhD, U. Calif., Riverside, 1972. Sci. tchr. Mountain View (Calif.) Acad., 1963-67; research asst. U. Calif., Riverside, 1967-72; asst. prof. biochemistry Loma Linda (Calif.) U., 1972-78, assoc. prof., 1978-85, prof., 1985—. Contbr. articles to profl. publs. Mem. AAAS, Am. Chem. Soc., Am. Assn. Dental Sch. (sec. 1985-86), Am. Assn. Dental Research, Internat. Assn. Dental Research, Acad. Soaring Club. Adventist. Avocations: flying, motorcycling, hiking, astronomy. Home: 2100 Cahuilla Colton CA 97324 Office: Loma Linda U Dept Biochemistry Loma Linda CA 92354

LESSMAN, DEBORAH ANN, air force officer, social worker; b. Plainfield, N.J., Feb. 3, 1961; d. Anthony Michael and Shirley Ann (Reinbold) L. B in Social Work, Kean Coll., 1983; MSW, Rutgers U., 1984. Family therapist Mental Health Clinic Ocean County, Tomsriver, N.J., 1984-85; commd. 2d lt. USAF, 1985, advanced through grades to 1st lt., 1985; clin. social worker USAF, Travis AFB, Calif., 1985—. Big sister Big Bro./Big Sister Program, Solono County, Calif., 1986—. Mem. Nat. Assn. Social Workers. Methodist. Avocations: skiing, camping, jogging, hiking, reading. Home: 270 Belair Dr Apt 33 Vacaville CA 95688 Office: Mental Health Clinic Travis AFB CA 94535

LESSNER, MARK M., pediatrician; b. Tucson, Oct. 10, 1948; s. Harold S. and Nettie W. Lessner; m. Evelyn J. Diehl, Aug., 1977 (div.); 1 child, Ameena May Diehl Lessner. BA in Chemistry with honors, U. Ariz., 1971, MD, 1975. Diplomate Am. Bd. Pediatrics, Nat. Bd. Med. Examiners. Intern Gorgas Fed. Hosp., Ancon, U.S. Canal Zone, 1975-76, Children's Hosp., Honolulu, 1976-77; resident Kaiser Hosp., Los Angeles, 1978-80; family planning fellow UCLA, 1980-81, genetics/mental retardation fellow, 1981-82; with genetics, devel. pediatrics U. Calif., Irvine, 1982-83; staff pediatrician Silas B. Hays Army Hosp., Ft. Ord, Calif., 1983-85; practice medicine specializing in pediatrics Stockton, Calif., 1985—. La. State U., Internat. Ctr. Med. Research and Tng. internat. health fellow, 1975. Mem. Los Angeles Pediatric Soc., E. Bay Pediatric Soc., Am. Soc. Human Genetics, Royal Soc. Tropical Medicine, Phi Kappa Phi. Avocations: clarinet, hiking.

LESTER, JOHN CLAYTON, life insurance company executive; b. Cheyenne, Wyo., Sept. 26, 1940; s. Arthur C. and Harleen E. (Gorman) L.; B.B.A., Wichita State U., 1965; m. Ruth A. Whatley, Nov. 21, 1959; children—John Clayton, Connie Sue. Office supr. State Farm Fire & Casualty Co., Greeley, Colo., 1965-69; agt. Equitable Life Assurance Soc., Greeley, 1969-70, dist. mgr., then agy. mgr., Denver, 1970-78, regional agy. v.p., 1978-84, agy. mgr., Woodland Hills, Calif., 1984—. Served with USN, 1958-61. C.L.U., 1977. Mem. Am. Soc. C.L.U.s, San Fernando Valley Life Underwriters, Gen. Agts. and Mgrs. Assn. (pres. San Fernando Valley chpt.). Republican. Home: 29372 Castlehill Dr Agoura Hills CA 91301 Office: Equitable Life Assurance Soc 21041 Burbank Blvd Suite 200 Woodland Hills CA 91365

LESTER, JOHN JAMES NATHANIEL, II, engineer, environmental analyst; b. Houston, May 7, 1952; s. John James Nathaniel Lester and Margaret Louise (Tisdale) Sharp; m. Leslie Ann Yarab, Oct. 5, 1980. Student, U. Tex., 1970, Lee Coll., 1971; AS, Grossmont Coll., 1979; BA in Behavioral Sci., Nat. U., 1987. Registered profl. stationary engr. Nuclear power specialist USN, various, 1971-77; microbiology lab. technician VA, San Diego, 1978; prin. engring. asst. San Diego Gas & Electric, 1979-85, engring. environ. analyst, 1985—. Logistics dir. and regional bd. mem. Gary Hart Presdl. Campaign, San Diego, 1984; founding mem. Inlet drug crisis ctr., Houston, 1970. Served with USN, 1971-77. Mem. ASME, IEEE (interim pres. and founding mem. San Diego region Ocean Engring. Soc. 1984-85), Mensa, Assn. Humanistic Psychology, Amnesty Internat., Hunger Project, Sierra Club. Democrat. Presbyterian. Clubs: BMW Car Club of Am. (tech. advisor 1985-86). Avocations: scuba diving, underwater photography, back-packing. Home: PO Box 4274 Carlsbad CA 92008 Office: San Diego Gas & Electric Co 4600 Carlsbad Blvd Carlsbad CA 92008

LESTER, WILLIAM ALEXANDER, JR., chemist, educator; b. Chgo., Apr. 24, 1937; s. William Alexander and Elizabeth Frances (Clark) L.; m. Rochelle Diane Reed, Dec. 27, 1959; children: William Alexander III, Allison Kimberleigh. B.S., U. Chgo., 1958, M.S., 1959; postgrad., Washington U., St. Louis, 1959-60; Ph.D., Cath. U. Am., 1964. Phys. chemist Nat. Bur. Standards, Washington, 1961-64; asst. dir. Theoretical Chemistry Inst. of U. Wis.-Madison, 1965-68; research staff mem. IBM Research Lab., San Jose, Calif., 1968-75; mgr. 1976-78; mem. tech. planning staff IBM T.J. Watson Research Center, Yorktown Heights, N.Y., 1975-76; dir. Nat. Resource for Computation in Chemistry, Lawrence Berkeley (Calif.) Lab., 1978-81, also assoc. dir., staff sr. scientist, 1978-81, faculty sr. scientist, 1981—; prof. chemistry U. Calif.-Berkeley, 1981—; lectr. chemistry U. Wis., 1966-68; cons. NSF, 1976-77, mem. chem. div. adv. panel, 1980-83, adv. com. Office Advanced Sci. Computing program, 1985—, chmn., 1987; mem. U.S. nat. com. Internat. Union Pure and Applied Chemistry, 1976-79; mem. com. on recommendations for U.S. Army Basic Sci. Research NRC, 1984-87; chemistry research evaluation panel AF Office Sci. Research, 1974-78; chmn. Gordon Conf. Atomic and Molecular Interactions, 1978; mem. NRC panel on chem. physics Nat. Bur. Standards, 1980-83; mem. com. to survey chem. scis. NRC, 1982-84. Editor: Procs. of Conf. on Potential Energy Surfaces in Chemistry, 1971; mem. editorial bd. Jour. Phys. Chemistry, 1979-81, Internat. Jour. Quantum Chemistry, 1979—, Jour. Computational Chemistry, 1980-87, Computer Physics Communications, 1981-86. Recipient Alumni award in sci. Cath. U. Am., 1983. Fellow Am. Phys. Soc. (chmn. div. chem. physics 1986); mem. Am. Chem. Soc. (sec.-treas. Wis. sect. 1967-68, chmn. div. phys. chemistry 1979, treas. div. computers in chemistry 1974-77), Nat. Orgn. Black Chemists and Chem. Engrs. (Percy L. Julian award 1979, Outstanding Tchr. award 1986, exec. bd. 1984-87), AAAS. Home: 4433 Briar Cliff Rd Oakland CA 94605 Office: Dept Chemistry U Calif-Berkeley Berkeley CA 94720

LESZYNSKI, STANLEY WILLIAM, instrumentation engineer; b. Hobart, Ind., Aug. 19, 1924; s. Stanley Matthew and Krystina Mary (Ziolo) L.; m. Marie Lois Erickson, Nov. 3, 1956; children: Stanley Jr., Christina, Linda, Patti. Communication specialist cert., N.C. State Coll., 1945; BSEE, Purdue U., 1947. Telephone design engr. Western Electric, Chgo., 1947-48; instrumentation engr. Boeing Aerospace Co., Seattle, 1949—; reviewer strain gage mfg. Fed. Republic Germany and Eng., 1957; with tech. support systems Saturn Rocket devel., Huntsville, Ala., 1966, Minuteman test, Valley City, N.D., 1966, Booster Engine test, El Paso, Tex., 1964-66, SRAM Missile test, Alamogordo, N.Mex., 1968-71, Cruise Missile test, San Leandro and Ontario, Calif., 1986. Patentee strain gage applicator, high-temperature strain gages. Founder Polish Christmas programs Seattle Mus. History and Industry, 1954-76; organized internat. cultural groups Seattle World Fair, 1962; mem. Wash. Com. Better City Govt.; scoutmaster Chief Seattle council Boy Scouts Am., 1969—. Served as cpl. U.S. Army, 1944-46. Democrat. Roman Catholic. Club: N.W. Folkdancers Inc. (Seattle) (dance dir. 1951-66, pres. 1960-61). Avocations: gardening, antique cars, trivia collector. Home: 75 157th Ave SE Bellevue WA 98008 Office: Boeing Aerospace Co PO Box 3999 Seattle WA 98124

LETENDRE, LORIN, publishing company executive; b. Mpls., Feb. 21, 1947; s. Douglas N. and Lola E. (Atwater) L.; A.B., U. Calif., Santa Barbara, 1968; M.A., 1969; m. Karen Barkley List, June 1, 1980; children—Dana Andre, Jason Michel. Instr. polit. sci. Santa Barbara City Coll., 1969-71; prof. polit. sci. San Diego Community Colls., 1971-73; with CTB/McGraw-Hill, Monterey, Calif., 1973-80, dir. new ventures, 1979-80; pres. Cons. Psychologists Press, Inc., Palo Alto, Calif., 1980—. Mem. Am. Assn. Counseling and Devel., Council Exceptional Children, Am. Mgmt. Assn., Am. Soc. Tng. and Devel. Author: Understanding American Politics Through Fiction, 1973, 2d edit., 1977. Office: 577 College Ave Palo Alto CA 94306

LETOURNEAU, DUANE JOHN, biochemist, educator; b. Stillwater, Minn., July 12, 1926; s. John Peter and Olga Margaret (Lange) LeTourneau; m. Phyllis Jean Kaercher, June 22, 1947; children: Bruce Duane, Diane Elaine, Keith George. B.S., U. Minn., 1948, M.S., 1951, Ph.D., 1954. Asst. prof., asst. agrl. chemist U. Idaho, Moscow, 1953-58; assoc. prof., asso. agrl. chemist U. Idaho, 1958-63; prof., biochemist 1963—; vis. prof. botany U. Sheffield (Eng.), 1973; vis. scientist Nat. Research Council Can., Saskatoon, 1981; Bd. dirs. Idaho Inst. Christian Edn., 1958-62, 73-75, v.p., 1959-62. Author research publs. on plant biochemistry. Bd. dirs. U. Idaho Luth. Campus Council, 1962-64, 73-75, chmn., 1963-64; trustee Farm House Internat. Found., 1974-80, chmn., 1976-80; trustee Gritman Meml. Hosp., 1969-82, v.p., 1977-80; bd. dirs. Latah County Hist. Soc., 1982—, pres. bd. dirs., 1984-87. Served with USAAF, 1945. Recipient Outstanding Faculty award Asso. Students U. Idaho, 1960-62, 87, Coll. Agr. Outstanding Instr. award, 1962, R.M. Wade Excellence in Teaching award, 1968, 78, Disting. Faculty award, 1982, Prof. of Yr. award, 1983; Citation for Disting. Achievement, U. Idaho, 1984; Nat. Acad. Scis.-NRC sr. postdoctoral fellow, 1964-65. Fellow AAAS, Am. Inst. Chemists; mem. AAUP (v.p. U. Idaho chpt. 1959-60, sec. 1984—), Am. Chem. Soc., Am. Soc. Plant Physiologists, Am. Inst. Biol. Scis., Am. Phytopath. Soc., Idaho Acad. Sci. (v.p. 1985-86, pres. 1986-87, editor jour. 1983—), Mycol. Soc. Am., Phytochem. Soc. N.Am., Am. Soc. Plant Physiologists, Sigma Xi, Alpha Zeta, Gamma Alpha, Gamma Sigma Delta (pres. U. Idaho chpt. 1979-80), Iron Wedge, Phi Kappa Phi, Phi Lambda Upsilon, Phi Sigma, Farm House Frat. (dir. Idaho 1957-62, 72-75, 82—, pres. 1957-62, 74, 82-85; nat. dir. 1960-64, nat. v.p. 1962-64). Lutheran (chmn. ch. council and congregation, 1966-69). Club: Lions (dir. Moscow Central club 1971-74, pres. 1973-74). Home: 479 Ridge Rd Moscow ID 83843

LETTA, DONALD RUSSELL, art director; b. Buffalo, Nov. 3, 1940; s. Thomas Alfred and Katherine Rose (Kistner) L. BA, Calif. State, Long Beach, 1961, MA, 1962; student, Accademia De Belle Arte, Palermo, Italy. Art dir. Max W. Becker Advt., Long Beach, Calif., 1962-68, San Francisco C. of C., 1968-75, Singer Corp., San Leandro, Calif., 1975-80, Hewlett-Packard, Palo Alto, Calif., 1980-83; pvt. practice art directing San Francisco, 1983-86; assoc. Doremus, Porter, Novelli, Russom, San Francisco, 1986—. Contbr. designs to profl. mags. Democratic. Club: A.D. (San Francisco). Avocations: painting, vintage autos, body building, traveling, counseling. Home: 1090 Eddy St #606 San Francisco CA 94109 Office: Russom & Co Pub Relations 350 Pacific Ave San Francisco CA 94111

LEUM, LEONARD, wholesale grocery company executive. Chmn. bd. dirs. Cert. Grocers of Calif., Ltd., Los Angeles. Office: Cert Grocers of California Ltd 2601 S Eastern Ave Los Angeles CA 90040 *

LEUNG, DANIEL KA-YIU, social worker; b. Hong Kong, Jan. 11, 1955; came to U.S., 1982; s. Hoi Wai and Po Chuen (Cheng) L; m. Lisa H.E. Hancock, June 2, 1984. BS, U. Melbourne, Australia, 1977, BSW, 1979; MSW, U. Hawaii, 1984. Asst. to dir. Anglican Ch. Dept. for Migrants, Refugees and Ethnic Affairs, Melbourne, 1980; social worker Hong Kong Christian Service, 1981-82, Child and Family Service Refugee Employment and Social Assistance Program, Honolulu, 1984-85; dir. Chinese Counseling Ctr., Honolulu, 1985—; bd. dirs. Lawyers for the People of Hawaii, Honolulu, 1985—, Indochinese Mut. Assistance Assns. Ctr., Honolulu, 1986—, East-West Ctr. Alumni Assn. Hawaii chpt., Honolulu, 1986—; mem. Refugee Assistance Program Mental Health Task Force, Honolulu, 1985—. Mem. Interagency Council for Immigrant Services, Honolulu, 1986—. East-West Ctr. grantee, Honolulu, 1982-84. Mem. Nat. Assn. Social Workers, Soc. Intercultural Edn. Tng. and Research. Episcopalian. Avocations: graphic design, ink drawing, photography. Home: 555 Hahaione St #7H Honolulu HI 96825 Office: Chinese Counseling Ctr 3627 Kilauea Ave Suite 408 Honolulu HI 96816

LEUNG, EDDIE MAN-WAI, engineer; b. Hong Kong, Oct. 2, 1953; came to U.S., 1976; s. Hee-Lit and Yee-Han (Wong) L.; m. Irene Wai-Yin Hui, Dec. 27, 1983; 1 child, Alicia Wing-Yee. BS in Engring. Physics, Queen's U., Kingston, Ont., Can., 1976; MS in Engring. Mgmt., Midwest Coll. Engring., 1982. Project engr. Fermi Nat. Accelerator Lab., Batavia, Ill., 1976-82; engring. specialist space systems div. Gen. Dynamics Corp., San Diego, 1982—. Contbr. articles to profl. jours. Recipient Russel B. Scott Cryogenic Engring. award Cryogenic Engring. Conf. Bd., San Diego, 1981. Mem. ASME (heat transfer div. K-18 com.). Club: Toastmasters (sgt. at arms, treas. 1977-79). Avocations: tennis, fishing, sailing, gardening. Home: 8170 Casa Blanca Pl San Diego CA 92126 Office: Gen Dynamics Space Systems Div PO Box 85990 MZ 92-7100 San Diego CA 92138

LEUSCHEN, DONALD M., energy company executive. BSEE, Mont. St. U., 1950. With Mont. Power Co. 1950—, groundman, Lewistown, 1950-51, jr. elec. engr., 1951-54; asst. elec. engr.,Missoula, 1954-57, Butte, 1957-58; asst. div. supt., Bozeman, 1958-60, Glasgow, 1958-63; dist. mgr., Glasgow, 1963-65; div. supt. Great Falls, 1965-66; div. mgr., Billings, 1966-74, Missoula, 1974-82; v.p. adminstrn., 1982-84, pres., 1984—, also dir. Served with USN, 1943-46. Office: Mont Power Co 40 E Broadway Butte MT 59701 *

LEUS MCFARLEN, PATRICIA CHERYL, water chemist; b. San Antonio, Mar. 12, 1954; d. Norman W. and Jacqueline S. (Deason) Leus; m. Randy N. McFarlen, June 28, 1986. AA, Highline Community Coll., 1974; BS in Chemistry, Eastern Wash. U., 1980. Lab. technician, oil analyst D.A. Lubricant, Vancouver, Wash., 1982-83; plant chemist Navajo Generating Sta., Page, Ariz., 1983—. Sci. judge Page Schs. Sci. Project Fair, 1985; chemist Navajo Generating Sta./Page Sch. Career Day, 1986. Mem. Am. Chem. Soc., Sigma Kappa (treas. 1976-78). Methodist. Avocations: sewing, hiking, snow skiing, archery, pilot. Office: Navajo Generating Sta Chem Dept PO Box W Page AZ 86040

LEVADA, WILLIAM JOSEPH, archbishop; b. Long Beach, Calif., June 15, 1936; s. Joseph and Lorraine (Nunez) L. B.A., St. John's Coll., 1958; S.T.L., Gregorian U., Rome, 1962, S.T.D., 1971. Ordained priest Roman Catholic Ch., 1961, consecrated bishop, 1983. Assoc. pastor Archdiocese of Los Angeles, 1962-67; prof. theology St. John's Sem., Camarillo, Calif., 1970-76; ofcl. Doctrinal Congregation, Vatican City, Italy, 1976-82; exec. dir. Calif. Cath. Conf., Sacramento, 1982-84; aux. bishop, vicar for Santa Barbara County Archdiocese of Los Angeles, 1983-86; archbishop Archdiocese of Portland in Oregon, 1986—. Bd. dirs. Calif. Assn. Cath. Hosps., Sacramento, from 1982; trustee Mt. St. Mary's Coll., Los Angeles, from 1983. Mem. Nat. Conf. Cath. Bishops (com. on doctrine, com. for pro-life activities, com. for pastoral research and practices, com. for pastoral letter on women in church and society), U.S. Cath. Conf., Cath. Theol. Soc. Am., Canon Law Soc. Am. Office: Archdiocese of Portland in Oreg 2838 E Burnside St Portland OR 97214 *

LEVAN, KEITH RICHARD, radar engineer, physical chemist, consultant; b. Williamsport, Pa., Dec. 11, 1955; s. Robert Lockwood and Lois Mae (Robinson) L.; m. Deborah Leigh Crain, Aug. 10, 1985. BS in Chemistry, Bloomsburg (Pa.) State Coll., 1977; MS in Chemistry, Bucknell U., 1979; PhD in Phys. Chem., UCLA, 1984. Postdoctoral researcher U. Calif., Irvine, 1984; systems engr. Hughes Aircraft Co., El Segundo, Calif., 1984—. Contbr. articles to profl. jours. Mem. Am. Chem. Soc., Am. Crystallographic Soc., U.S. Chess Fedn. Republican. Methodist. Avocation: chess. Office: Hughes Aircraft Co 1940 E Mariposa St El Segundo CA 90045

LEVANGER, JIM NEILS, food company executive, marketing professional; b. Caldwell, Idaho, Aug. 23, 1943; s. Neils Murry Levanger and Hazel Rachel (Hansen) Croshaw; m. Marilee Forsyth, July 28, 1967 (dec. Dec. 1982); children: Maria Lee, Jason Neils; m. Suzanne Josephine Pottenger, Oct. 5, 1985. AA in Acctg., Ricks Coll., 1963; BA in Polit. Sci., Brigham Young U., 1968, MBA, 1970. With brand mgmt. staff Proctor & Gamble, Cin., 1970-75; group product mgr. Laura Scudder's, Anaheim, Calif., 1975-77; dir. mktg. J.R. Simplot Co., Caldwell, 1977-83; v.p. mktg. Gourmet Brands, Salt Lake City, 1983—; practice cons., Salt Lake City, 1985—. Republican. Mormon. Avocations: computer science, gardening, fishing. Home: 465 W Honey Bee Circle Farmington UT 84025 Office: Gourmet Brands 699 E South Temple Salt Lake City UT 84102

LEVARY, ARNON, consulting engineer. BSME, U. Colo., 1975; MBA, U. Oreg., 1977. Registered profl. engr., Colo. Project mgr., cost analyst Solar Energy Research Inst., Golden, Colo., 1978-81; project mgr., engr. BHCD Engrs., Inc., Denver, 1981-85, Reiter Engring., Lakewood, Colo., 1985—; vice-chmn. Mech. Code Com., Denver, 1983—. Home: 14600 E Evans Ave Aurora CO 80014 Office: Reiter Engring Inc Lakewood CO 80226

LEVCHUK, GEORGE, mechanical-aeronautical consulting engineer; b. Poland, Nov. 27, 1907; s. Ioan Basili and Nadia Kornilia (Ferencewich) L.; came to U.S., 1949, naturalized, 1952. M.E., Warsaw (Poland) Inst. Tech., 1938, M.S., 1969; Ph.D., Kensington U., 1982. Polish State aircraft factory designer, 1932-38; engr. Polish Airlines, 1938-39; d essinatuer Leo-45 bomber, Argenteuil, France, 1940; interim prototype shop mgr. Turkish Air League, 1941-48; impact extrusion engr. Victor Metal Industries, Bklyn., 1949-50; engr. Chase Aircraft Co., Trenton, N.J., 1950-53; designer N.Am. Aviation Corp., 1953-60; mathematician-designer U.S. Steel Corp., 1960-61; re-entry flow engr. Hughes Aircraft Corp., 1962-63; aerodynamicist Aeronutronics-Ford subs. Aeronutronic, Newport Beach, Calif., 1965-66; research scientist Calif. Inst. Tech., Pasadena, 1967-70; B-1 structures engr. Rockwell Corp., Inglewood, Calif., 1970-72, shuttle stress engr., 1973-77; stress engr. McDonnell Douglas Corp., St. Louis, 1978-81, Bell Helicopter Textron, 1985-86; mech.-aero. cons. engr., Downey, Calif., 1982—. Served to lt. Polish Air Force, 1940-41, Eng. Mem. AIAA.

LEVEE, ARNOLD LEONARD, physician; b. N.Y.C., Oct. 1, 1932; s. Lazar and Irene (Rosen) L.; m. Linda Jean Sherman, June 7, 1959; children: James B., Lawrence N., Thomas M. Student, UCLA, 1950, 52-55; MD, U. So. Calif., 1959. Diplomate Am. Bd. Otolaryngology. Intern Harbor Gen. Hosp., Torrance, Calif.; resident Wadsworth VA Hosp., Los Angeles; physician Santa Monica, Calif. Served with USN, 1950-52. Democrat. Jewish. Lodge: Lions (zone chmn.). Avocations: sports, photography, travel. Home: 13636 Bayliss Rd Los Angeles CA 90049 Office: 1304 15th St # 324 Santa Monica CA 90404

LEVENSON, LEONARD LIONEL, physics educator, researcher; b. San Francisco, Sept. 18, 1928; s. Sidnel Levenson and Evelyn (Grossman) Marcus; m. Maryse Duprat Renaud, Dec. 21, 1957; children: Myriam, Michel, Claudine. AB in Physics, U. Calif., Berkeley, 1952, MSME, 1955; PhD in Physics, U. Paris, 1968. Physicist USN Test Sta., Inyokern, Calif., 1952; resident engr. U. Calif., Berkeley, 1952-58; physicist Lawrence Radiation Lab., Livermore, Calif., 1958-62, Nuclear Research Ctr., Saclay, France, 1962-68; prof. U. Mo., Rolla, 1968-81, dir. grad. ctr. materials research, 1975-81; prof. U. Colo., Colorado Springs, 1981—, chmn. dept. physics, 1981-84; vis. prof. Kyoto (Japan) U., 1986-87. Contbr. 70 articles to profl. jours.; patentee in field. Served with U.S. Army, 1946-48. Mem. Am. Vacuum Soc., Electrochem. Soc., Am. Phys. Soc., AAAS, Sierra Club (life), Sigma Xi, Phi Kappa Phi. Democrat. Unitarian. Office: U Colo PO Box 7150 Colorado Springs CO 80933

LEVENSON, MILTON, chemical engineer; b. St. Paul, Jan. 4, 1923; s. Harry and Fanny M. Levenson; m. Mary Beth Novick, Aug. 27, 1950; children: James L., Barbara G., Richard A., Scott D., Janet L. B.Ch.E., U. Minn., 1943. Jr. engr. Houdaille-Hershey Corp., Decatur, Ill., 1944; research engr. Oak Ridge Nat. Lab., 1944-48; with Argonne (Ill.) Nat. Lab., 1948-73, assoc. lab. dir., 1973; dir. nuclear power div. Electric Power Research Inst., Palo Alto, Calif., 1973-80; cons. to pres. Bechtel Power Corp., San Francisco, 1981—; lectr. in field. Contbr. articles to profl. jours., chpts. to books. Served with C.E. U.S. Army, 1944-46. Fellow Am. Inst. Chem. Engrs. (Robert E. Wilson award 1975), Am. Nuclear Soc. (pres. 1983-84); mem. AAAS, Nat. Acad. Engring. Patentee in field. Office: Bechtel Power Corp 50 Beale St San Francisco CA 94119

LEVENSTEIN, ROSLYN M., advertising consultant; b. N.Y.C., Mar. 26, 1920; d. Leo Rapoport and Stella Schimmel Rosenberg; m. Justin Seides, June 7, 1943 (div. 1948); 1 child, Leland Seides.; m. Lawrence Levenstein, June 25, 1961. BA in Advt., NYU, 1940. Sr. v.p., assoc. creative dir. Young and Rubicam, Inc., N.Y.C., 1962-79; cons. Young and Rubicam, Inc., Los Angeles and San Diego, 1979-83; advt. cons., writer La Jolla, Calif., 1979—. Creator: Excedrin Headache commls. (Andy awards 1967,

68, 69), I'm Only Here for the Beer (Cannes award 1970, Clio Jury award 1970). Recipient: Silver Lion award Cannes Film Festival, 1968, multiple advt. awards U.S. and Eng.; named one of YWCA Women of Yr., 1978. Mem. Charter 100, Women's Com. Brandeis U. Home: 5802 Corral Way La Jolla CA 92037

LEVENTHAL, RICHARD CHARLES, marketing educator; b. Bklyn., June 20, 1943; s. Harry and Rose (Smith) L.; m. Lynn Marie Crandell, Aug. 10, 1975. BS, Cornell U., 1966; MBA, San Francisco State U., 1972; PhD, U. Denver, 1978. Sales, mktg. mgr. Scott Paper Co., Phila., 1966-67, 71-73, Syntex Dental Co., Valley Forge, Pa., 1973-75; prof. mktg. Metro. State Coll., Denver, 1976—; cons. Leventhal Research, Inc., Evergreen, Colo., 1976—. Author: (instrs. manuals) Marketing by Mandel, 1985, Marketing by Kotler, 1986; author-editor, Readings in Sales Management, 1983, Reading in Retail Management, 1983. Pres. bd. trustees Double D Manor, Evergreen, Colo.; bd. dirs. Cen. Agy. Jewish Edn., Denver, Auraria Faculty Club, Denver. Served with USN, 1967-71. Mem. Am. Mktg. Assn., Assn. Instl. Research, So. Mktg. Assn., Southwestern Mktg. Assn., Am. Assn. Higher Edn. Avocations: photography, travel, reading. Office: 7744 Native Dancer Trail Evergreen CO 80439

LE VEQUE, MATTHEW KURT, state legislative consultant, marketing professional; b. Los Angeles, May 24, 1958; s. Edward Albert and Vera Eleanora (Behne) LeV. BA in Polit. Sci., UCLA, 1981. reapportionment cons. Calif. State Legislature, Sacramento, 1981; cons. Berman and D'Agostino Campaigns, Inc., Los Angeles, 1982—; coordinator Los Angeles Olympic com., 1984; spl. advisor Congressmen H. Waxman and H. Berman, Calif., 1983-85; sr. cons. Calif. State Senate, Los Angeles and Sacramento, 1985—; cons. Spillano Internat., Newport Beach, Calif., 1984—. Active numerous local and nat. Dem. polit. campaigns. Avocations: cycling, running. Office: Calif State Senate 1950 Sawtelle Blvd #210 Los Angeles CA 90025

LEVER, JANET RAE, sociology educator, TV talk show host; b. St. Louis, Dec. 5, 1946; d. Harry H. and Sophia (Goldberg) L. BA summa cum laude, Wash. U., St. Louis, 1968; M in Philosophy, Yale U., 1971, PhD, 1974. Instr. Yale U., New Haven, 1974; asst. prof. sociology Northwestern U., Evanston, Ill., 1974-82; vis. asst. prof. U. Calif. San Diego, La Jolla, 1983-85; vis. lectr. UCLA, 1985—; sr. analyst readers' sex survey Playboy Mag., Chgo., 1981-83; cons. Playboy Cable Channel, Los Angeles, 1983—, talk show host, 1983—. Author: Soccer Madness, 1983; co-author: Women at Yale, 1971. Mem. Am. Sociol. Assn., Nat. Women's Studies Assn., Internat. Com. Sociology of Sport, Phi Beta Kappa. Office: UCLA Dept Sociology 264 Haines Hall Los Angeles CA 90024

LE VESQUE, GERALDINE ALMA, bank executive; b. St. Paul, May 24, 1935; d. Joseph Arthur and Anna Charlotte (Kohls) Le V. Auditing officer Bank Calif., San Francisco, 1968-70, asst. auditor, 1970-79, asst. v.p., mgr. funds mgmt., 1979-81, asst. v.p., project leader corp. services, 1981-82, asst. v.p., mgr. payroll services, 1982—. Mem. Nat. Assn. Bank Women, Nat. Assn. Female Execs. Democrat. Lutheran. Club: Toastmasters. Avocation: oil painting.

LEVIN, ALVIN IRVING, educator, composer; b. N.Y.C., Dec. 22, 1921; s. David and Frances (Schloss) L.; B.M. in Edn., U. Miami (Fla.), 1941; M.A., Calif. State U., Los Angeles, 1955; Ed.D. with honors, UCLA, 1968; m. Beatrice Van Loon, June 5, 1976 (div. 1981). Composer, arranger for movies, TV, theater Allied Artists, Eagle-Lion Studios, Los Angeles, 1945-65; tng. and supervising tchr. Los Angeles City Schs., 1957-65, adult edn. instr., 1962-63; research specialist Los Angeles Office Supt. Edn., 1965-67; asst. prof. ednl. research Calif. State U., Los Angeles, 1968; asst. prof. elem. edn. Calif. State U., Northridge, 1969-73; founder, pres. Alvin Irving Levin Philanthropic Found., 1973—; ordained to ministry Ch. of Mind Sci., 1975; founder, pres. Divine Love Ch.-An Internat. Metaphys. Ch., 1977—, Meet Your New Personality, A Mind Expansion Program, 1975-77. Bd. overseers Calif. Sch. Profl. Psychology, 1974—; gen. chmn., producer Fiftieth Anniversary Pageant of North Hollywood Park, 1977. Composer: Symphony for Strings, 1984, Tone Poem for Male Chorus and Brass, 1984. Recipient plaque State of Calif., 1977, Golden Merit medal Rep. Presdl. Task Force, 1985. Named to Rep. Task Force Presdl. Commn., 1986. Mem. Nat. Soc. for Study Edn., AAUP, Am. Statis. Assn., Internat. Council Edn. for Teaching, Los Angeles World Affairs Council, Internat. Platform Assn., North Hollywood C. of C. (dir. 1976—), Phi Delta Kappa. Author: My Ivory Tower, 1950; (music-drama) Happy Land, 1971; Symposium: Values in Kaleidoscope, 1973; America, America! (TV series), 1978-79; (docu-drama) One World, 1980; Symphony for Strings, 1984; Tone Poem for Male Chorus and Brass, 1984; compiler and contbr. U.S. Dept. Edn. reports; Adult Counseling and Guidance, 1967, Parent Child Presch. Program, 1967, English Classes for Foreign Speaking Adult Profls., 1967. Home: 8612 Jellico Ave Northridge CA 91325

LEVIN, JACK, physician, educator; b. Newark, Oct. 11, 1932; s. Joseph and Anna (Greengold) L.; m. Francine Corthesy, Apr. 13, 1975. B.A. magna cum laude, Yale U., 1953, M.D. cum laude, 1957. Diplomate: Am. Bd. Internal Medicine. Intern in medicine Grace-New Haven Hosp., 1957-58, asst. resident in medicine, 1960-62; clin. assoc. Nat. Cancer Inst., Bethesda, Md., 1958-60; fellow in hematology Johns Hopkins Sch. Medicine, Balt., 1962-64; chief resident in medicine Yale-New Haven Med. Center, 1964-65; mem. faculty Johns Hopkins U. Sch. Medicine and Hosp., 1965-82, prof. medicine, 1978-82; prof. lab. medicine, prof. medicine U. Calif.-San Francisco Sch. Medicine, 1982—; dir. hematology lab. San Francisco VA Med. Ctr., 1982—; cons. in field. Author: (with P.D. Zieve) Disorders of Hemostasis, 1976; editor: (with E. Cohen and F.B. Bang) Biomedical Applications of the Horseshoe Crab (Limulidae), 1979, (with S.W. Watson and T.J. Novitsky) Endotoxins and Their Detection with the Limulus Amebocyte Lysate Test, 1982, Detection of Bacterial Endotoxins with The Limulus Amebocyte Lysate Test, 1987; (with others) Bacterial Endotoxins. Structure, Biomedical Significance, and Detection with the Limulus Amebocyte Lysate Test, 1985; mem. editorial bd. Blood Cells; contbr. numerous articles to profl. jours; developer (with F.B. Bang) Limulus test for bacterial endotoxins. Mem. Yale Alumni Schs. Com. for Md., 1967-82, for San Francisco, 1986—; mem. sci. adv. bd. Nat. Aquarium, Balt., 1978-82; mem. corp. Marine Biol. Lab. Served with USPHS, 1958-60. Markle scholar, 1968-73; Josiah Macy Jr. Found. faculty scholar, 1978-79; USPHS research career devel. awardee, 1970-75. Fellow ACP; mem. Am. Soc. Hematology, Am. Soc. Clin. Investigation, Internat. Soc. Hematology, Internat. Soc. Explt. Hematology, Assn. Am. Pathologists, Am. Fedn. Clin. Research, Soc. Exptl. Biology and Medicine, So. Soc. Clin. Investigation, Yale Assn. Md., Western Assn. Physicians, Soc. Invertebrate Pathology, Soc. Analytical Cytology, Cell Kinetics Soc., Calif. Acad. Medicine, Phi Beta Kappa, Sigma Xi. Clubs: 14 W Hamilton St, Tudor and Stuart; Yale (San Francisco).

LEVIN, KENNETH, marine engineer, writer; b. Chgo., June 2, 1943; s. Maurice Arthur and Goldie (Pepper) L.; m. Eileen Terry Powell, Sep. 24, 1976; children: Benjamin Joseph, Daniel Theodore. BA, Wash. U., 1966; MS, U.S. Naval Postgrad. Sch., 1972. Water safety instr. Skokie (Ill.) Park Dist., 1964-65; commd. ensign USN, 1966—; advanced through grades to commdr. 1978; ret. USN, 1981; cons. Springfield, Va., 1982; programs mgr., project engr. M. Rosenblatt & Son, Inc., San Francisco, 1982—; cons. Stanwick Corp., Washington, 1982, Norfolk (Va.) Shipbldg. and Dry Dock Corp.; adv. com. mem. Sec. of Navy, Washington, 1986—. Contbr. articles to profl. jours. Decorated Bronze Star with gold star, Purple Heart with gold star; Cross of Gallantry (Republic of Vietnam). Soc. Naval Architects and Marine Engrs., Am. Soc. Naval Engrs., U.S. Naval Inst., Disabled Am. Vets., Blind Vets. Assn., Ret. Officers Assn. Avocations: sailing, cooking, reading, travel.

LEVIN, MARTIN HOWARD, computer consultant, retired air force officer; b. Hazleton, Pa., Feb. 9, 1941; s. Benjamin and Selma Louise (Rosen) L.; B.S. in Bus. Adminstrn., Pa. State U., 1962; M.S. in Retailing, N.Y. U., 1963; m. Rosa Bernardina Fernandez Rosado, Aug. 15, 1965; children—Maya Ann, Richard Benjamin. Commd. 2d lt. U.S. Air Force, 1963, advanced through grades to maj., 1973; comdr. 825th Services Squadron, Little Rock AFB, Ark., 1968-69; commissary officer Anderson AFB, Guam, 1969-72; comdr. 635th Services Squadron, U-Tapao, Thailand, 1972-73; services staff officer Hdqrs. 15th Air Force, SAC, 1973-75; camp comdr. Anderson AFB Indochina Refugee Camp, 1975; dep. comdr. Korea Regional Exchange, Seoul, 1975-78; chief USAF Acad. Cadet Dining Hall, 1978-79; dir. housing and services Aerospace Def. Command, Colorado Springs, Colo., 1979-80; services requirements mgr. SAC, 1980-83; ret., 1983; course dir., instr. Am. Inst. Profl. Edn., Madison, N.J., 1982-84; pres. Levin and Assocs., Inc., Colorado Springs, 1984— ; sr. v.p. Tech. Internat. Corp., 1986—; cons. microcomputer applications and edn., 1982—; instr. Pikes Peak Community Coll., Colorado Springs, 1980-82. Decorated Air Force Commendation medal with 3 oak leaf clusters, Meritorious Service medal, Joint Service Commendation medal. Jewish. Home: 5850 Escapardo Way Colorado Springs CO 80917 Office: Levin & Assocs 2120 Academy Circle Executive Park Suite E Colorado Springs CO 80917

LEVIN, ROBERT N., cardiologist; b. Providence, June 13, 1954; s. Leonard M. and Eunice E. (Kaze) L. BS in Biology, Tufts U., 1976; MD, Brown U., 1980. Diplomate Am. Bd. Internal Medicine. Intern Newton-Wellesley Hosp., Boston, 1980-81, resident, 1981-83; cardiology fellow Harbor-UCLA Med. Ctr., Torrance, 1983—. Mem. ACP, AMA, Am. Soc. Internal Medicine, Am. Heart Assn., Am. Coll. Cardiology, Phi Beta Kappa, Sigma Xi, Psi Chi. Avocations: sailing, jogging, cycling, cross-country skiing. Home: 6 Whip O Will Dr Box 628 Hyannis MA 02601

LEVIN, THOMAS AUGUSTUS, health science association executive; b. Montgomery, Ala., Dec. 8, 1946; m. Carolyn Dahlgren; children: Daniel, Carey. BA, U. Ala., 1968; JD, U. N.C., 1971. Bar: N.C. 1971, D.C. 1972, N.Mex. 1974. Staff counsel N.Mex. Blue Cross & Blue Shield, Albuquerque, 1974-76, v.p. legal affairs, 1976-81, pres., chief exec. officer, 1981—; bd. dirs. First Interstate Bank; mem. exec. com., chmn. govtl. affairs com., bd. dirs. Blue Cross & Blue Shield Assn. Mem. bd. visitors U. N.Mex. Sch. Law, strategic planning com. U. N.Mex., Mayor's Task Force Alcohol Abuse. Served with U.S. Army, 1972-74. Mem. N.Mex. Bar Assn., Nat. Health Lawyers Assn., N.Mex. Hosp. Assn. (bd. dirs.), N.Mex. Health Systems Agy. (vice chmn. governing body), Albuquerque C. of C. Office: Blue Cross & Blue Shield N Mex Office of Pres 12800 Indian Sch Rd NE Albuquerque NM 87112

LEVIN, WAYNE ALLEN, photographer, educator; b. Los Angeles, Oct. 24, 1945; s. Melvin Harrington and Clarice (Hattenback) L. BFA, San Francisco Art Inst., 1979; MFA, Pratt Inst., 1982. Free lance photographer Honolulu, 1983—; lectr. photography U. Hawaii, Honolulu, 1983-85; lectr. Hawaii Loa Coll., Honolulu, 1986—; v.p. Image Found., Honolulu, 1985—; treas. Honolulu Printmakers, 1984-85; chmn., student councilor San Francisco Art Inst., 1978-79; artist-in-residence Hawaii Sch. for Girls, 1986-87, Dayton Art Inst., 1987-88. Author, photographer: Preservations, 1979; photography portfolio: Underwater Photographs, 1984, Kalaupapa, 1986; contbr. photographs to profl. jours.; one-man shows include Honolulu Acad. Arts, 1974, 1985, Camera Works Gallery, Los Angeles, 1976, Diego Rivera Gallery, San Francisco Art Inst., 1979, Focus Gallery, San Francisco, 1980, Pratt Inst., Bklyn., 1982, Arsenal Gallery, Gallery of N.Y. Dept. Parks, N.Y.C., 1983, Midtown Y Photo Gallery, N.Y.C., 1983, Art Loft, Honolulu, 1984, Orange Coast Coll., Costa Mesa, Calif., 1985, Equivalents Gallery, Seattle, 1985; exhibited in group shows at Pratt Inst. Exchange Exhibit, Tokyo, 1981, Artists of Hawaii, Honolulu Acad. Arts, 1983, Pratt Alumni Exhibition, Cayman Gallery, N.Y.C., 1984, Water, Blue Sky Gallery, Portland, Oreg., 1984, Edwynn Houk Gallery, Chgo., 1984, Morgan Gallery, Kansas City, Mo., 1984, Comtemporary Photographers of Hawaii, Honolulu Acad. Arts, 1985, Urban Photography, Kenyon (Ohio) Coll., 1985, New Photographics, U. Cen. Wash., 1985, Third Annual Woodstock (N.Y.) Nat. Exhibition, 1985, Gallery Picture, Osaka, Japan, 1986; represented in permanent collections Shakley Corp., Honolulu City Council, Honolulu Acad. Art., Hawaii State Found. for Culture and the Arts, Contemporary Arts Ctr., Honolulu, Soc. for Contemporary Photography, New Photographics Cen. Wash. U., Mus. Modern Art. Fellow Nat. Endowment for the Arts, 1984. Mem. Coll. Art. Assn., Soc. for Photographic Edn., Los Angeles Inst. for Creative Photography, Soc. for Contemporary Photography. Avocations: sailing, surfing. Home: 6801 Hapuna Pl Honolulu HI 96825

LEVINE, BEVERLY, nursing educator; b. Duluth, Minn., Jan. 17, 1928; d. Victor and Ida (Perfetto) L. BS in Nursing Edn., U. Minn., 1953; M in Nursing, U. Wash., 1964. RN, PHN. Instr. nursing edn. San Francisco State U., 1961-62, Foothill Coll., Los Altos, Calif., 1963-64, Chabot Coll., Hayward, Calif., 1964—; mem. adv. com. Am. Cancer Soc., Alameda County, Calif. chpt., 1975-80. Vol. Sta. KQED-TV, San Francisco, 1964-84. Avocations: jogging, tennis, hiking. Home: 6400 Valley View Rd Oakland CA 94611

LEVINE, DOUGLAS STEWART, physician scientist; b. Washington, June 27, 1952; s. Oscar and Betty (Palais) L; m. Barbara Sather, Nov. 19, 1981. BA, Boston U., 1974; MD, U. Mass., 1979. Intern in medicine R.I. Hosp., Providence, 1979-80, resident in medicine, 1980-82; fellow in gastroenterology U. Wash., Seattle, 1982-85, acting instr., 1985—. Contbr. articles to profl. jours. Recipient Nat. Research Service award, Pub. Health Service NIH, 1982-84. Mem. AAAS, Am. Gastroenterol. Assn., Am. Coll. Physicians, N.Y. Acad. Sci. Jewish. Home: 4509 NE 71st St Seattle WA 98115 Office: U Wash RG-24 NE Pacific Seattle WA 98195

LEVINE, MARK LEE, lawyer. GRI, U. Colo.; LLM, NYU; PAP, Northwestern U.; PhD in Bus. Adminstrn, Century U.; JD, U. Denver; BS in Bus. and Econs. magna cum laude, Colo. State U. Instr. tax, real estate U. Colo., 1969—; law clk. Goldsmith & Carter, 1966-68; dist. atty. clerkship 1967; with Arthur Young & Co., 1968-70; ptnr. Levine & Pitler, 1968—; chmn. bd. dirs. Levine, Ltd., Realtors; asst prof. Met. State Coll., 1969-75; prof. U. Denver, 1975—; tchr. U. No. Colo., Arapahoe Coll., Community Coll. Denver. Contbr. numerous articles to profl. jours. Mem. Arapahoe Community Coll. Adv. Bd. Mem. ABA, Nat. Assn. Realtors (cert., sr. prof.), Colo. Bar Assn., Am. Bus. Law Assn., Colo. Realtors Assn., Arapahoe Community Coll. Council for Paralegals, Greater Denver Tax Cousnels' Assn., Am. Assn. Cert. Appraisers (counselor), Colo. Soc. CPA's (instr.), Am. Soc. Real Estate Profls., Denver Bd. Realtors., Speaker's Bur., Beta Gamma Sigma. Home: 180 S Dahlia St Denver CO 80222 Office: U Denver Coll of Bus Adminstrn Room BA 321-A 2020 S Race St Denver CO 80208

LEVINE, MELDON EDISES, congressman, lawyer; b. Los Angeles, June 7, 1943; s. Sid B. and Shirley B. (Blum) L.; m. Jan Greenberg; children—Adam Paul, Jacob Caplan, Cara Emily. A.B., U. Calif.-Berkeley, 1964; M.P.A., Princeton U., 1966; J.D., Harvard U., 1969. Bar: Calif. 1970, D.C. 1972. Assoc. Wyman, Bautzer, Rothman & Kuchel, 1969-71; legis. asst. U.S. Senate, Washington, 1971-73; mem. Levine Krom & Unger, Beverly Hills, Calif., 1973-77, Calif. Assembly, Sacramento, 1977-82, 98th-100th Congresses from 27th Calif. dist., Washington, 1983—. Author: The Private Sector and the Common Market, 1968; contbr. articles to various publs. Mem. governing bd. So. Calif. chpt. Anti-Defamation League, So. Calif. chpt. Am. Jewish Com., So. Calif. chpt. Am. Jewish Congress, So. Calif. chpt. NAACP Legal Def. Fund, U. Judaism, City of Hope, U. Calif. Alumni Council. Mem. Calif. Bar Assn., Los Angeles Bar Assn. Office: Office of House Reps Washington DC 20515

LEVINE, MICHAEL, public relations executive; b. N.Y.C., Apr. 17, 1954; s. Arthur and Virgiaia (Gaylor) L. Student, Rutgers U., 1972-77. Owner, operator TV News Mag., Los Angeles, 1977-83; pres., owner Michael Levine Pub. Relations, Los Angeles, 1982—; mem. Gov.'s adv. bd. State Calif., Sacramento, 1980-82; pres., owner Aurora Pub., Los Angeles, 1986—. Author: The Address Book: How to Reach Anyone Who's Anyone, 1984, The New Address Book, 1986, The Corporate Address Book, 1987. Mem. Ronald Reagan Pres.'s Library, Rosey Grier's Are You Committed, Los Angeles, 1986—, Neil Bogart Labs. of Cancer Research, 1986—. Mem. TV Acad. Arts and Scis., Entertainemnt Industries Council, West Hollywood C. of C. (bd. dirs. 1980-82). Republican. Jewish. Office: 8730 Sunset Blvd 6th Floor Los Angeles CA 90069

LEVINE, MICHAEL JOSEPH, insurance company executive, managment consultant; b. Boston, Mar. 23, 1945; s. Sam and Helen Alice (Michelman) L.; m. Margaret Mary Gutierrez, Aug. 6, 1983. BA, Boston U., 1967. Supr. underwriting Comml. Union. Ins., Boston, 1969-73; mgr. Harris-Murtagh Ins., Boston, 1973-75, Cohen-Goldenberg Ins. Agy., Boston, 1975-77; v.p. Southwest Underwriters Ins., Deming, N.Mex., 1977-83, pres., 1983-86; pres. Consol. Ins. Cons., Deming, N.Mex., 1985—; mgr. Pollard Southwest Ins. Co., Deming, 1986—. V.p. Border Area Mental Health Services, So. N.Mex., 1978—; pres. Deming Arts Council, 1979-81; treas. Luna County (N.Mex.) Crimestoppers, Inc., 1979—. Mem. Mensa, Soc. CPCU's (cert.), Soc. Cert. Ins. Counselors (cert.), Ins. Mktg. Assocs., Luna County C. of C. (v.p. 1981-84), Ind. Ins. Agts. N.Mex. (state dir. 1985—), Southwest N.Mex. Ind. Ins. Agts. (treas. 1981-83, pres. 1983-85). Democrat. Jewish. Lodges: B'Nai Brith, Moose. Avocations: tennis, model railroads, computers, rock collecting. Home: 1920 S Silver St Deming NM 88030 Office: Pollard Southwest Ins Agy 120 W Pine St Deming NM 88031

LEVINE, MYRON LOUIS, optometrist; b. Los Angeles, Nov. 21, 1930; s. Jack and Jennie (Berman) L.; m. Nancy Lou Siegler Gambet, Aug. 15, 1953; children—Jeffrey Dean, Bradley Allen, Steven Mitchell. B.S., Pacific U., 1953, O.D., 1954. Lic. optometrist, Calif., Nev. Pvt. practice optometry, West Los Angeles, 1954-60, group practice, Beverly Hills, Calif., 1960-81, partnership practice, Los Angeles, 1982—; mem. staff Mt. Sinai Optometric Clinic, 1960-63, Queen of Angels Hosp., 1964—, Santa Marta Hosp., 1964—, contact lens clinic, 1982; lectr. various profl. groups. Recipient Los Angeles Service award, Dist. 4 Chain Maker award, Past Pres. Service award, B'nai B'rith. Mem. Los Angeles Optometric Assn. (Award of Merit 1966), Am. Optometric Assn. (charter mem. contact lens sect., multidisciplinary practice sect.). Democrat. Jewish. Clubs: Masons, B'nai B'rith (past pres.). Contbr. articles to profl. jours. Home: 10587 Holman Ave Los Angeles CA 90024 Office: 840 S Robertson Blvd Los Angeles CA 90035

LEVINE, WILLIAM HOWARD, real estate developer; b. Vancouver, B.C., Can., May 18, 1941; s. Moses Harry and Pearl L.; Dec. 23, 1967; children—Sarah, Anna. Grad. with honors in econs., U. B.C., 1963; MA in Bus. Adminstrn, Harvard U., 1965. Mgr. comml. loans Laurentide, Toronto, Ont., Can., 1965-70; corp. sec. to v.p. fin. and sec. Daon Devel. Corp., Vancouver, 1970-75; exec. v.p. Daon Devel. Corp. (now BCE Devel. Corp.), Vancouver, 1975—, now pres.; Mem. Vancouver Econ. Adv. Commn., 1980. Trustee Fraser Inst., 1979-80; bd. dirs. United Way Appeal, 1979-80. Club: Columbia Centre Squash. Office: BCE Devel Corp, 999 W Hastings St, Vancouver, BC Canada V6C 2W7 *

LEVINSKY, JANET BETH, designer and retailer; b. Indianapolis, Nov. 1, 1947; d. Samuel and Dora (Shuster) Levinsky; m. Marc Stein Prigozen, Mar. 16, 1980. B.F.A., U. Colo., 1969, M.F.A., 1971. Designer Wright, Porteous & Lowe, Indpls., 1970; design mgr. Witkin Homes, Denver, 1970-73; designer and sales staff Foliage Services, Inc., Denver, 1973-75; mgr. design ctr., Mission Viejo Co., Mission Viejo Calif., and Denver, 1975-76; store mgr. Dancewear Showcase, Denver, 1976-78; bus. mgr. Colo. Conservatory Ballet, Denver, 1976-78; owner, operator Denver Dance Shop, Denver, 1978—; assoc. ptnr. D. Waters Interiors, 1985—; freelance designer. Mem. exec. Bd. Coll. Contemporary Dance; mem. Children's Diabetes Guild, Jr. Symphony Guild, Denver Ballet Guild; sponsor David Taylor Dance Theatre; bd. dirs. Nat. Jewish Hosp. Mem. Am. Soc. Interior Designers, Nat. Landscape Inst., Nat. Soc. Interior Designers. Home: 4530 S Verbena Unit 336 Denver CO 80237

LEVINSON, ARTHUR DAVID, molecular biologist; b. Seattle, Mar. 31, 1950; s. Sol and Malvina (Lindsay) L.; m. Rita May Liff, Dec. 17, 1978; children: Jesse, Anya. BS, U. Wash., 1972; PhD, Princeton U., 1977. Postdoctoral fellow U. Calif., San Francisco, 1977-80; sr. scientist Genentech, South San Francisco, 1980-84, staff scientist, 1984—. Mem. AAAS, Am. Soc. Biol. Chemistry, N.Y. Acad. Sci. Office: Genentech Inc 460 Point San Bruno Blvd South San Francisco CA 94080

LEVINSON, KENNETH LEE, lawyer; b. Denver, Jan. 18, 1953; s. Julian Charles and Dorothy (Milzer) L.; m. Shauna Titus McCaffery, Dec. 21, 1986. B.A. with distinction, U. Colo.-Boulder, 1974; J.D., U. Denver, 1978. Bar: Colo. 1978, U.S. Ct. Appeals (10th cir.) 1978. Assoc. atty. Balaban & Lutz, Denver, 1979-83; shareholder Balaban & Levinson, Denver, 1984—. Contbr. articles to profl. jours. Pres., Dahlia House Condominium Assn., 1983-85; intern Reporters Com. For Freedom of the Press, Washington, 1977. Recipient Am. Jurisprudence award Lawyers Co-op., 1977. Mem. ABA, Denver Bar Assn., Colo. Bar Assn., Am. Arbitration Assn. (arbitrator), Internat. Platform Assn. Clubs: Denver Law, Denver Athletic.

LEVINTOW, LEON, microbiologist, virologist, educator, department chairman; b. Phila., Nov. 10, 1921; s. Benjamin Henry and Dora (Melnicoff) L.; m. Pearl Slutz, Feb. 6, 1946 (dec. Jan. 1955); m. Regina Goodman, Apr. 1, 1959; children: Michael, Stephen, Daniel, Robert Paul. BA, Haverford Coll., 1943; MD, Thomas Jefferson U., 1946. Research chemist Nat. Cancer Inst., Bethesda, Md., 1949-51, 52-56; research fellow Mass. Gen. Hosp., Boston, 1951-52; asst. lab. chief, lab. cell biology Nat. Inst. Allergy and Infectious Diseases div. NIH, Bethesda, 1956-61, asst. lab. chief, lab. biol. viruses, 1962-65; prof. microbiology U. Calif., San Francisco, 1965—, chmn. dept. microbiology and immunology, 1981—; Mem. Molecular Biology panel NSF, Washington, 1966-69; chmn. exptl. virology study sect. NIH, Bethesda, 1975-79; chmn. fellowship screening com. Am. Cancer Soc. Calif. div., 1980-83. Assoc. Editor Virology jour., 1961—. Served to capt. U.S. Army med. corps., 1943-49, USPHS, 1949-65, med. dir. Mem. Am. Chem. Soc., Am. Soc. Biol. Chemists, Am. Soc. Microbiology (chmn. virology div., 1969-70). Office: U Calif Sch Medicine Dept Microbiology and Immunology Rm S-412 San Francisco CA 94143

LEVITON, ALAN EDWARD, museum curator; b. N.Y.C., Jan. 11, 1930; s. David and Charlotte (Weber) L.; m. Gladys Ann Robertson, June 30, 1952; children: David A., Charlotte A. A.B., Stanford U., 1949, M.A., 1953, Ph.D., 1960; student, Columbia U., summers 1947, 48, 53, N.Y. U., 1948, U. Nebr., 1954. Asst. curator herpetology Calif. Acad. Scis., San Francisco, 1957-60; assoc. curator Calif. Acad. Scis., 1960-61, chmn., curator, 1962-82, curator, 1983—, coordinator computer services, 1983—; assoc. curator zool. collections Stanford, 1962-63; lectr. biol. sci. 1963-70; professorial lectr. Golden Gate U., 1953-63; adj. prof. biol. sci. San Francisco State U., 1967—. Author: North American Amphibians and Reptiles, 1972; contbr. numerous articles to sci., profl. jours. Am. Philos. Soc. grantee, 1960; NSF grantee, 1960-61, 77-79, 80-83; Belvedere Sci. Fund grantee, 1958-59, 1962. Fellow Calif. Acad. Scis., AAAS (council 1976—, com. council affairs 1983-85, sec.-treas. Pacific div. 1975-79, exec. dir. 1980—), Explorers Club; mem. Am. Soc. Ichthyologists and Herpetologists (bd. govs. 1960-84), Soc. Systematic Zoology (sec.-treas. Pacific sect. 1970-72), Herpetologists League (pres. 1961-62), Soc. Vertebrate Paleontologists, History of Sci. Soc., Geol. Soc. Am., Sigma Xi. Home: 571 Kingsley Ave Palo Alto CA 94301 Office: Calif Acad Scis Golden Gate Park San Francisco CA 94118

LEVITT, LAWRENCE DAVID, financial recovery services executive; b. Los Angeles, Apr. 18, 1944; s. Albert Herbert and Reva (Narvey) L.; m. Cinda Sue Coffee, Apr. 8, 1967; 1 child, Rachel Diane. AA, Solano Community Coll., 1970; B, U. San Francisco, 1976. Officer, detective Fairfield (Calif.) Police Dept., 1968-78; officer, supr. Douglas (Wyo.) Police Dept., 1978-79; comdr. Rock Springs (Wyo.) Police Dept., 1979-83, chief of police, 1983-86; owner CoServe, Rock Springs, 1986—; instr. Solano Community Coll., Fairfield, 1972-78, Western Wyo. Coll., Rock Springs, 1979—; mem. curriculum com. Wyo. Law Enforcement Acad., Douglas, 1985—. Mem. adv. bd. Youth Home, Inc., Rock Springs, 1980, S.W. Wyo. Alcohol Rehab. Assn., Rock Springs, 1984-86; mem. Upper Solano County Assn. For Retarded Children, Fairfield, 1974-78. Recipient Red Cross Life Saving award ARC, 1970; named Police Officer of Yr., Fairfield-Suisun Exchange Club, 1973. Mem. Internat. Assn. Chiefs of Police, Wyo. Assn. Chief's Police (v.p. 1985-86, chmn. edn. com. 1985—), Wyo. Peace Officers Assn., Rock Springs C. of C. Democrat. Jewish. Club: Wyo. Paint Horse (Douglas). Lodges: Lions, Shriners, Masons, Elks. Avocations: fly fishing, golf. Home: 248 Cherokee Dr Rock Springs WY 82901 Office: 409 Broadway Suite B PO Box 6109 Rock Springs WY 82901

LEVITT, RAYMOND ELLIOT, engineering educator; b. Johannesburg, Republic of South Africa, Aug. 7, 1949; came to U.S., 1972; s. Barnard and Riva Eleanor (Lazarus) L.; m. Kathleen Adele Sullivan, Nov. 26, 1976; children: Benjamin John, Joanna Maurine, Zoë Ellen. BSCE, U. Witwatersrand, Johannesburg, 1971; MSCE, Stanford U., 1973, PhDCE, 1975.

Project engr. Christiani & Neilsen, Cape Town, Republic of South Africa, 1971-72; asst. prof. civil engring. MIT, Cambridge, 1975-79, assoc. prof., 1979-80; assoc. prof. Stanford (Calif.) U., 1980—; bd. dirs. sci. advisors Egecon Italia, Rome and Milan; cons. IntelliCorp., Mountain View, Calif., 1985—; advisor U.S. Dept. Labor, Washington, 1976-77, Calif. Pub. Utilities Commn., San Francisco, 1982-84. Author: Howsafe Diagnostic System, 1986; co-author: Union and Open-Shop Construction, 1978, Construction Safety Management, 1987. Pres. Stanford Homeowners Assn., 1981-83. Recipient Marksman award Engring. News Record, N.Y.C., 1985. Mem. ASCE (Huber Prize award 1982), Am. Assn. Artificial Intelligence, Project Mgmt. Inst. Unitarian. Avocations: swimming, trout fishing, tennis, music. Office: Stanford U Dept Civil Engring Stanford CA 94305

LEVITT, THOMAS CHARLES, lawyer; b. Sioux City, Iowa, Nov. 12, 1954; s. David Jacob Levitt and Nancy Elaine (Rich); m. Elise Ann Parnes, June 25, 1977; children: Dana Rose, Jacob Kenneth. BS in Chem. Engring, U. Calif., Davis, 1976; JD, U. Calif., San Francisco, 1979; postgrad., U. Calif., Davis, 1983-85. Bar: Wash. 1979. Assoc. Layman, Mullin & Etter, Spokane, Wash., 1979-83; atty. Totem Pacific, Spokane, Wash., 1983—; exec. v.p. Totem Pacific Corp., Spokane, 1985—; of counsel Totem Pacific Corp. Mem. Am. Chem. Soc., Wash. State Trial Lawyers Assn. Avocation: family orchards. Home: 2720 Feather Pl Davis CA 95616 Office: E 8518 Green Bluff Rd Colbert WA 99005

LEVITZ, JOEL JACOB, community developer; b. Phila., Jan. 4, 1935; s. Milton and Sophia (Kurtz) L.; B.S., CCNY, 1958; M.A., Sacramento State Coll., 1964; postgrad CCNY, 1959-60, Columbia U., 1960-61, U. Denver, 1961-62; Ed.D., Temple U., 1973; m. Karen R. Bell, Sept. 17, 1977; children—Michael Seth, John, Susan, Robin, Michael Kimball. Tchr. emotionally disturbed children Hawthorne (N.Y.) Cedar Knolls, 1958-60; tng. supr., tech. rep. Am. Machine & Foundry, Stamford, Conn., 1960-62; engring. psychologist Aerojet Gen. Corp., Sacramento, 1962-64, Philco Ford, Willow Grove, Pa., 1964-66; program mgr. ednl. systems Burroughs Corp., Ardmore, Pa., 1966-70; dir. spl. support serviced Federal City Coll., Washington, 1970-71; v.p. mktg., Ill. and Ariz. ops. Environ. Devels., Inc., 1971-78; pres. Executive Homes Inc., Denver, 1977—, Calvan Properties Inc., 1978—, Paragon Realty (USA) Ltd., 1979—; pres. The Levitz Group, 1982—; mem. U.S. Senatorial Bus. Adv. Com. Mem. Human Factors Soc. (exec. council at large 1966-67), Am. Psychol. Assn., (asso.), Nat. Assn. Homebuilders, Nat. Assn. Realtors, Psi Chi, Phi Delta Kappa, Phi Theta Tau. Home: 3670 S Helena Way Aurora CO 80013 Office: 14001 E Iliff Ave Aurora CO 80014

LEVRAN, ALEXANDER, electrical engineer, educator; b. Potkamin, USSR, July 26, 1950; s. Tzvi and Hana Leber; m. Mala Kushnier, Apr. 13, 1973; children: Netta, Sivan, Annatte. BSc in Elec. Engring., Bengurion U., Beersheva, Israel, 1973; MSc in Elec. Engring., Technion, Haifa, Israel, 1979; PhD in Elec. Engring., Poly. Inst. of N.Y., 1982. Elec. engr. Israeli Industry, 1973-79; adj. instr. Technion, 1974-76; research fellow Poly. Inst. of N.Y., Bklyn., 1979-81; chief engr. Teledyne INET, Torrance, Calif., 1981—; vis. prof. Northrop U. and UCLA, 1985—; cons. in field, Los Angeles, 1985—. Mem. IEEE. Avocations: chess, tennis. Home: 12524 Indianapolis St Los Angeles CA 90066 Office: Teledyne INET Engring 2750 W Lomita Blvd Torrance CA 90509

LEVY, ALAN DAVID, real estate executive; b. St. Louis, July 19, 1938; s. I. Jack and Natalie (Yawitz) L.; grad. Sch. Real Estate, Washington U., 1960; m. Abby Jane Markowitz, May 12, 1968; children—Jennifer Lynn, Jacqueline Claire. Property mgr. Solon Gershman Inc., Realtors, Clayton, Mo., 1958-61; gen. mgr. Kodner Constrn. Co., St. Louis, 1961-63; regional mgr. Tishman Realty & Constrn. Co., Inc., N.Y.C., 1963-69, v.p., Los Angeles, 1969-77; exec. v.p., dir. Tishman West Mgmt. Corp., 1977—; dir. Metro-Plex Airline, Dallas; guest lectr. on real estate mgmt. to various forums. Mem. Los Angeles County Mus. Art; chmn. bd. trustees Westlake Sch. Mem. bldg. owners and mgrs. assns. Los Angeles (dir.), N.J. (co-founder, hon. dir.), Inst. Real Estate Mgmt. (cert. property mgr.), Urban Land Inst., Internat. Council Shopping Centers. Contbr. articles on property mgmt. to trade jours. Home: 10960 Wilshire Blvd Los Angeles CA 90024

LEVY, DAVID STEVEN, college administrator; b. Los Angeles, Mar. 9, 1955; s. Henry and Gloria Grace (Barouh) L.; m. Stephanie Brashears. B.A., Occidental Coll., 1977; M.A., 1979. Asst. dir. fin. aid Calif. State Coll., San Bernardino, 1978-79; fin. aid counselor Calif. State U.-Northridge, 1979-80; assoc. dir. student fin. aid Calif. State U.-Dominguez Hills, 1980-82; dir. fin. aid Occidental Coll., Los Angeles, 1982—; mem. Title IA Adv. Com. Calif., 1977—. Mem. life-long learning com. Calif. Postsecondary Edn. Commn., 1980—, mem. student fin. aid issues com., 1984—. Richter fellow Princeton U., 1976; Calif. State U. adminstrv. fellow, 1981—. Mem. Mortar Board Alumni Assn. (pres. 1977—), Calif. Assn. Student Fin. Aid Adminstrs. (ind. segmental rep. 1984, sec. 1985, treas. 1986), Western Assn. Student Fin. Aid Adminstrs., Nat. Assn. Student Fin. Aid Adminstrs., Phi Beta Kappa, Delta Phi Epsilon, Psi Chi, Phi Alpha Theta, Sigma Alpha Epsilon. Jewish. Coeditor Calif. Student Aid Commn. Student Aid Workbook, 1977—. Home: 41 Northwoods Ln La Crescenta CA 91214 Office: Occidental Coll 1600 Campus Rd Los Angeles CA 90041

LEVY, EUGENE HOWARD, planetary sciences educator, researcher; b. N.Y.C., May 6, 1944; s. Isaac Philip and Anita Harriet (Guttman) L.; m. Margaret Lyle Rader, Oct. 13, 1967; children—Roger P., Jonathan S., Benjamin H. A.B. in Physics with high honors, Rutgers U., 1966; Ph.D. in Physics, U. Chgo., 1971. Teaching asst. physics U. Chgo., 1966-69, research asst. Enrico Fermi Inst., 1969-71; postdoctoral fellow physics and astronomy U. Md., 1971-73; asst. prof. physics and astrophysics Bartol Research Found., Franklin Inst., Swarthmore, Pa., 1973-75; asst. prof., then assoc. prof. U. Ariz., Tucson, 1975-83, prof. planetary scis., 1983—, head dept., dir. lunar and planetary lab., 1983—; mem./chmn. numerous coms., adv. bds. NASA, Nat. Acad. Scis., 1976—; cons., invited lectr. in field; mem. ad hoc theory panel Space Sci. Bd., 1980; sci. cons. Rockwell Internat. Corp., 1980; disting. vis. scientist Jet Propulsion Lab., Calif. Inst. Tech., Pasadena, 1985—; mem. COSPAR Internat. Tech. Panel on Comets, 1980-82; mem. U.S.-NASA del. to discussions on internat. cooperation investigations of Comet Halley, Padua, Italy, 1981; mem. U.S.-NASA del. U.S.-USSR Joint Working Group on Near-Earth Space, the Moon and Planets, 1981; internat. program adv. bd. Internat. Conf. on Cometary Exploration, Budapest, Hungary, 1982; exec. com. univ.' space sci. working group Assn. Am. Univs., 1982-86; study panel U.S.-Soviet cooperation in space sci. U.S. Cong. Office of Tech. Assessment, 1984. Contbr. numerous articles to profl. jours.; author articles for gen. pub., reports for Congl. Record, abstracts, book reviews, others. NASA fellow U. Chgo., 1966-69; recipient Disting. Pub. Service medal NASA, 1983;grantee NASA, NSF. Mem. AAAS, Am. Astron. Soc., Am. Geophys. Union, Am. Phys. Soc., Internat. Astron. Union, Phi Beta Kappa, Sigma Xi. Home: 5442 E Burns St Tucson AZ 85711 Office: U Ariz Lunar and Planetary Lab Tucson AZ 85721

LEVY, HAROLD P., public relations cons.; b. Trinidad, Colo., Mar. 8, 1907; s. Phan and Fannie (Akerman) L.; A.B., U. Wash., 1929; m. Alice Klund, Sept. 9, 1938. Reporter, Seattle Union Record and Seattle Post-Intelligencer, 1926-29; reporter, editor Seattle Times, 1929-34; resident writer Henry St. Settlement, N.Y.C., 1934-35; dir. publicity Nat. Conf. Social Work, Columbus, Ohio, 1935-39; research assoc. Russell Sage Found., N.Y.C., 1939-45; nat. dir. pub. relations Commn. Community Interrelations, N.Y.C., 1945-47; founder, pres. Harold P. Levy Pub. Relations, Los Angeles, 1947—; faculty U. Calif. Extension, 1947-49. Bd. dirs. Tb and Health Assn. Los Angeles County, 1958-64, pres., 1962-63; bd. dirs. Calif. Orgn. Public Health Nursing, 1949-52, Pasadena Symphony Orch., 1981-84. Mem. Pub. Relations Soc. Am. (charter; nat. dir. 1954, chpt. dir. 1950-54), Sigma Delta Chi. Clubs: Assocs. of Calif. Inst. Tech., Athenaeum. Author: There Were Days Like That, 1985, Public Relations for Social Agencies, 1956; Building a Popular Movement, 1944; A Study in Public Relations, 1943; contbr. articles to profl. jours. Address: 2980 Edgewick Rd Glendale CA 91206

LEVY, JEROME, dermatologist; retired naval officer; b. Bklyn., Aug. 17, 1926; s. Alexander and Pauline (Wollkof) L.; m. Leona Elsie Eligator, June 6, 1948; children—Andrew B., Eric J., Peter C., David J. Student, Wesleyan U., 1944-45; postgrad., 1952-54; A.B., Yale U., 1947; M.D., Albany Med. Coll., 1958. Diplomate Am. Bd. Dermatology. Commd. ensign M.C., U.S. Navy, 1957, advanced through grades to capt., 1972; intern U.S. Naval Hosp., Newport, R.I., 1958-59; resident U.S. Naval Hosp., Phila., 1960-62, U. Pa. Grad. Sch. Medicine, Phila., 1962-63; chief dept. dermatology U.S. Naval Hosp., Memphis, 1963-67, Yokosuka, Japan, 1967-70, Long Beach, Calif., 1974-75; head outpatient dermatology clinic San Diego Naval Hosp., 1970-72; sr. med. officer Keflavik, Iceland, 1972-74; ret., 1975; med. dir. dermatology Westwood Pharm Co., Buffalo, 1975-82; acting chief dermatology dept. Buffalo Gen. Hosp., 1981-82; cons. Erie County Health Dept., 1979-82; clin. assoc. prof. SUNY, Buffalo Med. Sch., 1980-82; practice medicine specializing in dermatology, Coronado, Calif., 1982—. Contbr. articles to med. jours. Decorated Navy Commendation medal, Joint Service Commendation medal; Knight's Cross and Order of Falcon (Iceland). Fellow Am. Acad. Dermatology, ACP; mem. AMA, So. Med. Assn., Assn. Mil. Surgeons, U.S., Navy League, Alpha Omega Alpha. Republican. Jewish. Home: 3352 Lucinda St San Diego CA 92106 Office: 478 Orange Ave Coronado CA 92118

LEVY, MORTON FRANK, organic chemist; b. N.Y.C., May 31, 1925; s. Leo and Tillie (Pasternak) L.; divorced; children: Brooke Levy Greene, Drew Levy Irvin, Alisa. BS, Queens Coll., 1950; MA, Columbia U., 1951; PhD, Yale U., 1955. Organic chemist Argus Chem. Co., Bklyn., 1955-60, Wallace & Tiernan, Belleville, N.J., 1960-64; sr. chemistr IBM Corp., Endicott, N.Y., 1964-70, San Jose, Calif., 1970—. Editor and pub. Primary Lateral Sclerosis newsletter, also founder; contbr. articles to profl. jours.; patentee in field. Served with U.S. Army, 1943-46, ETO, ATO. Mem. AAAS, Am. Chem. Soc. Avocations: acting, directing, ceramics. Home: 105 Stacia St Los Gatos CA 95030 Office: IBM Corp 5600 Cottle Rd San Jose CA 95193

LEVY, PHILIP LAZARUS, physician, ophthalmologist; b. N.Y.C., Mar. 9, 1931; s. David Emanuel and Anna F. (Berstein) L. m. Roslyn Finkelstein, Dec. 19, 1954 (div. 1979); children: Leonard Robert, Amy Rachel; m. Lynn Marie Jenkins, June 12, 1983. BA in Biology, NYU, 1952; MD, N.Y. Med. Coll., 1956. Diplomate Am. Bd. Ophthalmology. Intern Michael Reese Hosp., Chgo., 1956-57; resident U. Pa., Phila., 1957-58, Wills Eye Hosp., Phila., 1960-62; practice medicine and surgery specializing in ophthalmology Sacramento, 1962—; clin. prof. ophthalmology Sch. Medicine U. Calif., Davis, 1979-85, clin. prof., 1985—; cons. USAF, 1962—, State of Calif., 1967—, U.S. HHS, 1968—; lectr. in field. Contbr. articles to profl. jours. Bd. dirs. Jewish Fedn., Sacramento, 1966-69, 72-78. Served to capt. MC., USAF, 1958-60. Recipient Cor et Manus Honor award N.Y. Med. Coll., 1956; Bausch & Lomb Co. grantee, 1978. Fellow ACS, Am. Acad. Ophthalmology, Kerato-Refractive Soc., Am. Intraocular Implant Soc. (founder), Calif. Assn. Ophthalmology (v.p. 1986—). Jewish. Office: Med Corp 77 Scripps Dr Suite 202 Sacramento CA 95825

LEVY, RICARDO BENJAMIN, chemical company executive; b. Quito, Ecuador, Jan. 11, 1945; came to U.S., 1962; s. Leopoldo and Kate (Bamberg) L.; m. Noella Luke, June 15, 1967; children: Tamara, Brian. BS, Stanford U., 1966, PhDChemE, 1972; MS, Princeton U., 1967. Gen. mgr. Sudamericana, Quito, 1967-70; research engr. Exxon Research & Engring. Corp. subs. Exxon Corp., Florham Park, N.J., 1972-74; v.p., co-founder Catalytica Assocs. Inc., Mountain View, Calif., 1974—. Co-Author: Catalysis in Coal Conversion; patentee in field. Mem. Am. Inst. Chem. Engrs., Comml. Devel. Assn., Phi Beta Kappa. Avocation: sailing. Office: Catalytica Assocs Inc 430 Ferguson Dr Bldg 3 Mountain View CA 94043

LEVY, SALOMON, mechanical engineer; b. Jerusalem, Apr. 4, 1926; came to U.S., 1945; s. Abraham Isaac and Sultana Claire (Elyachar) L.; m. Eileen Dolores Jaques, Oct. 14, 1951; children: Marshall Douglas, Linda C. BSME, U. Calif., Berkeley, 1949, MME, 1951, PhD in Mech. Engring., 1953. Engr. Gen. Electric Co., Schenectady, N.Y. and San Jose, Calif., 1953-59; mgr. heat transfer Gen. Electric Co., San Jose, 1959-66, mgr. systems engring., 1966-68, mgr. design engring., 1968-71, gen. mgr., 1971-75, gen. mgr. boiling water reactor ops., 1975-77; pres. S. Levy Inc., Campbell, Calif., 1977—; adj. prof. UCLA, 1986-87; Springer prof. U. Calif., Berkeley, 1979-80; bd. dirs. Iowa Electric Utilities, Cedar Rapids. Patentee in field. Fellow Am. Soc. Mech. Engrs. (chmn. heat transfer div. 1964-65, heat transfer meml. award 1966, heat transfer conf. award 1963); mem. Nat. Acad. Engring, Am. Nuclear Soc. (chmn. thermal hydraulics div. 1985-86). Democrat. Mem. Unitarian Ch. Avocations: racquetball, golf. Home: 1829 Dry Creek Rd San Jose CA 95124 Office: S Levy Inc 3425 S Bascom Ave Campbell CA 95008

LEVY, SAMUEL CHARLES, research chemist; b. Far Rockaway, N.Y., Jan. 5, 1937; s. Julius and Diana (Osias) L.; m. Cecile Peltz, Aug. 23, 1958; children: June Hope, Robert Scott. BA in Chemistry, Hofstra Coll., 1958; PhD in Inorganic Chemistry, Iowa State U., 1962. Mem. tech. staff Sandia Nat. Labs., Albuquerque, 1961—. Mem. Am. Chem. Soc., Electrochem. Soc. Avocations: photography, running. Office: Sandia Nat Labs Div 2523 PO Box 5800 Albuquerque NM 87185

LEVY, SHEILA ZELLA, school administrator, speech pathologist; b. Los Angeles, Feb. 16, 1950; s. Jack Louis and Paula Rose (Levine) L. BA, UCLA, Westwood, 1972; MA, Calif. State U., Long Beach, 1977. Speech lang. pathologist Long Beach VA Hosp., 1976-77, St. Jude Hosp., Fullerton, Calif., 1977-78; speech lang. specialist Santa Ana (Calif.) Unified Sch. Dist., 1978-86, coordinator com. handicapped, 1986—; guest lectr. Calif. State U., Long Beach, 1980-86; speech pathologist, cons. Bernard Landes and Assoc., Long Beach, 1976—. Producer/dir. (cable TV show) Story-Time, 1986. Mem. Am. Speech Lang. and Hearing Assn., Calif. Speech-Hearing Assn., Nat. Assn. Speech-Hearing Action.

LEW, CLEMENT, public relations executive; b. Laramie, Wyo., Feb. 13, 1960; s. Jeffrey James and Penelope (Young) L. AA, Santa Rosa Coll., 1980; BA, Calif. State U., Northridge. Mktg. specialist Fairchild/VSI, Sylmar, Calif., 1983; media communications mgr. Deutsch Corp., Los Angeles, 1983—. Director advt. program (award Marine Mktg. Excellence award 1984); contbr. articles to newspapers (award Calif. Soc. Jr. Colls. 1980). Mem. Sigma Delta Chi. Club: Sonoma Press (Santa Rosa, Calif.)(hon.). Office: Deutsch Corp 14800 S Figueroa Los Angeles CA 90248

LEWANDOWSKI, STANLEY RICHARD, JR., utility company executive; b. Hammond, Ind., Sept. 1, 1937; s. Stanley Richard Sr. and Helen (Owczarak) L.; m. Gayle Marcia Anderson, Nov. 2, 1967; children: Paula, Ann-Marie, John. AA, San Diego City Coll., 1960; BS, San Diego State U., 1962. Ops. analyst Rural Electric Adminstrn., Washington, 1962-66; regional rep. Rural Electric Adminstrn., Denver, 1966-71; exec. v.p. San Isabel Electric Co., Pueblo, Colo., 1971-72; gen. mgr. Intermountain Rural Electric Assn., Sedalia, Colo., 1972—; bd. dirs. Affiliated Littleton (Colo.) Nat. Bank. Served with USN, 1954-58. Mem. Am. Mgmt. Assn., Castle Rock C. of C., Parker C. of C., Douglas County Econ. Devel. Council, Teller County Econ. Devel. Council. Republican. Roman Catholic. Lodges: Rotary, Elks. Avocation: Poker playing. Home: 2426 S Zephyr Way Lakewood CO 80227 Office: Intermountain Rural Electric Assn 5496 N US Hwy 85 Sedalia CO 80135

LEWICKY, ROMAN TARAS, orthopedic surgeon; b. Sambir, Ukraine, Jan. 1, 1942; came to US., 1949; s. Witold G. and Irene (Antonowych) L.; m. Puka Therese Gizinski, June 26, 1965; children: Andrey, Yuri. B.S., Holy Cross Coll., Mass., 1964; M.D., Northwestern U., 1968. Diplomate Am. Bd. Orthopedic Surgery. Intern, Denver Gen. Hosp., 1968-69; resident in orthopedic surgery Northwestern U., Chgo., 1971-75; orthopedic surgeon No. Ariz. Orthopedics, Flagstaff, 1975—; cons. athletics No. Ariz. U., 1975—. Mem. pres.'s adv. council No. Ariz. U., 1982-84. Fellow ACS, Am. Acad. Orthopedic Surgeons; mem. Ariz. med. Assn. (Sports Medicine Physician of Yr. 1983), Am. Orthopaedick Sports Medicine Soc., Western Orthopedic Assn., AMA. Republican. Roman Catholic. Avocation: breeding Arabian horses. Home: Route 4 Box 711 Flagstaff AZ 86001 Office: No Ariz Orthopedics 1355 N Beaver St Flagstaff AZ 86001

LEWIN, CAROLYN GOOD, interior designer; b. Portland, Oreg., Jan. 30, 1952; d. Vernon Allen and Virginia Alberta (Davis) Good; m. Gary Andrew Lewin, June 21, 1978 (div. Apr. 1986); children: Rian Skye Good Lewin, Jordan Hart Good Lewin.. BS in Clothing, Textiles and Related Arts, Oreg. State U., 1975. Interior design cons. Benson's, Corvallis, Oreg., 1975-77; pvt. practice interior design Wearable Artist, Durango, Colo., 1982-85; interior designer Wannamakers, Durango, 1985-86; pvt. practice archtl. lighting design Durango, 1985—; color cons. Edgemont Ranch, Durango, 1985-86; designer/builder Clearview Mountain Lodge, Durango, 1984-86. Organizer Durango Art Ctr., 1978-79. Avocations: rock climbing, cross country skiing, fashion designing. Home and Office: 1012 Clearview Dr Durango CO 81301

LEWIS, BARBARA JIMMIE, artist; b. El Paso, Tex., Mar. 14, 1932; d. Frederick Howard and Mildred (Neilson) Cushing; m. Rollin C. Lewis, Oct. 27, 1951; children—Lynn, Bradley, David. Student, U. Tex.-El Paso, 1950-70, U. Nev., 1982—. Tchr., El Paso Pub. Schs., 1954-69; condr. various art classes, workshops; represented by Gallery " 20" , Farmington, N.Mex., Artistic License, Farmington. Exhibited in group shows in Salt Lake City, Las Vegas, Nev., Farmington, N.Mex.; nat. and regional shows in Calif., Utah, Tex., Nev., N.Mex. (first prize watercolor 1982) Mem. N.Mex. Watercolor Soc., Nev. Watercolor Soc., Am. Watercolor Assn. (assoc.), Nat. League Am. Penwomen, Watercolor West Assn. (assoc.), So. Ariz. Watercolor Guild.

LEWIS, CAROL REICHEL, research engineer, project manager; b. N.Y.C., June 19, 1956; d. Manny and Beatrice (Vogel) Reichel; m. Nathan Saul Lewis, May 31, 1981. BS in Chemistry, Yale U., 1977; PhD in Inorganic Chemistry, MIT, 1981. Research asst. Yale U., New Haven, Conn., 1976-77, Eastman Kodak, Rochester, N.Y., 1977, MIT, Cambridge, 1977-81; research engr. Varian Assocs., Palo Alto, Calif., 1981—. Contbr. articles on electronics and inorganic chemistry to profl. jours. Mem. Am. Chem. Soc., Electrochem. Soc., Sigma Xi. Office: Varian Assocs 611 Hansen Way Palo Alto CA 94303

LEWIS, DAVID EDWIN, trust banker; b. Los Angeles, Aug. 16, 1945; s. Edwin Norbert and Marie Lucy (Concenia) L.; m. Bonne Ann Ostroff, June 8, 1968. B.S. in Bus. Adminstrn. and Instl. Mgmt., U. Nev., 1968; A.A.S. in Money and Banking, Western Nev. Community Coll., 1976, A.A.S. in Law Enforcement, 1977; cert. Am. Inst. Banking, 1970-75; honor grad. Pacific Coast Banking Sch., U. Wash., 1982. Asst. cashier Pioneer Citizens Bank of Nev., Reno, 1970-74, asst. cashier, ops. officer Moana Lakeside br., 1974-75, asst. mgr., loan officer Moana-Lakeside br., 1975-76, trust officer, Reno, 1976-84, asst. v.p., mgr., trust officer, 1984-85, v.p., mgr., trust officer, 1985—. Active YMCA, Reno, 1979—; devel. com. Salvation Army, Reno, 1986—; mem. Fleischmann Scholarship Com. Reno/Sparks Campus, Western Nev. Community Coll., 1976-78. Served with U.S. Army, 1968-70. Mem. Estate Planning Council, Am. Inst. Banking, (pres. Sierra Nevada chpt. 1977-78, mem. No. Nev. Dist. Council 1978-80, Nev. state chmn.-elect 1981). Republican. Roman Catholic. Club: Lions. Home: PO Box 3023 Reno NV 89505 Office: PO Box 2351 Reno NV 89505

LEWIS, DAVID JOHN, electrical engineer; b. Denver, Mar. 16, 1930; s. John Phillip and Carol May (Greig) L.; m. Mary Gertrude Ayotte, Nov. 28, 1953; children: Robert Thomas, Garrett David. BSEE, MIT, 1955; MSEE, U. Pa., 1957. Research asst. U. Pa., Phila., 1955-57, research assoc., 1957-61; mem. tech. staff Hughes Aircraft Corp., Culver City, Calif., 1961-68, sect. head, 1968-71, sr. scientist, 1971—. Contbr. articles to profl. publs.; patentee in field. Served as 2d lt. U.S. Army, 1957. Democrat. Home: 4536 Royal Oak Dr Oceanside CA 92056

LEWIS, DENNIS CARROLL, public relations executive; b. Milw., Jan. 7, 1940; s. Carroll and Alyce Mae (Bryce) Lewis Paxton; m. Marie Benedicte Denizet, Nov. 1, 1973 (div. Dec. 1982); 1 son, Benoit. Student U. Wis. 1957-61; B.S., San Francisco State Coll., 1964. Computer programmer, analyst Levi Strauss, San Francisco, 1969-72; freelance book editor, San Francisco, 1972-73; book editor Miller Freeman Publishing Co., San Francisco, 1973-76; pub. relations account exec. Paul Purdom & Co., San Francisco, 1977-81; ptnr. Hi-Tech. Publicity, San Francisco, 1981-84; chmn., pres. Hi-Tech Pub. Relations, Inc., San Francisco, 1984—. Author: Sacred Tradition and Present Need, 1975; On the Way to Self-Knowledge, 1976. Also articles in newspapers and profl. jours. Co.-pub., editor Computer Publicity News, San Francisco, 1981—. Mem. Tech-Net (founding), Pub. Relations Soc. Am., Pub. Relations Round Table, Internat. Assn. Bus. Communicators, Bus. Profl. Adv. Assn. Democrat. Home: 523 Valley St San Francisco CA 94131 Office: Hi-Tech Pub Relations Inc 444 De Haro St San Francisco CA 94107

LEWIS, DEREK LAMONT, advertising sales executive; b. Los Angeles, May 28, 1956; s. Arthur Alexander Lewis and Maxine Kennedy; m. Elizabeth Aileene Campfield, July 11, 1981. BA in English, UCLA. With sales dept. Cal Stereo, West Los Angeles, Calif., 1978-79; pub. relations rep. CBS Television, Los Angeles, 1979-80; sales rep. Lewis Vending Co., Los Angeles, 1973-81; acct. exec. Sta. KACE, Los Angeles, 1981—. Mem. Nat. Assn. Broadcasters, So. Calif. Broadcasting Assn., So. Calif. Media Network, UCLA Alumni Assn. Democrat. Avocations: scuba diving, skiing, martial arts, reading, traveling. Office: Sta K-ACE Radio 1710 E 111th St Los Angeles CA 90059

LEWIS, EDWARD B., biology educator; b. Wilkes-Barre, Pa., May 20, 1918; s. Edward B. and Laura (Histed) L.; m. Pamela Harrah, Sept. 26, 1946; children—Hugh, Glenn (dec.), Keith. B.A., U. Minn., 1939; Ph.D., Calif. Inst. Tech., 1942; Phil.D., U. Umea, Sweden, 1982. Instr. biology Calif. Inst. Tech., Pasadena, 1946-48; asst. prof. Calif. Inst. Tech., 1949-56, prof., 1956-66, Thomas Hunt Morgan prof., 1966—; Rockefeller Found. fellow Sch. Botany, Cambridge U., Eng., 1948-49; mem. Nat. Adv. Com. Radiation, 1958-61; vis. prof. U. Copenhagen, 1975-76, 82. Editor: Genetics and Evolution, 1961. Served to capt. USAAF, 1942-46. Fellow AAAS; mem. Genetics Soc. Am. (sec. 1962-64, pres. 1967-69), Nat. Acad. Scis., Am. Acad. Arts and Scis. Research on developmental genetics, somatic effects of radiation. Home: 805 Winthrop Rd San Marino CA 91108 Office: Calif Inst Tech Div Biology Pasadena CA 91125

LEWIS, EDWIN REYNOLDS, biomedical engineering educator; b. Los Angeles, July 14, 1934; s. Edwin McMurtry and Sally Newman (Reynolds) L.; m. Elizabeth Louise McLean, June 11, 1960; children: Edwin McLean, Sarah Elizabeth. AB in Biol. Sci., Stanford U., 1956, MSEE, 1957, Engr., 1959, PhD in Elec. Engring., 1962. With research staff Librascope div. Gen. Precision Inc., Glendale, Calif., 1961-67; mem. faculty U. Calif., Berkeley, 1967—, prof. elec. engring. and computer scis., 1971—, assoc. dean grad. div., 1978-82; dir. Biomed. Engring. Tng. Program, U. Calif., Berkeley, 1969-77. Author: Network Models in Population Biology, 1977, (with others) Neural Modeling, 1977, The Vertebrate Inner Ear, 1985, also numerous articles. NSF, Nat. Aero. and Space Adminstrn. grantee, 1984, 87; Neurosci. Research Program fellow, 1966, 69; recipient Disting. Teaching award U. Calif., 1972; named Jacob Javits Neurosci. Investigator, NIH, 1984—. Fellow IEEE; mem. AAAS, Assn. Research in Otolaryngology, Acoustical Soc. Am., Sigma Xi. Club: Toastmasters (area lt. gov. 1966-67). Avocations: birding, diving, photography. Office: U Calif Dept EECS Berkeley CA 94720

LEWIS, FREDERICK THOMAS, insurance company executive; b. Tacoma, Apr. 1, 1941; s. Arthur Thomas and June Louise (Levenhagen) L.; m. Sarah Carolyn Boyette, Apr. 18, 1971; adopted children: Johanna, Elizabeth, Sarah, Jonathan, Matthew. Student, Concordia Coll., Portland, Oreg., 1959-61, Dominican Coll., San Rafael, Calif., 1967-71. Registered health underwriter. Enroute coordinator Trans World Airlines, N.Y.C., 1961-62, 64-66; customer service rep. Trans World Airlines, Oakland, Calif., 1966-75; dist. rep. Aid Assn. for Luths., Twin Falls, Idaho, 1975-84, dist. mgr., 1984—. Vocalist Oakland Symphony Chorus, 1972-75; soloist Magic Valley Chorale, Twin Falls, 1979-83. Cantor Immanuel Luth. Ch., Twin Falls, 1984—; organizer Theos of Magic Valley, Filer, Idaho, 1984. Served with U.S. Army, 1962-64. Recipient 1st Yr. Rep. Recognition award Aid Assn. Luths., 1976. Mem. Nat. Assn. Life Underwriters (tng. council fellow 1984, nat. quality award, nat. sales achievement award, health ins. quality award, 1978—), Million Dollar Round Table, So. Idaho Life Underwriters (pres. 1980-81, edn. chmn. 1984—), So. Idaho Health Underwriters (bd. dirs. 1986—), Idaho Fraternal Congress (ins. counselor 1976, bd. dirs. 1976—, pres. 1981-82). Republican. Lodges: Lions (local v.p. 1979-81, pres. 1982-83, organizer Women's aux. 1983, sec. 1986—). Avocations: ceramics, numismatics, gardening, music. Home: Rural Rt 2 Box 5902 Twin Falls ID

83301 Office: Aid Assn for Lutherans 1210 Addison Ave E Twin Falls ID 83301

LEWIS, GEORGE PAUL, news correspondent; b. Bakersfield, Calif., Apr. 16, 1943; s. George Ira and Beulah Ellen (Harris) L.; m. Jane Cranford Cook, Aug. 22, 1964; children: Sarah, Katherine. AB in Polit. Sci., San Diego State U., 1964. Reporter, newswriter Sta. KFMB-TV, San Diego, 1962-69; reporter Sta. KNBC-TV, Los Angeles, 1969-70; news corr. NBC News, Saigon, Socialist Republic of Vietnam, 1970-72, Houston, 1972-79, London, 1979-80, Washington, 1980-82, Los Angeles, 1982—. Recipient News Documentary Emmy award Nat. Acad. TV Arts and Scis., 1980, Silver medal N.Y. Internat. Film and TV Festival, 1968. Avocations: skiing, home computing, electronics. Office: NBC Network News 3000 W Alameda Ave Burbank CA 91523

LEWIS, GEORGE RAYMOND, social work administrator; b. Bridgeton, N.J., July 7, 1944; s. Raymond and Evelyn Rhoda (Mitchell) L.; m. Tenelia Kay Boykin, Sept. 3, 1966. BA, U. N.Mex., 1966; MSW, Our Lady of the Lake Coll., 1971. Cert. social worker. With N.Mex. Health and Social Services Dept., 1971—; dist. tng. officer N.Mex. Health and Social Services Dept., Roswell, 1972-73, field office mgr., 1973-75, social worker cons., 1975-84, dist. ops. mgr., 1984—; behavioral sci. specialist Community Guidance Ctr., San Antonio, 1971; adj. instr. N.Mex. State U., Las Cruces, 1971, 83, 85, Eastern N.Mex. U., Roswell, 1973-76; clin. dir. Chaves County 1st Offender Program, Roswell, 1974-77; field instr. Tex. Tech U., Lubbock, 1981; bd. dirs. Assurance Home Inc., Roswell. Bd. dirs. Chaves County Home Health Agy. Inc., Roswell, 1973-76, Parents Anonymous of N.Mex. Inc., 1978-79. Named an Outstanding Young Man of Am., U.S. Jaycees, 1978, 81. Mem. Nat. Assn. Social Workers, Acad. Cert. Social Workers, Order of the Arrow, Blue Key. Democrat. Baptist. Avocations: greenhouse gardening, camping, fishing, hunting. Home: 1018 N Plains Park Roswell NM 88201 Office: NMex Human Services Social Services Div 1101 S Main St Roswell NM 88201

LEWIS, GERALD JORGENSEN, judge; b. Perth Amboy, N.J., Sept. 9, 1933; s. Norman Francis and Blanche M. (Jorgensen) L.; m. Laura Susan McDonald, Dec. 15, 1973; children by previous marriage—Michael, Marc. A.B. magna cum laude, Tufts Coll., 1954; J.D., Harvard U., 1957. Bar: D.C. 1957, N.J. 1961, Calif. 1962, U.S. Supreme Ct. 1968. Atty. Gen. Atomic, LaJolla, Calif., 1961-63; ptnr. Haskins, Lewis, Nugent & Newnham, San Diego, 1963-77; judge Mcpl. Ct., El Cajon, Calif., 1977-79; judge Superior Ct., San Diego, 1979-84; assoc. justice, Calif. Ct. of Appeal, San Diego, 1984—; adj. prof. evidence Western State U. Sch. Law, San Diego, 1977—, exec. bd., 1977—; faculty San Diego Inn of Ct., 1979—, Am. Inn of Ct., 1984—. Cons. editor: California Civil Jury Instructions, 1984. City atty. Del Mar, Calif., 1963-74, Coronado, Calif., 1972-77; counsel Comprehensive Planning Orgn., San Diego, 1972-73; trustee San Diego Mus. Art., 1986—; bd. dirs. Air Pollution Control Dist., San Diego County, 1972-76; trustee San Diego Mus. Art, 1986—. Served to lt. comdr. USNR, 1957-61. Named Trial Judge of Yr., San Diego Trial Lawyers Assn., 1984. Mem. Am. Judicature Soc., Calif. Judges Assn., Soc. Inns of Ct. in Calif., Confrerie des Chevaliers du Tastevin, Friendly Sons of St. Patrick. Republican. Episcopalian. Clubs: LaJolla Country (dir. 1980-83); Honkers Hunting (Niland, Calif.); Prophets. Home: 6505 Caminito Blythfield LaJolla CA 92037 Office: Ct of Appeal 1350 Front St San Diego CA 92101

LEWIS, GLEN ALAN, manufacturing company executive; b. Willows, Calif., June 22, 1958; s. Lee and Carole (Carlile) L. BA, U. Calif., Los Angeles, 1979-80; postgrad., Harvard U., 1978, Calif. Poly. State U., 1976-78. Tech. supt. Container Corp. Am., Los Angeles, 1981-83, prodn. supt., 1983-85, prodn., tech. supt., 1985—. Mem. Nat. Rep. Congl. Com., Washington, 1982—; mem. Los Angeles World Affair Council. Served to capt. USAFR, 1980—. Walter Wells Meml. scholar Calif. Poly. State U., 1976. Mem. TAPPI, Am. Chem. Soc., Willows C. of C. (disting. citizen award 1972), Lambda Chi Alpha. Avocations: flying, sports, music. Office: PO Box 711 Willows CA 95988

LEWIS, JAMES B., state government official; b. Rosell, N.Mex., Nov. 30, 1947; m. Armandie Johnson; children: Terri, James Jr., Shedra, LaRon. BS in Edn., Bishop Coll., 1970; MA in Pub. Adminstrn., U. N.Mex., 1977, BS in Bus. Adminstrn., 1981. Coordinator, counselor pub. services careers program N.Mex. State Personnel Office, Albuquerque; adminstr. consumer affairs div., investigator white collar crime sect., then dir. purchasing div. Bernalillo County Dist. Atty.'s Office; adminstr., educator U. Albuquerque; county treas. Bernalillo County, 1982-85; state treas. State of N.Mex., 1985—. Mem. adv. bd. Victims of Domestic Violence; past chmn. Dem. precincts and ward, Albuquerque. Served with U.S. Army, 1970-72. Mem. Nat. State Treas.'s Assn., Pub. Employees Retirement Assn., Edn. Retirement Assn., Mortgage Fin. Authority, N.Mex. Assn. fo Counties (past pres. treas.'s affiliate), Nat. Assn. County Treas. and Fin. Officers (chmn. membership com., bd. dirs.), Am. Soc. for Pub. Adminstrn. (past treas. N.Mex. chpt.), NAACP, Am. GI Forum, Am. Legion, Internat. Alumni Assn. Bishop Coll., Taylor Ranch Neighborhood Assn., Omega Psi Phi (life). Lodges: Kiwanis, Masons. Office: Office State Treas PO Box 608 Villa Revera Bldg Santa Fe NM 87504

LEWIS, JAMES BRYAN, molecular biologist; b. York, Pa., Dec. 14, 1945; s. John Bryan and Mary Elizabeth (Eberle) L.; m. Anita Joyce Zappala, Sept. 2, 1967 (div. 1980); children: John Bryan, Christopher Michael. BA, U. Pa., 1967; MA, Harvard U., 1968, PhD, 1972. Postdoctoral assoc. Swiss Inst. Cancer Research, Lausanne, Switzerland, 1971-73; postdoctoral assoc. Cold Spring Harbor (N.Y.) Lab., 1973-74, staff investigator, 1974-75, sr. staff investigator, 1975-80; assoc. mem. Fred Hutchinson Cancer Inst., Seattle, 1980—; affiliate assoc. prof. dept. pathology, U. Wash. Med. Sch., Seattle, 1983—. Contbr. articles to profl. jours. Grantee NSF, Am. Cancer Soc., Rita Allen Found., Damon Runyon Found., Nat. Cancer Inst., 1971—. Mem. AAAS, Am. Soc. Microbiology, N.Y. Acad. Scis. Home: 7527 40th Ave NE Seattle WA 98115 Office: Fred Hutchinson Cancer Research Ctr 1124 Columbia St Seattle WA 98104

LEWIS, JAMES CHARLES, health services administrator; b. Columbus, Miss., Nov. 7, 1925; s. Charlie and Della (Williams) L.; m. Dorothy Chisholm, Feb. 5, 1966; children: Taradell, Lawrence. AB, Howard U., 1951; MSW, Denver U., 1959. Psychiat. social worker Dept. Mental Health, Calif., 1959-66; psychiat. social work supr. Los Angeles County Dept. Mental Health, 1966-70, tng. coordinator, 1970-72, mental health edn. cons., 1972-84, clin. mental helth program head, 1984—. Served with USMCR, 1944-46, PTO. Mem. Nat. Assn. Mental Workers, Am. Group Psychotherapy Assn. Home: 829 S Longwood Los Angeles CA 90005

LEWIS, JAMES JOSEPH, financial manager, retired naval officer; b. Harrisonville, Mo., Dec. 24, 1940; s. Samuel Theron and Pharis Zelda (Haynes) L.; m. Paula Jean Crose, Aug. 12, 1962; children—Lisa Lynne, Laura Lee, Lyndsey Anne. B.A., William Jewell Coll., 1962; M.B.A., U. San Francisco, 1975; M.S., Naval Postgrad. Sch., 1976. Commd. ensign, U.S. Navy, 1963, advanced through grades to comdr., 1978; inventory mgmt. officer USS White Plains, San Francisco, 1969-71; staff Naval Supply Ctr., Oakland, Calif., 1971-75, supply officer USS Tarawa, San Diego, 1977-79, dir. aviation dept. Naval Supply Ctr., Oakland, 1979-82; ret., 1982; ops. mgr. Pinne, Garvin, Herbers & Hock Inc., 1982—, chief fin. officer, 1983—, dir., 1984—; bd. dirs. Ad Exchange, Inc. Founding pres. Homeowners of Inverness Park, San Ramon, Calif., 1981-82. Mem. Am. Assn. Advt. Agys., Internat. Fedn. Advt. Agys., Mensa, Sigma Nu.

LEWIS, JAMES LUTHER, savs. and loan exec.; b. Bridgeport, Ohio, Sept. 29, 1912; s. William Luther and Gwen (Evans) L.; grad. Mercersburg Acad., 1931; B.A., Yale U., 1935; m. Mary Anne Glen, Oct. 26, 1943; children—William Luther II, Gwendolyn. Salesman, asst. sales dist. mgr. Chgo. Pneumatic Tool Co., 1935-43, asst. to pres., 1946-55; v.p., adminstrn. and sales, dir. Van Norman Industries, Inc., 1956; pres. Insuline Corp., 1956-58; v.p. corp. devel. Norris Thermador Corp., Los Angeles, 1959-65; chmn. bd., dir. Am. Savs. & Loan Assn., Reno, 1965—, Sierra Fin. Corp., 1968—; dir. Firth Sterling Steel Corp., 1956-58. Served to lt. USNR, 1943-46. Decorated Purple Heart, Presdl. Unit citation. Presbyterian. Home: 7755 Lakeside Dr Reno NV 89511 Office: 67 W Liberty St Reno NV 89501

LEWIS, JERRY, congressman; b. Oct. 21, 1934. B.A., UCLA, 1956. Life ins. underwriter; field rep. for former U.S. Rep. Jerry Pettis; mem. Calif. State Assembly, 1968-78; vice chmn. rules com., chmn. subcom. on air qualit; mem. 96th-100th congresses from 35th Calif. dist.; mem. appropriation com., ranking minority mem. legis. br. subcom. 96th-100th congresses, mem. fgn. ops. subcom., ind. agys. subcoms. HUD. Office: 326 Cannon House Office Bldg Washington DC 20515 *

LEWIS, JOANNE, English educator; b. Shreveport, La., Aug. 19, 1930; d. Alfred Raleigh Lewis and Alice Lorene (Featherstone) Barr; m. Arthur Whiting Lynn, Sept. 8, 1951 (div. 1979); children: Robin Lorene, Steven Andrew, Katherine Margaret. BA cum laude, Pomona Coll., 1952; MA, Calif. State U., Fullerton, 1965; PhD, U. Calif., Irvine, 1974. Instr. English Fullerton Coll., 1964-65; prof. English Calif. State U., Fullerton, 1965—; cons. Ednl. Testing Service, Calif. Contbr. articles to profl. jours. Mem. MLA, Am. Soc. 18th Century Studies, Western Soc. 18th Century Studies, Children's Lit. Assn., Philological Assn. of Pacific Coast. Democrat. Home: 31442 Holly Dr South Laguna CA 92677 Office: Calif State U Dept English Fullerton CA 92634

LEWIS, JOE T., marketing professional, consultant; b. Van Nuys, Calif., Mar. 19, 1958; s. Walter Rodrick and Lois (McDonald) L. AA in Mktg., Los Angeles Pearce Coll., 1978; BS in Mktg., Calif. State U., Northridge, 1984. Plant mgr. PPG Electronics, Van Nuys, 1979-82; acct., adminstrv. asst. CFT Credit Union, Burbank, Calif., 1979-82; acct. supr., data processing supr., mktg. dir. Burbank (Calif.) Fed. Credit Union, 1982—; chief fin. officer Burbank Family Fin. Ctr., Inc. subs. Burbank Fed. Credit Union, also bd. dirs. Mem. Fin. Mktg. Assn. So. Calif. Mktg. Roundtable, Mktg. Assn. Calif. (bd. dirs. 1986—). Office: Burbank Fed Credit Union 1715 W Magnolia Blvd PO Box 7767 Burbank CA 91510

LEWIS, JOHN CLARK, JR., manufacturing company executive; b. Livingston, Mont., Oct. 15, 1935; s. John Clark and Louise A. (Anderson) L.; m. Carolyn Jean Keesling, Sept. 4, 1960; children: Robert, Anne, James. BS, Fresno (Calif.) State U., 1957. With Service Bur. Corp., El Segundo, Calif., 1960-70, Computer Scis. Corp., 1970; with Xerox Corp., El Segundo, 1970-77, pres. bus. systems div., 1977; pres. Amdahl Corp., Sunnyvale, Calif., 1983—, chief exec. officer, 1983—. Served with USNR, 1957-60. Roman Catholic. Office: Amdahl Corp 1250 E Arques Ave Sunnyvale CA 94086 *

LEWIS, JOHN WILEY, III, bank export trading company executive; b. Birmingham, Ala., June 15, 1945; s. John Wiley Jr. and Mary Virginia (Marshall) L.; m. Nancy Hotchkiss, Oct. 11, 1968; children: Katherine, William. BS, Ga. Inst. Tech., 1966, MS, 1968, PhD, 1971. Asst. prof. Washington U., St. Louis, 1972-80; dir. info. systems Virginia Mason Med. Ctr., Seattle, 1980-84; v.p., mgr. Rainier Internat. Trading Co., Seattle, 1984—; chmn. ACM/SIGBIO Internat., 1981-84; judge tech. papers Med. Computing Conf., 1982-84. Contbr. articles to profl. jours. Chmn. Land Use Adv. Com., Bainbridge Island, Wash., 1985-86. Served to 1st lt. U.S. Army, 1971-72. Fellow World Student Fund ETH, Zürich, Switzerland, 1966-67. Mem. AAAS, IEEE, Am. Inst. Banking, Assn. Computing Machinery, Sigma Xi. Avocations: sailing, skiing. Home: 7754 NE Bergman Rd Bainbridge Island WA 98110 Office: Rainer Internat T23-4 PO Box 3966 Seattle WA 98124

LEWIS, JOHN WILSON, political scientist; b. King County, Wash., Nov. 16, 1930; s. Albert Lloyd and Clara (Lewis) Seeman; m. Jacquelyn Clark, June 19, 1954; children: Cynthia, Stephen, Amy. Student, Deep Springs Coll., 1947-49; A.B. with highest honors, UCLA, 1953, M.A., 1958, Ph.D., 1962; hon. degree, Morningside Coll., 1969, Lawrence U., 1986. Asst. prof. govt. Cornell U., 1961-64, assoc. prof., 1964-68; prof. polit. sci. Stanford U., 1968—, William Haas prof. Chinese politics, 1972—, co-dir. NE Asia U.S. Forum on Internat. Policy, co-dir. arms control and disarmament program, 1971-83, co-dir. Ctr. for Internat. Security and Arms Control; chmn. Internat. Strategic Inst. 2; chmn. joint com. on contemporary China Social Sci. Research Council-Am. Council Learned Socs., 1976-79; former vice chmn. and bd. dirs. Nat. Com. on U.S.-China Relations; cons. Senate Select Com. on Intelligence, 1977-81, Lawrence Livermore Nat. Lab.; chmn. com. advanced study in China Com. Scholarly Communication with People's Republic of China, 1979-82; mem. com. on internat. security and arms control Nat. Acad. Scis., 1980-83. Author: Leadership in Communist China, 1963, Major Doctrines of Communist China, 1964; co-author: The United States in Vietnam, 1967, Modernization by Design, 1969; editor: The City in Communist China, 1971, Party Leadership and Revolutionary Power in China, 1970, Peasant Rebellion and Communist Revolution in Asia, 1974; contbr.: Congress and Arms Control, 1978, China's Quest for Independence, 1979, others.; mem. editorial bd.: Chinese Law and Govt, China Quar., Survey, The Pacific Rev. Served with USN, 1954-57. Mem. Assn. Asian Studies, Am. Polit. Sci. Assn., Council Fgn. Relations, Phi Beta Kappa. Organized first univ. discussion arms control and internat. security matters Chinese People's Inst. Fgn. Affairs, 1978; negotiated first univ. tng. and exchange agreement People's Republic of China, 1978. Home: 541 San Juan St Stanford CA 94305 Office: Stanford U 320 Galvez St Stanford CA 94305

LEWIS, JOSEPH MARTIN, infosystems specialist; b. Cin., Feb. 6, 1924; s. Joseph J. and Sophia (Peters) L.; m. Mary Ruth Obryan; children: Robert J., Patrick F., Bryan M., Kathleen, Michelle. BS, U. Cin., 1948. Data processing mgr. Kroger Co., Cin., 1960-59; cons. Pullman Inc., Chgo., 1959-61; data processing mgr. Thiokol Chem., Brigham City, Utah, 1961-62; data processing cons. Gen. Electric, Schenectady, N.Y., 1963-65; corp. dir. Atlas Chem. Ind., Wilmington, Del., 1965-66; mgmt. infosystems mgr. City and County of Denver, 1966—; pres. GMIS, Denver, 1979-80, 85-86; bus. advisor computer tng. for handicapped Community Coll. of Denver, 1979—. Advisor Emily Griffith Opportunity Sch., Denver, 1980-86. Named Employee of Yr. Gen. Electric, 1964. Avocations: handcrafts. Home: 2906 S Moline Pl Aurora CO 80014 Office: City and County of Denver 3840-L York St Denver CO 80205

LEWIS, KENNETH, shipping executive; b. N.Y.C., Aug. 23, 1934; b. Nathaniel and Hana Evelyn (Kotler) L.; A.B., Princeton U., 1955; J.D., Harvard U., 1958; m. Carol Ann Schnitzer, Aug. 3, 1958 (div. 1982); children—Scott, Laurence, Kathleen; m. 2d, Colleen Anne Wesche, Nov. 27, 1983. Admitted to N.Y., Oreg. bars, 1959; law clk. to judge U.S. Dist. Ct., N.Y.C., 1958-59; asso. King, Miller, Anderson, Nash & Yerke, Portland, Oreg., 1959-61; gen. counsel Indsl. Air Products Co., Portland, 1961-63; v.p. to exec. v.p. Lasco Shipping Co., Portland, 1963-79, pres., 1979—; bd. dirs. Britannia Steam Ship Ins. Assn., Ltd., London, 1986—. Mem. Port of Portland Commn., 1974-81, treas., 1977, v.p., 1978, pres., 1979; trustee Lewis and Clark Coll., 1974-83; bd. dirs. Columbia River Maritime Mus., 1987—, Oreg. Community Found., 1982—, treas., 1986—; mem. Portland Met. Area Boundary Commn., 1974-74, Portland Met. Mass Transit Dist. Bd., 1973-74; pres. Portland Zool. Soc., 1970, World Affairs Council of Oreg., 1969. Mem. Am., Oreg. Bar Assns., Soc. Maritime Arbitrators, Inc., Portland Steamship Operators Assn. Democrat. Jewish. Clubs: Multnomah Athletic, Arlington, University, Masons, City (Portland). Office: Lasco Shipping Co 2880 NW Ariel Terrace Portland OR 97210

LEWIS, KRISTIN ANITRA, architect; b. Dallas, Jan. 31, 1949; d. Louis Wilson Lewis and Barbara Ann (Moen) Renton; m. Charles Stanley Forsman, June 10, 1972. BS, U. Calif., Davis, 1971; MArch., U. Calif., Berkeley, 1975. Licensed architect, Colo., N.Y. Designer, drafting Dominick Assocs., Denver, 1976; project architect Everett, Zeigel, Boulder, Colo., 1977-79, James, Stewart, Polshek, N.Y.C., 1979-81, Midyette Assocs., Boulder, 1981-82; prin. Kristin Lewis & Assocs., Boulder, 1982—; bd. dirs. Colo. Chautauqua Assocs., Boulder, Friendship City Projects, Boulder; pres. Architects and Planners of Boulder, 1983; vis. lectr. U. Colo., Boulder, 1983—. Contbr. chpts. to books, photographs to profl. pubs. Mem. AIA, Women in Architecture, Nat. Trust Hist. Preservation, Soc. Comml. Archaeology. Democrat. Avocations: traveling, photography. Home: 511 Pleasant St Boulder CO 80302 Office: 828 A Pearl St Boulder CO 80302

LEWIS, LORAINE RUTH, music teacher; b. Vernal, Utah, July 22, 1921; d. Perrie Benjamin and Hazel (Bentley) Galbreath; B.S.L., Missionary Bible Coll., Tabor, Iowa, 1947; B.S. in Edn., Marion (Ind.) Coll., 1949; postgrad. Walla Walla Coll., 1967-70, Eastern Wash. State Coll., 1970-81, Central Wash. State Coll., 1970-85, Whitworth Coll., 1975, Seattle Pacific U., 1976-83, Ft. Wright Coll., 1980-81, Gonzaga U., 1980-81, Pacific Luth. U., 1980-81, Wash. State U., 1983; m. Jesse Dale Lewis, Apr. 12, 1951; children—Nancy Loraine, Dale Delbert, Paul Jeffrey. Printer, linotype operator various printing and pub. cos., 1941-56; with Prosser Printing Co. (Wash.), 1956-66; tchr. Prosser (Wash.) Consol. Sch. Dist., 1966-86; pvt. music tchr., 1966—. Named Outstanding Female Linotype Operator Bus. and Profl. Women's Orgn., 1960; named Outstanding Woman Prosser Ch. of the Nazarene, 1978. Mem. NEA, Wash., Prosser edn. assns. Specialist in edn. for migrant children. Home and Office: 1914 Highland Dr Prosser WA 99350

LEWIS, MARY ANN, nurse practitioner, researcher, educator; b. Kansas City, Mo., Aug. 1, 1937; d. Michael and Pauline (Markese) Gurera; m. Charles Edwin Lewis, Dec. 27, 1963; children: Kevin, David, Matthew, Karen. BS in Nursing, U. Kans., 1962; MS in Nursing, Boston U., 1963; DrPH, UCLA, 1984. Instr. pub. health nursing U. Kans., Kansas City, Mo., 1963-66; coordinator pub. health nursing Children's Mercy Hosp., Kansas City, 1966-68; research health specialist UCLA, 1971-73, project dir. Primex Family Nurse Practice, 1972-76, adj. asst. prof. med. nursing, 1976-80, adj. assoc. prof. med. nursing, 1980—; cons. internat. health Health Resources Adminstrn., Washington, 1978—; bd. dirs. Maxicare Research and Edn. Found., Los Angeles; cons. Asthma and Allergy Found. Am., Washington, 1984—, Boehringer-Ingelheim Ltd., Ridgeville, Conn., 1985—. Author: Health Decision-Making, 1980; contbr. articles to profl. jours. Com. mem. AIDS Project, Los Angeles, 1986—. Mem. Am. Nursing Assn., Calif. Nursing Assn., Am. Pub. Health Assn., The Nurse Practitioner (bd. dirs., editorial bd. 1981—), Calif. Joint Practice Commn. (co-chmn. 1982—), Sigam Theta Tau. Office: UCLA Health Scis Ctr Dept Medicine Div Gim/HSR Los Angeles CA 90024

LEWIS, NANCY PATRICIA, speech-language pathologist; b. Miami, Fla., Sept. 23, 1956; d. James and Sara (Gilman) L. BS, U. Fla., 1978; MS, U. Ariz., 1980. Postgrad. fellow U. Tex. Med. Br., Galveston, 1979-80, speech lang. pathologist, 1980-81; speech lang. pathologist Albuquerque Pub. Schs., 1982-84; child devel. specialist Albuquerque Spl. Presch., 1984—; pvt. practice speech pathology Albuquerque, 1985—; speaker in field. Author (dianostic procedure) Khan-Lewis Phonological Analysis, 1986; (therapeutic materials) Familiar Objects and Actions, 1985. Bd. dirs. Vols. for the Outdoors, Albuquerque, 1984—. Fellow U. Tex. Med. Br., Galveston, 1981. Mem. Am. Speech Lang. and Hearing Assn., N.Mex. Speech Lang. and Hearing Assn. Democrat. Avocations: swimming, hiking, camping, hot springs. Office: Albuquerque Spl Presch 3501 Campus Blvd NE Albuquerque NM 87106

LEWIS, NORMAN, English language educator, author; b. N.Y.C., Dec. 30, 1912; s. Herman and Deborah (Nevins) L.; m. Mary Goldstein, July 28, 1934; children—Margery, Debra. B.A., CUNY, 1939; M.A., Columbia U., 1941. Instr., lectr CUNY, N.Y.C., 1943-52; assoc. prof. English NYU, N.Y.C., 1955-64; instr. Compton Coll., Calif., summers 1962-64, UCLA, 1962-69; prof. English Rio Hondo Coll., Whittier, Calif., 1964—, chmn. communications dept., 1964-75. Author: (with Wilfred Funk) Thirty Days to a More Powerful Vocabulary, 1942, rev., 1970, Power with Words, 1943, How to Read Better and Faster, 1944, rev. edit., 1978, The Lewis English Refresher and Vocabulary Builder, 1945, Better English, 1948, Word Power Made Easy, 1949, rev. edit., 1978, The Rapid Vocabulary Builder, 1951, rev. edit., 1980, How to Get More Out of Your Reading, 1951, Twenty Days to Better Spelling, 1953, The New Roget's Thesaurus in Dictionary Form, 1961, rev. edit., 1978, Dictionary of Correct Spelling, 1962, Correct Spelling Made Easy, 1963, rev. edit. 1987, Dictionary of Modern Pronunciation, 1963, New Guide to Word Power, 1963, The New Power with Words, 1964, Thirty Days to Better English, 1964, The Modern Thesaurus of Synonyms, 1965, RSVP-Reading, Spelling, Vocabulary, Pronunciation, elem. texts, I-III, 1966, coll. edit., 1977; See, Say, and Write!, books I and II, 1973, Instant Spelling Power, 1976, R.S.V.P. for College English Power, book II, 1978, book III, 1979, R.S.V.P. with Etymology, book I, 1980, book II, 1981, book III, 1982; R.S.V.P. books I-III, rev. edits., 1982-83, books A-B, 1985-86; Instant Word Power, 1981, Dictionary of Good English, 1987; also numerous articles in nat. mags. Home: 5140 Javalambre Dr Whittier CA 90601

LEWIS, ORME, JR., real estate company executive, natural resources company executive; b. Phoenix, Apr. 26, 1935; s. Orme and Barbara (Smith) L.; m. Elizabeth Bruening, Oct. 17, 1964; children: Orme Joseph, Elizabeth Blaise. BA, U. Ariz., 1958. Assoc. Coldwell Banker, Phoenix, 1959-64; v.p. Braggiotti Constrn., Phoenix, 1964-65; pvt. practice investment brokerage Phoenix, 1966-69, 73-78; dep. asst. sec. Dept. Interior, Washington, 1969-73; ptnr. World Resources Co., Phoenix and McLean, Va., 1978—; pres. Applewhite, Laflin and Lewis, Phoenix, 1979—; gen. ptnr. Equity Interests, Phoenix, 1982—; co-chmn. U.S. Adv. Com. Mining and Mineral Research, Washington, 1982—, mem. State Plant Site Transmission Line Com., Phoenix, 1974-85. Mem. Ariz. State Senate, 1966-69; bd. dirs. Phoenix Children's Hosp., 1981—, Polycystic Kidney Research Found., Kansas City, Mo., 1983—, Ariz. Community Found., 1986—, Ariz. Parks and Recreation Com., 1985—, Ariz. State U. Found., Tempe, 1981—. Republican. Clubs: Metropolitan (Washington); Ariz. Valley Field Riding and Polo (Phoenix); Paradise Valley Country (Scottsdale, Ariz.). Home: 4325 E Palo Verde Dr Phoenix AZ 85018-2784 Office: Applewhite Laflin and Lewis 4250 E Camelback Rd 175-K Phoenix AZ 85018-2784

LEWIS, RALPH JAY, III, management and human resources educator; b. Balt., Sept. 25, 1942; s. Ralph Jay and Ruth Elizabeth (Schmeltz) L. BS in Engring., Northwestern U., 1966; MS in Adminstrn., U. Calif., Irvine, 1968; PhD in Mgmt., UCLA, 1974. Research analyst Chgo. Area Expressway Surveillance Project, 1963-64, Gen. Am. Transp. Co., Chgo., 1965-66; assco. prof. mgmt. and human resources mgmt. Calif. State U., Long Beach, 1972—; cons. Rand Corp., Santa Monica, Calif., 1966-74, Air Can., Montreal, Que., 1972-73, Los Angeles Times, 1973;. Co-author: Studies in the Quality of LIfe, 1972; author instructional programs, monographs; co-designer freeway traffic control system. Bd. dirs. Project Quest, Los Angeles, 1969-71. Mem. AAAS, Am. Psychol. Assn., Assn. for Humanistic Psychology, The World Future Soc., Soc. of Mayflower Desc., SAR (Ill. soc.), Internat. Arabian Horse Assn., Sierra Club, Beta Gamma Sigma. Democrat. Office: Calif State U Dept Human Resources Mgmt Long Beach CA 90840

LEWIS, RALPH MILTON, real estate developer, accountant, lawyer; b. Johnstown, Pa., Nov. 9, 1919; s. Morris and Sarah (Galfond) L.; m. Goldy Sarah Kimmel, June 12, 1941; children: Richard Alan, Robert Edward, Roger Gordon, Randall Wayne. A.A., Los Angeles City Coll., 1939; B.S., UCLA, 1941; postgrad., U. So. Calif., 1945-48. Bar: Calif. 1952. Pvt. practice acctg. Los Angeles, 1945-55; practice law Los Angeles, 1953-55; founder Lewis Homes, 1957; chmn. bd. Lewis Construction Co., Upland, Calif., 1959—, Lewis Bldg. Co., Las Vegas, 1960—; Republic Sales Co., Inc. Lewis Bldg. Co., Upland, 1956—; dir., v.p. Kimmel Enterprises, Inc., 1959—; mng. partner Lewis Homes of Calif., 1973—, Lewis Homes of Nev., 1972—, Western Properties, Upland, 1972—, Foothill Investment Co., Las Vegas, 1971—, Republic Mgmt. Co., Upland, 1978-86; dir. Gen. Telephone Co. Calif.; mem. adv. bd. Inland div. Security Pacific Nat. Bank; instr. U. So. Calif., UCLA, Los Angeles City Coll., 1948-54, Dooley Law Rev. Course, 1953-54; guest lectr. numerous colls., univs. Contbr. articles to mags., jours. Mem., com. chmn. Calif. Commn. of Housing and Community Devel., 1965-67; mem. Calif. Gov.'s Task Force on the Home Bldg. and Construction Industry, 1967; pres. Bd. of Edn. Citrus Community Coll. Dist., Azusa, Calif., 1969, 73, mem., 1967-73; mem. Citizens Planning Council, Los Angeles County Regional Planning Commn., 1972-73, UCLA Found., Chancellor's Assoc.; mem. dean's council UCLA Grad. Sch. Architecture and Urban Planning.; bd. dirs. Regional Research Inst. So. Calif., 1983-84; chmn. land use and planning com. Citizens' Adv. Council, Calif. Senate Housing Com., 1983-84. Recipient Humanitarian award NCCJ, 1979; Builder of Year award Bldg. Industry Assn. So. Calif., 1970. Mem. Am. Bar Assn., Calif. Soc. C.P.A.'s, Nat. Assn. Home Builders (dir.), Calif. Bldg. Industry Assn. (dir., chmn. affordable housing task force 1978-80), Bldg. Industry Assn. So. Calif. (past treas., pres., dir., named to Hall of Fame 1987, Bldg. Industry Medal of Honor, 1987). Office: Lewis Homes 1156 N Mountain Ave Upland CA 91786

LEWIS, RANDOLPH VANCE, biochemistry educator; b. Powell, Wyo., Apr. 8, 1950; s. Jack F. and Evelyn J. (Vonburg) L.; m. Lorrie Dale Emery,

May 27, 1972; children: Brian, Daryl (dec.). BS, Calif. Inst. Tech., 1972; MS, U. Calif., San Diego, 1974; PhD, U. Calif., 1978. Postdoctoral fellow Roch Inst. Molecular Biology, Nutley, N.J., 1978-80; asst. prof. molecular biology U. Wyo., Laramie, 1980-84, assoc. prof., 1984—, head dept., 1986—; cons. Syntho Corp., La Jolla, Calif., 1983—, NIH, Bethesda, Md., 1985—. Contbr. articles to profl. jours. Sloan Found. fellow, 1985; recipient Research Career Devel. award NIH, 1985, Burlington-North Faculty award U. Wyo., 1986, Jr. Faculty award Am. Cancer Soc., 1985. Mem. Am. Chem. Soc., Am. Soc. Biol. Chemists, N.Y. Acad. Scis. Republican. Methodist. Avocations: fly fishing, bird hunting. Home: 635 Howe Rd Laramie WY 82070 Office: Univ Wyo PO Box 3944 University Sta Laramie WY 82071

LEWIS, RICHARD BOND, advertising executive; b. Atkinson, Nebr., Apr. 14, 1925; s. Monte Claire and Lulu Pearl (Bond) L.; m. Carol Ann Bigglestone, Nov. 23, 1948; children: Eric, Shannon, Carrie. Student U. Ariz., 1946-49; B.A., Art Center Coll. Design, 1953. Art dir., account exec. Hal Stebbins Inc. advt. agy., Los Angeles, 1953-64; account exec. Buxton Advt., Pasadena, Calif., 1964-65; account mgr. McCann-Erickson advt. agy., Los Angeles, 1965-71; pres. Richard Bond Lewis & Assocs., West Covina, Calif., 1971—. Bd. dirs., past pres. Vis. Nurses Assn., West Covina; commr. West Covina Personnel Dept.; vice chmn. West Covina Waste Mgmt. Commn.; presdl. appointee Selective Service Civilian Rev. Bd.; lay leader, del., mem. communications com. Pacific S.W. conf. United Methodist Ch., 1979-82. Served to staff sgt. U.S. Army, 1945-46. Recipient Camp Fire Girls special service award, 1979, West Covina resolution award for service, 1982. Mem. West Covina C. of C. (com. mem. of year 1971, 72, 76, pres. 1981-82, Dir. of Yr. 1982-83), Art Dirs. Club Los Angeles, West Covina Hist. Soc. (dir.), Lambda Chi Alpha. Republican. Club: Kiwanis (pres. West Covina club, 1986-87). Home and office: 1112 W Cameron Ave West Covina CA 91790

LEWIS, ROBERT HARRISON, JR., horse show judge, stable owner, trainer, equitation expert; b. Dallas, Sept. 14, 1914; s. Robert Harrison Sr. and Susan Elizabeth (Atwood) L.; m. Leila Barlow, July 15, 1942; children—Susan Elizabeth, Dinah L., Robert Allan, Amy-Leigh. Grad. pub. schs., Dallas, 1932. Owner-mgr. Bob Lewis Stables, Woodside, Calif., 1946—. Served with Tex. N.G., 1930-33; Utah NG, 1945-50; served to infantry capt. U.S. Army, 1941-45, ETO. Decorated Purple Heart. Mem. Am. Horse Shows Assn. (judge, symposium panel, various coms.), United Profl. Horseman's Assn. (charter, coms. Ill. chpt.), Internat. Arabian Horse Assn. (judge), Am. Morgan Horse Assn. (judge), Fedn. Equestre Canadienne (judge), Calif. Profl. Horseman's Assn. (charter, pres. No. Calif. chpt. 1964-66). Republican. Home: 555 Summit Dr Redwood City CA 94062 Office: Bob Lewis Stables Why Worry Farm 3603 Woodside Rd Woodside CA 94062

LEWIS, ROBERT LEE, III, health science facility executive; b. San Francisco, Sept. 20, 1949; s. Robert Lee Jr. and Dolores Patricia (Brady) L.; m. Kimberly G. Hawkins, June 24, 1972 (div. 1981). BS, Calif. State U., Fresno, 1971, MBA, 1978; cert. advanced mgmt., Stanford U., 1983. Ops. officer, adminstrv. asst. to v.p. Security Pacific Nat. Bank, Fresno, 1971-74; service chief County Health Dept., Fresno, 1974-79; adminstrv. dir. clin. labs. Stanford (Calif.) U. Hosp., 1979-84; pres. Western Div. Internat. Clin. Labs., Dublin, Calif., 1984-86; v.p. Performance Health Care, Inc., 1986—; mem. hiring bds. Calif., Fresno County, 1978-79; cons. Performance Health Care, 1986—, Abbott Diagnostics, 1984—, Nichols Inst. 1984, Syva Co. 1983-84, 86, hosp. mgmt. 1982—. Author: Optimizing Productivity: Capital Equipment Acquisition, 1985; mem. editorial bd. Syva Monitor, 1984. Mem. YMCA Century Club; officer Fresno County Council for Developmentally Disabled, 1975-79; mem. Mayor's Com. on Hiring Handicapped, 1976-79; mem. adv. bd. Goodwill Industries, 1977-78. Served with USNG, 1971-76. Mem. Calif. Clin. Lab. Assn. (bd. dirs. 1984-86), Clin. Lab. Mgmt. Assn. (founder No. Calif. chpt.), Calif. Assn. Rehab. Facilities (co-chmn. state conf. 1976), Fresno Assn. for Retarded (bd. dirs. (1975-78), Pi Omega Pi (v.p. 1970-71). Republican. Roman Catholic. Club: Stanford Buck. Avocations: tennis, racketball, collecting Southwest art. Home: 108 Durham St Menlo Park CA 94025 Office: ICL Western 6511 Golden Gate Dr Dublin CA 94568

LEWIS, ROBERT TURNER, psychologist; b. Taft, Calif., June 17, 1923; s. D. Arthur and Amy Belle (Turner) L.; m. Jane Badham, Mar. 23, 1946; children—Jane, William, Richard. B.A., U. So. Calif., 1947, M.A., 1950; Ph.D., U. Denver, 1952. Lic. psychologist, Calif. Chief psychologist Hollywood Presbyn. Hosp., Los Angeles, 1953-58; dir. psychol. services Salvation Army, Pasadena, Calif., 1958-68; dir. Pasadena Psychol. Ctr., 1964-74; successively asst. prof., assoc. prof. and prof., Calif. State U.-Los Angeles, 1952-83, prof. emeritus, 1984—; assoc. dir Cortical Function Lab., Los Angeles, 1972-84; clin. dir. Diagnostic Clinic, West Covina, Calif., 1983-85; dir. Job Stress Clinic, Santa Ana, Calif., 1985—. Author: Taking Chances, 1979; co-author: Money Madness, 1978; Human Behavior, 1974; The Psychology of Abnormal Behavior, 1961. Served to lt. (j.g.) USNR, 1943-46, PTO. Mem. Am. Psychol. Assn., Los Angeles County Psychol. Assn., Nat. Acad. Neuropsychology. Republican. Office: Job Stress Clinic 1200 N Main St #230 Santa Ana CA 92701

LEWIS, SAMELLA SANDERS, artist, educator; b. New Orleans, Feb. 27, 1924; d. Samuel and Rachel (Taylor) Sanders; m. Paul Gad Lewis, Dec. 22, 1948; children—Alan Stephen, Claude Anthony. Student, Dillard U., 1941-43; B.S., Hampton Inst., 1945; M.A., Ohio State U., 1947, Ph.D., 1951; postgrad., U. So. Calif., 1964-66; L.H.D. (hon.), Chapman Coll., 1976. Asst. prof. Hampton (Va.) Inst., 1945-47; asso. prof. art Morgan State Coll., 1950-52; chmn. dept. art, prof. Fla. A&M U., 1953-58; prof. SUNY, Plattsburgh, 1958-67; coordinator edn. Los Angeles County Mus. Art, 1968-69; prof. Asian, African, Afro-Am. Art History Scripps Coll., Claremont, Calif., 1970-84; prof. emerita Scripps Coll., 1984—; artistic cons. Producer five films on Black Am. artists; founder Mus. African Am. Art, Los Angeles, 1976; founder, dir., The Gallery, Los Angeles, 1969-79, Asanti Gallery, Pomona, Calif., 1980; Art editor Internat. Rev. African Am. Art, 1976—; One woman shows, Clark Mus., Claremont, Calif., 1979, Univ. Union Gallery, 1980, group shows include, Huntsville (Ala.) Mus., 1979, Smithsonion Instn. travelling exhbn., 1980-81; represented in permanent collections, Balt. Mus. Art, Oakland Mus. Art, High Mus., Atlanta, Palm Springs Mus., Va. Mus. Art. Fulbright fellow, 1962; NDEA post doctoral fellow, 1964-66; Ford Found. grantee, 1965, 81. Mem. Assn. Asian Studies, Nat. Conf. Artists, So. Calif. Art History Assn., Coll. Art Assn. Am. Home: 1237 S Masselin Ave Los Angeles CA 90019 Office: Museum African American Art 4005 Crenshaw Blvd 3d Floor Los Angeles CA 90008

LEWIS, SHELDON NOAH, chemical company executive; b. Chgo., July 1, 1934; s. Jacob Joseph and Evelyn (Mendelsohn) Iglowitz; m. Suzanne Joyce Goldberg, June 17, 1957; children: Sara Lynn, Matthew David, Rachel Ann. B.A. with honors, Northwestern U., 1956; M.S. (Univ. fellow), 1956; Ph.D. (Eastman Kodak fellow), UCLA, 1959; postgrad. (NSF fellow), U. Basel, Switzerland, 1959-60; postgrad. cert. in research mgmt, Indsl. Research Inst., Harvard U., 1973. With Rohm & Haas Co., 1960-78, head lab., 1963-68, research supr., 1968-73, dir. splty. chem. research, 1973-74; gen. mgr. DCL Lab. AG subs., Zurich, Switzerland, 1974-75; dir. European Labs. DCL Lab. AG subs., Valbonne, France, 1975-76; corp. dir. research and devel. worldwide for polymers, resins and monomers DCL Lab. AG subs., Spring House, Pa., 1976-78; with The Clorox Co., Oakland, Calif., 1978—; v.p. research and devel. The Clorox Co., 1978, 1978-84, exec. v.p., 1984—, also bd. dirs., profl. recruiter, univ liaison. Referee: Jour. Organic Chemistry; contbr. articles to profl. publs. Mem. World Affairs Council, UCLA Chemistry Adv. Council, Bay Area Sci. Fair Adv. Bd., Mills Coll. Adv. Council for Sci. and Math., NSF Indsl. Panel on Sci. and Tech. Recipient cert. in patent law Phila. Patent Law Assn., 1962, Roon award for coatings research Fedn. Socs. Coatings Tech., 1966, cert. of service Wayne State U. Polymer Conf. Series, 1967, cert. in mgmt. by objectives Am. Mgmt. Research, Inc., 1972. Mem. Soap and Detergent Assn. (bd. dirs.), Indsl. Research Inst., Am. Chem. Soc. (chmn. Phila. polymer sect. 1970-71), Soc. Chem. Industry London, Sigma Xi. Jewish. Patentee in field. Home: 3711 Rose Ct Lafayette CA 94549 Office: The Clorox Co 1221 Broadway Oakland CA 94612

LEWIS, SHIRLEY JEANE, educator; b. Phoenix, Aug. 23, 1937; d. Herman and Leavy (Hutchinson) Smith; A.A., Phoenix Community Coll., 1957; B.A., Ariz. State U., 1960; M.S., San Diego State U., 1975, M.A., 1986; M.A., Azusa Pacific U., 1982; Ph.D., U. So. Calif., 1983; m. Edgar Anthony Lewis, June 25, 1966 (div. May 1980); children—Edgar Anthony, Roshaun, Lucy Ann, Steven Glen. Recreation leader Phoenix Parks and Recreation Dept., 1957-62; columnist Ariz. Tribune, Phoenix, 1958-59; tchr. phys. edn. San Diego Unified Schs., 1962—; adult educator San Diego Community Colls., 1973—, instr. psychology, health, Black studies, 1977—, counselor, 1981—; community counselor S.E. Counseling and Cons. Services, and Narcotics Prevention and Edn. Systems, Inc., San Diego, 1973-77; counselor educator, counselor edn. dept. San Diego State U., 1974-77; marriage, family, child counselor Counseling and Cons. Center, San Diego, 1977—; inservice educator San Diego Unified and San Diego County Sch. Dists., 1973-77; lectr. in field. Girl Scout phys. fitness cons., Phoenix, 1960-62; vol. community tutor for high sch. students, San Diego, 1963; sponsor Tennis Club for Youth, San Diego, 1964-65; troop leader Girl Scouts U.S.A., Lemon Grove, Calif., 1972-74; vol. counselor USN Alcohol Rehab. Center, San Diego, 1978. Named Woman of Year, Phoenix, 1957, One of Outstanding Women of San Diego, 1980; recipient Phys. Fitness Sch. award and Demonstration Sch. award Pres.'s Council on Phys. Fitness, Taft Jr. High Sch., 1975; Delta Sigma Theta scholar, 1957-60; Alan Korrick scholar, 1956; certified tchr., Calif. Mem. NEA, Calif. Tchrs. Assn., San Diego Tchrs. Assn., Assn. Marriage and Family Counselors, Am. Personnel and Guidance Assn., Calif. Assn. Health, Phys. Edn. and Recreation, Am. Alliance of Health, Phys. Edn. and Recreation, Delta Sigma Theta. Democrat. Baptist. Contbr. articles to profl. jours. Home: 1226 Armacost Rd San Diego CA 92114 Office: 2630 B St San Diego CA 92102

LEWIS, THOMAS ANTHONY, mechanical designer; b. Hanford, Calif., Oct. 6, 1946; s. Thomas Anthony and Josephine Bernice (Bebereia) L.; m. Joan Marie Marfia, Nov. 12, 1966; children: Richard, Randall. AS, Gavilan Coll., 1976. Designer Holex, Inc., Hollister, Calif., 1965-69, BE-GE Mfg. Co., Gilroy, Calif., 1969-72; sr. designer Burke Industries, San Jose, Calif., 1972—; advisor vocational curriculum Gavilan Coll., Gilroy, 1977—. Com. mem. Monterey Corridor Project, San Jose, 1985, Leader Gilroy 4-H Club, 1968-84. Served with U.S. Army, 1967-68, Vietnam. Recipient Commendation award City of San Jose, 1985. Mem. Calif. Women for Agriculture, Gilroy C. of C., Internat. Mgmt. Council (chmn. chpt. devel. 1982-85, spl. recognition awards 1984, 85, 2 edn. awards, 1985), Santa Clara Valley chpt. of Internat. Mgmt. Council (cert. mgr. 1984, v.p. 1986—, edn. award 1986). Democrat. Roman Catholic. Club: Smalltowners (San Martin, Calif.) (pres. 1980-81). Avocations: photography, motorcycles, sports. Home: 8130 Oak Ct Gilroy CA 95020 Office: Burke Industries 2250 S 10th St San Jose CA 95112

LEWIS, THOMAS HOWARD, psychiatrist, educator; b. Red Lodge, Mont., July 28, 1919; s. William Michel and Charlotte Amanda (Johnson) L.; m. Ruth Danielson, May 5, 1944; children: William Richard, Daniel John, Thomas Morgan, Linda Ruth, David Gryffdd. BS, U. Wash., 1943; MD, Duke U., 1946. Commd. 2d. lt. USN, 1946, advanced through grades to capt., 1962; intern U.S. Naval Hosp. USN, Bethesda, Md., 1951-53; intern NIMH USN, 1960, dir. resident tng. in psychiatry Nat. Naval Med. Ctr., 1963-68, chief neurology and psychiatry, 1969-73, ret., 1973; prof. psychiatry Georgetown U., Washington, 1975—. Contbr. articles on medicine, anthropology, biology, ethnology and anatomy to profl. jours.; assoc. editor Am. Indian Quar., 1975—. Fellow ACP, Am. Psychiat. Assn.; mem. AMA, AAAS, Wash. Psychoanalytic Soc., Wash. Psychiat. Soc., N.Y. Acad. Sci., Sigma Xi, Phi Sigma. Democrat. Clubs: Cosmos, St. David's Soc. (Washington). Home and Office: Boyd MT 59013

LEWIS, THOMASINE ELIZABETH, magazine editor in chief; b. Manila, Phillipines, Sept. 20, 1958; d. Thomas Donald and Elizabeth Jane (Munson) L. Student, Broward Community Coll., 1977, Universidad de las Americas, Mexico City, 1977, U. Fla., Los Angeles Valley Coll., 1979, UCLA, 1984. Copy editor, reporter Mexico City News, 1979-80; mng. editor LF Pub., Los Angeles, 1980-82; editor Eton Pub., Hollywood, Calif., 1982-83; editor in chief Playgirl Mag., Santa Monica, Calif., 1983-86; exec. editor mag. devel. Petersen Pub., Hollywood, Calif., 1986—. Bd. dirs. Santa Monica Red Cross; mem. League of Women Voters, NOW. Mem. Hollywood Press Club. Avocations: skiing, traveling, writing, running.

LEWIS, WILLIAM, pathologist, educator; b. N.Y.C., Mar. 7, 1950; s. Joseph E. and Ruth (Franzblau) L. BS, U. Mich., 1971; MD, Boston U., 1975; intern in internal medicine, Boston VA Med. Ctr., 1975-76; resident in Pathology, Yale New Haven (Conn.) Hosp., 1976-78. Diplomate Am. Bd. Pathology; cert. Nat. Bd. Med. Examiners. Chief resident, fellow in pathology Mallory Inst. Boston City Hosp., 1978-80; fellow in cardiac pathology Mt. Sinai Med. Ctr., N.Y.C., 1980-83; asst. prof. pathology UCLA Sch. Medicine, 1983—. Mem. Am. Assn. Pathologists, Internat. Acad. Pathologists, Soc. Cardiovascular Pathologists, Am. Heart Assn. (council for basic sci.). Office: UCLA Sch Medicine Dept Pathology Los Angeles CA 90024

LEWITT, MILES MARTIN, computer engineering company executive; b. N.Y.C., July 14, 1952; s. George Herman and Barbara (Lin) L.; m. Susan Beth Orenstein, June 24, 1973. BS, CCNY Engring., 1973; MS, Ariz. State U., 1976. Software engr. Honeywell, Phoenix, 1973-78; software engr., architect irmx line ops. systems Intel Corp., Santa Clara, Calif., 1978; engring. mgr. Intel, Hillsboro, Oreg., 1978-80, 1981—, corp. strategic staff, 1981-82; engring. mgr. Intel, Israel, 1980-81; instr. Maricopa Tech. Coll., Phoenix, 1974-75. Contbr. articles to profl. jours. Recipient Engring. Alumni award CCNY, 1973, Eliza Ford Prize CCNY, 1973, Advanced Engring. Program award, Honeywell, 1976, Product of Yr. award Electronic Products Mag., 1976. Mem. IEEE Computer Soc., Assn. Computing Machinery (voting mem.). Democrat. Avocations: photography, internat. travel. Home: 720 SW Brookwood Ave Hillsboro OR 97123 Office: Intel Corp 5200 NE Elam Young Pkwy Hillsboro OR 97123

LEWITZKY, BELLA, choreographer; b. Los Angeles, Jan. 13, 1916; d. Joseph and Nina (Ossman) L.; m. Newell Taylor Reynolds, June 22, 1940; 1 dau., Nora Elizabeth. Student, San Bernardino Valley (Calif.) Jr. Coll., 1933-34; hon. doctorate, Calif. Inst. Arts, 1981, Occidental Coll., 1984. Chmn. contemporary dance dept. U. So. Calif., Idyllwild, 1956-72; adv. panel U. So. Calif., 1972—; founder Sch. Dance, Calif. Inst. Arts, 1969, dean, 1969-72; vice chmn. dance adv. panel Nat. Endowment Arts, 1974-77, mem. artists-in-schs. adv. panel, 1974-75; mem. Nat. Adv. Bd. Young Audiences, 1974—, Joint Commn. Dance and Theater Accreditation, 1979—; com. mem. Am. chpt. Internat. Dance Council of UNESCO, 1974—; bd. dirs. Am. Arts Alliance, 1977-82, Arts, Edn. and Americans, 1978—; trustee Nat. Found. Advancement Arts, 1982—, Lake Placid Ctr. for Arts, 1982-84, Calif. Arts Council, 1983-86, Calif. Assn. Dance Cos., 1976-81, Nat. Found. Advancement in Arts; trustee Idyllwild Sch. Music and the Arts, 1986—. Co-founder, co-dir., Dance Theatre, Los Angeles, 1946-50, founder, dir., Dance Assocs., Los Angeles, 1951-55, founder 1966; since artistic dir., Bella Lewitzky Dance Co., Los Angeles, choreographer, 1948—; founder, artistic dir. The Dance Gallery, Los Angeles; contbr. articles in field. Recipient ann. award Dance mag., 1978; Dir.'s award Calif. Dance Educators Assn., 1978; recipient YWCA achievement award, 1982; Mellon Found. grantee, 1975, 81, 86; Guggenheim Found. grantee, 1977-78; Nat. Endowments for Arts grantee, 1969-86.

LEYBA, MARTIN, aerospace engineer; b. Long Beach, Calif., Mar. 7, 1953; s. Frank and Adeline Connie (Galindo) L.; m. Susan Marie Chelius, Sept. 11, 1976; 1 child, Jessica Marie. AS in Physics, Long Beach City Coll., 1974; BS in Phys. Chemistry, UCLA, 1977. Switchman AT&SF R.R., Los Angeles, 1972-74, engine foreman, 1974-77; engr. Hughes Aircraft Co., El Segundo, Calif., 1977-80, engr., supr., 1980-83, engr., sect. head, 1983-85, asst. dept. mgr., 1985—. Sch. coordinator Youth Motivation Task Force, So. Calif., 1983—. Recipient Superior Performance award Hughes Aircraft Co., 1980. Republican. Home: 3706 Lime Ave Long Beach CA 90807 Office: Hughes Aircraft Co PO Box 92426 El Segundo CA 90009

LEYDA, JEAN CRAVENS (MRS. VIRGIL WILLIAM LEYDA), author, editor, club woman; b. Granby, Mo., Jan. 15, 1903; d. William A. and Lois (Harmon) Cravens; A.A., Stephens Coll., 1920; B.A., Mt. Holyoke Coll., 1923; M.A. in English Lit., U. Wis., 1930; m. Virgil William Leyda, Aug. 10, 1945; 1 foster son, Leonard Brechler. Tchr. English, Freeport (Ill.) High Sch., 1923-26, head English dept., 1926-27; head English dept. Mishawaka (Ind.) High Sch., 1929-45, dir. English, Mishawaka Jr. and Sr. High Schs., 1938-45; co-author lit. anthologies Scott, Foresman Co., Chgo., 1940-50, editorial staff, after 1945; now ret. Pres., Chandler (Ariz.) Woman's Club, 1954-55, chmn. community service com., 1961-63, hon. life mem.; edn. chmn. Ariz. Fedn. Women's Clubs, 1955-57. Mem. founding adv. bd. Chandler Pub. Library. Recipient alumnae achievement award Stephens Coll., 1956. Former mem., past pres. Ind. Council Tchrs. English. Mem. Ind. Ret. Tchrs. Assn., Nat. Ret. Tchrs. Assn., DAR, Colonial Dames 17th Century, PEO, Phi Theta Kappa. Democrat. Presbyn. (trustee 1951-53, life elder). Mem. Order Eastern Star, Daus. of Nile. Club: Desert (past pres.). Author: (with others) Enjoying Life through Literature, 1951; Exploring Life through Literature, 1951. Address: 400 N Hartford St Chandler AZ 85224

LEYDEN, DONALD ELLIOTT, chemistry educator; b. Gadsden, Ala., June 26, 1938; s. Elliott Hampton and Vivian Ione (Buckner) L.; m. Alice Jane Trowbridge, June 10, 1961; children: Mary Dawn, Sean Michael. B.S., Kent State U., Ohio, 1960; M.S., Emory U., 1961, Ph.D., 1964. Faculty U. Ga., Athens, 1965-76; Phillipson prof. environ. and mining chemistry U. Denver, 1976-81; prof. chemistry Colo. State U., Ft. Collins, 1981—. Editorial adv. bd.: Analytica Chimica Acta, 1977—, Internat. Jour. Environ. Analytical Chemistry, 1977—; editor Chemically Modified Surfaces, 1985—; Contbr. articles to profl. jours. NIH grantee, 1965-68; NSF grantee, 1970—; Phillip Morris Tobacco Co. grantee, 1973-74. Mem. Am. Chem. Soc., Soc. for Applied Spectroscopy. Home: 1324 Stonehenge Dr Fort Collins CO 80525 Office: Dept Chemistry Colo State U Fort Collins CO 80523

LEYDET, FRANÇOIS GUILLAUME, author; b. at Neuilly-sur-Seine, France, Aug. 26, 1927; s. Bruno and Dorothy (Lindsey) L.; A.B., Harvard, 1947, postgrad. Bus. Sch., 1952; postgrad. Johns Hopkins Sch. Advanced Internat. Studies, 1952-53; Bachelier-es-lettres-philosophie, U. Paris (France), 1945; m. Patience Abbe, June 17, 1955 (div.); step children—Catherine Abbe Geissler, Lisa Amanda O'Mahony; m. 2d, Roslyn Carney, June 14, 1970; step-children—Walter E. Robb IV, Rachel R. Avery, Holly H. Prunty, Mary-Peck Harris. Came to U.S., 1940, naturalized, 1956. Assoc. Fellow Peace and Common Security; bd. advisers Research Ranch, Elgin, Ariz., Am. Wilderness Alliance; past dir. Marin County Planned Parenthood Assn., Planned Parenthood Center Tucson. Served to 1st lt. French Army, 1947-48. Mem. Nat. Parks Assn., Wilderness Soc., Sierra Club, Nat. Audubon Soc., World Wildlife Fund, Am. Mus. Natural History, Union Concerned Scientists, Environ. Def. Fund, Friends of the Earth, Ariz.-Sonora Desert Mus., Ariz. Hist. Soc., Common Cause, World Affairs Council No. Calif., Western Writers Am., Western River Guides Assn. Clubs: Commonwealth, Harvard (San Francisco). Author: The Last Redwoods, 1963; Time and the River Flowing: Grand Canyon, 1964; The Coyote: Defiant Songdog of the West, 1977. Editor: Tomorrow's Wilderness, 1963; contbg. editor On Beyond War; contbr. to Nat. Geog. mag. Address: 183 Oak Ave San Anselmo CA 94960

LEYKIS, TOM, radio director; b. N.Y.C., Aug. 1, 1956; s. Harold Francis and Laura Grace (O'Mara) L.; m. Christine M. González, Mar. 1, 1986. Student, Fordham U., 1973-75, Hunter Coll., 1978. Radio talk host Sta. WBAI Radio, N.Y.C., 1979-80, Sta. WNWS Radio, Miami, Fla., 1984-85; researcher CBS-TV Alan Landsburg Productions, N.Y.C., 1980; producer Sta. WABC Radio, N.Y.C., 1981; program dir. Sta. WQBK Radio, Albany, N.Y., 1981-84; program dir., talk host Sta. KFYI Radio, Phoenix, 1985—. Producer (radio show) Simone Phone, 1979-80. Office: KFYI Radio 631 N 1st Ave Phoenix AZ 85003

LI, CHIA-CHUAN, engineer, consultant; b. Taipei, Republic of China, Dec. 29, 1946; came to U.S., 1971; s. Wei-Tong and San (Huang) L.; m. Clemencia Vasquez, Nov. 26, 1983; 1 child, Angie. BS, Nat. Taiwan U., Taipei, 1969; MS, Rutgers U., 1974; PhD, U. Mich., 1977; MBA, Pepperdine U., 1986. Sr. engr. Gen. Atomic Co., San Diego, 1977-84; staff engr. Hughes Aircraft Co., El Segundo, Calif., 1984-85; sr. project engr. Rockwell Internat. Corp., Anaheim, Calif., 1985—. Mem. Am. Soc. Metals, Sigma Xi. Democrat. Office: Rockwell Internat Corp 3370 Mira Loma Ave 031BD07 Anaheim CA 92803

LI, TU LEUNG, management executive; b. N.Y.C., Nov. 10, 1948; d. Gum Ming and Toa Moy (Wong) Lee; m. Ta M. Li, Dec. 31, 1969; 1 child, Ta Ming. B.S., U. Utah, 1977. Sr. cons. Aetna Ins. Co., Salt Lake City, 1977-78; advt. mgr. Assn. Surg. Technologist, Littleton, Colo., 1978-80; research mgr. MET-Research Co., Lakewood, Colo., 1980-82; pres., chief exec. officer Tatum & Assocs., Littleton, 1982-85; sr. acct. Martin Marietta Data Systems, Colo., 1985—; dir. Asian X-M Ltd, Loveland, Colo. Contbr. articles on computer mgmt. techniques to publs. Sec., Friends of Littleton Library, 1984. Mem. AAUW (bd. dirs. 1983-84). Club: Argonauts Investment (pres. 1982-83) (Littleton).

LI, VICTOR HAO, law educator, lawyer, institute administrator; b. 1941. B.A., Columbia U., 1961, J.D., 1964; LL.M., Harvard U., 1965; S.J.D., Harvard U., 1971. Bar: N.Y. 1965. Vis. asst. prof. U. Mich., 1967-69; asst. prof. Columbia U., 1969-72; assoc. prof. Stanford U Law Sch., 1972-74, Lewis Talbot and Nadine Hearn Shelton prof., 1974-81; pres. East-West Ctr., Honolulu, 1981—; vis. prof. U. Hawaii, 1977, UCLA, fall 1978. Office: East-West Center 1777 East-West Rd Honolulu HI 96848

LIANG, JASON CHIA, research chemist; b. Beijing, Peoples Republic China, Feb. 24, 1935; came to U.S., 1978, naturalized 1984; s. Tsang Truan and Shulin (Tang) L.; m. Joan Chorng Chen, June 11, 1960; children: Cheryl, Chuck. BS in Medicinal Chemistry, U. Beijing, 1957; postgrad., Pharm. Research Instn., Beijing, 1961; MS in Organic Chemistry, U. Oreg., 1980. Chemist Beijing Chem. Factory, 1961-71; research chemist Beijing Pharm. Factory, 1971-78; research chemist Tektronix Inc., Beaverton, Oreg., 1980-84, sr. chemist, 1985—. Contbr. articles to profl. jours.; patentee in field. Fellow Am. Inst. Chemists; mem. Am. Chem Soc. (organic chemistry div.), Internat. Union Pure and Applied Chemistry (affiliate). Office: Tektronix Inc PO Box 500 M/S 50-320 Beaverton OR 97077

LIBBEY, LEONARD MORTON, food science educator; b. Boston, Apr. 17, 1930; s. Leonard Frank Libbey and Eleanor (Jones) Miller; m. Janet May Young, Aug. 15, 1971. BVA, U. Mass., 1953; MS, U. Wis., 1954; PhD, Wash. State U., 1961. Asst. prof. food sci. Oreg. State U., Corvallis, 1961-68, assoc. prof., 1969-80, prof., 1981—; cons. to several food co.'s, Oreg., 1961—. Contbr. articles to profl. jours. Grantee NSF, 1979-84, Nat. Cancer Inst., 1979—. Mem. Am. Chem. Soc., Inst. Food Technologists, AAAS, Am. Oil Chemists Soc., N.Am. Truffling Soc., US Chess Fedn. Republican. Mem. Disciples of Christ Ch. Avocations: chess, photography, classical music, computers, sci. fiction. Home: 905 NW 30th St Corvallis OR 97330 Office: Oreg State U Dept Food Sci and Technology Corvallis OR 97331

LIBBY, PERRY BENJAMIN, water company owner; b. Westfield, Iowa, Aug. 25, 1936; s. Perry and Mary (Connelly) L.; m. Pauline Kay Orr, Sept. 3, 1971; children—Steven Wesley, Janice Louise. Student U. Nebr., Omaha, 1973-74. Foreman wastewater plant City of Blair (Nebr.), 1974-77; supr. water dept. City of Gillette (Wyo.), 1977-80; owner Libbys O & M Service Co., Gillette, 1980—; faculty Casper Coll., 1978-81. Served with USN, 1954-57, USAF, 1959-63. Recipient Wyo. Plant Ops. Merit award Rocky Mountain Pollution Control Assn., 1979; William D. Hatfield award Water Pollution Control Fedn., 1980. Mem. Am. Water Works Assn., Water Pollution Control Fedn., Nat. Safety Council, Wyo. Water Quality Pollution Control Assn. Address: 1304 Rawhide Dr Gillette WY 82716

LIBERMAN, DAVID ARTHUR, research physicist; b. Los Angeles, Nov. 8, 1926; s. Ernest and Blanche (Hyman) L.; m. Elisabeth F. Saam, Feb. 4, 1961. BS, Calif. Inst. Tech., 1949, PhD, 1955. Mem. staff Los Alamos (N.Mex.) Nat. Lab., 1955-84, cons., 1984—; physicist Lawrence Livermore (Calif.) Nat. Lab., 1984—. Contbr. articles to profl. jours. Served with USN, 1944-46. Fellow AAAS, Am. Phys. Soc. Home: 4126 Rennellwood Way Pleasanton CA 94566 Office: Lawrence Livermore Nat Lab PO Box 808 Livermore CA 94550

LIBERMAN, MARTIN JON, insurance company executive; b. Los Angeles, Sept. 27, 1944; s. Lester H. and Dina (Horwich) L. BA, Calif. State U., Los Angeles, 1967; JD, U. West Los Angeles, 1974. Asst. to divisional mdse. mgr. May Co., Los Angeles, 1966-69; with Transam. Occidental Life Ins. Co., Los Angeles, 1969—, credit ins. underwriter, 1970-75, mgr. credit ins. underwriting, 1975-85, dir. mktg. and adminstrn., 1986—. Treas. Transam. Employees' Fed. Credit Union, 1975, v.p., 1981, pres., 1982. Fellow Life Office Mgmt. Assn. Avocations: computers, photography, chess. Office: Transam Occidental Life Ins 1150 S Olive Room T-607 Los Angeles CA 90015

LIBERMAN, ROBERT PAUL, psychiatry educator, researcher, writer; b. Newark, Aug. 16, 1937; s. Harry and Gertrude (Galowitz) L.; m. Janet Marilyn Brown, Feb. 16, 1973; children—Peter, Sarah, Danica, Nathaniel, Annalisa. A.B. summa cum laude, Dartmouth Coll., 1959, diploma in medicine with honors, 1960; M.S. in Pharmacology, U. Calif.-San Francisco, 1961; M.D., Johns Hopkins U., 1963. Diplomate Nat. Bd. Med. Examiners, Am. Bd. Psychiatry and Neurology; cert. community coll. instr., Calif. Intern Bronx (N.Y.) Mcpl. Hosp.-Einstein Coll. Medicine, 1963-64; resident in psychiatry Mass. Mental Health Ctr., Boston, 1964-68; postdoctoral fellow in social psychiatry Harvard U., 1966-68, teaching fellow in psychiatry, 1964-68; mem. faculty group psychotherapy tng. program Washington Sch. Psychiatry, 1968-70; with Nat. Ctr. Mental Health Service, Tng. and Research, St. Elizabeths Hosp., also mem. NIMH Clin. and Research Assocs. Tng. Program, Washington, 1968-70; asst. clin. prof. psychiatry UCLA, 1970-72, assoc. clin. prof., 1972-73, assoc. research psychiatrist, 1973-76, research psychiatrist, 1976-77, prof. psychiatry in residence, 1977—; adj. faculty mem. Antioch Coll. West/U. Without Walls, 1971-73; lectr. Calif. Luth. Coll., 1973-74; cons. div. mental health and behavioral scis. edn. Sepulveda (Calif.) VA Hosp., 1975-80; cons. in psychiatry to hosps.; practice medicine specializing in psychiatry, Reston, Va., 1968-70, Thousand Oaks, Calif., 1977—; staff psychiatrist Fairfax Hosp., Falls Church, Va., 1968-70, Ventura County Mental Health Dept., 1970-75; staff psychiatrist Ventura County Gen. Hosp.; mem. med. staff UCLA Hosp., Ventura Gen. Hosp., Camarillo State Hosp., West Los Angeles VA Med. Ctr.; dir., prin. investigator Mental Health Clin. Research Ctr. for Schizophrenia and Psychiat. Rehabilitation, NIMH, 1977—; chief rehab. medicine service Brentwood div. Los Angeles VA Med. Ctr., 1980—; dir. clin. research unit Camarillo State Hosp., 1970—; dir. Rehab. Research and Tng. Ctr. Mental Illness, 1980-85. Bd. dirs. Lake Sherwood Community Assn., 1978—, pres., 1979-81; mem. Conejo Valley Citizens Adv. Bd., 1979-81. Served as surgeon USPHS, 1964-68. Research grantee. Mem. Assn. Advancement Behavior Therapy (exec. com. 1970-72, dir. 1972-79), Am. Psychiat. Assn., Assn. Clin. Psychosocial Research (exec. com. 1985—), Phi Beta Kappa. Author: (with King, DeRisi and McCann) Personal Effectiveness: Guiding People to Assert Their Feelings and Improve Their Social Skills, 1975; A Guide to Behavioral Analysis and Therapy, 1972; (with Wheeler, DeVisser, Kuehnel and Kuehnel) Handbook of Marital Therapy: An Educational Approach to Treating Troubled Relationships, 1980, Psychiatric Rehabilitation of Chronic Mental Patients, 1987; mem. editorial bd. Jour. Applied Behavior Analysis, 1972-78, Jour. Marriage and Family Counseling, 1974-78, Jour. Behavior Therapy and Exptl. Psychiatry, 1975—, Behavior Therapy, 1979—, Assessment and Intervention in Devel. Disabilities, 1980-85; assoc. editor Jour. Applied Behavior Analysis, 1976-78, Schizophrenia Bull., 1981—; contbr. over 200 articles to profl. jours., chpts. to books. Home: 528 E Potrero Rd Thousand Oaks CA 91361 Office: 11301 Wilshire Blvd Suite 691/B 117 Los Angeles CA 90073

LIBOV, MORT, television producer; b. Balt., Apr. 20, 1935; s. Irving and Hilda (Shapiro) L.; m. Susan Grant Mar. 11, 1978 (div. Dec. 1, 1978). Student, U. Md., 1953-57. Stock broker John C. Legg & Co., Balt., 1960-63; investment banker Goldman Sachs & Co., N.Y.C., 1963-66; advt. exec. Leon Golnick & Co., Los Angeles, 1966-68; prin. Mort Libov Prodns., Los Angeles, 1968—; cons. Westinghouse Group, N.Y.C. 1971-72; pres. Shoreham Towers, Los Angeles, 1980-86. bd. dirs. Boystown Jerusalem, Los Angeles, 1980-84. Served with USAF, 1958-59. Recipient Clio award, 1979, 3 Eiffie awards Am. Mktg. Assn. 1979. Mem. Dirs. Guild Am., Acad. TV Arts and Scis., Hollywood Hackers. Jewish. Clubs: Pips (Los Angeles), Atrium (N.Y.C.). Avocations: golf, tennis. Home: 8787 Shoreham Dr Los Angeles CA 90069 Office: 1438 N Gower St Suite 550 Hollywood CA 90028

LIBOVE, JOEL MICHAEL, research scientist, electrical engineer; b. Cleve., Apr. 11, 1954; s. Charles and Rosa (Greenspan) L.; m. Barbara Ellen Sacks, Dec. 26, 1983; 1 child, Robin Anne. BS, Cornell U., 1976; MS, U. Calif., Berkeley, 1978, PhD, 1981. With engring. co-op Sanders Assocs., Nashoa, N.H., 1974-75; research asst. U. Calif., Berkeley, 1977-79; chief engr. Dual Systems Corp, Berkeley, 1979-82, v.p. research, 1982—; cons. Berkeley, 1979—; mem. bd. tech. advisors VMEbus Systems Jour., Scottsdale, Ariz., 1985—. Contbr. tech. articles to profl. jours.; inventor and patentee in field. Earle C. Anthony fellow U. Calif., Berkeley, 1976. Mem. IEEE, AAAS, N.Y. Acad. Scis., Sigma Xi, Tau Beta Pi, Eta Kappa Nu. Democrat. Jewish. Home: 475 Yampa Way Fremont CA 94539 Office: Dual Systems Corp 2530 SAn Pablo Ave Berkeley CA 94702

LICHTE, FREDERICK ERVIN, research chemist; b. Reedsburg, Wis., Aug. 7, 1941; s. Erwin Martin and Erma (Mutch) L.; m. Julianne Mensing, Dec. 27, 1963; children: Erika Sue, Nathan Frederick, Gretchen Ann. BA, Wartburg Coll., 1963; PhD, Colo. State U., 1973. Chemist Sinclair Oil, Harvey, Ill., 1963-69; research chemist Atlantic Richfield Co., Harvey, 1973-74; group leader U. Mo., Columbia, 1974-76; research chemist U.S. Geol. Survey, Denver, 1977—; cons. Jarrell-Ash, Waltham, Mass., 1973, Monsanto, St. Louis, 1975-76, MHD Project, Butte, Mont., 1975. Contbr. articles to profl. jours. Mem. Arvada (Colo.) Community Ctr., 1977—. Mem. Soc. Applied Spectroscopy (chmn. Rocky Mountain Conf. 1978-80). Avocations: golf, fishing, hunting. Home: 8280 Garland Dr Arvada CO 80005 Office: US Geol Survey DFC M/S 92S Denver CO 80225

LICHTEN, STEVEN MICHAEL, environmental affairs specialist, educator; b. Encino, Calif., Oct. 30, 1959; s. Edward Barnett and Evelynne Merle (Freed) L. BS, Calif. State U., Northridge, 1983, MS, 1984. Cert. mgr. hazardous materials. Pulmonary function lab. technician VA Hosp., Sepulveda, Calif., 1980-82; adminstr. environ. and regulatory affairs Hughes Aircraft Co., El Segundo, Calif., 1982—; asst. prof. health sci. Calif. State U., Northridge, 1985—; tng. cons. Los Angeles County Fire Dept., 1984—. Recipient Cert. of Service Associated Students of Calif. State U., Northridge, 1982, Cert. of Recognition Orange County (Calif.) Disaster Preparedness Acad., 1986. Mem. Am. Chem. Soc., Am. Indsl. Hygiene Assn., Assn. Hazardous Materials Profls., Nat. Environ. Health Assn., Calif. State Firemans Assn., Environ. and Occupational Health Students Assn. (pres. Northridge chpt. 1982-83). Avocations: photography, combat target shooting, backpacking, flying. Office: Hughes Aircraft Co Electro-Optical/Data Systems Group PO Box 902 E8 G113 El Segundo CA 90245

LICHTENBERG, BRUCE CHARLES, insurance company executive; b. Champaign, Ill., Jan. 14, 1950; s. Wilbert Charles and Clair Mildred (Kiphart) L.; m. Karen Elizabeth Jones, Sept. 18, 1971 (div. 1979); children: Scott Wlliam, Kevin Charles; m. Karen Lee Williams, Sept. 29, 1984. Student, Coll. San Mateo, 1969-71. Dist. mgr. Westland Life Ins. Co., San Francisco, 1971-74; agt., supr. Standard Ins. Co., San Jose, Calif., 1974-79; supr. agy. Conn. Mut. Life Ins. Co., San Jose, 1979-83; v.p. employee benefits Klindt Fin. Group, Los Gatos, Calif., 1983—, also bd. dirs. Mem. Senate Commn. on Fin. and Ins., Calif., 1983. Mem. Nat. Assn. Life Underwriters, Calif. Assn. Life Underwriters (regional trustee 1985—), San Jose Assn. Life Underwriters (bd. dirs. 1975-85, Pres.'s Trophy 1984), Employee Benefits Council, Million Dollar Roundtable. Lodge: Kiwanis (numerous offices). Avocations: golf, boating, reading. Home: 3655 Brach Way Santa Clara CA 95051 Office: Klindt Fin Group PO Box 1670 233 N Santa Cruz Ave Los Gatos CA 95030

LICHTENBERG, LARRY RAY, chemist, consultant, researcher; b. Marceline, Mo., July 25, 1938; s. Kenneth Ray and Evelyn (Lauck) L.; m. Clarice Elaine Dameron, Dec. 23, 1961; children: Julia-Isabel Dameron. BS in Chemistry, Northeast Mo. State U., 1962. Chemist Bell & Howell, Chgo., 1962-62; jr. chem. engr. Magnavox Corp., Urbana, Ill., 1963-64; process engr. Gen. Electric Co., Bloomington, Ill., 1964-70; mfg. engr. Burr-Brown, Tucson, 1970-72; sr. staff engr. Motorola, Scottsdale, Ariz., 1972—; mem. corp. tech. council Motorola, Scottsdale, 1982—. Contbr. articles to profl. jours. Mem. Am. Chem. Soc., Internat. Soc. Hybrid Microelectronics (pres. Phoenix chpt. 1981-82). Republican. Baptist. Avocations: photography, sailing, amateur radio. Home: 13018 N 32 Ave Phoenix AZ 85029 Office: Motorola GEG 8220 E Roosevelt Rd Scottsdale AZ 85252

LICHTMANN, CHARLENE ANN, lawyer; b. Cin., Oct. 24, 1946; s. Carl Charles and Louceil (O'Neill) L.; m. George Hertrich, Jan. 13, 1967 (div. 1972); children—Daniel, David Hertrich. Student Boston Coll., 1966; B.A. cum laude, Ohio Dominican Coll., 1968; J.D., Golden Gate U., 1974. Bar: Alaska, 1980, U.S. Ct. Appeals (9th cir.) 1983, U.S. Dist. Ct. Alaska 1980. Atty., Alaska Ct. System, Anchorage, 1978-79, Pub. Defender Agy., Anchorage, 1979-80; master Alaska Ct. System, 1981; atty. Kay Christie Saville & Coffey, Anchorage, 1982-84, Alaska State Housing Authority, Anchorage, 1984-86; sole practice, Alaska, 1986—; instr. U. Alaska, 1980-85; staff atty. Alaska Jud. Council, 1978-79. Editor: Computerized Medical Studies, 1974. Dir. Head Start, Warren County, Ohio, 1973-74. Mem. Assn. Trial Lawyers Am., Nat. Assn. Criminal Def. Lawyers, Alaska Bar Assn., Anchorage Bar Assn. Democrat. Jewish. Home: 6530 Cimarron Circle Anchorage AK 99504 Office: 510 L St Suite 105 Anchorage AK 99504

LIDICKER, WILLIAM ZANDER, JR., zoologist; b. Evanston, Ill., Aug. 19, 1932; s. William Zander and Frida (Schroeter) L.; m. Naomi Ishino, Aug. 18, 1956 (div. Oct., 1982); children: Jeffrey Roger, Kenneth Paul. B.S., Cornell U., 1953; M.S., U. Ill., 1954, Ph.D., 1957. Instr. zoology, asst. curator mammals U. Calif., Berkeley, 1957-59; asst. prof., asst. curator U. Calif., 1959-65, assoc. prof., assoc. curator, 1965-69; assoc. dir. Mus. Vertebrate Zoology, 1968-81, acting dir., 1974-75, prof. zoology, curator mammals, 1969—. Contbr. articles to profl. jours. Bd. dirs. No. Calif. Com. for Environ. Info., 1971-77; bd. trustees BIOSIS, 1987—; N. Am. rep. steering com., sect. Mammalogy IUBS, UNESCO, 1978—; chmn. rodent specialist group Species Survival Commn., IUCN, 1980—. Fellow AAAS, Calif. Acad. Scis.; mem. Am. Soc. Mammalogists (dir., 2d v.p. 1974-76, pres. 1976-78, C.H. Merriam award 1986), Am. Soc. Naturalists, others. Club: Berkeley Folk Dancers (pres. 1969). Office: Mus of Vertebrate Zoology U Calif Berkeley CA 94720

LIE, KIAN JOE, medical parasitologist; b. Indonesia, Nov. 25, 1916; s. Siong Pin and How Nio (Tio) L.; came to U.S., 1964, naturalized, 1978; Ph.D., U. Indonesia, 1941, M.D., 1943; D.T.M.H., London Sch. Hygiene and Tropical Medicine, 1950; m. Luan Eng Injo, Apr. 18, 1948; children—Tiong, Tony. Lectr. pathology U. Indonesia Med. Sch., 1943-47; asst. research microbiologist Inst. Tropical Hygiene, Leyden, Netherlands, 1947-50; prof. parasitology and gen. pathology U. Indonesia, 1950-60; research parasitologist Hooper Found., U. Calif., San Francisco, 1960-81, adj. prof. parasitology, 1978-83, research assoc. Dept. Epidemiology and Internat. Health., 1983—. Recipient Eykman medal Dutch Soc. Tropical Medicine, 1948. Mem. AAAS, Am. Soc. Parasitologist, Am. Soc. Tropical Medicine and Hygiene, Soc. Invertebrate Pathology. Author numerous papers in field. Home: 30 Lansdale St San Francisco CA 94127 Office: Univ Calif Dept Epidemiology and Internat Health San Francisco CA 94143

LIEBER, RICHARD LOUIS, biomedical engineering scientist, educator; b. Walnut Creek, Calif., Dec. 14, 1956; s. Richard and Janet Elizabeth (Stone) L.; m. Deborah Jane Chippendale, Oct. 22, 1980; children: Katelyn Suzanne, Kristin Michelle. BS with honors, U. Calif., Davis, 1978, PhD, 1982. Biomed. engr. VA Med. Ctr., San Diego, 1983—; asst. prof. surgery U. Calif., San Diego, 1985—; cons. Mentor Corp., Mpls., 1983-84, Empi Corp., Fridley, Minn., 1984—, Medtronic Corp., Mpls., 1986—, Multacc Corp., 1987—. Contbr. sci. papers to profl. publs.; inventor surgical myometor, 1985. Faculty advisor Inter-Varsity Christian Fellowship, San Diego, 1984—. Recipient Presdl. award Am. Acad. Cerebral Palsy, 1984; State of Calif. Gov.'s scholar, 1974. Mem. IEEE, Orthopaedic Research Soc., Biophys. Soc. (Talbot award 1981), Rehab. Engring. Soc. N.Am., Soc. Neurosci. Republican. Avocations: long distance running, guitar playing. Home: 2816 Jacaranda Ave Carlsbad CA 92009 Office: U Calif Dept Orthopaedic Research V-151 San Diego CA 92161

LIEBERGALL, MICHAEL BARRY, marketing executive; b. Bklyn., May 4, 1946; s. Charles and Gertrude (Farb) L.; m. Judith Ann Marchyn, July 3, 1982. Pres. Lieberman Research West Inc., Los Angeles, 1976-82, Interviewing Service of Am., Inc., Los Angeles, 1982-86; chmn., chief exec. officer Am. Direct Response, Inc., Los Angeles, 1986—. Mem. Am. Mktg. Assn. Jewish. Office: Lieberman Research West 1900 Ave of Stars Los Angeles CA 90067

LIEBERMAN, ALVIN, manufacturing executive; b. Chgo., June 14, 1921; s. Louis and Jennie (Kuznetsky) L.; m. Tillie Bess Lavin, Aug. 24, 1947; children: Gary M., Harold A. BA, Cen. YMCA, Chgo., 1942; BS in Chem. Engring., Ill. Inst. Tech., 1948, MS in Chem. Engring., 1949. Research assoc. Alfred (N.Y.) U., 1949-51; mgr. engring. section Ill. Inst. Tech., Chgo., 1951-68; research and devel. dir. Royco Instruments, Menlo Park, Calif., 1968-83; tech. specialist Particle Measuring Systems, Boulder, Colo., 1983-85, 87—; chief scientist HIAC div. Royco Instrument, Menlo Park, 1985-87; cons., Menlo Park, 1968—. Contbr. articles to profl. jours. Served with U.S. Army, 1942-45, PTO. Mem. Am. Chem. Soc., Am. Inst. Chem. Engrs., Inst. Environ. Sci. (Whitfield award 1955), Fine Particle Soc. (pres. 1977-78, Hausner award 1983). Avocation: classical music. Home: 1943 Mount Vernon Ct 309 Mountain View CA 94040 Office: Particle Measuring Systems 46729 Fremont Blvd Fremont CA 94538

LIEBERMAN, GERALD J., statistics educator; b. N.Y.C., Dec. 31, 1925; s. Joseph and Ida (Margolis) L.; m. Helen Herbert, Oct. 27, 1950; children—Janet, Joanne, Michael, Diana. B.S. in Mech. Engring., Cooper Union, 1948; A.M. in Math. Stats., Columbia U., 1949; Ph.D., Stanford U., 1953. Math. statistician Nat. Bur. Standards, 1949-50; mem. faculty Stanford U., 1953—, prof. statistics and indsl. engring., 1959-67, prof. statistics and operations research, 1967—, chmn. dept. operations research, 1967-75, assoc. dean Sch. Humanities and Scis., 1975-77, acting v.p. and provost, 1979, vice provost, 1977-85, dean research, 1977-80, dean grad. studies and research, 1980-85; cons. to govt. and industry, 1953—. Author: (with A. H. Bowker) Engineering Statistics, 1959, 2d edit., 1972, (with F.S. Hillier) Introduction to Operations Research, 1967, 4th edit., 1986. Ctr. Advanced Studies in Behavioral Scis. fellow, 1985-86. Fellow Am. Statis. Assn., Inst. Math. Statistics, Am. Soc. Quality Control (Shewhart medal 1972), AAAS; mem. Nat. Acad. Engring., Inst. Mgmt. Sci. (pres. 1980-81), Ops. Research Soc. Am., Nat. Acad. Engring. (elected), Sigma Xi, Pi Tau Sigma. Home: 811 San Francisco Terr Stanford CA 94305

LIEBERMAN, JACK, physician; b. Chgo., Jan. 4, 1926; s. Louis and Molly (Sadowski) L.; m. Eleanor Weinstein, Oct. 18, 1955; children: Mila Ann, Debra Lynn, Martin Alan, Wayne Scott. BA, UCLA, 1949; MD, U. So. Calif., 1954. Diplomate Am. Bd. Internal Medicine. Clin. investigator VA, Long Beach, Calif., 1960-63, sect. chief, 1963-68; dir. respiratory disease VA, Sepulveda, Calif., 1976—; assoc. dir. respiratory disease City of Hope, Duarte, Calif., 1968-76. Author: Sarcoidosis, 1985; contbr. 150 articles to profl. jours. Served to cpl. USAF, 1944-45. NIH grantee, 1976-84, VA grantee 1976—. Fellow ACP, Am. Coll. Chest Physicians, mem. Western Assn. Physicians, Western Soc. Clin. Investigation, Am. Soc. Human Genetics. Jewish. Avocations: photography, tennis. Home: 17813 Lemarsh St Northridge CA 91325 Office: VA 16111 Plummer St Sepulveda CA 91343

LIEBERMAN, JAMES LANCE, chemistry educator; b. Newport News, Va., Nov. 26, 1952; s. Lawrence Lipman and Evelyn (Wilks) L. BS, U. Richmond, 1975. Lab. specialist U. Wis., Madison, 1976-78; chemist Vail (Colo.) Assocs., Inc., 1981-84, supr. sanitation ops., 1984-85; instr. celestial navigation Colo. Mountain Coll., Vail, 1981—; instr. skiing Vail/Beaver Creek Ski Sch., 1979-80. Mem. Vail Mountain Rescue Group, 1982—, local lic. bd., Vail, 1982-85. Named Instr. of Yr. Colo. Mountain Coll., 1984. Mem. Am. Chem. Soc., Internat. Ozone Assn. Jewish. Avocations: skiing, sailing, mountaineering. Home: PO Box 1990 Vail CO 81658 Office: Vail Assocs Inc PO Box 7 Vail CO 81657

LIEBERMAN, JEFFREY ALAN, chemist, microbiologist; b. Los Angeles, Dec. 9, 1956; s. George and Gloria (Brown) L. BA, Calif. State U., Northridge, 1984. Microbiologist Sun Labs., Los Angeles, 1982-83; chemist Woodard Labs., Van Nuys, Calif., 1983-85, Rachel Perry Inc., Chatsworth, Calif., 1985—. Mem. Am. Soc. Microbiology, Soc. Cosmetic Chemists. Avocation: mountaineering. Office: Rachel Perry Inc 9111 Mason Ave Chatsworth CA 91311

LIEBERSON, STANLEY, sociologist, educator; b. Montreal, Que., Can., Apr. 20, 1933; s. Jack and Ida (Cohen) L.; m. Patricia Ellen Beard, 1960; children—Rebecca, David, Miriam, Rachel. Student, Bklyn. Coll., 1950-52; M.A., U. Chgo., 1958, Ph.D., 1960. Asso. dir. Iowa Urban Community Research Center, U. Iowa, 1959-61, instr., asst. prof. sociology, 1959-61; asst. prof. sociology U. Wis., 1961-63, asso. prof., 1963-66, prof., 1966-67; prof. sociology U. Wash., 1967-71, dir. Center Studies Demography and Ecology, 1968-71; prof. sociology U. Chgo., 1971-74, assoc. dir. Population Research Center, 1971-74; prof. sociology U. Ariz., Tucson, 1974-83; head dept. U. Ariz., 1976-79; prof. sociology U. Calif.-Berkeley, 1983—; vis. prof. Stanford U., summer 1970; Claude Bissell disting. vis. prof. U. Toronto, 1979-80; mem. com. on sociolinguistics Social Sci. Research Council, 1964-70; mem. sociology panel NSF, 1978-81. Author: (with others) Metropolis and Region, 1960, Ethnic Patterns in American Cities, 1963; Editor: Explorations in Sociolinguistics, 1967, (with Beverly Duncan) Metropolis and Region in Transition, 1970, Language and Ethnic Relations in Canada, 1970, A Piece of the Pie, 1980, Language Diversity and Language Contact, 1981, Making It Count, 1985; assoc. editor: Social Problems, 1965-67, Sociol. Methods and Research, 1971—; editorial cons. Sociol. Inquiry, 1965-67; adv. editor: Am. Jour. Sociology, 1969-74; editorial bd. Lang. in Society, 1972-74, Internat. Jour. Sociology of Lang, 1974—, Canadian Jour. Sociology, 1975—, Social Forces, 1980-83; adv. council Sociol. Abstracts, 1972-73, Language Problems and Language Planning, 1984-87. Recipient Colver Rosenberger Ednl. prize, 1960; Guggenheim fellow, 1972-73. Fellow Am. Acad. Arts and Scis.; mem. Am. Sociol. Assn. (disting. contbn. to scholarship award 1982, commn. 1985-87), Population Assn. Am. (dir. 1969-72), Internat. Population Union, Pacific Sociol. Assn. (v.p. 1984-85, pres. 1986-87), Sociol. Research Assn. (exec. com. 1976-81, pres. 1981, pres.-elect 1986-87), Oakland Sociol. Assn. Home: 560 Valle Vista Ave Oakland CA 94610 Office: U Calif 442 Barrows Hall Berkeley CA 94720

LIEBHABER, FREDERICK JOSEPH, naval officer; b. Chgo., Nov. 14, 1959; s. Frank Bernard and Leanora Nancy (Scotese) L.; m. Lana Elaine Toombs, July 14, 1984. BS in Bus. and Econs., U. Ill., 1981. Commd. ensign USN, 1981, advanced through grades to lt., 1985; material support div. dir. Naval Air Rework Facility, Alameda, Calif., 1984—. Nominated for vice admiral Robert F. Batchelder; recipient Navy League award, 1985. Mem. Bay Area Supply Area Corps Assn. Republican. Roman Catholic. Avocations: golfing, fishing, hunting, camping, skiing. Home: 16612 SE 29th St Bellevue WA 98008

LIEN, WALLACE WAYNE, lawyer, land use consultant; b. McMinnville, Oreg., Aug. 19, 1949; s. Allen John and Elaine Eulala (Spafford) L.; m. Neala Gorgeen King, Mar. 14, 1966 (div. 1972); children: Stephen Brian, Wallace Wayne Jr.; m. Janet Kathleen MacInnes, Aug. 20, 1977; children: Elizabeth Andrea, Alexis Anne, Michael Allen. AS, Chemeketa Community Coll.; BS with honors, Oreg. Coll. Edn.; JD, Willamette U. Bar: Oreg. 1979, U.S. Supreme Ct. 1985. Ptnr. Lien, Lien & Hobson, Keizer, Oreg., 1979-81; asst. county counsel Marion County, Salem, Oreg., 1981-82; chief legal counsel Polk County, Dallas, Oreg., 1982-83; instr. Chemeketa Community Coll., Salem, 1980-85; ptnr. Paulus, Rhaten & Lien, Salem, 1983-86; sole practice Salem, 1986—. Mem. bd. dirs. Oreg. Econ. Inst., Portland, 1985; pres. Oreg. Community Coll. Student Assn., Salem, 1972-73; mem. Oreg. Bd. Edn., Salem, 1972. Western Interstate Commn. Higher Edn. scholar, U.S. Govt., 1976; recipient Col. Robertson award Willamette U., 1978, first pl. moot ct. award Willamette Law Sch., 1977. Mem. ABA, Oreg. State Bar Assn., Marion County Bar Assn., Am. Trial Lawyers Assn., Chemeketa Alumni Assn. Republican. Lodge: Elks. Avocation: water skiing. Home: 3678 Carmelle Ct NE Salem OR 97305 Office: 750 Front St NE Suite 100 Salem OR 97301

LIENAU, BONNIE L(OUISE) ROSZAK, surgical nurse adminstrator, consultant; b. Langley, Va., Aug. 9, 1944; d. Cleo Mitchell and Annie Christine (Brown) Groves; m. Rudy Roszak, July 1, 1966 (div.); 1 son, Christopher Thomas; m. Richard M. Lienau, Jan. 1, 1987. Diploma Gen. Hosp. Sch. Nursing, Nashville, 1965; B.S., Belmont Coll., 1969; postgrad. U. Colo., 1978, Calif. Coast U. Cert. ARC nurse. Staff nurse Vanderbilt U. Hosp., Nashville, 1966; head nurse Bapt. Hosp., Nashville, 1966-72; physician asst. Anesthesiology Assocs., Nashville, 1972-73, Middle Tenn. Anesthesiology, P.C., Nashville, 1973-75; head nurse Rose Med. Ctr., Denver, 1975-76, asst. dir. surgery, 1976-77, dir. surgery, 1977-78; dir. surgeries Good Samaritan Hosp., Corvallis, Oreg., 1978-80; dir. surg. services Santa Monica (Calif.) Hosp. Med. Ctr., 1980—; operating room cons. Pacific Health Resources, Los Angeles. Mem. Assn. of Operating Room Nurses (Los Angeles chpt.), Calif. Soc. Nursing Service Adminstrs., Internat. Assn. Quality Circles Office: Santa Monica Hosp Med Ctr 1225 15th St Santa Monica CA 90404

LIFF, SEYMOUR HERBERT, market researcher, management consultant, computer systems specialist; b. Bronx, N.Y., May 26, 1923; s. Joseph and Ida (Trotsky) L.; m. Dorothy Nell Bonis; children: Miriam Joan, Paul Jaime. AB, Bklyn. Coll., 1948; postgrad., Columbia U., 1948-49, NYU Am. U., 1949-51; MS in Engring., Stevens Inst. Tech., 1956. Computer info. specialist Rockwell, Anaheim-Downey, Calif., 1966-71; community devel. analyst County of Los Angeles, 1971-81; pres. DP Time Broker, Santa Ana, Calif., 1977-81, S.H. Liff Cons., Santa Ana, Calif., 1981-83; prin. TMP Cons., Santa Ana, Calif., 1983—. Contbr. articles to profl. jours. Research dir. Com. to Elect Wilson Riles, Calif., 1924. Served with USAF, 1942-45, ETO. Democrat. Jewish. Avocations: polit. activities. Office: TMP Cons 13361 Bow Pl Santa Ana CA 92705

LIFFICK, FENTON ARTHUR, manufacturing company executive; b. Terre Haute, Ind., Sept. 10, 1926; s. Roy H. and Ruby F. (Fox) L.; student Rose Poly. Inst., 1944-45, W.Va. U., 1945, Ind. U., 1947-49; m. Dorothy M. Luedemann, June 28, 1953; children: Jeffrey Alan, Gregory Gene, Cynthia Gay, Theresa Gail, Bradley James, Sheryl Ann. Gen. mgr. Keystone Processing & Engring. Co., Inc., North Hollywood, Calif., 1967-69; v.p. mfg. Cragar Industries, Inc., Compton, Calif., 1969-74; pres., gen. mgr. Ansen div. Whittaker Corp., Gardena, Calif., 1974-75; sr. v.p. mfg. and engring. Chemplate Corp., Los Angeles, 1975—, also dir.; pres. Fendor Truck Specialties, Sylmar, Calif., 1983—. Patentee in field. Served with U.S. Army, 1945-46. Mem. SAE (automotive bright trim com., Decorative Electroplating Task Force test methods and specifications subcom.). Republican. Lutheran. Home: 12449 Carol Pl Granada Hills CA 91344 Office: Chemplate Corp 4355 E Sheila St Los Angeles CA 90023

LIGEROS, M. SUE, transport refrigeration executive; b. Boulder, Colo., June 25, 1948; d. Michael George Ligeros and F. Evelyn (Summers) Leonard. Student Denver Woman's Coll. Mgr. Ohio Skate, Toledo, 1974-76; gen. mgr. M.G.L. Leasing Co., Denver, 1976-77, Thermo King Sales of Denver, 1977-81, pres., gen. mgr., 1982—; pres. Nissan Diesel Truck Sales of Denver, Inc., 1986—. Recipient Pres.'s award Thermo King Corp., 1982. Mem. Thermo King Dealer Adv. Council (sec.-treas. 1984-86). Republican. Greek Orthodox. Avocations: hiking; camping; outdoor sports. Office: Thermo King of Denver Inc 5455 E 52d Ave Commerce City CO 80022

LIGHT, RONALD LEWIS, audio visual producer; b. Los Angeles, Dec. 17, 1948; s. Hyman and Maxene Shirley (Okun) L.; m. Kenan Veeda Shapero, May 29, 1982. BA in Anthropology, San Francisco State U., 1971; MFA in Design, Calif. Inst. Arts, 1974. Media specialist Ramah (N.Mex.) Navajo Sch. Bd., 1974-76; photographer, designer Ctr. Anthropol. Studies, Albuquerque, 1977-78; cons. Navajo Area Sch. Bd. Assn., Window Rock, Ariz., 1978-80; prin. Ronald Light Studios, Albuquerque, 1981-84, San Francisco, 1984—. One-man show Gallup (N.Mex.) Pub. Library, 1976; exhibited in group show at Image Gallery, Aarhus, Denmark, 1979; contbr. photographs to La Confluencia, 1980, New Am.: A Rev., 1977. Mem. prodn. bd. dirs. Nat. Ednl. Film and Video Festival, Oakland, Calif., 1985—. Mem. Soc. Anthropology Visual Communication (S.W. regional contbg. editor Newsletter, 1978-79), Soc. hist. Archaeology (flim program organizer 13th ann. meeting 1980), Assn. Ind. Video and Flimmakers, Bay Area Video Coalition, Flim Arts Found.. Office: Ronald Light Studios PO Box 883683 San Francisco CA 94188

LIGHTER, ERIC AARON, real estate developer, consultant; b. Chico, Calif., Aug. 6, 1950; s. Bruce Clyde and Katherine Bernice (Stutsman) L.; m. Gitte Gadix, Dec. 18, 1976 (div. Feb. 1978); m. 2d, Janet Shellen Wong, Apr. 20, 1982 (div. July 1985). Grad. Grad. Realtors Inst., 1973; student U. Hawaii. Salesman Fin. Security Life, Honolulu, 1970; founder, treas. 3d Eye Prodns., Honolulu, 1974-76; pres. Home Rent Hawaii, Honolulu, 1976; pres. A. Lighter Cons., Graphic and Media, 1977—; pres. Lighter Properties Corp., Developers, Honolulu, 1978—; founder Quality Income Systems, Honolulu, 1983; mem. Honolulu Realtor Pub. Relation Com., 1983-84. Editor: Ke Alaka'i, 1984. Bd. dirs. Hawaii Alliance for Arts in Edn., 1984, Inst. Human Services, Honolulu, 1984; Hawaii Statue of Liberty Program Mgr., 1986; founder Diamond Cross Ministries, 1985, performing Gospel guitarist, 1985. Mem. Hawaii Assn. Realtors, Bldg. Industry Assn. Hawaii (Parade of Homes Award of Excellence 1983), Hawaii Jaycees (project initiator Silver Jubilee Project 1983, mgr. Outstanding Hawaii Jaycees program mgr., founding pres. Capital Dist. 1982, chaplin Honolulu Chinese 1982-84, King of King award 1982, 83), Nat. Assn. Bed and Breakfast. Republican. Episcopalian. Club: Scandinavian of Hawaii. Lodge: Lions (Honolulu) (var. offices, including treas.). Avocation: playing Gospel guitar. Home: Honolulu Inn 1045 Spencer St Honolulu HI 96813 Office: Lighter Properties Corp 1110 Richards St Honolulu HI 96813

LIGHTMAN, BERNARD VISE, educator; b. Toronto, Ont., Can., Apr. 30, 1950; s. Irwin and Selma (Vise) L.; m. Merle Rebecca Feldman, Sept. 18, 1975; 1 child, Matthew Benson. BA with honors, York U., Toronto, 1973, MA, 1974; PhD, Brandeis U., 1979. Asst. prof. European intellectual history Queen's U., Kingston, Ont., 1979-83; asst. prof. U. Oreg., Eugene, 1983—. Co-author: Victorian Science and Religion, 1984; author: The Origins of Agnosticism, 1987. Office: U Oreg Honors Coll Eugene OR 97403

LIGHTSEY, PAUL ALDEN, physics educator; b. Wray, Colo., Aug. 25, 1944; s. S.L. and Gwen Lee (Parker) L.; m. Carol Virginia Lewis, June 5, 1965; 1 child, Virginia Jean. BS, Colo. State U., 1966; MS, PhD, Cornell U., 1972. Vis. lectr. Beloit (Wis.) Coll., 1972-73; asst. prof. physics and math. U. Dallas, Irving, 1973-75; electrician Gt. Western Sugar Co., Longmont, Colo., 1975-76; assoc. prof. physics and math. Colo. Mountain Coll., Glenwood Springs, 1976-77; assoc. prof. physics U. No. Colo., Greeley, 1977—; scientist NOAA, Boulder, Colo., 1982-84; vis. scientist Nat. Ctr. Atmospheric Research, Boulder, 1986—; sr. ptnr. Ptnr.'s Inc., Greeley, 1980—; co-dir. honors workshop NSF, 1985. Contbr. articles to profl. jours. Vol. Greeley Sr. Ctr., 1983—; elder, deacon, bd. dirs. 1st Christian Ch., Greeley, 1978-84; bd. dirs. Community Christian Ch., Greeley, 1985—. Mem. Am. Assn. Physics Tchrs. (council mem. 1982—), Colo.-Wyo. Acad. Scis. (exec. bd. dirs. 1986—), Internat. Soc. Biomechanics in Sports, Optical Soc. Am., Soc. Photo-Instrumentation Engrs., Soc. Coll. Sci. Tchrs., Nat. Sci. Tchrs. Assn., Rocky Mountain Athletics Congress (race walking chmn. 1977-80), Sigma Xi (past local v.p., pres.), Phi Kappa Phi, Sigma Pi Sigma, Kappa Mu Epsilon. Democrat. Mem. Christian Ch. Club: Colo. Track (Boulder). Avocations: racewalking, backpacking, cross country skiing, owning pets. Home: 2400 E 16th St Greeley CO 80631 Office: U No Colo Dept Physics Greeley CO 80639

LIGRANI, LAWRENCE DENNIS, oil scout; b. Grand Junction, Colo., Nov. 24, 1955; s. Roxy Joseph and Frieda Lucilla (Phillips) L.; m. Judy Ann Elverman, Aug. 28, 1983. Student Mesa Coll., 1974-76, Colo. U., 1976-78; A.S., Community Coll. Denver, 1978, postgrad. U. Denver, 1986. Mudlogger, Analysts Schlumberger, Denver, 1978-80; cons. Rebco Petroleum Cons., Denver, 1980; nuclear magnetic residency technician, Amoco Prodn. Co., Denver, 1980-81, oil scout, 1981—. chief exec. officer Larco Investments. Mem. Internat. Oil Scouts, Am. Assn. Petroleum Geologists, Rocky Mountain Oil Scout Assn. (treas.). Club: Denver Petroleum. Office: Amoco Prodn Co 17th & Broadway Denver CO 80201

LIKENS, ROBERT LEE, computer manager, educator; b. Louisville, Mar. 7, 1949; s. Carl Robert and Thelma Lee (Gambrell) L.; m. Inja Um, July 12, 1971; children: Michelle Lee, Natalie Lynn. Student, Ohio State U., 1967-68, Electronic Computer Programming Inst., Columbus, Ohio, 1973-74; BS in Bus. Adminstrn., Franklin U., 1978. Computer analyst J.C. Penney Co., Columbus, 1974-80; asst. v.p. Security Pacific Automation Co., Brea, Calif., 1980—; instr. data processing N. Orange County Regional Occupational Programs, Anaheim, Calif., 1984—. Served to sgt. U.S. Army, 1969-71, Vietnam. Mem. Seven Tech. Users Forum (pres. 1984-86). Republican. Office: Security Pacific Automation Co 275 S Valencia Brea CA 92621

LIKENS, SUZANNE ALICIA, physiologist, researcher; b. Chgo., Nov. 12, 1945; d. Harry Ross and Sibyle Lovelett (Butler) L. BS in Biology, U. N.Mex., 1969, MS in Physiology, 1982. Research asst. biology dept. U. N.Mex, Albuquerque, 1969; sr. research technologist Inhalation Toxicology Research Inst., Albuquerque, 1974—. Mem. Costeau Soc., N.Mex. Zool. Soc., Humane Soc. of U.S., N.Mex. Herpetological Soc. (charter), Women in Sci. and Engring., AAAS, Ctr. Environ. Edn. Whale Protection Fund, Turkey Track Dressage Sch., Sigma Xi. Republican. Presbyterian. Avocations: riding, training horses (dressage), snakes, pub. speaking. Home: 1311 Dartmouth NE Albuquerque NM 87106 Office: Inhalation Toxicology Research Inst PO Box 5890 Albuquerque NM 87185

LIKUSKI, ROBERT KEITH, medical device company executive; b. Hillcrest, Alta., Can., Oct. 16, 1937; came to U.S., 1964; s. Henry Fredrick Charles and Nellie (Kropinak) L.; m. Ines Levy, July 1, 1971; children: David, Andrew. BS, U. Alta., 1959; MS, U. Ill., 1961, PhD, 1964. Asst. prof. elec. engring. U. Tex., Austin, 1965-70; staff scientist Micro-Bit Corp., Lexington, Mass., 1970-76; dir. research and devel. Cooper Med. Devices Corp., San Leandro, Calif., 1976-80; research mgr. Altex div. SmithKline Beckman Instruments, San Ramon, Calif., 1980—. Inventor in field. Mem. IEEE, Sigma Xi. Home: 4430 School Way Castro Valley CA 94546 Office: Altex div Beckman Instruments 2350 Camino Ramon San Ramon CA 94583-0701

LILIENTHAL, JEANETTE ROBERTA TRUJILLO, speech pathologist; b. Española, N.Mex., Mar. 21, 1950; d. Seferino and Geneva Ernestine (Baca) Trujillo; m. James Haworth Lilienthal, Mar. 30, 1970; children: Doenika Bridgit, Jason Haworth, Katy Rebecca. MS, U. N.Mex., 1983. Speech-lang. pathologist, cons. Española Mcpl. Schs., 1983-87, Santa Rosa (N.Mex.) Consolidated Schs., 1984-85, Springer (N.Mex.) Schs., 1985-87, N.Mex. Boys Sch., Springer, 1985-87, Headstart Programs, Santa Fe, El Rito, Springer, N.Mex., 1985—. Mem. Am. Speech Lang. Hearing Assn., N.Mex. Speech Lang. Hearing Assn. (sec. 1985-87). Democrat. Roman Catholic. Avocations: reading, landscaping, remodeling. Home and Office: Rt 10 PO Box 146 Santa Fe NM 87501

LILLIE, JOHN MITCHELL, retail executive; b. Chgo., Feb. 2, 1937; s. Walter Theodore and Mary Ann (Hatch) L.; children: Alissa Ann, Theodore Perry. B.S., Stanford U., 1959, M.S., M.B.A., 1962-64. Various positions including dir. systems devel., also asst. to pres. Boise Cascade Corp., 1964-68; v.p., chief financial officer Arcata Nat. Corp., Menlo Park, Calif., 1968-70; exec. v.p., chief operating officer Arcata Nat. Corp., 1970-72; pres., chief exec. officer Leslie Salt Co., Newark, Calif., 1972-79; exec. v.p. Lucky Stores Inc., Dublin, Calif., 1979-81, pres., 1981-86, chmn., chief exec. officer, 1986—, also dir.; dir. Spectra Physics Inc. Mem. Beta Theta Pi, Tau Beta Pi. Office: Lucky Stores Inc 6300 Clark Ave Dublin CA 94568

LILLO, JAMES ALLEN, manufacturing executive; b. Duluth, Minn., Jan. 19, 1950; s. Jerome Alvin and Margaret (Hansen) L.; m. Karen Lynn Lillo, Jan. 29, 1973 (div. Jan. 1986); children: Shilo B., Joshua C. Grad. high sch., Carson City, Nev. Mem. assembly staff Mallory, Inc., Carson City, 1972-74, service technician, 1974-75, nat. sales mgr., 1976-81, plant mgr., 1981-82, gen. mgr., 1982-87; v.p. sales and mktg. Weland Automotive Industries, Los Angeles, 1987—. Ambassador State Nev. Commn. Econ. Devel., Carson City, 1985-86. Served with U.S. Army, 1968-71, Vietnam. Avocations: softball, hunting, fishing, cars. Home: 4240 Sarah St Burbank CA 91505 Office: Weland Automotive Industries 2316 San Fernando Rd Los Angeles CA 90065

LILLY, GEORGE DAVID, broadcasting executive; b. Winchester, Mass., Nov. 3, 1934; s. George M. and Eleanor (Hamlin) L.; children: Brian, Kevin, Kristin. BS in Communication Arts, Boston U., 1956. Mgr. Sta. WGAN-TV, Portland, Maine, 1960-69, Sta. WIVB-TV, Buffalo, 1969-80; v.p. TV ops. Park TV, Ithaca, N.Y., 1980-83; prin., pres. BK&K, Inc., Syracuse, N.Y., 1986—, SJL, Inc., Billings, Mont., 1984—; prin., dir. Fayetteville, N.C., 1985—; pres. SJL Broadcast Mgmt. Corp., 1984—; owner Sta. KTVQ-TV, Billings, 1984—, Sta. WKFT-TV, Fayetteville, 1985—, Sta. WSTM-TV, Syracuse, 1986—, WGRZ-TV, Buffalo, 1986—; mem. CBS Affiliates Govt. Relations com., 1986. Mem. U.S. Olympic Com., Mont., 1986; bd. dirs. Billing Family YMCA, 1986, Eastern Mont. Coll. Found., Billings, 1986, U. Mont. Citizens Council, Missoula, 1986. Served with U.S. Army, 1957-59. Mem. Nat. Assn. Broadcasters. Avocations: skiing, pvt. pilot. Home: 5810 Sam Snead Dr Billings MT 59103 Office: Mont TV Network Station KTVQ Box 2557 Billings MT 59103

LILLY, LUELLA JEAN, university administrator; b. Newberg, Oreg., Aug. 23, 1937; d. David Hardy and Edith (Coleman) L. BS, Lewis and Clark Coll., 1959; postgrad., Portland State U., 1959-61; MS, U. Oreg., 1961; PhD, Tex. Woman's U., 1971; postgrad., various univs., 1959-72. Tchr. phys. edn. and health, dean girls Cen. Linn Jr.-Sr. High Sch., Halsey, Oreg., 1959-60; tchr. phys. edn. and health, swimming, tennis, golf coach Lake Oswego (Oreg.) High Sch., 1960-63; instr., intramural coach Oreg. State U., Corvallis, 1963-64; instr., intercollegiate coach Am. River Coll., Sacramento, 1964-69; dir. women's phys. edn., athletics U. Nev., Reno, 1969-73, dir. women's athletics, 1973-75, assoc. dir. athletics, 1975-76, assoc. prof. phys. edn., 1971-76; dir. women's intercollegiate athletics U. Calif., Berkeley, 1976—; organizer, coach Lue's Aquatic Club, 1962-64. Author: An Overview of Body Mechanics, 1966, 3d rev. edit., 1969. Vol. instr. ARC, 1951; vol. Heart Fund and Easter Seal, 1974-76; ofcl. Spl. Olympics, 1975; mem. Los Angeles Citizens Olympic Com., 1984. Mem. AAHPER (life), AAUW, Nat. Soc. Profs., Women's Athletic Caucus, Council Collegiate Women Athletics Adminstrs., Western Soc. Phys. Edn. Coll. Women (membership com. 1971-74, program adv. com. 1972, exec. bd. 1972-75), Western Assn. Intercollegiate Athletics for Women (exec. bd. dirs. 1973-75, 79-82), Oreg. Girls' Swimming Coaches Assn. (pres. 1960, 63), Cen. Calif. Bd. Women Ofcls. (basketnball chmn. 1968-69), Calif. Assn. Health, Phys. Edn. and Recreation (chmn.-elect jur. coll. sect. 1970), Nev. Bd. Women Ofcls. (chmn. bd., chmn. volleyball sect., chmn. basketball sect. 1969), No. Calif. Women's Intercollegiate Conf. (sec. 1970-71, basketball coordinator 1970-71), No. Calif. Intercollegiate Athletic Conf. (volleyball coordinator 1971-72), Nev. Assn. Health, Phys. Edn. and Recreation (state chmn. 1974—), No. Calif. Athletic Conf. (pres. 1979-82), Phi Kappa Phi, Theta Kappa. Mem. Soc. Friends. Lodge: Soroptimists. Home: 60 Margrave Ct Walnut Creek CA 94596 Office: U Calif 177 Hearst Gym Berkeley CA 94720

LILLY, MICHAEL ALEXANDER, lawyer; b. Honolulu, May 21, 1946; s. Percy Anthony, Jr. and Virginia Craig Lilly; children—Cary J., Laura B., Claire F. AA, Menlo Coll., Menlo Park, Calif., 1966; BA, U. Calif., Santa Cruz, 1968; JD with honors, U. of Pacific, 1974. Bar: Calif. 1974, U.S. Dist. Ct. (no., so. and ea. dists.) Calif. 1974, U.S. Ct. Appeals (9th cir.) 1974, Hawaii 1975, U.S. Dist. Ct. Hawaii 1975, U.S. Ct. Appeals (D.C. cir.) 1975, U.S. Supreme Ct. 1978, U.S. Ct. Appeals (7th cir.) 1979. Atty. Pacific Legal Found., Sacramento, 1974-75; dep. atty. gen. State of Hawaii, Honolulu, 1975-79, 1st dep. atty. gen., 1981-84, atty. gen., 1984-85; ptnr. Feeley & Lilly, San Jose, Calif., 1979-81, Green, Ning, Lilly & Jones, Honolulu, 1985—; faculty Hastings Litigation Trial Advocacy Sch., San Francisco, 1984; mem. U.S. Atty. Gen. Law Enforcement Coordinating Com., Honolulu. Alumni rep. U. Calif., Santa Cruz, 1982—, Menlo Coll.; div. leader sustaining membership drive YMCA, Honolulu, 1984—. Served to lt. USN, 1968-71, Vietnam; comdr. USNR. Named Hon. Ky. Col. Mem. Nat. Assn. Attys. Gen., Hawaii Law Enforcement Ofcls. Assn., Naval Res. Assn. (pres. 14th dist.), Navy League, Nat. Dist. Attys. Assn., Mothers Agains Drunk Drivers. Episcopalian. Club: Outrigger Canoe. Home: 2616 Pali Hwy Honolulu HI 96817 Office: Green Ning Lilly & Jones 1100 Pauahi Tower 1001 Bishop St Honolulu HI 96813

LIM, DANIEL, obstretrician-gynecologist, military officer; b. Yong Kang, Republic of Korea, May 29, 1930; came to U.S., 1958; s. Edward K. and Byung Kee (Kim) L.; m. Kumja Chang, Dec. 9, 1961; children: Eugene, Mona, Pauline. MD, Seoul Nat. U., Republic of Korea, 1958; diploma in Psychiatry, U. Manitoba, 1966. Diplomate Am. Bd. Ob-Gyn. Practice medicine specializing in obstetrics-gynecology Wise, Va., 1968-69, Davenport, Iowa, 1969-85, East Moline, Ill., 1979-85; commd. lt. col. U.S. Army, 1985—; mem. faculty Tripler Army Med. Ctr., Honolulu, 1985—. Fellow Am. Coll Ob-Gyns. Methodist. Lodge: Rotary. Home: 1031 Ala Napunani St #1202 Honolulu HI 96818 Office: Tripler Army Med Ctr Dept Ob-Gyn Honolulu HI 96859

LIM, VICTOR ALLEN, optometrist; b. San Francisco, May 14, 1944; s. Allen and Lilly (Chow) L.; m. Camille Chan, Apr. 22, 1967; children—Matthew, Brett. B.A., U. Calif.-Berkeley, O.D., 1970. Lic. optometrist, Calif., 1970. Optometrist San Bruno (Calif.) Med.-Optical Clinic, 1970-72; ptnr. pvt. practice Lim, Schrader and Helmus, 1972—. Chmn. City of Davis (Calif.) Personnel Bd.; mem. adv. bd. Yolo County (Calif.) Drug and Alcohol Abuse Commn., Los Ricos Community Coll.; active Boy Scouts Am.; mem. site council Davis High Sch.; chmn. personnel bd. City of Davis. Named Cub Master of Yr. Yolo County, Calif., 1985, Citizen of Yr. City of Davis, 1986. Mem. Am. Optometric Assn., Calif. Optometric Assn., Sacramento Valley Optometric Assn., C. of C. (bd. dirs., sec., Mem. of Year 1979), U. Calif. Optometry Sch. Alumni Assn. (v.p.). Democrat. Roman Catholic. Clubs: Chinese Fellowship of Davis (past pres.), Kiwanis (past pres.). Home: 4022 Almond Ln Davis CA 95616 Office: 1109 Kennedy Pl Davis CA 95616

LIMANDRI, CHARLES SALVATORE, lawyer; b. San Diego, Aug. 19, 1955; s. Joseph John and Florence Ann (Dippolito) LiM.; m. Nancine Belfiore, Oct. 20, 1984. BA, U. San Diego, 1977; Diploma in Internat. Law, U. Wales, 1980; JD, Georgetown U., 1983. Bar: Calif. 1983, D.C. 1984. Tchr. St. Augustine High Sch., Washington, 1978-79; assoc. Adams, Duque, Los Angeles, 1983-85, Lillick, McHose & Charles, San Diego, 1985—. Rotary Internat. grad. fellow U. Wales at Aberystwyth, 1980; recipient Hattie M. Strong Found. award, Washington, 1983. Mem. ABA, Assn. Trial Lawyers Am., San Diego County Bar Assn., Italian-Am. Lawyers Assn., U. San Diego Alumni Assn. (bd. dirs.), Thomas More Soc. Am. (bd. dirs. 1982-84), Sons of Italy. Democrat. Roman Catholic. Lodge: Rotary. Avocations: running, weight lifting, skiing, scuba diving. Home: 2755 Wyandotte Ave San Diego CA 92117 Office: Lillick McHose & Charles 101 W Broadway San Diego CA 92101

LIMBERHAND, LYNDA JOYCE, academic administrator; b. Spokane, Wash., Dec. 21, 1946; s. Walter Norvel and Doris (Wolftooth) Locher; m. Ben. L. Limberhand, Sept. 3, 1965 (dec.); children: Michelle, Bobbi Jo, Kelly, Rusty, Megan. BS, Eastern Mont. Coll., 1975; student, Mont. State U., 1985—. Tchr. Lame Deer (Mont.) Pub. Sch., 1969-75; dir. adult edn. Indian Action Program, Lame Deer, 1975-80; dean of instrn. Dull Knife Meml. Coll., Lame Deer, 1975-80, dir. devel., 1983-85, dir. spl. edn., 1985—; cons. Office of PUb. Instr., Helena, Mont., 1980-81; mem. adv. council Manpower Program, Billings, Mont., 1981-83, Tchr. Corp. Program, Lame Deer, 1975-80. Editor of manuscript evaluations of Indian edn. books, 1984. Chmn. sch. bd. Lame Deer Pub. Sch., 1981-83; mem. bd. dirs. Day Care Bd., Lame Deer Day Care, 1975-80; mem. task force Battered Spouses State of Mont., Colstrip, 1975-80; parent adv. com. Follow Through Project, Lame Deer, 1975-80; v.p. Parish Council, Lame Deer, 1983-84. Recipient Community Leadership award, Tchr. Corps Program, 1983; name Outstanding Sch. Bd. Mem., Lame Deer Pub. Sch., 1983. Mem. Council for Indian Edn. (bd.dirs. 1984), Nat. Adult Edn. Assn., Nat. Indian Adult Edn. Assn., No. Cheyenne Edn. Com., Council on Exceptional Children, Faculty Assn. (pres. 1985—). Democrat. Roman Catholic. Avocations: swimming, reading, golfing, writing, community devel. projects. Home: PO Box 254 Lame Deer MT 59043 Office: Dull Knife Meml Coll PO Box 98 Lame Deer MT 59043

LIMBS, DENNIS WAYNE, financial and investment counselor; b. Austin, Tex., June 7, 1944; s. Lee Andrew and Bessie Mae (Webb) L. Student, U. Chgo., 1965-67; AA, Phoenix Coll., 1970; B in Mgmt., U. Phoenix, 1980. With advt., mktg. depts. Nat. Publs. Sales, Inc., Chgo., 1966-68; from officer to supr. correctional programs Ariz. State Dept. Corrections, Ft. Grant, 1981-82; social worker, counselor human resources dept. City of Phoenix, 1974-85; assets mgr., salesman Jackson region A.L. Williams, Phoenix, 1985—. V.p., bd. dirs. Ebony House, Inc., Phoenix, 1982—; chmn. bd. dirs. So. Phoenix Community Med. Ctr., 1979-81; adv. and counselor, ANY-TOWN adv. com. Ariz. region, NCCJ, Phoenix, 1985—; mem. U.S. Mil. Acads. Selection Com., Phoenix, 1985; treas. dist. 23 Maricopa County Dems., Phoenix, 1980—; mem. precinct com. Maricopa County Dems., 1980—, also dep. registrar, 1980—; served as sgt. U.S. Army, 1959-62. Named Outstanding Employee of Yr. Human Resources Dept., Phoenix, 1980. Mem. Am. Mgmt. Assn., Am. Correctional Assn., Am. Legion, Am. Assn. Social Workers, U.S. Jaycees (bd. dirs. Phoenix chpt. 1978-81, Dir. of Yr. award 1979). Democrat. Methodist. Lodges: Elks, Masons. Avocations: golf, reading, genealogy, working with youth, horseback riding. Home: 1206 E Hunnington Dr Phoenix AZ 85040 Office: A L Williams Inc 40 W Baseline Suite 114 Tempe AZ 85282

LIN, ALEXANDER SHINNFU, radiologist, physicist; b. Tokyo, Oct. 26, 1942; came to U.S., 1968; s. J.G. and Shu-mei L.; m. Alice Weilung Lee, June 14, 1970; children: Carol, Margaret. BS in Physics, Nat. Taiwan U., Taipei, 1967; MS in Physics, U. Pitts., 1969; PhD in Applied Physics, Stanford U., 1974; MD, U. Miami, Fla., 1977. Diplomate Am. Bd. Radiology, Am. Bd. Nuclear Medicine, Nat. Bd. Med. Examiners. Postdoctoral research fellow Stanford (Calif.) Electronic Labs., 1975; intern Genesee Hosp., Rochester, N.Y., 1977-78; resident UCI Med. Ctr., Orange, Calif., 1978-81; fellow ultrasound and computerized tomography U. Calif. Med. Ctr., San Diego, 1981-82; fellow nuclear medicine UCLA, 1982-83; staff radiologist Western Pa. Hosp., Pitts., 1983-84, Costa Mesa (Calif.) Med. Ctr. Hosp., 1984—; asst. adj. prof. U. Calif., Irvine, 1979-80. Contbr. articles on physics, radiology and medicine to profl. jours. Mem. Radiol. Soc. N.Am., Soc. Nuclear Medicine, Am. Inst. Ultrasound in Medicine, Am. Phys. Soc. Republican. Home: 5225 Paseo Panorama Yorba Linda CA 92686 Office: Costa Mesa Med Ctr Hosp 301 Victoria St Costa Mesa CA 92627

LIN, CHWEN-HAO FRANCIS, structural engineer; b. Chiayi, Taiwan, Oct. 22, 1949; came to U.S., 1975; s. Chuan-Hsiang and Tsai-Hwei (Chao) L.; m. Jean Lung, Nov. 22, 1978; children: Christopher C., Stephanie Y. BS in Engring., Nat. Taiwan U., Taipei, 1973; MS in Engring., U. Calif., Berkeley, 1976. Registered profl. engr., Calif. Engr. Raymond Internat., Inc., San Francisco, 1977-78; research engr. Vetco Offshore, Inc., Ventura, Calif., 1979-80; mem. tech. staff Rockwell Internat. Corp., Canoga Park, Calif., 1980-81; sr. engr. Bechtel Group, Inc., San Francisco, 1981-85; research specialist Lockheed Missiles and Space Co., Inc., Sunnyvale, Calif., 1985—. Contbr. articles to profl. jours. Mem. Sigma Xi (research award 1977). Home: 2781 Boncheff Dr San Jose CA 95133 Office: Lockheed Missiles and Space Co 1111 Lockheed Way Sunnyvale CA 94089

LIN, HUN-CHI, molecular biologist; b. Yun-Lin, Taiwan, Republic of China, Nov. 8, 1953; came to U.S., 1980; s. Shun-Tsu and Yu-Hwa (Tsai) L.; m. Shau-Ping Lei, July 6, 1980; 1 child, Victoria Lei. BS, Nat. Taiwan U., Taipei, 1976, MS, 1978; PhD, UCLA, 1984. Teaching asst. UCLA, 1983; research scientist Ingene, Santa Monica, Calif., 1984-85, project dir., 1985-87, prin. investigator, 1985-87; research dir. Sinogen, Los Angeles, 1987—. Contbr. articles to profl. jours. Served to lt. Chinese Army, 1978-80. Mem. AAAS, Am. Soc. Microbiology. Office: Sinogen 11452 Clarkson Rd Los Angeles CA 90064

LIN, JIANN-TSYH, research chemist; b. Taoyuan, Taiwan, Jan. 15, 1940; came to U.S., 1965; s. Yuan-I and Mu-Mien (Tsou) L.; Su-Tsu Hsu, July 12, 1969; children: Robert, Jeffrey. BS, Chung-Hsing U., Taiwan, 1963; MS, U. Miss, 1967; PhD, Drexel U., 1971. Research assoc. U. Tenn., Memphis, 1971-72, U. Minn., Austin, 1972-76, U. Wash., Seattle, 1976-77; research chemist USDA, Albany, Calif., 1977—. Contbr. articles to profl. jours. Mem. Am. Chem. Soc., Am. Soc. Plant Physiologists. Office: USDA 800 Buchanan St Albany CA 94710

LIN, JUNG-TAI, civil engineer; b. Kweichow, China, Oct. 7, 1941; came to U.S., 1964, naturalized, 1974; s. Sheng-Heng and Yü-Piao (Wu) L.; m. Anne Liu, Sept. 11, 1966; children: Johnny W., Joann Y. BS, Nat. Taiwan U., Taipei, 1963; MS, Colo. State U., 1967, PhD, 1969. Registered profl. civil and mech. engr., Wash. Research asst., then research assoc. Colo. State U., Ft. Collins, 1965-69; research engr. Iowa Inst. Hydraulic Research, Iowa City, 1969-70; vis. scientist Nat. Ctr. Atmospheric Research, Boulder, Colo., 1970-71; dept. dir., sr. scientist Flow Industries Inc., Kent, Wash., 1971-78; pres. United Industries Corp., Bellevue, Wash., 1978—. Pres. Chinese Community Pub. Affairs Orgn., Seattle, 1985, Soc. Chinese Engrs., Seattle, 1982; commr. Storm and Surface Water Adv. Commn., Bellevue, 1986—. Mem. ASCE (chmn. energy conservation subcom.), ASHRAE. Avocation: choral music. Office: United Industries Corp 12835 Bell-Red Rd #120 Bellevue WA 98005

LIN, LAWRENCE SHUH LIANG, mental health executive; b. China, July 5, 1938; s. Wan Chow and Inn Chi Lin; came to U.S., 1967, naturalized, 1979; LL.B., Soochow U., 1963; M.B.A., Pepperdine U., 1970; m. Grace Yu, July 31, 1966; children—Ray, Lester. Spl. project acctg. supr. Motown Records, Hollywood, Calif., 1975; chief accountant Elektra/Asylum/Nonesuch Records, Beverly Hills, Calif., 1976-77, United Artists Music Pub. Group, Hollywood, 1977-80; controller-adminstr. Pasadena (Calif.) Guidance Clinics, 1980-86; v.p. Stew Kettle Corp., Los Angeles, 1986—. Mem. Nat. Accountants Assn. Baptist. Office: Stew Kettle Corp 1612 Montebello Town Ctr Dr Montebello CA 90640

LIN, PAUL YOUNG, electronics executive, consultant; b. Shanghai, Peoples Republic of China, Apr. 7, 1942; came to U.S., 1946; s. Tung Yen and Margaret (Kao) L.; m. M. Lois Wilcox, Apr. 15, 1967; children: Deanna, Kathryn, Erik. BSEE, U. Calif., Berkeley, 1964, MSEE, 1966. Cert. community coll. tchr. Mem. tech. staff Watkins Johnson, Palo Alto, Calif., 1966-69, 70-71, v.p., div. mgr., 1982—; sr. engr. Applied Tech., Palo Alto, 1969-70; sr. devel. engr Probe Systems, Sunnyvale, Calif., 1971-73; instr. Coll. San Mateo, Calif., 1973-76, div. dir., 1976-79; adv. com. mem. San Jose State U., 1981-82, Coll. San Mateo, 1980—, Am. River Coll., Sacramento, 1984—. Author: Essentials of Electric Circuits, 1982. Bd. dirs. Peninsula Symphony Assn., San Mateo, 1982. NSF fellowship, 1965. Mem. IEEE, Am. Mgmt. Assn., Assn. Old Crows, Delta Chi. Club: University. Avocation: photography, music, tennis, coin collecting. Office: Watkins Johnson 3333 Hillview Ave Palo Alto CA 94304

LIN, ROBERT I-SAN, pharmaceutical company executive; b. Fuchow, Republic of China, Oct. 9, 1942; came to U.S., 1962; s. Shuen and Kwei-Leu Lin; m. Cecile V. Fung, Dec. 12, 1971; children: Sylvia, Alva, Rose, David. BS, Nat. Taiwan U., 1961; MS, UCLA, 1965, PhD, 1968. Postdoctoral trainee Calif. Inst. Tech., Pasadena, 1968-70, MIT, Cambridge, 1970-71; v.p. RIA Products subs. Rohm & Haas Co., Waltham, Mass., 1971-75; chief scientist Frito-Lay Inc. subs. PepsiCo., Dallas, 1975-82; v.p. Natural Products div. Richardson-Vicks, Irvine, Calif., 1982-85; sr. v.p. Makers of Kal Corp., Woodland Hills, Calif., 1986—; vis. disting. prof. Tex. Women's U., Denton, 1981-82; sci. com. mem. Council for Responsible Nutrition, Washington, 1982-85. Contbr. articles to profl. jours.; patentee in field. Recipient Nat. award Advanced Studies, Republic of China, 1962-65. Mem. Am. Chem. Soc., N.Y. Acad. Scis. (life), Am. Coll. Nutrition, Am. Mgmt. Assn., Inst. Food Technologists, Orange County Chinese Culture Club, Sigma Xi (life). Avocation: application of traditional Chinese herbal medicine to modern diseases, nutrition and health enhancement. Home: 6 Silverfern Dr Irvine CA 92715

LIN, SHENG-RONG, aerospace technologist; b. Taipei, Taiwan, Republic of China, Sept. 20, 1940; came to U.S., 1964; s. H.J. and Wen I. (Chang) L.; m. Li-Lien Fang, Mar. 19, 1966; children: Gray T., Nancy T. BS, Nat. Taiwan U., 1961, MS, 1964; MS, Calif. Inst. Tech., 1965; PhD, UCLA, 1971, postdoctoral scholar, 1971-73. Project scientist Aerospace Research Assocs., West Covina, Calif., 1966-73; mem. tech. staff Structures Dept. Aerospace Corp., El Segundo, Calif., 1973-78, sect. mgr. Structures Dept., 1978-85, dir. Structural Tech. office, 1985—. Contbr. articles to profl. jours. Pres. Chinese Lang. Sch. So. Calif., Los Angeles, 1980. Mem. Sigma Xi, Phi Tau Phi (sec. 1985-87). Club: Toastmasters (El Segundo) (pres. 1979). Home:

1295 El Hito Circle Pacific Palisades CA 90272 Office: Aerospace Corp 2350 El Segundo Blvd El Segundo CA 90245

LIN, YI-CHING, electrical engineer, educator; b. Tounan, Taiwan, Republic of China, Sept. 8, 1949; came to U.S., 1974; s. Wun-Chang and Su-Jen (Sen) L.; m. Shiou-Ling Lieu, Aug. 24, 1977; children: Teresa Cynthia, Karen Alice. BSEE, Nat. Taiwan U., Taipei, 1972; MSEE, U. Houston, 1976; PhD, U. Calif., Berkeley, 1981. Testing engr. Acurex, Inc., Mt. View, Calif., 1976-77; research asst. U. Calif., Berkeley, 1977-81; mem. tech. staff Tex. Instruments, Dallas, 1981-84; engring. specialist Monolithic Memories, Santa Clara, Calif., 1984—; mem. faculty/lectr. San Jose (Calif.) State U., 1986—. Contbr. articles to profl. jours.; patentee in field. Served to 2d lt. Army Republic of China, 1972-74. Recipient Incentive award Tex. Instruments, Dallas, 1984. Mem. IEEE. Buddhist. Office: Monolithic Memories Inc 2175 Mission College Blvd Santa Clara CA 95050

LINCE, JEFFREY ROBERT, chemical physicist; b. Pasadena, Calif., July 19, 1957. BS in Chemistry, U. Calif., Berkeley, 1980; PhD in Chemistry, UCLA, 1985. Research asst. chemistry dept. UCLA, 1982-85; mem. tech. staff The Aerospace Corp., El Segundo, Calif., 1985—. Contbr. articles to profl. jours. Recipient chemistry dept. teaching award, UCLA, 1981, 82, Internat. Precious Metals Inst. award, 1985. Mem. Am. Phys. Soc., Am. Chem. Soc., Am. Vacuum Soc., Materials Research Soc. Office: The Aerospace Corp Surface Sci Dept 2350 El Segundo Blvd El Segundo CA 90245

LINCOLN, DAVID COLVILL, laser company executive; b. Cleve., Nov. 10, 1925; s. John Cromwell and Helen (Colville) L.; m. Joan Rechtin, July 29, 1950; children: Virginia, Kathryn, Carl, James. BS in Engring., Calif. Inst. Tech., 1946, MSEE, 1947; D of Laws (hon.), Soochow U., Taipei, Taiwan Republic of China, 1974; DSc (hon.), Ariz. State U., 1979. Engr. Gen. Dynamics Co., San Diego, 1947-49; head dept. engring. Sperry Gyroscope Co., Great Neck, N.Y., 1949-57; asst. to pres. Universal Wire Co., Cleve., 1957-59; pres. Bagdad Copper Corp., Phoenix, 1959-73, Vika Corp., Phoenix, 1971—; chmn. Lincoln Laser Co., Phoenix, 1974—; pres. Lincoln Found., Phoenix, 1959—, Lincoln Inst. Land Poly., Cambridge, Mass., 1974—; bd. dirs. Lincoln Electric Co., Cleve. Trustee John C. Lincoln Hosp., Phoenix, 1965—; bd. dirs. Am. Grad. Sch. Internat. Mgmt., Glendale, Ariz., 1975—. Recipient Chinese Order of Brilliant Star, Govt. Republic of China, Taipei, 1980, Disting. Citizen award U. Ariz., Tucson, 1978, Disting. Achievement award Ariz. State U., Tempe, 1975. Mem. IEEE, Am. Mgmt. Assn. (bd. dirs. 1981-84), Tau Beta Pi. Club: John Gardiner's Tennis Ranch (Phoenix). Office: Lincoln Laser Co 55 E Thomas Rd Phoenix AZ 85012

LINCOLN, SANDRA ELEANOR, chemistry educator; b. Holyoke, Mass., Mar. 11, 1939; d. Edwin Stanley and Evelyn Ida (Mackie) L. BA magna cum laude, Smith Coll., 1960; MSChem, Marquette U., 1970; PhD in Inorganic Chemistry, SUNY, Stony Brook, 1982. Tchr., prin. Oak Knoll Sch., Summit, N.J., 1964-74; tchr. Holy Child High Sch., Waukegan, Ill., 1974-76; lectr. chemistry, dir. fin. aid Rosemont (Pa.) Coll., 1976-78; teaching asst. SUNY, Stony Brook, 1978-82; asst. prof. chemistry U. Portland, Oreg., 1982—; researcher Oreg. Grad. Ctr., Beaverton, 1982—; bd. dirs. Portland Chemists for Pauling Symposium. Contbr. articles to profl. jours. Cath. sister Soc. Holy Child Jesus, 1963—. Recipient Pres.'s award for Teaching, SUNY, Stony Brook, 1981. Mem. Am. Chem. Soc., Phi Beta Kappa, Sigma Xi. Democrat. Home: 5431 N Strong St Portland OR 97203 Office: U Portland 5000 Willamette Blvd Portland OR 97203

LINCOLN, T(HOMAS) CRAIG, JR., graphic and image designer, educator; b. San Antonio, Feb. 14, 1942; s. Thomas Craig and Martha Jo (Nicholson) L.; m. Linda Lea Singer, Jan. 23, 1963; children: Thomas Craig III, Michael John. Cert. vocat. edn. tchr., Colo. Dir. art Sta. KENS-TV, San Antonio, 1965-66; dir. design HemisFair '68, San Antonio, 1966-68, Communications Cons., Santa Monica, Calif., 1968-70; owner Lincoln & Assocs., Hollywood, Calif., 1970-74, Ohman & Lincoln, Inc., Denver, 1974-77; vocat. educator Cherry Creek Schs., Englewood, Colo., 1977-86; prin. Design Cons., Aurora, Colo., 1980—. Mem. Colo. adv. coms. for Comml. Art, 1979—, Graphic Arts, 1979-83. Served with USAF, 1961-65. Recipient Quality Edn. award Littleton (Colo.) Pub. Schs., 1982, Excellence in Edn. award Cherry Creek Schs., 1986, Outstanding Service award Colo. Bd. Community Colls., 1985. Democrat. Roman Catholic. Avocations: World War II history, gardening, flying. Home: 1647 S Sedalia St Aurora CO 80017 Office: Cherry Creek Schs 9150 E Union Ave Englewood CO 80111

LIND, BRUCE ELVIN, land developer; b. Twin Falls, Idaho, June 25, 1941; s. Wyland Herman and Helen Eileen (Bailey) L.; B.S., Utah State U., 1967, B.S. in Bus. Edn., 1968, M.S. in Mktg., 1969; m. Patricia Zohner; children—Billie Jean, Bonita, Ben, Katy, Tyler, Tara, Corbin, Jess. Product mgr., wholesaler Boise Cascade Corp. (Idaho), 1968-70; asst. to nat. sales mgr. Tru-Joist Corp., Boise, 1970-71; founder, pres. A.M.R. Corp., Idaho Falls, Idaho, 1971—, chmn. bd., 1972—. Mem. Delta Phi Kappa. Club: Lions. Office: A M R Corp 244 Broadway Idaho Falls ID 83402

LIND, MAURICE DAVID, research physicist; b. Jamestown, N.Y., July 25, 1934; s. Paul William Frederick and Florence Rosemond (Hedstrom) L.: m. Carol Norma Dickson, Apr. 21, 1962; 1 child, Diana Nadine. BS, Otterbein Coll., 1957; PhD, Cornell U., 1962. Postdoctoral fellow Cornell U., Ithaca, N.Y., 1962-63; research scientist Union Oil Co., Brea, Calif., 1963-66, Rockwell Internat., Thousand Oaks, Calif., 1966—; vis. prof. applied physics Tech. U. Denmark, Lyngby, 1985. Contbr. articles to profl. jours. Recipient Pub. Service award NASA, 1976. Mem. Am. Phys. Soc., Am. Crystallographic Assn., Am. Assn. Crystal Growth, Metall. Soc., Sigma Xi. Home: 1690 Stoddard Ave Thousand Oaks CA 91360 Office: Rockwell Internat 1049 Camino Dos Rios Thousand Oaks CA 91360

LIND, TERRIE LEE, program administrator, speech pathologist; b. Spokane, Wash., June 5, 1948; d. Clifford and Edna Mae (Allenbach) Presnell; m. Stephen George Lind, Aug. 29, 1970 (div. Mar. 1981); children: Erica Rachel, Reid Christopher. BA cum laude, Wash. State U., 1970, MA, 1971. Cert. tchr., Wash., Ariz.; cert. in Porch Index Communicative Ability. Specialist communication disorders U. Tex., Houston, 1971-73; clin. supr. The Battin Clinic, Houston, 1973-76; specialist communication disorders Spokane Guilds Sch., 1980-82; program coordinator, adminstr. Fresno (Calif.) Community Hosp., 1982-87; program adminstr. Advantage 65* sr. access program Health Dimensions, Inc., San Jose, Calif., 1987—; cons. Adolescent Chem. Dependency Unit, Fresno, 1984—. Mem. Am. Speech and Hearing Assn. (cert., Continuing Edn. award 1985-86), Wash. Speech and Hearing Assn. (co-chmn. state conv. program com. 1981-82), AAUW (officer 1976-82). Club: Hobie Sailing Fleet (Fresno). Avocations: snow and water skiing, flying, sailing, gourmet cooking, traveling. Home: 866-D Apricot Ave Campbell CA 95008 Office: Health Dimensions Inc Advantage 65*sm 2005 W Hamilton Ave Suite 300 San Jose CA 95128

LINDAHL, ROGER MATHEWS, business editor; b. Orange, N.J., July 22, 1955; s. Melvin August and Barbara (Davenport) L.; m. Po-Yee Au, June 12, 1979; one child, Patricia Si-Ling. BA, Franklin and Marshall Coll., 1977; MBA, U. Mich., 1982. Research assoc. Bus. Internat. Asia/Pacific, Hong Kong, 1982-83; editor Daily Comml. News, San Francisco, 1984-86; bus. editor Diagnostic Imaging mag., San Francisco, 1986—. Trustee, elder Old 1st Presbyn. Ch., San Francisco, 1986—. Mem. Phi Beta Kappa. Democrat. Office: Miller Freeman Pubs 500 Howard St San Francisco CA 94105

LINDBLAD, WILLIAM JOHN, utility executive; b. Oakland, Calif., May 22, 1929; s. William N. and Johnina B. (Moore) L.; B.S. in Elec. Engring., U. Calif., Berkeley, 1951; m. Rosella J. Allender, July 4, 1953; children—Catherine, Nancy, Thomas, Christopher, Margaret, Michael, Therese, Paul. Various engring. and mgmt. positions Pacific Gas & Electric Co., San Francisco, 1954-77; v.p. engring. and constrn. Portland (Oreg.) Gen. Electric Co., 1977-80, pres., dir., 1980—; bd. dirs. Portland Gen. Corp., 1986—. . Mem. adv. bd. Providence Med. Center, 1981—; bd. dirs. Portland State U. Found., 1981—; trustee St. Mary's Acad., Served 1982-83. with USN, 1951-54. Registered profl. engr., Calif. Mem. ASME, Am. Soc. Naval Engrs., IEEE. Republican. Roman Catholic. Club: Univ. Office: Portland Gen Electric Co 121 SW Salmon St Portland OR 97204

LINDE, HANS ARTHUR, justice Oregon Supreme Court; b. Berlin, Germany, Apr. 15, 1924; came to U.S., 1939, naturalized, 1943; s. Bruno C. and Luise (Rosenhain) L.; m. Helen Tucker, Aug. 13, 1945; children: Lisa, David Tucker. B.A., Reed Coll., 1947; J.D., U. Calif., Berkeley, 1950. Bar: Oreg. 1951. Law clk. U.S. Supreme Ct. Justice William O. Douglas, 1950-51; atty. Office of Legal Adviser, Dept. State, 1951-53; individual practice law Portland, Oreg., 1953-54; legis. asst. U.S. Sen. Richard L. Neuberger, 1955-58; asso. prof., prof. U. Oreg. Law Sch., 1959-76; justice Oreg. Supreme Ct., Salem, 1977—; Fulbright lectr. Freiburg U., 1967-68, Hamburg U., 1975-76; cons. U.S. ACDA, Dept. Def., 1962-76; mem. Adminstrv. Conf. U.S., 1978-82. Author: (with George Bunn) Legislative and Administrative Processes, 1976. Mem. Oreg. Constl. Revision Commn., 1961-62. Served with U.S. Army, 1943-46. Fellow Acad. Arts and Scis.; mem. Am. Law Inst. (council), Order of Coif, Phi Beta Kappa. Office: Oreg Supreme Ct Salem OR 97310

LINDEN, JAMES CARL, professor, consultant; b. Greeley, Colo., Sept. 12, 1942; s. Carl W. and Dorthy (Gray) L.; m. Susan Chapman, Dec. 26, 1968; children: Diana, Christina. BS in Chemistry, Colo. State U., 1964; PhD in Biochemistry, Iowa State U., 1969. Postdoctoral U. Muenchen, Fed. Republic of Germany, 1969-71, U. St. Louis, 1971-72; project leader G.W. Sugar Co., Loveland, Colo., 1972-76; chemist Adolf Coors Co., Golden, Colo., 1976-77; research scientist Colo. State U., Ft. Collins, 1977-85, assoc. prof., 1985—; cons. ETH (Biotechnology), Zurich, Switzerland, 1980. Contbr. articles to profl. jours. Recipient Alexander von Humboldt Stipendiate award, Bonn, Fed. Republic of Germany, 1969-71, Research Faculty award, Colo. State U., 1982, 85. Mem. Am. Assn. Plant Physiologists, Am. Chem. Soc., Am. Inst. Chem. Engrs., Am. Soc. Microbiology, Soc. Indsl. Microbiology. Avocations: hiking, skiing. Office: Colo State U 109 Glover Fort Collins CO 80523

LINDEN, ROBERT DAVID, psychiatrist, psychopharmacologist; b. Cleve., Apr. 29, 1952; s. Milton J. and Francine J. (Lox) L.; m. Catherine Hwang, May 7, 1983. BA, Yale U., 1974; MD, Case Western Res. Sch. Med., 1978. Diplomate Am. Bd. Psychiatry and Neurology. Resident in psychiatry U. Chgo., 1982; fellow in psychopharmacology Mailman Research Ctr., Belmont, Mass., 1982-84; instr. psychiatry Harvard U. Med. Sch., Boston, 1982-86; ward chief of specialized treatment and research unit U. Calif. Med. Ctr., Irvine, 1985—, adj. asst. prof., 1985—; attending psychiatrist McLean Hosp., Belmont, 1982-84; asst. med. dir. Pembroke (Mass.) Hosp., 1984-85; bd. dirs. Mass. Council on Compulsive Gambling, 1984—. Contbr. articles to jours. and chpts. to books. Mem. Am. Psychiat. Assn., Orange County Psychiat. Soc. Office: U Calif Irvine Med Ctr 101 City Dr Orange CA 92668

LINDGREN, DON RICHARD, civil engineer; b. Huntington Park, Calif., June 21, 1944; s. Sterling Carl and Antonia (Cunico) L.; m. Marjorie Lynn Bullers, June 13, 1970; 1 child, Erica. BSCE, Calif. State U., Long Beach, 1968. Registered profl. civil engr., Calif. Engr. Los Angeles County Flood Control Dist., Los Angeles, 1968-78, VA, Inc., Irvine, Calif., 1978-81; prin., founding ptnr. Fuscoe, Williams, Lindgren and Short, Santa Ana, Calif., 1981—. Mem. ASCE, Calif. Council Civil Engrs. and Land Surveyors, Soc. Am. Mil. Engrs., Am. Pub. Works Assn. Avocations: snow skiing, camping, hiking.

LINDGREN, FRANK TYCKO, research biophysicist, lipoprotein methodologist; b. San Francisco, Apr. 14, 1924; s. Ty and Grace Orissa (Lund) L.; m. Helen Darrow, Aug. 8, 1953. BA in Physics, U. Calif., Berkeley, 1947, PhD in Biophysics, 1955. Asst. research biophysicist Donner Lab., U. Calif., Berkeley, 1955-56, research assoc., 1956-67, research biophysicist, 1967-78, sr. staff biophysicist, 1978—; lipids cons. NIH, 1972-80, reviewer Jour. Lipid Research, 1960—, reviewer grants, 1970—. Assoc. editor Lipids, 1966-76; contbr. numerous articles to profl. jours. V.p. and treas. Berkeley Dem. Club, 1960-76. Served to 1st lt. U.S. Army, 1943-47. Fellow Council on Arteriosclerosis of Am. Heart Assn.; mem. AAAS, Am. Oil Chemist Soc., AAAS, Sigma Xi, Phi Beta Kappa. Democrat. Club: U. Calif. Faculty (Berkeley). Avocations: hiking, classical piano playing. Home: 2707 Rose St Berkeley CA 94708 Office: U Calif 315 Donner Lab Berkeley CA 94720

LINDH, PATRICIA SULLIVAN, banker, former government official; b. Toledo, Oct. 2, 1928; d. Lawrence Walsh and Lillian Winifred (Devlin) Sullivan; m. H. Robert Lindh, Jr., Nov. 12, 1955; children: Sheila, Deborah, Robert. B.A., Trinity Coll., Washington, 1950, LL.D., 1975; LL.D., Walsh Coll., Canton, Ohio, 1975, U. Jacksonville, 1975. Adoption case worker Cath. Charities, Chgo., 1954-55; editor Singapore Am. Newspaper, 1957-62; spl. asst. to counsellor to Pres. 1974, spl. asst. to Pres., 1975-76; dep. asst. sec. state for ednl. and cultural affairs Dept. State, 1976-77; v.p., dir. corp. communications Bank Am., Los Angeles, 1978-84, World Banking P.R. Bank Am., San Francisco, 1985—. Trustee La. Arts and Sci. Center, 1970-73, Calif. Hosp. Med. Ctr.; bd. dirs. Jr. League of Baton Rouge, 1969, Children's Bur. Los Angeles, 1979, Rep. state vice chairwoman La., 1970-74, Rep. nat. committeewoman, La., 1974; mem. adv. panel Assn. Jr. Leagues, 1979—; mem. adv. bd. Jr. League Los Angeles, 1980—; bd. visitors Southwestern U. Sch. Law. Mem. Nat. Assn. Women Bus. Owners, Central City Assn. Roman Catholic. Home: 1916 Jackson St San Francisco CA 94109

LINDLEY, FRANCIS HAYNES, lawyer; b. Los Angeles, May 25, 1899; s. Walter and Florence (Haynes) L.; student Williams Coll., 1916-17; A.B., Harvard U., 1922; student U. So. Calif. Law Sch., 1923-26; LL.D., Claremont Grad. Sch.; m. Grace N. McCanne, Sept. 6, 1930; children—Francis Haynes, Walter. Admitted to Calif. bar, 1926, since practiced in Los Angeles; partner Chapman, Frazer, Lindley & Young, 1953-64; former dir. Safeco Co., Great Basins Petroleum Co., O. T. Johnson Corp., Compania Contratists de Costa Rica, Bolsa Corps.; dep. city atty. Los Angeles, 1927-36, asst. city atty., 1936-42, 45-46. Pres., Town Hall, 1952; dir. Christmas Seal Fund, 1950-52; former bd. dirs. Los Angeles Children's Bur.; mem. U.S. Regional Loyalty Bd., 1949-53; mem. Los Angeles Com. Fgn. Relations, Los Angeles Bd. Power and Water Commrs., 1965-67; v.p., trustee Hosp. Good Samaritan Med. Center, 1968-83, hon. trustee, 1983—; pres. Haynes Found., 1937-77, chmn. bd. trustees, 1977—; past pres. Friends Claremont Colls.; hon. trustee Claremont Univ. Center, Whittier Coll., Honnold Library Soc. of Clarement Colls.; bd. dirs., Hosp. Council So. Calif., 1970-76, English Speaking Union Los Angeles br., 1974-80. Mem. Am. Bar Assn. (chmn. sect. municipal law 1951-52), Los Angeles Bar Assn., Phi Delta Phi. Republican. Clubs: California, Lincoln, Men's Garden (Los Angeles); Harvard (So. Calif.). Home: 639 S June St Los Angeles CA 90005

LINDMAN, ELISABETH JACOBSEN (LISSE J WILSON), interior designer, consultant; b. Nyborg, Denmark, June 18, 1911; came to U.S., 1918, naturalized, 1932; d. Hans Christian and Ellen Maria Elisabeth La Cour (Siegumfeldt) Jacobsen; m. Guy Childers Wilson, June 18, 1936 (dec.); children—Richard Guy, Ellen Celia Wilson Ekedal; m. 2d, Bertram Herman Lindman, Aug. 10, 1974. B.A., U. Wash., 1934; student Art Ctr. Sch., Los Angeles, 1934; postgrad. U. Calif.-Riverside, 1970. Interior designer Robinson's, Los Angeles, 1934, Hildebrandt Interiors, Hollywood, Calif., 1935; sec., treas. Wilson Equipment Co., Redlands and Colton, Calif., 1954-66; interior designer Gibboney Interiors, Redlands, 1969, Robinson's, Santa Barbara, 1970; interior designer and originator interior design dept. Haywards, Santa Barbara, Calif., 1970; mem. adv. com. Santa Barbara City Coll.; career adviser U. Calif.-Santa Barbara. Bd. dirs. Trust for Hist. Preservation, Santa Barbara; chmn. scholarship com. Am. Scandinavian Found., Santa Barbara. Mem. Am. Soc. Interior Designers. Club: Ret. Officers Santa Barbara. Office: Haywards 1025 Santa Barbara St Santa Barbara CA 93101

LINDNER, DAVID GORDON, mechanical contractor; b. Phoenix, July 14, 1944; s. John Barton and Rosada Mary (Fritch) L.; m. Patricia Angeline Shannon, Feb. 14, 1967; children: Eric David, Jonas Scott. Student, Phoenix Coll.; diploma, Phoenix Tech. Journeyman Phoenix, 1968-75; pres., chief exec. officer Dave's Refrigeration and Heating, Inc., Phoenix, 1975—. Active Nat. Rep. Congress Com., 1982—; sound and mechanical cons. Strumming Amigos, 1984—. Mem. Electric. League Ariz. (bd. dirs. 1983—, Leadership award 1986), Blue Energy Inst. Ariz. (pres. 1983—), Gas Safety Fund for Blue Energy (bd. trustees 1983—), Ariz. Heat Pump Council, Aero Mech. Flying Club, Phoenix Metro C. of C. Episcopalian. Avocations: builder, developer, investor, aircraft owner and pilot, scuba diving. Office: Dave's Refrigeration & Heating Inc 7118 N 7th St Phoenix AZ 85020

LINDSAY, CHARMAINE CAROL, educator; b. Rock Springs, Wyo., Dec. 13, 1929; d. Oscar Wayne and Irene Ilah (Wakkila) Matson; m. Roy L. Lindsay, Aug. 21, 1949; children—Gregory M., Alison C., Wade W., Lisa A. Student, Linfield Coll., 1947-50; B.A., Portland State Coll., 1964; M.S.T., Portland State U., 1973. Lang. arts tchr., dept. chmn., tchr. evaluator Tigard (Oreg.) Sr. High Sch., 1968—, dept. chmn., tchr. evaluator, 1972—, tchr. lang. arts, 1968—. Chmn., Lloyd Johnson Meml. Scholarship Com., 1982—; alumni rep. Linfield Coll. Bd. Trustees, 1973-79. Mem. NEA, Assn. Supervision and Curriculum Devel., Nat. Council Tchrs. English, Oreg. Council Tchrs. English, Oreg. Edn. Assn., Tigard Edn. Assn., Phi Delta Kappa, Delta Kappa Gamma. Democrat. Methodist. Office: Tigard Sr High Sch 9000 SW Durham Rd Tigard OR 97224

LINDSAY, DALE RICHARD, research administrator; b. Bunker Hill, Kans., Aug. 9, 1913; s. Charles Edwin and Iva (Missimer) L.; m. Sybil Anne McCoy, June 6, 1937; children—Martha Lou Lindsay Cover, Judith Anne Lindsay Clapp, Patricia Dale. A.B., U. Kans., 1937, M.A., 1938, Ph.D., Iowa State Coll., 1943. Entomologist Dept. Agr., summers 1937-39; teaching fellow, instr., research asso. Iowa State Coll., 1938-43; commd. officer USPHS, 1943—, scientist dir., 1955; assigned malaria control in war areas 1943-45; entomologist charge operations Communicable Disease Center Activies, Pharr, Tex., 1945-48; chief Thomasville (Ga.) field sta. 1948-53; chief program evaluation sect., div. research grants NIH, 1953-55, asst. chief div., 1955-60, chief div., 1960-63; dep. to gen. dir. Mass. Gen. Hosp., Boston, 1963-65; spl. asst. to chancellor health scis. U. Calif. at Davis, 1965-67, asst. chancellor research and health scis., 1968-69; asso. commr. sci. FDA, 1969-71; asso. dir. med. and allied health edn. Duke U., 1971-75; asst. dir. for sci. coordination Nat. Center for Toxicol. Research, Jefferson, Ark., 1975-76; adj. prof. medicine U. Ark. Med. Sch., 1975-76; asso. dept. family and community medicine U. Ariz., 1977-82; Agrl. bd. Nat. Acad. Sci.-NRC, 1970-73; mem. exec. com., public trustee Nutrition Found., 1972-76, Environ. and Agrl. Found., 1974-79; chmn. sci. adv. bd. Nat. Center for Toxicol. Research, 1972-74. Fellow AAAS, Am. Public Health Assn.; mem. Entomol. Soc. Am. (gov. bd. 1958-62), Commd. Officer Assn. USPHS (treas. nat. exec. com. 1959-61) , Sigma Xi, Phi Kappa Phi, Gamma Sigma Delta.

LINDSAY, DONALD RANSOM, petroleum geologist; b. Oakland, Calif., Feb. 7, 1925; s. Frank Stanley and Louise Jeanette (Swartout) L.; m. Paula Helen Wilbur, June 12, 1947; children—Joan Lindsay Letlow, Barbara, Robert. B.S., Stanford U., 1948, M.A., UCLA, 1952. Registered profl. geologist, Calif. Staff geol. engr. Shell Oil Co., Calif., Wyo., N.Mex., Tex., 1951-78; geologist Occidental Geothermal, Inc., Bakersfield, Calif., 1978-84; sr. staff prodn. geologist Occidental Internat. Exploration and Prodn. Co., 1984—; dir. Geothermal Resources Council, Davis, Calif., 1977-78. Author: (with Weimer and Howard) Sandstone Depositional Environments, 1982; contbr. geothermal energy articles to profl. jours. Served to ensign USNR, 1943-46; Mem. Am. Assn. Petroleum Geologists, Count Dracula Soc. (v.p. 1973—), Acad. Sci. Fiction, Fantasy and Horror Films. Republican. Home: 501 Carr St Bakersfield CA 93309 Office: Occidental Geothermal Inc 5000 Stockdale Hwy Bakersfield CA 93309

LINDSAY, J. ARTHUR, industrial relations executive; b. Okemah, Okla., Mar. 19, 1930; s. Frank E. and Margaret E. (Barnes) L.; m. Katherine Sherman, Dec. 16, 1949 (div. 1960); children—Karen K., Brian G.; m. 2d, Willa B. Flowers, July 28, 1962; 1 son, Darrin C. B.B.A., U. Ga., 1955; M.B.A., San Francisco State U., 1968. Personnel mgr. Firemans Fund Ins. Co., Oakland, Calif., 1960-68, Argonaut Ins. Co., San Francisco, 1970-73; v.p. indsl. relations Soule' Steel Co., San Francisco, 1974-78; pres. Federated Employers, San Francisco, 1979—, Lindsay Oil Properties-Art Realty & Investments, Alameda, Calif., 1968—; gen. ptnr. Arjay Well Servicing Co., Cherryville, Kans., 1980—. Served to sgt. U.S. Army, 1948-52. Mem. Am. Soc. for Personnel Adminstrn., Nat. Soc. Pub. Accts., Nat. Assn. Real Estate Brokers, Delta Mu Delta. Club: San Francisco Commonwealth. Writer, editor, pub. newsletters and reference materials in field. Home: 1166 Otis Dr Alameda CA 94501 Office: Federated Employers 582 Market St Suite 412 San Francisco CA 94104

LINDSAY, ROBERT FORREST, geologist; b. Ogden, Utah, Nov. 9, 1948; s. Wallace Robert and Martha Lucille (Ramsay) L.; m. Deborah Marie Mischel, May 8, 1973; children—Jared, Julie, Janet, Jacob. B.S., Weber State Coll., Ogden, 1974; M.S., Brigham Young U., Provo, Utah, 1976. Geologist, supr. enhanced oil recovery Gulf Oil Exploration and Prodn. Co., Oklahoma City, 1976-83, sr. project geologist, Houston, 1983-85; carbonate petrographer Chevron U.S.A., Denver, 1985—; editor Oklahoma City Geol. Soc., 1981-83. Contbg. author books: 4th International Williston Basin Symposium, 1982; American Association Petroleum Geologists Memoir-Williston Basin, 1986; Scanning Electron Microscopy in Geology, 1986; Carbonate Petroleum Reservoirs, 1985. Mem. Geol. Soc. Am., Am. Assn. Petroleum Geologists, Soc. Econ. Paleontologists and Mineralogists. Home: 5316 S Olathe Circle Aurora CO 80015 Office: Chevron USA PO Box 599 Denver CO 80201

LINDSAY, SCOTT BRIAN, chemist; b. Seattle, Oct. 30, 1958; s. Walter Kay and LaVerne (Cowell) L.; m. Julie Ann Fletcher, Aug. 14, 1982; 1 child, Brooke. BA in Chemistry, Cen. Wash. U., Ellensburg, 1982. Chemist Olympic Sci., Seattle, 1983-84, Skagit Mining, Ltd., Sedro Woolley, Wash., 1984-85; insp. N.W. Indsl. Maintenance (contracted to Texaco), Anacortes, Wash., 1985-86; chemist, stock mgr. Northwestern (contracted to Texaco), Anacortes, 1986—. Mem. Assn. Ofcl. Analytical Chemists (assoc.). Lutheran.

LINDSAY, VICTOR ERNEST JOHN, aerospace engineer; b. San Francisco, Apr. 1, 1944; s. Victor Frank and Alicia Maryann (Martorella) L.; m. Barbara Marie Cressey, Feb. 9, 1969; children: Alicia Marie, Rena Kay. BS in Engring., Santa Clara U., 1966. Structural engr. Boeing Aerospace, Seattle, 1966-70, tech. lead, 1977—; pres. V.E. Lindsay Co. Inc., Soquel, Calif., 1970-75; regional sales engr. Union Metal Mfg., Fremont, Calif., 1975-77; ptnr. Lindsay & Assocs. polit. cons., Bellevue, Wash., 1982—. Rep. precinct committeeman, Bellevue, 1977—. Mem. Soc. Advancement Materials and Process Engring., AIAA. Republican. Episcopalian. Club: Corvair Soc. (Tukwila, Wash.). Avocations: vegetable gardens, auto restoration.

LINDSAY, WILLARD LYMAN, research soil science educator; b. Dingle, Idaho, Apr. 7, 1926; s. William Henry and Phoebe May (Humpherys) L.; m. Lorna Lance, Nov. 19, 1951; children: Diane, Janice, Cheryl, Calvin Willard. BS, Utah State U., 1952, MS, 1953; PhD, Cornell U., 1956. Grad. research asst. Utah State U., Logan, 1952-53; grad. research and teaching asst. Cornell U., Ithaca, N.Y., 1953-56; research soil chemist TVA, Muscle Shoals, Ala., 1956-60; from asst. prof. to prof. soil scientist Colo. State U., Ft. Collins, 1960-70, Centennial prof. agronomy, 1970—; cons. in field, 1966—. Author: Chemical Equilibria in Soils, 1979; contbr. articles to profl. jours.; author scientific papers. Served with USN, 1945-46. Fellow Geigy Travel, Scotland, 1966, Geigy Travel, Australia, 1968; recipient Andrew G. Clark award Colo. State U., 1970, Shepardson Outstanding Teaching award, 1983, Burlington Northern Faculty Achievement award 1985; nominee USDA Disting. Service award 1986. Fellow Am. Soc. Agronomy, Soil Sci. Soc. Am. (co-author: Micronutrients in Agriculture, 1972); mem. Internat. Soil Sci. Soc., Western Soil Sci. Soc., Soc. Environ. Geochem. and Health, Sigma Xi, Phi Kappa Phi, Gamma Sigma Delta, Delta Phi Kappa. Mormon. Home: 208 Tulane Dr Fort Collins CO 80525 Office: Colo State U Dept Agronomy Fort Collins CO 80523

LINDSEY, DAVID PARK, architectural firm executive; b. Sunnyside, Wash., July 26, 1949; s. Marvin L. and Louise (Park) L.; m. Susan Kearney, Sept. 7, 1974; children: Alexander, Hannah. BArch, U. Wash., 1972, MBA, 1979. Registered architect, Wash., Oreg., Colo., Idaho, Calif., Utah, N.Mex., Ariz., Hawaii, Md., Tex., Va., Washington. Mem. staff Callison Assocs., Seattle, 1973-75; dir. design Callison, Erickson, Hobble, Seattle, 1975-76; exec. v.p., treas. The Callison Partnership, Seattle, 1976—. mem. Bainbridge Island Planning Adv. Commn. Mem. AIA, Urban Land Inst., Soc. for Mktg. Profl. Services, Profl. Services Mgmt. Assn. Clubs: Wash. Athletic,

Harbor (Seattle). Office: The Callison Partnership Ltd 1423 Third Ave Suite 300 Seattle WA 98101

LINDSEY, JACK B., business executive; b. Taft, Calif., Nov. 20, 1925; student Fresno State Coll., 1943-44; B.Applied Sci. in Elec. Engring., U. Calif., at Berkeley, 1946; M.B.A., Stanford U., 1950; m. Jean Catherine O'Brien, Jan. 24, 1948 (dec. Mar. 1983); children—Daniel Lee, David Allan; m. Terryl Rae Stewart Lupien, May, 1984. Mktg. mgr. Carnation Co., Los Angeles, 1950-59; asst. to pres. Microdot, Inc., electronics, South Pasadena, Calif., 1959-61; pres. Lindsey-Westwood Assos., mgmt. cons., Los Angeles, 1961-64; v.p. mktg. Early Calif. Foods, Inc., Los Angeles, 1964-69, pres., 1971-74; v.p. Early Calif. Industries, Inc., Los Angeles, 1964-74; dir., 1964-75; pres., pub. Clarke Pub. Co., Portland, 1969-71; pres., chief exec. officer Sun Harbor Industries, San Diego, 1974-77, Point Adams Packing Co. (Oreg.), 1974-75, Sun Harbor-Caribe, Inc., P.R., 1974-77; chmn. bd., chief exec. officer Sun Belt Mgmt. Services, Inc., mgmt. cons., 1977—; chmn. Sun Belt Energy Corp.; founder, chief fin. officer Alaska Pacific Refining, Inc., 1986—, also bd. dirs.; dir. Alaska Pacific Refining, Inc., New Generation Foods, Inc. Legis. sec. to gov. of Calif., 1966-67; chmn. Favorite Son Com., 1968; alt. del. Republican Nat. Conv., 1968; candidate for Congress, 1969; mem. President's Round Table. Served to lt. (j.g.) USNR, 1943-47. San Francisco Advt. Club grantee, 1948. Mem. IEEE, Order of Golden Bear, Pres.'s Assn., Stanford Alumni Assn., Phi Gamma Delta. Christian Scientist. Club: San Diego Yacht. Home: 1594 Hacienda Dr El Cajon CA 92020

LINDSEY, JOHN HALL, JR., software company executive; b. Malvern, Ark., July 29, 1938; s. John Hall and Jeannette Francis (Stuart) L.; m. Renetta Louise Harms, July 14, 1962; children: Sabra, Lemecia, Lance. Student, Ark. Poly. U., 1956-58, Okla. State U., 1958-60; BS in Bus., U. Utah, 1964; MBA, U. So. Calif., 1968. Data base mgr. NCR corp., Rancho Bernardo, Calif., 1966-75; data base adminstr. Kal Kan Foods, Vernon, Calif., 1975-77; data base supr. Kaiser Steel, Fontana, Calif., 1977-79; mgr. data base and tech. support Western Gear, Lynwood, Calif., 1979-84; mgr., sr. cons. data base Citicorp/TTI, Santa Monica, Calif., 1984-86; prin. Lindsey & Assocs., Playa del Rey, Calif., 1986—; ptnr. Lindsey/Milligan Cos., Houston; mem. computer adv. com. Ontario/Montclaire Schs., Calif., 1980-82; mem. industry advisor Cullinet Corp., Westwood, Mass., 1986—; bd. dirs. IDMS User Assn., Westminster, chmn. large users adv. com., 1985—; bd. dirs. S.W. User Assn., Los Angeles; guest lectr. U. So. Calif., 1975-76. Author: IDMS DB Design Review, 1982. Elder local Presbyn. Ch., 1980-82; vol. Culver City (Calif.) YMCA, 1986, Santa Monica (Calif.) Real Soccer Club, 1985-86; pres. Mt. Baldy Swim Team, Upland, Calif., 1975-80; bd. dirs. Ontario Community Credit Union, 1979-80. Served with USNG, 1956-64. Mem. IDMS User Assn., S.W. Area IDMS User Assn. (chmn. 1982—), Assn. System Mgmt. (v.p. 1966-68), Soc. for Mgmt. Info. (co-founder 1979). Avocations: children's groups, personal computers, woodworking, writing, swimming. Home and Office: 7609 W 85th St Playa del Rey CA 90293

LINDSEY, WILLIAM FUSSELL, newspaper association executive; b. Rocky Mount, N.C., Mar. 22, 1923; s. Robert Penn and Wallolah (Fussell) L.; B.A. Westminster Coll., 1948; B.S., U. Colo., 1950; m. Gwen R. Caverly, Dec. 28, 1948; children—Charles Penn, Rebecca Ruth. Jr. acct. Redecker, Stanley & Alhberg, Denver, 1950-52; with Colo. Press Service, Denver, 1952-64; sec.-mgr. Colo. Press Assn., Denver, 1964—; Served with USAAF, World War II. Decorated D.F.C., Air medal with six oak leaf clusters; recipient Big Hat award U. Colo. Journalism Sch., 1982. Mem. Newspaper Assn. Mgrs. (pres. 1978), Nat. Newspaper Assn. (dir. 1978), Nat. Editorial Assn., Soc. Profl. Journalists, Advt. Club Denver, Colo. C. of C., Denver Press Club, Delta Tau Delta. Home: 405 Baseline at Gregory Canyon Boulder CO 80302 Office: Colo Press Assn Press Bldg 1336 Glenarm Pl Denver CO 80204

LINDSKOG, MARJORIE OTILDA, educator; b. Rochester, Minn., Oct. 13, 1937; d. Miles Emery and Otilda Elvina (Hagre) L. B.A., Colo. Coll., 1959, M.A. in Teaching, 1972. Field advisor/camp dir. Columbine Girl Scout Council, Pueblo, Colo., 1959-65; staff mem. Wyo. Girl Scout Camp, Casper, 1966; camp dir. Wyo. Girl Scout Camp, 1967; asst. camp dir. Pacific Peaks Girl Scouts, Olympia, Wash., 1968; camp dir. Pacific Peaks Girl Scouts, 1969; tchr. Dist. 60, Pueblo, Colo., 1966—; campcraft instr. Am. Camping Assn., 1969—, dir. instrs., 1975—, camp standards visitor, 1976—; instr. Jr. Great Books Program, 1981—; mem. credit com. Pueblo Tchr.'s Credit Union. Contbr. articles to profl. jours. Bd. dirs. Columbine Girl Scout Council, 1983-85, Dist. #60 Blood Bank, 1985—; area co-chmn. Channel 8 Pub. TV Auction, Pueblo, 1983—; mem. Pueblo Nature Ctr., 1981—. Recipient Thanks Badge award Girl Scouts of U.S. Mem. Colo. Archeol. Soc. (Pueblo chpt.), Bus. and Profl. Women, Assn. for Supervision and Curriculum Devel., Internat. Platform Assn., Intertel, Mensa, Alpha Phi, Phi Delta Kappa (v.p.). Lutheran. Club: Pueblo Country. Lodge: Sons of Norway. Home: 2810 7th Ave Pueblo CO 81003 Office: Sunset Park Sch 110 University Circle Pueblo CO 81005

LINDSTROM, DUAINE GERALD, engineering educator; b. Raymond, Wash., Jan. 18, 1937; s. Gunar Wilhelm Lindstrom and Margaret May (Bishop) Zimmerman; m. Vieno Rae Ojala, May 30, 1967. BS ChemE, U. Wash., 1959; PhD in Nuclear Engring., U. Wash, 1968; MS in Nuclear Engring., U. Mich., 1960. Registered profl. engr., Calif. Physics specialist Aerojet-Gen. Corp., Sacramento, 1968-71; lectr. Imperial Coll., London, 1971-75; assoc. prof. U. Okla., Norman, 1975-82; program coordinator for nuclear engring. and chem. engring. Tri-Cities Univ. Ctr., Richland, Wash., 1982—; cons. Kerr-McGee Corp., Oklahoma City, 1980, Battelle/Pacific N.W. Labs., Seattle, 1983-85. Recipient Faculty Profl. Devel. grant NSF, 1979. Mem. Am. Nuclear Soc., Brit. Nuclear Energy Soc., Am. Inst. Chem. Engrs., Health Physics Soc., Sigma Xi, Tau Beta Pi. Office: Tri Cities Univ Ctr 100 Sprout Rd Richland WA 99352

LINDZEY, GARDNER, educator, psychologist; b. Wilmington, Del., Nov. 27, 1920; s. James and Marguerite (Shotwell) L.; m. Andrea Lewis, Nov. 28, 1944; children—Jeffrey, Leslie, Gardner, David, Jonathan. A.B., Pa. State U., 1943, M.S., 1945; Ph.D., Harvard U., 1949. Research analyst OSRD, 1944-45; instr. psychology Pa. State U., 1945-46; teaching fellow Harvard U., 1946-47, research fellow, 1947-49, research assoc., asst. prof., 1949-53, lectr., chmn. psychol. clinic staff, 1953-56, prof., chmn. dept., 1972-73; prof. psychology Syracuse U., 1956-57, U. Minn., 1957-64; prof. psychology U. Tex., 1964-72, chmn., 1964-68, v.p. acad. affairs, 1968-70, v.p. ad interim, 1971, v.p., dean Grad. Studies, prof. psychology, 1973-75; dir. Ctr. for Advanced Study in Behavioral Scis., Stanford, Calif., 1975—; mem. psychopharmacology study sect. NIMH, 1958-62, mem. program-project com., 1963-67, mem. adv. com. on extramural research, 1968-71; mem. com. faculty research fellowships Social Sci. Research Council, 1960-63, bd. dirs., 1962-76, mem. com. problems and policy, 1963-70, 72-76, chmn., 1965-70, mem. exec. com., 1970-75, chmn., 1971-75, mem. com. genetics and behavior, 1961-67, chmn., 1961-65; mem. com. biol. bases social behavior, 1967—; mem. com. work and personality in middle years, 1972-77; mem. sociology and social psychology panel NSF, 1965-68, mem. spl. commn. social scis., 1968-69, mem. adv. com. research, 1974—, mem. Waterman award com., 1976—; mem. exec. com., assembly behavioral and social sci. Nat. Acad. Sci.-NRC, 1970—, mem. com. life sci. and pub. policy, 1968-74, mem. panel nat. needs for biomed. and behavioral research personnel, 1974—, mem. com. social sci. in NSF, 1975—, mem. Inst. Medicine, 1975—; mem. com. on drug abuse Office Sci. and Tech., 1962-63; mem. Presdl. Com. Nat. Medal Sci., 1966-69; bd. dirs. Found.'s Fund Research in Psychiatry, 1967-70; bd. dirs. Am. Psychol. Found., 1968-76, v.p., 1971-73, pres., 1974-76. Author: (with Hall) Theories of Personality, 1957, 70, 78; (with Allport and Vernon) Study of Values, 1951, 60; Projective Techniques and Cross-Cultural Research, 1961; (with J.C. Loehlin and J.N. Spuhler) Race Differences in Intelligence, 1975; (with C.S. Hall and R.F. Thompson) Psychology, 1975; also articles; editor: Handbook of Social Psychology, Vols. 1 and 2, 1954, Vols. 1-5, 1969, Assessment of Human Motives, 1958, Contemporary Psychology, 1967-73, History of Psychology in Autobiography, Vol. 6, 1974; assoc. editor Psychol. Abstracts, 1960-62, Ency. Social Scis., 1962-67; co-editor Century Psychology Series, 1960-74, Theories of Personality: Primary Sources and Research, 1965, History of Psychology in Autobiography, Vol. V, 1968, Behavioral Genetics: Methods and Research, 1969, Contributions to Behavior-Genetic Analysis, 1970. Fellow Ctr. Advanced Study Behavioral Scis., Stanford, 1955-56, 63-64, 71-72, Inst. Medicine, 1975—. Fellow Am. Psychol. Assn. (bd. dirs. 1962-68, 70-74, mem. publs. bd., 1956-59, 70-73, chmn. 1958-59, mem. council of reps. 1959-67, 68-74, pres. div. social and personality psychology 1963-64, mem. policy and planning 1975, 78, pres. assn. 1966-67, mem. council of editors 1968-73, chmn. com. sci. award 1968-69, pres. div. gen. psychology 1970-71), Am. Acad. Arts and Scis., Am. Philos. Soc., AAAS, Am. Sociol. Assn.; mem. Am. Eugenics Soc. (bd. dirs. 1962-70), Soc. Social Biology (bd. dirs. 1972—, pres. 1978—), Am. Psychol. Assn. (dir. ins. trust 1973—), Univs. Research Assn. (bd. dirs. 1973-75). Club: Cosmos. Home: 890 Robb Rd Palo Alto CA 94306

LINFORD, LAURANCE DEE, cultural organization administrator; b. Cheyenne, Wyo., Mar. 2, 1951; s. Dee Verl and Helen Grace (Bagley) L.; m. Karen Page Stephens, Nov. 23, 1971; children: Justin D., Micah Robert. BA, U. N.Mex., 1973; MA, U. Ariz., 1978. Archaeologist Sch. Am. Research, Santa Fe, 1967-75, Ariz. State Mus., Tucson, 1975-77, Nat. Park Service, Tucson, 1977-78, Navajo Nation, Window Rock, Ariz., 1978-82; exec. dir. Inter-Tribal Indian Ceremonial Assn., Gallup, N.Mex., 1982—; bd. dirs. St. Michaels (Ariz.) Hist. Mus., 1979-86. Author, editor; The Pinon Project, 1982. Pres. Indian Country Tourism Council, 1982-86; mem. tourism com. Gallup McKinnley County Chamber, 1985-86. Democrat. Avocations: cabinetry, woodwork, research of Am. frontier. Office: Inter-Tribal Indian Ceremonal Assn PO Box 1 Church Rock NM 87311

LINGREN, WESLEY EARL, chemistry educator; b. Pasadena, Calif., Aug. 27, 1930; s. Lawrence Earl and Dorothy (Green) L.; m. Merrilyn Elizabeth Summer, Feb. 24, 1961; children: Eric, Leslie. BS, Seattle Pacific Coll., 1952; MS, U. Wash., 1954, PhD, 1962. Asst. prof. chemistry Pasadena Coll., 1956-58; asst. prof. Seattle Pacific U., 1962-65, assoc. prof., 1965-67, prof., 1968—; NSF fellow Yale U., New Haven, Conn., 1967-68. Author: Inorganic Nomenclature, 1980, Essentials of Chemistry, 1986; contbr. articles to profl. jours. Served to sgt. M.C., U.S. Army, 1954-56. Fellow Am. Assn. Engring. Edn., Solar Energy Research, Golden, Colo., 1984. Mem. Am. Chem. Soc., Nat. Sci. Tchrs. Assn., U.S. Tennis Assn., Sigma Xi. Presbyterian. Avocation: tennis. Office: Seattle Pacific U Seattle WA 98119

LINN, BRIAN JAMES, lawyer; b. Seattle, July 8, 1947; s. Bruce Hugh and Jeanne De V. (Weidman) L.; m. Renee Diane Mousley; children—Kelly, Kareem, Kari. B.A. in Econs., U. Wash., 1972; J.D., Gonzaga Sch. Law, 1975. Bar: Wash. 1975. Mng. atty. Legal Services for Northwestern Pa., Franklin, 1975-76; staff atty. The Nat. Ctr. for Law and the Handicapped, U. Notre Dame Law Sch., South Bend, Ind., 1976-78; pvt. practice, Seattle, 1978—; lectr. Seattle U., 1980-85. Chmn. civil and legal rights subcom. Gov.'s Com. on Employment of the Handicapped; mem. Wash. State Devel. Disabilities Planning Council, 1980-83; trustee Community Service Ctr. for the Deaf and Hard of Hearing, Seattle, 1982-84; chmn. legal rights task force Epilepsy Found. Am., 1979-81. Editor Gonzaga Law Rev., 1973-75. Served with U.S. Army, 1967-69; Vietnam. Mem. Wash. State Bar Assn., Washington State Trial Lawyers Assn., Omicron Delta Epsilon. Democrat. Methodist. Hon. editor DePaul Law Rev., 1978; contbr. articles to profl. jours. Home: 21211 21st Ave S Seattle WA 98188 Office: 245 SW 152d St Seattle WA 98166

LINN, GEORGE BYRON, academic administrator, writer; b. Hillmont, Wyo., Aug. 19, 1913; s. George Toney and Laura Adelaide (Osborn) L.; m. Ruby Fonda, Aug. 6, 1938 (dec. Mar. 1973); 1 child, Kent Landen; m. Reta Nayoma Faler, June 28, 1977. BA, U. Wyo., 1936, MA, 1941; postgrad., U. Wash., 1955; EdD, U. So. Calif., 1965. Speech instr. U. Wyo., Laramie, 1937-38; tchr. various schs., Wyo., 1938-42; supt. various schs., Oreg. and Ak., 1942-1954; instr. U. Ariz., Tucson, 1946-47; speech clinician Santa Paula (Calif.) Sch. Dist., 1955-59; adminstr. Cerebral Palsy Sch., Santa Paula (Calif.) Sch. Dist., 1960-62; coordinator of spl. edn. South Bay Area Sch. Dists., Redondo Beach, Calif., 1962-66; dir. of spl. edn. Ventura County (Calif.) Supt. of Schs. Office, 1966-78; lectr. Calif. Luth. Coll., Thousand Oaks, 1975; ret. 1978. Author: Broadax Artists, 1984; contbr. articles to profl. jours. Recipient cert. of appreciation Ventura County Assn. for the Retarded, 1967, hon. membership Ventura County Council for Neurological Handicapped Children, 1968, award for service to exceptional Children Ventura County Council For Exceptional Children, 1977, Outstanding Service award Calif. State Dept. of Edn., 1978. Mem. NEA, Calif. Tchrs. Assn., AAAS, Am. Speech-Lang.-Hearing Assn., Calif. Speech and Hearing Assn., Delta Sigma Rho, Delta Epsilon. Democrat. Presbyterian. Lodges: Kiwanis (pres. East Ventura, Calif. Club 1974-75; lt. gov. 1977-78), Masons. Home: 1229 Woodland Dr Santa Paula CA 93060

LINN, STUART MICHAEL, biochemist, educator; b. Chgo., Dec. 16, 1940; s. Maurice S. and Pauline L.; m. Priscilla K. Cooper; children: Matthew S., Allison D., Meagan S. B.S. with honors in Chemistry, Calif. Inst. Tech., 1962; Ph.D. in Biochemistry, Stanford U., 1967. Asst. prof. biochemistry U. Calif., Berkeley, 1968-72; asso. prof. U. Calif., 1972-75, prof., 1975—. Mem. editorial bd.: Nucleic Acids Research, 1974—, Molecular and Cellular Biology, 1987—; mem. editorial bd.: Jour. Biol. Chemistry, 1975-80; contbr. articles to profl. jours., chpts. to books. Helen Hay Whitney fellow, 1966-68; John Simon Guggenheim fellow, 1974-75. Mem. Am. Soc. Biol. Chemists, Am. Soc. Microbiologists, AAAS. Office: Dept Biochemistry Univ Calif Berkeley CA 94720

LINNELL, ROBERT HARTLEY, institute administrator; b. Kalkaska, Mich., Aug. 15, 1922; s. Earl Dean and Constance (Hartley) L.; m. Myrle Elizabeth Talbot, June 17, 1950; children: Charlene LeGro, Lloyd Robert, Randa Ruth, Dean Maxfield. B.S., U. N.H., 1944, M.S., 1948; Ph.D., U. Rochester, 1950. Asst. instr. U. N.H., 1942-44, instr., 1947; asst. prof. chemistry Am. U., Beirut, 1950-52; assoc. prof., chmn. chemistry dept. Am. U., 1952-55; v.p. Tizon Chem. Corp., Flemington, N.J., 1955-58; assoc. prof. chemistry U. Vt., 1958-61; dir. Scott Research Labs., Plumsteadville, Pa., 1961-62; program dir. phys. chemistry NSF, 1962-65, planning assoc., 1965-67, program mgr. departmental sci. devel., 1967-69; dean Coll. Letters, Arts and Scis., U. So. Calif., Los Angeles, 1969-70; dir. Office Instl. Studies Coll. Letters, Arts and Scis., U. So. Calif., 1970-82, chmn. safety sci. dept., 1982-85, prof. emeritus, 1985—; pres. Harmony Inst., 1985—; cons. Reheis Corp., 1958-61, Coll. Chemistry Cons. Service, 1970-76, EPA, 1971-73, Lake Erie Environment Program, 1971-73. Author: Graduate Student Support and Manpower Resources in Graduate Science Education, 1968, Air Pollution, 1973, Hydrogen Bonding, 1971, Dollars and Scholars, 1982, Meeting The Needs of The Non-Smoking Traveler, 1986; contbr. articles to profl. jours. Served with USNR, 1944-46. Recipient Outstanding Achievement award Coll. Tech., U. N.H., 1969. Fellow AAAS; mem. Am. Chem. Soc. (program chmn. Washington 1968, program chmn. div. chem. edn. 1971), Am. Assn. Higher Edn., Assn. Instl. Research, Am. Soc. Safety Engrs., Nat. Safety Mgmt. Soc., AAUP, Am. Assn. Univ. Adminstrs. Patentee in chemistry field. Home: PO Box 99 Tollhouse CA 93667 Office: Harmony Institute Inc PO Box 210 Tollhouse CA 93667

LINNIHAN, PATRICIA CATHERINE, social worker; b. Mpls., Sept. 9, 1941; d. John Leo and Elizabeth Catherine (Halloran) L. BA in History, Rosary Coll., 1963; AM in Social Work, U. Chgo., 1969. Lic. clin. social worker. Sch. social worker Chgo. Bd. Edn., 1969-74; social work fellow Mt. Zion Hosp., San Francisco, 1974-75; asst. dir., cons. social worker Adolescent Day Treatment Ctr. of Children's Hosp., San Francisco, 1975—. Fellow Am. Orthopsychiat. Assn.; mem. Nat. Assn. Social Workers (cert.). Avocations: photography, writing, skiing, collecting children's books. Home: 485 Buena Vista E San Francisco CA 94117 Office: Childrens Hosp Adolescent Day Treatment Ctr 4319 Geary Blvd San Francisco CA 94118

LINSDAY, RICHARD H., insurance agent; b. Oak Park, Ill., Oct. 30, 1947; s. Herbert Robert and Margaret (Boyer) L.; m. Laura Jane Brink, June 16, 1979. BS in Bus., No. Ill. U., DeKalb, 1969. CLU, 1977; Chartered Fin. Cons., Am. Coll., Bryn Mawr, Pa., 1983. Brokerage rep., then mgr. Aetna Life Ins. Co., Los Angeles, 1972-78; brokerage mgr. Mfrs. Life Ins. Co., Los Angeles, 1978-86; sr. v.p. Integrated Fin., 1987—; pres. Lindsay Fin. Ins. Services, Inc. (formerly Richard H. Linsday & Assocs., Ltd.), Los Angeles, 1975—; tchr. adult edn. estate planning. Contbr. articles to profl. jours. Coordinator, W. Los Angeles Spl. Olympics, 1978-79. Served with USMC, 1969-72, Vietnam, maj. Res. Recipient cert. public service Joseph Kennedy Found., 1979. Mem. Nat. Assn. Life Underwriters (v.p. W. Los Angeles chpt. 1980, pres. 1982-83, Philip Grosser Meml. award 1982), Am. Soc. CLU's (dir. Los Angeles chpt. 1982-84, v.p. 1986, pres. 1987-88), Wilshire Estate Planning Council (v.p. 1981, pres. 1982-83), Calif. Assn. Life Underwriters (trustee region 6 1983-85), Cert. Fin. Planners Assn. Methodist. Home: 5540 Vista Canada Pl La Canada CA 91011 Office: Integrated Fin 16530 Ventura Blvd Encino CA 91436

LINSON, PATRICIA ANN, social worker; b. Guthrie, Okla., Aug. 25, 1937; d. Charles William and Clara Nadine (Conaway) Jones; m. Jerry Claude Linson, June 26, 1955 (div. Dec. 1973); children: Michael, Debra Parsons, Pam Gund, Marcia Dayton. BSW, Colo. State U., 1979; MSW, U. Denver, 1983. Cons. Alternatives for Battered Women, Inc., Loveland, Colo., 1983-84, dir., 1984—; cons. Loveland Police Dept., 1983—; regional rep. Colo. Domestic Violence Commn., 1984-85, co-chmn., 1986—, bd. dirs., 1985—; cons. Loveland Domestic Violence Commn., 1985—. Mem. Nat. Assn. Social Workers (regional rep. 1985), Colo. State Crime Prevention. Democrat. Avocations: cross country and downhill skiing, bridge, classical music concerts. Office: Alternatives for Battered Women 407 N Lincoln #107 Loveland CO 80537

LINSTONE, HAROLD ADRIAN, management and systems science educator; b. Hamburg, Fed. Republic Germany, June 15, 1924; came to U.S., 1936; s. Frederic and Ellen (Seligmann) L.; m. Hedy Schubach, June 16, 1946; children: Fred A., Clark R. BS, CCNY, 1944; MA, Columbia U., 1947; PhD, U. So. Calif., 1954. Sr. scientist Hughes Aircraft Co., Culver City, Calif., 1949-61, The Rand Corp., Santa Monica, Calif., 1961-63; assoc. dir. planning Lockheed Corp., Burbank, Calif., 1963-71; prof. Portland (Oreg.) State U., 1970—; pres. Systems Forecasting, Inc., Santa Monica, 1971—; cons. 1973—. Author: Multiple Perspectives, 1984; co-editor: The Delphi Method, 1975, Technological Substitution, 1976, Futures Research, 1977; editor-in-chief Technol. Forecasting Social Change, 1969—. NSF grantee, Washington, 1976, 79, 85. Mem. Inst. Mgmt. Scis., Ops. Research Soc. Avocation: photography. Office: Portland State U PO Box 751 Portland OR 97207

LIONAKIS, GEORGE, architect; b. West Hiawatha, Utah, Sept. 5, 1924; s. Pete and Andriani (Protopapadakis) L.; student Carbon Jr. Coll., 1942-43, 46-47; B. Arch., U. Oreg., 1951; m. Iva Oree Braddock, Dec. 30, 1951; 1 dau., Deborah Jo. With Corps Engrs., Walla Walla, Wash., 1951-54; architect Liske, Lionakis, Beaumont & Engberg, Sacramento, 1954—. Mem. Sacramento County Bd. Appeals, 1967—, chmn., 1969, 75, 76; pres. Sacramento Builders Exchange, 1976. Served with USAAF, 1943-46. Mem. AIA (pres. Central Valley chpt., 1972—), Constrn. Specifications Inst. (pres. Sacramento chpt., 1962; nat. awards, 1962, 63, 65), Sacramento C. of C. (code com., 1970—). Club: North Ridge Country (pres. 1987). Lodge: Rotarian (pres. East Sacramento 1978-79). Prin. works include Stockton (Calif.) Telephone Bldg., 1968, Chico (Calif.) Main Telephone Bldg., 1970, Mather AFB Exchange Complex Sacramento, 1970, Base Chapel Mather AFB, Sacramento, 1970, Woodridge Elementary Sch., Sacramento, 1970, Pacific Telephone Co. Operating Center Modesto, Calif., 1968, Sacramento, 1969, Marysville, Calif., 1970, Red Bluff, Calif., 1971, Wells Fargo Banks, Sacramento, 1968, Corning, Calif., 1969, Anderson, 1970, Beale AFB Exchange Complex, Marysville, 1971, Cosumnes River Coll., Sacramento, 1971, base exchanges at Bergstrom AFB, Austin, Tex., Sheppard AFB, Wichita Falls, Tex., Chanute AFB, Rantoul, Ill., McChord AFB, Tacoma, Wash., health center Chico State U., Sacramento County Adminstrn. Center, Sacramento Bee Newspaper Plant. Home: 160 Breckenwood Way Sacramento CA 95825 Office: Lionakis Beaumont Design Group 401 Watt Ave Sacramento CA 95864

LIOU, KUO-NAN, atmospheric science educator, researcher; b. Taipei, Taiwan, Republic of China, Nov. 16, 1943; m. Agnes L.Y. Hung, Aug. 3, 1968; 1 child, Julia C.C. BS, Taiwan U., 1965; MS, NYU, 1968, PhD, 1970. Research assoc. Goddard Inst. for Space Studies, N.Y.C., 1970-72; asst. prof. atmospheric sci. U. Wash., Seattle, 1972-74; assoc. prof. U. Utah, Salt Lake City, 1975-80, prof., 1980—, dir. grad. studies in meteorology, 1981-84; vis. prof. UCLA, 1981; vis. scholar Harvard U., Cambridge, Mass., 1985; cons. NASA Ames Research Ctr., Moffett Field, Calif., 1984—, Los Alamos (N.Mex.) Nat. Lab., 1984—. Author: An Introduction to Atmospheric Radiation, 1980; contbr. articles to profl. jours. Fellow NRC, Washington, 1970, David Gardner fellow U. Utah, Salt Lake City, 1978; recipient Founders Day award NYU, 1971, NSF grant, 1974—. Fellow Optical Soc. Am.; mem. AAAS, Am. Geophys. Union, Am. Meteorol. Soc. (chmn. radiation com. 1982-84). Home: 4480 Adonis Dr Salt Lake City UT 84114 Office: U Utah Dept Meteorology Salt Lake City UT 84112

LIPETZ, LIN, artist, interior designer; b. Bozeman, Mont., July 2, 1928; d. Frank Frances Kreher and Grace (Leona) Street; m. Harold Lipetz, Aug. 4, 1951 (dec. 1968); children: Janus, Bradford. BFA, U. Wash., 1951, MFA in Design, 1968; BS in Interior Design, Calif. State U., San Jose, 1985. Painter Seattle, 1959-69; founder, dir. The Factory of Visual Art, Seattle, 1969-78; designer Space Designs, Mountain View, Calif., 1983-85; painter San Jose, 1986—. Represented in permanent collections Seattle Art Mus., Bank of Am., Baba & Morrow, Monterey & Newport, Los Angeles Sheraton Hotels, Beverly Hills Banks of Commerce, PMI Ins. Co., Good Samaritan Corp., and numerous pvt. collections. Bd. dirs. Arts for Youth Adv. Council, Seattle, 1973-76; nat. trustee Am. Craft Council, N.Y.C., 1975-78; trustee World Craft Council, N.Y.C., 1977. Recipient Exceptional Leadership award Friends of Crafts, 1975, 1st prize for watercolor Seattle Art Mus., 1964. Presbyterian.

LIPKA, JAMES JOSEPH, chemist; b. Highland Park, Mich., Aug. 1, 1954; s. Bernard and Donalda (McDonough) L. BS in Chemistry, U. Mich., 1976; MA, Columbia U., 1977, PhD, 1982. Research assoc. Brookhaven Nat. Lab., Upton, N.Y., 1981-85, asst. chemist, 1985; asst. chemist VA Med. Ctr., San Francisco, 1985—. Mem. AAAS, Sigma Xi. Democrat. Avocations: photography, bicycling, swimming. Home: 628A Ivy San Francisco CA 94102 Office: VA Med Ctr 4150 Clement St San Francisco CA 94121

LIPKIN, ALAN, geography educator; b. N.Y.C., Dec. 23, 1944; s. Morris and Lena (Feldman) L.; m. Shirley Treger, June 27, 1970; children: Michal Lirit, Penina Rachel. BA, CUNY, 1969; MA, Columbia U., 1973, MPhil., 1975. Vis. asst. prof. Columbia U., N.Y.C., 1979k; asst. prof. Sonoma State U., Rohnert Park, Calif., 1975-81; vis. asst. prof. Sanoma State U., Rohnert Park, 1983—, U. Pitts., 1981-83, Santa Rosa (Calif.) Jr. Coll., 1983—; profl. philatelist The Stamp Den, Petaluma, Calif., 1983—. Pres. Congregation B'nai Israel, Petaluma, 1980-81. Served with U.S. Army, 1963-66. Mem. Assn. Am. Geographers, Am. Stamp Dealers Assn., Am. Philatelic Soc., Bur. Issues Assn. Democrat. Jewish. Office: The Stamp Den 6 Petaluma Blvd N Petaluma CA 94952

LIPKIN, EDWARD WALTER, research physician; b. St. Louis, Aug. 1, 1949; s. David and Shirley Belle (Douthitt) Lipkin. BA, Williams Coll., 1971; PhD, Case Western Res. U., 1977, MD, 1978. Diplomate Am. Bd. Internal Medicine, Am. Bd. Endocrinology and Metabolism. Intern Boston City Hosp., 1978-79, resident, 1979-81; instr. Sch. Medicine Boston U., 1980-81; instr. U. Wash., Seattle, 1982-84, asst. prof. medicine, 1984—; asst. dir. research Clin. Research Unit, U. Wash., 1985—; clin. assoc. physician NIH, 1984-87, new investigator, 1984-87. Mem. AAAS, Am. Fedn. Clin. Research, Am. Soc. Parenteral and Enteral Nutrition, Am. Soc. Clin. Nutrition.

LIPKIN, MARY CASTLEMAN DAVIS (MRS. ARTHUR BENNETT LIPKIN), former psychiat. social worker; b. Germantown, Pa., Mar. 4, 1907; d. Henry L. and Willie (Webb) Davis; student grad. sch. social work U. Wash., 1946-48; m. William F. Cavenaugh, Nov. 8, 1930 (div.); children—Molly C. (Mrs. Gary Oberbillig), William A.; m. 2d, Arthur Bennett Lipkin, Sept. 15, 1961 (dec. June 1974). Nursery sch. tchr. Miquon (Pa.) Sch., 1940-45; caseworker Family Soc. Seattle, 1948-49, Jewish Family and Child Service, Seattle, 1951-56; psychiat. social worker Stockton (Calif.) State Hosp., 1957-58; supr. social service Mental Health Research Inst., Fort Steilacoom, Wash., 1958-59; engaged in pvt. practice, Bellevue, Wash., 1959-61. Former mem. Phila. Com. on City Policy. Former diplomate and bd. mem. Conf. Advancement of Pvt. Practice in Social Work. Mem. Acad. Cert. Social Workers, Nat. Assn. Social Workers, Internat. Conf. Social Work, Menninger Found., Union Concerned Scientists, Physicians for Social Responsibility, Center for Sci. in Pub. Interest, Jr. League, Seattle Art Mus., Asian Art Council, Wing Lake Mus., Bellevue Art Mus., Pacific Sci. Center,

Western Wash. Solar Energy Assn., Nature Conservancy, Wilderness Soc., Sierra Club, Common Cause, ACLU, Pa. Acad. Fine Arts. Clubs: Cosmopolitan, Cricket (Phila.); Women's University (Seattle); Nassau (Princeton, N.J.). Home: 9102 N Mercer Way #101 Mercer Island WA 98040-3107

LIPMAN, JEANNE E., business educator; b. Billings, Mont., Apr. 29, 1948; d. Harry and Esther Ann (Niss) L.; m. David Michael Barnes, Oct. 22, 1982. A.B.A., Denver U., 1968; B.A., Bradley U., 1971; M.A., U. No. Colo., 1977; postgrad. Ariz. State U., 1982—. Type A teaching cert. and vocat. credential, Colo. Tchr., YWCA, Peoria, Ill., 1969-71; sec. Honeywell Inc., Denver, 1971-72; adminstrv. asst. Majestic Savs. Assn., Denver, 1972-73; tchr. Arickaree Schs., Anton, Colo., 1973-75; asst. prof. bus. U. No. Colo. Lab. Sch., Greeley, 1975—, chmn. dept., 1978—. Mem. Nat. Bus. Edn. Assn., Am. Vocat. Assn., Phi Delta Kappa, Delta Pi Epsilon. Democrat. Jewish. Office: University of Northern Colorado Laboratory School Greeley CO 80639

LIPOFSKY, MARVIN BENTLEY, art educator; b. Elgin, Ill., Sept. 1, 1938; s. Henry and Mildred (Hyman) L.; 1 child, Lisa Beth. BFA in Indsl. Design, U. Ill., 1961; MS, MFA in Sculpture, U. Wis., 1964. Instr. design U. Wis., Madison, 1964; asst. prof. design U. Calif., Berkeley, 1964-72; prof., chmn. glass dept. Calif. Coll. Arts and Crafts, Oakland, 1967-87, pres. faculty assembly, 1984-87; guest instr. Haystack Mountain Sch., Deer Isla, Maine, 1967, 73, 87, San Francisco Art Inst., 1968, Hunterdon Art Ctr., Clinton, N.J., 1973, Pilchuck Sch. Glass, Stanwood, Wash., 1974; vis. prof. Bazalel Acad. Art and Design, Jerusalem, 1971; pres. faculty assembly, 1984—. One-man shows include Richmond (Calif.) Art Ctr., 1965, Anneberg Gallery, San Francisco, 1966, Crocker Art Gallery, Sacramento, 1967, San Francisco Mus. Art, 1967, Mus. Contemporary Crafts, N.Y.C., 1969, U. Ga., Athens, 1969, Utah Mus. Fine Arts, U. Utah, Salt Lake City, 1969, Calif. Coll. Arts and Crafts, 1970, Stedelijke Mus., Amsterdam, The Netherlands, 1970, Galerie de Enndt, Amsterdam, 1970, Baxter Art Gallery, Calif. Inst. Tech., Pasadena, 1974, Ao Gallery, Tokyo, 1975, Yaw Gallery, Birmingham, Mich., 1976, 78, Gallery Marronnier, Kyoto, Japan, 1979, U. Del., Newark, 1979, Greenwood Gallery, Washington, 1980, SM Gallerie, Frankfurt, Fed. Republic Germany, 1981, Galerie L. Hamburg, Fed. Republic Germany, 1981, Betsy Rosenfield Gallery, Chgo., 1982, Robert Kidd Gallery, Birmingham, Mich., 1984, Holsten Galleries, Palm Beach, Fla., Maurine Littiety Gallery, Washington; vis. artist, critic Gerriet Rietveld Academie, Amsterdam; vis. artist Atheneium Sch. Art and Design, Helsinki, Finland, 1970, UCLA, 1973, Pilchuck Sch. Glass, 1977, 81, 84, Sommervail, Battle Mountain Glass Symposium, Vail, Colo. Trustee Calif. Coll. Arts and Crafts, Oakland, 1984—. NEA fellow, 1974, 76. Mem. Glass Art Soc. (pres. 1978-80, jour. editor 1976-80, advisor 1980—), Am. Craft Council (trustee 1986—). Office: Calif Coll Arts and Crafts Glass Dept 5212 Broadway Oakland CA 94618

LIPOW, MYRON, computer software engineer; b. Newark, Apr. 12, 1928; s. Sidney Samuel and Aline (Ackerman) L.; m. Susan-Lee Landisman, Aug. 27, 1950; children—Martin Edward, Stephen Kenneth. B.S. in Math., Calif. Inst. Tech., 1949; cert. quality, reliability engr., Am. Soc. Quality Control, 1972. Statistician Aerojet-Gen. Corp., Azusa, Calif., 1949-50, devel. engr., 1951-55, reliability engr., 1956-58; reliability sect. head TRW Systems Group, Redondo Beach, Calif., 1958-60, dept. mgr., 1961-67, product assurance mgr., 1967-71, sr. staff engr., 1972-79, subproject mgr. software product assurance, Electronics and Def., 1979-84; project mgr. Radar Systems Group Hughes Aircraft Co., 1984—; cons. in field. Recipient TRW good neighbor award, 1973. Assoc. fellow AIAA; sr. mem. IEEE (Computer Soc., Reliability Soc.), Math. Assn. Am. Jewish. Club: Los Verdes Men's. Co-author: Reliability: Management, Methods, and Mathematics, 1977; Characteristics of Software Quality, 1978; Software Reliability: A Study in Large Project Reality, 1978. Office: Hughes Aircraft Co Radar Systems Group El Segundo CA 90009

LIPPE, PHILIPP MARIA, neurosurgeon, educator; b. Vienna, Austria, May 17, 1929; s. Philipp and Maria (Goth) L.; came to U.S., 1938, naturalized, 1945; m. Gail B. Busch, 1977; children by previous marriage—Patricia Ann Marie, Philip Eric Andrew, Laura Lynne Elizabeth, Kenneth Anthony Ernst. Student Loyola U., Chgo., 1947-50; B.S. in Medicine, U. Ill. Coll. Medicine, 1952, M.D. with high honors, 1954. Rotating intern St. Francis Hosp., Evanston, Ill., 1954-55; asst. resident gen. surgery VA Hosp., Hines, Ill., 1955, 58-59; asst. resident neurology and neurol. surgery Neuropsychiat. Inst., U. Ill. Research and Ednl. Hosps., Chgo., 1959-60, chief resident, 1962-63, resident neuropathology, 1962, postgrad. trainee in electroencephalography, 1963; resident neurology and neurol. surgery Presbyn.-St. Luke's Hosp., Chgo., 1960-61; practice medicine, specializing in neurol. surgery, San Jose, Calif., 1963—; instr. neurology and neurol. surgery U. Ill., 1962-63; clin. instr. surgery and neurosurgery Stanford U., 1965-69, clin. asst. prof., 1969-74, clin. assoc. prof., 1974—; staff cons. in neurosurgery O'Connor Hosp., Santa Clara Valley Med. Center, San Jose Hosp., Good Samaritan Hosp., Los Gatos Community Hosp., El Camino Hosp. (all San Jose area); founder, exec. dir. Bay Area Pain Rehab. Center, San Jose, 1979—; clin. adviser to Joint Commn. on Accreditation of Hosps.; mem. dist. med. quality rev. com. Calif. Bd. Med. Quality Assurance, 1976—, chmn., 1976-77. Served to capt. USAF, 1956-58. Diplomate Am. Bd. Neurol. Surgery, Nat. Bd. Med. Examiners. Fellow ACS; mem. AMA (Ho. of Dels. 1981—), Calif. Med. Assn. (Ho. of Dels. 1976-80, sci. bd., council 1979-87, sec. 1981—), Santa Clara County Med. Soc. (council 1974-81, pres. 1978-79), Chgo. Med. Soc., Congress Neurol. Surgeons, Calif. Assn. Neurol. Surgeons (dir. 1974-82, v.p. 1975-76, pres. 1977-79), San Jose Surg. Soc., Am. Assn. Neurol. Surgeons (dir. 1983-86, 87—), Western Neurol. Soc., San Francisco Neurol. Soc., Santa Clara Valley Profl. Standards Rev. Orgn. (dir., v.p., dir. quality assurance 1975-83), Fedn. Western Socs. Neurol. Sci., Internat. Assn. for Study Pain, Am. Pain Soc. (founding mem.), Am. Acad. Algology (sec. 1983-86, pres.-elect 1986—), Alpha Omega Alpha, Phi Kappa Phi. Contbr. articles to profl. jours. Pioneered med. application centrifugal force using flight simulator. Office: 2100 Forest Ave Suite 106 San Jose CA 95128

LIPPERT, THOMAS RAY, corporate executive, director; b. New Ulm, Minn., Nov. 6, 1949; s. Raymond Thomas and Myra Louise (Witt) L.; m. Jean Corpula, Aug. 17, 1979. BA, St. John's U., Collegeville, Minn., 1971; JD, U. Notre Dame, 1974. Bus. mgr. Shultz Corp., Mpls., 1979-80; CEO Jenton Invt. Mkt., Mpls., 1980-83, Scandi Fashions, Inc., Salt Lake City, 1983-86; CEO St. Blaise Internat., Inc., Salt Lake City, 1986—, also cons. Pres. Elders Quorum Ch. Jesus Christ Latter-day Saints, Salt Lake City, 1985; employment counselor, 1986. Named Employee of Yr. Shultz Corp., Mpls., 1979; recipient Civic award Sand, Utah, 1985. Mem. ABA, Am. Mgmt. Assn., Am. Entrepreneurs Assn., Jaycees (pres. Sandstone, Minn. chpt. 1979, Jaycee of Yr. award 1978). Club: Toastmasters (Sandstone) (pres. 1979, Toastmaster of Yr. award 1978). Home: 1534 W Rhoda Ave West Jordan UT 84084-2416 Office: St Blaise Internat Inc PO Box 4042 Ogden UT 84402-4042

LIPPINCOTT, CHARLES M(YERS), JR., film marketing executive; b. Adams, Mass., Oct. 28, 1939; s. Charles Myers and Ruth Frances (Bayliss) L. BA in Anthropology, Northwestern U., 1961; postgrad., Georgetown U., 1962-64, U. So. Calif., 1964-70. V.p. Star Wars Corp., 1975-78; pres. Creative Movie Mktg., 1978-80, 83—; v.p. prodn. De Laurentiis Film Co., Beverly Hills, Calif., 1980-82; v.p. acquisitions MGM/United Artists, Culver City, Calif., 1982-83; cons. to Universal Film Studios, De Laurentiis Film Co., 1979-80; marketed Star Wars, Alien, Black Stallion, Coal Miner's Daughter, Flash Gordon, for 20th Century Film Studios, United Artists and Universal Film Studios, 1975-79; chmn. documentaries FILMEX, Los Angeles, 1975-84. Contbr. articles to mags. Fellow Am. Film Inst., 1968-69. Mem. Cinema Circulus U. So. Calif. (pres. 1985—). Avocation: collecting jazz and blues records. Office: Creative Movie Mktg 3511 6th St #15 Los Angeles CA 90020

LIPPITT, ELIZABETH CHARLOTTE, writer; b. San Francisco; d. Sidney Grant and Stella Lippitt; student Mills Coll., U. Calif.-Berkeley. Writer, performer own satirical monologues; contbr. articles to 85 newspapers including N.Y. Post, Los Angeles Examiner, Orlando Sentinel, Phoenix Republic, also advt. Recipient Congress of Freedom award, 1959, 71-73, 77, 78; writer on nat. and polit. affairs for 85 newspapers including Muncie Star, St. Louis Globe-Democrat, Washington Times, Utah Ind., Jackson News. Mem. Commn. for Free China, Conservative Caucus. Mem. Nat. Assn. R.R. Passengers, Nat. Trust for Hist. Preservation, Am. Security Council, Internat. Platform Assn., Am. Conservative Union, Nat. Antivivisection Soc., High Frontier, For Our Children, Childhelp U.S.A., Free Afghanistan Com., Humane Soc. U.S., Young Ams. for Freedom, 8 antivivisection orgns. Clubs: Metropolitan, Olympic, Commonwealth. Pop singer, recorder song album Songs From the Heart. Home: 2414 Pacific Ave San Francisco CA 94115

LIPPMAN, JOHN AARON, television executive; b. Chgo., Sept. 12, 1949; s. Jordan Howard and Kaleen Wool L.; m. Barbara Gay Heinen, Aug. 24, 1977 (div. 1980); 1 dau., Sarah Rosanne; m. Julie Jueling Neff, June 15, 1984; stepchildren: Britt Jueling, John David. A.B., Dartmouth Coll., 1971; postgrad. Wharton Sch., U. Pa., 1981-82, Am. Mgmt. Assn., 1982-83; Notre Dame, 1985. News writer, intern Sta. WBZ-TV, Boston, 1970; news reporter, anchorman Sta. KING-TV, Seattle, 1971-76; news and pub. affairs dir. Sta. KSTW-TV, Tacoma, Wash., 1976-79; v.p., TV news dir. Sta. KIRO-TV, Seattle, 1979-86, exec. v.p. news, 1986—. Active Leadership Tomorrow, Seattle, 1983-84, Downtown Seattle Assn., City Club Seattle; bd. dirs. Wash. Research Council, 1985—. Recipient Best Newscast in U.S.A. award, UPI, 1984, Better Understanding award Wash. Edn. Assn., 1978; Wash. Internat. fellow, 1986—. Mem. Radio TV News Dirs. Assn., Nat. Acad. TV Arts and Scis. (Emmy for news 1983, 84, 85), Wash. AP Broadcasters Assn. (pres. Seattle 1982-85). Club: Wash. Athletic. Office: KIRO-TV 2807 3rd Ave Seattle WA 98111

LIPPMAN, LOUIS GROMBACHER, psychology educator; b. Whittier, Calif., Jan. 10, 1941; s. Robert Weiler and Ruth Major (Grombacher) L.; m. Marcia Zoe Luehrs, Dec. 21, 1965; children: Leah N., David R. BA, Stanford U., 1962; MA, Mich. State U., 1963, PhD, 1966. Teaching asst. Mich. State U., East Lansing, 1962-66; asst. prof. psychology Western Wash. U., Bellingham, 1966-69, assoc. prof., 1969-74, prof., 1974—; vis. prof. San Diego State U., 1978. Author children's piano accompaniment book; editorial bd. mem. Jour. Irreproducible Results, 1984—; contbr. sci. and sci. humor articles to profl. jours. Mem. Psychonomic Soc., Rocky Mountain Psychol. Assn., Midwestern Psychol. Assn., Behavioral and Brain Scis. (assoc.), Am. Suzuki Assn., Sigma Xi, Psi Chi. Republican. Jewish. Avocations: walking, photography, piano and organ music. Office: Western Wash U Psychology Dept Bellingham WA 98225

LIPPOLD, ROLAND WILL, surgeon; b. Staunton, Ill., May 1, 1916; s. Frank Carl and Ella (Immenroth) L.; m. Margaret Cookson, June 1, 1947; children: Mary Ellen Lippold Elvick, Catherine Anne Lippold Rolf, Carol Sue Lippold Webber. Diplomate Am. Bd. Surgery. Intern Grant Hosp., Chgo., 1941-42, resident in surgery, 1942-43, 47-48; resident in surgery St. Francis Hosp., Evanston, Ill., 1946-47; fellow in pathology Cook County Hosp., Chgo., 1947-48, resident in surgery, 1949-50; practice medicine specializing in surgery Chgo., 1950-53; also asst. in anatomy U. Ill., Chgo., 1950-53; practice medicine specializing in surgery Sacramento, 1953-68; chief med. officer No. Reception Ctr.-Clinic, Calif. Youth Authority, Sacramento, 1954-68, chief med. services, 1968-79; cons. in med. care in correctional instns.; cons. Calif. State Personnel Bd. Contbr. articles to med. publs. Chmn. Calif. Expn. Hall of Health, 1971-72. Served to comdr. M.C., USNR, 1943-73, PTO. Mem. Sacramento Surg. Soc., Sacramento County Med. Soc., Calif. Med. Assn., AMA, Assn. Mil. Surgeons U.S., Am. Heart Assn., Audubon Soc., Sacramento Hist. Soc. (life). Republican. Lutheran. Home: 1811 Eastern Ave Sacramento CA 95864

LIPSCOMB, ANNA ROSE FEENY, hotel executive; b. Greensboro, N.C., Oct. 29, 1945; d. Nathan and Matilda (Carotenuto) L. B.A. in English and French summa cum laude, Queens Coll., 1977. Reservations agt. Am. Airlines, St. Louis, 1968-69, ticket agt., 1969-71; coll. rep. CBS, Holt Rinehart Winston, Providence, 1977-79, sr. acquisitions editor Dryden Press, Chgo., 1979-81; owner, mgr. Taos Inn, N.Mex., 1981—; bd. dirs. N.Mex. Hotel and Motel Assn., 1986—. Editor: Intermediate Accounting, 1980; Business Law, 1981. Contbr. articles to profl. jours. Bd. dirs., 1st v.p. Taos Arts Assn., 1982-85; founder, bd. dirs. Taos Spring Arts Celebration, 1983—; founder, dir. Meet-the-Artist Series, 1983—; bd. dirs. and co-founder Spring Arts N.Mex., 1986; founding mem. Assn. Hist. Hotels, Boulder, 1983—; organizer Internat. Symposium on Arts, 1985; bd. dirs. Arts in Taos, 1983, Taoschool, Inc., 1985—. Recipient Outstanding English Student of Yr. award Queens Coll., 1977; named Single Outstanding Contributor to the Arts in Taos, 1986. Mem. Millicent Rogers Mus. Assn., Taos Lodgers and Restaurant Assn., Taos County C. of C. (bd. dirs. 1987-90), Phi Beta Kappa. Democrat. Home: Talpa Route Taos NM 87571 Office: Taos Inn PO Drawer N Taos NM 87571

LIPSEY, ALLEN IRA, clinical and pediatric pathologist; b. Chgo., Apr. 9, 1938; s. William Wolf and Rae (Kramer) L.; m. Myra Joyce Kahn, Sept. 8, 1963; children: David Benjamin, Sarah Elizabeth. AB in Chemistry, U. Ill., 1958, MD, 1962; MS in Biometry, U. So. Calif., 1978, MEd, 1979. Assoc. pathologist Children's Hosp. Los Angeles, 1970-71, dir. clin. lab., 1971—; assoc. prof. clin. pathology U. So. Calif., Los Angeles; docent Los Angeles Zoo. Served to maj. USAR, 1962-71. Fellow Coll. Am. Pathologists, Am. Soc. Clin. Pathologists, Soc. Pediatric Pathology (sec. 1984—), Nat. Accrediting Agy. for Clin. Lab. Scis. (chmn. 1982-85). Office: Childrens Hosp Los Angeles 4650 Sunset Blvd Los Angeles CA 90027

LIPSTONE, HOWARD H., television production executive; b. Chgo., Apr. 28; s. Louis R. and Ruth B. (Fischer) L.; m. Jane A., Apr. 7, 1957; children—Lewis, Gregory. B.A. in Cinema, U. So. Calif., 1950. Asst. to gen. mgr. Sta. KTLA, Los Angeles, 1950-54; film and program dir. Sta. KABC-TV, Los Angeles, 1954-63; exec. asst. to pres., exec. producer Selmur Prodns. Inc. subs. ABC-TV, 1963-69; exec. v.p. Ivan Tors Films, Inc., 1969-70; pres. Alan Landsburg Prodns., Inc., Los Angeles, 1970-85; pres. The Landsburg Co., Los Angeles, 1985—. Mem. Soc. Motion Picture and TV Engrs., Acad. TV Arts and Scis., Motion Picture Acad. Arts and Scis. Office: The Landsburg Co 11811 Olympic Blvd Los Angeles CA 90064

LIPTON, MILTON A., electronics engineering consultant; b. N.Y.C., May 1, 1917; s. Max and Celia L.; m. Ruth M. Magid, June 20, 1943; children—William Victor L., Deborah Jane Lipton Kremsdorf. B.E.E., Cooper Union Inst. Tech., 1939, E.E. (hon.), 1946. Registered profl. engr., N.J. Elec. draftsman Lummus Co., N.Y.C., 1939-40; electronics engr. Dept. of Army, Fort Monmouth, N.J., 1940-72; engrng. cons. Gen. Systems Cons., West Long Branch, N.J., 1972-79, San Diego, 1978—. Pres. Friends Internat. Ctr., U. Calif.-San Diego, 1982-84. Ann. Milton A. Lipton engrng. excellence award established in his honor Dept. Army, Ft. Monmouth, N.J., 1984. Fellow AAAS; mem. IEEE (life). Home: 3161 Occidental St San Diego CA 92122

LIQUIDO, NICANOR JAVIER, entomology educator; b. Calamba, Philippines, Jan. 10, 1953; s. Francisco Lajara Liquido and Isidra (Mailom) Javier; m. Susan Heftel, Apr. 14, 1984. BS in Applied Zoology, Entomology and Microbiology, U. Philippines, 1975, MS in Entomology and Genetics, 1978; PhD in Entomology and Biometry, U. Hawaii, 1982. Instr. in biology and Entomology U. Philippines, Los Banos, 1976-77; sr. research asst. The Internat. Rice Research Inst., Los Banos, 1978-79; mem. research faculty U. Ill., Champaign, 1983-85; mem. grad. faculty U. Hawaii-Manoa, Honolulu, 1985—; research entomologist Agrl. Research Service USDA, Hilo, Hawaii, 1985—. Editor The Exuviae Quar. newsletter, 1978; corr. The Weekly Notes newsletter U. Philippines, 1977-78; contbr. articles to profl. jours. Fellow Ill. Natural Hist. Survey, Champaign, 1983-85; East-West Ctr. scholar, Honolulu, 1979-82; grantee Kasetsart U., Thailand, U. Hawaii, East-West Ctr., 1981. Mem. AAAS, Entomol. Soc. Am. (sec.-elect subsect. Cd, ecology, Bionomics and Behavior), Entomol. Soc. Can., Ecol. Soc. Am., Hawaiian Entomol. Soc., Am. Inst. Biol. Scis., Assn. Philippine Entomologists, Pest Control Council of Philippines, Hawaii Acad. Sci., N.Y. Acad. Scis., Sigma Xi, Gamma Sigma Delta, Phi Sigma. Roman Catholic. Club: Yacht (Hilo). Avocations: jogging, swimming, racquetball, paddling, developing ecol. computer models. Home: 2296 Kalanianaole Ave Hilo HI 96720 Office: Agrl Research Service USDA PO Box 4459 Hilo HI 96720

LISCHKA, LESLIE ELLEN, engineering executive, consultant; b. Washington, Apr. 26, 1942; d. Louis L. and Florence D. (Rosen) Lavine; 1 child, Tamara R. BA, U. Minn., 1964; MA, U. Ariz., 1967, PhD, 1975. Various engrng. and acad. positions, 1960-79; sr. group engr. Martin Marietta, Denver, 1979-82; mgr. systems computer software GTE, Westboro, Mass., 1982-84; mgr. Boston program office Merdan Group Inc., Burlington, Mass., 1984-86; pres. Systems and Software Assocs., Colorado Springs, Colo., 1986—. Contbr. articles to profl. jours. Mem. IEEE, Air Force Communications and Electronics Assn., Sigma Xi. Avocations: cross-country skiing; sailing; hiking; travel. Home and Office: 3604 Rocky Knoll Dr Colorado Springs CO 80918

LISOWSKI, GERALD THOMAS, analytical chemist; b. Pitts., May 9, 1945; s. Thomas Joseph and Josephine (Brentin) L.; m. Rizalina Brevia Puruganan, Jan. 21, 1978; 1 child, Jonathan Thomas. BS, MIT, 1967; PhD, U. Wis., 1975. Assoc. research chemist Stauffer Chem. Co., Richmond, Calif., 1975-76, research chemist, 1976-85, sr. research chemist, 1985—. Contbr. articles to profl. jours. NIH fellow, 1968; MIT scholar, 1963. Mem. Am. Chem. Soc., Assn. of Official Analytical Chemists, Interex. Avocations: mil. history, motorcycling, personal computers. Office: Stauffer Chem Co 1200 S 47th St Richmond CA 94804

LISS, KENNETH WAYNE, cabinet maker; b. San Francisco, Feb. 22, 1948; s. Max and Gladys (Howard) L.; m. Daniela Mostny, Dec. 5, 1970 (div. Jan. 1973); m. Dara Harnnarong, Nov. 5, 1975. Student, Coll. San Mateo, 1966-68, U. Calif., Berkeley, 1968-69. Park dir. Daly City (Calif.) Recreation Dept., 1966-69; warehousman Golden State Mat Mfg., San Francisco, 1970-72; prin. Taratilou Imports, San Rafael, Calif., 1973-75; cabinet maker West Coast Industies, San Francisco, 1976—. Served as pvt. USNG, 1970. Democrat. Avocations: mountaineering, body building, recreational travel. Home: 18 Skylark Dr #3 Larkspur CA 94939 Office: West Coast Industries 3150 18th St San Francisco CA 94107

LISSY, DAVID JEROME, photographer; b. Oak Park, Ill., July 6, 1950; s. Alfred E. and Eleanoretta (Mathews) L.; m. Carol Melissa Mather, Oct. 9, 1977; children—Brooke Melissa, Joel David, James Jerome. B.A. in Polit. Sci., No. Ill. U., 1972. Photographer, John Russell Photography Co., Aspen, Colo., 1976-79, Norm Clasen Photography, Aspen, 1979-80; freelance photographer David Lissy Photography, Golden, Colo., 1980—. Mem. Am. Soc. Mag. Photographers (cert.), Rocky Mountain Ski Writers, Assoc. Photographers Internat., U.S. Ski Writers (cert.). Contbr. photography to numerous popular mags. Office: 14472 Applewood Ridge Rd Golden CO 80401

LISTER, HUGH LAWRENCE, social work educator; b. Portland, Oreg., July 14, 1935; s. Hugh Lawrence and Honor Farrell (Youngson) L.; m. Constance Louise Clark, June 21, 1958; children: Jennifer Louise, Cheryl Ann. BA, Willamette U., 1957; MSW, U. Wash., 1959; DSW, Columbia U., 1970. Social worker Family Counseling Service, Portland, 1959-66; research assoc. psychiat. epidemiology research unit N.Y. State Psychiat. Inst., N.Y.C., 1966, 68-70; assoc. prof. U. Hawaii Sch. of Social Work, Honolulu, 1970-86, prof., 1986—; cons., Hawaii, 1970—; lectr., U.S. and Hawaii, 1970—. Editor: (with others) Human Sexuality in Medical Social Work, 1984, Human Sexuality, ETHNOCULTURE, and Social Work, 1986. Pres. The House, Inc., Honolulu, 1985—; active Am. Cancer Soc. Career teaching fellow Columbia U., 1968. Mem. AAUP, NEA, Nat. Assn. Social Workers. Democrat. Avocations: writing, health fitness sports. Home: 648 Paopua Loop Kailua HI 96734 Office: U Hawaii Sch Social Work 2500 Campus Rd Honolulu HI 96822

LISTOE, KIM MARIE, audiologist; b. Bozeman, Mont., Jan. 16, 1958; d. Merle Roy and Edna Marie (Rucker) L. BS in Speech Pathology, U. Wyo., 1980, MS in Audiology, 1982. Audiologist Edn. Resource Ctr., Riverton, Wyo., 1982—. Mem. Wyo Speech Hearing Assn. (sec. 1984-86, pres. 1987), Am. Speech Lang. and Hearing Assn. (cert.). Republican. Roman Catholic. Lodge: Soroptimists. Home: 319 S 2d West Riverton WY 82501 Office: Fremont County Sch Dist #25 121 N 5th West Riverton WY 82501

LISTON, ALBERT MORRIS, administrator, educator, investor; b. Carlinville, Ill., Aug. 6, 1940; s. Joseph Bostick and Hazel Marie (Smalley) L.; A.B. in Econs., U. Calif., Davis, 1963; M.A. in Govt., Calif. State U., Sacramento, 1970; m. Phyllis Clayton, Feb. 27, 1967 (div. July 1970). Research analyst Ombudsman Activities Project polit. sci. dept. U. Calif., Santa Barbara, 1970-72; asst. prof. polit. sci. dept. Calif. State U., Fullerton, 1973-79. Served to lt. Supply Corps, USN, 1963-66. Mem. Am. Polit. Sci. Assn., Am. Soc. for Public Adminstrn., Town Hall of Calif., Commonwealth Club Calif., Kappa Sigma, Phi Kappa Phi. Democrat. Contbr. chpt. to Executive Ombudsmen in the United States, 1973. Office: PO Box 1552 Sausalito CA 94966

LITCHFIELD, JEAN LOUISE, school librarian; b. Burlington, Kans., Nov. 26, 1932; s. Earl David Pantle and Helen Katharine (Townsend) Clark; m. Russell Orean Litchfield, June 7, 1952; children: Russell O. II, Rebecca L. Litchfield Blevins. Student, Washburn U., 1949-52; BA, San Diego State U., 1971, postgrad., 1978-80; postgrad., San Diego Evening Coll., 1976-78. Library services credential; Calif. tchrs. credential. Jr. clk. San Diego City Schs., 1972-78, library technician, 1976-78, librarian, 1980—. Mem. Calif. Media and Library Educators Assn., San Diego City Schs. Library Media Assn. (sec. 1983-84). Republican. Mem. United Ch. of Christ. Lodge: Order Eastern Star. Avocations: reading, dancing, cooking, plays, concerts. Home: 4111 Lymer Dr San Diego CA 92116 Office: Wangenheim Jr High Sch 9230 Gold Coast Dr San Diego CA 92126

LITIZZETTE, STANLEY VICTOR, lawyer; b. Helper, Utah, Aug. 25, 1920; s. Victor E. and Vera A. (Bottino) L.; B.A. magna cum laude, Notre Dame U., 1942; J.D., Georgetown U., 1949; A.A. (hon.), Coll. Eastern Utah, 1981; m. Edith Breznick, June 16, 1956; 1 son, Stanley Lawrence. With identification div. FBI, Washington, 1942; admitted to D.C. bar, 1949, Utah bar, 1949, U.S. Supreme Ct., 1977; since in pvt. practice at Helper, Utah; city atty. Helper, 1954-76; gen. counsel, dir. Helper State Bank, 1957-78. Chmn. bd. trustees Price River Water Improvement Dist., 1960-78; chmn. instl. council Coll. Eastern Utah, 1986-87; chmn. Carbon County Planning Commn., 1968-72, Coll. Eastern Utah Instnl. Council, 1986; bd. dirs. Carbon Water Conservancy Dist., 1986, Carbon Hosp., 1958-73. Served with USAAF, 1943-45. Mem. Eastern Utah Bar Assn. (pres. 1953, 1968, 74), Am. Bar Assn., Assn. Trial Lawyers Am., Am. Legion. Roman Catholic. Clubs: Elks, KC. Home: 26 S Main St Helper UT 84526 Office: 30 S Main St Helper UT 84526

LITTELL, KATHERINE MATHER, fine arts dealer, writer; b. Seattle, June 5, 1936; d. Norman M. and Katherine M. (Maher) Littell. B.A. Magna cum laude in English, Radcliffe Coll., 1958; postgrad. (German Exchange Service scholar) U. Munich, 1958-59; M.A. in German Lit., Harvard U., 1961; Ph.D. in Germanic Langs. and Lit., Columbia U., 1972. Instr. German, SUNY-New Paltz, 1965-66; instr. German lang. and lit. Tchrs. Coll., Columbia U., N.Y.C., 1966-69; instr. German and humanities SUNY-Stonybrook, 1968-69; asst. prof. Edinboro (Pa.) State Coll., 1969-70, assoc. prof., 1970-72, prof. methods of fgn. lang. teaching, German lit., 1972-76; asst. prof. dept. modern langs. Bucknell U., Lewisburg, Pa., 1976-78, research assoc., 1976-82; propr. Fine Arts Research Assoc., 1982—; lectr. Santa Rosa Jr. Coll., Yuba City Community Coll.; cons. bilingual edn. Central Susquehanna Intermediate Unit, 1972-76, dir. Bilingual Program. Author: Jeremiah Gotthelf's Die Kaserel in der Vehfeude, A Didactic Satire, 1977; contbr. articles to profl. jours., newspapers, mags. Nat. Inst. Edn. grantee, 1973; Bucknell U. Grantee, 1975; Pro Helvetia grantee, 1978, grantee Ministry Edn., People's Republic of China. Mem. Robert G. Sproul Assocs. U. Calif.-Berkeley, Harvard Club San Francisco, M.H. DeYoung Mus. Soc. Republican. Lutheran. Clubs: Sulgrave, Harvard Radcliffe of N.Y. Home: 20124 Forest Vista Dr Twain Harte CA 95383

LITTLE, BONITA CLAUDENE, home economics educator; b. Greenville, Tex., Aug. 21, 1952; d. Claude Edward and Bonnie Bell (Poteet) Little. Student Bethany Nazarene Coll., 1970-71; B.S. in Vocat. Home Econs. Edn., East Tex. State U., 1974, M.S. in Home Econs., 1979. Cert. tchr. vocat. home econs. edn., Tex. Tchr., coordinator Home Econs. Coop. Edn., Wolfe City (Tex.) Ind. Sch. Dist., 1975-78; asst. instr. home econs. East Tex. State U., Commerce, 1978-79, adj. instr., 1981; prof. home econs. edn. N.W. Nazarene Coll., Nampa, Idaho, 1981—; lectr. in field. Recipient Henson-Kickernick scholarship, East Tex. State U., 1972; named Outstanding Young Home Economist, State Idaho, 1986-87. Mem. Am. Home Econs. Assn.,

Idaho Home Econs. Assn., Am. Vocat. Assn., Idaho Vocat. Assn., Home Econs. Edn. Assn., Nat. Assn. Edn. of Young Children. Nazarene. Office: NW Nazarene Coll Nampa ID 83651

LITTLE, JUDITH MAURER, management consultant; b. Winston-Salem, N.C., July 4, 1946; d. William and Thelma (McKeithan) Maurer; m. John Anderson Little, Aug. 29, 1970 (div. Mar. 1977). BA, St. Andrews Coll., 1968; MA, Presbyn. Sch. of Christian Edn., 1970; MSW, U. N.C., 1975. Prin. Judith Little & Assocs., Chapel Hill, N.C., 1980-83; mgmt. devel. specialist Levi Strauss and Co., San Francisco, 1983-84, mgr. corp. tng. and devel., 1984-87; account exec. Emile Labadie & Assocs., Piedmont, Calif., 1987—. Mem. Am. Soc. Tng. and Devel. (Nat., Golden Gate chpts.), The Conf. Bd. (devel. council). Democrat. Home: 183 Carl St San Francisco CA 94117 Office: Emile Labadie & Assoc 183 Indian Rd Piedmont CA 94610

LITTLE, THOMAS ALLYN, construction company marketing executive; b. Portland, Oreg., Aug. 16, 1947; s. Carl Mize Little and Elizabeth (Rathbun) Herrin; m. Vicki Gayle Miles, June 14, 1969; children: Lindsey Taylor and Shawna Marie (twins). AA in Bus., Diablo Valley Coll., 1972; BBA, San Francisco State U., 1974. V.p. mktg. Albay Constn. Co., Martinez, Calif., 1970—, also bd. dirs. Served to sgt. USAF, 1965-70. Republican. Episcopalian. Avocations: fishing, camping, gardening, history. Office: Albay Constrn Co 865 Howe Rd Martinez CA 94553

LITTLE, WILLIAM JOHN, accountant; b. South Porcupine, Ont., Apr. 15, 1942; s. John Gorby and Jean (Wilson) L.; m. Tania Galichenko, Oct. 23, 1965; children—David, Deborah. B. Commerce, U. B.C., 1965. Controller Kootenay Forest Products, Nelson, 1967-70; treas. Wescorp. Industries Ltd., Vancouver, 1970-74; ptnr., v.p. Dunwoody & Co., Vancouver, 1974—, trustee in bankruptcy, 1978. Co-author: Insolvency Manual, 1980; National Insolvency Course, 1983. Mem. Inst. Chartered Accts. B.C., Can. Insolvency Assn. Club: Terminal City (Vancouver). Home: 5588 Willow St, Vancouver, BC Canada V5Z 3S4 Office: Dunwoody & Co, PO Box 49272, 1800-1055 Dunsmuir St, Vancouver, BC Canada V7X 1C5

LITTLEFIELD, LOIS COBURN, clinical social worker; b. Detroit, Oct. 22, 1917; d. Samuel Dixon and Mildred Miriam (Sloman) Coburn; m. William L. Lester, Aug. 28, 1941 (div. 1956); 1 child, Marilyn Jo; m. Donald Bruce Littlefield, Mar. 17, 1967; stepchildren: Robert B., Donald R. BA in Sociology, U. Mich., 1938, MSW, 1954. Social worker Pub. Welfare, Detroit, 1940-42; med. social worker Los Angeles County and U. So. Calif. Med. Ctr., 1942-45; social worker Vista Del Mar Child Care, Los Angeles, 1950-53; med. social worker Cedars Hosp., Hollywood, Calif., 1956-59; supr. adoptions Dept. Adoptions, Los Angeles, 1959-68; med. social worker cons. Dept. Pub. Social Services, Los Angeles, 1968-80; pvt. practice specializing in clin. social work Westlake Village, Calif., 1980—; cons., therapist Calabasas (Calif.) Acad., 1982-85; cons. Oxnard Manor Convalescent Hosp., 1986—; affiliate status mem. of med. staff, Westlake Village, 1984—; social worker Nat. Med. Homecare, 1986—, children's project Ventura County Mental Health and Ventura County Schs., 1986. Referee State Bar Ct., Ventura and Santa Barbara and San Luis Obisbo counties, Calif., 1980—, probation monitor, 1985—; care-giver Hospice of the Conejo, Thousand Oaks, Calif., 1984—; mem. adv. bd., bd. dirs. Ventura County Mental Health, 1980—. Fellow: Soc. Clin. Social Work (Continuing Edn. award 1981); mem. Nat. Assn. Social Workers (cert., register of clin. Social Workers adv. bd., counseling, Psychotherapy Service sec. 1985—, Continuing Edn. award 1982), med. staff Westlake Community Hosp. (affiliate), AAAS (book reviewer 1981—). Avocations: duplicate bridge, reading, swimming, traveling, socializing. Office: 2659 Townsgate Rd Suite 100 Westlake Village CA 91361

LITTLER, DONALD, electronics company executive; b. Pao Ting Fu, China, Oct. 6, 1930; s. Harold and Nellie (Fisher) L.; came to U.S., 1948, naturalized, 1954; student Coll. of Marin, 1950-51; B.S., U. Calif.-Berkeley, 1957; postgrad. San Jose State U., 1958-60, exec. program Stanford U., 1976; m. Gwen U. Davis, Aug. 13, 1955; children—Ralph, Raymond, Robert. Devel. engr. Sperry Gyroscope Co., Sunnyvale, Calif., 1957-63, R.S. Electronics, Sunnyvale, 1963; with Sylvania Electronic Systems, Mountain View, Calif., from 1963, dept. mgr., then bus. area mgr.; now v.p., gen. mgr. strategic elec. def. div., GTE Systems Corp., 1977. Bd. dirs. Casols Sch., Los Gatos, 1974—; asst. cubmaster Boy Scouts Am., San Jose, Calif., 1968-69. Served to staff sgt. AUS, 1951-54. Mem. IEEE, Assn. Old Crows. Republican. Lutheran. Patentee in field. Office: Sylvania Electronic Systems PO Box 188 Mountain View CA 94040

LITTMAN, RICHARD ANTON, psychologist, educator; b. N.Y.C., May 8, 1919; s. Joseph and Sarah (Feinberg) L.; m. Isabelle Cohen, Mar. 17, 1941; children—David, Barbara, Daniel, Rebecca. A.B., George Washington U., 1943; postgrad., Ind. U., 1943- 44; Ph.D., Ohio State U., 1948. Faculty U. Oreg., 1948—, prof. psychology, 1959—, chmn. dept., 1963-68, vice provost acad. planning and resources, 1971-73; Vis. scientist Nat. Inst. Mental Health, 1958-59. Contbr. articles to profl. jours. Sr. postdoctoral fellow NSF, U. Paris, 1966-67; sr. fellow Nat. Endowment for Humanities, U. London, 1973-74; Ford Found. fellow, 1952-53; recipient U. Oreg. Charles H. Johnson Meml. award, 1980. Mem. Am., Western, psychol. assns., Soc. Research and Child Devel., Psychonomics Soc., Animal Behavior Soc., Soc. Psychiat. Study of Social Issues, Internat. Soc. Developmental Psychobiology, History of Sci. Soc., Am. Philos. Assn., AAUP, Sigma Xi. Home: 3625 Glen Oak Dr Eugene OR 97405 Office: U Oreg Dept Psychology Eugene OR 97403

LITTRELL, ROBERT THOMAS, educator; b. Winfield, Kans., Nov. 6, 1926; s. Harold Hubert and Winifred (Davis) L.; B.S., U. Nebr., 1950, M.A., 1951, Ed.D., 1957; m. Shirley Clinkenbeard, Sept. 8, 1946; children—Gloria Ann, Allison; m. 2d, Agnes Cummings, Feb. 4, 1967; 1 son, Stephen Robert. Prin. pub. sch., Blue Hill, Nebr., 1951-53; dir. elementary edn., jr.-high edn. and tchr. edn. for the Govt. of Am. Samoa, Pago Pago, Samoa; also Tutuila, Samoa, 1953-55; counselor-trainer U. Nebr., Lincoln, 1956-57, research asst., 1955-56; test officer Long Beach State Coll., 1957-65, coordinator instnl. research, 1959-65, asst. prof., 1957-60, asso. prof. psychology, 1960-64, prof., 1964-71, dir. instl. research, 1971—; ltd. pvt. practice counseling and hypnotherapy; tax-shelter cons. Stout-Hall and Assocs., South Pasadena, Calif; dir. Coll. and Univ. Research Enterprises, Inc., Long Beach; ednl. cons. State Farm Ins. Co., Santa Ana, Calif., 1960-64. Served with USMCR, 1943-46. Decorated Purple Heart. Mem. Am. Psychol. Assn., Calif. Assn. Instl. Research (exec. com.), Psi Chi, Phi Delta Kappa, Phi Kappa Phi. Mason. Contbr. articles to profl. jours. Home: 1900 E Ocean Blvd Apt 916 Long Beach CA 90802 Office: 1250 Bellflower Blvd Long Beach CA 90840

LIU, ANNEMARY TZE-AN, chemist; b. Quebec City, Can., Dec. 13, 1959; d. Ignace D. and Rosaline C. (Soo) L.; m. John Robert Kern, Apr. 19, 1984. Student, U. Calif., Santa Barbara, 1977-80; BS, U. Calif., Santa Cruz, 1980-82; postgrad., Stanford U., 1983-84. Chemist, researcher SRI Internat., Menlo Park, Calif., 1982-84, Syntex Research, Palo Alto, Calif., 1984-85; chemist, asst. water quality supr. Calif. Water Service, San Jose, 1985—. Contbr. articles to profl. jours. Mem. Am. Chem. Soc., Soc. Environ. Toxicology and Chemistry, Chinese-Am. Chem. Soc., Assn. for Analytical Chemists, U. Calif. Alumni Assn., Am. Water Works Assn. Office: Calif Water Service Co 1720 N First St San Jose CA 95112

LIU, EDMUND KIN, research chemist; b. Honolulu, June 7, 1951; s. Young Wah and Shuk Kwan (Ho) L.; m. Edwina P. Wong, Sept. 6, 1980; children: Jennifer, Katherine. BS, U. Chgo., 1973; PhD, MIT, 1977. Mem. postdoctoral staff mem. Los Alamos (N. Mex.) Nat. Lab., 1978-79; chemistry specialist Aerojet Strategic Propulsion Co., Sacramento, 1979—. Mem. Am. Chem. Soc., Sigma Xi. Home: 904 Doheney Ct Roseville CA 95661 Office: Aerojet Strategic Propulsion Co PO Box 15699C Sacramento CA 95852-1699

LIU, GERALD HANMIN, cultural and educational administrator; b. San Francisco, Aug. 24, 1944; s. Howard Y. and Patricia Marian (Lee) Low; m. Jennifer Mei, Sept. 6, 1969. BA, U. Pacific, 1966; DDS, NYU, 1970; PhD, Union for Experimenting Colls. and Univ.'s, 1978. Lectr. U. Calif., San Francisco, 1974-75; exec. dir. Min An Health Ctr., San Francisco, 1979-82; pres. U.S.-China Ednl. Inst., San Francisco, 1978—, also bd. dirs.; bd. dirs. San Francisco-Shanghai Friendship City Com., 1983—; cons. W.K. Kellogg Found., Battle Creek, Mich., 1984—, MacArthur Found., Chgo., 1986—; mem. steering com. Kellog Internat. Fellowship program Mich. State U., East Lansing, 1985—; hon. advisor Shanghai Mental Health Ctr., People's Rep. China, 1987. Project dir. (textbook) Essential Book of Traditional Chinese Medicine, Vols. I and II, 1986. Served to capt. U.S. Army, 1971-73. Grantee Ednl. Found. Am., 1981-85, Ettinger Found., 1980, 86, Ednl. Comm. Fgn. Med. Grads., 1982, L.J. and M.C. Skaggs Found., 1985, W.K. Kellogg Found., 1986; named hon. advisor Shanghai 1st People's Hosp., People's Republic of China, 1985, Beijing Med. U., People's Republic of China, 1986. Mem. AAAS, Omicron Kappa Upsilon. Home: 1146 Pacific Ave San Francisco CA 94133 Office: US-China Ednl Inst 1146 Pacific Ave San Francisco CA 94133

LIU, KATHERINE CHANG, artist, art educator; b. Kiang-si, Peoples Republic of China; came to U.S., 1963; d. Ming-fan and Ying (Yuan) Chang; m. Yet-zen Liu; children: Alan S., Laura Y. MS, U. Calif., Berkeley, 1965. Staff instr. Conejo Valley Art Mus., Thousand Oaks, Calif., 1981-82; tchr. Tex. Watercolor Soc., Ohio Watercolor Soc., Ariz. Watercolor Assn., Rocky Mountain Watercolor Workshop, U. Va. extension, Longwood. Coll., Va. One-man shows include Harrison Mus., Utah State U., Riverside (Calif.) Art Mus., Ventura (Calif.) Coll., Roanoke (Va.) Mus. Fine Arts, Fla. A&M U., Louis Newman Galleries, Los Angeles, Lung-Men Gallery, Taipei, Republic of China; juror of award Watercolor West Nat., Calif., 1986, Western Fedn. Exhibition, Houston, 1986, San Diego Internat. Watercolor Exhbn., 1986, Ohio Watercolor Soc., 1986. Recipient Rex Brandt award San Diego Watercolor Internat., 1985, Purchase Selection award Watercolor USA and Springfield (Mo.) Art Mus., 1981, Gold Medal award Allied Arts Am. Nat. Arts Club, N.Y.C., 1986; NEA grantee, 1979-80. Mem. Nat. Watercolor Soc. (life, chmn. jury 1985, pres. 1983, Top award 1984), Watercolor USA Honor Soc., Nat. Soc. Painters in Case in and Acrylic (2d award 1985), Rocky Mountain Nat. Watermedia Soc. (juror 1984, awardee 1978, 80, 86), West Coast Watercolor Soc.

LIU, ROBERT SHING-HEI, chemistry educator, researcher; b. Shanghai, Peoples Republic of China, Aug. 1, 1938; came to U.S., 1958; s. George C.C. and Aline (Tang) L.; m. Regina S.L. Ro, Nov. 22, 1967; children: Corey Wei, Conan Chung. BA, Howard Payne Coll., 1961; PhD, Calif. Inst. Tech., 1965. Research chemist E.I. DuPont de Nemours & Co., Wilmington, Del., 1964-68; assoc. prof. U. Hawaii, Honolulu, 1968-72, prof. chemistry, 1972—; vis. research assoc. biol. lab. Harvard U., Cambridge, Mass., 1974-75: vis. researcher Royal Instn., London, 1975. Contbr. articles to profl. jours. Sloan fellow, 1970-72, Guggenheim fellow, 1974-75; Fujio Matsuda scholar U. Hawaii Found., 1985-86; Medal for Excellence in Research U. Hawaii Bd. Regents, 1986. Office: U Hawaii Chemistry Dept 2545 The Mall Honolulu HI 96822

LIU, ROGER KIM SING, accountant; b. Honolulu, July 25, 1934; s. Roger O.K. and Alice (Mar) L.; m. Sandra Jean Ching, Aug. 9, 1958; children—Rouen, RoJeanne, RoAnne, Ian, Royd. B.A., U. Hawaii, 1956; postgrad. Golden Gate U., 1957. C.P.A., Hawaii. Acct., sr. tax auditor Peat, Marwick, Mitchell, Honolulu, 1958-62; pvt. practice acctg., Honolulu, 1963—; account exec. E.A. Buck Co., Inc.; dir., officer Broadcast Services, Inc., Honolulu, Ellaric Corp., Honolulu. Bd. dirs. Cath. Youth Orgn., Honolulu, 1983; treas. PTA, Honolulu, 1981; treas. Hawaii Chinese History Ctr., 1983; pres. U. Hawaii Art Assn., 1984. Mem. Am. Inst. C.P.A.s, Hawaii Soc. C.P.A.s (chmn. edn. com., lect., taxation cons.), Nat. Fedn. Ind. Bus., Am. Assn. Ind. Investors (life). Republican. Roman Catholic. Clubs: Chinese Jaycees (dir. 1966-68), Newman Club (dir. 1954-56), Peng Hui (pres. 1954-56). Home: 1531 Ipukula St Honolulu HI 96821 Office: 1221 Kapiolani Blvd Penthouse Blackfield Bldg Honolulu HI 96814

LIU, SHIN-TSE, chemical consultant; b. Taipei, Republic of China, Sept. 27, 1932; s. Teng-mien and Alee (Chen) L. BSChemE, Taiwan Nat. U., Taipei, 1956; Diplom-Chemiker, Technische-Hochschule, Aachen, Fed. Republic Germany, 1962, Dr. rer. nat., 1966. Research chemist ITT Rayonier, Whippany, N.J., 1967-70, UCLA, 1970-72; research engr. Jet Propulsion Lab., Pasadena, Calif., 1972-73; pres. S.T. Liu & Co., Los Angeles, 1974—. Mem. Am. Chem Soc. Office: PO Box 17457 Los Angeles CA 90017

LIVERGOOD, NORMAN DAVID, information systems consultant, academic administrator, educator; b. Syracuse, Kans., Sept. 21, 1933; s. Donald and Bessie (Tucker) L.; m. Nanette Vawter, Apr. 17, 1976; children: Jamila, Brianna. BA, Phillips U., 1955; BD, Yale U., 1958, PhD, MA, 1962; M in Psychology, S. Ill. U., 1968. Assoc. prof. philosophy So. Ill. U., Edwardsville, 1965-69; acad dean Calif. Inst. Asian Studies, San Francisco, 1972-75; pres. Inst. Creative Learning, Santa Rosa, Calif., 1980-82; vice prin., computer coordinator Armstrong Preparatory Sch., El Cerrito, Calif., 1982-83; computer coordinator Head Royce Sch., Oakland, Calif., 1983-84; dir. undergrad. studies U. San Francisco, 1984-87; prof. program coordinator Nat. U., Los Angeles, 1987—. Author: Activity in Marx's Philosophy, 1967, Walter Lippmann and The Continuing American Revolution, 1976; developed intelligence tutoring system. Woodrow Wilson fellow Yale U., 1960. Mem. Am. Assn. Artificial Intelligence. Avocations: chess, badminton, writing. Home: 2453 Chelsea Pl #3 Santa Monica CA 90403 Office: Nat Univ 9920 S La Cienega Blvd Los Angeles CA 90301

LIVESAY, THOMAS ANDREW, museum administrator; b. Dallas, Feb. 1, 1945; s. Melvin Ewing Clay and Madge Almeda (Hall) L.; m. Jennifer Clark, 1985; children: Heather Marie, Russell Lee. B.F.A., U. Tex., Austin, 1968, M.F.A., 1972; postgrad., Harvard U. Inst. Arts Adminstrn., 1978. Curator Elisabet Ney Mus., Austin, 1971-73; dir. Longview (Tex.) Mus. and Arts Center, 1973-75; curator of art Amarillo (Tex.) Art Center, 1975-77, dir. center, 1977-80; asst. dir. for adminstrn. Dallas Mus. Fine Arts, 1980-85; dir. Mus. of N.Mex., Santa Fe, 1985—; mem. touring panel Tex. Commn. Arts; mem. panel Nat. Endowment Arts, Inst. Mus. Services. Author: Young Texas Artists Series, 1978, Made in Texas, 1979; editor: video tape American Images, 1979, Ruth Abrams, Paintings, 1940-85, NYU Press. Served with U.S. Army, 1969-71. Mem. Am. Assn. Museums (council 1986—), Tex. Assn. Museums (v.p. 1981, pres. 1983), N.Mex. State Records and Archives Commn. (chmn. 1986—). Office: PO Box 2087 Santa Fe NM 87504

LIVINGSTON, ALVIN JACOB, state official; b. New Orleans, June 12, 1929; s. Bernard and Annette H. (Steckler) L.; m. Rita Cornelia Powers, Oct. 29, 1961. B.S. with honors, UCLA, 1953. Spl. asst. to pres. So. Calif. Freight Lines, Los Angeles, 1954-57; v.p., gen. mgr. Torre Safety Devices, Los Angeles, 1957-59; v.p. fin. and adminstrn., sec.-treas., conglomerate of Twentieth Century Engrng. Corp., Radiant Industries Inc., Mammoth Mountain Inn Corp. and affiliates including Hurley & Grassini, Operation Gateway; pres. subs. Qualimetrics, Los Angeles, 1959-78; cons. fin., mgmt., pub. relations, career guidance, polit. campaign mgmt., Los Angeles, 1958-83; chief dep. dir. Calif. Dept. Motor Vehicles, Sacramento, 1983—. Past pres. Los Angeles Library Assn., Cedars-Sinai Med. Ctr. Young Men's Group, Fernando Awards Inc., various polit. orgns.; past officer, dir. United Chambers of San Fernando Valley, Pacific Lodge Boy's Home, Gt. Western Council Boy Scouts Am.; mem. 1972 Electoral Coll.; mem. exec. com. Sacramento Vol. Ctr. Mem. UCLA Alumni Assn. (life, former bd. dirs., pres. Class of 1953, mem. govt. affairs steering com., pres. 1985—). Republican. Jewish. Clubs: Optimists, Sacramento Yacht. Lodge: Masons. Editorial bd. Los Angeles County Guide to Govt. Almanac, 1964-83, chmn., 1971-75, editor, 1983; editor various polit. newspapers and bus. publs. Office: Dept Motor Vehicles 2415 1st Ave Sacramento CA 95818

LIVINGSTON, MYRA COHN, poet, writer, educator; b. Omaha, Nebr., Aug. 17, 1926; d. Mayer L. and Gertrude (Marks) Cohn; m. Richard Roland Livingston, Apr. 14, 1952; children: Joshua, Jonas Cohn, Jennie Marks. B.A., Sarah Lawrence Coll., 1948. Profl. horn player 1941-48; book reviewer Los Angeles Daily News, 1948-49, Los Angeles Mirror, 1949-50; asst. editor Campus Mag., 1949-50; various public relations positions and pvt. sec. to Hollywood (Calif.) personalities 1950-52; tchr. creative writing Dallas (Tex.) public library and schs., 1958-63; poet-in-residence Beverly Hills (Calif.) Unified Sch. Dist., 1966-84; sr. instr. UCLA Extension, 1973—; cons. to various sch. dists., 1966-84, cons. poetry to publishers children's lit., 1975—. Author: Whispers and Other Poems, 1958, Wide Awake and Other Poems, 1959, I'm Hiding, 1961, See What I Found, 1962, I Talk to Elephants, 1962, I'm Not Me, 1963, Happy Birthday, 1964, The Moon and a Star and Other Poems, 1965, I'm Waiting, 1966, Old Mrs. Twindlytart and Other Rhymes, 1967, A Crazy Flight and Other Poems, 1968, The Malibu and Other Poems, 1972, When You Are Alone/It Keeps You Capone: An Approach to Creative Writing with Children, 1973, Come Away, 1974, The Way Things Are and Other Poems, 1974, 4-Way Stop and Other Poems, 1976, A Lollygag of Limericks, 1978, O Sliver of Liver and Other Poems, 1979, No Way of Knowing: Dallas Poems, 1980, A Circle of Seasons, 1982, How Pleasant to Know Mr. Lear!, 1982, Sky Songs, 1984, A Song I Sang to You, 1984, Monkey Puzzle, 1984, The Child as Poet: Myth or Reality?, 1984, Celebrations, 1985, Worlds I Know and Other Poems, 1985, Sea Songs, 1986, Earth Songs, 1986, Higgledy-Piggledy, 1986 others; co-editor: The Scott-Foresman Anthology, 1984; Author: The Writing of Poetry; film strips; editor 16 anthologies of poetry; contbr. articles on children's lit. to ednl. publs., contbr., essays on lit. and reading in edn. to various books. Officer Beverly Hills PTA Council, 1966-75; pres. Friends of Beverly Hills Public Library, 1979-81; bd. dirs. Poetry Therapy Inst., 1975—, Reading is Fundamental of So. Calif., 1981—. Recipient Honor award N.Y. Herald Tribune Spring Book Festival, 1958, Excellence in Poetry award Nat. Council Tchrs. of English, 1980. Mem. Authors Guild, Internat. Reading Assn., Soc. Children's Book Writers (honor award 1975), Tex. Inst. Letters (awards 1961, 80), So. Calif. Council on Lit. for Children and Young People (Comprehensive Contribution award 1968, Notable Book award 1972), PEN. Club: Commonwealth of Calif. (award 1984). Address: 9308 Readcrest Dr Beverly Hills CA 90210

LIVINGSTON, PATRICIA ANN, marine biologist, researcher; b. Detroit, Dec. 10, 1954. BS, Mich. State U., 1976; MS, U. Wash., 1980, M in Pub. Adminstrn., 1987. Ecosystem modeller Nat. Marine Fish Service, Seattle, 1977-82, trophic interactions program leader, 1983—; mem. sci. and tech. bd. The Sea Use Council, Seattle, 1986—. Contbr. articles on ecosystem modelling and marine fish trophic interactions to profl. jours. Mem. Am. Fisheries Soc. (officer and regional fish corr. Marine Fish sect., 1982-84), AAAS. Office: NW and Alaska Fisheries Ctr 7600 Sand Point Way NE Bldg 4 Bin C15700 Seattle WA 98115

LIVINGSTON, ROBERT BURR, neuroscientist, educator; b. Boston, Oct. 9, 1918; s. William Kenneth and Ruth Forbes (Brown) L.; m. Mandana Beckner, Dec. 21, 1954 (div. 1977); children—Louise, Dana, Justyn. A.B., Stanford, 1940, M.D., 1944. Intern, asst. resident internal medicine Stanford Hosp., 1943-44; instr. physiology Yale Sch. Medicine, 1946-48, asst. prof., 1950-52; research asst. psychiatry Harvard Med. Sch., 1947-48; NRC sr. fellow neurology Inst. Physiology, Geneva, Switzerland, 1948-49; Wilhelm Gruber fellow neurophysiology Switzerland, France, Eng., 1949-50; exec. asst. to pres. Nat. Acad. Scis.-NRC, 1951-52; asso. prof. physiology and anatomy U. Calif. at Los Angeles, 1952-56, prof., 1956-57; dir. basic research NIMH and Nat. Inst. Neurol. Diseases and Blindness, 1956-61; chief neurobiology lab. NIMH, 1960-65; prof. dept. neuroscis. U. Calif. at San Diego Sch. Medicine, 1965—, chmn. dept., 1965-70; Gast prof. U. Zurich, Switzerland, 1971-72; Ernest Sachs lectr. Dartmouth Med. Sch., 1981; cons. NRC, VA, NASA, HEW, NSF, Dept. Def.; asso. neuroscis. research program Mass. Inst. Tech., 1963-76, hon. asso., 1976—. Adv. editorial bd.: Jour. Neurophysiology, 1959-65; editorial bd.: Internat. Jour. Psychobiology, 1970-80, Neurol. Research, 1979—; cons. editor: Jour. Neurosci. Research, 1975-85. Bd. dirs. Foundations' Fund for Research in Psychiatry, 1954-57; bd. incorporators Jour. History of Medicine and Allied Scis.; incorporator Inst. Policy Studies, 1963, Elmwood Inst., 1984. Served to lt. (j.g.) M.C. USNR, 1944-46. Decorated Bronze Star; recipient Award for Excellence Matrix: Midland Festival, 1981. Fellow AAAS (chmn. commn. sci. edn. 1968-71), Am. Acad. Arts and Scis.; mem. Am. Physiol. Soc., Am. Assn. Anatomists, Am. Neurol. Assn., Am. Acad. Neurology, Assn. for Research in Nervous and Mental Diseases, Am. Assn. Neurol. Surgeons, Soc. for Neurosci.

LIVSEY, ROBERT CALLISTER, lawyer; b. Salt Lake City, Aug. 7, 1936; s. Robert Frances and Rosezella Ann (Callister) L.; m. Renate Karla Guertler, Sept. 10, 1962; children: Scott, Rachel, Daniel, Benjamin. BS, U. Utah, 1962, JD, 1965; LLM, NYU, 1967. Bar: Utah 1965, Calif. 1967. Prof. Haile Selassie U., Addis Abbaba, Ethiopia, 1965-66; spl. asst. to chief counsel IRS, Washington, 1977-79; assoc., then ptnr. Brobeck, Phleger & Harrison, San Francisco, 1967—; adj. prof. U. San Francisco Law Sch., 1970-77; mem. adv. com. IRS Dist. Dirs., 1986—. Research editor U. Utah Law Rev., 1964-65; editor Tax Law Rev., 1966-67; contbr. articles to profl. jours. Dist. bd. dirs. adv. com. IRS; pres. tax litigation San Francisco Club, 1986-87. Mem. State Bar Calif. (chmn. taxation sect. 1984-85), ABA (chmn. subcom. real estate syndications, 1981-84), San Francisco Bar Assn. (chmn. taxation sect. 1982), Am. Law Inst., Tax Litigation Club (pres. 1986—), Order of Coif, Beta Gamma Sigma. Democrat. Mem. Evangelical Covenant Ch. Club: Commonwealth (San Francisco). Home: 128 LaSalle Ave Piedmont CA 94610 Office: Brobeck Phleger & Harrison Spear St Tower San Francisco CA 94105

LLEWELLYN, JOHN FREDERICK, cemetery executive; b. Los Angeles, Nov. 16, 1947; s. Frederick Eaton and Jane Elizabeth Llewellyn; divorced. BA, U. Redlands, 1970; MBA, U. So. Calif., 1972. Foreman Pacific T&T, Orange, Calif., 1970; underwriter Allstate Ins. Co., Santa Ana, Calif., 1971-72; asst. to controller Forest Lawn Co., Glendale, Calif., 1972-73, v.p., 1973-75, exec. v.p., 1976—, treas., chief fin. officer, 1978-83, sec., bd. dirs., 1983—; various offices, bds. dirs. divs. Forest Lawn Co., Glendale, Calif., 1974—; exec. v.p. Founders Fin. Corp., Glendale, 1974-75, pres. 1975-82, also bd. dirs.; chief exec. officer Met. Computer Ctr., Glendale, 1974-81, Upstairs Gallery Inc., Glendale, 1974—, also vice chmn. bd. dirs.; bd. dirs. Beneficial Standard Life Ins. Co., Los Angeles, Braille Inst., Los Angeles; trustee Glendale Meml. Hosp. Bd. dirs. Greater Los Angeles Visitors and Convention Bur., Glendale Devel. Council, Los Angeles area Council Boy Scouts Am., vice chmn., 1987.. Mem. Am. Cemetery Assn., (bd. dirs. 1977-81, 83-86, v.p. 1985-86, pres.-elect 1986-87), Internment Assn. Calif. (bd. dirs 1984—, state v.p. 1985—), Calif. Mortuary Alliance (bd. dirs.), Econ. Round Table (sec.-treas. 1983-85), Newcomer Soc. N.Am. Clubs: Calif., Lincoln (Los Angeles). Home: 1960 Wilson Ave Arcadia CA 91006 Office: Forest Lawn Meml-Parks and Mortuaries 1712 S Glendale Ave Glendale CA 91205

LLOYD, MCKINLEY, personnel director, municipal offical; b. Shreveport, La., Jan. 27, 1947; s. Harrison and Marie (Smith) L.; m. Patricia Laura Ann Lynn Lloyd, June 18, 1976; children: Ileidth, Parlisha, Doretha, Tony, Robert. BS, So. U. and A&M Coll., 1969; MA, Chapman Coll., 1979. Cert. community coll. tchr., Calif. Manpower planner City of Stockton, Calif., 1976-77, personnel analyst, 1977-80, personnel analyst, affirmative action specialist, 1980-86, dep. dir. personnel services, 1986—; dir. Iva's Internat. Skin Care and Cosmetics. Chmn. bd. dirs. OIC of San Joaquin County, Calif., 1982-83; mem. Leadership Stockton, 1983-84, Stockton Alumni Assn., 1984—. Served to capt. U.S. Army, 1969-75. Mem. Calif. Assn. Affirmative Action Officers, Calif. Pub. Employer Labor Relations Assn., Greater Stockton Area Personnel Assn., San Joaquin County Intercultural Assn. (founder 1979). Democrat. Baptist. Avocations: gourmet cooking, collecting jazz music, traveling. Home: 345 E Yorkshire Dr Stockton CA 95207 Office: City of Stockton Dept Personnel 425 N El Dorado St Stockton CA 95202

LLOYD, WILLIAM EMMONS, JR., lawyer; b. Richmond, Va., June 13, 1944; s. William Emmons and Alice Roberta (Hannah) L.; B. Chem. Engring. U. Va., 1967; J.D., Am. Univ., 1971; children—Jennifer Anne, Josena-June Clemens, Jason Damion, Jeannine Claudine, Danielle Ashley. Bar: U.S. Patent Office 1968, Va. 1971, U.S. Ct. Customs and Patent Appeals 1973, U.S. Ct. Appeals (9th cir.) 1979, U.S. Supreme Ct. 1977, Calif. 1980. Assoc. Kelly & Cogan, Santa Monica, Calif., 1983-86; sole practice, Los Angeles, 1986—. Served with USNR, 1964-67. Scholar Calif. State, 1962, U. Va., 1962-64. Mem. Alexandria, Va. Jaycees (dir. 1977-79), Calif. Bar Assn., Los Angeles Trial Lawyers Assn. (chmn. def. doctors bank 1981), Calif. Trial Lawyers Assn. (co-chmn. toxics subcom. of legis. liason com. 1986—), Assn. Trial Lawyers Am., Va. Bar Assn., Delta Theta Phi. Democrat. Episcopalian. Office: 11601 Wilshire Blvd Suite 1830 Los Angeles CA 90025

LO, SAMUEL NAI-MING, clinical psychologist; minister; b. Canton, China, Dec. 6, 1935; came to U.S., 1962; s. Tze-Kwai and Siu-Hing (Chan) L.; m. Helen Yeung, Dec. 23, 1966; children: Sharon, Amy, Bonnie. Diploma Chung Chi Coll., Hong Kong, 1959, Canton Bible Inst., Hong Kong, 1962; BDiv., Fuller Theol. Sem., 1965; PhD, Fuller Grad. Sch. Psychology, 1971.

Ordained to ministry Evangelical Free Ch. Am., 1966; lic. psychologist, lic. marriage family counselor. Clin. psychologist Rancho Los Amigos Hosp., Downey, Calif., 1970-78; asst. clin. prof. U. So. Calif., Los Angeles, 1978-82; community psychologist Asian Counseling Ctr., Los Angeles, 1978—; clin. asst. prof. Fuller Sch. Psychology, Pasadena, Calif., 1980-84; pvt. practice clin. psychology, Monterey Park, Calif., 1973—; pastor Chinese Evangelical Free Ch., Los Angeles, 1965-68; interim pastor Chinese Evang. Free Ch., Monterey Park, Calif., 1978-79. Mem. Am. Psychol. Assn., Asian Am. Psychol. Assn., Calif. State Psychol. Assn., Western Psychol. Assn., Pasadena Area Psychol. Assn. Office: 850 S Atlantic Blvd Suite 306 Monterey Park CA 91754

LO, WAITUCK, artist; b. Honolulu, June 9, 1919; s. Wai Tong and Kam T. Lo; m. Agnes Lo Ching; Jan. 4, 1958; children: Edwina, Felix, Lisa Ann. BS, Utopia U., Shanghai, China, 1942; postgrad., Yen Yu Inst. Fine Art, Shanghai, Ind. U. Exhibited in group shows at Assn. Honolulu Artists Jury Art Show, 1956, 57 (Most Decorative award 1956, 57), Assn. Honolulu Artists non-jury show, 1957 (Popular award 1957), Narcissus Festival Art Exhibition, 1960 (Kaiser award 1960, Most Popular award 1960), Maui County Fair Art Exhibition, 1963 (2d prize 1963). Recipient 1st Place Water Color award Assn. Honolulu Artists, 1965, 68, Hayward award Assn. Honolulu Artists, 1968, 1st Place Water Color award Home Builders Assn. Art Show, 1966; Honorable Mention in Oil and Water Color, Assn. Honolulu Artists, 1966, Internat. Assn. Artists, 1979. Club: Toastmasters (Honolulu) (pres. 1986). Home: 6080 Keoki Pl Honolulu HI 96821

LO, WILLIAM WEI-HSING, engineer, consultant; b. Hong Kong, People's Republic of China, Apr. 15, 1950; came to U.S., 1976; s. Tao-Haim and Fu-Shien (Hwang) L.; m. Emily Shiuh-Fang, Jan. 16, 1978; children: Jennifer, Benjamin Lo. BS, Taipei Inst. Tech., Republic of China, 1971; MS, Kans. State U., 1979. Sr. engr. Control Data Corp., Omaha, 1979-82; systems engr. Ibis System Inc., Westlake Village, Calif., 1982-85; prin. engr. Pertec Peripherals Corp., Chatsworth, Calif., 1985—, Amperif Corp., Chatsworth, 1986—; computer cons. Computest Internat. Co., Thousand Oaks, Calif., 1984—. Recipient Tech. Excellence award Control Data Corp., 1981. Mem. IEEE. Home: 2779 N Velarde Dr Thousand Oaks CA 91360 Office: Amperif Corp 9232 Eton Ave Chatsworth CA 91311

LOBB, CHARLES WILLIAM, electronics company executive; b. Kansas City, Mo., Dec. 10, 1932; s. Lloyd W. and Urazelle M. (Huhn) L.; m. Charlotte Jane Carter, Aug. 9, 1961; children: Carolyn Jane, Patricia Ann. BEE, U. Minn., 1955; MSEE, U. So Calif., 1968. Mem. engring. research and devel. staff Gen. Mills, Inc., Mpls., 1955-56; mem. tech. staff Hughes Aircraft Co., Culver City, Calif., 1958-68, group head, 1968-71, sect. head, 1971-78, dept. mgr., 1978-80, corp. dir., 1980—; instr. electronics, 1967-68; lectr. UCLA, 1982; asst. dir. Tech. Edn. Ctr., Los Angeles, 1980—; chmn. Alumni Relations U. So. Calif. Sch. Engring., 1985. Contbr. articles on computers to profl. jours. Co-chmn. Marathon Communications Summer Olympic Games, 1984; chmn. Los Angeles Area Council Amateur Radio Clubs, 1985. Served to capt. USAF, 1956-58. Hughes fellow, 1966-68. Mem. Am. Radio Relay League (asst. dir. southwestern div. 1985—), Quarter Century Wireless Assn., Am. Soc. Engring. Edn., U. So. Calif. Alumni Assn. (bd. govs. 1985—), U. So. Calif Assocs. (life), U. So. Calif. Dean's Circle (life). Home: 1843 244th St Lomita CA 90717 Office: Hughes Aircraft Co PO Box 45066 Los Angeles CA 90045-0066

LOBBAN, ROBERT PAUL, diversified electronics company executive; b. Boston, June 29, 1954; s. John Frederick and Audrey Ruth (Palmer) L. BS in Indsl. Engring., Northeastern U., 1977; MBA, Harvard U., 1981. Indsl. engr. Tex. Instruments, Attleboro, Mass., 1977-78, supr. material control, 1978-79; controller fiberloys div. Rogers (Conn.) Corp., 1981-82; controll flexible interconnections div. Rogers Corp., Chandler, Ariz., 1982-84, adminstrv. mgr. flexible interconnections div., 1984—. Mem. Am. Inst. Indsl. Engrs., Alpha Pi Mu (v.p. 1975-76, pres. 1976-77), Tau Beta Pi. Baptist. Avocations: golfing, skiing, swimming, boating. Home: 4346 E Ahwatukee Dr Phoenix AZ 85044 Office: Rogers Corp Box 700 Chandler AZ 85224

LOBERG, ARNOLD PALMER, manufacturing company executive; b. Poplar Hill, Alta., Can., May 30, 1933; s. Lars and Agnes (Brekke) L.; m. Helen Margaret Peterson; children—Kevin, Ian, Joanne. Student Augsburg Coll., 1955-56. Lic. pilot. Pres. Summit Drapery, Ltd. Prince George, B.C., Can., 1970—. Contbr. articles to newsletters. Speaker The Shepard Ch., Prince George; bd. dirs., adminstr. Office of Billy Graham Evangelistic Assn., Prince George, 1982, council of reference, 1984—; condr. seminars in field; bd. dirs. adv. council, resource person Christian Businessmen's Com. B.C., 1981-85, chmn. bd. dirs., 1984-85; bd. dirs. Christian Businessmen's Assn. Can., 1978-84; chmn. bd. Youth for Christ, 1977-80, Northwest Counseling Services, 1987—; bd. dirs. Partnership in Gospel Program, Luth. Ch. Can., 1964-65, Men's Brotherhood, Luth. Ch. Am., 1961-68, other religious orgns.; founding mem., B.C. Dept. Recreation and Sports, bd. dirs. Christian Counseling Ctr., 1978-82; chmn. B.C. Govt. safety standards com. on hang gliding, 1976-78. Mem. Western Guides and Outfitters Assn., Can. Owners and Pilots Assn., Christian Assn. Psychol. Studies. Club: Fred Bear Sports of Am. (charter). Address: 169 Riley Dr, Prince George, BC Canada V2M 3N9 Address: PO Box 346, Prince George, BC Canada V2L 4S2

LOBERG, ERIC LEWIS, orthodontist; b. Ithaca, N.Y., Apr. 18, 1946; s. Harry J. and Aline (Johnson) L.; m. Mary Elizabeth Fogarty, Dec. 21, 1968; children—Kristin, Erica, Dana. Student Cornell U., 1966; D.M.D., Tufts U., 1970; cert. in orthodontics Eastman Dental Ctr., Rochester, N.Y., 1973. Diplomate Am. Bd. Orthodontics. Pvt. practice orthodontics, Los Angeles, 1973—. Mem. Coll. Diplomates of Am. Bd. Orthodontics, Am. Assn. Orthodontists, Western Dental Soc., Pacific Coast Soc. Orthodontists, E.H. Angle Soc. Orthodontists, Westwood Acad. Medicine and Dentistry (pres. 1978), Beverly Hills Acad. Dentistry (bd. dirs. 1979-81). Republican. Clubs: Calif. Yacht (Marina del Rey), Rotary (pres. Westwood Village 1982-83). Home: 10793 Wellworth Ave Los Angeles CA 90024 Office: 10921 Wilshire Blvd Suite 1203 Los Angeles CA 90024

LOCATELLI, PAUL LEO, university administrator, educator; b. Santa Cruz, Calif., Sept. 16, 1938; s. Vincent Dino and Marie Josephine (Piccone) L. B.S., Santa Clara U., 1961; M. Div., Jesuit Sch. Theology, 1974; D.B.A., U. So. Calif., 1971. C.P.A., Calif. Ordained priest Roman Catholic Ch., 1974. Acct., Kasch, Lautze & Lautze, San Jose, Calif., 1960-61, Wolf & Co., San Francisco, 1973-74; prof. acctg. Santa Clara U., Calif., 1974-86, assoc. dean Sch. Bus., 1975-78, acad. v.p., 1978-86; sr. commr. Western Assn. Schs. and Colls., 1982—; rector, prof. acctg. Loyola Marymount U., Los Angeles, 1986—. Trustee, Bellarmine Coll. Prep., San Jose, 1975—, U. San Francisco, 1979-86, Seattle U., 1983—. Named Outstanding Tchr. of Yr., Santa Clara U., 1978. Mem. Calif. Soc. CPAs, Am. Inst. CPAs, Am. Acctg. Assn. Democrat. Club: Commonwealth (San Francisco). Office: Loyola Marymount U 7101 W 80th St Los Angeles CA 90045

LOCKART, BARBETTA, counselor, educator, researcher, writer; b. Sacramento, Calif., Feb. 28, 1947; d. Bernard Elwood and Naomi Joyce (Wilson) L.; m. Michael Stanley Ray, Dec. 29, 1982 (div). AA in English, Southwestern Coll., Chula Vista, Calif., 1974; BA, San Diego State U., 1975; MA in Edn. Adminstrn., N.Mex. State U., Las Cruces, 1979, MA in Counseling and Guidance, 1981. Sec., interim coordinator, tchr. Indian Edn. Project, Palm Springs (Calif.) Unified Sch. Dist., 1976-79; outreach counselor Tecumseh House/Boston Indian Council, 1980-81, asst. dir., 1981; acad. counselor, coordinator native Am. affairs Ea. N.Mex. U., Portales, 1981-82; ind. researcher in field of counseling, Albuquerque, 1982—; owner Dearwater Designs, Albuquerque; speaker in field of community edn., alcoholism, urban native Am. women. Rockefeller Found. fellow, 1978-79; Nat. Inst. Edn. fellow, 1979-80. Mem. NEA, Am. Indian Higher Edn. Council, Am. Personnel and Guidance Assn., N.Mex. Personnel and Guidance Assn. Author: Resolving Discipline Problems for Indian Students: A Preventative Approach, 1981, Auctions and Auction-Going: Make Them Pay Off for You; contbr. articles to profl. jours.

LOCKE, LOUIS GARFIELD, JR., chemical engineer; b. Everett, Wash., Jan. 22, 1945; s. Louis Garfield and Helen (Davis) L.; m. Carol Maxine Hansberry, Apr. 16, 1966; children: Greg Louis, Garret Daniel. Process engr. Reynold's Metals, Longview, Wash., 1970-73, asst. supt. cryolite, 1973-79, supt. cryolite, 1979-82, supt. cryolite/carbon, 1982—. Pres. Monticello Middle Sch. PTO, Longview, 1985; v.p. Longview Soccer Club, 1986; chmn. campaign Bob Williams for State Rep., 1978. Mem. Am. Inst. Chem. Engrs. (sec./treas. 1972-75). Republican. Baptist. Club: Toastmasters (Longview) (area gov. 1979). Avocations: hunting, bicycling, running, coaching youth sports. Home: 1818 Florence Ave Longview WA 98632 Office: Reynolds Metals Co PO Box 999 Longview WA 98632

LOCKE, RAYMOND KENNETH, podiatric physician, educator; b. Czestohowa, Poland, Oct. 28, 1909; s. Leon and Ceceilia (Opatowska) L.; m. Edith Cavell Bester, Sept. 10, 1939; children—Linda Locke Shirer, Steven Elliot. Student Ind. U.; D.P.M., Ohio Coll. Podiatric Medicine, 1931, D.Ed. (hon.), 1966. Diplomate Am. Bd. Podiatric Surgery. Practice podiatric medicine, Englewood, N.J., 1931-78, San Diego, 1978—; assoc. prof. Calif. Coll. Podiatric Medicine U. So. Calif., Los Angeles County Med. Ctr., 1978—; cons. podiatric medicine and surgery. Contbr. to textbooks, articles to profl. jours. Patentee medical instruments. Co-chmn. Rancho Bernardo Guild of San Diego Opera Assn., 1980-82; bd. dirs. San Diego State U. Opera Inst.; bd. dirs. Rancho Bernardo Recreation Council, 1979-84, pres., 1980-81; Mem. No. area com. Parks and Recreation Bd. San Diego. Recipient Disting. Alumni award Ohio Coll. Podiatric Medicine, 1981; research awards including Stickel award, 1964, 69, 1st prize Sci. Exhibits award, Western Podiatry Congress, 1960; 1st award sci. exhibit Am. Coll. Emergency Physicians, 1977; decorated for disting. service in medicine E.U.R., Rome, 1965. Fellow Am. Coll. Foot Surgeons (past pres. Eastern div.), Am. Coll. Podiatric Radiology, Am. Assn. Hosp. Podiatrists (past pres.); mem. Am. Podiatry Assn. (past bd. trustees, 4 gold medals, 1 silver medal sci. exhibits award, audio visual competition awards 1972, 73), Calif. Podiatric Med. Assn., San Diego Podiatric Med. Assn., World Med. Assn. (assoc.), U. So. Calif. Los Angeles Med. Staff Assn., Am. Med. Writers Assn., San Diego County Health Com. Health Systems Agy. Lodge: Rotary. Office: 16766 Bernardo Center Drive Rancho Bernardo CA 92128

LOCKE, SUSAN R., corporate art consultant; b. Detroit, Dec. 30, 1946; s. Maurice and Freda Molly (Glassman) Rubenstein. Student, Mich. Luth. Coll., 1964-65, U. Chgo., 1969-71; BA in Art History, San Francisco State U., 1976. Med. technologist various cos., Mich., Ill., Calif., and Eng., 1966-74; art cons. various cos. including Bank Am., Kaiser Hosp., Chevron Oil Corp., Pacific Bell Telephone, 1976—; owner Plaza Posters and Plaza Frames, San Francisco. Bd. dirs. Magnes Mus., Berkeley, Calif., 1976—, Ctr. Visual Arts, Oakland, Calif., 1979—, Ind. Living Project, San Francisco, 1981—. Mem. Profl. Bus. Women's Exchange (charter), Art Deco Soc. No. Calif., San Francisco Mus. Modern Art, Univ. Art Mus. Berkeley, Mu. Contemporary Art Los Angeles, Jewish Mus. of West. Democrat. Jewish. Home and Office: 201 Estate Dr Piedmont CA 94611

LOCKETT, JO ANN, diversified electronics company executive; b. Santa Monica, Calif., Dec. 6, 1938; d. William Alfred and Virginia (Snow) L. BA, UCLA, 1961; MS, West Coast U., 1974; postgrad., Smith Mgmt. Program, 1985-86. Systems analyst Rand Corp., Santa Monica, 1961-72, computer scientist, 1972-78; bus. planning mgr. Xerox Corp., El Segundo, Calif., 1978-82, program mgr., 1982—. Author: Algorithims, Graphs, Computers, 1970, Numerical Inversion of La Place Transform., 1966; contbr. articles to profl. jours. Mem. Assn. Computing Machinery (several local offices 1974—, conf. coms. 1974-81), Sigmetrics (nat. bd. dirs., 1981-82, local chmn. 1977-78), Digital Computer Assn., Am. Fedn. Info. Processing Socs. Mormon. Home: 3311 Cabrillo Rd Los Angeles CA 90066 Office: Xerox Corp 701 S Aviation Blvd El Segundo CA 90245

LOCKHART, KENNETH BURTON, architectural company executive; b. Charles City, Iowa, Oct. 2, 1916; s. Louis James and Dorothy Hildred (Hurst) L.; m. Mary Francis Coan, July 10, 1945 (div.): children: Brian, Leslie; m. Susan Jacobs, Sept. 27, 1964. Project adminstr. Fla. So. Coll., Lakeland, 1946-50; farm mgr. Frank Lloyd Wright Found., Spring Green, Wis., 1951-52, mem. staff, 1952-62; dir. quality assurance Taliesin Assoc. Architects, Spring Green and Scottsdale, Ariz., 1963—. Mem. Constrn. Specifications Inst. (cert. constrn. specifier, chmn. reg. tech. 1983—, spectext com. 1986-87, bd. dirs. Phoenix chpt. 1985-86, sec. Phoenix chpt. 1986-87, recipient Hon. Mention 1982, 83, 86, 87, Honor award 1984, Southwest region Dir.'s Citation 1986, Outstanding Profl. award 1986). Avocations: fly fishing, cross-country skiing, home brewing, wine making, bldg. own home. Home and Office: Frank Lloyd Wright Found 13900 N 108th St Scottsdale AZ 85261-4430

LOCKHART, KORALJKA, opera magazine editor, public relations consultant; b. Dubrovnik, Yugoslavia, May 30, 1932; came to U.S., 1965, naturalized, 1971; d. Zvonimir Peter and Lina (Kukuljica) Krstic; m. Keith M., Lockhart, July 26, 1966 (div. 1979). Student Music Sch., Dubrovnik, 1941-51, U. Zagreb (Yugoslavia), 1951-55. Music dir. Sta. KKHI-AM-FM, San Francisco, 1965-70; press rep. San Francisco Opera, 1970-74, mag. editor, pub. relations cons., 1981—; acting pub. relations dir. San Francisco Symphony, 1979-80; dir. promotion Com. for Arts and Lectures, U. Calif., Berkeley, 1974-78; cons. in field. Author: San Francisco Opera: The Adler Years, 1953-81, 1981; Opera Calendar, 1980-81. Home: 289 Lexington Rd Kensington CA 94707 Office: War Meml Opera House San Francisco CA 94102

LOCKWOOD, COURTNEY DANA, public relations executive; b. San Bernardino, Calif., Oct. 9, 1981; d. Carleton W. and Jeane M. Lockwood; m. David M. Kabashima, Jan. 1, 1976; children: Gregory, Dana. BA in English, Psychology, Occidental Coll., 1972. Pub. relations dir. San Fernando Valley Girl Scout Council, Reseda, Calif., 1975-78; pub. relations specialist CalComp, Anaheim, Calif., 1978-79; account supr. Harshe-Rotman & Druck, Los Angeles, 1979-81; group supr. The Bohle Co., Los Angeles, 1981-84; v.p. client services Carl Terzian Assocs., Los Angeles, 1984-86, sr. v.p., 1986—. Mem. Publicity Club of Los Angeles, (pres. 1986-87, PRO award, 1981), Pub. Relations Soc. Am. (sec. so. Pacific dist. 1987, PRISMS award 1982). Office: Carl Terzian Assocs 11726 San Vicente Blvd Suite 550 Los Angeles CA 90049

LOCKWOOD, JOHN PAUL, volcanologist; b. Bridgeport, Conn., Oct. 26, 1939; s. Paul Vincent and Arlene Gertrude (Pfalzgraf) L.; m. B. Martha Bell; children: Pamela, Glen. AB, U. Calif., Riverside, 1961; PhD, Princeton U., 1966. Exchange scientist Nat. Acad. Sci., Moscow, 1966; geologist U. S. Geol. Survey, Calif., 1966-73, Hawaii, 1974—; cons. to govt. agys., Indonesia, Colombia, Italy, Cameroon; bd. dirs. Volcano Art Ctr., Hawaii. Contbr. numerous articles to profl. jours. Fellow Geol. Soc. Am.; mem. Internat. Assn. Volcanology, Sigma Xi. Office: Hawiian Volcano Observatory PO Box 51 Hawaii National Park HI 96718

LOCKWOOD, JOHN SCHUYLER, music educator; b. Covington, Ky., July 31, 1946; s. John Piatt and Barbara (Duer) L.; m. Barbara Schmidt, Jan. 4, 1974; children: Maura Michelle, Heather Christine, Justin Thomas. B in Music Edn., Eastern Ky. U., 1969; M in Music Edn., Ariz. State U., 1975; PhD, U. Colo., 1985. Tchr. music Hulett (Wyo.) Pub. Schs., 1969-71, Chandler (Ariz.) Pub. Schs., 1973-75; music dir. Am. Internat., Duësseldorf, Fed. Republic of Germany, 1975-77; music tchr. Poudre Sch. Dist., Fort Collins, Colo., 1979-81; music instr. Aims Community Coll., Greeley, Colo., 1984; asst. prof. U. Wyo., Laramie, 1984—; mem. undergrad. curriculum com. U. Wyo., 1984—, liason curriculum and instrn. Music dept., 1984—; chmn. music edn. com., 1985—. Leader Awana Boys Club, Ft. Collins, 1985—. Mem. Music Educators Nat. Conf., Nat. Assn. Jazz Educators. Republican. Roman Catholic. Home: 1117 Clark St Fort Collins CO 80524 Office: U Wyo Dept Curriculum and Instrn Laramie WY 82071

LOCZI, BARBARA BIDDLE, marketing consultant; b. Rockford, Ill., Jan. 4, 1947; d. Herbert Dale and Lucille Edith (Philion) Biddle; m. Geza Anthony Loczi, July 5, 1969; children: Jennifer Paige, Magda Allyn, Zachary Robert. BA in Eng. Edn., Purdue U., 1969. Tchr. English, speech East Hills (Mich.) Jr. High Sch., 1969-78, Ferndale (Mich.) High Sch., 1969-78; mgr. promotions Avon Champ., Detroit, 1979-80; coordinator promotions Detroit Express Soccer, 1980; cons. communications Henredon Furniture, Morganton, S.C., 1981; advt. copywriter Ted Bates, Gothenberg, Sweden, 1983-84; pvt. practice advt., mktg. cons. Moorpark, Calif., 1984—; media cons. United Communication Service Task Force, Detroit, 1981-82. Mem. cons. United Communication Service Task Force Media Cons., Detroit, 1981-82, child sex abuse task force Children's Ctr., Detroit, 1982-83; leadership trainer Jr. League, Birmingham, Mich., 1972-83; bd. dirs. and pub. relations Women's Ctr., Birmingham, 1982-83; co-founder and media rep. Citizens for Accountability and Responsibility in Edn., Moorpark, 1986. Democrat. Roman Catholic. Avocations: custom needlepoint designs, tennis, running, baking. Home and Office: 4233 Laurelhurst Rd Moorpark CA 93021

LODGE, JAMES PIATT, JR., consulting chemist; b. Decatur, Ill., Feb. 4, 1926; s. James Piatt and Grace Marie (Carr) L.; m. Nancy Pickering Myers, Sept. 4, 1948; children: Martha P., Judith T., Susan P., Elizabeth H., Eric P. BS, U. Ill., 1947; PhD, U. Rochester, 1951. Asst. prof. chemistry Keuka Coll., Keuka Park, N.Y., 1950-52; research chemist U. Chgo., 1952-55; chief chem. research Robert A. Taft Sanitary Engring. Ctr. of USPHS, Cin., 1955-61; program scientist Nat. Ctr. Atmospheric Research, Boulder, Colo., 1961-74; cons. atmospheric chemistry Boulder, 1974—; adj. prof. La. State U., Baton Rouge, 1966-69; bd. dirs. Wright-Ingraham Inst., Colorado Springs, Colo. Co-Editor: Atmospheric Chemistry of Chlorine and Sulfur Compounds, 1959, The Smoke of London, 1969, Sulfur in the Atmosphere, 1978; editor Atmospheric Environment, 1958—, Jour. Aerosol Sci., 1985—; contbr. articles to profl jours. Mem. Gov.'s Adv. Com. Weather Control, Colo., 1963-66; mem. Colo. Air Pollution Variance Bd., Denver, 1966-70; chmn. Colo. Air Pollution Control Commn., Denver, 1970-76. Recipient Annual award PLAN, Boulder County, Colo., 1974. Fellow AAAS, N.Y. Acad. Scis.; mem. Am. Chem. Soc. (cert., citation 1970, Disting. Service 1973), Air Pollution Control Assn. Home: 801 Circle Dr Boulder CO 80302 Office: 385 Broadway Boulder CO 80303

LODMER, EMILY LEVIN, English language educator; b. Denver, Mar. 1, 1948; d. Nathaniel Ira and Selma Carolyn (Weintraub) Levin; m. Sheldon Ira Lodmer, Nov. 28, 1970; children: Abby Rebecca, Zachary Harris. Student, Universidad Nacional Autonoma de Mex., Mexico City, 1967; BA in Spanish and French, UCLA, 1969, MA in Applied Linguistics, 1979. Cert. secondary, community coll. tchr., Calif. Tchr. Los Angeles Children's Ctrs., 1969-70; tchr. Spanish, ESL Anaheim (Calif.) Union High Sch. Dist., 1970-75; tchr. Spanish, French Santa Monica (Calif.) Unified Sch. Dist., 1975-76; prof. ESL Santa Monica Coll., 1977—; mem. Santa Monica Coll. ESL Adv. Council, 1983—; presenter Jerusalem Conf. ESL, Eng. as a Fgn. Lang., Hebrew U., 1985, Catesol State Conf., 1986, Santa Monica Coll. ESL Consortium, 1986. Sch. Bd. pres. Malibu (Calif.) Jewish Ctr. and Synagogue, 1980-81. Mem. Calif. Tchrs. ESL (presenter conf. Oakland 1986), Calif. Community Colls. ESL. Avocations: cycling, aerobic dance, Spanish reading, marathon running, writing poetry. Office: Santa Monica Coll Dept English 1900 Pico Blvd Santa Monica CA 90405-1628

LOEB, JOYCE LICHTGARN, interior designer, civic worker; b. Portland, Oreg., May 20, 1936; d. Elias Lichtgarn and Sylvia Amy (Margulies) Freedman; m. Stanley Robinson Loeb, Aug. 14, 1960; children: Carl Eli, Eric Adam. Student U. Calif.-Berkeley, 1954-56; B.S., Lewis and Clark Coll., 1958; postgrad. art and architecture, Portland State U., 1976. Tchr. art David Douglas Sch. Dist., Portland, 1958-59, 61-64; tchr., chmn. art dept. Grant Union High Sch. Dist., Sacramento, 1959-60; designer, pres. Joyce Loeb Interior Design, Inc., Portland, 1976—; cons. designer to various developers of health care facilities. Chairperson fundraisers for civic orgns. and Jewish orgns.; bd. dirs. Met. Family Services, Portland, 1968-71, Young Audiences, Inc., Portland, 1970-76, 78-80, Portland Opera Assn., 1978-84, Arts Celebration, Inc., Portland, 1984—, Congregation Beth Israel, 1986—; chmn. Artquake Festival, 1985, Operaball, 1987; v.p. Beth Israel Sisterhood, 1981-83; trustee Congregation Beth Israel, 1986—, chmn. art interior design com. Mem. Inst. Bus. Designers, Nat. Council Jewish Women. Democrat. Club: Multnomah Athletic. Home: 1546 SW Upland Dr Portland OR 97221

LOEB, ROBERT GEORGE, electrical engineer; b. Phoenix, Jan. 31, 1949; s. Howard Meyers and Ruth (Osgood) L.; m. Kitty Loeb, Feb. 24, 1974 (div. Apr. 1982). BSEE, Carnegie Tech., 1971. Engr. Quadri Corp, Phoenix, 1971-72; pres. OPTIFAB Inc., Phoenix, 1972—. Lobbyist, Washington, 1986—. Mem. Assn. Corp. Growth, Ariz. Circuits Assn., IEEE, Internat. Comanche Soc., Am. Electronics Assn. (bd. dirs. Palo Alto, Calif. chpt. 1986—, v. chmn. Ariz. chpt. 1986—), Young Pres. Assn. Republican. Jewish. Avocations: flying, scuba, sailing, cross county skiing. Home: 3720 E Mountain View Phoenix AZ 85028 Office: OPTIFAB 1550 W VAn Buren Phoenix AZ 85007

LOEBER, LAWRENCE (LARRY) ERVIN, real estate developer, freelance photographer; b. Pasco, Wash., Feb. 19, 1943; s. Ervin Carl and Evelyn Grace (Farrand) L.; m. Kathleen Joy Mosteller, Aug. 23, 1969; children: Lincoln E., Krystal Joy. BABA, N.W. Nazarene Coll., 1967; postgrad., U. Oreg., 1970; Cert. in Photography, Sch. Photography, Portland, Oreg., 1971, 74, 80; Cert. in Retirement Housing, Nat. Real Estate Devel. Ctr., San Francisco, 1985; Cert. in Cumputer Constrn., Edmonds Community Coll., 1986. Prin. Prime Properties, Kennewick, Wash., 1976—, Laka Devel., Eugene, Oreg., 1968-76. Sec. bd. dirs. Ch. of Nazarene, Richland, Wash., 1977-86, also lay chmn, dir. Caravan Youth Program; regional dir. Pinewood Derby Caravan Youth Program, Eastern Wash., 1984-85; dir. jr. high sch. youth group, Eugene, Oreg., 1969-75. Recipient Best of Show award for photography, Benton-Franklin Fair, Kennewick, Wash., 1977, Driving Rodeo Champion award Connell, Wash., 1961. Mem. Urban Land Inst., Assn. Multi-image. Republican. Avocations: snow skiing, softball, racquetball. Home and Office: Prime Properties 8934 179th Pl SW Edmonds WA 98020

LOEBLICH, HELEN NINA TAPPAN, paleontologist, educator; b. Norman, Okla., Oct. 12, 1917; d. Frank Girard and Mary (Jenks) Tappan; m. Alfred Richard Loeblich, Jr., June 18, 1939; children—Alfred Richard III, Karen Elizabeth Loeblich McClelland, Judith Anne Loeblich Covey, Daryl Louise Loeblich Valenzuela. B.S., U. Okla., 1937, M.S., 1939; Ph.D., U. Chgo., 1942. Instr. geology Tulane U., 1942-43; geologist U.S. Geol. Survey, 1943-45, 47-59; mem. faculty UCLA, 1958—, prof. geology, 1966-84, prof. emeritus, 1985—, vice chmn. dept. geology, 1973-75; research assoc. Smithsonian Instn., 1954-57; assoc. editor Cushman Found. Foraminiferal Research, 1950-51, incorporator, hon. dir., 1950—. Author: (with A.R. Loeblich, Jr.) Treatise on Invertebrate Paleontology, part C, Protista 2, Foraminiferida, 2 vols, 1964; The Paleobiology of Plant Protists, 1980, also articles profl. jours., govt. publs., encys.; Editorial bd.: Palaeoecology, 1972-82, Paleobiology, 1975-81. Guggenheim fellow, 1953-54; named Woman of Yr. in Sci. Palm Springs Desert Mus., 1987. Fellow Geol. Soc. Am. (councilor 1979-81); mem. Paleontol. Soc. (pres. 1984-85, medal), UCLA Med. Ctr. Aux. (Woman of Yr. medal), AAUP, Soc. Econ. Paleontologists and Mineralogists (councilor for paleontology 1975-77, hon. mem. 1978—, R.C. Moore medal), Internat. Paleontological Assn., Paleontol. Research Inst., Am. Microscopical Soc., Am. Inst. Biol. Scis., Phi Beta Kappa, Sigma Xi. Home: 11427 Albata St Los Angeles CA 90049 Office: Dept Earth and Space Scis Univ Calif Los Angeles CA 90024

LOEBNER, EGON EZRIEL, physicist; b. Plzen, Czechoslovakia, Feb. 24, 1924; s. Emil and Josephine (Koeser) L.; came to U.S., 1947, naturalized, 1952; BA in Physics, U. Buffalo, 1950, PhD in Physics, 1955; m. Sonya S. Sajovics, June 18, 1950; children: Gary Emil, Benny Joseph, Mindy Sue. Draftsman, Danek & Co., Bolevec, Czechoslavakia, 1941-42, asst. to chief engr. Terezin Waterworks, 1942-44; sr. engr. Sylvania Electric Products, Inc., Buffalo and Boston, 1952-55; mem. tech. staff RCA Labs., Princeton, N.J., 1955-61; mgr., research specialist H.P. Assos., Palo Alto, Calif., 1961-65; dept. head, research adviser Hewlett-Packard Labs., 1965-74, lab. assoc., 1976-77, mgr. data base mgmt. systems dept., 1977-80, mgr. cognitive interface dept., 1980-85, counselor sci. and tech. 1985—; counselor sci. and technol. affairs U.S. embassy, Moscow, 1974-76; lectr. Stanford U., part-time 1968-74; lectr. U. Calif. at Santa Cruz, 1972-74. Mem. N.J. Commn. on Radiation Protection, 1960-62; mem. lay adv. com. on math. Unified Palo Alto Sch. Dist., 1964-66. Bd. dirs. Jewish Center, Princeton, 1957-59. Fellow Phys. Soc. London; mem. Am. Phys. Soc., IEEE, Semiotic Soc. Am., Am. Assn. Artificial Intelligence, Am. Optical Soc., NSPE, Calif. Soc. Profl. Engrs., AAAS, Sigma Xi, Assn. for Computing Machinery, Cognitive Sci. Soc., N.Y. Acad. Scis., Calif. Acad. Scis., Sigma Alpha Mu. Democrat. Jewish. Club: Palo Alto Hills Golf and Country, Commonwealth. Research in physics, chemistry, electronics, metalurgy, psychology, biophysics, cybernetics, math., sci. policy and linguistics data processing. Patentee in optoelectronics. Home: 2934 Alexis Dr Palo Alto CA 94304 Office: Hewlett Packard Labs 1501 Page Mill Rd Palo Alto CA 94304

LOEHMAN, RONALD ERNEST, materials scientist; b. San Antonio, Feb. 22, 1943; s. Roland Albert and Charlotte (Herweck) L.; m. Edna Tusak, June 26, 1965 (div. Oct. 1981), 1 child, Rachel Andrea; m. Ellen Louise Griffith, July 10, 1982; 1 child, Matthew Charles. BA, Rice U., 1964; PhD, Purdue U., 1969. Asst. prof. U. Fla., Gainesville, 1970-75, assoc. prof., 1975-78; sr. materials scientist SRI Internat., Menlo Park, Calif., 1978-82; mem. tech. staff Sandia Nat. Labs., Albuquerque, 1982-86, div. supr., 1986—. Contbr. articles to profl. jours.; patentee in field. Mem. AAAS, Am. Ceramic Soc. (Roland Snow award 1984), Nat. Inst. Ceramic Engrs., Sigma Xi. Office: Sandia Nat Labs PO Box 5800 Albuquerque NM 87185

LOEHR, JOHN GEORGE, management consultant; b. N.Y.C., Sept. 20, 1941; s. John Francis Loehr and Gertrude Alma (Sweetman) Thomas; m. Hazel Delores Duboise, Feb. 24, 1962 (div. May 1977); children: Lee Anna, John Joseph, Edward Francis, Rita Carmen Kemm, Sarah Veronica. BA, Highlands U., 1964; student, U. N.Mex., 1962-63, postgrad., 1978-82. Pres. Ind. Learning, San Rafael, Calif., 1970-76; supt. edn. Alamo Navajo Sch. Bd., Magdalena, N.Mex., 1978-80; dir. pub. affairs WSAF, Santa Fe, 1982-83; sr. ptnr. Vanguard Group, San Rafael, 1984—. Mem. Nat. Soc. Performance and Instruction. Democrat. Club: Plaza Vieja (Las Vegas, N.Mex.). Avocations: flying, rafting, fishing. Home: North Star Rt Box 1439 Corrales NM 87048 Office: Vanguard Group 41 Marinita Park San Rafael CA 94901

LOEPPKY, JACK ALBERT, physiologist, researcher; b. Saskatoon, Sask., Can., Jan. 14, 1944; came to U.S., 1967; s. George and Sarah (Martens) L.; m. Janet Sue By, Nov. 22, 1974; children—Kristopher, Ninya. B.A. with distinction, U. Sask., 1966; M.S., U. N.Mex., 1969, Ph.D., 1973; postgrad. Colo. State U., 1969-70. Instr., U. Sask., Saskatoon, 1966-67; technician Lovelace Med. Found., Albuquerque, 1968-69, research assoc., 1970-75, assoc. scientist, 1975—, head dept. cardiopulmonary physiology, 1981-83; head respiratory technologist Wellington (N.Z.) Hosp., 1975; adj. asst. prof. U. N.Mex., Albuquerque, 1982—. Editor: Oxygen Transport to Human Tissues, 1982; contbr. articles to profl. jours. Max Planck fellow physiology, 1983-84; NSF grantee, 1984. Mem. Am. Physiol. Soc. Club: N.Mex. Mountain (Albuquerque). Office: Lovelace Med Found 2425 Ridgecrest Dr SE Albuquerque NM 87108

LOESER, JOHN DAVID, neurosurgeon, educator; b. Newark, Dec. 14, 1935; s. Lewis Henry and Rhoda Sophie (Levy) L.; m. Susan Winifred Becker, June 11, 1961 (div. 1974); children: Sally Ann, Thomas Eric, Derek William; m. Karen Winslow, Dec. 29, 1977; 1 child, David Winslow. BA, Harvard U., 1957; MD, NYU, 1961. Diplomate Am. Bd. Neurol. Surgery; cert. Nat. Bd. Med. Examiners.; lic. neurosurgeon, Wash. Intern dept. surgery U. Calif., San Francisco, 1961-62; resident neurol. surgery U. Wash., Seattle, 1962-67; asst. prof. neurosurgery U. Calif., Irvine, 1967-68; asst. prof. neurol. surgery U. Wash., Seattle, 1969-75, assoc. prof., 1975-80, prof., 1980—, dir. MultidisciplinaryPain Clinic, 1983—. Contbr. articles to profl. jours. Served as maj. U.S. Army, 1968-70. Mem. Internat. Assn. Study of Pain (sec. 1985—), Am. Pain Soc. (treas. 1980-85, pres. 1986—), Am. Assn Neurol. Surgeons, AAAS, Am. Soc. Functional and Stereotactic Neurosurgery, N. Pacific Soc. of Neurology and Psychiatry, Wash. Assn. Neurosurgery, Western Neurosurg. Soc., Am. Acad. Algology, King County Med. Soc., Cong. Neurol. Surgeons, Phi Beta Kappa, Alpha Omega Alpha. Avocations: skiing, woodcarving. Home: 1142 38th Ave Seattle WA 98122 Office: U Wash RI-20 Dept Neurol Surgery Seattle WA 98195

LOEWY, OLIVIA ROCHELLE, personnel trainer, consultant; b. Calif., Nov. 14, 1946; d. Peter and Annette (Cohen) Markin; m. Aaron David Loewy, June 14, 1970; 1 child, Monika Haley. B.A., UCLA, 1969; M.A. in Ednl. Psychology, Calif. State U.-Northridge; Ph.D., U. So. Calif. Cert. marriage, family and child counselor, Calif. Dir. Full Circle Guidance Clinic, Glendale, Calif., 1977-80; cons., trainer Western region U.S. Dept. Labor, 1980—, U.S. Office Personnel Mgmt., 1982—; co-founder Personal Dimensions, Glendale, Calif.; hon. academic appointee Calif. Sch. Profl. Psychology. Mem. Am. Soc. Tng. and Devel., Calif. Assn. Marriage and Family Therapists. Writer numerous fed. funded grant proposals. Home: 3128 Brookdale Rd Studio City CA 91604 Office: 3128 Brookdale Rd Studio City CA 91204

LOFFT, WILLIAM ALFRED, corporation executive; b. N.Y.C., Feb. 19, 1947; s. William A. and Lenore (Morgan) L.; m. Susan Panell, Mar. 30, 1968; children: Nicole Kimberly, William A. III. BA, U. Calif., Santa Barbara, 1970; MBA, San Diego State U., 1973. Lectr. fin. San Diego State U., 1973-74; fin. analyst GA Techs., San Diego, 1973-78, mgr. treasury, 1978-81, treas., 1981—; treas. Pyro Power Corp. subs. GA Techs., San Diego, 1980-82. Bd. dirs. Internat. Adv. bd. City of San Diego, 1984-86; com. chmn. Scripps Ranch Civic Assn., San Diego, 1975-79. Mem. World Trade Assn. (pres. San Diego chpt. 1985—), Dist. Export Council San Diego, San Diego C. of C. (internat. adv. council 1985—), Cash Mgmt. Assn. Republican. Home: 10635 Atrium Dr San Diego CA 92131 Office: GA Techs Box 85608 San Diego CA 92138

LOFGREN, ZOE, county government official; b. San Mateo, Calif., Dec. 21, 1947; d. Milton R. and Mary Violet L.; m. John Marshall Collins, Oct. 22, 1978; children: Sheila Zoe Lofgren Collins, John Charles Lofgren Collins. BA in Polit. Sci., Stanford U., 1970; JD cum laude, U. Santa Clara, 1975. Bar: Calif. D.C. Adminstrv. asst. to Congressman Don Edwards, San Jose, Calif., 1970-79; ptnr. Webber and Lofgren, San Jose, 1979-81; mem. Santa Clara County Bd. Suprs., 1980—; part-time prof. Law, U. Santa Clara, 1978-80. Exec. dir. Community Housing Developers, Inc., 1979-80; trustee San Jose Community Coll. Dist., 1979-82; bd. dirs. Community Legal Services, 1978-81, San Jose Housing Service Ctr., 1978-79; pres. Calif. Voter Group, Inc., 1977, mem. adv. bd. 1978—; mem. steering com. sr. citizens housing referendum, 1978; del. Calif. State Bar Conv., 1979-82, Dem. Nat. Conv., 1976; active Assn. Immigration and Nationality Lawyers, 1976-82, Calif. State Dem. Cen. Com., 1975—, Santa Clara County Dem. Cen. Com., 1974-78, Notre Dame High Sch. Blue Ribbon Com., 1981—, Victim-Witness Adv. Bd., 1980—. Recipient Santa Clara Law Sch. Community Service award, 1979, Bancroft-Whitney award for Excellence in Criminal Procedure, 1973. Mem. Santa Clara County Bar Assn. (trustee 1979—), Santa Clara County Women Lawyers Com. (exec. bd. 1979-80), Sanata Clara Law Sch. Alumni Assn. (v.p. 1977, pres. 1978), Nat. Women's Polit. Caucus. Office: Bd Suprs 70 W Hedding St San Jose CA 95110

LOFLAND, JOHN FRANKLIN, sociologist, educator; b. Milford, Del., Mar. 4, 1936; s. John Purnell and Juanita (Jobe) L.; m. Lyn Hebert, Jan. 2, 1965. B.A., Swarthmore Coll., 1958; M.A., Columbia U., 1960; Ph.D., U. Calif., Berkeley, 1964. Asst. prof. sociology U. Mich., 1964-68; assoc. prof. sociology Calif. State U., Sonoma, 1968-70; asso. prof. sociology U. Calif., Davis, 1970-74; prof. U. Calif., 1974—. Author: Doomsday Cult, 1966, 77, Analyzing Social Settings, 1971, 2d edit. (with L. H. Lofland), 1984, Doing Social Life, 1976, Crowd Lobbying, 1982, (with M. Fink) Symbolic Sit-ins, 1982, Protest, 1985; founding editor: Contemporary Ethnography, 1970-74; contbr. articles and revs. to profl. lit. Mem. Am. Sociol. Assn. (chair sect. on collective behavior and social movements 1980-81), Pacific Sociol. Assn. (pres. 1980-81), Soc. Study Symbolic Interaction (pres. 1986-87). Home: 523 E St Davis CA 95616 Office: U Calif Sociology Dept Davis CA 95616

LOFSTROM, MARK D., public relations official, arts administrator, writer; management consultant; b. Mpls., May 11, 1953; s. Dennis E. and Dorothy Dee (Schreiber) L. BA in Art History, Carleton Coll., 1979. Editorial asst. CANTO: A Rev. of Arts, Andover, Mass., 1977-78; pub. relations asst. Honolulu Acad. Arts, 1979, pub. relations rep., 1980-84, pub. relations officer, 1984-85, sec. 1985-86, chmn. ways and means, 1986—; sec., bd. dirs. Arts Council Hawaii, pres. bd. dirs. Coordinator rep. program Carleton Coll. Alumni Assn., Hawaii, 1984—. Mem. Am. Assn. Mus., Pub. Relations and Communications Mgmt. Com., Hawaii Mus. Assn. (editor newsletter), Pub. Relations Soc. Am., Historic Hawaii Found., Nat. Trust for Historic Preservation, Hawaii Lit. Arts Council. Editor mag. on preservation; contbr. articles on current exhbns.; mem. editorial adv. bd. East-West mag. ann. Honolulu Gallery Guide; organizer artists and writers exhbn., 1981. Office: Honolulu Acad Arts 900 S Beretania St Honolulu HI 96814

LOFTHOUSE, ROBERT ELLIS, banker; b. Valley City, N.D., Nov. 10, 1950; s. John William and Elizabeth Ann (Swan) L.; m. Patricia Ann Kaczowka, June 21, 1980; 1 child, Jon Remington. Student, Pasadena City Coll., 1975-76, UCLA, 1980. Programmer NCR Corp., Los Angeles, 1974-75, First City Bank, Rosemead, Calif., 1975-76, Universal Computer Service, Lawndale, Calif., 1976-78; analyst Philips Bus. Systems, Los Angeles, 1978; founder, mgr. The Software Loft, Downey, Calif., 1978-81; mgr. systems and programming First Interstate Bank, Los Angeles, 1981-84, sr. systems project mgr., 1984—, asst. v.p. Author, editor articles to newspapers, 1968-70. Vol. Spl. Olympics of Calif., Los Angeles, 1986. Served as cpl. USMC, 1970-74. Mem. Data Processing Mgmt. Assn. (bd. dirs. 1982-83). Republican. Roman Catholic. Avocations: sailing, skiing, swimming, racquetball, softball.

LOFTHOUSE, RUSS WILBERT, schoolteacher; b. Chgo., Jan. 21, 1945; s. Russell Wilber and Anne Marie (Daker) L.; m. Pamlin I. Axelson, Aug. 7, 1976; one child, James. BA in Elem. Edn., U. Denver, 1971; MA in Elem. Edn., U. Colo., Denver, 1978. Cert. elem tchr., Colo. Tchr. Cherry Creek Schs., Englewood, Colo., 1971—; mem. adv. bd. Teaching and Computers, N.Y.C., 1986—. Recipient Disting. Tchr. award Cherry Creek Schs., 1985; named Colo. Tchr. of Yr., Colo. Dept. Edn., 1986. Mem. Assn. Supervision and Curriculum Devel., Am. Acad. and Inst. Human Reason (dir. community leaders and succesful schs.), Fulbrite Tchrs. Alumni Assn., NEA, Nat. State Tchs. of Yr., Phi Delta Kappa. Avocations: outdoor activities, reading, advising and consulting. Home: 6802 N Hillside Way Parker CO 80134 Office: Cherry Creek Sch Dist 4700 S Yosemite Englewood CO 80111

LOFTUS, THOMAS DANIEL, lawyer; b. Seattle, Nov. 8, 1930; s. Glendon Francis and Martha Helen (Wall) L. B.A., U. Wash., 1952, J.D., 1957. Bar: Wash. 1958, U.S. Ct. Appeals (9th cir.) 1958, U.S. Dist. Ct. Wash. 1958, U.S. Ct. Mil. Appeals, U.S. Supreme Ct. Trial atty. Northwestern Mut. Ins. Co., Seattle, 1958-62; sr. trial atty. Unigard Security Ins. Co., Seattle, 1962-68, asst. gen. counsel, 1969-83, govt. relations counsel, 1983—; mem. Wash. Commn. on Jud. Conduct (formerly Jud. Qualifications Commn.), 1982—, vice-chmn., 1987—; judge pro tem Seattle Mcpl. Ct., 1973-81. Sec., treas. Seattle Opera Assn., 1980—; pres., bd. dirs. Vis. Nurse Services, 1979—; pres., v.p. Salvation Army Adult Rehab. Ctr., 1979—; vice chmn. Young Republican Nat. Fedn., 1963-65; pres. Young Reps. King County, 1962-63; bd. dirs. Seattle Seafair, Inc., 1975; bd. dirs., gen. counsel Wash. Ins. Council, 1984-86, sec., 1986—; bd. dirs. Arson Alarm Found. Served to 1st lt. U.S. Army, 1952-54, to col. Res., 1954-83. Fellow Am. Bar Found.; mem. Am. Arbitration Assn. (nat. panel arbitrators 1965—), Wash. Bar Assn. (gov. 1981-84), Seattle King County Bar Assn. (sec., trustee 1977-82), ABA (ho. of dels. 1984—), Internat. Assn. Ins. Counsel, Def. Research Inst., Am. Judicature Soc., Res. Officers Assn., Wash. Ins. Council (v.p., sec., gen. counsel, bd. dirs. 1984—), U. Wash. Alumni Assn., Phi Delta Phi, Theta Delta Chi. Republican. Presbyterian. Clubs: Coll. of Seattle, Wash. Athletic. Home: 3515 Magnolia Blvd West Seattle WA 98199 Office: 1215 4th Ave 18th Floor Seattle WA 98161

LOGAN, GEORGIA HOLMAN, English educator; b. Chgo., May 29, 1937; s. Charles Montgomery and Marie Agnes (Dunoon) Holman; m. Larry Logan, Dec. 20, 1958 (div. June 1964). BA in History, Oberlin Coll., 1958; MA in English, Stanford U., 1961; MA in Rhetoric, U. Calif., Berkeley, 1974. Instr. English, Foothill Coll., Los Altos Hills, Calif., 1961-67; prof. English and speech De Anza Coll., Cupertino, Calif., 1967—, dir. chamber theater prodn., 1972-75, pres. elect. acad. senate, 1975-76, pres., 1976-77, coordinator The Writing Place, 1981-83, co-dir. Women's Studies, 1987—; cons. Tadlock Assocs. Anchorage Community Colls. and Seattle Community Colls., 1977-78; chief of conciliation Foothill Coll. Dist., 1978-81; co-dir. Teaching Resource Ctr., 1985-86. Author: Handbook for Part-Time Faculty at De Anza, 1984; author-editor Handbook for English 1A Teachers at Foothill, 1964; contbr. articles to profl. jours.; book reviewer various orgns. Stanford U. grantee, 1960. Mem. ACLU, Nat. Coalition to Ban Handguns, So. Poverty Law Ctr., Common Cause, Stanford Alumni Assn., Foothill-De Anza Faculty Assn., Faculty Assn. Calif. Community Colls. Democrat. Club: Sierra. Avocations: traveling, swimming, camping, theater, oral interpretation.

LOGAN, JAMES KENNETH, judge; b. Quenemo, Kans., Aug. 21, 1929; s. John Lysle and Esther Maurine (Price) L.; m. Beverly Jo Jennings, June 8, 1952; children: Daniel Jennings, Amy Katherine, Sarah Jane, Samuel Price. A.B., U. Kans., 1952; LL.B. magna cum laude, Harvard, 1955. Bar: Kans. 1955, Calif. 1956. Law clk. U.S. Circuit Judge Huxman, 1955-56; with firm Gibson, Dunn & Crutcher, Los Angeles, 1956-57; asst. prof. law U. Kans., 1957-61; prof., dean U. Kans. (Law Sch.), 1961-68; partner Payne and Jones, Olathe, Kans., 1968-77; judge U.S. Circuit Ct., 10th Circuit, 1977—; Ezra Ripley Thayer teaching fellow Harvard Law Sch., 1961- 62; vis. prof. U. Tex. Law Sch., 1964, Stanford, 1969, U. Mich., 1976; commr. U.S. Dist. Ct., 1964-67. Author: (with W.B. Leach) Future Interests and Estate Planning, 1961, Kansas Estate Administration, 5th edit., 1986, (with A.R. Martin) Kansas Corporate Law and Practice, 2d edit., 1979; also articles. Candidate for U.S. Senate, 1968. Served with AUS, 1947-48. Rhodes scholar, 1952; recipient Disting. Service citation U. Kans., 1986. Mem. Am., Kans. bar assns., Phi Beta Kappa, Order of Coif, Beta Gamma Sigma, Omicron Delta Kappa, Pi Sigma Alpha, Alpha Kappa Psi, Phi Delta Phi. Democrat. Presbyterian.

LOGAN, LEE ROBERT, orthodontist; b. Los Angeles, June 24, 1923; s. Melvin Duncan and Margaret (Seltzer) L.; B.S., UCLA; 1952; D.D.S., Northwestern U., 1956, M.S., 1961; m. Maxine Nadler, June 20, 1975; children—Fritz, Dean, Scott, Gigi, Chad, Casey. Gen. practice dentistry, Reseda, Calif., 1958-59; practice dentistry specializing in orthodontics, Northridge, Calif., 1961—; pres. Lee R. Logan D.D.S. Profl. Corp.; mem. staff Northridge Hosp., Tarzana Hosp.; owner Maxine's Talent Agy. Served to USNR, 1956-58. Diplomate Am. Bd. Orthodontics. Named (with wife) Couple of Yr. Austic Children Assn., 1986. Fellow Internat. Acad. Nutrition; mem. Am., San Fernando Valley dental assns., Am. Assn. Orthodontists, Pacific Coast Soc. Orthodontists (dir., pres. so. sect. 1974-75, chmn. membership 1981-83), Found. Orthodontic Research (charter mem.), Calif. Soc. Orthodontists (chmn. peer rev. 1982-86), G.U. Black Soc. (charter mem.), Angle Soc. Orthodontists (pres. 1986-87, bd. dirs. 1982-86, nat. pres. 1982-86), Xi Psi Phi. Club: U.S.C. Century. Contbr. articles to profl. jours. Home: 4830 Encino Ave Encino CA 91316 Office: 18250 Roscoe Blvd Northridge CA 91324

LOGAN, WILLIAM ALFRED, law enforcement agent; b. Spokane, Wash., Nov. 26, 1933; s. James William and Mary Ada (Farmer) L.; m. Anna Virginia Loomis, 1956 (div. 1976); children: Laura Louise, Karla Christine, Doris Elaine, Elmer Palo; m. Marilyn Kay Nay, Feb. 11, 1978; 1 child, Denise Ann Nay. ATA LE, Centralia Coll., 1974. Jailor, dispatcher Lewis County Sheriff's Office, Chehalis, Wash., 1963-65, records and identification officer, 1965-69, patrol dep., 1969-71, patrol sgt., 1971-78, patrol lt., 1978-86, sheriff, 1987—. Bd. dirs. Sch. Dist. 300, Onalaska, Wash., 1967, 69. Served to sgt. U.S. Army, 1953-61, Korea. Recipient Disting. Service award US Jaycees, Chehalis, 1968. Democrat. Lodge: Eagles. Avocations: diving, photography, shooting. Home: 285 SW 2d St Chehalis WA 98532 Office: Lewis County Sheriff's Office 345 Main St Chehalis WA 98532

LOGE, FRANK JEAN, II, hospital administrator; b. Redlands, Calif., May 28, 1945; s. J. Phillip Loge and Helen M. (Booker) Loge Power; m. Sharon Lee Entrekin, Dec. 11, 1967; children—Frank III, Christopher, Gregory. B.A., Claremont Men's Coll., Long Beach, Calif., 1967; M.B.A., Calif. State U.-Long Beach, 1969; postgrad., UCLA Sch. Pub. Health, 1972-73. Mgr. mgmt. analysis UCLA, 1972-73, asst. dir. fin., 1973-74; dir. fin. U. Calif. Davis Med. Ctr., Sacramento, 1975-79, dep. dir. hosp. and clinics, 1979-84, dir. hosp. and clinics, 1984—. Office: U Calif Davis Med Ctr 2315 Stockton Blvd Sacramento CA 95817

LOGSDON, D(ONALD) F(RANCIS), JR., educator, college administrator; b. Chgo., Mar. 7, 1940; s. Donald Francis Sr. and Wilma Theresa (Wax) L.; m. Nancy Colette Graham, Dec. 14, 1963; children: David Kenneth, Donald Christopher, Cynthia Lenore, Valory Joie. BA in Biology, Northwestern U., 1961; MS in Biology, Trinity U., 1970; PhD in Zoology, Colo. State U., 1975; BA in Psychology, Chapman Coll., 1980, MA in Edn., 1982, MS in Human Resources Mgmt./Devel., 1985, MA in Devel. Psychology, 1986; LLB, LaSalle Extension U., Chgo., 1972; BS in Med. Lab. Studies, Thomas A. Edison Coll., 1982. Research technician Argonne (Ill.) Nat. Lab., 1961-63; commd. 2d lt. USAF, 1963, advanced through grades to lt. col.; biomed. lab. officer USAF, various locations, 1963-78; resigned USAF, 1978; dir., prof. Chapman Coll., Sacramento, 1978—; provider continuing edn., Sacramento, 1976—; researcher social and cultural studies, Sacramento, 1984—. Contbr. over 350 research articles, manuals, revs. Serves as lt. col. USAFR, 1978—. Mem. AAAS, Soc. Armed Forces Med. Lab. Sci., Sigma Chi, Phi Delta Kappa. Democrat. Home: 7341 Spicer Dr Citrus Heights CA 95621 Office: Chapman Coll Edn Services Bldg 2500 Mather AFB CA 95655

LOHAFER, DOUGLAS ALLEN, chemical engineer; b. Holstein, Iowa, June 7, 1949; s. Walter Jessen and Dorothy Ann (Thies) L. AA, Waldorf Coll., 1975; BA in Biology, Chemistry, Luther Coll., 1977. Sr. satellite ops. engr. Lockheed Missiles & Space Co., Inc., Sunnyvale, Calif., 1978—. Active Gideons Internat. Mem. Calif. Acad. Scis., Nat. Eagle Scout Assn., Am. Chem. Soc. (assoc. Santa Clara Valley sect. 1979, div. biol. chemistry 1979, div. nuclear chemistry and tech. 1986), Health Physics Soc., N.Y. C.S. Lewis Soc., U.S.A. S—ren Kierkegaard Soc., Phi Theta Kappa. Democrat. Lutheran. Home: 403 Los Encinos Ave San Jose CA 95134 Office: Lockheed Missiles & Space Co 1111 Lockheed Way Sunnyvale CA 94086

LOHMAN, MARION BETH SIMPSON BECKER, educational administrator; b. Sheridan, Mont., Nov. 30, 1918; d. Thomas Alexander and Maude Murilla (Bullerdick) Simpson; m. Peter Wilson Becker, June 28, 1941 (dec.); children—Laura Lynn, Karen Lee, Joyce Lenore; m. 2d, Michael S. Lohman, July 12, 1976 (dec.). Teaching degree Mont. State Normal Coll., 1939; B.S., Gonzaga U., 1956, M.S., 1964. Cert. librarian, Calif. Tchr., Mont. State Orphans Home, Twin Bridges, 1939-41, Post Falls, Idaho, 1952-54; librarian Greenacres Jr. High Sch., Spokane, Wash., 1956-63; media coordinator Edison High Sch., Huntington Beach, Calif., 1963-87 ; exec. rep. Crescent Cement Co., Costa Mesa, Calif., 1977-83. Sponsor Chess Club (nat. championship 1975), other sch. clubs. Served to chief yeoman USCG, 1942-45. Mem. Calif. Tchrs. Assn., Nat. Curriculum, Assn. Supervision and Curriculum Devel., Am. Bus. Profl. Women. Republican. Lodge: Order Eastern Star (life). Home: 3244 New York Ave Costa Mesa CA 92626 Office: Edison High Sch 21400 Magnolia St Huntington Beach CA 92646

LOHNES, WALTER F. W., German language and literature educator; b. Frankfurt, Ger., Feb. 8, 1925; came to U.S., 1948, naturalized, 1954; s. Hans and Dina (Koch) L.; m. Claire Shane, 1950; children: Kristen, Peter, Claudia. Student, U. Frankfurt, 1945-48, Ohio Wesleyan U., 1948-49, U. Mo., 1949-50; Ph.D., Harvard U., 1961. Asst., Inst. German Folklore, U. Frankfurt, 1947-48; instr. in German, U. Mo., 1949-50; head dept. German, Phillips Acad., Andover, Mass., 1951-61; asst. prof. German, Stanford U., 1961-65, assoc. prof., 1965-68, prof., 1969—, dir. NDEA Inst. Advanced Study, 1961-68, chmn. dept. German studies, 1973-79, dir. Inst. Basic German, prin. investigator NEH grant, 1978-80; vis. prof. Woehler-Gymnasium, Frankfurt, 1956-57, Middlebury Coll., 1959, U. N.Mex., 1980, 81, 86; mem., chmn. various coms. examiners Ednl. Testing Service and Coll. Bd.; chmn. German Grad. Record Exam. Author: (with V. Nollendorfs) German Studies in the United States, 1976, (with F. W. Strothmann) German: A Structural Approach, 1968, 3d rev. edit., 1980; (with E.A. Hopkins) Contrastive Grammar of English and German, 1982, (with Martha Woodmansee) Erkennen und Deuten, 1983, (with J.A. Pfeffer) Grunddeutsch, Texte zur gesprochenen deutschen Gegenwartssprache, 3 vols., 1984; contbr. numerous articles to profl. jours.; editor; Unterrichtspraxis, 1971-74. Bd. dirs. Calif. Youth Symphony, 1977-78, Oakland (Calif.) Symphony Youth Orch., 1978-80. German Govt. grantee, 1975, 76, 78. Mem. Am. Assn. Tchrs. German (v.p. 1961-62, 70-71), MLA, Am. Assn. Applied Linguistics, Am. Council on Teaching Fgn. Langs., German Studies Assn., Internationale Vereinigung für Germanische Sprach- und Literaturwissenschaft. Home: 733 Covington Rd Los Altos CA 94022 Office: Dept German Studies Stanford U Stanford CA 94305

LOHR, GEORGE E., state supreme court justice; b. 1931. B.S., S.D. State U.; J.D., U. Mich. Bar: Colo. 1958, Calif. 1969. Former judge Colo. 9th Dist. Ct., Aspen; assoc. justice Colo. Supreme Ct., Denver, 1979—. Office: Colo Supreme Ct State Judicial Bldg 2 E 14th Ave Denver CO 80203

LOHRDING, RONALD KEITH, statistician, scientific analyst; b. Coldwater, Kans., Jan. 1, 1941; s. Fred Henry and M. LaVaun (Nichols) L.; m. Janet Kay Christopher, Aug. 11, 1962; children: Bradley Keith, Tami Kay. BA in Math., Southwestern Coll., Winfield, Kans., 1963; MS in Stats., Kans. State U., 1966, PhD in Stats., 1968. Mem. staff stats. group Los Alamos (N.Mex.) Nat. Lab., 1968-74, group leader stats. analysis and assessment group, 1974-78, alt. div. leader, systems, analysis and assessment div., 1978-79, dep. assoc. dir. environment and bioscis., 1979-81, dep. assoc. dir. internat. affairs and energy policy, 1981-83, asst. dir. indsl. and internat. initiatives, 1983-87, mgr. Cen. Am. energy and minerals program, 1984—, dir. energy and tech. program, 1987—; mem. sci. and tech. adv. com. State N.Mex., Santa Fe, 1982-85, sci. and tech. commn., 1985—; research fellow East-West Ctr., Honolulu, 1979, vis. prof. U. Hawaii, 1979; mem. task force Western Gov. Assn., Denver, 1986. Contbr. articles to profl. jours. Chmn. social concerns com. Bethlehem Luth. Ch., Los Alamos, 1971-75, council mem., 1974-77; vp. and bd. dirs. Los Alamos Group Home for Retarded Citizens, 1978—. Mem. AAAS, Los Alamos Assn. Retarded Citizens. Republican. Home: 2229 Loma Linda Los Alamos NM 87544 Office: Los Alamos Nat Lab MS P373-Energy and Tech Los Alamos NM 87545

LOKEY, R. EUGENE, legislative consultant; b. Washington, Ga., Sept. 3, 1944; s. Walter Eugene and Zelma (May) L. BA, San Jose State U., 1966, BA, 1968, MA, 1974. Pres., Calif. Planners & Cons., Sacramento, 1970—; ptnr. Patrick Andrews Advt. Co., San Jose, 1974-75; pres. Save-A-Bee, San Jose, 1975-83; dir. Physicians and Surgeons Ins. Exchange, Los Angeles, 1976—. Contbr. articles to profl. jours. Pres., San Jose Dem. Club, 1972, San Jose Community Theatre, 1973; bd. dirs. Frances Gulland Child Care Ctr., San Jose, 1974; mem. Data Confidentiality Commn., Santa Clara County, 1980; bd. dirs. Nat. Council Alternative Health Care Policy, 1984. Recipient La Torre award San Jose State U., 1968; Community Service award Nat. Assn. Social Workers, 1970. Mem. Am. Polit. Sci. Assn., Am. Assn. Polit. Cons., Tau Delta Phi, Psi Sigma Alpha. Home: 559 N San Pedro St San Jose CA 95110 Office: Calif Planners and Cons Inc 1029 K St Suite 48 Sacramento CA 95814

LOLLEY, RICHARD N., health science administrator, educator; b. Blaine, Kans., May 25, 1933; s. Loran Newton and Catherine Agnes (Caffrey) L.; m. Hazel Ruth Bauerrichter, June 4, 1959; children: Emily Ruth, Melissa Anne, Cybil Marie. BS in Pharmacy, U. Kans., 1955, PhD in Physiology, 1961. Registered pharmacist. Postdoctoral research fellow Maudsley Hosp., U. London, 1960-62; postdoctoral fellow in neuropathology McLean Hosp., Harvard U., Boston, 1962-64; research pharmacologist VA Med. Ctr., Sepulveda, Calif., 1965-71, assoc. chief staff research and devel., 1978-80, chief devel. neurology lab., 1971—; asst. prof. anatomy Sch. Medicine, UCLA, 1966-70, assoc. prof. anatomy, 1970-76, prof. anatomy, 1976—, cons. Jules Stein Eye Inst., 1972-78, mem. staff Jules Stein Eye Inst., 1981—, mem. med. scientist tng. program and med. sch. admissions; chmn. research and devel. com. VA Med. Ctr.; chmn. adv. com. geriatric research Edn. and Clin. Ctr., Sepulveda; mem. Nat. Adv. Eye Council, Nat. Eye Inst., 1979-84; mem. research scientist evaluation com. VA Cen. Office, Washington, 1981-84. Editor: Neurochemistry of the Retina, 1980; mem. editorial bd. Investigative Ophthamology and Visual Sci. Named Research Career Scientist, VA, 1979; research grantee, NSF, VA, Nat. Eye Inst., Nat, Retinitis Pigmentosa Found. Mem. AAAS, Assn. Research in Vision and Ophthamology (trustee), Soc. Neurosci., Am. Soc. Neurochemistry, Internat. Soc. Neurochemistry, Am. Soc. Anatomists, Internation Soc. Eye Research. Home: 1107 Vallejo Ave Simi Valley CA 93065 Office: VA Med Ctr Lab Devel Neurology Sepulveda CA 91343

LOLLI, ANDREW RALPH, industrial engineer, former army officer; b. Seatonville, Ill., Oct. 15, 1917; s. Joseph Fredrick and Adolfa (Fiocchi) L.; student Armed Forces Staff Coll., 1950, Nat. War Coll., 1957, N.Y. Inst. Fin., 1971; B.S., Dickinson Coll., 1952; postgrad. Fordham U., 1952; m. Mary H. Tatsapaugh, Jan. 14, 1983. Enlisted in U.S. Army, 1940, advanced through grades to maj. gen., 1960; chief plans and priorities Allied Forces So. Europe, 1952-56; comdr. Air Def. units, N.Y. and San Francisco, 1957-60; comdr. XX U.S.A. Corps, 1961-62, XV, 1962-63, comdr. Western

NORD Region, Hamilton AFB, Calif., 1963-66; ret., 1966; exec. asst. Hughes Aircraft Co., Fullerton, Calif., 1967; dir. gen. services State of Calif., Sacramento, 1967-70; v.p. Sigmatics, Newport Beach, Calif., 1970-73, Intercoast Investments Co., Sacramento, 1975-76; pres. Andrew R. Lolli Assos. Inc., San Francisco, 1973—, Lolman Inc., San Francisco, 1976—; pres. bd. trustees Commonwealth Equity Trust, 1974-80; vice chmn. Calif. Pub. Works bd., 1967-69; mem. adv. panel Nat. Acad. Scis. and Engring. in Research, Washington, 1968-70; mem. fed., state and local govt. adv. panel Fed. Gen. Services, Washington, 1968-69. Bd. dirs. Columbia Boys Park Club, San Francisco, Lab. for Survival, San Francisco. Decorated D.S.M., Legion of Merit with oak leaf cluster, Bronze Star with oak leaf cluster; named Man of Year, Italian Sons of Am., 1964. Mem. Nat. Assn. Uniformed Services, Assn. U.S. Army, Ret. Officers Assn. Roman Catholic. Clubs: Presidio San Francisco, Golf. Developed short notice inspection system for army air def. missiles, 1960. Home: 1050 North Point San Francisco CA 94109 Office: 286 Jefferson St San Francisco CA 94133

LOMAS, RAUL GEORGE, lawyer; b. Havana, Cuba, Apr. 7, 1952; came to U.S., 1962; s. Jose Raul and Gloria (Lozano) L. AA, Cypress Coll., 1972; BA, UCLA, 1974; JD, Western State U., Fullerton, Calif., 1980. Bar: Calif. 1982, U.S. Dist. Ct. (cen. dist.) Calif. Sole practice Pasadena, Calif., 1983—. Mem. Pasadena Bar Assn., San Gabriel Valley Bar Assn., Cuban-Am. Bar Assn., Los Angeles Trial Lawyers Assn., Assn. Trial Lawyers Am. Roman Catholic. Avocations: skiing, jazz, travel, football. Office: 484 E California #43 Pasadena CA 91101

LOMASH, MARGARET ELIZABETH, psychiatric social worker; b. Paterson, N.J., Jan. 17, 1961; d. Stephen and Adele (Ciukiewicz) L. BA in Psychology, Rutgers U., 1983; MSW, U. Chgo., 1985; cert. law program for community developers and social workers, John Marshall Law Sch., Chgo., 1984. Clin. and research intern Douglass Devel. Disabilities Ctr. Rutgers U., New Brunswick, N.J., 1981-83; intern Salvation Army Family Services Ctr., Chgo., 1983-84, Children's Meml. Hosp. Dept. Social Work, Chgo., 1984-85; asst. social worker St. Joseph's Home, Totowa, N.J., 1984; psychiat. social worker Patton (Calif.) State Hosp., 1985—; mem. research com. Patton State Hosp., 1985—, sec. quality assurance com., 1985—. Mem. Nat. Assn. Social Workers. Roman Catholic. Avocations: aerobics, dancing. Office: Patton State Hosp 3102 E Highland Ave Patton CA 92369

LOMBARD, CARYN ANDERSON, telecommunications company executive; b. Rochester, Minn., June 1, 1942; d. Bruce Murat and Caroline (Brown) Anderson; m. Russell Joseph Lombard, Jr., July 24, 1971; 1 son, Christian Murat. B.A., Stanford U., 1963; M.B.A., San Francisco State U., 1977. Asst. product mgr. Castle & Cooke, 1972-74; account exec. N.Y. Times Info. Service, 1976-78; consumer promotion mgr. MJB Co., 1978-80; sales promotion mgr. Calif. Canners & Growers, 1980-82; area mgr. priority mktg. Pacific Bell, San Francisco, 1982—; mktg. cons. Chmn. Mayor's Women's Adv. Com., 1980-82; exec. com. Mayor's Econ. Devel. Council, 1980-81; pres. Friends of Commn. on Status of Women, 1981-83; founding mem. Bay Area Women's Coalition; mem. Internat. Visitors Ctr. Bay Area, Embarcadero Ctr. Forum. Mem. Women in Advt. (dir. 1976-79), Women in Telecommunications, Merchandising Execs. Club (dir. 1980-82). Clubs: San Francisco Tennis, Les Amis du Vin, Commonwealth of Calif. (exec. com. internat. relations sect.).

LOMBARDI, JOHN HAROLD, educator; b. Chgo., Aug. 23, 1944; s. John and Lorraine Mae (Bending) L.; m. Donna Marie De Clue, Nov. 27, 1976. B in Writing, English. Lit., Elmhurst Coll., 1968; M, Chgo. State U., 1975, postgrad., 1975; PhD in Criminology, Fla. State U., 1981. Account exec. Shell Oil Co., Chgo., 1966-67; indsl. relations adminstr. AT&T, Chgo., 1970-72; chief warrant officer State of Ill., Chgo., 1973-77; asst. prof. criminology U. Ala., Birmingham, 1981-83, U. Nev., Reno, 1983—; chief exec. officer Lombardi, Bending, Winthrop and Mac Grail, Chartered Internat., Reno, 1983—. Contbr. articles to profl. jours; host Lombardi's Law Talk, Sta. 63 AM, Reno, 1984—. Bd. dirs. Nev. Dept. Corrections, Reno, 1984—. Served to lt. USMC, 1968-70. Fla. State U. fellow, 1978-81; teaching fellow Fla. State U., 1977. Mem. Acad. Security Educators and Trainers, Am. Soc. Indsl. Security, Acad. Criminal Justice Scis., Nev. Council Crime Prevention. Republican. Roman Catholic. Avocations: Romantic period poetry, writing, reading history. Home: 1885 Severn Dr Reno NV 89503

LOMELÍ, REFUGIO (JESSE), athletics educator; b. Aguascalientes, Mex., July 23, 1941; came to U.S., 1954, naturalized, 1965; s. J. Jesus and Maria Guadalupe (Ascencio) L.; m. Barbara L. McMinn, Aug. 24, 1968; children: Lorena, Maya, Marc. Assoc., Palomar Coll., 1962; B, U. of the Americas, Mexico City, 1965; M, San Diego State U., 1972; postgrad., U. Pitts., 1972-74. Firefighter U.S. Forest Service, So. Calif. region, 1962-66; tchr. Santana H.S., Santee, Calif., 1967-73; counselor, tchr., soccer coach Mira Costa Coll., Oceanside, Calif., 1973—. Named Community Coll. Soccer Coach of Yr., Pacific Coast Conf., 1985. Mem. Nat. Assn. Fgn. Student Advisors, Am. G.I. Forum. Lodge: KC. Home: 1250 Vista Colina Dr San Marcos CA 92069 Office: Mira Costa Coll 1 Barnard Dr Oceanside CA 92056

LOMEN, DAVID ORLANDO, mathematician, educator; b. Decorah, Iowa, May 11, 1937; s. Erlin Reuben and Ellen Dorthea (Jensen) L.; m. Constance Sylvia Treeck, Dec. 25, 1961; 1 dau., Catherine Ellen. B.A., Luther Coll., 1959; M.S., Iowa State U., 1962, Ph.D., 1964. Research asst. Socony Mobil Research Lab., Duncanville, Tex., summer 1960; design specialist Gen. Dynamics/Convair Co., San Diego, 1963-66; asst. prof. math. U. Ariz., Tucson, 1966-69; assoc. prof., 1969-74, prof., 1974—; vis. scientist dept. applied math. and theoretical physics U. Cambridge (Eng.), 1972-73; vis. scientist Inst. voor Cultuurtechniek en Waterhuishouding, Wageningen, The Netherlands, summer 1978; vis. prof. U. Oslo, 1980; cons. in field. Bd. dirs. Tucson chpt. Cystic Fibrosis Found., 1975-80. Recipient Creative Teaching award U. Ariz. Found., 1978; Marshall Fund Research award Am. Assn., Norway, 1980, 84. Mem. Am. Math Soc., Soc. Indsl. and Applied Math., Soil Sci. Soc. Am. Geophys. Union, European Geophys. Soc., Consortium for Math. and Application. Lutheran. Club: Nordmanns Forbundet. Research in math. modeling of water flow in soils and developing math. lessons for computer aided instrn. Contbr. numerous articles and research reports to Applied Math. Home: 6945 E Blue Lake Dr Tucson AZ 85715 Office: Math Dept U Ariz Tucson AZ 85721

LONDON, RAY WILLIAM, clinical, consulting and medical psychologist, researcher; b. Burley, Idaho, May 29, 1943; s. Loo Richard and Maycelle Jerry (Moore) L. A.S., Weber State Coll., 1965, B.Sc., 1967; M.S.W., U. So. Calif., 1973, Ph.D., 1976. Diplomate: Am. Bd. Psychol. Hypnosis (dir. 1984—), Am. Acad. Behavioral Medicine, Am. Bd. Psychotherapy, Am. Bd. Med. Psychotherapy, Am. Bd. Psychotherapy, Internat. Acad. Medicine and Psychology, Am. Bd. Profl. Neuropsychology, Am. Bd. Family Psychology, Am. Bd. Med. Psychotherapy; cert. Am. Assn. Sex Therapists, Soc. Med. Hypnosis. Congl. asst. U.S. Ho. of Reps., 1964-65; research assoc. Bus. Advs., Inc., Ogden, Utah, 1965-67; dir. counseling and consultation services Meaning Found., Riverside, Calif., 1966-69; mental health and mental retardation liaison San Bernardino County (Calif.) Social Services, 1968-72; clin. trainee VA Outpatient Clinic, Los Angeles, 1971-72, Children's Hosp., 1972-73, clin. fellow, 1973-74; clin. trainee Reiss Davis Child Study Ctr., Los Angeles, 1973-74, Los Angeles County-U. So. Calif. Med. Center, 1973; psychotherapist Benjamin Rush Neuropsychiat. Ctr., Orange, Calif., 1973-75; clin. psychology postdoctoral intern Orange County (Calif.) Mental Health, 1976-77; postdoctoral fellow U. Caif.-Irvine-Calif. Coll. Medicine, 1978; clin. psychologist Orange Police Dept., 1974-80; pvt. practice consultation and assessment, Santa Ana, Calif., 1974—; cons. to public schs., agys., hosps., bus., nationally and internationally, 1973—; pres. bd. govs. Human Factor Programs, Ltd., 1976—; pres. Internat. Bd. Medicine and Psychology, 1980—; mem. faculty UCLA, U. So. Calif., Calif. State U., U. Calif., Irvine, Calif. Coll. Medicine, Internat. Congress of Hypnosis and Psychosomatic Medicine, Soc. Clin. and Exptl. Hypnosis, Internat. Adv. Bd. European Congress Hypnosis and Psychosomatic Medicine; research assoc. Nat. Commn. for Protection of Human Subjects of Biomed. and Behavioral Research, 1976; fellow Inst. for Social Scientists on Neurobiology and Mental Illness, 1978. Editor: Internat. Bull. Medicine and Psychology, 1980, behavioral medicine Australian Jour., 1980, editorial cons. Internat. Jour. Clin. and Exptl. Hypnosis, 1981; cons. editor Internat. Jour. Psychosomatics, 1984; cons. Am. Jour. Forensic Psychology, 1986; pub.: London Behavioral Medicine Assessment, 1982; producer: TV series Being Human, 1980; contbg. author World Book Ency. and books; contbr. articles to profl. jours. Recipient Congl. recognition U.S. Ho. of Reps., 1978; named scholar laureate Erickson Advanced Inst., 1980. Fellow Internat. Acad. Medicine and Psychology (dir. 1981—), Soc. Clin. Social Work (dir. 1979-80), Royal Soc. Health, Am. Coll. Forensic Psychology, Soc. Clin and Experimental Hypnosis (bd. dirs. 1985—); mem. Acad. Psychosomatic Medicine, Am. Psychol. Assn., Am. Group Psychotherapy Assn., Am. Orthopsychiat. Assn., Am. Soc. Clin. Hypnosis, Internat. Soc. Hypnosis, N.Y. Acad. Sci., Soc. Behavioral Medicine, Internat. Psychosomatic Inst., Australian Coll. Pvt. Clin. Psychologists, Australian Psychol. Soc., Phi Delta Kappa, Delta Sigma Rho, Tau Kappa Alpha, Pi Rho Phi, Lambda Iota Tau. Club: Toastmasters. Office: 1125 E 17th St Suite E-209 Santa Ana CA 92701

LONERGAN, THOMAS FRANCIS, III, criminal justice consultant; b. Bklyn., July 28, 1942; s. Thomas Francis and Katherine Josephine (Roth) L.; B.A., Calif. State U., Long Beach, 1966, M.A., 1973; M.P.A., Pepperdine U., 1976; postgrad. U. So. Calif.; m. Irene L. Kaucher, Dec. 14, 1963; 1 son, Thomas F. Dep. sheriff Los Angeles County Sheriff's Dept., 1963-68; U.S. Govt. program analyst, 1968—; fgn. service officer USIA, Lima, Peru, 1970-71; dep. sheriff to lt. Los Angeles Sheriff's Office, 1971-76, aide lt. to div. chief, 1976-79; dir. Criminal Justice Cons., Downey, Calif., 1977—; cons. Public Adminstrv. Service, Chgo., 1972-75, Nat. Sheriff's Assn., 1978, 79; cons. Nat. Inst. Corrections, Washington, 1977—, coordinator jail ctr., 1981—; tchr. N. Calif. Regional Criminal Justice Acad., 1977-79; lectr. Nat. Corrections Acad., 1983—; spl. master, U.S. Dist. Ct. (no. dist.) Ohio, 1984-85, Santa Clara Superior Ct. (Calif.), 1983—, U.S. Dist. Ct. Ga., Atlanta, 1986—, U. S. Dist. Ct. (no. dist.) Calif., 1984—, U.S. Dist. Ct. (no. dist.) Idaho, 1986—; also ct. expert. Mem. Air Force Assn., U.S. Naval Inst., U.S. Strategic Inst., Nat. Jail Assn., Nat. Jail Mgrs. Assn., Nat. Sheriff's Assn., Am. Polit. Sci. Assn., Zeta Beta Tau. Democrat. Roman Catholic. Author: California-Past, Present & Future, 1968; Training-A Corrections Perspective, 1979; AIMS-Correctional Officer; Liability-A Correctional Perspective; Liability Law for Probation Administrators; Liability Reporter; Probation Liability Reporter. Study Guides.

LONETREE, GEORGIA L., rehabilitation counselor; b. Portage, Wis., Sept. 22, 1946; d. Edward and Minnie I. (Decorah) L.; children—Lucinda J., Aaron E. Yazzie. B.S. in Vocat. Rehab., U. Wis.-Stout, 1976, postgrad., 1976-77; M.S. in Vocat. Rehab. Counseling, U. Wis., 1981, postgrad., 1981-82. Team tchr. U. Wis.-Stout, 1976, Native Am. coordinator ednl. and cultural enrichment program, 1977-78; statewide specialist Indian edn. and community programs U. Wis. Extension, 1978-79; sec. to tribal atty. Wis. Winnebago Bus. Com., Madison, 1980; rehab. counselor intern Waisman Ctr. Mental Retardation and Human Devel., U. Wis., 1981, project evaluator Madison Indian parent com., 1981-82; vocat. evaluator, edn. coordinator Project Hogan Naa Nish, Navajo Vocat. Rehab. Program, Tuba City, Ariz., 1982-83; instr. rehab. edn. Navajo Community Coll., Tsaile, Ariz., 1983; homeliving specialist guidance dept. Shonto (Ariz.) Boarding Sch., 1984—. Vocat. adv. com. Tuba City High Sch., 1982; treas. Wisconsin Dells chpt. Native Am. Ch., 1979-80; sec.-treas. Ho-Chunk Housing Authority, Wis. Winnebago Bus. Com., Nekoosa, 1979-80; past officer, mem. Native Am. Awareness Club, U. Wis.-Stout, 1972-76. Continuing edn. scholar Dells Indian Club, Inc., 1982; Am. Indians into Grad. Edn. fellow, 1981-82; Advanced Opportunity fellow, 1980-81; recipient Am. Indian Scholarship award, 1976, Chancellor's award for high acad. achievement, 1975; Outstanding Alumni award U. Wis.-Stout, 1986. Mem. Am. Rehab. Counseling Assn., Am. Personnel and Guidance Assn. Home: 752 Spruce St PO Box 364 Shonto AZ 86054

LONG, ARTHUR DENNIS, public health engineer; b. Ventura, Calif., Feb. 24, 1952; s. Neville Stuart and Elizabeth Anne (Armstrong) L.; m. Lynellyn Dunstan Horne, Aug. 25, 1984. BS in Engring., Stanford U., 1973; MS in Ocean Engring., MIT, 1975; MS in Population Scis., Harvard U., 1977, DSc in Tropical Pub. Health, 1981. Ocean engr. Bechtel Corp., San Francisco, 1975, sr. scientist, 1981—; environ. engr. Pacific Gas & Electric Corp., San Francisco, 1975. Rockefeller fellow Harvard U., 1979-81; AAAS Sci.-Engring., and Diplomacy fellow U.S. AID, Washington, 1983-84. Mem. Sigma Xi. Episcopalian. Avocations: swimming, running. Home: 2687 McAllister St Apt #1 San Francisco CA 94118

LONG, FRANCIS MARK, electrical engineer, educator; b. Iowa City, Nov. 10, 1929; s. Frank B. and Hilda B. (Rohret) L.; m. Mary Ann Coyne, June 8, 1964; children: Ann Brett, Mary Bronwyn, Thomas Martin Carver, Caitlin Frances. B.S., U. Iowa, 1953, M.S., 1956; Ph.D., Iowa State U., 1961; NIH fellow, Stanford U. and Lawrence Livermore Lab, 1972-73. With Collins Radio Co., Cedar Rapids, Iowa, summers 1952, 55, Douglas Aircraft Co., Santa Monica, Calif., summer 1953, USNAMTC, Point Mugu, Calif., summer 1956, Good All Electric Co., Ogallala, Nebr., summer 1957, Lawrence Radiation Lab., Livermore, Calif., summer 1967, Globe Union Co., Milw., summer 1975; instr. U. Wyo., Laramie, 1956-58; prof. elec. engring. U. Wyo., 1960—, head elec. engring. dept., 1977—; instr. Iowa State U., 1958-60; dir. Wyo. Biotelemetry, Inc., Rocky Mountain Bioengring. Symposium; pres. Alliance for Engring. in Medicine and Biology, 1983, 84, mem. exec. com., 1979—; conf. chmn., procs. editor 1st, 2d, 3d and 5th Internat. Conf. on Wildlife Biotelemetry. Author: (with E.M. Lonsdale) Introductory Electrical Concepts, 1967, rev. edit., 1977; co-author: (with R.G. Jacquot) Introduction to Engineering Systems. Trustee St. Paul's Newman Center Parish, 1969-72; mem. City of Laramie Planning Commn., 1970-72. Served with C.E. U.S. Army, 1953-55. Decorated citation Republic of Korea Army C.E.; recipient G.D. Humphrey Outstanding Faculty award U. Wyo., 1973, Western Electric Fund award for engring. teaching, 1978. Mem. Am. Soc. Engring. Edn. (v.p., dir., 1st Outstanding Biomed. Engring. Educator award biomed. engring. div. 1981, chmn. Elec. Engring. Div. 1986-87), IEEE, Internat. Soc. for Hybrid Microelectronics, Sigma Xi. Democrat. Roman Catholic. Home: 507 S 24th St Laramie WY 82070 Office: Box 3295 University Sta Laramie WY 82071

LONG, GEORGE STEVENSON, JR., photographer; b. Indpls., June 12, 1923; s. George Stevenson and Hazel (Walker) L.; m. Marjorie Claire Carper, May 9, 1947; children—Steve, Bob, Timothy, Joan. Student Navy Photographic Sch., Pensicola, Fla. Photographer, UPI, Los Angeles, 1951-61; photographer Steve Hannigan, Sun Valley, Calif., 1948-51; owner Sheedy and Long Photography, 1961-75; owner Long Photography, Los Angeles, 1975—. Served in USN, 1943-46. Mem. Profl. Photographers Am., Los Angeles Press Photographers. Presbyterian. Work appears in Sports Illustrated (17 years), Time, Life, Fortune, Nat. Geog., U.S. News & World Reports. Home: 7514 Otto St Downey CA 90240 Office: 1265 S Cochran Ave Los Angeles CA 90019

LONG, GERALD DEAN, electrical engineer; b. Lehigh, Iowa, Mar. 8, 1934; s. Ronald Earl and Anna Geneva (Dosland) L.; married Aug. 17, 1953 (div. Feb. 1976); children: Ronald E., Debra A., Steven M.; m. Jexix Elizabeth Gibson, Dec. 28, 1977. Student, Iowa State U., 1951-53; BA in Physics, U. No. Iowa, 1957; MS in Tng. and Organic Devel., Eastern Wash. U., 1986. Project mgr. Bendix Aviation, Towson, Md., 1959-60; dir. cust. tng. Reliance Electric Co., Cleve., 1960-64; maint. supr. Kaiser Aluminum and Chemical Co., Trentwood, Wash., 1964-75, 78-85, mgr. tng., 1975-78, sr. elec. engr., 1985—. Contbr. articles to profl. jours. Served with U.S. Army, 1957-59. Mem. Am. Soc. Tng. and Devel. (treas. 1983). Democrat. Avocations: electronic repair, metalworking. Home: E 13014 8th Ave Spokane WA 99216 Office: Kaiser Aluminum and Chemical Corp Trentwood Works Spokane WA 99215

LONG, J. BRUCE, producer, educator; b. Spur, Tex., Apr. 25, 1937; s. Joe Bailey and Julia (Jennings) L.; m. H. Linda, Aug. 30, 1964 (div. Dec. 1982); childen: Jennifer Beth, Stacy Matthew; m. Patricia Lee Wisne, June 17, 1984. BA, Baylor, 1959; MA in Religion & Lit., U. Chgo., 1963, M in Hist. of Religion, 1965, PhD in Hist. of Religion, 1970. Asst. prof. Haverford (Pa.) Coll., 1968-72, Cornell U., Ithaca, N.Y., 1972-78; dir. Blaisdell Inst. World Cultures and Religions, Claremont, Calif., 1978-81; assoc. prof. Claremont Grad. Sch., 1982-83; founder, pres. Gemini Prodn., Santa Monica, Calif., 1983—; trustee, Zen Ctr. Los Angeles, 1979-81, Religion and the Humanities Publ., 1978—, Lumbini Project, Washington, 1985—; adv. bd. Re-Vision, Cambridge, Mass., 1981—. Meml. editor: Journal of Religion to Paul Tillich, 1966, Judaism and Christian Sem. Curriculum, 1966, Encounters With Shiva, 1984, The Mahabharata, 1976; contbr. articles on Hinduism and history of religions. U. Chgo. fellow, 1966, Am. Inst. Indian Studies jr. fellow, 1967, sr fellow, 1982; Ford Found. grantee, 1971, research grantee Cornell U., 1974, 75, 76. Mem. Am. Acad Religion, Assn. for Asian Studies, Internat. Documentary Assn., Internat. Soc. Comparative Study of Civilizations, Conf. on Religion in South India. Democrat. Episcopalian. Lodge: Rotary. Avocations: jogging, tennis, alto recorder, madrigal singing, gourmet cooking. Home and Office: 1044 7th St #10 Santa Monica CA 90403

LONG, JACQUELINE ANN, social worker; b. Denver, July 22, 1949; d. M. Milton Sr. and Thelma V. (Menifee) Long; m. Guy Darlan, May 19, 1973 (div. 1976). BSW, U. Kans., 1972, MSW, 1973; grad. family therapy tng. program, U. Denver, 1986. Clin. social worker Denver Pub. Schs., 1974—; educator, cons. Colo. Edn. Dept., 1979—; field instr. U. Denver Grad. Sch. Social Work, 1980—. Active Urban League, Denver, 1984. Recipient Walter Oliver award for Excellence in Edn., Denver Pub. Schs., 1985. Mem. NEA, Acad. Cert. Social Workers, Nat. Assn. Social Workers (clin. diplomate, bd. dirs.), Colo. Sch. Social Workers (pres. 1979-81), Colo. Edn. Assn., Denver Classroom Assn., Alpha Kappa Alpha. Avocations: tennis, swimming, skiing. Home: 4512 Abilene St Denver CO 80239 Office: John Amesse Elem. 5440 Scranton St Denver CO 80239

LONG, KATHY GOWANS, advertising executive; b. Tooele, Utah, Sept. 4, 1940; d. Robert Noel and Lydia (Bickmore) G.; m. Frederic Neil Arneman, Aug. 16, 1961 (div. Sept. 1979); children: Scott Neil, Kelly Ann; m. Elmer A. Long, Oct. 2, 1982. Student, Stevens-Henager Coll., 1959-60. Sec.-treas. Heritage Sales, Inc., Salt Lake City, 1972-77; v.p. Enterprise Newspaper Group, Salt Lake City, 1977—; bd. dirs. Western Bus. Newspapers, Phoenix. Mem. Utah Advt. Fedn. Republican. Presbyterian. Avocations: golf, winetasting. Home: 5954 Sandusky Salt Lake City UT 84123 Office: Enterprise Newspaper Group 500 Continental Bank Bldg Salt Lake City UT 84101

LONG, LYLE NORMAN, aerospace engineer, researcher; b. Fergus Falls, Minn., Apr. 7, 1954; s. Norman Laverne and Shirley Anne (Leeman) L.; m. Laura Jean Greuel, July 11, 1981; 1 child, David Alexander. BME, U. Minn., 1976; MS, Stanford U., 1978; DSc., George Washington U., 1983. Engring. intern Donaldson Co., Mpls., 1974-76; research asst. NASA/Stanford U., Moffett Field, Calif., 1977-78; research assoc. NASA/ George Washington U., Hampton, Va., 1979-83; research specialist Lockheed Calif., Burbank, 1983-85; staff scientist Lockheed Advanced Aerospace Co., Valencia, Calif., 1985—. Mem. AIAA, Am. Soc. Engring. Edn., Soc. Indsl. and Applied Math., Pi Tau Sigma, Sigma Xi. Avocations: backpacking, racquetball. Office: Lockheed ASG Research PO Box 551 Burbank CA 91520-7013

LONG, MICHAEL THOMAS, manufacturing executive; b. Heidelberg, Fed. Republic of Germany, May 21, 1953; came to U.S., 1954 (parents Am. citizens); s. Roger Lewis Long and Helene Christine (D'Ambrosio) Jinkens; m. Jill Ko, June 6, 1981. AB, U. Chgo., 1975. Engr. M/A-Com Power Hybrids, Inc., Torrance, Calif., 1977-79, 80-83, Hewlett-Packard, San Jose, Calif., 1979-80; pres. and founder Am. Microwave Technology, Inc., Fullerton, Calif., 1983—. Mem. IEEE. Republican. Roman Catholic. Avocations: running, biking, swimming. Home: 1915 Mathews Ave #4 Redondo Beach CA 90278 Office: Am Microwave Technology Inc 1127 S Placentia Ave Fullerton CA 92631

LONG, MICHELLE YVETTE, chemist; b. Montgomery, Ala., Nov. 3, 1960; d. Curtis and Ruby (Sankey) L.; 1 child, Chauntelle Renee. BS in Chemistry, Pacific Luth. U., 1984. Chemist N.W. Labs., Seattle, 1984-85; lab. supr. U.S. Oil and Refining Co., Tacoma, 1985—; bd. dirs. Minority in Engring. and Sci. Achievement, Tacoma, 1985—. Fusch-Harden scholar, 1983. Mem. Am. Chem. Soc. Democrat. Baptist. Avocations: volleyball, backgammon, jigsaw puzzles, piano playing, rollerskating. Office: US Oiland Refining Co 3001 Marshall Ave Tacoma WA 98421

LONG, PAUL ROBERT, real estate executive, economics educator; b. Hillsboro, Tex., May 28, 1949; s. Lee Watkin and Thelma Lee (Tunsel) L.; m. Sherry Ann Jones, July 20, 1970 (div. Nov. 1981); children—Betty, Jocelyn, Melissa, Yvette. B.A. in Psychology, Park Coll., Kansas City, Mo., 1972; M.A. in Pub. Adminstrn., U. No. Colo., Greeley, 1976; postgrad. U. Colo., Boulder, 1976—. Pres. Lonico Enterprises, Denver, 1979—; prof. econs. Auraria Community Coll., Denver, 1982-83, Park Coll., Denver, 1983—. Contbr. articles to profl. jours. Served with USAF, 1967-71. Colo. Energy and Research Inst. grantee, 1977. Mem. Am. Mgmt. Assn., VFW, Am. Legion, Disabled Am. Veterans, NAACP. Democrat. Methodist. Club: Soc. Saber & Quill (bd. dirs. 1971-72) (Kansas City). Home: 4435 Durham Ct Denver CO 80040 Office: Lonico Enterprises PO Box 55 Aurora CO 80040

LONG, ROBERT MERRILL, retail drug company executive; b. Oakland, Calif., May 19, 1938; s. Joseph Milton and Vera Mai (Skaggs) L.; m. Eliane Quilloux, Dec. 13, 1969. Student, Brown U., 1956-58; B.A., Claremont Men's Coll., 1960. With Longs Drug Stores Inc., Walnut Creek, Calif., 1960—, dir., 1968—, pres., 1975-77, pres., chief exec. officer, 1977—. Mem. Nat. Assn. Chain Drug Stores (dir.). Office: Longs Drug Stores California 141 N Civic Dr Walnut Creek CA 94596

LONG, ROGER ALDEN, aircraft company executive; b. Akron, Ohio, Oct. 14, 1921; s. Roger Meredith and Kathrine Rachael (Inglish) L.; m. Anne Agnes Olzeski, Feb. 19, 1959; children: Carolyn, Gayle, Richard, Robert. BS Chem. Engring., Ohio State U., 1943; LLB, Cleve. Marshall Law Sch., 1951; JD, Cleve. State U., 1969. Bar: Ohio 1952. Metallurgist Lockheed Vega Aircraft Corp., Burbank, Calif., 1943-45; chief metall. br. NACA Lewis Research Ctr., Cleve., 1946-53; div. mgr. Ferrotherm Co., Cleve., 1953-56; mgr. refractories research dept. Narmco Research and Devel. Co., San Diego, 1956-66; exec. asst., dir. materials and processing dept. Teledyne Ryan Aero. Co., San Diego, 1966—; owner Rancho Longacres Stables, Escondido, Calif.; cons. in field. Contbr. articles to profl. publs.; inventor in field. Mem. Am. Soc. Metals, Am. Ceramic Soc., AIAA, Ohio Bar Assn. Democrat. Methodist. Avocations: thoroughbred horse breeding and racing. Home: 2730 Verda Ave Escondido CA 92025 Office: Teledyne Ryan Aero Co 2701 Harbor Dr San Diego CA 92112

LONG, SARAH ANN, librarian; b. Atlanta, May 20, 1943; d. Jones Lloyd and Lelia Maria (Mitchell) Sanders; m. James Allen Long, 1961 (div. 1985); children: Andrew C., James Allen IV. BA, Oglethorpe U., 1966; M in Librarianship, Emory U., 1967. Asst. librarian Coll. of St. Matthias, Bristol, Eng., 1970-74; cons. State Library of Ohio, Columbus, 1975-77; coordinator Franklin County Pub. Library, Columbus, 1977-79, dir. Fairfield County Dist. Library, Lancaster, Ohio, 1979-82, Dauphin County Library System, Harrisburg, Pa., 1982-85, Multnomah County Library, Portland, Oreg., 1985—. Contbr. articles to profl. jours. Bd. dirs. Dauphin County Hist. Soc., Harrisburg, 1983-85, Keystone Area Council Boy Scouts Am., 1984—, ARC, Harrisburg, 1984-85; pres. Lancaster-Fairfield County YMCA, Lancaster, 1981-82; vice-chmn. govt. and edn. div. Lancaster-Fairfield County United Way, Lancaster, 1981-82; sec. Fairfield County Arts Council, 1981-82. Recipient Dir.'s award Ohio Program in Humanities, Columbus, 1982; Sarah Long Day Fairfield County, Lancaster, Bd. Commrs., 1982. Mem. Pa. Library Assn. (co-chmn. legis. com. 1983-84), Oreg. Library Assn. (task force chmn. 1985—), Pacific N.W. Library Assn., Pub. Library Assn., ALA, Pa. Citizens for Better Libraries, AAUW. Club: City (Portland). Lodge: Zonta. Office: Multnomah County Library 801 SW Tenth Ave Portland OR 97205

LONG, STANLEY BERNARD, designer; b. Youngstown, Ohio, July 2, 1954; s. Ross C. and Marie J. (Lantz) L. Student, Thomas Aquinas Coll., 1972; BA in Art, Calif. State U., Northridge, 1986. Sales rep. Polacheck's Jewelers, Glendale, Calif., 1974-77; mgr. Chandel Jewelers, Glendale, 1977-79; owner Ultracare Home Mgmt., Los Angeles, 1979—; prin. Stan Long Design Assocs., Los Angeles, 1986—. Mem. bldg. com. Gay and Lesbian Community Services Ctr., Hollywood, Calif., 1986—. Mem. Am. Soc. Interior Designers (local pres. 1986). Roman Catholic. Avocation: fine arts. Home and Office: 230 S Hyperion Ave Los Angeles CA 90027

LONG, WALTER, civil and envionmental engineer, consultant; b. Lomond, Alta., Can., Mar. 7, 1933; s. K.S. and Mrs. K.S. (Huey) L.; children: Shane

S., Renee J. BS, U. Alta., Edmonton, 1958; MA in Sci., U. Toronto, 1960. Registered profl. civil engr., Calif., Nev., Can. Dist. engr. City of Toronto, 1958-60; sr. engr. R.E. Winter & Assocs., Toronto, 1961-63, Carl Yoder & Assocs., Berkeley, 1963-69; prin. Walter Long & Assocs., Consulting Engrs., Berkeley, 1969—; mem. Project Coordinating com. East Bay Mcpl. Utilities Dist., 1980-86. Bd. dirs. Environ. com. El Cerrito, Calif., 1975-80. Mem. ASCE, Am. Pub. Works, Water Pollution Control Fedn. Republican. Office: Walter Long & Assocs 1409 5th St Berkeley CA 94710

LONG, WILLIAM E., hydrologist, geologist; b. Minot, N.D., Aug. 18, 1930; s. Fred Ellis and Meda Maud (Becker) L.; m. Sallie M. Rogers, Apr. 14, 1954 (div. Aug. 1971); children: William Ware, Brooke Ellis; m. Katherine M. Costigan, Sept. 10, 1971. BS in Geology, U. Nev., 1957; MSc in Geology, Ohio State U., 1961, PhD in Geology, 1964. Cert. profl. geologist. Planner, chief water reservoir sect. Alaska Matanuska-Susituc div. Geol. and Geophys. Surveys, Eagle River, Alaska, 1977—. Home: PO Box 1831 Palmer AK 99645 Office: Alaska Div Mining and Geology WRS PO Box 772116 Eagle River AK 99577

LONGACRE, WILLIAM ATLAS, anthropology educator; b. Hancock, Mich., Dec. 16, 1937; s. William A. and Doris L. Longacre. BA, U. Ill., 1959; MA, U. Chgo., 1962, PhD, 1963. Asst. prof. U. Ariz., Tucson, 1964-68, assoc. prof., 1968-74, prof. anthropology, 1974—; fellow Ctr. Advanced Study, Palo Alto, Calif., 1972-73; vis. prof. U. Philippines, Quezon City, 1975-76, 79-80, U. Hawaii, Honolulu, 1984-85; adv. panel mem. NSF, Washington, 1983—. Author numerous books, book chpts. and articles. Fellow: AAAS, Am. Anthropol. Assn.; mem. Soc. Am. Archaeology, Ariz. Acad. Sci (sec. anthropology sect. 1965-66), Sigma Xi. Home: 2133 W Window Rock Dr Tucson AZ 85745 Office: U Ariz Dept Anthropology Tucson AZ 85721

LONGERICH, MARY COATES, aphasiologist; b. Oklahoma City, Nov. 12, 1908; d. Roger Smith and Mayme (Surber) Coates; m. Edward Longerich (dec.). AB, U. Akron, 1931; MA, U. Wis., 1935; PhD, La. State U., 1942. Pvt. practice speech pathology specializing in aphasia Los Angeles, 1943—; cons. speech pathology Orthopaedic Hosp., Los Angeles, 1944—; dir. Logopaedic Clinic, Los Angeles and Pasadena, Calif., 1946-75; lectr. in logopaedics Loma Linda U., Los Angeles, 1949-50. Author: Manual for the Aphasia Patient, 1955, 2d rev. edit. 1958, Helping the Aphasic to Recover his Speech, 1955, 2d rev. edit. 1967; co-author Aphasia Therapeutics, 1954, 2d rev. edit. 1977. Fellow Am. Speech-Lang.-Hearing Assn. (cert.); mem. Am. Acad. Pvt. Practice in Speech Pathology, Calif. Speech Hearing Assn., Delta Gamma. Republican. Presbyterian. Home: 3355 Wilshire Blvd Los Angeles CA 90010 Office: Logopaedic Clinic Suite 1416 1930 Wilshire Blvd Los Angeles CA 90057

LONGLEY, BERNIQUE, painter, sculptor; b. Moline, Ill., Sept. 27, 1923; d. Eli James and Effie Marie (Coen) Wilderson; 1 child, Bernique Maria Glidden. Grad., Art Inst. Chgo., 1945. One-woman shows, Mus. N.Mex., 1947, 50, 52, Appleman Gallery, Denver, 1950, VanDieman-Lillienfield Galleries, N.Y.C., 1953, Knopp-Hunter Gallery, Santa Fe, 1954, 57, 58, Gallery Five, Santa Fe, 1964, 65, Coll. Santa Fe, 1967, Sanger-Harris, Dallas, 1968, Lars Laine Gallery, Palm Springs, Calif., 1969, Canyon Rd. Gallery, Santa Fe, 1972, Summer Gallery, Santa Fe, 1973, 74, 75, 76, Cushing Galleries, Dallas, 1977, Gov.'s Gallery, N.Mex. State Capitol, 1978, Santa Fe East, Austin, Tex., 1979, Santa Fe East Gallery, 1985, 86, Leslie Levy Gallery, 1985-86; group shows include, Denver Art Mus., 1948, N.Mex. Highlands U., 1957, Lars Laine Gallery, 1961, 63, Santa Fe Festival of Arts, 1977, 78, 79, 80, Leslie Levy Gallery, Scottsdale, Ariz., 1985-86, Santa Fe East, 1985-86, many others, retrospective exhbn., Santa Fe East Gallery, 1982; represented in permanent collections, Mus. N.Mex., Fine Arts Center, Colorado Springs, Coll. Santa Fe, also pvt. collections.; subject of book Bernique Longley-A Retrospective, 1982. Bryan Lathrop Fgn. Travelling fellow, 1945. Mem. Art Inst. Chgo. Alumni Assn., Artists Equity Assn. Home and. Studio: 427 Camino del Monte Sol Santa Fe NM 87501

LONGMIRE, PATRICK ANTHONY, geochemist; b. Los Alamos, N.Mex., July 15, 1952; s. Conrad Lee and Theresa (Izzo) L.; m. Shelley Boyer, Sept. 16, 1979. BS, U. N.Mex., 1976, MS, 1983, postgrad. Research geologist U. N.Mex., Albuquerque, 1976-79; geochemist Colo. Geol. Survey, Denver, 1979-80; staff geochemist N.Mex. Environ. Improvement Div., Santa Fe, 1980-86; sr. geochemist City of Albuquerque, 1986; hydrogeochemist Roy F. Weston Inc., Albuquerque, 1986—; cons. Nat. Acad. Scis., 1983, Lee Wilson and Assocs., Santa Fe, 1984-85. Contbr. articles to profl. publs. Lenard scholar, 1974; Colo. Sch. Mines fellow, 1978-79. Mem. Geochem. Soc., Internat. Geochem. Soc., Assn. Ground Water Scientists and Engrs., Am. Chem. Soc. Democrat. Avocations: music, skiing, oil painting. Home: 122 Placita de Oro Santa Fe NM 87501 Office: Roy F Weston Inc 5301 Central Ave NE Albuquerque NM 87108

LONGO, PATRICIA LACY, deputy mayor, advertising company executive; b. Anderson, Ind., Sept. 24, 1927; d. Flay Samuel and Arla Robbins (Begeman) Lacy; m. Charles Rudolph Longo, Jan. 19, 1952; children—Stephen, Christopher, Tracy. Student Brevard Coll., 1945, Ventura Coll., 1964-67, 75-76. Dir. pub. relations Gallaudet Coll. for the Deaf, Washington, 1958-61; field cons. Am. Nat. Red Cross, San Francisco, 1966-68; fund cons. Fiesta delas Rosas, San Jose, Calif., 1968-69; mgr. San Jose Symphony, 1969-71; mem. Ventura City Council, Calif., 1981—, dep. mayor; mem. community, econ. and human devel. com., 1981—, mem., transp. and communication com., 1981—. Commr. Ventura Redevel. Agy., 1981—; bd. dirs. South Coast Area Transit, 1981—, chmn., 1983—; chmn. Ventura County Repub. Cen. Com., 1982—; pres: Ventura Rep. Assembly; bd. dirs. Rape and Sexual Abuse Ctr. Ventura County; mem. Calif. Rep. exec. com., 1983—. Mem. Calif. Elected Women Assn. Edn. and Research, Ventura County Profl. Womens Network, Ventura C. of C. Club: PEO. Lodges: DAR, Am. Legion. Office: 501 Poli St PO Box 99 Ventura CA 93002

LONGRIGG, PAUL, electrical research engineer, consultant; b. Eng., Apr. 27, 1927; came to U.S., 1966, naturalized, 1983; s. Sidney and Mabel Alice (Sibson) L.; m. Mary-Anne Holdar, Nov., 1966; B.Sc. with honors, U. Wales, 1950, Lanchester Tech. U., Eng., 1958. Chartered profl. engr., Eng. Radar design engr. Hawker-Siddeley Dynamics, Stevenage, Eng., woomers, South Australia, 1958-66; sr. mfg. research engr. L.T.V. Aerospace Corp., Warren, Mich., 1967-69; research and devel. scientist Forney Engring. Co., Dallas, 1969-74; chief engr. Crompton-Ark. Mills, Morrilton, 1974-76; meteorologist N.Z. Meteorol. Service, Wellington, 1976-79; sr. research engr. Solar Energy Research Inst., Golden, Colo., 1980—; pres. Modus Tech. Cons. Inc., Dallas, Golden, Colo., 1973-85. Inventor coal combustion detection and laser systems. Tchr. Jr. Achievement, Warren, 1970, Adopt A Sch. Program, Denver, 1983; active Boy Scouts of Great Brit. Served to lt. Brit. Royal Navy, 1943-53. ETO, Korea. Recipient Energy Conservation award Brit. Petroleum, 1979. Fellow Brit. Interplanetary Soc.; mem. IEEE (sr.; chmn. subcom. 1980-85, del. to Peoples Republic of China, 1983). Mem. Ch. of Eng. Club: AX POW (Denver); Prestatyn Conservative Club.

LONGSTREET, RENEE SCHONFELD, tv writer, producer; b. Los Angeles, July 19, 1940; d. Morrey and Faye (Zeiler) Schonfeld; m. Jack Silas, Nov. 19, 1961 (div. Dec. 1973); children: Julie Lynne, Carolyn Jo, Sean Michael; m. Harry Stephen Longstreet, Jan. 9, 1977. BA in English, UCLA, 1961. Producer, writer Universal Studios, Los Angeles, 1982-83, 20th Century Fox, Inc., Los Angeles, 1983; supervising producer NBC Prodns., Los Angeles, 1984-85, Warner Bros. TV, Los Angeles, 1985; exec. producer, writer MGM-TV, Los Angeles, 1986—. Author: (screenplay) Gathering Part II, 1979, The Promise of Love, 1980, The Sky's No Limit, 1983. Chairperson of Listeners' Bur. Nat. Council for Families and TV, Los Angeles, 1982—, mem. steering com. Mem. Writers Guild of Am., Acad. TV Arts and Scis., Women in Film. Democrat. Jewish.

LONIGRO, VICTORIA MARIE, utility company executive; b. San Pedro, Calif., Nov. 3, 1947; d. Vincent and Madge Evelyn (Tatum) LoN. AA, Los Angeles Harbor Coll., 1967; BA in History, Calif. State U., Dominquez Hills, 1971; MA in Mgmt., U. Redlands, 1981. Customer service rep. Los Angeles Water and Power, 1967-73, sr. employee devel. specialist, 1984-87, administrv. mgr. water quality, 1987—; adminstrv. asst. Police Dept., Los Angeles, 1973-81; pension claims officer Fire and Police Pensions, Los Angeles, 1981-84; instr. human resource mgmt. West Coast U., Los Angeles, 1986—. Vice capt. USCG Aux., Long Beach, Calif., 1980—. Mem. So. Calif. Personnel Mgmt. Assn., Town Hall of Calif., Am. Soc. for Tng. and Devel., Whittier Hist. Soc., Windsor Sq. Hancock Park Hist. Soc. Roman Catholic. Avocations: boating, aviation, history, art, hist. preservation and renovation. Home: 5441 Mavis Ave Whittier CA 90601 Office: Dept Water and Power 111 N Hope St #A-18 Los Angeles CA 90012

LOOKABILL, LARRY LEE, accounting educator; b. Long Beach, Calif., Oct. 26, 1944; s. Lyle D. and Florence M. Lookabill; children: Erik, Anna. BS, Portland State U., 1968; MBA, U. Wash., 1969; PhD, Stanford U., 1975. CPA, Oreg. Asst. prof. acctg. U. Ill., Urbana, 1973-76, U. Oreg., Eugene, 1976-85; vis. reader U. Queensland, Brisbane, Australia, 1980-81; vis. lectr. U. Queensland, Brisbane, 1983; assoc. prof. Western Wash. U., Bellingham, 1985—; owner Profl. Edn. Seminars of Wash., Bellingham, 1986—. Doctoral Dissertation award Ernst & Whinney, 1972. Mem. Am. Acctg. Assn. (Competitive Manuscript award 1976). Home: 1207 Chuckanut Dr Bellingham WA 98226 Office: Western Wash U Dept Acctg Bellingham WA 98225

LOOMIS, MARY JEANETTE, editor-in-chief; b. Houston, July 21; d. Richard William and Mary Evelyn (Richards) Roby; m. Robert Lindsey Loomis, Feb. 10, 1965; children: Robert Duncan, Richard Roby. BA in Fine Art, Scripps Coll., 1966. Pres. Santa Monica (Calif.) Bay Printing and Pub. Co., 1983—; editor-in-chief L.A. West Mag., Santa Monica, 1985—. Editor, designer (datebooks) Datebook for Westsiders, 1982, Yesterday Tripping, 1984; contbr. articles to profl. jours. Mem. Civic Action Com., Pacific Palisades, Calif., 1983-85. Mem. Mag. Pubs. Assn., Western Pubs. Assn., Prodn. Club. Los Angeles. Republican. Roman Catholic. Office: Santa Monica Bay Printing & Pub 919 Santa Monica Blvd #245 Santa Monica CA 90272

LOOMIS, WILLIAM FARNSWORTH, biology educator; b. Boston, Sept. 17, 1940; s. William F. and Violet (Amory) L.; m. Patricia Hasegawa, Aug. 21, 1981; children: Catherine Amory, Emily Farnsworth. BS, Harvard U., 1962; PhD, MIT, 1965. Prof. biology U. Calif., San Diego. Author: Developmental Biology, 1986. Mem. Soc. Devel. Biology (pres.). Office: U Calif-San Diego Dept Biology B-022 La Jolla CA 92093

LOONEY, RALPH EDWIN, newspaper editor; b. Lexington, Ky., June 22, 1924; s. Arville Zone and Connie Elizabeth (Boyd) L.; m. Clarabel Richards, Dec. 7, 1944. B.A., U. Ky., 1948. Successively proof reader, photographer, chief photographer, sports writer, reporter Lexington Leader, 1943-52; reporter Albuquerque Tribune, 1953-54; reporter, copy editor, chief copy editor St. Louis Globe-Democrat, 1955-56; city editor Albuquerque Tribune, 1956-68, asst. mng. editor, 1968-73, editor, 1973-80; editor Rocky Mountain News, Denver, 1980—. Author: Haunted Highways, the Ghost Towns of New Mexico, 1969; contbr.: articles to mags. including Nat. Observer; others, photographs to mags. Founder, mem. N.Mex. Motion Picture Commn., 1967-76; v.p., dir. Albuquerque C. of C., 1971-75; bd. dirs. Albuquerque Indsl. Devel. Service, 1971-80; bd. advisors Lovelace Med. Center, Albuquerque, 1976-80; bd. advs. UPI, 1983-86; bd. dirs. Newspaper Features Council, 1984—; mem. exec. council St. Joseph Hosp., 1986—. Recipient N.Mex. medal of Merit, 1968, Robert F. Kennedy Journalism award, 1970, George Washington Honor Medal Freedoms Found., 1969, 19 E.H. Shaffer awards for editorial writing, reporting and photography N.Mex. Press Assn., 1965-80. Mem. N.Mex. Press Assn. (state pres. 1976), Colo. Press Assn. (bd. dirs. 1982-85), Sigma Delta Chi (state pres. 1960). Methodist. Office: Rocky Mountain News 400 W Colfax St Denver CO 80204

LOPER, D. ROGER, retired oil company executive; b. Mpls., Dec. 14, 1920; s. Donald Rust and Agnes (Yerxa) L.; m. Sylvia Lee Brainard, Aug. 16, 1946 (dec. Apr. 1973); children: Ann Kathleen, Michael Brainard, Joyce Elizabeth, Nancy Jean Loper Woods; m. Genevieve Jean Kusles, May 4, 1974. BSMetE, Carnegie Tech. Inst., 1947. Registered chem. engr., Calif. Div. supr. Standard Oil of Calif., San Francisco, 1958-64, asst. chief engr., 1964-74; gen. mgr. Chevron Petroleum, London, 1974-80; pres. Chevron Shale Oil Co., Denver, 1980-82; v.p. Chevron Overseas Petroleum, San Francisco, 1982-85; cons. Loper Assocs., Redwood City, Calif., 1985—. Inventor hydrocracking reactor, remote inspection device. Pres. Our Saviour Luth. Ch., Lafayette, Calif., 1971-72. Served to maj. U.S. Army, 1942-46. Republican. Home and Office: 4 Woodleaf Ave Redwood City CA 94061

LOPER, JAMES LEADERS, broadcasting executive; b. Phoenix, Sept. 4, 1931; s. John D. and Ellen Helen (Leaders) L.; m. Mary Louise Brion, Sept. 1, 1955; children: Elizabeth Margaret, James Leaders. BA, Ariz. State U., 1953; MA, U. Denver, 1957; PhD, U. So. Calif., 1967; DHL (hon.), Columbia Coll., 1973; LLD (hon.), Pepperdine U., 1978. Asst. dir. bur. broadcasting Ariz. State U., Tempe, 1953-59; news editor, announcer Sta. KTAR, Phoenix, 1955-56; dir. ednl. TV, Calif. State U., Los Angeles, 1960-64; v.p. Community TV So. Calif., Los Angeles, 1962-63; asst. to pres. Sta. KCET-Pub. TV, Los Angeles, 1963-65, sec., 1965-66, dir. ednl. services, 1964-65, asst. gen. mgr., 1965-66, v.p., gen. mgr., 1966-69, exec. v.p., gen. mgr., 1969-71, pres., gen. mgr., 1971-76, pres., chief exec. officer, 1976-82; exec. dir. Acad. TV Arts and Scis., 1983—; chmn. bd. Pub. Broadcasting Service, Washington, 1969-72; adj. prof. Sch. Cinema and TV Annenberg Sch. Communications U. So. Calif., 1984—; sr. lectr. U. So. Calif., Los Angeles, 1969-70; pres. Western Ednl. Network, 1968-70; mem. Gov.'s Ednl. TV and Radio Adv. Com., Calif., 1968-74; U.S. rep. CENTO Conf. Radio and TV, Turkey, 1978. Contbr. articles to profl. jours; contbr. to ETV: The Farther Vision, 1967, Broadcasting and Bargaining: Labor Relations in Radio and Television, 1970. Mem. adv. bd. Jr. League of Los Angeles, 1970-76, Jr. League of Pasadena, 1972-75, Los Angeles Jr. Arts Ctr., 1968-72; exec. v.p. Assocs. of Otis Art Inst., 1971-77, pres., 1975-77; chmn., dir. The Performing Tree, Los Angeles; bd. dirs. Los Angeles Civic Light Opera Co., 1974—, v.p., 1975—; bd. dirs. Sears-Roebuck Found., 1976-79; chmn. bd. visitors Annenburg Sch. Communications, U. So. Calif., 1975-80; trustee Poly. Sch., Pasadena. Recipient Disting. Alumnus award Ariz. State U., 1972; Alumni award of Merit, U. So. Calif., 1975; Gov's. award Hollywood chpt. Nat. Acad. TV Arts and Scis., 1975; Alumni Achievement award Phi Sigma Kappa, 1975. Mem. Acad. TV Arts and Scis. (past gov., v.p. Hollywood chpt., trustee nat. acad.), TV Acad. Found., Hollywood Radio and TV Soc. (treas., dir.), Western Ednl. Soc. Telecommunications (past pres.), Assn. Calif. Pub. TV Stas. (past pres.), Young Pres.'s Orgn., Phi Sigma Kappa, Pi Delta Epsilon, Alpha Delta Sigma, Sigma Delta Chi. Presbyterian (chmn. Mass Media Task Force So. Calif. synod 1969-75). Clubs: Valley Hunt (Pasadena), Bel-Air Bay, Los Angeles, 100 of Los Angeles, Valley of San Marino, Sunset, Calif. (Los Angeles). Office: Acad TV Arts and Scis 3500 W Olive Rd Burbank CA 91505

LOPER, WARREN EDWARD, computer scientist; b. Dallas, Aug. 2, 1929; s. Leon Edward and Belva (Fannin) L.; BS in Physics, U. Tex. at Austin, 1953, BA in Math. with honors, 1953; m. Ruth M. Wetzler, June 17, 1967; 1 dau., Mary Katherine Loper. Commd. ensign U.S. Navy, 1953, advanced through grades to lt., 1957; physicist U.S. Naval Ordnance Test Station, China Lake, Calif., 1956-61; operational programmer U.S. Navy Electronics Lab., San Diego, 1962-64; project leader, systems programming br., digital computer staff U.S. Fleet Missile Systems Analysis and Evaluation Group, Corona, 1964-65, sr. systems analyst digital computer staff U.S. Naval Ordnance Lab., Corona, 1965-69; head systems programming br. Naval Weapons Center, Corona Labs, 1969; computer specialist compiler and operating systems devel., Naval Electronics Lab. Center, San Diego, 1969-76; project leader langs., operating systems and graphics Naval Ocean Systems Ctr., San Diego, 1977—; Navy rep. on tech. subgroup Dept. Def. High Order Lang. Working Group, 1975-80. Recipient Disting. Service award Dept. Def., 1983. Mem. IEEE, Assn. Computer Machinery. Democrat. Roman Catholic. Home: 6542 Alcala Knolls Dr San Diego CA 92111 Office: Naval Ocean Systems Ctr/Code 424 271 Catalina Blvd San Diego CA 92152

LOPEZ, ANTHONY, social work educator, consultant; b. San Juan, P.R., July 12, 1943; s. Antonio and Octavia (Cordero) L.; m. Lorraine Mata, July 29, 1967; children—William III, Teresa, Orlando. B.A. in Sociology and Theology, So. Calif. Coll., 1971; M.S.W., U. So. Calif., 1973; postgrad. U. Denver, 1976—. Psychiat. social worker U. So. Calif. Med. Ctr., 1973-74, dir. tng. substance abuse program, 1974-76; intergovtl. relations coordinator III, drug abuse program Denver Regional Council Govts., 1978-79; prof./coordinator human services program Community Coll. Denver-Aurora, Denver, 1979—, interim div. dir. health and human services, 1986—; cons. in field. NIMH grantee, 1971-73; Council Social Work Edn. grantee, 1976-78. Mem. Nat. Assn. Social Workers, Nat. Orgn. Human Service Educators, Coalition Spanish-Speaking Mental Health Orgns., Nat. Orgn. Puerto Ricans Social and Drug Abuse Workers, Chicano Alliance, Hispanic Democratic Caucus. Mem. Assembly of God Ch. Office: Community Coll Denver-Auraria 1111 W Colfax Denver CO 80204

LOPEZ, JOSÉ MANUEL, aerospace engineer; b. Santurce, P.R., June 28, 1948; s. José Manuel and Eva Lygia (Reyes) L.; m. Lee Ana Trujillo, Sept. 24, 1983. BS in Aerospace Engring., St. Louis U., Cahokia, Ill., 1969; MS in Aerospace Engring., U. Tenn. Space Inst., 1971; postgrad., Armed Forces Staff Coll., Norfolk, 1982-83. Commd. USAF, Tullahoma, Tenn., 1969; advanced through grades to lt. col. USAF, 1986; with Space and Missile Systems Orgn., USAF, Norton AFB, 1971-75; with 19th surveillance squadron USAF, Diyarbakir, Turkey, 1975-76; with 2d communications squadron USAF, Denver, 1976-79; mem. tech. staff Hughes Aircraft Co., Denver, 1979-85, sr. project engr., 1985—; maj. def. logistics agy., Santa Ana, Calif., 1983—. Served to lt. col. USAF, Res. Masters scholar Air Force Inst. Tech., U. Tenn., 1970. Avocations: writing, computers. Office: Hughes Aircraft Co 8000 E Maplewood Ave Englewood CO 80111-4999

LOPEZ-AVILA, VIORICA, chemical engineer; b. Bucharest, Romania, June 7, 1949; came to U.S., 1975; d. Grigore and Maria (Neagu) Raducanu; m. Carlos Lopez, Apr. 19, 1969. Student in chem. engring., Poly. Inst., Bucharest, 1966-71; PhD, MIT, 1979. Chem. engr. Research Inst. Drugs, Bucharest, 1971-75; sr. chemist Midwest Research Inst., Kansas City, Mo., 1979-81; group leader Acurex Corp., Mountain View, Calif., 1981—. Contbr. articles to profl. jours. Mem. Am. Chem. Soc., Am. Soc. Mass Spectrometry, Soc. Environ. Toxicology and Chemistry (publs. com.), Bay Area Mass Spectrometry. Avocations: sewing, landscaping, camping. Office: Acurex Corp 485 Clyde Ave Mountain View CA 94039

LOPOUR, MARTHA JEANETTE (MRS. DAVID LEE), business exec., former county govt. ofcl.; b. El Paso, Tex., Nov. 18, 1937; d. Clarence Oren and Martha Belle (Denerson) Shirey; student N.Mex. Jr. Coll.; m. David Lee LoPour, July 6, 1956; children—Melissa Dianne, David Gregory. Dep. tax assessor Lea County Tax Assessor's Office, Lovington, N.Mex., 1957-61, dep. appraiser-tax assessor, 1968-76, data processing coordinator, 1976—; owner LoPour Ltd., 1982—; v.p. LoPour Storm Windows & Doors. Sec., Lovington Democratic Women, 1980, rec. sec., 1981; Lovington bd. dirs. March of Dimes Found., 1962, 78; bd. dirs. Lovington Blood Services; mem. Youth Ctr. Council, sponsor, 1981-82, Lovington Community Concert Assn. Council. Recipient cert. of nobility N.Mex. Sec. State, 1980; named one of Outstanding Young Women of Am. Mem. Internat. Assn. Assessing Officers (active 1972-81), Beta Sigma Phi (pres. 1981), Alpha Kappa (pres. 1965, 74, 81, preceptor 1981-86, Woman of Yr.), Xi Omicron. Baptist. Club: Lovington Woman's, Lovington Garden. Home and office: 802 W Gore Ave Lovington NM 88260

LOPPNOW, DAVID HUNT, radar engineer; b. Milw., Jan. 2, 1934; s. Lester Alfred and Irma Iva (Hunt) L.; m. Sharon Lee Gray, June 21, 1958; children: Jeffrey, Randall, Heather. AB, Ripon Coll., 1955; postgrad., U. Hawaii, 1958, UCLA, 1978, Ga. Tech., 1981, George Washington U., 1979-82. Sr. programming analyst System Devel. Corp., Santa Monica, Calif., 1959-62; engring. group leader Litton Data Systems, Canoga Park, Calif., 1962-66; sr. member tech. staff ITT Gilfillan, Van Nuys, Calif., 1966—. Author tech. papers. Served to lt. j.g. USN, 1955-59. Recipient Pres. Team award ITT Gilfillan Pres., 1984, ITT Quality citation, ITT World Hdqrs., 1985. Mem. IEEE (featured speaker 1985), Aerospace and Electronic Systems Soc., ITT Gilfillan Mgmt. Assn., Assn. Old Crows. Republican. Avocations: jogging, travel, theater, music, sailing. Home: 22577 Waterbury St Woodland Hills CA 91364 Office: ITT Gilfillan 7821 Orion Ave PO Box 7713 Van Nuys CA 91409

LORANCE, ELMER DONALD, organic chemistry educator; b. Tupelo, Okla., Jan. 18, 1940; s. Elmer Dewey and Imogene (Triplett) L.; m. Phyllis Ilene Miller, Aug. 31, 1969; children: Edward Donald, Jonathan Andrew. BA, Okla. State U., 1962; MS, Kansas State U., 1967; PhD, U. Okla., 1977. NIH research trainee Okla. U., Norman, 1966-70; asst. prof. organic chemistry So. Calif. Coll., Costa Mesa, 1970-73, assoc. prof., 1973-80, prof., 1980—, chmn. div. natural scis. and math., 1985—. Contbr. articles to profl. jours. Cons. Harbor Christian Sch., Costa Mesa, 1974. Mem. AAAS, Am. Chem. Soc., Internat. Union Pure and Applied Chemistry (assoc.), Am. Inst. Chemists, Am. Sci. Affiliation, Phi Lambda Upsilon. Republican. Mem. Ch. Assembly of God. Avocations: reading, gardening, music. Office: So Calif Coll 55 Fair Dr Costa Mesa CA 92626

LORBER, ROBERT L., small business owner, author; b. N.Y.C., July 26, 1947; s. Jules and Rose (Fleischman) L.; m. Sandra Elaine Wilson, May 11, 1974; children: Tracie Suzanne, Lindie Diane. BA in Sociology, U. Calif., Davis, 1969, MA in Sociology, 1971; PhD in Applied Behavioral Sci. and Organic Psychology, Union Grad. Sch., 1974. Gen. mgr. SAGA Adminstrn. Corp., 1969-71; dir., gen. mgr. RLS Assn., Inc., Sacramento, 1971-75; sr. v.p. CEC, Tustin, Calif., 1975-77; pres., chief exec. officer, founder Performance Systems Improvement, Santa Ana, Calif., 1977-83, Lorber Kamai Assocs., Orange, Calif., 1983—; bd. dirs. Sukut Constn., Anderson and Anderson Ins. Brokers. Author: (with Kenneth H. Blanchard) Putting the One Minute Manager to Work, (with Riaz Khadem) One Page Management; contbr. articles to profl. jours. Active exec. council Orange County, Calif., bd. dirs. Bus. Sch. U. Santa Clara; mem. World Affairs Council, Town Hall of Calif. Mem. Basic Am. Med., Inc. (bd. dirs.), Am. Mgmt. Assn., Am. Mgmt. Assn. President's Assn., Am. Productivity Mgmt. Assn., Am. Psychol. Assn. Avocations: skiing, reading, photography. Home: 19251 Canyon Dr Orange CA 92667 Office: Lorber Kamai Assocs 505 S Main St Suite 1017 Orange CA 92668

LORD, ARTHUR ABRAM, TV producer; b. N.Y.C., Mar. 3, 1942; s. Benjamin and Kathryn (Zucker) L.; m. Susan E. Tallman, Aug. 28, 1965; children: Michael, Sharon. Student, Ohio Wesleyan U., 1961; BS in Journalism, U. Fla., 1963. Newswriter NBC, N.Y.C., 1967-71; war corr. NBC, Saigon, Vietnam, 1971-73; S.W. bur. dir. NBC, Houston, 1973-79; network news dir. NBC, Burbank, Calif., 1979-82, producer, 1982—; cons. (TV movie) Special Bulletin, 1983. Producer news feature Heart Transplant, 1980 (Emmy award 1981): Writer news spl. Apollo to the Moon, 1970 (Emmy award 1970); contbr. articles to TV Guide. Served to capt. USAF, 1963-67. Recipient Nat. Merit award Houston Urban League, 1975, Peabody award, 1985. Mem. TV News Dirs. Assn. Jewish. Club: Mid Valley Athletic. Avocations: pvt. pilot, tennis, freelance writing. Office: NBC News 3000 W Alameda Burbank CA 91523

LORD, HAROLD WILBUR, consulting electronics engineer; b. Eureka, Calif., Aug. 20, 1905; s. Charles Wilbur and Rossina Camilla (Hansen) L.; B.S., Calif. Inst. Tech., 1926; m. Doris Shirley Huff, July 25, 1928; children—Joann Shirley (Mrs. Carl Cook Disbrow), Alan Wilbur, Nancy Louise (Mrs. Leslie Crandall), Harold Wayne. With Gen. Electric Co., Schenectady, 1926-66, electronics engr., 1960-66; pvt. cons. engr., Mill Valley, Calif., 1966—. Coffin Found. award Gen. Electric Co., 1933. Fellow IEEE (life, tech. v.p. 1962, Centennial medal 1984, IEEE Magnetics Soc. 1984 Achievement award). Contbr. articles to profl. jours. Patentee in field. Home and office: 336 Corte Madera Ave Mill Valley CA 94941

LORD, JACK, actor, director, artist, producer; b. N.Y.C., Dec. 30, 1930; s. William Lawrence and E. Josephine (O'Brien) Ryan; m. Marie de Narde, Apr. 1, 1952. B.S. in Fine Arts, N.Y. U., 1954. pres. Lord and Lady Enterprises, Inc., 1968—. Exhibited galleries, museums, including, Corcoran Gallery, Nat. Acad. Design, Whitney Mus., Bklyn. Mus., Met. Mus. Art, N.Y.C., Library of Congress, Brit. Mus., London, Bibliotheque Nationale, Paris, Mus. Modern Art, N.Y.C., Met. Mus. Art, Brit. Mus., Bklyn. Mus., Bibliotheque Nationale, Paris, Fogg Mus., Harvard U., Santa Barbara (Calif.) Mus. Art, John and Mable Ringling Mus. Art, Sarasota, Fla., Grunwald Graphic Arts Found., UCLA, Brooks Meml. Art Gallery, Memphis, Cin. Art Mus., Atkins Mus. Art, Kansas City, Mo., Fine Arts Gallery, San Diego, Colby Coll. Art Mus., Waterville, Maine, Ga. Mus. Art, U. Ga., Atlanta, DePauw U. Art Mus., Greencastle, Ind., Chouinard Art Inst., Los Angeles, Free Library Phila., Columbia U., N.Y.C., Lycoming

Coll., Williamsport, Pa., Rutgers U., New Brunswick, N.J., U. Maine, Orono; works represented in permanent collections, Dartmouth Coll., Hanover, N.H., Colgate U. Library, Hamilton, N.Y., Simmons Coll., Boston, Kalamazoo Inst. Arts, U. N.C., Chapel Hill, Evansville (Ind.) Mus. Arts, Massillon (Ohio) Mus., Hebrew Union Coll., Cin., N.Y.C., Los Angeles, Jerusalem, Flint (Mich.) Inst. Arts, Lehigh U. Coll. Arts, Bethlehem, Pa., Birmingham (Ala.) Mus. Art, Case Western Res. U., Cleve., Coll. of Wooster (Ohio), Calif. Inst. Arts; appeared on Broadway in Traveling Lady, Cat on a Hot Tin Roof, Flame-Out, The Illegitimist; star series Stoney Burke; producer, star series: series Hawaii Five-O; creator: TV shows The Hunter series; creator, dir., producer: TV motion picture M Station: Hawaii, 1980; writer original screenplay: Melissa, 1968; dir.: episodes Hawaii Five-O; appeared in: feature films The Court Marshall of Billy Mitchell, Williamsburg, The Story of a Patriot, Tip on a Dead Jockey, God's Little Acre, Man of the West, The Hangman, Walk Like a Dragon, Dr. No, Ride to Hangman's Tree, Doomsday Flight; leading TV roles include: Constitution series Omnibus, Playhouse 90, Goodyear Playhouse, Studio One, U.S. Steel Hour, Have Gun Will Travel, Untouchables, Naked City, Rawhide, Bonanza, Americans, Route 66, Gunsmoke, Stagecoach West, Dr. Kildare, Greatest Show on Earth, Combat, Chrysler Theater, 12 O'Clock High, Loner, Laredo, FBI, Invaders, Fugitive, Virginian, The Man from UNCLE, High Chaparral, Ironside, Alcoa Theatre, Loretta Young Show, The Millionaire, Checkmate, Climax, Kraft, Philco, Danger, Suspense, The Web, You Are There, Lineup, Grand Hotel, Kraft Suspense Theatre. Recipient St. Gauden's Artist award, 1948; Fame award, 1963; Spl. Law Enforcement award Am. Legion, 1973; Adminstr.'s award VA, 1980; Legend in His Own Time award State of Hawaii, 1980; named to Cowboy Hall of Fame, 1963. Office: c/o Lord & Lady Ent Inc 4999 Kahala Ave Honolulu HI 96816 also: care JW Hayes 132 S Rodeo Dr Beverly Hills CA 90212

LORD, JACKLYNN JEAN, student services representative; b. Sacramento, Feb. 2, 1940; d. Jasper Jackson and Celia (Moreno) Opdyke; m. Brent Andrew Nielsen, Aug. 6, 1966 (dec. Sept. 1974); 1 child, Taumie Celia; m. Mark William Lord, Mar. 5, 1983; 1 child, Jacklynn Michelle. Student, Sacramento State U., 1958-60, Cabrillo Coll., 1962-66, Sacred Coll. of Jamilian Theology and Div. Sch., Reno, 1976—. Communications cons. Pacific Telephone Co., San Jose, Calif., 1966-74, Nev. Bell Co., Reno, 1974-76; student services rep. for extension program Jamilian U. of Ordained, Reno, 1976—; asst. music dir. Internat. Community Christ, Reno, 1980—; choral instr. Jamilian Parochial Sch., Reno, 1976—; sexton Jamilian Handbell Choir, Reno, 1981—; organist Symphonietta, Reno, 1983—. Mem. Nat. League Concerned Clergywomen. Republican. Mem. Ch. Internat. Community Christ (ordained to ministry). Avocations: music, tennis, gardening, pvt. pilot. Home: 1990 Humboldt Reno NV 89509 Office: Internat Community Christ 643 Ralston St Reno NV 89503

LORDS, JAMES LAFAYETTE, biology educator, researcher; b. Salt Lake City, Apr. 5, 1928; s. Lafayette and Lenore (Coppin) L.; m. Katherine Reeves, June 4, 1955; children: Kevin James, John Lafayette. BS, U. Utah, 1950, MS, 1951, PhD, 1960. Research asst. U. Wis., Madison, 1960-61, research assoc., 1961-62; asst. prof. biology U. Utah, Salt Lake City, 1962-66, assoc. prof., 1966-75, prof., 1975—. Author: (with others) Instructional Methods in Experimental Biology, 1965; contbr. numerous articles to profl. jours.; patentee in field. Served as sgt., U.S. Army, 1951-53. Mem. AAAS, Bioelectromagnetic Soc. (bd. dirs. 1979-80), Am. Physiol. Soc., Sigma Xi (pres. Utah chpt. 1978-79). Home: 4190 Sovereign Way Salt Lake City UT 84124 Office: Univ Utah Dept Biology 200 S University St Salt Lake City UT 84112

LOREN, JOHN WALTER, utilities executive; b. Cleve., Mar. 29, 1949; s. John Walter and Lois (Eller) L.; m. Gwen Fisher, July 18, 1982. BS in Chemistry, Baylor U., 1971. Chief chemist Radio-Med, Rosemont, Ill., 1971-72; analytical coordinator Dearborn Chem. Co., Lake Zurich, Ill., 1972-75; regional mgr. H-O-H Chems., Palatine, Ill., 1975—; cons. chemist, Littleton, Colo., 1983—. Mem. ASHRAE, Nat. Assn. Corrosion Engrs., Am. Chem. Soc., ASTM. Club: Colo. Mountain (Denver). Avocations: rock and ice climbing, mountaineering, skiing. Home: 4952 S Iris St Littleton CO 80123 Office: H-O-H Chems Inc PO Box 24713 Denver CO 80224

LORENTZ, DAVID RICHARD, engineering specialist; b. Portland, Oreg., Apr. 29, 1957; s. John and Ann R. (Richard) L.; m. Sarah M. McQuade, Jan. 7, 1984; 1 child, Thomas David. BSME, Ariz. State U., 1979, MSME, 1980; cert. in program mgmt., West Coast U., 1985. Registered profl. engr., Calif. Research asst. Ariz. State U., Tempe, 1979-81; engr. Convair div. Gen. Dynamics, San Diego, 1981-84, sr. engr., 1984-85; engring. specialist Space Systems div. Gen. Dynamics, San Diego, 1985—. Contbr. tech. articles to profl. jours. Recipient Shell award Ariz. State U., 1978, Glasstone award Am. Nuclear Soc., 1978. Mem. AIAA. Republican. Roman Catholic. Avocations: skiing, tennis, basketball. Office: Gen Dynamics Space Systems Div PO Box 85990 San Diego CA 92138

LORENZ, SUSAN KATHERINE, information management executive; b. Pryor, Okla., Sept. 23, 1946. BA in Internat. Politics, George Washington U., 1968; MBA, Computer Sci., U. Hawaii, 1971; postgrad., Army Command and Staff Coll., 1979, Army War Coll., 1986—. Computer specialist various orgns., Honolulu, 1969-74; project mgr. U.S. Army Communications Command, Ft. Huachuca, Ariz., 1974-81, chief computer acquisitions, 1981-84; research cons. U.S. Army Info. Systems Command, Ft. Huachuca, Ariz., 1984-85, dep. chief of staff, 1985—. Mem. Phi Beta Kappa, Kappa Alpha Theta (chpt. pres.). Office: Commdr USAISC Attn AS-1M Fort Huachuca AZ 85613

LORENZEN, ROBERT FREDERICK, ophthalmologist; b. Toledo, Ohio, Mar. 20, 1924; s. Martin Robert and Pearl Adeline (Bush) L.; B.S., Duke, 1948, M.D., 1948; M.S., Tulane U., 1953; m. Lucy Logsdon, Feb. 14, 1970; children—Roberta Jo, Richard Martin, Elizabeth Anne. Intern, Presbyn. Hosp., Chgo., 1948-49; resident Duke Med. Center, 1949-51, Tulane U. Grad. Sch., 1951-53; practice medicine specializing in ophthalmology, Phoenix, 1953—; mem. staff St. Joseph's Hosp., St. Luke's Hosp., Good Samaritan Hosp., Maricopa County Hosp. Pres. Ophthalmic Scis. Found., 1970-73; chmn. bd. trustees Rockefeller and Abbe Prentice Eye Inst. of St. Luke's Hosp., 1975—. Recipient Gold Headed Cane award, 1974. Fellow Internat. Coll. Surgeons, A.C.S., Am. Acad. Ophthalmology and Otolaryngology, Soc. Eye Surgeons; mem. Am. Assn. Ophthalmology (sec. of ho. of dels. 1972-73, trustee 1973-76), Ariz. Ophthal. Soc., Royal Soc. Medicine. Republican. Lodge: Rotary (pres. Phoenix 1984-85). Editor-in-chief Ariz. Medicine, 1963-66, 69-70. Home: 2921 W Manor Dr Phoenix AZ 85014 Office: 367 E Virginia Ave Phoenix AZ 85004

LORMAN, WILLIAM RUDOLPH, civil engineer, retired naval officer; b. Cleve., Sept. 26, 1910; s. Rudolph Calman and Theresa Mary (Pollock) L.; m. Hulda Wanita Babel, May 2, 1936 (dec. May 1980); children: Jonathan, Timothy. BS, Case Western Res. U., 1933; MS, U. Colo., 1939, profl. degree CE, 1956. Asst. dep. engr. Cuyahoga County Engrs., Cleve., 1935-36; asst. engr. U.S. Bur. Reclamation, Denver and Redding, Calif., 1936-42; commd. lt. (j.g.) USN, 1942, advanced through grades to lt. comdr., 1948, ret., 1970; spl. projects officer USN, Calif. and Vanuatu, 1943-46; civil engr. USN, San Francisco, 1946-48; materials research engr. USN, Port Hueneme, Calif., Solomons, Md., 1948-82; cons. Dart Assocs. Inc., Oxnard, Calif., 1984—; USN liason DuBridge Oil Lease Panel, Los Angeles, 1969, Com. Status of Cement and Concrete Research in U.S., Washington, 1979-81. Contbr. articles to profl. jours. Fellow ASCE, Am. Concrete Inst.; mem. ASTM, The Ret. Officers Assn. (life, sec. Ventura County, Calif. chpt. 1983-87), Sigma Xi. Republican. Avocations: reading, music. Home: 510 Ivywood Dr Oxnard CA 93030

LORNE, SIMON MICHAEL, lawyer; b. Hampton, Eng., Feb. 1, 1946; came to U.S., 1952, naturalized, 1961; s. Henry Thomas and Daphne Mary (Brough) L.; A.B. cum laude, Occidental Coll., 1967; J.D. magna cum laude, U. Mich., 1970; m. Patricia Ann Coady, Aug. 12, 1967; children—Christopher, Michele, Allison, Nathan James, Katrina. Admitted to Calif. bar, 1971; assoc. firm Munger, Tolles & Olson, Los Angeles, 1970-72, ptnr., 1972—; vis. assoc. prof. law U. Pa., 1977-78, acting dir. Ctr. Study of Fin. Instns., 1977-78; lectr. in law, corp. fin. U. So. Calif., 1986—. Author: Acquisitions and Mergers: Negotiated and Contested Transactions, 1985. Mem. Los Angeles Mayor's Com. on Internat. Trade Devel., 1979-81; bd. dirs., sec. Los Angeles Internat. Trade Devel. Corp., 1982-85; mem. adv. com. to U.S. Senator S.I. Hayakawa on Internat. Trade, 1979-82; bd. govs. Econ. Literacy Council Calif., 1981—. Served with USMCR, 1967-68. Mem. Los Angeles Area C. of C. (exec. com., internat. commerce com., leadership mission to People's Republic of China, 1980), ABA, Los Angeles County Bar Assn. (exec. com. bus. and corps. law sect., chmn. 1984-85). Republican. Roman Catholic. Clubs: Jonathan; Stock Exchange; Lake Arrowhead Yacht. Office: Munger Tolles & Olson 355 S Grand Ave Los Angeles CA 90071

LORTS, JACK EDWARD, English educator, poet; b. Wichita, Kans., Sept. 4, 1940; s. Kenneth Warren and Doris Maxine (Hedberg) L.; m. Cecilia Ann Kennedy, Nov. 9, 1960; children: Jacqueline, Gerine, Virginia. BA, Calif. State U., Fullerton, 1962; MEd, U. Oreg., 1978. cert. secondary and elem. tchr., Calif., Oreg. Tchr. lang. arts El Rancho Sch. Dist., Pico Rivera, Calif., 1962-63, Valle Lindo Sch. Dist., South El Monte, Calif., 1963-68, 69-74, Medford (Oreg.) Sch. Dist., 1968-69, South Umpqua Sch. Dist., Myrtle Creek, Oreg., 1974—; tchr., cons. Oreg. Writing Project, 1983—; instr. lang. arts Umpqua Community Coll., Roseburg, Oreg., 1975—. Contbr. poems, articles to Ariz. Quar., Vis-a-Vis, English Jour., Kans. Quar., Oreg. English, others. NEH fellow Kenyon Coll., 1984. Mem. NEA, Nat. Council Tchrs. English, Assn. Supervision and Curriculum Devel. Democrat. Methodist. Lodge: Masons (master local lodge 1981, 83). Home: 991 Mason St PO Box 279 Myrtle Creek OR 97457 Office: South Umpqua High Sch 501 S W Chadwick Ln Myrtle Creek OR 97457

LOS BANOS, ALLAN, JR., contracting executive; b. Honolulu, Sept. 6, 1948; s. Allan and Aurora (Leonida) Los B.; m. Kirsten Kuuiponohea Soong, Nov. 23, 1974; children: Allan P., Aedward O., Alexander L., Andrea K. BA, U. Hawaii, PhD. Cert. tchr., Hawaii. Archaeologist State of Hawaii, Honolulu, 1970-71; lectr. Chaminade Coll., Honolulu, 1972-74; educator, counselor Palama Settlement, Honolulu, 1974-78; clin. supr. YMCA, Kailua, Hawaii, 1979-80; exec. dir. Gen. Contractors Assn., Honolulu, 1981—; cons. in field, Honolulu, 1978-80. Coach Pop Warner Football, Palama Settlement, 1974-76; youth companion Vols. in Pub. Service, Honolulu, 1977-78; mem. State Adult Edn. Adv. Council, Honolulu, 1981, youth adv. bd. Urban 4-H, Honolulu, 1985—; mgr. Glee Club, Honolulu, 1981—. Recipient Service to Community award, Kaneohe Bus. Assn., 1980. Mem. Apprenticeship and Tng. Coordinator Assn. Roman Catholic. Club: Golf (Honolulu) (sec. 1982—). Avocations: Hawaiian archaelogy, weight tng., horticulture, martial arts. Office: Gen Contractors Assn 1065 Ahua St Honolulu HI 96819

LOSEY, DEBRA ANN, librarian, information specialist; b. Ann Arbor, Mich., June 18, 1958; d. Roger Samuel Losey and Marilyn Joanne (Fiegel) Anderson. BS in Social Scis., Eastern Mich. U., 1980; MLS, U. Mich., 1982. Library clk. Saline (Mich.) Pub. Library, 1976-79; tech. services asst. Washtenaw County Library, Ann Arbor, 1979-80; library technician Great Lakes Environ. Research Lab. Library, Ann Arbor, 1980-82; info. specialist Nat. Ctr. Atmos. Research Library, Boulder, Colo., 1983; librarian U.S. Dept. Commerce NOAA-Mountain Adminstrv. Support Ctr., Boulder, 1982-84; tech. info. specialist Southwest Fisheries Ctr. Library U.S. Dept. Commerce NOAA-Nat. Marine Fisheries Service, La Jolla, Calif., 1984—. Mem. Internat. Assn. Marine Sci. and Info. Ctrs., So. Calif. Online Users Group, San Diego Online Users Group, Spl. Library Assn. Democrat. Clubs: Mourton Bay Fig Morris Dancers, Gesundheit German Dancers (San Diego). Avocations: folk dancing, drawing, textile arts, horseback riding, reading. Office: Southwest Fisheries Ctr Library PO Box 271 8604 La Jolla Shores Dr La Jolla CA 92038

LOTKER, MICHAEL, energy healthcare financier; b. N.Y.C., May 28, 1948; s. George Kenneth and Grace (Reinstein) L.; m. Carol Martha Siegel, Jan. 23, 1971; children—Howard Scott, Stefanie Ellen, Andrea Phyllis. B.A. in Physics, Queens Coll., 1970; M.S. in Physics, U. Ill., 1972. Sr. research scientist Northeast Utilities, Berlin, Conn., 1972-77; sr. assoc. Booz Allen Hamilton, Washington, 1977-79; v.p. DHR, Inc., Washington, 1979; exec. v.p. The Synectics Group, Washington, 1979-83; pres. Renewable Energy Ventures, Encino, Calif., 1983-85; v.p. Intellimed Corp., 1985—. U. Ill. fellow, 1971. Home: 1646 Folkstone Terrace Westlake Village CA 91361

LOTT, DAVIS NEWTON, advertising agency executive, publisher; b. San Antonio, May 8, 1913; s. James and Sissilla (Davis) L.; m. Arlene Marion Peterson Nov. 1, 1942; children—Vicki Arlene, Christy Sue, Laurie Ann. B.S., Northwestern U., 1935; post-grad. UCLA. With Better Homes and Gardens, Des Moines, Iowa, 1935-36; with Abbott, Labs., North Chicago, Ill., 1936-37; copywriter J. Walter Thompson, Chgo., 1938-39; owner and pres. Lott Advt. Agy., Los Angeles, 1939-41, 46—; owner Lott Pub. Co., Los Angeles, 1948—; pres. USA Corp., Marina del Ray, Calif.; pres. Western Publs., Santa Monica, Calif.; pub. Am. Buyers Rev., Am. Carwash Rev., Am. Personal Protection Rev.; dir. spl. projects Microlert Systems Internat. Past bd. dirs. Los Angeles Library Assn. Served to comdr. USNR, 1941-46, 1951-52, World War II, Korea. Named Assoc. Dean of Candy Industry, Nat. Candy Wholesalers Assn., 1974. Author: Rules of the Road, 1942; Emergency Shiphandling Manual, 1943; Collision Prevention, 1947; Treasure Trail, 1944; Star Spangled Broadcast, 1950; Mystery of Midnight Springs, 1954; Dodge City Justice, 1957; The Inaugural Addresses of the American Presidents, 1964; The Presidents Speak, 1965; See How They Ran 1972; The Presidents Illustrated, 1976; Jimmy Carter-And How He Won, 1976; co-author: (with Bruce Greenland) musical comedy The Music Room, 1982. Home: 13222 B Admiral Ave Marina del Rey CA 90291 Office: PO Lockbox 9669 Marina del Rey CA 90291

LOUDERBACK, TRUMAN EUGENE, environmental manager, consultant; b. Sterling, Colo., Jan. 17, 1946; s. George DeWayne and Lillian Louise (Harrach) L.; m. Dena Marie Chambers, June 1, 1985; 1 child, Nicole Marie. BS, Colo. State U., 1968; postgrad., U. Colo., 1974-75. Project investigator and biologist, research inst. Colo. Sch. Mines, Golden, 1972-78; adminstr. quality assurance Cleveland-Cliffs Iron Co., Casper, Wyo., 1979, dir. environ. affairs, 1980-83; dir. environ. affairs Cleveland-Cliffs Iron Co., Rifle, Colo., 1984—, Cliffs Engring., Inc., Rifle, Colo., 1984—; pvt. practice cons. Lakewood, Colo., 1978-79; chmn. environ. com. Pacific Shale Project, Rifle, 1983—, also mgr. environ. impact statement, 1983-84. Contbr. articles to profl. jours. Industry rep. Colo. Joint Rev. Process Team, Colo. Dept. Nat. Resources, 1983. Mem. Nat. Assn. Environmental Profls. (cert.), Rocky Mountain Assn. Environmental Profls. Republican. Methodist. Lodge: Rotary (bd. dirs. Rifle chpt. 1984), Masons. Avocations: travel, fishing, photography. Office: Cleveland-Cliffs Iron Co 818 Taughenbaugh Blvd Rifle CO 81650

LOUGHRAN, THOMAS PATRICK, JR., research oncologist; b. Darby, Pa., Nov. 12, 1953; s. Thomas P. Sr. and Margaret Mary (Boyle) L. BS in Biology with honors, Ursinus Coll., 1975; MD, Hahnemann U., 1979. Diplomate Am. Bd. Internal Medicine, Am. Bd. Oncology. Resident in medicine Thomas Jefferson U., Phila., 1979-82; fellow in oncology Fred Hutchinson Cancer Research Ctr., Seattle, 1982-85, assoc. clin. research, 1985-86, asst. mem., 1986—; mem. staff Pacific Med. Ctr., Seattle, 1984—. Contbr. articles to profl. jours. Fellow Leukemia Soc. Am., 1985-87, Spl. Fellow 1987—; fellow Am. Cancer Soc. 1984-85. Mem. AAAS. Republican. Roman Catholic. Avocation: golf. Office: Fred Hutchinson Cancer Research Ctr 1124 Columbia St Seattle WA 98104

LOUIE, JAMES SAM, physician, educator; b. Los Angeles, June 23, 1940; s. Willie Way Louie and Janice Leong; m. Roella Ching Hsieh, July 23, 1967; children: John, Andrew, Matthew. Student, Tulane U., 1958-61; MD, Washington U., St. Louis, 1965. Diplomate Am. Bd. Internal Medicine, Am. Bd. Rheumatology. Intern then resident Johns Hopkins U., Balt., 1965-67; chief resident UCLA, Los Angeles, 1971-72, asst. prof., 1972-80, assoc. prof., 1980-85, prof. medicine, 1985—. Author Renoir-His Art and his Arthritis (Internat. Rheumatology prize 1979). Served to capt. USAF, 1967-69. Named Disting. Tchr. Harbor UCLA, Torrance, 1982. Fellow ACP, Am. Rheumatology Assn.; mem. So. Calif. Rheumatology Assn., Arthritis Health Profls., Western Soc. Clin. Investigation. Republican. Presbyterian. Avocation: art. Office: Harbor Gen Hosp 1000 W Carson St Torrance CA 90509

LOUIE, MARCIA FUJIMOTO, tax lawyer; b. Papaaloa, Hawaii, July 10, 1951; d. Frank Shigeo and Shizue (Inomoto) Fujimoto; m. Martin Louie, June 2, 1978; 1 dau., Beth. B.B.A., U. Mich., 1973; J.D., 1978. Bar: Wash. 1978; C.P.A., Wash., Mich. Sr. auditor, Coopers & Lybrand, Detroit, 1973-78; EDP auditor State of Wash., Seattle, 1979-81; tax mgr. Deloitte Haskins & Sells, Seattle, 1981-84; pvt. practice, 1984—. Bd. dirs. Asian Mgmt. and Bus. Assn., Seattle, 1983-86, Women and Bus., Asian Counseling and Referral Service, Seattle, 1984-86. Mem. Wash. Soc. C.P.A.s, Wash. State Bar Assn., Wash. Women in Tax, Estate Planning Council, Seattle-King County Bar Assn. Office: 2525 First Interstate Ctr Seattle WA 98104

LOUIS, STEVEN, computer scientist; b. San Francisco, Mar. 8, 1953; s. Lou and Annette Geneva (Fisher) L.; m. Maurie Manning, Mar. 16, 1980; children—Brian Samuel, Erin Davies. A.B. in Computer Sci., U. Calif.-Berkeley, 1974. Computer scientist Nat. Magnetic Fusion Energy Computer Ctr., Lawrence Livermore Nat. Lab., Livermore, Calif., 1974-79, mem. staff Cen. Computer Systems Group, 1982-86, group leader File Storage Systems Group, 1986—; sr. analyst CalComp, Inc., Santa Clara, Calif., 1979-80; product mgr. Benson, Inc., San Jose, Calif., 1980-82. Mem. Assn. Computing Machinery, ACM Special Interest Group in Graphics, Nat. Computer Graphics Assn. (charter). Home: 1885 Helsinki Way Livermore CA 94550 Office: Lawrence Livermore Nat Lab PO Box 5509 L-561 Livermore CA 94550

LOUKE, SAMUEL FRANKLIN, electronic manufacturing engineer; b. Bakersfield, Calif., Mar. 27, 1956; s. Monzell Reed and Gladys Louke; m. Phyllis Ellen Avidan, July 2, 1978; children: Marissa, Jeremy. BSChemE, U. Calif., Santa Barbara, 1978. Engr. microelectronic mfg. Intel Corp., Hillsboro, Oreg., 1978-85, sr. staff engr., 1986—. Avocations: pilot, trombone player. Office: Intel Corp 5200 NE Elam YG Pkwy Hillsboro OR 97123

LOUP, CAROL LORIOUX, speech and language pathologist, consultant; b. Wichita, Kans., Oct. 12, 1957; d. Charles Amel and Carolyn Joy (Riley) Loup; m. Timothy Michael Murphy, July 15, 1978 (div. July 1984). BA, Wichita State U., 1980, MA, 1982. Speech therapist USD #500, Kansas City, 1982-84, Speech Plus, Inc., Wichita, 1985, Head Start Program, Seattle, 1985-86, Overlake Hosp., Seattle, 1985-86, Auburn (Wash.) Schs., 1986—. Mem. Am. Speech Hearing Assn. (cert. clin. competence 1983), Wash. Speech Hearing Assn., Nat. Student Speech-Lang. Hearing Assn. (sec. Wichita chpt. 1980), Grad. Students Colloquium (pres. 1981), Cascade Bike Club. Democrat. Baptist. Avocations: running, swimming, skiing, reading, music. Home: 206 31st Ave E Seattle WA 98112 Office: Auburn Sch Dist 915 4th St NE Auburn WA 98002

LOUTAS, SHIRLA MARIE, speech pathologist; b. Guthrie, Okla., Mar. 2, 1947; d. Melvin Henry and Verna Laurene (Myers) Swaim; m. Anastasios G. Loutas, Sept. 3, 1977. BA, Phillips U., 1968, MS, 1974. Speech pathologist Ednl. Service Unit 13, Ainsworth, Nebr., 1968-69, Community Speech and Hearing Ctr., Enid, Okla., 1970-73, Natrona County Sch. Dist. 1, Casper, Wyo., 1973-78, Casper Child Devel. Ctr., 1978-86, Natrona County Sch. Dist. 1, Casper, Wyo., 1986—. Mem. adv. bd. Natrona County Pub. Health Dept., 1979-83. Named one of Outstanding Young Women of Am., 1977. Mem. Am. Speech Lang. and Hearing Assn., Wyo. Speech Lang. and Hearing Assn. (sec. 1979). Avocations: gardening, reading.

LOUVAU, GORDON ERNEST, management consultant, educator; b. Oakland, Calif., May 29, 1928; s. Ernest and Ella Meta (Meins) L.; student U. Calif., 1946-49; postgrad. Calif. State U., Hayward, 1975-77; M.B.A., John F. Kennedy U., 1980; m. Lois Louvau Peterson, June 9, 1984; children—John Pierre, Tanya Lissette, Charles Frederic. Accountant, Oakland, 1950-59; asst. controller U.S. Leasing, Inc., San Francisco, 1960-61; pres. Louvau Systems Co., Oakland, 1962-66; v.p., gen. mgr. Prescolite div. U.S. Industries Co., San Leandro, Calif., 1966-68; cons. acctg. systems, 1969—; vis. prof. acctg. U. S.Africa, 1970-71; dir. Inst. Research and Bus. Devel., asst. prof. acctg. Calif. State U. at Hayward, 1972-80; asst. dean., asso. prof. mgmt., dir. acctg. programs J.F. Kennedy U., 1969-85. Cert. Quantitative Techniques for Adminstrs. and Accts, 1975, mgmt. acctg. Mem. Nat. Assn. Acct. (dir. 1972-74), Am. Acctg. Assn. Republican. Author: Financial Management of the Clinical Laboratory, 1974; Management and Cost Control Techniques for the Clinical Laboratory, 1977; Computers in Accountant's Offices, 1981. Office: PO Box 5808 Carmel CA 93921

LOUX, MARK WILLIAM, marketing executive; b. Beverly, Mass., Nov. 27, 1961; s. Gordon Dale and Elizabeth Ann Loux; m. Beth Ann Boot, Apr. 28, 1984. BA, Wheaton Coll., 1985. Mktg. adminstr. Holt Internat., Eugene, Oreg., 1984—. Mem. Oreg. Direct Mktg. Assn., Christian Ministries Mgmt. Assn. Republican. Baptist. Office: Holt Internat. Children's Services 1195 City View St Eugene OR 97402

LOVATT, ARTHUR KINGSBURY, JR., manufacturing company executive; b. Ventura, Calif., Mar. 12, 1920; s. Arthur Kingsbury and Flora (Mercedes) L.; B.S., U. So. Calif., 1941; M.B.A., Queens U., 1943; m. Juanita Gray, Feb. 1, 1946; children—Sherry Lynn, Tim Arthur. Leaseman, Shell Oil Co., Los Angeles, 1946-51; dir. indsl. relations Willys-Overland Motors, Inc., Los Angeles, 1952-55; asst. to pres. and gen. mgr. Pastushin Aviation Corp., Los Angeles, 1955-57; pres. Lovatt Assos., Los Angeles, 1957-66; chmn. bd., pres., gen. mgr. Lovatt Tech. Corp., Santa Fe Springs, Calif., 1966—, also dir.; chmn. bd. Lovatt Sci. Corp., Santa Fe Springs, Metal Ore Processes, Inc., Santa Fe Springs; dir. Lovatt Industries, Inc., others. Mem. Calif. Republican State Central Com., 1964—; state adviser U.S. Congl. Adv. Bd.; chartered mem. Republican Pres. Task Force. Served with U.S. Army, 1943-45. Mem. Am. Legion (post comdr. 1946), AAAS, Nat. Space Inst., Am. Soc. Metals, Los Angeles C. of C., U. So. Calif. Alumni Assn. (life), Nat. Hist. Soc. (founding assoc.), N.Y. Acad. Scis., Internat. Oceanographic Found., Smithsonian Assos., Am. Ordnance Assn., Disabled Am. Vets., U.S. Senatorial Club, Nat. Rifle Assn. Club: Masons (past master, Shriner). Inventor, developer tech. processes. Office: Lovatt Tech Corp 10106 Romandel Ave Santa Fe Springs CA 90670

LOVE, ALBERT, architect, consultant, poet; b. Phila., Jan. 20, 1927; s. Samuel and Esther (Israel) L.; m. Goldie Kramer (div.); children: Sherie Love Edelman, Michael; m. Lilly Bercovici, Nov. 15, 1964. BArch, Drexel U., 1953. Registered architect, Pa., Md., Calif.; cert. Nat. Council Archtl. Registration Bds., 1977. Archtl. designer Kling Partnership, Swinburne Assocs., Etc., Phila., 1953-65; project architect, specifications engr. Pereira Assocs., Luckman, Partnership, Ralph M. Parsons Co., Los Angeles, 1965-75; architect Northrop Corp., Pico Rivera, Calif., 1981—; archtl. cons. U.S. Postal Service, IBM Corp., Jet Propulsion Lab., others, Los Angeles, 1975-81. Served as sgt. U.S. Army, 1945-46. Mem. Soc. Am. Registered Architects (Architect of Month 1980), Constrn. Specifications Inst., Britannica Soc. (hon. Golden Poet award 1986). Republican. Jewish. Avocations: music, aerobics, travel. Home: PO Box 182 Pico Rivera CA 90660 Office: Northrop Corp 8900 E Washington Blvd Dept F553/ID Pico Rivera CA 90660

LOVE, CHARLES STEELE, systems manager; b. St. Louis, Aug. 19, 1961; s. Jack Wayne and Elizabeth (Vogt) L.; m. Barbara Porte, Oct. 18, 1986. Student, Gonzaga U., 1979-80; BA, Westmont Coll., 1984. Project engr. Love Med. Research, Santa Barbara, Calif., 1981-85; engring. systems mgr. Symetrics Inc., Newbury Park, Calif., 1985—. Republican. Roman Catholic. Avocations: flying, skiing, travelling. Home: 650 Ash St #D Carpinteria CA 93013 Office: Symetrics Inc 3353 Old Conejo Rd Newbury Park CA 91320

LOVE, JACK WAYNE, surgeon; b. Belleville, Ill., Sept. 20, 1930; s. Charles H. and Helen M. (Golden) L.; student Harvard, 1948-49, U.S. Mil. Acad., 1950-51, U. Ill., Chgo., 1951-52; MD cum laude, Yale U., 1958; D Philosphy (Rhodes scholar), Oxford U., Eng., 1956; m. Elizabeth J. Vogt, Nov. 19, 1960; children: Charles S., John W., Elizabeth P., Richard M., George F., Sarah L. Intern Barnes Hosp., St. Louis, 1959-60, resident in gen. surgery, 1960-61, fellow in thoracic surgery, 1961-63; resident in gen. surgery Walter Reed Gen. Hosp., Washington, 1963-65; practice medicine specializing in cardiovascular surgery; chief of thoracic surgery William Beaumont Gen. Hosp., El Paso, Tex., 1965-67, dir. intern tng., 1966-67; chief div. thoracic and cardiovascular surgery Balt. City Hosps., 1967-69; asso. prof. surgery

Johns Hopkins U. Sch. Medicine, Balt., 1967-70; staff surgeon Johns Hopkins Hosp., 1967-70, Greater Balt. Med. Center, 1969-70; Union Meml. Hosp., 1969-70, Md. Gen. Hosp., 1969-70; cons. thoracic surgeon Good Samaritan Hosp., 1969-70, Mt. Wilson State Hosp., 1969-70, Santa Barbara (Calif.) Cottage Hosp., 1970—, Goleta (Calif.) Valley Community Hosp., 1970—, attending thoracic surgeon Harbor Gen. Hosp., Los Angeles, 1974—; assoc. clin. prof. surgery U. Calif., Los Angeles, 1974— . Served from capt. to maj. U.S. Army, 1963-67. Diplomate Am. Bd. Surgery, Am. Bd. Thoracic Surgery. Fellow ACS, Am. Coll. Cardiology, Am. Coll. Chest Physicians; mem. Soc. for Vascular Surgery, Internat. Cardiovascular Soc., Am. Assn. Thoracic Surgery, Soc. of Thoracic Surgeons, Western Thoracic Surg. Assn., Pacific Coast Surg. Assn., N.Y. Acad. Scis., Am. Trauma Soc., Am. Gastroent. Assn., Sigma Xi, Alpha Omega Alpha. Republican. Roman Catholic. Contbr. numerous articles to med. jours.; editorial bd. Jour. AMA, 1973-77; patentee blood oxygenator, prosthetic heart valve. Home: 785 Carosam Rd Santa Barbara CA 93110 Office: Santa Barbara Med Found Clinic Santa Barbara CA 93110

LOVE, JOHN ARTHUR, lawyer; b. Gibson City, Ill., Nov. 29, 1916; s. Arthur C. and Mildred (Shaver) L.; m. Ann Daniels, Oct. 23, 1942; children: Dan, Andy, Becky. B.A., U. Denver, 1938, LL.B., 1941, LL.D., 1963; LL.D., Colo. Coll., 1964. Bar: Colo. 1941. Practice law Colorado Springs, Colo., 1945-62; ptnr. Love & Cole and predecessor firms, 1948-62; gov. State of Colo., Denver, 1962-73; head Office Energy Policy, asst. to pres., 1973; pres., chief exec. officer Ideal Basic Industries, Denver, 1974-85; of counsel Davis, Graham & Stubbs, Denver, 1985—. Served to lt. comdr. AC USNR, 1942-45. Decorated D.F.C. (2); decorated Air medal with 4 oakleaf clusters. Congregationalist. Lodge: Rotary. Home: 100 Lafayette St Denver CO 80218 Office: Davis Graham & Stubbs 370 17th St Suite 4700 Denver CO 80202

LOVE, RAYMOND ALLEN, financial company executive; b. San Francisco, Sept. 22, 1928; s. George Lorentis and Gladys Lenore (Buckley) L.; m. Patricia Mary Nedd, Feb. 25, 1951; children: David George, Jennifer Robin Love Hamilton. BSBA, U. San Francisco, 1949. Trust officer Crocker Bank, Monterey, Calif., 1960-69; mgr. trust office Crocker Bank, Fresno, Calif., 1969-76; mgr. employee benefits trust Calif. Can. Bank, San Francisco, 1976-80, mgr. trust adminstr., 1980-84, mgr. trust dept., 1984-85; mgr. trust dept. Barclays Bank, San Francisco, 1985—. Served to 1st lt. U.S. Army, 1951-53. Mem. San Francisco Estate Planning Council, Western Pension Conf., Mechanics Inst. Clubs: Commonwealth, Stock Exchange. Avocations: microcomputers, philately, swimming. Home: 2 Partridge Ct Novato CA 94947 Office: Barclays Bank 340 Pine St 3rd Floor San Francisco CA 94104

LOVE, (CATHERINE JANE) REEVE, educator; b. N.Y.C., Oct. 18, 1944; d. Claude Rolfe and Mary Sue (Jaynes) L. B.A., Duke U., 1965; M.A., U. Tex., 1971; postgrad. U. N.Mex., 1980—. Ednl. tech. writer S.W. Ednl. Devel. Lab., Austin, Tex., 1968-73; tchr. high sch. English, Am. Sch. Found., Mexico City, 1973-74; media technologist/tech. writer Ednl. Devel. Corp., Austin, 1974-75; tng. specialist Ctr. for Pub. Sch. Ethnic Studies, U. Tex., Austin, 1975-76; edn. cons. Intercultural Devel. Research Assn., San Antonio, 1976-80; lectr. Navajo tchr. edn. devel. program, Dept. Elem. Edn. U. N.Mex., Albuquerque, 1980-81, assoc. dir. sex equity tng. programs Dept. Tech. and Occupational Edn., 1981—; participant various nat., internat. ednl. confs., 1977—; cons. Tex. Edn. Agy., 1974-75, Air Force Human Resources Lab., Lackland AFB, 1975, U.S. Dept. Edn., 1983—, others. Nat. Merit scholar, 1961-65, Ives Meml. scholar, U.N.Mex., 1985-86; Tinker Found./U. N.Mex. research grantee in Latin Am. 1982, 85; Dolores Gonzales Meml. fellow U. N.Mex., 1982-83; Title VII Bilingual fellow, 1982-85; Millicent A. Rogers Found. fellow, 1983-84; Nelle Gooch Travelstead fellow, 1984-86, Fulbright fellow, U. N.Mex., 1985-86, Charles R. Spain fellow, U. N.Mex., 1985-86; Mellon Found. Inter-Am. field research grantee, 1983, 84. Mem. Nat. Assn. for Bilingual Edn., N.Mex. Assn. for Bilingual Edn., Internat. Transactional Analysis Assn., Latin Am. Studies Assn., Internat. Soc. Intercultural Edn., Tng. and Research, N.Mex. Assn. Bilingual, Phi Beta Kappa, Theta Alpha Phi. Democrat. Contbr. articles in field to profl. lit. Home: 824 Quincy St NE Albuquerque NM 87110 Office: U NMex Dept Tech and Occupational Edn Albuquerque NM 87131

LOVE, RODNEY J., food distribution executive; b. 1938. BS, Okla. State U., 1962. With IGA Co., 1956—, advt. mgr., buyer, tng. and sales mgr., 1962-73; asst. gen. mgr. Assoc. Grocers Colo., Denver, 1974-77, v.p. ops., exec. v.p., gen. mgr., 1977-78, pres., chief exec. officer, 1978—, also bd. dirs. Office: Assoc Grocers of Colo PO Box 5529 Denver CO 80217 *

LOVE, SAMUEL LESTER, photography educator, management consultant; b. Phila., May 4, 1922; s. Henry and Sarah (Green) L.; m. Maggie Dee Langley, Mar. 6, 1946 (dec.); children: Jeffrey, Deborah Jo; m. Helen Curtis Weiss, Mar. 20, 1969 (dec. 1975); m. Clementine Sheppard, Dec. 22, 1976. Student, U. Pa., 1942. Dir. apprentice tng. Metron Instrument Co., Denver, 1950-54; founder, chmn. bd. Nat. Camera, Inc. (formerly Nat. Camera Repair Sch., Inc.), 1955-77; mgr., gen. ptnr. Exec. Hangars, Denver, 1979—; cons. photography, edn., mgmt.; bd. dirs. Republic Nat. Bank, Englewood; v.p. Bike Lovers Place, 1983—. Author several books on camera craftsmanship, articles in field; editor, compiler Camera Repairman's Handbook; co-inventor electronic photographic test instruements; designer spl. camera repair tools, automatic density-altitude indicating instrument. Trustee Nat. Home Study Council, 1960-61; chmn. Englewood (Colo.) Bd. Adjustment and Appeals, 1961; mem. Englewood Planning Commn., 1962-63, Englewood Water Bd., 1964-66; chmn. adv. com. Colo. State Propietary Sch., 1967-70; chmn. pro-tem com. Arapahoe County (Colo.) Airport; mem. Englewood Sch. Bd.; councilman City of Englewood, 1961-66; mayor, 1964-66; pres. El Jebel Air Patrol, 1985. Served as sgt. USAF, 1943-45. Mem. Soc. Photog. Scientists and Engrs. (chpt. pres.), Soc. Motion Picture and TV Engrs., Soc. Photog. Instrumentation Engrs., Soc. Photo-Technologists (life, pres. 1961), Am. Soc. Tng. and Devel. (past chpt. pres.), Colo. Flight Instrs. Assn. (pres. 1969), Profl. Phogotraphers Am., Photog. Soc. Am., Mile High Epson Computer Users' Group (editor newsletter 1983—), Shrine Air Patrol (past pres.). Democrat. Club: Denver Pilots (sec.). Lodge: Lions (past pres. local chpt.), Mason, Shriners (potentates aide El Jebel club 1987). Home: 6261 S Crestbrook Dr Morrison CO 80465

LOVE, SANDRA RAE, info specialist; b. San Francisco, Feb. 20, 1947; d. Benjamin Raymond and Charlotte C. Martin; B.A. in English, Calif. State U., Hayward, 1968; M.S. in L.S., U. So. Calif., 1969; m. Michael D. Love, Feb. 14, 1971. Tech. info. specialist Lawrence Livermore (Calif.) Nat. Lab., 1969—. Mem. Spl. Libraries Assn. (sec. nuclear sci. div. 1980-82, chmn. 1983-84), Beta Sigma Phi. Democrat. Episcopalian. Office: Lawrence Livermore Nat Lab PO Box 808 L-389 Livermore CA 94550

LOVEJOY, DAVID WINSOR, outdoor recreation educator; b. Lynchburg, Va., Oct. 11, 1951; s. Albert E. and Eunice (Gaul) L. BA, Prescott Coll., 1973. Instr. sr. seminar E. High Sch., Denver, 1971; instr. Boujum Inst., San Diego, 1978; faculty Prescott (Ariz.) Coll., 1979—; instr. Colorado Outward Bound Sch., Denver, 1981, Pacific Crest Outward Bound Sch., Portland, Oreg., 1980-81; team leader Prescott Coll. Search and Rescue Team, 1979-86. Author, editor: Granite Mountain Climbing Guide, 1973; contbr. articles to profl. jours. Mem. Am. Profl. Mountain Guides Assn. (assoc.), Wester River Guides Assn., Assn. Exptl. Edn., Grand Canyon Natural History Assn. Club: Syndecato Granitica (flagstaff 1970—). Avocations: mountain climbing around the world, rafting, photography, geography, jazz music. Home: 308 Pine Dr. Prescott AZ 86301 Office: Prescott Coll 220 Grove Ave Prescott AZ 86301

LOVELACE, JON B., investment management company executive; b. Detroit, Feb. 6, 1927; s. Jonathan Bell and Marie (Andersen) L.; m. Lillian Pierson, Dec. 29, 1950; children: Carey, James, Jeffrey, Robert. A.B. cum laude, Princeton U., 1950. Personnel asst. Pacific Finance Co., 1950-51; with Capital Research & Mgmt. Co., Los Angeles, 1951—; treas. Capital Research & Mgmt. Co., 1955-62, v.p., 1957-62, exec. v.p., 1962-64, pres., 1964-75, 82-83, chmn. bd., 1975-82, 83—, also dir.; chmn. bd. Investment Co. Am., 1982—; dir. Capital Research Co., 1967—; chmn. bd. Am. Mut. Fund, Inc, 1971—; pres., dir. New Perspective Fund; vice chmn. Capital Group, Inc.; bd. dirs. Am. Pub. Radio. Trustee Claremont McKenna Coll.; mem. adv. bd. Stanford U. N.E. Asia/U.S. Forum on Internat. Policy; mem. adv. council Stanford U. Grad. Sch. Bus.; trustee Calif. Inst. Arts, chmn., 1983—; trustee Santa Barbara Med. Found. Clinic., J. Paul Getty Mus. Mem. Council on Fgn. Relations, Sierra Club. Clubs: Princeton (N.Y.C.), University (N.Y.C.); Calif. (Los Angeles). Home: 800 W 1st St Los Angeles CA 90012 also: Capital Research & Mgmt 780 El Bosque Rd Santa Barbara CA 93108 Office: 333 S Hope St Los Angeles CA 90071

LOVELESS, EDWARD EUGENE, educator, musician; b. Lafayette, Ind., July 29, 1919; s. Benjamin Moses and Belva Lucille (Bowles) L.; m. Jean Evelyn Skinner, May 18, 1941; children: Linda Louise Loveless Reeder, Kathleen Beal Loveless Bodine, Stephen Edward, Melissa Jane Loveless Campbell, Benjamin Warwick. B.S., Purdue U., 1940, M.S., 1941; Ed.D., Stanford U., 1960. Tchr., prin., supt. public schs. Ind., 1941-57; asst. Stanford U., 1957-60; prin. public schs. Palo Alto, Calif., 1961-65; asst. prof. sch. adminstrn. San Francisco State Coll. and assoc. prof. San Jose State Coll., 1960-65; assoc. prof. U. Nev., Reno, 1965-72; prof. U. Nev., 1972—; vis. prof. Purdue U., summers 1965, 68, 75; prof. exec. devel. program USAF, Crete, spring 1973; clarinetist, saxaphonist, vocalist Jean and Ed (musical duo), 1984—. Author: The Teacher and School Law; Cases and Materials in the Legal Foundations of Education, 1974, (with J. Clark Davis) The Administrator and Educational Facilities, 1982; contbr. articles to profl. jours.; editor: Who's Who in Northern Nevada Education, 1976; speaker on sch. vandalism; Musical tours Ms World Discoverer, Singapore, Borneo, Celebes, New Guinea, Western Samoa, Tonga, others, 1984-85; performance South Pacific Coll., Stanford U. Alumni Assn., 1985; command performance King Tauf-ahau Tupou IV, Tonga, 1985; commd. performance Trident submarine USS Nev., 1986. Commendation for providing benefit concerts and performances Sierra Health Care Ctr., 1985. Mem. NEA, Nev. Edn. Assn., Internat. Soc. Gen. Semantics, Nat. Soc. Profs., Kappa Sigma, Phi Delta Kappa (cert. for disting. service 1974, placque of appreciation Gamma Psi chpt. 1976). Democrat. Presbyterian (elder). Home: 2895 Moana Ln Reno NV 89509 Office: University of Nevada Reno NV 89509

LOVELESS, H. KEVIN, travel agency executive; b. Burley, Ind., June 10, 1954; s. Harold William and Evelyn (martin) L. Student, Boise State U., 1973-76. Travel cons. Global Travel, Boise, 1971-75, v.p., 1975—. Home: 115 Horizon Circle Boise ID 83702 Office: Global Travel 1111 Main St Boise ID 83702

LOVELL, EMILY KALLED, journalist; b. Grand Rapids, Mich., Feb. 25, 1920; d. Abdo Rham and Louise (Claussen) Kalled; student Grand Rapids Jr. Coll., 1937-39; B.A., Mich. State U., 1944; M.A., U. Ariz., 1971; m. Robert Edmund Lovell, July 4, 1947. Copywriter, asst. traffic mgr. Sta. WOOD, Grand Rapids, 1944-46; traffic mgr. KOPO, Tucson, 1946-47; reporter, city editor Alamogordo (N.Mex.) News, 1948-51; Alamogordo corr., feature writer Internat. News Service, Denver, 1950-54; Alamogordo corr., feature writer El Paso Herald-Post, 1954-65; Alamogordo news dir., feature writer Tularosa (N.Mex.) Basin Times, 1957-59; co-founder, editor, pub. Otero County Star, Alamogordo, 1961-65; newscaster KALG, Alamogordo, 1964-65; free lance feature writer Denver Post, N.Mex. Mag., 1949-69; corr. Electronics News, N.Y.C., 1959-63, 65-69; Sierra Vista (Ariz.) corr. Ariz. Republic, 1966; free lance editor N.Mex. Pioneer Interviews, 1967-69; asst. dir. English skills program Ariz. State U., 1976; free-lance editor, writer, 1977—; part-time tchr., lectr. U. Pacific, 1981-86; part-time interpreter Calif., 1983—, Interpreters Unlimited, Oakland, 1985—; sec., dir. Star Pub. Co., Inc., 1961-64, pres., 1964-65. 3d v.p., publicity chmn. Otero County Community Concert Assn., 1950-65; mem. Alamogordo Zoning Commn., 1955-57; mem. founding com. Alamogordo Central Youth Activities Com., 1957; vice chmn. Otero County chpt. Nat. Found. Infantile Paralysis, 1958-61; charter mem. N.M. Citizens Council for Traffic Safety, 1959-61; pres. Sierra Vista Hosp. Aux., 1966; pub. relations chmn. Ft. Huachuca chpt. ARC, 1966. Mem. nat. bd. Hospitalized Vets. Writing Project, 1972—. Recipient 1st Pl. awards N.Mex. Press Assn., 1961, 62. Pub. Interest award Nat. Safety Council, 1962. 1st Pl. award Nat. Fedn. Press Women, 1960, 62; named Woman of Year Alamogordo, 1960. Editor of Week Pubs. Aux., 1962, adm. N.Mex. Navy, 1962, col. a.d.c. Staff Gov. N.Mex., 1963, Woman of Yr., Ariz. Press Women, 1973. Mem. N.Mex. (past sec.), Ariz. (past pres.) press women, N.Mex. Fedn. Womens Clubs (past dist. pub. relations chmn.), N.Mex. Hist. Soc. (life), N.Mex. Fedn. Bus. and Profl. Womens Clubs (past pres.), Pan Am. Round Table Alamogordo, Theta Sigma Phi (past nat. 3d v.p.), Phi Kappa Phi. Democrat. Moslem. Author: A Personalized History of Otero County, New Mexico, 1963; Weekend Away, 1964; Lebanese Cooking, Streamlined, 1972; A Reference Handbook for Arabic Grammar, 1974, 77; contbg. author: The Muslim Community in North America, 1983. Home: PO Box 7152 Stockton CA 95207

LOVELL, JOHN STANLEY, oil service executive; b. West Hartlepool, England, May 17, 1943; came to U.S., 1980; s. Tom and Lizzie (Hatton) L.; m. Jocelyne Susan Pengelley, Dec. 17, 1966 (div. 1986); children: David Jonathan, Robert John. BS with honors, Southampton U., Hampshire, England, 1966; PhD, Royal Sch. Mines, London, 1979; diploma, Imperial Coll., London, 1974-79. Research ceramicist Royal Doulton China, Sunbury, England, 1965-66; mine geologist Amalgamated Tin Mine of Nigeria, Jos, Plateau, 1966-67; exploration geologist Anglo-Oriental (Australia), Brisbane, Queensland, 1967-73; sr. research asst. Royal Sch. Mines, London, 1974-79; research geologist Barringer Resources, Golden, Colo., 1979-84; v.p. Barringer Geoservice, Golden, Colo., 1984—. Author: Handbook of Geochemistry, 1986; contbr. articles to profl. jours. Mem. Assn. Exploration Geochemistry. Avocations: squash, volleyball, stained glass, skiing. Home: 12615 W Bayaud Ave #32 Lakewood CO 80220 Office: Barringer Geoservices 1500 W 6th Ave Golden CO 80401

LOVELY, RICHARD HERBERT, physiological psychologist; b. Santa Monica, Calif., Sept. 20, 1941; s. Herbert James and Vivian Cecilia (Kilner) L.; m. Sharon Diane Ogden, Dec. 18, 1970 (div. June 8, 1976). BA, Calif. State U., Northridge, 1965; MS, Cen. Wash. U., 1967; PhD, U. Wash., 1974. Instr. psychology Yakima (Wash.) Valley Coll., 1967-68; asst. prof. Calif. State U., Chico, 1972-73; instr. U. Wash., Seattle, 1974-75, asst. prof. Sch. Medicine, 1976-79; sr. research scientist Battelle Meml. Inst., Richland, Wash., 1979—, group leader neurosci., 1979—; exchange scientist Nat. Inst. Environ. Health U.S.-USSR, 1977-82; cons. Nat. Council Radiation Protection and Measurements, 1977-85. Editor: (with Dr. M.E. O'Connor) Electromagnetic Fields and Neurobehavioral Function, 1986. NSF fellow, 1979-80. Mem. AAAS, Bioelectromagnetics Soc. (charter, bd. dirs. 1985—), Am. Nat. Standards Inst., Soc. Neurosci., Psychonomics Soc., Nat. Council Radiation Protection and Measurements. Republican. Episcopalian. Avocations: fishing, water sports, sports cars. Office: Battelle Seattle Research Ctr 4000 NE 41st St Seattle WA 98105

LOVENTHAL, MILTON, librarian, author, playwright, lyricist; b. Jan. 19, 1923; m. Jennifer McDowell. BA, U. Calif., Berkeley, 1950, MLS, 1958; MA in Sociology, San Jose State U., 1969. Researcher Hoover Instn., Stanford, Calif., 1952-53; librarian San Diego Pub. Library, 1957-59; librarian, bibliographer San Jose (Calif.) State U., 1959—; tchr. writing workshops, poetry readings, 1969-73; co-producer lit. and culture radio show Sta. KALX, Berkeley, 1971-72. Author: Books on the USSR 1917-57, 1957, Black Politics, 1971, A Bibliography of Material Relating to the Chicano, 1971, Autobiographies of Women 1946-70, 1972, Blacks in America, 1972, The Survivors, 1972, Contemporary Women Poets an Anthology, 1977, Ronnie Goose Rhymes for Grown-Ups, 1984; co-author: (Off-Off-Broadway plays) The Estrogen Party To End War, 1986, Mack the Knife: Your Friendly Dentist, 1986, Betsy & Phyllis, 1986, The Oatmeal Party Comes to Order, 1986; co-writer: (musical comedy) Russia's Secret Plot to Take Back Alaska, 1987. Recipient Bill Casey award in Letters, 1980; grantee San Jose State U., 1962-63, 84. Mem. Assn. Calif. State Profs., Calif. Alumni Assn., Calif. Assn. Research Librarians, Calif. Theatre Council. Office: PO Box 5602 San Jose CA 95150

LOVETT, ROBERT ELIOT, management consultant; b. Washington, Feb. 14, 1926; s. Eliot Callender and Helen Lucetta (Thompson) L.; m. Glenna Beatrice Bartlett, Jan. 26, 1957; children—Sharon, Laura Lee, Robert Eliot. A.B., U. Mich., 1948; M.B.A., N.Y.U., 1950; Ph.D., U. So. Calif., 1965. Fin. rep. Jour. of Commerce, N.Y.C., 1948-49; pub. relations adminstr. N.Y.U., 1949-51; buyer Gladding-McBean, 1951-53; customer service cons., 1953-54; v.p., treas., mktg. dir. Boylhart, Lovett & Dean, Inc., 1954-76; pres. Nat. Research Center, 1966-76; ptnr. BLD Mgmt., 1960-76; pres., dir. Voice in Pasadena, Inc., Los Angeles, 1964-83; pres., chmn. Robert E. Lovett, Inc., Laguna Beach, Calif., 1976—; officer, dir. KRLA, Inc., Los Angeles, 1977-83; dir. Higgins, Marcus & Lovett, Inc., Los Angeles, 1979—; dir. C.W. Driver, Los Angeles, 1970—; dir. workshops on Mng. for Results, 1979—; lectr. mktg. and mgmt. U. So. Calif., UCLA, Pepperdine U., Calif. State U.-Fullerton, 1954—. Past mem. Calif. State Toll Bridge Authority, Orange County Citizens' Direction-Finding Commn.; regular mem. Pasadena Tournament of Roses Assn. Served with U.S. Army, Chem. Corps, USAAF, 1944-46. Mem. Am. Mktg. Assn., Nat. Assn. Realtors, Am. Arbitration Assn. (commercial arbitrator 1986—). Republican. Christian Scientist. Club: Jonathan (Los Angeles). Contbr. articles in field to profl. jours. Home: 396 Myrtle St Laguna Beach CA 92651 Office: PO Box 1483 Laguna Beach CA 92652

LOVETT, WENDELL HARPER, architect; b. Seattle, Apr. 2, 1922; s. Wallace Herman and Pearl (Harper) L.; m. Eileen Whitson, Sept. 3, 1947; children: Corrie, Clare. Student, Pasadena Jr. Coll., 1943-44; B.Arch., U. Wash., 1947; M.Arch., Mass. Inst. Tech., 1948. Architect, designer Naramore, Bain, Brady & Johanson, Seattle, 1948; architect, assoc. Bassetti & Morse, Seattle, 1948-51; pvt. practice architect Seattle, 1951—; instr. architecture U. Wash., 1948-51, asst. prof., 1951-60, assoc. prof., 1960-65, prof., 1965-83, prof. emeritus, 1983—; lectr. Technische Hochschule, Stuttgart, 1959-60. Prin. works include Nuclear Reactor bldg, U. Wash., 1959, Weyerhaeuser Ecology Center, 1970. Pres. Citizen's Planning Council, Seattle, 1968-71. Served with AUS, 1943-46. Recipient 2d prize Progressive Architecture U.S. Jr. C. of C., 1949; Internat. design award Decima Triennale di Milano, 1954; Arch. Record Homes awards, 1969, 72, 74; Interiors award, 1973; Sunset-AIA awards, 1959, 62, 69, 71; Fulbright grantee, 1959; AIA fellow, 1978. Mem. AIA (sec. Wash. chpt. 1953-54). Patentee in field. Home and office: 420 34th Ave Seattle WA 98122

LOVING, JEAN FRANKLIN, retired elementary school administrator, consultant; b. Kansas City, Kans., Sept. 28, 1925; d. James Wesley and Nine Jane (McMullen) L.; m. Betty Lou Pearsall, May 30, 1947; children: Janet Kay, Donald Franklin. BS in Edn., Ariz. State Coll., 1950, MA in Sch. Adminstrn., 1958; EdS in Sch. Adminstrn., No. Ariz. U., 1966. Cert. elem. tchr., Ariz. Tchr. Prescott (Ariz.) Pub. Schs., 1950-65; asst. supt. bus. Prescott Pub. Schs., 1972-74, elem. prin., 1974-85; adminstrv. asst. No. Ariz. U., 1965-66; asst. prin. Prescott Jr. High, 1966-72; cons. reading programs, Prescott, 1983; speaker Nat. Elem. Sch. Prins. Conv., Denver, 1985; creator edn. computer program, 1984; creator reading program Million Minutes of Reading, 1983. Scoutmaster Boy Scouts of Am., Prescott, 1950-60; active fund drives Big Brothers Big Sisters, Prescott, 1982-84; elder Church of Christ, Prescott, 1985. Served to staff sgt. U.S. Army Air Force 1943-45. No. Ariz. U. fellow, 1965-66. Mem. Ariz. Sch. Admins. (prof. growth com. 1985-86, speaker workshops, Ariz Disting. Elem. Prin. 1985), Nat. Elem. Sch. Adminstrs. (Nat. Disting. Elem. Prin. 1985). Republican. Church of Christ. Clubs: Smoki, Am. Bowling Congress (Prescott). Avocations: bowling, hiking, photography, woodworking, oil painting. Address: 519 Highland Ave Prescott AZ 86301

LOVINS, AMORY BLOCH, energy consultant; b. Washington, Nov. 13, 1947; s. Gerald Hershel and Miriam (Bloch) L.; m. L. Hunter Sheldon, Sept. 6, 1979. Student, Harvard U., 1964-65, 66-67, Magdalen Coll., Oxford, Eng., 1967-69; MA, Merton Coll., Oxford, 1969-71; DSc (hon.), Bates Coll., 1979, Williams Coll., 1981, Kalamazoo Coll., 1983, U. Maine, 1985; LLD (hon.), Ball State U., 1983. Jr. research fellow Merton Coll., 1969-71; Brit. rep., policy advisor Friends of the Earth, San Francisco, 1971-84; regent's lectr. U. Calif., Berkeley and Riverside, 1978, 81; v.p., dir. research Rocky Mountain Inst., Old Snowmass, Colo., 1982—; cons. physicist, 1963-68; govt. energy cons., 1971—. Author: (also layout artist and co-photographer) Eryri, The Mountains of Longing, 1971, The Stockholm Conference: Only One Earth, 1972, Openpit Mining, 1973, World Energy Strategies: Facts, Issues, and Options, 1975, Soft Energy Paths: Toward a Durable Peace, 1977; co-author: (with J. Price) Non-Nuclear Futures: The Case for an Ethical Energy Strategy, 1975, (with L.H. Lovins) Energy/War: Breaking the Nuclear Link, 1980, Brittle Power: Energy Strategy for National Security, 1982, (with L.H. Lovins, F. Krause, and W. Bach) Least-Cost Energy: Solving the CO2 Problem, 1982, (with P. O'Heffernan, sr. author, and L.H. Lovins) The First Nuclear World War, 1983, (with L.H. Lovins, sr. author, and S. Zuckerman) Energy Unbound: A Fable for America's Future; co-photographer (book) At Home in the Wild: New England's White Mountains, 1978; author numerous poems; contbr. articles to profl. jours., reports to tech. jours.; patentee in field. Recipient Right Livelihood award Right Livelihood Found., 1983, Sprout award Internat. Studies Assn., 1977, Pub. Edn. award Nat. Energy Resources Orgn., 1978, Pub. Service award Nat. Assn. Environ. Edn., 1980, Mitchell prize Mitchell Energy Found., 1982. Fellow AAAS, Lindisfarne Assn.; mem. Fedn. Am. Scientists. Avocations: mountaineering, photography, music. Home and Office: 1739 Snowmass Creek Rd Box 505 Old Snowmass CO 81654

LOVRET, JUANITA ROBINSON, magazine editor; b. Santa Ana, Calif., July 2, 1926; d. Robert Henry and Frances M. (Jones) Robinson; m. Edwin Clinton Lovret, June 27, 1953; children: Linda, Robert, Laurie. BA in Journalism, U. So. Calif., 1948. Cert. lifetime sec. tchr., Calif. Reporter Valley Times, North Hollywood, Calif., 1948-51; Eng. tchr. Garden Grove (Calif.) High Sch., 1952-54, Tustin (Calif.) High Sch., 1954-60; instr. creative writing Saddleback Coll., Leisure World, Calif., 1967-82; assoc. editor The Mcht. mag., Newport Beach, Calif., 1979—; editor Bldg. Products Digest, Newport Beach, 1982—. Contbr. articles to mags. Chmn. various coms. Assistance League of Santa Ana, 1976—. Mem. Western Pubs. Assn., Women in Communications, Alpha Omicron Pi. Republican. Roman Catholic. Avocations: tennis, gardening, reading, travel. Home: 13232 Bow Pl Santa Ana CA 92705 Office: Bldg Products Digest 4500 Campus Dr Suite 480 Newport Beach CA 92660

LOVRIN, DARIJA, administrator; b. Zadar, Yugoslavia, June 22, 1954; came to U.S., 1967; d. Dunat and Marija (Lukin) L. AA, Tacoma Community Coll., 1974; BA, U. Puget Sound, 1976; MS, Wash. State U., 1978. Asst. safety officer City of Tacoma, 1978-79; tech. adminstr. EBI Cos., Seattle, 1980-81; workers' compensation program adminstr. Tacoma Pub. Schs., 1981—. Mem. Am. Soc. Safety Engrs., Wash. Self-Insurers Assoc. (program com. mem. 1983—). Democrat. Roman Catholic. Avocations: stained glass, ceramics, photography, swimming. Office: Tacoma Pub Schs PO Box 1357 Tacoma WA 98401

LOVSKY, MARINA DAVID, physicist, material scientist; b. Moscow, Aug. 12, 1940; came to U.S., 1981; s. David Samuel and Ekaterina (Ivanov) L.; divorced; 1 child, Lev. MS, Moscow State U., 1964. Sr. engr. Spl. Design Bur., Moscow, 1964-77; group leader Inst. Info., Moscow, 1977-80; mfg. engr. Datagraphix, San Diego, 1981—. Contbr. articles to profl. jours. Mem. Soc. Info. Displays. Republican. Jewish.

LOVVIK, DARYL VAUGHN, consulting geologist; b. Eau Claire, Wis., July 26, 1941; s. Oscar W. and Pearl B. (Johnson) L.; m. Perla Ivonne Vargas; children: Alexander Wilhelm, Rodolfo, Sheila Najivi. B.S. in Geology, W. Tex. State U., 1975. Cert. profl. geologist; registered profl. geologist, Alaska, Ariz. Cons. geologist, Golden, Colo., 1975-77; exploration geologist Cotter Corp., Moab, Utah, 1977-79; pres. Southwestern Geol. Survey, Mesa, Ariz., 1979-86; water resource dir. Tohono O'Odham Nation, Sells, Ariz., 1986—. Author articles. Served with USAF, 1960-64; Far East. Mem. Am. Inst. Profl. Geologists, Geol. Soc. Am., Am. Assn. Petroleum Geologists, Soc. Mining Engrs. Republican. Episcopalian. Home: 410 E Beatryce St Tempe AZ 85281

LOW, KATHLEEN, reference librarian; b. Suisun, Calif., Aug. 22, 1956. BA, U. Calif., Davis, 1977; MLS, San Jose State U., 1978. Cataloger U. Calif., Davis, 1980-83; coordinator of online services Calif. Library Authority for Systems and Services, San Jose, Calif., 1983-84; online reference librarian Calif. State Library, Sacramento, 1984—. Book reviewer Lector mag., 1983; contbr. articles to profl. jours. Mem. ALA, Spl. Libraries Assn. (Sierra-Nev. chpt. newtorking chairperson, 1985—), No. Calif. Assn. Law Libraries, No. Calif. Tech. Processes Group (mem. nominating com. 1985—). Office: Calif State Library 914 Capitol Mall Sacramento CA 95814

LOWE, DORIS JEAN, social worker; b. Pompano, Fla., July 9, 1943; d. Richard Carl and Dorothy May (Malson) Ladeburg; m. Alfred Lewis Lowe, Aug. 29, 1964; children: Lorrie, Wayne. AA, Casper Coll., 1963; BSW, U. Wyo., 1979, MS in Counselor Edn., 1986. Sch. social worker Natrona Schs., Casper, Wyo., 1979—; mem. State Task Force on roles of counselors and social workers in schs., 1984, Forms Com. for Spl. Edn. in Natrona County Schs., 1983-86, Dist. Parent Ctr. Adv. Council, 1983—; liaison Natrona County Sch. Social Workers to Adminstrv. Com., 1983-85. Bd. dirs. Windy Cities Corp. for rehab. of the Developmentally Disabled, Natrona County, 1983—; bd. dirs. Overcomers Corp., 1974—; chairperson Natrona County Child Protection Team, 1986—, coordinator of first state wide meeting, 1985; mem. God's Fenced Flock prison ministry, 1985-86. Mem. Nat. Assn. Social Workers (1st v.p. and pres. Wyo. chpt.), NEA, AAUW (pres. 1984-85, 1st v.p. 1982-83), Natrona County Edn. Assn. (mem. negotiations com. 1985—, mem. grievance com. 1985—), Kappa Kappa Iota (pres. elect 1985-86, pres. 1986—). Democrat. Mem. Assemblies of God Ch. Avocation: singing. Home: 2919 Belmont Casper WY 82604 Office: Natrona County Sch Dist #1 970 Glenn Rd Casper WY 82601

LOWE, OARIONA, dentist; b. San Francisco, June 17, 1948; d. Van Lowe and Jenny (Go) Lowe-Silva; m. Evangelos Rossopoulos, Dec. 18, 1985. BS, U. Nev., Las Vegas, 1971; MA, George Washington U., 1977; DDS, Howard U., 1981; pediatric dental cert., UCLA, 1984. Instr. Coll. Allied Health Scis. Howard U., Washington, 1974-76, asst. prof., 1976-77; research asst. Howard U. Dental Sch., Washington, 1977-81; resident gen. practice Eastman Dental Ctr., Rochester, N.Y., 1981-82; dir. dental services City of Hope Med. Ctr., Duarte, Calif., 1984-86; vis. lectr. pediatric dentistry UCLA; mem. oral cancer task force Am. Cancer Soc., Pasadena, Calif., 1985—. Contbr. articles to profl. jours. Mem. ADA, Nat. Soc. Autistic Children, Calif. Dental Assn., Am. Acad. Pedodontics, Am. Soc. Dentistry Children, Sigma Xi, Alpha Omega. Republican. Presybterian. Avocations: cooking, bicycling, walking, aerobic dancing. Office: 11822 E Floral Dr Suite D Whittier CA 90601

LOWE, RICHARD GERALD, JR., computer programmer manager; b. Travis AFB, Calif., Nov. 8, 1960; s. Richard Gerald and Valerie Jean (Hoeffer) L. Student, San Bernardino Valley Coll., 1978-80. Tech. specialist Software Techniques Inc., Los Alamitos, Calif., 1980-82, sr. tech. specialist, 1982-84, mgr. tech. services, 1984-85; mgr. cons. services Software Techniques Inc., Cypress, Calif., 1985-86; sr. programmer BIF Accutel, Camarillo, Calif., 1986—, Beck Computer Systems, Long Beach, Calif., 1986—. Contbr. articles to profl. jours. Mem. Assn. Computing Machinery, Digital Equipment Corp. Users Group. Avocations: reading and writing sci. fiction, collecting movies. Office: BIF Accutel 1011 Avenida Acaso Camarillo CA 93010

LOWE, RICHARD NORMAN, food product executive; b. Portland, Oreg., Jan. 26, 1946; s. Forrest Adrian and Nona Irene (Masten) L.; m. Joanne Dee Alexander, Jan. 1, 1986; children from previous marriage: Jeffrey, Christopher, Stacie, Amy, Casey. BS in Microbiology, Wash. State U., Pullman, 1969. Mgr. quality control Western Farmers Assn., Seattle, 1969-71; sr. mgr. Gen. Foods Corp., Dover, Del., 1971-79; v.p. Pepsico Internat., Ft. Lauderdale, Fla., 1979-85; gen. mgr., chief exec. officer Copper River Fishermen's Cooperative, Seattle, 1986—; bd. dirs. Prince william Sound Aquaculture Corp. Contbr. articles to tech. jours. Fundraiser Del. Rep., Dover, 1977-79. Mem. Oreg. Coastal Zone Mgmt., Cordova C. of C. (bd. dirs.). Republican. Presbyterian. Avocations: computers, golf, skiing. Office: Copper River Fishermen's Cooperative 116 1/2 S Washington Seattle WA 98104

LOWE, WARREN, chemist; b. San Francisco, June 4, 1922; s. Lung and Jean Shee (Yee) L.; B.S., U. Calif. at Berkeley, 1945; m. Caroline Louie, Nov. 30, 1958. Research asst. Manhattan Project Radiation Lab., U. Calif. at Berkeley, 1943-45; sr. research assoc. chemist Chevron Research Co., Richmond, Calif., 1945—, project leader exploratory research work, 1964-69 . Mem. adv. com. Mt. Hermon Assn., Inc. 1972-80 ; youth counselor various orgns. Fellow Am. Inst. Chemists; mem. Am. Chem. Soc., AAAS, Tung Sen Benevolent Assn., U. Calif. Alumni Club, El Sobrante Boys' Club. Chinese-Am. Chem. Soc., Sigma Xi, Pi Alpha Phi. Presbyn. (pres. bd. trustees 1960-72, mem. nat. bd. missions 1970-79 , sec. ch. session 1952—, elder 1955—, chmn. missions dept. 1975-81 , pres. bd. missions Pacific Presbytery of Calif. 1976-84). Contbr. articles to profl. jours; holder over 170 patents in field. Home: 5619 Jordan Ave El Cerrito CA 94530

LOWEN, KENNETH MARTIN, electronics company executive; b. Chico, Calif., Nov. 12, 1945; s. Arthur and Jeanne (Carlisle) L.; m. Joy Carol Thorson, Nov. 10, 1979; children: Tiffany Joy, Krystle Cherie. BA in Communications, Brigham Young U., 1969. Dir. Sta. KREX-TV, Grand Junction, Colo., 1969-70; mgr. field ops. Mardix Corp., Mt. View, Calif., 1978-83; owner CPI Communications, San Jose, Calif., 1983—. Served with USAF, 1970-75, maj. Calif. Air N.G., 1977—. Recipient Sikorsky Helicipter Rescue award Sikorsky Aircraft, 1982. Mem. N.G. Assn., Sigma Delta Chi, Kappa Tau Alpha. Republican. Mormon. Avocations: computers, videos. Office: CPI Communications 404 Railroad Ave Milpitas CA 95035

LOWENSOHN, RICHARD IRWIN, medical educator, physician; b. Los Angeles, Jan. 1, 1944; s. Robert Henry and Judy Pearl (Kaplan) L.; m. Diane Loretta Martin, June 24, 1975; children: Erin, David, Joshua. BSEE, Stanford U., 1965; MD, U. So. Calif., 1970. Diplomate Am. Bd. Ob-Gyn; cert. maternal fetal medicine. Intern U. So. Calif.-Los Angeles County Med. Ctr., Los Angeles, 1970-71; resident in ob-gyn Women's Hosp. div. U. So. Calif.-Los Angeles County Med. Ctr., Los Angeles, 1971-75; asst. prof. ob-gyn U. So. Calif., Los Angeles, 1977-78, Pritzker Sch. Medicine, Chgo., 1978-83; perinatologist Alta Bates Hosp., Berkeley, Calif., 1983-86; assoc. prof. ob-gyn Oreg. Health Scis. U., Portland, 1986—; pres. RI Lowensohn MD Inc., Oakland, Calif., 1984-86. Fellow Am. Coll. Ob-Gyn; mem. IEEE, Soc. Perinatal Obstetricians, Oreg. Med. Assn., Western Perinatal Collaborative Group (sec., treas.), Tau Beta Pi. Democrat. Jewish. Avocations: computers, woodworking. Office: Oreg Health Scis U Dept Ob-Gyn 3181 SW Sam Jackson Pkwy Rd Portland OR 97201

LOWENTHAL, ARLINE MAE, marketing research executive; b. Buffalo, Aug. 8, 1931; d. Harry and Lena (Michaels) Jaffey; m. Richard Irwin Lowenthal, July 6, 1952 (div. 1975); children: Lauren Ileen, Robin Beth, Andrew Jaffey. BS in Psychology, U. Buffalo, 1953. Women's program dir. Sta. WXRA-Radio, Buffalo, 1953-57; v.p., co-founder Survey Service of Western N.Y., Buffalo, 1958-74; pres., chief exec. officer Analysis Research Ltd., San Diego, 1975—; co-founder, co-dir. Mercadotecnia Y Publicidad AP, Mex.; elected San Diego del. and vice chmn. to 1980 White House Conf. on Small Bus., elected del. San Diego White House Conf. com., 1986—; co-chmn. Govt. Procurement sect. for Calif. Conf. on Small Bus., 1986—. Contbr. articles to profl. jours. and chpts. to books on mktg. Trustee Ysidro U. Mem. Market Research Assn. (editor nat. profl. jour. Viewpoint, conf. chairperson, Ednl. Think Tank com., Pres.' award), Am. Mktg. Assn., Am. Assn. Pub. Opinion Researchers, Qualitative Research Cons. Assn., Soc. of the Quill. Avocations: travel, flower arranging, crafts. Office: Analysis/Research Ltd 4655 Ruffner St Suite 180 San Diego CA 92111

LOWERY, WILLIAM DAVID, congressman; b. San Diego, May 2, 1947; s. Thomas Henry and Eve (Howard) L.; m. Kathleen Ellen Brown, Sept. 7, 1968; children: Ashley Colleen, Alison Elizabeth, Thomas Harrington. Student, San Diego State Coll., 1965-69, Calif. Western Sch. Law, 1970. Self-employed 1973-77; with Calif. Group, 1977-79; councilman City of San Diego, 1977-80; dep. mayor 1980; mem. 97th-100th Congresses from 41st dist. Calif., 1981—; mem. Congl. adv. bd. Future Bus. Leaders Am., Grace Caucus. Art Caucus, Congl. Coalition for Soviet Jewry, Caucus for Ethiopian Jews, Environ. and Energy Study Conf., Travel and Tourism Caucus, Congl. Hispanic Caucus (hon.). Bd. dirs. Calif. Water Found., 1978-79; council liaison Unified Port Commn.; mem. Commn. Californias; founder, chmn. Calif. Concord Group; mem. San Diego Sch. Fin. Task Force; chmn. Calif. League Cities; dir. Aseltine sch. San Diego council Boy Scouts Am.; chmn. San Diego March of Dimes, 1981; active Republican orgns. Recipient YMCA Red Triangle award; Amigo de Distinction Mex. and Am. Found. Mem. Urban League San Diego, Navy League. Roman Catholic. Office: 225 Cannon House Office Bldg Washington DC 20515

LOWI, ALVIN, JR., mechanical engineer, consultant; b. Gadsden, Ala., July 21, 1929; s. Alvin R. and Janice (Haas) L.; m. Guillermina Gerardo Alverez, May 9, 1953; children: David Arthur, Rosamina, Edna Vivian, Alvin III. BME, Ga. Inst. Tech., 1951, MSME, 1955; postgrad., UCLA, 1956-61. Registered prof. engr., Calif. Design engr. Garrett Corp., Los Angeles, 1956-58; mem. tech. staff TRW, El Segundo, Calif., 1958-60, Aerospace Corp., El Segundo, 1960-66; prin. Alvin Lowi and Assocs., San Pedro, 1966—; pres. Terraqua Inc., San Pedro, Calif., 1968-76; v.p. Daeco Fuels and Engring. Co., Wilmington, Calif., 1978—; also bd. dirs. Daeco Fuels and Engring. Co.; vis. research prof. U. Pa., Phila, 1972-74; sr. lectr. Free Enterprise Inst., Monterey Park, Calif., 1961-71; bd. dirs. So. Calif. Tissue Bank; research assoc. Heather Found., San Pedro, 1966—. Contbr. articles to profl. jours.; patentee in field. Served to lt. USN, 1951-54, Korea. Fellow Inst. Humane Studies; mem. ASME, NSPE, Soc. Automotive Engrs., Soc. Am. Inventors, So. Bay Chamber Music Soc., Scabbard and Blade, Pi Tau Sigma. Jewish. Avocations: chamber music, jazz, photography, classic automobiles, motor sports, philosophy of science. Home and Office: 2146 Toscanini Dr San Pedro CA 90732

LOWRIE, RAYMOND LEE, government official; b. Alcoa, Tenn., Feb. 19, 1933. BS in Mining Engring., U. Tex., El Paso, 1960; MS in Mineral Econs., Colo. Sch. Mines, 1971. Registered profl. engr., Tex. Miner Climax (Colo.) Molybdenum Co., 1959; mining engr. Lone Star Steel Co., McAlester, Okla., 1960-62, U.S. Bur. Mines, Denver, 1962-64, Washington, 1964-67; supervisory mining engr. Bituminous Coal div. Denver, 1967-73; chief Intermountain Field Ops. Ctr. 1975-78; chief Reclamation div. Ohio Dept. Natural Resources, Columbus, 1973-74; regional dir. U.S. Office of Surface Mining Reclamation and Enforcement, Kansas City, Mo., 1978-82; adminstr. Eastern Tech. Ctr. Pitts., 1982-85; asst. dir. Western field ops. Denver, 1985—. Contbr. articles to profl. jours. Recipient Hubert E. Risser award, 1971. Mem. AIME. Office: US Office Surface Mining Reclamation and Enforcement Brooks Towers 1020 15th St Denver CO 80202

LOWRY, CANDACE E., human resource administrator, consultant; b. Miles City, Mont., Sept. 27, 1950; d. James A. and Nathlee (Azar) Zadick; m. Michael Roy Lowry, June 7, 1980; 1 child, Natalie. BSW with high honors, U. Mont., 1971; MSW with high honors, U. Iowa, 1975; DSW, U. Utah, 1984. Clin. social worker, Utah; cert. marriage and family therapist and supr. Inpatient social worker II U. Iowa Psychiat. Hosps., Iowa City, 1975-76, inpatient social worker III, 1976-79, coordinator, Iowa Autism Program, 1979-80; coordinator, social work specialist U. Utah Counseling Ctr., Salt Lake City, 1980-86, assoc. dir., 1986; program dir. adult unit Wasatch Canyons Hosp., Salt Lake City, 1986—; clin. instr. U. Utah, Salt Lake City, 1981—; ptnr., cons. Consultwest, Salt Lake City, 1983—. Co-author: Meeting the Needs of Autistic Children, 1980; contbr. articles to profl. jours. Mem. Nat. Assn. Social Workers, Acad. Cert. Social Workers (cert.), Nat. Register Clin. Social Workers, Am. Group Psychotherapy Assn., Salt Lake City C. of C. Avocations: running, piano, hiking. Home: 1742 S Stephenson Way Salt Lake City UT 84108 Office: Wasatch Canyons Hosp 5770 S 1500 W Salt Lake City UT 84123

LOWRY, LARRY LORN, management consulting company executive; b. Lima, Ohio, Apr. 12, 1947; s. Frank William and Viola Marie L.; m. Jean Carroll Greenbaum, June 23, 1973; 1 child, Alexandra Kristin. B.S. in E.E., MIT, 1969, M.S. in E.E., 1970; M.B.A., Harvard U., 1972. Mgr. Boston Consulting Group, Menlo Park, Calif., 1972-80; sr. v.p. Booz, Allen & Hamilton Inc, San Francisco, 1980—. Western Electric fellow, 1969, NASA fellow, 1970. Mem. Sigma Xi, Tau Beta Pi, Eta Kappa Nu. Presbyterian. Home: 137 Stockbridge Ave Atherton CA 94025

LOWRY, MIKE, congressman; b. St. John, Wash., Mar. 8, 1939; s. Robert M. and Helen (White) L.; m. Mary Carlson, Apr. 6, 1968; 1 dau., Diane. B.A., Wash. State U., Pullman, 1962. Chief fiscal analyst, staff dir. ways and means com. Wash. State Senate, 1969-73; govtl. affairs dir. Group Health Coop. Puget Sound, 1974-75; mem. council King County Govt., 1975-78, chmn., 1977; mem. 96th-100th congresses from 7th dist. Wash. Chmn. King County Housing and Community Devel. Block Grant Program, 1977; pres. Wash. Assn. Counties, 1978. Democrat. Address: 2454 Rayburn House Office Bldg Washington DC 20515 *

LOWTHER, FRANK EUGENE, research physicist; b. Orrville, Ohio, Feb. 3, 1929; s. John Finger and Mary Elizabeth (Mackey) L.; m. Elizabeth E. Koons, Apr. 21, 1951; children—Cynthia E., Victoria J., James A., Frank Eugene. Grad. Ohio State U., Columbus, 1952. Scientist missile systems div. Raytheon Corp., Boston, 1952-57, Gen. Electric Co., Syracuse, N.Y., and Daytona Beach, Fla., 1957-62; mgr. ozone research and devel. W.R. Grace Co., Curtis Bay, Md., 1972-75; sr. engring. assoc. Linde div. Union Carbide Corp., Tonawanda, N.Y., 1975-79; chief scientist, Purification Sci. Inc., 1979-81; chief scientist, Atlantic Richfield-Energy Conversion and Materials Lab, 1981-83; prin. scientist Atlantic Richfield-Corp. Tech., 1983-85, sci. adv., 1985—. Recipient Inventor of Yr. award Patent Law Assn. and Tech. Socs. Council, 1976. Assoc. fellow AIAA; mem. IEEE (sr.). Club: Masons. Patentee in field of ozone tech., plasma generators, solid state power devices, internal combustion engines, electro-desorption, thermoelectrics, virus and bacteria disinfection systems.

LOWTHORP, MARCUS MERROW, federal agency administrator; b. Devine, Tex., Feb. 20, 1932; s. James Wilson and Viola Etha (Hardcastle) L.; m. Patsy Jean Ray, Mar. 21, 1953; children: Marcus Ray, Michael James, Matthew Kyle. Student, San Antonio Coll., 1958; BS, Bible Bapt. Sem., 1962; postgrad., Arlington State Coll., 1962-63; LLD(hon.), Bethany Nazarene Coll., 1971. Account, auditing clk. Kelly AFB, San Antonio, 1954-56; bookkeeper Pak-Mor Mfg., San Antonio, 1956-57; rt. sales mgr. Coca-Cola Bottling Co., San Antonio, 1957-58; clk. Ft. Worth Army Depot, 1961-62, mgmt. technician, 1962-64; storage specialist Gen. Service Adminstrn., Ft. Worth, 1964-66; program ops. specialist HUD, Ft. Worth, 1966-67; grants mgmt. specialist HEW, Dallas, 1967-70; grants mgmt. specialist HEW, Seattle, 1970-74, edn. specialist, 1974-76; student aid br. chief U.S. Dept. Edn., Seattle, 1976-80, dep. regional adminstr., 1980-81, regional adminstr., 1981-87; western regional dir. U.S. Dept. Edn., San Francisco, 1987—; co-owner Yorkshire Antiques, Kirkland, Wash., 1984—; pres. Lowthorp Enterprises, Kirkland, 1976—. Assoc. pastor Milby Rd. Bapt. Ch., Arlington, 1959-61; pastor Berean Bapt. Ch., Arlington, 1961-62; loaned exec. Combined Fed. Campaign, Ft. Worth, 1965-67; rep. San Antonio River Theatre, 1957. Mem. Wash. Fin. Aid Assn., Oreg. Assn. Student Fin. Aid Adminstrs., Idaho Assn. Student Fin. Aid Adminstrs., Alaska Assn. Student Fin. Aid Adminstrs. Republican. Club: Puget Sound Pug (Seattle) (founder, v.p. 1972—). Lodge: Masons. Home: 308 Grayson Terr Pleasant Hill CA 94523 Office: US Dept Edn Office Student Fin Assistance 50 UN Plaza San Francisco CA 94102

LOYD, JOHN LEE, computer generalist; b. Carnegie, Okla., May 1, 1945; s. John and Ruby (Law) L.; divorced; children: Aldous, Jessica. B U. Studies, U. N.Mex., 1980. Programmer Bernalillo County, Albuquerque, 1973-75, sr. systems analyst, 1975-79, info. systems mgr., 1979-83; v.p. NIMCOS, Boulder, Colo., 1983-85, bd. dirs., 1983—; mgr. new product devel. BI, Inc., Boulder, 1985—. Patentee electronic home incarceration device. Served with U.S. Army, 1967-70. Avocations: handball, skiing, softball.

LOZANO, IGNACIO EUGENIO, JR., newspaper editor; b. San Antonio, Jan. 15, 1927; s. Ignacio E. and Alicia (E. de) L.; m. Martha Navarro, Feb. 24, 1951; children: Leticia Eugenia, José Ignacio, Monica Cecilia, Francisco Antonio. A.B. in Journalism, U. Notre Dame, 1947. Asst. pub. La Opinion, Los Angeles, 1947-53, pub., editor-in-chief, 1953-76, 77-86, editor-in-chief, 1986—; Am. ambassador to El Salvador 1976-77; bd. dirs. BankAmerica Corp., Bank of Am. NT & SA, Pacific Lighting Corp., The Walt Disney Co. Bd. dirs. Community TV of So. Calif., Los Angeles Council for Internat. Visitors, Los Angeles Philharm. Assn., Los Angeles World Affairs Council, Santa Anita Found., Youth Opportunity Found.; trustee Monterey Inst. Internat. Studies, Mus. Contemporary Art, U. Notre Dame; bd. govs. Calif. Community Found. Mem. Calif. Press Assn., Cath. Press Council of So. Calif., Greater Los Angeles Press Club, Inter-Am. Press Assn. (1st v.p.), Calif. Newspaper Publishers Assn. (dir.). Office: La Opinion 1436 S Main St Los Angeles CA 90015

LUBATTI, HENRY JOSEPH, physicist, educator; b. Oakland, Calif., Mar. 16, 1937; s. John and Pauline (Massimino) L.; m. Catherine Jeanne Berthe Ledoux, June 29, 1968; children: Karen E., Henry J., Stephen J.C. A.A., U. Calif.-Berkeley, 1957, A.B., 1960, Ph.D., 1966; M.S., U. Ill., 1963. Research assoc. Faculty Scis. U. Paris, Orsay, France, 1966-68; asst. prof. physics MIT, 1968-69; assoc. prof., sci. dir. visual techniques lab. U. Wash., 1969-74, prof., sci. dir. visual Techniques lab., 1974—; vis. lectr. Internat. Sch. Physics, Erice, Sicily, 1968, Herceg-Novi, Yugoslavia Internat. Sch., 1969, XII Cracow Sch. Theorectical Physics, Zapokane, Poland, 1972; vis. scientist CERN, Geneva, 1980-81; vis. staff Los Alamos Nat. Lab., 1983-86; mem. physics editorial adv. com. World Sci. Pub. Co. Ltd., 1982—. Contbr. numerous articles on high energy physics to profl. jours. Alfred P. Sloan research fellow, 1971-75. Fellow Am. Phys. Soc.; mem. Sigma Xi; mem Tau Beta Pi. Office: U Wash Visual Techniques Lab Physics FM 15 Seattle WA 98195

LUBECK, MARVIN JAY, physician; b. Cleve., Mar. 20, 1929; s. Charles D. and Lillian (Jay) L.; A.B., U. Mich., 1951, M.D., 1955, M.S., 1959; m. Arlene Sue Bitman, Dec. 28, 1955; children—David Mark, Daniel Jay, Robert Charles. Intern, U. Mich. Med. Center, 1955-56, resident ophthalmology, 1956-58, jr. clin. instr. ophthalmology, 1958-59; practice medicine, specializing in ophthalmology, Denver, 1961—; mem. staff Rose, Children's, Mercy, St. Luke's hosps.; asso. clin. prof. U. Colo. Med. Center; cons. ophthalmologist State of Colo. Served with U.S. Army, 1959-61. Diplomate Am. Bd. Opthalmology. Fellow ACS; mem. Am. Acad. Ophthalmology, Denver Med. Soc., Colo. Ophthalmol. Soc., Am. Intraocular Lens Implant Soc. Home: 590 S Harrison Ln Denver CO 80209 Office: 3865 Cherry Creek N Dr Denver CO 80209

LUBECK, STANLEY, podiatrist; b. Phila., Dec. 7, 1935; s. Abraham and Mollie L.; m. Rosalind Lubeck, Nov. 24, 1968; two children. Student, L.A. Coll., 1953-54; DPM, Temple U., 1958. Diplomate Am. Bd. Podiatric Orthopedics. Practice medicine specializing in podiatry Havertown, Pa., 1958-67, Phila., 1967-80; pvt. practice podiatric medicine Tempe, Ariz., 1981—; instr. Pa. Coll. Podiatric Medicine, Phila., 1965-71, asst. prof., 1975-78; cons. Grad. Hosp., Phila., 1961-63, Green's Nursing Home, Phila., 1968-70, Aldine Nursing Home, Phila., 1971-77, Our Lady Help of Christians Nursing Home, Phila., 1971-78, Adelphia Nursing Home, Phila. 1973-77, Mercy-Douglass Human Services Ctr., Phila., 1980, South Mountain Manor Nursing Ctr., Phoenix, 1985—, Desert Sunquest Rehab. and Care Ctr., Mesa, Ariz., 1986—; courtesy staff James C. Giuffre Med. Ctr., Phila., 1978-81; affiliate staff Camelback Hosp., Scottsdale, Ariz., 1982-84, cons. staff, 1984—, Village Green Nursing Home, Phoenix, 1986—, Casa Delmar of Scottsdale Nursing & Rehab. Ctr., 1986—; mem. clin. med. assisting adv. com. Phoenix Coll., 1985. Fellow AM. Soc. Podiatric Dermatology, Am. Soc. Podiatric Medicine, Am. Coll. Foot Orthopedists, Acad. Ambulatory Foot Surgery; mem. Am. Assn. Hosp. Podiatrists, Am. Pub. Health Assn., Ariz. Podiatric Med. Assn., Am. Podiatric Med. Assn., Pi Delta. Avocation: photography. Office: 2435 E Southern Ave Tempe AZ 85282

LUBIN, MARY LUELLA, nursing home administrator; b. Glastonbury, Conn., Apr. 24, 1932; d. Robert Harley and Luella (Sampson) Kellogg; m. Michael D. Lubin, Sept. 10, 1955; children: Elizabeth Lubin Hughes, James Kellogg. BS, Simmons Coll., 1954; MA, Calif. State U., 1970. Cert. gerontol. nurse. Pub. health nurse New Haven VNA and Sacramento Health Depts., 1954-56; lectr. pub. health. nursing Boston Coll., Chestnut Hill, Mass., 1965-67; rehab. nurse specialist Internat. Rehab. Assn., Atlanta, 1975-76; dir. staff devel. Nat. Health Enterprises, San Leandro, Calif., 1980-81; dir. nursing services Hillhaven Corp., Alameda, Calif., 1981-85, adminstr., 1985—; co-owner YRAM Applications Software, 1982—. Bd. dirs. L.I.T.A. Vol. Assn., Alameda; vol. leader United Way, Sacramento, 1976-80; nurse vol. USAF and ARC, Sacramento, 1958-64, Japan, 1970-72; organizing com. mem. Social Services for Elders, Oakland, Calif., 1986—. Mem. Am. Pub. Health Assn., Am. Nurses Assn., Am. Coll. Health Care Adminstrs. (cert.), Calif. Assn. Health Care Facilities, Alameda C. of C., DAR. Avocations: oriental art, antiques. Home: 1235 View Dr San Leandro CA 94577 Office: Hillhaven Alameda 516 Willow St Alameda CA 94501

LUCAS, DONALD LEO, private investor; b. Upland, Calif., Mar. 18, 1930; s. Leo J. and Mary G. (Schwamm) L.; B.A., Stanford U., 1951, M.B.A., 1953; m. Lygia de Soto Harrison, July 15, 1961; children—Nancy Maria, Alexandra Maria, Donald Alexander. Asso. corporate finance dept. Smith, Barney & Co., N.Y.C., 1956-59; gen., ltd. partner Draper, Gaither & Anderson, Palo Alto, Calif., 1959-66; pvt. investor, Menlo Park, Calif., 1966—; chmn. bd. Oracle Corp., Inc., Belmont, Calif.; dir. Data Card Corp., Mpls., HBO & Co., Atlanta, ICOT Corp., Mountain View, Liconix, Mountain View, Robinton Products, Inc., Sunnyvale, Calif., Kahler Corp., Tracor, Inc., Austin, Tex., SDA Systems, Santa Clara, Calif., Tri-Data Corp., Inc. Mem. bd. regents Bellarmine Coll. Prep., 1977—; regent emeritus U. Santa Clara, 1980—. Served to 1st lt., AUS, 1953-55. Mem. Am. Council for Capital Formation, Stanford U. Alumni Assn., Stanford Grad. Sch. Bus. Alumni Assn., Zeta Psi. Clubs: Commonwealth (San Francisco); Stanford Buck; Vintage (Indian Wells, Calif.); Menlo Country (Woodside, Calif.); Menlo Circus (Atherton, Calif.); Jackson Hole Golf. Home: 224 Park Ln Atherton CA 94025 Office: 3000 Sand Hill Rd #3 Menlo Park CA 94025

LUCAS, GEORGE W., JR., film director, producer, screeen writer; b. Modesto, Calif., 1944. Student, Modesto Jr. Coll; B.A., U. So. Calif., 1966. Asst. to Francis Ford Coppola on The Rain People; dir. documentary on making of Filmmaker; dir., co-writer: THX-1138, 1971, American Graffiti, 1973; dir., author screenplay: Star Wars, 1977; exec. producer: More American Graffiti, 1979, The Empire Strikes Back, 1980; Raiders of the Lost Ark, 1981; exec. producer, co-author screenplay: Return of the Jedi, 1983; exec. producer Indiana Jones and the Temple of Doom, 1984, Labyrinth, 1986; co-exec. producer Mishima, 1985. Recipient Grand Prize for film THX, Nat. Student Film Festival, 1967. Chmn. Lucasfilm, Ltd., San Rafael, Calif. Office: Lucasfilm Ltd PO Box 2009 San Rafael CA 94912*

LUCAS, JOHN EDWARD, public relations executive; b. Miami, Fla., Sept. 22, 1953; s. Joseph Stephen and Madeline (Lubert) L.; m. Christine Ann Listug, Aug. 14, 1982. AA, Santa Monica (Calif.) Coll., 1975; BA in Journalism, U. Calif., Berkeley, 1977. Accredited in pub. relations, Calif. Exec. asst. Bldg. Industry Assn., Novato, Calif., 1979-80; pub. relations staff David W. Evans, Inc., San Francisco, 1980-82, dir. pub. relations, 1983-84; mgr. mktg. and media relations Pacific Bell, San Francisco, 1984-85, dir. mktg. communications, 1986—. Mem. Am. Mktg. Assn., Pub. Relations Soc. Am. (Hon. mention for feature article No. Calif. chpts. 1983, Cert. of Honor No. Calif. chpts. 1986), Sales and Mktg. Exec. Assn. Democrat. Roman Catholic. Avcations: snow skiing, bicyling, film criticism, photography. Office: Pacific Bell 2600 Camino Ramon room 4S850 San Ramon CA 94583

LUCAS, MALCOLM MILLAR, chief state justice; b. Berkeley, Calif., Apr. 19, 1927; s. Robert and Georgina (Campbell) L.; m. Joan Fisher, June 23, 1956; children: Gregory, Lisa Georgina. B.A., U. So. Calif., 1950, LL.B., 1953. Bar: Calif. 1954. Partner firm Lucas, Deukmejian and Lucas, Long Beach, Calif., 1955-67; judge Superior Ct., Los Angeles, 1967-71, U.S. Dist. Ct., Central Dist., Calif., 1971-84; assoc. justice Calif. Supreme Ct., 1984-87, chief justice, 1987—. Office: Calif Supreme Ct 350 McAllister St San Francisco CA 94102 also: Calif Supreme Ct Sacramento CA 95814 *

LUCAS, ROBERT SCOTT, computer research engineer; b. Portland, Oreg., Aug. 28, 1961; s. Leonard Frank and Frances Jean (Martin) L. BSEE, U. Portland, 1982. Mem. research lab staff Oreg. Mus. Sci. and Industry, Portland, 1976-79, planetarium lectr., 1979-83; engring. computer specialist N.W. Natural Gas Co., Portland, 1983-84, computer research engr., 1984—; cons. in field, Portland, 1979—. Inventor in field. Mem. IEEE, NSPE. Roman Catholic. Avocations: astronomy, music, backpacking. Office: NW Natural Gas Co 220 NW Second Ave Portland OR 97209

LUCAS, SUZANNE, statistician; b. Baxter Springs, Kans., Jan. 16, 1939; d. Ralph Beaver and Marguerite (Sansocie) L.; B.A. in Math., Calif. State U., Fresno, 1967, M.A. in Ednl. Theory, 1969; M.S. in Stats., U. So. Calif., 1979; children—Patricia Sue Jennings, Neil Patric Jennings. Asst. to dir. NSF Inst., Calif. State U., Fresno, 1968; Tchr. secondary math. Fresno city schs., 1968-78; statistician corp. indsl. relations Hughes Aircraft Co., Los Angeles,

1979-80; personnel adminstr. Hughes Aircraft Co. Space and Communications Group, Los Angeles, 1981-82, mem. tech. staff in math., 1982-85, staff engr., 1986—; lectr. in biostats. U. So. Calif., 1979. Kiwanis scholar, 1958. Mem. Soc. Women Engrs., Am. Statis. Assn., Am. Psychol. Assn., Internat. Assn. Parametric Analysts, Inst. Cost Analysis, U. So. Calif. Alumni Assn. (life), Kappa Mu Epsilon. Home: 13430 Isis Ave Hawthorne CA 90250 Office: Hughes Aircraft Co PO Box 92919 Bldg S65 Mail Sta J324 Los Angeles CA 90009

LUCAVS, PAUL, mechanical designer; b. Jelgava, USSR, Dec. 27, 1932; came to U.S., 1979; s. Alfred Alexander and Valentina (Suts) L.; m. Joy Penelope, Jan. 12, 1957; children: Dawn, Louise, Jason, Paul. Student, George Brown Coll., Toronto, Ont., Can., Centennial Tech. Inst., Toronto, North Alta. Tech. Inst., Edmonton, Can. Cert. engrng. technician Ont., Can. Mech. designer Reid, Crowther and Ptnrs., Toronto, 1970-73; sr. mech. designer Stone and Webster Can., Toronto, 1973-76, Vinto Engrs. Ltd., Edmonton, 1976-79, Aetekton Engrs., San Diego, 1979—. Mem. ASHRAE, Heating Refrigeration and Air Conditioning Inst. Lutheran. Avocations: painting, photography, target shooting, fishing, inventing toys. Home: 9045 Westmore Rd San Diego CA 92126

LUCCHESI, RAYMOND JOHN, architect; b. Las Vegas, Aug. 26, 1954; s. Julio John and Angela Jean (Squatritto) L.; m. Catherine Ann Chaney, Nov. 16, 1985. BArch, Ariz. State U., 1979; postgrad., U. Nev., 1986—. Registered architect, Nevada. Architect Architronics, Las Vegas, 1979-81, JMA, Las Vegas, 1981-82, Lucchesi and Assocs., Las Vegas, 1982—; bd. dirs. U. Nev. Architecture Program, Las Vegas, 1982—. Mem. AIA, Las Vega Chpt. AIA (bd. dirs., pres. elect. 1984—, pres. 1987—). Republican. Avocations: skiing, photography. Office: Lucchesi and Assocs Inc 2770 S Maryland Pkwy #406 Las Vegas NV 89109

LUCENTE, ROSEMARY DOLORES, educational administrator; b. Renton, Wash., Jan. 11, 1935; d. Joseph Anthony and Erminia Antoinette (Argano) Lucente; B.A., Mt. St. Mary's Coll., 1956, M.S., 1963. Tchr. pub. schs., Los Angeles, 1956-65, supr. tchr., 1958-65, asst. prin., 1965-69, prin. elem. sch., 1969-85, 86—, dir. instrn., 1985-86; nat. cons., lectr. Dr. William Glasser's Educator Tng. Ctr., 1968—; nat. workshop leader Nat. Acad. for Sch. Execs.-Am. Assn. Sch. Adminstrs., 1980; Los Angeles Unified Sch. Dist. rep. for nat. pilot of Getty Inst. for Visual Arts, 1983-85, site coordinator, 1983-86. Recipient Golden Apple award Stanford Ave. Sch. PTA, Faculty and Community Adv. Council, 1976, resolution for outstanding service South Gate City Council, 1976. Mem. Nat. Assn. Elem. Sch. Prins., Los Angeles Elem. Prins. Orgn. (v.p. 1979-80), Assn. Calif. Sch. Adminstrs. (charter mem.), Assn. Elem. Sch. Adminstrs. (vice-chmn. chpt. 1972-75, city-wide exec. bd., steering com. 1972-75, 79-80), Asso. Adminstrs. Los Angeles (charter), Pi Theta Mu, Kappa Delta Pi (v.p. 1982-84), Delta Kappa Gamma. Democrat. Roman Catholic. Home: 6501 Lindenhurst Ave Los Angeles CA 90048 Office: Roscomare Rd Sch 2425 Roscomare Rd Los Angeles CA 90077

LUCERO, JUAN G., JR., engineer; b. San Clemente, Philippines, Oct. 6, 1947; came to U.S., 1970; s. Juan P. and Flordeliza (Galicia) L.; m. Edita Nafrada Toledo, Dec. 24, 1969; children: Jane, Jessica, JoAnne. BS in Mech. Engring., Feati U., Manila, 1969. Registered profl. engr., Utah. Mech. engr. Pullman-Torkelson, Salt Lake City, 1970-74; project engr. Devenco-Utah, Inc., Salt Lake City, 1974-78; sr. project engr. Kennecott, Salt Lake City, 1978-83; chief engr. Garb Oil Corp., Salt Lake City, 1983-85; engring. mgr. Newbery Engring. Corp., Salt Lake City, 1985—. Mem. Philippine Am. Assn. of Utah (pres. 1984—), Asian Assn. Utah (bd. dirs. 1984—), Asian Adv. Council (bd. dirs.). Democrat. Roman Catholic. Avocations: golf, fishing, bowling. Office: Newbery Engring Corp 1205 Wilmington Ave Salt Lake City UT 84106

LUCERO, LUIS, transportation company executive; b. Pecos, N.Mex., Aug. 1, 1938; s. Procopio and Eusevia (Martinez) L.; m. Barbara Rose Tippy; children: Marcos Luis, Angela Maria. BSME, N.Mex. State U., 1960. With Gen. Dynamics Corp., Groton, Conn., San Diego, 1960-70; chief weight control, mgr. design integration Litton Ship Systems, Culver City, Calif., 1970-72; engr. supr. Hughes Helicopters, Culver City, 1972-77, chief weights, 1977-82, mgr. weights, 1982-85; mgr. tech. McDonnell Helicopters, Tempe, Ariz., 1985—. Mem. Am. Helicopter Soc., Soc. Allied Weight Engrs. (tech. com., local chpt. bd. dirs.). Office: McDonnell Douglas Helicopter Co 5000 E McDowell Rd Mesa AZ 85205

LUCHAK, BARRY DALE, accountant; b. Barhead, Alta., Can., June 22, 1951; s. Victor and Rose (Pawliuk) L.; m. Donita Louise Johnson, July 28, 1973; children—Kristofer B.J., Gregory J. Student U. Calgary, 1971-72; B. Commerce, U. Alta., 1974; Chartered acct., Alta. Student in accountancy Deloitte, Haskins and Sells, Edmonton, Alta., 1974-75; staff chartered acct. Thorne Riddell, Edmonton, 1975-77; ptnr. Knull and Luchak, Leduc, Alta., 1978-80; mng. ptnr. Barry D. Luchak P.C., Leduc, 1981-87; mng. ptnr. Luchak and Wright, Chartered Accts., Leduc, 1987—; auditor City of Leduc, 1983—; dir. various pvt. corps., Leduc; adviser Govt. Alta. Hosps., Sr. Citizen Homes Acctg. Mgmt. Mem. Inst. Chartered Accts. Can., Inst. Chartered Accts. Alta. Progressive Conservative. Lodge: Elks (dir. advisor 1978-82). Office: Luchak and Wright, 4716-51 Ave Box 1255, Leduc, AB Canada T9E 2Y7

LUCHTEL, DANIEL LEE, environmental health educator; b. Carroll, Iowa, Jan. 13, 1942; s. Harry Henry and Irma Elizabeth (Onken) L. BS, St. Benedict's Coll., 1963; PhD, U. Wash., 1969. NIH postdoctoral fellow U. Wash., Seattle, 1969-71, research assoc., 1973-75, asst. prof., 1975-82, assoc. prof., 1982—; research fellow Hubrecht Lab., Utrecht, The Netherlands, 1972. Contbr. articles to profl. jours. Co-investigator research grantee NIH, 1973-76, 76-82, EPA, 1977-79; prin. investigator research grantee NIH, 1982-85. Mem. AAAS, Am. Inst. Biol. Scis., Electron Microscopy Soc. Am., Am. Soc. Cell Biology, Sigma Xi. Club: Seattle Mountaineers. Avocations: mountain climbing, skiing. Home: 6047 29th NE Seattle WA 98115 Office: U Wash Dept Environ Health SC-34 Seattle WA 98195

LUCHTERHAND, RALPH EDWARD, engineer; b. Portland, Oreg., Feb. 9, 1952; s. Otto Charles II and Evelyn Alice (Isaac) L.; m. JoAnn Denise Adams, Aug. 13, 1983; 1 dau., Anne Michelle. B.S., Portland State U., 1974, MBA, 1986. Registered profl. engr., Oreg., Wash. Mech. engr. Hyster Co., Portland, 1971-75, service engr., 1975-76; project engr. Lumber Systems Inc., Portland, 1976-79; prin. engr. Moore Internat., Portland, 1979-81, chief product engr., 1981-83; project engr. Irvington-Moore, Portland, 1983, chief engr., 1983-86; ind. cons. engr., 1986; engring. program mgr. Precision Castparts Corp., Portland, 1986—. Active Village Bapt. Ch., Beaverton, Oreg. Mem. ASME (pres. student chpt. 1973-74), Forest Products Research Soc., Assn. MBA Execs. Republican. Home: 3000 NW 178th Ave Portland OR 97229 Office: Precision Castparts Corp 4600 SE Harney Dr Portland OR 97206

LUCIANI, RALPH ANGELO, city official, educator; b. Albuquerque, Oct. 3, 1944; s. Ulisses Dominic and Theresa Cenovia (Trujillo) Garcia L.; m. Lynne Margaret Natland, Apr. 27, 1968 (div. Apr. 1982); children—Marcus Damon, Nicolus Dominic, Wendy Dyan. B.A. in History, Calif. State U.-Fullerton, 1967, M.Pub. Adminstrn., 1973. Adminstrv. asst. City of Garden Grove, Calif., 1970-74; asst. city mgr. City of Manhattan Beach, Calif., 1974—; instr. U. So. Calif., Los Angeles, 1980—, El Camino Coll., Gardena, Calif., 1981-82. Mem. Internat. City Mgmt. Assn., Internat. Personnel Mgmt. Assn., Mcpl. Mgmt. Assts. So. Calif. (pres. 1973-74), So. Calif. Pub. Labor Relations Council (bd. mem., pres. 1983), S.W. Ctr. for Tng. and Devel. (bd. mem., chmn. 1978), Phi Kappa Tau. Office: City of Manhattan Beach 1400 Highland Ave Manhattan Beach CA 90266

LUCKE, LOU, data processing executive; b. Havre, Mont., May 21, 1931; s. Alvin Jack and Jeanette Cronky (Shephard) L.; m. JoAnne (Cloninger), Apr. 2, 1954; children: Louis Alvin, Jean Elaine, Larry Lee. BS in Physics, Mont. State U., 1954, BS in Geology, 1975. Systems engr. IBM, Helena, Mont., 1960-62; programming supr. North Am. Aviation, Downey, Calif., 1962-66; exec. advisor McDonnell-Douglass, Huntington Beach, Calif., 1966-69; dir. computing services Mont. State U., Bozeman, 1969-81, No. Mont. Coll., Havre, 1981—. Contbr. articles to profl. jours. Recipient Spl. Achievement award, McDonnell Douglas-Astro', 1969, Supervisory Mgmt. award North Am. Aviation, 1965. Assn. for Computing Machinery (regional sec. 1959), Data Processing Mgmt. Assn. (indsl. rep. 1972-75), Mont. Data Processing Assn. (pres. 1979-81, exec. sec. 1982—). Club: Mont. State U. Flying Bobcats (Bozeman) (v.p. 1979). Lodge: Elks. Avocations: ranching, hunting, fishing, flying. Home: 900 Third Ave Havre MT 59501 Office: No Mont Coll Havre MT 59501

LUCKETT, BARBARA JEANINE, social worker; b. Portland, Maine, May 30, 1940; d. Lawrence H. and Elsie I. (Crockett) Spiller; m. Roland Hayes Luckett, July 25, 1964 (div. 1977); children: Jason, Josslyn. BA in Sociology, U. Maine, Orono, 1962; MSW, U. Hawaii, 1964. Lic. clin. social worker, Calif. Social worker Cath. Social Service, Honolulu, 1964-66; psychiat. social worker Calif. State Mental Hygiene Ctr., Los Angeles, 1966-73; clin. social worker Orange County Dept. Mental Health, South County, Calif., 1974—; pvt. practice clin. social work Irvine, Calif., 1982—; fieldwork instr. U. So. Calif. Sch. Social Work, Los Angeles, 1980-86. Organizer Conf. on Battered Women, Orange County, Calif., 1977. Mem. Nat. Assn. Social Workers. Democrat. Mem. United Ch. of Christ. Home: 11 Greenleaf Irvine CA 92714 Office: 15435 Jeffrey Rd Suite 132 Irvine CA 92714

LUCKEY, RICHARD ROY, hydrologist; b. Sterling, Colo., Dec. 19, 1945; s. Roy L. and Florence M. (Koenig) L.; m. Bonita M. Kellerhuis, Nov. 2, 1969 (div. June 1981); children: Brian R., Kristina M., Craig A.; m. Carole Valdez, Nov. 8, 1984. BA in Math., U. Colo., 1968. Hydrologist U.S. Geol. Survey, Lakewood, Colo., 1968-75, 78—, Rolla, Mo., 1975-78. Mem. Am. Geophys. Union, Am. Inst. Hydrology (cert.), Assn. Ground Water Scientists and Engrs., Nat. Water Wells Assn. (mem. ground water editorial bd. 1975-78, Best Paper Ground Water award 1974), Colo. Ground Water Assn. Office: US Geol Survey WRD PO Box 25046 MS 412 Lakewood CO 80225

LUDEMAN, KATE, human resources executive; b. San Antonio, Aug. 14, 1946; d. Ben and Annette (Martin) L.; 1 child from previous marriage, Catherine. BS in Engring., Tex. Tech U., 1967, MA in Psychology, 1972; postgrad., U. Tex., 1974-76; PhD in Psychology, Saybrook Inst., 1979. Project leader Control Data, Saigon, Socialist Republic of Vietnam, 1970-71; cons. Dallas, 1972-79; interviewer morning news ABC Tsa. WFAA-TV, Dallas, 1976-77; mgr. tng. and devel. Shaklee Corp., San Francisco, 1979-81; mgr. human resources Impell Corp., San Francisco, 1981-83; corp. v.p. human resources KLA Instruments, Santa Clara, Calif., 1984—; developer profl. stress mgmt. conf. for use in Dallas, Albuquerque, and Atlanta. Author: Stress Management and Allergy Handbook, 1979; contbr. articles to profl. jours. Chemstrand & Am. Dyers scholar Tex. Tech U., 1965-67. Mem. Am. Soc. Personnel Adminstrs., Am. Soc. Tng. and Devel., Semiconductor Equipment and Mfrs. (academis chmn. 1985-86), Tau Beta Phi. Home: 19644 Montevina Rd Los Gatos CA 95030 Office: KLA Instruments 3530 Bassett Rd Santa Clara CA 95054-0554

LUDIN, ROGER LOUIS, physics educator; b. Jersey City, June 13, 1944; s. Fredric E. and Gwendolyn C. (Rogers) L.; m. Diane E. Wilson, Aug. 26, 1966; children: Stephen L., Joyce E. BS in Physics, Brown U., 1966; MS in Physics, Worcester Polytech. Inst., 1968, PhD in Physics, 1969. Postdoctoral fellow Worcester (Mass.) Polytech. Inst., 1969-70; prof. Burlington County Coll., Pemberton, N.J., 1970-85; lectr. Calif. Poly. State U., San Luis Obispo, 1984—. Author lab. manuals for introductory physics. Active Medford Lakes (N.J.) Bd. Edn., 1976-84, pres. 1978-84; bd. dirs. Medford Lakes Athletic Assn., 1974-84; soccer coach Morro Bay (Calif.) High Sch., 1985—. Named Tchr. of Yr. Burlington County Coll., 1982, 83. Mem. Am. Assn. Physics Tchrs. (sec., treas. N.J. Jersey sect. 1976-84, named Outstanding Contbr. to Physics Edn., 1984, editor So. Calif. sect. 1985—), Am. Phys. Soc., AAAS, Sigma Xi. Lodge: Lions. Avocations: photography, coaching youth sports, camping, canoeing, acting. Home: 2691 Koa Ave Morro Bay CA 93442 Office: Calif Poly State U Physics Dept San Luis Obispo CA 93407

LUDWIG, GEORGE HARRY, physicist; b. Johnson County, Iowa, Nov. 13, 1927; s. George McKinley and Alice (Heim) L.; m. Rosalie F. Vickers, July 21, 1950; children: Barbara Rose, Sharon Lee, George Vickers, Kathy Ann Ramsay. B.A. cum laude, U. Iowa, 1956, M.S., 1959, Ph.D., 1960. Research asst. U. Iowa, 1956-60, research assoc., 1960; head fields and particles Instrumentation sect. Goddard Space Flight Center, NASA, 1960-65, chief info. processing div., 1965-71, assoc. dir. for data ops., 1971-72; dir. systems integration Nat. Environ. Satellite Service, 1972-75; dir. ops. U.S. Nat. Environ. Satellite System, 1975-80, tech. dir., 1980; sr. scientist Environ. Research Lab. NOAA, Boulder, Colo., 1980-81; dir. Environ. Research Lab. NOAA, 1981-83; asst. to chief scientist NASA, 1983-84, ind. cons. data mgmt. and space sta. design, 1983—; sr. research assoc. Lab. for Atmospheric and Space Physics U. Colo., 1985—; designer radiation detection instrumentation for numerous sci. spacecraft including Explorer I, 1956-65; overseer devel. and op. U.S. Nat. Environ. Satellite System, 1972-80; overseer environ. research program NOAA, 1981-83; co-discoverer Van Allen radiation belts; expert on NASA sci. and applications research data processing ; oversaw devel. and operation U.S. Nat. Environ. Satellite System, 1972-80; oversaw environ. research program Nat. Oceanic and Atmospheric Adminstrn., 1981-83. Served from pvt. to capt. USAF, 1946-52. Van Allen scholar, 1958; research fellow U.S. Steel Found., 1958-60; recipient Exceptional Service medal NASA, 1969, Program Adminstrn. and Mgmt. award NOAA, 1977, Exceptional Sci. Achievement medal NASA, 1984. Mem. AAAS, Am. Geophys. Union, IEEE (sr.), Am. Meteorol. Soc., Phi Beta Kappa, Sigma Xi, Phi Eta Sigma, Eta Kappa Nu. Lodge: Kiwanis. Home and Office: 880 Crescent Dr Boulder CO 80303

LUDWIG, GILDA MARY, retired social worker; b. Fall River, Mass., Dec. 15, 1926; d. Francisco Pacheco and Ethel (Souza) Da Silva; m. John Howard Ludwig, Nov. 9, 1946; children: Howard Russell, Robert William. Student, U. Md., 1953-55; AB, Boston U., 1957; MSW, Ohio State U., 1961. Tchr. Mt. Washington (Ohio) High Sch., 1957-59; social worker Dept. Social Services, Cin., 1961-63; sch. social worker Dept. Edn., Clermont County, Ohio, 1964-67; clin. social worker NIH, Bethesda, Md., 1968-70; adminstr. human services Dept. of Health and Human Resources, Washington, 1970-72; bd. dirs. Santa Barbara Mental Health Assn. (Vol. award 1983), ; chmn. Santa Barbara Mental Health Aux., 1984-86; bd. dirs., fund chmn. Santa Barbara unit Recording for the Blind, pres.-elect 1987-90. Neighborhood coordinator Newcomers, Santa Barbara, 1973-74; vol. registered Portuguese interpreter for local med. facilities. Mem. Nat. Assn. Social Workers (cert., co-chmn. 1981-83). Avocations: travelling, tennis. Home: 43 Alston Pl Santa Barbara CA 93108

LUDWIG, JOHN ROBERT, wildlife research biologist, consultant; b. West Reading, Pa., Mar. 14, 1943; s. Robert Mandon and Grace Elaine (Nice) L.; m. Barbara Ann Ely, Aug. 28, 1965; children—Todd Alan, Kristen Sue. B.S., Pa. State U., 1965; M.A., So. Ill. U., 1967, Ph.D., 1976. Research asst., grad. fellow, teaching asst. So. Ill. U., Carbondale, 1965-69, 71-73; research asst. N.C. State U., 1969-71; camp dir. Youth Conservation Corps, So. Ill. U., Carbondale, 1971, 72; deer, elk, black bear staff biologist Ont. Ministry Natural Resources, 1973-76; white-tailed deer and wild turkey research biologist Farmland Wildlife Population and Research Group, Minn. Dept. Natural Resources, Madelia, 1976-84; regional dir. Ducks Unltd., Nev., 1984—. Pa. State scholar, 1961-65; grantee Pope and Young Club, 1981, 82, 83, Minn. Archery Assn., 1981, 82. Mem. Wildlife Soc., Nev. Wildlife Fedn., Nat. Wildlife Fedn., Ducks Unltd., Nat. Wild Turkey Fedn. (grantee 1983), Nat. Rifle Assn., Nev. Orgn. for Wildlife, Nev. Rifle and Pistol Assn., Sigma Xi. Contbr. articles to profl. jours. Home and Office: 639 Thorobred Ave Gardnerville NV 89410

LUDWIG, ROLF MARTIN, internist; b. Bautzen, Germany, June 3, 1924; came to U.S., 1953; s. Martin Max and Doris (Metz) L.; m. Shirley Jean Ray, Oct. 26, 1956 (div. June 1983); 1 child, Mark Stephen. M.D., Eberhard Karls U. Tuebingen, Germany, 1953. Intern, Mary's Help Hosp., San Francisco, 1953-54, then resident in internal medicine; resident in internal medicine Franklin Hosp., San Francisco, Huntington Meml. Hosp., Pasadena, Calif., Wadsworth VA Gen. Hosp., Los Angeles, 1959-60. Internist, Kaiser/Permanente, Fontana, Calif., 1960-63, 73—; practice medicine specializing in internal medicine, Yucaipa, Calif., 1963-72; retired, 1987. Served to capt. M.C., U.S. Army, 1956-59. Mem. Am. Soc. Internal Medicine, Calif. Soc. Internal Medicine, Inland Soc. Internal Medicine, Union of Am. Physicians and Dentists. Republican. Lutheran. Home: 11711 Holmes St Yucaipa CA 92399 Office: So Calif Permanente Med Group 9985 Sierra Ave Fontana CA 92335

LUDWIG, WILLIAM ORLAND, sugar company executive, lawyer; b. Pontiac, Mich., Jan. 9, 1931; s. Austin Lewis and Nina C. (Wixon) L.; m. Maureen Condon, July 6, 1957; children—John, James, Kathryn, Andrew, Amy, Stephen. A.B., Alma Coll., 1952; J.D., Salmon P. Chase Coll. Law, 1964; LL.M. in Taxation, Boston U., 1972. Bar: Ohio 1964; C.P.A., Utah, cert. mgmt. accountant. Various fin. mgmt. positions Procter & Gamble Co., Cin., 1956-68; div. controller Polaroid Corp., Cambridge, Mass., 1968-72; controller The Kingsford Co. subs. Clorox Co., Oakland, Calif., 1972-78; v.p. fin. Amalgamated Sugar Co., Ogden, Utah, 1978-82; sr. v.p. fin., chief fin. officer Holly Sugar Corp., Colorado Springs, Colo., 1982—; lectr. law Chase Coll., 1965. Served to 1st lt. U.S. Army, 1952-56. Mem. Fin. Execs. Inst., Assn. U.S. Army, Nat. Assn. Accts., U. of Ams. Found., Inst. Cert. Mgmt. Accts. Republican. Methodist. Lodges: Masons, Shriners. Office: PO Box 1052 Colorado Springs CO 80901

LUEKER, GEORGE S., computer scientist, educator; b. Concordia, Mo., Mar. 26, 1949; s. Erwin L. and Anna Marie (Schick) L. BA, Valparaiso U., 1971; MA, Princeton U., 1973, PhD, 1975. Asst. prof. info. computer sci. U. Calif., Irvine, 1975-81, assoc. prof., 1981—, acting dept. chair, 1983-84, chair campus com. on research, 1986-87. NSF grantee, 1979-83, 1985—. Mem. AAAS, Assn. Computing Machinery, Sigma Xi. Avocations: electronic music, volleyball. Office: U Calif ICS Dept Irvine CA 92717

LUENBERGER, DAVID GILBERT, electrical engineer, educator; b. Los Angeles, Sept. 16, 1937; s. Frederick Otto and Marion (Crumly) L.; m. Nancy Ann Iversen, Jan. 7, 1962; children: Susan Ann, Robert Alden, Jill Alison, Jenna Emmy. B.S.E.E., Calif. Inst. Tech., 1959; M.S.E.E., Stanford U., 1961, Ph.D. in Elec. Engring., 1963. Asst. prof. elec. engring. Stanford U., Calif., 1963-67, assoc. prof. engring.-econ. systems, 1967-71, prof., 1971—, dept. chmn., 1980—; tech. asst. dir. U.S. Office Sci. and Tech., Exec. Office of Pres., Washington, 1971-72; vis. prof. MIT, Cambridge, 1976; dir. Optimization Tech., Inc., Auburn, Ala.; guest prof. Tech. U. of Denmark, Lyngby, 1986. Author: Optimization by Vector Space Methods, 1969, Linear and Nonlinear Programming, 1973, 2d edit., 1984, Introduction to Dynamic Systems, 1979; contbr. numerous articles to tech. publs. Fellow IEEE; mem. AAUP, Am. Fin. Assn., Econometric Soc., Soc. for Promotion Econ. Theory, Inst. Mgmt. Sci., Soc. Econ. Dynamics and Control (pres. 1987), Math Programming Soc., Palo Alto Camera Club, Sigma Xi, Tau Beta Pi. Lutheran. Office: Stanford U Dept Engring-Econ Systems Terman Ctr 306 Stanford CA 94305-4025

LUETGERT, JAMES HOWARD, geophysicist; b. Elmhurst, Ill., Dec. 12, 1944; s. Howard Arthur and Mary Ruth (Noble) L.; m. Christine Adele Beck, Dec. 31, 1983. BA, Oberlin Coll., 1966; postgrad., Carnegie Mellon U., 1966-68, U. Pitts., 1968-70; PhD, U. Wis., 1982. Geophysicist U.S. Geol. Survey, Menlo Park, Calif., 1982—. Contbr. articles to profl. jours. Mem. Am. Geophys. Union, Seismol. Soc. Am., Soc. Exploration Geophysicists, Sigma Xi. Office: US Geol Survey 345 Middlefield Rd Menlo Park CA 94025

LUEVANO, FRED, JR., computer systems executive; b. Alamogordo, N.Mex., June 21, 1943; s. Fred Macias and Margaret (Baca) L.; m. Lupe Olmos, July 11, 1964; children: Michael, James Paul. AA in bus., Fullerton Coll., 1975; BA in Mgmt., U. Redlands, 1979, MA in Mgmt., 1985. Cert. data processing mgr. Mgr. computer ops. Hoffman Electronics, El Monte, Calif., 1971-76; mgr. computer ops. and tech. services City of Anaheim, Calif., 1976-79; mgr. data processing Wyle Data Services, Huntington Beach, Calif., 1979-83; mgr. corp. computer ops. Northrop Corp., Hawthorne, Calif., 1983, mgr. corp. computing, 1985—, dir. disaster revovery program, 1983—; cons. info. systems, La Habra, Calif., 1971—. Cub master Boy Scouts Am., La Habra, 1979-84, chmn. com. 1975-79; councilman candidate City of La Habra Heights, Calif., 1982; pres. Red Coach Club, 1979-80; pres. La Habra Parents for Swimming Inc., 1986. Served with USN, 1961-65. Mem. Am. Mgmt. Assn., Telecommunications Assn., Assn. Computer Ops. Mgrs. (speaker 1983-86), Northrop Mgmt. Club. Republican. Roman Catholic. Avocations: fishing, basketball. Office: Northrop Corp 13020 Yukon Ave Hawthorne CA 90250

LUFT, HAROLD S., health economist; b. Newark, N.J., Jan. 6, 1947; s. George and Kay (Grossman) L.; m. Lorraine Ellin Levinson, May 24, 1970; children: Shira Levinson, Jana Levinson. A.B., Harvard U., 1968, AM, 1970, Ph.D., 1973. Systems analyst, research asst. Harvard Transport Research, Cambridge, Mass., 1965-68; systems analyst Harvard Econ. Research Project, Cambridge, Mass., 1968-72; instr. econs. Tufts U., Medford, Mass., 1972-73; postdoctoral fellow Harvard Ctr. Community Health, Boston, 1972-73; asst. prof. health econs. Stanford U., Calif., 1973-78; prof. health econs. Inst. Health Policy Studies, U. Calif., San Francisco, 1978—; cons. Applied Mgmt. Scis., Silver Spring, Md., 1979—, Robert Wood Johnson Found., Princeton, N.J., 1982—; study sect. Nat. Ctr. Health Services, Rockville, Md., 1981-83. Author: Poverty and Health, 1978; Health Maintenance Organization, 1981. Contbr. chpts. to books, articles to profl. jours. Advisor, fin. planning com. Mid-Peninsula Health Service, Palo Alto, Calif., 1984—. NSF fellow, Carnegie Found. fellow, Grad. Prize fellow Harvard U., 1968-72. Mem. Am. Pub. Health Assn., Am. Econ. Assn., Inst. Medicine, Western Econ. Assn. Home: 1020 Ramona St Palo Alto CA 94301 Office: Inst Health Policy Studies U Calif 1326 3d Ave San Francisco CA 94143

LUFT, RENE WILFRED, civil engineer; b. Santiago, Chile, Sept. 21, 1943; came to U.S., 1968; s. David and Malwina (Kelmy) L.; m. Monica Acevedo, Aug. 24, 1970; children: Deborah Elaine, Daniel Eduardo. CE, U. Chile, 1967; MS, MIT, 1969, DSc, 1971. Registered profl. engr., Alaska, Calif., Mass., N.H., R.I., Vt., Republic of Chile. Asst. prof. civil engring. U. Chile, 1967-68; research asst. MIT, Cambridge, Mass., 1969-71, vis. lectr., 1983-84; staff engr. Simpson, Gumpertz & Heger Inc., Arlington, Mass., 1971-74, sr. staff engr., 1975-78, assoc., 1978-83, sr. assoc., 1984-86; sr. assoc., asst. branch mgr. Simpson, Gumpertz & Heger Inc., San Francisco, 1986—; sec. seismic adv. com. Mass. Bldg. Code Commn., 1978-80, chmn., 1981-82; mem. Boston seismic instrumentation com. U.S. Geol. Survey. Contbr. articles to profl. jours. Mem. ASCE, Boston Soc. Civil Engrs. (chmn. seismic design adv. com. 1981-86, Clemens Herschel award for tech. paper 1980, pres.'s award for leadership in earthquake engring. 1984), Am. Concrete Inst., Earthquake Engring. Research Inst., Structural Engrs. Assn. Calif., NSPE (Young Engr. of Yr., 1979), Nat. Earthquake Hazards Reduction Program (design overview com., bldg. seismic safety council), Sigma Xi, Chi Epsilon. Home: 109 Ardith Dr Orinda CA 94563 Office: 221 Main St Suite 1500 San Francisco CA 94105

LUGTU, TITO ATENCION, chemist; b. Manila, Aug. 9, 1957; came to U.S., 1982; s. Gil Lacson and Laura Tuazon (Atencion) L. BS in Chemistry, U. Santo Thomas, Manila, 1978. Chemist Research and Devel. Ctr., San Miguel Corp., Makati, Philippines, 1980-82; methods devel. chemist Libby Labs., Berkeley, Calif., 1982—; cons. Thomas Lab., Hayward, Calif., 1985—. Inventor in field. Mem. Am. Chem. Soc., Assn. Ofcl. Analytical Chemist. Avocations: elec. and mech. works. Home: 2808 Oxford Ave Richmond CA 94806 Office: Libby Labs 1700 6th St Berkeley CA 94710

LUI, CHIU-LUN (ALLAN), dentist; b. Canton, Peoples Republic of China, Feb. 9, 1944; came to U.S., 1971; s. Dean and Fung (Eng) L.; m. Ching P. Lau, May 1, 1972; children: Jennie, Edward, Edwin. BDS, Nat. Def. Med. Ctr., Taipei, Taiwan Republic of China, 1971; DMD, Tufts U., 1975. Commd. U.S. Army, 1976, advanced through grades to lt. colonel, 1987; gen. dentist officer U.S. Army, Ft. Campbell, Ky., 1976-80; asst. officer in charge U.S. Army, Fed. Republic of Germany, 1980-82, acting comdr., 1982-83; with gen. dentist office Walter Reed Army Med. Ctr., Washington, 1983-84; gen. dentistry resident U.S. Army, Ft. Ord, Calif., 1984—86; chief fixed prosthodontics Chessen Dental Clinic, Ft. Polk, La., 1986—. Deacon, interpreter Salinas (Calif.) Chinese Christian Ch., 1984—. Mem. ADA, Acad. Gen. Dentistry. Office: US Army Dental Activity Fort Polk LA 71459

LUIS, MARTIN JAMES, plant manager; b. Salinas, Calif., July 26, 1953; s. James August and Alice Marie (Sousa) L.; m. Margaret Loree Crowl, Dec. 27, 1982; children: Shawn Haligan, Martin II, Matthew, Morgan. AS, Modesto Jr. Coll., 1973. Laborer James A. Luis, Stockton, Calif., 1966-70; v.p. Luis Farms, Stockton, 1970—; foreman Sousa Farms, Stockton, 1979-82; field rep. S.M.S. Briners, Stockton, 1977-79, asst. plant mgr., 1982-84, plant mgr., 1984—. Mem. Calif. Tomatoe Growers Assn., Pickle Packers Internat., Calif. Beet Growers Assn., Alpha Gama Sigma. Republican. Roman Catholic. Avocations: photography, gourmet foods, playing cards, traveling. Office: SMS Briners 17750 E Hwy 4 Stockton CA 95205

LUITEN, PETER HENRI, architectural engineer; b. The Hague, The Netherlands, Jan. 9, 1922; came to U.S., 1946; s. Johannnes P.A. and Catherina W. (Lafeber) L.; m. Johanna Theodora Brandsen, Jan. 10, 1948; children: Ted, Peter, Kathy, Thea, Ria, John, Rick, Vicky. Student, St. Joris Coll., Eindhoven, The Netherlands; BS in Archtl. Engring., HTS, s'Hertogenbosch, The Netherlands, 1942. Registered profl. engr., Calif. Structural designer Aerojet-Gen. Corp., Azusa, Calif., 1947-52; project mgr.rocket test facilities Aerojet, Aetron div., Covina, Calif., 1952-65, mgr. internat. ops., 1965-72; mktg., product mgr. Aerojet Envirogenics div., El Monte, Calif., 1972-75; cons. engr. PH Luiten & Assocs., Arcadia, Calif., 1975—; structural cons. engr., City of Monrovia, Calif., 1976—. Contbr. articles to profl. jours.; patentee in field. Served with M.I. Corps, U.S. Army, 1944-45, ETO. Republican. Roman Catholic. Avocation: fgn. langs. Office: 37 E Huntington Dr Arcadia CA 91006

LUJAN, MANUEL, JR., congressman; b. San Idlefonso, N.Mex., May 12, 1928; s. Manuel and Lorenzita (Romero) L.; m. Jean Kay Couchman, Nov. 18, 1948; children: Terra Kay Everett, James Manuel, Barbara Frae, Robert Jeffrey. B.A., Coll. Santa Fe, 1950; student, St. Mary's (Calif.) Coll., 1946-47. Engaged in ins. bus. Santa Fe and Albuquerque, from 1948; mem. 91st-100th congresses from 1st N.Mex. Dist.; mem. interior and insular affairs com., energy and environment subcom., mem. sci. and tech. com. Office: 1323 Longworth Office Bldg Washington DC 20515 *

LUKE, BRIAN THOMAS, theoretical chemist, researcher; b. Montreal, Que., Can., Oct. 12, 1953; came to U.S., 1958; s. Thomas Saunders and Joan Elliot (Husband) L.; m. Carole Anne Payot, Aug. 4, 1979. BS in Chemistry, BS in Biology, Calif. Inst. Tech., 1975; PhD in Chem. Physics, U. So. Calif., 1980. Postdoctoral fellow Carnegie-Mellon U., Pitts., 1981-83; research assoc. Molecular Research Inst., Palo Alto, Calif., 1983—; research scientist SRI Internat., Menlo Park, Calif., 1983—. Contbr. articles to profl. jours. Mem. Am. Chem. Soc., AAAS, N.Y. Acad. Sci. Office: SRI Internat 333 Ravenswood Ave Menlo Park CA 94025

LUKE, SAMUEL CUMMINS, insurance company executive; Honolulu, Mar. 11, 1935; s. Samuel S. and Pansy (Lee) L.; B.A., U. Hawaii, 1957; M. Martial Arts, Am. Jujitsu Inst., 1978; m. Florence W.N. Ng, June 17, 1955; children—Lance, Layne, Lorin, Larsen, Lisa. Office mgr. Pacific Ins. Co. Ltd., Honolulu, 1957-69; v.p. adminstrn. Hawaii Resort Industries, Honolulu, 1969-72; v.p. Western Underwriters Co., Honolulu, 1972; asst. v.p. dataprocessing Island Ins. Co. Ltd., Honolulu, 1972-78; v.p. adminstrn. Profl. Underwriters Corp., Honolulu, 1978-81; pres. VIP Underwriters Corp., 1981—; v.p. Kudlich Gen. Ins. Agy. Ltd., Economi Plan Ins., Inc.; v.p., sec. Orient Marine Underwriters, Ltd.; sec. Mahalo Farms Inc., sec.-treas. DSI Software Services, Inc. Pres. parish council St. John Vianney Catholic Ch.; pres. Cath. Social Service Adv. Bd.; chmn. adv. bd. Leeward Community Coll., mem. adv. bd. Kapiolani Community Coll. Lic. real estate agt., ins. gen. agt. Mem. Ins. Acctg. and Statis. Assn. (chpt. pres.), Data Processing Mgmt. Assn. (dir., regional v.p.). Assn. System Mgmt. (chpt. v.p.). System 3 Users Club, Honolulu Auto Club (v.p.), Am. Jujitsu Inst. (prof., black belt 7th degree), Kung Sheong Doo Soc. (bd. dirs.), Lukes of Hawaii (bd. dirs.). Home: 1274 Kuuna St Kailua HI 96734 Office: VIP Underwriters Corp 470 Nimitz Way Honolulu HI 96817

LUKENBILL, GREGG, real estate developer, professional basketball team executive. Mng. gen. ptnr. Sacramento Kings, Nat. Basketball Assn., 1984—. Office: care Sacramento Kings 1515 Sports Drive Sacramento CA 95834 *

LUKENS, HERBERT RICHARD, JR., chemist, researcher; b. Coquille, Oreg., May 19, 1921; s. Herbert R. Lukens and Mary C. (Cribbens) Mitchell; m. Edna Eleanor Varvel, Aug. 25, 1945; 1 child, Herbert Richard III. BA in Biochemistry, U. Calif., Berkeley, 1945; MA in Marriage and Family Counseling, U.S. Internat. U., 1975, PhD in Human Behavior, 1979. Chemist Alber's Milling Co., Oakland, Calif., 1945-46, Consumer's Yeast Co., Oakland, 1946-48, Tracerlab, Inc., Richmond, Calif., 1948-55, Shell Devel. Co., Emeryville, Calif., 1955-62; prin. scientist IRT Corp., San Diego, 1962—. Author: (with others) Radioisotope Applications Engineering, 1961; patentee in field. Counselor San Diego Youth and Community Services, 1976-79, bd. dirs. 1979-82. Mem. Am. Chem. Soc., AAAS, Am. Assn. Marriage and Family Therapists. Republican. Methodist. Office: IRT Corp PO Box 85317 San Diego CA 92138

LUM, HERMAN TSUI FAI, chief justice Hawaii Supreme Court; b. Honolulu, Nov. 5, 1926; s. K.P. and Helen (Tom) L.; m. Almira Ahn, June 17, 1949; children: Forrest K.K., Jonathan K.K. Student, U. Hawaii, 1945-46; LL.B., U. Mo., 1950. Bar: Hawaii 1950. Asst. public prosecutor City and County Honolulu, 1950-52; chief atty. Hawaii Ho. of Reps., 1955, chief clk., 1956-61; partner Suyenaga, Sakamoto & Lum, Honolulu, from 1956; U.S. atty. Dist. Hawaii, 1961-67; judge Circuit Ct. Honolulu, 1967-76, sr. judge Family Ct., 1977-80; assoc. justice Supreme Ct. Hawaii, 1980-83, chief justice, 1983—; Pres. Jr. Bar Assn. Hawaii, 1957. Mem. ABA, Bar Assn. Hawaii, Fed. Bar Assn. Hawaii (pres. 1963), Phi Delta Phi, Lambda Chi Alpha. Home: 2508 Makiki Heights Dr Honolulu HI 96822 Office: Supreme Ct of Hawaii PO Box 2560 Honolulu HI 96804 *

LUM, JEAN LOUI JIN, nurse educator; b. Honolulu, Sept. 5, 1938; d. Yee Nung and Pui Ki (Young) L. BS, U. Hawaii, Manoa, 1960; MS in Nursing, U. Calif., San Francisco, 1961; MA, U. Wash., 1969, PhD in Sociology, 1972. Registered nurse, Hawaii. From instr. to prof. Sch. Nursing U. Hawaii-Manoa, Honolulu, 1961—, acting dean, 1982, dean, 1982—; project coordinator Analysis and Planning Personnel Services, Western Interstate Commn. Higher Edn., 1977; extramural assoc. div. Research Grants NIH, 1978-79; mem. mgmt. adv. com. Honolulu County Hosp., 1982; mem. exec. bd. Pacific Health Research Inst., 1980-88; mem. health planning com. East Honolulu, 1978-81. Contbr. articles to profl. jours. Recipient Nurse of Yr. award Hawaii Nurses Assn., 1982; USPHS grantee, 1967-72. Fellow Am. Acad. Nursing; mem. Am. Nurses Assn., Am. Pacific Nursing Leaders Conf. (pres. 1983—), Council Nurse Researchers, Nat. League for Nursing (bd. rev. 1981—), Western Council Higher Edn. for Nurses (chmn. 1984-85), Western Soc. for Research in Nursing, Am. Sociol. Assn., Pacific Sociol. Assn., Assn. for Women in Sci., Hawaii Pub. Health Assn., Hawaii Med. Services Assn. (bd. dirs. 1985-86), Mortar Bd., Phi Kappa Phi, Sigma Theta Tau, Alpha Kappa Delta, Delta Kappa Gamma. Episcopalian. Office: U Hawaii at Manoa Sch Nursing Webster 416 2528 The Mall Honolulu HI 96822

LUM, KIM SIU, banker; b. Kwong Tung, China, Nov. 26, 1943; came to U.S., 1965, naturalized, 1970; d. Leung Yuke and Seung Mon (Lum) Luke; m. Kenneth Lum, Oct. 26, 1968; children—Keith Andrew, Selene Adina. Student in Bus. Edn., Sacramento City Coll., 1982, Cosumnes River Coll., 1983, U. Calif.-Davis, 1984—. Asst. v.p., asst. mgr. Sumitomo Bank Calif., Sacramento, 1966-82; v.p., mgr. Calif. Nat. Bank, Sacramento, 1982-84; exec. v.p. Covenant REIT, Inc., Sacramento, 1984—; dir. Covenant Advisors, Inc.; mem. adv. bd. United Bank, Sacramento, 1985. Bd. dirs. Chinese Am. Culture Ctr., Sacramento, 1984. Republican. Clubs: Sacramento Chinese Mandarin Cultural and Ednl. (bd. dirs.), Chinese Am. Republican of Sacramento (bd. dirs.). Office: Covenant REIT 1401 El Camino Ave Suite 350 Sacramento CA 95815

LUM, TERRI LYNN CAROL, social worker; b. Honolulu, Dec. 24, 1957; d. Walter T.C. and Phyllis Y. (Kawamoto) L. BA in Psychology, U. Hawaii, 1979; MSW, U. Wash., 1981. Social worker Dept. Social and Health Services, Seattle, 1981-82; social worker Cath. Social Services CSATP, Honolulu, 1982-84, supr., 1984-85; counselor, coordinator Sex Abuse Treatment Ctr., Honolulu, 1985—. Facilitator Parents United/Daus. and Sons United, Honolulu, 1982-85; vol. Shelter for Abused Spouses and Children, Honolulu, 1978-79, Vol. Info. and Referral Services/Suicide and Crisis Ctr., Honolulu, 1976-77. Mem. Nat. Assn. Social Workers (sec. Hawaii chpt. 1985—), Hawaii (sec. 1985—), Nat. Assn. Counsel for Children, Acad. Cert. Social Workers (cert.). Office: Kapiolani Womens and Children's Med Ctr Sex Abuse Treatment Ctr 1319 Punahou St Room 519 Honolulu HI 96826

LUMBY, MALCOLM EUGENE, JR., public relations executive, educator; b. Rome, N.Y., June 2, 1938; s. Malcolm Eugene and Henrietta (Zcah) L. A.A., Pasadena City Coll., 1970; B.A., Calif. State U.-Los Angeles, 1971; M.S., So. Ill. U., 1972, Ph.D., 1974, postgrad. UCLA, 1979. Minister, Internat. Assn. Bible Students, Ghana, also Calif., La., N.C., N.Y., 1957-68; student instr. Sch. Journalism, So. Ill. U., Carbondale, 1972-74; publs. coordinator, speech trainer Automobile Club So. Calif., Los Angeles, 1975-79; v.p. pub. relations First Interstate Bancorp, Los Angeles, 1979—; pub. relations instr. UCLA, 1978-79; instr. Grad. Sch. Bus. and Fin., Golden Gate U., Los Angeles, 1981—. Bd. dirs. Pasadena (Calif.) Heritage, 1981-85. Mem. Assn. for Edn. Journalism, Internat. Assn. Bus. Communicators (Golden Quill award 1982), Pub. Relations Soc. Am. (Prism award 1981), Soc. Profl. Journalists, Town Hall of Calif., Sigma Delta Chi. Republican. Club: Toastmasters (Century City pres. 1979, gov. Los Angeles area 1980). Contbr. articles to profl. jours. Office: First Interstate Bancorp 707 Wilshire Blvd Los Angeles CA 90017

LUMPKIN, PEGGY ANN LANZA, human resources executive; b. Lancing, Tenn., Jan. 22, 1948; d. K.R. and Shirley Elaine (Van Der Aue) Le Croy; m. Joseph A. Lanza, Dec. 21, 1968 (div. July 1982); children: Mario, Dei; m. F. Dale Lumpkin, July 19, 1986. Student, Lewis and Clark Coll., 1966-68; BA in English Lit., Secondary Edn., Portland State U., 1970. V.p. personnel First State Bank Oreg., Portland, 1970-79; personnel mgr. Dept. Environ. Quality State of Oreg., Portland, 1982-83; dir. human resources Oreg. Mut. Ins., McMinnville, 1983—. Bd. dirs. United Way, Yamhill County, Oreg., 1985—; mem. State of Oreg. Fair Dismissals Appeals Bd., Salem, 1977-81. Mem. Bank Adminstrn. Inst. (pres. Portland chpt. 1976), Oreg. Bankers Assn. (chmn. personnel com. 1977-78), Am. soc. Personnel Adminstrs. Republican. Home: 17701 SW Overlook Circle Lake Oswego OR 97034 Office: Oreg. Mut Ins 4th and Davis McMinnville OR 97128

LUNA, DENNIS R., lawyer; b. Los Angeles, Aug. 21, 1946; B.S. in Petroleum Engring., U. So. Calif., 1968, M.S. in Petroleum Engring., 1969, M.B.A., 1971; J.D., Harvard U., 1974. Bar: Calif. 1974; Assoc. firm McCutchen, Black, Verleger & Shea, Los Angeles, 1974-81, partner, 1981—. Commr. Bd. Recreation and Parks, City of Los Angeles, 1984—. Contbr. articles to legal jours. Registered profl. petroleum engr., Calif. Mem. Soc. Petroleum Engrs., ABA (sect. of corp., banking and business law, sect. natural resources law), State Bar of Calif. Office: 600 Wilshire Blvd Los Angeles CA 90017

LUNA, MAUREEN ANNETTE, investment broker; b. Elizabeth, N.J., Feb. 22, 1940; d. Thomas C. and Josephine (Pecesky) Branagan; m. Robert E. Luna, June 10, 1961; children—Robert Davis, Thomas Robert, Carol Maureen. A.B., Douglass Coll., Rutgers U., 1961; M.A., U. N.Mex., 1969. Cert. fin. planner. Tchr., Ewing Twp. (N.J.) pub. schs., 1961-63; exec. dir. Community Services for the Handicapped, Albuquerque, 1979; v.p., spl. ptnr. Boettcher & Co., Inc., Albuquerque, 1979—. Mem. Albuquerque Bd. Edn., 1973-79, pres., 1977-78; mem. governing bd. Albuquerque Tech.-Vocat. Inst., 1973-79, pres., 1973-77; chmn. community adv. bd. Pub. TV Sta. KNME-TV, 1979-83, mem. governing bd., 1983—; bd. dirs. N.Mex. Estate Planning Council. Mem. Internat. Assn. Fin. Planning (dir. 1983-84, 85-87), N.Mex. Sch. Bds. Assn. (exec. com., legis. com. 1975-79), Nat. Sch. Bds. Assn. (pres.'s task force 1977-78), AAUW (chpt. v.p. 1971-73), N.Mex. State Bar Assn. (fee arbitration com. 1985—). Democrat. Roman Catholic. Home: 4809 Northridge Ct NE Albuquerque NM 87109 Office: 1717 Louisiana Blvd NE Suite 121 Albuquerque NM 87110

LUNAS, JOHN PAUL, physician; b. Glen Ridge, N.J., Mar. 11, 1936; s. Lawrence John and Pauline Howell (MacGahan) L.; m. Frances Jean Jorgensen, Sept. 3, 1960 (div. Oct. 1984); children: William Alan, Terese Barrett, Lisa Kirsten, Fredric Warren; m. Sharron Leverne Sumrall, Oct. 18, 1984; children: William Louis, Colin Watson, Philip Leighton. BA, Johns Hopkins U., 1958; MD, Duke U., 1962. Cert. Am. Bd. Internal Medicine. Intern U. Pitts. Health Ctr. Hosps., 1963; resident in internal medicine U. Oreg., Portland, 1970; commd. surgeon USPHS, 1963, advanced through grades to asst. dir. grade, 1970; med. officer USPHS, various cities, Alaska, 1963-67; chief medicine USPHS, Mt. Edgecumbe, Alaska, 1970-71; practice medicine specializing in internal medicine Sitka, Alaska, 1971—; affiliate faculty mem. Advanced Cardiac Life Support, Alaska Heart Assn., 1979—; pres. Sitka Community Hosp. Med. staff, 1976-77. Pres. Alaska Heart Assn., 1979—; actor Baranof Little Theater, Sitka, 1976-83; singer Sitka Community Chorus. Named winner Islands Community Coll. Debating Pub. Forum, Sitka, 1983; poetry contest winner Southeast Alaska State Fair, 1983. Mem. ACP, AMA, Alaska Med. Assn., Sitka-Mt. Edgecumbe Med. Assn., Internat. Soc. for Philosophical Enquiry, Triple Nine Soc. Republican. Episcopalian. Lodges: Moose, Elks. Avocations: hunting, fishing, singing, Biblical studies. Home: 311 Erler St Sitka AK 99835 Office: Box 58 Sitka AK 99835

LUND, GERALD NIELS, school administrator, religious educator; b. Fountain Green, Utah, Sept. 12, 1939; s. Jewell Grover and Mary Evelyn (Mortenson) L.; m. Retta Lynn Stanard, June 5, 1963; children: Cynthia, Julie, Gerald S., Steven, Lori, Rebecca, Matthew. BA, Brigham Young U., 1965, MS, 1969; postgrad., Pepperdine U., 1970-72. Tchr. Latter Day Saints Ch. Ednl. System, Salt Lake City, 1965-74, curriculum writer, 1974-78, dir. curriculum, 1978-81, dir. instrn., 1981-83, dir. curriculum and instrn., 1983-86, zone adminstr., 1986—; lectr. Brigham Young U., Provo, Utah, 1978—, tour dir. to Middle East and Europe, 1977—. Author: The Coming of the Lord, 1971, This is Your World, 1973, One in Thine Hand, 1981, The Alliance, 1983, Leverage Point, 1985; numerous articles. Served with USAR, 1968-74. Recipient Excellence in Teaching award Brigham Young U., 1985. Home: 1097 E 1500 S Bountiful UT 84010 Office: Ch Ednl System 50 E N Temple St 9th Floor Salt Lake City UT 84150

LUND, STEVE, agronomist, research administrator; b. Exeland, Wis., Dec. 3, 1923; s. Robert Henry and Annie Belle (McHenry) L.; m. Gracemary Henrietta Bernskoetter, Jan. 29, 1946; children: Steve, John R., Thomas A., Cynthia M., Lisa A. BS, Clemson Coll., 1949; MS, U. Wis., 1951, PhD, 1953. Extension agronomist Clemson Coll., 1953-54; asst. research specialist Rutgers U., New Brunswick, N.J., 1954-57, assoc. research specialist, 1957-62, research prof., 1962-75, chmn. dept. soils and crops, 1971-75, prof. emeritus, 1975—; supt. and prof. Oreg. State U., Columbia Basin Agrl. Research Ctr., Pendleton, 1975-85; prof. emeritus Oreg. State U., Pendleton, 1985—. Contbr. articles to profl. jours. Served to 1st sgt. U.S. Army, 1943-46. Mem. Crop Sci. Soc. Am., Am. Soc. Agronomy, Western Soc. Crop Sci., Am. Phytopathology Soc., Sigma Xi, Alpha Zeta, Phi Kappa Phi, Phi Eta Sigma. Club: Pendleton Country. Lodge: Rotary. Avocations: golf, skiing. Home: 1201 SW 23d Pendleton OR 97801 Office: Columbia Basin Agrl Research 1201 SW 23d St Pendleton OR 97801

LUNDBERG, ERIC GWYNN, police officer, lawyer; b. Provo, Utah, Oct. 25, 1948; s. Lynne Jay and Elaine (Gwynn) L.; m. Susan W. Randall, May 17, 1969; children: Jennifer Elaine, Larry Jason, Jessica Mary. BS, San Jose State U., 1972; cert. No. Calif. Peace Officers Acad. (1st in class), 1975; M in Pub. Adminstrn., Golden Gate U., 1980; JD, U. of the Pacific, 1984. Bar: Calif. 1984. Truck driver Los Angeles Herald Examiner, 1968-69; research asst. Water Quality Control Bd., State Calif., 1973-74; field biologist fisheries Calif. Dept. Fish and Game, 1973-74; police officer City of Richmond, Calif., 1974-85; assoc. firm Archer, McComas & Lageson, Walnut Creek, Calif., 1984—; traffic investigator Richmond Police Dept., 1978-81, crime scene investigator, 1981-85, mem. underwater search and rescue team, 1977. Editorialist West County Times, 1983—. Advisor Golden Empire Council Boy Scouts Am. Recipient Triple Gold medals Calif. Police Olympics, 1976, Chiefs Commendation, Richmond Police Chief, 1979. Mem. Fed. Bar Assn., Calif. State Bar, Solano County Bar Assn., Contra Costa County Bar Assn., Am. Trial Lawyers Assn., Calif. Young Lawyers Assn. Office: Archer McComas & Lageson 2033 N Main St Suite 800 Walnut Creek CA 94596 Office: 1299 Newell Hill Pl Walnut Creek CA 94596

LUNDBERG, MERLE FRANKLIN, city official; b. Cedar Rapids, Iowa, May 23, 1926; s. Carl Oscar and Addie Lena (Reed) L.; B.S., U. Calif., Berkeley, 1950, M.B.A., 1956; m. Patricia Leslie, July 12, 1953; children—Michael Allen, Jeffrey Brian, James Robert, John Eric. Auditor, Haskins & Sells, C.P.A.'s, Los Angeles, 1952-57; asst. controller Earle C. Anthony, Inc., Los Angeles, 1957-60; sec.-treas. So. Calif. Water Co., Los Angeles, 1960-70; acctg. cons., Los Angeles, 1971-72; controller City of Beverly Hills (Calif.), 1972-75; dir. fin. Irvine (Calif.) Ranch Water Dist., 1975-77; dir. fin. City of Manhattan Beach (Calif.), 1977—. Troop treas. Boy Scouts Am., 1964-66, troop com. chmn., 1966-68; tribe chief Indian Y Guides, 1973-74; bd. mgrs. Wayfarers Chapel Portuguese Bend, Calif., 1964-84, chmn. bd., 1979-84; bd. dirs. Centinela-South Bay Credit Union, 1983—, chmn. bd., 1987—. Served with USNR, 1944-46. C.P.A., Calif. Mem. Am. Inst. C.P.A.'s, Calif. Soc. C.P.A.'s, Govt. Fin. Officers Am., Calif. Soc. Mcpl. Fin. Officers (bd. dirs. 1983-86). Republican. Mem. New Jerusalem Ch. Am. and Can. Office: City of Manhattan Beach 1400 Highland Ave Manhattan Beach CA 90266

LUNDE, DONALD THEODORE, physician; b. Milw., Mar. 2, 1937; m. Marilynn Krick; children: Montgomery, Christopher, Glenn, Evan, Bret. BA with distinction, Stanford U., 1958, MA in Psychology, 1964, MD, 1966. Diplomate Nat. Bd. Med. Examiners. Ward psychologist Palo Alto (Calif.) VA Hosp., 1965-66, chief resident in psychiatry, 1969-70, assoc. chief tng. and research sect., 1970-72, acting chief tng. and research sect., 1971-72; intern in internal medicine Palo Alto/Stanford Hosp., 1966-67; resident in psychiatry Stanford (Calif.) U. Sch. Medicine, 1967-69, instr. psychiatry, 1969-70, asst. prof. psychiatry, 1970-75, dir. med. sch. edn. in psychiatry, 1971-74, clin. assoc. prof. psychiatry, 1978—; staff physician Atascadero (Calif.) State Hosp., 1968. Author books and articles in field. Served with USN, 1958-61. Fellow Am. Psychiat. Assn.; mem. Am. Coll. Forensic Psychiatry, Am. Psychiat. Assn., No. Calif. Psychiat. Soc., Phi Beta Kappa, Alpha Omega Alpha. Office: Stanford U 900 Welch Rd #400 Palo Alto CA 94304

LUNDEEN, ELAINE SUSAN, social worker; b. Beruit, Lebanon, Jan. 7, 1956; came to U.S., 1957; d. Glen Albert and Barbara (Redlick) L. AA, Fresno City Coll., 1979; BA in Psychology, U. Calif., Santa Cruz, 1981; MSW, San Francisco State U., 1985. Social work intern Star Lodge Drug and Alcohol Treatment Ctr., Scotts Valley, Calif., 1983; with employees assistance program NASA, Moffett Field, Calif., 1983-84; psychiat. social worker intern Cath. Social Services Children's Counseling Ctr., Santa Clara, Calif., 1984, Kaiser Permente-Psychiatry, Redwood City, Calif., 1984-85; psychiat. social worker San Benito County Mental Health, Hollister, Calif., 1985—; cons. San Benito County Schs., 1985—. Mem. Nat. Assn. Social Workers. Democrat. Avocations: windsurfing, hiking, crafts. Home: 106A Village Dr Aptos CA 95003 Office: San Benito County Mental Health 471 Fourth St Hollister CA 95023

LUNDELL, WILLIAM GROBE, computer scientist executive; b. San Antonio, Tex., May 8, 1947; s. Virgil Vern and Betty Jane (Thorn) L.; 1 child, Hilary Katherine; m. Mary Jane Gibson, July 26, 1985. B.S.E.E., Stanford U., 1970, M.S.E.E., 1971. Electronics engr. Watkins-Johnson, Palo Alto, Calif., 1971-74; sr. application engr. Sci. Micro Systems, Sunnyvale, Calif., 1975-77; elec. cons. MicroComm, Santa Clara, Calif., 1977-79; sr. adv. engr. Shugart Assocs., Santa Clara, 1979-80; sr. project engr. Advanced Tech. Labs., Bellevue, Wash., 1980-83; v.p. research and devel. Applied Computer Scis., Kirkland, Wash., 1983-86; sr. project engr. Abbott Research, Bothell, Wash., 1986—; owner, cons. MicroComm., Kirkland, 1980—. Dir. disaster action ARC, Palo Alto, Calif., 1973-75, instr. first aid, 1974-76, dir. communications, 1974-78. Mem. Am. Mgmt. Assn., Profl. Engring. Soc., IEEE, N.W. Computing Soc., Mensa. Home: 5225 279th Ave NE Redmond WA 98053 Office: Microcomm 132 Central Way Kirkland WA 98033

LUNDEN, SAMUEL EUGENE, architect; b. Chgo., July 14, 1897; s. Albert Axel and Christina Eugenia (Erickson) L.; m. Leila Burton Allen, Mar. 13, 1925; children: Alice Marie, Robert Allen, Ardelle Leila. Student, Calif. Inst. Tech., Pasadena, 1918; SB in Architecture, MIT, 1921. Mem. Am. Students Reconstrn. Unit, Verdun, France, 1921; traveled and studied architecture in Europe, 1921, 51, 61, 68; asso. with office Cram & Ferguson, Boston, 1921-27; commenced practice of architecture in Los Angeles, 1928; partner Lunden, Hayward & O'Connor, 1949-57, Samuel E. Lunden-Joseph L. Johnson (architects), Los Angeles, 1960-78; cons. architect Lyon Assocs., Inc., Los Angeles, 1978-83; prin. Samuel E. Lunden FAIA Cons. Architect, 1983—. Author: Community Development Through an Exposition for Los Angeles, 1944; projects include Pacific Coast Stock Exchange (declared heritage cultural monument 1979), 1929; co-architect: interiors of St. Vincent de Paul Ch., 1928 (declared Heritage Cultural Monument 1978), Edward L. Doheny Meml. Library, U. So. Calif., 1932; cons. architect Allan Hancock Biol. Research Found. Bldg.; architect residence halls, U. So. Calif., Hosp. Good Samaritan Med. Center, Los Angeles, 1943-73, City Hall South, Civic Center, Los Angeles, 1954, master plan, Temple Urban Renewal Project, Los Angeles, 1958; Las Palmas Sch. Girls, Probation Dept. County Los Angeles, 1959; co-architect: Harbor Police Sta, City Los Angeles, 1961, Western Fed. Bldg.; complete modernization, 1964; cons. architect: VA Hosp, Phoenix, 1948; master plans and design sch. bldgs. Los Angeles Unified Sch. Dist; co-architect: master plans and design Univ. Ctr., Calif. State U. at Fullerton, 1975; master plans and design sch. bldgs. Vets. Meml. Regional County Park, County Los Angeles, Sylmar, Calif., 1976, Temple Israel, Hollywood, Calif., Heritage Cultural Monument, 1978; mem. planning commn. master plans and design sch. bldgs. Manhattan Beach, 1942-43. Bd. govs. Town Hall Calif., 1955-60, 62-68, pres., 1965, hon. life gov.; vice chmn. Citizens Traffic, Transp. Com., Los Angeles Area, 1954-55; mem. Am. Arbitration Assn., 1953—, Los Angeles adv. council, 1967-75; hon. sec. Mass. Inst. Tech., Alumni Assn., mem. alumni fund bd., 1967-70, mem. corp. devel. com., 1965—. Recipient first prize Am. Hosp. Assn. competition for design small community hosp. and med. ctr., 1945; certificate merit So. Calif. chpt. AIA; Town Hall award, 1960; Beaver award MIT, 1962; Marshall B. Dalton award, 1980; Kemper award AIA, 1963. Mem. AIA (v.p. 1945-47, pres. So. Calif. chpt. 1942-43, mem. Coll. Fellows 1945, dir. Calif. council 1965), Los Angeles Area C. of C. Clubs: M.I.T. of So. Calif. (pres. 1955), Life Assos. (U. So. Calif.); California (Los Angeles). Inventor conductive pad and system for discharging static charges for hosp. operating rooms. Home: 6205 Via Colinita Rancho Palos Verdes CA 90274

LUNDER, DENNIS ARNE, sales training executive, instructor; b. Sioux Falls, S.D., July 1, 1943; s. Arne C. and Avis O. (Rikansrud) L.; m. Bonnie L. Lommen, Aug. 10, 1969; 1 child, Lisa. BS in Math. and Physics, Augustana Coll., Sioux Falls, S.D., 1965; MS in Computer Sci., U. Okla., 1968; PhD in Math. Edn., U. Denver, 1978. Math. tchr. Fremont (Calif.) Unified High Sch., 1968-78; dir. ednl. tng. Fairchild C&I, Mountain View, Calif., 1978-81; corp. tng. mgr. North Star Computers, San Leandro, Calif., 1981-82; ednl. mgr. Fortune Systems, Belmont, Calif., 1982-84; nat. sales tng. dir. Epson Am., Torrance, Calif., 1984—; computer cons. Ohlone Coll., Fremont, 1982; math. and computer instr. various colls. Author: 101 Basic Games, 1975. Recipient Outstanding Young Educator award, 1975; HEW fellow U. Okla., 1967-68. Mem. Am. Mgmt. Assn. Republican. Lutheran. Avocations: raquetball, skiing, computers, teaching. Home: 4495 Emerald St Torrance CA 90503 Office: Epson Am Nat Sales Tng 2780 Lomita Blvd Torrance CA 90505

LUNDERVILLE, GERALD PAUL, English as second language educator; b. Springfield, Mass., Feb. 22, 1941; s. Leon Albert and Florence Marion (Jolivette) L.; m. Martha Ann Sumner, Mar. 26, 1966 (div. Aug. 1971); m. Bony Lek, June 30, 1984. BA cum laude, U. N.H., 1963; MA, Middlebury Coll., 1969, U. Rochester, 1973; postgrad., Calif. State U., Long Beach, 1981-84, 86—. Instr. Spanish Berwick Acad., South Berwick, Maine, 1963-64; tchr. French, Spanish Barnstable High Sch., Hyannis, Mass., 1967-68; instr. Spanish Cape Cod Community Coll., West Barnstable, Mass., 1968-71; tchr. French, Spanish Stevens High Sch. Annex, Claremont, N.H., 1973-74; tchr. English Centro de Estudios Norteamericanos, Valencia, Spain, 1974-75; dept. head fgn. langs. Merrimack High Sch., N.H., 1975-80; tchr. Spanish El

Camino Coll., Torrance, Calif., 1980-85; tchr. English as second lang. Wilson High Sch., Long Beach, Calif., 1980—. Contbr. articles to Am. Atheist Mag. Sec. Merrimack Tchrs. Assn., 1977-80; active Long Beach Area Citizens Peace, 1982—, Animal Protection Inst. Am., Sacramento., 1983—. Served with U.S. Army, 1964-67, Vietnam. Mem. ACLU, Nat. Assn. Tchrs. Spanish and Portuguese, NEA, Modern and Classical Lang. Assn. of So. Calif., Tchrs. of English as a Second Lang., Merrimack Tchrs. Assn. (sec. 1977-80), Lambda Pi. Avocations: cooking, tennis, guitar, reading, traveling. Home: 1740 Washington St Long Beach CA 90805

LUNDFELT, CHARLES EDWARD, fire chief, educator; b. N.Y.C., Mar. 7, 1944; s. Charles Edward and Marie Clotilde (Reilly) L.; m. Abigail Jane Cheney, Aug. 21, 1966 (div. 1973); 1 child, Christian August; m. 2d, Cathi Laird Carr, Mar. 9, 1973. Student, U. Alaska, 1965, Tanana Valley Community Coll., 1979—. Cert. paramedic Los Angeles County; cert. fire fighter program instr., Alaska. Owner, supt. Dunrite Constrn. Systems, Fairbanks, Alaska, 1974-80; fireman, paramedic Clear AFS Fire Dept., Anderson, Alaska, 1980-81; fire chief Chena Goldstream Fire Dept., Fairbanks, 1978-81; fire chief North Star Vol. Fire Dept., Fairbanks, 1981—; fire service instr. State of Alaska Dept. Edn., Fairbanks, 1981—. Pres., Greater Fairbanks Headstart Assn., 1974-75. Served to sgt. U.S. Army, 1966-69, Vietnam. Mem. Alaska Fire Chiefs' Assn. (sec.), Internat. Assn. Five Service Instrs., Tanana Valley Community Coll. Fire Sci. Adv. Bd. Democrat. Quaker. Author: (procedure manual) North Star Volunteer Fire Department, 1983. Home: PO Box 81349 College AK 99708 Office: North Star Vol Fire Dept SR 70116 Fairbanks AK 99701

LUNDGREN, JAMES REINHOLD, civil engineer, transportation association executive; b. Vancouver, B.C., Jan. 11, 1945; came to U.S., 1968; s. Nels Reinhold and Agnes May (Fulton) L.; m. Angela Andrian Plaza, Nov. 24, 1973; children: Steven, Douglas, Mary. BS, U. B.C., 1968; MS, U. Ill., 1970. Registered profl. engr., Que. Project engr., sr. project engr. Can. Nat. Rys., Montreal, 1971-76; mgr. FAST project Assn. Am. R.R.s, Pueblo, Colo., 1976-77, mgr. track research div., Chgo., 1977-78, dir. research, test ops., Pueblo, 1978-82, exec. dir. transp. test ctr., 1982-83, asst. v.p. research, test dept. transp. test ctr., 1983—. Contbr. articles to profl. jours.; editor, Technical Proceedings FAST Engineering Conference, 1981. Recipient scholarship Union Carbide Can., Ltd., Vancouver, 1963; Lafarge Cement Can., Ltd., U. B.C. 1967; Golder, Brauner Assocs., 1967; Nat. Research Council Canada, 1968. Mem. ASME, Am. Ry. Engring. Assn., Roadmasters and Maintenance of Way Assn., Car Dept. Officers Assn., Ry. Fuel and Operating Officers Assn., Pueblo C. of C. (hon. dir. 1982—). Presbyterian. Home: 1138 Bluestem Pueblo CO 81001 Office: Assn Am Railroads Transp Test Ctr PO Box 11130 Pueblo CO 81001

LUNDGREN, SUSAN ELAINE, social science educator, college program director, counselor; b. Martinez, Calif., May 31, 1949; d. Elmer Alfred and Shirley (Bright) L.; 1 child, Alicia Hadiya. AA, Diablo Valley Coll., 1969; BA in English, San Francisco State U., 1971, MA in Counseling, 1975; EdD, U. San Francisco, 1983. Instr. and counselor Diablo Valley Coll., Pleasant Hill, Calif., 1976-86; instr. and coordinator C.C.C.C. Dist., Martinez, Calif., 1986—; instr. Diablo Valley Coll., Pleasant Hill, Calif., 1982, dir. faculty, women's ctr., 1983-85; lectr. grad. career devel. dept. John F. Kennedy U., Orinda, Calif., 1984-85. Sec., bd. dirs. Rape Crisis Ctr. of C.C.C., Concord, Calif. Named participant in leadership devel. inst. AAUW and Nat. Assn. Community Colls., 1983. Mem. NOW (pres. and past pres. East Bay chpt., bd. dirs. Calif. chpt.), Calif. Advs. for Re-entry Edn., I-Pride, Eureka Consortium (conf. speaker 1986—). Avocations: travel, photography, camping, hiking. Home: 2015 Cedar Berkeley CA 94709 Office: Diablo Valley Coll 321 Golf Club Rd Pleasant Hill CA 94523

LUNDIN, ANN FRANCES, chemist, medical technologist; b. Dallas, Pa., Sept. 22, 1941; d. Walter Stanley and Frances Evelyn (Sholes) Black; m. Lars Norman Lundin, June 10, 1967; children: Lori, Terri, Wendy. BS in Chemistry, Coll. Misericordia, 1963; MS in Chemistry, Villanova U., 1967. Chem. asst. Worcester Found. for Exptl. Biology, Shrewsbury, Mass., 1963-67; research chemist Dow Chem. Co., Wayland, Mass., 1967-71; chem. technologist Children's Hosp., Boston, 1975-80, VA Med. Ctr., San Francisco, 1980-83; quality control chemist Nobel Sci., Alexandria, Va., 1983-84; chemist Nat. Health Labs., Englewood, Colo., 1984—; cons. sci. projects Randolph Mass., 1975-80,. Sec. Jr. League of Swedish Charitable Soc., Boston, 1970-72. Grantee NSF, 1959. Mem. Am. Chem. Soc. Democrat. Roman Catholic. Club: Gen. Fedn. Womens. Lodge: Order of Eastern Star, Ind. Order Vikings. Avocations: arts and crafts, photography, model railroading. Home: 11442 E Adriatic Pl Aurora CO 80014 Office: Nat Health Labs S Alton Way Englewood CO 80111

LUNDIN, RICHARD ALLEN, retired career military officer, federal government administrator; b. Holyoke, Mass., Feb. 19, 1937; s. Gustav Regner and Frances (Gaston) L.; m. Dolores Segovia, Nov. 19, 1962; children: Valerie Frances, Jeanie Elizabeth. AA, Am. River Jr. Coll., 1970; BA, Golden Gate U., 1973, MBA, 1976; diploma, Command and Gen. Staff Coll. U.S. Army, 1985. Cert. tchr., Calif.; instr. cert. U.S. Army. Commd. USAF, 1954, advanced through grades to lt. col., 1977; with res. USAR, Calif., 1962—; with Gen. Services Adminstrn. USN, USAF, Tex. and Calif.; cons. Family Fin. Planning Group, Benicia, Calif., 1982—; instr. USAR, 1985—; adj. profl. Golden Gate U., San Francisco, 1978—; cons. contracts, mktg., edn. Asst. chmn. Waterfront Planning Commn., Benicia, Calif. 1982-84; mem. Utility User Tax Com., Benicia, 1984; treas. Sister Cities Com., Benecia, 1982-86; active Calif. Rep. Assembly. Recipient Sister Cities Com. Appreciation award Mayor of Tula, Hidalgo, Mex., 1985, Benicia City Appreciation award, Mayor of Benicia, 1984. Mem. Res. Officers Assn. U.S. (pres.), Nat. Contracts Mgmt. Assn. (mem. chmn.), Golden Gate U. Alumni Assn., Benicia C. of C., VFW. Republican. Roman Catholic. Club: Yacht (Benicia). Lodge: K.C.

LUNDQUIST, VIOLET ELVIRA, agency administrator; b. Bristol, Conn., Jan. 28, 1912; d. Otto Nimrod and Mabel Elvira (Lindeen) Ebb; diploma music Augustana Coll., Rock Island, Ill., 1932; postgrad. mgmt. systems U. Mo., 1969; m. Vernon Arthur Lundquist, May 14, 1935; children—Karen Ebb, Jane Christine. Tchr. music, public schs., Olds, Iowa, 1932-35; editor Warsaw (Mo.) Times, 1935-45, Anthon (Iowa) Herald, 1945-57; field dir. Iowa Heart Assn., Des Moines, 1957-66; exec. dir. S.E. Iowa Community Action Program, Burlington, 1966-74; adminstrn. dir. S.E. Ariz. Govts. Orgn. Community Services, Bisbee, Ariz., 1975-77; statewide advocate developmentally disabled adults, 1977—; adminstr. Arizona City Med. Ctr., part-time, 1979-80; adminstr. Dist. V Council on Devel. Disabilities, 1980-87. Bd. dirs. Cen. Ariz. Health Systems Agy., 1979—, chmn., 1986—; chmn. Arizona City Home and Property Owners Assn., 1979-82; bd. dirs. Ariz. State Health Planning Council, 1986—; mem. Ariz. Statewide Health Coordinating Council, 1986—, Ariz. Dist. V Human and Legal Rights Com. Recipient Carol Lane award Nat. Safety Council, 1956, 1st place award Nat. Fedn. Press Women, 1952, 53, 55, 57; USPHS scholar, Columbia U., summers 1963, 64; cert. vocat. rehab. adminstr. Mem. Nat. Soc. Community Action Program Dirs. (dir. 1966-75), Ariz. Fedn. Press Women. Lutheran. Clubs: Zonta (area dir. 1984-86), Women of Moose. Home and Office: 609 W Cochise St PO Box 2265 Arizona City AZ 85223

LUNDSTROM, JEAN LOUISE, health care facility executive; b. Houston; d. Floyd Cornelius and Lois (Swinney) Tucker; m. Paul Hearell (dec.); 1 child, Stuart. RN, Saddleback Community Coll., 1975; BSN, Calif. State U., Fullerton, 1977, M in Pub. Adminstrn., 1979, PhN, 1979. Adminstr. Saddleback Hosp., Laguna Hills, Calif., 1968-83, Meml. Hosp. Ptnrs. in Care, Huntington Beach, Calif., 1983-84; pres. Saddlebay Health Enterprises, Dana Point, Calif., 1985—; founder, council pres. Orange County Council Home Health Agys., 1984-86; hostess local TV talk show "Healthwrap," 1986-87. Author: (symphony) Flight of the Whale, 1986. Mem. cast containment Gov.'s Commn., Sacramento, 1986; com. mem. Congl. Adv. Com. on Health and Aging, Washington, 1986. Mem. Calif. Assn. Health Services at Home (pres. 1984—).

LUNDSTROM, ROBERT JAMES, cardiologist, laboratory administrator; b. Berkeley, Calif., Apr. 15, 1945; s. James Willard and Erma (Capps) L.; m. Kathryne Ann Stoltz, Sept. 20, 1967 (div. June 1972); m. Mary Elizabeth Twieg, May 19, 1984. AB in Psychology, U. Calif., Berkeley, 1967; MD, UCLA, 1972. Diplomate Am. Bd. Internal Medicine, Am. Bd. Cardiovascular Diseases. Intern San Francisco Gen. Hosp., 1972-73; resident in medicine Kaiser Found. Hosp., San Francisco, 1973-75, dir. cardiac lab., 1981—; fellow in cardiology Pacific Presbyn. Med. Ctr., San Francisco, 1975-77; chief of cardiology Kaiser Found. Hosp., South San Francisco, Calif., 1977-81; sr. physician Kaiser Permanente Med. Group, San Francisco, 1979—. Fellow Council on Clin. Cardiology of Am. Heart Assn., Am. Coll. Cardiology. Democrat. Avocations: amateur radio, automobile restoration, woodworking. Home: 1347 Montero Ave Burlingame CA 94010 Office: Kaiser Permanente Med Group 2200 O'Farrell San Francisco CA 94115

LUNGERHAUSEN, RICHARD EARLE, data processing executive; b. Marinette, Wis., Feb. 14, 1952; s. Richard Thomas and Anne Louise (Earle) L.; m. Jean Ann Kennedy, Aug. 22, 1981. BS in Computer Sci., U. Mich., 1974; MBA in Fin., U. Colo., 1982. Programmer Inst. Social Research, Ann Arbor, Mich., 1974-75, programmer, analyst, 1975-77; system programmer Pub. Service Co., Denver, 1977-79, data processing planning analyst, 1980-81; prin., cons. Comcon Assocs., Denver, 1981-82; pres. Comcon Assocs., Golden, Colo., 1982—; lectr. Morino Assocs. Inc., Vienna, Va., 1984—. Mem. Ind. Computer Cons. Assn., Golden C. of C., Beta Gamma Sigma. Republican. Avocations: photography, back-packing, golfing, basketball, tennis. Office: Comcon Assocs Inc 910 12th St Golden CO 80401

LUNGREN, DANIEL EDWARD, congressman; b. Long Beach, Calif., Sept. 22, 1946; s. John Charles and Lorain Kathleen (Youngberg) L.; m. Barbara Kolls, Aug. 2, 1969; children: Jeffrey Edward, Kelly Christine, Kathleen Marie. A.B. cum laude, Notre Dame U., 1968; postgrad., U. So. Calif. Law Sch., 1968-69; J.D., Georgetown U., 1971. Bar: Calif. 1972. Staff asst. Sen. George Murphy, Sen. William Brock, 1969-71; spl. asst. to co-chmn. Republican Nat. Com.; dir. spl. programs Rep. Nat. Com., 1971-72; asso. firm Ball, Hunt, Hart, Brown & Baerwitz, Long Beach, 1971-78; partner Ball, Hunt, Hart, Brown & Baerwitz, 1978; mem. 96th-97th Congresses from 34th, 98th-99th Congresses from 42d Calif. Dist.; Mem. Rep. State Central Com. Calif., from 1974. Bd. dirs. Long Beach chpt. ARC; bd. dirs. Boy's Club. Recipient Good Samaritan award Los Angeles Council Mormon Chs., 1976. Republican. Roman Catholic. Office: 555 E Ocean Blvd Suite 505 Long Beach CA 90802 Office: 2440 Rayburn House Office Bldg Washington DC 20515

LUNIEWSKI, ALLEN WILLIAM, computer scientist; b. Pitts., Aug. 5, 1952; s. Alphonse and Helen (Ruszkowski) L.; m. Patsy Ann Fenerin, Nov. 19, 1983. BS in Math., Carnegie-Mellon U., 1974; SM in Computer Sci., Elect. Engring., MIT, 1979, PhD in Computer Sci., 1979. Devel. mgr. Xerox Corp., Palo Alto, Calif., 1979-86; research staff mem. IBM, San Jose, Calif., 1986—. Mem. Assn. Computing Machinery. Roman Catholic. Home: 1443 Falcon Ave Sunnyvale CA 94087 Office: IBM 650 Harry Rd San Jose CA 95120-6099

LUNINE, JONATHAN IRVING, planetary scientist, educator; b. N.Y.C., June 26, 1959. BS magna cum laude, U. Rochester, 1980; MS, Calif. Inst. Tech., 1983, PhD, 1985. Research assoc. U. Ariz., Tucson, 1984-86, asst. prof., 1986—; vis. asst. prof. U. Calif., Los Angeles, 1986; lectr. Flandrau Planetarium, Tucson, 1985, Sierra Vista (Ariz.) Astronomy Club, 1985. Contbr. articles to profl. jours. Mem. Am. Astronomical Soc., Am. Geophys. Union, Sigma Xi. Club: So. Ariz. Hiking (guide 1986—). Avocation: hiking. Office: U Ariz Lunar and Planetary Lab Tucson AZ 85721

LUNNEY, NANCY KAYE, non-profit organization executive; b. N.Y.C., June 25, 1940; d. Eugene and Muriel Kaye; m. David John Lunney, Aug. 26, 1963 (div. 1983); children: Elizabeth Andrea, Jennifer Alexandra. BA, NYU, 1962; MA, Pepperdine U., 1976. Free lance musical dir., vocal coach N.Y.C. and Los Angeles, 1962-77; psychotherapist Esalen Inst., Big Sur, Calif., 1977—, program dir., trustee, 1981—, pres., 1982-86; guest faculty Cornell U., Ithaca, N.Y., 1985—. Office: Esalen Inst Big Sur CA 93920

LUNNEY, ROBERT F., police chief. Chief of police City of Edmonton, Alta., Can. Office: Office of Chief of Police, 9620 103A Ave, Edmonton, AB Canada T5H 0H7 *

LUNT, OWEN RAYNAL, educator, biologist; b. El Paso, Tex., Apr. 8, 1921; s. Owen and Velma (Jackson) L.; m. Helen Hickman, Aug. 8, 1953; children: David, Carol, Janet. B.A. in Chemistry, 1947, Ph.D. in Agronomy, 1951. Mem. faculty UCLA, 1951—, prof. plant nutrition, 1964-72, prof. biology, 1972—, acting chmn. dept. biophysics, 1965-70; dir. Lab. Biomed. and Environ. Scis., 1968—. Served with USN, 1944-46. Fellow Am. Soc. Agronomy, Soil Sci. Soc. Am.; mem. Am. Soc. Plant Physiologists, Internat. Soc. Soil Sci., AAAS, Am. Nuclear Soc. (Los Angeles chpt.), Sigma Xi. Research in soil chemistry, fertility, plant physiology. Home: 1200 Roberto Ln Los Angeles CA 90077 Office: UCLA 900 Veteran Ave Los Angeles CA 90024

LUNTZ, RICHARD DAVID, medical device manufacturer; b. Los Angeles, July 19, 1940; s. David and Delia May (Sheehan) L.; m. Pamela Mae Evans, Sept. 5, 1964; children: Katharine Diane, Kurt Evan. AA, Pasadena City Coll., 1962; BSEE, Calif. State U., Los Angeles, 1968; MSME, U. Utah, 1972. Head system devel. Terra Tek Inc., Salt Lake City, 1970-74; assoc. dir. biomed. system lab. U. Utah, Salt Lake City, 1974-76; v.p. mfg. Motion Control Inc., Salt Lake City, 1976—, also bd. dirs.; adj. prof. surgery, adj. prof. mech. engring. U. Utah, 1975—. Patentee in field; contbr. numerous articles to profl. jours. Recipient Eagle Scout award Boy Scouts Am., San Gabriel, Calif., 1955. Mem. IEEE, ASME (various offices local program com. 1973-76), Soc. Exptl. Stress Analysis, Sigma Xi, Sigma Epsilon, Pi Tau Sigma. Republican. Avocations: stained glass, whitewater canoeing, hunting, camping, fishing.

LURIE, ROBERT A. (BOB LURIE), professional sports team executive. Businessman; owner San Francisco Giants (Nat. League) baseball team, 1976—, now chmn. Office: San Francisco Giants Candlestick Park San Francisco CA 94124 *

LURIE, RON, Mayor, city of Las Vegas, Nev., 1987—. Office: Office of the Mayor 400 E Stewart Ave Las Vegas NV 89101 *

LUST, PETER, JR., microwave engineer; b. Montreal, Que., Can., Apr. 21, 1960; came to U.S., 1975; s. Peter Clark and Evelyn (Heymanson) L.; m. Gloria Ruth Bingle, Apr. 5, 1985. Student, Lowry Tech. Tng. Ctr., Community Coll. A.F., Albuquerque, USAF Acad. Enlisted USAF, 1979, resigned, 1982; computer meterologist Electro Rent, Burbank, Calif., 1982-84; microwave engr. Transco Products, Camarillo, Calif., 1984—; prin. Electronic Note Enterprises, Port Hueneme, Calif., 1984—; cons. in field, Port Hueneme, 1984—. Recipient Technol. award USAF, 1980, Discovery award NASA, 1987. Republican. Club: Channel Islands Health (Port Hueneme). Avocations: hiking, swimming, making model airplanes. Office: Electronic Note Enterprises PO Box 460 Suite 16 Port Hueneme CA 93041

LUSTECK, CLAUDIA ANN DUFEK, curriculum specialist; b. Phoenix, Sept. 2, 1948; d. John Allen and Teresa Magdolin (Lazok) Dufek; m. Ronald James Lusteck, Nov. 30, 1968; 1 son, Ryan Alexander. BS, U. Ariz., 1971; MEd, 1974. High sch. tchr. Tucson Unified Sch. Dist., 1971-85; curriculum specialist Pueblo High Sch., Tucson, 1985—; tchr. adult edn. program Pima (Ariz.) Community Coll., 1974-75; workshop facilitator; lectr. in field. Author: Activity Guide for Guide to Good Food, 1982, Activity Guide for Housing Decisions, 1983. Mem. exec. bd. Tucson Boy's Chorus Parent's Assn., 1985—. Named Ariz. Tchr. of Yr., Ariz. Home Econs. Assn., 1981. Mem. Assn. for Supervision and Curriculum Devel., Phi Delta Kappa, Pi Lambda Theta. Office: Pueblo High Sch 3500 S 12th Ave Tucson AZ 85713

LUSTED, HUGH SHERBORNE, auditory physiologist, real estate developer; b. San Francisco, Mar. 18, 1953; s. Lee Browning and Winifred (Chamberlin) L; m. Anne Rodney, May 1, 1982 (div. Feb. 1986). BS, Stanford U., 1975; PhD, Stanford U. Sch. Medicine, 1980. Auditory research asst. U. Oreg., Portland, 1976; engring. research asst. Stanford (Calif.) U., 1977080; surg. research assoc. Stanford U., 1982—; post doctoral fellow U. London, 1981-82; auditory research cons., Stanford U., 1978—; owner real estate investment co., San Rafael, Calif., 1985—. Contbr. articles to profl. jours. Mem. AAAS, N.Y. Acad. Sci., Acoustical Soc. Am., European Neurosci. Assn., Assn. Research Otolaryngology, Fellowship of Friends (Renaissance, Calif.). Democrat. Methodist. Avocations: scuba diving, art and antique collecting, electronic music prodn. Office: Stanford U Sch Medicine ENT Div R-123 Stanford CA 94305

LUTER, JOHN, newsman, educator; b. Knoxville, Tenn., Jan. 17, 1919; s. John Thomas and Bertha Mae (Carver) L.; m. Mary Hickey, 1948 (dec.); 1 dau., Linda; m. Yvonne Spiegelberg, 1966 (div. 1971); m. Nan Hoyt Lawrence, 1974. B.A., St. Mary's U., Tex., 1939; postgrad. Coll. Law, St. Mary's U., 1939-42; fellow Time Inc, Sch. Advanced Internat. Studies, Washington, 1945. Reporter San Antonio Light, 1939-42, Washington Star, 1942-44; corr. Time mag., 1944-45; war corr. Time mag., Pacific, 1945; fgn. corr. Time and Life mags., Southeast Asia, 1945-46, Japan, 1946-47, Israel, 1948-49, Italy, 1949-54; asst. editor internat. edit. Life mag., 1954-56; reporter, writer CBS News, 1957-58; asso. editor Newsweek mag., 1958-61; radio news commentator stas. WQXR and QXR-FM Network, 1960-61; coordinator advanced internat. reporting program Columbia Grad. Sch. Journalism, 1961-72; dir. Maria Moors Cabot Prize Program, 1961-74; mem. profl. staff Bank St. Coll. Edn., 1973-74; prof., dir. journalism U. Hawaii, Honolulu, from 1974, now prof. and chmn. journalism dept. Adv. editor: Columbia Journalism Rev., 1961-72. Chmn. internat. relations com. N.Y.C. Protestant Council, 1968-71; chmn. adv. screening com. communications Sr. Fulbright Program, 1970-73; trustee Overseas Press Club Found., 1962-72, chmn., 1964-65; bd. dirs. UN Assn. N.Y., 1973-74; chmn. Honolulu Community Media Council, 1982-84. Mem. Assn. Edn. Journalism and Mass Communications, Assn. Schs. Journalism and Mass Communications, Honolulu Com. Fgn. Relations, Pacific and Asian Affairs Council, Sigma Delta Chi (mem. chpt. exec. council 1966-69), Japan Am. Soc. Clubs: Overseas Press (pres. N.Y.C. 1960-62), Honolulu Press, Outrigger Canoe. Home: 2442 Halekoa Dr Honolulu HI 96821 Office: U Hawaii 208 Crawford Hall 2550 Campus Rd Honolulu HI 96822

LUTHER, JOHN STAFFORD, biology educator, consultant; b. Los Angeles, April 5, 1943; s. John Andrew and Marcia (Stafford) L.; divorced; 1 son, David. BA, Beloit (Wis.) Coll., 1965; MA, Calif. State Coll., Hayward, 1968. Mem. faculty dept. biology Merritt Coll., Oakland, Calif., 1968-70; mem. faculty Coll. of Alameda (Calif.), 1970—, chmn. sci. and math. div., 1973-75; cons. Environ. Impacts Reports, 1972—; leader natural history trips, 1978—. Mem. Oakland (Calif.) Mus. Assn., 1972—; mem. Ednl. Use Adv. Com., East Bay Regional Park Dist., 1981—. Mem. Western Field Ornithologists (pres. 1978-81, dir. 1975—), Calif. Bird Records Com. (sec. 1976-81), Sierra Club, Nat. Audubon Soc., Am. Birding Assn., Golden Gate Audubon Soc., Nature Conservancy, Cooper Ornithol. Soc., Point Reyes Bird Obs. Contbr. articles to Western Birds; mem. editorial bd. Western Birds. Home: 6511 Exeter Dr Oakland CA 94611 Office: Coll of Alameda 555 Atlantic Ave Alameda CA 94501

LUTIN, DAVID LOUIS, real estate development and finance cons.; b. East Hartford, Conn., Apr. 18, 1919; s. Solomon and Esther (Newman) L.; A.B., Ohio No. U., 1946; M.B.A., Syracuse U., 1949; m. Dorothy Marmor, Dec. 3, 1944; children—Gary, Marnie (Mrs. George Wittig). Housing economist and field rep. HHFA, Washington, 1950-57; dir. urban renewal City of Brookline, Mass., 1957-58; cons. on urban renewal and housing Com. for Econ. Devel., N.Y.C., 1958-59; propr. David L. Lutin Assocs., real estate devel. and fin. cons., Rye, N.Y., 1959-73, Phoenix, 75—; v.p. real estate and mortgages Am. Bank and Trust Co., N.Y.C., 1973-75. Research assoc. Albert Farwell Bemis Found., M.I.T., 1951-52. Served to capt. AUS, 1942-46. Decorated Purple Heart. Mem. Am. Econ. Assn., Nat. Planning Assn., Mortgage Bankers Assn., Urban Land Inst., Am. Planning Assn., Am. Statis. Assn., Nat. Assn. Home Builders. Contbr. articles and reports on econs., housing and urban devel. to profl. jours. Home and office: 11419 N Century Ln Scottsdale AZ 85254

LUTSKY, SHELDON JAY, marketing consultant, writer; b. New Kensington, Pa., Jan. 13, 1943; s. Hyman I. and Rose S. (Schwartz) L.; B.S., Kent State U., 1967; postgrad. U. Colo., 1969-70. Chemist B.F. Goodrich, Akron, Ohio, 1966; with United Bank of Denver, 1968-75; founder Mountain States Ski Assn., pub. Mountain States Recreation, Denver, 1976-81; pres. Lutsky and Assocs., Denver, 1981—; instr. penny stocks Denver U. Bd. mem. Colo. 4-H Adv. Council. Recipient Burr Photog. Achievement award Kent State U., 1965. Mem. Denver C. of C., Denver Conv. Bur., Nat. Ski Writers Assn., Rocky Mountain Ski Writers Assn., Rocky Mountain Fin. Writers Assn. (pres. 1982-84). Developer Slope Scope, ski slope evaluation system. Home: 4807 S Zang Way Morrison CO 80465 Office: Lutsky & Assocs 2124 S Dayton St Denver CO 80231

LUTTRELL, MARY MILDRED, marketing management consultant; b. Kansas City, Mo., Oct. 19, 1946; d. Kryn T. and Mildred Miller (Smiser) Vyverberg; m. Richard LeGro Luttrell, May 29, 1982. BA, Purdue U., 1968; MSW, U. Calif., Berkeley, 1971. Counselor Eastfield Ctr., Campbell, Calif., 1968-69; with social service dept. Marin County (Calif.) Office Social Services, San Rafael, 1971-73; program advisor, therapist Mt. St. Joseph's, San Francisco, 1974-75; dir. Shalom Program, San Francisco, 1975-77; exec. dir. Lane Ctr., Sebastopol, Calif., 1977-81; owner Mgmt. Cons. Services, Santa Rosa, Calif., 1982—; instr. Sonoma State U., Rohnert Park, Calif., 1983, Santa Rosa Jr. Coll., 1984. Contbr. articles to profl. jours. Bd. dirs. Santa Rosa C. of C., 1986—, Vol. Ctr. of Sonoma County, Santa Rosa, 1985—. NIMH scholar, 1970. Office: Mgmt Cons Services 707 2d St Santa Rosa CA 95404

LUTVAK, MARK ALLEN, computer company marketing executive; b. Chgo., Feb. 9, 1939; s. Joseph Issac and Jeanette Nettie (Pollock) L.; B.S. in Elec. Engring., U. Mich., 1962; M.B.A., Wayne State U., Detroit, 1969; m. Gayle Helene Rotofsky, May 24, 1964; children—Jeffrey, Eric. Sales rep. IBM Corp., 1962-64; successively sales rep., product mktg. mgr., corp. product mgr. Burroughs Corp., Detroit, 1964-76; mgr. product mktg. Memorex Corp., Santa Clara, Calif., 1976-80, product program gen. mgr., 1980-81; dir. product mktg. Personal Computer div. Atari, Inc., Sunnyvale, Calif., 1981-83; dir. mktg., v.p. Durango Systems, San Jose, Calif., 1983-85; dir. mktg. ITTQUME Corp., San Jose, 1985—; prof. Applied Mgmt. Center, Wayne State U., 1967-72, Walsh U., Troy, Mich., 1974-76, West Valley Coll., Saratoga, Calif., 1977-78. Trustee, pres. brotherhood Temple Emanuel, San Jose, Calif., 1979-80. Mem. IEEE, Soc. Applied Math., Alpha Epsilon Pi. Home: 1364 Box Canyon Rd San Jose CA 95120

LUTZ, BARRY LAFEAN, astronomer; b. Windsor, Pa., Jan. 2, 1944; s. Ray Donald and Nina Capitola (Bull) L.; m. Karen Lee Witman, Sept. 3, 1966 (div. June 1981); m. Mary Susanna Maxwell, July 25, 1981. BS, Lebanon Valley Coll., 1965; NASA trainee, Princeton U., 1966-68, AM, 1967, PhD, 1968. Postdoctoral fellow Nat. Resource Council, Ottawa, Ont., Can., 1968-70; postdoctoral resident in astronomy Lick Obs. and U. Calif., Santa Cruz, 1970-71; sr. research assoc. SUNY, Stony Brook, 1971-77; astronomer Lowell Obs., Flagstaff, Ariz., 1977—; adj. asst. prof. SUNY, Stony Brook, 1971-74, adj. assoc. prof., 1974-81; adj. assoc. prof. physics Ariz. State U., Tempe, 1981-83, adj. prof. physics, 1983—; cons. Kitt Peak Nat. Obs., Tucson, 1973, Princeton U., N.J., 1974, Obs. de Meudon, France, 1979, U. Dijon, France, 1980; research com. NSF, 1972—. Contbr. articles to profl. jours. mem. Dem. County Com., Suffolk County, N.Y., 1972-80; nat. del. Dem. Midterm Conv., 1974. Research grantee NASA, 1975—. Mem. Am. Astron. Soc., Div. Planetary Scis., Astron. Soc. Pacific, Internat. Astron. Union, Sigma Xi. Home: 3330 Gillenwater Dr Flagstaff AZ 86001 Office: Lowell Obs Mars Hill Rd 1400 W Flagstaff AZ 86001

LUTZ, DAVID, psychologist; b. Denver, Sept. 20, 1953; s. Joseph Herbert and Eleanor Josephine (Canacari) L.; m. Ellen Scott McLean, Aug. 8, 1978; 1 child, Britton McLean. BA in Psychology and Sociology, U. Kans., 1975, MA in Psychology, 1978, PhD in Clin. Psychology, 1980. Therapist U. Kans. Psychol. Clinic, 1976-78; asst. instr. U. Kans., 1977-79; intern Vanderbilt-Peabody Internship in Profl. Psychology, 1979-80; assoc. prof. dept. psychology Calif. State U., San Bernardino, 1980—, supr. grad. students Community Counseling Ctr., 1980—, faculty cons. computer ctr., 1981-84, assoc. dean, 1984-86; therapist Inland Counties Family Learning Ctr., Grand Terrace, Calif., 1982—, Ctr. for Individual and Family Therapy, Colton, Calif., 1984—; Cons. Patton State Hosp., 1981-84, Omnitrans tranp. system, 1981-82, Behavior Mgmt. Cons., Inc. Contbr. articles to profl. jours. Active Social Sci. Research and Instrnl. Council, State of Calif., 1981-84;

active Univ. Planning and Adv. Council, Calif. State U., San Bernardino, 1983-84; senator Faculty Senate, Calif. State U., San Bernardino, 1983-86; bd.dirs. The Boys Club of San Bernardino, 1985-86. Mem. Am. Psychol. Assn. (mem. clin. psychology div., sec./treas. cons. psychology div. 1986—, research and sci. affairs com., psychologists in ind. practice), Assn. Advancement Psychology, Inland So. Caolf. Psychol. Assn., N.Am. Soc. for Psychology of Sport and Physical Activity, Western Psychol. Assn. Home: 6848 Rycroft Dr Riverside CA 92506 Office: Calif State U 5500 Univ Pkwy San Bernardino CA 92407

LUTZ, JOHN SHAFROTH, lawyer, investment company general counsel; b. San Francisco, Sept. 10, 1943; s. Frederick Henry and Helena Morrison (Shafroth) L.; m. Elizabeth Boschen, Dec. 14, 1968; children—John Shafroth, Victoria. B.A., Brown U., 1965; J.D., U. Denver, 1971. Bar: Colo. 1971, U.S. Dist. Ct. Colo. 1971, U.S. Ct. Appeals (2d cir.) 1975, D.C. 1976, U.S. Supreme Ct. 1976, U.S. Dist. Ct. (so. dist.) N.Y. 1977, U.S. Tax Ct. 1977, U.S. Ct. Appeals (10th cir.) 1979, N.Y. 1984. Trial atty. Denver regional office U.S. SEC, 1971-74; spl. atty. organized crime, racketeering sect. U.S. Dept. Justice, So. Dist. N.Y., 1974-77; atty. Kelly Stansfield and O'Donnell, Denver, 1977-78; gen. counsel Boettcher & Co., Denver, 1978—; allied mem. N.Y. Stock Exchange, 1978—. Bd. dirs. Cherry Creek Improvement Assn., 1980-84, Spalding Rehab. Hosp., 1986—. Served to lt. jg, USN, 1965-67. Mem. ABA, Colo. Bar Assn., Denver Bar Assn., Am. Law Inst., Securities Industry Assn. (state regulations com. 1982-86), Nat. Assn. Securites Dealers, Inc. (arbitration com.). Republican. Episcopalian. Clubs: Denver Law, Denver Country, Denver Tennis, Denver Athletic, Rocky Mountain Brown (founder, past pres.); Racquet and Tennis (N.Y.C.). Home: 144 Race St Denver CO 80206 Office: Boettcher & Co 828 17th St Denver CO 80202

LUTZ, JULIE HAYNES, astronomy educator; b. Mt. Vernon, Ohio, Dec. 17, 1944; d. Willard Damon and Julia Awilda (Way) Haynes; m. Thomas Edward Lutz, July 8, 1967; children: Melissa, Clea. BS, San Diego State U., 1965; MS, U. Ill., 1968, PhD, 1971. Asst. prof. astronomy Wash. State U., Pullman, 1972-78, asst. dean sci., 1978-79, assoc. prof., 1978-84, assoc. provost, 1981-82, prof., 1984—; research fellow Univ. Coll. London, England, 1976-77, 82-83. Contbr. articles on astron. research to profl. jours. Fellow Royal Astron. Soc.; mem. AAAS (mem. com. 1982-85), Am. Stron. Soc. (pubs. bd. 1986—), Internat. Astron. Union, Astron. Soc. Pacific. Avocations: cooking, backpacking, fishing. Home: NE1200 McGee Way Pullman WA 99163 Office: Wash State U Program in Astronomy Pullman WA 99164-2930

LUTZ, LOUISE MARIE, transportation company executive; b. Chgo., Aug. 17, 1949; d. Louis S. and Susan (Pereksta) Mattis; m. John F. Lutz, Jr.; 1 dau., Nicole Eileen. B.A., Calif. State U., 1971, postgrad. 1971-73. With Ampex Corp., Redwood City, Calif., 1971-73, Consol. Freightways, San Francisco, 1973-74, Allied Van Lines, San Francisco, 1974-75; with United Parcel Service, San Francisco, 1975—, personnel supr., Oakland, 1976-78, safety mgr., 1979, employment mgr., 1980—; exec. on loan New Oakland Com., 1981. Recipient Cert. of Achievement, Human Devel. Seminars, Inc., 1981. Mem. Nat. Assn. Female Execs., Assn. Personnel Profls. Oakland, Calif. Unemployment Ins. Council. Home: 968 Pizarro Ln Foster City CA 94404 Office: United Parcel Service 8400 Pardee Dr Oakland CA 94621

LUTZ, RICHARD L., clinical social worker; b. Gary, Ind., July 25, 1929; s. Charles D. and Mabel M. (Fast) L.; m. Mary A. Koreman; children: James, Judy, Anita, Sherry, David. BA, U. Chgo., 1953; MSW, Ind. U., Indpls., 1955; MA in Pub. Adminstrn., U. No. Colo., 1977. Social worker various cos. and orgns., 1953-69; div. dir. State Mental Hosp., Pueblo, Colo., 1969-77; supr. State Mental Hosp., Pendelton, Oreg., 1977-79; mental health coordinator West Salem Clinic, Salem, Oreg., 1979-83; pvt. practice clin. social worker Stayton, Oreg., 1983—. Author, narrator cassette tape series on relaxation, 1982. Mem. Acad. Cert. Social Workers (clin. cert. Oreg.), Nat. Assn. Social Workers. Home: 3820 Oak Hollow Ln SE Salem OR 97302 Office: Ctr for Improvement 223 W Locust Stayton OR 97383

LUTZ, THOMAS EDWARD, astronomy educator; b. Teaneck, N.J., Nov. 20, 1940; s. Harry Joseph and Mary Agnes (Farrell) L.; m. Julie Hollis Haynes, July 8, 1966; children: Melissa, Clea. BME, Manhattan Coll., 1962; MS, U. Ill., 1965, PhD, 1969. Asst. prof. astronomy Wash. State U., Pullman, 1969-75, assoc. prof., 1975-81, prof., 1981—; vis. asst. prof. U. Wash., Seattle, 1971; vis. astronomer Royal Greenwich Obs., East Sussex, Eng., 1976-77; hon. research fellow U. Coll., London, 1982-83; dir. Jewett Obs., Pullman, 1980—, program in astronomy Wash. State U., 1980—; bd. govs. Astrophys. Research Consortium, Seattle, 1984—. Contbr. articles to profl. jours. Fellow Royal Astron. Soc.; mem. AAAS, Am. Astron. Soc., Astronom. Soc. Pacific, Internat. Astronom. Union. Home: NE 1200 Mc Gee Pullman WA 99163-3818 Office: Wash State U Pullman WA 99164-2930

LU VALLE, JAMES ELLIS, retired chemistry educator; b. San Antonio, Nov. 10, 1912; s. James A.B. and Isabelle (Ellis) Lu V.; m. Dorothy Jean Long, Feb. 2, 1946; children: John, Phyllis, Michael. BS in Chemistry, UCLA, 1936, MS in Chemistry, 1937; PhD in Chemistry, Calif. Inst. Tech., 1940. Instr. Fisk U., Nashville, 1940-41; sr. research chemist Eastman Kodak Co., Rochester, N.Y., 1941-46, research assoc., 1946-53; sr. scientist Tech. Ops., Burlington, Mass., 1953-59; dir. research Fairchild Camera, Syosset, N.Y., 1959-68; with tech. div. SCM Labs., Skokie, Ill., 1968-69; dir. phys. and chem. research SCM Labs., Palo Alto, Calif., 1969-71, scientific coordinator, 1971-75; dir. undergrad. labs., dept. chemistry Stanford (Calif.) U., 1975-83; vis. lectr. Brandeis U., Waltham, Mass., 1957-59. Contbr. artilces to profl. jours.; patentee in field. Mem. Lexington (Mass.) Town Meeting, 1956-59, pres. 1957-59; chmn. troop com. Boy Scouts Am., Setauket, N.Y., 1963-68. Fellow Royal Soc. Chemistry; mem. Am. Chem. Soc., Am. Phys. Soc., Assn. for Computing Machines, Phi Beta Kappa, Sigma Xi, Phi Lambda Upsilon, Pi Mu Epsilon. Home: 3580 Evergreen Dr Palo Alto CA 94303 Office: Dept Chemistry Stanford U Stanford CA 94305

LWOWSKI, WALTER WILHELM GUSTAV, research chemist, educator; b. Garmisch, Bavaria, Federal Republic of Germany, Dec. 28, 1928; came to U.S., 1955; s. Hans and Anna (Hanstein) L. Diplom Chemiker, U. Heidelberg, Federal Republic of Germany, Dr. rer. nat, 1955. Postdoctoral fellow UCLA, 1955-57; Wissenschaftl. Asst. U. Heidelberg, 1957-59; postdoctoral fellow Harvard U., Cambridge, Mass., 1959-60; asst. prof. Yale U., New Haven, 1960-66; research prof. N.Mex. State U., Las Cruces, 1966—; bd. drs. Boehringer-Mannheim Corp. Editor books Nitrenes, 1970, Chemistry of Small and Large Heterocycles, 1984. Fellow N.Y. Acad. Sci., AAAS; mem. Am. Chem. Soc., Royal Soc. Chemistry (England), Gesellschaft Deutscher Chemiker. Avocations: music, hiking, electronics. Home: 905 Conway Ave Condo 20 Las Cruces NM 88005 Office: N Mex State U Dept Chemistry Box 3-C Las Cruces NM 88003

LYBARGER, SAM ALBERT, safety professional; b. Albuquerque, June 30, 1948; s. Edward L. and Faye G. (Glassman) L.; m. Judy K. Johnson, July 14, 1973. BS, U. N.Mex., 1970, postgrad., 1970-73; postgrad., U. Houston, 1978-80; E.Ed. in Secondary, Post Secondary and Vocat. Edn., U. Nev., Las Vegas, 1982. Tchr. Moriarty (S.D.) Mcpl. Sch., 1971-73; asst. dir. safety ARC, Albuquerque, 1973-75; safety tng. coordinator Lapata Offshore Drilling, Houston, 1975-76; sr. safety rep. Mundy Inst. Maintenance, Houston, 1976-80; occupational safety profl. Reynold Electric and Engring. Co., Las Vegas, 1980—; safety edn. cons. ARC, Phoenix, 1983—. Instr. Clark County (Nev.) ARC, also bd. dirs. Recipient awards Clark County ARC, 1985, 86. Mem. Am. Soc. Safety Engrs. (treas. So. Nev. chpt. 1986-87), Nev. Safety Council, Mustang Club of Las Vegas (pres. 1985-87), U. N.Mex. Alumni Assn. (pres. 1986-87). Avocations: racquetball, walking, swimming, restoring Mustang automobiles. Home: 1101 Woodbridge Las Vegas NV 89108 Office: Reynold Electric and Engring Co PO Box 14400 Las Vegas NV 89114-9969

LYDEN, FREMONT JAMES, political science educator; b. Pelican Rapids, Minn., Jan. 8, 1926; s. Gothard Ferdinand and Marie Caroline (Hanson) L. B.A., U. Wash., 1950, M.P.A. (Carnegie Found. fellow), 1952, Ph.D. (Health Info. Found. fellow), 1960; postgrad. (univ. fellow), Princeton U., 1955-56. Adminstrv. asst. Bur. Reclamation, Ephrata, Wash., 1952-53; position classifier, wage analyst 1953-55, mgmt. analyst, 1957; instr. polit. sci. U. Wash., Seattle, 1956-59; asst. prof. U. Wash. (Grad. Sch. Public Affairs), 1962-66, asso. prof. public adminstrn., 1966-75, prof., 1975—; research asso. Harvard U. Med. Sch., also Littauer Sch., Harvard Coll., Cambridge, Mass., 1960-62; cons. Bolt, Beranek & Newman, 1963-65, U.S. Bur. Land Mgmt., Washington, 1963-64, Grant County Public Utility Dist., Ephrata, 1972—, Zaring Corp., Bellevue, Wash., 1972, Souder, Clark, Griffin & Assos., 1974-75, Boeing Computer Services, Seattle, 1976, U.S. Forest Service, Washington, 1980. Author: (with E.G. Miller) Planning-Programming-Budgeting: A Systems Approach to Management, 1968, Japanese translation, 1969, 2d edit., 1972, Public Budgeting: Program Planning and Evaluation, 1978, Spanish translation, 1983, 2d edit., 1982, (with O.L. Peterson and H.J. Geiger) The Training of Good Physicians, 1968, (with G.A. Shipman and M. Kroll) Policies, Decisions and Organization, 1969, (with Marc Lindenberg) Public Budgeting in Theory and Practice, 1983, (with E.G. Miller) Presupuesto Publico, 1983; feature editor: Public Adminstrn. Rev., 1969-78. Mem. Gov.'s Task Force Public Assistance, 1966-69; adv. com. Seattle-King County Ad Hoc Com. on Health, 1970-71; mem. NSF Task Force on Weather Modification, 1966-67; mem. task force on ops. King County Dept. Assessment, 1984. Served with USNR, 1944-46. Mem. Am. Polit. Sci. Assn., Am. Sociol. Assn., Am. Soc. Public Adminstrn., Am. Pub. Health Assn., Phi Beta Kappa, Pi Sigma Alpha, Pan Xenia. Home: 8060 28th Ave NW Seattle WA 98117 Office: U Wash Grad Sch Pub Affairs M260 Smith Hall Seattle WA 98195

LYDICK, LAWRENCE TUPPER, judge; b. San Diego, June 22, 1916; s. Roy Telling and Geneva (Lydick) L.; m. Gretta Grant, Aug. 7, 1938; children: Gretta Grant, Lawrence Tupper; m. Martha Martinez, Oct. 1969; 1 son, Chip. A.B., Stanford U., 1938, LL.B. (Crothers law scholar), 1942; Sigma Nu exchange scholar, U. Freiburg, Germany, 1938-39; postgrad., Harvard U., 1943, Mass. Inst. Tech., 1943-44. Bar: Calif. 1946. Since practiced in Los Angeles; dir. disputes div. 10th region Nat. War Labor Bd., San Francisco, 1942-43; asst. to pres., gen. counsel U.S. Grant Export-Import, Ltd., Los Angeles, 1946-48; assoc. Adams, Duque & Hazeltine, Los Angeles, 1948-53; partner Adams, Duque & Hazeltine, 1953-71; U.S. dist. ct. judge Central Dist. Calif. 1971—. Bd. vis. Sanford Law Sch. Served from ensign to lt. USNR, 1943-46. Mem. Am. Law Inst., Sigma Nu. Republican. Congregationalist. Office: US Court House Los Angeles CA 90012

LYE, WILLIAM FRANK, university administrator; b. Kimberley, B.C., Can., Feb. 19, 1930; came to U.S., 1955, naturalized, 1981; s. Arthur Percy and Jessie Loretta (Prince) L.; m. Velda Campbell, Oct. 16, 1953; children—William Mark, Matthew Campbell, David Arthur, Victoria, Regina. Student Ricks Coll., 1953-55, Duke U., 1963; B.S., Utah State U., 1959; M.A., U. Calif.-Berkeley, 1959; Ph.D., UCLA, 1969. Instr. polit. sci. Ricks Coll., Rexburg, Idaho, 1959-63, 67-68, head dept. polit. sci., 1959-63; teaching asst. dept. history UCLA, 1964-65; asst. prof. Utah State U., Logan, 1968-69, acting head dept. history and geography, 1969-70, assoc. prof., head dept. history and geography, 1970-73, prof., head dept. history and geography, 1973-76, dean Coll. Humanities, Arts and Social Scis., 1976-83, v.p. for univ. relations, prof. dept. history and geography, 1983—; vis. lectr. dept. history Brigham Young U., Provo, Utah, 1970; temporary lectr. dept. history U. Cape Town, Republic of South Africa, 1974; social cons. for project design teams in land conservation, U.S. Agy. for Internat. Devel. Khartoum, Sudan, 1978, Maseru, Lesotho, 1979; mem. higher edn. taskforce on telecommunications, Utah; chmn. State of Utah Telecommunications Coop., Regents' Com. on Credit by Exam., Utah; mem. adv. com. Sta. KULC-TV, State Ednl. Telecommunications Operating Ctr.; pres.-elect Utah Alliance for Arts Edn. Author: (with Colin Murray) Transformations on the Highveld: The Tswana and Southern Sotho, 1980. Editor: Andrew Smith's Journal of His Expedition into the Interior of South Africa, 1834-36, 1975. Producer (TV series) Out of Africa, 1977, The God Seekers, 1978. Contbr. articles and book revs. to profl. publs. Chmn. State Day celebration, Logan, Utah, 1973, univ. drive for new Logan Regional Hosp. Recipient Leadership award Standard of Calif., 1957, Idea of Yr. award Utah State U., 1971, Faculty Service award Associated Students, Utah State U., 1977-78; Woodrow Wilson Nat. fellow 1958, Foreign Area fellow Social Sci. Research Council, Republic of South Africa, England, 1966-67, 67-68; faculty devel. grantee Utah State U., 1972, Human Sci. Research Council of South Africa publ. grantee, 1975, Mauerberger Trust grantee, 1976, 79. Mem. African Studies Assn., Royal African Soc., Western Assn. Africanists (program chmn. 1972-74, pres. 1974-76), Am. Soc. Landscape Architects (accreditation bd. 1967—), Council for Advancement and Support Edn., Phi Kappa Phi, Phi Alpha Theta. Mormon. Lodge: Rotary. Home: 696 E 400 N Logan UT 84321 Office: Utah State U Logan UT 84322-1440

LYGRE, DAVID GERALD, chemistry educator; b. Minot, N.D., Aug. 10, 1942; s. C. Gerald and Esther R. (Fossum) L.; m. Laurae Y. Johnson, Aug. 20, 1966; children: Jedd, Lindsay. BA, Concordia Coll., 1964; PhD, U. N.D., 1968. Postdoctoral fellow Case Western Res. U., Cleve., 1968-70; asst. prof. chemistry Cen. Wash. U., Ellensburg, 1970-73, assoc. prof., 1973-80, prof., 1980—, assoc. dean Coll. Letters, Arts and Scis., 1981—; vis. prof. U. York, Eng., 1976-77, U Wash., Seattle, 1983, U. Canterbury, Christchurch, New Zealand, 1983-84; reviewer manuscripts Wadsworth Pub. Co., Belmont, Calif., 1978-83. Author: Life Manipulation, 1979, Chemistry: A Contemporary Approach, 1987; contbr. articles to profl. jours. Grantee Research Corp., 1971. Mem. AAAS, Am. Chem. Soc., Sigma Xi. Avocations: long distance running, music. Home: 805 B St Ellensburg WA 98926 Office: Cen Wash U Office Dean Coll Letters Arts Scis Ellensburg WA 98926

LYKINS, JAY ARNOLD, economic development director; b. Shattuck, Okla., Feb. 13, 1947; s. George Eldridge and Lucy Lee (Croom) L.; m. (Mary) Lynn Turner, Jan. 3, 1970; children: Mary Lee and Amy Lynn (twins), Jason. BA, Covenant Coll., 1973; Masters, William Carey Internat. U., 1986. Credit specialist Gen. Electric Supply Co., Nashville, 1974-75; owner, mgr. Environment Control Co., Nashville, 1975-78; bus. adminstr. Youth for Christ, Atlanta, 1978-81; controller Young Life, Colorado Springs, Colo., 1981-82, internat. adminstr., 1982-85; exec. dir. Global Reach, Colorado Springs, 1985—; cons. Royal Donuts, Lima, Peru, Barnabas Group, Vancouver. B.C, Manna Corp., Bulawayo, Zimbabwe, Denver Bridge Corp. Author: Values in the Marketplace, 1986. Served with USN, 1966-68. Mem. Internat. Council for Small Bus., Am. Cons. League, Assn. MBA Execs., Ctr. Enterpreneurial Mgmt. Club: Nob Hill Country (Snellville, Ga.) (pres. 1980). Home: 3296 Bell Mountain Dr Colorado Springs CO 80918 Office: Global Reach PO Box 7000 Colorado Springs CO 80933

LYKKEN, CATHERINE TOWNLEY, social worker; b. Norman, Okla., Mar. 21, 1936; d. Thomas Lee and Marie Winnie (Nemecek) Townley; m. Jerry Don Farren, June 8, 1963 (div. Feb. 1970); m. Gary Lee Lykken, Nov. 28, 1974. BA, U. Okla., 1959. Lic. real estate broker. Children's worker Wesley Community House, Louisville, 1959-63; caseworker Weld County Dept. Social Services, Greeley, Colo., 1965-68; asst. dir. Weld County Services for Aging, Greeley, 1968-69; caseworker Routt County Social Services, Steamboat Springs, Colo., 1969-77, dir., 1977-85; instr. Colo. Mountain Coll., Steamboat Springs, 1985—; sec. Colo. County Dirs. Social Services Assn., 1982-84, Routt County Council Aging, Inc., 1975-78, bd. dirs. 1985—; sales assoc. Morrison & Assocs., Steamboat Springs, 1986—. Mem. Am. Soc. on Aging, Colo. Gerontol. Soc., LWV (pres. Routt County chpt. 1976-78, bd. dirs. 1985-86). Democrat. Avocations: gardening, skiing, cooking. Home: PO Box 399 Steamboat Springs CO 80477

LYM, GLENN ROBERT, architect; b. Berkeley, Calif., June 24, 1944; s. Glenn Dewey and Evelyn Marilyn (Glenchur) L.; m. Ruth Ethel Kwitko, July 15, 1970; 1 child: Mindy Shoshana. BArch, U. Calif., 1967; MA, Harvard U., 1971, PhD, 1975. Registered architect, Calif. Pvt. practice architecture San Francisco, 1977—; assoc. Esherick, Homsey, Dodge & Davis, San Francisco, 1978-86, also bd. dirs.; lectr. U. Calif., Berkeley, 1979-80. Author A Psychology of Building, 1980. Prin. works include Tibbetts House, Berkeley (Sunset AIA Western Home awards 1981), Lym House, San Francisco. Mem. AIA. Avocations: micro computers, skiing. Office: Esherick Homsey Dodge & Davis 332 Rutledge St San Francisco CA 94110

LYMAN, DONALD JOSEPH, materials science educator; b. Chgo., Nov. 5, 1926; s. Joseph Abner Lyman; m. Elizabeth C. Medvedeff, May 19, 1978; children: Nancy Carol, Barbara Ann. BS in Chemistry, U. Nev., 1949; MS in Chemistry, U. Del., 1951, PhD in Chemistry, 1952. Research chemist E.I. DuPont de Nemours Co., Wilmington, Del., 1952-61; sr. polymer chemist Stanford U. Research Inst., Menlo Park, Calif., 1961-69; prof. materials sci. and engring. U. Utah, Salt Lake City, 1969—, prof. bioengring., research assoc. prof. surgery, adj. prof. chemistry; pres. Vascular Internat., Inc., Salt Lake City, 1983—. Mem. editorial bds. Biomed. Polymer, 1985—, Annals of Biomed. Engring., 1985—, Jour. of Dialysis, 1975—, Jour. Biomed. Materials Research, 1967—; contbr. articles to profl. jours.; patentee in field. Recipient U. Utah Disting. Research award, 1982. Mem. AAAS, Am. Chem. Soc. (tour speaker 1967—, symposium chmn. 1966, 73, 74, 75), The Biomed. Engring. Soc., Soc. Biomaterials (founder, Clemson award 1982), Am. Soc. Artificial Internal Organs (program chmn. 1967, 68, fellow 1969), Internat. Soc. Artificial Organs. Avocations: music, woodworking, travel. Office: U Utah Dept Materials Sci 2008 MEB Salt Lake City UT 84112

LYMAN, JOHN, psychology and engineering educator; b. Santa Barbara, Calif., May 29, 1921; s. Oren Lee and Clara Augusta (Young) L. A.B. in Psychology and Math., UCLA, 1943, M.S., 1950, Ph.D. in Psychology, 1951. Research technician Lockheed Aircraft Corp., Burbank, Calif., 1940-43; mathematician Lockheed Aircraft Corp., 1943-44; with dept. psychology UCLA, 1947—, assoc. prof., 1957-63, prof., 1963—, from instr. to assoc. prof. Sch. Engring. and Applied Sci., 1950-63, prof. Sch. Engring. and Applied Sci., 1963—, chmn. engring. systems dept., 1978-84, head Biotech. Lab., 1958—; research engr. Inst. Traffic and Transp., 1967-73; vis. prof. bioengring. Technol. Inst., Delft, Netherlands, 1965; spl. cons. Nat. Acad. Scis., Washington, 1973; cons. VA, Los Angeles, 1962-66, 67-76, NIH, 1963-66, 68-73, med. devices div. FDA, 1976-78, Perceptronics, Inc., Woodland Hills, Calif., 1978—, other agys. and cos. Author chpts. in books, articles in profl. jours.; editor in field. Served to lt. (j.g.) U.S. Navy, 1944-46. Recipient numerous fellowships and grants. Fellow Am. Psychol. Assn., Soc. Engring. Psychologists, AAAS, Human Factors Soc. (Paul Fitts award 1971, pres. 1967-68); mem. Biomed. Engring. Soc. (pres. 1980-81), IEEE, Am. Soc. Engring. Edn., Am. Assn. Artificial Intelligence, Robotics Internat., Soc. Mfg. Engrs., Sigma Xi, Tau Beta Pi. Office: UCLA 6532 Boelter Hall U Calif Los Angeles CA 90024

LYMBURNER, SUMNER AUBREY, aerospace program executive; b. Castine, Maine, Feb. 18, 1942; s. Allen Clarence and Abbie Laura (Gray) L.; m. Jane Marie MacDonough, June 8, 1963 (div. Feb. 1971); 1 child, Anne Elizabeth. BSEE, U. Maine, 1963; postgrad., UCLA, 1981-83. Program engr. Gen. Electric Corp., Roanoke, Va., 1963-66; project engr. Hamilton Standard, Windsor Locks, Conn., 1966-74, Sundstrand Corp., Rockford, Ill., 1974-78, Lear Siegler, Cleve., 1978-80; program mgr. AESD-Garrett, Torrance, Calif., 1980—, Airesearch Electronics, Tucson, 1980—. Selectman East Windsor, 1971-72; mem. Rep. com. East Windsor, 1969-73; pres. scholarship assn. East Windsor, 1970. Mem. Parents Without Partners (pres., other offices 1972—). Republican. Lodge: Grange. Avocations: woodworking, tennis, swimming, skiing, traveling. Home: 1060 W Oleta Dr Tucson AZ 85704-3440 Office: AESD Garrett-Allied Signal 11100 N Oracle Tucson AZ 85704-9588

LYNCH, CHARLES ALLEN, express courier executive; b. Denver, Sept. 7, 1927; s. Laurence J. and Louanna (Robertson) L.; m. Linda Bennet, June 14, 1952; children: Charles A., Tara O'Hara, Casey Alexander. B.S., Yale U., 1950. With E.I. duPont de Nemours & Co., Inc., Wilmington, Del., 1950-69, dir. mktg., 1965-69; corp. v.p. SCOA Industries, Columbus, Ohio, 1969-72; corp. exec. v.p., also mem. rotating bd. W.R. Grace & Co., N.Y.C., 1972-78; chmn. bd., chief exec. officer Saga Corp., Menlo Park, Calif., 1978-86, also dir.; chmn., chief exec. officer DHL Airways, Inc., Redwood City, Calif., 1986—; bd. dirs. Pacific Mut. Life Ins. Co., Nordstrom, Inc., So. Pacific Transp. Co.; trustee Conf. Bd. Bd. dirs. San Francisco YMCA; vice chmn. Bay Area Council; former chmn. Calif. Roundtable; mem. adv. council Grad. Sch. Bus., Stanford U.; trustee Occidental Coll. Served with USNR, 1945. Republican. Clubs: Yale (N.Y.C.); Internat. Lawn Tennis; Menlo Country (Calif.), Menlo Circus (Calif.); Pacific Union (San Francisco); Ponte Vedra (Fla.); Beach and Tennis; Coral Beach and Tennis (Bermuda); Vintage (Indian Wells, Calif.). Office: DHL Airways Inc 333 Twin Dolphin Dr Redwood City CA 94065 *

LYNCH, CHARLES THOMAS, educator; b. Waterbury, Conn., Oct. 10, 1918; s. Charles Thomas and Sara (Carroll) L.; m. Helen Victoria Kaliss, Aug. 4, 1941; children: Charles Thomas III, Jean, Christopher. Student, U. Ala., 1935-37, Mich. State U., 1960; B.A., Western Mich. U., 1963, M.A., 1966; Ph.D., So. Ill. U., 1972. Announcer, producer, writer various radio stas. Conn., Pa., Fla., Mich., 1938-49; program dir., exec. producer Fetzer Broadcasting Co., Kalamazoo, 1949-67; asst. prof. radio-TV, sta. mgr. Sta. WSIU, So. Ill. U., 1967-74, asso. prof., chmn. dept. radio-TV, 1974-79; prof., chmn. dept. radio-TV-film Calif. State U., Northridge, 1979—. Author various documentaries, spl. broadcast programs; contbr. articles profl. jours. Pres. Kalamazoo Area PTA Council, 1960-61, Kalamazoo Civic Players, 1962-64, Community Theatre Assn. Mich., 1963-65, Am. Cancer Soc., Kalamazoo, 1965-67. Recipient Broadcast Preceptor award Broadcast Industry Conf., 1976. Mem. Hollywood Chpt. Acad. TV Arts and Scis., St. Louis Chpt. Nat. Acad. TV Arts and Scis., Am. Film Inst., Broadcast Edn. Assn., Soc. Profl. Journalists, Ill. News Broadcasters Assn., Hollywood Radio and TV Soc., Am. Women in Radio and TV (bd. dirs. So. Calif. chpt. 1985—), Broadcast Pioneers, Pacific Pioneer Broadcasters (bd. dirs. 1983-86), Sierra Club, Alpha Epsilon Rho, Phi Kappa Phi. Office: Radio TV Film Dept California State University Northridge CA 91330

LYNCH, DAVID DILLON, transportation executive, educator; b. Richmond Heights, Mo., July 24, 1940; s. David Dillon and Alice Ann (Eubank) L.; m. Judy Anton, Aug. 13, 1960; children: Gwynn, Christine, Jennifer. BSEE, Washington U., Clayton, Mo., 1962, MSEE, 1965; postgrad., Bklyn. Poly. Inst., 1966, UCLA, 1974, 84. Project engring. asst. Union Electric Co., St. Louis, 1961; project engr. Mo. Research Lab., St. Louis, 1962-64; mem. tech. staff Bell Labs., Murray Hill, N.J., 1964-65; group supr. Emerson Electric Co., St. Louis, 1966-70; program mgr., assoc. mgr. engring. div. Hughes Aircraft Co., Los Angeles, 1970—; instr. UCLA, 1971-76, U. So. Calif., Los Angeles, 1973-76; asst. prof. U. Mo., Rolla, 1964-67; cons. Evolving Technology, San Diego, 1973—. Co-author books on radar and signal processing; contbr. articles to profl. jours.; patentee in field. Recipient Hyland Patent award Hughes Aircraft Co., 1978. Mem. IEEE, Computer Soc. of IEEE (pres. and v.p. chpt.), Soc. Photo Optical Engrs., Hughes Mgmt. Club, Sigma Xi (assoc.), Phi Delta Theta. Episcopalian. Avocations: tech. climbing, running, triathalons, music, backpacking. Home: 18651 Gledhill St Northridge CA 91324 Office: Hughes Aircraft Co Radar Systems Group PO Box 92426 Los Angeles CA 90009

LYNCH, DELL MARIE RYAN, civic worker, writer, artist; b. Scranton, Pa.; d. Cornelius James and Alice Wall (Burke) Ryan; BA, Manhattanville Coll., 1922; m. James Merriman Lynch, Apr. 6, 1926 (dec. Feb. 1982); 1 child, Nathaniel Merriman. Exhibited in group shows Pala Art Show, Showcase of Arts, Bank Am. Exhibit, Fireside Restaurant Exhibit, Country Squire Exhibit; one-woman show Woman's Club, 1979; publicity chmn. Santa Barbara County Med. Aux., 1947-48; co-chmn. Garden sect. Palomar Meml. Hosp. Aux., 1958-61; bd. mem. Friends of Leonell Strong Cancer Found., 1969-70; v.p. Friends of Pala Indian Mission Sch., 1967-72, Friends of Escondido Library, 1972-73; chmn. Showcase of Arts Gallery, 1967-68; project chmn. Exceptional Girl Scouts U.S.A., 1957-58. Recipient award for over 20 yrs. vol. service Palomar Meml. Hosp., 1981; hon. mention state poetry award Women's Club, 1980. Mem. Felicita Found. (life), Escondido Hist. Soc. (life), Palomar Meml. Hosp. Aux. (life), Friends of Escondido Library (life), Escondido Art Assn. (life), Chaparral Poets, AAUW (life; area rep. for cultural interests 1964-65, courtesy chmn. 1968-77, cultural interests chmn. 1977-78, creative writing chmn. 1978-81, cert. of appreciation 1977-78). Clubs: Woman's (chmn. creative writing 1977-81, creative writing chmn. 1977-81, , cert. of appreciation 1977-78, 1st place poetry, writing contest 1978, 1st, 2d, 3d places poetry, 1979, 3 1st place awards for poetry, 2d place for prose 1980, 1st place and 2d place for poetry 1981), Escondido Garden (therapy co-chmn., Cert. Appreciation, 1986). Author numerous poems. Home: 810 Omar Dr Escondido CA 92025

LYNCH, EUGENE F., federal judge; b. 1931. B.S., U. Santa Clara, 1953; LL.B., U. Calif., 1958. Assoc. O'Connor, Moran, Cohn & Lynch, San Francisco, 1959-64, ptnr., 1964-71; judge Mcpl. Ct., San Francisco, 1971-74; justice Superior Ct. City and County San Francisco, 1974-82; judge U.S. Dist. Ct. (no. dist.) Calif., San Francisco, 1982—. Office: US Courthouse 450 Golden Gate Ave San Francisco CA 94102

LYNCH, FRANK WILLIAM, aerospace company executive; b. San Francisco, Nov. 26, 1921; s. James Garfield and Med (Kelly) L.; m. Marilyn Leona Hopwood, June 24, 1950; children: Kathyn Leona, Molly Louise. A.B., Stanford U., 1943, postgrad., 1946-48. Research engr. Boeing Airplane Co., Seattle, 1948-50; with Northrop Corp., Hawthorn, Calif., 1950-57, Los Angeles, 1959—; sr. v.p. ops. corp. hdqrs. Northrop Corp., 1974-78, sr. v.p. and group exec. Tactical and Electronic Systems Group, 1978-82, pres., chief operating officer, 1982-87, vice chmn. of bd., 1987—; div. v.p. engring. Lear-Siegler Corp., Anaheim, Calif., 1957-59. Served with AC U.S. Army, 1942-46. Mem. IEEE (sr. mem.), AIAA (sr. mem.), Assn. U.S. Army, Am. Def. Preparedness Assn., Air Force Assn., Navy League. Clubs: Balboa Yacht (Newport Beach, Calif.); Regency (Los Angeles); Center (Costa Mesa, Calif.). Home: 1933 Altura Dr Corona Del Mar CA 92625 Office: Northrop Corp 1840 Century Park E Los Angeles CA 90067

LYNCH, JOHN DANIEL, educator; b. Butte, Mont., Sept. 17, 1947; s. Leo and Queenie Veronica Lynch; m. Shannon Christine Crawford, May 7, 1983. B.S., West Mont. Coll., Rep., Mont. State Legislature, Helena, 1971-79, state senator, 1982—; tchr. Butte High Sch., Mont., 1970-78, Butte Vo-Tech, 1978—. Democrat. Roman Catholic. Lodge: Elks, KC.

LYNCH, LEO, mathematics educator, consultant; b. Winnipeg, Man., Can., Aug. 5, 1926; s. John Alfred and Elizabeth (O'Llary) L.; m. Angela Pollis, Oct. 22, 1961 (div. 1965). BS, U. Man., 1950; MS, Va. Poly. Inst. and State U., 1954, PhD, 1957. Cons. Booz-Allen, Los Angeles, 1965-71; freelance cons. Los Angeles, 1971—; instr. math. El Camino Coll., Torrance, Calif., 1975-79, Harbor Coll., Harbor City, Calif., 1976—; prof. math. Northrop U., Inglewood, Calif., 1979—; research assoc. U.S. Steel, Pitts., 1958-65, Can. Govt., Churchill, 1951-53, Va. Poly. Inst. and State U., 1955-57. Mem. Rep. Presdl. Task Force, Washington, 1983—, Ch. Orgns., Redondo Beach, Calif., 1971—, Cystic Fibrosis Orgn., Ann Arbor, Mich., 1975—. Served with Navy, 1944-46, Can. Recipient Cert. for Teaching. AIAA, 1983. Mem. Am. Math. Assn., Am. Statis. Assn., Am. Math. Soc., Nat. Novice Hockey Assn., Sigma Xi. Republican. Roman Catholic. Club: Victoria Golf (Carson, Calif.). Lodge: KC. Avocations: golf, hockey, collector classical records and books. Home: 902 Camino Real #102 Redondo Beach CA 90277 Office: Northrup U 5800 W Arbor Vitae Los Angeles CA 90045

LYNCH, MARY MEAD, administrative executive; b. San Francisco, Jan. 29, 1938; d. William Howard and Elizabeth (Crowell) Mead; children: William Mead, Michael J. II, James Anthony. Student, U. Colo., 1955-59, U. San Francisco, 1986-87. Dir. Project Head Start, Dell City, Tex., 1965; pub., editor Hudsepth County Herald, 1965-75; owner, operator Lyn-Mar Iris Gardens, Dell City, 1965-75; exec. dir. Insights El Paso Sci. Ctr. Inc., 1978-82; adminstr. Franklin Land and Resources, El Paso, 1982-85, Steeples Ranch Registered Charolais Cattle, 1970-72. Named one of Outstanding Young Women of Am., Jaycees, 1966; named Woman of Yr., Dell Valley C. of C., 1968, Vol. of Yr., Jr. League of El Paso, Inc., 1980, Vol. of Yr., United Way El Paso Vol. Bur., 1983. Republican. Episcopalian. Home: 2701 Larkin San Francisco CA 94109

LYNCH, PAUL VINCENT, safety engineer; b. Bklyn., Apr. 11, 1932; s. John Andrew and Mary Catherine L.; BA, St. Anselm's Coll., Manchester, N.H., 1954; postgrad. Fordham U. Law Sch., 1958-59, U. N.H., 1969-71; m. Muriel Dubuc, Jan. 25, 1956; children: David, Marianne. Corp. ins. specialist Allied Chem. Corp., 1959-66; asst. to dir. risk mgmt. Am. Metal Climax, Inc., N.Y.C., 1966-68; lectr. risk mgmt., adminstr. safety U. N.H., Durham, 1969-71; asso. prof. safety N.H. Vocat.-Tech. Coll., 1971-75; pres. Lynch Assocs., Inc., cons., Pittsfield, N.H., 1972-75; regional safety officer GSA, 1976-79; safety mgr. for Calif., U.S. Bur. Land Mgmt., Sacramento, 1979-86, safety mgr., 1986—; v.p. N.H. Safety Council, 1972-74; instr. safety mgmt. Am. River Coll., Sacramento, 1975-76. Active, Boy Scouts Am., 1962— , membership chmn., mem. exec. bd. Golden Empire Council, 1978—, dist. chmn., 1984-85. Served with U.S. Army, 1955-57. Recipient Silver Beaver award Boy Scouts Am., 1977. Mem. Am. Soc. Safety Engrs. (pres. Sacramento chpt. 1981-82; regional v.p.; nat. long range planning com.; chmn. legis. affairs com., adminstr. pub. sector div., named div. Safety Profl. of Yr. 1986, Sacramento chpt. safety com.), Am. Indsl. Hygiene Assn., Vets of Safety (pres. Sacramento chpt. 1984-85). Club: Pittsfield Rotary (sec. 1970-73). Author, editor govt. publs.

LYNCH, ROBERT BERGER, lawyer; b. LaCrosse, Wis., June 10, 1931; s. Jan P. and Eve (Berger) L.; B.S., U.S. Merchant Marine Acad., 1955; J.D., U. of the Pacific, 1967; m. Ann Godfrey, May 30, 1980; 1 son, Jan Fredrick. Sr. engr. Aerojet Gen. Corp., Sacramento, Calif., 1955-61, proposal mgr., 1961-63, asst. contract adminstrn. mgr., 1963-66, contract adminstrn. mgr., 1967-70; admitted to Calif. bar, 1969, U.S. Supreme Ct. bar, 1972; individual practice law. Rancho Cordova, Calif., 1969—; instr. bus. law Solano Community Coll., 1977-79, San Joaquin Delta Coll., 1978-79. Monthly columnist Mil. History Rev. Active various charity fund-raising campaigns in Sacramento Calif., 1966-68; mem. mission com. St. Clements Episcopal Ch., Rancho Cordova, Calif., 1967-68; trustee Los Rios Community Coll. Dist., Calif., 1971-79. Served with USCG, 1949-51. Fellow Brit. Interplanetary Soc.; mem. Am. Bar Assn., Assn. of Trial Lawyers of Am., Calif. Trial Lawyers Assn., IEEE, Calif. Wildlife Fedn., Internat. Turtle Club, Marines Meml. Assn., Am. Legion, Mensa. Home and Office: 10615 Coloma Rd Rancho Cordova CA 95670

LYNCH, SUZANNE HARVEY, lawyer; b. Hornell, N.Y., June 30, 1934; d. Leo Bernard and Eleanor (Leahy) Harvey; m. Daniel F. Lynch, Feb. 14, 1958 (div. Dec. 1980); children: Ann Lynch Steinfort, Daniel F. Jr., Eleanor H., John C. AB, Trinity Coll., 1955; JD, Georgetown U., 1958. Bar: Colo. 1960. Assoc. Martin & Johnson, Boulder, Colo., 1963-64; ptnr. Lynch, MacIntosh & Lynch, Denver, 1965-72; dep. dist. atty. City of Denver, 1973-75; trial atty. EEOC, Denver, 1976-78; dir. div. hearing officers State of Colo., Denver, 1979-82; sole practice Denver, 1982—. editor, co-pub. First Report, 1983—. Chmn. Colo. Com. Workmen's Compensation Procedures, 1981. Mem. Colo. Bar Assn., Colo. Women's Bar Assn. (bd. dirs. 1982-83), Am. Assn. Adminstrv. Law Judges. Democrat. Roman Catholic. Avocations: reading, skiing, bicycling, golf. Office: 950 S Cherry #915 Denver CO 80222

LYNCH, TIMOTHY BRUCE, not-for-profit organization administrator; b. Lewistown, Pa., Dec. 30, 1949; s. James F. and Elsie (Holloman) L.; m. Cecilia P. Resendez, Jan. 28, 1984; children: Dennis, Kelly, Johnny, Michael. BS in Biology, U. Calif., Riverside, 1971; MPA, Harvard U., 1984. Research asst. U. Calif., Riverside, 1971-72, spl. asst., 1985; campaign mgr. Brown for Congress, Riverside, 1972; legis. asst. Congressman George Brown, Washington, 1973-80, adminstrv. asst., 1980-84; exec. asst. Memel, Jacobs, Pierno, Gersh & Ellsworth, Los Angeles, 1985-87; membership dir. The Planetary Soc., Pasadena, Calif., 1987—. Active Riverside Press Council, 1973-74, Environ. Protection Com., Riverside, 1973-74; dir. Return Brown to Cong. campaign, San Bernardino, 1984. Mem. AAAS, U. Calif.-Riverside Alumni Assn. Democrat. Home: 12753 Emelita St North Hollywood CA 91607 Office: The Planetary Soc 65 N Catalina Ave Pasadena CA 91106

LYNCH, VIVIAN ELIZABETH, lawyer; b. Detroit, June 17, 1940; d. Edward Winemac and Winifred (Grant) L.; m. Robert L. Rubin, Sept. 18, 1963 (div. Aug. 1973); children: David B., Edward A., Ruth L. BA, Wayne State U., 1960, JD, 1962. Bar: Nev. 1985, U.S. Dist. Ct. Nev. 1985, U.S. Ct. Appeals (9th cir.) 1986. Ptnr., exec. dir. Club Tahoe, Incline Village, Nev., 1978-81; exec. adminstr. Harbor/Depoe Bay, Oreg., 1982; ptnr. Hamilton and Lynch, Reno, 1985—; cons. Oreg. Real Estate Div., Salem, 1982-83; conv. speaker Western Regional Assn. Regulatory Agys., Incline Village, 1983. Editor Survey/Mich. Law Rev., 1961. Wayne State U. scholar, 1961-62. Mem. Washoe County Bar Assn., Am. Trial Lawyers Assn., Nev. Trial Lawyers Assn. Republican. Roman Catholic. Avocations: songwriting, guitar, piano, aviation. Office: Hamilton and Lynch 317 S Arlington Ave Reno NV 89501

LYNCH-MAHONEY, MARGARET MARY, businesswoman, civic leader; b. San Francisco, Sept. 8, 1920; d. Jeremiah John Mahoney and Susan Marie McKeen-Mahoney; m. Joseph David Mahoney Lynch, June 10, 1945; children: Timothy Jeremiah, Suzanne Marie. Cert. real estate, U. Calif., San Francisco, 1966, D of Bus. Adminstrn., 1967. Clk. MahoneyEstates Co., San Francisco, 1945-50; mng. ptnr., owner, pres. Mahoney Corp., San Francisco, 1950-60; ptnr., owner, mgr. Mahoney Corp. Group, San Francisco, 1960-78; sr. ptnr, owner Mahoney Holding Group, San Francisco, 1978-87; chmn., chief exec. officer, sr. ptnr. Mahoney Realty Corp. Ltd., San Francisco, 1980-87; mem. White House Council of Advisors of U.S. Cabinet Council, U.S. adv. council Domestic or Fgn. Pub. Policies, Pres.' Adv. Bd. on Policy Matters; bd. dirs., mem. audit com. Bank of Am., San Francisco. Bd. dirs. Bus. Com. for Econ. Devel. of San Francisco, vice chmn. 1987; chmn. U.S.-Asian affairs com. World Affairs Council of No. Calif.; trustee San Francisco Opera Guild, San Francisco Mus. Modern Art; mem. Bay Area Council, 1980, social com. San Francisco Showcase, Rep. Nat. Com.; mem. San Francisco Mayor's coms. on internat. diplomacy, protocol, vis. dignitaries; bd. dirs. Upper Noe Valley Improvement Assn., 1980-87; various offices Boys' Town of Italy, San Francisco. Mem. Calif. Hotel/Motel Assn. (cons.), Golden Gate Hotel Assn. S.F., Calif. BAnkers Assn. (bd. dirs. 1980-87), Fin. Execs. Inst., Calif. Hotel Assn. (bus. coms. 1978-87), Apt. House Lessees Assn., Downtown Assn. San Francisco, San Francisco C. of C. (affiliate), N.Y. Council Fgn. Relations. Republican. Roman Catholic. Clubs: Palo Alto Women's, San Francisco Women's, San Francisco Theatrical. Avocations: gardening, opera guild, ballet, theatre, social entertaining. Home: 501 Forest Ave Palo Alto CA 94301 Office: Mahoney Realty Group Ltd 540 Jones St #211 San Francisco CA 94102

LYNN, CHARLES RANDAL, engineering executive; b. Dumas, Tex., July 18, 1954; s. Orden Jr. and Mildred Ruth (Johnson) L.; m. Susan Marie Barber, May 28, 1977; children: Patrick Randal, Christopher Charles. BSEE, Tex. Tech. U., 1977, MS in Indsl. Engring., 1979. Process engr. Phillips Petroleum Co., Borger, Tex., 1975-79; assoc. engr. IBM Corp., Tucson, 1979, mfg. mgr., 1980, quality assurance mgr., 1981, current products project mgr., 1983, adv. engr., mgr., 1985-86, devel. engr., mgr., 1986—. Deacon Palo Verde Ch. of Christ, 1986. Mem. IEEE (jr., v.p. 1976-77), AIEE (v.p. 1977-79), Alpha Pi Mu (sec. Lubbock, Tex. chpt. 1978-79), Tau Beta Pi (sec. Lubbock chpt. 1979). Home: 1401 N Arbor Circle Tucson AZ 85715

LYNN, JOHN WILLIAM, author, researcher; b. Grand Junction, Colo., June 27, 1952; s. Jack Norris and Janis Arline (Griffee) L. BA, Mesa Coll., 1983. Pres. Lynn Internat., Grand Junction, 1975—, Desert Hill Books, Grand Junction, 1979—, Lynn Research, Grand Junction, 1983—, Internat. Map Co., Grand Junction, 1985—. Author: numerous books including The Settling of West Central Colorado, 1980, The Story of Emmet Crawford, 1844-1886, 1981, Research Guide to Western Colorado, 1984, A History of the Grand Mesa, 1983. Mem. The Soc. of Cin., SAR, Soc. Mayflower Descendants. Democrat. Mormon. Avocations: golf, skiing, camping.

LYNN, KATHERINE LYN, materials engineer, chemist; b. Nagoya, Japan, June 25, 1954; (parents Am. citizens); d. Jimmie Frank and Barbara Sue (Whiteside) Sutton; m. Richard Shelly Lynn, Feb. 28, 1981. BS in Chemistry cum laude, Calif. State U., Fullerton, 1979. Technician U.S. Borax Corp., Anaheim, Calif., 1974-79; chemist Armstrong World Industries, Southgate, Calif., 1979-82; project engr. Hydril Co., Whittier, Calif., 1982-84; materials engr. So. Calif. Gas Co., Los Angeles, 1984—. Patentee fluorspar flotation. Mem. So. Calif. Thermal Analysis Group (sec. 1985-87), Soc. Plastic Engrs., N. Am. Thermal Analysis Soc., Am. Chem. Soc., Sierra Club. Mem. Christian Ch. Avocations: outdoor activities, backpacking, Nordic and Alpine skiing. Home: 5120 Faust St Lakewood CA 90713 Office: So Calif Gas Co Box 3249 Terminal Annex ML730B Los Angeles CA 90051

LYNN, WILLIAM MAX, church administrator; b. Fox, Okla., July 20, 1927; s. Warren A. and Mary (Johnston) L.; B.S., UCLA, 1952; m. Elinor Jane Treiber, Feb. 28, 1953; children—Kevin Edward-Holmes, Daniel Warren, Nancy Edith, Colleen Erin. Mem. publicity dept. Metro-Goldwyn-Mayer Studios, Culver City, Calif., 1952-53; dir. bus. and finance United Ch. of Religious Sci., Los Angeles, 1953-82, dir. devel., 1982—, asst. chief exec. officer, 1982-85, dir. devel., 1985—; lectr., cons. ch. adminstrn. Served with AUS, 1945-48. Mem. Am. Mgmt. Assn., Am. Soc. for Tng. and Devel., Conf. Bd., Nat. Assn. Ch. Bus. Adminstrs., Town Hall, Newcomen Soc. Am., Acacia. Republican. Club: City (San Marino). Lodge: Rotary. Mem. United Ch. Religious Sci. Home: 2100 El Molino Ave San Marino CA 91108 Office: United Ch of Religious Sci 3251 W 6th St Los Angeles CA 90020

LYON, DAVID WILLIAM, research and development executive; b. Lansing, Mich., Mar. 26, 1941; s. Herbert Reid and Mary Kathleen (Slack) L.; m. Catherine McHugh Dillon, July 8, 1967. B.S., Mich. State U., 1963; M. City and Regional Planning, U. Calif., Berkeley, 1966, Ph.D., 1972. Regional economist Fed. Res. Bank Phila., 1969-71; research dir. human and econ. resources The N.Y.C.-Rand Inst., 1972-75, v.p., 1975; sr. economist The Rand Corp., Santa Monica, Calif., 1975-77, dep. v.p., 1977-79, v.p. domestic research div., 1979—; dir. Coll. Environ. Design Council, U. Calif., Berkeley, 1979—; adj. prof. U. Pa., 1975. Contbr. articles to profl. jours. Bd. dirs. Sr. Health and Peer Counseling Ctr., Santa Monica, Calif., 1985—. Mellon fellow in city planning, 1966-68; Econ. Devel. Adminstrn. grad. fellow, 1966. Mem. AAAS, Am. Econ. Assn. Club: Riviera Tennis (Pacific Palisades CA). Office: The Rand Corp 1700 Main St Santa Monica CA 90406

LYON, J. HART, retail executive; b. 1913; married. B.S. in Mktg., NYU, 1934. With Carter Hawley Hale Stores, 1958—; exec. v.p. mdse. and sales promotion Broadway Dept. Stores, 1958-68; pres., chief exec. officer Weinstock's, 1968-72; chmn., chief exec. officer The Broadway, 1972-79; corp. exec. v.p., dir. Carter Hawley Hale Stores, Los Angeles, 1979—. Bd. dirs. Los Angeles Countil Boy Scouts Am.; trustee Boys Club of Los Angeles. Served with USAAD, 1942-45. Mem. Assocs. of Los Angeles C. of C. Office: Carter Hawley Hale Stores Inc 550 S Flower St Los Angeles CA 90071

LYON, JOHN DAVID, lawyer, businessman; b. Tulsa, Feb. 16, 1937; s. Buford Carl and Mary Louise (Cochrane) L.; m. Melinda Mitchell, June 16, 1972. B.A., U. Chgo., 1955; J.D., Harvard U., 1960. Bar: N.Y. 1961, Calif. 1974, N.Mex., 1986. Assoc., Paul, Weiss, Rifkind, Wharton & Garrison, 1961-65; with Tosco Corp. and predecessor firm The Oil Shale Corp., Los Angeles, 1965-83, v.p., gen. counsel, 1979-75, exec. v.p., 1975-83, dir., 1979—, chief operating officer Oil Shale div., 1980-82, chief operating officer Comml. Devel. div., 1982-83; of counsel Katsky & Hunt, Los Angeles, 1984—; pres. The Cogeneration Co., Los Angeles, 1984—; pres. Lion Oil Co., 1976-77. Served with USAR, 1960-66. Mem. State Bar Calif., Assn. Bar City N.Y. Office: 9200 Sunset Blvd Suite 618 Los Angeles CA 90069

LYON, KEITH GEOFFREY, systems engineer, physicist; b. Springfield, Ill., Dec. 31, 1951; s. Wolcott Norbert and Marjorie Ann (Ingham) L. BS in Physics, Eastern Ill. U., 1973; PhD in Solid State Physics, Iowa State U., 1978. Tennis coach Iowa State U., Ames, 1975-77, teaching asst., 1973-75; research asst Ames Lab., 1975-78; lab. scientist Hughes Aircraft Co., El Segundo, Calif., 1978—; propr. Home Programmers Inc., Playa del Rey, Calif., 1985—. Contbr. articles on thermal expansion of solids to profl. jours. Mem. Sigma Xi, Sigma Pi Sigma. Republican. Clubs: Hughes Waterski (treas. 1983—), Hughes Tennis (v.p. 1982)(El Segundo). Avocations: tennis, water skiing, snow skiing, golf, restoring old cars. Home: 8828 Pershing Dr #302 Playa del Rey CA 90293 Office: Hughes Aircraft Co Space and Communications Group PO Box 92919 S32/C331 Los Angeles CA 90009

LYONS, ROBERT E., data processing executive; b. N.Y.C., Sept. 2, 1950; s. Thomas J. and Edna J. (Doyle) L.; m. Luciana G. Lyons, Dec. 3, 1983; 1 child, Emily. BS, Long Island U., 1973. Mgr. Bankers Trust, N.Y.C., 1974-75; head ops. Citibank Corp., N.Y.C., 1975-77; dir. ops. Tymshare, Inc., Fremont, Calif., 1977-82; v.p., project leader in-house data processing Assocs. Corp., Pleasanton, Calif., 1982—, also internal cons., 1982-84. Author: (software packages) Credit Application, 1983, Check Automation, 1984, In-house Credit Card System, 1985. Republican. Roman Catholic. Home: 2900 Sombrero Circle San Ramon CA 94583

LYONS, ROBIN STERN, mathematician; b. Chgo., Oct. 11, 1948; d. Milton Morgan and Bessie (Lewis) Stern; m. Lawrence Robert Lyons, Sept. 28, 1969; children: Eric Harold, Daniel Joseph. BA, UCLA, 1969, MA, 1970; MS, U. Colo., 1983. Tchr. Boulder (Colo.) Valley Schs., 1979-80; mathematician wave propagation lab. NOAA, Boulder, 1980-83; mathematician U.S. Army Missile Command, Redstone Arsenal, Calif., 1983-84, Aerospace Corp., El Segundo, Calif., 1984-85, TRW, Redondo Beach, Calif., 1985—. Contbr. articles to profl. jours. Mem. Sigma Xi. Home: 456 Via El Chico Redondo Beach CA 90277

LYONS, TERRENCE ALLAN, diversified manufacturing company executive; b. Grande Prairie, Alta., Can., Aug. 1, 1949; s. Allan Lynnwood and Mildred Helen (Smith) L. B.Applied Sci., U. B.C., 1972; M.B.A., U. Western Ont., 1974. Registered profl. engr., B.C. Gen. mgr. Southwestern Drug Co., Vancouver, B.C., Can., 1975-76; mgr. planning Versatile Corp., Vancouver, 1976-83, asst. v.p., 1983-86, v.p., dir., 1986— . Author articles on mfg. tech. Bd. dirs. Vancouver Jr. Achievement, 1974-78. Mem. B.C. Water Polo Assn. (sec. 1978-80). Office: Bentall Centre, 3300 1055 Dunsmuir St Box 49153, Vancouver, BC Canada V7X 1K3

LYONS, WILLIAM DEAN, banker; b. Newton, Iowa, Feb. 3, 1930; s. Guy Lyons and Edna (Salaway) White; m. Elaine M. Hegele, Aug. 26, 1932; children—Lynda C. Lyons Boss, Steven W., Duane W. B.B.A., San Diego State U., 1952; postgrad. U. Va. Grad. Sch. Banking, 1970-72. Mgr., Pacific Fin. Corp., Escondido, Calif., 1953-62, dist. mgr., Los Angeles, 1962-64; asst. v.p. Union Bank, Torrance, Calif., 1964-77; v.p., mgr. City Nat. Bank, Torrance, 1977-80, regional v.p., 1980-84, sr. v.p., Beverly Hills, Calif., 1984; sr. v.p., mgr. South Bay hdqrs. div. 1st Bus. Bank, Los Angeles, 1984—. Bd. dirs. Torrance Meml. Hosp. 1981-82, UCLA Harbor Collegium, 1983-84. Mem. Delta Sigma Phi (v.p. 1949-52; Athletic award 1950). Democrat. Office: 1st Bus Bank Gateway III Bldg 970 W 190th St Torrance CA 90502

LYRA, SYNESIO, JR., minister, theology educator; b. Recife, Brazil, Aug. 24, 1938; s. Synesio and Nisia (Gueiros) L.; m. Louise Kline, Sept. 21, 1968; children: Hans Eric, Christina Marie. MDiv, Faith Theol. Sem., 1961; D of Theology, Free U., Amsterdam, The Netherlands, 1964; D of Religion, Newport U., 1981. Ordained to ministry Presbyn. Ch. Asst. prof. Shelton Coll., Cape May, N.J., 1965-69; prof. theology grad. sch. Columbia (S.C.) Grad. Sch., 1969-71; asst. prof. Covenant Theol. Sem., St. Louis, 1971-76; minister of edn. The Crystal Cathedral, Garden Grove, Calif., 1976-79, dean lay ministers tng. ctr., 1976-79; assoc. prof. theology Internat. Sch. Theology, San Bernardino, Calif., 1979—; pres. bd. dirs. Crystal Cath. Acad., Garden Grove, 1977-78, also bd. dirs.; minister Mayflower Ch., Laguna Hills, Calif., 1985—; lectr. in field. Contbr. articles to profl. jours., columnist; author (study manual and audio cassettes) A New Laity. Lodge: Rotary (past bd. dirs., Paul Harris Fellow 1985). Avocations: reding, piano playing, travelling, gardening. Home: 8571 Enault Ln Garden Grove CA 92641 Office: Internat Sch Theology Arrowhead Springs San Bernardino CA 92412

LYTLE, CARLAH ELIZABETH, social work consultant; b. Rawlins, Wyo., 1927; s. Charles C. and Carlah B. (Martin) L. BA, U. Wyo., 1949, MA, 1950; MSW, U. Denver, 1956. Chief social worker County Dept. Pub. Welfare, Butte, Mont., 1956-57; field cons. child welfare County Dept. Pub. Welfare, Helena, Mont., 1957-60; chief social worker Butte Mental Hygiene Clinic, 1960; chief social worker dept. psychiatry and behavioral scis. U. Wash. Sch. Medicine, Seattle, 1961-66, head social work tng. sect., div. child psychiatry, dept. psychiatry and behavioral scis., 1977-80; acting assoc. dir. social service dept. U. Wash. Hosp., Seattle, 1966-68, assoc. dir. social service dept., 1968-77, acting adminstrv. dir. child, adolescent and family programs, outpatient child psychiatry clinic., 1975-77; pvt. practice in social work Seattle and Bellvue, Wash., 1966-78, 85—; acting dir. behavioral scis. Children's Orthopedic Hosp. and Med. Ctr., Seattle, 1980-81, dir. dept. social work, 1981-85; clin. prof. dept. Psychiatry and Behavioral Scis. U. Wash. Sch. Medicine, 1980-85. Mem. Nat. Assn. Social Workers (cert., regional rep. Pacific Northwest Regional Inst. 1965-66, chairperson 1965-66), Am. Group Psychotherapy Assn., Am. Pub. Health Assn., Soc. Hosp. Social Work Dirs., Am. Hosp. Assn., Northwest Inst. Family Therapy, Inc., NOW, Am. Orthopsychiat. Assn., Wash. Advs. for the Mentally Ill. Home: 2627 107th NE Bellevue WA 98004

MA, GABRIEL WAI CHIU, orthopedic surgeon; b. Hong Kong, Dec. 17, 1927; came to U.S., 1947, naturalized, 1963; s. Chui Tsui and Yuet-Hing (Wong) M.; m. Frances C.H. Siu, Mar. 3, 1951; children: Michael James G.S., Anthony Shane B.S. BA, Adelphi Coll., 1949; MB, U. Sydney, Australia, 1958. Diplomate Am. Bd. Orthopedic Surgery. Intern Leisham Gen Hosp., Sydney, 1958-59; teaching fellow orthopedic surgery Tufts U., 1960; resident in orthopedic surgery Lahey Clinic, Boston, 1961-64; practice medicine specializing in orthopedic surgery Honolulu, 1965; clin. instr. orthopedic surgery U. Hawaii, Honolulu, 1967-74, asst. clin. prof. surgery, 1973-74; chief orthopedic service St. Francis Hosp., 1969-74; asst. chief dept. orthopedic surgery Queens Med. Ctr., 1970, chief dept. orthopedic surgery, 1971—; cons. Tripler Army Hosp., Honolulu, 1972-74. Fellow ACS, Am. Acad. Orthopedic Surgeons; mem. Australian Med. Assn., AMA, Hawaii Med. Assn., Pan-Pacific Surgery Assn., Western Orthopedic Assn., Honolulu County Med. Soc. (chmn. Medicare claims rev. com. 1970), Hawaii Acad. Sci., Sigma Xi. Home: 3502 Kahawalu Dr Honolulu HI 96817 Office: 1380 Lusitana St Suite 214 Honolulu HI 96813

MA, LUCY BELLE, college program director; b. Elk City, Okla., Nov. 3, 1921; d. Robert Lee and Irene (Middleton) Stokes; m. Jonathan Kai-Ling Ma, June 12, 1967. AA, Wayland Coll., 1944; BA, Baylor U., 1947; MRE, Southwestern Sem., 1949. Bookkeeper, cashier Woolworth Co., Albuquerque, 1938-43; missionary Fgn. Mission Bd., So. Baptist Conv., Japan, 1949-61; dir. Baptist Student Ctr. U. N.Mex., Albuquerque, 1961-67; coordinator community service and continuing edn. N.Mex. State U., Grants, 1972—. Mem. AAUW (various positions 1980-86, named Woman of Yr. 1983-84), Delta Kappa Gamma (sec. 1986). Avocations: reading, writing, cooking, planning parties. Office: NMex State U 1500 N 3d St Grants NM 87020

MA, SHAO-MU, physical chemist; b. Kiangdo, Republic of China, Feb. 5, 1934; came to U.S., 1960; s. Sue-Chen and Q.N. (Be) M.; m. Jane Kuo-chen Chi, Dec. 22, 1964; children: Grace Yu-Chun, John Yu-Chien. BS, Nat. Taiwan U., Taipei, 1956; PhD in Chemistry, U. Utah, 1964. Rheologist and surface chemist Gen. Mills. Inc., Mpls., 1964-72; research assoc. U. Utah, Salt Lake City, 1972-76, asst. research prof., 1976—. Contbr. articles to profl. jours. Active Salt Lake City Sch. Dist. Council on Sch. Boundaries and Secondary Sch. Edn., 1984—. Grantee NIH, 1984; recipient Cert. Recognition for Tech. Innovation NASA, 1982. Mem. Am. Chem. Soc., Soc. Rheology. Buddhist. Home: 2230 Blaine Ave Salt Lake City UT 84108 Office: U Utah Dept Anesthesiology 50 Medical Dr Salt Lake City UT 84108

MA, WAI-SAI, biotechnology company executive; b. Canton, Peoples Republic of China, Sept. 13, 1943; came to U.S., 1962; s. Shin-ming and Ping (Won) M.; m. Cheuk-ling Kam, May, 1972; children: Joseph, Fontane. BS in Chemistry, U. Cin., 1966; PhD in Biochemistry, SUNY, Albany, 1971. Postdoctoral fellow Kidney Disease Inst. N.Y. State Dept. Health, Albany, 1971-73; sr. research scientist Dome Labs. div. of Miles Labs., West Haven, Conn., 1974-77; group leader tech. support lab. Abbott Diagnostics, North Chicago, Ill., 1977-78; mgr. of research and devel. Nuclear Med. Lab. div. of Warner Lambert, Dallas, 1978-82; dir. product devel. Syngene Products and Research div. Tech Am., Ft. Collins, Colo., 1982-83; v.p. ops. Tech Am. Diagnostics, San Marcos, Calif., 1983-85; pres. Animal Biotech Corp. div. NMS Pharms., Newport Beach, Calif., 1985—; bd. dirs. Advance Allergy Research Ctrs., Los Angeles, 1986—. Contbr. articles to profl. jours. Mem. AAAS, Am. Chem. Soc., N.Y. Acad. Sci. Office: Animal Biotech Corp 1531 Monrovia Ave Newport Beach CA 92663

MAAS, DARRYL WAYNE, process engineer; b. Glasgow, Mont., July 29, 1960; s. Albert H. and Elaine A. (Stohl) M.; m. Beverly Ann Cordis, Mar. 19, 1983. BS in Chemistry, Mont. State U., 1983. Process engr. Gould AMISemiconductors, Pocatello, Idaho, 1984-86, Lattice Semiconductor Corp., Beaverton, Oreg., 1986—. Home: 19015 NW Rock Creek Blvd Portland OR 97229

MAAS, SALLY ANN, journalist; b. Portage, Wis., Apr. 10, 1947; d. Franklin Arthur and Mabel Gladys (Engen) Maas; m. Robert A. Marshall, Aug. 3, 1973. BJ, U. Wis., 1969. Reporter, The Paper, Oshkosh, Wis., 1969-70; feature writer The Press, Binghamton, N.Y., 1970-71; feature writer The Press-Enterprise, Riverside, Calif., 1971-76, lifestyle editor, 1976-83, feature editor, 1983-85, asst. mng. editor features and art, 1985—. Recipient Outstanding Woman of Achievement award Bus. and Profl. Women's Club, 1981. Mem. Soc. Newspaper Design, Women in Communications, LWV, Sigma Delta Chi. Club: Twin Cities Press (past pres.). Home: 26925 Ladera Redlands CA 92373 Office: The Press-Enterprise Co 3512 14th St Riverside CA 92502

MABEY, EDWARD MILO, ins. agy. exec.; b. Bountiful, Utah, Feb. 26, 1919; s. Charles Rendell and Afton (Rampton) M.; student U. Utah, 1936-38, 40, San Francisco Trade Sch., 1941-42, U. Tenn., 1944; m. Edrice Louise Haslam, July 23, 1940 (div.); children—James Edward, Afton Louise Mabey Wettstein, Charlynn Edrice Mabey Scharlow; m. 2d, Gun Sundberg, Aug. 27, 1979; 1 dau., Amanda Gun. Book salesman, mgr. Edward Brown & Sons Gen. Ins. Co., Oakland, Calif., 1940-41; pres., dir. Western Gen. Agy., Inc., Salt Lake City, 1947-81; pres. Brother Christopher Inc. Western Underwriters, Inc.; chmn. bd., dir. Investment Mgmt. Corp.; pres., chmn. bd. Western Indsl. Shares, Inc.; chmn. bd. Bountiful State Bank, 1965-68; pres., dir. Western Holding Corp., 1973-76; mng. dir. Internat. Guaranteed Fund, Ltd.; dir., owner-developer Oakridge Improvement Co., Farmington, Utah; mng. dir. Bahamian Investment Mgmt. Ltd.; dir. Natural Resources, Inc., New Hemisphere Life Ins. Co., Victoria Falls Enterprises, Inc., Bayview Park Devel. Co., Woods Cross, Utah, Zions First Nat. Bank, Bountiful, Four-square Fund, Boston. Exec. dir. Utah Opera Co., 1979, pres., 1980-82, chmn. bd., 1982-85. Served with USNR, World War II. Mem. Intercollegiate Knights, Beta Theta Pi. Republican. Mem. Ch. Jesus Christ of Latter-day Saints. Clubs: Ambassador, Oakridge Country (dir.). Address: 780 E South Temple Salt Lake City UT 84102

MABIE, RUTH MARIE, realtor; b. Pueblo, Colo., Feb. 7; d. Newton Everett and Florence Ellen Allen; M.B.A., La Jolla U., 1980, Ph.D., 1981; m. Richard O. Mabie, Nov. 29, 1946; 1 son, Ward A. Mgr., LaMont Modeling Sch., San Diego, 1962; tchr. Am. Bus. Coll., San Diego, 1964-66; fashion modeling, 1960-72; owner, broker Ruth Mabile Realty, San Diego, 1972—; asst. v.p. Skil-Bilt, Inc., 1976—; dir. Mabie & Mintz, Inc. Bd. dirs. Multiple Sclerosis Dr., 1971—. Mem. San Diego Bd. Realtors, Nat. Assn. Female Execs. Republican. Office: 2231 Camino del Rio So #302 San Diego CA 92108-3605

MACALLISTER, JACK ALFRED, telephone company executive; b. Humeston, Iowa, July 12, 1927; s. Maxwell A. and Opal E. (Caldwell) MacA.; m. Marilyn Anderson, June 12, 1950; children: Steven, James, Sue. B.Commerce, U. Iowa, 1950; student, Iowa State Tchrs. Coll., Cedar Rapids, 1947-48. With Northwestern Bell Telephone Co., 1950-65, 67-83; v.p. ops. Northwestern Bell Telephone Co., Omaha, 1974-75, pres., 1965-82, chmn., 1982-83; pres., chief exec. officer U.S. West, Inc., Englewood, Colo., 1984-86, chmn. bd. dirs., chief exec. officer, 1986—; mem. staff AT&T, N.Y.C., 1965-67; bd. dirs. 1st Interstate bank of Los Angeles, The St. Paul Cos., Western Strategy Ctr. for Regional Devel.; mem. adv. bd. U. Pa. Wharton Sch. Fishman-Davidson Ctr. for study of service sector; mem. nat. adv. bd. U. Ariz.; mem. internat. adv. bd. Stanford Research; mem. Pvt. Sector Adv. Panel on Infrastructure Financing; mem. The Conf. Bd.; mem. Bus. Higher Edn. Forum. Trustee com. for econ. devel., mem. exec. bd. Denver Area council Boy Scouts Am.; bd. dirs. U. Iowa Found. Mem. Bus. Higher Edn. Forum, Gov.'s Econ. Devel. Council (co-chmn. Colo. chpt.), The Bus. Roundtable. Office: US West Inc 7800 E Orchard Rd Englewood CO 80111

MACARTHUR, TIMOTHY WAYNE, banking executive; b. Denver, May 29, 1959; s. Charles Roy and Patricia Louis (Hazelett) MacA. BABA, Western State Coll., 1980. Ops. analyst Colo. Nat. Bank, Denver, 1980-81, work coordinator, 1981, account exec., 1981-82, sales rep., 1982-84, mgr. dept., 1984-85, mgr. div., 1985-86, asst. v.p. ops., 1986—; bd. dirs. Quality Castings, Inc., Englewood, Colo. Corp. advisor Jr. Achievement, Denver, 1985; sect. chmn. United Way, 1986—. Mem. Denver C. of C. (pres.'s club 1984-85, sect. chmn. 1986—). Republican. Presbyterian. Lodge: Optimists. Avocations: skiing, reading, traveling, golf. Home: 1020 15th St #21H Denver CO 80202 Office: Colo Nat Bank Denver 17th and Champa Sts Denver CO 80217

MACCALLUM, (EDYTHE) LORENE, pharmacist, consultant; b. Monte Vista, Colo., Nov. 29, 1928; d. Francis Whittier and Bernice Viola (Martin) Scott; m. David Robertson MacCallum, June 12, 1952; children: Suzanne Rae MacCallum Homiak and Roxanne Kay MacCallum Batezel (twins), Tracy Scott, Tamara Lee MacCallum Johnson, Shauna Marie MacCallum Bost. B.S. in Pharmacy, U. Colo., 1950. Registered pharmacist, Colo. Pharmacist Presbyn. Hosp., Denver, 1950, Corner Pharmacy, Lamar, Colo., 1950-53; research pharmacist Nat. Chlorophyll Co., Lamar, 1953; relief pharmacist, various stores, Delta, Colo., 1957-59, Farmington, N.Mex., 1960-62, 71-79, Aztec, N.Mex., 1971-79; mgr. Med. Arts Pharmacy, Farmington, 1966-67; cons. pharmacist Navajo Hosp., Brethren in Christ Mission, Farmington, 1967-77; sales agt. Norris Realty, Farmington, 1977-78; pharmacist, owner, mgr. Lorene's Pharmacy, Farmington, 1979—; tax cons. H&R Block, Farmington, 1968; cons. Pub. Service Co., N.Mex. Intermediate Clinic, Planned Parenthood, Farmington, mem. N.Mex. Bd. Pharmacy. Advisor Order Rainbow for Girls, Farmington, 1975-78. Mem. Nat. Assn. Bds. Pharmacy (com. on internship tng., com. edn.), Nat. Assn. Retail Druggists, N.Mex. Pharm. Assn. (mem. exec. council 1977-81). Presbyterian. Club: Order Eastern Star (Farmington). Home: 1301 Camino Sol Farmington NM 87401 Office: 901 W Apache Farmington NM 87401

MACCOLLAM, JOEL ALLAN, clergyman, consultant; b. Albany, N.Y., Dec. 19, 1946; s. Allan and Edith MacCollam; m. Jann M. Scherer, May 3, 1975. BA, Hamilton Coll., 1968; MDiv, Gen. Theol. Sem., 1972; LLD, Calif. Grad. Sch. Theology, 1987. Ordained in Episc. Ch. Assoc. rector St. James' Ch., Oneonta, N.Y., 1973-74; rector St. Stephen's Ch., Schuylerville, N.Y., 1974-78; assoc. rector St. Mark's Ch., Glendale, Calif., 1978-79; dir. devel. Door of Hope Internat., Glendale, 1981-82, cons., 1982—; v.p. Voice of Americanism, Glendale, 1982-85; pres. World Emergency Relief, Glendale, 1986—. Author: The Way Doctrine, 1977, Carnival of Souls, 1978. Cons. various Rep. and conservative causes. Mem. Nat. Soc. Fund Raising Execs., Christian Ministry Mgmt. Assn. Office: World Emergency Relief PO Box 977 Glendale CA 91209

MACCOLLUM, DAVID VICTOR, safety engineering consultant; b. Portland, Oreg., June 10, 1923; s. Victor White and Jane (Williams) MacC.; m. Anne McDonald, May 10, 1952; children: Sandra, Judith, William. BS, Oreg. State U., 1951. Registered profl. engr., Ariz., Calif.; cert. safety profl. Safety engr. Oreg. Indsl. Accident Commn., 1951-55, Portland Dist. C.E., 1955-61; dir. safety Dept. Army, Ft. Lewis, Tacoma, 1961-63, Dept. Army, Ft. Huachuca, Sierra Vista, Ariz., 1963-69, Army Communications, Ft. Huchuca, 1969-72; safety cons. D.V. MacCollum, Ltd., Sierra Vista, 1972—; mem. constrn. safety commn., U.S. Dept. Labor, Washington, 1969-72; expert witness State and Fed. Cts., nationwide, 1972—. Served with USN, 1942-45, PTO. Mem. NSPE (pres. Cochise chpt. 1965), Am. Soc. Safety Engrs. (pres. 1975-76), Human Factors Soc., Assn. Mining Engrs., System Safety Soc. Republican. Mem. United Ch. Christ. Lodges: Kiwanis, Rotary, Masons, Shriners. Home and Office: 1515 Hummingbird Ln Sierra Vista CA 85635

MACCORKINDALE, SIMON CHARLES PENDERED, actor; b. Ely, Cambridge, Eng., Feb. 12, 1952; came to U.S., 1981; s. Peter Bernard and Gilliver Mary (Pendered) MacC.; m. Fiona Elizabeth Fullerton, July 10, 1976 (div. Sept. 1983); m. Susan Melody George, Oct. 5, 1984. Student, Haileybury Coll., Hertford, Eng., 1965-70. Producer, dir. Amy Internat. Prodns., Inc., Los Angeles, 1984—, Amy Internat. Prodns., Ltd., Middlesex, Eng., 1987—. Appeared in feature films Juggernaut, 1974, Road to Mandalay, 1977, Death on the Nile, 1977, The Riddle of the Sands, 1978, The Quatermass Conclusion, 1978, Cabo Blanco, 1979, Outpost of Progress, 1981, The Sword & the Sorcerer, 1981, Falcon's Gold, 1982, Jaws 3-D, 1982; made for TV and mini-series Time and Again, 1974, Jesus of Nazareth, 1975, Three Weeks, 1976, Out of Battle, 1977, Quartermass, 1978, The Hammer House of Horror, 1980, The Mansions of America, 1980-81, Obsessive Love, 1984, Sincerely, Violet, 1986; TV series Hawkeye the Pathfinder, 1973, General Hospital, 1974, Skin Game, 1974, Sutherland's Law, 1975, Hunter's Walk, 1975, I, Claudius, 1976, Will Shakespeare, 1976, Romeo and Juliet, 1976, Baby for Beasts, 1976, Just William, 1977, Within These Walls, 1977, Doomdolt Chase, 1977, This is Your Life, 1977, Dukes of Hazzard, 1979, Scalpels, 1980, Fantasy Island, 1981, Macbeth, 1981, Hart to Hart, 1982, Dynasty, 1982, Manimal, 1983, Matt Houston, 1984, Falcon Crest, 1984-86, Future Probe II, 1985; theatre appearances include Journey's End, 1973, Getting On, 1973, Front Page, 1973, Bequest to the Nation, 1973, Back to Methuselah, 1973, Potsdam Quartet, 1973, Happiest Days of Your Life, 1974, Pygmalion, 1974, B-B-Que, 1974, Relatively Speaking, 1974, 77, French Without Tears, 1975, Dark Lady of the Sonnets, 1975, 77, Gayden Chronicles, 1980, Macbeth, 1980, A Merchant of Venice, 1981, A Doll House, 1982, Sleuth, 1982; appeared in one man show The Importance of Being Oscar, 1977, 80, 81, 82, 85. Named Most Promising Newcomer to Motion Pictures, Brit. Standard awards London, 1978. Mem. Acad. Motion Picture Arts and Scis., Brit. Acad. Film and TV Arts, Am. Film Inst., Acad. TV Arts and Scis., Stars Orgn. for Spastics, Screen Actors Guild, Dirs. Guild Am., Brit. Actors Equity. Club: St. James (London). Avocations: sports, photography, opera, travel. Office: Kaufman & Bernstein #2270 1900 Ave of the Stars Los Angeles CA 90067

MACCULLOUGH, ANN WINSLOW, community and social service executive; b. Washington; d. Joseph E. and Agnes B. Winslow; m. Craig C. MacCullough, 1963; children: Sharin, Andrew. Student State Tchrs. Coll., Towson, Md. Exec. sec. GAO, Washington, 1957-64, Design Premiums, Inc., Continuous Curve Contact Lenses, Inc., Zapata Ocean Resources and Travelodge-Trusthouse Forte, San Diego; officer, bus. mgr., adminstrv. asst. MacCullough Brown Assocs., San Francisco and San Diego, 1980-85; dir. family options program YMCA, San Diego, 1985—. Dir. canteen service Bethesda (Md.) Naval Med. Hosp., ARC, 1961-62; treas. Jaycee Wives, Bethesda, 1969-70; chmn. com. Parkwood Elem. Sch. PTA, 1973, 74, 75; sec. Parkwood Civic Assn., 1975-76; mem. San Carlos (Calif.) Protective Assn., 1980; mem. San Carlos Area Council, 1980, 81, 82, 83; 1st v.p., 1981-82, pres., 1982-85; key area supr. campaign for mayor of San Diego, 1983-84; mem. San Carlos Friends of Library; mem. cen. bd. San Diego Friends of Library; sec. Save Our Heritage Orgn., 1986-87; mem. citizen's adv. com. Sander Project, 1985-87; mem. San Diego County Commn. Status Women, 1985-87; co-chmn. Mayor's Council on Neighborhoods, 1985-86; bd. dirs. Navajo Community Planners, 1984-85, v.p. 1986-87; bd. dirs. Hillcrest Assn.; dir. vols. Dem. congl. campaign in 41st Calif. dist., San Diego, 1984. Mem. Save our Heritage Orgn. (sec. 1986-87). Clubs: Kenwood Golf and Country (Bethesda); San Carlos Swim and Racquet (San Diego); Porsche of Am.

MACDONALD, CRAIG CURRY, public relations executive; b. Oakland, Calif., Sept. 26, 1949; s. Franklin and Jane (Curry) MacD.; m. Debbie Stock, Nov. 5, 1980; 1 child, Christopher. BA in Social Sci., San Jose State U., 1971. Reporter The San Diego Union, 1972-79, columnist nationally syndicated newspaper, 1975-80; contbg. editor AirCal Mag., 1975-81; with public relations dept. Pacific Bell, Orange and Los Angeles, San Francisco and Calif., 1980—; dir. media relations 1984 Los Angeles Olympics Pacific Bell, 1983-84; subject of Pub. Relations Jour. cover story, 1984; guest lectr. various univs. Author: Charley Park Hurst, 1973, Ghost Town Glimpses, 1975, Leather 'N Lead, 1976, Gold, 1984, (poems) See The Train, 1985, The Strange West, 1986; editor: Operator 1982; co-composer record and music video: LA- Here's Lookin' At Ya, 1984. Served with USAR, 1972-77. Recipient First Place award Pub. Relations Soc. Am., 1982, Arthur Page award AT&T, 1983, Golden Reel award Internat. TV Assn., 1983, Pub. Relations Soc. Am. award, 1985, Consumer Affairs Reporting award J.C. Penney-U. Mo., 1974, Best Publ. award Orange County Press Club, 1987; Copley Newspapers fellow, 1972; nominee Pulitzer prize, 1974. Mem. ASCAP, Soc. Profl. Journalists, San Diego Press Club (charter), Phi Alpha Theta, Phi Kappa Phi. Club: San Diego Press (charter), Orange County Press, Internat. Assn. Bus. Communicators, Calif. Writer's.

MACDONALD, DIGBY DONALD, science administrator; b. Thames, New Zealand, Dec. 7, 1943; came to U.S., 1977; s. Leslie Graham and Francis Helena (Verry) MacD.; m. Mirna Urquidi, July 6, 1985; children: Leigh Vanessa, Matthew Digby, Duncan Paul. BS in Chemistry, U. Auckland, New Zealand, 1965; MS in Chemistry with honors, U. Auckland, 1966; PhD, U. Calgary, Alta., Can., 1969. Asst. research officer Atomic Energy of Can., Pinawa, Man., Can., 1969-72; lectr. Victoria U., Wellington, New Zealand, 1972-75; sr. research assoc., assoc prof. Alta. Sulfur Research U. Calgary, 1975-77; sr. metallurgist SRI Internat., Menlo Park, Calif., 1977-79; prof. metall. engring. Ohio State U., Columbus, Ohio, 1979-84; lab. dir. SRI Internat., Menlo Park, 1984—; adj. prof. Ohio State U., 1984; cons. in field. Author: Transient Techniques in Electrochemistry, 1977; contbr. numerous articles to profl. jours.; patentee in field. Nat. Research Council scholar, Ottawa, Can., 1967-69; recipient Research award Ohio State U., 1983. Mem. Electrochem. Soc. (div. editor 1982-84), Nat. Assn. Corrosion Engrs. (pub. com. 1982—), Metall. Soc. of AIME, Am. Chem. Soc. Clubs: Aero Squadron (Columbus), Stanford Flying (Palo Alto). Avocations: sailing, flying. Home: 44406 Arapaho Ave Fremont CA 94539 Office: SRI Internat 333 Ravenswood Ave Menlo Park CA 94025

MACDONALD, DOUGLAS ALAN, aerospace engineer; b. Seattle, Feb. 15, 1954; s. Rae Douglas and Katherine Laura (Shoaf) M. BS, Fla. State U., 1975; MS, Calif. Inst. Tech., 1981, PhD, 1984. Cons. Rand Corp., Santa Monica, Calif., 1977-81; mem. tech. staff Rockwell Internat., Anaheim, Calif., 1984—. Co-editor: Black Holes: The Membrane Paradigm, 1986. Mem. Am. Phys. Soc., Sigma Xi. Democrat. Avocations: volleyball, reading Shakespeare. Office: Rockwell Internat 3370 Mira Loma Ave Anaheim CA 92803

MAC DONALD, ELLEN KAYE, hospital corporation executive; b. Visalia, Calif., Oct. 9, 1950; d. Ian Dunbar and Claudine (Burch) Stubbs. M.P.H., UCLA, 1984. Dir. med. records AMI, Los Angeles, 1972-75, cons. AMI/Stat Records, 1975-78, v.p. Stat Records, 1978-82, pres., 1984—, corp. asst. v.p. AMI, 1982, v.p., 1983—. Author: (with others) Physician's Guide to DRGS, 1984, Hospital Coding Guidelines, 1984. Mem. So. Calif. Med. Records Assn. (pres. 1985-86), Calif. Med. Records Assn. (chmn. pub. relations 1984-85), Am. Med. Records Assn., Calif. Med. Records Assn., So. Calif. Soc. Hosp. Risk Mgrs., Nat. Assn. Med. Staff Coordinators. Avocations: tennis, aerobics, skiing, reading. Office: AMI/STAT Records Inc 9601 Wilshire Blvd Suite 744 Beverly Hills CA 90210

MACDONALD, J. HOWARD, petroleum company executive. Chmn., chief exec. officer, chief fin. officer, dir. Dome Petroleum Ltd., Calgary. Office: Dome Petroleum Ltd, 333 7th Ave SW, Calgary, AB Canada T2P 2Z1 *

MACDONALD, NORVAL WOODROW, safety engineer; b. Medford, Oreg., Dec. 8, 1913; s. Orion and Edith (Anderson) MacD.; m. Elizabeth Ann Clifford, Dec. 8, 1937; children: Linda (Mrs. Bob Comings), Peggy (Mrs. Don Lake), Kathleen. Student, U. So. Calif., 1932-34. Registered profl. safety engr., Calif. Safety engr. Todd Shipyards, San Pedro, Calif., 1942-44, Pacific Indemnity Ins. Co., San Francisco, 1944-50; area safety engring. mgr. Indsl. Ind., San Francisco, 1950-76; v.p. loss control Beaver Ins. Co., 1976—; tchr. adult evening classes U. San Francisco, 1960-63, Golden Gate U., 1969—. Contbr. articles to profl. jours. Mem. Am. Soc. Safety Engrs. (pres. 1958-59), Engrs. Club San Francisco. Methodist. Club: Las Posas Country (Camarillo, Calif.). Lodge: Masons. Home: 1710 E Shoreline Camarillo CA 93010 Office: Beaver Loss Control 100 California St San Francisco CA 94111

MACDONALD, PETER, SR., tribal official, electrical engineer; b. Teecnospos, Ariz., Dec. 16, 1928; s. Dyahthlni and Lucy (Ute) Begay; m. Wanda L. LeClere, June 1973; children: Hope Marie, Faith Ann, Charity Lynn; children by previous marriage: Linda, Peter. AA, Bacone Coll., 1952; BS, U. Okla., 1957. Project engr., mem. tech. staff Hughes Aircraft Co., El Segundo, Calif., 1957-63; dir. mgmt. and procedures Navajo Tribe, Window Rock, Ariz., 1963-65; exec. dir. Office of Navajo Econ. Opportunity, Ft. Defiance, Ariz., 1965-70; chmn. Navajo Tribal Council, 1970-82, 86—. Mem. N.Mex. Gov.'s Econ. Devel. Adv. Group, 1963-67, N.Mex. State Planning Com., 1963-67; mem. nat. task force for mgmt. and career devel. OEO, 1968-69; mem., v.p. Leadership Inst. for Community Devel., 1968; mem. Four Corners Regional N.Mex. tech. action panels, 1968; del. Rep. Nat. Conv., 1972. Served as cpl. USMC, 1944-46, PTO. Republican. Baptist. Office: Navajo Tribal Council PO Box 308 Window Rock AZ 86515 *

MACDONALD, RICHARD JOHN, engineering company executive, educator; b. Hudson, N.Y., Mar. 1, 1931; s. Duncan Stanislaus and Ann Marie (Dauner) M.; m. Gene Ann Simpson, Sept. 10, 1955 (dec. 1971); children—John, Jeff, James, David, Kevin; m. Carol Ann Lethbridge, Nov. 1, 1980; children—James, Teresa. B.S., UCLA, 1953; M.B.A., U. So. Calif., 1969. Mgmt. devel. Garrett, Los Angeles, 1956-67; mgmt. devel. McDonnell-Douglas, Long Beach, Calif., 1967-68; dir. tng. Transcon, El Segundo, Calif., 1968-75; mgmt. devel. Fluor, Irvine, Calif., 1975-78; mgr. personnel devel. Parsons, Pasadena, Calif., 1978—; instr. Cypress Coll., Calif., 1977-78, U. Phoenix, Costa Mesa, Calif., 1984—. Contbr. article to mag. Mem. Pasadena Pvt. Industry Council, 1984, exec. devel. group Calif. Inst. Tech., 1984, Pasadena City Coll. Adv. Bd., 1984. Mem. Am. Soc. Tng. and Devel. (lectr. 1983—). Republican. Roman Catholic. Home: 1969 Berkshire Dr Fullerton CA 92633 Office: Parsons 100 W Walnut St Pasadena CA 91124

MACDONALD, RODERICK LEE, business executive, botanical consultant, plant ecologist; b. Paw Paw, Mich., Oct. 11, 1949; s. Lee H. and Vivian Ella (Clark) M.; m. Wendy Kay Kinsel, May 22, 1971 (div. 1974); m. Maura Elizabeth Metz, May 21, 1983. B.S. in Biology with dept. honors magna cum laude, Alma Coll., 1971; M.S. in Botany, U. Calif.-Davis, 1974. Bot. cons., interior landscape maintenance, 1974—. Active creation of habitat, Fair Oaks, Calif., 1974-79. Danforth fellow, 1971-74. Mem. AAAS. Office: PO Box 4195 Davis CA 95617

MACDONALD, VIRGINIA BROOKS, architect; b. Denver, July 17, 1918; d. Emmet Earl and Lulu (Gatchel) Stoffel; widowed; m. Russell A. Apple, Oct. 18, 1981; children: Philip Brooks, Anne Brooks Hormann, Bill Brooks, Mike Brooks. BArch, Case Western Res. U., 1946. Registered architect, Hawaii. Dir. Timberline Camp., Honolulu, 1962-67; planner State of Hawaii, Honolulu, 1967-77; pvt. practice architecture Volcano, Hawaii, 1977—. Author: West Hawaii, 1972; (book/report) Na Ala Hele, 1973. Active Volcano Community Assn., 1980—. Recipient Innovative Energy award U.S. Dept. Energy, 1984, Energy Saving award State of Hawaii, 1984. Mem. AIA (pres. elect. local sect. 1986—), Sierra Club (past state bd. dirs), Hawaii Conservation Council (past state pres.). Avocations: snorkeling, hiking, cooking. Home and Office: PO Box 32 Hawaii National Park HI 96718

MACDONOUGH, ROBERT HOWARD, consulting engineer; b. Chgo., Jan. 24, 1941; s. John Haaf and Helen Margaret (McWilliams) MacD.; m. Joan Carol Rosecrants, Dec. 28, 1963 (div. Nov. 1975); children: John Haaf, Thomas William, Mark Peter. BS in Engring. Ops., Iowa State U., 1962; MA in Econ., Drake U., 1966. Registered profl. engr., Iowa. Assoc. Mgmt. Sci. Am., Palo Alto, Calif., 1969; mng. assoc. Theo. Barry & Assoc., Los Angeles, 1970-72; mgr. indsl. engring. Advanced Memory Systems, Sunnyvale, Calif., 1972-73; mgr. planning and engring. Signetics, Sunnyvale, 1973-75; pres. Facilities Cons., Mountain View, Calif., 1976—. Mem. Inst. Indsl. Engrs. (sr.), Am. Inst. Plant Engrs., Am. Contract Bridge League, Phi Gamma Delta. Republican.

MACDOUGALL, JOHN DOUGLAS, earth science educator; b. Toronto, Ont., Can., Mar. 9, 1944; s. Lorn Graham and Grace A. (Virtue) MacD.; m. Shiela Dawn Ward, June 8, 1968; children: Christopher David, Katherine Heather. BS, U. Toronto, 1967; MS, McMaster U., 1968; PhD, U. Calif.-San Diego, 1972. Asst. research geologist U. Calif., Berkeley, 1972-74; prof. earth scis. Scripps Inst. Oceanography U Calif.-San Diego, La Jolla, 1974—, chmn. geol. research div., 1985—. Contbr. articles to profl. jours. Mem. AAAS, Gochem. Soc., Meteoritical Soc., Am. Geophys. Union. Home: 534 Bonair St La Jolla CA 92037 Office: Scripps Inst Oceanography A-020 La Jolla CA 92093

MACE, JAMES PATRICK, social worker, educator, computer programmer; b. Sutton, W.Va., Oct. 9, 1949; s. Garland Deo and Georgia Maria Mace; m. Holly Marlene Rodgers, Aug. 24, 1985. BA in Psychology, W.Va. U., 1972, MSW, 1976. Lic. clin. social worker, Calif. Social worker II Spencer (W.Va.) State Hosp., 1972-75, dir. crisis unit, 1976-78; dir. Jackson County Guidance Clinic, Ravenswood, W.Va., 1978-81; group home supr. Ettie Lee Homes Inc., Baldwin Park, Calif., 1982-83; programmer UCLA Sch. Social Welfare, 1984-86, UCLA Sch. Nursing, 1986—; asst. prof. Calif. State U., Long Beach, 1986-87; programmer Los Angeles County Dept. Mental Health; bd. dirs. Roane County Sheltered Workshop, Spencer, 1973-76, Jackson County Sheltered Workshop, Ripley, W.Va., 1979-81. Mem. Nat. Assn. Social Workers, Sierra Club. Avocation: mountain climbing.

MACE, JOHN WELDON, physician; b. Buena Vista, Va., July 9, 1938; s. John Henry and Gladys Elizabeth (Edwards) M.; m. Janice Mace, Jan. 28, 1962; children—Karin E., John E., James E. B.A., Columbia Union Coll., 1960; M.D., Loma Linda U., 1964. Diplomate: Am. Bd. Pediatrics, Sub-bd. Pediatric Endocrinology. Intern U.S. Naval Hosp., San Diego, 1964-65; resident in pediatrics U.S. Naval Hosp., 1966-68; fellow in endocrinology and metabolism U. Colo., 1970-72; asst. prof. pediatrics Loma Linda (Calif.) U. Med. Center, 1972-75, prof., chmn. dept., 1975—; bd. dirs. Inland Counties Devel. Disabilities Services, 1970—. Contbr. articles to profl. jours. Treas. Found. for Med. Care, San Bernardino County, 1979-80, pres., 1980—; mem. Congl. Adb. Bd., 1984—; pres. So. Calif. affiliate Am. Diabetes Assn., 1985-86; mem. adv. bd. State Calif. Children's Services, 1986—. Served with USN, 1962-70. Mem. N.Y. Acad. Scis., AAAS, Calif. Med. Soc. (adv. panel genetic diseases State Calif. 1975—), Am. Diabetes Assn. So. Calif. (dir. 1980—), Western Soc. Pediatric Research, Lawson Wilkens Pediatric Endocrine Soc., Assn. Med. Pediatric Dept. Chairmen, Sigma Xi, Alpha Omega Alpha. Office: Loma Linda U Dept Pediatrics Med Center Barton & Anderson Sts Loma Linda CA 92350

MACELWEE, MRS. IRVIN REED (HELENE C. MACELWEE), civic worker, club woman, business executive; b. Stevens Point, Wis.; d. Joseph Victor and Jeannette M. (Gasche) Collins; B.E., U. Wis., Stevens Point; postgrad. Carroll Coll.; B.Lit. Sci., U. Wis., Madison, 1918; m. Irvin Reed MacElwee, Dec. 29, 1927; children—Marilyn Jean Macelwee Throckmorton, Donald Beall. Dir. Fibremold, Inc., Woburn, Mass. Apptd. to 1960 Assay Commn. Mem. bd. Phila. Cancer Dr., 1954-64; hon. pres. St. Christopher's Hosp. Auxiliary, 1957-61. Mem. advisory com. Phila. Com. on Alcoholism. Pres. Pa. Council Republican Women, 1960-62; pres. Rep. Women Pa., 1954-60; mem. bd. Nat. Fedn. Rep. Women, 1960-64, mem. exec. bd., 1962-64; alternate del. Rep. Nat. Conv., 1972, 76. Bd. dirs. Soc. Retarded Children, March of Dimes, Phila., Women's Soc. Prevention Cruelty to Animals; active Tucson Symphony, 1978-82, Ariz. Theater Co. Recipient Plaque for citizenship work in Swarthmore, Lions Club, 1966; Alumni Achievement award, U. Wis., 1969. Mem. D.A.R. (Phila. chpt. regent 1956-59, state program chmn. 1957-67), Am. Acad. Polit. and Social Scis., Los Angeles Mus. Art, Daus. 17th Century, Colonial Dames Am., Needlework Guild Am. (dir. Swarthmore br. 1935-79), Woman's Med. Coll. Aux., Sons and Daus. Pilgrims, Soc. Preservation Old Landmarks, AAUW, Am. Contract Bridge Assn., Nat. Geog. Soc., U. Wis. Phila. Alumni Assn. (v.p. 1958-61, 64-69), Internat. Platform Assn., Smithsonian Assocs., Strawberry Mansion and Com. of 1926, Delta Zeta (dir. eastern region 1926-34). Presbyterian. Clubs: Nat. Travel; Union League; Springhaven Golf (Wallingford, Pa.); Capitol Hill (Washington). Home: 861 Camino del Monte Green Valley AZ 85614

MACFARLANE, GORDON FREDERICK, telephone company executive; b. Victoria, B.C., Can., Sept. 21, 1925; s. Frederick Randolph and Nora Margaret (La Fortune) MacF.; m. Hazel Louise Major, June 1946; children: Michael, Gordon, Ann L. McFarlane Patterson, Katherine M. McFarlane Bernard. B.S.E.E., U. B.C. Chief engr., dir. plant services B.C. Telephone Co., Vancouver, 1966-67, v.p. ops., 1967-70, v.p. corp. devel., 1970-76, v.p. adminstr., 1976; chmn., chief exec. officer B.C. Telephone Co., Burnaby, 1977—; pres., chief exec. officer GTE Automatic Elec., Brockville, Ont., Can., 1976-77; chmn. Microtel Ltd.; chmn., pres. chief exec. officer North-West Telephone Co., Telecom Leasing Can. (TLC) Ltd.; dir. Microtel Pacific Research Ltd., B.C. Forest Products Ltd., Can. Telephones and Supplies

Ltd., Bank of N.S., Inland Natural Gas Co. Ltd. Past pres., mem. bd. govs. Vancouver Pub. Aquarium Assn. Mem. IEEE (McNaughton medal 1982), Assn. Profl. Engrs. B.C., Telephone Pioneers Am. Office: BC Telephone, 21-3777 Kingsway, Burnaby, BC Canada V5H 3Z7

MACFARLANE, ROBERT BRUCE, research biological oceanographer; b. Greensburg, Pa., Jan. 24, 1947; s. Samuel and Elizabeth Mae (Ramsey) MacF.; m. Christine Anne Stuart. Dec. 10, 1968. BS, Pa. State U., 1968; MS, Fla. State U., 1970, PhD, 1980. Research asst. Dept. Food and Dairy Sci., Pa. State U., 1967-68; research asst. Dept. Oceanography, Fla. State U., Tallahassee, 1968-70, 75-76, teaching asst., 1976-77, instr., 1978-80; research oceanographer NOAA, Tiburon, Calif., 1980—; tech. advisor Calif. Water Resources Control Bd., Sacramento, 1982—, EPA San Francisco Bay Delta Project, San Francisco, 1987. Contbr. numerous articles to profl. jours. Served to capt. USAF, 1970-75. Recipient Quality Step Increase award NOAA and Dept. Commerce, 1984, Sustained Superior Performance award NOAA and Dept. Commerce, 1985. Mem. AAAS, Am. Chem. Soc., Am. Soc. Zoologists, Am. Fisheries Soc., Am. Inst. Fisheries Research Biologists, Sierra Club, Sigma Xi. Democrat. Avocations: skiing, tennis, backpacking, flying, fishing. Home: 55 San Joaquin Pl Novato CA 94947 Office: NOAA 3150 Paradise Dr Tiburon CA 94920

MACGILL, TERI LYNN, internal auditor; b. Brewster, Wash., Aug. 27, 1953; d. Vincent Vidger and Eileen Phyllis (Lynch) Wehmeyer; m. Robert Edward MacGill, July 2, 1975; children—Jennifer Anne, Charles Bryson. B.A. in Bus. Adminstrn. and Acctg., U. Wash., 1975. C.P.A., Wash., Alaska, Oreg.; cert. internal auditor, info. systems auditor. Revenue auditor State of Wash., Seattle, 1975-78, State of Alaska, Anchorage, 1978-81; Internal auditor State of Alaska, 1981; internal audit dir. Anchorage Sch. Dist., 1981-83; internal auditor Blue Cross/Blue Shield of Oreg., Portland, 1984—; pvt. practice pub. acctg., Dundee, Oreg., 1983—. Bd. dirs. Hillcrest Day Care Ctr., Inc., Anchorage, 1980-82. Named Citizen of Day, No. Lights Broadcasting, Anchorage, 1982. Mem. Am. Inst. C.P.A.s, Inst. Internal Auditors, EDP Auditors Assn. Democrat. Episcopalian. Home: PO Box 213 Dundee OR 97115 Office: Blue Cross/Blue Shield of Oreg 100 SW Market St Portland OR 97201

MACGINITIE, WALTER HAROLD, psychologist; b. Carmel, Calif., Aug. 14, 1928; s. George Eber and Nettie Lorene (Murray) MacG.; m. Ruth Olive Kilpatrick, Sept. 2, 1950; children: Mary Catherine, Laura Anne. B.A., UCLA, 1949; A.M., Stanford U., 1950; Ph.D., Columbia U., 1960. Tchr. Long Beach (Calif.) Unified Sch. Dist., 1950, 1955-56; mem. faculty Columbia U. Tchrs. Coll., 1959-80, prof. psychology and edn., 1970-80; Lansdowne scholar, prof. edn. U. Victoria, B.C., Can., 1980-84; research assoc. Lexington Sch. Deaf, N.Y.C., 1963-69. Co-author: Gates-MacGinitie Reading Tests, 1965, 78, Psychological Foundations of Education, 1968; Editor: Assessment Problems in Reading, 1972; co-editor: Verbal Behavior of the Deaf Child, 1969. Life mem. Calif. PTA. Served with USAF, 1950-54. Fellow Am. Psychol. Assn., AAAS, Nat. Conf. Research English, N.Y. Acad. Scis.; mem. Internat. Reading Assn. (pres. 1976-77), Reading Hall of Fame. Home and Office: PO Box 1728 Friday Harbor WA 98250

MACGREGOR, DONALD LANE, JR., banker; b. Duluth, Minn., June 21, 1931; s. Donald Lane and Julia (Waldo) MacG.; m. Mary Jo Rouse, Sept. 27, 1959; children—Jeffrey Lane, Steven Scott, John Rouse. Student, Carleton Coll., 1948-51; B.A. in Econs., Macalester Coll., 1956. Asst. cashier 1st Nat. Bank of Mpls., 1956-61; v.p. United Calif. Bank, San Francisco, 1961-69; pres. Ormand Industries, Dallas, 1969-70; v.p. United Calif. Bank, Los Angeles, 1970-71; pres., chief operating officer Am. Security Bank (name now Interstate Bank of Hawaii), Honolulu, 1972-83, pres., chief exec. officer, 1983—. Bd. dirs. Aloha council Boy Scouts Am., Hawaii, 1974—; hon. trustee Hawaii Army Mus. Soc., Honolulu, 1978—; bd. regents Chaminade U., Honolulu. Served to capt. USAF, 1951-55. Mem. Am. Bankers Assn. (leadership del. 1984-86), Hawaii Bankers Assn. (pres. 1986-87), Hawaii C. of C. (bd. dirs. 1985—). Republican. Clubs: Outrigger Canoe, Pacific, Waialae Country (Honolulu). Office: First Interstate Bank of Hawaii 1314 S King St Honolulu HI 96814

MACHIDA, CURTIS A., research molecular neurobiologist; b. San Francisco, Apr. 1, 1954. AB, U. Calif., Berkeley, 1976; PhD, Oreg. Health Scis. U., 1982. Postdoctoral scientist Oreg. Health Scis. U., Portland, 1982—. Editorial cons. Oreg. Health Scis. U. News, 1984-87; contbr. articles to profl. jours. NIH fellow 1980-82, 85-87; recipient Leukemia Assn. award, 1981, Tartar award Med. Research Found. Oreg., 1980. Mem. AAAS, Am. Soc. Microbiology. Office: Oreg Health Scis U Inst Advanced Biomed Research L 474 Portland OR 97201

MACHIDA, EILEEN MARIE, software engineer, consultant; b. Los Angeles, July 25, 1954; d. Edward and Ayako (Nomura) M. BS, UCLA, 1978. Systems programmer UCLA, 1979-82, Transaction Tech. Inc., Santa Monica, Calif., 1982-83; software engr. Interactive Systems, Santa Monica, 1983—; cons. Megadyne Info. Systems, Santa Monica, 1983-85. Mem. Assn. for Computing Machinery, AAAS, IEEE (affiliate). Avocations: writing, political research, music, bridge. Office: Interactive Systems Corp 2401 Colorado Santa Monica CA 90405

MACHO, KENNETH JOHN, geologist; b. Whittier, Calif., Apr. 3, 1948; s. Cecil Mark and Muriel (Ross) M. B.S. in Geology, Kans. State U., 1970. Geologist, Gulf Oil, Morgan City, La., 1970-74; geol. engr. Tenneco Oil, Oklahoma City, 1975-77, sr. engr., project geol. engr., Midland and San Antonio, Tex., 1977-79, geol. supr., Denver, 1979-80, div. geol. engr., Denver and Bakersfield, Calif., 1980—, geol. cons., 1986—. Served with U.S. Army, USAF, 1971-77. Mem. Am. Assn. Petroleum Geologists, Soc. Profl. Well Log Analysts, Soc. Petroleum Engrs., Sigma Gamma Epsilon. Republican. Roman Catholic. Home: 3008 Bralorne Ct Bakersfield CA 93309 Office: Tenneco Oil Co 10000 Ming Ave Bakersfield CA 93389

MACHUGA, ADAM J., math and engineering educator; b. Erie, Pa., Jan. 24, 1920; s. Stephen and Anna (Dufala) M.; m. Virginia B. Peters, June 6, 1942; children: James A., Ric S. Student, Lawrence Inst. Tech.; BSAE, Tri State U., 1942; MA in Indl. Tech., Cornell U., 1969; MA, Calif. State U., Chico. Engrng. supr. Gen. Dynamics Corp., Pomona, Calif., 1952-65; instr. math. and engrng. Citrus Coll., Glendora, Calif., 1963-64, Calif. State U., Chico, 1966-68; instr. math. and engrng., coordinator Butte Coll., Oroville, Calif., 1968—; instr. Manpower Devel. Tng. Act, Glendora, 1963-64, instr. engrng. documentation and problem solving. Author: Technical Sketch, 1969, Simplified C.A.D., 1986; reviewer for tech. pubs. in field. Served with USN, 1944-45. Mem. NEA, Calif. Tchrs. Assn. (clk. 1984-85). Republican. Avocations: airplanes, automobiles, construction. Home: 6710 Machuga Ln Paradise CA 95965 Office: Butte Coll Dept Math and Engrng 3536 Campus Dr Oroville CA 95969

MACIAS, AMELIA, leasing company executive; b. Las Cruces, N.Mex., June 10, 1950; d. Jesus Tostado and Maria Teresa (Huizar) M. A.B., U. San Francisco, 1980. Chief planner Calif. Office Small Bus., Sacramento, 1976-78; v.p. Tech. Leasing Corp., Oakland, Calif, 1979-82, sr. v.p., 1982-84, chief ops. officer, 1984—, also bd. dirs.; bd. dirs. Gaylor Constrn., Oakland. Served as staff sgt. USAF, 1975-79. Recipient Design award Community Design Assocs., 1984. Mem. Oakland C. of C., Mexican-Am. C. of C. (v.p. 1980) Western Assn. Equipment. Democrat. Mormon. Avocation: interior decorating. Office: Tech Leasing Corp 621 MacArthur Blvd Oakland CA 94610

MACIEL, RONALD JOHN, lawyer; b. Hanford, Calif., Nov. 25, 1943; s. John J. and Ludrie (Mendes) M.; m. Shirley Lucchesi, July 8, 1967; children: Virginia, Jennifer, Rosemarie. BS, UCLA, 1966; JD, Loyola U., Los Angeles, 1973. Bar: Calif. 1974, U.S. Tax Ct. 1980, U.S. Supreme Ct. 1981, U.S. Ct. Appeals (9th cir.) 1982. Agt., IRS, Los Angeles, 1966-76; sole practice law, Hanford, 1976—; pres. RJM Electronics, Inc. Mem. Kings County Cabillo Civic Club, Hanford; trustee Kings County Law Library. Mem. AAAS, N.Y. Acad. Scis., ABA, Fed. Bar Assn., Kings County Bar Assn., Am. Assn. Atty.-CPA's, Christian Legal Soc., Am. Film Inst. Office: 104 E 7th St Hanford CA 93230

MACINKO, GEORGE, geography educator; b. Nesquehoning, Pa., Jan. 19, 1931; s. Stephen and Anna (Kowatch) M.; m. Mary Ann Tuttle, June 20, 1954; children: Joe Russell, Seth Stephen. BA, U. Idaho, 1953; MA, U. Mich., 1957, PhD, 1961. Instr. geology, geography U. Idaho, Moscow, 1958-61; from asst. prof. to assoc. prof. U. Del., Newark, 1961-67; from assoc. prof. to prof. Cen. Wash. U., Ellensburg, 1967—; vis. prof. Dartmouth Coll., 1969-70, 77-78, Cornell U., 1971. Co-editor: Sourcebook on the Environment, 1978, Beyond the Urban Fringe, 1983; contbr. articles to sci. jours. Served to 1st lt. USAF, 1954-56. Woodrow Wilson fellow, 1953-54, NSF fellow, 1965-66. Mem. AAAS, Assn. Am. Geographics (chmn. environ. studies commn. 1975-77), Phi Beta Kappa, Sigma Xi. Avocations: amateur wrestling, barbershop singing. Home: 1202 Craig Ave Ellensburg WA 98926 Office: Central Wash U Ellensburg WA 98926

MACK, BRENDA LEE, sociologist, public relations consulting company executive; b. Peoria, Ill., Mar. 24; d. William James and Virginia Julia (Pickett) Palmer; A.A., Los Angeles City Coll.; B.A. in Sociology, Calif. State U., Los Angeles, 1980; m. Rozene Mack, Jan. 13 (div.); 1 child, Kevin Anthony. Ct. clk. City of Blythe, Calif.; partner Mack Trucking Co., Blythe; ombudsman, sec. bus facilities So. Calif. Rapid Transit Dist., Los Angeles, 1974-81; owner Brenda Mack Enterprises, Los Angeles, 1981—; lectr., writer, radio and TV personality; co-originator advt. concept Vee/Dee Project. Past bd. dirs. Narcotic Symposium, Los Angeles. Served with U.S. WAC. Mem. Women For, Calif. State U. Los Angeles Alumni. Home: 8749 Cattaraugus Ave Los Angeles CA 90034 Office: Brenda Mack Enterprises PO Box 5942 Los Angeles CA 90055

MACK, CHARLES DANIEL, III, labor union executive; b. Oakland, Calif., Apr. 16, 1942; s. Charles Daniel and Bernadine Zoe (Ferguson) M.; m. Marlene Helen Fagundes, Oct. 15, 1960; children—Tammy, Kelly, Kerry, Shannon. B.A., San Francisco State Coll., 1964. Truck driver Garrett Freight Lines, Emergyville, Calif., 1962-66; bus. agt. Teamsters Local No. 70, Oakland, 1966-70, sec.-treas., 1972—; legis. rep. Calif. Teamsters Pub. Affairs Council, Sacramento, 1970-71; trustee Western Conf. Teamsters Pension Trust Fund, 1980—, mem. policy com., 1980-82, pres. joint council, San Francisco, 1982—; rep. Internat. Botherhood Teamsters, Chauffeurs, Warehousemen & Helpers of Am., 1984—. Bd. dirs. Econ. Devel. Corp. of Oakland, 1980—, Pvt. Industry Council, Oakland, 1983-84, Children's Hosp. of East Bay, 1981-83, Calif. Compensation Ins. Fund, San Francisco, 1980-86, Alameda County Easter Seals, 1983-85, United Way, 1978-82. Democrat. Roman Catholic. Office: Teamsters Union Local No 7 Executive Pk Blvd Suite 2900 San Francisco CA 94134

MACK, DONALD JEROME, federal agency administrator; b. Wailuku, Hawaii, June 4, 1939; s. Jerome Peter and Verda Asayo (Inouye) M.; m. Susan Yoshiko Miyamoto, Dec. 30, 1961; children: Kirby Bryce, Alissa Jodie. BA, UCLA, 1961; diploma, Indsl. Coll. Armed Forces, 1979, Air Force War Coll., 1981; MA, Cen. Mich. U., 1985. Commd. 2d lt. U.S. Army, 1961, advanced through grades to maj., resigned, 1968; stock broker DuPont Walston, Inc., Honolulu, 1968-73; personnel officer Army Res. Technician Group, Ft. DeRussy, Hawaii, 1973-81; supervisory personnel staffing specialist Pub. Works Ctr., Honolulu, 1981—. Coach Am. Youth Soccer Orgn., Kaneohe, Hawaii, 1979-81; bd. dirs. Child & Family Service, Honolulu, 1971-75. Served to col. USAR, 1970—. Recipient Gov.'s Award plaques Commn. on Handicapped, Honolulu, 1982-85, Commendation Pres.'s Com. Employment of Handicapped, 1983, Commendation VA, Honolulu, 1984. Mem. Assn. of U.S. Army, Res. Officers Assn., Scabbard and Blade (pres. Los Angeles chpt. 1960-61), Nat. Mil. Honor Soc., Eta Lambda Kappa. Avocations: football, soccer, raising Belgian sheepdogs. Home: 46-193 Alaloa St Kaneohe HI 96744-4009 Office: Navy Pub Works Ctr Consolidated Civilian Personnel Office 4300 Radford Dr Honolulu HI 96818-3298

MACK, EDWARD SEMMEL, dentist; b. San Francisco, Feb. 8, 1918; s. David and Anita (Semmel) M.; student Stanford, 1935-37; D.D.S., San Francisco Coll. of Phys. and Surgs., 1942; m. Susan Tabor Brand, Aug. 5, 1945; children—Ronald Brand, Bruce Edward, Kevin Lee. Practice dentistry specializing in pedodontics, San Francisco, 1949—; asst. clin. prof. Coll. Phys. and Surgs., San Francisco, 1949-51, 63—; mem. dental staff Mt. Zion Hosp., San Francisco, 1955-59, 65—. Mem. Patrons of Art and Music of Calif. Palace of Legion of Honor; patron H.M.S. De Young Mus. Served as lt. USNR, 1942-46. Diplomate Am. Bd. Pedodontics. Fellow Am. Coll. Dentists; mem. Am., Calif. dental assns., Am. Soc. Dentistry for Children (pres. 1974), Calif. Soc. Pediatric Dentists (pres. 1977-78), San Francisco Assn. Mental Health, Acad. Dentistry for Handicapped, Pub. Health League Calif., San Francisco Amateur Astronomers, Sierra Club. Club: Concordia (San Francisco). Contbr. articles to profl. jours. Home: 80 Chumasero Dr San Francisco CA 94132 Office: 2022 Taraval St #5401 San Francisco CA 94116

MACK, ROBERT LEONARD, hospital engineer; b. Watertown, S.D., July 12, 1929; s. Nicholas Peter and Eleanor (Heyn) M. Plant supt. Alexian Bros. Hosp., St. Louis, 1962-64, San Jose, Calif., 1964-70; adminstrv. engr. San Jose Hosp. and Health Ctr., 1970—. Bd. dirs., pres. Home Helpers, Inc., San Jose. Mem. Am. Soc. Hosp. Engrng. (past dir., past pres.), Calif. Soc. Hosp. Engring., Nat. Fire Protection Assn. Office: 675 E Santa Clara St San Jose CA 95112

MACK, RONALD BRAND, dentist; b. San Francisco, Feb. 20, 1948; s. Edward Semmel and Susan Tabor (Brand) M.; m. Janet Berringer, July 12, 1986; children by previous marriage: Joshua Hamilton, Aaron Edward. Diplomate Am. Bd. Pediatric Dentistry. BS, U. Calif., Davis, 1969; DDS, U. Pacific, 1973; cert. pediatric dentistry Ind. U., 1975. Practice dentistry specializing in pediatric dentistry, San Francisco, 1975—; instr., mem. staff, Oakland (Calif.) Children's Hosp., 1976-82; instr. gen. practice residency Mt. Zion Hosp., San Francisco, 1978—; adj. assoc. prof. pediatric dentistry, U. Pacific Sch. Dentistry, 1983—. United Cerebral Palsy clinical fellow, 1973, 74; G.R. Baker fellow, 1975. Fellow Internat. Coll. Dentists, Am. Coll. Dentists, Am. Acad. Pediatric Dentistry, Acad. Dentistry for Handicapped, Am. Soc. Dentistry for Children; mem. San Francisco Dental Soc., Bay Area Dental Guidance Council for the Disabled (co-founder, 1977), U. Pacific Sch. Dentistry Alumni Assn., Calif. Dental Assn., Coll. Diplomates of Am. Bd. Pediatric Dentistry, Calif. Soc. Pediatric Dentists (bd. dirs. 1979-81), Calif. Soc. Dentistry for Children (pres. 1981-82), ADA, Am. Soc. Dentistry for Children, Ind. U. Pediatric Dentistry Alumni Assn. (bd. dirs. 1981—), Bay Area Pediatric Dentistry Study Club (pres. 1983-84), Am. Med. Joggers Assn., Nat. Running and Fitness Assn., Internat. Assn. Dentistry for Children, Internat. Assn. Dentistry for the Handicapped, Tau Kappa Omega, Alpha Omega (pres. San Francisco alumni chpt. 1977-78). Sr. editor, contbg. author: Essentials of Clinical Pediatric Dentistry; contbr. articles to profl. jours., chpts. to books. Home: 6 Locksley Ave Apt 8C N Tower San Francisco CA 94122 Office: 800 Santiago St San Francisco CA 94116

MACK, ZELLA EDITH, writer, real estate investor; b. Jonesville, Mich.; d. George Melvin and Edith Mae (Brown) Kennedy; m. Frank Patrick Mack, Sept. 15, 1945. B.A. in Polit. Sci., U. Calif.-Berkeley, 1944. Cert. legal asst. Nat. Assn. Legal Assts. Legal sec. various law firms, San Francisco, Boston and Sacramento, 1939-52, Calif. Atty. Gen.'s Office, Sacramento, 1952-63; aide to assoc. justice Calif. Ct. Appeals Third Dist., Sacramento, 1963-77; free-lance writer, Sacramento, 1977—; tchr. legal secs., legal assts. Mem. exec. bd. Camellia Soc. Sacramento. Mem. Calif. Writers Club, Nat. Assn. Legal Assts., Inc., Nat. Fedn. Paralegal Assns., Sacramento Assn. Legal Assts. (assoc.), Legal Secs. Inc., Sacramento Legal Secs. Assn., Sacramento Women's Network, Am. Camellia Soc. Roman Catholic. Club: Sutter Lawn Tennis (Sacramento). Author: California Paralegal's Guide, 1977, 3d edit., 1987, columnist daily newspaper; contbr. various mags.

MACKAY, ALEXANDER RUSSELL, retired physician; b. Bottineau, N.D., Oct. 8, 1911; s. Alexander Russell and Eleanor (Watson) M.; B.S., Northwestern U., 1932, M.D., 1936; M.S. in Surgery, U. Minn., 1940; m. Marjorie Andres, July 16, 1941; children—Andrea, Alexander Russell. Intern, Med. Center, Jersey City, 1935-37; fellow in surgery Mayo Clinic, Rochester, Minn. 1937-41; practiced medicine specializing in gen. surgery, Spokane, Wash., 1941-82, now ret.; former staff Deaconess, Sacred Heart hosps., Spokane. Served from lt. to capt., M.C., AUS, 1942-45. Diplomate Am. Bd. Surgery. Fellow ACS; mem. Spokane Surg. Soc., North Pacific Surg. Assn., Alpha Omega Alpha, Phi Delta Theta, Nu Sigma Nu, Phi Beta Kappa. Home: E 540 Rockwood Blvd Spokane WA 99202

MACKAY, DOUGLAS MCDUFF, educator, researcher; b. North Kingstown, R.I., Nov. 13, 1948; s. Douglas Severance and Rosa Jo (McDuff) M.; m. Linda LeMoyne Hall, June 10, 1972 (div. July 1978). BS, Stanford U., 1970, MS, 1973, PhD, 1981. Environ. engr. EPA, Washington, San Francisco, 1973-75; research asst. Cornell U., Ithaca, N.Y., 1976-77; research asst. Stanford (Calif.) U., 1977-1981, research assoc., 1981-85; asst. prof. UCLA Sch. Pub. Health, 1986—; cons. U.S. EPA/UAREP (Univs. Assoc. for Research and Edn., Inc.), San Francisco, 1984-85; cons. asst. prof., Stanford U., 1986—; lectr. various programs U. Calif., Davis, 1985—; expert witness U.S. House Reps., W. Covina, Calif., 1983, U.S. Senate, Washington, 1986. Contbr. articles to profl. jours. and newspapers. Participant regulation devel. Calif. Dept. Health Services, Berkeley and Sacramento, Calif., 1981-82, Calif. Office Appropriate Tech., Sacramento, 1981-82; collaborator Environ. Def. Fund, Washington, 1986. Served with USN. Marx-Moreno fellow, 1980. Mem. AAAS, ASCE, Am. Chem. Soc., Am. Geophys. Union (assoc.), Nat. Water Well Assn., Sigma Xi. Democrat. Office: UCLA Sch Pub Health Environ Sci and Engring Los Angeles CA 90024

MACKE, DAVID LYNN, geologist; b. Terre Haute, Ind., Nov. 18, 1951; s. Arnold Chester and Mary Ellen (Spittler) M. BS, U. Ill., 1973; MS, Colo. State U., 1977. Geologist Wyo. State Hwy. Dept., Cheyenne, 1975, U.S. Geol. Survey, Denver, 1975—. Author (geophys. map) Aeroradiometric Map N.E. Wyo., 1978; co-author (geol. maps) Tertiary Geology, 1986; editor RMS-SEPM Field Trip Guidebook, 1985. Mem. Soc. Econ. Paleontologists and Mineralogists, Rocky Mountain Sect. of Soc. Econ. Paleontologists and Mineralogists (publ. com. 1986), Am. Geophys. Union, Sigma Xi. Avocations: cooking, gardening. Office: US Geol Survey PO Box 25046 MS 916 Denver CO 80225

MACKELLAR, WILLIAM FISHER, analytical chemistry; b. Youngstown, Ohio, May 19, 1950; s. William Henry and Anetta LaVerne (Fisher) MacK.; m. Sandra Harley, Sept. 21, 1972; 1 child, Sean Harley. BA in Biology, Kent State U., 1977, BS in Chemistry, 1979. Chemist S.D. Meyers Inc., Cuyaloga Falls, Ohio, 1977-81; lab. supr. IMCC, Carlsbad, N.Mex., 1981—. Served with U.S. Army, 1972-74. Mem. Am. Chem. Soc. Republican. Lodge: Elks. Avocations: skiing, tennis, racketball, bicycling, camping. Office: Internat Minerals and Chems PO Box 71 Carlsbad NM 88220

MACKENNA, CRAIG A., computer scientist; b. Milw., Dec. 12, 1944; s. Kenneth Stuart McKenna and Anne Louise (Kempa) Sanger; m. Merikay Goede, Jan. 31, 1966; children: Deidre, Gilbert. BS, U. Wis., Milw., 1966. Supr. systems and procedures Computer Ctr. U. Wis., Milw., 1966-68; supr. digital systems Badger Meter Mfg. Co., Brown Deer, Wis., 1968-70; mgr. software Venture Computer Systems, New Berlin, Wis., 1970-73; mgr. engrng. Astronautics Corp. Am., Milw., 1973-78; mgr. mktg. Mostek Corp., Carrollton, Tex., 1978-83; mgr. architecture Signetics Corp., Sunnyvale, Calif., 1983—. Mem. IEEE (microprocessor standards com. 1985—, P1014 working group 1983—, U.S. del to IEC, Stockholm, 1986, contbr. to Jour.). Avocations: sci. fiction reading and writing, tennis, golf. Home: 101 Fremont Ct Los Gatos CA 95030 Office: Signetics Corp MB 76 811 E Arques Ave Sunnyvale CA 95030

MACKENROTH, JOYCE ELLEN, teacher; b. Portland, Oreg., June 22, 1946; d. Ferrel Adelbert and Ellen Ellenora (Setala) McKinney; m. Glen MacKenroth, Sept. 21, 1968; 1 child, Tonia Lynn. BS, Western Oreg. State Coll., 1968; postgrad. U. Oreg., 1980, 81, 83, 85, Portland State U., 1984. Cert. elem. tchr., Oreg. Salesperson Avon, Tucson, Toledo, 1969-70, 73-77; tchr. Lincoln County Sch. Dist., Newport, Oreg., 1970—; bd. dirs. Curriculum Coordinating Council, Newport; computer instr. and coordinator Lincoln County Sch. Dist., 1984—; mem. various lang. arts and writing coms., 1981—. Sec. State Assn. Pagent Bds., Seaside, Oreg., 1984-85; active Miss Lincoln County Scholarship Pagent, Toledo, Oreg., 1979—. Mem. Internat. Reading Assn., Oreg. Reading Assn., Seacoast Reading Assn., Oreg. Edn. Assn. (uniserv treas. 1979-81, bd. dirs. 1981-82), Lincoln County Edn. Assn. (sec. 1974, v.p. 1975, pres. 1976, 81), NEA, Beta Sigma Phi (sec. 1983-84, v.p. 1985-86, pres. 1986—). Democrat. Avocations: reading, community service, computer operations, piano. Home: 264 NE 1st Toledo OR 97391 Office: Arcadia Elem Sch 1811 Arcadia Dr Toledo OR 97391

MACKENZIE, ELLYN GERDA, educator; b. Chgo., Dec. 18, 1942; d. Charles Audley and Fahreda Juanita (Booth) Simms. BS in Secondary Edn., U. Nev., 1964, MA in Edn. Adminstrn., 1978. Cert. elem. and secondary tchr., ednl. adminstr., Nev. Elem. and mid. sch. tchr. Washoe Sch. Dist., Reno, 1964-66, 69-85, academically talented students tchr., program coordinator, 1985—; elem. and jr. high sch. tchr. Granite Sch. Dist., Salt Lake City, 1966-69. Active Washoe County Tchrs. in Politics, 1970—; mem. Nev. Dem. Cen. Com., 1986—, precinct capt., Reno, 1971; co-chmn. Murphy for Senate campaign, Reno, 1976; active Robert List for Gov. campaign, Washoe County, 1978-82. Mem. AAUW, Internat. Reading Assn., Academically Talented Parents Orgn., No. Nev. Writing Project, Nev. Network Women in Edn., Westerners Internat. Corral, Delta Kappa Gamma (local pres. 1975, 77), Phi Delta Kappa. Avocations: snow and water skiing, driving, reading, hist. research. Home: 1107 Spanish Springs Rd Sparks NV 89431 Office: E O Vaughn Mid Sch 1200 Bresson Reno NV 89502

MACKETT, DAVID JAMES, fishery biologist, research administrator; b. Milw., June 3, 1937; s. James August and Loretta A. (Thranow) M.; m. Marilyn Jahnke, June 20, 1959; children: Scott Ross, Todd Cole. BS, Oreg. State U., 1959; postgrad., UCLA, 1961-64. Biologist Calif. Dept. Fish and Game, 1960-62, statistician, supr., 1962-69; chief FAO Fishery Data Ctr., Rome, 1969-72; planning officer Nat. Marine Fisheries Service, La Jolla, Calif., 1972—; cons. of fisheries devel. Poland, Brazil, Peru, Argentina, South Vietnam, Indonesia. Recipient Spl. Achievement award Nat. Marine Fisheries Service, 1973, Merit Pay award Nat. Marine Fisheries Service, 1981-86. Mem. Inst. Mgmt. Scis., Am. Inst. Fishery Research Biologists, Soc. Gen. Systems Research. Office: 8604 La Jolla Shores Dr La Jolla CA 92037

MACKEY, DONALD R., veterinarian, livestock industry consultant; b. La Salle, Colo., July 6, 1919; s. Raymond E. and Mary F. (Pumphrey) M.; m. Ruth L., Sept. 6, 1941; children—Donald Jack, Lawrence Ray. B.S., Colo. State U., D.V.M., 1942. Registered veterinarian, Colo., 1942. Owner, operator Mackey's Veterinary Service, 1942—. Recipient T-Bone Club Award for Outstanding Service to the Livestock Industry, 1970. Mem. Profl. Veterinary Supply (pres.), Colo. Veterinary Med. Assn. (past pres.), Colo. State Veterinary Soc., Am. Veterinary Assn., Am. Assn. Bovine Practitioners, Agrl. Cons. Soc., Nat. Fedn. Ind. Businessmen. Republican. Presbyterian. Clubs: Elks, Lions, T-Bone, Greeley, Colo. Contbg. editor Feedlot Mgmt., Dairy Herd Mgmt. Home: 4704 13th St Greeley CO 80631 Office: 4704 13th St PO Box 57 Greeley CO 80632

MACKIE, DIANE MAREE, psychology educator; b. Auckland, New Zealand, Dec. 10, 1955; came to U.S., 1980; d. David Harold and Joan (Casey) M. BA, U. Auckland, 1977, MA, 1978; MA, Princeton U., 1982, PhD in Social Psychology, 1984. Jr. lectr. U. Auckland, 1978; research scholar Université de Genève, Geneva, 1979; asst. prof. psychology U. Calif., Santa Barbara, 1984—. Ad hoc reviewer Jour. Personality and Social Psychology, Jour. Exptl. Social Psychology, Jour. Cross Cultural Psychology, Personality and Social Psychology Bulletin; contbr. articles to profl. jours. Recipient Dissertation award Soc. Exptl. Social Psychology, 1985, Fulbright Travel award, 1980, Fowlds Meml. Prize U. Auckland, 1978; Harold W. Dodds Honorific fellow, 1983-84, Swiss Fed. scholar, 1979-80, sr. scholar U. Auckland, 1976, New Zealand Jr. scholar, 1973; grantee Acad. Senate Gen. Research, 1984, 85. Mem. Soc. Exptl. Social Psychology (mem. editorial bd. Jour. Exptl. Social Psychology 1987), Am. Psychol. Assn., Soc. Personality and Social Psychology div. Am. Psychol. Assn., Sos. Consumer Behavior div. Am. Psychol. Assn., Internat. Fedn. Univ. Women. Office: U Calif Dept Psychology Santa Barbara CA 93106

MACKIN, DANIEL EDWARD, advertising executive; b. Pasadena, Calif., Apr. 21, 1948; s. Howard James and Gladys (Barbara) M.; m. Doris Elizabeth Banister, Sept. 20, 1985. BA, Universidad De Las Americas,

Puebla, Mexico, 1985, MA summa cum laude, 1986. Cert. tchr. Cons., instr. Exterior Dept. Commerce, Puebla, 1974-75; instr., dir. Calif. State U., Fullerton, 1976-81; sales dir. Preview Channel, Venice, Calif., 1981-82; mktg. dir. Satellite Shopping Network, Venice, 1982-84; media supr. Grey Advt., San Francisco, 1984-85; mgr. East/West Network, San Francisco, 1985—. Served with USN, 1968-71, Vietnam. Mem. Mag. Pubs. Reps., Nat. Assn. Bilingual Edn. (chmn. for conv. planning), Alaska Visitors Assn., Swan Owners Assn., Travel and Tourism Research Assn. Republican. Roman Catholic. Avocations: water color painting, sailing, diving,. Home: 2621 Via Cascadita San Clemente CA 92672 Office: East/West Network 369 Pine St 620 San Francisco CA 94104

MACKIN, DOROTHY MAE, hotel executive, writer, play producer; b. Hayden, Colo., July 16, 1917; d. Earl Glen and Ruth Lillian (Stacy) Mabee; m. Wayne S. Mackin, Mar. 5, 1946; children—Stephen Kirk, Susan Diane Mackin Lever, Jeffrey Wayne. Student pub. schs., Salamanca, N.Y. Sec., payroll clk. London Gold Mine, Alma, Colo., 1936-37; sec., saleswoman, buyer, officer mgr. Nobel Merc. Co., Denver, 1937-39; owner Intermountain Food Brokerage Co., Denver, 1939-43; co-owner, mgr., producer, dir. Imperial Hotel and Imperial Players, Cripple Creek, Colo., 1946—; guest dir. Star Bar Players, Colorado Springs, Colo., 1982. Trustee, pres. Cripple Creek Dist. Mus. Recipient (with Wayne Mackin) Larry Tijari Drama award, 1967; Gov.'s Hospitality award, 1981. Mem. Internat. Platform Assn., Rocky Mountain Writers Guild. Episcopalian. Club: Balboa (Mazatlan, Mex.). Author: The Imperial, 1977, Melodrama Classics: Six Plays and How To Stage Them, 1982, Memories and Memorials, 1985.

MACKINNON, PEGGY LOUISE, public relations executive; b. Florence, Ariz., June 18, 1945; d. Lacy Donald Gay and Goldie Louise (Trotter) Martin; m. Ian Dixon Mackinnon, Oct. 20, 1973. BA, San Jose State U., 1967, postgrad., 1968. Cert. secondary tchr., Calif. Tchr. Las Lomas High Sch., Walnut Creek, Calif., 1968-69; edn. officer Ormond Sch., Sydney, Australia, 1970-72; tchr. Belconnen High Sch., Canberra, Australia, 1972-73; temp. exec. sec. various orgns., London, 1973-75; mktg. mgr. Roadtown Wholesale, Tortola, British Virgin Islands, 1975-80; v.p. Hill & Knowlton Inc., Denver, 1981—. Bd. dirs. Rocky Mountain Poison and Drug Found., Denver, 1984-87. Mem. Pub. Relations Soc. Am. (accredited). Avocations: tennis, squash, skiing, sewing, cooking. Home: 9200 Cherry Creek Dr S #21 Denver CO 80231 Office: Hill & Knowlton Inc 1050 17th St Suite 2200 Denver CO 80265

MACKINNON, ROBERT LOUIS, amusement park executive; b. Dracut, Mass., May 12, 1925; s. Daniel Finley and Grace Elizabeth (Pushee) MacK.; m. Helen Adele Menger, Aug. 21, 1945; children—Robert C., Patricia L., Susan A., Robin A., Jeanne L. Student Mich. State U., 1943, Fla. So. U., 1950; student in Archtl. Engring., U. Colo., 1950; B.A. in Cinema, U. So. Calif., 1959. Commd. 2d lt. U.S. Air Force, 1943, advanced through grades to lt. col., 1963, served as pilot, 1943-59, producer, dir., exec. producer Lookout Mountain, Hollywood, Calif., 1959-65, ret., 1965; capt. ABC Airlines, Los Angeles, 1965; mgr. entertainment and ops. Disneyland, Anaheim, Calif., 1965-74, dir. bus. affairs, 1974-87; tournament dir. Walt Disney World Open Golf Tournament, Profl. Golf Assn., Orlando, Fla., 1971, 72. Producer, dir. film Water Safety-Guam, 1963 (1st pl. Venice Film Festival 1964). Deacon First Presbyterian Ch., Orange, Calif., 1983-84. Mem. Soc. Motion Picture and TV Engrs., Anaheim C. of C. (pres. and chmn. bd. 1984-85), Phi Beta Kappa, Delta Kappa Alpha. Republican. Lodge: Optimists (pres. Anaheim 1967-68).

MACKINTOSH, FREDERICK ROY, oncologist; b. Miami, Fla., Oct. 4, 1943; s. John Harris and Mary Carlotta (King) MacK.; m. Judith Jane Parnell, Oct. 2, 1961 (div. Aug. 1977); children: Lisa Lynn, Wendy Sue; m. Claudia Lizanne Flournoy, Jan. 7, 1984. BS, MIT, 1964, PhD, 1968; MD, U. Miami, 1976. Intern then resident in gen. medicine Stanford (Calif.) U., 1976-78, fellow in oncology, 1978-81; asst. prof. med. U. Nev., Reno, 1981-85, assoc. prof., 1985—. Contbr. articles to profl. jours. Fellow ACP; mem. Am. Soc. Clin. Oncology, Am. Cancer Soc. (pres.-elect Nev. div. 1985), No. Nev. Cancer Council (bd. dirs. 1981—), No. Calif. Cancer Program (bd. dirs. alt. 1983—). Avocation: bicycling. Office: Nev Med Group 781 Mill St Reno NV 89502

MACKINTOSH, JOHN BRUCE, college official; b. Seattle, Dec. 2, 1946; s. John Almon and Bernice Emma (Marlowe) M.; m. Candace Eileen Shopbell, Sept. 3, 1981 (div. 1986); 1 child, Leah Nicole. Student U. Wash., 1965-66; B.A., Parsons Coll., 1969; M.A.Ed., U. No. Iowa, 1973. Asst. dir. student activities Parsons Coll., Fairfield, Iowa, 1969-71; program asst. Student Union, U. No. Iowa, Cedar Falls, 1971-73; registrar Met. Jr. Coll., Mpls., 1973; coordinator student activities, Highline Community Coll., Midway, Wash., 1974—. Pres. bd. Eternal Temple Truth and Light, Kent, Wash., 1983—. Mem. Am. Soc. Tng. and Devel., Wash. Assn. Community Coll. Student Activities Personnel (pres.). Office: Highline Community Coll Midway WA 98032

MACKLIN, JENENNE ROBERTA, clinical social worker; b. Omaha, Nov. 3, 1954; d. Robert Joseph and Mary Adaline (Andrew) M. B, Whittier Coll., 1977; M, Calif. State U., Sacramento, 1979. Social worker Deseret Youth Ctr., Riverside, Calif., 1979-81; probation counselor Orange (Calif.) County Juvenile Hall, 1982-83; social worker McKinley Home for Boys, San Dimas, Calif., 1983—; exec. dir. Adolescent Mgmt. Systems, Inc., Gardena, Calif., 1984-86. Served with USNR, 1982-84. Mem. Nat. Assn. Social Workers (cert.), Assn. Black Social Workers, Calif. Child Youth Family Coalition, VFW. Club: Inglewood Democratic. Home: 8218 S Crenshaw Blvd Inglewood CA 90305

MACLACHLAN, JAMES CRAWFORD, geology educator; b. Detroit, Jan. 13, 1923; s. Hughey James and Verna Gertrude (Crawford) McL.; m. Marjorie Elizabeth Hindle, Oct. 21, 1950. BA, Wayne State U., 1948; MA, Princeton U., 1951, PhD, 1952. Geologist U.S. Geol. Survey, Denver, 1952-56; cons. geologist Ministerio de Minas e Hidrocarburos, Caracas, Venezuela, 1949-55; sr. exploration geologist Phillips Petroleum Co., Denver, 1957-62; geologist, cons., treas. Shallow Well Exploration Co., Denver, 1962-67; prof. geology Met. State Coll., Denver, 1967. Contbr. articles to profl. jours. Served as sgt. U.S. Army, 1943-46. Mem. Geol. Soc. Am., Am. Assn. Geologists, Colo. Sci. Soc., U.S. Naval Inst., St. Andrew Soc., Sigma Xi. Republican. Club: St. Andrew Soc. (Denver) (treas., vice-chmn. 1971-75). Avocations: shooting, collecting antiques, mil. history. Office: Met State Coll 1006 11th St Earth Sci Dept Denver CO 80204

MACLAREN, WALTER ROGERS, allergist, educator; b. Yokohama, Japan, Dec. 7, 1910; s. Walter Wallace and Zaidee (Rogers) McL.; m. Dorothy Agnes Goodwin, June 1942 (div. 1970); children: Walter Jr., Jean, Anne, Elizabeth, Catherine; m. Dorothy Hamblen, July 7, 1971. BA, Queens U., 1933; MD, Harvard U., 1938. Diplomate Am. Bd. Allergy and Immunology (bd. dirs., sec. 1978-83). Practice medicine specializing in asthma, allergy and immunology Pasadena, Calif., 1947—; clin. prof. medicine U. So. Calif. Sch. Med., Los Angeles, 1948—; dir. Allergy and Immunology Cons. Labs., Inc., Pasadena, 1978—. Contbr. 32 articles to profl. jours. Bd. dirs. Pasadena Symphony Orch., 1976-82, Pasadena Chamber Orch., 1984-86. Fellow Am. Acad. Allergy and Immunology, Am. Coll. Allergists, Assn. Clin. Immunology and Allergy (pres.), Sigma Xi. Republican. Club: Valley Hunt (Pasadena). Office: U So Calif 94 N Madison Ave Pasadena CA 91101

MACLAUCHLIN, ROBERT KERWIN, communications artist, educator; b. Framingham, Mass., Oct. 8, 1931; s. Charles Lewis MacLauchlin and Elinor Frances Kerwin; m. Elizabeth D'Ann Willson, June 13, 1964. BA in Sociology, U. Mass., Amherst, 1954; MEd, Bridgewater State Coll., 1958; MS in Radio and TV, Syracuse U., 1959; PhD in Speech, Radio, TV, Mich. State U., 1969. Personnel trainee Nat. Security Agy., Washington, 1954-55; elem. sch. tchr. Mattapoisett (Mass.) Pub. Schs., 1957-58; asst. prof., dir. programming Maine Ednl. TV Network, Orono, 1959-66; assoc. prof. Speech Communications, dir. TV-Radio instrn. Colo. State U., Ft. Collins, 1969-76, prof., 1976—; cons. U. Maine, Orono, 1968, Ft. Collins Presbyn. Ch., 1976-78, Sta. KCOL-AM-FM, Ft. Collins, 1978, Pub. Health Assn., Ft. Collins, 1985; archives program guest Maine Pub. Broadcast, Orono, 1983. Served with inf. U.S. Army, 1955-57. Named Disting. Vis. Prof. U. Vt., Burlington, 1983, A Teacher Who Makes A Difference Denver's Rocky Mountain News, KCNC-TV; recipient Friend of broadcasting award, 1985. Mem. Colo. Broadcasters Assn. (edn. com. 1972—, Hall of Fame com. 1980—, Friend of Broadcast award 1985), Western Speech Communications Assn., Speech Communications Assn., Broadcast Edn. Assn. Industry State (chmn. 1981-86), State Assn. Communications (chmn. 1981-86). Republican. Lodge: Kiwanis (Ft. Collins chpt. Disting. Past Pres. 1979-80). Avocations: outdoor activities. Home: 1407 Country Club Rd Fort Collins CO 80524 Office: Colo State U Dept Speech Communication Fort Collins CO 80523

MACLAY, DONALD TRACY, communications consultant; b. Buffalo, Mar. 20, 1933; s. Donald Edwin and Barbara (Tracy) M.; m. Caroline Ann Pedersen, Dec. 23, 1967; children—Nelson Donald, Tracy Anne, Craig Aksel. B.Mech. Engring., Cornell U., 1956; postgrad. exec. program Stanford U., 1977. Engr., plant mgr. Warren Wire Co., Pownal, Vt., Santa Barbara, Calif., 1959-63; plant mgr. Gen. Cable Corp., Santa Barbara, Calif., 1963-65; cons., assoc., v.p. Booz Allen & Hamilton, Los Angeles, Australia, Thailand, Korea, 1965-77; gen. mgr. Thai Zinc, Inc., Bangkok, 1977-78; pres. Tel-Max, 1977-86; v.p. ViTel Internat. Inc. Telecommunications, 1986—; communications cons. and western sales orgn. for Via Titus, Inc., Los Angeles, 1977-86, v.p., 1979-86. Chmn., Santa Monica Unified Spl. Com. for Sch. Desegregation, 1978-79; chmn. troop com. Boy Scouts Am., 1980-82; bd. dirs. Point Dume Property Owners, 1980-81, Point Dune Community Ctr. Assn., 1982—. Republican. Office: 1801 Ave of the Stars Suite 401 Los Angeles CA 90067

MACLEISH-JENSEN, LINDA, management consulting firm executive; b. Wiesbaden, Germany, Apr. 11, 1951; d. Thomas Robert and Gisela Elizabeth (Gonnerman) MacLeish; m. Stephen Anton Jensen, Oct. 4, 1981. A.A. in Bus. Adminstrn. cum laude, Wesley Coll., 1974; B.S. in Bus. Adminstrn. cum laude, Del. State Coll., 1980, postgrad., 1982—. Clk.-typist Del. State Fire Sch., 1971-73, sec., 1973-76, adminstrv. asst., 1976-78, adminstrv. officer, 1978-81; pres., propr. Linda MacLeish-Jensen Assocs., Phoenix, 1981—; tech. asst., cons. U.S. Fire Adminstrn., 1976—. Pres. bd. dirs. YWCA of Maricopa County; mem. reproductive choice com. LWV. Mem. Am. Soc. Tng. and Devel., Internat. Soc. Fire Service Instrs., Nat. Fire and Burn Edn. Assn. (bd. dirs.). Roman Catholic. Contbr. articles to profl. jours.

MACLEOD, (J.M.) JACK, oil company executive; b. Beddeck, N.S., Can., 1931; m. Beverley Ann Thurston; children: Heather, Carol, Sandra. Alan. B in Engring., Tech. U. N.S., Halifax, 1954, D in Engring. (hon.), 1982. Petroleum engr. Shell Can. Ltd., Calgary, Alta., Can., 1954-69, mgr. dept. prodn., 1969-71, gen. mgr. frontier div., exploration and prodn., 1971-72, gen. mgr. prodn., 1972-73; gen. mgr. supply & logistics Shell Can. Ltd., Toronto, Ont., Can., 1973-75; v.p. corp. planning and pub. affairs Shell Can. Ltd., Calgary, 1975-77, v.p. exploration and prodn., sr. v.p. resources, 1977-82, exec. v.p., 1982-83, pres., chief exec. officer, fir., 1985—; coordinator natural gas Shell Internat. Petroleum Co., London, 1983-85; bd. dirs. C.D. Howe Inst. Bd. dirs. Calgary Philharmonic Soc., The Council for Can. Unity, The Council for Bus. and the Arts in Can. Mem. Assn. Profl. Engrs. Geologists and Geophysicists Alta., Can. Inst. Mining and Metallurgy, Bus. Council on Nat. Issues. Clubs: Calgary Petroleum, Calgary Golf and Country, Mississauga Golf and Country. Avocations: skiing, gardening. Office: Shell Can Ltd, 400 4th Ave SW, Calgary, AB Canada T2P 0J4

MACLEOD, KRISTI LEE, social service director; b. Oakland, Calif., Sept. 16, 1947; d. Grover Harrington and Lucele Emma (Vaught) MacL. BA, U. Calif., Berkeley, MSW. Oncology clin. social worker Mt. Diablo Hosp., Concord, Calif., 1979-80; dir. social services Rideout Meml. Hosp., Marysville, Calif., 1977-79, Providence Hosp., Oakland, 1980—; field instr. Calif. State U., Chico, 1977-78, San Francisco State U. Sch. Social Work Edn., 1982-85, U. Calif., Berkeley, 1986-87. Mem. Soc. Hosp. Social Work Dirs. (sec. 1982, membership chmn. 1984-85), Vis. Nurses Assn. (profl. adv. com. 1983-85). Democrat. Club: Toastmasters (Oakland). Avocations: theater, hiking, backpacking, aerobics. Office: Providence Hosp 3100 Summit Oakland CA 94623

MACLISE, JAMES RAYMOND, educator, writer; b. Newark, Dec. 14, 1935; s. Deming Gerow and Vivian Ruth (Jackson) M.; m. Lura Elizabeth Geyser, Aug. 24, 1968; 1 son, Daniel Ross. B.A., U. Calif.-Davis, 1957; M.A., U. San Francisco, 1971. Cert. secondary and community coll. tchr., Calif. Lectr. U. San Francisco, 1971-72; tchr. English, Lodi High Sch., Calif., 1972—. Author articles. Served with U.S. Army, 1959-60. Mem. Soc. to Preserve Hist. Radio Program Materials. Democrat. Roman Catholic.

MACMEEKEN, JOHN PEEBLES, lawyer; b. Glen Ridge, N.J., Aug. 15, 1924; s. John West and Esther (Strong) M.; m. Mary Swanberg, Nov. 26, 1949; children—Carol B. Macmeeken Luther, John W., Susan G. Student U. Calif., Berkeley, 1941-43, Ind. U., 1943-44; J.D., Harvard U., 1948. Bar: Calif. 1948. Assoc. Chickering & Gregory, San Francisco, 1948-60, ptnr., 1960-82; ptnr. Pettit & Martin, San Francisco, 1982—; dir. Lanark West Corp., Vice-pres. Oakland-Dalian Peoples Friendship City Assn.; pres. Found. for Books for China. Served to sgt. U.S. Army, 1943-45. Mem. ABA, Calif. Bar Assn., San Francisco Bar Assn. Republican. Congregationalist. Clubs: Golden Gateway Tennis, Berkeley Tennis; World Trade (Lakeview). Home: 5708 Glenbrook Dr Oakland CA 94618 Office: Pettit & Martin 101 California St San Francisco CA 94111

MACMILLAN, ROBERT SMITH, electronics engr.; b. Los Angeles, Aug. 28, 1924; s. Andrew James and Moneta (Smith) M.; B.S. in Physics, Calif. Inst. Tech., 1948, M.S. in Elec. Engring., 1949, Ph.D. in Elec. Engring. and Physics cum laude, 1954; m. Barbara Macmillan, Aug. 18, 1962; 1 son, Robert G. Research engr. Jet Propulsion lab. Calif. Inst. Tech., Pasadena, 1951-55, asst. prof. elec. engring., 1955-58; asso. prof. elec. engring. U. So. Calif., Los Angeles, 1958-70; mem. sr. tech. staff Litton Systems, Inc., Van Nuys, Calif., 1969-79; dir. systems engring. Litton Data Command Systems, Agoura Hills, Calif., 1979—; treas., v.p. Video Color Corp., Inglewood, 1965-66. Cons. fgn. tech. div. USAF, Wright-Patterson AFB, Ohio, 1957-74, Space Tech. Labs., Inglewood, Calif., 1956-60, Space Gen. Corp., El Monte, Calif., 1960-63. Served with USAAF, 1943-46. Mem. IEEE, Am. Inst. Physics, Am. Phys. Soc., Sigma Xi, Tau Beta Pi, Eta Kappa Nu. Research in ionospheric, radio-wave, propagation; very low frequency radio-transmitting antennas; optical coherence and statist. optics. Home: 350 Starlight Crest Dr La Canada CA 91011 Office: Litton Data Command Systems 29851 Agoura Rd Agoura Hills CA 91301

MACMULLEN, DOUGLAS BURGOYNE, writer, publisher, editor, retired army officer; b. Berkeley, Calif., Dec. 26, 1919; s. T. Douglas and Florence (Burgoyne) MacM.; ed. San Francisco State U., 1937-41, Stanford U., U. Calif., Fgn. Service Inst., Air War Coll., Army Mgmt. Sch.; m. Sherry Bernice Auerbach, Mar. 11, 1942; 1 son, Douglas Burgoyne. Commd. 2d lt. F.A. Res. U.S. Army, 1941; advanced through grades to col. M.I., 1967; army gen. staff, Psychol. Ops., fgn. service, Pacific, ret., 1972; exec. editor Am. Research Assoc., Sherman Oaks, Calif.; cons. in communication; accredited corr. Def. Dept. Bd. govs. Monte Vista Grove Homes, Pasadena, Calif.; pres. Clan MacMillan Soc. N.Am., 1973-77, trustee, 1975—; mem. Los Angeles Olympics Citizens Adv. Commn., 1982-84; bd. dirs. Masonic Press Club, Los Angeles, 1975, 84—; mem. steering com. Mayor Los Angeles Council Internat. Visitors and Sister Cities, 1969; chmn. Los Angeles-Glasgow Sister Cities Ad Hoc Com.; former mem. San Francisco Mayor's Mil. and Naval Affairs Com.; mem. wills and gifts com. Shriners Hosp. Crippled Children, Al Malaikah Temple, Los Angeles, 1974-80; cons. com. on pub. info. Masons of Calif. Decorated Legion of Merit, Army Commendation medal (U.S.); knight Royal Order Scotland. Mem. Internat. Inst. Strategic Studies, Nat. Mil. Intelligence Assn., Assn. Former Intelligence Officers (pres. chpt.), U.S. Naval Inst., Assn. U.S. Army, Company Mil. Historians, Am. Def. Preparedness Assn., St. Andrew's Soc. Los Angeles (past pres., trustee), Air Force Assn., Stanford U. Alumni Assn., Calif. Newspaper Pubs. Assn., Nat. Def. Exec. Res., Sigma Delta Chi. Republican. Presbyterian (deacon). Clubs: Press, Caledonian (London); San Francisco Press. Lodges: Masons (32 deg.), K.T., Shriners (editor, pub. The Al Malaikahan), Quatuor Coronati C.C. Co-author: Psychological Profile of Cambodia, 1971; also numerous other publs. and articles; radio commentator and newspaper columnist on mil., polit. and internat. affairs. Address: PO Box 5201 Sherman Oaks CA 91413

MACNAUGHTON, ANGUS ATHOLE, financial company executive; b. Montreal, Que., Can., July 15, 1931; s. Athole Austin and Emily Kidder (MacLean) MacN.; children—Gillian Heather, Angus Andrew. Student, Lower Can. Coll., Montreal, 1947-48, McGill U., 1949-54. Auditor Coopers & Lybrand, Montreal, 1949-55; acct. Genstar Ltd., Montreal, 1955; asst. treas. Genstar Ltd., 1956-61, treas., 1961-64, v.p., 1964-70, exec. v.p., 1970-73, pres., 1973-76, vice chmn., chief exec. officer, 1976-81, chmn., pres., chief exec. officer, 1981-86; pres. Genstar Investment Corp., 1987—; dir. Can. Pacific Ltd., Sun Life Assurance Co. Can. Ltd., Am. Barrick Resources Corp., Varian Assocs. Inc. Bd. govs. Lakefield Coll. Sch.; sr. mem. Conf. Bd. N.Y.; bd. dirs. San Francisco Bay Area Council. Mem. Tax Execs. Inst. (past pres. Montreal chpt.). Clubs: Pacific Union, World Trade (San Francisco); Mount Royal, St. James, Montreal Badminton and Squash, Toronto. Office: Suite 3800 4 Embarcadero Center San Francisco CA 94111 *

MAC NEIL, JOSEPH NEIL, archbishop; b. Sydney, N.S., Can., Apr. 15, 1924; s. John Martin and Kate (Mac Lean) Mac N. B.A., St. Francis Xavier U., Antigonish, N.S., 1944; postgrad., Holy Heart Sem., Halifax, N.S., 1944-48, U. Perugia, 1956, U. Chgo., 1964; J.C.D., U. St. Thomas, Rome, 1958. Ordained priest Roman Catholic Ch., 1948; pastor parishes in N.S., 1948-55; officialis Chancery Office, Antigonish, 1958-59; adminstrn. Diocese of Antigonish, 1959-60; rector Cathedral Antigonish, 1961; dir. extension dept. St. Francis Xavier U., Antigonish, 1961-69; v.p. St. Francis Xavier U., 1962-69; bishop St. John, N.B., Can., 1969-73; archbishop of Edmonton, Alta., 1973—; chancellor U. St. Thomas, Fredericton, N.B., 1969-73. Vice chmn. N.S. Voluntary Econ. Planning Bd., 1965-69; exec. Atlantic Provinces Econ. Council, 1968-73, Can. Council Rural Devel., 1965-75; dir. Program and Planning Agy. N.S. Govt., 1969. Mem. Canadian Assn. Adult Edn. (past pres. N.S.), Canadian Assn. Dirs. Univ. Extension and Summer Schs. (past pres.), Inst. Research on Public Policy (founding mem.), Can. Conf. Cath. Bishops (pres. 1979-81), Futures Secretariat (bd. dirs.). Address: Archbishop of Edmonton 10044 113th St, Edmonton, AB Canada T5K 1N8

MACNEILL, C(HARLES) DON, museum curator, systematic entomologist; b. San Francisco, Dec. 3, 1924; s. Charles Donald and Miriam Elizabeth (Mecredy) MacN.; m. Grace Florence Beckberger, Mar. 8, 1945 (div. 1981); children—Nora Liese MacNeill Manss, Daren Alison MacNeill Collins, Linn Margaret MacNeill Harris. B.S., U. Calif.-Berkeley, 1950, Ph.D., 1960. Teaching asst. entomology U. Calif.-Berkeley, 1952-55; asst. curator, entomologist Calif. Acad. Sci., San Francisco, 1957-65; cataloger, nat. sci. Oakland Mus., Calif., 1965-67, assoc. curator I, 1967-68, assoc. curator II, 1968-71, sr. curator nat. sci., 1971—; mem. adv. com. Lawrence Hall of Sci., U. Calif.-Berkeley, 1972-75. Author: The skippers of the genus Hesperia, 1964; The Hesperiidae of North America, 1975; contbr. articles to sci. jours. Trustees Nature Conservancy, 1968-74; bd. dirs. Calif. Natural Areas Coordination Council, 1967, 68, 79—; bd. dirs., v.p. Biol. Inst. Tropical Am., 1982—; mem. adv. com. land resources E. Bay Mcpl. Utilities Dist., Oakland, 1969-71, mem. adv. com. edn., 1971—; mem. adv. com. U. Calif. Bot. Garden, Berkeley, 1979-83, U. Calif. Press, Berkeley, 1984—. Mem. Pacific Coast Entomol. Soc. (pres. 1966), Lepidopterists Soc. (exec. council 1948—), Calif. Acad. Scis., Brit. Ecol. Soc., Biosystematists. Democrat. Club: Explorers (N.Y. and Calif.). Office: Dept Natural Scis Oakland Mus 1000 Oak St Oakland CA 94607

MACOMBER, JAMES DALE, systems analyst, chemistry consultant; b. Albany, Calif., June 23, 1939; s. Kenneth Dale and Pauline (Marr) M.; m. Christine Cecelia Platt, Feb. 6, 1960 (div. Oct. 1962); m. Cynthia Fraser Nelson, June 12, 1963; children: Heidi Nelson, Heather Cecile, Marcia Fraser, Benjamin Dale. BS in Chemistry, U. Calif., 1960; PhD in Phys. Chemistry, MIT, 1965. Phys. chemist Gen. Electric Research Labs., Schenectady, N.Y., 1960; from asst. prof. to assoc. prof. chemistry La. State U., Baton Rouge, 1967-76; from assoc. prof. to full prof. U. Petroleum and Minerals, Dhahran, Saudi Arabia, 1976-85; systems analyst Gifford Fong Assocs., Walnut Creek, Calif., 1985—; cons. DuPont Engring. Res. Labs., Wilmington, Del., 1969, U. Tex. Chemistry Dept., Austin, 1971, Odom Offshore Surveys, Baton Rouge, 1974-75. Author: Dynamics of Spectroscopic Transitions, 1976; editor Arabian Jour. Sci. Engring., 1978-81; contbr. articles to sci. jours. Past. pres. ACLU, Baton Rouge. Served to capt. Chem. Corps, U.S. Army, 1965-67. Grantee NIH, 1967-70, U. Petroleum and Minerals, 1977-85. Mem. Am. Chem. Soc. (Petroleum Research Fund grantee 1967), Optical Soc. Am., Sigma Xi. Republican. Avocation: genealogy. Home: 1408 Babel Ln Concord CA 94518 Office: Gifford Fong Assocs 1600 Riviera Ave Suite 285 Walnut Creek CA 94596

MACOVSKI, ALBERT, educator; b. N.Y.C., May 2, 1929; s. Philip and Rose (Winogr) M.; m. Adelaide Paris, Aug. 5, 1950; children—Michael, Nancy. B.E.E., City Coll. N.Y., 1950; M.E.E., Poly. Inst. Bklyn., 1953; Ph.D., Stanford U., 1968. Mem. tech. staff RCA Labs., Princeton, N.J., 1950-57; asst. prof., then asso. prof. Poly. Inst. Bklyn., 1957-60; staff scientist Stanford Research Inst., Menlo Park, Calif., 1960-71; fellow U. Calif. Med. Center San Francisco, 1971-72; prof. elec. engring. and radiology Stanford U., 1972—; dir. Magnetic Resonance Systems Research Lab.; cons. to industry. Author. Recipient Achievement award RCA Labs., 1952, 54; award for color TV circuits Inst. Radio Engrs., 1958; NIH spl. fellow, 1971. Fellow IEEE (Zworykin award 1973), Optical Soc. Am.; mem. Am. Assn. Physicists in Medicine, Soc. Magnetic Resonance in Medicine, Sigma Xi, Eta Kappa Nu. Jewish. Patentee in field. Home: 2505 Alpine Rd Menlo Park CA 94025 Office: Stanford U Dept Elec Engring Stanford CA 94305

MACPHERSON, BARRY LEE, psychologist; b. Lamar, Colo., Oct. 26, 1946; s. Wallace Alexander and Lillian (Rowe) M. A.A. in Psychology, Los Angeles Harbor Coll., 1967; B.A. in Psychology, Calif. State U.-Long Beach, 1969, M.A. in Ednl. Psychology, 1971. Cert. sch. psychologist, Calif.; lic. ednl. psychologist, Calif.; lic. marriage family child therapist, Calif. Teaching asst. Seal Beach Sch. Dist., 1970; psychometric asst. Savannah Sch. Dist., 1971; sch. psychology intern Long Beach (Calif.) Unified Sch. Dist., 1971; dist. psychologist Newport-Mesa (Calif.) Unified Sch. Dist., 1972, psychologist spl. edn., 1980; ednl. psychologist, marriage/family/child therapist in pvt. practice, 1977—; oral commr. ednl. psychologist lic. bd. Recipient WHO award Calif. Tchrs. Assn., 1980. Mem. Newport/Mesa Psychol. Assn. (pres. 1980-82), Am. Psychol. Assn., NEA, Calif. Assn. Lic. Ednl. Psychologists, Orange County Assn. Ednl. Psychologists, Newport/Mesa Tchrs. Assn.. Home: 515 35th St Newport Beach CA 92663 Office: 425 East 18th St Costa Mesa CA 92627

MAC QUEEN, ROBERT MOFFAT, solar physicist; b. Memphis, Mar. 28, 1938; s. Marion Leigh and Grace (Gilfillan) MacQ.; m. Caroline Gibbs, June 25, 1960; children: Andrew, Marjorie. BS, Rhodes Coll., 1960; PhD, Johns Hopkins U., 1968. Asst. prof. physics Rhodes Coll., 1961-63; instr. physics and astronomy Goucher Coll., Towson, Md., 1964-66; sr. research scientist Nat. Center for Atmospheric Research, Boulder, Colo., 1967—; dir. High Altitude Obs. Nat. Center for Atmospheric Research, 1979-86; asst. dir. Nat. Ctr. for Atmospheric Research, 1986—; prin. investigator NASA Apollo program, 1971-75, NASA Skylab program, 1970-76, NASA Solar Maximum Mission, 1976-79, NASA/ESA Internat. Solar Polar Mission, 1978-83; lectr. U. Colo., 1968-79, adj. prof., 1979—; mem. com. on space astronomy Nat. Acad. Scis., 1973-76, mem. com. on space physics, 1977-79; mem. Space Sci. Bd., 1983-86. Recipient Exceptional Sci. Achievement medal NASA, 1974. Fellow Optical Soc. Am.; mem. Am. Astron. Soc. (chmn. solar physics div. 1976-78), Assn. Univ. Research Astronomy (dir.-at-large 1984—), Am. Assn. Physics Tchrs., Sigma Xi. Home: 1366 Northridge Ct Boulder CO 80302 Office: Nat Ctr Atmospheric Research PO Box 3000 1850 Table Mesa Dr Boulder CO 80307

MACQUITTY, JONATHAN JAMES, biotechnology executive; b. London, June 15, 1952; came to U.S., 1980; s. William Baird and Betty Edna (Bastin) M.; m. Laurie Newcomb Hunter, Sept. 15, 1984. BA in Chemistry, Oxford (Eng.) U., 1974; PhD, Sussex (Eng.) U., 1977; MBA, Stanford U., 1982. Research chemist Exxon Chems., Brussels, 1977-79; tech. coordinator Exxon Chems., Oxford, Eng., 1979-80; assoc. cons. Boston Cons. Group, London, 1981; mgr. indsl. mktg. Genentech Inc., South San Francisco, 1982-83; comml. dir. Genencor Inc., South San Francisco, 1983-86, v.p., 1986—; bd. dirs. Stanford (Calif.) Ctr. for Entrepreneurship. Patentee in field; contbr. articles to profl. jours. Scholar De La Rue Co., 1970-74, NATO, 1976. Mem. Royal Soc. of Arts, Royal Soc. Chemistry (cert.), Am. Chem. Soc.,

Inst. Food Technologists. Avocations: running, contract bridge, opera, wine tasting. Office: Genencor Inc 180 Kimball Way South San Francisco CA 94080

MACUMBER, JOHN PAUL, insurance company executive; b. Macon, Mo., Jan. 21, 1940; s. Rolland Deardorf and Althea Villa (Cason) M.; B.A., Central Meth. Coll., Fayette, Mo., 1962; Asso. in Risk Mgmt., Ins. Inst. Am., 1978; m. Marilyn Sue Ashe, Nov. 10, 1962; children—Leanne, Cheryl. Casualty underwriter U.S. Fidelity & Guaranty Co., St. Louis, 1962-66; automobile underwriter Am. Indemnity Co., Galveston, Tex., 1966-69; auto casualty underwriter St. Paul Cos., New Orleans, 1969-73; sr. comml. casualty underwriter Chubb/Pacific Indemnity, Portland, Oreg., 1973-75; casualty underwriter Interstate Nat. Corp., Los Angeles, 1975-76, underwriting supr., 1976-78, v.p., br. mgr., Mpls., 1978-82, also v.p. subs. Chgo. Ins. Co.; umbrella/spl. risk supr. Guaranty Nat. Ins. Co., Englewood, Colo., 1982-85; br. mgr. Burns & Wilcox, Ltd.-West, Salt Lake City, 1985—. Served with USAF, 1962-68. Nat. Methodist scholar, 1958. Mem. Minn. Assn. Spl. Risk Underwriters, Ins. Assn. Utah, Profl. Ins. Agts. Utah, Ind. Ins. Agts. Utah, Surplus Line Assn. Utah, Nat. Assn. Profl. Surplus Lines Offices. Republican. Mem. Unity Ch. (sec. bd. dirs. 1979). Lodges: Optimists (charter pres. 1968) (Friendswood, Tex.); Kiwanis (charter pres. 1979) (Bloomington, Minn.). Clubs: Ins., Blue Goose (Mpls.). Home: 9683 S Buttonwood Dr Sandy UT 84092 Office: 455 E South Temple Suite 101 Salt Lake City UT 84111

MAC VICAR, ROBERT WILLIAM, university president emeritus; b. Princeton, Minn., Sept. 28, 1918; s. George William and Elizabeth (Brennan) MacV.; m. Clarice Chambers, Dec. 23, 1948; children—Miriam J., John R. B.A., U. Wyo., 1939, LL.D., 1977; M.S., Okla. State U., 1940; Ph.D., U. Wis., 1946; D.Sci. (hon.), Dankook U., Korea, 1980. Assoc. prof., prof. biochemistry Okla. State U., 1946-64, dean grad. sch., 1953-64, v.p. acad. affairs, 1957-64; v.p. acad. affairs So. Ill. U., Carbondale, 1964-68; chancellor So. Ill. U., 1968-70; pres. Oreg. State U., Corvallis, 1970-84; pres. emeritus Oreg. State U., 1984—; acting pres. Coll. of Ganado, Ariz., 1985; founding mem., bd. dirs. Central Ednl. Midwest Research Lab., chmn. exec. com., 1969-70. Served with U.S. Army, 1939-45. Rhodes scholar, 1939. Mem. Am. Soc. Biol. Chemists, Am. Chem. Soc., Am. Inst. Nutrition, Okla. Acad. Sci., Phi Beta Kappa, Sigma Xi, Phi Kappa Phi. Presbyterian. Home: 1440 NW 14th St Corvallis OR 97330 Office: Oreg State U Corvallis OR 97331

MADDEN, DAVID WILLIAM, English language educator; b. San Francisco, Sept. 10, 1950; s. John Joseph and Esther Calvert (Pearce) M.; m. Mary Virginia Davis, Mar. 19, 1977; children: Anne Elizabeth, Margaret Kathleen. Student, St. Mary's Coll., Moraga, Calif., 1968-70; BA, U. Calif., Davis, 1972, MA, 1974, PhD, 1980. Lectr. U. Calif., Davis, 1980-82; asst. prof. Calif. State U., Sacramento, 1982-85, assoc. prof., 1985—. Contbr. articles to profl. jours. Active Am. Cancer Soc., Sacramento, 1986—. Recipient Exceptional Merit Service award Calif. State U., Sacramento, 1984, Fulbright grantee, 1977-78. Mem. Western Lit. Assn., Am. Com. Irish Studies, Phi Kappa Phi. Democrat. Home: 3201 Lemitar Way Sacramento CA 95833 Office: Calif State U Dept English 6000 J St Sacramento CA 95819

MADDEN, DIANE S., public information officer; b. N.Y.C., Sept. 6, 1945; d. Mortimer Schachter and Betty (Jessel) Lewis; m. John William Madden, July 4, 1981 (div. Sept. 1985); children: Victoria, Melanie, Ashleigh. BA, Goddard Coll., 1974; EdM, U. Ariz., 1976. With exec. sales dept. House Beautiful mag., N.Y.C., 1971-72; gen. mgr. Stas. KWFM-KEVT Radio, Tucson, 1973-74; interventionist, counselor Suicide Prevention Crisis Ctr., Tucson, 1976-77; pres., therapist Advs. in Counseling., Tucson, 1977-78; dir. fellowships Hand Surgery, Ltd., Tucson, 1978-84; dir. community relations Pima County Dept. Transp. and Flood Control Dist., Tucson, 1984—; bd. dirs. P.I.M.A., Tucson. Comr. Tucson Women's Commn., 1984-86; precinct person Pima County Reps., Tucson, 1984-85, bd. dirs. Pima Coll. Pub. Relations Group. Recipient Copper Letter award City of Tucson, 1986, cert. recognition YWCA Women on the Move, Tucson, 1985, cert. appreciation U. Ariz. Pres. club, 1986. Mem. AAUW, Tucson C. of C. (bd. dirs. Leadership Tucson com. 1984—), Leadership Alumni Assn. Avocations: running, weight tng., theater, metaphysics, dance. Home: 260 E Limberlost Rd Tucson AZ 85705 Office: Pima County Dept Transp 1313 S Mission Rd Tucson AZ 85713

MADDEN, PAUL R., lawyer; b. St. Paul, Nov. 13, 1926; s. Ray Joseph and Margaret (Meyer) M.; student St. Thomas Coll., 1944; A.B., U. Minn., 1948; J.D., Georgetown U., 1951; m. Rosemary R. Sorel, Aug. 7, 1974; children—Margaret Jane, William, James Patrick, Derek R. Sorel, Lisa T. Sorel. Admitted to Ariz., Minn., D.C. bars; asso. firm Hamilton & Hamilton, Washington, 1951-55; legal asst. to commr. S.C., Washington, 1955-56; asso. Lewis and Roca, Phoenix, 1957-59, partner, 1959—; counsel to The Indsl Devel. Authority of City of Phoenix; asso. gen. counsel Blood Systems, Inc., Scottsdale, Ariz. Sec. Minn. Fedn. Coll. Rep. Clubs, 1947-48; chmn. 4th dist. Minn. Young Rep. Club, 1948; nat. co-chmn. Youth for Eisenhower, 1951-52; mem. Ariz. Rep. Com., 1960-62; bd. dirs., past pres. Ariz. Club, Phoenix, Mesa Airlines, Farmington, N.Mex.; bd. dirs., past chmn. Found. for Sr. Living, Phoenix; bd. dirs., vice chmn., Cen. Ariz. chpt. ARC; bd. dirs., past pres. Jr. Achievement Cen. Ariz., Inc.; bd. dirs. Camelback Mental Health Systems, Inc., Scottsdale. Served with USNR, 1946-48. Mem. Am., Ariz., Maricopa County, Fed. Bar Assns., Phoenix Soc. Fin. Analysts, Internat. Assn. Ins. Counsel, Fedn. Ins. Counsel, Nat. Health Lawyers Assn., Am. Soc. Hosp. Attys., Nat. Assn. Bond Lawyers, Ariz. Assn. for Indsl. Devel., Phi Delta Phi. Clubs: The Barristers (Washington). Home: 3732 E Pierson St Phoenix AZ 85018 Office: 100 W Washington Phoenix AZ 85003

MADDEN, RICHARD BLAINE, forest products executive, educator; b. Short Hills, N.J., Apr. 27, 1929; s. James L. and Irma (Twining) M.; m. Joan Fairbairn, May 24, 1958; children: John Richard, Lynn Marie, Kathryn Ann, Andrew Twining. B.S., Princeton U., 1951; J.D., U. Mich., 1956; M.B.A., NYU, 1959. Bar: Mich. 1956, N.Y. 1958. Gen. asst. treas.'s dept. Socony Mobil Oil Corp., N.Y.C., 1956-57; spl. asst. Socony Mobil Oil Corp., 1958-59, fin. rep., 1960; asst. to pres. Mobil Chem. Co.; also dir. Mobil Chems. Ltd. of Eng., 1960-63; exec. v.p., gen. mgr. Kordite Corp.; also v.p. Mobil Plastics, 1963-66; v.p. Mobil Chem. Co., N.Y.C., 1966-68; group v.p. Mobil Chem. Co., 1968-70; asst. treas. Mobil Oil Corp., 1970-71; chmn. Mobil Oil Estates Ltd., 1970-71; pres., chief exec. to chmn., chief exec. officer Potlatch Corp., San Francisco, 1971—; dir. Pacific Gas and Electric Co., AMFAC, Inc.; from lectr. to adj. asso. prof. fin. NYU, 1960-63. Bd. dirs. Am. Paper Inst., Georgetown U., Nat. Park Found., C. of C. of U.S.; vice-chmn. Bay Area Council; trustee, exec. com. Am. Enterprise Inst.; bd. govs. San Francisco Symphony; bd. dirs. San Francisco Opera Assn.; mem. distbn. com. San Francisco Found. Served to lt (j.g.) USNR, 1951-54. Mem. N.Y., Mich. bar assns. Roman Catholic. Clubs: University (N.Y.C.); Pacific Union (San Francisco), Bohemian (San Francisco); Lagunitas (Ross, Calif.); Metropolitan (Washington).

MADDEN, SARA LEE, educator; b. Spearville, Kans., Mar. 24, 1928; d. Delbert Dewey and Arva Allene (Clark) Imel; m. Gerald Houk, Sept. 1948 (dec. Dec. 1972); 1 son, Robert Dewey; m. 2d, Donald Madden, Dec. 28, 1967 (dec. July 1979). B.S. in Bus. Adminstrn./Edn., U. Wichita, 1964. Cert. tchr., Calif. Sec., Office of Vets. Affairs, Salina, Kans., 1949-50; sec. engring. dept. Kans. State Coll., Manhattan, 1951-52; exec. sec. Transport Co. of Tex., Kwajalein, M.I., 1958-61; tchr. Wichitan High Sch. West, Wichita, Kans., 1964; tchr. bus. and office edn. Franklin High Sch., Stockton, Calif., 1964—, chmn. dept., 1967—; tchr. adult edn. San Joaquin Delta Community Coll., Stockton, 1965-82; mem. Adv. Com. for Vocat. Edn., mem. Adv. Com. for Regional Occupational Ctr. Mem. Nat. Bus. Edn. Assn., NEA, Calif. Bus. Edn. Assn., Western Bus. Edn. Assn., Am. Vocat. Assn., Calif. Assn. Vocat. Edn., Calif. Tchrs. Assn., Stockton Tchrs. Assn., AAUW, Kappa Delta Pi, Delta Kappa Gamma. Republican. Lodge: Order Eastern Star. Home: 3503 Harpers Ferry Dr Stockton CA 95209 Office: 300 N Gertrude Ave Stockton CA 95205

MADDOX, JACKSON PAUL, safety and health director; b. Charleston, S.C., Sept. 5, 1944; s. Jackson Lee and Doris Evelyn (Camp) M.; m. Hope Dianne Nordloh, Nov. 20, 1965; children: Terra Jennifer, Jason Paul. BS in Bus., U. Nev., 1973, MBA, 1975. Registered profl. engr., Calif.; cert. safety prof., cert. hazard control mgr., cert. assoc. risk mgr. Safety inspector REE Co., Las Vegas, Nev., 1964-66; safety engr. EG&G Energy Measurements, Inc., Las Vegas, 1966-74, safety adminstr., 1974-76, office mgr., 1976-78, dept. mgr., 1978-80, div. dir., 1980—; mem. exec. com. Nev. Safety Council, Las Vegas, 1985. Named Safety Profl. of Yr. Nev. Safety Council, 1983. Mem. Am. Soc. Safety Engrs. (pres. So. Nev. chpt. 1979-80, 87—, Safety Profl. of Yr. 1983). Democrat. Avocations: racquetball, snowmobiling, fishing. Office: EG&G Energy Measurements Inc PO Box 1912 Las Vegas NV 89125

MADDUX, PARKER AHRENS, lawyer; b. San Francisco, May 23, 1939; s. Jackson Walker and Jeanette Ahrens M.; m. Mathilde G.M. Landman, Mar. 20, 1966; 1 child, Jackson Wilhelmus Quentin. A.B., U. Calif., 1961; J.D., Harvard U., 1964. Bar: Calif. 1965, U.S. Dist. Ct. (no. and ea. dist.) Calif. 1965, U.S. Ct. Apls. (9th cir.) 1972, U.S. Ct. Clms., 1974, N.Y. 1981, U.S. Supreme Ct. 1982, Assoc., Pillsbury, Madison & Sutro, San Francisco, 1965-72, ptnr., 1973—; lectr. in field. Bd. dirs. Friends of Recreation and Parks, San Francisco; trustee Coll. Preparatory Sch., Oakland, Calif. Fulbright fellow, 1964-65. Mem. ABA (chmn. antitrust legis. subcom. of litigation subcom.), Calif. Bar Assn., San Francisco Bar Assn. Republican. Unitarian. Clubs: St. Francis Yacht (San Francisco); Harvard (N.Y.C.). Contbr. articles to profl. jours. Office: Pillsbury Madison & Sutro 225 Bush St San Francisco CA 94104

MADDY, KENNETH LEON, state senator, lawyer; b. Santa Monica, Calif., May 22, 1934; s. Russell T. and Anna M. (Balzer) M.; m. Beverly Ann Chinello, 1957; children—Deanna G., Donald P., Marilyn M.; m.2d, Norma Foster, 1981. B.S., Fresno State Coll., 1957; J.D., UCLA, 1963. Ptnr., Chinello, Chinello, Maddy & Shelton, Fresno, Calif., after 1963; now of counsel Law Office of D.A. Jackson; mem. Calif. State Assembly from Dist. 30, 1971-78, now mem. Calif. State Senate. Del. Republican Nat. Conv., 1976, 80, 84. Served to 1st lt., USAF, 1957-60; capt. Res. Mem. Calif. Bar Assn., Jaycees, Fresno C. of C., Blue Key, Sigma Nu, Phi Delta Phi. Lodge Rotary. Office: Calif State Senate Sacramento CA 95814

MADER, KELLY FORBES, real estate broker, senator; b. Sheridan, Wyo., Jan. 21, 1952; s. Richard August and Ena Cora (Forbes) M.; m. Nancy Gay Murray, Nov. 16, 1975; children: Amy, Angie, Ian. Student, Bob Jones U., 1970-71, Grace Coll., 1971-72, Tex. A&M U. Owner, pres. Kelly F. Mader & Assocs., Gillette, Wyo., 1973—; rep. Wyo. State Legis., Cheyenne, 1982-84, senator, 1984—. Officer Campbell County Sheriffs Res., Gillette, 1981—, Campbell County Search and Rescue Team, Gillette 1981—. Named one of Outstanding Young Men of Am., 1982, 85. Mem. Am. Legis. Exchange Council (state chmn. 1984—), Nat. Rifle Assn. Republican. Avocations: golf, shooting.

MADERA, JOSEPH J., bishop; b. San Francisco, Nov. 27, 1927. Ed., Domus Studiorum of the Missionaries of the Holy Spirit, Coyoacan, D.F., Mexico. Ordained priest Roman Cath. Ch., 1957; ordained coadjutor bishop of Fresno, Calif., 1980; bishop of Fresno, 1980—. Office: PO Box 1668 Fresno CA 93717

MADILL, EDWIN JOSEPH, consultant, former foreign service officer; b. Charlevoix, Mich., Feb. 19, 1911; s. Robert G. and Elaine J. (Orlowski) M.; m. Margaret A. Shea, May 9, 1934; children: Margaret Ann Madill Baptie, Mary Paula Madill Jarrett, Edwin Joseph, Michael Shea. Student, Georgetown U., 1929-32, Columbus U., 1936-37, 41-42; grad., U.S. Army War Coll., 1957, Breveted Brig. Gen., 1972. Tax analyst Mich. Tax Commn., 1933-34; asst. supt. HOLC, 1934-36; successively acct., tech. adviser, classification agt., personnel dir. Office of Treas. U.S. Treasury Dept., 1936-45; asst. dir. Office Contract Selttlement Exec. Office of Pres., 1945-46, spl. adminstrv. cons., 1946; mgmt. analyst U.S. Dept. State, 1946-48; mem. civil service com. expert examiners 1948, spl. liaison officer to Brit. and Can. govts. on emergency planning problems, 1947-56; spl. rep. to Paris U.S. Dept. State, 1948, 50, spl. rep. to Rome and London, 1949, spl. rep. to Philippines, Thailand and India, 1949, spl. rep. to Rome and Geneva, 1950, spl. rep. to Panama, France, Germany, Austria, Italy, 1952, spl. rep. to France, Italy, Saudi Arabia, East Africa, 1953, spl. rep. to Italy, 1954, spl. rep. to Italy, Austria, France, Eng., Germany, Spain, Greece, Turkey, Lebanon, 1955, spl. asst. to adminstr. Bur. Security and Consular Affairs, 1955-56, spl. coordinator to Italy, Lebanon, Syria, Jordan, Israel, Cyprus, Egypt, Iraq, 1956-57; U.S. Consul Calgary, Alta., Can., 1957-63; dean Calgary Consular Corps, U.S. Consul Auckland, N.Z., 1963-64; ret. 1964; cons. pub. relations adminstrn. and mgmt. engring. Author: Position Classification in the Federal Service, 2d edit., 1945; Manual on Emergency Procedures and Practices, 1950, edits. 1952-56, History of Emergency Planning, 1957, Genealogy of Five Families, 1977, The Madill Chronicles, 5 vols., 1983, Verse & Worse, 6 vols., Madill's 20th Century, 7 vols. Mem. Canukeena Club (hon.), Lord Strathcona's Horse, The Queen's Own Rifles, King's Own Armored Regt., H.M.C.S. Tecumseh, Sarcee Tribe (hon. chief). Clubs: Ranchmen's (Calgary), Royal N.Z. Yacht Squadron, Auckland, Northern. Lodges: KC. Home: 5630 E Calle Del Paisano Phoenix AZ 85018

MADNI, ASAD MOHAMED, engineering executive; b. Bombay, India, Sept. 8, 1947; came to U.S., 1966; s. Mohamed Taher and Sara Taher (Wadiwalla) M.; Gowhartaj Shahnawaz, Nov. 11, 1976; 1 child, Jamal Asad. Cert. in gen. edn., U. Cambridge, Bombay, 1964; AAS, RCA Insts., Inc., 1968, AS in Electronics, 1968; BS in Engring., UCLA, 1969, MS in Engring., 1972; postgrad., Stanford U., 1984; PhD, Calif. Inst. Tech., 1987. Sr. instr. Pacific States U., Los Angeles, 1969-71; electronics auditor Pertec Corp., Chatsworth, Calif., 1973-75; project engr., sr. engr., program mgr., dir. advanced programs Microwave div. Systron Donner, Van Nuys, Calif., 1975-82, dir. enring., 1982—, gen. mgr., 1985—; tech. advisor Test and Measurement World, Boston, 19806. Mem. editorial rev. bd., West coast chmn. Microwave Systems News and Communications Tech., 1982—; contbr. articles to mags. and jours.; patentee in field. Mem. IEEE (sr.), Assn. Old Crows, Nat. Rifle Assn., Calif. Rifle and Pistol Assn. Home: 3582 Greenfield Ave Los Angeles CA 90034 Office: Systron Donner Corp Microwave Div 14844 Oxnard St Van Nuys CA 91409

MADONNA, LEAH, editor mining periodical, writer, photographer; b. Birmingham, Ala., Nov. 20, 1937; d. Julian Clarence and Lillian Lee (Wall) Harper; m. James Albert Madonna, Feb. 14, 1976; children: Riska, Kimberley, Michael, Niki. Student, St. Mary's Jr. Coll., Birmingham, Ala., Newark Sch. Design, 1963-64, U. Alaska, 1972-75, 84-86. Cons. fashions White Lakes and J.C. Penneys dept. stores, Topeka, 1963; pvt. practice fashion designer Fairbanks, Alaska, 1965-74; inventory controller N C Co., Fairbanks, 1974-76; editor, mgr. Alaskan Prospectors Pub., Fairbanks, 1980-86; gen. mgr. Alaskan Prospectors Supply Stores, Anchorage and Fairbanks, 1976—; travel dir. Alaska/Australia Mines and Cultural tour, 1986. Prin. design works include: costume for Miss Alaska Universe, 1971 (1st nat. prize, 1971, also co-designer, 1972 (1st nat. prize 1972)), graphics design Alaskan Prospector mag. logo, 1978; co-contbr. Alaskan Mineral Exhibit display at Internat. Airport, Fairbanks; contbr. articles and photos to Alaska N.W. Pubs. Mem. Alaska Miners Assn. (supr. conf. trade show 1970-85), Placer Miners Alaska (bd. dirs. 1984-85), Alaska Women in Mining (pres. 1985-86). Republican. Clubs: Alaska Press, Far North Press. Avocations: photojournalism, Alaskan mining history, Australian history and culture. Home and Office: 504 College Rd Fairbanks AK 99701

MADRID, JOE HERNANDEZ, speech pathologist; b. Artesia, N.Mex., Mar. 21, 1944; s. Felix Rodriquez and Senaida Brito (Hernandez) M.; m. Linda Gayle Jacobs, Oct. 15, 1966; children: Valerie Jane, Kelley Joe, Donicio Jose. BS, Eastern N.Mex. U., 1968; MA, Western Mich. U., 1970. Speech pathologist Del. County Schs., Manchester, Iowa, 1970-73, U. Mont., Missoula, 1971-72; speech and hearing supr. Porter County Spl. Edn., Valparaiso, Ind., 1973-79; exec. dir. TDTC, Inc., Roswell, N.Mex., 1979—. Participant Leadership Roswell, 1984-85. Served with U.S. Army, 1968-69. Office of Edn. fellow Western Mich. U., 1969. Mem. Am. Speech and Hearing Assn. (cert.), Council N.Mex. Services to Handicapped, Nat. Rifle Assn., Nat. Wild Turkey Fedn., Roswell Interagy. Council. Democrat. Roman Catholic. Lodges: Eagles, Kiwanis. Avocations: reading, hunting, fishing, racquetball, home remodeling. Office: TDTC Inc 337 E 6th St Roswell NM 88201

MADSEN, ELIZABETH KARLENE, librarian, educator; b. Swarthmore, Pa., Aug. 16, 1944; d. Roy Harding and Katharine (Walters) Madsen. BA, Western Wash. State U., 1966; MLS, U. Hawaii, 1972, postgrad. 1981—; AM, Stanford U., 1985. Editor Kodiak Daily Mirror, Alaska, 1967-68; outreach librarian Fairbanks N. Star, 1972; asst. librarian A. Holmes Johnson Library, Kodiak, 1973-74, King County Library, Bothell, Wash., 1974-76; community coll. librarian Matanuska Susitna Community Coll., Palmer, Alaska, 1976—. Chmn. Friends of Library, Bothell, 1976; bd. dirs. Alaska Pub. TV, Anchorage, 1978-80; del. Gov.'s Conf. on Libraries, 1979; chmn. Alaska State Collection Devel. Steering Com., 1986; intern Stanford Inst. Intercultural Communication, summer 1981. Recipient Outstanding Program award Matanuska-Susitna Community Coll., 1983. Mem. ALA, Alaska Library Assn. (treas. 1979-80), Mensa., Stanford U. Alumni Assn. Republican. Home: PO Box 499 Palmer AK 99645 Office: Mantanuska Susitna Community Coll Pouch 5001 Trunk Rd Palmer AK 99645

MADSEN, HAROLD STANLEY, linguistics educator; b. Salt Lake City, Apr. 23, 1926; s. Harold J. and Helen Anna (Sanders) M.; m. Mona Eloise Darton; children: Suzanne, Larry, Debra, Denise, Marcia, Harold Jay. BA, U. Utah, 1953, MA, 1960; PhD, U. Colo., 1965. Prof. Brigham Young U., Provo, Utah, 1956-66, 1970—; assoc. prof. Haile Sellassie I U., Addis Ababa, Ethiopia, 1966-70. Author: (with J.D. Bowen) Adaptation in Language Teaching, 1978, Techniques in Teaching Testing, 1983, TESOL (with J.D. Bowen & A. Hilferty) Techniques and Procedures, 1985. Bd. govs. Am. Community Sch., Addis Ababa, 1969-70. Served with U.S. Army, 1944-46. Recipient Karl G. Maeser Research and Creative Arts award, Brigham Young U., 1979. Mem. Intermountain Tchrs. English to Speakers of Other Langs. (pres. 1973-75, Disting. Service award 1983). Republican. Mormon. Home: 176 E 4635 N Provo UT 84604 Office: Brigham Young U Dept Linguistics 2129 JKHB Provo UT 84602

MADSEN, JACK ENOCH, III, architect, educator; b. Los Angeles, Jan. 31, 1948; s. Jack Enoch Jr. and Vivian (Brooksby) M.; m. Charlotte Ann Davis, July 30, 1970; children: Jennifer Michelle, Kimberlee Ann, Terresa Lee, Jack Enoch IV, Nicholas William. Student, Mt. San Antonio Coll., 1966-68, 71, Brigham Young U., 1969-70, Calif. State Poly. U., Pomona, 1971-74. Registered profl. architect, Ariz., Calif.; cert. Nat. Council Archtl. Registration Bds. Archtl. coordinator Bank of Am., Los Angeles, 1974-76; prin., designer Jack E. Madsen Design, Claremont, Calif., 1978—; dir. project mgmt. and archtl. services Cannell & Chaffin Comml. Interiors, Los Angeles, 1984-86; project architect HMC Architects, Inc., Ontario, Calif., 1986—; asst. v.p. store planning Bullock's Dept. Stores, Los Angeles, 1976-78; assoc. designer Jasper and Assocs., Pasadena, Calif., 1979-82; pres., corp. architect Miller-Madsen Corp., Claremont, 1982—; prof. design and tech. Mt. San Antonio Coll., Walnut Calif., 1983-84, mem. steering com., 1984—; geotechture (subterranean architecture) researcher. Cub master Boy Scouts Am. Claremont council, 1978, exec. troop com., 1981-83; asst. coach Am. Youth Soccer Orgn., Claremont, 1983. Mem. AIA (long range planning com. 1984, minute man polit. program 1978-83), Calif. Council AIA, Foothill Chpt. AIA, Los Angeles Chpt. AIA, Inst. Store Planners. Democrat. Mormon. Avocations: dirt motorcycle riding, water skiing, scuba diving, boating, fishing. Home: 1521 N Webster Ave Claremont CA 91711 Office: HMC Architects Inc 500 East E St Ontario CA 91764

MADSEN, ROGER BRYAN, lawyer; b. Logan, Utah, Dec. 1, 1947; s. Louis Linden and Edith Louise (Gundersen) M.; m. Leslie Sheryl Roberts, 1972; children: Rebecca, Deborah, Bryan, Benjamin, Melanie. B.A. in Polit. Sci. and French with distinction, Wash. State U., 1971; M.A. in Polit. Sci., Brigham Young U., 1972, J.D., 1976; M. Internat. Mgmt., Am. Grad. Sch. Internat. Mgmt., 1973. Bar: Idaho 1976, U.S. Dist. Ct. Idaho 1976. Jud. intern U.S. Supreme Ct., Washington, 1974; legal intern JAG's Sch., U. Va. Law Sch., Charlottesville, 1974, Wash. State Atty. Gen.'s Office, Pullman, 1975; asst. atty. gen. Idaho Atty. Gen.'s Office, Boise, 1976-80; dist. mgr. Gibbens Co., Inc., Boise, 1980-83; sole practice, Boise, 1983—. Contbr. numerous articles on employment law to profl. jours. Vice chmn. Idaho del. to White Ho. Conf. on Families, Los Angeles, 1980; mem. planning com., bus. lobbyist, mgmt. cons. Idaho Celebration of Bicentennial of U.S. Constn., 1986; chmn. Idaho Gov.'s Task Force on Unemployment Ins., 1983-84, Mayor-County Commn. Task Force on Pub. Housing Authority Investigation, 1986; mem. Gov.'s Workers Compensation Adv. Council, 1986—; polit. activist, fund-raiser; bd. dirs. Idaho Allied Civic Forces, Boise, 1981—; alumni ednl. counselor Am. Grad. Sch. Internat. Mgmt., Glendale, Ariz., 1974—; Mormon missionary in France and Belgium, 1986—, high council Ch. of Jesus Christ of Latter-day Saints, exec. sec. stake; gen. counsel Idaho Assn. Counties. Mem. Wash. State U. Alumni Assn. (bd. dirs., com. chmn.), J. Reuben Clark Law Soc. (charter), Idaho Bar Assn., Idaho Assn. Commerce and Industry. Republican. Home: 7842 Desert Ave Boise ID 83709 Office: 3775 Cassia St Boise ID 83705

MADSEN, WILLIAM DANIEL, public affairs executive; b. Denver, Apr. 28, 1913; s. Emil Thomas and Mabel (Wessel) M.; B.S., Colo. State U., 1939; m. Mary Evelyn O'Connor, Jan. 11, 1947; children—William Daniel, Karen Elaine. Asst. to supt. Swift & Co., Denver, 1939-42; adj. Colo. Wing CAP, 1942-46; pres. Rocky Mountain Air Shows, 1946-53; air photo instr. U.S. Air Force, Lowry AFB, 1953-58; charter mgr. Vest Aircraft Co., Denver, 1958-62; pub. affairs specialist U.S. Air Force, USAF Acad., Colorado Springs, 1962—; tchr. photography Pikes Peak Community Coll., 1974—. Bd. dirs. Alumni Found., Colo. State U. Served with USAF, 1942-44. Named Sr. Mem. of Yr., CAP, 1981; named to Colo. Aviation Hall of Fame, 1982, CAP Hall of Honor, 1985; recipient Brewer Meml. Aerospace award, 1982, Crown Circle award Nat. Congress on Aerospace Edn., 1983; Category V Brewer Meml. Aerospace award, 1984. Mem. Cross and Cockade, Aerospace Historians, OX-5 Aviation Pioneers, Aircraft Owners and Pilots Assn., Comml. Pilots Assn., Air Force Assn., Profl. Photographers Assn., Colo. Pilots Assn., Colo. Aviation Hist. Soc. (pres. 1979-86), Colo. Aviation Assn. (pres. 1982), Colorado Springs Press Assn., Colorado Springs C. of C. (visitors promotion com.), Sigma Chi, Alpha Lambda Epsilon. Episcopalian. Clubs: Denver Pilots, Colo. Silver Wings. Editor, pub: The Aircraft Bluebook, 1958-63. Home: 1327 Kern St Colorado Springs CO 80915 Office: USAF Acad Harmon Hall Room 324 Colorado Springs CO 80840

MADWAY, DAVID MAGEN, lawyer; b. Phila., July 23, 1939; s. Harry and Beatrice (Brod) M.; m. Nancy Ashworth, June 15, 1963; children: Jesse B., Gabriel A. Bar: N.Y. 1966, Calif. 1970. Assoc. Herzfeld & Rubin, N.Y.C., 1964-66, Poletti, Friedin, Prashker, Feldman & Gartner, N.Y.C., 1966-69; atty. Nat. Housing Law Project, Berkeley, Calif., 1969-77, exec. dir., 1977-86; ptnr. Madway, Blumberg, Farber and Smith, Berkeley, 1986—; Calif. commr. Nat conf. Commrs. Uniform State Laws, Chgo., 1976-78; bd. dirs. Nat. Low-Income Housing Coalition, Washington. Mem. State Bar Calif. Democrat. Home: 5676 Oak Grove Ave Oakland CA 94618 Office: Madway Blumberg Farber & Smith 1950 Addison St Berkeley CA 94704

MAEDA, JAMES HIROSHI, state agency radio dispatcher; b. El Paso, Tex., Dec. 6, 1960; s. Fumio and Yoriko (Takahashi) M. BA, U. Hawaii, 1983. Communications cons. Pacific Teletec, Waipahu, Hawaii, 1983-85; account clk. Bank of Hawaii, Honolulu, 1985; clerk-typist State of Hawaii, Honolulu, 1985-86, radio dispatcher, 1986—.

MAEHL, WILLIAM HARVEY, historian, educator; b. Bklyn., May 28, 1915; s. William Henry and Antoinette Rose (Salamone) M.; m. Josephine Scholl McAllister, Dec. 29, 1941; children: Madeleine, Kathleen. BSc, Northwestern U., 1937, MA, 1939; PhD, U. Chgo., 1946. Asst. prof. history St. Louis U., 1941-42, Tex. A&M U., College Sta., 1943, De Paul U., Chgo., 1944-49; historian Dept. of Def., Karlsruhe, Stuttgart, Fed. Rep. Germany, 1950-52; chief briefing office U.S. hdqrs. EUCOM, Frankfurt, Fed. Rep. Germany, 1952-53; chief historian Artillery Sci. Ft. Sill, Okla., 1954, war plans office Hdqrs. NAMAE, USAF, Burtonwood, Eng., 1954-55; assoc. prof. European history Nebr. Wesleyan U., Lincoln, 1955-57, prof., 1958-62, 65-68; prof. German history Auburn (Ala.) U., 1968-81, prof. emeritus, 1981—; vis. prof. U. Nebr., 1962, U. Auckland, New Zealand, 1963-64, Midwestern U., Wichita Falls, Tex., 1965. Author: German Militarism and Socialism, 1968, History of Germany in Western Civilization, 1979, A World History Syllabus, 3 vols., 1980, August Bebel, Shadow Emperor of the German Workers, 1980, The German Socialist Party: Champion of the First Republic, 1918-33, 1986; monographs, chpts. to books; contbr. articles to profl. jours. Grantee Nebr. Wesleyan U., 1959, Auburn U., 1969-73, 79-80, Am. Philosophical Soc., 1973-74, Deutscher Akademischer Austauschdienst, 1978. Mem. Am. Hist. Assn., Phi Kappa Phi, Phi Alpha Theta.

MAEL, ROD(NEY) ERNEST, industrial engineer; b. Spokane, Wash., Dec. 24, 1949; s. Ernest Elmer and Georgia Marie (Lower) M.; m. Sandra Lee Farrish, Sept. 17, 1969 (div. June 1984); children: Gina, Anthony, Lisa; m. Teresa Joan Pringle. Dec. 8, 1984. Cert. broadcasting, Columbia Sch. Broadcasting, San Francisco, 1972; BSBA, City U., Seattle, 1979. Disc jockey/radio announcer Federal Way, Wash., 1969-75; mgr. dept. White Front Stores, Inc., Burien, Wash., 1972-73; indsl. engr., mgr. Boeing Airplane Co., Seattle, 1973—; cons., tchr. mgmt. programs Boeing Airplane Co., Seattle, 1985—. Area coordinator, loaned exec. Assn. Wash. Bus.'s, Cen. Wash. U., 1985-86. Avocations: playing guitar, writing music, study hypnosis, home computing, motorcycling. Office: Boeing Devel Mfg PO Box 3707 M/S 1R-37 Seattle WA 98124-2207

MAES, CHARLES JOSEPH, chemist; b. Santa Fe, Oct. 1, 1957; s. Eloy and Ruby (Martinez) M.; m. Bernice Marie Holm, May 16, 1980; 1 child, Dominic Charles. BS, Grand Canyon Coll., 1979. Tech. service asst. ICI Americas Inc., Phoenix, 1980-82, lab. supr., 1982-86, supr. accounts and tech. services, 1986—. Am. Legion Scholar, 1975. Mem. Am. Chem. Soc., AIME. Republican. Roman Catholic. Club: Volvo Tennis League (Phoenix). Avocations: tennis, jogging, bicycling, golf. Home: 2440 W Redfield Rd Phoenix AZ 85023 Office: ICI Americas Inc 50 S 45th Ave Phoenix AZ 85043

MAFFIA, PAUL MARIE, internal controls and finance consultant; b. Chgo., July 14, 1936; s. Anthony and Clara (Leo) M.; m. Mary Ellen McLane, June 25, 1960; children: Timothy, Felicia. BS in Commerce, Loyola U., Chgo., 1958; MBA, U. Wash., 1974. Sales clk. Montgomery Ward and Co., Chgo., 1955-58; internal auditor The Boeing Co., Seattle, 1962-70; state examiner Office of State Auditor, Olympia, Wash., 1975-81; cons. Bainbridge Island, Wash., 1981—. Served to 1st lt. U.S. Army, 1958-62. Recipient Silver medal Chgo. Tribune, 1956, 58. Mem. Assn. MBA Execs., Inst. Cert. Fin. Planners (cert.), Inst. Internal Auditors (cert., gov., CIA chmn., audit chmn.). Roman Catholic. Avocations: philatey, photography, collecting old radio programs. Home and Office: 4574 Crystal Springs Dr NE Bainbridge Island WA 98110

MAGA, JOSEPH ANDREW, food science educator; b. New Kensington, Pa., Dec. 25, 1940; s. John and Rose Maga; m. Andrea H. Vorperian, June 13, 1964; children: Elizabeth, John. BS, Pa. State U., 1962, MS, 1964; PhD, Kans. State U., 1970. Project leader Borden Foods Co., Syracuse, N.Y., 1964-66; group leader Cen. Soya Co., Chgo., 1966-68; asst. prof. Colo. State U., Ft. Collins, Colo., 1970-72, assoc. prof., 1972-74, prof. food sci., 1974—. Contbr. numerous articles to profl. jours. Mem. Inst. Food Technologists, Am. Chem. Soc., Am. Dairy Sci. Assn., Am. Assn. Cereal Scientists, Am. Soc. Wine Educators. Office: Dept Food Sci and Nutrition Colo State U Fort Collins CO 80523

MAGALOUSIS, NICHOLAS MICHAEL, anthropology, archaeology educator; b. Gadsden, Ala., Nov. 10, 1945; s. Chris Nick and Angela Ann (Chacos) M. BA in Anthropology, Archeology, Calif. State U., Fullerton, 1973, MA in Anthropology, Archeology, 1974; postgrad., UCLA, 1976-78, U. Calif., Irvine, %. Instr. Cypress (Calif.) Coll., 1975-76; asst. prof. Calif. State U., Long Beach, 1975-76; instr. U. Calif., Irvine, 1977-81, Santa Ana (Calif.) Coll., 1981; adj. prof. Chapman Coll., Orange, Calif., 1975—; dir. Interdisciplinary Research, Laguna Beach, Calif., 1977—, dir. Anthropol. and Archeol. Research, San Juan Capistrano, Calif., 1979—; dir. San Juan Capistrano Mission Mus., 1979—; dir. Ednl. Travel Tours, Laguna Beach., 1981-82. Contbr. articles to profl. jours. Served as sgt. USAF, 1966-70. Grantee Irvine Found., 1984, Disneyland Found., 1983, Community Service, City of San Juan Capistrano, 1983-87, Nat. Endowment for Humanities, 1986, Ahmanson Found., 1986-87. Mem. Nat. History Found. of Orange County, Soc. Archaeol. Sci., Soc. Calif. Archaeology, San Juan Capistrano Hist. Soc. (bd. dirs. 1986—), Calif. Mission Studies Assn. (exec. bd. chmn. 1984—), Laguna Beach Hist. Soc. (exec. bd. mem. 1984-85, DAR (lectr. 1979—), C. of C. (lectr. 1979—). Democrat. Greek Orthodox. Lodge: Rotary. Avocation: traveling. Office: Chapman Coll Orange CA 92666

MAGEE, JOE WILTON, JR., chemical engineer, thermodynamics consultant; b. Meridian, Miss., June 9, 1955; s. Joey Wilton and Faye (Rose) M. BS, Ga. Inst. Tech., 1978; MS, Rice U., 1981, PhD ChemE, 1983. Postdoctoral chem. engr. Rice U., Houston, 1983-84; postdoctoral fellow Nat. Bur. Standards, Boulder, Colo., 1984-86, chem. engr. thermophysics div., 1986—; thermodynamics cons. Boulder indsl. consortium, 1984-86. Contbr. numerous articles to sci. publs. Patron Denver Art Mus. and Denver Mus. Natural History, 1984-86. Fellow Nat. Research Council, Washington, 1984. Mem. Am. Inst. Chem. Engrs., Am. Chem. Soc., Calorimetry Soc. Episcopalian. Avocations: fgn. travel, mountain hiking, symphony music. Home: PO Box 3053 Boulder CO 80307 Office: Nat Bur Standards Thermophysics Div 774 03 325 Broadway Boulder CO 80303

MAGEL, DONALD GEORGE, social work educator, academic administrator; b. Brush Valley, Pa., Aug. 27, 1937; s. George Joseph and Lucille (Solomon) M.; children: Keith, Sidney, Karl; m. Rose Marie Langer, Nov. 2, 1985. AA, Vallejo Jr. Coll., 1962; BA, Calif. State U., 1962; MSW, U. Calif., Berkeley, 1964; PhD, U. Pitts., 1975. Instr. U. Pitts., 1968-71; asst. prof. W.Va. U., Morgantown, 1971-73, U. W. Fla., Pensacola, 1973-75, U. Evansville, Ind., 1975-78; assoc. prof. Ariz. State U., Tempe, 1978—, dir. undergrad. programs, 1986—; social service dir. Nev. Mental Health, Sparks, 1984-85. contbr. articles to profl. jours. Served with USAF, 1955-58. Avocations: hiking, backpacking, fishing, shooting. Home: 206 E 14th St Tempe AZ 85281 Office: Ariz State U Sch of Social Work Tempe AZ 85287

MAGELLI, PAUL JOHN, college president, economics consultant; b. Mt. Clare, Ill., June 28, 1931; s. Biagio and Mary (Mareta) M.; m. Karolyn Jane Bodznick, Sept. 1, 1958; children—Paul, Jr., Merrell A. B.A. in Econs., U. Ill., 1959, M.S. in Econs., 1960, Ph.D. in Econs., 1965. Asst. to dean U. Ill., Urbana, 1959-65, asst. dir. Midwest Univs. Consortium for Internat. Services, 1966-67; dean Fairmount Coll. Liberal Arts and Scis., Wichita State U., Kans., 1969-83; v.p. acad. adminstrn. Drake U., Des Moines, 1983-85; pres. Metro. State Coll., Denver, 1985—; cons. Am. Nat. Bank, Assn. Midwest Colls., State of Ill. Higher Edn. Assistance Corp.; v.p. acad. affairs at U. Ill., Chgo. Circle. Author: The Problem and the Promise, 1981; The Humane Administrator, 1986. Bd. dirs. Am. Heart Assn., Wichita, Goodwill Inds., Inc., Wichita, 1975-78, Denver Partnership, 1985—. Mem. Am. Assn. Higher Edn., Am. Council on Edn., Assn. Am. Colls., Council Colls. of Arts and Scis. (pres. 1983, bd. dirs. 1980-84), Denver C. of C. (bd. dirs. small bus. council 1985—). Roman Catholic. Club: Denver Athletic. Lodge: Rotary. Avocations: ice skating; jogging; flower gardening. Home: 1301 Speer Blvd Apr 805 Denver CO 80204 Office: Metro State Coll 1006 11th St Denver CO 80204 *

MAGID, GAIL AVRUM, neurosurgery educator; b. Chgo., Oct. 15, 1934; s. Harry M. and Henrietta (Busch) M.; m. Janet Louise Reinhardt, June 15, 1962 (div.); children: Allison Drew, Jonathan Alward; m. Roseanne Cipra Muirhead, Sept. 4, 1982; children: Heather Marie, John Scott IV, Mark Andrew. BSc, U. Ill., 1954; MD, Chgo. Med. Sch., 1958. Diplomate Am. Bd. Neurol. Surgery. Intern Cook County Hosp., Chgo., 1958-59; resident, then fellow neurol. surgery Mayo Clinic, Rochester, Minn., 1959-61, 63-65; clin. instr. neurosurgery U. Calif., San Francisco, 1965-70, asst. clin. prof., 1970-79, assoc. prof., 1979—; chmn. Dominican Neurol. Inst., Santa Cruz, Calif., 1975—, bd. dirs. Dominican Found.; sr. v.p. Frank Magid Assocs., Cedar Rapids, Iowa; cons. neurosurgery U.S. Army; cons. neurosurgeon San Francisco Gen. Hosp. Assoc. editor: Clinical Neurosurgery, 1974. Bd. dirs. Santa Cruz Symphony Assn., 1983-85, U. Calif. Friends of Arts, Santa Cruz, 1985-86. Served to lt. comdr. USN, 1961-63. Fellow ACS, Internat. Coll. Surgeons; mem. AMA, Calif. Med. Assn., Internat. Soc. Pediatric Neurosurgeons, Am. Assn. Neurol. Surgeons, Western Neurosurg. Soc., Cong. Neurol. Surgeons. Republican. Club: St. Francis Yacht (San Francisco). Home: 241 4th Ave Santa Cruz CA 95062 Office: 1661 Soquel Dr Santa Cruz CA 95065

MAGNESS, BOB JOHN, telecommunications executive; b. Clinton, Okla., 1924. Attended, South Western State Coll. Chmn. Tele-Communications, Inc., Denver. Office: Tele-Communications Inc PO Box 22595 Wellshire Sta Denver CO 80222 *

MAGNUSON, ALAN DOUGLAS, banking executive; b. Valparaiso, Ind., Jan. 22, 1942; s. Douglas Harold and Alice Elizabeth (Burch) M.; m. Rose Becerra, Apr. 25, 1971; children: Lori, Kathi, Juli. Diploma, South Bend Coll. Commerce, 1962. Officer trainee Crocker-Citizens Bank, Los Angeles, 1967-70, ops. officer, 1967-70; ops. officer So. Calif. 1st Nat. Bank, San Diego, 1970-73; loan officer 1st Nat. Bank Nev., Las Vegas, 1973-80; br. mgr. 1st Interstate Nev., Las Vegas, 1980-82, v.p., 1984—; instr. Clark County Community Coll., Las Vegas; speaker SBA, Las Vegas. Served as sgt. U.S. Army, 1960-63. Mem. Am. Inst. Banking (gov. So. Nev. chpt. 1971-77, plaque 1977), Bank Adminstrn. Inst. (pres. So. Nev. chpt. 1982-83, plaque 1983), Henderson C. of C., Boulder City C. of C. (v.p. 1980-81), North Las Vegas C. of C. (comml. com., chmn. audit com., chmn. fairshow, chmn. funds appropriation subcom., import-export com., chmn. fin. subcom., pub. relations com.). Republican. Lodge: Lions (chmn. Nev. zone 1982-83, sec. Nev. cabinet 1983-84, gov. Nev. dist. 1985-86, chmn. council govs. Calif./Nev. 1985-86). Office: 1st Interstate Nev PO Box 98588 Las Vegas NV 89193-8588

MAGNUSON, GUSTAV DONALD, physicist; b. Chgo., Aug. 22, 1926; s. Gust and Anna (Sjostrand) M.; m. Phyllis Elaine Mason, Mar. 18, 1950; children: Randal B., Donald G., Erik J., Scott K. PhB, U. Chgo., 1949, BS, 1950; MS, U. Ill., 1952, PhD, 1957. Lifetime teaching cert., Calif. Sr. staff scientist Gen. Dynamics/Convair, San Diego, 1957-66, staff scientist, 1976—; research assoc. prof. U. Va., Charlottesville, 1966-69; staff scientist Gulf Gen. Atomic, San Diego, 1969-72, IRT Corp., San Diego, 1972-76; inst. San Diego Community Coll., San Diego State U.; judge San Diego Sci. Fair. Contbr. articles to profl. jours. Served with U.S. Army, 1946-47. Mem. Am. Phys. Soc., Am. Assn. Physics Tchrs., AAAS, Nat. Assn. Clock and Watch Collectors, Sigma Xi. Republican. Roman Catholic. Home: 1755 Catalina Blvd San Diego CA 92107 Office: Gen Dynamics/Convair PO Box 80847 MZ 41-6850 San Diego CA 92138

MAGOWAN, PETER ALDEN, grocery chain executive; b. N.Y.C., Apr. 5, 1942; s. Robert Anderson and Doris (Merrill) M.; m. Jill Tarlau (div. July 1982; children—Kimberley, Margot, Hilary; m. Deborah Johnston, Aug. 14, 1982. B.A., Stanford U.; M.A., Oxford U., Eng.; postgrad., Johns Hopkins U. Store mgr. Safeway Stores, Inc., Washington, 1968-70; dist. mgr. Safeway Stores, Inc., Houston, 1970-71; retail ops. mgr. Safeway Stores, Inc., Phoenix, 1971-72; div. mgr. Safeway Stores, Inc., Tulsa, 1973-76; mgr. internat. div. Safeway Stores, Inc., Toronto, Ont., Can., 1976-78; mgr. western region Safeway Stores, Inc., San Francisco, 1978-79; chmn. bd., chief exec. officer Safeway Stores, Inc., Oakland, Calif., 1980—; bd. dirs. Pacific Gas and Electric, Chrysler Corp. Mem. U.S. C. of C., Food Mktg. Inst. (bd. dirs.), Bus. Roundtable. Office: Safeway Stores Inc 201 4th St Oakland CA 94660

MAGUIRE, JOHN DAVID, educator, university president; b. Montgomery, Ala., Aug. 7, 1932; s. John Henry and Clyde (Merrill) M.; m. Lillian Louise Parrish, Aug. 29, 1953; children—Catherine Merrill, Mary Elizabeth, Anne King. A.B. magna cum laude, Washington and Lee U., 1953, Litt.D. (hon.), 1979; Fulbright scholar, Edinburgh (Scotland) U., 1953-54; B.D. summa cum laude, Yale, 1956, Ph.D., 1960; postdoctoral research, Yale U. and U. Tübingen, Germany, 1964-65, Univ. of Calif.-Berkeley, 1968-69, Silliman U., Philippines, 1976-77. Acting chaplain Washington and Lee Univ., 1952-53; acting dir. Internat. Student Center, New Haven, 1956-58; asst. in instrn. systematic theology Yale U. Div. Sch., 1958-59; mem. faculty Wesleyan U., Middletown, Conn., 1960-70; asso. provost Wesleyan U., 1967-68; vis. lectr. Pacific School Religion and Grad. Theol. Union, Berkeley, 1968-69; pres. SUNY Coll. at Old Westbury, 1970-81, Claremont (Calif.) U. Center and Grad. Sch., 1981—. Author: The Dance of the Pilgrim: A Christian Style of Life for Today, 1967; also numerous articles. Mem. Conn. adv. com. U.S. Commn. Civil Rights, 1961-70; participant White House Conf. on Civil Rights, 1966; permanent trustee and 1st chmn. bd. dirs. Martin Luther King Center for Social Change, Atlanta, 1968—; bd. dirs. Nassau County Health and Welfare Council, 1971-81, pres., 1974-76; trustee United Bd. Christian Higher Edn. in Asia, 1975-81, Inst. Internat. Edn., 1980-86, Thacher Sch., Ojai, Calif., 1982—, The Tomás Rivera Ctr., Claremont, Calif., 1984—, Assn. Ind. Calif. Colls. and Univers., 1985—, The Calif. Achievement Council, 1985—; bd. dirs. Assn. Am. Colls., 1981-86, chmn., 1984-85; bd. dirs. west coast div. NAACP Legal Def. and Edn. Fund, 1981—; mem. Am. Com. East-West Accord, 1981—, Blue Ribbon Calif. Commn. on Teaching Profession, 1984-86; mem. governing council Aspen Inst. Wye Faculty Seminar, 1984—, mem. Council on Fgn. Relations, 1983—, Los Angeles Humanitas Council, 1986—; sr. fellow Inst. Trustee Leadership, Assn. Governing Bds., 1985—. Recipient Julia A. Archibald High Scholarship award Yale Div. Sch., 1956; Day fellow Yale Grad. Sch., 1956-57; Kent fellow, 1957-60; Howard Found. postdoctoral fellow Brown U. Grad. Sch., 1964-65; Fenn lectr., 7 Asian countries, 1976-77; recipient Conn. Prince Hall Masons' award outstanding contbns. human rights in Conn., 1965; E. Harris Harbison Gt. Tchr. prize Danforth Found., 1968. Fellow Soc. Values Higher Edn. (pres. 1974-81); mem. Phi Beta Kappa, Omicron Delta Kappa. Democrat. Office: Office of President Claremont Univ Center and Grad Sch Claremont CA 91711-6165

MAGUIRE, JOHN FRANCIS, physical chemist; b. Dungannon, Ireland, July 18, 1951; came to U.S., 1977; s. Francis Joseph and Margaret Mary (Conway) M.; m. Maureen O'Neill, Aug. 22, 1973; children: Neil, Una, Sean, Claire. BS, U. Ulster, Coleraine, Ireland, 1973, PhD, 1977. Postdoctoral scholar UCLA, 1977-78; sr. research assoc. Vant Hoff Inst. U. Amsterdam, Holland, 1979-81; mgr., sr. engr. Gen. Electric Aero. Engine Bus. Group, Albuquerque, 1984—; indsl. assoc. Lear Fan Ltd., N. Ireland, 1981-83; lectr. U. Ulster, 1983-84. Contbr. articles to profl. publs. Mem. Royal Soc. Chemistry, Am. Chem. Soc., AAAS. Avocation: hill walking. Home: 6805 Glendora Dr NE Albuquerque NM 87109 Office: Gen Electric Co 336 Woodward Rd SE Albuquerque NM 87109

MAGUIRE, LAURIE ANN, marketing consultant; b. San Jose, Calif., Sept. 30, 1951; Edward Paul and Velva Blanche (Leazer) M.; 1 child, Paul Nicholas Falzon IV. AA, Riverside City Coll., 1975; BA, U. Calif., Riverside, 1977, MBA, 1980. Research analyst Carnation Co., Los Angeles, 1980-81; mng. dir. Mktg. Research Inst., Riverside, 1981-83; v.p. MUSE Cons. Inc., Riverside, 1983—; founding mem. Resource Ctr. for Tech. Tng., Glendora, Calif., 1986. Grad. Opportunity fellow U. Calif., Riverside, 1979-80; recipient Eric P. Ziegler award Ziegler Found., Riverside, 1981. Mem. Am. Mktg. Assn., Bus. Devel. Assn. Home: 1567 Alta Redlands CA 92374 Office: MUSE Cons Inc 3780 12th St Suite B Riverside CA 92501

MAH, JOHN JENIEN, SR., real estate executive, investment consultant; b. Ning-Po City, Peoples Republic of China, Sept. 2, 1934; s. Luchen Chon-Chow and Fushow Shaw-Tsai (Hu) M.; m. Helen Theresa Wu, July 1, 1962; children: Jacqueline Janine, John Jenien Jr. BA, Emporia Coll., 1961; MBA, NYU, 1967; PhD (hon.), Tamkang U., Taipei, Republic of China, 1972. Cert. data processor; cert. tchr., Fla. Sr. staff Lockheed Corp., NASA, Houston, 1967-69; fin. specialist Eastern/Nat. Airlines, Miami, Fla., 1969-76; prin. cons. Dade County Schs., Miami, 1976-78; sr. planner Bechtel Corp., San Francisco, 1978-80; founder, chief exec. officer JM & Assocs., Seattle, 1980—; trust officer Chase Manhattan Bank, N.Y.C., 1961-64; treas. staff Gen. Motors Corp., N.Y.C. , 1964-65; engring. analyst Western Electric/AT&T, N.Y.C., 1965-67; cons. Internat. Trade, Inc., Taipei, 1980—; bd. dirs. Golden Horse Investment, Seattle, 1983—. Author: Far East Trade, 1981, Pacific Rims Countries, 1984; editor Far East Bus. Jour., 1971 (editor of yr. 1970). Vol. first original Peace Corps, 1961; bd. dirs. United Way King County, Seattle, 1981-83; sr. cons. Walnut Green Assn., Walnut Creek, Calif., 1978-80; campaign mgr. for U.S. Pres. Lyndon B. Johnson, Emporia, Kans., 1960-61; chmn. Miami Springs (Fla.) Planning and Zoning Bd., 1974-78. Served to capt. U.S. Army, 1957-59. Recipient Businessman award Fla. Bus. Soc., Miami, 1977; named Businessman of Yr., SBA, 1985; Asian fellow Asian Found., Taipei, 1959. Mem. Nat. Mgmt. Found., Am. Mgmt. Assn., Data Processing Mgmt. Assn., Am. Bus. Broker Club, Nat. Real Estate Bd. Republican. Roman Catholic. Clubs: Foster Country (treas. 1980-81), University (Seattle) (v.p. 1982-83). Lodge: Shriners. Avocations: travelling, reading, music. Home: 5310 S 166th St Seattle WA 98188 Office: JM & Assocs 16400 South Center Pkwy Seattle WA 98188

MAH, ROBERT, microbiology educator; b. Fresno, Calif.. BA, U. Calif., Davis, 1957, MA, 1958, PhD, 1963. Asst. prof. environ. microbiology Calif. State U., Northridge, Calif., 1962-64; asst. prof. biology U. N.C., Chapel Hill, 1964-67, assoc. prof., 1967-71; assoc. prof.environ. microbiology UCLA pub. health dept., 1971-74, prof., 1974—; referee Sci., Archives for Microbiology, Applied Environ. Microbiology, Jour. Bacteriology. Co-author book chpts., articles; bd. editors Applied and Environ. Microbiology, 1969-78. Mem. NSF, EPA, Am. Soc. Microbiology, Gas Research Inst., Sigma Xi, Phi Kappa Phi, Delta Omega. Office: UCLA Sch Pub Health Los Angeles CA 90024

MAHAFFAY, WILLIAM EDWARD, mechanical engineer. s. James W. and Ida (Hyink) M.; m. Carolyn Dahlquist, Oct. 15, 1935; 1 son, John W. B.S., Northwestern U., 1933. Registered engr., Ind. Various positions Internat. Harvester Co., 1935-42; plant engr. Internat. Harvester Co. (Refrigeration div.), 1942-45, chief engr. advanced engring sect., 1945-51; exec. engr. Whirlpool Corp., St. Joseph, Mich., 1951-53; dir. engring. and research Whirlpool Corp., 1953-56, v.p. engring. and research, 1956-65, group v.p., 1965-70; Dir. Robbins & Myers Inc., Dayton, Ohio, Ranco Inc., Columbus, O.; Engring. cons.; adj. prof. U. Mich., 1970—; vis. prof. Purdue.; Life regent Northwestern U.; tech. adv. com. Purdue U. Mem. ASHRAE, ASME, Acacia, Northwestern U. Alumni Assn., Instrument Soc. Am., Sigma Xi, Tau Beta Pi, Pi Tau Sigma. Clubs: Union League (Chgo.); Paradise Valley Country (Scottsdale). Home: 86 Colonia Miramonte Scottsdale AZ 85253

MAHAFFEY, JOAN, nurse, association executive; b. Richmond, Utah, Feb. 7, 1926; d. Joseph Perry and Annie Marie (Christofferson) Peart; R.N., Meth. Hosp., Los Angeles, 1950; B.S. in Health Sci., Calif. State U., Northridge, 1971, M.P.H., 1976; m. J.B. Mahaffey, June 5, 1949 (div. Jan. 1967). Hosp. and office nurse, Calif., 1951-72; mem. staff Calif. Nurses Assn., 1972-81, regional dir. epicenter region 3, Van Nuys, 1981-83, pres. region 3, 1983-85; dir. registry Epicenter Region Nurses Profl. Registry Inc., 1974—; cons., speaker in field. Mem. Am. Nurses Assn., Valley Nursing Edn. Council. Democrat. Mormon. Clubs: Soroptimist, San Fernando Emblem 37. Home: 6620 Glade Ave Canoga Park CA 91303 Office: Epicenter Region Nurses Profl Registry Inc 7 Van Nuys Blvd Suite O Van Nuys CA 91405

MAHAJAN, CHANDRAKANT DAYARAM, manufacturing company executive; b. Yawal, India, Jan. 9, 1941; came to U.S., 1965; s. Dayaram A. and Laxmibai D. (Chaudhary) M.; m. Jyoti Anand Sarode, Dec. 25, 1971; children: Niraj, Nita. BS, Utah State U., 1967; MS, U. So. Calif., 1971; MBA, Pepperdine U., 1984. With Price Pfister Corp., Pacoima, Calif., 1967—, methods and procedures analyst, 1971-73, sr. systems analyst, 1973-76, product and inventory control mgr., 1976—, mfg. system mgr., 1984—. Mem. Am. Prodn. and Inventory Control Soc., Alpha Pi Nu. Home: 17083 Goya St Granada Hills CA 91344 Office: Price Pfister Corp 13500 Paxton St Pacoima CA 91331

MAHALINGAM, R., chemical engineering educator, consultant. BS in Chemistry with honors, Bombay (India) U., 1957; DIIScChemE, Indian Inst. Sci., Bangalore, 1959; MSChemE, Purdue U., 1963; PhDChemE, U. Newcastle/Tyne, England, 1966. Chem. engr. Century Rayon, Bombay, 1959-61, Monsanto Chem. Co., Ruabon, Wales, 1966-67, Sci. Design Co., N.Y.C., 1967-69; mem. summer faculty Battelle Labs., Richland, Wash., summers 1973, 74, Dept. Energy, Morgantown, W.Va., summers 1979, 80; prof. chem. engring. Wash. State U., Pullman, 1969—, courtesy appointment prof. materials sci. and engring.; cons. UN, Ciba-Geigy, Energy Resources Co., Mittelhauser Corp., Mar-Tech. Inc., Ashland Chemical, Olin Corp., Aerojet Energy Conv. Co., Am. Carbon & Chem. Co., Battelle Labs., Hittman-Westinghouse Co., Weyerhauser Corp., Energy Resources Co. Inc., Petrobas, Brazil, 1972—. Mem. editorial bd. Environ. Progress Jour., 1981—; contbr. chpts. to books, articles to profl. jours. Recipient Faculty Research Excellence award Wash. State U. Coll. Engring., 1984; research grantee NSF, U.S. Dept. Energy, Electric Power Research Inst., others, 1970—. Mem. Am. Chem. Soc. (research grantee), Am. Inst. Chem. Engrs. (mem. research com. 1983—), Environ. div. Am. Inst. Chem. Engrs. (sec. 1985). Lodge: Kiwanis. Office: Wash State U Chem Engring Dept Pullman WA 99164-2710

MAHER, JOHN FRANCIS, investment banker; b. Berkeley, Calif., Apr. 25, 1943; s. Edward John and Emilia A. (Radovan) M.; m. Ann Elizabeth Breeden (div. 1975); children: Edward John II, Elizabeth Ann; m. Helen Lee Stillman, Mar. 20, 1976; children: Michael Stillman, Helen Cathline. BS, Menlo Coll., 1965; MBA, U. Pa., 1967. Gen. ptnr. Eastman Dillon, Los Angeles, 1971; 1st v.p. Blyth Eastman Dillon, Los Angeles, 1972, exec. v.p., 1976-79; exec. v.p., chief fin. officer Gt. Western Fin., Beverly Hills, Calif., 1973-76, also bd. dirs.; mng. dir. Shearson Lehman Bros., Los Angeles, 1979-86; pres., chief operating officer Great Western Fin. Corp., Beverly Hills, 1986—; bd. dirs. Gt. Western Savs., Beverly Hills, IRT Corp. Bd. dirs. Los Angeles Big Bros., Inc., 1984—. Joseph Wharton fellow U. Pa., 1965-67. Mem. Pacific Coast Elec. Assn. (bd. dirs. 1985—). Office: Great Western Fin Corp 8484 Wilshire Blvd 10th Floor Beverly Hills CA 90211-3212

MAHER, LEO THOMAS, bishop; b. Mt. Union, Iowa, July 1, 1915; s. Thomas and Mary (Teberg) M. Ed., St. Joseph's Coll., Mountain View, Calif., St. Patrick's Sem., Menlo Park, Calif. Ordained priest Roman Catholic Ch.; asst. pastor in San Francisco, 1944-47, sec. archbishop of, 1947-61; chancellor Archdiocese San Francisco, 1956-62, dir. vocations, 1957-62, archdiocesan consultor, 1959-62; apptd. domestic prelate 1954; bishop Santa Rosa, Calif., 1962-69; 3d bishop of San Diego, 1969—; prior Western Lieutenancy of Knights and Ladies of Holy Sepulchre. Bd. dirs. Soc. Propagation of Faith, Youth's Director, Cath. Youth Orgn.; chmn. bd. trustees U. San Diego; Del. Ecumenical Council, Rome, Italy, 1962, 63, 64, 65. Home: 2031 Sunset Blvd San Diego CA 92103 Office: Diocesan Office Alcala Park San Diego CA 92110

MAHER, WILLIAM JAMES, entertainment industry executive; b. Chgo., Feb. 23, 1937; s. Alexander E. and Merle G. M.; B.B.A., Marquette U., 1961. Merchandising exec. Montgomery Ward & Co., Inc., Chgo., 1962-68; mgmt. cons. Cresap, McCormack & Paget, N.Y.C., 1968-69; v.p., treas. Solar Prodns., Inc., Hollywood, Calif., 1969-72; v.p., sec., treas. Creative Mgmt. Assocs., Los Angeles, 1972-74; v.p., dir. Josephson Internat., Inc., Los Angeles, 1974-83; pres. Tipperary Prodns., Inc., Beverly Hills, Calif., 1983—. Office: Tipperary Prodns Inc 1930 N Beverly Dr Beverly Hills CA 90210

MAHEU, MARLENE MURIEL, psychologist; b. Hartford, Conn., June 1, 1954; d. Robert Joseph and Claire (Boivin) M. BA summa cum laude, U. Hartford, 1977; MA, PhD in Clin. Psychology, Calif. Sch. Profl. Psychology, 1985. Psychol. intern Mid-City Community Clinic, San Diego, 1982-83, Cath. Community Services, San Diego, 1983-84, San Diego Police Dept., 1984-85; pvt. practice psychology San Diego, 1984—; researcher, cons. Gen. Dynamics, Rohr Industries, Pacific Southwest Airlines, San Diego, 1984—. Author health maintenance program Ex-Smokers for LIfe, 1986. Mem. Am. Psychol. Assn., Acad. San Diego Psychologists, NOW, Sigma Xi, Psy Chi, Alpha Chi. Avocations: traveling, reading, gardening. Home: 6019 Caminito Del Deste San Diego CA 92111 Office: 3519 Front St San Diego CA 92103

MAHLER, DANIEL ARTHUR, health association administrator; b. Salt Lake City, Apr. 20, 1950; s. Anton and Elfriede (Butchereit) M.; m. Lisa R. Goodroad, Mar. 7, 1981; children: P. Simon, Sarah. BS in Sociology, Social Welfare, U. Utah, 1973, MSW, 1975. Group counselor, supr. Neighborhood House, Salt Lake City, 1970-73; social service worker Bur. Indian Affairs, Fairbanks, Alaska, 1974; unit dir. N. Idaho Children's Home, Lewiston, 1975-78, dir. residential services, 1978-85; exec. dir. Christie Sch., Marylhurst, Oreg., 1985—; lit. reviewer Child Welfare Resource Exchange, Washington, 1978-80; foster parent trainer Boise (Idaho) State U., 1978-80; instr. Lewis Clark State Coll., Lewiston, 1980-85. Named Disting. Employee N. Idaho Children's Home, 1980, 81. Mem. Nat. Assn. Social Workers (pres. Idaho chpt. 1982-85, Social Worker Yr., 1982), Am. Assn Children's Residential Ctrs. Avocations: reading, running, phys. excercise activities. Home: 16890 SW Cortez Ct Lake Oswego OR 97035 Office: Christie Sch Marylhurst OR 97036

MAHLER, DAVID, chem. co. exec.; b. San Francisco; s. John and Jennie (Morgan) M.; Ph.C., U. So. Calif., 1932; children—Darrell, Glenn. Pres.,

United Drug Co., Glendale, Calif., 1934-37, Blue Cross Labs., Inc., Saugus, Calif., 1937—. Active Fund for Animals, Friends of Animals, Com. for Humane Legislations; patron Huntington Hartford Theatre, Hollywood, Calif. Mem. Packaging and Research Devel. Inst. (hon.), Anti-Defamation League, Skull and Daggar, Rho Pi Phi. Office: 26411 N Golden Valley Rd Saugus CA 91350

MAHLER, RICHARD JOSEPH, physican, hospital administrator; b. N.Y.C., Mar. 4, 1934; s. Jacob and Naomi (Feder) M.; m. Ida May Adler, Aug. 23, 1960; children: Susan Toba, Jonathan David. BA, NYU, 1955; MD, N.Y. Med. Coll., 1959. Diplomate Am. Bd. Internal Medicine. Intern New Rochelle (N.Y.) Hosp., 1960; resident in internal medicine N.Y. Med. Coll., N.Y.C., 1960-63, metabolic research fellow, 1962-63, instr. medicine, 1964-67, asst. prof., 1967-70, assoc. prof., 1970-71; traveling fellow N.Y. Acad. Medicine, 1963-64; practice medicine specializing in internal medicine N.Y.C., 1964-71; chief sect. on diabetes Met. Hosp., N.Y.C., 1968-71; assoc. dir. dept. metabolism and endocrinology City of Hope Med. Ctr., 1971-73; dir. dept. metabolism and endocrinology Eisenhower Med. Ctr., Palm Desert, Calif., 1973—, mem. med. staff, 1973—, pres., 1976—; med. cons. to Merck and Co., Rahway, N.J., 1971—, U.S. Vitamin Corp., N.Y.C., 1973—; spl. cons. to FDA, 1972. Contbr. articles on metabolic research and diabetes to profl. jours., chpts. to med. books; assoc. editor Hormone and Metabolic Research, 1969-76, co-editor, 1976—. Bd. dirs. Palm Valley Sch., 1975—. Fellow ACP; mem. Endocrine Soc., Am. Diabetes Assn. (Devel. award 1966-67), Am. Fedn. Clin. Research, Diabetes Assn. So. Calif., Western Soc. Clin. Research, Am. Physiol. Soc., N.Y. Acad. Scis., Royal Soc. Medicine, Assn. Am. Med. Colls., Alpha Omega Alpha. Jewish. Clubs: Racquet of Palm Springs. Home: 2367 Yosemite Dr Palm Springs CA 92264 Office: 39000 Bob Hope Dr Rancho Mirage CA 92270

MAHONEY, CAROLYN MARIE, hospital adminstrator; b. San Francisco, Mar. 23, 1946; d. Frank Wensinger and Florence E. (Shipsey) M. BS, U. San Francisco, 1968; MS, Calif. State U., Sonoma, 1978; MBA, Pepperdine U., 1978. Cert. med. technologist, Calif. Mgr. lab. Palm Drive Hosp., Sebastopol, Calif., 1972-77, dir. profl. services, 1977-79; mgr. lab. Am. Med. Internat., Los Angeles, 1979-81; mgr. lab. Alta Bates Hosp., Berkeley, Calif., 1981-83, dir. clin. services, 1983-85, v.p., 1985—; chmn. examination com. Nat. Certifying Agy. Med. Lab. Personnel, Washington, 1980-83. Named one of Outstanding Young Women of Am. Isaac Montoya of Medicus Corp. Mem. Am. Soc. Med. Tech. (pres. chpt. 1975-76), Am. Coll. Health Care Execs. (nominee). Office: Alta Bates Hosp 3001 Colby St Berkeley CA 94705

MAHONEY, JAMES P., bishop; b. Saskatoon, Sask., Can., Dec. 7, 1927. Ordained priest Roman Catholic Ch., 1952; bishop Saskatoon, 1967—. Office: Chancery Office, 106 5th Ave N, Saskatoon, SK Canada S7K 2N7 *

MAHONEY, WILLIAM ANTHONY, marketing professional, sales executive; b. Bklyn., July 15, 1942; s. William and Shirley (Williams) M.; m. Sandra L. Benton, Dec. 2, 1967; children: Emily, Melissa. AAS, Bklyn. Community Coll., 1963; BSCE, U. Ill., 1967. Asst. sales engr. Westinghouse Electric Co., Chgo., 1967-69; sales engr. Westinghouse Electric Co., Peoria, Ill., 1969-70; regional sales mgr. Hitachi Am., Indpls., 1970-73; sales mgr. Hitachi Am., San Francisco, 1973-79; mktg. mgr. Hitachi Am., Tarrytown, N.Y., 1979-84, Intelledex Corp., Corvallis, Oreg., 1984—. Mem. Robotics Industries Assn., Am. Nat. Standards Inst. Roman Catholic. Home: 5855 NW Highland Pl Corvallis OR 97330

MAHONY, ROGER MICHAEL, archbishop; b. Hollywood, Calif., Feb. 27, 1936; s. Victory James and Loretta Marie (Baron) M. A.A., Our Lady of Queen of Angles Sem., 1956; B.A., St. John's Sem. Coll., 1958, B.S.T., 1962; M.S.W., Catholic U. Am., 1964. Ordained priest Roman Cath. Ch., 1962, ordained bishop, 1975. Asst. pastor St. John's Cathedral, Fresno, Calif., 1962, 68-73, rector, 1973—; residence St. Genevieve's Parish, Fresno, Calif., 1964—, adminstr., 1964-67, pastor, 1967-68; titular bishop of Tamascani, aux. bishop of Fresno 1975-80; chancellor Diocese of Fresno, 1970, vicar gen., 1975-80; bishop Diocese of Stockton (Calif.), 1980-85; archbishop Diocese of Los Angeles, 1985—; diocesan dir. Cath. Charities and Social Service Fresno, 1964-70, exec. dir. Cath. Welfare Bur., 1964-70; exec. dir. Cath. Welfare Bur. Infant of Prague Adoption Service, 1964-70; chaplain St. Vincent de Paul Soc., Fresno, 1964-70; named chaplain to Pope Paul VI, 1967; mem. faculty extension div. Fresno State U., 1965-67; sec. U.S. Cath. bishops ad hoc com. on farm labor Nat. Conf. Bishops, 1970-75; chmn. com. on pub. welfare and income maintenance Nat. Conf. Cath. Charities, 1969-70; bd. dirs. West Coast Regional Office Bishops Com. for Spanish-Speaking, 1967-70; chmn. Calif. Assn. Cath. Charities Dirs., 1965-69; trustee St. Patrick's Sem., Archdiocese of San Francisco, 1974-75. Mem. Urban Coalition of Fresno, 1968-72; mem. Fresno County Econ. Opportunities Commn., 1964-65, Fresno County Alcoholic Rehab. Com., 1966-67, Fresno City Charter Rev. Com., 1968-70, Mexican-Am. Council for Better Housing, 1968-72, Fresno Redevel. Agy., 1970-75; bd. dirs. Fresno Community Workshop, 1965-67; trustee St. Agnes Hosp., Fresno. Named Young Man of Yr. Fresno Jr. C. of C., 1967. Mem. Canon Law Soc. Am., Nat. Assn. Social Workers. Home: 114 E 2d St Los Angeles CA 90012 Office: Archdiocese of Los Angeles 1531 N 9th St Los Angeles CA 90012 *

MAI, HAROLD LEVERNE, judge; b. Casper, Wyo., Apr. 5, 1928. B.A., U. Wyo., 1950, J.D., 1952. Bar: Wyo. 1952, U.S. Supreme Ct. 1963. Sole practice, Cheyenne, Wyo., 1953-62, 67-71; judge Juvenile Ct., Cheyenne, 1962-67; U.S. bankruptcy judge, Cheyenne, 1971—. Mem. adv. bd. Salvation Army. Wyo. Mem. ABA, Wyo. Bar Assn., Laramie County Bar Assn., Nat. Conf. Bankruptcy Judges. Home: 5428 Walker Rd Cheyenne WY 82009 Office: US Courthouse 2120 Capital Ave Cheyenne WY 82001

MAIBAUM, MATTHEW, behavioral scientist, writer; b. Chgo., Aug. 14, 1946; s. Richard W. and Sylvia M. AB summa cum laude, U. Calif. Berkeley, 1969; MA in Pub. Adminstrn., UCLA, 1973; PhD, Calif. Sch. Profl. Psychology, 1975; PhD in Polit. Sci., Claremont Grad. Sch., 1980. Diplomate Am. Bd. Psychotherapy, Internat. Acad. Profl. Counseling and Psychotherapy; lic. psychologist, Calif. Intern Met. State Hosp., Norwalk, Calif., 1973-74, postdoctoral intern, 1977-78; postdoctoral intern Pacific State Hosp., Pomona, Calif., 1976-77; pvt. practice cons. Los Angeles, 1978—; instr. various Calif. Univs., Los Angeles area, 1976—; cons. to orgns., Los Angeles area, 1969—; lectr. social sci., various univs. Los Angeles area, 1970—. Author (play) Sly Times, 1984; contbr. articles to profl. jours. Recipient Merit award San Fernando Valley Engrs.' Council, 1984. Mem. Am. Coll. Forensic Psychology (candidate for cert.), Authors Guild Am., Dramatists Guild Am. (assoc.), Sigma Xi, Phi Kappa Phi, Pi Gamma Mu. Club: Amity Circle (Los Angeles). Home: 826 Greentree Rd Pacific Palisades CA 90272

MAIER, CORNELL C., aluminum and chemical company executive; b. Herreid, S.D., Jan. 12, 1925; s. Phillip and Ann (Riedlinger) M. B.S. in Engring, U. Calif. at Berkeley, 1949. With Kaiser Aluminum & Chem. Corp., Oakland, Calif., 1949-87; v.p., mgr. European region Kaiser Aluminum Internat., 1963-68; v.p., gen. mgr. European region Kaiser Aluminum Internat. (Mill Products div. parent co.), 1969; v.p., gen. mgr. European region Kaiser Aluminum Internat. (N.Am. aluminum ops.), 1969-70, exec. v.p., 1970-72; corp. gen. mgr. Kaiser Aluminum and Chem. Corp., Oakland, Calif., 1971-72; pres. Kaiser Aluminum and Chem. Corp., Oakland, 1972-82; chief exec. officer Kaiser Aluminum and Chem. Corp., 1972-87, chmn. bd., 1978-87, also dir.; dir. Anglesey Aluminum (London) Metal Ltd., Bank of Am. N.T. & S.A., Volta Aluminum Co. Ltd., BankAm. Corp.; mem. Bus. Roundtable. Co-chmn. Calif. Commn. on Campaign Financing; mem. adv. bd. U. Calif. Sch. Bus., Berkeley; bd. dirs., bd. dirs., mem. exec. com. Bay Area Council Inc.; bd. dirs. Calif. Econ. Devel. Corp. Served with USAAF, 1943-45. Named Mfr. of Yr., Calif. Mfrs. Assn., 1983. Mem. Calif. C. of C. (dir.), Aluminum Assn. (chmn. adv. council). Clubs: Round Hill Country, Alamo, Silverado Country, Pacific Union. Office: Kaiser Aluminum & Chem Corp Kaiser Center 300 Lakeside Dr Oakland CA 94643

MAIER, PAUL VICTOR, pharmaceutical executive; b. Seattle, Nov. 6, 1947; s. Norman Alvin and Rosalie (Godek) M.; m. Shirley Diehl, Aug. 11, 1979. Lic. Dept. Real Estate, Calif. Fin. analyst Greyhound Corp, Phoenix, 1975-76; asst. mgr. Wells Service Wells Fargo Bank, San Francisco, 1976-78; v.p. Fin. Cummins Service and Sales, Los Angeles, 1978-84; v.p. fin. SPI Pharms., Inc., Costa Mesa, Calif., 1984d—. Chmn. hosp. div. United Way Region V, Los Angeles, 1983-84. Served with USNR, 1969—. Mem. Fin. Execs. Inst., The Athletic Congress, The Pa. State Club of Los Angeles, Harvard Bus. Sch. Assn. of So. Calif., Ctr. for Non-Profit Mgmt., Vis. Nurse Assn. of Los Angeles (bd. dirs. 1979—, past pres.), Protection Mutual Inst. (west coast adv. bd. 1985). Republican. Roman Catholic. Club: Los Angeles Athletic, Port Fermin Flyers (San Pedro). Office: ICN Pharms Inc 3300 Hyland Ave Costa Mesa CA 92626

MAIER, ROBERT OSCAR, mathematics educator; b. Wilkes-Barre, Pa., Feb. 24, 1924; s. Jacob and Katherine (Reng) M.; m. Lorraine Alison Kay, Aug. 28, 1949; children: Michael, Claire, Teresa, James, Phillip, Mary. BA, UCLA, 1950, EdD, 1972; MA, Calif. State U., Los Angeles, 1957. Research engr. Northrop Aircraft Co., Hawthorne, Calif., 1950-55; prof. math. El Camino Coll., Torrance, Calif., 1955—; dean of students Maui Community Coll., Kahului, Hawaii, 1967-68. Author: Statistics and Probability Simplified, 1981. Treas. Torrance Community Theater, 1982. Served with U.S. Army, 1943-46, ETO. Biostats. grantee Sch. Pub. Health U. Calif., Berkeley, 1962. Mem. The Planetary Soc., Nat. Geog. Soc., Internat. Wildlife Orgn., Acad. Magical Arts (life). Clubs: Magic Castle (Hollywood, Calif.); Chapel Theatre (Lomita, Calif.). Avocations: actor community theatre, magician. Home: 920 Knob Hill Ave Redondo Beach CA 90277 Office: El Camino Coll 16007 Crenshaw Blvd Torrance CA 90506

MAIL, PATRICIA DAVISON, public health specialist; b. Kamloops, B.C., Can., Dec. 10, 1940; d. George Allen and Constance (Davison) M.; B.S., U. Ariz., 1963, M.A., 1970; M.S., Smith Coll., 1965; M.P.H., Yale U., 1967; postgrad. Seattle U., 1974. Commd. officer USPHS, 1970—, chief health edn. br. Portland Indian Health Service, 1979-86, dep. chief field ops. Nat. Health Service Corps., 1986-87, spl. asst. to dir., 1987— ; mem. faculty Seattle U., 1974-78. Recipient Early Career award Public Health Edn. sect. Am. Public Health Assn., 1979; USPHS Service Plaque, 1979, 86; USPHS Commendation medal, 1981, 86, Outstanding Service medal, 1986; USPHS trainee Yale U., 1965-67; NDEA grantee, 1968-70. Mem. Am. Public Health Assn., Soc. Public Health Edn., Med. Anthropology Soc., Soc. Applied Anthropology, Am. Sch. Health Assn., AAAS, AAHPER, Commd. Officers Assn. USPHS, Smith Coll. Alumnae Assn. Episcopalian. Club: Dorian Group. Author: (with D.R. McDonald) Tulapai to Tokay, 1980; editor SOPHE Sounds, 1976-86; contbr. articles to profl. jours. Home: 35214 28th Ave S Federal Way WA 98003 Office: Nat Health Service Corp 7A39 Parklawn Bldg 5600 Fishers Ln Rockville MD 20857

MAIN, RICHARD BREWSTER, marketing professional; b. San Diego, July 27, 1949; s. Richard Gilbert Main and Irene Elanor (Johnson) Chisholm; m. Susan Mary Acosta, Apr. 17, 1969 (div.); 1 child, Richard Tony; m. Rita Denise Graef, Dec. 27, 1975; children: Richard Michael, Andrew Christopher. BS in Computer Sci., SUNY, Albany, 1984, BS in Mktg., 1985; MBA, San Jose State U., 1985, MS in Computer Engring., 1986; JD, Santa Clara U., 1986—. Chief engr. Univ. Engring. Systems, Pleasanton, Calif., 1972-76; systems engr. Ford Aerospace, Palo Alto, Calif., 1976-77; engring. mgr. Neptune UES, Pleasanton, 1977-79; pres. Zendex Corp., Dublin, Calif., 1979-82; engring. mgr. Signetics Corp., Sunnyvale, Calif., 1983-84; pres. ZEBU Research Corp., Sunnyvale, 1981—; exec. sec. VMEbus Mfg. Group, Sunnyvale, 1983. Active Rep. Nat. Com., Washington, 1983—. Mem. IEEE. Mem. Unitarian Ch. Avocations: numismatics, ancient history and civilizations. Home: 663 S Bernardo Sunnyvale CA 94087

MAIN, ROBERT GAIL, communications and training cons., television and film producer, educator, former army officer; b. Bucklin, Mo., Sept. 30, 1932; s. Raymond M. and Inez L. (Olinger) M.; m. Anita Sue Thoroughman, Jan. 31, 1955; children: Robert Bruce, David Keith, Leslie Lorraine. BS magna cum laude, U. Mo., 1954; grad. with honors, Army Command and Gen. Staff Coll., 1967; MA magna cum laude in Communications, Stanford U., 1968; PhD, U. Md., 1978. Commd. 2d lt. U.S. Army, 1954, advanced through grades to lt. col., 1968; various command and staff assignments field arty., 1954-64; sr. instr. and div. chief Pershing missile div. U.S. Army Arty. and Missile Sch., Ft. Sill, Okla., 1964-66; mem. faculty U.S. Army Command and Gen. Staff Coll., 1968-70; chief speechwriting and info. materials div. U.S. Army Info. Office, 1971, chief broadcast and film div., 1972-73; dir. def. audiovisual activities Office of Info. for Armed Forces, 1973-76, ret., 1976; prof., grad. adv. Coll. Communications, Calif. State U., Chico, 1976-87; pres. Grant & Main, Inc., corp. communications and tng. cons. Author: Radio Station Handbook, 1973; contbr. articles on audiovisual communications to profl. publs.; producer: Walking Wounded, TV documentary, 1983; producer army info. films, army radio series, 1972-73. Decorated Legion of Merit, Meritorious Service medal, Commendation medal with oak leaf cluster, combat Inf. Badge; Vietnamese Cross of Gallantry; recipient Freedom Found. awards, 1972, 73, 74; Bronze medal Atlanta Film Festival, 1972; Best of Show award Balt. Film Festival, 1973; Creativity award Chgo. Indsl. Film Festival, 1973; Cine gold award Internat. Film Producers Assn., 1974. Mem. Assn. for Ednl. Communications Tech., Am. Soc. of Curriculum Developers, Nat. Assn. Ednl. Broadcasters, Phi Eta Sigma, Alpha Zeta, Phi Delta Gamma, Omicron Delta Kappa, Alpha Gamma Rho. Mem. Christian Ch.

MAINES, CLIFFORD BRUCE, ins. co. exec.; b. Tacoma, Wash., Aug. 14, 1926; s. Clifford McLean and Ida Vera (Wardall) M.; m. Mary Jean Marshall, Sept. 4, 1948; children—Molly, Janet Lynn. Student, Central Coll., Fayette, Mo., 1944-45, U. Mich., 1945-46; B.S., U. Wash., 1948, LL.B., 1949, J.D., 1949. Bar: Wash. bar 1950. Mem. legal staff Safeco Corp., Seattle, 1950-62, asso. gen. counsel, 1962-66, gen. counsel, 1966-68, v.p., gen. counsel, 1968-74, sr. v.p., 1974-81, pres., 1981—, pres., chief exec. officer, 1986—, dir., 1977—; exec. v.p., chief operating officer, dir. Gen. Ins. Co. Am., 1974-77, pres., 1977-81; now dir.; exec. v.p. 1st Nat. Ins. Co. Am., 1974-77, pres., 1977-81; now dir.; exec. v.p. Safeco Ins. Co., 1974-77, pres., 1977-81, now dir.; dir. Safeco Life Ins. Co.; exec. v.p. GSL. Served with USNR, 1944-46. Mem. ABA, Wash. Bar Assn., Seattle-King County Bar Assn. (past trustee), Wash. Ins. Council (past pres.), Pacific Ins. and Surety Conf., Beta Theta Pi. Methodist (past chmn. bd.). Clubs: Washington Athletic, Broadmoor Golf, Seattle Golf, Columbia Tower (Seattle). Lodge: Lions. Office: Safeco Corp Safeco Plaza Seattle WA 98185

MAING, I. YOUNG, food company executive; b. Seoul, Republic of Korea, July 9, 1942; came to U.S., 1968, naturalized, 1968; s. Kwang Ho Maing and In Sun Lee; m. Jeanne Lee, Aug. 12, 1968; children: Michelle, Juhn-Michael. BS, Seoul Nat. U., 1967; MS, U. Ga., 1970; PhD, U. Wis., 1972. Sr. food technologist Armour Foods, Oak Brook, Ill., 1974-75; project leader Gen. Foods, Tarrytown, N.Y., 1975-77, group leader, 1977-79, sr. research specialist, 1980-82; exec. mgr. Gen. Foods Internat., Honolulu, 1982—; also bd. dirs. Gen. Foods Internat., Seoul; dir. USDA, Washington, 1980-82; exec. dir. Korea Indsl. Research Inst., Seoul, 1982—, strategy and policy com. Gen. Foods, Korea, 1985—; invited scientist German Research Inst., Kulmbech, 1972-74. Inventor in field. Mem. Rep. Presdl. Task Force, Washington, 1984, Statue of Liberty Ellis Island Found., N.Y.C., 1984. Grantee Internat. Child Health Found., N.Y.C., 1969; FDA fellow U. Ga., Athens, 1967. Mem. Am. Cereal Chemists Soc., Inst. Food Technologists (counselor 1984—), Am. Chem. Soc., Korean-Am. Food Scientists Assn. (chmn. 1978). Avocations: collecting paintings and antiques. Home: 1519 Kamole St Honolulu HI 96821 Office: Gen Foods Internat Asia/Pacific Div 615 Piikoi St Honolulu HI 96814

MAINTHIA, JAY SUCHACK, marketing professional; b. Surat, Gujarat, India, Sept. 5, 1949; s. Jadavkumar and Jayman J. (Thakkar) M.; m. Jyoti Mainthia; children: Anushri, Rajshri. BBA, U. Bombay, India, 1970; BS, U. Ark., 1971; MSJ, Northwestern U., 1972; MBA, NYU, 1980. Asst. account exec. Ogilvy & Mather, N.Y.C., 1973-75; account supr. William Esty Co., N.Y.C., 1975-77; asst. product mgr. Legg's Products, Winston- Salem, N.C., 1977-79; sr. product mgr. Welch Foods, Westfield, N.Y., 1979-83; dir. mktg. Ogden Food Products, City of Commerce, Calif., 1983—. Home: 2600 Winrow Ct Rowland Heights CA 91748 Office: Ogden Food Products 7030 Slauson Ave City of Commerce CA 90040

MAISEL, TERRI LYNN, organization administrator; b. Tucson, Dec. 28, 1951; d. John Louis and Irene (Ellis) Gunby; m. Albert Lloyd Maisel, Feb. 11, 1978. Student, U. N.Mex., 1975-80; cert., Inst. Orgn. Mgmt., 1985. New accounts rep. SunWest Bank, Albuquerque, 1971-74, employment adminstr., 1974-76, communications dir., 1976-78; pub. info. dir. Albuquerque C. of C., 1978-81, gen. mgr., 1981-83, exec. v.p., 1983—; pres. N.Mex. C. of C. Execs. Assn., 1986-87, bd. dirs. 1980—; bd. dirs. populous regional com. U.S. Chamber Com. Recipient Bus. Devel. award Expn. Mgmt. Inc., 1985, Women on Move award YWCA, 1986; named one of Outstanding Women of Am., 1984. Mem. Am. Chamber Execs. (bd. dirs. 1986—), U.S. Chamber of Commerce. Republican. Avocations: golf, reading, gymnastics. Office: Greater Albuquerque C of C PO Box 25100 Albuquerque NM 87125

MAISH, F(REDERIC) MICHAEL, electrical engineer; b. Bedford, Ind., Sept. 28, 1943; s. Frederic F. and Helen Lucile (Robinette) M.; m. Melanie Louise Barnes, June 24, 1972; children: Scott, Lara. BSEE, Purdue U., 1965; MSEE, U. Colo., 1973. Registered profl. engr., Colo. Research and devel. engr. Emerson Electric Co., St. Louis, 1965-66; research scientist U.S. Dept. Commerce, Boulder, Colo., 1967-83; supervisory engr. Nat. Bur. Standards, Boulder, 1984—; Am.-Soviet exchange scientist NSF Office Polar Programs, Washington, 1969. Bd. dirs. Historic Boulder; mem. troop com. Boy Scouts Am., Boulder, 1985. Recipient Soviet 150th Antarctic Anniversary medal Artic and Antarctic Inst., 1970. Mem. IEEE, Assn. Computing Machinery, L-5 Soc., Theta Alpha Phi, Theta Xi (bd. dirs. Colo. Ednl. Found., 1975). Republican. Avocations: skiing, mountain climbing, fencing, Antarctic antiquarian. Home: 2314 Dennison Ln Boulder CO 80303 Office: Nat Bur Standards 325 Broadway Boulder CO 80303

MAITZEN, DOLORES ANN, educator; b. Chgo., Nov. 2, 1952; d. Joseph Thomas and Angeline G. (Butz) Svacik; student John Robert Powers Modeling Sch., 1975-76; B.S., Ill. State U., 1973; M.S., Chgo. State U., 1976; m. Robert H. Maitzen, Jr., Apr. 15, 1978. Tchr., Josephinum High Sch., Chgo., 1973-75, Queen of Peace High Sch., Burbank, Ill., 1976-79; coordinator home econs. related occupations and tchr. home econs. North High Sch., Phoenix Union Dist., 1979-81; asst. prof. Ariz. State U., 1981—. tchr. fashion merchandising Paradise Valley High Sch. Mem. Ariz. Assn. Vocat. Home Econs. Educators (state membership chmn. 1981-83, pres. 1986-87), Am. Vocat. Assn. (del. nat. conf.), Ariz. Vocat. Assn. (sec. 1983-84, bd. dirs., exec. bd.), Am. Home Econs. Assn., Ariz. Home Econs. Assn. (profl. awards chmn. 1983-86, profl. recognition award 1982, Elem.-Secondary Adult Edn. award 1982), Ill. State U. Alumni Assn., Ariz. State U. Women's Faculty Assn., Ariz. State Home Econs. Adv. Council, Nat. Restaurant Assn., Assn. Supervision and Curriculum Devel., Chgo. State U. Alumni Assn., Alpha Gamma Delta, NEA, Ariz. Edn. Assn. Club: Young Ladies of St. Joseph Ch. Home: 3702 E Dahlia Dr Phoenix AZ 85032 Office: Dept Home Econs Ariz State U Tempe AZ 85287

MAJOR, MARGUERITE LOUISE, magazine editor; b. Kansas City, Mo., Jan. 26, 1929; d. Ray Clark and Celia Marguerite (Fowler) M. AB in Journalism, San Jose State U., 1950. Reporter, editor Sunnyvale (Calif.) Standard, 1951-52; alumni dir. San Jose State U., 1953-57; pubs. dir. Santa Clara (Calif.) U., 1957-60, news dir., 1960-78, pub. affairs dir., 1978-83; editor Santa Clara Today, Santa Clara U., 1983-86, Santa Clara mag., Santa Clara U., 1986—. Mem. Pub. Relations Soc. Am. (accredited), Council for Advancement and Support of Edn. (trustee 1975-77), Am. Coll. Pub. Relations Assn. (regional dir. 1974-75). Republican. Episcopalian. Avocations: reading, sports gardening, travel. Home: 7135 Via Solano San Jose CA 95135 Office: Santa Clara U Santa Clara CA 95053

MAKANSI, TAREK, electrical engineer; b. Wilmington, Del., Oct. 21, 1957. BSEE, Cornell U., 1980; MSEE, U. Calif., Berkeley, 1982, PhD in Elec. Engring., 1985. Coop. engr. Gen. Elec., Schenectady, N.Y., 1978-80; teaching asst. U. Calif., Berkeley, 1980-82, research asst., 1982-84; engr. Ampex Corp., Redwood City, Calif., summers 1981, 82; staff engr. IBM, San Jose, Calif., 1985-86, mgr., 1986—; cons. SRI Internat., Menlo Park, Calif., 1984; cons., chmn. bd. dirs. Digital Kinetics Corp., Danville, Calif. Scholar McMullen Dean Cornell U., 1976, Earl C. Anthony, U. Calif., Berkeley, 1980. Mem. IEEE, Communications Soc. IEEE, Control Sytems Soc. IEEE, Tau Beta Pi, Eta Kappa Nu. Avocations: tennis, swimming, camping, corp. history. Office: IBM Corp 5600 Cottle Rd San Jose CA 95193

MAKEPEACE, DARRYL LEE, manufacturing company executive, management educator; b. Pitts., Oct. 24, 1941; s. Thomas Henry Makepeace and Nevada Ruth (Wagner) Desin; m. Maryanne Stright, Aug. 16, 1977; children: Krisanne, Erin. BS in Indsl. Engring., Pa. State U., 1969; MBA, Pepperdine U., 1982. Dept. mgr. Procter & Gamble, Cin., 1969-72; plant mgr. CBS Mus. Instruments, Fullerton, Calif., 1972-76; dir. mfg. Frigid Coil/Wolf, Whittier, Calif., 1977-79; mgr. materials mgmt. Nat. Supply, Los Nietos, Calif., 1979-85, mgr. mfg., 1985-86; program mgr. Armed Cumberland Group, Middletown, Ohio, 1986—. Contbr. articles to profl. jours. Served with U.S. Army, 1960-61. Named to Honorable Order of Ky. Cols. Mem. Am. Prodn. and Inventory Control Soc., Petroleum Soc., Inst. Indsl. Engrs., Alpha Pi Mu, Tau Beta Pi. Avocation: reading. Home: 10541 Frederick Dr Villa Park CA 92667

MAKI, KAZUMI, physicist, educator; b. Takamatsu, Japan, Jan. 27, 1936; s. Toshio and Hideko M.; m. Masako Tanaka, Sept. 21, 1969. B.S., Kyoto U., 1959, Ph.D., 1964. Research asso. Inst. for Math. Scis., Kyoto U., 1964; research asso. Fermi Inst., U. Chgo., 1964-65; asst. prof. physics U. Calif., San Diego, 1965-67; prof. Tohoku U., Sendai, Japan, 1967-74; vis. prof. Universite Paris-Sud, Orsay, France, 1969-70; prof. physics U. So. Calif., Los Angeles, 1974—; vis. prof. Inst. Laue-Langevin, U. Paris-Sud, France, 1979-80, Max-Planck Inst. für Fetkörper Forschung, Stuttgart, Fed. Republic of Germany. Assoc. editor Jour. Low Temperature Physics, 1969—; contbr. articles to profl. jours. Recipient Nishina prize, 1972, Alexander von Humboldt award, 1986-87; Fulbright scholar, 1964-65; Guggenheim fellow, 1979-80. Fellow Am. Phys. Soc.; Mem. Phys. Soc. Japan, AAAS. Office: Physics Dept U So Calif Los Angeles CA 90089

MAKINA, JAMILA TATU, mathematics, science, computer educator; b. Somerset City, Md., Mar. 16, 1943. BS, Morgan State U., 1966; postgrad., U. San Francisco, 1973, U. Calif., Berkeley, 1976-80; MS, Calif. State U., Haward, 1982. Cert. jr. coll. tchr., Calif., cert. secondary tchr., Calif., cert. adminstrv., cert. sch. bus. mgmt. Tchr. Balt. City Pub. Schs., 1968-70, Overseas Dependent Sch., Kenitra, Morrocco, 1970-72, Emery Unified Schs., Emeryville, Calif., 1973—; tax preparer H & R Block, Oakland, Calif., 1985—; pres. J.A.M. Enterprize, Oakland, 1984—. Mem. NEA, Nat. Tchrs. Math. Council, Calif. Math. Council, Calif. Sci. Tchrs. Assn., Calif. Tchrs. Assn. (chairperson affirmative action com. 1984—, legis. coordinator 1985—, Outstanding Educator 1984), Emery Tchrs. Assn. (pres. 1983-84), Phi Delta Kappa, Alpha Kappa Alpha (chairperson 1986—). Home: PO BOx 3293 Berkeley CA 94703 OFfice: J.A.M. Enterprize 1948 89th Ave Oakland CA 94621

MAKOWSKI, EDGAR LEONARD, obstetrician and gynecologist; b. Milw., Oct. 27, 1927; s. Adam and Ernestine (Horn) M.; m. Patricia M. Nock, Nov. 1, 1952; children: Peter, James, Ann, Mary, Thomas, Paul. B.S., Marquette U., 1951, M.D., 1954. Intern Deaconess Hosp., Milw., 1954-55; resident in Ob/Gyn U. Minn., Mpls., 1955-59; asst. prof. U. Minn., 1959-66, asso. prof., 1966; asso. prof. Ob/Gyn U. Colo., Denver, 1966-69; prof. U. Colo., 1969—, chmn. dept., 1976—. Contbr. articles to sci. jours., chpts. to books. Served with AUS, 1946-47. NIH spl. fellow in physiology Yale U., 1963. Mem. Am. Gynecol. and Obstet. Soc. (pres.), Am. Gynecol. Soc., Am. Coll. Obstetricians and Gynecologists, Soc. Gynecol. Investigators, Central Assn. Obstetricians and Gynecologists, Colo. Soc. Ob/Gyn. Roman Catholic. Club: Brown Palace. Office: U Colo Sch Medicine 4200 E 9th Ave Denver CO 80262

MAKOWSKI, PETER EDGAR, hosp. exec.; b. Milw., Nov. 21, 1953; s. Edgar Leonard and Patricia Mae (Nock) M.; m. Cynthia Renee Edgerly, Apr. 7, 1979. B.A. in Polit. Sci., Whittier Coll., 1976; M.P.H., UCLA, 1980. Adminstrv. intern Calif. Hosp. Med. Center, Los Angeles, 1977, unit mgr. emergency dept., 1977-78; adminstrv. resident Presbyn. Intercommunity Hosp., Whittier, Calif., 1979-80, adminstrv. dir. support services, 1980-82, v.p. ambulatory/spl. services, 1982-84, v.p. diagnostic/therapeutic services, 1984-85; sr. v.p. Calif. Med. Ctr., Los Angeles, 1985-86; exec. v.p. Queen of the Valley Hosp., West Covina, Calif., 1986—. Mem. adv. council San Gabriel Valley Area Health Edn. Ctr., 1983-84; vice-chmn. adv. com. Trauma Hosp., Los Angeles County, 1987—. Mem. Am. Cancer Soc. (Long

Beach SE unit, bd. dirs. 1984-85), Am. Hosp. Assn., Am. Coll. Hosp. Adminstrs. (student assoc.), Health Care Execs. So. Calif., UCLA Hosp. Adminstrn. Alumni Assn., Nat. Honor Soc, Whittier Alumni Assn. (bd. dirs. 1984—). Republican. Roman Catholic. Club: Whittier Host Lions. Home: 1308 Calle Galante San Dimas CA 91773 Office: 1115 S Sunset Ave West Covina CA 91790

MAKUCH, ANDREW LUBOMIR, librarian; b. Jaroslaw, Poland, Jan. 14, 1928; came to U.S., 1949; s. Simon and Sofia (Kuroczka) M. BA, U. Ill., 1951; MLS, U. Mich., 1955, MA, 1963. Reference librarian Detroit Pub. Library, 1955-56; head librarian N.Mex. Mil. Inst., Roswell, 1956-58; librarian book selection U. Mich., Ann Arbor, 1958-64; bibliographer for collection devel. U. Ariz., Tucson, 1964—. Served with U.S. Army, 1951-53. Mem. ALA, Seminar on Acquisition of Latin Am., Library Materials. Republican. Roman Catholic. Avocations: piano, collecting first edition books by contemporary authors. Home: 1301 E Mabel Tucson AZ 85719 Office: U Ariz Library Tucson AZ 85721

MALACHOWSKI, MICHAEL JON, biophysicist, educator; b. Chgo., Sept. 4, 1945; s. Thaddeus Antony and Natalie Constance (Kryczewski) M.; m. Cynthia Louise Hamer; 1 child, Jessica Lynn. Student, Colo. Coll., 1963-65; AB in Physics and EE, U. Calif., Berkeley, 1968, PhD in Biophysics and Health Sci., 1978. Cert. instr., Calif. Engr. Coherent Radiation Lab., Palo Alto, Calif., 1966-67; v.p. Centurion Enterprises, Berkeley, Calif., 1968-72; research assoc. Lawrence Berkeley Labs., 1973-77; NRC fellow U. Western Ont., London, Can., 1977-80; chief exec. officer Cellulose Conversion Enterprises, Berkeley, 1980—; assoc. NASA, Moffett Field, Calif., 1975-80, cons. Berkeley, 1981—; instr. biophysics U. Calif., San Francisco, 1981; mem. student body pres. council, U. Calif., Berkeley, 1974-76, chmn. grad. assembly, 1976. Colo. Coll. scholar, 1963; biophysics tng. grantee NIH, 1972-76. Office: Cellulose Conversion Enterprises Box 9315 Berkeley CA 94709

MALCOLM, GERALD LINDBURG, elec. co. exec.; b. Genola, Utah, Dec. 18, 1927; s. John Leo and Rhoda (Steele) M.; student U. Utah, Salt Lake City, 1957-59; m. Edith Jackson, Oct. 4, 1952; children—Guy David, Roger Allan, JoAnn, Tracy Dale, Gerald Leo, Edith Christine. Electrician, Excel Neon Sign Co., Salt Lake City, 1946-48; owner, operator Malcolm Electric Co., Santaquin, Utah, 1948-52; journeyman electrician Dept. Army, Dugway Proving Grounds, Utah, 1952-60; sr. constrn. foreman A, Thiokol Chem. Corp., Tremonton, Utah, 1960-62; electrician leader VA Med. Center, Salt Lake City, 1962-73, constrn. mgr., 1973-81; owner, operator Malcolm Electric Co., Salt Lake City, 1965—; instr. Utah Tech. Coll., Salt Lake City, 1974-76; lectr. in field. Active Soil Conservation, Utah County, U.S. Dept. Agr., 1950-51. Master electrician, Utah, also elec. contractor license. Mem. Ch. Jesus Christ Latter-Day Saints. Home: 1549 S 1300 W Salt Lake City UT 84104 Office: Malcolm Electric Co 1549 S 1300 W Salt Lake City UT 84104

MALECHA, MARVIN JOHN, architect, academic administrator; b. Lonsdale, Mich., June 26, 1949; s. George and Barbara Malecha; m. Cynthia Marie Miller, Aug. 8, 1970; children: Peter, Michelle. Student, St. Thomas Coll.; BArch, U. Minn.; M in Design, Harvard U. Registered architect, Calif. Designer Wallace and Mundt Architects, Edina, Minn., 1969-73, Hugh Stubbins and Assocs., Cambridge, Mass., 1973-76; instr. Cambridge Urban Awareness Program, 1973-76, Boston Archtl. Ctr., 1974-76; asst. chmn., asst. prof. dept. architecture Sch. Environ. Design, Calif. State Poly. U., Pomona, 1976-77, chmn., assoc. prof., 1979-82, prof., dean Sch. Environ. Design, 1982—; chmn. Assn. Collegiate Sch. Architecture Adminstrs Conf., Washington, Dec. 1985, Univ. Fall Conf. com. Calif. State Poly. U., 1984; mem. steering com. Architects for Social Responsibility; mem. bd. advisors Tchrs. cert. program City Bldg. Edn. Program, planning com. So. Calif. Assn. Govts.; vis. critic UCLA, 1985, U. Minn., 1981-83, U. So. Calif., 1980, 82, 83, 84, 85, Calif. Poly. State U., San Luis Obispo, 1979, 82, 83; lectr. to schs. and archtl. assns.; cons. in architecture and research, Claremont, Calif., 1976—; master juror Nat. Council Archtl. Registration Bds.; mem. edn. equity com. Calif. State U. System, 1985-86. Contbr. aticles to profl. jours. Mem. Art and Liturgy com. Our Lady Assumption Ch., Claremont, Calif. Recipient Ellerbe Archtl. award, 1972, Hon. Mention Mass. Housing Dept., 1976; Rotch scholar, 1980. Mem. AIA (bd. dirs. Los Angeles chpt. 1982-83, chmn. state and nat. awards coms. 1983-85, chmn. Monterey design conf. com., Henry Adams award 1973), Soc. Am. Registered Architects, Calif. Council of Archtl. Edn. (bd. dirs.). Home: 4143 Las Casas Claremont CA 91711 Office: Calif State Poly U Sch Environ Design 3801 W Temple Ave Pomona CA 91768

MALEK, LINDA JOAN, marketing professional; b. New Haven, Conn., Feb. 29, 1952; d. Jack H. and Myra Malek. Student, UCLA, 1970-73; BA in Clin. Psychology cum laude, Calif. State U., Dominguez Hills, 1980. Account exec. Berkhemer & Kline, Los Angeles, 1975-78; mktg. coordinator MDT Corp., Los Angeles, 1978-79; mktg. mgr. Sanjon, Inc., Los Angeles, 1979-82; mktg. dir. Marineland, Los Angeles, 1982—; bd. dirs. Palos Verdes Marine Animal Care Found., Los Angeles; cons. J.D. Inc., Los Angeles. Mem. Am. Mktg. Assn., Los Angeles Advt. Club, Nat. Travel Industry Am., Calif. Travel Industry Am. Avocations: jazz dance, water and snow skiing. Office: Marineland 6610 Palos Verdes Dr S Rancho Palos Verdes CA 90274

MALERNEE, JAMES KENT, JR., management consultant; b. Durango, Colo., June 15, 1947; s. James Kent and Norma Virginia (Calhoon) M.; BS in Engring., U. Tex., Austin, 1970, PhD in Bus. Adminstrn., 1977; MBA, So. Meth. U., 1972; m. Charlean Ann Born, Aug. 21, 1971. Petroleum engr. Tex. R.R. Commn., 1970-71; instr. in fin. U. Tex., 1973-75; lectr. fin. U. Tulsa, 1975-76; sr. asso. Mgmt. Analysis Center, Northbrook, Ill. and Palo Alto, Calif. 1977-80, v.p., 1980—; sr. v.p. The MAC Group, 1987—, also bd. dirs.; lectr. mgmt. Stanford Grad. Sch. Bus., 1983; leader seminars on mergers and acquisitions and corp. strategy; guest speaker in field of strategy. Named Outstanding Young Man of Am., U.S. Jaycees, 1977. Mem. Fin. Mgmt. Assn. (v.p. 1981-82, dir. 1983-85), Assn. Corp. Growth. Methodist. Author: Skiing The West; contbr. articles on ins., leasing and other subjects to profl. jours. Home: 25 Buckland Ct San Carlos CA 94070 Office: The MAC Group 1000 El Camino Real #250 Menlo Park CA 94025

MALÈS, RENÉ HENRI, research executive; b. Paris, Sept. 24, 1932; came to U.S., 1940; s. Henri and Vera (Danford) M.; m. Barbara Young, Aug. 7, 1954; children: Eric Henri, Kerstin Renée, Melissa Gail. BA in Math, French, Ripon Coll., 1954; postgrad., U. Chgo., 1954; MBA, Northwestern U., 1956. Mgr. gen. services Commonwealth Edison Co., Chgo., 1956-76; v.p. Electric Power Research Inst., Palo Alto, Calif., 1976-86; sr. v.p. Decision Focus Inc., Los Altos, Calif., 1986—; chmn. adv. com. Brookhaven Nat. Lab., Upton, N.Y., 1977-82; mem. adv. com. Oak Ridge (Tenn.) Nat. Lab., 1976-81, Fed. Power Commn. Nat. Power Survey, Washington, 1970, 74. Co-author: Load Management, 1982. Mem. adv. com. Chgo. Urban League, 1972-76. Served with U.S. Army, 1956-58. Mem. AAAS, Internat. Energy Econs. Assn., Nat. Assn. Bus. Economists (founder Chgo. chpt. 1968). Office: Decision Focus Inc 4984 El Camino Real Los Altos CA 94022

MALEY, SAMUEL WAYNE, educator; b. Sidney, Neb., Mar. 1, 1928; s. Samuel Raymond and Inez (Moore) M.; m. Elizabeth Anne Green, June 11, 1963; children—Karen Margaret, Laura Elaine. B.S., U. Colo., 1952, M.S., 1957, Ph.D., 1959; student, U. N.M., 1957-58. Geophysicist Stanolind Oil Co., Lubbock, Tex., 1952; design engr. Beach Aircraft Corp., Wichita, Kan., 1952-53, Dynalectron Corp., Cheyenne, Wyo., 1953-56; research scientist U. Colo., 1959-60, vis. lectr., 1960-61, asst. prof., 1961-62, asso. prof. elec. engring., 1962-67, prof., 1967—; cons. Nat. Center Atmospheric Research, 1964, Automation Industries Research Div., Boulder, Colo., 1960-71, Midwec Corp., Ogallala, Neb., 1969-70, IBM, Boulder, 1969—. Author: Combinational Logic Circuits, 1969. Served with AUS, 1946-47; Served with USAF, 1947-48. Mem. I.E.E.E., Am. Assn. U. Profs., A.A.A.S., Soc. Indsl. and Applied Math. Methodist. Research electromagnetic theory; communication theory; computer design. Home: 3760 N 57th St Boulder CO 80301

MALI, DINESH BHAGWANI, mechanical engineer; b. Karachi, West Pakistan, Jan. 9, 1946; s. Bhagwanji and Shanta Beni Mali; m. Aruna Gorajia, Dec. 27, 1970 (div. July 1980); children: Sandip, Sonal; m. Purnima D. Amarkotia, July 19, 1980; children: Ketan, Milan. BSME, U. Mo., 1969; MSME, Wash. U., St. Louis, 1976. Registered profl engr., Mo., Ill., Calif. Design engr. Bendy Engring. Co., St. Louis, 1970-73; mech. designer William Tao & Assoc., St. Louis, 1973-74; mech. engr. Erwin-Colnon Corp., St. Louis, 1974-76; proj. engr. Allen & Garcia Co., Chgo., 1976-79, D.R. Warren Co., Los Angeles, 1979; mgr. Shanta Engring. Co. Inc., Cerritos, Calif., 1979-80, pres., 1980—. Mem. Calif. Mining Assn. (assoc.), Alaska Mining Assn. (assoc.), Colo. Mining Assn. (assoc.), Utah Mining Assn. (assoc.), Pi Tau Sigma. Hindu. Office: Shanta Engring Co 11110-C Artesia Blvd Cerritos CA 90701

MALIAN, IDA MARGUERITE, educator; b. Detroit, Mar. 25, 1950; d. Artin Ghevont and Agavnie Agnes (Eknayan) M. BA, Oakland U., 1970; MA, U. Mich., 1971, PhD, 1977. Dir. ednl. tng. Children's Psychiat. Hosp., Ann Arbor, Mich., 1974-75; instr. U. Mich., Ann Arbor, 1974-75; behavior mgmt. cons. Med. Ctr. U. Nebr., Omaha, 1975-78, asst. prof., 1975-78; assoc. prof. dept. elem. edn. San Diego State U., 1978—; state hearing officer Legal Officer State Dept., Sacramento, 1979-83; state mediator State Legal Office, 1980-83; cosn. San Diego City Schs., 1979-81. Author: (with C.M. Charles) Special Student: Practical Help for the Classroom Teacher, 1980; contbr. articles to profl. jours. Bur. Edn. Handicapped grantee, 1975, fellow, 1973. Mem. Council for Exceptional Children, Council for Behavior Disorders (regional dir. 1980-82), Ctr. for Study of Sensory Integrative Dysfunction (dir. 1982-83). Democrat. Eastern Orthodox. Home: 5405 Baltimore Dr #78 La Mesa CA 92042 Office: San Diego State U Dept Elem Edn San Diego CA 92182

MALICH, KENNETH ANTONE, marine equipment technician; b. Tacoma, Feb. 7, 1946; s. Marco Jasper and Minnie (Modun) M.; m. Kitty Carlotta Miller, Jan. 7, 1978 (div. June 1982); 1 child, Matthew Michael. AS, Olympic Coll., 1984, AA, 1985, A Gen. Studies, 1986. Comml. fisherman various locations, Wash. and Alaska, 1961-82; engring. technician Puget Sound Naval Shipyard, Bremerton, Wash., 1982-83, marine mechanic, 1984—. Councilman Town of Gig Harbor, Wash., 1976-80. Served with U.S. Army, 1967-70, Vietnam. Mem. AAAS, Planetary Soc., Puget Sound Gullnetters Assn. (bd. dirs. 1978-82). Roman Catholic. Lodge: Eagles. Avocations: computers, snow skiing, jogging.

MALICK, JOHN DAVID, architect, urban planner; b. Pitts., Apr. 3, 1951; s. Franklin Sherrick and Maude Helen (Steene) M.; m. Susan Lord Dillard, May 31, 1975; children: Andrew, Molly, Nichols. BS, Yale U., 1972, MArch, 1975. Licensed architect, Oreg., Calif. Assoc. architect SOM, Portland, Oreg., 1975-83, San Francisco, 1983-85; assoc. architect Hall, Goodhue, Haisley and Barker, San Francisco, 1985—. Mem. AIA. Episcopalian. Home: 138 Wildwood Ave Piedmont CA 94610 Office: Hall Goodhue Haisley & Barker 282 2d St San Francisco CA 94105

MALIN, DANIEL DAVID, construction executive; b. Hartford, Conn., Sept. 12, 1949; s. Daniel and Anne (Delekta) Malinguaggi; 1 child, Kyle Leigh. BS, Cen. Conn. State Coll., 1971. Cert. secondary tchr., Conn. Tchr. pub. schs., East Hartford, Conn., 1971-72; computer processor Comtec, New Britain, Conn., 1972-73; surveyor Luches & Beckerman, Glastonbury, Conn., 1973-75; engring. technician Golden Valley Electrir, Fairbanks, Alaska, 1975; with constrn. dept. Trans Alaskan Pipeline, 1975-77; owner, pres. Uptight Siding, Inc., Fairbanks, 1976—; sales mgr. San-Alaska and The Plans Room, Fairbanks, 1985—. Tournament organizer Easter Seals/Fairbanks Businessmen, 1986. Recipient Leadership award Keep Am. Beautiful, Inc., Fairbanks, 1986. Mem. No. Lights Jaycees, Fairbanks C. of C. Republican. Club: Golf & Country (Fairbanks) (tournament com. 1985—). Lodge: Moose. Avocations: golf, racquetball, waterskiing, reading, stock analysis. Home: 311 Slater Dr Fairbanks AK 99701 Office: Uptight Siding Inc PO Box 74685 Fairbanks AK 99707

MALIN, MICHAEL CHARLES, geology educator; b. Burbank, Calif., May 10, 1950; s. Jack and Beatryce (Solomon) M. AB, U. Calif., Berkeley, 1971; PhD, Calif. Inst. Tech., 1975. Sr. scientist Jet Propulsion Lab., Pasadena, Calif., 1975-78, mem. tech. staff, 1978-79; asst. prof. geology Ariz. State U., Tempe, 1979-82, assoc. prof., 1982-87, prof., 1987—. Co-author: Earthlike Planets, 1981; contbr. articles to profl. jours. Mem. Am. Geophys. Union, Am. Astron. Soc. (div. Planetary Scis.). Office: Ariz State U Dept Geology Tempe AZ 85237

MALINOWSKI, JAY WAYNE, public relations executive, educator; b. Brownsville, Tex., Apr. 12, 1945; s. Raymond and Phyllis Roseline (Moore) M.; m. Dorene Marie Ludwig, Dec. 20, 1968 (div. Jan. 1986). AA, U. S. Fla., 1970; BA in Sociology, Calif State U., Los Angeles, 1976, MA in Pub. Adminstrn., 1978. Editor Tampa mag. Tampa C. of C., 1970-72; dir. pub. affairs Cerritos Coll., Norwalk, Calif., 1972-80; asst dir. pub. affairs Met. Water Dist., Los Angeles, 1980—; instr. Pasadena (Calif.) City Coll., Calif. State U., Northridge. Served with USAF, 1965-68. Recipient Silver Six award Internat. Assn. Bus. Communicators, 1984. Mem. Pub. Relations Soc. Am. (accredited), Town Hall Los Angeles (chmn. pub. relations sect. 1986), Mgmt. Devel. (pres. 1985-86), Mensa, Soaring Soc. Am. Democrat. Avocations: sailplane piloting, phtography. Home: 120 Sierra Madre Blvd Pasadena CA 91107 Office: Metro Water Dist 1111 Sunset Blvd Los Angeles CA 90012

MALIYACKEL, ANTHONY CHERU, chemist, research associate; b. Edathuruthy, India, Dec. 24, 1948; came to U.S., 1983; s. Cheru K. and Mary K. Maliyackel; m. Baby Paul Mavely, June 5, 1977; children: Marian, Christie. BSc, Christ Coll., Kerala, India, 1969; MSc, U. Bombay, 1973; PhD, U. Saskatchewan, Can., 1984. Chemist Bhabha Atomic Research Ctr., Bombay, 1972-77; research assoc. Lawrence Berkeley (Calif.) Lab., 1983—. Contbr. articles to profl. jours. Gerhard Herzberg fellow U. Saskatchewan, 1979-80; grad. fellow U. Saskatchewan, 1979-83. Roman Catholic. Office: Lawrence Berkeley Lab Chem Biodynamics #3 Berkeley CA 94720

MALKAN, MATTHEW ARNOLD, astronomy educator; b. N.Y.C., June 4, 1956; s. Arnold George and Audrey Jane (Hubbard) M. AB summa cum laude, Harvard U., 1977, AM, 1977; C.P.G.S., Cambridge U., Eng., 1978; PhD, Calif. Inst. Tech., 1983. Research assoc. Calif. Inst. Tech., Pasadena, 1983, U. Ariz., Tucson, 1983-84; asst. prof. UCLA, 1984—. Contbr. articles to astrophysics jours. Marshall scholar Cambridge U., 1977-78; Fannie and John Hertz Found. fellow Calif. Inst. Tech., 1979-83; NSF predoctoral fellow, 1978-79, Presdl. Young Investigator research grantee at UCLA, 1986—. Mem. Am. Astron. Soc. Episcopalian. Home: 827 Levering Apt #505 Los Angeles CA 90024 Office: Univ Calif at Los Angeles Dept Astronomy Los Angeles CA 90024

MALKOFF, JUDY D., psychotherapist; b. Altoona, Pa., Apr. 8, 1933; d. Joseph L. and Edna R. (Brett) Sherman; m. Jack Malkoff, Dec. 19, 1954; children—Laurie, Robbie, Gregg, Scott. B.S., Pa. State U., 1954; M.S. in Counseling, Youngstown State U., 1976. Cert. interactional psychotherapist, Ariz. Assertiveness tng. leader YWCA, Altoona, 1977-79; therapist Family Service Agy., Scottsdale, Ariz., 1980-81, CIGNA Health Plan, Phoenix, 1981—; group leader assertiveness tng. Paradise Valley Community Edn. Program, Phoenix, 1979. Vice pres. LWV, Youngstown, Ohio; Mem. Am. Personnel and Guidance Assn., Am. Mental Health Counselors Assn., Assn. Specialists in Group Work, Ariz. Personnel and Guidance Assn.

MALLER, JUDY BATMAN, public relations company executive; b. Bridgeport, Conn., Jan. 3, 1939; s. Homer C. and Margaret (Evvard) Batman; m. Jonathan Cromwell, June 11, 1960 (div. 1968); 1 child, Kimberly Cromwell Lopez; m. John M. Maller, June 24, 1971. BA, Manhattanville Coll., 1960; MS, UCLA, 1967. V.p. Penney & Bennett, Los Angeles, 1967-72; account exec. Laurence Laurie, Los Angeles, 1972-73, account supr., 1974-81; dir. pub. relations Charles Luckman, Los Angeles, 1973-74; pvt. practice pub. relations Los Angeles, 1981—. Pres. The Crippled Children's Soc. So. Calif., Los Angeles, 1984—. Home and Office: 1108 Somera Rd Los Angeles CA 90077

MALLETTE, LEO ALBERT, aerospace company executive; b. Detroit, May 26, 1953; s. Albert Gedeon and Dolores Marguerite (Carriere) M.; m. Kathryn Joan Abrahamzon, Aug. 10, 1985; 1 child, Andrea. BEE, U. Cen. Fla., 1975, MEE, 1977; MBA, Pepperdine U., 1985. Instr. U. Cen. Fla., Orlando, 1977-78; cons. Martin Marietta, Orlando, 1977, USN, Orlando, 1978; engr., mgr. Hughes Aircraft Co., Los Angeles, 1978—; bd. dirs. Aerospace Applications Conf., MTS Assocs. Contbr. articles to profl. jours.; patentee in field. Mem. IEEE (sr., many coms.). Republican. Roman Catholic. Avocations: coins, genealogy, gardening. Home: 2309 S Santa Anita Ave Arcadia CA 91006 Office: Hughes Aircraft Co PO Box 92919 S41-B322 Los Angeles CA 90009

MALLORY, DANIEL HENRY, optometrist; b. Washington, May 5, 1954; s. Herbert Dean and Dorothy Marie (Graber) M.; 1 dau., Aimee Ranai. B.S. in Biol. Scis., U. Calif.-Irvine, 1977; O.D., So. Calif. Coll. Optometry, 1981. Pvt. practice optometry, Ridgecrest and Lake Isabella, Calif., 1982—. Methodist. Club: Rotary. Office: PO Box 2953 5109-B Lake Isabella Blvd Lake Isabella CA 93240 Office: #2 722 E North Norma Ridgecrest CA 53107

MALLOTT, BYRON IVAR, holding corporation executive; b. Yakutat, Alaska, Apr. 6, 1943; s. Jay B. and Emma M. (Brown) M.; m. Evelyn Anderson Converse, 1964 (div. 1971); children: Byron, Meredith; m. Antoinette Mary Evans, May 7, 1972; children: Anthony, Joseph. Student, Eastern Wash. State Coll., 1961-62, Western Wash. State Coll., 1962-64. Spl. asst. U.S. Senator Mike Gravel, 1969; exec. dir. Rural Alaska Action Program, Anchorage, 1970; dir. State of Alaska Local Affairs Agy., Juneau, 1971, commr. State Dept. Community and Regional Affairs, 1972-74; chmn. SeaLaska Corp., Juneau, from 1976, chief exec. officer, 1982—; co-owner Alaska Native Mgmt., Yakutat, 1974-80; dir. B.M. Behrends Bank, Juneau, 1978—, Alaska Airlines Inc., Seattle, 1982—, Alaska Permanent Fund, Juneau, 1982—, Fed. Res. Bank, Seattle, 1983—. Mayor City of Yakutat, 1965; mem. Alaska Reapportionment Bd., Juneau, 1980—, chmn., 1980; mem. U. Alaska Found., Fairbanks, 1981—. Recipient Gov.'s award Alaskan of Year Com., 1982. Mem. Alaska Fedn. Natives (Citizen of Year 1982). Democrat. Roman Catholic. Club: Alaska Native Brotherhood (v.p. 1968-69). Office: SeaLaska Corp 1 SeaLaska Plaza Juneau AK 99801 *

MALM, DONALD BURNELL, marketing executive; b. Erie, Pa., Nov. 12, 1933; s. John Sigurd and Manghild Svea (Johnson) M.; m. Janice Helen Driscoll, June 6, 1964; children—Barbara Jan, Dion John. B.S. in Journalism, Northwestern U., 1956. Traffic mgr. Young & Rubicam, N.Y.C., 1962-64; advt. and sales promotion mgr. Royal Typewriter Co., N.Y.C., 1964-69; advt. mgr. Plus Products, Irvine, Calif., 1969-75; owner DBM Advt., San Clemente, Calif., 1975-80; v.p. mktg. Radiance Products Inc., City of Industry, Calif., 1980-85; owner The Duck Press, San Clemente, 1985—. Served with AUS, 1955-58. Montgomery Ward scholar, 1956. Mem. Mensa. Republican. Methodist.

MALM, ROYCE ELLIOTT, musician; b. Los Angeles, Nov. 22, 1929; s. Albin Nils and Mildred Elizabeth (Aden) M.; Mus.B., U. So. Calif., 1952, M.Mus. in Composition, 1954; m. Ruth Emilie Eggert, Dec. 1, 1962; 1 dau., Lorraine Elise. Tchr. public schs. in Calif., 1957—; tchr. secondary choral music and music appreciation Burbank (Calif.) Unified Sch. Dist., 1964—; mem. Burbank Symphony Assn., 1971—, pres., 1975-78, exec. dir., 1979—; dir. ch. choirs, 1953-73; v.p. Burbank Community Concerts Assn., 1973-75, Symphony League Los Angeles County, 1978—, Performing Arts Fedn. Burbank, 1977-78. Composer: Reflections, 1980; others. Served with AUS, 1954-56. Mem. Music Educators Nat. Conf., NEA, Burbank Tchrs. Assn., Calif. Tchrs. Assn., Choral Conductors Guild Calif., So. Calif. Vocal Assn., Pro Musica Sana, Sir Thomas Beecham Soc., Pi Kappa Lambda, Phi Mu Alpha. Democrat. Presbyterian. Home: 924 Tufts Ave Burbank CA 91504 Office: 420 S Mariposa St Burbank CA 91506

MALMBERG, JOHN HOLMES, physics educator; b. Gettysburg, Pa., July 5, 1927; s. Constantine F. and Margaret Eloise (Dysinger) M.; m. Vilma Ruth Martinus, June 21, 1952; children: David Gabriel, Lori Ann. BE, Ill. State U., 1949; MS in Physics, U. Ill., 1951, PhD in Physics, 1957. Research, teaching asst. U. Ill., Champaign, 1949-57; staff mem. Gulf Gen. Atomic, San Diego, 1957-69; prof. physics U. Calif., San Diego, 1967—. Contbr. numerous sci. articles to jours.; patentee in field. Served with U.S. Army, 1946. Recipient Tech. Innovation award NASA. Fellow Am. Phys. Soc. (Maxwell prize in plasma physics 1985); mem. Sigma Psi. Home: 445 Van Dyke Del Mar CA 92014 Office: U Calif San Diego Dept Physics B 019 La Jolla CA 92093

MALMSTADT, HOWARD VINCENT, university provost; b. Marinette, Wis., Feb. 17, 1922; s. Guy August and Nellie (Rusch) M.; B.S., U. Wis., 1943, M.S., 1948, Ph.D., 1950; m. Carolyn Gay Hart, Aug. 3, 1947; children—Cynthia Sue, Alice Ann, Jonathan Howard. Postdoctoral research asso. U. Wis., 1950-51; mem. faculty U. Ill., 1951—, prof. chemistry, 1961-78, emeritus, 1978—, dir. electronics insts., 1960-74; dean sci. and tech., provost, sr. v.p. acad. affairs Pacific and Asia Christian U., Kona, Hawaii, 1978—; Fulbright-Hays disting. prof., Romania, 1978; cons. to govt. and industry. Served as officer USNR, 1943-46. Recipient award in edn. Instrument Soc. Am., 1970, Outstanding Analytical Chemist award Pitts. Conf. Analytical Chemistry and Applied Spectroscopy, 1978, ISCO award contbns. biochem. instrumentation, 1980; Guggenheim fellow, 1960; grantee NSF, 1965-78, NIH, 1975-80; recipient Outstanding Contbns. in Chemistry award ANACHEM, 1987. Mem. Am. Chem. Soc. (award instrumentation 1963, award analytical chemistry 1976, award for excellence in teaching 1984), Optical Soc. Am., Soc. Applied Spectroscopy, Am. Assn. Clin. Chemists. Author textbooks, articles in field; adv. bds. profl. jours. Patentee sci. instruments. Home: 75-5786 Niau Pl Kailua-Kona HI 96740 Office: PAC Univ Box YWAM Kailua-Kona HI 96740

MALMSTROM, LAURIE SUZANNE, food service marketing executive; b. Salt Lake City, Oct. 7, 1949; d. Wayne W. and Clair (Ford) M. Student, U. Utah, 1968-72. Region mktg. mgr. Burger King-Pillsbury Co., Santa Clara, Calif., 1978-80; acct. supr. Dailey and Assocs. Advt., San Francisco, 1980; nat. field mktg. mgr. Foodmaker-Ralston-Purina, San Diego, 1980-83; western div. market mgr. Taco Bell subs. PepsiCo, Santa Ana, Calif., 1983-85; v.p. mktg. Straw Hat Restaurants, Dublin, Calif., 1985—; pres./owner Momentum Mktg., San Diego, 1985—; advt. cons., San Francisco. Creator full page black and white ad for nat. mags. (Gold award 1978), radio advertisement (Gold award 1978). Recipient 1st Place award for creativity and execution for consumer premiumsAdvt. Specialties Co., 1986. Mem. Ad Club (Salt Lake City, San Diego and San Francisco chpts.). Democrat. Avocations: tennis, water sports, reading, travel, watercolors. Office: Straw Hat 6400 Village Pkwy Dublin CA 94568

MALONE, JAMES MICHAEL, vascular surgeon, educator; b. Berkeley, Calif., Sept. 13, 1946; s. George Edward and Lucille Marie (Gay) M.; m. Karla Kay Fraker, May 19, 1983; children: Jenifer Suzanne, Melissa Jill, James Anthony. Student, U. Calif., Berkeley, 1964-67; B in Med. Sci., U. Calif., San Francisco, 1968; MD, U. Calif., 1971. Diplomate Am. Bd. Surgery; cert. competence in vascular surgery. Asst. prof. surgery U. Ariz., Tucson, 1977-83, assoc. prof. surgery, 1984-87; chief vascular surgery Tucson VA Med. Ctr., 1981-87; chmn. dept. surgery Maricopa Med. Ctr., Phoenix, 1987—. Contbr. articles on surgery, amputation and vascular research to profl. jours. Recipient Career Devel. award VA, Tucson, 1977. Mem. ACS, Soc. Vascular Surgery, Internat. Soc. Cardiovascular Surgery, Assn. Acad. Surgeons, Soc. Univ. Surgeons, Phi Beta Kappa, Alpha Omega Alpha. Republican. Roman Catholic. Office: Maricopa Med Ctr Dept Surgery PO Box 5099 Phoenix AZ 85010

MALONE, JOHN C., telecommunications executive; b. 1941. Attended, Yale U., Johns Hopkins U. Formerly pres. Jerrold Electronics Corp.; now pres. Tele-Communications, Inc., Denver. Office: Tele-Communications Inc 5455 S Valentia Way Denver CO 80111 *

MALONEY, JEAN KAE, interior designer; b. St. Paul, Nebr., May 29, 1944; d. Isadore Joseph and Lydia Lillian (Trubl) Kezeor; m. Edward Stephan Maloney, July 27, 1968; children: Darren T., E. Stephen, Meghan. Student, Diablo Valley Coll., Concord, Calif., 1982, U. Calif., 1971, U. Nebr., 1966; BA, Duchesne Coll., Omaha, 1966. Tchr. Cathedral of Risen Christ, Lincoln, Nebr., 1966-67; counselor Neighborhood Youth Corps., Lincoln, %; tchr. Sacramento Unified Sch. Dist., Sacramento, Calif., 1967-68, Mt. Diablo Sch. System, Concord, Calif., 1968-70; interior designer Comprehensive Design, Walnut Creek, Calif., 1976-80, Suisun, Calif., 1980-

84, Napa, Calif., 1984-86; designer Napa Valley Showhouse, 1986. Publisher: Hotel and Restaurant Design Mag., 1986, Designers West, 1987. Treas. John Muir Hosp. Auxiliary, Walnut Creek, 1973; mem. AAUW, 1969, 70, 76. Republican. Roman Catholic. Avocations: tennis, skiing.

MALONEY, KENNETH LONG, fuels scientist, consultant; b. Wilkes-Barre, Pa., Oct. 1, 1945; s. Kenneth Francis and Lois (Long) M.; m. Sharon Sandelin, Dec. 23, 1979; children: Ryan Matthew, Jeffrey Conor, Leigh-Erin Charlotte. BS in Chemistry, Wilkes Coll., 1967; PhD in Fuel Sci., Pa. State U., 1971. Postdoctoral research Drexel U., Phila., 1971-72, Princeton U., N.J., 1972-73; sr. scientist Ultrasystems, Irvine, Calif., 1973-74; mgr. product devel. KVB, Inc., Irvine, 1974-83; v.p. Calpenn Assocs., Inc., Laguna Beach, Calif., 1983-85, pres., 1985—; coal expert U.S. Marshal's Office, San Francisco, 1981-85; combustion expert A.E. Staley Co., Decatur, Ill., 1984-85; pulverizer expert Electric Power Research Inst., Palo Alto, Calif., and Delmarva Power Co., Wilmington, Del., 1985-86. Author tech. publs.; patentee in field. King Fifth Wheel Corp. scholar, Mountain Top, Pa., 1963-67,research assistantship Pa. State U., 1967-71, spl. recognition award Fuller Internat. Inc. Quest Contest, Bethlehem, Pa., 1985. Mem. Am. Chem. Soc., Combustion Inst., Air Pollution Control Assn., Nat. Forensic Ctr. (Lexis and Nexus), Sigma Xi. Republican. Avocations: tennis, running, gourmet cooking. Office: Calpenn Assocs Inc 433 Locust St Laguna Beach CA 92651

MALONEY, WILLIAM JOSEPH, television producer; b. Chgo., Aug. 28, 1930; s. Joseph A. and Marie V. (McCarron) M.; children: Melanie, Russell, Aimee, William, Jr. BA, U. Ill., 1950; student, Northwestern U. TV producer Foote, Cone, Belding Advt., Chgo., 1954-64; v.p. Clinton E. Frank Advt., Chgo., 1964-74; account supr. BBDO Advt., Detroit, 1974-84; pres. Motorsports TV Prodns., Inc., Huntington Beach, Calif., 1984—. Editor: Competition Press, 1965-69; producer (TV series) Motorsports International, 1968-70 (nominated Chgo. Emmy), (TV spl.) Cars and Stars, 1973, (home video) Home Auto Show, 1985-86, numerous radio shows in the Midwest; exec. producer Tune Up America, 1987. Served to lt. (j.g.) USN, 1943-45, PTO. Named sports car racing champion Central Div. SposrtsCar Club Am., 1967. Mem. Am Mktg. Assn., Am. Auto Racing Writers and Broadcasters Assn. (best TV script 1968), Internat. Motor Press Assn. Republican. Roman Catholic. Avocations: auto racing, writing. Home: 21551 Brookhurst St Huntington Beach CA 92645 Office: Motorsports Prodns Inc 18782 Main St Huntington Beach CA 92648

MALOOF, GILES WILSON, mathematics educator; b. San Bernardino, Calif., Jan. 4, 1932; s. Joseph Peters and Georgia (Wilson) M.; m. Mary Anne Ziniker, Sept. 5, 1958 (dec. Oct. 1976); children—Mary Jane, Margery Jo. B.A., U. Calif. at Berkeley, 1953; M.A., U. Oreg., 1958; Ph.D., Oreg. State U., 1962. Petroleum reservoir engr. Creole Petroleum Corp., Venezuela, 1953-54; mathematician electronics div. research dept. U.S. Naval Ordnance Research Lab., Corona, Calif., 1958-59; asst. prof. math. Oreg. State U., Corvallis, 1962-68, research assoc. dept. oceanography, 1963-68, vis. prof. math., 1977-78; prof. math. Boise (Idaho) State U., 1968—, head dept., 1968-75, dean grad. sch., 1970-75; project dir. Dept. Energy Citizens' Workshop Energy Environment Simulator for Eastern Oreg., No. Nev. and Idaho, 1976—. Served with Ordnance Corps, AUS, 1954-56. Recipient Carter award, 1963, Mosser prize, 1966, Oreg. State U. Mem. Math. Assn. Am., Am. Math. Soc., Soc. Indsl. and Applied Math., Northwest Coll. and Univ. Assn. for Sci. (dir. 1973—), Northwest Sci. Assn. (trustee 1977-80), Sigma Xi, Pi Mu Epsilon, Phi Kappa Phi. Editor Ida. Council of Tchrs. of Math. Newspaper, 1971-73. Home: 1400 Longmont Ave Boise ID 83706

MALORRUS, FARLEY MARTIN, astrologer; b. St. Louis, Aug. 11, 1948; s. Fred Max and Beatrice (Cuttler) M. B.A. in Speech, Drama and English, Central Meth. Coll., Fayette, Mo., 1970; postgrad. in English, UCLA, 1974, in Astrology, 1974-76. Pvt. practice astrology, Culver City, Calif., 1975—; ship's astrologer, lectr. Sun Princess, Queen Elizabeth 2, Sitmar, Cunard, Princess and Carnival Cruise Lines, 1980—; columnist Redondo Beach (Calif.) Community Network News, 1982—; astrologer Sta. KROQ-FM, 1983—; ships astrologer Holland Am. Cruise lines, 1985—; dir., host astrology series for cable TV, 1983; astrologer various TV shows, 1983-86; host Astrology Hour, Sta. KFOX-FM, 1983—, Astrology and You, Sta. KIEV-AM, 1983—; ship astrologer S.S. Rotterdam, 1985, Nieu Amsterdam, 1986; sports astrologer Los Angeles Times, 1985; guest lectr. United Astrology Congress, 1986. Address: PO Box 2988 Culver City CA 90230

MALOSH, JAMES BOYD, mechanical engineering educator, consultant; b. Licking, Ill., July 30, 1943; s. John Andrew and Nadean Gertrude (Crandall) M.; m. Sandra Sue Bowne, June 22, 1963 (div. 1971); children—Jeffrey, Brian, Ronald; m. 2d, Helen Fay Kangas, Oct. 22, 1973; 1 dau., Melanie. B.S.M.E., Wayne State U., 1966; M.S. in Engring. Mechanics, Mich. Tech. U., 1969, Ph.D. in Engring. Mechanics, 1980. Registered profl. engr., Mich., Ohio, Pa., Alaska, Calif. Acoustical engr. Walker Research Lab., Grass Lake, Mich., 1969-70; research assoc. Mich. Tech. U., Houghton, 1970-75; sr. research engr. U.S. Steel Research Labs., Monroeville, Pa., 1975-80; prin. research scientist Battelle Meml. Labs., Columbus, Ohio, 1980-81; assoc. prof. mech. engring. U. Alaska, Fairbanks, 1981-83; sr. cons. in engring. acoustics, San Francisco, 1984-85; mech. engr. Pacific Gas and Electric Co., San Ramon, Calif., 1985-86; sr. research engr., Whirlpool Corp., Benton Harbor, Mich., 1986—; acoustical cons. Arctic Designers; prin. investigator Alaska Dept. Transp. Wayne State U. Bd. Govs. scholar, 1966; NSF trainee, 1968, 70, 71. Mem. ASME, Nat. Soc. Profl. Engrs., Soc. Automotive Engrs., Acoustical Soc. Am., Inst. Noise Control Engrs., Sigma Xi, Tau Beta Pi, Pi Tau Sigma. Lutheran. Patentee automotive silencer, blast furnace stove burner to reduce pulsations.

MALOTT, ALAN MARC, lawyer; b. Bklyn., Jan. 18, 1953; s. Irving and Diana (Goldenberg) M.; m. Linda Ellen McNeil, Aug. 23, 1981; 1 child, Brian Joel. B.S. in Criminal Justice, Ariz. State U., 1976; J.D., U. N.Mex., 1979. Bar: N.M. 1979, U.S. Ct. Appeals (10th cir.) 1980. Assoc. Shaffer Law Firm, Albuquerque, 1979-81, Harold B. Albert, P.A., Albuquerque, 1981; sole practice, Albuquerque, 1981—; legal counsel N.Mex. Chiropractic Assn., 1983—. Contbr. articles to profl. jours. Mem. Huning Highlands Hist. Assn., 1983—. Recipient Criminal Procedure plaque Bancroft-Whitney Pubs., 1978, Equity Practice plaque, 1978. Mem. Ct. Practice Inst. (diplomate), Assn. Trial Lawyers Am. Democrat. Jewish. Office: 112 Edith NE Albuquerque NM 87102

MALOTT, DWIGHT RALPH, accountant; b. Medford, Oreg., Mar. 24, 1947; s. Ralph Joseph and Eugenia (Romanchuk) M.; m. Janet Gail Born, June 28, 1975; children—Jennifer, Paul, Michelle. A.Tech. Arts, Everett Jr. Coll., 1967; B.B.A., U. Wash., 1969. C.P.A., Wash. Acct. Main Hurdman, Everett, Wash., 1973-81; controller Shaffer Crane, Inc., Everett, 1981-83; prin. acct. Dwight Malott & Co., P.S., Arlington, Wash., 1983—. Loaned exec. United Way of Snohomish County, Everett, 1977, mem. allocations panel, 1980, 81, 82; bd. dirs. Lions Sight and Hearing Found. of Snohomish County, Everett, 1979—; mem. acctg. adv. com. Everett Community Coll., 1979—. Served to staff sgt. USAF, 1969-73. Mem. Wash. Soc. C.P.A.s, Am. Inst. C.P.A.s, Smokey Point C. of C., U. Wash. Alumni Assn. (life), Beta Alpha Psi. Democrat. Lodge: Lions (local pres. 1981-82). Office: Suite 103 Dwight Malott & Co PS CPA 3326 Smokey Point Dr Arlington WA 98223

MALOTT, JAMES RAYMOND, JR., lawyer; b. Globe, Ariz., Feb. 23, 1917; s. James Raymond and Edith (Spencer) M.; m. Carol Hover, Sept. 9, 1939 (div. Sept. 1948); children—James Spencer, Lucinda; m. Barbara Farr, Feb. 20, 1949 (div. Jan. 1974); m. Ruth Austin, Jan. 10, 1975 (dec. Jan. 1986). Student, U. Ariz., 1934-36; A.B., Stanford U., 1938, LL.B., 1941. Bar: Ariz. 1940. Dep. county atty. Gila County, 1943; practice in Globe, 1945—; mem. firm Morris & Malott, 1948—. Served to 2d lt. USAAF, 1944-45. Mem. State Bar Ariz. (bd. govs. 1955-60, v.p. 1959-60). Home: 1220 Skyline St Globe AZ 85501 Office: 1450 South St Globe AZ 85501

MALOTT, TIMOTHY GERALD, banker; b. Rochester, Ind., Feb. 11, 1953; s. Ronald Dean and Loa Eleanor (Leininger) M.; divorced; children—Daniel Kevin, Andrew Joseph. B.S. in Bus. Adminstrn., Valparaiso U., 1974. C.P.A., Calif. Mgr., Crowe, Chizek & Co., Michigan City, Ind., 1975-80; pres. First Nat. Bank of Crown Point, Ind., 1980-81; exec. v.p., chief fin. officer Bank of Commerce, San Diego, 1981—, also bd. dirs. Exec. com. Kearney-Mesa Planning Group; pres. LaPorte County Sheltered Workshop, Inc., Michigan City, 1980; chmn. adv. council Salvation Army Adult Rehab. Program, San Diego, 1984-85; treas. Jim Rady for City Council campaign, 1984. Mem. Ind. Soc. C.P.A.s (chpt. pres. 1978-79), Am. Inst. C.P.A.s, Nat. Assn. Accts. Republican. Methodist. Club: Exchange (pres. 1983-84, sec., dir. Child Abuse Prevention Ctr. San Diego, Exchangite of Yr. Michigan City 1979). Home: 14059A Mango Dr Del Mar CA 92014 Office: Bank of Commerce 8920 Miramar Rd Suite C San Diego CA 92126

MALOY, DANITA LOYE, marketing professional; b. Okmulgee, Okla., Sept. 17, 1946; d. Bud Ira and Gladys Laverne (Franz) Burkhart; m. Robert Albert Maloy, Mar. 15, 1974. BMus, U. Ark., 1969; MBA, Pepperdine U., 1982. Mktg. rep. Honeywell Info. Systems Inc. subs. Honeywell, Inc., Orange, Calif., 1976-77; field sales engr. Tex. Instruments, Irvine, Calif., 1977-81; product mgr. Lear Siegler, Anaheim, Calif., 1981-82; mgr. sales support Printronix, Irvine, 1982-83; mgr. mktg. support CIE Terminals Corp., Irvine, 1983-85, mgr. mktg. research, 1986—. Mem. Festival Singers (publicity chmn. 1985-86). Democrat. Club: Toastmasters (Costa Mesa, Calif.) (v.p. adminstrn. 1979-80). Avocations: singing, reading, tennis. Home: 26251 Buscador Mission Viejo CA 92692 Office: CIE Terminals 2505 McCabe Irvine CA 92714

MALPHURS, ROGER EDWARD, insurance company executive; b. Lake Worth, Fla., Dec. 15, 1933; s. Cecil Edward and Muriel Thelma (Ward) M.; m. Carolyn Sue Calapp, Feb. 2, 1963; children: Steven, Brian, Darren, Regina, Victoria. BS, U. Utah, 1961. Cert. med. technologist. Supr. spl. chemistry Cen. Pathology Lab., Santa Rosa, Calif., 1968-73; mgr. lab. Community Hosp., Santa Rosa, 1973-76; supr. chem., staff asst. Meml. Hosp., Santa Rosa, 1976-85; pres., chief exec. officer R.E. Malphurs Co., Sunnyvale, Calif., 1972—; owner, developer REMCO Mktg. Assocs., Santa Rosa, 1970-72, Better Bus. Forms and Typeset, Santa Rosa, 1977-81. Author: A New, Simple Way to Win at Blackjack, 1972. Served as squadron commdr. CAP USAF Aux., 1982-84. Mem. Am. Chiropractic Assn , Calif. Chiropractic Assn. Republican. Club: Optomists Internat. (Santa Rosa)(youth awards chmn. 1969-74). Avocations: flying, computers, pistol shooting, oil painting.

MALPHUS, EDWARD THOMAS, mechanical engineer; b. Phila., Dec. 3, 1956; s. Thomas Edward and Constance (Bavits) M.; m. Erin Ilene Johnson, Mar. 29, 1980; 1 child, Richard Octavius. Student, Mesa Jr. Coll., 1983—. Journeyman Water Sports, Inc., Memphis, 1976-80; robotics engring. aide Cipher Data Products, Inc., San Diego, 1984-86, assoc. engr. robotics, 1986—; modelmaker Promax Machine, San Diego, 1980—. Author: Death of a Species, 1983, Bred into Extinction, 1984; patentee in field. Served with USN, 1980-84. Avocations: archery, soccer, camping, reading. Home: 1375 Hemlock St Imperial Beach CA 92032 Office: Ciper Data Products Inc 10225 Willow Creek Rd San Diego CA 92032

MALTBY, HAZEL FARROW, weaver; b. San Francisco, Dec. 26, 1917; d. Richard Harry and Effie Isabelle (Hardin) Johnstone; student San Francisco State Coll., 1935-36; m. Jack Allen Maltby, Nov. 11, 1974; children—Charlene Sue McAuley, Claudia Jane Polzl. Tchr.-lectr. weaving Foothill Community Coll., Los Altos, Calif., De Anza Coll., Cupertino, Calif., 1973-74, Nat. Conf. Handweavers, San Francisco, 1974; pvt. tchr., 1970—; one-woman exhbns. include Menlo Park Civic Center, libraries and banks in Palo Alto, Woodside, Los Altos, San Jose, Calif., 1972-75, also exhibited San Jose Fine Art Mus., Triton Mus., San Jose, Calif. Art Festival, Nat. Conf. Handweavers, No. Calif. Handweavers Conf., Bay Area Arts and Crafts, Internat. Weaving exhbn., others; author: Painting Warps, 1974; group exhbns. include Los Vegas Art League, 1971, Tex. Fine Arts League, 1974, Internat. Weaving Exhbn., Kouvola, Finland, 1977; commd. to do 6 large tapestries Epiphany Episc. Ch., San Carlos; now weaving tapestries for indsl. firms. Mem. Palo Alto Art Club (v.p.), Trampornus Weaving Guild (past pres.), Handweavers Guild Am., Calif. PTA (hon. life; past pres. San Carlos). Clubs: Order Eastern Star, Order Jobs Daus. Address: 118 Plazoleta St Los Gatos CA 95030

MALTIN, FREDA, univ. adminstr.; b. Calgary, Alta., Can., June 4, 1923; d. Meyers Wolfe and Ida (Kohn) Rosen; came to U.S., 1958; diploma Garbutt's Bus. Coll., Calgary, 1942; m. Manny Nayton Maltin, Aug. 25, 1950; 1 son, Richard Allan. Various secretarial and bookkeeping positions, 1951-61; mem. adminstrv. staff U. So. Calif., 1961—, asst. to Dir. Center for Futures Research, Grad. Sch. Bus. Adminstrn., 1981—. Mem. Exec. Women International. Club: U. So. Calif. Staff (charter). Office: U So Calif Bridge 401 University Park Los Angeles CA 90089-1421

MALVEAUX, JULIANNE MARIE, economist; b. San Francisco, Sept. 22, 1953; d. Paul and Proteone Marie (Alexandria) M. BA, Boston Coll., 1974, MA, 1975; PhD, MIT, 1980. Jr. staff economist Council Econ. Advisor The White House, Washington, 1977-78; research fellow Rockefeller Found., N.Y.C., 1978-80; asst. prof. New Sch. Social Research, N.Y.C., 1980-81, San Francisco State U., 1981-85; vis. scholar U. Calif., Berkeley, 1985—; cons. women's issues, labor, edn. devel., 1981—. Contbg. editor: Essence mag., 1984—; co-editor Slipping Through the Cracks: Status of Black Women; contbr. articles to profl. jours. Founder, chmn. San Francisco Anti-Apartheid com., 1985-86; bd. dirs. Coleman Advs. Children Youth, San Francisco, 1985, Nat. Rainbow Coalition, Washington, 1986, NAACP, San Francisco, 1984, Dem. Women's Forum, San Francisco, 1983. Named one of Am.'s Top 100 Black Bus. and Profl. Women, Dollar and Sense Mag., 1985; postdoctoral fellow NRC, 1985-86. Mem. Comparable Worth Project (v.p. 1984-86). Roman Catholic. Home: 226 Kingston St San Francisco CA 94110 Office: U Calif Inst Indsl Relations 2521 Channing Way Berkeley CA 94570

MAMMEN, WILLIAM PATTERSON, architect; b. Shelbyville, Ill., Apr. 28, 1949; s. William Ernest and Dorothy June (Patterson) M.; m. Kay Elizabeth Morrison, Dec. 21, 1973; children - Taylor Gilbert, Kyle Patterson, Jenni Elizabeth, Hillary Joyce. B.S., MIT, 1971; M. Arch., U. Wash., 1978. Registered architect, Calif., Wash., Utah. Project architect Allen Knowles & Miller, Santa Ana, Calif., 1971-73; jr. assoc. Lee Knell & Assocs., Provo, Utah, 1973-75; dir. architecture Carothers & Assoc., Seattle, 1975-76; research asst. U. Wash. Sch. Architecture, Seattle, 1976-78; project architect Knowles & LaBonte, Irvine, Calif., 1978-79; co-founder, pres. Mammen Assoc. Architecture, Inc. (formerly Reynolds & Mammen), Park City, Utah, 1979-86, prin. Mammen Assocs. for Advancement of Architecture, 1986—; dir. A/E Design Group Utah, Park City, 1982-83; cons. Mem. Park City Planning Commn., Utah, 1980-82; commr. Park City Hist. Dist., 1980-82; del. Summit County Rep. Conv., Utah, 1982-86; active Boy Scouts Am. Recipient Owens-Corning Energy award, 1975, others. Mem. AIA, Tau Sigma Delta. Republican. Mormon. Office: 613 Main St PO Box 1720 Park City UT 84060

MAN, GUY KEE, aerospace and mechanical engineer; b. Kowloon, Hong Kong, May 27, 1951; came to U.S., 1970, naturalized, 1985; s. Hon Kwong and Sau Ching (Luk) M.; B.S., U. Redlands, 1974; M.S., Stanford U., 1975, M.E., Ph.D., 1979; m. Debra Y. K. Ching, Dec. 15, 1979. Sr. engr. guidance and control sect. Jet Propulsion Lab., Calif. Inst. Tech., Pasadena, Calif., 1979-82, tech. group leader, 1982-83, tech. group, supr. guidance and control analysis group, 1982-86, tech. group supt. system design and integration guidance and control sect., 1986—; cons. in dynamics, kinematics, controls, automation, seismic analysis and software devel., 1982-84. Registered profl. engr., Calif. Mem. AIAA, ASME, Calif. Soc. Profl. Engrs., Nat. Soc. Profl. Engrs., Sigma Xi. Contbr. tech. articles to various publs. Home: 2158 Valentine Pl San Marino CA 91108

MANAGO, GARY HIDEO, food service instructor; b. Honolulu, Nov. 14, 1954; s. Harry Yoshinori and Nancy Hisae (Yonemura) M. BEd, U. Hawaii, 1977. Asst. mgr. Plaza Coffee Shop, Honolulu, 1977-80, gen. mgr., 1981-82; mgr. Summery Coffee Shop, Honolulu, 1980-81; instr. Kapiolani Community Coll., Honolulu, 1982—; asst. Maitre d'Maile Restaurant, Honolulu, 1983—; cons. KC Drive In-Manoa, Honolulu, 1984-85. Mem. Soc. Wine Educators, Profl. Cooks Hawaii (sec. 1984-85), Hawaii Vocat. Assn., German Wine Soc., Nat. Restaurant Assn. Avocations: golfing, bowling. Home: 1641 St Louis Dr Honolulu HI 96816 Office: U Hawaii Kapiolani Community Coll 620 Pensacola St Honolulu HI 96814

MANALO, PACITA BARBAZA, physician, pathology educator; b. Manila, Philippines, May 17, 1932; d. Carlos and Magalena (Barbaza) M.; m. Hector C. De Los Santos, Aug. 5, 1982. A.A., U. Santo Tomas, Manila, 1950; M.D., U. Santo Tomas, Manila, 1955; M.S. in Pathology, Northwestern U., Chgo., 1963. Diplomate Am. Bd. Pathology. Rotating intern General Rose Meml. Hosp., Univ. Colo., Denver, 1955-56; resident in pathology St. Joseph's Hosp., Denver, 1956-59; resident clin. pathology Evanston (Ill.) Hosp. and Northwestern Univ., 1959-60, Postdoctoral fellow in pathology, 1960-61; pathologist anatomic surg. pathology, cytopathology VA Med Ctr., Reno, Nev., 1975-83, chief anatomic pathology service, 1983—; attending pathology Evanston Hosp., Ill., 1961-75, dir. cytology, cytogenetics, 1961-75, dir. Blood Bank, 1967-75, dir. Sch. Med. Tech., 1970-75, instr. pathology residency tng. program in anatomical and clin. pathology, 1961-75; mem. staff Washoe Med. Ctr., St. Mary's Hosp., Reno. Instr. pathology Northwestern Univ. Med. Sch., Chgo., 1960-67, asst. prof. pathology, 1967-74, assoc. prof. pathlogy, 1974-75; vis. prof. pathology Karolinska Inst. and Huddinge Hosp., Sweden, 1974; assoc. prof. pathology U. Nev. Sch. Medicine, Reno, 1975—, acting chmn. dept. lab. medicine and pathology, 1982-84, med. dir. med. tech. program, 1980-84. Contbr. numerous articles to various publs. Mem. blood donor recruitment program Northsuburban Blood Center, Northbrook, Ill., 1971-75, mem. med. adv. bd., 1971-75; mem. commn. allied health fields Washoe County Med. Soc., 1979-80; mem. clin. com. No. Nev. Cancer Council, 1977—; mem. med. adv. com. Reno Planned Parenthood No. Nev., Reno, 1981—; chmn. advance gifts com., med. dir. Easter Seal Treatment Ctr., Sparks, Nev., 1976-79, 1979-80; bd. dirs. Easter Seal Soc. Crippled Children Nev., Sparks, 1976-79; chmn., coordinator tumor bd., cancer bd. VA Med. Ctr., 1978—; mem. med. students admissions com. U. Nevada, Sch. Medicine, Reno, 1975—; bd. dirs. Nev. Easter Seal Soc., Reno, 1976-79. Research grantee Chgo. and Ill. Heart Assn., 1964-72, G. D. Searle & Co., Chgo., 1968-69, Eli Lilly Co., Indpls., 1969-71, Reno Cancer Center, 1980-81. Republican. Roman Catholic. Home: 3455 San Mateo Ave Reno NV 89509 Office: VA Med Ctr 1000 Locust St Reno NV 89520 Office: U Nev Sch Medicine Manville Bldg Reno NV 89557

MANARY, RICHARD DEANE, manufacturing executive; b. Des Moines, Nov. 11, 1944; s. Robert Claude and Veronica (Cornwell) M.; m. Eileen Cecile, Aug. 16, 1986; children: (Erica (dec.), Matthew, Stephen. AA in Indsl. Engring., Southwestern Coll., 1976; BA in History, Calif. State U., San Diego, 1967, BS in Edn., 1973. Registered profl. engr., Calif. Mfg. engr. Rohr Industries, San Diego, 1967-78; chief research and devel. Rohr Industries, Riverside, Calif., 1978-80, project mfg. mgr., 1980-84; dep. program mgr. Rohr Industries, Wichita, Kans., 1984-87; program mgr. Rohr Industries, Riverside, 1987—. Contbr. articles to profl. jours. Chmn. Rohr Industries Co. Employee and Community Assistance Program, Riverside, 1981-85; adv. Jr. Achievement, Riverside chpt., 1978-79. Mem. Soc. Mfg. Engrs. (sr., assoc., chmn. 1978-79), Soc. Automotive Engrs., Soc. Material and Process Engrs., Am. Soc. Metals, Nat. Mgmt. Assn. (chmn. 1980-81). Democrat. Roman Catholic. Avocations: backpacking, skiing, stamp collecting, travel. Home: 23816 Cold Spring Rd Moreno Valley CA 92388 Office: Rohr Industries PO Box 878 Chula Vista CA 92012

MANAUT, FRANK J., banker; b. 1924; married. B.S., UCLA, 1947. With Standard Oil Co., 1947-50; with Bank of Hawaii, 1950—, chmn. bd., chief exec. officer, dir.; chmn. bd., chief exec. officer Bancorp Hawaii, 1980—. Office: Bank of Hawaii Inc 111 S King St Box 2900 Honolulu HI 96813 *

MANCERA, FERNANDO ORTEGA, packing and recycling company executive; b. Mexico City, June 25, 1958; came to U.S., 1959; s. Fernando Mancera Vélez and Josefina (Mancera) Ortega. Student, CETYS, Mexicali Baja, Mex., 1974-76, CETYS, Mexicali Baja, Mex., 1976-80. Fund raising supr. Centro de Enseñanza Tecnica y Superior, 1978-80, fund raising program dir., 1980-82; pres. Procesador de Chatarra, Mexicali Baja, 1982—; vice chmn. Palmar Santa Anita, Mexicali Baja, 1982—. Sponsor CETYS, Mexicali, 1982—, bd. dirs. Roman Catholic. Avocations: horse back riding, water and snow skiing, hunting. Home: Viena 152 VillaFontana, Mexicali Baja Mexico Office: Procesador de Chatarra PO Box 2751 Calexico CA 92231 also: Ap P1-943, Mexicali Baja Mexico

MANCH, RICHARD ALAN, physician; b. Buffalo, Jan. 6, 1944; s. Joseph R. and Dorothy (Strom) M.; m. Raimonde Bastine Harriman, July 9, 1974; children: Eric Scott, Allison Rebecca. BA magna cum laude, SUNY, Buffalo, 1965, MD, 1971; fellow in gastroenterology, U. N.Mex., 1974-76. Diplomate Am. Bd. Internal Medicine, Nat. Bd. Med. Examiners. Intern in Internal Medicine SUNY, Buffalo, 1971-72; resident in Internal Medicine Maricopa Med. Ctr., Phoenix, 1972-74; practice medicine specializing in gastrontology Phoenix, 1976—; dir. gastroenterology fellowship Good Samaritan Med. Ctr., Phoenix, 1985—, cons., 1976—, chmn. Samaritan Health Plan, 1985—, chief of medicine, 1985—; clin. asst. prof. medicine U. Ariz., Phoenix, 1986—; cons. in gastroenterology Humana Hosp., Phoenix, 1976—, St. Lukes Hosp., Phoenix, 1976, St. Josephs Hosp., Phoenix, 1980—. Mem. AMA, ACP, AM. Gastroenterol. Assn., Am. Soc. Gastrointestinal Endoscopy, Ariz. State Med. Assn., Phi Beta Kappa. Jewish. Mem. AMA, Ariz. State Med. Assn., Am. Soc. Gastrointestinal Endoscopy, Am. Gastroenterol. Assn., Am. Coll. Physicians, Phi Beta Kappa. Home: 3116 N 52d St Phoenix AZ 85018 Office: Gastrointestinal Assn PA 1300 N 12th St #610 Phoenix AZ 85006

MANCHESTER, SCOTT OWEN, social worker; b. Mpls., Dec. 4, 1951; s. Owen Russell and Carol Ruth (Johnson) M. BA, Northwestern U., 1973; MSW, Portland State U., 1978. TB control worker Peace Corps, Jecheon, Republic of Korea, 1974-76; sr. planner Eastern Oreg. Health Systems Agy., Redmond, 1979-84; health systems analyst Northwest Oreg. Health Systems, Portland, 1978-79, State Health Planning and Devel. Agy., Salem, Oreg., 1984—. Mem. Nat. Assn. Social Workers (state bd. dirs. 1985—, legis. action com. chmn. 1984—), Sierra Club. Democrat. Soc. Friends. Avocations: backpacking, cross-country skiing. Office: State Health Planning and Devel Agy 3886 Beverly NE Suite 19 Salem OR 97305

MANCINELLI, JACOB EMIL, corp. exec., consultant; b. Smock, Pa., Oct. 1, 1919; s. Joseph and Claudia (Di Russo) M.; B.A., Harvard U., 1948; m. Sumiko Ogura; children—Teresa Ann, Kathryn Jean, Robin. With fin. dept. Gen. Electric Co. and G.E. C.C., Louisville, 1948-62; sr. v.p. U.S. Leasing Corp., San Francisco, 1962-69; sec., dir. Silver State Leasing Corp.; v.p., dir. Air Lease Corp., Barrel Leasing Corp., Cargo Vans Ltd., Comml. Pacific Corp., Fleet Leasing Corp., San Francisco, 1962-69; pres., dir. Compass Fin. Corp. (formerly Whittaker Leasing Corp.), Burlingame, Calif., 1969-73; pres., dir. TRE Fin. Corp., San Mateo, Calif., 1973-74; chmn. bd., pres. Dome Fin. Corp., Burlingame, 1974—; chmn. bd. Highridge, Inc., Redwood City, Calif., 1974-81; owner The Dome Co., Dome Realty, San Mateo, Calif., 1980—; instr. U. Calif. Extension. Pres., Foster City (Calif.) Home Improvement Assn., 1964-66; mem. Foster City Park and Recreation Commn., 1968—; chmn. Foster City Com. for Better Govt., 1973—; chmn. bd. United Assn. Union City, 1986-87; exec. bd. San Mateo council Boy Scouts Am.; bd. dirs. Foster City Community Assn., 1972—, pres., 1973—; chmn. bd. United Assn. Union City, 1986—. Served as officer USAF, 1939-54. Decorated Air medal with 2 clusters, Presdl. citation. Mem. Nat. Comml. Fin. Conf. (dir. 1967—), Greater San Francisco (mcpl. legis. com. 1967-69), Foster City (dir. 1972) chambers commerce, Internat. Platform Assn., Res. Officers Assn. Roman Catholic (council 1972—). Clubs: Commonwealth of Calif., Marina Point Tennis (pres.), Arnhem 1944 Vets. Author: Love Thoughts and Other Things, 1980. Home: 4927 Antioch Loop Union City CA 94587 Office: PO Box 381 Union City CA 94587

MANCINO, JOHN GREGORY, software company executive; b. N.Y.C., Nov. 14, 1946; s. John D. and Carmela A. Mancino; B.A., Colgate U., 1968. Chief appraiser Rusciano Appraisers & Cons., N.Y.C., 1968-70; v.p. Pisces Prodns., Boulder, Colo., 1971-73; v.p. ops. Celestial Seasonings Inc., Boulder, 1973-84, also dir.; bd. dirs. Computer Connection, Inc., Mr. Software, Inc., Spruce St. Mktg., Inc., Fortune 44 Co., Inc.; pres., bd. dirs. Decision Makers Software, 1984—; chmn. Generation 5 Tech., 1985—, Preferred Bus. Investments, Ltd., 1986—. Home: Mount Mead Boulder CO 80302 Office: 1910 Joslyn Pl Boulder CO 80302

MANDEBERG, JEAN ANN, artist, art educator; b. Detroit, Aug. 7, 1950; d. Mitchell Raymond and Nancy Elizabeth (Markus) M.; m. Joel Greene, July 27, 1986. BA, U. Mich., 1972; MFA, Idaho State U., 1977. Mem. fine arts Faculty The Evergreen State Coll., Olympia, Wash., 1978—. Recipient Art in Pub. Places award Wash. State Arts Com., Seattle, 1986; grantee The Evergreen Found., 1984. Mem. Am. Craft Council, Soc. N.Am. Goldsmiths, N.W. Designer Craftsmen. Office: Evergreen State Coll Olympia WA 98505

MANDEL, BENJAMIN JORGE, dentist, consultant; b. Mexico City, May 13, 1944; s. Maurice and Victoria (Eskenazi) M.; m. Olga Sherr, Dec. 27, 1970; children—Joshua, Jonathan. B.S. in Chemistry, U. Calif.-Berkeley, 1966; M.S. in Chemistry, C.I.E.A.-I.P.N., Mexico City, 1969; D.D.S., NYU, 1975. Research asst. C.I.E.A.-I.P.N., 1967-69; research assoc. U. Wis.-Madison, 1970-71, Hoffman La Roche, Nutley, N.J., 1971-72; gen. practice resident VA Hosp., Martinez, Calif., 1975-76; gen. practice dentistry, San Jose, Calif., 1976—; cons. Mission Convalescent Home, San Jose, 1976, Child Health and Disability Prevention Program, San Jose, 1978-80; lectr. profl. meetings. Author: Dentistry for the 21st Century. Vol. Kron Health Fair, San Jose, 1977; TV guest People and Progress Show, 1985. Recipient appreciation award Mexican Ctr. for Research and Oral Rehab., 1984; Herman Muehlstein scholar, 1974. Mem. ADA, Calif. Dental Assn. (lectr. annual meetings 1984—, presenter ann. meeting 1986), Santa Clara County Dental Soc. (hosp. and dental health com. 1978-81), Am. Soc. Clin. Hypnosis, Western Soc. Periodontology (bd. dirs. 1982—), Am. Acad. Gnathological Orthopedics, Santa Clara Periodontics Study Club (founder, chmn. 1980—), Internat. Platfrom Assn., Alpha Omega. Republican. Office: 74 Harold Ave San Jose CA 95117

MANDEL, WILLIAM JAY, cardiologist; b. N.Y.C., Apr. 18, 1937; s. Nathan and Vera (Ferguson) M.; m. Diane Marilyn Isaacs, June 23, 1963; children: Stacey Pamela, William Jay Jr. BA, U. Va., 1958; MD, Downstate Med. Ctr., 1962. Intern Downstate Med. Ctr., N.Y.C., 1962-63, jr. asst. resident, 1963-64, chief med. resident, 1967-68; research fellow electrophysiology Upstate Med. Ctr., Syracuse, N.Y., 1966-67, Columbia U. Coll. of Physicians and Surgeons, N.Y.C., 1968-70; dir. clin. electrophysiology Cedars Sinai Med. Ctr., Los Angeles, 1980—; prof. medicine UCLA Sch. Medicine, 1982—. Editor: (med. textbook) Cardiac Arrhythms, 1981, 2d rev. edit. 1986; contbr. numerous articles to profl. jours. Served to capt. M.C., U.S. Army, 1964-66. Fellow Am. Coll. Cardiology, ACP, Am. Coll. Chest Physicians, Council Clin. Cardiology of Am. Heart Assn. Democrat. Mem. Soc. Friends. Club: Hillcrest. Avocation: golf. Office: 414 N Camden Dr Beverly Hills CA 90210

MANDELBAUM, KIM IRENE, lawyer; b. Las Vegas, Nev., Sept. 5, 1956; d. Jack Mandelbaum and Ruby Edith Young; m. Lawrence M. Allen, Nov. 29, 1986. BA in Polit. Sci., U. San Diego, 1978; JD, Calif. Western Sch. Law, 1983. Bar: Nev. 1984. Assoc. Gifford & Vernon, Las Vegas, 1984—. State and County del. Dem. party, 1986; mem. Young Dems. Clark County, 1986. Mem. ABA, Clark County Bar Assn., Nev. State Bar Assn., Nev. Trial Lawyers Assn., Assn. Trial Lawyers Am., Attys. Without Wives (founder), Planned Parenthood (bd. dirs. So. Nev. chpt.). Avocations: golf, softball, big-game fishing. Office: Gifford & Vernon 601 S Rancho Suite C23 Las Vegas NV 89106

MANDELL, GORDON KEITH, aerospace engineer; b. N.Y.C., Mar. 6, 1947; s. Bertram Herman and Maria Catherine (O'Hagan) M. BS, MIT, 1969, MS, 1970. Research aerospace engr. MIT, Cambridge, Mass., 1970-72; aero. cons. Eagle River, Alaska, 1972-76, designated engring. rep., 1976-82; aerospace engr. FAA, Anchorage, 1982—. Author/editor: Topics in Advanced Model Rocketry, 1973; mng. editor Model Rocketry mag., Cambridge, 1968-72; contbr. articles to profl. jours. NSF fellow, MIT, 1969; scholar Grumman Aerospace Corp., MIT, 1965. Mem. Nat. Assn. Rocketry, Sigma Xi, Sigma Gamma Tau, Tau Beta Pi. Buddhist. Avocations: rural living, model building, home computing. Home: PO Box 1061 Eagle River AK 99577 Office: FAA Aircraft Cert ANM-100A 701 C St Box 14 Anchorage AK 99513

MANDELL, WAYNE ALAN, petroleum geologist; b. Plainfield, N.J., Jan. 4, 1947; s. Arthur Andrew and Dorothy Louise (Wiess) M.; m. Sharon Lee Zeillmann, Mar. 30, 1968 (div. Dec. 1979); children—Heather Ann, Christopher Wayne; m. Linda Louise Van Kleef, 1985. B.A. in Geology, U. Louisville, 1973; M.S. in Geology, Eastern Ky. U., 1975. Cert. petroleum geologist. Geologist IV, Mobil Oil Co., New Orleans, 1975-81; sr. geologist Natomas N.Am., Denver, 1981-84; profl. geologist Amerada Hess, Denver, 1984-86; cons. to Marschang Engrs. and Columbine Resources, Denver, 1986—. Author: Transition of Environments Across Silvro-Ordivician Boundary; West Side of Cincinnati Arch, 1975. Mem. Young Republicans, Denver. Served with USCG, 1967-71. Mem. Am. Assn. Petroleum Geologists, Rocky Mountain Assn. Geologists, Soc. Econ. Paleontologists and Mineralogists, Am. Legion. Lutheran. Club: KodoKan (Tokyo). Home and Office: 1200 S Forest St Denver CO 80222

MANDLER, GEORGE, psychologist; b. Vienna, Austria, June 11, 1924; came to U.S., 1940, naturalized, 1943; s. Richard and Hede (Goldschmied) M.; m. Jean Matter, Jan. 19, 1957; children: Peter Clark, Michael Allen. B.A., NYU, 1949; M.S., Yale U., 1950, Ph.D., 1953; postgrad., U. Basel, Switzerland, 1947-48. Asst. prof. Harvard U., 1953-57, lectr., 1957-60; prof. U. Toronto, Ont., Can., 1960-65; prof. psychology, dir. Ctr. Human Info. Processing U. Calif.-San Diego, 1965—, chmn. dept. psychology, 1965-70. Author: books the most recent being Mind and Emotion, 1975, (German edit.), 1980, Mind and Body, 1984, Cognitive Psychology, 1985; contbr. articles and revs. to profl. jours.; editor: Psychol. Rev., 1970-76. Served with U.S. Army, 1943-46. Fellow Ctr. for Advanced Study in Behavioral Scis., 1959-60; vis. fellow Oxford U., Eng., 1971-72, 78; Guggenheim fellow, 1971-72; hon. research fellow Univ. Coll., London U., 1977-78, 82—. Fellow AAAS; mem. Am. Assn. Advancement Psychology (trustee 1974-82), Psychonomic Soc. (governing bd., chmn. 1983), Am. Psychol. Assn. (pres. div. exptl. psychology 1978-79, pres. div. gen psychology 1982-83, mem. council reps. 1978-82, William James prize 1986), Internat. Union Psychol. Scis. (U.S. com. 1985—), Soc. Exptl. Psychologists, Fedn. Behavioral Psychol. and Cognitive Scis. (pres. 1981), AAUP. Home: 1406 La Jolla Knoll La Jolla CA 92037 Office: U Calif San Diego Dept Psychology La Jolla CA 92093

MANDRA, YORK T., geology educator; b. N.Y.C., Nov. 24, 1922; s. Raymond and Irene (Farruggio) M.; m. Highohi Kechijian, Jan. 26, 1946. BA, U. Calif., Berkeley, 1947, MA in Paleontology, 1949; PhD in Geology, Stanford U., 1958. From instr. to assoc. prof. geology San Francisco State U., 1950-63, prof., 1964—, head geology sect., chmn. dept. 1960-67; vis. prof. U. Aix-Marseille, France, 1959, Syracuse U., summer 1963, U. Maine, summer 1969, U. Calif., Santa Barbara, summers 1972—; research assoc. U. Glasgow, 1959, Calif. Acad. Scis., 1966—; vis. scientist New Zealand Geol. Survey, fall 1970. Contbr. numerous articles to profl. jours. Pres. David S. Sohigian Found., 1975—. Served with USAAF, 1942-46. Teaching fellow Danforth Found., 1958, NSF, 1959; research grantee NSF, 1967-77; recipient Neil Miner Disting. Coll. Teaching award, 1984. Fellow Calif. Acad. Scis., Geol. Soc. Am., AAAS; mem. Nat. Assn. Geology Tchrs. (pres. Far Western sect. 1953-54, 73-74, Robert Wallace Webb award 1977), Paleontol. Soc., Soc. Econ. Mineralogists and Paleontologists, Soc. for Environ. Geochemistry and Health. Avocations: walking, reading, music. Home: 8 Bucareli Dr San Francisco CA 94132 Office: San Francisco State U Dept Geoscis 1600 Holloway Ave San Francisco CA 94132

MANDT, DOUGLAS KERMIT, chemist, educator, lab safety consultant; b. Chgo., Sept. 8, 1935; s. Konrad Ingman and Myrtle (Moen) M.; m. Carol Lynn Breece, June 8, 1958; children: Laurel Kay, Eric Douglas. BA, Pacific Luth. U., 1957; MS, U. Wis., 1962. Cert. secondary tchr., Wash. Quality control technician Monsanto Chem. Co., Seattle, 1957; tchr. math. and sci. Boisfort High Sch., Klaber, Wash., 1957-58; tchr. chemistry and dist. sci. coordinator Summer (Wash.) Sch. Dist., 1958—; instr. sci. methods Pacific Luth. U., Tacoma, Wash., 1969, U. Puget Sound, Tacoma, 1975-77, chemistry edn. U. Wash., Seattle, 1985-86, chemistry Ft. Steilacoom Community Coll., 1977-79; computer rep. Tex. Instruments, Dallas, 1981-83. Author: CHEM13 Cycle of Copper; co-author Guidelines and Recommendations for Teaching Chemistry, 1983, Guidelines for Science Education in the State of Washington, 1985. Recipient Pres. Recognition award Wash. State, 1983; named Dreyfus Master Tchr. Dreyfus Found. and Woodrow Wilson Nat. Fellowship Found., 1984; NIH Centenniel teacher, State of Wash., 1987. Mem. Am. Chem. Soc. (Outstanding Chemistry Tchr. award Puget Sound sect. 1983, regional award for chemistry teaching Northwest region 1984), Nat. Sci. Tchrs. Assn., Wash. Edn. Assn., Nat. Sci. Suprs. Assn., Nat. Assn. Biology Tchrs., NEA, Wash. Sci. Teachers Assn., Phi Delta Kappa. Avocations: photography, fishing, reading. Home: 4525 126th Ave Ct E Sumner WA 98390 Office: Sumner Sr High Sch 1707 Main St Sumner WA 98390

MANEA-MANOLIU, MARIA ION, linguistics educator; b. Galatz, Romania, Mar. 12, 1934; came to U.S., 1978; d. Ion T. and Ana S. (Codescu) Manoliu; m. Ion S. Manea, Nov. 26, 1968. BA, French Coll., Galatz, 1951; MA, U. Bucharest, Romania, 1955, PhD, 1966. Asst. prof. linguistics U. Bucharest, 1957-61, assoc. prof., 1961-68; prof. U. Calif., Davis, 1978—; vis. prof. U. Chgo., 1972-74; cons. NEH, 1980—; mem. adv. bd. Romance Philology, Berkeley, Calif., 1984—. Author: Sistematica Substitutelor, 1968 (Ministry of Edn. award 1968), Gramatica Comparată, 1971, El Estructuralismo Lingüistico, 1979, Tipología e Historia, 1985; editor-in chief Bull. de la S.R.L.R., Bucharest, 1975-78; corresponding editor Revue Romane, Copenhagen, 1972—; contbr. articles to profl. jours. Grantee Internat. Com. Linguists, 1972, Fulbright, 1972-74, U. Calif., 1979—. Mem. Am. Romanian Acad. (pres. 1982—), Soc. de Linguistique Romane, Soc. Roumaine de Linguistique Romane (v.p. 1974-78), Internat. Assn. Hist. Linguistics, MLA, Linguistics Soc. Am. Avocations: tourism, gardening, knitting. Office: U Calif Dept French and Italian 506 Sproul Hall Davis CA 95616

MANEATIS, GEORGE A., utility company executive; b. 1926. BS in Elec. Engring., Stanford U., 1949, MS in Elec. Engring., 1950. With Gen. Elec. Co., 1950-53; with Pacific Gas & Elec. Co., San Francisco, 1953—, v.p., 1979-81, sr. v.p., 1981-82, exec. v.p., 1982-86, pres., 1986—, also dir. Office: Pacific Gas & Electric Co 77 Beale St San Francisco CA 94106 *

MANEVAL, DAVID RICHARD, mineral beneficiation educator, consultant; b. Williamsport, Pa., Dec. 18, 1928; s. Paul D. and Julia (Heisler) M.; m. Lyne Page Heisley, Feb. 25, 1951; children—David Richard Jr., Michael, Holly Maneval McDonaugh, Laurie Maneval Zellers. B.S., Pa. State U., 1950, M.S., 1957, Ph.D., 1961. Asst. prof. mineral preparation Pa. State U., State College, 1961-63; dir. research Pa. Dept. Mines, Harrisburg, 1963-69; dep. sec. Pa. Dept. Environment, Harrisburg, 1969-70; sci. advisor Appalachian Regional Com., Washington, D.C., 1971-78; asst. dir. Office Surface Mining, Washington, D.C., 1979-81; prof. mineral beneficiation U. Alaska, Fairbanks, 1981—; freelance cons., 1961—. Contbr. articles and chpts. to profl. publs. Mem. Coll. Area Sch. Bd., State College, Pa., 1957-63; chmn. adv. com. Bur. Land Mgmt. Fairbanks dist. 1983—, mem. Fairbanks Council Boy Scouts Am. Served with U.S. Army, 1950-52. Recipient Superior Service award U.S. Dept. Interior, 1979. Mem. Am. Chem. Soc., AIME (recipient environ. conservation disting. service award 1980), Alaska Miners Assn., Sigma Xi. Republican. Presbyterian. Lodges: Rotary (bd. dirs. 1983, sec. 1985), Elks. Home: 460 Lone Pine Dr Fairbanks AK 99709 Office: Univ Alaska Sch Mineral Engring Fairbanks AK 99775

MANG, JOHN CHUNG YUEN, mechanical engineer; b. Canton, People's Republic of China, Apr. 10, 1944; came to U.S., 1972; s. Tim Yau and Wai Yee (Poon) M.; m. Carmelita Setero Chu, June 16, 1972; children: Emily Suzanne, Olivia Carol. BSc, U. Hong Kong, 1969, diploma mgmt. studies, 1972; MS in Indsl. and Systems Engring., U. So. Calif., 1976, MS in Ops. Research, 1978. Registered profl. engr., Calif. Mgr. engring. Progressive Indsl. Co., Hong Kong, 1969-72; mgr. quality control Romalite, Inc., Compton, Calif., 1972-80; supr. quality engring. Hughes Helicopters, Inc., Culver City, Calif., 1980-82; sr. project engr. Hughes Aircraft Co., El Segundo, Calif., 1982—. Mem. Am. Soc. Quality Control (cert.), Soc. Mfg. Engrs. (cert.). Home: 6413 W 80th Pl Los Angeles CA 90045 Office: Hughes Aircraft Co El Segundo CA 90245

MANGALIK, AROOP, medical oncology educator; b. Agra, India, Oct. 10, 1935; came to U.S., 1976; s. Vanmali Saran and Parvati (Mithal) M.; m. Asha Lata Gupta, Jan. 25, 1959 (div. Aug. 22, 1986); 1 child, Saurabh. BS in Medicine, Surgery, King George's Med. Coll., Lucknow, India, 1958; MD, All India Inst. Med. Scis., New Delhi, 1962. Asst. prof. oncology All India Inst. Med. Scis., 1966-71, assoc. prof., 1971-76; asst. prof. U. Colo., Denver, 1976-81; adj. clin. prof. U. N.Mex., Albuquerque, 1982—; cons. Nat. Cancer Inst., Bethesda, Md., 1979—. Author: Follow up of Cancer Patients, 1982; also articles to profl. jours. V.p. Zero Popluation Growth, Denver, 1980, Physicians for Social Responsibility, Albuquerque, 1986. Mem. Am. Soc. Hematology, Am. Soc. Clin. Oncology. Home: 1415 Quincy NE Albuquerque NM 87110 Office: U NMex Cancer Ctr 900 Camino de Salud NE Albuquerque NM 87131

MANGAN, PAUL CHARLES, real estate executive; b. Lynn. Mass., Jan. 19, 1946; s. James Lawrence and Mary Patricia M.; cert. in real estate Cerritos (Calif.) Coll., 1976; m. Deborah Mary; children—Kivi Anne, Krishawn Annette. Service adv. Chaffee Motors Co., Hawthorne, Calif., 1968-73; salesman Red Carpet Realtors, Cerritos, 1973-74; owner, realtor The Great Am. Real Estate Co., Cerritos, 1975-78, Mangan & Assn. Realtors, 1978-84; v.p., gen. mgr. Bishop Hawk Comml. Indsl. Real Estate Brokers, Costa Mesa, Calif., 1984-86; dir. tng. and investments Century 21 Region V, Inc., West Covina, Calif., 1986—. Commr. Los Angeles Citizens Adv. Commn. on Community Devel.; bd. dirs. Rancho Los Cerritos Bd. Realtors, 1979-81, now v.p. Cert. tchr. real estate, Calif. Commr. Los Angeles County- Cerritos Regional Park Authority. Served with USMC, 1964-68. Mem. Bldg. Industry Assn. (treas. comml./indsl. council Orange County chpt.), Cerritos C. of C. (pres. 1977-78), Nat. Assn. Realtors, Cerritos Jaycees (past dir.), Calif. Assn. Realtors (dir., regional liaison local govtl. realtions com.). Roman Catholic. Lodge: Optimists. Home: 18725 Alfred St Cerritos CA 90701 Office: 100 N Citrus Ave West Covina CA 91791

MANGAN, TERENCE JOSEPH, police chief; b. Utica, N.Y., Feb. 17, 1938; s. Lawrence and Eloise (Roth) M.; m. Charlotte Mauss, June 19, 1971; children—Sean, Megan. B.A., St. Mary's Coll., Norwalk, Conn., 1961; M.A., St. Albert's Coll., 1965; postgrad. in Pub. Adminstrn., Adminstrn. Justice, U. So. Calif., 1972-76; Grad. FBI Nat. Acad. Cert. Wash. State Criminal Justice Tng. Commn., Calif. Peace Officers Standards and Tng. Commn.; grad. Northwest Law Enforcement Exec. Command Coll., 1986; cert. Gov.'s Rev. Tean Child Abuse Services, 1986. With Seaside (Calif.) Police Dept., 1968-72; with Lakewood (Calif.) Police Dept., 1972-76, chief, dir. community safety, to 1976; chief Bellingham (Wash.) Police Dept., 1976—; chmn. Wash. State Criminal Justice Tng. Commn.; mem. Mgmt. Adv. Group Organized Crime and Narcotics Enforcement; lectr. FBI Acad. Pres., bd. dirs. United way, Whatcom County, Calif.; mem. archdiocesan steering com. 1982 Ann. Catholic Appeal. Recipient Disting. Service award City of Seaside, 1972; citation U.S. Secret Service, 1969; Congressional Com. Internal Security, 1971; Disting. Service award City of Lakewood, also Wash. Assn. Sheriffs and Police Chiefs, 1978-81; Law Enforcement Officer of Yr. award Wash. VFW, 1980; Community Service award Wash. Toastmasters Internat., 1980; Pres. award Pacific Lutheran U., 1981; Paul Harris fellow Rotary Internat., 1986. Mem. Internat. Assn. Chiefs Police, Nat. Council Crime and Delinquency, Wash. Assn. Sheriffs and Police Chiefs (past pres.), Internat. Peace Arch Law Enforcement Council. Roman Catholic. Office: Police Dept Hdqtrs 210 Lottie St Bellingham WA 98225

MANGEL, LEROY DWIGHT, information systems professional; b. Westby, Mont., Oct. 18, 1945; s. Ervin LeRoy and Phyllis Delphine (Hereim) M.; m. Jane Irene Wisness, Dec. 27, 1969; children: Lisa Jane, Lori Jo. AS in Data Processing, N.D. State Sch. of Sci., 1969; BS in Computer Mgmt. Sci., Met. State Coll., Denver, 1985. Cert. systems profl. Programmer Blue Cross/Blue Shield, Fargo, N.D., 1969-72; programmer analyst Northwestern Nat. Ins. Corp., Milw., 1972-74; systems analyst Green Giant Co., Le Sueur, Minn., 1974-79; systems and programming mgr. Homestake Mining Co., Golden, Colo., 1979-81, system planning and support mgr., 1982-85, computer systems mgr., 1985—. Served with USAF, 1963-67. Mem. Data Processing Mgmt. Assn., Golden Key Nat. Hon. Soc. (life). Lutheran. Avocations: fishing, camping, woodworking, antique and classic automobiles. Office: Homestake Mining Co 1726 Cole Blvd Golden CO 80401

MANGELS, BARBARA JEAN, speech and language pathologist; b. Phila., Nov. 27, 1947; d. Alfred P. and Jean (Chute) M. BA, Mary Washington Coll., 1969; MEd, U. Va., 1970. Outpatient speech and language pathologist Glendale (Calif.) Adventist Med. Ctr., 1975-76; dir. speech pathology Bay Harbor Hosp., Harbor City, Calif., 1976-83; pvt. practice speech and language pathology Torrance, Calif., 1983—. Mem. Am. Speech and Hearing Assn., Calif. Speech and Hearing Assn., South Bay Speech Pathologists, Nat. Stuttering Project. Home: 3553 Emerald St #315 Torrance CA 90503 Office: 3400 W Lomita Blvd Suite 209 Torrance CA 90505

MANGELS, JOHN DONALD, banker; b. Victoria, B.C., Can., Apr. 14, 1926; s. August and Marguerite E. M.; m. Mary Ann Hahn, Nov. 25, 1954; children: Susan, Meg, John Donald. B.A. in Bus. and Econs, U. Wash., 1950. With Rainier Nat. Bank (and affiliates), Seattle, 1950—; vice chmn. Rainier Bancorp., Seattle, 1975-84, pres., 1984—; pres. Rainier Nat. Bank, Seattle, 1976-86, chmn. bd. dirs., 1986—; dir. PEFCO, ISC Systems, Inc., Rainier Realty Investors. Trustee Downtown Seattle Assn., 1976, Corp. Council for Arts, 1979, United Way of King County, 1978, 5th Ave. Theatre Assn., 1981, Seattle-King County Econ. Devel. Council, 1984. Served with USAAF, 1944-46. Mem. Wash. Inst. C.P.A.s, Assn. Res. City Bankers, Robert Morris Assos. Presbyterian. Clubs: Rainier, Broadmoor Golf.

MANGIO, FRANK JOSEPH, advertising executive; b. Boston, Feb. 1, 1938; s. James Joseph and Mary (Sisto) M.; m. Mary Kay Hoffman, Mar. 20, 1977; children: Ronald, Lynda, Sandra. BA, San Diego State U., 1973. Announcer Sta. KLAN-AM, Fresno, Calif., 1962-67; program dir. Sta. KMLO-AM, Vista, Calif., 1967-74; account exec. Cambion Advt., San Diego, 1974-76; pres. Mangio Profl. Communications, San Diego, 1977—; tchr. Ctr. Communication Arts, San Diego, 1985—. Author: The Merchants Manual, 1986. Mem. mktg. and membership com. YMCA, Encinitas, Calif., 1984—, Boys and Girls Club, Solana Beach, 1983—. Served with U.S. Army, 1957-60. Recipient Cert. Appreciation Marine Corps, San Diego, 1983, YMCA, Encinitas, 1986, Small Bus. of Yr. award Greater Solana Beach Area, 1986-87. Mem. Am. Mktg. Assn., Internat. Council of Shopping Ctrs., Solana Beach C. of C. (bd. dirs. 1986—). Avocations: photography, flying. Office: Mangio Profl Communications 11772 Sorrento Valley Rd Suite 112 San Diego CA 92121

MANGLONA, BENJAMIN T., commonwealth senator; b. Rota, Mariana Islands; s. Prudencio M. and Maria T. M.; m. Magdalena Manglona, 1959; children: Lillian Manglona Matsumoto, Rebecca Manglona Taisague, Theodore, Marie, Joann, Benjamin M., Jr., Harold M., Debra M., Selina M. Grad., Surveyor's Sch., Palua, 1957; student Internat. Correspondence Sch., Scranton, Pa., 1964-65, Honolulu Community Coll., 1966-67; AS in Civic Engring. Tech., U. Guam, 1973. Registered profl. land surveyor. Jr. engring. aide Rota Dist. Adminstrn., 1957, sr. engring. aide, 1958, supr. engring., 1958-59, asst. surveyor and cartographic engr., 1959-68, asst. clk. ct., 1962-66, sta. mgr. Air Micronesia, Rota, 1968-69; pub. works office, Rota, 1970-75; pres. Rota Petroleum Co., B & M Constrn. Co., Rota Community Project Assn.; mem. Mariana Islands Dist. Legislature, 1963-65; mem. Ho. of Reps. Congress of Micronesia, 1965-70, chmn. resources and devel. com. 1969-70; mem. Mariana Islands Dist. Legislature, 1975; mem. No. Marianas Legislature, 1976-78; mem. No. Mariana Islands Commonwealth Legislature (Senate), 1978—, chmn. senate fiscal affairs com., 1978-85, 86—, v.p. 1980-84, v.p., legis. sec., 1984—; mem. Congress of Micronesia Joint Commn. on Polit. Status, 1969-70. Mem. Rota Mcpl. Scholarship Bd., 1969-75; mem. Trust Terr. Bd. of Land Surveying Examiners, 1972-75; 1st v.p. No. Marianan Constl. Conv., 1976. Home: Songsong Village Rota CM 96951 Office: PO Box 120 Saipan CM 96950

MANGOLD, WILLIAM JOHNSON, plastic surgeon, lawyer; b. Mar. 21, 1943. BA, U. Tex., 1967, JD, 1969, MD, 1973. Staff plastic surgeon Audie Murphy Vet. Hosp., San Antonio, 1979-80; asst. prof. U. Tex. Health Sch., San Antonio, 1979-80; vis. prof. Tex. Tech. U. Med. Sch., Lubbock, 1972-74; pvt. practice family medicine Lockney, 1974-75; pvt. practice specializing in plastic and reconstructive surgery Tucson, 1980—; bd. dirs. Mut. Ins. Co. Ariz. Contbr. articles to profl. jour. Chmn., bd. dirs. Ariz. Med. Polit. Action Com.; bd. dirs. Ariz. Repertory Singers, 1984—. Mem. Pima County Med. Soc. (chmn. legis. com. 1983—, bd. dirs. 1985—), Am. Coll. Legal Medicine, AMA, ABA, Ariz. Med. Assn. (bd. dirs. 1986—), Met. Tucson C. of C. (bd. dirs. com. on local govt. 1987—). Democrat. Club: So. AE Roadrunners (Tucson) (pres. 1982-84). Office: Plastic & Reconstructive Surgery 2001 W Orange Grove Rd#308 Tucson AZ 85704

MANGUM, PETER GORDON, minister; b. Eureka, Calif., Mar. 21, 1957; s. Paul Daniel and Geraldine Edna (Webb) M.; m. Sally Jean Leep, May 22, 1982; children: Amanda Rae, Daniel Ray. Student, Point Loma Coll., 1975-77; BA in Religion, N.W. Nazarene Coll., 1979. Ordained to ministry Ch. of Nazarene, 1978. Youth pastor Biltmore Ch. of Nazarene, Phoenix, 1976; jr. high pastor Coll. Ch. of Nazarene, Nampa, Idaho, 1977-78; assoc. pastor North Nampa Ch. of Nazarene, Nampa, 1978-79; minister youth and Christian edn. Omaha Cen. Ch. of Nazarene, 1983-84, Seattle First Ch. of Nazarene, 1984—; dir. coll. career ministries Wash. Pacific Dist. Nazarene Youth Internat., 1984—; chmn. bd. Christian life Chattanooga Ch. of Nazarene, 1982-83; del. internat. inst. Phila. Dist. Ch. of Nazarene, 1974. Named one of Outstanding Young Men of Am., 1982. Mem. Nazarene Multiple Staff Assn., Point Loma Coll. Alumni Assn., N.W. Nazarene Coll. Alumni Assn. Republican. Avocations: organized and leisure sports, table games. Home: 23327 12th Pl W Bothell WA 98012 Office: Seattle First Ch of Nazarene 4401 Second Ave NE Seattle WA 98105

MANIERI, MICHAEL JOSEPH, JR., industrial hygienist, safety engineer; b. Jersey City, Dec. 16, 1951; s. Michael Joseph and Lucille (De Luca) M.; m. Lori Frances Thresher, Oct. 6, 1984. B.S., N.Y. Inst. Tech., 1973; M.S. in Indsl. Hygiene, Wayne State U. Sch. Medicine, 1976. Indsl. hygienist, research analyst SRI Internat. (formerly Stanford Research Inst.), Menlo Park, Calif., 1976-77; corp. indsl. hygienist Employees Benefits Ins. Cos., San Jose, Calif., 1977-80; assoc. indsl. hygienist Calif. Dept. Occupational Safety and Health, San Jose, 1980-81; corp. mgr. indsl. hygiene safety AVANTEK, Inc., Santa Clara, Calif., 1981-83; corp. indsl. hygienist, occupational safety specialist Applied Materials, Inc., Santa Clara, 1983-84; program mgr. occupational and environ. health services, Safety Specialists, Inc., Sacramento, 1984-85; assoc. safety engr., Calif. Occupational Safety and Health Standards Bd., Sacramento, 1985—. Commr. City of Sacramento Toxic Substances Commn., 1985—. Mem. Am. Electronics Assn., Am. Indsl. Hygiene Assn. (symposium com. No. Calif. sect. 1983, contbr. Hygienic Guide Series 1976-78), Am. Soc. Safety Engrs., Peninsula Indsl. Bus. Assn., Bay Area Electronics Safety Group, Soc. Bio-Med. Scis., Nat. Off-Rd. Bicycle Assn., Sacramento Sports Assn., Sacramento Bike Hikers, Sierra Club, U.S. Far West Ski Assn., Tau Epsilon Phi. Roman Catholic. Contbr. articles to profl. jours. Home: 7042 Charolais Way Citrus Heights CA 95610 Office: State Calif Occupational Safety and Health Standards Bd 1006 4th St 3d Floor Sacramento CA 95834

MANKAU, SAROJAM KURUDAMANNIL, biology educator; b. Kottayam, Kerala, India, June 5, 1930; m. Reinhold Mankau; children: Ashok, Alisha. BA, Women's Christian Coll., Madras, India, 1949; MA, U. Ill., 1952, PhD, 1956. Research assoc. U. Ill., Urbana, 1953-56, instr. travel and research, 1956-58; instr. U. Redlands, Calif., 1958-59; assoc. C.E.S. U. Riverside, Calif., 1959, asst. prof. biology, 1959-62; prof. Calif. State U., San Bernardino, 1966—, chmn. dept., 1985—. Contbr. articles to profl. jours. Mem. Am. Soc. Parasitologists, Am. Microscopical Soc., Phi Sigma. Home: 449 E Blaine St Riverside CA 92507 Office: Calif State U 5500 University Pkwy San Bernardino CA 92407

MANKIEWICZ, ANGELA CONSOLO, computer systems designer/manager, consultant; b. Bklyn., May 26, 1944; d. Michael and Josephine (Comande) Consolo; m. Richard Chester Mankiewicz, Feb. 25, 1972. B.A. in Rhetorical Theory, Calif. State U.-Los Angeles, 1966, postgrad. 1966-67. Tng. co-ordinator, systems analyst United Mchts. and Mfrs., Los Angeles, 1966-72; cons. data processing, Los Angeles; sr. systems analyst Proto Tool Co., Los Angeles, 1973-75; tech. services mgr. Pacific Stock Exchange, Los Angeles, 1976-77; project leader Warner Bros., Burbank, Calif., 1977-79; mgr. comml. distbn. and fin. software Xerox Computer Services, Los Angeles, 1979—. Author: Speaker and Gavel, 1967. Mem. Assn. Systems Mgmt., Council Logistics Mgmt., Phys. Distbn. Mgmt. Bus. and Profl.

Women's Fedn., Data Processing Mgmt. Assn., ACLU, Computer Profls. for Social Responsibility, NOW. Office: Xerox Computer Services 5310 Beethoven St Suite MA-33 Los Angeles CA 90066

MANKINS, JOHN CARLTON, aerospace systems manager; b. Santa Maria, Calif., Mar. 27, 1956; s. James Carlton Mankins and Sarah Belle (Forrester) Keane; m. Kathleen Frances Forbes, Aug. 4, 1984. BS in Physics, Harvey Mudd Coll., 1978; MS in Physics, UCLA, 1983; MBA, Claremont (Calif.) Grad. Sch., 1987. Sr. field engr. Bendix, Pasadena, Calif., 1980-82; mem. tech. staff Jet Propulsion Lab., Pasadena, 1982-85, mem. space sta. tech. advocacy group, 1984-87, acting technologist systems div., 1985-87, mgr. space sta. requirements analysis, 1985-87; Mem. space sta. mission integration panel Johnson Space Ctr., Houston, 1985-86; tech. bd. Jet Propulsion Lab., 1985-87, tech. planning Mars Rover and Sample Return Mission, 1987—. Merit fellow, Claremont Grad. Sch., 1983, 84, 85, 86; NASA Group Achievement award, 1981. Mem. AIAA (soc. and aerospace tech. com.), AAAS, Jet Propulsion Lab. Astronomy Club (sec. 1981-82), Sigma Xi. Republican. Baptist. Avocations: modeling, gardening. Home: 1617 Finecroft Dr Claremont CA 91711 Office: Jet Propulsion Lab 4800 Oak Grove Dr Pasadena CA 91109

MANLEY, WILL, library director. Dir. Tempe (Ariz.) Pub. Library; columnist Wilson Library Bull. Office: Tempe Public Library 3500 S Rural Rd Tempe AZ 85282 *

MANLY, PHILIP JAMES, manufacturing executive; b. Cin., Apr. 12, 1944; s. Richard Samuel and Marian (LeFevre) M.; m. Jean Angela Maron, Mar. 25, 1967; children: Charlotte, Fred, Peter, Elizabeth. BS, MIT, 1967; MS, Rensselaer Poly. Inst., 1971. Head tech. div. Pearl Harbor Naval Shipyard, Honolulu, 1972-74, health physicist, 1974, head tng. div., 1974-78; pres. Gamma Corp., Wahiawa, Hawaii, 1978—, Osteon Inc., Wahiawa, 1984—. Patentee in field. Mem. Health Physics Soc., Am. Nuclear Soc. Home: 228 Plum St Wahiawa HI 96786 Office: Osteon Inc 410 Kilani Ave #202 Wahiawa HI 96786

MANN, ANDREA KILMER, speech pathologist; b. Auburn, N.Y., June 23, 1953; d. Elmer and Shirley Eunice (Trowbridge) Kilmer; m. Thomas Leonard Mann, Nov. 29, 1980. MA in Speech Pathology, SUNY, Geneseo, 1976. Speech pathologist Newark (N.Y.) Devel. Ctr., 1977-79, Rochester (N.Y.) City Schs., 1979-80, United Cerebral Palsy Assn., Denver, 1980-85, Boulder (Colo.) Meml. Hosp., 1985—; cons. Colo. Dept. Edn., Denver, 1983—; coordinator Rocky Mountain Regional Ctr. Augmentative Communication Boulder Meml. Hosp., 1985—. Mem. Internat. Soc. Augmentative and Alternative Communication, Rocky Mountain Communication Group (co-founder, sec. 1984-85, v.p. 1986—), Colo. Speech, Lang. and Hearing Assn., Am. Speech Lang. and Hearing Assn. (cert.). Lodge: Sertoma. Office: Boulder Meml Hosp 311 Mapleton Ave Boulder CO 80302

MANN, GORDON LEE, JR., ins. broker; b. Taylor, Tex., May 5, 1921; s. Gordon L. and Ruth (Kirkpatrick) M.; student U. Calif. at Los Angeles, 1939, Sch. Law, Loyola U., Los Angeles, 1961. Claims mgr. Traders and Gen. Ins. Co., Los Angeles, 1948-52, Fireman's Fund Am. Ins. Cos., 1952-70; account exec., claims cons. Behrendt-Levy Ins. Agy., 1970-72; asst. div. mgr. Argonaut Ins. Co., Los Angeles, 1972-78; v.p. Frank B. Hall & Co., Los Angeles; 1978—. Served to lt. USNR, 1946. Recipient Meritorious Pub. Service citation Dept. Navy, 1965; Nat. Scroll of Honor, Navy League, 1968. C.P.C.U. Mem. Am. Soc. C.P.C.U.'s (pres. Los Angeles chpt. 1972, gen. chmn. nat. conv. 1970), Navy League U.S. (nat. dir. 1963-75, v.p. for adminstrn. 11th region 1974-75, pres. Los Angeles council 1962, state pres. 1965), Am. Legion (past comdr.) Nat. Soc. Colonial Wars (gov. Calif. soc. 1967, nat. dep. gov. gen. 1969), Children Am. Revolution (past nat. com. chmn.), S.R., Mil. Order World Wars, Men of All Saints' Soc. (past pres.), Naval Order U.S. Republican. Episcopalian (past vestryman). Clubs: Masons, Los Angeles; American (London). Speaker and writer on ins. and patriotic subjects. Home: 435 S Curson Ave Los Angeles CA 90036 Office: 3200 Wilshire Blvd Los Angeles CA 90010

MANN, LLOYD GODFREY, experimental physicist; b. Sterling, Mass., July 2, 1922; s. Walter and Ethel May (Godfrey) M.; m. Patricia Ann Barraclough, Mar. 7, 1959; children: Martha Louise, Lorraine Frances, Douglas Lloyd. BS, Worcester Poly. Inst., 1944; MS, U. Ill., 1947, PhD, 1950. Mem. staff radiation lab. MIT, Cambridge, 1944-45; instr. physics Stanford U., Palo Alto, Calif., 1950-53; physicist Lawrence Livermore (Calif.) Nat. Lab., 1953—. Fellow Am. Phys. Soc.; mem. AAAS. Democrat. Avocations: music, sports. Office: Lawrence Livermore Nat Lab PO Box 808 Livermore CA 94550

MANN, MARY ANNEETA, author; b. Rockhampton, Queensland, Australia; came to U.S., 1965; d. Willie Augustus and Dorothy Louisa M.; 1 child, Attica Andrew. BA, Sydney U., Australia, 1964; MA, U. Calif., Berkeley, 1970; PhD, U. So. Calif., 1982. Author: Los Angeles Theatre Book, 1978, Los Angeles Theatre Book, 1984, The Construction of Tragedy, 1985; author plays: Tortoise Shell, Diana Devereaux, The Senator's Daughter, Maria and the Comet, 1983, Anzac I and II, 1984. Mem. Australian Soc. Accts.

MANNEL, CHARLES HOWARD, educational administrator; b. Balt., Feb. 5, 1929; s. Charles and Kathleen Agnes (McCrea) M.; B.P.A., U. Md., 1957; B.S. in Edn., U. Minn., 1958, M.A., 1965; m. Rose Janice Schumann, Feb. 26, 1953; children—Charles Howard, Laura Kay, Kurt John. Tchr. Balt. public schs., 1957-58, Duluth (Minn.) public schs., 1959-61; with Investors Diversified, Inc., 1961-62; faculty U. Minn., Duluth, 1962-64; placement dir. U. Minn., Duluth, 1965-67; dir. placement U. Minn., Mpls., 1967-69, asst. dean programs and adminstrn., 1969-73, dir. student services and alumni, 1973-76; dir. career services Am. Grad. Sch. of Internat. Mgmt., Thunderbird campus, Glendale, Ariz., 1976-81, v.p. corp. relations, 1981-86, v.p. external affairs, 1986—; cons. in field; cons. Personnel Decision Inc., 1968—. Active fund raising, YMCA, Boy Scouts Am., Indian Guides; mem. CAP, 1967-76, regional dir. aerospace edn. N.Central Region, 1971-76. Served with USAF, 1950-54, Res., 1955-83. Decorated Air Force Commendation medal, Meritorious Service medal; recipient Outstanding Faculty Staff award U. Minn., 1964, 67; Frank G. Brewer award Nat. Recognition Aerospace Edn., 1975; Frank B. Kokesh award for student service, 1976. Mem. Aircraft Owners and Pilots Assn., Air Force Res. Assn., Council for Advancement and Support of Edn. Republican. Methodist. Lodges: Masons, Kiwanis. Contbr. articles to profl. jours. Home: 4633 W Frier Dr Glendale AZ 85301 Office: Am Grad Sch Internat Mgmt Thunderbird Campus Glendale AZ 85306

MANNELLY, KATHY OLSON, associate dean, consultant, lecturer; b. Lawrence, Mich., Jan. 24, 1945; d. William Edward and Marjorie Ellen Olson; m. Patrick Kevin Mannelly, Apr. 9, 1980; stepchildren—Brian, Michael. A.B., Grand Rapids Jr. Coll., 1971; B.S. in Psychology, Grand Valley State Coll., 1973; postgrad. Pacific Luth. U., 1982. Lic. social worker, Mich. Coordinator edn., coordinator Sunrise Program, Project REHAB, Grand Rapids, Mich., 1974-75, supr. employee assistance resource, 1975-77, v.p. personnel and mktg., 1977-78; program analyst Dept. Mgmt. and Budget, State of Mich., Lansing, 1978-80; dir. coop. edn., govtl. grants officer Pacific Luth. U., Tacoma, 1980-83, assoc. dean for student life, 1983—; trainer, cons. Dymaxion Corp., Lansing, Profl. Update, Seahurst, Wash., 1975-82; lectr. in hiring practices. Recipient various awards. Mem. Am. Soc. Tng. and Devel., Coop. Edn. Assn., Nat. Assn. Student Personnel Adminstrs., Nat. Assn. Women Deans, Adminstrs. and Counselors, Nat. Orientation Dirs. Assn. (bd. dirs. 1986—), Office: Pacific Luth Univ Tacoma WA 98447

MANNING, MARLOU, psychotherapist; b. Tucson, June 2, 1956; d. William Herman and Carole Eleanor (Musgrove) McBratney. BA U. Ariz., 1981; MA Calif. Grad. Inst., 1983, PhD, 1987. Lic. marriage, family and child counselor. Asst. to pres. Western Psychol. Services, Los Angeles, 1978-81; crisis counselor Cedars-Sinai Med. Ctr., Los Angeles, 1980-84; counselor South Bay Therapeutic Clinic, Hawthorne, Calif., 1982-84; psychotherapist PMC Treatment Systems, Los Angeles, 1984-85, Beverly Hills Counseling Ctr., 1984-85, Comprehensive Care Corp., Los Angeles, 1985-86; pvt. practice, Los Angeles, 1986—; counselor Brotman Med. Ctr., Los Angeles, 1982-83, Julia Ann Singer Ctr., Los Angeles, 1984; bd. dirs. Los Angeles Commn. Assualts Against Women. Mem. AAUW, Am. Orthopsychiat. Assn., N.Y. Acad. Scis., Women in Health, Am. Anorexia-Bulimia Assn., Nat. Assn. Female Execs., Calif. State Psychol. Assn., Calif. Assn. Marriage and Family Therapists. Democrat. Office: 9911 W Pico Blvd Suite 670 Los Angeles CA 90035

MANNING, WALTER THOMAS, construction and marketing company executive; b. Drumheller, Alta., Can., May 18, 1941; s. Thomas Sorley and Ellen Catherine (Burke) M.; m. Doris Hillar, Aug. 29, 1964 (div. 1970); children—Brenda, Barry; m. Janice Isabelle Fritz, Apr. 21, 1973; children—Richard, Ryan. M.Elec. Engring., U. Calgary, 1968. Electrician, Alta., 1966-67; electrician supr. Plain Constn., Alta., 1967-73; pres., gen. mgr. Aarvak Electric Ltd., Alta., 1973—. Patentee electronic annunciator, 1978, Mannings Relish, Mannings Pudding Sauce, 1979. Mem. Can. Gas Processors Supplies Assn., Can. Legion. Lodge: Elks. Home: PO Box 1256, Airdrie, AB Canada T0M 0B0

MANNINO, J. DAVIS, psychotherapist; b. Patchoque, N.Y., Sept. 27, 1949; s. Joseph I. and Adrienne Adele (Davis) M. BA magna cum laude, SUNY, Stony Brook, 1971; MSW summa cum laude, San Francisco State U., 1974; EdD in COunseling and Ednl. Psychology, U. San Francisco, 1987. Lic. psychotherapist, Calif. Instr. U. Molaysia, 1974-76; dir. refugee programs City San Francisco, 1979-82; instr. U. San Francisco, 1979—; pvt. practice specializing in psychology San Francisco, 1979—; cons. foster care Calif. State Legislature, 1980, community relations, San Francisco Police Dept., 1982—; forensic task force on A.I.D.S., San Francisco Pub. Health Dept., 1984-85; child abuse investigation supr. City of San Francisco, 1986. Contbr. articles to profl. jours.; local psychology columnist, 1986—. Mem. Am. Psychol. Assn., Nat. Assn. Social Workers (diplomate clin. social work), Orthopsychiat. Assn., Am. Assn. Counseling and Devel., Calif. Assn. Marriage Family and Child Therapists, Golden Gate Bus. Assn. (ethics com. 1986, Disting. Service award, 1985). Lodge: Lions (bd. dirs. San Francisco chpt. 1986). Avocations: running, weight lifting, writing, gardening. Home: 1030 Noe St San Francisco CA 94114

MANNIX, DAVID KEVIN, motion picture and television studio executive; b. Bklyn., Oct. 24, 1952; s. Thomas Edward and Catherine (Canning) M.; m. Antoinette Marie Farrugia, Apr. 7, 1979; children, David Jr., Steven. BS in Acctg., Fordham U., 1976; Masters degree, Pepperdine U., 1983. Mgr. fin. analysis Paramount Pictures, Los Angeles, 1977-78, asst. studio controller, 1978-79, dir. prod. ops., 1979-81, exec. dir. studio ops., 1981-83, v.p. adminstrn., 1983-85, v.p. studio ops., 1985—. Roman Catholic. Home: 23604 Real Ct Valencia CA 91355 Office: Paramount Pictures Corp 5555 Melrose Ave Los Angeles CA 90038

MANN-LAMBERT, SANDRA MARIE, information systems security consultant; b. Los Angeles, Nov. 29, 1946; d. Carl Albert and Bertha Martha (Michalek) Mann; m. J. Louis Lambert, Nov. 16, 1985. BA, Mt. St. Mary's Coll., Los Angeles, 1968; MS in Math., U. So. Calif., 1972; MBA, Pepperdine U., 1979. Cert. data processing; cert info. systems auditor. Office mgr. Ralph Williams Ford, Encino, Calif., 1968-73; sr. EDP auditor The Larwin Group, Inc., Beverly Hills, Calif., 1973-75, Hughes Aircraft Co., Los Angeles, 1975-76; v.p., security mgr. Security Pacific Nat. Bank, Los Angeles, 1976—, cons., 1985—; lectr. on data security mgmt. various orgns., 1975—; chmn. data security com Bank Adminstrn Inst., Rolling Meadows, Ill., 1984-86. Contbr. articles to profl. jours. Mem. Info. Systems Security Assn. (co-founder, first pres.). Avocations: tennis, photography, painting, flying.

MANSAGER, ERIK DONN, state agency administrator; b. Montevideo, Minn., Feb. 19, 1955; s. DeWane Earle and Wynona Mary (Tucker) M.; m. Helen Adams, Nov. 1, 1980; children: Ryan Adam, Alyssa Drew. BA, St. Thomas Theol. Sem., 1977; MA, U. Ariz., 1981. Human service specialist State Ariz. Dept. Econ. Security, Casa Grande, 1978-81; supr. State Ariz. Dept. Econ. Security, Coolidge, 1983-86; trainer State Ariz. Dept. Econ. Security, Phoenix, 1984—, child sexual abuse prevention specialist, 1986—; teaching parent Children's Behavioral Services, Las Vegas, Nev., 1981-83; cons. Gila River Indian Community, Sacaton, Ariz., 1985—. Author tng. pamphlet Everything about Team Staffing, 1984. Co-chmn. Youth Issues Council, Coolidge, 1985-86. Mem. Am.'s Inst. Adlerian Studies (cert. profl. studies), N. Am. Soc. Adlerian Psychology, Adlerian Soc. Ariz. (pres. 1986-87, editor newletter 1986—). Democrat. Roman Catholic. Avocations: profl. guitarist, tech. writings, theol./psychol. studies. Home: OMSR PO Box 2073 Oracle AZ 85623 Office: Ariz Dept Econ Security 1346 N Stone Tucson AZ 85705

MANSHARDT, THOMAS BREWSTER, concert pianist, educator; b. Wai, India, Mar. 23, 1927; s. Clifford George and Agnes Helene (Lloyd) M.; B.Mus., Oberlin Coll., 1953; tutored by Alfred Cortot, Lausanne, Switzerland, 1957-62. Debuts include Vienna, 1954; London, 1955; Bonn, Germany, 1956; Los Angeles, 1964; N.Y.C., 1965; concert tours include Germany, Austria, India, Pakistan, U.S., Canada; numerous radio and TV appearances; prof. music U. Regina, Sask., Can., 1966—. Served with AUS, 1945-46. Home: 1830 College Ave, Apt 1301, Regina, SK Canada S4P 1C2 Office: Dept Music U Regina, Regina, SK Canada S4S 0A2

MANSON, IRA REXON, publisher; b. Los Angeles, Dec. 15, 1936; s. Morse Packard and Kathryn (Rexon) M.; m. Sarah Fay Isbitz, May 2, 1969; children—Karen, Jeffrey. B.S., Calif. State U., Los Angeles, 1965; M.B.A., UCLA, 1966. With Manson Western Corp., Los Angeles, 1957—; pres. Manson Western Corp., 1967—; founder Human Behavior mag., 1972. Mem. Calif. Democratic Central Com., Los Angeles County Dem. Central Com.; pres. Westwood Dem. Club, 1970; benefactor John Wayne Cancer Clinic UCLA. Served with AUS, 1959-60. Mem. Am. Arbitration Assn., Los Angeles World Affairs Council, Los Angeles Town Hall, Direct Mktg. Advt. Assn. Address: 12031 Wilshire Blvd Los Angeles CA 90025

MANSOUR, TAG ELDIN, pharmacologist; b. Belkas, Eqypt, Nov. 6, 1924; came to U.S., 1951, naturalized, 1956; s. Elsayed and Rokaya (Elzayat) M.; m. Joan Adela MacKinnon, Aug. 6, 1955; children—Suzanne, Jeanne, Dean. B.Sc., Cairo U., 1946; PH.D., U. Birmingham, Eng., 1949, D.Sc., 1974. Lectr. U. Cairo, 1950-51; Fulbright instr. physiology Howard U., Washington, 1951-52; sr. instr. pharmacology Western Res. U., 1952-54; asst. prof., assoc. prof. pharmacology La. State U. Med. Sch., New Orleans, 1954-61; assoc. prof., prof. pharmacology Stanford U. Sch. Medicine, 1961—, Donald E. Baxter prof., chmn. dept. pharmacology, 1977—; cons. USPHS, WHO, Nat. Acad. Scis.; Mem. adv. bd. Med. Sch., Kuwait U.; Heath Clarke lectr. London Sch. Hygiene and Tropical Medicine, 1981. Contrbr. sci. articles to profl. jours. Commonwealth Fund fellow, 1965; Macy Found. scholar NIMR, 1982. Fellow AAAS; mem. Am. Soc. Pharmacology and Exptl. Therapeutics, Am. Soc Biol. Chemists, Am. Heart Assn., World Affairs Council, Sierra Club, Sigma Xi. Club: Stanford Faculty. Office: 300 Pasteur Dr Stanford CA 94305

MANUELE, PAMELA JEAN, nurse; b. Des Moines, Aug. 24, 1945; d. Robert Charles and F. Arleen (Murphy) Ferren; m. James Carl Manuele, May 20, 1967; children: James, Alyson. Diploma, Mercy Hosp. Sch. Nursing, Des Moines, 1966; BSN, Am. U., 1976. RN. Charge nurse intensive care unit Dewitt Army Hosp., Ft. Belvoir, Va., 1969-75; nurse coordinator Sleepy Hollow, Annandale, Va., 1976; in-service dir. Cushing Meml. Hosp., Leavenworth, Kans., 1976-79; nurse practitioner Acoma State Clinic, Denver, 1985—; sec. treas. firm Ferren-Manuele and Assocs., Inc., Aurora, Colo. Organizer People Against Reckless Spending, 1986. Served to 1st lt. U.S. Army, 1966-69. Mem. Colo. Nurses Assn., Nurse Practitioner Spl. Interest Group (sec. 1985-86), Am. Nurses Assn. Republican. Avocations: sewing, knitting, crocheting, crewel, needlepoint.

MANZO, ANTHONY JOSEPH, painter; b. Saddle Brook, N.J., Apr. 25, 1928; s. Michael and Jennie (Spinneli) M.; m. Ruth Hendricks, Jan. 27, 1956; children—Kathleen, Joanne. Student NAD, N.Y.C., 1946-49, Phoenix Sch. Design, N.Y.C., 1955-58; studied privately with Salvatore Lascari, 1945-65. Freelance comml. illustrator, 1956-59; painter and sculptor, 1958—; instr. pvt. art classes Renaissance Sch. Art, N.J. Served with U.S. Army, 1950-52. Recipient Ray A. Jones award N.J. Painters and Sculptors Soc., 1976. Am. Artist Profl. League fellow. Mem. Am. Artist Profl. League, Salmagundi Club. Roman Catholic. Address: Box 2708 Taos NM 87571

MAPELLI, ROLAND LAWRENCE, cattle company executive; b. Denver, June 10, 1922; s. Herman M. and Della (Borelli) M.; m. Neoma Robinson, Apr. 1942; children—Terralyn Mapelli DeMoney, Geraldine Mapelli. Student, Regis Coll., 1959-61. Former pres., then co-chmn. Monfort Colo., Inc., Greeley, chmn. bd., sr. v.p., 1971—, also dir.; pres. Monfort Food Distbg. Co., Greeley, 1969—; owner, operator Mapelli Farms, Eaton, Colo., 1974—; chmn. bd. Denver Union Stock Yards Co., 1969-70; dir. United Banks Colo., Greeley. Mem. Gov.'s 100-Man Local Affairs Commn., 1962-66; div. chmn. 1962 Mile High United Fund campaign; mem. Colo. Bd. Agr.'s Frozen Food Provisioners Bd., 1967-71, Colo. Agrl. Adv. Com., 1966-73; chmn. Denver Off-Street Parking Commn., 1960-72; mem. Denver City Council, 1955-59, Colo. Ho. of Reps. (to fill vacancy), 1961, Colo. Senate, 1962-66; state fin. chmn. Dem. Party, 1963-66; mem. adv. bd. Ft. Logan Mental Health Ctr., 1961-64; bd. dirs. North Denver Civic Assn., 1955-65, Better Bus. Bur., 1966-69; mem. bd. ambassadors Loretto Heights Coll., 1960-65; adv. bd. St. Anthony's Hosp., 1960-65; bd. dirs., exec. com. Nat. Western Stock Show, 1966—. Served to 2d lt. USAF, 1942-45, ETO. Recipient Knute Rockne award for outstanding civic achievement, 1961; Water for Colo. Environ. Leadership award, 1986. Mem. Colo. Meat Dealers Assn. (pres. 1968-69), Colo. Cattlemen's Assn., Colo. Cattlefeeders Assn., Colo.-Wyo. Restaurant Assn., Nat. Assn. Meat Purveyors. Roman Catholic. Clubs: Cherry Hills Country (Denver); Greeley Country; Thunderbird Country (Rancho Mirage, Calif.). Lodge: Rotary. Home: 18979 Weld County Rd 78 Eaton CO 80615 Office: Monfort of Colo Inc 1930 AA St Box G Greeley CO 80632 *

MARAFINO, VINCENT NORMAN, aerospace executive; b. Boston, June 8, 1930; m. Doris Marilyn Vernall, June 15, 1958; children: Marli Ann, Sheri Louise, Wendi Joan. A.B. in Acctg. and Econs., San Jose State Coll., 1951; M.B.A., Santa Clara U., 1964. Chief acct. Am. Standard Advance Tech. Lab., Mountain View, Calif., 1956-59; with Lockheed Missiles & Space Co., Sunnyvale, Calif., 1959-70; chief accountant Lockheed Missiles & Space Co., 1967-68, dir. fin. mgmt. and controls, research and devel. div., also asst. dir. fin. ops., 1968-70; asst. controller Lockheed Corp., Burbank, Calif., 1970-71, v.p., controller, 1971-77; sr. v.p. fin. Lockheed Corp., 1977-83, exec. v.p., chief fin. and administrv. officer, 1983—, also dir.; chmn. bd. Lockheed Fin. Corp.; dir. Lockheed Missiles & Space Co., Inc., Fluorocarbon Co., Laguna Niguel, Calif., Dataproducts Corp., Woodland Hills, Calif., Newport Corp., Fountain Valley, Calif. Trustee Holy Cross Hosp., Mission Hills, Calif, Harvey Mudd Coll., Claremont, Calif. Served with USAF, 1953-56. Mem. Fin. Execs. Inst., Am. Inst. CPAs. Club: Jonathan, North Ranch Country (Village, Calif.). Office: Lockheed Corp 4500 Park Granada Blvd Calabasas CA 91399

MARAGONI, PAUL CAESAR, mechanical engineer; b. Toronto, Ont., Canada, Aug. 19, 1956; came to U.S., 1957; s. Ralph and Jessie (Chietera) M. AS in Engring., Reedley Jr. Coll., 1976; BME, Calif. State U., Fresno, 1978. Registered mech. engr., Calif. Mech. designer SWF Mfg., Sanger, Calif., 1979-80; assoc. mech. engr. FMC Corp., San Jose, Calif., 1980, assoc. test engr., 1980-81, facilities engr., 1981-82, mech. engr., 1982—. Youth leader, elder, treas. Sanger (Calif.) Foursquare Ch., 1979-80; leader singles home group Calvary Community Ch., San Jose, 1980-84, The Home Ch., San Jose, 1985—. Mem. Soc. Automotive Engrs., ASME. Republican. Lodges: Lions, Masons. Avocations: skiing, photography, sports. Home: 5149 Vera Ln San Jose CA 95111 Office: FMC Corp 1105 Coleman Ave PO Box 1201 San Jose CA 95108

MARANGONI, ANNE LOUISE, podiatrist; b. Palo Alto, Calif., Aug. 19, 1957; d. Louis Dommenic and Phyllis (Garver) M. BA in Biol. Sci., San Jose State U., 1979; DPM, Calif. Coll. Podiatric Medicine, 1983. Diplomate Nat. Bd. Podiatry Examiners. Resident in podiatry Meml. Hosp. Hawthorne, Calif., 1983-84; practice podiatry Menlo Park, Calif., 1984-85, Pacific Grove, Calif., 1985—. Contbr. newspaper articles to Monterey Bay Tribune. Named Pacific Grove Young Career Woman, Bus. and Profl. Women's Club, 1985. Mem. Calif. Podiatric Med. Assn., LWV (luncheon coordinator 1985-86), Padre Trails Camera Club, Jaycees (Monterey Peninsula club). Democrat. Lodge: Zonta. Avocations: scuba diving, photography. Office: 648 Pine Ave Pacific Grove CA 93950

MARAVICH, MARY LOUISE, realtor; b. Fort Knox, Ky., Jan. 4, 1951; d. John and Bonnie (Balandzic) M. A.A. in Office Adminstrn., U. Nev., Las Vegas, 1970, B.A. in Sociology and Psychology, U. So. Calif., 1972; grad. Realtors Inst. Cert. residential specialist. Adminstrv. asst. dept. history U. So. Calif., Los Angeles, 1972-73; asst. personnel supr. Corral Coin Co., Las Vegas, 1973-80; Realtor, Americana Group div. Better Homes and Gardens, Las Vegas, 1980-85, Jack Matthews and Co., 1985—. Mem. Nev. Assn. Realtors (cert. realtors inst.), Las Vegas Bd. Realtors, Nat. Assn. Realtors, Women's Council of Realtors, Am. Bus. Women's Assn., Nat. Assn. Female Execs. Club: Million Dollar, Pres.'s. Office: 3100 S Valley View Blvd Las Vegas NV 89102

MARCELYNAS, RICHARD CHADWICK, manufacturing company manager; b. New London, Conn., Aug. 21, 1937; s. Anthony F. and Elizabeth A. (Chadwick) M.; m. Betty A. Forray, July 1, 1961; children: Michael R., Thomas R. B.A. in Bus. Adminstrn., U. Wash., 1961; postgrad. Seattle U., 1971-72. Mgmt. trainee, installation foreman Pacific Bell, Fullerton, Calif., 1964-65; cost acct. Scott Paper Co., Everett, Wash., 1965-68; asst. v.p. personnel and adminstrn. Nat. Pub. Service Ins. Co., Seattle, 1968-77; mgr. indsl. relations Heath Tecna Precision Structures Inc., Kent, Wash., 1978-85; mgmt. con. Pilon Mgmt. Co., Seattle, 1985— ; cons., lectr. Active youth soccer and Jr. Achievement programs. Served to maj. USMCR, 1961-77. Decorated commendations for bravery and tech. expertise, 1962, 63, 64; recipient Seattle Pacific N.W. Personnel Mgrs. Assn. Bd. Dirs. award, 1975. Mem. Am. Soc. Personnel Adminstrs., Pacific N.W. Personnel Mgrs. Assn. (past pres. Tacoma chpt.), Am. Soc. Safety Engrs. Republican. Roman Catholic. Lodge: Elks. Office: Tower Bldg Seattle WA 98101

MARCH, STEVEN LAWRENCE, engineering manager; b. N.Y.C., Aug. 24, 1943; s. Elliot Q. and Florence (Jacobs) M.; m. Gail Ellen Mahar, Sept. 13, 1963; children: Steven E., Michael J., Robert C. BSEE, Rensselaer Poly. Inst., 1965; MS in Electrophysics, Poly. Inst. Bklyn., 1970. Program mgr. ASC Systems, Rockville, Conn., 1974-77; sr. specialist E-Systems Inc., Garland, Tex., 1978-81; dir. engring. Compact Software, Palo Alto, Calif., 1981-85, Calif. Amplifier, Camarillo, 1985-86; engring. mgr. Maury Microwave Corp., Cucamonga, Calif., 1986—; lectr. in field, 1981—; cons. in field, 1984—. Contbg. editor Microwaves and RF Mag., 1981—; mem. editorial rev. bd. Microwave Jour., 1981—; mem. tech. rev. bd. Microwave Systems News, 1981-84; contbr. articles to profl. jours. Supt. ch. sch. Ellington (Conn.) Congl. Ch., 1975; chmn. pack com. Cub Scouts/Boy Scouts Am., Ellington, 1974. Mem. IEEE (sr., Outstanding Achievement award 1980), Microwave Theory and Techniques Soc. of IEEE (mem. adminstrv. com., treas. 1984-86, mem. awards com. 1984-85, editor newsletter 1981-83), Internat. Microwave Symposium (chmn. steering com. 1987—). Presbyterian. Lodge: Elks. Avocations: golf, philately, photography. Home: 6387 Sapphire St Alta Loma CA 91701 Office: Maury Microwave Corp 8610 Helms Ave Cucamonga CA 91730

MARCHAND, FREDERIC ELLSWORTH, aeronautical engineer; b. McPherson, Kans. March 3, 1933; s. George Earl and Dorothy Helen (McConkey) M.; m. Mary Charlotte Owen, Feb. 14, 1958; children—Nicole, Michel Frederic. B.S. in Aero. Engring., U. Wichita, 1956; M.S. in Aero. Engineering, U. So. Calif., 1961. Engr. North Am. Aviation, Downey, Calif., 1956, 1958-63; prin. engr. Ford Aerospace & Communications Corp., Newport, Beach, Calif., 1963-78, electro-optical systems supr., 1978-83, new bus. devel. mgr., program mgr., 1983—. Contbr. articles to profl. jours. Vice pres. Laguna Beach Civic League, Calif., 1972; mem. Main Beach com., Laguna Beach, 1972. Served to capt., USAFR, 1956-58, . Mem. Am. Rocket Soc., Am. Defense Preparedness Assn., Nat. Mgmt. Assn., Nat. Security Indsl. Assn. AIAA. Republican. Home: 2085 Temple Hills Dr Laguna Beach CA 92651 Office: Ford Aerospace and Communications Corp Ford Rd Newport Beach CA 92660

MARCHAND, JEAN-PAUL, mathematician, educator; b. Murten, Switzerland, Mar. 25, 1933; came to U.S., 1967; s. Charles and Johanna (Schnyder)

M. MS in Math., U. Bern, Switzerland, 1958; PhD in Physics, U. Geneva, Switzerland, 1963. Lectr. in physics U. Bern, Switzerland, 1965-66; asst. prof. math U. Denver, 1967-69, assoc. prof. math., 1969-79, prof. math., 1979—. Author: Distributions, 1962; editor: Scattering Theory, 1974; contbr. articles to profl. jours. Served to 1st lt. Swiss Army, 1953-67. NSF grantee, 1969. Mem. Internat. Assn. Math Physics. Avocation: music.

MARCHAND, JOANN, laboratory technician; b. Cañon City, Colo., June 5, 1941; d. Lawerence Eugene and Helen Lucille (Giem) M. BS, Colo. State U., 1962, MS, 1967. Vol. Peace Corps, Nepal, 1962-64; grad. research asst. Colo. State U., Ft. Collins, 1965-57, lab. technician II botany dept., 1967—; cons. Sci. Tchr.'s Workshop, Kathmandu, Nepal, 1963, cons. for research Mission Hosp., Tansen Palpa, West Nepal, 1963. Contbr. articles to profl. jours. Mem. Colo. Assn. Pub. Employees, Nat. Little Britches Rodeo Assn. (photographer), Audobon Soc., Nature Conservancy, Nat. Rifle Assn., Pentax Owners Club, Sigma Xi, Gamma Sigma Delta. Avocations: hunting, sculpture, bicycling, jogging, gardening. Home: 4908 E County Rd 60 Wellington CO 80549 Office: Colo State U Botany Dept Fort Collins CO 80523

MARCHANT, MAURICE PETERSON, librarian, educator; b. Peoa, Utah, Apr. 20, 1927; s. Stephen C. and Beatrice (Peterson) M.; m. Gerda VaLoy Hansen, June 3, 1949; children: Catherine, Barrie, Alan, Roxanne, Claudia, David, Theresa. B.A., U. Utah, 1949, M.S., 1953; A.M. in L.S, U. Mich., 1966, M.A., 1968, Ph.D., 1970. High sch. tchr. Altamont, Utah, 1949-50; high sch. librarian Salt Lake City and Preston, Idaho, 1950-53; chief tech. librarian Dugway (Utah) Proving Ground, 1953-58; librarian Carnegie Free Library, Ogden, Utah, 1958-66; mem. faculty Brigham Young U., Provo, Utah, 1969—; prof. library and info. scis. Brigham Young U., 1976—; dir. Brigham Young U. (Sch. Library and Info. Scis.), 1975-82; exec. dir. Nat. Library Week, Utah, 1961-62. Author: Participative Management in Academic Libraries, 1976, SPSS as a Library Research Tool, 1977, also articles. Served with USN, 1945-46. Mid-career fellow Council Library Resources, 1972. Mem. ALA (research paper award Library Research Round Table 1975), Mountain Plains Library Assn., Utah Library Assn. (pres. 1964-65, Disting. Service award 1986), AAUP.

MARCHESE, LAMAR V., broadcasting executive; b. Tampa, Fla., Dec. 11, 1943; s. Thomas and Catherine (Palmer) M.; m. Patricia Davis, June 23, 1966; children: Peter, Julia. BA, U. So. Fla., 1964; MA, U. Fla., 1971. Media specialist Morehead (Ky). State U., 1969-72; program coordinator Clark County Library Dist., Las Vegas, Nev., 1972-78; gen. mgr. Sta. KNPR-FM, Las Vegas, 1979—; mem. adv. com. Legis. Subcom. on Pub. Broadcasting, Carson City, Nev., 1983-85; bd. dirs. Sta. KUNV, Las Vegas; acting chmn. Nev. Pub. Broadcasting Assn., 1986—. Pres. Nev. Alliance for the Arts, Las Vegas, 1983-86; chmn. Citizens Against 12, Las Vegas, 1984; mem. steering com. Library Bond Election, Las Vegas, 1985. Recipient Gov.'s Arts award Nev. State Council on Arts, 1985; named Outstanding Fundraising Exec., Nat. Soc. Fund Raising Execs., Las Vegas, 1985. Democrat. Office: Sta KNPR (FM) 5151 Boulder Hwy Las Vegas NV 89122

MARCHI, GARY MICHAEL, futurist, business market development consultant; b. San Francisco, Feb. 25, 1953. Cert., B.L. Internat. Corp. Bus. Sch., Aervoe/Dynamin Corp. Bus. Sch., San Francisco, 1974. Bus. and market devel. cons. Califa Corp., San Francisco; fund raising cons. Leo Fund Raising Services div., San Francisco, 1972-73; owner, operator, bus. market devel. advisor Spirit of the Future Unltd., San Francisco, 1974—; pub. relations, promotion advisor Media Network Systems div., San Francisco, 1979—; founder, dir. Spirit of the Future Creative Inst., 1976—; mktg. advisor Centergy Innerprises, 1985. Author: Consultants Contract Kit, 1983, Re-Establishing the U.S. Constitution and Clearly Defining the Free Enterprise System; Creator-producer FUTURE CONSUMER, weekly radio and TV documentary series, 1979—. Chmn. Ruff Community Forum, 1980-82. Mem. Nat. Health Fedn. (advisor, promoter 1979—), Constl. Patriots Assn. (advisor, promoter 1982—), Venture Devel. Assn. (co-founder, pres. 1981-82).

MARCHI, JON, cattle rancher, former investment brokerage exec.; b. Ann Arbor, Mich., Aug. 6, 1946; s. John Robert and Joan Trimble (Toole) M.; m. Mary Stewart Sale, Aug. 12, 1972; children: Aphia Jessica, Jon Jacob. Student Claremont Men's Coll., 1964-65; BS, U. Mont., 1968, MS, 1972. Sec., treas. Marchi, Marchi & Marchi, Inc., Morris, Ill., 1968-69; account exec. D. A. Davidson & Co., Billings, Mont., 1972-75, asst. v.p., office mgr., 1976-77, v.p. mktg. and adminstrn., Great Falls, Mont., 1977—; sec., dir., v.p. fin. services and exec. devel., D. A. Davidson Realty Corp., Great Falls, 1978-85, chmn. research com., 1980; cattle rancher, Polson, Mont., 1985—; bd. dirs. Big Sky Airlines, Billings, Mont., Energy Overthrust Found., Mansfield Found., Mont. Beverages. Chmn. Mont. Gov.'s Subcom. for Venture Capital Devel.; chmn. investment com., State of Mont. Sci. and Tech. Alliance, 1985—; chmn. seed capital com. State of Mont.; mem. Mont. Peoples Action; sec.-treas. Valley View Assn., 1987—. Served with U.S. Army, 1969-71. Mem. Nat. Cattlemen's Assn., Securities Industry Assn., Mont. Stock Growers Assn., Polson C. of C. Episcopalian. Clubs: Leadership Great Falls, Ski, Mont., Helena Wilderness Riders. Lodge: Rotary. Home: Rte 1 Box 175A Polson MT 59860 Office: Marchi Ranch Valley View Polson MT 59860-0437 Address: PO Box 437 Polson MT 59860-0437

MARCKWARDT, HAROLD THOMAS, assn. exec.; b. Chgo., May 4, 1920; s. Herman and Carrie (Polachek) M.; AB, U. So. Calif., 1949, AM, 1953; MS, U. Calif., 1970, postgrad., 1970—; m. Patricia Ann Hoffman, Apr. 7, 1945; children: Craig, Diana, Brad, Glenn. Tool and machinery designer Douglas Aircraft, Santa Monica, Cal., 1939-43; playground leader County Los Angeles, 1946-47; community program dir. Hollywood (Calif.) YMCA, 1947-51, dir. community program and bldg., 1952-55; exec. dir. Westchester YMCA, Los Angeles, 1955-63; area dir. Nat. Council YMCA, 1963-66, pres. Western Center Assocs., Los Angeles, 1966—; internat. mgmt. cons., Indonesia, 1985-86; field assoc. Internat. Exec. Service Corps, 1987. Exec. dir. Calif. Youth and Govt. Statewide Com., 1965, del. seminar UN, 1959. Colliver lectr. U. Pacific, 1965. Trainer, Leadership Devel. Camp, Los Angeles, 1959; mem. Mayor's Steering Com., 1973-75, chmn. Mayor's Facilitators com. Conf. Children, Youth and Sr. Citizens, 1974; mem. employment and tng. subcom. Los Angeles County Task Force, 1977; mem. Task Force on Equity for Women in Employment, 1976-77. Served to 1st lt., USAAF, 1943-46, USAF, 1950-52. Recipient One of Hollywood's Top Ten Young Men award, 1954. Mem. Am. Soc. Tool Engrs. (charter mem.), Pacific S.W. Area YMCA Assn. Profl. Dirs. (pres. 1963-66), Orgn. Devel. Network, Airplane Owner's and Pilots Assn., Am. Soc. Tng. and Devel. (v.p. 1979, pres. 1980), Internat. Fedn. Tng. and Devel. Orgns., Pacific Area Travel Assn., Assn. for Humanistic Psychology. Democrat. Author: The Leader Makes The Difference, 1968; Leading Discussion Groups, 1972; How to Make Executive Decisions About Training, 1976; 16 Steps to the Job You Want, 1979; The Quality Circles Kit, 1982. Home: 4216 Colbath Sherman Oaks CA 91423 Office: 13323 Moorpark St Sherman Oaks CA 91423

MARCUS, AARON, graphic artist; b. Omaha, May 22, 1943; s. Nathan and Libbie (Burstein) M.; m. Susan Wightman Douglas, Sept. 9, 1968; children: Joshua, Elisheva; m. Leslie Becker, Dec. 15, 1985. BFA, MFA, Yale U., 1968; BA, Princeton U., 1985. Asst. prof. Princeton (N.J.) U., 1969-77; research fellow East-West Ctr., Honolulu, 1978; lectr. U. Calif., Berkeley, 1979-80; staff scientist Lawrence Berkeley Lab., 1980-82; prin. Aaron Marcus and Assocs., Berkeley, 1983—. Mem. Nat. Computer Graphics Assn., Human Factors Soc., Am. Inst. Graphic Arts, Spl. Interest Group on Computer Graphics and Interactive Techniques of Assn. Computing Machinery, Spl. Interest Group on Computer and Human Interaction of Assn. Computing Machinery. Democrat. Jewish. Home and Office: Aaron Marcus and Assocs 1196 Euclid Ave Berkeley CA 94708-1640

MARCUS, BECCA NIMMER, psychotherapist; b. Los Angeles, Aug. 6, 1948; d. Melville Bernard and Gloria Dee (Madoff) Nimmer; m. Paul Marcus, Dec. 22, 1968; children: Emily Nimmer, Beth Nimmer. Cert. de Français, École Internat. de Genève, 1966; BA summa cum laude, UCLA, 1970; MSW, U. Ill., 1982. Tchr. Los Angeles City Schs., 1970-73; intern therapist Champaign (Ill.) County Mental Health Ctr., 1982; adj. faculty mem., counselor San Diego State U., 1983; family therapist Adlerian Family Counseling, Tucson, 1983-86; pvt. practice psychotherapy Tucson, 1986—. Mem. adv. com. sex. edn. Catalina Foothills Sch. Dist., 1984; bd. dirs. Champaign County Mental Health Ctr., 1979-82; interviewer Adult Diversion Program, Champaign, 1976-77. Mem. Nat. Assn. Social Workers, Ariz. Assn. Social Workers, Adlerian Soc. Ariz., Alpha Delta Mu. Avocations: travel. Office: 1625 N Alvernon Way Tucson AZ 85712

MARCUS, GEORGE MATHEW, real estate executive; b. Limni, Greece, Aug. 15, 1941; s. John and Mary (Moutsanas) M.; m. Judith A. Otten, June 26, 1965; children: Mary Jane, John, Demetra, Alexandra. BA in Econ., San Francisco State U., 1965. Founder, chmn. Marcus & Millichap, Inc. and affiliate cos., Palo Alto, Calif.; founder Plaza Bank of Commerce, San Jose, Calif.; bd. dirs. Mid Peninsula Bank. Trustee Calif. State U. system; bd. dirs. San Francisco Internat. Film Festival; mem. Urban Land Inst.; mem. Policy Adv. Bd. Ctr. for Real Estate and Urban Econs., U. Calif., Berkeley; mem. San Francisco Host Com.; mem. Calif. Syndication Forum; bd. dirs. Greek Orthodox Fellowship of Santa Clara County. Club: Fremont Hills Country. Home: Black Mountain Rd Los Altos Hills CA 94022 Office: Marcus & Millichap 2626 Hanover St Palo Alto CA 94304

MARCUS, JEFFREY HOWARD, security company executive; b. Albany, N.Y., June 4, 1950; s. Paul and Phyllis (Zippert) M.; m. Claudia Kramlich, Aug. 22, 1981. BS in Elec. Engrng. and Computer Sci., U. Colo., Denver, 1977; MBA, U. Phoenix, Denver, 1985. Specialist counter intelligence U.S. Army, Washington, 1971-73; v.p. engrng. Securus (formerly Photo-Scan of Colo.), Denver, 1977-84, pres., 1984—, also bd. dirs.; Bd. dirs. Marcham Controls, Inc., Denver; bd. dirs. PSA Fin. Services, Inc., Westminster, PSA Eyewitness Security Systems, Westminster, also tech. com. Democrat. Jewish. Avocations: traveling, skiing, snorkeling, photography. Office: Photo-Scan of Colo Inc 12411 E 37th Ave Denver CO 80239

MARCUS, ROBERT, aluminum company executive; b. Arlington, Mass., Feb. 24, 1925; s. Hymen David and Etta (Arbetter) M.; children: Lawrence Brian, Janie Sue, Clifford Scott, Emily. A.B., Harvard U., 1947; M.B.A., U. Mich., 1949; M.Ed., Tufts U., 1950. Market analyst Govt. Commodity Exchange, N.Y.C., 1952-54; mkt. research analyst Gen. Electric Co., 1954-55; corp. mkt. analyst Amax Inc., N.Y.C., 1955-62; staff mkt. mgr. aluminum group Amax Inc., 1962-65, pres. internat. aluminum div., 1965-70, v.p., 1970-71; exec. v.p. Amax Pacific Corp., San Mateo, Calif., 1971-72; exec. v.p., dir. Alumax Inc., San Mateo, 1973-82, pres., chief exec. officer, dir., 1982-86; bd. dirs. Domtar, Inc., Montreal. Trustee World Affairs Council, 1974—; bd. dirs. Japan Soc. Coyote Point Mus., 1982-84, Bay Area Council. Served with USN, 1943-46. Mem. Japan Soc. (bd. dirs.). Clubs: Harvard (N.Y.C.); University, Bankers, Commonwealth, (San Francisco). Home: 2645 Scott St San Francisco CA 94123

MARCUS, RUDOLPH ARTHUR, chemist; b. Montreal, Que., Can., July 21, 1923; came to U.S., 1949, naturalized, 1958; s. Myer and Esther (Cohen) M.; m. Laura Hearne, Aug. 27, 1949; children: Alan Rudolph, Kenneth Hearne, Raymond Arthur. B.S., McGill U., 1943, Ph.D., 1946; D.Sc. (hon.), U. Chgo., 1983, Poly. U., 1986. Postdoctoral research assoc. NRC of Can., Ottawa, Ont., 1946-49, U. N.C., 1949-51; asst. prof. Poly. Inst. Bklyn., 1951-54, assoc. prof., 1954-58, prof., 1958-64; prof. U. Ill., Urbana, 1964-78; Arthur Amos Noyes prof. chemistry Calif. Inst. Tech., Pasadena, 1978—; temp. mem. Courant Inst. Math. Scis., N.Y. U., 1960-61; trustee Gordon Research Confs., 1966-69, chmn. bd., 1968-69, mem. council, 1965-68; mem. rev. panel Argonne Nat. Lab., 1966-72, chmn., 1967-68; mem. rev. panel Brookhaven Nat. Lab., 1971-74; mem. rev. com. Radiation Lab., U. Notre Dame, 1975-80; mem. panel on atmospheric chemistry climatic impact com. Nat. Acad. Scis.-NRC, 1975-78, mem. com. kinetics of chem. reactions, 1973-77, chmn., 1975-77, mem. com. chem. scis., 1977-79, mem. com. to survey opportunities in chem. scis., 1982-86; adv. council in chemistry Princeton U., 1972-78; vis. com. div. chemistry and chem. engring. Calif. Inst. Tech., 1977-78; adv. council chemistry Poly. Inst. N.Y., 1977-80; adv. com. for chemistry NSF, 1977-80; vis. prof. theoretical chemistry U. Oxford, Eng., 1975-76; also professorial fellow Univ. Coll. Mem. editorial bd. Jour. Chem. Physics, 1964-66, Ann. Rev. Phys. Chemistry, 1964-69, Jour. Phys. Chemistry, 1968-72, 80-84, Accounts of Chem. Research, 1968-73, Internat. Jour. Chem. Kinetics, 1976-80, Molecular Physics, 1977-80, Chem. Physics Letters, 1980—, Laser Chemistry, 1982—; Advances in Chem. Physics, 1984—, Theoretica Chimica Acta, 1985—, World Sci. Pub., 1987—; contbr. articles to profl. jours. Recipient Anne Molson prize in chemistry McGill U., 1943, Alexander von Humboldt Found. Sr. U.S. Scientist award, 1976, Robinson medal Faraday div. Royal Soc. Chemistry, 1982, Chandler medal Columbia U., 1983, Wolf prize in chemistry, 1984-85; Alfred P. Sloan fellow, 1960-63; NSF sr. postdoctoral fellow, 1960-61; sr. Fulbright-Hays scholar, 1972. Fellow Am. Acad. Arts and Scis. (exec. com. Western sect., co-chmn. 1981-84); mem. Nat. Acad. Scis., Am. Chem. Soc. (past div. chmn., mem. exec. com., mem. adv. bd. petroleum research fund, Irving Langmuir award Chem. Physics 1978), Am. Phys. Soc. (exec. com. div. chem. physics), AAUP, Alpha Chi Sigma. Home: 331 S Hill Ave Pasadena CA 91106

MARCUS, (GAIL) SUE, furniture company representative; b. Montclair, N.J., Aug. 12, 1962; d. Alan Jay and Carole Maxine (Gass) M. BS, Boston U., 1984. Sales rep. O'Asian Designs, Compton, Calif., 1984-85, Am. of Martinsville, Los Angeles, 1985, The Thomas Charles Group, Los Angeles, 1985—. Jewish. Avocations: photography, tennis. Home and Office: 5801 E 2d St Long Beach CA 90803

MAREE, ANDREW MORGAN, III, business management and investment advisor; b. Detroit, Mar. 9, 1927; s. Andrew Morgan, Jr., and Elizabeth Lathrop (Cady) M.; B.A., Claremont Men's Coll., 1950; M.B.A., U. Chgo., 1951; J.D., Whittier Coll., 1982; m. Wendy Patricia Haymes, Dec. 20, 1980; children—Samantha, Andrew Morgan, IV. Trust analyst Hanover Bank & Trust Co., N.Y.C., 1951-52; pres. A. Morgan Maree, Jr., & Assocs. Inc., Los Angeles, 1952-86, chmn. bd., 1987—; dir. Carson Estate Co. Served with USNR, 1944-46. Mem. Acad. Motion Picture Arts and Scis., The Players, Am. Film Inst. Office: Suite 600 6363 Wilshire Blvd Los Angeles CA 90048

MAREI, IBRAHIM, medical technologist; b. Marowe, Sudan, Dec. 6, 1939; s. Hassan and Shafika (Mohamed) M. BS in Chemistry, U. Cairo, 1966; MS in Med. Tech., Calif. State U., 1980. Lic. clinical chemist tech., Calif., clinical lab. tech., Calif. Clinical chemist Biosci. Lab., Van Nuys, Calif., 1969-71; supr. ctr. critically ill lab. Hollywood Presbyn. Med. Ctr., Los Angeles, 1971-75; sr. toxicologist, clin. chemist spl. chemistry dept. Refrence Labs., Newbury Park, Calif., 1975—, instr. on the job tng. and edn. new students, tech. staff, 1980—. Mem. Am. Soc. Clinical Pathologists (cert.), Am. Chem. Soc., Am. Assn. Clinical Chemists (cert.), Am. Pub. Health Assn. Calif. Assn. for Med. Lab. Tech. Home: 384 E Wilbur Rd Apt 102 Thousand Oaks CA 91360 Office: Reference Labs 1011 Rancho Conejo Blvd Newbury Park CA 91360

MARES, FRANK JAMES, ophthalmologist; b. El Paso, Tex., Oct. 1, 1951; s. Presciliano Percy and Ascencion Maria (Sisneros) M.; m. Barbara Jean Sais, Feb. 27, 1977. B.S., Colo. State U., 1973; M.D., U. N.Mex., 1977. Diplomate Am. Bd. Ophthalmology. Intern Good Samaritan Hosp., Portland, Oreg., 1977-78; resident in ophthalmology Oreg. Health Scis. U., Portland, 1978-81, fell in pediatric ophthalmology, 1981-82, fell in glaucoma, 1983; chief ophthalmology VA Hosp., Albuquerque, 1982-83; practice medicine specializing in ophthalmology and glaucoma, Albuquerque, 1983—; council mem. Nat. Inst. Gen. Med. Scis., NIH, Bethesda, Md., 1974-78; asst. clin. prof. Oreg. Health Scis. Ctr., Portland, 1981-82, 83, U. N.Mex. Med. Ctr., Albuquerque, 1983—. Fellow Am. Acad. Ophthalmology; mem. Bernalillo County Med. Assn., N.Mex. Ophthalmol. Soc., Alpha Omega Alpha, Alpha Kappa Phi. Democrat. Roman Catholic. Office: Eye Assocs of NMex 806 Grand NE Albuquerque NM 87102

MARESCA, JOSEPH WILLIAM, JR., physical oceanographer; b. Tampa, Fla., Feb. 5, 1946; s. Joseph William and Mary (Cueto) M.; B.S. in Civil Engring., Lehigh U., 1968; M.S., Stanford U., 1969; M.S. in Oceanic Sci., U. Mich., 1973, Ph.D., 1975; m. Noreen Mary Angiola, June 27, 1970; children—Michele Eileen, Craig Robert. Sr. oceanographer, program mgr. SRI Internat. (formerly Stanford Research Inst.), Menlo Park, Calif., 1975-84; v.p. Vista Research, Inc., Mountain View, Calif., 1984—. Served with C.E., U.S. Army, 1969-72. NSF trainee, 1972-74; NDEA Title IV fellow, 1974-75. Mem. Marine Tech. Soc., Am. Geophys. Union, Sigma Xi, Tau Beta Pi, Chi Epsilon. Roman Catholic. Contbr. articles to profl. jours. Home: 780 Fife Way Sunnyvale CA 94087 Office: Vista Research Inc 100 View St PO Box 998 Mountain View CA 94042

MARG, ELWIN, physiological optics, optometry educator; b. San Francisco, Mar. 23, 1918; s. Sigmund and Fannie (Sockolov) M.; m. Helen Eugenia Kelly, Apr. 1, 1942; 1 child, Tamia. AB, U. Calif., Berkeley, 1940, PhD, 1950. Asst. prof. physiol. optics and optometry U. Calif., Berkeley, 1950-56, assoc. prof., 1956-62, prof., 1962—; Bd. dirs. Eyetronics, Inc., 1984—, Berkeley, Minerva Found., Berkeley. Author: Computer Assisted Eye Examination, 1980; also articles. Served to lt. col. USAF, 1941-46, 50-52, ETO. NSF fellow, Nobel Inst. Scockholm, 1957, Guggenheim, Madrid, 1964; recipient Miller Research Professorship U. Calif.-Berkeley, 1967. Fellow: AAAS, Optical Soc. Am., Am. Acad. Optometry; mem. Soc. Neurosci., Assn. Research Vision and Ophthalmology. Office: U Calif Dept Physiol Optics and Optometry Berkeley CA 94720

MARGERUM, J(OHN) DAVID, chemist; b. St. Louis, Oct. 20, 1929; s. Donald Cameron and Ida Lee (Nunley) M.; m. Virginia Bolen, June 5, 1954; children: John Steven, Kris Alan, Julie Ellen. A.B., S.E. Mo. State Coll., 1950; Ph.D., Northwestern U., 1956. Research chemist Shell Oil Co., Wood River, Ill., 1945-55; chief spectroscopy sect. U.S. Army QMR&E Center, Natick, Mass., 1957-59; research specialist Sundstrand Corp., Pacoima, Calif., 1959-62; with Hughes Research Labs., Malibu, Calif., 1962—, sr. scientist, head chemistry sect., 1967—. Contbr. articles to profl. jours.; patentee in field. Served with U.S. Army, 1955-57. Recipient Holley medal ASME, 1977. Fellow AAAS; mem. Am. Chem. Soc., Electrochem. Soc., Soc. Info. Display, Inter-Am. Photochem. Soc., Sigma Xi. Democrat. Unitarian. Home: 5433 Rozie Ave Woodland Hills CA 91367 Office: 3011 Malibu Canyon Rd Malibu CA 90265

MARGOLES, MICHAEL STUART, orthopedic surgeon; b. Milw., Aug. 14, 1942; s. Sidney Regal and Sylvia (Posner) M.; student San Jose State U., 1961-63; B.A., U. Calif., Berkeley, 1965; M.D., U. Calif., Irvine, 1969; m. Michelle Stratton Church, July 2, 1967; children—Shaynah Stratton, Honey Elizabeth. Intern, Hosp. for Joint Disease and Med. Center, N.Y.C., 1969-70, resident in orthopedic surgery, 1970-74; practice medicine specializing in orthopedic surgery and pain therapy, San Jose, Calif., 1977—. Contbr. to Pain Measurement and Assessment, also articles to profl. jours. Diplomate Am. Bd. Orthopedic Surgery. Fellow Am. Acad. Neurol. and Orthopedic Surgeons; mem. AMA, Santa Clara County Med. Soc., Calif. Med. Assn., Internat. Assn. Study of Pain, Am. Pain Soc., Am. Back Soc., Western U.S.A. Pain Soc., Am. Acad. Algology, Phi Delta Epsilon. Home: 5018 New Trier Ave San Jose CA 95136 Office: Cambrian Park Plaza 14438 Union Ave San Jose CA 95124

MARGOLIS, ESTHER LUTERMAN, court administrator; b. Pitts., Jan. 12, 1939; d. Nathan and Belle (Fogel) Luterman; B.S., Ariz. State U., 1976, M.S., 1978; m. Herbert Marvin Margolis, Apr. 15, 1962; children: Ruth Lys, Judith Lyn. Statistician, court planners office Ariz. Supreme Ct., 1976-77; planner Ariz. Dept. Corrections, 1979; adminstrv. asst. planning and research bur. Phoenix Police Dept., 1979-82, police research analyst, 1982-83; ct. mgmt. analyst Calif. Jud. Council, Adminstrv. Office of Cts., San Francisco, 1983-84; asst. ct. adminstr., jury commr. Contra Costa County Superior Ct., 1984—; instr. Phoenix Community Coll., 1980-82; presenter paper ann. meeting Acad. Criminal Justice Scis., Phila., 1981. Mem. textbook selection com. Roosevelt Sch. Dist., Phoenix, 1975; chmn. bd. YMCA, South Mountain br., 1977-81; bd. mgrs. Phoenix and Valley of the Sun YMCA, 1978-81; pres. bd. dirs. Do it Now Found., 1978-80; bd. dirs. Boys' Clubs Phoenix, 1982-83; fin. officer Pinole Ridge Homeowners Assn., 1986—, pres., 1987. Mem. Am. Soc. Public Adminstrn. (program com., panel coordinator regional conf. 1983; panel discussant ann. meeting N.Y.C. 1983), Am. Soc. Criminology, Nat. Council Crime and Delinquency, Nat. Assn. Women in Criminal Justice, Profl. Women for Kennedy. Editor ann. report Phoenix Police Dept., 1979-82. Home: 1417 Greenfield Circle Pinole CA 94564 Office: 725 Court St Room 124 Martinez CA 94553

MARGON, BRUCE HENRY, astrophysicist; b. N.Y.C., Jan. 7, 1948; s. Leon and Maxine E. (Margon) Siegelbaum; m. Carolyn J. Bloom, May 8, 1976; 1 dau., Pamela. A.B., Columbia U., 1968; M.A., U. Calif.-Berkeley, 1971, Ph.d., 1973. Asst. researcher astronomer U. Calif.-Berkeley, 1973-76; assoc. prof. astronomy UCLA, 1976-80; chmn., prof. astronomy U. Wash., Seattle, 1980—; chmn. bd. govs. ARC, Inc., Seattle; dir. Aura, Inc., Washington; co-investigator Space Telescope, NASA, Washington, 1977—. NATO postdoctoral fellow, 1973-74; Sloan Found. research fellow, 1979-83. Mem. Internat. Astron. Union, Am. Astron. Soc. (Pierce Prize 1981), Am. Phys. Soc., AAAS, Royal Astron. Soc. Office: U Wash Astronomy Dept FM 20 Seattle WA 98195

MARGULIES, CAL, interior designer; b. Los Angeles, May 29, 1932; s. Henry David and Anna (Wolfstone) M.; m. Harriet Dolores Mathews, June 17, 1951; children—Susan Denise Miyamoto, Laura Diane Morgan, Catherine Lynn Takata. A.A., Los Angeles City Coll., 1956; student Calif. State U.-Los Angeles, 1956-60, Calif. State U. Poly., 1979-80. Cert. Nat. Council Interior Design, 1974. Interior designer, sales mgr., gen. mgr. Miller Desk div. Household Internat. Corp., Los Angeles, 1956-67; gen. mgr. Cannel & Chaffin, Inc., Los Angeles, 1968-69; pres. Custom Industries Inc., Covina, Calif., 1969-77, Corp. Interiors, Inc., Los Angeles, 1977-79, Corona Pacific Designs, Irvine, Calif., 1979-81; prin. Cal Margulies & Assocs., Costa Mesa, Calif., 1979-81, Margulies, Bentley & Assocs., Inc., 1981—; instr. Interior Designers Guild, 1982—, Sch. Interior Design, 1982—. Pres., bd. dirs. Hope House for Multiple Handicapped, 1965-80; bd. dirs. San Gabriel Valley YMCA, 1972; pres. Covina Republican Club, 1968; mem. Capital Improvements Com. Covina, 1970; v.p. Calif. Legis. Conf. on Interior Design. Mem. Sales and Mktg. Execs. Internat. (Outstanding Achievement award 1971, Merit award 1972), Am. Soc. Interior Designers, Inst. Bus. Designers. Republican. Seventh-day Adventist. Clubs: Acad. Magical Arts and Scis., Masons, Rotary. Contbr. designs to various jours. Office: 3300 Irvine Ave Ste 235 Newport Beach CA 92660

MARGULIES, TODD DAVID, environmental scientist, geochemist; b. Sioux Falls, S.D, Oct. 28, 1959; s. Donald Lee and Carolyn (Caplan) M. Student, U. Miami, Coral Gables, Fla., 1977-78, Augustana Coll., 1978-79; B in Geology, U. No. Colo., 1982, M in Environ. Sci. and Geochemistry, 1987. Geologist Dynatech Corp., Lakewood, Colo., 1982-83; geotechnologist Cone Geochem., Lakewood, 1983, Omenex Resources, Golden, Colo., 1983-84, Q.C. Data Collectors, Denver, 1984-86; geochemist and environ. scientist Environ. Sci. and Engring., Inc., Englewood, Colo., 1986—. Mem. Am. Assn. Petroleum Geologists (assoc.), Environ. Sci. and Tech. Assn. Jewish. Home: 17491 W 16th Ave #2-110 Golden CO 80401 Office: Environ Sci and Engring Inc 7332 S Alton Way #H Englewood CO 80112

MARGULIS, ROBERT JOEL, infosystems specialist; b. N.Y.C., 1948. BA in English with honors, CUNY, S.I., 1973. Infosystems mgr. Group Health Coop. of Puget Sound, Seattle, 1979—. Avocations: mountaineering, cruising. Office: Group Health Coop Infosystems 300 Elliott Ave W Seattle WA 98119

MARIAN, TERESA, aerospace materials engineer, consultant; b. Yokohama, Japan, June 18, 1955; came to U.S., 1956, parents U.S. citizens; d. Paul John and Josephine Hiroko (Tokita) M.; m. Robert Clyde Oakes, June 18, 1979. BSChemE, U. Nev., Reno, 1981. Materials and process and structural cert. engr. Lear Fan Co., Reno, 1980-84; cons. Advanced Composite Techs., Reno and Los Angeles, 1984—; cons. Avtek Corp., Camarillo, Calif., 1985—, Quiet Nacelle, Miami, Fla., Avtek Def., Murdock Engring. Co., Irving Tex. Abarix, Reno. Mem. Soc. Advancement of Materials and Process Engring. Republican. Roman Catholic. Home and Office: Advanced Composite Techs 1155 W Huffaker Ln Reno NV 98511

MARICH, KENNETH WILLIAM, medical equipment company marketing executive; b. Chgo., July 1, 1939; s. Samuel Steven and Annabel Marie (Janovsky) M.; m. Barbara Jean Gronbach, Apr. 27, 1961; children—Kenneth David, Deborah Jean. B.S., Roosevelt Univ., 1961; M.B.A., U. of Santa Clara, 1974. Registered medical tech., Am. Soc. Clin. Pathology. Research analyst U. of Calif., Davis, 1962-68; research assoc. Stanford Med. Sch., Calif., 1968-73; sr. research analyst Stanford Research Inst., Menlo Park,

Calif., 1973-75; instr. Central Oreg. Community Coll., Bend, 1975-79; biomedical engring. mgr. SRI Internat., Menlo Park, 1979-81; mktg. mgr. Diasonics Inc., Milpitas, Calif., 1981—; bus. cons. Advanced Bus. Mgmt., Bend, 1977-79; health cons. SRI Internat., Menlo Park, 1983; mktg. instr. DeAnza Coll., Cupertino, Calif., 1983; clinical instr. U. of Calif., San Francisco, 1984. Author: Clinics in Diagnostic Ultrasound, 1984. Co-author articles in field. Cubmaster, scoutmaster Boy Scouts of Am., Ill., Oreg., Calif., 1959-76; edn. judge Distributive Edn. Clubs of Am., Bend, 1978-79. Scholar Am. Soc. Clin. Pathologists, 1961; Sci. grantee NIH, 1975. Mem. Am. Inst. Ultrasound in Medicine, Soc. Non-Invasive Vascular Tech., Tau Kappa Epsilon, Tri Beta. Republican. Home: 2810 Pruneridge Ave Santa Clara CA 95051 Office: Diasonics Inc 1656 McCarthy Blvd Milpitas CA 95035

MARIEL, photographer, former fabrication company executive; b. Pasadena, Calif., Aug. 5, 1938; d. Oscar Branche and Mary Lincoln (Hicks) Jackson; adopted dau. William Nathan Turner; m. Donald E. Coombes, June 13, 1957 (div. June 1972); children—William Cullen, Anna Maria, Joel Howard; 1 son by previous marriage, Scott Craig Goodwin. Co-incorporator, Mineral Harvesters Inc., Salem, Oreg., 1966-71, Ariz. Custom Mfg. Inc., Phoenix, 1971-81, bus. mgr., pres., 1972-81; pres. Ariz. Custom Steel, Phoenix, 1976-81, Eagle Erectors, Phoenix, 1979-81; now with Lazarus Enterprises; former co-owner WCS Constrn., Inc. Asst. dist. coordinator Oreg. Republican Party, 1964. Mem. Nat. Assn. Women Bus. Owners, Nat. Assn. Female Execs., Ariz. Network Profl. Women, Women Emerging, Internat. Platform Assn., Tolsum Farm Homeowners Assn., Ariz. Steel Fabricators Assn. (past pres.). Republican. Mem. Reorganized Ch. Jesus Christ of Latter-day Saints. Clubs: Intertel, Mensa. Home: PO Box 69325 Portland OR 97201

MARIELLA, RAYMOND P., chemistry educator, consultant; b. Phila., Sept. 5, 1919; s. Angelo Raphael and Sophia (Peel) M.; m. Miriam Margaret McMahon, Nov. 26, 1943; children: Miriam Margaret, Raymond P., Anne Marie, Patricia Sue. B.S., U. Pa., 1941; M.S., Carnegie Inst. Tech., 1942, D.Sc., 1945; postdoctoral fellow, U. Wis., 1946. Instr., then asst. prof. chemistry Northwestern U., 1946-51; mem. faculty Loyola U., Chgo., 1951-77; prof. chem. Loyola U., 1955-77, chmn. dept., 1951-70; asso. dean Loyola U. (Grad. Sch.), dir. grad. sci. programs, 1968-69, dean, 1969-77, sci. cons. indsl. orgns., 1951-77; assoc. exec. dir. Am. Chem. Soc., 1977, exec. dir., 1978-82; Sec.-treas. Midwestern Assn. Grad. Schs., 1972-77; exec. com. Council of Grad. Schs., 1972-74; Scientific adviser to gov. Ill. Producer, performer sci. TV shows Chgo. networks, 1956-65; Author: Laboratory Manual of Organic Chemistry and Biochemistry, 1953, Inorganic Qualitative Analysis, (with J. L. Huston), 1958, Chemistry of Life Processes, (with Rose Blau), 1968, Selected Laboratory Experiments for Chemistry of Life Processes, 1968, also articles. Recipient McCormack Freud Hon. lectr. award chemistry and chem. engring. Omicron chpt. Phi Lambda Upsilon, 1961; Merit award Chgo. Tech. Socs. Council, 1962. Mem. Am. Chem. Soc. (chmn. Chgo. 1960-61, nat. councilor 1956-82, chmn. bd. com. on profl. relations 1974-75, cons. to chmn. bd.), AAAS, N.Y. Acad. Scis., Sigma Xi (pres. Loyola chpt. 1956-57), Phi Kappa Phi, Alpha Chi Sigma, Phi Lambda Upsilon, Lambda Chi Sigma, Sigma Delta. Home and Office: 21215 123d Dr Sun City West AZ 85375

MARIETTA, MARY BLACKFORD, clinical social worker; b. Gallup, N.Mex., Mar. 17, 1929; d. Clyde Walter and Edna (Elder) Blackford; m. Wallace Cameron Sweat, Aug. 31, 1951 (div. Mar. 1958); children: Eric Kevin (dec.), Cynthia Eileen Moriarty; m. George Albert Marietta, June 18, 1967. BS, Ariz. State U., 1951; MSW, UCLA, 1967. Lic. clin. social worker, Calif. Social worker Los Angeles County Dept. Welfare, 1953-57; probation officer Los Angeles Dept. Probation, 1957-70, clin. social worker, 1967-70; social services dir. Epworth Village, York, Nebr., 1970-71; clin. social worker Mental Health Ctr., Lincoln, Nebr., 1971-77; child protective services social worker San Diego County Dept. Social Services, Oceanside, Calif., 1977—; pvt. practice clin. social worker Oceanside, 1977—; cons. Group Home for Girls, Lincoln, 1972-77; field instr. U. Nebr., Lincoln, 1970-77. Mem. Nat. Assn. Social Workers, Nat. Assn. Social Workers Clin. Registry, N. County Child Abuse Coalition (treas. 1986), Sierra Club. Baha'i. Avocations: dancing, reading, gardening, sewing, music. Home: 851 Loma Alta Terrace Vista CA 92054 Office: San Diego County Dept Social Ser 1701-C Mission Ave Oceanside CA 92054

MARINI, GIACOMO, electronics company executive; b. Cugnoli, Italy, June 30, 1951; s. Mario and Nice (Di Domizio) M.; m. Barbara Galanzino, Aug. 19, 1980 (div.). B, U. Pisa, Italy, 1974. Mem. research staff IBM Corp., Pisa, 1974-76, Venice, 1976-78; mgr. software devel. Olivetti Co., Ivrea, Italy, 1978-81; pres. Logitech SRL, Ivrea, 1981-83; v.p. engring. Logitech, Inc., Redwood City, Calif., 1983—, also bd. dirs.; bd. dirs. Algol Logitech SPA, Milan, Logitech Far East Ltd., Hsinchu, Republic of China. Contbr. articles to profl. jours. Mem. Computer Soc. IEEE, Assn. Computing Machinery, Associazione Italiana di Calcolo Automatico. Home: 1983 Euclid Ave Menlo Park CA 94025-2626 Office: Logitech Inc 805 Veterans Blvd Redwood City CA 94063

MARINO, DEAN FRANK, research chemist; b. Albany, Calif., Apr. 26, 1952; s. Frank and Orien Juanita (Forster) M.; m. Sandra Bishop, June 17, 1973 (div. Jan. 1976); m. Joan Evans Carver, June 19, 1976; children: Bryan Earendil, Dylan Feanor, Megan Arwen. BS, Calif. State U., Fresno, 1974, MS, 1976; PhD, Oreg. State U., 1980. Research chemist E.I. DuPont de Nemours Co., Wilmington, Del., 1980-81; project leader Dow Chem. Co., Walnut Creek, Calif., 1981—. Contbr. articles to profl. jours. Republican. Jewish. Home: 3001 Camby Antioch CA 94509 Office: Dow Chem Western Div 2800 Mitchell Walnut Creek CA 94589

MARION, DOUGLAS WELCH, magazine editor; b. Des Moines, May 9, 1944; s. Francis Orville and Alice Virginia (Welch) M.; m. Patricia Fisher, Sept. 2, 1967; children—Douglas Welch, Anne Welch. B.A., Parsons Coll., 1970; postgrad., Fresno State U., 1970. Staff editor Argus Publs., Los Angeles, 1975—, editor Super Chevy Mag., 1980—; cons. in field. Contbr. articles to profl. jours. Named Man of Yr., Classic Chevy Club, Dearborn, Mich., 1981. Republican. Avocations: sports; golf; music; auto racing; photography. Office: Super Chevy Mag 12301 Wilshire Blvd Suite 316 Los Angeles CA 90025

MARK, DAVID FU-CHI, molecular biologist; b. Hong Kong, Dec. 10, 1950; came to U.S., 1970; s. Hua Cheuk and Patricia Li M.; m. Joyce Lai-Jean Yee, July 1, 1973; children: Jonathan, Jennifer, Andrew. BA summa cum laude, U. Mass., 1973; PhD, Harvard U., 1977. Postdoctoral fellow Stanford (Calif.) Med. Sch., 1977-79; scientist Cetus Corp., Emeryville, Calif., 1979-83, project mgr., 1981—; dir. molecular biology Cetus Corp., 1982—, sr. scientist, 1983—; sci. advisor China Nat. Ctr. for Biotech. Devel., Beijing, 1984. Contbr. articles to profl. jours.; patentee in field. Named Outstanding Young Scientist, Sci. Digest mag., N.Y.C., 1984, Inventor of Yr. Intellectual Property Owners, Washington, 1986; Commonwealth of Mass. scholar U. of Mass., 1971-73. Mem. AAAS, Am. Soc. for Microbiology, Am. Assn. Immunologists. Republican. Baptist. Office: Cetus Corp 1400 53d Emeryville CA 94608

MARKEN, WILLIAM RILEY, magazine editor; b. San Jose, Calif., Sept. 2, 1942; s. Harry L. and Emma Catherine (Kraus) M.; m. Marilyn Tonascia, Aug. 30, 1964; children—Catherine, Elizabeth, Michael, Paul. Student, Occidental Coll., 1960-62; B.A., U. Calif.-Berkeley, 1964. Writer, mng. editor, now editor-in-chief and v.p. Sunset Mag., Menlo Park, Calif., 1964—. Bd. dirs. Calif. Tomorrow, 1979-83. Democrat. Avocations: tennis; skiing; basketball. Office: Sunset Mag Lane Pub Co 80 Willow Rd Menlo Park CA 94025

MARKER, MARC LINTHACUM, lawyer, leasing company executive; b. Los Angeles, July 19, 1941; s. Clifford Harry and Voris (Linthacum) M.; m. Sandra Yocom, Aug. 29, 1965; children—Victor, Gwendolyn. B.A. in Econs. and Geography, U. Calif.-Riverside, 1964; J.D., U. So. Calif., 1967. Bar: Calif. 1971, U.S. Dist. Ct. (cen. dist.) Calif. 1971, U.S. Tax Ct. 1972, U.S. Dist. Ct. (ea. dist.) Calif. 1977, U.S. Ct. Appeals (D.C. cir.) 1977, U.S. Ct. Appeals (9th cir.) 1978, U.S. Dist. Ct. (no. and so. dists.) Calif. 1984. Asst. v.p., asst. sec. Security Pacific Nat. Bank, Los Angeles, 1970-73; sr. v.p., chief counsel, sec. Security Pacific Leasing Corp., San Francisco, 1973—; pres. Security Pacific Leasing Services Corp., San Francisco, 1977-85, dir., 1977—; bd. dirs., sec. Voris, Inc., 1973-86; bd. dirs. Refiners Petroleum Corp., 1977-81, Security Pacific Leasing Singapore Ptc Ltd., 1983-85; lectr. in field. Served to comdr. USCGR. Mem. ABA, Calif. Bar Assn., San Francisco Bar Assn., Am. Assn. Equipment Lessors. Republican. Lutheran. Club: University (Los Angeles). Office: Security Pacific Leasing Corp 4 Embarcadero Ctr #1200 San Francisco CA 94111

MARKEY, JOSEPH WILLIAM, physician, health administrator; b. Eaton, Ohio, Aug. 7, 1929; s. John Frances and Pauline (Gaul) M.; m. Margaret Ann Buckley, Mar. 2, 1957; children: Rebecca, Sean. BS, U. Cin., 1951, MD, 1955. Diplomate Am. Bd. Psychiatry and Neurology. Staff physician Boulder (Colo.) Med. Ctr., 1961-68, staff neurologist, 1972-81; staff neurologist Charlotte (N.C.) Rehab. Hosp., 1981-83; dir. pain rehab. Boulder Meml. Hosp., 1983—. Bd. dirs. Boulder County Dept. Health, 1984—. Served to lt. M.C., USNR, 1956-58, PTO. Mem. Am. Assn. for Study of Headaches, Am. Pain Soc., Am. Acad. Neurology, Colo. Med. Soc. (v.p. jud. council 1975-81), Boulder County Med. Soc. (pres. 1967-68). Democrat. Roman Catholic. Office: Meml Hosp 311 Mapleton Ave Boulder CO 80302

MARKLAND, FRANCIS SWABY, JR., biochemist, educator; b. Phila., Jan. 15, 1936; s. Francis Swaby Sr. and Willie Lawrence (Averritt) M.; m. Barbara Blake, June 23, 1957; children—Cathleen Blake, Francis Swaby. B.S., Pa. State U., 1957; Ph.D., Johns Hopkins U., 1964. Postdoctoral fellow UCLA, 1964-66, asst. prof. biochemistry, 1966-73; vis. asst. prof. U. So. Calif., Los Angeles, 1973-74, assoc. prof., 1974-83, prof., 1983—, acting chmn. dept. biochemistry, 1986—; cons. Clin. Lab. Med. Group, Los Angeles, 1977—, Cortech, Inc., Denver, 1983—. Contbr. articles, chpts. and abstracts to profl. publs. Mem. Masterworks Choral, Northridge, Calif. Served to capt. USNR. Recipient NIH research career devel. award USPHS, NIH, 1968-73; research grantee NCI, 1979—, Nat. Heart Lung and Blood Inst., 1984—. Mem. Am. Soc. Biol. Chemists, Am. Chem. Soc., Internat. Soc. on Toxinology, Endocrine Soc., Internat. Soc. on Thrombosis and Haemostasis, Am. Assn. Cancer Research, Biochem. Endocrinology Study sect. NIH, 1986—; Am. Heart Assn. (thrombosis council), Am. Soc. Hematology, Sigma Xi, Alpha Zeta. Avocations: singing; jogging; skiing; tennis; aerobics. Office: U So Calif Sch Medicine Cancer Research Lab Room 106 1303 N Mission Rd Los Angeles CA 90033

MARKOE, M. ALLEN, leasing company executive; b. St. Paul, Feb. 23, 1927; s. Julius and Bernice (Jacobson) M.; student Drake, 1947-48; B.S. U. Wis., 1950; m. Joan B. Lewensohn, Aug. 7, 1949; children—Guy Leigh, Sara Lynne, Robin Dawn. Owner, Diversified Bus., Milw., 1950-54; dir. mgmt. adv. services Profit Counselors, Inc., Chgo., N.Y.C., 1954-60; pres. Pacific Am. Leasing Corp., Phoenix, 1961-80; ret., 1980; founder, pres. Markoe Fin. Group, Markoe Leasing; pres. AM Leasing Ltd., Phoenix; chmn., chief operating officer Shillelagh Ventures, Chartered Pub. Co., Phoenix. Served with AUS, 1945-46. Mem. Am. Indsl. Devel. Council, Ariz. Assn. Mfrs., Soc. for Advancement Mgmt., N.Am. Soc. Sci. Mgmt. (symposium dir.), Assn. Equipment Lessors, Western Assn. Lessors, Phoenix C. of C., Am. Legion, Frat. Order Police (assoc.). Republican. Jewish. Clubs: Ariz. Aikido Kai, Lions. Home: 7050 N Wilder Rd Phoenix AZ 85021 Office: 5815 N Black Canyon Hwy Phoenix AZ 85015

MARKOVITZ, RICHARD TYLER, motion picture marketing executive; b. Phila., June 9, 1951; s. Victor Seymour and Anita (Rosenthal) M.; B.A. in English, Trinity Coll., 1973. Account exec. Spiro & Assocs., Advt. Agy., Phila., 1973-75; publicist Columbia Pictures, Universal Studios, Phila., 1976-77; account exec. Grey Advt. Co., N.Y.C., 1977-78; account supr. D'Arcy, MacManus & Masius Co., Los Angeles, 1979-80; dir. advt. RASTAR Prodns., Burbank, Calif., 1980-82; v.p. internat. mktg. Lorimar Inc., Culver City, Calif., 1982-85 ; v.p. account dir. J. Walter Thompson Entertainment, Los Angeles, 1986—; lectr. in field. Mem. Acad. Motion Pictures Arts and Sci. Club: Harmony (N.Y.C.).

MARKS, DOROTHY LIND, mathematics tutor; b. N.Y.C., Apr. 30, 1900; d. Alfred Daniel and Martha (Herzog) Lind; m. Norman Lincoln Marks, May 29, 1923 (dec. 1959); 1 son, Alfred Lind (dec. 1980). B.A., Barnard Coll., 1921. Substitute tchr. N.Y. high schs., 1921-28; math tutor The Brearley Sch., N.Y.C., 1953-62, The Marlborough Sch., Los Angeles, 1973—, pvt. and pub. secondary schs., Los Angeles, 1973—, NYU, 1965-72; chmn. math dept. The Lenox Sch., N.Y.C., 1960-70. Bd. dirs. women's orgn. Temple Rodeph Sholem, N.Y.C., 1925-50, fin. sec., 1925-47. Mem. Phi Beta Kappa (recipient Kohn Math. Prize 1921, sec.-treas. Barnard chpt. 1925-50, chartermem. alumnae in N.Y.). Republican. Jewish. Avocations: reading, music, theatre, concerts, ballet.

MARKS, JAY GLENN, geologist; b. Los Angeles, Aug. 7, 1916; s. Jasper Glenn and Florence (Pixley) M.; A.B., Stanford, 1938, A.M., 1941, Ph.D., 1951; m. Consuelo Beers Plaza, Dec. 12, 1942; children—Jay Glenn, John Pixley, Brian Robert. Paleontologist-geologist Internat. Petroleum Corp., Ecuador, 1941-46; sr. paleontologist-geologist Creole Petroleum Corp., Venezuela, 1948-57; profl. geologist Exxon Co., Los Angeles, also Denver, 1957-75. Fellow Geol. Soc. Am.; mem. Am. Assn. Petroleum Geologists, Soc. Econ. Paleontologists and Mineralogists, Am. Inst. Profl. Geologists (pres. Calif. sect. 1968-69), Paleontol. Research Instn., Rocky Mountain Assn. Geologists. Contbr. articles to profl. jours. Home and office: 3900 S Clermont St Englewood CO 80110

MARKS, JOE ANGEL, JR., construction company executive; b. Brownsville, Tex., Feb. 10, 1941; s. José Angel and Olivia (Cisneros) M.; m. Gloria Yzaguirre, Apr. 8, 1978; children: Jo Anna, Desiree, Joe A. III. BEE, Tex. A&I U., 1967. Registered profl. engr., Wash., Alaska, Tex. Chief engr. Brown and Root, Anchorage, 1973-76; pres. Marks Engring., Anchorage, 1976—, Marenco, Inc., Anchorage, 1980—. Served with USAF, 1959-63. Mem. Sigma Tau. Home and Office: 13961 Jarvi Anchorage AK 99515

MARKS, MICHAEL BRUCE, management consultant; b. Charlotte, N.C., Nov. 1, 1940; s. Leo Mitchell Marks and Jeanne (Fine) Seeman; m. Susan Roy, Dec. 27, 1985; children: Leo Mitchell, Zachary Lewellyn. BS in Psychology, Stanford U., 1961. Nat. accounts mgr. Sperry-Rand-Unival Corp., Los Angeles, 1967-77; pres. Universal Cons., Los Angeles, 1976—, Martronics Corp., Los Angeles, 1977-81, Overseas Unltd., Los Angeles, 1981—; pres., bd. dirs. OUA of Idaho Inc.; bd. dirs. TRT, Inc., , Overseas Councel. Served as 1st lt. U.S. Army, 1961-63. Mem. Children's Mus. Los Angeles (trustee 1984—), Am. Diabetes Assn. (bd. dirs. 1985—). Jewish. Avocation: contract bridge. Office: Overseas Unlimited Agy Inc 3460 Wilshire Blvd Los Angeles CA 90010

MARKS, MILTON, state senator; b. San Francisco, July 22, 1920; s. Milton and Olita M. (Meyer) M.; B.A., Stanford U., 1940; LL.B., San Francisco Law Sch., 1949; m. Carolene Wachenheimer, Aug. 14, 1955; children—Carol, Milton, Edward David. Mem. Calif. Assembly, from 1959; judge mcpl. ct., San Francisco, 1966-67; mem. Calif. Senate, 1967—, chmn. election coms., select com. on maritime industry, com. on disabled. Bd. dirs. Nat. Council on Alcoholism, Calif. League for Handicapped, St. Anthony's Dining Room, Mex. Am. Polit. Assn., Chinese-Am. Citizens Alliance. Served with U.S. Army, World War II. Recipient numerous awards including: Bronze Key award Nat. Council on Alcoholism; Man of Yr. award Council for Civic Unity of San Francisco Bay Area, 1973; Legislator of Yr. award Calif. Assn. Physically Handicapped, 1973; Consumer Legislator of Yr. award, 1981; Calif. Preservation award, 1982; Legislator of Yr. award Students of Calif. State Univ. System; Legislator of Yr. award Planning and Conservation League Calif., 1984. Mem. Am. Legion, VFW. Democrat. Jewish. Club: Press Club (San Francisco). Lodge: Lions. Office: State Capitol Room 5035 Sacramento CA 95814

MARKS, PETER AMASA, technical company administrator; b. Passaic, N.J., Dec. 5, 1948; s. Amasa A. and Eunice L. (Irwin) M.; B.S. in Design Engring., U. Cin., 1972, M.A. in Media Communications, 1973, postgrad. in human factors engring. Research asst. dept. mech. engring. U. Cin., 1972; sr. engr. Ford Motor Co., Sharonville, Ohio, 1972-75; prin. Design Insight Cin., 1976—; mng. dir. SDRC TEC Services, Milford, Ohio, 1978-84, dir. product planning and devel., SDRC, Inc., Milford, 1981-84; sr. v.p. ops. Automation Tech., Campbell, Calif., 1985—; lectr., cons. on product design tech. implementation, U.S., Asia, Europe, also for Am. Mgmt. Assns. Grad. fellow; Gen. Motors grantee in design, 1970; winner nat., internat. competitions for tech. programs. Mem. ASME, Soc. Mfg. Engrs., Soc. for Tech. Communication, Computer and Automated Systems Assn., Mensa. Author books, articles and films in field. Home: 55 Church St PO Box 2080 Los Gatos CA 95031 Office: Automation Tech Products 1671 Dell Ave Campbell CA 95008

MARKS, RICHARD, film editor; b. N.Y.C., Nov. 10, 1943; s. Ben and Irene (Epstein) Marks; m. Barbara Joan Fallick, Jan. 15, 1967; 1 child, Leslie Sharon. Student, NYU; BA, CCNY. Freelance film editor N.Y.C. and Los Angeles, 1964—. Mem. Motion Picture Acad. Arts and Scis., American Cinema Editors.

MARKS, ROBERT JACKSON, electrical engineer; b. Sutton, W.Va., Aug. 25, 1950; s. Robert Jackson and Lenore Ethyl (Hersman) M.; m. Connie Lynn Jewett, July 28, 1974; children: Jeremiah Jackson Jewett, Joshua Jackson Jewett. BSEE, Rose-Hulman Inst. Tech., 1972, MSEE, 1973; PhD in Elec. Engring., Tex. Tech U., 1977. Reliability engr. Naval Weapons Ctr., Crane, Ind., 1973-74; research asst. Tex. Tech U., Lubbock, 1974-77; asst. prof. elec. engring. U. Wash., Seattle, 1978-82, assoc. prof., 1982—; cons. Applied Physics Lab., Seattle, 1978-79, Appa Systems Inc., Bellevue, Wash., 1981-82, Tech. Arts Corp., Seattle, 1983-84. Contbr. articles to profl. jours. Mem. IEEE (sr. mem.; Centennial medal and cert. 1984, outstanding br. councilor-advisor award 1982), Optical Soc. Am., Soc. Photo-optical Instrumentation Engrs., Sigma Xi, Eta Kappa Nu. Republican. Home: 16515 Ashworth Ave N Seattle WA 98133 Office: U Wash Dept Elec Engring Seattle WA 98195

MARKS, SHERYL ANN, fitness center executive, association executive; b. Inglewood, Calif., Feb. 19, 1955; d. Hal R. and Ann Louise (DeBoer) M.; m. Craig Hamilton Perry, Sept. 11, 1974 (div. Dec. 1984). A.A., Grossmont Community Coll., 1976; B.A., San Diego State U., 1978. Speaker, Pacific Telephone at Disneyland, 1973-74; adminstr. Sch. for Internat. Tng., 1975-76; tchr. Calif. Aerobic Dance, 1976, San Diego State U., 1977; instr., lectr. Green Mountain Weight Control Community, Poultney, Vt., 1979; dir. Applied Fitness Systems, San Diego, 1979; technician, instr., nutrition counselor San Diego State U., Exercise Physiology Lab., 1977-79; curriculum cons., tchr. regional occupation program San Diego City Schs., 1979-80; dir. Gen. Dynamics Corp., Health Fitness Ctr., Convair Recreation Assn., San Diego, 1980-84; bd. advisors Internat. Dance Exercise Assn., San Diego, 1983-84, assoc. dir., 1984-85, exec. dir., chmn. bd. dirs. 1986—; bd. advisors U. Calif.-San Diego, 1984—, Reebok Nat., 1986—; bd. experts Standards and Malpractice Reporter; project advisor Health Media Strategies, Inc., 1985—; cons., speaker bus. and community groups, San Diego, 1982—; advisor health promotion curriculum com. San Diego State U., 1983—; instr. corp. fitness programs Nat. U., 1982, U. Calif.-San Diego, 1984. Mem. com. on quality assurance of health promotion programs at worksite Calif. State Health Dept., 1984—. Author: Shape Up Workbook, 3d edit., 1984. Mem. heart in industry com. San Diego chpt. Am. Heart Assn., 1980-84. Recipient Innovative Ednl. Program award Nat. Am. Coll. Testing-Nat. Univ. Continuing Edn. Award Competition, 1982; Outstanding Community Service award Options Drug Abuse Prevention Program, 1983; named one of Outstanding Young Women of Am., 1984. Mem. Nat. Mgmt. Assn. (outstanding service award 1983), Am. Coll. Sports Medicine, Assn. for Fitness in Bus. (outstanding service award 1983, 84, profl. jour. com. 1982-83, pres. S.W. region 1982-83). Home: 4085-188 Pte La Paz San Diego CA 92122 Office: Internat Dance Exercise Assn 2431 Morena BlvdSuite 2D San Diego CA 92110

MARKSTEIN, DAVID LIBERMAN, fin. cons., author; b. New Orleans, Jan. 8, 1920; s. Joseph Carl and Genevieve (Liberman) M.; student La. State U.; m. Elizabeth Gough, Feb. 14, 1944; children—Donald D., Genevieve Markstein Jones, Anne Markstein, Robert G. Pvt. practice as investment counselor, formerly in New Orleans, now in Scottsdale, Ariz., 1972—; co-chmn., moderator 8 public investment seminars Loyola U.; chmn., prin. speaker fin. seminars in Des Moines, Phoenix, Cleve., Cheyenne, Wyo., Phoenix, Scottsdale, Ariz.; speaker before prin. clubs and groups in New Orleans, Phoenix, Scottsdale and Sun City, Ariz.; instr. Loyola U., New Orleans, Phoenix Coll., Scottsdale Coll.; appeared on numerous talk shows. Active Boy Scouts Am., St. Vincent de Paul Soc. Served with USNR, 1942-45. Mem. Authors Guild Am., Phoenix Press Club, Fin. Analysts New Orleans (past pres.). Author: How to Chart Your Way to Stock Market Profits, 1966, How to Make Money With Mutual Funds, 1967, How You Can Beat Inflation, 1968, Nine Roads to Wealth, 1969, Manage Your Money and Live Better, 1969, Practical Ways to Build A Fortune in the Stock Market, 1968, Six Steps to Investing Success, 1970, How to Make Your Money Do More, 1970, Investing in the Seventies, 1972, Retire Rich, 1973, Money Raising and Planning for the Small Business, 1974, Markstein's Guide to Much Bigger Investment Income, 1976, Double Your Money, Dow Jones-Irwin, 1986; editor-pub. Markstein Letter, 1967-75; contbg. editor nat. mags.; contbr articles to mags. and newspapers. Home and Office: 8208 E Vista Dr Scottsdale AZ 85253

MARKUS, SHARYN KATHRYN, educator. BA, Eastern Ill. U., 1971; MA, U. Colo., Colorado Springs, 1982. Tchr. Sacred Heart and Ursuline Acad., Springfield, Ill., 1972-75, Colo. Pub. Sch. Dist. 20, Colorado Springs, 1977—; adj. instr. Colorado Springs Bus. Coll., 1977-78; exec. dir. Colorado Springs Dental Soc., 1976—; asst. dir. yearbook workshop Eastern Ill. U., Charleston, 1983; presenter various workshops and profl. meetings, 1980—; bd. dirs. Southeastern Colo. Health Systems Agy., 1983-86. Author: (booklet) 10-Minute Writing Assignments, 1980 (Ednl. Resources Info. Ctr. award 1980), others; editor jour. Colo. Reading Assn., 1982-83; editor newspaper The Vol. Lawman, 1986—. Youth group leader St. Patrick's Ch., Colorado Springs, 1981; res. police officer, Colorado Springs Police Dept., 1984—, active Neighborhood Watch program, 1986—, Nat. Grammar Hotline, 1987—. Mem. Res. Law Officers Am., Colo. Lang. Arts Soc., Nat. Council Tchrs. English, Am. Soc. Dental Execs. Republican. Roman Catholic. Avocations: reading, freelance writing. Address: Colorado Springs Dental Society 1304 N Academy Blvd #203 Colorado Springs CO 80909

MARLENEE, RONALD CHARLES, Congressman; b. Scobey, Mont., Aug. 8, 1935; m. Cynthia Tiemann; children—Sheila, Casey, Allison. Student, Mont. State U., U. Mont., Reisch Sch. Auctioneering. Farmer, rancher; mem. 95th-100th Congresses from 2d Mont. Dist., 1977—; congressional committeeman 2d Congressional dist. Mont., 1975-76. Mem. Mont. Stockgrowers Assn., Daniels County Farm Bur., Daniels Fair Assn., Mont. Beef Performance Assn., Mont. Grain Growers Assn. Republican. Lutheran. Clubs: Masons, Lions. Office: 2465 Rayburn House Office Bldg Washington DC 20515

MARLER, STEVE JOHN, protective services official; b. Mission City, B.C., Can., July 11, 1959; s. Edward William and Edna Eleanor (Kilback) M.; m. Karen Theodora Carson, Mar. 20, 1982; 1 child, Stephanie Virginia. Student, Columbia Coll., 1977-79, Modesto Jr. Coll., 1979-83, Santa Rosa Jr. Coll., 1983—. Firefighter Tuolumne County Fire Dept., Moccasin, Calif., 1977-79, City of Ceres Fire Dept., Calif., 1979-83; capt. City of Sonoma Fire Dept., Calif., 1983—. Mem. Sonoma County Fire Prevention Officers, Norcal Fire Prevention Officers Assn. Republican. Roman Catholic. Avocations: camping, boating. Office: City of Sonoma Fire Dept 32 Patten St Sonoma CA 95476

MARLOW, CHRISTINE RUTH, social science educator; b. Redruth, Cornwall, England, Oct. 11, 1949; came to U.S., 1972; d. Edward Arthur (James) and Janet Marion (Archer) M. BS in Anthropology, Sociology magna cum laude, U. Wales, Swansea, 1972; MA in Social Work, U. Chgo., 1979, PhD in Social Work, 1983. Community social worker Bureau Mental Retardation, Rockland, Maine, 1975-77; research asst. various, 1977-81; research assoc. U. Chgo., 1981-83; asst. prof. social work Ind. State U., Terre Haute, 1984-85, N.Mex. State U., Las Cruces, 1985—; cons. Planned Parenthood, 1984-86; organizer Literacy Vols., 1973-77. Contbr. articles to profl. jours. Named one of Outstanding Young Women Am., Ind. State U., 1985; research grantee Ind. State U., 1985. Mem. Nat. Assn. Social Workers, Council Social Work Edn. Avocations: running, gardening, backpacking. Home: 5010 Dunn Dr Las Cruces NM 88005 Office: N Mex State U Dept Social Work Box 35W Las Cruces NM 88003

MARLOW, JERRY W., hotel management executive, real estate investor; b. Atoka, Okla., Sept. 1, 1939; s. Ervin L. and Buelah A. (Darst) M.; m. Donna G. Harbolt, June 3, 1962; children: Leslie K., Darcy L. BS, Okla. State U., 1962. Pres. Lodgeco., Inc., Seattle, 1972-75; sr. v.p. Metro Inn Mgmt. Co., Dallas, 1975-76; pres. Hotel Mgmt. Assn., Beaverton, Oreg., 1976—. Served with USN, 1962-64. Mem. Oreg. Hotel-Motel Assn. (pres. 1986—), Small Luxury Hotels (vice chmn. 1986—), Portland C. of C. (bd. dirs. 1986—). Republican. Baptist. Club: Oswego Country, Mountain Park Racquet, City. Avocations: golf, tennis. Home: 2371 Palisades Crest Dr Lake Oswego OR 97034

MARLOW, KEITH WINTON, physicist; b. Madison, Kans., Nov. 14, 1928; s. Marcus Augustus Marlow and Erma Delila (Chew) Rivers; m. Betty Lou Warren, Oct. 21, 1951; children: Susan Elaine, April Louise, Kevin Gaylord (dec.). BS, Kans. State U., 1951; PhD, U. Md., 1966. Research physicist Naval Research Lab., Washington, 1951-68, head reactors br., 1968-70, head radiation detection group, 1970-84; mem. tech. staff Sandia Nat. Labs., Albuquerque, 1984—; vis. scientist Inst. Nuclear Research, Amsterdam, The Netherlands, 1967-68. Recipient E.O. Hulburt Ann. Sci. award Naval Research Lab., 1981. Mem. AAAS, Am. Phys. Soc., Sigma Xi. Mem. Unitarian Ch. Avocations: golf, skiing. Home: 9405 Oakmont Rd NE Albuquerque NM 87111 Office: Sandia Nat Labs Div 9112 Albuquerque NM 87185

MARMARELIS, VASILIS ZISSIS, engineering educator; b. Mytilini, Greece, Nov. 16, 1949; came to U.S., 1972; s. Zissis P. and Elpis V. (Galinos) M. Diploma in elec. and mech. engring., Nat. Tech. U. of Athens, Greece, 1972; MS in Info. Sci., Calif. Inst. Tech., 1973, PhD in Engring. Sci., 1976. Research fellow Calif. Inst. Tech., Pasadena, 1976-78; asst. prof. U. So. Calif., Los Angeles, 1978-83, assoc. prof., 1983—, also dir. biomed. simulations resource, 1985—. Author: Analysis of Physiological Systems, 1978; contbr. articles to profl. jours. Mem. AAAS, IEEE, Internat. Fedn. Automatic Control, Biomed. Engring. Soc. Office: U So Calif OHE 500 Los Angeles CA 90089-1451

MARMOR, JUDD, psychiatrist, educator; b. London, May 1, 1910; came to U.S., 1911, naturalized, 1916; s. Clement K. and Sarah (Levene) M.; m. Katherine Stern, May 1, 1938; 1 son, Michael Franklin. A.B., Columbia U., 1930, M.D., 1933; D.H.L., Hebrew Union Coll., Los Angeles, 1972. Diplomate: Am. Bd. Psychiatry and Neurology, Nat. Bd. Med. Examiners. Intern St. Elizabeth Hosp., Washington, 1933-35; resident neurologist Montefiore Hosp., N.Y.C., 1935-37; psychiatrist Bklyn. State Hosp., 1937; psychoanalytic tng. N.Y. Psychoanalytic Inst., N.Y.C., 1937-41; pvt. practice psychiatry, psychoanalysis and neurology N.Y.C., 1937-46, Los Angeles, 1946—; instr. assoc. in neurology Columbia Coll. Physicians and Surgeons, 1938-40; adj. neurologist, neurologist-in-charge clinic Mt. Sinai Hosp., N.Y.C., 1939-46; lectr. New Sch. Social Research, N.Y.C., 1942-43; instr. Am. Inst. Psychoanalysis, N.Y.C., 1943; lectr. psychiatry N.Y. Med. Coll., 1944-46; lectr. social welfare UCLA, 1948-49, vis. prof. social welfare, 1949-64, clin. prof. psychiatry Sch. Medicine, 1953—, adj. prof. psychiatry, 1980—; vis. prof. psychology U. So. Calif., 1946-49; tng. analyst, also pres. So. Calif. Psychoanalytic Inst., 1955-57; sr. attending psychiatrist Los Angeles County Gen. Hosp., 1954—; dir. divs. psychiatry Cedars-Sinai Med. Center, Los Angeles, 1965-72; Franz Alexander prof. psychiatry U. So. Calif. Sch. Medicine, 1972-80, emeritus, 1980—; sr. cons. regional office social service VA, Los Angeles, 1946-50; cons. psychiatry Brentwood VA Hosp., Calif., 1955-65; mem. Council Mental Health of Western Interstate Commn. Higher Edn.; Bd. dirs. Human Interaction Research Inst., Behavioral Sci. Research Found.; v.p. Psychosomatic Research Found. Editor: Sexual Inversion-The Multiple Roots of Homosexuality, Modern Psychoanalysis: New Directions and Perspectives, Psychiatry in Transition: Selected Papers of Judd Marmor, Homosexual Behavior: A Modern Reappraisal, (with S. Woods) The Interface Between the Psychodynamic and Behavioral Therapies; editorial bd.: Jour. Sex and Marital Therapy, Am. Jour. Psychoanalysis, Contemporary Psychoanalysis, Psychiatry Digest, Archives Sexual Behavior, Am. Jour. Community Psychology; contbr. articles in field to profl. jours. Bd. dirs. Neumeyer Found. Served as sr. attending surgeon USPHS USNR, 1944-45. Fellow Am. Psychiat. Assn. (life mem., pres. 1975-76), N.Y. Acad. Medicine (life mem.), Am. Acad. Psychoanalysis (pres. 1965-66), Am. Orthopsychiat. Assn. (dir. 1968-71), AAAS, Am. Coll. Psychiatrists; mem. AMA, Calif. Med. Assn., Group for Advancement Psychiatry (dir. 1968-70, pres. 1973-75), Am. Fund for Psychiatry (dir. 1955-57), So. Calif. Psychiat. Soc., So. Calif. Psychoanalytic Soc. (pres. 1960-61), Am. Psychoanalytic Assn., Los Angeles County Med. Soc., Phi Beta Kappa, Alpha Omega Alpha. Home: 655 Sarbonne Rd Los Angeles CA 90077 Office: 10889 Wilshire Blvd Suite 909 Los Angeles CA 90024

MARNELL, ANTHONY AUSTIN, II, architect; b. Riverside, Calif., Mar. 30, 1949; s. Anthony Austin and Ida Marie (Comforti) M.; B.Arch., U. So. Calif., 1972; m. Sandra Jean Graf, June 24, 1972; children—Anthony, Alisa. Architect, draftsman firms in Calif. and Nev., 1969-72; project coordinator Zuni Constrn. Co., Las Vegas, Nev., 1973-74; office mgr., architect Corrao Constrn. Co., Inc., Las Vegas, 1974-82; chmn. bd. Marnell Corrao Assos., Las Vegas, 1976—; pres. Marinelli Internat., Inc., 1978—, A.A. Marnell II, Architect, 1980—, Air Continental Jet Charter, Inc., 1980—; mem. ethics com. Nev. Bd. Architects, 1974; prin. works include: additions to Caesar's Palace Las Vegas, Maxim Hotel, Sundance Hotel, additions to Desert Inn and Sands Hotel (all Las Vegas), Caesar's Boardwalk Regency, Atlantic City, others. Mem. Nat. Council Archtl. Registration Bds., Post Tensioning Inst. Roman Catholic. Office: Marnell Corrao Assoc Inc 4495 S Polaris Ave Las Vegas NV 89103

MARON, MILFORD ALVIN, judge; b. Chgo., Jan. 21, 1926; s. Martin and Anna (Newman) M.; B.A. cum laude, U. So. Calif., 1949, M.A., 1953, LL.B., 1954, LL.M., 1958; m. Esther Kass, Dec. 24, 1966; children—Steven, Dean, Melissa, Adam. Admitted to Calif. bar, 1955; dep. commr. corps. Calif. Div. Corps., Los Angeles, 1955-57; trial counsel SEC, Los Angeles, 1957-61, Calif. Div. Labor Law Enforcement, 1961-63; adminstrv. law judge Calif. Office Adminstrv. Hearings, Los Angeles, 1963—. Served with AUS, 1944-46. Mem. Bar Assn. Calif. Democrat. Jewish. Office: Calif Office Adminstrv Hearings 314 W 1st St Los Angeles CA 90012

MARONDE, ROBERT FRANCIS, internist, clin. pharmacologist, educator; b. Monterey Park, Calif., Jan. 13, 1920; s. John August and Emma Florence (Palmer) M.; m. Yolanda Cerda, Apr. 15, 1970; children—Robert George, Donna F. Maronde Varnau, James Augustus, Craig DeWald. B.A., U. So. Calif., 1941, M.D., 1944. Diplomate: Am. Bd. Internal Medicine. Intern Los Angeles County-U. So. Calif. Med. Center, 1943-44, resident, 1944-45, 47-48; asst. prof. physiology U. So. Calif., Los Angeles, 1948-49; asst. clin. prof. medicine U. So. Calif., 1949-60, asso. clin. prof. medicine, 1960-65, asso. prof. medicine and pharmacology, 1965-67, prof., 1968—; cons. FDA, 1973. Served to lt. (j.g.) USNR, 1945-47. Fellow ACP; mem. Am. Soc. Clin. Pharmacology and Therapeutics, Alpha Omega Alpha. Home: 785 Ridgecrest St Monterey Park CA 91754 Office: U So Calif 2025 Zonal Ave Los Angeles CA 90033

MAROVICH, JAMES MICHAEL, hospital administrator; b. Gary, Ind., Aug. 12, 1949; s. Donald M. and Vinnie J. (Cimino) M.; m. Barbara J. Hlodnicki, Aug. 22, 1969; 1 child, Jaime. BS, Ind. U., 1971; MBA, U. Fla., 1977. Indsl. engring. cost anlayst U.S. Steel, Gary, 1969-75; adminstrv. resident St. Joseph's Hosp., Tucson, 1977, asst. adminstr., 1977-81; adminstr., chief exec. officer Navapache Hosp., Show Low, Ariz., 1981—; chmn. Family Health Plan of Northeastern Ariz., Show Low, 1983—. Chmn. Pinetop-Lakeside (Ariz.) Econ. Devel. Commn., 1986. Foster McGaw scholar, 1976. Mem. Ariz. Hosp. Assn. (chmn. elect. 1986-87, chmn. 1987-88, Roland Wilpitz award 1983) No. Ariz. Hosp. Council (pres. 1982—), Am. Coll. Healthcare Execs., Pinteop-Lakeside C. of C. (bd. dirs. 1983-86). Lodge: Rotary (Show Low club pres. 1984-85). Avocations: snow skiing, running, softball, acting, theater. Home: Rt 2 Box 2251 N Lakeside AZ 85929 Office: Navapache Hosp 2200 Show Low Lake Rd Show Low AZ 85901

MARQUARDT, TERRY TYRONE, optometrist; b. Alamogordo, N.Mex., Nov. 20, 1949; s. Oscar Henry and June Lavonne (Weaver) M.; children—Tyrone, Todd. B.S., U. N.Mex., 1970; O.D., So. Coll. Optometry, 1974; lic. optometrist. Assoc. Drs. Marquardt & Marquardt, Alamogordo, 1974-78; pvt. practice optometry, Ruidoso N.Mex., 1978—; low vision cons. N.Mex. Services for the Blind, N.Mex. Sch. Visually Handicapped, 1975-76. Coach Seratoma Little League Basketball. Bausch & Lomb Contact Lens Research fellow 1973. Mem. Am. Optometric Assn., Optometric Extension Program Found., Council on Sports Vision, Republican. Lutheran. Club: Rotary (dir. 1980). Home: PO Box 3596 Ruidoso NM 88345 Office: Sierra Professional Ctr 123 Mescalero Trail Ruidoso NM 88345

MARQUESS, LAWRENCE WADE, lawyer; b. Bloomington, Ind., Mar. 2, 1950; s. Earl Lawrence and Mary Louise (Coberly) M.; m. Barbara Ann Bailey, June 17, 1978; children: Alexander Lawrence, Michael Wade. B.S. in Elec. Engring., Purdue U., 1973; J.D., W.Va. U., 1977. Bar: W.Va. 1977, U.S. Dist. Ct. (so. dist.) W.Va. 1977, Tex. 1977, U.S. Dist. Ct. (no. dist.) Tex. 1977, Colo. 1980, U.S. Dist. Ct. Colo. 1980, U.S. Ct. Appeals (10th cir.) 1980, U.S. Supreme Ct. 1984. Assoc. Johnson, Bromberg, Leeds & Riggs, Dallas, 1977-79; assoc. Bradley, Campbell & Carney, Golden, Colo., 1979-82, ptnr., 1983-84; assoc. Stettner, Miller & Cohn P.C., Denver, 1984-85, ptnr., 1985—. Mem faculty Am. Law Inst.-ABA Advanced Labor and Employment Law Course, 1986, 87. Mem. ABA (labor and litigation sects.), Colo. Bar Assn. (program com., labor law com.), Denver Bar Assn. (program com., labor law com.), 1st Jud. Dist. Bar Assn. Sierra Club, Nat. Ry. Hist. Soc., ACLU. Democrat. Methodist. Home: 2293 Yellowstone St Golden CO 80401 Office: Stettner Miller & Cohn PC 1380 Lawrence St Suite 1000 Denver CO 80204

MARQUEZ, RICARDO, architect; b. Mexico City, Sept. 3, 1948; came to U.S., 1978; s. Flavio and Amalia (Orozco) M.; m. Mary Joel, Mar. 22, 1980. BArch., U. Mex., Mex. City; MA in Solar Tech., Ariz. State U. Registered architect. Architect Toor, Mexico City, 1975-77, Gilbert Honanie, Phoenix, 1978-82, IPESA, Mex., 1982-83, Design Group, Scottsdale, Ariz., 1984-85; pvt. practice architecture Fountain Hills, Ariz., 1985—. Author: Como Organizar El FBA, 1982, Futbol Americano Inf., 1986. head coach U. Mex., Mexico City, 1969-77; coach kicking and specialty teams Outlaws USFL, Phoenix, 1985—; def. coordinator Aguilas U. N.Mex., 1982-83; jr. varsity head coach Ariz. State U., Tempe, 1978-80. Named Coach of Yr. Pop Warner Coll., 1975, 81; DuBois Found. scholar, 1978. Mem. AIA (assoc.), ASHRAE, Constn. Surveyors Inst. Avocation: model bldg.

MARQUEZ-OROZCO, RICARDO, architect, football coach; b. Mexico City, Mexico, Sept. 3, 1948; came to U.S., 1977, naturalized, 1981; s. Flavio and Amalia (Orozco Mendez) Marquez de la Fuente; m. Mary Joel Machrol, Mar. 22, 1980. B.Arch., U. Mexico, 1975; grad. in solar tech., Ariz. State U., 1980. Football coach U. Mexico, 1975-77; architect TORACT, Mexico City, 1975-77; football coach Ariz. State U., Tempe, 1978-79, 80—; architect/planner Ricardo Marquez, Architect, Tempe, 1978—; asst tchr. U. Mexico Coll. Architecture, 1976-77; cons. Mexican archtl. firms Ipesa, U.N.A.M.; prof. summer courses U. Mex., Mexico City Coll. Architecture. Named Coach of Yr., U. Mexico, 1976; Dubois Orgn. scholar, 1978-79. Mem. AIA (assoc.), Constrn. Specifications Inst., ASHRAE. Roman Catholic. Author: Como Organizar un Equipo de F.B.A., 1980. Home: 17044 Armour Circle Fountain Hills AZ 85268

MARQUIS, EMANUEL, purchasing executive; b. Pittsfield, Mass., Jan. 19, 1942; s. Kieve Carl and Evelyn (Markell) M.; m. Rochelle Rakovsky, Nov. 11, 1968; children: Jacqueline, Daniel Maxwell. A., Berkshire Community Coll., Pittsfield, Mass., 1962; B., U. N.D., 1965. Buyer Pratt & Whitney, East Hartford, Conn., 1966-71, Converse Rubber, Wilmington, Mass., 1972-77; sr. buyer Dalmo Victor, San Carlos, Calif., 1977-79; sr. buyer, subcontract adminstr. Ford Aerospace Lab., Palo Alto, Calif., 1979—. Founder town meeting, 1977. Mem. Purchasing Mgmt. Assn. of Silicon Valley (pres. 1983). Democrat. Jewish. Avocations: reading, golf.

MARQUIS, ROBERT B., architect; b. Stuttgart, Ger., July 9, 1927; came to U.S., 1937, naturalized, 1943; s. Paul Charles and Marianne (Gutstein) M.; m. Ellen Godfrey, Dec. 20, 1950; children—Lisa Leeds, Tessa, David. Student, Sch. Architecture, U. So. Calif., 1946-49, Acad. di Belle Art, Florence, Italy, 1949-50. Founder Marquis Assocs. Architects, San Francisco, 1953-56; pres. Marquis & Stoller, Architects and Planners, San Francisco and N.Y.C., 1956-74, Marquis Assocs., San Francisco and N.Y.C., 1974—; vis. critic Stanford U.; Thomas Jefferson prof. architecture U. Va., 1980—; lectr. various univs. Prin. works include Novato (Calif.) Library (Design award), Sonoma State Coll. Cafeteria, (Instn. Mags. award), housing for elderly (Design awards), St. Francis Sq. Co-op, (Design awards), St. Francis Yacht Club, San Francisco (Design awards); energy-conserving Calif. Dept. Justice Office Bldg, Sacramento (Owens Corning Energy award); Am. embassy, San Jose, Costa Rica, Braun Music Bldg, Stanford U., Primate Ctr. San Francisco Zoo, Aaron Copland Sch. Music Queens Coll., N.Y.C., Rosa Parks Sr. Citizens Housing, San Francisco, south terminal modernization San Francisco Internat. Airport; numerous pvt. residences and restoration projects, Works included in publs., exhibited museums. Thomas Jefferson prof. architecture U. Va.; Grantee Nat. Endowment Arts; recipient Albert J. Evers Environ. award; No. Calif. AIA, 1975; Calif. Council AIA Firm award, 1984, 50 other design awards. Fellow AIA (past pres. chpt., past nat. dir., past internat. relations com., bd. dirs., trustee AIA Found. 1984-86). Address: 243 Vallejo St San Francisco CA 94111

MARR, LUTHER REESE, film co. exec.; b. Kansas City, June 23, 1925; s. Luther Dow and Aileen (Shimfessel) M.; m. Christelle Lois Taylor, July 12, 1956; children—Michelle Lois, Stephen Luther, Christelle Elizabeth. A.B., U. Calif. at Los Angeles, 1946; J.D., U. So. Calif., 1950. Bar: Calif. bar 1951. With firm Hasbrouck & Melby, Glendale, 1952-54; atty. The Walt Disney Co., Burbank, Calif., 1954—; corp. sec. The Walt Disney Co., 1957-78, v.p. corp. and shareholder affairs, 1978—; also officer, dir. The Walt Disney Co. (subs.'s.). Trustee Le Lycée Français de Los Angeles. Served with USNR, 1946-47. Mem. Am. Soc. Corp. Secs., Calif., Los Angeles bar assns., Phi Beta Kappa, Phi Alpha Delta. Republican. Methodist. Home: 2323 Via Saldivar Glendale CA 91208 Office: 500 S Buena Vista St Burbank CA 91521

MARRA, P(ETER) GERALD, manufacturers representative distributor firm executive; b. Cranbrook, B.C., Can., June 29, 1940; came to U.S., 1964, naturalized, 1973; s. John and Angela Rose Marra; B.Sc., U. B.C., 1963, postgrad., 1963-64; m. Eileen Elizabeth Sowerby, Feb. 11, 1967 (div. 1987); children: Amber Eileen, Anne-Marie Geraldine. Computer engr. Canadair Ltd., Montreal, Que., 1962-63; research engr. Boeing Corp., Seattle, 1964-68; hardware specialist Computer Sci. Corp., Toronto, Ont., Can., 1969; pres., gen. mgr. D.I.S.C., Seattle, 1970-74; sales mgr. Hayes Tech. Co., Seattle, 1975; owner, pres. Marra & Assocs., Bellevue, Wash., 1976—; cons. small bus., 1970—. Republican party platform chmn. King County, 1976-78, legis. dist. chmn., 1978; pres., dir. fundraising for U. B.C., Friends of U. B.C., 1975—; asst. chmn. archery com. Wash. State Sportsmen's Council, 1980, chmn., 1981-83, chmn. big game com. 1981-83; mem. Mt. Rainier Wildlife Com., 1981—. IBM scholar, 1964. Mem. Can. Soc. of Northwest (exec. com. 1985—), U. B.C. Alumni (pres. Seattle, Pacific N.W. chpt. 1974—). Club: Cedar River Bowman Archery. Home: 1739 172d Pl NE Bellevue WA 98008

MARROW, MARVA JAN, photographer; b. Denver, Apr. 22, 1948; d. Sydney and Helen Berniece (Garber) M.; m. Michael Eschger, Jan. 26, 1985. Student, Carnegie-Mellon U., 1965-67. Singer, songwriter RCA Records, Italy, 1972-77; pvt. practice photography Italy and U.S., 1976—; represented by Gamma Liaison, Shooting Star Agencies, USA, Franco Masi Fotoservizi, Italy; correspondent, photographer Italian TV Guide, Milan, 1979—; collaborator, photographer for other U.S. And Italian publs. Author numerous songs for Italian pop artists, including: Lucio Battisti, Battiato, Premiata Forneria Marconi (PFM), Patty Pravo, 1972—; contbr. photographs for covers and articles to nat. and internat. mags. Mem. Motion Picture Assn. of Am., Fgn. Press Assn. Democrat. Avocations: cooking, travelling, people animals. Home and Office: 1267 Boston St Altadena CA 91001 Office: Gamma Liaison Agy 6606 Sunset Blvd Suite 201 Los Angeles CA 90026

MARRS, LEO RICHARD, JR., materials manager; b. Birmingham, Ala., June 29, 1949; s. Leo Richard Sr. and Oma Lee (Stone) M.; m. Penny Ann Boals, Dec. 26, 1971; children: Hilary Anne, Thomas Richard. BA, U. So. Ala., 1974; MBA, U. Phoenix, 1985. Lab. asst. U. So. Ala., Mobile, 1973-75; rep. Marrs Electric Co., Tarrant, Ala., 1975-79; buyer Magma Copper Co., San Manuel, Ariz., 1979-81; sr. buyer Magma Copper Co., San Manuel, 1981-85, materials control supr., 1985-86, chief warehouse supr., 1986, warehouseing mgr., 1986—. Mem. Nat. Assn. Purchasing Mgmt., Purchasing Mgmt. Assn. So. Ariz., Am. Prodn. and Inventory Control Soc. Methodist. Avocations: reading, flyfishing, flytying. Home: 7911 N Hopdown Ave Tucson AZ 85741 Office: Magma Copper Co PO Box M State Hwy 77 San Manuel AZ 85631

MARSCHALL, EKKEHARD PAUL, mechanical engineering educator; b. Hermsdorf, Schlesien, Germany, Apr. 18, 1935; Came to U.S. in 1967; s. Gerhard and Ruth (Lachmann) M.; m. Sieglinde F. Franke, Aug. 28, 1960; children: Jochen, Anne. Dipl.-Ing., U. Hannover, Fed. Replublic Germany, 1962, Dr.-Ing., 1967. Research assoc. U. Stuttgart, Stuttgart, Fed. Republic of Germany, 1968-69; prof. mech. engring. U. Calif., Santa Barbara, 1969—. Contbr. numerous articles to profl. jours. NATO fellow, 1967-68. Mem. Am. Soc. Mech. Engrs., Am. Inst. Chem. Engrs., Am. Assn. U. Profs., Sigma Xi. Home: 367 El Gaucho Rd Santa Barbara CA 93111 Office: U Calif Dept Mech Engring Santa Barbara CA 93106

MARSDEN, GUY TALBOT, technokinetic artist, electronics engineer, consultant; b. Boston, May 19, 1955; s. Peter Bernard and Jo Mary (Horry) M. BFA, Md. Inst. Coll. Art, 1976. Display engr. Md. Sci. Ctr., Balt., 1977-79; pvt. practice spl. effects tech., various films Los Angeles, 1979-85, cons. display engring., 1985—; technokinetic artist 1986—. Prin. works include electronic-kinetic shows Mus. Neon Art, Los Angeles, 1985, Neon and On exhibit, Ariz., 1986. Avocation: building high-voltage Tesla Coils.

MARSH, DEBRA ROSE RANIERE, speech-language pathologist; b. Weisbaden, Republic of Germany, Nov. 27, 1955; came to U.S., 1956; d. Lawrence Charles and Philomena Marie (LaQuaglia) Raniere; m. John Harrison Marsh, June 18, 1977; 1 child, Jennifer Rose. BA in Communication Scis. and Disorders, Oreg. State U., 1977; MS in Speech-Lang. Pathology, Western Oreg. State Coll., 1980-83. Service rep. Gen. Telephone Co. of the N.W., Tigard, Oreg., 1977-78, sales rep., 1978-79; speech-lang. pathologist Reedville Sch. Dist., Aloha, Oreg., 1979—; vol. clinician Crestwood Speech Camp, Salem, Oreg., 1984; mem. orientation and adv. com. Commn. for Status of Women. Campaign rep. United Good Neighbor, Aloha, 1980-83; block leader March of Dimes, Beaverton, Oreg., 1984-85; vol. Neil Goldschmidt for Gov., Portland, Oreg., 1986—; active Oreg. Environ. Council., 1986—, Oreg. Natural Resources Council, 1986—. Recipient Most Valuable Staffer award News and Observer Newspaper, 1973. Mem. Am. Speech-Lang.-Hearing Assn., Oreg. Speech-Lang.-Hearing Assn. (mem. program com.), Oreg. Winegrowers Assn., Great Lovers of Wine, Alpha Delta Pi (hostess, Panhellenic Bagatelle Luncheon), Zeta Phi Eta (sec. 1976-77), Kappa Delta Pi. Avocations: snow skiing, sewing, gourmet cooking, antiques, aerobics. Office: Reedville Sch Dist #29 2425 SW 219th Aloha OR 97006

MARSH, MARCUS MARLENE, mathematics educator; b. Birmingham, Ala., Jan. 15, 1948; s. Guss Marcus Marsh and Ida Lee (Keenam) Joiner; m. Dorothy Davis Sherling, Oct. 13, 1973 (div. 1979); m. Marilee Elizabeth Richter, Jan. 11, 1986. BS in Math., Auburn U., 1970; MS, U. Houston, 1976, PhD in Math., 1981. Assoc. prof. math. Calif. State U., Sacramento, 1981—. Contbr. articles to profl. jours. Served to ensign USN, 1970-71. Recipient Assigned Time Research grant Calif. State U., Sacramento, 1984-85, 85-86, 86-87. Mem. Am. Math. Soc., Math. Assn. Am., N.Y. Acad. Scis. Democrat.

MARSH, RICHARD NORMAN, electrical engineer; b. Hartford, Conn., June 22, 1946; s. Norman Frank and Virginia E. (Corey) M.; m. Barbara Lea Sweeney, Aug. 12, 1984; 1 child, Dean Michael. BSEE, Sacramento State Coll., 1966. With Lawrence Livermore Nat. Lab., Livermore, Calif., 1966—, computer systems engr. calibration and measurements Standards Lab., 1966-79, tech. coordinator prompt diagnostics nuclear test research and devel. labs., 1979-82, sr. elec. engr. tech. coordinator fusion energy and beam research, 1982—. Mem. noise abatement com. City of Livermore, 1977. Served with U.S. Army, 1969-72. Mem. Audio Engring. Soc., So. Audio Cons., No. Calif. Audio Soc. Republican. Home: 3301 Fallen Tree Ct Sacramento CA 95827 Office: PO Box 808 Livermore CA 94550

MARSHALL, ARTHUR K., lawyer, judge, arbitrator, educator, writer; b. N.Y.C., Oct. 7, 1911. B.S., CCNY, 1933; LL.B., St. John's U., N.Y.C., 1936; LL.M., U. So. Calif., 1952. Bar: N.Y. State 1937, Calif. 1947. Practice law N.Y.C., 1937-43, Los Angeles, 1947-50; atty. VA, Los Angeles, 1947-50; tax counsel Calif. Bd. Equalization, Sacramento, 1950-51; inheritance tax atty. State Controller, Los Angeles, 1951-53; commr. Superior Ct. Los Angeles County, 1953-62; judge Municipal Ct., Los Angeles jud. dist., 1962-63, Superior Ct., Los Angeles, 1963-81; supervising judge probate dept. Superior Ct., 1968-69, appellate dept., 1973-77; presiding judge Appellate Dept., 1976-77; pvt. practice 1981—, arbitrator, referee, judge protem, 1981—; Acting asst. prof. law U. Calif. at Los Angeles, 1954-59; mem. grad. faculty U. So. Calif., 1955-75; lectr. Continuing Edn. of Bar; vice chmn. Calif. Law Revision Commn., 1984-86, chmn. 1986—. Author: Joint Tenancy Taxwise & Otherwise, 1953, Branch Courts, 1959, California State and Local Taxation, Text, 2 vols, 1962, rev. edit., 1969, supplement, 1979, 2d edit., 1981, California State and Local Taxation Forms, 2 vols, 1961-75, rev. edit., 1979, California Probate Procedure, 1961, 9th rev. edit., 1986, Guide to Procedure Before Trial, 1975. Served with AUS, 1943-46; lt. col. Res. ret. Named Judge of Yr. Lawyers Club of Los Angeles County, 1975; Arthur K. Marshall Award established by estate planning, trust and probate sect. Los Angeles Bar Assn., 1981; Disting. Jud. Career award Los Angeles Lawyers Club. Fellow Am. Bar Found.; mem. Internat. Acad. Estate and Trust Law (academician, founder, 1st pres., now chancellor), ABA (probate litigation com. real property, probate and trust sect.), Calif. State Bar (adv. to exec. com. estate planning, probate and trust sect. 1970-83), Santa Monica Bar Assn. (pres. 1960), Westwood Bar Assn. (pres. 1959), Los Angeles Bar Assn., Lawyers Club, Am. Judicature Soc., Am. Legion (comdr. 1971-72), U. So. Calif. Law Alumni Assn. (pres. 1969-70), Phi Alpha Delta (1st justice alumni chpt. 1976-77). Office: 300 S Grand Ave 29th Floor Los Angeles CA 90071

MARSHALL, CHARLEEN IRENE, interior designer; b. Rosemead, Calif., Dec. 25, 1940; d. Charles Richard and Alice Irene (Miller) Guess; m. Thomas Lee Marshall Sr., Nov. 28, 1959; children: Thomas Jr., Sheri Lynn, Charles Howard. AA magna cum laude, Fashion Inst. of Design and Merchandising, Los Angeles, 1974. Showroom mgr. Sinclaire Wallcoverings, Los Angeles, 1975-78; owner, designer New Surroundings, Inc., Westlake Village, Calif., 1978-81; assoc. project designer Cannell and Chaffin, Los Angeles, 1981-85; exec. showroom mgr. Pindler and Pindler, Los Angeles, 1985—; designer Met. Water Dist., Los Angeles, 1984, City of Simi Valley (Calif.) Dept. Human Resources, 1985. Designer Showcase House, 1979. Mem. Calif. State Hist. Soc. (hist. site design cons. The Stage Coach Inn, Thousand Oaks, Calif., 1979-81), Nat. Hist. Preservation. Republican. Roman Catholic. Club: Exec. Women (Los Angeles). Avocation: raising miniature horses. Office: Pindler & Pindler Inc 145 N Robertson Blvd Los Angeles CA 90025

MARSHALL, DENNIS LEHR, gen. contractor, home bldg. exec.; b. Denver, Feb. 13, 1943; s. Howard Leonard and Gloria Elise (Larkin) M.; student LaSalle Extension U., 1963; m. Jeanette Burnett, Aug. 28, 1960; children—Randy Lee, Donna Jean. Carpenter foreman Ray Delcamp Gen. Contractor, Denver, 1960-64; sub contractor Marshall Constrn., Denver, 1965-67; with Vantage Builders Wheat Ridge, Colo., 1967—, creator Vantage Custom Homes, 1968, pres., 1970—; founder Vantage Enterprises, 1973. Mem. Bd. Rev., Jefferson County, 1972-86; coach Little League Football, 1969-77; mem. Residential Energy Com., 1979-82, chmn. Codes and Standards Com.; chmn., gov.'s appointee Colo. State Housing Bd.; 1st. chmn. Colo. loan program and loan com. Colo. Div. Housing, 1985-86. Recipient Builder of Year award Home Builders Assn. Met. Denver, 1977, 78; Outstanding Service award Colo. Assn. Home Builders, 1978. Mem. Nat. Assn. Home Builders (life bd. dirs.), Colo. Assn. Home Builders (bd. dirs.), Home Builders Assn. Met. Denver (past pres.). Republican. Baptist. Club: Beech Areo; Toastmaster. Home: 1051 S Foothill Dr Lakewood CO 80228

MARSHALL, HAL GEORGE, atmospheric scientist; b. Twin Falls, July 17, 1955; s. James J. and Shirley A. (Moyes) M.; m. Marianne T. Wuchner, June 18, 1977; children: Andrew, Jacob. BS in Physics magna cum laude, Calif. Poly. Inst., Pomona, 1977; MS in Physics, Iowa State U., 1979, PhD in Meteorology, 1983. Postdoctoral scholar U. Mich., Ann Arbor, 1983-84, research fellow, 1984-85; asst. prof. Wash. State U., Pullman, 1985—; cons. N.W.I.M. Weather, Twin Falls, Idaho. Contbr. articles on atmospheric dynamics to profl. jours. Recipient Pace award, Iowa State U., 1979. Mem. AAAS, Am. Meteorol. Soc., Am. Geophys. Soc., Phi Kappa Phi, Sigma Pi Sigma. Home: 1835B Lamont St NW Pullman WA 99163 Office: Wash State U Lab for Atmospheric Research Pullman WA 99164-2730

MARSHALL, JAMES KENNETH, academic administrator; b. Providence, Dec. 25, 1952; s. James William and Eileen Frances (O'Connell) M. BA in Chemistry, SUNY, Plattsburgh, 1974; MBA in Fin., U. R.I., 1977; postgrad., U. Wash., 1978-79. Fin. instr. U. R.I., Kingston, 1978; teaching assoc. U. Wash., Seattle, 1978-79; asst. dir. facilities mgmt. U. Colo., Boulder, 1979-86, dir. buying and contracting, 1986—; honorarium instr. U. Colo., Denver, 1981—. Recipient Job Well Done award U. Colo. Boulder Dept. Facilities Mgmt., 1983. Mem. Rocky Mountain Assn. Phys. Plant Adminstrs., Assn. Phys. Plant Adminstrs., Internat. Facilities Mgmt. Assn. (research com. 1984-86), Beta Gamma Sigma, Phi Kappa Phi. Avocations: skiing, climbing, fishing, golf. Office: U Colo Campus Box 380 Dept Buying & Contracting Boulder CO 80309

MARSHALL, JOSEPHINE RETTMAN, insurance auditor; b. Dallas, July 24, 1937; d. Robert Henry and Sophie Elizabeth (Barnard) R.; m. Charles Roy Foord, Oct. 2, 1971 (dec. Mar. 1974); m. 2d, Alden Edgar Marshall Jr., June 26, 1976. B.S. in Bus. Adminstrn., North Tex. State U., 1962. Sr. audit reviewer Fireman's Fund Ins. Group, Dallas, 1962-65; premium audit supr. Hartford Ins. Group, San Francisco, Reno and Los Angeles, 1965-75; regional premium audit mgr. C.G./Aetna Ins. Co., Los Angeles, 1975-82; controller designate Argonaut Ins. Co., Fullerton, Calif., 1982—; regional premium audit mgr. Argonaut Ins. Cos., Los Angeles, 1985—; fin. planner, audio visual editor, planner; mktg. researcher, forecaster; fashion model. Active Los Angeles County Mus. Art, San Francisco Ballet, Am. Heart Assn.; organizing com. Reno Air Show. Recipient Hartford Ins. Group Spl. Achievement award, 1971, C.G./Aetna Ins. Co. Affirmative Action award, 1982. Mem. Nat. Soc. Ins. Premium Auditors (pres. 1986), Colonial Dames Am., Fashion Models Internat., Ins. Auditors Assn. West (pres. 1984, 1st v.p., Achievement Recognition award 1983), Calif. Ins. Audit Mgrs. Assn., Internat. Environ. Edn. for Whale Protection. Republican. Roman Catholic. Club: Toastmistress Internat. Contbr. material to profl. publs. Office: 425 Shatto Place Los Angeles CA 90020

MARSHALL, L. B., medical technologist; b. Chgo., Feb. 10; s. Gillman and Ethel (Robinson) M.; B.S., U. Puget Sound; postgrad. San Francisco State U., City Coll. San Francisco; Sc.D.; m. Esther Wood, Sept. 28, 1961; 1 dau., Lelani. Pres., Med. Offices Health Services Group Inc., San Francisco, 1964—. Served with U.S. Army, 1947-53. Decorated Bronze Star, Med. Combat Badge. Recipient certificate of appreciation Pres. Nixon, 1973, Urban League, 1973, Calif. Dept. Human Resources, 1973. Mem. Am., Calif. assns. med. technologists, NAACP (life). Club: Oyster Point Yacht. Author poetry.

MARSHALL, MAUREEN GRETA, management company executive; b. Yorkshire, Eng., Aug. 14, 1921; d. George Cyril and Greta Beatrice (Hall) Stevenson; came to U.S., 1952; B.A. with distinction, U. Calif. at Berkeley, 1969, M.A., 1970; m. Sherwood Barnett Marshall, Nov. 1, 1952; 1 dau., Virginia Maureen Marshall Lang. Vice pres. Alameda (Calif.) Convalescent Hosp., 1968-70, Sonoma (Calif.) Convalescent Hosp., 1970-74; gen. ptnr. Valley View Lodge, Walnut Creek, Calif., 1974-82; exec. v.p. SAV Service Corp., Walnut Creek, 1975—; pres. Tri-County Supply Inc., Walnut Creek, 1978—; v.p. Kristina Odysseys, Ltd., Del., 1979. Served with Canadian Women's Army Corps, World War II. Mem. San Francisco Women's Artists (pres. 1977-79), Phi Beta Kappa. Episcopalian. Paintings exhibited at Calif. Inst. Art, Mus. Modern Art, San Francisco, Worth Ryder Gallery, San Francisco, U. Calif. at Berkeley, San Francisco Art Commn. Gallery, St. Mary's Coll., Moraga, Calif., Internat. Ctr. for Contemporary Art, Paris, 1983, Percy Basse Gallery, London, 1985, also at juried shows. Office: care Seiler & Co 120 Montgomery St Suite 2250 San Francisco CA 94104

MARSHALL, ROBERT OWEN, JR., municipal official; b. Tulsa, Oct. 9, 1936; s. Robert Owen and Esther Dell (Dixon) M.; m. Linda Kay Mercer, Oct. 21, 1956; children: Robert Owen III, Natalie Kay Pebles. AS, Casper Coll., student. Cert. law enforcement instr. Peace Officer Standards Commn., Cheyenne, Wyo, 1975—. Lt. Casper (Wyo.) Police Dept., 1959-79; adminstr. of corrections Natrona County Sheriff's Dept., Casper, 1979-81, chief investigations, 1981—. Mem. Wyo. Peace Officers Assn. Republican. Lutheran. Avocations: running, photography, painting. Home: 3700 E 18th St Casper WY 82609

MARSHALL, VAUGHN GILES, neuroradiologist, researcher; b. Oklahoma City, Okla., Sept. 26, 1948; s. Charles Edward and Marguerite (Walker) M.; m. René Purcell, Aug. 14, 1971; 1 child, Vaughn Charles. BS, Okla. State U., 1970; MD, U. Okla., 1974. Cert. Am. Bd. Radiology. Staff radiologist USN, San Diego, 1978-82; radiologist The Duluth (Minn.) Clinic, 1983-85; fellow in imaging Huntington Med. Research Inst., Pasadena, Calif., 1985-86; fellow in nueroradiology Los Angeles County Hosp., U. So. Calif., 1985-87; cons. radiologist U. Calif., San Diego, 1979-82. Served with USNR, 1971-82. Mem. AMA, Radiol. Soc. N.Am., Am. Coll. Radiology. Republican. Avocations: skiing, golf, racquetball. Home: 909 Vista Mesa Ct Duarte CA 91010 Office: U So Calif Med Ctr Los Angeles County Hosp 1200 N State St Los Angeles CA 90033

MARSHALL-GRATRIX, WILLIAM JEREMY DAVID, airline pilot, lawyer; b. Hale, Cheshire, Eng., Aug. 22, 1931; came to U.S., 1964, naturalized, 1968; s. William Henry and Nellie (Patterson) M.-G.; m. Diane Kathleen Hearne, July 9, 1975. BS, Queen's Coll., Cambridge U., 1954; MA, Hon. Soc. Lincoln's Inn., 1958, barrister, 1958; solicitor, Law Soc. B.C., 1960, barrister, 1961. Cert. test pilot, exptl. test pilot. Asst. prosecutor City of Vancouver, B.C., Can., 1960-64; airline capt. United Air Lines, Reno, 1964—; flying instr. and cons. Served with RAF and RCAF, 1955-60. Mem. Guild of Air Pilots, Air Line Pilots Assn., Lawyer-Pilots Bar Assn. Mem. Ch. of Eng. Lodge: Masons. Home: 304 Bret Harte Ave Reno NV 89509

MARSHALL-WALKER, ROBERT WILLIAM, financial consultant, economist, tax lawyer; b. San Marcos, Tex., July 4, 1945; s. Robert William and Martha Ann (Westenbarger) W. BA, Calif. State U., 1969; postgrad., U. Calif.-Davis, 1969-72, Calif. State U., San Francisco; JD, New Coll. Sch. Law, 1984. Bar: Calif. 1965; U.S. Dist. Ct. (9th cir.), U.S. Dist. Ct. Appeals (9th cir.), U.S. Tax Ct.; lic. real estate broker, Calif. With African Tradeways, Inc., San Francisco, 1973-86 , pres., 1976-86 ; mng. ptnr. Marshall-Walker Assocs., San Francisco, 1977—; chief exec. officer Diversified Real Estate Investments Am., San Francisco, Fresno, Calif. and Tokyo, 1980—; prin. Grannis-Cox-Walker Assocs., Fresno and Patterson, Calif., 1980—; trainer Motivation Services, San Francisco, 1975-79; cons. Govt. Mali, Agrl. Trade Devel., 1979-81; cons. Somiex, Mali, 1980-82. Richard M. Weaver fellow, 1969; Arthur Mellinger Found. Fellow, 1969. Mem. Am. Philatelic Soc., Bar Assn. San Francisco, The Barristers Club, Fresno County Bar Assn., Bay Area Lawyers for the Arts, U. Calif. San Francisco Alumni Faculty Club, King Hall Counselors, Am. Numismatic Soc., ABA (com. taxation, com. real property, com. probate and trust law). Office: PO Box 352 San Francisco CA 94101

MARSI, KENNETH L., chemist, educator; b. Los Banos, Calif., Dec. 13, 1928; s. Sam and Wilma Evelyn (Soper) M.; m. Gertrude Irene Gutschenritter, Mar. 5, 1955; children: Marianne, Kenneth Scott, Brian Geoffrey, Teresa Jeanne. AB, San Jose State U., 1951; PhD, U. Kans., 1955. Sr. research chemist The Sherwin-Williams Co., Chgo., 1955-57; from asst. prof. to assoc. prof. chemistry Kans. State U., Ft. Hays, 1957-61, Calif. State U., Long Beach, 1961—; chemist Douglas Aircraft, Santa Monica, Calif., 1964-67; cons. S-cubed, San Diego, 1983—. Author: Problems in Organic Chemistry, 1968; reviewer Prentice-Hall, Inc., Englewood Cliffs, N.J., 1961—; abstractor Chem. Abstracts, Columbus, Ohio, 1958-67; contbr. articles to profl. jours. Named Outstanding Prof. Calif. State U.,Long Beach, 1984, Trustees Outstanding Prof. Calif. State U. System, 1985. Mem. Am. Chem. Soc. (com. mem. 1962—), Organic Sect. Am. Chem. Soc., Phi Beta Kappa, Sigma Xi (treas. Kans. chpt. 1954-55), Phi Lambda Upsilon (pres. 1954). Democrat. Episcopalian. Avocations: gardening, reading, biking, backpacking. Home: 1517 Vuelta Grande Long Beach CA 90815 Office: Calif State U Dept Chemistry 1250 Bellflower Blvd Long Beach CA 90840

MARSOLEK, L. GENE, manufacturer's representative; b. Denver, Apr. 2, 1942; s. Paul Robert and Tillie Marie (Richter) M.; m. Judith Kay Busch, Dec. 26, 1970; 1 son, Eric Lee. Student U. Colo., 1965. Mgr. Marsolek's Hardware & Appliance Store, 1961-65, 67-68; mfr.'s rep. John Brickell Co., Denver, 1970-74; owner, pres. L. Gene Marsolek Co., Inc., Denver, 1975—. Served with Colo. Air N.G., 1965-69; Korea. Mem. Assoc. Rep. of Mfrs. (past pres.), Mfr. Agt. Nat. Assn. Presbyterian. Clubs: El Jebel Mariners, Shriners, Masons. Home: 6314 S Monaco Ct Englewood CO 80111 Office: L Gene Marsolek Co Inc 2186 S Holly St Suite 206A Denver CO 80222

MARSOT, ALAIN GERARD, political science educator; b. Saigon, Republic Vietnam, Apr. 16, 1935; came to U.S., 1968; s. Henri Gustave and Colette (Brau) M.; m. Afaf Lutfi al-Sayyid, July 31, 1964; children: Vanina, Vanessa. Licence en droit, Faculty of Law, Paris, 1959, MA in Polit. Sci., 1961, PhD, 1964; BLitt., Oxford (Eng.) U., 1969. Bar: Paris 1961. Attaché Ministry Affaires Étrangères, Paris, 1959-60; chargé de mission Cen. Bank West Africa, Paris, 1960-61; lectr. Reading (Eng.) U., 1962-64; instr. Faculty of Law, Dijon, France, 1964-65; asst. prof. Am. U., Cairo, 1965-68; prof. Polit. Sci. Calif. State U., Long Beach, 1968—; vis. asst. prof. Cairo Nat. U., 1968; vis. prof. UCLA, 1979-81, 85, 87. Co-author/editor Southeast Asia Under New Balance of Power, 1974; contbr. articles to polit. sci. jours. Oxford U. scholar, 1961-64. Mem. Assn. for Asian Studies, World Future Soc. Democrat. Avocations: classical music, swimming. Office: Calif State U Dept Polit Sci 1250 Bellflower Blvd Long Beach CA 90840

MARSTON, MICHAEL, urban economic consultant; b. Oakland, Calif., Dec. 4, 1936; s. Lester Woodbury and Josephine (Janovic) M.; B.A., U. Calif. at Berkeley, 1959; postgrad. London Sch. Econs., 1961-63; m. Alexandra Lynn Geyer, Apr. 30, 1966. Vice pres. Larry Smith & Co., San Francisco, 1969-72, exec. v.p. urban econ. div., 1969-72; chmn. bd. Keyser Marston Assocs., Inc., San Francisco, 1973—; gen. partner The Sequoia Partnership, 1979—; pres. Marston Vineyards and Winery, 1982—, Marston Assocs., Inc., 1982—. Chmn., San Francisco Waterfront Com., 1969-86; chmn. fin. com., bd. dirs., mem. exec. com., treas. San Francisco Planning and Urban Research Assn., 1976-87; trustee Cathedral Sch. for Boys, 1981-82, Marin Country Day Sch., 1984—, St. Luke's Sch., 1986—; pres. Presidio Heights Assn. of Neighbors, 1983-84; v.p., bd. dirs., mem. exec. com. People for Open Space, 1972-87; mem. Gov.'s Issue Analysis Com. and Speakers Bur., 1966; mem. speakers bur. Am. embassy, London, 1961-63; v.p., bd. dirs. Democratic Forum, 1968-72; v.p., trustee Youth for Service. Served to lt. USNR. Mem. Urban Land Inst., Order of Golden Bear, Lambda Alpha, Sigma Chi. Home: 3375 Jackson St San Francisco CA 94118 Office: 55 Pacific Ave Mall San Francisco CA 94111

MARTELLO, MICHAEL EDWARD, lawyer; b. Quantico, Va., Dec. 14, 1941; s. Salvatore Frank and Vivian Patricia M.; B.S. in Acctg., Fairleigh Dickinson U., 1965; M.B.A. in Taxation, Pace U., 1969; J.D., Seton Hall U., 1979; LL.M. in Taxation, NYU, 1983; m. Marie Gloria Inzalaco, Dec. 23, 1962; children—Michael, Matthew, Michele, Marc. Bar: N.J. 1980. Tax acct. Worthington Corp., 1962-66, Martin Marietta Corp., 1966-68, Abex Corp., N.Y.C., 1968-69; asst. tax mgr. Foster Wheeler Corp., Livingston, N.J., 1969-71, tax mgr., 1971-77, dir. taxes, 1977-81, corp. tax counsel, 1981-82; asst. controller and mgr. taxes Bechtel Corp., San Francisco, 1982—. Mem. ABA, N.J. Bar Assn., Tax Execs. Inst. Roman Catholic. Home: 1732 Oro Valley Circle Walnut Creek CA 94596 Office: 50 Beale St San Francisco CA 94105

MARTENS, DAVID BAKER, publishing executive; b. St. Paul, June 3, 1942; s. Henry C. and Harriette C. (Baker) M.; m. Mary Jo Noack, Aug. 22, 1969; children: Jennifer Jo, Patrick Henry. BA, Mich. State U., 1965. Regional mgr. Times Mirror Cable, San Clemente, Calif., 1971-72; pub. The Advertiser-Tribune, Tiffin, Ohio, 1973-78; pub. York (Pa.) Daily Record, 1978-83, pres., 1983—; v.p. Buckner News Alliance, Seattle, Wash., 1983—; also bd. dirs. Buckner News Alliance, Bellingham, Wash.; mem. adv. bd. Am. Press Inst., Reston, Va., 1985—. Presbyterian. Avocations: sailing, travel, reading. Office: Buckner News Alliance 221 First Ave W Suite 315 Seattle WA 98119

MARTENS, HERMAN HELLMUTH, retired analytical chemist; b. Hamburg, Federal Republic of Germany, Mar. 23, 1923; came to U.S., 1936; s. Hellmuth Heinrich and Ottilie (Hirschfeld) M.; m. Agnes Rose Galligan, Apr. 25, 1942; children: Margaret R., Carol A., Janice M., Linda K. BS in Chemistry, St. Mary's U., San Antonio, 1952. Analytical chemist S.W. Research Inst., San Antonio, 1952-56; scientist III Biochem. Inst. U. Tex., Austin, 1956-57; research chemist Am. Potash and Chem. Co., Los Angeles, 1957-59; supr. quality control lab. Lockheed Propulsion Co., Redlands, Calif., 1959-61; research chemist Aerojet Gen. Corp., Azusa, Calif., 1961-66; project mgr. USAF/AFSC-AFRPL, Edwards AFB, Calif., 1966-83; cons. in field, Sparks, Nev., 1983—. Contbr. articles to profl. jours.; inventor dogbone testerin. Served as cpl. USAAF, 1943-45, ETO. Mem. AAAS, Am. Chem. Soc. (sec.-treas. Sierra Nev. sect. 1986), Am. Inst. Chem. Engrs. (assoc.), Nat. Assn. Ret. Fed. Employees (2d v.p., program chmn. 1986), Sigma Xi. Republican. Avocations: photography, audiophile. Home: 863 E Greenbrae Dr Sparks NV 89431

MARTENS, ROY CHARLES, computer company executive; b. Chgo., Sept. 9, 1928; s. Le Roy Peter and Alice Faye (Bacon) M.; m. Sari Belle Rosenstein, Sept. 28, 1970; children: Mark D., Dane C., Julie S. BS, Northwestern U., 1955. Mgr. product mktg. Hughes Aircraft Corp., Los Angeles, 1956-61; mgr. western sales Hayden Pubs., N.Y.C., 1961-66; ptnr. T.Jones Advt. Agy., Los Altos, Calif., 1966-70; dir. advt. AMI Corp., Cupertino, Calif., 1970-72; pres. Mountain View (Calif.) Press, 1972—, also bd. dirs.; pres. Forth Vendors Group, Los Angeles, 1983-85. Pub. Forth Dimensions mag., 1979-84. Served as sgt. USAF, 1950-54. Republican. Jewish. Avocations: fishing, traveling, gardening, cooking. Home: 135 Waverly Pl Mountain View CA 94040 Office: Mountain View Press Drawer X Mountain View CA 94040

MARTI, MANUEL, architect; b. Havana, Cuba, Aug. 6, 1940; came to U.S., 1967; s. Manuel Antonio and Olga (Munoz) M.; m. Patricia Damm, Apr. 15, 1967 (div. Dec. 1973); children—Patricia, Manuel Alberto, Michelle; m. Patricia A. Stillman, Aug. 25, 1978. BArch., Nat. U. of Mex., 1966, M in Archaeology, 1967. Registered architect, Ariz., Fla., Wis. Designer, Barry Sugerman Architects, Miami, Fla., 1967-73; project mgr. Potter, Lawson, & Pawlowsky, Madison, Wis., 1973-81; project mgr., assoc. Anderson DeBartolo Pan, Inc., Tucson, 1981—. Author: Space Operational Analysis, 1981; No Place to Hide, 1984. Recipient Medal of Merit, Nat. U. Mex. Mem. AIA, Constrn. Specifications Inst., World Future Soc., Ariz. Soc. Architects. Democrat. Home: 6121 N Camino Padre Isidoro Tucson AZ 85718 Office: Anderson DeBartolo Pan Inc 2480 N Arcadia Ave Tucson AZ 85712

MARTI, MARIAN JEAN, educator; b. Cheboygan, Mich., Apr. 21, 1946; d. Floyd Elwood and Isabelle Jean (Adlam) Sampson. AA with honors, Macomb County Community Coll., 1973; BS with honors, Wayne State U., 1975; MEd with honors, Colo. State U., 1980. Cert. tchr., Colo., Utah, Mich. Med. sec., office mgr. A.K. Shaalan, Detroit, 1970-73; med. sec., bookkeeper Steamboat Orthopaedics, Steamboat Springs, Colo., 1973-76; tchr. Steamboat Springs High Sch., 1977—, Colo. Mountain Coll., Steamboat Springs, 1980-84; mktg. adminstr. HGM Med. Laser Systems Inc., Salt Lake City, 1985-86; advisor Three Wire Winter Mag., Steamboat Springs, 1984-85, 86-87; advisor high sch. class Steamboat Springs High Sch., 1977-84; project dir. local history project and title IV-C grant Steamboat Springs High Sch., 1977-79. Author: Local History an Oral History Program, 1979. Avocations: horses, skiing, camping, traveling, reading. Office: Steamboat Springs High Sch 45 E Maple Steamboat Springs CO 80477

MARTIN, ALICE LOUISE MCCLURE, purchasing executive; b. Ottumwa, Iowa, Mar. 23, 1926; d. Floyd Edgar and Lena Olive (Shepherd) McClure; student Iowa State Coll., 1946-47; m. George Kenneth Martin, Oct. 19, 1947; 1 child, Douglas Bruce. Draftsman, engrng. dept. Ottumwa Iron Works (Iowa), 1944-46; order receiver John Morrell & Co., Ottumwa, 1946-50; clk. prodn. control Proto Tool div. Ingersoll-Rand Co., Portland, Oreg., 1970-72, steel inventory planner, 1972-77, steel buyer, 1978-83, parts and steel buyer, 1983-84; parts and steel buyer Stanley-Photo Indsl. Tools, 1984-86, material control analyst, 1986—. Mem. Clackamas County Election Bd., 1961-70; pres. women's assn. Oak Hills Presbyn. Ch., 1965-66. Mem. Nat. Assn. Female Execs., Inc., Sigma Kappa. Republican. Presbyterian. Home: 5332 SE El Centro Way Portland OR 97267 Office: 10330 SE 32d Ave Portland OR 97222

MARTIN, BERNARD LEE, college dean; b. Dayton, Ohio, May 29, 1923; s. Harley L. and Clare (Murphy) M.; m. Mary Patricia McDonald, Nov. 23, 1950; children: Joseph, Mary, David, Patrick, Paul, Timothy, Michael, Christopher. B.A., Athenaeum of Ohio, 1941-45; M.A. in History, Xavier U., 1950, M.B.A., 1955; Ph.D. in Econs, U. Cin., 1963; Ph.D. honoris causa, Canisius Coll., 1978. Mem. faculty Xavier U., Cin., 1948-65; asst. prof. bus. adminstrn. Xavier U., 1955-62, assoc. prof. mktg., 1962-65, chmn. mktg. dept., 1961; chmn., prof. mktg. Eastern Mich. U., Ypsilanti, 1965-66; dean Sch. Bus. Adminstrn., Canisius Coll., Buffalo, 1966-71; acting acad. v.p. Sch. Bus. Adminstrn., Canisius Coll., 1971-73, dean sch. bus. adminstrn., 1973-78; dean McLaren Coll. Bus. Adminstrn., U. San Francisco, 1978-86; prof. mktg. U. San Francisco, 1986—. Author: (with others) Contemporary Economic Problems and Issues, 3d edit, 1973. Ford Found. grantee Harvard, 1964. Mem. Am. Mktg. Assn., Am. Econ. Assn. Club: Rotary Internat. Home: 224 Greenview Dr Daly City CA 94014 Office: 2130 Fulton St San Francisco CA 94117

MARTIN, BOYD ARCHER, emeritus political science educator; b. Cottonwood, Idaho, Mar. 3, 1911; s. Archer Olmstead and Norah Claudine (Imbler) M.; m. Grace Charlotte Swingler, Dec. 29, 1933; children: Michael Archer, William Archer. Student, U. Idaho, 1929-30, 35-36, B.S., 1936; student, Pasadena Jr. Coll., 1931-32, U. Calif. at Los Angeles, summer 1934; A.M., Stanford, 1937, Ph.D., 1943. Research asst. Stanford U., 1936-37, teaching asst., 1937-38; instr. polit. sci. U. Idaho, 1938-39; acting instr. polit. sci. Stanford U., 1939-40; John M. Switzer fellow, summer 1939-40; chief personnel officer Walter Butler Constrn. Co., Farragut Naval Tng. Center, summer 1942; instr. polit. sci. U. Idaho, 1940-43, asst. prof. polit. sci., 1943-44, asso. prof. polit. sci., 1944-47; prof., head dept. social sci., asst. dean U. Idaho (Coll. Letters and Sci.), 1947-55, dean, 1955-70, Borah Distinguished prof. polit. sci., 1970-73, prof., dean emeritus, 1973—; Vis. prof. Stanford U., summer 1946, spring 1952, U. Calif., 1962-63; affiliate Center for Study Higher Edn., Berkeley, 1962-63; mem. steering com. N.W. Conf. on Higher Edn., 1960-67, pres. conf., 1966-67; mem. bd. Am. Assn. of Partners of Alliance for Progress; chmn. Idaho Adv. Council on Higher Edn.; del. Gt. Plains UNESCO Conf., Denver, 1947; chmn. bd. William E. Borah Found. on Causes of War and Conditions of Peace, 1947-55; mem. Commn. to Study Orgn. Peace; dir. Bur. Pub. Affair Research, 1959-73, dir. emeritus, 1973—; dir. Inst. Human Behavior, 1970—. Author: The Direct Primary in Idaho, 1947, (with others) Introduction to Political Science, 1950, (with other) Western Politics, 1968, Politics in the American West, 1969, (with Sydney Duncombe) Recent Elections in Idaho (1964-70), 1972, Idaho Voting Trends: Party Realignment and Percentage of Voters for Candidates, Parties and Elections, 1890-1974, 1975, In Search of Peace: Starting From October 19, 1980, 1980, Why the Democrats Lost in 1980, 1980; Editor: The Responsibilities of Colleges and Universities, 1967; Contbr. to: Ency. Britannica, 1974; also articles in polit. sci. to reviews. Mem. Am. Polit. Sci. Assn. (exec. council 1952-53), Nat. Municipal League, Am. Soc. Pub. Adminstrn., Fgn. Policy Assn., UN Assn., AAUP, Western Polit. Sci. Assn. (pres. 1950), Phi Beta Kappa, Pi Gamma Mu, Kappa Delta Pi, Pi Sigma Alpha. Home: 516 Eisenhower Moscow ID 83843

MARTIN, B(RUCE) MORGAN, product manager; b. Corpus Christi, Tex., Aug. 22, 1949; s. Joseph Morgan and Jane Maureen (Harriss) M. BS in Math., U. Tex., Arlington, 1971; postgrad., U. Tex., Austin, 1972-76. Mgr. tech. ops. Metromedia, Los Angeles, 1976-78; mgr. West Coast Rupert Neve Inc., Los Angeles, 1979-85; product mgr. SoundDroid The Droid Works, San Rafael, Calif., 1986—. Mem. Soc. Motion Picture and TV Engrs., Audio Engrng. Soc., Nat. Gay Rights Assn. Democrat. Presbyterian. Avocations: photography, travel, computers, hiking. Home: 1846 N Ave 50 Los Angeles CA 90042 Office: The Droid Works PO Box CS 8180 San Rafael CA 94912

MARTIN, CARL ERNEST, urban planner, civil designer; b. Germany, July 25, 1933; came to U.S., 1955; s. Johann and Paula (Moehrle) M.; m. Laura Dominguez, June 28, 1956 (div. Nov. 1959); children: Diana, Yvonne; m. Anneliese Horn; Nov. 28, 1966; 1 child, Tanja. Grad. high sch., Mindelheim, Germany. Draftsman City of Regina, Sask., Can., 1953-55; planner CST Engrng., Los Angeles, 1955-82; planner, draftsman Engrng. Tech., Los Angeles, 1982-85; prin. Delineation Tech., Culver City, Calif., 1985—. Served with U.S. Army, 1956-58. Republican. Roman Catholic. Avocations: photography, skiing, bicycling. Home and Office: 4832 Salem Village Pl Culver City CA 90230

MARTIN, CLYDE VERNE, psychiatrist; b. Coffeyville, Kans., Apr. 7, 1933; s. Howard Verne and Elfrieda Louise (Moehn) M.; m. Barbara Jean McNeilly, June 24, 1956; children—Kent Clyde, Kristin Claire, Kerry Constance, Kyle Curtis. Student Coffeyville Coll., 1951-52; A.B., U. Kans., 1955; M.D., 1958; M.A., Webster Coll., St. Louis, 1977; J.D., Thomas Jefferson Coll. Law, Los Angeles, 1985. Diplomate Am. Bd. Psychiatry and Neurology. Intern, Lewis Gale Hosp., Roanoke, Va., 1958-59; resident in psychiatry U. Kans. Med. Ctr., Kansas City, 1959-62, Fresno br. U. Calif.-San Francisco, 1978; staff psychiatrist Neurol. Hosp., Kansas City, 1962; practice medicine specializing in psychiatry, Kansas City, Mo., 1964-84; founder, med. dir., pres. bd. dirs. Mid-Continent Psychiat. Hosp., Olathe, Kans., 1972-84; adj. prof. psychology Baker U., Baldwin City, Kans., 1969-84; staff psychiatrist Atascadero State Hosp., Calif., 1984-85; clin. prof. psychiatry U. Calif., Berkeley, 1985—; chief psychiatrist Calif. Med. Facility, Vacaville, 1985—; pres., editor Corrective and Social Psychiatry, Olathe, 1970-84, Atascadero, 1984—. Contbr. articles to profl. jours. Bd. dirs. Meth. Youthville, Newton, Kans. 1965-75, Spofford Home, Kansas City, 1974-78. Served to capt. USAF, 1962-64, col. USAFR. Fellow Royal Soc. Health, Am. Assn. Mental Health Profls. in Corrections, World Assn. Social Psychiatry, Am. Orthopsychiat. Assn.; mem. AMA, Am. Psychiat. Assn., Assn. for Advancement Psychotherapy, Am. Assn. Sex Educators, Counselors and Therapists (cert.), Assn. Mental Health Adminstrs. (cert.), N.Y. Acad. Sci., Phi Beta Pi, Pi Kappa Alpha. Methodist (del. Kans. East Conf. 1972-80, bd. global ministries 1974-80). Clubs: Carriage; Kansas City. Lodge: Mason. Office: PO Box 3365 Fairfield CA 94533

MARTIN, DAVID LEE, health and social service administrator; b. Deer Lodge, Mont., Jan. 13, 1939; s. David Wesley and Nellie Elouise (McMillan) M.; m. Maxine Marie Monson, June 16, 1962; children: Beth, Debby. BS, N.W. Christian Coll., 1963; MDiv, Tex. Christian U., 1966; MSW, U. Nebr., 1969. Cert. social worker, Idaho; lic. vocat. rehab. counselor, Wash. Resident caseworker Child Inst., Omaha, summers 1966-69; program coordinator Mentah Health Ctr., Moscow, Idaho, 1969-79; regional mgr. Community Rehab. Programs, Coeur d'Alene, Idaho, 1979-81; regional program dir. Adult/Child Devel. Ctr., Coeur d'Alene, 1981—; vis. faculty U. Idaho, 1971, 77; adj. clin. prof. Wash. State U., Pullman, 1970-73; mem. faculty continuing edn., N. Idaho Coll., Coeur d'Alene, 1981-83; cons. NIH fellow, 1967-69; grantee FDA, Idaho Dept. Human Services, Vista; named one of OUtstanding Young Men Am. Mem. Nat. Assn. Social Workers (cert., pres. Idaho chpt. 1970-72). Democrat. Mem. Christian Ch. Avocations: cross country skiing, sailing, building sailboats.

MARTIN, DAVID LOUIS, financial systems analyst; b. Oak Park, Ill., Dec. 20, 1950; s. Donald Maxwell and Marian Sylvia (Goers) M.; m. Norma Kay Allen, June 7, 1975. BA, Calif. State U., Fullerton, 1972. Mgr. programming Mortgage Systems, Anaheim, Calif., 1974-79; sr. programmer McDonnell Douglas, Huntington Beach, Calif., 1979-80; systems analyst Downey Savs., Costa Mesa, Calif., 1980-83; sr. systems analyst Columbia Savs., Irvine, Calif., 1983—; cons., Santa Ana, Calif., 1973—. Mem. Orange

County Mortgage Banker Assn. Lutheran. Avocations: guitar, martial arts, stained glass. Home: 2041 N Ross Santa Ana CA 92706 Office: Columbia Savs and Loan 17911 Von Karman Ave Irvine CA 92714

MARTIN, DAVID UHL, engineer, applied mathematics researcher; b. Canton, Ohio, Oct. 4, 1947; s. Curtis Chapman and Jennie Pauline (Uhl) M.; m. Phyllis Eileen Golloway, Sept. 18, 1972; children: Michael Chapman, Ryan Corey. BS, Ohio State U., 1969; PhD, Calif. Inst. Tech., 1981. Software engr. TRW, Redondo Beach, Calif., 1973-77, fluid mechanics researcher, 1977-82; systems engr. TRW, San Diego, 1982-86; computer aided design engr. GE Calma, San Diego, 1986—. Contbr. articles to profl. jours. Fellow Woodrow Wilson Found., 1969, NSF, 1969; Calif. State fellow, 1971. Mem. Am. Assn. Artificial Intelligence, Spl. Interest Group in Artificial Intelligence, Phi Beta Kappa. Avocations: music, bicycle and horseback riding, hiking, surfing, skiing. Home: 13415 Sawtooth Rd San Diego CA 92129 Office: Calma Co 9805 Scranton Rd San Diego CA 92121

MARTIN, DAVID WILLIAM, psychology educator; b. Indpls., June 28, 1943; s. Daniel William and Martha (Parker) M. BA, Hanover Coll., 1965; MA, Ohio State U., 1966, PhD, 1969. Asst. prof. N.Mex. State U., Las Cruces, 1969-75, assoc. prof., 1975-83, head dept. psychology, 1981—, prof. psychology, 1983—, chmn. faculty senate, 1980-81. Author: Doing Psychology Experiments, 2d rev. edit., 1985; contbr. articles to profl. jours. Mem. Rocky Mountian Psychol. Assn. (pres. 1984-85), Am. Psychol. Assn., Rio Grande Human Factors Soc. (pres. 1986), Human Factors Soc., Psychonomic Soc. Lodge: Sertoma (pres. Las Cruces club 1977-78). Avocations: stockcar racing, scuba diving. Home: 3251 Solar Ridge Las Cruces NM 88001 Office: New Mex State U Dept Psychology Las Cruces NM 88003

MARTIN, DAVID WILLIAM, JR., medical corporation executive, medical educator; b. West Palm Beach, Fla., Jan. 15, 1941; s. David W. Sr. and Joanna (Law) M.; m. Kathleen McKinnon, Aug. 22, 1964; children: David McKinnon, Gillian Hope. Student, MIT, 1958-60; MD, Duke U., 1964. Research assoc. lab. molecular biology, G. M. Tomkins U. Calif., San Francisco, 1966-69, asst. prof. medicine, chief med. genetics service, 1970-75, investigator Howard Hughes Med. Inst., 1974-82, assoc. prof. medicine and biochemistry, 1975-79, prof. medicine and biochemistry in residence, 1979-82; v.p. research Genentech, Inc., South San Francisco, 1983—; adj. prof. medicine and biochemistry U. Calif., San Francisco, 1983—; mem. DNA adv. bd. com. NIH, 1981-85, Cystic Fibrosis Found., 1983—, Duke U. Comprehensive Cancer Ctr., 1985—, U. Calif. Biotech. Research and Edn. Program 1986—, UCLA Symposia, 1986—. Editor Harper's Rev. Biochemistry, 1979-85, Sci. Yr., 1981-86, Jour. Biol. Chemistry, 1983—; contbr. articles to profl. jours. Mem. Am. Fedn. Clin. Research, Western Soc. Clin. Research., Am. Soc. Biol. Chemists, Am. Soc. Clin. Investigation, Assn. Am. Physicians, Western Assn. Physicians, Alpha Omega Alpha. Office: Genentech Inc 460 Point San Bruno Blvd South San Francisco CA 94080

MARTIN, DONALD WALTER, editor, writer; b. Grants Pass, Oreg., Apr. 22, 1934; s. George E. and Irma Ann (Dallas) M.; m. Kathleen Elizabeth Murphy, July, 1970 (div. May 1979); children: Daniel Clayton, Kimberly Ann; m. Betty Woo, Mar. 18, 1985. Enlisted USMC, 1952; advanced through grades to staff sgt. USMC, Japan, Republic of Korea, Republic of China, 1956-61; with Blade-Tribune, Oceanside, Calif., 1961-65; entertainment editor Press-Courier, Oxnard, Calif., 1965-69; mng. editor Argus-Courier, Petaluma, Calif., 1969-70; assoc. editor Motorland Mag., San Francisco, 1970—. Author: Best of San Francisco, 1986, Best of the Gold Country, 1987; contbr. articles on travel to publs. Recipient Diane Seely award Ventura County Theatre Council, 1968. Republican. Avocations: traveling, hiking, swimming, biking. Home: 587 Europa Ct Walnut Creek CA 94598 Office: Motorland Mag 150 Van Ness Ave San Francisco CA 94102

MARTIN, DOUGLAS RICHARD, educational administrator; b. Wadena, Minn., Oct. 16, 1940; s. Richard Oskar and Myrtle Jessie (Carter) M.; m. Anita Jo Friedrichs, June 29, 1963; children—Richard Norman, Jennifer Elizabeth. B.A., Concordia Coll., 1963; M.A., U. So. Calif., 1969, Ed.D., 1974. Tchr., adminstrv. intern Los Angeles Unified Sch. Dist., 1963-71, administrv. dean, 1971-73; vice prin. Paso Robles (Calif.) Pub. Schs., 1973-79; prin. Lindsay (Calif.) Unified Sch. Dist., 1979-82; supt. Esparto (Calif.) Unified Sch. Dist., 1982-85; personnel dir. Paramount (Calif.) Unified Sch. Dist., 1985—. Scoutmaster, dist. commr., council tng. chmn. Boy Scouts Am., 1979-85; pres. Long Beach Ballet Guild, 1985—. Recipient Kiwanis Disting. Pres.'s award, 1977; IDEA fellow, 1982. Mem. Assn. Calif. Sch. Administrs., Calif. Assn. Sch. Bus. Ofcls., Assn. Supervision and Curriculum Devel., Phi Delta Kappa. Republican. Lutheran. Clubs: Paramount (Calif.) Rotary; Lions; Kiwanis. Home: 9 Compass Ct Long Beach CA 90703 Office: Paramount Unified Sch Dist 15110 S California Ave Paramount CA 90803

MARTIN, FRED KENNETH, JR., solar energy and real estate executive; b. Fresno, Calif., Nov. 21, 1942; s. Fred K. and Emma B. (Balmer) M.; m. Maria Armanno, June 5, 1976; children: Kenneth, Mario. AA, Fresno City Coll., 1964; Sec. of the Navy nomination to US Naval Acad., 1965; student, U. Santa Clara, 1986. With Travelers Corp., San Jose Calif. and Hartford, Conn., 1967-72, regional sales dir. L.H. & F.S., prodn. mgr., 1972-75; with Fafco Inc., Menlo Park, Calif., 1976—, nat. comml. sales mgr., 1971-78, gen. mgr., Bay Area Distbn. Co., 1978; pres., Fafco Solar Systems, 1979-83; dir., v.p. Solar Energy Sales, Inc.; pres., chmn. bd. Martin & Mickle Ins. and Fin. Corp., 1983-85; exec. v.p. Century 21 Bonus Realty, 1986—, also bd. dirs.; mem. Century 21 Brokers Council and Advt. Com.; solar energy advisor Pacific Gas & Utility Co., U.S. Congressman Pete McCloskey, Calif. Solar Energy Commn., 1983-84. Served with USMCR, 1960-68. Mem. Calif. Solar Energy Soc. (state bd. dirs.), Calif. Solar Energy Industries Assn., Calif. Insulation Contractors Assn. (div., chmn. govtl. affairs, chmn. polit. action com.), Internat. Solar Energy Soc. Republican. Lutheran.

MARTIN, GIFFORD LYLE, SR., engineer; b. Newberg, Oreg., Nov. 28, 1912; s. George Archie and Flora Sara (Batson) M.; m. Jewell Natalie Penley, Mar. 27, 1949; children: Gifford L., Janet Lynn, Douglas Charles. BA, Berea Coll., 1936. Registered profl. engr., Calif. Chemist Charlton Labs., Portland, Oreg., 1939-41; chief chemist, supr. Northwest Chemonite Corp., Portland, 1941-48, asst. mgr., 1948-49; pres., mgr. Gen. Testing & Inspection, Portland, 1949-71; chmn. bd., tech. dir. Timber Products Inspection, Portland, 1971-82, chmn. bd., cons., 1982-85. Mem. Am. Chem. Soc. (chmn. profl. relations com. 1983-86), Am. Soc. for Testing Materials, Am. Wood Preservers Assn., Am. Inst. Timber Constrn. (cons. tech. adv. com.). Republican. Presbyterian. Home: 1990 NW 113th Ave Portland OR 97229

MARTIN, GLEN LEROY, civil engineer; b. Devils Lake, N.D., Jan. 21, 1932; s. Roy Lee and Alma Elizabeth (Aronson) M; m. Theolyn Margaret Johnson, Aug. 22, 1954; children: Timothy Glen, Carrie Elizabeth, Mary Ellen. BSCE, N.D. State U., 1957; MSCE, Oreg. State U., 1961; PhDCE, U. Ariz., 1965. Registered profl. engr. Oreg., Calif., Mont. Instr. civil engring. Oreg. State U., Corvallis, 1957-61; asst. prof. civil engring. Oreg. State U., 1961-62; assoc. prof., head dept. civil engring. Mont. State U., Bozeman, 1969-70, prof., head dept. civil engring. and engring. mechanics, 1970-75; dean coll. of engring., prof. civil engring. San Diego State U., 1975-70; dir. organized design CH2M Hill, Corvallis and Denver, 1979—; cons. engr. in field. Contbr. numerous articles to profl. jours. Served with U.S. Army, 1951-52, Korea, N.G., 1952-56. Recipient numerous grants and fellowships. Fellow ASCE, Am. Soc. Elec. Engrs., Am. Soc. Engring. Edn.; mem. Am. Rd. and Transp. Buidlers' Assn., Nat. Soc. Profl. Engrs., Accreditation Bd. for Engring. and Tech. (chmn. continuing edn. planning com., 1980—), Am. Soc. Engring. Mgmt., U. Alaska Sch. Engring. Adv. Council, Mont. State U. Engring. Adv. Council, Sigma Xi, Chi Epsilon, Tau Beta Pi. Lutheran. Lodge: Elks. Avocations: fishing, photography, travel, golf. Home: 6011 S Emporia Circle Englewood CO 80111 Office: CH2M Hill PO Box 22508 Denver CO 80222

MARTIN, HARRY (JOE), JR., advertising executive; b. Detroit, July 19, 1931; s. Harry M. and Irene Louis (McClung) M.; m. Linda Garn, Feb. 15, 1976; children—Monique, Michael, Jeffrey. BA, Mich. State U., 1957. Advt. mgr. Gate City Sash & Door Co., Ft. Lauderdale, Fla., 1955-56; advt. brand mgr. Coca Cola Co., 1958-59; founder, pres. Martin Advt., Inc., Tustin, Calif., 1960—. Served with USCGR, 1953-55. Pres. Tustin area Republican Assembly, 1967-68. Mem. Pub. Relations Soc. Am., Western States Advt. Assn. Am. (bd. dirs.), Nat. Assn. Home Builders, Bldg. Industry Assn., Sales and Mktg. Council, The Constrn. Industries Alliance for City of Hope (v.p. Orange County chpt.). Clubs: Lincoln, Pacific, Center, Balboa Bay, Shark Island Yacht, Irvin Racquet. Avocations: sailing, photography. Office: 18141 Irvine Blvd Tustin CA 92680

MARTIN, JACK EDWARD, beef cattle nutritionist; b. Carroll County, Mo., June 4, 1931; s. Raymond L. and Myra R. (Kingery) M.; m. Norma Remley, Apr. 21, 1955; children: Keith E., Grant A., Paul N. BS, U. Mo., 1953, MS, 1961; PhD, U. Fla., 1963. Product supr. Monsanto Co., St. Louis, 1963-67; research cons. Ralston Purina Co., St. Louis, 1967-69; nutritionist Ceres Land Co., Sterling, Colo., 1969-71; pres., nutritionist Sterling Nutritional Service Inc., 1971—. Elder First Christian Ch., Sterling, 1983-85, 86—, bd. dirs. 1985—. Mem. Am. Soc. Agrl. Cons. (v.p. 1980-81, 84-85, sec.-treas. 1983-84, pres.-elect 1985-86, pres. 1986-87), Am. Soc. Animal Sci., Council Agrl. Sci. and Tech., Sigma Xi. Republican. Mem. Christian Ch. Club: Sterling Country (bd. dirs. 1985—). Lodge: Masons (jr. wardon Wakanda club 1954). Avocations: gardening, skiing, fishing, reading, traveling. Home and Office: Rt 4 407 Highland Dr Sterling CO 80751

MARTIN, JAMES JOHN, consulting research firm executive, systems analyst; b. Paterson, N.J., Feb. 3, 1936; s. James John and Lillian (Lea) M.; m. Lydia Elizabeth Bent, June 11, 1954; children—David, Peter, Laura, Daniel, Lucas. B.A., U. Wis.-Madison, 1955; postgrad., Div. Sch., Harvard U., 1955-57; M.S., Navy Postgrad. Sch., 1963; Ph.D., MIT, 1965. Commd. ensign U.S. Navy, 1957; advanced through grades to comdr. 1971, ret., 1977; sr. v.p. Sci. Applications Internat. Corp., La Jolla, Calif., 1977—. Author: Bayesian Decision Problems and Markov Chains, 1967; also articles on nuclear strategy. Decorated Legion of Merit. Mem. Internat. Inst. Strategic Studies, Ops. Research Soc. Am., Mil. Ops. Research Soc. (bd. dirs. 1974-77). Republican. Avocation: cooking. Home: 6603 Aranda Ave La Jolla CA 92037 Office: Sci Applications Internat Corp 10260 Campus Point Dr PO Box 2351 San Diego CA 92121

MARTIN, JAMES LEE, senator; b. Las Vegas, N.Mex., July 4, 1948; s. Willard Franklin and Florence Ruth (Wesner) M. AA, N.Mex. Mil. Inst., 1967; student, U. N.Mex., 1967-70. Mgr. Martin Auto Supply, Socorro, N.Mex., 1971-85; supr. Aerojet Ordnance Co., Socorro, 1985—; mem. U.S. Ho. Reps., N.Mex., 1976-84; U.S. senator from N.Mex. 1984—. Named Hon. Alumnus, N.Mex. Inst. Mining and Tech., 1980. Republican. Lodge: Lions. Avocations: boating, motorcycling, racquetball. Home: PO Box 1006 Socorro NM 87801

MARTIN, JON WINTHROP, aerospace scientist; b. Los Angeles, Jan. 14, 1936; s. Ernest Winthrop and Marguerite (Taylor) M.; m. Jan E. Taylor, June 15, 1957; children: Craig, Kimberly. BS, Calif. State U., San Francisco, 1959, MS, 1963; MBA, Calif. State U., Long Beach, 1981. Research scientist Shell Chem. co., Torrance, Calif., 1963-69; sr. scientist TRW, Redondo Beach, Calif., 1969—. Contbr. articles to profl. publs.; patentee in field. Recipient Simon Ramo Tech. award TRW, 1985, Tech. Innovation awards NASA, 1976-85. Mem. Am. Chem. Soc. (rubber div.). Methodist. Avocations: stamps, music. Office: TRW One Space Park 01-2010 Redondo Beach CA 90278

MARTIN, JOSEPH, JR., lawyer, diplomat; b. San Francisco, May 21, 1915; m. Ellen Chamberlain Martin, July 5, 1946; children: Luther Greene, Ellen Myers. AB, Yale U., 1936, LLB, 1939. Assoc. Cadwalader, Wickersham & Taft, N.Y.C., 1939-41; ptnr. Wallace, Garrison, Norton & Ray, San Francisco, 1946-55, Pettit & Martin, San Francisco, 1955-70, 73—; gen. counsel FTC, Washington, 1970-71; ambassador, U.S. rep. Disarmament Conf., Geneva, 1971-76; mem. Pres.'s Adv. Com. for Arms Control and Disarmament, 1974-78; bd. dirs. Arcata Corp., Shaughnessy Holdings Inc., Astec Industries, Inc. Pres. Pub. Utilities Commn., San Francisco, 1956-60; Rep. nat. committeeman for Calif., 1960-64; treas. Rep. Party Calif., 1956-58; bd. dirs. Patrons of Art and Music, Calif. Palace of Legion of Honor, 1958-70, pres., 1963-68; bd. dirs. Arms Control Assn., 1977—; pres. Friends of Legal Assistance to Elderly, 1983—. Served to lt. comdr. USNR, 1941-46. Recipient Ofcl. commendation for Outstanding Service as Gen. Counsel FTC, 1973, Distinguished Honor award U.S. ACDA, 1973, Lifetime Achievement award Legal Assistance to the Elderly, 1981. Fellow Am. Bar Found. Clubs: Burlingame Country, Pacific Union. Home: 2580 Broadway San Francisco CA 94115 Office: 101 California St San Francisco CA 94111

MARTIN, JUNE JOHNSON CALDWELL, journalist; b. Toledo, Oct. 6; d. John Franklin and Eunice Imogene (Fish) Johnson; A.A., Phoenix Jr. Coll., 1939-41; B.A., U. Ariz., 1941-43, 53-59; student Ariz. State U., 1939, 40; m. Erskine Caldwell, Dec. 21, 1942 (div. Dec. 1955); 1 son, Jay Erskine; m. 2d, Keith Martin, May 5, 1966. Free-lance writer, 1944—; columnist Ariz. Daily Star, 1956-59; editor Ariz. Alumnus mag., Tucson, 1959-70; book editor, gen. feature writer Ariz. Daily Star, Tucson, 1970—; panelist, co-producer TV news show Tucson Press Club, 1954-55, pres., 1958; mem. editorial bd. Clarion, women's issues newspaper. Contbg. author: Rocky Mountain Cities, 1949; contbr. articles to World Book Ency., and various mags. Mem. Tucson CD Com., 1961; vol. campaigns of Samuel Goddard, U.S. Rep. Morris Udall, U.S. ambassador and Ariz. gov. Raul Castro. Recipient award Nat. Headliners Club, 1959, Ariz. Press Club award, 1957-59, Am. Alumni Council, 1966, 70. Mem. Jr. League of Tucson, Tucson Urban League, Pi Beta Phi. Democrat. Methodist. Club: Tucson Press. Home: PO Box 2631 Tucson AZ 85702 Office: PO Box 26807 Tucson AZ 85726

MARTIN, LARRY L., engineer; b. Mt. Pleasant, Mich., Sept. 18, 1941; s. David Leon and Irma Bessie (Trussel) M.; m. Celia Kellam, June 5, 1971; children: Jeffrey Alan, Debra Lynnea. BS in Gen. Engring., U. Wyo., 1972. Registered profl. engr., Wyo., Colo., Nebr. Maintenance engr. Hilton Hotels, St. Paul, 1966-68; v.p. Mortan Inc, Torrington, Wyo., 1972-74; indsl. devel. State of Wyo., Cheyenne, 1974-76; v.p. Willard Given & Assoc., Cheyenne, 1976-80; pres. Martin & Jones, Cheyenne, 1980—; v.p. Wyo. Assn. Cons. Engrs. and Surveyors, Riverton, 1984—. Chmn. bd. appeals City of Cheyenne, 1976—; mem. Gov's. Com. on Ins., Cheyenne, 1985. Served with USN, 1962-66. Mem. Nat. Soc. Profl. Engrs., ASHRAE, Wyo. Soc. Profl. Engrs. (pres. Cheyenne chpt. 1979-80), Wyo. Assn. Cons. Engrs. and Surveyors (v.p. 1985-86). Republican. Presbyterian. Lodges: Elks, Masons, Shriners, Consistory. Avocations: skiing, camping, hunting, auto restoration. Home: 3719 Dover Rd Cheyenne WY 82001 Office: Martin & Jones 1780 Westland Rd Cheyenne WY 82001

MARTIN, LOUIS HAROLD, labor relations executive; b. Joplin, Mo., Apr. 30, 1916; s. John L. and Mabel (Smith) M.; ed. pub. schs., Joplin; m. Vineta R. Babb, June 16, 1936. Founder Contra Costa Labor News, editor, pub., 1960-78; founder, adminstr. Contra Costa Labor Blood Bank, 1959-78; founder, exec. sec. Contra Costa Labor Health & Welfare Council, 1956-78; service officer Contra Costa Bldg. Trades Council, 1953-78, sec. emeritus, 1978—; ret., 1979; founder Martinez Health Center, Inc., exec. treas., 1971-76; founder Martinez Med. Arts Bldgs., Inc., exec. treas., 1972-76; founder Pre-Paid Comprehensive Health Services Corp., exec. treas., 1972-76; vice chmn. adv. com. Adobe Savs. & Loan Assn., 1978-81, v.p., dir., 1983—; cons. editor Contra Costa, Napa-Solano Labor News, 1979—. U.S. marshall No. Dist. Calif., 1968-69; pres., dir. West Contra Costa Water Dist., 1955-59. Pres., Richmond Boys Club, 1959, Martinez Boys Club, 1962-65. Bd. dirs. Martinez Community Hosp., 1967-73. Served with USMC, 1942-45. Recipient medallion and silver keystone, Boys Clubs of Am., 1962-65; resolution and commendation, Calif. Legislature, 1966, 73, 79; award of merit Fraternal Order of Eagles, 1967; commendation U.S. Dept. Justice, 1969, U.S. Bur. Prisons, 1969; resolution of commendation Calif. Legislature, 1979; cert. of commendation Contra Costa County Bd. Supr., 1979; proclamation of appreciation City of Martinez, 1979; named Labor Man of Year, Contra Costa County, 1973; First Man of Year, Martinez, 1972. Lodge: Elks (exalted ruler Richmond, Calif. 1962-63). Home: 320 Lindsey Dr Martinez CA 94553

MARTIN, PAUL DEAN, English language educator; b. East Meadow, N.Y., Aug. 2, 1949; s. James Andrew and Marie (Bing) M.; m. Beverly Ann Rollins, Sept. 12, 1981; children: Joshua, Jasmine. Student, Nassau Community Coll., 1968; AA, Long Beach City Coll., 1974; BA in English, Calif. State U., Long Beach, 1976, M in Pub. Adminstrn., 1978. Social sci. component coordinator Calif. State U., Long Beach, 1976-77, instr. ESL, 1978—; tutorial program coordinator student services Long Beach City Coll., 1979-81; instr. lang. skills program Calif. State U., Long Beach, 1977-85; sales and tng. mgr. Orbit Satellites, Ont., Can., 1985-86; listing agt. Vista Mobile Homes, Ont., 1986—. Editor Orbit Satellite Tng. Manual, 1985. Served with USMC, 1970-72, USAFR, 1982—. Mem. Calif. Assn. Tchrs. Eng. to Speakers Other Langs. Democrat. Club: Strokin' Tennis (Long Beach) (pres. 1977-79). Avocations: writing, sketching, chess, racquetball, cyling. Home: 1140 Mahanna Ave Long Beach CA 90813 Office: Long Beach City Coll 1305 E Pacific Coast Hwy Long Beach CA 90804

MARTIN, PRESTON, savings and loan executive; b. Los Angeles, Dec. 5, 1923; s. Oscar and Gaynell (Horne) M.; 1 son, Pier Preston. BS in Fin., U. So. Calif., 1947, MBA, 1948; PhD in Monetary Econs., U. Ind., 1952. Research fellow U. Ind., Bloomington, 1948-49; prin. in housebldg. firm 1952-56; with mortgage fin. and consumer fin. instns., 1954-57; prop. econ. research group specializing in savs. and loan matters, 1956-66; developer, adminstr. Pakistan Project for Grad. Bus. Edn., Los Angeles, 1960-63; developer, dir. Programs for Bus. and Govt. Execs. U. So. Calif., Los Angeles, 1959-63; commr. savs. and loan State of Calif., 1967-69; chmn. Fed. Home Loan Bank Bd., Washington, 1969-72; chmn., chief exec. officer PMI Mortgage Ins. Co., 1972-80; chmn., chief exec. officer Seraco Group subs. Sears, Roebuck & Co., 1980-81, also dir. parent co.; chmn., chief exec. officer H.F. Holdings, Inc., San Francisco, 1986—; mem. Fed. Res. Bd., Washington, 1982-86. Author: Principles and Practices of Real Estate, 1959; contbr. articles to profl. jours. Mem. Rep. Assembly, Los Angeles, 1959-60, Joint Ctr. Urban Studies MIT; sr. advisor Reagan Adminstrn. Commn. on Housing, 1980-81. Served with AUS, 1943-46. Recipient House and Home award, 1969, award Engring. News Record, 1971, NAHB Turntable award, 1973. Mem. Am. Econs. Assn., Am. Fin. Assn., Lambda Chi Alpha. Presbyterian. *

MARTIN, RICHARD FRANCIS, construction company executive, consultant; b. Newburgh, N.Y., Mar. 19, 1920; s. Roland Francis and Marion (Hall) M.; m. Phyllis Jane Norton, Nov. 20, 1951; children—Richard Francis, Pamela J. Martin Gilmore, William F., Thomas S. B.S.B.A. magna cum laude, Syracuse U., 1949. With Gen. Electric Co., Schenectady, 1937-51; personnel mgr. Fairmont Foods Co., Omaha, 1951-64; adminstrv. v.p. Fairmont Foods Co., Phila., 1964-69; pres. Martin Mgmt. Services, Denver, 1969-72, Scottsdale, Ariz, 1972—; exec. v.p. The Tanner Cos., Phoenix, 1972—, also dir.; dir. Tanner S.W., Phoenix. Contbr. articles to profl. jours. Bd. commrs. Valley Forge Park, Pa., 1966-69; chmn. bd., bd. dirs., com. chmn. YMCA Phoenix and Valley of Sch., 1974—; bd. dirs. Hahneman Hosp., Phila., 1966-69. Recipient award for article Soc. Advancement Mgmt., 1950. Mem. Phoenix Exec. Club (bd. dirs. 1981-84, treas. 1981-82), Assn. Gen. Contractors (chmn. edn. com. Ariz. chpt.), Beta Gamma Sigma. Republican. Methodist. Lodge: Toastmasters (internat. bd. dirs. 1963-65, past pres. local club). Avocations: bridge; pewter collecting; old books collecting; public speaking. Office: The Tanner Cos PO Box 20128 Phoenix AZ 85036

MARTIN, RICHARD LINDEN, general contractor; b. Arlington Heights, Mass., June 18, 1913; s. Richard Joseph and Alice Linden (Yorke) M.; m. Mary Martha Streamer, Aug. 14, 1946; children: Mary, Richard Jr., Susan, Cathryn, John, Sarah. BA, Harvard U., 1936. Mfg. supr. Am. Can Co., N.Y.C., 1937-42; aide-de-camp U.S. Mil. Acad., West Point, N.Y., 1942-46; pres. Richard L. Martin Inc., Lake Oswego, Oreg., 1946—. Pres. Lake Oswego water bd., 1960-66; mem. curriculum com. Lake Oswego Sch. Bd., 1962-64. Served to maj. C.E., U.S. Army, 1942-46. Mem. Associated Gen. Contractors Am. Republican. Avocations: gardening, sailing. Office: PO Box 999 Lake Oswego OR 97034

MARTIN, ROBERT BLAIR, humorous illustrator, greeting card artist; b. Chgo., July 13, 1950; s. Robert Danial and Bonnie J. (Blair) M.; m. Rhonda K. Gideo, Nov. 1, 1975. BFA, Ariz. State U., 1972. V.p., owner SHR Graphic Design, Phoenix, 1972-75; freelance designer Scottsdale, Ariz., 1975-77; art dir. Best Western Hotels, Phoenix, 1977-79; creative v.p. Structural Graphics, Essec, Conn., 1979-80; stylist, sr. designer Hallmark Cards Inc., Colorado Springs, Colo., 1982—. Illustrator: Teaching For Competence, 1983, (film strips) Dept. HEW; designer/illustrator greeting cards, posters, puzzles, others. Served to capt. USAR, 1967-80. Recipient Crown Zellerbach award, 1974, Gold medal for Humorous Illustration, Phoenix Soc. Visual Arts, 1973. Mem. Sigma Nu. Republican. Avocations: camping, hiking, cross-country skiing, photography. Office: Hallmark Humor Group 628 N Weber Colorado Springs CO 80903

MARTIN, ROBERT BRUCE, engineer, researcher, educator; b. Harrisburg, Pa., July 17, 1940; s. Robert Earl and Helen Margaret (Beauman) M.; m. Cora Sue Pitzer (div. Aug. 1980); 1 child, Benjamin Delbert; m. Ann Gail Peterson, July 10, 1983; children: Christopher Andrew, Daniel Patrick. BS, W.Va. U., 1966, MS, 1969, PhD, 1970. From instr. orthopedics to prof. orthopedic surgery and dir. research W.Va. U., Morgantown, 1970-84; prof. and dir. research U. Calif., Davis, 1984—; expert witness, cons. in orthopedics and biomechanics. Reviewer Jour. biomechanics and other sci. jours, NSF grant proposals; contbr. articles to sci. publs., chpts. to books. Served with USN, 1960-64. Mem. ASME, Orthopedic Research Soc., Am. Soc. Biomechanics (founding), Sierra Club (knapsack com. Sacramento chpt. 1983—). Avocations: backpacking, hiking, wilderness preservation. Home: 2340 Bueno Dr Davis CA 95616 Office: U Calif Orthopedic Research Lab TB-150 Davis CA 95616

MARTIN, ROBERT EDWARD, JR., forestry educator, scientist, researcher; b. Flint, Mich., Jan. 9, 1931; s. Robert Edward and Sarah Catherine (Royal) M.; m. Patricia Ann Meyer, Nov. 7, 1953; children—Steven Francis, Michael Philip, Kathleen Marie. B.S. in Physics, Marquette U., 1953; B.S. in Forestry, U. Mich., 1958, M. in Forestry, 1959, Ph.D., 1963. Researcher forester Forest Service, U.S. Dept. Agr., Macon, Ga., 1960-63; from asst. prof. to prof. Va. Poly. Inst., Blacksburg, Va., 1963-71; prof., research physicist Forest Service, U.S. Dept. Agr. and U. Wash., Seattle, 1971-75; research forester Forest Service, U.S. Dept. Agr., Bend, Oreg., 1975-82; prof. forestry U. Calif.-Berkeley, 1982—; forestry cons. REMAR, Oakland, Calif., 1984—. Served to lt. USN, 1953-56. Mem. Soc. Am. Foresters, AAAS, Soc. Range Mgmt., Sigma Xi, Phi Kappa Phi, Xi Sigma Pi. Club: Toastmasters (Berkeley). Avocations: cross country skiing; photography; biking. Home: 75 Chadbourne Way Oakland CA 94619 Office: U Calif-Berkeley Dept Forestry and Research Mgmt 145 Mulford Hall Berkeley CA 94720

MARTIN, ROBERT GREGORY, chemist; b. Denver, Apr. 24, 1959; s. Harold Gregory and Margaret C. (Mayer) M. BS, U. Denver, 1982. Computer distbr. Tronics Sales Corp., Ft. Worth, 1983; lab. technician Hager Labs., Denver, 1983-84, chem. analyst I, 1984-85, chem. analyst II, 1985-86, chem. analyst III, 1986—. Recipient Hornbeck award U. Denver, 1982; scholar U. Denver, 1982. Mem. AAAS, Am. Chem. Soc., Am. Indsl. Hygiene Assn., Am. Inst. Chemists, The Planetary Soc., Gold Key, Alpha Lambda Delta, Alpha Epsilon Delta. Roman Catholic. Avocations: microcomputers, reading, bicycling, photography. Home: 1370 Oneida St Denver CO 80220 Office: Hager Labs 11234 Caley A Englewood CO 80111

MARTIN, STEPHEN GEORGE, environmental engineer, executive; b. Eagle Grove, Iowa, Sept. 20, 1941; s. George Alfred and Thelma Helen (Sundheim) M.; m. Kathyanne Lio, Mar. 24, 1984; children: Lance Douglas, Tamsen Heather. BS, U. Wis., 1964, MS, 1967; PhD, Oreg. State U., 1970. Asst. prof. Colo. State U., Ft. Collins, 1970-73, affiliate faculty, 1973—; v.p. Environ. Research & Tech., Inc., Ft. Collins, 1970—; chmn. Univ. Nat. Bank, Ft. Collins, 1980—. Contbr. articles to profl. jours. Pres. Ft. Collins Audubon Soc., 1975-76. Mem. The Wildlife Soc. (cert. wildlife biologist), Ecol. Soc. Am. (cert. sr. ecologist), Am. Ornithologists Union, Cooper Ornithol. Soc. (Howell award 1970), The Wilson Ornithol. Soc. Avocations: archery, gardening, bird watching, travel. Home: 7121 N County Rd 9 Wellington CO 80549 Office: Environ Research & Tech 1716 Heath Pkwy Fort Collins CO 80524

MARTIN, SUSAN KAYE, speech-language pathologist; b. Quinter, Kans., Mar. 10, 1954; d. Lyle Keith and Rose Kathryn (Mai) M. BA magna cum laude, Adams State Coll., 1976, MA, 1977. Grad. teaching asst. Adams State Coll., Alamosa, Colo., 1976-77; speech-lang. specialist Sch. Dist. Eleven, Colorado Springs, Colo., 1977—, strategic planning com. mem., 1985—; cons. Gifted/Talented Edn. Pikes Peak Region, Colo., 1980—, Creative Dramatics, Very Spl. Arts Colo., Denver, 1979— (Commendation 1985). Author: (manual) Parent Teacher Inservice Guide for Special Education, 1985. Regional coordinator Pikes Peak Arts for the Handicapped, Colorado Slprings, 1983-85; co-coordinator Mayor's Conf. on Spl. Arts., Colorado Springs, 1984, 85. Recipient Achievement award Colo. Arts for the Handicapped, 1985. Mem. Am. Speech-Lang.-Hearing Assn., Council for Exceptional Children: Colorado Springs Tchr.'s Assn., Phi Delta Kappa. Avocations: visual arts, theatre. Home: 4842 Evening Sun Ln Colorado Springs CO 80917 Office: Madison Elem Sch 4120 Constitution Ave Colorado Springs CO 80909

MARTIN, SUSAN VELMA, lawyer; b. Abington, Pa., Oct. 18, 1946; d. Charles Dennis and Velma (Smith) Martin. BA in History, Beaver Coll., 1968; MA in History, West Chester State Coll., 1971; JD, U. Denver, 1983. Bar: Colo. 1983, U.S. Ct. Appeals (10th cir.) 1983, U.S. Dist. Ct. Colo. 1983. Tchr. Western cultures, also coach field hockey and basketball Marple Newton Sr. High Sch., Newtown Square, Pa., 1969-72; office mgr., scuba diving instr. Colo. Divers' World, Denver, 1972-74; assoc. Silver and Hayes, P.C., Denver, 1982—; adv. bd. paralegal program Community Coll. Denver; lectr. Small Claims Ct. Vol. fund agt. Beaver Coll.; also vol. United Fund, YMCA fundraising com., Denver Symphony Orchestra fundraising com., March of Dimes fundraising com., Dale Tooley Cancer Research Ctr.; mgr. campaign Paul W. Powers for state senate. Mem. ABA, Assn. Trial Lawyers Am., Colo. Trial Lawyers Assn., Colo. Bar Assn., Colo. Women's Bar Assn., Denver Bar Assn. (lectr.). Republican. Club: Law. Office: Silver & Hayes PC Bank Western Bldg 9th fl 210 University Blvd Denver CO 80206

MARTIN, SUZANNE LUCILLE, educational administrator, archaeologist; b. Chgo., Dec. 5, 1947; d. John Hugh and Jean (Morrison) M. B.A., Chatham Coll., 1969; M.A., U. Minn., 1972, Ph.D., 1976. Assoc. dean students, asst. prof. history Whitman Coll., Walla Walla, Wash., 1978—; staff mem. UMME archaeol. excavation, Nichoria, Greece, 1971-76. Co-author: UMME Excavation at Nichoria, vol. 2, 1987. Pres. Archeol. Soc., Walla Walla, 1980-84. Ford Found. Archeol. trainee, 1971, 72; recipient Frances E. Andrews award Mpls. Found., 1975; Carnegie Adminstrv. intern, Salem Coll., 1977-78. Mem. Archeol. Inst. Am., Nat. Acad. Advising Assn., Nat. Assn. Women Deans, Adminstrs. and Counselors. Home: 538 E Alder St Walla Walla WA 99362 Office: Whitman Coll Walla Walla WA 99362

MARTIN, TED LOUIS, realtor; b. Phoenix, Jan. 3, 1943; s. John Paul and Augusta May (Metcalf) M.; student Phoenix Coll., 1960. Sales mgr. Red Carpet Realty, Phoenix, 1972-74; instr. Phoenix Community Coll., 1974-75; state dir. Red Carpet Corp. of Am., Phoenix, 1974-76; exec. dir. Century 21 of Southwest, Inc., 1976-79; pres. Allied Realty, Inc., Phoenix, 1979—, broker Century 21 Allied Realty, Phoenix, 1979—; bd. dirs. Phoenix Bd. Realtors, Inc., 1984-85. Served with USAF, 1964-71. Mem. Glendale-West Maricopa Bd. Realtors (pres. 1983), Maricopa County Brokers Council (dir. 1983, pres. 1983, 86, v.p. 1985), Ariz. Realtors Inst. (bd. govs. 1975-81), Nat. Mktg. Inst., Phoenix Bd. Realtors Inc. (bd. dirs. 1984-85). Author: Arizona Real Estate Finance, 1974. Office: 8718 N 35th Ave Phoenix AZ 85051

MARTIN, WAYNE H., state education testing coordinator; b. Benton Harbor, Mich., Dec. 21, 1945; s. Warren H. and Leona Rachel (Scherer) M.; m. Mary Ellen Lee, Apr. 29, 1967; children: Doreen P., Michael G., Matthew S. BA, U. Mich., 1968; MA, U. Conn., 1970, postgrad., 1968-71. Research assoc. evaluation and testing dept. Ednl. Research Council of Am., Cleve., 1971-72; math. analyst Nat. Assessment of Ednl. Progress, Denver, 1972-75, tech. info. coordinator, 1975-79, pub. info. officer, 1979-83; planning and evaluations specialist Colo. Dept. Edn., Denver, 1984-85, state testing coordinator, 1985—; cons. Ednl. Research Council Am., 1973-74, various state and local dist. testing programs., 1974-80, Ednl. Testing Service, Princeton, N.J., 1983-84, Cherry Creek Sch. Dist., Englewood, Colo., 1984. Contbr. articles to profl. jours. Bd. dirs. Catholic Community Services, Denver, 1977-84. Mem. Am. Ednl. Research Assn., Pub. Relations Soc. Am., Assn. Colo. Endl. Evaluators. Avocations: bridge, rebuses, trivial pursuit, reading fiction, computer programming. Home: 2832 S Wabash Circle Denver CO 80231 Office: Colo Dept Edn 201 E Colfax Ave Denver CO 80231

MARTIN, WILLIAM CHARLES, lawyer; b. Shenandoah, Iowa, May 25, 1923; s. J. Stuart and Chloe Irene (Anderson) M.; m. Marilyn Forbes, Oct. 18, 1947 (div. 1979); children—Ann, James; m. 2d, Kathryn Ann Fehr, Sept. 17, 1979. B.A., U. Iowa, 1946, J.D., 1947. Bar: Iowa 1947, Oreg. 1948. Sr. ptnr. Martin Bischoff, Templeton, Biggs & Ericsson, Portland, Oreg., 1951—; mem. Oreg. Bd. Bar Examiners, 1966-69; instr. Lewis and Clark Coll. Law, 1973-75. Bd. dirs. Eastmoreland Gen. Hosp., Portland, 1960-84, chmn., 1978-81; mem. Lawyers Com. for Civil Rights Under Law, Jackson, Miss., 1965; bd. dirs. Lake Oswego (Oreg.) Pub. Library, 1981-84, chmn., 1982-84. Served to 1st lt. USAAF, World War II. Mem. Iowa State Bar, Oreg. State Bar, ABA, Phi Delta Phi, Sigma Nu. Democrat. Presbyterian. Clubs: University (Portland); Mt. Park Tennis, Portland Heights. Home: 3915 S Shore Blvd Lake Oswego OR 97034 Office: Martin Bischoff Templeton Biggs & Ericsson 2908 1st Interstate Tower Portland OR 97201

MARTIN, WILLIAM WILEY, health services executive, psychologist; b. Albany, Ga., Mar. 24, 1951; s. William W. and Lynne (Durham) M.; m. Diana Susanne Place, Nov. 7, 1981; 1 son, Christopher William. A.A. in Liberal Arts, Clayton Jr. Coll., 1973; B.S. in Counseling Psychology, Ga. State U. 1975; postgrad. in clin. psychology Chapman Coll., 1978; postgrad. Calif. State U., 1978-80; M.A. in Marriage, Family and Child Counseling, Pepperdine U., 1980; Ph.D. in Clin. Psychology, Internat. Coll., Los Angeles, 1983. Cert. tchr., counselor, Calif.; lic. marriage, family and child counselor, clin. psychologist, Calif.; cert. rational emotive psychotherapist, N.Y.; cert reality therapist, Calif.; cert. sex educator, counselor, Washington; cert. alcohol and drug abuse counselor, Calif.; cert vocat. cons., Calif., Ga. Psychotherapist, group facilitator Ctr. for Dynamic Therapy, Los Alamitos, Calif., 1977-78, Cypress Counseling Ctr. (Calif.), 1978-80; rehab. bur. liaison, vocat. counselor Internat. Rehab. Assn. Inc., Anaheim, Calif., 1978-80; sr. vocat. counselor Internat. Rehab. Assn. Inc., Norcross, Ga., 1980-82; psychotherapist, group facilitator Buckhead Counseling Ctr., Atlanta, 1980-82; pres., exec. dir. Consol. health Services. Inc., Atlanta, 1982—, Huntington Beach, Calif., 1984—, Clin. Psychology Group, Los Alamitos, Calif., Assessment and Psychotherapy Ctr., Calif., Vocat. Exploration Services, Inc., Calif.; pvt. practice psychotherapy Comprehensive Vocat. Services, Los Alamitos, Huntington Beach, and Tustin, Calif.; Mem. Am. Psychol. Assn., Calif. Psychol. Assn., Am. Marriage, Family and Child Therapist Assn., Am. Assn. Sex Educators, Counselors and Therapists, Calif. Assn. Marriage and Family Therapists, Nat. Rehab. Assn., Calif. Assn. Rehab. Profls., Counselors of Alcohol and Addiction Related Dependencies. Democrat. Unitarian. Home: 3530 Marna Ave Long Beach CA 90808 Office: 3772 Katella Ave Suite 212 Los Alamitos CA 90720 Other: 16052 Beach Blvd Suite 228 Huntington Beach CA 92647 Office: 14751 Plaza Dr Suite P Tustin CA 92680

MARTINDALE, ALLEN P., diversified company executive. BBA, UCLA. CPA. Acct. Lybrand, Ross and Montgomery, 1954-64; with, past pres. Arden Mayfair Groceries, 1964-70; exec. v.p. Smith's Mgmt. Corp., Salt Lake City, 1970—, later chief operating officer, exec. v.p., now chmn. bd. dirs., also bd. dirs. Office: Smiths Mgmt Corp 1544 S Redwood Rd Salt Lake City UT 84104 *

MARTINDALE, DAVID L., science laboratory administrator; b. Burley, Idaho, Jan. 16, 1936; s. Lyman Lenore and Cleora Olive (Peterson) M.; m. Margaret Joan Ferguson, June 30, 1960; children: Robert, Margaret Lynn, Anthony. BSME, Brigham Young U.; postgrad., UCLA, 1962-63, San Diego State U., 1963-64. Registered profl. engr., Calif., registered mech. engr., Calif., registered mfg. engr., Calif. Design group engr. Gen. Dynamics/Convair, San Diego, 1959-66; mgr. cyrogenic systems Ametek/Straza, El Cajon, Calif., 1966-72; emissions specialist engr. San Diego Gas and Electric Co., 1959-66; gen. mgr. Cyrolab Inc., San Luis Obispo, Calif., 1973—. Patentee in field. Pres. Airport Area Property Owners Assn., San Luis Obispo, 1985—. Served with USNG, 1953. Mem. Soc. Profl. and Registered Engrs., ASME, Cyrogenic Soc. Am., Vacuum Soc. Am. Republican. Mormon. Lodges: Elks, Lions (pres. 1983-84). Avocations: flying, skiing, golfing. Home: 2101 Lariat Los Osos CA 93402 Office: Cyrolab Inc 4175 Santa Fe Rd San Luis Obispo CA 93401

MARTINE, LAWRENCE PAUL, marketing and advertising consultant; b. Rahway, N.J., Aug. 21, 1958; s. Lawrence Ferdinand and Henrietta Marie (Senerote) M. BS in Mktg., U. Colo., 1980; MBA in Mktg. cum laude, U. Denver, 1986. Comml. actor, represented by Shirley Hamilton Agy. (Chgo.), Sarah Norton Agy. (Dallas), Plaza 3 (Phoenix), and Vannoy Talent (Denver), 1980-84; free-lance copywriter Mefford-Weir, Inc., Denver, 1984; free-lance advt. and mktg. cons. Denver, 1984—. Mem. Mu Kappa Tau. Roman Catholic. Avocations: consumerism, graphics, languages, sports, arts. Home and Office: 8825 W 93rd Ave Broomfield CO 80020

MARTINETTI, RONALD ANTHONY, lawyer; b. N.Y.C., Aug. 13, 1945; s. Alfred Joseph and Frances Ann (Battipaglia) M. JD, U. So. Calif., 1981, U. Chgo. Law Sch., 1981-82. Bar: Calif. 1982, U.S. Dist. Ct. (cen. and no. dists.) Calif. 1982, U.S. Ct. Appeals (9th cir.) 1982. Ptnr. Brakefield & Kazanjian, Glendale, Calif., 1984—. Author: James Dean Story, 1975; contbr. articles to profl. jours. Mem. Calif. Bar Assn., Los Angeles Bar Assn., Samuel Williston Soc. Found. (chmn. 1981—). Roman Catholic. Home: 3700 Los Feliz Blvd Los Angeles CA 90005 Office: Brakefield & Kazanjian 225 W Broadway Glendale CA 91204

MARTINEZ, CAMILLA MARIA, lawyer; b. Santa Fe, Feb. 26, 1954; d. Eloy A. and Frances (Roybal) M. BS, U. N.Mex., 1975, MA with honors, 1978; JD, U. Denver, 1985. Classroom tchr. Albuquerque Pub. Schs., 1975-82; with staff Martinez Bail Bond Co., Santa Fe, 1975-82; with legal staff Willis A. Belford, Jr. Law Offices, Colorado Springs, Colo., 1985—. Reader Mother of God Catholic Ch., Denver, 1983—, eucharistic minister, 1985—. Named one of Outstanding Young Women Am., 1985. Mem. Am. Trial Lawyers Assn., Colo. Trial Lawyers Assn., Student Am. Bar Assn., Mexican-Am. Law Students Assn., Phi Alpha Delta. Democrat. Avocations: sports, stamp collecting, photography, tutoring children. Home: 412 Alta Vista Santa Fe NM 87501

MARTINEZ, DAVID JOSEPH, municipal official, energy consultant; b. Loma Linda, Calif., May 1, 1950; s. Joseph S. and Annie (Trevino) M.; m. Nadine G. Luine, Spt. 27, 1971; children: Robbie A., Ryan J. AA, San Bernardino Valley Coll., 1982; cert., Riverside City Coll., 1984. Bldg. advisor City of Redlands, Calif., 1972-76; bldg. inspector II Riverside (Calif.) County, 1976-79, plans examiner, 1979-84; prin. D.J.'s Energy Cons., Redlands, 1979—; sr. plans examiner Riverside (Calif.) County, 1984-85; bldg. inspector Willdan & Assoc., San Bernardino, 1985-86; bldg. official City of Claremont, Calif., 1986—. Served with USMC, 1969-71, Vietnam. Named Citizen of Yr., Nat. Rifle Assn., 1984. Mem. Internat. Conf. Bldg. Officials (Riverside chpt. parliamentarian 1986, Foothill chpt. sec.-treas. 1987). Democrat. Presbyterian. Avocations: fishing, hunting, travel, racquetball. Office: City of Claremont 207 Harvard Ave Claremont CA 91711

MARTINEZ, EDWARD RAY, civil engineer; b. Brighton, Colo., Feb. 18, 1961; s. Raymond F. and Mary E. Martinez. BArch, Civil Engring., U. Colo., 1983. Introduction engr. Peak Engring. Co., Inc., Colorado Springs, Colo., 1983-84; hwy. engr. State of Colo., Denver, 1984—; owner Frameworks, 1985. Mem. Soc. Hispanic Profl. Engrs., Nat. Soc. Archtl. Engrs., ASCE, Colo, Profl. Land Surveyors. Avocations: Seibukan karate, skiing, running, photography. Office: State of Colo DOH 4201 E Arkansas Denver CO 80222

MARTINEZ, ELUID LEVI, water resources engineer; b. Cordova, N.Mex., Apr. 26, 1944; s. Plajeres and Eliria (Lopez) M.; m. Suzanne Cecilia Robinson, Aug. 26, 1967; children—Adrian, Trina, Pamela. B.S.C.E., N.Mex. State U., 1968. Registered profl. engr., land surveyor, N.Mex. Computer systems engr. N.Mex. Hwy. Dept., Santa Fe, 1968-71; chief hydrographic survey sect. N.Mex. State Engrs. Office, Santa Fe, 1971-84, chief tech. div., 1984—, hearing examiner, 1984—. Author: What is a New Mexico Santo?, 1978. Chmn., Santa Fe Bd. Edn., 1978-84; chmn. bd. City of Santa Fe Planning Commn., 1973-83, City/County of Santa Fe Extraterritorial Zoning Commn., 1982, Santa Fe Bd. Adjustment, 1980, Hist. Styles Com., 1978. Mem. Chi Epsilon, Sigma Tau, Sigma Chi Rho. Roman Catholic. Club: Caballero de Vargas. Office: N Mex State Engr Office Bataan Bldg Santa Fe NM 87501

MARTINEZ, GLENN ADAM, graphic, architectural, industrial designer; b. Mt. Kisco, N.Y., Mar. 12, 1957; s. John Robert and Violet Mary (Vallejo) M.; m. Colleen Ann Schuman, Aug. 16, 1985. Student, Parsons Sch. Design, 1965, Maryland Inst. Coll. Art, 1973-74, Kans. City Art Inst., 1974-75, San Francisco Art Inst., 1975-76. Art dir. Calif. Builder and Engring. Mag., Palo Alto, 1976-77, Sonoma Bus. Mag., Santa Rosa, Calif., 1977; owner, designer Glenn Martinez & Assocs., Santa Rosa, 1977—; owner Zenitram Gallery, Santa Rosa, 1985—; owner, designer Zenitram Design Modern, Santa Rosa, 1985—; bd. dirs. Profl. Communications Design, Santa Rosa, 1982—. Prin. works include designs for Calif. Cooler, 1985, Safeway Stores, 1986, Christian Bros., 1986, Lucky Stores, 1986. Mem. Am. Inst. Graphic Artists, Sant Rosa C. of C. Club: Sonoma County Ad. Avocations: reading, flying, skiing. Office: Glenn Martinez & Assocs. 15 Third St Santa Rosa CA 95401

MARTINEZ, JOSE FLAMINIO, data processing executive; b. Bernalillo, N.Mex., Apr. 16, 1944; s. Barbara D. (Gutierrez) M. AA in Computer Sci., Pasadena City Coll., 1968. Tech. rep. Burroughs Corp., City of Industry, Calif., 1966-75; dir. data processing Lovelace Med. Ctr., Albuquerque, 1975-78; pres. Data Mgmt. Services, Albuquerque, 1978-86, Unltd. System Solutions Inc., Albuquerque, 1986—. Named Outstanding Young Man of Yr., U.S. Jaycees, 1979. Mem. Rio Grande Burroughs Users Group (pres. 1980), Cert. Systems Profls. Democrat. Roman Catholic. Avocations: writing poetry, softball, fishing. Home: 6304 Colleen NE Albuquerque NM 87109

MARTINEZ, MATTHEW GILBERT, congressman; b. Walsenburg, Colo., Feb. 14, 1929; children: Matthew, Diane, Susan, Michael, Carol Ann. Cert of competence, Los Angeles Trade Tech. Sch., 1959. Small businessman and bldg. contracto; mem. 97th-99th Congresses from 30th dist. Calif. Mem. Monterey Park Planning Commn., 1971-74; mayor City of Monterey park, 1974-75; mem. Monterey Park City Council, 1974-80, Calif. State Assembly, 1980-82; bd. dirs. San Gabriel Valley YMCA. Served with USMC, 1947-50. Mem. Congl. Hispanic Caucus, Hispanic Am. Democrats, Nat. Assn. Latino Elected and Apptd. Ofcls., Communications Workers Am., VFW, Am. Legion, Latin Bus. Assn., Monterey Park C. of C., Navy League (dir.). Democrat. Lodge: Rotary. Office: 109 Cannon House Office Bldg Washington DC 20515 *

MARTÍNEZ-MAZA, OTONIEL, research immunologist; b. Cardenas, Cuba, Jan. 28, 1954; came to U.S., 1961; s. Otoniel Martinez-Alba and Aida (Maza) Martinez; m. Jeannie C. Stallings, May 9, 1981; children: Duncan, Anna. BS, U. Calif., Irvine, 1975; postgrad., Stanford U., 1975-76; PhD, UCLA, 1981. NIH-Swedish Med. Research Council postdoctoral fellow Karolinska Inst., Stockholm, 1981-82, NATO postdoctoral fellow, 1982-83; Pasteur ADIP postdoctoral fellow Pasteur Inst., Paris, 1983; postdoctoral scholar Sch. Medicine, UCLA, 1984-86, asst. research immunologist, 1986—. Contbr. articles to sci. jours. Will Rogers Meml fellow, 1986—. Mem. Am. Assn. Immunology, Scandinavian Soc. Immunology, Sigma Xi. Republican. Avocation: cycling. Office: UCLA Sch Medicine Dept Microbiology and Immunology Los Angeles CA 90024

MARTINI, EMIL P., JR., wholesale pharmaceutical distribution company executive; b. Teaneck, N.J., 1928. Grad., Purdue U., 1950. With Bergen Brunswig Corp., Los Angeles, 1952—, now chmn., chief exec. officer; pres., mgr. Bergen Drug Co. div., Los Angeles, 1956-69, corp. pres., chief exec. officer, from 1969, also dir.; dir. Bro-Dart Industries, David Jamison Carlyle Corp. Office: Bergen Brunswig Corp 4000 Metropolitan Dr Orange CA 92668 *

MARTINI, ROBERT E., wholesale pharmaceutical and related products company executive; b. Hackensack, N.J., 1932. B.S., Ohio State U., 1954. With Bergen Brunswig Corp., Orange, Calif., 1956—, v.p., 1962-69, exec. v.p., 1969-81, pres., chief operating officer, dir., 1981—. Served to capt. USAF, 1954. Office: Bergen Brunswig Corp 4000 Metropolitan Dr Orange CA 92668

MARTINSON, CONSTANCE FRYE, television program hostess, producer; b. Boston, Apr. 11, 1932; d. Edward and Rosalind Helen (Sperber) Frye; m. Leslie Herbert Martinson, Sept. 24, 1955; 1 child, Julianna Martinson Carner. BA in English Lit., Wellesley Coll., 1953. Dir. pub. relations Coro Found., Los Angeles, 1974-79; producer/host KHJ Dimensions, Los Angeles, 1979-81, Connie Martinson Talks Books, Los Angeles, 1981—; instr. dept. humanities UCLA, 1981—; celebrity advisor Book Fair-Music Ctr., Los Angeles, 1986. Author Dramatization of Wellesley After Images, 1974; book editor, columnist Calif. Press Bur. Syndicate, 1986—. Pres. Mayor's adv. council on volunteerism, Los Angeles, 1981-82; chmn. community affairs dept. Town Hall of Calif., Los Angeles, 1981-85; bd. dirs. legal def. fund NAACP, Los Angeles, 1981-84. Mem. Women in Cable, Am. Film Inst., Jewish TV Network (bd. dirs. 1985—). Democrat. Jewish. Club: Wellesley Coll. (pres. 1979-81). Avocations: tennis, theater, reading. Home and Office: 2288 Coldwater Canyon Beverly Hills CA 90210

MARTON, LAURENCE JAY, clinical pathologist, educator, researcher; b. Bklyn., Jan. 14, 1944; s. Bernard Dov and Sylvia (Silberstein) M.; m. Marlene Lesser, June 27, 1967; 1 child, Eric Nolan. B.A., Yeshiva U., 1965; M.D., Albert Einstein Coll. Medicine, 1969. Intern Los Angeles County-Harbor Gen. Hosp., 1969-70; resident in neurosurgery U. Calif.-San Francisco, 1970-71, resident in lab. medicine, 1973-75, asst. research biochemist, 1973-74, asst. clin. prof. depts. lab. medicine and neurosurgery, 1974-75, asst. prof., 1975-78, assoc. prof., 1978-79, prof., 1979—, asst. dir. div. clin. chemistry, dept. lab. medicine, 1974-75, dir. div., 1975-79, acting chmn. dept., 1978-79, chmn. dept., 1979—. Co-editor: Polyamines in Biology and Medicine, 1981; Liquid Chromatography in Clinical Analysis, 1981; Clinical Liquid Chromatography, vol. 1, 1984, vol. 2, 1984. Served with USPHS, NIH, 1971-73. Recipient Research Career Devel. award Nat. Cancer Inst. Mem. Am. Assn. Cancer Research, Am. Assn. Clin. Chemistry, AAAS, Acad. Clin. Lab. Physicians and Scientists, Assn. Pathology Chairmen, Am. Assn. Pathologists, San Francisco Med. Soc., Calif. Med. Assn., Alpha Omega Alpha. Jewish. Avocations: photography; art; music; travel; sports. Home: 69 Aloha Ave San Francisco CA 94122 Office: U Calif Dept Lab Medicine San Francisco CA 94143

MARTY, RAYMOND, physician; b. Bklyn., Oct. 26, 1929; s. Harry Kenneth and Pearl (Bailin) M.; B.A., UCLA, 1952; M.D., U. Lausanne (Switzerland), 1959; m. Carole M. Perry, Jan. 25, 1960. Intern, Hosp. Good Samaritan, Los Angeles, 1960-61; resident in diagnostic radiology Albert Einstein Sch. Medicine, Bronx, N.Y., 1962; fellow radiation therapy Stanford Med. Sch., 1962-63; dir. out patient clinic St. Joseph's Hosp., San Francisco, 1963-65; fellow Tumor Inst., Seattle, 1965-66, mem. staff, 1966—, dir nuclear medicine/ultrasound, 1967—; assoc. clin. prof. nuclear medicine tech. Seattle U. Med. Sch., 1972—; asst. clin. prof. nuclear medicine U. Wash. Med. Sch., Seattle, 1974—. Mem. AMA, Am. Coll. Radiology, Radiol. Soc. N.Am., Am. Coll. Nuclear Physicians, Soc. Nuclear Medicine, N.Y. Acad. Scis., Fedn. Am. Scientists, AAAS. Clubs: Seattle Yacht, La Chaine des Rotisseurs; Lahaina Yacht (Maui, Hawaii). Contbr. articles to profl. jours. Home: 4607 103rd Ln NE Kirkland WA 98033 Office: 1229 Madison St Suite 1150 Seattle WA 98104

MARTZ, CARL SCOTT, aerospace engr.; b. Grand Rapids, Mich., June 18, 1958; s. Kenneth Wayne and Edwina Pauline (Goodheart) M. BS in Biol. Sci., U. Calif., Irvine, 1981. Mem. tech. staff Rockwell Internat., Downey, Calif., 1981—. judge Los Angeles Sci. Fair, 1984, 85. Mem. Nat. Space Soc., Smithsonian Inst., U. Calif. Irvine Century Club. Democrat. Avocations: rock climbing, astronomy, fitness, music. Home: 21513 Juan Ave #2 Haw Gardens CA 90716 Office: Rockwell Internat 12214 Lakewood Blvd MLS FA19 Downey CA 90241

MARTZ, PHILIP REID, artificial intelligence engineer; b. Grand Rapids, Mich., Feb. 1, 1952; s. Kenneth W. and Edwina P. (Goodheart) M.; m. Laurie F. Tilton, May 21, 1985; 1 child, Henry Russell. BS in Biology, U. Calif., Irvine, 1975. Engr. artificial intelligence Beckman Instruments, Inc., Fullerton, Calif., 1982—. Mem. Am. Assn. Artificial Intelligence, Am. Chem. Soc. Avocation: mountaineering. Home: 2225 N Spinnaker Santa Ana CA 92706 Office: Beckman Instruments 2500 Harbor Fullerton CA 92624

MARUSKA, JOHN HANS, marketing and management consultant; b. Trenton, N.J., Feb. 5, 1946; s. John Howard and Ruth Anne (Peterson) M.; BS, N.Mex. State U., 1968; MA, U. N.Mex., 1976; diploma Am. Inst. Banking, 1972; MA, N.Mex. Highlands U., 1981; m. Evelyn D. Martinez, Sept. 3, 1966; children: Jacquelyn, Kristin. With Fed. Land Bank, Albuquerque, 1971-72, Valley Nat. Bank, Espanola, N.Mex., 1972-73; with N.Mex. Parks and Recreation Commn., Santa Fe, 1973—, dir. Bur. Planning and Devel., 1975—; propr. Magnum Enterprises, cons.; owner welding excavation bus. Dir. N.Mex. Manufactured Housing Dept., 1984-85; chmn. La Acequia de Los Chicos Irrigation Commn., 1978; dir. N.Mex. Soil and Water Conservation Commn., 1981-83; past mem. N.Mex. Coal Surface Mining Commn. Chmn. adv. bd. Embudo (N.Mex.) Presbyn. Hosp., 1972-75. Served with USN, 1969-71. Mem. Nat. Recreation and Park Assn., N.Mex. Park and Recreation Assn., N.Mex. Solar Energy Assn. Democrat. Roman Catholic. Lodge: Rotary (dir. Espanola 1971-73). Home: PO Box 252 Velarde NM 87582 Office: PO Box 9151 Santa Fe NM 87504

MARUYAMA, MAGOROH, business researcher, consultant; b. Tokyo, Apr. 2, 1929; came to U.S., 1950; s. Sinsaku and Toyoko (Takashima) M.; m. Pierrette Duriez, Apr. 1966 (div. 1974); 1 child, Yukon; m. Kuniko Sakakibara, July 23, 1976; 1 child, Yuki. BA in Math., U. Calif., Berkeley, 1951; postgrad., U. Munich, U. Heidelberg, Fed. Republic of Germany, 1954-55, U. Copenhagen, 1955-57; PhD, U. Lund, Sweden, 1959. Asst. prof. U. Calif., Berkeley, 1960-62; research assoc. Stanford U., Calif., 1962-64; assoc. prof. San Francisco State U., 1965-70; prof. Antioch Coll., 1971-72, Portland (Oreg.) State U., 1973-76; vis. prof. U. Ill., Urbana, 1976-77, U. Uppsala, Sweden, 1982, UCLA, 1983, Nat. U., Singapore, 1983-84; research prof. U. Hawaii, Honolulu, 1984—; cons. U.S. Dept. Commerce, 1971, Can. Fed. Ministry Urban Affairs, 1974, NASA, 1975, Monsanto Chems., 1980, Volvo, Sweden, 1982, Fed. Motors of Indonesia, 1984, Technopolises Japan, 1984, MITI of Japan., 1985. Served to sgt. USMC, 1952-54. NSF, NIMH, Dept. Energy grantee, 1965-86. Fellow AAAS, mem. Am. Psychol. Assn., Acad. Internat. Bus., Internat. Cons. Found, Acad. Mgmt., Sigma Xi, Pi Mu Epsilon. Avocations: garden design, African and Asian folkore, architecture. Office: Pacific Asian Mgmt Inst 2404 Maile Way Honolulu HI 96822

MARVEL, CARL SHIPP, retired chemistry educator; b. Waynesville, Ill., Sept. 11, 1894; s. John Thomas and Mary Lucy (Wasson) M.; m. Nelle Beggs, June 1918 (div. 1933); m. Alberta Hughes, Dec. 16, 1933; children: Mary Catharine, John Thomas. AB, MS, Ill. Wesleyan U., 1915; AM, U. Ill., 1916, PhD, 1920; DSc (hon.), Ill. Wesleyan U., 1946, U. Ill., 1963, Poly. Inst. N.Y., 1983, U. Louvain, Belgium, 1970. Instr. chemistry U. Ill., Urbana, 1920-21, assoc., 1921-23, asst. prof., 1923-27, assoc. prof., 1927-30, prof. organic chemistry, 1930-53; prof. chemistry U. Ariz., Tucson, 1953-78; cons. E.I. DuPont Co., Wilmington, Del., 1928—. Author: An Introduction to the Organic Chemistry of High Polymers, 1959. Recipient Plastic Sci. Engring. award Soc. Plastic Engrs. Internat., 1964, Perkin medal Am Sect. Soc. Chem. Industry, 1965, Achievement award U. Ill. Alumni Assn., 1976, Creative Sci. award U. Ariz. Found., 1978, Nat. Medal of Sci., U.S. Govt., 1986; inducted into Plastics Hall of Fame, 1986. Mem. Am. Chem. Soc. (pres. 1945-46, Nichols medal N.Y. sect. 1944, Willard Gibbs medal Chgo. sect. 1950, Priestly medal 1956, Polymer Chemistry award 1964, Madison Marshall award North Ala. sect. 1966, Chemistry of Plastics and Coatings award 1973, 40 Yrs. Service Council Mem. award 1980, Chem. Edn. award 1984, 45 Yrs. Service Council Mem. award 1985), Am. Acad. Arts and Scis., Nat. Acad. Scis., Am. Inst. Chemists (Gold medal 1955), Am. Philos. Soc., Alpha Chi Sigma (John R. Kuebler award 1970). Club: Cosmos. Avocation: bird watching. Home: 2332 E 9th St Tucson AZ 85719 Office: U Ariz Chemistry Dept CSML Bldg #37 Tucson AZ 85721

MARVEL, ORIN EDWARD, chief scientist, educator; b. White Plains, N.Y., Sept. 23, 1940; s. Orin Edward Marvel and Elenore (Knatis) Van Duren; m. JoAnn Vinson, June 1, 1964; children: Terry, Kelly, Dawn, Robby. BEE, Ga. Tech., 1964, MEE, 1965; M in Math., Calif. Poly., 1984; D in Engring., U. Ill., Champaign, 1970. Prin. fellow Honeywell, West Covina, Calif., 1970-85; chief scientist Hughes, Fullerton, Calif., 1985—; adj. prof. U. South Fla., Tampa, 1971-75, Calif. Poly. Pamona, 1978-82, 84—, George Washington U., 1983. Mem. IEEE (sect. chmn. 1982, Congl. fellow 1983, Centennial award 1984). Republican. Presbyterian. Avocations: ham radio, motorcycling. Home: 5948 W View Dr Orange CA 92669 Office: Hughes PO Box 3310 Fullerton CA 92634

MARVIN, RICHARD FREDERICK, geologist; b. Bozeman, Mont., May 1, 1926; s. Guy E. and LaVern (Birkett) M.; m. Lillian Esther Kabes, Nov. 1, 1955; children: Ellen, Eric. BS, Mont. Sch. Mines, 1950, MS, 1952. Geologist U.S. Geol. Survey, Washington and Denver, 1952—. Mem. AAAS, Geol. Soc. Am., Am. Geophys. Union. Methodist. Avocations: hiking, reading, ping pong.

MARX, JAY NEIL, physicist; b. N.Y.C., Nov. 30, 1945; s. Leo and Lila (Weil) M.; m. Katya Michelle Hope, July 7, 1977; 1 child Elena Hope. AB, Columbia U., 1966, MS, 1969, PhD, 1970. Mem. faculty Yale U., New Haven, 1970-75; with sci. staff Lawrence Berkeley (Calif.) Lab., 1975—. Mem. AAAS, Am. Phys. Soc., Sigma Xi. Office: Lawrence Berkeley Lab 1 Cyclotron Rd Berkeley CA 94720

MARX, LARRY FRANK, environmental consultant; b. Los Angeles, Mar. 6, 1955; s. Curt Arthur and Ruth Ellen (Ziegler) M. BA, U. Calif., Berkeley, 1976; MS, U. So. Calif., 1978. Staff researcher U. So. Calif., Los Angeles, 1976-78; staff engr. Rockwell Internat., Newbury Park, Calif., 1978-81; dir. Tetra Tech Inc. subs. Honeywell Inc., Bellevue, Wash., 1981—. Patentee in field. Mem. ASCE (mem. 2 subcoms.), Nat. Assn. Environ. Profls., Am. Chem. Soc., Marine Tech. Soc. Democrat. Jewish. Avocations: running, backpacking, golf. Home: 3830 165th Pl SE Bellevue WA 98008 Office: Tetra Tech Inc 11820 Northrup Way Bellevue WA 98005

MARX, ROBERT PHILLIP, lawyer; b. Oregon City, Oreg., Jan. 23, 1949; s. Joseph Wesley and Louise Roseline (Belen) M.; m. Paula Jayne Fisher, Sept. 14, 1968; children: Rachel Elizabeth, Justin Robert, Jordan Thomas. BS in Polit. Sci., Oreg. State U., 1971; JD, Northwestern U., 1979. Bar: Hawaii, 1980. Rep. Oreg. State Legis., Salem, 1973-79, vice chmn. com. on revenue, 1974-75, co-chmn. interim com. on judiciary, 1975; sole practice Hilo, Hawaii, 1980—. Recipient Star and Lamp Key award Phi Kappa Phi, Corvallis, Oreg., 1968; named Sr. Advocate of Yr., Nat. Retired Tchrs. Assn. and Am. Assn. Retired People, 1978. Mem. ABA, Assn. Trial Lawyers Am. Democrat. Office: 688 Kinoole St Suite 105B Hilo HI 96720

MARYLANDER, STUART JEROME, hospital administrator; b. Oakland, Calif., Nov. 13, 1931; s. Philip and Lilyan (Wolf) M.; m. Judith Rosenblatt, June 3, 1956; children: Steven Mark, Grant. M.P.H. in Hosp. Adminstrn, U. Calif.-Berkeley, 1956. Research asst. med. care adminstrn. Sch. Pub. Health, U. Calif.-Berkeley, 1955-56; adminstrv. resident Mt. Zion Hosp., San Francisco, 1956-57; asst. adminstr. Cedars of Lebanon Hosp., Los Angeles, 1957-62; adminstr. Mt. Sinai Hosp. div. Cedars-Sinai Med. Center, Los Angeles, 1963-64; adminstrv. dir. center Mt. Sinai Hosp. div. Cedars-Sinai Med. Center, 1964-66, asso. exec. dir. and adminstrv. dir., 1967-71, exec. dir., 1971-74, exec. v.p., 1974-78, pres., 1979—; instr. U. So. Calif. Sch. Pub. Adminstrn., 1965-70; bd. dirs. Vol. Hosps. Am. Bd. dirs. Commn. Adminstrv. Services to Hosps., 1967-76; bd. dirs. Hosp. Council So. Calif., 1968-76, pres., 1975-76; chmn. Council Teaching Hosps., 1980-81, mem. adminstrv. bd., 1977-82. Served with AUS, 1953-55. Fellow Am. Pub. Health Assn., Royal Soc. of Health (Eng.), Am. Coll. Hosp. Adminstrs.; mem. Am. Hosp. Assn. (, bd. trustees 1987—, rep. to ho. of dels. 1983-88), Calif. Hosp. Assn. (dir. 1974-80, chmn. 1979), Assn. Am. Med. Colls. (mem. assembly 1977-82, exec. council 1979-82), Nat. Assn. Biomed. Research (bd. dirs. 1986—), Internat. Hosp. Fedn., Sigma Alpha Mu. Office: 8700 Beverly Blvd Los Angeles CA 90048

MASAKI, BECKIE UTA, social worker, artist; b. Sacramento, Dec. 9, 1957; d. Akito and Emi (Yamada) M. BA in Psychology, BA in Art, U. Calif., Berkeley, 1980, M in Social Welfare, 1983. Advisor Ednl. Guidance Ctr., Berkeley, 1981-82; co-dir. Tng. in Community Services program, Berkeley, 1982-83; vol./outreach program coordinator La Casa De Las Madres, San Francisco, 1983-85; head counselor for women Upward Bound/Ptnrship., U. Calif., Berkeley, 1985; transfer ctr. coordinator Calif. State U., Hayward, 1985—; cons. Nat. Action Against Rape, Oakland, 1985, Action Com. Against Rape, 1985. One woman show Ohana Cultural Ctr., Oakland, 1986, Tygress 50 Gallery, San Francisco, 1986. Bd. dirs. Berkeley Community YWCA, also pres., 1984—. Grad. fellow U. Calif., Berkeley, 1982. Mem. Calif. Women of Color Against Domestic Violence, Nat. Assn. Social Workers, Asian Battered Women's Shelter Project (organizing com., program com. chair 1985—), Phi Beta Kappa. Buddhist. Office: Calif State U Office Admissions and Records Hayward CA 94542

MASCHGAN, MARILYN GAIL, audiologist; b. Sharon, Pa., Dec. 7, 1953; d. Oswald and Eleanor (Christie) M. BS, Pa. State U., 1975; MA, San Diego State U., 1979. Cert. clin. competence. Audiologist Ross-Loos Med. Group, Orange, Calif., 1980-81, Audiology Group, Las Vegas, Nev., 1981-85, Charles J. Abdo, M.D., Speech and Hearing Ctr., Las Vegas, 1985—. Mem. Am. Speech Lang. Hearing Assn., Nev. Hearing Aid Dealers Assn. (sec. 1985—). Mem. Eastern Orthodox Ch. Avocation: aerobics. Office: Charles J Abdo MD Speech and Hearing Ctr 801 S Rancho #D2 Las Vegas NV 89106

MASCHO, GEORGE LEROY, educator; b. Warsaw, N.Y., Feb. 5, 1925; s. Clayton Leroy and Dorothy Emma (Bailey) M. B.Ed., SUNY, Geneseo, 1948; M.A., Stanford U., 1950; Ed.D., Ind. U., 1961. Tchr. Ontario (N.Y.) Jr. High Sch., 1948-49, Burris Lab. Sch., Muncie, Ind., 1950-61; mem. faculty Ball State U., Muncie, 1961-85; prof. edn. Ball State U., 1967-85, prof. emeritus, 1985—. Contbr. articles to profl. jours. Bd. dirs., treas. United Day Care Center, 1977—; mem. nat. com. developing Head Start program, 1965-66. Served with inf. U.S. Army, 1943-46. Mem. Nat. Assn. Edn. Young Children, Ind. Assn. Edn. Young Children (chmn. legis. com. 1968-70), Assn. Childhood Edn., Maui Ret. Tchrs. Assn. (dir. 1985—), Ind. Arabian Horse Assn. (dir. 1968-73), Phi Delta Kappa. Republican. Home: 2792 Aina Lani Dr Pukalani HI 96768

MASHAW, BIJAN, information systems educator, consultant; b. Tehran, Iran, June 1, 1943; came to U.S., 1971.; s. Ali and Fateme (Haidari) Mashayekhi; m. Faraneh Attarchi, Aug. 15, 1972 (div. June 1979); 1 child, Arsheeya Mashayekhi. BS, Tehran U., 1966, MS, 1968; PhD, Clemson U., 1976; diploma indsl. engring., Carl Duisberg Inst., Fed. Republic of Germany, 1971. Systems analyst Telephone Co., Tehran, 1965-66; dept. supr. Brass Co., Tehran, 1966-69; instrumentation design engr. Siemens Co., Berlin, 1969-71; mem. faculty Cen. Mich. U., Mount Pleasant, 1977-84, assoc. prof. info. systems and analysis, 1977-84; vis. prof. Calif. State U., Hayward, 1982-83, prof. info. systems, 1984—; cons. in field. Author: Programming Byte By Byte Structured Fortran 77, 1983, Structured Basic, 1985; contbr. articles to profl. jours. Mem. Assn. Computing Machinery, Am. Inst. Decision Scis., Data Processing Mgmt. Assn. Home: 5511 Wisteria Way Livermore CA 94550 Office: Calif State U Hayward CA 94532

MASILAMONEY, SAM, not-for-profit foundation administrator, minister; b. Palayamkottai, Madras, India, May 17, 1944; came to U.S., 1977; s. Thachanamoorthi and Nancy (Arumainayagam) Thangiah; m. Leona Pushpa Prasangi, Dec. 29, 1970; children: Bonnie Josephine, Daniel Paul. BS, U. Madras, 1965; ThD, Calcutta Bible Coll., India, 1970; BTh, Allahabad Bible Sem., India, 1975; DD, Am. Bible Sem., 1979; PhD, Western Evang. Sch. Theology, 1985. Area dir. Collegiate Ambassadors, Calcutta, 1970-75; missions dir. N.Am. Evangelistic Assn., Everett, Wash., 1976-79; founder, dir. Operation India Internat., Watsonville, Calif., 1979—; asst. supt. N.Am. Evangelistic Assn., 1979—; prof. San Jose Bible Coll., Calif., 1986; bd. dirs. Multi-Cultural Bible Inst., San Jose. Author: Christ Changed My Karma, 1971; editor Action mag., 1972. Pastor home mission dept. East Indian Bapt. Mission So. Bapt. Conv. Mem. Evang. for Social Action, Am. Council of Counselors and Educators. Lodge: Rotary (editor newsletter Asanol, India chpt. 1977, chmn. 3H program Kailua-Kona, Hawaii chpt. 1978). Avocations: still and action photography, documentary movie-making. Home and Office: Operation India Internat Inc 130 Sudden St PO Box 1015 Watsonville CA 95077

MASON, CHARLES THOMAS, JR., taxonomy educator; b. Joliet, Ill., Mar. 26, 1918; s. Charles T. and Alphie (Longley) M.; m. Patricia Bovyer, June 26, 1943; 1 child, Charles T. III. BS, U. Chgo., 1940; MA, U. Calif., Berkeley, 1942, PhD, 1949. Tchr. secondary schs. Long Beach, Calif., 1942-47; instr. U. Wis., Madison, 1949-53; asst. prof. U. Ariz., Tucson, 1953-58, assoc. prof., 1958-62, prof. taxonomy, curator herbarium, 1962—. Fellow AAAS; mem. Internat. Soc. Plant Taxonomy, Am. Assn. Plant Taxonomy, Am. Inst. Biol. Scis., Calif. Bot. Soc., Sigma Xi, Phi Kappa Phi, Gamma Sigma Delta. Lodges: Masons (grandmaster 1983-84). Home: 2945 N Bear Canyon Rd Tucson AZ 85749 Office: Herbarium U Ariz Tucson AZ 85721

MASON, DAVID LAUN, gas company executive; b. Salt Lake City, July 21, 1943; s. Laun H. and Betty Jane (Ross) M.; m. Connie Criddle, Dec. 28, 1967; children: Anthony, Elizabeth, Katherine, Jonathan, Megan. BBA, U. Utah; postgrad., Brigham Young U. Staff auditor Utah Power and Light Co., Salt Lake City, 1970-73; supr. staff auditor Mountain Fuel Supply co., Salt Lake City, 1973-76, dir. purchasing, warehousing, 1976-78, dir. materials, equipment and office services, 1978-80, mgmt. cons. in material mgmt., 1978-80; mgr. adminstrv. services Mountain Fuel Resources Inc., Salt Lake City, 1980—; assoc. instr. U. Utah, Salt Lake City, 1975-78. Contbr. articles to profl. jours. Chmn. Rep. Voting Dist., Salt Lake City, 1981; councilman Holladay (Utah) Community, 1985, chmn. Holladay Boy's Baseball Assn., 1982-83; scoutmaster Boy Scouts Am., Holladay, 1984—; chmn. planning United Way, Greater Salt Lake, chmn. allocation coms. 1982—. Served as sgt. USNG, 1960-67. Nominated Young Man of Yr., Jaycees, Salt Lake City, 1972. Mem. Pacific Coast Gas Assn. (chmn. materials mgmt. 1979-80), Am. Gas Assn. (chmn. materials mgmt. 1984-85), Salt Lake City Area C. of C. (edn. com. 1985-86, pres's. club 1982-86, pres. plaque 1983).,. Mormon. Office: Mountain Fuel Resources Inc 79 S State Salt Lake City UT 84147

MASON, DEAN TOWLE, cardiologist; b. Berkeley, Calif., Sept. 20, 1932; s. Ira Jenckes and Florence Mabel (Towle) M.; m. Maureen O'Brien, June 22, 1957; children: Kathleen, Alison. B.A. in Chemistry, Duke U., 1954, M.D., 1958. Diplomate: Nat. Bd. Med. Examiners, Am. Bd. Internal Medicine (cardiovascular diseases). Intern, then resident in medicine Johns Hopkins Hosp., 1958-61; clin. asso. cardiology br., sr. asst. surgeon USPHS, Nat. Heart Inst., NIH, 1961-63, asst. sect. dir. cardiovascular diagnosis, attending physician, sr. investigator cardiology br., 1963-68; prof. medicine, prof. physiology, chief cardiovascular medicine U. Calif. Med. Sch., Davis-Sacramento Med. Center, 1968-82; dir. cardiac ctr. Cedars Med. Ctr., Miami, Fla., 1982-83; physician-in chief Western Heart Inst., San Francisco, 1983—; chmn. dept. cardiovascular medicine St. Mary's Med. Ctr., San Francisco, 1986—; co-chmn. cardiovascular-renal drugs U.S. Pharmacopeia Com. Revision, 1970-75; mem. life scis. com. NASA; med. research rev. bd. VA, NIH; vis. prof. numerous univs., cons. in field; mem. Am. Cardiovascular Splty. Certification Bd., 1972-78. Author: Cardiovascular Management, 1974, Congestive Heart Failure, 1976, Advances in Heart Disease, Vol. 1, 1977, Vol. 2, 1978, Vol. 3, 1980, Cardiovascular Emergencies, 1978, Principles of Noninvasive Cardiac Imaging, 1980, Myocardial Revascularization, 1981, Cardiology, 1981, 82, 83, 84, 85, 86, Clinical Nuclear Cardiology, 1981, Love Your Heart, 1982; also numerous articles.; Editor: Clin. Cardiol. Jour; editor-in-chief: Am. Heart Jour; mem. editorial bds. sci. jours. Recipient Research award Am. Therapeutic Soc., 1965; Theodore and Susan B. Cummings Humanitarian award State Dept.-Am. Coll. Cardiology, 1972, 73, 75, 78; Skylab Achievement award NASA, 1974; U. Calif. Faculty Research award, 1978; named Outstanding Prof. U. Calif. Med. Sch., Davis, 1972. Fellow Am. Coll. Cardiology (pres. 1977-78), A.C.P., Am. Heart Assn., Am. Coll. Chest Physicians, Royal Soc. Medicine; mem. Am. Soc. Clin. Investigation, Am. Physiol. Soc., Am. Soc. Pharmacology and Exptl. Therapeutics (Exptl. Therapeutics award 1973), Am. Fedn. Clin. Research, N.Y. Acad. Scis., Am. Assn. U. Cardiologists, Am. Soc. Clin. Pharmacology and Therapeutics, Western Assn. Physicians, AAUP, Western Soc. Clin. Research (past pres.), Phi Beta Kappa, Alpha Omega Alpha. Republican. Methodist. Club: El Marcero Country. Home: 3015 Country Club Dr El Macero CA 95618 Office: Western Heart Inst St Mary's Med Ctr 450 Stanyan St San Francisco CA 94117

MASON, GEORGE HAMPTON, public relations company executive; b. Napa, Calif., Dec. 12, 1946; s. George Hampton and Betty Jean (Conner) M.; m. Salli Jane Slaughter, May 6, 1978; children: Samantha Caitlin Slaughter-Mason. BA, San Francisco State U., 1970. Team leader Nueva Learning Ctr., Hillsborough, Calif., 1972-79; writer Western Regional Resource Ctr., Anchorage, 1980-81; community unit dir. Family Connection, Anchorage, 1983-85; account exec. pub. relations Murray, Bradley & Peterson Inc., Anchorage, 1985, account supr. pub. relations, 1986, v.p. pub. relations, 1986—; instr. NSF, San Jose, Calif., 1975-76; cons./writer Mason Jenkins & Assocs., Anchorage, 1981-84. Author: (manual) Man to Man, 1982; co-author Laboratory Laughter, 1974, Developmental Language, 1981; contbr. articles to profl. jours. Chmn. Mayor's Community Devel. Block Grant Task Force, Anchorage, 1985—; bd. dirs. Neighbor to Neighbor Community Fund, Anchorage, 1985—, Alaska Wildlife Alliance, Anchorage, 1984. Mem. Pub. Relations Soc. Am. (pres.-elect Alaska chpt. 1986, bd. dirs. 1984-85), Alaska Hybrid Wolf Assn. (pres. 1983). Democrat. Avocations: outdoor activities, raising exotic animals, collecting animal skulls from around the world. Home: 2606 W 29th Anchorage AK 99503 Office: Murray Bradley & Peterson 1840 S Bragaw Anchorage AK 99508

MASON, GEORGE ROBERT, surgeon, educator; b. Rochester, N.Y., June 10, 1932; s. George Mitchell and Marjorie Louise (Hooper) M.; m. Grace Louise Bransfield, Feb. 4, 1956; children—Douglas Richard, Marcia Jean, David William. B.A., Oberlin Coll., 1955; M.D. with honors, U. Chgo., 1957; Ph.D. in Physiology (Giannini fellow 1966-67), Stanford U., 1968. Diplomate: Am. Bd. Surgery (examiner 1977-80, dir. 1980-86), Bd. Thoracic Surgery. Tchg. asst. pathology U. Chgo., 1954-56; rotating intern U. Chgo. Clinics, 1957-58; tchg. asst. surgery, NIH postdoctoral fellow, USPHS fellow surgery Stanford U., 1960-62; from asst. resident in surgery to sr. and chief resident in surgery Stanford U. Hosps., 1962-66; mem. faculty Stanford Med. Sch., 1965-71, asso. prof., 1970-71; prof., chmn. dept. surgery U. Md. Med. Sch., Balt., 1971-80; also prof. physiology; prof., chmn. dept. surgery U. Calif., Irvine, 1980—. Contbr. to profl. jours., med. textbooks. Served to capt. M.C. USAF, 1958-60. Recipient Markle scholarship in acad. medicine, 1968-74. Mem. Am. Assn. Thoracic Surgery, AAUP, Am. Coll. Chest Physicians, A.C.S., AMA, Am. Physiol. Soc., Am. Gastroent. Assn., Pacific Coast Surg. Assn., Assn. Acad. Surgery, Balt. Acad. Surgery, Los Angeles Surg. Soc., Halsted Soc., Chesapeake Vascular Soc., Soc. Internat. de Chirurgie, Soc. Clin. Surgery, Soc. Surgery Alimentary Tract, Soc. U. Surgeons, Sigma Xi, Alpha Omega Alpha. Home: 18712 Via Torino Irvine CA 92715 Office: Dept Surgery U Calif Irvine CA 92717

MASON, HAROLD FREDERICK, oil company executive, retired; b. Porterville, Calif., Feb. 15, 1925; s. Arthur Charles and Mary Grace (McConchie) M.; m. Marian Elizabeth Caldwell, Jan. 30, 1954; children: Charles, Richard, Catharine. B in Chem. Engring., Cornell U., 1950; PhD, U. Wis., 1955. Chem. engr. Rohm and Haas Co., Bristol, Pa., 1950-51; research chemist Chevron Research Co., Richmond, Calif., 1954-65; sects. supr. Chevron Research Co., Richmond, 1965-67, research div. mgr., 1967-86; ret. 1986. Inventor; researcher in petroleum processing. Sr. Warden St. Anselms Ch., Lafayette, Calif., 1976-77. Served to 2nd lt. USAAF, 1944-46. Mem. Am. Chem. Soc., Am. Inst. Chem. Engrs. Republican. Avocations: photography, hiking, backpacking, travel. Home: 36 Ashford Pl Moraga CA 94556

MASON, JAMES ALBERT, university dean; b. Eureka, Utah, 1929; married, 1956; 3 children. BA, Brigham Young U., 1955, MA, 1957; EdD, Ariz. State U., 1970. Cons., clinician in fine arts, 1955—; former chmn. dept. music Brigham Young U., Provo, now dean Coll. Fine Arts and Communications; vis. prof., lectr. Ind. U., Northwestern U., Cin. Coll.-Conservatory, U. Tex., Central Conservatory, Beijing, Internat. Soc. Music Edn., Warsaw; chmn. nat. symposium Applications of Psychology to the Teaching and Learning of Music; co-founder, 1st pres. Utah Valley Symphony Orch.; past condr. Utah Valley Youth Orch. Editor: The Instrumentalist, Orch. News, Utah Music Educator, Research News column, Jour. Research in Music Edn. Bd. dirs. Presser Found. Mem. Music Educators Nat. Conf. (past nat. pres., council), Nat. Music Council (bd. dirs.), Am. Music Conf. (bd. dirs.). Address: Brigham Young U Coll Fine Arts and Communications A-410 Harris Fine Arts Ctr Provo UT 84602

MASON, J.D., oil company executive; b. Deadwood, S.D., Feb. 17, 1943; m. Barbara H. Jones, Aug. 21, 1964; children: Stephanie R., Nora C. BFA, U. S.D., 1967, MBA, 1968. Staff acct. Peat, Marwick, Mitchell & Co., Chgo. and Denver, 1968-69; v.p., treas. Love Oil Co., Sheridan, Wyo. and Scottsdale, Ariz., 1969-72, also bd. dirs.; pres. Love Oil Co., Inc., Denver, 1976—, also bd. dirs.; mng. dir. Pacific Regional Exploration N.L., Melbourne, Australia, 1970-73; pres. Petro Futures, Inc., Phoenix, 1973-74; owner The Carefree Traveler of Carefree (Ariz.), 1973-78; research assoc. U. S.D., Sioux Falls, 1974-76; pres. Dakota Research Assocs., Ltd., Sioux Falls, 1974-76; dir. Dakota Exploration, Ltd., 1976—; dir. Adv. Council Vocat. Edn., 1974-76. Bertelero scholar, 1961; named Disting. Alumni Lectr., 1971; Alumni of Yr., 1982. Mem. Am. Assn. Petroleum Geologists, Am. Assn. Petroleum Landman, The Geol. Soc. Am., Rocky Mountain Assn. Geologists, N.W. Petroleum Assn., Wyo. Geol. Assn., N.Mex. Geol. Assn., Four Corners Assn. Petroleum Landmen, Beta Gamma Sigma. Methodist. Clubs: Athletic (Denver), Petroleum (Denver). Avocations: rare books, antique prints, bronze art, photography, fly fishing.

MASON, KATHERINE MOLER, health science facility administrator; b. Martinsburg, W.Va., Mar. 8, 1935; s. D. Grove and Katherine (Hirst) M.; m. Howard Merritt, July 7, 1956; children—Katherine, Virginia, Ellen. B.S. in S.W., W.Va. U., 1956; M.S.W., U. Utah, 1971; postgrad. U. Utah, 1973-75. Group worker YWCA, Washington, 1956-59; child welfare worker Utah Div. Family Services, 1965-71, program specialist, 1971-74, cordinator mental retardation program, 1974-76; dept. dir. Office Family, Children and Adult Services, Dept. Social and Health Services State of Wash., Olympia, 1976-78, asst. dir. program and adminstrn. div. developmental disabilities, 1979-80; asst. dir. Santa Clara County Dept. Social Services, San Jose, Calif., 1980-82; adminstr. client services San Andreas Regional Ctr., San Jose, 1982-84; owner The Marshall Group—K. Mason & Assocs. Personnel Service, 1984-85; govt. programs dir. HealthAm., 1985-87; ops. dir. San Mateo Health Commn., 1987—. Mem. AAUW (dir. San Jose br. 1981-85), Am. Pub. Welfare Assn. (dir. 1980-82, nat. membership chairperson 1980-82, regional membership chairperson 1975-80), Nat. Assn. Personnel Cons., W.Va. U. Alumni Assn. Democrat. Episcopalian. Club: Toastmasters Contbr. in field. Home: 1096 Prevost Ct San Jose CA 95125 Office: 4655 Old Ironsides Dr Suite 220 Santa Clara CA 95054

MASON, ROBERT STEVEN, forest products executive; b. DeFuniak Springs, Fla., May 30, 1930; s. Nance Edward and Lola (Brackin) M.; m. Joyce Martens, Mar. 24, 1984. B.S., U. Ala., 1957. Brand mgr. Gen. Mills, Inc., Mpls., 1957-60; advt. mgr. Ralston Purina Co., St. Louis, 1960-64; v.p., gen. mgr. Internat. Minerals & Chems., Skokie, Ill., 1964-71; pres. Accent Internat., Skokie, 1971-72; v.p. Potlatch Corp., San Francisco, 1972-84; pres., chief operating officer Pope & Talbot, Inc., Portland, Oreg., 1984—, also dir. Served with USAF, 1950-54, ETO. Republican. Unitarian. Avocations: flying; boating; golf. Home: 1930 Egan Way Lake Oswego OR 97034 Office: Pope & Talbot Inc 1500 SW 1st Ave Portland OR 97201

MASON, RODNEY JACKSON, physicist, research scientist; b. N.Y.C., Feb. 27, 1939; s. Rodney Jackson and Elizabeth Lorraine (Maher) M.; stepson Alexander R. Weismuller; m. Caroline Faith Vibert Pearce, Feb. 1, 1969; children: Vanessa Jane, Rosalind Jennifer. BA in Physics with honors, Cornell U., 1960, PhD in Aerospace Engring., 1964. Fullbright Found. fellow in plasmaphysics Inst. für Plasmaphysik, Garching, Fed. Republic Germany, 1964-65; Ford Found. postdoctoral fellow, assistant prof. MIT, 1965-67; mem. tech. staff Bell Telephone Labs., Whippany, N.J., 1967-72; staff mem. Los Alamos (N.Mex.) Nat. Lab., 1972—; cons. Can. Nat. Scis. and Engring. Research Council, 1982—; vis. fellow Imperial Coll., London, 1984. Contbr. articles to profl. jours. Recipient Disting. Performance award Los Alamos Nat. Lab, 1981; scientist astronaut finalist NASA, Houston, 1967. Fellow Am. Phys. Soc., mem. IEEE (sr.), AAAS. Home: 148 Piedra Loop Los Alamos NM 87544 Office: Los Alamos Nat Lab X-1 MS-E531 Los Alamos NM 87545

MASON, WILLIAM A(LVIN), psychologist, educator, researcher; b. Mountain View, Calif., Mar. 28, 1926; s. Alvin Frank and Ruth Sabina (Erwin) M.; m. Virginia Joan Carmichael, June 27, 1948; children—Todd, Paula, Nicole, Hunter. B.A., Stanford U., 1950, M.S., 1952, Ph.D., 1954. Asst. prof. U. Wis.-Madison, 1954-59; research assoc. Yerkes Labs. Primate Biology, Orange Park, Fla., 1959-63; head dept. behavioral sci. Delta Primate Research Ctr., Tulane U., Covington, La., 1963-71; prof. psychology, research psychologist U. Calif.-Davis, 1971—; cons. USPHS, 1968-75; leader behavioral biology unit Calif. Primate Research Ctr., Davis, 1972-85; bd. dirs. Jane Goodall Inst., 1979—, Karisoke Research Ctr., 1980-86. Contbr. numerous chpts., articles to profl. publs.; editorial bd. Animal Learning and Behavior, 1973-76, Infant Behavior and Devel., 1976—, Internat. Jour. Primatology, 1980—. Served with USMC, 1946-48. USPHS spl. fellow, 1963-64. Fellow Am. Psychol. Assn. (pres. Div. 6 1982), AAAS, Animal Behavior Soc.; mem. Internat. Primatological Soc. (pres. 1976-80, 81-84), Am. Soc. Primatologists (pres.-elect 1986—), Internat. Soc. Devel. Psychobiology (pres. 1971-72, Best Paper of Yr. award 1976), Sigma Xi. Home: 2809 Anza Ave Davis CA 95616 Office: Dept Psychology U Calif Davis CA 95616

MASRI, SAMI F(AIZ), civil and mechanical engineering educator, consultant; b. Beirut, Dec. 9, 1939; came to U.S., 1956; B.S. in Aerospace Engring., U. Tex., 1960, M.S. in Aerospace Engring., 1961; M.S. in Mech. Engring., Calif. Inst. Tech., 1962, Ph.D. in Mech. Engring., 1965. Research fellow Calif. Inst. Tech., Pasadena, 1965-66; asst. prof. civil and mech. engring. U. So. Calif., Los Angeles, 1966-69; assoc. prof. U. So. Calif., 1969-76, prof., 1976—. Contbr. articles to profl. jours. Research grantee NSF, NASA, NRC. Mem. AIAA, ASME, IEEE, AAAS, Sigma Xi. Office: U So Calif Civil Engring Dept MC 0242 Los Angeles CA 90089

MASS, SHARON, social worker; b. Bklyn., Jan. 29, 1945; d. Jack and Rose Mass; m. Samuel Achs, June 16, 1976. BA, Bklyn. Coll., 1968; MSW, Hunter Sch. Social Work, 1975; PhD, U. So. Calif. Sch. Social Work, 1985. Lic. clin. social worker. Reference librarian Donaldson, Lufkin & Jenrette, Inc., N.Y.C., 1968-73; clin. social worker Jewish Hosp. and Med. Ctr., N.Y.C., 1975-79; dir. social services United Western Med. Ctr., Santa Ana, Calif., 1979—; mem. faculty sch. of social work U. So. Calif., Los Angeles, 1985—; cons. Western Med. Ctr., 1982—; adv. bd. U. So. Calif. Tri County Branch Sch. Social Work, 1985—, Vis. Nurses Assn. Hospice, Orange County, Calif., 1982—. Fellow: Soc. Clin. Social Workers, Nat. Assn. Social Workers; mem. Soc. Hosp. Social Workers. Democrat. Jewish. Avocations: swimming, fishing, cooking, piano. Home: 395 S Old Bridge Rd Anaheim CA 92808 Office: Western Med Ctr 1001 N Tustin Ave Santa Ana CA 92705

MASSELL, THEODORE BENEDICT, retired vascular surgeon, consultant; b. Boston, May 26, 1907; s. James Hirsch and Regina Goldie (Chaloff) M.; m. Helen C. Weinberg, Dec. 5, 1930 (dec. 1971); m. Margaret A. Hansen, Mar. 17, 1973; 1 child, Diane Massell Edmisten. AB, Harvard U., 1926, MD, 1931, AM, 1934. Practice medicine specializing in surgery Worcester, Mass., 1937-41; chief vascular surgery Birmingham VA Hosp., Van Nuys, Calif., 1946-49; practice medicine specializing in vascular surgery Los Angeles, 1950-86; cons. Calif. Dept. Health, 1973-78; chief vascular surgery Cedars-Sinai Med. Ctr., 1955-71; asst. prof. surgery Coll. Med. Evangelists, 1947-57; ind. med. examiner Workmen's Appeal Bd., 1975—; med. cons. Calif. Dept. Rehab., 1978—. Assoc. editor Angiology, 1967-70; contbr. articles to med. jours. Served to maj. AUS, 1942-46. Mem. Internat. Cardiovascualr Soc., Am. Coll. Angiology (past pres.), Internat. Coll. Angiology (past v.p.), Phi Beta Kappa, Alpha Omega Alpha. Club: Beach. Home: 2175 S Beverly Glen Los Angeles CA 90025

MASSETTI, CECILIA ANN, curriculum director, school psychologist, administrator, consultant; b. Madera, Calif., May 24, 1954; d. Fred Carroll and Evelyn Marie (Bergon) Massetti. B.S., St. Mary's Coll., 1976, M.A., 1977; M.A. in Ednl. Adminstrn., U. San Francisco, 1981. Psychologist, counselor Woodland (Calif.) Joint Unified Sch. Dist., 1978; intern psychologist Sacramento Med. Ctr., 1978-79; sch. psychologist Madera County Dept. Edn., 1979—, cons., coordinator, 1982—, dir. curriculum and pupil personnel services, 1986—; trainer human devel. tng. inst. programs; chmn. Madera County spelling championships, Madera County acad. decathlon; v.p. and exec. bd. Madera unit Am. Cancer Soc., also bd. dirs.; mem. St. Joachim's Parish Council, 1982-86. Mem. Calif. Assn. Sch. Psychologists, Assn. Calif. Sch. Adminstrs., Madera Hist. Soc., Assn. Supervision and Curriculum Devel., AAUW (pres. local chpt. 1985-86), St. Mary's Coll. Alumni Assn. (pres. Fresno chpt. 1985-87). Republican. Roman Catholic. Lodge: soroptimists. Home: 8256 Road 26 Madera CA 93637 Office: Madera County Dept Education 28123 Ave 14 Madera CA 93638

MASSEY, JERRY LEROY, data processing executive; b. Salina, Kans., Feb. 2, 1940; s. Chester C. and Geraldine L. (Tapanna) m. Barbara L. Nold, Feb. 25, 1960 (div. June 1966); children: James, Bruce, Patti; m. Camille Jezewski, Sept. 16, 1982. BEE, U. Tex., El Paso, 1964. Instr. ITT Corp., Europe and Asia, 1966-68; data processor Bendix, Goldstone, Calif., 1968-73; customer engr. Digital Equipment, Santa Clara, Calif., 1973-80; pres. SMCOE, Redwood City, Calif., 1980—. Inventor of Massey Method, 1982. Democrat. Methodist. Home: 2670 Derby Dr San Ramon CA 94583 Office: San Mateo County Office Edn 333 Main St Redwood City CA 94063

MASSEY, KALA DENISE, banker; b. Seminole, Tex., Oct. 14, 1953; d. Billy Clifton and Barbara June (Wallace) Ward; m. Gregory Lee Massey, June 11, 1977. Student N.Mex. Jr. Coll., 1972-73. Asst. mgr. Comml. Credit, Hobbs, N.Mex., 1973-80; asst. v.p. First Interstate Bank, 1980—. Bd. dirs., chpt. chmn. March of Dimes, 1983—. Baptist. Home: 1101 N Llano Hobbs NM 88240 Office: First Interstate Bank PO Box 5210 Hobbs NM 88240

MASSIER, PAUL FERDINAND, mechanical engineer; b. Pocatello, Idaho, July 22, 1923; s. John and Kathryn (Arki) M.; m. Miriam Parks, May 1, 1948 (dec. Aug. 1975); children: Marilyn Massier Schwegler, Paulette Massier Holden; m. Dorothy Hedlund, Sept. 12, 1978. Cert. engring., U. Idaho, 1943; BSME, U. Colo., 1948; MSME, MIT, 1949. Engr. Pan-Am. Refining Corp., Texas City, Tex., 1948; design engr. Maytag Co., Newton, Iowa, 1949-50; research engr. Boeing Co., Seattle, 1951-55; sr. research engr. and supr. dep. sect. mgr. Jet Propulsion Lab. Calif. Inst. Tech., Pasadena, 1955-84, task mgr., 1984—. Contbr. article to profl. jours. Mem. Arcadia High Sch. Music Club, 1966-71. Served with U.S. Army, 1943-46. Recipient Apollo Achievement award NASA, 1969, Basic Noise Research award NASA, 1980, Life Mem. Service award Calif. PTA, 1970. Fellow AIAA (assoc., Sustained Service award 1980-81), Am. Biog. Inst. Research Assn., Internat. Biographical Assn.; mem. AAAS, Planetary Soc., Sigma Xi, Tau Beta Pi, Pi Tau Sigma, Sigma Tau. Congregationalist. Avocations: producer of motion picture travelogs, antiques, coins, stamps. Home: 1000 N First Ave Arcadia CA 91006 Office: Jet Propulsion lab 4800 Oak Grove Dr Pasadena CA 91109

MASSY, PATRICIA GRAHAM BIBBS (MRS. RICHARD OUTRAM MASSY), social worker, author; b. Newbury, Eng., Mar. 21, 1918; came to U.S., 1963, naturalized, 1969; d. Oswald Graham and Dorothy (French) Bibbs; m. Richard Outram Massy, July 22, 1944 (div. Aug. 1986); children: Patricia Lynn Massy Holmes, Julie Suzanne, Shaun Adele Massy Brink. BA, U. B.C., 1941, MSW, 1962. With B.C. Welfare Field Service, Vancouver, Kamloops, Abbottsford, 1942-44; social worker Brandon Welfare Dept., Man., Can., 1945; with Children's Aid Soc., Vancouver, 1948-62; supr. Dept. Pub. Social Service, Los Angeles, 1963-70, staff devel. specialist-mgmt., 1970-77; lectr. colls. and seminars Author: A Study Guide for a Course in Miracles, 1984; One, 1985. Mem. AAUW (treas. 1970), Nat. Assn. Social Workers, Alpha Phi. Mem. Religious Sci. Ch. Home: 18936 Upper Cow Creek Rd Azalea OR 97410

MAST, TERRYL JANE, toxicologist; b. Providence, July 21, 1946; d. Jack Lester and Alma (Twist) Rice; m. William Hubbard Mast, June, 1976; children: Karen Irene McCrea, Eric McCrea. BS in Biochemistry, U. Calif., Davis, 1974, MS in Environ. Chemistry, 1979, PhD in Environ. Chemistry, 1983. Lectr. U. Calif., Davis, 1978-83, research assoc., 1984-85; sr. research scientist Battelle Meml. Inst., Richland, Wash., 1986—; instr. Am. AID Program to Egypt, 1982, U. Calif., Univ. Extension, 1983-84. Contbr. articles to profl. jours. Speaker Sacramento Lung Assn., 1985. Mem. Am. Chem. Soc. (program com. agrochem. div. 1985—), Soc. Toxicology, Pacific N.W. Assn. Toxicologists, AAAS. Avocations: hiking, skiing, woodworking. Office: Battelle NW Biology Dept PO Box 99 Richland WA 99352

MASTERS, WALLACE ELLSWORTH, manufacturing executive; b. Cottage Grove, Oreg., June 4, 1937; s. Roy Franklin and Sonia (Hackstead) M.; m. Shirley Ileen Murrey, June 27, 1959; children: Gregory, Nancy. BS in Engring., Oreg. State U., 1959. Indsl. engr. Boeing co., Seattle, 1959-63; prodn. mgr. Tektronix, Inc., Beaverton, Oreg., 1963-78; producibility engring. mgr. Electro Sci. Industries, Portland, Oreg., 1978-80, mfg. mgr., 1980-82, v.p. mfg., 1982—. Republican. Presbyterian. Office: Electro Sci Industries 13900 NW Sience Park Dr Portland OR 97229

MASTERSON, WILLIAM LLOYD, real estate development company executive, management consultant, grain company executive; b. Chgo., Aug. 19, 1949; s. Lawrence and Lorraine Mae (Shaw) M. Student pub. schs., Chgo. Organizer United Farm Workers, various locations, 1968-72; innkeeper Holiday Inns, Skokie, Ill., 1972-74; sec. Ill. Racing Bd., Chgo., 1974-79; gen. mgr. Maywood Park (Ill.) Race Track, 1979-83; pres. N.Am. Grain Co., Chgo.; gen. mgr. Racing Assn. Cen. Iowa; sr. project mgr. The JNC Cos., v.p. devel., 1987; lectr. U. Ariz. Civic leader tour USAF, 1986. Recipient Outstanding Achievement award Chgo. div. Horsemen's Benevolent and Protective Assn., 1976. Mem. Nat. Assn. State Racing Commrs. (hon. life), Amnesty Internat., Harness Tracks of Am. (bd. dirs. 1979-83), Am. Horse Council, Chgo. Symphony Soc., Irish Am. Cultural Inst., Art Inst. Chgo. Democrat. Lutheran. Club: Irish Fellowship (Chgo.). Home: 7604 E Callisto Circle #16 Tucson AZ 85715 Office: 5780 N Swan Rd Tucson AZ 85718

MASTRINI, JANE REED, social worker, consultant; b. Lincoln, Nebr., July 23, 1948; d. William Scott and Ellen (Daly) Cromwell; m. Charles James Mastrini, July 19, 1969. BA, Western State Coll., Gunnison, Colo., 1970; MSW, U. Denver, 1980. Cert. alcoholism counselor. Tchr. Flandreau (S.D.) Indian Sch., 1970; social worker S.D. Dept. Welfare, Pierre, 1970-75; child care worker Sacred Heart Home, Pueblo, Colo., 1975-76; counselor Fisher Peak Alcohol Treatment Ctr., Trinidad, Colo., 1976-77; family therapist West Nebr. Gen. Hosp., Scottsbluff, 1980-81; adolescent coordinator St. Luke's Hosp., Denver, 1981-86; dir. treatment New Beginnings At Denver, Lakewood, Colo., 1986—; cons. Colo. Counseling Consortium, Denver, 1984—; field work supr. U. Denver, 1983—. Lectr., group leader Colo. Teen Inst., Denver, 1984-85. Mem. Nat. Assn. Social Workers (cert.), Mile High Council on Alcoholism, P.E.O. (pres. 1984-87). Democrat. Episcopalian. Avocations: hiking, camping, skiing. Home: 8972 W Cooper Ave Littleton CO 80123 Office: New Beginnings at Denver 1325 Everett Ct Lakewood CO 80215

MASTROLIA, LILYAN SPITZER, educator; b. Blkyn., Mar. 28, 1934; d. Samuel R. and Lena (Rosenbaum) Spitzer; m. Edmund J. Mastrolia, Aug. 28, 1956; children: John Alan, Philip Louis. BS in Chemistry, Bklyn. Coll., 1955; postgrad., U. So. Calif., 1955-56; MEd, Calif. State U., Los Angeles, 1957; postgrad., Calif. State U., Sacramento, 1959-60, 80-81. Tchr. Los Angeles Unified Sch. Dist., 1957-58, Folsom Unified Sch. Dist., 1958-63, San Juan Unified Sch. Dist., Carmichael, Calif., 1967—; sci. chmn. Barrett Intermediate Sch., Carmichael, 1970-84, Mills Jr. High Sch., Rancho Cordova, Calif., 1959-63. Author poetry and book revs.; co-author Physical Science, 1979; contbr. articles to profl. jours. Facilitator reachig out Drug Abuse Prevention, 1984. Grantee NSF, 1960, 83, 84, Am. Cancer Soc. 1984. Mem. Nat. Sci. Tchrs. Assn., Nat. Writers Club, Computer Writers Assn., Nat. League Am. Penwomen (pres. 1985), Calif. Writers Club (pres. 1981-82). Avocation: tennis. Home: 4706 Cameron Ranch Dr Sacramento CA 95841 Office: Barrett Intermediate Sch 4243 Barrett Rd Carmichael CA 95608

MASUMOTO-FULTON, PAT, training and speech professional; b. Lahaina, Hawaii, Nov. 29, 1939; d. George K. and Florence (Fujikawa) Hasegawa; m. Stephen J. Fulton, July 8, 1984. BA, Oberlin Coll., 1961; M in Edn., U. Hawaii, Honolulu, 1975. Marriage and family counselor Intimate Communication Unltd., Honolulu, 1975—; pres. Video Instant Playback Labs., Honolulu, 1980—; also speaker, trainer IUC, VIP Labs., Honolulu, %. Author: (poems) Inside-Out, 1984. Bd. dirs. The Halfway House, Honolulu, 1977-78, Friends of the Ballet, Honolulu, 1984—, Pacific Film Inst., 1984—. Named Vol. of the Yr., Oahu Community Correctional Ctr., 1977. Mem. Nat. Speakers Assn. (Hawaii vis.'s bur.), Hawaii Speakers Assn. (pres. 1985). Avocations: filmmaking, writing, painting. Office: Video Instant Playback Labs 3732 Lurline Dr Honolulu HI 96816

MASURSKY, HAROLD, geologist; b. Fort Wayne, Ind., Dec. 23, 1923; s. Louis and Celia (Ochstein) M.; 4 children. B.S. in Geology, Yale U., 1943, M.S., 1951; D.Sc. (hon.), No. Ariz. U., 1981. With U.S. Geol. Survey, 1951—, chief astrogeologic studies br., 1967-71; chief scientist U.S. Geol. Survey (Center Astrogeology), Flagstaff, Ariz., 1971-75; sr. scientist U.S. Geol. Survey (Center Astrogeology), 1975—; lunar orbiter Surveyor Missions, 1965-67; team leader, prin. investigator TV experiment (Mariner Mars), 1971; co-investigator Apollo field geol. team Apollo 16 and 17, also mem. Apollo orbital sci. photog. team, Apollo site selection group; leader Viking Mars Missions Site Selection and cert. team, 1975; mem. imaging teams Voyager (Jupiter, Saturn, Uranus, Neptune), 1977; chmn. mission ops. group Venus Pioneer Mission 1978, co-chmn. mission operational group Galileo Mission, 1981, mission ops. leader, radar team Magellan mission Magellan Mission, 1981—; mem. camera team Mars observer, 1986; mem. Space Sci. Adv. Com., 1978-81, solar system exploration com., 1980-86; mem. Space Sci. Bd., 1982-85; pres. intedisc com. B, COSPAR; sec. Coordinating Com. of Moon and Planets. Assoc. editor: Icarus, Geophys. Rev. Letters, Geodynamics. Served with AUS, 1943-46. Fellow Geol. Soc. Am. (assoc. editor bull., pres. planetary geol. div.), AAAS, Am. Geophys. Union (pres. nomenclature workgroup), Internat. Astron. Union (exec. com. compar planet interan. Union Geol. Sci.), Am. Astron. Assn. Address: US Geol Survey 2255 N Gemini St Flagstaff AZ 86001

MATA, SARA ISABEL, industrial engineer, real estate broker, insurance agent; b. Ocotal, Nicaragua, May 1, 1951; came to U.S., 1978; d. Ricardo Andres and Emilia M. (Barrios) Lopez; m. Gilberto Suarez, Aug. 28, 1971 (div. Sept. 1978); 1 child, Ricardo; m. David Mata, Dec. 2, 1982. BSChemE, BS in Indsl. Engring., U. Cen. Am., Managua, Nicaragua, 1975; MBA in Fin., U. San Francisco, 1984. Prodn. mgr. Jaboneria Prigo, Granada, Nicaragua, 1977-78; tech. cons. Cen. Bank Nicaragua, Managua, 1978; project engr. Bechtel Corp., San Francisco, 1980-82; indsl. engr. Shaklee Corp., San Francisco, 1979-80, Def. Logistic Agy., San Bruno, Calif., 1984—. Mem. Am. Inst. Indsl. Engrs. Roman Catholic. Lodge: Soroptomists. Avocation: camping. Home: 819 Masson Ave San Bruno CA 94066 Office: Def Logistic Agy 1250 Bayhill Dr San Bruno CA 94066

MATAN, LILLIAN KATHLEEN, designer, home economics educator; b. Boston, Aug. 18, 1937; d. George Frances and Lillian May (Herbert) Archambault; m. M. Joseph Anthony Matan, Aug. 6, 1960; children—Maria, Meg, Tony, Liz, Joan. B.S. in Home Econs., Seton Hill Coll., postgrad. Tex. A&I, 1971, U. Tex., 1972, Towson State U., 1973; Rudolph Schaeffer Sch. Design, 1977-80; M.A. in Home Econs., San Francisco State U., 1985. Cert. tchr., Md. Tchr. home econs. Surrattsville High Sch., Md., 1960-61; edn. cons. Head Start, Frederick, Md., 1971-72; head home econ. dept. Brunswick High Sch., Md., 1972-73, tchr. adult edn., 1973-74; designer Dudley Kelly & Assocs., San Francisco, 1977-82; designer, prin. Kay Matan Antiques & Interiors, Ross, Calif., 1983—. Bd. dirs. Cath. Social Services, Marin County, Calif., 1984—, Parnow Friendship House, Marin County, 1984—, Cath. Charities, Archdiocese San Francisco, 1987—, McGucken House, 1987—; del. Joint Community County Wide Plan, Marin County, 1984—; active in Marin Ecumenical Assn. Housing, 1981-83, Ross Valley Ecumenical Housing, Marin County, 1981-83. Mem. Women in Design, Home Economists Bus., Am. Assn. Home Economists, Am. Assn. Housing Educators, Calif. Assn. Home Economists, Environ. Forum of Marin, Marin Conservation League.

MATAS, MYRA DOROTHEA, interior designer, consultant; b. San Francisco, Mar. 21, 1938; d. Arthur Joseph and Marjorie Dorothy (Johnson) Anderson; m. Michael Richard Matas Jr., Mar. 15, 1958; children—Michael Richard III, Kenneth Scott. Cert. interior design, Canada Coll.; cert. interior design, Calif. Owner, operator Miquel's Antiques Co., Millbrae, Calif., 1969-70, Miguel's Antiques & Interiors Co., Burlingame, Calif., 1970-79, Country Elegance Antiques & Interiors Co., Menlo Park, Calif., 1979-84, La France Boutique Co., 1979-84, Myra D. Matas Interior Design, San Francisco, 1984—; mgr. La France Imports, Inc., 1982—; instr. interior design dept. Canada Coll. Mem. Nat. Home Fashion League, Am. Soc. Interior Designers (asso.), Menlo Park C. of C. Contbr. articles in field to profl. jours. Office: 200 Kansas St San Francisco CA 94103 Office: 1209 Bellevue Ave #S Burlingame CA 94010

MATAYOSHI, HERBERT TATSUO, corporate executive, former mayor; b. Hilo, Hawaii, Nov. 21, 1928; s. Zenko and Midori (Shiraishi) M.; m. Mary Yuriko, Feb. 9, 1951; children—Jerold, Ronald, Eric, Kathryn. B.S., U. Mich., 1950; postgrad. Temple U.; M.B.A., U. Hawaii, 1980. Mem. Hawaii County Bd. Suprs., 1962-68, Hawaii County Council, 1968-74, chmn., 1970-72; mayor County of Hawaii, Hilo, 1974-84; pres. Matayoshi, Inc., 1985—; v.p., treas. Camp Cable TV; mgr. Francis I. duPont & Co., Hilo; owner-mgr. Hilo Investors Service. Chmn. Am. del., mem. exec. com. Japan-Am. Conf. Mayors and C. of C. Presidents; chmn. County Hosp. System Com.; vice chmn. state adv. bd. Comprehensive Health Program; chmn. Hawaii Econ. Devel. Dist. Com.; gov.'s steering com. Hawaii State Conf. on Employment; vice chmn. supervisory bd. Hawaii Law Enforcement and Juvenile Delinquency Planning Agy.; chmn. CETA Consortium of Hawaii; dir. Natural Energy Lab. of Hawaii; mem. Japanese C. of C. and Industry of Hawaii; past pres. Hui Okinawa. Democrat. Congregationalist. Clubs: Y Men's, East Hawaii Kiwanis (past pres.), U. Hawaii at Hilo Athletic Booster, Hilo Rotary (hon.). Office: 25 Aupuni St Hilo HI 96720

MATHAI, CHIRATHALAKAL VARUGHESE, environmental scientist; b. Tiruvalla, Kerala, India, Mar. 21, 1945; came to U.S., 1969, naturalized, 1986; s. C. Varughese and Mary (Mathai) C.; m. Susy I. Kurien, Aug. 28, 1972; children—Suma-Mary, Sabu-George. B.Sc., Kerala U., 1965; M.Sc., M.S. U., Baroda, India, 1968; M.S., U. Minn., 1973; Ph.D., U. Okla., 1976. Lectr., Calicut U., Kerala, 1968-69; research assoc. U. Calgary, Can., 1977-80; sr. scientist AeroVironment, Inc., Pasadena, 1980-84, cons., 1984—; sr. environ. cons. Ariz. Pub. Service Co., Phoenix, 1984—; speaker in field. Contbr. articles to profl. jours. Inventor control device for airborne particles. Bd. dirs. Minn. Internat. Ctr. for Students and Visitors, 1971-72. AEC merit scholar, Bombay, India, 1968. Mem. Air Pollution Control Assn., Am. Assn. for Aerosol Research, Am. Phys. Soc. Eastern Orthodox. Home: 2717 W Gila Ln Chandler AZ 85224 Office: Ariz Pub Service Co 2216 W Peoria Phoenix AZ 85029

MATHENY, RAYMOND THOMAS, archeologist; b. Los Angeles, Feb. 15, 1925; s. Raymond Thomas and Edna Margarite (Ryan) M.; m. Deanne Louise Gurr, Oct. 18, 1979. B.A., Brigham Young U., 1960, M.A., 1962; Ph.D., U. Oreg., 1968. Field researcher Campeche, El Aguacatal, Xcalumkin, Dzibilnocac, Santa Rosa Xtampak, 1961-74, Chiapas, Mexico, Upper Grijalva Basin, 1976-78, El Mirador, Guatemala, 1979-83; asst. prof. Brigham Young U., Provo, Utah, 1964, prof. anthropology and archeology, 1978—; archeol. adv. Bur. Land Mgmt., Nat. Parks, 1967-77; mem. antiquities com. Utah Gov.'s Hist. and Cultural Sites Com., 1971—. Served with USAAF, 1942-45; Served with USAF, 1951-57. Decorated Air medal; Nat. Sci. and Nat. Geog. Soc. research grantee, 1974-83. Fellow Explorers Club, Soc. Am. Archeology (steering com. public archeology 1971-78), Am. Anthrop. Assn., Current Anthropology; mem. Sociedad de Antropologia Mexicana, Sigma Xi. Mem. Ch. Jesus Christ of Latter-day Saints. Home: 1746 N 760 W Orem UT 84057 Office: Brigham Young U Dept Anthropology Provo UT 84602

MATHENY, RICHARD EDWIN, educational administrator, consultant; b. Spokane, Wash., June 22, 1940; s. Fredrick Elwin and Ethel Christine (Hanson) M.; m. Phyllis Ann Cheever, June 10, 1961; children—Richelle Ann, Dwight, Richard. B.A., Wash. State U., 1962; M.P.A., U. So. Calif.-Los Angeles, 1973; postgrad. Harvard U., summer 1982; Ed.D., Gonzaga U., 1985. Sr. real estate agt. County of Orange, Santa Ana, Calif., 1962-73; exec. v.p. Internat. Right of Way Assn., Los Angeles, 1973-77, Whitworth Found., Spokane, Wash., 1977-81, v.p., 1981-84; now assoc. vice chancellor U. Calif.-Irvine; ednl. cons. Lilly Endowment, Indpls., Northwest Area Found., St. Paul, Z. Smith Reynolds Found., N.C., 1980—. Author: Creating Charitable Trusts with Real Estate, 1982; contbr. articles on mgmt. to profl. jours. Bd. dirs. Presbyn. Ministries Inc., Seattle; bd. govs. Holy Family Hosp., Spokane. Recipient Journalism award Am. Soc. Assn. Execs., 1977. Mem. Council Advancement and Support of Edn. Office: U Calif-Irvine Office Assoc Vice Chancellor Irvine CA 92717

MATHER, PORTIA ANN, episcopal priest; b. Port Townsend, Wash., June 10, 1949; d. Howard Lester and Portia Davis (Bentley) M. BA, U. Oreg., 1972; postgrad., Ripon Coll. Cuddesdon, Oxford, Eng., 1982-83; MDiv., Ch. Div. Sch. of Pacific, 1984. Ordained to ministry Episcopal Ch. as deacon, 1984, as priest, 1985. Dir. religious edn. St. Thomas Episcopal Ch., Eugene, Oreg., 1975-78; adminstrv. sec. Campus Interfaith Ministry U. Oreg., Eugene, 1978-79; sec. Christian edn. Diocese of Oreg., Portland, 1979-80; curate All Saints Episcopal Ch., Palo Alto, Calif., 1984—; convenor Santa Clara Deanery Christian Educators Diocese of El Camino Real, Calif., 1985-86. Mem. Episcopal Women's Caucus. Avocations: cooking, fishing, travelling, needlepoint, reading. Office: All Saints Episcopal Ch 555 Waverley St Palo Alto CA 94301

MATHES, STEPHEN JOHN, plastic and reconstructive surgeon, educator; b. New Orleans, Aug. 17, 1943; s. John Ernest and Norma (Deutsch) M.; m. Jennifer Tandy Woodbridge, Nov. 26, 1966; children: David, Brian, Edward. BS, La. State U., 1964; MD, La. State U., New Orleans, 1968. Diplomate Am. Bd. Surgery, Am. Bd. Plastic Surgery. Asst. prof. surgery Wash. U., St. Louis, 1977-78; assoc. prof. U. Calif., San Francisco, 1978-84, prof., 1984, prof. surgery, anatomy and cell biology, 1984-85, also bd. dirs. craniofacial anomalies; head plastic surgery sect. U. Mich., Ann Arbor, 1984-85, prof. surgery, 1984-85, head plastic and reconstructive surgery div., 1985—. Author: (textbook) Clinical Applications for Muscle and Musculocutaneous Flaps, 1983 (Best Med. Book award Physician's category, Am. Med. Writer's Assn., 1983); contbr. articles to profl. jours. Recipient 1st prize plastic surgery scholarship contest, Plastic Surgery Edn. Found., 1981, 83, 84, 86; grantee NIH, 1982-85, 86—. Fellow ACS; mem. Am. Assn. Plastic Surgery, Plastic Surgery Research Council (pres.-elect 1986), Am. Soc. Surgery of Hand, Soc. Univ. Surgeons. Republican. Episcopalian. Avocations: gardening, tennis. Home: 30 Trophy Ct Hillsborough CA Office: U Calif Div Plastic Surgery U-147 San Francisco CA 94143

MATHESON, STUART NEIL, bearing engineer; b. Los Angeles, Dec. 31, 1934; s. Roy Douglas and Nellie Beatrice (Kidston) M.; m. Ruth Maryln Kurkowske, July 21, 1956; children: Karen, Marilyn, James, Linda, Paul. BS, UCLA, 1959. Chief engr. Bearing Inspection Inc., Santa Fe Springs, Calif., 1959—, v.p., 1984—; expert witness for various cts., 1972—. Inventor bearing analyzer. Served with U.S. Army, 1954-59. Mem. Am. Soc. Lubrication Engrs. Republican. Baptist. Avocation: flying. Home: 7151 Walker St La Palma CA 90623 Office: Bearing Inspection Inc 10041 Shoemaker Ave Santa Fe Springs CA 90670

MATHEWS, CHARLES ANDERSON, electronics company executive; b. Cardiff, Wales, Feb. 23, 1938; came to U.S., 1969, naturalized 1984; s. Mervyn Charles and Bertha Annie (Farrow) M.; m. Stephanie Rose, Aug. 30, 1980; children: Charles, Clare, Vicki. BS, Imperial Coll. Sci., London, 1960. Project dir. ITT, London, 1965-69; asst. controller ITT Gilfillan, Van Nuys, Calif., 1969-71; dir. ops. ITT Cannon Electric, Santa Ana, Calif., 1971-73; dir. tech. services Plessey Co., Ltd., London, 1973-76; v.p. Plessey, Inc., Plessey Trading Corp., Plessey Materials; pres. Plessey Peripheral Systems Inc., 1976-84; pres., chief operating officer, bd. dirs. Cipher Data Products, Inc., San Diego, 1984-85, Sci. Micro Systems Inc., Mountain View, Calif., 1985—; bd. dirs. Micro Systems Ltd., Sci. Micro Systems GmbH. Home: 585 Joandra Ct Los Altos CA 94022 Office: Sci Micro Systems Inc 339 N Bernardo Ave PO Box 7777 Mountain View CA 94039

MATHEWS, CHERI RENE, speech pathologist; b. Salmon, Idaho, Sept. 19, 1958; d. Howard Eugene and Ruth Ellen (Billings) Van Komen; m. James William Mathews, Sept. 10, 1983. BS in Speech and Hearing Pathology, Northwest Nazarene Coll.; MS in Speech Pathology, Idaho State U. Speech/lang. pathologist Humboldt County (Nev.) Sch. Dist., Winnemucca, 1982-83; speech/lang. specialist Washoe County (Nev.) Sch. Dist., Reno, 1983—. Sec. Neighborhood Watch Program, Reno, 1984—. Mem. Am. Speech Lang. and Hearing Assn. (cert. clin. competance), Nev. Speech and Hearing Assn., No. Nev. Speech and Hearing Assn. Club: Merry Mainstreamers Square Dance (Reno) (sec. 1984-85). Avocations: stained glass, needlework, reading, gardening. Home: 9375 Pagoda Way Reno NV 89506

MATHEWS, LEE MORRIS, petroleum engineer; b. East Lake, Colo., Dec. 7, 1924; s. Lloyd E. and Eva (Stucka) M.; m. L. Maxine Gorden, Sept. 26, 1948; children—Wayne, Janet, Susan, Mark, Kent, Lynne. Diploma in petroleum engring., Colo. Sch. Mines, 1942-48, diploma in advanced mgmt., Harvard Bus. Sch., 1973. Registered profl engr., Wyo., Can. Dist. engr. Marathon Oil Co., Cody, Wyo., 1950-55, Calgary, Alta., Can., 1955-60, engring. mgr. Findlay, Ohio, 1960-67; resident mgr. Marathon Australia, Brisbane, 1967-70; mgr. internat. ops. Marathon Internat. Oil Co., Findlay, Ohio, 1970-77; dir. applied tech. Marathon Research, Littleton, Ohio, 1977—; counselor Australian Petroleum Assn., Brisbane, 1967-70. Served with USN, 1944-46, PTO. Mem. Soc. Petroleum Engrs., Rocky Mountain Oil and Gas Assn. (bd. dirs. 1980—), Am. Petroleum Inst. Republican. Presbyterian. Club: Denver Petroleum. Home: 1410 E Easter Ave Littleton CO 80122 Office: Marathon Oil Co Box 269 Littleton CO 80160

MATHEWS, LINDA MCVEIGH, journalist; b. Redlands, Calif., Mar. 14, 1946; d. Glenard Ralph and Edith Lorene (Humphrey) McVeigh; m. Thomas Jay Mathews, June 15, 1967; children—Joseph, Peter, Katherine. B.A., Radcliffe Coll., 1967; J.D., Harvard U., 1972. Gen. assignment reporter Los Angeles Times, 1967-69, Supreme Ct. corr., 1972-76, corr., Hong Kong, 1977-79, China corr., Peking, 1979-80, op-ed page editor, 1980-81, dep. nat. editor, 1981-84, dep. fgn. editor, 1985—; corr. Wall St. Jour., Hong Kong, 1976-77; lectr.; freelance writer; books include: (with others) Journey Into China, 1982; One Billion: A China Chronicle, 1983. Mem. Women's Legal Def. Fund, 1972-76; co-founder, pres. Hong Kong Montessori Sch., 1977-79; docent Pasadena Heritage, 1982—. Mem. Fgn. Corrs. Club Hong Kong, Am. Soc. Newspaper Editors. Office: Los Angeles Times Times Mirror Sq Los Angeles CA 90053

MATHEWSON, KAY LOUISE, adoption consultant; b. Madison, Wis., Apr. 9, 1942; d. Keith Q. and Gladys L. (Kollmeyer) Kellicutt; m. Rodney Mathewson, Sept. 6, 1969 (div. Mar. 1976); children: Christopher, Daniel, Linda Kay. BS, U. Wis., 1965. Cert. Am. child protection. Day care cons. State of Wyo. div. pub. assistance social service, Cheyenne, 1969-73, day care dir., 1974-75, social service cons., 1979-85, adoption cons., 1985—; cons. Model Cities Program Day Care, Cheyenne, 1973. Charter chmn. Nutrition and Child Devel., Casper, Wyo., 1977; bd. dirs. Head Start, Casper, 1979, Rocky Mountain Planned Parenthood, Denver, 1984-85. Mem. Wyo. Human Resources Confederation. Democrat. Avocations: sewing, reading. Home: 7236 Bomar Dr Cheyenne WY 82001 Office: SD-PASS Hathaway Bldg 345 Cheyenne WY 82001

MATHIAS, BETTY JANE, communications and community affairs consultant, writer, editor, lecturer; b. East Ely, Nev., Oct. 22, 1923; d. Royal F. and Dollie B. (Bowman) M.; student Merritt Bus. Sch., 1941, 42, San Francisco State U., 1941-42; 1 dau., Dona Bett. Asst. publicity dir. Oakland (Calif.) Area War Chest and Community Chest, 1943-46; pub. relations Am. Legion, Oakland, 1946-47; asst. to pub. relations dir. Cen. Bank of Oakland, 1947-49; pub. relations dir. East Bay chpt. of Nat. Safety Council, 1949-51; propr., mgr. Mathias Public Relations Agy., Oakland, 1951-60; gen. assignment reporter and teen news editor Daily Rev., Hayward, Calif., 1960-62; freelance pub. relations and writing, Oakland, 1962-66, 67-69; dir. corp. communications Systech Fin. Corp., Walnut Creek, Calif., 1969-71; v.p. corp. communications Consol. Capital companies, Oakland, 1972-79, v.p. community affairs, Emeryville, Calif., 1981-84, v.p. spl. projects, 1984-85; v.p., dir. Consol. Capital Realty Services, Inc., Oakland, 1973-77; v.p., dir.

Centennial Adv. Corp., Oakland, 1976-77; communications cons., 1979—; cons. Mountain Air Realty, Shingle Springs, Calif., 1986—; lectr. in field; bd. dirs. Oakland YWCA, 1944-45, ARC, Oakland, So. Alameda County chpt., 1967-69, Family Ctr., Children's Hosp. Med. Ctr. No. Calif., 1982-85, also mem. adv. bd., 1986—, March of Dimes, 1983-85, Equestrian Ctr. of Walnut Creek, Calif., 1983-84, also sec.; adult and publs. adv. Internat. Order of the Rainbow for Girls, 1953-78; communications arts adv. com. Ohlone (Calif.) Coll., 1979-85, chmn., 1982-84; mem. adv. bd. dept. mass communications Calif. State U.-Hayward, 1985; pres. San Francisco Bay Area chpt. Nat. Reyes Syndrome Found., 1981-86; vol. staff Columbia Actors' Repertory, Columbia, Calif., 1986—; mem. exec. bd., editor newsletter Tuolumne County Dem. Club, 1987—. Recipient Grand Cross of Color award Internat. Order of Rainbow for Girls, 1955. Order Eastern Star (publicity chmn. Calif. state 1955). Editor East Bay Mag., 1966-67, TIA Traveler, 1969, Concepts, 1979-83. Home: 20575 Gopher Dr Sonora CA 95370

MATHIAS, CORINNE FLORENCE, consultant company executive; b. Buffalo, June 10, 1926; d. Sidney and Florence (Vincent) O'Neill; m. Richard Charles Mathias, Sept. 6, 1947 (dec. Apr. 20, 1972); children—Richard Charles, Micheal William, Corinne Mary, Marc Francis. A.A., Citrus Coll., 1979. Dir. Universal Product Code and Direct Store Set-UP, Vons Grocery Co., El Monte, Calif., 1958-78; pres., owner Direct Delivery Data, Glendora, Calif., 1978—. Author receiving clerk's manual, 1966. Fellow mem. Los Angeles Art Mus., 1984—, Com. Against Govt. Waste, Washington, 1984—, Redlands Community Music Assn., Calif., 1984—. Women in Mgmt. scholar, 1979. Fellow So. Calif. Grocers Assn., Bus. and Profl. Women. Democrat. Roman Catholic. Avocations: bridge; golf; tennis; travel; photography.

MATHUR, ASHOK, telecommunications engineer, educator, researcher; b. Gorakhpur, Uttar Pradesh, India; came to U.S., 1979; s. Raj Swarup and Savitri Mathur; m. Jayanti Srivastava, May 31, 1978; children: Menka, Puja. BS, U. Agra, India, 1963, MS, 1965; PhD, U. Southampton, Hampshire, Eng., 1974. Cert. telecommunications engr., Calif., tchr., Calif. Lectr. upper atmospheric physics Kanpur, India, 1965-68; doctoral researcher U. Southampton, 1968-73; postdoctoral research fellow U. Poitiers, Vienne, France, 1973-74; assoc. prof., research supr U. Kanpur, 1974-79; mem. tech. staff telecommunications sci. and engring. div. Jet Propulsion Lab. Calif. Inst. Tech., Pasadena, 1979—. Contbr. articles to profl. jours.; mem. editorial bd. Acta Ciencia Indica Jour., 1975-78. Recipient 5-Year Service award Jet Propulsion Lab. Calif. Inst. Tech., 1984. Mem. IEEE, AIAA, The European Phys. Soc., Calif. Inst. Tech. Mgmt. Club., Armed Forces Communications and Electronics Assn. Republican. Hindu. Avocations: photography, traveling, reading. Home: 1923-B Huntington Dr Duarte CA 91010 Office: Jet Propulsion Lab Calif Inst Tech 4800 Oak Grove Dr MS 126-322 Pasadena CA 91109

MATIN, ABDUL, microbiology educator, consultant; b. Delhi, India, May 8, 1941; came to U.S., 1964, naturalized, 1983; s. Mohammed and Zohra (Begum) Said; m. Mimi Keyhan, June 21, 1968. BS, U. Karachi, Pakistan, 1960, MS, 1962; PhD, UCLA, 1969. Lectr. St. Joseph's Coll., Karachi, 1962-64; research assoc. UCLA, 1964-71; sci. officer U. Groningen, Kerklaan, The Netherlands, 1971-75; from asst. to assoc. prof. microbiology Stanford U., Calif., 1975—; cons. Engenics, 1982-84, Monsanto, 1984—. Contbr. numerous publs. to sci. jours. Fellow Fulbright Found., 1964, NSF, 1981—, Ctr. for Biotech. Research, 1981-85, EPA, 1981-84. Mem. AAAS, AAUP, Am. Soc. Microbiology, Soc. Gen. Microbiology, Soc. Indsl. Microbiology, Biophys. Soc. Avocations: reading, music, walking. Home: 690 Coronado Ave Stanford CA 94305 Office: Stanford U Med Microbiology Fairchild Sci Bldg Stanford CA 94305

MATIS, HOWARD SCOTT, physics researcher; b. N.Y.C., Sept. 19, 1948; s. Irving and Bea (Lieberman) M.; m. Mary Smith, Jan. 15, 1977; children: Kenneth, Justin. BS, Rensselaer Poly. Inst., 1970; SM, U. Chgo., 1971, PhD, 1976. Research assoc. U. Chgo., Ill., 1976-78; postdoctoral fellow Los Alamos (N.M.) Nat. Lab., 1978-80, mem. staff, 1980-83; staff scientist Lawrence Berkeley Lab., Berkeley, Calif., 1983—. Contbr. various articles to profl. jours. mem. Kaiser Sch. Improvement Program, Oakland, Calif., 1985—. Mem. AAAS, Am. Physical Soc. Home: 6824 Sherwick Dr Berkeley CA 94705 Office: Lawrence Berkeley Lab MS 70A-3307 Berkeley CA 94720

MATKINS, ROBERT EDWIN, SR., financial executive; b. Spencer, Ind., Sept. 28, 1934; s. John Robert Matkins and Wilma Fay (Need) Harmon; m. Fran Kathryn Kilpatrick, Aug. 16, 1963; children: David Dean, Robert Edwin Jr. BS in Physics, Ind. U., 1959. Sr. systems engr. Ford Aerospace and Communications Corp., Billings, Mont., 1969-75, program mgr., 1975-79; project mgr. Ford Aerospace and Communications Corp., Butte, Mont., 1979; asst. facility div. mgr. MERDI, Butte, 1979-80; project control mgr. MSE, Inc., Butte, 1980-83, chief fin. officer, 1983—. Served to sgt. USAF, 1952-56. Mem. IEEE (sr.; sect. chmn. 1975). Democrat. Presbyterian. Avocations: genealogy, personal computers, civil war history. Home: 3120 Quincy St Butte MT 59701 Office: MSE Inc 505 Centennial St Butte MT 59701

MATLACK, GEORGE MILLER, radiochemist; b. Pitts., June 14, 1921; s. Allyn Wolcott and Mildred Narcissa (Miller) M.; m. Meredith Mildred Madsen, Sept. 4, 1943; children—Nancy Christine, Martin, Allyn. A.B., Grinell Coll., 1943; M.S., State U. Iowa, 1947, Ph.D., 1949. Prin. chemist Iowa Geol. Survey, Iowa City, 1943-46; research asst. State U. Iowa, 1946-49; sect. leader, analytical chemistry Los Alamos (N.Mex.) Nat. Lab., 1949-82, assoc. group leader analytical chemistry div., 1983—. Contbr. articles to profl. jours. Pres., Los Alamos Choral Soc., 1961-62, Los Alamos Sinfonietta, 1967-69. Fellow Am. Inst. Chemists, AAAS; mem. Am. Chem. Soc., Am. Nuclear Soc., N.Y. Acad. Scis., Iowa Acad. Scis., Four-Fifths Mus. Soc. Lodges: Masons, Eastern Star. Home: 254 San Juan Dr Los Alamos NM 87544 Office: Los Alamos Nat Lab PO Box 1663 MS-G740 Chemistry Div Los Alamos NM 87545

MATOSIAN, JACKLINE, market research executive, corporate professional; b. Tehran, Iran, Nov. 13, 1939; came to U.S., 1953; d. Haroutiun Vartevar and Armenouhi (Demirian) Minassian; m. Michael S. Matosian, Sept. 5, 1964; 1 child, Ani Lucene. AA, Pasadena (Calif.) City Coll., 1959; BA, UCLA, 1961; MBA, Pepperdine U., 1978. Survey analyst Los Angeles Times, 1964-67; sr. mktg. officer United Calif. Bank, Los Angeles, 1967-73; sr. research coordinator Atlantic Richfield Co., Los Angeles, 1973-75; market research mgr. So. Calif. Rapid Transit Dist., Los Angeles, 1975—. Advisor Armenian Ch. Youth Orgn., 1984—. Recipient MARSY award So. Calif. chpt. Am. Mktg. Assn., 1978. Mem. So. Calif. Research Soc. Democrat. Avocations: calligraphy, needlepoint, reading, crossword puzzles. Home: 1629 Oak Knoll Ave San Marino CA 91108 Office: So Calif Rapid Transit Dist 425 S Main St Los Angeles CA 90013

MATSEN, JEFFREY ROBERT, lawyer; b. Salt Lake City, Nov. 24, 1939; s. John Martin and Bessie (Jackson) M.; B.A. cum laude, Brigham Young U., Provo, Utah, 1964; J.D. with honors, UCLA, 1967; m. Susan Davis, July 27, 1973; children—Gregory David, Melinda Kaye, Brian Robert, Jeffrey Lamont, Kristin Sue, Nicole, Brett Richard. Admitted to Calif. bar, 1968, also U.S. Supreme Ct., U.S. Tax Ct., D.C. Ct. Appeals bars; practice in Los Angeles, 1968, Newport Beach, 1971—; mng. ptnr. firm Jeffrey R. Matsen & Assocs., 1978—; prof. law Western State U. Coll. Law, Fullerton, Calif., 1969—; instr. Golden Gate U. Grad. Taxation Program, 1978—. Served as capt. USMCR, 1968-71. Decorated Navy Commendation medal. Mem. Am. Bar Assn., State Bar Calif. (certified taxation specialist), Order of Coif. Mormon. Author: Business Planning for California Closely-Held Enterprises. Contbr. articles to legal jours. Office: 4000 MacArthur Blvd Suite 600 Newport Beach CA 92660

MATSUDA, FUJIO, research organization executive; b. Honolulu, Oct. 18, 1924; s. Yoshio and Shimo (Iwasaki) M.; m. Amy M. Saiki, June 11, 1949; children: Bailey Koki, Thomas Junji, Sherry Noriko, Joan Yuuko, Ann Mitsuyo, Richard Hideo. B.S. in Civil Engring., Rose Poly. Inst., 1949; D.Sc., Mass. Inst. Tech., 1952; D. Engring. (hon.), Rose Hulman Inst. Tech., 1975. Research engr. Mass. Inst. Tech., 1952-54; research asst. prof. engring. U. Ill., Urbana, 1954-55; asst. prof. engring. U. Hawaii, Honolulu, 1955-57; assoc. prof. U. Hawaii, 1957-62, chmn. dept. civil engring., 1960-63, prof., 1962-65, 74-84, dir. engring. expt. sta., 1962-63, v.p. bus. affairs, 1973-74, pres., 1974-84; exec. dir. Research Corp. U. Hawaii, 1984—; dir. Hawaii Dept. Transp., Honolulu, 1963-73; v.p. Park & Yee, Ltd., Honolulu, 1956-58; pres. SMS & Assos., Inc., 1960-63; pvt. practice as structural engr., 1958-60; dir. C. Brewer & Co., Ltd., Hawaiian Electric Co., Allegis Corp. (formerly UAL, Inc.), First Hawaiian Bank, Pacific Internat. Ctr. for High Tech. Research, Kuakini Health System and Kuakini Geriatric Care, Inc.; adv. bd. Duty Free Shoppers Ltd.; mem. Bd. Water Supply, Honolulu, 1963-73; mem. Airport Ops. Council Internat., 1968-73; pres. Pacific Coast Assn. Port Authorities, 1969; mem. sci. bd. Dept. Army, 1978-80; mem. U.S. Army Civilian Adv. Group, 1978—; bd. dirs. Hawaii Inst. Electronic Research; mem. exec. com. transp. research bd. NRC, 1982-86. Bd. dirs. Aloha United Way, 1976-79; trustee Kuakini Health Systems, 1984-86; trustee Nature Conservancy. Served with AUS, 1943-45. Recipient Honor Alumnus award Rose Poly. Inst., 1971; recipient Disting. Service award Airport Ops. Council Internat., 1973, Disting. Alumnus award U. Hawaii, 1974; named Hawaii Engr. of Yr., 1972. Mem. ASCE, Nat. Acad. Engring., Nat. Soc. Profl. Engrs., Social Sci. Assn., Western Coll. Assn. (exec. com. 1977-84, pres. 1980-82), Japanese-Am. Soc. Honolulu (trustee 1976-84, adv. council 1984—), Beta Gamma Sigma, Sigma Xi, Tau Beta Pi. Office: Research Corp of the UH 1110 University Ave Rm 408 Honolulu HI 96826

MATSUI, ROBERT TAKEO, congressman; b. Sacramento, Sept. 17, 1941; s. Yasuji and Alice (Nagata) M.; m. Doris Kazue Okada, Sept. 17, 1966; 1 child, Brian Robert. A.B. in Polit. Sci, U. Calif.-Berkeley, 1963; J.D., Hastings Coll. Law, U. Calif., San Francisco, 1966. Bar: Calif. 1967. Practiced law Sacramento, 1967-78; mem. Sacramento City Council, 1971-78, vice mayor, 1977; mem. 96th-100th Congresses from 3d Dist. Calif., mem. ways and means com.; chmn. profl. bus. forum Dem. Congl. Campaign Com.; congl. liaison nat. fin. council Dem. Nat. Com.; mem. adv. council on fiscal policy Am. Enterprise Inst. chmn. Profl. Bus. Forum of the Dem. Congl. Co. and Com.; congl. liaison Nat. Fin. Council, Dem. Nat. Com.; mem. Am. Enterprise Inst. Adv. Council on Fiscal Policy. Named Young Man of Yr. Jr. C. of C., 1973; recipient Disting. Service award, 1973. Mem. Sacramento Japanese Am. Citizens League (pres. 1969), Sacramento Met. C. of C. (dir. 1976). Democrat. Clubs: 20-30 (Sacramento) (pres. 1972), Rotary (Sacramento). Office: 2419 Rayburn House Office Bldg Washington DC 20515

MATSUMOTO, HARUYOSHI, acoustic scientist, consultant; b. Matsuyama, Japan, July 27, 1952; came to U.S., 1976; s. Toshio and Hiroko (Sugimoto) M.; m. Gale Yurie Harada, July 12, 1980. BS, Tokai U., 1975; MS, U. Hawaii, 1978, PhD, 1984. Elec. engr. Hawaii Inst. Geophysics, U. Hawaii, Honolulu, 1977-78, research asst., 1982-83, acoustic scientist, 1984—; cons. Oceanit Lab., Hawaii. Contbr. articles to profl. jours. Grantee East-West Ctr., Honolulu, 1978-82. Mem. Acoustical Soc. Am., Oceanog. Soc. Japan, Am. Geophysical Union. Office: U Hawaii Hawaii Inst Geophysics 2525 Correa Rd Honolulu HI 96816

MATSUMOTO, SHIGEMI, soprano, educator; b. Denver; d. Moriichi and Suki Matsumoto; B.A. in Mus. Performance, Calif. State U., Northridge; m. Martin J. Stark, Apr. 27, 1967. Performances with opera companies in Brussels, San Francisco, Phila., Portland, Oreg., Wolf Trap, Va., Kansas City, Mo., Tucson, San Antonio, Toledo/Dayton, Ohio, Augusta, Ga., Little Rock, Lake George, N.Y., also Spring Opera Theatre; with symphonies in Antwerp, Belgium, Lourdes, France, Mexico City, San Francisco, Mpls., Pitts., St. Louis, Houston, Denver, New Orleans, Memphis and Wichita, other cities; numerous internat. recitals including Tokyo, Washington, Chgo., Los Angeles, San Francisco, Houston, Vancouver, B.C., Kansas City, San Antonio, Milw.; lectr. demonstrations, master classes coll. campuses; guest artist, lectr. Can. Fedn. Music Tchrs.; guest soloist 25th Anniversary Celebration Founding UN, 1970. Bd. dirs. So. Calif. Opera Guild, 1986—. Recipient 1st prize Western Regional Met. Opera Auditions, 1967; grand winner San Francisco Nat. Opera Auditions, 1968; award winner Geneva Internat. Music Competitions, 1971; grantee Nat. Opera Inst., Internat. Inst. Edn., Los Angeles Bur. Music; named Japanese Woman of Year in So. Calif., Japanese-Am. Soc., 1969-70. Mem. Am. Guild Mus. Artists. Republican. Presbyterian. Home: 18342 Chatham Ln Northridge CA 91326 Other: 18142 Arminta St Reseda CA 91335

MATSUNAGA, SPARK MASAYUKI, U.S. senator; b. Kauai, Hawaii, Oct. 8, 1916; s. Kingoro and Chiyono (Fukushima) M.; m. Helene Hatsumi Tokunaga, Aug. 6, 1948; children: Karen (Mrs. Hardman), Keene, Diane, Merle, Matthew. Ed.B. with honors, U. Hawaii, 1941; J.D., Harvard U., 1951; LL.D. (hon.), Soochow U., 1973, St. John's U., 1977, Eastern Ill. U., 1978, U. Md., 1979; H.L.D., Lincoln U., 1979. Bar: Hawaii 1952. Vets. counsellor U.S. Dept. Interior, 1945-47; chief priority claimants div. War Assets Adminstrn., 1947-48; asst. pub. pros. City and County of Honolulu, 1952-54; practice of law Honolulu, 1954-62; mem. Hawaii Ho. of Reps., 1954-59, majority leader, 1959; mem. U.S. Ho. Reps. 88th-94th Congresses; mem. Rules, Aging, Steering and Policy coms., dep. majority whip; U.S. senator from Hawaii, 1976—; mem. Fin., Energy and Natural Resources, Vets.' Affairs coms., chief dep. whip.; Mem. Hawaii statehood delegations to Congress, 1950, 54, Pacific War Meml. Commn., 1959-62; adv. com. Honolulu Redevel. Agy., 1953-54. Author: Rulemakers of The House, 1976. Chmn. bd. Kaimuki YMCA; pres. Naturalization Encouragement Assn. Honolulu; Bd. dirs. World Brotherhood. Soc. Crippled Children and Adults, Honolulu Council Social Agys. Served from 2d lt. to capt., inf. AUS, 1941-45; ret. lt. col. JAGC 1969. Decorated Bronze Star with valor clasp, Purple Heart with oak leaf cluster. Mem. Am., Hawaii bar assns., D.A.V., V.F.W., Japan-Am. Soc., U. Hawaii Alumni Assn. Democrat. Episcopalian. Clubs: Lions (Honolulu), 100 (Honolulu). Office: 109 Hart Senate Office Bldg Washington DC 20510 *

MATSUO, FUMISUKE, physician, educator; b. Iida, Japan, Dec. 24, 1942; came to U.S., 1969; s. Riichi and Utako (Sasaki) M.; m. Ruth Ann Smith, May 24, 1975; children: Jocelyn, Bryan. MD, Kyoto (Japan) Prefectural U. Medicine, 1968. Asst. prof. U. Iowa, Iowa City, 1975; asst. prof. U. Utah, Salt Lake City, 1975-79, assoc. prof., 1979—; dir. EEG Lab. Univ. Hosp., Salt Lake City, 1975—. Contbr. articles to profl. jours. Fellow Am. Acad. Neurology, Am. EEG Soc.; mem. AMA, Soc. Neurosci., Am. Epilepsy Soc., Epilepsy Assn. Utah (bd. dirs. 1978-81), Western EEG Soc. (bd. dirs. 1983-86). Home: 615 Matterhorn Dr Summit Park UT 84060 Office: U Utah Med Ctr 50 N Medical Dr Salt Lake City UT 84132

MATSUO, WAYNE, public official; b. Honolulu, Aug. 27, 1943; s. Tatsuro and Harriet Haruko (Eguchi) M.; m. Gail Yukiko Harada, Aug. 17, 1968;children: Lianne Akiko, Stacy Haruko. BA, U. Hawaii, 1967, MA, 1976. Group worker Palama Settlement House, Honolulu, 1965-67; social worker Dept. Social Services and Housing, Honolulu, 1968-71, adminstr., 1971-81; adminstr. U. Hawaii, Honolulu, 1981-83, Office of the Ombudsman, Honolulu, 1983—. Avocations: woodworking, ocean activities. Office: Office of Ombudsman 465 S King St 4th Floor Honolulu HI 96813

MATSUSHITA, TATSUO, chemical executive, research scientist; b. Kearny, N.J., July 29, 1937; s. Riutaro and Shige (Yamaguchi) M.; m. Geraldine Carmen Russomano, June 25, 1967 (div. July 1981); 1 child, Robert Martin; m. Vicki Lynne Williams, Aug. 31, 1984. BA in Chemistry, Cornell U., 1960; PhD in Biochemistry, Rutgers U., 1970. Math. tchr. Kearney (N.J.) High Sch., 1963-64; research assoc. Princeton (N.J.) U., 1969-72; geneticist Argonne (Ill.) Nat. Lab., 1972-82; dir. Syngene Products and Research, Ft. Collins, CO, 1982—; cons. Becton Dickinson Labware Div., Oxnard, Calif., 1980. Published 40 papers and abstracts in DNA replication, cell biology, genetic toxicology, photobiology and antibodies. Pres. Downers Grove (Ill.) Tennis Assn., 1977; mem. governing bd. Ft. Collins Tennis Assn., 1984-86. Served to lt. (j.g.) USN, 1960-63. Mem. Am. Assn. Advancement Sci., Am. Mgmt. Assn. Democrat. Presbyterian. Avocations: tennis, skiing, windsurfing. Home: 2219 Kiowa Ct Fort Collins CO 80525 Office: Syngene Products and Research 225 Commerce Dr Fort Collins CO 80524

MATSUYAMA, WAYNE SUSUMU, optometrist; b. Honolulu, Oct. 23, 1952; s. Toshio and Ellen Kimie (Hashizume) M.; m. Judy Sayeko Morimoto, June 4, 1977. Student Chaminade Coll., Honolulu, 1968-70, U. So. Calif., 1970-72, U. Hawaii, 1972-73; O.D., Ill. Coll. Optometry, 1977. Lic. optometrist, Hawaii, Ill. Mem. corp. Terada, Matsuyama & Matsuyama, O.D., Inc., Honolulu, 1977—. Pub. edn. chmn. Am. Cancer Soc., 1979-80; bd. mgrs. YMCA, 1982—, bd. dirs. 1987—. Mem. Hawaii Optometric Assn. (bd. dirs. 1979—, corr. sec. 1979-81, 1st v.p. 1981-82, pres. 1983-84, conv. com. 1986, Man of Yr. 1981), Am. Optometric Assn. (del. to congress contact lens sect. 1982), Kaimuki Bus. and Profl. Assn. (bd. dirs. 1979-81, 2d v.p. 1982-83, co-chmn. Christmas Parade 1980-82). Lodges: Optimists (charter, external v.p. Honolulu club 1986-87), Lions (pres.). Home: 98-1358 Hoohonua St Pearl City HI 96782 Office: Terada Matsuyama & Matsuyama OD Inc 1109 12th Ave Honolulu HI 96816

MATTESON, FREDERICK HAROLD, engineer, stockbroker; b. Bad Axe, Mich., July 22, 1925; s. Harold M. and E. Mildred (Matson) M. B in Aero. Engring., Ga. Tech. U., 1946; MS in Mech. Engring., Stanford U., 1949, PhD in Indsl. Engring., 1974. Registered profl. mech. engr., Calif. Aero. research scientist Nat. Advisory Com. for Aeronautics, Moffett Field, Calif., 1946-54; aero. engr. USAF, Wiesbaden, Federal Republic of Germany, 1954-56, Hiller Aircraft Co., Menlo Park, Calif., 1957-66; pvt. practice aero. engring. Hollister, Calif., 1974—; chief engr. Weatherly Aviation Co., Inc., Hollister, 1982—; lectr. San Jose (Calif.) State U., 1968-74; bd. dirs. Am. Poly-Therm, Sacramento. Author: American Soaring Handbook, 1971, Analysis of In-flight Disintegration Accidents, 1974. Served to lt. (j.g.) USNR, 1943-56. Recipient Excellence in Design award Design News mag., Boston, 1981. Avocation: bicycling. Home: 1874 Cushman St Hollister CA 95023 Office: Weatherly Aviation Co Inc 2304 San Felipe Rd Hollister CA 95023

MATTEUCCI, DOMINICK VINCENT, real estate developer; b. Trenton, N.J., Oct. 19, 1924; s. Vincent Joseph and Anna Marie (Zoda) M.; B.S., Coll. of William and Mary, 1948; B.S., Mass. Inst. Tech., 1950; m. Emma Irene DeGuia, Mar. 2, 1968; children—Felisa Anna, Vincent Eriberto. Owner, Matteucci Devel. Co., Newport Beach, Calif.; pres. Nat. Investment Brokerage Co., Newport Beach. Served with USAAC, 1943-46. Recipient NASA achievement award, 1974; registered profl. engr., Calif.; lic. gen. bldg. contractor, real estate broker. Home: 2104 Felipe Newport Beach CA 92660 Office: PO Box 8328 Newport Beach CA 92660

MATTHES, JOHN JAY, broadcasting executive; b. Mpls., July 6, 1952; s. John Francis and Barbara (Sime) M. BS, U. So. Calif., 1974, MBA, 1980. Jr. research assoc. NBC, Burbank, Calif., 1974-75; research assoc. NBC, Burbank, 1975-76, sr. analyst, 1976-77, adminstr. program research, 1977-78, mgr. concept research, 1978-79, dir. program research, 1979—; guest lectr. to univs. and orgns.; mem. panel Blue Ribbon Emmy Award, 1976, 77, 84, 85. Mem. Am. Mktg. Assn. (Outstanding Service award 1978), Am. Mgmt. Assn., Acad. TV Arts and Scis., Am. Film Inst. Roman Catholic. Avocations: archery, photography, skiing. Home: 2028 Sanborn Hollywood CA 90027 Office: NBC 3000 W Alameda Ave Burbank CA 91523

MATTHES, STEVEN ALLEN, analytical chemist; b. Charlottesville, Va., Oct. 5, 1950; s. Albert Jacob and Mary Louise (Dyer) M.; m. Margaret Ann Latshaw, Oct. 31, 1975; children: Ethan, Megan, Leah, Adam. BS in Chemistry, Oreg. State U., 1977. Grad. teaching asst. Oreg. State U., Corvallis, 1974-77, asst. dir. bands, 1974—; pvt. music tchr. Corvallis, 1974—; research chemist Bur. Mines, Alabany, Oreg., 1977—. Dir. Corvallis Community Band, 1980—; prin. clarinetist Oreg. State U. Symphony Orch., 1976—; clarinetist Dr. Jon's Jazz Band, Jefferson, Oreg., 1983—. Mem. Am. Chem. Soc., Soc. for Applied Spectroscopy, Am. Fedn. Musicians, Oreg. Music Tchrs. Assn. Republican. Presbyterian. Avocations: classical and jazz musician. Office: US Dept Interior 1450 Queen Ave SW Albany OR 97321

MATTHEW, LYN, art marketing consultant and educator; b. Long Beach, Calif., Dec. 15, 1936; d. Harold G. and Beatrice (Hunt) M.; m. Wayne Thomas Castleberry, Aug. 12, 1961 (div. Jan. 1976); children—Melanie, Cheryl, Nicole, Matthew. B.S., U. Calif.-Davis, 1958; M.A., Ariz. State U., 1979. Pres., Davlyn Cons. Found., Scottsdale, Ariz., 1979-82; cons. The Art Business, Scottsdale, 1982—; vis. prof. Maricopa Community Coll., Phoenix, 1979—, Ariz. State U., Tempe, 1980-83; cons. Women's Caucus for Art, Phoenix, 1983—, The Art Bus., Scottsdale. Bd. dirs. Rossom Ho.- Heritage Square Found., Phoenix, 1987—. Author: The Business Aspects of Art, Book I, 1979, Book II, 1979; Marketing Strategies for the Creative Artist, 1985. Mem. Women Image Now (Achievement and Contbn. in Visual Arts award 1983), Women in Higher Edn., Nat. Women's Caucus for Art (v.p. 1981-83), Ariz. Women's Caucus for Art (pres. 1980-82, hon. advisor 1986-87), Vocat. Edn. Assn. (sec. 1978-80), Ariz. Visionary Artists (treas. 1987).

MATTHEWS, DARYL BRUCE, psychiatrist; b. Cleve., Sept. 26, 1947; s. David Earle and Esther Ann (Seifter) M.; m. Esther Solomon, Dec. 24, 1979; children: Max, Jacob. BA in Human Biology, Johns Hopkins U., 1969, MD, 1973, PhD in Sociology, 1977. Diplomate Am. Bd. Psychiatry and Neurology, Am. Bd. Forensic Psychiatry. Asst. prof. psychiatry Boston U., 1976-81; assoc. prof. U. Va., Charlottesville, 1981-82; assoc. clin. prof. U. Hawaii, Honolulu, 1982—. Author: Disposable Patients, 1981; contbr. articles to profl. jours. Jewish. Office: U Hawaii 4370 Kukui Grove St Suite 209 Lihue, Kauai HI 96766

MATTHEWS, HARRY ROY, biochemistry educator; b. Faversham, Kent, Eng., May 25, 1942; came to U.S., 1980; s. Elton Roy and Mavis (Sheppard) M.; m. Margaret Jean Wynne, Sept. 15, 1965 (div. May 1979); m. Iris Mary, May 16, 1979. BS, Kings Coll. U. London, 1963; postgrad., U. Hong Kong, 1963-64; PhD, Kings Coll. U. London, 1968. From lectr. to sr. lectr. Portsmouth (Eng.) Poly. U., 1967-80; guest investigator Rockefeller U., N.Y.C., 1975-79; assoc. prof. U. Calif., Davis, 1979-85, prof., 1985—. Author: Fractionation of Nucleic Acids and Oligonucleotides, 1975, DNA Chromatin and Chromosomes, 1981; contbr. articles to profl. jours. Sci. Research Council grantee, 1973-80, NIH grantee, 1983—, Am. Cancer Soc. grantee, 1984—. Mem. Am. Soc. Biol. Chemists. Home: 619 Filmore St Davis CA 95616 Office: U Calif Dept Biological Chemistry Davis CA 95616

MATTHEWS, JACK EDWARD, real estate executive; b. El Paso, Oct. 29, 1928; s. Jack C. and Helen (Guidry) M.; A.A., Los Angeles City Coll., 1951, U. So. Calif., 1953; m. Willa Blaine Davis, May 29, 1948; children—Jon E., Vikki. Gen. sales mgr. Volk-McLain Co., San Diego, 1956-60; co-owner Brent-Matthews & Co., San Diego, 1960-62; v.p. Am. Savs. & Loan, No. Calif., 1962-67; sr. v.p. 1st Western Savs. & Loan, Las Vegas, Nev., 1967-69; pres. Jack Matthews & Co., Realtors, Las Vegas, 1969-80, Merrill Lynch Realty/Jack Matthews, 1981-84; prin. Jack Matthews Co., Las Vegas, 1984—; chmn. bd. Continental Nat. Bank, Las Vegas, 1983—. Pres. Lions Club, 1975-76, named Lion of Year, 1976; state baseball chmn. Am. Legion. Served with USNR, 1946-48; PTO. Mem. Nat. Homebuilders Assn. (Sales Mgr. of Year 1959), Realtors Inst. (cert. residential specialist, designation), Nat. Assn. Realtors (cert. residential broker, bd. dirs. 1978-85, nat. regional v.p. 1985, Realtor of Yr. 1984, State Realtor or Yr. 1985), Nev. Assn. Realtors (pres. 1982), Las Vegas Bd. Realtors (pres. 1976), Reno Bd. Realtors, Bay Area Sales Mgrs. Club (charter), Las Vegas Execs. Club. Democrat. Club: Las Vegas Country. Office: 3100 S Valley View St Las Vegas NV 89102

MATTHEWS, JOHN LOUIS, air national guard officer, educator; b. Copperton, Utah, June 27, 1932; m. Darlene Davis, 1956; 3 children. B.S. in Geology, Brigham Young U., 1955, M.Ed. in Ednl. Adminstrn., 1967; Air War Coll. Grad., 1976. Commd. 2d lt. U.S. Air Force, 1954; advanced through grades to instr. pilot, Laredo, Tex., 1955-58; mem. Utah Air N.G., 1959—, Colo. Air N.G., 1961-62, commdr. 151st Air Refueling Group, asst. adj. gen. for Air, 1981-82, Chief of Staff, 1982, adj. gen. State of Utah, 1982—; instr. pilot United Airlines, Denver, 1962—; tchr. math. sci. Dixon Jr. High Sch., Provo, Utah, 1962-67, prin., 1967-73; prin. Timpview High Sch., Provo, 1976-79. Decorated Air Force Commendation medal, State of Utah Medal of Merit, Vietnam Service medal, Nat. Def. Service medal, others. Mem. N.G. Assn. Utah, N.G. Assn. of U.S., Adjs. Gen. Assn. of U.S., Air Force Assn., Assn. U.S. Army. Lodge: Rotary.

MATTHEWS, KEITH BOYD, labor relations executive; b. Salt Lake City, Jan. 14, 1930; s. Clarence E. and Connie (Thompson) M.; B.S. in Polit. Sci., Brigham Young U., 1953; cert. indsl. relations U. Utah, 1964; m. Shirley Louise Ferguson, Feb. 12, 1953; children—Adrienne Lee, Lindsey Dee, Keith Kyle. Supr. indsl. relations Utah copper div. Kennecott Copper Corp., Salt

Lake City, 1957-67; mgr. indsl. relations Utah Internat., Inc., San Francisco, 1967—. Served to capt. USN, 1948-49, 53-56. Mem. Am. Soc. Personnel Adminstrn., Indsl. Relations Research Assn., Naval Res. Assn. Club: Commonwealth (San Francisco). Home: 2635 Via Verde Walnut Creek CA 94598 Office: Utah Internat Inc 550 California St San Francisco CA 94104

MATTHEWS, LEONARD LOUIS, academic principal; b. New Orleans, Dec. 4, 1930; s. Alex and Angie (Bell) M.; m. Dolores B. Madere, Dec. 29, 1952; 1 child, Mallory Louis. BS, BS in Bus. and Edn., So. U., Baton Rouge, 1959; postgrad., Calif. State U., Los Angeles, 1964-65, UCLA, 1970-72, Pepperdine U., 1973-74; MEd, Calif. State U., Dominquez Hill, 1974. Cert. pupil personnel services adult edn., elem., secondary. Elem. prin. St. John Sch. Dist., Reserve, La., 1952-59; drama specialist, master tchr. Los Angeles Unified Sch. Dist., 1959-70, counselor, 1970-74; secondary prin. Inglewood (Calif.) Unified Sch. Dist., 1974—. Author: Black Students Self Image, 1974, (manuals) New Math Concepts, 1962, Guide for Playacting and Story Telling, 1968. Organizer Citizens Against Prostitution, Inglewood, 1982-84, Citizens Against Crime and Drugs, Inglewood, 1984-86, Dr. Martin L. King Jr. Meml., Inglewood, 1983-86; pres. St. Eugene's Ch., Inglewood, 1984-86. Served with U.S. Army, 1976-78. Recipient Service award Assn. Calif. Adminstrs., 1982, Recognition award Project INVEST, 1978. Mem. Inglewood Mgmt. Assn. (v.p. 1986, plaque 1985), Calif. Continuation Edn. Assn., YMCA (membership chmn. 1981-85, cert. 1981-86), PTA (6th v.p. 1985-86, plaque 1985), Alpha Phi Alpha (sec. 1963-64, plaque 1964). Democrat. Roman Catholic. Club: 5th Ave Block (Inglewood). Home: 9626 5th Ave Inglewood CA 90305 Office: Hillcrest High Sch 441 W Hillcrest Blvd Inglewood CA 90301

MATTHEWS, LISE, architect, product designer; b. New Orleans, Oct. 26, 1948; d. Edward De Saunhac and Martha Lise (McDonough) M.; m. James J. McNamara, Apr. 10, 1972 (div. Oct. 1982); 1 child, James J. III. BA, Tulane U., 1969; BArch, So. Calif. Inst. Architecture, 1979. Registered architect, Calif. Designer Gruen & Assocs., Los Angeles, 1979-80, Coy Howard & Co., Los Angeles, 1980-82; prin. Lise Matthews & Assocs., Venice, Calif., 1983—. Prin. works include planning kits Plan-a-Flex Home Designer, 1984, Plan-aFlex Bath Designer, 1985, Plan-a-Flex Kitchen Designer, 1985, Plan-a-Flex Landscape Designer, 1986. Mem. hist. rev. bd. Los Angeles Conservancy, also docent walking tours, 1986. Recipient citation Progressive Architecture mag., 1977. Mem. AIA (profl. practice com. 1985-86), Am. Soc. Interior Designers (bd. dirs. 1986—). Democrat. Office: 1508 W Washington Blvd Venice CA 90291

MATTHEWS, MALLORY LOUIS, school system administrator; b. New Orleans, Mar. 29, 1953; s. Leonard Louis and Dolores (Madere) M. BA in Psychology, UCLA, 1975; MA in Edn. and Adminstrn., Pepperdine U., 1977, postgrad., 1982—. Basketball coach Mt. Carmel High Sch., Los Angeles, 1974-76; counselor autism project Los Angeles County, summer 1975; counselor, tchr. Averitt Youth Home/Probation Ctr., Los Angeles, summer 1975; tchr. social studies and life sci. Archdiocese of Los Angeles, 1977-79, youth field rep., 1977-79; dir. activities, student counseling advisor Inglewood (Calif.) Unified Sch. Dist., 1976-79, sch. dist. cons., 1979-81, adult edn. coordinator, asst. principal, 1980—; dir. counselling services Serra High Sch., Gardena, Calif., summer 1979; adminstrv. supr. Sierra High Sch., Gardena, Calif., 1976-79. Author: The Effects of Stress on the Anxiety Level of High School Graduating Female Seniors, 1973, How Black and White High School Students Rate Speakers of Black English vs. Standard English, 1975, Self-Image in Black High School Students, 1975, An Anthology of Political and Sociological Readings, 1977. Mem. Sch. bd. St. Mary's Acad., Inglewood, 1980-82, City of Inglewood Parks and Recreation Commn., 1984-87, Inglewood Neighborhood Housing Services, Inc., 1982-87, YMCA, Inglewood, Inglewood Dem. Assn., St. Eugene's Ch., Inglewood. Recipient commendation congressman Mel Levine, 1984, 86, congressman Julian Dixon, 1984, 86, sen. Diane Watson, 1984, 86, Inglewood Mayor Edward Vincent, 1984, 86, others. Mem. Assn. Calif. Sch. Adminstrs., Calif. Activities Dirs. Assn., Calif. Tchrs. Assn., Nat.Assn. Secondary Sch. Principals, Inglewood Mgmt. Assn., Phi Eta Sigma. Roman Catholic. Club: 5th Ave. Block (Inglewood). Home: 9626 5th Ave Inglewood CA 90305 Office: Inglewood Unified Sch Dist 401 S Inglewood Ave Inglewood CA 90301

MATTHEWS, MARY LOIS, educator; b. Pasadena, Calif., July 22, 1958; d. Kermit Dean and Mary Roman (Sparks) M. BA in Psychology, Pomona Coll., 1980; MA in Elem. Edn., U. No. Colo., 1981. Cert. elem. tchr., Calif., Colo. Asst. dir. YMCA Day Camp, Covina, Calif., 1980; tchr. kindergarten-2d grade Tres Pinos (Calif.) Sch. Dist., 1983-84; elem. tchr. Cucamonga Sch. Dist., Rancho Cucamong, Calif., 1984—. Mem. Cucamonga Tchrs. Assn. (negotiatior 1985—), Phi Delta Kappa, Phi Lambda Theta. Republican. Avocations: crafts, music, hiking, puppetry, ch. activities.

MATTHEWS, NORMAN SHERWOOD, JR., ins. co. executive; b. San Antonio, Tex., Apr. 23, 1944; s. Norman Sherwood and Alice Ann (Hathaway) M.; student Middle Tenn. State U., 1962-64, Ventura Coll., 1965, Calif. State U., 1965-66, U. Md., 1968-70; B.B.A., U. Tex., 1972; postgrad. U. Hawaii, 1977-79; m. Masayo Nakamura, Sept. 1, 1970; children—Debbie Ann, Scott Tsuyoshi. Research asst. State Farm Ins. Co., Murfreesboro, Tenn., 1963-64; inventory control analyst Minn. Mining & Mfg. Co., Camarillo, Calif., 1964-65; sr. acct. Peat, Marwick, Mitchell & Co., Honolulu, 1973-75; dir. mgmt. analysis Hawaii Med. Service Assn., Honolulu, 1975—. Served with USAF, 1966-70. Decorated Air medal with 8 oak leaf clusters. C.P.A., Hawaii; cert. internal auditor. Mem. Am. Inst. C.P.A.s, Hawaii Soc. C.P.A.s, Nat. Assn. Accts., Am. Acctg. Assn., Inst. Internal Auditors, EDP Auditors Assn., Am. Mgmt. Assn. Home: 2525 Date St Apt 2001 Honolulu HI 96826 Office: Hawaii Med Service Assn 818 Keeaumoku St Honolulu HI 96814

MATTHEWS, PATRICIA ANN, retail company executive; b. Victorville, Calif., Jan. 8, 1957; d. Samual Rosevelt Jones and Rose Marie (Hasty) Jones Williams; m. Richard Patrick Matthews, Nov. 24, 1978; children—Angela Lynne, Sonnie James, Richard Paul Samual. Student in psychology U. N.Mex., 1982-84. Personnel specialist Lovelace Med. Ctr., Albuquerque, 1977-79; personnel dir. Richardson Med. Ctr., Tex., 1979-80; asst. mgr. Lionel Playworld, San Antonio, 1980-81; zone mgr. Circle K Corp., Albuquerque, 1981-84, dist. mgr., Farmington, N.Mex., 1984—. Fundraising coordinator Muscular Dystrophy, Albuquerque, 1982-84, United Cerebral Palsy, Farmington, 1984—. Recipient awards Circle K Corp., 1983. Mem. Nat. Assn. Female Execs., Bloomfield C. of C., U.S. C. of C. Republican. Roman Catholic. Avocation: physical conditioning. Home: 4301 Windsor Dr Farmington NM 87401 Office: Circle K Corp 110 N 4th St Suite 2 Bloomfield NM 87413

MATTHEWS, ROBERT LLOYD, banker; b. Omaha, Sept. 23, 1937; s. Lloyd Dale and Henrietta Anna (Voss) M.; m. Elizabeth Ann Martell, Feb. 17, 1962; children: Charles Robert, John Lloyd. B.A., U. Nebr.-Omaha, 1959; grad., Am. Inst. Banking, 1968, Pacific Coast Banking Sch., 1970. With Ariz. Bank, Phoenix, 1959—; beginning as mgmt. trainee, successively loan officer, br. mgr., loan supr., asst. to pres., exec. v.p. charge loan div. Ariz. Bank, 1959-75, exec. v.p. charge earning assets div., 1975-77, pres., 1978—; dir., past chmn. Pacific Coast Banking Sch. Bd. dirs., adv. dir. former pres. Valley Big Bros.; mem. Phoenix Thunderbirds, Fiesta Bowl Adv. Bd.; mem. bd. regents, Brophy Prep. Coll.; adv. bd. Sun Angel Found.; trustee St. Lukes Health Systems; bd. dirs. Pheonix Community Alliance, Compas, Desert Bot. Gardens, Heard Mus., Phoenix Civic Ctr., Phoenix Together; mem. adv. council Engring. Sch., Ariz. State U. Served with Air N.G., 1959-65. Mem. Robert Morris Assos. (past pres.), Ariz. Bankers Assn. (dir., past pres.), Am. Bankers Assn. (past council), Phoenix Met. C. of C. (dir., past chmn.). Republican. Roman Catholic. Office: Ariz Bank PO Box 2511 Phoenix AZ 85002

MATTHEWS, WARREN WAYNE, state supreme court justice; b. Santa Cruz, Calif., Apr. 5, 1939; s. Warren Wayne and Ruth Ann (Maginnis) M.; m. Donna Stearns, Aug. 17, 1963; children: Holly Maginnis, Meredith Sample. A.B., Stanford U., 1961; LL.B., Harvard U., 1964. Bar: Alaska 1965. Assoc. firm Burr, Boney & Pease, Anchorage, 1964-69, Matthews & Dunn, Matthews, Dunn and Baily, Anchorage, 1969-77; justice Alaska Supreme Ct., Anchorage, 1977—. Bd. dirs. Alaska Legal Services Corp., 1969-70. Mem. Alaska Bar Assn. (bd. govs. 1974-77), ABA, Anchorage Bar Assn., Assn. Trial Laywers Am. Office: Alaska Supreme Ct Juneau AK 99811

MATTHEWS, WILLIAM JOHN, small business owner; b. Croswell, Mich., Jan. 1, 1919; s. Silas Oliphant and Lois O. (Arnot) M.; divorced; children: Lois, Carol, James, John, Robert. B of Music, U. Calif., Santa Barbara, 1941; student, Florence Conservatory, Italy. Owner, operator Wm. J. Matthews Piano Studio, Long Beach, Calif., 1946—. Author: Matthews Modern Music Methods for Piano and Organ (6 vol.), 1965—. Served to sgt. Signal Corps, U.S. Army, 1942-46. Republican. Avocation: outdoor activities.

MATTHIAS, JUDSON STILLMAN, civil engineering educator, consultant; b. Scofield Barracks, Hawaii, Oct. 6, 1931; s. Norman Arthur and Charlotte Aleta (Stillman) M.; m. Georgia Stewart, June 9, 1956; children: Mary, Elizabeth, Judson Jr., Anne. BS, grad. U.S. Mil. Acad., 1954; MSCE, Oreg. State U., 1963; PhD, Purdue U., 1967. Commd. 2d lt. U.S. Army, 1954, resigned, 1961; instr. Oreg. State U., Corvallis, 1962-64, Purdue U., West Lafayette, Ind., 1964-67; prof. civil engring. Ariz. State U., Tempe, 1967—. Contbr. articles to profl. jours. Mem. Traffic Accident Reduction Program, Phoenix, 1982-85, Valley Forward, Phoenix, 1972-84. Grantee Fed. Hwy. Adminstrn., Evanston, Ill., 1980, Washington, D.C., 1982; elected Outstanding Engr. of Yr., Ariz. Soc. Profl. Engrs., 1986. Fellow Inst. Transp. Engrs.; mem. ASCE (hwy. and traffic safety), Am. Rd. and Transp. Builders Assn. (pres. ednl. div. 1984-185, bd. dirs. 1984-85), Transp. Research Bd. of Nat. Acad. of Scis. (univ. rep. 1971—). Home: 2032 E Laguna Dr Tempe AZ 85282 Office: Arizona State U Civil Engring Dept Tempe AZ 85287

MATTHYS, ERIC FRANCOIS, educator; b. Brussels, Feb. 22, 1956; came to U.S., 1979; s. Roger and Elise (Wesly) M. Degree in mech. and elec. engring., Brussels U., 1978; MSME, Calif. Inst. Tech., 1980, PhDME, 1985. Engr. Poly. Sch., Brussels, 1978-79; researcher NSF, Belgium, 1981-85; prof. U. Calif., Santa Barbara, 1985. Contbr. revs. and articles to profl. jours. Fellow several profl. founds. Mem. ASME, Soc. Rheology, Sigma Xi.

MATTICE, JACK SHAFER, environmental scientist, ecologist; b. Hobart, N.Y., Aug. 25, 1941; s. Henry Bellinger Mattice and Kathryn (Shafer) Bellinger; m. Elizabeth Sara Lench, July 2, 1967. BS in Biology, SUNY, Stonybrook, 1963; PhD in Invertebrate Zoology, Syracuse U., 1971. Tchr. biology Mattituck (N.Y.) High Sch., 1963-65; research assoc. Oak Ridge (Tenn.) Nat. Lab., 1972-76, research ecologist, 1976-81; project mgr. Elec. Power Research Inst., Palo Alto, Calif., 1981—; adj. asst. prof. Tenn. Technol. U., Cookeville, 1980-81. Contbr. articles to profl. jours. Exchange fellow U.S. Nat. Acad. Sci. and Polish Acad. Sci. Warsaw, Poland, 1971-72. Mem. ASTM, Am. Fisheries Soc., Soc. Environmental Toxicology and Chemistry, Ecol. Soc. Am., N.Am. Benthol. Soc. Avocations: team sports, fishing. Office: Electric Power Research Inst 3412 Hillview Ave Palo Alto CA 94303

MATTICE, NANCY JEAN, university foundation executive; b. Batavia, N.Y., July 14, 1942; d. Simeon Grant and Jean Gladys (Mason) M. AB, SUNY, Fredonia, 1964; MA, Syracuse U., 1966; PhD, UCLA, 1983. Asst. dean students Pitzer Coll., 1966-69; activities coordinator Calif. State U., Long Beach, 1970-75; research assoc. Higher Edn. Research Inst., Los Angeles, 1976-77; research asst. UCLA, 1975-76, 77-79; research analyst Los Angeles Community Coll. Dist., 1980; research assoc. Ctr. For the Study of Community Colls., Los Angeles, 1980-82; instl. research assoc. U. Hartford, 1983; dir. research Calif. State U. Found., Long Beach, 1984—; evaluator Fund Improvement Postsec. Edn., 1977; tech. writer Computer Scis. Corp., Los Angeles, 1979; cons. System Devel. Corp., Los Angeles, 1981. Named Good Citizen of the Yr. DAR, 1960; N.Y. State Regents scholar,1960-64, Calif. State Scholar, 1975. Mem. Am. Assn. Higher Edn., Assn. Inst. Research, Sierra Club, Pi Lambda Theta. Avocations: designing houses, hiking. Office: Calif State U Found 400 Golden Shore Long Beach CA 90802

MATTINGLEY, ANN, publishing executive; b. Bloomington, Ind., Aug. 21, 1941; d. Ray Herrell and Betty Ann (Bender) Mattingley; m. Robert Joseph Galavitz, June 24, 1960 (div. Nov. 1978); children: Rowena, Renata; m. Torrance Edward Campbell, July 4, 1984 (di. Mar. 1987). Student, East Stroudsburg State Coll., 1969-72. Asst. mgr. Consumers Land Abstract, Stroudsburg, Pa., 1980-84; asst. editor/co-pub. TEST Engring. and Mgmt., Oakhurst, N.J. and Oakland, Calif., 1984—. Mem. Soc. Tech. Communication. Office: The Mattingley Pub Co Inc 3756 Grand Ave Suite 205 Oakland CA 94610

MATTINGLEY-HANNIGAN, EVE, publishing executive, editor; b. Long Branch, N.J., Nov. 14, 1944; d. Ray Herrell and Betty Ann (Bender) Mattingley; m. John Tyler Hannigan, Apr. 6, 1968 (div. Feb. 1975); 1 child, Ben Mattingley; m. Stephen James Poelma, Apr. 14, 1985. Student, Phila. Mus. Coll. Art, 1962-64. Editorial asst. TEST Engring. and Mgmt., Oakhurst, N.J., 1964-66, asst. editor, 1966-71, buyers' guide editor, 1968-71, assoc. editor, 1971-84, editor, co-pub., 1984-85; editor, co-pub. TEST Engring. and Mgmt., Oakland, Calif., 1985—. Home: 3347 68th Ave Oakland CA 94605 Office: The Mattingley Pub Co Inc 3756 Grand Ave Suite 205 Oakland CA 94610

MATTIS, NOEMI PERELMAN, psychologist, educator; b. Lodz, Poland, Oct. 16, 1936; came to U.S., 1958; d. Chaim Pinchas and Fela Estera (Liwer) Perelman; m. Daniel Charles Mattis, Nov. 9, 1958; children—Michael, Olivia. B.A., Free U., Brussels, 1955, J.D., 1958; M.A., Columbia U., 1963, Ph.D., 1973. Lic. psychologist, N.Y., Utah. Instr. French lit. Briarcliff Coll., 1960-62; psychologist Cage Teen Ctr., White Plains, N.Y., 1973-76; pvt. practice, Scarsdale, N.Y., 1976-80, Salt Lake City, 1981—; psychologist, adj. asst. prof. dept. ednl. psychology, Women's Resource Ctr., U. Utah, Salt Lake City, 1980-83, clin. asst. prof. dept. psychology, 1980-85; mem. Gov.'s Commn. on the Status of Women, 1986—. Mem. Utah Women's Forum, 1987—, Utahns United Against Nuclear Arms Race, 1986—, Women Concerned about Nuclear War, 1985—; bd. dirs. YWCA, 1981-86, Salt Lake Acting Co., 1984—. Mem. Am. Psychol. Assn., Utah Psychol. Assn. (bd. dirs. 1984), Soc. Psychol. Study Social Issues, Utah Psychologists in Pvt. Practice (pres. 1984), Westchester Psychol. Assn. (past dir.), Alliance Française (hon.), Psi Chi, Kappa Lambda Pi, Pi Lambda Theta. Address: 299 Federal Heights Circle Salt Lake City UT 84103

MATTISON, ELISA SHERI, industrial psychologist; b. Grand Rapids, Mich., Apr. 24, 1952; d. Andrew and Lorraine R. Wierenga; m. John H. Mattison, Sept. 29, 1978. B.S. cum laude, Western Mich. U., 1974, M.A., 1979. Trainer No. Inst., Anchorage, 1980; mgmt. cons.,trainer Alaska Assocs. Human Devel. Inc., Anchorage, 1980-82; job devel. specialist Collins, Weed and Assocs., Anchorage, 1982-83; owner Matheson & Assocs., Anchorage; mem. adj. faculty Anchorage Community Coll., 1981-82; work environment and design coordinator ARCO Alaska Inc., 1983-86; cons. Employee Assts. Cons. Alaska, Anchorage, 1982; v.p. Human Resource Mgmt. and Mktg. Alaskan Fed. Credit Union, 1986—. Mem. Am. Soc. Tng. and Devel., Am. Soc. Personnel Adminstrs., Credit Union Execs. Soc. Contbr. articles to profl. publs. Office: 3400 La Touche St Anchorage AK 99508

MATTISON, JEFFREY RICHARD, consulting engineering company executive, mechanical engineer; b. Springville, N.Y., Apr. 16, 1949; s. Kenneth D. and Beatrice M. (Smock) M.; m. Beverly J. Gerard, Apr. 21, 1972; children: Dawn M., Bradley S. Student Glendale Community Coll., 1967-69, U. Colo., 1969-71. Registered profl. engr., Ariz. Designer LSW Engring. Co., Phoenix, 1971-78, v.p., project mgr. and design engr., 1982-87; v.p., chief mech. engr. LSW Engring. Co., San Diego, 1987—; design engr. Schreiber Engring. Co., Phoenix, 1979-82; com. mem. City of Phoenix Plumbing Code, 1982; com. mem. City of Phoenix Bldg. Safety Adv. Bd., 1986-87. Mem. ASHRAE, Am. Soc. Profl. Engrs., Am. Soc. Plumbing Engrs. (pres. Phoenix chpt. 1981-83). Republican. Roman Catholic. Office: LSW Engring Co Inc 5560 Ruffin Rd San Diego CA 92123

MATTIVI, DON V(ERN), JR., small business owner, title consultant; b. Denver, Nov. 7, 1948; s. Donald V. and Mary (Rediess) M.; m. Julia F., Apr. 10, 1982 (div. Jan. 1986). BS, Colo. State U., 1970; MA in Bus., Western State Coll., 1975. Sales rep. Hilti, Inc., Pueblo, Colo., 1976-78; landman Wheatley Oil, Denver, 1978-81; owner, operator Mattivi Land Services, Central City, Colo., 1981—. Com. mem. Blackhawk (Colo.) Sch. Bd., 1985. Served with USAF, 1970-74. Mem. Land Title Assn. Colo., Denver Assn. Petroleum Landmen, Am. Assn. Petroleum Landmen. Republican. Lodge: Elks (Central City) (named Elk of Yr. 1984). Avocations: golf, fishing, basketball, collecting stamps. Home and Office: 106 1st E High St Central City CO 80427-0643

MATTOON, DARREL NOLAN, insurance company executive; b. Forest Grove, Oreg., Dec. 28, 1944; s. Oliver P. and Elsie R. (Harper) M.; m. Janice M. Kindel, Jan. 18, 1969; children: Michelle D., Kimberley A. Cert. in computer programming, Electronic Computer Programming Inst., Portland, Oreg., 1970; student, Portland Community Coll., various years. V.p. adminstrn., dir. corp. data processing North-West Ins. Co., Portland, 1970-84, asst. to receiver, 1984—; ptnr. Complete Software Services, Hillsboro, Oreg., 1983—. Pres. Thirty Eight Roundtable Resources Info. for Interested Customers, 1983 (founder), St. Matthews Sch. Bd., Hillsboro, 1977-84. Served with USCG, 1963-67. Roman Catholic. Lodge: Elks, Rotary (Portland bd. dirs.). Avocations: model railroading, camping, water skiing. Home: 1469 NE Jackson Sch Rd Hillsboro OR 97124 Office: The North-West Ins Co 720 SW Washington #350 Portland OR 97205-3586

MATTSON, FRED HUGH, chemical researcher; b. Spokane, Wash., Dec. 16, 1918; s. Fred Duane and Lucille (McShane) M.; m. Lucile M. Larkey, Sept 7, 1943 (dec. Mar. 1985); children: Mary Jean Mattson Hayes, Elizabeth Mattson Dennison, Rosemary, James, Virginia. BS, Loyola U., Los Angeles, 1940; MS, U. So. Calif., 1942, PhD, 1948. Research chemist Procter & Gamble Co., Cin., 1948-78; adj. prof. medicine U. Cin., 1965-78, U. Calif.-San Diego, La Jolla, 1978—. Served to capt. AC, 1942-53, ETO. Mem. Am. Heart Assn., Am. Inst. Nutrition (mem. fin. com.), Am. Chem. Soc. (Chemist of Yr. 1968). Home: 3582 Mercer Ln San Diego CA 92122 Office: U Calif San Diego M-013D La Jolla CA 92093

MATTSON, HOMER ALPHIN, vocational education consultant; b. Braham, Minn., Apr. 29, 1922; s. Alphin E. and Ida C. (Amnell) M.; m. Joyce B. Anderson, Apr. 6, 1946; children—Brian, Drew, Lee, Faye. B.S., St. Cloud State U., 1951; M.A., U. No. Colo., 1959; Ed.D., U. Nebr., 1970. Cert. tchr., vocat. dir., Wash. Sec. treas. Mattson Builders Inc., Mpls., 1951-58; indsl. arts tchr. Omaha pub. schs., 1959-61, supr. trade and indsl. edn., 1961-69; vocat. dir. Spokane Sch. Dist. 81, from 1969; now Peace Corps vocat. edn. adviser W.I. Ministry of Edn., St. Vincent; cons. Burroughs Corp., No. Natural Gas. Author: Proparation for Teaching, 1986. Past pres., bd. dirs. Riverview Terr. Served with AUS, 1943-46. Recipient Spokane Bd. Edn. Cert. Merit, 1982; named Wash. State Adminstr. of Year, 1982. Mem. Am. Vocat. Assn., Wash. Vocat. Assn., Nat. Council Local Adminstrs., Am. Indsl. Arts Assn., Phi Delta Kappa. Author articles for profl. publs.; creator stained glass windows. Home: 6527 113th Pl SE Rento WA 98056

MATTSON, JAMES ALLEN, clinical psychologist; b. Seattle, July 4, 1949; s. Glenn Arthur and Lillian B. (Schnaidt) M.; m. Charyl B. Thurber, July 22, 1972; children: Robert Charles, David James. BS in Psychology, U. Wash., 1971; PhD in Clin. Psychology, U. Tex., Austin, 1975. Lic. psychologist, Wash. Assoc. dir. planning and evaluation N. Cen. Community Mental Health Ctr., Columbus, 1975-78; exec. dir. Drug Abuse Council, Everett, Wash., 1978—; co-founder Substance Abuse Treatment Assn.; mgr. Creative Investments. pres. Wash. Assn. TASC programs, United Way Agy. Exec. Dirs. Assn. Mem. Am. Psychol. Assn. Unitarian. Office: Drug Abuse Council 2720 Rucker Everett WA 98201

MATTSON, ROY HENRY, engring. educator; b. Chisholm, Minn., Dec. 26, 1927; s. Gust and Hilma (Appel) M.; m. June Eileen Lindstrom, June 14, 1948; children—Kristi Lynn, Lisa Kay, Greta Lee, Linnea Jean, Marla Jo, Brent Anders, Brian Alan. B.Elec. Engring., U. Minn., 1951, M.S. in Elec. Engring, 1952; Ph.D., Iowa State U., 1959. Registered profl. engr. Mem. tech. staff Bell Telephone Labs., Inc., 1952-56; asst. prof., then asso. prof. Iowa State U., 1956-61; asso. prof. U. Minn., 1961-66; prof. elec. engring., head dept. U. Ariz., 1966-86, prof. elect, comp. engring,, 1986—; Del. to A.S. Popov Congress, Moscow, USSR, 1972; non-govt. observer to UN Conf. on Human Environment, Stockholm, 1972; chmn. grad. faculty, acad. exec. com. Nat. Tech. U., 1986—. Author: Basic Junction Devices and Circuits, 1963, Electronics, 1966, also articles. Mem. Amphitheater Bd. Sch. Trustees, 1971-76, pres., 1976. Served with USNR, 1946-47. Fellow IEEE (editor Transactions on Edn. 1970-73, chmn. validation of ednl. achievement program 1976-82), AAAS; mem. Am. Soc. Engring. Edn., Sigma Xi, Theta Tau, Eta Kappa Nu, Tau Beta Pi. Patentee in field. Home: 9060 N Riviera Dr Tucson AZ 85704 Office: U Ariz Dept Elec Computer Engring Tucson AZ 85721

MATTSON, VERNON WILLIAMS, theology educator; b. Salt Lake City, Jan. 15, 1934; s. Vernon W. and Ellen (Williams) M.; m. Georgia M. Jensen, Dec. 19, 1958; children—Anna, Denise, Shane, David, Paul, Steven. B.S., Brigham Young U., 1960, M.R.E., 1969. Tchr., Ch. Jesus Christ of Latter-day Saints, Salt Lake City, 1960—, lectr., 1977—; pres. Buried Records Prodns., Salt Lake City, 1978—. Author: The Dead Sea Scrolls and Other Important Discoveries, 1979. Served with USN, 1952-54. Mem. Am. Schs. Oriental Research, Soc. Early Hist. Archeology, Found. Ancient Research and Mormon Studies. Republican. Home: 3439 W 7260 S West Jordan UT 84084

MATZENAUER, JAMES OTIS, aerospace engineer; b. Tacoma, Wash., Nov. 7, 1917; s. Charles S. and Edna Alice (Otis) M.; m. Shirley McKee, Oct. 6, 1946; children—Victoria Borden, Alison Rondone, Cathy Gavriliadis. B.S. in Aero. Engring., U. Wash., 1941; postgrad. UCLA, U. So. Calif., 1947-60. Lic. mech. engr., Calif. Power plant test and devel. engr. Douglas Aircraft, Santa Monica, Calif., 1946-47; power plant devel. supr. N.Am. Aviation, Los Angeles, 1947-57; rocket engine preliminary design engr., supr. applications engring., chief engr. spl. projects Rocketdyne div. Rockwell, Canoga Park, Calif., 1957-62; mgr. advanced lunar systems studies, proposal and study mgr. advanced systems Rockwell Space Div., Downey, Calif., 1962-79; acting mgr. shuttle engring., launch vehicles payload integration Aerospace Corp., El Segundo, Calif., 1979-81, project engr. system requirements and analysis, 1981—. Served to maj. USAFR, 1940-51. Mem. AIAA (chmn. Los Angeles tech. com. 1983), Am. Rocket Soc., Inst. Aerospace Sci., Am. Astronautical Soc. Republican. Roman Catholic. Clubs: Aerospace Gun, Nat. Rifle Assn. Contbr. articles to profl. jours.; patentee in field. Office: Aerospace Corp 2350 E El Segundo Blvd M5-557 El Segundo CA 90245

MAUCH, GENE W., baseball manager; b. Salina, Kans., Nov. 18, 1925; s. George W. and Mamie (Peterson) M.; m. Nina Lee Taylor, Dec. 15, 1945; 1 child, Leanne. Profl. baseball player Bklyn. Dodgers, Pitts. Pirates, Chgo. Cubs, Boston Braves, St. Louis Cardinals, Chgo. White Sox; mgr. Atlanta Baseball Club, then Mpls. Club, 1958-60, Phila. Phillies, 1960-68, Montreal Expos, 1969-75, Minn. Twins, 1976-80; coach Calif. Angels, 1980-81, mgr., 1981-82, dir. player personnel, 1983-84, mgr., 1985—. Named Mgr. of Yr., 1973; AP Mgr. of Yr., 1964. Office: care Calif Angels Anaheim Stadium 2000 State College Blvd Anaheim CA 92806 *

MAUDERLY, JOE LLOYD, veterinary respiratory physiologist; b. Strong City, Kans., Aug. 31, 1943; s. Joseph Park and Violet May (Cox) M.; m. Cheryl Gaines, Jan. 31, 1965; children: Laurie Jean, Jennifer Lynn. BS, Kans. State U., 1965, DVM, 1967. Respiratory physiologist Lovelace Inhalation Toxicology Research Inst., Albuquerque, 1967-76, supr. pathophysiology group, 1976—; cons. in field. Contbr. articles to profl. jours., chpts. to books. Served to capt. USAF, 1967-69. Mem. AAAS, Am. Soc. Vet. Physiologists and Pharmacologists, Am. Assn. Aerosol Research, World Assn. Vet. Physiologists Pharmacologists and Biochemists, Comparative Respiratory Soc., Am. Thoracic Soc. (program com.), Am. Physiol. Soc., Am. Vet. Med. Assn., N.Mex. Vet. Med. Assn., Exptl. Aircraft Assn. Republican. Avocations: aviation, exptl. aircraft constrn. Home: 4517 Banff NE Alubquerque NM 87111 Office: Lovelace Inhalation Toxicology Research Inst PO Box 5890 Albuquerque NM 87195

MAUGHAN, EDWIN KELLY, geologist; b. Glendale, Calif., Oct. 13, 1926; s. Thomas Adamson and Irene (Kelly) M.; B.S. with honors, Utah State U., 1950; postgrad. UCLA, 1950-51, U. Colo. Grad. Sch., 1956-57, Colo. Sch. Mines, 1977; m. Fae Lewis, June 8, 1951 (div. 1971); children—Kenneth

Lewis, Gordon Lewis, Laura Anne, Evan Lewis; m. 2d, Jayne Kessler, Nov. 15, 1975 (div. 1977). Geologist U.S. Corps Engrs., Los Angeles, 1951, U.S. Geol. Survey, Denver, 1951-67; tech. adviser U.S. Geol. Survey & Agy. for Internat. Devel., Bogota, Colombia, 1967-69; geologist U.S. Geol. Survey, Middlesboro, Ky., 1969-72, Denver, 1972—. Served with USNR, 1945-46. Fellow Geol. Soc. Am.; mem. Soc. Econ. Paleontologists and Mineralogists (v.p. Rocky Mountain sect. 1983-84, pres. 1985-86), Am. Assn. Petroleum Geologists, Colo. Chorale (dir. 1976-80), Men's Orgn. Denver Symphony Orch., Sigma Gamma Epsilon, Phi Kappa Phi. Mem. Ch. of Jesus Christ of Latter-day Saints (br. pres. 1968-69). Author, co-author numerous articles on Upper Paleozoic stratigraphy, paleogeography, and petroleum source rocks in northern Rocky Mountains and Great Basin; areal geology in central Mont., Wyo. and southeastern Ky.; and Cretaceous phosphorite deposits in Colombia. Home: 1317 Yank St Golden CO 80401 Office: US Geol Survey Fed Center Denver CO 80225

MAUK, THOMAS GREGORY, city manager; b. Oakland, Calif., Oct. 21, 1943; s. James R. and Constance Ivy (Jensen) Nourse; m. Rebecca V. Mauk, Mar. 18, 1968; children—Donald, Katherine, Laura, Danielle. B.B.A., Calif. State U.-Pomona, 1966; M.P.A., U. So. Calif., 1972. Adminstrv. analyst City of Los Angeles, 1967-70; asst. city adminstr. City of Montclair (Calif.), 1970-76; city mgr. City of Norco (Calif.), 1976-80, City of Whittier (Calif.), 1980—; pub. speaker; tchr. Named Man of Yr., Norco C. of C., 1977. Mem. Internat. City Mgrs. Assn., Los Angeles World Affairs Council, Town Hall of Calif. Club: Lions. Home: 10015 Santa Gertrudes St Whittier CA 90603 Office: City of Whittier 13230 Penn St Whittier CA 90601

MAUL, TERRY LEE, psychologist, educator; b. San Francisco, May 6, 1946; s. Chester Lloyd and Clella Lucille (Hobbs) M.; AB, U. Calif., Berkeley, 1967, MA, 1968, PhD, 1970; student Coll. San Mateo, 1964-65; m. Gail Ann Retallick, June 27, 1970 (div. Dec. 1986); 1 son, Andrew Eliot. Assoc. prof. psychology San Bernardino Valley Coll., San Bernardino, Calif., 1970—, chmn. dept., 1979-82; researcher self-actualization. Mem. Am. Psychol. Assn., AAUP (chpt. pres. 1971-73), Audubon Soc., Mensa, Nature Conservancy, Rachel Carson Council, Wilderness Soc., Sierra Club. Democrat. Author: (with Eva Conrad) Introduction to Experimental Psychology, 1981; (with Gail Maul) Beyond Limit: Ways to Growth and Freedom, 1983; contbg. author other psychol. texts. Home: 6155 Bluffwood Dr Riverside CA 92506 Office: San Bernardino Valley Coll 701 S Mount Vernon Ave San Bernardino CA 92410

MAULDIN, JEAN HUMPHRIES, aviation co. exec.; b. Gordonville, Tex., Aug. 16, 1923; d. James Wiley and Lena Leota (Noel-Crain) Humphries; B.S., Hardin Simmons U., 1943; M.S., U. So. Calif., 1961; postgrad. Westfield Coll., U. London, 1977-78, Warnborough Coll., Oxford, Eng., 1977-78; m. William Henry Mauldin, Feb. 28, 1942; children—Bruce Patrick, William Timothy III. Psychol. counselor social services 1st Baptist Ch., 1953-57; pres. Mauldin and Staff, public relations, Los Angeles, 1957-78; pres. Stardust Aviation, Inc., Santa Ana, Calif., 1962—. Mem. Calif. Democratic Council, 1953-83; mem. exec. bd. Calif. Dem. Central com., 1957—, Orange County Dem. Central Com., 1960—; mem. U.S. Congl. Peace Adv. Bd., 1981—; del. Dem. Nat. Conv., 1974, 78; mem. nat. advisor U.S. Congl. Adv. Bd. Am. Security Council; pres. Santa Ana Friends of Public Library, 1973-76, McFadden Friends of Library, Santa Ana, 1976-80; chmn. cancer crusade Am. Cancer Soc., Orange County, 1974; mem. exec. bd. Lisa Hist. Preservation Soc., 1970—; lay leader Protestant Episcopal Ch. Am., Trinity Ch., Tustin, Calif. Named Woman of Yr., Key Woman in Politics, Calif. Dem. Party, 1960-80. Am. Mgmt. Assn. (pres.'s club), Bus. and Profl. Women Am., Exptl. Aircraft and Pilots Assn., Nat. Women's Polit. Caucus, Dem. Coalition Central Coms., Calif. Friends of Library (life), Women's Missionary Soc. (chmn.), LWV, Nat. Fedn. Dem. Women, Calif. Fedn. County Central Com. Mems., Internat. Platform Assn., Peace Through Strength, Oceanic Soc., Nat. Audubon Soc., Sierra Club, Nat. Wildlife Fedn., Internat. Amnesty Assn., Am. Security Council, Nat. Women's Pilot. Club: U. So. Calif. Ski, Town Hall of Calif. Author: Cliff Winters, The Pilot, The Man, 1961; The consummate Barnstormer, 1962; The Daredevil Clown, 1965. Home: 1013 W Elliott Pl Santa Ana CA 92704 Home: 102 E 45th St Savannah GA 31405 Home: 112 8th St Seal Beach CA 90740 Office: 16542 Mount Kibby St Fountain Valley CA 92708

MAUND, GAY ELIZABETH, audiologist; b. Phila.; d. Walter Thomas and Eleanor Claire (Logan) Maund. B.A., Marymount Coll., 1963-67; M.A., U. So. Calif., 1969. Lic. audiologist, Calif. Audiologist, VA Outpatient Clinic, Los Angeles, 1970—, coordinator, hearing aid program, 1978—, pub. relations officer, 1979—, adminstrv. officer drug dependency program, 1985-86; part-time faculty Calif. State U.-Los Angeles, Calif. State U.-Northridge; lectr. in field. Mem. Los Angeles City Council for the Handicapped, 1982-83. Recipient VA Bronze Pin Spl. Award for Excellence in Improving Communications and Service to Pub., 1975, VA Quality Increase Performance award, 1977, Cert. of Appreciation, 1980, Spl. Contbn. award, 1982, others. Mem. Am. Speech and Hearing Assn. Address: 425 S Hill St Los Angeles CA 90013

MAUNDER, RICHARD JOHN, physician, researcher; b. Lansing, Mich., Nov. 30, 1949; s. Robert Howard and Margaret (McCrimmon) M.; m. Lucinda Robbins Rudell, Sept. 25, 1971; children: Cary, Carlotta. Student, Kalamazoo Coll., 1967-70; AB in Psychology, U. Calif., Berkeley, 1972; MD, George Washington U., 1977. Diplomate Am. Bd. Internal Medicine. Intern then resident Yale U. Hosp., New Haven, 1977-80, chief resident in medicine, 1980-81, instr., 1980-81; asst. prof. U. Wash., Seattle, 1984—, pulmonary fellow, 1981-84; practice medicine specializing in pulmonary and critical care medicine Harborview Med. Ctr., Seattle, 1984—. Contbr. articles to profl. jours. Moderator Pilgrim Congl. Ch., Seattle, 1986—. Mem. AAAS, Am. Thoracic Soc., ACP, Am. Coll. Chest Physicians, Am. Physiol. Soc., Phi Beta Kappa, Alpha Omega Alpha. Home: 1135 20th Ave E Seattle WA 98112 Office: Harborview Med Ctr 325 Ninth Ave Seattle WA 98104

MAUPIN, PAUL HUTSELL, research chemist; b. Cleve., Sept. 20, 1954; s. Paul H. and Ruth (Morrison) M. BS in Chemistry, U. Tenn., 1976; PhD in Chemistry, Rice U., 1983. Chemist Oak Ridge (Tenn.) Nat. Lab., 1976-78; sr. research chemist Envirogenic Systems, El Monte, Calif., 1983-85, Hydranautics, San Diego, 1985—. Active Environ. Affairs Com., San Diego, 1985—. Robert Welsh fellow, 1978-82. Mem. Am. Chem. Soc. (San Diego chpt. com. chmn., awards chmn. 1986). Republican. Methodist. Office: Hydranautics 11111 Flintkote Suite B San Diego CA 92121

MAURER, ERNEST WILLIAM, college dean, astronautics and computer educator, consultant; b. Lakewood, Ohio, Aug. 11, 1951; s. Ernest Edward and Cynthia Bell (Muir) M. A.A., Cuyahoga Community Coll., Ohio, 1972; B.S. in Edn., Kent (Ohio) State U., 1973, M.A. in Tech., 1976; PhD in Edn. UCLA, 1986. Cert. tchr., Calif.; lic. pilot and flight instr., FAA. Mechanic, service mgr., asst. store mgr., various Goodyear tire ctrs. Cleve., 1971-73; indsl. arts tchr., Lakewood (Ohio) High School, 1973-76, Fontana Junior High School, Ohio, 1976-77; prof. astronautics and computer literacy Coast Community Coll. Dist., Costa Mesa, Calif., 1977—; cons. to Taiwan Ministry Edn. in tchr. edn. and indsl. automation. Mem. Nat. Space Council, AIAA, Univ. Aviation Assn., Flying Tchrs., Aircraft Owners and Pilots Assn., Theta Tau. Contbr. articles to profl. books and jours. Home: 7611 Rhone Ln Huntington Beach CA 92647 Office: Orange Coast Coll 2701 Fairview Rd Coast Mesa CA 92626

MAURO, RICHARD FRANK, lawyer, educator, businessman; b. Hawthorne, Nev., July 21, 1945; s. Frank Joseph and Dolores D. (Kreimeyer) M.; m. LaVonne M. Madden, Aug. 28, 1965; 1 child, Lindsay Anne. AB, Brown U., 1967; JD summa cum laude, U. Denver, 1970. Bar: Colo. 1970. Assoc. Dawson, Nagel, Sherman & Howard, Denver, 1970-72; assoc. Van Cise, Freeman, Tooley & McClearn, Denver, 1972-73, ptnr., 1973-74; ptnr. Hall & Evans, Denver, 1974-81, Morrison & Forester, Denver, 1981-84, Parcel, Mauro, Hultin & Spaanstra, Denver, 1984—; pres. Sundance Oil Exploration Co., 1985—; adj. prof. U. Denver Coll. Law, 1981—. Symposium editor: Denver Law Jour., 1969-70; editor: Colorado Corporation Systems Manual; contbr. articles to legal jours. Pres. Colo. Open Space Council, 1974. Francis Wayland scholar, 1967; recipient various Am. jurisprudence awards. Mem. ABA, Colo. Bar Assn., Denver Bar Assn., Colo. Assn. Corp. Counsel. (pres. 1974-75), Am. Arbitration Assn. (comml. arbitrator), Order St. Ives. Club: Denver Athletic (bd. dirs. 1986—). Home: 3264 Taft Ct Wheat Ridge CO 80033 Office: 1801 California St Suite 3600 Denver CO 80202

MAURY, MARIO ANDREU, JR., electronics business executive, microwave engineer; b. Havana, Cuba, July 21, 1936; came to U.S., 1945; s. Mario A. and Angela (Wandel) M.; m. Janet M. Batteau, Mar. 5, 1960; children: Mario, Donna, Beth, Michele. AA, Mt. San Antonio Coll., 1957; student, Citrus Coll., 1956-57, Los Angeles State Coll., 1958-59. Jr. engr. Convair Corp., Pomona, Calif., 1955-57; v.p. Maury & Assocs., Montclair, Calif., 1957-1963; design engr. Gen. Dynamics Corp., Pomona, 1958-61; pres. Maury Microwave Corp., Cucamonga, Calif., 1963—. Editor (spl. issue) Microwave Jour., 1982; contbr. articles to profl. jours. Com. chmn. Boy Scouts Am., Upland, Calif. Served with U.S. Army, 1959. Recipient Honored Contbr. award Hewlett Packard Co., 1984. Mem. IEEE (sr.) Microwave Techniques and Theory Soc. of ADCOM, Automatic Radio Frequency Techniques Group (pres. 1980-82, mem. exec. com., Service award 1980, Disting. Service award 1983). Democrat. Roman Catholic. Home: 719 Dalton Ct Upland CA 91786 Office: Maury Microwave Corp 8610 Helms Ave Cucamonga CA 91730

MAUS, JOHN ANDREW, computer systems engineer; b. Whittier, Calif., July 13, 1945; s. Kenneth Waring and Bertha Estella (Eckman) M.; M. Diana Barba, May 16, 1977 (div. May 1, 1983); m. Colette An Moschelle, Nov. 23, 1985; stepchildren: BreAnn, Adam. BA in Physics, U. Calif., Riverside, 1963-67; MS in Physics, San Diego State U., 1967-70. Cert. data processor, 1983. Programmer, analyst San Diego State Found., 1970-72; instr. bus. San Diego State U., 1971-73; systems programmer San Diego State U., San Diego, 1971-74; data processing mgr. M.H. Golden Co., San Diego, 1974-79; computer systems engr. Hewlett-Packard Co., Spokane, Wash., 1979—; physics lab. asst. USDA Salinity Lab., Riverside, Calif., 1965-67; underwater acoustics programmer Naval Undersea Ctr., San Diego, 1967-70; programmer San Diego Inst. Pathology, 1972-76. Co-author: Chemical Physics Letters, 1971, Electronic and Atomic Collisions, 1971. Merit badge counselor Spokane chpt. Boy Scouts Am., 1983—. Mem. Assn. Computing Machinery (founder Spokane chpt., chpt. chmn. 1980-82, service award 1981). Avocations: internat. travel, skiing, horses. Home: N 16922 Tamarac Ln Nine Mile Falls WA 99026 Office: Hewlett-Packard Co N 1225 Argonne Rd Spokane WA 99212-2657

MAUTER, WARREN EUGENE, chemist, business development consultant; b. Denver, Aug. 27, 1951; s. Jacob Martin and Harriette June (Kaiser) M.; m. Deborah Lee Long, Jan. 22, 1983. BS in Chemistry, Met. State Coll., 1976; MBA, U. Colo., 1986. Research chemist Manville Corp., Denver, 1973-80, group leader, 1980-83; applications mgr. Cardinal Chem., Columbia, S.C., 1983-84; prin. Alpine Cons., Denver, 1984—; instr. econs. and finance U. Colo. Coll. Engring, 1987—; mem. bd. advs. Shuck Found., 1986—. Bd. reviewers Jour. Vinyl Tech., 1981-83; contbr. articles to profl. jours. Sci. and Tech. Colo. scholar Met. State Coll., 1972-75. Mem. ASTM, Soc. Plastics Engrs. (bd. dirs. vinyl div. 1982-86), Nat. Sanitation Found. (industry adv. bd. 1980-84), Am. Chem. Soc., Am. Mgmt. Assn. Republican. Clubs: Colo. Mountain, U. Colo. Exec. (Denver). Avocations: mountaineering, sailing, competitive running. Home: 1649 S Marion St Denver CO 80210 Office: Alpine Cons PO Box 10374 Denver CO 80210

MAVEETY, PATRICK JOHN JOSEPH, curator; b. San Diego, June 17, 1930; s. Herman Matthew and Sylvia (Kolk) M.; m. Darle Ann Hermann, May 31, 1958; children—Matthew, Mary. A.B. in Design, Stanford U., 1951, M.A. in Oriental Art, 1975. Commd. ensign, U.S. Navy, 1951, advanced through grades to lt. comdr., 1961, ret. 1972; curator Asian Art Stanford U. Mus. Art, Stanford, Calif., 1978—; adv. bd. N.W. Regional China Council, Portland, Oreg., 1984—, San Francisco Crafts and Folk Art Mus., 1984—. Author exhbn. catalogues. Decorated Joint Services Commendation medal. Mem. Asia Soc., Nat. Trust for Hist. Preservation, Ret. Officers Assn., Oriental Ceramic Soc. London. Home: 22 Rhododendron Ln Salishan Gleneden Beach OR 97388 Office: Stanford Univ Mus Art Stanford CA 94305

MAWHINNEY, JOHN THOMAS, state senator; b. Phila., May 27, 1937; s. James Joseph and Helen Grace (Maguire) M.; m. Margaret Jane Cybulski, June 21, 1958; children—Helen Marie, John Thomas II, Katherine Elizabeth. Student parochial schs., Phila. Enlisted USAF, 1954, advanced through grades to maj., 1966; ret., 1966; pilot, flight engr. Pan Am. Airways, 1966-85; pilot United Airlines, 1985—; mem. flight engrs. bd. adjustment, N.Y.C., 1974—; referee Pima County Juvenile Ct., 1977—; mem. Ariz. Senate, 1979—, majority whip, 1981—, asst. majority leader, 1983—, chmn. rules com., 1985—. Fire commr. Manalapan (N.J.) 1 Fire Dist., 1973; mem. Ariz. Groundwater Study Commn., 1979. Decorated Air medal with 4 oak leaf clusters. Mem. Airline Pilots Assn., Flight Engrs. Internat. Assn., Am. Legion, Mil. Order World Wars. Republican. Home: PO Box 35536 Tucson AZ 85740 Office: PO Box 35536 Tucson AZ 85740

MAWLA, SHAMIL ANTANEOUS, chemist; b. Mosuel, Iraq, Mar. 2, 1952; came to U.S., 1977; s. Antaneous A. and Salma D. Mawla; m. Carol C. Ibrahim, Dec. 27, 1980; children: Jacqueline, Christine. BS, U. Baghdad, Iraq, 1975. Chemist Ampex Corp., Redwood City, Calif., 1977-79, sr. chemist, 1979-84; process mgr. IMC, Santa Clara, Calif., 1984—. Inventor in field. Avocations: sports, reading, gardening. Office: IMC 2875 Northwestern Pkwy Santa Clara CA 95051

MAX, WENDY BARBARA, economics educator; b. Newark, Feb. 15, 1954; d. Robert and Shirley (Biller) Max; m. Robert David Siegel, Sept. 4, 1983. BA, Stanford U., 1976; MA, U. Colo., 1981, PhD, 1983. Policy analyst Colo. Dept. Health, Denver, 1979-80; economist Solar Energy Research Inst, Golden, Colo., 1980-81; asst. prof. econs. Calif. State U., Hayward, 1984—; affiliated faculty and research assoc. U. Calif. Inst. for Health and Aging, San Francisco, 1984—; cons. U.S. Forest Service, San Francisco, 1986. Contbr. articles to prof. jours. Grantee Resources for the Future, 1981-82. Mem. Am. Econ. Assn., Western Econ. Assn., Soc. Am. Foresters. Democrat. Avocations: swimming, gardening, backpacking, hiking, jogging. Office: Calif State U Econs Dept Hayward CA 94542

MAXEY, VALERIE KRIZ, writer, communications consultant; b. Berkeley, Calif., Oct. 16, 1954; d. Leland Calvin and Rita Rose (Webber) Kriz; m. Lyle Denny Maxey, June 2, 1979. B.A. in Communication, Stanford U., 1976. Analyst parts & service div. Ford Motor Co. Pico Rivera, Calif., 1977-79; account coordinator Bozell & Jacobs, Inc., Newport Beach, Calif., 1979-81, account exec., 1981, account supr., 1981-82; corp. pub. relations mgr. Smith Internat., Inc., Newport Beach, 1982-86 . Chmn. Stanford U. Ann. Fund, Orange County (Calif.), 1982-86 . Mem. Pub. Relations Soc. Am., Women in Communications, Nat. Assn. Female Execs.

MAXON, JAMES CLARK, archaeologist, environmental education specialist; b. Alamosa, Colo., Dec. 19, 1935; s. Leo Gilbert and Mary Edith (Taylor) M.; student U.S. Mil. Acad., 1954; B.A. in Anthropology, U. Denver, 1958; M.A. in Archaeology, U. Wis., 1969; m. Sharon Kay Sullivan, Aug. 16, 1958; children—Kevin Joseph, Clark Christopher, Dianne Marie; m. 2d, Kristin Jane Lenning, Jan. 3, 1982. Archaeologist, Aztec Ruins Nat. Monument, 1958-61, Bandelier Nat. Monument, 1961-67; environ. edn. specialist Lake Mead Nat. Recreation Area, 1967-74; instr. continuing edn. U. Nev., Las Vegas, 1972—; with U.S. Bur. Reclamation, Lower Colo. River region, Boulder City, Nev., 1975-85, regional archaeologist, 1976-85, chief archaeologist, Denver, 1986—. Pres. Nev. Environ. Edn. Council 1974—. Mem. Soc. Am. Archeology, Am. Soc. Conservation Archeology, Nev. Hist. Soc., Boulder City First Nighters. Author: Indians of the Lake Mead Country, 1971; Boating Guide to Lake Mohave, 1971; Lake Mead: The Story Behind the Scenery, 1980. Home: Lakewood CO 80215 Office: US Bur Reclamation Engring and Research Ctr DFC PO Box 25007 Denver CO 80225

MAXWELL, COLIN, Canadian provincial cabinet minister; b. Tillicoultry, Scotland, Dec. 16, 1943; arrived in Can., 1966; s. Colin and Molly (Drummond) M.; m. Cherry Harvey, July 6, 1966; children—Ashley, Kirstin, Brigham. Grad. Jordanhill Coll., 1965, Grad. diploma in Edn., 1966; B.Edn., U. Regina, 1975. Cert. tchr., Scotland, Sask. Tchr., Sturgis Sch. Dist., Preeceville, Sask., 1966-67; prin. Nipawin Sch. Dist., Smeaton, Sask., 1968; phys. edn. tchr. Melville, Sask., 1968-74; univ. lectr. U. Regina, 1974-76; prin. Spiritwood High Sch., Sask., 1976-82; head coach Legion Track and Field Camp., Sask., 1974-75. Mayor Spiritwood Town Council, 1978-82; mem. legis. assembly Conservative Govt. Sask. Legislation, Regina, 1982—; re-elected mem. Turtleford Constituency, 1986; cabinet minister of advanced edn. and manpower, 1983, cabinet minister of parks and renewable resources, Regina, 1985. Pres. Melville local Sask. Tchrs. Fedn., 1970-72, councillor, 1970-74, Mem. Commonwealth Parliamentary Assn. Lutheran. Lodges: Lions, Masons. Office: Legis Bldg, Room 340, Regina, SK Canada S4S 0B3

MAXWELL, DONALD STANLEY, controller, publishing executive; b. Los Angeles, May 30, 1930; s. Harold Stanley and Margaret (Trenam) M.; m. Martha Helen Winn, Dec. 5, 1952; children: Sylvia Louise, Cynthia Lynn, Bruce Stanley, Bradley Erl, Walter James, Wesley Richard, Amy Bernice. Student, Long Beach City Coll., 1948-50; B.B.A., Woodbury Coll., 1956. C.P.A. Ptnr. Robert McDavid & Co. (C.P.A.'s), Los Angeles, 1955-61; controller Petersen Pub. Co., Los Angeles, 1961-68; v.p. fin. Petersen Pub. Co., 1969; controller Los Angeles Times, 1969-79, v.p., 1977-79, v.p. fin., 1979-81; asst. treas. Times Mirror Co., 1971-82, v.p., controller, 1982—. Trustee Woodbury U., 1981—, chmn. bd. trustees, 1984—. Served with AUS, 1950-52. Mem. Fin. Execs. Inst. (dir. 1979—, pres. Los Angeles chpt. 1973-74), Inst. Newspaper Controllers and Fin. Officers (dir. 1978-82, pres. 1980-81), Am. Inst. C.P.A.s, Calif. Soc. C.P.A.s, Am. Horse Council, Internat. Arabian Horse Assn., Arabian Horse Assn. So. Calif. Republican. Baptist. Club: Friendly Hills Country (Whittier, Calif.). Home: 2160 LeFlore Dr La Habra Heights CA 90631 Office: Times Mirror Sq Los Angeles CA 90053

MAXWELL, KENNETH LEROY, political science educator; b. Wilkinsburg, Pa., May 26, 1913; s. Benjamin Harrison and Anna Belle (Park) M.; m. Miriam Alice Young, 1936 (dec. 1940); m. Marian Jean Carslon, 1941 (div. 1974); m. Janet Elizabeth King, 1974 (div. 1981); m. Mary Pepys McGraw, Aug. 10, 1985; children: Carol Irene Kolsti, Marshall Kenneth, Elizabeth Anne. BA, Denison U., 1935, DD (hon.), 1966; MDiv, Colgate Rochester Div. Sch., 1938; PhD, Yale U., 1953. Ordained to ministry. Pastor Am. Bapt. Chs., Conn., Ohio, 1939-55; exec. dir. dept. Internat. Affairs Nat. Council Chs., N.Y.C., 1955-66; prof. polit. sci. Rider coll., Lawrenceville, N.J., 1966-78, founder, chair Grad. Program for Adminstrs., 1970-78; vis. prof. Sch. Bus. Adminstrn. Clarion (Pa.) U., 1978-79; prof. polit. sci. Trenton (N.J.) State Coll., 1979-83; adj. prof. Ariz. State U., Tempe, 1984—; prof. internat. studies Thunderbird Am. Grad. Sch. Internat. Mgmt., Tempe, 1987—; vis. fellow Woodrow Wilson Sch. Pub. and Internat. Affairs, Princeton (N.J.) U., 1966-67; rep. UN, 1955-66. Co-editor: Paths to World Order, 1967; author: Seek Peace and Pursue It, 1983; contbr. articles to profl. jours. Founder, bd. dirs. Nat. Council UN Assn., 1964—; mem. exec. com. U.S. Com. for UNICEF, N.Y.C., 1957-66; pres. Council of Orgns. on UN, 1961-63; del. UN Conf. on Human Environment, Stockholm, 1972; observer for UN Devel. Programme UNESCO Conf., Brussels, 1972; del. World Council of Chs. Gen. Assemblies, Evanston, Ill., New Delhi, Uppsala, 1954, 1962, 68; trustee Westminster Choir Coll., Princeton, 1965-83; hon. chair Ariz. UN Day, 1986. Scholar Cambridge (Eng.) U., 1938-39. Mem. Am. Acad. Polit. and Social Sci., Am. Polit. Sci. Assn., Internat. Studies Assn., Am. Soc. Pub. Adminstrn., Soc. for Values in Higher Edn., UN Assn. USA (pres. Phoenix chpt. 1987—, bd. dirs. Ariz. div. 1986—), Kappa Sigma, Tau Kappa Alpha. Republican. Avocations: classical music, running, swimming, walking, traveling. Home: 222 The Terrace 16724 Gunsite Dr Fountain Hills AZ 85268 Ofice: Ariz State U Dept Polit Sci Tempe AZ 85287

MAXWELL, LEROY MAHLON, construction company executive, consultant; b. Sheridan, Wyo., May 23, 1935; s. James Alfred and Blanche Edith (Stallings) M.; m. Joan Gierisch (div. 1974); children: Sheree Maxwell Bench, Daniel, David, Kerri, Jonathon. C.E., Colo. State U., 1959. Constrn. mgr. Lloyd M. Hill, Inc., Salem, Oreg., 1968-71, Cabax Mills, Eugene, Oreg., 1971-78; owner, mgr. Maxwell Cons., Eugene, 1978-80; v.p., mgr. Gen. Constrn. Co. of Hawaii, Honolulu, 1980-82; v.p., ops. mgr. Arctic Slope/Wright Schuchart Constrn. Co., Anchorage, 1982—; v.p. Keystone Devels., Inc., Anchorage, 1985—, Frontier Equipment Co., Anchorage, 1985—; owner, mgr. Image Seminars, Anchorage; owner C&M Enterprises, Anchorage; cons. U.S. Forest Service. Mem. Pres.'s Republican Task Force (charter), U.S. Senatorial Club. Mem. Am. Mgmt. Assn. Republican. Clubs: Plaza (Honolulu); Elks (Eugene). Office: Frontier Cos of Alaska Box 101616 Anchorage AK 99510

MAXWELL, MARY SUSANNA, psychology educator; b. Dallas, Mar. 28, 1948; d. Otis Allen and Emma Vee (Dunlap) M.; m. Barry Lafean Lutz, July 25, 1981. BA, U. Tex., 1970, PhD, 1978. Lic. psychologist, Ariz. Asst. prof. psychology No. Ariz. U., Flagstaff, 1978-84, dir. sch. psychology programs, 1979-85, assoc. prof., 1984—, cons. personnel dept., 1984-86, coordinator ednl. psychology, 1985—; editorial cons. Holt, Rinehart & Winston, 1980-81, MacMillan, 1984. Mem. editorial bd. Sch. Psychology Rev., 1983—. Recipient Pres.'s award for Outstanding Faculty, 1986. Mem. Am. Psychol. Assn., Nat. Assn. Sch. Psychologists, Ariz. Assn. Sch. Psychologists (exec. bd. 1983, No. regional dir. Pres. award 1983), Council Dirs. Sch. Psychology Programs (exec. bd. 1984—). Democrat. Avocations: cross-country skiing, travel, photography. Home: 3330 Gillenwater Flagstaff AZ 86001

MAXWELL, NEAL A., church official. m. Colleen Hinckley; four children. B in Polit. Sci., M in Polit. Sci., U. Utah, LLD (hon.); LLD (hon.), Brigham Young U.; LittD (hon.), Westminster Coll.; HHD (hon.), Utah State U. Legis. asst. U.S. sen. Wallace F. Bennett, Utah; various adminstrv. and teaching positions U. Utah, Salt Lake City; various secular positions including bishop Salt Lake City's Univ. Sixth Ward, mem. gen. bd. youth orgn., adult correlation com. and one of first REgional Reps. of the Twelve; elder Ch. Jesus Christ Latter Day Sts., Asst. to the Council of Twelve, 1974-76, mem. of Presidency of First Quorum of the Seventy, 1976-81, mem. of Council of Twelve Apostles, 1981—; bd. dirs. Quester Corp., Deseret News Pub. Co., Zions First Nat. Bank. Mem. Quorum of the Twelve Ch. of Jesus Christ of Latter-Day Saints, Salt Lake City. Recipient Liberty Bell award Utah State Bar, 1967; named Pub. Adminstr. of Yr. Inst. Govt. Service Brigham Young U., 1973. Office: Quorum of the Twelve 50 E N Temple St Salt Lake City UT 84150

MAXWELL, SHARON LEE REYNOLDS, government official, consultant; b. Taft, Calif., Mar. 2, 1939; d. Theodore Roosevelt Reynolds and Adelaide Velma (Johnson) Reynolds Sikola; B.A., U. Ariz., 1966, M.A., 1969; divorced; children—Maurynne Ruth, Edward Stuart. Asst. cataloger Tucson Public Schs., 1966-68, tchr., librarian, 1968-72; teaching asst. U. Ariz., 1969-70; with City of Tucson, 1972—, citizen participation adminstr., 1978—. Mem. Pima area adv. group Health Systems Agy. So. Ariz., 1978-80, mem. governing body, 1979-84; mem. adv. com. Community Mediation Program, 1985—. Mem. Internat. Reading Assn., NEA, AAUW, Tucson Community Food Bank, Ariz. Edn. Assn., Am. Soc. Public Adminstrn., Am. Soc. Tng. and Devel., Nat. Assn. Female Execs., Exec. Women's Council of So. Ariz., Altrusa Internat., Pi Lambda Theta. Avocations: music; reading; counseling. Home: PO Box 13388 Tucson AZ 85732 Office: City of Tucson PO Box 27210 Tucson AZ 85726

MAXWELL, SONIA L., social worker; b. Kokomo, Ind., Dec. 15, 1947; s. Charles Clayton and Bernice Louise (Tyrrell) M.; m. Roger E. Armstrong, July 14, 1984. BA, Washburn U., 1970; MSW, U. Kans., 1974. Probation officer Pima County Juvenile Ct., Tucson, 1974-75; clin. social worker St. Mary's Hosp., Tucson, 1975-79, dir. social work, 1979-83; prin. Counseling, Therapy, and Mediation Assocs., Tucson, 1984—. Service and rehab. vol. Am. Cancer Soc., Tucson, 1980—, bd. dirs. 1981-84; chmn. Pima Unit Rehab. and Service Com., Tucson, 1982-83; conf. participant Ariz.-Sonora Commn., 1982; mem. allocations com. Tucson United Way, 1984-85. Mem. Nat. Assn. Social Workers, Acad. Cert. Social Workers (cert.). Avocations: swimming, reading, tennis, weight-lifting. Home: 2310 N Madelyn Circle Tucson AZ 85712 Office: Counseling Therapy & Mediation Assocs 1540 N Tucson Blvd Tucson AZ 85716

MAXWELL, SY, insurance broker; b. N.Y.C., Apr. 5, 1929; s. Jack and Stella (LeBow) M.; m. Charlotte Edelstone, Jan. 10, 1954; children—Leslie, Bruce, Robin, Tracy. B.A., U. Mich., 1950. Pres., Triangle Ins., Inc.,

Sherman Oaks, Calif., 1955—; founder, dir. Lincoln Nat. Bank, 1982-84. Pres. 500 Club of City of Hope, 1983; sec. Ins. Council, City of Hope; bd. dirs. II ABC, 1986—, Boys and Girls Club of San Fernando Valley, 1986—. Served with USNR, 1947-57. Mem. Beverly Hills Bus. and Profl. Men's Assn. (pres. 1962), Ind. Ins. Agts. and Brokers Assn. Calif. (pres. San Fernando Valley chpt. 1969-70, chmn. govt. affairs com. 1982-84). Democrat. Office: Triangle Ins Inc 4340 Fulton Ave Sherman Oaks CA 91423

MAY, DEAN LOWE, history educator; b. Worland, Wyo., Apr. 6, 1938; s. Frank Peter May and Wanda (Lowe) Rockhill; married; children: Timothy Dean, Caroline Elizabeth, Thaddeus James. BA with highest honors, Brigham Young U., 1964; MA, Harvard U., 1968; PhD, Brown U., 1974. Research historian Ch. Jesus Christ Latter-day Sts., Salt Lake City, 1974-77; dir. Ctr. for Hist. Population Studies U. Utah, Salt Lake City, 1977-83, asst. prof. history, 1977-84, assoc. prof., 1984—; mem. adv. com. Charles Redd Ctr. Western Studies, Brigham Young U., Provo, Utah, 1972—. Co-author: Building the City of God: Community and Cooperation Among the Mormons, 1976 (Mormon History Assn. Best Book award); author: From New Deal to New Economics: The American Liberal Response to the Recession of 1937, 1981; writer, presenter Peoples' History of Utah, twenty part TV series and book, 1983-88. Mem. Utah State History Bd., Salt Lake City, 1983—. Fellow Fulbright, U. Cologne, Fed. Republic of Germany, 1964-65, Woodrow Wilson, Harvard U., 1965-66, Huntington Haynes, Huntington Library, 1986. Mem. Orgn. Am. Historians, Social Sci. History Assn., Western History Assn. (program com. 1981), Mormon History Assn. (program com. 1986, editor jour. 1981-85). Democrat. Avocations: swimming, music, skiing, gardening. Home: 1130 Sherman Ave Salt Lake City UT 84105 Office: U Utah Dept History Salt Lake City UT 84112

MAY, GERALD WILLIAM, university administrator, civil engineering consultant; b. Kenya, Jan. 2, 1941; s. William and Ruth (Koch) M.; m. Mary Joyce Pool, July 27, 1963; children: Erica Ruth, Christian William, Heidi Clara. B.S., Bradley U., 1962; M.S., U. Colo., 1964, Ph.D., 1967. Registered profl. engr., N.Mex. Civil engr. Ill. Hwy. Dept., Peoria, summer 1959-63; instr. U. Colo., Boulder, 1964-67; asst. prof. to prof. engring. U. N.Mex., Albuquerque, 1967-77; dean Coll. Engring., U. N.Mex., Albuquerque, 1980-86; pres. U. N.Mex., Albuquerque, 1986—; dir. accident study program, Albuquerque, 1970-75, cons. to corps., govtl. agys. Contbr. articles to profl. jours., chpts. to books. Recipient Borden Freshman award Bradley U., 1958. Mem. ASCE (pres. N.Mex. sect. 1982-83), Am. Soc. Engring. Edn. (Outstanding Young Faculty award 1973), Nat. Soc. Profl. Engrs., Sigma Xi, Chi Epsilon, Tau Beta Pi, Phi Eta Sigma. Office: Office of Pres U New Mex Albuquerque NM 87131

MAY, GRACE BUCKNER (MRS. MICHAEL HUGO MAY), civic worker; b. Los Angeles; d. Manfred R. and Jean Ann (Naftalin) Buckner; student UCLA, 1946-49; B.A., Los Angeles State Coll., 1955; m. Michael Hugo May, Dec. 23, 1948; children—Carolyn Estherlee, Michael Werner, Jonathan Gustav. Docent, Los Angeles County Mus. Natural History; mem. art council UCLA; tour guide George C. Page Mus. Bd. dirs. Helping Hand, Los Angeles. Home: 4917 San Feliciano Dr Woodland Hills CA 91364

MAY, JERRY RUSSELL, psycholotgist; b. Seattle, Apr. 24, 1942; s. Harold Russell May and Anne Margret (Jones) DeGolier; m. Carolyn Marlene May; children: Darin, Christopher, Laurel. Student, Sorbonne U., Paris, 1961-62; BA, Western Wash. U., 1966; PhD, Bowling Green State U., 1974. Prof. psychiatry sch. medicine U. Nev., Reno, 1974—, dean admissions sch. medicine, 1977—; cons. VA Med. Ctr., Reno, 1974—, U.S. Olympic Sports Medicine Program, Colorado Springs, Colo., 1977—; pvt. practice clin. psychology, Reno, 1977—; team psychologist U.S. Ski Team, Park City, Utah, 1977—; chmn. U.S. Olympic Psychology Com., Colorado Springs, 1985—; mem. U.S. Olympic Sports Medicine Council, Colorado Springs, 1985—. Author/editor: Sports Psychology: The Psychological Health of the Athlete, 1986; contbr. articles to profl. jours., chpts. to books. Pres. West Coast Group on Student Affairs, 1981-82. Served to lt. USN, 1968-71. Mem. No. Nev. Assn. Cert. Psychologists (pres. 1979-82), Am. Psychol. Assn., Western Psychol. Assn., Am. Assn. Med. Colls., Nev. Psychol. Assn. Home: PO Box 2661 Truckee CA 95734 Office: U Nev Sch Medicine Reno NV 89557

MAY, MICHAEL WAYNE, broadcast school executive; b. Springhill, La., Mar. 31, 1949; s. Willie Wilmer and Ethel Florene (Sigler) M.; student So. Ark. U., 1968-70, La. Tech. U., 1970-71. Prodn. dir. Sta. KKAM, Pueblo, Colo., 1973-75; quality control dir. Sta. KBOZ, Bozeman, Mont., 1975-78; music dir., dir. research, disk jockey Sta. KOOK, Billings, Mont., 1978-80; founder, operator May Sch. Broadcasting, Billings, 1980—. Mem. Nat. Assn. Trade and Tech. Schs. (Key mem. for Mont.). Author: Building with the Basics: Radio Personality Development, 1979. Home: 80 Skyline Dr Billings MT 59105 Office: PO Box 127 Billings MT 59103

MAY, RONALD VARNELLE, county official, historic archaeologist; b. Salt Lake City, Oct., 26, 1946; s. Russell Varnelle and Dorothy (Jensen) M.; m. Dale Ellen Ballou, May 8, 1983. A.A., Mesa Coll., 1967; B.A., San Diego State U., 1970; postgrad., 1972-75, 85—. Dist. liason archaeologist Calif. Div. Hwys. San Diego County, 1970-73; supervisory archaeologist San Diego State U. Found., San Diego County, 1971, 73; archeol. cons. pvt. contractor, Calif., 1971—; sr. archaeologist David D. Smith & Assocs., So. Calif., 1972-74; anthropology instr. Mesa Coll., San Diego, 1976-77; environ. mgmt. specialist II County San Diego, 1974—. Contbr. articles on Spanish fortifications, shore-whaling and Calif. Indian pottery to acad. and history jours.; editor Fort Guijarros Quar.; chmn. bd. dirs. Fort Guijarros Mus. Found., San Diego, 1981—; mem. staff County Hist. Site Bd., 1986—. Recipient Award of Merit Inst. History, 1982; San Diego Community Found. conservation grant, 1983, Cabrillo award for Maritime History Inst. of History, 1985, Community Service award Peninsula C. of C., 1987, Mark Raymond Harrington award for Conservation Archaeology, 1987. Mem. E Clampus Vitus (Clamper of Yr. 1985), Soc. Am. Archaeology, Soc. Profl. Archaeologists; Assn. Conservation Archaeology, Soc. Hist. Archaeology, San Diego County Archeol. Soc. (pres. 1980-82), Soc. Calif. Archaeology (v.p., ethics chmn., editor 1977-82; Spl. Achievement award 1983), Archeol. Resource Mgmt. Soc. (treas., fund raising chmn. 1980-82), Nature Conservancy, Greenpeace, San Diego Maritime Soc., Sigma Xi. Republican. Clubs: San Diego State U. Anthro. Soc. (pres. 1969, 72), Council on Am. Mil. Past. Office: Planning Dept County San Diego 5201 Ruffin Rd Suite 5B San Diego CA 92123

MAY, WANDA LOU, real estate corporation officer, small business owner; b. Pierce, Okla., Mar. 16, 1934; d. Edd and Inez Beasley (Wheeler) B.; m. Carl Ben May, July 7, 1951; children: Gary Lynn, Cheryl Ann Stephan. Grad. high sch., Okla. Credified residential broker and cert. real estate broker, Ariz. Cashier Phoenix Title, 1955-60; sales assoc. J. French, Sun City, Ariz., 1969-73, John D. Noble, Sun City, 1973-77; prin., broker May & Assocs., Glendale, Ariz., 1977—. Bd. dirs. West Valley YMCA, Phoenix, 1974-78, Downtown Glendale Devel. Corp., 1984-85. Mem. Women's Council Realtors (gov. Glendale chpt. 1981-82, pres. Ariz. chpt. 1980, Omega award 1982), Glendale Bd. Realtors (pres. 1981), Ariz. State Realtors Assn., Nat. Assn. Realtors (gov. 1981-82), Women's Council Realtors, Realtors Nat. Mktg. Inst., West Phoenix C. of C. (bd. dirs.), Omega Tau Rho. Republican. Baptist. Lodge: Soroptimist (pres. Glendale chpt. 1985-86). Avocation: travel. Home: 5545 N 83 Ave Glendale AZ 85303 Office: May & Assocs 5534 W Palmaire Glendale AZ 85301

MAYALL, BRIAN HOLDEN, science laboratory administrator, educator; b. Nelson, Lancashire, Eng., Nov. 14, 1932; Came to U.S., 1962; m. Susan M. Hayter, 1955; children: 3 daus., 1 son. BA, U. Cambridge, Eng., 1954, MA, 1958; MD, U. Western Ont., London, Can., 1961. Sr. staff scientist Lawrence Livermore (Calif.) Nat. Lab., 1972—; dir. program analytical cytology U. Calif., San Francisco, 1982—, prof. lab. medicine, 1982—. Served with RAF. Mem. Soc. Analytical Cytology (editor jour.), AAAS. Avocations: skiing, swimming, hiking. Office: Lawrence Livermore Nat Lab Dept Biomed Scis PO Box 5507 Livermore CA 94550

MAYALL, BROUN HUNT, news executive; b. Oklahoma City, Jan. 21, 1908; s. Roy Winfield and Loutilla (Hunt) M.; m. Geneva Ann Holmes, June 1, 1927; children—Donald H., Russell H.; m. Melba Maurine White, Apr. 15, 1945; children—Nancy Sue May, Elizabeth Ann Mayall Straka, Sally Lou Brasher. B.A., Central State U., 1927; M.Ed., Okla. U., 1935. Registrar, Southeastern State Coll., Durant, Okla., 1927-28; registrar, dir. pub. relations Okla. Coll. for Women, Chickasha, 1928-42; nat. dir. USAF Ground Observer Corps, Colorado Springs, Colo., 1953-57; command dir. info. Air Def. Command, Colorado Springs, 1957-61; v.p. mktg. Colorado Springs Nat. Bank, 1961-74; pres. Mayall Assocs., Colo. Springs, 1974—; dir. Miller High Life News Bur. Olympic Tng. Ctr., Colorado Springs, 1982—; cons. pub. relations Nat. Carvers Mus. Mem. devel. council Nat. Benevolent Assn.; bd. dirs. Colo. Christian Home, 1977-81; mem. Pikes Peak council Boy Scouts Am., Pikes Peak Council Chs.; mem. Colo. Commn. on Aging, 1977-84, chmn., 1979-81; mem. ofcl. bd. 1st Christian Ch. Served to col. USAF, 1942-61. Decorated Legion of Merit, Commendation medal with 2 oak leaf clusters. Mem. Pub. Relations Soc. Am., Phi Delta Kappa. Democrat. Mem. Disciples of Christ Ch. Clubs: Lions, Garden of the Gods, El Paso, Plaza (Colorado Springs). Author numerous articles on sr. citizens programs and aging. Home: 2403 Constellation Dr Colorado Springs CO 80906 Office: 1750 E Boulder St Colorado Springs CO 80909

MAYBEE, JOE THOMAS, software engineer; b. Tokyo, Nov. 22, 1954; s. Joe Thomas and Ruth Eloise (Lyons) M.; m. Valorie Kathleen Fisher, Sept. 2, 1977 (div. Nov. 1981). BS in Computer Sci., Wash. State U., 1978. Electronics engr. Tektronix, Wilsonville, Oreg., 1978-80; software engr. Tektronix, Wilsonville, Oreg., 1982—; systems analyst Wash. State U., Pullman, 1980-82. Mem. ACLU, Mensa. Buddhist. Lodge: Masons. Avocations: skiing, hiking. Home: 4735 SW Luradel Apt 52 Portland OR 97219 Office: Textronix PO Box 1000 Wilsonville OR 97070

MAYBERRY, FRANK DAVID, aerospace company executive; b. Pratt, Kans., Jan. 7, 1936; s. Clyde Theron Mabry and Mary Rosemond (Brehm) Mayberry Wells Reed; m. Eve Catherine Cholerton, July 9, 1960; children: Kari Kristin, Tristan David. BS, USAF Acad., 1960; MS, U. So. Miss., 1965. Commd. 2d lt. USAF, 1960, advanced through grades to lt. col., 1976, ret., 1980; staff engr. Martin-Marietta Corp., Waterton, Colo., 1980-82; systems engr. Hughes Aircraft Co., Englewood, Colo., 1982-85; sr. systems engr. TRW, Aurora, Colo., 1985—; sec., treas., bd. dirs. Am. Service Corp., Littleton, Colo., 1982—, also cons., real estate investor. Sec. Woodridge Homeowners' Assn., Littleton, 1981, v.p., 1982; pres. Wesley Community Ch. Council, Littleton, 1982, v.p., 1983. Decorated Bronze Star; Honor Medal first class (Republic of Vietnam); named World Class Runner Boston Marathon, 1979; 4th pl. Siebenthal (Republic of Germany) Marathon, 1974; 10th pl. Athens Marathon, 1977; 1st pl. Denver Gr. Beerathon, 1982. Republican. Avocations: genealogy, running. Home: 7924 S Marion Ct Littleton CO 80122

MAYEDA, CRAIG SHIGERU, farmers cooperative manager; b. Honolulu, Feb. 27, 1953; s. Jack Noboru and Helen Kazuko (Meguro) M.; m. Charmain Yim, June 21, 1980. B.S., U. Hawaii, 1975, M.S., 1978. Office supr., night auditor Ala Moana Hotel, Honolulu, 1971-79; night auditor Hyatt Regency Hotel, Honolulu, 1977-78; gen. mgr. Koolau Farmers Coop. Ltd., Kaneohe, Hawaii, 1979-85; sales mgr. Hiromi's Nursery, Waimaniaolo, Hawaii, 1985—; instr. Dale Carnegie Courses, Honolulu, 1986—; host garden program Sta. KHVH, Honolulu. Mem. Soil and Water Conservation Bd. S. Oahu County; chmn. community affairs Kaneohe Bus. Group, dir., 1983-85; pres., charter mem. Kaneohe Jaycees, 1983-84; dist. dir. Hawaii Jaycees, 1984-85, region dir., 1985-86, state pres., 1986-87. Home: 2825 S King St Apt 301 Honolulu HI 96826 Office: Hiromi's Nursery 41-782 Kakaina St Waimanalo HI 96795

MAYER, HERBERT CARLETON, JR., management information systems educator; b. Newton, Mass., Aug. 2, 1922; s. Herbert Carleton and Elsie Marie (Hauser) M.; m. Maryetta Brodkord, Aug. 21, 1948; children: Judith Marie, Christine Louise. BS, Parsons Coll., 1943; MS, U. Iowa, 1947; PhD, U. So. Calif., 1975. Instr. math. U. Idaho, Moscow, 1947-48, U. Utah, Salt Lake City, 1949-51; edn. adminstr. Gen. Electric co., Richland, Wash., 1951-59; systems engr., univ. industry specialist IBM, Chgo., 1959-81; assoc. prof. Wash. State U., Pullman, 1980-82, U. Wis.-Parkside, Kenosha, 1982-85, Eastern Wash. U., Cheney, 1985—; adj. prof. mgmt. U. Tex., El Paso, 1976-78. Pres. Tri-City Heights Assn., Kennewick, Wash., 1956-58, PTA, Kennewick, 1957-58; v.p. Kennewick Sch. Bd., 1958, pres., 1959. Mem. Math. Assn. Am., Assn. Ednl. Data Systems, Am. Soc. Engring. Edn., Data Processing Mgmt. Assn., Phi Delta Kappa. Home: S 3334 Bernard Spokane WA 99203 Office: Eastern Wash U 316 Kingston Hall Cheney WA 99004

MAYER, MELANIE JUEL, psychology educator; b. Hamilton, Ohio, Feb. 25, 1945; d. Edward J. and T. Jewel (Bond) M. BA in Chemistry, Cornell U., 1967; MA in Exptl. Psychology, U. Wis., 1968; PhD in Exptl. Psychology, U. Calif.-San Diego, La Jolla, 1973. Assoc. prof. psychology and psychobiology U. Calif., Santa Cruz., 1972—. Author: Demonstration of Sensory Perception, 1982; editor: Instructor's Guide to Psychology Today, 1970. Grantee NIH, Nat. Eye Inst.; recipient Research Career Devel. award, NIH Nat. Eye Inst., 1983—. Mem. AAAS, Am. Phys. Soc., Optical Soc. Am., Assn. Research in Vision and Ophthalmology. Home: 246 High St Santa Cruz CA 95060

MAYERS, LESLIE LEE, marketing executive; b. Los Angeles, Jan. 30, 1945; s. Louis Spencer and Helen Septima (Grossman) M.; m. Kathy Ann Kent, July 3, 1977; 1 child, Samantha Lee. BS, U. So. Calif., 1967. Acct. exec. trainee Doyle, Dane, Bernbach, Los Angeles, 1967-68; nat. sales mgr. Monogram Industries, Inc., Los Angeles, 1968-73; Western sales mgr. Meyers Mfg. Co., N.Y.C., 1976-81; pres. Les Mayers & Co., Los Angeles, 1975—; pres., chief exec. officer Gen. Merchandising Corp., Los Angeles, 1985—. Jewish. Avocations: photography, sailing, tennis, painting, sculpture.

MAYFIELD, DAVID MERKLEY, library administrator; b. Salt Lake City, Nov. 29, 1942; s. Orson Smith and Isabell (Merkley) M.; m. Judy Rae White, Dec. 17, 1965; children—Celeste, Melody, Michael, Paul, Nathan, Heather, Christopher, Benjamin. B.A. in German, U. Utah, 1967, M.A. in German, 1969; M.L.S., UCLA, 1971. Instr. Brigham Young U., Provo, Utah, 1971-72; mgr., dir. hist. dept., mem. and stats. records dept., info. systems dept. Ch. of Jesus Christ of Latter-day Saints, Salt Lake City, 1972-80; dir. genealogical library of Ch. of Jesus Christ of Latter-day Saints, Salt Lake City, 1980—. Contbr. articles to profl. jours. Fellow NDEA, 1967, HEW Title II, 1970. Mem. Internat. Fedn. Library Assns. and Insts. (voting del.), Nat. Geneal. Soc. (chmn. inst. services com. 1983-85), ALA, Nat. Soc. Sons of Utah Pioneers (v.p. 1982-83), Phi Beta Kappa. Republican. Mormon. Office: Genealogical Library 50 E N Temple Salt Lake City UT 84150

MAYNARD, HAL BRUCE, utility company executive, infosystems specialist; b. Dandridge, Tenn., June 1, 1926; s. Robert Bruce and Carrie Lee (Irwin) M.; m. Mary LaVerne Wolfe, Feb. 17, 1946; children: Diana, Laura, Karen. Student, Carson-Newman Coll., 1958-59; AA, U. Tenn., 1960; student, Troy State U., 1973-74. Office mgr. Appalachian Electric Co., Jefferson City, Tenn., 1950-66; asst. mgr. Co-Mo Electric Co., Tipton, Mo., 1967-70; office mgr. Cen. Ala. Electric Co., Prattville, 1970-80; mgr. office and staff Orcas Power and Light Co., Eastsound, Wash., 1980—; lectr. Digital Systems, Inc., Columbia, S.C., 1984, N.W. Pub. Power, Vancouver, Wash., 1985, Nat. Rural Electric Co., Washington, 1986. Author: (pamphlets) Info. Handbooks, 1962, 85. Mem. Inst. Indsl. Engrs. (sr. pres. 1966-67, 73-74, Award of Excellence 1967, 74, Outstanding Service award 1974), Soc. Advancement Mgmt. (v.p. Montgomery, Ala. chpt. 1976-79, historian Knoxville, Tenn. chpt., 1962), Jaycees (pres. Jefferson City chpt., 1959). Republican. Lutheran. Lodges: Lions (Lion Tamer Eastsound club 1985-86), Masons (sec. 1950-54). Avocations: antique collecting and restoration. Home: Rt 1 Box 123A Eastsound WA 98245 Office: Orcas Power and Light Co Mt Baker Rd PO Box 187 Eastsound WA 98245

MAYNARD, JOHN B., health care executive; b. Camp McCoy, Wis., Oct. 14, 1944; s. John B. and Fern (Barber) M.; m. A. Susan Perry, Aug. 23, 1981; stepchildren: Dana Perry, Seth Perry; 1 child, Christopher Maynard. BS in Chemistry, Colo. Coll., 1966; MA in Rehab. Counseling, U. No. Colo., 1974; PhD in Counseling, U. Colo., 1983. Rehab psychologist Boulder (Colo.) Mental Health Ctr., 1974-77; pres. Employee Assistance Programs, Inc., Boulder, 1977-86; dir. behavioral health AMI Rocky Mountain Healthcare System, Denver, 1986—; dir. EAP, Inc., Boulder, 1977—; cons. in field. Trustee CFPWD Found., Boulder, 1985—. Served to 1st lt. U.S. Army, 1966-68. Grantee Colo. Health Dept. Mem. Am. Soc. Personnel Adminstrn., Assn. of Labor Mgmt. Adminstrs. and Cons. on Alcoholism, Boulder Area Personnel Assn. Avocations: photography, running. Home: 258 Spruce St Boulder CO 80302 Office: AMI Rocky Mountain Healthcare System 160 E 19th Ave Denver CO 80203

MAYNARD, NORMAN LEE, architect; b. Warwick, R.I., Apr. 17, 1958; s. Mozart Maynard and Bettye Louise (Adams) M.; m. Mary Jo Bates, Oct. 28, 1983. BS, Cath. U. Am., 1981. Architect Lawrence Livermore (Calif.) Lab., 1981-83, Spilsted & Assocs., San Francisco, 1983-86, Gensler & Assocs., San Francisco, 1986—. Mem. Nat. Trust for Historic Preservation, Mus. Modern Art, Tau Beta Pi. Office: Gensler & Assocs 550 Kearny St San Francisco CA 94104

MAYNARD, ROBERT CLYVE, journalist; b. Bklyn., June 17, 1937; s. Samuel Christopher and Robertine Isola (Greaves) M.; m. Nancy Hicks, Jan. 1, 1975; children: Dori J., David H., Alex Caldwell. Student (Nieman fellow), Harvard U., 1966; D.H.L. (hon.), York Coll., 1984; D.F.A. (hon.), Calif. Coll. Arts and Crafts, 1985. Reporter Afro-Am. News, Balt., 1956; reporter York (Pa.) Gazette and Daily, 1961-67; reporter Washington Post, 1967-72, assoc. editor/ombudsman, 1972-74, editorial writer, 1974-77; editor, pub. Oakland (Calif.) Tribune, 1979—, owner, 1983—; former chmn. Inst. Journalism Edn.; Syndicated columnist Universal Press Syndicate; dir. AP; mem. Pulitzer Prize Bd. bd. dirs. Ctr. Law and Politics Marcus Foster Ednl. Inst., Bay Area Council, Pulitzer Prize Bd.; nat. bd. govs. Media and Society Seminars.; trustee Rockefeller Found., Pacific Sch. Religion, Found. Am. Communications. Mem. Am. Newspaper Pubs. Assn. (govt. affairs com.), Am. Press Inst. (Western region adv. bd.), Newspaper Advt. Bur. (bd. dirs.), Council on Fgn. Relations., U.S. Supreme Ct. Hist. Soc., Sigma Delta Chi. Club: Commonwealth (bd. govs.). Office: The Tribune Tower Oakland CA 94612

MAYO, FRANK JOSEPH, charitable organization administrator; b. Tacoma, Wash., Dec. 26, 1925; s. Willis and Arvilla Marchetta (Anderson) M.; diploma Simpson Coll., 1949; postgrad. UCLA, 1965, Kennedy Sinclaire Estate Planning Sch., 1966, 72, 78; m. Ruth Rustad, July 18, 1947 (div. Sept. 1983); children—Karen Ruth, Sharon Darlene, Rebekah Kay, Deborah Jean; m. 2d Virginia Faith Cole Bubna, Jan. 13, 1984; stepchildren—Kurt, Kevin, Kraig, Kimberly. Ordained to ministry Christian and Missionary Alliance, 1951; pastor chs., Wolf Creek, Oreg., Boise, Idaho, Ellensberg, Wash., Dallas, Oreg., Sherman Oaks, Calif.; field rep. planned gifts Christian and Missionary Alliance, Western U.S. area, 1966-72; v.p. planned giving Le Tourneau Coll. Fund, Longview, Tex., 1972-76; planned gifts cons. Western ter. Salvation Army, Rancho Palos Verdes, Calif., 1976-84; v.p. St. Joseph Med. Center Found., Burbank, Calif., 1984—; pres. Frank Mayo and Co., planned giving consultants, 1980—; pres. So. Calif. Planned Giving Roundtable, 1984-87. Bd. dirs. Simpson Coll. Found., 1974-79; trustee Simpson Coll., San Francisco, 1963-79. Served with USAF, 1944-46. Mem. Nat. Assn. for Hosp. Devel. (legis. chmn. region 10). Home: 9714 Cabanas Ave Tujunga CA 91042 Office: Buena Vista and Alameda Sts Burbank CA 91505

MAYO, SAMUEL H., history educator, academic administrator; b. Los Angeles, Mar. 31, 1932; s. Isaac and Hanna (Torf) M.; m. Sandra Louise Lytle, July 14, 1967 (div. May 1977); children: Robert Francis, Jennifer Elise; m. Leslee Louise Lockhart, May 29, 1977. AA, Los Angeles City Coll.; BA, MA, Calif. State U., Los Angeles; postgrad., Calif. State U., U. Mex., Mexico City, 1961, Inst. Mex. and Am. Cultural Relations, Mexico City, 1962; postgrad. in philosophy, UCLA, 1972. Treas. House of Props., Los Angeles, 1956-58; tchr. Van Nuys (Calif.) High Sch., 1958-65; assoc. prof. history UCLA, 1966-67; prof. history Los Angeles Valley Coll., Van Nuys, 1965—, dir. sch. relations, 1985—, asst. dean of admissions and records, 1987—; pres., owner Amerind Press, 1977—. Author: History of Mexico, 1970, History of Mexico Study Guide, 1979; author/narrator TV series History of Mexico, 1977 (awards Los Angeles City Council, Los Angeles Bd. Suprs., Calif. State Assembly, Calif. State Senate, Hubert Herring Meml. award), El Espejo, 1981. Served with U.S. Army, 1954-56. Mem. Latin Am. Historians Assn. (bd. dirs. Pacific Coast Conf. on Latin Am. Studies), Calif. Hist. Soc., Ephebian Honor Soc. (pres. 1963-74), Toy Train Operating Soc. Democrat. Avocations: collecting and repairing toy trains, antique clocks and gramophones, skiing. Office: Los Angeles Valley Coll 5800 Fulton Ave Los Angles CA 91401

MAYOL, RICHARD THOMAS, advertising executive, political consultant; b. Springfield, Ill., Oct. 30, 1949; s. Richard McFaren and Marjorie (Maddox) M. AA, Springfield Coll., 1969; BS, U. Tulsa, 1972. Co-owner First Tuesday Inc., Phoenix, 1976-85; pres. The Victory Group Inc., Phoenix, 1985—; cons. Dem. candidates, Western U.S., 1976—, Mo Udall for Congress, Tucson, 1982—, Mayor Terry Goddard, Phoenix, Senator John Melcher, Mont. Mem. Phoenix Film Commn., 1985—. Mem. Am. Assn. Polit. Cons. Avocations: photography, writing, horseback riding. Home: 2329 N 57th Pl Scottsdale AZ 85257-1907 Office: The Victory Group Great Am Tower 3200 N Central #1530 Phoenix AZ 85012

MAYOR, ROBERTA ADRIAN, educational administrator; b. Honolulu, June 13, 1944; d. Robert David and Alice (Park) Phillips; m. Richard Lee Mayor, Dec. 17, 1965; children—Regina Helene, Robert William. B.A. in English, U. Hawaii, 1966, M. in Ednl. Adminstrn., 1981. Cert. tchr., sch. adminstr., Hawaii. Tchr. English, Waipahu (Hawaii) High Sch., 1966-78, dept. chmn., 1972-75; vice-prin. Kahuku (Hawaii) High Sch., Elem. Sch., 1977, Pearl City (Hawaii) High Sch., 1978-80; prin. Waianae (Hawaii) Intermediate Sch., 1980, Waipahu (Hawaii) Intermediate Sch., 1980-82, Waianae (Hawaii) High Sch., 1982-85; dep. dist. supt. Honolulu Dist. Schs., 1985—; mem. Supt.'s Task Force on Intermediate Sch., Learning Ctrs.; mem. Leeward Dist. Civil Rights Complaint Bd. Vice-pres., Pearl City Community Assn.; mem. Waianae Mil.-Civilian Adv. Council. NEH fellow, 1981. Mem. Nat. Assn. Secondary Sch. Prins., Hawaii Assn. Secondary Sch. Prins., Assn. Supervision and Curriculum Devel.

MAYRAND, LIONEL EDMOND, JR., accountant, consultant; b. Dover, N.H., Dec. 27, 1942; s. Lionel Edmond Sr. and Eileen V. (Kelley) M.; m. Barbara J. Douglas, Mar. 7, 1975 (div. Oct. 1979); children: Cynthia L., Jennifer L. Grad., Burdett Coll., 1962; student, U. N.H., 1963-68. Pvt. practice acctg. Dover, 1963-65; dep. dir. Strafford Community Action Program, Dover, 1965-67; dir. Operation Mainstream, York County Community Action Program, Biddeford, Maine, 1967-69; dir. Headstart, York County Community Action Program, Waterbro, Maine, 1969-70; chief fin. officer York County Community Action Program, Alfred, Maine, 1970-73; pvt. practice acct., cons. Rochester, N.H., 1973-74; mgmt. acctg. specialist New Eng. Gerontology Ctr., Durham, N.H., 1974-79, staff assoc., 1977-79; assoc. dir. New Eng. Gerontology Ctr. and New Eng. Ctr. for Continuing Edn., Durham, 1979-81; chief program ops. Adminstrn. Aging Region IX, HHS, 1981; officer fiscal operation HHS OHDS RIX, 1982-84; acct. Comprehensive Bus. Service, San Francisco, 1984—. Author various gvt. reference books. Mem. adv. bd. Comprehensive Acctg. Corp.; mem. Nat. Awareness Fund. Named one of Outstanding Young Men Am., U.S. Jaycees, 1974; recipient Adv. for Elders award Miss. Council Aging, 1981, Outstanding Service award HHS, 1985. Democrat. Roman Catholic. Lodge: Lions. Avocations: stamp collecting. Home: 1911 Eddy St #3 San Francisco CA 94115 Office: Comprehensive Bus Service 1320 Divisidero St San Francisco CA 94115

MAYRSOHN, WILLIAM, metals acquisitions consultant, geologist; b. N.Y.C., June 29, 1931; s. Charles M., M. Natalie Ruth Engerman, Feb. 6, 1953; children—Cheryl L., Valerie A. M.A., Kans. U., 1957; M.B.A., NYU, 1971. Geologist, Skelly Oil Co., Wichita, Bismarck, 1957-63; Belco Petroleum Co., N.Y.C., 1963-66; fin. analyst. Conoco Oil Co., N.Y.C., 1966-67, sr. fin. analyst Kennecott Copper, N.Y., 1967-74; treas. Rosario Resources, N.Y.C., 1974-77, v.p. materials, 1977-80; mgr. mktg. Minerals Div., v.p. mktg. Copper Range Div., La. Land & Exploration Co., Lakewood, Colo., 1980-84; precious metals acquisitions cons., 1984-85; cons. in field; mgr. metals and concentrate mktg. Asamera Minerals (U.S.), Inc., Denver, 1986—. Mem. Am. Assn. Petroleum Geologists, AIME, Colo. Mining Assn. Home: 9241 W Hialeah Pl Littleton CO 80123

MAYS, CHARLES WILLIAM, radiation physicist; b. Corsicana, Tex., Feb. 17, 1930; s. Charles William and Fay (Lockhart) M.; m. Evelyn Ekker, June 21, 1951 (div. Jan. 1969); children: Shelby Marie Box, Sharon Eve McGough, Susan Fay Kinsel; m. Desiree McMahon, Oct. 18, 1972; children: David Charles, Rory Michael. Student, U. Mo., 1947-48; BS in Physics, U. Utah, 1951, PhD in Physics, 1958. Asst. research prof. anatomy U. Utah, Salt Lake City, 1962-66, assoc. research prof., 1966-75, research prof., 1975-82, adj. prof. physics, 1975-83, research prof. pharmacology, 1979-86, research prof. Sch. of Medicine, 1986—; cons. GAO, Washington, 1978-81, EPA, Washington, 1982—; chmn. adv. com. U.S. Transuranium, Richland, Wash., 1978-83. Editor-in-chief: Delayed Effects of Bone-Seeking Radionuclides, 1969; co-editor: Some Aspects of Internal Radiation, 1962; editor: Biological Effects of Ra-224 and Thorotrast, 1978; inventor improved radiation detector. Dep. radiation def. officer Utah Civil Def., 1957-65; mem. Utahns United Against the Nuclear Arms Race, 1982—. Served to 1st lt. U.S. Army, 1951-54, Korea. Decorated Bronze Star; recipient Disting. Teaching award U. Utah, 1977. Mem. U.S. Nat. Council on Radiation Protection, Health Physics Soc. (cert. health physicist), Radiation Research Soc., AAAS. Avocations: long distance running, skiing, arrowhead chipping, swimming, hiking. Home: 2410 Emerson Ave Salt Lake City UT 84108 Office: U Utah Radiobiolgy Div Bldg 351 Salt Lake City UT 84112

MAZELIS, MENDEL, plant biochemist, educator, researcher; b. Chgo., Aug. 31, 1922; s. Jacob and Anna (Brvarnick) M.; m. Noreen Beimer, Mar. 24, 1969; 1 son, Jacob Russell. B.S., U. Calif.-Berkeley, 1943, Ph.D., 1954. Jr. research biochemist U. Calif.-Berkeley, 1954-55; research assoc., instr. U. Chgo., 1955-57; assoc. chemist Western Regional Research Lab., Albany, Calif., 1957-61; asst. prof. U. Calif.-Davis, 1961-64, assoc. prof., 1964-73, prof., 1973—. Served to lt. (j.g.) USN, 1943-46. Mem. Am. Soc. Plant Physiologists, Am. Soc. Biol. Chemists, Biochem. Soc. London, Phytochem. Soc. N.Am., Phytochem. Soc. Europe, Inst. Food Technologists. Office: U Calif Dept Food Sci/Tech 1480 Chemistry Annex Davis CA 95616

MAZENKO, DONALD MICHAEL, spacecraft materials engineer, consultant; b. Benld, Ill., July 11, 1925; s. Mike George and Anna Agnes (Kozak) M.; m. Joyce Christine Patrick, Apr. 22, 1950; children: Donna Nijmeh, Joyce Ann, Martha Jane. Student, Mont. Sch. Mineral Sci. and Tech., 1944, U. Wash., 1945-46; BSME, U. Ill., 1949; MBA, U. Santa Clara, 1965. Tech. supt. Reynolds Metals Co., Listerhill, Ala., 1949-62; sr. staff engr. Lockheed Missles and Space Co., Sunnyvale, Calif., 1962—; cons. Saratoga, Calif., 1976—; instr. De Anza Community Coll., Cupertino, Calif. 1973—. Contbr. articles to profl. jours. Served to lt. USNR, 1947-67, PTO. Fellow Soc. Adv. Material and Process Engring. (various offices); mem. Soc. Automotive Engrs., Aero. Material Specifications. Republican. Roman Catholic. Club: Ascension Men's (Saratoga, Calif.). Lodge: KC (dep. grand knight 1958-62). Avocations: bowling, golf, fishing, swimming, tennis. Home: 19361 Bellwood Dr Saratoga CA 95070 Office: Lockheed Missles and Space Co Inc 1111 Lockheed Way Sunnyvale CA 94088

MAZIA, JUDITH ANN, lawyer; b. Boise, Nov. 21, 1943; d. Daniel and Gertrude Mazia. B.A., U. Calif.-Berkeley, 1966; postgrad. in urban planning Columbia U. and Hunter Coll., 1966-67; J.D., Hastings Coll. Law, 1974. Bar Calif. 1974, U.S. Dist. Ct. (no. dist.) Calif. 1974, U.S. Ct. Appeals (9th cir.) 1981. Law clk. Office of Zaide Kirtley, San Francisco, 1972-74; ptnr. firm Kirtley, Levinson & Mazia, San Francisco, 1975-77; sole practice, San Francisco, 1977—. Bd. dirs., pres. North of Market Child Devel. Ctr. (formerly Hastings Child Care Ctr.), San Francisco, 1982—. Recipient Commendation San Francisco Bd. Supervisors, 1984; Rosentiel Found. fellow, 1966-67. Mem. Phi Beta Kappa. Office: 1188 Franklin St Suite 201 San Francisco CA 94109-6839 Home: 5316 Golden Gate Ave Oakland CA 94618

MAZINGO, SHERRIE LEE, writer, educator; b. Spokane, Wash., Apr. 8, 1947; d. Anthony Von and Erma Louise (Brown) M. BA, Howard U., 1965; postgrad., U. Minn., 1968-69; MS, Syracuse U., 1971; PhD, Mich. State U., 1975. Reporter The Mpls. Star and Tribune, 1965-72; writer, producer NBC TV Network News, N.Y.C., 1976-77; producer NBC TV Network News, Atlanta, 1977-83; prof. journalism U. So. Calif., Los Angeles, 1983—; nat. media cons., 1978—; cons. U.S. Office Edn., Washington, 1972-75, U.S. Info. Agy., Washington, 1973-74, The Mott Inst., Grand Rapids, Mich., 1974-75, Western Newspaper Pub., Sacramento, 1985—. Assoc. editor International Communication Yearbook, 1985; mem. editorial bd. Jour. Mass Media Ethics, 1985—; contbr. articles to profl. pubs. Recipient Disting. Reporting award The Am. Pol. Sci. Assn., 1972; named one of Outstanding Young Women in Am., 1983; research grantee Nat. Assn. Broadcasters, 1975, The Ford Found., 1975; Wash. Journalism Ctr. fellow, 1970. Mem. Assn. Edn. in Journalism, Nat. Assn. Black Journalists (cons.), Syracuse Alumni Assn. So. Calif. (v.p. 1984—), Ebonics Support Group U. So. Calif. (bd. dirs. 1985—). Baptist. Home: 5925 Canterbury Dr Los Angeles CA 90230 Office: U So Calif Los Angeles CA 90089-1695

MAZO, ROBERT MARC, chemistry educator; b. Bklyn., Oct. 3, 1930; s. Nathan and Rose Marion (Mazo) M.; m. Joan Ruth Spector, Sept. 5, 1954; children: Ruth, Jeffrey, Daniel. B.A., Harvard U., 1952; M.S., Yale U., 1953, Ph.D., 1955. Research assoc. U. Chgo., 1956-58; asst. prof. Calif. Inst. Tech., 1958-62; assoc. prof. U. Oreg., Eugene, 1962-65; prof. chemistry U. Oreg., 1965—, head chemistry dept., 1978-81, dir. Inst. Theoretical Sci., 1964-67, 84—, assoc. dean Grad. Sch., 1967-71; program dir NSF, 1977-78; Alfred P. Sloan fellow, NSF Sr. Postdoctoral fellow, vis. prof. U. Libre de Bruxelles, Belgium, 1968-69; vis. prof. Technische Hochschule Aachen, Weizmann Inst., Rehovoth, Israel, 1981-82. Author: Statistical Mechanical Theories of Transport Processes, 1967; also research articles. NSF Postdoctoral fellow U. Amsterdam, Netherlands, 1955-56. Mem. Am. Chem. Soc., Am. Phys. Soc., AAAS, AAUP. Home: 2460 Charnelton St Eugene OR 97405 Office: U Oreg Inst Theoretical Sci Eugene OR 97403

MAZUMDER, AMITABHA, physician, researcher; b. Calcutta, India, Oct. 28, 1952; s. Bibhuti and Nilima (Deb Chcudhury) M.; m. Shibani Ray, June 29, 1979; 1 child, Nikhilesh. BA, Johns Hopkins U., 1973, MD, 1977. Internship and residency Baylor Coll. of Med., Houston, 1977-79; asst. prof. Baylor Coll. Med., Houston, 1983-85; clin. assoc. Nat. Cancer Inst., Bethesda, Md., 1979-82, investigator, 1982-83; asst. prof. M.D. Anderson Hosp., Houston, 1983-85; asst. prof. U. So. Calif. Med. Sch., Los Angeles, 1985—, dir. bone marrow transplantation unit, dept. hematology, 1985—, mem. med. student research com., 1985—, assoc. prof., 1987—. Contbr. articles to profl. jours., chpts. to books. V.p. Med. Student Govt., Balt., 1977; pres. Youth Forum, Balt., 1976. Served to capt. USPHS, 1979-83. Mem. AAAS, ACP, Am. Assn. Immunologists, Am. Assn. Cancer Research, Am. Soc. Clin. Oncology, Indian Orgns. (Houston chpt. sec. 1979, Balt. sec. 1980-81), Phi Beta Kappa, Alpha Omega Alpha. Democrat. Hindu. Avocations: musician, traveling. Home: 1950 E Mountain Pasadena CA 91104 Office: Norris Cancer Ctr Room 162 1441 E Lake Ave Los Angeles CA 90033-0804

MAZUR, MARGIE ELLA HANDLEY MEREDITH, reading educator; b. Tulsa, Mar. 27, 1941; d. Joyce Samuel and MaryPaul (Ellsworth) Handley; m. Don Leroy Mazur, Aug. 31, 1962 (div. Nov. 1974); children: Susan Diane, Michael. B.A. in Art, U. Tulsa, 1962, M.Teaching Arts in Spl. Edn., 1967; postgrad. Calif. State U.-Los Angeles, UCLA, Purdue U.-Calumet, Ind., San Jose State U. Accredited tchr., reading specialist, adminstr., Calif. Classroom tchr. Tulsa Pub. Schs., 1963-65; fellow, clinician, diagnostician, instr. Mabee Reading Clinic, U. Tulsa, 1965-67; instr. So. Meth. U. Reading Clinic, Dallas, fall 1969; classroom tchr. Los Angeles Unified Sch. Dist., 1975-76; reading specialist Sierramont Middle Sch., Berryessa Union Sch. Dist., San Jose, Calif., 1976—; pvt. tutor, San Jose, 1976—; owner, operator Eastside Learning Ctr. and Reading Clinic, San Jose, 1978-82. Cons., activist in women's and children's rights in child-support enforcement; chmn. child-support enforcement task force San Jose-South Bay chpt. NOW, 1984-85. Entrance Exam. scholar U. Tulsa, 1959, John Mabee grad. fellow, 1966. Mem. Santa Clara County Reading Council, Calif. Reading Assn., Internat. Reading Assn., Women Leaders in Edn., Lantern Hon. Soc., Scroll Hon. Soc., Mortar Bd., Alpha Delta Kappa, Kappa Alpha Theta (chpt. pres. 1961-62). Mem. Bahái Faith, San Jose Community. Avocations: ballroom dancing; skiing; sailing; reading; sewing. Home: PO Box 32744 San Jose CA 95152 Office: Sierramont Middle Sch 3155 Kimlee Dr San Jose CA 95132

MAZUROWSKI, PAUL RICHARD, distributing company executive; b. Buffalo, Jan. 13, 1952; s. Richard Edward and Marcia Telka (Gusch) M. BS in Gen. Studies, USAF Acad., 1973. Commd. 2d lt. USAF, 1975, advanced through grades to capt., resigned, 1979; v.p. Meyer Distbg. Co., 1980—. organist, choir dir. Cath. Choir, Norton AFB, 1975-82, St. Anthony's Ch., Upland, Calif., 1983—. Mem. Nat. Orgn. Pastoral Musicians. Democrat. Roman Catholic. Avocations: flying, music. Office: Meyer Distbg Co Inc 305 N Central PO Box 1150 Upland CA 91763

MAZZA, ROBERT BRADLEY, public relations executive; b. San Luis Obispo, Calif., Mar. 23, 1948; s. Alfred and Ester Ellen (Haden) M. B.A. in Journ., Pepperdine U., 1971. Asst. press sec. to county supr. Los Angeles County, 1972-74; publicity dir. San Antonio Spurs, Am. Basketball Assn., 1974; with publicity dept. MGM-TV Studios, Los Angeles, 1976-80; owner-ptnr. Cottman/Mazza Pub. Relations, Los Angeles, 1980-84; owner Mazza Mktg. & Pub. Relations, 1984—; lectr. UCLA Extension, Pepperdine U. Active in publicity Los Angeles Free Clinic. Mem. Am. Mktg. Assn. (publicity chmn. chpt.), Los Angeles Advt. Club, Acad. TV Arts and Scis., So. Calif. Book Publicists. Office: Mazza Mkgt Pub Relations 1900 S Sepulveda 3rd Floor Los Angeles CA 90025

MAZZEI, SANDO ERNEST, school administrator; b. Tacoma, Wash., Apr. 21, 1926; s. Peter and Clara M.; m. Jean Margaret Williams, Aug. 1, 1962. B.A., U. Puget Sound, 1952, B.E., 1954, M.E., 1958; postgrad. Ohio State U., Seattle U. Tchr., 1952-58; asst. prin. Jason Lee Jr. High Sch., 1958-62; asst. prin. Stadium High Sch., 1962-65; adminstr. secondary edn., Tacoma Pub. Schs., 1965-80, dir. grants mgmt., 1980-82; cons. adminstrv. services, Tacoma, 1982—. Served with USNR, 1944-46. John Hay fellow, 1963. Mem. Wash. Edn. Assn., NEA, Phi Delta Kappa. Clubs: Kiwanis, Lakewood Racquet, Elks, Oakbrook Golf and Country. Home: 7414 Onyx Dr SW Tacoma WA 98498

MCALLISTER, JAMES ADDAMS, electrical, computer and ocean engineering educator, retired naval officer, archaeology photographer; b. Covington, Va., Dec. 16, 1915; s. Hugh Maffit and Evaline (Long) McA.; m. Bernice Jacklyn Lyons, June 26, 1942; children—Bruce Hugh, John Milton. B.S. in Engring., U.S. Naval Acad., 1939; M.S. in Physics, UCLA, 1949. Commd. ensign U.S. Navy, 1939, advanced through grades to capt., 1958; officer of the deck USS Md., Pearl Harbor, 1941; rep. U.S. Navy Electronic Labs., Am. Mgmt. Assn. Conf., N.Y., 1958; asst. dir. Ship Electronic div. Navy Dept., Washington, 1952-54; electronic and radiol. safety officer San Francisco Naval Shipyard, 1954-56; asst. dir. Navy Electronics Lab., San Diego, 1956-59; asst. dir. Supreme Allied Command Atlantic Antisubmarine Warfare Research Ctr., La Spezia, Italy, 1959-61; dir. underseas research and devel. Navy Dept., Washington, 1962; ret., 1962; asst. prof. physics Calif. Western U., San Diego, 1962-64; assoc. prof. elec., computer and ocean engring. Calif. State Poly. U., Pomona, 1964—, assoc. dean engring., 1967-69; crew photographer archeol. excavation crews, Cucamonga, Temecula, Calico, Calif., Korea, Italy, Turkey and other Asian, Middle East and European sites; lectr., cons. in field; protocol chmn. Internat. Starboat Races, San Diego, 1958; dir. ocean engring. and electronics engring. exhibits Los Angeles County Fair, 1977. Contbr. articles to profl. jours. Co-inventor Gunnery Star-Shell Computer WW II. Recipient Letter of Appreciation Calif. State Legis., 1958, Letter of Commendation, Am. Soc. Engring. Edn., 1971; Letter of Appreciation Lord Louis Mountbatten, First Sea Lord Great Britain, 1958. Mem. IEEE, Am. Soc. Engring. Edn., Acoustical Soc. Am., Am. Inst. Physics, U.S. Naval Acad. Alumni Assn., Ret. Officers Assn., Calif. Poly. U. Alumni Assn. (hon.), NEA, Calif. Tchrs. Assn., Calif. State Employees Assn., Archaeol. Survey Assn. Clubs: Long Beach Navy Yacht (Calif.); Naval Officers Yacht (La Spezia); San Diego Yacht. Office: Calif State Poly Univ 3801 W Temple Ave Pomona CA 91768

MCALLISTER, JUDITH ELAINE, clinical social worker; b. Flagstaff, Ariz., July 17, 1936; d. Ray Waldo and Eleanor Mahon (Hughes) Ragsdale; m. Merle Douglas Lehman, Aug. 26, 1956 (div. Apr. 1974); children: Debra Feather Morning, Rebecca Jean Migdal, Christina Lynn Lehman, Liesl Lee Jacobson; m. Mark Thomas McAllister, Aug. 12, 1981; 1 child, Joshua Michael David. BA, DePauw U., 1958; MSW, San Diego State U., 1980. Drug counselor Substance Abuse Control Services, Riverside, Calif., 1973-78; counseling intern U. Calif. Psychol. Services, San Diego, 1978-79; counselor, coordinator Conquest Ctr., Edmonds, Wash., 1981; social worker HEW, Jerome, Idaho, 1982; social work cons. HEW, Twin Falls, Idaho, 1982-85; pvt. practice psychotherapy The Relationship Place, Twin Falls, 1984—; group leader singles club dir. Riverside Growth Ctr., 1974-75; group therapist Sexual Abuse Treatment Group, Twin Falls, 1985-86. Dir. children's social services YWCA, Greencastle, Ind., 1957-58; chmn. Set the Date com. to End Vietnam War, Riverside, 1968; dist. trainer bd. edn. Meth. Ch., Riverside, 1969-70, ch. sch. supt., Riverside, Los Angeles, 1966-72; fund-raising chmn. Vols. Against Violence, Twin Falls, 1986. Recipient Service award Rubidoux, Calif. Rotary, 1976; PEO Continuing Edn. Fund grantee, 1978. Mem. Nat. Assn. Social Workers. Democrat. Avocations: fishing, hiking, camping, backpacking, gardening. Home: 615 Fillmore St Twin Falls ID 83301 Office: The Relationship Place 404 7th Ave N Twin Falls ID 83301

MCALLISTER, WILLIAM JOSEPH, JR., physician; b. Ft. Riley, Kans., Sept. 21, 1940; s. William Joseph and Oga (Somer) M.; m. Janet Louise Smith, Mar. 21, 1975. B.S. in Chemistry, U. Fla., 1962, M.D., 1966. Resident in internal medicine U. Colo., Denver, 1967-70; practice medicine specializing in internal medicine, San Rafael, Calif., 1972—. Mem. Republican Central Com., 1984—. Served as maj. M.C., USAF, 1970-72. Mem. ACP, AMA, Marin County Med. Assn., Calif. Med. Assn., Am. Coll. Geriatrics. Roman Catholic. Office: Marin Medical Group Inc 11 Professional Center Parkway San Rafael CA 94903

MCALPINE, STEPHEN, state official, lawyer; b. Yakima, Wash., May 23, 1949; s. Robert Eugene and Myrtle B. (Loomis) McA.; m. Dana Sue Hill, Jan. 15, 1982; 1 child, Sean Michael. B.A., U. Wash., 1972; J.D., U. Puget Sound, 1976. Bar: Alaska. With Alaska Dept. Health and Social Services, Valdez, 1972-73; contracts adminstr. Fluor Alaska, Valdez, 1974-75; assoc. Law Offices James Ginotti, Valdez, 1977-80; pres. Ginotti & McAlpine, Valdez, 1980-82; lt. gov. State of Alaska, Juneau, 1982—; mem. Alaska Resource Devel. Council, 1978—. Mem. Valdez City Council, 1979-82; mayor City of Valdez, 1980-82; bd. dirs. Alaska Mcpl. League, 1979-82. Served with USAR, 1968-71. Named Young Alaskan of Yr., Anchorage Jaycees, 1982. Mem. Alaska Bar Assn., ABA, Assn. Trial Lawyers Am., Valdez Fisheries Devel. Assn., Alaska Native Brotherhood, Am. Legion. Democrat. Roman Catholic. Lodges: Elks, Moose. Avocations: hunting; fishing; skiing; baseball; hiking. Office: Office of Lt Gov PO Box AA Juneau AK 99811

MCALPINE, TERRY LYNN, public information officer; b. Lynwood, Calif., Jan. 5, 1952; d. Max N. and Mary H. (Mozingo) McA.; m. Louis A. Palmer, June 26, 1982. B.A. in Journalism, Pepperdine U., 1974. Pub. info. officer Norwalk-La Mirada Unified Sch. Dist., Norwalk, Calif., 1975-84, ABC Unified Sch. Dist., Cerritos, Calif., 1984—. Mem. Nat. Sch. Pub. Relations Assn., Pub. Relations Soc. Am., ABC Adminstrs. Assn., So. Calif. Sch. Pub. Relations Assn. (past pres.). Home: 9602 Walthall Ave Whittier CA 90605 Office: ABC Unified School District 16700 S Norwalk Blvd Cerritos CA 90701

MC ANALLY, DON, editor-publisher; b. Sewell, N.J., Oct. 27, 1913; s. James C. and Ina (MacLeod) McA.; grad. high sch.; m. Edith P. McKinney, Dec. 11, 1934; 1 dau., Shirley M. English. Reporter, Woodbury (N.J.) Daily Times, 1932-45; editor Owens-Ill. Co. publs. in N.J. and Ohio, 1945-47; asst. advt. mgr. Libbey-Owens-Ford Glass Co., also Libbey-Owens-Ford Glass Fibers Co., Toledo, 1947-59; editor Pacific Oil Marketer, Los Angeles, 1960-66; editor-publisher O&A Marketing News, La Canada, Calif., 1966—, The Automotive Booster of Calif., 1974—, Calif. Sr. Citizen News, La Canada, 1977-84, CAlif. Businesswoman, 1978; Good Neighbor award Toledo, 1948; award Western Oil Industry, 1971; Man of Yr. award Pacific Oil Conf., 1977, Diamond Pin award Pacific Oil Conf., 1986; awards Douglas Oil Co., 1978, Automotive Affiliated Reps., 1979, So. Calif. Petroleum Industry Golf and Tennis Tournament, 1984, Intermountain Oil Marketers Assn., 1985. Mem. Calif. Ind. Oil Marketers Assn., Am. Petroleum Inst. (basin chpt.), Automotive Hall of Fame (v.p. So. Calif. chpt. 1984), OX5 Aviation Pioneers, Nat. Speakers Assn., Internat. Platform Assn., Petroleum Writers of Am. Clubs: Lions, Masquers, Gabby, Silver Dollar, Roorag (Los Angeles), Greater Los Angeles Press, Hollywood Press. Home: 4409 Indiana Ave La Canada CA 91011 Office: PO Box 765 La Canada CA 91011

MCANDREWS, JOHN FRANCIS, SR., fire department administrator; b. Three Forks, Mont., July 18, 1927; s. George Francis and Mary (Saffell) McA.; m. Beverly JoAnne True, June 27, 1947; children: Patricia, Barbara, Mary, John Jr., Sharon, Susan, Jeffery. Student in acctg., Kinman Bus. U., 1969. Credit mgr. Tire Co., Spokane, Wash., 1969-71; acctg. clk. Traffic Engring., Spokane, 1971-74, City of Spokane Cen. Garage, 1974-76; acct. I City of Spokane Acctg. Dept., 1976-78; acct. II City of Spokane Park Dept., 1978-79; adminstrv. asst. City of Spokane Fire Dept., 1979—; sec. Credit Union Bd., Spokane, 1985—. Served with USN, 1944-46. Mem. Nat. mgmt. Assn. (v.p. 1985), Fire Service Secs., Govtl. Fin. Officers, Wash. Fin. Officers, Am. Legion. Avocations: reading, travel, photography. Office: Spokane Fire Dept W 44 Riverside Ave Spokane WA 99201

MCANINCH, RUTH, journalist, newspaper editor; b. N.Y.C., Apr. 10, 1925; m. M. Merl McAninch, May 6, 1965; children: Joan, Marcia, Tracy. Student CCNY, New Sch. for Social Research. With advt. dept. N.Y. Times, N.Y.C., 1958-68; feature columnist Foster City Progress, Calif., 1976-81, entertainment editor, display advt. mgr., 1981-85; mem. staff Boutique & Villager, Hillsborough and Burlingame, Calif., 1981-87, entertainment editor; hostess TV show Burlingame Magazine, 1983. Former mem. Foster City Art and Culture Com.; former dir. Foster City Beauty Pageant; bd. dirs. Bay Area chpt. USO, Nat. Kidney Found. Recipient numerous awards, certs. of recognition and appreciation from Easter Seals, Foster City City Council, Kidney Found., Am. Cancer Soc. Office: Fucha Publs 1755 Rollins Rd Burlingame CA 94010

MCANUFF, DES, artistic director; b. Princeton, Ill., June 19, 1952; s. John Nelson and Ellen Boyd; m. Susan Berman, Jan. 1, 1984. founding mem. Dodger Prodsn.; former faculty Julliard Sch.; now adj. prof. theatre U. Calif. San Diego. Dir. off-Broadway plays including Gimme Shelter (Soho Arts award 1980), Mary Stuart, How It All Began, Henry IV Part One, The Death of Von Richthofen as Witnessed from Earth (Villager award 1982), N.Y. Shakespeare Festival; A Mad World My Masters, Romeo & Juliet, As You Like It (San Diego Critics Circle award), The Sea Gull, Shout Up A Morning, Gillette, The Matchmaker, La Jolla Playhouse; Macbeth, Stratford Festival Can.; Big River on Broadway (Tony award 1985, Boston Circle Critics award); A Walk in the Woods, Yale Repertory Theatre author plays including Leave it to Beaver is Dead (Soho Arts award), The Death of Von Richthofen as Witnessed from Earth (Villager and Bay Area Circle Critics awards), Troll, A Lime in the Morning, Silent Edward. Can. Council grantee, Rockefeller grantee. Mem. Theatre Communications Group (past bd. dirs.). Office: La Jolla Playhouse PO Box 12039 La Jolla CA 92037

MCARTHUR, ROBERT BRUCE, systems analyst; b. Toledo, Sept. 14, 1938; s. James Arnold and Dorella Bertha (McAran) Mc A.; m. Elizabeth Rosar, Jan. 7, 1961 (div. June 1983); children: Lori Ann, Lynn Marie; m. Linda Lou Bartley, May 15, 1985; children: Julie Lynn, Lisa Anne. Cert. computer sci., Davis Bus. Coll., 1969. Lab. technician Owens of Ill., Inc., Toledo, 1962-67, programmer, 1969-76, systems analyst, 1976-85; systems analyst S.D. Warren Co., Muskegon, Mich., 1985—. Inventor composite can vaccum pack, 1962. Republican. Lutheran. Home: 1725 Gaylord Dr Muskegon MI 49445 Office: SD Warren Co 2400 Lakeshore Dr Muskegon MI 49441

MCAULIFFE, CLAYTON DOYLE, chemist; b. Chappell, Nebr., Aug. 18, 1918; s. John F. and Emma Elizabeth (Stenger) McA.; m. Irene Opal Pickering, Sept. 5, 1943; children: Carol Ann McAuliffe Krenek, Clifford Andrew, Douglas Clayton, Thomas Frank. A.B., Nebr. Wesleyan U., 1941; M.A., U. Minn., 1942; Ph.D., Cornell U., 1948. Lab. asst. Nebr. Wesleyan U., 1939-41; research chemist Manhattan Project, 1943-46; cons. Dept. Agrl., 1947-48; research assoc. Cornell U., 1948-50; research assoc. prof. N.C. State U., 1950-56; sr. research chemist Chevron Oil Field Research Co., La Habra, Calif., 1946-67, sr. research assoc., 1967-86; pres. Clayton McAuliffe and Assocs., Inc., 1986—; mem. steering com. petroleum in marine environ. Nat. Acad. Scis., 1972-75, com. energy and environ. 1974-76, com. dispersnat effectiveness, 1985-87; mem. Ocean Scis. Bd., 1975-77; cons. in field. Contbr. articles to profl. jours., chpts. to books; patentee in field. U. Minn. fellow, 1941-42; Cornell U. fellow, 1942-43, 46-48; NSF grantee; duPont Co. grantee; AEC grantee. Fellow AAAS; mem. Am. Chem. Soc., Soc. Petroleum Engrs., Am. Soc. Agronomy, Soil Sci. Soc. Am., Am. Assn. Petroleum Geologists. Republican. Methodist. Home: 1220 Frances Ave Fullerton CA 92631 Office: PO Box 446 La Habra CA 90631

MCAUSLAND, THOMAS DENNIS, office products executive; b. N.Y.C., Dec. 4, 1932; s. Thomas and Mary (Friel) M.; m. Vivian Holleran, April 23, 1960 (div. May 1968); 1 child, David John; m. Catherine Desmoulins, April 30, 1969; 1 child: David John. BS in Mech. Engring., Columbia U., 1958. Project engr. W.L. Maxson Corp., N.Y.C., 1958-59; applications engr. Hazeltine Corp., Little Neck, N.Y., 1959-62; dir. European ops. Hughes Aircraft Co., Paris, 1962-69; div. market mgr. Hughes Aircraft Co., Fullerton, Calif., 1969-72; dir. European ops. Litton Industries, Brussels, 1972-78; v.p. bus. devel. Litton Industries, Los Angeles, 1978—; mem. North Atlantic Treaty Orgn. Indsl. Adv. Group, Brussels, 1982— (chmn. 1983-86). Mem. Electronics Industry Assn., Navy League, Am. Def. Preparedness Assn., Air Force Assn. Republican. Roman Catholic. Club: Capital Hill (Washington). Avocations: sailing, golf. Home: 4411 Portico Pl Encino CA 91316 Office: Litton Data System 8000 Woodley Ave Van Nuys CA 91406

MCBANE, BRUCE NEWTON, consultant, retired chemist; b. Nampa, Idaho, Oct. 25, 1917; s. Daniel L. and Adah Lillian (Newton) McB.; m. H. Ruth Lynch, Aug. 29, 1939 (dec. Feb. 1986); children: Bonnie M. Huntley, Caroline L. Hlavsa, Brian M. BS, Coll. Idaho, 1939; MS, U. Wis., 1941. Chemist Pittsburgh Plate Glass Co. (now called PPG Industries, Inc., Milw., 1941-48; mgr. auto coatings PPG Industries Inc., Springdale, Pa., 1959-70; dir. ind. ctng. devel. PPG Industries Inc., Allison Park, Pa., 1971-80; asst. tech. dir. Ditzler Color Co., Detroit, 1948-59; cons. in field 1981—. Author book chpts.; patentee in field. Mem. AAAS, Am. Chem. Soc. Presbyterian. Avocations: lapidary, astronomy, music. Home and Office: 1214 Perion Dr Belen NM 87002

MC BATH, JAMES HARVEY, speech educator; b. Watertown, S.D., Oct. 24, 1922; s. Earl A. and Edna (Harvey) McB.; m. Jean Bloomquist, July 6, 1963 (dec. Oct. 1979); children: Margot, Douglas, Janet. B.S., Northwestern U., 1947, M.A., 1948, Ph.D., 1950; fellow, Inst. Hist. Research, U. London, 1952-53. Asst. prof. speech U. N.Mex., 1950-52, U. Iowa, 1953-54, U. Md. European Program, 1954-56; mem. faculty U. So. Calif., 1956—, prof. speech communication, 1963—, chmn. dept., 1965-78, pres. faculty senate, 1977-78, vice chmn. pres.'s adv. council, 1978-80; cons. Am. Student Found., 1961-64, Calif. Office Econ. Opportunity, 1972, City of Hope, 1973, RAND Corp., 1973-78, Nat. Endowment for Humanities, 1973-75, Tokyo Inst. English Lang., 1977—, Nat. Center Ednl. Stats., 1975-78; mem. U.S. Dist. Ct. Com. Sch. Integration, 1978-79. Co-author: Guidebook for Speech Practice, 1961, British Public Addresses, 1828-1960, 1971, Guidebook for Speech Communication, 1973, Communication Education For Careers, 1975. Editor: Essays in Forensics, 1970, Forensics as Communication: The Argumentative Perspective, 1975, Argumentation and Debate, 1963, Jour. Am. Forensic Assn, 1966-68; assoc. editor: Quar. Jour. Speech, 1967-69; contbr.: Ency. of Edn, 1971; mem. editorial bd.: The Rhetoric of Protest and Reform, 1980. Trustee Pasadena Methodist Found., 1985—; mem. bd. edn. Pasadena Unified Sch. Dist., 1985—. Served with Psychol. Research Unit USAAF, 1943-46. Mem. Speech Communication Assn. (exec. council 1966-70, chmn. bicentennial coordinating com. 1971-76, legis. council 1977-79, chmn. Winans-Wichelns award com. 1978-79, dissertation awards com. 1983, nominating com. 1983, adminstrv. com., 1983-87, chmn. fin. bd. 1986-87), Am. Forensic Assn. (pres. 1960-62), Western Speech Assn. (pres. 1968-69), Calif. Speech Assn., Assn. Communication Adminstrn. (pres. 1975-76), World Communication Assn., Am. Inst. Parliamentarians, English-Speaking Union, Brit. Hist. Assn., AAUP, Am. Assn. Higher Edn., Assn. Coll. Honor Socs. (nat. council 1975—), Communication Assn. Pacific (adv. bd. 1972—), Phi Kappa Phi, Phi Delta Kappa, Delta Sigma Rho-Tau Kappa Alpha (pres. 1969-72, disting. alumni award 1983). Methodist. Home: 395 S San Marino

Ave Pasadena CA 91107 Office: U So Calif Dept Communication Arts and Scis Los Angeles CA 90089

MCBEATH, GERALD ALAN, political science educator, researcher; b. Mpls., Sept. 13, 1942; s. Gordon Stanley and Astrid Elvira (Hjelmeir) McB.; m. Jenifer Huang, June 7, 1970; children—Bowen, Rowena. B.A., U. Chgo., 1963, M.A., 1964; Ph.D., U. Calif.-Berkeley, 1970. Vis. asst. prof. polit. sci. Rutgers Coll., New Brunswick, N.J., 1970-72; asst. prof. John Jay Coll., CUNY, N.Y.C., 1972-74, 75-76; assoc. prof. Nat. Chengchi U., Mucha, Taipei, Taiwan, 1974-75; prof. U. Alaska, Fairbanks, 1976—; cons. Inst. Social and Econ. Research, Anchorage, 1976-77; contract researcher Alaska Dept. Natural Resources, Alaska Dept. Edn., Nat. Inst. Edn., others; staff dir. task force on internat. trade policy Rep. Conf., U.S. Senate. Sr. author: Dynamics of Alaska Native Self-Government, 1980; author monograph: North Slope Borough Government and Policymaking, 1981; jr. author: Alaska's Urban and Rural Governments, 1984; sr. editor Alaska State Government and Politics, 1987; editor: Alaska's Rural Development, 1982. Mem. bd. edn. Fairbanks North Star Borough, 1986—. Named Outstanding Faculty Mem., Assn. Students U. Alaska, Fairbanks, 1979, Alumni Assn. U. Alaska, Fairbanks, 1981; grantee Nat. Inst. Edn., 1980-83, Alaska Council on Sci. and Tech., 1982-84. Mem. Asian Studies on Pacific Coast (program chmn. 1983, bd. dirs. 1982-83), Assn. Asian Studies, Western Polit. Sci. Assn., Am. Polit. Sci. Assn., Am. Soc. Pub. Adminstrn., Fairbanks N. Star Borough Bd. Edn. Democrat. Home: 1777 Red Fox Dr Fairbanks AK 99709 Office: U Alaska Dept Polit Sci Fairbanks AK 99701

MCBEATH, MICHAEL KEVIN, research engineer; b. Istanbul, Turkey, Apr. 23, 1955; came to U.S., 1959; s. Bernard Charles and Pearl Marcia (Loebenstein) McB.; m. Karen Ann Haymond, Sept. 4, 1983. ABEE and Psychology, Brown U., 1977; MS in Instrumentation, U. Calif., Santa Barbara, 1979; postgrad., Stanford U., 1985—. Engr. Burroughs Corp., Santa Barbara, 1978; design engr. Microface, Torrence, Calif., 1979; software engr. Milcom, Arlington, Va., 1980; research engr. Washington U., St. Louis, 1980-85, NASA/Ames, Mountain View, Calif., 1986—; researcher McDonnell Lab. for Psychical Research, St. Louis U., 1980-85, Dept. Psychology Stanford U., 1985—. Contbr. articles to profl. jours. Stanford U. fellow, 1985. Mem. IEEE, AAAS, Am. Soc. Psychical Research, Parapsychol. Assn., Soc. for Study of Philosphy and Psychology, ACLU, Common Cause, Union of Concerned Scientists. Avocations: playing sports, skiing, camping, music. Home: Abrams 4-C Escondido Village Stanford CA 94305 Office: Stanford U Psychology Dept Jordan Hall Bldg 420 Stanford CA 94305

MCBEE, RICHARD HARDING, retired lay worker, microbiologist; b. Eugene, Oreg., May 15, 1916; s. Elmer Francis and Cora Cochrane (Clow) McB.; m. Virginia Helen Brown, June 15, 1940; children: Gail Elizabeth, Richard Harding Jr., Christopher Alan, Anne Katherine. Student, U. Oreg., 1934-36; BS in Chemistry, Oreg. State U., 1938, MS, 1940; postgrad., U. Md., 1939-41; PhD in Bacteriology, Wash. State U., 1948. Diplomate Am. Bd. Med. Microbiology. Bacteriologist Md. State Dept. Health, 1941-43; asst. prof. microbiology Mont. State U., Bozeman, 1949-51, assoc. prof., 1951-55, prof., 1955-76, prof. emeritus, 1976—, head dept. botany and microbiology, 1964-68, dean Coll. Letters and Sci., 1968-74; vestry and sr. warden St. James Ch., Bozeman, Mont., 1950-78; mem. commn. on ministry Diocese of Mont., Helena, 1970-76, mem. commn. on evangelism, 1979-82; mem. diocesan council Diocese of Mont., 1979-81; mem. commn. on lay ministry Diocese of Eastern Oreg., The Dalles, 1982—, mem. commn. on ministry, 1984—, mem. standing com., 1984—, pres., 1986—; dir. McBee Lab., Oreg., 1952—; research assoc. Rowett Research Inst., Bucksburn, Aberdeenshire, Scotland, 1960; cons. in microbiology Anaconda Copper Mining, Inc., Frito-Lay, Inc., Midwest Research Inst., 1952—, Nat. Sci. Found., Antarctica Office Naval Research, 1956-57; reader gen. ordination examinations, 1986-87. Co-author: General Bacteriology, 1955, 2d ed. 1962, Introductory Microbiology, 1973; contbr. numerous articles to sci. and religious jours.; patentee anaerobic tube roller. Mem. Hood River (Oreg.) Sch. Bd., 1985—. Served to capt. U.S. Army, 1943-46. Fellow NRC, 1948-49; research grantee NSF, 1951-74, NIH, 1953-57. Fellow AAAS, Am. Acad. Microbiology; mem. Am. Soc. Microbiology (pres. N.W. br. 1960, councilor 1962). Republican. Lodges: Rotary, Elks. Home: 3599 Belmont Rd Hood River OR 97031

MCBRIDE, DOUGLAS LADSON, JR., oil company executive; b. Wichita Falls, Tex., Sept. 19, 1926; s. Douglas Ladson McBride and Beulah Irene (Tanner) McBride Hanson; children—Sue Hanson McBride Rose, Julie McBride Roach, Douglas Ladson III; m. Barbara Joyce Anson, Oct. 16, 1978. B.A., N.Mex. Mil. Inst., 1946. B.S., Tex. Tech U., 1951. Regis. profl. geologist, Calif. Geologist Hanson Oil Co., Roswell, N.Mex., 1951-54, pres., owner, 1973—; ind. cons. geologist, Luling, Tex., 1954-73; pres., owner Ladson Operating Co., Luling, 1969-73, Ladson Oil Corp., Roswell, 1980—, Hanlad Oil Corp., Roswell, 1973—, Hanson Operating Co., Roswell, 1982—, White Mountain Devel. Co., Ruidoso, N.Mex., 1973—; gen. ptnr. Hanson-McBride Petroleum Co., Roswell, 1981—. Served to lt. gen. USNG, 1977-83. Decorated DSM, Legion of Merit; Bronze Star, others.; named to Inf. Hall of Fame, Ft. Benning, Ga., Hall of Fame, N.Mex. Mil. Inst. Mem. Am. Assn. Petroleum Geologists, Soc. Am. Mil. Engrs., Res. Officers Assn., Am. Petroleum Inst., Ret. Officers Assn., N.G. Assn., Assn. U.S. Army, Soc. Ind. Profl. Earth Scientists, Am. Legion. Republican. Baptist. Lodges: Masons (32d degree), Shriners. Home: PO Box 2104 Roswell NM 88201 Office: Hanson Oil Corp PO Box 1515 Roswell NM 88201

MC BRIDE, GUY THORNTON, JR., college president emeritus; b. Austin, Tex., Dec. 12, 1919; s. Guy Thornton and Imogene (Thrasher) McB.; m. Rebekah Jane Bush, Sept. 2, 1942; children: Rebekah Ann, William Howard, Ellen McBride McCarty. B.S. in Chem. Engring., U. Tex., 1940; Sc.D., MIT, 1948; D.P.S. (hon.), Regis Coll., 1979; D.Engring. (hon.), Colo. Sch. Mines, 1984. Registered profl. engr., Tex. La., N.Y., Colo. Instr. chem. engring. Mass. Inst. Tech., 1942-44, research assoc., 1946-48; job engr. Standard Oil Co. Calif., 1944-46; asst. prof. chem. engring Rice Inst., 1948-55, assoc. dean students, 1950-57, dean, 1957-58, assoc. prof., 1955-58; cons. Tex. Gulf Sulphur Co., 1950-58, asst. mgr. research dept., 1958-59, mgr., 1959-60, v.p., mgr. research, 1960-63; v.p. Tex. Gulf Sulphur Co. (Phosphate div.), 1963-70, gen. mgr., 1966-70; pres. Colo. Sch. Mines, Golden, 1970-84; dir. Halliburton Co., Kerr-McGee Corp., Hercules, Inc.; hon. dir. Texasgulf Inc. Mem. Am. Chem. Soc., Am. Inst. Chem. Engrs., Nat. Soc. Profl. Engrs., Sigma Xi, Phi Lambda Upsilon, Tau Beta Pi. Club: Mile High (Denver). Home: 2615 Oak Dr #13 Lakewood CO 80215

MCBRIDE, JOHN STEVEN, architect; b. Cheyenne, Wyo., July 16, 1948; s. John A. and Ruth D. (Brown) McB.; m. Sherilyn L. Taylor, Mar. 15, 1975 (div. Dec. 1980); 1 child, John Robert. B.S.C.E. with archtl. option, U. Wyo., 1970. Lic. architect, Wyo. Serviceman, Greyhound Bus Lines, Cheyenne, summers 1966-69; engr. Cheyenne Community Redevel. Agy., 1971-75; devel. adminstr. Cheyenne Dept. Community Devel., 1975-77; architect Kemper Architects, P.C., Cheyenne, 1977—; mem. design rev. bd. Old Town Mall; mem. adv. com. Cheyenne Mcpl. Bldg., 1977-79. Coach YMCA baseball, 1984-85; coach Cheyenne Soccer Assn., 1985-87. Served with U.S. Army N.G., 1970-76. Mem. AIA (assocs. rep. Wyo. chpt. 1984-86), Cheyenne Design Group. Democrat. Methodist. Lodge: Kiwanis. Home: 417 E 20th St Cheyenne WY 82001 Office: Kemper Architects 3822 Dillon Ave Cheyenne WY 82001

MCBRIDE, MICHAEL JOHN, political science educator; b. Jersey City, Nov. 2, 1945; s. Herschel Vernon and Deane (Eager) McB.; m. Gail Granat, Jan. 27, 1968; children: Jennifer, Kathleen. BA, Purdue U., 1966, MA, 1967, PhD, 1969. Asst. prof. Whittier (Calif.) Coll., 1969-74, assoc. prof., 1974-80, prof. polit. sci., 1980—, dean of advisement, 1981-85, dir. internat. studies, 1981—. Contbr. articles on Soviet politics to profl. jours. Fellow David Ross Purdue U., 1968, Haynes Found., 1970. Mem. Am. Polit. Sci. Assn., Model U.N. of the Far West Corp. Bd. (pres. 1986-87). Democrat. Avocations: women's softball coach, baseball research. Office: Whittier Coll Whittier CA 90608

MCBRIDE, RODNEY LESTER, investment counselor; b. Denver, Sept. 1, 1941; s. Laurence Thomas and Harriet Alvina (Primmer) McB.; m. Nancy Faye Davenport, Mar. 21, 1964 (div. June 1984); children: Douglas L., Cheryl L. BS in Mktg., U. Colo., 1963; MBA, U. Calif., Berkeley, 1976. Cert. investment counselor Investment Counsel Assn. Am.; chartered investment counselor Fin. Analysts Fedn. Indsl. salesman Fibreboard Corp., San Diego and San Francisco, 1963-66; investment counselor Shuman, Agnew & Co., San Francisco, 1966-71; investment counselor, co-founder capital counseling service Bank of Am., San Francisco, 1971-75; investment counselor Scudder, Stevens and Clark, San Francisco, 1975-76; sr. v.p., office mgr. Crocker Investment Mgmt. Corp., Los Angeles, 1977-84; sr. v.p., dir. portfolio mgmt., chmn. equity strategy com. Crocker Investment Mgmt. Corp., San Francisco, 1984—. Pres., coach Palos Verdes (Calif.) Basketball Assn., 1982-83. Mem. Los Angeles Soc. Fin. Analysts (sec., bd. dirs. 1984, treas. 1983, chmn. seminar com. 1982-83), San Francisco Soc. Fin. Analysts, Western Pension Conf., U. Colo. Alumni Assn., U. Calif. Alumni Assn., Alpha Kappa Psi (treas. 1963). Republican. Methodist. Club: Black Hawk Country. Avocations: golf, tennis, volleyball, duck hunting, fishing. Home: 172 Field Point Rd #2 Greenwich CT 06830 Office: Crocker Investment Mgmt Corp 595 Market St San Francisco CA 94105

MCBRIDE, SHERRY (SHARON) LOUEEN, magazine editor; b. Eureka, Kans., Aug. 1, 1937; d. Marvin Chester and Vera Minnie Shaw; m. William Thomas McBride Jr., Sept. 12, 1959 (div. Apr. 1972); children: Erin, Sean. BA, UCLA, 1964. Mng. editor Hi-Way Herald Trailer Life Enterprises Inc., Agoura, Calif., 1979-81, editor Hi-Way Herald, 1981-83, mng. editor MotorHome mag., 1983-84, sr. editor MotorHome and Trailer Life mags., 1984—. Mng. editor: Trailer Life's RV Campground and Services Directory, 1980, 81. Mem. Western Publs. Assn. Democrat. Avocations: golf, square dancing.

MC BRIDE, THOMAS FREDERICK, university dean, former government official; b. Elgin, Ill., Feb. 8, 1929; s. Thomas Wallace and Sarah Rosalie (Pierce) McB.; m. Catherine Higgs Milton, Aug. 23, 1975; children: Matthew (dec.), Elizabeth, John, Raphael, Luke. B.A., NYU, 1952; LL.B., Columbia U., 1956. Bar: N.Y. 1956, D.C. 1966, U.S. Supreme Ct. 1963. Asst. dist. atty. N.Y. County, 1956-59; trial atty. organized crime sect. Dept. Justice, 1961-65; adviser to Home Ministry, Govt. India, 1964; ofcl. Peace Corps, 1965-68; dep. chief counsel select com. on crime Ho. of Reps., 1969-70; assoc. dir., staff dir. Police Found., 1970-73; assoc. spl. prosecutor Watergate, 1973-75; dir. bur. enforcement CAB, 1975-77; insp. gen. U.S. Dept. Agr., Washington, 1977-81, U.S. Dept. Labor, Washington, 1981-82; assoc. dean Stanford Law Sch. (Calif.), 1982—; mem. Pres.'s Commn. Organized Crime, 1983-86, Calif. Council on Mental Health, 1986—. Co-author: Team Policing, 1973. Served with AUS, 1946-47. Mem. D.C. Bar Assn. Home: 837 Cedro Way Stanford CA 94305 Office: Stanford U Sch Law Stanford CA 94305

MCBRIDE, WILLIAM, corporate safety administrator; b. Pitts., June 21, 1928; s. Albert Sr. and Mabelle (Danhart) McB.; m. Jennie Francis Pelloni, Sept. 30, 1960; children: Blair A. Weaver, Dale W. Weaver, Scott R. Weaver, Lorraine D. BA, U. Pitts., 1953; JD, Dickinson Sch. Law, 1956. Safety inspector U.S. Steel Corp., Ellwood City, Pa., 1957-60; tng. rep. N. Am. Aviation, Anaheim, Calif., 1960-65; mgr. personnel services Food Giant Markets, Santa Fe Springs, Calif., 1965-66; adminstr. employee relations Auto Club So. Calif., Los Angeles, 1967-71, asst. mgr. safety and security, 1971-83, adminstr. safety, 1983—; instr. N. Orange County Jr. Coll. Dist., Anaheim, Calif., 1965-70, Cerritos Coll., Norwalk, Calif., 1968. Dist. chmn. Boy Scouts Am., Ellwood City, 1957-59; petitioner Various Civic Causes, Los Angeles, 1975—; communicator State and Fed. Reps., Sacramento and Washington, 1975—; mem. bus. adv. com. Rep. Assemblyman Frank Hill, 1986—; donor Heritage Found., Washington, 1983—, Rep. Presdl. Task Force, Washington, 1980—. Served to sgt. USAF, 1946-53, PTO. Mem. Am. Soc. Safety Engrs. Lodges: Masons, Shriners (life). Avocations: investments, sales, reading, gardening, golf. Office: Auto Club So Calif 2601 S Figueroa St Los Angeles CA 90007

MCBROOM, SUSAN JO, health care administrator; b. LaGrange, Ind., Aug. 20, 1952; d. Truman G. and Jeanne Marie (Rowan) Schmidt. BS in Nursing, Ariz. State U., 1974; MS, Coll. St. Francis, 1985. Staff nurse St. Joseph's Hosp., Phoenix, 1974-75; dir. nursing Southwood Mental Health Ctr., Chula Vista, Calif., 1975-78; asst. adminstr. St. Luke's Behavioral Health Ctr., Phoenix, 1978-86, corp. dir. mktg., 1986—; adminstr./developer St. Luke's Ctr. Behavioral Health and Law, Phoenix, 1984—; chief exec. officer Youth Health Resources, Inc., Phoenix, 1985—. Mem. Adv. Coalition for Comprehensive Children's Mental Health Services; vice chmn. child mental health task force Govs. Office of Children, 1986; cons. Orgnl. Devel. Product Line Mgmt. and Evaluation, 1985—. Mem. San Diego County Nursing Dir. Council, 1976-78; Orchestrator Community Task Force Committment Law, Ariz., 1985; mem. Rep. Caucas; bd. advisors Maricopa County Youth Service Bur., Ariz., 1978-80; planner/presenter South Bay Planning Council Nursing Continuing Edn., 1976-78. Citation County of Pima Office Pub. Defender, 1986. Mem. Ariz. Assn. Family and Conciliation Cts. (v.p. 1985), Ariz. Council Ctrs. for Children and Adolescents (pres. 1984-85). Roman Catholic. Avocations: sailing, traveling, biking, sewing, reading. Home: 517 W Palm Ln Phoenix AZ 85003 Office: St Luke's Behavioral Health Ctr 1800 E Van Buren Phoenix AZ 85006

MCCABE, DONALD LEE, physician; b. Phila., Nov. 5, 1925; s. Joseph Grant and Agnes Muriel (Lee) McC.; student Ursinus Coll., 1944-45, Haverford Coll., 1946; D.O., Phila. Coll. Osteo. Medicine, 1950; D. Social Sci., World U., 1983; m. Jean Smallwood, June 25, 1977; children—Geoffrey, Timothy, Karen, Ellie, Derek, Traill. Intern, Phila. Osteo. Hosp., 1950-51; resident in psychiatry Del. Valley Mental Health Found., 1973-74; individual practice medicine, specializing in gen. practice, Towanda, Pa., 1951-68, specializing in psychoanalysis, gen. medicine, Harrisburg, Pa., 1968-71; psychiatrist Harrisburg State Hosp., also Delaware Valley Mental Health Found., 1970-73; individual practice medicine specializing in gen. practice and psychiatry, 1974—; faculty Phila. Coll. Osteo. Medicine, 1971; preceptor Mich. State Osteo. Med. Coll., 1978; founder Coll. Osteo. Medicine of Pacific, 1979; cons. in field. Original clin. research and publs. on kryptopyrroles. Lic. physician Calif. Fellow Am. Public Health Assn., Acad. Psychosomatic Medicine, Am. Coll. Gen. Practitioners in Osteo. Medicine and Surgery (pres. Pa. 1968-71, nat. dir. 1970-71, pres. Calif. Soc., 1977); mem. Osteo. Physicians and Surgeons Calif. (pres. 1979) editor jour. 1975-79), Calif. Soc. Orthomolecular Medicine (founding), Am. Osteo. Assn. (Calif. del. 1978-79), Am. Coll. Neuropsychiatry, AAAS, Academie Internationale de Lausanne, other orgns. Club: Vallejo Yacht (Calif.). Office: 3530 Auburn Blvd Suite 3 Sacramento CA 95821

MCCABE, JOHN LEE, engineer, educator; b. Fond du Lac, Wis., Mar. 26, 1923; s. Arthur Lee and Florence Gertrude (Molleson) McC.; m. M. Leora Harvey, Mar. 17, 1946; 1 child, Steven Lee. Student, Western Mich. U., 1941-42, U. Colo., 1946-47; Community Coll. Aurora, 1984-85. Designer project assignments, Denver, 1947-50; archtl. engr. The Austin Co., Denver, 1950-52; resident engr. Peter Kiewit Sons Co., Portsmouth, Ohio, 1953; dist. mgr. Hugh J. Baker Co., Evansville, Ind., 1953-56; engr. Lauren Burt Inc., Denver, 1956-58; project mgr. Denver Steel Products Co., Commerce City, Colo., 1958-66; pres. corp. McCabe and Co., Aurora, Colo., 1966-75; master tchr. high sch. Sch. Dist. 50, Westminster, Colo., 1975-83; tchr. Aurora pub. schs., 1983—. Author: Word Problems Simplified, 1986. Served with USAAF, 1943-46; PTO. Mem. Colo. Soc. Engrs. Roman Catholic. Lodge: Optimists. Home: 750 S Clinton St Denver CO 80231 Office: Aurora Pub Schs 500 Buckley Rd Aurora CO 80011

MCCAIN, JOHN SIDNEY, III, senator from Ariz.; b. Panama Canal Zone, Aug. 29, 1936; s. John Sidney and Roberta (Wright) McC.; m. Cindy Hensley, May 17. 1980; children: Douglas, Andrew, Sidney, Meghan, Jack. Grad. U.S. Naval Acad., 1958; grad., Nat. War Coll., 1973. Commd. ensign U.S. Navy, 1958, capt., 1977; prisoner of war, Vietnam, 1967-73; dir. Navy Senate Liaison Office, Washington, 1977-81; mem. 98th-99th Congress from 1st Ariz. Dist.; U.S. senator from Ariz. 1987—. Bd. dirs. Community Assistance League, Phoenix, 1981-82. Decorated Legion of Merit; decorated Silver Star, Bronze Star, Purple Heart, D.F.C., Vietnamese Legion of Honor. Mem. Soc. of the Cin., Am. Legion, VFW. Republican. Episcopalian. Office: US Senate Office Senate Members 210 Hart Bldg Washington DC 20510

MCCAIN, KENNETH GARY, marketing educator; b. Riverside, Calif., Nov. 5, 1945; s. Kenneth E. and Mary (Holman) McC.; m. Evelynn R. Pehrson, Jan. 9, 1970; children: Darren, Amy, Jared. BA, Eastern Wash. U., 1969, MBA, 1971; PhD in Mktg., U. Oreg., 1977. Instr. mktg. Eastern Wash. U., Cheney, 1971-73; grad. asst. U. Oreg., Eugene, 1973-77; asst. prof. Kans. State U., Manhattan, 1977-79; assoc. prof. Boise (Idaho) State U., 1979—; cons. U.S. Mass Transp. Adminstrn., Washington, 1984—. Contbr. articles to profl. jours. Scoutmaster Boise council Boy Scouts Am., 1983-85. Named Top Researcher of Yr. Boise State U. Dept. Mktg., 1982-83. Mem. Am. Mktg. Assn., Acad. Mktg. Scis., Western Mktg. Educators Assn. Mormon. Avocations: flyfishing, reading, basketball. Home: 3857 Barstow Ct Boise ID 83709 Office: Boise State U Dept Mktg 1910 University Dr Boise ID 83725

MCCAIN, WARREN EARL, supermarket company executive; b. Logan, Kans., 1925. A.A., Oreg. State U., 1948. Supr. sales Mountain States Wholesale Co., 1951-59; with Albertson's Inc., Boise, Idaho, owner, operator supermarkets, 1959—, became mgr. non-foods, 1959, mgr. store, 1962-65, supr. merchandise, 1965-67, dir. intermountain region, 1967-68, v.p. ops., 1968-72, exec. v.p., 1972-74, pres., 1974-84, chmn. bd., chief exec. officer, 1976—, also dir.; dir. Idaho 1st Nat. Bank. Office: Albertson's Inc 250 Parkcenter Blvd Boise ID 83726 *

MCCALL, JAMES ANDREW, data processing executive; b. Paterson, N.J., Apr. 1, 1947; s. James Andrew and Grace Marie (Schultheis) McC.; m. Carol Cox, July 25, 1981; children: Andy, Julianne, Christopher. BS in Engring., U.S. Mil. Acad., 1969; MS in Ops. Research, MS in Engring.-Econs., Stanford U., 1971. Commd. U.S Army, 1969, advanced through grades to capt.; co. comdr. U.S Army, Vietnam, 1971-72; ADP officer U.S Army, Ft. Belvoir, Va., 1972-75; resigned U.S Army, 1975; infosystems analyst Gen. Electric Space div., Sunnyvale, Calif., 1975-79; mgr. techn. programs Gen. Electric Space div., Sunnyvale, 1979-82; mgr. software sect. SAIC, La Jolla, Calif., 1982-84, v.p., 1985—. Co-Author: Software Quality Management, 1979; contbr. articles to profl. jours. Mem. IEEE, Assn. Computing Machinery. Avocations: sports, camping. Home: 3132 Verde Ave Carlsbad CA 92008 Office: SAIC 1200 Prospect St La Jolla CA 92038

MCCALL, NELDA DUNN, economist; b. Dayton, Ohio, Nov. 28, 1945; s. Wilson Alexander and Marie Geraldine (Fanning) McC.; m. Steven Snyder, June 6, 1970. BA in Econs., Cath. U. Am., 1967; MA in Econs., Georgetown U., 1971. Assoc. programmer Fed. Systems Div. IBM Research Found., Gaithersburg, Md., 1967-70; research assoc. Palo Alto (Calif.) Med. Clinic, 1970-77; sr. analyst Control Analysis Corp., Palo Alto, 1977; founder, dir. health policy research SRI Internat., Menlo Park, Calif., 1977—; mem. Nat. Ctr. for Health Services Research, Health Services Devel. Grants Review Subcom. Study Sect., 1984—; mem. Calif. Health Policy and Data Adv. Com., 1985—. Contbr. articles on financing and delivery of med. care to profl. jours. Mem. Am. Pub. Health Assn. (governing council), Am. Econ. Assn., Assn. for Health Services Rev., Assn. Social Services and Health. Home: 1803 Laguna St San Francisco CA 94115 Office: SRI Internat 333 Ravenswood Ave BN346 Menlo Park CA 94025

MCCALL, SHARON LEE, registered nurse; b. Bremerton, Wash., May 17, 1943; s. Lester Mack and Mildred Gladys (Boyer) Grippin; m. Kelvin Scott Jones, OCt. 20, 1962 (div.); children: Shawn Scott, Jill Celeste. AS, Coll. So. Idaho, 1973; BS, Pacific-Christian Coll., 1978; MS, Georgetowne U., Sacramento, 1985. Lic. registered nurse; cert. quality assurance profl. Dental asst. Dr. Jack ADams, Jerome, Idaho, 1965-68; charge nurse St. Benedicts Hosp., Jerome, Idaho, 1969-75; staff nurse Greater Sacramento PSRO, 1977-80; health care services nurse State of Calif. Dept. Mental Health, Sacramento, 1980-84; asst. mng. dir. utilization rev. Sharp Meml. Hosp., San Diego, 1984-85; dir. utilization mgmt. and quality assurance Coordinated Health Care Systems, San Diego, 1985—; edn. cons. Intelligent Images Inc., San Diego. Recipient St. Benedicts-Sister Martina Clin. Excellence award, 1973. Mem. Calif. Assn. Quality Assurance Profl. (cert., regional rep. 1983-85), Nat. Assn. Quality Assurance Profls. (regional rep. 1983-85, nominating com. chmn. 1982), Coll. So. Idaho Nursing Alumni (pres. 1973-75), Beta Sigma Phi. Republican. Presbyterian. Avocation: gourmet cooking. Office: Coordinated Health Care Systems 12651 High Bluff Dr Suite 300 San Diego CA 92130

MCCALL, W. CALDER, oil and chemical company executive; b. Hoquiam, Wash., Feb. 1, 1906; s. Dougall Hugh and Hughena (Calder) McC.; m. Mar. 22, 1946; children—Ernest, Robert. Student U. Oreg., 1924-28. Chmn. McCall Oil & Chem. Corp., Portland, Oreg., 1939—, Gt. Western Chem. Co., Portland, 1955—. Republican. Episcopalian. Office: McCall Oil & Chem Corp 808 SW 15th Ave Portland OR 97205

MCCALLEY, RODERICK CANFIELD, chemist; b. Portland, Oreg., Aug. 2, 1943; s. Roderick Gilbert and Esther Drew (Canfield) McC.; m. Peggy Ann Hock, Dec. 11, 1976; children: Roderick Hock, Carmody Kathryn. BS, Calif. Inst. Tech., 1964; PhD, Harvard U., 1971. Postdoctoral fellow Stanford (Calif.) U., 1971-72; asst. prof. chemistry Dartmouth Coll., Hanover, N.H., 1972-79; research scientist Lockheed Missile and Space Co., Palo Alto, Calif., 1979—. Mem. Am. Chem. Soc., Sigma Xi. Avocations: chess, backpacking. Home: 3489 Cowper St Palo Alto CA 94306 Office: Lockheed Missile & Space Co 0/93-50 B/204 3251 Hanover St Palo Alto CA 94304

MCCALLON, LARRY KEITH, aerospace company executive; b. Mayfield, Ky., Oct. 21, 1939; s. Clyde Dawson and Annie Dee (Burnett) McC.; m. Su-Chun Lee, Apr. 10, 1981; children: James, Bryan, David, Monica. BS in Engring. Math. and Aero. Engring., U. Mich., 1962; MSin Aero. Engring., Air Force Inst. Tech., 1963. Commd. 2d lt. USAF, 1962, advanced through grades to maj., 1972; research assoc. Lawrence Radiation Lab., Livermore, Calif., 1966-69; br. chief USAF Weapons Lab., Albuquerque, 1969-71; chief research and devel. div. U.S. Mil. Assistance Group, Seoul, Republic of Korea, 1975-81; br. chief program office USAF Space Div., Los Angeles, 1981-83; ret. USAF, 1983; mgr. strategic missile program office, electronics div. Northrop Corp., Hawthorne, Calif., 1983—; pres., chief exec. officer McFam Corp., Huntington Beach, Calif., 1984—. Decorated Bronze Star. Mem. Air Force Assn., Am. Def. Preparedness Assn., Tau Beta Pi. Republican. Avocations: bridge, gardening.

MCCALLUM, BARBARA EILAND, lawyer; b. Fresno, Calif., Jan. 1, 1938; d. Edward Marvin Walker and Alma Bernice (Pratt) Rubes; m. Murray Lee Eiland, Feb. 25, 1955 (div. 1965); m. Donald George McCallum, Apr. 28, 1970. JD, U. Pacific, 1967. Bar: Calif., U.S. Dist. Ct. (no. and ea. dists.) Calif. 1967, U.S. Ct. Appeals (9th cir.). Atty. Coben & Eiland, Sacramento, 1967-68; sole practice Sacramento, 1968-70; ptnr. Wong, McCallum & McCallum, Sacramento, 1970-74, McCallum & McCallum, Sacramento, 1974—; atty. State Bar Vol. Legal Services, Sacramento, 1984—. Columnist: The Ethics Corner, Family Law News, 1970s. Mem., parliamentarian El Dorado Dem. Cen. Com., 1974-78; chairperson El Dorado County Commn. on Status of Women, 1978-79, 85—; mem. Calif. Senate Select Com. on Long Range Planning's Indsl. Competitiveness Task Force, 1985-86; mem. Nat. Panel Arbitrators Better Bus. Bur. Recipient Soroptomist Women Helping Women award, 1977, 79-80, 85-86. Mem. Women Lawyers Sacramento (past. pres.), Placerville Bus. and Profl. Women (pres. 1977-78), Capital Dist. Bus. and Profl. Women (pres. 1981-82, Woman of Achievement award 1980), El Dorado Women's Info. Ctr. (pres. 1979-84), Sacramento Community Commn. Women (past pres.), Calif. Legis. Roundtable (past vice chair), Nat. Women Lawyers, Calif. Women Lawyers, Sacramento County Bar Assn. (council mem. 1971-72, 80-82), Internat. Women Lawyers (past world council mem.), Calif. Fedn. Bus. Profl. Women (writer, editor newsletter 1980, writer legis. column 1980-85, writer newspaper 1986, legis. adv. 1975—). Club: Comstock (Calif.). Avocations: legis. advocacy, reading, oil painting, rug making. Office: 901 H St Suite 310 Sacramento CA 95814

MCCALLUM, MALCOLM ERNEST, geology educator; b. Springfield, Mass., July 28, 1934; s. Henry Hardy and Edith Agnes (Vanderpoel) McC.; m. Cecilia Louise Paradis, Sept. 7, 1963; children: Gregory Richard, Eleanor Edith. AB, Middlebury Coll., Vermont, 1956; MS, U. Tenn., 1958; PhD, U. Wyo., 1964. Grad. teaching asst. U. Tenn., Knoxville, 1956-58; instr. geol. field camp Miss So. Coll., Held M East, Tenn., 1958; grad. teaching asst. U. Wyo., 1958-61; from asst. prof. to prof. geology Colo. State U., Ft. Collins, 1962—; part-time research geologist, U.S. Geol. Survey, 1956—, Wyo. Geol. Survey, 1960-61; lectr. Nat. Park Service, Estes Park, Colo., 1966-69; instr. spl. short courses for mining cos., 1980, 81. Contbr. numerous articles to profl. jours. Active Hist. Soc., Ft. Collins. Grantee NSF, U.S. Office of

Water Research, Winston Found., South African Research Council; recipient Best Tech. Publ. award, U.S. Geol. Survey, 1965; named Outstanding Educator, Colo. State U. and Outstanding Educators of Am., 1975. Fellow Geol. Soc. Am., Mineral Soc. Am.; mem. Mineral. Soc. Can., Geochem. Soc., AAAS, Soc. Exploration Geochemists. Avocations: fishing, gardening, traveling, sports. Home: 1421 Rollingwood Ln Fort Collins CO 80525 Office: Colo State U Dept Earth Resources Fort Collins CO 80523

MCCALMON, SANDRA ANN, educator; b. Denver, Aug. 7, 1944; d. Jordan Edward and Verna Rose (Hair) Gagnon; m. Robert Thomas McCalmon Jr., Mar. 20, 1976; 1 child, Scott. BS, U. Colo., 1966; BA, U. Denver, 1978. Tchr. Denver Pub. Schs., 1967-68; tchr. Aurora (Colo.) Pub. Schs., 1968-78, staff devel. liaison, 1978-79, learning coordinator, 1980-82, reading specialist, 1982; presenter Math. Conf., Denver, 1978; dir. Gifted Edn. Workshop, Aurora, 1978, Metric Edn. Workshop, Aurora, 1978-79. Author: Teaching Ethnicity, 1979. Mem. Jr. League Denver, 1977—, Jr. Symphony Guild, Denver, 1985; bd. dirs. Denver Ctr. Performing Arts, 1970-72; founder, past chmn., com. mem. Denver Arts, 1974. Mem. Internat. Reading Assn. (Colo. chpt.), Phi Delta Kappa. Republican. Presbyterian. Clubs: Denver Country, Denver Athletic. Avocations: skiing, needlework, performing arts. Home: 325 Ivanhoe St Denver CO 80220 Office: Aurora Pub Schs 1085 Peoria St Aurora CO 80011

MCCAMMON, BOB, professional hockey coach. Coach Vancouver Canucks, 1987—. Address: care Vancouver Canucks, Pacific Coliseum, 100 N Renfrew St, Vancouver, BC Canada V5K 3N7 *

MC CANDLESS, ALFRED A., congressman; b. Brawley, Calif., July 23, 1927; s. Max T. and Fleta (Beaty) McCandless; m. Gail W. Glass, Nov. 26, 1982; children: Cristina, Alfred A., Craig, Blaine, Ward. B.A. in Polit. Sci. and Pub. Adminstrn., UCLA, 1951. Mem. Riverside County Bd. Suprs., Calif., 1971-82, chmn. bd., 1971-72, 80-81; founder McCandless Motors, Indio, Calif., 1953-75; mem. 98th-100th congresses from 37th dist. Calif. Founding mem. South Coast Air Quality Mgmt. Dist.; mem. Riverside County Housing Authority; founding mem. Sunline Transit Agy.; founder Coachella Valley Assn. Govts.; exec. com., dir. County Suprs. Assn. Calif. Served to capt. USMC, 1945-46, 50-52. Mem. Indio Co. of C. (hon. life), Greater Riverside C. of C. Lodge: Indio Rotary (past pres.). Office: 435 Cannon House Office Bldg Washington DC 20515 *

MCCANN, GERALD ALOYSIUS (KEVIN COSTELLO), playwright, journalist; b. N.Y.C.; s. Aloysius Joseph and Ann (Granaghan) McC.; B.A., M.A. San Jose State U.; student Lincoln U. Law Sch.; m. Angelina Palomino, Sept. 17, 1954 (div.); 1 child, Kevin Carlos; m. Phronsa Kay Buck; 1 child, Kerry. Editor, pub. Downtowner Weekly, Ft. Worth, 1950-51; section editor El Universal, Mexico City, 1955, 57-59; editor, pub. Curtain Call Mag., Harlingen, Tex., 1956-57; staff KGBT-TV, Harlingen, KATR, Corpus Christi, Tex., 1959; editor CSEU Union Call, San Francisco, 1961-62; dir., founder Pacific Internat. Press Service, Palo Alto, Calif.; columnist It Takes all Kinds, 1959—, Dateline-Mount Olympus, 1962—, Del Companario (Spanish), 1979—. Mem. staff Remedial Phonetic Tng. Center, San Francisco, 1966—. Recipient Phelan award, 1980, 84. Mem. Am. Judicature Soc., Am. Nat. Theatre Assn., Nat. Writers Union, Mensa Internat. (intelligencer, Los Gatos, Calif., 1973), Sindicato Nacional de Redactores de la Prensa Mexico City, Alpha Phi Omega. Club: Nat. Press. Author: (plays) The Cross of Bonaventure, Viva la Quince Brigada 1967, One Step Enough for Me; (fiction) Command Decision, Long Ago and Far Away, The Specialist, The Immortal Soul of Tommy O', The Small Victories of M. Fynaut; (essay) Democracy and The Court System. Contbr. short stories and articles in English and Spanish to numerous mags. Address: PO Box 421980 San Francisco CA 94142

MCCANN, JACK ARLAND, former construction and mining equipment company executive, consultant; b. Chestnut, Ill., Apr. 16, 1926; s. Keith Ogden and Miriam Imogene McC.; m. Marian Adele Gordon, Mar. 31, 1956; 1 son, Christopher John. A.B., Bradley U., 1950. Mgr. Washington Office, R.G. LeTourneau Inc., 1950-53; mgr. def. and spl. products Westinghouse Air Brake Co., 1958-64, mgr. nat. accounts, 1964-67, mng. dir. Belgian plant and European mktg., 1967-70; gen. sales mgr. WABCO div. Am. Standard Inc., Peoria, Ill., 1970-73, v.p. mktg., 1973-80, v.p. staff, 1980-82; ret., 1982; now cons. Served with USNR, 1944-46. Decorated chevalier Ordre de la Couronne (Belgium). Mem. Nat. Def. Transp. Assn. (life), U.S. C. of C., Am. Legion. Clubs: Bradley Chiefs, Old Pueblo. Lodges: Shriners, Masons.

MCCANN, STEVE ARNOLD, chemist; b. Havre, Mont., Apr. 28, 1944; s. Clarence Leo and Helena (Krocker) McC.; m. Rose Marie Deppmeier, June 13, 1965; children: Patrick Steven, Rachelle Marie. BS, No. Mont. Coll., 1966; MNS, U. Idaho, 1970. Biology tchr. Lincoln High Sch., Eureka, Mont., 1966-67; sci. dept. head Inverness (Mont.) High Sch., 1967-69, Roundup (Mont.) High Sch., 1970-75; profl. cons. Mont. Lung Assn., Helena, 1975-77; chief chemist ASARCO, East Helena, Mont., 1977-85, chief chemist smelting and refining div., 1985—. Author: Small Mammal and Reclamation, 1977. Scouting coordinator United Meth. Men, Helena; scoutmaster Boy Scouts Am., Helena, 1982-85, dist. commr., 1984, roundtable commr., 1984—, team coach, 1985—. Grantee Mont. Dept. Fish and Game, 1971-76. Mem. ASTM (com. mem. 1985—), Mont. Acad. Scis., Am. Soc. Mammalogists, Am. Soc. Chemists, Idaho Acad. Scis. Avocations: hunting, fishing, gardening. Home: 1110 Peosta Helena MT 59601 Office: ASARCO Box G East Helena MT 59635

MC CARDLE, RANDALL RAYMOND, realtor; b. Phila., Sept. 2, 1931; s. Russell Henry and Ruth Hertha (Snyder) McC.; A.A., Orange Coast Coll., 1956; B.A., Chapman Coll., 1958, M.A., 1966; Ph.D., Western Colo. U., 1974; 1 son, Mark. Real estate broker, Newport Beach, Calif., 1953-61; founder, pres. The Real Estaters, Orange County, Calif., 1961—, Treeco Escrow Co., Inc., Costa Mesa, Calif., 1971—; founder Bank of Costa Mesa, 1972, dir. bus. devel., 1973—; also newspaper columnist, lectr., investment counselor. Fund-raising chmn. Boys' Club of Am., Harbor area, 1979-80; bd. dirs. Boys Club Harbor Area; mem. adv. com. Orange Coast Coll., 1964—, Golden West Coll., 1969—. Served with USNR, 1950-53. Recipient Appreciation award Bd. Realtors, 1967, 68, 70, 76, 80; inducted into Orange Coast Coll. Hall of Fame, 1983. Mem. Calif. Assn. Realtors (state dir. 1963-67), Calif. Assn. Real Estate Tchrs. (state dir. 1966-80), Orange County Coast Assn. (dir. 1974—), C. of C., Nat. Assn. Real Estate Appraisers, Bd. Realtors (pres. 1966-67 long-range planning com. 1981), U. So. Calif. Faculty Assn., Red Baron Flying Club. Mason (Shriner). Contbr. articles to various publs. Home: 1828 Jamaica St Costa Mesa CA 92626 Office: 1525 Mesa Verde Dr Suite 116 Costa Mesa CA 92626

MCCARROLL, MARY BARBARA, social services adminstrator; b. Canton, Ohio, May 16, 1927; d. Donald Lester and Mildred (Troll) McC. BA, Ohio Wesleyan U., 1949; MSW, U. Mich., 1959. Dir. health, phys. edn. and recreation YWCA, Canton, 1950-55, Lansing, Mich., 1955-58; br. exec. YWCA, Detroit, 1959-74, assoc. exec. dir., 1974-79; exec. dir. YWCA, San Diego, 1979—; mem. nominating com. U.S. YWCA, 1985-88. Bd. dirs. San Diego County United Way, 1984-86, mem. Par Council, 1982-86. Mem. Nat. Assn. Social Work, Agy. Exec. Assn. (pres. 1984-86), Nat. Assn. YWCA Execs. (nominating com. 1986—), Altrusa (pres. San Diego chpt. 1983-85). Methodist. Avocations: swimming, outdoor activities, needlework. Home: 5129 Abuela Dr San Diego CA 92124 Office: YWCA of San Diego County 1012 C St San Diego CA 92101

MCCART, SHARON RAE, chemist, researcher; b. Berkeley, Calif., July 3, 1953; d. Stanley James and Virginia Ruth (Butler) Gollery; m. J. Dale McCart, June 17, 1972; 1 child, Matthew Paul. BA, Calif. State U., Fullerton, 1978. Chemist Winning Labs., Santa Ana, Calif., 1978-81; assoc. chemist Dynachem Corp., Tustin, Calif., 1981—. Mem. Am. Chem. Soc. Democrat. Methodist. Avocations: camping, sewing, gardening. Office: Dynachem Corp 2631 Michelle Dr Tustin CA 92720

MCCARTHY, BRIAN, municipal administrator; b. Boston, Oct. 8, 1932; s. Charles Jeremiah and Anne Terese (Winston) McC; m. Donna Marilyn Sprague, Jan. 1, 1968; children: Christopher, Mattec. BS in Social Sci., St. Peter's Coll., 1962. Reporter UPI, Atlanta, 1961-62; with U.S. Peace Corps, Sabah, Malaysia, 1964-67; pub. affairs officer USN, Yokohama, Japan, 1967-68; pub. relations officer Motion Picture Assn., Manila, Philippines, 1968-70; assoc. adminstrv. analyst Office San Diego City Clerk, 1974—. Contbr. articles to Mission Beach Star and San Diego Star News. Mem. Mission Beach Town Council, San Diego, 1974—, officer Mission Beach Precise Plan com., 1983-85, mem. Mission Bay Com., 1984-87; mem. Save the Coaster Com., 1980-86. Served with USN, 1952-56; Hawaii. Mem. AMA. Roman Catholic. Avocations: violin, surfing. Home: 811 Kingston Ct San Diego CA 92109 Office: San Diego City Clerk 202 C St San Diego CA 92101

MCCARTHY, BRIAN NELSON, investment banker; b. Detroit, May 24, 1945; s. Andrew Nelson and Ruth Elizabeth (Hill) McC.; m. Linda Lang, Aug. 10, 1974; children—Amanda Lang, Kelly Elizabeth, Meghan Virginia. B.S. in Engring. Sci., Oakland U., Rochester, Mich., 1966; M.B.A., Harvard U., 1972. Cons. engr. Gen. Motors Corp., Pontiac, Mich., 1965-67; co-owner Sound Wave Systems, Costa Mesa, Calif., 1971-78; chief fin. officer, controller A&W Gershenson Co., Farmington, Mich., 1972-75; chief operating officer Devel. Group, Southfield, Mich., 1975-81; chief exec. officer Brichard & Co., San Francisco, 1982-86; exec. v.p. Am. Resource Corp., 1986— ; nat. rep. BK Advt. Council, Miami, Fla., 1979-80. Regional dir. Burger King Corp.-Polit. Action Com., Miami, 1980. Served to lt. USNR, 1967-70; commdr. Res. Recipient Navy Commendation medal with gold star. Mem. Internat. Council Shopping Ctrs., Nat. Assn. Realtors, Real Estate Securities and Syndications Inst., Nat. Assn. Security Dealers. Republican. Clubs: Harvard Business of No. Calif., Commonwealth (San Francisco). Office: Am Resource Corp 1925 Century Park East 17th Los Angeles CA 90067

MCCARTHY, DANIEL DONALD, III, advertising executive; b. Delmar, N.Y., Apr. 8, 1944; s. Daniel D. and Gail Mary (Langley) McC.; m. Diane Patricia Ehlman, Nov. 30, 1968; children: Siobhan Gail, Meghan Elsbeth. BS in Econs. cum laude, Niagara U., 1967. Account supr. Rumrill-Hoyt Inc., Rochester, N.Y., 1968-75; v.p. mktg. Winterkorn & Lillis, Rochester, 1975-81; v.p., media dir. Bozell & Jacobs, Phoenix, 1981-82; pres., chief exec. officer Thelen & McCarthy, Phoenix, 1982-85, McCarthy Advt., Phoenix, 1985—. Served to 2nd lt. USMC, 1986—. Mem. Phoenix Advt. Golf Assn. Roman Catholic. Club: Locust Hill Country (Rochester). Avocation: golf. Office: McCarthy Advt Inc 1430 E Missouri #160 Phoenix AZ 85014

MCCARTHY, GRACE MARY, Canadian provincial government official; b. Vancouver, B.C., Can., Oct. 14, 1927; d. George and Allrietta (McCloy) Winterbottom; m. Raymond McCarthy, June 23, 1948; children—Mary, Calvin. Pres. Grayce Florists, Vancouver; mem. legis. assembly province of B.C., Victoria, 1966—, dep. premier, provincial sec., minister of recreation and travel industry, 1976-78, dep. premier, minister of human resources, 1978-83, minister human resources, B.C. transit, 1983-86; provincial sec. and and Minister of Govt. Services, 1986, dep. premier and minister of Econ. Devel., 1986—; commr. Bd. Parks and Pub. Recreation, 1961-66. Past pres. Vancouver Credit Women's Bus. Club, B.C. Social Credit Party; chmn. Capt. Cook Bicentennial Com., 1978, Yr. of Child, 1979; mem. nat. adv. bd. Salvation Army; bd. dirs. Can. Assn. Christians and Jews. Recipient Pres.'s award Greater Victoria Tourist Assn., Medal of Distinction Internat. Assn. Lions Clubs, H.J. Merilees award of Yr., Greater Vancouver Conv. and Visitors Assn., Marketer of Yr. award Internat. Sales and Mktg. Execs.; Silver medal Can. Govt. Fellow Coll. Fellows Royal Archtl. Inst. Can. (hon.); mem. Hastings C. of C. (1st women pres.); hon. mem. Vancouver Aquarium Assn., Florists' Transworld Delivery Service, Northwest Florist Assn., Vancouver Tourist Assn., B.C. Chefs Assn., B.C. Motels, Resorts and Trailer Parks Assn., Victoria Acadamie of Chefs de Cuisine, Van Dusen Bot. Gardens Assn. Anglican. Club: Variety Internat. (first woman mem.). Lodge: Daus. of Nile. Office: Parliament Bldgs, Victoria, BC Canada

MCCARTHY, JACK DANIEL, surgeon, educator; b. Chgo., Mar. 13, 1927; s. Elmer Vincent and Helen Vanda (Rogal) McC.; m. Victoria Maria de la Riva, May 9, 1953; children: Lellie Anna, Silvia Rose. PhB, U. Chgo., 1946, MD, 1951. Diplomate Am. Bd. Surgery. Intern then resident in surgery U. Chgo. Clinics, 1951-53, 55-57; resident in surgery U. Mich., Ann Arbor, 1957-59; surgeon Lovelace Med. Ctr., Albuquerque, 1961—; chmn. dept. surgery Lovelace Med. Ctr., 1968; clin. prof. surgery U. N.Mex., 1976—. Contbr. articles to profl. jours. Guggenheim fellow, 1959. Fellow ACS (state cancer liason fellow 1964-82), Southwestern Surg. Cong. (state councillor 1978-86); mem. Western Surg. Assn., F.A. Coller Surg. Soc. (council mem. 1974-76). Libertarian. Office: Lovelace Med Ctr 5400 Gibson Blvd Albuquerque NM 87108

MCCARTHY, JOANNE ELIZABETH, educator, consultant; b. Allentown, Pa., May 6, 1943; d. Robert Franklin and Sarah Elizabeth (Knauss) Schall; m. William James McCarthy, June 21, 1969. B.A., UCLA, 1968; M.Ed., U. Rochester, 1974; M.S., U. LaVerne, 1981; M.A., Mills Coll., 1983. Elem. tchr. Centralia Sch. Dist., Buena Park, Calif., 1968-70; reading specialist elem. sch. Spencerport (N.Y.) Sch. Dist., 1973-74, Wayne Central Sch. Dist., Ontario, N.Y., 1974-75; tchr. State Demonstration Project, Pittsburg (Calif.) Unified Sch. Dist., 1977-78; English and reading tchr. Vallejo (Calif.) City Unified Sch. Dist., 1978—; staff devel. cons. Profl. Devel. Ctr. Mem. NEA, Assn. Supervision and Curriculum Devel., Calif. Assn. Tchrs. English, Nat. Council Tchrs. English, Phi Delta Kappa, Pi Lambda Theta; Nat. Audubon Soc. Author publ. in field. Home: 105 Poshard St Pleasant Hill CA 94523 Office: Vallejo City Unified School District 840 Nebraska St Vallejo CA 94591

MCCARTHY, KARLIN, newspaper editor, freelance writer; b. Pitts., July 11, 1959; d. William Steele and Virginia Margaret (Schott) Cutler. BA, Colo. State U., 1982. Legis. aide Colo. Gen. Assembly, Denver, 1981; legis. liaison Colo. Gen. Assembly and Colo. State U., Denver, 1981-82; closing asst. Cabin Country, Inc., Ft. Collins, Colo., 1982-83; asst. to pub., media resource person Gen. Communications, Inc., Denver, 1983; asst. to editor The Denver Post/Empire mag., 1983-86; publicity counsel, Tempe, Ariz., 1987—; dir. pub. relations Stricklan Communications, Inc., Scottsdale, Ariz., 1986. Contbr. articles to profl. security jours. Bd. dirs. March of Dimes, Phoenix, Juvenile Diabetes Found., Phoenix, Patten Inst. Arts, Bus. and Arts Council; vol. childrens' vis. unit Poudre Valley Hosp., Ft. Collisn, 1979, campaign to re-elect Pat Schroder, Denver, 1976; precinct capt. Campaign to re-elect Gary Hart to Senate, Ft. Collins, 1982; past mem. Hadassah; active Colo. Dems. Mem. Pub. Relations Soc. Am. Office: The Denver Post 650 15th St Denver CO 80202

MCCARTHY, KEVIN JOSEPH, music educator, academic dean, researcher, consultant; b. Lakewood, Ohio, July 24, 1938; s. John Joseph and Ruth Hazel (Leary) McC.; m. Maureen Marilyn Spellacy, May 25, 1966; children: Michaela, Mary, Matthew. B in Music Edn., U. Notre Dame, 1960; MusM, Mich. State U., 1961; PhD in Music Edn., Case Western Res. U., 1969. Cert. elem. and secondary tchr., Colo. Dir. music dept. Chanel High Sch., Bedford, Ohio, 1961-62, St. John Coll., Cleve., 1962-66, Roxboro Jr. High Sch. and Cleveland Heights High Sch., Cleve., 1966-67; music dir., prof. Fairmont (W.Va.) State Coll., 1967-69; assoc. prof., assoc. dean music U. Colo., 1969—. Editor Cultural Resource Guide for Colo. Tchrs. (U.S. Dept. Edn.), 1985; contbr. articles on music research to profl. jours. Pres. Boulder (Colo.) Assembly on Arts 1976-79; participator in KGNU-FM Radio weekly classical music show, 1979-80; dir. various ch. choirs. Recipient Disting. Service award Nat. Alliance Arts Edn. Kennedy Ctr. Washington, 1985, Van Gogh Arts award Jefferson County, Colo., 1986. Mem. Colo. Alliance Arts Edn. (chmn. 1983-86), Colo. Music Educators Assn. (editor jour. 1970-80, editorial service award 1980, pres. 1980-82, Disting. Service award 1982).

MCCARTHY, LEO TARCISIUS, state lieutenant governor; b. Auckland, N.Z., Aug. 15, 1930; came to U.S., 1934, naturalized, 1942; s. Daniel and Nora Teresa (Roche) McC.; m. Jacqueline Lee Burke, Dec. 17, 1955; children: Sharon, Conna, Adam, Niall. B.S., U. San Francisco, 1955; J.D., San Francisco Law Sch., 1961. Bar: Calif. 1963. Supr. Bd. of Supr., City of San Francisco, 1964-68; assemblyman Calif. State Legislature, Sacramento, 1969-82, assembly speaker, 1974-80; lt. gov. State of Calif., Sacramento, 1983—. Chmn. Econ. Devel. Commn. of Calif., 1983—; regent U. Calif., 1983—; trustee State Coll. and Univ. System Calif., 1983—; chmn. Task Force on Nursing Home Care, Calif., 1982—; mem. Democratic State Central Com., 1969—. Served with USAF, 1951-52. Named Outstanding Legislator Planning and Conservation League of Calif., 1971; named Outstanding Legislator in U.S. Nat. Council Sr. Citizens, 1972; recipient Torch of Liberty award B'nai B'rith, 1976. Roman Catholic. Address: Lt Govs Office State Capitol Room 1028 Sacramento CA 95814 *

MCCARTHY, MARJORIE CHRISTINE, information systems company executive, consultant; b. Laurium, Mich., Jan. 23, 1942; d. Henry Matthew and Mabel (Haataja) Honkanen; m. Brian W. McCarthy, Aug. 19, 1967 (div. Dec. 1978). B.S. in Math., Mich. Tech. U., 1964. Systems analyst Gen. Research Corp., Santa Barbara, Calif., 1972-73; project leader GTE Sylvania, Mountain View, Calif., 1974-75; mgr. systems U. Fla., Gainesville, 1975-76; project mgr. Montgomery Ward, Chgo., 1977-80; systems mgr. FMC Corp., Chgo., 1980-82; sr. cons. Applied Info. Devel., Phoenix, 1983—. Contbr. articles to profl. jours. Active in Scottsdale Ctr. Arts, 1983—. Mem. Assn. Computing Machinery (sec. 1980-82, chmn. 1985-86), IEEE Computer Soc., Mensa. Club: Toastmasters. Democrat. Home: 7749 E Rose Ln Scottsdale AZ 85253

MCCARTHY, MARY ELLEN, speech-language pathologist; b. Prescott, Ariz., Aug. 26, 1934; d. David Joseph and Elsie Louise (Shupp) Dougherty; m. George Edwin McCarthy, June 22, 1957; children: George Robert, Bryan Patrick. BA with honors, U. Calif., Santa Barbara, 1957; postgrad., Long Beach State Coll., 1958—, San Jose State U., Santa Clara U. Tchr. Anaheim (Calif.) Unified Sch. Dist., 1957-58; speech pathologist Garden Grove Elementary Schs., Garden Grove, Calif., 1958-60, San Luis Obispo (Calif.) County Schs., 1960-64, Morgan Hill (Calif.) Unified Sch. Dist., 1967—; master clinician for student tchrs., 1986—. Sch. bd. mem. Lutheran Ch., San Jose, 1984—. Mem. Am. Speech-Lang.-Hearing Assn. (cert.), Calif. Speech and Hearing Assn. , Santa Clara County Speech and Hearing Assn. (pres. 1979-80), Council of Exceptional Children, Calif. Assn. Neurologically Handicapped Children, Am. Fedn. Tchrs. Avocations: traveling, camping, sewing crafts. Home: 717 Bolivar Dr San Jose CA 95123 Office: Morgan Hill Unified Sch Dist PO Box 927 Morgan Hill CA 95037

MCCARTHY, MARY PHYLLIS MASCITTI, social worker, nun; b. Leominster, Mass., Oct. 12, 1928; d. Pelino and Anna (DiNino) Mascitti; m. Walter Joseph McCarthy, May 21, 1955 (dec.). B.A., UCLA, 1954; M.S.W., Cath. U. Am., 1963; Ph.D., Bryn Mawr Coll., 1976. Joined Order Sisters in Social Service, Roman Catholic Ch., 1959; psychometrist UCLA, 1953-55; caseworker Cath. Social Services, Vallejo, 1959-61; instr. Immaculate Heart Coll., Hollywood, Calif., 1963-65, St. Mary's Coll., Los Angeles, 1966-68; casework dir. Holy Family Adoption Service, Los Angeles, 1963-71; counselor Rosemont (Pa.) Coll., 1971-75; liaison Los Angeles Archdiocese Dept. Health and Hosps./Cedars-Sinai Med. Ctr., 1975-80; assoc. dir. counseling and psychotherapy Cath. Charities, Archdiocese of Los Angeles; dir. Quo Vadis Family Ctr., Torrance, Calif., 1980—; social systems analyst, Los Angeles, 1976—. Mem. com. on community devel. services in child welfare Los Angeles Welfare Planning Council, 1966-71; mem. study task force services to unmarried parents Calif. Social Welfare Bd., 1968-69; local dir. Sisters of Social Service, Los Angeles, 1968-71, del., 1967, chmn. edn. commn., 1968; treas. gen. council Sisters of Social Service, 1976-78. Bd. dirs. Natural Family Planning, St. Joseph Hosp., Orange, Calif., 1981—. NIMH grantee, 1962, 71; NIH co-prin. investigator Cedars Sinai Med. Ctr., 1976-79. Mem. Nat. Assn. Social Workers, Acad. Cert. Social Workers, Calif. Clin. Social Workers, Nat. Conf. Social Welfare, Internat. Conf. Social Welfare, Am. Assn. Social Welfare History, Nat. Conf. Cath. Charities, Sigma Kappa. Author: Drastic Social Change of a Closed Community, 1977. Home: 1120 Westchester Pl Los Angeles CA 90019 Office: 3715 W Lomita Blvd #129 Torrance CA 90505

MCCARTHY, PATRICK KENNY MICHAEL, lawyer; b. Huntington, N.Y., May 4, 1948; s. John F. and Marion A. (Casey) McC. BA, U. Calif., Berkeley, 1975; JD, San Francisco Law Sch., 1982. Trial atty. Marin County Dist. Atty.'s Office, San Rafael, Calif., 1983-84, Moore, Clifford, Oakland, Calif., 1985—. Office: Moore Clifford 300 Lakeside Dr Kaiser Bldg 17th Floor Oakland CA 94604

MCCARTY, DORAN CHESTER, religious educator; b. Bolivar, Mo., Feb. 3, 1931; s. Bartie Lee and Donta Marian (Russell) McC.; m. Gloria Jean Laffoon, June 14, 1952; children: Gaye, Risë, Marletta, Leslie. AA, Southwest Bapt. Coll., 1950; AB, William Jewell Coll., 1952; BD, So. Bapt. Theol. Sem, 1956, PhD, 1963. Pastor 1st Bapt. Ch., Switz City, Ind., 1956-62, Pleasant Hill, Mo., 1962-65; pastor Susquehanna Bapt. Ch., Independence, Mo., 1965-67; prof. Midwestern Bapt. Theol. Sem., Kansas City, Mo., 1967-81, Golden Gate Bapt. Theol. Sem., Mill Valley, Calif., 1981—; cons. Bapt. Home Mission Bd., 1981—. Author: Rightly Dividing the Word, 1973, Teilhard de Chardin, 1976, The Supervision of Ministry Students, 1978, The Supervision of Mission Personnel, 1983, The Inner Heart of Ministry, 1985, Working With People, 1987; editor: Key Resources, 5 vols., Broadman Leadership Series, 16 vols. Recipient Life Service award Southwest Bapt. U., Bolivar, 1973, William Jewell Coll. Achievement citation, 1987. Mem. Assn. for Theol. Field Edn. (chairperson 1979-81), Inst. Theol. Reflection (exec. dir. 1978-86), Fellowship In Service Guidance Dirs. (pres. 1986-87). Home: 562 Storer Mill Valley CA 94941 Office: Golden Gate Bapt Theol Sem Strawberry Point Mill Valley CA 94941

MCCARTY, SHIRLEY CAROLYN, aerospace executive; b. Minot, N.D., May 2, 1934; d. Harry and Cecelia Marie (Engene) Wolhowe; m. John Myron McCarty, Apr. 3, 1958. BS in Bus. Administrn., U. N.D., 1958. Mem. tech. staff Douglas Aircraft, El Segundo, Calif., 1960-62; mem. tech. staff The Aerospace Corp., El Segundo, 1962-72, mgr., 1972-73, dir., 1973-79, prin. dir., 1979—; mem. adv. council Calif. State U., Northridge, 1979—, chmn., 1984—; mem. indsl. adv. bd. Purdue U., West Lafayette, Ind., 1979-82, 1985—. Named Woman of Yr. The Aerospace Corp., 1976; recipient Spl. Judges Award for Leadership, Los Angeles YWCA, 1977, Sioux Alumni Award, U. N.D, 1982. Mem. IEEE, Assn. for Computing Machinery, Soc. Women Engrs., Bus. and Profl. Women (Woman of Achievement 1984, Golden Nike award 1985), Women in Bus., Women in Computing (founding mem., bd. dirs.). Avocations: raising and training Siberian Huskies, traveling, writing. Home: 357 Valley St El Segundo CA 90245 Office: The Aerospace Corp 2350 E El Segundo Blvd El Segundo CA 90245

MCCASLIN, ROSEMARY, social welfare educator; b. Houston, Oct. 18, 1948; d. James Bea andMiriam Rosa Lee (White) McC. BA with honors, U. Tex., 1970; AM, U. Chgo., 1973, PhD, 1980. Child care worker Brown Schs., Austin, Tex., 1970; research asst. Baylor Coll. Med., Houston, 1971; dir. sr. info. services Tex. Research Inst. Mental Scis., Houston, 1973-76; lectr. U. Chgo., 1977-80; asst. prof., sch. social work U. Tex., Austin, 1980-84; asst. prof., sch. social welfare U. Calif., Berkeley, 1984—; numerous consultantships, workshops, and lectures; adv. com. Acad. Geriatric Resource Program U. Calif., Berkeley, 1985—; founding mem., treas. Nat. Com. Gerontology in Social Work Edn., 1983—, also bd. dirs.; founding mem. Waterloo Counseling Ctr., Austin, 1983-84; pres. Council Info. and Referral Services, Houston, 1974-76. Editor: (book) The Older Person as a Mental Health Worker, 1983; contbr. articles to profl. jours. Recipient Tex. Excellence in Teaching award U. Tex. Alumni Assn., 1982, Teaching award U. Tex. Sch. Social Work, 1982; Regents' Jr. Faculty fellow U. Calif., 1985. Fellow Gerontolog. Soc. Am.; mem. Nat. Assn. Social Workers, Council on Social Work Edn. Office: U Calif Sch Social Welfare 120 Haviland Hall Berkeley CA 94720

MCCAUGHEY, MARY HILL, public relations executive; b. Los Angeles, Sept. 3, 1959; d. Thomas Milton and Helen Christina (Deghi) Hill; m. William Carroll McCaughey, Oct. 8, 1983. BA, Loyola Marymount, 1981. Pub. relations asst. Laird Internat. Studio, Culver City, Calif., 1979-82; dir. pub. relations San Bernardino (Calif.) Community Hosp., 1982-86, Kaiser Permanente Inland Counties, Fontana, Calif., 1986—. Bd. dirs. Alvord Edn. Found., Riverside, Calif., 1986—. Mem. Am. Mktg. Assn., Pub. Relations Soc. Am. (bd. dirs. 1986—), Healthcare Pub. Relations and Mktg. Assn., Fontana C. of C., San Bernardino Area C. of C. Lodge: PEO. Avocations: running, skiing, antiques, reading. Office: Kaiser Permanente Med Ctr 9961 Sierra Ave Fontana CA 92335

MCCAUGHEY, TIMOTHY HOYT, university dean, educator; b. Oakland, Calif., May 21, 1944; s. Hamilton McCaughey and Roberta Charlotte (Hoyt) Bradshaw; m. Sarah Ann Griffin, Feb. 17, 1973; children—Brian Gallagher,

Katherine Hoyt. A.A., City Coll. of San Francisco, 1965; B.S. in Bus. Adminstrn., U. Denver, 1966, M.B.A., 1967; D.B.A., U. Colo., 1975. Teaching asst. U. Denver, 1966-67; grad. asst. U. Colo., Boulder, 1968-70; prof. bus. Humboldt State U., Arcata, Calif., 1971—, dean acad. planning, 1981-86, univ. bus. mgr., 1987—; cons. in field, 1966—. Co-author: Economic Development Strategies, 1978. Contbr. articles to profl. jours. Developer computer software systems. Bd. dirs. Arcata Christian Sch., 1979-83, Arcata Econ. Devel. Corp., 1978—; v.p. Congress Faculty Assns., Arcata, 1980-81. Mem. Fin. Mgmt. Assn., Fin. Analysis Fedn., Nat. Assn. Coll. and Univ. Bus. Officers, Beta Gamma Sigma, Sigma Iota Epsilon, Theta Chi. Democrat. Baptist. Home: 63 E 15th St Arcata CA 95521 Office: Humboldt State U SH 216 Arcata CA 95521

MC CAULEY, BRUCE GORDON, investment advisor; b. St. Louis; s. William Maurice and Evylin Adele (Halbert) McC.; m. Barbara Allen Stevens, Mar. 16, 1945 (dec.); children: David S., Sharon; m. Gwen Crumpton Cummings, Nov. 25, 1967. Student, U. Mo., 1939-41, Yale, 1944; B.S. in Engring, U. Calif. at Berkeley, 1948, M.B.A., 1949, M.S. in Indsl. Engring, 1952. Registered profl. engr., N.Y., Calif., Hawaii. Asst. purchasing agt. Curtis Mfg. Co., St. Louis, 1941-43; teaching asst. U. Calif. at Berkeley, 1948-49, asst. prof. mech. engring., 1950-56, chmn. indsl. engring. inst., 1954-55; design engr. Standard Oil Co. of Calif., 1949-50; sr. partner McCauley & Dunmire, San Francisco, 1952-56; v.p. Shand & Jurs Co., Berkeley, 1956-58; dir. Shand & Jurs Co., 1957-60, exec. v.p., 1958-60; asst. to pres. Honolulu Star- Bulletin, 1960-62; gen. mgr. Christian Sci. Pub. Soc., Boston, pubs. Christian Science Monitor, Christian Sci. Jour., Christian Sci. Sentinel; gen. mgr., sec. New York News, Inc., N.Y.C., 1969-74; v.p. New York News, Inc., 1971-73, sr. v.p., 1973-75, asst. to pres., 1974-75, also dir., 1971-75; v.p. Daseke & Co., Inc., Westport, Conn., 1975-77; sr. v.p. Daseke & Co., Inc., 1977—, mgr. West Coast office, 1978—. Bd. dirs. Better Bus. Bur., N.Y.C., 1973-77, N.Y.C. Conv. and Visitors Bur., 1974-77, Albert Baker Fund, 1979—, Asher Found., 1983—. Served as capt. USAAF, 1943-46, PTO. Mem. Nat. Assn. Security Dealers (registered prin.), Am. Inst. Indsl. Engrs., ASME, Nat. Assn. Accountants, Nat. Soc. Profl. Engrs., U. Calif. Alumni Assn., Principia Alumni Assn., Sigma Xi, Tau Beta Pi, Beta Gamma Sigma, Pi Mu Epsilon. Christian Scientist. Clubs: Bankers (San Francisco); Masons (32 deg.). Home: 194 Stewart Dr Tiburon CA 94920 Office: Bruce G McCauley 3266 Ptarmigan Dr 3B Walnut Creek CA 94595

MCCLAIN, WILLIAM RICHARD, marketing professional; b. Cleve., May 7, 1958; s. George H. and Joyce (Cotner) McC. BS, W.Va. Wesleyan Coll., 1979; MBA, U. Pitts., 1980. Mktg. asst. Calif. and Wash. Co., Burlingame, Calif., 1982-83, asst. mktg. mgr., 1983-85, mktg. mgr., 1985—. Mem. No. Calif. Frozen Food Council, Ariz. Frozen Food Council. Avocations: photography, backpacking, canoeing, racquetball. Home: 88 Corte Lenosa Greenbrae CA 94904 Office: Calif & Wash Co 1575 Old Bayshore Hwy Burlingame CA 94010

MCCLANAHAN, CRAIG RANDALL, engineer; b. Salem, Oreg., Jan. 20, 1953; s. Mark C. and V. Faye (Wheeler) McC.; m. Ruth Cooper, July 13, 1974; children: Matthew Eli, Amanda Ruth. BSBA, U. Puget Sound, 1975. Systems engr. Data Gen. Corp., Portland, Oreg., 1976-80; pres. Omega Software Systems, Inc., Portland, 1980-83; dir. tech. services Dial-A-Truck, Inc., Portland, 1983—. Republican. Avocations: golfing, skiing, photography. Home: 22164 SW Pinto Dr Tualatin OR 97062 Office: Dial-A-Truck Inc 10210 N Vancouver Way Portland OR 97211

MCCLARY, RICHARD LEE, physicist, engineer; b. Klamath Falls, Oreg., Oct. 29, 1952; s. George Joseph and Emma Marie (Monter) McC. BS, UCLA, 1974, MS, 1976, PhD, 1982. Mem. tech. staff TRW, Inc., Redondo Beach, Calif., 1982-84; engring. specialist Northrop Corp., Pico Rivera, Calif., 1984—. Mem. Am. Phys. Soc. Democrat. Avocations: skiing, hiking. Home: 941 W Carson #203 Torrance CA 90502 Office: Northrop Corp 8900 E Washington Blvd Pico Rivera CA 90660

MCCLATCHY, CHARLES KENNY, editor; b. Fresno, Calif., Mar. 25, 1927; s. Carlos Kelly and Phebe (Briggs) McC.; m. Grace Kennan, Mar. 1, 1958 (div. 1968); children—Charles, Adair, Kevin. Grad., Deerfield Acad., Mass., 1945; B.A., Stanford, 1950. Reporter Washington Post, 1953-55, Washington news bur. ABC-TV, 1957-58, Sacramento Bee, 1958-63; assoc. editor McClatchy Newspapers, Sacramento, 1963-68; exec. editor McClatchy Newspapers, 1968-74, editor, 1974—, corp. v.p., 1969-78, pres., 1978—; mem. Pulitzer Prize Bd.; bd. dirs. Newspaper Advt. Bur.; trustee Washington Journalism Ctr. Asst. press sec. Adlai Stevenson Presdl. campaign, 1956. Served to 1st lt. AUS, 1951-53. Mem. Am. Press Inst. (bd. dirs.). Clubs: Sutter (Sacramento); Bohemian (San Francisco). Home: 2124 U St Sacramento CA 95818 Office: 21st and Q Sts Sacramento CA 95816

MCCLATCHY, JAMES B., editor, publisher; b. Sacramento; s. Carlos K. and Phebe (Briggs) McC.; m. Susan Brewster; children: Carlos F., William B. B.A., Stanford U.; M.S., Columbia U. Reporter, editor Sacramento Bee; reporter, editor Fresno Bee, Calif.; pub. Tahoe World, Calif.; chmn. bd. McClatchy Newspapers, Sacramento. Pres. French Am. Bilingual Sch., 1974-76, Lake Tahoe Area Council, 1969-71. Served as pilot USAF, 50-52. Mem. InterAm. Press Assn. (bd. dirs.), Calif. Nature Conservancy (bd. dirs.). Office: McClatchy Newspapers 21st and Q Sts Sacramento CA 95813

MCCLATCHY, JOSEPH KENNETH, medical laboratory director, microbiologist; b. Brownwood, Tex., July 5, 1939; s. Glynn Emerson and Mary Ellen (Thompson) McC.; m. Martha Galbreath, July 17, 1960 (div. Jan. 1980); children: Melissa, Marsha, Michael, Jessica; m. Anna Y. Tsang, June 20, 1986. BS, Tex. Tech U., 1961; MA, U. Tex., 1963, PhD, 1966. Postdoctoral fellow Ind. U., Bloomington, Ind., 1965-66; postdoctoral fellow Nat. Jewish Hosp., Denver, 1966-67, lab. dir., 1967-81; lab. dir. Colo. Clin. Lab., Denver, 1981—; bd. dirs. Mile High Transplant Bank, Microtech Med. Systems; cons. U.S. Army, Denver, 1977-81; prin. investigator Nat. Inst. Health Grants, Denver, 1967-84. Author: Anti-mycobacterial Drugs, 1985; contbr. articles to profl. jours. Served with USAR, 1957-64. Mem. Am. Soc. Microbiology (O.B. Williams award Tex. br. 1962), AAAS, Conf. Pub. Health Labs., Am. Assn. Bioanalysts. Democrat. Presbyterian. Avocations: music, fishing, camping, hiking, drama. Home: 7925 W Layton #310 Littleton CO 80123 Office: Colo Clin Labs 3705 E Colfax #301 Denver CO 80123

MCCLEARY, HERBERT ELWOOD, advertising executive; b. Bridgewater, Maine, Mar. 29, 1931; s. Richard James and Madeline Adora (Allen) McC.; m. Elaine Alice Nordell, July 12, 1952; children—Karen, Richard, Brian, Rhonda. B.A. in Indsl. Arts, San Diego State U., 1959. Ind. newspaper account exec., San Diego, 1962-66; advt. mgr. Mayfair Markets, San Diego, 1966-69; asst. advt. dir., Handyman Inc., San Diego, 1969-74; advt. dir. United Sporting Goods, Los Angeles, 1974-77; advt. mgr. Handy Dan/ Angels, Los Angeles, 1977-78; v.p. advt. Pay N Pak Stores Inc., Kent, Wash., 1978—. Served with USN, 1951-55. Republican. Home: 32520 1st Pl S Federal Way WA 98003 Office: Pay N Pack Stores Inc 1209 S Central Kent WA 98032

MCCLEARY, LEILA O'BRIEN, clinical; b. Seattle, Sept. 23, 1944; d. William Lee and Kathryn (Williams) O'Brien; m. Henry G. McCleary. BA in Chemistry, Whitman Coll., 1966; PhD in Biochemistry, U. Wash., 1971. Chemistry technologist St. Peter Hosp., Olympia, Wash., 1971-77; clin. chemist Olympia Med. Lab., 1977—. Mem. AAAS, Am. Assn. Clin. Chemistry, Am. Chem. Soc., Clin. Ligand Assay Soc. Avocations: music, travel, reading, shooting, farming.

MCCLEARY, LLOYD E(VERALD), educator; b. Bradley, Ill., May 10, 1924; s. Hal and Pearl McC.; m. Iva Dene Carter, June 13, 1971; children: Joan Kay, Victoria Lea. Student, Kans. U., 1941-42; B.S., U. Ill., 1948, M.S., 1950, D.Ed., 1956; postgrad., Sorbonne, Paris, 1946. Tchr., asst. prin. Portland (Oreg.) Public Schs., 1949-51; asst. prin. Univ. High Sch., Urbana, Ill., 1951-52; prin. Univ. High Sch., 1953-56; asst. supt. Evanston Twp. (Ill.) High Sch., 1956-60; assoc. Roosevelt U., 1957-69; mem. faculty U. Mich., summers, 1958-59; prof. ednl. adminstrn. U. Utah, 1969—, chmn. dept., 1969-74; assoc. CFK Ltd. Found., 1971-76; dir. projects in Latin Am. for AID, World Bank, Ford Found., Bolivian Govt.; dir. Nat. Sch. Prin. Study, 1976-79; edn. rep. to Utah People to People Program; Keynoter Asian Conf. Edn., 1985; edn. adviser Office of the Queen, Jordan, 1985-86. Author: Organizational Analysis X-Change, 1975, Politics and Power in Education, 1976, The Senior High School Principalship, 1980, Educational Administration, Today, 1984. Served with inf. AUS, 1941-46. Decorated Bronze Star with oak leaf cluster, Army Commendation medal; S.D. Shankland fellow, 1956; Ford Found. grantee, 1968, 72; AID grantee, 1966, 67, 70, 72, 74, 76; CFK Ltd. grantee, 1970-74; Rockefeller Family Found. grantee, 1979-80; Nat. Assn. Secondary Sch. Prins. grantee, 1969, 77, 86—; U.S. Dept. State grantee, 1981, 86-87; U.S. Dept. Def. grantee, 1986-87. Mem. Nat. Assn. Secondary Sch. Prins. (cert. of merit 1978), Assn. Supervision and Curriculum Devel., Nat. Assn. Elem. Sch. Prins., Phi Delta Kappa, Kappa Delta Pi. Methodist. Home: 1470 Wilton Way Salt Lake City UT 84108 Office: 339 MBH University of Utah Salt Lake City UT 84112

MCCLELLAN, ROBERT EDWARD, consulting engineer, technology executive; b. Atlanta, Feb. 27, 1922; s. Robert Edward and Maria Elizabeth (Ameln) McC.; m. Mary Margaret Billetter, Oct. 21, 1944; children: Kathleen Mary, Mary Elizabeth, Patricia Maura, Eileen Mary, Robert Edward III, Mary Margaret, Thomas Francis. BCE, U. So. Calif., 1947, MSCE, 1956, PhD in Engring., 1970. Registered profl. civil and structural engr., Calif. Gen. supr. design Rocketdyne, Canoga Park, Calif., 1959-62; mem. tech. staff The Aerospace Corp., El Segundo, Calif., 1962-69, mgr. strategic studies, 1980-85; chief tech. staff The Ralph M. Parsons Co., Pasadena, Calif., 1969-80; v.p. research and devel. Apollo Systems Tech., Canyon Country, Calif., 1985—, also bd. dirs. Served to lt. (j.g.) USN, 1943-46, PTO. Mem. AIAA, Am. Def. Preparedness Assn., Structural Engrs. Assn. So. Calif., Am. Soc. Indsl. Security, Tau Beta Pi, Sigma Xi, Chi Epsilon. Republican. Roman Catholic. Club: Los Angeles Athletic. Office: PO Box 6186 Woodland Hills CA 91365

MCCLELLAN, ROGER ORVILLE, toxicologist; b. Tracy, Minn., Jan. 5, 1937; s. Orville and Gladys (Paulson) McC.; m. Kathleen Mary Dunagan, June 23, 1962; children—Eric John, Elizabeth Christine, Katherine Ruth. D.V.M. with highest honors, Wash. State U., 1960; M.Mgmt., U. N.Mex., 1980; diplomate Am. Bd. Vet. Toxicology, cert. Am. Bd. Toxicology. From biol. scientist to sr. scientist Gen. Electric Co., Richland, Wash., 1957-64; sr. scientist biology dept. Pacific N.W. Labs., Richland, Wash., 1965; scientist med. research br. div. biology and medicine AEC, Washington, 1965-66; asst. dir. research, dir. fission product inhalation program Lovelace Found. Med. Edn. and Research, Albuquerque, 1966-73; v.p., dir. research adminstrn., dir. Lovelace Inhalation Toxicology Research Inst., Albuquerque, 1973-76, pres., dir., 1976—; mem. research com. Health Effects Inst., 1981—; bd. dirs. Toxicology Lab. Accreditation Bd., 1982—, treas., 1984—; adj. prof. Wash. State U., 1980—, U. Ark., 1970—; clin. assoc. U. N.Mex., 1971—; mem. dose assessment adv. group U.S. Dept. Energy, 1980-87, mem. health and environ. research adv. com., 1984-85; mem. exec. com. sci. adv. bd. EPA, 1974—, mem. environ. health com., 1980-83, chmn., 1982-83, chmn. radionuclide emissions rev. com., 1984-85; mem. com. on toxicology Nat. Acad. Sci.-NRC, 1979-87, chmn., 1980-87, ad hoc mem. bd. environ. studies and toxicology, 1980-87; pres. Am. Bd. Vet. Toxicology, 1970-73; mem. adv. council Ctr. for Risk Mgmt., Resources for the Future, 1987—. Contbr. articles to profl. jours. Editorial bd. Jour. Toxicology and Environ. Health, 1980—, assoc. editor, 1982—; editorial bd. Fundamental and Applied Toxicology, 1984—, assoc. editor, 1987—; editorial bd. Toxicology and Indsl. Health, 1984—. Recipient Herbert E. Stokinger award Am. Conf. Govtl. Indsl. Hygienists, 1985, Alumni Achievement award Wash. State U., 1987. Fellow AAAS, Am. Acad. Vet. and Comparative Toxicology; mem. Radiation Research Soc. (sec.-treas. 1982-84, chmn. fin. com. 1979-82), Health Physics Soc. (chmn. program com. 1972, Elda E. Anderson award 1974), Soc. Toxicology (v.p.-elect to pres. 1987-90; inhalation specialty sect. v.p. to pres. 1983-86; bd. publs. 1983-86, chmn. 1983-85), Am. Assn. Aerosol Research (bd. dirs. 1982—, treas. 1986—), Soc. Risk Analysis, Gesellschaft fur Aerosolforschung, Sigma Xi, Phi Kappa Phi, Phi Zeta. Republican. Lutheran. Home: 1111 Cuatro Cerros SE Albuquerque NM 87123 Office: Lovelace Inhalation Toxicology Research Inst PO Box 5890 Albuquerque NM 87185

MCCLELLAND, CHARLES EDGAR, III, history educator; b. San Antonio, July 29, 1940; s. Charles Edgar Jr. and Frances (Hobbs) McC.; m. Muriel Becker, Mar. 25, 1965 (div. 1975); 1 child, Gabrielle. AB, Princeton U., 1962; MA, Yale U., 1963, PhD, 1967. Instr. history Princeton (N.J.) U., 1966-68; asst. prof. U. Pa., 1968-74; prof. U. N.Mex., Albuquerque, 1974—. Author: The German Historians and England, 1971, State, Society and University in Germany, 1980; editor (book) Postwar German Culture, 1974, rev. edit., 1980; contbr. numerous articles to profl. jours. Grantee NEH, 1972-73, Alexander von Humboldt Found., 1982. Mem. German Studies Assn. (exec. com. 1985—), Conf. Group on Cen. European History of Am. Hist. Assn. Democrat. Episcopalian. Home: 1002 Richmond Dr NE Albuquerque NM 87106

MCCLELLAND, GEORGE ANDERSON HUGH, entomology educator; b. Bushey, Eng., May 12, 1931; came to U.S., 1962; s. Hugh and Victoria May (George) McC.; m. Patricia A. Wheatley, May 23, 1958 (div. July 1975); children: Alison Victoria, Hugh Mackie; m. Karen Elizabeth Loeblich, Nov. 7, 1975; children: Alekxandra Oella, Anastassia Tatiana. BA, Cambridge (Eng.) U., 1955; PhD, U. London, 1962. Sci. officer E. Africa Virus Research Inst., Entebbe, Uganda, 1955-59; research assoc. U. Notre Dame, Ind., 1962-63; asst. prof. entomology U. Calif., Davis, 1963-69, assoc. prof., 1969-75, prof., 1975—; vis. assoc. prof. Kalamazoo (Mich.) Coll., 1975; project leader, mem. research unit WHO, Dar-es-Salaam, Tanzania, 1969-70. Grantee NIH, 1972-75. Fellow Royal Entomol. Soc. London, Zool. Soc. London; mem. Royal Soc. Tropical Medicine and Hygiene (Eng.), Am. Soc. Tropical Medicine and Hygiene, Am. Soc. Naturalists. Democrat. Avocations: gardening, music, travel, computer programming. Home: 909 Sierra Madre Way Davis CA 95616 Office: U Calif Dept Entomology Davis CA 95616

MCCLELLAND, JANE (SUDEKKUM), public relations consultant; b. Tempe, Ariz., Feb. 1, 1922; d. Robert Henry and Ellen Josephine (Cantrell) Sudekum; m. Bruce Alden McClelland, Aug. 31, 1946; children: Bruce Alden II, Kirk Alan. BA, Stanford U., 1944. Reporter Phoenix Gazette, 1940-41, Ariz. Republic, Phoenix, 1941-43; writer Sta. KTAR, Phoenix, 1943; reporter Times, Palo Alto, Calif., 1943-44, News/Scripps-Howard, San Francisco, 1944-52; owner McClelland Agy., San Jose, Calif., 1961—. Bd. dirs. San Jose Day Nursery, 1963-86, pres., 1980-82, Happy Hollow Corp., San Jose, 1960-72, pres. 1970; mem. Parks and Recreation Commn., San Jose, 1968-76, vice chmn., 1975; mem. Goals com., City of San Jose, 1968. Recipient All Am. City award, City of San Jose, 1961, Disting. Citizen award, City of San Jose Exchange Club, 1986. Mem. San Jose Advt. Club (bd. dirs. 1964-67), South Bay Pub. Relations Roundtable (v.p. 1974), Pub. Relations Soc. Am. (South Bay chpt. sec. 1973). Avocation: gardening. Office: McClelland Agy 1642 El Dorado Ave San Jose CA 95126-1527

MCCLELLAND, JOHN MORRIS, publishing executive; b. Rogers, Ark., May 31, 1915; s. John Morgan and Adlyn (Morris) McC.; m. Burdette Craig, June 28, 1939; children: John M. III, Genevieve Sue. BA, Stanford U., 1937. Editor, pub. Daily News, Longview, Wash., 1950-77; founder, editor, pub. Jour.-Am., Bellevue, Wash., 1976-86; pres. Evergreen Pub. Co., Seattle, 1984—. Author: R.A. Long's Planned City-Longview, 1971, Cowlitz Corridor, 1964. Chmn. State Parks and Recreation Commn., Washington, 1952-56; mem. Wash. Bd. Geographic Names, 1978—; bd. dirs. Health and Hosp. Services, Bellevue, 1977—, N.W. Kidney Ctr., Seattle, 1979—, Annie Wright Sch., Tacoma, 1986—. Served to lt. USNR, 1942-45. Named Internat. Boss of Yr., Nat. Secs. Assn., 1968; named to Wash. Newspaper Hall of Honor, Wash. State U., 1984. Fellow Soc. Profl. Journalists; mem. Am. Soc. Newspaper Editors, Am. Antiquarian Soc., Wash. State Hist. Soc. (pres. 1982—), AP (bd. dirs. 1968-71, 72-81), Am. Legion, Golf Collectors Soc., Sigma Delta Chi, Kappa Sigma. Clubs: Royal and Ancient Golf of St. Andrews (Scotland); Seattle Golf. Lodge: Elks. Avocations: boating, travel. Office: Evergreen Pub Co 901 Lenora Seattle WA 98121

MC CLELLAND, JOHN PETER, winery executive; b. N.Y.C., Aug. 17, 1933; s. Harold Stanley and Helen Lucille (Gardner) McC.; m. Ann Carolyn Campbell, Aug. 27, 1954; children: John, Kristen. Student, UCLA, 1951-53. With Almadén Vineyards, Inc., San Jose, Calif., 1958-83; v.p. sales, then v.p. mktg. Almadén Vineyards, Inc., 1970-76, pres., 1976-83; chmn. bd., chief exec. officer Geyser Peak Winery, 1983—. Served with AUS, 1954-56. Mem. Wine Inst. (chmn. public relations com. 1977—, exec. com. 1979—, chmn. 1986-87), Sonoma County Wine Bd. Republican. Presbyterian.

MCCLENATHAN, ROBERT VINCENT, aerospace engineer; b. Dunkirk, N.Y., Dec. 10, 1957; s. Robert Edward and Janet Mae (Bentley) McC. BSME, U. Ky., 1981. Cert. mfg. engr. Tool designer Georgetown (Ky.) Metal Products, 1980-81; desing engr. Gray Tool Co., Houston, 1981-83; project engr. Universal Propulsion Co. Inc., Phoenix, 1983—; engring. cons. Mac Engring., Phoenix, 1984—. Designer Micro Rocket Motors, 1984, Flow Measurement Piping Connections, 1983. Mem. AIAA, Am. Soc. Metals, Soc. Mfg. Engrs. Republican. Roman Catholic. Avocations: golf, tennis, softball, basketball, traveling. Home: 18626-3 N 33d Dr Phoenix AZ 85027 Office: Talley Industries Inc Universal Propulsion Co Inc Phoenix AZ 85029

MCCLENDON, IRVIN LEE, SR., technical writer, editor; b. Waco, Tex., June 12, 1945; s. Irvin Nicholas and Evelyn Lucile (Maycumber) McC.; m. Mary Helen Burrell Swanson, June 26, 1982; 1 son, Richard Lester children by previous marriage—Michael Boyd, Irvin Lee Jr., Laura Ann, Paul Nicholas; stepchildren—Brenda Irene, Kevin Ray, Perry Lee. Student El Camino Coll., 1961-63, U. So. Calif., 1962-66; B.A. in Math., Calif. State U.-Fullerton, 1970, postgrad. in bus. adminstrn., 1971-76; cert. nat. security mgmt. Indsl. Coll. Armed Forces, 1974; postgrad. in religion Summit Sch. Theology, 1982-84. Engring. lab. asst. Rockwell Internat. Corp., Anaheim, Calif., 1967-68, test data analyst, 1968, assoc. computer programmer, 1968-70, mem. tech. staff, 1970-82; systems programmer A-Auto-trol Tech. Corp., Denver, 1982-84, sr. tech. writer, 1984-86; sr. tech. writer, editor Colo. Data Systems, Inc., Englewood, Colo., 1986—. Sec. of governing bd. Yorba Linda Library Dist., 1972-77; trustee Ch. of God (Seventh Day), Bloomington, Calif., 1979-81, treas., 1980-81, mem. Calif. State U. and Coll. Statewide Alumni Council, 1976-77; 2d v.p. Orange County chpt. Calif. Spl. Dists. Assn., 1976, pres., 1977; mem. Adams County Rep. Cen. Com., 1984—, vice-chmn. 32d House Dist. Vacancy com., 1984-86, chmn., 1986—. Served with USAFR, 1967-71. USAF Nat. Merit scholar, 1963-67. Mem. Calif. Assn. Library Trustees and Commrs. (exec. bd., So. Calif. rep. 1976-77), Assn. Computing Machinery, Air Force Assn., Nat. Eagle Scout Assn., Calif. State U.-Fullerton Alumni Assn. (dir. 1975-77). Republican. Mem. Ch. of God (Seventh Day). Home: 9835 Pennsylvania Dr Thornton CO 80229-2117 Office: 3301 W Hampden Ave Unit C Englewood CO 80110

MCCLENDON, ROBERT FRANK, architect; b. Seattle, Feb. 26, 1946; s. Don and Gracey (Carmicle) Whittemore; m. Meredith R. McClendon, Mar. 26, 1970; children: Anna Michel, Ian Robert. BArch, Wash. state U., 1970; MEd magna cum laude, Yale U., 1972; Assoc. MBA, Harvard U., 1972. Assoc. Ibsen Nelsen, Seattle, 1972-76; lead designer TRA, Seattle, 1976-78; dir. design and planning Media 5, Honolulu, 1978-80; dir. office CDA, Seattle, 1980-82; v.p. and gen. mgr. mgmt. services CADI, Seattle, 1982—; ptnr. Pacific Fin. Group, Bellevue, Wash., 1982—. Contbr. articles to profl. jours. Recipient Platz BoBo Peace award, France, 1972; Progressive Architecture Design award, 1978, 80, Progressive Architecture South Lake Union Master Plan award, Plastics Inst. award, Italy, 1973, Golden Nugget award, Kako Master Plan for Honolulu award, Bagdad Internat. Design award; named to U.S. Olympic Swim Team, 1964, All-Am. Swimmer, 1966, 67. Mem. AIA, AICP. Republican. Clubs: Tower, Coll., Washington Athletic (Seattle). Office: CADI 627 Wash Bldg Seattle WA

MCCLINTICK, ROBERT ROY, insurance company executive; b. Walnut, Kans., Nov. 19, 1924; s. A.W. and Louella (Burnett) McC.; m. Hazel Jean Wathen, Aug. 12, 1950; children—Suzanne McClintick Dinsmore, Stephanie. B.S., U. Kans., 1949; postgrad. U. Kansas City, 1950-52. C.P.C.U., C.L.U. With Farmers Ins. Group, Kansas City, 1949-51, Austin, Tex., 1952-55, underwriting mgr., Merced, Calif., 1956-58, gen. underwriting mgr., Los Angeles, 1959-62, dir. underwriting adminstrn. and personal lines, 1963-68, regional mgr. Pacific Northwest, 1969-74, v.p., mgr. Great Lakes region, 1975-76, v.p. claims, Los Angeles, 1977-78, v.p. field ops., 1979-84, sr. v.p. property and casualty ops., 1985—; pres. Fire Underwriters Assn., Los Angeles, 1982—; also dir.; dir. Farmers Underwriters Assn., Truck Underwriters Assn., Mid-Century Ins. Co., A.I.F. Holding Co.; mem. Farmers Ins. Group Safety Found. Investment Com.; v.p., gen. mgr. Farmers Ins. Co. of Wash., 1969-74; pres. Farmers Ins. Co. Oreg., 1969-74, Ill. Farmers Ins. Co., 1974-76; chmn. Oreg. steering com. Western Ins. Info. Service, 1973-74; dir. Oreg. Ins. Guaranty Assn., Assn. Oreg. Industries, Ill. Ins. Info. Service. Mem. U.S. C. of C., Portland C. of C. (legis. com.), Aurora C. of C., Nat. Mgmt. Assn., C.P.C.U. (Los Angeles chpt.). Office: Farmers Group Inc 4680 Wilshire Blvd Los Angeles CA 90010

MC CLINTOCK, ARCHIE GLENN, semi-retired State attorney general, lawyer; b. Sheridan, Wyo., Mar. 26, 1911; s. James Porter and Martie E. (Glenn) McC.; m. Ina Jean Robinson, May 27, 1939 (dec. 1974); children: Ellery, Jeffry, Kathleen. B.A., U. Wyo., 1933, LL.B., 1935. Bar: Wyo. 1935, Calif. 1982. Pvt. practice law Cheyenne, Wyo., 1935-73, 81-83; justice Wyo. Supreme Ct., Cheyenne, 1973-81; atty. gen. State of Wyo., 1982-87; semi-ret. Mem. Wyo. Fair Employment Practices Commn., 1965-71. Served with USNR, 1944-45. Mem. Wyo. State Bar (pres. 1950-51), Am. Judicature Soc., Sigma Nu. Democrat. Club: Elks. Home: 1211 Richardson Ct Cheyenne WY 82001

MCCLOSKEY, CHESTER MARTIN, chemical manufacturing company executive; b. Fresno, Calif., July 21, 1918; s. Mandeville Alfred and Moneta (Martin) McC.; m. Olive Jordan, June 30, 1944; children: Marilyn, Wallace. BA in Chemistry, Whittier Coll., 1940; MS in Organic Chemistry, U. Iowa, 1941, PhD in Organic Chemistry, 1944. Registered patent agt. Chief chemist Alexander Kerr & Co., Los Angeles, 1946-48, 48—; chemist Office Naval Research, Pasadena, Calif., 1948-55, chief scientist, 1955-57; exec. dir. indsl. assocs. Calif. Inst. Tech., Pasadena, 1957-62; pres. Norac Co. Inc., Azusa, Calif., 1962—; co-chmn. steering com. So. sect. Calif. State Indsl. Safety Conf.; cons. in field. Contbr. articles to profl. jours.; patentee in field. Asst. scout master Boy Scouts Am., Pasadena, 1964-69, scout master, 1970, asst. post advisor, 1971-74; elder Westminster Presbyn. Ch., Pasadena. Sr. research fellow Calif. Inst. Tech., 1945-46, 1957-62. Mem. Am. Chem. Soc., Am. Rocket Soc. (pres. So. Calif. sect. 1955), Soc. Plastics Industry (chmn. organic peroxide producers safety div. 1971, bd. dirs. 1971), Nat. Fire Prevention Assn. Republican. Presbyterian. Avocation: farming. Home: 1981 Sinaloa Ave Altadena CA 91001 Office: Norac Co Inc PO Box F Azusa CA 91702

MCCLOUD, PEGGY, painting contracting company executive; b. Ft. Worth, Apr. 27, 1954; d. Leland Webb and Carolyn (Schmitz) McC. B.A. in Psychology, U. Calif.-Davis, 1975; M.A. in Psychology, Humboldt State U., 1985. Plant mgr. S&W, Buena Park, Calif., 1978-82; prodn. control mgr. Inter-Am., Costa Mesa, Calif., 1982-83; owner, operator Jill of all Trades, Buena Park, 1983—; speaker women's conf. Mem. Women in Mgmt., Women in Bus., Nat. Assn. Women Bus. Owners. Democrat. Home: 5345 Humboldt Dr Buena Park CA 90621

MCCLURE, ALLAN HOWARD, space contamination specialist, space materials consultant; b. Phila., Mar. 29, 1925; s. C. Howard and Edda Cherry (Speirs) McC.; m. Jean Florence Hall, May 31, 1947; children: Joyce Ann, Allan Hall. BS, Widener U., 1949; postgrad., Command & Gen. Staff Coll., 1972. Chemist Am. Cyanamid, Pitts., 1950-52; materials engr. Piasecki/Vertol Helicopter Co., Morton, Pa., 1952-59; lead engr. Boeing Aerospace Co., Seattle, 1959-71; sr. specialist engr. Boeing Aerospace Co., Kent, Wash., 1974-85; tech. cons. Adhesive Engring. Co., San Carlos, Calif., 1971-74. Author, investigator spacecraft contamination control documents and govt. reports. Pres. Seattle Crime Prevention League, 1974-84. Served to maj. U.S. Army, 1943-46, ETO, PTO; sec. Boeing Employees Amateur Radio Soc., 1984; membership chmn. Amateur Radio Emergency Services, 1984-85. Recipient Silver Beaver award and William H. Spurgeon III award Boy Scouts Am., Seattle, 1964. Mem. Am. Chem. Soc., Soc. for Advancement of Material and Process Engring. (nat. dir., pres. Seattle chpt.), Rainier C. of C., Res. Officers Assn. (life). Republican. Avocations: amateur radio, hiking, coin collecting, canoeing, photography. Home: 5249 S Mayflower St Seattle WA 98118

MCCLURE, ELDON RAY, mechanical engineer; b. Carson, N.D., Dec. 31, 1933; s. Clarence N. and Rose Magdeline (Anderson) McC.; m. Amelia Lillian Cesar, June 16, 1956; children: Michael Dean, Steven Scott. BSME, Wash. State U., 1955; MSME, Ohio State U., 1959; DEng, U. Calif., Berkeley, 1969. Registered profl. engr., Calif. Mech. engr. Boeing Airplane Co., Seattle, 1955-57, Battelle Meml. Inst., Columbus, Ohio, 1957-58; asst. prof. Oregon State U., Corvallis, 1957-63; mech. engr., deputy dept. head, div. leader Lawrence Livermore Nat. Lab., Livermore, Calif., 1965-78, precision engr., program leader, 1979—, also chmn. steering com. machine tool task force, 1978-80; mem. machine tool panel Nat. Acad. Engrs., Washington, 1980-83; mem. adv. bd., adj. prof. precision engring. lab. N.C. State U., Raleigh, 1984—. Contbr. numerous articles to profl. jours. NSF fellow. Mem. ASME (sr.), Soc. Mfg. Engrs., AAAS, Japan Soc. Precision Engring., Am. Nat. Standards Inst. (vice chmn. standards com. B46 1979—), Nat. Tooling and Machine Assn. (Disting. Service award 1986). Republican. Roman Catholic. Home: 5721 Crestmont Ave Livermore CA 94550 Office: Lawrence Livermore Nat Lab Precision Engring Program 7000 East Ave PO Box 808 Livermore CA 94550

MC CLURE, JAMES A., senator; b. Payette, Idaho, Dec. 27, 1924; s. W. R. and Marie McC.; m. Louise Miller; children: Marilyn, Kenneth, David. J.D., U. Idaho, 1950; J.D. hon. doctorate, 1981; DL (hon.), Coll. Idaho, 1986. Mem. Idaho State Senate, 1961-66; asst. majority leader 1965-66; city atty. City of Payette (Idaho); pros. atty. Payette County; Mem. 90th-92d Congresses from 1st Idaho Dist., 1967-73; U.S. Senator from Idaho 1973—; Energy and Natural Resources Com.; mem. Com. on Rules and Adminstrn., Com. on Appropriations; subcom. on Interior and related agys.; mem. subcoms. on agrl., def., energy/water devel. Bd. visitors U.S. Mil. Acad., Sch. Forestry and Environ. Studies of Duke U.; trustee Kennedy Center; bd. govs. Council of Nat. Policy. Mem. Phi Alpha Delta. Methodist (trustee). Clubs: Elks, Masons, Kiwanis. Office: 309 Hart Senate Bldg Washington DC 20510 *

MCCLURE, LLOYD WILLIAM, chemical engineer; b. Billings, Mont., Oct. 9, 1950; s. Jack and Jean Irene (Welzenbach) McC.; Rita Kay Brumley, Sept. 19, 1970; children: Brandi Lee, Cody Lyn. BSChemE, Mont. State U., 1972; MSChemE, U. Idaho, 1979. Research engr. Allied Chem. Corp., Idaho Falls, Idaho, 1972-77; mgr. process verification Exxon Nuclear Idaho Co., Inc., Idaho Falls, 1977-84; mgr. process devel. Westinghouse Idaho Nuclear Co., Inc., Idaho Falls, 1984—. Mem. Nat. Ski Patrol, Kelly Canyon, Idaho, 1974—. Mem. Am. Nuclear Soc. (active various coms. 1978—). Avocations: fishing, camping, snow skiing. Home: 1885 Sabin Dr Idaho Falls ID 83401 Office: Westinghouse Idaho Nuclear Co PO Box 4000 Idaho Falls ID 83403

MCCLURE, PAUL THOMAS, stained glass company executive; b. Detroit, Feb. 18, 1943; s. Jack Cloer and Helen Maureen (Green) McC.; B.S., Calif. Western U., 1964; M.P.A., U. So. Calif., 1968, Ph.D., 1972; m. Elizabeth McCullough, Dec. 25, 1979; children—Shauna, Erin, Scott. Adminstrv. analyst Los Angeles Internat. Airport, 1966-68; policy analyst Rand Corp., Santa Monica, Calif., 1968-73; adj. prof. Golden Gate U., San Francisco, 1973—; artist/owner Am. Art Glass Co., Adelanto, Calif., 1973—. Mem. Adelanto Sch. Bd., 1973-83, pres., 1976-79; mem. Adelanto Planning Commn., 1973-75, chmn., 1973-75; mem. bd. property and fin. Brookside Free Meth. Ch., 1985—; co-chmn. United Way Campaign, 1986, bd. dirs. Redlands area United Way, 1985—; pres. YMCA Found. Bd. dirs. 1985—. RAND fellow, 1972. TV host bus. profile Inland Empire Illustrated KVCR-TV, PBS, 1984—; stained glass commns. include: Campus Hill Seventh-day Adventist Ch., Loma Linda, Calif., 10th Ave. Bapt. Ch., Los Angeles, Assembly of God Ch., Hesperia, Calif., Living Waters Chapel, Apple Valley, Calif. Lodge: Rotary. Office: Am Art Glass Co 15444 7th St Victorville CA 92392

MCCOLLOR, ROBERT LAWRENCE, engineer, physicist, consultant; b. Ocheyedan, Iowa, Feb. 20, 1922; s. Lawrence Patrick and Jennie Lee (Rumelhart) M.; m. Betty Jeanne Ebert, March 25, 1949; children—Virginia Marie, Lisa Edna Jeanne. A.S. in Mech. Engring., N.D. Agrl. Coll., Fargo, 1944; B.A. in Math. and Physics, Morningside Coll., Sioux City, Iowa, 1949; cert. Nat. Security Mgmt. Indsl. Coll. of the Armed Forces, Washington; M.S. in Mgmt. Engring., Kensington U., Glendale, Calif., 1977, Ph.D. in Physics, 1978. Registered profl. engr., Mass., N.H. Design engr. RCA Corp., Camden, N.J., 1952-54; engring. mgr. RCA, 1954-61; engring. mgr. RCA, Burlington, Mass., 1961-71, sr. engring. scientist, 1971-74; prin. engr. Support Systems Assocs., Inc., Valencia, Calif., 1975-83; sr. project engr. M&T Co., Valencia, 1983—. Served with U.S. Army, 1942-46. Mem. AAAS, AIAA. Contbr. articles to profl. jours. Home: 42944 Amoy St Lancaster CA 93534

MCCOLLOUGH, W. VANCE, electrical engineer, educator; b. Pitts., Feb. 16, 1947; s. Robert G. and Joan (Vance) McCollough. BSEE, Carnegie Mellon U., 1969; MSEE, U. R.I., 1973, PhDEE, 1977. Research assoc. U. R.I., Kingston, 1973-77; sr. engr. Raytheon Corp., Portsmouth, R.I., 1977-85; sr. staff engr. Hughes Aircraft, Englewood, Colo., 1985-86, head systems analysis sect., 1986—; adj. prof. U. R.I., 1977-85, Denver U., 1985—. Contbr. articles to profl. jours. Co-chmn. United Way, Raytheon Corp., 1982-84. Mem. IEEE (sr., lectr., student chpt. advisor, exec. com. 1985—), Soc. Photo-Optical Instrumentation Engrs., Eta Kappa Nu, Phi Kappa Phi. Clubs: Newport (R.I.) Yacht (race com. chmn. 1980-84); So. Colo. Yacht (Pueblo); U.S. Yacht Racing Union (sr. race officer 1985—). Avocations: sailing, golf, tennis. Office: Hughes Aircraft Co MS600 8000 E Maplewood Ave Englewood CO 80111

MCCOLLUM, PATRICIA JUNE, hospital administrator; b. Atlanta, Nov. 22, 1932; d. Ernest Emory and Gladys (Darrington) Hambrick; widowed; children: Melissa McCollum Mix, Shelley McCollum Ralston; m. Khider Ali El Zein, May 11, 1979 (div. Mar. 1982). BS, Loma Linda U., 1968; post-grad., U. Mo., Kansas City. Dir. med. records Good Samaritan Hosp., Portland, Oreg., 1969-72; cons. WHO, Geneva, 1972-77, United Arab Emirates Ministry of Health, Abu Dhabi, 1978-79; asst. prof. allied health scis. Kans. U., Kansas City, 1979-81; dir. med. records, outpatient clinic King Khalid U. Hosp., Riyadh, Saudi Arabia, 1982-84; asst. prof. allied health scis. Kuwait U., Kuwait, 1984-85; dir. med. records McKenzie-Willamette Hosp., Springfield, Oreg., 1985—; cons. Oreg. Dept. Health, Salem, 1970; adminstrv. advisor Cen. Oreg. Community Coll., Bend, 1986—. Contbr. articles to profl. jours. Recipient Outstanding Service award CARE-MEDICO, N.Y.C., 1975, Merit award U. Philippines, Manila, 1976. Mem. Am. Med. Record Assn. (research com. 1980-82), Oreg. Med. Record Assn. (chmn. edn. com. 1971, pres. elect 1972). Bahai. Avocations: gardening, piano. Home: 8401 Old Stage Rd Apt 86 Central Point OR 97502 Office: McKenzie-Willamette Hosp 1460 G St Springfield OR 97477

MCCOMAS, JOHN LAWRENCE, safety engineer; b. Huntington, W.Va., Apr. 3, 1940; s. Lawrence Gerald and Aileen Jane (Jeffery) McC.; m. Beatrice Anne Harris, Jan. 28, 1959; m. Amalia Maria Bonnemaison, Feb. 28, 1980; children—Valerie Anne Munoz, Jeffrey Scott; 1 stepchild, Rafael Alonso. B.S.M.E., Milw. Sch. Engring., 1969; M.S. with honors in Health Sci., Calif. State U., 1978. Lic. profl. engr., Calif. Loss control engr. Aetna Life and Casualty, Fresno, Calif., 1969-72; dist. mgr. Calif. Div. Indsl. Safety, San Francisco and Bakersfield, 1972-76; North slope project engr. SOHIO/BP Constrn. Co., San Francisco, 1976-79; assoc. mgr. safety engring. Occidental Petroleum Exploration and Prodn. Co., Bakersfield, 1979-83; western regional safety engr. Cities Service Oil & Gas Corp., Bakersfield, 1983—; assoc. prof. safety and fire protection engring. Calif. State U.-Fresno; instr. safety and loss control mgmt. Bakersfield Coll. Served with USN, 1958-62. Mem. Am. Petroleum Inst. (com. safety and fire protection), Western Oil and Gas Assn. (fire, safety and health com.), Am. Soc. Safety Engrs., System Safety Soc. Republican. Presbyterian.

MCCOMB, KARLA JOANN, staff development coordinator; b. Tacoma, July 23, 1937; d. John Frank and Lorraine Beatrice (Winters) Bohac; m. Russell Marshall McComb, Nov. 27, 1959 (div.); children—Marsha McComb Hayes, Kathleen Ann. Cert. instr. French, U. Paris, 1958; B.A., Calif. State U.-Sacramento, 1960; M.S., Nova U., 1984. Cert. secondary tchr., Nev. Tchr. French and music Sacramento Waldorf Sch., 1960-62; tchr. French, Red Bluff High Sch., 1967-68; tchr. French and music Pocatello (Idaho) Schs., 1969-71; tchr., chairperson dept. Clark County Sch. Dist., 1971-76; curriculum cons. social sci., fgn. lang., profl. growth, Las Vegas, 1976-84; cons. staff devel. and profl. growth, 1984—; cons. Taft Inst. Govt., Salt Lake City, 1977—. Tchr. Inservice, Follett Pub. Co., 1980-81; coordinator Nev. Close-Up Program, 1980—. Mem. Sacramento Symphony Orch., 1954-66, Nev. Humanities Com.; bd. dirs. Love All People Youth Group, supt. Love All People Sch., 1983—, producer staff devel. films, 1986—. Mem. Clark County Fgn. Lang. Tchrs. Assn. (pres.), Nat. Council Social Studies, Social Studies Suprs. Assn., Nev. Fgn. Lang. Tchrs. Assn. (pres.-elect), AAUW, Phi Theta Kappa, Mu Phi Epsilon, Alpha Delta Kappa. Democrat. Clubs: Vegas Valley Dog Obedience (pres.), Jackpot Obedience Assn. (pres.). Author: A Cultural Celebration, 1980; editor: The Nevada Holocaust Curriculum, 1987. Home: 409 A N Lamb Blvd Las Vegas NV 89110 Office: 600 N 9th St Las Vegas NV 89101

MCCOMBS, RICHARD N., wine company executive; b. Moorestown, N.J., Apr. 22, 1946; s. Thomas Lloyd and Elizabeth (Klauter) McC.; m. Patricia Cummings, June 21, 1980; children: Michael, Sara, Emily. BA in Econs., Amherst Coll., 1969; MBA, Stanford U., 1979. Cons. mgr. Touche Ross & Co., San Francisco, 1979-83; pres. ISC Wines of Calif., San Francisco, 1983—. Clubs: St. Francis Yacht (San Francisco); Mill Valley Tennis. Avocation: ocean racing.

MCCOMBS, ROLLIN KOENIG, radiation oncologist; b. Denver, Aug. 17, 1919; s. Curtis and Emma Elizabeth (Koenig) McC.; m. Judy Louise Bacon, Dept. 20, 1952; children: David, Daniel, Susan, Kathleen, Michael. BA in Chemistry, U. Colo., 1941, MA in Physics, 1944; MD, Stanford U., 1954. Diplomate Am. Bd. Radiology, Am. Bd. Nuclear Medicine. Research fellow, assoc. physician Donner Lab. Med. Physics, Berkeley, Calif., 1954-57; resident VA Hosp., Long Beach, Calif., 1957-67, staff; dir. radiation oncology Long Beach Community Hosp., 1967-86; instr. physics U. Colo., Boulder, 1942-48; asst. clin. prof. radiology U. So. Calif. Sch. Medicine, Los Angeles, 1978-84, assoc. clin. prof. radiology, 1984—. Contbr. articles to profl. jours. Recipient Chmn's. award U. So. Calif. Sch. Medicine, 1983. Mem. AMA, Am. Coll. Radiology, Soc. Nuclear Medicine, Brit. Inst. Radiology, Am. Assn. Physicists in Medicine, Am. Soc. Therapeutic Radiology and Oncology, Sigma Xi, Phi Beta Kappa. Democrat. Presbyterian. Avocations: electronics, model railroading, target and trap shooting. Home: 1802 Tulane Ave Long Bech CA 90815

MCCONAGHY, DAVID CHARLES, systems manager; b. Clarkston, Wash., July 19, 1950; s. John A. and Jo Ann (Shafer) McC.; m. Janet Sue Wallace, Aug. 8, 1970; children: Coral Ann, Kellie Noel. BA in Math., U. Wash., 1972; MS in Systems Mgmt., U. So. Calif., 1980. Commd. ensign NOAA, 1972, advanced through grades to lt. comdr., 1983; comdg. officer Townsen Cromwell Ship NOAA, Honolulu, 1985—; pres. Microstrategies, Honolulu, 1984—. Contbr. articles to profl. jours. Avocations: boating, sailing. Home: 397 Opihikao Pl Honolulu HI 96825 Office: NOAA Ship Townsend Cromwell 1 Sand Island Access Rd Honolulu HI 96819

MCCONNELL, CALVIN DALE, clergyman; b. Monte Vista, Colo., Dec. 3, 1928; s. Roy and Leota Fern (Taylor) McC.; m. Mary Caroline Bamberg, Sept. 2, 1952 (dec. Apr. 1986); children: David William, Mark Andrew. B.A., U. Denver, 1951; M.Div., Iliff Sch. Theology, 1954; S.T.M., Andover Newton Theol. Sem. Ordained to ministry United Meth. Ch.; pastor Meth. Ch., Williams, Calif., 1955-58, 1st United Meth. Ch., Palo Alto, Calif. and Stanford U. Wesley Found., 1958-61; chaplain and asst. prof. religion Willamette U., Salem, Oreg., 1961-67; pastor Christ United Meth. Ch., Denver, 1968-72; pastor 1st United Meth. Ch., Boulder, Colo., 1972-79, Colorado Springs, Colo., 1979-80; bishop of United Meth. Ch., Portland Area, 1980—. Trustee Iliff Sch. Theology, Denver, Willamette U., Salem, Alaska Pacific U., Anchorage. Club: Rotary. Office: 1505 SW 18th Ave Portland OR 97201

MCCONNELL, CHARLES P., science teacher; b. Wayne, Nebr., Mar. 3, 1942; s. Charlie Irving and Truma (Prescott) M.; m. Cathie Dianne Harris, Aug. 22, 1964; children: Stefanie Michele, John Edward. BS, U. Nebr., 1964, MS, 1967. Sci. tchr. Fresno (Calif.) Unified Sch. Dist., 1967—. Active Boy Scouts Am. Mem. Nat. Sci. Tchrs. Assn., NEA (life), Calif. Tchrs. Assn., Fresno Tchrs. Assn. (life), Sigma Xi (assoc.). Republican. Lutheran. Avocation: amateur radio. Home: 1658 W Mesa Ave Fresno CA 93711 Office: Wawona Middle Sch 4524 N. Thorne Fresno CA 93704

MCCONNELL, HAROLD BOYD, JR., science educator; b. Trinidad, Colo., Apr. 18, 1933; s. Harold B. Sr. and Helen Louise (Craddock) McC. AA, Pueblo Jr. Coll., 1954; BA, U. Denver, 1956; MS, Webster U., 1968; PhD, Susan B. Anthony U., 1979. Cert. sci. tchr., Colo. Tchr. sci., math Crowley (Colo.) Schs., 1957-59; tchr. sci. Pueblo (Colo.) Pub. Schs., 1959—, pres. science resource, 1968-70, co-chmn. curriculum for middle sch. sci., 1972-73; chmn. sci. dept. Roncalli Middle Sch., Pueblo, Colo., 1971-76, 83—; tech. resource tchr. Roncalli Middle Sch., 1984—; bd. dirs. Colo. Sci. Olympiad. Mem. Environ. Adv. Com., Pueblo City Govt., 1979, chmn. 1982. Recipient Service award for Drama Pueblo Jr. Coll., 1954; Susan B. Anthony U. grantee, 1967. Fellow Internat. Oceanographic Soc.; mem. NEA, Colo. Assn. Sci. Tchrs. (presenter 1984), Nat. Assn. Sci. Tchrs. (presider 1984), Ind. Space Research Group, Profl. Assn. Diving Instrs. (instr. 1974-80), Colo. Gypsy Divers (pres. 1966, 77). Avocation: scuba diving. Home: 2624 Vinewood Ln Pueblo CO 81005

MC CONNELL, JOHN DOUGLAS, corporate executive; b. Dimboola, Victoria, Australia, May 13, 1932; s. William Thomas and Ada Maud (Gardner) McC.; came to U.S., 1964; B.A., Melbourne U., 1954; Ph.D., Stanford U., 1967; m. Gloria Ann Revak, Oct. 12, 1968; children—Joanne Patricia, Meredith Lorraine. Asst. to mng. dir. Automotive & Gen. Industries Ltd., Melbourne, 1954-59; mgr. Eagle M.R. Service Pty. Ltd., Melbourne, 1959-64; dir. mgmt. systems SRI Internat., Washington, 1975-77, dir. mgmt. econs. Europe and Middle East, 1977-78, dir. mgmt. services group, Menlo Park, Calif., 1978-80, dir. Food and Forest Products Ctr., 1980-83; v.p. Sungene Techs. Corp., Palo Alto, 1983-85; dir. fin. services ctr. SRI Internat., 1986—, Palo Alto; vis. lectr. U. Bradford (Eng.); lectr. San Francisco State U. Contbr. articles to profl. mags. Life gov. Royal Victorian Inst. Blind, 1957—; mem. exec. bd. Stanford Area Council Boy Scouts Am. Alfred P. Sloan Fellow, 1964-65; Gen. Electric Co. fellow, 1966. Fellow Australian Inst. Mgmt., Advt. Inst. Australia; mem. Am. Mktg. Assn., Royal Scottish Country Dance Soc. Presbyterian. Clubs: St. Andrews Soc. San Francisco, The Queen's, Army and Navy. Lodge: Masons. Home: 4174 Oak Hill Ave Palo Alto CA 94306 Office: SRI Internat 333 Ravenswood Ave Palo Alto CA 94304

MCCONNELL-MCCRORY, SUSAN MICHELE, product engineer, materials scientist; b. Twentynine Palms, Calif., Sept. 9, 1962; d. Dale Marvin and Patricia Ellen (Kennedy) McC.; m. Rudolph Anthony Montalvo, July 19, 1986. BS in Materials Engring., BS in Physics, U. Utah, 1983. Lab asst. U. Utah, Salt Lake City, 1981-83, research asst., 1983-84, lab. supr., 1983; engr. Abbott Critical Care, Salt Lake City, 1984—. Pres. scholar U. Utah, 1980. Mem. Phi Kappa Phi, Tau Beta Pi, Phi Eta Sigma. Democrat. Roman Catholic. Office: Abbott Critical Care 4455 Atherton Dr Salt Lake City UT 84123

MCCORKLE, CHESTER OLIVER, JR., agricultural and environmental sciences educator; b. Gilroy, Calif., Jan. 18, 1925; s. Chester Oliver and Avis Jacqueline (Kickham) McC.; m. Nina Grace Mathews, June 11, 1945; children: Sandra Lee, Kenneth Carl, Timothy Kevin. Student, Calif. Poly. State U., San Luis Obispo, 1941-43, U. Redlands, 1943-44; BS, U. Calif., Berkeley, 1947, MS, 1948, PhD, 1952. Research asst. U. Calif., Berkeley, 1947-48, asst. specialist, 1949-51; agrl. analyst Bank of Am., San Francisco, 1948-49; from research asst. to dean Coll. Agrl. and Environ. Scis. U. Calif., Davis, 1952-70, prof. agrl. econs., 1978—; v.p. Universitywide Office, Berkeley, 1970-78; research economist Ctr. for Econ. Research, Athens, Greece, 1961-62; econ. cons. Ministry Coordination, Kingdom of Greece, 1965; chmn. agr. and renewable resources bd. NRC-Nat. Acad. Scis., 1977-80, mem. commn. on natural resources, 1976-81. Served with USMCR, 1943-46, 51-52. Mem. AAAS, AAUP, Am. Western Agrl. Econ. Assn. (past pres.). Club: Bohemian (San Francisco). Home: 637 Eisenhower St Davis CA 95616 Office: U Calif Voorhies Hall Room 210 Davis CA 95616

MCCORMAC, BILLY MURRAY, physicist, research institution executive, former army officer; b. Zanesville, Ohio, Sept. 8, 1920; 1948, 69; 5 children. B.S., Ohio State U., 1943; M.S., U. Va., 1956, Ph.D. in Nuclear Physics, 1957. Commd. officer U.S. Army, 1943; advanced through grades to lt. col.; physicist U.S. Army (Office Spl. Weapons Devel.), 1957-60; scientist U.S. Army (Office of Chief of Staff), 1960-61; physicist U.S. Army (Def. Atomic Support Agy.), 1961-62, chief electromagnetic br., 1962-63; ret. 1963; sci. advisor Ill. Inst. Tech. Research Inst., 1963, dir. div. geophysics, 1963-68; sr. cons. scientist Lockheed Research Labs., Palo Alto, Calif., 1968-69, mgr. Radiation Physics Lab., 1969-74, mgr. Electro-optics Lab., 1974-76, mgr. solar and optics physics, 1976—; Chmn. radiation trapped in earth's magnetic field Adv. Study Inst., Norway, 1965, chmn. aurora and airglow, Eng., 1966, Norway, 1968, Can., 1970, chmn. physics and chemistry of atmospheres, France, 1972, Belgium, 1974, chmn. earth's particles and fields, Germany, 1967, Calif., 1969, Italy, 1971, Eng., 1973, Austria, 1975; chmn. Shuttle Environment and Ops.-I, Washington, 1983, -II, Houston, 1985; chmn. Space Station in 21st Century, Reno, 1986. Now editor: Jour. Water, Air and Soil Pollution; editor: Geophysics and Astrophysics Monographs. Fellow Am. Inst. Aero. and Astronautics (asso.); mem. A.A.A.S., Am. Astronautical Soc. (sr.), Am. Phys. Soc., Am. Geophys. Union, Marine Tech. Soc., Am. Astron. Soc., Am. Ordnance Assn. Home: 12861 Alta Tierra Rd Los Altos Hills CA 94022 Office: 3251 Hanover St Palo Alto CA 94304

MC CORMAC, WESTON ARTHUR, ret. educator, ret. army officer; b. Tacoma, Mar. 5, 1911; s. Jesse Carney and Jessie (Myron) McC.; B.A., Golden Gate U., M.B.A., 1968; diploma Nat. War Coll., 1956; M.P.A., U. So. Calif., 1972; M.A., Calif. Poly. State U., 1975. m. Mary Jeanne Rapp, Sept. 5, 1940. Account exec. Merrill, Lynch, Pierce, Fenner & Beane, Tacoma, Seattle, 1929-40; commd. lt. U.S. Army, 1940, advanced through grades to col., 1946; asst. chief of staff 7th Army G 1, 1952-54; comdg. officer 35th F.A. Group, Germany, 1956-58; dep. chief of staff V Corps, 1958-60, asst. chief of staff G 1, Pacific, 1962-65; ret., 1966; prof. bus., dept. chmn. Calif. Poly. State U., San Luis Obispo, 1968-80, ret., 1980. Decorated Legion of Merit with 2 oak leaf clusters, Silver Star, Bronze Star medal, Commendation medal with oak leaf cluster. Fellow Fin. Analysts Fedn.; mem. Los Angeles Soc. Fin. Analysts. Club: San Luis Obispo Golf and Country. Home: 176 Country Club San Luis Obispo CA 93401

MCCORMACK, DENNIS K., clinical psychologist. children: Kelly, Karen. BA in Math., Calif. Western U., 1969; MA, U.S. Internat. U., 1971, PhD in Leadership and Human Behavior, PhD in Psychology, 1974, 78. Diplomate Internat. Council Profl. Counseling and Psychotherapy, Am. Inst. Counseling and Psychotherapy, Internat. Acad. Health Care Profls. Pvt. practice family therapist Coronado, Calif.; guest speaker at numerous clubs, lodges and local orgns. Contbr. articles to profl. jours. Mem. Sr. Citizen Adv. Com., 1982—, Land Use Adv. Com., Coronado, 1979-80; chmn. Coronado Planning Commn., 1978-83, St. Paul's United Meth. Ch., 1978-81, personnel com., 1978-81, mem. adminstrv. bd., 1983—; pres. Coronado Coordinating Council, 1983—; mem. adv. bd. Mil. Affairs Com., 1984—; bd. dirs. Vietnam Vets. Leadership Program, 1984—; mem. Southbay Chember Exec. Com., 1986—, Coronado Visitor Promotion Bd., 1986—. Fellow Internat. Council of Sex Edn. and Parenthood of Am. U., Am. Bd. Med. Psychotherapists (clin. assoc.), Coronado C. of C. (pres. 1986—). Office: 1017 Isabella Ave PO Box 583 Coronado CA 92118

MCCORMACK, MIKE, professional football team executive. Pres., gen. mgr. Seattle Seahawks, NFL. Office: Seattle Seahawks 11220 NE 53d St Kirkland WA 98033

MCCORMICK, ADELE VON RÜST, psychotherapist; b. San Francisco, Dec. 11, 1929; d. George Washington and Adele E. von Rüst; clin. cert. Moreno Inst., SUNY, 1968; Ph.D. in Psychology, Columbia Pacific U., 1980; m. Thomas E. McCormick, Dec. 11, 1971; 1 child, Deborah. Profl. actress with Warner Bros., 1958-62; appeared in films including My Enemy The Sea, 1961, Days of Wine and Roses, 1962; co-founder Charila Found., San Francisco, 1968; instr. psychiat. residents Agnews (Calif.) State Hosp., 1966-72; cons. in psychotherapy Belmont Psychiat. Center, 1972-75; founder, dir. Psychotherapy Inst., San Francisco, 1970, dir., 1970-81; exec. dir. Clin. Psychotherapy Inst., 1983—; condr. clin. workshops in group dynamics and psychodrama in Switzerland, Eng., Spain, U.S., 1971-78; hon. prof. U. Madrid, 1977; founder, exec. dir. adult and adolescent treatment units McCormick Found., Inc., 1979—; founder Equine Therapy for the Psychosis, 1985—. Recipient Medal of Honor, U. Madrid, 1977. Mem. Soc. Analytic Psychotherapy, Internat. Assn. Group Psychotherapy, Orthopsychiat. Soc., Friends of the Psychoanalytic Soc. Republican. Episcopalian. Contbr. articles on group psychotherapy to profl. publs. Home: 9000 Franz Valley Rd Calistoga CA 94515 Office: 227 Indian Creek Santa Rosa CA 94903

MCCORMICK, CHARLES PERRY, JR., food products company executive; b. Balt., May 29, 1928; s. Charles P. and Marion (Hinds) McM.; m. Marlene Darby Hicks, July 29, 1950 (div. 1980); children: Charles P. III, William C., Linda M., Gail P.; m. Jimi Helen Faulk, July 1, 1980. Student, Johns Hopkins U., 1946-47, Duke U., 1948-49. V.p. new products McCormick Co., Inc., Hunt Valley, Md., 1962-70; v.p. corp. devel. McCormick Co., Inc., Hunt Valley, 1970-81, v.p. packaging group, 1986—; chmn., pres. Setco, Inc., Anaheim, Calif., 1981—, Tubed Products Inc., Easthampton, Mass., 1985—. Republican. Clubs: Annapolis Yacht, Newport Beach Country. Avocations: sailing, racing, golf, tennis. Office: Setco Inc 4875 Hunter Ave Anaheim CA 92817-0808

MCCORMICK, FLOYD GUY, JR., educator; b. Center, Colo., July 3, 1927; s. Floyd Guy and Gladys (Weir) McC.; m. Constance P. Slane, Sept. 18, 1965; children: Angela Lynn, Craig Alan, Kim Ann, Robert Guy. B.S., Colo. State U., 1950, M.Ed., 1959; Ph.D., Ohio State U., 1964. Tchr. vocat. agr. State Colo., 1956-62; asst. prof. agrl. edn. Ohio State U., 1964-67; mem. com. agr. edn. Commn. Edn. in Agr. and Natural Resources, Nat. Acad. Sci., 1967-69; prof. agrl. edn., head dept. U. Ariz., 1967—; cons. in-service edn., div. vocat. edn. Ohio Dept. Edn., 1963-64; vis. prof. Colo. State U., 1973; external examiner U. Sierra Leone, 1984, 85, 87; adv. trustee Am. Inst. Cooperatives, Washington, 1985—; mem. Nat. Council Vocat. and Tech. Edn. in Agriculture, Washington, 1985—. Co-author Teacher Education in Agriculture, 1982, Supervised Occupational Experience Handbook, 1982; Author instructional units, tech. bulls., articles in profl. jours.; Spl. editor: Agrl. Edn. mag, 1970-74. Trustee Nat. FFA Found. Served with USNR, 1945-46. Named hon. state farmer Colo., 1958, hon. state farmer Ariz., 1968; Hon. Am. Farmer, 1972; Outstanding Educator in Am., 1972; recipient Centennial award Ohio State U., 1970; E.B. Knight award NACTA Jour., 1980. Mem. Am. Vocat. Assn. (mem. policy com. agrl. edn. div. 1976-79, v.p. div. 1985—, chmn. membership com. 1980-83, sec. agrl. edn. div. 1983-86, pres. 1985—), Nat. Vocat. Agr. Tchrs. Assn. (life; Outstanding Service award Region I 1974, 83), Am. Assn. Tchr. Educators in Agr. (disting. lectr. 1984, editor newsletter 1975-76, pres. 1976-77, Disting. Service award 1978), Alpha Zeta, Alpha Tau Alpha (hon.), Gamma Sigma Delta, Phi Delta Kappa. Home: 6933 Paseo San Andres Tucson AZ 85710

MC CORMICK, HAROLD L., motion picture theatre company executive, state senator; b. Florence, Colo., May 16, 1918; s. B. P. and Anna L. (Hoffman) McC.; m. Jeanne E. Rolfes, Jan. 8, 1941; children—Brian, Carole, Ellen. B.S., U. Denver, 1940. Owner, operator McCormick Theatres, Colo., N. Mex., 1940—; mem. Colo. Gen. Assembly, 1961-72; mem. Colo. Senate, 1973—, pres. pro tem.; candidate for Congress, 1980. Trustee St. Thomas Hosp.; elder Presbyn. Ch. Served to capt. U.S. Army, 1942-47; col. USAF ret. Decorated Air Force Commendation medal, Presidential citation; named Legislator of Yr. DAV; Citizen on Yr. Jr. C. of C. Mem. Am. Legion, VFW, Footprinters, Omicron Delta Kappa, Beta Theta Pi. Republican. Presbyterian. Club: Masons. Address: 927 Ebenezer St Canon City CO 81212

MCCORMICK, MICHAEL STUART, social worker; b. Colorado Springs, Colo., Aug. 3, 1952; s. Dale Wallace and Anna Rose (Kipp) McC.; m. Jackie Lou Moore, Oct. 11, 1975; children: Kelly Reid, Brock Thomas. BS in Psychology, Colo. State U., 1974; MSW, U. Denver, 1979. Group home counselor Vision Quest, Tucson, 1974-75; youth worker State of Colo. Div. Youth Services, Golden, 1975-80; asst. dir. Teton County Youth Services, Wilson, Wyo., 1980-83; family therapist Shawnee Mental Health, Coal Grove, Ohio, 1983-84; supr. III Garfield County Dept. Social Services, Rifle, Colo., 1984-86; pvt. practice social work White River Counseling, Rifle,

Colo., 1985—; program dir. Western Acad., Rifle, 1986—; bd. dirs., treas. Family Visitor Program, Glenwood Springs, 1984—. Mem. Nat. Assn. Social Workers (mem. Wyo. chpt. Pub. Relations com. 1982-83), Psi Chi. Episcopalian. Avocations: swimming, hiking, camping, fishing. Home: 995 Wamsley Way Rifle CO 81650 Office: Western Acad PO Box 1342 Rifle CO 81650

MCCORMICK, THOMAS EVERETT, psychiatrist; b. Tacoma, Wash., Oct. 13, 1924; s. Thomas Everett and Margaret Louise (Whidden) McC.; B.S., St. Martins Coll., 1949; M.D., U. Oreg., 1955; m. Adele von Ryst, Dec. 11, 1971. Intern, St. Josephs Hosp. and Maricopa County Hosp., Phoenix, 1955-56; gen. practice medicine, Coolidge, Ariz., 1956-59, San Rafael, Calif., 1959-67; resident in psychiatry Pacific Med. Center, San Francisco, 1967-69, Herrick Meml. Hosp., Berkeley, 1969-70; practice medicine specializing in psychiatry, Kentfield, Calif., 1970—; chief psychiat. sect. Ross (Calif.) Gen. Hosp., 1973-75; med. dir. San Francisco Psythotherapy and Psychodrama Inst., 1970-82. Exec. dir. McCormick Found. Inc., 1979; pres. Clin. Psychotherapy Inst., 1980-85. Served with M.C., USNR, 1943-46; PTO. Recipient Medal of Honor dept. psychology Autonomous U. Madrid, 1976. Mem. AMA, Calif. Med. Assn., Marin County Med. Assn. (mem. exec. bd. 1974-75), Am. Psychiat. Assn., Am. Group Psychotherapy Assn., Internat. Assn. Group Psychotherapy, Calif. Psychiat. Assn., Sonoma County Med. Soc., Redwood Psychiat. Soc., Moreno Acad., Phi Beta Phi. Republican. Episcopalian. Office: 1044 Sir Francis Drake Blvd Kentfield CA 94904 Office: 9000 Franz Valley Rd Calistoga CA 94515

MCCORMICK, WILLIAM MALLORY, financial services company executive; b. Hartford, Conn., Aug. 21, 1940; s. Ernest W. and Esther M. McCormick; B.S., Yale U., 1962; M.S., George Washington U., 1967; children—James and Skye (twins). Mgmt. cons. McKinsey & Co., N.Y.C., 1967-72; investment banker Donaldson, Lufkin & Jenrette, N.Y.C., 1972-75; with Am. Express Internat. Banking Corp., 1975-78, sr. v.p. fin., systems and ops., 1977-78; sr. v.p. fin. and planning card div. Am. Express Co., 1978-79, pres. travel div., 1979-80, pres. card div., 1980-81, pres. consumer fin. services group, 1981-82, pres. travel related services, 1982-83; chmn., chief exec. officer Fireman's Fund Ins. Co., 1984—; bd. dirs. SRI Adv. Council, Bay Area Council; mem. adv. bd. Nat. Ctr. on Fin. Services. Served to lt. USNR, 1962-67. Mem. Commonwealth Club, Calif. Roundtable. Address: Fireman's Fund Insurance Co 777 San Marin Dr Novato CA 94998 *

MCCORQUODALE, DAN A., state senator; b. Longville, La., Dec. 17, 1934; s. Dan A. and Lallah Mae (Thornton) McC.; m. Jean A. Botsford; children—Mike, Sharon, Dan. B.Edn., San Diego State U., 1962. Mem. Chula Vista City Council, Calif., 1960-64, mayor, 1964-68; tchr. elem. sch., National City and San Jose, Calif., 1962-72; rep. Santa Clara County Bd. Suprs., Calif., 1972-82; mem. Calif. Senate, 1982—, vice-chmn. agr. and water com. Founder, pres. Santa Clara County Consumers Protection and Edn. Council; chmn. Santa Clara County Consumer Protection Conf.; sec. adv. bd. Napa State Hosp.; chmn. Area VII Planning Bd. for Developmentally Disabled; rep. Statewide Homeowners Assn., others. Served to sgt. USMC, 1953-57; Pacific. Democrat.

MCCOWN, ANNE ROYAL, insurance company executive; b. Rapid City, S.D., June 23, 1954; d. Robert E. and Edoris (Stauffer) Royal; m. Eddie E. McCown, Oct. 2, 1982; 1 child, Garrett Edward. BS, Eastern Ill. U., 1976; postgrad. (AA), Orange Coast Coll., 1981. Div. mgr. Sears Roebuck and Co., Elkhart, Ind., 1976-77; loss control rep. Safeco Ins. Co., Fountain Valley, Calif., 1980-81; sr. loss control rep. CIGNA Corp., Orange, Calif., 1981-86, loss control br. mgr., 1986—. Mem. Am. Soc. Safety Engrs. Avocations: swimming, designing clothes. Home: 12 Sanderling Irvine CA 92714 Office: CIGNA Corp 1120 W LaVeta Orange CA 92668

MCCOY, GEORGE A., comptroller; b. Leavenworth, Wash., Sept. 13, 1926; s. John Wesley and Bessie Marian (Horn) McCoy; m. Shirley Ruth Mitchell, Feb. 14, 1956 (div. June 1982); children: Marcus G., Matthew M., Marian R., Martha J. BBA, U. Wash., 1951. Clk. Alcoa, Wenatchee, Wash., 1952; office mgr. Alcoa Exp. Co., Pitts., 1952-54; office mgr. Peshastin (Wash.) Fruit Growers, 1958-68, comptroller, 1971-76; asst. mgr. Trout Inc., Chelan, Wash., 1968-71; comptroller Skookum Inc., Wenatchee, 1976—. Mem. Nat. Soc. Accts. for Coops. Republican. Lodges: Kiwanis (pres. Peshastin club 1961), Lions. Avocations: fishing, cruising, hiking, plant and animal studies. Home: 201 S Elliott #5 Wenatchee WA 98801 Office: Skookum Inc PO Box 1987 Wenatchee WA 98801

MCCOY, LESTER BLAINE, laboratory manager, consultant; b. Evansville, Ind., Mar. 10, 1953; s. William Harold and Alberta Ellen (Gerard) McC.; m. Michele Faye Murphy, Dec. 26, 1981 (div. Apr. 1986). B in Microbiology, Ind. U., 1978. Field engr. Alaskan Resource Scis. Corp., Fairbanks, 1975-77; chemist City of Hood River, Oreg., 1978-81; environ. chemist Martin Marietta Aluminum Inc., The Dalles, Oreg., 1981-83; lab. mgr. Commonwealth Aluminum, Goldendale, Wash., 1983—; cons. Mt. Hood (Oreg.) Meadows, 1980—, City of Mosier, Oreg., 1981-82. Named Eagle Scout, Boy Scouts Am., 1968. Mem. Am. Chem. Soc. Democrat. Presbyterian. Lodge: Elks. Avocations: kayaking, water and snow skiing. Home: PO Box 61 Goldendale WA 98620 Office: Commonwealth Aluminum 85 John Day Dam Rd Goldendale WA 98620-9302

MCCOY, WILLIAM EDWARD, III, electronics engineer; b. Oakland, Calif., Jan. 9, 1939; s. William Edward and Mary Venable (Tuckerman) McC. AA with honors, Umpqua Community Coll., 1974; BS in Gen. Sci., BS. in Math. with high scholastic honors, Oreg. State U., 1977, BS in Computer Sci., 1980; MS in Computer Sci., Calif. State U., Chico, 1982; postgrad., UCLA, 1984-85. Logic designer, research asst. Hughes Aircraft Co., Culver City, Calif., 1962-64, asst. data processing analyst, 1964-65; programmer Bulter Publs., Hawthorne, Calif., 1966-67; data processing, systems analyst Atlantic Richfield Co., Los Angeles, 1968-69, Autographics, Monterey Park, Calif., 1969-71; electronics engr. Naval Weapons Ctr., China Lake, Calif., 1980-81; engr. EDP applications SP Communications, Burlingame, Calif., 1981-83; engr. GTE Sprint Communications Corp., 1983; mem. tech. staff Rockwell Internat., Lakewood, Calif., 1983-86; engring. specialist Applied Techs. div. Litton, San Jose, Calif., 1986—; cons. computer tech., 1971. Pres. Indian Wells Valley Pro-Life Com., 1981. Served with USAF, 1956-60. Mem. AAAS, AIAA, IEEE (chmn. membership devel. China Lake sect.), Am. Assn. Artificial Intelligence, Assn. Computing Machinery, Soc. Computer Simulation, Profl. Software Programmers Assn. (chmn. cert. com. 1983-84, product reviewer 1984-86), Calif. Assn. Physically Handicapped (life, parliamentarian Ridgecrest chpt. 1981), Buena Park Jaycees (treas. 1964), Hawthorne Jaycees (state dir. 1966), Southside Jayees (v.p. 1968), DAV, Assn. Old Crows, NAACP (1981-82), Phi Kappa Phi (life). Clubs: Toastmasters (China Lake) (treas. 1980, sec. 1981); Applied Orators (pres. 1986-87, asst. area gov. 1987, area gov. 1983-84, named able toastmaster 1983). Lodges: K.C. (chancellor Ridgecrest council 1980-81, dep. grand knight 1981), Masons. Home: 1736 Arroyo De Oro San Jose CA 95116-1350

MCCOY, WILLIAM HARRISON, physical chemist; b. Nelsenville, Ohio, May 28, 1925; s. McKinley and Pearl (Gerhardt) McC.; m. Joyce Esther Garman, June 6, 1959. BS, Youngstown U., 1950; PhD, U. Pitts., 1955. Asst. prof. phys. chemistry Washington and Jefferson Coll., Washington, Pa., 1955-56, Tex. A&M U., College Station, 1956-57; assoc. prof. Youngstown (Ohio) U., 1957-63; sr. scientist U.S. Dept. Interior, Washington, 1963-83; phys. scientist U.S. Dept. Interior, Yuma, Ariz., 1983-86. Editor: Water, 1975; contbr. articles to profl. jours. Served as sgt. AUS, 1943-45, ETO. Recipient Honor Achievement award U.S. Dept. Interior, Washington, 1971. Mem. Am. Chem. Soc., Sigma Xi, Phi Lambda Upsilon. Republican. Baptist. Avocations: photography, Civil War history. Home: 1461 W 16th Pl Yuma AZ 85364

MCCRADY, HOWARD C., bank holding company executive; b. 1931; married. B.S., U. So. Calif., 1953. Fin. analyst U.S. Steel Corp., 1956-61; fin. cons. Robert Heller & Assocs., 1961-64; mgr. EDP cost planning Mohasco Industries, 1964-67; sr. v.p. ops. and control 1st Western Bank & Trust, 1967-74; sr. v.p., chief fin. officer Valley Nat. Bank Ariz., Phoenix, 1974-78, exec. v.p. mktg., chief fin. officer, 1978-82, vice chmn., 1982-83, chmn. bd., chief exec. officer, 1983—; exec. v.p. Valley Nat. Corp., Phoenix, 1981-82, pres., 1982-83, chmn. bd., chief exec. officer, 1983—. Served with U.S. Army, 1954-55. Office: Valley Nat Corp PO Box 71 Phoenix AZ 85002 *

MC CRAKEN, ROBERT STANTON, newspaper and broadcasting exec.; b. Washington, June 1, 1924; s. Tracy Stephenson and Lillian G. (Davis) McC.; m. A. Anne Wright, May 6, 1960; children—Michael, Cindy. Student, Washington and Lee U., 1945, U. Denver, 1946; B.A., U. Wyo., 1948. Reporter Rawlins (Wyo.) Daily Times, 1948-50; promotion mgr. Cheyenne (Wyo.) Newspapers, Inc.; pubs. Wyo. Eagle, Wyo. State Tribune, Wyo. Tribune Eagle, 1950-54, asso. pub., 1955-58, pres., pub., 1958—; pres. Frontier Broadcasting Co., Cheyenne; chmn. bd. Laramie Newspapers, Inc., Rawlins Newspapers, Inc., Rock Springs Newspapers, Inc., Big Horn Basin Newspapers, Inc.; dir. Wyo. Broadcasting Co., Cheyenne Nat. Bank. Trustee U. Wyo., 1961-67. Served with AUS, World War II. Mem. Internat. Platform Assn., Cheyenne C. of C., Kappa Sigma. Presbyterian. Clubs: Elks, Kiwanis. Office: Wyo Eagle 702 W Lincolnway Cheyenne WY 82001

MCCRALEY, THOMAS LUE, superintendent schools; b. Taft, Calif., June 28, 1940; s. Don F. and Ethel M. (Roy) McC.; m. Frances L. Fawbush, June 19, 1973; children—Thomas M., Todd R., Timothy L., Tia L. B.S. in Edn., U. Ariz., 1964; M.A. in Edn., No. Ariz. U., 1970, Ed.D., 1975. Cert. tchr., supt., Ariz. Tchr., Bisbee Pub. Schs., Ariz., 1964-65, Bullhead City Schs., Ariz., 1966-68, asst. prin., 1969-70, supt., 1972-78; supt. Yuma Sch. Dist. No. 1, Ariz., 1978—; adj. prof. No. Ariz. U., Flagstaff, 1977—, presenter at mgmt. workshop, 1980-83;. Author: An Investigative Study of the Traditional versus Year-Round School Plan, 1975; contbr. articles to profl. jours. Mem., officer Yuma Group, 1980—, United Way Yuma, 1979—; mem. state adv. council NAU Ctr. for Excellence in Edn., 1984—; mem. supt.'s adv. council Ariz. State Bd. Edn., 1985—. Recipient Disting. Service award Bullhead City Jaycees, 1972; award Yuma chpt. Freedom's Found., 1984; named AAEA Art Advocate of Yr., 1985. Mem. Am. Assn. Sch. Adminstrs. (presenter conv.), Assn. Sch. Bus. Ofcls. (presenter conv.), Ariz. Assn. Sch. Adminstrs. (sec.-treas. 1983-84, pres.-elect 1984—), Nat. Orgn. on Legal Problems, Yuma Leadership, Phi Delta Kappa. Democrat. Mem. Ch. of Jesus Christ of Latter-day Saints. Lodges: Elks (officer, exalted ruler Bullhead City 1973-74), Rotary (officer). Home: 2420 W 11th St Yuma AZ 85364 Office: Yuma Sch Dist No 1 450 W 6th St Yuma AZ 85364

MCCRARY, ELIZABETH ADELLE, aerospace engineer, archaeologist, educator; b. Burbank, Calif., May 15, 1948; d. William Harry and Olene Adelle (Dunham) McC. BA, UCLA, 1969, MA, 1971, MS, Northrup U., 1979, BS, Calif. State U., 1983. Cert. community coll. instr., Calif. Asst. to dir. dept. inventory control U.S. Naval Supply Ctr., Long Beach, Calif., 1971-73; archaeologist U. Calif., Santa Barbara, 1974; pub. affairs dir., archaeologist Northridge (Calif.) Archaeol. Research Ctr., 1973-76; customer services rep. Wings West, Inc., Santa Monica, Calif., 1977-79; prof. Los Angeles Southwest Coll., 1973-85; mem. tech. staff Hughes Aircraft Co., El Segundo, Calif., 1980-86, sr. mem. tech. staff, 1986—; cons. in field. Mem. IEEE, AAAS, Assn. Computing Machinery. Republican. Club: PEO Sisterhood. Home: 6656 E Rosecrans Ave #S26 Paramount CA 90723 Office: Hughes Aircraft Co Bldg El M/S B146 2000 E El Segundo Blvd El Segundo CA 90245

MC CRAVEN, CARL CLARKE, health services administrator; b. Des Moines, May 27, 1926; s. Marcus Henry and Buena Vista (Rollins) McC.; B.S. in Elec. Engring., Howard U., 1950; M.S. in Health Services Adminstrn., Calif. State U.-Northridge, 1976; m. Eva Louise Stewart, Mar. 18, 1978; 1 son, Carl B. Radiation physicist Nat. Bur. Standards, 1951-55; research engr. Lockheed Calif. Co., 1955-63; mem. tech. staff TRW Systems, 1963-72; assoc. adminstr. Pacoima Meml. Hosp., Lakeview Terrace, Calif., 1972-74; pres. and chief exec. officer Hillview Mental Health Ctr., Inc., Lakeview Terrace, 1974—; asst. prof. Calif. State U., Northridge, 1976-78. Regent Casa Loma Coll.; bd. dirs. San Fernando Valley Girl Scout Council, Pledgerville Sr. Citizens Villa; bd. dirs., mem. budget rev. com. United Way; bd. dirs. ARC; treas. San Fernando Valley Mental Health Assn. Recipient citation Calif. Senate, 1971, Calif. Assembly, 1971, City of Los Angeles, 1971, 78. Fellow Assn. Mental Health Adminstrs.; mem. Am. Public Health Assn., Am. Mgmt. Assn., Nat. Assn. Health Services Execs., NAACP (pres. so. area Calif. conf. 1967-71, nat. dir. 1970-76), Sigma Pi Phi. Lodge: North San Fernando Valley Rotary (pres.). Home: 17233 Chatsworth St Granada Hills CA 91344

MCCRAVEN, EVA STEWART MAPES, health service adminstr.; b. Los Angeles, Sept. 26, 1936; d. Paul Melvin and Wilma Zech (Ziegler) Stewart; B.S. magna cum laude, Calif. State U., Northridge, 1974, M.S., 1976; m. Carl Clarke McCraven, Mar. 18, 1978; children—David Anthony, Lawrence James, Maria Lynn Mapes. Dir. spl. projects Pacoima Meml. Hosp., 1969-71, dir. health edn., 1971-74; asst. exec. dir. Hillview Community Mental Health Center, Lakeview Terrace, Calif., 1974—; past dir. dept. consultation and edn. Hillview Ctr., developer, mgr. long-term residential program, 1986—. Pres. San Fernando Valley Coordinating Council Area Assn., Sunland-Tujunga Coordinating Council; bd. dirs. N.E. Valley Health Corp., 1970-73, Golden State Community Mental Health Ctr., 1970-73. Fellow Assn. Mental Health Adminstrs.; mem. Am. Pub. Health Assn., Women in Health Adminstrn., Health Services Adminstrn. Alumni Assn. (v.p.), Bus. and Profl. Women, LWV. Office: Hillview Community Mental Health Ctr 11600 Eldridge Ave Lake View Terrace CA 91342

MCCREADY, DONALD LLOYD, JR., food supplement, cosmetics and household products executive; b. Columbus, Ohio, Feb. 12, 1926; s. Donald Lloyd and Helen (Smith) McC; student Newberry Coll., 1955, U. Ga., 1945, Ohio State U., 1945-47; m. June Williams, Jan. 6, 1956 (div.); children—Terry Lee, Donald Lloyd III, Deidre June; m. Sandra Lou Galbraith, Aug. 8, 1978; 1 dau., Dona Diana. Plastics engr. Battelle Meml. Inst., Columbus, 1947-50; chief packaging devel. U.S. Army Chem. Corps, Army Chem. Ctr., Md., 1952-56; packaging coordinator Continental Can Co., Mt. Vernon, Ohio, 1956-58, customer research cons., 1958-64, mgr. product devel., N.Y.C., 1964-68; dir. packaging devel. Parke, Davis & Co., Detroit, 1968-70; mgr. packaging systems Am. Hosp. Supply Corp., Glendale, Calif., 1970-74; dir. packaging systems Improved Tech. Corp., Los Angeles, 1974-76; mgr. packaging devel. Shaklee Corp., Hayward, Calif., 1976—; lectr. Sch. Packaging, Mich. State U., 1966—, Nat. Hosp. Packaging Conf., N.Y.U., 1973; mem. Nat. Def. Exec. Res., 1969—; assoc. dir. pub. speaking and human relationships Balt. Inst., 1953-54. Mem. Mt. Vernon 7th Day Adventists Sch. Bd.; chmn. Community Christmas Concert, Civic Christmas Lighting and Decorating Com.; bd. dirs. Mohaven Wild Life Found., 1960-61; mem. Nat. Def. Exec. Res., 1969—; bd. dirs. Western Packaging Edn. Found., 1981—; mem. packaging adv. bd; San Jose State U., 1981—; mem. Nat. Republican Senatorial Com., 1978—, Nat. Rep. Congl. Com., 1981—. Served with USNR, 1944-48; with Chem. Corps, AUS, 1950-52. Mem. Soc. Plastics Engrs., Soc. Packaging and Handling Engrs., Packaging Inst., ASTM (gen. sec. com. F-2 1962-64), Potato Chip Inst. Internat. (chmn. packaging com. 1963-64), Nat. Flexible Packaging Assn. (chmn. taste and odor test com. 1958-59). Mem. Seventh Day Adventist Ch. Contbr. articles to profl. jours. Patentee thermal bonding skin packaging. Home: 4650 Wente Ct Oakley CA 94561 Office: 1992 Alpine Way Hayward CA 94545

MCCREERY, JOHN THOMAS, architect; b. Muncie, Ind., July 28, 1948; s. Gene Sharp and Mary Jane (Robbins) McC.; m. Susan Richards, Feb. 22, 1970 (div. 1976); m. Sarah Hendry Fuller, May 31, 1977; children: Jennifer Robbins, Zacharia Quinton Fuller-McCreery. Student, Haile Selassie U., Addis Ababa, Ethiopia, 1968; BS in Polit. Sci., U. Utah, 1972, MArch, 1974. Registered architect, Oreg., Wash., Calif. Apprentice Lawrence Halprin & Assocs., San Francisco, 1975-76, Kroker Architects, Portland, Oreg., 1977-78, Fisher, Walling and Long, Portland, 1978-79; practice architecture Portland, 1979-84; ptnr. McCreery Martindale, Portland, 1984—; bd. dirs. Mental Health Services West. Active Oreg. for Neil Goldschmidt, Portland, 1986. Served to 2d lt. USNG, 1969-75. Recipient Best in Show photography award Skamania (Wash.) County Fair Bd., 1984. Mem. AIA, Nat. Council Archtl. Registration Bds., Portland Art Assn., Oreg. Mus. Sci. and Industry. Republican. Avocations: photography, sailing, pingpong, tennis, squash. Office: McCreery Martindale Architects 1220 SW Morrison Suite 1200 Portland OR 97205

MCCREIGHT, LOUIS R(ALPH), materials scientist; b. Zion, Ill., Nov. 26, 1922; s. Ralph B. and Phronia Etta (Benckendorf) McC.; m. Malvina Eloris Smith, Oct. 15, 1949; children—Brian R., Barbara L. B.S. in Ceramic Engring., U. Ill., 1946, M.S., 1949. Research asst. U. Chgo. and MIT, 1944-45; research asst., research assoc. U. Ill., Urbana, 1945-49; ceramic engr. Knolls Atomic Power Lab., Schenectady, 1949-55; mgr. materials research and devel. Gen. Electric Missiles and Space Div., Phila., 1955-81; dir. materials sci. lab. Aerospace Corp., El Segundo, Calif., 1981-84, sr. engr., engring. div., 1984—; mem. research adv. com. on materials NASA, Washington, 1959-69, chmn., 1965-67; mem. Nat. Materials Adv. Bd., NRC, 1966-70. Co-author: Ceramic and Graphite Fibers and Whiskers, 1965, 2d edit., 1968; contbr. articles to profl. jours.; patentee in field. Pres., Chester County council Boy Scouts Am., 1979-81; v.p. Upper Main Line YMCA, 1973-81. Fellow Am. Ceramic Soc. (officer); mem. Materials Research Soc., ASTM (research com. 1963-70). Republican. Presbyterian. Home: 2763 San Ramon Dr Rancho Palos Verdes CA 90274 Office: Aerospace Corp PO Box 92957 MS M4/966 Los Angeles CA 90009

MC CRONE, ALISTAIR WILLIAM, university president; b. Regina, Sask., Can., Oct. 7, 1931; came to U.S., 1953, naturalized, 1963; s. Hugh McMillan and Kathleen Maude Tallent (Forth) McCrone; m. Judith Ann Saari, May 8, 1958; children: Bruce, Craig, Mary. B.A., U. Sask., 1953; M.S. (Shell fellow), U. Nebr., 1955; Ph.D., U. Kans., 1961. Instr. geology NYU, 1959-61, asst. prof., 1961-64, assoc. prof., 1964-69, prof., 1969-70; chmn. dept. geology N.Y. U., 1966-69; assoc. dean NYU Grad. Sch. Arts and Scis., 1969-70; acad. v.p. U. of Pacific, Stockton, Calif., 1970-74; prof. geology U. of Pacific, 1970-74; pres., prof. geology Humboldt State U., Arcata, Calif., 1974—; bd. dirs. Redwood Empire Assoc., 1983—; Lectr. geology CBS-TV network, 1969-70; editorial cons. sci. series Harcourt-Brace-Jovanovich pub., 1971, 73, 77; mem. com. on environment Am. Assn. State Colls. and Univs., 1974-82. Contbr. articles to profl. jours. Trustee Pacific Med. Center, San Francisco, 1971-74; mem. Calif. Council for Humanities., 1978-82. Recipient Erasmus Haworth Honors award U. Kans., 1957; named Danforth Assos. convenor N.Y. U., 1966-68, Outstanding Educator of Am., 1975. Fellow Geol. Soc. Am., AAAS, Calif. Acad. Sci.; mem. Am. Assn. Petroleum Geologists, Soc. Econ. Paleontologists and Mineralogists, Am. Assn. Univ. Adminstrs. (bd. dirs. 1986—), St. Andrews Soc. of N.Y., Sigma Xi. Presbyterian. Club: Univ. of San Francisco. Lodge: Rotary. Office: Humboldt State U Univ Campus Arcata CA 95521

MCCRURY, PHILLIP WAYNE, lawyer; b. St. Peter, Minn., Aug. 29, 1944; s. Charles Floyd and Norine (Jagers) McC. BA, U. Tex., 1966, LLB, 1968; LLM, So. Meth. U., Dallas, 1978. Bar: Tex. 1968, Okla. 1978, Colo. 1985. Asst. dist. atty. Nueces County, Tex., 1969-72; ptnr. Auforth, Nebrat, Corpus Cristi, Tex., 1972-77; tax mgr. Phillips Petroleum, Bartlesville, Okla., 1978-85; ptnr. Kutak Rock & Campbell, Denver, 1985—. Pres. S. Tex. Lighthouse for Blind, 1974-77; bd. dirs. Nueces County Juvenile Ct., 1973-74, Nat. Industries for Blind, N.Y.C., 1974-76. Mem. Colo. Bar Assn., Okla. Bar Assn., Tex. Bar Assn. Home: 8122 E Phillips Circle Englewood CO 80112 Office: Kutak Rock & Campbell 707 17th St 2400 Arco Tower Denver CO 80202

MCCULLOCH, FRANK WALTER, JR., editor; b. Fernley, Nev., Jan. 26, 1920; s. Frank Walter and Frieda (Sieke) McC.; m. Jakie Caldwell, Mar. 1, 1942; children—Michaele Lee McCulloch Parman, Candace Sue, David Caldwell. B.A. in Journalism, U. Nev., 1941. With UP, San Francisco, 1941-42; with San Francisco Chronicle, 1945-46; gen. assignment reporter, legis. reporter, sports editor Reno Evening Gazette, 1946-53, Time Inc., 1953-60, 63-72; bur. chief Time Life News Service, Dallas, 1954-56, Los Angeles, 1957-60; mng. editor Los Angeles Times, 1960-64; bur. chief Time Life, Hong Kong and Saigon, 1964-68, Life, Washington, 1968-69, Time-Life, N.Y.C., 1969-72; v.p., editor Learning Mag., Palo Alto, Calif., 1972-75; mng. editor Sacramento Bee, 1975-80; dir. McClatchy Newspapers, Sacramento, 1978-85, exec. editor, 1980-85; mng. editor San Francisco Examiner, 1985—. Served with USMCR, 1942-45. Mem. Sigma Delta Chi, Phi Kappa Phi, Kappa Tau Alpha, Sigma Nu. Office: San Francisco Examiner 110 5th St PO Box 7260 San Francisco CA 94120

MCCULLOUGH, COLIN DAVID, publisher; b. Windsor, Ont., Can., Oct. 11, 1929; s. Samuel J. and Elizabeth R. McC.; m. Regina M. Ratinskas, Feb. 12, 1958; 1 dau., Katharine R. B.A., Detroit Inst. Tech., 1951. Asst. dir. personnel relations Hiram Walker & Sons, Walkerville, Ont., 1951-53; fgn. corr. in Peking, 1968-69, London, 1971-73; asst. pub. The Globe and Mail, Toronto, 1974-79; pub. Times-Colonist, Victoria, B.C., 1979—. Author: Stranger in China, 1972, Insider's London, 1973. Trustee Art Gallery of Victoria. Mem. Can. Daily Newspaper Pubs. Assn. (dir.), Can. Press Assn. (dir.), Commonwealth Press Union, Am. Newspaper Pubs. Assn. Anglican. Clubs: Victoria Golf, Union. Home: 194 Denison Rd, Victoria, BC Canada Office: 2621 Douglas St, Victoria, BC Canada V8W 2N4

MCCULLOUGH, HENRY FREDERICK, aircraft company executive; b. Vancouver, B.C., Can., Sept. 18, 1926 (parents Am. citizens); s. John Andrew and Beatrice Victoria (Warburton) McC.; m. Constance Agnes Van Nes, Feb. 27, 1951; children—Linda, Katherine, Cynthia, John, Pamela, Lucille. Grad., Sch. Mgmt., UCLA. Cert. quality engr., Am. Soc. Quality Control, 1966. Aircraft specialist Boeing of Can., Vancouver, 1943-45; quality control preflight insp. Boeing Co., Seattle, 1945-49, 53—, quality control chief 707-727 system test, 1955-68, quality control mgr. 747 program, 1968—. Pres., commr. King County Water Dist. #107, 1965; past pres. and bd. dirs. Wash. State Assn. Water/Wastewater dists., chmn. legis. and membership coms.; charter mem. Presdl. Task Force, 1982-86, trustee, 1986; mem. Presdl. Commn., 1986; vol. crime prevention unit precinct III King County Police. Served with USAF, 1949-53. Decorated Air medal; recipient Silver Beaver award Boy Scouts Am., 1978; Golden Acorn, PTA, 1977; cert. Nat. Ct. of Honor for Life Saving, 1974. Fellow Am. Soc. Quality Control; mem. Am. Water Works Assn., Water Pollution Control Fedn., Boeing Mgmt. Assn. (life), Nat. Rifle Assn. (life). Republican. Episcopalian. Clubs: Meydenbauer Bay Yacht, Newport Hills Community (past pres., dir.), Renton Fishing and Game. Home: 6808 128th Ave SE Bellevue WA 98006

MCCUNE, BERNARD EDWARD, construction and land development company executive; b. Gresham, Nebr., Mar. 24, 1921; s. Irvin E. and Catherine (Harris) McC.; B.S. in Civil Engring., U. So. Calif., 1951; m. Genevieve Ruth Reeves, July 4, 1941; children—Garen Lee, Bernard Lynn, Steven Jon. Dep. city engr., Long Beach, Calif., 1945-58; self-employed in heavy constrn. contracting, 1958-61; sr. v.p. Shapell Industries, Inc., Beverly Hills, Calif., 1961-77, 84—, vice chmn. bd. dirs., 1973—; chmn. bd. Kylcor Devel. Corp., Empire Cable TV; dir. Palm Desert Nat. Bank, Council Environment, Employment, Economy and Devel., Orange County, Calif. Past pres. Bixby Hill Community Assn.; past mem. Calif. Senate Interim Com.; chmn. adv. bd. Salvation Army, Long Beach, Calif., 1968, now hon. dir.; past bd. dirs., vice chmn. exec. com. Long Beach chpt. A.R.C.; pres. bd. dirs. Pacific Hosp., Long Beach, 1971-73, Boys Clubs Long Beach, 1971-72; bd. dirs. NCCJ; mem. 100 Club of Boy Scouts Am. Served to maj. C.E., AUS, 1940-45. Decorated Bronze Star with oak leaf cluster. Purple Heart; named Honor Citizen of Year, NCCJ, 1974; recipient Golden Man and Boy award Boys Clubs Am., 1973; also various resolutions. Registered profl. engr., Calif. Mem. Am. Assn. Engrs., Nat. Soc. Profl. Engrs., Am. Mil. Engrs. Assn., Bldg. Industry Assn. Calif. (past chpt. treas.), Long Beach (past bd. dirs., past chmn. sts. and hwys. com.), Orange County, Westminster, Garden Grove, Seal Beach, Cerritos, Huntington Beach chambers commerce, Navy League, Am. Legion, mil. orders Purple Heart, World Wars. Methodist. Clubs: Long Beach Exchange (past pres.), Internat. City, Mission Hills Country, Industry Hill Country. Lodges: Masons, Elks (past exalted ruler), Old Ranch Country, Shadow Mountain Country. Home: 6219 Riviera Circle Long Beach CA 90815 Office: 5170 E Colorado St Long Beach CA 90814

MCCUNE, DONALD PATRICK, oilfield service company official; b. Olds, Alta., Can., Feb. 1, 1950; s. Donald D. and Emma (Miller) McC.; m. Beverly Ann Walper, Aug. 11, 1972 (div. Jan. 1974); m. Lesley E. Graham, Sept. 29, 1979; children: Gennyne Evonne, Marcia-Dawn Victoria. BS, U. Calgary, 1974. Salesman Massey Ferguson, Alta., 1974-78, sales mgr., 1978-80; salesman Genco Pressure Control Ltd., Calgary, 1980-81, gen. mgr., 1981—. Vice-chmn. ops. Calgary Olympic Organizing Com., 1984—; sr. assoc. Calgary Stampede Board; mem. Calgary Stampede Reception Com., 1985—; chmn. manpower and recruitment Calgary Olympic Organizing Com. Mem. United Ch. Can. Office: Genco Pressure Control Ltd, 2216 27th Ave NE, Calgary, AB Canada T2T 4K3

MCCUNE, ELLIS E., university president; b. Houston, July 17, 1921; s. Ellis E. and Ruth (Mason) McC.; m. Hilda May Whiteman, Feb. 8, 1946; 1 son, James Donald. Student, Sam Houston State U., 1940-42; B.A., UCLA, 1948, Ph.D., 1957. Teaching asst. UCLA, 1949-51; instr. polit. sci. Occidental Coll., Los Angeles, 1951-56; asst. prof., chmn. applied politics and econs. curriculum Occidental Coll., 1956-59, assoc. prof., 1959; asst. prof. Calif. State U., Northridge, 1959-61; assoc. prof., chmn. dept. polit. sci. Calif. State U., 1961-63, prof., 1963, dean letters and sci., 1963; dean acad. planning Calif. State Univs. and Colls., 1963-67; pres. Calif. State U., Hayward, 1967—; cons. govtl. units and agys.; lectr., panelist; mem. Calif. State Scholarship and Loan Commn., 1964-68, chmn., 1967-68; pres. Govtl. Adminstrn. Group Los Angeles, 1959. Chmn. univs. and colls. div. United Bay Area Crusade, 1969-70, 73-74; bd. dirs. Oakland (Calif.) Museum Assn., 1974-77, 86—, mem. arts adv. council, 1986—; trustee Calif. Council Econ. Edn.; sec. bd. dirs. Eden Community Found., 1978-79. Served with USAAF, 1942-46. Mem. Am. Council on Edn. (adv. com. inst. coll. and univ. adminstrs. 1970-74, bd. dirs. 1985-86), Western Assn. Schs. and Colls. (accrediting commn. sr. colls. and univs. 1974-78, chmn., 1978-82, pres. 1979-81), N.W. Assn. Schs. and Colls. (commn. colls. 1974-80), Assn. Am. Colls. (bd. dirs. 1972-75, vice chmn. 1975-76), Assn. Western Univs. (bd. dirs.), Council on Postsecondary Accreditation (bd. dirs. 1977—, exec. com. 1979—, chmn. 1985—, chmn. com. recognition 1982-84), Am. Assn. State Colls. and Univs. (chmn. accreditation com. 1983-86), Calif. Council Edn. (trustee), Western Polit. Sci. Assn. (exec. council 1958-61), Hayward C. of C. (dir. 1968-71, 73-76, 77-80, 82-85, 86—), Regional Assn. East Bay Colls. and Univs. (exec. com. 1974—, sec. 1975-76, vice chmn. 1976-77, 84-85, chmn. 1977-79, 85-86), Phi Beta Kappa, Pi Gamma Mu, Pi Sigma Alpha. Clubs: Bohemian, Commonwealth (San Francisco). Lodge: Rotary. Office: Calif State U Hayward CA 94542

MCCUNE, RONALD WILLIAM, biochemistry educator; b. Glade, Kans., Sept. 23, 1938; s. Francis W. and Orpha McCune; m. Mary Joan Huxley, June 7, 1965; children: Anna Orpha, Heather Jean. BS, Kans. State U., 1961; MS, Purdue U., 1964, PhD, 1966. Postgrad. research biochemist UCLA, 1966-70; asst. professor biochemistry Idaho State U., Pocatello, 1970-73, assoc. prof., 1973-79, prof., 1979—; reviewer grant requests NSF, 1975, 77-79; biochemical researcher U. Calif., San Diego, 1977-78. Contbr. articles to profl. publs. Grantee NSF, 1976, 81, Idaho State U., 1982, 84. Mem. AAAS, Am. Chem. Soc., Am. Soc. Microbiology (pres. Intermountain br. 1976-77, 85-86), N.Y. Acad. Scis., Nat. Assn. Advisors for Health Professions, Western. Assn. Advisors for Health Professions (pres. 1975-77). Presbyterian. Home: 30 Colgate Pocatello ID 83201 Office: Idaho State U Dept Biol Scis Box 8007 Pocatello ID 83209-0009

MCCURDY, JOHN ANDREW, JR., physician; b. Kingsville, Tex., July 17, 1945; s. John Andrew and Elizabeth (Smith) McC.; A.B. in Chemistry, Duke U., 1967; M.D., Wake Forest U., Winston-Salem, N.C., 1971; divorced; children—John Andrew, Elizabeth Anne. Intern, Letterman Gen. Hosp., San Francisco, 1971-72; resident Madigan Army Med. Ctr., Tacoma, 1972-76; practice medicine specializing in cosmetic surgery, Wailuku, Hawaii, 1979—; mem. staff Tripler Army Med. Ctr., Maui Meml. Hosp., Castle Meml. Hosp.; asst. clin. prof. surgery U. Hawaii Med. Sch. Served to lt. col. M.C., USAR, 1971-79. Decorated Army Commendation medal; diplomate Am. Bd. Cosmetic Surgery. Fellow ACS, Am. Acad. Facial Otolaryngology, Am. Bd. Cosmetic Surgery, Am. Acad. Head and Neck Surgery. Plastic and Reconstructive Surgery, Am. Acad. Author: The Complete Guide to Cosmetic Facial Surgery, 1981, Beautiful Eyes, 1984, Sculpturing Your Body: Diet, Exercise and Lipo Suction, 1987. Home: 3126 Mapu Kihei HI 96753 Office: 1063 E Main St Suite 225 Wailuku HI 96793 Office: 1188 Bishop St Suite 2402 Honolulu HI 96813

MCCUSKER, ANDREW JOHN, IV, environmental specialist; b. Hartford, Conn., Aug. 9, 1947; s. Andrew John III and Marion (Cook) McC.; m. Deborah Rae Seraphin, Oct. 15, 1966; children: Andrew John V (dec.), Carrie Ann, Erinn Heather, Ethan Raymond. BA in Biol. Sci., U. Conn., 1970; MS in Zoology and Marine Ecology, U. N.H., 1972. Biologist U. N.H., Durham, 1972-74; research assoc., then mgr. offshore services Normandeau Assocs., Bedford, N.H., 1974-81; regional mgr. Alaska EG&G Environ. Cons., Anchorage, 1981-83; mgr. environ. services Earth Tech. Group, Anchorage, 1984-85; environ./regulatory mgr. Harding Lawson Assocs., Anchorage, 1985—; environ. cons. Alaska Railroad Co., Suneel Alaska Coal Co. Program developer Chugach Jr. Cross Country Boosters-All Alaska Running Camp, Anchorage, 1985-86. Mem. Nat. Assn. Environ. Profls., Alaska Assn. Environ. Profls. (founder, chmn. bd. dirs. 1985—), Marine Tech. Soc. Avocations: Nordic ski racing, basketball, soccer coaching, hiking, fishing. Home: 10421 Lone Tree Dr Anchorage AK 99516 Office: Harding Lawson Assocs 601 E 57th Pl Anchorage AK 99518

MCDADE, MATT COMPTON, public relations executive; b. Hillsborough, N.C., Dec. 29, 1923; s. Carl Compton McDade and Leslie Haley. AB in Journalism, U. N.C., 1944; postgrad., Am. Inst. Banking. Gen. reporter Washington Post, 1951-55; writer, editor Nat. Geographic mag., Washington, 1955-68; mgr. corp. publs. Litton Industries, Beverly Hills, Calif., 1968-76; v.p., dir. communications Bank of Am., N.Y.C., 1979-83; sr. pub. relations officer Bank of Am., San Francisco, 1983—; adj. prof. Pace U., N.Y.C., 1971-72. Author: (with others) Shrdlu, 1964, Land of Alfalfa, 1963; editor (assoc.) Stars and Stripes, 1944-45. Served to capt. U.S. Army, 1943-46. Mem. Pub. Relations Soc. Am., Internat. Assn. Bus. Communicators. Republican. Roman Catholic. Clubs: Players (N.Y.), City Tavern (Washington), Nat. Press (Washington). Avocations: films, tennis, traveling. Home: 336 8th Ave Apt 1 San Francisco CA 94118 Office: Bank of Am Dept 3120 555 California St San Francisco CA 94118

MCDANAL, LINDA LOUISE, insurance company manager; b. Manhattan, Kans., July 10, 1947; d. Robert G. and Alma A. (Rueschhoff) Mosier; m. Michael A. McDanal, June 15, 1968. Student Colo. State U., 1965-68. With Equitable Life Assurance Soc., Denver, 1968—, new bus. mgr., 1980—, also instr. new agts. Active Republican party, Denver Symphony. Named West Central Employee, Equitable Fin. Cos., 1981. Roman Catholic. Home: 10075 E Caley Pl Englewood CO 80111 Office: 370 17th St Suite 4950 Denver CO 80202

MCDANIEL, BRUCE WILLIAMS, army officer; b. Hartford, Conn., Mar. 28, 1960; s. Albert Wilson and Tracy (Foss) McD. BS in Advt., Journalism, U. Colo., Boulder, 1982. Commd. U.S. Army, 1982, advanced through grades to capt., 1986; platoon leader U.S. Army, Camp Red Cloud, Republic of Korea, 1983-84; flight sect. leader U.S. Army, K-16, Republic of Korea, 1984; exec. officer HHC CAB U.S. Army, Ft. Ord, Calif., 1984-86, exec. officer 206th AHC, 1986—. Mem. Sports Car Club of Am. (announcer 1985—), Monterey Navy Flying Club. Home: 237 Montecito #1 Monterey CA 93940

MCDANIELS, DAVID KEITH, physics educator; b. Hoquiam, Wash., May 21, 1929; s. Forest Leo and Grace Elizabeth (Law) McD.; m. Patricia Rosenberg, Apr. 9, 1966; children: Keith Alan, Kevin Patrick, David Douglas. BS, Wash. State U., 1951; PhD, U. Wash., 1960. Physicist Hanfor Atomic Products, Richland, Wash., 1951-54; prof. physics U. Oreg., Eugene, 1963—. Author: The Sun: Our Future Energy Source, 1984, 2d ed., 1986; contbr. articles to profl. jours. Served with U.S. Army, 1954-55. Fellow NSF, 1962. Mem. AAAS, Am. Phys. Soc., Am. Assn. Physics Tchrs., Internat. Solar Energy Soc. Democrat. Avocation: golf.

MCDANNEL, JOHN DAVIS, physician's assistant, medical technician; b. Anchorage, Oct. 12, 1948; s. John D. McDannel and M. Shirley (Teague) Wallace; divorced; 1 child, Ian. Med. tng., U.S. Army, 1966; student, El Camino Coll., 1969-71, Calif. State Coll., Dominguez Hills, 1971-72; spl. forces tng., Ft. Bragg, Ft. Sam Houston and Ft. Benning, 1972-73; AA in Physician Asst. Program, Acad. Health Scis. Baylor U., 1976; BA, NYU, Albany, 1980; postgrad., Alaska Pacific U. Cert. physician asst., Alaska; cert. audiometrist; cert. emergency med. technician I, II and III, Alaska; cert. emergency med. technician instr. I, II and III, Alaska; cert. Occupational Health and Safety Adminstrn. advanced first aid instr., Alaska; cert. CPR instr. Am. Heart Assn.; cert. advanced cardiac life support Am. Heart Assn., cert. advanced trauma life support Am. Heart Assn. Enlisted U.S. Army, 1966, advanced through grades to chief warrant officer 2d class, 1985; with M.C. U.S. Army, Ft. Benning, Ga., South Vietnam and Thailand, 1966-69; sr. team medic Spl. Forces, San Antonio, Tex. and Ft. Bragg, N.C., 1972-74; staff physician asst., ward officer alcohol detoxification unit Salvation Army, Anchorage, 1978; bn. surgeon U.S. Army, Uijonbu, Republic of Korea, 1976-77; physician asst. M.C., bn. surgeon U.S. Army, Ft. Richardson, Alaska, 1977-80; sta. med. technician Campion, and Murphy Dome Air Force Sta., 1980; physician asst. Arco Oil Co., Kuparuk, Alaska, 1980-81, Sohio Oil Co., Prodhoe Bay, Alaska, 1981-83; sta. med. technician RCA/OMS Cold Bay Air Force Sta., Cape Lisburne, Alaska, 1983; physician asst. Open Door Med. Clinic, Anchorage, 1983, med. dir., 1985; med. dir. Whittier (Alaska) Med. Clinic, 1984; bn. surgeon 5/297 Inf. Alaska N.G., 1985, spl. staff officer to chief of staff HTLV III Project, 1983-86; oil explorer, weather researcher, med. dispensary Fairweather Inc., 1985-86; owner, clinic dir. Anchor Med. Clinic, Anchorage, 1986—; counselor Vietnam Vets. Counseling Ctr., Anchorage, 1981-83; certifying officer Emergency Med. Technician, State of Alaska; service officer AMVETS. Editor Northwest Mil. Physician Assts. Assn. newspaper, 1975; contbr. Sound of Prince William Newspaper, 1984. Vol. Vietnam Vets. Fink for Gov. Alaska, 1983, Vietnam Vets. Knowles for Mayor, City of Anchorage, 1982; rep. dist. 17 Dem. S. Cen. Campaign, Wasilla, Alaska, 1984; bd. dirs. ARC, Anchorage, Vietnam Vets. Leadership Program; commr. Municipality of Anchorage Commn. Vets. Affairs; mem. Mayors Task Force on Vets. Affairs. Decorated Combat Med. Badge, Army Commendation medal for Valor with 2 oak leaf clusters, Nat. Def. Ribbon; recipient Cert. of Appreciation Vietnam Vets. Am., 1982. Mem. Alaska Acad. Physician Assts. (bd. dirs., nat. del. to Am. Acad. Physician Assts.), Soc. Army Physician Assts., Am. Assn. Physician Assts., Northwest Mil. Physician Assts. Assn., Non-commd. Officers Assn., Warrant Officer Assn., Spl. Forces Decade Assn., Jaycees, Vietnam Vets. of Alaska, Vietnam Vets. of America, AMVETS, Chi Gamma Iota. Lodges: Masons, Order DeMolay. Conducted weather research in Navarrin Basin of Bering Sea leading to on site fixed position data. Avocations: mountain climbing, fishing, kayaking, skiing. Home: 328 Boniface Suite 2259 Anchorage AK 99504 Office: Anchor Med Clinic 218 E 4th Ave Anchorage AK 99501

MCDERMOTT, DENNIS MICHAEL, association executive; b. Akron, Ohio, Jan. 9, 1947; s. Gerard J. and Irene C. (Lenz) M.; m. Margaret M. Hayden, Dec. 14, 1968 (div.); children—Martin Jerome, Kathleen Marie; m. Margaret Amberg Egan, Apr. 30, 1983. B.S. in Journalism, Kent State U., 1969, postgrad., 1973-76; postgrad. Chapman Coll., 1971-72. Reporter Akron Beacon Jour., 1967-69; conv. mgr. Am. Sch. Health Assn., Kent, Ohio, 1973-74, asst. exec. dir., 1974-77; exec. dir. Emergency Nurses Assn., Chgo., 1977-80, Oakland (Calif.) Bd. Realtors (exec. v.p. 1980-83); v.p. Calif. Assn. Realtors, Los Angeles, 1983-86; pres., Dennis McDermott Assn. Mgmt., 1986—; lectr.; cons. Served with USAF, 1969-72. Mem. Am. Soc. Assn. Execs., Pub. Relations Soc. Am., Soc. Profl. Journalists/Sigma Delta Chi. Office: Dennis McDermott Assn Mgmt PO Box 3716 South Pasadena CA 91030-6716

MCDERMOTT, MICHAEL JAMES, mariner, firefighter, maritime safety specialist, writer; b. San Francisco, June 16, 1956; s. James Edward and June Ester (Noyes) McD. BS, Calif. State Maritime Acad., Vallejo, 1979; postgrad. Maritime Inst. Tech. and Grad. Studies, 1984; cert. firefighter I & II, Hancock Coll. Fire Acad., 1985. Profl. mariner, lic. deck officer U.S. Mcht. Marine, 1979-85; firefighter Santa Barbara (Calif.) Fire Dept., 1985—. Served with USCG, 1974-75. Mem. Order of Golden Shellback, Internat. Assn. Firefighters, Nat. Fire Protection Assn., Internat. Orgn. Masters, Mates and Pilots, N.Am. Catamaran Racing Assn. Club: Dolphin Rowing (San Francisco).

MCDERMOTT, VINCENT, music composer, educator, ethnomusicologist; b. Atlantic City, Sept. 5, 1933; s. Joseph Vincent and Praxeda (Wassick) McD.; m. Charlene Senape, Sept. 10, 1959 (div. 1976); children: Robert C., Lise G., Jamie C.; m. Judith Bokor, Nov. 24, 1983; 1 child, Tristam Joseph. BFA, U. Pa., 1959, PhD, 1966; MA, U. Calif., Berkeley, 1961. Asst. prof. music Hampton (Va.) Inst., 1966-67; faculty and various adminstrv. positions Wis. Conservatory Music, Milw., 1967-77; prof. Lewis & Clark Coll., Portland, Oreg., 1977—. Composer some 30 musical works for orch., chorus, solo, chamber and electronics performance throughout U.S., Europe and Asia; named Mus. Dir. gamelan orch. Venerable Showers of Beauty, 1980—. Served with U.S. Army, 1953-55. Fellow Fulbright-Hays Commn., 1978, Oreg. Arts Commn., 1979; music commn. Nat. Endowment Arts, 1985, 87. Mem. Soc. Asian Music, N.Y. chpt. Composers Forum, Am. Soc. Univ. Composers. Home: 1501 SE Holly Portland OR 97214 Office: Lewis & Clark Coll Music Dept Portland OR 97214

MCDONALD, ALLAN JAMES, engineering administrator; b. Cody, Wyo., July 9, 1937; s. John William and Eva Marie (Gingras) M.; m. Linda Rae Zuchetto, Apr. 20, 1963; children—Gregory Allan, Lisa Marie, Lora Lynn, Meghan Rae. B.S. in Chem. Engring, Mont. State U., 1959, D. in Engring. (hon.), 1986; M.S. in Engring. Adminstrn., U. Utah, 1967. Engr. Wasatch div. Morton Thiokol Inc., Brigham City, Utah, 1959-67, project engr. solid rocket motor programs, 1967-74, mgr. devel. project dept., 1974-76, mgr. propellant devel. dept. 1976-79, mgr. project engring. div., 1979-84, dir. space shuttle solid rocket motor project, 1984-86, dir. space shuttle solid rocket motor verification task force, 1986—; mem. Air Force Space Tech. Propulsion Panel, 1982—. Judge sci. fair com. Weber State Coll., 1978—; bd. dirs. St. Joseph High Sch., 1976—, trustee, 1981—, pres. 1976-79; coach Little League Football, 1972-75; coach Little League Baseball, 1971-72, pres., 1972-74; pres. CCD program St. James Catholic Ch., 1976-79. Named Outstanding Engr. of Utah, AIAA, 1971, 86; Eastern Mont. Coll. scholar, 1955-57; Mont. State U. scholar, 1958-59. Fellow AIAA (assoc., past chmn. Utah sect., mem. solid rocket tech. com. 1979-83, chmn., 1984-86, space task force, 1986—, Shuttle Flag award 1984); mem. Tau Beta Pi, Phi Kappa Phi, Sigma Chi. Republican. Clubs: K.C., Elks, Ogden Athletic. Patentee solid rocket, pyrotechnic systems; contbr. articles to profl. jours., publs. Home: 4050 N 900 W Pleasant View UT 84404 Office: Morton Thiokol Wasatch Div PO Box 524 m/s EOO Brigham City UT 84302

MCDONALD, DANIEL ROBERT, senator; b. Seattle, Feb. 4, 1944; s. Robert William and Josephine Dorothy (Quigley) McD.; m. Norah Jane Cornwall, Dec. 28, 1966; children: Tod Robert, Evan Daniel. BSME, U. Wash., 1965, MA in Econs., 1975. Registered profl. engr., Calif., Wash. Mem. Wash. Ho. of Reps., Olympia, 1979-83, floor leader, 1983; mem. Wash. Senate, Olympia, 1983—, floor leader, 1985-86; mem. revenue forecast council, Olympia, 1984—, chmn. 1984-85; mem. legis. evaluation and accountability program, Olympia, 1983—; commr. exec. bd. Western Interstate Com. on Higher Edn., 1983—. Mem. Seattle/King County Drug Commn., 1978-79, Mcpl. League, Seattle, 1979—. Served to lt. (j.g.) USN, 1966-69, Vietnam. Mem. Am. Pub. Works Assn., Am. Waterworks Assn., Bellevue (Wash.) C. of C. Republican. Presbyterian. Lodge: Rotary. Home: 4650 92nd NE Bellevue WA 98004 Office: Wash State Senate 207 Institutions Bldg Olympia WA 98504

MCDONALD, JAMES WALLACE, university management trainer, consultant; b. Myrtle Beach, S.C., Oct. 11, 1943; s. James Joseph and Edna Ruth (Wallace) McD.; m. Cheryl Susanne Spurgeon, Feb. 2, 1974; children: Joshua James, Kevin Matthew. BA, Calif. State U., Sacramento, 1965; MSW with distinction, Calif. State U., Fresno, 1977; M in Divinity, Seabury Western Sem., 1968. Cert. mgmt. trainer; lic. clin. social worker (Calif.); ordained priest, Episcopal Ch., 1968. Vicar Episc. Ch., Anderson, Calif., 1968-72; priest Episc. Ch., Fresno, 1972—, assoc. rector, 1972-74; social worker Social Service Dept., Fresno, 1974-78; psychotherapist Family Service Ctr., Fresno, 1978-81; employee assistance program mgr. Community Hosps. Cen. Calif., Fresno, 1981-85; tng. officer Calif. State U., Fresno, 1985—; pvt. practice psychotherapy Fresno, 1978—. Bd. dirs. Golden Valley council Girl Scouts U.S., 1982-84, Holy Family Day Care Ctr., Fresno, 1985—; mem. edn. com. Mental Health Assn., Fresno, 1982-86. Profl. devel. grantee Calif. State U., 1986. Mem. Nat. Assn. Social Workers (diplomate in clin. social work), Am. Soc. Tng. and Devel., Phi Kappa Phi. Democrat. Avocations: travel, family, model railroading. Home: 6035 N 9th St Fresno CA 93710 Office: Calif State U Maple at Shaw Fresno CA 93740

MC DONALD, JEANNE GRAY (MRS. JOHN B.), television producer; b. Seattle, Sept. 11, 1917; d. George Patrick and Mary Edna (Gray) Murphy; m. John B. Mc Donald, June 30, 1951; children: Gregory Roland Stoner, Margaret Jeanne Eve. Student, Columbia U., 1940, Art Students League, 1940-43, Nat. Acad. Dramatic Art, 1945. Radio producer, commentator The Woman's Voice Sta. KMPC, Los Angeles, 1947-50; TV producer, commentator, writer The Woman's Voice Sta. KTTV-CBS, Los Angeles, 1950-51; TV producer, commentator The Jeanne Gray Show Sta. KNXT-TV CBS, Los Angeles, 1951-53; West Coast editor Home Show NBC network, Los Angeles, 1955-56; TV film producer documentaries and travelogues Virgonian Prodns., Los Angeles, 1953—. Author: The Power of Belonging, 1978. Women's chmn. Los Angeles Beautiful, 1971; mem. Women's Aux. St. John's Hosp.; trustee Freedoms Found. at Valley Forge, 1966—, founder, pres. women's chpt., Los Angeles County chpt., 1965-66, Western dir. women's chpt., 1967-68, nat. chmn. 1968-71, nat. chmn. women vols., 1973-75, hon life mem. Recipient Francis Holmes Outstanding Achievement award, 1949, Silver Mike award, 1948, Emmy award Acad. TV Arts and Scis., 1951, Lulu award Los Angeles Advt. Women, 1952, Genii award Radio and TV Women, 1956, George Washington Honor award Freedoms Found. Valley Forge, 1967, honor cert., 1972, Morale award Christians and Jews for Law and Morality, 1968, Exceptional Service award Freedoms Found., 1975, Liberty Belle award Rep. Women's Club, 1975, Leadership award Los Angeles City Schs., 1976, Theodore Roosevelt award USN League, 1986. Mem. Am. Women in Radio and TV, Radio and TV Women So. Calif. (hon. life, founder, 1st pres. 1952), Footlighters (v.p. 1958-59), Los Angeles C. of C. (dir. women's div. 1948-54, mem. exec. bd., women's div. 1954-66, pres. women's div. 1963-64, hon. past pres. women's div. 1979), Los Angeles Orphanage Guild, DAR, The Muses. Clubs: Bel Air Garden, Calif. Yacht. Home: 910 Stradella Rd Bel Air Los Angeles CA 90077

MCDONALD, MARIANNE, classicist; b. Chgo., Jan. 2, 1937; d. Eugene Francis and Inez (Riddle) McD.; B.A. magna cum laude, Bryn Mawr Coll., 1958; M.A., U. Chgo., 1960; Ph.D., U. Calif., Irvine, 1975; children—Eugene, Conrad, Bryan, Bridget, Kirstie, Hiroshi. Teaching asst. classics U. Calif., Irvine, 1972-74, instr. Greek, Latin and English, mythology, modern cinema, 1975-79, researcher Thesaurus Linguae Graecae Project, 1979—; dir. Centrum. Bd. dirs. Am. Coll. of Greece, 1981—, Scripps Hosp., 1981—, Am. Sch. Classical Studies, 1986—; ; mem. bd. overseers U. Calif. San Diego, 1985—; nat. bd. advisors Am. Biog. Inst., 1982—. Recipient Ellen Browning Scripps Humanitarian award, 1975; Disting. Service award U. Calif.-Irvine, 1982; named Philanthropist of Yr. Honorary Nat. Conf. Christians and Jews, 1986. Mem. Am. Philol. Assn., Am. Classical League, Philol. Assn. Pacific Coast, MLA, Am. Comparative Lit. Assn., Modern and Classical Lang. Assn. So. Calif., AAUP, Hellenic Soc., Calif. Fgn. Lang. Tchrs. Assn., Internat. Platform Assn. Republican. Greek Orthodox. Clubs: KPBS Producers, Hellenic Univ. (dir.). Author: Terms for Happiness in Euripides, 1978; Semilemmatized Concordances to Euripides' Alcestis, 1977; Cyclops, Andromache, Medea, 1978; Heraclidae, Hippolytus, 1979; Hecuba, 1982; Euripides in Cinema: The Heart Made Visible, 1983; Hercules Furers, 1984, Electra, 1985, Ion, 1985; translator: The Cost of Kindness and Other Fabulous Tales (Shinichi Hoshi), 1986; contbr. numerous articles to profl. jours. Home: Box 929 Rancho Santa Fe CA 92067 Office: Thesaurus Linguae Gracae Project U Calif Irvine CA 92717

MCDONALD, STEPHAN RICH, electronics specialist; b. Logan, Utah, Apr. 23, 1939; s. Walter Rich and Martha (Cook) M.; m. Emily Carol Hubbard, June 28, 1963; children—Brent Rich, Leslee. Cert. in trade and tech., Idaho State U., 1964. Sr. electronic technician E.G.&G., Inc., Las Vegas, Nev., 1964-69, Indsl. Computer Lab., Salt Lake City, 1969, Stabro Labs., 1969-71; electronic technician Utah Power & Light Co., 1971—. Mem. Instrument Soc. Am. (sec. Las Vegas chpt. 1969), Am. Numis. Assn., Am. Radio Relay League. Republican. Mormon. Home: 1570 E 1425 North Logan UT 84321 Office: Utah Power and Light Co 2813 Wall Ave Ogden UT 84401

MCDONALD, THOMAS EDWIN, JR., electrical engineer; b. Wapanucka, Okla., June 19, 1939; s. Thomas Edwin and Rosamond Bell (Enoch) McD.; m. Myrna Kay Booth, Sept. 10, 1961; children: Stephen Thomas, Jennifer Kay, Sarah Lynn. BSEE, U. Okla., 1962, MSEE, 1963; PhDEE, U. Colo., 1969. Asst. prof. elec. engring. U. Okla., Norman, 1969-70; planning engr. Okla. Gas and Electric Co., Oklahoma City, 1970-72; staff mem. Los Alamos (N.Mex.) Nat. Lab., 1972-82, group leader, 1974-80, program mgr., 1980—; adj. prof. elec. engring. U. Okla., 1970-72; cons. Los Alamos Tech. Assocs., 1980—. Contbr. articles to profl. jours. Bd. dirs. Christian Ch. Los Alamos, 1982-85. Served. to capt. U.S. Army, 1963-67. Mem. IEEE, Los Alamos Gymnastics Club (treas., bd. dirs. 1984-86), Sigma Xi, Eta Kappa Nu. Republican. Avocation: computer sci. Home: 4200 Ridgeway Dr Los Alamos NM 87544 Office: Los Alamos Nat Lab PO Box 1663 Los Alamos NM 87544

MCDONALD, WILLIAM BENNETT, computer software executive; b. Boise, Idaho, June 1, 1938; s. William Eugene and Lucille (Bennett) McDonald; m. Cherry Ann Rhoads, Oct. 30, 1971 ; children: Andrea Leslie, Jessica Lee. BA, U. Utah, 1962, postgrad.; postgrad., Stanford U. With IBM, 1963—; proj. mgr. IBM, White Plains, N.Y., 1976-78; devel. mgr. IBM, Palo Alto and Menlo Park, Calif., 1978-84; knowledge systems mgr. IBM, Menlo Park, 1984-86; dir. product mktg. Teknowledge Inc., Palo Alto, 1986—; pres. Abraxas Inc., Salt Lake City, 1972-85; pvt. practice software devel., Mountain View, Calif., 1983—. Developer numerous IBM software products and publs., 1978—. Programmer Utah Election Service, Salt Lake City, 1964; poll mgr. Wayne Owens congl. campaign, Salt Lake City, 1972. Fellow Am. Prodn. and Inventory Control Soc. (cert., material requirements planning com. chmn. 1978-84, cert. coordination com. 1984—). Democrat. Avocations: skiing, stained glass, reading, poetry, music. Home: 3382 Tryna Dr Mountain View CA 94040 Office: Teknowledge 1850 E Embarcadero Rd Palo Alto CA 94303

MCDONNEL, WILLIAM GEORGE, scientific instrumentation company executive; b. Rabat, French Morocco, May 10, 1952; came to U.S., 1953; s. Harold Albert and Anna (Yoos) McD.; B.S. in Chemistry/Biochemistry, Calif. State U., Fullerton, 1974, MBA Pepperdine U., 1987; m. Nancy Ann Hopwood, Aug. 27, 1977; children—Melissa, Allison Roe. Product specialist Process Instruments div. Beckman Instruments, Inc., Fullerton, 1974; sr. tech. specialist ion selective electrodes Lab. Products div. Orion Research Inc., Cambridge, Mass., 1975—; speaker in field. Mem. Am. Chem. Soc., Am. Electroplaters Soc., Phi Kappa Tau. Republican. Home: 27412 Cenajo Mission Viejo CA 92691 Office: Orion Research Inc 529 Main St Boston MA 02129

MCDONNELL, EDWARD JOE, business educator; b. Borger, Tex., Mar. 11, 1936; s. Lloyd Clyde and Edlina (Roscoe) McD.; m. Sharon Snyder, Dec. 30, 1958 (div. Jan. 1964); 1 child, Brian Edward. AA, East Los Angeles Coll., 1966; BS, Pepperdine U., 1969; MBA, U. So. Calif., 1970; postgrad., U.S. Internat. U. Sales rep. Standard Register Co., Long Beach, Calif., 1960-63; sales rep., contract mgr. Soulé Steel Co., Los Angeles, 1963-67; dist. sales rep., contract mgr. Allison Steel Co., Santa Fe Springs, Calif., 1967-68; mem. faculty Los Angeles City Coll., 1970—, instr., 1970-71; area adminstr. Los Angeles City Coll., Taiwan and Phillipines, 1971-72; prof. bus. adminstrn. Los Angeles City Coll., 1972—. Mem. Acad. Mgmt., Strategic Mgmt. Assn., Calif. Ednl. Computing Consortium. Home: 5335 Via San Delarro Los Angeles CA 90022 Office: Los Angeles City Coll 855 N Vermont Los Angeles CA 90029

MC DONNELL, EDWARD LAURENCE, real estate devel. co. exec.; b. Great Falls, Mont., May 13, 1912; s. George Edward and Clara Lucinda (Woodward) McD.; student Gonzaga U., Spokane, 1934; m. Evelyn Marie Cutz, Aug. 1, 1935; children—Thomas C., Victoria M., Virginia D. Mgr., Mont. Mustard Seed Co., Power, 1935-39; partner McDonnell Seed Co., Spokane, 1940-47; organizer, owner, mgr. E.L. McDonnell & Co., Spokane, 1947-60; pres. Trans-World Seeds, Ltd., Shelby, Mont., 1960-66; organizer, owner, mgr. Agro Supply, Billings, Mont., 1966-77; partner McBorg Properties, Billings, 1978-80, GEL Properties, Billings, 1980—; organizer, 1st pres. Pacific N.W. Pea Growers and Dealers Assn., 1949-53. Republican. Roman Catholic. Club: K.C. Author articles. Developer comml. fertilizer applicator equipment. Address: 3440 Winchell Ln Billings MT 59102

MCDONOUGH, JAMES MICHAEL, engineering educator; b. Springfield, Ohio, Dec. 10, 1945; s. James Michael and Marjorie Ann (Brandle) McD.; m. Mei Tsuo Huang, Feb. 19, 1983. BS in Aero. and Astronautical Engring., Ohio State U., 1968; MA in Applied Math., UCLA, 1975, PhD in Engring., 1980. Engr., scientist McDonnell-Douglas Co., Santa Monica,

Calif., 1968-72; staff mathematician Prose, Inc., Los Angeles, 1973-76; mem. tech. staff Aerospace Corp., El Segundo, Calif., 1980—; adj. asst. prof. UCLA, 1980—. Contbr. articles to profl. jours. Mem. AAAS, Am. Math. Soc., Am. Phys. Soc., Soc. Indsl. Applied Math., N.Y. Acad. Scis. Avocations: piano, basketball, model railroading. Home: 5812 Canterbury Dr Culver City CA 90230

MCDONOUGH, LESLIE MARVIN, research chemist; b. Tacoma, July 2, 1930; s. William Joseph McDonough and Kathlyn Lester; m. Olive Ellen Parks, June 3, 1950 (div. Mar. 1976); children: Kathlyn M. Maeda, Jennifer C. BS, U. Puget Sound, 1954; PhD, U. Wash., 1960. Research chemist E.I. du Pont De Nemours, Circleville, Ohio, 1960-64; assoc. research chemist Midwest Research Inst., Kansas City, Mo., 1964-65; research leader USDA Agrl. Research Service, Yakima, Wash., 1965—; assoc. entomologist/chemist Wash. State U., Pullman, 1980—. Contbr. numerous articles to profl. jours. Mem. Am. Chem. Soc., Entomol. Soc. Am., Sigma Xi. Avocations: classical piano, hiking, skiing. Home: 408 N 57th Ave Yakima WA 98908 Office: USDA Agrl Research Service 3706 W Nob Hill Blvd Yakima WA 98902

MCDORMAN, THOMAS WILLIAM, mechanical engineering executive; b. Los Angeles, July 17, 1956; s. Norbert William and Eileen (Harte) McD.; m. Julie Ann Deborba, Sept. 1979 (div. June 1981); m. Julie Anne Lewandowski, June 2, 1984. BSME, Calif. Poly. State U., San Luis Obispo, 1979. Engr. Martin Marrieta Corp., Vandenburg AFB, Calif., 1979-81, ISS Sperry Univac, Santa Clara, Calif., 1981-82; program mgr. Internat. Memories Inc., Cupertino, Calif., 1982-84, Computer Memories Inc., Chatsworth, Calif., 1984-85; dir. mfg. engr. Seagate Tech., Scotts Valley, Calif., 1985—. Patentee in field. Mem. Ronald Reagan Rep. Task Force, Washington, 1985-86. Office: Seagate Tech 915 Disc Dr Scotts Valley CA 95066

MCDOUGAL, GENEVIEVE GUERRA, government official; b. Las Cruces, N.Mex., Jan. 24, 1947; d. Augustine Arthur and Adela Miranda (Montoya) Guerra; m. Bruce Darrell McDougal, Sept. 21, 1968; children: Christina Marie, Michael Shawn. Student N.Mex. State U., 1980-83. Sales clk. Budget Shop, Stork Ctr., Las Cruces, 1963-65; sec. Home Edn. Livelihood Program, State of N.Mex., Las Cruces, 1966; with White Sands Missile Range, N.Mex., 1966-86, sr. mgmt. analyst, test and evaluation command mgmt. engring. office western team, 1983-86, chief mgmt. engring., work reception and systems br. Resources Mgmt. div. Facilities Engring. Directorate, 1979-83; program analyst MCAS Comml. Activities, El Toro, Calif., 1986—. Area coordinator cookie sales Girl Scouts U.S.A., 1979-84. Recipient numerous performance awards White Sands Missile Range, 1966-86. Mem. Am. Soc. Mil. Comptrollers, Assn. U.S. Army, Fed. Mgrs. Assn., Internat. Tng. and Communication (formerly Internat. Toastmistress Clubs, named Toastmistress of Yr. 1980). Democrat. Roman Catholic. Home: 27911 Paseo Nicole San Juan Capistrano CA 92675 Office: Marine Corp Air Sta Comptroller Code 1FE2 A&R Div Programs Br Santa Ana CA 92709

MCDOUGAL, WILLIAM GEORGE, civil engineering educator; b. Chico, Calif., Oct. 27, 1951; s. George Alvin and Donna Louise (Staffelbach) McD.; m. Joan Florence Davis, Dec. 30, 1972; children: Tobbie Anna, Ryan Marie. BS in Oceanography, BS Environ. Engring., Humboldt State U., 1976; MCE, U. Del., 1979; PhD in Civil Engring., Oreg. State U., 1982. Oceanographer EPA, Corvallis, Oreg., 1978-79; asst. prof. civil engring. Oreg. State U., Corvallis, 1981-85, chmn. ocean engr., 1984-85, assoc. prof., 1985—; cons. 1980-85. Contbr. articles to profl. jours. Mem. steering com. Philomath (Oreg.) Rodeo, 1983-85. Mem. ASME, ASCE (assoc., mem. pubs. com. 1983—, research com. 1985—), Am. Geophys. Union, Sigma Xi. Republican. Office: Oreg State U Dept Civil Engring Corvallis OR 97331

MCDOUGALL, GEORGE DOUGLAS, consultant; b. Indpls., July 20, 1930; s. Shirley Alton and Deborah Cleveland (Hall) McD.; student Asbury Coll., 1949-51, Mt. San Antonio Coll., 1960-61, Milw. Sch. Engring., 1977, Calif. State Poly. U., 1978; m. Maria Celia Velasquez, Aug. 4, 1956. Surveyor, Tidelands Exploration Co., Houston, 1954; with Vard, Inc., Pasadena, Calif., 1954-60, Gen. Dynamics, Pomona, Calif., 1960-62; researcher Aerojet Gen. Corp., Azusa, Calif., 1962-68; engr. Davidson Optonics, West Covina, Calif., 1968-69; mfg. mgr. Angeles Metal Systems, Los Angeles, 1969-79; cons. Fremont Gen. Corp., Los Angeles, 1979—; mem. automation research project Inst. Indsl. Relations, U. So. Calif., 1966-68; mem. research team U.S. Govt./U. So. Calif., 1979-81. Adv. bd. Automobile Club So. Calif., 1966-71; bd. dirs. St. Martha's Episcopal Sch., West Covina, 1978-81; lic. lay reader Episcopal Diocese of Los Angeles; vestryman St. Martha's Episc. Ch., West Covina, 1969-70, 77-79, 81-83; mem. U.S. Congl. Adv. Bd., 1982—; gen. conv. del. Episc. Diocese of Los Angeles, 1970-78; instnl. rep. Boy Scouts Am., 1978-79, coordinator San Gabriel Valley council, 1978-79. Served with JAGC, AUS, 1951-53; Korea. Cert. in mfg. engring., Canadian Council Profl. Cert., 1977; registered profl. engr., Calif. Fellow Internat. Biog. Assn.; mem. Soc. Engrs. (exec. council, sec. 1982; cert.), Computer and Automated Systems Assn. (charter), Nat. Soc. Profl. Engrs., Am. Soc. Safety Engrs., Calif. Soc. Profl. Engrs. (v.p.), Clan MacDougall Soc. U.S. and Can. (life), Highlands Clans and Family Soc. (exec. council 1982), St. Andrews Soc. Los Angeles (life), 101st Airborne Div. Assn. (life), Am. Legion, SAR. Republican. Clubs: Town Hall of Calif., Masons (life), Shriners. Home: PO Box 848 Azusa CA 91702 Office: Fremont Gen Corp 9 W 8th St Los Angeles CA 90017

MCDOUGALL, JOHN RICHARD, defense systems executive; b. Breckenridge, Minn., Nov. 21, 1939; s. John Nelson and Etta (Beving) McD.; m. Louise A. Southard, June 11, 1966; children: Amanda L., Kevin John. AS, N.D. State Sch. Sci., 1959; BSME with honors, N.D. State U., 1961; MS in Nuclear Engring., U. Wash., 1962. Registered profl. nuclear engr., Calif. Asst. dept. mgr. TRW, Redondo Beach, Calif., 1963-72; corp. v.p., ops. mgr. Sci. Applications Inc., La Jolla, Calif., 1972-81; dir., co-founder, pres. Titan Systems, La Jolla, 1981—. Mem. Phi Kappa Phi, Tau Beta Pi, Pi Tau Sigma. Republican. Presbyterian. Avocations: tennis, golf, racquetball, travel. Home: 7667 Pepita Way LaJolla CA 92037 Office: Titan Systems Inc 9191 Towne Centre Dr 500 San Diego CA 92122

MCDOUGALL, WALTER ALLAN, history educator; b. Washington, Dec. 3, 1946; s. Dugald Stewart and Carol Alberta (Brueggeman) McD.; m. Elizabeth Nuttall Swoope, Aug. 8, 1970 (div. 1979). BA, Amherst Coll., 1968; MA, U. Chgo., 1971, PhD, 1974. Asst. prof. U. Calif., Berkeley, 1975-83, assoc. prof. history, 1983-87, prof., 1987—; vis. scholar Hoover Inst., Stanford, Calif., 1986; mem. adv. panel Office Tech. Assessment, U.S. Congress, 1982-84, Harvard/Carnegie Study on Prevention of Nuclear War, 1985-86; witness House Sci. Tech. Com., U.S. Congress, 1985. Author: France's Rhineland Diplomacy, 1914-24. The Last Bid for a Balance of Power in Europe, 1978, The Grenada Papers, 1984, The Heavens and the Earth. A Political History of the Space Age, 1985 (Pulitzer prize 1986); contbr. numerous articles to profl. and scholarly jours. Vestryman St. Peter's Episcopal Ch., Oakland, Calif, 1984—. Served as sgt. U.S. Army, 1968-70, Vietnam. Recipient Men and Women Under 40 Who are Changing Am. award Esquire Mag., 1984, Dexter Prize award for History of Tech., 1986; resident fellow Wilson Ctr. Smithsonian, 1981-82, Nat. Air and Space Mus., 1982. Mem. Hoover Instn., Delta Kappa Epsilon. Republican. Anglican. Avocations: baseball, all selections music. Office: U Calif Dept History Berkeley CA 94720

MCDOWELL, ANGELA PARISI, small business owner, speech pathologist; b. Cleve., Feb. 5, 1940; d. Pasquale and Sylvia (Lombardi) P.; m. Ronald F. McDowell, July 3, 1965; 1 child, Natalie. BA, U. Ohio, 1962; postgrad., Calif. State U., Long Beach, 1966. Speech pathologist Ohio Crippled Children Assn., 1962, Mich. Sch. Dist., St. Clare, 1962-63, Santa Monica (Calif.) Unified Sch. Dist., 1963-72; pvt. practice in speech therapy Rancho Palos Verdes, Calif., 1972-78; speech therapist San Pedro (Calif.) Peninsula Hosp., 1978-79; owner, operator Palos Verdes Awards, Rancho Palos Verdes, 1979—; cons. speech pathologist, San Pedro, 1975-78. Creater awards presented to Johnny Cash, Loretta Lynn, Mr. Peter of Peter Principal. Mem. Am. Speech Lang. Hearing Assn., Palos Verdes Peninsula C. of C., Community Assn. of Peninsula, Leads. Lodge: Soroptomists. Avocations: race-walking, soccer. Home and Office: 28925 Geronimo Dr Rancho Palos Verdes CA 90274

MCDOWELL, HARDING KEITH, research laboratory administrator; b. High Point, N.C., Feb. 5, 1944; s. Harding Atlas and Evangeline (Hawks) McD.; m. Janet Stallings, June 14, 1975; children: Andrew Keith, John Harding. BS, Wake Forest U., 1966; PhD, Harvard U., 1972. Research assoc. SUNY, Stony Brook, 1972-74; asst. prof. chem. physics Clemson (S.C.) U., 1974-78, assoc. prof., 1978-83; group leader Los Alamos (N.Mex.) Nat. Lab., 1983—; vis. staff mem. Los Alamos Nat. Lab., 1979-83. Alfred P. Sloan fellow 1978-80. Mem. Am. Chem. Soc., Am. Phys. Soc. Republican. Office: Los Alamos Nat Lab CLS-2 Ms G738 Los Alamos NM 87545

MCDOWELL, JENNIFER, sociologist, composer, playwright; b. Albuquerque, May 19, 1936; d. Willard A. and Margaret Frances (Garrison) McD.; m. Milton Loventhal, July 2, 1973. B.A., U. Calif., 1957, M.L.S., 1963; M.A., San Diego State U., 1958; Ph.D., U. Oreg., 1973. Tchr. English Abraham Lincoln High Sch., San Jose, Calif., 1960-61; freelance editor Soviet field, Berkeley, Calif., 1961-63; research asst. sociology U. Oreg., Eugene, 1964-66; editor, pub. Merlin Papers, San Jose, 1969—, Merlin Press, San Jose, 1973—; research cons. sociology San Jose, 1973—; music pub. Lipstick and Toy Balloons Pub. Co., San Jose, 1978—; composer Paramount Pictures, 1982—; tchr. writing workshops; poetry readings, 1969-73; co-producer radio show lit. and culture Sta. KALX, Berkeley, 1971-72. Author: Black Politics: A Study and Annotated Bibliography of the Mississippi Freedom Democratic Party, 1971, Contemporary Women Poets: An Anthology of California Poets, 1977; co-author (plays) Betsy and Phyllis, 1986, Mack The Knife Your Friendly Dentist, 1986, The Estrogen Party to End War, 1986, The Oatmeal Party Comes to Order, 1986; contbr. poems, essays, short stories, book revs. to lit. mags., 1969; researcher women's autobiog. writings, contemporary writings in poetry, Soviet studies, civil rights movement and George Orwell, 1962—; writer: (songs) Money Makes A Woman Free, 1976, 3 songs featured in Parade of Am. Music; co-creator: musical comedy Russia's Secret Plot to Take Back Alaska, 1983. Recipient 8 awards Am. Song Festival, 1976-79, Bill Casey award in Letters, 1980; AAUW doctoral fellow, 1971-73; grantee Calif. Arts Council, 1976-77. Mem. Am. Sociol. Assn., Soc. Sci. Study of Religion, Soc. Study of Religion under Communism, Poetry Orgn. for Women, Dramatists Guild, Phi Beta Kappa, Sigma Alpha Iota, Beta Phi Mu, Kappa Kappa Gamma. Democrat. Office: Merlin Press PO Box 5602 San Jose CA 95150

MCDOWELL, ROBERT ALAN, research fisheries biologist; b. Casper, Wyo., Mar. 21, 1945; s. Lyle Wilton and Mildred Elizabeth (Jones) McD.; m. Patricia Kay Huffman, May 28, 1967; children: Michael Roddy, Kelly Lynn. AS in Forestry, Casper Jr. Coll., 1968; BS in Biology, U. Wyo., 1971, MS in zoology, physiology, 1973. Asst. fisheries biologist Wyo. Game & Fish Dept., Jackson, 1968; asst. fisheries biologist Wyo. Game & Fish Dept., Laramie, 1969-72, fisheries mgmt. research specialist, project leader, 1973-85; fisheries mgmt. research specialist I Wyo. Game & Fish Dept., Buffalo, 1985—; chmn. 1980 fish div. meeting workshop Wyo. Game and Fish Dept., Laramie; advisor Wyo. Outdoor Council Platte River Task Force, Saratoga, 1977-79. Contbr. articles to profl. jours. Mem. Am. Fisheries Soc. (chmn. award of excellence com. Colo./Wyo. div. 1978, chmn., editor proceedings 20th ann. meeting Colo./Wyo. chpt. 1984, Best Paper in Fish Mgmt. award 1976, 81), Wyo. Wildlife Fedn., Ducks Unltd., Sigma Xi. Democrat. Lutheran. Avocations: river rafting, photography, landscaping, amateur carpentry and constrn. Home: 902 Delaware PO Box 172 Buffalo WY 82834 Office: Wyo Game and Fish Dept Box F Buffalo WY 82834

MCDOWELL, ROBIN SCOTT, physical chemist; b. Greenwich, Conn., Nov. 14, 1934; s. James Duffil and Aimee Marguerite (Lavers) McD.; m. Arlene R. Egertsen, Nov. 23, 1963; children: Jennifer Ellen, Allison Elizabeth. BA, Haverford Coll., 1956; PhD, MIT, 1960. Mem. staff Los Alamos (N.Mex.) Nat. Lab., 1960-81, asst. group leader, 1981-82, fellow, 1983—. Contbr. articles to profl. jours. Chmn. Los Alamos County Library Bd., 1981-82. Mem. AAAS, N.Mex. Acad. Sci., Optical Soc. Am., Coblentz Soc., Inc. (pres. 1987—), Soc. Applied Spectroscopy, Sigma Xi. Avocations: photography, hiking, genealogy. Home: 885 Camino Encantado Los Alamos NM 87544 Office: Los Alamos Nat Lab Los Alamos NM 87545

MCEDWARD, CHUCK THOMAS, communications company executive; b. Bremerton, Wash., July 8, 1956; s. Clarence Norman McEdward and Blanche Irene (Griffith) McEdward Timborski; m. Beverly Kay Sandstrom, May 7, 1974 (div. 1976); children—Jason Thomas, Heather Marie. Student Olympic Coll. Video sales technician J.A. Smith Video, Bremerton, 1981-84;nat. sales and mktg. mgr. Wash. Satellite, Bremerton, 1984—; owner, pres. Olympic Satellite Broadcasting, Port Orchard, Wash., 1984—. Lobbyist, Inventors Workshop Internat., 1982. Recipient Bus. Devel. award SBA, Seattle, 1980. Mem. Am. Film Inst., Inventors Workshop Internat. (chmn. Bremerton chpt. 1980-83, service award, 1983). Democrat.

MCELROY, LEO FRANCIS, communications consultant journalist; b. Los Angeles, Oct. 12, 1932; s. Leo Francis and Helen Evelyn (Silliman) McE.; m. Dorothy Frances Montgomery, Nov. 3, 1956 (div. 1981); children—James, Maureen, Michael, Kathleen. B.S. in English, Loyola U., Los Angeles, 1953. News dir. KFI, KRLA, KABC Radio, Los Angeles, 1964-72; pub. affairs host Sta. KCET, Pub. TV, Los Angeles, 1967-74; v.p. Sta. KROQ AM/FM, Los Angeles, 1972-74; polit. editor Sta. KABC-TV, Los Angeles, 1974-81; pres. McElroy Communications, Los Angeles and Sacramento, 1981—; pres. sec. Lt. Gov.'s Office, Sacramento, 1983-84; chmn. Calif. AP Broadcasters, 1972-74; cons. State Office Migrant Edn., Sacramento, 1974, Californians for Water, Los Angeles, 1982, Calif. Water Protection Council, Sacramento, 1982. Author: Uneasy Partners, 1984; author plays: Mermaid Tavern, 1956, To Bury Caesar (Christopher award 1952), 1952. State del. Western Am. Assembly on Prison Reform, Berkeley, Calif., 1973; chmn. State Disaster Info. Task Force, Calif., 1973-74; campaign media dir. statewide issues, various candidates, Sacramento, Los Angeles, 1981-86; dir. Vols. In Victim Assistance, Sacramento, 1984. Recipient Gabriel award Catholic Archdiocese, Los Angeles, 1972; Golden Mike award Radio-TV News Assn., Los Angeles, 1973; Writing award Los Angeles Press Club, 1981; Hon. Resolution, Calif. State Assembly, Sacramento, 1981. Mem. ASCAP, AFTRA, Greater Los Angeles Press Club, Catholic Press Council. Republican. Roman Catholic. Home: 1325 O St Apt 2 Sacramento CA 95814-5928 Office: McElroy Communications 2410 K St Suite C Sacramento CA 95816 Office: 603 Green St Suite 200 Pasadena CA 91101

MC ELWAIN, JOSEPH ARTHUR, retired power company executive; b. Deer Lodge, Mont., Nov. 13, 1919; s. Lee Chaffee and Johanna (Petersen) McE.; m. Mary Cleaver Witt, Mar. 8, 1945; children—Lee William and Lori Louise (twins). B.A., U. Mont., 1943, LL.B., 1947. Bar: Mont. 1947. Individual practice law Deer Lodge, 1947-63; Washington legis. counsel Mont. Power Co., Butte, 1954-63; counsel Mont. Power Co., 1963-65, asst. to pres., 1965-67, v.p., 1967-70, exec. v.p., dir., 1970, then chmn., chief exec. officer, now ret.; dir. Mont. Bower Co., First Bank System 1975-84, Devel. Credit Corp. Mont.; MHD Devel. Corp. 1986—; mem. U.S. nat. com. World Energy Conf.; Mont. dir. for U.S. Savs. Bonds, 1980-81; cons. in field. Mem. Mont. Pub. Land Law Rev. Adv. Com. City atty. Deer Lodge, 1950-57, 60-63; mem. Mont. Ho. of Reps., 1949-55, majority floor leader, 1951; mem. Mont. State Senate, 1962-64; state chmn. Republican Central Com., Mont., 1952-54; mem. adv. com. Edison Electric Inst., U. Mont. Found., Missoula, Rocky Mountain Coll., Billings; bd. dirs. Mont. Internat. Trade Commn. Served with AUS, World War II and Korea. Recipient Judstin Miller award, 1947. Mem. Mont., Am. bar assns. Episcopalian. Clubs: Masons, Shriners, Kiwanis. Home: 40 E Broadway Butte MT 59701

MCENCROE, PAUL ROGER, restaurant executive; b. Chgo., Dec. 4, 1922; s. John James and Irene Violet (Blake) McE.; m. Donna Marie Zipprich, July 1, 1950; children—John, Andy, Linda, Anne. B.S. in Mktg., Northwestern U., 1947; postgrad. in fin. Denver U., 1964. Salesman, Burroughs Corp., Chgo., 1947-48, Snapout Forms Co., Chgo., 1948-50, Am. Seating Co., San Diego, 1951-52, Duplex Products Co., Milw., 1953-57; restaurant mgr. El Rancho Colo. Co., 1958—; condr. seminars Colo. Mountain Coll. System. Fin. chmn. Colo. Philharm., 1968-69; mem. Jefferson County (Colo.) Sch. Bd., 1969-77; adv. bd. St. Anthony Hosp. "Flight for Life," 1973-77; mem. Lookout Mountain dist. fire protection bd., 1978-82; mem. Colo. Tourism Bd.; chmn. 1986—; mem. El Rancho Met. Water and Sewer Dist. Bd., 1985. Served with USAAF, 1943-45. Decorated Air medal; named Lakewood (Colo.) Sentinel Man of Year, 1977. Mem. Colo. Wyo. Restaurant Assn. (Disting. Service award 1981). Democrat. Office: El Rancho Rural Br Denver/El Rancho CO 80401

MCENERNEY, MICHAEL THOMAS, accountant, taxation educator; b. Fargo, N.D., Sept. 13, 1948; s. John Joseph and Ellen Louise (Bakke) McE.; m. Irene Kazuyo Yanamura, Aug. 21, 1972; children: John-David K., William-James K., Thomas-Joseph K., Jason-Edward K. BS, Wis. State U., 1970; MBA, U. Hawaii, 1971; JD, Northwestern U., 1976. Bar: Ill., Hawaii, U.S. Tax Ct.; CPA, Ill., Hawaii. Mem. tax staff Alexander Grant & Co., Chgo., 1976-77, 79-80; vis. asst. prof. acctg. U. Hawaii, Honolulu, 1977-79; head tax dept. Jack Tyrell & Co. CPA's, Honolulu, 1980-84; ptnr. McEnerney & Shimabukuro CPA's, Honolulu, 1984—; instr. Hawaii Assn. Pub. Accts., Honolulu. Author annual tax course textbook, 1982, 5th rev. edit., 1986. Served with U.S. Army, 1971-73. Mem. Hawaii State Bar Assn., Hawaii Soc. CPA's (instr. 1978—), Am. Inst. CPA's, ABA, Hawaii Bar Assn., Ill. Bar Assn., Nat. Assn. Pub. Accountants. Club: Pacific (Honolulu). Office: McEnerney & Shimabukuro CPA's 165 S King St #1104 Honolulu HI 96813

MCENERY, THOMAS, mayor; b. San Jose, Calif., Sept. 23, 1945; s. John Patrick and Margaret (Sellers) McE.; m. Jill Rodrick, Sept. 21, 1971; children—Sarah, Erin, Molly. B.A. in Sci. and Commerce, U. Santa Clara, 1967, M.A. in History, 1969. Tchr. St. Joseph's Middle Sch., San Jose, 1970-71; pres. Farmers Union Corp., San Jose, 1974-82; mayor City of San Jose, San Jose, 1983—. Author: California Cavalier-The Journal of Captain Thomas Fallon, 1978. Mem. of hist. renovation and downtown planning coms., San Jose. Fellow U. Santa Clara Bd. of Fellows; mem. U.S. Conf. of Mayors. Democrat. Roman Catholic. Avocations: reading; history; movies; light writing; tennis. Office: San Jose Mayor's Office 801 N First St San Jose CA 95110 *

MCEVOY, PAMELA THOMPSON, psychotherapist; b. Forest Hills, N.Y., Mar. 8, 1937; d. Renny T. and Pamela Shipley (Sweeny) McE.; B.A., U. La Verne, 1978, M.S., 1980; Ph.D., U.S. Internat. U., 1982; children—Michael B. Anderson, Jeffery A. Thomas, Candy L. Anderson Anderson-Smith, Kenneth L. Anderson. Data processing coordinator Ernest Righetti High Sch., Santa Maria, Calif., 1974-78; instr. psychology-sociology Allan Hancock Coll., Santa Maria, 1977-78; mental health asst. Santa Barbara City Alcoholism Dept., 1977-78; gen. mgr. Profl. Suites, San Diego, 1978-81; therapist Chula Vista (Calif.) Community Counseling Ctr., San Diego, 1978-85; research asst. U.S. Internat. U., 1979-82; research coordinator Mil. Family research Ctr., San Diego, 1981-82; assoc. dir. Acad. Assoc. Psychotherapists, 1982-86; pvt. practice, San Diego, 1982—; bd. dirs. Women's Internat. Ctr., 1984-86. Bd. dirs. San Diego County Mental Health Assn., 1978-80; pres. Chula Vista Counseling Ctr., 1978; mem. Delinquency Prevention Commn., 1978. State fellow, 1979, 80, 81, 82, Calif. State scholar, 1976-77. Mem. Am. Psychol. Assn., Am. Assn. Marriage and Family Therapists, Calif. Assn. Marriage and Family Therapists. Republican. Roman Catholic. Home: PO Box 8946 Rancho Sante Fe CA 92067 Office: 4401 Manchester Ave #101 Encinitas CA 92024

MCEWAN, ANTHONY JOHNSON, aeronautical engineer; b. Stamford, Conn., Sept. 14, 1944; s. Allerton James and Ruth Juliet (Bell) McE.; B.S.E., Princeton U., 1966; M.S. in Aero. Engring., U. So. Calif., 1970. Student engr. ONERA, Chatillon-sous-Bagneux, France, 1965; assoc. engr. aircraft div. Northrop Corp., Hawthorne, Calif., 1966-67, engr. Ventura div., 1967-69, sr. engr., 1969-74, engr. specialist, 1974-81, mgr. aerodynamics propulsion and thermal analysis, 1981-82, mgr. engring. analysis, 1982, mgr. engring. design, 1982-83, mgr. vehicle design, 1983-86, tech. asst. to v.p. engring., 1986—; mem. launch dynamics panel USN Aeroballistics Com., 1980—. Assoc. fellow AIAA (vice chmn. Ventura Pacific sect. 1978, chmn. 1979, nat. membership com. 1980-82); mem. Assn. Unmanned Vehicle Systems. Democrat. Clubs: Princeton (So. Calif., Los Angeles), Malibu Yacht (bd. dirs. 1981-86). Contbr. articles to tech. publs. Home: 3931 Latigo Canyon Rd Malibu CA 90265 Office: Northrop Corp 1515 Rancho Conejo Blvd Newbury Park CA 91320

MCEWAN, STEPHANIE ANNE, lawyer; b. Buffalo, Aug. 22, 1958; d. Kenneth Harry and Patricia Anne (Coffey) McE. BA in Classical Civilization and Philosophy, U. Calif., Irvine, 1980, BS in Physics, 1980; JD summa cum laude, Am. Coll., Brea, Calif., 1984; postgrad. (Royal fellow), Cambridge U., London, 1980; postgrad. in radiology U. Calif.-Irvine Sch. Medicine. Med. physicist, Am. Diagnostics, Newport Beach, Calif., 1979-80; nuclear physicist U. Calif. Neutrino Physics Group, 1979-80; assoc. EIP/Cushman Corp., Newport Beach, 1980; law clk. Keenan & Tobin, Los Angeles, 1981-82; v.p. law, chief fin. officer Champion Plastics Corp., Orange, Calif., 1982-86; assoc. Connolly Law Offices, Costa Mesa, Calif., 1986—; clin. asst. prof. medicine U. Calif., Irvine, 1986—; legis. fellow U.S. Senator Pete Wilson. Author: The Cryogenic Principles of Experimental Cryosurgery; The Challenge of Space Law, 1980. Articles editor: Internat. Law Jour., 1980. Served to lt. USNR and USMCR, 1983—. Fellow Royal Astron. Soc.; mem. Assn. Trial Lawyers Am., U.S. Naval Inst., Aerospace Med. Assn., ABA, Sigma Xi, Sigma Delta Chi, Sigma Phi Sigma, Eta Sigma Phi, Delta Delta Delta, Phi Alpha Delta. Republican. Roman Catholic. Home: 29 Briarglen Irvine CA 92714 Office: Connolly Law Offices 3151 Airway Blvd Suite H-3 Costa Mesa CA 92626

MCEWEN, TERENCE A(LEXANDER), opera company executive. Student in pre-law, Sir George Williams Coll., Montreal. With Decca Records, London, Paris, 1950-80, London Records div. N.Y.C., 1959-80. With San Francisco Opera, 1980—, gen. dir. 1982—. Office: San Francisco Opera War Meml Opera House San Francisco CA 94102 *

MCEWEN, WILLIAM JAMES, advertising agency executive; b. Montclair, N.J., Aug. 14, 1943; s. Lester Vincent McEwen and Harriet Eleanor (Toner) McEwen Mitchell; m. Florence Marie Witkop, Aug. 21, 1965; children: James Garrett, Megan Alicia. BA, St. Anselm Coll., 1965; MA, Mich. State U., 1967, PhD, 1969. Assoc. prof. U. Conn., Storrs, 1970-76; research supr. Needham Harper, Chgo., 1976-77; pres., San Francisco office D'Arcy-MacManus, 1977-82; sr. v.p., dir. research Foote, Cone & Belding, Chgo., 1983-84; sr. v.p., dir. stategic planning McCann-Erickson, San Francisco, 1984—; adj. prof. U. So. Calif., 1979-80; cons. Ctr. for Environment and Man, Hartford, Conn., 1974-77. Co-author: Communication and Behavior, 1978; also contbr. articles to profl. jours. Mem. Coventry (Conn.) Town Council, 1974-75; mem. Dem. Town Com, Coventry, 1974-75; scoutmaster Boy Scouts Am., Barrington , Ill. 1983-84. Mem. Am. Mktg. Assn. (local v.p. programs 1980-81, pres. 1985-87, exec. fellow in residence 1986). Republican. Avocations: travel, tennis. Home: 238 Reed Blvd Mill Valley CA 94941 Office: McCann-Erickson 201 California San Francisco CA 94111

MCFADDEN, BRUCE ALDEN, biochemistry educator; b. La Grande, Oreg., Sept. 23, 1930; s. Eugene Field and Mary Elizabeth (McMaster) McF.; m. Roberta Ray Wilson, June 14, 1958; children: Paul, David, John. AB in Chemistry with honors, Whitman Coll., 1952, DSc (hon.), 1978; PhD in Biochemistry, UCLA, 1956. From instr. to prof. chemistry Wash. State U., Pullman, 1956-66, prof. biochemistry, 1974—, dir. sci. devel., 1974-78, chmn. dept. biochemistry, 1978-84; vis. prof. U. Leicester, Eng., 1972-73, U. Florence, Italy, 1980, Tech. U. Munich, 1980-81; mem. study sect. NIH, Bethesda, Md., 1978-79, 82; panelist research grants U.S. Dept. Energy, 1983, Frasch grants Am. Chem. Soc., 1982—; cons. to numerous jours. and agys., Pullman, 1966—. Contbr. articles to profl. jours.; patentee in field. Pres. Sunnyside Sch. PTA, Pullman, 1972; chmn 1984 and Beyond Citizens' com., Pullman Sch. Bd., 1983-84. Recipient Sr. Scientist award Humboldt Found. Tech. U. Munich, 1980-81; fellow Guggenheim Found., 1972-73, NIH, 1963-69,73; numerous others. Fellow AAAS; mem. Am. Chem. Soc. (pres. Wash.-Idaho Border sect. 1963-64), Am. Soc. Biol. Chemists (elected, nat. correspondant 1971—), Am. Soc. Microbiologists, Pacific Slope Biochem. Soc. (pres. 1973-74), Am. Soc. Plant Physiologists, Sigma Xi, Phi Kappa Phi, Phi Lambda Upsilon (pres. 1955). Democrat. Home: SW 1465 Wadleigh Dr Pullman WA 99163 Office: Wash State U Biochemistry Dept Pullman WA 99164

MCFADDEN, HUGH BARTLEY, JR., lawyer; b. Columbus, Ohio, July 24, 1942; s. Hugh Bartley and Marjorie Kathleen (Priest) McF.; m. Mary Bell Guthrie, June 6, 1964 (div. 1978); 1 child, Bartley; m. Carol Lea Hunter, Oct. 15, 1978; children: Michael, Benjamin. BA, U. Wyo., 1964, JD, 1968. Bar: Wyo. 1968, U.S. Ct. Appeals (10th cir.) 1976. Asst. atty. gen. Atty. Gen. Wyo., Cheyenne, 1968-70; ptnr. Corthell & King, Laramie, Wyo., 1970—; lectr. in law U. Wyo., Laramie, 1979. Chmn. Albany County

Library Bd. Trustees, 1974-80, Albany County Dem. Party, Laramie, 1983-84, Albany County Fair Bd., 1980-86. Mem. AAAS, Assn. Trial Lawyers Am., Wyo. Bar Assn. Democrat. Avocations: horses, boating, fishing, reading, writing. Office: Corthell & King 221 S 2d St Laramie WY 82070

MCFADDEN, LEON LAMBERT, artist, inventor; b. St. Paul, Apr. 19, 1925; s. Frank Grover and Irene Manilla Lambert (Deane) McF. Student, several colls., univs., art insts. Prin. McFadden Commercial Studios, 1946-50; with McFadden-Kaump Art Service, 1952-54; pres. McFadden Advt. (merger with Sundial Services, Inc.), 1954-70; mktg. dir. Kinelogic Corp. (now Echoscience Corp.), Mountain View, Calif., 1965-70; held position in research and devel. proprietary patents Sundial Systems div. Sundial Services, Inc., 1968-70; art instr. various Calif. community colls., 1972-74; minority bus. cons. VISTA/ACTION, 1974-75. Inventor, patentee seventeen mechanical tools and devices. Prin. artistic works include large assemblage painting of Statue of Liberty, found image works (represented in White House spl. collection). Served with USN, 1942-46, PTO. Mem. IEEE, AIAA, AAAS, N.Mex. Solar Energy Assn., Mensa, Artists Equity Assn. Inc., Artists Equity Assn. of N.Y., Siskiyou Artists Assn., Oakland Ctr. for Visual Arts, Sierra Club (life). Home: 418 3d St Yreka CA 96097 Studio: Liberty Painting Corp 6725 Old Hwy 99 Yreka CA 96097

MC FADDEN, WILMOT CURNOW HAMM, librarian; b. Lead, S.D., Oct. 30, 1919; d. William and Ingeborg (Christianson) Curnow; student S.D. State Coll., 1938-41; m. Kenneth G. Hamm, Jan. 8, 1944 (div. 1963); 1 dau., Wilmot Christine (Mrs. Charles Bice); m. John Stinson McFadden, Mar. 1965. Asst. librarian Rock Springs (Wyo.) Pub. Library, 1947-48, head librarian, 1953-86; appointed to mayoral adminstrv. bd. Rock Springs, 1987—. State committeewoman Dem. Party, 1952-74, also state vice chmn., del. Dem. State Conv., 1970, 72; del. Dem. Nat. Conv., 1956, 64; adv. bd. Fed. Commn. Civil Rights, 1963—; treas. Sch. Bd. Dist. 4, 1966-69, clk. dist. 1, 1969-77; bd. dirs. State Library, Archives, Hist. Bd.; adv. bd. Western Wyo. Community Coll.; mem. Wyo. Citizens for Arts, 1977—; mem. Wyo. Community Coll. Commn., 1983-85, mem. literacy com., 1986; mem. Wes. Recipient Nat. Grolier award Nat. Library Week, 1969, Librarian Service award Eagles Aux., 1982, cert. of commendation Western Wyo. Community Coll., 1985. Mem. Federated Woman's Club, Am. Legion Aux., Mountain Plains (exec. bd. 1967—, pres. 1972-73), ALA, Wyo. Library Assn. (chmn. conf. 1966, 70, pres. 1958-59, 72-73; Librarian of Yr. 1977, Georgia Shovlain Spl. Projects award 1980, Wyo.'s Outstanding Librarian 1985), Zonta (charter), Am. Library Trustees Assn., Wyo. Sch. Bds. Assn. (life; commendation 1979), Alpha Delta Kappa. Author: Handbook Wyoming Library Trustees. Home: 28 Cedar St Rock Springs WY 82901 Office: 400 C St Rock Springs WY 82901

MC FARLAND, NORMAN FRANCIS, bishop; b. Martinez, Calif., Feb. 21, 1922; student St. Patrick's Sem., Menlo Park, Calif.; J.C.D., Cath. U. Am. Ordained priest Roman Catholic Ch., 1946, consecrated bishop, 1970; titular bishop of Bida and aux. bishop of San Francisco, 1970-74; apostolic adminstr. Diocese of Reno, 1974-76; bishop Diocese of Reno-Las Vegas, 1976-87, Diocese of Orange, Calif., 1987—. Office: 2811 E Villa Real Dr Orange CA 92667

MCFARLAND, SHARRON RENEE DUNCAN, librarian; b. Corpus Christi, Tex., Aug. 30, 1939; d. Laurence Edwin and Doris Alice (Ross) Duncan; m. James Walter McFarland, Aug. 8, 1958; children: James Jr., Scott. BA, U. Tex., 1974, MLS, 1976. Indexer, records mgr. U. Tex., Austin, 1975-76; abstractor Congl. Info. Service, Bethesda, Md., 1977; head library services Nat. Rehab. Info. Ctrs., Washington, 1977-85; grad. sch. lectr. Cath. Univ. Sch. Library Info. Sci., Washington, 1983-84; community relations coordinator Stockton/San Joaquin County Pub. Library, Calif., 1986—; cons. Nat. Rehab. Info. Ctr., Washington, 1985—. Author: REHABDATA: A Selective Subject Catalog, 1984; editor: REHABDATA: A Selective Subject Catalog, 1982, 83; REHABDATA: Thesaurus of NARIC Descriptions, 1981, 83; editor ALA reference books bulletin; contbr. articles to profl. jours.. Vol. coordinator Sharpe Army Depot Library, Lathrop, Calif., 1985—. Grantee Tex. Rehab. Commn., 1975-76. Mem. ALA, Spl. Libraries Assn., Associated Info. Mgrs., Assn. Records Mgrs. and Adminstrs., Am. Soc. Indesers, Tex. Ex-students Assn., Phi Kappa Phi, Beta Phi Mu. Club: Civilian/Mil. Women's (Lathrop) (hon. pres. 1985—). Home: 26-700 E Roth Rd French Camp CA 95231 Office: Stockton/San Joaquin County Pub Lib 605 N Eldorado Stockton CA 95202

MCFARLANE, GREGORY ALAN, advertising executive; b. Salt Lake City, Aug. 15, 1956; s. Alan Garland and Alice (DiPietro) McF.; m. Linda Jo Fishburn, May 20, 1981. BA in English, U. Utah, 1978. Layout artist Grand Cen. Advt., Salt Lake City, 1978, copywriter, 1978-79; writer, producer Ross Jurney Advt., Salt Lake City, 1979-81, Gillham Advt., Salt Lake City, 1981-83; creative dir. Scopes-Garcia Advt., Salt Lake City, 1984; dir. advt. Evans & Sutherland Corp., Salt Lake City, 1985—. Writer, producer (TV comml.) Dick Nose, 1983 (N.Y. Film Festival 1983), others 1979-85. Avocations: playing and building guitars, photography, pottery, skiing, bicycling. Office: Evans & Sutherland 580 Arapeen Dr Salt Lake City UT 84108

MCGAGH, WILLIAM GILBERT, aerospace company financial executive; b. Boston, May 29, 1929; s. Thomas A. and Mary M. (McDonough) McG.; m. Sarah Ann McQuigg, Sept. 23, 1961; children: Margaret Ellen, Sarah Elizabeth. B.S., Boston Coll., 1950; M.B.A., Harvard U., 1952; M.S. (Sloan fellow), MIT, 1965. Fin. analyst Ford Motor Co., Dearborn, Mich., 1953-55; mem. staff treas. office Chrysler Corp., Detroit, 1955-64; comptroller, treas. Chrysler Can. Ltd., Windsor, 1965-67; staff exec.-fin. Latin Am. ops., Detroit, 1967-68; asst. treas. Chrysler Corp., 1968-75, treas., 1975-76, v.p., treas., 1976-80; sr. v.p. fin. and dir. Northrop Corp., Los Angeles, 1980—; also dir. Northrop Corp.; dir. Pacific Am. Income Shares, Inc. Bd. dirs. Greater Los Angeles Zoo Assn., Ind. Colls. of So. Calif., KCET Pub. TV. Served as 2d lt. USAF, 1952-53. Mem. Fin. Execs. Inst. (pres. Detroit chpt. 1979-80). Clubs: Detroit Athletic, Orchard Lake Country; Harvard (N.Y.C.); Beach (Santa Monica, Calif.); Los Angeles Country, California (Los Angeles). Home: 2189 Century Hill Los Angeles CA 90067 Office: 1840 Century Park E Century City Los Angeles CA 90067

MCGANN, ANTHONY FRANCIS, business educator; b. Newark, Oct. 4, 1941; s. Harold K. and Mary E. (Lydon) McG.; m. Waltraud K. Dafferneiter, July 25, 1965 (dec. Nov. 1980); m. Esther Mae Kunkel, Feb. 2, 1983; children: Celeste, Christopher, Kevin, Angelica. BS in Mil. Engring., U.S. Mil. Acad., 1963; MBA, U. Mo., 1968, PhD in Mktg., 1971. Commd. 2d lt. USAF, 1963; advanced through grades to capt. USAF, various locations, 1967; resigned USAF, 1969; from instr. to prof. bus. adminstrn. U. Wyo., Laramie, 1971-78, prof., 1978—; vis. prof. adminstrn. U. Ga., Athens, 1978-79; cons. Fed. Intermediate Credit Bank, Omaha, 1974-80, Adolph Coors Co., Golden, Colo., 1978. Co-author: Introduction to Business, 1979, Advertising Media, 1981; editor Jour. of Advt., 1983—. Mem. Am. Mktg. Assn., Am. Acad. Advt., Am. Council Consumer Interests (research award 1973), Mkt. Research Soc. Republican. Roman Catholic. Avocations: flyfishing, skiing. Home: 1416 Baker St Laramie WY 82071 Office: U Wyo Coll Commerce and Industry Laramie WY 82071

MCGANN, JOHN MILTON, real estate manager; b. Omaha, Mar. 18, 1948; s. John Byron and Donna M. (Rehnquist) McG.; m. Barbara June Scott, June 2, 1978. BSBA, cert. real estate, U. Nebr., Omaha, 1971. Property mgr. Boetel & Co., Omaha, 1971-73; asst. office bldg. mgr. The Irvine Co., Newport Beach, Calif., 1973-74; property mgr. Harbor Investment Co., Corona Del Mar, Calif., 1974-76, Robert A. McNeil Corp., Santa Ana, Calif., 1976-78; gen. mgr. Daon Mgmt., Newport Beach, 1978-80; v.p. August Mgmt. Inc., Long Beach, Calif., 1980-82, Calif. Fed. Asst. Mgmt., Los Angeles, 1982-83; pres. Wespac Mgmt. Realty Corp., Newport Beach, 1983-87; v.p., dir. due diligence and asset mgmt. Calif. Fed. Syndications, Los Angeles, 1987—. Mem. Inst. Real Estate Mgmt. (Orange County chpt.), Internat. Council Shopping Ctrs., Lambda Chi Alpha, Delta Sigma Pi, Rho Epsilon (pres.). Republican. Mem. Christian Sci. Ch. Home: 284 Robinhood Ln Costa Mesa CA 92627 Office: Calif Fed Syndications 5670 Wilshire Blvd Suite 2200 Los Angeles CA 90036

MCGARRITY, JACK JOHNSTON, architect, interior designer; b. Rocksprings, Wyo., Nov. 12, 1936; s. Carl A. Hawks and Dess (Johnston) Steuart. Registered architect, Hawaii, Calif., Ariz., Oreg., Tex., N.Mex., Colo., Wyo., Wash., Fla., Fiji. Architect, Jack J. McGarrity AIA, Honolulu, 1968—; interior designer Interspace Ltd., Honolulu, 1972—; resort developer Johnston Hawks Ltd., Honolulu, 1978—; architect, pres. Jack J. McGarrity AIA Assocs. Ltd., Honolulu, 1971— . Mem. Design Profl. Conciliation Panel, State of Hawaii, 1983—. Mem. AIA, Societas Damien (gov. gen. 1984—), Pacific Fleet Submarine Meml. Assn. (life, bd. dirs. 1984—). Episcopalian. Lodge: Rotary (sec. 1978; Paul Harris fellow, 1979). Home: PO Box 15697 Honolulu HI 96830-5697 Office: Jack J McGarrity AIA Assocs Ltd 1600 Kapiolani Blvd 524 Honolulu HI 96814

MC GAUGH, JAMES LAFAYETTE, psychobiologist; b. Long Beach, Calif., Dec. 17, 1931; s. William Rufus and Daphne (Hermes) McG.; m. Carol J. Becker, Mar. 15, 1952; children: Douglas, Janice, Linda. B.A., San Jose State U., 1953; Ph.D. (Abraham Rosenberg fellow), U. Calif. - Berkeley, 1959; sr. postdoctoral fellow, Nat. Acad. Scis.-NRC, Istituto Superiore di Sanita, Rome, 1961-62. Asst. prof., assoc. prof. psychology San Jose State U., 1957-61; assoc. prof. psychology U. Oreg., 1961-64; assoc. prof. U. Calif., Irvine, 1964-66, founding chmn. dept. psychobiology, 1964-67, 71-74, 86—, prof., 1966—; dean Sch. Biol. Sci. U. Calif. at Irvine, 1967-70, vice chancellor acad. affairs, 1975-77, exec. vice chancellor, 1978-82, dir. Ctr. Neurobiology of Learning and Memory, 1983—; Mem. adv. coms. NIMH, 1965-78. Author: (with J.B. Cooper) Integrating Principles of Social Psychology, 1963, (with H.F. Harlow, R.F. Thompson) Psychology, 1971, (with M.J. Herz) Memory Consolidation, 1972, Learning and Memory: An Introduction, 1973, (with R.F. Thompson and T. Nelson) Psychology I, 1977, (with C. Cotman) Behavioral Neuroscience, 1980; editor: (with N.M. Weinberger, R.E. Whalen) Psychobiology, 1966, Psychobiology-Behavior from a Biological Perspective, 1971, The Chemistry of Mood, Motivation and Memory, 1972, (with M. Fink, S.S. Kety, T.A. Williams) Psychobiology of Convulsive Therapy, 1974, (with L.F. Petrinovich) Knowing, Thinking, and Believing, 1976, (with R.R. Drucker-Colín) Neurobiology of Sleep and Memory, 1977, (with S.B. Kiesler) Aging, Biology and Behavior, 1981, (with G. Lynch and N. M. Weinberger) Neurobiology of Learning and Memory, 1984, Memory Systems of the Brain, 1985; editor Behavioral Biology, 1972-78, Behavioral and Neural Biology, 1979—. Fellow Am. Psychol. Assn. (chief sci. advisor 1986—, Disting. Sci. Contbn. award 1981), AAAS; mem. Internat. Brain Research Orgn., Soc. Neurosci., Am. Coll. Neuropsychopharmacology, Psychonomic Soc., Phi Beta Kappa, Sigma Xi. Office: Center Neurobiology of Learning and Memo U Calif Irvine CA 92717

MCGAUGHEY, CHARLES GILBERT, retired research biochemist; b. San Diego, Sept. 8, 1925; s. Gilbert Arthur and Louisa Ellen (Inskeep) McG. BA, U. Calif., Berkeley, 1950; MA, U. So. Calif., 1952. Diplomate Am. Inst. Oral Biology. Scientist radiol. hazards evaluation U.S. Naval Radiol. Def. Lab., San Francisco, 1952; research biochemist VA Med. Ctr., Long Beach, Calif., 1953-81; prin. investigator studies dental caries and oral cancer Oral Diseases Research Lab., 1978-81. Contbr. articles to profl. jours. Grantee Nat. Inst. Dental Research, 1965. Mem. AAAS. Republican. Home: 337 Winnipeg Pl Long Beach CA 90814

MCGAUGHEY, DENNIS EMMETT, banker; b. Los Angeles, Sept. 12, 1944; s. Emmett Connell and Mary Etta (Freese) McG.; m. Charlene Lynn Scarratt, Aug. 19, 1967; children: Lori Elisabeth, Karyn Ashley. BS in Fin., U. So. Calif., 1970, postgrad., 1977-78; postgrad. Stanford U., 1981. Trainee Union Bank, Los Angeles, 1970, loan officer, Beverly Hills, Calif., 1972-74, asst. v.p., 1974-75, v.p., 1975-80, regional v.p., North Hollywood, Calif., 1980-84; sr. v.p. Bank of Industry, North Hollywood, 1984-85; sr. v.p. Lincoln Nat. Bank, 1985—. Bd. dirs. Commerce Assocs. U. So. Calif., 1977-83. Served with U.S. Army, 1964-66. Mem. U. So. Calif. Alumni Assn., Chi Phi. Club: California (Los Angeles). Lodges: Masons, Shriners. Home: 6600 Langdon Ave Van Nuys CA 91406 Office: Lincoln Nat Bank 16030 Ventura Blvd Encino CA 91436

MC GAW, SIDNEY EDWIN, ednl. cons.; b. Toronto, Ont., Can., Sept. 21, 1908; s. Sidney Anson and May (Bigelow) McG.; student Fresno State Coll., 1928-31; B.S., U. Calif. at Berkeley, 1944, M.A., 1948, Ed.D., 1952; m. Clara E. Eca da Silva, June 15, 1931; children—Bruce A., Laurie A., Kathleen C. (Mrs. Richard Chylinski). Instr., counselor pub. schs., Oakland, Calif., 1941-47; asst. supr. trade and tech. tchr. tng. Calif. State Dept. Edn., 1947-50, regional supr., 1950-65; dean instrn. San Jose City Coll., 1965-74; ednl. cons., 1974—; lectr. U. Calif. at Berkeley, summers 1948-66; workshop lectr. U. Nev., summers 1955-56. Pres., Calif. League for Nursing, 1967-69; chmn. edn. and tng. commn. Redwood Region Conservation Council, 1953-65. Mem. Nat. League Nursing (bd. dirs. 1967-69). Lodge: Rotary (bd. dirs. West San Jose 1969-70). Club: Commonwealth of Calif. (San Francisco). Home: 1023 Ordway St Albany CA 94706

MCGEE, DAVID RAY, plant genetic engineering company executive; b. Shreveport, La., July 8, 1949; s. Horace Wright and Florence (Hilyard) McG.; m. Barbara Aitkens, May 16, 1976; children: Matthew, Kathryn. BS, La. State U., 1971, MS, 1977, PhD, 1981. Instr. La. State U., Baton Rouge, 1979-82; v.p. Sungene Techs. Corp., Palo Alto, Calif., 1982—. Author: Zoology Laboratory Handbook for Graduate Teaching Assistants, 1980; also articles to profl. jours. Served to capt. USMC, 1972-74. Named Eagle Scout, Boy Scouts Am., Casper, Wyo., 1965. Mem. Genetics Soc. Am., La. Acad. Scis., Sigma Xi (assoc.). Republican. Episcopalian. Office: Sungene Techs Corp 3330 Hillview Ave Palo Alto CA 94304

MCGEE, MICHAEL JAY, fire marshal, educator; b. Ft. Worth, June 9, 1952; s. Cecil Carl and Helen Ruth (Peeples) McG.; m. Carol Lee Garbarino, Sept. 18, 1982; children: Megan Rose, John Michael. Student, U. Tex., 1970-73, Colo. Mountain Coll., 1977—, Western Oreg. State U., 1983—. Driver Massengale Co., Austin, Tex., 1970-73; gen. mgr. Sundae Palace, Austin, 1973-74; staff mem. Young Life, Colorado Springs, Colo., 1970-75; mgr. Broadmoor Mgmt. Co., Vail, Colo., 1974-76; technician Vail Cable Communications, 1976-77; fire marshal Vail Fire Dept., 1977—; dist. rep. Joint Council Fire Dist. Colo., 1983-85; co-chmn. Eagle County Hazardous Materials, 1984-85. ARC Eagle County chpt. chmn., 1980-83, disaster chmn., 1977-80. Mem. Nat. Fire Protection Assn., Colo. State Fire Marshals Assn., Colo. State Fire Chiefs Assn. Office: Vail Fire Dept 42 W Meadow Dr Vail CO 81657

MCGEE, MICHAEL SEAN, aerospace engineer; b. Sacramento, Dec. 24, 1956; s. Gerald E. and Therese M. McGee; m. Sandra L. Hansen, June 28, 1986. BS in Indsl. Engring., Purdue U., 1978; MBA, U. Denver, 1984. Engr. Martin Marietta Co., Denver, 1978-80, sr. engr., 1981—; field engr. Schlumberger, Bakersfield, Calif., 1980-81; bd. dirs. Ecotech Inc., Littleton, Colo. Bd. dirs. Colony Homeowners Assn., Denver, 1986—. Mem. Am. Def. Preparedness Assn. Republican. Roman Catholic. Avocations: softball, volleyball. Home: 4720 S Dudley #22 Littleton CO 80123 Office: Martin Marietta PO Box 179 Denver CO 80201

MCGEE, PATRICIA ANN, computer management consultant; b. N.Y.C., July 22, 1939; d. Patrick James and Bridget Mary (O'Leary) Brennan; B.A., CCNY, 1961; 1 dau., Ayn Maureen. Sr. cons., analyst Western Ops., Inc., San Francisco, 1968-71; data processing mgr. R. H. Lapin & Co., San Francisco, 1971-73; project leader, systems analyst Transamerica Corp., San Francisco, 1973-74; systems analyst United Vintners, Inc., San Francisco, 1974-75; systems planner Fiberboard Corp., 1975-76; customer rep. Computer Scis. Corp., 1976-78; project mgr. Crocker Nat. Bank, 1978-80; cons. Bechtel Co., 1980, Mason-McDuffie & Co., 1980, Pacific Telephone Co., 1980-81; partner The Profls., San Francisco, 1981-83; computer cons. Risk Mgmt. Applications, San Francisco, 1983-84; cons. Bank of Am., Wells Fargo Realty Fin., 1985. Mem. Am. Mgmt. Assn., Republican Women San Francisco, Women Entrepreneurs, World Affairs Trade Council, Profl. Women's Network, Assn. System Mgrs. Republican. Roman Catholic. Clubs: Commonwealth of California; San Francisco Bay. Home: 430-10th Ave San Francisco CA 94118 Office: 430-10th Ave San Francisco CA 94118

MCGEEHON, CAROL LOUISE, librarian; b. Cottage Grove, Oreg., July 14, 1955; m. Michael J. McGeehon, Sept. 1, 1973. AA, Umpqua Community Coll., 1975; BA, U. Oreg., 1977, MLS, 1978. Reference librarian Douglas County (Oreg.) Library System, Roseburg, 1979—; instr. Umpqua Community Coll., spring 1981, Douglas County Library, 1981. Author: If You Like Tolkien, 1984; numerous book revs., 1984—. Mem. Oreg. Library Assn. (chmn. jr. mems. roundtable 1982-83, speaker 1987). Democrat. Avocations: astronomy, sci. fiction. Home: 516 Orchard Ln Roseburg OR 97470 Office: Douglas County Library System County Courthouse Roseburg OR 97470

MCGETTIGAN, CHARLES CARROLL, JR., investment banker; b. San Francisco, Mar. 28, 1945; s. Charles Carroll McGettigan and Molly (Fay) McGettigan Pedley; m. Katharine Havard King, Nov. 1, 1975 (div. 1981); m. Meriwether Lewis Stovall, Aug. 6, 1983; 1 child, Meriwether Lewis Fay. A.B. in Govt., Georgetown U., 1966; M.B.A. in Finance, Wharton Sch., U. Pa., 1969. Assoc., asst. v.p., v.p. Blyth Eastman Dillon, N.Y.C., 1970-75, 1st v.p., 1975-78, sr. v.p., San Francisco, 1978-80; sr. v.p. Dillon Read & Co., San Francisco, 1980-83; gen. ptnr. Woodman Kirkpatrick & Gilbreath, San Francisco, 1983-84; prin. corp. fin. Hambrecht & Quist, Inc., San Francisco, 1984—; dir. Circadian, Inc., San Jose, Calif., 1980-84; adv. dir. Chesapeake Ventures, Balt., 1984—. Trustee St. Francis Meml. Hosp., San Francisco, 1980-86; mem. United San Francisco Rep. fin. com., 1983—, steering com., 1986—; adv. bd. dirs. Leavey Sch. Bus. Adminstrn., Santa Clara U., Calif., 1984—. Served with USN, 1966. Republican. Roman Catholic. Clubs: Brook, Racquet and Tennis (N.Y.); Pacific Union, Bohemian (San Francisco); Burlingame Country (Hillsborough, Calif.); California (Los Angeles); Boston (New Orleans); Piping Rock (Locust Valley, N.Y.). Home: 3375 Clay St San Francisco CA 94118 Office: Hambrecht & Quist Inc 235 Montgomery St Suite 500 San Francisco CA 94104

MCGILL, SANDRA SAAREM, chemical engineer; b. Los Angeles, Calif., Sept. 18, 1955; d. Myrl John and Marjorie Ann (Mullin) Saarem; m. Daniel Bruce McGill, Jan. 3, 1976; children: Matthew, Kevin, Michael. BSCE, U. Nev., 1982, MS in Metall. Engr., 1985. Engr. in tng., Nev. Chem. engr. U.S. Bur. Mines, Reno, 1984—; cons. Nimbus Engrs., Sparks, Nev., 1984-85. Den leader Cub Scouts Am., Sparks, 1986—; vol. Am. Cancer Soc., Reno, 1983—, Am. Lung Assn., Reno, 1983—;. Mem. Am. Chem. Soc., Am. Inst. Mining Metall. and Petroleum Engrs. (chmn. annual meeting session 1985, local sect. treas. 1986—), Kappa Alpha Theta (local treas. 1980-82). Avocations: skiing, camping, composing music, guitar, piano. Home: 1451 Alvin Ct Sparks NV 89431 Office: U S Bur Mines 1605 Evans Ave Reno NV 89512

MCGILVRAY, DENNIS BEATON, anthropology educator; b. Palo Alto, Calif., Aug. 16, 1943; s. Alexander Seawall and Susan (Hays) McG.; m. Beth Fippinger, June 21, 1973; children: Cameron Hays, Grant Righter. BA, Reed Coll., 1965; MA, U. Chgo., 1968, PhD, 1974; MA (hon.), Cambridge U., Eng., 1973. Asst. prof. U. Santa Clara, Calif., 1972-73; asst. lectr. Cambridge U., 1973-78; A.W. Mellon postdoctoral fellow Cornell U., Ithaca, N.Y., 1978-80; assoc. prof. anthropology U. Colo., Boulder, 1980—. Editor: Caste Ideology and Interaction, 1982; contbr. articles to profl. jours., chpts. to books. Grantee Am. Inst. Indian Studies, 1983, Social Sci. Research Council, 1984. Fellow Am. Anthropol. Assn., Royal Anthropol. Inst.; mem. Assn. Social Anthropologists, Am. Ethnol. Soc., Assn. Asian Studies, Phi Beta Kappa. Avocations: photography, cello. Home: 1315 5th St Boulder CO 80302 Office: U Colo Dept Anthropology Boulder CO 80309-0233

MCGINLEY, WILLIAM HUGH, psychology educator; b. Los Angeles, Sept. 16, 1935; s. Daniel Leo and Hazel Mae (Dailey) McG.; m. Pathy Ruth Howard, Apr. 24, 1964 (div. May 1986); children: Bryan Keith, Laura Michelle. AA, Long Beach City Coll., 1959; BA, UCLA, 1961; MA, Calif. State U., Long Beach, 1964; PhD, U. Ky., 1968. Lic. psychologist, Wyo. Co. rep. Bendix Corp., Teterboro, N.J., 1961-62; social worker Los Angeles County, Long Beach, 1964; asst. prof. psychology U. Man., Winnipeg, Can., 1968-70; prof. U. Wyo., Laramie, 1970—; cons. HPM Psychol. Services, Laramie, 1976—. Contbr. articles to profl. jours. Vice-mayor City of Laramie, 1980-87, councilman, 1978—, mem. land use planning commn., 1982—; mem. goals com. Wyo. Assn. Municipalities, 1983—. Served as sgt. USAF, 1953-56. Fellow NIH, 1964-66; grantee NIH, 1971-73, State of Wyo., 1976-78, Can. Council, 1968-70. Mem. Am. Psychology and Law Soc., Psychonomic Soc., Soc. Personality Assessment, Soc. for Personality and Social Psychology, Cognitive Sci. Soc. Avocations: skiing, hiking, fishing. Home: 3411 Alta Vista Dr Laramie WY 82070 Office: U Wyo Dept Psychology Laramie WY 82071

MCGINNIS, ROBERT WILLIAM, electronics company executive; b. Modesto, Calif., Oct. 31, 1936; s. George Crawford and Lola May (Provis) McG.; B.S. in Elec. Engring. with highest honors, U. Calif., Berkeley, 1962; postgrad. N.Y. U., 1962-63; m. Sondra Elaine Hurley, Mar. 1, 1964; children—Michael Fredrick, Traci Anne, Patrick William. Mem. tech. staff Bell Telephone Labs, Murray Hill, N.J., 1961-63; devel. engr., engring. mgr., product mgr., ops. mgr. Motorola Semiconductor Group, Phoenix, 1963-73, ops. mgr. for hybrid circuits group, communications div., Fort Lauderdale, Fla., 1973-76, solar ops. mgr., 1976-79; v.p., gen. mgr. Photowatt Internat., Inc., Tempe, Ariz., 1979-83; gen. mgr. SAFT Electronic Systems Div., 1983-85, pres., Safe Power Systems, Inc., Tempe, 1985—. Mem. Ariz. Solar Energy Commn., 1977-83; chmn. photovoltaic subcom. Am. Nat. Standards Inst., 1978-83; mem. coordinating council Solar Energy Research Inst. Standards, 1977-82. Served with USNR, 1955-58. Mem. IEEE, Phi Beta Kappa, Tau Beta Pi, Eta Kappa Nu. Republican. Methodist. Contbr. articles in field to profl. jours. Home: 7887 Via Bonita Scottsdale AZ 85258 Office: Safe Power Systems Inc 528 W 21st Tempe AZ 85202

MCGIRR, RICHARD JOHN, importing and manufacturing executive; b. Norwalk, Conn., May 30, 1946; s. John Paul and Aileen (Lohrke) McG.; m. Elizabeth McCabe, June 14, 1968 (div.); m. Shelby Louise Wilson, Apr. 24, 1976; 1 child, Andree Lorette, Richard James. BA, Fairfield U., 1968. Sales rep. Owens-Corning, Los Angeles, 1973-78; regional mgr. Halsey Taylor Div., Freeport, Ill., 1978-79; mktg. mgr. Colton-Wartsila, Colton, Calif., 1979-85; dir. sales and mktg. Intercontinental Ceramics, Stamford, Conn., 1985—. Mem. Los Angeles County Art Mus. Served to maj. USMC, 1968-72, Vietnam, lt. col Res. Mem. Am. Soc. Plumbing Engrs., Am. Nat. Standards Inst. (subcom. vitreous chiva plumbing fixtures). Republican. Roman Catholic. Avocations: distance running, skiing, scuba diving, flying. Office: Interncontinental Ceramics Corp 444 W Katella Orange CA 92667

MCGLASSON, JAMES DEAN, publishing executive; b. Roswell, N.Mex., Mar. 22, 1944; s. Dean A. and Nadean (McPherson) McG.; m. Christine Gail Dawson, Feb. 17, 1966 (div. Jan. 1980); m. Linda Renee Horn, Sept. 1, 1981; children: Kimberly Ann, Patrick Dean. Student, Mira Costa Coll. Dir. advt. Daily Tribune, Greeley, Colo., 1977-81; v.p. sales and mktg. Tahoe Tribune, South Lake Tahoe, Calif., 1981-82; v.p., pub. Press-Courier Pub. Co., Vista, Calif., 1982-85; v.p., gen. mgr. Newhall (Calif.) Signal, 1985—; pres. Newhall (Calif.) Printing, 1985—. Bd. dirs. Boys Club of Vista, 1983—; bd. dirs. YMCA, Vista, 1984-85. Served with USN, 1966-68. Mem. Calif. Newspaper Advt. Execs. Assn., Calif. Newspaper Pubs. Assn. Club: Civitan (Vista). Lodges: Rotary, Masons. Home: 25314 Via Oriol Valencia CA 91355 Office: Newhall Signal/Newhall Printing 24000 Creekside Rd PO Box 877 Valencia CA 91355

MCGONIGLE, MAC DWIGHT, computer systems executive; b. Hutchinson, Kans., Sept. 24, 1944; s. James Key McGonigle and Constance Pauline (Grace) Hoag; m. Connie Jean Cannon, June 23, 1967; children: Carrie, Darin, Mark. AA in Data Processing, Fullerton Jr. Coll., 1966; BS in Data Processing, Calif. State Poly. U., Pomona, 1968; MBA, Calif. Poly. State U., Pomona, 1981. Programmer Fleetwood Enterprises, Riverside, Calif., 1973-76, lead programmer, 1976-79, systems devel. supr., 1979-83, systems devel. mgr., 1983—. Served with USAF, 1969-73. Named Most Valuable Person, Fullerton Jr. Coll., 1966. Republican. Mem. Christian Ch. Avocations: gardening, photography. Office: Fleetwood Enterprises 3125 Myers St Riverside CA 92523

MCGOODWIN, JAMES RUSSELL, anthropology educator; b. Houston, Dec. 26, 1941; s. James V. and Tina (Wait) McG. BBA, U. Tex., 1964, MBA, 1965, PhD, 1973. Assoc. prof. anthropology U. Colo., Boulder, 1973—; expert in fisheries and developing nations FAO, Rome, 1983—. Editor: The Colo. Bowhunter mag., 1986—; contbr. articles to profl. jours. Served to 1st lt. U.S. Army, 1965-67, Vietnam. Decorated Bronze Star, Purple Heart; research fellow Woods Hole Oceanographic Instn., 1978-79. Mem. Rocky Mountain Elk Found. (chmn. coordinating com. Denver chpt. 1985-86), The Wildlife Soc., Soc. Applied Anthropology, Sigma Xi. Avocations: hunting, backpacking, fishing, photography. Office: U Colorado Dept Anthropology Campus Box 233 Boulder CO 80309

MCGOON, CLIFFORD DUANE, publisher; b. Bismarck, N.D., Dec. 18, 1939; s. Clifford D. and Norma S. McGoon; m. Nancy Schonfeld, May 31, 1986; 1 child from previous marriage, Amie. BS in Communication, U. Ill., 1963. Publs. mgr. Hercules Inc., Wilmington, Del., 1968-76; dir. Big Brothers/Big Sisters Lake County, Calif., 1976-78; v.p. communication Internat. Assn. Bus. Communicators, San Francisco, 1978—; editor, publisher Communication World Mag., San Francisco, 1978—. Served to capt. USAF, 1963-68. Recipient Maggie award Western Publs. Assn., Los Angeles, 1984, 86. Mem. Am. Soc. Assn. Execs. (Gold Circle award 1983, 84, 85, 86), Pub. Relations Soc. Am. Office: Internat Assn Bus Communicators 870 Market St Suite 940 San Francisco CA 94102

MCGOVERAN, DAVID ORNAN, consulting firm executive, automation systems consultant; b. Pittsburg, Calif., Mar. 17, 1952; s. Lowell Benage and Tressie Jane (Sanders) McGoveran; m. Mary Louise Rhodes, July 7, 1978; 1 dau., Lauren Rachel. Student Diablo Valley Coll., 1970-73; A.B. in Physics, U. Chgo., 1976; postgrad. Stanford U., 1978-79. Physics assoc. Stanford Research Inst., Menlo Park, Calif., 1976-79; electronics engring. instr. Profl. Engring. Inst., Belmont, Calif., 1978-79; prof. dept. chmn. computer sci. and bus. mgmt. Condie Coll., San Jose, Calif., 1979-80; sales support mgr. GCA Corp., Santa Clara, Calif., 1980-82; CAM system mgr. Synertek, Santa Cruz, Calif., 1982-83; pres. Alternative Technologies, Santa Cruz, Calif., 1976—; vis. scholar Stanford U., 1986-87. Author: Electronics Engineering Technicians Handbook, 1980; Night Moods, 1982. Editor: Contributions to Combinatorial Physics, 1984; Discrete Approaches to Natural Philosophy, 1985. Contbr. articles to jours. and books. Inventor cable connecting tool, slide tube, FASTTRACK semiconductor automation system, algorithmic prediction of catalytic behaviour, constructive differential topology. U. Chgo. Merit scholar, 1974, 75, AAUW scholar, 1970; Richards Meml. scholar, 1973; Supplementary Ednl. Opportunity grantee, 1974. Fellow Meninger Found., 1979; research assoc. Inst. Noetic Scis., 1976; mem. Calif. Scholarship Found., 1970; sec. Electronics Experimenters League, 1969-70. Mem. IEEE, Assn. Computing Machinery, Condie Coll. Profl. Assn., Inst. for Advancement Noetics (pres., chmn. bd. 1975-78), Alternative Natural Philosophy Assn. (sec., treas., dir. 1978—), N.Y. Acad. Scis., Data Processing Mgmt. Assn., U. Chgo. Alumni Schs. Assn., Assn. Humanistic Psychology, AAAS, Md. Neurol. Soc., Delta Rocket Soc. (founding pres. 1966). Office: Alternative Technologies 150 Felker St Suite E Santa Cruz CA 95060

MCGOVERN, MICHAEL PATRICK, computer systems coordinator; b. Santa Monica, Calif., Nov. 17, 1951; s. Patrick Francis and Marilyn Lucille (Taylor) McG. BA in Econs., U. Calif., San Diego, 1973. Pres., owner Fern Forest Exports, Hilo, Hawaii, 1973-77; leasing adminstr., asst. controller Eurocars of Hawaii Ltd., Honolulu, 1976-80; computer systems mgr. Daiei (USA), Inc., Honolulu, 1980-85; systems coordinator Holmes & Narver, Inc., Honolulu, 1985—; cons. BMW of Honolulu Ltd., 1980—. Mem. Hawaii S/38 User Groups (bd. dirs. 1983-85). Republican. Clubs: Windward Orchid Soc. (Honolulu); Chicken Alice Group. Avocations: sailing, landscaping, orchids, cars. Home: 930 Kaheka St Apt 2904 Honolulu HI 96814 Office: Holmes & Narver Inc Pacific Ops PO Box 29939 Bldg T-3225 Hickam AFB HI 96820

MCGOVERN, REBECCA MAPLES, chamber of commerce executive; b. West Frankfort, Ill., July 3, 1934; d. Joseph Edward and Celia Belle (Gill) McG. B.A. magna cum laude, So. Ill. U., 1956; postgrad. Boston U., 1956-57. Advt. mgr. Beacon Press., Boston, 1962-65; dir. press mktg. MIT, Cambridge, Mass., 1965-74; pres. Mariposa Enterprises, San Juan Bautista, Calif., 1974-82; mgr. San Juan Bautista C. of C., 1976—; mktg. dir. San Juan Magazette, San Juan Bautista, 1982—. Bd. dirs. San Benito Econ. Devel. Corp., Chamber Music San Juan Found., Cabrillo Music Festival. Home: 102-104 The Alameda San Juan Bautista CA 95045 Office: 201 3d St San Juan Bautista CA 95045

MCGOVERN, RICKY JAMES, architect, educator; b. Tacoma, June 16, 1948; s. James Patrick and Betty Irene (Baxter) McG.; m. Kathleen Joy Kerrone, June 14, 1968; children—Jamie Francis, Brandon James. B.Arch., Wash. State U., 1973, B.S., 1973. Registered architect, Wash. Architect Burr Assocs., Tacoma, 1973-79, Erickson-Hogenson Architects, Tacoma, 1979-81; ptnr. Erickson-McGovern Architects, Tacoma, 1981—; instr. Tacoma Community Coll., 1979-85; vocat. advisor Bethel Sch. Dist., Spanaway, Wash., 1981—; sec. Avitar Inc., Tacoma, 1980—; bd. dirs. Sound Ventures, Inc., Plaza Hall. Co-chmn. Clearwood Community Assn., Pierce County, Wash., 1976-82; designer Bethel Community Daffodil Float, Spanaway, 1983-84. Recipient appreciation award Clearwood Community Assn., 1982. Mem. AIA, Council Ednl. Facilities Planning, Soc. Am. Value Engrs. (bd. dirs. 1982-83), Shelter Industry Coalition (vice chmn. 1983—), Parkland-Spanaway C. of C. (chmn. Community Days 1984, v.p. 1986, citizen of yr. award 1985, 86), Winner's Circle (v.p. 1983—). Clubs: Plaza Hall (bd. dirs. 1985—) City. Lodge: Kiwanis (pres. 1984-85, Kiwanian of Yr. award 1982, 83, 84). Office: Erickson-McGovern Architects 130 S 131st St Tacoma WA 98444

MC GOVERN, WALTER T., judge; b. Seattle, May 24, 1922; s. C. Arthur and Anne Marie (Thies) McG.; m. Rita Marie Olsen, June 29, 1946; children: Katrina M., Shawn E., A. Renee. B.A., U. Wash., 1949, LL.B., 1950. Bar: Wash. 1950. Practiced law in Seattle, 1950-59; mem. firm Kerr, McCord, Greenleaf & Moen; judge Municipal Ct., Seattle, 1959-65, Superior Ct., Wash., 1965-68, Wash. Supreme Ct., 1968-71, U.S. Dist. Ct. (we. dist.) Wash., 1971—; chief judge 1975—; mem. subcom. on supporting personnel Jud. Conf. U.S., 1981—, chmn. subcom., 1983, mem. adminstrn. com., 1983. Mem. Am. Judicature Soc., Wash. State Superior Ct. Judges Assn., Seattle King County Bar Assn. (treas.), Phi Delta Phi. Club: Seattle Tennis (pres. 1968). Office: 705 US Courthouse Seattle WA 98104

MCGOWAN, CHARLES DAVID, city official, housing developer; b. San Francisco, Dec. 20, 1949; s. William Charles and Pauline (Krisfalusy) McG. B.A., U. Notre Dame, 1971; M. Urban Planning, San Jose State U., 1982. Cons., City of Gilroy, San Jose, Calif., 1976-77, housing and community devel. grant coordinator, 1977-80; devel. officer Housing Authority County of Santa Clara, San Jose, 1980-86; project mgr. Redevel. Agy. of City of San Jose, Calif., 1986—. Mem. adv. council Council on Aging Santa Clara County, 1981-84. Served with USN, 1971-74. Calif. State scholar, 1967; U. Santa Clara scholar 1967. Mem. Am. Planning Assn., Am. Inst. Cert. Planners. Democrat. Club: Notre Dame of San Jose (bd. dirs.), Calif. Winetasters Guild (pres. 1982-83).

MC GRATH, RICHARD WILLIAM, osteopathic physician; b. Hartford, Conn., Nov. 17, 1943; s. William Paul and Stephanie Gertrude (Romash) McG.; B.S., St. Ambrose Coll., 1965; D.Osteo. Medicine and Surgery, Coll. Osteo. Medicine and Surgery, Des Moines, 1971; m. Mariette VanLancker, June 24, 1967; children—Shaun, Megan, Kelley. Osteo. physician Weld County Gen. Hosp., Greeley, Colo., 1971-72, Granby (Colo.) Clinic, 1972-75, Timberline Med. Ctr., P.C., Granby, 1975—; pres. Timberline Med. Center, 1976—, Bighorn Properties Inc., 1978—, Thia of Am. Corp., 1980—; med. coordinator/dir. regional emergency systems Colo. State Health Dept., 1978-79; mem. Colo. Comprehensive Health Planning Agy., 1975-77; assoc. prof. clin. medicine Tex. Coll. Osteo. Medicine; med. advisor Grand County Ambulance System, 1977—; vice chief staff Kremmling Meml. Hosp.; bd. dirs. M&L Bus. Machine Co., Denver, Sun-Flo Internat., Inc., Silver Creek Devel. Co. and Ski Area. Mem. steering com. to develop Colo. Western Slope Health System Agy., 1975-76, bd. dirs., 1977—; bd. dirs. St. Anthony Hosp. Systems Emergency Rooms, 1984—; med. dir. Community Hosp. and Emergency Ctr., Cranby; officer, police surgeon Grand Lake and Granby, 1977—; mem. parent adv. bd. Granby Sch. System, 1975-76; chmn. East Grand County Safety Council, 1974-76; dep. coroner Grand County, 1973-75; med. advisor Grand County Rescue Team, 1974-78. Recipient award Ohio State U. Coll. Medicine, 1977. Mem. AMA, ACS (com. on trauma), Am. Coll. Emergency Physicians, Western Slope Physicians Alliance Assn., Colo. State Emergency Med. Technicians (med. chmn. 1982-84), Colo. Union of Physicians (dir.), C. of C. of Granby, Grand Lake and Fraser Valley. Republican. Roman Catholic. Home: PO Box 706 Granby CO 80446 Office: PO Box 857 Granby CO 80446

MCGRAW, JOHN PATRICK, journalist, music critic; b. Omaha, Mar. 20, 1947; s. Mac and Margaret (Higgins) McG.; m. Connie Ann Vondy, Sept. 12, 1976 (div. 1986); children—Charla, Colin. B.S. in Journalism, U. Colo. Staff writer Denver Post, 1969—, music critic, 1974-87; show host KLZ radio, Denver, 1987; contbg. writer Compuserve Info. Service, Columbus, Ohio, 1984-85. Chmn. Students for Kennedy, Colo., 1960. Recipient Story of Yr. award AP, Colo., 1984. Named to Colo. Country Music Hall of Fame, 1985. Mem. Country Mus. Assn., Colo. Country Music Assn., Bluegrass Music Assn. Colo., NAACP, Sigma Delta Chi. Democrat. Roman Catholic. Club: Denver Press (News Story of Yr. award 1984). Office: Denver Post Box 1709 Denver CO 80201

MCGUGIN, DEANNA S., audiologist; b. Satanta, Kans., July 13, 1955; d. Marvin Ray and Carolyn Jane (Winsted) Schwertfeger; m. Terry Curtis McGugin, July 5, 1975; 1 child, Tara Kristelle. BA, U. Denver, 1981; MA, Kans. State U., 1983. Audiologist Audiology Ctr., Manhattan, Kans., 1983, Assocs. of Otolaryngology, Denver, 1984—. Mem. Am. Speech Lang. Hearing Assn. (cert. clin. competence), Communication Assn. of Colo., Phi Kappa Phi. Republican. Methodist. Avocations: reading, tennis, skiing, walking. Home: 5970 S Tabor St Littleton CO 80127

MCGUIRE, DAVID KELTY, holding company executive; b. Pitts., Dec. 18, 1934; s. Paul John and Dorothy Joan (Power) McG.; m. Meredith Anne Black, Dec. 27, 1965 (Div. Feb. 1983); children: Daniel, Rachel, Kieran. BS in Chemistry, St. Vincent Coll., 1957; PhD in Chemistry, U. Pitts., 1964. Postdoctoral fellow Brookhaven Nat. Lab., Upton, N.Y., 1964-65; asst. prof. Rider Coll., Lawrenceville, N.J., 1965-67; asst. prof., assoc. prof. Upsala Coll., East Orange, N.J., 1967-83; dir. licensing Patlex Corp., Westfield, N.J., 1983-85; asst. to pres. then pres. Apollo Lasers, Inc., Chatsworth, Calif., 1985-86; asst. to chmn. bd. Patlex Corp., Chatsworth, Calif., 1987—. Contbr. articles to profl. jours. Mem. AAAS, Am. Chem. Soc. Democrat. Roman Catholic. Avocations: hiking, tennis, reading, music, movies. Office: Patlex Corp 20415 Nordhoff St Chatsworth CA 91311

MCGUIRE, JAMES CHARLES, aircraft company executive; b. St. Louis, Aug. 8, 1917; s. John Patrick and Anna Beulah (Erbar) McG.; A.B., Washington U., St. Louis, 1949, M.A. (Univ. fellow), 1953, Ph.D., 1954; m. Ingrid Elisabeth Getreu, Sept. 16, 1954. Research assoc. Ohio State U., 1953-56; research psychologist Aeromed. Lab., Wright-Patterson AFB, Ohio, 1956-59; group supr. Boeing Airplane Co., Seattle, 1959-61; dept. mgr. Internat. Electric Corp., Paramus, N.J., 1961-62; sr. human factors scientist System Devel. Corp., Santa Monica, Calif., 1962-67; v.p. Booz-Allen Applied Research, Saigon, Vietnam, 1967-72; v.p. Assoc. Cons. Internat., Saigon, 1972-75, Bethesda, Md., 1975-78; br. chief Human Factors, System Tech. Devel., 1978-82 prin. staff engr. tech. modernization methodology Douglas Aircraft Co., Long Beach, Calif., 1982-85; program mgr. cockpit automation tech. program, Northrop Aircraft div., Hawthorne, Calif., 1985—; lectr. Nat. Def. Coll., Vietnamese Armed Forces, Saigon, 1971. Served with AUS, 1940-46. Decorated Bronze Star medal with oak leaf cluster. Mem. Am. Def. Preparedness Assn., Assn. U.S. Army, Am. Psychol. Assn., AAAS, IEEE, Human Factors Soc., Am. Assn. Artificial Intelligence, Assn. Computing Machinery, Computer and Automated Systems Assn., Soc. Mfg. Engrs., Phi Beta Kappa, Sigma Xi. Republican. Club: Monarch Bay. Home: 23201 Mindanao Circle Laguna Niguel CA 92677 Office: Northrop Aircraft Div 1 Northrop Ave Hawthorne CA 90250-3277

MCGUIRE, MICHAEL DENNIS, mining engineer; b. Olympia, Wash., Oct. 30, 1937; s. Harvey Everet and Ann (Kruse) McG.; m. Gwendolyn Elizabeth James, July, 1958 (div. Oct. 1970); children: Heidi Ann, David Michael, Anne Elizabeth; m. Sheryl Sue Anson, Sept. 25, 1971. Grad., Colo. Sch. Mines, 1959. Registered profl. engr., Colo. Surveyor Mont. Phos. Product Co., Garrison, 1961-63; various mgmt. positions Climax (Colo.) Molybdenum Co., 1963-69; mining engr. U.S. Dept. Interior Mining Enforcement and Safety Adminstrn., Bellevue, Wash., 1969-75, U.S. Dept. of Labor Mine Safety and Health Adminstrn. (formerly U.S. Dept. Interior Mining Enforcement and Safety Adminstrn.), Denver, 1978-80, 83—; sr. safety supr. oil shale div. Tosco Corp., Aurora, Colo., 1980-83. Sec. Amberwick Homeowners Assn., Golden, 1984, 1st v.p., 1985, pres. 1986. Served to 2d lt. USAR, 1959-60. Mem. Soc. Mining Engrs., Am. Soc. Safety Engrs. Republican. Avocations: skiing, mountaineering, flying. Office: MSHA Safety and Health Tech Ctr Indsl and Elec Safety div PO Box 25367-DFC Denver CO 80225

MC GUIRE, MICHAEL JOHN, environ. engr.; b. San Antonio, June 29, 1947; s. James Brendan and Opal Mary (Brady) McG.; B.S. in Civil Engring., U. Pa., 1969; M.S. in Environ Engring., Drexel U., 1972, Ph.D. in Environ. Engring., 1977; diplomate Am. Acad. Environ. Engring.; m. Deborah Marrow, June 19, 1971; children: David, Anna. San. engr. Phila. Water Dept., 1969-73; research assoc. Drexel U., Phila., 1976-77; prin. engr. Brown & Caldwell Cons. Engrs., Pasadena, Calif., 1977-79; water quality engr. Met. Water Dist. of So. Calif., Los Angeles, 1979-84, water quality mgr., 1984-86, dir. water quality, 1986—; cons. environ. engr., 1979—; instr. Temple U., Phila., 1974; cons. to subcom. on absorbents, safe drinking water com. Nat. Acad. Scis., 1978-79. Registered profl. engr., Pa., N.J., Calif. Mem. Am. Water Works Assn. (Acad. Achievement award 1978, edn. div. chmn. 1982-83, chmn. Calif.-Nev. sect. water quality and resources div. 1982-83, governing bd. 1984—, trustee Research Found. 1983-86), Am. Acad. Environ. Engrs. (diplomate), Am. Chem. Soc., ASCE, Water Pollution Control Fedn., Sigma Xi, Sigma Nu, Sigma Tau. Editor: (with I.H. Suffet) Activated Carbon Adsorption of Organics From the Aqueous Phase, 2 vols., 1980; Treatment of Water by Granular Activated Carbon, 1983; contbr. articles to profl. jours. Office: Met Water Dist of So Calif PO Box 54153 Los Angeles CA 90054

MCGUIRK, PAUL RAYMOND, college administrator; b. Irvington, N.J., Aug. 23, 1947; s. Edward Francis and Ann Margaret (Rudolph) McG. BS in Mgmt., Fairleigh Dickinson U., 1969, MBA, 1981. Cert. adminstr., div. Vocat. Edn. Calif. Dept. Edn. Program mgr. Prudential Ins. Co., Newark, 1970-72; dir. fin. aid Bell & Howell Edn. Group, Woodbridge, N.J., 1972-75; dean of students DeVry Tech. Inst., Woodbridge, 1975-83; pres. DeVry Tech. Inst., Industry, Calif., 1983—. Mem. City of Industry Mfrs. Council, 1983-86. Mem. Am. Mgmt. Assn., Nat. Assn. Student Personnel Adminstrs., Nat. Assn. Student Fin. Aid Adminstrs., Nat. Assn. Trade and Tech. Schs. (publs. com.), North Cen. Regional Accreditation Task Force. Republican. Club: Suburban Country (Union, N.J.) (admissions com.). Home: 5122 Alder Irvine CA 92715 Office: DeVry Inst Tech 12801 Crossroads Park S Industry CA 91744

MCHARDY, JOHN, research electrochemist; b. Leicester, Eng., July 10, 1940; s. Leo John and Mary Dorothy (Jones) McH.; m. Marilyn Sue Jeffries, Nov. 24, 1965; children: Lang Joseph, Ian Howard. BA, U. Cambridge, Eng., 1962, MA (hon.), 1966; PhD, U. Pa., 1972. Research engr. ALCOA, New Kensington, Pa., 1963-66; research fellow U. Pa., Phila., 1966-72; research assoc. United Techs. Inc., Middletown, Conn., 1972-75; group leader EIC Labs. Inc., Newton, Mass., 1975-80; mgr. exploratory research Koppers Co., Monroeville, Pa., 1980-83; sr. staff engr. Hughes Aircraft Co., El Segundo, Calif., 1983—; cons. Eastman Kodak Co., Rochester, N.Y., 1971, Leeds & Northrup Co., N. Wales, Pa., 1983. Contbr. chpts. to textbooks. Chmn. fund raising com. Carnegie Sci. and Tech. Library, Pitts., 1980-83. U. Pa. research fellow, 1966-72. Mem. Electrochem. Soc., Sigma Xi. Presbyterian. Avocations: tennis, golf, bridge, reading, pc programming. Home: 2338 Stormcroft Ct Westlake Village CA 91361 Office: Hughes Aircraft Co EDSG 2000 E El Segundo Blvd El Segundo CA 90245

MCHENRY, CHARLES STEVEN, biochemistry, molecular biology researcher; b. Indpls., Jan. 1, 1948; s. William H. and Barbara A. (Hayes) McH.; m. Mary Michele Herzogenrath; 1 child, Patrick Venzke. BS in Chemistry, Purdue U., 1970; PhD, U. Calif., Santa Barbara and San Francisco, 1974. Postdoctoral fellow Stanford U., Palo Alto, Calif., 1974-76; asst. prof. biochemistry and molecular biology U. Tex. Med. Sch., Houston, 1976-82, assoc. prof., 1982-85; prof. U. Colo. Sch. Medicine, Denver, 1985—; vis. prof. U. Basel, Switzerland, 1984. Contbr. articles to profl. jours. Guggenheim fellow, 1984, Cystic Fibrosis Found. fellow, 1974-76; Evan Scholars Found. scholar, 1966-70. Mem. AAAS, Am. Chem. Soc., Am. Soc. Biol. Chemistry, Am. Soc. Microbiology. Office: U Colo Sch Medicine B-121 4200 E 9th Ave Denver CO 80262

MCHENRY, HENRY MALCOLM, anthropologist, educator; b. Los Angeles, May 19, 1944; s. Dean Eugene and Emma Jane (Snyder) McH.; m. Linda Jean Conway, June 25, 1966; children: Lindsay Jean, Annalisa Jane. BA, U. Calif., Davis, 1966, MA, 1967; PhD, Harvard U., 1972. Asst. prof. anthropology U. Calif., Davis, 1971-76, assoc. prof. anthropology, 1976-81, prof. anthropology, 1981—, chmn. dept. anthropology, 1984—. Fellow Am. Anthrop. Assn.; mem. Am. Assn. Phys. Anthropologists (exec. com. 1981-85), Soc. Study Evolution, Vertebrate Paleontology Soc., Human Biology Council, Phi Beta Kappa, Phi Kappa Phi. Democrat. Buddhist. Avocation: wine making. Home: 330 11th St Davis CA 95616 Office: Univ of Calif Davis Dept of Anthropology Davis CA 95616

MCHENRY, ROBERT WILLIAM, JR., English language professional, educator; b. Panama City, Fla., Aug. 27, 1943; s. Robert William Sr. and Frances (Boatner) McH.; m. Patricia Jane Frantz, Dec. 29, 1972; children: Elizabeth, Margaret. AB, Boston U., 1965, MA, 1967; PhD, U. Mich., 1972. Lectr. English U. Mich., Flint, 1969-70; asst. prof. U. Hawaii, Manoa, Honolulu, 1970-77, assoc. prof., 1977-85, prof., 1985—, dir. research relations, 1986—. Author: Contexts 3: Absalom and Achitophel, 1986; contbr. articles to profl. jours. Pres. St. Louis Heights Community Assn., Honolulu, 1985. Research grantee William Andrews Clark Library, Los Angeles, 1981. Mem. Am. Soc. 18th Century Studies, Philol. Assn. of Pacific Coast. Home: 1510 Bertram St Honolulu HI 96816 Office: U Hawaii Bachman Hall 2444 Dole St Honolulu HI 96822

MCHENRY, VERE A., ednl. adminstr.; b. Murray, Utah, Jan. 5, 1928; s. Samuel B. and Florence Jane (McGhie) McH.; m. Barbara Jean Oliver, July 19, 1948; children—Debra Kaye Flink, Charles Kevin, Barbara Deon Kleinendorst, Samuel Scott. B.S., U. Utah, 1950, M.S., 1954, Ed.D., 1965; postgrad. Stanford U., 1960-61. Social studies tchr. Murray (Utah) High Sch., 1949-51, 53-54; elem. sch. prin., Murray, 1954-60; adminstrv. asst. Sunnyvale (Calif.) Sch. Dist., 1960-61; prin. jr. high sch., Murray, 1961-65; dir. curriculum Murray Sch. Dist., 1965; tchr. edn. and profl. relations Utah State Office Edn., 1965-69, adminstr., coordinator staff devel., 1969—; cons. program devel. and profl. practices. Mem. Murray City Bd. Edn., 1968-76; mem. Murray Community Council, 1970-76. Served with USAF, 1951-53, to lt. col. USAFR, 1953-81. Decorated Disting. Service medal; recipient Tchr. Educator of Year award Utah Assn. Tchr. Educators, 1981. Mem. Assn. Tchr. Educators, Nat. Assn. State Dirs. Tchr. Edn. and Cert., NEA, Utah Edn. Assn., Phi Delta Kappa. Mormon. Club: Lions. Contbr. numerous articles to ednl. jours.

MC HUGH, MARGARET ANN GLOE, psychologist; b. Salt Lake City, Nov. 8, 1920; d. Harold Henry and Olive (Warenski) Gloe; B.A., U. Utah, 1942; M.A. in Counseling and Guidance, Idaho State U., 1964; Ph.D. in Counseling Psychology, U. Oreg., 1970; lic. psychologist; nat. cert. counselor; m. William T. McHugh, Oct. 1, 1943; children—Mary Margaret McHugh-Shuford, William Michael, Michelle. Tchr. kindergarten, Idaho Falls, Idaho, 1951-62, tchr. high sch. English, 1962-63; counselor Counseling Center, Idaho State U., Pocatello, 1964-67; instr. U. Oreg., Eugene, 1967-70; asst. prof. U. Victoria, B.C., Can., 1970-76; therapist Peninsula Counseling Center, Port Angeles and Sequim, Wash., 1976-81, McHugh & Assocs. Counseling Center, 1981—. Served with WAVES, 1943-44. Mem. Am. Psychol. Assn., Am. Assn. for Counseling and Devel., Am. Assn. Marriage and Family Therapy, Wash. Psychol. Assn. Research on women in relationships, also depression and women, sexual abuse. Home: 249 F Cameron Rd Sequim WA 98382

MCHUGH, STEVEN JAMES, lawyer; b. Encino, Calif., Apr. 6, 1956; s. Frank A. and Jeanne D. (Dickinson) McH.; m. Debra Anne Macdonald, Dec. 21, 1981. AA in Adminstrn. of Justice with honors, Coll. San Mateo, 1976; BS in Criminal Justice Adminstrn. and Polit. Sci. with highest honors, Calif. State U., San Jose, 1978; JD, U. Hawaii, 1984. Bar: Hawaii 1984, U.S. Dist. Ct. Hawaii 1984. Pvt. investigator Burns Internat., San Francisco, 1977-78; daily spl. investigator Narcotics Investigation and Enforcement unit Dept. of Justice, Calif., 1978; law clk. Prosecuting Atty.'s Office, Honolulu, 1982; intern Pub. Defender's Office, Honolulu, 1983; law clk. Hoddick, Reinwald, O'Connor and Marrack, Honolulu, 1983-84; assoc. Reinwald, O'Connor and Marrack, Honolulu, 1984—; bd. dirs. Hawaii Council Am. Indian Nations, Inc., Am. Indian Services Corp., Red Cloud Enterprises; pres. Delta Investigative Research Co., Honolulu, 1983—; cons. Gavin de Becker, Inc., Los Angeles, 1980—. Casenote author: U. Hawaii Law Rev., 1983. Recipient Excellence in Corp. Law award Am. Jurisprudence, 1983, Outstanding Achievement award Am. Legion, 1970. Mem. ABA (founder, editor Newsbrief 1983, Silver Key award 1983), Hawaii State Bar Assn., Am. Trial Lawyers Assn., Am. Judicature Soc., Phi Delta Phi, Phi Kappa Phi. Avocations: archery, tennis, scuba diving, oil painting, model aircraft bldg. Home: PO Box 88314 Honolulu HI 96830 Office: Reinwald O'Connor et al 733 Bishop St #2400 Honolulu HI 96813

MCHUGH, STUART LAWRENCE, research scientist; b. San Francisco, Nov. 7, 1949; s. James and Ruth McHugh. BSc in Geophysics with high distinction, U. Nev., 1971, BSc in Geol. Engring. with high distinction, 1972; MS in Geophysics, Stanford U., 1974, MS in Materials Sci., 1976, PhD in Geophysics, 1977. Seismol. asst. U. Nev., Reno, 1971-72; intern, student geophysicist Humble Oil Co., New Orleans, summer 1972; geophysicist U.S. Geol. Survey, Menlo Park, Calif., 1973-77, cons., 1977—; geophysicist SRI, Internat., Menlo Park, 1977-81, cons., 1981—; research scientist Lockheed Missiles & Space Co., Palo Alto, Calif., 1981—. Contbr. articles to profl. jours. Mem. Service League of San Mateo County (Calif.), Redwood City, 1982—. Recipient traineeship NSF, 1972-73; named MacKay Sch. Mines Outstanding Geologist, U. Nev., Reno, 1972. Mem. AAAS, Internat. Soc. Math. Modeling, Am. Geophys. Union, Am. Phys. Soc. (human rights com. 1982—), Phi Kappa Phi. Republican. Avocations: teaching history, fgn. lang. studies, jogging. Office: Lockheed Missiles & Space Co B 204 0/9330 3521 Hanover St Palo Alto CA 94304

MCHUGH, WILLIAM FLEMING, government agency administrator; b. Chgo., Jan. 27, 1941; s. John Charles Sr. and Eleanor Marie (Fleming) McH.; student DePaul U., 1959, Laval U., 1960, U. Minn., 1961; B.A. summa cum laude, St. Mary's Coll., 1962; A.M., Stanford U., 1963; postgrad. Cornell U., 1969-70. Intern in personnel mgmt. U.S. Dept. Labor, Washington, 1963-65, program analyst, manpower admnstrn., 1966-71, program analyst, chief div. of evaluation systems design Occupational Safety and Health Adminstrn., 1971-75, spl. asst. to admnstr., acting br. chief, acting div. dir., Pension and Welfare Benefit Programs, 1975-77; dep. assoc. regional adminstr. Job Corps, Employment and Tng. Admnstrn., San Francisco, 1977-79, fed. rep., 1979-84; equal opportunity specialist, acting regional dir. Office of Civil Rights, 1984-86; manpower devel. specialist Employment and Tng. Adminstrn., 1986—; instr. history St. Mary's Coll., Winona, Minn., 1965-66. Served to lt. USNR, 1963-73. Woodrow Wilson fellow Stanford U., 1962; Pullman Found. grantee St. Mary's Coll., 1958, 59, 60, 61; Brunet grantee Laval U., 1960; Nat. Inst. Pub. Affairs fellow Cornell U., 1969; recipient superior performance awards, U.S. Dept. Labor, 1972, 75, 76, 80, 83. Mem. Am. Hist. Assn., Am. Soc. Pub. Admnstrn., Am. Cath. Hist. Assn. Roman Catholic. Club: Marines Meml. Occasional panelist Quiz Kids radio and TV show, 1949-52; contbr. article on labor statistics to profl. organization. Home: 1111 Bay St Apt 205 San Francisco CA 94123 Office: 450 Golden Gate Ave San Francisco CA 94102

MC ILHANY, STERLING FISHER, publishing company executive; b. San Gabriel, Calif., Apr. 12, 1930; s. William Wallace and Julia (Fisher) M. B.F.A. with high honors, U. Tex., 1953; postgrad. UCLA, 1953-54, 55-57, Universita per Stranieri, Perugia, Italy, 1957, Accademia delle Belle Arti, Rome, 1957-58. Teaching asst. in art history UCLA, 1953-54, 55-57; art supr. Kamehameha Prep. Sch., Honolulu, 1954-55; instr. Honolulu Acad. Arts, 1955; assoc. editor Am. Artist mag., N.Y.C., 1958-61, editor, 1969-70; host Books and the Artist network series Sta. WRVR, N.Y.C., 1961-62; sr. editor Reinhold Book Corp., N.Y.C., 1962-69; pres. IFOTA Inc., Los Angeles, 1981—; instr. Sch. Visual Arts, N.Y.C., 1961-69. Author: Banners and Hangings, 1966; Art as Design—Design as Art, 1970; Wood Inlay, 1972; Simbari, 1975; also articles. Recipient First award tour European art ctrs. Students Internat. Travel Assn., 1952; Rotary fellow Accademia delle Belle Arti, 1957-58. Mem. Nat. Soc. Lit. and Arts. Roman Catholic. Address: 6376 Yucca St Los Angeles CA 90028

MCILROY, J. CRAIG, financial planner; b. Phoenix, Sept. 9, 1953; s. James Rudolph and Bertha Odell (Craig) McI., m. Bertha Hiskey, Feb. 18, 1977. B.A. in Communications, Brigham Young U., 1978. Adminstrv. asst. pub. relations Brigham Young U., Provo, 1976-77, asst. dir. performance scheduling, 1977-80, asst. dir. pub. relations, 1980-82, dir. hosting services, 1982-85; ptnr. McIlroy, Darais, Bowie, pub. relations cons. firm, 1983-85. Bd. dirs. Utah Valley Indsl. Devel. Assn., 1980-85, Utah County Conv. and Vis. Bur., 1980-85. Mem. Pub. Relations Soc. Am., Council for Advancement and Support of Edn., Orem, Utah C. of C. (dir. 1980-82, v.p. pub. relations 1982-85). Republican. Mormon. Office: Mony Fin Services 416 E 500 S Salt Lake City UT 84111

MCILWRAITH, C. WAYNE, veterinary surgery educator; b. Oamaru, New Zealand, Dec. 12, 1947; came to U.S., 1975; s. Cyril Alfred and Kathleen Avaca (O'Grady) McI.; m. Nancy Lynn Goodman, June 22, 1984. DVM, Massey U., Palmerston North, New Zealand, 1970; MS, Purdue U., 1977, PhD, 1979. Diplomate Am. Coll. Vet. Surgeons. Resident in vet. surgery Purdue U., West Lafayette, Ind., 1975-77, instr., 1977-79; asst. prof. equine surgery Colo. State U., Ft. Collins, 1979-81, assoc. prof., 1981-86, prof., 1986—; cons. surgeon. equine vet. practices, 1981—. Author: (textbook) Techniques in Large Animal Surgery ,1982; Diagnostic and Surgical Arthroscopy in the Horse, 1984, Advanced Techniques in Equine Surgery, 1986; pioneered the technique of arhtroscopic surgery in the horse. Recipient Colo. State U. AAEP Faculty award for Teaching Equine Medicine and Surgery, 1982, Colo. State U. Alumni Outstanding Faculty award, 1983. Mem. AVMA, Royal Coll. Vet. Surgeons, Am. Assn. Vet. Surgeons, Colo. Vet. Med. Assn., Vet. Orthopedic Soc. Avocations: rock climbing, skiing, scuba diving. Home: 108 Blueridge Ct Fort Collins CO 80524 Office: Colo State U Vet Teaching Hosp 300 W Drake Fort Collins CO 80523

MCINERNEY, WILLIAM DAVID, litigation cons.; b. Northampton, Mass., Dec. 27, 1925; s. Joseph Morgan and Mary Theresa (Mercure) McI.; student U. Rochester, 1954, Eastern Ky. U., 1972, U. Ky., 1972, 73, U. Louisville, 1975; m. Sandra Jean Schultz, June 6, 1959; children—Patricia, Eileen, William, Maura, Megan, Erin, Shannon. Archtl. hardware cons. Edward Hines Lumber Co., Skokie, Ill., 1957-64; sales engr. Prison Equipment, Herrick Pacific Corp., Hayward, Calif., 1964-68; v.p., gen. mgr. Muni-Quip Corp. div. Duncan Industries, Elk Grove Village, Ill., 1968-71; asst. dir. Nat. Crime Prevention Inst., Sch. Police Adminstrn., U. Louisville, 1971-76; mktg. and tech. cons., Anchorage, Ky., 1976-78; phys. security specialist, civil engring. lab. U.S. Navy, Port Hueneme, Calif., 1978—; expert witness in litigation involving security matters; nat. and internat. lectr. Apptd. mem. Ky. Bldg. Security Study Commn., 1975. Served with USMC, WW II and Korea. Mem. Am. Mgmt. Assn. (crimes against bus. council 1977), Associated Locksmiths of Am. (charter), Comml. and Indsl. Equipment Users Adv. Conf., Underwriters Labs. Inc., Soc. Archtl. Hardware Consultants, ASTM, Am. Soc. Indsl. Security (charter mem., cert. protection profl.), Security Equipment Industry Assn., Internat. Soc. Crime Prevention Practitioners, Internat. Assn. Chiefs of Police, Nat. Sheriffs Assn., Am. Correctional Assn., Door and Hardware Inst., Am. Legion, Order Ky. Cols. Republican. Club: Elks. Contbr. articles to profl. jours. Home: 3711 Tiller Dr Oxnard CA 93030 Office: Security Engring Div US Naval Civil Engring Lab Port Hueneme CA 93043

MCINNES, GILBERT, III, defense equipment and systems manufacturing specialist; b. Pitts., Mar. 3, 1946; s. Gilbert and Florence (Heinlein) McI.; m. Vera Ellen Kovalich, Sept. 25, 1971. B.S. in Bus. Adminstrn., Pa. State U., 1968, M.B.A., 1971. Programming cons. Pa. State U., State College, 1968, programmer, analyst, grad. asst., 1970-71; traffic analyst Procter and Gamble Co., Cin., 1971-73; logistics info. systems mgr. Massey-Ferguson Ltd., Toronto, Ont., Can., 1973-77; projects mgr.-comptrollers Massey-Ferguson, Inc, Des Moines, 1977-79, fin. systems mgr., 1979, gen. bus. systems mgr., 1979-82, gen. systems devel. mgr. N.Am., 1982-85; Mgmt. Info. Systems mgr. Ordnance div. FMC Corp., San Jose, Calif., 1985—. Served with U.S. Army, 1968-70. Republican. Avocations: travel; biking; tennis; swimming. Office: FMC Corp Ordnance Div 1105 Coleman Ave Box 1201 San Jose CA 95109

MCINNES-STINE, PAMELA MARGARET, reporter; b. Auckland, New Zealand, Jan. 11, 1948; came to U.S., 1971; s. Angus Ross and Joyce Ann (Mackrell) McI.; m. Oliver Charles Stine, May 19, 1979; 1 child, Brittany Jo. Student, Perugia U., Italy, 1969. Cert. librarian, comml. pilot. Librarian Auckland Mus., 1967-69; news researcher BBC, London, 1969-71; dir. flight ops. Great Atlantic and Pacific, Van Nuys, Calif., 1973-76; pilot/traffic reporter Sta. KGIL, Los Angeles, 1976-79, Sta. KMPC and Sta. KUTE, Los Angeles, 1979—. Speaker career days pub. schs., service clubs, orgns. Recipient Commendation Los Angeles Police Dept., 1984. Mem. AFTRA, Aircraft Owners and Pilots Assn., 99's (vice chmn. 1975-76, Service award 1976). Presbyterian. Avocations: photography, gardening, motor racing. Office: Sta KMPC/KUTE Radio 5858 Sunset Blvd Hollywood CA 90028

MCINNIS, RAYMOND GEORGE, reference librarian; b. Wishart, Sask., Can., Nov. 1, 1936; s. George and Phyllis (Fensom) McI.; m. Karen Ewbank; children: Michael Scott, Erin Michelle. Student, U. Alta., Can., 1960; BA, U. B.C., 1960; MLS, U. Wash., 1961. Bibliographer U. Wash., Seattle, 1961-62; county librarian Grays Harbor County Library, Montesano, Wash., 1962-65; reference librarian Western Wash. U., Bellingham, 1965-68, head reference librarian, 1968—. Author: New Perspectives for Reference Service in Academic Libraries, 1978, Research Guide for Psychology, 1982; gen. editor (series) Reference Sources in the Social Scis. and Humanities, 1980—. Home: 3400 Taylor Bellingham WA 98225 Office: Western Wash Univ Reference Dept Wilson Library Bellingham WA 98225

MCINTOSH, LOWRIE WENDELL, management consultant; b. Denver, Sept. 5, 1926; s. Lee Roy and Pearl O. (Jones) McI.; children: David, Lisa, Patricia. BS, U. Denver, 1951; MBA, NYU, 1958. Registered profl. engr., cert. records mgr. Project indsl. engr. tech. cons. prodn. control Pitney-Bowes, Stamford, Ct., 1953-58; mng. assoc. Arthur Young & Co., Los Angeles, 1958-65; v.p. adminstrn. No. Trust Co., Chgo., 1965-69; corp. v.p. mgmt. info. systems Lone Star Industries, Greenwich, Conn., 1969-72; pres. Informaco, Inc., N.Y.C., 1972-78, Infologics, Inc., Pasadena, Calif., 1978—; instr. Bridgeport (Conn.) Engring. Inst., 1952-55; adj. prof. mgmt. NYU, 1955-58. Contbr. articles to profl. jours. Served with USN, 1944-46, 51-52 PTO. Mem. Newcomen Soc., Soc. Mgmt. Info. Systems, Fin. Execs. Inst., Am. Inst. Indsl. Engrs. (sr.). Club: Jonathan (Los Angeles). Avocations: golf, biking. Home: 190 Arroyo Terr #104 Pasadena CA 91103 Office: Infologics Inc 221 E Walnut St Suite 250 Pasadena CA 91101

MC INTYRE, DONALD B., geologist, educator; b. Edinburgh, Scotland, Aug. 15, 1923; s. Robert E. and Mary (Darling) McI.; m. Ann I. Alexander, Dec. 23, 1957; 1 child, Ranald Ewen. B.Sc., U. Edinburgh, 1945, Ph.D., 1947, D.Sc., 1951. Postdoctoral fellow U. Neuchatel, Switzerland, 1947-48; lectr. petrology U. Edinburgh, 1948-54; faculty Pomona Coll., Claremont, Calif., 1954—; prof. geology Pomona Coll., 1957—; Matthew Vassar lectr. Vassar Coll., 1969; Swiney lectr. (Brit. Mus.) Edinburgh U., 1969, 71, 83; cons. IBM Sci. Center, Phila., 1971, State Seismol. Bur., Beijing, China, 1985; Disting. lectr. Am. Assn. Petroleum Geologists, 1977-78; Roberts lectr. Colo. Coll.; nat. lectr. Assn. Computing Machinery, 1986. Named Calif. Coll.-Univ. Prof. of Yr., Council Advancement and Support of Edn., 1985; Guggenheim fellow, 1969-70. Mem. Royal Soc. Edinburgh Geol. Soc., Am. Geol. Soc., Edinburgh Geol. Soc., Assn. Computing Machinery (nat. lectr. 1985—), AAAS, Sigma Xi (nat. lectr. 1968). Home: 625 W 12th St Claremont CA 91711

MCINTYRE, GARY ALLEN, plant pathology educator; b. Portland, Oreg., July 16, 1938; s. John H. and Onie Marie (Meihoff) McI.; m. Loene Beneva, Sept. 1, 1963; children: Paula Lynn, Laura Ann. BS, Oreg. State U., 1960, PhD, 1964. Asst. prof. botany and plant pathology U. Maine, Orono, 1963-68, assoc prof., 1968-73, prof., 1973-75, chmn. botany, plant pathology dept., 1969-75; prof., chmn. botany, plant pathology Colo. State U., Ft. Collins, 1975-84, prof., head plant pathology and weed sci. dept., 1984—; Coordinator Western Regional Integrated Pest Mgmt. program, 1978—. Mem. Am. Photopathol. Soc., Potato Assn. Office: Colo State U Dept Plant Pathology/Weed Sci Fort Collins CO 80523

MCINTYRE, ROBERT MALCOLM, utility company executive; b. Portland, Oreg., Dec. 18, 1923; married. B.A., UCLA, 1950. Gen. sales mgr. So. Counties Gas Co. Calif., 1952-70; with So. Calif. Gas Co. (subs. Pacific Lighting Corp.), Los Angeles, 1970—, v.p., asst. to chmn., then sr. v.p., 1974-80, former pres., from 1980, now chmn., chief exec. officer, also dir. Office: So Calif Gas Co 810 S Flower St Los Angeles CA 90017 *

MCKAMEY, LAURA JO, speech and language pathologist; b. Great Falls, Mont., Sept. 21, 1957; s. David James and Olive Wyoma (Heckmann) Parker; m. Alvin George McKamey, June 17, 1980; children: Brandon, Russell, Sandra Jo, Alvin James. BS, Brigham Young U., 1979; MS, Utah State U., 1984. Cert. tchr., Mont.; lic. speech pathologist, Mont. Tchr. A.J. Winters Sch., Montpelier, Idaho, 1979-80; speech pathologist Cen. Mont. Learning Resource Ctr. Coop., Lewistown, 1984-86; speech/language theapist Headstart Presch. Program, Great Falls, Mont., 1986—. Mem. Am. Speech Lang. Hearing Assn. (cert.). Mormon. Avocations: sewing, reading, cooking, oil painting. Home: 1671 Millegan Rd Great Falls MT 59405

MC KASSON, ROBERT EDWARD, JR., insurance sales executive; b. Los Angeles, Feb. 3, 1945; s. Robert E. and Verda C. (White) McK.; A.A., Fullerton Coll., 1967. Salesman various life ins. cos., 1967—; pres., chmn. bd. Ind. Bankers Ins. Services, Newport Beach, Calif., 1977—. Recipient Gold medal ins. sales awards, 1976, 78; Bronze medal Investors Guaranty Life, 1979. Mem. 6 Million Dollar Forum. Club: 20-30. Featured in Nat. Underwriter, Aug. 1983. Home and Office: 124-31st St Newport Beach CA 92663-3004

MC KAUGHAN, HOWARD PAUL, linguistics educator; b. Canoga Park, Calif., July 5, 1922; s. Paul and Edith (Barton) McK.; A.B., UCLA, 1945; M.Th., Dallas Theol. Sem., 1946; M.A., Cornell U., 1952, Ph.D., 1957; m. Barbara Jean Budroe, Dec. 25, 1943; children—Edith (Mrs. Daniel Skene Santoro), Charlotte (Mrs. Martin Douglas Barnhart), Patricia (Mrs. Stephen B. Pike), Barbara (Mrs. Ronald Chester Bell), Judith (Mrs. Frank L. Achilles III). Mem. linguistic research team Summer Inst. Linguistics, Mexico, 1946-52; asso. dir. Summer Inst. Linguistics, Philippines, also assoc. dir. summer sessions U. N.D., 1952-57, dir. Philippine br., 1957-61; research asst. prof. anthropology U. Wash., 1961-62; research assoc. prof., 1962-63; assoc. prof. linguistics U. Hawaii, 1963-64, prof. linguistics, 1964—, chmn. dept., 1963-66, dir. Pacific and Asian Linguistics Inst., 1964, 1966-69, assoc. dean grad. div., 1965-72, dean grad. div., dir. research, 1972-79, acting chancellor, 1979, interim vice chancellor acad. affairs, 1981-82, acting dir research, 1982-84, acting dean grad. div., 1982—; lectr. linguistics U. Philippines, summers, 1954, 60; Fulbright vis. prof. Philippine Normal Coll.-Ateneo Consortium, Philippines, 1977; prin. Wycliffe Sch. Linguistics, summers 1953, 61; vis. prof. Australian Nat. U., Canberra, 1970; adj. prof. linguistics U. Okla., summers 1984, 85, 86. Sr. scholar East-West Center, Honolulu, 1964; NDEA Maranao-Philippines research grantee, 1963-65; Office of Edn. Hawaii English grantee, 1965-66; NSF Jeh Language of South Vietnam grantee, 1969-70, Maranao Linguistic Studies, 1971-72, numerous other research grants. Mem. linguistic socs. Am., Philippines, Western Assn. Grad. Schs. (pres. 1978), Hawaii, Linguistic Circle N.Y., Philippine Assn. Lang. Tchrs., Hawaii Govt. Employees Assn., Phi Beta Kappa, Phi Kappa Phi. Author (with B. McKaughan): Chatino Dictionary, 1951; (with J. Forster) Ilocano: An Intensive Language Course, 1952; The Inflection and Syntax of Maranao Verbs, 1959; (with B. Macaraya): A Maranao Dictionary, 1967. Editor: Pali Language Texts: Philippines, 21 vols., 1971; The Languages of the Eastern Family of the East New Guinea Highlands Stock, 1973. Contbr. articles, chpts. to books, sci. jours. Home: 3670 Alani Dr Honolulu HI 96822

MCKAY, D. BRIAN, lawyer, attorney general; b. Billings, Mont., Jan. 18, 1945. A.B., Colgate U., 1971; J.D., Albany Law Sch., 1974. Bar: Nev., U.S. Dist. Ct. Nev., N.Y., U.S. Dist. Ct. (no. dist.) N.Y., U.S. Ct. Appeals (9th cir.) 1978, U.S. Supreme Ct. Former mem. Sully, McKay & Lenhard, Las Vegas, Nev.; atty. gen. State of Nev., Carson City, 1983—; mem. adv. policy bd. Nat. Crime Info. Ctr., 1986—. Alt. mem. Western States Water Council, from 1978; mem. Clark County Air Pollution Control Bd., from 1979, adv. policy bd. Nat. Crime Info. Ctr., 1986—. Served with USAF, 1966-69. Mem. ABA, State Bar Nev., N.Y. State Bar Assn. Office: Office Atty Gen Heroes Meml Bdlg 198 S Carson St Capitol Complex Carson City NV 89710

MCKAY, DALE ROBERT, chemical company administrator, physicist; b. Oakland, Calif., Oct. 26, 1946; s. Leonard Dale and Marion Ada (Greensill) McK.; m. Christine Marie Zuponovich, Sept. 20, 1969 (div. Nov. 1976); m. Karen Ann LaBonte, Nov. 19, 1976; 1 child, Erin Jean LaBonte. BA in Physics, Calif. State U., Hayward, 1968; PhD in Physics, U. Wyo., 1980. Research assoc. Colo. State U., Ft. Collins, 1979-83; product mgr. Chemagnetics, Ft. Collins, 1983-85, ops. mgr., 1985—; cons. in field. Mem. AAAS. Democrat. Avocations: cars, backpacking, sailing. Home: 1560 Quail Hollow Fort Collins CO 80525 Office: Chemagnetics 208 Commerce Fort Collins CO 80524

MCKEAN, BONNIE JOYCE, advertising executive; b. San Bernadino, Calif., July 19, 1945; d. H.H. and Rose M. Parrell; children: Robert, David. BA, U. Calif., Berkeley, 1966; MA, U. Redlands, 1979. Account exec. IPD, San Jose, Calif., 1976-79; pres. Reflections, Alameda, Calif., 1979-83; sales mgr. CCC Publ., Walnut Creek, Calif., 1983-86; advt. dir. Calif. Monthly Mag., Berkeley, 1984—; account exec. Donnelly Info. Publ., Lafayette, Calif., 1986-87; pub., owner Alameda Directory Co., 1987—; acct. exec. Guestinformant, 1986. Pres. Mt. Diablo Child Care Advs., Concord, Calif., 1976-78; bd. dirs. Concord Children's Council, 1976-78. Mem. Calif. Alumni Assn. (pres. 1983), Alameda C. of C. (bd. dirs. 1980-83).

MCKEAN, JOSEPH JED, safety professional; b. Salt Lake City, Apr. 21, 1946; s. Joseph Boyd and Lea Jacquene (Whitlock) McK.; m. Carolyn Hoggard, Aug. 13, 1977; 1 child, Annette. AS, Coll. Eastern Utah, 1970, Assoc. in Mining. Tech., 1974; BS in Occupational Safety and Health, Cen. Wash. U., 1982. Cert. safety profl., Utah. Coal miner U.S. Steel, East Carbon, Utah, 1972-80; research asst. Safety Ctr. Cen. Wash. U., Ellensberg, 1981-82; safety officer McNally Pitts. Inc., Tulsa, 1983-84, corp. field safety supr., 1984-85; coordinating safety fire protector Intermountain Power Agy., Delta, Utah, 1985—; safety specialist Delta 7th Ward, 1986—; counselor of safety and fire for Boy Scouts Am., Ellensberg, 1982-83; instr. first aide ARC, Delta, 1983—. Author: (manuals) Fork Lift Operators, 1981, Fork Lift Training, 1981. Pres. Young Republicans, 1967-68. Served with U.S. Army, 1970-71. Mem. Am. Soc. Safety Engrs. (pres. 1981-82), World Safety Orgn. Mormons. Home: 840 E Bristle Cone Ln #22-5 Delta UT 84624 Office: Intermountain Power Agy Rt 1 Box 824 Delta UT 84624

MCKECHNIE, C. LOGAN, lawyer; b. Monticello, Ky., Sept. 29, 1942; s. Glenn Logan and Jean Alva (Eads) McK.; m. Barbara J. Allen, Apr. 3, 1971; children—B. Roxanne, Amanda J. Student W. Tex. State U., 1960-61, Amarillo Coll., 1961, Goethe Inst., Fed. Republic Germany, 1964-67; L.L.B., J.D., Western State U., San Diego, 1977. Reporter, editor News-Texan, Grand Prairie, Tex., 1959-60, KGNC-TV, Globe News, Amarillo, Tex., 1960-61; cryptologist Army Security Agy., Nat. Security Agy., 1962-64; corr. UPI, Europe, 1964-67; reporter Ariz. Republic, Phoenix, 1967-71; reporter, editor The Tribune, San Diego, 1971-72; spl. asst. to dist. atty., San Diego, 1972-80; sole practice, San Diego, 1981—; lectr. San Diego State U., Western State U., San Diego, Nat. Coll. Dist. Attys., U. Houston. Contbr. articles to Am., European and S.Am. mags. Pres. Tierrasanta Community Council, San Diego, 1974; life mem., advisor, counsel Tierrasanta Friends of Library, San Diego, 1979—; advisor Mudd for Judge Campaign, San Diego, 1984, Calif. Legis. Sports Law Com., 1983—; bd. dirs. Lakeside Cityhood Com., 1987—, East County Bus. Council. Served to capt. U.S. Army, 1961-67. Recipient cert. of Merit, U.S. Jaycees, 1969, Appreciation award Santee Lions Club, 1983. Mem. ABA (sports and entertainment com., vice chmn. criminal justice subcom. 1985—, disting. pub. service award 1970), Nat. Dist. Attys. Assn., Calif. Bar Assn., Calif. Dist. Attys. Assn., San Diego Bar Assn., Foothills Bar Assn., Trial Lawyers Assn., Lakeside C. of C. (bd. dirs. 1987—), Nu Beta Epsilon. Republican. Lodges: Lions (pres. Lakeside club 1984, officer 1985—), Kiwanis. Home: 11875 Rocoso Rd Lakeside CA 92040 Office: 9820 Maine Ave Lakeside CA 92040

MC KEE, JOHN ANGUS, oil company executive; b. Toronto, Ont., Can., Aug. 31, 1935; s. John William and Margaret Enid (Phippen) McK.; m. Susan Elizabeth Harley, May 30, 1970; children: John Andrew, Mary Susan. Student, U. Toronto, 1954-58. With Dominion Securities Corp. Ltd., Toronto, 1958-61; v.p. Patino Mining Corp., Toronto and London, Eng., 1962-72; pres. J. Angus McKee & Assos. Ltd., 1973-83; pres., chief exec. officer Can. Occidental Petroleum Ltd., 1983—; dir. Teradyne Can. Ltd., Stone & Webster Can. Ltd., Cullman Ventures Inc., others.; Mng. dir. Consol. Tin Smelters Ltd., 1968-71. Bd. govs. Trinity Coll. Sch. Mem. Alpha Delta Phi. Clubs: Toronto, York, Badminton and Racquet; Knickerbocker (N.Y.C.). Office: Can Occidental Petroleum, 1600-700 4th Ave SW, Calgary, AB Canada T2P 3J5 *

MC KEE, JOHN CAROTHERS, industrial psychologist; b. San Diego, Apr. 25, 1912; s. John Joseph and Margaret (Giesman) McK.; B.A., U. So. Calif., 1935, M.A., 1937; Ph.D., Tulane U., 1947; m. Gladys Irene Michel, Jan. 10, 1941 (dec. Feb. 1968); children—John Michael, Hillary Barbara; m. 2d, Sara Forman, June 25, 1968; one son, Evan. Gen. mgr. Hotel Royal, La Ceiba, Honduras, 1932-33; mgmt. cons. Douglas Aircraft Co., Long Beach, Calif., 1942-67, exec. adviser, dir. operations control, 1967—, also pres. mgmt. assn. Douglas Space Systems Center; exec. adviser fin. mgmt. McDonnell Douglas Astronautics, v.p. Santa Monica Health Spot Shoe Corp., 1949—; pres. McKee Mgmt. Center, Volumetrics, Inc., Mentron Corp.; exec. v.p. Consearch Inc.; pres. McKee Mgmt. Center, Stanton, Calif., Quantek Internat. Inc.; partner McKee & Wright and Assn., Stanton; v.p. Advion Corp.; lectr. Acad. of Justice, Riverside, Calif.; cons. Space Systems Center, Huntington Beach, Calif., 1964—; cons. Hanford, Orange, Cypress police depts. (all Calif.); dir. Consultron, Inc. Author: Law Enforcement Manager's Handbook. Pres. sports council YMCA; bd. dirs. Long Beach YMCA. Asso. dir. Mgmt. Center, Chapman Coll.; bd. dirs. McKee Wright La Verne Coll. Mgmt. Center, Cavaliers Fencing Schs., 1935—, Law Enforcement Mgmt. Center, Calif.; mgr. Stanton Bd. Trade, 1978—; Olympic fencing coach, 1984; pres. Ctr. for Strategic Planning, Orange County, Calif.; mem. fed. res. adv. bd. Recipient Personagraph Speaker of Yr. award Indsl Mgmt. Assn,; Outstanding Law Enforcement Work award Calif. Atty. Gen., 1984; named to Am. Police Hall of Fame, 1984; Charles R. Able citation for co. mgmt., Certificate of Merit, Amateur Fencers League Am.; Citizen of Yr. award Calif. Office Atty. Gen., 1984; resolution of thanks for work with police City of Hartford; Resolution of Excellence Hartford City Council; Calif. Gov.'s award for civilian service to law enforcement; named Cavalier Fencing Coach of Yr., 1982; named to Pub. Hall of Fame, 1985; Nat. Police Hall of Fame, 1985; cert. instr. Calif. Dept. Justice POST program. Mem. Internat. Platform Assn., Am. Statis. Assn. (past pres., mem. nat. council). Nat. Mgmt. Assn. (recipient Silver Knight of Mgmt., 1961, v.p. area council), Nat. Assn. Chiefs of Police, Internat. Assn. Chiefs Police, Calif. Assn. Police Tng. Officers, Fedn. Internationale D'Esgrime, Amateur Fencers League Am., AAAS, C. of C. (mem. research com. of Los Angeles), Inst. Mgmt. Scis., Am. Assn. Indsl. Editors, Internat. Council Indsl. Editors, So. Calif. Indsl. Editors Assn., Nat. Assn. Bus. Economists, Orange County Econ. Roundtable (Exec. of Year award, pres.), Calif. Adminstrn. Justice Educators, Calif. Assn. Peace Officers, Phi Beta Kappa. Author: Learning Curves, Quantity-Cost Curves, Estimating Engineering Costs, Systems Analysis, Cost and Budgeting Analysis and Statistics for Non-Mathematical Managers; Zero Base Budgeting; The Fencer's Work Book; Fiscal Management; The Police Chief's Financial Handbook. Home: 16509 Harbour Lane Huntington Beach CA 92649 Office: Law Enforcement Mgmt Ctr 10801 Dale St Stanton CA 90680

MCKEE, JOSEPH FULTON, engineering and construction executive; b. Placerville, Calif., Apr. 28, 1921; s. Joseph Fulton and Pearl Margarite (Varroza) McK.; m. Eva Deane Adcock, Mar. 15, 1949 (dec.); m. Sharon Lucille Ricketts Adamson, Jan. 23, 1982; children—Robert Deane, Renne E. Hackbarth. B.C.E., U. Santa Clara, 1947. Constrn. engr. Western Contracting Corp., 1947-50; supt., project engr., gen. supt. constrn. Morrison-Knudsen Co., Western U.S., 1950-54; project engr., constrn. mgr. Morrison-Knudsen Co., Western U.S., Morocco, 1954-57; constrn. mgr. Morrison-Knudsen Co., Western U.S., Iran, 1957-60, worldwide, 1960-65; area mgr. Morrison-Knudsen Co., Western U.S., Australia, 1965-73; v.p. Morrison-Knudsen Co., Western U.S., Europe, Africa, Mid-East, 1973-77; sr. v.p. Morrison-Knudsen Co., Western U.S., Tehran, 1977-80, Boise, Idaho, 1981-81; project dir. Cerrejon Coal Project, Colombia, 1981-85; exec. v.p. internat. Morrison-Knudsen Engrs., San Francisco, 1985-86, ret., 1986. Served to lt. C.E., USN, 1943-46. Mem. ASCE, Chi Epsilon, Tau Beta Pi. Republican. Roman Catholic. Office: 4781 Rivervista Pl Boise ID 83703

MCKEE, KATHRYN DIAN GRANT, bank holding company executive; b. Los Angeles, Sept. 12, 1937; d. Clifford William and Amelia Rosalia (Shacher) Grant; m. Paul Eugene McKee, June 17, 1961; children: Scott Alexander, Grant Christopher. BA, U. Calif., Santa Barbara, 1959; grad. Sch. Mgmt. Exec. Program, UCLA, 1979. Accredited compensation and benefits. Mgr., Mattel, Inc., Hawthorne, Calif., 1963-74; dir. Twentieth Century Fox Film Corp., Los Angeles, 1975-80; sr. v.p. First Interstate Bancorp, Los Angeles, 1980—; treas. Personnel Accreditation Inst., 1983-86, pres., 1986. Contbr. articles to profl. jours. Pres. GEM Theatre Guild, Garden Grove, Calif., 1984-86; bd. dirs. Vis. Nurses Assn., Los Angeles, 1984—, ASPA, 1986—, trustee Garden Grove Assn. for Arts, 1985—. Recipient Sr. Honor Key, U. Calif., Santa Barbara, 1959; named Outstanding Sr. Woman, 1959. Mem. Internat. Assn. Personnel Women (various offices, past nat. pres., Mem. of Yr. 1986), Orgn. Women Execs., Women in Bus., Am. Compensation Assn. (William Winter award 1986). Club: Los Angeles Athletic. Office: First Interstate Bancorp 707 Wilshire Blvd Los Angeles CA 90017

MC KEE, RAYMOND WALTER, accountant; b. Joplin, Mo., Dec. 24, 1899; s. Charles Edward and Sarah Ellen (Epperson) McK.; student pub. schs., Joplin; m. Frances Ida Howe, Nov. 1, 1947; children—Michael, David, Roderick, Duncan, Malcolm, Brude. Acct., Price, Waterhouse & Co., 1923-25, Haskins & Sells, 1925-26; pvt. practice acctg., La Puente, Calif., 1964—; lectr. St. Louis U., 1923-24; v.p. Richfield Oil Corp., Pan Am. Petroleum Corp., 1928-30; sec. West Coast Air Transport, 1926-30; sec.-treas. West Coast div. Anchor Hocking Corp.; dir., v.p. Maywood Mut. Water Co.; pres. Cross Water Co. Co-founder Nat. Paraplegia Found. (name now Nat. Spinal Cord Found.), 1947. C.P.A., Calif. Mem. Petroleum Accts. Soc. (co-founder). Club: Lions. Author: Accounting for Petroleum Industry, 1925; Petroleum Accounting, 1938; Saludos California, 1947; Book of McKee, 1959. Home and office: 738 S 3d Ave La Puente CA 91746

MCKEE, RICHARD PHILIP, advertising/broadcasting executive, consultant; b. N.Y.C., June 10, 1930; s. Joseph V. and Cornelia (Kraft) Mck.; m. Virginia C. Alicoate, Oct. 16, 1954; children—Michael, Christopher, Matthew, Teresa, Stephen. B.S.S., Georgetown U., 1952. Gen. mgr. Sta. KOB-AM & FM, Albuquerque, 1969-74; pres. Aloha Broadcasting Co., Honolulu, 1975-77; gen. mgr. Sta. KRKE AM/FM, Albuquerque, 1977-80; v.p. Summit Communications Okla. Inc., Oklahoma City, 1981; mgr. pub. info. Jacobs Engring. Group, Albuquerque, 1982; v.p. Sandia Advt., Albuquerque, 1983-86; pres. Dick McKee & Assocs. Media Cons., 1974—. Commr., Bernalillo County (N.Mex.), 1974; pres. bd. trustees Bernalillo County Mental Health Ctr., 1979. Served with Signal Corps, U.S. Army, 1952-54. Named Broadcaster of Year, N.Mex. Broadcasters Assn., 1980. Mem. Pub. Relations Soc. Am. Republican. Roman Catholic. Home and Office: 4208 Marla Dr NE Albuquerque NM 87109

MCKEEL, R. BRUCE, investment banker; b. Oregon City, Oreg., Apr. 13, 1942; s. Ralph Orman and Gladys Anna (Palmer) McK.; m. Lynn E. Mackey, Feb. 14, 1976; children: Amber Lynn, Elizabeth Ann, Janette Kathryn, Tiffany Lane. B.A., U. Oreg., 1964. Investment banker Davis Skaggs & Co., San Francisco, 1968-73; v.p. HBE Leasing Corp., San Francisco, 1973-75; v.p. leverage leasing Equilease Corp. subs. Eltra Corp., San Francisco, 1975-77; pres., founder, dir. Qartel Corp., San Francisco, 1977-79; v.p. leverage leasing, spl. fin. project Prescott Ball & Turben, San Francisco, 1979-80; founder, chmn. bd., pres. McKeel & Co. Inc. and subs., 1980—; spl. project fin. cons. to various nat. cos., 1979—. Vice chmn. spl. gifts United Crusade, 1978. Recipient cert. distinction N.Y. Inst. Fin., 1968. Mem. Western Assn. Equipment Lessors (past officer, dir.), Am. Assn. Equipment Lessors. Republican. Episcopalian. Clubs: Olympic of San Francisco, Family, Mchts. Exchange, San Francisco Bond, San Francisco Comml., Hillsborough Racquet. Home: 560 Hayne Rd Hillsborough CA 94010 Office: 465 California St San Francisco CA 94104

MCKELL, CYRUS M., biotechnology company executive; b. Payson, Utah, Mar. 19, 1926; s. Robert D. and Mary C. (Ellsworth) McK.; m. Betty Johnson; children: Meredith Sue, Brian Marcus, John Cyrus. BS, U. Utah, 1949, MS, 1950; PhD, Oreg. State U., 1956; postdoctoral student, U. Calif., Davis, 1957. Instr. botany Oreg. State U., Corvallis, 1955-56; research plant physiologist U. Calif. USDA-Agrl. Research Service, Davis, 1956-60; prof., dept. chmn. U. Calif., Riverside, 1960-69; prof. dept. head., dir. Utah State U., Logan, 1969-80; v.p. research NPI, Salt Lake City, 1980—; cons. Ford Found. 1968-72, Rockefeller Found., 1964-70, U.N., 1978, Nat. Acad. Sci., 1980, USAID, 1972. Editor Grass Biology and Utilization, 1971, Useful Wildland Shrubs, 1972, Rehabilitation of Western Wildlife Habitat, 1978, Paradoxes of Western Energy Development, 1984, Resource Inventory and Baseline Study Methods for Developing Countries, 1983, Shrub Biology and Utilization, 1987; contbr. numerous articles to profl. jours. Chmn. Cache County Planning Commn., Logan, 1974-79; active Energy Conservation and Devel. Council, Salt Lake City, 1976-79; active Commn. of the Californias, Riverside, 1965-68. Served to 1st lt. USAF, 1951-53. Fulbright scholar, 1967-68; World Travel grantee Rockefeller Found., 1964. Fellow AAAS (com. chmn. 1979—, sci. exchange to china grantee 1984-85); mem. Am. Soc. Agronomy, Soc. Range Mgmt. (pres. Calif. sect. 1965, pres. Utah sect. 1982). Mormon. Avocations: travel, photography. Home: 2248 E 4000 S Salt Lake City UT 84124 Office: NPI 417 Wakara Way Salt Lake City UT 84108

MCKELVEY, GEORGE IRWIN, III, college executive; b. Glen Ridge, N.J., May 5, 1925; s. George Irwin, Jr., and Florence (Samuel) McK.; m. Velma E. Vergara, June 28, 1959; 1 son, George Stuart. A.B. in History, U. Rochester, 1950, M.A. in govt., 1958. Exec. sec. Alumni Assn. U. Rochester, N.Y., 1950-56, Alumni Fedn., U. Rochester, 1953-56, dir. alumni relations, 1955-56; assoc. dir. Am. Alumni Council, Washington, 1956-57; dir. devel. Harvey Mudd Coll., Claremont, Calif., 1957-68, v.p. devel. and planning, 1968—. Trustee Raymond M. Alf Mus., Claremont, 1982—; bd. dirs. Bates Found. for Aero. Edn., Claremont. Served with USN, 1943-46. Mem. Council for Advancement and Support of Edn., Psi Upsilon. Republican. Presbyterian. Club: University (Los Angeles). Office: Harvey Mudd Coll 12th St Claremont CA 91711

MCKENNA, PATRICK JAMES, management consultant; b. Edson, Alta., Can., Oct. 31, 1951; s. James Edward and Madeline (Watson) McK.; C.I.M., Can. Inst. Mgmt., Toronto, Ont., 1979, P. Mgr., 1977, M.B.A., 1982, I.C.I.A., 1985. Asst. div. mgr. Hudsons Bay Co., Edmonton, Alta., 1973-75; gen. mgr. Alta. C. of C. Edmonton, 1975-78; mng. dir. QCTV Ltd., Edmonton, 1978-81; v.p. Achieve Enterprises Ltd., Edmonton, 1981-83; pres. Edge Cons. Assocs., Inc., Edmonton, 1983—; dir. Nebula Holdings Ltd., Edmonton, 1980—, Can. Inst. Mgmt., 1981-85. Editor: The Enterprizer Quar., 1976. Contbr. articles to profl. jours. Advisor on bus. administrn. Lakeland Coll., Lloydminister, Sask., 1984; bd. dirs. Jr. Achievement of Alta., 1984; dir. Edmonton Ctr. P.C. Party Assn., Alberta, 1984. Mem. Can. Inst. Mgmt. (bd. dirs. 1981-84), Guild ICIA (chmn. 1986-87), Am. Mktg. Assn., Internat. Assn. Strategic Planning Cons. (founding mem.), Canadian Bar Assn., ABA, Alta. Entrepreneurs Assn. (founding mem.), Alta. Conf. Soc. (founding mem.). Conservative. Club: Royal Glenora (Edmonton). Home: 4242 111th Ave, Edmonton, AB Canada T5W 0K2

MCKENNA, ROBERT CHARLES, civil engineer; b. Portsmouth, N.H., May 1, 1936; s. Charles T. and Priscilla (Greenaway) McK.; m. Harriet Koutrelakos, Sept. 8, 1957; children—Douglas, Beth, Charles. B.S.C.E., U. N.H., 1959; M.Resource Adminstrn., U. Mont., 1975. Registered profl. engr., Mont., N.H., Wash. Project engr. Wright & Pierce, Portsmouth, 1962-65; supt. pub. works City of Portsmouth, 1965-66; project engr. USAF, Pease AFB, N.H., 1966-68; cons. engr. McKenna Assocs., Portsmouth, 1968-75, Helena, 1983—; civil engr., resource mgr. Mont. Dept. Fish, Wildlife and Parks, Helena, 1976-83; cons. engr. McKenna Assocs., Helena, 1983—. Contbr. articles to profl. jours. Pres. Canyon Ferry Recreation Assn., Helena, 1984-85; mem. core group Helena Cursillo Movement, 1983-85; mem. parish council Sts. Cyril-Methodius Parish, 1980-83; mem. fin. com. St. Helena Cathedral, 1984—. Served to 1st lt. USAF, 1959-62. Recipient disting. contbn. award Canyon Ferry Recreation Assn., 1983. Mem. ASCE (editor nat. surveying and mapping newsletter 1970-73), Assn. Conservation Engrs. (chmn. nat. spl. action com. 1981-82; Dedicated Service award 1982), NSPE, Cons. Engring. Council Mont., Mont. Tech. Council, Helena C. of C. Democrat. Roman Catholic. Club: Mont. Home: 916 N Park Ave Helena MT 59601

MCKENZIE, CHRISTINE ANN, social worker; b. Balt., Nov. 27, 1952; d. Charles Henry and Lenora Frances (Miller) McK. BA, Cath. U., Washington, 1974; MSW, U. So. Calif., 1978, PhD, 1986. Lic. clin. social worker, Calif. Social worker intake/group home Five Acres, Altadena, Calif., 1977-80, dir. devel., 1980-83, dir. community services, 1985—; pvt. practice psychotherapy Pasadena, Calif., 1980—; psychotherapist Foothill Family Service, Pasadena, 1983-84; specialist orgn. devel. U. So. Calif., Los Angeles, 1983-84, tchr. med. sch., 1984—. Mem. Nat. Assn. Social Workers (cert.), Bus. and Profl. Women (editor newsletter 1983—), Phi Delta Epsilon. Avocations: outdoor sports. Home: 138 W Laurel Altadena CA 91001 Office: Five Acres 690 E Green St 211A Pasadena CA 91101

MCKENZIE, MARCIA WILLOUGHBY, business educator; b. Yreka, Calif.; d. William Sherwood and Agnes Evelyn (Sly) Swigart; m. Robert Ernest McKenzie, Aug. 15, 1948; children: Dawn Renee, Marta Lin, Tamara Lee McKenzie Bryan. BA, Calif. State U., Chico, 1949, MA, 1977. Cert. secondary tchr., Calif.; cert. adminstr., Calif. Instr. bus. Galileo High Sch., San Francisco, 1951-56, Shasta Coll., Redding, Calif., 1970—. Mem. and clk. Redding Elem. Sch. Bd., 1963-67; pres. Sierra Cascade council Girl Scouts U.S., Chico, 1967-71, Family Service Agy., Redding, 1965-66, Cypress PTA, Redding, 1961-62. Named Green Angel, Girl Scouts U.S., 1972; hon. life mem. Calif. PTA. Mem. Calif. Bus. Edn. Assn. (pres. 1986-87, pres. elect 1985-86, treas. 1984-85, sec. 1982-83, pres. no. sect. 1981-82), Western Bus. Edn. Assn., Internat. Soc. Bus. Edn., AAUW (pres. Redding br. 1962-64, Edn. Found. honoree 1984), Nat. Bus. Edn. Assn., Community Concert Assn. (membership chmn.), Learn and Earn Club. Republican. Methodist. Club: Newcomers (Redding). Avocations: cross-country skiing, gourmet cooking. Home: 3530 Scenic Dr Redding CA 96001 Office: Shasta Coll PO Box 6006 Redding CA 96099

MCKENZIE, MERLE, aerospace engineer; b. Denver, Aug. 30, 1954; s. Keith Edward and Betsy Louise (Vogel) Gehrke. BS, Calif. Inst. Tech., 1977; postgrad., U. So. Calif., 1985-86. Engr. Jet Propulsion Lab., Pasadena, Calif., 1976-79, sr. engr., 1979-81, group leader, 1981-83, group supr., 1983—, mgr. space sta. software issues, 1986-87, mgr. space sta. info. system analysis, 1987—; cons. aerospace and telecommunications orgns., 1986—. Reviewer Engring. Mgmt. Internat. jour., 1984—; contbr. articles to profl. jours. Scholar Calif. Inst. Tech., 1972-76, Boettcher, 1972, U. Colo., 1972. Mem. AIAA (chmn. econs. tech. com., publs. subcom. 1983-86, chmn. econs. standards com. 1986—, nat. and Los Angeles sect. pub. policy com. 1983—), Sigma Xi. Avocations: skiing, writing, motorcycling, flying, piano. Office: Jet Propulsion Lab MS 301-375 4800 Oak Grove Dr Pasadena CA 91109

MCKERNAN, THOMAS VINCENT, JR., automobile club executive; b. Alexandria, La., June 20, 1944; s. Thomas Vincent and Mae Marie (Gassiott) McK.; m. Judith Havenner, Mar. 27, 1971; children: Megan, Shannon. BS, Calif. State U., Los Angeles, 1981, MBA, 1985. Cert. data processor; cert. systems profl. Computer programmer Automobile Club of So. Calif., Los Angeles, 1969-71, systems analyst, 1971-72, supr. programming, 1972-75, mgr. systems, 1975-80, dir. data processing, 1980-83, asst. v.p. fin. and adminstrn., 1983-85, v.p. fin. and adminstrn., 1985—; mem. adv. com. Calif. State U. Los Angeles, Calif. State U. Long Beach. Mem. Fin. Exec. Inst., Soc. for Mgmt. Info. Systems. Republican. Roman Catholic. Office: Automobile Club So Calif 2601 S Figueroa St Los Angeles CA 90007

MCKILLOP, WILLIAM LAWIE, forest economics educator; b. Aberdeen, Scotland, June 3, 1933; came to U.S., 1961; s. William L.M. and Isabella (Morrison) McK.; m. Kathleen Jessie Smith, Feb. 15, 1958; children: Lesley, Robin, Aileen, Valerie. BS, U. Aberdeen, 1954; MS, U. N.B., Can., 1959; MA, PhD, U. Calif., Berkeley, 1965. Forest economist Can. Forestry Service, Ottawa, Ont., 1958-61; mem. faculty U. Calif., Berkeley, 1964-75, prof. forest econs., 1975—. Contbr. articles to profl. jours. Served to lt. C.E., Brit. Army, 1954-56. Mem. Soc. Am. Foresters, Am. Econ. Assn. Home: 40 Sleepy Hollow Ln Orinda CA 94563 Office: Univ of Calif Dept Forestry & Resource Mgmt Berkeley CA 94720

MCKINLAY, (DONALD) BRUCE, research center director; b. Colorado Springs, Colo., June 9, 1936; s. Donald R. and Mabel (Davies) McK.; children: Kate, Donald. BS, U. Oreg., 1958, MA, 1967, PhD, 1971. Tch. Gresham (Oreg.) High Sch., 1958-59; personnel mgr. Snider Farms, Troutdale, Oreg., 1959; labor economist Dept. Employment, 1960-69; research assoc. U. Oreg., Eugene, 1970-72, research ctr. dir., 1972—; cons., 1972—. Developer computer aided career planning systems, 1969, 72, 86 (Chavrid award 1977). Com. chmn. Human Rights Commn., Eugene, 1968-70, Gov.'s Vocat. Edn. Council, Oreg., 1973-75; chmn. Univ. Patent Policies Commn., Eugene, 1974—; mem. Community Goals Com., Eugene, 1967. Mem. Am. Econ. Assn., Am. Assn. for Counseling and Devel., Assn. of Computer-based Systems for Career Info. (sec./treas. 1986). Episcopalian. Office: Career Info System 1787 Agate St Eugene OR 97403

MC KINLEY, ROYCE BALDWIN, business executive, lawyer; b. Ann Arbor, Mich., Feb. 20, 1921; s. Earle B. and Leola (Royce) McK.; m. Roberta Schreck, Apr. 15, 1943; 1 dau., Martha Lee; m. Anne de Beixedon, July 7, 1973. Student, Harvard U., 1938-40; A.B., U. Mich., 1942; J.D., Harvard U., 1948; LL.M., George Washington U., 1951. Bar: D.C. 1949, Mo. 1953, Ill. 1959. Practiced in Washington 1948-52; counsel Ralston Purina Co., St. Louis, 1952-55; assoc. McKinsey & Co., Inc., Chgo. and London, 1955-60; v.p., sec. Electro-Sci.-Investors, Inc., Dallas, 1960-63; v.p. finance and adminstrn. Space Gen. Corp., El Monte, Calif., 1963-66; asst. dir. mgmt. systems TRW, Inc., Redondo Beach, Calif., 1967-68; v.p. fin., sec.-treas. Santa Anita Consol., Inc., Los Angeles, 1968-73; exec. v.p., chief operating officer Santa Anita Consol., Inc., 1973-79; also dir.; pres., chief exec. officer Santa Anita Realty Enterprises, Inc., Los Angeles, 1980—, also dir.; dir. Santa Anita Operating Co., Arcadia, Calif., Los Angeles Turf Club, Arcadia, Minn. Racetrack Inc. Served to lt. (j.g.) USNR, 1943-46. Mem. Nat. Assn. Real Estate Investment Trusts (bd. govs. 1981—, pres. 1985-86). Club: California (Los Angeles). Home: 262 S Orange Dr Los Angeles CA 90036 Office: Santa Anita Realty Enterprises Inc 1 Wilshire Bldg Suite 2303 Los Angeles CA 90017

MCKINNEY, BERNIE OLIN, II, military officer; b. Wichita, Kans., Nov. 21, 1953; s. Bernie Olin and Thelma Lucille (Burrows) McK. BS in Chem. Engring., U. Fla., 1981; MEE, Northrop U., 1987. Commd. USAF, 1981, advanced through grades to capt., 1985; devel. and research engr. USAF, Los Angeles, 1981-86; missile launch officer USAF, Cheyenne, Wyo., 1986—. Mem. Am. Inst. of Chem. Engrs., AAAS, Air Force Assn. Democrat. Avocations: reading, electronics. Home: 5709 Education Dr Apt #206 Cheyenne WY 82009

MCKINNEY, ELOISE VAUGHN, English language educator; b. Greensboro, N.C., Dec. 7, 1926; d. Theophilus Elisha and Martha Virginia (Lloyd) McK.; divorced; 1 child, Myron Herman Johnson Jr. AB, Spelman Coll., 1947; AM, Boston U., 1948; postgrad., Johnson C. Smith U., 1950, U. Wis., 1950-51, U. Colo., 1953, U. Calif., 1966-67, 70, U. Pacific, 1970, San Francisco City Coll., 1971, San Francisco State U., 1976; cert. African Heritage course, U. Ife, Nigeria, 1970; cert. publishing course, Stanford U., 1986. Instr. English Laney Coll., 1975—, No. Peralta Community Coll., 1973-75; instr., chmn. dept. English Peralta Coll., 1971-73; tchr. San Francisco Community Coll., 1966-71; lectr. John Adams Adult Sch., 1966; reader English San Francisco Unified Sch. Dist., 1965-67, educator, 1965; assoc. prof. N.C. Agrl. Tech. State U., 1961-65; from instr. to asst. prof. Morehouse Coll., 1953-61; instr. Carver Mcpl. Jr. Coll., 1951, Winston Salem State Coll., 1948-52; bd. dirs. San Francisco Acad. World Studies; Mother's Day speaker Morehouse Coll., 1959. Contbr. articles to profl. pubs. Trustee San Francisco African Am. Hist. and Cultural Soc. Merrill Faculty fellow Morehouse Coll., 1959, grantee Laney Coll., 1976. Mem. AAUW (life), Nat. Council Tchrs. English (Study Abroad cert. 1959), Calif. Assn. Tchrs. of English, LWV, NAACP (life), No. Calif. Spelman Coll. Club, Nat. Assn. Speech and Dramatic Arts, San Francisco chpt. of the UN Assn., Coll. Lang. Assn. (life), Assn. Study Afro-Am. Life and History (life), Alpha Kappa Alpha, various other orgns. Office: Dept of English Laney Coll 900 Fallon St Oakland CA 94607

MCKINNEY, JOE CHARLES, architectural planner; b. McKinney, Tex., June 28, 1939; s. Joe Majers and Chloe Grace (Chestnutt) McK.; m. Mary Edna Pierce, Jan. 26, 1962; 1 child, Charles Collin. B in Architecture, Tex. Tech. U., 1965. Planner III City of Albuquerque, 1965-67; sr. planner Chambers & Campbell, Inc., Albuquerque, 1967-68, prin. planner, 1968-69; univ. planner U. N.Mex., Albuquerque, 1969—; cons. State Soc. Architects, Morelia, Michoacan, Mex., 1979—. Contbr. articles to profl. jours. Co-chmn. Albuquerque Urban Progress, 1974—; vice-chmn. Old Town Archts. Rev. Bd., City of Albuquerque, 1972-78; bd. dirs. Nob Hill Main St. USA, Inc., Albuquerque, 1985—, Mus. Albuquerque, 1970-73; mem. S.W. council bd. Boy Scouts Am., Albuquerque, 1970-76; vice-chmn. N.Mex. Emergency Services Council, Santa Fe, 1976-78; dir. sr. programs Civil Air Patrol N.Mex., Kirtland AFB, Albuquerque, 1981—. Recipient Award Merit Boy Scouts Am., North Brunswick, N.J., 1976, Meritorious Service award Nat. Bd. Civil Air Patrol, 1983, Loening Aerospace award Nat. Bd. Civil Air Patrol, 1984, Applied Research award Progressive Architecture, 1984. Fellow Nat. Assn. for Search and Rescue Coordinators (bd. dirs. 1973-75); mem. Soc. Coll. and Univ. Planning, N.Mex. Sect. Ptnrs. of the Am.'s (com. chmn. 1979—). Republican. Methodist. Club: U. N.Mex. Faculty (bd. dirs. 1972-74). Avocations: photography, classical music, sports car racing, vintage sports cars, amateur radio. Office: U NMex Office of Architect 1841 Lomas Blvd NE Albuquerque NM 87131

MC KINNEY, JOHN ADAMS, retired construction company executive; b. Huntsville, Tex., Nov. 9, 1923; s. Andrew Todd and Myra (Adams) McK.; m. Cleo Turner, Aug. 31, 1946; children: John Adams, Todd T. B.S., U.S. Naval Acad., 1945; J.D., Georgetown U., 1951. Bar: D.C. 1951, Colo. 1976. Examiner U.S. Patent Office, 1947-51; chief patent counsel Manville Corp., Denver, 1957-71, v.p. legal services, 1971-74, sr. v.p., corp. sec., dir., 1974-76, pres., dir., 1976-86, chief exec. officer, 1977-86, chmn. bd., 1979-86. Served to ensign U.S. Navy, 1945-47. Mem. Am., D.C. bar assns., Am. Patent Law Assn., Licensing Execs. Soc. Office: Ken-Caryl Ranch PO Box 5108 Denver CO 80217

MC KINNEY, MONTGOMERY NELSON, advertising executive; b. Chgo., June 20, 1910; s. William Ayer and Roberta (Montgomery) McK.; m. Virginia Dickey, Nov. 2, 1957; children by previous marriage: Jane McKinney McDonald, William; children: Beth McKinney Lavarn, Robert. B.A., Oberlin Coll., 1934. Sales, sales promotion, advt., treas. Kitchen Art Foods, Inc., Chgo., 1934-40; v.p. Earle Ludgin & Co., Chgo., 1940-55; account supr. Leo Burnett Co., Inc., 1956; v.p. Doyle-Dane Bernbach, Inc., Los Angeles, 1957-69; sr. v.p. client services Doyle-Dane Bernbach, Inc., 1969-75; exec. v.p., dir. client services Chiat/Day, Inc., Los Angeles, 1975-76; chmn. bd. Chiat/Day, Inc., 1976-83; chmn. Doyle Dane Bernbach/West, 1983-86; chmn. DDB Needham West 1986—; mem. faculty Inst. Advanced Advt. Studies, 1964-68. Chmn. campaign Winnetka (Ill.) Community Chest, 1950, pres., 1952; trustee John Thomas Dye Sch., Bel Air, Calif., 1966-75, pres., 1973-75; trustee Oberlin Coll., 1971-85, emeritus trustee, 1986— ; trustee, chmn. fin. com. Winnetka Congregational Ch., 1950-56. Served to lt. USNR, 1944-46. Recipient silver medal Am. Advt. Fedn., 1983. Mem. Am. Assn. Advt. Agys. (gov. So. Calif. council 1972-76, sec.-treas. 1972, vice chmn. 1973, chmn. 1974-75, nat. dir. 1981-83), West States Assn. Advt. Agys. (dir. 1978-83, Advt. Leader of Yr. 1980), Los Angeles Advt. Club. Methodist (trustee 1970-74, vice chmn. 1973-74). Clubs: Riviera Country (Pacific Palisades, Calif.); Los Angeles Athletic. Home: 140 Ocean Park Blvd #625 Santa Monica CA 90405 Office: DDB Needham 5900 Wilshire Blvd Los Angeles CA 90036

MCKINNEY, RITA ESTELLE, needlework designer, instructor; b. Los Angeles, Oct. 25, 1946; d. Virgil William and Herticina (Russell) McCue; m. Edward Derrell McKinney, Mar. 20, 1969; 1 child, Jason Bowden. Student Cerritos Coll., Calif., 1970-71, El Camino Coll., Torrance, Calif., 1966-68; cert. of completion Acad. of Arts, San Francisco, 1965. Asst. art dir. Kierulff Electronics, Los Angeles, 1970-76; prodn. mgr. EPI Advt., Los Angeles, 1972-76; artist, designer The Garden, Downey, Calif., 1976-79; owner, artist, designer Etcetera Designs, Los Angeles, Hanford, Visalia, Calif., 1979-82, Rita Designs, Tulare, Calif., 1982—; pub. relations dir. SDA Orgn., Kings County, Calif., 1980-83. Contbr. articles to Sun Newspapers. Mem. Embroiderers Guild Am., Am. Needlepoint Guild. Home and office: Rita Designs 448 W Allstar Ave Tulare CA 93274

MCKINNON, JAMES BUCKNER, real estate salesman, writer; b. Tacoma, Dec. 5, 1916; s. James Mitchell and Rochelle Lenore (Buckner) McK.; m. Marylyn Adelle Coote, Mar. 12, 1967 (div. May 1977); 1 child, Michelyn; m. Martha Sackmann, June 12, 1977. BA, U. Wash., 1983. Police detective Los Angeles Police Dept., 1946-50; bn. security officer 1st med. bn. 1st Marine div. Fleet Marine Force, 1950-53; owner, operator, mgr. The Saucy Dog Drive-In, Venice, Calif., 1953-63; salesman new car sales and leasing Burien Mercury, Seattle, 1963-66; real estate salesman and appraiser various firms Seattle, 1966—; instr., lectr. U.S. Naval Support Activity, Sandpoint, Wash., 1964-74; mem., lectr. NRC 11-8, Naval Postgrad. Sch., Monterey, Calif., 1975-76. Published poetry in anthologies. Served with USN, 1939-53, PTO, Korea. Recipient Wilmer Culver Meml. award Culver Alumni Fictioneers, Seattle, 1979; Occidental Coll. scholar, 1935, Golden Poet award, 1985-86. Mem. U.S. Naval Inst., N.W. Writers Conf., Ret. Officers Assn. (life). Republican. Club: Am. Mensa Ltd. Lodges: KP, Masons. Home: 2312 41st Ave SW Seattle WA 98116

MCKINZIE, CARL WAYNE, laywer; b. Lubbock, Tex., Dec. 3, 1939; s. J. Clyde and Flora (Cates) McK.; m. Rowena Ann Williams; children: Wayne, Clinton, Morgan. BBA, Tex. Tech U., 1962, MBA, 1963; JD, So. Meth. U., 1966. From assoc. to ptnr. Nossaman, Guthner & Knox, Los Angeles, 1966-80; prin. Riordan & McKinzie, Los Angeles, 1980—. Contbr. articles to law jours. Bd. visitors So. Meth. U. Law Sch., Dallas, 1979-83, bd. dirs. 1970-73, 84—. Served to capt. USAF, 1967-70. Mem. ABA (chmn. current devel. subcom., com. tax problems, 1978-80), Calif. Bar Assn., Los Angeles County Bar Assn. Republican. Clubs: Jonathan, Los Angeles Athletic. Home: 527 21st Pl Santa Monica CA 90402 Office: Riordan & McKinzie 300 S Grand 29th Floor Los Angeles CA 90071

MCKITTRICK, JOSEPH TERRENCE, school administrator, educator; b. Memphis, Aug. 30, 1935; s. Joseph Terrence and Grace Louise (Werner) McK.; m. Donna J. Newman, Aug. 22, 1963 (div. 1964); m. Nancy Joan Christopher, July 3, 1965; children—Michele Tresa, Christopher William. B.A. in Philosophy, Quincy Coll., 1960; M.A. in Edn., Calif. Coast U., 1977, Ph.D. in Edn., 1979. Tchr., coach Cath. High Sch., Memphis, 1960-63; tchr., coach, counselor Dinuba High Sch., Calif., 1963-74; prin. Lovell High Sch., Orosi, Calif., 1974—; instr. Calif. State U.-Fresno, 1980—. Chmn. Dinuba Planning Commn., 1972-75; candidate Dinuba City Council, 1980. Recipient Tchr. in Politics award, 1974; Disting. Pres.'s pin and award Kiwanis Internat., 1980; Cert. of Merit for Outstanding Service in Sch. Dist., 1982; Nat. Appreciation award Soc. Disting. Am. High Sch. Students, 1982. Mem. Calif. Continuation Edn. Assn. (pres. 1976-77, plaque 1978), Assn. Calif. Sch. Adminstrs., Western Assn. Schs. and Coll., State Continuation Adv. Bd. (cert. of appreciation 1978), Phi Delta Kappa. Democrat. Methodist. Home: 636 Davis Dr Dinuba CA 93618 Office: Lovell High Sch 41855 Rd 128 Orosi CA 93647

MC KNIGHT, LENORE RAVIN, child psychiatrist; b. Denver, May 15, 1943; d. Abe and Rose (Steed) Ravin; student Occidental Coll., 1961-63; B.A., U. Colo., 1965, postgrad. in medicine, 1965-67; M.D., U. Calif., San Francisco, 1969; m. Robert Lee McKnight, July 22, 1967; children—Richard Rex, Janet Rose. Cert. adult and child psychiatrist Am. Bd. Psychiatry. Intern pediatrics Children's Hosp., San Francisco, 1969-70; resident in gen. psychiatry Langley Porter Neuropsychiat. Inst., 1970-73, fellow child psychiatry, 1972-74; child psychiatrist Youth Guidance Center, San Francisco, 1974-74; pvt. practice medicine specializing in child psychiatry, Walnut Creek, Calif., 1974—; asst. clin. prof. Langley Porter Neuropsychiat. Inst., 1974—; asst. clin. prof. psychiatry U. Calif. San Francisco Med. Center. Diplomate Am. Bd. Psychiatry and Neurology. Internat. Insts. Edn. fellow U. Edinburgh, summer 1964; NIH grantee to study childhood nutrition, summer 1966. Mem. Am. Acad. Child Psychiatry, Am. Psychiat. Assn., Psychiat. Assn. No. Calif., Am. Med. Women's Assn., Internat., Diablo arabian horse assns. Breeder Arabian horses. Home: 3441 Echo Springs Rd Lafayette CA 94549 Office: 130 LaCasa Via Walnut Creek CA 94598

MCKNIGHT, RALPH GLEDHILL, mining laboratory executive, mining chemist, art retail specialist; b. Provo, Utah, Sept. 21, 1948; s. H. Neil and Utahna (Gledhill) McK.; m. Marianne Wilson, Aug. 23, 1976; children: Nathan, Spencer, Heather, Angela, Bonnie. Student, Oreg. State U., 1966-67; BS, Brigham Young U., 1973; postgrad., U. Utah, 1977, Sierra Coll., 1981, 83-84, U. Calif., 1986. Chief chemist U.S. Nat. Metals, Salt Lake City, 1973-76; geochemist Kennecott Exploration Inc., Salt Lake City, 1976-77; chief metallurgist Internat. Metals, Tooele, Utah, 1977-79; mining cons. Mesa, Ariz., 1979-80; lab. mgr. Sierra Properties Corp., North San Juan, Calif., 1981-83; owner, mgr. Sierra Mineral Analysis, Grass Valley, Calif., 1984—; ptnr. McKnight & Smeaton-Paintings by the Old Masters, San Francisco, 1987—. Inventor electric assay furnace. Active Boy Scouts Am. Brigham Young U. scholar, 1970. Mem. Soc. Mining Engrs. of AIME, Am. Chem. Soc. Mormon. Avocations: photography, genealogy. Office: Sierra Mineral Analysis 13046 Loma Rica Dr #4 PO Box 2524 Grass Valley CA 95945

MC KNIGHT, ROBERT KELLOGG, anthropology educator; b. Sendai, Japan, Jan. 10, 1924; s. William Quay and Mary (Kellogg) McKnight (parents Am. citizens); m. Veronica Margaret Schwartz, Nov. 7, 1947; children: William K., Victoria McKnight Labarge. B.A. cum laude in Psychology, Miami U., Oxford, Ohio, 1951; M.A. in Social Psychology, Ohio State U., 1954, Ph.D. in Anthropology, 1960. Dist. anthropologist Trust Ter. Govt., Palau, Micronesia, 1958-63; community devel. officer Trust Ter. Govt., Saipan, Micronesia, 1963-65; assoc. prof. anthropology U. Wis.-Milw., 1965-66; prof. anthropology Calif. State U., Hayward, 1966-87; chmn. dept. Calif. State U., 1969-74, prof. emeritus, 1987—. Author: (with J. Bennett and H. Passin) In Search of Identity, 1960; contbr. profl. jours. Served with AUS, 1943-46, 51-52. Mem. Am. Anthrop. Assn., AAAS, Am. Ethnol. Soc., Assn. Social Anthropology in Oceania, Internat. House (Japan). Home: 25681 Barnard St Hayward CA 94545 Office: Calif State U Dept Anthropology Hayward CA 94542

MC KOY, BASIL VINCENT CHARLES, theoretical chemist, educator; b. Trinidad, W.I., Mar. 25, 1938; came to U.S., 1960, naturalized, 1973; s. Allan Cecil and Doris Augusta McK.; m. Anne Ellen Shannon, Mar. 18, 1967; 1 son, Christopher Allan. B.Chem. Eng., N.S. Tech. U., 1960; Ph.D. in Chemistry (Univ. fellow), Yale U., 1964. Instr. chemistry Calif. Inst. Tech., 1964-66, asst. prof. chemistry, 1966-69, asso. prof., 1969-75, prof. theoretical chemistry, 1975—, chmn. of faculty, 1985-87; cons. Lawrence Livermore Lab., U. Calif., Livermore, 1974—, Inst. Def. Analysis, 1984—; vis. prof. Max Planck Inst., Munich, Ger., 1976—, U. Paris, 1968—, U. Campinas, Brazil, 1976—; lectr. Nobel Symposium, Goteborg, Sweden, 1979. Contbr. articles to Jour. Physics, London, Chem. Physics Letters, Phys. Rev., Jour. Chem. Physics.; bd. editors: Chem. Physics Jour., 1977-79; co-editor: Electron-Molecule and Photon-Molecule Collisions, 1979, 83, Swarm Studies and Inelastic Electron-Molecule Collisions, 1986; co-author: Electron-Molecule Collisions and Photoionization Processes, 1982. Recipient medal Gov.-Gen. Can., 1960; Alfred P. Sloan Found. fellow, 1969-73; Guggenheim fellow, 1973-74. Fellow Am. Phys. Soc. Home: 3855 Keswick Rd Flintridge CA 91011 Office: Div Chemistry Calif Inst Tech Pasadena CA 91125

MCLACHLAN, CLAUDIA PEARSON, social worker; b. Portland, Oreg., Apr. 9, 1952; d. Keith Milo and Lila Jean (Hartvigsen) Pearson; m. Mark Cooper McLachlan, Jan. 4, 1974; children: Adam Pearson, Erika Jean. BS in Sociology, U. Utah, 1978, MSW, 1986, cert. social welfare, 1978. Foster care caseworker Utah State Family Services, Salt Lake City, 1980-82, assure caseworker, 1983-87; guidance counselor Granite Sch. Dist., Salt Lake City, 1987—. Vol. to organize, develop and act as chmn. for Family Resource Vol. Program div. Family Services, 1981-85. Mem. Nat. Assn. Social Workers, Phi Kappa Phi. Democrat. Mormon. Avocations: jogging, skiing, traveling, gardening. Home: 1758 S 2600 E Salt Lake City UT 84108

MCLAIN, BARBARA RUTH, nurse, educator; b. Holyoke, Mass., Feb. 10, 1947; d. Vincent Russell and Ruth Elizabeth (Williams) McL. BS, U. Mass., 1969; MS, Boston U., 1974; EdD, U. San Francisco, 1985. From staff nurse to head nurse and clin. specialist Beth Israel Hosp., Boston, 1977; sr. instr. nursing U. Colo., Denver, 1977-78; assoc. clin. prof. nursing U. Calif., San Francisco, 1978—; clin. instr. Boston State Coll., 1975-77; assoc. dir. family nurse practitioner program U. Calif., San Francisco, 1981—; commr. Calif. Joint Practice Commn.; pres., bd. dirs. Southeast San Francisco Area Health Edn. Ctr., 1983-85. Contbr. articles to profl. jours. HHS grantee, 1980—, Calif. Health Manpower Policy Commn. grantee, 1980—, NIH grantee, 1984-85. Mem. Am. Nurses Assn., Sigma Theta Tau. Club: Dolphi South End Runners (San Francisco). Office: U Calif San Francisco Sch Nursing 513 Parnassus Ave San Francisco CA 94143

MCLAIN, WILLIAM ALLEN, lawyer; b. Chgo., Oct. 19, 1942; s. William Rex and Wilma L. (Raschka) McL.; m. Cynthia Lee Szatkowski, Sept. 3, 1966; children—William A., David M., Heather A. B.S., So. Ill. U., 1966; J.D., Loyola U., Chgo., 1971. Bar: Ill. 1971, U.S. Dist. Ct. (no. dist.) Ill. 1971, U.S. Ct. Appeals (7th cir.) 1971, Colo. 1975, U.S. Dist. Ct. Colo. 1975, U.S. Ct. Appeals (10th cir.) 1975. Law clk. U.S. Dist. Ct. (no. dist.) Ill., Chgo., 1971-72; assoc. Sidley & Austin, Chgo., 1972-75; ptnr. Welborn, Dufford, Brown & Tooley, Denver, 1975-86; pres. William A. McLain PC, 1986—, Interact, Inc., 1986—. Mem. Dist. 10 Legis. Vacancy Commn., Denver, 1984-86. Served with U.S. Army, 1966-68. Recipient Leadership and Scholastic Achievement award Loyola U. Alumni Assn., 1971. Mem. ABA, Colo. Bar Assn. (lobbyist 1983-85), Denver Bar Assn., Assn. Trial Lawyers Am., Colo. Assn. Commerce and Industry (legis. policy council 1983—), Colo. Mining Assn. (state and local affairs com. 1978—). Republican. Clubs: Denver Athletic; Pueblo Country (Colo.), Roundup Riders of the Rockies. Lodges: Masons, Shriners, Scottish Rite, York Rite. Home: 8679 Doane Pl Denver CO 80231 Office: 1700 Broadway Suite 500 Denver CO 80290

MCLANE, SUSAN MARGARET, investment company executive; b. San Francisco, Feb. 4, 1956; d. Roy E. and Sally McLane; m. Robert N. Block, Mar. 8, 1980. Student with honors, San Jose State U., 1974-76; BA with honors, UCLA, 1979, MBA, 1987. Acct. Kendall & Warner, CPA's, Los Angeles, 1981; v.p., treas. Pacific Fin. Research, Beverly Hills, Calif., 1981—; treas. Clipper Fund, Inc., Beverly Hills, 1984—, also bd. dirs., 1984—. Mem. Phi Beta Kappa, Beta Gamma Sigma, Alpha Phi. Avocations: dance, theatre, lit. Home: 7941 Electra Dr Los Angeles CA 90046 Office: Pacific Fin Research 9601 Wilshire Blvd Suite 828 Beverly Hills CA 90210

MCLAREN, CYNTHIA JANE, marketing professional; b. Ames, Iowa, Nov. 29, 1946; d. John D. and Elizabeth Jane (Little) Kaufman. BA, U. Minn., 1968, MA, 1970. Supr. research Campbell-Mithun Advt., Mpls., 1970-71; project analyst Applied Mgmt. Scis., Silver Springs, Md., 1972; analyst ops. research EPA, Washington, 1973-76; v.p. The NPD Group, Rosemont, Ill., 1976-85; sr. v.p., regional mgr. Info. Resources, Inc., Los Angeles, 1985—. Co-editor Decision-Maker's Guide to Solid Waste Management., 1975. Mem. Am. Mktg. Assn. (Los Angeles and San Francisco chpts.). Club: Los Angeles Ad. Avocations: tennis, skiing, attending ballet. Home: 5512 Pacific Ave Marina del Rey CA 90292 Office: Info Resources Inc 4551 Glencoe Ave Suite 225 Marina del Rey CA 90292

MCLARNAN, DONALD EDWARD, banker, corporation executive; b. Nashua, Iowa, Dec. 19, 1906; s. Samuel and Grace (Prudhon) McL.; m. Virginia Rickard, May 5, 1939; children: Marilyn, Marcia, Roxane. A.B., U. So. Calif., 1930; grad., Southwestern U. Law Sch., 1933; postgrad., Cambridge U. Trust appraiser, property mgr. Security-Pacific Nat. Bank, Los Angeles, 1935-54; regional dir. SBA for, So. Calif., Ariz., Nev., 1954-61; area adminstr. SBA for, Alaska, Western U.S., Hawaii, Guam, Samoa, U.S. Trust Terr., 1969-73; pres. Am. MARC, Inc. (offshore oil drillers and mfr. diesel engines), 1961-63, Terminal Drilling & Prodn. Co., Haney & Williams Drilling Co., Western Offshore, 1961-63; v.p., dir. Edgemar Dairy, Santa Monica Dairy Co., 1954-70; founder, pres., chmn. bd. Mission Nat. Bank, 1963-67; pres. Demco Trading Co., Mut. Trading Co.; dir. Coast Fed. Savs. & Loan; cons. numerous corps.; guest lectr. various univs. Contbr. articles on mgmt. and fin. to profl. jours. Chmn. fed. agys. div. Community Chest, 1956; nat. pres. Teachers Day, 1956; bd. councillors U. So. Calif.; founder, chmn., pres. Soc. Care and Protection Injured Innocent; adv. bd. Los Angeles City Coll.; bd. dirs. Calif. Easter Seal Soc.; nat. chmn. U. So. Calif. Drug Abuse Program. Recipient Los Angeles City and County Civic Leadership award, 1959. Mem. Nat. Assn. People with Disabilities (pres.); Mem. Skull and Dagger, Delta Chi. Clubs: Mason (Los Angeles) (K.T., Shriner), Los Angeles (Los Angeles), Jonathan (Los Angeles). Home: 135 S Norton Ave Los Angeles CA 90004 Office: 1111 S Crenshaw Blvd Los Angeles CA 90019

MCLAUGHLIN, CALVIN STURGIS, biochemistry educator; b. St. Joseph, Mo., May 29, 1936; s. Calvin Sturgis and Agnes Jane McLaughlin; m. Chin Helen Moy, Sept. 7, 1960; children—Heather Chin Chu, Christine Leng Oy, Andrew Calvin Moy. B.S., King Coll., 1958; postgrad., Yale U., 1958-59; Ph.D., MIT, 1960. Postdoctoral fellow Institut de Biologie Physico-Chimique, Paris, 1964-66; prof. biochemistry U. Calif., Irvine, 1966—, dir. Cancer Research Inst., 1981-83; vis. prof. Sch. Botany Oxford U., Eng., 1976, 80; mem. peer rev. panels Am. Cancer Soc., NSF, NIH, VA. Contbr. numerous articles to profl. jours.; mem. editorial bds. Jour. Bacteriology, 1975-80, Exptl. Mycology, 1980-86; reviewer profl. jours. Bd. dirs. Am. Cancer Soc., Orange County, 1980—; mem. Traffic Affairs Com., Newport Beach, Calif., 1972-78. Named Outstanding Tchr. U. Calif.-Irvine, 1978, Gabriel Lester Meml. Lectr. Reed Coll., 1979; fellow Rockefeller Found., 1958-59, Upjohn Found., 1959-60, Nutrition Found., 1960-61, NIH, 1961-64, Am. Cancer Soc., 1964-66. Mem. Genetics Soc. Am., Am. Soc. Biol. Chemistry, Am. Soc. Microbiology, Am. Soc. Mycology, Am. Soc. for Cell Biology, Yeast Genetics and Molecular Biology Soc. Am. (co-chair 1986—). Presbyterian. Office: U Calif-Irvine Dept Biol Chemistry Irvine CA 92717

MCLAUGHLIN, CONSTANCE NETHKEN, science educator; b. Elkins, W.Va., Feb. 3, 1949; d. Ralph David and Helen Irene (Shreve) Nethken; m. Terry Walthall McLaughlin, May 23, 1970; 1 child, Veronica Lynn. BS in Chemistry, W.Va. U., 1971; MA in Sci. Edn., U. No. Colo., 1980. Cert. tchr., Colo. Tchr. Jefferson County Schs., Lakewood, Colo., 1982—; participant Personal Consultation Cadre Jefferson County Schs. Methodist. Avocations: woodworking, camping.

MCLAUGHLIN, HAROLD JOSEPH, management consultant; b. Dearborn, Mich., Aug. 21, 1932; s. Harold Liman and Josephine Rose (Kneip) McL.; m. Beverly Jo Kinsman, Oct. 8, 1955; children—Jacqueline Ann, Michael Joseph. E.E., Elec. Inst. Tech., 1957; Ph.D., U. Beverly Hills, 1980. Sr. project engr. Bryant Computer Products, Walled Lake, Mich., 1960-63; sales mgr. mnemotrom div. TMC, Stamford, Conn., 1964; various mktg. positions Digital Devel. Corp., San Diego, 1965-71; nat. sales mgr. Pacific Nat. Micronetics, San Diego, 1971-72; product mgr. Data Disc., Inc., Sunnyvale, Calif., 1972-74; dir. mktg. Memory Byte Tech., Santa Clara, Calif., 1974; mktg. mgr. Fairchild Memory Systems, San Jose, Calif., 1976-77; mktg. mgr. peripheral products div. Electronic Memories and Magnetics, San Jose, 1977-79; cons. Bus. Research Cons., Inc., San Jose, 1974-76, 1979—. Author: Building Your Business Plan, A Step By Step Approach, 1984. Contbr. articles to profl. jours. Patentee in field. Served with U.S. Army, 1952-54. Mem. IEEE, IEEE Computer Soc., Profl. Tech. Cons. Assn. Home and Office: Bus Research Cons Inc 971 Yarmouth Way San Jose CA 95120

MCLAUGHLIN, JAMES DANIEL, architect; b. Spokane, Wash., Oct. 2, 1947; s. Robert Francis and Patricia (O'Connel) McL.; B.Arch., U. Idaho, 1971; m. Willa Kay Pace, Aug. 19, 1972; children—Jamie Marie, Robert James. Project architect Neil M. Wright, Architect, AIA, Sun Valley, Idaho, 1971-74, McMillan & Hayes, Architects, Sun Valley, 1974-75; now pres., prin. McLaughlin Architects Chartered, Sun Valley. Prin. works include Oakridge Apts., Moscow, Idaho (Excellence in Design award AIA), Walnut Ave. Mall, Ketchum, Idaho (Excellence in Design award AIA, 1987), McMahan Residence, Sun Valley (Excellence in Design award AIA, 1987). Chmn., Ketchum Planning and Zoning Commn., Ketchum Planning Commn., Ketchum Zoning Commn.; vice chmn. Sun Valley Planning and Zoning Commn. Served to 1st lt. U.S. Army. Registered architect, 8 states including Idaho. Mem. AIA (award of Excellence for Walnut Ave. Mall in Sun Valley, award of Excellence for William McMahan Residence in Sun Valley 1987), Nat. Council Archtl. Registration Bds., Nat. Home Builders Assn., Ketchum-Sun Valley C. of C. (dir.). Roman Catholic. Club: Rotary. Prin. archtl. works include James West Residence, First Fed. Savs., Fox Bldg. Rehab., Walnut Ave. Mall, First St. Office Bldg. Home: Lot #5 Red Cliffs Subdivision Box 6 Ketchum ID 83340 Office: McLaughlin Architects Chartered PO Box 479 Sun Valley ID 83353

MCLAUGHLIN, MARGUERITE P., state senator, logging company executive; m. Bruce McLaughlin; 3 children. Owner, operator contract logging firm, Orofino, Idaho; former mem. Idaho Ho. of Reps.; now mem. Idaho Senate. Trustee Joint Sch. Dist. 171; pres. Orofino Celebration, Inc. Democrat. Offfice: Idaho State Senate Boise ID 83720

MCLAUGHLIN, RICHARD H., retail executive; b. Butte, Mont., July 31, 1947; s. Donald J. Sr. and Mary E. (Edsall) McL.; m. Karen L. Bennetts; children: Brittany, John. BA in Math., U. Mont., 1970. Tchr. Helena (Mont.) Jr. High, 1970-74; Sales rep. Don's Office Machine Co., Butte, 1974-79, pres., 1979—. Convention chmn. Western Office Machine Dealers Assn., Denver, 1985. Mem. C. of C. (bd. dirs. Butte Silver Bow Co. 1986), Mont. Office Machine Dealers Assn. (pres. 1984). Club: Exchange. Avocations: fishing, skiing, sports. Office: Dons Office machine Co 2009 Harrison Ave Butte MT 59701

MCLAUGHLIN, VANESSA LEE, marketing consultant company executive; b. Eugene, Oreg., Aug. 27, 1956; d. Jerald P. and Gloria J. Totman; m. Todd S. McLaughlin, Mar. 27, 1982; children: Colin Bryce, Gavin Taggart. Student U. Ariz., 1975-77; B.S. in real Estate Fin., U. Oreg., 1979. Account exec. Sta. KYES, Roseburg, Oreg., 1981; account exec. KRSB-FM, Roseburg, 1982; account exec. Sta. KPNW-AM-FM, 1982; owner AdSpectrum Mktg. Cons., Roseburg, 1982—; dir. pub. relations, bd. dirs. Consumer Credit Counseling. Mem. brochure com. Visitors and Conv. Bur., Roseburg; bd. dirs. Umpqua Valley Arts Assn., 1984. Mem. Bus. and Profl. Women (Young Careerist award Douglas County chpt., 1983), Mid-Oreg. Advt. Club (Woody Award of Excellence, 1985), Roseburg C. of C. (pub. relations com., 1986—, pioneer award com., 1986—, greeter's com.), Umpqua Valley Rep. Women. Club: Roseburg Country. Home: 338 W Riverside Dr Roseburg OR 97470 Office: PO Box 2098 Roseburg OR 97470

MCLAUGHLIN, WILLIAM IRVING, space technical manager; b. Oak Park, Ill., Mar. 6, 1935; s. William Lahey and Eileen (Irving) McL.; student Calif. Inst. Tech., 1953-57; B.S., U. Calif.-Berkeley, 1963, M.A., 1966, Ph.D., 1968; m. Karen Bjorneby, Aug. 20, 1960; children—William, Margot, Walter, Eileen. Mem. tech. staff Bellcomm, Inc., 1968-71; mem. tech. staff Jet Propulsion Lab., Pasadena, Calif., 1971—; supr. terrestrial planets mission design group, 1981-83, mission design mgr. for Infrared Astron. Satellite, 1982-83, mgr. flight engring. office for Voyager/Uranus project, 1983-86; mgr. mission profile and sequencing sect., 1986—. Served with USMC, 1957-60. Recipient Apollo Achievement award, 1969, Exceptional Service medal NASA, 1984, Outstanding Leadership medal NASA, 1986. Fellow Brit. Interplanetary Soc.; mem. Internat. Acad. Astros., Phi Beta Kappa, Sigma Xi. Monthly columnist Spaceflight mag., 1982—. Home: 4626 Janvier Way LaCrescenta CA 91214 Office: 4800 Oak Grove Dr Pasadena CA 91109

MC LAURIN, FRANCIS WALLIN (FRANK), radio broadcasting exec.; b. Sioux Falls, S.D., Sept. 24, 1923; s. Archibald A. and Clementine B. (Wallin) McL.; student Calif. Jr. Coll., 1941-42; m. Barbara Lee Jones, May 26, 1956; 1 dau., Barbara Lyn. Announcer sta. KGGM, Albuquerque, 1946; in prodn., sta. KFXM, San Bernardino, Calif., 1947-51; gen. mgr. sta. KWRN, Reno, 1951-52; account exec. KFMB TV, San Diego, 1953-54; gen. mgr. sta. KSRO, Santa Rosa, Calif., 1954—; dir., v.p. Finley Broadcasting Co., Santa Rosa. Mem. broadcast adv. bd. UPI. Bd. dirs. Boy Scouts Am. Recipient Young Man of Yr. award, Santa Rosa Jr. C. of C., 1957; Calif. Broadcasters Disting. award, 1984. Mem. Calif. Broadcasters Assn. (dir., past chmn.), Nat. Assn. Broadcasters (dir.), Santa Rosa C. of C. (pres. 1960). Republican. Presbyterian. Rotarian (pres. 1966-67). Home: 1708 Pamela Dr Santa Rosa CA 95404 Office: Sta KSRO College Ave Santa Rosa CA 95403

MCLEAN, HUGH ANGUS, management consultant; b. Salt Lake City, Feb. 19, 1925; s. George Mark and Rose (Powell) McL.; m. Martha Lane Green, Nov. 23, 1949; children: Michael Hugh, Merrie Smithson. Student, U. Kans., 1943-44; BSME, Iowa State U., 1946; postgrad., U. Utah, 1946, 61-66. Registered profl. engr., Utah. With Utah Oil Refining Co., Boise, Idaho, Twin Falls, Idaho and Salt Lake City, 1953-61, Am. Oil Co., Salt Lake City and 11 western states, 1961-66; cons. Standard Oil (Ind.), Chgo., 1966-69; v.p. Mahler Assocs., Midland Park, N.J., 1969-76; pres. McLean Mgmt. Systems, Wyckoff, N.J., 1976-84, Heber City, Utah, 1984—. Author: There is a Better Way to Manage, 1982, Developmental Dialogues, 1972, Career Planning Program, 1975; creator, host (TV) live shows and commls., 1956-57. Rep. election judge, Salt Lake City, 1964, Operation Eagle Eye, Chgo., 1968; pub. communications dir. Ch. Jesus Christ Latter-day Saints, N.Y. metro area, 1981-84. Served to lt. (j.g.) USNR, 1943-46. Recipient Silver award Am. Petroleum Inst., 1957. Mem. Am. Soc. Tng. Devel. (chmn. N.Y. metro chpt. field trips 1972-74). Home: 3384 S Mill Rd Heber City UT 84032 Office: McLean Mgmt Systems PO Box 251 Heber City UT 84032

MCLEAN, RICHARD CAMERON, judge; b. Denver, Nov. 6, 1931; s. Leslie Robert and Alberta Martha (Payne) McL.; m. Carolyn Lee Lindseth, May 28, 1955 (div. 1977); children: Scott Cameron, Joan McLean-Braun. BA, Stanford U., 1954; LLB, U. Colo., 1958. Bar: Colo. Law clk. U.S. Courts, Denver, 1959; ptnr. Bayer, McLean & Carey, Denver, 1960-80; judge 20th Jud. Dist., Boulder, Colo., 1980—. Mem. city council, Boulder, 1970-73, Mayor, 1972-73, open space trustee, 1978-80. Served to 1st lt. U.S. Army, 1955-57. Fellow Am. Coll. Trial Lawyers; mem. ABA, Colo. Bar Assn., Boulder Bar Assn. Democrat. Avocations: amateur astronomy, skiing, scuba diving. Home: 2059 Hardscrabble Dr Boulder CO 80303 Office: PO Box 471 Boulder CO 80306

MCLEAN, ROBERT GEORGE, ecologist, epidemiologist, researcher; b. Warren, Ohio, Jan. 10, 1938; s. Francis Horace and Dorothy Ellen (Sells) McL.; m. Carol Lenore Toth, Sept 10, 1960; children: Jennifer Ellen, Caroline Beth. BS in Edn., BS, Bowling Green State U., 1961, MA, 1963; PhD, Pa. State U., 1966. Cheif parasitology br. 3d U.S. Army Med. Lab., Ft. McPherson, Ga., 1966-68; biology instr. Ga. State U., Atlanta, 1967-68; research ecologist rabies control unit Ctrs. Disease Control, Lawrenceville, Ga., 1968-73; research ecologist vertebrate ecology and arbovirus ecology brs. Ctrs. Disease Control, Ft. Collins, Colo., 1973-82, research ecologist arbovirus ecology br., 1984—; research ecologist med. entomology research and tng. unit Ctrs. Disease Control, Guatemala City, Guatemala, 1982-84; mem. faculty dept. zoology Colo State U., Ft. Collins, 1974—. Editor: (asst.) Profl. Journal Wildlife Diseases, 1984—; contbr. articles to profl. jours. Chmn. bd. dirs. Parent Adv. Bds. Pub. Schs., Ft. Collins, 1974-82. Served to capt. U.S. Army, 1966-68. Recipient Outstanding Service award Ctrs. Disease Control, 1975. Mem. Wildlife Disease Assn. (com. chmn. 1975, 81, 87), Am. Soc. Tropical Medicine and Hygiene, Ecol. Soc. Am., Am. Soc. Mammalogists, Assn. Tropical Biology, Western Bird Banding Assn. Avocations: sports, hiking, photography, travel, camping. Home: 318 N Shields Fort Collins CO 80521 Office: Ctrs Disease Control Arbovirus Ecology Br Box 2087 Fort Collins CO 80522-2087

MCLEAN, ROBIN JENNIFER, marketing professional; b. Denver, Dec. 15, 1960; d. Robert Earl and Marjorie Lee (Worland) McL. BA, U. Denver, 1983, postgrad., 1986—. Prodn. asst. Sta. KOA, Denver; advt. intern Colle & McVoy, Englewood, Colo.; advt. sales rep. Dow Jones & Co., Inc., Englewood, 1983-85; acct. exec. Univ. Graphics, Inc., Englewood, 1985-86; mktg. asst. MPS, Inc., Denver, 1986—; v.p. Columbine Mktg., Denver, 1986—; advisor U. Denver, 1985—. Mem. Internat. Assn. Bus. Communicators, Bus./Profl. Advt. Assn., Denver Art Mus., Nat. Hist. Preservation Soc. Republican. Roman Catholic. Avocations: skiing, swimming, hiking, dancing, reading. Home: 1601 Hudson St Denver CO 80220 Office: Columbine Mktg 255 Clayton St Denver CO 80206

MCLEAN, STEPHEN RUSSELL, mechanical, environmental engineering educator; b. Columbia, Mo., May 21, 1949; s. Eugene Otis and Marjorie Inez (Russell) McL.; m. Valerie Jean Phillips, Aug. 10, 1973; children: Lee Anthony, Sarah Elizabeth. BS, Miami U., Oxford, Ohio, 1971; PhD, U. Wash., 1976. Postdoctoral fellow U. Wash., Seattle, 1976-78; research scientist U. Kiel, Fed. Republic Germany, 1978-80; asst. prof. mech., environ. engring. U. Calif., Santa Barbara, 1980-86, assoc. prof., 1986—; cons. VSE Corp., Camarillo, Calif., 1985-86. Contbr. articles to profl. jours. Mem. AAAS, ASME, Am. Geophys. Union. Mem. Ch. of Christ. Home: 476 Pintura Dr Santa Barbara CA 93111 Office: U Calif Dept Mech Environ Engring Santa Barbara CA 93106

MCLEOD, DOUGLAS KENNETH, civil and structural engineer, consultant; b. Huntington Park, Calif., May 22, 1944; s. Reginald George Anderson and Joan E. (McDonald) Larrison; m. Kathleen Featherstone, June 3, 1969; 1 child, Elizabeth Kim. Student, U. Alaska, 1971-73, BSCE, 1975; student, U. Hawaii, Manoa, 1973-75. Registered profl. engr., Alaska, Oreg. Comml. pilot Kenai (Alaska) Air Service, 1968-70, Kodiak (Alaska) Airways, 1970-71; civil engr. Philleo Engring. and Archtl. Service, Fairbanks, Alaska, 1975-78; prin. Arctic Designers, Fairbanks, 1978—; chief engr. Kalen and Assocs., Fairbanks, 1982—; cons. City of Fairbanks, Fairbanks North Star Borough, U. Alaska Facilities Planning and Constrn. Pres. Chena Goldstream Fire and Rescue, Fairbanks, 1983-85; ruling elder Univ. Community Presbyn. Ch., Fairbanks, 1980-85; mem. Interior Adoptive Parents, Faribanks, 1983—; mem. Fairbanks Light Opera Theater, 1978—, tech. dirs. for Oliver, set designer for Oliver, Music Man and Mikado. Served with U.S. Army, 1965-67. Mem. ASCE (pres. 1977-78 Alaska chpt., Pres.'s Citation, 1978), Internat. Conf. Bldg. Officals Alaska, NSPE, Earthquake Engring. Inst., Seismol. Soc. Am., Instn. Civil Engrs. (Great Britain, grad.) Tau Beta Pi. Club: Wash. Athletic. Avocations: flying (fixed wing and helicopters), performance in mus. theater and ch. choir, cross country skiing, swimming. Office: Arctic Designers PO Box 82190 Fairbanks AK 99708

MCLEOD, JOHN HUGH, JR., mechanical and electrical engineer; b. Hattiesburg, Miss., Feb. 27, 1911; s. John Hugh and Martha (Caldwell) McL.; m. Suzette Boutell, June 23, 1951; children—John Hugh III, Robert Boutell. B.S., Tulane U., 1933. Registered profl. engr., Calif. Engr. various firms, 1933-39; field engr. Taylor Instrument Co., Rochester, N.Y., 1940-42; research and devel. engr. Leeds & Northrup Co., Pa., 1943-47; sect. head guidance systems and guided missiles U.S. Naval Air Missile Test Ctr., Point Mugu, Calif., 1947-56; design specialist Gen. Dynamics/Astronautics, San Diego, 1956-63, cons., 1963-64; pvt. practice mech. and elec. engring. cons., La Jolla, Calif., 1964—; mem. exec. com. Fall Joint Computer Conf. Am. Fedn. Info. Processing Socs., 1965. Author: Simulation: The Dynamic Modeling of Ideas and Systems with Computers, 1968, Computer Modeling and Simulation: Principles of Good Practice, 1982; editor, pub.: Simulation Council Newsletter, 1952-55, editor, 1955—; editor: Simulation, 1963—; editor Simulation in the Service of Soc., 1971—; co-author: Large-Sclae Models for Policy Evaluation, 1977. Recipient Sr. Sci. Simulation award Electronic Assocs., Inc., 1965, TIMS award, 1986; NEH, NSF grantee, 1983. Mem. IEEE, Soc. Computer Simulation. Home: 8484 La Jolla Shores Dr La Jolla CA 92037 Office: Soc Computer Simulation PO Box 17900 San Diego CA 92117

MCLEOD, LESLIE ANN, public relations executive, writer; b. St. Louis, Mar. 11, 1960; d. Russell W. and Ruth E. King; m. Daniel S. McLeod, Sept. 7, 1985. AA, Pasadena City Coll., 1978-80; BS, Calif. State Poly. U., Pomona, 1983. Pub. relations coordinator Pomona Valley Community Hosp., 1982—. Contbr. articles to bus. mags. Named one of Outstanding Young Women Am., 1981. Mem. Internat. Assn. Bus. Communicators, Pub. Relations Soc. Am., So. Calif. Soc. Hosp. Pub. Relations (writer, program coordinator, Best in State award 1983), Portfolio (publicity coordinator 1983-84), Phi Kappa Phi.

MCLEOD, W(ILLIAM) CURTIS, civil engineer; b. North Bend, Oreg., Feb. 12, 1935; s. William Rhue and Alice Eliza (Curtis) McL.; m. Janet Johnson, June 23, 1956; children: Deborah D. Wolfgram, Pamela L. BSCE, Oreg. State U., 1957; MS in Mechanics and Hydraulics, U. Iowa, 1959. Registered profl. engr., Calif., Colo. Iowa, Oreg., Wash. Engr. Bechtel Corp., San Francisco, 1959-65, Stanley Cons., Muscatine, Iowa, 1965-67; project mgr. CH2M Hill, Corvallis, Oreg., 1967-80; regional chief engr. CH2M Hill, Denver, 1980—. Advisor Jr. Achievement, Denver, 1985. Mem. NSPE, Am. Acad. Environ. Engrs., Am. Pub. Works Assn., Am. Water Works Assn., Water Pollution Control Fedn. Republican. Home: 5760 Green Oaks Dr Littleton CO 80121 Office: CH2M Hill PO Box 22508 Denver CO 80222

MCLIN, STEPHEN T., banker; b. St. Louis, Nov. 11, 1946; s. Leonard Dale and Hazel (Goodlett) McL.; m. Rebecca Missen, Dec. 26, 1965 (div. 1975); children: Cynthia Jeanne, Stephen Dale; m. Catherine Anne Crespi, Oct. 12, 1981; children: Scott Thomas, Stephanie Therese. BS in Chem. Engring., U. Ill.-Urbana, 1968; MS in Mech. Engring., Stanford U., 1970, MBA, 1972. Research engr. Atlantic Richfield Corp., Anaheim, Calif., 1968-69; staff officer First Chgo. Corp., 1972-74; asst. v.p. Bank of Am., San Francisco, 1972-75, v.p., 1975-81, sr. v.p., 1979-86, exec. v.p., 1986-87; pres. Am. First Fin. Corp., San Francisco, 1987—; professorial lectr. Golden Gate U., San Francisco, 1976-82. Bd. regents JFK U., Orinda, Calif., 1977-81. Recipient Disting. Service award Golden Gate U., 1982. Mem. Council Planning Execs., Assn. Corp. Growth. Clubs: San Francisco Golf, Bankers (San Francisco); Contra Costa Country (Pleasant Hill, Calif.); Blackhawk (Calif.) Country. Office: Am First Fin Corp 555 California St PO Box 1725 San Francisco CA 94101

MC LURE, CHARLES E., JR., economist; b. Sierra Blanca, Tex., Apr. 14, 1940; s. Charles E. and Dessie (Evans) McL.; m. Patsy Nell Carroll, Sept. 17, 1962. B.A., U. Kans., 1962; M.A., Princeton U., 1964, Ph.D., 1966. Asst. prof. econs. Rice U., Houston, 1965-69, assoc. prof., 1969-72, prof., 1972-79, Allyn R. and Gladys M. Cline prof. econs., 1973-79; exec. dir. for research Nat. Bur. Econ. Research, Cambridge, Mass., 1977-78, v.p., 1978-81; sr. fellow Hoover Instn., Stanford U., 1981—; dep. asst. sec. Dept. Treasury, 1983-85; sr. staff economist Council Econ. Advisers, Washington, 1969-70; vis. lectr. U. Wyo., 1972; vis. prof. Stanford U., 1973; cons. U.S. Treasury Dept., Labor Dept., World Bank, UN, Com. Econ. Devel., IMF, govts. Can., Colombia, Malaysia, Panama, Jamaica, Bolivia, Indonesia. Author: Fiscal Failure: Lessons of the Sixties, 1972, (with N. Ture) Value Added Tax: Two Views, 1972, (with M. Gillis) La Reforma Tributaria Colombiana de 1974, 1977, Must Corporate Income Be Taxed Twice?, 1979, Economic Perperspective on State Taxation of Multijurisdictional Corporations, 1986, The Value Added Tax: Key to Deficit Reduction, 1987; also numerous articles on econs. and public finance. Ford Found. faculty research fellow, 1967-68. Mem. Am. Econ. Assn., Nat. Tax Assn. (dir.), editorial bd. jour.), Beta Theta Pi. Home: 250 Yerba Santa Ave Los Altos CA 94022 Office: Hoover Instn Stanford CA 94305

MCMAHAN, CELESTE TINA, architectural and construction manager; b. Denver, Jan. 1, 1948; d. Frank McMahan and Jean Dolores (Graves) Kauno; m. George Cardinal Richards, Dec. 2, 1977. B.S. in Urban Studies, U. Colo., 1976, M.S. in Urban and Regional Planning, 1977, postgrad. in architecture, 1977. Lic. real estate salesman Colo. Housing sales coordinator Gt. Western United, Colorado City, Colo., 1970-74; dir. parks and recreation City of Edgewater, Colo., 1975-76; intern WICHE, 1976; intern planner City of Aurora, Colo., 1976-77; project mgr./architect Stanford U., Calif., 1977-79; designer, facilities planner Sacramento Savs., 1979-80; project mgr. Crocker Bank, San Francisco, 1980-81, Bank of Am., San Francisco, 1981—, team mgr. No. Calif. project devel., 1987—; owner McMahan Assocs., Vallejo, Calif., 1979—. Author: A Market Analysis of Downtown, 1976; Housing Market and Population Projections, 1976; Tales From the Old Country, 1984. Photographer. Mem. archtl. com. San Francisco Traditional Jazz Found., 1985; commr. Archtl. Rev. Bd., Menlo Park, Calif., 1978; mem. com. Gov.'s Housing Policy Com., Rural Subcom. on Housing Legis., Social Concerns Legis. Com., Denver, liason com. to form Aurora Community Devel. Corp., 1976; bd. dirs. Bay Area Lawyers for the Arts, Women's Evening Orgn., 1986; mem. congl. council Grace Cathedral, 1987, devel. com., 1986-87; San Francisco Friends of Arts, 1984. Recipient 1st place award Music Educators Assn. Ensemble Festival, 1965; ednl. grantee U. Colo., 1974-77. Mem. Orgn. Women Architects, AIA, Nat. Assn. Women in Constrn., Women Evening Orgn. (v.p.), Grace Cathedral Devel. Com., Bay Area Lawyers for the Arts (bd. dirs.), Nat. Assn. Corp. Real Estate,

Downtown Aurora Mchts. Assn. (hon.), Internat. Acad. Lymphology (Cert.),, Internat. Platform Assn., Stanford U. Alumni Assn. Episcopalian. Club: Commonwealth (San Francisco). Home: PO Box 26084 San Francisco CA 94126-6084 Office: Bank of Am Corporate Real Estate Dept 560 Davis San Francisco CA 94111

MCMAHON, JAMES PATRICK, ecologist; b. Chgo., July 10, 1951; s. James Patrick and Helen Margaret (Walter) McM. B in Ecology, U. Ill., 1974; postgrad., Cen. Wash. U., 1975-76. Prin. Seattle Recycling, Inc., 1978-79; project mgr. City of Seattle, 1979-80, Fibres Internat., Bellevue, Wash., 1980-85; prin. Environ. Enhancement Group, Lynnwood, Wash., 1985—. Exec. producer (video) Recycling in Washington State, 1985, conducted numerous bus. seminars. Mem. survey and nat. conf. coms. Dept. Ecology, 1985-86; bd. dirs. Nat. Recycling Coalition, 1983-86. Mem. Wash. State Recycling Assn. (v.p. 1984-85), Nature Conservancy, Greater Seattle C. of C., Mcpl. League. Club: Trout Unltd. Avocations: skiing, fly fishing. Home and Office: 4920 200th SW A 305 Lynnwood WA 98036

MCMAHON, RICHARD EARL, manufacturing company executive; b. Delaware, Ohio, Feb. 8, 1940; s. Thomas Henry and Evelyn Ruth (Milligan) McM.; m. Rebecca Ann Piper, Dec. 31, 1966; children: Kimberly Shawn, Ricky Thomas, Kerri Dionne. Diploma in sci., Riverside Mil. Acad., 1958; AA in Law, Glendale (Ariz.) Community Coll., 1974; BS in Scis., BS in Bus., Grand Canyon Coll., 1977. Sr. quality engr. Gen. Electric Co., Phoenix, 1963-70; sr. indsl. engr. Honeywell Corp., Phoenix, 1970-80; mgr. mfg. engring. Sperry Flights Systems subs. Sperry Co., Phoenix, 1980-83; mgr. prodn. Cal Comp, Phoenix, 1983—; owner McMahon Enterprises, Phoenix, 1963—. Coach Sunnyslope Soccer Club, Phoenix. Served as cpl. USMC, 1958-62. Recipient Leatherneck High Rifle award Leatherneck mag., Paris Island, S.C., 1958. Mem. MME, Am. Soc. Quality Control, Am. Legion, Goju Ryu Kai (instr. 1960-77), Kung Fu Atado (black belt). Avocations: karate, basketball, track, gymnastics, soccer. Home: 9402 N 17th St Phoenix AZ 85020 Office: Cal Comp 14555 N 82d St Scottsdale AZ 85260

MCMANIGAL, PAUL GABRIEL, aerospace executive, physicist; b. Los Angeles, Apr. 15, 1936; s. Robert Moore and Evelyn Lenore (Moulin) McM.; m. Penny Ann Hineman, Aug. 22, 1959; children: Lisa, Scott. BA, Pomona Coll., 1958; PhD, U. Calif., Berkeley, 1963; cert., UCLA Grad. Sch. Mgmt, 1985. Mgr. missile systems engring. Ford Aerospace and Communications Corp., Newport Beach, Calif., 1963-71, dir. devel. planning, 1973-81, v.p. tech., 1981-84, mgr. advanced sensors, 1984—; dir. advanced sensors Def. Adv. Resource Projects Agy., Washington, 1971-73. Patentee in field. Mem. Assn. U.S. Army, Am. Def. Preparedness Assn. Home: 16 Inverness Ln Newport Beach CA 92660-5110 Office: Ford Aerospace and Communications Corp PO Box A Newport Beach CA 92658-9983

MCMANUS, HUGH LESLIE NICHOLAS, aerospace engineer; b. Boston, Feb. 11, 1958; s. Hugh and M. Jean (Millar) McM. BS, MIT, 1980, MS, 1981. Research engr. Kaman Avidyne, Burlington, Mass., 1981-84; structures engr. Lockheed Missiles and Space Corp., Sunnyvale, Calif., 1984—. DuPont fellow MIT, 1980. Mem. AIAA. Avocations: cycling, sailing, skiing. Home: 11 Patterson Ave Menlo Park CA 94025 Office: Lockheed Missiles and Space Corp PO Box 3504 Sunnyvale CA 94088-3504

MCMASTER, JOANNE TRUNICK, theater educator; b. Ventura, Calif., June 13, 1934; d. Franklin Silas and Ruth Berniece (Walton) Trunick; m. Donald Albert McMaster, Aug. 27, 1954; children: Terrence, Christopher, Jeffrey, Deron. BA, UCLA, 1956, MA, 1965, MFA, 1972. Scenic artist theater dept. UCLA, 1968-75, asst. prof. theater dept., 1975-86, assoc. prof. dept. theater, film and TV, 1986—, chmn. exec. com. Coll. Fine Arts, 1986—; free lance scene designer Theater 40, Beverly Hills, Calif., 1982-86; resident designer RBI Prodns., La'Mirada Civic Theatre, 1986—. Mem. U.S. Inst. Theater Tech. Avocation: painting. Office: UCLA Dept Theater Film and TV 405 Hilgard Ave Los Angeles CA 90024

MCMATH, CARROLL BARTON, JR., former coll. adminstr., ret. army officer; b. Godfrey, Wash., Sept. 18, 1910; s. Carroll Barton and Grace Jenness (Matthews) McM.; B.S., Ore. State U., 1932; M.S. (A. Olson Research scholar), N.Y. U., 1936; m. Betty Ruth Thompson, Nov. 26, 1937; children—Robert Thompson, Carol. With Sacramento Bee Newspaper, 1932-35; jr. exec. Lord & Taylor, N.Y.C., 1936-39; head dept. bus. Boise (Ida.) Jr. Coll., 1939-40; Res. officer on active duty U.S. Army, 1940-46, assigned gen. staff War Dept., 1943-45; commd. capt. regular U.S. Army 1947, advanced through grades to lt. col., assigned Joint Chiefs of Staff, 1951-53, Office Sec. of Army, 1953-55, ret., 1963; campaigns include Okinawa, Korea, Vietnam; mem. faculty U. Hawaii, Honolulu, 1964-77, asst. to dir. research, profl. adviser to faculty on research, 1964-77; faculty Indsl. Coll. of Armed Forces, Washington, 1945-46; asst. prof. retailing N.Y. U., N.Y.C., 1946-47. Mem. Assn. U.S. Army, AAAS, AAUP, Ret. Officers Assn., Honolulu Acad. Arts, Hawaiian Hist. Soc., Am. Theatre Organ Soc., Hawaii Found. History and Humanities, Scabbard and Blade, Alpha Delta Sigma, Alpha Kappa Psi, Eta Mu Pi Democrat. Elk. Club: Koa Anuenue. Home: 1624 Kanunu St PH-B Honolulu HI 96814

MCMILLAN, CAROL ANN, anthropology instructor, researcher; b. Berkeley, Calif., May 21, 1944; d. Frank Matthew and Frances Jean (Clay) McM.; m. Peter Feuille, Aug. 19, 1972 (div. 1977); m. William Gerard Christman, Jr., July 10, 1982; stepchildren: Emilie, Jebediah. BA, U. Colo., 1966; MA, U. Calif., Berkeley, 1971, SUNY, Buffalo, 1978; PhD, SUNY, Buffalo, 1982. Cert. elem. tchr.; comml. art cert. Tchr. elem. schs. Oakland, Calif., 1968-71, Eugene, Oreg., 1971-74, Kenmore, N.Y., 1974-76; grad. research asst. SUNY, Buffalo, 1977-80; dir. research project Caribbean Primate Research Ctr., Punta Santiago, P.R., 1980-81; illustrator N.Y. State Archeology, Buffalo, 1981-82; instr. Wenatchee Valley Coll. N., Omak, Wash., 1983—. Bd. dirs. Okanogan River COOP, Tonasket, Wash., 1983-85; adv. Red Rd. Assn., Omak, 1985—; mem. N. Valley Peacemakers, Ellisforde, Wash., 1983-86. Nat. Tchrs. Assn. fellow, 1969; research grantee and grad. fellow, SUNY, 1980. Mem. Am. Assn. Phys. Anthropologists (S. Washburn prize 1979, Juan Comas award 1982), Am. Soc. Primatologists, Am. Anthropol. Assn., Sigma Xi (Willard B. Elliot award 1982). Avocations: hiking, photography, farming, animal behavior observations. Home: Rt 2 Box 698 Oroville WA 98844 Office: Wenatchee Valley Coll North PO Box 2058 Omak WA 98841

MCMILLAN, DAVID ROBERT, business executive; b. Montebello, Calif., Mar. 28, 1957; s. Robert Harold and Olga (Lipinski) McM; m. Patricia J. Jacob, Sept. 21, 1985. B.A., U. Calif.-Riverside, 1979. Salesman, Brinkerhoff Realty, Riverside, Calif., 1976-79; account rep. EDP, Burroughs Corp., San Bernardino, Calif., 1979-83; br. mgr. Thor Agys., Santa Ana, Calif., 1983—. Chmn. parade com. Helping Others Scholarship Orgn., Riverside, 1981. Named one of Outstanding Young Men Am., 1982. Mem. Data Processing Mgmt. Assn., Assn. Info. Systems Profls., Palm Springs Jaycees, Orange County C. of C. Club: Toastmasters (treas. 1982-83). Home: 1621 Toyon Pl Corona CA 91720 Office: Thor Agy 2080 N Tustin Santa Ana CA 92701

MCMILLAN, DONALD ERNEST, research facility director; b. San Francisco, Dec. 13, 1931; s. George Ernest and Agnes Josephine (McGaffigan) McM.; m. Marilyn Marshal, June 23, 1956; children: David, Mark, Kathleen, Robert, Bruce, Rhannon. AB with distinction, Stanford U., 1953, MD, 1957. Diplomate Am. Bd. of Internal Medicine, Am. Bd. of Endocrinology and Metabolism. Intern USPHS Hosp., San Francisco, 1957-58; resident USPHS Hosp., New Orleans, San Francisco, 1959-63, dir. metabolic service, 1965-68, assoc. chief of medicine, endocrinology, 1972-82; chief endocrine and diabetes clinics Sansum Med. Clinic, Inc., Santa Barbara, Calif., 1968-82, lab. dir., 1972-82; dir. research Hal B. Wallis Research Facility, Rancho Mirage, Calif., 1982—; dir. Diabetes Research Sansum Med. Research Found., 1968-72; spl. reviewer NIH Spl. Study Sect., 1980-81; clin. prof. of medicine, U. So. Calif., 1980; cons. numerous agys. and founds. Reviewer numerous sci. jours.; contbr. articles to profl. jours. Recipient USPHS Clin. Soc. Research Prize, 1963, Mary Jane Kugel award Juvenile Diabetes Found., 1982; fellow U. Calif. Med. Ctr., San Francisco, 1963-65. mem. AAAS, Am. Diabetes Assn. (pres. So. Calif. Affiliate 1982-83, bd. dirs. 1984-87), Am. Fedn. for Clinical Research, AMA, Am. Physiological Soc., Biorheology Soc., Endocrine Soc., Glycoconjugate Soc., Microcirculatory Soc., Sigma Xi, Phi Beta Kappa. Republican. Roman Catholic. Avocations: body surfing, back packing, camping. Home: 45-395 Chocta Circle Indian Wells CA 92210 Office: Hal B Wallis Research Facility Eisenhower Med Ctr 39000 Bob Hope Dr Rancho Mirage CA 92270

MC MILLAN, EDWIN MATTISON, physicist, educator; b. Redondo Beach, Calif., Sept. 18, 1907; s. Edwin Harbaugh and Anna Marie (Mattison) McM.; m. Elsie Walford Blumer, June 7, 1941; children—Ann B., David M., Stephen W. B.S., Calif. Inst. Tech., 1928, M.S., 1929; Ph.D., Princeton U., 1932; D.Sc., Rensselaer Poly. Inst., 1961, Gustavus Adolphus Coll., 1963. Nat. research fellow U. Calif. at Berkeley, 1932-34, research asso., 1934-35, instr. in physics, 1935-36, asst. prof. physics, 1936-41, asso. prof., 1941-46, prof. physics, 1946-73, emeritus, 1973—; mem. staff Lawrence Radiation Lab., 1934—, asso. dir., 1954-58, dir., 1958-73; on leave for def. research at Mass. Inst. Tech. Radiation Lab., U.S. Navy Radio and Sound Lab., San Diego, and Los Alamos Sci. Lab., 1940-45; mem. gen. adv. com. AEC, 1954-58; mem. commn. high energy physics Internat. Union Pure and Applied Physics, 1960-67; mem. sci. policy com. Stanford Linear Accelerator Center, 1962-66; mem. physics adv. com. Nat. Accelerator Lab., 1967-69; chmn. 13th Internat. Conf. on High Energy Physics, 1966; guest prof. CERN, Geneva, 1974. Trustee Rand Corp., 1959-69; Bd. dirs. San Francisco Palace Arts and Scis. Found., 1968—; trustee Univs. Research Assn., 1969-74. Recipient Research Corp. Sci. award, 1951; with Glenn T. Seaborg) Nobel prize in chemistry, 1951; with Vladimir I. Veksler) Atoms for Peace award, 1963; Alumni Distinguished Service award Calif. Inst. Tech., 1966; Centennial citation U. Calif. at Berkeley, 1968; Faculty Research lectr. U. Calif. at Berkeley, 1955. Fellow Am. Acad. Arts and Scis., Am. Phys. Soc.; mem. Nat. Acad. Scis. (chmn. class I 1968-71), Am. Philos. Soc., Sigma Xi, Tau Beta Pi. Address: Lawrence Berkeley Lab Univ of Calif Berkeley CA 94720

MCMILLAN, FRANK M., chemical consultant, writer; b. Swanwick, Ill., Jan. 14, 1914; s. Will B. and Rose B. (McCurdy) McM.; m. Frances Jean Clay, July 9, 1937; children: Jean P. Bennett, Carol Ann. BS, Monmouth Coll., 1934, DSc (hon.), 1961; PhD, Stanford U., 1937. Research chemist Shell Devel. Co., Emeryville, Calif., 1937-54; tech. asst. to pres. Shell Devel. Co., N.Y.C., 1954-56; dept. head Shell Devel. Co., Emeryville, 1957-59, mgr. research econs., 1965-71; mgr. research and devel. Shell Chem. Co., N.Y.C., 1959-62, mgr. bus. devel., 1965; cons. SRI Internat., Calsec Cons. Author: The Chain Straighteners, 1981, (poems) Pilgrim's Regress, 1981, If We But Loved, 1985; contbr. articles to profl. jours.; patentee in field. Pres. Orinda (Calif.) Hist. Soc., 1982-83. Mem. AAAS, Am. Chem. Soc. Avocations: woodworking, photography, rock working, golf. Home and Office: 99 Tara Rd Orinda CA 94563

MCMULLEN, SUNNY VAZQUEZ RON, educator, bilingual resource specialist; b. San Mateo, Calif., Dec. 29, 1942; d. John and Auria (Vazquez Ron) Gishe; m. Richard James McMullen, Nov. 27, 1968; children—Spencer, Neil. B.A., Calif. State U.-San Francisco, 1964; M.A., Calif. State U.-Northridge, 1976; postgrad. U. So. Calif., 1983—. Tchr., Portola Valley Sch. Dist., Calif., 1964, Millbrae Unified Sch. Dist., Calif., 1964-68, Burbank Unified Sch., Calif., 1969-72; guest lectr. Calif. State U., Northridge, 1974-76; tchr. Los Angeles Unified Sch. Dist., 1972-84, acad. adminstrv. devel. program intern, 1983-84, dist. inservice instr., 1980—, mem. curriculum alignment team, 1983—. Author: Snail Trail Games, 1975. Dir. CCD, Los Angeles Cath. Archdiocese, Malibu Lake, Calif., 1978-80, pres. parish council, 1982-83, sec., 1981-82, CCD vol. tchr., St. Bernardine Cath. Ch., Woodland Hills, Calif., 1981-82. Mem. Calif. Fgn. Lang. Tchrs. Assn., San Fernando Valley Reading Assn., Mexican Am. Educators Assn., Educare, AAUW (internat. relations rep. 1978-79), Phi Delta Kappa. Republican. Roman Catholic. Home: 5155 Llano Dr Woodland Hills CA 91364

MCMULLEN, TERENCE PERRY, health care company executive; b. Modesto, Calif., Nov. 11, 1942; s. Charles Carter and Loma Leis (Lavender) McM.; m. Grace Davidson Calfee, Apr. 3, 1971; children: Stuart, Audrey. BA, Stanford U., 1964, MBA, 1970. Gen. mgr. Citibank Internat., Chgo., 1970-79; pres. ADF Internat. Fin. Inc., Los Altos, Calif., 1979-81; v.p. Nat. Med. Enterprises Inc., Los Angeles, 1981—. Served to lt. USN, 1964-68, Vietnam. Delta Kappa Epsilon. Club: Porter Valley Country (Northridge, Calif.). Office: Nat Med Enterprises Inc 11620 Wilshire Blvd Los Angeles CA 90025

MCMURDO, REGINALD WAYNE, business executive; b. Kalispell, Mont., Sept. 24, 1945; s. David Rex and Vera Fern (Everhart) McM.; m. Carol Ann Benson, Aug. 20, 1966; children—Wendy Sue, Kevin James, Jesse Allen. Student pub. schs., Whitefish, Mont. Elec. constrn. with various firms, 1964-80; exec. bd. Local Union 768 IBEW, Kalispell, Mont., 1974-80, bus. mgr., 1980—; pres. Western Mont. Bldg. and Constrn. Trades Council, Missoula, 1983—; com. mem. Mont. Joint Apprenticeship and Tng. Com., Helena, 1981—; adv. trustee 8th Dist. Pension Trust, Denver, 1980—; trustee Mont. Electricians Health and Accident Trust, Billing, 1982—. Mem. Mont. Bldg. Codes Adv. Council, 1983, Nat. Elec. Codemaking Panel, 1984—. Mem. Mont. Sheriffs and Peace Officers Assn. (hon. mem.). Democrat. Clubs: Nat. Rifle Assn., Whitefish Rifle and Pistol. Home: 101 Washington Ave Whitefish MT 59937 Office: Local Union 768 IBEW PO Box 786 Kalispell MT 59901

MCMURRAY, ROBERT DAVID, newspaper editor; b. New Westminster, B.C., Can., June 26, 1926; s. Murdoch and Lillian Ethel (Wray) McM.; m. Kathryn Grace McMillan, Aug. 5, 1955; children: Mark Colin, Janet Lynn, Grant David. Grad., high sch., Burnaby, B.C. Reporter The Province, Vancouver, B.C., Can., 1945-55, asst. city editor, 1955-60, bus. editor, 1961-76, city editor, 1976-78, asst. mng. editor, 1978-84, mng. editor, 1984-85, editor, 1985—. Club: Terminal City (Vancouver). Office: The Province, 2250 Granville St, Vancouver, BC Canada V6H 3G2

MCMURTRY, BURTON JOHN, venture capital investor, electrical engineer; b. Houston, Mar. 26, 1935; s. James G. and Alberta Elizabeth (Matteson) McM.; m. Ann Kathryn Meck, June 9, 1956; children—Cathryn Ann, John Eric. B.A., Rice U., 1956, B.S.E.E., 1957; M.S.E.E., Stanford U., 1959, Ph.D. in Elec. Engring. (Raytheon fellow), 1962. Engr. Microwave Tube div. Sylvania, Mountain View, Calif., 1957-62; research asst. Stanford U., 1960-62; head lab. research and devel. in electro-optics GTE, Sylvania, Mountain View, 1962-66; mgr. Equipment Engring. Labs., 1967-68; dir., gen. mgr. electro-optics orgn. Sylvania Electronic Systems, 1968-69; asso. Jack L. Melchor (personal venture capital investment bus.), Los Altos, Calif., 1969-70; pres. Palo Alto Investment Co., Calif., 1970-73; gen. partner Dennis, Jamieson & McMurtry, Menlo Park, Calif., 1973—, TVI Mgmt., TVI Mgmt.-2, TVI Mgmt.-3, Menlo Park, 1980—; past dir. NBI, Inc., KLA Instruments, ROLM, Triad Systems Corp.; dir. Cadnetix, DAVID Systems, USX Telectrs., Veri-Fone. Contbr. articles, chpts. to electronics publs., mainly on microwave tubes, lasers, optical detectors. Bd. dirs. El Camino Hosp. Found.; elder Menlo Park Presbyn. Ch.; mem. major gifts com. Stanford U.; mem. Sproul Assocs., Berkeley. Recipient Alfred Noble prize, 1964. Mem. Nat. Venture Capital Assn. (pres.-elect, bd. dirs.), Western Assn. Venture Capitalists (pres. 1972-73), Am. Phys. Soc., Optical Soc. Am., Sigma Xi (sr. award 1957), Sigma Tau, Tau Beta Pi. Home: 7 Coalmine View Portola Valley CA 94025 Office: Tech Venture Investors 3000 Sand Hill Rd Menlo Park CA 94025

MCMURTRY, GARY MICHAEL, geochemist, research director; b. Upland, Calif., Feb. 25, 1950; s. James Samuel and Grace Marietta (Tomlinson) McM.; m. Francine Emy Yagawa, Mar. 3, 1979. BS with honors, U. Calif., Riverside, 1972; MS, U. Hawaii, 1975, PhD, 1979. Research geologist U. Calif., San Diego, 1979-80; asst. geochemist U. Hawaii, Honolulu, 1980-86, assoc. geochemist, 1986—; sci. dir. Hawaii Undersea research Lab., Honolulu, 1982—; grad. faculty mem. U. Hawaii, Honolulu, 1982—; cons. TRW Corp., Redondo Beach, Calif., 1979-80; assoc. dir. Electron Microscopy Lab., Honolulu, 1983-86; panelist Nat. Undersea research program NOAA, Washington, 1985—. Contbr. articles to profl. jours. Recipient Antarctic Service medal NSF, 1979. Mem. AAAS, Am. Geophys. Union, Hawaii Acad. Sci., Marine Tech. Soc., Soc. Econ. Paleontologists and Mineralogists, The Planetary Soc., Sigma Xi. Avocations: tennis, surfing, computing. Office: Hawaii Inst Geophysics 1000 Pope Rd Honolulu HI 96822

MCNALL, CLO ANN, newspaper executive; b. Goodland, Kans., July 18, 1933; d. Lloyd Cecil and Mary Alice (Haller) Wilkins; m. John Mark McNall, Oct. 19, 1951; children—Lynette, Diane, Marcie. Trainee, Gazette Telegraph, Colorado Springs, Colo., 1950-53; co-pub. Eastern Colo. Plainsman, Hugo, 1954-61, Chewelah Ind., Wash., 1966-69; editor, co-pub. Clearwater Tribune, Orofino, Idaho, 1969—, pub., 1984. Office: PO Box 71 Orofino ID 83544

MCNALLY, BRUCE EDWARD, aerospace company executive; b. N.Y.C., June 14, 1937; s. Joseph Gerard and Dorothy Margaret (Ruth) McN.; m. Florence Margaret Martin, Jan. 8, 1966; children: Daniel Joseph, Michael Stephen. Student, Villanova U., 1955-58; BBA, St. John's U., Jamaica, N.Y., 1962; MBA, U. Hawaii annex, Tokyo, 1970. Dir. Pan Am. World Airways Inc., Uganda, Japan, and Europe, 1962-75; cons. Pan Am. World Airways Inc., N.Y.C. and worldwide, 1985—; v.p. Alaska Airlines, Seattle, 1975-77; gen. mgr. Boeing Co., Tehran, Iran, 1977-80; v.p. Rogerson Aircraft, Irvine, Calif., 1980-84; pres. Eagle Enterprises Inc., Seattle, 1984—; bd. dirs. Azure Blue, Seattle, Anchor Equity Corp., N.Y.C.; lectr. Makerere U., Kampala, Uganda, 1970-73. Coach Mercer Island Youth Sports Leagues; bd. dirs. Mercer Island Boys & Girls Club. Served to capt. U.S. Army, 1958-60. Recipient Internat. Assistance award Makerere U., 1973, Coaches Recognition award Mercer Island Boys & Girls Club, 1983. Mem. Mus. Flight, Aerospace Mgmt. Assn. Republican. Roman Catholic. Club: Wings (N.Y.C.). Lodge: Rotary (local bd. dirs.). Avocations: golfing, skin diving, flying light aircraft. Home: 6847 SE 33d St Mercer Island WA 98040 Office: Eagle Enterprises Inc 5729 Lakeview Dr NE Kirkland WA 98033

MCNALLY, DAVID JOHN, mechanical engineer; b. Schenectady, N.Y., Aug. 14, 1961; s. John J. and Anita G. (Brault) McN. BSME, LaFayette Coll., 1983. Engr. Hercules Aerospace, Magna, Utah, 1983-84; regional sales mgr. Phys. Acoustics Corp., Princeton, N.J., 1984-85; mgr. sensor products western div. EDO Corp., Salt Lake City, 1985—. Active Big Bros. Am., Easton, Pa., 1980-83, March of Dimes fundraising, Salt Lake City, 1986. Named Eagle Scout Boy Scouts Am., Wilton, Conn., 1975; C. Homewood scholar Instrument Soc. Am., 1982. Mem. ASME, Soc. Mfg. Engrs. Republican. Roman Catholic. Avocations: skiing, camping, gen. fitness. Home: 992 Well Spring Rd #21J Midvale UT 84047 Office: EDO Corp Western Div 2645 S 300 W Salt Lake City UT 84115

MCNALLY, GERALD, JR., lawyer; b. Kalamazoo, Dec. 28, 1947; s. Gerald and Elizabeth Louise (Lake) McN.; m. Barbara Frances Robinson, Mar. 17, 1979; children: Charles Patrick Ritchie, Fiona Kathleen. Student, Mich. State U., 1965-67; JD, Whittier Coll., 1984. Bar: Calif., 1984. Treas. Ch. of Scientology, San Diego, 1971-74; customer service rep. Xerox Corp., Los Angeles, 1974-78; acct., enrolled agt. Los Angeles, 1978-84; sole practice Glendale, Calif., 1984—. Served with USN, 1967-71. Mem. ABA, Glendale Bar Assn., Am. Trial Lawyers Assn., Sierra Club, Assn. for Childbirth at Home Internat. (bd. dirs. 1980). Republican. Avocations: computers. Home: 4849 Aldama St Los Angeles CA 90042 Office: 803 East Broadway F Glendale CA 91205

MCNALLY, VERN LEROY, marriage and family counselor; b. Midland, S.D., May 15, 1939; s. Frederick H. and Alma L. (Phillips) McN.; m. Dorothy M. Briles, May 30, 1959; children: Randal G., James L., Penn J. BA, Cen. Bible Coll., 1961; MA, Calif. Grad. Sch. of Theology, 1982, PhD, 1986. Pastor Assembly of God Ch., Willard, Mo., 1960-61; missionary to Sioux Indians Sisseton, S.D., 1961-64; sr. pastor First Assembly of God Ch., Haysville, Kans., 1964-69, Las Cruces, N.Mex., 1969-71; assoc. pastor The Stone Ch., Chgo., 1971-72; sr. pastor New Life Ctr., Tulsa, 1972-77; sr. pastor Evangel Community Ch., Seattle, 1977-79, Little Rock, 1979-81; admisions officer Phoenix Inst. Tech., 1981-82; assoc. pastor Trinity Ch., Scottsdale, Ariz., 1982-84; dir. Insight Counseling Ctr., Scottsdale, Ariz., 1984—; Ariz. dir. Berean Coll. of the Assemblies of God; Phoenix extension dir. Calif. Grad. Sch. Theology; tng. instr. Trinity Broadcasting Newtork telephone counselor; organizer, host Ark. Paryer Breakfast; bd. dir. Parents Without Ptnrs., Little Rock; pres. Ministerial Assn., Haysville, Las Cruces, Tulsa; Nat. Bibile Quizmaster; Dist. Youth v.p., Kans.; Jr. High Camp dir. Chmn. Task Force for Relocation of Viet Nam War Refugees, Okla.; chmn. ARC, Roberts County, S.D. Mem. Christian Assn. for Psychol. Studies Internat. Republican. Office: Insight Counseling Ctr 3501 N Scottsdale Suite 234 Scottsdale AZ 85251

MC NAMARA, JOHN J., educator; b. Rochelle, Ill., Dec. 6, 1909; s. John and Grace (Campbell) McN.; B.E., No. Ill. U.; M.A., U. Iowa; Ph.D., Purdue U.; m. Hazel D. Dionne, Aug. 11, 1936; children—John, Denise, Carole, Michael, Terrence, Kevin. Tchr., St. Albans Acad., Sycamore, Ill., 1932-34; faculty St. Viator Coll., Kankakee, Ill., 1934-37; asso. prof. U. Detroit, 1937-43; head tng. div. Republic Aviation Corp., 1943-45; pres. M & M Cendy, Hackettstown, N.J., 1945-59; dir. M & M Mars (now Mars Inc.), McLean, Va., 1952-62; chmn. bd. Uncle Ben's Rice, Houston, 1959-62; corp. mktg. adv. Warner Lambert Pharm. Co., Morris Plains, N.J., 1966-67; prof. No. Ill. U., DeKalb, 1970-78; prof. dept. mktg. Calif. State Coll., Bakersfield, 1978-80. Calcot-Kennedy disting. prof., 1980—. Recipient Chick Evans award and service award No. Ill. U., 1971; inducted into NYU Football Hall of Fame, 1984. Mem. Am. Assn. Advt. Agys. Sigma Xi, Phi Delta Kappa. Club: Stockdale Country. Contbr. articles to profl. publs. Home: 508 Malibu Ct Bakersfield CA 93309 Office: 9001 Stockdale Hwy Bakersfield CA 93309

MC NAMARA, JOSEPH DONALD, chief of police; b. N.Y.C., Dec. 16, 1934; s. Michael and Eleanor (Shepherd) McN.; m. Rochelle Wall, Jan. 25, 1964; children—Donald, Laura, Karen. B.S., John Jay Coll., 1968; fellow, Harvard Law Sch., 1970; D.P.A. (Littauer fellow), Harvard U., 1973. Served to dep. insp. Police Dept., N.Y.C., 1956-73; police chief Kansas City, Mo., 1973-76, San Jose, Calif., 1976—; adj. instr. Northeastern U., 1972, John Jay Coll., 1973, Rockhurst Coll., 1975-76, San Jose State U., 1980; cons. U.S. Civil Rights Commn., 1978; lectr., appearances on nat. TV; apptd. nat. adv. bd. U.S. Bur. Justice Stats., 1980. Author: (non-fiction) Safe and Sane Fawcett, 1984, (novel) The First Directive Crown, 1985, Fatal Command, 1987. Contbr. articles to profl. publs. Active NCCJ. Served with U.S. Army, 1958-60. Named one of 200 Young Am. Leaders Time mag., 1975; recipient disting. alumni award John Jay Coll., 1979, Western Soc. Criminology pres.'s award, 1979. Mem. Internat. Assn. Chiefs of Police, Calif. Police Chiefs Assn., Calif. Peace Officers Assn., Major Cities Police Chiefs Assn., Police Exec. Research Forum (dir.). Kansas City police named best in country by Nat. Newspaper Enterprises, 1974, San Jose Police Dept. named nat. model U.S. Civil Rights Commn., 1980. Office: 201 W Mission San Jose CA 95510

MCNEAL, DALE WILLIAM, JR., educator; b. Kansas City, Kans., Nov. 23, 1939; s. Dale William and Geraldine Estelle (Reed) McN.; m. Arlene Joyce Purvis, Feb. 26, 1966. B.A., Colo. Coll., 1962; M.S., Syracuse U., 1964; Ph.D., Wash. State U., 1969. Asst. prof. dept. biol. scis. U. Pacific, Stockton, Calif., 1969-74; asso. prof. U. Pacific, 1974-79, prof., 1979—, chmn. dept., 1978-84. Contbr. articles to profl. jours. Served with U.S. Army, 1964-66. Mem. Am. Bot. Soc., Am. Soc. Plant Taxonomists, Internat. Soc. Plant Taxonomy, Calif. Acad. Scis., Sigma Xi. Republican. Episcopalian. Office: U Pacific Dept Biol Scis Stockton CA 95211

MC NEAR, DENMAN KITTREDGE, transportation company executive; b. San Francisco, July 20, 1925; s. E. Denman and Mary H. (Kittredge) McN.; m. Susan L. Anderson, Jan. 27, 1962; children: Denman K., Stephen A., George D. BSCE, MIT, 1948; MBA, Stanford U., 1950. Registered profl. engr., Calif., Ariz., N.Mex., Tex. With So. Pacific Transp. Co., San Francisco, 1948—, asst. to pres., 1963-67, v.p., 1967-75, v.p. ops., 1975-76, pres., 1976—, chmn. bd., chief exec. officer, 1982—, also bd. dirs.; chmn., pres. St. Louis Southwestern Ry. Co., 1983. Mem. corp. MIT, Cambridge; bd. dirs. Jr. Achievement, Inc. Served with USN, 1944-46. Mem. Assn. Am. R.R.s (bd. dirs.), ASCE, Econ. Literacy Council Calif. (pres. 1975-78, bd. govs.). Republican. Clubs: Bohemian, Pacific-Union, Stock Exchange. Office: So Pacific Transportation Co So Pacific Bldg 1 Market Plaza San Francisco CA 94105

MC NEELY, E. L., manufacturing company executive; b. Pattonsburg, Mo., Oct. 5, 1918; s. Ralph H. and Viola (Vogel) McN.; m. Alice Elaine Hall, Sept. 18, 1948; children: Sandra (Mrs. Ronald Gessl), Gregory, Mark, Kevin. Student, Central Bus. Coll., Kansas City, Mo., 1935-36, U. Mo., 1936-37; A.B., No. Mo. State U., Kirksville, 1940; student, Rockhurst Coll., Kansas City, Mo., 1942. With Montgomery Ward & Co., 1940-64, divisional mdse. mgr., 1961-64; dir. marketing Wickes Corp., Saginaw, Mich.,

1964-65; sr. v.p. Wickes Corp., 1965-69, pres., 1969-74, chief exec. officer, chmn., 1974-80; chmn. bd., chief exec. officer Wickes Cos., Inc., 1980-82, also dir.; chmn., chief exec. officer Oak Industries Inc.; dir. Dayco Internat., Fed. Mogul Corp., Nat. Bank LaJolla, Pacific Tel. & Tel. Co., Transam. Corp. Served as officer USNR, 1942-46, PTO. Mem. Beta Gamma Sigma, Alpha Phi Omega. Republican. Presbyterian. Clubs: Saginaw; Union League, Metropolitan (Chgo.); La Jolla Country; Fairbanks Ranch Country, Cuyamaca (San Diego; San Francisco Golf; Deepdale Golf (N.Y.). Office: 7910 Ivanhoe Ave Suite 110 La Jolla CA 92037 *

MCNEILL, FREDERICK WALLACE, lawyer, writer, aviation consultant, pilot; b. Chgo., Jan. 4, 1932; s. James Joseph and Irene Gertrude (Stevenson) McN.; m. Judith Carol Austin, Feb. 9, 1957; children: Marjorie, Tamelyn, Kenneth, Patricia, Darcy, Sean, Meghan. BBA, U. Ariz., 1974, JD, 1977. Bar: Ariz. 1977, U.S. Dist. Ct. Ariz., 1977. Served to maj. USAF, 1949-73; ret., 1973; bus. mgr. Engring. & Research Assocs., Inc., Tucson, 1973-74; mng. ptnr. ERA Shopping Ctr., Tucson, 1973-75; chief pilot, spl. agt. Narcotics Strike Force, Ariz., 1975-77; dep. county atty. Pima County, Ariz., 1977-79; atty. Ariz. Drug Control Dist., 1977-79; ptnr. Rees & McNeill, Tucson, 1979-84; writer, 1984—; lectr. air smuggling seminars, organized crime seminars, Ariz., 1977-79. Vice pres. Indian Ridge Homeowners Assn., 1980-82; bd. dirs. Tucson Boys Chorus Bldg. Fund Com., 1972-74. Decorated DFC, Air medal (5), Air Force Commendation medal (2). Mem. ABA, Ariz. Bar Assn., Pima County Bar Assn., Assn. Trial Lawyers Am., Ariz. Trial Lawyers Assn., Lawyer Pilots Bar Assn., Ret. Officers Assn., Air Force Assn. Club: Order of Daedelians. Office: PSC Box 845 APO Miami FL 34002

MCNEILL, VICKI S., mayor. m. James P. McNeill; 2 children. Appointed mem. Spokane (Wash.) City Council, 1982, elected mem., 1983-85; mayor City of Spokane, 1985—. Pres. Wash. State Pavilion Fund; trustee Spokane Symphony Soc., Spokane C. of C., Spokane Centennial Commn. Recipient Golden Deeds award Exchange Club, 1975, Distinction award Women in Communications, 1979, Outstanding Achievement Leadership award YWCA, 1983. Address: Office of Mayor W 808 Spokane Falls Blvd Spokane WA 99201

MCNELIS, PETER JAMES, social worker, military officer; b. Erie, Pa., Jan. 20, 1940; s. Gerald Augustine and Katherine Marie (Judermanns) McN.; m. Nancy Lee Killmeyer, June 15, 1963; children: Peter Brian, Sean Brandon, Michele Marie. BA, Gannon U., 1961; MSW, Fordham U., 1963; DSW, Tulane U., 1972; postgrad., U.S. Army Command and Gen. Staff Coll., 1983. Commd. 2d lt. U.S. Army, 1961, advanced through grades to col., 1985; chief social work service U.S. Army, Augsburg, Fed. Republic of Germany, 1966-69, U.S. Army Hosp., Ft. Campbell, Ky., 1973-74; social work cons. to chief surgeon U.S. Army, Heidelberg, Fed. Republic of Germany, 1974-78; chief social work service Tripler (U.S.) Army Med. Ctr., Honolulu, 1978-82; dir. mil. family resource ctr. Office of Asst. Sec. Def., Washington, 1982-85; program mgr., contracting officer Letterman Army Inst. Research, San Francisco, 1985—; instr. U. Md., 1967-68, Tulane U., New Orleans, 1971, Western Ky. U., Ft. Campbell, 1973; asst. prof. U. Hawaii, Honolulu, 1978-82. Contbr. articles to profl. jours. Coordinator U.S. Mil. State of Hawaii Family Advocacy Programs, 1980-82. Mem. Nat. Assn. Social Workers (European chpt. pres. 1974-78, editorial bds., task force 1978—), Internat. Council on Social Welfare (U.S. com. 1975-77), Am. Hosp. Assn. (pres., bd. dirs. Hawaii Soc. Hosp. Social Work Dirs. 1978-81), Nat. Ctr. Child Abuse and Neglect (adv. bd. 1982-85). Democrat. Roman Catholic. Avocation: writing. Home: 510 B Simonds Loop Presidio San Francisco CA 94129 Office: Letterman Army Inst Research Presidio San Francisco CA 94129

MCNELLY, WILLIS E(VERETT), English educator; b. Waupun, Wis., Dec. 16, 1920; s. Willis E. Sr. and Mary (Creighton) McN.; m. Genevieve Marie Skilondz, Jan. 22, 1944; children: Peter, Patrick, Margaret, James , Jean. BA, Cen. YMCA Coll., Chgo., 1942; MA, Loyola U., Chgo., 1948; PhD, Northwestern U., 1957. Asst. prof. English Loyola U., Chgo., 1947-50, 51-52; chmn. dept. English. Rich Twp. High Sch., Park Forest, Ill., 1952-58; asst. prof. English Santa Ana (Calif.) Coll., 1958-61; from asst. prof. to assoc. prof. Calif. State U., Fullerton, 1961-68, prof., 1968—; vis. lectr. St. Joseph's Coll., Orange, Calif., 1961-63. Editor: (anthologies) Mars, We Love You, 1971, 3d rev. ed., 1975, Science Fiction Novellas, 1974; (with L. Stover) Above the Human Landscape, 1973; (essays) Science Fiction: The Academic Awakening, 1972; author, editor: The Dune Encyclopedia, 1984; also articles, reviews, and forewords to various novels. Co-sec. Christian Family Movement, Los Angeles, 1963-65, co-chmn., 1965-67; chmn., bd. dirs. St. Joseph's Coll. Lecture Series, 1960-68; faculty advisor Newman Assn., 1961—. Served to 1st lt. Q.M.C., U.S. Army, 1942-46, 50-51, PTO. Named Outstanding Prof. of Yr., Calif. State U., Fullerton, 1975, Bd. Trustees of Calif. State U. System, 1975. Mem. Western Assn. Schs. and Colls. (accrediting team 1974—), Alpha Phi Omega. Democrat. Roman Catholic. Avocations: photography, camping, travel. Home: 2007 E Union Ave Fullerton CA 92631-3011 Office: Calif State U Dept English Fullerton CA 92634

MCNERNEY, JAMES FRANCIS, electronics company executive; b. Lancaster, Pa., Apr. 15, 1928; s. Michael Joseph and Mina Leone (Harding) McN.; m. Norma Adeline Neumann, May 30, 1952; children: Stephen R., David J. BS in Naval Sci., U.S. Naval Acad., 1951; BS in Aerospace Engring., USN PG Sch., 1958; MS in Aerospace Engring., MIT, 1959. Commd. ensign USN, 1951, advanced through grades to capt., ret., 1974; mgr. Rohr Marine Inc., Chula Vista, Calif., 1975-78, Gen. Dynamics Convair Div., San Diego, 1978-85; mgr. advanced systems TRW, San Diego, 1985—. Mem. AIAA (mem. tech. com 1984—), Navy League, Am. Def. Preparedness Assn., Sigma Xi. Republican. Roman Catholic. Lodge: Kiwanis (bd. dirs. Tierrasanta club 1984—). Home: 10808 Via Cascabel San Diego CA 92124 Office: TRW Mil Electronics Div One Rancho Carmel San Diego CA 92128

MCNETT, THOMAS LEE, physician; b. Los Angeles, July 18, 1940; s. Thomas Edward and Helen Marie McN.; 1 child, Teresa Lee; m. Elizabeth Lenyo, Apr. 4, 1981; 1 child, Stephanie Marie. BA, UCLA, 1963, MA, 1965; MD, Mich. State U., 1972. Intern Mercy Hosp. and Med. Ctr., San Diego, 1972-73; resident U. Calif. Davis Med. Ctr., Sacramento, 1973-76, mem. clin. faculty, emergency physician, 1983—; emergency physician Lodi (Calif.) Meml. Hosp., 1976-83; dir. emergency dept. and Medi-Flight/No. Calif., Meml. Hosp. North, Modesto, 1985—. Producer film: Trepanation, East Africa, 1968. Mem. Am. Coll. Emergency Medicine. Office: Meml Hosp North Emergency Dept 1700 Coffee Rd Modesto CA 95355

MCNEW, GEORGE LEE, plant pathologist; b. Alamogordo, N.Mex., Aug. 22, 1908; s. William Henry and Nettie Belzora (Fry) McN.; m. Elizabeth Anne Mehlop, May 28, 1932; 1 child, Freda Louise. BS in Agr., N.Mex. State U., 1930, DSc (hon.); MS in Plant Pathology, Iowa State U., 1931, PhD in Plant Pathology, 1935. Biol. research scientist Rockefeller Inst. for Med. Research, Princeton, N.J., 1935-39; research scientist N.Y. Agrl. Exptl. Sta., Geneva, 1939-43; mgr. research and devel. in agrl. chemistry U.S. Rubber Co., Naugatuck, Conn., 1943-47; prof., head dept. botany Iowa State U., Ames, 1947-49; mng. dir. Boyce Thompson Inst., Yonkers, N.Y., 1949-78; scientist N.Mex. State U., Las Cruces, 1978—; cons. USDA, Washington, 1975-78, N.Mex. State U., 1978-86. Contbr. articles to profl. jours.; patentee in field. Named Disting. Alumnus N.Mex. State U., 1973, Disting. Alumnus Iowa State U., 1977. Fellow Am. Phytopathol. Soc. (pres.); mem. AAAS (bd. dirs. 1959-62), Am. Inst. biol. Scis. (pres. 1970), Am. Chem. Soc. (pres. N.Y. div.). Republican. Presbyterian. Club: Torrey Bot. (pres. 1965). Home: 1406 Georgianna Ct Las Cruces NM 88005 Office: NMex State U Dept Entomology/Plant Pathology Las Cruces NM 88003

MCNICHOLS, ROBERT J., federal judge; b. 1922. Student, Wash. State U., 1946-48; J.D., Gonzaga U., 1952. Bar: Wash. 1952. Chief judge U.S. Dist. Ct. for Eastern Dist. Wash., Spokane. Office: US Dist Ct PO Box 2136 Spokane WA 99210

MCNICHOLS, STEPHEN LUCID ROBERT, JR., lawyer; b. Denver, June 5, 1943; s. Stephen Lucid Robert and Marjorie Roberta (Hart) McN.; children: Justin, Chelsea. Student, Monterey Inst. Fgn. Studies, 1964-65; BA, Pomona Coll., 1965; JD, U. Calif., Berkeley, 1968. Bar: Colo. 1968, Calif. 1969. Dep. dist. atty. San Luis Obispo County, Calif., 1970-73; assoc. Varni, Fraser, Hartwell & Van Blois, Hayward, Calif., 1973-76; ptnr. Varni, Fraser, Hartwell, McNichols & Rodgers, Hayward, 1976-86, McNichols, McCann, Seibel & Inderb, San Ramon, Calif., 1987—. Mem. Morro Bay (Calif.) Planning Commn., 1970-72, chmn. 1972; bd. dirs. Children's Hosp. Found., 1980-83. Mem. ABA (litigation sect.), Calif. Bar Assn. (adminstrn. justice com.), Alameda County (Calif.) Bar Assn. (bd. dirs. 1986—), So. Alameda County Bar Assn. (bd. dirs. 1978-80), Assn. Trial Laywers Am., Calif. Trial Lawyers Assn., Alameda-Contra Costa County Trial Lawyers Assn. (bd. dirs. 1977-78). Democrat. Club: Barristers (Alameda County)(bd. dirs. 1974-77); Blackhawk Country (Calif.). Avocations: skiing, running, golfing. Home: 947 Redwood Dr Danville CA 94526 Office: McNichols McCann Seibel & Inderbitzen 18 Crow Canyon Ct Suite 395 San Ramon CA 94583

MCNICOL, PAUL BRIGGS, real estate consultant; b. East Liverpool, Ohio, July 4, 1918; s. Daniel Bertram and Edna (Briggs) McN.; m. Barbara Gould, Oct. 6, 1945 (dec. July 1975); m. 2d, Laura Holsinger, Dec. 1, 1976; children—Lauren, Kathryn, Kevin, Donald, Dana, Jonathan, Steven, Elsibeth, Reginald, Madra. B.S./B.A., Boston U., 1940; M.B.A., Harvard U., 1953. Commd. USMC, 1940, advanced through grades to col.; served ETO, PTO; co-designer USMC computer systems, Washington; ret., 1962; dir. fin. ops. Ford/Philco Aerospace, 1962-64; v.p. Cemland, 1965; v.p. Louis Allen Assocs., 1966-75; pres. McNicol Mgmt. Services, 1975-83; pres. MacReal Properties, Los Altos, Calif., 1979—; instr. U. Md., U. Calif. extension, West Valley Coll., DeAnza Coll., Foothill Coll., 1976-83. Author 2 books. contbr. articles to profl. jours. Pres. Am. Real Estate Acad., Los Altos, Calif., 1979—; mem. capital improvement com. City of Los Altos; mem. econ. devel. commn. Santa Clara County, Calif. Mem. Los Altos Bd. Realtors. Roman Catholic. Club: Harvard Bus. Sch. Office: 334 State St PO Box 901 Los Altos CA 94022

MCNULTY, IRVING BAZIL, biology educator; b. Salt Lake City, Jan. 6, 1918; s. Irving Monroe and Svea Melvina (Lindegren) McN.; m. Elizabeth Lund, Dec. 24, 1943 (div. 1967); children: Michael, Marc, Michelle; m. Joyce Reeder, Mar. 21, 1980. BA, U. Utah, 1942, MS, 1947; PhD, Ohio State U., 1952. From instr. to prof. biology U. Utah, Salt Lake City, 1947—. Chmn. adv. bd. State Arboretum Utah, Salt Lake City, 1981—. Served to 2d lt. USAF, 1943-45. Mem. AAUP, AAAS, Am. Soc. Plant Physiologists, Bot. Soc. Am. Democrat. Avocations: camping, hunting, skiing. Office: U Utah Biology Dept Salt Lake City UT 84112

MCNULTY, JOHN KENT, lawyer, educator; b. Buffalo, Oct. 13, 1934; s. Robert William and Margaret Ellen (Duthie) McN.; m. Linda Conner, Aug. 20, 1955 (div. Feb. 1977); children: Martha Jane, Jennifer, John K. Jr.; m. Babette B. Barton, Mar. 23, 1978. A.B. with high honors, Swarthmore Coll., 1956; LL.B., Yale U., 1959. Bar: Ohio 1961, U.S. Supreme Ct. 1964. Law clk. Justice Hugo L. Black, U.S. Supreme Ct., Washington, 1959-60; vis. prof. Sch. Law, U. Tex., summer 1960; asso. firm Jones, Day, Cockley & Reavis, Cleve., 1960-64; prof. law Sch. Law, U. Calif., Berkeley, 1964—; of counsel Baker & McKenzie, San Francisco, 1974-75; acad. visitor London Sch. Econs., 1985; lectr. univs. Cologne, Hamburg, London, Munich, Tokyo, Tilburg, Amsterdam, Rotterdam, Econs. U. Vienna, also others; mem. adv. bd. Carolina Acad. Press. Author: (with Kragen) Federal Income Taxation (Individuals, Corporations, Partnerships), 1985, 4th edit., Federal Income Taxation of Individuals, 3d edit., 1983, Federal Estate and Gift Taxation, 3d edit., 1983; mem. adv. bd. Carolina Academic Press. Guggenheim fellow, 1977. Mem. Am. Bar Assn., Am. Law Inst., Internat. Fiscal Assn. (council U.S. br.), Internat. Tax and Bus. Lawyers (mem. bd. overseers), Order of Coif, Phi Beta Kappa. Home: 620 Spruce St Berkeley CA 94707 Office: 389 Boalt Hall Sch of Law U Calif Berkeley CA 94720

MCNUTT, STEPHEN RUSSELL, volcanologist, geophysical scientist; b. Hartford, Conn., Dec. 21, 1954; s. Elmer Ellsworth and Leona (LaPointe) McN. BA, Wesleyan U., Middletown, Conn., 1977; MA, Columbia U., 1982, MPhil, 1984, PhD, 1985. Sr. seismologist Calif. Div. Mines and Geology, Sacramento, 1984-86, 1986—; cons. U. Costa Rica, San José, 1982-83. Contbr. articles to profl. jours. Mem. AAAS, Seismol. Soc. Am., Am. Geophys. Union, Internat. Assn. Volcanology and Chemistry of Earth Interior. Democrat. Roman Catholic. Club: Buffalo Chips Running (Sacramento) (bd. dirs. 1986—). Avocations: running, skiing, music, philately, drawing cartoons. Office: Calif Div Mines and Geology 630 Bercut Dr Sacramento CA 95814

MCPARTLAND, THOMAS JOSEPH, historian, educator; b. Oakland, Calif., July 30, 1945; s. Richard Joseph and Anne Josephine (Calmes) McP. BA, U. Santa Clara, 1967; MA, U. Wash., 1969, PhD, 1976. Acting asst. prof. U. Wash., Seattle, 1976-79; lectr. Pacific Luth. U., Tacoma, 1977, U. Wash., Seattle, 1985; instr. Bellevue (Wash.) Community Coll., 1981—; cons. to psychotherapists, Seattle, 1977—; instr. Telos, Clyde Hill, Wash., 1985-86, Issaquah, Wash., 1986—. Contbr. articles to profl. jours. Recipient scholarship Calif. State Scholarship Fedn., 1983-87; grantee for lecture Santa Clara U., 1985, Lonergan Workshop of Boston Coll., 1986. Mem. West Coast Methods Inst. Office: Bellevue Community Coll Dept Hist 3000 Landerholm Circle SE PO Box 92700 Bellevue WA 98009-2037

MCPHERSON, DAVID CARLTON, English language educator; b. Jayton, Tex., Jan. 19, 1935; s. Fred and Gladys Jefferson (Carlton) McP.; m. Francis Joyce Read, Oct. 15, 1961; children: Laurie Gail, Kathryn Read. BA, Hardin-Simmons U., 1957; MA, U. Tex., 1962, PhD, 1966. Asst. prof. U. Calif., Santa Barbara, 1966-72; assoc. prof. U. N.Mex., Albuquerque, 1972-77, prof., 1977—, dept. chmn., 1986—. Editor: Ben Jonson: Selected Works, 1972; contbr. articles to profl. jours. Served to capt. U.S. Army, 1958, 61-62. Fulbright-Kommission grantee, 1985-86. Mem. MLA. Democrat. Unitarian. Avocation: farming. Home: PO Box 335 Corrales NM 87048 Office: U NMex Dept English Albuquerque NM 87131

MCPHERSON, GALEN LOCKE, loss prevention engineer, consultant; b. Denver, July 30, 1933; s. Lawrence Theodore and Blanche (Graebing) McP.; m. Anne Elaine Werner, Feb. 16, 1966 (div. 1971); m. Nada Rapelje Arnett, Dec. 22, 1984. B.S. in Chem. Engring., U. Denver, 1955. Registered profl. engr., Colo. Profl. philatelist, Denver, 1958-66; sr. engr. Factory Mut. Engring., Chgo., 1966-72; acct. engr. large risk specialist FMI Ltd., London, 1972-78; sr. loss prevention specialist, Orange, Calif., 1978—; instr. UCLA Extension, 1984—. Mem. Soc. Fire Protection Engrs., Fire Protection Assn., Am. Inst. Chem. Engrs., Am. Philatelic Soc., Trans Mississippi Philatelic Soc. Unitarian. Home: 444 W Huntington Dr Apt #120 Arcadia CA 91006 Office: Factory Mutual Engring 505 City Parkway West Orange CA 92668

MCPHERSON, MALCOLM JOHN, mining engineering educator; b. Larkhall, Lanarkshire, Scotland, Feb. 16, 1937; s. Malcolm and Jeannie McPherson; m. Shirley Wass, July 28, 1958; children: Malcolm Stewart, Alison Dawn. BSc with honors, U. Nottingham, Eng., 1962, PhD, 1965. Lectr., sen. lectr. U. Nottingham, 1965-80; prof. mining engring. U. Calif., Berkeley, 1981—; pres. Mine Ventilation Services, Inc., Lafayette, Calif., 1982—. Co-author: Computer Methods for the 80's in the Mineral Industry, 1979, Environmental Engineering in South African Mines, 1982; contbr. articles to profl. jours. Fellow Instn. Mining and Metallurgy (Consolidated Goldfields Gold medal 1982, Mine Ventilation Soc. S. Africa (Gold Medal 1972), Instn. Mining. Engring. (mem. council 1980—, Silver Medal 1977); mem. Am. Inst. Mining Engrs. (ventilation com. 1982—, Henry Krumb Lectr. 1983), Engring. Council of U.K. (chartered). Avocations: music, photography. Office: U Calif Dept Materials Sci Mineral Engring Hearst Mining Bldg Berkeley CA 94549

MC PHERSON, ROLF KENNEDY, clergyman, church official; b. Providence, Mar. 23, 1913; s. Harold S. and Aimee Elizabeth (Semple) McP.; m. Lorna De Smith, July 21, 1931; children—Marlene (dec.), Kay. Graduate, So. Cal. Radio Inst., 1933; D.D. (hon.), L.I.F.E. Bible Coll., 1944. Ordained to ministry Internat. Ch. Foursquare Gospel, 1940, pres., dir., 1944—; Pres., dir. Echo Park Evangelistic Assn., L.I.F.E. Bible Coll., Inc.; bd. adminstrn. Pentecostal Fellowship N.Am., 1948—. Office: 1100 Glendale Blvd Los Angeles CA 90026

MCQUILLIN, MAHLON (LON) BRICE, II, TV producer, director; b. Chgo., Apr. 3, 1950; s. Brice and Eleanor Valey (Lindskog) McQ. AA, Coll. San Mateo, 1970. Mem. advt .dept. San Mateo (Calif.) Times, 1970-71; audio systems mgr. Foremans Co., San Mateo, 1971-73; video systems mgr. Brooks Co., San Francisco, 1973-76; pres. gen. mgr. MicroVision Systems, San Mateo, 1976—; owner, cons. McQ Prodns.; owner, cons. McQ Prodns.; producer, dir., editor TV programs for broadcast, corp. communications, syndication, commls.; dir. cable series Comedy Showcase; instr. Coll. San Mateo, 1981-84; faculty mem. N.Am. TV Inst.; bd. dirs. San Francisco Film/Tape Council, sec., 1986—. Author: The Video Production Guide 1983, Computers in Video Production, 1986; (with others) The Handbook of Private Television, 1982; designer MicroVision 20 videotape editing system; developer computer software; editor Internat. TV News, 1975-79; contbg. editor Video Systems mag., 1978-81; contbr. articles to industry publs. Active Poplar Ctr., San Mateo. Served with USAFR, 1970-73. Winner Silver and Bronze awards Internat. Film and TV Festival of N.Y., 1979, 81, 82, Gold award Internat. Film and TV Festival of N.Y., 1983. Mem. Internat. TV Assn. (Golden Reel of Excellence), Soc. Motion Picture and TV Engrs., Nat. Acad. TV Arts and Scis. Office: PO Box 1676 San Mateo CA 94401

MCQUISTON, MICHAEL CHARLES, mining safety administrator; b. Nevada City, Calif., Apr. 24, 1944; s. Frank Wood and Frances (Haseltine) M.; m. Judith P. Price, Dec. 23, 1972; 1 child, Michael Scott; m. Helen Louise Sitterly, Jan. 23, 1982; 1 child, Apryl Dawn. A.A.S. in Indsl. Engring., Western Piedmont Community Coll., Morganton, N.C., 1972; A.A.S. in Liberal Studies, Central Ariz. Community Coll., 1975. Safety engr. Magma Copper Co., San Manuel, Ariz., 1972-77; dir. safety and environ. Smoky Valley Mining div. Copper Range Co., Round Mountain, Nev., 1978-79; supt. safety, tng. and personnel Westcoast Oil and Gas Corp., Sparks, Nev., 1979-81; site inspection controller Cementation of Am. Inc., Carlsbad, N.Mex., 1981-83; self-employed, 1983-84; safety adminstr. EG&G, Pleasanton, Calif., 1984—. Served with U.S. Army, 1968-70. Decorated Purple Heart. Mem. Am. Soc. Safety Engrs., Soc. Mining Engrs. AIME. Methodist. Home: 3121 Kittery Ave San Ramon CA 94583

MCRAE, FRANCES ELEANOR MOORMAN, nursing administrator; b. St. Brieux, Sask., Can., May 11, 1933; d. Stanley Degolia Moorman and Ruby Frances (Smith) Moorman Mullins; m. Robert D. McRae, Aug. 14, 1955 (div. Aug. 1963); children: Theresa Louise, Heather Jeanine, Robert D. Jr. Student, U. Lethbridge, Alta., Can., 1962-63, Vanderbilt U., 1979; BS, Walla Walla Coll., 1955; MS, Loma Linda U., 1979. Cert. advanced nursing adminstrn. Staff nurse St. Mary's Hosp., Walla Walla, Wash. and Our Lady of Lourdes, Pasco, Wash., 1955-63; instr. Columbia Basin Coll., Pasco, 1963-70, Galt Sch. of Nursing, Lethbridge, 1970-73, Kelsey Inst., Saskatoon, Sask., 1975-77; staff nurse Loma Linda (Calif.) U., 1973-75, head nurse, 1977-78; asst. adminstr. nursing Madison (Tenn.) Hosp., 1978-79; dir. nursing Tillamook (Oreg.) County Gen. Hosp., 1979—. V.p. Am. Cancer Soc., Tillamook, 1980-86. Recipient nursing Am. Nurses Assn., 1984. Mem. Assn. Seventh Day Adventist Nurses, Nat. League for Nursing, Willamette Council Oreg. Orgn. Nurse Execs. (sec.,treas. 1986—), Oreg. Nurse Execs., Bus. and Profl. Women, Sigma Theta Tau. Republican. Club: Toastmasters. Avocations: photography, gardening, camping, writing. Home: 7450 Vaughn Rd Tillamook OR 97141 Office: 1000 3d st Tillamook OR 97141

MCRAE, HAMILTON EUGENE, III, lawyer; b. Midland, Tex., Oct. 29, 1937; s. Hamilton Eugene and Adrian (Hagaman) McR.; m. Betty Hawkins, Aug. 27, 1960; children—Elizabeth Ann, Stephanie Adrian, Scott Hawkins. BSEE, U. Ariz., 1961; student, USAF Electronics Sch., 1961-62; postgrad., U. Redlands, Calif., 1962-63; JD with honors and distinction, U. Ariz., 1967. Bar: Ariz. 1967, U.S. Supreme Ct. 1979. Elec. engr. Salt River Project, Phoenix, 1961; assoc. Jennings, Strouss & Salmon, Phoenix, 1967-71, ptnr., 1971-85, chmn. real estate dept., 1980-85, mem. policy com., 1982-85, mem. fin. com., 1981-85, chmn. bus. devel. com., 1982-85; ptnr. and co-founder Stuckey & McRae, Phoenix, 1985—; co-founder, chmn. bd. Republic Cos., Phoenix, 1985—; magistrate Paradise Valley, Ariz., 1983-85; juvenile referee Superior Ct., 1983-85; pres., dir. Phoenix Realty & Trust Co., 1970—; officer Indsl. Devel. Corp. Maricopa County, 1972-86; instr. and lectr. in real estate; officer, bd. dirs. other corps. Contbr. articles to profl. jours. Elder Valley Presbyterian Ch., Scottsdale, Ariz., 1973-75, 82-85, corp. pres., 1974-75, 84-85, trustee, 1973-75, 82-85, chmn. exec. com., 1984; trustee Upward Found., Phoenix, 1977-80, Valley Presbyn. Found., 1982-83, Ariz. Acad., 1971—; trustee, mem. exec. com. Phi Gamma Delta Ednl. Found., Washington, 1974-84; trustee Phi Gamma Delta Internat., 1984-86, Archon, 1986-87, bd. dirs.; founder, trustee McRae Found.; trustee, mem. exec. com. Ariz. Mus. Sci. and Tech., 1984—, 1st v.p., 1985-86, pres., 1986—; vol. fund raiser YMCA, Salvation Army, others; mem. Taliesin Council, Frank Lloyd Wright Found., 1985—; dir. Food for Hungry (Internat. Relief), 1985—, exec. com., 1986—, chmn. bd. dirs. 1987—; mem. Ariz. State U. Council of 100, 1985—, investment com., 1985—; U. Ariz. Pres.'s Club, 1984—. Served with USAF, 1961-64. Recipient various mil. awards. Mem. ABA, Ariz. Bar Assn., Maricopa County Bar Assn., AIME, Ariz. Acad., U. Ariz. Alumni Assn., Clan McRae Soc. N.Am., Tau Beta Pi. Republican. Clubs: Phoenix Exec., Phoenix Country, Arizona, Continental Country; Jackson Hole Racquet (Wyo.). Home: 8101 N 47th St Paradise Valley AZ 85253 Office: Republic Cos 5500 N 24th St Phoenix AZ 85016

MC REYNOLDS, MARY BARBARA, educator; b. Los Angeles, Feb. 18, 1930; d. Clyde C. and Dorothy (Slaten) McCulloh; B.A., U. N.Mex., 1951, M.A., 1972, Edn. Specialist, 1975, postgrad., 1981—; m. Zachariah A. McReynolds, Feb. 9, 1952 (dec.); children—Gregg Clyde, Barbara, Zachariah A. Dept. sec. USAF Intelligence, Wiesbaden, W. Ger., 1953-54; tchr. Annandale (Va.) Elem. Sch., 1962-65, supr. adult edn., 1965-66; tchr. Albuquerque High Sch., 1968-75, 77—, social studies curriculum dir., 1973-75; instr. U. N.Mex., Albuquerque, 1975-76, decathlon coach Albuquerque High Sch., 1986—; evaluator N. Central Assn., 1970-81, dir. Cultural Awareness Workshop, 1976, 79; coordinator Sex Equality, 1979, 80. Bd. dirs. Greater U. N.Mex. Fund, 1978-79, 79-80, fund raiser, 1976-81, pres. club, 1977-80; campaign mgr. state senatorial campaign, 1976; exec. sec. Civic Assn., 1958-60; sponsor Black Student Union, 1978-80; sponsor Boys and Girls State, 1968-75; rep. Am. Fedn. Tchrs., 1982-86; precinct chmn. Democratic Party, Albuquerque, 1985-86. Indian research and tuition edn. grantee, 1971; grantee U. N.Mex., 1975-76, others. Mem. Assn. Supervision and Curriculum Devel., Nat. Social Studies Council, N.Mex. Social Studies Council, Phi Kappa Phi, Phi Delta Kappa, Pi Alpha Theta, Kappa Kappa Gamma. Democrat. Episcopalian. Clubs: N.Mex. Democratic Women, Air Force Officers Wives, Kappa Kappa Gamma Alumni. Condr. research in field. Home: 15 Plaza Olas Altas Albuquerque NM 87109

MCREYNOLDS, NEIL LAWRENCE, electric utility company executive; b. Seattle, July 27, 1934; s. Dorr E. and Margaret (Gillies) McR.; m. Nancy Joyce Drew, June 21, 1957; children: Christopher, Bonnie. BA in Journalism, U. Wash., 1956. Assoc. editor Bellevue (Wash.) Am., Wash., 1956-60, editor, 1960-67; press sec. to gov. Dan Evans State of Wash., Olympia, 1967-73; northwest regional mgr. for corp. relations ITT Corp., Seattle, 1973-80; v.p. corp. relations Puget Sound Power and Light, Bellevue, 1980-87, sr. v.p., 1987—; bd. dirs. Contential Savs. Bank, Seattle; chmn. communications exec. adv. com. Edison Electric Inst., 1983-84; mem. communications adv. com. Electric Power Research Inst., 1985—. Bd. dirs. Seattle Symphony, 1981—, Pub. Affairs Council, 1981—, Nature Conservancy, 1985—, Ind. Colls. of Wash., 1984—, Assn. Wash. Bus., 1985—, Corp. Council for Arts, 1985—, Fred Hutchison Cancer Research Ctr., 1987—; chmn. bd. Leadership Tomorrow, Seattle, 1987—; v.p. Seattle Rotary Service Found., 1986-87, Electric Info. Council, 1987—. Named Citizen of Yr., Bellevue, 1963, One of Wash. State's Three Outstanding Young Men, 1965. Mem. Profl. Journalists, Public Relations Soc. Am. (accredited), Sigma Delta Chi. Republican. Episcopalian. Clubs: Rainier (Seattle); Overlake Golf & Country (Medina, Wash.); Bellevue Athletic. Lodge: Rotary. Avocations: golf, hiking, skiing, photography. Home: 4502 Elizabeth St #5 Cudahy CA 90201 Office: Puget Sound Power & Light Co PO Box 97034 Bellevue WA 98009

MCSWEENEY, FRANCES KAYE, psychology educator; b. Rochester, N.Y., Feb. 6, 1948; d. Edward William and Elsie Winifred (Kingston) McS. BA, Smith Coll., 1969; MA, Harvard U., 1972, PhD, 1974. Lectr. McMaster U., Hamilton, Ont., Can., 1973-74; asst. prof. Wash. State U., Pullman, 1974-79, assoc. prof., 1979-83, prof. psychology, 1983—, chmn. dept. psychology, 1986—; cons. in field. Contbr. articles to profl. jours. Woodrow Wilson fellow, Sloan Fellow, 1968-69; NSF fellow, 1970-72; NIMH fellow, 1973. Mem. Am. Psychol. Assn., Western Psychol. Assn.,

Psychonomic Soc., Assn. Behavior Analysis, Phi Beta Kappa, Sigma Xi. Home: NW 90 Thomas-D Pullman WA 99163 Office: Wash State U Dept Psychology Pullman WA 99164

MCSWEENY, WILLIAM FRANCIS, petroleum company executive; b. Haverhill, Mass., Mar. 31, 1929; s. William Francis and Mary Florence (Doyle) McS.; m. Dorothy Pierce, Jan. 20, 1969; children—William Francis III, Cathy Ann, Ethan Madden Maverick, Terrell Pierce. Reporter, columnist, fgn. corr. Hearst Newspapers, 1943-67; dep. chmn., dir. pub. affairs Democratic Nat. Com., 1967-68; spl. asst. to White House Chief of Staff, 1968-69; sr. exec. v.p. Occidental Internat. Corp., Washington, 1969-76, pres., 1976—; exec. v.p., bd. dirs. Occidental Petroleum Corp.; dir. Fin. Gen. Bankshares Co., Washington, 1978-82, Chevy Chase Savs. and Loan, 1985—. Author: Go Up for Glory, 1965, Violence Every Sunday, 1966, The Impossible Dream, 1967; also articles. Bd. visitors Fletcher Sch. Law and Diplomacy, Tufts U.; bd. advisors Karl F. Landegger Program Internat. Bus. Diplomacy, Sch. Fgn. Service, Georgetown U.; chmn. Meridan House Internat.; v.p. Middle East Inst.; bd. dirs. Washington Soc. Performing Arts, Nat. Arts for Handicapped, Arena Stage, Corcoran Gallery Art, Am. Com. on East-West Accord, Arms Control Assn., Africare, Fed. City Council, Washington Opera, Ford Theater, Folger Shakespeare Theater, Cities in Schs. Capital Children's Mus.; v.p. Ct. of the Mary Rose, Portsmouth, Eng.; mem. Pres.'s Commn. Exec. Interchange; mem. U.S. Commn. UNESCO; trustee Holton Arms Sch., Washington Episcopal Sch. Served to maj. AUS, 1950-53. Decorated Combat Inf. badge; recipient Outstanding Young Man award Boston Jaycees, 1961, U.S. Disting. Service award, 1968, outstanding service spl. award, 1969, D.C. disting. citizen, 1981, Paul Hill award Kenedy Ctr., 1983; numerous awards for domestic reporting, awards for reporting from Vietnam and Middle East. mem. nat. adv. com. The Smithsonian Instn.; spl. counsel Speaker of Ho. of Reps., 1971-72; Presdl. Commn., 1976-80; mem. Pres.'s Inaugural Com., 1980, 84, Pres.'s Korean War Meml. Commn., 1987; Pres.'s Spl. ambassador to Bolivia, 1982; Pres.'s rep. to USSR, 1980; Presdl. spl. rep. to Oman, 1979. Clubs: Nat. Press, Cosmos, 1925 F Street, Internat. (Washington); Lotos (N.Y.C.). Office: Occidental Internat Corp 1747 Pennsylvania Ave NW Suite 375 Washington DC 20006

MCTATE, GABRIELLA ANGEL, clinical social worker; b. Cin., Mar. 6, 1948; d. Eli and Hazel (Gentry) Angel; m. David McTate, Oct. 11, 1975; 1 child, Emily. BA, Ohio State U., 1970; MSW, Tulane U., 1974. Social worker Dept. Pub. Welfare, Cin., 1970-75, Family Services, Omaha, 1975-78; social worker supr. Isfar U. Nebr. Med. Ctr., Omaha, 1978-80; clin. social worker, adminstr. Family Enrichment, Omaha, 1980—; bd. dirs. Child Saving Inst., Omaha, 1984—; cons. St. Pio's and St. Leo's Schs., Omaha, 1982—. Mem. Jr. League, Omaha, 1979—. Fellow Am. Orthopsychiat. Assn.; mem. Nat. Assn. Social Workers (treas. Nebr. chpt. 1982-84, named Social Worker of Yr. 1984). Avocation: swimming. Office: Family Enrichment 5002 Dodge Omaha NB 68132

MCVEIGH-PETTIGREW, SHARON CHRISTINE, communications company executive; b. San Francisco, Feb. 6, 1949; d. Martin Allen and Frances (Roddy) McVeigh; m. John Wallace Pettigrew, Mar. 27, 1971; children: Benjamin Thomas, Margaret Mary. B.A. with honors, U. Calif.-Berkeley, 1971; diploma of edn. Monash U., Australia, 1975; M.B.A., Golden Gate U., 1985. Tchr., adminstr. Victorian Edn. Dept., Victoria, Australia, 1972-79; supr. Network Control Ctr., GTE Sprint Communications, Burlingame, Calif., 1979-81, mgr. customer assistance, 1981-84, mgr. state legis. ops., 1984-85, dir. revenue programs, 1986—; telecommunications speaker Dept. Consumer Affairs, Sacramento, 1984. Panelist Wash. Gov.'s Citizens Council, 1984; founding mem. Maroondah Women's Shelter, Victoria, 1978; organizer nat. conf. Bus. Women and the Polit. Process, New Orleans, 1986;mem. sch. bd. Boronia Tech. Sch., Victoria, 1979; active Friends to Parents, South San Francisco, 1981—, NOW, San Mateo, Calif., 1982—. Recipient Tchr. Spl. Responsibilities award Victoria Edn. Dept., 1979. Mem. Women in Telecommunications (panel moderator San Francisco 1984), Am. Mgmt. Assn. Democrat. Roman Catholic. Office: US Sprint Communications PO Box 974 Burlingame CA 94010

MCVEY, MARCIA ALICE, educational administrator; b. San Jose, Calif., Aug. 31, 1934; d. Charles Thurston and Thelma (Hackett) McV.; B.A., Pomona Coll., 1955; M.A., Claremont Grad. Sch., 1959; Ed.D. (Delta Kappa Gamma Scholar), U. So. Calif., 1978. Tchr., Glendora Sch. Dist., 1955-59; tchr. Covina Valley Unified Sch. Dist., 1959-65, counselor, jr. high sch., 1965-67, asst. prin. jr. high, 1967-68, prin., 1968-72, 73-79; dir. curriculum and instruction Norwalk (Calif.) LaMirada Unified Sch. Dist., 1979-83; asst. supt. Centralia Sch. Dist., Buena Park (Calif.), 1983-86, Duarte Unified Sch. Dist., Calif., 1986—; ednl. cons.; mem. Calif. Dept. Edn. task force on conflict resolution in secondary schs., 1972-73. Bd. dirs. HEAR Center, Pasadena, 1976—; community vol. Pomona Coll. Assocs.; mem. Calif. Curriculum Devel. and Supplemental Materials Commn., 1984—. Kettering IDEA fellow, 1981. Mem. Assn. Calif. Sch. Adminstrs., Calif. Assn. Gifted, Profl. Advocates for Gifted Edn., Assn. Supervision and Curriculum Devel., AAUW, Phi Delta Kappa, Delta Kappa Gamma. Contbr. articles to profl. jours. Office: 1427 Buena Vista Ave Duarte CA 91010

MCVICKER, DAWSON SCOTT, energy resources engineer; b. Lincoln, Nebr., May 3, 1952; s. Dwight Sidney and Jean (Steven) McV. AA in Chemistry, Pasadena City Coll., 1973; BSChemE, U. Colo., 1977; MSChemE, U. Wyo., 1980; MBA in Energy Mgmt., U. Denver, 1986. Chem. engr. Harris & Assocs. Engrs. Inc., Laramie, Wyo., 1979-81; engr. Keplinger & Assocs., Denver, 1981-84, EG&G Wash. Analytical Services Ctr., Laramie, 1984—; cons. in field, 1979—. Mem. Soc. Petroleum Engrs., Am. Inst. Chem. Engrs., AAAS, Sigma Xi, Phi Delta Theta. Democrat. Methodist. Avocations: hunting, fishing, racquetball, flying.

MCWALTER, J(OHN) BRYCE, stockbroker, financial planner; b. Seattle, Oct. 28, 1949; s. Jack and Marie C. (Bryce) McW.; m. Maureen B. Pereira, Aug. 11, 1973; children: John Michael, Jaclyn Marie, Jason Bryce. BA, Seattle U., 1972; MBA, Pepperdine U.-Honolulu, 1974. Cert. fin. planner. Account exec. Dean Witter Reynolds, Inc., Seattle, 1976-83, asst. br. mgr., Northgate, Seattle, 1983-86, assoc. v.p. dowtown Seattle office, 1986—; lectr. Chaminade U. Honolulu, 1974-76; instr. U. Puget Sound, 1980-82. Rep. precinct committeeman, King County, Seattle, 1980-84, 1986—; coach Interbay 7-11 Men's Softball Team, 1977-84; chmn. prize com. Cystic Fibrosis Celebrity Golf Tournament, 1986, putting contest, 1987. Served to capt. U.S. Army, 1972-76, maj. Res. Mem. Jaycees (pres. treas. Interbay 1977-80, Honolulu Jaycee of Month, 1975, Keyman award 1976), Inst. Fin. Planners, Seattle U. Alumni Assn. (bd. govs.), Res. Officers Assn., Ballard C. of C., U.S. Golf Assn. Roman Catholic. Club: College (Seattle). Home: 2621 27th St W Seattle WA 98199 Office: Dean Witter Reynolds Inc 1301 5th Ave 2800 Rainier Bank Tower Seattle WA 98101

MC WILLIAMS, ROBERT HUGH, judge; b. Salina, Kans., Apr. 27, 1916; s. Robert Hugh and Laura (Nicholson) McW.; m. Catherine Ann Cooper, Nov. 4, 1942 (dec.); 1 son, Edward Cooper; m. Joan Harcourt, Mar. 8, 1986. A.B., U. Denver, 1938, LL.B., 1941. Bar: Colo. bar 1941. Colo. dist. judge Denver, 1952-60; justice Colo. Supreme Ct., 1961-68, chief justice, 1969-70; judge 10th Circuit Ct. Appeals 1970—. Served with AUS, World War II. Mem. Phi Beta Kappa, Omicron Delta Kappa, Phi Delta Phi, Kappa Sigma. Republican. Episcopalian. Home: 137 Jersey St Denver CO 80220 Office: US Courthouse 1929 Stout St Denver CO 80294

MEACHAM, CRAIG LEI, police chief; b. Pasadena, Calif., Mar. 5, 1931; s. William Albert and Edna May (Hornbeck) M.; m. Carolyn June Stentz, Feb. 22, 1971; children—Alan, Pamela, Craig, Janelle, Cynthia. A.A., Rio Hondo Coll., 1964; B.A., Calif. Western U., 1976, M.A., 1976. With Whittier (Calif.) Police Dept., 1955-69, div. comdr., until 1969; cons. criminal justice Gov. Ronald Reagan, 1969-70; dep. chief West Covina Police Dept., 1970-78, chief of police, 1978—, pub. safety div. mgr., 1981—; instr. Rio Hondo Coll. Served with USAF, 1950-54. Mem. Los Angeles County Chiefs of Police Assn. (pres. 1982), San Gabriel Valley Police Chiefs Assn. (pres.), Calif. Police Chiefs Assn. (v.p.), Peace Officers Assn. Los Angeles County (pres. 1986—), San Gabriel Valley Peace Officers Assn. (pres. 1983), West Covina C. of C. (legis. com.). Club: West Covina Lions. Office: 1444 W Garvey St West Covina CA 91790

MEACHAM, MARGIE MILLHONE, judge; b. Omaha, Feb. 4, 1930; d. Paul L. and Margaret M. (Griffith) Millhone. B.S., U. Wyo., 1952, J.D., 1954. Bar: Wyo. 1954, U.S. Dist. Ct. Wyo. 1967, U.S. Ct. Appeals (10th cir.) 1967, U.S. Supreme Ct. 1980. Law librarian, instr. U. Wyo., 1953-55; assoc. Jerry W. Housel, Cody, Wyo., 1955-56, 62-68; sole practice, Cody, 1968-73; justice of peace Carbon County, Wyo., 1974-83; mcpl. judge City of Cody, 1968-73, City of Rawlins (Wyo.), 1978-82; judge County Ct., Rawlins, 1983—; sec. County Ct. Judges div. Wyo. Jud. Council; mem. Jud. Planning Com. State of Wyo., 1978—. Sec., bd. dirs. Carbon County Counseling Ctr.; bd. dirs. Wyo. Law Enforcement Acad., 1972-73; past dir. Cody Boy Scouts Am. Mem. ABA (exec. bd. conf. spl. ct. judges, jud. adminstrn. div., 1981—), Wyo. Bar Assn., Park County Bar Assn. (pres. 1965-66), Am. Judges Assn., Am. Judicature Soc., Nat. Assn. Women Judges (nat. membership chmn. 1982-83, dist. dir. 1985—), Wyo. Judges of Cts. of Ltd. Jurisdiction Assn. (pres. 1980-82), Na.t Ctr. for State Cts. (bd. dirs. 1986—). Address: 1124 8th St Rawlins WY 82301

MEAD, HYRUM ANDERSON, JR., business executive; b. Pueblo, Colo., Mar. 24, 1947; s. Hyrum A. and Opal E. (Jarrell) M.; m. G. Rosemary Dunn, Jan. 2, 1974; children: Hyrum Brandon, Heather Rose, Holly Mary. BS, Brigham Young U., 1971; MBA, Utah State U., 1973. Cert. in vocat. edn., Colo. Missionary, Japan, 1966-69; instr. Midwest Bus. Coll., Pueblo, 1973; account rep. IBM, Denver, 1974-80; v.p. sales and mktg. Electro Controls, Inc., Salt Lake City, 1980-84, chief operating officer, 1984-86, pres. 1986—; bus. cons., 1975—; speaker lighting industry. Co-author: The Life of James Anderson, 1973; also sales manuals. Dist. commr. Boy Scouts Am., 1983-84; neighborhood coordinator State Emergency Preparedness Program, 1983-84. Recipient Presdl. citation, 1980. Mem. Illuminating Engring. Soc. (speaker), Nat. Assn. Broadcasters, Am. Theatre Assn., U.S. Inst. Theatre Tech., Nat. Home Builders Assn. Republican. Mormon. Home: 232 S Constitution Way North Salt Lake UT 84054 Office: Electro Controls Inc 2975 S 300 W Salt Lake City UT 84115

MEAD, JERRY DALE, wine expert, writer; b. Rogers, Ark., May 14, 1939; s. Lloyd Willard and Mary Frances (Boyd) M.; m. Linda Elizabeth Gallentine, Aug. 31, 1957; children—Loretta Jean, Jerry Dion, Sean Darren. Wine expert, cons. and writer, San Francisco, 1969—; founder Wine Investigation for Novices and Oenophiles (WINO). Chmn. judges panel Orange County Fair com. wine competition; program chmn. ann. wine festival, Laguna Niguel, Calif. Recipient Perpetual Trophy for Excellence in Wine Writing, Calif. Assn. Winegrape Growers, 1985. Mem. Bay Area Wine Writers. Author syndicated column Mead on Wine; pub. WINO newsletter, WINO trader; contbr. numerous articles to nat. and regional publs.

MEAD, ROBERT ALLEN, state agency administrator, cartographer; b. Oregon City, Oreg., Sept. 19, 1931; s. George Linwood and Dollie Ada (Mclendon) M.; m. Dora Marion Johnson, Dec. 11, 1932; children: Susan Annette, Deanna Gail Bathke. Student, U. Oreg., 1956-58. Surveyor U.S. Naval Postgrad. Sch., Annapolis, Md., 1951-55; cartographer Oreg. Dept. Revenue, Salem, 1955-57, mgr. projects, 1958-72, mgr. mapping, 1972—; cons. Costa Rica, 1983-85. Author: Cadastral Map Standards, Concepts, Cartographic Procedures, 1979, 2d rev. edit., 1981; designer first computer-ized cadastral map system. Served with USN, 1951-55. Mem. Nat. Computer Graphics Assn., Gov.'s State Map Adv. Com. Republican. Presbyterian. Club: Sports Car of Am. (Oreg.) (dep. exec. steward 1970-86). Avocations: Ham radio, oil and watercolor painting, fishing, sports car racing, photography. Home: 2480 Fisher Rd NE Salem OR 97305 Office: Oreg Dept Revenue 955 Center St Salem OR 97310

MEAD, ROBERT L., grocery company executive. Chmn. Assoc. Grocers Inc., Seattle. Office: Associated Grocers Inc 3301 S Norfolk St Seattle WA 98118 *

MEADE, ROBERT HEBER, geologist; b. Bklyn., Dec. 27, 1930; s. Robert Heber Meade and Billie (Temple) White; m. Mereth Ellenor Mueller, June 17, 1956; children: Alexander, Stephanie, Eric. BS in Geology, U. Okla., 1952; MS in Geology, Stanford U., 1957, PhD in Geology, 1960. Geologist, hydrologist U.S. Geol. Survey, Menlo Park, Calif., 1957-63, Woods Hole, Mass., 1963-74, Denver, 1974—; adj. prof. SUNY, Stony Brook, 1975-83; ground-water cons. Town of Falmouth, Mass., 1969-71, Town of Harwich, Mass., 1973-74. Assoc. editor Jour. Geophys. Research, 1974-77; contbr. articles to profl. jours. Elected rep., Town Meeting Falmouth, Mass., 1969-72; pres. Falmouth Music Assn., 1965-67, program chmn., 1969-70; bd. dirs. Cape Cod Conservatory of Music and Art, Barnstable, Mass., 1968-71. Served to lt. USNR, 1952-55. Recipient Meritorious Service award U.S. Dept. Interior, 1985. Fellow Geol. Soc. Am.; mem. Am. Geophys. Union, Internat. Assn. Sedimentologists, ASCE, AAAS, Soc. Economic Paleontologists and Mineralogists. Avocations: singing, acting. Office: US Geol Survey MS 413 Box 25046 Fed Ctr Denver CO 80225

MEADE, STEPHEN ALAN, insurance company executive; b. Boston, Nov. 22, 1949; s. Richard Alan and Rosemary (Coakley) M.; m. Donna Marie Dianto, Sept. 12, 1971 (div. Mar. 1981); m. Mary Lou Fountain, Apr. 23, 1983; children: Christine, Michelle. BS, Boston State Coll., 1971. CPCU. Planning dir. Fireman's Fund Ins. Co., San Francisco, 1977-78, sr. project dir., 1978-81; asst. v.p. San Francisco Reins. Co., 1981-85; v.p. Balboa Ins. Group, Irvine, Calif., 1985-86, sr. v.p., 1986—; bd. dirs. Avco Fin. Ins. Group, Irvine, 1986—. Served with USNG, 1970-76. Recipient Acad. Excellence award Ins. Inst. Am., 1981. Episcopalian. Avocations: photography, tennis, piano, racquetball. Home: 2329 N Linwood Ave Santa Ana CA 92701 Office: Balboa Ins Group 3347 Michelson Dr Suite 400 Irvine CA 92715

MEADER, JONATHAN GRANT (ASCIAN KYTHE), artist; b. Orange, N.J., Aug. 29, 1943; s. William Granville and Audrey Meader. One-man shows Corcoran Dupont Center, 1969, Lunn Gallery, Washington, 1972, Pyramid Gallery, Washington, 1973, 74, Plum Gallery, Md., 1976, 78, 78, Klein-Vogel Gallery, Mich., 1976, Harlan Gallery, Tucson, 1977, Swearingen Gallery, Ky., 1977, Schoolhouse Gallery, Fla., 1978, 83, Ethel Putterman Gallery, Mass., 1978, Washington Project for Arts, 1981, Galerie Grüner Panther, Frankfurt, W. Ger., 1982, Illuminarium Gallery, Los Angeles, 1985, Illuminarium Gallery, Larkspur, Calif., 1985; Illuminarium, Mill Valley, Calif., 1982, 83, Gallery Show, Tokyo, 1985, Kraskin Gallery, Potomac, Md., 1986, Midtown Gallery, Washington, 1986; group shows include Corcoran Gallery Art, Washington, 1972, Balt. Mus. Traveling Show, 1972, Phillips Collection, Washington, 1972, Iowa U. Mus., 1975, Plum Gallery, 1975; represented in permanent collections, Whitney Mus. Am. Art, N.Y.C., Met. Mus. Art, N.Y.C., Nat. Gallery, Washington, Hirshhorn Mus., Washington. Wurlitzer Found. grantee, 1967; Stern Family grantee, 1970; Nat. Endowment Arts grantee, 1974. Address: 758 Marin Drive Mill Valley CA 94941

MEADOR, ROBERT LYMAN, dentist; b. Portland, Oreg., Jan. 20, 1934; m. Sharon Lynn Caillouet, Apr. 10, 1967 (div. June 1978); m. Charlotte Ann Dodson, Sept. 14, 1985. BS, U. Oreg., 1957; DMD, U. Oreg., Portland, 1959. Lic. dentist, Calif., N.Mex., Oreg. Chief, attending dental staff Orange (Calif.) County Med. Ctr., 1966-67, chief, restorative dental service, 1971-77; assoc. prof. dentistry Loma Linda (Calif.) U., 1969-70; clin. assoc. prof. diagnostic scis., oral diagnosis and emergency clinic. U. So. Calif., Los Angeles, 1981-83, clin. assoc. prof.; dir., gen. practice residency and clin. restorative service U. Calif., Irving, 1974-77; chief, attending dental staff Fullerton (Calif.) Community Hosp., 1982-83. Contbr. articles to profl. jours. Mem. Am. Heart Assn. (bd. dirs. Orange County chpts. 1981—, active dental CPR program 1975—, chmn. emergency services com. 1975—, co-chmn. hypertension control com. 1975-78); active Allied Health Profls., Yorba Linda City Planning Commn.; pres. Richard M. Nixon Birthplace Found., 1982-86. Served to Capt. USAF, 1959-62. Named one of Outstanding Young Men Am., 1966, Outstanding State Dir., Calif. Jaycees, 1965; Paul Harris fellow, Yorba Linda Rotary club, 1980. Mem. Acad. Gen. Dentistry (mastership 1984), Am. Assn. Hosp. Denstists (Calif. vice-chmn. 1974-80), Am. Dental Assn. and Local Components, Am. Dental Soc. of Anesthesiology, Am. Edodontic Soc., Calif. Soc. Anesthesiology (pres.-elect 1983-84, pres. 1984-85), Orange County Dental Soc. (chmn. continuing edn. com. 1973-74, chmn. children's dental clinic com 1970-71), Yorba Linda C. of C. (pres. 1971-72), North Orange County Jaycees (dist. gov. state of Calif., 1968-69, outstanding dist. chmn. 1966), Yorba Linda Jaycees (pres. 1966-67, disting. service award 1967, Kay Man award 1967).

MEADOWS, BONNIE JEAN, publishing executive; b. Cheverly, Md., Apr. 12, 1949; d. Wilbur Irving and Angela (Aiello) Duvall; m. Russell Meadows III, Feb. 16, 1964. Student, Loretta Heights Coll., Denver, Colo. U. Publs. dir. North Suburban Printing and Pub., Westminster, Colo., 1979-86; v.p. The Pubs. House, Inc., Westminster, 1986—. Monthly columnist Westminster Window, 1987;. Recipient Best Ad award Colo. Press Assn., 1979, Graphic Excellence award Butler Paper, 1984, Star award Colo. Wildlife Mag., 1985. Mem. Nat. Writer's Club, Met. North C. of C. Republican. Avocations: horseback riding, reading, fiction writing. Office: The Pub House Inc PO Box 215 Westminster CO 80030

MEADS, ARTHUR RALPH, college adminstrator, artist; b. Lethbridge, Alta., Can., Oct. 7, 1947; s. Arthur Ernest and Violet Ruth (Hanson) M.; m. Alice May Mansell, July 12, 1980; children—Tara, Lauren. B.A., U. B.C., Vancouver, 1971; diploma Vancouver Sch. Art, 1971. Artist City of Vancouver (B.C., Can.); display artist Hudson's Bay, Calgary, Alta., 1975-77; lectr. U. Calgary, 1977-78; program coordinator Alta. Coll. Art, Calgary, 1978-82, acad. supr., 1982-83, head, 1983-85, acting pres., 1985, v.p., acad. dean. 1985—. Office: Alta Coll Art, 1407 14th Ave NW, Calgary, AB Canada T2N 4R3

MEAGHER, JAMES FOSTER, interior and architectural designer; b. Richmond, Va., Aug. 16, 1942; s. John Joseph and Catherine Estelle (Eck) M. BFA, Va. Commonwealth U., 1964. Owner, designer Color Control, San Francisco, 1971-79; prin. Foster Meagher Enterprises, Los Angeles, Houston, 1979—; nat. spokesman Nat. Paint and Coatings Assn., Washington, 1981-85, dir. restoration, 1985; designer Ford Found., N.Y.C., 1982, Local Initiatives Support Corp., NYC, 1982-83, South Bronx Devel. Orgn. Inc. Painter/designer (comml. projects) Ninfa's Fajita's Restaurant, Houston, The Cliff House, San Francisco, La Piazza Restaurant, San Francisco, 1st Fed. Savs. and Loan, San Francisco; (residential projects) Steven Spielberg, Malibu, Calif., Cissy King, Beverly Hills, Calif., Joan Darling, Boston, Mass., others. Mem. Am. Soc. Interior Designers, Color Mktg. Group. Republican. Home and Office: 1836 Courtney Terr Los Angeles CA 90046

MEANS, ROBERT EARL, consulting chemical engineer; b. Cordova, Alaska, Sept. 25, 1925; s. George Earl and Genevieve Means; m. Mary Morency, Dec. 30, 1949; children: Joseph, Rosemary, Louise, Paul, Claire, Margaret. BS ChemE, U. Wash., 1951. Chem. engr. Dawes Products, Chgo., 1947-48; mgr. engring. West, Hooker Chem., Tacoma, 1950-68; v.p. engring. Pacific Cons. Inc., Seattle, 1968-70; v.p. chem. Bouillon, Christofferson & Schairer, Seattle, 1970-78; project mgr. ABAM Engrs., Federal Way, Wash., 1978-80; pres. R.E. Means, P.E., Tacoma, 1980—. Mem. adv. council Bonnevill Power Adminstrn., Portland, 1961-72; chmn. indsl. bur. Tacoma C. of C., 1963. Served to lt. (j.g.) USN, 1944-46. Mem. Am. Inst. Chem. Engrs. (chmn. Puget Sound sect. 1960—), Am. Chem. Soc., The Chlorine Inst. Roman Catholic. Home and Office: 1013 Corona Dr Tacoma WA 98466

MEANY, HERBERT JOHN, manufacturing company executive; b. Prescott, Ariz., Mar. 12, 1923; s. Herbert John and Alice Louise (Vallett) M.; children: Herbert J., Claudine Meany Moore, Deborah Meany de Santos. AA cum laude, East Los Angeles Jr. Coll., 1949; BS in Engring. magna cum laude U. So. Calif., 1951. Registered profl. engr., Calif. With NI Industries, Inc., Los Angeles, 1945—, engr., 1951-53, chief engr., 1953-56, div. mgr., 1956-60, corp. v.p., 1960-67, group v.p., 1967-72, exec. v.p., 1972-75, pres., chief exec. officer, 1975-81, chmn., pres., 1981-85, chmn., chief exec. officer, 1985—; bd. dirs. Farr Co., Electronic Scales Internat. Councilor U. So. Calif. Grad. Sch. Bus. Adminstrn. Served with U.S. Army, 1941-45. Mem. Elec. Industries Assn. Calif. (pres. 1963; Man of Yr. 1973), Mchts. and Mfrs. Assn. (bd. dirs., mem. exec. com.), ASME, Newcomen Soc. Clubs: Calif., Jonathan. Office: NI Industries Inc One Golden Shore Longbeach CA 90802 *

MEARNS, ALAN JOHN, ecologist, marine scientist; b. Los Angeles, Oct. 4, 1943; s. John and Agnes (Sandor) M.; m. Bonnie L. Mearns; children: Michelle Ann, Michael Alan. BS, Calif. State U., Long Beach, 1965, MA, 1967; PhD, U. Wash., 1971. Environ. specialist So. Calif. Coast Water Research Project, Long Beach, 1971-73, leader biology div., 1973-80; ecologist NOAA, Seattle, 1980—. Contbr. articles to profl. jours. Named Outstanding Alumni in Biology Calif. State U. Dept. Biol. Scis., Long Beach, 1985. Mem. AAAS, Am. Fisheries Soc., Am. Inst. Fisheries Research Biologists (sec./treas. 1976-78, vice dir. Los Angeles chpt. 1979, Seattle chpt. 1982-83), So. Calif. Acad. Scis. (control bd. 1979-80). Avocations: travel, writing. Office: NOAA Div Ocean Assessment 7600 Sand Point Way NE Seattle WA 98115

MEARS, BRAINERD, JR., geology educator; b. Williamstown, Mass., June 24, 1921; s. Brainerd and Sally Worthington (Bliss) M.; m. Anne Gardner Carter, June 5, 1948; children: Alison Bliss, Holly Cordary. BA, Williams Coll., 1943; PhD, Columbia U., 1950. From asst. prof. to full prof. geology U. Wyo., Laramie, 1949—. Author: The Changing Earth, 1970, Essential of Geology, 1978; editor, author: The Nature of Geology, 1970. Served with USMC, 1942-45. Fellow AAAS, Geol. Soc. Am. Club: Nakomis (Laramie). Home: PO Box 3692 Laramie WY 82071 Office: U Wyo Dept Geology Laramie WY 82071

MEAYS, BARTON RICHARDS, governmental association administrator; b. Newark, Apr. 7, 1935; s. Barton Taylor and Sarah E. (Richards) M.; m. Marilyn A. Water, June 14, 1958 (div. June 1977); children: Janet Meays Silva, Diana; m. Elba Noemi Burgueño, May 29, 1981; 1 child, James. BS in Urban Planning, U. Ill., 1958; postgrad., Calif. State U., Sacramento, 1961-62, U. So. Calif., 1985. Prin. planner Sacramento County, Calif., 1958-68; dir. planning City of Los Gatos, Calif., 1968-70; dep. dir. planning So. Calif. Assn. Govt., Los Angeles, 1970-72, dir. fin. and adminstrn., 1972-74, dep. exec. dir., 1974-85, exec. dir., 1976, adminstr., 1985—; adj. prof. pub. adminstrn. Calif. State U., Long Beach, 1976-84, Dominguez Hills, 1986—. Mem. blue ribbon panel Sacramento Unified Sch. Dist., 1964; sec.-treas. Rancho Cordova (Calif.) Community Council, 1966; bd. dirs. Wilshire Ctr. Community Involvement Assn. Mem. Internat. City Mgmt. Assn., Am. Soc. Pub. Adminstrn. (pres. Los Angeles chpt. 1984-85), Pub. Employees Roundtable (chmn. local chpt. 1985-86), Delta Upsilon. Republican. Methodist. Avocation: sailing. Home: 9303 N Marina Pacifica Dr Long Beach CA 90803 Office: So Calif Assn Govts 600 S Commonwealth Los Angeles CA 90005

MECH, WILLIAM PAUL, mathematics educator, director honors program; b. La Crosse, Wis., Mar. 10, 1942; s. Stephen John and Eunice (Sampson) M.; m. Mary Ethel Bayne, Feb. 2, 1964 (div. Dec. 1980); children: Elizabeth Ann, Kathryn Marie, Stephen Glen; m. Victoria Craig, Aug. 4, 1983; m. Victoria Craig Hunt, Aug. 4, 1983. BA, Wash. State U., 1964; MS, U. Ill., 1965, PhD, 1970. Instr. math. U. Ill., Urbana, 1967-69; asst. prof. Boise (Idaho) State U., 1970-73, assoc. prof., 1973-77, prof., 1977—, dir. honors program, 1971—; cons. Hanford Engring. Devel. Labs., Richland, Wash., 1976, Capital Computer Corp., Boise, 1982. Contbr. articles on honors programs to profl. jours. Vol. coordinator Partners in Edn., Boise schs., 1985-86; active Council on Fgn. Relations, Boise, 1974—. Grantee NSF, 1980. Mem. AAAS, Am. Math. Soc., Math. Assn. Am., Nat. Coll. Honors Council (pres. 1981-82), Sigma Xi, Phi Beta Kappa, Phi Kappa Phi (chpt. pres. 1973-75). Home: 325 McGuffin Ln Boise ID 83712 Office: Boise State U Honors Program 1910 University Dr Boise ID 83725

MECHAM, EVAN, state governor; b. Duchesne, Utah, May 12, 1924; m. Florence Lambert; seven children. Student, Utah State U., 1942-43, Ariz. State U., 1947-50. Owner Pontiac agy. franchise, Ajo, Ariz., 1950-54, Glendale, Ariz., 1954—; sen. State of Ariz., 1961-62, gov., 1987—; past pub. Am. Newspaper Group. Author: Come Back America, 1982. Active Ch. Jesus Christ of Latter-day Sts. Served with USAF, 1943-46, prisoner of war, Germany. Office: Office of the Gov State Capitol Phoenix AZ 85007

MECHAM, GLENN JEFFERSON, lawyer; b. Logan, Utah, Dec. 11, 1935; s. Everett H. and Lillie (Dunford) M.; B.S., Utah State U., 1957; J.D., U. Utah, 1961; m. Mae Parson, June 5, 1957; children—Jeff B., Scott R., Marcia, Suzanne. Admitted to Utah bar, 1961, Supreme Ct. U.S., U.S. Ct. Appeals 10th Circuit, U.S. Dist. Ct. Utah, U.S. Ct. Claims; engaged in gen. practice, Roy, Utah, 1961-65; Duchesne County atty., 1962, Duchesne City atty., 1962; city judge Roy City, 1963-66; judge City of Ogden, Utah, 1966-69; lectr.-in-law and govt. Stevens-Henager Coll., Ogden, 1963-75; asst. U.S. atty. Dist. Utah, 1969-72; ptnr. Mecham & Richards, Ogden, Utah, 1972-82; pres. Penn Mountain Mining Co., South Pacific Internat. Bank, Ltd.; mem. Bur. Justice Stats. Adv. Bd., U.S. Dept. Justice. Chmn. Ogden City Housing Authority; chmn. instl. council Utah State U.; asst. mayor City of Ogden; pres. Utah League Cities and Towns, 1981-82. Served to col. USAF, 1957. Mem. Weber County (pres. 1966-68), Am., Utah bar assns., Am. Judicature Soc., Weber County Bar Legal Services (chmn. bd. trustees 1966-69), Utah Assn. Mcpl. Judges (sec.), Sigma Chi, Phi Alpha Delta. Home: 1748 Victoria Ct Ogden UT 84403

MECHAM, STEVEN RAY, educational administrator; b. Salt Lake City, Oct. 10, 1938; s. Milton Claudius and Marjorie (White) M.; m. Donna Jean Johnson, Jan. 22, 1943; children: Brian Paul, Allan LeRoy. AS, Weber State Coll., 1958; BS, U. Utah, 1963; MA, Tchrs. Coll., Columbia U., 1965; postgrad. McGill U.; PhD U. Santa Barbara, Calif., 1981. Prin., Montreal (Que.) Oral Sch., 1966-70; state dir. hearing impaired Conn. Dept. Edn., 1970-71; dir. guidance Lexington Sch. for the Deaf, N.Y.C., 1971-72; prin. Exton Elem. Jr. High Sch., Mexico City, 1972-77; coordinator spl. edn. Weber Sch. Dist., Ogden, Utah, 1977-78; prin. Roosevelt Elem. Sch., Ogden, 1978-82; asst. supt. Weber County Schs., Ogden, 1982—; instr. U. Utah, 1965-66, St. Joseph Coll., Hartford, Conn., 1970-71; adj. prof. McGill U.; instr. Tchrs. Coll., Columbia U., 1968-70; acting chmn. dept. edn. U. Americas, Mexico City, 1976-77; cons. Far West Labs., San Francisco. Bd. dirs. Instituto Mexicano Norte Americano de Relaciones Culturales, Mexico City, 1975-76; bishop Ch. Jesus Christ of Latter-day Saints, chmn. Cancer Crusade; pres. Finnish Mission Ch. Jesus Christ of Latter-day Saints; bd. dirs. Am. Cancer Soc. Weber County. Mem. Am. Orgn. Educators of Hearing Impaired (pres.), Can. Hearing Soc. (dir.), Utah Assn. Elem. Sch. Prins., Nat. Assn. Elem. Sch. Prins., Internat. Reading Assn., Am. Assn. Sch. Adminstrs., Alexander Graham Bell Assn. Club: Rotary. Contbr. articles to profl. jours. Home: 2163 E Jennifer St Ogden UT 84403 Office: Weber County Schs 5320 S Adams Ogden UT 84405-6998

MECHEM, EDWIN LEARD, judge; b. Alamogordo, N.Mex., July 2, 1912; s. Edwin and Eunice (Leard) M.; Dorothy Heller, Dec. 30, 1932 (dec. 1972); children—Martha M. Vigil, John H., Jesse (dec. 1968), Walter M.; m. Josephine Donavan, May 28, 1976. L.L.B., U. Ark., 1939; L.L.D. (hon.), N.Mex. State U., 1975. Bar: N.Mex. 1939, U.S. Dist. Ct. N.Mex. 1939. Lawyer Las Cruces and Albuquerque, 1939-70; now judge U.S. Dist. Ct. N.Mex., Albuquerque; spl. agt. FBI Dept. Justice, various locations, 1942-45; mem. legislature State of N.Mex., 1947-48, gov., 1951-54, 57-58, 61-62; senator U.S. Govt., Washington, 1963-64. Mem. ABA, N.Mex. Bar Assn., Am. Law Inst. Republican. Methodist. Avocation: travel. Office: 500 Gold SW Albuquerque NM 87103

MECKLENBURG, DIANNE JORGI, speech pathologist, audiologist; b. Los Angeles, Feb. 22, 1945; d. Ralph Anthony Mecklenburg and Pauline Rae (Sherman) Sherman. BA, Calif. State U., Los Angeles, 1971, MA, 1972; PhD, Bowling Green State U., 1977. Trainee VA, Los Angeles, 1971; research asst. Wayne State Med. Hosp., Detroit, 1976-77; lectr. audiology U. Melbourne, Australia, 1978-80; pres. Cavale Cons., Boulder, Colo., 1980-86; clin. coordinator Cochlear Corp., Englewood, Colo., 1980-85, dir. clin. studies, children's program, 1986—; lectr. continuing edn. Fla. Lang. Speech and Hearing Assn., Calif. Speech and Hearing Assn., 1985—. Asst. editor Australian Jour. Speech and Hearing, 1979-80; contbr. articles to profl. jours. Grad. assistantship Calif. State U., 1971; fellow Bowling Green (Ohio) State U., 1973-76. Mem. Am. Speech Lang. and Hearing Assn., Am. Auditory Soc., Rehab. Engring. soc. N.Am., Alexander Graham Bell Soc., Assn. Research in Otolaryngology. Home: 975 Eighth St Boulder CO 80302 Office: Cochlear Corp 61 Inverness Dr Englewood CO 80112

MEDIGOVICH, WILLIAM MITCHELL, state emergency services official; b. Marysville, Calif., Mar. 2, 1940; s. Mitchell Vaso and Olga (Mojsich) M.; m. Kyla Celeste Houston, May 4, 1963; children—Mitchell Kyle, Jeffrey William. B.A., San Francisco State U., 1962; M.A., Monterey Inst. Internat. Studies, 1967. Staff officer CIA, Washington, 1967-74; adminstr. Calif. Dept. Justice, Sacramento, 1974-80; chief law enforcement div. Gov.'s Office Emergency Services, Sacramento, 1980-83, dir., 1983—. Bd. dirs. Sacramento Safety Council, 1983. Served with ASA, 1962-65. Mem. Calif. Peace Officers Assn., Res. Officers Assn., Assn. Former Intelligence Officers, Nat. Emergency Mgmt. Assn., Calif. Fire Chief's Assn. Republican. Office: Office Emergency Services 2800 Meadowview Rd Sacramento CA 95832

MEDITCH, JAMES STEPHEN, electrical engineering educator; b. Indpls., July 30, 1934; s. Vladimir Stephen and Alexandra (Gogeff) M.; m. Theresa Claire Scott, Apr. 4, 1964; children: James Stephen Jr., Sandra Anne. B.S. in Elec. Engring, Purdue U., 1956, Ph.D., 1961; S.M., M.I.T., 1957. Staff engr. Aerospace Corp., Los Angeles, 1961-65; assoc. prof. elec. engring. Northwestern U., 1965-67; mem. tech. staff Boeing Sci. Research Labs., Seattle, 1967-70; prof. U. Calif., Irvine, 1970-77; prof. U. Wash., 1977—, chmn. dept. elec. engring., 1977-85. Author: Stochastic Optimal Linear Estimation and Control, 1969; co-editor: Computer Communications Networks, 1984. Fellow IEEE (disting. mem. control systems soc., 1983, editor proceedures jour, 1983-85, Centennial medal 1984); mem. AAAS, Am. Soc. Engring. Edn., Assn. for Computer Machinery. Office: Dept Elec Engring FT-10 U Wash Seattle WA 98195

MEDLEY, DONALD BRUCE, computer educator, consultant; b. Monroe, Mich., Sept. 20, 1932; s. Hugh Lloyd and Nurnie (Clawson) M.; m. Louise Spencer, Sept. 1, 1956; children: Brian, Sherrie, Anthony. BVE, Calif. State Coll., Los Angeles, 1971, MA, Calif. State U., Los Angeles, 1972; EdD, Brigham Young U., 1976. Sr. machine operator Willys Motors, Inc., 1956-57; supr. data processing Kobacker Stores, Inc., 1957-59; programmer Hughes Aircraft, 1959-60; mgr. data processing ops. Telecomputing Corp., 1960-62; sr. computing analyst Rocketdyne Div., N.Am., 1962-67; sr. mgmt. systems designer Xerox Data Systems, 1968-70; instr. data processing, coop. work experience coordinator Moorpark Coll., 1963-82; pres. Evaluation Techniques Consortium, Inc. Chatsworth, Calif., 1977-81; staff computer specialist U.S. Dept. Agr. Beltsville, Md., 1980-81; prof. computer info. systems, dir. classroom computing support Calif. State Poly. U., Pomona, 1981—; cons. in field. Co-author: Programming Principles with Cobol I, 1984; co-author: Programming Principles with Cobol II, 1985, Advanced Office Systems, 1986, Computer Information Systems: Planning and Management Decision Making, 1987, Computer Information Systems: Information Resource Management, 1987. Contbr. papers to profl. jours. Mem. Ops. Com. for Office Automation Cons., 1984; mem. program com. Nat. Computer Conf., 1978, program chmn., 1980, gen. chmn., 1983, com. mem., 1984—. Served with USAF, 1952-56. Mem. Data Processing Mgmt. Assn. (grant rev. com., chmn. mgmt. curriculum devel. com.), Calif. Soc. IEEE, Assn. Computing Machinery, Soc. Data Educators, So. Calif. Soc. for Info. Mgmt. Republican. Club: Optimist. Office: Calif Poly U Dept Info Systems 3801 W Temple Ave Pomona CA 91768

MEDLEY, NANCY MAY, nurse; b. Knoxville, Oct. 8, 1948; d. Donald Raymond and Josephine Ruth (Blakley) M. A.A., Riverside City Coll., 1970. R.N., Calif. Staff nurse in medicine Riverside Gen. Hosp., Calif., 1970-71; staff nurse neonatal unit Kaiser Permanente Hosp., Hollywood, Calif., 1971-72; critical care nurse neuro unit Harbor-UCLA Hosp., Torrance, 1972-78, head nurse CCU, 1978—. Mem. Am. Heart Assn. Republican. Presbyterian. Home: 636 Manhatten Ave Apt C Hermosa Beach CA 90254 Office: Harbor-UCLA Hosp 1000 Carson St Torrance CA 90502

MEDNICK, SCOTT ALAN, graphic design executive; b. Boston, Mar. 19, 1956; s. Arthur William and Phyllis (Greenberg) M.; m. Michele Susan Goldberg, Sept. 19, 1981 (div. Sept. 1985). BFA, R.I. Sch. Design, 1978. Co-dir. Market House Designers, Providence, 1977-79; creative dir. DBD&M, Los Angeles, 1979-84; pres. Scott Mednick & Assocs., Los Angeles, 1984—; judge Los Angeles Art Dirs. Club Ann. Exhibition, 1985, Los Angeles Advt. Women Ann. LuLu Awards, 1986. Exhibited in one-man show Kresge Art Mus., Mich. State U.; group exhibitions include Art Dirs. Club N.Y.C., Am. Inst. Graphic Arts, N.Y.C., Los Angeles, San Francisco, Art Dirs. Club Traveling Exhibit, Atlanta, St. Louis, Salt Lake City, Los Angeles, Honolulu, N.Y.C., Seattle, Japan, Fed. Republic Germany, Switzerland, Australia, Soc. Typographic Arts, Chgo., N.Y.C., others; lectures include Art Dirs. and Artists Club Sacramento, Art Dirs. Club Los Angeles, Art Dirs. Club Boston, Art Ctr. Coll. of Design, Otis/Parsons of Los Angeles, Parsons of N.Y.C., others; featured in many mags. and jours. Advisor United Synagogue Am., N.Y.C., 1976; regional bd. dirs. New Eng. United Synogogue, 1973; youth group advisor Temple Emanuel, Providence, 1975-77. Recipient Cert. of Recognition Nat. Tb Soc., 1974. Mem. Am. Inst. Graphic Arts, Art Dirs. Club N.Y., Art Dirs. Club Los Angeles (advisor 1980-86). Jewish. Avocations: music composition, writing, photography. Home: 18090 Karen Dr Encino CA 91316 Office: Scott Mednick & Assocs 7412 Beverly Blvd Los Angeles CA 90036

MEDSGER, THOMAS LAURENCE, art director; b. Greenport, N.Y., July 1, 1940; s. William Francis and Doris Gould (Brigden) M.; B.F.A. cum laude (Dean's medal advt. design), Pratt Inst., Bklyn., 1962. Art dir. R. Ptak, advt., Phoenix, 1962-63, Cole, Fisher, Rogow, Inc., advt., Beverly Hills, Calif., 1965-67; art dir. Frank M. Hiteshew & Assos., publishers spl. interest mags., Beverly Hills, 1967-82; art dir., asst. editor Western's World, in-flight mag., Beverly Hills, 1970-82; art dir., package designer Mattel Electronics, 1982-84; art dir. Brentwood Pub. Corp., pubs. spl. interest mags., Los Angeles, 1984—; guest lectr. UCLA, San Diego State U. Served with U.S. Army, 1963-65. Decorated Army Commendation medal; recipient cert. merit Soc. Illustrators Los Angeles, 1970, 72. Office: 1640 5th St Santa Monica CA 90401

MEDUSKI, JERZY WINCENTY, nutritionist, biochemist; b. Kalusz, Poland, Oct. 29, 1918; s. Dobieslaw Antoni and Katarzyna (Barbowska) M.; came to U.S., 1962, naturalized, 1969; M.D., Warsaw (Poland) Med. Sch., 1946; Ph.D. in Biochemistry, U. Lodz (Poland), 1951; 1 son, Jerzy Dobieslaw. Organizer, chief pharmacology labs. Polish Nat. Inst. Hygiene, Warsaw, 1945-52, organizer, head lab. of intermediary metabolism, 1952-59; asso. prof. biochemistry Warsaw Med. Sch., 1955-59; asst. prof. neurology U. So. Calif. Sch. Medicine, Los Angeles, 1973—; pres. Nutritional Cons. Group, Inc. Mem. Los Angeles County Bd. Suprs. Task Force on Nutrition. WHO fellow, Holland, Scotland, 1948-49; research grantee, USSR, 1956. Mem. Polish Acad. Sci. (sci. sec. biochem. com. 1952-59), Polish Med. Assn. (sci. sec. nat. bd. 1958-59), Polish Biochem. Soc. (founding mem.), Biochem. Soc. London, Chem. Soc. London, Internat. Soc. on Toxinology, AAAS, Am. Soc. Microbiology, Internat. Soc. on Oxygen Transport to Tissues, Sigma Xi. Author 3 books on biochemistry; contbr. more than 80 articles to internat. jours.; author textbook on nutritional biochemistry, 1977. Home: 1066 S Genesee Ave Los Angeles CA 90019 Office: U So Calif Sch Medicine 2025 Zonal Ave Los Angeles CA 90033

MEDVIDOFSKY, NATHAN H., real estate appraisal company executive, software development appraiser; b. Keene, N.H., Aug. 27, 1950; s. Charles and Lona (Williams) M.; m. Evelyn Heimbach, Feb. 6, 1971; children—Joshua, Sol. Student Met. State Coll., Denver, 1981. Real estate salesman Harvest Realty/Medvidofsky & Son, Keene, N.H., 1971-75; appraiser World Savings Co., Denver, 1975-79; v.p. Silverado Savs. Co., Denver, 1979-80; pres. Valuation Research Corp., Denver, 1980-82, chief exec. officer, 1982—; dir. profl. practice com. Soc. Real Estate Appraisers, chpt. 9, 1986—. S.R.A. appraisal designation awarded 1984. Author (with others) appraisal software, 1983. Treas./dir. East Lakewood Sanitation Dist., Colo., 1982-86. Office: Valuation Research Corp 9590 W 14th Ave Lakewood CO 80215

MEECHAN, ROBERT JOHN, medical educator; b. Newport, Wash., Aug. 25, 1926; s. Robert John Meechan and Katharine M. (Battick) Williams; m. K. Brenda Hanrahan, Dec. 27, 1952; children: Robert D., Patrick J., Peter T. BA, Oreg. State Coll., 1949; MA, MD, U. Oreg., 1953. Diplomate Am. Bd. Pediatrics. Instr. pediatrics Oreg. Health Science U., Portland, 1956-62, asst. prof., 1962-68, assoc. prof., 1968-72, prof. pediatrics, 1972—, asst. dean admissions, 1976—. Served with USN, 1944-46. Recipient Disting. Service award Alumni Oreg. Health Sci. Ctr., 1986. Mem. Ambulatory Pediatric Assn., Oreg. Acad. Pediatrics, North Pacific Pediatric Soc., Portland Acad. Pediatrics (sec., treas. 1962-65, pres. 1965). Democrat. Roman Catholic. Home: 12040 SE Foster Pl Portland OR 97266 Office: Oreg Health Sci U 3181 SW Sam Jackson Park Rd Portland OR 97201

MEEHAN, PAULA KENT, cosmetic company executive; b. West Los Angeles, Calif., Aug. 9, 1931; d. Richard Moorehead and Lois Evelyn (Martin) Bear; m. John Edwin Meehan, Apr. 20, 1973; children: Michael D. Miller, Chris Meehan, Matthew Meehan. Extension student, UCLA. Founder 1960; since pres., chmn. bd. Redken Labs. Inc., Canoga Park, Calif. Bd. regents Loyola U., Los Angeles. Republican. Address: 6625 Variel Ave Canoga Park CA 91303

MEEK, CHARLES RONALD, banker, former community college president, agriculture educator; b. Sherman, Tex., Sept. 3, 1943; s. Marion Harold and Doris Ethyl (Keller) M.; m. Connie Marie Meek; children—Charles Ronald, II, Janyth Cheryll, Beau Joshua Keller, Jason Richard. A.A.S., Central Tex. Coll., 1965; B.S., East Tex. State U., 1970, M.Ed., 1971, D.Ed., 1975; B. Agrl. Mgmt., Am. Tech. U., 1976. Cert tchr., Tex.; lic. pilot, Tex. Asst. instr. East Tex. State U., 1970-71; dir. agr., dir. men's dormitory Grayson County Coll., 1971-73; dir. student affairs, registrar Central Tex. Coll., 1974, adminstrv. aide to v.p., 1975-76, exec. dean Overseas Europe, 1978-80, dep. chancellor program devel. and evaluation, 1980-81; dir. adminstrv. services, registrar Am. Tech. U., 1974-75, chmn. agri-mgmt. dept., 1975-76, dean of students, 1975-77; dean mil. and vets. affairs Am. Ednl. Complex Consortium, 1976, exec. dean Ft. Hood ops., 1976-78; supt. Am. Prep. Inst., 1977-78; pres. Pueblo (Colo.) Community Coll., 1981-84; exec. v.p. Pueblo Bank and Trust Co., 1984—. Pres. Pueblo Met. Mus. Bd.; bd. dirs. Boy Scouts Am., Camp Fire Girls, Prison Vocat. Tng.; mem. Pueblo Econ. Devel. Corp. Served with USAF, 1963-66. Mem. Nat. Rehab. Assn., Colo. Vocat. Assn., Aircraft Owners and Pilots Assn., Am. Assn. Community and Jr. Colls. (Pres.'s Acad.), Pueblo C. of C. (bd. dirs.), Phi Delta Kappa, Alpha Gamma Who. Club: Rotary. Designer individualized skill tng. programs for U.S. mil. personnel. Office: Pueblo Bank and Trust Co 5th and court Sts Pueblo CO 81002

MEEK, DANIEL ERWIN, pharmaceutical company executive; b. McMinnville, Oreg., May 7, 1946; s. Calvin L. and Mildred R. (Flansberg) M.; m. Katharine Marie Thomas, Dec. 5, 1970; children: Lisa Marie, Jonathan Thomas. AA, Chaffey Coll., 1967; BA in English, Calif. State U., Fullerton, 1969; MA in Mktg. Mgmt., Claremont Grad. Sch., 1979, MBA, 1986; grad. Med. Mktg. Program, UCLA, 1987. Sales rep., trainer, mktg. specialist Westwood Pharms. div. Bristol Myers Co., Los Angeles, 1971-79; product mgr. Bourns Med. Systems, Riverside, Calif., 1979-80; mgr. mktg. research CR Bard Inc., Rancho Cucamonga, Calif., 1980-82; mgr. mktg. research and planning Am. Edwards Labs., Irvine, Calif., 1982-83; mgr. new bus. devel. IOLAB Corp div. Johnson and Johnson Co., Claremont, 1983-86; product dir. IOLAB Pharms., Claremont, 1986—; mktg. adv. com. campaign for preeminence Claremont (Calif.) Grad. Sch., 1985-86. Advisor on dist.-wide survey regarding overcrowding of schs. Chino (Calif.) Unified Sch. Dist., 1986—. Mem. Western Mktg. Research Council (program chmn. for edn. 1986—), Conf. Bd., So. Calif. Corp. Planners, Am. Mktg. Assn., Med. Mktg. Assn., Claremont Corp. Roundtable. Republican. Mem. Calvary Christian Reformed Ch. Avocations: photography, tennis, hiking, fishing. Home: 12773 Kumquat Ave Chino CA 91710 Office: IOLAB Pharms div Johnson & Johnson Co 500 IOLAB Dr Claremont CA 91711

MEEK, LOYAL GEORGE, editor (retired); b. Cedar Rapids, Iowa, Sept. 10, 1918; s. Charles William and Mina (Armstrong) M.; A.B., Coe Coll., Cedar Rapids, 1940; m. Lois Tankersley, Sept. 28, 1941; children—Jeremy, Andrew, Geoffrey, Margaret. Reporter, state editor, editorial writer Cedar Rapids Gazette, 1940-60; spl. asst. to U.S. Senator Jack Miller, 1961-62; editorial writer, then chief editorial writer Milw. Sentinel, 1962-73; editor Phoenix Gazette, 1973-84. Bd. dirs. Friends of Phoenix Public Library, Ariz. Clean and Beautiful. Service with AUS, 1942-46. Mem. Nat. Conf. Editorial Writers, Am. Soc. Newspaper Editors. Club: Phoenix Press, Univ. Office: PO Box 1950 Phoenix AZ 85001

MEEKER, DAVID REILEY, judge, lawyer; b. San Bernardino, Calif., May 28, 1941; s. Melvin Mansuer and Wanda Leontene (Burke) M.; m. Sharon Kay, Aug. 26, 1965 (div. Feb. 1977); m. Linda Jeanne Danziger Meeker, Apr. 16, 1983; children—Kurt, Lisa, Marc, Genevieve. B.A. in Govt., U. Redlands, 1964; postgrad. UCLA Law Sch., 1964-66; J.D., Western State U., 1973. Bar: Calif. 1973. With U.S. Peace Corps, Liberia, West Africa, also Nigeria, 1964-66; instr. Cabrillo Pacific Law Sch., San Diego, 1974; atty. Calif. Legislature, Sacramento, 1975-77; litigation atty. State of Calif., Sacramento, 1977-81; adminstrv. law judge State of Calif., Sacramento, 1981—; real estate developer, subdiv. investor, San Bernardino, Sacramento, San Luis Obispo, Calif., also San Diego, 1969—. chaperone Am. Field Service, N.Y.C., 1963, 66; chmn. selection com. for chaperones Drew U., Madison, N.J., 1964; facilitator Sage Corp., Sacramento, 1984. Mem. ABA, Phi Beta Phi. Home: 1037 9th Ave Sacramento CA 95818 Office: Unemployment Ins Appeals Bd 714 P St Sacramento CA 95814

MEEKER, M(ORETON) DAVID, theatre educator; b. Phoenix, Nov. 22, 1932; s. Russell Y. and Lucy H. (Axline) M.; m. Brenda A. Cole, Oct. 19, 1963; children: Rachel E., Jennifer K., Hannah N., Joshua D. BA in Music, U Ariz., 1954, MMEd, 1956. Cert. community coll. tchr., Ariz. Profl. singer Roger Wagner Chorale, Los Angeles, 1958-60; profl. singer, actor various cos., N.Y.C., 1960-64; profl. artist N.Y.C., Calif., and Ariz., 1960—; instr. music, art, and drama Buena High Sch., Sierra Vista, Ariz., 1964-75; prof. art, music, drama Cochise Coll., Douglas, Ariz., 1975—, coordinator cultural activities, 1983—; dir., producer Buena Musical Theatre, Sierra Vista, 1964-75, Cochise Community Theatre, Sierra Vista, 1975—. Annual one-man show of paintings, Sierra Vista, 1965—. Chmn. Cochise Alliance Supporting the Arts, 1983—. Recipient numerous art awards, N.Y. and Ariz., 1962-86. Mem. Sierra Vista Booster Club (named Outstanding Citizen 1975). Republican. Mem. United Ch. Christ. Avocation: church activities. Home: 99 Cargill Dr NE Sierra Vista AZ 85635 Office: Cochise Coll 901 Colombo Sierra Vista AZ 85635

MEEKER, RICHARD HALLIDAY, publisher, lawyer; b. Washington, Jan. 20, 1949; s. Leonard Carpenter and Christine Rhoda (Halliday) M.; m. Ellen Frances Rosenblum, June 13, 1982; 1 child, Catherine Lily Rosenblum. BA, Amherst Coll., 1970; JD, U. Oreg., 1974. Author Ticknor & Fields, N.Y.C., 1980-83; editor Willamette Week, Portland, Oreg., 1977-80, pub., 1983—. Author: Newspaperman, 1983. Mem. Assn. Alternative Newsweeklies (promotions chmn. 1984—). Democrat. Office: Willamette Week 2 NW Second Ave Portland OR 97209

MEEKER, ROBERT THOMAS, architecture educator; b. Columbia, Mo., Mar. 28, 1944; s. Clifford Reznor and Frances Laura (Patterson) M.; m. Cynthia Lee Hefner, Mar. 28, 1972; children: Emma, Guthrie. BArch, Cornell U., 1968; MA in City Planning, MA in Urban Design, Harvard U., 1974. Lic. profl. architect, Tex.; cert. Nat. Council Archtl. Registration Bds. Project mgr. John Sharratt & Assocs., Boston, 1974-76; asst. prof. architecture Tex. A&M U., Bryan-College Station, Tex., 1976-78; asst. prof. U. Ill., Urbana-Champaign, 1978-81; project designer Celli-Flynn & Assocs., Pitts., 1981-83; assoc. prof. Mont. State U., Bozeman, 1983—; prin. Robert T. Meeker & Assocs., Bozeman, 1977—. Contbr. articles to profl. jours. Recipient Arthur Ross award Classical Am., N.Y.C., 1986. Democrat. Home: 314 E Olive St Bozeman MT 59715 Office: Mont State U Sch Architecture Bozeman MT 59717

MEEKS, HENRY SPIENGLER, III, metallurgist; b. Queens, N.Y., Feb. 6, 1949; s. Henry S. and Barbara (Wenzel) M.; m. Janet Anne Hirner, May 2, 1970; children: Jessica, Jonathan, Alison. AS in Design Engring., Acad. Aeronautics, 1970; BS in Engring. Materials, Calif. State U., Long Beach, 1974. Plant metallurgist Valeron Corp., Riverside, Calif., 1974-82; plant mgr., metallurgist GTE/Valeron Corp., Monument, Colo., 1982-86; dir. ops. and tech. Advanced Materials Group Nat. Forge Co., Colorado Springs, Colo., 1986—; v.p. mfg. and tech. Champion Horseshoe Co., Pound Ridge, N.Y., 1986—; cons. Surface Tech., Ft. Collins, Colo., 1983-86, MimTech., Denver, 1986—. Mem. Am. Soc. Metals, Am. Inst. Metall. Engrs., Soc. Carbide and Tool. Engrs., Metal Powder Industries Fedn.f. Mormon. Avocations: backpacking, fishing, hunting. Office: VCI 4975 N 30th St Colorado Springs CO 80919

MEEKS, JAMES DONALD, librarian, educator; b. Kansas City, Mo., May 10, 1920; s. Walter James and Mary Elizabeth (Mershon) M.; B.A. in English Lit., U. Kansas City, 1941; B.S. in Library Sci., U. Denver, 1946; M.S., Columbia U., 1951; m. Patricia Ann Lowe, Feb. 27, 1953 (div.); children—Mary, Ann, Robert. Head reference dept., then asst. library dir. Yonkers Pub. Library (N.Y.), 1947-49; dir. library services USIS, Calcutta, India, 1949-50; br. asst. Bklyn. Pub. Library, 1950-51; dir. Enid Pub. Library (Okla.), 1951-53, St. Joseph Pub. Library (Mo.), 1953-55, Dallas Pub. Library, 1955-61; library coordinator Cherry Creek Sch. Dist., Englewood, Colo., 1962-69; instr. U. Denver, 1963-69; dir. Colo. State Library, 1969-74; mem. faculty U. Denver, 1974-75; city librarian, Eugene, Oreg., 1975—; mem. faculty U. Oreg. Sch. Librarianship; vis. prof. Grad. Sch. Library Studies, U. Hawaii, Manoa, fall 1982. Mem. Tex. Library Assn. (pres. 1960), Colo. Library Assn. (pres. 1970), Oreg. Library Assn. (pres. 1980), ALA. Served with AUS, 1942-45. Mem. Pacific N.W. Library Assn. Episcopalian. Home: 1162 Charnelton St Apt 5 Eugene OR 97401 Office: 100 W 13th Ave Eugene OR 97401

MEENAN, PATRICK HENRY, state legislator; b. Casper, Wyo., Sept. 24, 1927; s. Hugh Martin and Margaret (Kelly) M.; B.S. cum laude, U. Notre Dame, 1949; m. Shirley Louise Byron, Dec. 30, 1950; children—Mauryа Ann, Kevin Patrick, Michael James, Patricia Kelly. CPA Raab, Roush & Gaymon, Casper, 1949-53, partner 1960-68; asst. treas. Williston Oil & Gas Co., 1953-55; partner Meenan & Higgins, Casper, 1955-60; pres. KATI-AM & FM, Casper, 1963-81, KAWY Stero Radio, 1967-81; ptnr. Meenan, Miracle & Sherrill, C.P.A.'s, 1975-76; sec. dir. Bank of Casper, 1980—; pres. PM Enterprises, Inc., 1981—; Erin Corp. Councilman City of Casper, 1956-65, v.p., 1961, mayor, 1962, 65; mem. Wyo. Ho. of Reps., 1969—, majority floor leader, 1983-85, Speaker Pro Tem, 1985-87, Speaker of the House, 1987—, chmn. house-rules com., chmn. mgmt. council, 1987—. Named Young Man of Year, Jr. C. of C., Casper, 1962; Boss of Year, 1965; Distinguished Pub. Servant award City of Casper. Mem. Am. Inst. C.P.A.'s, Notre Dame Alumni (nat. dir. 1972-75), Wyo. Soc. C.P.A.'s, Nat., Wyo. assns. broadcasters. Elk, K.C. Republican. Roman Catholic. Home: 3070 E 4th St Casper WY 82609 Office: PM Enterprises Inc 300 Country Club Rd Suite 211 Hilltop Nat Tower PO Box 9727 Casper WY 82609

MEENK, ROBERT JAMES, real estate developer, consultant; b. Everett, Wash., Jan. 3, 1938; s. Ernest Franklin and Elise C. (Troost) M.; m. Ruth H. Lewis, Sept. 27, 1960; children: Robert James Jr., Ruth Lisa, Regna L., Theodore E. BA in Bus., Wash. State U., 1963. Cert. real estate brokerage mgr. Dist. rep. GM Acceptance Corp., Tacoma, 1966-73; div. mgr., v.p. C.S. Lewis, Inc., Portland, Oreg., 1973-75; assoc. broker Whitfield Bernhardt, Vancouver, Wash., 1975-80; designated broker, mgr. STROUT, Washington, Oreg., 1980-85; owner, broker Pacific Slope, Olympia, Wash., 1985—; owner, cons. mgr. Northwest Associated Brokers, Olympia, 1980—. Vol. Econ. Devel. Council Olympia, 1985—, numerous polit. campaigns, Vancouver and Olympia, 1975-85. Served to lt. USMC, 1963-66. Mem. Olympia C. of C., Nat. Assn. Realtors, Wash. Assn. Realtors. Club: Columbia Tower (Seattle). Lodge: Lions. Office: Pacific Slope Properties 2637 12th Ct SW PO Box 6136 Olympia WA 98502

MEESE, CELIA EDWARDS, pharmaceutical and nutritional supplement company executive; b. San Diego, May 10, 1938; d. Roy Clifford Edwards and Bessie Lucille (Lang) Hill; m. Jed D. Meese, July 6, 1963; 1 son, Scott Edwards. Student U. Calif.-Sacramento, 1958-60; B.A., U. Wis., 1964; B.A. (hon.), U. Taiwan, 1965. Office mgr. Pacific Telephone, San Jose, Calif., 1965-72; pres. Vitaline Corp., Incline Village, Nev., 1972—; v.p. RenalChem, Inc., San Jose, Calif., 1982—, Formulations Tech., Inc., Oakdale, Calif., 1982—; dir. Spectra Diagnostics, San Jose. Bd. dirs. Sierra Council on Alcoholism, Kings Beach, Calif., 1980—. English-Chinese Exchange Council, Taipei, 1964-65; vol. Brandon House, San Jose, 1965—, Children's Home Soc., San Jose, 1965—; mem. steering com. U.S. Rep. Mineta, Calif., 1974.

Mem. Pharm. Mfrs. Assn., Am. Soc. Bariatric Physicians, Mensa (proctor 1985). Home: PO Box 4772 Incline Village NV 89450 Office: Vitaline Corp PO Box 6757 Incline Village NV 89450

MEEUSE, BASTIAAN JACOB DIRK, biologist, educator, researcher; b. Sukabumi, Indonesia, May 9, 1916; came to U.S., 1947; s. Adrianus Dirkszoon and Jannigje (Kruithof) M.; m. Johanne Roberta ten Have, Aug. 28, 1942; children: Karen Barbara, Peter Nicholas. BSc in Biology, U. Leiden, The Netherlands, 1936, M, 1939; D in Tech. Sci., U. Delft, The Netherlands, 1943. Tchr. Hort. Inst., Boskoop, The Netherlands, 1939-42; asst. lectr. U. Delft, 1942-46, chief asst. lectr., 1946-49, lectr., 1949-52; asst. prof. U. Wash., Seattle, 1952-55, assoc. prof., 1955-60, prof. botany, 1960—; corr. Royal Dutch Acad. Scis., Amsterdam, The Netherlands, 1965—; vis. prof. U. Nijmegen, The Netherlands, 1985; cons. Shell Devel. Co., Modesto, Calif., 1986—. Author: The Story of Pollination, 1961, The Sex Life of Flowers, 1984; contbr. articles to profl. jours. Fellow NSF, 1962-63, Rockefeller Found., 1947-49. Mem. Royal Dutch Bot. Soc., Am. Soc. Plant Physiologists, Am. Bot. Soc., Japanese Soc. Plant Physiologists, Native Plant Soc., Sigma Xi. Club: Holland-America (Seattle). Avocations: photography, hiking, showing films, lecturing. Office: U Wash Botany Dept KB-15 Seattle WA 98195

MEGAS, EUGENE ALEXANDER, system safety specialist; b. Marysville, Calif., Dec. 1, 1931; s. Christopher A. and Emilie (Herder) M.; m. Joyce Evelyn Heintschel, Sept. 16, 1951; children: Emilie Marie Megas Santana, Alexander Christopher. AS, Antelope Valley Coll., 1975. Electrician aircraft div. Northrop Aircraft Corp., Hawthorne, Calif., 1951-60; crew chief aircraft div. Northrop Aircraft Corp., El Paso, Tex., 1960-61; tech. rep. Northrop Aircraft Corp., Hawthorne, 1962-72, system safety and reliability specialist, 1972—; liason rep. System Safety, Norton AFB, Calif., 1976—; accident investigator System Safety, Hawthorne, 1976—. Contbr. articles to profl. jours. Republican. Avocations: photography, model aircraft, sewing. Office: Northrop Corp System Safety Div MS 3891/82 One Northrop Ave Hawthorne CA 90250

MEGRAW, ROBERT ELLIS, clinical chemist; b. Phila., Feb. 10, 1930; s. John Jr. and Florence (Ellis) Megraw; m. Sally Caroline Lexow, Aug. 1956 (div. July 1971); children: Jennifer, Timothy, Jason, Tobias, Jeremy; m. Clara Josephine Caccavale, Aug. 7, 1971; 1 child, Gina. BA, Fla. State U., 1956, MS, 1960; PhD, Iowa State U., 1964. Diplomate, Am. Bd. Clin. Chemistry. Postdoctoral fellow Albert Einstein Med. Ctr., Phila., 1964-66; scientist Gen. Diagnostics, Morris Plains, N.J., 1966-71; research biochemist Sigma Chem. Co., St. Louis, 1971-73; mgr., asst. dir. Bio-Dynamics, Indpls., 1973-80; research mgr. Ortho Diagnostics, Irvine, Calif., 1981-83; tech. dir. Bio-Rad Labs., Anaheim, Calif., 1983—; lectr. chemistry Butler U., Indpls., 1981. contbr. articles to profl. jours. Served as staff sgt. USAF, 1948-52. Mem. AAAS, Am. Assn. Clin. Chemistry, Am. Chem. Soc, Sigma Xi. Republican. Episcopalian. Avocation: running. Home: 18651 Ervin Ln Santa Ana CA 92705 Office: Bio Rad Labs ECS Div 3700 E Miraloma Anaheim CA 92806

MEGY, JOSEPH ALLEN, research chemist, technical director; b. Spokane, Wash., Aug. 12, 1945; s. Lehman C. and Jeanne Clarice (Taylor) M.; m. Kristin Elaine Harbaugh, Dec. 4, 1965; children: Devin, Jeffrey, Sean. BS in Math., Oreg. State U., 1967, PhD in Chemistry, 1975; postgrad., MIT, 1977; PhD in Chemistry (hon.), U. Mex. City, 1982. Chemist, research engr. Teledyne WahChang, Albany, Oreg., 1971-78; group leader, project mgr. Occidental Research Co., Irvine, Calif., 1978-83; tech. dir. Albany (Oreg.) Titanium, Inc., 1983—; metallurgy adv. com. Linn Benton Community Coll. Contbr. articles to profl. jours.; patentee in field. Mem. Am. chem. Soc., Am. Inst. Metallurgical Engring., Am. Inst. Chem. Engring.. Republican. Clubs: Albany Bridge, Corvallis (Oreg.) Golf, ALTi Golf (Albany). Avocations: skiing, golf, bridge, piano, guitar. Home: 3740 NW Chiquapin Pl Corvallis OR 97330 Office: Albany Titanium Inc 840 30th St Albany OR 97321

MEHALCHIN, JOHN JOSEPH, financial executive; b. Hazleton, Pa., Aug. 8, 1937; s. Charles and Susan (Korba) M.; divorced; 1 child, Martin. B.S. with honors, Temple U., 1964; M.B.A., U. Calif., Berkeley, 1965; Student U. Chgo., 1964; Supr. costs Winchester-Western, New Haven, Conn., 1965-67; mgmt. cons. Booz-Allen & Hamilton, N.Y.C., 1967-68; mgr. planning TWA, N.Y.C., 1968-70; 2d v.p. Smith, Barney, N.Y.C. and Paris, 1970-74; chief fin. officer, pres. leasing co. Storage Tech. Corp., Louisville, Colo., 1974-79; sr. v.p. Heizer Corp., 1979; pres., founder Highline Fin. Services, Inc. and subs., Boulder, Colo., 1979—. Served with AUS, 1958-61. U. Calif. fellow, Berkeley, 1964; U. Chgo. scholar, 1964. Mem. Fin. Execs. Inst., Am. Assn. Equipment Lessors, Beta Gamma Sigma, Omicron Delta Epsilon. Home and Office: Highline Fin Services Inc 1881 9th St Suite 320 Canyon Ctr Boulder CO 80302

MEHLMANN, MARYBETH AMES, speech pathologist; b. Jersey City, Sept. 27, 1951; d. William Emmett and Gloria (McGuinn) Ames; m. Gregory Karl Mehlmann, Aug. 30, 1976; children: Gregory Karl Jr., Nicholas Ames. BA, Colo. State U., 1974; MA, U. No. Colo., 1976. Speech pathologist pub. schs. Denver, 1976-82, Englewood, Colo., 1982-85; instr. Cherry Creek Staff Devel., Englewood, 1984-85; coordinator Intensive Treatment of Stuttering Program, 1983-85. Co-Author: Proofwriter, 1984; author: Wuzzles Step By Step, 1985; contbr. articles to mags. Active Jr. League Denver, 1980-85. Grantee U. Denver and Cherry Creek Sch. Dist., 1985. Mem. Am. Speech and Hearing Assn. (cert.), Colo. Speech and Hearing Assn., Council Exceptional Children, Council Learning Disabilities. Office: Cherry Creek Schs 4700 S Yosemite St Englewood CO 80111

MEHLUM, JOHAN ARNT, banker; b. Trondheim, Norway, Nov. 11, 1928; came to U.S., 1950, naturalized, 1955; s. Hans Aage and Olga (Nygaard) M.; diploma Norwegian Bus. Coll., 1946, Grad. Sch. Banking, Rutgers U., 1971; m. Ladona Marie Christensen, May 30, 1951 (dec. 1983); children—Ann Marie, Katherine, Susan Jane, Rolf Erik. Clk., Forretningsbanken, Trondheim, 1946-50, First Nat. Bank Oreg., Astoria and Corvallis, 1952-57; cashier, mgr. Bank of Shedd, Brownsville, Oreg., 1958-63; pres., chmn. Siuslaw Valley Bank, Forence, Oreg., 1963—; chmn. bd. Community Bank Creswell (Oreg.), 1970-79; founding dir., pres. Western Banker Service Corp., 1983-84; dir. Siuslaw Valley Plaza, Inc., 1966—. Mayor, Dunes City, Oreg., 1973-75. Trustee Lane Community Coll. Found., 1971-78; chmn. bd. dirs. NW Intermediate Banking Sch., Lewis and Clark Coll., Portland, Oreg., 1975-77; trustee, past chmn. Western Lane County Found., 1976-82. Served with Royal Norwegian Army, 1948-49. Named Jr. First Citizen, Astoria, 1955, First Citizen, Brownsville, 1962; recipient internat. relations award U.S. Jr. C. of C., 1960. Mem. Western Ind. Bankers (mem. exec. council 1970-74), Am. Bankers Assn. (mem. exec. com. community bankers div. 1976-78, governing council 1982-84), Oreg. Bankers Assn. (exec. council 1977-83, pres. 1981-82), Florence Area C. of C. (pres. 1970), Banking Profession Polit. Action Com. (state chmn. 1973-76), Sons of Norway. Clubs: Elks, Rotary (pres. 1967-68), Norsemen's League (pres. 1954). Home: PO Box 131 Florence OR 97439 Office: PO Box 280 Florence OR 97439

MEHREN, LAWRENCE LINDSAY, investment company executive; b. Phoenix, May 26, 1944; s. Lawrence and Mary Teresa (Stelzer) M.; B.A., U. Ariz., 1966; M.A., U. Ariz., 1968; m. Lynn Athon McEvers, June 5, 1965; children—Lawrence Lindsay, John Eskridge. Bus. mgr. Rancho Santa Maria, Peoria, Ariz., 1968-69; traffic mgr. Glen-Mar Mfg. Co., Phoenix, 1969-70; account exec. Merrill Lynch, Pierce, Fenner and Smith, Inc., Phoenix, 1970-77, sr. account exec., 1977-78, asst. v.p., 1978-80, v.p., 1980-82; v.p. Harbor Equity Funds, Inc., 1982-84; sr. v.p. Harbor Fin. Group, Inc., Phoenix, 1984—. Mem. Maricopa County Citizens Action Com., Charter Govt. Com.; chmn. Madison Citizens Adv. Com., 1973-74; bd. dirs. Planned Parenthood, 1972-75, Brophy Coll. Prep. Sch., 1981—, Prescott Coll., 1984-85. Recipient award Ariz. Hist. Found., 1968. Mem. Phoenix Stock and Bond Club (dir. 1979-82), Ariz. Acad. Public Affairs, Phoenix C. of C., Internat. Wine and Food Soc., Phi Alpha Theta, Beta Theta Pi. Club: Valley Field Riding and Polo. Home: 7215 N Central Ave Phoenix AZ 85020 Office: 2525 E Ariz Biltmore Circle Phoenix AZ 85016

MEHRING, CLINTON WARREN, engineering executive; b. New Haven, Ind., Feb. 14, 1924; s. Fred Emmett and Florence Edith (Hutson) M.; m. Carol Jane Adams, Mar. 9, 1946; children—James Warren, Charles David, John Steven (dec.), Martha Jane. B.S., Case Inst. Tech., 1950; M.S., U. Colo., 1956. Registered profl. engr., Wyo., Colo., Nev. Design engr. U. S. Bur Reclamation, Denver, 1950-56; design engr. Tipton & Kalmbach, Denver, 1956-58; asst. resident engr. Tipton & Kalmbach, Quito, Equador, 1959-61; asst. chief design engr. Tipton & Kalmbach, Lahore, Pakistan, 1962-65; v.p. Tipton & Kalmbach, Denver, 1966-73, exec. v.p., 1973-79, pres., 1979—, also bd. dirs. Served with AUS, 1943-45. Recipient Theta Tau award as outstanding grad. Case Inst. Tech., 1950. Fellow ASCE; mem. Am. Cons. Engrs. Council, Colo. Soc. Engrs., U.S. Com. on Large Dams, Am. Concrete Inst. (life), U.S. Com. Irrigation and Drainage, Sigma Xi, Tau Beta Pi, Theta Tau, Sigma Chi, Blue Key. Methodist. Club: Denver Athletic. Home: 1821 Mt Zion Dr Golden CO 80401 Office: 1331 17th St Denver CO 80202

MEHURON, WILLIAM OTTO, electronics company executive; b. Hammond, Ind., Nov. 30, 1937; s. Arthur and Margaret Irene (Soroka) M.; m. Charlotte Anne Nyheim, Aug. 26, 1982; children: Kimberly Anne, Kristine Lynn. BSEE, Purdue U., 1959; MSEE, U. Pa., 1962, PhD, 1966. Tech. staff RCA, Moorestown, N.J., 1959-64, Gen. Electric, Phila., 1964-68; group leader Mitre Corp., McLean, Va., 1969-74; tech. dir. naval intellegence Dept. Navy, Washington, 1974-81; dir. research and engring. Nat. Security Agy., Ft. Meade, Md., 1981-85; v.p., gen. mgr. data systems div. Ampex Corp. subs. Allied-Signal Co., Redwood City, Calif., 1985-86; v.p. product ops. Daisy Systems Corp., Mountain View, Calif., 1986—. Mem. IEEE, AAAS, Armed Forces Communication and Electronics Assn., Soc. Motion Picture and TV Engrs., Assn. Electronics Warfare, Security Affairs Support Assn. Avocations: amateur radio (W4XM), running, tennis, cooking, antiques. Home: 2332 Warner Range Ave Menlo Park CA 94025 Office: Daisy Systems Corp 700 E Middlefield Rd Mountain View CA 94039

MEIER, ALLEN LEE, research chemist; b. Sidney, Nebr., Apr. 9, 1942; s. Edgar Nicholous and Merna Mary (Crow) M.; m. Margaret Mary Wright, Sept. 30, 1967; children: Susan, Karen, Sharon. BS, Colo. State U., 1964. Research chemist U.S. Geol. Survey, Denver, 1966—. Served to 1st lt. U.S. Army, 1964-66. Mem. Shenandoah Corp. Club (pres. 1984—). Avocations: fishing, hunting, boating. Home: 6742 Urban Ct Arvada CO 80004 Office: US Geol Survey PO Box 25046 MS 955 Denver CO 80225

MEIER, CHARLES OSBORNE, sales executive; b. Nashville, Apr. 22, 1956; s. John Gabriel and Muriel Helen (Osborne) M. BA, U. Calif., Berkeley, 1980. Adminstrv. asst. Eldex Labs., Menlo Park, Calif., 1981-82, asst. sales mgr., 1982-84; sales mgr. Elder Labs., San Carlos, Calif., 1984—. Avocations: classical piano, bicycling. Home: 914 9th Ave San Mateo CA 94402 Office: Eldex Labs Inc 831 Bransten Rd San Carlos CA 94070

MEIER, DENNIS RAY, nuclear engineering consultant; b. College Station, Tex., Feb. 20, 1954; s. Walter and Ruby Lee (Poehl) M. BS in Nuclear Engring., Tex. A&M U., 1976, MS in Nuclear Engring., 1977. Engr. EG&G Idaho, Inc., Idaho Falls, 1977-80; sr. engr. Energy Inc., Idaho Falls, 1980-83; co-founder Sage Software, Idaho Falls, 1983-84; software quality assurance engr. Boeing Corp., Seattle, 1984-85; cons. engr. Scientech Inc., Idaho Falls, 1985—; cons. Exxon Nuclear, Richland, Wash. and Idaho Falls, 1985—. Mem. Am. Nuclear Soc., Am. Soc. of Quality Control. Avocations: writing fiction, skiing, bicycling, running. Office: Scientech Inc PO Box 1406 Idaho Falls ID 83403

MEIER, MARGARET SHELTON, music educator, composer; b. N.Y.C., Mar. 7, 1936; s. Hans and Margaret Meier; divorced; children: Karl Shelton, Robert Shelton. MusB, Eastman Sch. Music, 1958; MA, Calif. State U., Los Angeles, 1972; PhD, UCLA, 1983. Instr. Pasadena Christian Sch., 1958-68; teaching assoc. UCLA, 1975-80; lectr. Calif. State U., San Bernardino, 1977-79; instr. Mt. San Antonio Coll., Walnut, Calif., 1980—; dir. music Trinity United Meth. Ch., Pomona, Calif., 1982—. Composer: Mythical Muliebrity (orchestral variations), 1972, This Child, 1977 (Axel-Stordahl Commn. award 1977), The Catherine Wheel (chamber music song-cycle), 1977, (solo cantata) The Spanish Gypsy, 1983, Te Deum, 1986. Stephen minister Trinity United Meth. Ch., Pomona, 1986—. George Eastman scholar, 1954-58; recipient Atwater Kent composition award, 1980, Atwater Kent musicology award, 1980. Mem. Am. Women Composers, Inc., 1983— (v.p. west coast 1984—), ASCAP, Nat. Assn. Composers USA, Music Tchrs. Assn. Calif. (Pomona br. pres. 1984—, composition state composers' chmn. 1974-76), Internat. Congress on Women in Music, Internat. League of Women Composers. Office: Mt San Antonio Coll 1100 N Grand Walnut CA 91789

MEIER, THOMAS JOSEPH, engineering geologist, consulting engineering firm executive; b. Superior, Nebr., June 16, 1948; s. Hugh Milton and Stella Bella (Dugas) M.; student U. Kans., 1966-69, U.S. Army Engr. Sch., 1969, Met. State Coll., 1976-78; BA in Geology, U. Colo., 1980; m. Jo Ann Weeks, June 4, 1968; 1 child, Nicole Victoria. Office mgr. Testing & Engring. Services, Inc., Colorado Springs, Colo., 1972-74; v.p. Thomas E. Summerlee & Assos., Inc., Vail, Colo., 1974-76; mktg. exec. Fox & Assocs., Inc., Phoenix, Denver, 1976-84, v.p. mktg. corp. hdqrs., Denver, 1984—, dir., 1982—; tech. services rep., geologist, Phoenix, 1981-84; dir. Thomas E. Summerlee & Assos., 1975-76. Rep. Dist. Committeeman, Jefferson County, Colo., 1980. Served with C.E., U.S. Army, 1969-72. Decorated Bronze Star; recipient Meritorious Service award Lai Kae Orphanage, Lai Kae, S.Vietnam, 1970. Mem. Soc. Mktg. Profl. Services, Denver Info. Network, Industries for Jeffco, Soc. Am. Mil. Engrs. (past pres. Phoenix), Am. Mgmt. Assn., U. Kans. Alumni Assn., U. Colo. Alumni Assn., Denver C. of C., Colo. Assn. Commerce and Industry, Metro North C. of C., Nat. Assn. Indsl. and Office Parks, Colo. Mining Assn., Cons. Engrs. Council. Roman Catholic. Contbr. articles to profl. publs. Author: Environmental Geology Digest, 2 vols. Home: 7535 South Jasmine Ct Englewood CO 80112 Office: 4765 Independence St Wheat Ridge CO 80033

MEIGS, RICHARD JOHN, banking executive; b. Redmond, Oreg., July 18, 1950; s. Sylvester Harrison and Gladys Emily (Smith)) M.; m. Frances Elaine Hampton, Aug. 14, 1976; children: Ryan John, Christopher David. Student, Portland Community Coll., 1973, Marylhurst Coll., 1985. Adminstrv. asst. First Interstate Bank, Portland, Oreg., 1975-76, asst. v.p., 1976-81, v.p., 1981—; v.p. curriculum U. Wis. Sch. Bank Adminstrn., Madison, 1982-84. Author: A Prayer Journal, 1978, (software program) A Garden Journal, 1984. Del. Oreg. Rep. Cen. Com., 1979; Deacon Lincoln St. Baptist Ch., Portland, 1978—; bd. dirs. NW Baptist Found., Portland, 1984—, chmn. investment com., 1985—; Del., So. Baptist Conv. Commn. on Bds., Nashville, 1985-86. Avocations: backpacking, gardening, reading, family history.

MEIJERS, FRANK BART, JR., manufacturing company executive; b. Vlissingen, Zeeland, The Netherlands, Aug. 29, 1938; came to U.S., 1968; s. Frank B. and Marie (Lute) M.; m. Jeanine J. Vanderhayden, July 17, 1959; children: Victor L., Eeke J. BSChemE, Tech. U., Delft, The Netherlands, 1960; BSEE summa cum laude, Northeastern U., 1974. Mgr. product mgmt. Control Data Corp., Mpls., 1974-76; v.p. ops. CFI Memorex, Anaheim, Calif., 1976-78; v.p. tech. ops. Three Phoenix Co., 1978; v.p. ops. Pace Industries Inc., Phoenix, 1978-80; pres., chief exec. officer Luctor Corp., Phoenix, 1980—. Served to 1st lt. Royal Netherlands Air Force, 1959-65. Mem. Am. Nat. Standards Inst. (chmn. disk test methods standards com. 1985—), IEEE, Assn. Corp. Growth. Club: Eagle (Aruba, Netherlands Antilles) (chmn. 1967-68). Lodge: Kiwanis (sec. Scottsdale club 1981-82). Avocations: photography, jazz. Home: 9136 N 81 St Scottsdale AZ 85258 Office: Luctor Corp 2311-104 W Royal Palm Rd Phoenix AZ 85021

MEIKLEJOHN, ALVIN J., JR., state senator, lawyer, acct.; b. Omaha, June 18, 1923; B.S., J.D., U. Denver, 1951; m. Lorraine J. Meiklejohn; children—Pamela Ann, Shelley Lou, Bruce Ian, Scott Alvin. Mem. Colo. Senate from 19th dist., 1976—, chmn. com.; edn.; mem. Edn. Commn. of States, 1981—. Mem. Jefferson Sch. Dist. No. R-1 Bd. Edn., 1971-77, pres., 1973-77. Served to capt. U.S. Army, 1940-46; to maj. USAF, 1947-51. Mem. Colo. Bar Assn., Denver Bar Assn., Colo. Soc. C.P.A., Arvada C. of C. Republican. Clubs: Masons, Shriners. Home: 7540 Kline Dr Arvada CO 80005 Office: Jones Meiklejohn Kehl & Lyons 1600 Lincoln Ctr Bldg Denver CO 80264

MEILACH, DONA ZWEIGORON, author, lecturer, consultant; b. Chgo.; s. Juluis and Rose (Don) Zweigoron; m. Melvin M. Meilach, Feb. 15, 1948; children; Susan Seligman, Allen. Student, Art Inst. Chgo. and Chgo. Jr. Colls., 1958-64, Palomar Jr. Coll., 1979-81; PhB, U. Chgo., 1946; MA in Art History, Norhtwestern U., 1969. Tchr. Evergreen Park (Ill.) High Sch., 1958-65; tchr. fundamentals of art Moraine Valley Jr. Coll., Palos Park, Ill., 1970-71; instr. art history and crafts Purdue U., Hammond, Ind., 1969-71; lectr. arts and crafts at various colls. and workshops in U.S. and Can. 1970—; appeared in various radio and TV programs including: Arlene Francis Show, 1972, Good Morning Show, 1973, Not For Women Only, 1975, Sun-Up San Diego, 1979. Author books on art-crafts, 1964—, including Creating Modern Furniture, 1975, Decorative and Sculptural Ironwork, 1977, Exotic Needlework, 1978, Basketry Today, 1979, Ethnic Jewelry, 1981; books on other subjects include: Art of Belly Dancing, 1975, Jazzercise 1978, How to Relieve Your Aching Back, 1979, Homemade Liqueurs, 1979, Homemade Cream Liquors, 1986; books on computers include Before You Buy a Computer, 1983, Before You By Word Processing Software, 1984, Before You Buy a Used Computer, 1985, 1985, Dynamics of Computer Graphics, 1986; contbr. numerous articles to various newspapers and mags. including: Chgo. Sun-Times, N.Y. Times, Redbook, Cosmopolitan mag., Today's Health mag., PC mag., Bus. Software and others; contbr. articles to World Book Ency.; syndicated columnist Creative Crafts, 1974-77; editor Sphere mag., 1973; contbr. numerous photographs to various newspapers and mags. Judge Oreg. State Fair, 1976, So. Calif. Expn. State Fair, 1977, Crocker Art Gallery, 1979; colleague San Diego County Dept. Edn., 1986, 87; arts commr. City of Carlsbad, Calif., 1986—. Mem. Author's Guild Am., Nat. Assn. Sci. Writers, Am. Craft Council, Artist-Blacksmith Assn. of N.Am., Nat. Computer Graphics Assn., SIGGRAPH, Sigma Delta Chi. Address: 2018 Saliente Way Carlsbad CA 92009

MEILAHN-WHITE, KRISTINE, speech pathologist; b. Kewaskum, Wis., Dec. 7, 1955; d. Carl Albert and Caroline Philliphine (Klumb) M.; m. Bruce T. White, Mar. 29, 1986. BS, U. Wis., Oshkosh, 1978; MS, U. Oreg., 1979. Cert. speech pathologist, communication disorders specialist; cert. neuro devel. treatment. Speech, lang. pathologist Children's Clinic and Presch., Seattle, 1979-84; communication disorders specialist Bellevue (Wash.) Pub. Schs., 1984-86, Pediatric Diagnostic and Treatment Ctr., Providence Hosp., Everett, Wash., 1986—. Mem. Pacific Northwest Non Vocal Communication Group (video coordinator 1985—, mailing library chair 1984-85), Bellevue Pub. Schs. Student Adv. Council, Kappa Delta Phi. Avocations: hammered dulicimer, recorder, traveling, photography. Home: 20701 NE 79th Redmond WA 98052 Office: Pediatric Diagnostic & Treatment Ctr The Luther Child Ctr Campus 4526 Federal Everett WA 98201

MEINDL, JAMES DONALD, electrical engineer; b. Pitts., Apr. 20, 1933; s. Louis M. and Elizabeth F. (Steinhauser) M.; m. Frederica Ziegler, May 21, 1961; children: Peter James, Candace Ann. B.S., Carnegie Mellon U., 1955, M.S., 1956, Ph.D., 1958. Engr. Autonetics Co., Downey, Calif., 1957, Westinghouse Co., Pitts., 1958-59; head sect. microelectronics U.S. Army Electronics Command, Ft. Monmouth, N.J., 1959-62; chief br. semicondr. and microelectronics U.S. Army Electronics Command, 1962-65, dir. div. integrated electronics, 1965-67; assoc. prof. elec. engring. Stanford U., 1967-70, prof., 1970-84, John M. Fluke prof. elec. engring., 1984-86, assoc. dean research, 1984-86, dir. integrated circuits lab., 1967-84, dir. Electronics Labs.,, 1972-86, dir. Ctr. Integrated Systems, 1981-86; v.p. acad. affairs, provost, dean Rensselaer Poly. Inst., Troy, N.Y., 1986—; dir. Telesensory Systems Inc., Palo Alto, Calif., 1971-84; cons. to govt., industry. Author: Micropower Circuits, 1969; contbr. numerous articles to profl. publs. Served to 1st lt. AUS, 1959-61. Recipient Arthur S. Flemming Commn. award Washington Jr. C. of C., 1967; J.J. Ebers award IEEE Electron Devices Soc., 1980. Fellow IEEE (editor Jour. Solid State Circuits 1966-71, Internat. Solid-State Circuits Conf. Outstanding Paper award 1970, 75, 76, 77, 78), AAAS; mem. Nat. Acad. Engring., Electrochem. Soc., Biomed. Engring. Soc. (co-editor Annals of Biomed. Engring. 1976-80), AAUP, Sigma Xi, Tau Beta Pi, Eta Kappa Nu, Phi Kappa Phi. Patentee integrated circuit field.

MEISTER, FREDERICK WILLIAM, state official, lawyer; b. Waterbury, Conn., May 21, 1938; s. William Frederick and Marion Callender (Tracy) M.; m. Joanne Marie Babich, June 12, 1982. B.A., Swarthmore Coll., 1960; M.B.A., Harvard U., 1962; J.D., U. Pitts., 1975. Bar: Pa. 1975, D.C. 1980. Fin. analyst First Pa. Bank, Phila., 1966-67; asst. comptroller Am. Friends Service Com., Phila., 1967-72; program analyst HEW, Washington, 1976-77; project mgr., program analyst Health Care Financing Adminstrn., Balt., 1977-82; chief Bur. of Fiscal and Contract Mgmt., Ariz. Health Care Cost Containment System, Phoenix, 1982-84, chief policy, planning and research, 1984—. Founding chmn. troop com. Valley Forge council Boy Scouts Am., Media, Pa., 1966-68; bd. dirs., mem. bus. com. Fellowship House and Farm, Inc., Phila., 1968-72; county dir. U.S. Senate Primary Campaign for H. John Heinz, Montgomery County, Pa., 1976., mem. fin. com. Am. Friends Sevice Com., Balt., 1980-82; mem. contracts task force Ariz. Dept. Health Services, Phoenix, 1983-84. Served to lt. USNR, 1962-65. Recipient Bur. Dirs. citation Bur. Quality Control, Health Care Financing Adminstrn., 1982. Mem. ABA, Fed. Bar Assn., Am. Soc. Pub. Adminstrn. Republican. Mem. Soc. Friends. Club: Harvard Bus. Sch., Harvard of Phoenix, Phoenix City. Home: 1722 W Earll Dr Phoenix AZ 85015 Office: Ariz Health Care Cost Containment System 801 E Jefferson St Phoenix AZ 85034

MEISTER, JOHN EDWARD, JR., electronics engineer; b. Elgin, Ill., Nov. 17, 1956; s. John Edward and Marilyn Barbara (Futter) M.; m. Rebecca Marie Buehner, Nov. 15, 1975; children: Christine Marie, Mark Christopher. AA, Cen. Tex. Coll., 1979, U. Md., 1980; BS cum laude, U. Md., 1981; postgrad., Western Conservative Baptist Sem., 1982-83. Enlisted U.S. Army, 1974, advance through grades to staff sgt., 1980; electronics technician Frankfurt, Fed. Republic of Germany, 1974-77; maintenance supr. Darmstadt, Fed. Republic of Germany, 1978-81; transferred from 232d Signal Co. Telecommunications, 1981; sr. instr. U.S. Army Signal Sch., Ft. Gordon, Ga., 1981-82; resigned U.S. Army, 1982; sr. electronics instr. ITT Tech. Inst., Portland, Oreg., 1982-83; equipment engr. Services Tech., Aloha, Oreg., 1983-85; electronic designer Boeing Electronics Co., Everett, Wash., 1985—; electronics engr. Innovative Designs and Electronic Systems Techs., Portland, 1982-85. Mem. Apollo Domain User's Soc., First Osborne Users Group. Republican. Baptist. Avocations: computers, stained glass, automotive mechanics, writing, real estate investments. Home: 12819 2d St SE Lake Stevens WA 98258 Office: Boeing Electronics Co M/S OU-10 PO Box 24969 Seattle WA 98124

MEJIA, BARBARA OVIEDO, chemistry educator; b. San Francisco, Apr. 14, 1946; s. Louis Jerome and Alice May (Beall) O.; m. Michael Scot Ellison, June 7, 1969 (div. Jan. 1977); m. Richard S. Mejia, Sept. 15, 1982. AA, Sierra Coll., 1967; BS, U. Calif., Davis, 1969, PhD, 1973. Cert. community coll. tchr., Calif. Lectr. U. Calif., Davis, summer 1977; lectr. Calif. State U., Chico, 1973-76, asst. prof., 1976-80, assoc. prof., 1980-85, prof., 1985—. Contbr. articles to profl. jours. Judge Cen. Valley Sci./Engring. Fair, Chico, 1977, 80, 81, 82, bd. dirs. 1978-79; judge Butte County Sci. Fair, Chico, 1985-86. Mem. AAAS, Am. Chem. Soc., Congress of Faculty Assns., Cal Aggie Alumni Assn., Sigma Xi. Home: 4 Jasper Dr Chico CA 95928 Office: Calif State U Dept Chemistry Chico CA 95929-0210

MEJIA, KAREN GAYLE, registered nurse; b. Grass Valley, Calif., Aug. 6, 1942; s. Eric August and Catherine Marie (Baun) Schindhelm; m. Michael Robert Mejia, 1962; children: Steven, David, Dawn. BS in Nursing, Chico State U., 1965. RN. Positions as nurse various hosps., Calif., 1966-77; charge nurse coronary care unit Santa Rosa (Calif.) Meml. Hosp., 1970-73, 77-79; staff nurse II Community Hosp. Sonoma County, Santa Rosa, 1979—; staff nurse Specialty Emergency Services, 1981—; Active Amway, Amsoil, Neolife, Royal Am.'s Food Co., Pre-paid Legal Services, Forever Living Products, Windberg Line. Editor Hosp. Communication Publ. newsletter Prognewsis, 1984—. Mem. Am. Heart Assn., Am. Cancer Soc., Am. Lung Assn., Girl Scouts Am. (assoc.), Calif. Scholarship Fedn. Democrat. Roman Catholic. Lodge: Job's Daughter. Avocations: gardening, sewing, flute, travel, organ.

MEKURIA, GIRMA, consulting company executive; b. Dire Dawa, Ethiopia, Sept. 28, 1940; came to U.S., 1973; s. Mekuria Muluneh and Shewaye Agonafir; m. Margaret Mekuria; children: Tamirat, Elizabeth. BS, Haile Selassie U., 1965; MS, Syracuse U., 1970. Registered profl. engr. Ill., Wash., Alaska, Calif., Oreg., Colo. Field engr. Harza Engring. Co., Finchaa, Ethiopia, 1970-72; design engr. Harza Engring. Co., Chgo., 1973-78; supervising engr. R.W. Beck & Assocs., Seattle, 1978-80, prin. engr., 1980-84, exec. engr., 1984—. Contbr. articles to profl. jours. Home: 3028 NW 59th St Seattle WA 98107 Office: R W Beck & Assocs 2121 Fourth Ave Seattle WA 98121

MELAND, WANDA MARIE, counselor; b. Havre, Mont., Oct. 30, 1950; d. Sigurd Elmer and Mary Thelma (Ulven) Meland. A.A., Waldorf Luth. Jr. Coll., 1970; B.A., B.S., Eastern Mont. Coll., 1973; M.S., No. Mont. Coll., 1977. Cert. profl. in psychology, Mont. Dept. Insts.; cert. guidance, phys. edn. tchr., Mont. Alt. houseparent Yellowstone Boys and Girls Ranch, Billings, Mont., 1973-75; therapist, dir. day treatment ctr. Northcentral Community Mental Health Ctr., Havre, 1975-77; elem. counselor Chinook (Mont.) Pub. Schs., 1977-84; rehab. specialist Internat. Rehab. Assocs., 1985—. Mem. Am. Personnel and Guidance Assn., Mont. Personnel and Guidance Assn., Am. Mental Health Counselors Assn., Mont. School Counselors Assn. Democrat. Lutheran. Club: Sons of Norway. Home: Rt 1 Box 3 Chinook MT 59523

MELBY, ALAN KENNETH, linguist, educator; b. Murray, Utah, Mar. 25, 1948; s. Kenneth O. and Charolette (Bryner) M.; B.S., Brigham Young U., 1973, M.A., 1974, Ph.D., 1976; m. Ulla-Britta L. Sandholm, Aug. 14, 1970; children—Eric, Roland, Irene, Philippe, Yvette, Vivianne. Assoc. prof. linguistics Brigham Young U., Provo, Utah, 1977—; v.p. Mgmt. Acctg., Inc. Mem. Linguistic Soc. Am., ACM, Assn. Computational Linguistics, Linguistic Assn. Can. and U.S., Acoustical Soc. Am., Am. Translators Assn. Republican. Mormon. Contbr. articles to profl. jours. Home: 1223 Aspen Ave Provo UT 84604 Office: Linguistics Dept Brigham Young Univ Provo UT 84602

MELCHER, JOHN, U.S. senator; b. Sioux City, Iowa, Sept. 6, 1924; m. Ruth Klein, Dec. 1, 1945; children: Terry, Joan, Mary, Robert, John. Student, U. Minn., 1942-43; D.V.M., Iowa State U., 1950. Ptnr. Yellowstone Valley Vet. Clinic, Forsyth, Mont., operator cattle feed lot, 1953-55; alderman City of Forsyth, 1953-55; mayor City of Foryth, 1955-61; mem. Mont. Ho. of Reps. from Rosebud County, 1961-62, 69, Mont. Senate, 1963-67, 91st-94th congresses from 2d Mont. Dist., 1969-77; U.S. senator from Mont. 1977—; Former mem. Mont. Legis. Council. Democratic candidate for U.S. Ho. of Reps., 1966. Served with AUS, 1943-45, ETO. Decorated Purple Heart, Bronze Star, Combat Infantryman's Badge; recipient Disting. Service award Nat. Assn. Conservation Dists., 1985, Centennial medal U. Pa. Sch. Vet. Medicine, 1984. Democrat. Office: 730 Hart Senate Office Bldg Washington DC 20510

MELCHIOR, IB JORGEN, director, author; b. Copenhagen, Denmark, Sept. 17, 1917; s. Lauritz and Inger (Nathansen) M.; came to U.S., 1938, naturalized, 1944; grad. Stenhus Coll., Holbaek, Denmark, 1936; Cand.Phil., U. Copenhagen, 1937; m. Harriet Hathaway Kale, Mar. 15, 1942 (div. 1960); 1 child, Leif; m. Cleo Baldon, Jan. 18, 1964; 1 stepson, Dirk Arin. Actor, stage mgr., co-dir. The English Players, 1937-39; stage mgr. Radio City Music Hall and Center Theatre, N.Y.C., 1941-42; actor and writer, N.Y.C., 1947-50; TV dir. Perry Como Show, 1951-54, Eddy Arnold Show, 1952; TV's Top Tunes, 1953, March of Medicine, 1955-56; assoc. producer G-L Enterprises, 1952-53; free-lance writer, dir., producer, 1957—; writer, dir, feature films, documentary films, plays, TV shows. Mem. adv. com. Narcotics Information Clinic Program, Los Angeles, 1971. Served with AUS, 1942-45; ETO. Decorated Bronze Star; King Christian X Erindrings medal (Denmark); knight comdr. Cross Mil. Order St. Brigitte (Sweden); brig. gen. Medal Merit, Old Guard (Phila.); recipient Hamlet award for excellence in playwriting Hour of Vengeance, Shakespeare Soc. Am., 1982. Mem. Dirs. Guild Am., Poets, Essayists and Novelists, Writers Guild Am. West, Authors Guild, Manuscript Soc., Acad. Sci. Fiction Films (hon. mem., Golden Scroll award for best writing 1976), Royal Danish Guard Assn. Calif., Danish-Am. Club (founding pres. 1962-65), Am.-Scandinavian Found. Danish Luncheon Club (dir. 1967). Adventurers. Author: Order of Battle, 1972; Sleeper Agent, 1975; The Haigerloch Project, 1977; The Watchdogs of Abaddon, 1979; The Marcus Device, 1980; The Tombstone Cipher, 1983; Eva, 1984; V-3, 1985; Code Name: Grand Guignol, 1987; translator, narrator cassette album of Hans Christian Andersen stories, 1986; also numerous articles. Address: 8228 Marmont Ln Los Angeles CA 90069

MELENDEZ, SYLVIA JEAN, accountant; b. Puyallup, Wash., Apr. 12, 1948; d. Wilford Arthur and Lorna Lotus (Torrey) Holdren; m. William Francis Culbert, Feb. 13, 1966 (div. May 1978); m. Christopher Joseph Melendez, July 29, 1978. Grad. high sch., Carson, Calif. Acct., mgr. office Stem Search Co., Torrance, Calif., 1973-77, Kopy-King Inc., Ventura, Calif., 1977-79; acctg. mgr. FCD-Tecon Pacific, West Sacramento, 1979-82; acct. Greve, Clifford et al, Sacramento, 1983-84; adminstrv. mgr. Calif. Builders Supply, Sacramento, 1984—; acct. Custom Truck and Trailer, Sacramento, 1985—. Mem. Blue Canyon Western Hist. Preservation Soc. (sec.-treas. 1980-81). Republican. Adventist. Avocations: computer programming, skiing, darts, knitting, crocheting. Office: Calif Builders Supply Co PO Box 13457 Sacramento CA 95813

MELIA, DANIEL FREDERICK, Celtic studies and rhetoric educator, educational administrator, consultant; b. Fall River, Mass., Mar. 2, 1944; s. Daniel John and Rita Ann (Lough) M.; m. Nancy Ruth Geist, Sept. 7, 1966 (div.); m. 2d, Teresa A. Donovan, July 30, 1983; 1 child, Daniel Thomas. A.B. magna cum laude in English, Harvard U., 1966, M.A. in Celtic, 1970, Ph.D. in Celtic Langs. and Lit., 1972. Teaching fellow Harvard U., Cambridge, Mass., 1968-72, asst. prof. dept. Celtic, summer 1974; asst. prof. rhetoric and folklore U. Calif., Berkeley, 1972-78, assoc. prof., 1978—, assoc. dean Coll. Letters and Sci., 1981-83, assoc. dean grad. div., 1984-87, assoc. dir. study ctr., Eng. and Ireland, 1987—, humanities faculty research fellow, 1978-79. Vis. asst. prof. English dept. UCLA, 1973; lang. cons. Harvard Grad. Prize Fellow, 1969-72; jr. summer research fellow Nat. Endowment for Humanities, 1975. Fellow Medieval Acad. Ireland; mem. Medieval Acad. Am., Medieval Assn. of the Pacific, MLA, Celtic Studies Assn. N.Am. (pres. 1985-87). Club: Harvard of N.Y.C. Author: (with D. Calder et al) Sources and Analogues of Old English Poetry, Vol. II, 1983; contbr. articles in field to pubs. including Brit. Archaeological Reports, Studia Hibernica, Philological Quar. Home: 196 Bellingdon Rd, Chesham, Buckinghamshire England Office: Study Ctr U Calif, 21 Strutton Ground, London SW1 England Office: U Calif Dept Rhetoric Berkeley CA 94720

MELLISH, DONALD LEROY, banker; b. Fairbanks, Alaska, Nov. 1, 1927; s. William and Monica (Hugg) M.; m. Susan H. Schmelzer; children: Gabriele, John, Robert. Student, U. B.C., Can.), Vancouver, 1946-47; grad., Pacific Coast Banking Sch., 1963. With Nat. Bank of Alaska, Anchorage, 1953—; exec. v.p. Nat. Bank of Alaska, 1962-65, pres., 1965-75, chmn. exec. com., 1975—; dir. Seattle br. Fed. Res. Bank San Francisco, 1978-82, Alascom Inc., MAPCO, Inc., Tulsa, Northwest Capital Corp.; mem. Nat. Export Expansion Council, Small Bus. Adv. Council, Regional Adv. Com. on Banking Policies and Practices, 1968-69. Chmn. Alaska Radio Free Europe, 1971-74. Mem. Am. Bankers Assn., Alaska Nippon Kai. Office: PO Box 600 Anchorage AK 99510

MELLO, DONALD R., state senator; b. Owensboro, Ky., June 22, 1934; s. Jack and Gladys (Jasper) M.; student U. Nev.; grad. B.F. Goodrich Co. Mgmt. Sch., Sacramento; m. Barbara Jane Woodhall; children—Donald, David. Condr., S.P. Co.; mem. Nev. Assembly from 30th Dist., 1963-, chmn. Interim Finance com., 1975-77, chmn. Legis. Commn., 1973-74, chmn. Ways and Means com., 1973-80, sr. Democratic assemblyman, 1973-81, sr. assemblyman, 1977-82, Nev. state senator, 1983—; chmn. com. on transp., 1985—, vice chmn. com. on fin., 1985—. Mem. adv. com. Title III, Nev. Dept. Edn. Mem. Washoe County Democratic Central Com., 1968—; mem. Pres.'s Club United Transp. Union, PTA (life). Served with USNR. Recipient Friend of Edn. award Washoe County Tchrs. Assn., 1974, Appreciation award Nev. N.G., 1973-75, Assembly Speaker's award, 1977, Appreciation award Ret. Public Employees Nev., 1979, award Clark County Classroom Tchrs., 1981, appreciation award United Transp. Union, 1981, Pres.' award Nev. State Edn. Assn., 1981, 85, Nev. AFL-CIO, 1981; commd. hon. Ky. col.; named One of 10 Outstanding Legislators in U.S., Assembly State Govtl. Employees, 1976; Don Mello Sports Complex named in his honor City of Sparks (Nev.). Democrat. Lodge: Masons. Office: 2590 Oppio St Sparks NV 89431

MELLOR, TONY (CLINTON LEE), JR., public relations/advertising executive; b. Phila., Apr. 23, 1942; s. Clinton Lee and Catherine Eugena (Stroud) M.; children—Christine Tawn, Gabriel Ballenger, Dawn Irish. B.S., U. Ariz., 1964. Salesman Sta. KGUN, ABC-TV, Tucson, 1968-74; account exec. Sta. KZAZ-TV, Tucson, 1974-76, Sta. KOLD, CBS-TV, Tucson, 1976-78; div. mgr. Uni-Lab Corp., Tucson, 1979-82; dir. pub. relations Pima County Fairgrounds, Tucson, 1982-85, Cactus Recreation Ctrs., 1985—. State bd. dirs. Ariz. Mental Health Assn.; bd. dirs. Mental Health Assn. Greater Tucson; mem. La Fiesta de los Vaqueros Rodeo Promotion Com. Mem. Internat. Rodeo Writers Club, Tucson Advt. Club, N.W. Businessmen's Club, Alpha Gamma Rho Alumni. Republican. Episcopalian. Office: 1601 S Alvernon Tucson AZ 85711

MELOAN, TAYLOR WELLS, marketing educator; b. St. Louis, July 31, 1919; s. Taylor Wells and Edith (Graham) M.; m. Anna Geraldine Leukering, Dec. 17, 1944 (div. 1974); children: Michael David, Steven Lee; m. Jane Innes Bierlich, Jan. 30, 1975. B.S. cum laude, St. Louis U., 1949; M.B.A., Washington U., St. Louis, 1950; D.B.A., Ind. U., 1953. Advt. mgr. Herz Corp., St. Louis, 1941-42; sales promotion supr. Liggett & Myers Tobacco Co., St. Louis, 1942-43; asst. prof. mktg. U. Okla., Norman, 1953; from asst. prof. to assoc. prof. mktg. Ind. U., Bloomington, 1953-59; prof., chmn. dept. mktg. U. So. Calif., Los Angeles, 1959-69; dean Sch. Bus. Adminstrn. U. So. Calif., 1969-71, assoc. v.p. acad. adminstrn. and research, 1971-81, prof. mktg., 1959—; prof. bus. adminstrn. U. Karachi, Pakistan, 1962; vis. prof. mktg. Istituto Post U. Per Lo Studio Dell Organizzazione Aziendale, Turin, Italy, 1964; Disting. vis. prof. U. Witwatersrand, Johannesburg, 1978; editorial adviser bus. adminstrn. Houghton Mifflin Co., Boston, 1959-73; cons. to industry and govt., 1953—; bd. dirs. Council Better Bus. Burs., Inc., 1978-84, Nat. Advt. Rev. Bd., 1985—. Author: New Career Opportunities, 1978, Innovation Strategy and Management, 1979, Direct Marketing: Vehicle for Department Store Expansion, 1984, Preparing the Exporting Entrepreneur, 1986; co-author: Managerial Marketing, 1970, Internationalizing the Business Curriculum, 1968, Handbook of Modern Marketing, contbg. author, 1986; bd. editors: Jour. Mktg., 1965-72. Served with USNR, 1943-46. Mem. Newcomen Soc. N.Am., Am. Mktg. Assn. (pres. Los Angeles chpt. 1963-64), Order of Artus, Beta Gamma Sigma, Delta Pi Epsilon. Clubs: Calif. Yacht, University (Los Angeles). Lodge: Rotary. Home: 639 Burlingame Ave Los Angeles CA 90049 Office: U So Calif Los Angeles CA 90007

MELONE, MARGIE RUTH, health care co. exec.; b. Shawnee, Okla., Oct. 9, 1933; d. Jonah H. and Barbara Nancy (Krause) Haze; vocat. nurse diploma Fairmont Hosp., San Leandro, Calif., 1965; postgrad. Chabot Coll., U. Calif.; m. Victor P. Melone, Apr. 26, 1952; children—Victor P., Terri R. Vocat. nurse Barrett Convalescent Hosp., Hayward, Calif., 1965-68; v.p. La-Mar Co., Hayward, 1968—, Hunt-Malone Enterprises, Hayward, 1968-78; v.p. True Care, Inc., Hayward, 1970-77, Embassy House, Walnut Creek, Calif., 1970—; pres., adminstr. Barrett Convalscent Hosp., Inc., 1968-75, owner, adminstrv. cons., 1978—; trustee Barret Rest Home, Inc.; co-chmn. Adv. Bd. Mentally Ill and Retarded, 1973. Mem. So. Alameda County Commn. Aging, Am. Health Care Assn., Alameda County Mentally Retarded Assn., Calif. Assn. Health Facilities. Clubs: Met. Yacht, Order Eastern Star. Author articles, short story, poetry. Home: 1535 Denton Ave Hayward CA 94545 Office: 1625 Denton Ave Hayward CA 94545

MELOY, HARRIETT CRUTTENDEN, historian, librarian; b. Inkster, N.D., June 23, 1916; d. Coran Henry and Muriel Gladys (Jones) C.; m. Peter George Meloy, July 23, 1941; children—Peter Michael, Timothy John, Steven Henry, Kerry Meloy Massucco, Mark Kingsley. B.A., Jamestown Coll., 1937; LLD (hon.), Carroll Coll., 1986. Researcher, librarian Mont. Hist. Soc., Helena, 1957-77; mem. Mont. Bd. Pub. Edn., 1970-85, chair, 1975-77, 78-79, 83-84; bd. dirs. LWV, Helena, 1950—; v.p. Mont. Dem. Women, 1959-60; state rep. Nat. Com. Support Pub. Schs., 1965-77; rev. panelist U.S. Dept. Edn. Elem. Sch. Recognition Program, 1985-86. Recipient Golden Apple award Mont. Edn. Assn., 1975, Cliff Worthen award Phi Delta Kappa, 1978, Silver Apple award Helena Edn. Assn., 1972, Am.'s Women of Distinction award Soroptimist Internat., 1986. Mem. Mont. Library Assn., Nat. Assn. State Bds. Edn., AAUW (state div. pres. 1972-74), Delta Kappa Gamma (hon.).

MELSHEIMER, GAYNET ELIN, construction company executive; b. Portland, Oreg., May 22, 1941; d. Harold V. and Ellen Beldin; m. Sam Melsheimer, Aug. 27, 1983; children: Steve Duarte, Anamarie Duarte. BBA, Merritt Coll., 1962. Lease mgr. Elder Equipment, Portland, 1978-83; pres. Gaynetco, Inc., Portland, 1983—. Author: Things I Like, 1984. Mem. Am. Buswomens. Assn. (pres., sec. 1985, nat. Top Ten award 1985), Women in Constrn. (sec. 1986), Assn. Women Contractors (sec., treas. 1986), Am. Gen. Contractors (bd. dirs. 1984-86, exec. com. 1985-86). Lodge: Women of Elk (pres. 1975-76). Home: 16675 SE Bush Portland OR 97256 Office: Gaynetco Inc 10416 NE Marx Portland OR 97220

MELTON, BILLY ALEXANDER, crop and soil science educator; b. Wheeler, Tex., Aug. 21, 1932; s. Billy A. and Margaret (Moore) M.; m. Lois McKinley, Sept. 4, 1951; children: Kathy, Deborah. BS, N.Mex. A&MA, 1954; MS, U. Ill., 1956, PhD, 1958. Alfalfa breeder N.Mex. State U., Las Cruces, 1958—, asst. prof. crop and soil sci., 1958-62, assoc. prof., 1962-66, prof., 1966—. Contbr. numerous articles to profl. jours. Named Disting. Researcher, N.K. & Co., 1965, Disting. Researcher, N.Mex. State U., 1969; grantee in field. Fellow Am. Soc. Crop Sci., Am. Soc. Agronomy; mem. Western Soc. Crop Sci., Nat. Alfalfa Improvement Conf., Western Alfalfa Improvement Conf., Am. Grassland Council, Sigma Xi, Phi Kappa Phi. Home: 2805 Huntington Las Cruces NM 88001

MELTON, JEANNE LESLIE, social worker; b. Charleston, W.Va., Oct. 9, 1942; d. George Creevey and Gladys Arlene (Lockhart) Leslie; m. Melvin Kay Melton, Sept. 11, 1965; children: Wendy Elizabeth, Rachel Leslie. BA, DePauw U., 1964; MSW, Smith Coll., 1966. Social worker Va. Treatment Ctr., Richmond, 1966-67, Family Bur., Winnipeg, Can., 1967-69, Family and Children's Services, St. Louis, 1969-70, Washington U. Child Guidance Clinic, St. Louis, 1970-71, Christian Children's Ranch, Eagle, Idaho, 1978-85; therapist Warm Springs Ctr., Boise, 1985; pvt. practice, Boise, 1984-85; group facilitator Parents United, Boise, 1984—. Tchr., cons. Boise Valley Christian Communion, 1976—. Mem. Nat. Assn. Social Workers, Am. Assn. Counseling and Devel., Task Force on Adolescent Suicide Prevention. Democrat. Avocations: sewing, walking, cross country skiing, bicycling, back packing. Home: 3202 Camrose Ln Boise ID 83706

MELVILLE, ROBERT FRANCIS, JR., artifical intelligence systems company executive; b. Chgo., Dec. 13, 1936; s. Robert Francis Sr. and Bellma Katherine (Krueger) M.; m. Joan Ann Denton, Sept. 7, 1958 (div. June 1974); children—Lori, Scott, Kimberly, Dennis; m. Elizabeth Louise Masterson, Aug. 31, 1974; 1 child, Diane. Student Wright Jr. Coll., 1955, U. Ill., 1956; B.S. in Mktg., San Diego State U., 1959. PERT analyst Litton Data Systems, Canoga Park, Calif., 1961-62; master programmer Hughes Aircraft Co., Culver City, Calif., 1962-63; program control adminstr. TRW System Inc., Redondo Beach, Calif., 1963-64; project control supr. Hughes Aircraft Co., Canoga Park, 1964-68; asst. dir. master scheduling Litton Ship Systems, Culver City, 1968-72; adminstrv. ops. Xerox Artifical Intelligence Systems, Pasadena, Calif., 1972—, mgr. adminstr./product ops.; guest speaker planning and control systems Loyola U., Los Angeles, 1970. Sect. chmn. United Way, Pasadena, 1981; counselor Jr. Achievement, Culver City, 1970-71; alt. com. mem. Republican Party, Conoga Park, 1965. Recipient Cert. Spl. Achievement Indsl. Coll. Armed Forces, 1963. Mem. Nat. Mgmt. Assn. (sec. 1979-80, arrangements chmn. 1978-79, pub. relations chmn. 1977-78, Excellent award, 1979, 80, 84), Assn. Old Crows. Baptist. Office: Xerox Artificial Intelligence Systems 250 N Halstead St Pasadena CA 91107

MELVIN, RITA ANNE, clinical social worker; b. Ironton, Ohio, June 21, 1947; d. Jonathan Albert and Edna Lucille (Cromley) M. BS, Columbia Union Coll., 1969; postgrad. tng. family and community devel., U. Md., 1972-74; MSW, UCLA, 1980. Discharge planning coordinator Washington Adventist Hosp., Takoma Park, Md., 1974-76, St. Francis Med. Ctr., Lynwood, Calif., 1976-78; clin. social worker St. Francis Med. Ctr., Lynwood, 1980-86; social work supr. in maternal, child health Huntington Meml. Hosp., Pasadena, Calif., 1986—; mem. adv. bd. Project Family, Los Angeles, 1980-86, Perinatal Mental Health Group, Los Angeles, 1985; chairperson Perinatal Social Work Group, Los Angeles County, 1984—; subcom. co-chairperson High Risk Task Force, Los Angeles, 1986—. Contbr. articles to profl. jours. Active Southeast Council on Child Abuse, Lynwood, Southeast Council on Services to Elderly, Southeast Los Angeles County. Mem. Nat. Assn. Perinatal Social Workers, (state rep. 1984-85, nat. conf. planner, chairperson 1987, Region IX liaison 1985-86, bd. dirs.), Nat. Assn. Social Workers, Calif. Perinatal Assn., Nat. Perinatal Assn., Lawrence County Geneal. Soc., So. Calif. Br. of Ohio Geneal. Assn. Mem. Seventh-Day Adventists. Avocations: photography, travel, camping, genealogy. Home: 12558 Brookshire Ave #3 Downey CA 90242 Office: Huntington Meml Hosp Dept Patient Services 100 Congress St Pasadena CA 91109-7013

MELZER, SARA ELIZABETH, French educator; b. Los Angeles, Aug. 5, 1947; d. Lester and Mildred (Mahlin) M. BA, U. Wis., 1969; MA, U. Chgo., 1970, PhD, 1975. Asst. prof. Duke U., Durham, N.C., 1975-78; assoc. prof. French UCLA, 1978—. Author: Discourses of The Fall: A Study of Pascal's Pensées, 1986. Home: 674 Kelton Ave Los Angeles CA 90024 Office: UCLA French Dept Hilgard Ave Los Angeles CA 90024

MENCONI, DORITA ELENA, chemist, marketing professional; b. Redwood City, Calif., Feb. 21, 1959; d. Alfred Anthony and Elizabeth Eileen (Whitcomb) Langone; m. David Alan Menconi, June 30, 1984; 1 child, Janine Elana. BS in Chemistry, San Jose State U., 1981, MS in Chemistry, 1984. Chemist Sierra Chem. Co., Milpitas, Calif., 1981-85; mktg. coordinator Telos Labs. Inc., Fremont, Calif., 1985-87; tech. info. coordinator Monoclonal Antibodies, Sunnyvale, Calif., 1987—. Mem. Am. Chem. Soc. (cert.). Avocations: cross country skiing, racquetball, hiking, swimming. Home: 357 Spring Valley Ln Milpitas CA 95035 Office: Telo Labs Inc 45725 Northport Loop W Fremont CA 94538

MENDELSON, ALAN CHARLES, lawyer; b. San Francisco, Mar. 27, 1948; s. Samuel Mendelson and Rita Rosalie (Spindel) Brown; divorced; children: Jonathan Daniel, David Gary. BA with great distinction, U. Calif., Berkeley, 1969; JD cum laude, Harvard U., 1973. Bar: Calif. 1973. Assoc. Cooley, Godward et al., San Francisco, 1973-80; ptnr. Cooley, Godward, Castro, Huddleson & Tatum, Palo Alto, Calif., 1980—; bd. dirs. Sanmina Corp., San Jose, Calif.; sec, Acuson, Mountain View, Calif., 1982—, Chisholm, Campbell, Calif., 1985—, Zoran Corp., Santa Clara, Calif., 1983—. Chmn. Piedmont (Calif.) Civil Service Commn., 1978-80; den leader Boy Scouts Am., Menlo Park, Calif.; coach Menlo Park Little League, 1982—; mem. exec. com., bd. dirs. No. Calif. chpt. Nat. Kidney Found. Served with USAR, 1969-75. Named U. Calif. Berkeley Alumni scholar, 1966, Scaife Found. scholar, 1966. Mem. Harvard U. Law Sch. Alumni Assn. (area rep. funds com. 1978—), Phi Beta Kappa. Democrat. Jewish. Avocations: golf, tennis, softball, basketball, photography. Home: 665 San Mateo Dr Menlo Park CA 94025 Office: Cooley Godward Castro et al 5 Palo Alto Sq 400 Palo Alto CA 94306

MENDELSON, MARTIN, physician, educator; b. N.Y.C., Apr. 16, 1937; s. Moses and Pauline (Freundel) M.; divorced; children: Kathryn, Christopher. AB, Cornell U., 1958; PhD, Calif. Inst. Tech., 1962; MD, SUNY, Stony Brook, 1976. Diplomate Am. Bd. Family Practice. Resident Emanuel Hosp., Portland, Oreg., 1979; assoc. prof. physiology N.Y.U. Med. Sch., N.Y.C., 1963-71, SUNY, Stony Brook, 1971-76; gen. practice medicine Columbia Health Assn., St. Helens, Oreg., 1979-81; asst. prof. family practice U. Calif. Med. Sch., Davis, 1981-85; clin. assoc. prof. Tacoma (Wash.) Family Medicine, 1985—; del. Oreg. Acad. Family Physicians, Portland, 1978-79; alt. del. Oreg. Med. Assn.; grant reviewer NSF, Washington, 1969-71; investigator Marine Biol. Lab., Woods Hole, Mass., 1964-71; program com. MUMPS User's Group, Wash., 1985—. Contbr. articles on neurophysiology, med. computing to profl. jours. Grass Found. fellow in neurophysiology, 1962; NIH research grantee, 1964-71; HHS tng. grantee, 1982-85. Fellow Am. Acad. Family Physicians; mem. AAAS, Am. Assn. Med. Systems and Informatics, Soc. Gen. Physiologists (treas. 1967-69), Wash. Med. Assn., N.Y. Acad. Sci.Sigma Xi. Club: Tacoma Osbourne Group. Avocations: scuba diving, sailing, skiing, bicycling, computer programming. Office: Tacoma Family Medicine 721 S Fawcett Tacoma WA 98402

MENDENHALL, CARROL CLAY, physician, surgeon; b. Missouri Valley, Iowa, July 26, 1916; s. Clay and Maude (Watts) M.; student U. So. Calif., 1942-43, Chapman Coll., 1946-47, Los Angeles City Coll., 1947-48; D.O., Coll. Osteo. Physicians and Surgeons, 1952; M.D., Calif. Coll. Medicine, 1962; m. Lucille Yvonne Bonvouloir, June 14, 1946 (div. July 1957); 1 son, Gregory Bruce; m. 2d, Barbara Marilyn Huggett-Davis, Sept. 28, 1974. Intern, Los Angeles County Osteo. Hosp., 1952-53; gen. practice medicine, 1953-82, specializing in weight control, Gardena, Calif., 1961-74, specializing in stress disorders and psychosomatic medicine, Ft. Worth, 1974-78, specializing in integral medicine and surgery, Santa Clara, Calif., 1978—; med. dir. Green's Pharms., Long Beach, Calif., 1956-64; v.p. Internat. Pharm. Mfg. Co., Inc., San Pedro, Calif., 1965-66; pres. Chemico of Gardena, Inc., 1964-69; staff Gardena Hosp.; active staff O'Connor Hosp., San Jose, Calif., 1979—; tchr., lectr. biofeedback, prevention and treatment of stress, creative thought; founder, dir. Eclectic Weight Control Workshop, 1971-74, Longevity Learning, Longevity Learning Seminars, 1980; past mem. adv. bd. dirs. Los Angeles Nat. Bank. Cadre med. dir. Gardena Civil Def., 1953-54, asst. to chief med. dir., 1954-60, chief med. and first aid services, 1960-64. Served as pharmacist's mate USNR, 1944-46. Fellow Royal Soc. Health, Am. Acad. Med. Preventics, Am. Acad. Homeopathic Medicine; mem. Calif. Med. Assn., Santa Clara County Med. Soc., Acupuncture Research Inst. (also alumni assn.), Los Aficionados de Los Angeles (pres. 1964-66), Am. Soc. Clin. Hypnosis. Flamenco Soc. No. Calif. (treas., bd. dirs. 1986—). Republican. Address: 255 Crestview Dr Santa Clara CA 95050

MENDENHALL, DONNA MACMILLAN, information scientist; b. Calif., Aug. 2, 1925; d. Robert S. and Emma E. (Nikkel) MacMillan; 1 son. BS, So. Conn. State Coll., 1972, MS, 1975; cert., Rutgers U., 1978. Librarian Uniroyal Chem. Co., Naugatuck, Conn., 1967-80; sr. info. scientist Oxirane Internat., Princeton, N.J., 1980; tech. info. and patent specialist ARCO Chem. Co., Phila., 1981; supr. ARCO Metals, Louisville, 1982; mgr. tech. info. TRW Corp., Redondo Beach, Calif., 1983—. Contbr. articles to profl. jours. Pres. West Hill Condominium Assn., Naugatuck, 1975-76; mem. Met. Opera Guild. Mem. AIAA, AAUW, Am. Chem. Soc., Am. Soc. Info. Sci., Indsl. Tech. Info. Mgrs. Group, So. Calif. Online Users Group, Am. Def. Preparedness Assn., N.Y. Acad. Scis. Avocations: music, tech. writing. Home: 1958 Rolling Vista Dr Lomita CA 90717 Office: TRW Corp Tech Info Ctr 1 Space Park S/1930 Redondo Beach CA 90278

MENDENHALL, JOHN, graphic design educator; b. Hindsdale, Ill., Nov. 17, 1950; s. George and Kveta M. BFA, U. Ill., 1972; MA, Stanford U., 1973. Designer Agy. Internat. Devel., 1972-73; lectr. Ill. Wesleyan U., Bloomington, 1974-75, Pa. State U., College Station, 1975-76; vis. asst. prof. Ariz. State U., Tempe, 1976-80; prof. art Calif. Poly State U., San Luis Obispo, 1980—; pvt. practice graphic designer, San Luis Obispo, 1980—. Author: American Trademarks 1930-1950, Vol. 1, 1983, Vol. 2, 1986, High Tech Trademarks, 1985. Mem. Am. Inst. Graphic Arts. Office: Calif Poly State U San Luis Obispo CA 93407

MENDEZ, CELESTINO GALO, mathematics educator; b. Havana, Cuba, Oct. 16, 1944; s. Celestino Andres and Georgina (Fernandez) M.; came to U.S., 1962, naturalized, 1970; B.A., Benedictine Coll., 1965; M.A., U. Colo., 1968, Ph.D., 1974, M.B.A., 1979; m. Mary Ann Koplau, Aug. 21, 1971; children—Mark Michael, Matthew Maximilian. Asst. prof. math. scis. Met. State Coll., Denver, 1971-77, assoc. prof., 1977-82, prof., 1982—, chmn. dept. math. scis., 1980-82. Mem. advt. rev. bd. Met. Denver, 1973-79; parish outreach rep. S.E. deanery, Denver Cath. Community Services, 1976-78; mem. social ministries com. St. Thomas More Cath. Ch., Denver, 1976-78, vice chmn., 1977-78, mem. parish council, 1977-78; del. Adams County Republican Conv., 1972, 74, Colo. 4th Congl. Dist. Conv., 1974, Colo. Rep. Conv., 1982; alt. del. Colo. Rep. Conv., 1974, 76, 5th Congl. dist. conv., 1976; del. Douglas County Rep. Conv., 1976, 78, 80, 82, mem. rules com., 1978, 80, precinct committeeman Douglas County Rep. Com., 1976-78, mem. central com., 1976-78; bd. dirs. Rocky Mountain Better Bus. Bur., 1975-79, Rowley Downs Homeowners Assn., 1976-78; mem. exec. bd., v.p. Assoc. Faculties of State Inst. Higher Edn. in Colo., 1971-73; trustee Hispanic U. Am., 1975-78; councilman Town of Parker (Colo.), 1981-84, chmn.

budget and fin. com. 1981-84; chmn. joint budget com. Town of Parker-Parker Water and Sanitation Dist. Bds., 1982-84. Recipient U. Colo. Grad. Sch. excellence in teaching award, 1965-67; Benedictine Coll. grantee, 1964-65. Mem. Math. Assn. Am., Am. Math. Soc., Nat. Council Tchrs. of Math., Colo. Council Tchrs. of Math., Colo. Internat. Edn. Assn., Asso. Faculties of State Insts. Higher Edn. in Colo. (v.p. 1971-73). Republican. Roman Catholic. Contbr. articles to profl. jours. and newspapers. Home: 11482 S Regency Pl Parker CO 80134 Office: 1006 11th St Denver CO 80204

MENDOZA, CAROLYN COREY, educator; b. Canton, Ohio, June 26, 1949; d. Frederick Constantine and Dorothy (Stauff) Corey; m. Salvador Leo Mendoza, Aug. 7, 1971. BA in Psychology, Calif State U., Fullerton, 1972; MS in Edn. and Reading, Calif State U., 1982. Cert. secondary tchr. ESL and reading, Calif. ESL, Spanish tchr. Fullerton Elem. Sch. Dist., 1972-74, cultural resources tchr., 1974-75; ESL/ reading tchr. Santa Ana (Calif.) Unified Sch. Dist., 1976—, chairperson dept. reading, 1983—. Vol. Children's Hosp. of Orange County, Calif., 1985-86; sec. Mexican-Am. Arts Council Bowers Mus., Santa Ana, 1985-86. Classroom Tchr. Instructional Improvement Program grantee Santa Ana Unified Sch. Dist., 1985; writing fellow U. Calif. Irvine, 1982—. Mem. Internat. Reading Assn., Orange County Reading Assn., Nat. Educators Assn., Cal-State Fullerton Alumni Assn., Learned Laides. Republican. Avocations: reading, tennis, travel, computers. Office: Santa Ana High Sch 520 W Walnut Santa Ana CA 92705

MENDOZA, SALLY PATRICIA, psychology educator; b. Santa Fe, Sept. 24, 1951; d. David John Rhodes and Jennifer Margaret (Fields) Peacock; m. Israel David Mendoza, June 22, 1971 (div. Feb. 1974). Student, Wash. State U., 1969-71; BA, The Evergreen State Coll., 1974; PhD with distinction, Stanford U., 1978; postdoctoral, U. Calif., Davis, 1981-84. Research assoc. Stanford (Calif.) U., 1978, 80-81; instr. The Evergreen State Coll., Olympia, Wash., 1979-80; postdoctoral fellow U. Calif., Davis, 1981-84, asst. research scientist, 1984—, asst. prof. psychology, 1986—. Co-editor: Social Cohesion: Essays Toward a Sociophysiological Perspective; contbr. articles to jours. and chpts. to books. Organizer United Farm Workers Union, Dallas, 1971-72. Recipient Nat. Research Service award Nat. Inst. Child Health and Human Devel., 1981-84; fellow William Caldwell Young Mem., West Coast Sex Soc., 1977, Biol. Scis. Tng., NIMH, 1974-77. Mem. AAAS, Am. Psychol. Assn., Am. Soc. Primatologists (program chmn. 1984—) Animal Behavior Soc., Internat. Primatol. Soc., Sigma Xi. Office: U Calif Primate Research Ctr Davis CA 95616

MENDOZA, SYLVIA ANN, speech pathologist; b. Montebello, Calif., Jan. 18, 1958; d. Ramon and Lupe (Valdez) M.; m. Michael David Driebe, Feb. 16, 1985. BA, U. So. Calif., 1980; MA, Whittier Coll., 1982. Speech pathologist Almansor Edn. Ctr., Alhambra, Calif., 1982-84, Cedars-Sinai Hosp., Los Angeles, 1982—; bilingual cons. La Habra (Calif.) Rehab. Assn., 1981—; speech cons. Indleside Mental Health Ctr., Los Angeles, 1983—. Getty Oil scholar, 1982. Mem. Am. Speech Lang. and Hearing Assn. (cert., Continuing Edn. award 1986), Calif Speech Lang. and Hearing Assn. Avocations: sailing, running. Home: 5503 Eglise Ave Pico Rivera CA 90660 Office: Cedars-Sinai Hosp 8700 Beverly Blvd Los Angeles CA 90049

MENEFEE, BARRY EUGENE, medical manufacturing executive; b. Sacramento, Oct. 15, 1947; s. Stephen Franklin and Jessie California (McGrath) M.; m. Jacqueline Julie Beaulieu, Dec. 26, 1969; children: Kristin Stephenie, Jenifer Lauren, Courtney Megan. BS, U. Ariz., 1973, MS, 1977, PhD in Molecular Biology, 1979. Sr. chemist Sigma Chem. Co., St. Louis, 1979-80; prodn. mgr. Tago Inc., San Francisco, 1980-81; founder, pres. Am. Qualex Co., Los Angeles, 1981-86; v.p. tech. ops. Am. Bioclin. Corp., Portland, Oreg., 1986—; prin. Cons. for Biotech., Riverside, Calif., 1985—. Served with USAF, 1965-68, Vietnam. Mem. AAAS, N.Y. Acad. Sci., Am. Soc. Microbiologists. Republican. Roman Catholic. Lodge: KC (grand knight 1984-85). Avocations: automotive restoration, computer scis. Home: 5568 Wentworth Dr Riverside CA 92505

MENG, PAUL CHING-LING, infosystems specialist; b. Nanking, Peoples Republic of China, Nov. 5, 1946; came to U.S., 1969; s. Mark T.F. and Mary M.W. (Lee) M.; m. Cynthia W. Huang, July 3, 1971 (div. Dec. 1981); m. Christine H. Hsu, May 9, 1982; children: Oliver T., Teresa S., Anita N., Victor D. PhD, Northeastern U., 1976. Sr. engr. Digital Equipment Corp., Maynard, Mass., 1976-77; research specialist Prime Computer, Inc., Wellesley, Mass., 1977-79; system specialist Ford Aerospace Corp., Sunnyvale, Calif., 1979-81; mgr. data communications dept. Citicorp/TTI, Santa Monica, Calif., 1981—. Prin. tech. works include Smart Card, Data Encryption Device,local area computer networking; contbr. tech. articles to data communication mags.; patentee in field. Fellow IEEE; mem. Am. Nat. Standard Inst. (X9A6 com.), Am. Mgmt. Assn., Tunghai U. Alumni Assn. (pres. Los Angeles chpt.), Conejo Chinese Culture Assn. (sr. tchr.), Joint Chinese Univ. Alumni Assn. So. Calif. (bd. dirs. 1986—), Phi Kappa Phi. Republican. Roman Catholic. Avocations: music, camping, racquetball. Office: Citicorp/TTI 3100 Ocean Park Blvd Santa Monica CA 90405

MENGERS, SUE, motion picture talent agent; b. Hamburg, Germany, Sept. 2, 1938; came to U.S., 1938; s. Eugene and Ruth Sender; m. Jean-Claude Tramont, May 5, 1973. Student public schs., N.Y.C. Agent Korman & Assos., N.Y.C., 1963-68; with Creative Mgmt. (name now Internat. Creative Mgmt.), Los Angeles, 1968—; sr. v.p., co-chmn. dept. motion pictures Creative Mgmt. (name now Internat. Creative Mgmt.), 1977—; mem. bd. advisers Horizon Mag., Ladies Blue Ribbon 400. Office: Internat Creative Mgmt 8899 Beverly Blvd Suite 721 Los Angeles CA 90048

MENKES, JOHN, pediatric neurologist; b. Vienna, Austria, Dec. 20, 1928; came to U.S., 1940; s. Karl and Valerie (Tupler) M.; m. Miriam Trief, Apr. 14, 1957 (div. Feb. 1978); m. Joan Simon Feld, Sept. 28, 1980; children: Simon, Tamara, Rafael C. AB, U. So. Calif., 1947, MS, 1951; MD, Johns Hopkins U., 1952. Diplomate Am. Bd. Pediatrics, Am. Bd. Neurology. Intern, jr. asst. resident Children's Med. Ctr., Boston, 1952-54; asst. resident pediatrics Bellevue Hosp., N.Y.C., 1956-57; resident neurology, trainee pediatric neurology Columbia-Presbyn. Med. Ctr., Neurological Inst. N.Y., N.Y.C., 1957-60; asst. prof. pediatrics Johns Hopkins U., Balt., 1960-63, assoc. prof., 1963-66, asst. prof. neurology, 1964-66, chief pediatric neurology div., 1964-66; prof. pediatrics and neurology UCLA, 1966-74, chief pediatric neurology div., 1966-70, prof. psychiatry, 1970-74; chief Neurology-Neurochem. Lab. Brentwood (Calif.) VA Hosp., 1970-74; clin. prof. psychiatry, neurology and pediatrics UCLA, 1974-77, clin. prof. pediatrics and neurology, 1977-84, prof. pediatrics and neurology, 1985—; mem. metabolism study sect. NIH, 1966-70, project com. 1969-70; mem. adv. com. Nat. Inst. Child Health and Human Devel., 1985-87; mem. Genetically Handicapped Persons Program, Dept. Health Services, Calif., 1980—; mem. adv. bds. Hereditary Disease Found., Council Child Neurology Soc., Dysautonomia Found; bd. trustees Dystonia Med. Research Found., Vancouver, Can., 1985—. Author: Textbook of Child Neurology, 1985; (play) The Last Inquisitor, 1985 (Drama Logue Critics award 1985); contbr. numerous articles to pediatric jours. Served with USAF, 1954-56. Mem. Am. Acad. Neurology, Am. Acad. Pediatrics, Am. Chem. Soc., Soc. for Pediatric Research, Sociedad Peruana de Neuro-Psychiatria (hon.), Am. Neurochem. Soc., Am. Neurol. Assn., Am. Pediatric Soc., Child Neurology Soc. (Hower award 1980), editorial bds. of related jours., Dramatist Guild. Jewish. Home: 548 Green Craig Rd Los Angeles CA 90049 Office: UCLA Reed Neurologic Research Ctr Los Angeles CA 90024

MENN, DONALD EDWARD, publisher, consultant, writer; b. Kansas City, Mo., Sept. 24, 1945; s. Roy Thorpe and Helen Lockwood (Miller) M.; m. Mary Ellen Culver, Nov. 25, 1968 (div.); children—Gretchen Elizabeth, Kirsten Alexandra. A.A., Met. Jr. Coll. Kansas City, 1965; B.A., Leland Stanford Jr. U., 1972. Actor various plays and films internationally 1960—; copy boy, editorial asst. Kansas City Star, Mo., 1962-67; freelance writer 1967—; from editorial asst. to editor-in-chief Guitar Player Mag., GPI Publs., Inc., Cupertino, Calif., 1973-81; assoc. pub. Guitar Player Mag., GPI Publs., Inc., 1981—, chief fin. officer, dir. fin., analysis acquisitions, 1985—; chief exec. officer Arcturus Palo Alto, Calif., 1981—; editor-cons. numerous articles, records and books primarily on music. Contbr. stories, poems, screenplays and songs. Active Amnesty Internat., Handgun Control, So. Poverty Law Ctr., Mothers Against Drunk Driving, SANE, Union of Concerned Scientists, Citizens for a Better Environment and other polit. and charitable orgns. Recipient 1st place award for Journalism, Mo. Interscholastic Newswriting Contest, 1962, Commendation, So. Poverty Law Ctr., 1984. Mem. Fulfillment Mgrs. Assn., Nat. Assn. Jazz Educators, Western Pubs. Assn. (recipient several Maggie awards 1975—), Mag. Pubs. Assn. Club: French Cine (Palo Alto) (dir. 1970—). Avocations: music; running; swimming; biking; writing. Office: GPI Publs 20085 Stevens Creek Blvd Cupertino CA 95014

MENNELLA, VINCENT ALFRED, automotive manufacturing and airplane company executive; b. Teaneck, N.J., Oct. 7, 1922; s. Francis Anthony and Henrietta Vernard (Dickson) M.; B.A. in Acctg., U. Wash., 1948; m. Madeleine Olson, Aug. 18, 1945; children - Bruce, Cynthia, Mark, Scott, Chris. Sales and bus. mgmt. positions Ford div. Ford Motor Co., 1949-55; founder, pres. Southgate Ford, Seattle, 1955-80; pres., Flightcraft, Inc., Seattle, 1973-86; Chmn. bd Stanley Garage Door Co., 1981-86. Former chmn. March of Dimes. Served to capt. USNR, 1942-45. Republican. Roman Catholic. Clubs: Rainier Golf, Seattle Tennis, Wash. Athletic, Rotary (past pres.). Home: 1400 SW 171st PL Seattle WA 98166

MENNIG, JAN COLLINS, police chief; b. Pasadena, Calif., Oct. 9, 1927; s. Christian and Lucile (Collins) M.; m. Mary Ann Harmelink, June 9, 1979; 1 dau., Lucy Marie. B.S. in Pub. Adminstrn., U. So. Calif., 1959, M.S., 1964; Ph.D. in Polit. Sci., Pacific Western U., 1983; postgrad., U.S. Army Command and Staff Coll., 1972; postgrad. Indsl. Coll. Armed Forces, 1977; postgrad. Air War Coll., 1978. Cert. logistician, U.S. Army. With Pasadena (Calif.) Police Dept., 1950-65; with Culver City (Calif.) Police Dept., 1965—, asst. police chief, 1965-69, 76—, chief, 1970-75; cons. and lectr. in field. Chmn. Los Angeles Regional Criminal Justice Planning Bd., 1974-75; bd. mgrs. Culver Palms YMCA, chmn., 1970, 71; mem. Culver City Edn. Com., chmn., moderator, 1970. Served to col. USAR, 1944-82, World War II, Korea. Decorated Legion of Merit, others; recipient YMCA Man of Yr. award, 1971, Adult Leadership award Los Angeles United Way, 1984, Golden Book of Disting. Service award Los Angeles Met. YMCA, 1985. Mem. Internat. Assn. Chiefs of Police, Fed. Criminal Investigators Assn., Los Angeles County Peace Officers Assn., Am. Soc. for Pub. Adminstrn., internat. Police Assn., Calif. Police Chiefs Assn. (past mem. exec. com.), Calif. Peace Officers Assn., Res. Officers Assn. U.S., Mil. Order World Wars, Scapa Praetors, Pi Sigma Alpha. Republican. Clubs: Lions; Masons, Scottish Rite, York Rite, Elks (Culver City), Shriners (Los Angeles). Author: Elements of Police Supervision, 2d edit., 1978; others. Office: PO Box 808 Culver City CA 90232

MENNIS, EDMUND ADDI, investment management consultant; b. Allentown, Pa., Aug. 12, 1919; s. William Henry and Grace (Addi) M.; m. Selma Adinoff, Sept. 25, 1945; children: Ardith Grace, Daniel Liam. B.A., CCNY, 1941; M.A., Columbia U., 1946; Ph.D., NYU, 1961. Security analyst Eastman, Dillon & Co., N.Y.C., 1945-46; sr. research asst. Am. Inst. Econ. Research, Great Barrington, Mass., 1946-50; security analyst Wellington Mgmt. Co., Phila., 1950-61; dir. research Wellington Mgmt. Co., 1958-61, v.p., mem. investment com., 1958-66, economist, 1953-66; sr. v.p., chmn. trust investment com. Republic Nat. Bank, Dallas, 1966-72; sr. v.p., chmn. investment policy com. Security Pacific Nat. Bank, Los Angeles, 1972-81; pres., dir. Bunker Hill Income Securities, Inc., 1973-81; chmn. bd. Security Pacific Investment Mgrs., Inc., 1977-81; ind. cons. to investment mgmt. orgns. 1982—; Tech. cons. Bus. Council, Washington, 1962-66, 72-77, 79-81; econ. adviser sec. commerce, 1967-68; mem. investment adv. panel Pension Benefit Guaranty Corp., 1981-83. Assoc. editor: Financial Analysts Jour, 1960—; editor: C.F.A. Digest, 1971-86, Bus. Econs., 1985—; author books, chpts., numerous articles in field of econs. and investments. Trustee Fin. Analysts Research Found., 1981-86. Served to 1st lt. USAAF, 1942-45; to capt. USAF, 1951-53. Fellow Nat. Assn. Bus. Economists (council 1967-69), Fin. Analysts Fedn. (dir. 1970-72, Graham and Dodd award 1971, Molodovsky award 1972); mem. Am. Econ. Assn., Am. Fin. Assn., Am. Statis. Assn., N.Y. Soc. Security Analysts, Los Angeles Soc. Fin. Analysts, Conf. Bus. Economists (vice chmn. 1977, chmn. 1978), Inst. Chartered Fin. Analysts (pres. 1970-72, trustee 1968-74, C. Stewart Sheppard award 1978). Home: 721 Paseo Del Mar Palos Verdes Estates CA 90274 Office: 405 Via Chico Suite 7 Palos Verdes Estates CA 90274

MENOR, BENJAMIN, state supreme court justice. Justice Hawaii Supreme Ct., Honolulu. Office: Supreme Ct of Hawaii 417 S King St Honolulu HI 96813 *

MENSER, HARRY ALVIN, agriculturalist, researcher; b. Pitts., Dec. 30, 1930; s. Harry Alvin and Hazel Alma (Ross) M.; m. Elizabeth Jean Colvin, June 18, 1960; children: Daniel John, Molly Jean. BS, U. Del., 1954; MS, U. Md., 1959, PhD, 1963. Agrl. extension agt. U. Md., Upper Marlboro, 1955-57; grad. asst. U. Md., College Park, 1957-59; research technician Agrl. Research Service, USDA, Beltsville, Md., 1959-62, plant physiologist, 1962-80; plant physiologist Agrl. Research Service, USDA, Morgantown, W.Va., 1974-80; supt., extension research horticulturalist U. Idaho, Sandpoint, 1980—. Contbr. numerous articles to profl. jours. Served with USAF, 1951-52. Mem. Am. Soc. Agronomy, Am. Soc. Horticultural Scis., Sigma Xi, Phi Kappa Phi, Alpha Zeta. Methodist. Avocations: water sports, skiing, hiking, gardening. Home: 6370 Kaniksu Shore Cir Sandpoint ID 83864 Office: U Idaho Research and Extension Ctr 2105 N Boyer Ave Sandpoint ID 83864

MENSINGER, PEGGY BOOTHE, mayor; b. Modesto, Calif., Feb. 18, 1923; d. Dyas Power and Margaret (Stewart) Boothe; m. John Logan Mensinger, May 25, 1952; children: John B., Stewart I., Susan B. A.B. in Polit. Sci, Stanford U., 1944. Reporter San Francisco Red Cross Chpt. News Bur., 1944; acting mgr. Boothe Fruit Co., Modesto, Calif., 1945; asst. dir. Stanford (Calif.) Alumni Assn., 1947; exec. sec. public exercises com. Stanford U., 1949-51; mem. Modesto City Council, 1973-79, mayor, 1979—; bd. dirs. League of Calif. Cities; chmn. air quality subcom. U.S. Conf. of Mayors; pres. Stanford Assocs., 1985-87. Bd. dirs. Nat. council Girl Scouts U.S.A., 1978-87; chmn. Citizens Com. for Internat. Students, 1965-70; pres. Modesto PTA Council, 1967-69, Modesto chpt. Am. Field Service, 1969-70, Stanislaus County Hist. Soc., 1970-71, state bd. Common Cause, 1973-75; chmn. Modesto City Cultural Commn., 1968-73; del. White House Conf. on Families, Los Angeles, 1980; chmn. Stanislaus Area Assn. Govts., 1976-77. Recipient Woman of Year award VFW Aux., 1980. Mem. Nat. League Am. Pen Women (asso.), LWV (hon.), Calif. Elected Women's Assn. for Edn. and Research, AAUW (grant honoree Edn. Found. 1978), Stanford Assos., Phi Beta Kappa, Gamma Phi Beta. Unitarian. Club: Soroptimist (hon.; Women of Achievement award 1980). Home: 1320 Magnolia Ave Modesto CA 95350 Office: 801 11th St Modesto CA 95354

MENZIES, JEAN STORKE (MRS. ERNEST F. MENZIES), retired newspaperwoman; b. Santa Barbara, Calif., Dec. 30, 1904; d. Thomas More and Elsie (Smith) Storke; B.A., Vassar Coll., 1927; M.A. in Physics, Stanford, 1931; m. Ernest F. Menzies, Oct. 20, 1937; children—Jean Storke (Mrs. Dennis Wayne Vaughan), Thomas More. Teaching asst. dept. physics Stanford, 1927-29; instr. of physics Vassar Coll., 1929-30; tchr. math., chemistry, gen. sci. Sarah Dix Hamlin Sch., San Francisco, 1931-34; sec. to Dr. and Mrs. Samuel T. Orton, N.Y.C., 1935-36; press reporter, spl. writer Santa Barbara News-Press, 1954-63. Rec. sec. nat. YWCA, India, Burma and Ceylon, 1941-42; rec. sec., Calcutta YWCA, 1942-47, v.p., 1949-51; sec. Tri-County adv. council Children's Home Soc., Santa Barbara, 1952-54; founding dir., sec. corp. Santa Barbara Film Soc., Inc., 1960-66. Bd. dirs. Santa Barbara County chpt. Am. Assn. UN, 1954-59, Friends U. Calif. at Santa Barbara Library, 1970-74, Small Wilderness Area Preservation, 1971-79; sec. bd. trustees Crane Country Day Sch., 1955-57; trustee Mental Hygiene Clinic of Santa Barbara, 1956-60, U. Calif. Santa Barbara Found., 1974-80, Santa Barbara Mus. Natural History, 1977-81; adv. council Santa Barbara Citizens Adult Edn., 1958-62, v.p., 1960-62; bd. dirs. Internat. Social Sci. Inst., sec., 1963-68, mem. adv. bd., 1969; bd. dirs. Planned Parenthood Santa Barbara County, Inc., 1964-65, adv. council, 1966-67; trustee Santa Barbara Botanic Garden, 1967-81, hon. trustee, 1981—; trustee. Santa Barbara Trust for Historic Preservation, 1967-68, 72-77; mem. affiliates bd. dirs. U. Calif. at Santa Barbara, 1960-61, 67-70, 72-77; sec. Santa Barbara Mission Archive-Library, 1967—; mem. Santa Barbara Found., 1977-81. Mem. Santa Barbara Hist. Soc. (dir. 1957-62, founding mem. women's projects com. 1959-63, sec. 1961-62), Channel City Women's Forum (v.p. 1969-73, bd. dirs. 1973—), Phi Beta Kappa, Sigma Xi. Club: Vassar of Santa Barbara and the Tri-Counties (1st v.p., founding com. 1956-57, 2d v.p. 1959-61, chmn. publicity com. 1961-73). Home: 2298 Featherhill Rd Santa Barbara CA 93108

MENZIES, THOMAS NEAL, art consultant, art critic; b. Long Beach, Calif., Mar. 1, 1945; s. Thomas Warren and Frances (Starks) M. BA, U. Calif., Irvine, 1972. Library dir. Parsons Sch. Design, Los Angeles, 1980-82; art coordinator Hirsch/Bedner & Assocs., Santa Monica, Calif., 1982-84; pres. Neal Menzies Contemporary Art Inc., Los Angeles, 1984—. Contbg. editor ARTWEEK mag., Oakland, Calif., 1979-83. Founder Mus. Contemporary Art, Los Angeles; docent Venice (Calif.) Art Walk, 1986. Mem. So. Calif. Art Writers Assn., Los Angeles Contemporary Exhibitions (friend), Los Angeles County Mus. Art. Home: 2719 Griffith Park Blvd Los Angeles CA 90027 Office: Neal Menzies Contemporary Art 170 S LaBrea Ave Los Angeles CA 90036

MERCADO, JOSEPH ZACARIAS, social worker; b. Sacramento, July 7, 1948; s. Jose and Grace (Esparza) M.; m. Sally Boe, Apr 11, 1970; children: Dawn Marie, Jennifer Lynn, David Anthony, Christopher Rayn, John Andrew. AA in Social Sci., West Valley Coll., 1980; BA in Psychology, San Jose State U., 1983. Counseling intern Inst. for Community as Extended Family, San Jose, Calif., 1985-86; from eligibility worker I to III Santa Clara County Social Service Dept., San Jose, 1975-78, eligibility work supr. I, 1978—; religious edn. tchr. St. Lucy's Cath. Ch., Campbell, Calif., 1980-84, St. John Vianney, San Jose, 1984—. Contbr. articles to profl. jour. Recipient Outstanding Vol. Cert. Appreciation Vol. Action Ctr. Jur. League San Jose, 1978, Award of Merit Parent Participation Nursery Sch. Mgmt. Assn., 1985. Mem. Internat. Soc. for Prevention of Child Abuse and Neglect, Nat. Assn. Social Workers (cert.), Alpha Gamma Sigma (cert. achievement 1979). Democrat. Avocation: reading. Home: 2541 Coconut Dr San Jose CA 95148 Office: Santa Clara County Dept Social Services 1880 Pruneridge Ave Santa Clara CA 95050

MERCEDES HARDEN, M(ARCIAL) S(USAN), social worker, social program director; b. Watertown, N.Y., Aug. 9, 1947; d. Elmer Verner and Jean (Anderson) Stark; m. James Harden, Mar. 15, 1986. BA in English, St. Lawrence U., 1969; MSW Adminstrn., U. Denver, 1985. Tchr. Auburn High Sch., Syracuse, N.Y., 1970-71; health care specialist Women's Health Services, Colorado Springs, Colo., 1975-79, exec. dir., 1979-83; program dir. El Paso County Health Dept., Colorado Springs, 1985—; Bd. dirs. Women's Health Services; U.S. del. to WHO Conf. on Women, Geneva, Switzerland, 1981. Democrat. Roman Catholic. Avocations: bicycling, writing poetry, singing. Home: 1121 Sunset Rd Colorado Springs CO 80909 Office: El Paso County Health Dept 710 S Tejon Colorado Springs CO 80903

MERCER, ASHISHA (MARIJANE), editor, illustrator; b. Vallejo, Calif., Sept. 8, 1944; d. Lyle Russell Mercer and Louise Katherine (Bertuzzi) Brooks. B.A. in English and Art, San Hose State U., 1966, MA, secondary teaching credentials, 1967. Tchr. Campbell Union High Sch., San Jose, Calif., 1967-78 ; stage mgr. Foothill Theatre Co., Nevada City, Calif., 1980-82; mng. editor, illustrator Mothering Publs., Santa Fe, 1982 -; ptnr. High Mesa Press, Taos, N. Mex., 1985 -. Editor, illustrator: I Come as a Brother, 1985. Served with Peace Corps, 1971-73, Republic of Korea. Club: N. Mex. Press Women. Avocations: hiking, biking, jogging, outdoors activities. Home: PO box 2938 Taos NM 87571 Office: Mothering Publs 733 Galisteo St. Santa Fe NM 87501

MERCER, FRANK WOODWARD, chemist, researcher; b. Alameda, Calif., Apr. 29, 1953; s. E.O. and G. Joyce (Woodward) M.; m. Kristin Dahl, Aug. 17, 1975. BS in Chemistry, San Jose State U., 1975; PhD in Chemistry, U. Calif., Irvine, 1979. Sr. chemist 3M Co., St. Paul, 1979-81, Aerojet Gen., Sacramento, 1981-83; sr. staff scientist Raychem Corp., Menlo Park, Calif., 1983—. Contbr. articles to profl. jours.; patentee high temperature polymers. Mem. Am. Chem. Soc. Office: Raychem Corp 300 Constitution Dr Menlo Park CA 94025

MERCER, JOSEPH HENRY, lawyer, former state senator; b. Peoria, Ill., Feb. 1, 1937; s. Maurice D. and Dorothy J. M.; me. JoAnn Swicegood, July 21, 1967; children—Stephen, Jennifer, Matthew. B.A., U. N. Mex., 1961; J.D., Harvard U., 1964. Bar: N. Mex. 1966. With Hanna and Mercer, Mercer and Carpenter, Mercer and McCash, to 1980; ptnr. Mercer, Lock, and Keating, Albuquerque, 1980-86, Mercer Profl. Assn., Albuquerque, 1986—; mem. N.Mex. Ho. of Reps., 1975-76; mem. N. Mex. Senate, 1977-84, minority floor leader, 1980-84. Chmn. Albuquerque Com. on Fgn. Relations, 1975-76, mem., 1967-84, judicial council, 1981-84; mem. Gov.'s Organized Crime Prevention Commn., 1986—, oversight com., 1981-84. Served to 1st lt. arty U.S. Army, 1955-58. Mem. N. Mex. State Bar (Outstanding Service award 1974), Albuquerque Bar Assn. (dir. 1977-78). Republican. Episcopalian. Office: 5400 Phoenix NE Suite 100 Albuquerque NM 87110

MERCER, ROBERT LEE, association executive; b. Spring Coulee, Alta., Can., July 8, 1926; s. James Lee and Catherine Ela (Coombs) M.; m. Beverley Knowlton, Sept. 2, 1953; children—Robin Lee, Cherie, Catherine Jo, Jeffrey Robert. B.Sc., Brigham Young U., 1949, postgrad., 1952-53; M.S., U. Maine, 1956. Researcher, U.S. Steel Co., Prov, Utah, 1956-57; field mgr. R.T. French Co., Shelley, Idaho, 1957-72; dir. Nat. Potato Promotion Bd., Denver, 1972—; internat. authority and speaker on potatoes. Mem. Idaho Potato Commn., 1969-72. Contbr. articles to profl. jours. U. Maine fellow, 1954; Outstanding Jaycee, State Idaho, 1960; recipient Highest Merit cert. Gov. Idaho, 1972; named Potato Man of Yr., Vance Publ. Corp., 1982. Mem. Potato Assn. Am. (pres. 1974-75), Produce Mkg. Assn. (dir. 1979-82), United Fresh Fruit and Vegetable Assn., AAAS, Potato Processos Idaho (pres. 1967-68). Republican. Mormon. Home: 4706 Tule Lake Dr Littleton CO 80123 Office: The Potato Bd 1385 S Colorado Blvd Denver CO 80222

MERCHANT, ROLAND SAMUEL, SR., hospital administrator, educator; b. N.Y.C., Apr. 18, 1929; s. Samuel and Eleta (McLvmont) M.; m. Audrey Bartley, June 6, 1970; children—Orelia Eleta, Roland Samuel, Huey Bartley. B.A., N.Y.U., 1957, M.A., 1960; M.S., Columbia U., 1963, M.S.H.A., 1974. Asst. statistician N.Y.C. Dept. Health, 1957-60, statistician, 1960-63; statistician N.Y. TB and Health Assn., N.Y.C., 1963-65; biostatistician, adminstrv. coordinator Inst. Surg. Studies, Montefiore Hosp., Bronx, N.Y., 1965-72; resident in adminstrn. Roosevelt Hosp., N.Y.C., 1973-74; dir. health and hosp. mgmt. Dept. Health, City of N.Y., 1974-76; from asst. adminstr. to adminstr. West Adams Community Hosp., Los Angeles, 1976; spl. asst. to assoc. v.p. for med. affairs Stanford U. Hosp., Calif., 1977-82, dir. office mgmt. and strategic planning, 1982-85, dir. mgmt. planning, 1986—; clin. assoc. prof. dept. Family, Community and Preventive Medicine Stanford U., 1986—. Served with U.S. Army. 1951-53. USPHS fellow. Fellow Am. Coll. Healthcare Execs., Am. Pub. Health Assn.; mem. Am. Hosp. Assn., Nat. Assn. Health Services Execs., N.Y. Acad. Scis. Home: 953 Cheswick Dr San Jose CA 95121 Office: Stanford U Hosp Stanford CA 94305

MERCURIO, EDWARD PETER, natural science educator; b. Orange, Calif., Dec. 28, 1944; s. Peter Amadeo and Jeanne (Monteleone) M.; m. Jeanne Roussel Gable, Oct. 18, 1980 (div. Dec. 1984); 1 child, Katherine Roussel; m. Patricia Ann Kahler, Apr. 12, 1987. BA, UCLA, 1967, MA, 1970, CPhil, 1978. Research asst. UCLA, 1971, teaching asst., 1968-71; instructional assoc. Golden West Coll., Huntington Beach, Calif., 1972-73; cons. Monterey County Planning Dept., Salinas, Calif., 1980; prof. Hartnell Coll., Salinas, Calif., 1973—; photographer in field, Calif., 1961—; lectr. in field, Calif., 1970—; cons. in field, 1980—. Fellow Woodrow Wilson Nat. Fellowship Found., 1967. Mem. AAAS, Sierra Club. Democrat. Avocations: writing and performing original songs, hiking, backpacking, plant and animal breeding, long range weather forcasting. Home: 647 Wilson St Salinas CA 93901 Office: Hartnell Coll 156 Homestead Ave Salinas CA 93901

MERECICKY, FRANK STEPHEN, advertising executive; b. Cleve., Sept. 4, 1950; s. Anthony Joseph and Helen Marie (Vasileff) M.; m. Lilia Rose Olivero, Mar. 21, 1976; 1 child: Laura Jane. BSBA, Bowling Green U., 1972. Advt. mgr. Joy Mfg., Colorado Springs, Colo., 1978-83; pres. Merecicky Mktg., Colorado Springs, 1983-85, mktg. cons., 1983-85; v.p. account service, prin. Bulloch & Haggart Advt., Colorado Springs, 1985—. Mem. mktg. task force Econ. Devel. Council, Colorado Springs, 1985—; sustaining mem. Pikes Peak YMCA, Colorado Springs, 1984—; com. mem. mktg. curriculum com. Pikes Peak Community Coll., Colorado Springs, 1986—; mem. Downtown Colorado Springs; active Pvt. Industry Council, 1985. Recipient 1st Pl. award, Pikes Peak Advt. Fedn., 1985—. Mem. Pikes Peak Advt. Fedn., Am. Mktg. Assn., Colorado Springs C. of C. Republican. Avocations: skiing, running, tennis, river rafting, sailing. Office: Bulloch & Haggart Advt 226 E Monument Colorado Springs CO 80903

MEREDITH, GEOFFREY EVAN, advertising executive; b. Pitts., Mar. 18, 1943; s. Thomas Niel and Helen (Campe) M.; m. Valerie Joan Mohr, Aug. 30, 1969; children: Christopher, Leigh. BA, Princeton U., 1965; MBA, Stanford U., 1970. Account mgr. Ketchum Advt., San Francisco, 1970-83; sr. v.p. Hal Riney & Ptnrs., San Francisco, 1983—; mem. permanent staff Am. Assn. Advt. Agys. Inst. Advanced Advt., San Francisco, 1978—. Served to 1st lt. U.S. Army, 1966-68. Avocations: painting, chess. Office: 735 Battery St San Francisco CA 94111

MERIGAN, THOMAS CHARLES, JR., physician, med. researcher, educator; b. San Francisco, Jan. 18, 1934; s. Thomas C. and Helen M. (Greeley) M.; m. Joan Mary Freeborn, Oct. 3, 1959; 1 son, Thomas Charles III. B.A. with honors, U. Calif., Berkeley, 1955; M.D., U. Calif., San Francisco, 1958. Diplomate: Am. Bd. Internal Medicine. Intern in medicine 2d and 4th Harvard med. services Boston City Hosp., 1958-59, asst. resident medicine, 1959-60; clin. assoc. Nat. Heart Inst., NIH, Bethesda, Md., 1960-62; asso. Lab. Molecular Biology, Nat. Inst. Arthritis and Metabolic Diseases, NIH, 1962-63; practice medicine specializing in internal medicine and infectious diseases Stanford, Calif., 1963—; asst. prof. medicine Stanford U. Sch. Medicine, 1963-67, assoc. prof. medicine, 1967-72, head div. infectious diseases, 1966—, prof. medicine, 1972—, George E. and Lucy Becker prof. medicine, 1980—; dir. Diagnostic Microbiology Lab., Univ. Hosp., 1966-72, Diagnostic Virology Lab., 1969—; hosp. epidemiologist; mem. microbiology research tng. grants com. NIH, 1969-73, virology study sect., 1974-78; cons. antiviral substances program Nat. Inst. Allergy and Infectious Diseases, 1970—; mem. Virology Task Force, 1976-78, bd. sci. counselors, 1980-85; mem. U.S. Hepatitis panel U.S. and Japan Cooperative Med. Sci. Program, 1979—; co-chmn. interferon evaluation Group Am. Cancer Soc., 1978-81; mem. vaccines and related biol. products adv. com. Ctr. for Drugs and Biols., FDA, 1984—; mem. AIDS clin. drug devel. commn. NIAID; mem. internat. adv. com. on biol. sci. Sci. Council, Singapore, 1985—; mem. adv. com. J.A. Hartford Found., 1979-84; mem. Albert Lasker awards jury, 1981-84; mem. peer review panel U.S. Army Med. Research and Devel. Com., 1986—. Contbr. numerous articles on infectious diseases, virology and immunology to sci. jours.; editor: Antivirals with Clinical Potential, 1976, Antivirals and Virus Diseases of Man, 1979, 2d edit., 1984, Regulatory Functions of Interferon, 1980, 2d. edit., 1984, Interferons, 1982, Interferons as Cell Growth Inhibitors, 1986; assoc. editor: Virology, 1975-78, Cancer Research, 1987—; co-editor: monograph series Current Topics in Infectious Diseases, 1975—; editorial bd.: Archives Internal Medicine, 1971-81, Jour. Gen. Virology, 1972-77, Infection and Immunity, 1973-81, Intervirology, 1973-85, Proc. Soc. Expt. Biology and Medicine, 1978-87, Reviews of Infectious Diseases, 1979—, Jour. Interferon Research, 1980—, Antiviral Research, 1980-86, Jour. Antimicrobial Chemotherapy, 1981—, Molecular and Cellular Biochemistry, 1982—, AIDS Research, 1983—, Jour. Virology, 1984—. Recipient Borden award for Outstanding Research Am. Assn. Med. Colls., 1973; Guggenheim Meml. fellow, 1972. Mem. Assn. Am. Physicians, Western Assn. Physicians, Am. Soc. Microbiology, Am. Soc. Clin. Investigation (council 1977-80), Am. Assn. Immunologists, Am. Fedn. Clin. Research, Western Soc. Clin. Research, Soc. Exptl. Biology and Medicine (publ. com. 1985—), Infectious Diseases Soc. Am.; mem. Am. Soc. Virology; Mem. Inst. Medicine; mem. Pan Am. Group for Rapid Viral Diagnosis; Mem. AMA; mem. Internat. Soc. Interferon Research (council 1983—); Mem. Calif. Med. Assn., Santa Clara County Med. Soc., Calif. Acad. Medicine, Royal Soc. Medicine, AAAS, Alpha Omega Alpha. Home: 148 Goya Rd Portola Valley CA 94025 Office: Div Infectious Diseases Stanford Univ Sch Medicine Stanford CA 94305

MERIWETHER, MARGARET KATHERINE, historian; b. Lodi, Calif., July 22, 1921; d. George M. and Theresa L. (Dillonberg) Gannon; m. Richard Derling Meriwether, Nov. 18, 1945; children—Thomas Joseph, Theresa Lois. Cert. tchr. Calif. Elem. tchr., Glendale, Calif., 1943-45; docent Gamble House, Pasadena, Calif., 1969-74, organizer Greene & Greene Library, 1969-70, chmn., 1970-74; research historian Pasadena Cultural Heritage Com.; vol. reference dept. Pasadena Pub. Library, 1974—; cons. archtl. history Pasadena. Founding mem. Friends of Pasadena Pub. Library, bd. dirs., 1974-75. Recipient Pasadena Pub. Library and Cultural Heritage Com. spl. award for extraordinary service, 1982, Pasadena Heritage cert. appreciation, 1983. Mem. Gamble House Docent Council, Soc. Archtl. Historians (So. Calif. chpt.), Pasadena Heritage, Pasadena Assistance League, Alpha Chi Omega. Republican. Roman Catholic. Club: Annandale Golf (Pasadena). Author bibliographies and indexes on Pasadena history and architecture. Home: 1055 Stoneridge Dr Pasadena CA 91105

MERKEL, ALFRED WILLIAM, publishing executive; b. Lafayette, Ind., Mar. 29, 1929; s. Charles Daniel and Lillian Mae (Bennett) M.; m. Marlowe Marcia Graves, Sept. 2, 1955; children: Jennifer, Todd, Carolyn. BS, Purdue U., 1952. Indsl. engr. R.R. Donnelly, Crawfordsville, Ind., 1952-53; v.p. sch. div. Jostens, Mpls., 1958-72; v.p. Am. Can Co., Indpls., 1972-75; pres. Times Mirror Press, Los Angeles, 1975—. Area chmn. United Way, Los Angeles, 1983; mem. ALISO-PICO Businessmen's Council, Los Angeles, 1981—. Served to capt. USAF, 1953-58. Mem. Printing Industries So. Calif. (pres. 1980, Man of Yr., 1980), Printing Industries of Am. (vice chmn. 1983—). Lutheran. Club: Oakmont (Glendale, Calif.),. Avocations: golf, fishing, gardening. Office: Times Mirror Press 1115 S Boyle Ave Los Angeles CA 90023

MERLO, HARRY ANGELO, forest products executive; b. Stirling City, Calif., Mar. 5, 1925; s. Joseph Angelo and Clotilde (Camussa) M.; 1 son, Harry A. B.S., U. Calif.-Berkeley, 1949, postgrad., 1949. Vice pres. Rockport Redwood Co., Cloverdale, Calif., 1967; v.p. No. Calif. div. Ga.-Pacific Corp., Samoa, Calif., 1967-69; v.p. Western lumber div. Ga.-Pacific Corp., Portland, Oreg., 1969-71, exec. v.p. Western timber, plywood and lumber operations, 1971-73; pres., chmn. bd. La.-Pacific Corp., Portland, 1973—; adv. bd. Sch. Bus. Adminstrn. U. Calif., Berkeley; bd. dirs. World Forestry Ctr., IC Industries. Mem. Pres.'s Council, Columbia Pacific council Boy Scouts Am.; former mem. nat. adv. council Salvation Army; trustee Hugh O'Brian Youth Found., Oreg. Mus. Sci. and Industry, Goodwill Industries; past chmn. bd. Am. Acad. Achievement; Western fin. chmn. U.S. Olympic commn.; dir., adv. bd. Salvation Army, Portland; bd. dirs. Marshall U. Soc. Yeager Scholars. Served to lt. USMCR. Named Man of Year Ga.-Pacific Corp., 1969; recipient Golden Plate award Am. Acad. Achievement, 1974; Horatio Alger award, 1980, Gold award for forest products industry The Wall St. Transcript, 1982, 83, Disting. Service award La. Tech. U., 1984, Aubrey Watzek award Lewis and Clark Coll., 1984, Citizen of Merit award Assoc. Builders and Contractors, 1986. Mem. Calif. Redwood Assn. (past pres., dir.), Am. Paper Inst. (dir.), Knights of the Vine. Clubs: Founders (bd. dirs.), Waverly Country, Arlington, Multnomah Athletic, Ingomar, West Hills Racquet. Office: Louisiana-Pacific Corp 111 SW 5th Ave Portland OR 97204

MERRELL, ROBERT BRUCE, oil company executive; b. Brigham City, Utah, Dec. 20, 1945; s. Elliott Hepworth and Doris (Jensen) M.; BS in Indsl. Engring., U. Utah, 1969, MEA, 1973; m. Lynne McDermott, Apr. 4, 1968; children: Melissa Ann, Jason Matthew, David Bruce, Jeffrey Todd. Sales rep. Shell Oil Co., Portland, Oreg., Seattle, 1969-70, 72-74, head office rep., Houston, 1974-75; v.p., treas., dir. Lilyblad Petroleum Co., Tacoma, 1975-77, also bd. dirs.; dir. mktg. Pacific No. Oil Corp., Seattle, 1975-77, exec. v.p., gen. mgr., 1977, pres., chief exec. officer, 1977—, also dir. pres., chief exec. officer Pacific No. Marine Corp., 1980-83. Mem. exec. bd. dirs. Chief Seattle council Boy Scouts Am., 1984—; bd. dirs. Seattle Urban League, Sea Fair; chmn. Latter-day Sts. relationship com., 1984—. Served to capt. USAR, 1970-71. Decorated Bronze Star. Recipient Council Merit award Boy Scouts Am., 1985. Mem. Seattle C. of C. Mormon. Clubs: Washington Athletic, Columbia Tower (Seattle); Overlake Golf and Country (Bellevue, Wash.); Mercer Island Country (Wash.). Office: Pacific No Oil Corp 100 W Harrison N Tower #200 Seattle WA 98119

MERRICK, LEW, mechanical engineer; b. Washington, Oct. 29, 1953; s. Ivan Edward and Barbara Alice (Jones) M.; m. Sharon Ann Bisnett, Apr. 1, 1983; children: Shawna Lynn, Heather Alyse. Registered profl. engr. Engr. The Boeing Co., Seattle, 1978-81; sr. engr. Martin Marietta, New Orleans, 1981-82; contract engr. Tangent Engring., Lynnwood, Wash., 1982—. Mem. ASME, Am. Soc. Metals, Forth Interest Group, C User's Group, German Machinist's Guild.

MERRICK, ROBERT GREGORY, manufacturing company executive; b. Oakland, Calif., July 29, 1932; s. Roy Birchard Merrick and Elizabeth Aileen Mulgrew; m. Letha M. Merrill, July 11, 1959; children—Anne Elizabeth, Katherine Clare, John Patrick. A.A., U. Calif.-Berkeley, 1952, B.A., 1954. Asst. advt. mgr. Gen. Metals Corp., San Francisco, 1958-60; product advt. mgr. Fairchild Semicondr., Mountain View, Calif., 1960-66; account exec. Hal Lawrence Advt. Agy., Palo Alto, Calif., 1966-68; founder, chief exec. officer Merrick Industries, Inc., Sunnyvale, Calif., 1968—; founder, dir. Pioneer Savs. & Loan, San Jose, Calif., 1973-81. Inventor transparent watch calendar, 1968, slide rule calculator, 1965, bus. card punch, 1984. Del. White House Conf. on Small Bus., 1980. Served to lt. comdr. USNR, 1955-58, 61-62, Vietnam. Mem. Am. Mktg. Assn., Calif. Inventors Council (pres. 1979-80, bd. dirs. 1973-83), Delta Upsilon. Roman Catholic. Lodge: Elks. (Palo Alto). Office: Merrick Industries Inc Merrick Bldg 690 W Fremont Ave Sunnyvale CA 94087

MERRIFIELD, WILLIAM POWERS, lawyer, real estate broker; b. Carmel, Calif., Mar. 11, 1941; s. Charles Wellington and Clara Louise (Power) M.; m. Viola Mae Lucero, 1960 (div. 1970); children; Catherine Lynn, Gregory Todd. Student, Stanford U., 1958-59; BA in Econs., Calif. State U., Long Beach, 1966; JD, Pepperdine U., 1975. Bar: Calif. 1978. Research engr. Rockwell Internat., Los Angeles, 1960-66, contract mgr., 1966-80; components engr. CTS Keene, Paso Robles, Calif., 1981; real estate broker The Real Estate Group, San Luis Obispo, Calif., 1982-85; sole practice law, real estate broker San Luis Obispo, 1986—. Campaign supr. Marlaine Hubbard for City Council, San Luis Obispo, 1986. Served with U.S. Marine Corps Res., 1959-65. Mem. Calif. Assn. Realtors, San Luis Bd. Realtors (ethics com.), Nat. Assn. Realtors, Calif. Bar Assn., ABA, Kern County Bar Assn. Republican. Congregationalist. Clubs: Sea Hawks Swim, Slo Skiers (San Luis Obispo). Avocations: jogging, triathlons. Home: 8200 Kroll Way Apt #81 Bakersfield CA 93311

MERRILL, CHARLES MERTON, U.S. judge; b. Honolulu, Dec. 11, 1907; s. Arthur M. and Grace Graydon (Dickey) M.; m. Mary Luita Sherman, Aug. 28, 1931 (dec.); children: Julia Booth Stoddard, Charles McKinney. AB, U. Calif., 1928; LLB, Harvard, 1931. Bar: Calif. 1931, Nev. 1932. Sole practice Reno, 1932-50; judge Nev. Supreme Ct., 1951-59, chief justice, 1955-56, 59; judge U.S. Ct. of Appeals (9th cir.), San Francisco, 1959-74, sr. judge, 1974—. Mem. ABA, State Bar Nev. (gov. 1947-50), Am. Law Inst. (council 1960—). Office: US Ct of Appeals San Francisco CA 94101

MERRILL, FRANK HARRISON, data processing executive, consultant; b. Pitts., June 20, 1953; s. Edgar Frank and Harriet Margaret (Gallagher) M.; m. Rita Alice Mae Murray, May 27, 1977; 1 child, Laura Dawn. BSMetE, Colo. Sch. Mines., 1971-76; postgrad. in data processing, U. Denver. Cert. systems profl. Metall. engr. Inspiration Copper Co., Miami, Ariz., 1979-80, Cominco Am., Inc., Bixby, Mo., 1980-81; programmer, analyst M.L. Foss, Inc., Denver, 1981-83, Titsch & Assocs., Denver, 1983; data processing mgr. PBI/BAXA, Inc., Denver, 1983-86; owner (systems cons.) Dynamic Solutions, Denver, 1986—; cons. in field, Denver, 1985—; instr. continuing edn. User's Group, Denver, 1985—. Adult leader Boy Scouts Am., Denver and Globe, Ariz., 1973—; mem. Marriage Encounter Interfaith Bd., Denver. Served to 2d lt. U.S. Army, 1977-79. Mem. Assn. Systems Mgmt. (profl.), Colo. Pick Users' Group (edn. chmn. 1984—). Republican. Free Methodist (God and Service award 1984). Club: Rocky Mountain Wanderers. Avocations: model railroading, model rocketry, hiking, camping, mountaineering.

MERRILL, HARVIE MARTIN, manufacturing executive; b. Detroit, Apr. 26, 1921; s. Harvie and Helen (Nelson) M.; m. Mardelle Merrill; children—Susan, Linda. B.S. in Chem. Engring, Purdue U., 1942. Devel. engr. Sinclair Refining Co., 1946-47; research and gen. mgr. 3M Co., St. Paul, 1947-65; v.p. fabricated products Plastics div. Stauffer Chem. Co., N.Y.C., 1965-69; with Hexcel Corp., San Francisco, 1969-86; pres., chief exec. officer Hexcel Corp., 1969-86, chmn. bd., 1976—; dir. Nimbus Inc., Rancho Cordova, Calif., Upright Inc., Berkeley, Calif., Vendo Co., Fresno, Calif. Trustee Grace Cathedral, Children's Hosp. Found., French-Am. Internat. Sch., all San Francisco. Served with USAF, 1942-46. Clubs: Pacific-Union, Bohemian (San Francisco); Links (N.Y.C.). Home: 1170 Sacramento St San Francisco CA 94108 Office: Hexcel Corporation 650 California St Suite 1400 San Francisco CA 94108

MERRILL, ROBERT EDWARD, spl. machinery mfg. co. exec.; b. Columbus, Ohio, Oct. 21, 1933; s. Robert Ray and Myrna Ione (Rinehart) M.; student Ohio State U., 1954-56 M.B.A., Pepperdine U.; m. Donna Rae Bernstein, Mar. 19, 1967; children—Robert Edward, Aaron Jay, Jonathan Cyrus, Raquel Naomi. Pres., PSM Corp., San Jose, Calif., 1974—. Served with AUS, 1950-51; Korea. Mem. Soc. Mfg. Engrs., Am. Soc. Metals, Soc. of Plastics Industry. Patentee in pneumatic applications for indsl. press machinery. Home: 858 Fieldwood Ct San Jose CA 95120 Office: Box 5156 San Jose CA 95150

MERRILL, SHARON MARES, speech pathologist; b. Oceanside, Calif., Jan. 7, 1948; d. James Hart and Margaret Mary (O'Connell) Pope; m. Fidencio Manual Mares, June 10, 1972 (div. Jan. 1974); m. Robert Odgen Merrill, Aug. 22, 1981; children: Kathryn Janes, James Whitney. BA, Fresno State U., 1970; MA, Calif. State U., Los Angeles, 1976. Speech/lang. specialist Kings Canyon Unified Sch. Dist., Reedley, Calif., 1971-72; speech/lang. specialist Los Angeles County Supt. Schs., Downey, Calif., 1972-78, bilingual assessment program specialist for people Spanish test project, 1979-81; speech pathologist Daniel Freeman Hosp., Inglewood, Calif., 1978-79; coordinator spl. edn. ABC Unified Sch. Dist., Cerritos, Calif., 1981-83; pvt. practice speech pathology Long Beach, Calif., 1983—; cons. North Orange County Spl. Edn. Consortium, Anaheim, Calif., 1983-85, Capistrano (Calif.) Unified Sch. Dist., 1983-85, Chula Vista (Calif.) Unified Sch. Dist., 1985, Ednl. Service Ctr. Region 17, Lubbock, Tex., 1980. Mem. Am. Speech-Lang. and Hearing Assn. (cert.), Calif. Speech and Hearing Assn., Council Exceptional Children. Avocations: painting, sewing, gardening, reading. Home and Office: 6461 Mantova St Long Beach CA 90815

MERRILL, STEPHEN ALEXANDER, university official, lecturer; b. Phoenix, Dec. 9, 1948; s. Bruce and Virginia Mae (Walters) M.; m. Colette Duckett, May 24, 1974; children: Jason, Jonathan, Wade, Jessie, Hillary. BS in Fin., Ariz. State U., 1974. Mgr. Am. Cable TV, Phoenix, 1972-76, v.p., 1976-78; telecommunications analyst U. Utah, Salt Lake City, 1978-80, telecommunications adminstr., 1980—; pres. Merrill & Assocs., Salt Lake City, 1979—. Contbr. articles to profl. jours. Sheriff dep. Maricopa County Divers Possee, Phoenix, 1970-76. Served with U.S. NG, 1970-76. Mem. Assn. Coll. Univ. Telecommunications Adminstrs., Utah Telecommunications Mgmt Assn. (founder, pres. 1983-84, bd. dirs. 1982—, chmn. bd. 1984-85). Republican. Mormon. Home: 1909 E Falcon Way Sandy UT 84092 Office: U Utah Telecommunications 1085 Annex Salt Lake City UT 84112

MERRILL, THOMAS SELFRIDGE, clinical psychologist, consultant; b. Honolulu, Feb. 17, 1940; s. William Dickey and Evelyn Merriman (Selfridge) M.; m. Kathleen Morrissey, Jan. 16, 1965; children—Lisa Lani, Kirsten Elizabeth, Kimberly Alexander. B.A., U. Colo., 1963; M.Ed., U. Hawaii, 1977; Ph.D., U. Tex., 1981. Lic. psychologist, Hawaii; diplomate Am. Bd. Med. Psychotherapists, Am. Bd. Psychotherapy. Div. adminstrv. mgr. Kaiser Aluminum and Chem. Corp., Oakland, Calif., 1965-68; mktg./advt. mgr. Trans Internat. Airlines, Transamerica Corp., Alameda, Calif., 1968-70; sr. v.p. Fawcett McDermott Cavanagh Advt., Honolulu, 1970-77; dir. Peck, Sims, Mueller Advt.; pvt. practice cons., Austin and Honolulu, 1977—; clin. psychologist in pvt. practice, Honolulu, 1981—. Bd. dirs., treas. Ptnrs. in Health, Honolulu; bd. dirs. Hawaii Epilepsy Soc.; trustee Hawaiian Mission Children's Soc. Mem. Am. Psychol. Assn., Hawaii Psychol. Assn. (pres. 1984-85), Tex. Psychol. Assn., Am. Group Psychotherapy Assn., Am. Soc. Clin. Hypnosis, Soc. Exptl. and Clin. Hypnosis, Running Psychologists, Am. Soc. Composers and Publishers, Am. Acad. Neuropsychologists, Am. Coll. Forensic Psychologists, Pacific Acad. Neuropsychologists (founder). Club: Outrigger Canoe (Honolulu). Composer music and lyrics including Bottles & Cans, 1973. Home: 2657 Terrace Dr Honolulu HI 96822 Office: 1441 Kapiolani Blvd Suite 909A Honolulu HI 96814

MERRIN, EDWARD LOUIS, psychiatry educator, researcher; b. Los Angeles, Apr. 11, 1946; s. Sam and Rose Ann (Katz) M.; m. Linda Gayle Davis, Dec. 11, 1974 (div. June 1979); m. Judith Ann Quinn, Mar. 7, 1981; children: Elizabeth, Kristina. AB, UCLA, 1967; MD, U. Calif., San Francisco, 1971. Diplomate Am. Bd. Psychiatry and Neurology. Psychiat. resident Dartmouth Coll. Sch. Medicine, Hanover, N.H., 1972-74; chief resident psychiatry Highland Hosp., Oakland, Calif., 1975; staff psychiatrist Palo Alto VA Hosp., Menlo Park, Calif., 1975-76; chief psychiat. emergency VA Med. Ctr., San Francisco, 1976-84, chief psychiat. inpatient unit, 1984—; asst. prof. psychiatry U. Calif. Sch. Medicine, San Francisco, 1981—. Contbr. articles to profl. jours., chpt. to books. Regents scholar UCLA, 1965-67, U. Calif. San Francisco, 1967-71; recipient VA Merit rev., San Francisco VA Ctr., 1984—. Mem. AAAS, N.Y. Acad. Scis., Am. Psychiat. Assn., Phi Beta Kappa. Avocations: photography, computer programming, blues and jazz guitar music. Office: VA Med Ctr 4150 Clement St San Francisco CA 94121

MERRITT, MARYTHERESE, exploration oil scout; b. Detroit, July 21, 1933; s. James F. William and Berenice Columbia (Franchere) Best; m. Z.S. Merritt, July 12, 1956 (div. Dec. 1978); children: Aline Elizabeth, Dennis Samuel. BS in Geology, U. Wyo., 1956. Geologist GeoScout Petroleum Service, Salt Lake City, 1964-66, Wolf Ridge Minerals, Glenwood Springs, Colo., 1967-68; cons. landman Inexco, Casper, Wyo., 1968-70; geologist, asst. mgr., chief scout Hotline Energy Reports, Casper, 1978-80; Rx. mountain regional scout Marathon Oil Co., Casper, 1980—. Active League Women Voters, Casper, 1985, Friends Natrona County Library, Casper, 1986, Nicolayson Mus. Friends, Casper, 1986. Mem. Internat. Oil Scouts Assn. (bd. dirs., v.p. 1986—), Rocky Mountain Oil Scouts Assn., Powder River Oil Scouts Assn. (treas. 1984—), Am. Assn. Petroleum Geologists, Wyo. Assn. Petroleum Geologists, Rocky Mountain Assn. Geologists, Rocky Mountain Sect. Soc. Econ. Paleontologists and Mineralogists, Computer Oriented Geol. Soc., Phi Beta Kappa, Phi Kappa Phi. Republican. Roman Catholic. Avocations: archeology, camping. Office: Marathon Oil Co 159 N Wolcott Casper WY 82601

MERRITT, MELVIN L(EROY), physicist; b. Juneau, Alaska, Nov. 12, 1921; s. Melvin L. and Nellie Isobell (Brown) M.; m. Thelma Dinwiddie, Dec. 29, 1949; children: Melvin III, Audrey, Linda, Jeannine. BS in Physics, Calif. Inst. Tech., 1943, PhD in Physics, 1950. Engr. Gen. Electric Co., Syracuse, N.Y., 1943-46; mem. tech. staff Sandia Nat. Lab., Albuquerque, 1950—, div. supr., 1951-84, mem. mgmt. staff, 1984—. Co-author, prin. editor: The Environment of Amchitka Island, Alaska, 1977. Fellow Am. Phys. Soc.; mem. AAAS, Am. Assn. Physics Tchrs., Arctic Inst. N. Am., Health Physics Soc. (sec.-treas. local chpt. 1984-86). Democrat. Mem. United Ch. Christ. Office: Sandia Nat Labs Orgn 400 Albuquerque NM 87185

MERROW, TONI SUE, secretary; b. Springfield, Mo., Mar. 24, 1940; d. Haldene Kemp and Ruth Darlene (Jordan) Holt; m. Maesil LeGrand Merrow, May 13, 1961; children—Dene O., Scott J., Regina L. Student pub. schs., Denver. Exec. sec. Colo. Brick Co., Denver, 1959-60; sec. Stanley Aviation, Denver, 1960-61; sec. to service specialist Ford Motor, Tractor div., Denver, 1961-77; sec. to v.p. advt. communications KWAL Paints, Inc., Denver, 1979-84; sec., asst. to v.p. Intermountain Network, Denver, 1985—; pub. relations cons. The Osburn Band, Denver, 1977—. Vice pres. Hallet Sch. PTA, Denver, 1971-73; active various charitable orgns.; mem., pub. relations cons. Blue Knights Drum and Bugle Corps Parents Orgn., Littleton, 1983-84; historian, pub. relations cons. Highland High Sch. Booster Assn., Thornton, 1983-84. Cert. of Commendation, City of Thornton, 1975. Mem. Nat. Assn. Female Execs., Scholastic Gold Key. Avocations: antiques; geneology; reading; camping. Home: 2502 E 90th Pl Thornton CO 80229

MERRYMAN, HOLT WALLACE, finance company executive; b. Los Angeles, Nov. 26, 1927; s. Emmett and Annette (Wallace) M.; m. Fantine Elizabeth Holley, Apr. 24, 1949; children—Lloyd, Elizabeth (Mrs. Bruce W. Lorber), Craig. B.S., U. Calif. at Los Angeles, 1952; postgrad., U. Hawaii, 1962. C.P.A., Calif. With Seaboard Finance Co., Los Angeles, 1956-67; pres. Seaboard Finance Co., 1969-71, Avco Fin. Services, Inc. (merger Seaboard Fin. Co. and Avco Delta Corp.), Newport Beach, Calif., from 1971; chmn. bd. Avco Fin. Services, Inc. (merger Seaboard Fin. Co. and Avco Delta Corp.), 1975—, also bd. dirs.; dir. Collins Foods Internat., Inc. Mem. Chancellor's club; bd. dirs. Orange County council Boy Scouts Am., past pres., mem. exec. com., dir. Orange County council; trustee U. Calif. at Irvine Calif. Coll. Medicine. Served with USNR, 1945-48. Club: Canyon Country. Office: Arco Fin Services Inc 3349 Michelson Dr Irvine CA 92715

MERTA, PAUL JAMES, cartoonist, photographer, engr., restauranteur, real estate developer; b. Bakersfield, Calif., July 16, 1939; s. Stanley Franklin and Mary Ann (Herman) M.; A.A., Bakersfield Jr. Coll., 1962; B.S. in Engring., San Jose State Coll., 1962. Cartoonist nat. mags., 1959—; civilian electronics engr. Air Force/Missiles, San Bernardino, Calif., 1962-65; electronics countermeasures engr., acquisition program mgr. Air Logistics Command, Sacramento, 1965—; TV film animator, producer, owner Merge Films, 1965—; photographer, owner The Photo Poster Factory, Sacramento, 1971—; owner restaurant La Rosa Blanca, Sacramento, 1980—; ptnr. Kolinski and Merta Hawaiian Estates, 1981—; polit. cartoonist Calif. Jour., 1958-59, Sacramento Union Newspaper, 1979—, Sacramento Legal Jour., 1979. Home: 4831 Myrtle Ave #8 Sacramento CA 95841 Office: 1005 12th St Sacramento CA 95814

MERTOL, ATILA, mechanical engineer; b. Adana, Turkey, Dec. 17, 1953; came to U.S., 1977; s. Ahmet and Devlet (Bilsel) M.; m. Nilgun Orta, Sept. 29, 1984. BSc, Middle Eastern Tech. U., Ankara, Turkey, 1976; MSc, U. Calif., Berkeley, 1978, PhD, 1980. Staff scientist Lawrence Berkeley (Calif.) Lab., 1979-85, Sci. Applications Internat., Corp., Los Altos, Calif., 1985—. Contbr. articles to profl. jours., chpts. to books. Grantee Sci. and Tech. Research Council of Turkey, 1971-76, Florence M. Lankershim Found., 1977, Earl C. Anthony Fund, 1977-78; NATO fellow, 1978-80. Mem. ASME, Internat. Solar Energy Soc., Chamber of Mech. Engrs. in Turkey, Turkish Soc. for Thermal Scis., ASHRAE. Home: 333 Escuela Ave #241 Mountain View CA 94040 Office: Sci Applications Internat Corp 5150 El Camino Real Suite C-31 Los Altos CA 94022

MERWIN, EDWIN PRESTON, health planning and development consultant; b. Revere, Mass., Oct. 13, 1927; s. George Preston and Edith Charlotte (Miller) M.; m. Marylynn Joy Bicknell, Nov. 3, 1979; 1 son by previous marriage, Ralph Edwin; stepchildren—Charles John Burns, Patrick Edward Burns, Stephen Allen Burns. B.S., U. So.Calif., 1955, postgrad. Law Sch., 1955-57; postgrad., San Fernando Valley State Coll., 1965-66; M.P.H. (USPHS fellow), U. Calif. at Berkeley, 1970; Ph.D., Brantridge Forest (Eng.), 1971. Tng. officer Camarillo (Calif.) State Hosp., 1961-66; asst. coordinator Mental Retardation Programs, State of Cal., Sacramento, 1966-67; project dir. Calif. Council Retarded Children, Sacramento, 1967-69; asst. dir. Golden Empire Comprehensive Health Council, Sacramento, 1970-76, health care cons., 1976-77; cons. Calif. Dept. Health, 1977-78; cons. Calif. Office Statewide Health Planning and Devel., 1978-79; chief Health Professions Career Opportunity Program State of Calif., Sacramento, 1979-81; chief Health Personnel Info. and Analysis Sect., Office of Statewide Health Planning and Devel., 1981-82, asst. div. chief div. Health Professions Devel., 1982-84, asst. dep. dir., 1984-86; project dir. Alzheimers Disease Insts., Calif., 1986—; tchr. Ventura (Calif.) Coll., 1962-66, Merritt Coll., Oakland, Calif., 1969; sr. adj. prof. Golden Gate U., 1976—; lectr. continuing edn. program U. Calif. at Berkeley; instr. Los Rios Community Coll. Dist., 1982—; cons. NIMH, HEW, Calif. Assn. Health Facilities. Mem. health adv. council San Juan Sch. Dist., 1972-73; treas. Calif. Camping and Recreation Council, 1972-73. Bd. dirs. Sacramento Rehab. Facility, 1970—, v.p., 1973-76, bd dirs. Sacramento Vocational Services, 1986—. Recipient Pres.'s award Golden Gate U., 1982. Mem. Am. Assn. Mental Deficiency, Calif. Pub. Health Assn., Sacramento Mental Health Assn., Sacramento Assn. Retarded (life mem., dir., service award 1984), Nat. Assn. for Retarded Children, DAV (life), Am. Legion, Marines Meml. Assn. (life), AAAS,

SCAPA Praetors. Founder, editor: T. Patrick Heck Meml. Case Studies, 1982; co-author textbook: Written Case Analysis, 1982; contbr. articles to profl. lit. Home: 8008 Archer Ave Fair Oaks CA 95628 Office: 1600 9th St Sacramento CA 95814

MERZ, PAUL LOUIS, organic polymer chemist; b. New Haven, June 1, 1918; s. Paul and Marie Louise (Schumacher) M.; m. Esther Jane Simson, Aug. 21, 1950; children: Charles, Brian, Bruce, Cheryl. BS in Chemistry, Union Coll., 1940; PhD in Organic Chemistry, Yale U., 1951. Research and devel. chemist Beech-Nut Packing Co., Canajoharie, N.Y., 1940-43, head polymer lab., 1945-47, cons., 1947-51; group leader, project dir. U.S. Rubber Co., Naugatuck, Conn., 1951-62; sr. plastics chemist Lawrence Livermore (Calif.) Lab., 1962-64; staff scientist, sr. engrng. specialist Gen. Dynamics Convair, San Diego, 1964-82; cons. Merz Research, Ophir, Oreg., 1982—. Contbr. articles to profl. jours.; patentee in field. Scout master Boy Scouts Am., La Jolla, Calif., 1966-69; chmn. Commn. Christian Edn. Meth. Ch., La Jolla, 1971-72. Served as cpl. U.S. Army, 1943-45, ETO. Mem. AAAS (emeritus), Am. Chem. Soc. (emeritus), Sigma Xi (emeritus). Republican. Presbyterian. Avocations: camping, swimming, diving. Home: 94454 Williams St Gold Beach CA 97444 Office: Merz Research PO Box 33 Orphir OR 97464

MESCUS, PATRICIA IONA, electronics technician; b. Roadtown, Tortola, B.V.I., Sept. 14, 1956; came to U.S., 1958, naturalized, 1968; d. John Alexander and Kathleen Dorothy (Phillip) M. Student Los Angeles City Coll., 1976, Ventura Coll., 1980—. Electrician, Grumman Aerospace, Point Mugu, Calif., 1979, electronics technician range instrumentation systems dept., 1979-83; electronics technician Naval Ship Weapon Systems Engrng. Sta., Port Hueneme, Calif., 1983—. Served with USN, 1975-79. Mem. Nat. Assn. Female Execs., Blacks in Govt., Ventura County Navy Women's Assn. Home: PO Box 1228 Port Hueneme CA 93041 Office: Combat System Test Dept Code 4-J30 Port Hueneme CA 93043

MESEC, DONALD FRANCIS, psychiatrist, neurologist; b. Waukegan, Ill., Aug. 29, 1936; s. Joseph Mesec and Johanna (Setnicar) M.; m. Francesca Auditore, June 20, 1964; 1 child, Steven Francis. B.S. cum laude, U. Notre Dame, 1958; M.D., N.Y. Med. Coll., 1963. Diplomate Am. Bd. Psychiatry and Neurology. Resident in psychiatry and neurology N.Y. Med. Coll.-Manhattan State Hosp., N.Y.C., 1964-67; chief of service Manhattan Psychiat. Ctr., N.Y.C., 1970-76, dir. psychiat. research, 1974-75, dir. Meyer Manhattan Alcohol Rehab. Ctr., 1975; med. dir. Meyer Day Ctr., N.Y.C., 1976-77; staff psychiatrist Asheville VA Hosp., N.C., 1977-78; practice medicine specializing in psychiatry, Phoenix, 1978—; instr. clin. psychiatry Columbia U., N.Y.C., 1972-77; dir. psychiat. edn. St. Joseph's Hosp., Phoenix, 1982—, co-dir. pain program, 1982—, vice chmn. dept. psychiatry, 1984—. Served with USPHS, 1963-64. Mem. New York County Med. Soc., Ariz. Med. Assn., Maricopa County Med. Soc., Ariz. Psychiat. Soc., AMA, Am. Psychiat. Assn. Office: 350 W Thomas Rd Phoenix AZ 85001

MESGHALI, FARID, electrical engineer; b. Tehran, Iran, Aug. 23, 1952; came to U.S., 1974; s. Ahmad and Ashraf (Shahroudi) M.; m. Homa Hesari, Dec. 24, 1984. BS, Sharif U. of Tech., Tehran, 1974; MS, U. Dayton, 1976; engrng. degree, UCLA, 1980, PhD, 1984. From teaching asst. to fellow 1980-84, postgrad. researcher, 1982-84; sr. MIC engr. Systron Donner Corp. Microwave div., Van Nuys, Calif., 1984—; vis. prof. UCLA, 1984—. Mem. IEEE. Office: UCLA PO Box 24357 Los Angeles CA 90024

MESNICK, CHARLES S., social work administrator; b. Cleve., Mar. 7, 1914; s. Abraham and Rose (Schaffer) M.; m. Dora Gewirtz, May 23, 1937; children: Michael, Richard. AB, Case Western Reserve U., 1934; MSW, U. So. Calif., 1944. Registered social worker. Supr. Works Progress Adminstrn., Cleve., 1935-36, State Relief Adminstrn., Los Angeles, 1937-40; dir. emigrè resettlement com. Fedn. Jewish Welfare Orgn., 1940-41; dir. USO, Jewish Welfare Bd., Salt Lake City, 1941-42; unit dir. Jewish Ctrs. Assn., Los Angeles, 1943-64, asst. exec. dir., 1964-67, exec. dir., 1967-76; founder, pres. Jewish Communal Retirees Assn., Los Angeles, 1977—. Contbr. 20 articles on communal work trends to profl. jours. Mem. Gov.'s Com. on Service to the Aged, Mayor's Community Adv. Com., Recreation and Youth Services Planning Council, 1960's. Participated in various other community events. Served with USN, 1944-46. Recipient Community Service award for 50 years' service, Los Angeles Bd. Supervisors and City Council, 1985. Mem. Nat. Assn. Social Workers, Assn. Jewish Community Orgn. Persons, Assn. Jewish Ctrs. Workers (pres. Western states div. 1965), Jewish Fedn. Council, So. Calif. Jewish Hist. Soc., Hebrew Union Coll., Sch. Jewish Communal Services (vol.). Democrat. Avocation: travel. Home: 1828 Holmby Ave Los Angeles CA 90025

MESQUITA, ROSALYN E., artist, educator; b. Belen, N.Mex., Aug. 21, 1935; d. Trinidad Jose and Margaret Oliva (Aragon) Anaya; m. Theodore Richard Mesquita, Jan. 14, 1956; children: John, Richard, Larry, Thresa. BA, Calif. State U., Northridge, 1974; MFA, Calif. State U., Irvine, 1976. Cert. community coll. credential, Calif. Prof. Los Angeles City Coll., Van Nuys, Calif., 1965-81; curator State of N.Mex., Santa Fe, 1968-72; lectr. Los Angeles Hist. Soc., 1978—; prof. Pasadena (Calif.) City Coll., 1981—; lectr. Non Govtl. Orgn. UN Planning Com., Nairobi, Kenya, and N.Y., 1985—; curator, participant Am. Women in Art, UN World Conf., Nairobi, 1985; curator Mus. Natural History, Los Angeles, 1978. Lectr. Los Angeles BiCentennial and 1985 Olympic Com., 1976-84. Recipient Col.-Aide-De Camp award Gov. David F. Cargo, 1972; Ford Found. fellow, 1975. Mem. Coll. Art Assn., Nat. Womens Caucus for Art (affirmative action officer 1980-83, honorarium 1983), Hispanic Faculty Assn. (treas. 1980—), Assn. Latin Am. Artists (pres. 1982—), Los Angeles La Raza Faculty Assn. (sec. 1979-85). Democrat. Roman Catholic. Avocation: traveling. Home: 13426 Vanowen St Van Nuys CA 91405 Office: Pasadena City Coll 1570 Colorado Blvd Pasadena CA 91106

MESSENGER, GEORGE CLEMENT, engineering consultant; b. Bellows Falls, Vt., July 20, 1930; s. Clement George and Ethel Mildred (Farrar) M.; m. Priscilla Betty Norris, June 19, 1954; children—Michael Todd, Steven Barry, Bonnie Lynn. BS in Physics, Worcester Poly. U., 1951; MSEE, U. Pa., 1957; PhD in Engrng., Calif. Coast U., 1986. Research scientist Philco Corp., Phila., 1951-59; engrng. mgr. Hughes Semicondr., Newport Beach, Calif., 1959-61; div. mgr. Transitron Corp., Wakefield, Mass., 1961-63; staff scientist Northrop Corp., Hawthorne, Calif., 1963-68; cons. engr., Las Vegas, Nev., 1968—; lectr. UCLA, 1969-75; v.p., dir. Am. Inst. Fin., Grafton, Mass., 1970-78; gen. ptnr. Dargon Fund, Anaheim, Calif., 1983—. Coauthor: The Effects of Radiation on Electronic Systems, 1986; contbg. author: Fundamentals of Nuclear Hardening, 1972; contbr. numerous articles to tech. jours.; patentee microwave diode, hardened semicondrs. Recipient Naval Research Lab. Alan Berman award, 1982; Best Paper award Heart Conf., 1983, Spl. Merit award Heart Conf., 1983; fellow IEEE, 1976, annual merit award 1986. Mem. Research Soc. Am., Am. Phys. Soc. Congregationalist. Club: Balboa Bay. Home and Office: 3111 Bel Air Apt 7F Las Vegas NV 89109

MESSER, DONALD EDWARD, theological school president; b. Kimball, S.D., Mar. 5, 1941; s. George Marcus and Grace E. (Foltz) M.; m. Bonnie Jeanne Nagel, Aug. 30, 1964; children—Christine Marie, Kent Donald. B.A. cum laude Dakota Wesleyan U., 1963; M. Divinity magna cum laude Boston U., 1966, Ph.D., 1969. L.H.D. (hon.), Dakota Wesleyan U., 1977. Asst. to commr. Mass. Commn. Against Discrimination, Boston, 1968-69; asst. prof. Augustana Coll., Sioux Falls, S.D., 1969-71; assoc. pastor 1st United Methodist Ch., Sioux Falls, 1969-71; pres. Dakota Wesleyan U., Mitchell, S.D., 1971-81, The Iliff Sch. Theology, Denver, 1981—. Author: Christian Ethics and Political Action, 1984. Contbr. articles to Face To Face, The Christian Century, The Christian Ministry. Active Edn. Commn. of U.S., 1973-79; co-chmn. Citizens Commn. Corrections, 1975-76; vice chmn. S.D. Commn. on Humanities, 1979-81. Dempster fellow, 1967-68; Rockefeller fellow, 1968-69. Mem. Soc. Christian Ethics, Am. Acad. Religion, Assn. United Methodist Theol. Schs. (v.p. 1986—). Democrat. Office: Iliff Sch Theology 2201 S University Blvd Denver CO 80210

MESSICK, RANDALL LYN, artistic director performance company, actor; b. Lawton, Okla., Nov. 4, 1955; s. Otis William and Alpha Jean (Strother) M.; m. Darlene Michelle Morton, Nov. 26, 1983. BA in Theatre, Calif. State U., Fresno, 1981; MFA in Dramatic Art, U. Calif., Davis, 1983. Actor Monterey (Calif.) Shakespeare Fest., 1980-81; instr. acting Monterey Peninsula Coll., 1980; actor Edinburgh (Scotland) Fringe Festival, 1980; instr., dir. Bakersfield (Calif.) Coll., 1983—; artistic dir. Kern Shakespeare Festival, Bakersfield, 1984—. Served with USCG, 1974-77. Avocations: motorcycling, composing music. Home: 1419 Baker St Bakersfield CA 93305 Office: Bakersfield Coll 1801 Panorama Dr Bakersfield CA 93305

MESSMER, LOUIS WILLIAM, retired biology educator, consultant; b. Forsyth, Mont., June 5, 1920; s. Fred George and Helen Catherine (Holmes) M.; m. Anna Henrietta Kovar, July 31, 1944; children: William, James, John, Maryann, Robert, Karen. AS, Grays Harbor Coll., 1939; BS, U. Wash., 1942, MS, 1951. Tchr. biology Kelso (Wash.) High Sch., 1951-53; chmn. life scis. dept. Grays Harbor Coll., Aberdeen, Wash., 1953-86; cons. U.S. Army C.E., Wash. State Dept. Ecology, others, Western Washington, 1968—. Served to lt. USNR, 1942-45, PTO. Mem. Pacific Estuarine Research Soc., Nat. Assn. Marine Educators, Pacific sect. Am. Bot. Soc., NEA, Wash. Ednl. Assn., The Nature Conservancy (state bd. 1975-81), Wash. Native Plant Soc. (state bd. 1976—). Democrat. Roman Catholic. Avocations: hiking, fishing, photography, gardening. Home: Rt 1 Box 17 Aberdeen WA 98520 Office: Grays Harbor Coll Aberdeen WA 98520

MESSNER, KATHRYN HERTZOG, civic worker; b. Glendale, Calif., May 27, 1915; d. Walter Sylvester and Sadie (Dinger) Hertzog; B.A., UCLA, 1936, M.A., 1951; m. Ernest Lincoln, Jan. 1, 1942; children—Ernest Lincoln, Martha Allison Messner Cloran. Tchr. social studies Los Angeles schs., 1937-46; mem. Los Angeles County Grand Jury, 1961. Mem. exec. bd. Los Angeles Family Service, 1959-62; dist. atty.'s adv. com., 1965-71, dist. atty.'s adv. council, 1971-82; mem. San Marino Community Council; chmn. San Marino chpt. Am. Cancer Soc.; bd. dirs. Pasadena Rep. Women's Club, 1960-62, San Marino dist. council Girl Scouts U.S.A., 1959-68; pres. San Marino High Sch. PTA, 1964-65; bd. mem. Pasadena Vol. Placement Bur., 1962-68; mem. adv. bd. Univ. YWCA, 1956—; co-chmn. Dist. Atty.'s Adv. Bd. Young Citizens Council, 1968-72; mem. San Marino Red Cross Council, 1966—, chmn., 1969-71, vice chmn., 1971-74; mem. San Marino bd. Am. Field Service; mem. atty. gen.'s vol. adv. com., 1971-80; bd. dirs. Los Angeles Women's Philharm. Com., 1974—, Beverly Hills-West Los Angeles YWCA, 1974-85, Los Angeles YWCA, 1975-84, Los Angeles Lawyers Wives Club, 1974—, Pacificulture Art Mus., 1976-80, Reachout Com., Music Center, Vol. Action Center, West Los Angeles, Calif., 1980-85, Stevens House, 1980—, Pasadena Philharm. Com., 1980—, Friends Outside, 1983—, Internat. Christian Scholarship Found., 1984—; hon. bd. dirs. Pasadena chpt. ARC, 1978-82. Recipient spl. commendation Am. Cancer Soc., 1961; Community Service award UCLA, 1981. Mem. Pasadena Philharmonic, Las Floristas, Huntington Meml. Clinic Aux., Nat. Charity League, Pasadena Dispensary Aux., Gold Shield (co-founder), Pi Lambda Theta, Pi Gamma Mu, Mortar Bd., Prytanean Soc. Home: 1786 Kelton Ave Los Angeles CA 90024

MESTER, JORGE, conductor; b. Mexico City, Apr. 10, 1935; came to U.S., 1946, naturalized, 1968; s. Victor and Margarita (Knöpfler) M. B.S., Juilliard Sch. Music, 1957, M.S., 1958; studied conducting with, Jean Morel, Leonard Bernstein., Albert Wolff. Faculty Juilliard Sch. Music, 1956-68, chmn. conducting studies, 1980—. Also condr., Juilliard Theatre Orch., 1961-62, Beaux Arts Trio, 1961-65; mus. dir., Louisville Orch., Greenwich Village Symphony, 1961-62, mus. dir., condr., Louisville Orch., 1967-79, artistic adviser, Kansas City Philharmonic, 1971-72, then music dir., Kansas City Philharmonic, 1973-77, music dir., Aspen Music Festival, 1970—, Festival Casals, 1978-85; music dir. Pasadena Symphony, 1984—; prin. guest condr., St. Paul Chamber Orch., 1978-79, guest condr., Orquesta Sinfonica Nacional de Mexico, Philharmonica Triestina, Spoleto Festival Orch., Japan Philharmonic, Yomiuri Nippon Symphony, Boston Symphony, Pitts. Symphony, New Orleans Philharmonic, Indpls. Symphony, N.Y.C. Opera, Phila. Orch., London Royal Philharmonic, Denver Symphony, Bach Aria Group, Cin. Orch., Rochester Philharmonic, Utah Symphony, Oreg. Symphony, Cin. Symphony, others; condr. dance season, Spoleto Festival, Grant Park, Chgo., Tanglewood, Mass., Harkness Dance Festival, 1964, Cosi Fan Tutte, 1964, L'Elisir D'Amore, rec. with, Columbia, Vanguard, Mercury, Desto, CRI, Cambridge records, also, Louisville 1st Edit. Recs. Named Ky. col., 1967; recipient Naumburg award, 1968, Ditson Condrs. award, 1985. Office: care Aspen Music Festival 250 W 54th St 10th Floor East New York NY 10019 also: PO Box AA Aspen CO 81612

METCALF, EDGAR ODEN, oil company manager; b. Lake Charles, La., Dec. 8, 1937; s. Edgar Vernham and Inez (Oden) M.; m. Earlyne Davis, June 3, 1961; children: Eric Davis, Erin Virginia. BSEE, Lamar U., 1961. Registered profl. engr., Tex.; cert. safety mgr., safety exec. Sr. engr. Boeing Aerospace Co., Seattle and Houston, 1961-73; engrng. supr. Boeing Aerospace Co., Houston, 1973-78; safety cons. Boeing Engrng. and Constrn. Co., London, 1978-80; engrng. supr. Boeing Aerospace Co., Houston, 1980-81; mgr. safety adminstrn. Occidental Oil and Gas Corp., Bakersfield, Calif., 1981—. Named one of Outstanding Young Men of Am., 1962. Mem. World Safety Orgn. (cert.), Am. Soc. Safety Engrs., Nat. Safety Council (exec. com. Petroleum sect.), Tex. Safety Assn., System Safety Soc. Methodist. Home: 6245 S Knoxville Tulsa OK 74136 Office: Occidental Oil and Gas Corp 5000 Stockdale Hwy Bakersfield CA 93309

METCALF, JACK, state senator; b. Marysville, Wash., Nov. 30, 1927; s. John Read and Eunice (Grannis) M.; student U. Wash., 1944-48; B.A., B.Ed., Pacific Luth. U., 1951; m. Norma Jean Grant, Oct. 3, 1948; children—Marta Jean, Gayle Marie, Lea Lynn, Beverlee Ann. Tchr., Elma (Wash.) pub. schs., 1951-52, Everett (Wash.) pub. schs., 1952-81; mem. Wash. Ho. of Reps., 1960-64; mem. Wash. Senate, 1966-74, 80—. Chmn. Honest Money for Am. Mem. Council State Govts., Wash. Edn. Assn. (dir. 1959-61), Wash. Assn. Profl. Educators (state v.p. 1979-81, state pres. 1977-79). Republican. Club: South Whidbey Kiwanis. Office: 106A Institutions Bldg Olympic WA 98504

METCALFE, JAMES E., health science facility administrator; b. Monterey, Calif., June 24, 1933; married; children: Nanette, Elliott, Michael. AA, Monterey Peninsula Coll.; BS in Bus. and Indsl. Mgmt., San Jose State Coll., 1959; MHA, U. Calif., Berkeley, 1961. Intern Santa Monica (Calif.) Hosp., 1959-60; resident Santa Barbara (Calif.) Cottage Hosp., 1961-62, asst. adminstr., 1961-70; asst. adminstr. St. Mary's Hosp. and Med. Ctr., San Francisco, 1971-74, assoc. adminstr., v.p., 1974-81, pres., chief exec. officer, 1981—; pres., chief exec. officer Mercy Services Corp., Mercy Profl. Bldg., Inc., Mercy Terr. Corp., MSC Ambulatory Services, Inc., MSC Psychiat. Services, Inc., St. Mary's Found.; pres. Affiliated Hosps. San Francisco, 1982-84, bd. trustees, 1981-84, chmn. 1985, PRSO adv. com., chmn. 1980. Mem. Am. Coll. Hosp. Adminstrs., Am. Hosp. Assn., Calif. Hosp. Assn. (adv. com. statewide PSRO council, com. on health facilities planning and licensure 1983-85, com. on regulations 1985, PRO adv. task force 1985), Hosp. Council No. Calif. (bd. dirs. hosp. services corp., futures com., mgmt. com., planning com., publ affairs com.), San Francisco PSRO (bd. dirs. 1983-84), West Bay Hosp. Conf. (bd. dirs. 1983-84, pres.-elect 1985, chmn. San Francisco Hosps., 1985). Home: 2075 Laguna Vista Dr Novato CA 94947 Office: St Marys Hosp & Med Ctr 450 Stanyan St San Francisco CA 94117

METHENY, STEVEN MARK, electrical engineer; b. Albuqueque, Oct. 22, 1957; s. William James and Ann (Rogers) M.; m. Phoebe Downs, Aug. 3, 1979; 1 child, Sara. BEE, N.Mex. State U., 1981; MEE, U. Colo., Boulder, 1987. Registered profl. engr., Colo. Engrng. technician Salt River Project, Phoenix, 1979-80; night service clk. El Paso Electric Co., Las Cruces, N.Mex., 1980-81; mgr. engrng. Delta-Montrose Electric Assn., Montrose, Colo., 1981—. Contbr. articles to profl. jours. Mem. IEEE, NSPE, Montrose County C. of C.. Republican. Baptist. Avocations: sports, fishing, photography. Office: Delta-Montrose Electric Assn PO Box 59 Delta CO 81416

METHNER, SIDNEY KONRAD, financial analyst; b. Ithaca, N.Y., Apr. 12, 1956; s. Harry Wolfgang and Ruth (Heuman) M. BA in Econs., U. Colo., 1978; MBA in Fin. and Acctg. with Honors, Regis Coll., 1984. Test analyst Auto-trol Tech., Denver, 1978-79, lead test analyst, 1979-81, software support specialist, 1981-84, adminstrv. asst., 1984-86, asset mgr., 1986-87; cons. Denver, 1987—. Pres. Timber Condo Assn., Arvada, Colo., 1983—; mem. Jefferson County (Colo.) Statutory Grand Jury, 1985. Mem. Nat. Assn. Investment Clubs (regional dir. 1984—). Democrat. Jewish. Avocations: personal investing, skiing, sports cars. Home and Office: 8488 C Everett Way Arvada CO 80005

METHVEN, MARGARET PETERSON, speech pathologist, school principal; b. Norfolk, Va., Dec. 24, 1918; d. Ward E. and Marguerite (Helm) Peterson; B.A., Washburn U., Topeka, 1940; M.A., U. Denver, 1960, Ed.D., 1976; m. William Charles Methven, Jan. 2, 1947: children—William Charles, Robert Ward. High sch. tchr., Burlingame, Kans., 1940-42; speech/lang. specialist Boettcher Sch. Physically Handicapped and Fairmont Sch., Denver Public Schs., 1959—; past prin. Force Elem. Sch., now prin. Barnum Elem. Sch. Mem. Am., Colo. (past treas.) speech and hearing assns., Nat. Orgn. Legal Problems Edn., Denver Elem. Prins. Assn., Kappa Delta Pi, Delta Kappa Gamma (pres. 1978-80, State Parliamentarian 1979—), Alpha Phi., Phi Delta Kappa. Presbyterian. Office: Barnum Elem Sch 85 Hooker St Denver CO 80219

METTLER, MARY A., newspaper agency executive; b. Akron, Ohio, Oct. 9, 1937; d. William M. and E. (Young) M.; B.A. with distinction in Econs., Stanford U., 1959; postgrad. program in bus. adminstrn. Harvard U.-Radcliffe Coll., 1960; M.B.A., Am. U., 1962. Dir. research Ferris & Co., Washington, 1960-63; systems engr. IBM, San Francisco, 1964-68; pres. Western Ops., Inc., San Francisco, 1968-74; dir. fin. United Vintners, San Francisco, 1975-79; sr. v.p., chief fin. officer Lawrence Systems Inc., San Francisco, 1979-84; v.p. fin. San Francisco Newspaper Agy., 1984—. Recipient Elijah Watt Sells award, 1974. Club: Commonwealth of Calif. Home: 4462 24th St San Francisco CA 94114 Office: San Francisco Newspaper Agy 925 Mission St San Francisco CA 94103

METTLER, RUBEN FREDERICK, electronics and engineering company executive; b. Shafter, Calif., Feb. 23, 1924; s. Henry Frederick and Lydia M.; m. Donna Jean Smith, May 1, 1955; children: Matthew Frederick, Daniel Frederick. Student, Stanford, 1941-43; BSEE, Calif. Inst. Tech., 1944, MS, 1947, PhD in Elec. and Aero. Engrng, 1949. Registered profl. engr., Calif. Assoc. div. dir. systems research and devel. Hughes Aircraft Co., 1949-54; spl. cons. to asst. sec. def. 1954-55; asst. gen. mgr. guided missile research div. Ramo-Wooldridge Corp., 1955-58; pres. Space Tech. Labs., Inc., Los Angeles, 1962-65, TRW Systems Group, 1965-68; exec. v.p., dir. TRW Inc. (formerly Thompson Ramo Wooldridge, Inc.), 1965, asst. pres., 1968-69, pres., 1969-77, chmn. bd., chief exec. officer, 1977—; dir. Bank Am. Corp., Merck & Co.; past vice-chmn. Ind. adv. council Dept. Def. Author reports airborne electronic systems. Nat. campaign chmn. United Negro Coll. Fund, 1980, 81; chmn. Pres.' Sci. Policy Task Force, 1969; mem. Pres.' Blue Ribbon Def. Panel, 1969-70, Emergency Com. for Am. Trade; chmn. Nat. Alliance Business, 1978-79; chmn. bd. trustees Calif. Inst. Tech.; trustee Com. Economic Devel., Cleve. Clinic Found.; bd. dirs. Nat. Action Council for Minorities in Engrng. Served with USNR, 1942-46. Named 1 of 10 Outstanding Young Men of Am., U.S. Jr. C. of C., 1955, So. Calif.'s Engr. of Year, 1964; recipient Meritorious Civilian Service award Dept. Def., 1969, Nat. Human Relations award NCCJ, 1979, Excellence in Mgmt. award Industry Week Mag., 1979. Fellow IEEE, AIAA; mem. Sci. Research Soc. Am., Bus. Roundtable (chmn. 1982-84), Conf. Bd. (trustee 1982—), Bus. Council (vice chmn. 1981-82, chmn. 1986-87), Nat. Acad. Engrng., The Japan Soc. (bd. dirs.), Sigma Xi, Eta Kappa Nu (Nation's Outstanding Young Elec. Engr. 1954), Tau Beta Pi, Theta Xi. Clubs: Cosmos (Washington); Union (Cleve.), 50 (Cleve.). Patentee interceptor fire control systems. Home: 1900 Richmond Rd Cleveland OH 44124 Office: TRW Inc 1 Space Park Redondo Beach CA 90278

METZ, MARY SEAWELL, college president; b. Rockhill, S.C., May 7, 1937; d. Columbus Jackson and Mary (Dunlap) Seawell; m. F. Eugene Metz, Dec. 21, 1957; 1 dau., Mary Eugena. B.A. summa cum laude in French and English, Furman U., 1958; postgrad., Institut Phonetique, Paris, 1962-63, Sorbonne, Paris, 1962-63; Ph.D. magna cum laude in French, La. State U., 1966; H.H.D. (hon.), Furman U., 1984; LL.D. (hon.), Chapman Coll., 1985. Instr. French La. State U., 1965-66, asst. prof., 1966-67, 1968-72, assoc. prof., 1972-76, dir. elem. and intermediate French programs, 1966-74, spl. asst. to chancellor, 1974-75, asst. to chancellor, 1975-76; prof. French Hood Coll., Frederick, Md., 1976-81, provost, dean acad. affairs, 1976-81; pres. Mills Coll., Oakland, Calif., 1981—; vis. asst. prof. U. Calif.-Berkeley, 1967-68; mem. commn. on leadership devel. Am. Council on Edn., 1981—; mem. adv. council SRI, 1985—; assoc. Gannett Ctr. for Media Studies, 1985—; bd. dirs. PG&E, Lucky Stores, Pacific Telesis, PacTel & PacBell, Rosenberg Found. Author: Reflets du monde francais, 1971, 78, Cahier d'exercices: Reflets du monde francais, 1972, 78, (with Helstrom) Le Francais a decouvrir, 1972, 78, Le Francais a vivre, 1972, 78, Cahier d'exercices: Le Francais a vivre, 1972, 78; standardized tests; mem. editorial bd.: Liberal Edn., 1982—. bd. dirs. Rosenberg Fedn., 1985-87. NDEA fellow, 1960-62,, 1963-64; Fulbright fellow, 1962-63; Am. Council Edn. fellow, 1974-75. Mem. Western Coll. Assn. (v.p. 1982-84, pres. 1984-86), Assn. Ind. Calif. Colls. and Univs. (exec. com. 1982), Nat. Assn. Ind. Colls. and Univs. (govt. relations adv. council 1982-85), So. Conf. Lang. Teaching (chmn. 1976-77), World Affairs Council No. Calif. (dir. 1984—), Bus.-Higher Edn. Forum, Women's Forum West, Women's Coll. Coalition (exec. com. 1984—), Phi Kappa Phi, Phi Beta Kappa. Office: Mills College Oakland CA 94613

METZ, ROBERT ALLEN, mining geologist; b. Cleve., Dec. 22, 1932; s. Allen Andrew and Beatrice Marie (Schlitter) M.; m. Victoria Eugenia Hopper, Dec. 17, 1961 (div. Feb. 1972); children: James A.; Thomas C., Lori A., David A.; m. Sarah Jocelyn Wallace, Dec. 23, 1973. Degree in Geol. Engrng., Colo. Sch. Mines, 1955. Registered profl. geologist. Asst. geologist Kennecott Copper Corp., Santa Rita, N.Mex., 1955-59; geologist Ray Mines div. Hayden, Ariz., 1959-68; chief mine geologist Duval Sierrita Corp., Tucson, 1968-69, sr. geologist, 1969-70, dist. geologist, 1970-78, mgr. evaluation sect., 1978-85; sr. geologist evaluation Battle Mountain Gold Co., Tucson, 1985—. Author: Arizona Geological Society Guidebook III, 1968, SPOT Simulations Applications Handbook, 1985, Geology of the Porphyry Copper Deposits of Southwestern North America, 1966; editor Applied Mining Geology: Problems of Sampling and Grade Control, 1985. Mem. Soc. Mining Engrs. of AIME (chmn. Tucson sect. 1984, chmn. Western region sect. reps. 1986), Soc. Econ. Geologists, Ariz. Geol. Soc. (treas. 1972), N.Mex. Geol. Soc., Mining Club of S.W. Republican. Lodge: Elks. Avocations: tennis, bicycling, hunting, fishing, mineral collecting. Office: Battle Mountain Gold Co 4715 E Fort Lowell Rd Tucson AZ 85712

METZENBACHER, GARY WILLIAM, library administrator; b. Erie, Pa., May 30, 1953; s. William Wallace and Joyce Ann (Kestel) M. B.A. in Bibl. Lit., Taylor U., 1975; N.H.A. diploma, Ind. U.-Indpls., 1976; M.A. in Theology, Western Evang. Sem., 1979; M.L.S., Ind. U., Bloomington, 1983. Ordained to ministry Evangelical Ch., 1976. Nursing home adminstr. Community Care Ctr., Decatur, Ind., 1976; pastor Arcadia Bible Ch., Ind., 1976, Washington Valley, Cambridge Springs, Pa., 1977; assoc. pastor Collins View Ch., Portland, Oreg., 1978-82; singles pastor Valley View Ch., Portland, 1982—; library dir. Western Evang. Sem., Portland, 1982—; library cons. Azuza Pacific U., Calif., 1983, Warner Pacific Coll., Portland, 1984. Author: Church Growth Through TEE, 1979; contbr. articles to profl. jours. Mem. ALA, Am. Theol. Library Assn., Assn. Christian Librarians, Wesleyan Theol. Soc., Assn. for Profl Edn. for Ministry, Assn. Coll. and Research Libraries, NW Assn. Christian Librarians. Republican. Home: 4200 SE Jennings Ave Portland OR 97267

METZGER, ALBERT EMANUEL, space scientist, nuclear chemist; b. N.Y.C., Sept. 10, 1928; s. Frederic and Hortense (Abrams) M.; m. Avra Judith Friedman, Nov. 27, 1958 (div. 1981). BA, Cornell U., 1949; MS, Columbia U., 1951, PhD, 1958. Chemist Sylvania Electric Co., Bayside, N.Y., 1951-54; scientist Jet Propulsion Lab., Pasadena, Calif., 1959-61, sr. scientist, 1961-63, supr. research group, 1964-83, mem. tech. staff, 1983—. Contbr. articles to profl. jours. Recipient Exceptional Sci. medal NASA, 1975, Apollo Experiment Team award NASA. Fellow AAAS; mem. Am. Phys. Soc., Am. Geophys. Soc., Am. Astron. Soc., Sci., Math. and Environ. Info. Analysis Ctr. (pres. 1975-78), Phi Lambda Upsilon. Avocations: music, theater, reading, hiking. Office: Jet Propulsion Lab 4800 Oak Grove Dr Pasadena CA 91109

METZGER, FRANK JOSEPH, physician, internist; b. Springfield, Ill., July 8, 1949; s. Frank Fred Metzger and Mary Catherine (Shofner) Dahlkamp; m. Meredith Kay Spaeth, July 13, 1974; children: Frank Carl, Amy Marie,

Stephanie Ann. BS in Pharmacy, U. Ariz., 1972; DO, U. Health Scis., Kansas City, Mo., 1978. Diplomate Am. Coll. Osteo. Internists. Intern Mt. Clemens (Mich.) Gen. Hosp., 1978-79; resident in internal medicine Okla. Osteopathic Hosp., Tulsa, 1981-84; clin. pharmacist Mesa (Ariz.) Luth. Hosp., 1972-74; gen. practice medicine Grand Junction, Colo., 1979-81; practice medicine specializing in internal medicine Mesa, 1984—; Dir. pain ctr. Mesa Gen. Hosp., 1984—, Home Health Agy. Summit Corp., Mesa, 1985—; clin. prof. Coll. Osteo. Medicine of Pacific, Pomona, Calif., 1985—. Mem. Am. Coll. Osteo. Internists, Am. Osteo. Assn., Ariz. Osteo. Med. Assn., Psi Sigma Alpha, Rho Chi. Republican. Home: 1656 S Los Alamos Circle Mesa AZ 85204 Office: 455 N Mesa Dr Suite 16 Mesa AZ 85201

METZGER, H(OWELL) PETER, publicist, essayist; b. N.Y.C., Feb. 22, 1931; s. Julius Radley and Gertrude (Fuller) M.; m. Frances Windham, June 30, 1956; children: John, James, Lisa, Suzanne. B.A., Brandeis U., 1953; Ph.D., Columbia U., 1965. Mgr. advanced programs Ball Bros. Research Corp., Boulder, 1968-70; research assoc. Dept. Chemistry, U. Colo., Boulder, 1966-68; sr. research scientist N.Y. State Psychiat. Inst., N.Y.C., 1965-66; syndicated columnist N.Y. Times Syndicate, 1972-74, Science Critic, Newspaper Enterprise Assn., 1974-76; sci. editor Rocky Mt. News, Denver, 1973-77; mgr. public affairs planning Public Service Co. Colo., Denver, 1977—; cons. Environ. Instrumentation, 1970-72; dir. Colspan Environ. Systems, Inc., Boulder, Colo., 1969-72. Author: The Atomic Establishment, 1972; Contbr. articles in field to profl. jours., nat. mags. Pres. Colo. Com. for Environ. Info., Boulder, 1968-72; mem. Colo. Gov.'s State Health Planning Council, 1969-72, Colo. Gov.'s Adv. Com. Underground Nuclear Explosions, 1971-74; mem. spl. project on energy policy mgmt. Heritage Found., 1980; mem. 1981 Presdl. Rank Rev. Bd. U.S. Office Personnel Mgmt., 1981; Bd. dirs. Wildlife-2000, 1970-72, Colo. Def. Council, 1972—. USPHS fellow, 1959-65; prin. investigator, 1968; archivee Hoover Instn. Stanford U., 1982. Mem. ACLU (state bd. 1968-71), Sigma Xi, Phi Lambda Upsilon. Clubs: Denver Athletic, Denver Press; Am. Alpine (N.Y.C.). Address: 2595 Stanford Ave Boulder CO 80303

METZGER, LAWRENCE, psychologist, educator; b. Oceanside, N.Y., Jan. 9, 1933; s. Jerome and Fay (Gerber) M.; m. Martha Engle Bilsing, Dec. 24, 1970 (div.). B.A., Trinity Coll., 1955; M.S.W., U. Mich., 1970; Ph.D., Saybrook Inst., San Francisco, 1976; lic. clin. social worker Calif. Social work intern Ypsilanti (Mich.) State Hosp., 1968-69, VA Hosp., Battle Creek, Mich., 1969-70; psychiat. social worker San Francisco Dept. Pub. Health, 1970-71; tng. supr. staff devel. Alameda County Human Resources Agy., Oakland, Calif., 1971-73; psychiat. social worker Alameda County Health Care Services, Oakland, 1973-75; pvt. practice psychotherapy, Oakland, 1975—; mem. faculty U. Calif. Extension, Berkeley, Santa Cruz, Santa Barbara, Irvine, 1975-86; mem. field faculty Lone Mountain Coll., San Francisco, 1976-79; dir. clin. services Vista de la Vida, Tiburon, Calif., 1979-81; staff psychologist, publicity dir. Inst. Rational Living, San Francisco, 1981; cons. in field. Author: From Denial to Recovery: Counseling Problem Drinkers, Alcoholics and Their Families; 1987. Mem. legis. task force unmet needs of children Nat. Assn. Social Workers, 1974; mem. San Francisco Mental Health Assn., 1975. Served with USN, 1955-57. Mem. Am. Psychol. Assn., Psychotherapy Inst., Assn. Family Therapists, Nat. Council Alcoholism (edn. com.). Contbr. articles to profl. jours. Home and Office: 5463 Manila Ave Oakland CA 94618

METZGER, ROBERT OWEN, banking consultant, educator, writer; b. N.Y.C., Oct. 22, 1939; s. Homer P. and Catherine Dale (Owen) M.; m. Dorothee Benkenstein, Apr. 25, 1968; 1 child, Joelle Laurence Owen. BS in Econs., U. Md. Overseas Coll., 1963; PMD, Harvard U., 1969; PhD in Bus. Adminstrn., U. Beverly Hills, 1981. Staff exec. IT&T, 1970-72; chief exec. officer Faber Merlin Ltd., Hong Kong, 1973; sr. mgr. McSweeney & Assocs., Newport Beach, Calif., 1974-75; founder, chmn., mag. prin. Metzger & Assocs., Santa Ana, Calif., 1976—; adj. prof. mgmt. and orgn. Grad. Sch. Bus. Adminstrn. U. So. Calif., Los Angeles, 1984—; assoc. dir. Ctr. for Ops. Mgmt., Edn. and Tng., 1982—. Author: Organizational Issues to Strategic Planning in the Commercial Banking Industry, 1981, Consulting to Management, 1983; editorial rev. bd. and contbr. editor: Fin. Mgrs. Statement Quar., Orgn. and Group Studies, Bankers Monthly; editorial rev. bd.: Jour. Retail Banking, Jour. Mgmt. Cons.; contbr. numerous articles on bank mgmt. to profl. jours. Served with USAF, 1958-62. Mem. Inst. Mgmt. Cons., Berkshire Sch. Alumni Assn. (founder, pres. So. Calif. chpt.), Astron. Soc. Pacific. Club: Harvard Bus. Sch. So. Calif.

METZGER, ROBERT PHILIP, biochemistry, science educator; b. San Jose, Calif., Jan. 28, 1940; s. Ralph Anderson and Marie Odile (Wenz) M.; m. Silvia Adriana Arnone, Dec. 28, 1968; children: Marco E., André G. BS in Chemistry, UCLA, 1961; MS in Chemistry, San Diego State U., 1963; PhD in Chemistry, U. Calif. (San Diego) and San Diego State U., 1967. Lectr. chemistry San Diego State U., 1963-68, asst. prof. phys. sci., 1968-71, assoc. prof., 1971-75, prof. natural sci., 1975—; vis. scientist U. Genoa, Italy, 1979—, Johns Hopkins U., 1980, U. Calif., San Diego, 1986-87. Contbr. articles to profl. jours. Fellow AAAS; mem. Am. Chem. Soc. (chmn. San Diego sect. 1980, 85), Am. Diabetes Assn., Royal Soc. Chemistry, N.Y. Acad. Sci., Sigma Xi (pres. San Diego chpt. 1975-77). Roman Catholic. Avocations: model trains, photography, pen and ink drawings. Office: San Diego State U Dept Natural Sci San Diego CA 92182-0324

METZGER, RODNEY CRAIG, sociology educator; b. Richarton, N.D., Apr. 6, 1943; s. Edwin Arthur and Meta Dora (Fuchs) M.; m. Anne Christensen, June 29, 1973; 1 child, Brady S. BA, U. Mont., 1965, MA, 1968. Vocat. rehab. counselor Dept. Vocat. Rehab., Missoula, Mont., 1965-66; research analyst and program dir. War on Poverty, Missoula, 1966-68; asst. prof. sociology Lane Community Coll., Eugene, Oreg., 1969—; pvt. practice family crisis cons. Eugene, 1980—; curriculum developer WHO, N.Y.C., 1972; book reviewer for numerous pubs.,1978—; instr. course devel. Med. Soc. Nurses, 1972. bd. dirs. Lane County Youth Care Ctrs., Eugene, 1974-77; bd. dirs. Am. Youth Soccer Orgn., 1983—, commr. region 53, 1986—. Mem. Pacific Sociol. Assn., Clin. Sociol. Assn. Republican. Mem. Ch. of Christ. Avocations: remote control aircraft, water skiing, wood sculpture, horses. Home: 209 Carthage Ave Eugene OR 97404 Office: Lane Community Coll Social Sci Dept 4000 E 30th Ave Eugene OR 97405

METZGER, VERNON ARTHUR, educator; b. Baldwin Park, Calif., Aug 13, 1918; s. Vernon and Nellie C. (Ross) M.; B.S., U. Calif., Berkeley, 1947, M.B.A., 1948; m. Beth Arlene Metzger, Feb. 19, 1955; children—Susan, Linda, 1 step-son, David. Estimating engr. C. F. Braun & Co., 1949; prof. mgmt. Calif. State U. at Long Beach, 1949—, founder Sch. Bus.; mgmt. cons., 1949—. Mem. Fire Commn. Fountain Valley, Calif., 1959-60; pres. Orange County Democratic League, 1967-68; mem. State Dept. mgmt. task force to promote modern mgmt. in Yugoslavia, 1977; mem. State of Calif. Fair Polit. Practices Commn., Orange County Transit Com. Served with USNR, 1942-45. Recipient Outstanding Citizens award Orange County (Calif.) Bd. Suprs. Fellow Soc. for Advancement of Mgmt. (life; dir.); mem. Acad. Mgmt., Orange County Indsl. Relations Research Assn. (v.p.), Beta Gamma Sigma, Alpha Kappa Psi, Tau Kappa Upsilon. Home: 1938 Balearic Dr Costa Mesa CA 92626 Office: 1250 Bellflower Blvd Long Beach CA 90804

METZLER, JERRY DON, nursing adminstrator; b. Mishawaka, Ind., Mar. 6, 1935; s. Gerald Donald and Cleota Christabell (Dowell) M.; m. Dorothy J. Masters, Aug. 18, 1962. BS, Ariz. State U., 1962, MA in Edn., 1967; BS, San Diego State U., 1973; MS, U. Ariz., Tucson, 1980. Sci. tchr. Washington Sch., Sanger, Calif., 1963-68; tchr. biology San Jacinto (Calif.) High Sch., 1968-70; staff nurse Maricopa County Hosp., Phoenix, 1973-76; staff nurse St. Luke's Hosp., Phoenix, 1976-77; nursing instr., dept. head Gila Pueblo Coll., Globe, Ariz., 1977-78; nurse educator, asst. dir. nursing USPHS Indian Hosp., Tuba City, Ariz., 1980-84; asst. nursing service mgr. Phoenix Indian Med. Ctr., 1984-85; pub. health educator Phoenix Indian Med. Ctr., 1985—. Served with USN, 1956-60, USPHS, 1980—; Mem. Res. Officers Assn., Am. Nurses Assn., Am. Assn. Critical Care Nurses. Republican. Methodist. Lodge: Masons. Home: 3413 N 44th Pl Phoenix AZ 85018 Office: Phoenix Indian Med Ctr Phoenix AZ 85016

METZLER, MICHAEL, chamber of commerce executive. Pres. Greater Santa Ana C. of C., Santa Ana, Calif. Office: Greater Santa Ana C of C PO Box 205 Santa Ana CA 92702 *

METZLER, YVONNE LEETE, travel agt.; b. Bishop, Calif., Jan. 25, 1930; d. Ben Ford and Gladys Edna (Johnson) Leete; student U. Calif., Berkeley, 1949; m. Richard Harvey Metzler, June 2, 1950; children—David Grant, Regan M., Erin E. Vocat. instr. Ukiah (Calif.) Jr. Acad., 1962-63; bookkeeper Sid Beamer Volkswagen, Ukiah, 1963-64; acct. Ukiah Convalescent Hosp., 1964, Walter Woodard P.A., Ukiah, 1964-66; asso. dir. Fashion Two Twenty, Ukiah, 1966-67, dir., Santa Rosa, Calif., 1967-71; acct. P.K. Marsh, M.D., Ukiah, 1971-72, Walter Woodard P.A. and Clarence White C.P.A., Ukiah, 1972-74; partner, travel agt. Redwood Travel Agy., Ukiah, 1973-76; owner, mgr. A-1 Travel Planners, Ukiah, 1976—; owner A-1 Travel Planners of Willits, Willits, Calif., 1979—. Commr., Ukiah City Planning Commn., 1979-84 , chmn., 1981-83; mem. Republican County Central Com., 1978-80. Mem. Ukiah C. of C. (1st v.p. 1980, pres. 1981-82), Mendocino County C. of C. (dir. 1981). Clubs: Soroptimist (pres. 1977-78), Bus. and Profl. Women (treas. 1977-78, named Woman of the 80's). Office: 505 E Perkins St Ukiah CA 95482

METZNER, RICHARD JOEL, psychiatrist, computer systems designer, media producer, educator; b. Los Angeles, Feb. 15, 1942; s. Robert Gerson and Esther Rebecca (Groper) M.; B.A., Stanford U., 1963; M.D., Johns Hopkins U., 1967; m. Linda Susan Nordlinger, Sept. 22, 1968; children—Jeffrey Anthony, David Jonathan. Intern, Roosevelt Hosp., N.Y.C., 1967-68; resident in psychiatry Stanford U. Med. Center, 1968-71; staff psychiatrist div. manpower and tng. NIMH-St. Elizabeths Hosp., Washington, 1971-73; chief audiovisual edn. system VA Med. Center Brentwood, Los Angeles, 1973-79, chmn. VA Dist. 26 Ednl. Task Force, 1976-78; asst. prof. psychiatry UCLA Neuropsychiat. Inst., 1973-80, asso. clin. prof., 1980—, lectr. Sch. Social Welfare, 1975-84; pvt. practice medicine specializing in psychiatry, Bethesda, Md., 1972-73, Los Angeles, 1973—; dir. Western Inst. Psychiatry, Los Angeles, 1977—; pres. Psychiat. Resource Network, Inc., 1984—; Served with USPHS, 1968-71. Recipient 6 awards for film and videotape prodns., 1976-80; diplomate Am. Bd. Psychiatry and Neurology (cons. 1974-78, producer audiovisual exam. programs 1975-77). Mem. Am. Psychiat. Assn., So. Calif. Psychiat. Soc., Mental Health Careerists Assn. (chmn. 1972-73), AAAS, Am. Film Inst., Phi Beta Kappa. Democrat. Jewish. Contbr. numerous articles to profl. publs., 1963—; producer, writer numerous ednl. films and videotapes, 1970—; developer videoscan treatment technique in psychiatry. Home and Office: 2711 Forrester Dr Los Angeles CA 90064

MEUNIER, ROBERT RAYMOND, research electrical engineer, optical engineer; b. Hollywood, Calif., Mar. 27, 1957; s. Raymond Robert and Anna Marie (Rapp) M. Student, Calif. State Poly. U., Pomona, Pasadena City Coll. Assoc. engr. Jet Propulsion Lab., Pasadena, Calif., 1984-85; research engr. Rockwell Internat., Seal Beach, Calif., 1985—. Mem. Laser Inst. Am., Soc. Photo-optical Instrumentation Engrs., Los Angeles Collegiate Council (alumnus), Inter Organizational Council (founder, chmn. 1981-82), Sigma Pi. Republican. Roman Catholic. Office: Rockwell Internat 2600 Westminster Blvd PO Box 3644 Seal Beach CA 90740

MEURER, GORDON C., civil engineering company executive; b. Rocky Mountain, N.C., Feb. 26, 1946; s. Malcolm Reede and Queen Elizabeth (Harper) M.; m. Shirley Jean Famularo, June 24, 1967; children: Alicia Elan, Jeffrey Curtis. BS in Civil Engring., Colo. State U., 1969; MBA, U. Colo., 1977. Registered profl. engr., Colo., N. Mex., Wyo., Kans., Mont. Jr. engr. Boyle Engring. Co., Santa Ana, Calif., 1969-71; prin., v.p., design engr., project mgr. Meurer, Serafini & Meurer, Denver, 1971-78; pres. Meurer & Assocs., Lakewood, Colo., 1970—. Mem. ASCE, Am. Water Works Assn., Water Pollution Control Adminstrn. Republican. Methodist. Club: Denver Athletic (bd. dirs. 1984-87, pres. 1987—). Avocations: handball, golf, running, photography. Home: 10 Skyline Dr Denver CO 80215 Office: Meurer & Assocs 700 Kipling St Suite 4000 Lakewood CO 80215

MEWHINNEY, JAMES ALBERT, radiobiologist, researcher; b. Dayton, July 19, 1939; s. Albert Bauer Mewhinney and Florence Jean (Potts) Salisbury; m. Patricia Lou Stady, June 11, 1965 (div. Apr. 1980); children: Brent Allan, Lori Ann, Greg Robert; m. Carla Jo Freeman, July 12, 1985. BA, Wabash Coll., 1961; PhD, Purdue U., 1971. Health physicist Lovelace Found., Albuquerque, 1965-67; radiobiologist Inhalation Toxicology Research Inst., Albuquerque, 1971—. Contbr. articles to profl. jours. Avocations: golf, antique model airplanes. Home: 9705 Toltec NE Albuquerque NM 87111 Office: Inhalation Toxicology Research Inst PO Box 5890 Albuquerque NM 87185

MEYER, AUGUST CHRISTOPHER, JR., broadcasting company executive, lawyer; b. Champaign, Ill., Aug. 14, 1937; s. August C. and Clara (Rocke) M.; m. Karen Haugh Hassett, Dec. 28, 1960; children: August Christopher, Elisabeth Hassett. A.B. cum laude, Harvard U., 1959, LL.B., 1962. Bar: Ill. 1962. Partner firm Meyer, Capel, Hirschfeld, Muncy, Jahn and Aldeen, Champaign, Ill., 1962—; dir., officer Midwest Television, Inc., owner Sta. KFMB-TV-AM-FM, San Diego, Sta. WCIA-TV, Champaign, Ill. , Sta. WMBD-TV-AM, WKZW, Peoria, Ill., 1968—; pres. Sta. KFMB-TV-AM-FM, San Diego, Sta. WCIA-TV, Champaign, Ill. , Sta. WMBD-TV-AM, WKZW, 1976—; dir. Bank of Ill.; spl. asst. atty. gen. Ill., 1968-76. Chmn. bd. trustees Carle Found. Hosp., Urbana, Ill. Mem. Ill., Champaign County bar assns. Club: Champaign County. Home: 106 Greencroft Champaign IL 61820 Office: 509 S Neil Champaign IL 61820 also: 7677 Engineer Rd San Diego CA 92111

MEYER, CHARLES FRANKLIN, electrical engineer; b. El Paso, Tex., Jan. 18, 1922; s. Charles Franklin and Annis Belle (Ford) M.; m. Alice B. Longbottom, Apr. 24, 1942; children: C. Richard, D. Lee, Barbara. BSEE, N.Mex. State U., 1942; MS, U. Ariz., 1955; postgrad., Stanford U., 1956. Engr. Gen. Electric Co., Pa., N.Y., Conn., and N.Mex., 1942-44, 45-49; sr. project leader Motorola Research Lab., Phoenix, 1949-56; engring. specialist and program mgr. Sylvania Electronic Def. Lab., Mountain View, Calif., 1956-63; mem. tech. staff, program mgr. Gen. Electric. Ctr. for Advanced Studies, Santa Barbara, Calif., 1963-81; sr. scientist Kaman Scis. Corp., Santa Barbara, 1982—; cons. in advanced energy systems, Santa Barbara, 1981-82; cons. electronic warfare specialist, analyst, 1982—. Contbr. articles to profl. jours. Commr. Santa Barbara City Bd. Water Commrs., 1974—. Served with USNR, 1944-45. Mem. IEEE, Am. Geophys. Union, Assn. Old Crows, Winchester Canyon Gun Club (bd. dirs. 1977-83), Nat. Rifle Assn., Sigma Xi, Sigma Tau. Avocations: shooting, photography, computers. Office: Kaman Tempo PO Drawer QQ Santa Barbara CA 93102

MEYER, CHARLES STANTON, electrical engineer; b. San Rafael, Calif., Apr. 27, 1959; s. Robert Stanton and Frances Joan (Deaton) M.; m. Sophia Katherine Brown, Aug. 17, 1985. BEE, U. Calif., Berkeley, 1981, MEE, 1982. Engr. Atari/Cyan Engring., Grass Valley, Calif., summers 1979-81, staff engr., 1983-84; design engr. Fairchild Semiconductor, Mountain View, Calif., 1982-83; staff engr. Grass Valley Group, 1984-86; v.p. engring. Applied Design Labs., Grass Valley, 1986—; tech. cons. Calif. corps. Inventor video optimized modem, 1985, switched capacitator QAM modulator, 1985. Fellow Tektronix Found. U. Calif., Berkeley, 1981. Mem. IEEE, Phi Beta Kappa, Tau Beta Pi. Republican. Presbyterian. Avocations: skiing, stained glass, photography, audio. Home: 12806 Pasquale Rd Nevada City CA 95959 Office: Applied Design Labs PO Box 2405 Grass Valley CA 95945

MEYER, DONALD ROBERT, banker, lawyer; b. Phoenix, June 4, 1942; s. Donald Duncan and Eleanor M.; m. Virginia Whitesel, Sept. 3, 1966; 2 children. AB, U. Calif., Berkeley, 1964, JD, 1967; postgrad. Harvard U. Sch. Bus. Adminstrn., 1968. Bar: Calif. 1972. Lectr. Seoul Nat. Univ., Korea, 1969-70; assoc. Graham & James, San Francisco, 1971-76; asst. sec. Calif. First Bank, San Francisco, 1973—, v.p., 1976-78, gen. counsel, 1976—, sr. v.p., 1978—. Contbr.: Intro to the Law & Legal System of Korea, 1983. Mem. World Affairs Council, San Francisco, Sierra Club; co-chmn. San Francisco/Seoul Sister City Com.; mem. Asian Art Commn. of San Francisco, 1985—. Recipient Key to Seoul, Korea, 1984. Mem. Am. Bankers Assn. (v.p. Calif. State 1982-83), Calif. Bankers Assn. (chmn. legal affairs com. 1982-84), Korean-Am. C. of C. (San Francisco sec., bd. dirs. 1974—), Soc. Calif. Pioneers. Republican. Episcopalian. Club: University. Office: California First Bank 350 California St San Francisco CA 94104-1476

MEYER, EDMOND GERALD, energy and natural resources educator; b. Albuquerque, Nov. 2, 1919; s. Leopold and Beatrice (Ilfeld) M.; m. Betty F. Knobloch, July 4, 1941; children: Lee Gordon, Terry Gene, David Gary. B.S. in Chemistry, Carnegie Mellon U., 1940, M.S., 1942; Ph.D. (research fellow), U. N.Mex., 1950. Chemist Harbison Walker Refractories Co., 1940-41; instr. Carnegie Mellon U., 1941-42; asst. phys. chemist Bur. Mines, 1942-44; chemist research div. N.Mex. Inst. Mining and Tech., 1946-48; head dept. sci. U. Albuquerque, 1950-52; head dept. chemistry N.Mex. Highlands U., 1952-59; dir. N.Mex. Highlands U. (Inst. Sci. Research), 1957-63; dean N.Mex. Highlands U. (Grad. Sch.), 1961-63; dean Coll. Arts and Sci., U. Wyo., 1963-75, v.p., 1974-80, prof. energy and natural resources, 1981—; exec. cons. Diamond Shamrock Corp., 1980; chmn. Carbon Fuels Corp., 1981—; chmn. Am. Nat. Bank, Laramie, 1980—; Sci. adviser Gov. Wyo.; cons. Los Alamos Nat. Lab., NSF, HHS, GAO, Diamond Shamrock Corp., Wyo. Bancorp.; contract investigator Research Corp., Dept. Interior, AEC, NIH, NSF, Dept. Energy, Dept. Edn.; Fulbright exchange prof. U. Concepcion, Chile, 1959. Co-author: Chemistry-Survey of Principles, 1963, Legal Rights of Chemists and Engineers, 1977, Industrial Research & Development Management, 1982; Contbr. articles to profl. jours. Served with USNR, 1944-46. Recipient Disting. service award Jaycees. Fellow AAAS, Am. Inst. Chemists (dir.); mem. Asso. Western Univs. (chmn. 1973-74), Am. Chem. Soc. (councilor), Chilean Chem. Soc., Biophys. Soc., Council Coll. Arts and Scis. (pres. 1971, sec.-treas. 1972-75, dir. Washington office 1973), C. of C. (pres. 1984), Sigma Xi. Home: 1058 Colina Dr Laramie WY 82070 Office: Arts and Scis Bldg U Wyo Laramie WY 82071

MEYER, ERIC G., orchestra administrator; b. Washington, May 7, 1953; s. Rauer H. and Evelyn (Glad) M; m. Pamela Sue Placeway, Nov. 27, 1976; children: Andrew Douglas, Bronwyn Elizabeth. B.S. in Econs., Coll. of Wooster, 1975. Asst. mgr. Tucson Symphony Orch., 1977-80, dir. devel., 1978-80, gen. mgr., 1980. Mem. exec. com. Tucson Commn. on Arts, 1983, grants award com., 1984—. Mem. Am. Symphony Orch. League (bd. dirs. 1985), Met. Orch. Mgrs. Assn. (pres. 1986-87). Democrat. Presbyterian. Lodge: Rotary. Office: Tucson Symphony Soc 443 S Stone Ave Tucson AZ 85701

MEYER, GARY MILTON, artist; b. Boonville, Mo., May 13, 1934; s. Milton Simon and Anna Margaret (Davis) Meyer; m. Hiroko Julie Ii, Feb. 26, 1960; 1 son, Allan Gary Yoshio. B.P.A. with honors, Art Ctr. Coll. Design, Pasadena, Calif., 1959; postgrad. Chouinard Art Inst., 1962. Prodn. illustrator Universal Studios, Universal City, Calif., 1966-68; illus. Macco, Newport Beach, Calif., 1968-69; v.p. Recretects, Costa Mesa, Calif., 1970-71; illus., prin. Gary Meyer Illustration, Santa Monica and Burbank, Calif., 1972-78; pres. Gary Meyer Inc., Santa Monica, 1978—; documentary artist U.S. Air Force, 1967—. One man shows: Burbank Bd. Edn., 1952, J. Walter Thompson, Chgo., 1984; numerous group shows, including N.Am. Sculpture Exhbn., Golden, Colo., 1981, 83, Illus. West, Los Angeles County Mus. Sci. and Industry, 1983, Ill. West, 1984, Keys Art Exhbn., 1984; represented in permanent collections Smithsonian Air and Space Mus., USAF, Washington; prin. works include Roaring Head bronze sculpture (N.Am. Sculpture exhbn. Art Castings of Colo. award 1981), Fathead bronze sculpture (N.Am. Sculpture exhbn. Beyond Bronze award 1983). Served to sgt. USMC, 1952-55; Korea. Recipient 1st and 3d Pl. awards Tech. Illustration Mgmt. Assn., 1962, 1st Pl. award Tech. Illustration Mgmt. Assn., 1963, award of excellence CA-80, Communication Arts Mag., 1980, 1st prize European category Hollywood Reporter Mag. Key Arts Awards, 1983, Silver medal Illustration West 24 mag., 1985, also numerous award certs. Mem. Soc. Illustrators, Soc. Illustrators Los Angeles (2 Spl. Judges awards 1982, Best of Show award 1983, Best of Category award 1983, Spl. Judges award 1983, Best of Category award), Soc. Art Ctr. Alumni (sec. 1974-75). Democrat. Mem. Unity Ch. Home and Studio: 227 W Channel Rd Santa Monica CA 90402

MEYER, HARRY JOHN (JACK), geologist; b. Portland, Oreg., June 15, 1946; s. Raymond John and Esther Kay (Kopetski) M.; m. Rosa Maria Soto, Oct. 17, 1971; children—Thomas, Steven, Rosalie, Rebecca. B.S. in Geology, Portland State U., 1968, postgrad. in geology, 1972-76. Registered geologist, Oreg. Geol. field asst. Tom Beard & Assoc., El Paso, Tex.; gas supply supr. N.W. Nat. Gas Co., Portland, 1973-77, geothermal geologist, Portland, 1977-81, petroleum geologist, 1981—. Served with U.S. Army, 1968-71. Mem. Gresham Youth Soccer, Oreg. Mem. Portland C. of C. (chmn. mineral resources com. 1983-85), Am. Assn. Petroleum Geologists (Pacific sect., energy minerals div.), Geol. Soc. Am., N.W. Petroleum Assn. Democrat. Office: NW Nat Gas Co 220 NW 2d Ave Portland OR 97209

MEYER, HERBERT FREDERICK REICHERT, motel executive; b. Glendale, N.Y., July 1, 1914; s. Henry Gerard and Maria Regina (Reichert) M.; m. Ellen Elizabeth Crowell, Apr. 5, 1939 (dec. Jan. 25, 1946); m. 2d, Frances Helen Lengfeld, Sept. 20, 1947; children—Diana, Barbara, Christina, Herbert Jr. B.S., Columbia Coll., 1936. With R.H. Macy and Co., N.Y.C., 1936-56, mdsg. v.p., Calif., 1956; pres. Meyer Motels Inc. (now Meyer Motels Ltd.), Redding, Calif., 1956—. Served to lt. USNR, 1942-45. Republican. Lutheran. Club: San Mateo Rotary (pres. 1968, sec. 1969-72). Home: 4480 Plumas Reno NV 89509 Office: 2059 Hilltop Dr Redding CA 96002

MEYER, HOWARD ROBERT, JR., military officer, chemistry educator; b. Bolling AFB, Md., Nov. 16, 1955; s. Howard Robert Meyer and Mamie Irene (Blackwell) Meyer-Franceschini; stepfather Walter Adrian Franceschini; m. Mary Evelyn Corley, June 4, 1977; children: Rachel Eileen, Hannah Ruth. BS, USAF Acad., 1977; MS in Chemistry, U. Wyo., 1983. Commd. 2d lt. USAF, 1977, advanced through grades to capt., 1981; missile crew comdr., alt. command post missile crew comdr. USAF, F.E. Warren AFB, Wyo., 1977-80, officer code controller Wing Code div., 1981-82, chief code handler tng. br. Strategic Missile Wing, 1982; instr. chemistry USAF Acad., Colo., 1983-86, course dir. dept. chemistry, 1985, asst. prof., 1986—. Instr., coordinator ARC swimming program, F.E. Warren AFB, 1978-81; tchr., youth coordinator Protestant Chapel Program, F.E. Warren AFB, 1978-82; Sunday Sch. supt. Christ Community Ch., Colorado Springs, Colo., 1985—. Scholar U. Wyo., 1986. Mem. Am. Chem. Soc., Am. Sci. Affiliation, Electrochem. Soc. Republican. Mem. Ch. Christian and Missionary Alliance. Avocations: computers, woodworking, swimming, outdoor sports. Home: 2521 Overland Rd Laramie WY 82070 Office: Univ Wyoming Dept Chemistry AFIT/CIS Laramie WY 82070

MEYER, IVAH GENE, social worker; b. Decatur, Ill., Nov. 18, 1935; d. Anthony and Nona Alice (Gamble) Viccone; A.A. with distinction, Phoenix Coll., 1964; B.S. with distinction, Ariz. State U., 1966, M.S.W., 1969; postgrad. U.S. Internat. U.; m. Richard Anthony Meyer, Feb. 7, 1954; children—Steven Anthony, Stuart Allen, Scott Arthur. Social worker Florence Crittendon Home, Phoenix, 1969-70; social worker Family Service of Phoenix, 1970-73; faculty asso. Ariz. State U., 1973; field supr. Pitzer Coll., Claremont, Calif., 1977—; social worker Family Service of Pomona Valley, Pomona, Calif., 1975—; field supr. Grad. Sch. Social Services, U. So. Calif., 1978—; pvt. practice Chino (Calif.) Counseling Center. Lic. clin. social worker, Calif. Mem. Nat. Assn. Social Workers, Acad. Cert. Social Workers. Republican. Roman Catholic. Home: 778 Via Montevideo Claremont CA 91711 Office: 12632 Central Ave Chino CA 91710

MEYER, J. DEAN, executive search company executive; b. St. Louis, Feb. 8, 1918; s. Joseph C. and Ros T. (Patterman) M.; m. Ruth F. Heidt, June 21, 1941; 1 son, John Dean. B.S. in Adminstrv. Engring., Purdue U., 1939. With Bendix Corp., South Bend, Ind., 1942-61, dir. sales, 1951-61; asst. dir. mktg. Martin Co., Balt., 1961-63; v.p. Menasco Mfg. Co., Burbank, Calif., 1963-73; exec. v.p. Am. Safety Equipment Corp., Encino, Calif., 1973-77, dir., 1975—; pres. J.E. Fowler & Assocs., Burbank, 1977—, dir., 1982—; dir. Flight Systems, Inc., Universal Mfg. Corp. Mem. Soc. Automotive Engrs., AIAA, Burbank C. of C., Purdue Alumni (past pres. South Bend). Club: Town Hall. Home: 2032 Hillsbury Rd Westlake Village CA 91361 Office: 255 E Orange Grove Ave Suite B Burbank CA 91502

MEYER, JAMES HENRY, university chancellor; b. Fenn, Idaho, Apr. 13, 1922; s. Carl A. and Anita (de Coursey) M.; m. Mary Regan, Aug. 20, 1980; children by previous marriage: Stephen J., Susan T., Gary C., Joan K., Teresa A. B.S. in Agr. U. Idaho, 1947; M.S. in Nutrition (fellow Wis. Alumni Research Found.), U. Wis., 1949, Ph.D., 1951. Research asst. U. Wis., 1949-51; faculty U. Calif., Davis, 1951—; prof. animal husbandry U. Calif., 1960—, chmn. dept., 1960-63; dean U. Calif. (Coll. Agr. and Environment), 1963-69, chancellor univ., 1969—; Mem. Commn. Undergrad. Edn. in Biology, 1964-69. Editorial bd.: Jour. Animal Sci, 1961-65. Mem.

Western Coll. Sr. Accrediting Commn., 1982—. Served with USMCR, 1942-46. Recipient Am. Feed Mfr.'s award in nutrition, 1960. Mem. AAAS, Am. Soc. Animal Prodn., Nat. Assn. State Univs. and Land Grant Colls., Western Coll. Assn. (exec. com. 1971-74), Sigma Xi.

MEYER, JAROLD ALAN, oil company research executive; b. Phoenix, July 28, 1938; s. Lester M. and Anita (Walker) M.; m. Diane Louise Wheeler; children: Ronald Alan, Sharon Lynne. BSChemE, Calif. Inst. Tech., 1960, MS, 1961. Mgr. process devel. Chevron Research, Richmond, Calif., 1978-82; tech. mgr. Chevron U.S.A., El Segundo, Calif., 1982-84; v.p. process research Chevron Research, Richmond, 1984-86, pres., 1986—; bd. dirs. Solvent Refined Coal Internat., Inc., San Francisco. Inventor petroleum catalysts; contbr. articles to profl. jours. Bd. visitors U. Calif., Davis, 1983—. Mem. Am. Chem. Soc., Nat. Petroleum Refining Assn., Tau Beta Pi, Sigma Xi. Avocations: electronics design and constrn., photography. Office: Chevron Research Co 576 Standard Ave Richmond CA 94802

MEYER, JEFFERY WILSON, chemical marketing executive; b. San Francisco, June 22, 1923; s. Wilson and Mabel Marian (Wilson) M.; m. Janet Busse, Jan. 28, 1945; children—Pamela Meyer McLaughlin Elizabeth Meyer Helman. B.S., U. Calif.-Berkeley, 1948. With Wilson & George Meyer, San Francisco, 1948—, mgr. coke dept., 1952-56, v.p. agrl. dept., 1956-59, pres., dir., 1959—, chmn. bd., chief exec. officer, 1973—; fish collector for Steinhart Aquarium. Past pres. Norwegian Am. C. of C.; trustee, chmn. Calif. Acad. Scis. Served to lt. AUS, 1942-46, 50-52; PTO. Decorated Bronze Star; recipient Order of St. Olav Knight 1st class, Norway; Clubs: Bohemian, Pacific Union, Cercle de l'Union, St. Francis Yacht (San Francisco); Menlo Country (Redwood City); San Francisco Yacht (Tiburon). Home: 25 St Francis Rd Hillsborough CA 94010 Office: Wilson & George Meyer 270 Lawrence Ave South San Francisco CA 94080

MEYER, JEROME J., company executive; b. Caledonia, Minn., Feb. 18, 1938; s. Herbert J. and Edna (Staggemeyer) M.; m. Sandra Ann Beaudoin, June 18, 1960; children—Randall Lee, Lisa Ann, Michelle Lynn. Student, Hamline U., 1956-58; B.A., U. Minn., 1960. Devel. engr. Firestone Tire & Rubber Co., Akron, Ohio, 1960-61; v.p., gen. mgr. Sperry Univac, St. Paul, 1961-79; group v.p. Honeywell, Inc., Mpls., 1979-84; pres., cheif operating officer, dir. Varian Assocs., Palo Alto, Calif., 1984—; dir. Magnetic Data Inc., Mpls., Keycom Electronic Pub. Co., Chgo., Honeywell Erickson Devel. Co., Anaheim, Calif. Bd. dirs. YMCA, West St. Paul, Minn., 1977. Clubs: Southview Country (West St. Paul) Palo Alto Hills Country, Mission Viejo Country. Avocation: golf.

MEYER, JOAN MARIE, podiatrist; b. Waucoma, Iowa, Nov. 18, 1948; d. Matthew Joseph and Sophie Theresa (Heinz) Blong; Dan W. Meyer, June 26, 1972. BA in Med. Tech., U. No. Iowa, 1972; D Podiatric Medicine, Ill. Coll. Podriatric Medicine, 1980. Technician, instr. U. Minn. Blood Bank, Mpls., 1974-76; resident in podiatry Northlake (Ill.) Hosp., 1980-81; practice podiatry Escondido, Calif., 1981—. Mem. Am. Podiatric Med. Assn., San Diego Podiatric Med. Assn., Nat. Assn. Female Execs. (local coordinator 1984—). Avocations: jogging, gardening. Office: 735 E Ohio St Suite 102 Escondido CA 92025

MEYER, JOSEPH B., state attorney general; b. Casper, Wyo., 1941; m. Mary Meyer; children: Vincent, Warren. Student, Colo. Sch. Mines; BA, U. Wyo., 1964, JD, 1967; postgrad., Northwestern U., 1968. Dep. county atty. Fremont County, Wyo., 1967-69; ptnr. Smith and Meyer, 1968-71; asst. dir. legis. service office State of Wyo., Cheyenne, 1971-87, atty. gen., 1987—; conductor numerous govt. studies on state codes including Wyo. probate, criminal, state adminstrn., banking, domestic relations, game and fish, state instn., employment security, worker's compensation, motor vehicle, others; conductor legis. rev. of adminstrv. rules; negotiator with Office of Surface Mining for Wyo. state preemption; instr. Wyo. Coll. Law, fall 1986; lectr. Rocky Mountain Mineral Law Found., 1977. Bd. dirs. Cheyenne Jr. League, 1982-85, Jessup PTO, 1980-81; instr. Boy Scouts Am. Congregationalist. Club: Cheyenne Country. Lodge: Rotary. Avocations: golf, tennis, gardening, wood carving, rock hunting. Office: Attorney Generals Office 123 Capitol Building Cheyenne WY 82002

MEYER, LEE GORDON, attorney, fuel company executive; b. Washington, Oct. 22, 1943; s. Edmond Gerald and Betty (Knobloch) M.; m. Lynn Nix, Mar. 14, 1980; children—Veronica, Victoria, David. B.S. in Chemistry, U. Wyo., 1966, M.B.A., 1969, J.D. (hon.), 1973. Bar: Wyo. 1973, Tex. 1973, Ohio 1981, Ky. 1982, Colo. 1985, U.S. Patent Office, U.S. Supreme Ct. Patent atty. Texaco Corp., Austin, Tex., 1974-77; chief patent and trademark counsel Alcan Aluminum Co., Cleve., 1977-79; gen. counsel Donn, Inc., Cleve., 1979-81; asst. gen. counsel Diamond Shamrock Co., Lexington, Ky., 1981-83; v.p. fin. and adminstrn. Fort Union Coal Co., Denver, 1983-84; pres., chief exec. officer Carbon Fuels Corp., Denver, 1984—. Patentee in field. Mem. ABA, Am. Mgmt. Assn., Am. Chem. Soc., Licensing Exec. Soc., Ops. Research Soc., Denver C. of C. Republican. Home: 10487 E Ida Ave Englewood CO 80111 Office: Carbon Fuels Corp 5105 DTC Pkwy #317 Englewood CO 80111

MEYER, LHARY, electronics company executive; b. N.Y.C., May 25, 1947; s. Alfred P. and Shirley Meyer; m. Debra L. McFeron, 1982. Engr. Jefferson Airplane, San Francisco, 1970-72, Fantasy Films, Berkeley, Calif., 1978-79; mgr. elec., spl. effects Lucasfilm Ltd., San Rafael, Calif., 1979-81; owner, mgr. Albedo Engring., Novato, Calif., 1981—; v.p. Stereographics, San Rafael, 1983—, also bd. dirs. Patentee in field. Mem. IEEE, Soc. Motion Picture and TV Engrs. Avocations: ham radio, fishing.

MEYER, NATALIE, state official; b. Henderson, N.C., May 20, 1930; d. Ranie Thomas and Mary Osborne (Johnson) Clayton; m. Harold Meyer, June 17, 1951; children—Mary, Becky, Amy. Student in bus. and edn., U. No. Iowa, 1951. Formerly tchr. pub. schs. Jefferson County; past tchr. and prin. Ascension Luth. Ch. Midweek Sch.; past leasing mgr. for office comple; sec. of state State of Colo., Denver, 1982—. past vice chairperson Arapahoe County Republicans, Colo.; mgr. Senator Bill Armstrong's 1974 Fifth Congl. Campaign; exec. dir. Pres. Reagan's 1976 Colo. Campaign; dir. Ted Strickland's 1978 Gubernatorial Race; mgr. Phil Winn's race for Rep. state chmn., 1978; author, adminstr. Colo. program for Rep. legis. races, 1980, other statewide campaign plans; coordinator Draft Phil Winn effort. Avocations: bridge; reading; golf. Office: Colo State Dept 1560 Broadway Suite 200 Denver CO 80202 *

MEYER, RICHARD SCHLOMER, food company executive; b. Rapid City, S.D., Dec. 31, 1945; s. Harm Henry Schlomer and Marie Charolette (Hoffman) Meyer; m. Bonnie June Francis, July 15, 1970; children: Jennifer June, Christina Francis. BS, Wash. State U., 1968, MS, 1970; PhD, Cornell U., 1974. Sr. scientist Nestle Co., New Milford, Conn., 1974-76; mgr. research and devel. Armour & Co., Scottsdale, Ariz., 1976-81; v.p. and tech. mgr. research and devel. Griffith Labs., Alsip, Ill., 1981-82; v.p. tech. dir. research and devel. Kitchens of Sara Lee, Deerfield, Ill., 1982-84, Nalley's Curtice-Burns div. Agway, Tacoma, 1984—; mem. strategic planning com. N.W. Food Processor's Assn., Portland, Oreg., 1985—. Contbr. articles to profl. jours.; patentee in field. Mem. exec. com. Cornell U., 1973-74; mem. bd. edn. New Milford Pub. Schs., 1975-81; bd. regents Wash. State U., 1969-70; Rep. state committeeman and precinct capt., Phoenix, 1979-81. NIH fellow, 1971, 72. Mem. Inst. Food Technologists, Nutrition Today Soc., Can. Inst. Food Sci. and Tech., Am. Meat Sci. Assn., World Poultry Sci. Assn., Phi Kappa Phi, Alpha Zeta. Mem. Christian Ch. Lodges: Shriners, Masons. Office: Nalley's/Agway 3303 S 35th Tacoma WA 98411

MEYER, THOMAS ROBERT, TV product executive; b. Buffalo, Apr. 20, 1936; s. Amel Robert and Mildred Lucille M.; m. Dawn E. Shaffer, 1985. Student Purdue U., 1953-55, Alexander Hamilton Inst. Bus., 1960-62, West Coast U., 1969-72; children—Helen, Robyn, Sharon, Robert. Sect. chief wideband systems engring. Ground Elec. Engring. and Installation Agy., Dept. Air Force, 1960-66; product mgr., systems engr. RCA Corp., Burbank, Calif., 1966-71; systems cons. Hubert Wilke, Inc., Los Angeles, 1971-72; product mgr. Telemation, Inc., Salt Lake City, 1972-77; v.p. engring. Dynair Electronics, San Diego, 1977—. Served with USAF, 1955-59. Decorated Legion of Merit; recipient Bronze Zero Defects award Dept. Air Force, 1966. Fellow Soc. Motion Picture and TV Engrs. (chmn. subcom. digital control, co-chmn. SMPTE/European Broadcast Union task force for remote control); mem. Soc. Broadcast Engrs. (sr.), Computer Soc. of IEEE, Soc. St. Paul (sr.), Am. Electronics Assn.. Republican. Episcopalian. Research and publs. on color TV tech. and optics, TV equipment and systems, application of computer to TV systems. Office: Dynair Electronics 5275 Market St San Diego CA 92114

MEYER, URSULA, library director; b. Free City of Danzig, Nov. 6, 1927; d. Herman S. and Gertrude (Rosenfeld) M.; B.A., UCLA, 1949; M.L.S., U. So. Calif., 1953; postgrad. U. Wis., 1969. Librarian, Butte County (Calif.) Library, 1961-68; asst. pub. libraries, div. library devel. N.Y. State Library, Albany, 1969-72; coordinator Mountain Valley Coop. System, Sacramento, 1972-73; chmn. 49-99 Coop. Library System, Stockton, Calif., 1974-85; dir. library service Stockton (Calif.)-San Joaquin County Pub. Library, 1974—. Higher Edn. Title II fellow, 1968-69. Mem. Common Cause, NOW, Am. Assn. Pub. Adminstrs., ALA (mem. council 1979-83, chmn. nominating com. 1982-83, mem. legis. com. 1985-87), Calif. Library Assn. (pres. 1978), Sierra Club, Freedom to Read Found., AAUW, LWV. Lodge: Soroptimists. Office: Stockton-San Joaquin County Pub Library 605 N El Dorado St Stockton CA 95202

MEYER, WILLIAM TRENHOLM, electronics company official, real estate executive, former army officer; b. Ancon, C.Z., May 28, 1937; s. Trenholm Jones and Virginia Blanche (Morgan) M.; m. Erna Charlotte Albert, Dec. 14, 1961; children—Cynthia L., Bonnie A., Christopher T., Tori L. B.S., U. Nebr., 1965; grad. U.S. Army Command and Gen. Staff Coll., 1973. Commd. 2d lt. U.S. Army, 1961, advanced through grades to lt. col., 1976, ret., 1981; sr. engr. ManTech Internat. Corp., Sierra Vista, Ariz., 1981-82; mgr. field ops. RCA, Sierra Vista, 1982—; gen. ptnr., dir. Southwestern Investment Ltd. Partnership, Sierra Vista, 1983—. Sustaining mem. Republican Nat. Com., 1983—. Mem. Assn. Old Crows (regional dir. 1984—, chpt. pres. 1983-84, Internat. Electronic Warfare-Intelligence medal 1983), Armed Forces Communications and Electronics Assn., Ret. Officers Assn., Assn. U.S. Army. Roman Catholic. Clubs: Kings Tennis (pres. 1980, 87), Aquatic (pres. 1981) (Sierra Vista). Home: 1902 San Diego Circle Sierra Vista AZ 85635 Office: GE 2700 Fry Blvd Suite B-3 Sierra Vista AZ 85635

MEYERS, CHARLES WARREN, engineering consulting company executive; b. Watertown, S.D., Aug. 5, 1926; s. Jacob William and Jennie (Taube) M.; m. Gladys Arlene Kasal, Aug. 15, 1953; children: Karie Ann, Jeffrey Randall, Roger William, Jane Elizabeth. BSEE, S.D. Sch. Mines and Tech., 1950. Registered profl. engr., Colo., Wyo., Nebr., Kans., Tex. N.Mex., Utah, Alaska, Idaho, Fla., Oreg., S.D., Wash. Engr. Miner and Miner, Cons. Engrs., Inc., Greeley, Colo., 1950-69, pres., dir., 1969—; pres., dir. Miner and Miner Internat., Greeley, 1959—, Miner & Miner Internat. Engrs., Ltd., Greeley, 1963—; dir. Hydraulics Unltd., Eaton, Colo., 1967-86; adv. dir. Westen Fed. Savs. and Loan, Greeley, 1983-86. Bd. dirs. North Colo. Med. Ctr. Greeley, 1974-83. Served with AUS, 1944-46; ETO. Recipient Service award Profl. Engrs. Colo., 1967. Mem. Nat. Soc. Profl. Engrs. (chpt. pres. 1964), IEEE, Am. Cons. Engrs. Council (state v.p. 1980-81), Theta Tau. Club: Kiwanis (pres. 1968) (Greeley). Home: 1470 71st Ave Greeley CO 80634 Office: Miner and Miner Cons Engrs Inc 910 27th Ave Greeley CO 80632

MEYERS, JOSEPH ROBERT, technical writer, essayist, technical publication manager; b. Milw., Oct. 22, 1944; s. Albert R. and Viola H. Meyers; m. Melissa A. Biggs, June 18, 1977; 1 child, Benjamin G. Cert., Brown Inst. Electronics, Mpls., 1968; BA in Philosophy, Mount St. Paul Coll., Waukesha, Wis., 1969; BS in Math., U. Calif., San Jose, 1977. Tech. writer drive div. Ampex Disk, Sunnyvale, Calif., 1973-76; sr. tech. writer Ball Computer Products, Sunnyvale, Calif., 1976-78, Olivetti Corp., Ivrea, Italy, 1978-80, Apple Computer Inc., Cupertino, Calif., 1980-84; mgr. tech. pubs. Analog Design Tools Inc., Menlo Park, Calif., 1984—. Author: Apple IIe Owner's Manual, 1982, Apple IIc Reference Manual, 1984. Bd. dirs. Palo Alto Community Child Care System, Calif., 1984—. Mem. Soc. Tech. Communication. Home: 301 Bryant St Palo Alto CA 94301

MEYERS, MEL CHARLES, aerospace company executive; b. Toledo, Oct. 27, 1934; s. Stanley Steven and Clara Wanda (Pocwiercz) Czajkowski; m. Barbara Ann Coker, Dec. 29, 1956; children: Mark Vincent, Michelle Rene, Matthew Thomas. BBA, U. Toledo, 1957. Subcontract adminstr. Hughes Aircraft Co., Tucson, 1971-79, procurement mgr., 1980-84; procurement mgr. Hughes Aircraft Co., Canoga Park, Calif., 1979-80; materiel mgr. Hughes Aircraft Co., Fullerton, Calif., 1984—. Served with Signal Corps, U.S. Army, 1956-58. Recipient Million Dollar Cost Savs. award Hughes Aircraft Co., 1979. Mem. Nat. Contract Mgmt. Assn. Republican. Roman Catholic. Club: Mgmt. (Tucson) (bd. dirs. 1980—). Lodge: Elks. Home: 7320 Paseo Laredo Anaheim CA 92808

MEYERS, RICHARD STUART, college president; b. Chgo., Sept. 6, 1938; m. Yasuko Kamata, Sept. 15, 1965; children—Anne Akiko, Toni Takiko. B.M., DePaul U., 1961; M.S., U. So. Calif., 1963, Ph.D., 1971. With Inglewood Unified Sch. Dist., Calif., 1967-68; with Dept. Def. Overseas Sch. System, Tokyo, 1964-67; jr. and sr. high sch. tchr. Palos Verdes Peninsula Unified Sch. Dist., Palos Verdes, Calif., 1962-64; instr. media coordinator Grossmont Coll., El Cajon, Calif., 1968-72; dean instrn. Cerro Coso Community Coll., Ridgecrest, Calif., 1972-75, pres., 1975-78; sec. to bd. trustees, supt. and pres. Pasadena City Coll., Calif., 1978-83; pres. Western Oreg. State Coll., Monmouth, 1983—; speaker; cons. Contbr. articles to profl. jours. Bd. dirs. United Way, Salem, Oreg., 1984—; mem. Oreg. Internat. Trade Commn., 1983—, bd. dirs. Oreg. Symphony Assn., 1985—. Fulbright scholar, Egypt, 1975. Mem. Am. Assn. State Colls. and Univs., Pi Gamma Mu. Republican. Presbyterian. Lodge: Rotary. Home: 395 College St S Monmouth OR 97361 Office: Western Oreg State Coll 345 N Monmouth Ave Monmouth OR 97361

MEYERS, THEODORE RICHARD, fish pathologist; b. Kane, Pa., Sept. 22, 1950; s. Pauline Mae (Smith) Meyers; m. Patti Ann Sochia, June 6, 1970; 1 child, Montana Mae. AAS, Paul Smith's Coll., 1970; BS, Utah State U., 1972; MS, Oreg. State U., 1974; PhD, Cornell U., 1980. Fish pathologist Environ. Concern Inc., St. Michaels, Md., 1974; environ. project reviewer Md. Fisheries Adminstrn., Wye Mills, 1975; trainee aquatic vet. pathology Cornell U., Ithaca, N.Y., 1975-79; research assoc., fish pathologist Oreg. State U., Corvallis, 1980-82; asst. prof. fisheries U. Alaska, Juneau, 1982-85, affiliate asst. prof., 1985—; chief fish pathologist III Alaska Dept. Fish and Game, Juneau, 1985—. Contbr. articles to profl. jours. NDEA fellow Oreg. State U., 1973; grantee U. Alaska, Juneau, 1983-84, State of Alaska, 1983-85, NOAA, 1984-85. Mem. Am. Fisheries Soc. (cert. fish health sect.), Soc. Invertebrate Pathology, Phi Kappa Phi, Xi Sigma Pi. Avocations: fishing, hunting. Home: 3010 Glacierwood Dr Juneau AK 99801 Office: Alaska Dept Fish and Game PO Box 3-2000 Juneau AK 99802

MIANO, RICHARD JAMES, electrical manufacturing executive; b. Arlington, Mass., Dec. 13, 1936; s. Richard J. and Ruth A. (McPhail) M. Student Boston U., 1956-57, Northwestern U., 1962-63, U. Denver, 1978—, U. Pa., 1981, Regis Coll., 1986-87. Dist. mgr. Thomas & Betts Corp., Seattle, 1969-74, regional mktg. mgr., San Francisco, 1974, regional mgr., Denver, 1974—. Mem. Big Bros. of Seattle, 1972-73, Denver, 1978; counselor Boy Scouts Am., 1973; active Hunger Project of San Francisco, 1977—; mem. exec. com. Colo. State Reps. Served with USNR. Mem. Elec. Reps. Club of Denver, Ariz. Elec. League of Phoenix, Colo. Power Council (bd. dirs., sec. treas. 1985, v.p. 1986, pres.-elect 1987, chmn. econ. devel. com. 1987), Rocky Mountain Elec. League of Denver, Denver C. of C. (econ. and devel. council, pres.'s club), Snake River Valley Elec. Assn., Idaho Electric League, Intermountain Electric Assn. Pacific Northwest Elec. Assn. (dir.), Idaho Electric League, Intermountain Electric Assn., Internat. Facilities Mgrs. Assn., Internat. Assn. Elec. Insps. (assoc.), Pacific Northwest Electric League (scholarship chmn. 1972-73, bd. dirs. 1972), Southwest Elec., Colo. Assn. Commerce and Industry (econ. devel. adv. counsel 1987). Club. Clubs: Vail Racquet (bd. dirs. 1984-85, 86-87); N.Mex. Elec. Reps. Republican. Home: 4675 S Yosemite St Denver CO 80237 Office: 1660 S Albion Suite 907 Denver CO 80222

MICELI, MOTHER IGNATIUS, missionary sister; b. N.Y.C., Mar. 14, 1918; d. Joseph and Celelia (Torres) M. BS, Regis Coll.; MEd, Loyola U., New Orleans; M Religious Edn., Seattle U.; postgrad., U. Denver, 1968-69. Coordinator religious programs All Souls Ch., Englewood, Colo., 1968-71, dir. home instr. for adults, 1971-72, dir. adult edn., 1972—; dir. religious edn. Assumption, Welby, Colo., 1973-77, Holy Cross, Thorton, Colo., 1971-73; instr. religion various missions, 1968—. Author: (poems) Leaves Of Thought, 1980, Random Thoughts and Meditations, 1968. Mem. Internat. Bibl. Assn., Religious Edn. Assn. U.S., Reiligious Edn. Assn. Can., Kappa Delta Phi. Avocations: photography, camping, hiking, fishing, jeeping. Home: Cabrini Shrine Golden CO 80401 Office: All Souls Ch Religious Edn Office 435 Pennwood Circle Englewood CO 80110

MICHAEL, CAROL LYNN, computer executive; b. Chgo., Feb. 2, 1953; d. Jay Holden Simpson and Mabel (Blevins) French; m. Gregory Clark Michael, Jan. 1, 1984; children: Jillian Nicole, Lowell Evan. AS in Computer Sci., Pikes Peak Community Coll., 1978; cert. profl. mgmt. Mountain States Employer Council, 1982; BS in Tech. Mgmt., Regis Coll., 1986. Programmer City of Colorado Springs, 1978-79; programmer, analyst Colo. Dept. of Correction, Colorado Springs, 1979-80 software specialist Digital, Colordo Springs, 1980-81, sr. systems analyst, 1981-82, project mgr., 1983, staff mgr., 1983, mgr. of info. systems, 1983—; speaker Colo. State Bd. Edn., Colorado Springs, 1983, Colo. State Edn. Adv. Council, Colorado Springs, 1982; condr. bus. seminar for profl. sales people, Colorado Springs, 1978. Host SAT-UP Breakfast Local Bus. Community, Colorado Springs, 1978. Recipient Outstanding Achievement in Data Processing award Pikes Peak Community Coll., 1977-78, Exemplary Student award, 1978, Outstanding Bus. Student award, Wall Street Jour., 1978, Software Services Excellence award Digital, 1981, Achievement award Digital Info. Systems, 1984, 85; named Outstanding Young Woman of Am., 1984. Mem. Assn. Computing Machinery, Data Processng Mgmt. Assn. (bd. dirs.), Nat. Assn. Female Execs., Salesman with a Purpose, Phi Theta Kappa. Home: 5085 Cliff Point Circle E Colorado Springs CO 80907

MICHAEL, DONALD NELSON, social scientist, educator; b. Chgo., Jan. 24, 1923; s. Albert Abraham and Jean (Lewis) M.; m. Margot Jean Murphy, Apr. 7, 1956; 1 child, Geoffrey William. S.B., Harvard U., 1946, Ph.D., 1952; M.A., U. Chgo., 1948; D.Sc. (hon.), Marlboro Coll., 1964. Staff social scientist Weapons Systems Evaluation Group U.S., Joint Chiefs Staff, Washington, 1953-54; adviser Office Spl. Studies NSF, Washington, 1954-56; sr. research asso. Dunlap & Assos., Stanford, Conn., 1956-59; sr. staff mem. Brookings Instn., Washington, 1959-61; dir. Peace Research Inst., Washington, 1961-63; resident fellow Inst. Policy Studies, Washington, 1963-66; prof. planning and pub. policy, program dir. Center Research Utilization Sci. Knowledge, Inst. Social Research, prof. psychology U. Mich., Ann Arbor, 1966-82, prof. emeritus, 1982—, NIMH spl. research fellow, 1968-70; sr. mgmt. cons. SRI Internat., 1980-84; vis. fellow Inst. Internat. Studies U. Calif.-Berkeley, 1972-73; lectr. John Dewey Soc., 1967; mem. Commn. Study Orgn. Peace, 1965-74; fellow Sch. Mgmt. and Strategic Studies, Western Behavioral Sci. Inst., La Jolla, Calif., 1981—. Author: Proposed Studies on the Implications of Peaceful Space Activities for Human Affairs, 1961, Cybernation: The Silent Conquest, 1962, The Next Generation, 1965, The Unprepared Society, 1968, On Learning to Plan —And Planning to Learn, 1973. Co-vice chmn. nat. bd. U.S. Assn. for Club of Rome, 1978—; mem. nat. bd. Citizen Involvement Network, 1975; mem. nat. bd. Girl Scouts U.S.A., 1969-72, Congl. Inst. for Future. Served with AUS, 1943-46. Fellow Inst. Soc. Ethics Life Scis., AAAS, Am. Psychol. Assn., Soc. Psychol. Study Social Issues; mem. Club of Rome, N.Y. Acad. Sci., Am. Soc. Cybernetics (founding bd. 1964-68), Sigma Xi. Club: Cosmos. Office: 1472 Filbert St 511 San Francisco CA 94109

MICHAEL, ELLA ROSE SMITH, social worker; b. Ocean City, N.J., July 14, 1925; d. Harvey and Eva Barbara (Abel) Marts; m. Richard Franklin Smith, Jan. 20, 1946 (div. Feb. 1959); children: Barbara Jean Harrington, Patricia Ann Williams, George Allen; m. Russell Henry Michael, May 11, 1960 (dec. 1985); 1 child: Elizabeth Sue Svedberg. Diploma in nursing, Jewish Hosp. Sch. Nursing, 1945; AA, Palomar Jr. Coll., 1970; BA in Social Welfare, San Diego State U., 1972, MSW, 1973. RN, cert. rehab. counselor, ins. rehab. specialist. Nurse Office of Dr. Donald Tompkins, MD, Torrance, Calif., 1959-62, Office of Dr. Roy Palmateer, MD, Oceanside, Calif., 1968-69; contract social worker Vis. Nurse Assn. San Diego, 1974-77; program coordinator Olympic Area Agy. Aging, Montesano, Wash., 1978-79; census enumerator U.S Census Bur., Olympia, Wash., 1980; vocat. rehab. counselor Comprehensive Rehab. Service, Tacoma, 1980-85; rehab. counselor Office Worker's Compensation U.S. Dept. Labor, 1985-87; vocat. rehab. counselor Pacific Peronnel Mgmt., Federal Way, 1986—; social work cons. Olympic Peninsula End Stage Renal Disease Assn., Port Angeles, Wash., 1978-80. Asst. troop leader Girl Scouts U.S., Inglewood, Calif., 1955-58; den mother Boy Scouts Am., Encinitas, Calif., 1964-66; vol. counselor Planned Parenthood, San Diego, 1972-76. Mem. Clallam County Geneol. Assn., End Stage Renal Disease Assn., Nat. Assn. Social Workers, Pvt. Rehab. Orgns, Wash., Kappa Phi Kappa, Alpha Gamma Sigma. Lutheran. Avocations: animal husbandry, sewing, crocheting, reading, family research. Home and Office: 230 Lotzgesell Rd Sequim WA 98382

MICHAEL, GARY, artist, author; b. Denver, Apr. 17, 1937; s. Harold Jay and Florence (Tober) Spitzer; m. Jill Michael, Jan. 26, 1983. BA, Denver U., 1959; MA in Philosophy, U. Colo., 1961, MA in English, 1967; PhD in Humanities, Syracuse U., 1969. Prof. English U. Colo., Boulder, 1965-68, instr. painting, 1975-76; prof. philosophy Met. State U., Denver, 1970-73; lectr. demonstrator Grumbacher, N.Y., 1977—. Represented in permanent collection Denver Pub. Library, Denver Art Mus., Mus. Natural History, Denver, Colorado Springs (Colo.) Fine Arts Ctr., Miron Collection, Poughkeepsie, N.Y.; commd. murals: Perlmack Corp., Regent Plaza, Denver, 1975; bus. panel design, Bill and Dorothy Harmsen Collection, Denver, 1978; one-man shows: First of Denver, Farragimous V, 1976, United Bank, Denver, 1975, 76; No. Colo. Invitational Art Exhbn., 1979; Pastel Soc. Am., N.Y.C., 1979; Faces an d Places, Denver Nat. Bank, 1982; demonstrating artist Spree Arts Festival, 1975. Contbr. articles to profl. jours. Committeeman Democratic Party, Denver, 1980. Mem. Pastel Soc. Am. (Popular Vote aware 1979), Oil Pastel Assn. (Merit award 1983), Colo. Art Assn. Home: 3009 E 9th Ave Denver CO 80206

MICHAEL, JERROLD MARK, public health specialist, university dean, educator; b. Richmond, Va., Aug. 3, 1927; s. Joseph Leon and Esther Leah M.; m. Lynn Y. Simon, Mar. 17, 1951; children: Scott J., Nelson L. B.C.E., George Washington U., 1949; M.S.E., Johns Hopkins U., 1950; M.P.H., U. Calif., Berkeley, 1957; Dr. P.H., Mahidol U., 1983; Sc.D., Tulane U., 1984. Commd. ensign USPHS, 1950, advanced through grades to rear adm., asst. surgeon gen., 1966; ret. 1970; dean, prof. pub. health Sch. Pub. Health, U. Hawaii, Honolulu, 1971—; Bd. dirs. Nat. Health Council, 1967-78, Nat. Center for Health Edn., 1977—; mem. nat. adv. council on health professions edn., 1978-81; chmn. bd. dirs. Kuakini Med. Ctr., Honolulu. Contbr. articles to profl. jours.; assoc. editor Jour. Environ. Health, 1958—. Served with USNR, 1945-47. Recipient J.S. Billings award for mil. medicine, 1964; Walter Mangold award, 1961, gold medal Hebrew U. of Jerusalem, 1982, chair in pub. health named in his honor, 1985; decorated D.S.M., others. Fellow Am. Public Health Assn.; mem. Am. Acad. Health Adminstrn., Am. Soc. Cert. Sanitarians, Nat. Environ. Health Assn., Am. Acad. Environ. Engrs. Democrat. Jewish. Club: Masons. Office: 1960 East-West Rd Honolulu HI 96822

MICHAEL, STEPHEN WILLIAM, electrical engineer; b. El Centro, Calif., Sept. 22, 1946; s. William Eugene and Anna Mae (Lunceford) M.; A.A., Napa Coll., 1971; B.S., U. Calif. at Davis, 1973; m. Joanne Francis Frings, June 10, 1978. Product engr. Nat. Semiconductor Corp., Santa Clara, Calif., 1973-76, supervising product engr., 1976-79; mgr. div. engring. Fairchild Camera and Instrument, Mountain View, Calif., 1979-83; v.p. research and devel. engring. GE Intersil, Cupertino, Calif., 1983-87. Lt., Alameda County Underwater Recovery Unit, 1976-81; chmn. San Jose Young Reps., 1976-83; active Calif. Rep. Assembly, 1976—, treas. Los Gatos-Saratoga chpt., 1978; asso. mem. Rep. State Central Com. Calif., 1977-80; mem. Santa Clara County Rep. Central Com., 1978-80; airport commr. San Jose Mcpl. Airport, 1978—, vice chmn. commn., 1981-82, chmn., 1982-83; bd. dirs. Happy Hollow Park and Baby Zoo, 1978—, treas., v.p., 1979, pres., 1982-84; vice chmn. Santa Clara County Young Reps., 1978-79; mem. Rep. State Central Com. Calif., 1980-83; bd. dirs. Santa Clara and Santa Cruz Counties of Campfire, 1978-81. Served with USCG, 1966-70. Mem. Soc. Automotive Engring., IEEE, San Jose Jaycees (pres. 1979, internat. senator 1982), Aero

Club of No. Calif., Internat. Platform Assn., Mormon. Club: San Jose Rotary. Home: 5905 Royal Ann Dr San Jose CA 95129 Address: 10710 N Tantau Ave Cupertino CA 95014

MICHAELS, PATRICK FRANCIS, broadcasting company executive; b. Superior, Wis., Nov. 5, 1925; s. Julian and Kathryn Elizabeth (Keating) M.; A.A., U. Melbourne, 1943; B.A., Golden State U., 1954; Ph.D., London U., 1964; m. Paula Naomi Bowen, May 1, 1960; children—Stephanie Michelle, Patricia Erin. War corr. CBS; news editor King Broadcasting, 1945-50; war corr. Mid-East Internat. News Service, 1947-49; war corr. MBS, Korea, 1950-53; news dir. Sta. WDSU-AM-FM-TV, 1953-54; fgn. corr. NBC, S. Am., 1954-56; news dir. Sta. KWIZ, 1956-59; commentator ABC, Los Angeles, 1959-62; fgn. corr. Am. News Services, London, 1962-64; news commentator McFadden Bartell Sta. KCBQ, 1964-68; news commentator ABC, San Francisco, 1968-70; news dir. Sta. KWIZ, Santa Ana, Calif., 1970-74, station mgr., 1974-81; pres. Sta. KWRM, Corona, Calif., KQLH, San Bernardino, Calif., 1981—. Bd. dirs. Econ. Devel. Corp. Mem. Calif. Broadcasters Assn. (bd. dirs.), Nat. Assn. Radio Broadcasters (legis. liaison com.), Am. Fedn. TV and Radio Artists, Orange County Broadcasters Assn. (pres.), Sigma Delta Chi (ethics com.). Republican. Clubs: Rotary, Balboa Bay (bd. govs.), South Shore Yacht, Internat. Yachting Fellowship of Rotarians (staff commodore). Home: 4521 Cortland Dr Corona del Mar CA 92625 Office: Sta KQLH FM Box 100 Corona CA 91718

MICHAELS, SEAN KENNEDY, data processing administrator; b. Springfield, Mass., Nov. 29, 1952; s. William Edwin and Helen Virginia (Kennedy) M.; m. Susan Bennet Hills, Mar. 25, 1977 (div. Oct. 1983). Cert. in mgmt., Los Medanos Coll., 1985; cert. in data processing, Diablo Valley, 1986. Data processing analyst Aetna Life and Casualty, Hartford, Conn., 1972-81; data processing administr. Aetna Life and Casualty, Walnut Creek, Calif., 1981—. Vol. Red Cross; coach youth football and baseball. Democrat. Roman Catholic. Lodge: KC (local sec. 1979, dep. grand knight 1980). Home: 3081 N Main ST Apt. #1 Walnut Creek CA 94596 Office: Aetna Life and Casualty 201 N Civic Dr Suite 300 Walnut Creek CA 94596

MICHAELSON, RICHARD DEORR DELOS, social worker; b. Brigham City, Utah, Oct. 29, 1944; s. Dr. Chauncey DeOrr and Dena (Donaldson) M.; m. Shanah Goodman, June 5, 1964; children: Richard, Zachary. BS in Sociology, Weber State Coll., 1967; MSW, U. Utah, 1972. Social service aid Bur. Indian Affairs, Anchorage, 1971; social work specialist Youth Rehab., Nampa, Idaho, 1972-74, Region IV Community Mental Health Ctr., Boise, Idaho, 1974-76, Region III Community Mental Health Ctr., Caldwell, Idaho, 1976-79; unit I mgr. Idaho State Sch. and Hosp., Nampa, 1979—; clin. program cons. Channel Enterprises, Boise, 1976-78; pvt. practive parent effectiveness tng. instr., Nampa, 1976-79; cons. Gem State Homes, Meridian, Idaho, 1981. Bd. dirs. Community Involvement Programs, Nampa, 1972-74; pres. Sunnyridge Water Dist., Nampa, 1973—; state chmn. Inter-team Council on Substance Abuse, Boise, 1973-74. HEW grantee, 1973. Mem. Nat. Assn. Social Workers (cert.), Am. Assn. Mental Deficiency. Avocations: skiing, running, tennis, photography, carpentry. Office: Idaho State Sch and Hosp 3100 11th Ave N Nampa ID 83651

MICHALAK, LAURENCE O., anthropologist; b. Woodland, Calif., Oct. 10, 1942; s. Joseph Laurence and California (Flowers) M.; m. Karen Francis Trocki, June 25, 1977; children: Michael David, Nadia Helene. BA, Stanford U., 1964; MA, U. of London, 1970; PhD, U. of Calif., Berkeley, 1983. English tchr. Peace Corps, Tunis, Tunisia, 1964-66, assoc. dir., 1967-69; english tchr. St. Mary's Middle Sch., Pitts., 1971-72; instr. U. Pitts., 1972-73; grad. asst. Anthropology Dept. U. Calif., Berkeley, 1973-79, vice chmn. ctr. for Middle Eastern Studies, 1979—. Editor: Social Legislation in the Contemporary Middle East, 1986; contbr. articles to profl. jours. Grantee French Ministry External Relations, 1985, Social Sci. Research Council, 1977-79; Fulbright scholar, 1977-79. Mem. Middle East Studies Assn., Am. Anthrop. Assn., Middle East Research Group in Anthrop., (sec., treas. 1981—), Am. Inst. for Maghribi Studies, (bd. dirs. 1984-85, travel grantee 1985). Democrat. Roman Catholic. Avocations: winemaking. Office: U Calif Ctr for Middle Eastern Studies 215 Moses Hall Berkeley CA 94720

MICHALIK, JOHN JAMES, bar association executive; b. Bemidji, Minn., Aug. 1, 1945; s. John and Margaret Helen (Pafko) M.; m. Diane Marie Olson, Dec. 21, 1968; children: Matthew John, Nicole, Shane. BA, U. Minn., 1967, JD, 1970. Legal editor Lawyers Coop. Publishing Co., Rochester, N.Y., 1970-75; dir. continuing legal edn. Wash. State Bar Assn., Seattle, 1975-81, exec. dir., 1981—. Mem. Am. Soc. Assn. Execs., Nat. Assn. Bar Execs., Am. Mgmt. Assn., Am. Judicature Soc. Lutheran. Club: Seattle Coll. Office: Wash State Bar Assn 2001 6th Ave Seattle WA 98121-2599

MICHEL, PEGGY HUNTER, clinical social worker; b. Sidney, Mont., Nov. 15, 1949; d. Donald Lenny and Martha Elizabeth (Moore) Hunter; m. Steven R. Michel, Dec. 1, 1973 (div. June 1985). BA in Music, German, Rocky Mountain Coll., 1973; MSW, U. Utah, 1981. Oncology social worker LDS Hosp., Salt Lake City, 1981—; profl. adv. bd. IHC Home Health, Salt Lake City, 1984—. Bd. dirs. Utah div. Am. Cancer Soc., Salt Lake City, 1985—. Cert. Merit Outstanding Patient Service, Am. Cancer Soc., 1983-84. Mem. Nat. Assn. Oncology Social Workers, Nat. Assn. Social Workers. Mem. Unitarian Univeralist Ch. Avocations: guided imagery, meditation, golfing, swimming, hiking. Office: LDS Hosp Intermountain Health Care 325 8th Ave Salt Lake City UT 84143

MICHEL, VICTOR JAMES, JR., retired librarian; b. St. Louis, Feb. 2, 1927; s. Victor James and Bernadette (Fox) M.; student St. Louis U., 1946-48; m. Margaret A. Renaud, Feb. 3, 1951; children: Dennis W., Daniel J., Catherine A., Denise M. Asst. librarian McDonnell Aircraft Corp., St. Louis, 1948-55; mgr. Anaheim (Calif.) Information Center, Electronics Ops., Rockwell Internat. Corp., 1955-84; pres. V.J. Michel Inc., Grass Valley, Calif., 1986—; sec. Placentia Devel. Co., 1964-71. Charter mem. Placentia-Tlaquepaque Sister City Orgn., 1964-84; founder, pres. Placentia chpt. St. Louis Browns Fan Club. Planning commr., Placentia, Calif., 1957-60, city councilman, 1960-70, vice-mayor, 1960-64, mayor, 1964-68. Trustee Placentia Library Dist., 1970-79, pres., 1974-79; city historian, Placentia, 1976-84, city treas., 1980-84; chmn. Placentia Fine Arts Commn., 1978-80. Served from pvt. to staff sgt. AUS, 1945-46. Named Placentia Citizen of Yr., 1979. Mem. Placentia C. of C. (v.p. 1960), Placentia Jaycees (hon. life), Calif., Orange County (pres. 1976) library assns. Democrat. Roman Catholic. Club: West Atwood Yacht (hon. yeoman emeritus with citation 1970, ship's librarian). Author: Pictorial History of the West Atwood Yacht Club, 1966; Placentia—Around the World, 1970; also articles in profl. jours. Home: 107 Bernadine Ct Grass Valley CA 95949

MICHELIS, JAY, broadcaster, educator, consultant; b. Livermore, Calif., Oct. 24, 1937; s. John Robert and Eileen Mary (Scullion) M. B.A. in Humanities, San Jose State U., 1959; postgrad. Stanford U., 1959. Page, NBC, Hollywood, Calif., 1959-61, page supr., 1961-63, mgr. guest relations, 1963-64, coordinator promotion, 1964, adminstr. promotion, 1964-66, mgr. promotion, 1966-70, dir. nat. promotion, 1970-72, exec. dir. nat. promotion, N.Y.C., 1972-78, v.p. talent relations, 1978-79, v.p. creative services, 1979-81, v.p. talent relations and creative services, 1981-83, v.p. corp. creative services, Burbank, Calif., 1983-86, v.p. corp. and media relations, 1986—; lectr. in field; bd. dirs. NBC Employees Fed. Credit Union. Mem. Acad. TV Arts and Scis., Pasadena Hist. Soc., Big Sur Hist. Soc., Monterey Bay Aquarium Found. Democrat. Roman Catholic. Club: Am. Surfing Assn. Home: 912 Glen Oaks Blvd Pasadena CA 91105 Home: Grey Wolf Lodge Palo Colorado Canyon Big Sur CA 93923 Office: 3000 W Alameda Ave Suite C-195 Burbank CA 91523

MICHELSEN, THEODORE WILLIAM, marketing professional; b. Bklyn., Nov. 24, 1944; s. Warren Gerard and Maude Leanore (Smith) M.; m. Carol Lynn Steinkraus, June 18, 1967; children: Janet Lynn, Jennifer Lynn. BS in Chemistry, Rensselaer Poly. Inst., 1967, PhD in Inorganic Chemistry, 1971. Research chemist Manville Sales Corp., Denver, 1970-77, sr. research chemist, 1977-79, project. mgr., 1979-81, research mgr., 1981-83, mgr. mktg. engring. services, 1983-86, v.p., dir. research engring. services, 1986—; instr. Roofing Industry Ednl. Inst., Englewood, Colo., 1985—, Better Understanding of Roofing Systems Inst., Denver, 1983—. Mem. Ch. council Luth. Ch. Resurrection, Denver, 1975-80, chmn. Christian edn., 1978-80. Mem. Asphalt Roofing Mfr's. Assn. (roofing systems tech. com. 1983—, built-up roofing com. 1983—, chmn. built-up roofing com. 1986—), Am. Chem. Soc. Club: Rocky Mountain 99ers (Denver) (v.p. 1983-84, pres. 1984-85). Avocations: wood working, computers. Home: 1812 S Yank Ct Lakewood CO 80228 Office: Manville Sales Corp PO Box 5108 Denver CO 80217-5108

MICHELSON, DOUGLAS JEROME, state senator; b. Albuquerque, Feb. 17, 1942; s. Jack and Mildred (Bell) M. Student U. Ariz., 1959-61; B.S., U. N.Mex., student Indsl. Coll. Armed Forces, 1970. Civilian sales research and product devel. Sunbell Corp., Albuquerque, 1963-67, v.p., 1967-69, v.p. fin. and capital expenditure, 1969-71; with Rembrandt Investments, Albuquerque, 1972-76, Michelson Metals, 1976—; mem. N.Mex. Senate, vice chmn. pub. affairs com. Mem. N.Mex. Amigos. Democrat. Jewish. Home: 611 Lead SW #307 Albuquerque NM 87102 Office: 1503 Central St NW Suite 2 Albuquerque NM 87104

MICKELSON, ALAN ROLF, electrical engineering educator, optoelectronics researcher; b. Westport, Conn., May 2, 1950; s. Siegfried Thor and Maybelle (Brown) M.; m. Ann Karin Sumstad; 1 child, Lars S. BSEE, U. Tex., 1973; MS, Calif. Inst. Tech., 1974, PhD, 1978. Postdoctoral fellow Calif. Inst. Tech., Pasadena, 1978-79; vis. scientist Byurakan (Armenian S.S.R.) Obs., 1979-80; research scientist, electronics lab. Norwegian Inst. Tech., Trondheim, 1980-83; asst. prof. elec. engring. U. Colo., Boulder, 1984-86, assoc. prof., 1986—. Contbr. more than 20 sci. articles to profl. jours. Mem. IEEE, Antennas and Propogation Soc. of IEEE, Optical Soc. Am. (hon. mention best paper 1979), AAAS. Office: Univ Colo Elec Engring Dept Campus Box 425 Boulder CO 80309

MICKUS, MARIAN SUZANNE, financial executive; b. Chgo.; d. Frank J. and Santa (Polli) Mickus; B.S. in Fin., Calif. State U., 1979; M.B.A., Loyola U., 1981. Ops. mgr. consumer fin. subs. St. Paul Ins. Co., 1968-78; asst. treas. fin. planning Fremont Gen. Corp., Los Angeles, 1978—. Mem. Friends of the Joffrey Ballet, Decorative Arts Council Los Angeles Mus. Art. Mem. AAUW, The Planning Forum, Internat. Soc. for Planning and Strategic Mgmt., Nat. Assn. Female Execs., Los Angeles Jaycees, Nat. Assn. Ins. Women, Town Hall Calif., Women in Bus., Orgn. Women Execs. Clubs: Marina City, Los Angeles Athletic. Office: Fremont Gen Corp 1633 26th St Santa Monica CA 90404

MICSAK, STEPHANIE BIRES, speech pathologist, health facility administrator; b. Lorain, Ohio, Jan. 14, 1955; d. Stephen Lawrence and Mary (Angelos) Bires; m. Robert William Micsak, Sept. 3, 1977; 1 child, Robert Victor III. BS in Communications, Ohio State U., 1976, MA in Speech Pathology, 1977. Speech pathologist Walpole (Mass.) Pub. Schs., 1977-78; speech pathologist Rivendell Sch., Denver, 1978-81, dir. speech, 1979-81; dir. speech pathology and audiology, mgr. therapautic intervention services Wheatridge (Colo.) Regional Ctr., 1981—. tchr. skiing to hancicapped, Winter Park, Colo., 1979—. Fellow Colo. Speech and Hearing Dirs.; mem. Am. Speech Lang. and Hearing Assn. Democrat. Greek Orthodox. Avocations: downhill skiing, traveling, reading. Home: 8947 W Glasgow Pl Littleton CO 80123 Office: Wheatridge Regional Ctr 10285 Ridge Rd Wheatridge CO 80033

MIDDLEBROOK, GRACE IRENE, nurse/educator; b. Los Angeles, Mar. 5, 1927; d. Joel P. and Betty (Larson) Soderberg; dip. West Suburban Hosp., 1950; B.S. in Nursing, Wheaton Coll., 1951; M.A. in Edn., Ariz. State U., 1965, Ed.D., 1970; m. Albert William Middlebrook, July 7, 1950; children—Alberta Elizabeth, Jo Anne. Office nurse, Dr. G.A. Hemwall, Chgo., 1950-51; supr. Bates Meml. Hosp., Bentonville, Ark., 1955-58; instr. Sparks Meml. Hosp. Sch. Nursing, Ft. Smith, Ark., 1959-61; instr., coordinator med.-surg. nursing Sch. of Nursing, Good Samaritan Hosp., Phoenix, 1961-64, asst. dir. Sch. Nursing, 1964-73, dir. edn. and tng., 1968-80; corp. dir. edn. Samaritan Health Service, Phoenix, 1969—; adj. prof. Samaritan Coll. Nursing, Grand Canyon Coll. Mem. speakers bur. Sch. Career Days, 1970—. Recipient award for leadership co-op programs Phoenix Union High Sch., 1980, Sammy award Samaritan Health Service and Samaritan Med. Found., 1981. Mem. Ariz. Nurses in Mgmt. (bd. dirs. 1983-85), Am. Hosp. Assn., Nat. League Nursing, Ariz. League for Nursing, Adult Edn. Assn., Ariz. Heart Assn. (instr.), Pi Lambda Theta, Kappa Delta Pi, Sigma Theta Tau. Home: 4242 N 15th Dr Phoenix AZ 85015 Office: Samaritan Health Service Edn Center 1500 E Thomas Rd Phoenix AZ 85014

MIDDLEKAUFF, ROBERT LAWRENCE, historical educator, administrator; b. Yakima, Wash., July 5, 1929; s. Harold and Katherine Ruth (Horne) M.; m. Beverly Jo Martin, July 11, 1952; children: Samuel John, Holly Ruth. B.A., U. Wash., 1952; Ph.D., Yale U., 1961. Instr. history Yale U., New Haven, Conn., 1959-62; asst. prof. history U. Calif.-Berkeley, 1962-66, assoc. prof., 1966-70, prof., 1970-80, Margaret Byrne prof. history, 1980-83; dir. Huntington Library, Art Gallery and Bot. Gardens, San Marino, Calif., 1983—; mem. council Inst. Early Am. History and Culture, Williamsburg, Va., 1974-76. Author: Ancients and Axioms, 1963, The Mathers, 1971, The Glorious Cause: The American Revolution, 1763-1789, 1982. Served to 1st lt. USMC, 1952-54, Korea. Recipient Bancroft prize, 1972; recipient Commonwealth Club Gold medal, 1983; fellow Am. Council Learned Socs., 1965, NEH, 1973, Huntington Library, 1977. Fellow Am. Acad. Arts and Scis.; mem. Am. Hist. Assn., Orgn. Am. Historians, Soc. Am. Historians, Am. Antiquarian Soc., Assocs. Early Am. History and Culture (mem. exec. com.), Colonial Soc. Mass. (corr.). Home: 1650 Orlando Rd San Marino CA 91108 Office: Huntington Library Art Gallery and Bot Gardens 1151 Oxford Rd San Marino CA 91108

MIDDLETON, ANTHONY WAYNE, JR., urologist; b. Salt Lake City, May 6, 1939; s. Anthony Wayne and Dolores Caravena (Lowry) M.; BS, U. Utah, 1963; MD, Cornell U., 1966; m. Carol Samuelson, Oct. 23, 1970; children: Anthony Wayne, Suzanne, Kathryn, Jane, Michelle. Intern, U. Utah Hosps., Salt Lake City, 1966-67; resident in urology Mass. Gen. Hosp., Boston, 1970-74; practice urology Middleton Urol. Assos., Salt Lake City, 1974—; mem. staff Primary Children's Hosp., staff pres., 1981-82; mem. staff Latter-Day Saints Hosp., Holy Cross Hosp.; asst. clin. prof. surgery U. Utah Med. Coll., 1977—; vice chmn. bd. govs. Utah Med. Self-Ins. Assn., 1980-81, chmn. 1985-87. Bd. dirs. Utah chpt. Am. Cancer Soc., 1978-86; bishop Ch. Jesus Christ Latter-day Saints; vice chmn. Utah Med. Polit. Action Com., 1978-81, chmn., 1981-83; chmn. Utah Physicians for Reagan, 1983-84; mem. U. Utah Coll. Medicine Dean's Search Com., 1983-84; bd. dirs. Utah Symphony, 1985—. Served as capt. USAF, 1968-70. Mem. ACS, Utah State Med. Assn. (pres.-elect 1986-87), Am. Urologic Assn., AMA, Salt Lake County Med. Assn. (sec. 1965-67, pres. liaison com. 1980-81, pres.-elect 1981-83, pres. 1984), Utah Urol. Assn. (pres. 1976-77), Salt Lake Surg. Soc. (treas. 1977-78), Phi Beta Kappa, Alpha Omega Alpha, Beta Theta Pi. Republican. Contbr. articles to profl. jours. Home: 2798 Chancellor Pl Salt Lake City UT 84108 Office: 1060 E 1st S Salt Lake City UT 84102

MIDDLETON, CHARLES RONALD, educator, academic dean; b. Hays, Kans., Sept. 16, 1944; s. Charles Buster and Dorothy Bryant (Parsons) M.; m. Sandra Leigh Paulson, Dec. 19, 1964 (div. Jan. 1979); children: Charles Christopher, Kevin Andrew, Kathryn Gillian. AB with honors, Fla. State U., 1965; MA, Duke U., 1967, PhD, 1969. Asst. prof. U. Colo., Boulder, 1969-77, assoc. prof., 1977-85, asst. dean, 1979-80, prof. history, 1985—, assoc. dean Coll. Arts and Scis., 1980—. Contbr. articles to profl. jours. Bd. dirs. Found. for World Health, Denver and Boulder, 1985—. Recipient Faculty Teaching Excellence award U. Colo., Boulder, 1978; research grantee Am. Philos. Soc., 1977, U. Colo., 1972. Mem. N.Am. Conf. on Brit. Studies, Western Conf. on Brit. Studies (pres.-elect 1985-86, pres. 1986—), Am. Hist. Assn., Am. Com. for Irish Studies, Brit. Politics Group. Democrat. Avocations: fishing, skiing, gardening. Home: 4391 Butler Circle Boulder CO 80303 Office: U Colo Arts and Scis Adminstrn Box 275 Boulder CO 80309-0275

MIDDLETON, MICHAEL CHARLES, electrical engineer; b. Flint, Mich., Oct. 8, 1937; s. Leo C. and Vivian Marie (Peterson) M.; m. Marsha R. Gustafson, June 26, 1960; children: Bonnie, Lisa. BSBA, U. Phoenix, 1982. Electronic technician Gen. Electric, Phoenix, 1965-66, Motorola Corp., Phoenix, 1966-67; sr. elec. engr. Honeywell, Phoenix, 1967-84; elec. engr., chief exec. officer Wirebenders, Phoenix, 1984—; cons. THESYS Memory Systems, Scottsdale, Ariz., 1983-85. Contbr. articles to profl. mags.; inventor computer sequencing. Served with USAF, 1956-60. Mem. Ariz. Bicycle Club (pres. 1965-75). Republican. Presbyterian. Avocations: backpacking, bicycling. Home: 1713 W Eva Phoenix AZ 85021 Office: Wirebenders Inc 2440 W Mission Ln #9 Phoenix AZ 85021

MIDDLETON, RENEE COLLEEN, marketing executive; b. North Platte, Nebr., Mar. 6, 1961; d. Ralph Clarence and Dorothy Jeanne (Glade) M. BS in Journalism, U. Wyo. Editor/sales rep. Trader's Printing and Pub. Co., Cheyenne, Wyo., 1983-85; advt. mgr. H J & Assocs./Communication, Cheyenne, 1985; pres. Taco John's Internat., Cheyenne, 1986—; v.p. mktg. Cheyenne Melodrama, 1984—. Mem. membership com., newsletter staff Cheyenne Symphony Orch., 1985-86; big sister Spl. Friends Orgn., Cheyenne, 1984-86; chmn. publicity com. AMC and Am. Cancer Soc., Cheyenne. Mem. Socj. Profl. Journalists, Am. Advt. Fedn., Phi Beta Kappa. Republican. Lutheran. Avocations: skiing, softball, sewing, jigsaw puzzles. Home: 4431 E 17th St Cheyenne WY 82001 Office: Taco Johns Internat 808 W 20th St Cheyenne WY 82001

MIDDLETON, ROBERT GORDON, engineer, lecturer, author; b. Watsonville, Calif., May 31, 1908; s. Winton Gordon and Carrie (Leonard) M.; student U. Calif., 1928-31, U. Conn., 1944, N.Y. U., 1945; m. Teresa Emilson, June 29, 1940. Lectr., chief field engr. Simpson Electric Co., Chgo., 1954-57; internat. dir. tech. div. Radio Electronic TV Sch., Inc., Detroit, 1957-60. Mem. IEEE (life), Nat. Ret. Tchrs. Assn., Friends of U. Calif. at Santa Cruz Library. Club: Elks. Author 100 tech. books, the latest including: Transistor TV Servicing Guide, 1969; Transistor Color TV Servicing Guide, 1969; Tape Recorder Servicing Guide, 1970; Using Scopes in Color TV, 1970; Color-TV Waveform Analysis, 1970; Using Scopes in Transistor Circuits, 1970; Electronic Organ Servicing Guide, 1971; Audel's Television Service Manual, rev. edit., 1977; Audel's Radioman's Guide, rev. edit., 1977; Basic Electricity, 1974; Digital Equipment Servicing Guide, 1975; Handbook of Electronic Circuit Design, 1978; Handbook of Electronic System Design, 1978; Handbook of Audio Circuit Design, 1978; Acoustic Troubleshooting of Audio Systems, 1979; Understanding Microprocessors, 1980; Effectively Using the Oscilloscope, 1981; Understanding Digital Logic Circuits, 1982; Digital Logic Tests and Analysis, 1982; New Ways to Use Test Meters, 1983; New Digital Troubleshooting Techniques, 1984; Troubleshooting Electronic Equipment without Service Data, 1984; New Handbook of Troubleshooting Techniques for Microprocessors and Microcomputers, 1985; Designing Electronic Circuits, 1985, Handbook of Electronic Tables and Formulas, 1986, Rob Middleton's Handbook of Electronic Time-Savers and Shortcuts, 1987. Address: PO Box 594 Santa Cruz CA 95061

MIDDLETON, VINCENT FRANCIS, manufacturing company executive; b. N.Y.C., June 24, 1951; s. Vincent Aloysius and Mary Hilda (Lehane) M.; m. Collette Carolyn Peters, July 26, 1986. BSCE, So. Meth. U., 1974; MBA in Mgmt., Golden Gate U., 1986. Registered profl. civil engr., Calif. Structural engr. Bechtel Inc., San Francisco, 1974-77; project mgr. Fisher Devel. Inc., San Francisco, 1977-80; mgr. projects Ecodyne Corp., Santa Rosa, Calif., 1980-81, dir. constrn., 1981-84; mgr. engring. and constrn. Custodis-Ecodyne Inc., Santa Rosa, 1984-86, mgr. devel., construction, 1986—. Bd. dirs. Jr. Achievement, Sonoma County, Calif., 1986, MESA, Sonoma County, 1986. Engr. scholar So. Meth. U., Dallas, 1969; Tex. pub. Works scholar, 1973; grad. fellow So. Meth. U., 1974. Mem. ASCE, Am. Concrete Inst., Nat. Asbestos Council, Sigma Tau, Tau Beta Pi, Chi Epsilon. Republican. Roman Catholic. Avocation: writing. Home: 1945 Knolls Dr Santa Rosa CA 95405 Office: Custodis-Ecodyne Inc PO Box 1267 Santa Rosa CA 95402

MIDDLEWOOD, MARTIN EUGENE, technical communications specialist, writer, consultant; b. Galesburg, Ill., Mar. 21, 1947; s. Martin and Bernetta Maxine (Henderson) M.; m. Mona Marie Jarmer, Sept. 10, 1971; children: Erin, Martha, Emily, Margaret. BA, Eastern Wash. U., 1973, MA, 1980. Writer tech. manuals Tektronix, Inc., Beaverton, Oreg., 1976-77, tech. writer, 1977-79, sr. tech. writer, 1979-82, supr. pub. relations, 1982-84; mgr. pub. relations Tektronix, Inc., Vacouver, Wash., 1984-85, mgr. mktg. communications, 1985-87; account exec. The Waggener Group, Portland, Oreg., 1987—; chmn. adv. bd. sci. and tech. writing, Clark Coll., Vancouver, 1984—; owner communications cons. firm, Vancouver, 1978—. Author: (ednl. brochure series) Oscilloscope Measurements, 1979 (award of excellence Willamette Valley chpt. Soc. Tech. Communication, 1980); contbr. articles to profl. jours. Served with USMC, 1967-70. Recipient Cert. Recognition Clark Coll., Vancouver, 1984, 86; award of Excellence Pacific N.W. chpt. Internat. Assn. Bus. Communicators, 1985. Mem. Soc. Tech. Communication (sr.; pres. Willamette Valley chpt. 1983-85, award of recognition 1986, chpt. pub. achievement award 1985, 2 awards of distinction 1981). Avocation: photography. Home: 113 W 37th St Vancouver WA 98660 Office: The Waggener Group 6915 SW Macadam Ave Suite 300 Portland OR 97219

MIDKIFF, ROBERT RICHARDS, banker; b. Honolulu, Sept. 24, 1920; s. Frank E. and Ruth (Richards) M.; m. Evanita Sumner, July 24, 1948; children: Mary L., Robin S., Shelley S., Robert Richards, David W. B.A., Yale U., 1942. Asst. sec. Hawaiian Trust Co., 1951-56, asst. v.p., 1956-57, v.p., 1957-65; dir. Am. Factors, Ltd., 1954-65; v.p. Amfac, Inc., 1965-68; exec. v.p., dir. Am. Security Bank, Honolulu, 1968-69, pres., dir., 1969-71; pres., dir. Am. Trust Co. Hawaii, Honolulu, 1971—; chmn. bd. Bishop Trust Co. Ltd., Honolulu, 1984—; bd. dirs. Persis Corp., Honolulu, Kuakini Found., Honolulu. Co-chmn. Gov.'s Archtl. Adv. Com. on State Capitol, 1960-65; co-chmn. Gov.'s Adv. Com. on Fine Arts for State Capitol, 1965-69; past chmn., bd. dirs. Hawaii Visitors Bur.; past pres., bd. dirs. Downtown Improvement Assn.; bd. dirs. Lahaina Restoration Found., Samuel N. and Mary Castle Found., Atherton Family Found., Friends of Iolani Palace, Honolulu, 1972-79; past chmn. Profit Sharing Research Found., Aloha United Way, Honolulu, 1982, Hawaii Visitors Bur., Honolulu, 1964-66. Served to 1st lt. AUS, 1943-46. Mem. Council on Founds., Employee Stock Ownership Plan Assn. Am. (bd. dirs.), Profit Sharing Council Am., Profit Sharing Research Found. (past. chmn.), Honolulu C. of C. (dir.), Phi Beta Kappa. Democrat. Episcopalian. Clubs: Pacific, Waialae Golf, Oahu Country (Honolulu). Office: Am Fin Services 841 Bishop St #1203 Honolulu HI 96813

MIEL, VICKY ANN, municipal government executive; b. South Bend, Ind., June 20, 1951; d. Lawrence Paul Miel and Virginia Ann (Yeagley) Hernandez. BS, Ariz. State U., 1985. Word processing coordinator City of Phoenix, 1977-78, word processing adminstr., 1978-83, chief dep. city clk., 1983—; assoc. prof. Phoenix Community Coll., 1982-83, Mesa (Ariz.) Community Coll., 1983; speaker in field, Boston, Santa Fe, Los Angeles, N.Y.C. and St. Paul, 1980—. Author: Phoenix Document Request Form, 1985, Developing Successful Systems Users, 1986. Judge Future Bus. Leaders Am. at Ariz. State U., Tempe, 1984; bd. dirs. Fire and Life Safety League, Phoenix, 1984. Recipient Gold Plaque, Work Processing Systems Mag., Mpls., 1980, Green Light Productivity award City of Phoenix, 1981, Honor Soc. Achievement award Internat. Word Processing Assn., Willow Grove, Pa., 1981. Mem. Assn. Info. Systems Profls. (internat. dir. 1982-84), Internat. Inst. Mcpl. Clks. (cert.), Am. Records Mgrs. Assn., Assn. Image Mgmt., Am. Soc. Pub. Adminstrs., Am. Mgmt. Assn. Lodge: Soroptimists. Office: City of Phoenix 251 W Washington Phoenix AZ 85003

MIELKE, CLARENCE HAROLD, JR., hematologist; b. Spokane, Wash., June 18, 1936; s. Clarence Harold and Marie Katherine (Gillespie) M.; B.S., Wash. State U., 1959; M.D., U. Louisville, 1963; m. Marcia Rae, July 5, 1964; children—Elisa, John, Tina. Intern, San Francisco Gen. Hosp., 1963-64; resident in medicine Portland VA Hosp., 1964-65, San Francisco Gen. Hosp., 1965-67; fellow in hematology U. So. Calif., 1967-68; teaching fellow, asst. physician, instr. Tufts-New Eng. Med. Center Hosps., Boston, 1968-71; sr. scientist, dir. hematology Inst. Med. Scis., San Francisco, 1971—; chief hematology Presbyn. Hosp., San Francisco, 1971—; asst. clin. prof. medicine U. Calif. Sch. Medicine, San Francisco, 1971-80, assoc. clin. prof., 1979—, dir. Inst. Cancer Research; trustee, bd. dirs. Med. Research Inst. San Francisco. NIH grantee, 1973—. Fellow ACP, Internat. Soc. Hematology, Am. Coll. Angiology; mem. Am. Soc. Internal Medicine, Internat. Soc. Thrombosis and Hemostasis, Am. Heart Assn., N.Y. Acad. Scis., AMA, San Francisco Med. Soc., Am. Thoracic Soc., AAAS, Internat. Soc. Angiology. Editor, Jour. Clin. Aphersis, 1981; contbr. chpts. to books, articles to med. jours. Office: Inst of Cancer Research 2200 Webster St San Francisco CA 94115

MIELKE, FREDERICK WILLIAM, JR., retired utility company executive; b. N.Y.C., Mar. 19, 1921; s. Frederick William and Cressida (Flynn) M.; m. Lorraine Roberts, 1947; children: Bruce Frederick, Neal Russell. A.B., U. Calif., 1943; J.D., Stanford U., 1949. Bar: Calif. 1950. Law clk. to Assoc. Justice John W. Shenk, Calif. Supreme Ct., 1949-51; with Pacific Gas and Electric Co., San Francisco, 1951-86; exec. v.p. Pacific Gas and Electric Co., 1976-79, chmn. bd., chief exec. officer, 1979-86, now bd. dirs.; bd. dirs. Pacific Gas Transmission Co., Amfac Inc., SRI Internat., Alta. Natural Gas Co. Ltd. Edison Electric Inst., 1979-82. Trustee Stanford U., 1977-87, Golden Gate U., 1977-79; mem. adv. council Stanford Grad. Sch. Bus.; bd. dirs. Calif. C. of C., 1979-85, San Francisco C. of C., 1977-79, Ind. Colls. No. Calif., 1969-79; pres. United Way of Bay Area, 1986—. Served with USN, 1943-46. Mem. ABA, Calif. Bar Assn., Pacific Coast Elec. Assn., Pacific Coast Gas Assn. Club: Electric of San Francisco. Office: Pacific Gas and Electric Co 245 Market St San Francisco CA 94106

MIES, WILLARD ESDOHR, newsletter editor; b. Chgo., Jan. 27, 1947; s. Willard G. and Grace A. (Esdohr) M.; m. Julia S. Harding, Oct. 6, 1979; 1 child, Virginia. BA, U. Ariz., 1969; MA, Stanford U., 1970. Reporter San Diego Union, 1970-71; assoc. editor Walker's Weekly Newsletter, San Francisco, 1971-74; exec. news editor Pulp & Paper mag., San Francisco, 1974—; editor Pulp & Paper Week newsletter, San Francisco, 1979—; editorial dir. Nonwoven's World Mag., 1987—. Author, editor numerous books and articles on paper industry. Mem. Stanford Alumni Assn., Soc. Profl. Journalists, Sigma Delta Chi. Avocations: running, gardening. Home: 6201 Contra Costa Ave Oakland CA 94618 Office: Miller Freeman Publs Inc 500 Howard St San Francisco CA 94618

MIGLIORE, LEONARD ROBERT, industrial laser technologist; b. N.Y.C., Oct. 16, 1944; s. Joseph and Josephine (D'Onofrio) M.; m. Susan Elise Yellin, Aug. 29, 1968. BSMetE, Columbia U., 1968. Project engr. Arwood Corp., Tilton, N.H., 1968-78, Precision Founders, San Leandro, Calif., 1978-79; application engr. Spectra-Physics, San Jose, Calif., 1979—; laser mktg. specialist Spectra-Physics, San Jose, 1985—. Mem. Am. Soc. Metals (exec. com. 1984—), Laser Inst. Am. Avocations: music, photography. Home: 3617 Louis Rd Palo Alto CA 94303 Office: Spectra-Physics 3333 N 1st St San Jose CA 95134

MIGUÉLEZ, G. ARMANDO, language professor; b. Santibáñez de la Isla, León, Spain, Dec. 25, 1951; s. Andrés and Erundina Martínez M.; m. Cynthia Sue Giambruno, July 10, 1976; children: Xana, Ariana, Armando. Diploma in Common Studies, Universidad de Salamanca, Spain, 1972; MA, Universidad Complutense, Madrid, 1975; PhD, Ariz. State U., 1981. Assoc. faculty Pima Community Coll., Tucson, 1976-78; asst. prof. U. Ariz., Tucson, 1980-86; vis. lectr. MIT, Cambridge, 1987. Co-author: Jauja: Método Integral de Español para Bilingues, 1986, De la Nueva España, A Aztlán:; contbr. articles on Chicano lit. in profl. jours.; cons., researcher, writer "Reflexiones" segment KUAT TV Tucson, 1982-87; corr. El Imparcial, Hermosillo, Mex. Organizer Encuentros Culturales Hispanos de Tucson, 1982-86; bd. dirs. Teatro Carmen, Tucson, 1980-87. Recipient Teatro Carmen award Teatro Carmen, 1984. Mem. MLA, Nat. Assn Chicano Studies. Avocations: books, writing poetry, travel. Office: MIT Fgn Languages Dept 14N-207 77 Massachusetts Ave Cambridge MA 02139

MIHAN, RICHARD, dermatologist; b. Los Angeles, Dec. 20, 1925; s. Arnold and Virginia Catharine (O'Reilly) M.; student U. So. Calif., 1945; M.D., St. Louis U., 1949. Rotating intern Los Angeles County Gen. Hosp., 1949-51, resident in dermatology, 1954-57; practice medicine specializing in dermatology, Los Angeles, 1957—; clin. prof. dept. medicine, dermatology and syphilology U. So. Calif. Served as lt. (j.g.) M.C., USNR, 1951-53, ret. as lt. comdr. Diplomate Am. Bd. Dermatology. Fellow ACP; mem. Internat. Soc. Tropical Dermatology, Soc. Investigative Dermatology, Pacific Dermatologic Assn. (exec. bd. 1971-74), Calif. Med. Assn. (chmn. dermatologic sect. 1973-74), AMA, Los Angeles Dermatol. Soc. (pres. 1975-76), Am. Acad. Dermatology. Office: 1245 Wilshire Blvd Los Angeles CA 90017

MIHOLITS, ERNEST MARTIN, consulting civil engineer; b. Evanston, Ill., Oct. 15, 1934; s. Frank Xavier and Mary (Kanz) M.; m. Joan Bartlett, Aug. 19, 1967. BSCE, Northwestern U., 1957, MSCE, 1961; PhDCE, U. Tex., 1966. Registered profl. engr., Calif., N.Y., Tex. Asst. prof. civil engring. San Jose (Calif.) State U., 1966-68, Rensselaer Poly. Inst., Troy, N.Y., 1968-70; sr. sanitary engr. Kaiser Engrs., Oakland, Calif., 1970-73; engring. mgr. Bechtel Nat., Inc., San Francisco, 1973-85; owner, pres. e(m)2 Engring. Cons., Foster City, Calif., 1985—; guest seminar speaker on nuclear and hazardous materials SDI, 1981—. Contbr. articles to profl. jours. Bd. dirs. Homeowners Assn., Foster City, 1982-84. Served with U.S. Army, 1958, comdr. USPHSR, 1964—. USPHS fellow, 1960-61, 63-66. Mem. ASCE, AAAS, Assn. Mil. Surgeons of U.S., Reserve Officers Assn. of U.S. (v.p., bd. dirs. 1983-85, pres. 1985-86, Meritorious Service award 1986), Am. Mgmt. Assn., Sigma Xi. Republican. Home and Office: PO Box 4265 Foster City CA 94404-0265

MIKALOW, ALFRED ALEXANDER, II, deep sea diver, marine surveyor; b. N.Y.C., Jan. 19, 1921; student Rutgers U., 1940; M.S., U. Calif.-Berkeley, 1948; M.A., Rochdale U. (Can.), 1950; m. Janice Brenner, Aug. 1, 1960; children—Alfred Alexander, Jon Alfred. Owner, Coastal Diving Co., Oakland, Calif., 1950—, Divers Supply, Oakland, 1952—; dir. Coastal Sch. Deep Sea Diving, Oakland, 1950—; capt. and master research vessel Coastal Researcher I; mem. Marine Inspection Bur., Oakland. marine diving contractor, cons. Mem. adv. bd. Medic Alert Found., Turlock, Calif., 1960—. Served with USN, 1941-47, 49-50. Decorated Purple Heart, Silver Star. Mem. Divers Assn. Am. (pres. 1970-74), Treasury Recovery Inc. (pres. 1972-75), Internat. Assn. Profl. Divers, Assn. Diving Contractors, Calif. Assn. Pvt. Edn. (no. v.p. 1971-72), Authors Guild, Internat. Game Fish Assn., U.S. Navy League, U.S. Res. Officers Assn., Tailhook Assn., Explorer Club (San Francisco). Clubs: Masons, Lions. Author: Fell's Guide to Sunken Treasure Ships of the World, 1972; (with H.Rieseberg) The Knight from Maine, 1974. Office: 320 29th Ave Oakland CA 94601

MIKEL, THOMAS KELLY, JR, laboratory administrator; b. East Chicago, Ind., Aug. 27, 1946; s. Thomas Kelly and Anne Katherine (Vrazo) M.; B.A., San Jose State U., 1973; M.A., U. Calif.-Santa Barbara, 1975. Asst. dir. Santa Barbara Underseas Found., 1975-76; marine biologist PJB Labs., Ventura, Calif., 1976-81; lab. dir. CRL Environ., Ventura, 1981—; instr. oceanography Ventura Coll., 1980-81. Served with U.S. Army, 1968-70. Mem. Assn. Environ. Profls., Soc. Population Ecologists, ASTME (research contbr. 10th ann. symposium 1986). Biol. coordinator Anacapa Underwater Natural trail U.S. Nat. Park Service, 1976; designer ecol. restoration program of upper Newport Bay, Orange County, Calif., 1978; research contbr. 3d Internat. Artificial Reef Conf., Newport Beach, Calif., 1983. Democrat.

MIKESH, DAVID LEONARD, geologist; b. Cresco, Iowa, Nov. 3, 1941; s. Leonard and Gladys (Springer) M.; B.A., U. Iowa, 1963, M.S., 1965, Ph.D., 1968. Research asso. U. Ga. Marine Inst., Sapelo Island, 1968-69; with Amoco Prodn. Co., Denver, 1970-74, Koch Exploration Co., Denver, 1974-75, TransOcean Oil, Denver, 1975-76, Webb Resources, Denver, 1976-77, Laguna Petroleum Co., Denver, 1977-80; exec. v.p. exploration and geology Mallon Oil Co., Denver., 1980—; asst. prof. geology U. Iowa, Iowa City, 1969. Mem. Am. Assn. Petroleum Geologists, Am. Inst. Profl. Geologists, Soc. Econ. Paleontologists and Mineralogists, Sigma Xi. Club: Mensa. Home: 7993 S Trenton St Englewood CO 80112 Office: 1090 18th St Suite 2750 Denver CO 80202

MIKHAIL, MARY ATTALLA, computer systems development executive; b. Cairo, Eqypt, Apr. 2, 1945; came to U.S., 1980.; d. Attalla Shehata and Soad (Kamel) Abd-El-Malek; m. Ibrahim Fahmy Mikhail, May 1 ,1967; 1 child, Ireny. BS in Math. and Physics, U. Assiut, Egypt, 1965; MS in Math. and Computer Sci., U. Clausthal, Fed. Republic Germany, 1973; PhD in Math., U. Tuebingen, Fed. Republic Germany, 1976. Lectr. Math. Inst., Assiut, Egypt, 1965-67; from instr. to asst. prof. Math. Inst., Tuebingen, Fed. Republic Germany, 1973-78; cons., project mgr. Datel, Fed. Republic Germany, 1978-80; planner, systems analyst C.F. Braun, Alhambra, Calif., 1980-82; optic dept. mgr. Burroughs Corp., City of Industry, Calif., 1982—. Contbr. articles to profl. jours. Mem. IEEE (standards for software error, faults and failures com., standards for quality metrics com.), Am. Mgmt. Assn. Mem. Coptic Orthodox Ch.

MIKLOVIC, DANIEL THOMAS, electrical engineering educator, marketing manager; b. St. Louis, Oct. 1, 1950; s. John Joseph and Ruby Irene (Cloyd) M.; m. Linda Lois Pinkley, July 12, 1975; 1 child, Aimee Linette. AS in Nuclear Tech., Air Force Community Coll., Randolph AFB, Tex., 1977; BSEE, U. Mo., 1979; MS in Systems Mgmt., U. So. Calif., 1986. Engr. Weyerhaeuser, Raymond, Wash., 1979-82, Scott Paper, Skowhegan, Maine, 1982-83; researcher Weyerhaeuser, Tacoma, 1983-86, mktg. mgr., 1986—. Chmn. Pierce Coll. Vocat. Adv. Com., Puyallup, Wash., 1985-86. Served as sgt. USAF, 1973-77. Mem. IEEE, Instrument Soc. Am., Soc. Mfg. Engrs., Tech. Assn. Pulp and Paper Industry, Tau Beta Pi, Eta Kappa Nu, Delta Tau Delta. Office: Weyerhaeuser Tech Ctr Dept Research and Devel 1E19 Tacoma WA 98477

MIKNIS, FRANCIS PAUL, chemist, researcher; b. DuBois, Pa., Jan. 31, 1940; s. Frank A. and Mary L. (Markievich) M.; m. Carolyn Marie Bennett, Aug. 27, 1960; children: Patricia, Gregory, Robert, Christine. BS, U. Wyo., 1961, PhD, 1967. Sr. scientist Aeronutronics, Newport Beach, Calif., 1966-67; research chemist Dept. Energy, Laramie, Wyo., 1967-83; sr. staff research scientist Western Research Inst., Laramie, 1983—. Editor: Geochemistry and Chemistry of Oil Shales, 1983. Mem. Geochemistry Div. of Am. Chem. Soc. (chmn. 1983), Sigma Xi. Democrat. Roman Catholic. Office: Western Research Inst Box 3395 Univ Station Laramie WY 82071

MIKULKA, BOHUSLAV EDUARD, battery separators company executive; b. Velka Bystrice, Czechoslovakia, Apr. 7, 1925; s. Bohuslav and Anna (Langer) M.; B.S., U. Tharandt, Eberswalde, Germany, 1942-44; postgrad. U. Brno, Czechoslovakia, 1945-48; M. Forest Engring., Hochschule fur Bodenkultur, Vienna, Austria, 1951; Ph.D., Swiss Fed. Inst. Tech., Zurich, 1955, Inst. Wood Tech., Munich and Braunschweig, Germany, 1955; m. Maja Doris Eimer, July 25, 1956; 1 dau., Ann Elizabeth. Came to U.S., 1955, naturalized, 1961. Research assoc. Swiss Fed. Inst. Tech., 1951-55; with Temple Industries, Inc., Diboll, Tex., 1956-65; with Evans Products Co., Evanite, Inc., 1965—, dir. research and devel., mgr., Doswell, Va., 1969-71, mgr. tech. and engring. center, Corvallis, Oreg., 1971-77, dir. tech., 1977-79, v.p., dir. tech., dir. licensing, 1979—. Mem. tech. com. Insulation Bd. Inst., 1959-60; pres. Student Assn. Brno, 1947-49, Czechoslovakia Student Assn., Zurich, 1951-55, U. Free Europe, Strasbourg, France, 1953-55. Mem. Forest Products Research Soc., Nat. Particleboard Assn. (tech. com. 1964-65), Am. Hardboard Assn. (tech. com. 1971—). Home: 2917 NW Angelica Corvallis OR 97330

MIKUNI, RONALD YOSHIAKI, chemist; b. Fresno, Calif., Aug. 10, 1949; s. John Shigeo and Amy Yemiko (Takeuchi) M.; m. Donna Eiko Aoki, Oct. 21, 1978; children: Aaron, Russell. BS, Fresno State U., 1972. Plant chemist Stauffer Chem. Co., Richmond, Calif., 1973-78; sr. research chemist Western Research Ctr., Richmond, 1979—. Mem. Japanese Am. Citizens League, Am. Chem. Soc., Young Buddhist Assn. (pres. Sanger, Calif. chpt. 1968-69), Phi Kappa Phi. Republican. Buddhist. Office: Stauffer Chem Co 1200 S 47th St Box 4023 Richmond CA 94804-0023

MILAM, KATHRYN MARIE, medical researcher; b. Seattle, Aug. 21, 1951; d. James Robert and Beverly Jean (Greenwood) M. BS, U. Wash., 1975; MS, PhD, U. Calif., Davis, 1978, 1981. Postdoctoral fellow dept. toxicology U. Calif., Davis, 1981-82; postdoctoral fellow dept. radiobiology U. Calif., San Francisco, 1982-84, asst. researcher Brain Tumor Research Ctr., 1984—. Contbr. articles to profl. jours. Grantee NSF, 1975-78. Mem. AAAS, Genetic and Environ. Toxicology Assn. Republican. Avocation: pianist. Office: U Calif Brain Tumor Research Ctr San Francisco CA 94143

MILAM, WILLIAM JEROME, mech. engr.; b. St. Paul, Jan. 16, 1924; s. James Perkins and Evelyn Verleen (McQue) M.; B.S. in Mech. Engring., U. Minn., 1948; m. Violet Gouras, Jan. 5, 1946; children—Suzanne, Billie. Mech. engr. Ellerbe & Assos., St. Paul, 1948-53, Welton Becket & Assos., Los Angeles, 1953-62, Rocketdyne div. N. Am. Aviation Co., 1962-67; chief mech. engr. Hughes Tool Co., Culver City, Calif., 1967-73; sr. plant engr. ITT Gilfillan Co., Van Nuys, Calif., 1973-78, Litton Systems Inc., Woodland Hills, Calif., 1978-79; sr. mech. engr. Lockheed Corp., Burbank, Calif., 1979—; cons. in field. Served with USAAF, 1942-44; ETO. Decorated Silver Star, Purple Heart, Air medal; recipient engring. merit award San Fernando Valley Engrs. Council, 1983. Mem. Am. Inst. Plant Engrs., DAV. Contbr. articles to profl. publs. Address: 8350 Hillview Ave Canoga Park CA 91304

MILANI, CYRUS SAEED, pathologist, administrator, clinician; b. Mashad, Iran, May 14, 1941; came to U.S., 1968, naturalized, 1980; s. Boyouk and Habibeh (Sadaghiani) Sadeghi; m. Afsaneh Khavas, Aug. 25, 1966; children—Natalie B., Natasha B. M.D., Pahlavi U., Shiraz, Iran, 1966. Diplomate Am. Bd. Pathology, Am. Bd. Anatomic Pathology, Am. Bd. Clin. Pathology. Intern, Ellis Hosp., Schenectady, 1968-69; resident Hosp. U. Pa., 1969-72, chief resident, 1972-73; Pathologist Assoc. Hosp. U. Pa., Phila., 1973-74, Cantonal Univ Hosp., Lausanne, Switzerland, 1974-75; asst. prof. Teheran U., Iran, 1975-77; dir. Central Diagnostic Lab., Tarzana, Calif., 1977—, Preventive Clinic Am., Woodland Hills, Calif., 1981—; dir. Valley Cryobank div. Tissue Preservation Inst., Woodland Hills, 1981-87; vol. physician Olympic Games, 1984. Bd. dirs. French Am. Sch., Van Nuys, Calif., 1979—, Am. Cancer Soc., Van Nuys, 1981-82, Am. Heart Assn., Studio City, Calif., 1982. Mem. Am. Assn. Immunologists, Coll. Am. Pathologists, Am. Soc. Clin. Pathologists, AAAS.

MILANOVICH, NORMA JOANNE, occupational educator; b. Littlefork, Minn., June 4, 1945; d. Lyle Albert and Loretta (Leona) Drake; m. Rudolph William Milanovich, Mar. 18, 1943; 1 child, Rudolph William Jr. BS in Home Econs., U. Wis., Stout, 1968; MA in Curriculum and Instrn., U. Houston, 1973, EdD in Curriculum and Program Devel., 1982. Instr. human services U. Houston, 1971-75; dir. videos project U. N.Mex., Albuquerque, 1976-78, dir. vocat. edn. equity ctr., 1978-84, asst. prof. tech. occupational edn., 1982—, coordinator occupational vocat. edn. programs, 1983-85, dir. consortium research and devel. in occupational edn., 1984—. Author: Handbook for Vocational-Technical Certification in New Mexico, 1985, Model Equitable Behavior in the Classroom, 1983, Frustration Is...; editor: A Handbook for Handling Conflict in the Classroom, 1983, Choosing What's Best for You, 1982. Bd. dirs. Albuquerque Single Parent Occupational Scholarship Program, 1984-86; del. Youth for Understanding Internat. Program, 1985-87; tour dir. Interatn. Studies Tours Abroad to Japan, Australia, Eng., Korea, Mex., and Germany, 1984-86; mem. adv. bd. Southwestern Indian Poly. Inst., 1984-86; com. mem. Region VI Consumer Exchange Com., 1982-84. Grantee N.Mex. Dept. Edn., 1976-78, 78-86, 83-86, HEW. Mem. Nat. Assn. Female Execs., Am. Vocat. Assn., Vocat. Edn. Equity Council, Nat. Coalition for Sex Equity Edn., Am. Home Econs. Assn., N.Mex. Home Econs. Assn., Phi Delta Kappa, Phi Upsilon Omicron, Phi Theta Kappa. Democrat. Roman Catholic.

MILAVSKY, HAROLD PHILLIP, real estate executive; b. Limerick, Sask., Can., Jan. 25, 1931; s. Jack and Clara Milavsky. B in Commerce, U. Sask., Saskatoon, Can., 1953. Chief acct., treas., controller Loram Internat. Ltd. div. Mannix Co. Ltd., Calgary, Alta., Can., 1956-65; v.p., chief fin. officer Power Corp. Devels. Ltd., Calgary, Alta., Can., 1965-60; exec. v.p., bd. dirs. Great West Internat. Equities Ltd. (now Trizec Corp. Ltd.), Calgary, Alta., Can., 1969-76; former pres., now chmn., chief exec. officer, bd. dirs. Trizec Corp. Ltd., Calgary, Alta., Can., 1976—; bd. dirs. Trizec Corp. related cos., Brascan Ltd., Toronto, Can., Carena-Bancorp Inc., Toronto, The Rouse Co., Columbia, Md., Revelstoke Cos. Ltd., Calgary, London Life Ins. Co., Bramlea Ltd., Toronto, Dome Petroleum Ltd., Calgary. Dir. Terry Fox Humanitarian Award Program, Conf. Bd. Can.; gov., Acctg. Edn. Found. Alta.; mem. Bd. Govs. and Chancellor's Club, U. Calgary. Fellow Inst. Chartered Accts. Alta.; mem. Inst. Chartered Accts. Sask., Can. Inst. Pub. Real Estate Cos. (past pres., bd. dirs.), Can. C. of C. (past chmn.). Clubs: Petroleum, Ranchmen's, Glenmore Racquet (Calgary). Avocations: skiing, tennis. Office: Trizec Corp Ltd, 700 2d St SW #3000, Calgary, AB Canada T2P 2W2 *

MILAZZO, DAVID YOUNG, architect, interior designer; b. Bakersfield, Calif., Feb. 27, 1945; s. Anthony Alfred and Reeba Allen (Young) M.; m. Linda Lynn Gold, Aug. 21, 1968; 1 child, David Anthony. AA, Bakersfield Coll., 1970; BArch, Calif. Poly. State U., San Luis Obispo, 1974. Registered architect, Calif., N.Mex. Draftsman, designer Fisher and Wilde Architects, Ventura, Calif., 1974-75, Ken Sorensen Architect, Bakersfield, 1975-76; prin. designer Clemment/Milazzo and Assocs., Bakersfield, 1976-83; prin. Milazzo and Assocs., Bakersfield, 1983—. Positions held with the City of Bakersfield include bd. dirs. design rev. bd., 1982—, cons. zoning adv. com., 1981-82; city planning commr., 1982—; bd. dirs., chmn. bldg. com. Bakersfield Art Found., 1986—. Served as staff agt. USAF, 1965-69, Vietnam. Recipient Most Attractive Comml. Bldg. award Bakersfield C. of C., 1982, 83, 84, 85, Hon. Mention Comml. Office Category, Bakersfield C. of C., 1982, Most Attractive Comml. Landscaping award Bakersfield C. of C., 1983. Mem. AIA (Design of Excellence award Golden Empire chpt. 1981, Award of Merit, Golden Empire chpt. 1984, Citation award Golden Empire chpt. 1984), Kern County Execs. Assn. (bd. dirs. 1984-85), Italian Heritage Dante Assn. (bd. dirs. 1980—). Republican. Home: 2525 22d St Bakersfield CA 93301 Office: Milazzo and Assocs Architects AIA 3300 Truxtun Ave Suite 300 Bakersfield CA 93301

MILBY, THOMAS HUTCHINSON, physician, consultant, researcher, educator; b. South Bend, Ind., Feb. 7, 1931; s. Terry Hutchinson and Evelyn Luciel (Hecht) M.; m. Marilyn Monarch, June 1, 1953 (div. 1973); m. Rachel Natera, May 19, 1973; children—David, Steven, Nancy, Dalia. B.S., Purdue U., 1953, M.D., U. Cin., 1957, M.S., 1965; M.P.H., U. Calif-Berkeley, 1966. Diplomate Am. Bd. Preventive Medicine. Chief Bur. Occupational and Environ. Health, Dept. Health, State of Calif., Berkeley, 1962-75; sr. med. scientist SRI Internat., Menlo Park, Calif., 1975-77; med. cons. occupational and environ. medicine, Berkeley, 1977—; adj. assoc. prof. occupational medicine U. Calif.-Berkeley. Served to lt. comdr. USPHS, 1959-62. Fellow Am. Acad. Occupational Medicine, Am. Coll. Epidemiology; mem. N.Y. Acad. Sci. Contbr. articles to profl. jours. Home: One Aspen Ct Lafayette CA 94549 Office: 3687 Mt Diablo Blvd Suite 320 Lafayette CA 94549

MILDENHALL, JOSEPH NELSON, software company executive; b. Salt Lake City, May 14, 1953; s. Glen T. and D. Rae (Nelson) M.; m. Mary Alice Ord, Apr. 9, 1976; children: Thomas Ord, Kelly Jane, Brooke Anne. BS in Acctg., Brigham Young U., 1979. Programmer analyst J&K Computer Systems Inc., Salt Lake City, 1979-82, mgr. system 38 devel., 1982-85, v.p. systems, 1985—. Co-author software. Mormon. Club: Cougar Athletic. Avocations: skiing, racquetball. Office: J&K Computer Systems Inc 5505 S 900 E #300 Salt Lake City UT 84117

MILDON, JAMES LEE, author, photojournalist; b. San Francisco, Jan. 5, 1936; s. James Lee and Jeannette Marie (Balandras) M.; B.A. cum laude, Calif. State U. at San Francisco, 1963; M.A., U. Nev. at Reno, 1970; m. Marie Roberta Wilson, Sept. 17, 1958; children—Laura Marie Jeannette. Owner Jim Mildon: Images, Ink, Reno, 1969—; v.p. Frank & Mildon, Assos., Reno, 1971—; mgmt. cons. Western Electric Co., 1972; devel. cons. Vacation Plan Ltd., 1971—; instr. photojournalism U. Nev., 1974-83. Served with Army Security Agy., AUS, 1959-60. Mem. Profl. Photographers Assn. Am., Nat. Profl. Photographers Assn., Phi Kappa Phi, Alpha Kappa Nu, Beta Phi Gamma. Author: (with others) Portland, The City Across the River, 1972. Pub., editor, co-author: My World to Share, 1982. Illustrator: Newswriting: From Lead to 30, 1977. Address: 9135 Spearhead Way Reno NV 89506

MILES, GEORGE THOMAS, engineering educator; b. Gillingham, Kent, Eng., Mar. 29, 1925; came to U.S., 1953; s. George J. and Rosina M. (Roper) M.; divorced; children: Glenn Tracey, Kathryn Yvonne, Ronald George. BS, U. London, 1947; AA, Mt. San Antonio Coll., 1965. Cert. community coll. tchr., Calif. Design analyst Jet Propulsion Lab., Pasadena, Calif., 1960-62; chief standards engr. Aerojet-Gen., Azusa, Calif., 1963-68; sr. engr. Westinghouse, Sunnyvale, Calif., 1969-72; configuration mgr. TRW, Hawthorne, Calif., 1973-79; mgr. engring. services BASF, Fountain Valley, Calif., 1980-83; tchr. CEDU Sch., Running Springs, Calif., 1984—; tchr. El Camino Coll., Torrance, Calif., 1975—, Cerritos (Calif.) Coll., 1980-83; counselor/tchr. Coop. Career Edn., Torrance, 1982; rep. Nat. Aerospace Standards Com. and E20 Com. Soc. Automotive Engrs., 1963, 68. Editor LASER, 1964. Bd. dirs. Hawthorne C. of C., 1978; mem. Coll. Adv. Coms., Torrance, 1982—. Served with ednl. corps English Army, 1947-49. Recipient Founding Mem. award Vocat. Indsl. Clubs Am., 1975, Cert. Appreciation, Calif. Indsl. Edn. Assn., 1978. Mem. Standards Engrs. Soc. (publicity chmn. 1964), U.S. Metric Assn. (Cert. Appreciation, 1964). Republican. Episcopalian. Avocations: sailing, oil painting. Home: 1349 W 135th St #12 Gardena CA 90247 Office: El Camino Coll 16007 Crenshaw Blvd Torrance CA 90506

MILES, JACKIE DWAIN, electrician, building contractor; b. Soper, Okla., Feb. 16, 1932; s. Audley Odell and Ruby Loraine (LaRue) M.; m. Wilma June Holcomb, Dec. 30, 1952; children: Cynthia Deanne Miles Thompson, Stanley Kevin. Student Solano Coll., 1956-58; A.A., Sacramento State U., 1961. Supr. U.S. Civil Service, Fairfield, Calif., 1956-65; ptnr., dir., contractor B & M Electric, Suisun, Calif., 1965-71; owner, contractor All-Cal Electric, Suisun, 1971—; v.p., dir. developer, builder Casa Grande Homes, Fairfield, 1973—; ptnr., cons., contractor Tri-Co. Electric, Suisun; ptnr., cons., builder Mariah Builders, Fairfield, 1982—; ptnr., cons. Audie Electric Contractors, Fairfield, 1983—, Energy Seal Window Mfrs., Fairfield, 1985—, The Lighting Warehouse, Fairfield, 1985—. Inventor electromech. valve, 1963 (cert. 1964). Served with USAF, 1952-56. Mem. Napa/Solan Builders Exchange. Republican. Club: Exchange (Suisun). Lodges: Elks, Moose. Home: 4319 Green Valley Rd Suisun CA 94585 Office: All-Cal Electric 209 Main St Suisun CA 94585

MILES, LAWRENCE EDWARD, naval officer; b. Salina, Kans., July 8, 1955; s. Lewis George and Phyllis Roberta (Blank) M. BA, Lewis and Clark Coll., 1977; MA, U. Kans., 1982. Tchr. elem. schs. Olathe, Kans., 1980-81; chemist Hercules Inc., DeSoto, Kans., 1981-82; commd. ensign USN, 1982, advanced through grades to lt., 1985; substance abuse counselor USN, Guam, 1984-85. Mem. Am. Chem. Soc., U.S. Naval Inst. Republican. Mem. Ch. of Christ. Avocations: photography, sailing, marksmanship, deep sea fishing. Home: 2521 N Brynwood Santa Ana CA 92701 Office: USS Kirk (FF 1087) FPO San Francisco CA 96670

MILES, MAURICE JARVIS, chemist, consultant; b. St. George, Utah, Nov. 24, 1907; s. George Edmond and Josephine (Victoria) Jarvis; m. Mary Lyon; children: Mary, Howard, Daniel, Helen, Robert, Douglas, Carol, William, John, Clark. AB, Brigham Young U., 1930; MA, U. Utah, 1933; postgrad., U. Calif., Berkeley, 1935, U. Ill., 1939, U. Chgo., 1945. Dir. phys. sci. Dixie Coll., St. George, Utah, 1933-53; chief chemist Timet, Henderson, Nev., 1953-70, cons., 1980-86; research chemist U. Nev., Boulder City, 1976-80; pres. Miles Assocs., Inc., Henderson, 1980—. Contbr. articles on analytical chemistry to profl. jours. Mem. City Council St. George (Utah) City Corp., 1947-52. Mem. AAAS, Am. Chem. Soc. Home: 135 Elm St Henderson NV 89015 Office: Miles Assocs Inc Henderson NV 89015

MILES, MELVIN HENRY, research chemist; b. St. George, Utah, Jan. 18, 1937; s. Maurice Jarvis and Mary (Lyon) M.; m. V. Joyce Miles, July 22, 1962; children: David Lyon, Jolene Carol, Melinda Marie, Samuel Jarvis. Student, Dixie Coll., 1955-57; BA, Brigham Young U., 1962; PhD, U. Utah, 1966. Research chemist Naval Ordnance Lab., Corona, Calif., 1967-69; assoc. prof. chemistry Middle Tenn. State U., Murfreesboro, 1969-78; research chemist Naval Weapons Ctr., China Lake, Calif., 1978—; vis. scientist Brookhaven Nat. Lab., N.Y., summers, 1974, 75. Contbr. numerous articles to profl. jours.; patentee in field. Recipient Outstanding Performance award Naval Weapons Ctr., 1979, 84, 86; NATO fellow Tech. U., Munich, 1965-66. Mem. Am. Chem. Soc., Electrochem. Soc., Sigma Xi (Best Sci. Paper of Yr. award 1985). Republican. Mormon. Avocations: sports, gardening, hiking. Home: 807 Mamie Ave Ridgecrest CA 93555 Office: Naval Weapons Ctr Code 3852 China Lake CA 93555

MILES, OWEN PHILIPS, JR., consulting geologist; b. Freeport, Ill., June 15, 1928; s. Owen Philips and Helen (Minard) M.; m. Madelyn Larsen, Sept. 2, 1951; children—Lisa, Aimie. B.S., Beloit Coll., 1950; postgrad. U. Colo.-Boulder, 1950-51. Jr. geologist Magnolia Petroleum Co., Oklahoma City, 1950, Mobil Producing Co., Big Piney and Basin Wyo., 1951-53; instr. U.S. U.S. Army Petroleum Product Analysis Sch., Ft. Lee, Va., 1953-55; sr. geologist Mobil Oil Co., Casper, Wyo., 1955-64; self-employed cons. geologist, Casper, 1964—. Author: (guidebook) Kummerfeld Field, 1963; coauthor Bur. Mines report. Mem. Am. Assn. Petroleum Geologists, Am. Inst. Profl. Geologists (pres. Wyo. sect. 1965-67), Wyo. Geol. Assn., Casper Petroleum Club. Republican. Home: 3803 Alpine Dr Casper WY 82601 Office: PO Box 1786 Casper WY 82602

MILES, PAUL JAMES, advertising agency executive; b. Bklyn., Aug. 27, 1949; s. John Wallace and Catherine Rita (Martin) M.; m. Kathleen Margot Ward, June 2, 1984. AA, Kennesaw Coll., 1972; BBA, W. Ga. Coll., 1974. Account exec. Atlanta Jour. Constitution, 1974-77, WGST AM Radio, Atlanta, 1977-78; western regional mgr. Sawyer Ferguson Walker, San Francisco, 1978-81; acct. exec. KMPX FM Radio, San Francisco, 1981-83; advt. dir. IABC Communication World, San Francisco, 1983—; pub. relations dir. Atlanta Jaycees, 1974-75, NOVA Artists Assn., San Francisco, 1982-85; creative dir. The Jester, San Francisco, 1981—. Mem. Homestead Valley Civic Authority, Mill Valley, Calif., 1985—. Mem. Advt. Golf Assn. of No. Calif., U.S. Golf Assn. Republican. Roman Catholic. Avocations: golf, scuba diving, camping, writing, bicycling. Home: 210 Melrose Ave Mill Valley CA 94941 Office: IABC Communication World Mag 870 Market St San Francisco CA 94102

MILES, RALPH EARL, sr. statistician, systems research executive; b. San Antonio, Oct. 4, 1949; s. John and Bernice (Mapp) M.; BA, Calif. State U., Los Angeles, 1972; MPH, UCLA, 1976; postgrad. in research methods U. San Francisco; m. Theresa Paul Williams, Apr. 4, 1970; children: Tracy, Ahbani, Ralph Earl, Sabriya, Halima. Statistician dept. community medicine Drew Med. Sch., Los Angeles, 1973-75, systems mgr. dept. SIMS, 1985—; statistician programmer Fanon Research and Devel. Ctr., Los Angeles, 1975-77, sr. statistician dept. psychiatry, 1977—, corp. dir. research and data analysis, 1977—; cons., lectr. in field. Mem. Health Sci. Minority Com., Chancelor UCLA, 1973, 74; bd. dirs. Southside YMCA. Mem. Am. Statis. Assn., Math. Assn. Am., Am. Pub. Health Assn. Democrat. Roman Catholic. Researcher pineal gland calcification, cycle phenomena, social factor in stress; also articles. Home: 827 Virginia Blvd San Antonio TX 73203 Office: Scientific Info Mgmt Systems Office of Research 1720 E 120th St Los Angeles CA 90059

MILES, SAMUEL ISRAEL, psychiatrist; b. Munich, Mar. 4, 1949; came to U.S., 1949; s. Henry and Renee (Ringel) M.; m. Denise Marie Robey, June 26, 1977; children: Jonathan David, Justin Alexander. BS, CCNY, 1970; MD, N.Y. Med. Coll., 1974; PhD, So. Calif. Psychoanalytic Inst., 1986. Diplomate Am. Bd. Psychiatry and Neurology. Intern D.C. Gen. Hosp., Washington, 1974-75; resident in psychiatry Cedars-Sinai Med. Ctr., Los Angeles, 1975-78; practice medicine specializing in psychiatry Los Angeles, 1978—; ind. med. examiner Calif. Dept. Indsl. Relations, 1984—; asst. clin. prof. psychiatry UCLA Sch. Medicine, 1978—; attending psychiatrist Cedars-Sinai Med. Ctr., 1978—, co-chmn. utilization rev. and quality assurance commn., 1984—, mem. input adv. com., 1983-85, psychiatry adv. com., 1984—; attending psychiatrist Brotman Med. Ctr., Culver City, Calif., 1978—; faculty mem. So. Calif. Psychoanalytic Inst., 1986—. Fellow Am. Acad. Psychoanalysis, Am. Orthopsychiat. Assn.; mem. Acad. Psychiatry and the Law, So. Calif. Psychiat. Soc. (council rep. 1985—), So. Calif. Soc. Adolescent Psychiatry (treas. 1980-81), So. Calif. Psychoanalytic Inst. (pres. clin. assocs. orgn. 1981-82). Jewish. Avocations: flying, swimming. Office: 8631 W Third St #425E Los Angeles CA 90048

MILFORD, HOMER ERNEST, biology educator; b. Eau Clair, Wis., June 16, 1938; s. Homer Carter and Winifred J. (Remington) M.; m. Vivian Nora Grelick, June 6, 1961 (div. Jan. 1977); children: Elizabeth, David; m. Deborah Ann Garvey, May 15, 1978. BS, U. N.Mex., 1961; MS, U. Idaho, 1963; postgrad., SUNY, Bklyn., 1963-65. Asst. prof. U. Albuquerque, 1967-73, assoc. prof., 1973, 1973—, chmn. biology dept., 1978-81, chmn. sci. dept., 1985—; mem. adv. bd. Rio Grande Nature Ctr., Albuquerque, 1983—; cons. Comprehensive Plan, Bernalillo County, N.Mex., 1973. Bd. dirs. N.Mex. chpt. of Nature Conservancy, Albuquerque, 1975-83; pres. Open Space task force, Albuquerque, 1985; mem. Dem. Cent. Com. Bernalillo County, 1982—. Grantee NSF, 1973, fellowship, 1963; grantee USPHS, 1970, fellowship, 1964. Fellow N.Mex. Acad. Sci; mem. N.Mex. Zool. Soc. (bd. dirs. 1972—), N.Mex. Natural History Inst. (bd. dirs. 1979—), Ecol. Soc. Am., Am. Land Resource Assn., Bosque del Rio Grande Nature Preserve Soc., Phi Sigma, Sigma Xi. Home: 2828 Candelaria NW Albuquerque NM 87107 Office: U Albuquerque St Joseph Pl NW Albuquerque NM 87140

MILHOUS, PAUL B., newspaper printing company executive; b. 1938; married. Owner Milhous Auto Sales, 1960-65; with B&B Advt. Co., Stanton, Calif., 1965-67; now pres. Treasure Chest Advt. Co., Glendora, Calif., also bd. dirs. Office: Treasure Chest Advt Co Inc 511 W Citrus Edge Glendora CA 91740 *

MILHOUS, ROBERT E., advertising executive; b. 1937; married. BS, Purdue U., 1960. Advt. salesman Gen. Telephone Co., Calif., 1960-63; with B&B Advt. Co., Stanton, Calif., 1963-68; now chmn. bd. dirs., chief exec. officer Treasure Chest Advt. Co., Glendora, Calif., also bd. dirs. Served U.S. Army, 1958-60. Office: Treasure Chest Advt Co Inc 511 W Citrus Edge Glendora CA 91740 *

MILLARD, BARBARA JEANNE, business executive; b. Oakland, Calif., Jan. 8, 1958; d. William H. and Patricia (Nolder) M. Dir. IMS Assocs. Inc., from 1979, v.p. fin., 1982-83, pres., 1983, from 1985, chmn., from 1986; div. pres. ComputerLand Corp., Hayward, Calif., 1983-84, pres., chief operating officer, 1984-85. Bd. dirs. Millard Family Found. Club: Lakeview. Office: PO Box 75CHRB Saipan CM 96950

MILLARD, GEORGE RICHARD, bishop; b. Dunsmuir, Calif., Oct. 2, 1914; s. George Ellis and Constance (Rainsberry) M.; m. Mary Louise Gessling, June 29, 1939; children: George, Martha, Joseph. A.B., U. Calif.-Berkeley, 1936; B.D., Episcopal Theol. Sch., Cambridge, Mass., 1938; S.T.M., Pacific Sch. Religion, 1958; D.D., Ch. Div. Sch. Pacific, 1960; M.A., U. Santa Clara, 1983. Ordained priest Episc. Ch., 1938; asst. in N.Y.C., 1938-39, Waterbury, Conn., 1930-40; rector in Danbury, Conn., 1940-50, Alameda, Calif., 1951-59; suffragan bishop Episc. Diocese Calif., 1960-76; bishop of San Jose, 1969-76; exec., venture in mission program, exec. council Episc. Ch., 1977-78; bishop in charge Am. Chs. in Europe, 1978-80, bishop in charge ch. divinity sch. pacific exec. office for alumni/ae affairs, 1978-80; dean Convocation of Oakland, Calif., 1957-60; chmn. dept. missions Diocese Calif., 1958-60; mem. Joint Commn. on Structure, Episc. Ch., 1967-76; pres. bd. Strong Environ. Center. Mem. pres.'s council San Jose State Coll.; chmn. Maria Kip Orphange; chmn. devel. program U. Calif. at Berkeley Student Coop. Assn., 1966; coordinator Ch. Div. Sch. Pacific Alumni Affairs.

MILLARD, KENNETH REIMANN, city planning consultant, architect; b. Salt Lake City, May 26, 1930; s. Vern Bryan and Laura Aurelia (Reimann) M.; m. Patricia Jordan Walton, Nov. 25, 1958 (div. Feb. 1977); children: Kenneth R. Jr., Vern Dyke, John Walton, Patricia Jacqueline, Jennifer Michelle; m. Carolyn Lee Sorensen, Dec. 29, 1977; children: Noel Yvette, Lee Sorensen. BFA, U. Utah, 1954, BArch., 1958; student, U. Wash., 1954-55; M in Regional Planning, Cornell U., 1960. Registered architect, Utah. Dir. planning and engring. Provo (Utah) Mcpl. Corp., 1960-61; dir. planning S.W. Snohomish County (Wash.) Joint Planning Council, 1962; sr. planner Williams & Mocine, San Francisco, 1963-64; constrn. supr. Mormon Ch., France and Belgium, 1964-66; resident architect Nauvoo (Ill.) Restoration, 1966-67; pres. cons. Millard Cons., Salt Lake City, 1967—; adj. prof. Brigham Young U., Provo, 1968-78. Author/editor Master Plans for numerous municipalities., counties, and Great Salt Lake, 1960—, Land Development Code for Utah Counties and Municipalities, 1973—. City councilman N. Salt Lake City Corp., 1984—. Served with U.S. Army, 1956-57. Mem. AIA, Am. Inst. Cert. Planners. Republican. Mormon. Club: Utah-Bolivia Ptnrs. (pres.-elect). Lodge: Rotary (2d v.p. Salt Lake City club 1983-84, 85-86). Avocation: photography. Home: 745 Independence Way North Salt Lake UT 84054 Office: Millard Cons 2200 S 9th East St Salt Lake City UT 84106-1836

MILLARD, LAVERGNE HARRIET, freelance artist; b. Chgo., July 8, 1925; d. Lewis and Julia (Smolk) Bassmire; student Chgo. Art Inst., 1937-39; m. Samuel Costales, 1943 (div. 1957); m. Bailey Millard, Mar. 9, 1958 (div.); children—Bryan Lewis Costales, Julianne, Juanita Crump, Candace Lynn Millard. Cocktail waitress Verdis, Grant Street, Concord, Calif., 1955-61; mgr. used book shop Joyce Book Shop, Concord, 1964-79, seller art works, own prints; freelance artist, 1979—. Recipient ribbons local fairs, art shows. Republican. Copyright holder for pastel art work. Home and Office: 1890 Farm Bureau Rd Apt 11 Concord CA 94519

MILLARD, NEAL STEVEN, lawyer; b. Dallas, June 6, 1947; s. Bernard and Adele (Marks) M.; m. Holly Ann Hinman, Dec. 30, 1970. BA cum laude, UCLA, 1969; JD, U. Chgo., 1972. Bar: Calif. 1972, U.S. Dist. Ct. (cen. dist.) Calif. 1973, U.S. Tax Ct. 1973, U.S. Ct. Appeals (9th cir.) 1987. Assoc. Willis, Butler & Schiefly, Los Angeles, 1972-75; ptnr. Morrison & Foerster, Los Angeles, 1975-84, Jones, Day, Reavis & Pogue, Los Angeles, 1984—; instr. Calif. State Coll., San Bernardino, 1975-76; lectr. Practising Law Inst., N.Y.C., 1983—. Mem. citizens adv. com. Los Angeles Olympics, 1982-84; trustee Altadena (Calif.) Library Dist., 1985—; bd. dirs. Woodcraft Rangers, Los Angeles, 1982—. Served to capt. U.S. Army, 1970-72. Mem. ABA, Calif. Bar Assn., Los Angeles County Bar Assn. (trustee 1985—), Pub. Counsel (bd. dirs. 1984—), U. Chgo. Law Alumni Assn. (So. Calif. chpt. bd. dirs. 1981—), Phi Beta Kappa, Pi Gamma Mu, Phi Delta Phi. Clubs: Los Angeles Athletic; Altadena Town and County. Office: Jones Day Reavis & Pogue 355 S Grand Ave Los Angeles CA 90071

MILLER, ANNE KATHLEEN, manufacturing equipment company executive; b. Denver, Sept. 15, 1942; d. John Henry and Kathryn Elizabeth (Doherty) Meyer; m. Edgar Earle Miller, Aug. 20, 1966 (div. Aug. 1976); children: Sheila Anne, Rebecca Elizabeth; m. Warren Ross Landry, Dec. 11, 1982. BS in Chemistry, St. Mary Coll., Leavenworth, Kans., 1964. Cert. jr. coll., secondary tchr., Calif. Lectr. San Jose (Calif.) U., 1978-82; product mgr. Jasco Chem., Mountain View, Calif., 1979-82; v.p., gen. mgr. Micropel, Hayward, Calif., 1982-84; product mgr. Cambridge Instruments, Santa Clara, Calif., 1984-86; product mktg. mgr. KLA Instruments, Santa Clara, 1986—; v.p., cons. engr. Meyland Enterprises, Redwood City, Calif. 1982—. Inventor formation of optical film. Mem. Soc. Photo Optical Instrumentation Engrs., Am. Chem. Soc., Semiconductor Industry Equipment Materials Inst. Office: KLA Instruments Corp 3530 Bassett St Santa Clara CA 95054

MILLER, ARNOLD, electronics executive; b. N.Y.C., May 8, 1928; s. Sam and Mina (Krutalow) M.; m. Beverly Shayne, Feb. 5, 1950; children—Debra Lynn, Marla Jo, Linda Sue. B.S. in Chemistry, UCLA, 1948, Ph.D. in Phys. Chemistry, 1951. Registered profl. engr., Calif. Research phys. chemist Wrigley Research Co., Chgo., 1951; supr. phys. chemistry Armour Research Found., Chgo., 1951-54, mgr. chemistry and metals, 1954-56; chief materials sci. dept. Borg-Warner Research Ctr., Des Plaines, Ill., 1956-59; dir. research Rockwell Corp., Anaheim, Calif., 1959-66, dir. microelec. ops., 1967-68; group exec. materials ops. Whittaker Corp., Los Angeles, 1968-70; pres. Theta Sensors, Orange, Calif., 1970-72; mgr. xeroradiography Xerox Corp., Pasadena, Calif., 1972-75; corp. dir. research and adv. devel. Xerox Corp., Stamford, Conn., 1975-78; corp. dir. research and adv. devel. Xerox Corp., El Segundo, Calif., 1978-81, v.p. electronics div., 1981-84, pres. electronics div., 1984-87; corp. officer Xerox Corp., Stamford, 1984-87; pres. Tech. Strategy Group, Fullerton, Calif., 1987—; dir. Spectro Diode Labs, San Jose, Calif.; mem. vis. com. on materials sci. U. So. Calif., Los Angeles, 1966-68; bd. dirs. Semicondr. Research Corp.; mem. U. Calif. Micro Bd., 1984—. Editorial adv. bd. Advances in Solid State Chemistry; contbr. numerous articles to profl. jours. and monographs; patentee in field. Mem. civilian adv. group Dept. Commerce, 1959-60; mem. 5th decade com., also adv. com. on engring. and mgmt. program UCLA, 1984—; mem. com. on scholarly communication with People's Republic of China, Tech. Transfer Task Force, Nat. Acad. Sci., Washington, 1985—; bd. dirs. Orange County Pacific Symphony, Fullerton, Calif., 1982—; mem. pres.'s adv. bd. Calif. State U.-Fullerton, 1986—. Recipient sci. merit award Navy Bur. Ordnance/Armour Research Found., 1952, IR-100 award, 1964, 69. Mem. IEEE, AIME, Am. Chem. Soc., Soc. Photog. and Instrumentation Engrs. and Scientists, Elec. Industry Assn. (past chmn. microelectronics), Phi Beta Kappa, Sigma Xi, Phi Lamda Upsilon. Home: 505 Westchester Pl Fullerton CA 92635 Office: Tech Strategy Group 1370 Brea Blvd Suite 212 Fullerton CA 92635

MILLER, ARTHUR JOSEPH, neurophysiology and craniofacial biology educator; b. San Francisco, Jan. 18, 1943; s. Arthur Joseph and Theresa (Walczak) M.; m. Marilyn Loushin, Aug. 21, 1965; children: Garreth, Ashleigh, Heath. BA, San Jose State U., 1965; PhD, UCLA, 1970. Asst. prof. U. Ill., Chgo., 1970-75; asst. prof. growth, devel., physiology U. Calif., San Francisco, 1975-78, assoc. prof., 1978-84, prof., 1984—; bd. dirs. Ctr. for Craniofacial Anomalies, San Francisco. Contbr. articles to profl. jours. Mem. ADA, Am. Physiol. Soc., Neurosci. Soc., Internat. Assn. for Dental Research, Internat. Brain Research Assn., Native Sons of the Golden West. Democrat. Roman Catholic. Home: 160 Leslie Dr San Carlos CA 94070 Office: U Calif Ctr for Craniofacial Anomalies S-747 San Francisco CA 94143

MILLER, BARBARA STALLCUP, medical foundation administrator; b. Montague, Calif., Sept. 4, 1919; d. Joseph Nathaniel and Maybelle (Needham) Stallcup; m. Leland F. Miller, May 16, 1946; children—Paula Kay, Susan Lee, Daniel Joseph, Alison Jean. B.A., U. Oreg., 1942. Women's editor Eugene (Oreg.) Daily News, 1941-43; law clk. to J. Everett Barr, Yreka, Calif., 1943-45; mgr. Yreka C. of C., 1945-46; Northwest supr. Louis Harris and Assocs., Portland, Oreg., 1959-62; dir. pub. relations and fund raising Columbia River council Girl Scouts U.S.A., 1962-67; pvt. practice pub. relations cons., Portland, 1967-72; adviser of student publs., asst. prof. communications U. Portland, 1967-72, dir. pub. relations and info., asst. prof. communications, 1972-78, dir. devel., 1978-79, exec. dir. devel., 1979-83; assoc. dir. St. Vincent Med. Found., 1983—. Pres. bd. dirs. Vols. of Am. of Oreg., Inc., 1980-84, pres. regional adv. bd., 1982-84; chmn. bd. dirs. S.E. Mental Health Network, 1984—, Oreg. Black History Project; nat. bd. dirs. Vols. of Am., Inc., 1984—. Recipient Presdl. Citation, Oreg. Communicators Assn., 1973, Matrix award, 1976, 80, Miltner award U. Portland, 1977. Mem. Nat. Assn. Hosp. Devel., Nat. Soc. Fundraising Execs., Women in Communications (NW regional v.p. 1973-75), Nat. Fedn. Press Women, Oreg. Press Women (dist. dir.), Pub. Relations Soc. Am. (dir. local chpt.), Oreg. Fedn. Womens Clubs (communications chmn. 1978-80), Alpha Xi Delta. Unitarian. Clubs: Portland Zenith (pres. 1975-76, 81-82), City Club of Portland. Contbr. articles to profl. jours. Home: 5930 SW Meadows Rd Lake Oswego OR 97035 Office: 9205 SW Barnes Rd Portland OR 97225

MILLER, BETSY SOTZIN, hospital volunteer services official, management consultant; b. Washington, Nov. 10, 1925; d. Heber A. and Ann Henretta S.; m. Jack Edward Miller, 1949; 1 son, John Allen. B.A., Stanford U., 1947. Buyer, Roos Bros., Inc., 1947-51; profl. vol., 1951-69; dir. vol. services USPHS Hosp., San Francisco, 1969-81, St. Mary's Hosp., San Francisco, 1981—. Bd. dirs. Vol. Ctr., San Francisco, 1978—, pres., 1980-82; bd. dirs. Easter Seal Soc. San Francisco, 1978-81. Mem. No. Calif. Assn. Dirs. Vol. Service (pres. 1976-77), Assn. Vol. Adminstrn., Am. Soc. Dirs. Vol. Service (dir. 1979-82, pres. 1983), Chi Omega, Stanford U. Alumni Assn. Club: Stanford Women's (San Francisco). Home: 261 Santa Paula Ave San Francisco CA 94127 Office: Saint Marys Hosp 450 Stanyan St San Francisco CA 94117

MILLER, BILL, management and marketing consultant; b. Jersey City, Mar. 6, 1933; Children: Valerie, Lynn, Lori, Michael, Billy Joe. MBA, La Jolla U., 1980. Cert. (life) coll. level tchr. psychology, bus. mgmt. and mktg., mgmt. orgn. and human relations, Calif. Enlisted USMC, 1948, ret., 1967; instr. karate, judo and mob control N.J. and Calif. Police Depts.; dist. sales mgr. Syntex Labs., Palo Alto, Calif., 1968-75; owner, pres. Bill Miller and Assocs., Inc., 1976—, Mgmt. Dynamics; cons. to mgmt. in healthcare, exec. search; presenter mgmt. seminars; instr. psychology, bus. mgmt. and mktg., mgmt. orgn. and human relations U. Calif.-La Jolla and Nat. U., San Diego. Sponsor, founder Ann. Rancho Bernardo (Calif.) Half Marathon. Avocations: marathon athletic events. Home: 12696 Pacato Circle N Rancho Bernardo CA 92128

MILLER, BLAKE DELANE, marketing professional; b. Santa Monica, Calif., July 15, 1957; s. Robert Delane Miller and Florence Elizabeth (Kiessig) Jacobs; m. Jeryl Ann Byerly, Dec. 27, 1980; 1 child, Luke Edward Christian. BS, UCLA, 1980; MS, Stanford U., 1982. Mktg. mgr. Hewlett Packard, McMinnville, Oreg., 1982-84, Marcom mgr., 1984-85; markets mgr. Hewlett Packard, Vancouver, Wash., 1985—. Mem. Stanford Alumni Assn. Republican. Mem. Christian Ch. Avocation: running. Office: Hewlett Packard 18110 SE 34th St Camas WA 98607

MILLER, BRENT CARLTON, family studies educator, researcher; b. Logan, Utah, Jan. 11, 1947; s. Kae V. and Leona (Hatch) M.; m. Kevon Costley, Sept. 11, 1969; children: Clay, Micah, Erin. BS, Weber State Coll., 1971; MS, Utah State U., 1972; PhD, U. Minn., 1975. Asst. prof. U. Tenn., Knoxville, 1975-79; asst. prof. Utah State U., Logan, 1979-81, assoc. prof., 1981-85, prof. family studies, 1985—; cons. Kennedy Found., Washington, 1985—, Dept. Health and Human Services, Washington, 1984-86. Author: Family Research Methods, 1986; co-author: Marriage and Family Development, 1985; co-editor: Family Studies Rev. Yrbook, 3d edit., 1985; contbr. articles to profl. jours. Named Researcher of Yr., Coll. Family Life, 1981, 85. Mem. Nat. Council on Family Relations (pub. v.p. 1985-86, bd. dirs. 1981-83, 85-86), Am. Sociol. Assn., Soc. Research on Adolescence. Mormon. Avocations: handball, trout fishing. Home: 1370 E 1980 N Logan UT 84321 Office: Utah State U Dept Family and Human Devel Logan UT 84322-2905

MILLER, CARL WILLIAM, molecular biologist, researcher; b. Peoria, Ill., Oct. 7, 1951; s. Vincent Allen and Margaret Jane (Ellis) M.; m. Kay Deeney, July, 15, 1985; 1 child, Bob F. BA, Vassar Coll., 1974; PhD, Columbia U., 1983. Research assoc. dept. medicine UCLA, 1983—; bd. dirs. DARE Assn., Cambridge, Mass., 1980. Bank of Am. Giannini Found. fellow, 1985. Mem. AAAS. Home: 1417 S Westgate Ave Los Angeles CA 90025

MILLER, CAROLE ANN LYONS, editor, publisher, advertising specialist; b. Newton, Mass., Aug. 1, 1943; d. Markham Harold and Ursula Patricia (Foley) Lyons; m. Francis John Tucker, Dec. 28, 1968; m. David Thomas Miller, July 4, 1978. B.A., Boston U., 1964; bus. cert., Hickox Sch., Boston, 1964; cert. advt. and mktg. profl. UCLA, 1973; cert. retail mgmt. profl. Ind. U., 1976. Editor Triangle Topics, Pacific Telephone, Los Angeles; programmer Los Angeles Central Area Speakers' Bur., 1964-66; mng. editor/mktg. dir. Teen mag., Los Angeles and N.Y.C., 1966-76; advt. dir. L.S. Ayres & Co., Indpls., 1976-78; v.p. mktg. The Denver, 1978-79; founder, editor, pub. Clockwise mag., Ventura, Calif., 1979-85; spl. events mktg. mgr., mgr. pub. relations and spl. events Robinson's Dept. Stores, Los Angeles, 1985—; instr. retail advt. Ind. U., 1977-78. Recipient Pres.'s award Advt. Women of N.Y., 1974; Seklemian award 1977; Pub. Service Addy award, 1978. Mem. Advt. Women N.Y., Advt. Club Los Angeles, Ventura County Profl. Women's Network (founding), UCLA Alumni Assn. Editor: Sek Says, 1979. Home: 2554 Spinnaker Ave Port Hueneme CA 93041 Office: 600 W 7th St Los Angeles CA 90017

MILLER, CAROLYN JEAN, educator; b. Detroit, Sept. 23, 1939; d. John and Clara E. Miller; A.A. with honors, Pasadena (Calif.) City Coll., 1960; B.A. with high honors, U. Calif., 1962; M.A. in Edn. (Experienced Tchr. fellow), Stanford U., 1967. Tchr., Pasadena (Calif.) Unified Schs., 1962—, discovery room tchr., 1974, lang. arts resource tchr., 1976-78, project coordinator Sch. Improvement Program, 1978-79, tchr. Saturday tutorial program, 1979-80, reading resource tchr., 1979-81, coordinator Hoffman Reading Center, 1980-81, adminstrv. mgmt. intern, 1981, project coordinator Title I and sch. improvement programs, 1981-85, curriculum resource tchr., 1982—, adminstrv. mgmt. intern, 1985-86, project dir. Wilson Middle Sch., 1986—; Chmn. bd. dirs. Worthington Manor. Cert. tchr., Calif. Mem. Assn. Supervision and Curriculum Devel., Calif. Reading Assn., Internat. Reading Assn., Angeles Crest Reading Assn. (charter, pres.), Calif. Math. Council, Assn. Calif. Ach. Adminstrs., Calif. Assn. Compensatory Edn., Stanford Alumni Assn., Phi Delta Kappa, Delta Kappa Gamma. Home: 1801 Fair Oaks St Apt G South Pasadena CA 91030 Office: care Pasadena Sch Dist 351 S Hudson St Pasadena CA 91109

MILLER, CHARLES D., business exec.; b. Hartford, Conn., 1928; (married). Grad., Johns Hopkins U. Sales mgr. Yale & Towne Mfg. Co., 1955-59; asso. Booz, Allen & Hamilton, 1959-64; with Avery Internat. Corp., Pasadena, Calif., 1964—, group v.p., 1969-72, exec. v.p. ops., 1972-75, pres., 1975-77, chief exec. officer, 1977—, now also chmn., dir. Office: Avery Internat 150 N Orange Grove Blvd Pasadena CA 91103

MILLER, CHARLES MILTON, chemistry researcher; b. Richland, Wash., Jan. 18, 1954; s. Robert Dunlap and Ruth (Kelsey) M.; m. Marlene Vaughn, June 11, 1983. BS, Wash. State U., 1976; MA, Columbia U., 1977; PhD, Stanford U., 1980. Postdoctoral fellow Los Alamos (N.Mex.) Nat. Lab., 1980-82, staff mem., 1982-85, asst. group leader, 1985—. Contbr. articles to chem. jours. NSF fellow, 1976-79. Mem. Am. Chem. Soc., Am. Soc. Mass Spectrometry. Office: Los Alamos Nat Lab MS J-514 Los Alamos NM 87545

MILLER, CHESTER WAYNE, cement and concrete technologist; b. Sullivan County, Ind., Sept. 10, 1924; s. Garrett Hobert and Geneva Blanche (Walters) M.; m. Rose Mary Sligar, Sept. 20, 1945; children—Reginald, David; m. Ruth L. McCoy, June 14, 1969; children—Phyllis, James, Debra. B.S., Butler U., Ind., 1949; M.S., Purdue U., 1951; postgrad. in measurement and evaluation, U. Ariz., 1965. Supr. Kingan & Co., Indpls., 1951-52; lab. technician Ariz. Portland Cement Co., Phoenix, 1952-53, mix chemist, 1954-55, plant chemist, 1956-67, kiln foreman, 1965-66, combustion control, new product devel., tech. service engr., 1968-82, dir. tech. services, 1982-84, mgr. tech. services, 1984—; concrete and concrete prodn. technician U. Colo., 1968; cons., lectr. in field. Flotilla comdr., USCG Aux., 1979-80; comdr. Rio Salado Power Squadron, 1982—. Served as pharmacist mate, USN, 1943-46. Decorated Purple Heart with 1 gold star. Mem. Am. Concret Inst., AIME, Structural Engrs. Assn. Ariz., Ariz. Masonry Guild, Portland Cement Assn. (gen. tech. com.), ASTM, Sigma Xi, Phi Eta Sigma. Republican. Club: Civitan. Contbr. articles to profl. jours. Home: 5325 N 61st Dr Glendale AZ 85301 Office: 2400 N Central Suite 308 Phoenix AZ 85004

MILLER, CRAIG RUSSELL, management company executive; b. Chgo., Jan. 21, 1949; s. Daniel M. and Harriet (Rosen) M.; m. Isabel Jane Anderson, Nov. 27, 1979; children: Dylan, Sean. BSBA, U. Denver, 1971. Cost acct. Stephens Constrn., Bellvue, Nebr., 1971-73; pres. Token Prodns., Omaha, 1973-74; midwest exec. sgt. Joynus Music, Mill Valley, Calif., 1974-75; pres. The Miller Agy., San Francisco, 1975-77, C. M. Mgmt., Los Angeles, 1977—; cons. Warner bors. Records, Los Angeles, 1980-85; lectr. music bus., San Francisco, 1977—. Democrat. Jewish. Avocations: sports, music, video.

MILLER, DALE EDWARD, dentist; b. Klamath Falls, Oreg., Aug. 11, 1937; s. Warren Siler and Virginia Margarete (Adams) M.; m. Ann Marie Fenn, Sept. 17, 1960; children: Dale Edward Jr., Erik Charles, Jeffry William, Leslie Ann. DDS, U. Wash., 1961. Gen. practice dentistry Yakima, Wash., 1963—; mem. staff St. Elizabeth Med. Ctr., Yakima Valley Meml. Hosp. Bd. dirs. Yakima Sch. Dist. 7, 1975-85. Served to lt. USN, 1961-63. Recipient Citizen of Edn. award Citizens Edn. Ctr. N.W., Seattle, 1985. Fellow Internat. Coll. Dentists; mem. Wash. State Dental Assn. (chmn. membership com. 1984—, house of dels., exec. council 1971-75, 79—, other coms.), Yakima Valley Dental Assn. (sec., v.p., pres. 1969-71, Dentist Citizen of Yr., 1985). Avocations: fishing, racquetball, bicycling. Home: 5711 Richey Rd Yakima WA 98902 Office: Saint Elizabeth Med Ctr 110 S 9th Ave Yakima WA 98902

MILLER, DANIEL HOLMES, steel company executive; b. Berkeley, Calif., May 5, 1932; s. Alden Holmes and Virginia Elizabeth (Dove) M.; m. Dorothy Natalie Cake, June 30, 1955; children—Dana Jeanne (Mrs. Gregory Blair), Robert Holmes. B.S., U. Calif.-Berkeley, 1955; cert. exec. program Stanford U., 1980. Various tech. and supervisory positions Bethlehem Steel, South San Francisco, Calif., 1957-64, mill supt. 1964-75, plant mgr., 1975-77, Seattle, 1977-84; mgr. primary ops. Seattle Steel, Inc., 1985; dir. Incintech Am. Corp., Fresno, Calif., 1986—. Served to lt. (j.g.) USN, 1955-57. Mem. Am. Iron and Steel Inst., Assn. Iron and Steel Engrs. (sect. chmn. 1975-76, nat. dir. 1977, 83), Chi Psi (chpt. pres. 1954). Club: Rainier (Seattle). Lodge: Rotary. Home: 3169 W Alluvial Ave Fresno CA 93711 Office: Incintech Am Corp 5108 E Clinton Way Suite 113 Fresno CA 93727

MILLER, DAVID BRUCE, oil company executive; b. Dallas, Feb. 17, 1950; s. Van Roy and Fay Ann (Luther) M.; m. Mary Lee Filgo, May 27, 1972;

children: Kyle, Meredith. BBA, So. Meth. U., 1972, MBA, 1973. V.p. Republic Bank Dallas, 1973-78; v.p., mgr. Republic Energy Fin. Corp. subs. Republic Bank, Denver, 1978-81; chmn., chief exec. officer MAZE Exploration Inc., Englewood, Colo., 1981-86; pres. MKM Energy Corp., Dallas, 1987—; bd. dirs. Seismic Prospecting of Denver, Inc., Englewood. Mem. adv. bd. and exec. com. St. Andrew United Meth. Ch., 1987—. Mem. Ind. Petroleum Assn. Am., Ind. Petroleum Assn. Mountain States (bd. dirs. 1984—), Tex. Ind. Producers and Royalty Owners Assn., So. Meth. U. Alumni Assn. (bd. dirs. 1974-84, pres. Denver chpt. 1979-84)., So. Meth. U. Letterman's Assn. (bd. dirs. 1977-78). Republican. Methodist. Clubs: Metro Denver Executives, Denver Assocs. (pres. 1985-86); So. Meth. U. Mustang (Dallas) (bd. dirs. 1976-78). Avocations: tennis, skiing.

MILLER, DAVID HARRIS, health care facility executive; b. Oakland, Calif., Jan. 10, 1942; s. Robert D. and Pauline (Rappoport) M.; m. Jennifer M. Young, Aug. 25, 1968; children: Judith M., Rebecca S., Joshua S. BS, U. Calif., Davis, 1965, MS, 1967; PhD, U. Sydney, Australia, 1972. Prin. Miller Restorations, Sydney, 1969-72; tech. coordinator Hosp. Systems, Oakland, 1972-75, v.p. ops., 1975-79, pres., chief exec. officer, 1979—. Mem. Nat. Fire Protective Assn. Avocation: motorcar restoration. Home: PO Box 4164 Walnut Creek CA 94596 Office: Hosp Systems 5301 Adeline St Oakland CA 94608

MILLER, DONALD E., rubber company executive; b. Denver, Dec. 17, 1930; s. Alex H. and Nina A. (Schlatter) M.; m. Barbara J. Rehm, June 15, 1952; children: Steven, David. Grad., Colo. Sch. Mines, 1953. With Gates Rubber Co., Denver, 1963—; field sales mgr. idsl. sales Gates Rubber Co., 1963-66, v.p. mfg., 1966-69, v.p. auto-hardware sales, 1969-73, v.p. mktg., 1973-81, group v.p. automotive, 1981-82, pres., 1982—. 1st lt. U.S. Army, 1954-56. Presbyterian. Home: 5965 E Princeton Circle Englewood CO 80111 Office: Gates Rubber Co 999 S Broadway P O Box 5887 Denver CO 80209 *

MILLER, DONALD WICKS, rancher; b. Chgo.; s. Donald Jameson and Warner Louise (Wicks) M.; children: Donald, Dori. BBA, Los Angeles City Coll., 1950; postgrad., Citrus Coll., Azusa, Calif., 1960. Supr. Dept. Water and Power, Los Angeles, 1965-78; adminstr. Box G Ranch, Lancaster, Calif., 1952—; appraiser fine furniture and real estate Ins. Cos. Inspection Bur. Inc. Mem. Am. Way, Calif. Council for Blind. Served with USCG, 1942-46, ETO, PTO. Home: 3251 W Ave I Lancaster CA 93534

MILLER, ELVA RUBY CONNES (MRS. JOHN R. MILLER), civic worker; b. Joplin, Mo.; d. Edward and Ada (Martin) Connes; student Pomona Coll., part-time, 1936-56; m. John R. Miller, Jan. 17, 1934 (dec. Nov. 1968). Entertainer various night clubs, supper clubs, also Hollywood Bowl, 1967; TV appearances; rec. artist Capitol Records, 1966—, Amaret Records, 1969—; appeared in motion pictures. Active Girl Scouts U.S.A., 1933-58; hon. mem. Mayor's Com. for Sr. Citizens, Los Angeles, 1966; mem. Disabled Am. Vets. Comdrs. Club, Los Angeles County Mus. Art, Music Ctr. Los Angeles County. Recipient awards including Thanks badge Girl Scouts U.S.A., 1956, Key to City, Mayor San Diego, 1967, plaque Dept. of Def. for trip to Vietnam, 1967. Mem. Gen. Alumni Assn. U. So. Calif. (life). Republican. Presbyterian. Home: 9585 Reseda Blvd Northridge CA 91324

MILLER, EMERSON WALDO, accountant, tax, financial, business and management consultant; b. Green Island, Jamaica, W.I., Jan. 27, 1920; s. Adolphus Eustace and Catherine Sarah (Dixon) M.; m. Olive Claire Ford, Apr. 10, 1945; children—Cheryll, Hellena, Emerson, Oliver, Donald, Selwyn. Student U. Toronto (Ont., Can.), 1938-41, U. Calif.-Berkeley, 1950-61. Came to U.S., 1950, naturalized, 1957. Cost accountant Poierier & McLane Corp., N.Y.C., 1941-42; prin. Emerson Miller & Co., Kingston, Jamaica, 1942-49; lectr. accounting and bus. law Jamaica Sch. Commerce, Kingston, 1945-48; tax examiner, conferee Internat. Revenue Service, San Francisco, 1963-64; chief financial and accounting aspects transp. and communications services programs Gen. Services Adminstrn., San Francisco, 1965-70, chief maj. segment financial mgmt. activities, 1970-84; prin. Emerson W. Miller Tax, Fin., Bus. and Mgmt. Services, 1984—; instr. govt. accounting, 1966-69. Fed. Govt. Accountants Assn. rep. mgmt. improvement com. Fed. Exec. Bd., San Francisco, 1973-74. Chmn. credit com. VARO Fed. Credit Union, San Francisco, 1969-81, treas., dir., 1981—. Recipient Disting. Service award Toastmasters Internat., 1968, Commendable Service award Gen. Services Adminstrn., 1968, Spl. Achievement award, 1969; Faithful Service award VARO-SF Fed. Credit Union, 1974. Mem. Am. Accounting Assn., Nat. Assn. Accountants, Fed. Govt. Accountants Assn. (chpt. pres.), Am. Mgmt. Assn., Financial Mgmt. Assn., Brit. Inst. Mgmt., Am. Judicature Soc., Royal Econ. Soc. (Cambridge), U. Calif. Alumni Assn., Internat. Platform Assn., Acad. Polit. and Social Sci., AAAS, N.Y. Acad. Scis. Clubs: Toastmasters Internat. (ednl. v.p.), (San Francisco), No. Calif. Cricket (San Anselmo); Brit. Social and Athletic (Los Angeles). Home: 505 Coventry Rd Kensington CA 94707 Office: PO Box 471 Berkeley CA 94701

MILLER, EUGENIA PORRETTA, educational and training specialist, researcher; b. Silver Creek, Pa., July 12, 1928; d. Vincent James and Pietrina (Calabrese) Porretta; m. George David Miller, Oct. 15, 1966 (dec. July 1980). B.S., Mansfield U., 1950; M.S., SUNY-Albany, 1956; profl. diploma Columbia U., 1965; Ph.D., U. N.Mex., 1979. Cert. sch. dist. adminstr., tchr. English, French, Spanish, English supr., N.Y. Tchr. Stratford Sch. Dist., N.Y., 1950-55, Johnstown High Sch., N.Y., 1955-56; tchr. Clarkstown Sch. Dist., New City, N.Y., 1956-60, chmn. English dept., 1960-68, sch. adminstr., 1968-78; ednl. specialist BDM Corp., Albuquerque, 1980—; cons. in field, 1960-75; researcher S.W. Research, Albuquerque, 1976-77. Author: (children's book) Pedro and Tony, 1950; author, dir. films: Detour, 1963; The Junk Yard, 1964, Fiesta and Siesta, 1972. Active United Way, Albuquerque, 1982. Edn. Profl. Devel. Act grantee U. Iowa, Iowa City, 1969; N.Y. State grantee Columbia U., 1963. Mem. Am. Soc. Tng. and Devel., Nat. Soc. for Performance Inst., Querque Crows, Alpha Psi Omega, Kappa Delta Pi, Phi Delta Kappa. Republican. Roman Catholic. Home: 1801 Sunset Rd Rio Rancho NM 87124 Office: BDM Corp 1801 Randolph Rd Albuquerque NM 87106

MILLER, FOREST LEONARD, JR., statistician; b. Cin., June 18, 1936; s. Forest Leonard and Virginia Brasier (Peters) M.; m. Mitzi Lu Gwyn, May 25, 1961; children: Mark, Nathaniel, David. BS, Purdue U., 1958, MS, 1959; PhD, N.C. State U., 1975. Statistician Oak Ridge (Tenn.) Nat. Lab., 1958-79; research prof. Desert Research Inst., Las Vegas, Nev., 1979—. Contbr. articles to profl. jours. Commr. Boy Scouts of Am., Las Vegas, 1981—; instr. Hunter Safety, Las Vegas, 1980—. Mem. Am. Statis. Assn., Biometrics Soc., Inst. Math. Stats., Royal Statis. Soc., Health Physics Soc. (chpt. pres. 1984-85). Avocations: caving, hunting, camping, hiking, fishing. Home: 5275 Somerset Dr Las Vegas NV 89120 Office: Desert Research Inst 2505 Chandler Ave Suite 1 Las Vegas NV 89120

MILLER, FRANKLIN EMRICK, software engineer; b. Greenville, Ohio, Aug. 12, 1946; s. Rollin Linde and E. Evelyn (Emrick) M.; m. Sandra Lewis, Dec. 20, 1969; children—William Rollin, Rose Mary. B.S., Otterbein Coll., 1969; M.Ed. in Ednl. Psychology and Counseling, Wayne State U., 1975; PhD, U. Denver, 1984. Lic. pvt. pilot FAA. Commd. U.S. Air Force, 1969, advanced through grades to capt.; space surveillance officer, Maine, 1970-71, Thule, Greenland, 1971-72; chief instr./systems analyst, Correlation Ctr., McGuire AFB, N.J., 1972-73; site space surveillance officer, Aviano, Italy, 1973-75; chief support programming unit, Colo., 1975-79; chief applications support programming, South Australia, 1979-81; software engr. Aerojet Electro Systems Corp., Aurora, Colo., 1981—. Bd. dirs. Aurora Community Mental Health Ctr., 1976-79; vol. counselor Comitis Crisis Ctr., YMCA, Aurora, 1976-78. Mem. Am. Psychol. Assn., Phi Delta Kappa. Republican. Author: The Preliminary Online Rorschach Test Manual, 1980; contbr. article to profl. jour. Office: PO Box 31657 Aurora CO 80041

MILLER, GEORGE, congressman; b. Richmond, Calif., May 17, 1945; s. George and Dorothy (Rumsey) M.; m. Cynthia Caccavo, 1964; children: George, Stephen. B.A., San Francisco State Coll., 1968; J.D., U. Calif., Davis, 1972. Legis. counsel Calif. senate majority leader 1969-73; mem. 94th-100th Congresses from 7th Calif. Dist. Chmn. Contra Costa County (Calif.) Democratic Central Com., 1969-70. Mem. Calif. Bar Assn. Democrat. Club: Martinez Dem. (past pres.). Office: 2228 Rayburn House Office Bldg Washington DC 20515 *

MILLER, GREGORY JOHN, sales and marketing executive; b. Phila., June 14, 1946; s. John Henry and Patricia (McLaughlin) M.; m. Carolyn Hanson, Aug. 2, 1974; children: Keith, Kevin and Casey (twins). BA in Sociology, New England U., 1969. Dir. mktg. and sales Classic Towns, Braintree, Mass., 1975-79; v.p. mktg. J&D Expo Products, Canoga Park, Calif., 1979-84; western region mng. Trade Wind Tours, Simi Valley, Calif., 1984-86; pres., owner Gregory Miller & Assocs., Simi Valley, Calif., 1985—. Coach Simi Youth Baseball, 1983—. Mem. Am. Soc. Travel Agts., U.S. Town Operators Assn., Nat. Assn. Exposition Mgrs. Roman Catholic. Avocations: all sports. Home: 2205 E Knollhaven Simi Valley CA 93065

MILLER, HAROLD LEWIS, physician; b. Scipio, Utah, Oct. 13, 1924; s. Henry and Josie Ella (Peterson) M.; m. Laura Jean Chambers, June 13, 1951; children—Leslie Ann, Barbara Lee, Harold Craig, Steven Arnell, Lorenzo Kay and Ronald Kim (twins). B.S., U. Utah, 1949, M.D., 1953. Diplomate Am. Bd. Family Practice. Intern, Univ. Hosp., Ann Arbor, Mich., 1951-52, resident, 1952-53; practice family medicine, Henderson, Nev., 1953—; past chief of staff St. Rose de Lima Hosp., Henderson. Active Boy Scouts Am.; adv. trustee Henderson City Pub. Trust; Served with U.S. Army, 1943-46; PTO. Fellow Am. Acad. Family Practice (past del.; charter); mem. AMA, Nev. Med. Soc. Democrat. Mormon. Office: 106 Lake Mead Dr Henderson NV 89015

MILLER, HAROLD WILLIAM, nuclear geochemist; b. Walton, N.Y., Apr. 21, 1920; s. Harold Frank and Vera Leona (Simons) M. BS in Chemistry, U. Mich., 1943; MS in Chemistry, U. Colo., 1948, postgrad. Control chemist Linde Air Products Co., Buffalo, 1943-46; analytical research chemist Gen. Electric Co., Richland, Wash., 1948-51; research chemist Phillips Petroleum Co., Idaho Falls, Idaho, 1953-56; with Anaconda (Mont.) Copper Co., 1956; tech. dir., v.p. U.S. Yttrium Co., Laramie, Wyo., 1956-57; tech. dir. Colo. div. The Wah Chang Co., Boulder, Colo., 1957-58; analytical chemist The Climax (Colo.) Molybdenum Co., 1959; with research and devel. The Colo. Sch. of Mines Research Found., Golden, 1960-62; cons. Boulder, 1960—; sr. research physicist Dow Chem. Co., Golden, 1963-73; bd. dirs. Sweeney Mining and Milling Corp., Boulder; cons. Hendrick Mining and Milling Co., Boulder; instr. nuclear physics and nuclear chemistry Rocky Flats Plant, U. Colo. Contbr. numerous articles to profl. jours. Mem. Sigma Xi. Avocations: mineralogy, western U.S. mining history. Home and Office: Box 1092 Boulder CO 80306

MILLER, HARRIET SANDERS, art center director; b. N.Y.C., Apr. 18, 1926; d. Herman and Dorothy (Silbert) S.; m. Milton H. Miller, June 27, 1948; children—Bruce, Jeffrey, Marcie. B.A., Ind. U., 1947; M.A., Columbia U., 1949; M.S., U. Wis., 1962, M.F.A., 1967. Dir. art sch. Madison Art Ctr., Wis., 1963-72; acting dir. Center for Continuing Edn., Vancouver, B.C., 1975-76; mem. fine arts faculty Douglas Coll., Vancouver, 1972-78; exec. dir. Palos Verdes Arts Center, Calif., 1978-84; dir. Junior Arts Center, Los Angeles, 1984—; one woman exhibits at Gallery 7, Vancouver, 1978, Gallery 1, Toronto, Ont., 1977, Linda Farris Gallery, Seattle, 1975, Galerie Allen, Vancouver, 1973. Mem. Calif. Art Edn. Assn., Calif. Confedn. of Arts, Museum Educators of So. Calif., Arts and Humanities Symposium. Office: Junior Arts Ctr 4814 Hollywood Blvd Los Angeles CA 90027

MILLER, HAYDEN RAY, art museum director; b. Butler, Mo., Mar. 28, 1920; s. John Calvin and Martha Marie (Ray) M.; m. Maxine Smith, July 8, 1941; children: Connie Marlene, Mark Hayden, Scott Smith. BS, Cen. Mo. State U., 1942; MA, Calif. State U., Los Angeles, 1952. Cert. tchr., Calif. Sheet metal contractor Rays Tin Shop, Butler, 1946-48; art tchr. Mountain View Sch. Dist., El Monte, Calif., 1948-50; art cons. Whittier (Calif.) City Sch., 1950-55; dir. fine arts Riverside (Calif.) Unified Sch. Dist., 1955-81; exec. dir. Riverside Art Mus., 1981—; tchr. art edn. Whittier Coll., 1950-55; artist, musician, tchr. various colls., Whittier, Riverside, 1955—. Chmn. urban design and environment com. Riverside Downtown Assn., 1986. Served to sgt. U.S. Army, ETO. Mem. Calif. Retired Tchrs. Assn., Am. Assn. Mus., Riverside C. of C. Republican. Office: Riverside Art Ctr and Mus 3425 Seventh St Riverside CA 92501

MILLER, HOWARD ROSS, sales, marketing executive; b. Bklyn., Oct. 25, 1949; s. Bert M. and Phyllis Nightingale. BA, Antioch U., 1973, MA, 1975. Research analyst U. So. Calif., Los Angeles, 1976-77; instr. UCLA, 1978-79; adminstrv. asst. City of Irvine, Calif., 1980-81; comml. sales mgr. Storer Broadcasting Corp., Laguna Niguel, Calif., 1982-83; nat. sales mgr. Richard Soong and Co., Irvine, 1983-84; v.p. Equus Communications, Inc., Fountain Valley, Calif., 1985—. treas. Ind. Found., Los Angeles, 1970-80; instr. Learning Network, Garden Grove, Calif., 1986. Home: 144 Orchard Irvine CA 92720

MILLER, JAMES GRIER, psychiatrist, psychologist; b. Pitts., July 17, 1916; s. Earl Dalton and Mary Rebecca (Grier) M.; m. Jessie Louise Luthi, Sept. 3, 1938; children: John Grier, Thomas Christian. Student, Columbia Bible Coll., S.C., U. S.C., 1933-34, U. Mich., 1934-35; AB summa cum laude, Harvard U., 1937; AM, Harvard, 1938; MD cum laude, Harvard U., 1942, PhD, 1943. Diplomate Am. Bd. Examiners Profl. Psychology, Am. Bd. Psychiatry and Neurology. Asst. and tutor psychology Harvard U., Cambridge, Mass., 1937-38, mem. Soc. Fellows, 1938-44, asst. psychiatry Med. Sch., 1943-44; med. intern. Mass. Gen. Hosp., Boston, 1942-43, asst. resident, then resident in psychiatry, 1943-44; Lowell lectr. Boston, 1944; mem. and chief assessment program OSS, 1944-46; asst. prof. clin. psychology (on leave) Harvard U., 1946-47; chief clin. psychology sect. VA, Washington, 1946-47; prof., chmn. dept. psychology U. Chgo., 1948-55; clin. instr. in psychiatry U. Ill. Med. Sch., Chgo., 1952-55; lectr. Northwestern U. Med. Sch., 1953-55; prof. psychiatry and psychology, dir. Mental Research Inst. U. Mich., Ann Arbor, 1955-67; exec. dir. EDUCOM (Interuniv. Communications Council), Princeton, N.J., 1964-66, v.p., prin. scientist, 1966-70, trustee, 1970-81; trustee emeritus EDUCOM (Interuniv. Communications Counci), Princeton, N.J., 1981—; chmn. bd. EDUCOM (Interuniv. Communications Council), Princeton, N.J., 1976; v.p. for acad affairs Cleve. State U., 1967-70, provost, 1970-71; v.p. Acad. Ednl. Devel., Washington, 1971-73; lectr. psychiatry and behavioral scis. Johns Hopkins U., Balt., 1971-73; pres. U. Louisville, 1973-80, Robert Maynard Hutchins Ctr. for Study Democratic Instns., Santa Barbara, Calif., 1980-82; vis. prof. psychiatry UCLA, 1981-83, adj. prof., 1983—; adj. prof. psychology U. Calif., Santa Barbara, 1981—; chmn. bd. U. of the World, 1982—. Author: Unconsciousness, 1942, Living Systems, 1978; co-author: Assessment of Men, 1948; editor: Behavioral Science, 1956—; dept. editor in psychology: Ency. Brit., 1952-58; co-editor: Drugs and Behavior, 1960; contbr. articles to profl. jours. Served to capt. M.C. AUS, 1944-46. Fellow Internat. Inst. Applied Systems Analysis, Vienna, Austria, summers 1973-74. Fellow Am. Psychol. Assn. (pres. div. clin. psychology 1958-59), Am. Psychiat. Assn., Am. Coll. Neuropsychopharmacology, Am. Coll. Psychiatrists, Am. Coll. Clin. Pharmacology and Therapeutics, (charter); mem. AAAS, AMA, Am. Soc. Cybernetics (charter), Soc. Gen. Systems Research (pres. 1973-74), Phi Beta Kappa, Sigma Xi. Episcopalian. Clubs: Cosmos, Metropolitan (Washington); Century, Harvard (N.Y.C.). Avocations: philately, computers. Office: 1055 Torry Pines Rd Suite 203 La Jolla CA 92037

MILLER, JEANIE, account executive, real estate broker; b. Clovis, Calif., June 26, 1946; d. Kenneth Lynn and Vida Bessie (Wilkinson) Harris; m. Drake Boyce Edward, Sept. 4, 1965 (div. Apr. 1978); children—Steve, Cyndy; m. John Allen Miller, July 16, 1983. Student Fresno City Coll., 1964-66, U. So. Calif., 1980-81, MIT, 1984-85. Real estate broker, Calif. Service rep. Pacific Telephone, Fresno, 1965-75; owner Calif. Design Assoc., Fresno, 1976-77; realtor assoc. Rana Mead Real Estate, Fresno, 1977-81; real estate broker Central Real Estate, Fresno, 1981-82; account exec. ATT, Fresno, 1982-86; loan officer First Interstate Mortgage, 1986—; owner Miller Real Estate, Clovis, 1982—. Mem. Nat. Assn. Female Execs., Fresno C. of C., Western States Corvette Council (bd. dirs. 1982-84), Fresno Bd. Realtors. Democrat. Clubs: Corvettes of Fresno, Women in Bus. Lodge: Jobs Daus. Avocations: car shows; charity events; racquetball; aerobics. Home: 1476 W Locust St Fresno CA 93711

MILLER, JEFFREY VEACH, research biochemist; b. Schenectady, N.Y., Apr. 11, 1955; s. Ray H. and Donna L. (Veach) M. BA, U. Calif., Berkeley, 1978. Biochemist Syva Co., Palo Alto, Calif., 1979-81, Genentech Inc., South San Francisco, 1981-83, Genencor Inc., South San Francisco, 1983—. Contbr. articles to profl. jours.; patentee in field. Avocation: yacht racing. Office: Genencor Inc 180 Kimball Way South San Francisco CA 94080

MILLER, JERRY ALAN, pharmacologist; b. Petersburg, Va., July 6, 1955; s. James Albert and Jean Elizabeth (White) M. BS in Biology, Lehigh U., 1977; PhD in Pharmacology, Ind. U., 1984. Technician Am. Cyanamid, Bound Brook, N.J., 1977-78; instr. chemistry Somerset (N.J.) County Coll., 1978-79; instr. biology Marian Coll., Indpls., 1982-83; pharmacologist U. Colo. Health Sci. Ctr., Denver, 1984—. Author: Instrumentation Manual for Chemical Laboratory Technology, 1980; contbr. articles to profl. publs. Research grantee Lehigh U., 1976, 77; Ind. U. assistantship, 1980-82. Mem. AAAS, N.Am. Soc. Neurosci., Sigma Xi. Avocations: chess, computers, lit., sailing, camping. Home: 774 Ash St Denver CO 80220 Office: U Colo Health Sci Ctr 4200 E 9th Ave Box C-236 Denver CO 80262

MILLER, JERRY WATSON, architect; b. Boulder, Colo., Sept. 30, 1949; s. Joseph Baylor and Genevieve (Hall) M.; m. Mildred Marie Meador, Feb. 13, 1983. Student, U. Wyo., 1967-68, Colo. State Coll., 1968-69; BArch, U. Colo., 1973. Architect Boulder County, Colo., 1974-79; project architect Wallace D. Palmer Assocs., Boulder, 1979-81, Midyette Assocs., Boulder, 1981-83; prin. architect J.W. Miller Assocs., Longmont, Colo., 1983—; chmn. Master Bd. Appeals, Longmont, 1985—. Recipient Recreational Bldg. of Yr. award Braden Steel Corp., 1976. Mem. Constrn. Specifications Inst., Longmont C. of C. (pub. affairs council 1984—, chmn. site devel. com. 1986—), Sigma Chi. Democrat. Avocations: photography, astronomy. Office: 601 3d Ave Suite 206 Longmont CO 80501

MILLER, JOANNE MARIE, academic business instructor; b. Greenwood, Wis., Apr. 21, 1937; s. Arno A. and Lillian (Decker) M. BEd, U. Wis., Whitewater, 1959; MA, U. No. Colo., 1963. Bus. instr. Sheboygan (Wis.) High Sch., 1959-61, Evanston (Ill.) Township High Sch., 1961-64; instr. No. Ariz. U., Flagstaff, 1964-66, 68-72; teaching assoc. Ind. U., Bloomington, 1966-68; prof. bus. Hartnell Community Coll., Salinas, Calif., 1972—. Author: Support Staff Procedures in the Electronic Office, 1986; contbr. articles to profl. publs., chpts. to books. Grantee Career Edn., State of Ariz., 1971, Navajo Workshop, State of Ariz., 1970, Manpower Devel. Tng. Act, U.S. Govt., 1969. Mem. Calif. Bus. Edn. Assn. (area sec., v.p., treas., chmn. 1959—), Profl. Secs. Internat. (chmn. 1973-78), AAUW (treas. 1975-77), Reading is Fundamental (treas. 1976-78), Ariz. Bus. Edn. Assn. (program chmn. 1970-72), Nat. Bus. Edn. Assn., Delta Pi Epsilon. Democrat. Office: Hartnell Coll 156 Homestead Ave Salinas CA 93901

MILLER, JOHN R., congressman; b. N.Y.C., May 23, 1938; m. June Marion Hamula. B.A., Bucknell U., 1959; M.A., Yale U., 1964, J.D., 1964. Bar: Wash. Asst. atty. gen. State of Wash., 1965-68; practice law 1968-72; pres. Seattle City Council, 1972-80; adj. prof. govt. law U. Puget Sound, 1981-84; mem. 99th, 100th Congresses from 1st Wash. Dist. Mem. Wash. State Bar Assn. Office: care Postmaster Office of House of Reps Washington DC 20515 *

MILLER, JON HAMILTON, wood products company executive; b. Des Moines, Jan. 22, 1938; s. Victor George and Virginia Adelaide (Hamilton) M.; m. Sydney Gail Fernald, June 4, 1966; children: Emily, Sara. A.B. in Econs., Stanford U., 1959, M.B.A. in Mktg. and Finance, 1961. Asst. to pres. Boise Cascade Corp., 1961-62, prodn. service mgr., 1962-65; sr. v.p. bus. products and services and packaging Boise Cascade Corp., Portland, 1971-74; exec. v.p. paper and paper products Boise Cascade Corp., Boise, Idaho, 1974-76; exec. v.p. timber/wood products/bldg. materials Boise Cascade Corp., 1976-78, pres. and chief operating officer, 1978—, also dir.; dir. Northwestern Mut. Life Ins. Co. chmn. bd. dirs. St. Luke's Regional Med. Ctr. Served with U.S. Army, 1959-60. Mem. Greater Boise C. of C. (pres. 1977). Methodist. Clubs: Arid (Boise); Multnomah Athletic (Portland). Home: 3330 Mountain View Dr Boise ID 83704 Office: Boise Cascade Corp One Jefferson Sq Boise ID 83728

MILLER, JOSEPH ANTHONY, military professional; b. Kinston, N.C., July 13, 1959; s. Gordon and Mavis Grey (Brown) M.; m. Karolyn Mae DeGroot, June 12, 1982; children: Jeromy Paul, Sarah Elizabeth. AA, Coastal Carolina Community Coll., 1979; cert. in human communications, Eastern Wash. U., 1984; diploma, Non-Commd. Officers Leadership Sch., 1985. Commd. USAF, 1979; missile maintenance technician USAF, Grand Forks AFB, N.D., 1979-82, missile maintenance instr., 1982-83, missile wing scheduler, 1983-84, missile wing job controller, 1984-85; missile handling team chief USAF, Malmstrom AFB, Mont., 1985-87, missile handling team instr., 1987—. Vol. Salvation Army, Grand Forks, 1979-81, Big Bro. program; child sponsor World Vision Internat., 1982—. Named one of Outstanding Young Men of Am., 1985. Mem. Internat. Order Foresters, Air Force Sgts. Assn., Non-Commd. Officers Club. Mem. Christian Ch. Home: 2716 Central Ave Great Falls MT 59401 Office: 341 Organizational Missile Maintenance Squadron USAF Malmstrom AFB MT 59405

MILLER, KALMAN JOSEPH, service company executive; b. York, Pa., Nov. 17, 1940; s. David M. and Reva (Getz) M.; m. Barbara Ila Silver, Oct. 19, 1963; children: Deborah Lynn, Sarah Beth, Ellen Sue. BSChemE, U. Ariz., 1962, MSChemE, 1964. Registered profl. engr., Calif., Ariz. Research engr. Rockwell Internat., Canoga Park, Calif., 1964-69, sr. research engr., 1969-74, project mgr., 1974-79; v.p. S.W. Recreation Internat., Phoenix, 1979-82; pres. Milco Enterprises Inc., Phoenix, 1982—. Mem. Am. Nuclear Soc., Am. Chem. Soc. Lodge: Kiwanis. Avocations: hiking, biking, gardening. Home: 118 W Northview Ave Phoenix AZ 85021 Office: Milco Enterprises Inc 3344 W Flower Ave Phoenix AZ 85017

MILLER, KATHLEEN ELIZABETH, college administrator; b. Missoula, Mont., Oct. 12, 1942; s. Lyman Wellington and Kathryn Henrietta (Freyler) M. BS, Syracuse U., 1964; MS, U. Iowa, 1966, PhD, 1971. Instr. Western State U., Gunnison, Colo., 1964-65; from instr. to asst. prof. U. Iowa, Iowa City, 1966-70, 71-77; from asst. to prof. U. Mont., Missoula, 1977-85, acting dean sch. edn., 1985—, prof., 1986—; cons. Police Officer Standards and Tng. div. Dept. Justice, Helena, Mont., 1980—. Contbr. articles to profl. jours. Grantee Mont. Dept. Highways, 1985. Mem. Am. Alliance for Health, Phys. Edn., Recreation and Dance, Internat. Soc. Biomechanics for Sports, Sch. Adminstrs. Mont., Western. Mont. Sch. Adminstrs., Mont. Assn. for Health, Phys. Edn., Recreation and Dance. Avocations: fishing, hunting, hiking, gardening. Office: U Montana LA 136 Missoula MT 59812

MILLER, KATHLEEN MARIE, experimental scientist; b. Pitts., Feb. 22, 1956; d. William Mervin and Rita Elaine (Smyth) M. BS, U. Ill., 1978; PhD, UCLA, 1983. Mem. tech. staff TRW Inc., Redondo Beach, Calif., 1983—. Co-author articles in field. Mem. Am. Chem. Soc., Am. Phys. Soc., Am. Crystallographic Assn., U. Ill. Alumni Assn. (bd. dirs. 1984-86), Phi Beta Kappa. Club: TRW Tennis (Los Angeles). Avocations: tennis, downhill skiing, music. Home: 415 Herondo St #329 Hermosa Beach CA 90254 Office: TRW Inc One Space Park Redondo Beach CA 90278

MILLER, KATHY GROSS, transportation company executive; b. Englewood, N.J., Aug. 15, 1951; d. Charles Otto and Catherine Elizabeth (Reith) Gross; m. Daniel Russell Miller, May 29, 1976. BA in Econs., George Washington U., 1973, MBA, 1976. Statistician Assn. Am. Railroads, Washington, 1974-77; mgr. U.S. Railway Assn., Washington, 1977-81; economist Ariz. Pub. Service Co., Phoenix, 1983; mgr. Greyhound Leasing and Fin. Corp., Phoenix, 1984-86, dir. asset mgmt., 1987—; bd. dirs. Commercial State Bank, Phoenix; cons. Snavely, King and Assocs., 1981-82. Pres. First Presbyn. Ch., Phoenix, 1986, bd. stewards. Mem. Women's Transp. Seminar (treas. 1977-78, pres. Washington chpt. 1979-80, pres. Phoenix chpt. 1985-86, Mem. of Yr. 1980). Republican. Avocations: traveling, swimming, horticulture. Office: Greyhound Leasing and Fin Corp 111 W Clarendon Ave Phoenix AZ 85077

MILLER, KENNETH EDWARD, consulting engineer; b. Weymouth, Mass., Dec. 24, 1951; s. Edward Francis and Lena Joan (Trotta) M.; m. Florence Gay Wilson, Sept. 18, 1976; children: Nicole Elizabeth, Brent Edward. BSME, Northeastern U., 1974; MS in Systems Mgmt., U. So. Calif., 1982. Registered profl. engr., N.Y., N.H., Ariz., Nev.; registered land surveyor, Ariz. Test engr. Stone & Webster Engring., Boston, 1974-76; plant engr. N.Y. State Power Authority, Buchanan, 1976-80; maintenance engr. Pub. Service Co. of N.H., Seabrook, 1980-82; cons. engr. Helios Engring. Inc., Litchfield Park, Ariz., 1982—. Mem. Ariz. Profl. Land Surveyor. Republican. Roman Catholic. Avocations: piloting, scuba diving. Home and Office: 360 Ancora Dr Litchfield Park AZ 85340

MILLER, KENNETH RUSSELL, JR., financial planner; b. Bellevue, Pa., Mar. 7, 1946; s. Kenneth R. Sr. and Velma Jean (Barto) M.; divorced. Registered rep. Nat. Assn. Securities Dealers; lic. broker, SEC. Announcer various radio and TV stas., Calif. and Idaho, 1967-70; mgr. Alltrans Trucking, Watsonville, Calif., 1970-72, Bekins Moving & Storage Co., Burlingame, Calif., 1972-73; ins. agt. Mass. Mut. Life Ins. Co., San Jose, Calif., 1973-79; prin. Personalized Estate Planners, Sunnyvale, Calif., 1979-81, Money Concepts/Santa Clara County, Sunnyvale, Calif., 1982—. Served as cpl. USMC, 1964-67, Vietnam. Mem. Internat. Assn. Fin. Planners, San Jose Life Underwriters Assn., San Jose Real Estate Bd. Assn. Lodge: Eagles. Avocation: organic gardening. Home: 3765 SE 25th St Gresham OR 98080 Office: PO Box 61556 Sunnyvale CA 94088

MILLER, KENT DUNKERTON, physics and computer science educator; b. Duluth, Minn., Apr. 17, 1941; s. Paul Theodore and Melba D. (Dunkerton) M.; children: Kendra, Jeffrey. BA in Physics, Ariz. State U., 1964, MA in Physics, 1965. Physics tchr. Claremont (Calif.) Sch. Dist., 1964-79, computer instr., cons., 1979—; astronomy tchr. Citrus Coll., Glendora, Calif., 1969-85; computer edn. and staff devel. cons., So. Calif., 1980-85; planetarium presentor Citrus Coll., 1975-85. Recipient McLuhan Disting. Educator award Marshall McLuhan Ctr. on Global Communications, 1984. Mem. AAAS, NEA, Am. Assn. Physics Tchrs., Calif. Tchrs. Assn. Democrat. Presbyterian. Home: 1166 Eileen Ct Upland CA 91786 Office: Claremont Sch Dist 1601 N Indian Hill Blvd Claremont CA 91711

MILLER, LARRY JAMES, engineering staff consultant; b. Preston, Idaho, Sept. 9, 1936; s. Fred Kenneth and Guelda (Johnson) M.; m. Elwayna Jensen, Mar. 25, 1966; children: Michael, Shane, Shawn, Randall, Kirsten, Wanonie. BS, Brigham Young U., 1962; postgrad., Makerere Coll., Kampla, Uganda, 1963. Officer Ministry of Edn., Tanga, Tanzania, 1963-65; tchr. Granite Sch. Dist., Salt Lake City, 1965-66; engr. Sperry Utah Co., Salt Lake City, 1966-70; profl. sci. engr. Sperry Def. Systems Div., Salt Lake City, 1983-85; cons. engring. Sperry DSD, Salt Lake City, 1985—; sr. engr. Univac, Salt Lake City, 1970-74, prin. engr., 1974-80, staff engr., 1980-83; Mem. various co. coms., including Sperry Corp. Tech. Com., Tech. Red Team, Advanced Silicon Com., Processor Selection Group. Patentee in field. Recipient Top Ten Cost Reduction award Sperry DSD, 1984. Mem. Mentor User's Group. Republican. Mormon. Avocations: gardening, hunting, fishing, racquetball. Office: Sperry Corp 640 N Sperry Way Salt Lake City UT 84116

MILLER, LAURIE, science editor; b. Fed. Republic Germany, May 7, 1960; came to U.S., 1961; d. Thomas Walter and Jacquelyn (Jolley) M. Student, U. Minn., 1979-80; BA in Psychology, Scripps Coll., 1983; postgrad., UCLA. Programmer specialist Control Data Corp., San Diego, 1982, asst. mgr. software retail store, 1983-84; support technician Ashton-Tate, Torrance, Calif., 1984, editor-in-chief, 1985-87; dir. mktg. and publishing, head writer Tom Rettig Assocs., Beverly Hills, Calif., 1987—; ind. contractor, Calif. Tech. editor Addison-Wesley books; contbr. column to monthly mag., 1985-87. Mem. Los Angeles chpt. Soc. Tech. Communication, Pi Beta Phi (asst. treas. 1980). Democrat. Methodist. Avocations: classical piano, writing, bicycling. Office: Tom Rettig Assocs 9300 Wilshire Blvd Suite 470 Beverly Hills CA 90212

MILLER, LEROY JESSE, chemist; b. Lebanon, Pa., Aug. 12, 1933; s. Jesse Royer and Elsie Mae (Light) M.; m. LaRue Mary Smeltzer, July 10, 1954; children: Eric Lee, Kurt Alan, Karl Russell. BS, Elizabethtown Coll., 1954; MS, U. Del., 1957, PhD, 1959. Sr. research engr. Atomics Internat., Canoga Park, Calif., 1958-60; sr. research chemist Sundstrand Corp, Pacoima, Calif., 1960-62; staff engr. Hughes Aircraft Co., Culver City, Calif., 1962-72; staff engr. Hughes Aircraft Co., Malibu, Calif., 1972-78, sect. head., 1978—. Contbr. articles to profl. jours; patentee in field. Mem. AAAS, Am. Chem. Soc., Soc. Photographic Scientists and Engrs., Electrochem. Soc., Sigma Xi. Democrat. Home: 8313 Hillary Dr Canoga Park CA 91304 Office: Hughes Research Labs 3011 Mailbu Canyon Rd Malibu CA 90265

MILLER, LEWIS DONALD, educator; b. San Francisco, Jan. 19, 1930; s. Charles Hymie and Rose (Keller) M.; m. Elizabeth Rose Bein, Aug. 1, 1956; children: Jesse Reid, Thomas Joel. AB in Physics, U. Calif., Berkeley, 1951; MA in Physics, San Jose State U., 1962; PhD in Materials Sci., Stanford U., 1969. Physicist USN Ordance Test Station, China Lake, Calif., 1951-52; sr. scientist USN Radiol. Def. Lab., San Francisco, 1952-70; materials scientist Chromatix, Mountain View, Calif., 1970-71; instr., coordinator Can. Coll., Redwood City, Calif., 1971—; computer cons., Redwood City, 1980—. Mem. Sigma Xi. Republican. Jewish. Avocations: astronomy, photography, stamps. Office: Can Coll 4200 Farm Hill Blvd Redwood City CA 94061

MILLER, MARVIN MERLE, office automation consultant; b. Kirkwood, Ill., Aug. 30, 1928; s. Bert Harold and Rheba Mae (Haines) M.; m. Dorothy Elizabeth Sanetel, Aug. 14, 1953; children: Michael, Patrick, Mark, Matthew. Student Portland State Coll., 1953-61. Mgr. Crown Zellerbach, San Francisco, 1955-82; cons., info. specialist, San Francisco, 1983-84; value added reseller, Concord, Calif., 1985—. Served with U.S. Army, 1948-52. Home and Office: 991 Stimel Dr Concord CA 94518

MILLER, MICHAEL DAVID, gynecologist, obstetrician; b. Nyack, N.Y., Feb. 12, 1935; s. Joseph Samuel Arluck and Sarah Elizabeth (Carpin) M.; m. Merle Judith Jablin, Aug. 16, 1959; children: Nicole Gabrielle, Steven Paul. BSc, Union Coll., Schenectady, N.Y., 1957; MD, Albert Einstein U., 1962. Diplomate Am. Bd. Ob-Gyn, Am. Bd. Med. Examiners. Intern, then resident in ob-gyn Downstate Med. Ctr., N.Y.C., 1962-1967; obstetrician, gynecologist Permanente Med. Group, San Francisco, 1969—, perinatologist, 1979—; Mem. former chmn. Kaiser Found. Hosp. perinatal rev. com. (former chmn.), San Francisco, 1969—. Served to maj. U.S. Army, 1967-69. Fellow Am. Coll. Obstetricians and Gynecologists; mem. Soc. of Perinatal Obstetricians, Calif. Perinatal Soc., Hellman Obstet. and Gynecol. Soc., San Francisco Med. Soc. Avocations: harpsichord, photography, tennis, skiing, hiking. Home: 26 Mount Wittenburg Ct San Rafael CA 94903 Office: Permanente Med Group Dept OB-Gyn 2200 O'Farrell St San Francisco CA 94115

MILLER, MICHAEL LEWIS, clinical psychologist, educator; b. Milwaukee, Oct. 27, 1947; s. David Manfred and Beatrice (Cohen) M. B.A., U. Calif., Berkeley, 1969, Ph.D., 1976; lic. psychologist Wash.; cert. Nat. Register of Health Service Providers, 1979. Clin. supr., dir. inservice tng. Youth Eastside Services, psychotherapist Applied Psychol. Services, Seattle, 1977-78; clin. instr. dept. psychiatry and behavioral scis. U. Wash., Seattle, 1977-79, clin. asst. prof. dept. psychiatry and behavioral scis. and dept. psychology, 1980-86, clin. assoc. prof. depts. psychiatry and behavioral scis. and psychology, 1986—; pvt. practice in clin. psychology, Seattle, 1978—; cons. Dept. Youth Services, King County, Wash.; mem. exec. bd. North Community Mental Health Ctr., pres. bd., 1984-85. Mem. Am. Psychol. Assn., Wash. State Psychol. Assn. (exec. bd., pres. King county chpt., 1980), Assn. Advancement Psychology, Soc. Adolescent Medicine, Psychoanalytic Assn. Seattle, Phi Beta Kappa. Democrat. Jewish. Contbr. articles to profl. jours. Office: 4026 NE 55th St Suite B Seattle WA 98105

MILLER, MILTON DAVID, agronomist, educator; b. Melmont, Wash., Nov. 27, 1911; s. Milton and Katie Virginia (Manney) M.; m. Mary Eleanor McGraw, July 24, 1932; children: Mary Lee Varone, Judith Marie Zone. BS, U. Calif., Davis, 1935, MS, 1960. Cert. profl. agronomist; cert. profl. crop specialist. Extension agronomist U. Calif., Davis, 1936-74; tech. advisor Calif. Rice Research Bd., (disting. service award 1974), Yuba City, Calif., 1970-82; cons. World Bank, Romania, 1975, US Aid, Egypt, 1977. Served to lt. col. Q.M.C., 1941-46. Recipient Legion of Merit award U.S. Army, 1949. Fellow AAAS, Am. Soc. Agronomy, Am. Crop Sci. Soc.; mem. Sigma Xi, Alpha Zeta, Alpha Gamma Rho. Republican. Club: Commonwealth of Calif. Lodges: Rotary, Masons. Avocations: model rail roading. Home: 624 Oak Ave Davis CA 95616

MILLER, NORMAN, psychology educator, researcher; b. N.Y.C., Nov. 29, 1933; s. Arthur and Pearl (Doudera) M.; divorced 1975; 1 dau., Carrie Ellen. B.A., Antioch Coll., Yellow Springs, Ohio, 1956; M.S., Northwestern U., 1957; Ph.D., 1959. Asst. prof. Yale U., New Haven, 1959-65; assoc. prof. U. Calif., Riverside, 1966-68; assoc. prof. U. Minn., Mpls., 1966-68, prof., 1968-70; prof. psychology U. So. Calif., Los Angeles, 1970—, now Mendel B. Silverberg prof. Office: Dept Psychology U So Calif University Park Los Angeles CA 90089

MILLER, PAUL ALBERT, utility holding company executive; b. San Francisco, Oct. 30, 1924; s. Robert W. and Elizabeth (Folger) M.; children: Robert L., Charles B., Christian F., Gordon E., Alejandro C., Juan J. BA, Harvard U., 1946. Staff aide So. Calif. Gas Co., Los Angeles, 1948-52; treas., dir. Pacific Lighting Corp., San Francisco, 1952-58, v.p., treas., 1958-66, exec. v.p., 1966-68, pres., chief exec. officer, 1968-72, chmn. bd., chief exec. officer, 1972—; bd. dirs. Wells Fargo & Co., Wells Fargo Bank, Newhall Mgmt. Corp.; trustee Mut. Life Ins. Co. N.Y. Bd. dirs. Civic Light Opera Assn., Los Angeles World Affairs Council, United Way, Los Angeles, Music Ctr. Opera Assn., Los Angeles, Calif. Bus. Roundtable, United Way, Inc., Los Angeles; trustee Am. Enterprise Inst., Washington, U. So. Calif.; hon. dir. John Douglas French Found. for Alzheimer's Disease. Served with U.S. Army, 1943-46. Mem. Am. Gas Assn., Pacific Coast Gas Assn., Calif. C. of C. (bd. dirs. 1968—). Clubs: Los Angeles, Calif.; Pacific Union, Bohemian (San Francisco); Brook, Racquet and Tennis (N.Y.C.); The Regency; Regency Whist. London, Portland; White's; Aspinall's; Mark's. Office: Pacific Lighting Corp 810 S Flower St Los Angeles CA 90017

MILLER, PETER S., anthropologist; b. Middleboro, Mass., June 14, 1937; s. George W. Miller and Helen Frances (Springer) Bouchard; m. Peggy Lynn Baker, Sept. 5, 1981 (div. Aug. 1985); m. Lynn Ruth Osborne, Dec. 26, 1985; children: Colin, Alison, Matthew. BA, U. Nebr., 1962; MA, U. Ariz., 1967, PhD, 1969. Research prof. anthropology Western Carolina U., Cullowhee, N.C., 1976-77; chief anthropology service Iroquois Research, Fairfax, Va., 1977-78; dir. Agy. for Conservation Archeology, Portales, N.Mex., 1979-80; prin. Powder River Cons., Gillette, Wyo., 1980-83; archaeologist State of S.D., 1983-85; assoc. prof. archaeology U. Vermillion, S.D., 1984-85; forensic anthropologist US Army Cen. Identification Lab., Ft. Shafter, Hawaii, 1986—. Editor, contbr.: Who Owns the Ancestors, 1987. Fellow Am. Anthropol. Assn., Am. Assn. Phys. Anthropologists; mem. Soc. Profl. Archeologists, Soc. Conservation Archaeology (sec. 1985—), Am. Acad. Forensic Scis. (provisional), Sigma Xi. Episcopalian. Avocation: long distance running. Office: US Army Cen ID Lab Fort Shafter HI 96858

MILLER, RALPH HENRY, business educator, consultant; b. Berkeley, Calif., Nov. 4, 1944; s. Russell Sparks and Ruth Elizabeth (Bailey) M., m. Linnea Ann Pregler, Jan. 27, 1968 (div.); m. 2d, Nancy Sabin Root, Sept. 29, 1979. B.A. in Psychology, U. Calif.-Berkeley, 1967; M.A., San Jose State U., 1969; Ph.D. (NDEA fellow 1970-73), Claremont Grad. Sch., 1979. Cert. personnel testing, Calif. Asst. dir. Ctr. Applied Social Research Claremont (Calif.) Grad. Sch., 1973-76; lectr. ops. mgmt. dept. Sch. Bus., Calif. State Poly. U., Pomona, 1976-79; asst. prof. ops. mgmt. dept., 1979-83, assoc. prof., 1983—; v.p. Alice Inc., Los Angeles, 1978-84. Bd. dirs. Willow Sch., Rancho Cucamonga, Calif., 1980-81. Named Outstanding Educator, Calif. State Poly. U., 1982. Mem. Common Cause, Am. Psychol. Assn., Western Psychol. Assn., AAAS, Decision Scis. Inst. Home: 1725 Finecroft Dr Claremont CA 91711 Office: Calif State Poly U 3801 W Temple Ave Pomona CA 91768

MILLER, RANDALL ROBERT, college official; b. Harrisburg, Pa., July 26, 1949; s. Robert Amelious and Corrine Isabel (Miller) M.; m. Susan Elizabeth Hazen, Mar. 18, 1972. BA, Dickinson Coll., 1971; MPA, U. Alaska, 1975; cert. advanced study Harvard U., 1983; EdD, U. So. Calif., 1986. Registration officer U. Alaska, Anchorage, 1975, dir. records, 1975-78; dir. admissions and records Anchorage Community Coll., 1978-83, assoc. dean students, 1983-84, asst. to chancellor, 1984-85; dean of coll. relations, 1985—; chmn. United Way campaign, 1983-86; chmn. bd. dirs. Deacons Presbyn. Ch. Served to 1st lt. U.S. Army, 1971-75. Mem. Pacific Assn. Collegiate Registrars and Admissions Officers, Am. Assn. Collegiate Registrars and Admissions Officers, Pub. Relations Soc. Alaska, Advt. Fedn. Alaska (Best of North Advt. award), Anchorage C. of C. (chmn. edn. com. 1986-87), Pi Gamma Mu, Phi Delta Kappa (treas.), Sigma Alpha Epsilon. Republican. Home: 6348 Citadel Ln Anchorage AK 99504 Office: Anchorage Community Coll 2533 Providence Dr Anchorage AK 99508

MILLER, RICHARD AUSTIN, state official; b. Albany, Oreg., Feb. 1, 1923; s. Algra Pete and Lela Marceil (Buckler) M.; m. Mary Ann Woods, Aug. 22, 1976; children by previous marriage: David, Anne Marie, Cathy Miller Hosmer, Janie. B.S. in Edn, Oreg. State U., 1948, M.Ed., 1959; grad. various mil. schs. Tchr.-coach Grants Pass (Oreg.) High Sch., 1948-49, St. Helen's (Oreg.) High Sch., 1949-53, Hillsboro (Oreg.) High Sch., 1953-54; successively tchr.-coach, dir. athletics, vice prin., prin. David Douglas High Sch., Portland, Oreg., 1954-73; adj. gen. Mil. Dept. State of Oreg., 1973—. Bd. dirs. Willamette chpt. ARC, United Way, The Inn, Home for Boys, Marion-Polk Counties, Urban League of Portland; trustee Oreg. State U. Found.; mem. Gov.'s adv. com. Info. Systems; regional v.p. Army War Coll. Found. Served with AUS, 1943-46; joined Oreg. N.G., 1947; advanced through grades to maj. gen. 1974; exec. officer, then dep. comdr. 41st Brigade 1970-72. Decorated Bronze star, Legion of Merit with oak leaf cluster, Meritorious Service medal, Combat Infantryman's badge, various N.G. medals; recipient Disting. Community Service award Anti-Defamation League, B'nai B'rith. Mem. Multnomah County Schoolmasters (pres. 1959-60), Oreg. High Sch. Coaches Assn. (pres. 1961-62), Multnomah County Adminstrs. Assn. (pres. 1967-68), N.G. Assn. U.S. (treas. 1972-76, pres. 1976-78), N.G. Assn. Oreg. (dir. 1963-64), Oreg. Secondary Sch. Prins. Assn. (exec. bd. 1971-73), Assn. Secondary and High Schs. (permanent chmn. program com. 1971-72), Inter-League Council High Schs. in Portland Met. Area (pres. 1969-73), Oreg. Sch. Activities Assn. (mem. del. assembly 1970-73), Oreg. State U. Dad's Club (treas. 1968-69), David Douglas Edn. Assn., Air Force Assn., Assn. U.S. Army (adv. dir.), Phi Delta Theta. Presbyterian. Clubs: Kiwanis (pres. Greater SE club 1968-69), Elks. Home: Camp Withycombe Clackamas OR 97015 Office: Mil Dept Oreg 2150 Fairgrounds Rd NE Salem OR 97303 *

MILLER, RICHARD FRANKLIN, educator, researcher, educational administrator; b. San Francisco, Sept. 9, 1927; s. Henry G. and Hulda M. M. A.B., San Francisco State U., 1950; M.A., U. Calif.-Berkeley, 1964, Ed.D., 1970. Cert. secondary tchr., gen. supr. Calif. With San Francisco Unified Sch. Dist., 1956—, tchr. bus. edn., econs. and social studies Mission High Sch., 1967—, adminstr. career edn. program, 1970-80. Mem. San Francisco Symphony, Fine Arts Mus. Soc. Served to sgt., U.S. Army, 1952-54. Fellow in edn. U. Calif.-Berkeley, 1974-75. Mem. Assn. Supervision and Curriculum Devel., San Francisco Fedn. Tchrs., Phi Delta Kappa. Democrat. Unitarian. Office: 3750 18th St San Francisco CA 94114

MILLER, ROBERT CHRISTIAN, structural technician; b. Youngstown, Ohio, Feb. 5, 1943; s. Paul M. and Marian V. (Lambert) M.; m. Becky J. Fager, June 27, 1965; children: Kevin C., Brenda J., Kylie. AA, Kans. Tech. Inst., 1968. Cert. engring. technician. Constrn. mgr. Black & Veatch Engrs. Architects, Bismarck, N.D., 1978-79, project field mgr., 1980-82; project field mgr. Black & Veatch Engrs. Architects, Delta, Utah, 1982—. Dist. advancement chmn. Boy Scouts Am., Provo, Utah, 1986. Served with USAF, 1961-66, Korea. Mem. Am. Soc. Cert. Engring. Technicians, Nat. Eagle Scout Assn. Republican. Methodist. Avocations: woodworking, camping, softball. Home: 1555 W 1250 N Provo UT 84604 Office: Black & Veatch Engrs Architects Rural Rt 1 Box 985 Delta UT 84624

MILLER, ROBERT DAVID, insurance company consultant; b. Oak Park, Ill., Jan. 9, 1932; s. David R. and Louise (Reed) M.; B.S., Okla. State U., 1956; M.B.A., Ill. State U., Normal, 1970; m. Sharon Anderson, July 6, 1956; 1 son, Jay-James. Acctg. clk. Country Mut. Ins. Co., Bloomington, Ill., 1956-57, sr. acct., 1957-61, chief acct., 1961-68; controller Country Mut. Ins. Co., County Casualty, Mid-Am., Preferred ins. cos., Bloomington, 1968-79, dir. ops., 1979-83 ; v.p., dir. field ops. Kramer Capital Cons., Inc., N.Y.C., 1983—; pres., dir. Nat. Am. Ins. Co. Calif., Long Beach, 1985—; sec.-treas., dir. Westminster Village, Bloomington, dir. Ill. Ins. Guaranty Fund. lectr. in field. Active United Way, 1977-83; sec. bd. trustees 2d. Presbyn. Ch., Bloomington, 1978-81, elder, 1982-85. Served with USNR, 1952-54. Recipient Alumni Achievement award Ill. State U., 1980. Mem. McLean County (Ill.) Assn. Commerce and Industry (chmn. tax com. 1977-82), Ins. Acctg. and Systems Assn. (pres. 1979-80), Fin. Execs. Inst., Nat. Assn. Accts., Nat. Assn. Ind. Insurers (chmn. tax com. 1975-82), Mut. Ins. Com. Fed. Taxation (treas. 1973—), Data Processing Mgmt. Assn. (pres., internat. dir. 1973-75), Nat. Assn. Mut. Ins. Cos. (tax com. chmn. 1972-76, Presdl. award 1973), Adminstrv. Mgmt. Soc. Clubs: Bloomington Country, Masons, Shriners, Elks. Contbr. articles to profl. jours. Home: 1303 E Vernon Ave Normal IL 61761-3240 Office: Nat Am Ins Co Calif 19100 Susana PO Box 5810 Long Beach CA 90805 Office: Kramer Capital Cons 1 Greenwich Plaza Greenwich CT 06836

MILLER, ROBERT HYLAND, optical physicist; b. Balt.; s. Theodore Hyland and Emma Louise (Kahmer) M.; B.A. in Physics, Johns Hopkins U., 1962; M.S., Stevens Inst. Tech., N.J., 1968. Supr. lab. Keuffel & Esser Co., Morristown, N.J., 1962-72; tech. dir. Valtec Corp., Holliston, Mass., 1972-77; sr. research scientist Optical Coating Lab., Inc., 1977-80; sr. optical physicist Nanometrics, Sunnyvale, Calif., 1980-81; pres. Stanford Tech. Assoc., Santa Rosa, Calif., 1981-84; process devel. physicist 3M Co. (optical recording), Mountain View, Calif., 1984—; cons. to cos. including LTV Corp., Allied Corp., Teledyne, and Siemens. Recipient Hon. Sci. award Bausch & Lomb, 1956. Mem. Optical Soc. Am., Am. Vacuum Soc., Materials Research Soc., Soc. Photo-Optical Instrumentation Engrs., IEEE, Mus. Soc. San Francisco. Home: 1816 Arroyo Sierra Ct Santa Rosa CA 95405 Office: 420 Bernardo Ave Mountain View CA 94043

MILLER, ROBERT JOSEPH, lieutenant governor of Nevada, lawyer; b. Evanston, Ill., Mar. 30, 1945; s. Ross Wendell and Coletta Jane (Doyle) M.; m. Sandra Ann Searles, Oct. 17, 1949; children: Ross, Corrine. BA in Polit. Sci., U. Santa Clara, 1967; JD, Loyola U., Los Angeles, 1971. First legal advisor Las Vegas (Nev.) Met. Police Dept., 1973-75; justice of the peace Las Vegas Twp., 1975-78; dist. atty. Clark County, Las Vegas, 1979-86; lt. gov. State of Nev., 1987—. Chmn. Nev. Commn. on Econ. Devel., Carson City, 1987—, Nev. Commn. on Tourism, Carson City, 1987—; mem. Pres. Reagan's Task Force on Victims of Crime, 1982. Mem. Nat. Dist. Atty.'s Assn. (pres. 1984-85), Nev. Dist. Atty.'s Assn. (pres. 1979, 83). Democrat. Roman Catholic. Office: State of Nev Office of Lt Gov Capitol Complex Carson City NV 89710

MILLER, ROBERT SCOTT, not-for-profit organization administrator, social worker; b. Seattle, Dec. 12, 1947; s. Bert Lester and Carol Theresa (Gustafson) M.; m. Karen Ann Staake, Nov. 12, 1977; children: Sarah, Megan, Emily. BA in Sociology, Seattle Pacific U., 1970; AM in Social Work, U. Chgo., 1972; MA in Human Resources Mgmt., Pepperdine U., 1977. Br. supr. Wash. State Dept. Social and Health Services, Oak Harbor and Anacortes, 1975-78; lectr., coordinator rural community mental health project U. Wash., Seattle, 1978-83; exec. dir. Armed Services YMCA, Oak Harbor, 1984-86; area dir. United Way of Island County, Oak Harbor, 1986—. Recipient outstanding service award Armed Services YMCA of U.S., Dallas, 1985, two program merit awards McDonald's Corp., Oak Harbor, 1986. Mem. Nat. Assn. Social Workers (cert., bd. dirs. Wash. chpt. 1982-85), Wash. Assn. Social Welfare (pres. 1975-76), Bus. and Profl. Women (v.p. Oak Harbor chpt. 1985-86, pres. 1986-87). Lutheran. Lodge: Lions (sec. 1987—). Avocations: reading, camping, fishing. Office: United Way of Island County Navy Family Service Ctr Seaplane Base Bldg 20 PO Box 798 Oak Harbor WA 98277

MILLER, RONALD LEE, chemical engineering educator; b. Rawlins, Wyo., June 29, 1954; s. Walter Richard and Marian Lois (Miller) M.; m. Cynthia Mae Langston, Aug. 17, 1985. BSChemE, U. Wyo., 1977, MSChemE, 1979; PhD in Chem. Engring. and Petroleum Refining, Colo. Sch. Mines, 1982. Engr. Amoco Oil Co., Powell, Wyo., 1977; asst. prof. chem. engring. U. Wyo., Laramie, 1982-86; research asst. prof. Colo. Sch. Mines, Golden, 1986—; tech adv. Synthetic Fossil Fuels Co., Laramie, 1980-85; cons. In-Situ, Inc., Laramie, 1982-85, Western Research Inst., Laramie, 1984-86, Carbon Resources, Inc., Wheatridge, Colo., 1986—. Contbr. articles to profl. jours.; patentee in field. Research grantee Electric Power Research, 1982-86, Dept. Energy, 1986—. Mem. Am. Inst. Chem. Engrs., Am. Chem. Soc., Sigma Xi, Tau Beta Pi. Home: PO Box 1179 Golden CO 80402 Office: Colo Sch Mines Golden CO 80401

MILLER, RONALD THOMAS, utility co. exec.; b. Burke, Idaho, Aug. 6, 1919; s. Dale D. and Mary E. (Dunphy) M.; m. Betty Loretta Bergman, Mar. 7, 1942; children—Mary L. (Mrs. John A. Rhine, Jr.), Margaret A. (Mrs. Jan E. Monroe). B.S., Oreg. State U., 1941. Registered profl. engr., Oreg. Insp. fed. diking project U.S. C.E., Deer Island, Oreg., 1941; with N.W. Natural Gas Co., Portland, 1947—; chief engr. N.W. Natural Gas Co., 1968-71, v.p. engring. and gas control, 1971-73, exec. v.p., 1973-75, pres., chief exec. officer, from 1975, also dir., now chmn.; v.p., dir. Asso. Oreg. Industries, Blue Cross Oreg. Pres. Lake Oswego (Oreg.) P.T.A., 1963, Am. Field Service, Lake Oswego, 1966-67; bd. dirs. Portland Better Bus. Bur., Columbia-Pacific council Boy Scouts Am. Served to capt. C.E. AUS, 1942-47, PTO. Mem. Am. Gas Assn. (chmn. liquefied natural gas com. 1972-73, dir. 1979—), Am. Soc. M.E., Nat. Soc. Profl. Engrs., Profl. Engrs. Oreg. (award of merit 1968, chpt. sec. 1968), Pacific Coast Gas Assn. (gen. chmn. operating sect. 1972-73, dir. 1976—, 2d vice chmn. 1979—), Portland C. of C. (dir. 1979—), Alpha Sigma Phi. Republican. Roman Catholic. Clubs: Waverley Country (Portland); Arlington, Rotary. Office: Northwest Natural Gas Co 220 NW Second Ave Portland OR 97209 *

MILLER, ROY FRANKLIN, mgmt. cons.; b. Salt Lake City, Feb. 3, 1912; s. Roy F. and Cassie A. Miller; BBA, U. Wash., Seattle, 1934; m. Lena C. Clifford, May 26, 1935; children: Roy Franklin, III, Richard C., Virginia Moody. Chmn. bd. Kirchner Miller Agy., Inc., Pocatello, 1980; Devel. Assocs., Pocatello, 1967, Miller and Miller Land Devel. Co., Pocatello, 1968; past dir. South Idaho Med. Service Corp.; bd. dirs. Blue Cross of Idaho Health Services, Inc.; mem. Eastern Idaho Council Industry and Energy. past pres. Med. Dental Hosp. Burs. Am.; past mem. Idaho Health Planning Council. Bd. dirs. Idaho Spl. Olympics, Idaho Youth Ranch, Idaho Scottish Rite Found., Acacia Ednl. Found., Idaho DeMolay Found.; chmn. fin. com. Acacia Nat. Com., bd. dirs. Central Pacific Conf., United Ch. Christ; past chmn. bd. Pocatello Library; past chmn. Bannock County Republican Party; del. Rep. Nat. Conv., 1976; bd. dirs. Idaho Youth Ranch Found.; bd. dirs. Eastern Idaho Industry and Energy Commn.; chmn. president's adv. com. on health sci. edn. Idaho State U. Recipient Stanley R. Mauck award Med. Dental Hosp. Burs. Am., 1970; recipient various certs. merit. Mem. Fort Hall Water Users Assn., Am. Collectors Assn. (charter mem., past dir.), Nat. Fedn. Ind. Bus., Idaho Collectors Assn. (past pres.), Idaho Assn. Commerce and Industry, Pocatello C. of C. Clubs: Pocatello Rotary, Masons (33 deg., treas. bldg. bd., chmn. adv. conf. Scottish Rite bodies, Pocatello), Shriners. Home: 91 Foothill Blvd Box 1090 Pocatello ID 83204 Office: 836 E Center St Suite D Pocatello ID 83201

MILLER, R(USSELL) BRYAN, chemistry professor; b. Tyler, Tex., May 31, 1940; s. Ernest Barger and Dorothy (Bryan) M.; m. Francesca Elizabeth Rappole, Aug. 22, 1969; children: Francesca Leona Wellman, Arthur Albert Wellman. BS in Chemistry, Washington and Lee U., 1962; PhD in Chemistry, Rice U., 1967. Postdoctoral researcher Columbia U., N.Y.C., 1966-68; asst. prof. chemistry U. Calif., Davis, 1968-75, assoc. prof., 1975-81, prof., 1981—, chmn. chemistry dept., 1985—. Editor: Annual Reports in Organic Synthesis, 1970-73, 75-77; contbr. articles to profl. jours. Mem. Am. Chem. Soc. Office: U Calif Dept Chemistry Davis CA 95616

MILLER, RUSSELL TUTTLE, realtor; b. Spokane, Dec. 10, 1922; s. Russell Tuttle and Claudia (Lewis) M.; B.S., Mass. Inst. Tech., 1948; postgrad. Colo. Sch. Mines, 1950; m. Georgette Thioliere, Apr. 17, 1948. Pres., Golden West Enterprises, Cambridge, Mass., 1939-48;pres., New World Exploration Corp., Los Angeles, 1948-56; cons. mineral engring., Los Angeles, 1956-58; pres. Tech. Mktg. Assos., Los Angeles, 1959-73; pres. Titan Realty Corp., Los Angeles, 1959—, Worldwide Properties, Ltd., Newport Beach, Calif., 1976—, Sepol, Ltd., Irvine, Calif., 1976—, Internat. Fin. Cons., Newport Beach, Calif., 1972—. Served in U.S. Army, 1942-45. Decorated Purple

Heart. Mem. Am. Inst. Mining and Metall. Engrs., Am. Inst. Mining Engrs., Am. Inst. Chem. Engrs., Soc. Exploration Geophysicists. Episcopalian. Clubs: Calif. Yacht, Riviera Country, Marina City, Balboa Bay. Home and office: 1210 Park Newport #413 Newport Beach CA 92660

MILLER, SALLY M., history educator; b. Chgo., Apr. 13, 1937; d. Robert and Clara (Nixon) M. BA, U. Ill., 1958; AM, U. Chgo., 1963; PhD, U. Toronto, 1966. Prof. history Mich. State U., East Lansing, 1965-67, U. Pacific, Stockton, Calif., 1967—; vis. prof. U. Warwick, England, 1978-79. Author: The Radical Immigrant, 1974, Victor Berger, 1973; editor Flawed Liberation, 1981, Kate Richards O'Hare: Selected Writings and Speeches, 1982, Ethnic Press in the U.S., 1987; mng. editor Pacific Historian, 1985. Recipient Fulbright award U.S. Info. Agy., 1986. Mem. S.W. Labor Studies Assn. (pres. 1986—), Am. Hist. Assn., Immigration History Soc. (mem. exec. bd. 1985—), Orgn. Am. Historians, AAUP. Office: U Pacific History Dept Stockton CA 95211

MILLER, SAMUEL LEE, real estate exec.; b. Maywood, Ill., Apr. 22, 1912; s. Samuel Lee and Clarissa (Buck) M.; Ph.B., U. Chgo., 1935; m. Sally Ann Walton, June 24, 1939 (dec.); 1 dau., Sally Ann (Mrs. David Roth); m. 2d, Irene A. Reed, 1973. Foreman mfg. Am. Can Co., Maywood, 1933-42; adminstrv. mgr. George S. May Co., San Francisco, 1942-47; gen. sales mgr. Hunt Foods and Industries, Fullerton, Calif., 1947-58; with H.M. Parker and Son, wholesale automobile parts co., 1958-68, v.p., gen. mgr., North Hollywood, Calif., 1962-68, bd. dirs., 1959-68; pres. Am. Parts Systems, Inc., North Hollywood, 1968-69, regional sales promotion mgr., 1970-71, gen. mgr., Fairfield, Calif., 1972-76; pres. Roth & Miller Realty, Inc., 1977-85. Mem. Theta Delta Chi. Republican. Methodist. Mason. Home: 248 Cheyenne Dr Vacaville CA 95688

MILLER, SCOTT ALLAN, III, engineering physicist, consultant; b. Lincoln, Sept. 6, 1955; s. Scott Allan Jr. and Helen (Nelsen) M. Test engr. Beech Aerospace, Boulder, 1977-78; systems engr. Phoenix Geophysics, Toronto, 1978-80; dir. research and devel. Neomed Industries, Boulder, 1980-85; sr. engr. ValleyLab, Boulder, 1986—; cons. in field. Contbr. articles to profl. jours.; patentee in field. Grantee Engring. Devel. U. Colo., 1973, Colo. Ednl., 1974. Mem. AAAS, Assn. Advancement of Med. Instrumentation (faculty mem. 1984) Internat. Electro-tech. Commn. (U.S. rep. 1984-85), Mensa, Tau Beta Pi (treas. 1975-76), Sigma Pi Sigma. Office: Valley Lab Inc 5920 Longbow Boulder CO 80301

MILLER, SELAINA AUNOA LEVI, employment and training executive; b. Apia, Western Samoa, May 5, 1946; came to U.S., 1962, naturalized, 1969; d. Arius and Avasa (Niu) Levi; m. Charles M. Miller, Dec. 14, 1974; 1 child, Jamila Atamai. AA, Chabot Coll., 1969; BA, Calif. State U., Hayward, 1971. Cert. tchr., Calif. Program developer/coordinator Alameda County Assn. Mentally Retarded, Oakland, Calif., 1969-71; program dir., tchr. Contra Costa Assn. Retarded/Richmond Calif. Sch. Dist., Walnut Creek, Calif., 1971-74; mgr. regional services MidWillamette Jobs Council, Pvt. Industry Council, Salem, Oreg., 1975—; mem. adv. bd. study on unemployment problems of Samoans, N.W. Regional edn. Lab., Portland, Oreg., 1982-83; participant vocation extern program for tchrs. and trainers Oreg. State U. and Oreg. Alliance for Program Improvement, Corvallis, 1985-86. Participant region 9-Oreg. Joint Action for Community Service, 1982-85; bd. dirs. Green Thumb Agy. for Older Workers, Oreg.-Wash., 1985-86, Community Action Orgn. Info. and Referral, Stayton, 1985-86; mem. community adv. bd. spl. programs for students Salem-Keizer Sch Dist., 1986-87; active Metro Work Experience Coordinators Orgn., 1986-87. Mem. Soc. for Training Devel., Nat. Assn. Female Execs., Oreg. Employment and Tng. Assn. Avocations: sewing, gardening, swimming, volleyball, travel. Home: 18874 Old Mehama Rd SE Stayton OR 97383 Office: Mid Willamette Jobs Council 1495 Edgewater NW Suite 225 Salem OR 97304

MILLER, SOL, bioscience consultant; b. Akron, Ohio, June 3, 1914; s. Phillip and Mollie (Drutz) M.; m. Rosalyn Raful, Dec. 28, 1937; children—Barbara Claire Miller Olschwang, Kenneth Arnold. B.A., Akron U., 1936; M.S., Ohio State U., 1939; Ph.D., Sussex U., Eng., 1975. Cert. specialist Nat. Registry Microbiologists; cert. hazard control mgr.; cert. profl. chemist. Bacteriologist Ohio Dept. Health, 1939-42; chief chemist Q.O. Ordnance Corp., Grand Island, Nebr., 1942-43; research assoc. Children's Fund of Mich., Detroit, 1944-54; bacteriologist James Labs., Chgo., 1954-55; group leader, research bacteriologist IIT Research Inst., Chgo., 1955-72; corp. biohazard control Abbott Labs., North Chicago, Ill., 1972-84; biosci. cons. Safety Systems and Services Inc., Fairfield, Calif., 1984—; adj. instr. Chgo. Med. Sch., 1973-84, adj. asst. prof., 1984—; mem. exec. com. tng. chmn. research and devel. sect. Nat. Safety Council, 1974—. Contbr. articles to profl. jours. Recipient Tanner-Shaughnessy Merit award, 1981. Fellow Am. Inst. Chemists, Am. Acad. Microbiology; mem. Am. Inst. Biol. Scis., Am. Chem. Soc., Am. Soc. for Microbiology, Am. Soc. Indsl. Microbiology, Ill. Soc. for Microbiology, Am. Assn. Clin. Chemists, Am. Indsl. Hygiene Assn., Sigma Xi. Lodge: B'nai B'rith (past pres. Lodge 1455). Home: 315 Wayne Pl Apt 401 Oakland CA 94608 Office: 2499 Martin Rd Fairfield CA 94533

MILLER, STANLEY ALLEN, environmental scientist; b. Spokane, Wash., May 23, 1947; s. Stanley Joaquin and Barbara Ann (Hopp); m. Georgia Maureen Freeley, June 10, 1972. BA in Edn., Cen. Wash. U., 1969, BA in Chemistry, 1971; MS in Environ. Sci., Wash. State U., 1978. Tchr. Coulee City (Wash.) Schs., 1969-75; environ. specialist Spokane (Wash.) County, 1977-82, program mgr. ground water quality mgmt. program, 1982—. Editor: (newsletter) Rathdrum/Spokane Aquifer, 1985—; contbr. articles profl. jours. Recipient water quality planning grants Wash. Dept. Ecology, 1982—, Achievement award Nat. Assn. of Counties, 1982, 86. Mem. AAAS, N.Am. Lake Mgmt. Soc., Pacific Northwest and Pollution Control Assn. (session presider 1986), Am. Water Resources Assn. (dir. 1987). Avocations: outdoor activities, backpacking, photography, winemaking. Office: Spokane County Engrs N 811 Jefferson Spokane WA 99260

MILLER, STEPHEN DEWAYNE, computer engineer; b. Pochantas, Ark., Sept. 19, 1956; s. Tommy Joe and Patricia Ann (Edington) M. BA in Computer Sci., Webster U., 1978. Software engr. Hurletron Altair, Danville, Ill., 1981-82; sr. software engr. Cushman Electronics, San Jose, Calif., 1982-85; sr. test engr. Telenova, Los Gatos, Calif., 1983-85; sr. software engr. FMC, San Jose, 1985—. Mem. Am. Assn. Artificial Intelligence. Avocations: chess, backgammon, flying. Home: 2077 Foxhall Loop San Jose CA 95125

MILLER, STEPHEN HERSCHEL, surgery educator; b. N.Y.C., Jan. 12, 1941; s. Morris Louis and Mildred Lily (Beller) M.; m. Carol Susan Shapiro, Dec. 18, 1965; children: Mark, David. BS, UCLA, 1960, MD, 1964. Diplomate Am. Bd. Surgery, Am. Bd. Plastic Surgery (mem. exec. com. 1985—, chmn. written examination sect. 1985—, bd. dirs. 1984—). Asst. prof. surgery U. Calif., San Francisco, 1973-74; from asst. prof. to prof. surgery Milton S. Hershey Med. Ctr., Hershey, Pa., 1974-78; chief div. plastic surgery Oreg. Health Scis. U., Portland, 1979—. Physician advisor Boy Scouts Am., dist. chmn. scoutmaster exec. council, 1983-84; bd. dirs. Temple Beth Israel, Portland, 1984-86. Recipient Physician Recognition award, 1976; grantee Med. Research Found. of Oreg., 1980, Oreg. Health Scis. U., 1980. Mem. ACS (chmn. program com. 1983—), Am. Soc. Plastic and Reconstructive Surgery (bd. dirs. 1980—, v.p. 1985-86, pres.-elect 1986-87, grantee 1976), Am. Assn. Plastic Surgeons (chmn. research com. 1983-84), Assn. Acad. Chmn. Plastic Surgery (sec./treas. 1985—). Avocations: reading, tennis. Home: 3 Dover Way Lake Oswego OR 97034 Office: Oreg Health Scis U 3181 SW Sam Jackson Park Rd Portland OR 97206

MILLER, STEPHEN JOSEPH, research chemist; b. Glendale, Calif., Sept. 11, 1945; s. Leon Raymond and Grace (Kobrin) M.; m. Taska Barton, July 1, 1977; children: Joseph, Aaron, Lee. BS, UCLA, 1967; MS, U. Ill., 1972, PhD, 1974. Research chemist Chevron Research, Richmond, Calif., 1974-78, sr. research chemist, 1978-83, sr. research assoc., 1983—. Patentee in field. V.P. B'nai B'rith, Oakland, Calif., 1979. Served with U.S. Army, 1969-71. Mem. Am. Chem. Soc., Sigma Xi, Alpha Chi Sigma. Democrat. Jewish. Avocations: thoroughbred breeding and racing, classical singing. Home: 520 45th Ave San Francisco CA 94121 Office: Chevron Research Co 576 Standard Ave Richmond CA 94802

MILLER, STEPHEN PAUL, oceanographer, consultant; b. Lynwood, Calif., June 17, 1947; s. Paul and Valeria (Mangan) Miller. BS in Physics, U. Calif., 1965-69; MS in Geophysics, MIT, 1969-73. Specialist in marine physics Scripps Inst. Oceanography, La Jolla, Calif., 1973-80; specialist in geophysics U. Calif., Santa Barbara, 1980—; cons. geophys. research and computing, Santa Barbara, 1982—. Author numerous journal articles. Recipient Newcomb-Cleve. prize AAAS, 1980; MIT grantee, 1969. Fellow Royal Astrono. Soc.; mem. Am. Geophys. Union, Soc. of Exploration Geophysicists, Assn. for Computing Machinery, Porsche Owners Club of Los Angeles. Democrat. Avocations: porsche racing, photography, painting, world traveling. Home: 256 Big Sur Dr Goleta CA 93117 Office: U Calif Dept Geolo Sci Santa Barbara CA 93106

MILLER, STUART CREIGHTON, professor, author; b. N.Y.C., June 2, 1927; s. Stewart Gillespie and Susanna Morrow (Dunleavy) M.; m. Naomi Esterowitz, June 11, 1955; children: Sarah, Peter Isaac. BA, Colgate U., 1950; MA, Columbia U., 1955, PhD, 1966. Instr. history Columbia U., N.Y., 1958-62; asst. prof. San Francisco State U., 1962-66, assoc. prof., 1966-71, prof. social sci., history, 1971—; cons., evaluator U. Calif. Press, Berkeley, Calif., 1970-77; vis. assoc. prof. history, Smith Coll., Northampton, Mass., 1968; cons. Angel Island Project NEH, San Francisco, 1983-85, other NEH projects, Washington, 1970—; commentator radio programs world affairs council, Calif. Times/ Calif. History Humanities, 1964-85. Author: Unwelcome Immigrant: American Image of Chinese '69, Benevolent Assimilation: American Conquest Philippines '82; contbr. articles and essays to profl. jours. Organizer Sausalito (Calif.) Environ. Assn., 1974, research dir., 1974-80; mem. China Missionary Symposium Ford-AHA, Cambridge, Curnavaca, 1970-71, Philippine-Am. History Project Luce Found., Harvard, Cambridge, 1977-78. Served to lt. comdr. USN, 1944-47, 51-53. Recipient Research Leave award State of Calif., 1968, Meritorious Profl. Performance award NEH, 1985; NSF grantee, 1971, Am. Philos. Soc. grantee, 1972. Mem. Am. Hist. Assn., Orgn. Am. Historians, Immigration History Soc., Chinese Hist. Soc. Am., Sausalito and Truro (Mass.) Hist. Socs., Am Profs. for Peace Middle East. Democrat. Episcopalian. Club: Academica Judaica (San Francisco). Avocations: oil painting, tennis, sculling, board surfing, swimming. Home: 181 San Carlos Ave Sausalito CA 94965 Office: San Francisco State U 1600 Holloway San Francisco CA 94132

MILLER, THOMAS CECIL, private investigator; b. Los Angeles, Jan. 27, 1951; s. Thomas Cecil Miller and Oetta Elizabeth (Buckman) Harrison; m. Michele Marie Autin, Aug. 23, 1986. BA in History and Journalism, Metro State Coll., 1974; BA in Classical Langs., U. Denver, 1985; MA in English, Middlebury Coll., 1985. Freelance writer, journalist Denver; prin. Investigative Reporting Services, Denver, 1983—. Author numerous poems. Pub. relation dir. John Fuhr for Gov., Colo., 1982; del. Denver County Reps., 1984, alt., 1986. Mem. Profl. Pvt. Investigators Assn. Colo., Colo. Press. Assn., Denver C. of C. Roman Catholic. Avocations: skiing, target shooting, hunting, martial arts, fgn. langs. Office: Investigative Reporting Services PO Box 10844 Denver CO 80209

MILLER, THOMAS EUGENE, legal editor, writer; b. Bryan, Tex., Jan. 4, 1929; s. Eugene Adam and Ella Lucille (Schroeder) M. B.A., Tex. A&M U., 1950; M.A., U. Tex., 1956, J.D., 1966; postgrad. U. Houston, 1957-58, U Calif.-Berkeley, 1983. Bar: Tex. 1966. Research technician M.D. Anderson Hosp., Houston, 1956-58; claims examiner trainee Soc. Security Adminstrn., New Orleans, 1964; trademark examiner trainee Dept. Commerce, Washington, 1966; editor Bancroft-Whitney Co., San Francisco, 1966—; author book under pseudonym. Contbg. mem. Democratic Nat. Com., 1981-87. Fellow Internat. Biog. Assn. (life); mem. ABA, Internat. Platform Assn., Phi Kappa Phi, Psi Chi, Phi Eta Sigma. Methodist. Clubs: Nat. Writers, Press, Commonwealth. Home: 2293 Turk Blvd Apt 5 San Francisco CA 94118 Office: Bancroft-Whitney Co 301 Brannan St San Francisco CA 94107

MILLER, THOMAS JAMES, podiatrist; b. Titusville, Pa., Dec. 23, 1936; s. Charles Edward and Dorothy Irene (Patterson) M.; divorced; children: Thomas James II, Jessica Lynn. Degee in med. tech., Carnegie Inst.; B in Med. Tech., Waynesburg Coll.; D in Podiat. Medicine, Ohio Coll. Podiat. Medicine, 1963. Gen. practice podiat. medicine Cleve., 1964-79, Laramie, Wyo., 1980—; instr. surgery Ohio Coll. Podiat. Medicine, Cleve., 1975-77. Contbr. articles to profl. jours. Mem. Am. Podiat. Med. Assn. (treas. internat. region 1982—), Wyo. Podiat. Med. Assn. (pres. 1981-84, chmn. bd. 1984—). Lodges: Kiwanis (pres. Cleve. club 1972), Masons, Shriners. Avocations: oil painting, piano. Office: Laramie Foot Clinic 504 Lyons St Laramie WY 82070

MILLER, TIM LEE, chemist; b. Iowa City, Oct. 28, 1955; s. Melvin Curtis and Mary Agnes (Denton) M. BS in Chemistry, U. N.Mex., 1977. Vol. chemistry instr. U.S. Peace Corps, Fiji, 1977-79; asst. assayer Gold Fields Operating Co.-Ortiz, Santa Fe, 1979-82, assayer, 1982-83, chief assayer, 1983-85; chief chemist Gold Fields Operating Co.-Mesquite, Brawley, Calif., 1985—. NSF Research grantee, 1976. Mem. AAAS, Am. Chem. Soc. Roman Catholic. Avocations: archery, astronomy, hunting. Home: 1745 W 26th Dr Yuma AZ 85364 Office: Gold Fields Operating Co Mesquite HCR76 Glamis 100 Brawley CA 92227

MILLER, WARREN EDWARD, political scientist; b. Hawarden, Iowa, Mar. 26, 1924; s. John Carroll and Mildred Ovedia (Lien) M.; m. Ruth S. Jones, May 1981; children by previous marriage: Jeffrey Ralph, Jennifer Louise. B.S., U. Oreg., 1948, M.S., 1950; Ph.D., Maxwell Sch. Citizenship and Public Affairs, Syracuse U., 1954; Ph.D. (hon.), U. Goteborg, Sweden, 1972. Asst. study dir. Survey Research Ctr., Inst. Social Research, U. Mich., 1951-53, study dir., 1953-56, research assoc., 1956-59, program dir., 1959-68, research coordinator polit. behavior program, 1968-70, prin. investigator nat. election studies, 1977—; dir. Ctr. Polit. Studies, Inst. Social Research, 1970-81; program dir. Ctr. Polit. Studies, 1982—; asst. prof. polit. sci. Ctr. Polit. Studies, Inst. Social Research, 1956-58, asso. prof., 1958-63, prof., 1963—, Arthur W. Bromage prof. polit. sci., 1981-82; prof. polit. sci. Ariz. State U., 1981—; fellow Center Advanced Study in Behavioral Scis., 1961-62; exec. dir. Inter-univ. Consortium for Polit. and Social Research, 1962-70, assoc. dir., 1978—; vis. prof. U. Tilburg, Netherlands, 1973, U. Geneva, 1973, European U. Inst., Florence, Italy, 1979; vis. Disting. prof. Ariz. State U., 1981; trustee Inst. Am. Univs., 1970—. Author: (with others) books including The Voters Decide, 1954, American Voter, 1960, with T.E. Levitin) Leadership and Change: Presidential Elections from 1952-1976, 1977, (with M.K. Jennings) Parties in Transition, 1986, (with others) The American National Election Studies Data Sourcebook, 1952-1978, 1980; contbr. (with others) articles to profl. publs.; editorial bd.: (with others) Am. Polit. Sci. Rev, 1966-71, Computers and the Humanities, 1969-71, Social Science History, 1976, Social Science Review, 1978; editorial adv. bd.: (with others) Sage Electoral Studies Yearbook, 1974—. Served with USAAF, 1943-46. Recipient Disting. Alumnus award Maxwell Sch. Citizenship and Public Affairs, Syracuse U., 1974, Disting. Faculty Achievement award U. Mich., 1977. Fellow AAAS; mem. Am. Polit. Sci. Assn. (pres. 1979-80), Internat. Polit. Sci. Assn. (council 1969-73), M.W. Polit. Sci. Assn., Internat. Soc. Polit. Psychology, So. Polit. Sci. Assn., Social Sci. History Assn. (pres. 1979-80). Office: Ariz State U Dept of Polit Sci Tempe AZ 85287

MILLER, WENDELL SMITH, chemist, consultant; b. Columbus, Ohio, Sept. 26, 1925; s. Wendell Pierce and Emma Josephine (Smith) M.; B.A., Pomona Coll., 1944; M.S., U. Calif. at Los Angeles, 1952; m. Dorothy Marie Pagen, Aug. 18, 1949; children—William Ross, Wendell Roger. Chemist U.S. Rubber Co., Torrance, Calif., 1944; sr. chemist Carbide & Carbon Chemicals Corp., Oak Ridge, 1944-48; partner Kellogg & Miller, Los Angeles, 1949-56; patent coordinator Electro Optical Systems, Inc., Pasadena, Calif., 1956-59; v.p. Intertech. Corp. optical and optoelectronic system devel., North Hollywood, Calif., 1960-66, dir., 1966—; assoc. Ctr. for Study of Evolution and Origin of Life, UCLA. Commr., Great Western Council Boy Scouts Am., 1960-65. Served with AUS, 1944-46. Decorated Army Commendation medal. Mem. Los Angeles Patent Law Assn., IEEE, AAAS, 20th Century Round Table, Sigma Xi, Phi Beta Kappa, Pi Mu Epsilon. Numerous patents in field. Home: 1341 Comstock Ave Los Angeles CA 90024

MILLER, WILLIAM ELWOOD, mining co. exec.; b. Bend, Oreg., May 9, 1919; s. Harry Adelbert and Sarah (Heyburn) M.; B.A., Stanford, 1941, M.B.A., 1947; m. Constance Alban Crosby, July 2, 1955; children—William, Constance, Harold, Mary, Sarah Crosby, Charles Crosby, Helen, Harry. Owner and operator Central Oregon Pumice Co., Bend, 1948—; pres. The Miller Lumber Co., Bend, The Miller Ranch Co., Bend. Commr., City of Bend, 1959-62, mayor, 1960. Bd. dirs. Central Oreg. Coll.; pres. Central Oreg. Coll. Found., 1956-57; dir. Central Oregon Coll. Area Ednl. Dist., 1961-65, chmn., 1964-65; bd. govs. Ore. Dept. Geology and Mineral Industries, 1971-75. Served with A.C., USNR, 1942-45. Decorated D.F.C., Air medal. Mem. Central Oreg. (v.p. 1954), Bend (pres. 1954) chambers commerce, Kappa Sigma. Republican. Episcopalian. Rotarian (dir. Bend 1955-56). Club: Bend Golf. Home: 527 NW Congress St Bend OR 97701 Office: 5 NW Greenwood Ave Bend OR 97701

MILLER, WILLIAM FREDERICK, scientist, executive; b. Vincennes, Ind., Nov. 19, 1925; s. William and Elsie M. (Everts) M.; m. Patty J. Smith, June 19, 1949; 1 son, Rodney Wayne. Student, Vincennes U., 1946-47; B.S., Purdue U., 1949, M.S., 1951, Ph.D., 1956; D.Sc., 1972. Mem. staff Argonne Nat. Lab., 1955-64, assoc. physicist, 1956-59, dir. applied math. div., 1959-64; prof. computer sci. Stanford U., Palo Alto, Calif., 1965—; Herbert Hoover prof. pub. and pvt. mgmt. Stanford U., 1979—, assoc. provost for computing, 1968-70, v.p. for research, 1970-71, v.p., provost, 1971-78; mem. Stanford Assocs., 1972—; pres., chief exec. officer SRI Internat., Menlo Park, Calif., 1979—; chmn. bd., chief exec. officer SRI Devel. Co., Menlo Park, David Sarnoff Research Ctr., Inc., Princeton, N.J.; profl. lectr. applied math. U. Chgo., 1962-64; vis. prof. math. Purdue U., 1962-63; vis. scholar Center for Advanced Study in Behavioral Scis., 1976; bd. dirs. Fireman's Fund Ins. Co., Ann. Revs. Inc., Varian Assos. Inc., 1st Interstate Bancorp, 1st Interstate Bank of Calif., Pacific Gas and Electric Co., Nat. Sci. Bd.RESOLVE, Ctr. for Environ. conflict Resolution, SIAM Inst. Math. in Soc.; mem. computer sci. and engring. bd. Nat. Acad. Sci., 1968-71; mem. corp. com. on computers in edn. Brown U., 1972-79; mem. policy bd. EDUCOM Planning Council on Computing in Edn., 1974-79, chmn., 1974-76; ednl. adv. bd. Guggenheim Meml. Found., 1976-80; com. postdoctoral and doctoral research staff NRC, 1977-80. Assoc. editor: Pattern Recognition Jour, 1968—, Jour. Computational Physics, 1970-74. Served to 2d lt. F.A. AUS, 1943-46. Fellow IEEE, Am. Acad. Arts and Scis., AAAS; mem. Am. Math. Soc., Am. Phys. Soc., Soc. Indsl. and Applied Math. (trustee), Assn. Computing Machinery, Nat. Acad. Engring., Sigma Xi. Office: SRI Internat 333 Ravenswood Ave Menlo Park CA 94025

MILLER, WILLIAM HUGHES, theoretical chemist, educator; b. Kosciusko, Miss., Mar. 16, 1941; s. Weldon Howard and Jewel Irene (Hughes) M.; m. Margaret Ann Westbrook, June 4, 1966; children: Alison Leslie, Emily Sinclaire. B.S., Ga. Inst. Tech., 1963; A.M., Harvard U., 1964, Ph.D., 1967. Jr. fellow Harvard U., 1967-69; NATO postdoctoral fellow Freiburg (Germany) U., 1967-68; asst. prof. chemistry U. Calif.-Berkeley, 1969-72, assoc. prof., 1972-74, prof., 1974—; fellow Churchill Coll., Cambridge (Eng.) U., 1975-76. Recipient Ann. prize Internat. Acad. Quantum Molecular Sci., 1974; Alfred P. Sloan fellow, 1970-72; Camille and Henry Dreyfus fellow, 1973-78; Guggenheim fellow, 1975-76; Alexander von Humboldt-Stiftung U.S. Sr. Scientist award, 1981-82; Ernest Orlando Lawrence Meml. award, 1985. Fellow AAAS., Am. Phys. Soc., Internat. Acad. Quantum Molecular Sci. Research, numerous publs. in field. Office: Dept Chemistry U Calif Berkeley CA 94720

MILLER, WILLIAM THOMAS, military officer; b. St. Louis, Oct. 3, 1950; s. William and LaVerne Wilma (Niles) M.; m. Deborah Marie Clymer, July 13, 1973; 1 child, Jamie Mariah. BS in Aero. Engring., USAF Acad., 1973; MS in Aero. Engring., Air Force Inst. Tech., 1981. Commd. 2d lt. USAF, 1969, advanced through grades to maj., 1985, pilot instr., 1975-80; mech. engr., attrition modeleer 544 Strategic Intelligence Wing, Offutt AFB, 1982-85; flight commdr. 92 Air Refuel Squadron, Fairchild AFB, 1985—. Mem. Am. Inst. Aeros. and Astronautics. Roman Catholic. Avocations: computer programming, camping, flying. Home: S 922 Pierce Rd Spokane WA 99206 Office: USAF 92 Air Refueling Squadron Fairchild AFB WA 99011

MILLER, WILLIAM WALTER, chemist; b. Oakland, Calif., Sept. 17, 1941; s. John C. and Margrethe (Lauridsen) M.; m. Ramona Shadi Miller, Aug. 6, 1963; children: Shawn N., Alisa C. BS, U. Calif., Berkeley, 1963; PhD, Calif. Inst. Tech., 1967. Research chemist E.I. DuPont de Nemours, Wilmington, Del., 1967-73; mgr. research and devel. Beckman Inst., Fullerton, Calif., 1973-83, Cardiovascular Devices, Inc., Irvine, Calif., 1983—. Mem. Am. Assn. Clin. Chemists, Am. Chem. Soc. Republican. Avocations: skiing, racquetball, backpacking. Home: 9782 Sunderland St Santa Ana CA 92705 Office: Cardiovascular Devices Inc 2801 Barranca St Irvine CA 92714

MILLER, ZOYA DICKINS (MRS. HILLIARD EVE MILLER, JR.), civic worker; b. Washington, July 15, 1923; d. Randolph and Zoya Pavlovna (Klementinovska) Dickins; grad. Stuart Sch. Costume Design, Washington, 1942; student Sophie Newcomb Coll., 1944, New Eng. Conservatory Music, 1946; grad. Internat. Sch. Reading, 1969; m. Hilliard Eve Miller, Jr., Dec. 6, 1943; children: Jeffrey Arnot, Hilliard Eve III. Fashion coordinator, cons. Mademoiselle mag., 1942-44; instr. Stuart Summer Sch. Costume Design, Washington, 1942; fashion coordinator Julius Garfinckel, Washington, 1942-43; star TV show Cowbelle Kitchen, 1957-58, Flair for Living, 1958-59; model mags. and comml. films, also nat. comml. recs., 1956—; dir. program devel. Webb-Waring Lung Inst., Denver, 1973—. Mem. exec. com., bd. dirs. El Paso County chpt. Am. Lung Assn., 1954-63; mem. exec. com. Am. Lung Assn. Colo., 1965—, bd. dirs. 1965-84, chmn. radio and TV council, 1963-70, mem. med. affairs com., 1965-70, pres., 1961-68, procurer fund. funds, 1965-70; developer nat. radio ednl. prodns. for internat. use Nat. Tb and Respiratory Disease Assn., Am. Lung Assn., 1963-70, coordinator statewide screening programs Colo., other states, 1965-72; chmn. benefit fund raising El Paso County Cancer Soc., 1963; founder, coordinator Colorado Springs Debutante Ball, 1967—; coordinator Nat. Gov.'s Conf. Ball, 1969; mem. exec. com. Colo. Gov.'s Comprehensive Health Planning Council, 1967-74, chmn., 1972-73; chmn. Colo. Chronic Care Com., 1969-73, chmn. fund raising, 1970-72, chmn. spl. com. congressional studies on nat. health bills, 1971-73; mem. Colo.-Wyo. Regional Med. Program Adv. Council, 1969-73; mem. Colo. Med. Found. Consumers Adv. Council, 1972-78; mem. decorative arts com. Colorado Springs Fine Arts Ctr., 1972-75; founder, state coordinator Nov. Noel Pediatrics Benefit Am. Lung Assn., 1973—. Recipient James J. Waring award Colo. Conf. on Respiratory Disease Workers, 1963; Zoya Dickins Miller Vol. of Yr. award established Am. Lung Assn. of Colo., 1979; Nat. Pub. Relations award Am. Lung Assn., 1979, Gold Double Bar Cross award, 1980, 83; named Humanitarian of Yr., Am. Lung Assn. of Colo., 1987. Lic. pvt. pilot. Mem. Nat. (chmn. nat. father of year contest 1956-57), Colo., El Paso County (pres. 1954, TV chmn. 1954-59) cowbelle assns. Club: Broadmoor Garden (ways and means chmn. 1967-69, civic chmn. 1970-71, publicity chmn. 1972)(Colorado Springs, Colo.). Contbr. articles, lectures on health care systems. Home: 74 W Cheyenne Mountain Blvd Colorado Springs CO 80906

MILLHAM, CHARLES BLANCHARD, computer scientist, environmental scientist, educator, consultant; b. Liberal, Kans., Nov. 1, 1936; s. Charles B. and Abbie Estella (Lowrance) M.; 1 child, Michael Blanchard; m. BOnnie May Miller; 3 step-children. Student Carlton Coll., 1954-56; BA, Iowa State U., 1958, MS, 1961, PhD, 1962. Instr. math. Iowa State U., 1962-64, asst. prof., 1964-66; asst. prof. Wash. State U., Pullman, 1966-69, assoc. prof., 1969-74, prof., 1974, former chmn. environ. sci. and regional planning; profl. cons. Recipient citation Royal Sci. Soc. Jordan; Fulbright grantee U. Jordan, Amman, 1976-77. Mem. Soc. Indsl. and Applied Math., Math. Programming Soc., Ops. Research Soc., Am. Econ. Assn., Assn. Research Profs. Wash. State U. (founding mem., past pres.). Roman Catholic. Contbr. articles to profl. jours., chpts. to books. Home: 475 Larry St Pullman WA 99163 Office: Computer Sci 1079 Wash State U Pullman WA 99164

MILLHOUSE, O. EUGENE, neuroanatomist, educator; b. Westerville, Ohio, Aug. 21, 1941; s. Oliver Clarence and Dorothy Mae (Thompson) M.; m. Andrea C. Adams, Feb. 12, 1982. B.Sc., Ohio State U., 1963; PhD., UCLA, 1967. Teaching asst. physiology Ohio State U., Columbus, 1962; USPH fellow in anatomy UCLA, 1963-67; prof. anatomy and neurology U. Utah, Salt Lake City, 1969—; kulia tutor in neuroanatomy U. Hawaii, Honolulu, 1976—. Harvard Med. Sch. fellow, 1967-69, Danish Med. Research Council fellow, 1980-81; recipient Disting. Teaching award U. Utah, 1973, Disting. Teaching award U. Utah Sch. Medicine, 1973—. Mem. AAAS, Am. Assn. Anatomists, Sigma Xi (Utah chpt. sec., treas. 1981—, pres. 1985—). Home: 6220 Antelope Ave Cheyenne WY 82009 Office: U Utah 50 N Med Dr Salt Lake City UT 84132

MILLICAN, DAVID NEWTON, municipal finance executive; b. Kansas City, Mo., Oct. 16, 1948; s. Ossie Lassiter and Alta Maxine (Kelley) M.; m. Patricia Lee Morgan, May 26, 1974 (div. Jan. 1984); children: Elisabeth Sierra, Michael Morgan. BS in Acctg., U. Calif., Berkeley, 1969. CPA. Supr. Peat, Marwick, Mithcell & Co., San Francisco, 1970-76; dir. fin. City of Burlingame, Calif., 1977-78, City of South Lake Tahoe, Calif., 1978-83; v.p. Infocomp Systems, Inc., Colorado Springs, Colo., 1983-86; fin. dir., treas. City of Fremont, Calif., 1986—. Mem. Govt. Fin. Officers Assn., Calif. Soc. Mcpl. Fin. Officers (chmn. local chpt. 1982, 83). Office: City of Fremont 39700 Civic Ctr Dr PO Box 5006 Fremont CA 94537

MILLIGAN, ALICE JUNE NELSON, educator, consultant; b. Farmington, N.Mex., June 26, 1937; d. Bailey W. and Alice (Lindsey) Nelson; 1 dau., Deborah Jean. A.A., Colo. Woman's Coll., 1957; B.S., U N.Mex., 1959; postgrad. U. Oslo, 1961, U. Guam, 1963-64; cert. in library sci. Ariz. State U., 1972. Tchr. pub. schs., Calif., N.Mex., N.C., Tex., 1959-63; ednl. cons. Govt. of Guam, 1963-65; prin. U.S. Navy Schs., Guam, 1965-68; program supr. Nat. Child Care Ctrs., Phoenix, 1969-71; tchr. of gifted Washington Sch. Dist., 1976—; owner Serendepity Seminars, Phoenix, 1981—. Mem. Am. Assn. Bus. and Profl. Women, NEA, Women Emerging, Ariz. Authors Assn., Nat. Spakers Assn., AAUW, Kappa Alpha Theta, Delta Tau Kappa. Republican. Mem. Science of Mind Ch. Author: The Island, 1981. Home and Office: 8225 N Central Ave Phoenix AZ 85020

MILLIGAN, CARINA MARCIA HARGIS, family counselor, school psychologist; b. Chgo., May 31, 1955; d. Ira Clair and Geraldine Marie (Kelley) Hargis; m. Dennis Edward Milligan, Aug. 22, 1981. B.S. in Psychology and English, U. Central Ark., 1977; M.S. in Counseling and Sch. Psychology, U. Fullerton, 1980. Lic. marriage, family and child counselor, Calif., 1982. Counselor, Buena Park High Sch., Calif., 1977-78, Centralia Sch. Dist., Buena Park, 1978-80, Cornelia Connelly High Sch., Anaheim, Calif., 1980-82; marriage, family and child counselor in pvt. practice, Buena Park, 1982—; sr. social worker Orange County Social Services, 1983—. Mem. Am. Psychol. Assn., Am. Personnel and Guidance Assn., Calif. Personnel and Guidance Assn., Calif. Assn. Marriage and Family Therapists. Roman Catholic.

MILLIGAN, MARSHALL, banker; b. Oxnard, Calif., Nov. 9, 1951; s. Arthur Achille and Jeanne (Welch) M.; m. Gretchen Hartnack, Sept. 20, 1980; children: Lucy Elizabeth, Claire Catherine. BA, Yale U., 1973; MBA, Stanford U., 1976. Asst. v.p. corp. banking Wells Fargo Bank, San Francisco, 1976-79; exec. v.p., chief exec. officer Bank of A. Levy, Oxnard, Calif., 1979—; trustee Real Estate Investment Trust of Calif., Santa Monica, 1982—. Office: Levy Bancorp 143 W 5th St PO Box 272 Oxnard CA 93030

MILLIGAN, ROBERT HUGH, electronics industry executive; b. Winston Salem, N.C., Dec. 21, 1948; s. Roy Hugh and Isabel (Michalski) M.; m. Diane Alane Neffson, Apr. 13, 1984. BS in Engring. Math., U. Ariz., 1971, BBA, 1973, MS in Mgmt., 1975. Instr. U. Ariz., Tucson, 1974-75; indsl. engr. Barker Mfg. Co., Portland, Oreg., 1975-76, Hughes Aircraft Co., Tucson, 1976; mgr., indsl. and mfg. engr. Gates Learjet Corp., Tucson, 1976-81; mgr. indsl. engring. facilities services Nat. Semicondr. Corp., Tucson, 1981—. Contbr. articles to profl. jours. Mem. Inst. Indsl. Engrs. (sr., chpt. v.p. 1977-78, bd. dirs. 1978-79), Assn. Energy Engrs. Office: Nat Semicondr Corp 5901 S Calle Santa Cruz Rd Tucson AZ 85746

MILLIKAN, CLARK HAROLD, physician; b. Freeport, Ill., Mar. 2, 1915; s. William Clarance and Louise (Chamberlain) M.; m. Gayle Margaret Gross, May 2, 1942 (div. Apr. 1966); children—Terri, Clark William, Jeffry Brent; m. Janet T. Holmes, July 21, 1966. Student, Parsons (Kans.) Jr. Coll., 1935; M.D., U. Kans., 1939. Diplomate: Kans., Bd. Psychiatry and Neurology (dir., chmn. exams. com.). Intern St. Luke's Hosp., Clev., 1939-40; asst. resident medicine St. Luke's Hosp., 1940-41; from resident neurology to asst. prof. neurology State U. Iowa, Ames, 1941-49; staff Mayo Clinic, Rochester, Minn., 1949—; cons. neurology Mayo Clinic, 1958—; dir. Mayo Center for Clin. Research in Cerebrovascular Disease; prof. neurology Mayo Sch. Medicine; physician-in-chief pro tem Cleve. Clinic, 1970; prof. neurology U. Utah Sch. Medicine, Salt Lake City, 1976-87, U. Miami (Fla.) Sch. Medicine, 1987—; Asst. chmn., editor trans. 2d Princeton Conf. Cerebrovascular Disease, 1957, chmn. confs., 1961, 64; chmn. com. classification and nomenclature cerebrovascular disease USPHS, 1955-69; mem. council Nat. Inst. Neurologic Diseases and Blindness, NIH, USPHS, 1961-65, div. regional med. program, 1965-68; A.O.A. lectr. Baylor U., Waco, Tex., 1952; James Mawer Pearson Meml. lectr., Vancouver, B.C., Can., 1958; Conner Meml. lectr. Am. Heart Assn., 1961; Peter T. Bohan lectr. U. Kans., 1965, 73. Editor: Jour. Stroke, 1970-76; asso. editor, 1976—. Recipient Outstanding Alumnus award U. Kans., 1973. Fellow A.C.P., Am. Acad. Neurology, Royal Soc. Medicine; mem. Assn. Research Nervous and Mental Disease (pres. 1961), Am. Neurol. Assn. (1st v.p. 1969-70, pres. 1973-74), Am., Minn. med. assns., Four County Med. Soc. South Minn., AAUP, Central Neuropsychiat. Assn., AAAS, N.Y. Acad. Scis., Am. Heart Assn. (chmn. council cerebrovascular disease 1967-68, Gold Heart award 1976, Spl. Merit award 1981), Sigma Xi.

MILLIKEN, JOHN GORDON, research economist; b. Denver, May 12, 1927; s. William Boyd and Margaret Irene (Marsh) M.; m. Marie Violet Machell, June 13, 1953; children: Karen Marie, Douglas Gordon, David Tait, Anne Alain. B.S., Yale U., 1949, B.Eng., 1950; M.S., U. Colo., 1966, D.B.A., 1969. Registered profl. engr., Colo. Engr. U.S. Bur. Reclamation, Denver, 1950-55; asst. to plant mgr. Stanley Aviation Corp., Denver, 1955-56; prin. mgmt. engr., dept. mgr. Martin-Marietta Aerospace Div., Denver, 1956-64; mgmt. engr. Safeway Stores, Inc., Denver, 1964-66; sr. research economist, prof., assoc. div. head U. Denver Research Inst., 1966-86; pres. Univ. Senate, 1980-81; prin. Milliken Chapman Research Group, Inc., 1986—; vis. fellow sci. policy research unit U. Sussex, Eng., 1975-76; dir. Sci. Mgmt. Corp., Cogenco Internat., Inc., LIK Securities, Inc.; cons. mgmt. engr. Author: Aerospace Management Techniques, 1971, Federal Incentives for Innovation, 1974, Recycling Municipal Wastewater, 1977, Water and Energy in Colorado's Future, 1981, Technological Innovation and Economic Vitality, 1983, Metropolitan Water Management, 1981; others; contbr. articles to profl. jours. Bd. dirs. Southeast Englewood Water Dist., 1962—, South Englewood San. Dist., 1965—, South Suburban Met. Recreation and Park Dist., 1971—; chmn. Democratic Com. of Arapahoe County, 1969-71, 5th Congl. Dist. Colo., 1972-73, 74-75; mem. exec. com. Colo. Faculty Adv. Council, 1981-85; mem. Garrison Diversion Unit Commn., 1984. Served with M.C. AUS, 1945-46. Recipient Adlai E. Stevenson Meml. award, 1981. Mem. Acad. Mgmt., Nat. Assn. Bus. Economists, Yale Sci. and Engring. Assn., Am. Water Works Assn., Sigma Xi, Tau Beta Pi, Beta Gamma Sigma, Sigma Iota Epsilon. Congregationalist. Home: 6502 S Ogden St Littleton CO 80121 Office: Milliken Chapman Research Group Inc 6631 S University Blvd Littleton CO 80121

MILLIMAN, JOAN ANN, management consultant in arts; b. Glendale, Calif., Jan. 27, 1937; d. Kenneth Miles and Blanche (Christine (Fitch) M. B.A., Occidental Coll., 1959; M.A. (hon.), Cambridge (Eng.) U., 1972; Ph.D. in Musicology, U. So. Calif., 1977. Secondary tchr. English and music Los Angeles City Schs., 1960-67, adult tchr. Am. lit., 1962-65; teaching asst. dept. music history U. So. Calif., 1968-71; asst. prof. music Humboldt State U., spring 1975; tech. writer/editor Laventhol & Horwath, C.P.A.s, Los Angeles, 1978, cons. and adminstrv. supr. dept. mgmt. adv. services Leisure Time Industries Group, 1979-83; lectr. div. inter-arts and cultural studies Sch. Performing Arts, U. So. Calif., 1981-83; music reviewer and feature writer Star News, Pasadena, Calif., 1979-80; cons. to arts orgns., 1980—; panelist Artreach, 1980, Bus. Vols. for Arts, Los Angeles, 1981, U.S. Nat. Commn. for UNESCO, Washington, 1981. AAUW research fellow Cambridge U., 1971-73. Mem. Assn. Coll., Univ. and Community Arts Adminstrs., Am. Musicol. Soc., Am. Council for Arts, Am. Mgmt. Assn., Calif. Confedn. for Arts. Home: 901 N Ave 66 Los Angeles CA 90042

MILLION, RUTH HATFIELD, music educator; b. Altus, Okla., Sept. 13, 1923; d. Charles and Carrie Bliss (Aulick) Hatfield; m. Elmer Garr Million, June 30, 1944; children: Charlotte, Stephen, Deborah, Carolyn, Janet. BA, Georgetown (Ky.) Coll., 1943; postgrad., Coll. Music, 1943-44, Temple U., 1964-65; MusM, Am. Conservatory Music, 1946. Instr. Am. Conservatory Music, Chgo., 1946-50; from instr. to assoc. prof. music Western Oreg. State Coll., Monmouth, 1966—; organist Plymouth Valley Bapt. Ch., Norristown, Pa., 1961-65, 1st Presbyn. Ch., McMinnville, Oreg., 1973-85, Salem, Oreg., 1985—. Mem. Music Tchrs. Nat. Assn. (cert. chmn. N.W. div. 1982—), Oreg. Music Tchrs. Assn. (v.p. 1974-76, pres. 1976-78, legis. chmn. 1980-82). Democrat. Hoe: 13270 NE Brookside LN Carlton OR 97111 Office: Western Oreg State Coll Monmouth OR 97361

MILLNER, DIANNE MAXINE, lawyer; b. Columbus, Ohio, Mar. 21, 1949; d. Charles Nelson and Barbara Rose Millner. A.A., Pasadena City Coll., 1970; A.B.,U. Calif.-Berkeley, 1972; J.D., Stanford U., 1975. Bar: Calif. 1975, U.S. Dist. Ct. (no. dist.) Calif. 1975. Assoc. Pillsbury, Madison & Sutro, San Francisco, 1975-80; ptnr. Alexander, Millner & McGee and predecessor firm Alexander, Burris, Millner & McGee, San Francisco, 1980—; legal intern Calif. Supreme Ct., San Francisco, 1974; bar exam. grader State Bar Calif., San Francisco, 1976-78. Bd. dirs. Youth for Service, San Francisco, 1977-80. NEH summer fellow, 1978. Mem. William Hastie Lawyers Assn. (bd. dirs. 1980-82), Nat. Bar Assn. (women lawyers div. Presdl. award 1980), Charles Houston Bar Assn., Bar Assn. San Francisco, Black Women Lawyers No. Calif., Black Writers Workshop, Phi Beta Kappa. Office: Alexander Millner & McGee 353 Sacramento St Suite 1500 San Francisco CA 94111-3626

MILLS, BARTON FAY, architect; b. Portland, Oreg., July 14, 1956; s. Fay Wilkinson and Elda (Garfield) M.; m. Joanne Williams, June 28, 1985. BA, Brigham Young U., 1981; MArch, U. Utah, 1985. Designer Hallet Hermanson, Salt Lake City, 1984-85, Yost, Grube & Hall, Portland, 1985—. Contbr. articles to profl. jours.; design work presented at MIT, Cambridge, U. Md., College Park, U. Wash., Seattle, U. Oreg., Eugene, Oreg. Sch. Design, Portland. Missionary Ch. Jesus Christ Latter-Day Saints, Baton Rouge, 1976-77. Avocations: tennis, racquetball, marine aquarist, sketching. Home: 100 Kerr Pkwy #43 Lake Oswego OR 97035 Office: Yost Grube Hall 1211 SW 5th Ave Suite 2700 Portland OR 97204-3782

MILLS, CAROL MARGARET, trucking company executive; b. Salt Lake City, Aug. 31, 1943; d. Samuel Lawrence and Beth (Neilson) M.; B.S. magna cum laude, U. Utah, 1965. With W.S. Hatch Co., Woods Cross, Utah, 1965—, corp. sec., 1970—, traffic mgr., 1969—, dir. publicity, 1974—; dir. Hatch Service Corp., Nat. Tank Truck Carriers, Inc., Washington; bd. dirs. Intermountain Tariff Bur. Inc., 1978—, chmn., 1981-82,reelected 1986—; chmn. bd. Fund raiser March of Dimes, Am. Cancer Soc., Am. Heart Assn.; active senatorial campaign, 1976, gubernatorial campaign, 1984; witness transp. com. Utah State Legislature, 1984, 85; apptd. by gov. as trustee Utah Tech. Fin. Corp., 1986; mem. Pioneer Theater Guild, 1985—. Recipient service awards W. S. Hatch Co., 1971, 80; appointed gov. Utah to bd. trustees Utah Tech. Fin. Corp., 1986; mem. Pioneer Theatre Guild, 1985. Mem. Nat. Tank Truck Carriers, Transp. Club Salt Lake City, Am. Trucking Assn. (public relations council), Utah Motor Transport Assn. (dir. 1982—), Internat. Platform Assn., Beta Gamma Sigma, Phi Kappa Phi, Phi Chi Theta. Home: 77 Edgecombe Dr Salt Lake City UT 84103 Office: W S Hatch Co 643 S 800 W Woods Cross UT 84087

MILLS, CARROLL BING, physicist, consultant; b. Huntington, W.Va., Aug. 8, 1916; s. Otto Herbert and Edith Marie (Bing) M.; m. Anita Margery Hodgson, Feb. 17, 1944; children—Kenneth, Elissa, Ivy, Valerie. A.B., Marshall U., 1938; M.S., U. Hawaii, 1941. Physicist U.S. Engring. Dept., Honolulu, 1941-43, U. Calif.-Berkeley, 1943-47, Oak Ridge Nat. Lab., 1947-54, Curtiss Wright Corp., Woodridge, N.J., 1954-56, Los Alamos Nat. Lab., 1956—, cons., Santa Fe, 1974—; cons. Energy Conversion Systems, Ottawa, Ont., Can., 1974—. Contbr. articles to profl. publs. Patentee in field. Mem. Am. Phys. Soc., Am. Nuclear Soc. (chmn. Trinity sect. 1966), AAAS (hon.). Republican. Mem. Ch. of Jesus Christ of Latter-day Saints. Club: Toastmasters dist. gov. 1966). Home and Office: PO Box 802 155 Greene St Kenwood CA 95452

MILLS, DON HARPER, pathology and psychiatry educator; b. Peking, Republic of China, July 27, 1927; came to U.S., 1928; s. Clarence Alonzo and Edith Clarissa (Parott) M.; m. Lillian Frances Snyder, June 11, 1949; children: Frances Jo, Jon Snyder. BS, U. Cin., 1950, MD, 1953; JD, U. So. Calif., 1958. Diplomate Am. Bd. Law in Medicine. Intern Los Angeles County Gen. Hosp., 1953-54, admitting physician, 1954-57, attending staff pathologist, 1959—; pathology fellow U. So. Calif., Los Angeles, 1954-55, instr. pathology, 1958-62, asst. clin. prof., 1962-65, assoc. clin. prof., 1965-69, clin. prof., 1969—, clin. prof. psychiatry and behavioral sci., 1986—; asst. in pathology Hosp. Good Samatarian, Los Angeles, 1956-65, cons. staff, 1962-72, affiliating staff, 1972—; dep. med. examiner Office of Los Angeles County Med. Examiner, 1957-61; instr. legal medicine Loma Linda (Calif.) U. Sch. Medicine, 1960-66, assoc. clin. prof. humanities, 1966—; cons. HEW, 1972-73, 75-76, Dept. of Def., 1975-80; bd. dirs. Am. Bd. Law in Medicine, Inc., Chgo., 1980-86. Column editor Newsletter of the Long Beach Med. Assn., 1960-75, Jour. Am. Osteopathic Assn., 1965-77, Ortho Panel, 1970-78; exec. editor Trauma, 1964—; mem. editorial bd. Aspects of Med. Practice, 1972—, Med. Alert Communications, 1973-75, Am. Jour. Forensic Medicine and Pathology, 1979-87, Hosp. Risk Control, 1981—; contbr. numerous articles to profl. jours. Fellow Am. Coll. Legal Medicine (pres. 1974-76, bd. govs. 1970-78, v.p. 1972-74, chmn. malpractice com. 1973-74, mem. jour. editorial bd. 1984—), Am. Acad. Forensic Scis. (pres. 1986-87, v.p. 1984-85, exec. com. 1971-74, gen. program chmn. 1966-67, chmn. jurisprudence sect. 1966-67, 73-74, mem. jour. editorial bd. 1965-79); mem. AMA (mem. jour. editorial bd. 1973-77), Calif. Med. Assn., Los Angeles County Med. Assn., AAAS, ABA, State Bar Calif., Los Angeles County Bar Assn., Am. Judicature Soc., Drug Info. Assn., Am. Soc. Hosp. Attys., Calif. Soc. Hosp. Attys. Office: 1141 Los Altos Ave Long Beach CA 90815

MILLS, ESTHER RAY, academic administrator; b. Grand Coulee, Wash., June 10, 1940; d. Albert L. and Helen Audrey (Christenson) Ray; m. Derek Maitland Mills, Feb. 19, 1972; children: Soren Anselm, Graham Christenson. BA, Whitworth Coll., 1962; MA, U. Wash., 1967, PhD, 1976. Instr. Idaho State U., Pocatello, 1965-67; lectr. U. Wash., Seattle, 1967-74, asst. dir. testing program, 1970-73; asst. prof. Seattle U., 1974—, dir. Inst. Pub. Service, 1981—, interim dir. admissions, 1985-86, spl. asst. to acad. v.p., 1986—; instl. rep. Nat. Assn. Schs. Pub. Affairs and Adminstrn., 1982—; cons. Seafirst Corp., Seattle, 1979—, Acad. for Contemporary Problems, Columbus, Ohio, 1976-77; sr. assoc. Mills Cons. Group, Inc.1978—; assoc. Enrolment Mgmt.; assoc. Enrolment Mgmt. Cons. Mem. Organizational Behavior Teaching Soc., Am. Soc. Pub. Adminstrn. Home: 14339 22nd Ave NE Seattle WA 98125 Office: Seattle U Inst Pub Service Seattle WA 98122

MILLS, LAWRENCE, lawyer, trucking co. exec.; b. Salt Lake City, Aug. 15, 1932; s. Samuel L. and Beth (Neilson) M.; B.S., U. Utah, 1955, J.D., 1956. Admitted to Utah bar, 1956, U.S. Supreme Ct. bar, 1963; with W.S. Hatch Co. Inc., Woods Cross, Utah, 1947—, gen. mgr., 1963—, v.p., 1970—, also dir.; dir. Nat. Tank Truck Carriers, Inc., Washington, 1963—, pres., 1974-75, chmn. bd., 1975-76; mem. motor carrier adv. com. Utah State Dept. Transp., 1979; keynote speaker Rocky Mountain Safety Supervisors Conf., 1976. Del. to County and State Convs., Utah, 1970-72; v.p. Utah Safety Council, 1979-82, bd. dirs., 1979—, pres., 1983; mem. Utah Gov's Adv. Com. on Small Bus. Recipient Safety Dir.; award Nat. Tank Carriers Co., 1967, Trophy award W.S. Hatch Co., 1975. Mem. Salt Lake County Bar Assn., Utah Motor Transport Assn. (dir. 1967—, pres. 1974-76), Utah Hwy. Users Assn. (dir. 1981—), Indsl. Relations Council (dir. 1974—), Utah Safety Council (bd. dirs. 1979—), Salt Lake City C. of C., U.S. Jaycees (life Senator 1969—, ambassador 1977—, pres. Utah Senate 1979-80). Contbr. articles to legal publs. Club: Silver Tank. Home: 77 Edgecombe Dr Salt Lake City UT 84103 Office: 643 S 800 West Woods Cross UT 84087

MILLS, RICHARD ALAN, electronics executive, educator; b. Salt Lake City, Apr. 22, 1950; s. Joseph Lorraine and Katherine (Frazier) M.; m. Devie Wagstaff, Dec. 15, 1972; children: Shelly, Kimberly, Gregory, Brian, Jeff. BSEE, U. Utah, 1974; MSEE, Stanford U., 1976, MS in Engring. Mgmt., 1980. Prodn. engr. Hewlett Packard Co., Palo Alto, Calif., 1976-78, project mgr. research and devel., 1978-79; sect. mgr., mfg. Hewlett Packard Co., Spokane, Wash. and Palo Alto, 1979-83; prodn. mgr., mfg. Hewlett Packard Co., Spokane, 1983-85; product line mgr.-Europe, Hewlett Packard Co., Amsterdam, 1985—; adj. prof. Gonzaga U., Spokane, 1982-83, 85-86, Eastern Wash. U., Spokane, 1986; pvt. practice cons. Spokane and Palo Alto, 1976—. Coach Valley Soccer Assn., Spokane, 1981-86, YMCA Basketball, Spokane 1985-86, Valley Shrimp Softball, Spokane, 1981-83. Mem. Am. Prodn. and Inventory Control Soc. Republican. Mormon. Avocation: reading. Home: E 11614 36th Spokane WA 99206 Office: Hewlett Pakard Co E 24001 Mission Ave Spokane WA 99220

MILLS, ROBERT LEROY, retired chemist; b. Canton, Ohio, June 6, 1922; s. Clarence Cornelius and Elizabeth Ardena (Mills) M.; m. Rene Scott, June 9, 1945; children: Sandra, Christopher A., Jonathan S., Teresa. BS, Washington and Jefferson Coll., 1943; MS, Calif. Inst. Tech., 1948; PhD, Stanford U., 1950. With Los Alamos (N.Mex.) Nat. Lab., 1950—, asst. group leader, 1975-83, fellow, 1983—, cons., 1985—; cons. Teltech Research Network, Mpls., 1985—. Contbr. articles to profl. jours.; patentee in field. Fellow AAAS, Am. Inst. Chemists (cert.); mem. Am. Chem. Soc. Democrat. Club: 10th St. Tennis (Los Alamos). Avocations: skiing, stream fishing, tennis, painting. Home: 3126 Walnut St Los Alamos NM 87544 Office: Los Alamos Nat Lab PO Box 1663 Los Alamos NM 87545

MILLS, ROBERT STUART, analytical chemist; b. San Francisco, May 17, 1952; s. Robert E. and Doris Ann (Ulrickson) M.; m. Jacqueline Ann Cates, May 27, 1978; children: Robert Stuart III, Heather Ann. AA, Normandale Community Coll., 1972; BS, U. Minn., 1975, MAgr, 1984. Asst. mgr. McDonalds Restaurant, Mpls., 1978-79; from chemist I to chemist III Land-O-Lakes, Inc., Mpls., 1979-85; sr. analytical chemist Nalley's Fine Foods, Inc., Tacoma, 1985—. Mem. Inst. Food Tech. (profl.), Am. Chem. Soc., Minn. Chromatography Forum, Internat. Union Pure and Applied Chemistry (affiliate). Roman Catholic. Office: Nalley's Fine Foods 3303 S 35th St Tacoma WA 98411

MILLS, THOMAS DEAN, national guard officer; b. Denver, Oct. 23, 1947; s. William Samual and Alice Elizabeth (Brehm) M.; m. Linda Darlene Miller, Aug. 30, 1969; children: Thomas Dean II, Timothy Scott. BA, Met. State Coll., 1974. Cert. tchr., Colo. Enlisted USAR, 1966; transferred to USNG, Golden, Colo., 1969, advanced through grades to maj., 1986; tng. officer 5th Spl. Forces Battalion 19th Spl. Forces Group, Golden, Colo., 1977-79, adminstrv. officer, 1979-82; tng. officer Troop Command Colo. Army N.G., Golden, Colo., 1982-86, logistics officer, 1986, ops. officer, 1986—. Pres. Foothills Christian Ch., Wheatridge, Colo., 1984-85; pres. bd. dirs. Campbell Stone Meml. Residence, Denver, 1983-84. Mem. N.G. Assn. Avocations: chess, golfing, skiing, softball. Home: 12231 W 60th Ave Arvada CO 80004 Office: Detachment 1 State Area Command Co Camp George West Golden CO 80401

MILOSZ, CZESLAW, poet, author, educator; b. Lithuania, June 30, 1911; came to U.S., 1960, naturalized, 1970; s. Aleksander and Weronika (Kunat) M. M.Juris, U. Wilno, Lithuania, 1934; Litt.D. (hon.), U. Mich., 1977. Programmer Polish Nat. Radio, 1935-39; diplomatic service Polish Fgn. Affairs Ministry, Warsaw, 1945-50; vis. lectr. U. Calif., Berkeley, 1960-61; prof. Slavic langs. and lits. U. Calif., 1961-78, prof. emeritus, 1978—. Author: The Captive Mind, 1953, Native Realm, 1968, Post-War Polish Poetry, 1965, The History of Polish Literature, 1969, Selected Poems, 1972, Bells in Winter, 1978, The Issa Valley, 1981, Separate Notebooks, 1984, The Land of Ulro, 1984, The Unattainable Earth, 1985. Recipient Prix Littéraire Européen Les Guildes du Livre, Geneva, 1953, Neustadt Internat. prize for lit. U. Okla., 1978, citation U. Calif., Berkeley, 1978, Nobel prize for lit., 1980; Nat. Culture Fund fellow, 1934-35; Guggenheim fellow, 1976. Mem. Am. Inst. Arts and Scis., Polish Inst. Letters and Scis. in Am., PEN Club in Exile. Office: U Calif Dept Slavic Langs and Lits Berkeley CA 94720

MILROD, LINDA JANE, museum director; b. St. John, N.B., Can., Mar. 4, 1953; d. Samuel and Joyce (Levine) M. BA in Art History, U. Toronto, Ont., Can., 1975. Curatorial asst. Agnes Etherington Art Ctr., Kingston, Ont., 1975-79; dir. Dalhousie Art Gallery, Halifax, N.S., Can., 1979-84, Mendel Art Gallery, Saskatoon, Sask., Can., 1984—. J. Paul Getty Trust scholar, 1986. Mem. Can. Mus. Assn. (councillor 1983-86, chmn. conf. planning com. 1985-86), Sask. Arts Alliance (sec. 1985, v.p. 1986), Western Can. Art Assn. (exec. 1985), Can. Art Mus. Dirs. Orgn., Council Assoc. Mus. Dirs., Sask. Mus. Assn. Office: Mendel Art Gallery, 950 Spadina Crescent E, Box 569, Saskatoon, SK Canada S7K 3L6

MILROY, WILLIAM CHARLES, health care executive; b. Ludlow, Mass., Oct. 16, 1940; s. William Gordon and Mary (Moncrief) M.; m. Gail Carolyn Feicha, Aug. 4, 1962 (div. 1986); 1 child, Amy Elizabeth. BA, Am. Internat. Coll., 1962; MD, Johns Hopkins U., 1966; MS, U. Rochester, 1970, PhD, 1972. Diplomate Am. Bd. Preventive Medicine. Commd. USN, 1965, advanced through grades capt., retired, 1985; mgr. occupational medicine Hanford Environ. Health Found., Richland, Wash., 1985—; instr. Yale U., New Haven, Conn., 1981-85; vis. prof. Med. Coll. N.Y., Valhalla, 1982-85; clin. assoc. prof. U. Wash., 1987—. Contbr. articles to profl. jours. Recipient Alumni Achievement award Am. Internat. Coll., Springfield, Mass., 1985. Fellow Am. Acad. Occupational Medicine, Am. Occupational Med. Assn., Aerospace Med. Assn. (assoc.); mem. Sigma Xi, Assn. Mil. Surgeons U.S. Avocations: sailing, scuba diving, skiing. Office: Hanford Environ Health Found 3080 George Washington Way Richland WA 99352

MILSTEIN, JERROLD MARSHALL, child neurologist, educator; b. Mpls., Apr. 21, 1939; s. Joe and Minnie (Nolman) M., m. Leslie Joan Howard, Aug. 8. 1962; children: David S., Jonathan W. BA, U. Minn., 1960, BS, MD, 1964. Diplomate Am. Bd. Pediatrics, Am. Bd. Psychiatry and Neurology. Intern U. Calif. Affiliated Hosps., Los Angeles, 1964-65; resident in pediatrics and neurology U. Minn., 1965-68; clin. instr. U. Calif., Davis, 1968-70; spl. fellow in neurology U. Minn., 1970-71; asst. prof. U. Minn. Med. Sch., Mpls., 1971-77; assoc. prof. neurology U. Wash. Med. Sch., Seattle, 1977—; dir. child neurology Children's Orthopedic Hosp. and Med. Ctr., Seattle, 1977—. Bd. dirs. Jewish Community Ctr., Mpls., 1974-77. Served to capt. USAF, 1968-70. USPHS fellow 1970-71. Fellow Am. Acad. Neurology; mem. Profs. Child Neurology (sec.-treas. 1982-86), Child Neurology Soc., Internat. Neurochemistry Soc., Am. Epilepsy Soc. Home: 15930 SE 43d Bellevue WA 98006 Office: Children's Orthopedic Hosp Med Ctr 4800 Sand Point Way NE Seattle WA 98105

MILTNER, JOHN ROBERT, university official; b. Conneaut, Ohio, Sept. 6, 1946; s. Robert John and Grace Evelyn (Hall) M.; m. Carol Lee Herd, Oct. 27, 1973; children—William, Kelli, Bryan, Tiffany, Robert. B.S., Bowling Green U., 1968; M.B.A., Pace U., 1981. Cert. fundraising exec. Exploring dir. Boy Scouts Am., Toledo, 1968-72, dir. exploring, N.Y.C., 1975-76, dir. devel., 1977-79, exec. dir. devel. and communications Greater N.Y. councils, 1979-80; mktg. mgr. IBM, Toledo, 1972-73; regional mktg. mgr. Docutel Corp., Boston, 1974; dir. devel. Meml. Sloan-Kettering Cancer Ctr., N.Y.C., 1980-83; vice chancellor U. Calif.-Irvine, 1983—. Mem. exec. com. Irvine Med. Ctr., vice chmn.; bd. dirs. Orange County Performing Arts Ctr. Fraternity, Irvine Community Found., 1986—, Indsl. League Orange County, 1986-87, Orange County Council Boy Scouts Am.; mem. Charitable Giving Council Orange County, 1986—. Mem. Nat. Soc. Fund Raising Execs. (cert.; dir. 1977—, v.p. 1979-81, pres. 1981-82, vice chmn. nat. bd. 1982—, chmn.-elect 1985, chmn. 1986). Mem. Ref. Ch. Am. Clubs: Princeton (N.Y.C.); Balboa Bay (Newport Beach, Calif.); Center (Costa Mesa, Calif.); Pacific, Lincoln Ctr. of Orange County. Home: 33382 Breezy Pl Dana Point CA 92629 Office: 555 Adminstrn Bldg U Calif Irvine CA 92717

MINAMI, ISAMU, farmer; b. Guadalupe, Calif., July 21, 1922; s. Henry Yaemon and Kuni (Yamasaki) M.; student Santa Maria (Calif.) Jr. Coll., 1942; m. Grace Misao Yamamoto, May 6, 1950; children: Sammy Yahe, Susan Kuniye. Engaged in vegetable farming, Guadalupe, 1944—; owner Security Farms, 1944—; past pres., bd. dirs. Santa Barbara County Fair Bd. Bd. dirs. Santa Maria Assn. Retarded, Boys Club Santa Maria Valley; past bd. dirs. bldg. fund Sisters Hosp., Santa Maria; mem. comdr.'s liaison group Vandenburg AFB; bd. regents Santa Clara U.; mem. subcom. Calif. State Bd. Food and Agr.; mem. Santa Maria Valley Water Study Com.; bd. dirs. Marian Hosp. Found.; mem. community adv. com. Valley Community Hosp.; past mem. spl. adv. com. Senator S.I. Hayakawa of Calif. Mem. Nisei Farmers League, United Fresh Fruit Assn., Iceberg Lettuce Research Assn. (dir.), Grower-Shippers Assn. (bd. dirs., past pres.), Western Growers Assn.

(dir.), Calif.-Ariz. Growers Assn. (dir.), Calif. Farm Bur. Assn., Calif. C. of C., Santa Barbara County Taxpayers Assn., Santa Maria Valley C. of C. (dir.; Citizen of Year award 1980), Santa Maria Valley Developers (dir.), Friends of Santa Barbara County, Japan Am. Soc. So. Calif., Japanese Am. Citizens League, Santa Maria Valley Farmers Assn. (past pres.). Republican. Buddhist. Clubs: Guadalupe Rotary, 36th Congl., Republican Century, Santa Maria Elks. Office: PO Box 818 Guadalupe CA 93434

MINC, HENRYK, mathematics educator; b. Lodz, Poland, Nov. 12, 1919; came to U.S., 1960, naturalized, 1966; s. Izrael and Haja (Zyngler) M.; m. Catherine Taylor Duncan, Apr. 16, 1943; children—Robert Henry, Ralph Edward, Raymond. M.A. with honors, Edinburgh U. (Scotland), 1955, Ph.D., 1959. Lectr., Dundee Tech. Coll., Scotland, 1956-58, U. B.C., Vancouver, Can., 1958-59, asst. prof., 1959-60; assoc. prof. U. Fla., Gainesville, 1960-63; vis. prof. Technion Israel Inst. Tech., Haifa, 1969-80; prof. U. Calif.-Santa Barbara, 1963—; referee and reviewer for math. jours. Author: A Survey of Matrix Theory and Matrix Inequalities, 1964, translated into Russian, 1972; Introduction to Linear Algebra, 1965, translated into Spanish, 1968; Modern University Algebra, 1966; Elementary Linear Algebra, 1968, translated into Spanish, 1971; New College Algebra, 1968; Elementary Functions and Coordinate Geometry, 1969; Algebra and Trigonometry, 1970; College Algebra, 1970; College Trigonometry, 1971; Integrated Analytic Geometry and Algebra with Circular Functions, 1973; Nonnegative Matrices, 1974; Permanents, 1978, translated into Russian, 1980. Contbr. over 75 research papers and other pubs. to profl. jours. Served to 2d. lt. Polish Army, 1940-48. Recipient Lester Ford award Math. Assn. Am., 1966, research contract Office of Naval Research, 1985—. Air Force Office Sci. Research grantee, 1960-82, Lady Davis Fellow, 1975, 78. Mem. Am. Math Soc., Polskie Towarzystwo Matematyczne, Soc. Ancient Numismatics, Inst. Antiquity and Christianity (adv. bd.), N.Y. Acad. Scis., Israel Exploration Soc., Am. Numismatic Soc., Am. Schs. Oriental Research. Democrat. Jewish. Home: 4076 Naranjo Dr Santa Barbara CA 93110 Office: Dept Math U Calif Santa Barbara CA 93106

MINCKLER, TATE M., physician; b. Kalispell, Mont., Apr. 1, 1934; s. Jeff and Dona Rae (Bond) M.; m. Barbara Jean Scarff, June 19, 1956; children: Tye V., Kathryn T., Meghan J., Kimberly J., Christie Ann. BA, Reed Coll., 1955; MD, U. Oreg., 1959. Diplomate Nat. Bd. Med. Examiners, Anatomic Pathology Bd., Clin. Pathology Bd. Intern Jackson Meml. Hosp., Miami, Fla., 1959-60, resident in pathology, 1960-61; resident in pathology Gen. Rose Meml. Hosp., Denver, 1961-63, USPHS Nat. Cancer Inst., Bethesda, Md., 1963-64; pathologist Nat. Cancer Inst. NIH, Washington, 1963-65, head. tissue pathology unit, 1964-65; asst. prof. pathology, asst. pathologist Univ. Tex. Anderson Hosp. and Tumor Inst., Houston, 1965-69; head dept. med. automation The Presbyn. Med. Ctr., Denver, 1969-71; assoc. prof. and dir. computer div. dept. lab. medicine U. Wash., Seattle, 1971-75; adminstr. Mad River Community Hosp., Arcata, Calif., 1975-76, pathologist and dir. clin. labs., 1975-80; chief. pathology Al Hada Hosp. and Rehab. Ctr., Taif, Saudi Arabia, 1981-84; pathologist, med. dir. of lab. services The Gen. Hosp., Eureka, Calif., 1984—; med. dir. No. Calif. Community Blood Bank, Eureka, 1985—; cons. in field. contbr. articles to profl. jours. Served to lt. comdr. USPHS, 1963-65. Mem. AMA, AAAS, Am. Soc. Clin. Pathologists, Coll. Am. Pathologists, Soc. Computer Medicine, Soc. Cryobiology, The N.Y. Acad. Scis., Humboldt-Del Norte County Med. Soc., Calif. Med. Assn. Republican. Avocation: flying. Office: The Gen Hosp 2200 Harrison Ave Eureka CA 95501

MINDEL, LAURENCE BRISKER, restaurateur; b. Toledo, Oct. 27, 1937; s. Seymour Stewart and Eleanor (Brisker) M.; B.A., U. Mich., 1959; m. Deborah Dudley, Oct. 20, 1978; children: Katherine Dudley, Nicolas Laurence; children by previous marriage—Michael Laurence, Laura Beth, Anthony Jay. Gen. mgr. Western Coffee Instants, Inc., Burlingame, Cal., 1962-64, dir., partner, 1964, chmn. and chief exec. officer, 1964-70; pres., chief exec. officer Caswell Coffee Co., San Francisco; v.p., dir. Coffee Instants, Inc., Long Island City, N.Y., 1966-70; v.p. Superior Tea and Coffee Co., 1970-72; chmn., chief exec. officer Spectrum Foods, Inc., 1970-85; pres. Restaurant Group Saga Corp., Menlo Park, Calif., 1985-86, chmn., chief exec. officer, 1987—; chmn., chief exec. officer Il Fornaio (Am.) Corp., 1987—. Bd. dirs. Bay Area Easter Seal Soc.; trustee The Branson Sch. Mem. San Francisco Mus. Art, Young Pres. Orgn. Internat. Club: The Concordia-Argonaut (San Francisco). Home: 86 San Carlos Ave Sausalito CA 94965 Office: Il Fornaio Am Corp 725 Greenwich St San Francisco CA 94133

MINDELL, EARL LAWRENCE, nutritionist, pharmacist, author; b. St. Boniface, Man., Can., Jan. 20, 1940; s. William and Minerva Sybil (Galsky) M.; came to U.S., 1965, naturalized, 1972; BS in Pharmacy, N.D. State U., 1963; PhD in Nutrition, U. Beverly Hills, 1980; m. Gail Andrea Jaffe, May 16, 1971; children: Evan Louis-Ashley, Alanna Dayan. Pres. Adanac Mgmt. Inc., 1979—, Compact Disc-Count, Inc.; instr. Dale Carnegie course; lectr. on nutrition, radio and TV. Mem. Beverly Hills, Rancho Park, Western Los Angeles (dir.) regional chambers commerce, Calif., Am. pharm. assns., Am. Acad. Gen. Pharm. Practice, Am. Inst. for History of Pharmacy, Am. Nutrition Soc., Internat. Coll. Applied Nutrition, Nutrition Found., Nat. Health Fedn., Am. Dieticians Assn., Orthomolecular Med. Assn., Internat. Acad. Preventive Medicine. Clubs: City of Hope, Masons, Shriners. Author: Earl Mindell's Vitamin Bible, Earl Mindell's Vitamin Bible for your Kid, Earl Mindell's Quick and Easy Guide to Better Health, Earl Mindell's Pill Bible, Earl Mindell's Shaping Up with Vitamins, Earl Mindell's Unsafe At Any Meal; columnist Let's Live mag., The Vitamin Supplement, Better Health and Living mag.; contbr. articles on nutrition to profl. jours. Home: 709 N Hillcrest Rd Beverly Hills CA 90210 Office: 10739 W Pico Blvd West Los Angeles CA 90064

MINDS, ARTHUR JAMES, real estate management executive, lawyer; b. Phillipsburg, Pa., May 11, 1950; s. J. Arthur and Ruth Elizabeth (Sklar) M. B.S. in Acctg., Pa. State U., 1972; J.D., Duke U., 1976. Bar: Colo. 1976. Audit staff acct. Arthur Andersen & Co., N.Y.C., 1971-72; sole practice, Boulder, Colo., 1976-78; staff atty. U. Denver Sch. Law, 1978-79; pres. Condomgmt. Concepts Inc., Boulder, 1979-84; v.p. fin. services Profl. Community Mgmt., Denver, 1984-85; nat. v.p. ops. David H. Murdock Mgmt. Co., Los Angeles, 1985-86; asset mgr. M. David Paul & Assocs., Santa Monica, Calif, 1986—. Contbr. articles to profl. jours. Bd. dirs. Colo. Pub. Interest Research Group, Boulder, 1976-77. Republican. Home: 10401 Wilshire Blvd #209 Los Angeles CA 90024 Office: PCM of Colorado Inc 5340 S Quebec #290 Englewood CO 80111-1905

MINEKE, LAURENE DEE, clothing store owner; b. Grangeville, Idaho, Nov. 14, 1941; d. Lawrence Reed and Iris Velna (Clark) Hayes; m. Rodney Howard Mineke, Aug. 3, 1963; 1 child, Melina Dee. AA, Columbia Basin Coll., 1961; BA in English, Edn., Wash. State U., 1963; postgrad., U. Oreg., 1964-67. Caseworker Multnomah County Children's Dept., Portland, Oreg., 1964-67; substitute tchr. Pasco/Kennewick (Wash.) Sch. Dist., 1968-76; tchr. Kamiakin High Sch., Kennewick, 1976-80; owner Just Friends, Pasco, 1980—; pres. Riverview Shopping Ctr. Mchts. Assn., Pasco, 1985-86. Sec. Pasco Hometown USA, 1986; active Tri-Cities Indsl. Devel. Council; adv. com. Home and Family Life, Pasco, 1985-86, Deca Mktg. Mgmt., Tri-Cities, 1985-86; adv. com. fashion merchandising Columbia Basin Coll., Pasco, 1985-86. Mem. Greater Pasco C. of C. (edn. chmn. 1985—). Avocations: skiing, collecting antiques. Home: 4620 W Nixon Pasco WA 99301

MINEKE, RODNEY HOWARD, utility company administrator; b. Rolette, N.D., July 30, 1936; s. Vernon Howard and Esther Elaine (Longton) Mineke; m. Laurene Dee Hayes, Aug. 3, 1963; 1 child, Melina Dee. AA, Columbia Basin Coll., 1971. Rate auditor Garrett Freightlines, Portland, Oreg., 1957-67; traffic specialist Atlantic Richfield, Richland, Wash., 1967-75; supr. traffic, warehousing Wash. Pub. Power Supply System, Richland, 1975—. Mem. Nat. Mgmt. Assn. (bd. dirs. 1981—), Tri-City Transp. Club (pres., sec., bd. dirs. 1960—), Nat. Indsl. Traffic League, Supply System Employees Assn. (pres. 1977). Lodge: Kiwanis (program chmn.). Avocations: snowskiing, woodworking. Home: 4620 W Nixon Pasco WA 99301 Office: Wash Pub Power Supply System 3000 George Washington Way Richland WA 99352

MINER, JOHN MOREY, banker; b. Plainfield, N.J., May 24, 1922; s. Vincent Bernard and Laura Elizabeth (Morey) M.; m. Jeanne Louise Smith, 1947; children: Wendy, Forest; m. 2d, Anne Elaine Merritt, 1954; children: Kent, Kim, Grant. AB, Princeton U., 1946. With Princeton (N.J.) Bank and Trust, 1946-48; with Fidelity Bank, Phila., 1949-78, v.p. loan adminstrn., 1960-65, exec. v.p. Nat. div., 1965-70, sr. exec. v.p., 1970-73, dir., chmn. credit policy com., 1973-78; sr. v.p., chmn. risk mgmt. com. Crocker Nat. Bank, Los Angeles, 1978-85; pvt. practice fin. cons., 1985—; dir. Atlantic Electric Co., Pleasantville, N.J. Served with U.S. Army, World War II, Korea. Recipient Spl. Corp. Citizenship award Phila. Tribune, 1972; named hon. alumnus U. Mich., 1944. Clubs: Union League (Phila.); Univ. (Los Angeles). Office: 2340 Coniston Pl San Marino CA 91108

MINES, RICHARD LEE, realtor; b. Los Angeles, Feb. 5, 1939; s. Nathan and Theresa Minsberg; BS, Calif. State U., Los Angeles, 1961; m. Eileen Silverman, Jan. 21, 1968; 1 child, Todd. With Abbey Rents div. Consol. Foods, Inc., 1962-68; dir. ops. United Rent-All, Inc. div. Internat. Industries Inc., 1968-75; real estate broker, San Fernando Valley, Calif., 1975-77; pres. Kaye, Mines & Weatherby, Inc. aka KRW Properties, Beverly Hills, Calif., 1977-78; mgr. Brown Realtors, Thousand Oaks, Calif., 1978-79; v.p., sales mgr. Fred Sands Realtors, Westlake Village (Calif.) br., 1979-83, corp. v.p., Los Angeles, 1983—. Mem. Los Angeles Bd. Realtors, San. Fernando Bd. Realtors. Republican. Home: 16601 Adlon Rd Encino CA 91436 Office: Ptnrs Affiliate Home Fed Savs & Loan 15301 Ventura Blvd Sherman Oaks CA 91403

MINETA, NORMAN Y., congressman; b. San Jose, Calif., Nov. 12, 1931; children: David, K., Stuart S. B.S., U. Calif.-Berkeley. Agt./broker Mineta Ins. Agy., San Jose, 1956—; mem. adv. bd. Bank of Tokyo in Calif., 1961-75; mem. San Jose City Council, 1967-71; vice mayor San Jose, 1969-71; mayor 1971-75; mem. 94th-100th Congresses from 13th Calif. dist.; chmn. House Com. on Pub. Works and Transp., subcom. aviatio; mem. Com. on Sci., Space and Tech., Select Com. on Intelligence 94th-98th Congresses from 13th Calif. dist., dep. Dem. whip; Chmn. fin. com. Santa Clara County Council Chs., 1960-62; commr. San Jose Human Relations Commn., 1962-64, San Jose Housing Authority, 1966—. Precinct chmn. Community Theater Bond Issue, 1964; mem. spl. gifts com. Santa Clara County council Boy Scouts Am., 1967; sec. Santa Clara County Grand Jury, 1964; bd. dirs. Wesley Found., San Jose State Coll., 1956-58, Pacific Neighbors, Community Council Central Santa Clara County, Japan Soc., San Francisco, Santa Clara County chpt. NCCJ, Mexican-Am. Community Services Agy.; mem. exec. bd. No. Calif.-Western Nev. dist. council Japanese Am. Citizens League, 1960-62, pres. San Jose chpt., 1957-59; bd. regents Smithsonian Instn., 1979—; chmn. Smithsonian vis. com. for Freer Gallery, 1981—. Served to lt. AUS, 1954-56. Mem. Greater San Jose C. of C., Nat. Assn. Indsl. Ins. Agts., Calif. Assn. Indsl. Ins. Agts., San Jose Assn. Indsl. Ins. Agts. (dir. 1960-62), North San Jose Optimists Club (chpt. pres. 1956-58), Jackson-Taylor Bus. and Profl. Assn. (dir. 1963). Methodist. Office: 2350 Rayburn House Office Bldg Washington DC 20515

MINGER, TERRELL JOHN, state official; b. Canton, Ohio, Oct. 7, 1942; s. John Wilson and Margaret Rose M.; B.A., Baker U., 1966; M.P.A., Kans. U., 1969; Urban Exec. Program, M.I.T., 1975; Loeb fellow Harvard U., 1976-77; Exec. Devel. Program, Stanford U., 1979; M.B.A., U. Colo., 1983; m. Judith R. Arnold, Aug. 7, 1965; 1 dau., Gabriella Sophia. Asst. dir. admissions Baker U., 1966-67; asst. city mgr. City of Boulder, Colo., 1968-69; city mgr. City of Vail, Colo., 1969-79; pres., chief exec. officer Whistler Village Land Co., Vancouver, B.C., Can., 1979-81; v.p., gen. mgr. Cumberland Southwest Inc., Denver, 1981-83; exec. asst., dep. chief of staff to Gov. Colo., 1983—; adj. prof. Grad. Sch. Pub. Affairs U. Colo., 1983—; bd. dirs. Colo. Open Lands, Inc., 1986—. Spl. del. UN Habitat Conf. Human Settlements; founder Vail Symposium; co-founder, bd. dirs. Colo. Park Found., 1985—. Nat. finalist White House Fellowship, 1978; named one of B.C.'s Top Bus. Leaders for the '80's, 1980. Mem. Urban Land Inst., Colo. City Mgmt. Assn., Internat. City Mgrs. Assn. (Mgmt. Innovation award 1974-76), Western Gov.'s Assn. (staff council, chmn. adv. com. 1985-86). Editor: Vail Symposium Papers, 1970-79; author, editor: Growth Alternatives for Rocky Mountain West, 1976; Future of Human Settlements in the West, 1977. Club: Denver Athletic. Home: 785 6th St Boulder CO 80302 Office: Office of Governor State Capitol Denver CO 80203

MINGIS, FRANK EDWARD, interior designer; b. Chester, Pa., June 1, 1940; s. Frank Edward Mingis and Edna (Rae) Rush. Student, Phila. Coll. of Art, 1964-67, Memphis Acad., 1980-81. Mgr. design Thonet Industries, N.Y.C., 1967-73; dir. design Simmons Co., Chgo., 1974-75; sr. project designer Sheraton Corp., Boston, 1975-79; mgr. design Holiday Inns Inc., Memphis, 1979-81; sr. project designer Hirsch/Bedner Assoc., Santa Monica, Calif., 1981-87; prin. Mingus Design Group, San Francisco, 1987—. Home: 1436 Brockton Ave #8 Los Angeles CA 90025 Office: Mingis Design Group 240 Stockton St San Francisco CA 90404

MINHINNETT, THOMAS EDWARD, fire department administrator; b. Calgary, Alta., Can., Jan. 7, 1929; s. George Thomas and Mabel Gertrude (Sanderson) M.; m. Delores Etteline Smith, May 10, 1952; children: Glen Thomas, Marlene Delores. Diploma in Pub. Adminstrn., Mount Royal Coll., 1978. Joined Calgary Fire Dept., 1951, advanced through grades to fire chief, 1983—. Mem. Alta. Provincial Fire Chiefs Assn., Can. Assn. Fire Chiefs, Internat. Assn. Fire Chiefs (Can. div. provincial v.p.), Nat. Fire Protection Assn. (dir. Fire Service sect.). Conservative. Anglican. Lodge: Masons. Office: Calgary Fire Dept, 4124 11th St SE, Calgary, AB Canada T2G 3H2

MINISCE, RICHARD ANTHONY, college dean, management consultant; b. Rochester, N.Y., Sept. 16, 1942; s. Anthony J. and Albertine C. (Elman) M.; m. Louise J. Schliessman, Aug. 14, 1971; children—Heather, Holly, Courtney, Anthony. B.S. in Sociology, St. John Fisher Coll., 1964; M.A. in Sociology, Boston Coll., 1968; postgrad. New Sch. for Social Research, 1969-72, Wash. State U., 1978-79. Asst. to area supr. Bur. Recreation, Rochester, N.Y., 1961-64; instr. sociology Kings Coll., Wilkes Barre, Pa., 1965; asst. prof. St. Lawrence U., Canton, N.Y., 1966-68; prof. Suffolk County Community Coll., Selden, N.Y., 1969-81; dean of instrn. Tillamook Bay Community Coll., Bay City, Oreg., 1981—; pres. RAM Assocs., Mgmt. Services, 1983—; chief exec. officer Diversified Ventures Enterprise Group, Inc.; pres. Tillamook Burner Co. Inc.; chief of security, policeman, park ranger. reviewer coll. texts; cons. criminologist, sociologist. Chmn. bd. dirs., Tillamook County Vol. Bur., 1983-84; fireman, mem budget com. Bay City Vol. Fire Dept.; treas. Clatsop-Tillamook Fire Dept. Adv. Group; sr. warden, vestry St. Albans Ch., Tillamook, Oreg., 1983-84; chmn. personnel com. Bay City City Council, 1983—. Named Jaycee of Yr. Canton, N.Y., 1966; recipient Kiwanis Ruby K award, 1982. Mem. Oreg. Council Instructional Adminstrs., Nat. Council Community Services and Continuing Edn., Oreg. Assn. Community Edn. Deans and Dirs., Am. Sociol. Assn., Am. Vocat. Assn., Oreg. Assn. Criminal Justice Educators, Am. Assn. Community and Jr. Colls., Nat. Council Local Adminstrs., Oreg. Community Edn. Assn. Club: Tillamook Kiwanis (dir. 1983-84).

MINNICH, TAMELA ANN, social worker; b. Bartlesville, Okla., Feb. 24, 1949; d. Herbert Spenser and Eleanor Louise (Baily) M.; m. Richard Fralin; 1 child, Juanita Elena. B in Social Welfare, Fla. State U., 1970; MSW, U. Mich., 1972. Dir. day treatment program Washtenaw County Mental Health, Ann Arbor, Mich., 1972-74; spl. edn. social worker Albuquerque Pub. Schs., 1975—. Voter registrar Bernalillo County, Albuquerque, 1984—; precinct chmn. Dem. Party, Albuquerque, 1985—. Mem. Am. Fedn. Tchrs., Nat. Assn. Social Workers (state bd. mem. 1978-79), Phi Alpha, Delta Tau Kappa. Unitarian. Avocations: photography, hiking, bicycling, reading. Office: Albuquerque Pub Schs Dist Diagnostic Ctr 2700 Arizona NE Albuquerque NM 87110

MINNIE, MARY VIRGINIA, social worker, educator; b. Eau Claire, Wis., Feb. 16, 1922; d. Herman Joseph and Virginia Martha (Strong) M. BA, U. Wis., 1944; MA, U. Chgo., 1949, Case Western Reserve U., 1956. Lic. clin. social worker, Calif. Supr. day care Wis. Children Youth, Madison, 1949-57; coordinator child study project Child Guidance Clinic, Grand Rapids, Mich., 1957-60; faculty, community services Pacific Oaks Coll., Pasadena, Calif., 1960-70; pvt. practice specializing in social work various, Calif., 1970-78; cons., educator So. Calif. Health Care, North Hollywood, Calif., 1978—; med. social worker Kaiser Permanente Home Health, Downey, Calif., 1985—; pres. Midwest Assn. Nursery Edn., Grand Rapids, 1958-60; bd. dirs., sec. So. Calif. Health Care, North Hollywood; bd. dirs., v.p. Baby Sitters Guild Inc., Los Angeles; cons. project Head Start Office Econ. Opportunity, Washington, 1965-70. Mem. Soc. Clin. Social Workers, Nat. Assn. Social Workers, Nat. Assn. Edn. Young Children (1960-62). Democrat. Club: Altrusa (Laguna Beach, Calif.) (pres. 1984-87). Avocations: music, travel, tennis, swimming, walking. Home: 31342 Campana Way Laguna Niguel CA 92677 Office: Kaiser Permanente Home Health 9449 Imperial Hwy Downey CA 90242

MINNIEAR, DIANE ROBERTA, advertising executive; b. Long Beach, Calif., Feb. 24, 1941; d. Robert W. and Esther (Beckenstein) Nasworthy; m. Roger W. Minniear, Apr. 10, 1964 (div.). Student, Pacific Christian Coll., 1958-59, Long Beach City Coll., 1960, Minn. Bible Coll., 1961-62, Calif. State U., 1962-64. Sales exec. GTE Directories Corp., Los Alamitos, Calif., 1970-77; Yellow Pages account exec. with various advt. agys., Calif., 1977-78; ind. contractor Nat. Yellow Pages, 1978-79; mgr. Nat. Yellow Pages Budget Rent A Car, Western region, 1979-82; dir. Yellow Pages advt. Transamerica Mktg. Services, Los Angeles, 1982-85; exec. v.p. BMW Advt. Inc., 1985—; Yellow Page advt. cons., sales trainer. Named GTE Yellow Pages Sales All Star, 1975. Republican.

MINOR, JAMES ERNEST, research executive, chemical engineer; b. Davenport, Wash., Apr. 10, 1919; s. Ernest and Matilda (Hardin) M.; m. Dorothy Ann Sabro, Jan. 28, 1950; children: Ann Louise, James Craig, Carl Steven. BCE, Wash. State U., 1941; PhD in Physical Chemistry, U. Wash., 1950. Registered profl. engr., Wash. Research chemist Proctor and Gamble, Cin., 1950-52; research scientist, sect. mgr. Gen. Electric Co., Richland, Wash., 1952-65; research mgr. Battelle NW, Richland, 1965—. Contbr. articles to profl. jours. Mem. Richland City Council, 1956; chmn. Richland Sch. Bd., 1972-74; chmn. bd. trustees Columbia Basin Coll., Pasco, Wash., 1977-82. Served to maj. U.S. Army, 1941-46, ETO. Mem. Am. Soc. for Metals, Sigma Xi, Alpha Chi Sigma. Democrat. Presbyterian. Avocations: reading, fishing. Home: 2105 Symons Richland WA 99352 Office: Battelle NW PO Box 999 Richland WA 99352

MINSKER, MARILYN, speech, language pathologist; b. Jamestown, N.Y., Apr. 26; d. Frank and Ahsnah Ray (Otberg) M. BS in Edn., SUNY, Fredonia, 1973, MS, 1976. Lic. private therapist, Calif., cert. clin. competence, Calif., N.Y. Therapist Unified Sch. Dist., Adams-Friendship, Wis., 1975-76, Richard's Therapy and Edn. Ctr., Riverside, Calif., 1980-81, San Bernadino (Calif.) Sch. Dist., 1978-83; speech, lang. therapist Unified Sch. Dist., Palm Springs, Calif., 1985-86; pvt. practice therapy Palm Springs, Calif.; speech and language pathologist Creative Home Programs, Riverside, Calif., 1986—; speech and lang. pathologist Cucamonga (Calif.) Unified Sch. Dist., 1986—. Mem. Am. Speech, Lang., Hearing Assn., Calif. Speech, Lang., Hearing Assn. Buddhist. Avocations: aerobics, singing, traveling, attending concerts and plays.

MINTURN, WILLIAM OLIVER, physician, surgeon; b. Chgo., June 16, 1926; s. Benjamin Earl and Jeannette (Tate) M.; B.S., Trinity Coll., Conn., 1948; M.D., Yale U., 1952; m. Shirley Alice Moseley, June 15, 1952; children—Sarah Louise, David Bruce, Laura Ann. Intern, Cook County Hosp., Chgo., 1952-53; instr. surgery Wayne U., Detroit, 1953-57; resident in gen. surgery Detroit Receiving Hosp., 1953-57; resident in chest surgery Ingham Chest Hosp., Lansing, Mich., 1957-58, Roswell Park Cancer Inst. and Buffalo Children's Hosp., 1958-59; chief thoracic surgery VA Hosp., Phoenix, 1959-60; chief surgery Glendale (Ariz.) Samaritan Hosp., 1961-70; pvt. practice medicine, specializing in gen. and chest surgery, Sun City, Ariz., 1961—; founder, pres. Sun City Med. Clinic, 1961—; mem. staffs Boswell Meml., Glendale Samaritan, Maryvale Samaritan, Phoenix Bapt., John C. Lincoln hosps. Bd. dirs. Sun City chpt. Am. Cancer Soc. Served with USNR, 1943-45. Recipient merit award as founding mem. Boswell Hosp., Sun City, 1976; Faces in Crowd award Sports Illustrated mag., 1981. Diplomate Am. Bd. Surgery. Fellow Am. Coll. Chest Physicians; mem. AMA (named to Over-50 Sports Hall of Fame, 1984), Phoenix, Ariz. surg. assns., Pan Am. Med. Assn., SAR, Ariz. Marathon Soc., Delta Phi, Alpha Kappa Kappa. Republican. Episcopalian. Clubs: Rotary; Medics, Match Point Tennis (Phoenix); Prescott Country. Contbr. articles to Road Racers Am., Yale Medicine. Home: 6034 N 38th Pl Paradise Valley AZ 85253 Office: 10222 Coggins Dr Sun City AZ 85351

MINTZ, RONALD EARL, artist, art conservator, chromotechnics scientist; b. Rocky Mount, N.C., Jan. 21, 1926; m. Mildred Tilson, Dec. 18, 1948; children—Richard, Robert. A.B., U. N.C., 1948; student under Griesche and Liese, London and Garmische-Obermmergau, 1953-56; M.S., George Washington U., 1964; Ph.D., Jackson State U., 1975. Dep. commr. revenue State of N.C., Greenville, 1950-52; artist, art conservator, Washington, 1956-58, various locations, Tex., Fla., Maine, Wash., Ala., Nebr. and Calif., 1958-74; prin. firm Macropaedia Conservation, conservation hist. and artistic works, Chapel Hill, N.C., 1974-80; exhibited in one man shows, Chapel Hill, 1978, 80, Seattle, 1981-84; exhibited in group shows, Bellevue, Wash., 1982, New Orleans, 1982-83, Palm Beach, Fla., 1982-83. Helped establish N.C. State Mus. Art, 1949-51. Served to col. USAF, 1951-74. Decorated Legion of Merit, Meritorious Service medal. Developer abstract art form technique of Chromoformism. Currently semi-retired. Address: 14510 SE 167th St Fairwood Greens Renton WA 98058

MINUDRI, REGINA URSULA, librarian, consultant, lecturer; b. San Francisco, May 9, 1937; d. John C. and Molly (Halter) M. B.A., San Francisco Coll. for Women, 1958; M.L.S., U. Calif.-Berkeley, 1959. Reference librarian Menlo Park (Calif.) Pub. Library, 1959-62; regional librarian Santa Clara County (Calif.) Library, 1962-68; project coordinator Fed. Young Adult Library Services Project, Mountain View, Calif., 1968-71; dir. profl. services Alameda County (Calif.) Library, 1971, asst. county librarian, 1972-77; library dir. Berkeley Pub. Library, 1977—; lectr. U. San Francisco, 1970-72, U. Calif., Berkeley, 1977-81; cons., 1975—. Mem. ALA (pres. 1986—, exec. bd. 1980—, council 1979-83, Grolier award 1974), Calif. Library Assn. (pres. 1981, council 1965-69, 79-82), LWV (dir. Berkeley chpt. 1980-81). Author: Getting It Together, A Young Adult Bibliography, 1970; contbr. articles to publs. including School Library Jour., Wilson Library Bulletin. Office: Berkeley Pub Library 2090 Kittredge St Berkeley CA 94704

MINZNER, DEAN FREDERICK, aviation company executive; b. Winchester, Mass., July 20, 1945; s. Frederick Louis and Winifred (Hughes) M.; B.A., Franklin and Marshall Coll., 1967; M.B.A., Columbia U., 1972. Dist. exec. Greater N.Y. councils Boy Scouts Am., N.Y.C., 1972-76; sales exec. Coast Avia, Long Beach, Calif., 1976-78, Performance Aircraft, Inc., Hayward, Calif., 1978; owner, pres. Western Aviation Consultants, Inc., Hayward, 1978-82, Cal-Pacific Assocs., Inc., Hayward, 1979—, Cal-Pacific Enterprises, Hayward, 1982—. Mem. Assn. M.B.A. Execs., Columbia U. Grad. Sch. Bus. Alumni Assn., Aircraft Owners and Pilots Assn. Office: PO Box 6206 Hayward CA 94540

MIR, QUI-CHEE, chemisty educator; b. Cha-yi, Taiwan, Republic of China, Sept. 16, 1951; came to U.S., 1974; d. Dick and Huei-Chen (Chang) Wang; m. Muhammad Saeed Mir, Oct. 27, 1977; 1 child, Hasan. BS, Chung-Yuan Coll., People's Republic of China, 1973; MS, Portland State U., 1980; PhD, U. Idaho, 1980. Asst. prof. Hendrix Coll., Conway, Ark., 1980-81; vis. asst. prof. Alfatah U., Tripoli, Libya, 1981-82; research assoc. Clemson (S.C.) U., 1982-83; instr. chemistry Yakima (Wash.) Valley Coll., 1983—. Inventor in field. Mem. Am. Chem. Soc., Am. Soc. Chem. Edn. Avocations: reading, travel. Home: 1500 W Mead #86 Yakima WA 98902 Office: Yakima Valley Coll 16th and Nobhill Yakima WA 98907

MIRACLE, BRIAN FLOYD, psychologist; b. Casper, Wyo., June 9, 1933; s. Evert Arnold and Ann Alice (Nelson) M.; BA, U. Wyo., 1959, MA, 1964, EdD, 1965; m. Nancy; children: Robert Lowell, Jennifer Janet. Pvt. practice psychology, Lander, Wyo., 1965—; chmn. Wyo. State Parole Bd., Rawlins, 1971-78. Trustee U. Wyo., 1978—. Served with U.S. Army, 1950-52. Decorated Purple Heart. Mem. Wyo. Peace Officers Assn. Republican. Episcopalian. Lodges: Elks, Rotary, Masons, Shriners. Author: (with Carl Delacato) Neurological Organization and Reading, 1966. Office: 560 S 2d St Lander WY 82520

MIRACLE, ROBERT WARREN, banker; b. Casper, Wyo.; m. Maggie Miracle; children—Mark, John. B.S. in Law, U. Wyo., 1951; grad. with honors, Pacific Coast Banking Sch., 1960. With Norwest Bank Casper N.A.

(formerly Wyo. Nat. Bank of Casper), Wyo., 1954—, exec. v.p., 1967, pres., chief exec. officer, 1968—, chmn., 1983—; also dir. Norwest Bank Casper N.A. (formerly Wyo. Nat. Bank of Casper), Norwest Bank Gillette; pres., chief exec. officer, dir. Affiliated Bank Corp. Wyo. (formerly Wyo. Nat. Corp.), Casper, 1970—; Bd. dir. Norwest Bank East Casper, Norwest Bank West Casper N.A., Norwest Bank Cheyenne, Norwest Bank East Cheyenne, Norwest Bank Gillette. Bd. dirs. United Fund of Natrona County, Wyo., 1963-65, campaign co-chmn., 1973-78; trustee The Myra Fox Skelton Found., 1963—; bd. dirs. Investment in Casper, pres., 1967-70; Wyo. treas. Radio Free Europe, 1967-72; trustee Casper Coll. Found., 1967—, pres. 1973-75, 85—; trustee U. Wyo. Found., 1972—; chmn. Casper Downtown Improvement Assn., 1974-75; bd. dirs. Central Wyo. Fair Bd., 1974-79, pres. 1977-78. Served to capt. USMC. Recipient James C. Scarboro Meml. award Colo. Sch. Banking., 1977; Disting. Service in Bus. award U. Wyo. Coll. Commerce and Industry, 1980. Mem. Wyo. Bankers Assn. (chmn. legis. com. 1969-80, pres. 1974-75), Am. Bankers Assn. (mem. governing council 1974-75, 81-83), Am. Mgmt. Assn., Rocky Mountain Oil and Gas Assn., Newcomen Soc. in N.Am., Casper C. of C. (pres. 1965-66, Disting. Service award 1981), VFW. Clubs: Casper Petroleum, Casper Country. Lodge: Masons, Lions. Office: Affiliated Bank Corp Wyo PO Box 2799 Casper WY 82602

MIRAMONTES, JOHN S., architect; b. Los Angeles, Jan. 31, 1955; s. Salvador H. and Adelina (Lara) M. AA, Cerritos Coll., 1977; BS, Calif. Poly. U., Pomona, 1981. City planner Baldwin Park (Calif.) City Hall, 1979-80; project mgr. A.K. Ngai and Assocs., Los Angeles, 1980-85; cadd mgr. Corbin, Yamafuji & Ptnrs., Irvine, Calif., 1985—; coordinator Norwalk Christian Ctr., Calif., 1984—, Heritage Internt. Fellowship, 1984—. Mem. AIA (coordinator BEEP program Los Angeles chpt. 1986, lectr.), Am. Planning Assn. Republican. Avocations: writing, traveling, sports, music, art. Home: 14707 Gridley Rd Norwalk CA 90650 Office: Corbin Yamafuji & Ptnrs 17992 Mitchell S Irvine CA 92714

MIRELS, HAROLD, aerospace engineer; b. N.Y.C., July 29, 1924; s. Hyman and Lily (Efron) M.; m. Nell Segal, Oct. 4, 1953; children: Lily, Laurence Franklin, Jeremy Mark. BSME, Cooper U., 1944; MSME, Case Inst. Tech., 1949; PhD in Aero. Engring., Cornell U., 1953. Sect. head NACA, Cleve., 1944-57; br. chief NASA, Cleve., 1957-61; dept. head Aerospace Corp., El Segundo, Calif., 1961-78, assoc. dir., 1978-84, prin. scientist, 1984—. Co-inventor continuous wave chem. laser. Recipient Tech. Achievement award Cleve. Tech. Socs., 1960. Fellow AIAA, Am. Phys. Soc.; mem. Nat. Acad. Engring. Home: 3 Seahurst Rd Rolling Hills Estates CA 90274 Office: The Aerospace Corp Aerophysics Lab PO Box 92957 Los Angeles CA 90009

MIRKES, PHILIP EDMUND, developmental biologist; b. Oshkosh, Wis., May 8, 1943; s. Norman Valentine and Clara Barbara (Schoenberger) M.; m. Donna Zuk, June 8, 1968; children: Sean Philip, Trevor Ray. BS, St. Norbert Coll., 1965; MS, U. Mich., 1967, PhD, 1970. Postdoctoral fellow U. Wash., Seattle, 1970-73, research asst. prof., 1979-83, research assoc. prof., 1983—; asst. prof. U. S.C., Columbia, 1973-79; cons. Oak Ridge EPA, 1982—. Contbr. articles to profl. jours. Cons. adv. com. March of Dimes Repro. Hazards in the Workplace, 1985—; pres. Challenge Parents Assn., Lynnwood, Wash., 1985; coach Little League, Lynnwood, 1979—. Brown Hazen research grantee, 1975-79, NSF grantee, 1978-81, NIH grantee, 1979—. Mem. AAAS, Teratology Soc., Soc. Devel. Biology, Pacific N.W. Assn. Toxicologists. Avocations: reading, golfing, fishing, stamp collecting. Office: U Wash Dept Pediatrics Seattle WA 98195

MIROWSKI, PAUL JOSEPH, lawyer; b. Jackson, Mich., Feb. 16, 1954; s. Edward John and Elizabeth (Kapisinski) M. BS, Mich. State U., 1977; JD, U. San Francisco, 1982. Bar: Calif. 1982, U.S. Dist. Ct. (so. dist.) Calif. 1983, U.S. Ct. Appeals (9th cir.) 1983. Sole practice San Diego, 1983-85; ptnr. Seckelman & Mirowski, San Diego, 1986—; instr. Street Law, San Francisco, 1981. Mem. ABA, San Diego County Bar Assn., Assn. San Diego County Trial Lawyers. Clubs: Lawyers, Barrister. Avocations: music, skiing, travel. Office: 110 West C St Suite 1411 San Diego CA 92101

MISA, KENNETH FRANKLIN, management consultant; b. Jamaica, N.Y., Sept. 24, 1939; s. Frank J. and Mary M. (Soszka) M.; BS cum laude in Psychology, Fairfield U., 1961; MS in Psychology, Purdue U., 1963; PhD in Psychology (Fellow 1963-66), St. John's U., 1966. Staff psychologist Rohrer, Hibler & Replogle, Los Angeles, 1966-67; assoc. A.T. Kearney, Inc., Los Angeles, 1968-71, sr. assoc., 1972-74, prin., 1975-78, v.p., partner, 1979-86; pres. HR Cons. Group, 1987—. Cert. mgmt. cons.; lic. psychologist, Calif. Mem. Am. Psychol. Assn., Calif. Psychol. Assn., Los Angeles County Psychol. Assn., Am. Soc. for Tng. and Devel., Human Resources Planning Soc., Acad. of Mgmt., Indsl. Relations Research Assn. Internat. Assn. Applied Psychology, World Affairs Council of Los Angeles, Town Hall of So. Calif., Los Angeles C. of C. Republican. Roman Catholic. Clubs: Jonathan. Home: 924C S Orange Grove Blvd Pasadena CA 91105 Office: AT Kearney Inc 100 N Brand Blvd Suite 209 Glendale CA 91203

MISCH, PETER, geology educator; b. Berlin, Aug. 30, 1909; came to U.S., 1946, naturalized 1952; s. Georg and Clara (Dilthey) M.; m. Susan Maier-Leibnitz, 1934 (dec. 1942); 1 child, Hanna French-Misch; m. Nicoletta Rosenthal, 1947; children: Felix George, Anthony Arthur. PhD, U. Göttingen, Fed. Republic of Germany, 1932. Geologist Himalayan Expdn. to Nanga Parbat, 1934; prof. structural geology Nat. Sun Yat-sen U., Canton, Peoples Republic of China, 1935-38; adviser Geol. Surveys, Kwangtung and Yunnan, 1936-46; prof. structural geology Nat. Sun Yat-sen U., Yunnan, Peoples Republic of China, 1938-40; prof. Nat. Peking U. (inc. into Nat. S.W. Assoc. U.), Kunming, Yunnan, 1940-46; asst. prof. U. Wash., Seattle, 1947-48, assoc. prof., 1948-50, prof., 1950-80, prof. emeritus, 1980—. Guggenheim fellow, 1954-55. Mem. Geol. Soc. Am. (past. chmn. Cordilleran sect.), Geol. Assn. Can. (hon. mem. Cordilleran Sect.), Am. Geophys. Union , Am. Assn. Petroleum Geologists (disting. lectr. 1953, assoc. editor 1965-76), Mineral. Soc. Am., Geochem. Soc., Mineral. Assn. Can., Geol. Soc. London, Geologische Vereinigung, N.W. Sci. Assn. (Outstanding Scientist award 1979), Sigma Xi. Club: Am. Alpine. Home: 5726 NE 60th St Seattle WA 98115 Office: U Wash Dept Geol Scis Seattle WA 98195

MISCHLER, JANET KATHRYN, nursing educator; b. Boston, Sept. 30, 1939; d. Frederick Joseph and Eileen A. M. R.N., Boston City Hosp., 1960; B.S. in Nursing, Boston U., 1969; M.S., U. Calif.-San Francisco, 1970; Ed.D., U. So. Calif., 1982. Lic. R.N., Calif., Mass., Alaska; vocat. trade and tech. teaching in nursing edn. (life), Calif.; community coll. adminstr. and instr. (life), Calif. Staff nurse Boston City Hosp., 1960-64, instr. Sch. Practical Nursing, 1966-67; sr. staff nurse Boston U. Med. Ctr., 1964-66; instr. Solano Coll., Suisun City, Calif., 1971-82; asst. prof. nursing U. Alaska, Anchorage, 1982—, also mem. adminstrv. council, co-chmn. curriculum com. Co-chmn. disaster preparedness com. Vallejo-Multi-Hosp., 1972-76; trustee, chmn. pub. edn. Solano-Napa County br. Am. Heart Assn., 1974-76; mem. Solano County Emergency Med. Care Com., 1973-76; mem., sec., exec. com. Anchorage Area Emergency Mgmt. Adv. Com.; mem. trauma com. Providence Hosp., 1982; mem. disaster preparedness and nursing com. Anchorage chpt. ARC, 1982—; trustee Hospice of Anchorage; mem. ASPCA, Humane Soc., Alaska Sled Dog Racing Assn., Montana Creek Dog Mushers; mem., vol. Iditarod Trail Com. Middlesex County (Mass.) Women's Med. Assn. scholar, 1957-58; Allstate scholar, 1967; HEW trainee, 1968, 69-70; U. So. Calif. scholar, summers 1978, 80, 81. Mem. Alaska Nurses Assn., Nat. League Nursing, Western Soc. Research in Nursing, Phi Delta Kappa, Sigma Theta Tau. Home: PO Box 670223 Chugiak AK 99567 Office: Univ Alaska 3211 Providence Dr Anchorage AK 99508

MISER, MARTHA ARDEN, social worker; b. Ft. Worth, Apr. 14, 1935; d. Tarleton Alonzo Jenkins and Nedra Irene Cooper; m. Gainer Allen Jeffreys, Aug. 24, 1954 (dec. Apr. 1966); children: Sara Dyck, Susan; m. Frank Donald Miser, July 4, 1970. BA, U. Tex., 1956; MSW, U. So. Calif., 1969. Lic. clin. social worker, Calif. Social worker Los Angeles County, Compton, Calif., 1964-66, child welfare worker, 1967; child welfare worker Los Angeles County, Long Beach, Calif., 1969-70; med. social worker Kaiser Permanente, Bell Flower, Calif., 1972-75; social caseworker Concept 7, Tustin, Calif., 1977-85, supr., 1986—. Mem. Nat. Assn. Social Workers (cert.), AAUW. Republican. Methodist. Club: Toastmasters. Avocations: jogging, gourmet cooking, travel.

MISKIMEN, JOHN ANDREW, financial cons.; b. Phoenix, Aug. 12, 1932; s. Carl W. and Violette (Phillips) M.; A.B., Harvard U., 1954; M.B.A., Golden Gate U., 1967; m. Marilyn J. Howard, Aug. 30, 1952 (div. 1984); children—Debra L., John Andrew, Anne K.; m. Charlene M. Simon, Apr. 25, 1985. Dir. research Irving Lundborg & Co., San Francisco, 1959-65; sr. analyst Mitchum, Jones & Templeton, Inc., San Francisco, 1965-67; v.p. William Hutchinson & Co., Inc., San Francisco, 1967-72; v.p., treas. Manalytics, Inc., San Francisco, 1977-78; sr. v.p. Kelso & Co. Inc., 1978-81; pres. Corp. Procedures, Inc., 1981—. Mem. city council, San Rafael, Calif., 1967-83, Planning Commn., 1964-67. Bd. dirs. Bay Area Air Pollution Control Dist., 1968-70. Served to 1st lt. arty. AUS, 1954-56. Republican. Episcopalian. Home: 24 Dominican Dr San Rafael CA 94901 Office: PO Box 1201 San Rafael CA 94915

MISKUS, MICHAEL ANTHONY, electrical engineer, consultant; b. East Chicago, Ind., Dec. 10, 1950; s. Paul and Josephine Miskus; BS, Purdue U., 1972; AAS in Elec. Engring. Tech., Purdue U., Indpls., 1972; cert. mgmt. Ind. U., 1972, Ind. Central Coll., 1974; m. Jeannie Ellen Dolmanni, Nov. 4, 1972. Service engr. Reliance Electric & Engring. Co., Hammond, Ind., 1972-73; maintenance supr., maintenance mgr. Diamond Chain Co./AMSTED Industries, Indpls., 1973-76; primary and facilities elec. engr. Johnson & Johnson Baby Products Co., Park Forest South, Ill., 1976-81; prin. Miskus Cons., indsl./comml. elec. cons., 1979—; plant and facilities engring. mgr. Sherwin Williams Co., Chgo. Emulsion Plant, Chgo., 1981-85; with Miscon Assocs., Riverside, Calif., 1985—; acting dir. plant and facilities engring. Bourns Inc., 1982—; instr., lectr. EET program Moraine Valley Community Coll., Palos Hills, Ill., 1979; lectr. energy engring., bldg. automation systems Prairie State Coll., Chicago Heights, Ill., 1980—; mem. adj. faculty, faculty adv. bd. Orange Coast Coll., Costa Mesa, Calif.; mem. Elec. Industry Evaluation Panel. Mem. faculty adv. bd. Moraine Valley Community Coll., 1980—. Mem. IEEE, Assn. Energy Engrs., Assn. Energy Engrs. (sr., So. Calif. chpt.), Illuminating Engring. Soc. N.Am., Internat. Platform Assn., Riverside C. of C. Club: Purdue of Los Angeles. Office: Miscon Assocs PO Box 55353 Riverside CA 92517

MISNER, DEWAYNE ALAN, safety engineering specialist; b. Sapulpa, Okla., May 20, 1955; s. Harold W. and Patty E. (Dillon) M.; m. Lani L. Gorman, July 14, 1979; children: Jannette, Jared. BS in Safety Edn., Cen. State U., Edmond, Okla., 1978. Employee relations clerk Kerr McGee Corp., Oklahoma City, 1978-79; safety asst. Kerr McGee Coal Co., Gillette, Wyo., 1979-80; safety engr. Kerr McGee Chem. Corp., Trona, Calif., 1980-83, supt. safety and health, 1983—. Mem. Am. Soc. Safety Engrs. Baptist. AvocationsL snow and water skiing, softball. Home: 1107 N Las Posas Ridgecrest CA 93555 Office: Kerr McGee Chem Co PO Box 367 Trona CA 93562

MISRA, JAY, telecommunications executive, educator; b. Cuttack, India, Dec. 7, 1956; came to U.S., 1968; s. Jaga and Suprava Misra. BS, MS, U. Pitts., 1978; MBA, Harvard U., 1982. Product mgr. Intel Corp., Santa Clara, Calif., 1982-84; mktg. mgr. Rolm Corp., Santa Clara, 1984—; prof. mktg., telecommunications San Jose State, Calif., 1982—. Author: Business Telematics, 1986, Business Telecommunications, 1987. Mem. IEEE, Alpha Pi Mu. Avocations: tennis, squash, racquetball. Home: 707 Continental Circle #317 Mountain View CA 94040 Office: Rolm Corp 4900 Old Ironsides Santa Clara CA 95054

MISRA, MOHAN SWAROOP, metallurgical engineer; b. Veranasi, India, Nov. 30, 1944; came to U.S., 1967; s. Hari Krishna and Chandra Kanta (Kapuria) M.; m. Shikha Jhingaran M., Nov. 20, 1971; children: Rishi Dave, Anuska. BS in Metall. Engring., Banaras U., India, 1966; MS, U. Wash., 1970; PhD in Metallurgical Engring, Colo. Sch. Mines, 1986. Asst. prof. U. Roorkee, India, 1966-67; teaching asst. U. Wash., Seattle, 1967-70; research engr. Advance Structures and Tech., Santa Ana, Calif., 1971-72; sr. engr. Northrop Aircraft, Hawthorne, Calif., 1972-75; mgr. advance materials tech. Martin Marietta Aerospace, Denver, 1975—. Contbr. articles to profl. jours.; patentee in field. Recipient Inventor of Yr. award Martin Marietta Corp., 1982, Jefferson Cup for Outstanding Performance, 1982. Mem. Am. Soc. Metals, The Metall. Soc. (research com. mem. 1978), Am. Foundrymen's Soc. (research com. mem. 1980, Outstanding Tech. Achievement award, 1980). Avocations: tennis, travel, tech. and scientific reading. Home: 1066 S Foothills Dr Lakewood CO 80228 Office: Martin Marietta Aerospace M0487 PO Box 179 Denver CO 80201

MISSIMORE, PHILLIP GLENN, journalist; b. Santa Monica, Calif., Feb. 1, 1950; s. Lester Glenn and Elizabeth Patricia (Randle) M.; m. Judy Ellen Kaplan, Jan. 5, 1975; children: Ethan James, Adam David, Cory Alexander. BA in Journalism, Calif. State U., Northridge, 1971; postgrad., Pepperdine U., 1986—. Sr. editor Bldg. News, Los Angeles, 1975-77; editor Skateboard Industry News, Los Angeles, 1977-78; acct. exec. Kresser Craig, Los Angeles, 1978-79, J.B. Talmadge, Woodland Hills, Calif., 1979-81; assoc. pub., editor-in-chief Computer Reseller Monthly, Los Angeles, 1981—; mem. editorial adv. bd. Informart, Dallas, 1985—, Interface Group, Framingham, Mass., 1984—. Mem. Info. Industry Assn., Assn. Bus. Pubs. Home: 978 Meadowcrest St Newbury Park CA 91320 Office: CES Pub 3550 Wilshire Blvd Los Angeles CA 90010

MITCHAM, PATRICIA ANN HAMILTON, educator; b. El Paso, Tex., Sept. 8, 1942; d. Leverett Chandler and Annabelle Hamilton; m. Eugene Louis Mitcham III, Apr. 20, 1968; children: Shirley Dianne, Steven Craig. BA, Tex. Western Coll., 1964; postgrad., U. Calif., Irvine, 1983-85. Educator U. Tex., El Paso, 1964-66; instr. Hardin Simmons U., Abilene, Tex., 1966-67; educator El Paso Pub. Schs., 1968-70, 74-59; English instr. Los Angeles Unified Sch. Dist., 1979—; tng. supr. of vols. Army Community Service, Ft. Bliss, Tex., 1971-73, asst. supr., 1973-74. Mem. DAR, Assn. Supervision and Curriculum Devel., Internat. Platform Assn., Am. Bus. Women's Assn. (corresponding sec. 1986), Nat. Council Tchrs. of English, Computer Using Educators. Republican. Episcopalian. Avocations: painting, writing. Home: 6082 Hardwick Circle Huntington Beach CA 92647 Office: Gardena High Sch 1301 182d St Gardena CA 90248

MITCHELL, ADRIENNE HISCOX, fraternal organization executive; b. San Mateo, Calif., July 6, 1927; d. Richard G. and Lucy Woodbridge (Means) Hiscox; m. Bruce Tyson Mitchell, Oct. 14, 1951; 1 child, Mark Means. AB, U. Kans., 1948. Research chemist Del Monte Co., San Francisco, 1948-52. Precinct chmn. Rep. Party, Hillsborough, Calif., 1965-77, mem. Rep. State Cen. Com., 1972-76; pres. Children's Health Home Aux., San Mateo, Calif., 1965. Mem. Am. Chem. Soc., Am. Assn. Univ. Women (br. pres. 1969-70), Alumnae Panhellenic (pres. 1962), Pi Beta Phi (pres. alumnae club 1958-59, province pres. 1975-77, dir. acad. standards 1977-79, grand v.p. collegians 1979-85, grand v.p. philanthropies 1985—). Mem. United Ch. Christ. Home: 165 Redwood Dr Hillsborough CA 94010

MITCHELL, BETTY JO, writer, publisher; b. Coin, Iowa, May 2, 1931; d. Edith Darrah McWilliams; B.A., S.W. Mo. State U., Springfield; M.S.L.S., U. So. Calif. Asst. acquisitions librarian Calif. State U., Northridge, 1967-69, librarian for personnel and fin., 1969-71, acting asso. library dir., 1971-72, asso. dir. univ. libraries, 1972-81; owner Viewpoint Press, Tehachapi, Calif.; cons. Western Interstate Commn. for Higher Edn. USOE Inst. for Tng. in Staff Devel. Problem Solving; participant workshops in field. Bd. dirs. San Fernando Valley council Girl Scouts U.S.A., 1974-77, employed personnel com., 1979—; bd. dirs. Bear Valley Springs Condominium Owners Assn., 1978, Empyrean Found., 1978—. Mem. ALA (mem., chmn. various coms.), Nat. Library Assn., Calif. Library Assn., Assn. Calif. State U. Profs. (sec., exec. com., 1971-72), AAUP, Pi Beta Chi, Alpha Mu Gamma. Co-author: Cost Analysis of Library Functions: A Total System Approach, 1978; author: ALMS: A Budget Based Library Management System, 1982; co-author: How to See the U.S. on $12 a Day; speaker profl. confs.; contbr. writings to profl. publs.; editor Staff Development column in Special Libraries, 1975-76. Home: Star Route 3 Box 4600-7 Tehachapi CA 93561 Office: PO Box P Tehachapi CA 93561

MITCHELL, CARL GENE, religion and psychology educator; b. Santa Paula, Calif., July 29, 1926; s. Hubert R. and Isophine (McCalister) M.; m. Frances C. Rotramel, Feb. 8, 1953; children: Mickey S., Cary L., Michelle Mitchell Glover. BS in Ednl. Psychology, Pepperdine U., 1949, MA in Religion, 1966; diploma in Italian, U. Florence, Italy, 1960; PhD in Ednl. Psychology, U. So. Calif., 1967. Ordained to ministry Ch. of Christ, 1949; lic. marriage, family and child therapist, Calif. Minister Ch. of Christ, various locations, Calif., Ark., Italy, 1949—; prof. religion and psychology Pepperdine U., Malibu, Calif., 1955-80, chmn. dept. religion, 1976-80, also dean student affairs, 1984-87; prof., asst. dir. Italy program Harding U., Searcy, Ark., 1980-84; dir. Florence, Italy programs Pepperdine U., 1987—; lectr., U.S., Europe, Cen. Am., South Am. Author: Christian Evidence, 1958, Christian Psychology, 1958; (monograph) Vocational Evangelism, 1982. Bd. dirs. African Christian Hosp. Found., Searcy, 1978—, Calif. Christian Sch., Sepulveda, 1965—, Christian Childrens Services, Santa Fe Springs, Calif., 1985—. Mem. Am. Psychol. Assn., Am. Assn. Marriage and Family Therapists, World Mental Health Assn. Republican. Avocations: tennis, golfing, travelling. Home: 24327 Baxter Dr Malibu CA 90265 Office: Pepperdine U Pacific Coast Hwy Malibu CA 90265

MITCHELL, CHERYL RUTH, research chemist; b. Pomptain Plains, N.J., Dec. 4, 1954; d. William Alexander and Ruth (Cobbey) M.; m. Pat Richard Mitchell, Dec. 31, 1980; children: Sarah, Catherine. BS in Chemistry, Bethany Coll., 1976; PhD in Chemistry, Tex. A&M U., 1980. Asst. prof. chemistry Calif. State U., Sacramento, 1980-82; head research and devel. Calif. Natural Products, Manteca, 1982—. Patentee in field. Welsh fellow Tex. A&M U., College Station, 1976-80. Mem. Inst. Food Tech. (profl.). Home: 446 N Powers Manteca CA 95336 Office: Calif Natural Products PO Box 139 Manteca CA 95336

MITCHELL, DAVID GLEN, research aerospace engineer; b. Malvern, Ark., July 26, 1954; s. Jewell Delois Mitchell and Ruby Rachel (Reid) Moore; m. Holly Ann Gretsch, June 17, 1984. BS in Engring., UCLA, 1977; MS in Aerospace Engring., Northrop U., 1987. Aerospace engring. trainee NASA Dryden Flight Research Ctr., Edwards, Calif., 1973-76; staff engr. Systems Tech. Inc., Hawthorne, Calif., 1977—. Contbr. articles to profl. jours. Sec. So. Calif. Skeptics. Mem. AIAA, AAAS, Aircraft Owners and Pilots Assn., Am. Helicopter Soc. Avocations: pilot, magic, skiing. Office: Systems Tech Inc 13766 S Hawthorne Blvd Hawthorne CA 90250

MITCHELL, EARLENE CARRIER, educator; b. Salt Lake City; d. Earl M. and Alma (Shelton) C.; m. Dale Wally; children: Denise Boulanger, Allen, Jennifer Beal, Sheila, Rollin. BA in English with honors, U. Utah, 1967, MA, 1981, postgrad., 1981—. Cert. secondary tchr., Utah. Teaching asst. dept. English U. Utah, Salt Lake City, 1967-68, teaching asst. dept. edn., 1984-85; tchr. Hillcrest High Sch., Midvale, Utah, 1968—. Contbr. articles to profl. jours. Mem. Utah Council for Humanities Edn. (pres. 1983-86), Nat. Humanities Faculty, Assn. Supervision and Curriculum Devel., Utah Endowment for Humanities (grantee 1983-85, curriculum cons.), Phi Beta Kappa, Phi Kappa Phi. Democrat. Unitarian. Avocations: music, photography, skiing, running. Office: Hillcrest High Sch 7350 S 9th E Midvale UT 84047

MITCHELL, GENEVA BROOKE, hypnotherapist; b. Ringgold, Tex., Feb. 15, 1929; d. Roy Banks and Willie Jewel (Lemons) Shaw; m. Roy David Mitchell, Nov. 30, 1947; children: Ronald, Donald, Joel, Pamela, Annette. Cert. master hypnotist Hypnosis Tng. Inst., Los Angeles, 1980, cert. hypnotherapist, 1983; cert. in advanced investigative and forensic hypnosis Tex. A&M U., 1982. Chiropractic asst. Alamogordo, N.Mex., 1962-79; hypnotherapist Alamogordo Hypnosis and Counseling Ctr., 1980—; mng. ptnr. Shaw, Mitchell & Mallory, Albuquerque, 1986; hypnotherapist M&M Horses Corp., Tularosa, N.Mex., 1985—; pres. N.Mex. Chiropractic Aux., 1984-85; mem. Am. Council Hypnotist Examiners, 1980-85; hypnotist for tape series. Charter pres. La Sertoma, Alamogordo, 1957; pres. Oregon sch. PTA, Alamogordo, 1958, La Luz Sch. Parents Club, N.Mex., 1962; sec. N.Mex. Jr. Rodeo Assn., 1964; co-founder Pre-Sch. La Luz, 1969; mem. N.Mex. Gov.'s Council on Youth, 1969; bd. dirs. Otero County Jr. Rodeo Assn., N.Mex., 1968; dir. self-hypnosis sch. Recipient Speakers award Life Found., 1984. Mem. Am Assn. Profl. Hypnotherapists, Ladies for Life (appreciation award 1984), N.Mex. Ladies Life Fellowship (pres. 1983, bd. dirs. 1985). Avocations: golf; painting; swimming; martial arts. Office: Alamogordo Hypnosis and Counseling Ctr 9th and Porto Rico Alamogordo NM 88310

MITCHELL, GORDON LYNN, electrical engineer; b. Spokane, Wash., Dec. 20, 1942; s. Frank Leonard and Vesta Dorothy (Shaw) M.; m. Skaidrite Liesma Iesalnieks, July 17, 1966; children: Douglas, Adele, Vicki. BS, U. Wash., 1964, PhD, 1974. Registered profl. elect. engr., Wash., Oreg., Calif., Minn. Mem. research faculty U. Wash., Seattle, 1974-78; prin. research scientist, fiber optics group leader Honeywell Inc., Mpls., 1978-83; dir. research and devel. Tech. Dynamics, Woodinville, Wash., 1983—; comml. arbitrator. Contbr. articles to profl. jours.; patentee in field. Served with USN, 1964-69. Research grantee NSF, 1974-78, Technicon, 1975. Mem. IEEE (sr.), Optical Soc. Am., U.S. Strategic Inst. Home: 14724 NE 177th St Woodinville WA 98072 Office: Tech Dynamics 18800 142d Ave NE Woodinville WA 98072

MITCHELL, HARRY E., educator, mayor; b. Phoenix, July 18, 1940; s. Harry Casey and Irene Gladys (Childres) M.; m. Marianne Prevratil, May 5, 1962; children—Amy, Mark. B.A., Ariz. State U., 1962, M.P.A., 1981. Tchr. Tempe High Sch., Ariz., 1964—; councilman City of Tempe, 1970-76, vice mayor, 1976-78, mayor, 1978—. Bd. dirs. Tempe Sister City; trustee Tempe St. Lukes Hosp., Rio Salado Devel. Dist.; state rep. Sister Cities Internat., Washington; mem. Ariz. State U. Liberal Arts Alumni Adv. Bd., Adv. Council Ctr. Pub. Affairs, Ariz. Commn. Post Secondary Edn. Recipient Disting. Service award Tempe Jaycees. Mem. Ariz. State U. Alumni Bd. (chmn.), Ariz. State U. Advanced Pub. Exec. Program. Democrat. Roman Catholic. Office: City of Tempe 31 E 5th St Tempe AZ 85281 *

MITCHELL, JOSEPH NATHAN, real estate company executive; b. Winnipeg, Man., Can., Oct. 10, 1922; came to U.S., 1931, naturalized, 1936; s. Edward David and Anna (Copp) M.; m. Beverly Edna Henigson, Oct. 27, 1946; children: Jonathan Edward, Jan Ellen, Karin Helene. Student, UCLA, 1940-42. Pres. Beneficial Standard Corp., 1967-85; chmn., chief exec. officer EDM Equities, Inc., 1985—; mem. internat. bd. Ampal-Am. Israel Corp., N.Y.C.; dir. Pacific Lighting Corp., mem. compensation com., exec. com.; v.p. Jackson-Mitchell Pharms., Inc., Santa Barbara, Calif. Chmn. Los Angeles Appeal, State of Israel Bonds, 1967, also past mem. exec. com., cabinet; mem. Mayor's Steering Com. on Urban Coalition, Mayor's Ad Hoc Com. on Aging, 1980, Los Angeles Citizens Olympic Adv. Commn., 980-81, Dist. Atty.'s Adv. Council; past mem. bd. dirs., exec. com., nat. campaign cabinet United Jewish Appeal; mem. exec., investment, fin., planning, bldg., endowment funds, nominating and resource devel. coms. Cedars-Sinai Med. Center, also ad hoc com. on restructuring, chmn. exec. personnel com., bd. dirs.; past mem. exec. com. Jewish Fedn.-Council Greater Los Angeles; bd. dirs., past v.p., gen. chmn. United Jewish Welfare Fund, 1952; mem. Greater Los Angeles Urban Coalition; trustee, mem. adv. bd., past v.p. Jewish Community Found.; bd. dirs. ops. mgmt. council United Way, 1972-73, exec. com.; chmn. United Crusade Los Angeles; trustee, sec., treas. Edward D. and Anna Mitchell Family Found.; vice chmn. bd. govs. Performing Arts Council, 1980-81; chmn. Music Center Unified Fund Campaign, 1981. Served with AUS, 1942-46, ETO. Mem. Am. Technion Soc. (past nat. v.p., bd. govs.), U.S. C. of C., Calif.-Israel C. of C., Los Angeles C. of C. (dir., chmn. bd. 1980, pres. 1979), Calif. Roundtable (dir.). Clubs: Hillcrest Country (Los Angeles) (past treas., dir.), Los Angeles (Los Angeles); Tamarisk Country (Palm Springs, Calif.), Tennis (Palm Springs, Calif.). Office: 3700 Wilshire Blvd Los Angeles CA 90010

MITCHELL, JOSEPH PATRICK, architect; b. Bellingham, Wash., Sept. 29, 1939; s. Joseph Henry and Jessie Delila (Smith) M.; student Western Wash. State Coll., 1957-59; B.A., U. Wash., 1963, B.Arch., 1965; m. Marilyn Ruth Jorgenson, June 23, 1962; children—Amy Evangeline, Kirk Patrick, Scott Henry. Asso. designer, draftsman, project architect Beckwith Spangler Davis, Bellevue, Wash., 1965-70; prin. J. Patrick Mitchell, AIA & Assos./Architects/Planners/Cons., Kirkland, Wash., 1970—. Chmn. long range planning com. Lake Retreat Camp, 1965—; bldg. chmn. Northshore Baptist Ch., 1980—, elder, 1984—; mem. bd. extension and central com. Columbia Baptist Conf., 1977-83. Cert. Nat. Council Archtl. Registration Bds. Mem. AIA, Constrn. Specification Inst., Interfaith Forum Religion, Art, and Architecture, Nat. Fedn. Ind. Bus., Unltd. Hydroplane Hall of Fame Mus.

Christian Camping Internat., Woodinville C. of C. Republican. Office: 12620 120th Ave NE Suite 208 Kirkland WA 98033

MITCHELL, JUDITH MARIE, research associate, counselor; b. Los Angeles, Oct. 1, 1950; d. Glen H. and Carla Jane (Bilderback) Taylor; m. Paul Francis Mitchell, Dec. 29, 1969 (div.); 1 child, Jennifer Ann. BA, Calif. State U., Northridge, 1976, MA, 1980; PhD UCLA, 1980—. Research and data mgmt. asst. County Office Alcohol Abuse, Los Angeles, 1977-78; vocat. youth counselor, statis. reporter Seventh Step Found., Los Angeles, 1978-79; rehab. counselor San Fernando (Calif.) Valley Assn. for Retarded, 1979-80; vocat. counselor, VA Hosp., Sepulveda, Calif., 1980-81; staff research assoc. Neuropsychiat. Inst. UCLA, 1981-85; postgrad. research assoc. Sch. Pub. Health UCLA, 1986—. Contbr. articles to profl. jours. Fellow Mabel W. Richards Assn., 1974-77, Calif. State U., Northridge, 1974-76, U. Women's Club, 1978, UCLA, 1981-84, 85-86. Mem. Am. Psychol. Assn. Home: PO Box 5064 Mission Hills CA 91345 Office: UCLA Grad Sch Edn Counseling Psychology Los Angeles CA 90026

MITCHELL, KATHLEEN ANN, illustrator, graphic designer; b. Cin., July 27, 1948; d. Gerald Paige and Velma Alice (Bleier) Clary; m. Terence Nigel Mitchell, Feb. 2, 1977. BSc in Design, U. Cin., 1971. Graphic designer Lippincott & Margulies, N.Y.C., 1971, Allied Internat., London, 1972, Moura-George Briggs, London, 1973-75; art dir., photographer Phonograph Record Mag., Los Angeles, 1976-77; ptnr. Walter Morgan Assocs., Santa Monica, Calif., 1977-80; illustrator Artists Internat., Los Angeles and N.Y.C., 1983—. Illustrator: The Snow Queen, 1982, Jane Eyre, 1983, Once Upon A Cat, 1983, Alice in Wonderland, 1986, The Wizard of Oz, 1986, A Bible Alphabet, 1986, The Secret Garden, 1986. Democrat. Avocations: art, antiques. Home: 828 21st St #6 Santa Monica CA 90403

MITCHELL, LAURA ANN, lawyer; b. Miles City, Mont., Oct. 21, 1952; d. Wilmer Ashford and Avis Jean (Baldwin) M.; m. John Walker Ross, Nov. 21, 1981. BA in Polit. Sci. with high honors, U. Mont., Missoula, 1975; JD with honors, George Washington U., 1978. Bar: Mont. 1978. Law clk., U.S. Dist. Ct. for Mont., Billings, 1978-79; assoc. Crowley, Haughey, Hanson, Toole & Dietrich, Billings, 1979-83; ptnr. Crowley, Haughey, Hanson, Toole & Dietrich, 1983—. Mem. adv. panel spl. projects Mont. Arts Council, 1980-82. Mem. Am. Judicature Soc., ABA, Mont. Bar Assn., Yellowstone County Bar Assn. Office: Crowley Haughey Hanson Toole & Dietrich 500 Transwestern Plaza II 490 N 31st St Billings MT 59101

MITCHELL, MELINDA ANN, clinical social worker; b. St. Petersburg, Va., Aug. 1, 1950; d. Roy Gaylord and Abbie Mercedes (Browning) M. BA, Wheaton Coll., 1972; MSW, Fla. State U., 1975; M in Pub. Adminstrn., U. Okla., 1980; student, U. Denver, 1983—. Clin. social worker USAF, 1975—; asst. prof. USAF Acad., Colorado Springs, 1981-84; instr. U. Neb., Wichita Falls, Tex., 1975-79; cons. Easter Seal Rehab. Ctr., Wichita Falls, 1978-79; asst. prof. Pikes Peak Community Coll., Colorado Springs, 1983-84; command clin. social worker USAF Acad., Colorado Springs, 1984—. contbr. articles to profl. jours. Vol. Big Sisters, Denver, Wichita Falls, 1968-78, Head Start, Denver, 1968, Easter Seal Rehab. Ctr., Colorado Springs, 1985; mem. civic choir, Wichita Falls, 1976-79., 1976-79. Denver Classroom Tchrs. scholar, 1968; NIMH grantee, 1974; named Outstanding Women of Am., 1978, 81. Mem. Nat. Assn. Social Workers, LWV. Avocations: reading, hiking, gardening, handcrafts. Office: USAD Acad Hosp SGHMA Colorado Springs CO 80840

MITCHELL, NANCY EVELYN, advertising executive; b. Wakefield, Mich., June 15, 1942; d. Uno Emil and Thyra Evelyn (Maki) Hill; m. George Albert Mitchell, June 10, 1962; children: Michael Spense, Martha Leigh, Thomas William. AA, Suomi Coll., 1962; BBA, Mich. Tech. U., 1965; moyenne degree, Alliance Francaise Ecole Pegue, Geneva, 1978. Service rep. Bell Telephone Co. of Can., Sudbury, Ontario, 1962-63; advt. rep. Network mag., Salt Lake City, 1982; dir. advt. Webster Pub., Salt Lake City, 1983—. Ambassador Ballet West, Salt Lake City, 1985—; pres. troop com. 268 Boy Scouts of Am., Salt Lake City, 1985—. Mem. Utah chpt. Women in Communications, Inc. (pres. 1985—), Utah Advt. Fedn. (bd. dirs.), Utah Assn. Women Bus. Owners (bd. dirs.), Women in Bus. (com. bd.), Women's Info. Network, AAUW (Salt Lake City chpt). Home: 3747 S Forest Hills Dr Salt Lake City UT 84106 Office: Webster Publishing 349 S 600 East Salt Lake City UT 84102

MITCHELL, PAMELA HOLSCLAW, nursing educator, researcher; b. Denver, June 27, 1940; d. Harold Leslie and Maurine Agnes (Boatman) Holsclaw; m. Donald Waldo Mitchell, Sept. 17, 1966; children: Robert Edward, Kenneth Pearce, Andrew David. BS in Nursing, U. Wash., 1962; MS, U. Calif., 1965. Diplomate Am. Bd. Neurosci. Nurses. Asst. head nurse Mass. Gen. Hosp., Boston, 1962-64; pub. health nurse II Dane County Health Dept., Madison, Wis., 1966-67; nursing instr. Emory U., Atlanta, 1967-68; asst. prof. U. Wash., Seattle, 1970-71, 72-78, assoc. prof., 1977-82, prof. physiol. nursing, 1982—; research affiliate Wash. Regional Primate Ctr., Seattle, 1978-82; specialist U. Wash. div. Neurology, 1978—; acting chmn. physiologic nursing U. Wash., 1984-85;project dir. Am. Assn. Critical Care Nurses, Newport Beach, Calif., 1986—. Co-author: Neurological Assessment for Nursing Practice, 1984 (Am. Jour. Nursing Book of Yr. award 1984); author: Concept Basic to Nursing, 1973, 77, 81, translated to Norwegian, Danish, Spanish; contbr. articles to jours. Mem. adv. bd. local chpt. Nat. Multiple Sclerosis Soc., Seattle, 1977—, ARC, 1979—. Recipient Disting. Writing award Wash. and Am. jours. nursing, 1983; Am. Acad. Nursing fellow, 1980. Mem. Am. Assn. Neurosci. Nurses (chmn. clin. reference 1983—), Am. Assn. Critical Care Nurses (recipient Disting. Research award 1984), Am. Nurses Assn., Am. Councils of Nurse Researchers, Clin. Nurse Specialists, Med. Surg. Practice. Democrat. Congregationalist. Avocations: hiking, cross country skiing. Home: 6016 Upland Terr S Seattle WA 98118 Office: U Wash Dept Physiol Nursing SM 28 Seattle WA 98195

MITCHELL, PATRICIA ANN, education educator; b. Washington, Sept. 17, 1946; d. James Garnell and Ruth Estella (Harper) Turner; m. Larry Wayne Mitchell, June 29, 1977; children—Candyce, Jason, Jeremy. B.S. in Edn., Morgan State Coll., 1968; M.S. in Edn. (fellow), So. Ill. U., 1970; Ph.D. (fellow), Cath. U. Am., 1978. Cert. pub. sch., jr. coll. tchr., Calif., Md. Tchr. 1st grade Prince George's County (Md.) Pub. Schs., 1968, reading specialist, 1970-77; instr. U. San Francisco, 1977-78, asst. prof. edn., 1978—; coordinator Elem. edn. program, 1987—. Bd. dirs. Sem Yeta chpt. Camp Fire Inc.; mem. edn. com. Am. Cancer Soc. Solano County. Mem. NAACP, Nat. Urban League. Mem. Am. Ednl. Research Assn., Nat. Assn. Female Execs., Internat. Reading Assn., Calif. Women in Higher Edn. Assn., Coll. Reading Assn., Alpha Kappa Alpha. Democrat. Baptist. Office: Sch Edn U San Francisco 2130 Fulton St San Francisco CA 94117

MITCHELL, ROBERT CAMPBELL, nuclear engineering executive; b. West Point, N.Y., Mar. 28, 1940; s. Herbert V. and Beatrice Cheeseman (Campbell) M.; m. Mardeene Burr, Aug. 19, 1963 (div. Dec. 1983); children: Wendolyn, Dawnelle. BEngring., Stevens Inst. Tech., 1962; MEE, Rensselaer Poly. Inst., 1965. Registered profl. engr., Calif. Design engr. Knolls Atomic Power Lab., Schenectady, N.Y., 1962-65, sr. reactor operator, 1965-67; prin. tng. engr. Nuclear Energy Div. Gen. Electric Co., San Jose, Calif., 1967-72, project engr., 1972-75, mgr. advanced projects, 1975-77, project mgr., 1977—. Contbr. articles to profl. jours. Nominee White House fellow Gen. Electric Co., San Jose, 1973. Mem. Elfun Soc. Republican. Episcopalian. Avocations: photography, racquetball, bridge. Home: 5188 Meridian Ave San Jose CA 95118 Office: Gen Electric Co 175 Curtner Ave San Jose CA 95124

MITCHELL, ROBERT R., banker; b. 1923; married. Grad., Pacific Coast Sch. Banking, 1960; grad. exec. program, Stanford U., 1972. With U.S. Nat. Bank Oreg., Portland, 1945—, mgr. Lombard-Emerald br., 1959-62, mgr. Hollywood br., 1962-66, mgr. met. br., 1966-68, v.p. mgr. N.W. region, 1968-69, sr. v.p., mgr. orgn. and personnel div., 1969-71, sr. v.p., mgr. br. banking group, 1971-73, exec. v.p. gen. banking, 1973-74, pres., 1974—, dir.; exec. v.p., dir. U.S. Bancorp. Office: US Bancorp Tower T-31 111 SW 5th Ave PO Box 4412 Portland OR 97208

MITCHELL, WALLACE CLARK, entomologist, educator; b. Ames, Iowa, Nov. 12, 1920; s. Paul Decatur and Edna Ellen (Clarke) M.; m. Shizuko Maeda, June 27, 1958; children: Teri Ellen, Pamela Sue, Janyce Rae. BS, Iowa State U., 1947, MS, 1949, PhD, 1955. Registered profl. entomologist. Prof. entomology U. Hawaii, Honolulu, 1965-80; prof. emeritus of entomology U. Hawaii, 1985—; chmn. dept. entomology U. Hawaii, Honolulu, 1968-78, acting dean coll. tropical agr., 1975-76, assoc. dean acad. affairs, 1980-85; vice-chmn. bd. Consortium for Internat. Crop Protection, College Park, Md., 1984—. Contbr. articles to profl. jours., chpts. to books. Served with USN, 1943-46. Grantee USDA, 1982-87, Secondary Sci. Tng. Program NSF, Washington, 1967-68. Mem. Entomol. Soc. Am. (pres. Pacific br. 1984-85), Hawaii Acad. of Sci. (pres. 1972), Hawaii Trail and Mountain Hiking Club, Honolulu Amateur Radio Club (treas. 1985—), Sigma Xi (pres. Hawaii chpt. 1986), Gamma Sigma Delta (pres. Hawaii chpt. 1968), Phi Kappa Phi, Hawaiin Trail and Mountain Club. Methodist. Clubs: Honolulu Amateur Radio, Honolulu, (treas. 1985—). Lodge: Elks. Avocations: amateur radio, hiking, photography. Home: 2417 Parker Pl Honolulu HI 96822 Office: U Hawaii Dept Entomology 3050 Maile Way Honolulu HI 96822

MITCHELL, WAYNE LEE, educator, social worker; b. Rapid City, S.D., Mar. 25, 1937; s. Albert C. and Elizabeth Isabelle (Nagel) M.; B.A., U. Redlands (Calif.), 1959; M.S.W., Ariz. State U., 1970, Ed.D., 1979. Profl. social worker various county, state, and fed. agencies, 1962-70, Bur. Indian Affairs, Phoenix, 1970-77, USPHS, 1977-79; asst. prof. Ariz. State U., 1979-84; with USPHS, Phoenix, 1984—. Bd. dirs. Phoenix Indian Community Sch., 1973-75; bd. dirs. Phoenix Indian Center, 1974-79, Community Service award, 1977; mem. Phoenix Area Health Adv. Bd., 1975; mem. Community Behavioral Mental Health Bd., 1976-80; lectr. in field. Bd. dirs. Central Ariz. Health Systems Agy.; mem. Fgn. Relations Com. Phoenix. Served with USCG, 1960-62. Recipient Community Service award Ariz. Temple of Islam, 1980. Mem. Nat. Congress Am. Indians, UN Assn., Nat. Assn. Social Workers, Am. Orthopsychiat. Assn., NAACP, Internat. Platform Assn., Asia Soc., U.S.-China Assn., Kappa Delta Pi, Phi Delta Kappa, Chi Sigma Chi. Congregationalist. Democrat. Contbr. articles to publs. Home: PO Box 61 Phoenix AZ 85001 Office: 4212 N 16th St Phoenix AZ 85016

MITHUN, MARIANNE, linguist, researcher, educator; b. Bremerton, Wash., Apr. 8, 1946; d. Omer Lloyd George and Ruth Eleonor (Trueblood) M.; m. Wallace L. Chafe, Jan. 25, 1985. BA, Pomona Coll., 1969; MA, Yale U., 1972, M Philosophy, 1972, PhD, 1974. Prof. linguistics SUNY, Albany, 1973-85, U. Calif., Santa Barbara, 1986—; vis. prof. Université du Quebec, Can., 1973-83, Yale U., New Haven, 1980, Wake Forest U., Winston-Salem, N.C., 1975, U. Calif., Berkeley, 1981-86. Author: The Languages of Native America, 1979, Montague, Grammar, Philosophy and Linguistics, 1979; contbr. numerous articles on linguistics to profl. jours. Fellow Am. Anthrop. Assn. (bd. dirs., mem. exec. com., adminstrn. adv. com. 1982—); mem. Linguistic Soc. Am., Soc. Study Indigenous Langs. of Ams. (mem. Exec. bd. 1982—), Soc. Linguistic Antropology (pres. 1982-85), Linguistic Soc. Am. Office: U Calif Dept Linguistics Santa Barbara CA 93106

MITLER, MERRILL MORRIS, psychologist, researcher; b. Racine, Wis., Jan. 6, 1945; s. Benjamin and Dorothy Ann (Farrell) M.; m. Karin Helen Yock, Jan. 1968 (div. July 1976); m. Elizabeth A., Aug. 27, 1976; children: Marc Harold, Morris Henry, Maximillian Edward. BA in Psychology, U. Wis., 1967; MA in Psychology, Mich. State U., 1968, PhD in Psychology, 1970; postdoctoral cert., Stanford U. Med. Sch., 1973. Lic. psychologist, N.Y., Calif. Instr. psychology Stanford (Calif.) U., 1970-78, research assoc. med. sch., 1973-78; research prof. SUNY, Stony Brook, 1978-83; sr. scientist Scripps Clinic and Research Found., La Jolla, Calif., 1983—; prof. U. Calif., San Diego, 1985—; pres. Wakefulness-Sleep Edn. and Research Found., Del Mar, Calif., 1981—; mem. med. adv. bd. Am. Health mag. N.Y.C., 1977—; mem. U.S. Congl. Testimony Sleep Disorders and Health Policy, 1985-86. Contbr. articles to profl. jours. Mem. Rep. Senatorial Inner Circle, Washington, 1983—. NIH research grantee, 1970—; recipient Travel award for Presentations, Internat. Congress of Chrono-Pharmacology, Montreaux, Switzerland, 1986. Fellow Clin. Sleep Soc./Assn. Sleep Disorders Ctrs. exec. sec./treas. 1977—, Nathan Kleitman prize 1985); mem. Am. Psychol. Assn., AAAS, Internat. Soc. Chronobiology, Am. Assn. Automotive Medicine, Am. Narcolepsy Assn. (bd. dirs. 1985—), Assn. Profl. Sleep Socs. (bd. dirs. 1985—). Jewish. Avocations: computer sci., polit. sci., nat. govt. Home: 4820 Rancho Viejo Dr Del Mar CA 92014 Office: Scripps Clinic & Research Found 10666 N Torrey Pines Rd La Jolla CA 92037

MITTAL, MANMOHAN, electronics engineer; b. Muzaffarnagar, India, Sept. 5, 1950; came to U.S., 1981; s. Kedar Nath and Prakash (Wati) M.; m. Shashi Rani, Jan 28, 1976; children: Vivek, Vibhav. BSEE, Inst. Tech., Varanasi, India, 1971; MASEE, U. Ottawa, Ont., Can., 1981; PhD in Elec. and Computer Engring., Wash. State U., 1984. Electronics engr. IIMS, BHU, Varanasi, 1971-73; design engr. Bharat Heavy Elecs. Ltd., Haridwar, India, 1973-79; grad. research/teaching asst. Wash. State U., Pullman and U. Ottawa, 1979-84; DA mgr. CAE design automation Silicon Systems, Inc., Tustin, Calif., 1984—; sole proprietor Intercontinental Softrm Integrators, Irvine, Calif., 1986—. Contbr. tech. papers to profl. jours. Judge Calif. State Sci. Fair, Los Angeles, 1986, Los Angeles County Sci. Fair, 1986. Fellow U. Ottawa, 1979; grantee Wash. State U., 1982. Mem. IEEE (sr., sec. exec. com. Orange County chpt. 1985—, mem. tech. program com., bipolar circuits and tech. conf. 1985—), N.Y. Acad. Scis., Assn. Computing Machines, Sigma Xi, Tau Beta Pi. Hindu. Avocations: traveling, badminton, tennis. Office: Silicon Systems 14351 Myford Rd Tustin CA 92680

MITTERER, ADOLPH VICTOR, mining company executive; b. Denver, Aug. 24, 1927; s. Adolph Victor Sr. and Louise (Halverson) M.; m. Shirley Ann Brown, Aug. 25, 1951; children: Steven A., Thomas R. Engr. of mines, Colo. Sch. Mines, 1952; postgrad., MIT, 1974. Registered profl. engr., N.Mex., Colo., Utah, Wyo. Chief mining engr. Internat. Minerals and Chems., Carlsbad, N.Mex. and Skokie, Ill., 1954-68; mgr. mining and milling, minerals dept. Conoco, Inc., Denver, 1968-78; v.p. Rocky Mountain Energy, Broomfield, Colo., 1978—; mem. Minerals Availability Com., Am. Mining Congress, Washington, 1985—. Uranium processing patentee; contbr. numerous articles on mining to profl. jours. Served to lt. C.E., U.S. Army, 1945-47, ETO. Named Met. Exec. of Yr., Nat. Secs. Assn., Denver, 1973. Mem. Soc. of Mining Engrs. of AIME, Colo. Mining Assn. (bd. dirs. 1982—), Can. Inst. Mining and Metallurgy, Mining Club of Southwest, Northwest Mining Assn., Nev. Mining Assn., Utah Mining Assn., Colo. Sch. Mines Research Inst., Colo. Sch. Mines Alumni Assn. (bd. dirs. 1985—). Republican. Club: Denver Athletic. Avocations: wine making, photography, home renovation. Home: 12000 W 22nd Pl Lakewood CO 80215 Office: Rocky Mountain Energy Co 10 Longs Peak Dr PO Box 2000 Broomfield CO 80020

MITTS, THOMAS FREDERICK, plastic and reconstructive surgeon; b. Atlanta, Dec. 13, 1947; s. Russell Thomas Mitts; m. Andrea Gene Turnage, June 27, 1976 (div. Aug. 1984); m. Linda Kay Taylor, Nov. 2, 1986. MD, Loma Linda U., 1973. Diplomate Am. Bd. Surgery, Am. Bd. Plastic Surgery. Intern Loma Linda Med. Ctr., Calif., 1973-74, resident in gen. surgery, 1974-77; fellow in oncologic surgery City of Hope, Duarte, Calif., 1977-78; resident in plastic and reconstructive surgery U. Pitts., 1978-80; practice medicine specializing in plastic and reconstructive surgery, Visalia, Calif., 1980—; dir. Cranio Facial Panel, Visalia. Fellow ACS; mem. Am. Soc. Plastic and Reconstructive Surgeons, Am. Soc. for Aesthetic Surgery, AMA. Office: 300 E Mineral King #101 Visalia CA 93291

MITZELFELT, H. VINCENT, medical director, orchestral conductor; b. Chgo., Jan. 13, 1934; s. Harold Ezra and Sylvia June (Straw) M.; m. Karin M. Mitzelfelt, Jan. 11, 1980; children: Ramona Lynn, Dawna Kathryn, Bradley Vincent, (stepdaughter) Pia. BA, Union Coll., 1955; MD, Loma Linda U., 1960. Condr. Union Coll. Orch., Lincoln, Nebr., 1954-55, Loma Linda (Calif.) U. Chorus, 1955-56, Los Angeles Bach Festival, 1961-64; founder, condr. Mitzelfelt Chorale, Los Angeles, 1957-73; condr., instr. Immaculate Heart Coll. Orch., Hollywood, Calif., 1975-78; founder, condr. Los Angeles Orch. and Chorus, 1973-85; med. dir. Los Angeles div. So. Pacific Med. Services, 1969-70, Belcrest Med. Group, Inglewood, Calif., 1979-82, Metro Med. Ctr., Los Angeles, 1985—; chief of staff Suburban Hosp., South Gate, Calif., 1968-70. Recorded: Anthems of Praise and Rejoicing, 1959, Music of Faith and Inspiration, 1962, Beethoven's Ode to Joy, 1978, Flute and Harp Concerto, 1981; conducted European tours 1976, 78, 80, Mexico, 1980. Recording grantee Nat. Endowment Arts, 1982. Mem. AMA. Republican. Adventist. Home: 23203 Yvette Ln Valencia CA 91355 Office: Metro Med Ctr 639 S Spring St Los Angeles CA 90014

MIURA, MIKE YUKO, design engineer; b. Wahiawa, Hawaii, Oct. 11, 1931; s. Thomas Mitsuo and May Shizue (Ishida) M.; m. Janet Akemi Fukusaki, Dec. 29, 1964; children: Kurtis Yukio, Kyle Masami. BSCE, U. Hawaii, 1954. Registered profl. engr., Hawaii. Asst. hwy. engr. Calif. Div. Hwys., Stockton, 1954-56; topog. surveyor C.E., U.S. Army, Libya, North Africa, 1957-58; civil engr. III, Ter. Hawaii, Honolulu, 1959; constrn. mgmt. engr. USN, Pearl Harbor, Hawaii, 1960, project mgr. pub. works ctr., 1985—; head hwy. design engr. Hawaii Dept. Transp., Honolulu, 1960-85; trustee State Employees Retirement System, Honolulu, 1984-85. Pres. Hongwanji Mission Sch. PTA, Honolulu, 1975-76; mem. adv. bd. Hawaii Coastal Zone Mgmt., Honolulu, 1979; vice chmn., bd. mem. Aiea Neighborhood No. 20, Hawaii, 1977—; chmn. Selective Service Draft Bd. No. 5, Aiea, 1983—. Mem. ASCE, Am. Fedn. State, County and Mcpl. Employees, Hawaii Govt. Employees Assn. (state pres., sci. and profl. bargaining unit 13, 1982-85). Democrat. Home: 99-656 Aliipoe Dr Aiea HI 96701 Office: USN Pub Works Ctr Pearl Harbor HI 96860

MIURA, ROBERT MITSURU, mathematician, researcher, educator; b. Selma, Calif., Sept. 12, 1938; emigrated to Can., 1975; s. Richard Katsuki and Frances Yoneko (Yukutake) M.; children: Derek Katsuki, Brian Robert. B.S., U. Calif.-Berkeley, 1960, M.S., 1962; M.A., Princeton U., 1964, Ph.D., 1966. Research assoc. Princeton U. Plasma Physics Lab., 1965-67; assoc. research scientist Courant Inst. Math. Sci., N.Y.C., 1967-68; asst. prof. math. NYU, 1968-71; assoc. prof. math. Vanderbilt U., 1971-75; assoc. prof. math. U. B.C., Vancouver, B.C., Can., 1975-78, prof., 1978—; chmn. joint com. on math. in life scis. Am. Math. Soc.-Soc. Indsl. and Applied Math., 1981-84. Contbr. articles to profl. jours.; editor: Backlund Transformations, 1976, Nonlinear Phenomena in Physics and Biology, 1981, Some Mathematical Questions in Biology-Neurobiology, 1982, Muscle Physiology, 1986, DNA sequence Analysis, 1986, Plant Biology, 1986. John Simon Guggenheim fellow, 1980-81; U. B.C. hon. Killam fellow, 1980-81. Mem. Am. Math. Soc., Soc. Indsl. and Applied Math., Can. Applied Math. Soc., Can. Math. Soc. Office: Dept Math U BC, 1984 Mathematics Rd, Vancouver, BC Canada V6T 1Y4

MIURA, STEVEN YASUO, communications educator; b. Lihue, Hawaii, Mar. 6, 1953; s. Masayoshi and Chiyoko (Sahara) M.; m. Eva Mari Sunabe, Aug. 11, 1984. BA, Wash. State U., 1975, PhD, 1979; MA, U. Hawaii Manoa, Honolulu, 1976. Grad. asst. U. Hawaii Manoa, Honolulu, 1975-76, Wash. State U., Pullman, 1976-79; assoc. prof. communication U. Hawaii, Hilo, 1979—, dir. upward bound, 1982-84; communications con. office econ. opportunities County of Hawaii, Hilo, 1980-81, mass. transit agy, 1982, housing and community development, 1982-83, civil service dept., 1986—. Contbr. articles to profl. jours. Recipient Travel awards U. Hawaii System, 1979, 85, 86; co-author Upward Bound grant Dept. Edn., 1983. Mem. Internat. Communication Assn., Speech Communication Assn., World Communication Assn., Western Speech Communication Assn., NEA. Avocations: gardening, golf. Home: 1222 Puhau Pl Hilo HI 96720 Office: U Hawaii Hilo HI 96720

MIX, CONNIE LEE JACOBSEN BROWER, dental hygienist, consultant; b. Audubon, Iowa, Nov. 6, 1948; d. Richard Eugene and Edna Arnvig (Faaborg) Jacobsen; m. Lowell Alan Brower, Sept. 6, 1969 (dec. Oct. 1970); m. 2d, J. Steven Mix, Apr. 2, 1978; children—Chad Jacob, Jonathan Jacob. Grad. Shoreline Dental Hygiene Sch., 1970. Registered dental hygienist, Wash. Clin. hygienist various dentists, 1970-77; hygienist dental health program Federal Way (Wash.) Sch. Dist., Wash., 1973-74; dental health cons. Wash. State Health Dept., 1977—. Mem. Downs Syndrome Congress, Oak Park, Ill., 1978. Recipient cert. outstanding service Federal Way Sch. Dist., 1974; cert. of appreciation Benton Franklin County Dental Soc., 1981. Mem. Health Edn. Alliance, Wash. Pub. Health Assn., Wash. Dental Hygiene Component, Nutrition and Dental Health Consortium, Healthy Mothers Healthy Babies, Eta Sigma Gamma. Lutheran. Contbr. articles to mags. and profl. jours. Office: Dental Health Program Mailstop LC-11B Olympia WA 98504

MIYAMOTO, CRAIG TOYOKI, advertising and public relations company executive; b. Joliet, Ill., Oct. 14, 1944; s. Robert Mitsuo and Dorothy Toyoko (Okumura) M.; BBA, Woodbury Coll., 1967; MA, U. So. Calif., 1972; m. Diana Chie Ueda, Mar. 24, 1966; children: James Anthony Kazuyuki, Carleton Alan Yasuo. Reporter, Alhambra (Calif.) Post-Advocate, 1968-70; editor Monterey Park Californian, 1970-71; mng. editor So. Calif. Pub. Co., 1971-72; dep. pub. relations dir. Honolulu Bd. Water Supply, 1972-76, pub. relations dir., 1976-77; pres. Miyamoto Advt./Pub. Relations, Honolulu, 1977—, Pineapple Post, Honolulu, 1977—, Aura Publs., Honolulu, 1980-83, instr. pub. relations U. Hawaii, 1978-80. Pres., Honolulu Jaycees, 1975-76; mem. exec. com. 50th State Fair, 1974-76; dir. pub. relations Hawaii Jaycees, 1974-75, Monterey Park C. of C., 1970-71; bd. dirs. San Gabriel Valley YMCA, 1971-72, Garfield Community Sch. Bd., 1971-72; mem. Jaycees Internat. Senate, 1976—. Named Man of Yr., Honolulu, 1974, John Armbruster award, 1974; State Service award Hawaii Jaycees, 1974. Mem. Am. Advt. Fedn., Pub. Relations Soc. Am. (accredited, bd. dirs. Hawaii chpt., sec. Hawaii chpt.), Hawaii Advt. Fedn. (bd. dirs.), Mensa, Am. Philatelic Soc., Am. First Day Cover Soc., Am. Topical Assn., Internat. Soc. for Japanese Philately, Bur. Issues Assn., Hawaiian Philatelic Soc., Am. Assn. Polar Philatelists, Hawaii Stamp and Coin Dealers Assn. (v.p.). Democrat. Author: How to Earn $2,000 or More Without Hardly Working At All, 1979; The Pineapple Post Catalogue, 1984. Office: 657 Kapiolani Blvd Suite 7 Honolulu HI 96813

MIYASAKI, SHUICHI, lawyer; b. Paauilo, Hawaii, Aug. 6, 1928; s. Torakichi and Teyo (Kimura) M.; m. Pearl Takeko Saiki, Sept. 11, 1954; children—Joy Michiko, Miles Tadashi, Jan Keiko, Ann Yoshie. B.S.C.E., U. Hawaii-Honolulu, 1951; J.D., U. Minn., 1957; LL.M. in Taxation, Georgetown U., 1959; grad. Army War Coll., 1973. Bar: Minn. 1957, Hawaii 1959, U.S. Supreme Ct. 1980. Examiner, U.S. Patent Office, 1957-59; dep. atty. gen. State of Hawaii, 1960-61; mem., dir., treas. Okumura Takushi Funaki & Wee, Honolulu, 1961—; atty. Hawaii Senate, 1961, chief counsel ways and means com., 1962, chief counsel judiciary com., 1967-70; civil engr. Japan Constrn. Agy., Tokyo, 1953-54; staff judge adv., col. USAR, Ft. DeRussy, Hawaii, 1968-79; local legal counsel Jaycees, 1962. Legis. chmn. armed services com. C. of C. of Hawaii, 1973; instl. rep. Aloha council Boy Scouts Am., 1963-78; exec. com., sec., dir. Legal Aid Soc. Hawaii, 1970-72; state v.p. Hawaii Jaycees, 1964-65; dir., legal counsel St. Louis Heights Community Assn., 1963, 65, 73; dir., legal counsel Citizens Study Club for Naturalization of Citizens, 1963-68; life mem. Res. Officers Assn. U.S. Served to 1st lt., AUS, 1951-54. Decorated Meritorious Service medal with oak leaf cluster. Mem. ABA, Hawaii Bar Assn., U.S. Patent Office Soc., Hawaii Estate Planning Council, Phi Delta Phi. Clubs: Central YMCA, Waikiki Athletic, Elks, Army Golf Assn. Address: 1552 Bertram St Honolulu HI 96816

MIYASHIRO, ROBERT YOSHIHARU, physical education educator; b. Honolulu, Apr. 4, 1936; s. Herbert and Esther (Tamanaha) M. AA, Santa Rosa (Calif.) Jr. Coll., 1957; BA, U. Calif.-Santa Barbara, Goleta, 1958. Cert. tchr., Calif. Tchr. Harmony Union Sch., Occidental, Calif., 1961-64, Santa Rosa (Calif.) High Sch. Dist., 1964-70; instr. phys. edn. Santa Rosa Jr. Coll., 1970—; swimming team coach Santa Rosa Jr. Coll. Mem. Am. Swim Coaches Assn., Calif. Community Coll. Aquatic Coaches Assn. (pres. 1986-87, Coach of Yr. 1981). Avocations: gardening, koi. Office: Santa Rosa Jr Coll 1501 Mendocino Ave Santa Rosa CA 95401

MIZE, ROBERT HERBERT, JR., bishop; b. Emporia, Kans., Feb. 4, 1907; s. Robert Herbert and Margaret Talman (Moore) M. B.A., U. Kans., 1928 grad. Gen. Theol. Sem., N.Y.C., 1932, S.T.D., 1960. Vicar ch. missions Episcopal Ch., Hays Kans., 1932-41, Wakeeney, Kans., 1941-45; founder, dir. St. Francis Boys' Homes, Ellsworth and Salina, Kans., 1945-60; bishop of Damaraland Anglican Ch., Windhoek, Southwest Africa, 1960-68, asst. bishop, Gaberone, Botswana, 1968-70, 73-76; vicar Trinity Episcopal Ch., Marshall, Mo, 1970-73; assisting bishop Episcopal Ch. Diocese of San

Joaquin, Fresno, Calif., 1978—; dir. Gen. Theol. Seminary's Assoc. Mission, Hays, 1933-41; vicar St. Raphael's Episcopal Ch., Oakhurst, Calif., 1977-81. Mem. Phi Beta Kappa, Sigma Delta Chi, Phi Delta Theta. Office: Episcopal Ch Diocese of San Joaquin 4159 E Dakota Ave Fresno CA 93726

MIZER, CYNTHIA LEE, publishing executive; b. Vermillion, S.D., Dec. 7, 1958; d. Walter George and Shirlee (Perry) M. Student, U. Grenoble, France, 1980-81; BA, U. Calif., Santa Barbara, 1981. Asst. producer U. Calif., Santa Barbara, 1978-80; dir. Edn. Exchange, Grenoble, 1980-81; recruiter Assoc. Recruiters, San Diego, 1981-82; dir. promotion and advt. Coronado Publs./HBJ, San Diego, 1982—. Producer (video) Wheels of Change, 1986. Mem. San Diego League, MS Brunch Soc., Am. Theatre Heritage (dir. programs 1985—). Home: 3940 Gresham St Suite 334 San Diego CA 92109

MLCOCH, ROGER GILBERT, engineer; b. Grafton, N.D., Apr. 13, 1947; s. Gilbert Frank and Ellen Gladys (Nelson) M.; m. Judy Ann Sitta, Apr. 24, 1965; children: Sherri Lynn, Tami Kay. BSChemE, Calif. State Poly U., Pomona, 1973. Process engr. Xerox, Pomona, 1969-73; dir. engring. Bell Industries, Santa Ana, Calif., 1973—. Mem. Calif. Cirs. Assn., Am. Electroplaters Soc., Am. Chem. Soc., Inst. Interconnecting and Packaging Electronic Cirs. Avocations: racquetball, fishing, camping. Office: Bell Industries 1831 S Ritchey St Santa Ana CA 92705

MOBERLY, LINDEN EMERY, educational administrator; b. Laramie, Wyo., Jan. 4, 1923; s. Linden E. and Ruth (Gathercole) M.; B.S., Coll. Emporia, 1952; M.S., Kans. State Tchrs. Coll., 1954; m. Viola F. Mosher, Apr. 29, 1949. Tchr. sci., Florence, Kans., 1952-54, Concordia, Kans., 1954-56, Grand Junction, Colo., 1957-60; asst. prin. Orchard Mesa Jr. High Sch., Grand Junction, 1960-66, prin., 1967-84; field cons. Nat. Assn. Secondary Sch. Prins., 1985—. Served to sgt. USMC, 1941-46. Recipient Outstanding Secondary Prin. award Colo. Assn. Sch. Execs., 1978. Mem. NEA, Nat. Assn. Secondary Prins. (dir. 1979-83), Colo. Edn. Assn. (dir. 1968-71), Colo. North Central Assn. Colls. and Secondary Schs., Colo. Assn. Secondary Sch. Prins. (dir. 1974-77). Club: Lions.

MOBLEY, KEITH FREDERICKE, project engineer, geotechnical consultant; b. Boulder, Colo., July 16, 1953; s. Emory V. and Eleonore M. M. (Panzenhagen) M. BSCE, Mont. State U., 1976. Staff engr. San Dieguito Engr., Rancho Sante Fe, Calif., 1977-80, Ted Forsi & Assocs., Anchorage, 1980-81; project engr. Woodward-Clyde, Anchorage, 1981—. Mem. ASCE (activities com. 1986—), Can. Geotech. Soc., Internat. Soc. Soil Mechanics and Found. Engring. Avocations: ocean kayaking, photography, woodworking, symphony, opera. Home: PO Box 111882 Anchorage AK 99511 Office: Woodward Clyde 701 Sesame St Anchorage AK 99503

MOCCIA, MARY KATHRYN, social worker; b. Harrisburg, Pa., Jan. 28, 1951; d. John Joseph and Winifred Louise (Alexander) Trephan. BEd magna cum laude, U. Hawaii, 1978, MSW summa cum laude, 1980; postgrad., Fuller Theol. Sem. Intern Koko Head Mental Health Clinic, Honolulu, 1978-79, Dept. Social Services and Housing, Honolulu, 1979-80; vol. worker, group co-leader Waikiki Mental Health Ctr., Honolulu, 1979, social worker, 1980; workshop facilitator St. Louis-Chaminade Edn. Ctr. Dept. Insts. and Workshops, Honolulu, 1980-83; founding mem. Anorexia and Bulimia Ctr. Hawaii, Honolulu, 1983, pvt. practice psychotherapy and cons., 1983—; personal counselor Chaminade U. Honolulu, 1980—; guest lectr. U. Hawaii Sch. Social Work, Honolulu, 1980-81; vol. telephone specialist Suicide and Crisis Ctr. and Info. and Referral Service, Honolulu, 1981-83; condr. various workshops on anorexia and bulimia. Guest appearances on local tv and radio programs. Mem. Manoa Valley Ch. Mem. Nat. Assn. Social Workers, Nat. Assn. Christians in Social Work, Hawaii Personnel and Guidance Assn., Mortar Bd. (pres., nat. del.), Phi Kappa Phi, Pi Lambda Theta, Alpha Tau Delta (pres.). Avocations: traveling, dancing, swimming, lifting weights, Bible study. Office: Chaminade U 3140 Waiaha Ave Honolulu HI 96816

MOCK, THEODORE JAYE, accounting educator; b. Traverse City, Mich., May 28, 1941; s. Raymond Doris and Georgeann (Lardie) M.; m. Mary Jo Icenhower, Mar. 25, 1962; children—Christopher, Cameron. B.S. in Math., Ohio State U., 1963, M.B.A. in Fin., 1964; Ph.D. in Bus. Adminstrn., U. Calif.-Berkeley, 1969. Dir. AIS Research Ctr. UCLA, 1969-73, 82—; dir. Ctr. Acctg. Research, Arthur Andersen Alumni prof. acctg. U. So. Calif., 1982—. Author monographs: Risk Assessment, 1985, Internal Accounting Control (Am. Acctg. Assn. Wildman medal), 1983, Measurement and Accounting Information Criteria, 1976; mem. editorial bd. Auditing: A Jour. of Practice and Theory, 1982—, The Acctg. Rev., 1972-73, 73-78. Recipient C.P.A. Faculty Excellence award Calif. C.P.A. Found. for Edn. and Research, 1983. Mem. Acctg., Organs. and Soc. (editorial bd. 1978—), New Mgmt. (editorial bd. 1982—), Am. Acctg. Assn. (dir. research 1982-84). Office: Univ So Calif Sch of Acctg Los Angeles CA 90089-1421

MODAFFERI, GARY ANTHONY, lawyer; b. Denver, July 27, 1959; s. Anthony Carl and Ethel Pauline (Scarpelli) M. BA, Seton Hall U., 1980; JD, Suffolk U., 1983. Bar: Hawaii 1983, U.S. Dist. Ct. Hawaii 1983, U.S. Ct. Appeals (9th cir.) 1983. Law clk. U.S. States Atty., Boston, 1980-83; dep. prosecutor Dept. Prosecuting Atty., Honolulu, 1983—; supr. narcotic trial team, Honolulu, 1985—. Mem. ABA, Hawaii Bar Assn., Am. Trial Lawyers Assn. Avocation: tennis. Office: Dept Prosecuting Atty 1164 Bishop St Honolulu HI 96813

MODE, VINCENT ALAN, research executive, computer scientist; b. Gilroy, Calif., May 25, 1940; s. Vincent Allan and Jewel (Clary) M.; m. Sue A. Oleson, Feb. 14, 1964 (div. Feb. 1975); 1 child, Nicolle A.; m. Jackie Sue Hill, Dec. 23, 1976. BA magna cum laude, Whitman Coll., 1962; PhD in Inorganic Chemistry, U. Ill., 1965; MBA, Golden Gate U., 1980. Chemist Lawrence Livermore Nat. Lab., Livermore, Calif., 1965-69, group leader, 1969-72, sect. leader, 1972-80, facility mgr., 1984-85, dep. assoc. dir., 1985—; exec. dir. B.C. Research, Vancouver, Can., 1980-84; B.C. Sci Council, Vancouver, 1982-84; mem. B.C. Research Council, Vancouver, 1984—. Also lectr. sci. presentations. Contbr. articles to profl. jours. Named one of Outstanding Young Men Am., 1972; Alfred P. Sloan Nat. Scholar Whitman Coll., 1958-62, Ford Teaching fellow Whitman Coll., 1960-62. Mem. Soc. Computer Simulation (chmn. northwest region, 1982-84, vice-chmn. W. region, 1985-86), Interactive Fin. Planning System Users Assn., Sigma Xi. Avocations: sailing, gardening, woodworking. Home: 2610 Gapwall Ct Pleasanton CA 94566 Office: Lawrence Livermore Nat Lab PO Box 808 Livermore CA 94550

MODUGNO, VICTOR JOSEPH, actuary; b. N.Y.C., Sept. 27, 1949; s. Joseph and Romola (Erriquez) M. BA magna cum laude, Queens Coll., Flushing, N.Y., 1971. Actuarial assoc. Met. Life. Ins. Co., N.Y.C., 1971-80; asst. actuary Pacific Mut. Life Ins. Co., Newport Beach, Calif., 1980-86; actuary Exec. Life Ins. Corp. subs. 1st Exec. Corp., Los Angeles, 1986—. Fellow Soc. Actuaries; mem. Am. Acad. Actuaries, Los Angeles Actuaries Club. Republican. Roman Catholic. Avocation: running. Home: 140 The Village #407 Redondo Beach CA 90277 Office: Exec Life Ins Co 11444 W Olympic Blvd Los Angeles CA 90064

MOE, ANDREW IRVING, veterinarian; b. Tacoma, Jan. 2, 1927; s. Ole Andrew and Ingeborg (Gordham) M.; B.S. in Biology, U. Puget Sound, 1949; B.A., Wash. State U., 1953, D.V.M. 1954; m. Dorothy Clara Becker, June 25, 1950; children—Sylvia Moe McGowan, Pamela Moe Barker, Joyce. Meat cutter Art Hansen, Tacoma, 1943-48; gen. practice as veterinarian Baronti Vet. Hosp., Eugene, Oreg., 1956-57; veterinarian, regulatory Calif. Animal Health br. Calif. Dept. Food and Agr. Resident veterinarian II, Modesto, Calif., 1957-64, acting veterinarian-in-charge Modesto Dist. Office (veterinarian III), 1976-77. Watersafety instr. ARC, 1958-61. Served from 1st lt. to capt., Vet. Corps., 1954-56, 62; comdr. 417th Med. Service Flight Res. (AFRES), 1965-66, 71-73; lt. col. Biomed. Scis. Corps USAF, ret., 1982. Recipient Chief Veterinarian badge, 1975. Mem. Am., Calif., No. San Joaquin (pres. 1979) vet. med. assns., Calif. Acad. Vet. Medicine (charter), Res. Officers Assn. (life), Assn. Mil. Surgeons U.S., U.S. Animal Health Assn., Sons of Norway, Theta Chi. Alpha Psi. Lutheran (del. 102d Synod 1961). Club: Masons (Illustrious Master Modesto council 1983, Allied Masonic Degrees), Shriners. Home: 161 Norwegian Ave Modesto CA 95350 Office: 1800 Coffee Rd Suite L82 Modesto CA 95355

MOE, DOUGLAS EDWIN, professional basketball coach; b. Bklyn., Sept. 21, 1938; m. Jane M.; 2 children. Student, U. N.C. Player Italian Basketball League, Padua, 1965-67; player Am. Basketball Assn., New Orleans, 1967-68, Oakland, 1968-69; player Carolina Cougars, Am. Basketball Assn., 1969-70, Va. Squires, Am. Basketball Assn., 1970-72; coach San Antonio Spurs, NBA, 1976-80, Denver Nuggets, 1980—. Mem. All-Star Team, 1968-70, Championship Team, Am. Basketball Assn., 1969. Office: Denver Nuggets McNichols Sports Arena 1635 Clay St Denver CO 80204 *

MOE, ROY DEAN, social worker; b. Ft. Collins, Colo., Oct. 1, 1942; s. Robert Mahlon and Edna Mae (Cottrill) M.; m. Millicent Hegsted; children: Deena, Eric, Ryan. AA, Wenatchee Valley Coll., 1964; BA, Whitworth Coll., 1967; MSW, Eastern Wash. U., 1983. Lic. social worker. Social caseworker I, Idaho Dept. Health and Welfare, Sandpoint, 1967-69, social caseworker II, 1969-71, social caseworker III, 1971-75, sr. social worker, 1975-78, social work supr., 1978—; cons. Children's Network, Sandpoint, 1984—, Northwest Fedn. Human Services, Seattle; instr. Eastern Wash. U., Cheney, 1984; speaker Wash. Child Welfare Conf., Spokane, 1985. Pres. Washington Sch. PTA, Sandpoint, 1972; bd. dirs. Community Awareness, Sandpoint, 1978-81. Mem. Nat. Assn. Social Workers (sec. far North br. 1983—, Idaho Social Worker of Yr. award 1984), Alpha Delta Mu. Democrat. Presbyterian. Avocations: hunting, fishing, backpacking. Office: Idaho Dept Health and Welfare PO Box 1029 Sandpoint ID 83864

MOEL, STEVEN ALLEN, ophthalmalogist; b. Charleston, W.Va., Sept. 18, 1943; s. Harry and Ruth (Lee) M.; m. Susan Gayle Dill, Aug. 13, 1981; children: Andrew, Erin. AB, U. Miami, Fla., 1965; MD, W.Va. U., 1970. Diplomate Am. Bd. Ophthalmology. Intern Gen. Rose Meml. Hosp., U. Colo., Denver, 1970-71; resident in ophthalmology La. State U., New Orleans, 1971-75; research fellowship in ophthalmology U. Ill. Eye and Ear Care Infirmary, Chgo., 1973-74; pvt. practice medicine specializing in ophthalmology Monterey Park, Calif., 1980—; v.p., bd. dirs. Akorn Inc., New Orleans. Contbr. articles to profl. jours. Fellow Am. Acad. Ophthalmology. Office: 500 N Garfield Suite 100 Monterey Park CA 91754

MOELLER, ROBERT CHARLES (BUD), management consultant; b. Washington, Sept. 5, 1954; s. Charles Edward and Ann Joan (Federico) M.; m. Carol Elizabeth Buchanan, June 19, 1976; children: Melaine Elizabeth, Robert Kehne. BChemE, Ga. Inst. Tech., 1976; MBA, Harvard U., 1978. Cons. ERT, Concord, Mass., 1977-78; assoc. Booz, Allen & Hamilton, Bethesda, Md., 1978-81, sr. assoc., 1981-83; prin. Booz, Allen & Hamilton, San Francisco, 1983—; chmn. bd. dirs. Nat. Capital YFC, Olney, Md., 1981-83. Contbr. articles to energy pubs. Chmn. bd. dirs. East Bay Youth for Christ, Concord, Calif., 1983—; mem. Rep. Presdl. Task Force, Washington, 1984-86; adv. Montgomery County (Md.) Health Dept., 1981. Mem. Am. Inst. Chem. Engrs., Ferrari Owners Club, Mensa. Republican. Mem. Evangelical Free Ch. Club: HBS (San Francisco). Avocation: profl. auto racing. Home: 225 Clyde Dr Walnut Creek CA 94598 Office: Booz Allen & Hamilton 555 Montgomery St San Francisco CA 94111

MOFFATT, JOHN GILBERT, research chemist; b. Victoria, B.C., Can., Sept. 19, 1930; came to U.S., 1960; s. William James and Esthr Christine (Shankey) M.; m. June Collinson, Aug. 15, 1953; children: Susan, Vicki, Janet, Karen. BA, U. B.C., Vancouver, 1952, MSc, 1953, PhD, 1956. Tech. officer Can. Nat. Def. Research Bd., Ottawa, Ont., 1953-54; research assoc. B.C. Research Council, Vancouver, 1956-60; sect. leader Calif. Corp. Biochemical Research, Los Angeles, 1960-61; dept. head to v.p. and dir. Inst. Bio-organic Chemistry-Syntex Research, Palo Alto, Calif., 1961-87; cons. in biotech. Calif., 1987—. Contbr. articles to profl. jours. Mem. Am. Chem. Soc., Royal Soc Chemistry, Am. Soc. Biol. Chemists. Home: 495 S Clark Ave Los Altos CA 94022

MOFFATT, ROBERT HENRY, accountant, publisher, writer, consultant; b. Montreal, Que., Can., June 30, 1930; came to U.S., 1968, naturalized, 1973; s. James Bigelow and Edwige Edith M.; m. Constance Marie Lipka, June 20, 1959; children—Christopher, Timothy, Elizabeth. Student Loyola Coll., Montreal, Que., 1948-52, Acadia U., 1962, UCLA, 1970, 72. Lic. in air navigation, Can.; enrolled agt., Dept. Treasury. Mng. editor, pub. Kings-Annapolis Wings, 1961-66; pres., Valley Pubs. Ltd., Kingston, N.S., Can., 1961-67 exec. dir. Maritime Motor Transport Assn. and editor Maritime Truck Transport Rev., Moncton, N.B., Can., 1967-68; dir. spl. products div. Wolf-Brown Inc., Los Angeles, 1968-77; newsletter pub, writer, 1980—; pvt. practice acctg., tax acctg., Los Angeles, 1970—; tchr. continuing edn. for accts. West Los Angeles Coll. Community Services. Columnist, author editorials in mags., 1960s. Clk., author constn. Village of Greenwood, N.S., 1961-63; chmn. bd. commrs., 1963-66; publicity chmn. Voluntary Econ. Planning Program, province N.S., 1965-66. Served to lt. Can. Air Force, 1954-60. Mem. Nat. Assn. Enrolled Agts. (newsletter editor, bd. dirs.), Nat. Soc. Pub. Accts (accredited in taxation), Calif. Soc. Enrolled Agts. (bd. dirs. Los Angeles chpt.). Lodges: Rotary, Toastmasters, Lions (bd. dirs., newsletter editor, pres.). Home: 7509 W 88th St Los Angeles CA 90045 Office: 8939 S Sepulveda Blvd Suite 430 Los Angeles CA 90045

MOFFET, JUDITH LYNN, elementary teacher; b. Los Angeles, June 14, 1942; d. Clifford S. and Evelyn G. (Bender) Blocker; m. Clifford B. Moffet; 1 child, John C. BA in Ednl. Psychology, Pomona Coll., 1963; MA in Edn., Claremont Grad. Sch., 1972. Tchr. Child View Found., Cherry Valley, Calif., 1963-64, Pomona (Calif.) Unified Sch. Dist., 1967-69; tchr. educationally handicapped Claremont (Calif.) Unified Sch. Dist., 1969-78; tchr. Carden Hall, Newport Beach, Calif., 1979-84, Blind Children's Learning Ctr., Santa Ana, Calif., 1984-85, Sierra Vista Elem. Sch., Upland (Calif.) Sch. Dist., 1986—. Mem. Claremont Symphony, 1985—. Recipient World of Poetry Golden Poet award, 1985, 86. Home: 1013 Lake Forest Dr Claremont CA 91711

MOFFETT, CALVIN GARY, computer researcher; b. Farmington, N.Mex., Dec. 16, 1954; s. Gary Horace and Nedra Jean (Smith) M.; m. Debra Myra Hirschy, Sept. 1, 1979; children: Heidi, Anthony, Andrew. BS cum laude, with high honors, Brigham Young U., 1980. Computer programmer Phone Directories, Inc., Provo, Utah, 1978; computer cons. Data/Word, Provo, 1979; project mgr. Weidner Communications, Provo, 1979-84; program devel. mgr. Exec. Communication Systems, Provo, 1984-86; sr. systems programmer ALP Systems, Salt Lake City, 1986—; pres., ptnr. Micro-Comp, Payson, Utah, 1984—. Vol. Utah County Rep. Campaign, Provo, 1976; del. to State Dem. Conv., Salt Lake City, 1982; quorum pres. Mormon Ch., Provo, 1985-87. Democrat. Avocations: French and Russian lit., hiking, stock market analysis. Home: 1723 South 2000 E Salt Lake City UT 84108 Office: ALP Systems 295 Chipeta Way PO Box 8719 Salt Lake City UT 84108

MOFFETT, CHRISTINE FAYE, bank executive, real estate investor; b. Erie, Pa., May 29, 1951; d. Charles Byron and Joan Elizabeth (Whiting) Miller; m. Robert Neal Moffett, June 20, 1969; children—Jason Neal, Adam David, Matthew Robert. Student Long Beach City Coll., 1972-73; corr. student Mortgage Bankers Assn., 1975—. Asst. v.p. Utah Mortgage Corp., Albuquerque, 1975-81; v.p. and mgr. mortgage loan dept. Western Commerce Bank, Carlsbad, N.Mex., 1981—; instr. real estate fin. N.Mex. State U., Carlsbad, 1982—. Mem. N.Mex. Mortgage Bankers, Womens Council Realtors, Carlsbad Bd. Realtors, Pecos Valley Home Builders, Carlsbad C. of C. (retirement com.). Republican. Lutheran. Home: 1101 S Country Club Circle Carlsbad NM 88220 Office: Western Commerce Bank 501 N Canal Carlsbad NM 88220

MOFFETT, FRANK CARDWELL, architect, civil engineer; b. Houston, Dec. 9, 1931; s. Ferrell Orlando and Jewell Bernice (Williams) M.; B.Arch., U. Tex., 1958; m. Annie Doris Thorn, Aug. 1, 1952 (div.); children: David Cardwell (dec.), Douglas Howard; m. Darlene Adele Alm Sayan, June 7, 1985. Architect with archtl. firms, Seattle, Harmon, Pray & Detrich, Arnold G. Gangnes, Ralf E. Decker, Roland Terry & Assos., 1958-64; partner Heideman & Moffett, AIA, Seattle, 1964-71; chief architect Wash. State Dept. Hwys., Olympia, 1971-77, Wash. State Dept. Transp., 1977—; advisor Wash. State Bldg. Code Adv. Council, 1975—; instr. civil engring. tech. Olympia Tech. Community Coll., 1975-77; adv. mem. archtl. barriers subcom. Internat. Conf. Building Ofcls.; archtl. works include hdqrs. Gen. Telephone Directory Co., Everett, Wash., 1964; Edmonds Unitarian Ch., 1966; tenant devel. Seattle Hdqrs. Office, Seattle-First Nat. Bank, 1968-70; Wash. State Dept. Transp. Area Hdqrs. Offices, Mt. Vernon, Selah, Raymond & Colfax 1973-85, Materials Lab., Spokane, Wash., 1974; archtl. barriers cons. State of Alaska, 1978. Chmn. Planning Commn. of Mountlake Terr., Wash., 1963, 64, mem., 1961-67; mem. State of Wash. Gov.'s Task Force on Wilderness, 1972-75, Heritage Park Task Force, Olympia, Wash., 1986; trustee Cascade Symphony Orch., 1971; incorporating pres. United Singles, Olympia, 1978-79. Served with USN, 1951-54. Registered architect, Alaska, Calif., Wash., profl. engr., Wash.; cert. Nat. Council Archtl. Registration Bds., U.S. Dept. Def., Fallout Shelter Analysis, environ. engring. Mem. AIA (dir. S.W. Wash. chpt. 1980-82, pres.-elect 1985, pres. 1986, architects in govt. nat. com. 1978—), Am. Public Works Assn., Inst. Bldgs. and Grounds, ASCE, Constrn. Specifications Inst., Am. Arbitration Assn. (invited panelist), Gen. Soc. Mayflower Descs. (gov. Wash. Soc. 1982-83), Nat. Huguenot Soc. (pres. Wash. Soc. 1981-83, 85-87), Olympia Geneal. Soc. (pres. 1978-80), SAR (state treas. 1984-85), SCV, Sons and Daus. of Pilgrims, (gov. Wash. Soc. 1984), Order of Magna Charta. Republican. Unitarian. Clubs: Rotary Internat. (pres. Edmonds, 1969-70), Coll. of Seattle, Olympia Yacht, Olympia Country and Golf. Co-author: An Illustrated Handbook for Barrier-Free Design, 2d edit., 1984. Home: PO Box 2422 Olympia WA 98507 Office: Transportation Bldg KF-01 Olympia WA 98504

MOFFETT, JANE DANIELS, psychiatric social worker, dance therapist; b. St. Paul, Minn., July 7, 1949; s. John Hancock and Martha Hill (Williams) D.; married; children: Kate Serena, Charles Locke. BA, Sarah Lawrence Coll., 1971; MA, Goddard Coll., 1974; MSW, Fordham U., 1980. Intern Grand Street Settlement, N.Y.C., 1978-79, N.Y. State Psychiatric Inst., 1979-80; social worker The Cath. Guardian Soc. Bklyn., 1980-81; dir. for intakes Family Ctr. for Mental Health Inc., 1982-83; dance therapist various hosps. and ctrs., San Francisco area, 1972-78; now co-dir. Maternity Network, San Francisco. Mem. Nat. Assn. Social Workers, Am. Dance Therapy Assn., Inst. Nonverbal Communication Research.

MOFFETT, KENNETH LEE, superintendent schools; b. Mt. Vernon, Wash., May 6, 1935; s. Charles R. and Edith May (Barker) M.; m. Diane Muriel Buckley, July 30, 1966; children: Kendis Charlene, Patrick Charles. BA, Western Wash. State U., 1957; MA, Calif. State U., Los Angeles, 1958-60; EdD, U. So. Calif., 1972. Tchr. pub. schs., Inglewood, Calif., 1957-61, 63-65, asst. prin., 1965-69, prin., 1969-73; tchr. U.S. Dependent Sch., Pirmasens, Fed. Republic Germany, 1961-62, asst. prin., Erlangen, Fed. Republic Germany, 1962-63; asst. supt. Inglewood Sch. Dist., Calif., 1973-76; supt. Lennox Sch. Dist., Calif., 1976-86; supt. ABC Unified Sch. Dist., Cerritos, Calif., 1986—; mem. adv. bd. Ad Hoc Com. on Mental Health for Tchrs., Los Angeles, 1980-81; chmn. scholarship com. Bank of Am., 1979-84. Mem. adv. com. Los Angeles Area council Boy Scouts Am., 1981-83; mem. support group for U. So. Calif., 1978-84; bd. dirs. Centinela Valley Guidance Clinic, Inglewood, 1978-82. Recipient Service awards PTA, Inglewood, 1973, Lennox, 1982. Mem. Centinela Valley Adminstrs. Assn. (charter pres. 1979-80), Assn. Calif. Sch. Adminstrs. (region chmn. 1980-82, Service award 1982), Centinela Valley Supts. Group (chmn. 1980-84), Centinela Valley Trustees and Adminstrs. Assn. (sec.-treas. 1977-78). Republican. Methodist. Office: ABC Unified Sch Dist 16700 Norwalk Blvd Cerritos CA 90701

MOFFITT, CHARLES TUTHILL, publishing executive; b. Orange, Calif., Oct. 21, 1942; s. Robert Lovering and Martha Eleanor (Tuthill) M.; m. Gina Gilbert, May 12, 1979; children: Emily, Julia. BA, UCLA, 1964; MA, U. Wash., 1966. Exec. asst. to mayor City of Los Angeles, 1973-75; officer United Calif. Bank, Los Angeles, 1975-79; exec. v.p. Cen. Los Angeles Trading, 1979-81; pres. Digital Hydraulics, Inc., Costa Mesa, Calif., 1984, ST Internat., Inc., Huntington Beach, Calif., 1983-86, Lester/Moffitt, Inc., Los Angeles, 1986—; bd. dirs. ST Internat., Inc., AMCAT Corp., Huntington Beach. Dir. K.I. Children's Ctr., Los Angeles, 1985—. Mem. Los Angeles Com. Fgn. Relations. Office: Lester/Moffitt Inc 100 Barrington Walk Los Angeles CA 90049

MOFFITT, GINA GILBERT, architect; b. Highland Park, Ill., Apr. 11, 1954; d. Henry Alfred Gilbert and Patti L. (Friedman) Schleussner; m. Charles Tuthill Moffitt, May 12, 1979; children: Julia Tuthill, Emily Gilbert. BArch summa cum laude, U. Calif., Berkeley, 1976. Registered architect, Calif.; cert. architect Nat. Chartered Architects Registragion Bd. Project architect Bruce Becket & Assocs., Los Angeles, 1978-81, Winner Orgn., Los Angeles, 1981-82; practice architect self-employed, Los Angeles, 1982-83; project architect, chief prodn. McCune, Gerwin & Ptnrs., Los Angeles, 1983-86; dir. prodn. EDC, Inc., 1986—. Mem. AIA, Assn. Women in Architecture, Constrn. Specifications Inst., Nat. Trust Hist. Preservation, Los Angeles Conservancy, Phi Beta Kappa. Democrat. Jewish. Club: Twins and Triplets Mothers (Los Angeles).

MOFFITT, HAROLD ROGER, entomologist, consultant; b. Ukiah, Calif., Aug. 8, 1934; s. Harold Eugene Moffitt and Olga (Miller) Wirt; m. Celesta Ann Beutler, Nov. 27, 1954; children: Michael, Patrick, Karen. BS, U. Calif., Davis, 1957; MS, U. Calif., Riverside, 1963, PhD, 1967. Lab. technician U. Calif., Riverside, 1957-63, research asst., 1963-67; research entomologist USDA Agrl. Research Service, Wenatchee, Wash., 1967-69; research entomologist USDA Agrl. Research Service, Yakima, Wash., 1969—, research leader, 1972-80, location leader, 1972-77; cons. Internat. Atomic Energy Agy., Vienna, Austria, 1973-78; vis. scientist Dept. Sci. and Indsl. Research, Auckland, New Zealand, 1980-81. Contbr. articles to profl. jours. Recipient Performance award USDA Agrl. Research Service, 1982. Mem. AAAS, Entomol. Soc. Am., Entomol. Soc. Can. Home: 10 N 59th Ave Yakima WA 98908 Office: USDA Agrl Research Service 3706 W Nob Hill Blvd Yakima WA 98902

MOFFORD, ROSE, state official; b. Globe, Ariz., June 10, 1922. Attended pub. schs. Sec. to Joe Hunt, Ariz. State Treas., 1941-43, Ariz. State Tax Commr., 1943-54, Wesley Bolin, Ariz. Sec. of State, 1954-55; asst. sec. of state State of Ariz., Phoenix, 1955-75; asst. dir. of revenue State of Ariz., 1975-77, sec. of state, 1977—. Democrat. Office: Office of Sec of State West Wing State Capitol Phoenix AZ 85007 *

MOGG, DONALD WHITEHEAD, chemist; b. La Grange, Ill., Feb. 11, 1924; s. Harold William and Margaret (Whitehead) M.; B.S., Allegheny Coll., 1944; postgrad. Harvard U., 1946-47. Asst. chemist Gt. Lakes Carbon Corp., Morton Grove, Ill., 1947-48, chemist, 1948-53, research chemist, 1953-56, project supr., 1956-59, sect. head, 1959-63; sect. head Gt. Lakes Research Corp., Elizabethton, Tenn., 1963-66; research and devel. mgr. bldg. products div. Grefco, Inc., Torrance, Calif., 1966-68, corp. research and devel. mgr., 1968-72, group mgr., 1972-81, sr. research assoc., 1981-82. Served with U.S. Army, 1944-46. Mem. Am. Chem. Soc., AAAS, Phi Beta Kappa, Phi Kappa Psi. Presbyterian. U.S. and fgn. patentee in field of bldg. products. Home: 3823 Ingraham St Apt B202 San Diego CA 92109

MOHAMMAD, SYED FAZAL, biochemist, researcher; b. Lucknow, U.P., India, Sept. 2, 1942; came to U.S., 1972; s. Shafi and Nisa (Choudhry) M.; m. Rani F. Failbus. Feb. 27, 1969; children: Zeenat, Habeeb. BSc, U. Lucknow, India, 1961, MSc, 1963; PhD, All India Inst. Med. Scis., New Delhi, 1972. Postdoctoral fellow U. N.C., Chapel Hill, 1972-75; instr. clin. pathology Brown U., Providence, 1976-77; asst. prof. U. South Fla., Tampa, 1977-79; research asst. prof. U. Utah, Salt Lake City, 1979-80, research assoc. prof., 1981—; cons. U. Mo., Rolla, 1981-84; dir. hematology div. artificial organs U. Utah, 1986—. Campaign organizer Democratic Party R.I., 1976. Directorate Gen. Health Services, India nat. scholar, 1965-67. Mem. AAAS, Am. Assn. Pathologist, Am. Soc. Artificial Internal Organs, Internat. Thrombosis and Hemostasis Soc., N.Y. Acad. Scis. Democrat. Office: U Utah Sch Medicine Dept Pathology Salt Lake City UT 84132 Office: Artificial Heart Research Lab 803 N 300 W Salt Lake City UT 84103

MOHAN, CHANDRA, research biochemistry educator; b. Lucknow, India, Aug. 3, 1950; came to U.S., 1977; s. Prithivi Nath and Tara Rani (Sharma) Shastri; m. Nirmala Devi Sharma, July 23, 1978; 1 child, Deepak. BS, Bangalore (India) U., 1970, MS, 1972, PhD, 1976. Research assoc. U. So.

Calif. Med. Sch., Los Angeles, 1977-83, asst. prof., 1983—. Mem. editorial bd. Biochem. Medicine, Los Angeles, 1986—; contbr. articles to profl. jours. Recipient BRSG award U. So. Calif., 1983. Mem. Am. Diabetes Assn., N.Y. Acad. Scis., Am. Chem. Soc., Soc. Exptl. Biology and Medicine. Hindu. Avocations: photography, coin collecting. Home: 13638 E Dickey St Whittier CA 90605 Office: U So Calif Med Sch 2025 Zonal Ave Los Angeles CA 90033

MOHAR, JOHN MICHAEL, building contractor; b. Vallejo, Calif., July 12, 1949; s. Rudolph Michael and Ruth Elizabeth (Hauge) M.; m. Kathryn Ann Johnson, Sept. 16, 1974; children: Laura Leigh, Ian Michael. B.S., U. Utah, 1973. Warehouseman, Global Co., Oakland, Calif., 1964-74; carpenter Tierra Homes, Salt Lake City, 1974-75; survey chief U.S. Forest Service, Libby, Mont., 1976-77; solar cons. AERO, Billings, Mont., 1981; carpenter Solarium Homes, Libby, Mont., 1977-82; bldg. contractor John Mohar Constrn. Co., Troy, Mont., 1981—. State sen. Mont., 1983-86; chmn. Dem. Cen. Com. Lincoln County, 1982—; mem. bd. McCormick Rural Fire Dept., Troy, 1981-86.

MOHENO, PHILLIP BERTRAND BERKEY, science educator, biomedical researcher; b. Los Angeles, Sept. 16, 1952; s. Bernard and Flora (Moheno) Berkey; m. Yolanda Peraza, Aug. 30, 1980; 1 child Karla Rose. BS, UCLA, 1974, postgrad., 1976; PhD, U. Calif., Santa Barbara, 1985. Cert. community coll. instr. Research asst. Salk Inst. Biol. Studies, La Jolla, Calif., 1970-73; grad. researcher, dept. chemistry UCLA, 1975-78; research asst. La Jolla Cancer Research Found., 1979; instr. biology Oxnard (Calif.) Coll. and Santa Barbara (Calif.) City Coll., 1980-85; supr. tchr. edn. U. Calif., Santa Barbara, 1982-85; asst. dir. MESA program Calif. State Coll., Bakersfield, 1985—; assoc. Organizational Designs in Communications, Santa Barbara, 1984—. Fellow Ford Found. UCLA, 1974-78; grantee Patent Acad. Senate U. Calif. Santa Barbara, 1985. Mem. Nat. Sci. Tchrs. Assn., Sigma Xi. Democrat. Mem. Soc. Friends. Avocations: Gestalt psychology, travel. Home: 100 N El Rio Dr #38 Bakersfield CA 93309-1277 Office: Calif State Coll 9001 Stockdale Hwy Bakersfield CA 93311-1099

MOHOLY, NOEL FRANCIS, clergyman; b. San Francisco, May 26, 1916; s. John Joseph and Eva Gertrude (Cippa) M.; grad. St. Anthony's Sem., Santa Barbara; S.T.D., Faculte de Theologie, Universite Laval, Quebec, Que., Can., 1948. Joined Franciscan Friars, 1935; ordained priest Roman Catholic Ch., 1941; tchr. fundamental theology Old Mission Santa Barbara, 1942-43, sacred theology, 1947-58; tchr. langs. St. Anthony's Sem., 1943-44; Am. adminstr. (handling affairs of the cause in U.S.) Cause of Padre Junipero Serra, 1950-55, vice postulator, 1958—; retreat master San Damiano Retreat, Danville, Calif., 1964-67. Mem. Ann. Assay Commn. U.S. Mint, 1964. Occupied numerous pulpits, assisted in several Franciscan Retreat Houses; condr. series illustrated lectrs. on cause of canonization of Padre Junipero Serra to students of all Franciscan study houses in U.S., summer 1952, also speaker in field at various clubs of Serra Internat. in U.S., Europe and Far East, on CBS, ABC broadcasts and conducted own local TV series. Exec. dir., treas. Old Mission Restoration Project, 1954-58; mem. Calif. Hist. Landmarks Adv. Com., 1962-71, Calif. Hist. Resources Commn., 1971-76, Calif. Bicentennial Celebration Commn., 1967-70; pres. Serra Bicentennial commn., 1983-86. Nat. and internat. authority on mariology, Calif. history (particularly history of Father Serra). Decorated Knight comdr. Order of Isabella the Catholic. Pres. Father Junipero Serra 250th Anniversary Assn., Inc., 1964—. Named hon. citizen Petra de Mallora, 1969, Palma de Mallorca, 1976. Mem. Cath. Theol. Soc. Am., Mariol. Soc. Am., Native Sons Golden West, Associacion de los Amigos de Padre Serra, K.C. Author: Our Last Chance, 1931; Saint Irenaeus; the Father of Mariology, 1952; The California Mission Story, 1975; The First Californian, 1976; co-author (with Don DeNevi) Junipero Serra, 1985; producer phonograph records Songs of the California Missions, 1951, Christmas at Mission Santa Barbara, 1953, St. Francis Peace Record, 1957; producer The Founding Father of the West, 1976. Home: St Boniface Friary 133 Golden Gate Ave San Francisco CA 94102 Office: Serra Cause Old Mission Santa Barbara CA 93105

MOHR, DIANE LOUISE, librarian; b. Fairbanks, Alaska, Nov. 24, 1951; d. Dean Burgette and Mary Louise (Leonard) Mohr. Deuxieme degree, Alliance Francais, Brussels, 1971; BA in Black Studies Calif. State U., Long Beach, 1977; MLS, U. So. Calif. 1978. Indexer/reviewer Litigation Support Services, Getty Oil Co., Los Angeles, 1978-79; librarian in charge Woodcrest br., Los Angeles County Pub. Library, 1979-82, View Park br., 1982-83; sr. librarian-in-charge Compton br. Los Angeles County Pub. Library, 1983—. Mem. Vesta Bruena Scholarship Bd., 1980-83. Mem. ALA, Calif. Black Librarians Caucus, U. So. Calif. Alumni, The Links Inc., Alpha Kappa Alpha, Phi Kappa Phi. Democrat. Episcopalian. Home: 2354 N Indian Hill Blvd Claremont CA 91711 Office: Compton Pub Library 240 W Compton Blvd Compton CA 90220

MOHR, JOHN LUTHER, biologist, environmental consultant; b. Reading, Pa., Dec. 1, 1911; s. Luther Seth and Anna Elizabeth (Davis) M.; m. Frances Edith Christensen, Nov. 23, 1939; children: Jeremy John, Christopher Charles. A.B. in Biology, Bucknell U., 1933; student, Oberlin Coll., 1933-34; Ph.D. in Zoology, U. Calif. at Berkeley, 1939. Research asso. Pacific Islands Research, Stanford, 1942-44; research asso. Allan Hancock Found., U. So. Calif., 1944-46, asst. prof., 1946-47, asst. prof. dept. biology, 1947-54, asso. prof., 1954-57, prof., 1957-77, prof. emeritus, 1977—, chmn. dept., 1959-62; marine borer and pollution surveys harbors So. Calif., 1948-51, arctic marine biol. research, 1952-71; chief marine zool. group U.S. Antarctic research ship Eltanin in Drake Passage, 1962, in South Pacific sector, 1965; research asso. malacology Los Angeles County Mus. of Natural History, ethics of academics and scientists, 1971—, problems with offshore drilling discharges and oil spill dispersants, 1978—. Mem. Biol. Stain Commn., 1948—, trustee, 1971-81, emeritus trustee, 1981—, v.p., 1976-80. Recipient Guggenheim fellowship, 1957-58. Fellow AAAS (council 1964-73), So. Calif. Acad. Sci., Sigma Xi (exec. com. 1964-67, 68, 69, chpt.-at-large bd. 1968-69); mem. Marine Biol. Assn. U.K. (life), Am. Microscopical Soc., Am. Soc. Parasitologists, Am. Micros. Soc., Western Soc. Naturalists (pres. 1960-61), Soc. Protozoologists, Am. Soc. Tropical Medicine and Hygiene, Am. Soc. Zoologists, Ecol. Soc. Am., Calif. Native Plants Soc., Common Cause, Huxleyan, Phi Sigma, Theta Upsilon Omega. Home: 3819 Chanson Dr Los Angeles CA 90043

MOHR, SELBY, ophthalmologist; b. San Francisco, Mar. 11, 1918; s. Selby and Henrietta (Foorman) M.; A.B., Stanford U., 1938, M.D., 1942; m. Marian Buckley, June 10, 1950; children—Selby, John Vincent, Adrianne E., Gregory P. Asst. resident in ophthalmology U. Calif. Hosp. 1942-43; pvt. practice ophthalmology, San Francisco, 1947—; mem. past pres. med. staff Marshall Hale Meml. Hosp.; mem. staff Mt. Zion Hosp., St Francis Meml. Hosp. Dir. Sweet Water Co., Mound Farms, Inc., Mound Farms Oil & Gas, Inc. Served from lt. (j.g.) to lt. USNR, 1943-46; PTO. Diplomate Am. Bd. Ophthalmology. Fellow Am. Acad. Ophthalmology and Otolarngology; mem. AMA, Calif., San Francisco med. socs., Pan-Pacific Surg. Soc., Pan-Am. Assn. Ophthalmology, Pacific Coast Oto-Ophthalmol. Soc., Pan-Am. Med. Soc. Home: 160 Sea Cliff Ave San Francisco CA 94121 Office: 450 Sutter St San Francisco CA 94108

MOHR, WILLIAM L(UDWIG), electronics company executive; b. Furth, Fed. Republic Germany, Feb. 22, 1935; came to U.S., 1940; s. Ernest Jacob and Gusty (Midas) M.; m. Harriet Baris, Oct. 26, 1962; 1 child, Tara Sophia. BEE, Poly. Inst. N.Y., 1956; MS, Rensselaer Poly. Inst., 1959. Engring. supr. Pratt & Whitney Aircraft Co., East Hartford, Conn., 1956-61; project engr. Gerber Sci., South Windsor, Conn., 1961-63; dept. mgr. Philco Ford, Palo Alto, Calif., 1963-70; product mgr. Motorola Corp., Tel Aviv, 1971; mfg., quality mgr. Hewlett Packard Co., Sunnyvale, Calif., 1971—. Author with Harriet Mohr: Quality Circles: Changing Images of People at Work, 1983. Served to 1st lt. USAR, 1957-64. Mem. IEEE, Internat. Assn. Quality Circles (bd. dirs. 1983—), Am. Soc. Quality Control, Computer and Automated Systems Assn. (sr.), N.Y. Acad. Sci. (hon.), Eta Kappa Nu, Tau Beta Pi. Avocations: tennis, swimming, photography. Office: Hewlett Packard Fin Remktg Div 972 E Arques Sunnyvale CA 94086

MOIR, RALPH WAYNE, physicist; b. Bellingham, Wash., Jan. 21, 1940; s. Francis LeRoy and Florence Augusta (Hershey) M.; m. Elizabeth Grace Branstead, June 9, 1963; children: Sara Louise, Steven Hershey, Christina Elizabeth. BS, U. Calif., Berkeley, 1962; ScD, MIT, 1967. Registered profl. nuclear engr., Calif. Postdoctoral researcher Ctr. Nuclear Studies, AEC, Fontenay-Aux-Roses, France, 1967-68; group leader Lawrence Livermore (Calif.) Nat. Lab., 1968-79, head fusion breeder program, 1979—. Contbr. articles to profl. jours. Committeeman Boy Scouts Am., 1980-85; bd. dirs. Interfaith Housing, Inc., Livermore, 1985—. Named Eagle Scout Boy Scouts Am., 1958; AEC fellow, 1962-65. Fellow Am. Phys. Soc.; mem. Am. Nuclear Soc. (exec. com. 1982-85), Sigma Xi, Delta Chi. Republican. Unitarian. Home: 1730 Murdell Ln Livermore CA 94550 Office: Lawrence Livermore Nat Lab L-644 PO Box 5511 Livermore CA 94550

MOISE, BETH MAXWELL, organizational behavior specialist, consultant; b. Champaign, Ill., Feb. 21, 1945; d. Harry P. and Virginia May (Jameson) Maxwell; m. Steven K. Moise, June 2, 1968; children—Adam, Grant. B.A., U. Colo., 1967, M.A., 1969; Ph.D. with distinction, U. N.Mex., 1977. With Foley's Dept. Store, 1967-68, May D & F., 1969-71; instr. U. N.Mex., Albuquerque, 1976-86; orgn. behavior specialist U.S. West, Albuquerque, 1981—; pvt. practice cons., 1974—; adj. prof. Sch. Bus., U. N.Mex. Bd. dirs. YWCA, 1979-81; mem. Nat. Women's Polit. Caucus, NOW, Mayor's Adv. Com. for Women in City Govt., 1979-81, Nat. Council on Alcoholism Adv. Bd., 1983; v.p. bd. trustees Albuquerque Acad., pres. bd., 1986—. Mem. Am. Soc. Tng. and Devel., N.Mex. Personnel Assn., N.Mex. Psychol. Assn. Home: 6611 Guadalupe Trail NW Albuquerque NM 87107 Office: Mountain Bell 400 Tijeras NW Station 677 Albuquerque NM 87103

MOISE, STEVEN KAHN, lawyer; b. Lubbock, Tex., July 28, 1944; s. Joseph J. and Marguerite K. Moise; B.A., U. Colo., Boulder, 1966, J.D., 1969; m. Beth Maxwell, June 2, 1968; children—Adam M., Grant S. Admitted to Colo. bar, 1969, N.Mex. bar, 1971; atty. firm Rothgerber, Appel & Powers, Denver, 1969-71; atty. firm Sutin, Thayer & Browne, P.C., Albuquerque, 1971—, pres., chief exec. officer 1984—, also bd. dirs.; Southwest Nat. Bank, Albuquerque, 1974-85; N.Mex. Symphony Orch., 1973-78, pres., 1977-78; trustee Presbyn. Health Care Found., Albuquerque, 1980—, U. Colo. Found., 1969-79, United Way, 1979-84, Congregation Albert, Albuquerque, 1977-85, v.p., 1979-80, pres., 1981-82; trustee Manzano Day Sch., Albuquerque, 1979-86, U. N.Mex. Robert O. Anderson Sch. Mgmt. Found., 1979-85, Albuquerque Econ. Devel., 1982—, sec., 1984-86, v.p. 1986—; trustee, v.p. Albuquerque Community Found., 1982-84, pres., 1984—; sec. Albuqerque All Seasons Corp., 1986—; N.Mex. Amigos, 1986—. mem. adv. council Robert O Anderson Sch. Mgmt. Mem. ABA, N.Mex. Bar Assn., Colo. Bar Assn., Albuquerque Bar Assn., Denver Bar Assn. Democrat. Home: 6611 Guadalupe Trail NW Albuquerque NM 87107 Office: PO Box 1945 Albuquerque NM 87103

MOK, WILLIAM SHU-LAI, research engineer; b. Hong Kong, Jan. 3, 1959; came to U.S., 1977; m. Jacqueline Chang, July 21, 1984. BS, Whittier Coll., 1980; MS in Engring., Princeton U., 1982. Research assoc. U. Hawaii, Honolulu, 1982—. Contbr. articles to profl. jours. Mem. AAAS. Episcopalian. Home: 94-550 Kuaie St Mililani HI 96789 Office: U Hawaii Natural Energy Inst 2540 Dole St Honolulu HI 96822

MOLDANADO, SWARNALATHA ADUSUMILLI, nursing educator, researcher; b. Vijayawada, Andhra, India; came to U.S., 1977; d. Punnaih and Nagaratna (Chintapally) A.; m. Alexander Moldanado, Dec. 23, 1979; 1 child, Arjun. Registered nurse and midwife, Ill. Lectr. Postgrad. Inst. of Medical Edn. and Research, Chandigarh, India, 1971-77; research assoc., teaching asst. U. Ill. Coll. of Nursing, Chgo., 1977-81; tchr. practice Rush U. Coll of Nursing, Chgo., 1981-82; assoc. prof., chairman dept. nursing Rockford Coll., Ill., 1982-85; prof., Calif. State U., San Bernardino, 1985—. Mem., vol. Hunger Watch Com. Am. Assn. Univ. Women, 1983-84. Mem. Am. Pub. Health Assn., Ill. Sigma Xi Research Soc., Sigma Theta Tau. Avocations: music; gardening. Office: Calif State U 5500 University Pkwy San Bernardino CA 92407

MOLDAVE, KIVIE, academic administrator, biochemist; b. Kiev, USSR, Oct. 22, 1923; came to U.S., 1937; s. James and Lucille (Shapiro) M.; m. Rose H. Moldave, June 5, 1949; children: Peter Mahlon, Anne Lisa. BA in Biochemistry, U. Calif., Berkeley, 1947; MS in Biochemistry, U. So. Calif., 1950; PhD, U. Southern Calif., 1952. Prof. biochemistry Tufts U. Sch. Medicine, Medford, Mass., 1964-66; William S. McElroy Prof. biochemistry, chmn. dept. U. Pitts. Sch. Medicine, 1966-70; prof. biochemistry U. Calif. Coll. Medicine, Irvine, 1970-84, chmn. dept., 1970-80, acting grad. dean, 1982; acad. vice chancellor U. Calif., Santa Cruz, 1984—; mem. biochemistry com. Nat. Bd. Med. Examiners, 1976; mem. VA Research Service Merit rev. bd. in basic scis., 1972-76. Editor Methods in Enzymology-Nucleic Acids series, 1967—; co-editor Progress in Nucleic Acid, 1983—; mem. editorial adv. bd. Jour. Biochemistry, 1971-76, Jour. Biol. Chemistry, 1971-75, 77-79. USPHS research fellow, NIH, U. Paris, 1953-54, U. Wis., 1952-53; recipient research career award USPHS, Tufts U., 1963-66. Mem. AAAS, Am. Chem. Soc. (nat. program chmn. div. biol. chemistry 1969-72, chmn. Pitts. sect. 1968-69), Am. Soc. Biol. Chemistry (rep. chem. sect. AAAS 1978—, mem. editorial bd. jour. 1971-79), Am. Cancer Soc. (chmn. sci. adv. com. 1976, mem. adv. council research and clin. invest awards 1976—, scholar 1973), NIH (Mem. Physiol. Chemistry Study Sect., 1967-71), Nat. Inst. Aging (rev. com. 1977-81), Alpha Omega Alpha. Home: 119 Carbonera Ct Santa Cruz CA 95060 Office: U Santa Calif Office Acad Vice Chancellor 299 McHenry Library Santa Cruz CA 95064

MOLDOWAN, J(OHN) MICHAEL, research organic chemist; b. Detroit, Nov. 4, 1946; s. John Francis and Hazel Marie (Ouellette) M.; m. Mary Allison Thomson, Aug. 16, 1966; children: Shaun Michael, Jaime Joshua, Adam Gardner. BS in Chemistry, Wayne State U., 1968; PhD in Organic Chemistry, U. Mich., 1972. Postdoctoral fellow Stanford (Calif.) U., 1972-74; research chemist Chevron Oil Field Research Co., Richmond, Calif., 1974-80, sr. research chemist, 1980-85, sr. research assoc., 1985—; session chmn. Gordon Research Conf. on Organic Geochemistry, Plymouth, N.H., 1984. Contbr. articles to profl. jours. Fellow NSF 1968, NIH 1972-74. Mem. Am. Chem. Soc., Geochemistry div. Am. Chem. Soc. (chmn.-elect 1985, chmn. 1986), Bay Area Mass Spectrometry, Am. Assn. Petroleum Geologists. Office: Chevron Oil Field Research Co 576 Standard Ave Richmond CA 94802-0627

MOLINA, MARIO JOSE, physical chemist, educator; b. Mexico City, Mexico, Mar. 19, 1943; came to U.S., 1968; s. Roberto Molina-Pasquel and Leonor Henríquez; m. Luisa Y. Tan, July 12, 1973; 1 child, Felipe. Bachillerato, Acad. Hispano Mexicana, Mexico City, 1959; Ingeniero Químico, U. Nacional Autónoma de México, 1965; postgrad., U. Freiburg, Germany, 1966-67; Ph.D., U. Calif. at Berkeley, 1972. Asst. prof. U. Nacional Autónoma de México, 1967-68; research assoc. U. Calif.-Berkeley, 1972-73; research assoc. U. Calif.-Irvine, 1973-75, asst. prof. phys. chemistry, 1975-79, assoc. prof., 1979-82; sr. research scientist Jet Propulsion Lab., 1983—. Recipient Tyler Ecology award, 1983, Esselen award, 1987. Mem. Am. Chem. Soc., Am. Phys. Soc., Am. Geophys. Union, Sigma Xi. Discoverer the theory that fluorocarbons deplete ozone layer of stratosphere. Home: 1415 Sugar Loaf Dr La Canada CA 91011 Office: Jet Propulsion Lab Calif Inst Tech 4800 Oak Grove Dr Pasadena CA 91109

MOLINARE, LORNA MARGARET, social worker, family therapist; b. Fayette, Mich., Feb. 2, 1921; d. Rupert Donald and Anna (MacDonald) Greene; m. Peter Bartley Molinare, May 6, 1942 (dec. May 1950); 1 child, Peter Rupert; m. Donald Alexander Hume, Oct. 23, 1966. BS, U. Ariz., 1953; MSW, Ind. U., 1955; postgrad., Mental Research Inst., 1965. Social worker Phoenix VA Hosp., 1955-57, asst. chief social work service, 1957-69; pvt. practice marriage and family therapy Phoenix, 1969—; tchr. marriage and family therapy Ariz. State U., Tempe, 1969—; lectr. and presenter work shops various agys., instns. and orgns. throughout southwest U.S. Mem. Nat. Assn. Social Workers (cert.). Democrat. Avocations: polit. activism. Home: 1409 W Myrtle Phoenix AZ 85021 Office: 8015 N 12th St Phoenix AZ 85020

MOLINARI, TIMOTHY MARK, special events consultant; b. Portland, Oreg., May 9, 1957; s. Thomas Joseph and Marie A. (Schallberger) M. AA, Umpqua Community Coll., 1977; BA, Oreg. State U., 1982. Promotin mgr. Up With People, Tucson, 1980-83; material logistics dir. Los Angeles Olympic Organizing Com., 1984; advance dir. White House, Washington, 1984-85; state logistics dir. Hands Across Am., Dallas, 1986; cons. spl. events Sutherlin, Oreg., 1987—. Named to Eagle Scouts Boy Scouts Am., 1975. Mem. Los Angeles Amateur Athletic Found. (charter), Phi Kappa Phi. Republican. Roman Catholic. Home and Office: PO Box 619 Sutherlin OR 97479

MOLITOR, GARY WILLIAM, artist; b. Modesto, Calif., July 12, 1940; s. Milton William and Louise Emily (Kneppler) M. AA, San Francisco City Coll., 1961; BA, San Francisco State U., 1963, MA, 1965. Lectr. arts. U. Calif., Davis, 1967-69; asst. prof. Sonoma State U., Rohnert Park, Calif., 1970-73; assoc. prof. U. Nev., Las Vegas, 1972-73; sales supr. W.E. Mushet Co., San Francisco, 1973-84; exec. dir. Tifari, Sausalito, Calif., 1984-85; prodn. mgr. Ryan Paint Co., Oakland, Calif., 1985-87; mktg. dir. Aervoe-Pacific, San Leandro, Calif., 1987—. Artist (sculpture) The Dilexi Years 1958-70; artist ceramic sculpture Cerama-Rama, 1977, Calif. Ceramics and Glass, 1974; artist mixed media sculpture Molitor, 1967, Funk Show, 1967. Recipient award Nat. Council Arts and Humanities, 1966 . Mem. Fedn. Socs. Coatings Tech., Golden Gate Soc. Coating Tech., Soc. for Advancement of Material and Process Engring., Am. Crafts Council, Archaeol. Inst. Am., U.S. Parachute Assn. Democrat. Home: 18 Van Sicklen Pl Oakland CA 94610 Office: AERVOE-PACIFIC 14864 Wicks Blvd San Leandro CA 94577

MOLLET, JUDITH A., research entomologist; b. Lexington, Ky., Mar. 31, 1954; d. Howard William and Mary Dean (Abbott) M.; m. Jeffrey Richard Bloomquist, Sept. 21, 1985. BS, U. Calif., Riverside, 1975, PhD, 1984; MS, U. Ill., 1977. Plant and pesticide specialist State of Ill., Springfield, 1978-79; assoc. entomologist Eli Lilly and Co., Greenfield, Ind., 1979-81; sr. research entomologist Merck & Co., Inc., Fresno, Calif., 1984—. Mem. Entomol. Soc. Am., Am. Soc. Horicultural Sci. Home and Office: 303 E Bullard #141 Fresno CA 93710

MOLLOY, PETER MICHAEL, museum director; b. N.Y.C., Aug. 16, 1942; s. Peter Francis and Helen (O'Keefe) M.; m. Katherine Ann Molloy, Feb. 5, 1977; children: Rebecca, Heidi, Michael. ScB, U.S. Naval Acad., 1964; MA, Brown U., 1971, PhD, 1975. Commd. 2d lt. USMCR, 1964, advanced through grades to col.; curator Merrimack Valley Textile Mus., North Andover, Mass., 1973-76; dir. Western Mus. Mining and Industry, Colorado Springs, 1976—. Author: Haer Survey of Industrial Sites in the Merrimack Valley, 1975; contbr. articles to profl. jours. Fellow Brown U., 1968-72, Woodrow Wilson Found., 1970-71. Mem. Am. Assn. Mus., Soc. Indsl. Archaeology, Am. Soc. State and Local History, Colorado Springs C. of C. Lodge: Sertoma. Home: 6660 Grey Eagle Terr Colorado Springs CO 80919 Office: Western Mus of Mining & Ind 4520 North Park Dr Colorado Springs CO 80907

MOLLOY, WILLIAM FRANCIS, management consulting company executive; b. Orange, N.J., June 23, 1945; s. Corneilius John and Jean Ann (Marquier) M.; m. Lorraine Madeline La Pointe, Jan. 26, 1979; children—Heather Ann, Michael Francis. B.A. in History, Stonehill Coll., 1968; M.Ed. in Counseling and Personnel Services, U. Md., 1973. Tchr., coach Mackin High Sch., Washington, 1968-69; tchr., coach, counselor Red Bank (N.J.) Cath. High Sch., 1969-70; counselor, dir. devel. DeMatha High Sch., Hyattsville, Md., 1970-75; fin. planner Waddell & Reed, Washington, 1974-75; dealer mgr. Royal Bus. Machines, Pitts., 1975-77; successively mktg. mgr., regional mgr., v.p. Western region Devel. Dimensions Internat., Los Angeles, 1977—; guest speaker, lectr. in field. Vice pres. Fox Hills Pines Home Owners Assn., 1979-80. Mem. Am. Soc. Tng. and Devel. (leadership devel. com. 1985—), Am. Youth Soccer Orgn. (bd. dirs. region 7), Los Angeles C. of C. Contbr. articles to profl. publs. Home: 5879 W 77th Pl Los Angeles CA 90045

MOLNAR, RONALD JOHN, electrical packaging engineering manager; b. Whittier, Calif., Nov. 2, 1950; s. John and Maralee Viola (Wallin) M.; m. Carole Ann Danilson, June 24, 1978; children—Kelly Elizabeth, Melanie Ann. B.S.E.E., U. Calif.-Berkeley, 1973. Product engr. Monsanto Co., Palo Alto, Calif., 1973-78; mfg. engring. mgr. optoelectronics div. Siemens Components, Inc., Cupertino, Calif., 1978-86; plastic package engring. mgr. VLSI Tech., Inc., San Jose, Calif., 1986—. Served with USCGR, 1969-74. Mem. IEEE, Microelectronic Plastic Packaging Engrs., Internat. Soc. Hybrid Microelectronics, No. Calif. Golf Assn., U. Calif. Alumni Assn. Office: VLSI Tech Inc 1109 McKay Dr San Jose CA 95131

MOLTENI, BETTY PHILLIPS, painter; b. Norfolk, Va., Dec. 15, 1913; d. William Henry and Margaret (Brownley) Phillips; A.B., Coll. William and Mary, 1938; student art U. Nev., Reno, 1966-71; m. Peter G. Molteni, Jr., July 22, 1939; children—Peter G. III, Margaret Elizabeth, Christopher Phillips, Marianne Stephanie. Founder, chmn. Armed Forces Art Show Hawaii, 1962; one woman shows Artist Co-op., Reno, 1978, 81, Mother Lode Nat. Art Exhbn., Sonora, Calif., 1977, 79, Delta Art Assn. Show, Antioch, Calif., 1978; exhibited group shows Nev. Women Art Show Las Vegas, 1976, Nat. League Am. Pen Women, Salt Lake City, 1973, Sacramento, 1978, Washington, 1984, Lodi Art Ann., Acampo, Calif., 1979, 84, Tahoe Erhman Mansion Arts Festival, 1979-80, Sierra Nev. Mus., 1983, Nev. Watercolor Soc., 1984, New Artists Gallery, Las Vegas Mus., 1986, Brewery Art Ctr., Carson City, Nev., 1986; represented in pvt. collections, also Sierra Nev. Mus. Art, Reno. Bd. dirs. Nev. Art Gallery, 1975-78; del. Sierra Arts Assembly, 1977-78, 80-81. Mem. Nat. League Am. Pen Women (v.p. 1973, treas. Reno br. 1979, pres. 1980, state pres. 1982-84), Soc. Western Artists, Latimer Art Club (art scholarship chmn., pres. 1971, treas. 1978), Carson City Alliance (charter), Nev. Artists Assn., Nev. Art Gallery, Sierra Arts Assembly, Artist Co-op. (charter, v.p. 1983), Sierra Nevada Mus. Arts Aux., Reno Philharmonic League, Cath. Daus. Republican. Roman Catholic. Home: 1130 Alpine Circle Reno NV 89509

MOLTZ, DENNIS MICHAEL, nuclear science researcher; b. San Antonio, Oct. 2, 1952; s. Ellis Edward and Alice Rose (Wagner) M.; m. Rosette Margaret Ajemian; children: Andrew Michael, Christopher Gabriel. BS in Chemistry, BS in Math., Tex. A&M U., 1974; PhD in Chemistry, U. Calif., Berkeley, 1979. Postdoctoral nuclear researcher Oak Ridge (Tenn.) Nat. Lab., 1979-82, U.S.C., Columbia, 1982-84; staff scientist Lawrence Berkeley (Calif.) Lab., 1984—. Tutor Knox County (Tenn.) Reading Program, 1980-84. Mem. AAAS, Am. Chem. Soc., Am. Phys. Soc., Sigma Xi. Republican. Lutheran. Avocations: sports, gardening. Home: 500 Grizzly Peak Berkeley CA 94708 Office: U Calif Lawrence Berkeley Lab MS88 Berkeley CA 94720

MOMMAERTS, WILFRIED FRANCIS HENRY MARIA, physiologist, educator; b. Broechem, Belgium, Mar. 4, 1917; came to U.S., 1948, naturalized, 1956; s. Hendrik David and Maria (van Damme) M.; m. Elizabeth Barbara Batyka, July 29, 1944 (dec.); children—Robert Wilfried Anthony, Edina Maria, Quentin Francis. Student, U. Leiden, Netherlands, 1934-39; Ph.D., Kolozsvar, Hungary, 1943; Dr. honoris causa, U. Dijon, 1976. Faculty Am. U., Beirut, 1945-48, Duke U., 1948-53, Western Res. U., 1953-56; coordinator Commonwealth Fund Med. Curriculum Expt., 1955-56; spl. Rockefeller fellow U. Coll., London, 1956; prof. medicine, physiology, dir. Los Angeles County Heart Assn. Cardiovascular Research Lab. U. Calif., Los Angeles, 1956—; chmn. dept. physiology UCLA, 1966—; Mem. Roger Wagner Los Angeles Master Chorale.; Commonwealth Fund fellow Centre des Recherches sur les Macromolecules, Strasbourg, 1963-64; chmn. physiology tng. com. NIH, 1967—; vis. prof. U. Dijon, 1973-74; Mem. Internat. Commn. on Genetic Experimentation, 1980—. Author: Muscular Contraction, a Topic in Molecular Physiology, 1950; contbr. articles to profl. jours. Recipient award for outstanding contbn. to sci. knowledge Los Angeles County Heart Assn., 1967, award of merit, 1972; Samuel Racz medal, Budapest, 1985, Alexander von Humboldt award, 1987. Mem. Am. Physiol. Soc., Am. Soc. Biol. Chemists, Biophys. Soc., Am. Acad. Arts and Scis., Royal Belgian Acad. Medicine, Hungarian Physiol. Soc. (hon.), others. Address: U Calif Dept Physiology 405 Hilgard Ave Los Angeles CA 90024

MONACO, ALBERT MARION, JR., sports association executive; b. San Francisco, July 2, 1938; s. Albert Marion and Marie Francis (Grondona) M.; m. Loretta Tuck, Sept. 25, 1965; children: Richard Albert, Marie Loretta. BS, U. Calif., Berkeley, 1960, LLD, 1963. Assoc. Heller, Ehrman, White & McAuliffe, San Francisco, 1963-68; v.p. Atlas Heating, San Francisco, 1968-73; exec. dir. U.S. Volleyball Assn., Colorado Springs, Colo., 1973—; mem. U.S. Info. Agy. Sports Com., Fedn. Internationale de Volleyball Sports Commn. Contbr. Ency. Britannica Book of the Yr., 1975—; editor Volleyball USA, 1973—. Organizer volley ball competition Los Angeles

Olympic Games. Served to capt. U.S. Army, 1963-65. Recipient Leader in Volleyball award U.S. Volleyball Assn., 1985. Mem. Calif. Bar Assn., North Cen. Am. and Carribean Volleyball Confederation. Club: Olympic (San Francisco). Lodge: Rotary. Office: US Volleyball Assn 1750 E Boulder St Colorado Springs CO 80909

MONAHAN, JEANNETTE, hospital management development specialist; b. Dallas, May 9, 1949; d. John I. and Julia M. (Galloway) Welsh; m. Terence F. Meany, Mar. 17, 1977; 1 dau., Theresa K. Monahan. B.A. in English, U. Tex.-Austin, 1971; M.P.A., U. Colo., 1975; diploma of competency in systems renewal consultation Internat. Inst. for Study of Systems Renewal, Seattle, 1981. Intern, City of Boulder (Colo.), summer 1975, Dept. Regulatory Agys., State of Colo., Denver, summer 1976; tng. specialist Municipality of Met. Seattle, 1977-78; mgr. employee tng. and devel. U. Wash. Hosps., Seattle, 1978-82; dir. mgmt. devel. Virginia Mason Med. Ctr., Seattle, 1982—. Recipient Suggestion award Municipality of Met. Seattle, 1978. Mem. Am. Soc. for Tng. and Devel. (recipient outstanding contbn. award 1977, 78, mem. region VIII conf. planning com. 1983), Am. Soc. Healthcare Edn. and Tng. (nat. program planning com. 1982, 83). Democrat. Roman Catholic. Club: Toastmasters Internat. Contbr. articles on organizational devel. to profl. jours. Office: Virginia Mason Med Ctr 925 Seneca St PO Box 1930 Seattle WA 98111

MONARCHI, DAVID EDWARD, management scientist, information scientist, educator; b. Miami Beach, Fla., July 31, 1944; s. Joseph Louis and Elizabeth Rose (Muller) M.; B.S. in Engring. Physics, Colo. Sch. of Mines, 1966; Ph.D. (NDEA fellow), U. Ariz., 1972; 1 son by previous marriage, David Edward. Asst. dir. of Bus. Research Div., U. Colo., Boulder, 1972-75, asst. prof. mgmt. sci./info. systems, 1972-75, assoc. prof. mgmt. sci. and info. systems, 1975-84; assoc. dir. Bus. Research Div., 1975—, dir. Div. Info. Sci. Research, 1982-84; prin. investigator of socio-econ. environ. systems for govtl. agys., and local govt. orgns., State of Colo., also info. systems for pvt. firms, 1972-77. Mem. Gov.'s Energy Task Force Com., 1974. Mem. IEEE, Inst. for Mgmt. Sci., Ops. Research Soc. Am., Am. Inst. for Decision Scis., Assn. Computing Machinery. Contbr. numerous articles on socio-econ. modeling to profl. jours. Avocations: modeling, artificial intelligence. Home: 32 Benthaven Place Boulder CO 80303 Office: Grad Sch Bus Univ of Colorado Boulder CO 80309

MONDAVI, ROBERT, winery executive. Chmn. Robert Mondavi Winery, Oakville, Calif. Office: Robert Mondavi Winery 7801 St Helena Hwy Oakville CA 94562 *

MONDL, MARK CHRISTOPHER, military officer, environmental program administrator; b. Akron, Ohio, Feb. 16, 1948; s. Adam James and Mildred Irene (Denton) M.; m. Frieda Diann Isom, Nov. 28, 1980; 1 child, Adam Christopher. BS, Bowling Green State U., 1969, MA, 1971; postgrad., Wake Fores U., 1975-80. Commd. USAF, 1971, advanced through grades to maj., 1986; disaster preparedness officer USAF, McClellan AFB, Calif., 1971-73, Udorn RT AFB, Thailand, 1973-74; NORAD planning officer USAF, Malmstrom AFB, Mont., 1974-75; peacekeeper missile biologist USAF, Washington, 1980-84; environ. space shuttle program mgr. USAF, Los Angeles, 1984-86, mgr. environ. strategic defense initiative program, 1986—. Contbr. articles to profl. jours. Deacon Knollwood Bapt. Ch., Burke, Va., 1983-84. Mem. Am. Soc. Parasitologists, Sigma Xi. Republican. Avocations: marathon running, camping, hiking, photography. Home: 1029 Marshall Pl Long Beach CA 90807

MONE, LOUIS CARMEN, clin. social worker; b. Bklyn., July 10, 1936; s. Louis Anthony and Carmella (Guidone) M.; BA, U. Ariz., 1962; MSW, Rutgers U., 1965; PhD in Clin. Social Work, 1985; m. Elinor Sypniewski, Sept. 28, 1958; children—Marc, Lisa. Detention supr. Pima County Detention Home, Tucson, 1959-60; social worker N.J. Neuro-Psychiat. Inst., Princeton, 1961-63; psychiat. social worker Alcoholism Treatment Center, Roosevelt Hosp. Metuchen, N.J., 1963-66; caseworker Family Counseling Service of Somerset County, Bound Brook, N.J., 1965-67, group cons., 1965-69; prin. psychiat. social worker Raritan Bay Mental Health Center, Middlesex County Mental Health Clinic, Perth Amboy, N.J., 1966-69; social work cons. Borough of Spotswood, Spotswood (N.J.) Pub. Schs., 1967-69; pilot project dir., group therapist Heart Assn. Middlesex County, Edison, N.J., 1968-69; chief psychiat. social worker Insts. Religion and Health, N.Y.C., 1969-71; pvt. practice adolescent and adult psychotherapy, marriage and family counseling, East Brunswick, N.J., 1965-71, Del Mar, Calif., 1972-78, individual, marriage, family and child therapy, San Diego, 1973-78, La Jolla, Calif., 1978-86, San Diego, Del Mar, Calif., 1986—; instr. nursing programs Rutgers U., New Brunswick, N.J., 1970; dir. profl. services Family Services Assn. San Diego, 1971-75; instr. Calif. Sch. Profl. Psychology, 1974, 76-80. Served with AUS, 1955-57. Mem. Am. Group Psychotherapy Assn., Nat. Assn. Social Workers, San Diego Group Psychotherapy Soc., Delta Chi. Club: Calif. Ensenada Yacht. Author: Private Practice: A Professional Business. Home and Office: 3555 5th Ave San Diego CA 92103

MONFORT, ELIAS RIGGS, III, management consultant; b. Chgo., Sept. 6, 1929; s. Elias Riggs and Elizabeth (Sebald) M.; B.S., Purdue U., 1952; m. Hathalie Jean Ward, June 8, 1957; children—Stephen, Scott, Jonathan, Christoper. Liaison engr. Douglas Aircraft Co., Santa Monica, Calif., 1952; internat. regional mgr. Cessna Aircraft Co., Wichita, Kans., 1958-64; long-range planning service Stanford Research Inst., Sunnyvale, Calif., 1964-77, strategic mgmt., 1978—. Bd. regents Cogswell Engring. Coll. Served to capt. USAF, 1952-57; Korea. Mem. Soc. Automotive Engrs., Exptl. Aircraft Assn., Internat. Aerobatic Club, Corp. Planners Assn. (founding), Nat. Assn. Corp. Planners. Republican. Episcopalian. Clubs: Sequoia Woods Golf and Country. Home: 1609 Honfleur Dr Sunnyvale CA 94087 Office: 333 Ravenswood Menlo Park CA 94025

MONFORT, KENNETH, cattle production and meat processing company executive; b. 1928. Mem. Colo. Ho. of Reps., 1965-69; pres. Monfort of Colo. Inc., Greeley, 1969—, co-chmn., sr. v.p., 1976, pres., chief exec. officer, 1980—, also bd. dirs. Office: Monfort of Colo Inc PO Box G Greeley CO 80632 *

MONFORTON, MARY ELLEN, artist, educator; b. Memphis, June 15, 1944; d. Martin Joseph and Carolyn Elizabeth (Butin) Travers; m. Gerald P. Monforton; children: Matthew Gerald, Jason Allen, Timothy Michael. Student Okla. U.-Norman, 1962-63; B.S. in Art, Memphis State U., 1967. Cert. tchr., Tenn. Tchr., Memphis Pub. Schs., 1967-75; one woman show: The Four Pheasants, Kalispell, Mont., 1979; group shows include: Ligoa Duncan Arts, N.Y.C., 1977, Winner's Circle Gallery, Van Nuys, Calif., Palm Beach Art Galleries, Houston, 1984; represented in pvt. collections; sang with Memphis Community Choir, 1972-73. Recipient Prix de Paris, Ligoa Duncan Arts, 1977; Salon des Surindependants, Les Surindependants, Paris, 1977. Mem. NEA, Tenn. Edn. Assn., Memphis Edn. Assn., West Tenn. Edn. Assn., West Tenn. Vocal Music Edn. Assn. (treas. 1967-69), Music Educators Nat. Conf., Memphis Art Edn. Assn. (asst. sec. inservice tng. 1973-74), Art Edn. Assn., Am. Choral Dirs. Assn., Mont. Choral Dirs. Assn., Internat. Soc. Artists, Les Surindependants, Internat. Fine Arts Guild, Alpha Gamma Delta, Mu Phi Epsilon. Home: 1012 1st Ave W Kalispell MT 59901

MONICAL, STUART DEAN, consulting engineer; b. Cin., Apr. 13, 1951; s. Robert Duane and Carol Arnetha (Dean) M.; m. Jeannette Leonor Ferrand, Oct. 1, 1978; children: Jessica Carol, Amanda Kate. BSME, Purdue U., 1973. V.p. McFall, Konkel & Kimball, Denver, 1973—. Bd. dirs. Arapahoe Estates Water, Littleton, Colo., 1984—. Mem. ASHRAE, Am. Soc. Plumbing Engrs., Nat. Fire Protection Assn., Constrn. Specifications Inst., Inst. Environ. Scis., Am. Cons. Engring. Council, Cons. Engring. Council Colo. Home: 3383 E Euclid Pl Littleton CO 80121 Office: McFall Konkel & Kimball 2160 S Clermont St Denver CO 80222

MONROE, JAMES WARREN, federal government executive; b. Winnemucca, Nev., July 13, 1935; s. Warren L. and Mary Kathleen (Johnstone) M.; m. Joanne Lambert, Dec. 20, 1958; children: James, Michael, Eric, Mary. Student, U. Utah, 1953-57. Press sec. U.S. Senate, Washington, 1965-68; mgr. pub. affairs U.S. Dept. Interior, Washington, 1968-73; asst. dir. Bur. Land Mgmt., Washington, 1973-83; dist. mgr. Bur. Land Mgmt., Casper, Wyo., 1983—. Bd. dirs. Wyo. Futures Project, Inc., Casper, 1986—; mem. Utah Ho. Reps., Salt Lake City, 1963-64. Mem. Soc. Profl. Journalists. Lodge: Rotary (bd. dirs. Casper club 1985—). Avocations: sportsmanship, golfing.

MONROE, NANCY, bank auditor; b. Wyoming, Pa., Mar. 24, 1936; d. Arthur Mitchell and Anna Elizabeth (Jones) Fritz; m. Edward Allan Hearn Sr., Nov. 22, 1956 (div. Oct. 1971); children—Diane Lynn Hearn Thurmond, Edward Allan Jr.; m. Robert Hamilton Monroe, Feb. 23, 1980. Student, Am. Inst. Banking, Las Vegas, 1969-71; cert. compliance banking U. Okla., 1986. From teller to utility clk. First Nat. Bank, Las Vegas, 1963-72; from utility clk. to ops. officer Pioneer Citizens Bank of Nev., Las Vegas, 1972-74, ops. officer, Reno, 1978 -86, compliance officer, 1986—; from loan sec. to loan mgr. First Valley Bank, Kingston, Pa., 1974-78; asst. to the auditor Nev. Bankers Assn., Reno, 1983. Mem. Am. Inst. Banking. Republican. Baptist. Avocations: bowling; crocheting; bicycling. Office: Pioneer Citizens Bank of Nev 10 State St Reno NV 89505

MONROE, SHULA HELEN SCHWARTZ, librarian; b. Beirut, Lebanon, Mar. 24, 1927 (parents Am. citizens); d. Morris and Tania (Lurie) Leibson; m. Ralph Schwartz, Apr. 12, 1947 (div. Apr. 1970); children: Deborah Ruth Isgur, Jerrold Alan, Harris Ray; m. Harris Goodman Monroe, Aug. 22, 1978. BJ, Northwestern U., 1946; MLS, Tex. Woman's U., 1967. Cert. community coll. librarian, community coll. instr., Calif. Reference librarian L-T-V Inc., Dallas, 1954-62; mgr. T.I. Cen. Library Services, Dallas, 1962-70; head pub. services El Centro Community Coll., Dallas, 1970-72; assoc. dir. U. D.C., 1972-74; coordinator media proc. No. Va. Community Coll., Springfield, Va., 1975-78; city librarian National City Pub. Library, Calif., 1979—; cons. Swift & Assocs., Rockville, Md., 1974-75; instr. Dallas County Community Coll., 1969-71, Grossmont Coll., San Diego, 1979-80; lectr. U.D.C., 1972-74. Editor: Guidelines for Book Cataloging, 1977; An Evaluation ... of ... G.P.O., 1978. Pres. National City Community Action Network, 1987—. Mem. Spl. Libraries Assn. (pres. Tex. chpt. 1965-66), Dallas County Library Assn. (pres. 1971-72), Calif. Library Assn., ALA, Congress of Calif Pub. Library Systems (chmn. 1985, chmn.-elect chpt. on literacy 1987—). Democrat. Jewish. Home: 5015 Santa Cruz Ave San Diego CA 92107 Office: National City Pub Library 200 E 12 St National City CA 92050

MONROE, STANLEY EDWIN, surgeon; b. Bangor, Mich., June 26, 1902; s. Samuel E. and Ella (Monroe) M.; A.B., U. Mich., 1925; M.D., U. Chgo./ Rush Med. Coll., 1936; m. Ruth Williams, June 14, 1932 (dec. 1981); m. 2d, Flora Doss, Aug. 6, 1982. Intern, Evanston (Ill.) Hosp., 1935-36, resident surgeon, 1936-37, asst. surgeon, 1940-41; clin. asst. surgeon Northwestern U., 1938-39, instr. surgery, 1940-41; asst. to Dr. Frederick Christopher, 1937-41; chief surgery VA Hosp., Tucson, 1947-49; surgeon ARAMCO, Saudi Arabia, 1950; pvt. practice, Chula Vista, Calif., 1952-82; staff Paradise Valley Hosp., Mercy Hosp. (San Diego); founder Monroe Clinic. Served from capt. to maj. AUS, 1942-47; PTO. Diplomate Am. Bd. Surgery. Fellow Soc. for Academic Achievement, Internat. Coll. Surgeons; mem. Soc. Gen. Surgeons of San Diego, Am. Med. Writers Assn., Assn. Mil. Surgeons, Am. Soc. Abdominal Surgeons (founding), Alpha Omega Alpha, Phi Beta Pi. Author: Medical Phrase Book with Vocabulary (also Spanish edit.). Office: 2 Palomar Dr Chula Vista CA 92011

MONROE, YVONNE LIS, marketing executive; b. Amsterdam, N.Y., June 14, 1957; d. Charles John and Rose Emily Lis; B.S. cum laude, SUNY, Albany, 1978; M.B.A., San Francisco State U., 1979. Adminstrv. asst. Office Lt. Gov. N.Y. State, Albany, 1975-78; price adminstrn. supr. Intel Corp., Santa Clara, Calif., 1979-80, corp. planner, 1980-81, customer mktg. engr., 1981-82; product mktg. mgr. Shugart Corp., Sunnyvale, Calif., 1982-84; product line mgr. Ampex Corp., Cupertino, Calif., 1984-85; product mgr. Fujitsu Am. Inc., San Jose, Calif., 1985—. Mem. Am. Mktg. Assn., Assn. M.B.A. Execs. Roman Catholic. Office: Fujitsu Am Inc 3055 Orchard Dr San Jose CA 95134

MONSEN, ELAINE RANKER, educator, nutritionist, editor; b. Oakland, Calif., June 6, 1935; d. Emery R. and Irene Stewart (Thorley) Ranker; m. Raymond Joseph Monsen, Jr., Jan. 21, 1959; 1 dau., Maren Ranker. B.A., U. Utah, 1956; M.S. (Mead Johnson grad. scholar), U. Calif., Berkeley, 1959, Ph.D. (NSF fellow), 1961; postgrad. NSF sci. faculty fellow, Harvard U., 1968-69. Dietetic intern Mass. Gen. Hosp., Boston, 1956-57; asst. prof. nutrition, lectr. biochemistry Brigham Young U., Provo, Utah, 1960-63; mem. faculty U. Wash., Seattle, 1963—; prof. nutrition and medicine U. Wash., 1976-84, chmn. div. human nutrition, dietetics and foods, 1977-82; chmn. Nutrition Studies Commn., 1969-83; vis. scholar Stanford U., 1971-72; mem. sci. adv. com. food fortification Pan-Am. Health Orgn., São Paulo, Brazil, 1972; tng. grant coordinator NIH, 1976—. Editor Jour. Am. Dietetic Assn., 1983—; author research papers on lipid metabolism, iron absorption; author: PCA Building Code Requirements for Reinforced Concrete, 1984, Partial Prestressing, From Theory to Practice, 1986. Bd. dirs. A Contemporary Theatre, Seattle, 1969-72; trustee, bd. dirs. Seattle Found., 1978—, vice chmn., 1987—; pres. Seattle bd. Santa Fe Chamber Music Festival, 1984-85. Grantee Nutrition Found., 1965-68, Agrl. Research Service, 1969—, Center Research Oral Biology, 1970-72. Mem. Am. Inst. Nutrition, Am. Soc. Clin. Nutrition (sec. 1987—), Am. Dietetic Assn., Soc. Nutrition Edn., Am. Soc. Parenteral and Enteral Nutrition, Wash. Heart Assn. (nutrition council 1973-76), Phi Beta Kappa, Phi Kappa Phi. Office: Human Nutrition Univ Wash DL-10 Seattle WA 98195

MONSON, DAVID SMITH, former congressman; b. Salt Lake City, June 20, 1945; s. Smith Weston and Dorothy (Brammer) M.; m. Julianne Johnson, Feb. 4, 1971; children: David Johnson, Traci Lyn, Marianne, Kari, Smith Douglas. BS in Acctg., U. Utah, 1970. C.P.A., Utah. Acct. Elmer Fox and Co., Salt Lake City, 1970-72; auditor State of Utah, Salt Lake City, 1973-76; lt. gov. State of Utah, 1977-84; mem. 99th Congress; mem. exec. com. Nat. Conf. Lt. Govs., 1978-84 mem. State Bd. Regents, 1981-84. Bd. dirs. Utah Soc. to Prevent Blindness; chmn. Utah Cancer Crusade, 1979-80; chmn. bd. Salt Lake County unit Am. Cancer Soc., 1980-81; govt. group chmn. United Way, 1979, assoc. campaign chmn., 1981, campaign chmn., 1982; treas. Utah Rep. party, 1975-76; trustee Ballet West, 1977-81, Travis Found., 1977-84; bd. dirs. Osmond Found., 1982-84. Recipient Outstanding Young Man Am. award, 1977, 81; named One of 3 Outstanding Young Men Utah Jaycees, 1980-81. Mem. Council State Govts. (v.p. Western conf. 1974-75). Republican. Mem. Ch. Jesus Christ Latter Day Saints. Home: 792 Northview Dr Salt Lake City UT 84103 Office: 445 E 200 S #44 Salt Lake City UT 84111 *

MONSON, MARCIA LELAND, geriatric social services administrator; b. Albert Lea, Minn., Jan. 13, 1959; d. Leon J. and Ann L. (Carney) L.; m. Lynn E. Monson, Aug. 18, 1984; 1 child, Daniel Leland. BA, Bethany Coll., 1981. Dir. admissions Good Samaritan Village, Hastings, Nebr., 1981-82, dir. social services, 1982—; mem. peer assistance cons. team Nebr. Health Care Assn., Hastings, 1983-86. Day camp dir. The Salvation Army, Hutchinson, Kans., 1981; advocate for task force to study Alzheimer's disease, Lincoln, Nebr., 1986. Mem. Nat. Assn. Social Workers. Democrat. Lutheran. Avocations: aerobic dancing, racquetball, bicycling, reading.

MONSON, THOMAS SPENCER, church ofcl., publishing co. exec.; b. Salt Lake City, Aug. 21, 1927; s. George Spencer and Gladys (Condie) M.; m. Frances Beverly Johnson, Oct. 7, 1948; children—Thomas L., Ann Frances, Clark Spencer. B.S. with honors in mktg, U. Utah, 1948; M.B.A., Brigham Young U., 1974, LL.D. (hon.), 1981. With Deseret News Press, Salt Lake City, 1948-64; mgr. Deseret News Press, 1962-64; mem. Council Twelve Apostles, Ch. of Jesus Christ of Latter Day Saints, 1963—, bishop, 1950-55; pres. Canadian Mission, 1959-62; pres., chmn. bd. Deseret News Pub. Co., 1977—; dir. Beneficial Life Ins. Co., Mountain States Tel. & Tel., Comml. Security Bank, Deseret Mgmt. Corp., Continental Western Life Ins. Co., Western Am. Life Ins. Co.; Utah bd. advisers Mountain States Tel. & Tel; pres. Printing Industry Utah, 1958; bd. dirs. Printing Industry Am., 1958-64. Mem. Utah State Bd. Regents; nat. exec. bd. Boy Scouts Am.; Trustee Brigham Young U.; mem. 1st Presidency The Ch. of Jesus Christ of the Latter Day Saints, 1985—, council Twelve Apostles, 1963-85. Served with USNR, 1945-46. Recipient Recognition award, 1964, Disting. Alumnus award U. Utah, 1966; Silver Beaver award Boy Scouts Am., 1971; Silver Buffalo award, 1978. Mem. Utah Assn. Sales Execs., U. Utah Alumni Assn. (dir.), Salt Lake Advt. Club, Alpha Kappa Psi. Club: Exchange (Salt Lake City). Office: 47 East S Temple St Salt Lake City UT 84111

MONTAG, DAVID MOSES, computer company executive; b. Los Angeles, Apr. 30, 1939; s. Gustave and Esther (Kessler) M.; student UCLA, 1957-61; m. Beverly Edythe Bowden, Sept. 24, 1967; children: Daniel Gershon, Esther Yael, Michael Menachem. Tech. writer L.H. Butcher Co., Los Angeles, 1961; phys. sci. lab. technician East Los Angeles Coll., Monterey Park, 1961—, planetarium lectr., 1963—; owner EDUCOMP, Monterey Park, Calif., 1980—; mktg. cons. Aquinas Computer Corp.; ednl. cons. for computer-assisted instrn. Bd. dirs. Or Chadash, Inc., Monterey Park, 1968—; v.p., bd. dirs. Coll. Religious Conf., 1968—. Mem. Assn. of Orthodox Jewish Scientists, Laser Inst. Am., AIAA. Home: 729 N Spaulding Ave Los Angeles CA 90046 Office: Box 384 Monterey Park CA 91754

MONTAGUE, JEAN LOUISE, speech and language pathologist; b. Northampton, Mass., July 23, 1951; d. Alfred Dwight Montague and Claire Louise (Healy) Smith. BA, U. Mass., 1974; MS, Ill. State U., 1978. Cert. speech pathologist, Colo., Mass. Speech language pathologist Green Bay (Wis.) Pub. Schs., 1978-81, Jefferson County Community Ctr., Arvada, Colo., 1981-86, Glasrock Home Health Care, Lakewood, Colo., 1986—. Bd. dirs. Cerebral Palsy Inc. of Northeastern Wis., Green Bay, 1979-81, United Cerebral Palsy of Denver, 1983-87. Mem. Am. Speech Lang. and Hearing Assn. (cert.), Colo. Speech Lang. and Hearing Assn., Kappa Delta Pi. Democrat. Mem. United Ch. of Christ. Avocations: skiing, hiking, swimming, travel. Office: Glasrock Home Health Care 1841 Wadsworth Blvd Lakewood CO 80215

MONTAGUE, PATRICK VINCENT, architect, educator; b. Santa Monica, Calif., June 14, 1955; s. Patrick Raymond Montague and Patricia Julia Ryan. A.A., Los Angeles Pierce Coll., 1979; student U.S. Naval Acad., 1973-74; student in Engring., Calif. State U.-Northridge, 1975-77; student Los Angeles Pierce Coll., 1977-79; Salesman, estimator Terry Bldg. Ctr., Tarzana, Calif., 1976-78; archtl. draftsman Gensler & Assocs., Architects, Los Angeles, 1979-81; archtl. job capt. Walker Assocs. Inc., Los Angeles, 1981-85; draftsman, job. capt. Gensler and Assoc., Irvine, Calif., 1985— ; Recipient award archtl. restoration for Los Angeles Olympic Com., Inst. Bus. Designers, Los Angeles, 1984. Mem. AIA (assoc.). Democrat. Roman Catholic. Home: 167 Esplanade Irvine CA 92715 Office: Gensler & Assocs 18201 Von Karman Ave Irvine CA 92714

MONTANA, JOSEPH C., professional football player; b. New Eagke, Pa., June 11, 1956; m. Jennifer Wallace; 1 child, Alexandra. B.B.A. in Mktg., U. Notre Dame, 1978. Quarterback San Francisco 49ers, 1979—; player NFC Championship Game, 1982, 84, 85, NFL All-Star Game, 1981, 83, 84, Super Bowl, 1982, 85, Pro Bowl, 1982-85; mem. NFL Championship Team, 1982, 85. Named Most Valuable Player Super Bowl, 1982, 85. Address: care San Francisco 49ers 711 Nevada St Redwood City CA 94061 *

MONTEITH, LEE ELMER, chemist; b. Nampa, Idaho, June 30, 1929; s. Frank E. and Alice B. (Wilkins) M.; m. Gretchen Denton Surry, June 12, 1954; children: David K., Daniel B. BS, U. Wash., 1951, MS, 1956. Diplomate Am. Bd. Indsl. Hygiene. Tech. graduate program Gen. Electric Hanford Works, Richland, Wash., 1952; research chemist Lawrence Radiation Lab. (now Lawrence Livermore Nat. Lab.), Livermore, Calif., 1956-62; bioscientist Bioastros. div. Boeing Co., Seattle, 1962-65; lectr. dept. environ. health U. Wash., Seattle, 1965—. Contbr. articles to profl. jours. Merit badge counselor, scoutmaster Boy Scouts Am., Seattle, 1969—; hunter safety instr. Wash. State Game Dept., Seattle, 1976—. Served to col. USAR, 1951-81. Recipient Silver Beaver award Chief SEattle Council Boy Scouts Am., 1980. Mem. AAAS, Am. Chem. Soc., Am. Indsl. Hygiene Assn. (pacific northwest sect. sec./treas. 1969, Disting. Indsl. Hygiene award 1985), Husky Alumni Marching Band, Order of the Arrow. Presbyterian. Lodge: Elks. Home: 1400 Bigelow Ave No Seattle WA 98109

MONTERMOSO, JUAN PABLO, computer company executive, consultant; b. Washington, Jan. 22, 1949; s. Juan Cargado and Anita Enriquez (Pablo) M.; m. Susana Bernardo Ramos, Dec. 29, 1970; children—Juan-Antonio, Kara-Noelle. B.S., Yale U., 1969; M.S., Harvard U., 1970; D.B.A., Harvard U., 1977. Acctg. systems mgr. Hewlett-Packard, Palo Alto, Calif., 1975-78, product mgr., Cupertino, Calif., 1981-83, intercontinental market devel. mgr., Palo Alto, 1983-86, mgr. bus. systems mktg. ctr., Cupertino, Calif., 1986—; v.p. mgmt. info. systems First Philippine Holdings, Metro Manila, 1978-81; asst. prof. Ateneo U., Metro Manila, 1970-71, 79-80; assoc. cons. SGV Group, Metro Manila, 1970-71; cons. Devel. Acad. of Philippines, Metro Manila, 1980-81, dir. EVSA Corp., Metro Manila. Contbr. articles to profl. jours. Pres. Resurrection Sch. Bd., Sunnyvale, Calif., 1983-85. Recipient Homecoming Scientist award Philippine Nat. Sci. Devel. Bd., 1978. Mem. Assn. Computing Machinery, Am. Prodn. and Inventory Control Soc., Tau Beta Pi. Democrat. Roman Catholic. Home: 715 Jura Way Sunnyvale CA 94087 Office: Hewlett-Packard 19091 Pruneridge Ave Bldg 46113 Cupertino CA 95014

MONTERO, DARREL MARTIN, sociologist, educator; b. Sacramento, Mar. 4, 1946; s. Tony and Evelyn (Hash) M.; m. Tara Kathleen McLaughlin, July 6, 1975; children: David Paul, Lynn Elizabeth, Laura Ann. AB, Calif. State U., 1970; MA, UCLA, 1972, PhD, 1974. Postgrad. researcher Japanese-Am. Research Project UCLA, 1971-73, dir. research, 1973-75; assoc. head Program on Comparative Ethnic Studies, Survey Research Ctr. UCLA, 1973-75; asst. prof. sociology Case Western Res. U., Cleve., 1975-76; asst. prof. urban studies, research sociologist Pub. Opinion Survey, dir. urban ethnic research program U. Md., College Park, 1976-79; assoc. prof., dir, urban ethnic research program Ariz. State U., Tempe, 1979—; cons. research sect. Viewer Sponsored TV Found., Los Angeles, Berrien E. Moore Law Office, Inc., Gardena, Calif., 1973. Author: Japanese Americans: Changing Patterns of Ethnic Affiliation Over Three Generations, 1980, Urban Studies, 1978, Vietnamese Americans: Patterns of Resettlement and Socioeconomic Adaptation in the United States, 1979, Social Problems; mem. editorial bd. Humanity and Society, 1978—. Served with U.S. Army, 1966-72. Mem. Am. Sociol. Assn., Am. Assn. Pub. Opinion Research (exec. council, standards com.), Am. Ednl. Research Assn., Council of Social Work Edn., Soc. Study of Social Problems, D.C. Sociol. Soc., Am. Soc. Pub. Adminstrn., Nat. Assn. social Workers. Home: 1444 W Kiva Ave Mesa AZ 85202 Office: Ariz State U Sch Social Work Tempe AZ 85281

MONTEVERDI, JOHN PAUL, meteorology educator; b. San Francisco, Apr. 7, 1946; s. John Alphonse and Anna Rita (Piatanesi) M. AB in Geology, U. Calif., Berkeley, 1968, MA in Geography, 1970, PhD in Climatology, 1978. Research assoc. dept. geography U. Calif., Berkeley, 1968-78, lectr. dept. geography, 1978-80; lectr. U. Calif., Davis, 1978; cons. Enviros, Inc., Los Altos, Calif., 1972-76; assoc. prof. meteorology San Francisco State U., 1978—, chmn. dept. Geoscis., 1986—; cons. meteorologist, Oakland, 1978—. Contbr. articles to profl. jours. Mem. Calif. Acad. Sci., Am. Meteorol. Soc. (chpt. officer 1979-83, chmn. 1981, treas. 1982). Club: East Bay Striders (Oakland) (treas.). Avocations: running, model trains, bicycle riding, severe thunder storm chasing. Home: 4425 View St Oakland CA 94611 Office: San Francisco State U Dept Geoscis 1600 Holloway Ave San Francisco CA 94132

MONTGOMERY, DOUGLAS CARTER, industrial engineering educator; b. Roanoke, Va., June 5, 1943; s. Gordon Ashby and Gladys (Reed) M.; m. Martha Ellen Price, Aug. 7, 1965 (div. July 1982); children: Meredith, Colin, Neil. BSIE, Va. Poly. Inst., 1965, MS, 1967, PhD, 1969. Prof. indsl. systems engring. Ga. Inst. Tech., Atlanta, 1969-84; prof. mfg. engring., dir. indsl. engring. U. Wash., Seattle, 1984—, John M. Fluke disting. prof. mfg. engring., 1985—; cons. IBM, various locations, 1976—, Coca-Cola Co., Atlanta, 1970-84, Boeing Electronics Co., Seattle, 1984—, other mfg. companies. Author 6 books including: Intoduction to Statistical Quality Control, 1985, Design and Analysis of Experiments, 2d edition, 1984. Named John M. Fluke Disting. Prof. of Mfg. U. Wash., 1985. Mem. Inst. Indsl. Engrs., Soc. Mfg. Engrs., Am. Statistical Assn., Am. Soc. Quality Control, Ops. Research Soc. Am. Avocation: golf. Home: 9555 45th Ave NE Seattle WA 98115 Office: U Wash Dept Mech Engring FU-10 Seattle WA 98195

MONTGOMERY, GERALD WILLIAM, clergyman, consultant; b. Wright County, Minn., Apr. 29, 1939; s. Joseph Arthur and Marie Maude (Ritter) M.; m. Ruth Ann Huntsinger, Dec. 30, 1960; children—Lisa, Eric. B.A., Macalester Coll., 1961; Ph.D., Calif. Coast U., 1976; postgrad. United Theol. Sem. Twin Cities, 1965-67, Vancouver Sch. Theology, 1982, Claremont Sch. Theology, 1983. Ordained to ministry United Ch. of Christ, 1984; reporter UPI, Mpls., 1960; reporter, editor St. Paul Pioneer Press, 1960-69; mng. editor Port Angeles Daily News, Wash., 1969; reporter The Seattle Times, 1969-72; dir. King County Wash. Emergency Med. Services, 1973-75; pres. Communications Assn., Seattle, 1976-78; dir. communications URS Engrs., Seattle, 1978-81; owner Montgomery Communications, Seattle, 1980-83; pastor Shepherd of the Lakes, Tacoma, 1983-87; sr. pastor First Congl. Ch., Oakland, 1987—; adj. prof. bus. adminstrn. Central Wash. U., Edmonds, 1983; pres. Minn. Rescue and First Aid Assn., 1966; mem. exec. com. Am. Heart Assn. Wash., 1973-83; mem. No. Calif. Conf. United Ch. of Christ, 1987—; chaplain Olympia Police Dept. Author: The Selling of You, 1980, Are You Man Enough, 1973. Served with USNR, 1960-66. Robert Wood Johnson Found. grantee in emergency med. services, 1974.

MONTGOMERY, JAMES E., protective services official. m. Sheran Hill; children: Brooke, Scott. BS, U. Louisville, 1973, MS, 1977. With Nat. Exec. Inst.-Police Found., Idaho, 1978-80, Law Enforcement Exec. Devel. Seminar, Idaho, 1985, Idaho Peace Officer's Standards and Tng. Council, 1984, 85, 86. Chmn. Buechel Christian Sch. Bd., Louisville; past elder governing bd. 1st Alliance Ch., Louisville. Office: Boise Police Dept 7200 Barrister Drive Boise ID 83704

MONTGOMERY, JUDITH KOVACICH, school system administrator, speech-language pathologist. BS in Speech Pathology, U. Wis., Milw., 1969; MA in Speech Pathology, Calif. State U., Long Beach, 1973; PhD in Edn., Claremont Grad. Sch., 1986. Cert. tchr., community coll. tchr., physically handicapped tchr., ednl. adminstr., Calif; lic. speech pathologist, Calif. Speech therapist Los Angeles City Sch. Dist., 1969-70; speech-lang. specialist Santa Ana (Calif.) Unified Sch. Dist., 1970-72; speech-lang. pathologist Plavan Sch. Orthopedically and Multiple-Handicapped Students Fountain Valley (Calif.) Sch. Dist., 1972-77, program dir. Plavan Sch. Orthopedically and Multiple-Handicapped Students, 1977-80, elem. sch. prin. Cox Sch., 1980-84, dir. program/student services, 1984—; pvt. practice speech-lang. pathology, Newport Beach, Calif., 1974-79; instr. Golden West Coll., 1976, Calif. State U., Long Beach, 1976—, Calif. Luth. Coll., 1980-82, Santa Ana Coll., 1982—; vis. lectr. U. Calif., Irvine, 1980—. Author: (TV documentary) To Say I Am, 1980; contbr. articles to profl. jours. Mem. citizen's adv. com. Los Angeles Olympic Organizing Com., 1982-84; mem. project devel. com. Jr. League, Newport Harbor, Calif., 1983, chairperson tng. corps, 1984, mem. future planning com., 1985; active Discovery Mus. Orange County, Calif., 1985—; bd. dirs. Fountain Valley Ednl. Found., 1982—, Vols. in Action, 1982-84; chair Foster Care Video Commn., 1986; chief fin. officer Ct. Appointed Spl. Advocates, 1987. Named Orange County (Calif.) Outstanding Educator of Yr., 1975. Fellow Am. Speech-Lang.-Hearing Assn. (cert., assoc. materials editor jour. 1981-85, editorial cons. Jour. Speech and Hearing Disorders 1981-84, legis. council, chair credentials com. of legis. council 1982-83, Cert. Clin. Competence standards validation rev. adv. com. 1985—, numerous other coms. and adv. councils, 1st Place Media award 1980), Calif. Speech-Lang.-Hearing Assn. (master clinician's subcom., chair ann. conf. 1976, chair southwest regional conf. 1977, dist. dir. 1978-80, state bd. dirs. 1978-84, commr. confs. and programs 1980-84, pres.-elect 1985-87, pres. 1987-89, several other coms. and panels); mem. Internat. Project Communication Aids for Speech Impaired (U.S. adv. group), Internat. Soc. Augmentative & Alternative Communication (editorial cons. jour. 1984—, conf. program com. 1984), Alexander Graham Bell Assn., Assn. Edn. Severely Handicapped, Council Exceptional Children (v.p. Calif. chpt. communication disorders div. 1980, gifted edn. div., lang. com., counselor DCCD), So. Calif. Communication Group (advocacy com. 1977, bd. dirs. 1979-82, chair. ann. conf. 1981), Inst. Study Severely Handicapped, Assn. Calif. Sch. Adminstrs. (pupil personnel com. 1984-85, research presenter 1984), Fountain Valley Leadership Assn. (pupil personnel and spl. edn. com., 1984-86). Avocations: traveling, sailing, reading, tennis, aerobics. Home: 35 Lakeview Irvine CA 92714 Office: Fountain Valley Pub Schs 17210 Oak St Fountain Valley CA 92708

MONTGOMERY, LARRY DALE, biologist; b. Longview, Wash., Feb. 24, 1950; s. Edward Dale and Wanda Lea (Collins) M.; m. Linda Fay Hensley, Nov. 17, 1978 (div. Dec. 1980). BA in Biol. Scis., Cen. Wash. State Coll., 1973. Lic. fissionable material handler; cert. pool/spa operator. Radiochemistry technician Westingtonhouse Hanford, Richland, Wash., 1974-76; research asst. Pacific Northwest Labs., Richland, 1976-81; prin. code enforcement officer Municipality of Anchorage, 1982-83, environ. sanitarian, 1985—; engring. tech. Alaska Environ. Control Services, Anchorage, 1983, dir. environ. service, 1984-85. Contbr. articles to profl. jours. Mem. Internat. Assn. Milk, Food, and Environ. Sanitarians, AAAS, Am. Pub. Health Assn., Nat. Environ. Health Assn. (registered sanitarian), Nat. Geog. Soc., N.Y. Acad. Scis., Conf. for Food Protection. Democrat. Baptist. Home: 2630 N Tahiti Loop Anchorage AK 99507 Office: Dept Health Human Services Municipality of Anchorage 825 L St Anchorage AK 99519

MONTGOMERY, MAX COLLIER, civil engineer, consultant; b. Pryor, Okla., July 26, 1937; s. Collier Max and Ruby (Davis) M.; m. Arlene Gail Altizer, June 8, 1958; children—Monty, Mark. A.A., Sheridan Jr. Coll., 1958; B.S., U. Wyo., 1960. Registered profl. engr., Calif., Idaho, Nev., Wyo.; cert. in land surveying, Idaho; cert. water rights surveyor, Nev. Civil engr. Dept. Agr. Forest Service, San Bernardino, Calif., 1969-72, St. Anthony, Idaho, 1972-75, Challis, Idaho, 1975-78, Reno, Nev., 1978-83; owner, operating Peak Engring. Inc., Sparks, Nev., 1980—; civil engr. Nev. Health Div., Carson City, 1984-85; sr. civil engr. Chilton Engring., 1985-86, Nev. Dept. Prisons, 1987—; bd. dirs. Nev. Internat. Trade Exchange, Sparks, 1981—. Mem. Nat. Soc. Profl. Engrs. (bd. dirs. Nev. chpt. 1982—). Designer solar homes; inventor dry gold processor.

MONTGOMERY, ROBERT LOUIS, systems engineer, physical chemist; b. San Francisco, Nov. 20, 1935; s. Louis Clyde and Fay Elythe (Myers) M.; m. Patricia Helen Cook, Mar. 17, 1962; children: Cynthia Elaine, Jeanette Louise, Cecelia Irene, Howard Edwin. BS in Chemistry, U. Calif., Berkeley, 1956; PhD in Phys. Chemistry, Okla. State U., 1975. Registered profl. engr., Kans., Tex., Colo. Phys. chemist U.S. Bur. Mines, Reno, 1956-62; NSF predoctoral fellow Okla. State U., Stillwater, 1963-66; sr. engr. Boeing Co., Wichita, Kans., 1966-75; postdoctoral fellow Rice U., Houston, 1975-77, sr. research assoc., 1982-84; tech. data engr. M.W. Kellogg Co., Houston, 1977-82; staff engr. Martin Marietta, Denver, 1984—. Contbr. articles to profl. jours. Mem. Am. Chem. Soc., Profl. Engrs. Colo., Am. Soc. for Metals, AIAA, Sigma Xi. Lodge: Moose. Avocations: amateur radio, skiing. Home: 9933 Fairwood St Littleton CO 80125 Office: Martin Marietta Denver Aerospace PO Box 179 Denver CO 80201

MONTGOMERY, ROBERT NEAL, human resource development consultant; b. San Francisco, May 1, 1947; s. Daniel George and Helen Elizabeth (Groskopf) M.; m. Jane Murel Franklin, May 29, 1967; children: Matthew, Joshua. AA, San Mateo Jr. Coll., 1967; BA, Calif. State U., San Francisco, 1970; MS, Calif. State U., Hayward, 1972; postgrad., The Fielding Inst., 1984—. Field mgr. passenger services TransWorld Airlines, San Francisco, 1978-83; coordinator profl. devel. tng. TransWorld Airlines, Kansas City, Mo., 1976-83; sr. facilitator quality circles Monolithic Memories Inc., Santa Clara, Calif., 1983-85; mgr. improvement programs Monolithic Memories, Santa Clara, Calif., 1985—. Mem. Internat. Assn. Quality Circles (pres. 1984-86, chpt. achievement award 1984, 85), Bay Area Orgn. Devel. Network, Am. Soc. Tng. Devel. Democrat. Roman Catholic. Avocations: snow skiing, snorkeling, bicycling, traveling. Home: 420 Nimitz Ave Redwood City CA 94061 Office: Monolithic Memories 2175 Mission College Blvd Santa Clara CA 95054

MONTGOMERY, ROGER, architecture educator; b. N.Y.C., May 28, 1925; s. Graham Livingston and Ann Katharine (Cook) M.; m. Mary Elizabeth Hoyt, Apr. 23, 1949 (dec. Feb. 1980); children: Richard W., Thomas V., John G., Peter G. Student, Oberlin Coll., 1942-44, 47, N.C. State U., 1953-55; MArch, Harvard U., 1957. Architect Zeller & Hunter, Springfield, Ohio, 1948-53; assoc. prof. architecture Washington U., St. Louis, 1957-64, prof. architecture, 1964-67; architect, planner Anselevicius & Montgomery, St. Louis, 1957-70; prof. U. Calif., Berkeley, 1967—, assoc. dean environ. design, 1976-79, 81-84; pres. Calif. Council on Archtl. Edn., 1986, bd. dirs., 1983-87. Co-author: Architecture in State of Washington, 1980; co-editor: Housing in America, 1979, Housing Policy of the 1980's; contbr. articles to profl. jours. mem. Redevel. Commn., Berkeley, 1978-80, pres. 1980. Served as pvt. U.S. Army, 1945-47. Mem. Am. Planning Assn., Urban Land Inst., Planning Network. Office: Univ Calif 228 Wurster Hall Berkeley CA 94720

MONTGOMERY, VERNON CHARLES, training systems administrator; b. Lake Charles, La., Oct. 30, 1943; s. Vernon Charles and Rae (Houston) M.; m. Joan Lynn Tremblay, June 16, 1973. B.S. in Bus. Adminstrn., La. State U., 1966. Sales mgr. Goodwill Industries, Sacramento, Calif., 1973-76; field rep. Southland Corp., Sacramento, 1976-79, zone tng. mgr., 1979-80, div. tng. mgr., Seattle, 1980—. Served to capt. USAF, 1966-78, Vietnam. Named Outstanding staff mem. North Pacific div. Southland Corp., 1983. Mem. Am. Soc. Tng. and Devel., Scabbard and Blade, Sigma Chi. Republican. Presbyterian. Home: 14724 169 Ave SE Renton WA 98056 Office: Southland Corp 1035 Andover Park W Tukwila WA 98188

MONTGOMERY, WILLIAM FREDRIC, accountant; b. Los Angeles, Aug. 25, 1921; s. Raymond R. and Cora L. (Dock) M.; student, Sawyer Bus. Coll., 1946-47; student law LaSalle U., 1948-50; m. Ave Maria T. Devine, Oct. 13, 1946; children—Ave Maria, Sarah Maria, Margaret Mary, Kathleen B., William Fredric. Accounting trainee Paul E. Bain & Asso., Pasadena, Calif., 1947-49; comptroller Diggins Enterprize Corp., 1949-53; mgr., tax cons. Bookkeepers Bus. Service Co., 1953-57; pub. accountant, tax cons. William F. Montgomery, Pub. Accountant, Sacramento, 1957—. Served with AUS, 1942-45. C.P.A., Calif. Mem. Soc. Am. Accountants, Am. Soc. Fed. Tax Accountants, Nat. Soc. C.P.A.'s, Soc. Calif. Accountants, Sacramento Exchange Club, Holy Name Soc. (treas.). Moose, Woodmen, K.C. (3 deg.) Club: Valley Hi Country. Home: 42 Nurata Ave Sacramento CA 95823 Office: 3823 V St Sacramento CA 95817

MONTONI, ANDREA MANGINO, publishing executive; b. Portland, Maine, Feb. 22, 1956; d. Samuel Albert and Pauline (Beem) Mangino; m. Richard Alphonse Montoni, June 25, 1982. BS, Emerson Coll., 1978. Retail promotion dir. for New Eng. A&M Records, Inc., Boston, 1978-79; regional promotion and publicity mgr. Columbia Pictures, N.Y.C., 1980-82; pub. relations and spl. events dir. May D&F, Denver, 1982-83; promotion dir. KPKE-FM Radio, Denver, 1983-84; pub. relations mgr. The Denver Post, 1984—. Pub. relations vol. Rocky Mountain Adoption Exchange, Denver, 1983-84; bd. dirs. Child Abuse Prevention Vols., Inc., Denver, 1986—. Recipient Outstanding Promotion Efforts award A&M Records, Inc., Los Angeles, 1978. Mem. Denver Advt. Fedn., Denver Internat. Film Soc. (bd. dirs. 1986—), Internat. Assn. Bus. Communicators (Silver Quill award of merit 1986, award of excellence 1986, Gold Quill award of excellence 1987), Pub. Relations Soc. Am., Internat. Alliance Theatrical Stage Employees, Publicists Guild Am. Roman Catholic. Avocations: skiing, bicycling, phys. fitness. Office: The Denver Post Inc 650 15th St Denver CO 80202

MONTOYA, JOSEPH B., state senator; b. Rocky Ford, Colo., Apr. 30, 1939; s. Joseph Sacramento and Rosalia Maria (Santisteban) M.; m. Pilar Gonzalez, Mar. 19, 1960; children—Cristina, Pilar, Joseph III, Marisa. A.A., Mt. San Antonio Coll.; B.A., UCLA. Mem. City Council, LaPuente, Calif., 1968-70, mayor, 1970-72; mem. Calif. Assembly, 1972-78; mem. Calif. Senate, 1978—; mem. presdl. commn. U.S. Ct. Appeals (9th cir.), 1978-80. Bd. dirs., trustee Walter Kaitz Found., Crippled Children's Soc. Served with USAF, 1957-61. Democrat. Roman Catholic. Office: State Capitol Room 5064 Sacramento CA 95814

MONTOYA, MARY ANN, federal agency employee; b. Albuquerque, Mar. 2, 1942; d. Joseph M. and Connie Montoya. B in Art Edn., U. N.Mex., 1971. Freelance photographer Albuquerque, 1972-73; with Social Security Adminstrn., Albuquerque, 1973—; pres., owner Interior Cons., Albuquerque, 1983—. Mem. Federally Employed Women (pres. 1985-86), N.Mex. Minority Devel. Council, Albuquerque Women in Bus. Roman Catholic. Avocations: tennis, skiing, photography, designing, writing.

MONTOYA, STEVE LEO, social worker, consultant; b. Guadalupita, N.Mex., Oct. 26, 1949; s. Steve and Angie (Martinez) M.; m. Erlinda Gloria Telles, July 30, 1977; 1 child, Raquel Telles. BA, Coll. Santa Fe, 1973; MSW, U. Chgo., 1975. Cert. social worker, N.Mex. Social worker Albuquerque Pub. Schs., 1975-84; clin. social worker Albuquerque Family and Child Guidance Ctr., 1984—; clin. assoc. U. N.Mex. Dept. Psychiatry, Albuquerque, 1984—, minority cons., 1985—. Mem. Nat. Assn. Social Workers (peer rev. cons., treas. N.Mex. chpt. 1985—), Acad. Cert. Social Workers (clin. diplomate), Pi Gamma Mu. Democrat. Roman Catholic. Avocations: jogging, poetry writing, photography.

MONTOYA, SUSAN MARIE, infosystems specialist; b. Milw., Oct. 22, 1948; d. Ralph Walter and Beatrice (Zeimet) Mann; m. Emmanuel L. Montoya, Sept. 5, 1970; 1 child, Christina Marie. BSBA, U. So. Colo., 1982. Controller Am. Appraisal, Milw., 1967-68; mgr. acctg. Indsl. Gas Products & Supply, Inc., Pueblo, 1981-84; mgr. personnel Indsl. Gas Product & Supply, Inc., Pueblo, 1974-84, systems analyst, 1982—, mgr. info. systems, 1982—. Bd. dirs. YMCA, Pueblo, 1984-86. Mem. Adminstrv. Mgmt. Soc. (v.p. 1985—). Office: Indsl Gas Prod Supp 500 W 3d Pueblo CO 81003

MONTROSE, DONALD W., bishop; b. Denver, May 13, 1923. Student, St. John's Sem., Calif. Ordained priest Roman Catholic Ch., 1949. Aux. bishop Roman Cath. Ch., Los Angeles, 1983; bishop Diocese of Stockton, Calif., 1985—. Office: Diocese of Stockton 1105 N Lincoln St Stockton CA 95203 *

MONZINGO, ROBERT ALLEN, electrical engineer; b. Santa Monica, Calif., July 18, 1938; s. Carroll Willard Monzingo and Hollis Ruth (Gilliem) Foster; m. Mary Helen Hanf, Mar. 16, 1974; children: David, Darren. BS, Stanford U., 1960; MS, U. Ariz., 1962; ScD, Wash. U., 1966. Registered prof. engr., Calif. Project engr. Sperry Flight Systems, Phoenix, 1962-63; staff engr. Hughes Aircraft Co., Los Angeles, 1966-69, sr. scientist, 1971—; dir. research Sycom Inc., Anaheim, Calif., 1969-71. Co-author: Introduction to Adaptive Arrays, 1980. Mem. IEEE (sr.), N.Y. Acad. Scis., Sigma Xi. Democrat. Unitarian. Avocations: piano playing, running. Office: Hughes Aircraft Co PO Box 92919 Airport Sta Los Angeles CA 90009

MOODY, GEORGE FRANKLIN, banker; b. Riverside, Calif., July 28, 1930; s. William Clifford and Mildred R. (Scott) M.; m. Mary Jane Plank, Jan. 19, 1950; children: Jeffrey George, Jane Ellen Moody Fowler, John Franklin, Joseph William. Student, Riverside City Coll., 1948-50; grad. with honors, Pacific Coast Banking Sch., 1963. Bus. officer U. Calif., Riverside, 1950-52; with Security Pacific Nat. Bank, Los Angeles, 1953—, dir. personnel, v.p., 1970-71, sr. v.p. inland div. adminstrn., 1971-73, exec. v.p., 1973-78, vice chmn., 1978-80, pres., chief exec. officer, 1985—; pres., chief operating officer Security Pacific Corp., Los Angeles, 1985—, also bd. dirs. Chief prin. officer, mem. nat. bd. govs., ARC, chmn. exec. com. 1979-80; bd. dirs. Found., U.S. Olympic Com., chmn. Western region, 1981-84; trustee Calif. Neighborhood Housing Service Found., Jr. Achievement So. Calif.; trustee, mem. exec. com. Pomona Coll.; pres. Los Angeles area council Boy Scouts Am., 1980—; past bd. dirs. Los Angeles Music Ctr. Operating Co., Los Angeles United Way, Calif. Econ. Devel. Corp.; past. bd. dirs., past v.p. Hollywood Presbyn. Med. Ctr., Calif. Econ. Devel. Corp.; past chmn. Music Ctr. Unified Fund, Invest-In-Am.; past trustee Calif. Mus. Found., Com. for Econ. Devel., Washington; past. mem. bd. govs. Calif. Community Found. Mem. Los Angeles C. of C. (past pres.), U.S. C. of C. (bd. dirs.), Colorado River Assn. (pres.), Am. Bankers Assn. (bd. dirs.), Calif. Bankers Assn., Assn. Res. City Bankers, Merchants and Mfrs. Assn. (past chmn.), Performing Arts Council (former gov.). Republican. Clubs: California, Los Angeles Country, Hacienda Country. Address: Security Pacific Corp 333 S Hope St Los Angeles CA 90071

MOODY, KENTON JAMES, nuclear chemist; b. Vallejo, Calif., Dec. 5, 1954; s. James Henry and Arleen Marie (Taylor) M.; m. Zoe Dominique Randolph, Aug. 25, 1982; 1 child, James Alexander. AA, Ventura Coll., 1975; BS, U. Calif., Santa Barbara, 1977; PhD, U. Calif., Berkeley, 1983. Research asst. U. Calif., Berkeley, 1978-83; staff scientist Lawrence Berkeley Lab., 1983, Gesellschaft für Schwerionforschung, Darmstadt, Fed. Republic Germany, 1983-85; nuclear chemist Lawrence Livermore Nat. Lab., Livermore, Calif., 1985—. Contbr. numerous articles to profl. jours. Mem. AAAS, Am. Phys. Soc. Office: Lawrence Livermore Nat Lab L-232 PO Box 808 Livermore CA 94550

MOODY, THOMAS MONROE, wildlife supervisor; b. Santa Fe, Nov. 7, 1946; s. Tom and Juanita Fern (Page) M.; m. Delpha Jeanne Glover, May 30, 1969; children—Thomas R., Norman Clay, Sterling Levi. B.S., N.Mex. State U., 1968, M.S., 1970. Cert. law enforcement officer, N.Mex. Conservation officer N.Mex. Dept. Game and Fish, Los Alamos, 1970-72, fisheries mgr., Roswell, 1972-75, hatchery mgr., Jemez Springs, 1975-77, hatchery biologist, Santa Fe, 1977-79, asst. chief hatcheries, 1979-84, asst. chief law enforcement, 1984—. Recipient Big Horn Sheep award N.Mex. State U. chpt. Wildlife Soc., 1967. Mem. Am. Fisheries Soc., Am. Fisheries Soc. (pres. Ariz.-N.Mex. chpt. 1982-83). Democrat. Mem. Christian Ch. Home: 2451 Camino Capitan Santa Fe NM 87505 Office: NM Dept Game and Fish State Capitol Villagra Bldg Santa Fe NM 87503

MOON, FREDERICK FRANKLIN, college administrator; b. N.Y.C., Aug. 12, 1942; s. F. Franklin and Julia (Andrus) M.; m. Louise Rix; children: Elizabeth, Julia. BA, Amherst Coll., 1964; MBA, Harvard U., 1966. Asst. treas. Morgan Guaranty Trust, N.Y.C., 1966-81; treas. Emma Willard Sch., Troy, N.Y., 1971; v.p. Pomona Coll., Claremont, Calif., 1975—; bd. dirs. Investor Responsibility Research Ctr., Washington, 1980—. Pres. Padua Hills Inc., Claremont, 1982—; trustee Mt. San Antonio Gardens, Claremont, 1980—; bd. dirs. Julia Dyckman Andrus Meml., 1986—, John E. Andrus Meml., 1986—, Tina C. Found. Mem. Assn. Calif. Colls. and Univs. Fin. Services Corp. (chmn. bd. 1982—). Home: 137 N College Ave Claremont CA 91711 Office: Pomona Coll 333 College Way Claremont CA 91711

MOON, LYNNE HARA, personnel and training executive; b. Honolulu, Dec. 3, 1950; d. James and Gladys (Nakama) Hara. B.A. in Communications and Sociology magna cum laude, U. Wash., 1972; M.A., U. Hawaii, 1979. Research assoc. Hawaii Employers Council, Honolulu, 1976-77; personnel/tng. mgr. Liberty House, Honolulu, 1979-80, employee relations mgr., 1980-81; employee relations and mgmt. devel. mgr. Duty Free Shoppers, Honolulu, 1981-82, corp. dir. tng. and devel., 1982—. Bd. dirs. Jr. Achievement, Honolulu, 1982-84, advisor, 1976; coach J. Roger Basketball League, Honolulu, 1973. Wash. Advt. Scholar, 1972; East-West Ctr. degree scholar, 1972-74. Mem. Women in Communications, Am. Soc. Personnel Adminstrs., Am. Soc. Tng. and Devel., Internat. Platform Assn., Phi Beta Kappa, Alpha Kappa Delta, Alpha Lambda Delta. Democrat. Address: 5340 Liwai St Honolulu HI 96821 Office: Duty Free Shoppers 655 Montgomery 18th Floor San Francisco CA 94111 Office: 655 Montgomery St 18th Floor San Francisco CA 94111

MOON, MARJORIE RUTH, former state treasurer; b. Pocatello, Idaho, June 16, 1926; d. Clark Blakeley and Ruth Eleanor (Gerhart) M. Student, Pacific U., 1944-46; A.B. in Journalism cum laude, U. Wash., 1948. Reporter, Pocatello Tribune, 1944; Reporter Caldwell (Idaho) News-Tribune, 1948-50; Salt Lake City bur. chief Deseret News, Boise, Idaho, 1950-52; owner, operator Idaho Pioneer Statewide (weekly newspaper), Boise, 1952-55; founder, pub. Garden City (Idaho) Gazette, 1954-68; partner Sawtooth Lodge, Grandjean, Idaho, 1958-60, Modern Press, Boise, 1958-61; treas. State of Idaho, Boise, 1963-86. Chmn. Idaho Commn. on Women's Programs, 1971-74; del. Dem. Nat. Nominating Conv., 1972, 76, 80, 84; Dem. candidate Lt. Gov., Idaho, 1986. Mem. Nat. Assn. State Treas. (sec.-treas. 1976-78, regional v.p. 1978-79, 84-85), Nat. Fedn. Press Women, Idaho Press Women (past pres.). Congregationalist. Clubs: Soroptimists (Boise) (pres. club 1971-73), Women's Ltd. (Boise) (pres. 1984, dir. 1983-84). dir.). Office: 2227 Heights Dr Boise ID 83702

MOON, THOMAS EDWARD, epidemiologist, biometrician, educator; b. Pontiac, Mich., Aug. 16, 1943; m. Rebecca Ruth Fossdal, Sept. 5, 1964; 1 child, Avery Moon. BS in Math., No. Ill. U., 1965; MS in Stats., U. Chgo., 1967; PhD in Biostats. and Epidemiology, U. Calif., Berkeley, 1973. Asst. prof. biometrics MD Anderson Hosp., Houston, 1973-77; asst. dir. Ariz. Cancer Ctr., Tucson, 1977-86, head biometry computing and epidemiology unit, 1977-86, research prof. dept. family and community medicine, internal medicine, 1983-86, chief epidemiology and biometry sect., dept. family and community medicine, 1986—; mem. rev. com. cancer control intervention NCI, Washington, 1982—; mem. biostats. com. Mulitcenter Diltiazem Post Infarction Trials, 1982-86. Mem. Am. Cancer Soc. (bd. dirs. Ariz. chpt 1976-83), Am. Soc. Clin. Oncology, Am. Assn. Cancer Research, Soc. Epidemiology Research, Sigma Xi. Home: 770 W Las Lomitas Tucson AZ 85704 Office: Ariz Cancer Ctr 1501 N Campbell Ave Tucson AZ 85724

MOONEY, PATRICK JOSEPH, research gerontologist, biochemist; b. Chgo., July 21, 1930; s. Hugh Nicholas and Dorothy (Montgomery) M.; B.Sc., Roosevelt U., Chgo., 1965; children—Mary Kimera, Michael Kevin, Mary Kathleen. Constrn. and devel. engr., Chgo., 1950-64; archtl. supt. U. Ill., Chgo., 1964-67; bus. mgmt. systems cons., Chgo. and San Diego, Calif., 1969-76; co-founder, pres. Supernutrition Life-Extension Research, Inc., San Francisco, 1976—, Forever Young, San Francisco, 1977—; research and teaching assoc. Am. Inst. Biosocial Research, Tacoma, 1979—; founder, dir. Inst. Human Ecology, San Francisco, 1980-81; cons. balancing body chemistry for life-extension. Recipient award for outstanding contbns. to field of nutrition, Internat. Coll. Applied Nutrition, 1980, Manilla Med. Soc., 1984. Author: Supernutrition, the Answer to Aging, Wrinkles and the Degenerative Diseases, 1978; (with Hans J. Kugler) A Computerized Diet Analysis and Health Risk Evaluation, 1979. Office: 531 44th Ave San Francisco CA 94121

MOORE, ANDREW BROOKS, quality assurance scientist; b. Walton County, Ga., June 27, 1952; s. Ulysses Grand and Clare (Steward) M. BS, U. Ga., 1973, MS, 1976; PhD, U. Mass., 1980. Staff scientist Grocery Mfrs. Am., Washington, 1980-85; quality assurance auditor Dole Processed Foods, San Jose, Calif., 1985—. Mem. Inst. Food Technologists, Can. Inst. Food Sci. and Tech., Am. Chem. Soc., Am. Pub. Health Assn., Am. Soc. Microbiology. Republican. Methodist. Home: 516 N 4th St San Jose CA 95112 Office: Dole Processed Foods 100 Park Plaza Ctr San Jose CA 95113

MOORE, BEVERLY BARRETT, library director; b. Evanston, Ill., Mar. 17, 1934; d. James Henry and Louise (Miller) Barrett; m. James O. Moore, Oct. 6, 1957 (div. Sept. 1967); children: Louis Barrett, Ann Louise Cushman. AA, Hutchinson Jr. Coll., 1954; BA, U. No. Colo., 1970; MA in Library Scis., Denver U. Br. librarian Pueblo (Colo.) Library Dist., 1966-70; documents librarian U. So. Colo., Pueblo, 1970-74, head catalog librarian, 1974-76, library dir., 1970—; co-chair Colo. Acad. Library com., 1982—; treas. Arkansas Valley Regional Library Services System, 1984—. Coauthor: Colorado Academic Master Plan, 1985. Mem. Colo. Library Assn. (pres. 1985), ALA, LWV, AAUW, Beta Phi Mu. Democrat. Congregationalist. Avocations: needlepoint, reading, travel. Home: 1719 Jerry Murphy Rd Pueblo CO 81001 Office: Univ Southern Colo Pueblo CO 81001-4901

MOORE, BRUCE WALLACE, county ofcl.; b. LaJolla, Calif., Feb. 23, 1937; s. George R. and Katherine E. M.; B.S., Calif. State U., Fresno, 1970, M.B.A., 1970; m. Verna Christoffersen children—Katherine, Laura, Ian. Asst. mgr. Fresno (Calif.) Flood Control Dist., 1972-73; dep. exec. dir. Fresno Housing Authority, 1973-75, exec. dir., 1975-77; exec. dir. Monterey County (Calif.) Housing Authority, 1977—. Served with Army N.G., 1959. Mem. Nat. Assn. Housing and Redevel. Ofcls. (past pres. Pacific S.W. region), No. Calif. Exec. Dirs. Assn. (past v.p.), Housing Law Inst. (bd. dirs.), Housing for the Homeless, Inc. (bd. dirs.). Lodge: Rotary. Office: 134 E Rossi St Salinas CA 93901

MOORE, CARLETON BRYANT, geochemistry educator; b. N.Y.C., Sept. 1, 1932; s. Eldridge Carleton and Mabel Florence (Drake) M.; m. Jane Elizabeth Strouse, July 25, 1959; children—Barbara Jeanne, Robert Carleton. B.S., Alfred U., 1954, D.Sc. (hon.), 1977; Ph.D., Cal. Inst. Tech., 1960. Asst. prof. geology Wesleyan U., Middletown, Conn., 1959-61; mem.

faculty Ariz. State U., Tempe, 1961—; now prof., dir. Center for Meteorite Studies; vis. prof. Stanford U., 1974; Prin. investigator Apollo 11-17; preliminary exam. team Lunar Receiving Lab., Apollo, 12-17. Author: Cosmic Debris, 1969, Meteorites, 1971, Principles of Geochemistry, 1982, Grundzügeder Geochemie, 1985. Editor: Researches on Meteorites, 1961, Jour. Meteoritical Soc.; contbr. articles to profl. jours. Fellow Ariz.-Nev. Acad. Sci. (pres. 1979-80), Meteoritical Soc. (pres. 1966-68), Geol. Soc. Am., Mineral. Soc. Am., AAAS (council 1967-70); mem. Geochem. Soc., Am. Chem. Soc., Am. Ceramic Soc., Sigma Xi. Home: 507 E Del Rio Dr Tempe AZ 85282

MOORE, CHARLES WILLARD, architect, educator; b. Benton Harbor, Mich., Oct. 31, 1925; s. Charles Ephraim and Nanette Kathryn (Almendinger) M. B.Arch., U. Mich., 1947; M.F.A., Princeton U., 1956, Ph.D., 1957; M.A. (hon.), Yale U., 1965. Architect Mario Corbett (Architect), 1947-48, Joseph Allen Stein (Architect), 1948-49, Clark & Beuttler (Architects), 1949; asst. prof. U. Utah, 1950-52; asst. prof. architecture Princeton U., 1957-59; asso. prof. U. Calif., Berkeley, 1959-65; chmn. dept. architecture U. Calif., 1962-65, Yale U., New Haven, 1965-69; dean Yale U., 1969-71, prof., 1971-75; prof. architecture UCLA, 1975—, head dept., 1976-77, 77-80; architect Moore Lyndon Turnbull Whitaker (Architects), 1961-64, Moore Turnbull, San Francisco and New Haven, 1964-70, Charles Moore Assos., Essex, Conn., 1970-76, Moore Grover Harper, Essex, Conn., and Moore Ruble Yudell, Los Angeles, 1976—; O'Neil Ford Centennial prof. architecture U. Tex., Austin, 1985—. Author: The Place of Houses, 1974, Dimensions, 1975, Body Memory and Architecture, 1977. Served to capt. U.S. Army, 1952-54. Nat. Endowment Arts grantee, 1975; Guggenheim grantee, 1976-77. Fellow AIA. Democrat.

MOORE, DEAN ARLIN, telephone company executive; b. Hiawatha, Kans., Jan. 22, 1931; s. George Washington and Marion Ennis (Jones) M.; m. Lois Lovelle Stogdill, Sept. 14, 1973; children—Deborah M., Sheryl D., Julie A., Margo L., Bradley D. Student, Ry. Communications Tng. Sch., 1949-50, Southeastern Signal Sch., 1951-52, Dakota Bus. Coll., 1954-59. Agt., Gt. No. R.R., Minot, N.D., 1951-61; gen. mgr. Rainbow Telephone Coop., Everest, Kans., 1961-68; gen. mgr. Citizens Mut. Telephone Co., Bloomfield, Iowa, 1968-77; gen. mgr. West Iowa Telephone Co., from 1977; gen. mgr. Cordova Telephone Coop. Inc., Alaska; now gen. mgr. Copper Valley Telephone Coop., Valdez, Alaska. Mem. Lightning Protection Com., Nat. Fire Protection Assn., Nat. Safety Council; bd. dirs. Bloomfield Indsl. Devel. Commn. Served with U.S. Army, 1951-53. Recipient Cert. of Appreciation, Nat. Safety Council. Mem. Ind. Telephone Pioneers Am., S.D. Mgrs. Assn. (pres. 1981), S.E. Iowa Pioneer Club, Remsen C. of C. (bd. dirs.). Democrat. Methodist. Clubs: Elks, Lions, VFW, Masons. Office: PO Box 1932 Valdez AK 99686

MOORE, DIANNE LEA, data processing company executive; b. North Tonawanda, N.Y., Jan. 30, 1949; d. Donald Robert and Dorothy (Ghise) Wilke; m. William Lewis Tremont, Aug. 21, 1966 (div. Apr. 1973); children: Eric, Michelle; m. Allen Charles Moore, July 11, 1981. AA, Scottsdale Community Coll., 1978; student, Ariz. State U., 1978-81. Powder paint troubleshooter McGraw Edison, Phoenix, 1980-81; v.p., mgr. Cereus Recording, Tempe, Ariz., 1981-86; adminstrv. asst. McKesson, Phoenix, 1982-83; owner, mgr. Cereus Letter Processing, Tempe, 1983—. Pres. Aid Assn. for Luths. br. 5555, Scottsdale; treas. Chapel of the Cross, Scottsdale. Mem. Soc. Profl. Audio Recording Studios, Nat. Fedn. Ind. Businessmen. Democrat. Avocations: reading, running, traveling, personal computers. Office: Cereus Letter Processing 1733 E McKellips Suite 7 Tempe AZ 85281

MOORE, DONALD L., educator; b. Blythedale, Mo., Feb. 16, 1932; s. Harry Leonard and Bessie Lee (Hale) M. BS, N.W. Mo. State U., 1958; MA, U. No. Colo., 1965, PhD, 1972. Cert. tchr., Colo., Mo. Instr. bus. Corning High Sch., Iowa, 1958-59; instr. bus., prin. Edison Sch., Yoder, Colo., 1959-61; instr. bus. Pikes Peak Community Coll., Colorado Springs, Colo., 1972—; lectr. edn. Colo. Coll., Colorado Springs, 1975—; tchr. Sch. Dist. 11, Colorado Springs, 1961—; tchr. corps vol. NEA/AID, Addis Ababa, Ethiopia, summer 1970, Kathmandu, Nepal, summer 1975; sec.-treas. Policies Commn. for Bus. and Econ. Edn., 1983-86. Asst. venue coordinator-volleyball Nat. Sports Festival V, 1983; vol. Nat. Sports Festivals I and II, Colorado Springs, 1979, 80. Served with U.S. Army, 1952-54. Mem. Nat. Bus. Edn. Assn. (state membership dir. 1983-86, program dir. Nat. Conv. 1988), Mountain-Plains Bus. Edn. Assn. (treas. 1986—), Colo. Educators for/about Bus. (pres. 1978-81, Service award 1981, Merit award 1984), Am. Vocat. Assn., Colo. Vocat. Assn., NEA, Colo. Edn. Assn., Colorado Springs Tchrs. Assn., Phi Delta Kappa, Delta Pi Epsilon (chpt. pres. 1970-72). Democrat. Home: PO Box 1122 Colorado Springs CO 80901 Office: 1590 W Fillmore Colorado Springs CO 80904

MOORE, DOROTHY MARIE, social studies educator; b. Seattle, Dec. 19, 1944; d. Sidney W. and Edith Clara (Ruddell) M. B.A., Alaska Meth. U., 1967; M.Div., So. Bapt. Theol. Sem., 1974. Cert. pub. sch. tchr., Alaska. Tchr. pub. sch., Homer, Alaska, 1967-69; missionary journeyman sch. tchr., Santiago, Dominican Republic, 1969-71; teamster Bechtel Constrn. Co. Trans-Alaska Pipeline, Valdez, 1975-77; warehouseman Alyeska Pipeline, Valdez, 1977-81; tchr. social studies Gilson Jr. High Sch., Valdez, 1981—. Chmn. Heritage Bd. Mem. NEA, Delta Kappa Gamma. Club: Pioneers of Alaska (trustee, sec., pres.). Office: Gilson Jr High Sch Valdez AK 99686

MOORE, GARY RICHARD NIELSEN, lawyer; b. San Francisco, Aug. 28, 1944; 9. C. Earle (stepfather) and Gerda (Nielsen) Cavins; m. Lynn Elizabeth Sheerer, Sept. 25, 1982; children: Lindsey, Kirsten. BA cum laude, San Jose State U., 1966; JD, U. Calif., San Francisco, 1969. Atty. Boccardo Law Offices, San Jose, Calif., 1970-75, jr. ptnr., 1975-77; ptnr. Toff, Toff, Newton & Moore, San Jose, 1977-79, Moore & Toff, San Jose, 1979-80; sr. ptnr. Gary R.N. Moore Inc., San Jose, 1980—; judge pro tem, arbitrator Santa Clara County Superior Ct., 1984—. Pres. Cypress Point Homeowners Assn., Mountain View, Calif., 1975; candidate Mountain View City Council, 1978. Named Eagle Scout, Boy Scouts Am., 1958. Mem. Calif. Trial Lawyers Assn. (lectr. 1984, Recognition Experience award 1980), Santa Clara County Bar Assn. (trustee 1984-85, ethics com. 1982, torts com. 1982—), Calif. Bar Assn., Santa Clara County Trial Lawyers Assn., Phi Alpha Delta. Republican. Clubs: San Jose Athletic, Santa Teresa Golf; Cypress Point Tennis (Mountain View) (pres. 1977). Home: 20081 Chateau Dr Saratoga CA 95070 Office: 84 W Santa Clara #888 San Jose CA 95113

MOORE, GEORGE EUGENE, surgeon; b. Minn., Feb. 22, 1920; s. Jesse and Elizabeth (MacRae) M.; m. Lorraine Hammell, Feb. 22, 1945; children—Allan, Laurie, Linda, Cathy, Donald. B.A., U. Minn., 1942, M.A., 1943, B.S., 1944, B.M., 1946, M.D., 1947, Ph.D. in Surgery, 1950. Intern surgery U. Minn. Hosps., 1946-47; med. fellow gen. surgery 1947, dir. tumor clinic, 1951-53; sr. research fellow USHPS, 1947-48; faculty U. Minn. Med. Sch., 1948-53, cancer coordinator, 1951-53; chief surgery Roswell Park Meml. Inst., Buffalo, 1953-72; dir. Roswell Park Meml. Inst., 1953-67; dir. pub. health research N.Y. State Health Dept., Albany, 1967-73; clin. prof. surgery State U. N.Y. at Buffalo, 1962-73, also prof. research biology, 1955-69; dir. surg. oncology Denver Gen. Hosp., 1973—; prof. surgery U. Colo., 1973—. Author: Diagnosis and Localization of Brain Tumors, 1950, Cancerous Diseases, 1970; contbr. 600 articles to profl. jours. Recipient Outstanding Citizen award Buffalo Evening News, 1958; Outstanding Sci. Achievement award, 1959; Distinguished Achievement award Modern Medicine mag., 1962; Chancellor's medal U. Buffalo, 1963; Charles Evans Hughes award pub. adminstrn. Albany, 1963; Bronfman prize Am. Pub. Health Assn., 1964. Mem. Soc. U. Surgs., Halsted Soc., Am. Surg. Assn., Colo. Oncology Found. (pres.). Home: 12048 Blackhawk Dr Conifer CO 80433 Office: Denver Gen Hosp 645 Bannock St PO Box 1806 Denver CO 80204

MOORE, GEORGE W(ILLIAM), geologist; b. Palo Alto, Calif., June 7, 1928; s. George Raymond and Grace Amy (Hauch) M.; m. Ellen Louise James, Nov. 27, 1960; children: Leslie Ann, Geoffrey. BS, Stanford U., 1950, MS, 1951; PhD, Yale U., 1960. Geologist U.S. Geol. Survey, Menlo Park, Calif., 1951—; courtesy prof. geology, Oreg. State U., Corvallis, 1987—; geologist in charge La Jolla (Calif.) Marine Geology Lab., 1966-75; research assoc. Scripps Instn. Oceanography, La Jolla, 1972-75; participant Deep Sea Drilling Project, Japan, 1977; dep. chmn. marine geosci. Circum-Pacific Map Project, 1979—; invited lectr. USSR Acad. Scis., 1980, Indonesian Marine Geol. Inst. and Nat. Petroleum Co., 1986; rapporteur UN com. for coordination of offshore prospecting, Peoples Republic of China, 1985; advisor Calif. Coastal Commn., 1970-75; chmn. Earth and Space Scis. Awards, Internat. Sci. Fair, 1978. Author: Speleology, 1978 (Sci. Book Club award 1978); editor Geodynamic Map of the Circum-Pacific Region, 1985. Exhibit com. mem. San Diego Natural History Mus., 1968-75. Fellow AAAS, Geol. Soc. Am.; mem. Nat. Speleol. Soc. (hon., pres. 1963), Am. Assn. Petroleum Geologists (com. chmn. 1977), Am. Geophys. Union, Palo Alto Hist. Assn., Peninsula Geol. Soc. (pres. 1986). Democrat. Home: 3324 SW Chintimini Ave Corvallis OR 97333 Office: Dept Geology Oreg State U Corvallis OR 97331

MOORE, GORDON E., electronics company executive; b. San Francisco, Jan. 3, 1929; s. Walter Harold and Florence Almira (Williamson) M.; m. Betty I. Whittaker, Sept. 9, 1950; children: Kenneth, Steven. B.S. in Chemistry, U. Calif., 1950; Ph.D. in Chemistry and Physics, Calif. Inst. Tech., 1954. Mem. tech. staff Shockley Semicondr. Lab., 1956-57; mgr. engrng. Fairchild Camera & Instrument Corp., 1957-59, dir. research and devel., 1959-68; exec. v.p. Intel Corp., Santa Clara, Calif., 1968-75; pres., chief exec. officer Intel Corp., 1975-79, chmn., chief exec. officer, 1979-87, chmn., 1987—; dir. Micro Mask Inc., Varian Assocs. Inc., Transamerica Corp. Fellow IEEE; mem. Nat. Acad. Engrng., Am. Phys. Soc., Electrochem. Soc. Office: Intel Corp 3065 Bowers Ave Santa Clara CA 95051

MOORE, GWEN ANN, archivist; b. Little Rock, Feb. 21, 1957; d. Glenn R. Moore and B. Ann (Gertsch) Busterud. BA in History, Ouachita Bapt. U., 1980; postgrad., Westminster Coll., Salt Lake City, 1983-87. Records technician Utah State Archives, Salt Lake City, 1980-84, records analyst, 1984-85, cert. records mgr. tng. coordinator, 1985—. Mem. Assn. Records Mgrs. and Adminstrs. (pres. 1986-87, v.p. programs 1985-86, v.p. membership 1984-85, Chpt. Mem. Yr. 1986), Conf. Intermountain Archivists, Soc. Am. Archivists, Nat. Assn. Govt. Archivists and Records Adminstrs. Office: Utah State Archives State Capitol Archives Bldg Salt Lake City UT 84114

MOORE, HAROLD BEVERIDGE, microbiology educator; b. Alix, Arkansas, Sept. 11, 1928; s. Harold Moore and Irene (Beveridge) Pherson; m. Marion Elizabeth Tanner, Aug. 26, 1950; children: Diane Marie, Linda Jean. AB in Zoology, San Diego State U., 1951; MA in Microbiology, UCLA, 1955, PhD in Microbiology, 1958. Med. microbiologist Sharp Meml. Hosp., San Diego, 1957-60, microbiology cons., 1960-86; asst. prof. San Diego State U., 1960-64, assoc. prof., 1964-67, prof. microbiology, 1967—; cons. Palomar Hosp., Excondido, Calif., 1964—, Mercy Hosp., San Diego, 1976-84, Pomerado Hosp., Poway, Calif., 1980—. Co-author Lab Manual for Medical Bacteriology, 1971; contbr. articles to profl. jours. Fellow Am. Acad. Microbiology; mem. Am. Soc. Microbiology, So. Calif. Am. Soc. Microbiology, Sigma Xi. Democrat. Presbyterian. Home: 1776 Avenida CHerylita El Cajon CA 92020 Office: San Diego State U Dept Biology San Diego CA 92182

MOORE, HARVIELEE ANN, educator; b. Deming, N.Mex., June 8, 1948; d. Ira Joe and Louella Carolyn (Chandler) Offutt; m. Samuel Tolbert Moore, July 23, 1977. BA cum laude, McMurry Coll., 1967; MA, Western N.Mex. U., 1975. Lic. tchr. English, Spanish, History and Writing. Tchr. writing and Spanish Deming High Sch., 1967-69, 70-86, chmn. dept. English, 1969-70, 80-87; tchr. English Einstein High Sch., Seattle, 1969-70; tchr. continuing edn. Western N.Mex. U., Silver City, 1975-86; tchr., cons. for tchrs. teaching tchrs. N.Mex. State U., Las Cruces, 1986. Founder, sponsoring editor The Sunburst Mag., 1968 (1st Pl. award 1985); editor The Roadrunner newsletter, 1976-79; co-author Deming High Sch. Writing Program, 1983 (Grand Prize 1984). Mem. NEA, Deming Edn. Assn. (pres. 1978-79, Tchr. of Yr. 1979-80), N. Mex. Council Tchrs. of English (program presenter 1986), Nat. Council Tchrs. of English (program presenter 1985), Delta Kappa Gamma (pres. 1980-82), Phi Delta Kappa. Democrat. Methodist. Club: Drama (Deming) (bd. dirs. 1970-75, 78-82). Avocations: writing, collecting antiques, reading, traveling. Home: PO Box 763 1601 S 8th St Deming NM 88031 Office: Deming High Sch 1100 S Nickel Ave Deming NM 88030

MOORE, JAMES ALLAM, agricultural engineering educator, researcher; b. Fresno, Calif., Mar. 11, 1939; s. E. Dale and Anne Moore; m. Janet Rae Robles, Dec. 19, 1960; children: Catherine, Kimberly, Donald, Dennis, Korinna. BSAE, Calif. State Poly. U., 1962; MSAE, U. Ariz., 1964; PhD in Agrl. Engring., U. Minn., 1975. Registered profl. engr., Oreg. Research engr. agrl. engring. dept. U. Calif., Davis, 1964-68; from instr. to asst. prof. agrl. engring. U. Minn., Mpls./St. Paul, 1968-79; assoc. prof. agrl. engring. Oreg. State U., Corvallis, 1979-85, prof., 1985—, acting head dept. agrl. engring., 1983-84; forward planning com. Dept. Agrl. Engring., 1973, instruction com., 1973, 75. chmn. recruiting com, 1973-79, chmn. student activities, 1974-75; mem. steering com. Experiment Station Waste Mgmt., 1975-79, grad. com. 1979; mem. Midwest Plan Service Com. on Waste Mgmt., 1975-78; bd. dirs. Oreg. State U. Water Resources Research Inst., 1983-85. Contbr. numerous articles to profl. jours. Recipient Superior State award USDA, 1983. Fellow Am. Soc. Agrl. Engrs. (tech. dir. 1979-81, various editorial positions, Blue Ribbon award 1983, 84, G.B. Gunlogson Countryside Engring. award, 1985), mem. Soil Conservation Soc. Am., AM. Soc. Agrl. Engrs., Council for Agrl. Sci. and Tech., Sigma Xi, Gamma Sigma Delta, Alpha Epsilon. Avocations: hunting, fishing. *

MOORE, JAMES MAVOR, writer, actor. director; b. Mar. 8, 1919; s. Francis John and Dora (Mavor) M.; m. Darwina Faessler, 1943; 4 daus.; m. Phyllis Langstaff Grosskurth, 1969; m. Alexandra Browning, 1982; 1. B.A., U. Toronto, 1941; D.Litt. (hon.), York U., 1969; LL.D. (hon.), Mt. Alison U., 1982. Feature producer Can. Broadcasting Co., Toronto, 1941-42; chief producer internat. service Montreal and Pacific region producer, Vancouver, 1945-46; tchr. Acad. Radio Arts, Toronto, 1946-49; mng. producer New Play Soc., Toronto, 1946-50, 54-57; radio dir. CBC, 1946-50; mem. UN info. div., N.Y.C., 1947, 49; exec. TV producer UN info. div., 1954-60; chief producer CBC-TV, Toronto, 1950-54; chmn. Can. Theatre Centre, 1957-58; gen. dir. Confedn. Centre, Charlottetown, P.E.I., 1963-65; founder, artistic dir. Charlottetown Festival, 1964-67; gen. dir. St. Lawrence Centre for Arts, Toronto, 1965-70; prof. theatre York U., Toronto, from 1970; now prof theatre U. Victoria, B.C.; chmn. Can. Council, Ottawa, from 1980; bd. dirs. Stratford (Ont.) Festival, from 1953; bd. govs. Nat. Theatre Sch., Montreal, from 1958; drama critic Toronto Telegram, 1958-60; stage dir. Can. Opera Co., Toronto, 1959-61; pres. Mavor Moore Prodns. Ltd., Toronto, from 1961. Author: Spring Thaw, 1947, Who's Who, 1948, The Hero of Mariposa, 1954; adaptor The Optimist as musical comedy The Best of All Possible Worlds, 1956; author: The Ottawa Man, 1958, And What Do You Do? A Short Guide to the Trade and Professions; poetry, 1960; opera Louis Riel, 1967; translator Yesterday the Children Were Dancing, 1967; author musical comedy Johnny Belinda, 1968; editor: The Awkward Stage: The Ontario Theatre Study, 1969, Getting In, 1970, The Pile, 1970, Inside Out, 1971, The Store, 1972, Come Away, Come Away, 1972, Four Canadian Playwrights, 1973, An Anthology of Canadian Plays, 1973, A Collection of Canadian Plays, vol. II, 1973, The Roncarelli Affair, 1974. Recipient Molson Prize (Canada Council), 1986. Recipient Peabody awards. Office: Univ Victoria, Dept Theatre, Victoria, BC Canada V8W 2Y2 *

MOORE, JOHN D., consultant; b. Mt. Pleasant, Iowa, Apr. 7, 1937; s. Burris P. and Esther I. (Copenhaver) M.; A.B., Muscatine Community Coll., 1961; B.B.A., Augustana Coll., 1966; postgrad. U. Iowa, 1966-68; m. Karen K. Kriegel, June 19, 1957; children—Charles A., Michael J., Susan K., David J. Office mgr. Stanley Engring., Muscatine, Iowa, 1956-64; personnel mgr. Oscar Mayer & Co., Davenport and Perry, Iowa, 1964-68; Midwest regional mgr. A. S. Hansen, Lake Bluff, Ill., 1968-73; legal adminstr. Gardner, Carton & Douglas, Chgo., 1973-78, Heller Ehrman White & McAuliffe, San Francisco, 1978-84; v.p. and dir. Hildebrandt, Inc., Walnut Creek, Calif., 1984—. Pres., Libertyville (Ill.) High Sch. Bd., 1974, Libertyville Ecumenical Council, 1975; bd. dirs. Libertyville YMCA, 1969-71. Recipient Muscatine Disting. Service award, 1963; named Outstanding State V.P., Iowa Jaycees, 1964; Outstanding Nat. Dir., U.S. Jaycees, 1965. Mem. Assn. of Legal Adminstrs. (regional v.p. 1977-78, nat. v.p. 1979-81, nat. pres. 1982-83), Perry C. of C. (v.p. 1967), Am. Mgmt. Assn., Adminstrv. Mgmt. Soc., Found. Assn. of Legal Adminstrs. (pres. 1986—), Golden Gate Assn. Legal Adminstrs. Republican. Methodist. Home: 2632 Quiet Place Dr Walnut Creek CA 94598 Office: 2855 Mitchell Dr Suite 130 Walnut Creek CA 94598

MOORE, JOHN GREENWOOD, physician, internist, educator; b. Mpls., Nov. 8, 1935; s. Perry Randolph and Mary Gertrude (Clay) M.; m. Lisa Madelyn Sampinos, June 1, 1983; children: Camilla, Suzanna. MD, U. Utah, 1981. Diplomate Am. Bd. Internal Medicine, Am. Bd. Gastroenterology. Intern, then resident St. Louis City Hosp. and U. Utah, 1963-66; from instr. to assoc. prof. medicine U. Utah, Salt Lake City, 1968—; staff physician Salt Lake City VA Med. Ctr., 1968—. Contbr. articles to profl. jours. Served to capt. U.S. Army, 1966-68, Vietnam. Decorated Bronze Star Medal. Fellow ACP; mem. Am. Gastroenterol. Assn., Internat. Chronobiology Soc. Avocations: sports, chess, reading. Office: VA Med Ctr 500 Foothill Blvd Salt Lake City UT 84148

MOORE, JOHN HAMPTON, research administrator; b. Grand Forks, N.D., Apr. 19, 1935; s. Charles Harold and Marie (Lindberg) M.; m. Barbara Sue Corbett, Feb. 23, 1963; children—John Randolph, Matthew Corbett. B.S.E., U. Mich., 1958, M.B.A., 1959; Ph.D. in Econs., U. Va., Charlottesville, 1966. Research chemist Procter & Gamble Co., 1959-63; asst. prof. econs. U. Va.-Charlottesville, 1966-70, assoc. prof. econs., 1970-77; assoc. dir., research prof. Law and Econs. Ctr., U. Miami, Fla., 1977-80; assoc dir., prof. econs. Law and Econs. Ctr., Emory U., Atlanta, 1980; assoc. dir., sr. fellow Hoover Instn., Stanford U., Calif., 1981—, acting dep. dir., 1983-84; dep. dir. NSF, Washington, 1985—; sr. assoc. mem. St. Antony's Coll. Oxford U., Eng., 1973; mem. Nat. Sci. Bd., Washington, 1982-85. Author: Growth with Self-Management: Yugoslav Industrialization, 1952-75, 1980; co-translator, co-author: Stalinist Planning for Economic Growth, 1933-52, 1980; editor: To Promote Prosperity, 1984; contbr. articles to profl. jours. Nat. adv. bd. Ctr. for Studies in Free Enterprise 1983—; bd. dirs. Thomas Jefferson Ctr. Found. 1972—. NASA fellow, 1963-66; Hoover Instn. fellow, 1975-76. Mem. Am. Econ. Assn., Mont Pelerin Soc., Raven Soc., So. Econ. Assn., Philadelphia Soc., Phi Eta Sigma, Tau Beta Pi, Omicron Delta Kappa. Home: 6516 Bradley Blvd Bethesda MD 20817 Office: NSF 1800 G St NW Washington DC 20050

MOORE, JUDITH MARIE, nurse; b. Evanston, Ill., June 2, 1947; d. Herbert Potter and Irene Ellen (Wagner) M.; B.S., Loma Linda (Calif.) U., 1970. Mem. staff White Meml. Med. Center, Los Angeles, 1970-80, coordinator edn. tng. MacPherson Applied Physiology Lab., 1979-80; critical care nurse Critical Care Services, Inc., Los Angeles 1980; dir. health edn. and rehab. tng. St. Helena Hosp. and Health Center, Deer Park, Calif., 1981—; bd. dirs. Napa County chpt. Am. Heart Assn., 1980—, McDougall program, 1981-86; speaker in field. Mem. Am. Assn. Critical Care Nurses, Am. Heart Assn., Calif. Soc. Cardiac Rehab. Seventh-day Adventist. Home: PO Box 154 Deer Park CA 94576 Office: St Helena Hosp and Health Ctr Deer Park CA 94576

MOORE, JUSTIN EDWARD, data processing executive; b. West Hartford, Conn., June 17, 1952; s. Walter Joseph and Victoria Mary (Calcagni) M. BS in Mgmt. Sci., Fla. Inst. Tech., 1974. Systems assoc. Travelers Ins., Hartford, Conn., 1974-77; data processing programmer R.J. Reynolds Inc., Winston-Salem, N.C., 1977-78; programmer, analyst Sea-Land Service, Elizabeth, N.J., 1978-79; mgr. market analysis Sea-Land Service, Oakland, Calif., 1979-82; asst. v.p., dir. application systems Fox Capital Mgmt. Corp., Foster City, Calif., 1982-86; mgr. bus. services dept mktg. and pricing Am. Pres. Cos., Ltd., Oakland, 1987—. Democrat. Roman Catholic. Avocations: golf, personal computing, investment mgmt. Home: 5214 Jomar Dr Concord CA 94521 Office: Am Pres Cos Ltd 1800 Harrison St Oakland CA 94612

MOORE, LEONARD WENGERT, corporate executive, engineer; b. Independence, Iowa, Nov. 26, 1933; s. Leonard Dewey and Lillian Teresa (Wengert) M.; m. Martha Floyd Monger, June 16, 1956; children—Leonard Anthony, John Nicholas, Christopher Scott. B.S. in Elec. Engring., Iowa State Coll., 1956. Registered profl. engr., Calif. Test equipment liaison Hughes Aircraft, Culver City, Calif., 1956; project engr. Swanson Engring. Co., Inglewood, Calif., 1956-59; v.p. Ronan Engring. Co., Woodland Hills, Calif., 1959-67; project mgr. Waugh Controls, Chatsworth, Calif., 1967-68; pres., chief exec. officer Moore Industries-Pacific, Inc., 1968—; pres. Moore Industries-Europe, Electromagnetics, Moore Industries Internat. Inc. Active Republican Club; patron YMCA; mem. Pres.'s Circle, Los Angeles County Mus.; bd. dirs. Bur. Bus. Services, also Research-Advanced Tech. Inst., Calif. State U.-Northridge. Mem. Calif. Mfrs. Assn., Mchts. and Mfrs. Assn., Instrument Soc. Am. (sr.). Clubs: Regency, Mountain Gate Country, Los Angeles. Patentee in field of process instrumentation. Office: 16650 Schoenborn St Sepulveda CA 91343

MOORE, LOUIS ROBERT, III, systems analyst; b. Columbus, Ga., Feb. 24, 1948; s. Louis Robert and Maria Loftus (Stephens) M.; m. Barbara Elizabeth Billo, Aug. 14, 1982. BS in Math., Villanova U., 1970; MS in Stats., U. N.C., 1978, PhD in Stats., 1979. Asst. prof. quantitative methods bus. sch. U. N.C., Chapel Hill, 1978-85; systems analyst Rand Corp., Santa Monica, Calif., 1985—; cons. CACI Inc., Arlington, Va., 1983—. Contbr. articles to profl. jours. Served with USNR, 1972-75. Mem. Inst. Mgmt. Sci. (newsletter editor 1985-86), Inst. Math. Stats., Am. Statis. Assn., Ops. Research Soc. Am. Avocations: sailing, slow pitch softball. Home: 1597 Via Bajada Thousand Oaks CA 91360

MOORE, MARVIN E(VERARD), Canadian provincial official, farmer, businessman; b. Grande Prairie, Alta., Can., Aug. 31, 1938; s. Charlie S. and Winifred L. (DeBolt) M.; m. Frances Bodeker, Feb. 20, 1959; children—Kerry, Lonny, Bernice. Student schs., Grande Prairie, Alta. Elected Provincial Council Alta., 1971, minister of agr., 1975-79, minister of mcpl. affairs, 1979-82, minister of transp., 1982-86; minister hosps. and med. care, 1986—; farmer, DeBolt, Alta. Office: 423 Legislature Bldg, Edmonton, AB Canada T5K 2B6

MOORE, MARY FRENCH (MUFFY), potter, community activist; b. N.Y.C., Feb. 25, 1938; d. John and Rhoda (Teagle) Walker French; B.A. cum laude, Colo. U., 1964; m. Alan Baird Minier, Oct. 9, 1982; children—Jonathan Corbet, Jennifer Corbet, Michael Corbet. Ceramics mfr., Wilson, Wyo., 1969-82, Cheyenne, Wyo., 1982—; commr. County of Teton (Wyo.), 1976-83, chmn. bd. commrs., 1981, 83, mem. dept. public assistance and social service, 1976-82, mem. recreation bd., 1978-81, water quality adv. bd., 1976-82. Bd. dirs. Teton Sci. Sch., 1968-83, vice chmn., 1979-81, chmn., 1982; bd. dirs. Teton Energy Council, 1978-83; mem. water quality adv. bd. Wyo. Dept. Environ. Quality, 1979-83; Democratic precinct committeewoman, 1978-81; mem. Wyo. Dem. Central Com., 1981-83; vice chmn. Laramie County Dem. Central Com., 1983-84, chmn. 1987—; Wyo. Dem. nat. committeewoman, 1984-87; del. Dem. Nat. Conv., 1984, mem. fairness commn. Dem. Nat. Com., 1985, vice-chairwoman western caucus, 1986—; chmn. platform com. Wyo. Dem. Conv., 1982; mem. Wyo. Dept. Environ. Quality Land Quality Adv. Bd., 1983-84; mem. Gov.'s Steering Com. on Troubled Youth, 1982, Compliance Assistance Commn., 1986—; legis. aide for Gov. Wyo., 1985, 86; project coordinator Gov.'s Com. on Childrens' Services, 1985-86; bd. dirs. Wyo. Outdoor Council, 1984-85. Recipient Woman of Yr. award Jackson Hole Bus. and Profl. Women, 1981. Mem. Jackson Hole Art Assn. (bd. dirs., vice chmn. 1981, chmn. 1982), Pi Sigma Alpha. Home: 8907 Cowpoke Rd Cheyenne WY 82009

MOORE, MARY JANE, biological anthropologist; b. Memphis, July 5, 1939; d. Carey Moffett and Jane (Cockrill) M. BA, Agnes Scott Coll., 1961; BS, U. Tenn., 1962; PhD, U. Wis., 1972. Asst. prof. San Diego State U., 1972-76, assoc. prof. anthropology, 1978—; vis. asst. prof. U. Kans., Lawrence, 1976-77, vis. assoc. prof., 1977-78. Contbr. articles and book revs. to profl. publs., chptrs. to books. Faculty Research grantee San Diego State U., 1974, 75, 81, biomed. research support grantee 1985. Mem. Am. Assn. Phys. Anthropology, Am. Soc. Human Genetics, Am. Anthropol. Assn., Soc. Med. Anthropology, Human Biology Council, Assn. Anthropology and Gerontology (exec. bd. 1983-85, membership chair 1983-85). Home: 6145 Broadmoor Dr La Mesa CA 92042 Office: San Diego State U Dept Anthropology San Diego CA 92182

MOORE, MONICA MARGARET, real estate appraiser; b. East St. Louis, Ill., Mar. 12, 1942; d. Howard R. and Lela Catherine (Howard) M.; m. David Grover Fish, Jan. 8, 1977; stepchildren: David Joseph, Mary Kathryn, Robert Norman. BEd, Webster U., 1964; MS, So. Ill. U., 1970. Cert. tchr., Mo. Music tchr. East St. Louis Schs., 1964-70; social worker Children & Family Services, East St. Louis, 1970-73; administrator Sr. citizen Program, Lewis County, Wash., 1973-74, County of Orange, Calif., 1974-77; pres., chief exec. officer Fish & Moore Appraisers Inc., Corona Del Mar, Calif., 1977—. Chmn. 15th and 20th Coll. Reunion Webster U., 1979-84. Mem. Soc. Real Estate Appraisers (vice chmn. internat. chpt. services com. 1987—, vice gov. dist. 5 1983—, vice chmn. Calif. legis. steering com. govtl. regulation of appraiser 1985—), Sigma Alpha Iota. Democrat. Presbyterian. Home and Office: Fish & Moore Appraisers Inc 429 Marigold Ave Corona del Mar CA 92625

MOORE, PHILIP ARNOLD, accountant, consultant; b. Lake Wales, Fla., July 4, 1941; s. Edgar Arnold and Elizabeth (Cody) M.; m. Harriett Hope Hatfield, Apr. 6, 1962; children: Richard, Dwight, Dianna. BBA in Econs., U. Ga., 1967, MA in Econs., 1968; MBA in Fin., U. S.C., 1974. CPA, S.C. Mgr. fin. Westinghouse, various locations, 1968-75; mgr. acctg. Rocky Mountain Energy, Denver, 1975-76; mgr. cost/budget Allied Chem., Macon, Ga., 1976-78; mgmt. cons. Peat, Marwick & Mitchell, Denver, 1978-80; corp. controller Dencor PWI, Inc., Denver, 1980-83; pvt. practice acct., tax, bus. cons. Littleton, Colo., 1983—; instr. U. Ga., Athens, 1967-68, Wesleyan Coll., Rocky Mountain, N.C., 1970-71, Arapahoe Coll., Littleton, 1980-84; lectr., cons. various orgns. on acctg., fin. mgmt., computers. Mem. Nat. Assn. Accts., Colo. Soc. Pub. Accts., Planning Execs. Inst., Nat. Soc. Pub. Accts., Inst. Mgmt. Accts., Arnold Air Soc., Omicron Delta Epsilon. Republican. Office: Columbine Valley Bank Bldg 6901 S Pierce St Suite 120 Littleton CO 80123

MOORE, PHYLLIS CLARK, library director; b. Binghamton, N.Y., Jan. 31, 1927; d. John Oscar and Gladys Jeanette (Tilbury) Clark; B.A., Hartwick Coll., 1949; M.A., Syracuse U., 1952, M.S., 1954; Ph.D., U. Wis., 1971; Litt.D., Colo. State U., 1973; m. Roberts Scott Wellington Moore, Sept. 14, 1954. Librarian Free Library Phila., 1954-57; Librarian-adminstr. GS-9 main reference/Interloan Center, dir. 22 spl. services libraries met. Stuttgart, U.S. Govt. Spl. Services Europe, 1957-62; dept. Head young adult, fine arts, audiovisual, reference Yonkers (N.Y.) Pub. Library, 1962-67; dir. Hastings-on-Hudson (N.Y.) Pub. Library, 1967-68; cons. audio-visual services Westchester County (N.Y.) Library System, 1968-721; dir. Falls Church (Va.) Pub. Library, 1972-77, Alameda (Calif.) Free Library, 1978-84; library supr. Ojai (Calif.) Unified Sch. Dist., 1984—; cons. in field; research dir. underwater sealabs, Bremerhaven, W. Ger., 1960-61; tech. advisor Community Action Program Yonkers, N.Y., 1965-68. Chancel choir Ojai Presbyn. Ch. Active Nat. Humane Soc., Recording Service for Visually Handicapped. Mem. ALA (exec. council 1975-79), Internat. Oceanographic Found., Nat. Assn. Sch. and Media Librarians, Mask and Lute (pres. 1974), Nat. Health and Welfare Assn. (exec. bd.), Defenders of Wildlife (adv. council), Bay Area Library and Info. System (chairperson 1978-79), Audio Philharmonic Soc. (pres. 1983-84). Author: (play) Beneath the Sea, 1974; Command Performance, 1975; Blues in the Bibliotheque, 1979; A Catchy Title, 1980; Beyond the Blues, 1981; Girls of Yesteryear, 1983-84 (nat. TV prodn. award). Contbr. articles to profl. publs. Home: 25 Juniper Lane Ojai CA 93023 Office: Ojai Unified School District 1401 Maricopa Hwy Ojai CA 93023

MOORE, RANDOLPH GRAVES, real estate executive; b. Honolulu, Feb. 12, 1939; s. Howard Hoffman and Mary May (Phillips) M.; m. Lynne Johnson, Nov. 8, 1979; children: Allison, Juliet. BA, Swarthmore Coll., 1961; MBA, Stanford U., 1963. Vol. Peace Corps, Brenerville, Liberia, 1963-65; fin. analyst Castle & Cooke, Inc., Honolulu, 1966-70, treas., 1970-74, group controller, 1974-77; from sr. v.p. to exec. v.p. Oceanic Properties, Inc., Honolulu, 1977-84, pres., 1984-86; pres. Molokai Ranch, Ltd., 1986—. Home: 59-161 Ke Nui Rd Haleiwa HI 96712 Mailing: Molokai Ranch Ltd PO Box 4039 Honolulu HI 96812 Office: Molokai Ranch Ltd 810 Richards St #755 Honolulu HI 96813

MOORE, RAYMOND ARTHUR, JR., manufacturing engineer; b. Lancaster, Pa., Mar. 8, 1943; s. Raymond Arthur and Dorothy May (Beck) M.; m. Elizabeth Sharon Ballagh, June 13, 1965; children: Diane Michelle, Linda Eileen. AA, San Jose City Coll., 1972; BS in Indsl. Tech., Calif. State U., San Jose, 1975. Cert. mfg. engr., Calif. Electronic technician Data Products Inc., Mountain View, Calif., 1966-68; assoc. electronic engr. Gen. Electric Co., San Jose, 1968-77; supr. United Techs., San Jose, 1977-81; sr. mfg. engr. Amdahl Corp., Sunnyvale, Calif., 1981-85, AMEX Systems Inc., Compton, Calif., 1985—. Chmn. bd. Christian edn. Apostles Luth. Ch. and Sch., San Jose, 1977-80, elder, 1981-84. Served with USAF, 1962-66. Mem. Soc. Mfg. Engrs. (sr., treas. chpt. 1985, 86, 3d vice chmn. 1984), Instrument Soc. Am. (sr., standards rev. bd.), Am. Mgmt. Assn. Republican. Avocations: playing french horn, fishing. Home: 15851 Rochester St Westminster CA 92683 Office: AMEX Systems Inc Electronics Systems Div Allied Bendix Aeros pace Co 107 W Carob St Compton CA 90220

MOORE, ROBERT MULLINS, III, chemical company executive; b. Dallas, Sept. 14, 1947; s. Robert Mullins and Mary Nelle (Landrum) M.; m. Carolyn Francis, Mar. 13, 1981; children: Robert Mullins IV, Megan Francis. BA in Chemistry, Tex. Christian U., 1969; MS in Chemistry, U. Tex., Arlington, 1971. Sr. scientist Alcon Labs., Ft. Worth, 1971-76; mgr. product devel. Cooper Vision, Mountain View, Calif., 1977-81; project mgr. Bausch and Lomb, Rochester, N.Y., 1981-83; corp. v.p. Tech. Network, Peoria, Ariz., 1983—, tech. cons., 1983—; mgr. product devel. Carter Glogau Labs., Phoenix, 1985—; ophthalmic lectr., speaker Cooper Labs., Mountain View, Calif., 1980-81. Contbr. articles to profl. jours.; patentee in field. Advisor explorers Boy Scouts Am., Ft. Worth, 1974-76. Mem. Am. Chem. Soc., Pharm. Mfg. Soc. Methodist. Avocations: tennis, fine ship building, cooking. Home: 8729 N 104th Ave Peoria AZ 85345 Office: Carter Glogau Labs 620 N 51st Ave Phoenix AZ 85043

MOORE, RODERICK ALAN, podiatrist; b. Long Beach, Calif., Oct. 4, 1952; s. Robert Anthony and Ouida Kathleen (O'Neil) M.; m. Shirley Ann Kleyn, Aug. 28, 1976; 1 child, Lauren Ann. BS in Biology, So. Oreg. State Coll., 1977; DPM, Calif. Coll. Podiatric Medicine, 1981. Resident in surgery Waldo Gen. Hosp., Seattle, 1981-83, foot clin. dir., 1984-85, dir. podiatric residency program, 1985—; Mem. exec. com. podiatric staff 5th Ave. Med. Ctr., Seattle. Served with U.S. Army, 1972-74. Mem. Am. Podiatric Med. Assn., Wash. State Podiatric Med. Assn., Pi Delta, so. Oreg. State Coll. Honor Soc. (pres. 1976-77). Mem. Ch. of Christ. Office: 17401 135th Ave NE #3 Woodinville WA 98072

MOORE, RONALD MARVIN, internist, cardiologist; b. Loma Linda, Calif., May 13, 1929; s. Marvin Harrison and Ethel Marie (Wagner) M.; m. Orlene Stricker, Aug. 3, 1950 (div. 1973); children—Janet Lynne, Ronald Marvin, William Wilbur; m. Anne Marie Tolmosoff, Aug. 23, 1973. B.A. in Chemistry, Union Coll., 1952; M.D., Loma Linda U., 1958. Diplomate Am. Bd. Internal Medicine. Intern Los Angeles County Hosp., 1958-59, resident in internal medicine, 1959-61, sr. resident in internal medicine, 1962-63; fellow in cardiology White Meml. Hosp., Los Angeles, 1961-62; practice medicine specializing in internal medicine and cardiology, Fresno, Calif., 1963—; chmn. dept. medicine Fresno Community Hosp., 1974-75. Served with M.C., U.S. Army, 1952-54. Fellow Am. Coll. Cardiology; mem. AMA, Calif. Med. Assn., Fresno-Madera Med. Soc. (v.p. 1983-84, treas. 1978-79, bd. govs. 1976-79), Am. Soc. Internal Medicine, Calif. Soc. Internal Medicine, Fresno Soc. Internal Medicine (pres. 1977-78), Alpha Omega Alpha. Republican. Adventist. Office: 3636 N First Suite 141 Fresno CA 93726-6883

MOORE, RUTH, author; b. St. Louis; d. William Dunn and Ethel (Sledd) M.; m. Raymond W. Garbe. AB, MA, Washington U., St. Louis; DLitt., McMurray Coll., 1955. Staff writer Chgo. Sun-Times newspaper, 1943-70, Washington corr., 1943-50. Author: Man, Time, and Fossils, 1953, Charles Darwin-A Great Life in Brief, 1955, The Earth We Live On, 1956, The Coil of Life, 1961, Evolution, 1962, Niels Bohr: His LIfe, His Science and the World They Changed, 1966, (with Sherwood L. Washburn) Ape Into Man, 1973, rev. edit, Ape Into Human, 1980, Man in the Environment, 1975. Chmn. Prarie Ave. Historic Dist., 1974-82; mem. Commn. on Chgo. Hist. and Archtl. Landmarks, 1974-86; pres. women's bd. U. Chgo., 1973-77; pres. Chgo. Architecture Found., 1978-80; trustee Washington U. Recipient ann. award Friends of Lit., 1955, Alumni citation, Washington U., 1963, Champion Fighter for a Better Chgo. award Met. Housing and Planning Council, $1 million endowment Ruth and Norman Moore Professorship in Architecture and Urban Design Washington U., St. Louis, 1986; named Chgo. Preservationist of Yr., 1981. Mem. AIA (hon.), AAAS (standing com. on pub. understanding sci.), Phi Beta Kappa. Clubs: Women's Nat. Press (Washington); Fortnightly (Chgo.). Home: 2190 Washington St San Francisco CA 94109

MOORE, TERRY LEE, mechanical engineer; b. Pendleton, Oreg., Apr. 2, 1950; s. Delmar Lee and Emma Maybelle (Baker) M.; BS, Oreg. State U., 1973. Registered profl. engr., Wash. Project engr. Crown Zellerbach, Omak, Wash., 1978-81, prodn. supt., 1981-83, plant engr., 1983-86; pres., owner, operator Moore Constrn., 1986—; dir. N.W. Wood Products Clinic, Spokane, Wash., 1983-85. Author: (with others) operating manual revision Nuclear Instrumentation Maintenance Procedures, 1975. Served to lt. USN, 1973-78. Mem. Soc. Automotive Engrs., Omak C. of C. (bd. dirs. 1983-85), Theta Xi. Republican. Lodges: Elks, Kiwanis (dir. 1983). Home and Office: 1645 E Thomas Rd Apt 10 Phoenix AZ 85016

MOORE, WILLIS HENRY ALLPHIN, state official; b. N.Y.C., Dec. 14, 1940; s. Carl Allphin and Mary Catherine (Moody) M.; children: Patrick Kakela, Michael Kirby, Catherine Malia. BA Letters, U. Okla., 1962; MEd in Adminstrn., U. Hawaii, 1971. Teaching asst. dept. history U. Hawaii, 1962-64; dir. edn. Bernice P. Bishop Museum, Honolulu, 1967-76; pres., chief cartographer Hawaii Geog. Soc., Honolulu, 1976-78, exec. sec., 1978—; mem. Hawaii Com. for Humanities, 1976—; producer, narrator film-lecture programs Nat. Aududon Soc. and travelogue forums; instr. in Hawaiian culture and Hawaiian studies Hawaii Loa Coll. and U. Hawaii system, 1970—, Chaminade U. of Honolulu, 1987—; lectr. in field. Contbr. articles to Honolulu Advertiser, Pacific Daily News, Guam, Pacific Mag., Honolulu Star-Bull. U.S. Info. Service Honolulu Reception Ctr. escort, 1962—; mem. Hawaii Council for Culture and Arts. Mem. Pacific Sci. Assn., Hawaii Museum Assn. (pres. 1972-74), Pacific Area Travel Assn., Am. Guild Organists (v.p. Hawaii chpt.), Sierra Club (chmn. Hawaii chpt. 1973-75), Hawaiian Hist. Soc. Republican. Club: Honolulu Press, NSAL (Honolulu). Office: PO Box 1698 Honolulu HI 96806

MOORHEAD, CARLOS J., congressman; b. Long Beach, Calif., May 6, 1922; m. Valery Joan Tyler; children: Theresa, Catharine, Steven, Teri, Paul. B.A., UCLA, 1943; J.D., U. So. Calif., 1949. Bar: Calif. 1949, U.S. Supreme Ct. 1973. Dir. Lawyers Reference Service, Glendale Bar Assn.; mem. 93d-100th congresses from 22d Dist.Calif., Judiciary Com., Energy and Commerce Com.; dean Calif. Rep. Delegation. Pres. Glendale Hi-Twelve Club; mem. Verdugo Hills council Boy Scouts Am.; mem. Calif. Assembly, 1967-72; mem. Calif. Law Revision Commn., 1971-72; pres. 43d Dist. Republican Assembly, Glendale Young Republicans; mem. Los Angeles County Rep. Central Com., Calif. Rep. Central Com.; dean Calif. Congressional Rep. Delegation; pres. Glendale La Crescenta Camp Fire Girls, Inc. Served to lt. col. AUS, 1942-46. Recipient Man of Yr. award USO, 1979. Mem. Calif. Bar Assn., Angeles County Bar Assn., Glendale Bar Assn. (past pres.), C. of C. Clubs: Masons, Shriners, Lions, Elks. Office: 2346 Rayburn House Office Bldg Washington DC 20515

MOORTY, S. S., English language educator; b. Madanapalle, India; came to U.S., 1970, naturalized, 1984; s. Lakshmi N. and Annapoorna (Ayyagari) Sikha; m. Vijayalakshmi Viswanatha, May 16, 1968; children—Naresh, Neela. B. Commerce, Osmania U., 1956; M.A., Delhi U., India, 1966; Ph.D. in English, U. Utah, 1976. Adminstrv. asst. Council of Sci. and Indsl. Research, New Delhi, India, 1957-67; lectr. English, Shri Ram Coll. Commerce, Delhi U., 1967-70; teaching asst. dept. English, U. Utah, Salt Lake City, 1970-74; instr. English, Westminster Coll., Salt Lake City, 1970-71; asst. prof. English, So. Utah State Coll., Cedar City, 1975-80, assoc. prof., 1980—, dir. composition, 1982—; faculty adviser lit. mag., 1977-82; lectr. Shakespeare high schs. and community groups. Author anthology of poetry. Contbr. articles, book revs. to profl. jours. Assoc. mem. South Asian Area Ctr., U. Wis. Recipient numerous awards for debating and writing and acad. excellence; Am. Studies Research Ctr. grantee, 1970; fellow NEH, 1984. Mem. MLA (dir. Asian Langs. and Lit. sect), Rocky Mountain MLA (dir. Asian Langs. and Lit. sect.), Utah Acad. Scis., Arts and Letters (sect. leader gen. lit. 1977, 80, Disting. Coll. Teaching award 1986), Western Lit. Assn., Western Social Sci. Assn., European Assn. Commonwealth Lang. and Lit., Internat. Shakespeare Assn. (Stratford-upon-Avon), Assn. Mormon Letters, Phi Delta Kappa (pres. So. Utah chpt. 1984-85). Hindu. Home: 1178 Mountain View Dr Cedar City UT 84720 Office: So Utah State Coll Dept English Cedar City UT 84720

MOOS, RICHARD EUGENE, environmental sciences consultant; b. Kalispell, Mont., June 23, 1938; s. Louis M. and Mary Opal (Tucker) M.; m. Eileen A. Grosfield, Aug. 1961; children: David E., Alan R., Kevin E. BS, Mont. State U., 1961; MS, U. S.D., 1965, PhD, 1978. Sci. tchr. Cut Bank (Mont.) Jr. High Sch., 1961-64; asst. prof. St. Mary's Coll., Winona, Minn., 1970-73; project mgr. environ. scis. Tex. Instruments, Inc., Dallas, 1973-81; mgr. environ. scis. and project mgr. CH2M Hill, Denver, 1981—, also aquatic ecologist; field researcher U.S. Fish and Wildlife Services, Yankton, S.D., 1967-69. Mem. rev. task force Colo. Water Quality Control Commn., Denver, 1985-86. Mem. Am. Fisheries Soc., Nat. Assn. Environ. Profls., Sigma Xi. Home: 8250 Lakeview Dr Parker CO 80134 Office: CH2M Hill Orchard Place I Office Bldg 5995 Greenwood Plaza Blvd Englewood CO 80111

MOOSE, BRIAN DAVID, illustrator, art director; b. San Mateo, Calif., July 30, 1958; s. Irvin Russel and Gene (Thompson) M. AA in Comml. Art, Coll. of San Mateo, 1981; BFA in Illustration, Calif. State U., Long Beach, 1984. Pvt. practice illustrator San Mateo, 1977-81, Long Beach, 1981—; creative cons. Walt Disney Prodns., Anaheim, Calif., 1981-84; sr. model builder Walt Disney Co., Anaheim, 1984—; art dir. Am. Space Meml. Found. Inc., Anaheim, 1986—. Represented in permanent collection Smithsonian Inst., 1984; exhibited in shows of N.Y. Soc. Illustrators, N.Y.C., 1985. Mem. Graphic Artist Guild, Western Art Dirs. Club, OASIS L5 Soc. Republican. Avocations: sailing, sculling, sketching. Home: 134 McLellan Ave San Mateo CA 94403 Office: Walt Disney Co 1313 Harbor Blvd Anaheim CA 92803

MORADO, JOSEPH FRANK, research biologist, consultant; b. Greeley, Colo., Nov. 5, 1950; s. Lucio and Dominga (Hinojosa) M.; children from previous marriage: Jennifer Renee, Kathryn Marie; m. Maralee Benton, Oct. 28, 1983. BS, Colo. State U., 1974, U. Wash., 1978; MS, U. Wash., 1982. Research technician Colo. State U., Ft. Collins, 1974-75; research bacteriologist Physio-Control, Redmond, Va., 1975; research technician U. Wash., Seattle, 1976-78; fisheries research biologist Nat. Marine Fisheries Service, Seattle, 1979—. Fellow U. Wash., 1978, NSF, 1979; John N. Cobb scholar U. Wash., 1982. Mem. AAAS, Internat. Soc. Devel. Comparative Immunology, Nat. Soc. Histotechnologists, Am. Soc. Zoologists, Nat. Shellfisheries Assn., Soc. Invertebrate Pathology. Office: Nat Marine Fisheries Service 7600 Sand Point Way NE Seattle WA 98115

MORAFKA, DAVID JOSEPH, biology educator; b. San Francisco, Sept. 18, 1945; s. Aaron and Dorothy (Warner) M.; divorced. BA in Zoology, U. Calif., Berkeley, 1967; PhD in Biology, U. So. Calif., 1974. Prof. biology Calif. State U.-Dominquez Hills, Carson, 1972—; mem. nat. coll. bd. Edn. Testing Service, Princeton, N.J., 1978-80. Author: Biographical Analysis, 1977; contbr. articles to profl. jours. Advisor Friend of Madrona Marsh, Torrance, Calif., 1973—. Grantee, NIH, 1985-89, NSF, 1980, 82, 85, World WIldlife Fund, Office of Endangered Species. Fellow Inst. de Ecologia de Mexico (editor 1978—). Republican. Jewish. Avocations: tropical fish, hiking, jogging. Home: 3255 Glendon Ave Los Angeles CA 90034 Office: Calif State U-Dominguez Hills 1000 E Victoria St Carson CA 90747

MORAIN, MARY STONE DEWING, assn. exec.; b. Boston, Mar. 18, 1911; d. Arthur S. and Frances (Hall Rousmaniere) Dewing; student Radcliffe Coll., 1930-33; BS, Simmons Sch. Social Work, 1934; MA, U. Chgo., 1937; cert. social work U. So. Calif., 1941; m. Lloyd L. Morain, July 6, 1946. Social worker, Calif., N.Y.C., 1941-45; tchr. social scis. Keuka Coll., N.Y., 1945-46; v.p. LWV, Boston, 1946-53; bd. dirs., v.p. Planned Parenthood League Mass., 1948-52; bd. dirs., pres. Planned Parenthood Assn. San Francisco, 1953-60; bd. dirs. Internat. Humanist and Ethical Union, 1953-65; bd. dirs., v.p. Assn. Vol. Sterilization, 1963-77, 79—, UNESCO Assn. U.S.A., 1977—, Monterey YWCA, 1975-80, UN Assn. San Francisco, 1961-69; pres. Internat. Soc. Gen. Semantics, 1976—; bd. dir. Tor House Found., 1984—, Hidden Valley Inst. of the Arts, 1983—. Fellow World Acad. Art and Sci.; mem. Am. Assn. Social Workers. Club: Altrusa. Author: (with Lloyd Morain) Humanism as the Next Step, 1954; contbr. articles to profl. jours. Editor: Teaching General Semantics, 1969; Classroom Exercises in General Semantics, 1980; Bridging Worlds through General Semantics, 1984; Enriching Professional Skills Through General Semantics, 1986. Home: PO Box 7190 Carmel CA 93921 Office: PO Box 2469 San Francisco CA 94126

MORALES, ARMANDO, psychotherapist, mental health educator; b. Los Angeles, Sept. 18, 1932; s. Roberto Torres and Lupe (Acevedo) M.; m. Rebecca Gonzales, Aug. 27, 1955 (div. Apr. 1980); children: Roland Victor, Gary Vincent. AA, East Los Angeles Jr. Coll., 1955; BA, Los Angeles State Coll., 1957; MSW, U. So. Calif. Sch. Social Work, 1963, DSW, 1971. Gang group worker Los Angeles Times Boys Club, 1954-57; sr. dep. probation officer Los Angeles County Probation Dept., 1957-63; supervising psychiat. social worker, mental health cons. Las Palmas Sch. for Girls, 1963-66, Los Angeles County Dept. Mental Health, 1966-71; prof., chief clin. social work dept., dir. Spanish speaking psychosocial clinic Neuropsychiat. Inst. UCLA Sch. Medicine, 1971—; cons. Calif. Youth Authority, East Los Angeles, 1977—; speaker in field. Author: Ando Sangrando: A Study of Mexican American-Police Conflict, 1972, Social Work: A Profession of Many Faces, 4th edit. 1977, 1980, 1983, 1986; co-editor The Psychosocial Development of Minority Group Children, 1983; composer ethnic songs. pres. Western Ctr. on Law and Poverty, Inc., Los Angeles, 1975-77, bd. dirs., 1968-78; vice chmn. Citizens Adv. Council, Calif. Dept. Mental Health, 1977-82. Served as sgt. USAF, 1951-54. Appointed to Pres.' Commn. on Mental Health Task Panel on Legal and Ethical Issues, 1977-78; fellow NIMH, 1962, 69, 77; named Far East Air Force Bantamweight Champion, 1952, 53. Mem. Nat. Assn. Social Workers (cert.), Trabajadores de La Raza, Council on Mental Health Western Interstate Commn. for Higher Edn., 1976-78 (chmn.), Commn. Human Relations (commr., v.p. 1975-78). Democrat. Roman Catholic. Avocations: classical and flamenco guitar playing, Mexican and Am. folk singing, jogging, roller skating. Office: Neuropsychiatric Inst Sch of Medicine UCLA 760 Westwood Plaza Los Angeles CA 90024

MORALES, DOROTHY ANN, social services coordinator; b. El Paso, Tex., Dec. 1, 1943; d. Pete S. and Isabel (Peña) Hernandez; m. Manuel M. Morales, Oct. 9, 1960; children: Don, Susan. BSW, N.Mex. State U., 1979; MSW, U. Tex., Austin, 1984. Social worker Meml. Hosp., Las Cruces, N.Mex., 1977-78, also bd. dirs., 1982—; dir. Cath. Social Service, Las Cruces, 1979—, Immaculate Heart of Mary Cathedral, Las Cruces, 1979—; bd. dirs. La Casa, Las Cruces, 1982—, So. N.Mex. Human Devel., Las Cruces, 1985—. Recipient Appreciation award State of N.Mex., 1980, Whole Enchilada award City of Las Cruces, 1983; Am. Bus. Women scholar, 1979. Mem. Nat. Assn. Social Workers, N.Am. Christians in Social Work. Democrat. Avocations: sports, outdoor activities. Home: 1308 Delano Dr Las Cruces NM 88001 Office: Immaculate Heart Mary Cathedral 1240 S Espina Las Cruces NM 88001

MORALES, MARY LOU, business educator, real estate broker; b. San Antonio, Aug. 26, 1934; d. T. N. and Maria Angel Martinez; m. Rudy Morales, June 6, 1954; 1 dau., Jean Elizabeth. B.A., Tex. Woman's U., 1954; M.A., Loma Linda U., 1967. Tchr. bus. edn., Colo., 1954-57, Calif., 1957—, Alvord Unified Sch. Dist., 1959—, Notre Vista High Sch., 1959-76, Alvord Continuation High Sch., 1976-82, La Sierra High Sch., Riverside, Calif., 1982—; mentor tchr. Alvord Unified Schs., 1985-86, 86-87. Mem. state com. Dem. party, 1971-74; mem. re-election com. ednl. chmn. Congressman George Brown, 1971-72; mem. task force by bus. edn. unit Calif. State Dept. Edn., 1986-87, adv. com., 1987. Mem. NEA, Assn. Sch. Curriculum Devel., Calif. Tchrs. Assn. (area polit. chmn. 1973-76), Calif. Bus. Edn. Assn. Democrat. Roman Catholic. Office: 4145 La Sierra Ave Riverside CA 92505

MORALES, MILCIADES SEGUNDO, clinical social worker, consultant; b. Managua, Nicaragua, June 8, 1941; came to U.S., 1947; s. Milciades Hernandez and Constanza Josefa (Gomez) M.; m. Cleo Fawn Foran, Jan. 7, 1967; children: Sara Fawn, Calvin Milciades. BA, Calif. State U., San Francisco, 1965; MSW, Calif. State U., Sacramento, 1974. Lic. clin. social worker. Social worker Solano County, Vallejo, Calif., 1966, Imperial County, El Centro, Calif., 1967-69, Contra Costa County, Pittsburg, Calif., 1969-74; family therapist Children's Hosp. Med. Ctr., Oakland, Calif., 1974-80; counseling coordinator Family Stress Ctr., Pleasant Hill, Calif., 1980—; pvt. practice Antioch (Calif.) Counseling Ctr., 1981—; cons. Berkeley Planning Assn., Calif., 1981, No. Calif. Family Ctr., Walnut Creek, 1985; coordinator Families United Martinez (Calif.), East County Project, 1981; trainer Ctr. Human Devel., Lafayette, Calif., 1984. Co-founder, pres. Multi-Cultural Coordinating Council, Oakland, 1978—; bd. dirs. ACLU, Contra Costa, 1975-77, Bay Area Crisis Nursery, Concord, Calif., 1981—, Mental Health Adv. Bd., Martinez, 1981-86. Mem. Nat. Assn. Social Workers. Democrat. Avocations: backpacking, gardening, reading, bicycling. Office: Family Stress Ctr 200 A Harriet Dr Pleasant Hill CA 94523

MORAN, H. DANA, engineering research administrator; b. Quincy, Mass., Jan. 19, 1927; s. Herbert Claude and Mildred Lorraine (Davidson) M.; m. Shirley Doreen Moran, Nov. 5, 1955; 1 child, Kelly Doreen. BS in Aeros., Northrop U., 1960; MS in Engrng. Mgmt., UCLA, 1964. Preliminary design engr. Northrop Aircraft Corp., Hawthorne, Calif., 1951-56; mgr. engrg. Aerospace Industries Assn., Los Angeles, 1956-61; asst. to pres. Weber Aircraft Co., Burbank, Calif., 1961-63; program mgr. west coast div. Battelle-Columbus (Ohio) Labs., 1963-77; asst. to dir. Solar Energy Research Inst., Golden, Colo., 1977—; cons. mktg., Los Angeles, 1958-61. Contbr. articles to profl. jours. Pres. Foothills Art Ctr., Golden, 1982-85; v.p. Industries for Jefferson County, Colo., 1983—; bd. dirs. Golden C. of C., 1984—; trustee Colo. Innovation Found., Golden, 1984—. Named Outstanding Alumnus Northrop U., Inglewood, Cailf., 1969; recipient Personal Service award Solar Energy Industries Assn., Washington, 1985, Disting. Staff Service award Solar Energy Research Inst., Golden, 1986. Fellow AIAA (assoc., bd. dirs. 1974-76, Disting. Service award 1970), AAAS; mem. Am. Solar Energy Soc., Nat. Model Railroad Assn., Aircraft Owners and Pilots Assn., Tau Beta Pi. Republican. Lodge: Rotary (v.p. 1986). Avocations: pvt. pilot, woodworking, model railroading. Home: 1037 Dogwood Dr Golden CO 80401 Office: Solar Energy Research Inst 1617 Cole Blvd Golden CO 80401

MORAN, SUE, infosystems specialist; b. W.Va., Sept. 23, 1942. MS, U. Calif., Irvine, 1977. Dir. adminstrn. infosystems U. Calif., Irvine, 1980—. Office: U Calif AIS Irvine CA 92717

MORAN, THOMAS HARRY, university administrator; b. Milw., Oct. 21, 1937; s. Harry Edward and Edna Agnes Moran; B.S., U. Wis., 1964, M.A., 1972, Ph.D., 1974; m. Barbara Ellen Saklad, June 10, 1969; children—David Thomas, Karen Ellen. Dir. capital budgeting Wis. Dept. Adminstrn., 1962-64; exec. dir. Wis. Higher Ednl. Aids Bd., 1964-69; spl. cons. tax policy Wis. Dept. Revenue, 1973-74; dep. dir. Wis. Manpower Council, Office of Gov., 1974-76; v.p. bus. and fin., treas. U. Detroit, 1976-78; exec. assoc. v.p. health affairs U. So. Calif., Los Angeles, 1979—. USN fellow, 1957-59; U.S. Office Edn. research fellow, 1973. Mem. Am. Assn. Higher Edn., Phi Kappa Phi. Office: U So Calif 349 Adminstrn Bldg University Park Los Angeles CA 90007

MORAND, BLAISE E., bishop; b. Tecumseh, Ont., Can., Sept. 12, 1932. Ordained priest Roman Cath. Ch., 1958. Ordained coadjutor bishop Diocese of Prince Albert, Sask., Can., 1981, bishop, 1983—. Office: 1415 4th Ave W, Prince Albert, SK Canada S6V 5H1 *

MORANDO, JEANNE BUTLER, savings and loan association executive; b. Crystal River, Fla., Feb. 17, 1928; d. James Taylor and Lucile (Sparkman) Butler; student St. Helen's Hall Jr. Coll., 1945, U. Oreg. Extension Center, Portland, 1949-51, San Joaquin Delta Coll., 1963-65; m. Herbert O. Hope, June 12, 1951 (dec. 1958); m. 2d, Sil S. Morando, Jan. 13, 1961; children—Marta Lucile Hope Morando, James William Hope Morando. Asst. buyer Olds & Kings Western Dept. Stores, Inc., Portland, 1948-51; gen. mgr.

Hadley's Inc., Stockton, Calif., 1958-61; with World Savs. and Loan Assn., 1972-77, regional mgr., Oakland and Stockton, Calif., 1974-76, mktg. coordinator, Oakland, 1977; v.p., savs. adminstr., mktg. dir. Stockton Savs. & Loan Assn., 1977—; bd. dirs. Stockton Advt., Mktg. Media Club, Inc. Bd. govs. Stockton Civic Theatre, 1967-69, chmn. public relations and publicity, mem. steering com., 1967-69, 71-72, trustee, 1982-86; mem. adv. bd. U. Coll. of U. Pacific; bd. dirs. San Joaquin County (Calif.) United Way, 1979—, v.p., 1981-85, pres. and 1st v.p., 1985-86, pres., 1986-87, chmn. bd. trustees, 1987—; bd. dirs. Friends of Chamber Music, Jr. Achievement San Joaquin County, 1984—; mem. San Joaquin County Crime Awareness and Prevention Com., 1980; trustee Friends of Chamber Music, 1983—, bd. dirs., chmn. Artist Selection com. and booking. Lic. real estate broker, Calif. Mem. Savs. Instn. Mktg. Soc. Am. (basic mktg. sch. cert.), San Joaquin County Zool. Soc. (life). Republican. Lutheran. Club: Exec. Women (Stockton). Home: 1202 McClellan Way Stockton CA 95207 Office: 131 N San Joaquin St Stockton CA 95201

MORANDO, MARTA LUCILE HOPE, lawyer; b. Portland, Oreg., June 20, 1952; d. Sil. S. and Jeanne Hope (Butler) M. AB summa cum laude, U. Calif., Berkeley, 1972, JD, 1975. Bar: Calif. 1975. Assoc. Ware & Freidenrich, Palo Alto, Calif., 1975-80, ptnr., 1980—, mem. exec. com., 1983-86; lectr. on various legal topics. Mem. ABA, Calif. Bar Assn., Calif. Women's Lawyers Assn. Republican. Lutheran. Office: Ware & Freidenrich 400 Hamilton Ave Palo Alto CA 94301

MORARI, MANFRED, educator, engineering consultant; b. Graz, Austria, May 13, 1951; came to U.S., 1975; s. Manfred and Hilde (Florian) M.; m. Marina Korchynsky, May 12, 1984. Diploma Chem. Engring., Eidgenoessische Technische Hochschule, Zurich, Switzerland, 1974; PhD in Chem. Engring., U. Minn., 1977. Assoc. prof. U. Wis., Madison, 1977-83; prof. Calif. Inst. Tech., Pasadena, 1983—. Recipient D.P. Eckman award Am. Automatic Control Council, 1980. Mem. IEEE, Am. Inst. Chem. Engrs. (A.P. Colburn award 1984), Am. Chem. Soc. Home: 2735 Ardmore Rd San Marino CA 91108-1768 Office: Calif Inst Tech Dept Chem Engring 206-41 Pasadena CA 91125

MORATTO, MICHAEL JAMES, research company executive; b. Medford, Oreg., Sept. 9, 1943; s. Joseph and Berta Adele (Cassel) M.; m. Marilyn Elmira Nardi, Sept. 14, 1964 (div. 1975); 1 child, James Michael; m. Lynn Marie Riley, Jan. 17, 1976; children: Jennifer Lynn, Patricia Ann. AA, Santa Rosa Jr. Coll., 1965; BA, San Francisco State U., 1966; MA, U. Oreg., 1969, PhD, 1972. Prof. San Francisco State U., 1969-78, mus. dir., 1969-72; archaeologist U.S. Govt., Idaho and Calif., 1978-80; mgr. INFOTEC Devel., Costa Mesa, Calif., 1980-84; pres. INFOTEC Research, Sonora, Calif., 1984—, also bd. dirs.; cons. archaeologist, San Francisco, 1969-78. Author: Calif. Archaeology, 1984; contbr. articles to profl. jours. Fellow U. Oreg., 1966-69, Calif. Acad. Scis., 1976—. Fellow Am. Anthropol. Assn. (nominations com. 1980-82); mem. Am. Soc. for Conservation Archaeology (pres. 1981-82), Soc. for Calif. Archaeology (pres. 1972-73, M. Harrington award 1986), Soc. Am. Archaeology, Soc. Profl. Archaeologists (standards bd. 1978-80).

MORDENTI, JOYCE JENNEY, drug testing company administrator, pharmaceutical scientist; b. Oakville, Conn., May 18, 1952; d. Walter and Margaret (Jenney) M.; m. Jim Pohl, Dec. 24, 1981. BS cum laude, U. Conn., 1975, PhD, 1983. Registered pharmacist, Calif., Conn. Clin. pharm. and exptl. therapeutics fellow U. Calif., San Francisco, 1983-85, assoc. dir. drug studies unit, 1985—. Sect. editor Jour. Pharmacokinetics and Biopharmaceutics, 1986—; contbr. articles to profl. jours. Fellow U. Conn. Research Found., 1981-82; J.K. Lilly Meml. fellow Am. Found. Pharm. Edn., 1978-81. Mem. Am. Assn. Pharm. Scientists (publicity com. 1986—), Am. Med. Writers Assn., Am. Pharm. Assn., Am. Soc. Clin. Pharmocology and Therapeutics, Am. Soc. Microbiology (Cleverdon award 1983), Sierra Club, Sigma Xi, Phi Kappa Phi, Rho Chi. Avocations: motorcycles, classic cars. Home: 21 Longview Ct San Francisco CA 94131 Office: U Calif Sch Pharmacy Drug Studies Unit San Francisco CA 94143-0446

MOREHEAD, DOUGLAS CHARLES, property management executive; b. St. Joseph, Mo., June 18, 1946; s. Raymond Warren and Dorothy M. (Gurley) M.; m. Susan Starr, May 12, 1984. BS, Ariz. State U., 1971. Mgr. Hyatt Hotels Corp., Anaheim, Calif/., 1968-70; ptnr. Timely Products Corp., Anaheim, 1970-74; regional mgr. R&B Enterprises, Los Angeles and Houston, 1974-82; v.p. property mgmt. Triton National Co., Irvine, Calif., 1983—. Chmn., founder No-Name Invitational Charity Golf Tournament, Palm Springs, Calif., 1983—; bd. dirs. Aid to the Adoption of Spl. Kids. Mem. Building Owners and Mgrs. Assn. Orange County (Calif.), Comml. Indsl. Devel. Assn. Republican. Presbyterian. Lodge: Masons. Avocation: golf. Home: 425 Via Lido Nord Newport Beach CA 92663

MOREL, BENOIT FERDINAND, physicist; b. Meaux, France, Aug. 8, 1949; came to U.S., 1983; s. Bernard Ferdinand and Nicole Valentine (Deymie) M.; m. Penelope Ann Simmonds, Sept. 6, 1980; children; Alexandra, Christine. MS in Physics, U. Geneva, 1971, PhD in Physics, 1976. Postdoctoral fellow Harvard U., Cambridge, Mass., 1978-80; maitre-assistant U. Geneva, Switzerland, 1980-83; research fellow Calif. Inst. Tech., Pasadena, 1983-85; sci. fellow Stanford (Calif.) U., 1985—. Contbr. articles to profl. jours. Grantee Carnegie Inst., 1985. Home: 4004 Farmhill Blvd 205 Redwood City CA 94061 Office: Ctr for Arms Controls 320 Galvez St Stanford CA 94305

MORELAND, RONALD WILLIAM, insurance company executive; b. Decatur, Ill., Dec. 14, 1940; s. John William and Susan Irene (Daniels) M.; m. Jean Ann Cloyd, June 15, 1963 (div. 1976); children: Michael, Susan; m. Randi Elaine Thompson, June 3, 1984. BEd, Eastern Ill. U., 1962; MEd, U. Ill., 1963. CLU. Group mgr. Prudential Ins. Co., Chgo., 1963-68; regional mgr. Prudential Ins. Co., San Francisco, 1968-71; dir. group ins. Prudential Ins. Co., Newark, 1971-73, N.Y.C., 1973-78; v.p. group ins. Prudential Ins. Co., Los Angeles, 1978-83; exec. v.p. Transamerica Occidental Life Ins. Co., Los Angeles, 1983—. Clubs: Jonathan (Los Angeles); Beverly Hills Country (Cheviot Hills, Calif.). Avocations: tennis, golf, scuba, jogging. Office: Transamerica Occidental Life Ins Co Hill and Olive at 12th St Los Angeles CA 90015

MORELLI, AL, technical management company executive; b. Feb. 20, 1953; s. A.A. and S. Morelli; m. Sarah A. Decartert, 1978; children: William, Diana. BS in Indsl. Engring., Calif. Poly. State U., San Luis Obispo, 1977; MS in Indsl. Engring., U. So. Calif., 1981. Pres. Morelli Internat., Downey, Calif., 1977-84, Searchtec, Costa Mesa, Calif., 1984—; adj. prof. Calif. State Poly. U., Pomona; chmn. productivity and mgmt. program Calif. State U., Fullerton. Mem. Inst. Indsl. Engrs. (past pres., bd. dirs.), Soc. Advancement of Mgmt., Soc. Mfg. Engrs. Republican. Office: Searchtec 1421 Shamrock Costa Mesa CA 92626

MOREL-SEYTOUX, HUBERT JEAN, civil engineer, educator; b. Calais, Artois, France, Oct. 6, 1932; came to U.S., 1956; s. Aimé and Suzanne Claire (Rousseau) M.-S.; m. Margery K. Keyes, Apr. 16, 1960; children: Aimée, Claire, Sylvie, Marie-Jeanne. MS, Ecole Nationale des Ponts et Chaussées, Paris, 1956; PhD, Stanford U., 1962. Research engr. Chevron Oil Field Research Co., La Habra, Calif., 1962-66; prof. Colo. State U., Ft. Collins, 1966—; chargé de recherches U. Grenoble, France, 1972-73; maitre de recherces Ecole des Mines de Paris, Fontainebleau, France, 1982; cons. AID, Dakar, Senegal, 1985-86, Ministry of Agriculture and Water, Riyadh, Saudi Arabia, 1978-83, City of Thornton, Colo., 1986. Editor: Hydrology Days, 1981-86, 3d Internat. Hydrology Symposium, 1977. Pres. Internat. Ctr., Ft. Collins, 1984-86. Served to lt. French Army Marine Corps Engrs., 1959-62. Recipient Abell Faculty Research award Colo. State U. Coll. Engring., 1985. Mem. Am. Geophys. Union, ASCE, Soc. Petroleum Engrs., Am. Meteorol. Soc., Am. Soc. Agrl. Engrs. Home: 1005 Country Club Rd Fort Collins CO 80524 Office: Colo State U Fort Collins CO 80523

MOREN, ULF VILHELM, manufacturing company executive; b. Gothenburg, Sweden, May 10, 1940; came to U.S., 1966; s. Curt Vilhelm and Britt Moren; 1 child, Erik. BE, Gothenburg Tech. Coll., Sweden; MBA, Armstrong U., Berkeley, Calif. Lic. real estate broker. Overseas delivery Volvo AB, Gothenburg, Sweden, 1961-66; product mgr. Ledu Lamp Corp., Stamford, Conn., 1966-69; prodn. and purchasing mgr. Levi Strauss & Co., San Francisco, 1970-79; broker Bank St. Realtors, San Rafael, Calif., 1979-83; pres. Supercool USA Inc., San Rafael, 1983; bd. dirs. Supercool AB, Sweden, MAC Enterprises, Sonoma, Calif., Overseas Marine Ltd., Corte Madera, Calif., Bank St. Realtors, San Rafael. Contbr. articles to profl. jours. Mem. Rep. Presdl. Task Force, Washington, 1984—. Served to sgt. Swedish Army, 1959-61. Mem. Nat. Assn. Realtors, Calif. Assn. Realtors, Marin County Bd. Realtors, Homes for Living Network. Republican. Lutheran. Club: Royal Yacht (Gothenburg). Avocations: sailing, tennis, skiing. Home: 254 Bungalow Ave San Rafael CA 94901 Office: Supercool USA Inc 1004 Irwin St San Rafael CA 94901

MORENG, ROBERT EDWARD, educator, poultry scientist; b. N.Y.C., Jan. 29, 1922; s. Joseph and Martha Ida (Schlosser) M.; m. Miriam Trowbridge Tittmann, Aug. 12, 1950; children—George R., Nathan T., Jon C., Diane M., Michael Q., Charles C., Joseph P.H. B.S., U. Md., College Park, 1944, M.S., 1948, Ph.D., 1950. Asst. prof. N.D. State U., Fargo, 1950-55; prof. avian sci. Colo. State U., Ft. Collins, 1955-72, 78—, chmn. poultry dept., 1955-72, dir. research Coll. of Agrl. Scis., 1972-78, asst. dir. Expt. Sta., 1972-85; farmer, rancher. Served with AUS, 1944-46; ETO. Decorated Bronze Star. Recipient Teaching award Poultry Sci. Assn., 1967; Disting. Service award Colo. State U., 1968; Golden Turkey award Colo. Turkey Assn., 1966, 69. Fellow AAAS, Poultry Sci. Assn.; mem. N.Y. Acad. Sci., Soc. for Exptl. Biology and Medicine, Am. Genetics Assn., Am. Inst. Biol. Scis. Author: (with John S. Avens) Poultry Science and Production, 1985. Contbr. articles on stress-oriented selection in chickens and turkeys, high altitude reprodn. and gen. poultry mgmt. to profl. jours. and periodicals. Home: 6221 N Country Rd 15 Fort Collins CO 80524 Office: Dept Animal Scis Colo State Univ Fort Collins CO 80523

MORENO, JOHN A., tax consultant; b. Washington, Oct. 27, 1908; s. Aristides and Margaret Bell (Field) M.; m. Marian Stuart Groner, Nov. 25, 1933; 1 dau., Janet M. B.S., U.S. Naval Acad., 1930; M.Engring. Adminstrn., George Washington U., 1959; postgrad. Army Navy Staff Coll., 1944, San Diego State U., 1964. Commd. officer U.S. Navy, 1930, advanced through grades to capt., 1945, ret., 1960; comdg. officer USS San Jacinto, USS Floyds Bay; asst. plans officer Utah Assault Force (Normandy), 1944, So. France Assault and Lingayen Bay Assault, 1944; asst. dir. strategic plans Joint Staff, Joint Chiefs of Staff, 1956-59; mem. faculty San Diego City Coll., 1964-74; income tax cons., mgr. H & R Block, Coronado, Calif. 1978-83. Decorated Legion of Merit, Bronze Star (2). Mem. U.S. Naval Acad. Alumni Assn., George Washington U. Alumni Assn. Republican. Episcopalian. Club: Rotary. Address: 1214 Fifth St Coronado CA 92118

MORENO, MANUEL D., bishop. Educ. Univ. of Calif., Los Angeles, St. John's Sem., Camarillo, Calif. Ordained priest Roman Cath. church, 1961. Ordained aux. bishop of Los Angeles, titular bishop of Tanagra, 1977; installed as bishop of Tucson, 1982. Office: 192 S Stone Ave PO Box 31 Tucson AZ 85702 *

MORENO, RICHARD MILLS, fire chief; b. Tucson, June 30, 1938; s. Fred Elias and Lupe (Mills) M.; m. Yolanda Bertha Rodriquez, Sept. 3, 1960; children—Richard, Robert, Sonya, Rene. B.A, U. Ariz., 1976. With Tucson Fire Dept., 1959—, fire chief, 1982—; mem. adj. faculty Nat. Fire Acad. Md., 1978-79. Contbr. articles to profl. jours. Tng. chmn. Tucson Boy Scouts. Served with USMC, 1956-59. Mem. Internat. Fire Chiefs Assn., Nat. Fire Protection Assn., Ariz. Fire Chiefs Assn. Democrat. Roman Catholic. Club: Centurions. Office: Tucson Fire Dept 265 S Church St Tucson AZ 85701 *

MORENS, DAVID MICHAEL, epidemiologist, tropical medicine investigator; b. Detroit, Mar. 7, 1948; s. Ralph Michael and Martha Louise (Wright) M.; m. Darlene Lin Sun Luke, May 26, 1974 (div. Sept. 1977); children: Bryan Scott Kum Chan, Benjamin Michael Kum Chin. AB, U. Mich., 1969, MD, 1973. Epidemic Intelligence Service officer U.S. Ctrs. Disease Control, Atlanta, 1976-78; med. officer Bur. Labs. U.S. Ctrs. Disease Control, Atlanta, Ga. and Sierra Leone, 1978-81, chief respiratory and spl. pathogens br., 1981-82; assoc. prof. tropical medicine U. Hawaii, Honolulu, 1982-86, prof., chmn. dept. family practice and community health, 1987—, assoc. prof. pub. health, 1986—; Cons. WHO, govts. Egypt, Israel, Sierra Leone, Liberia, Indonesia, Vietnam, 1977—; med. dir. of labs. Leahi Hosp., Honolulu, 1982—. Co-author textbook chpts.; contbr. over 80 articles to profl. jours. Served to commdr. USPHS, 1976-82. Grantee NIH, WHO, Rockefeller Found., others. Mem. Am. Pub. Health Assn., Soc. Epidemiologic Research, Am. Com. Arthropod-Borne Viruses, Am. Soc. Tropical Med. Hygiene, Am. Soc. Microbiology. Avocations: music, hiking, scuba diving, travel, Pacific/Asian cultures. Home: 3636 Kilauea Ave Honolulu HI 96816-2318 Office: U Hawaii Dept Tropical Medicine Leahi Hosp 3675 Kilauea Ave Honolulu HI 96816 Address: U Hawaii Dept Pub Health Scis Sch Pub Health 1960 East-West Rd Honolulu HI 96822

MORENZONI, RICHARD A., microbiologist; b. Sonoma, Calif., Sept. 30, 1946; s. Anthony Vincent and Josephine Emily (Noli) M.; m. Dana Bianca, July 13, 1974; 1 child, Matt Michael. BS, U. Calif., Davis, 1968, PhD, 1973. Microbiologist E/J Gallo Winery, Modesto, Calif. Office: E/J Gallo Winery Modesto CA 95353

MORETTI, AUGUST JOSEPH, lawyer; b. Elmira, N.Y., Aug. 18, 1950; s. John Anthony and Dorothy M. (De Blasio) M.; m. Audrey B Kavka, Nov. 8, 1981;children: David Anthony, Matthew Alexander. BA, Princeton U., 1972; JD, Harvard U., 1975. Assoc. Heller, Ehrman, White and McAuliffe, San Francisco, 1976-82; ptnr. Heller, Ehrman, Whitey and McAuliffe, San Francisco, 1982—; lectr. bus. adminstrn. U. Calif. Berkeley, 1977-79. Mem. ABA. Office: Heller Ehrman White & McAuliffe 525 University Ave Palo Alto CA 94301

MOREWITZ, HARRY ALAN, engineering consultant; b. Newport News, Va., June 2, 1923; s. Jacob Louis and Sallie Florence (Rome) M.; m. Myra Kalkin, June 20, 1948; children: Ralph Steven, Dara Beth. BS, William and Mary Coll., 1943; MA, Columbia U., 1949; PhD, NYU, 1953. Project engr. Metavac, Inc., Long Island City, N.Y., 1952-53; supervising scientist Westinghouse Electric Co., Pitts., 1953-59; sr. staff engr. Rockwell Internat., Canoga Park, Calif., 1959-82; pres. H.M. Assocs., Ltd., Tarzana, Calif., 1982—; mem. adv. com. on reactor physics USAEC, Washington, 1969-72; instr. dept. radiology UCLA, 1967-72; cons. Nuclear Safety Analysis Ctr., Palo Alto, Calif. 1979-82. Contbr. scientific and engring. papers to profl. jours.; patentee nuclear safety fuse, 1961. Served to 1st lt. USMCR, 1943-46, PTO. Mem. Am. Phys. Soc., Am. Nuclear Soc., Health Physics Soc., Am. Geophys. Union, N.Y. Acad. Sci., Sigma Xi. Office: H M Assocs Ltd 5300 Bothwell Rd Tarzana CA 91356

MOREY, BOOKER WILLIAMS, technical and science consultant; b. Rochester, N.Y., May 12, 1941; s. Donald Roger and Nancy Lee Morey; m. Ann Intili, Aug. 1969 (div. Dec. 1984). BS in Mineral Engring., Pa. State U., 1963, MS in Mineral Engring., 1965; PhD in Mineral Engring., Stanford U., 1969. Registered profl. engr., Calif., Mass. Group leader separations Occidental Research, La Verne, Calif., 1969-78; dir. advanced tech. Envirotech Corp., Menlo Park, Calif., 1978-81; v.p. new bus. Waste Energy Tech., Bedford, Mass., 1982-84; sr. cons. SRI Internat., Menlo Park, 1984—. Patentee in field. Mem. AIME (v.p., dir. 1981-84), Filtration Soc., Brit. Inst. Mining and Metallurgy, Internat. Precious Metals Inst. Office: SRI Internat 333 Ravenswood Ave Menlo Park CA 94025

MORFITT, JOHN WINSLOW, laboratory director; b. Malden, Mass., July 4, 1920; s. John Henry and Gertrude (Winslow) M.; m. Elizabeth Nan Hale, Feb. 1, 1947; children: Carolyn E., Susan L., Craig W. BSChemE, Northeastern U., 1943; PhD in Physics, U. Tenn., 1953. Chem. engr., supr. Carbon and Carbide Chem. Co., Oak Ridge, Tenn., 1943-46, 52-55, nuclear criticality experimentalist, 1946-52; mgr. nuclear engring. Gen. Electric Co., Cin. and Idaho Falls, Idaho, 1955-67; mgr. project engring. Idaho Nat. Engring. Lab., Idaho Falls, 1967-76; lab. mgr., chief scientist EG&G, Idaho Falls, 1976—; nuclear criticality cons. Dept. Energy, Oak Ridge and Portsmouth, Ohio, 1955—. Contbr. articles to profl. jours. Bd. dirs. United Way, Idaho Falls, 1969-75, pres. 1975; bd. dirs. Head Start Program, Idaho Falls, 1978-83; chmn. of trustees Presbyn. Ch. Synod of Pacific, San Francisco, 1974-80. Fellow Am. Nuclear Soc. (bd. dirs. 1972-75); mem. Am. Phys. Soc., Sigma Xi. Avocations: hiking, fishing, writing, speaking. Home: 353 Westmoreland Dr Idaho Falls ID 83402 Office: EG&G Idaho PO Box 1625 Idaho Falls ID 83415

MORGAL, JOHN WILLIAM, chemical engineer; b. Lafayette, Ind., Aug. 22, 1943; s. Paul Walter and Dorothy Ann (Poore) M.; m. Carleen M., Apr. 12, 1975; children: Christy, Tracy, Cindy. BS, U. Calif., Berkeley, 1970. Registered profl. engr., Calif. Ordnance engr. Aerojet Gen., Downey, Calif., 1966-67; v.p. prodn. Teel Boat Works, Wilmington, Calif., 1970-72; engr., sales C.F. Braun Engrs., Alahambra, Calif., 1972-80; project mgmt. Fluor Engrs. and Constructors, Irvine, Calif., 1980—. Served to sgt. USMC, 1964-70. Republican. Office: Fluor Engrs Inc 3333 Michelson Irvine CA 92730

MORGAN, ANDREW LANE, urologist; b. Honolulu May 13, 1920; s. James Albert and Elsie Edna (Johnson) M.; B.A., Dartmouth Coll., 1942; M.D., Cornell U., 1945; m. Miriam Cleary, June 9, 1951; children—Andrew Lane, Christine, Martha, James. Diplomate Am. Bd. Urology. Intern, Lenox Hill Hosp., N.Y.C., 1945-46; resident, Queen's Med. Ctr., Honolulu, 1948-50, Yale U., 1950-52; practice medicine, specializing in urology, Honolulu, 1952—; chmn. dept. surgery Queen's Med. Ctr., 1979; clin. prof. urology John Burns Sch. Medicine, U. Hawaii. Served to capt., AUS, 1946-48. Fellow ACS; mem. Am. Urol. Assn. (past pres. Western sect.), Hawaii Med. Assn., Societe Internationale d'Urologie, Honolulu County Med. Soc. (bd. govs. 1970-76, treas. 1978-79). Episcopalian. Clubs: Plaza, Pacific (Honolulu). Home: 4022 Nuuanu Pali Dr Honolulu HI 96817 Office: 1380 Lusitana St Room 1008 Honolulu HI 96813

MORGAN, AUDREY, architect; b. Neenah, Wis., Oct. 19, 1931; d. Andrew John Charles Hopfensperger and Melda Lily (Radtke) Anderson; m. Earl Adrian Morgan (div); children: Michael A., Susan Lynn Heiner, Nancy Lee, Diana Morgan Lucio. B.A., U. Wash., 1955. Registered architect, Wash.; cert. NCARB. Project mgr. The Austin Co., Renton, Wash., 1972-75; med. facilities architect The NBBJ Group, Seattle, 1975-79; architect constrn. rev. unit Wash. State Dept. Social and Health Services, Olympia, 1979-81; project dir., med. planner John Graham & Co., Seattle, 1981-83; pvt. practice architecture, Seattle, 1983—, also health care facility cons., code analyst. Contbr. articles to profl. jours. and govt. papers; prin. works include quality assurance coordinator for design phase Madigan Army Med. Ctr., Ft. Lewis, Wash.; med. planner and code analyst Rockwood Clinic, Spokane, Wash. Cons. on property mgmt. Totem council Girl Scouts U.S.A., Seattle, 1969-84, troop leader, cons., trainer, 1961-74. Mem. AIA (subcoms. codes and standards, health planning and mental health of nat. com. on architecture for health 1980—, and numerous other coms., founding mem. Wash. council for health panel 1981—, recorder 1981-84, bd. dirs. S.W. Wash. chpt. 1983-84, vice chmn. 1987), Soc. Am. Value Engrs., Am. Hosp. Assn., Assn. Western Hosps., Wash. State Hosp. Assn., Seattle Womens Sailing Assn., Audubon Soc., Alpha Omicron Pi. Lutheran. Clubs: Coronado 25 Fleet 13 (Seattle) (past sec., bull. editor); GSA 25 Plus.

MORGAN, CHARLES EDWARD PHILLIP, banker; b. Wichita, Kans., Nov. 3, 1916; s. Wells C. Morgan and Mary E. (Brown) Allredge; m. Elizabeth Ann Brown, Oct. 14, 1943 (div. Dec. 1972); children—Valerie Donahue, Renee Tompkins. Student U. Wichita, 1935; student bus. adminstrn., U. Calif.-Berkeley, 1963. Teller First Nat. Bank, Santa Fe, 1938-42; safety officer Libby-McNeil-Libby, Sacramento, 1946-48; from teller to v.p./br. mgr. Wells Fargo Bank, Sacramento, 1948-76; sr. v.p. Capitol Bank of Commerce, Sacramento, 1976—. Served to 1st lt. USAF, 1942-45. Democrat. Mem. Christian Ch. Lodges: Masons, Shriners, Elks. Home: 6371 Granger's Dairy Dr Sacramento CA 95831

MORGAN, CHERYL JEAN, flight attendant; b. Ft. Collins, Colo., Mar. 14, 1947; s. Irwin Leroy and Shirley (Liggett) Johnson; m. Russ Morgan, July 5, 1981. B, U. No. Colo., 1969. Cert. elem. and music edn. tchr. Tchr. Poudre RI Schs., Ft. Collins, 1969-83; owner Welcome Welcome of Colo., Ft. Collins, 1983-85; flight attendant, tour dir. Ports of Call/Skyworld, Denver, 1985—; grad. asst. Dale Carnegie Inst., Ft. Collins, 1986—; piano tuner and repair person, 1986—. Accompanist ch. choir, Ft. Collins, 1981—, dir. Sweet Adelines, 1983-86. Mem. Sweet Adelines (dir. 1983—). Avocations: macrame, music, reading, traveling, watersports. Home: 1413 W Mulberry Fort Collins CO 80521

MORGAN, CLAYTON CALKINS, physician; b. Ontario, Oreg., Oct. 9, 1927; s. Frank Theodore and Jessie Margarete (Calkins) M.; m. Patricia Elaine Bolander, Dec. 19, 1947; children: Cathleen, Michael, Frank, Thomas. BS, U. Oreg., 1949, MD, 1952. Diplomate Am. Bd. Family Physicians, Am. Bd. Quality Assurance and Utilization Rev. Intern Madigan Army Hosp., 1952-53; practice medicine specializing in general medicine Nyssa, Oreg., 1955-59, Boise, Idaho, 1959—; chief of staff St. Luke's Hosp., 1971-73, dir., 1969-73; med. dir. Idaho Medicare Profl. Rev. Orgn., 1985-86. Editorial adv. bd. The Hosp. Med. Staff, 1970-75. Pres. health sci. adv. bd., med. advisor Sch. Nursing, Boise State U.; pres., bd. dirs. Boise Ind. Sch. Dist., 1973-80, pres., 1978-80; bd. dirs. Family Practice Residency S.W. Idaho, 1975—, bd. pres., 1979-82; cons. Blue Cross of Idaho, 1977—, med. dir., 1985—. Served with USAF, 1952-55. Recipient Star Garnet award Idaho Hosp. Assn., 1975, A.N. Robbins Community Service award, 1980. Fellow Am. Acad. Family Physicians (charter), Royal Soc. Health; mem. AMA, Idaho Med. Assn. (pres. 1981-82), ADA County Med. Soc. (past pres., dir.), Am. Hosp. Assn. (bd. dirs. 1983—, mem. ho. dels., vice chmn. com. physicians, physician mem. regional adv. bd.). Home: 2622 Alamo Rd Boise ID 83704 Office: 6613 Ustick Rd Boise ID 83704

MORGAN, DAVID FORBES, minister, Episcopal Church; b. Toronto, Ont., Can., Aug. 3, 1930; came to U.S., 1954; s. Forbes Alexander and Ruth (Bamford) M.; m. Delores Mae Storhaug, Sept. 7, 1956; children—Roxanne Ruth, David Forbes. B.A., Rocky Mt. Coll.; Th.B., Coll. of the Rockies, M.Div.; postgrad. Bishop's Sch. Theology; Litt.D. (hon.), Temple Coll., 1956, D.C. Nat. Coll. Ordained priest. Pres., Coll. of the Rockies, Denver, 1960-73; prior Order of Christ Centered Ministries, Denver, 1973—; canon pastor St. John's Cathedral, Denver, 1982—; dir. Alpha Inc., Denver., 1981—. Author: Christ Centered Ministries, A Response to God's Call, 1973; Songs with A Message, 1956. Clubs: Oxford, Denver Botanic Garden. Home: 740 Clarkson Denver CO 80218 Office: Saint Johns Cathedral 1313 Clarkson Denver CO 80218

MORGAN, DAVID GRIFFITH, neurobiologist, educator; b. Cin., Nov. 25, 1952; s. David Griffith Jr. and Polly Ann (Pauly) M. BA, Northwestern U., 1974, MS, 1978, PhD, 1981. Postdoctoral fellow U. So. Calif., Los Angeles, 1981-83, res. assoc., 1983-85, asst. prof., 1985—; instr. Calif. State U. Dominguez Hills, Caron, 1982; vis. sci. U. Umea, Sweden, 1984. Contbr. articles to sci. jours. Recipient New Investigator award Am. Geriatrics Soc., 1985; Potamkin-Lerner fellow Orentreich Found., 1983-85, French Found. fellow, 1985—, Nathan Shock award, Gerontol. Soc. Am., 1986. Mem. Soc. Neurosci., Am. Fedn. Aging Research, Internat. Congress Biomed. Gerontology. Democrat. Avocations: football, gardening, volleyball, auto restoration, carpentry. Office: U So Calif Gerontology Ctr Los Angeles CA 90089-0191

MORGAN, HAROLD THOMAS, physicist; b. Salt Lake City, Apr. 4, 1954; s. Athel Collier and Beverly Jean (Smith) M.; m. Barbara Jean Davie, Aug. 11, 1978; 1 child, Harold Thomas Jr. BS in Physics, Clark Coll., 1978. Engr. Hercules Aerospace, Magna, Utah, 1978-80, sr. engr., 1980-84; project engr. Aerojet Strategic Propulsion, Sacramento, 1984-85; program engr. Atlantic Research Corp., Gainesville, Va., 1986—. RCA scholar in sci. RCA Corp., Atlanta, 1976-77. Mem. Am. Soc. Non Destructive Testing. Democrat. Baptist.

MORGAN, JACK M., lawyer, state senator; b. Portales, N.Mex., Jan. 15, 1924; s. George Albert and Mary Rosana (Baker) M.; B.B.A., U. Tex., 1948; LL.B., 1950; m. Peggy Flynn Cummings, 1947; children—Marilyn, Rebecca, Claudia, Jack. Admitted to N.Mex. bar, 1950; sole practice law, Farmington, N.Mex., 1956—; mem. N.Mex. State Senate, 1973—. Served with USN, 1942-46. Mem. Am. Bar Assn., N.Mex. Bar Assn., S.W. Regional Energy Council (past chmn.). Republican. Clubs: Kiwanis, Elks. Office: PO Box 2151 Farmington NM 87499

MORGAN, JACK RICHARD, chemistry educator; b. Tinley Park, Ill., Jan. 24, 1956; s. Calvin Raymond and Elsie Betty (Klinke) M.; m. Tamba Jean McIntire, Aug. 12, 1978 (div. Dec. 1985); 1 child, Gregory. BS with high distinction, U. Ill., Urbana, 1978; PhD, UCLA, 1983. Postdoctoral fellow U. Calif., Berkeley, 1984-85; asst. prof. chemistry U. Nev., Reno, 1985—. Contbr. articles to profl. jours. Mem. Am. Chem. Soc., Am. Phys. Soc. Home: 330 Talus Way Apt A Reno NV 89503 Office: U Nev Dept Chemistry Reno NV 89557

MORGAN, JEFFREY WAYNE, process engineer, chemist; b. Oceanside, Calif., July 29, 1959; s. John Anthony and Barbara Ann (Hand) M.; m. Suzanne Elizabeth Wort, June 26, 1983. BS in Chemistry, Rose-Hulman Inst. Tech.; MS in Chemistry, U. Calif., Irvine. Chemist Am. Hosp. Supply, Irwindale, Calif., 1981-82; research asst. U. Calif., Irvine, 1981-85; mem. tech. staff Hughes Aircraft, Irvine, 1985—. Named Eagle Scout Boy Scouts Am., 1973. Mem. Am. Chem. Soc. Democrat. Methodist. Avocations: backpacking, rock climbing, photography. Office: Hughes Aircraft 2601 Campus Dr Irvine CA 92715

MORGAN, JIM LEE, business educator; b. Little Rock, Apr. 14, 1943; s. James Charles and Lois Marie (McPherson) M.; BS, BA, U. Ark., 1961, MEd, 1968; MPA, U. So. Calif., 1980. Asst. city mgr. City of Beverly Hills, Calif., 1972-74; dir. Human Service Planning, Simi Valley, Calif., 1975-76; prof. bus. and mgmt. West Los Angeles Coll., 1975—, pres. acad. senate, 1975—; lectr. in field. Bd. advisors U. So. Calif. Traffic Safety Center, 1974-75; bd. dirs. Beverly Hills Chamber Orch., 1973-75, West Los Angeles chpt. ARC, 1972-75; founder, hon. chmn. Ann. Festival of Arts, City of Beverly Hills, 1972-75; founding mem. Research Coordinating Forum of Ventura County, 1976—; v.p. dist. senate Los Angeles Community Coll., 1978-80; treas. Acad. Senate, Calif. Community Colls., 1980-81, fin. task force commn. Chancellor's Office, 1980—. Served to capt. USAF, 1967-72. Decorated Air Force Commendation medal; honored by Jim Lee Morgan Day, City of Beverly Hills, Apr. 14, 1974; named Air Force Systems Command Personnel Officer of the Yr., 1970. Mem. Internat. City Mgrs. Assn., So. Calif. Assn. Human Resources Dirs., Am. Soc. Planning Ofcls., Am. Mgmt. Assn., Phi Delta Kappa, Blue Key, Beta Gamma Sigma. Author: Social Planning for the City, 1975; Business of Management, 1982; Study Guide to Management, 1982; editor Community Services Newsletter, 1974-75, Customer Relations: Policy and Procedures, 1975, Human Services Directory, City of Simi Valley, 1976, Rev. mag., 1972-74. Home: 2601 E 19th St Apt #5 Signal Hill CA 90804 Office: West Los Angeles Coll 4800 Freshman Dr Culver City CA 90230

MORGAN, JOHN DERALD, electrical engineer; b. Hays, Kans., Mar. 15, 1939; s. John Baber and Avis Ruth (Wolf) M.; m. Elizabeth June McKneely, June 23, 1962; children: Laura Elizabeth, Kimberly Ann, Rebecca Ruth, John Derald. B.S. in Elec. Enging, La. Tech. U., 1962; M.S., U. Mo., Rolla, 1965; Ph.D., Ariz. State U., 1968. Registered profl. engr., Mo., N.Mex. Elec. engr. Tex. Eastman div. Eastman Kodak Co., 1962-63; instr. U. Mo., Rolla, 1963-65, Ariz. State U., 1965-68; asso. prof. elec. enging. U. Mo., Rolla, 1968-72; Alcoa Found. prof. elec. enging. U. Mo., 1972-75, chmn. elec. enging., 1978-85, assoc. dir. Ctr. Internat. Programs, 1970-78, Emerson Electric Co. prof., 1975-85; dean enging. N.Mex. State U., 1985—; cons. to industry. Author: Power Apparatus Testing Techniques, 1969, Computer Monitoring and Control of Electric Utility Systems, 1972, Control and Distribution of Megawatts Through Man-Machine Interaction, 1973, Electromechanical and Electromagnetic Machines and Devices, 1986; also articles. Pres. bd. trustees First Meth. Ch., Rolla, 1971-73; pres. adminstrv. bd. First United Meth. Ch. Rolla 1978-79; v.p., mem. bd. adminstrn. People to People, 1976; bd. dirs., cubmaster Ozarks dist. Boy Scouts Am., 1968-79, asst. dist. commr., 1971-73; dist. chmn. Meramec dist., 1978-80; bd. dirs. Mo. Partners of the Americas. Recipient Scouters Key award Ozarks council Boy Scouts Am., 1971, District award of merit Ozarks council Boy Scouts Am., 1977, Silver Beaver award Ozarks council Boy Scouts Am., 1982; T.H. Harris scholar, 1959-61; John H. Horton scholar, 1961-62. Fellow IEEE (chmn. internat. practices subcom. 1972-79, sec. PSE com., vice chmn., chmn. 1979-85, chmn. ednl. resources subcom. 1973-78, elected, award of Merit, St. Louis sect., Educators award St. Louis sect., honor award St. Louis sect., Centennial award 1984); mem. Am. Soc. Enging. Edn., Nat., Mo. socs. profl. engrs., ASTM Sigma Xi, Tau Beta Pi, Eta Kappa Nu, Omicron Delta Kappa, Phi Kappa Phi. Home: 2425 Janet Ann Ln Las Cruces NM 88005 Office: New Mexico State U Main Campus College of Engineering PO Box 3AA Las Cruces NM 88003

MORGAN, JOHN MCDOWELL, research neuroscience educator; b. Little Rock, June 15, 1938; s. Artis M. and Gladys (McDowell) M.; m. Dorothy Jeanne Schroeder, Dec. 18, 1965; children: Timothy Patrick, Katheleen Elizabeth. BA, Cardinal Glennon Coll., 1960; MA, So. Ill. U., 1967; PhD, Kans. State U., 1969. Prof. neurosci. Humboldt State U., Arcata, Calif., 1969—; vis. research scholar Northwestern U., Evanston, Ill., 1975-76; vis. prof. U. Leuven, Belgium, 1982-83; counselor North Coast Mental Health Clinic, McKinleyville, Calif., 1978-84. Contbr. articles to profl. jours. NIH fellow, Bethesda, Md., 1966-69; UNESCO Internat. Brain Research grantee, Paris, 1983. Mem. AAAS, BioFeedback Soc. Am., BioFeedback Soc. Calif., Internat. Soc. Study of Pain, Phychophysiology Soc. Avocations: computers, wood working. Home: 715 Fickle Hill Rd Arcata CA 95521 Office: Humboldt State U Dept Psychology Arcata CA 95521

MORGAN, LUCIAN LLOYD, aerospace engineering executive; b. Wichita Falls, Tex., Dec. 22, 1928; s. Jasper Hugh and Myrtle Irene (Huffman) M.; m. Dorothy Rea Dill, Sept. 14, 1950. B.S. in Chem. Enging., Tex. A&M U., 1949; M.S. in Nuclear Enging., So. Meth. U., 1958; postgrad. Stanford U., 1964-65; M.S. in Systems Mgmt., U. So. Calif., 1975. Registered profl. engr., Calif., Tex. Supr. U.S. Gypsum Co., Sweetwater, Tex., 1949-50; engr. supr. General Dynamics Co., San Diego, 1950-54, asst. chief chemist, 1954-57, project nuclear engr., 1957-60, supr. propulsion and analysis, 1960-62; project leader Lockheed Missiles and Space Co., Sunnyvale, Calif., 1962-81, mgr. systems enging., 1981-85, chief systems enging., 1985—. Served to capt. U.S. Army, 1952-53. Recipient NASA Pub. Service award for contbrs. to space shuttle, 1982. Mem. AIAA, Air Force Assn., Nat. Mgmt. Assn. Republican. Mem. Ch. of Christ. Home: 2029 Kent Dr Los Altos CA 94022 Office: Orgn 51-31 Bldg 586 PO Box 504 Sunnyvale CA 94088

MORGAN, MARK QUENTEN, astronomer, astrophysics educator; b. Topeka, Dec. 27, 1950; s. Walter Quenten and Barbara Gene (Haynes) M. BA in Astronomy, San Diego State U., 1972; PhD in Astronomy, U. Addison, Ont., Can., 1976. Jr. power plant engr. N.Am. Aviation, Palmdale, Calif., 1966-68; astron. observer San Diego State U., 1970-74; engr., solar observer U. Md.-Clark Lake Radio Obs., Borrego Springs, Calif., 1978-82; engr., lectr. Sci. Atlanta, San Diego, 1979—. Inventor continuous wave laser, 1965. Mem. Inst. Environ. Scis., Acoustic Soc. Am., Astrophys. Soc. Am., Union Concerned Scientists, Planetary Soc.

MORGAN, NEIL, author, editor, lecturer, columnist; b. Smithfield, N.C., Feb. 27, 1924; s. Samuel Lewis and Isabelle (Robeson) M.; m. Caryl Lawrence, 1945 (div. 1954); m. Katharine Starkey, 1955 (div. 1962); m. Judith Blakely, 1964; 1 child, Jill. A.B., Wake Forest Coll., 1943. Columnist San Diego Daily Jour., 1946-50; columnist San Diego Evening Tribune, 1950—, asso. editor, 1977-81, editor, 1981—; syndicated columnist Morgan Jour., Copley News Service, 1958—; lectr.; cons. on Calif. affairs Bank of Am., Sunset mag. Author: My San Diego, 1951, It Began With a Roar, 1953, Know Your Doctor, 1954, Crosstown, 1955, My San Diego 1960, 1959, Westward Tilt, 1963, Neil Morgan's San Diego, 1964, The Pacific States, 1967, The California Syndrome, 1969, (with Robert Witty) Marines of the Margarita, 1970, The Unconventional City, 1972, (with Tom Blair) Yesterday's San Diego, 1976, This Great Land, 1983; contbr.: nonfiction articles to Nat. Geog., Esquire, Redbook, Reader's Digest, Holiday, Harper's, Travel and Leisure, Ency. Brit. Served to lt. USNR, 1943-46. Recipient Ernie Pyle Meml. award, 1957, Bill Corum Meml. award, 1961, Disting. Service citation Wake Forest U., 1966; Grand award for travel writing Pacific Area Travel Assn., 1972, 78; co-recipient Ellen and Roger Revelle award, 1986; named Outstanding Young Man of Year San Diego, 1959. Mem. Authors Guild, Am. Soc. Newspaper Editors, Soc. Profl. Journalists, Explorers Club, Phi Beta Kappa, Omicron Delta Kappa. Club: Bohemian, Cuyamaca. Home: 7930 Prospect Pl La Jolla CA 92037 Office: PO Box 191 San Diego CA 92112

MORGAN, ROBERT FARBER, psychologist, academic administrator; b. Buffalo, Jan. 24, 1941; s. Brenn Joel and Evelyn Eliot (Farber) M.; children—Animaulda, Charles, Robert, Michael, Julia, Cinnamon, Angel Kwan-Yin. Student Clarkson Coll., Potsdam, N.Y., 1958-60; B.A., Mich. State U., 1962, M.A., 1964, Ph.D., 1965. Research fellow Mich. State U., 1963-65; clin. psychology, program dir. Hawaii State Hosp., Kaneohe, 1965-67; assoc. prof. psychology St. Bonaventure U., Olean, N.Y.; 1967-69; assoc. prof. psychology Acadia U., Wolfeville, N.S., Can., 1969-71; founding faculty, dean Calif. Sch. Profl. Psychology, San Francisco, 1971-75; prof. psychology, chmn. dept. U. So. Colo., Pueblo, 1975-78; chief human services edn. State of Nev., Reno, 1977-79; cons., tchr. San Diego State U., 1979-80; prof., chmn. dept. psychology Wilfrid Laurier U., Waterloo, Ont., 1980-82; acad. dean, prof. psychology Calif. Sch. Profl. Psychology, Fresno, 1982-86; acad. v.p. Pacific Grad. Sch. Psychology, Menlo Park, Calif., 1986—. Author: The Iatrogenics Handbook: A Critical Look at Research and Practice in the Helping Professions, 1983; Growing Younger: Measurement and Control of Body Age, 1983; Training the Time Sense: Hypnotic and Conditioning Approaches, 1983; Electric Shock, 1985. Contbr. numerous articles to various publs. Human relations commr. City East Lansing, Mich., 1963-64. Recipient Mayors Citation for Excellent Service, 1964. Named Man of Year AAUP, 1969; NIMH Pre-doctoral Research fellow, 1963-65. Mem. Internat. Council Psychologists, Am. Psychol. Assn., Internat. Assn. Applied Psychologists (div. pres.), Gerontol. Soc. Office: 431 Burgess Dr Menlo Park CA 94025

MORGAN, ROBERT STERLING, forest supervisor; b. Choteau, Mont., Aug. 27, 1922; s. James Clarence and Alma Zay (Adams) M.; m. Catharine Adriance Riley, May 17, 1947; children—Douglas, Gail, Richard, Catharine. B.S. in Forest Mgmt., U. Mont., 1948. Forest Ranger Forest Service, St. Joe Nat. Forest, St. Maries, Idaho, 1951-54, Moscow, Idaho, 1954-56; asst. forest supr. Flathead Nat. Forest, U.S. Forest Service, Kalispell, Mont., 1956-60, safety tng. officer Forest Service Region 4, Ogden, Utah, 1960-62, forest supr. Helena Nat. Forest, Mont., 1962-74, Bitteroot Nat. Forest, Hamilton, Mont., 1974—. Recipient Outstanding Environ. Achievement award Romcoe, Denver, 1972, Cert. of Merit Dept. Agr., 1980, Superior Service award Dept. Agr., 1981. Fellow Soc. Am. Foresters; mem. Helena C. of C. (bd. dirs. 1970-74), Bitteroot C. of C. (bd. dirs. 1978-83). Episcopalian. Lodge: Rotary (pres. Helena 1972-73, bd. dirs. Hamilton 1982—). Office: Bitteroot Nat Forest 316 N 3d St Hamilton MT 59840

MORGAN, SHELLEY TAYLOR, actress; b. Charleston, W.Va.; d. Leon Herman and Cleonne Sheila (Mandell) Stein. Grad. high sch., Los Angeles. Actress Gen. Hosp., ABC-TV, Hollywood, Calif., 1984—. Appeared in feature films My Tutor, The Sword and the Sorcerer. Vol. Animal Alliance, W. Los Angeles, Love Is Feeding Everyone, Los Angeles. Mem. Screen Actors Guild, AFTRA, Actors Equity Assn. Avocations: weight tng., English riding and jumping, swimming.

MORGAN, THOMAS LOGAN, science research associate; b. Oakland, Calif., June 18, 1953; s. Thomas Logan Jr. and June Eleanor (Hollister) M.; m. Mary-Frances O'Connor, Sept. 29, 1984. BS in Biology, U. Calif., Irvine, 1975, BA in Chemistry, 1976, MS in Radiol. Sci., 1979, PhD in Radiol. Sci., 1983. Postdoctoral fellow Mich. State U., East Lansing, 1983-86; Hanford fellow Battelle Labs., Richland, Wash., 1986—; sr. reactor operator U. Calif., Irvine, 1977-83. Recipient Nat. Research Service award NIH, 1983-85; Earl C. Anthony fellow U. Calif., Irvine, 1977-78. Mem. AAAS, Radiation Research Soc., Am. Assn. Microbiology. Home: 2405 Mark Ave Richland WA 99352

MORGAN, TIMOTHY STEWART, architect; b. Berwyn, Ill., June 21, 1947; s. Howard Pendlton and Rachel Mae (Stewart) M.; m. Lucinda Mary Bellmar, Dec. 28, 1975. Student, U. Ill., 1965-69; B.Arch., Ariz. State U., 1971. Registered architect, Colo., Nebr., Kans.; cert. Nat. Council Archtl. Registration Bds.; lic. pilot. Architect in tng. Eisteadt/Narcisi, Roselle, Ill., 1967-68; airport planner United Airlines, Elk Grove, Ill., 1969-70; architect in tng. Richard John Frank, Denver, 1971-72; project architect assoc. Seracuse Lawler & Ptnrs., Inc., Denver, 1972-78; project mgr. Cillessen Constrn. Co., Golden, Colo., 1978-81; pres. Heskin/Morgan Architects, Inc., Westminster, Colo., 1981—; sec., treas. Stratton Bancshares, Inc., Colo., 1984—; v.p. Design Build Concepts, Inc., Westminster, Colo., 1983-87, chmn. archtl. control com. Van Aire Skyport Corp., Brighton, Colo., 1982—; dir. Retreat Condo Homeowner's Assn., Breckenridge, Colo., 1984—, pres., 1985—. Recipient Eagle Scout award, God and Country award Boy Scouts of Am., Americans Abroad Program, Am. Field Service, Canberra, Australia, 1963-64. Mem. AIA, Brighton C. of C. Club: Fly-in-for-Lunch-Bunch (Denver).

MORGAN, WAYNE PHILIP, art exhibition producer; b. Dunnville, Ont., Can., Apr. 1, 1942. Cert., Sch. Art, Regina Coll., 1963; B.A., U. Sask., Can., 1966; student, Emma Lake Artists Workshop, Sask.; student of, Jules Olitski, 1964, Lawrence Alloway, 1966, Frank Stella, 1967, Don Judd, 1968. Community resident artist Weyburn (Sask.) Arts Council, 1967-70; dir./curator Dunlop Art Gallery, Regina (Sask.) Public Library, 1970-84; head curatorial services div. Winnipeg Art Gallery, Man., Can., 1984-85; ind. exhbn. producer 1985—; juror various art shows, 1970—; mem. Can. Council Explorations Jury, 1977-79; secretariat mem. Regina Arts Commn., 1979—; chmn. visual arts sub-com. Ottawa-Carleton Adv. Com. for the Arts. Mem. Western Can. Art Assn. (founding mem.), Sask. Museums Assn. (bd. dirs. 1978-80, pres. 1982-84), Sask. Craft Council (founding), Can. Museums Assn. (bd. dirs. 1984-86, chmn. profl. devel. standards com. 1985-86).

MORGAN, WILLIAM ROBERT, lawyer; b. Arkansas City, Kans., Jan. 6, 1924; s. Louis and Betty (Starner) M.; m. Willa June Hall, Mar. 11, 1945; children: Marilyn, Robert. A.A., Arkansas City Jr. Coll., 1942; postgrad., U. Okla., 1942-43, Susquehanna U., 1943; B.A., Stanford U., 1948, LL.B., 1949. Bar: Calif. 1949, U.S. Supreme Ct. 1953. Assoc. Johnson, Morgan, Thorne, Speed & Bamford, San Jose, Calif., 1949-52; founder, partner Morgan, Beauzay, Hammer, Ezgar, Bledsoe & Rucka (and predecessors), San Jose, 1952-78; sr. ptnr. Morgan & Towery, San Jose, 1978—; pres., chmn. bd. Triton Corp.; owner, operator Sta. KRAD, Perry, Okla. Author: Chairman Mao's Big Red Book, 1976, Justin Morgan, Founder of the Breed, 1987, Morgan Horse of the West, 1985; editor Labor Code Annotated, 1960—, Twenty-Four Dramatic Cases of the International Academy of Trial Lawyers, 1974. Chmn. San Jose Fine Arts Commn., 1960-63; chmn., bd. dirs. Triton Mus. Art, 1963; mem. central com. Santa Clara County Democratic Party, 1958-60; campaign mgr. numerous Calif. Democrats; mem. San Martin Planning Commn., 1981, Calif. Jud. Council, 1980-83; Gideon elder Presbyn. Ch. Served with U.S. Army, 1943-46. W. Robert Morgan day proclaimed on March 14, 1972 by resolution of Calif. Senate. Mem. ABA (Bus. Frauds and Their Complexities, 1986), Calif. Bar Assn. (bd. govs. 1977-80), Santa Clara County Bar Assn. (pres.), Santa Clara County Bar Assn. (pres. sr. lawyers club 1986-87), Calif. State Bar (v.p. 1979-80, exec. bd. law office mgmt. sect. 1980—), Assn. Trial Lawyers Am. (jud. council), Internat. Acad. Trial Lawyers (past pres., past sec., Am. nat. dir. at large), No. Calif. Morgan Horse Clubs, Geranium Soc. Presbyterian (elder). Clubs: Masons, Shriners (v.p. club), Eastern Star, Rotary, Kiwanis. Home: 9500 New Ave PO Box 1507 Gilroy CA 95020 Office: 1651 N 1st St San Jose CA 95112

MORGENSEN, JERRY LYNN, construction company executive; b. Lubbock, Tex., July 9, 1942; s. J.J. and Zelline (Butler) M.; m. Linda Dee Austin, Apr. 17, 1965; children: Angela, Nicole. BCE, Tex. Tech U., 1965. Area engr. E.I. Dupont Co., Orange, Tex., 1965-67; div. engr. E.I. Dupont Co., La Place, La., 1967-73; project mgr. Hensel Phelps Constrn. Co., Greeley, Colo., 1973-78, area mgr., 1978-80, v.p., 1980-85, pres., 1985—. Office: Hensel Phelps Constrn Co 420 Sixth Ave PO Box O Greeley CO 80632

MORGENSTERN, MATTHEW, computer scientist; b. N.Y.C.. BSEE, Columbia U., 1968, MSEE and Computer Sci., 1970; MS in Computer Sci. and Mgmt., MIT, 1975, PhD in Computer Sci., 1976. Asst. prof. computer sci. Rutgers U., New Brunswick, N.J., 1976-82; research computer scientist Info. Scis. Inst., U. So. Calif., Los Angeles, 1982-84; sr. computer scientist SRI Internat., Menlo Park, Calif., 1984—. Contbr. articles to profl. jours. Mem. IEEE, Am. Assn. Artificial Intelligence, Assn. Computing Machinery, Sigma Xi, Tau Beta Pi, Eta Kappa Nu. Office: SRI Internat 333 Ravenswood Ave Menlo Park CA 94025

MORGENSTERN, NORBERT RUBIN, civil engineering educator, educator; b. Toronto, Ont., Can., May 25, 1935; s. Joel and Bella (Skornik) M.; m. Patricia Elizabeth Gooderham, Dec. 28, 1960; children: Sarah Alexandra, Katherine Victoria, David Michael Gooderham. B.A.Sc., U. Toronto, 1956, D.Sc. h.c., 1983; D.I.C., Imperial Coll. Sci., 1964; Ph.D., U. London, 1964. Research asst., lectr. civil enging. Imperial Coll. Sci. and Tech., London, 1958-68; prof. civil enging. U. Alta. (Can.), Edmonton, 1968-83, Univ. prof., 1983—; cons. engr., 1961—. Contbr. articles to profl. jours. Bd. dirs. Young Naturalists Found., 1977-82, Edmonton Symphony Soc., 1978-85. Athlone fellow, 1956; recipient prize Brit. Geotech. Soc., 1961, 66; Huber prize ASCE, 1971; Legget award Can. Geotech. Soc., 1979; others. Fellow Royal Soc. Can.; mem. Canadian Geosci. Council (pres. 1983), various other profl. assns. Club: Royal Glenora. Home: 106 Laurier Dr, Edmonton, AB Canada T5R 5P6 Office: U Alta, Edmonton, AB Canada T6G 2G7

MORGENTHALER, JON EVERETT, medical technologist; b. Gt. Bend, Kans., July 14, 1955; s. Charles Edward and Mary Lee (Willis) M.; m. Karen Ann Shea, Mar. 7, 1981; 1 child, Erin Kathleen. BA in Biology, Western State Coll., 1978; BS in Med. Tech., U. Colo., 1980; cert. completion in electronics tech., Denver Inst. Tech., 1983. Med. technologist Montrose (Colo.) Hosp., 1980-81; microbiologist COBE Labs., Lakewood, Colo., 1981-83, research and devel. technologist, 1983—. Mem. AAAS, Am. Soc. Clin. Pathology (cert.), Am. Soc. Microbiology. Lutheran. Avocations: home brewing, electronics, photography, bike riding. Home: 2709 S Franklin St Denver CO 80210 Office: COBE Labs Inc 1185 Oak St Lakewood CO 80215

MORGER, KELLY MICHELE, flight test engineer; b. Ephrata, Wash., Sept. 10, 1959; d. Robert Marvin and Janice Lee (Pinney) M. BS in Aerospace Enging., Tex. A&M U., 1982; postgrad., U. Phoenix, 1985—. Acting project engr. Hughes Helicopters, Inc., Culver City, Calif., 1982-84; flight test engr. McDonnell Douglas Helicopter Co., Mesa, Ariz., 1984—. Contbr. articles to profl. jours. Mem. AIAA (flight test tech. com., McDonnell Douglas Helicopter rep.), Am. Helicopter Soc. (v.p. Ariz. chpt. 1985-86), Soc. Flight Test Engrs., Mensa. Avocations: racquetball, Swedish, swimming, motorcycling, reading. Home: 6662 E Heather Dr Mesa AZ 85205 Office: McDonnell Douglas Helicopter Co 5000 E McDowell Rd Bldg 562 Mesa AZ 85205

MORIARTY, DONALD PETER, II, engineering executive, military officer; b. Alexandria, La., Jan. 26, 1935; s. Donald P. and Catherine G. (Stafford) M.; children by previous marriage: Erin, Donald P. III; m. Diana Mary Blackburn, Feb. 4, 1984. BS, La. State U., 1957; MA, Fla. Atlantic U., 1973; diploma, U.S Army Comdr. and Gen. Staff Coll., 1977. Commd. 2d lt. U.S. Army, 1957, advanced through grades to lt. col., 1978; artillery officer U.S. Army, various, 1957-74; head tactical plans sect. Army Air Def. Command, Darmstadt, Federal Republic of Germany, 1975-77; dir. C3I div. Army Air Def. Ctr., Ft. Bliss, Tex., 1977-80; retired Army Air Def. Ctr., 1980; sr. system engr. Hughes Aircraft Co., Fullerton, Calif., 1980-82, mgr. engr. design dept., 1982-84, project mgr., 1984—; U.S. Army Rep. to Tactical Airpower Com. NATO hdqrs., Brussels, 1977-79, Tri-Service Group on Air Def., NATO, 1978-80, Air Def. Electronic Equipment Com., NATO, 1978-80; lead systems engr. Hughes Aircraft Co., Fullerton, 1980-83; Strategic Def. Initiative Program Coordinator Systems Div. Hughes Aircraft Co., 1985—. Author: The U.S. Army Officer as Military Statesman, 1973. Parade chmn. South Fla. Fair Assn., West Palm Beach, 1971; staff commr. Boy Scouts Am., Kaiserslautern, Federal Republic of Germany, 1974-76; sr. warden Episcopal Ch., Kaiserslautern, 1975, Wiesbaden, Federal Republic of Germany, 1977, Placentia, Calif., 1985-88. Decorated Vietnamese Cross of Gallantry with Palm, Air medal with two oak leaf clusters, Bronze Star with one oak leaf cluster, Legion of Merit; recipient Wood Badge award Boy Scouts Am., Newburgh, N.Y., 1969. Mem. AIAA, Assn. U.S. Army, Armed Forces Com.-Elect Assn., Am. Electronics Assn., SAR, Gen. Soc. Mayflower Descendants, Phi Alpha Theta, Acacia. Republican. Avocations: cosmology, genealogy. Home: 626 E Riverview Ave Orange CA 92665 Office: Hughes Aircraft Co 1901 W Malvern St Fullerton CA 92634

MORIARTY, JOHN, opera administrator; b. Fall River, Mass., Sept. 30, 1930; s. John J. and Fabiola Marie (Ripeau) M. MusB summa cum laude, New Engl. Conservatory, 1952. Artistic adminstr. Opera Soc. of Washington, 1960-62, Santa Fe Opera, N.Mex., 1962-65; dir. Wolf Trap Co., Vienna, Va., 1972-77; prin. condr. Central City Opera, Denver, 1978—, artistic dir., 1982—; panelist Nat. Inst. Music Theater, 1985, 86, 87, Conn. Arts Council, 1982, 84; adjudicator various contests including Met. Opera auditions, 1965—. Author: Diction, 1975. Trustee Boston Concert Opera. Recipient Frank Huntington Beebe award, Boston, 1954; Disting. Alumni award New Engl. Conservatory Alumni Assn., 1982. Mem. Nat. Opera Assn., Sigma Alpha Iota, Delta Omnicron, Pi Kappa Lambda. Office: Central City Opera House Assn 1615 California St Denver CO 80202 Office: New Eng Conservatory Opera Dept 290 Huntington Ave Boston MA 02155

MORIMOTO, CARL NOBORU, computer system engineer; b. Hiroshima, Japan, Mar. 31, 1942; came to U.S., 1957, naturalized, 1965; s. Toshiyuki and Teruko (Hirano) M.; m. Helen Kiyomi Yoshizaki, June 28, 1969; children: Matthew Ken, Justin Ray. B.A., U. Hawaii, 1965; Ph.D., U. Wash., 1970. Research assoc. dept. chemistry Mich. State U., East lansing, 1970-72; postdoctoral fellow dept. biochemistry and biophysics Tex. A&M U., College Station, 1972-75; sr. sci. programmer Syntex Analytical Instruments Inc., Cupertino, Calif., 1975-78; prin. programmer analyst, software enging. mgr. Control Data Corp., Sunnyvale, Calif., 1978-83; mem. profl. staff Space System div. Gen. Electric Co., San Jose, Calif., 1983—. Mem. Am. Crystallographic Assn., Assn. Computing Machinery, Am. Chem. Soc., Sigma Xi. Am. Baptist. Home: 4003 Hamilton Park Dr San Jose CA 95130

MORITA, JAMES MASAMI, banker, lawyer; b. Kealakekua, South Kona, Hawaii, July 18, 1913; s. Ushima and Kichi (Yamamoto) M.; m. Aiko Nagakura, Jan. 12, 1957; children: Caryn Sami, Marie Michiko. B.A., U. Hawaii, 1936; LL.B., Georgetown U., 1940; grad., Stonier Grad. Sch. Banking, 1970. Bar: Hawaii, D.C. 1940, U.S. Supreme Ct. 1949. Partner firm Fukushima & Morita, Honolulu, 1941-50; 1st asst. pub. prosecutor Honolulu, 1951-52; atty. City-County Honolulu, 1953-55, spl. counsel, 1956-57; atty. Morita, Kamo & Sakai, Honolulu, 1960-70; chmn. bd., chief exec. officer City Bank; Chmn. bd., pres. CB Bancshares, Inc.; bd. dirs. Citibank Properties, All Hawaii Investment Corp., New Otani Kaimana Beach Hotel, Tony Hawaii Corp, Pacific Olds GMC, Kanebo Cosmetics Hawaii, Inc. Nat. trustee Nat. Jewish Hosp. and Research Center, 1977, Hawaii Loa Coll., 1980; active Boy Scouts Am. Decorated Order of Rising Sun 3d class (Japan); recipient Outstanding award Nat. Jewish Hosp., 1976; recipient 75th Anniversary Rainbow award to disting alumni U. Hawaii, 1982, Freedom Symbol award Sertoma Club, 1983. Mem. Bar Assn. Hawaii, Am. Bankers Assn. (Stonier adv. bd.), Hawaii Bankers Assn., Assn. U.S. Army, Mid-Pacific, Georgetown U. alumni assns., Japan-Hawaii Econ. Council, Japan-Am. Soc. Honolulu., Hawaii Soc. Corp. Planners, Hawaii C. of C. (bd. dirs), U. Hawaii Alumni Assn. Democrat. Clubs: Waialae Country, 200, Honolulu Internat. Country (gov.), U. Hawaii Pres.'s, Plaza. Office: 810 Richards St City Bank Box 3709 Honolulu HI 96811

MORITA, RICHARD YUKIO, microbiology and oceanography educator, researcher; b. Pasadena, Calif., Mar. 27, 1923; s. Jiro and Reiko (Yamamoto) M.; m. Toshiko Nishihara, May 29, 1926; children—Sally Jean, Ellen Jane, Peter Wayne. B.S., U. Nebr., 1947; M.S., U. So. Calif., 1949; Ph.D., U. Calif., 1954. Postdoctoral fellow U. Calif., Scripps Inst. Oceanography, 1954-55; asst. prof. U. Houston, 1955-58; asst. prof., assoc. prof. U. Neb., 1958-62; prof. microbiology and oceanography Oreg. State U., Corvallis, 1962—; program dir. biochemistry NSF, 1968-69; cons. NIH, 1968-70; researcher in field. Contbr. articles to sci. lit. Patentee in field. Served with U.S. Army, 1944-46. Grantee NSF, 1962—, NIH, 1960-68, NASA, 1967-72, Office Naval Research, 1966-70, Dept. Interior, 1968-72, NOAA, 1975-82, Bur. Land Mgmt., 1982, EPA, 1986—; recipient awards including King Fredericus IX Medal and Ribbon, 1954, Sr. Queen Elizabeth II Fellowship, 1973-74, Hotpack lectr. and award Can. Soc. Office: Oreg State Univ Dept Microbiology Corvallis OR 97331

MORITSUGU, TOSHIO, sugar technologist, researcher; b. Honolulu, Apr. 2, 1925; s. Yasuichi and Yoshiko (Sumida) M.; m. Dorothy Yoshie Hoshide, Feb. 27, 1959; children: Alison Kay, Jon Stuart. BS, U. Louisville, 1949; MS, Ohio State U., 1951, PhD, 1954. Research fellow Ohio State U., Columbus, 1954-55; sugar technologist Hawaiian Sugar Planters Assn., Honolulu, 1955—. Contbr. articles to profl. jours. Fellow AAAS, Am. Inst. Chemists; mem. Am. Chem. Soc., Internat. Commn. Uniform Methods Sugar Analysis (referee), Sigma Xi. Republican. Methodist. Avocations: coin collecting, stamp collection, photography, jogging. Home: 3664 Loulu St Honolulu HI 96822 Office: Hawaiian Sugar Planters Assn Exptl Sta 99-193 Aiea Hts Dr Aiea HI 96701

MORLOCK, MARK JONATHAN, economics educator, consultant; b. Cedar Rapids, Iowa, June 13, 1948; s. Mark Jonathan and Paula Wilhamina (Reinking) M. BA, Calif. State U., Chico, 1973; MA, Wash. State U., 1976, PhD, 1978. Research assoc. Wash. State U., Pullman, 1977-78; asst. prof. econs. U. Tenn., Knoxville, 1978-79, Weber State Coll., Ogden, Utah, 1979-80; asst. prof. econs. Calif. State U., Chico, 1980-84, assoc. prof. econs., 1984—, chmn. dept. econs., 1985—; field research assoc. Princeton U., 1980-82, WESTAT, Inc., Rockville, Md., 1983-85. Mem. Butte County (Calif.) Pvt. Industry Council, 1984—. Served with U.S. Army, 1969-70. Grantee USDA, 1977, Econ. Lit. Council Calif., 1985, Calif. State Dept. Edn., 1985. Mem. Am. Econ. Assn., Western Social Sci. Assn. Democrat. Home: 1402 Heather Circle Chico CA 95926 Office: Calif State U Dept Econs Chico CA 95929

MOROSO, MICHAEL JOSEPH, aerospace engineer; b. Centerville, Iowa, Jan. 26, 1923; s. John and Antonietta (Sartor) M.; m. Jody Mary Scripter, June 16, 1951; children—Barbara, Michael, Robert, Philip. B.S.M.E., U. Wis., 1952. Designer Douglas Aircraft Co., Santa Monica, Calif., 1952-65; engr., scientist McDonnell Douglas launch ctr. Vandenberg AFB, Calif., 1965-70; engr., sci. specialist McDonnell Douglas Astronautics Co., Huntington Beach, Calif., 1970-76; sr. propulsion engr. Northrop Corp., Hawthorne, Calif., 1976-79; customer engr. Douglas Aircraft Co., Long Beach, Calif., 1979—. Served to lt. USN, 1943-47. Mem. advancement com. Boy Scouts Am., Santa Maria, Calif., 1966-69; Little League mgr., coach, Santa Maria, 1967-69. Assoc. fellow AIAA; mem. So. Calif. Profl. Engrs. Assn., Am. Legion (adjutant, fin. officer 1950-65), Douglas Mgmt. Club. Democrat. Roman Catholic. Home: 964 Lansing Ln Costa Mesa CA 92626 Office: 3855 Lakewood Blvd Long Beach CA 90846

MORRELL, CLYDE RAY, treasurer; b. Brigham City, Utah, Jan. 24, 1948; s. Lyman D. and Florence (Nichols) M.; m. Rose Marie Vavricka, Dec. 29, 1969; children: Krista, Malissa, Julie, Joseph, Mark, Thomas. BS, M in Acctg., Brigham Young U., 1973. CPA, Utah, Calif., Oreg. Mgr. Deloitte, Haskins & Sells, San Francisco, 1973-77; v.p., asst. controller U.S. Bancorp, Portland, Oreg., 1977-81; v.p., controller Bank of the West, San Francisco, 1981-83; controller Am. Express, Salt Lake City, 1983-86; treas. Brigham Young U., 1986—. Author: Dollars in Motion, 1977. Mem. steering com. Community Planning Orgn., Portland, 1979-80; pres. Latter Day Sts. Ch. Stake Mission, Salt Lake City and San Ramon, Calif., 1981-85, PTA, San Ramon, 1982-83, Latter Day Sts. Sunday Sch., Salt Lake City, 1983-86. Served to staff sgt. USAR. Mem. Am. Inst. CPA's, Utah Assn. CPA's, Nat. Assn. Accts. Republican. Avocations: German, personal computers, music. Home: 385 W 800 S Orem UT 84058 Office: Brigham Young U 305 ASB Provo UT 84602

MORRICE, RUTH FILL, educator, author, consultant; b. Tonawanda, N.Y., Feb. 15, 1914; d. William Louis Allen and Grace Lillian Maude (Bates) Fill; m. Charles Elmer Conklin, Dec. 8, 1930; 1 dau., Mary Ruth Fill Conklin Mailey; m. John Buchan Morrice, Oct. 19, 1946; children: John Fill Morrice, Christina Forbes Morrice Reynolds, Eleanor Wylde Morrice, George Niven Morrice. BA, Boston U., 1942, MA, 1943, postgrad., 1945-47; postgrad., Monterey Coll., San Jose State U., U. Calif.-Santa Cruz, U. Calif.-Berkeley. Asst. to English dept. Boston U., 1942-47; tchr. Hinsdale (Ill.) High Sch., 1943-45, head dept. English; instr. English Coll. William and Mary, Williamsburg, Va., 1947; instr. English and creative writing Culver Stockton Coll., Canton, Mo., 1948-49; faculty English and social studies Hartnell Coll., Salinas, Calif., 1967; teaching prin., counselor Olympia Sch., San Benito County, (Calif.) 1969-70; spl. tchr. Pacific Grove (Calif.) Unified Sch. Dist., 1964-76; ednl. cons., counselor, Carmel, Calif.; free lance writer, artist; sec. to Edward Rowe Snow, 1946, 47. Author: The Poetry of George Santayana, 1943, A Definition of the Novel 1920 to present, 1981, A Study of Santayana and Ruskin, 1981, ...Personal Biography, 1981; editor: A Pilgrim Returns to Cape Cod (Edward Rowe Snow), 1946-47, Photographs and Thoughts from My Journeying in the Orient, 1979. Bd. dirs., supt. Bible Sch., Tustin (Calif.) Congl. Ch., 1964; den mother, pack and dist. leader San Fernando Valley council Boy Scouts Am.; mem. sch. bd. Montague Sch., Los Angeles; active parent groups, Heart Fund, ch. and other choirs. Mem. AAUP, Coll. English Assn. (sec.-treas. 1947-48), Nat. Tchrs. Assn., Calif. Tchrs. Assn., Alpha Phi. Republican. Congregationalist. Home and Office: 3508 Trevis Way Carmel CA 93923

MORRILL, PETER WARREN, TV producer; b. Greenwich, Conn.; s. Grant Anthony II and Marjorie (Moore) M. BA in Communications, Bowling Green State U., 1978. Producer, dir. Sta. WBGU-TV (Pub. Broadcasting Service), Bowling Green, Ohio, 1976-78; producer, dir. Sta. KAID-TV (Pub. Broadcasting Service), Boise, Idaho, 1981-86, dir., 1978-81; exec. dir. Idaho Pub. TV, Boise, 1986—. Producer, dir. (film) Truth Soviet Style, 1985, (TV program) Outdoor Idaho, 1986, (TV documentary) The New Senate, 1981 (CPB Nat. award 1981). Recipient Silver award Internat. Film TV Festival, 1984, 1st Place award Internat. Assn. for Conservation Info., 1984. Mem. Rocky Mountain Acad. TV Art Scis. Episcopalian. Club: Idaho Press. Home: 1306 N 15th St Boise ID 83702 Office: Idaho Pub TV 1910 University Dr Boise ID 83725

MORRIN, VIRGINIA WHITE, educator; b. Escondido, Calif., May 16, 1913; d. Harry Parmalee and Ethel Norine (Nutting) Rising; B.S., Oreg. State Coll., 1952; M.Ed., Oreg. State U., 1957; m. Raymond Bennett White, 1933 (dec. 1953); children: Katherine Anne, Marjorie Virginia, William Raymond; m. 2d, Laurence Morrin, 1959 (dec. 1972). Social caseworker Los Angeles County, Los Angeles, 1934-40, 61-64; acctg. clk. War Dept., Ft. MacArthur, Calif., 1940-42; prin. clk. USAAF, Las Vegas, Nev., 1942-44; high sch. tchr., North Bend-Coos Bay, Oreg., 1952-56, Mojave, Calif., 1957-60; instr. Antelope Valley Coll., Lancaster, Calif., 1961-73; ret., 1974. Treas., Humane Soc. Antelope Valley, Inc., 1968—. Mem. Nat. Aero. Assn., Calif. State Sheriffs' Assn. (charter assoc.), Oreg. State U. Alumni Assn. (life). Office: PO Box 570 Lancaster CA 93539

MORRIS, ALVIN LEE, retired consulting corporation executive, meteorologist; b. Kim, Colo., June 7, 1920; s. Roy E. and Eva Edna (James) M.; B.S. in Meteorology (U.S. Weather Bur. fellow), U. Chgo., 1942; M.S., U.S. Navy Postgrad. Sch., 1954; m. Nadean Davidson, Jan. 16, 1979; children—Andrew N., Nancy L., Mildred M., Ann E., Jane C. Meteorologist Pacific Gas and Electric Co., San Francisco, 1947-50; commd. U.S. Navy, 1942, advanced through grades to capt., USNR, 1962, assignments including staff, comdr. 7th Fleet, ret., 1958; dir. research Navy Weather Research Facility, Norfolk, Va., 1958-62; facilities coordinator, mgr. sci. balloon facility, Nat. Center for Atmospheric Research Boulder, Colo., 1963-75; pres. Ambient Analysis Inc., Internat. Cons., Boulder, 1975-86. Treas. Home Hospitality for Fgn. Students Program, U. Colo., 1969-70; del. People to People Del. on Environment; Peoples Republic of China, 1984. Served with USN, 1942-46, 50-58. Mem. Am. Meteorol. Soc. (cert. cons. meteorologist), Am. Geophys. Union, ASTM, Ret. Officers Assn., Nat. Fedn. Ind. Bus. Club: Boulder County Knife and Fork. Editor Handbook of Scientific Ballooning, 1975; assoc. editor Jour. Oceanic and Atmospheric Tech.; contbr. articles to profl. jours.; convenor, editor proceedings ASTM conf. Home: 880 Sunshine Canyon Boulder CO 80302

MORRIS, CAROLE SUE, housing program manager; b. Arlington, Calif., May 28, 1940; d. Aubrey and Rose Marie (Graves) Luker; m. Thomas Earl Couts, Feb. 3, 1958; children—Thomas Earl, Donnie Roy; m. 2d, Bob J. Morris, Oct. 24, 1970. Student Valley Coll., 1973. Clk.-typist, County of San Bernardino (Calif.), 1959-60, Norton AFB, Calif., 1960-62; clk. II, Exptl. Housing Allowance Program, San Bernardino, 1973-75; transition counselor Housing Authority of County of San Bernardino, 1975-78, housing mgr., 1978—. Mem. Nat. Assn. Female Execs., NOW. Office: Housing Authority of County of San Bernardino 802 N E St San Bernardino CA 92410

MORRIS, DAVID EDWIN, research chemist; b. Toledo, July 14, 1956. BS, N.C. State U., 1978, PhD, 1984. Research asst. N.C. State U., Raleigh, 1978-84; postdoctoral fellow U. Tex., Austin, 1984; postdoctoral fellow Los Alamos (N.Mex.) Nat. Lab., 1984-86, staff scientist, 1986—. Contbr. articles to sci. jours. Fellow NSF, 1977, U. Colo., 1978-79, Robert A. Welch Found., U. Tex., 1984. Mem. Am. Chem. Soc., Phi Kappa Phi, Phi Lambda Upsilon (chpt. pres. 1983). Democrat. Roman Catholic. Avocations: snow skiing, golfing, tennis, bridge, reading. Home: 3711 11 Gold St Los Alamos NM 87544 Office: Los Alamos Nat Lab PO Box 1663 Los Alamos NM 87545

MORRIS, DAVID JOHN, mining engineer, consultant, mining executive; b. Seattle, May 6, 1945; s. Jack Abraham and Alice Jean (Hanson) M.; m. Melania F. Kearney, July 28, 1978; children: Whitney Elizabeth, Benton James, Sienna Elise. BA in Math. and Physics, Whitman Coll., 1968; BS in Mining Engring., Columbia U., 1968. Registered profl. engr., Colo., Utah, Wash. Mining engr. Union Oil of Calif., Los Angeles, 1968-69; mining engr. John T. Boyd Co., Denver, 1974-76, sr. mining engr., 1976-78, v.p., mgr., 1978—; mng. ptnr. Palmer Coking Coal Co., Black Diamond, Wash., 1976-82, pres. Pacific Coast Coal Co., Black Diamond, 1982—. Mem. Bd. Overseers Whitman Coll., Walla Walla, Wash., 1986—, chmn. Rep. camapign for Whitman, Denver, 1985. Served as lt. USN, 1969-74, Vietnam. Henry Krumb scholar Columbia U., N.Y.C., 1967-68. Mem. NSPE, Soc. Mining Engrs. (admissions com. 1985—, Howard Eavenson award com. 1984—), Western Rugby Football Union (sec. 1980). Republican. Clubs: Denver Athletic, Denver Country. Avocations: golf, hunting, fishing, gardening, rugby. Home: 860 Vine Denver CO 80206 Office: John T Boyd Co 1860 Lincoln #1028 Denver CO 80295

MORRIS, DAVID KEITH, cultural organization administrator; b. Glendale, Calif., July 8, 1941; s. Douglas Kent and Rose (Bosen) M.; m. Judith Louise Marek, Sept. 8, 1964; children: Carolyn, Erin. BS, San Jose State U., 1964. Park ranger, biologist Hawaii Volcanoes Nat. Park, 1965-70; park planner Nat. Park Service, Denver, 1970-74, San Francisco, 1976-78; park planner Dept. Nat. Parks and Wildlife, Lilongwe, Republic of South Africa, 1974-76; mgmt. trainee U.S. Nat. Park Services, Washington, 1978-79; park mgr. U.S. Nat. Park Services, King Salmon, Alaska, 1979—. Chmn. Bd. Health, Nakuek, Alaska, 1982—. Lodge: Lions (pres. Bristol Bay club 1985—). Avocations: sports, fishing, photography. Office: Katmai Nat Park and Preserve Office of Supt Box 7 King Salmon AK 99613

MORRIS, DAVID LENNOX, II, marketing and insurance executive; b. Indpls., Apr. 9, 1946; s. David Lennox and Clara Rose (Hess) M.; m. Christine Jenny Kline, Nov. 29, 1969 (div. July 1973). BS, Ind. U., 1969. Dir. safety Baldwin and Lyons, Indpls., 1971-77; risk adminstr. City of Pasadena, Calif., 1977-78; risk mgr. Fleetwood Enterprises, Riverside, Calif., 1978-79; sr. analyst Atlantic Richfield Co., Los Angeles, 1980-85; sr. v.p. Pacific Mktg. Systems Ltd., Anaheim, Calif., 1985—; corp. ins. mgr. Am. Contracting Services, Inc., Anaheim, 1987—; v.p., bd. dirs. Living Green Inc., Anaheim. Mem. Pasadena Tournament of Roses, 1978—. Served to 1st lt. U.S. Army, 1969-71, Vietnam. Decorated Bronze Star; named an Assoc. in Risk Mgmt., Ins. Inst. Am., 1981. Mem. Ind. Motor Truck Assn. (chmn. 1973-74), Risk and Ins. Mgmt. Soc. Republican. Avocations: skiing, photography, hydroponics, reading, stamps. Home: 19974 Ridge Manor Way Yorba Linda CA 92686 Office: Pacific Mktg Systems Ltd 430 B North Lakeview Anaheim CA 92807

MORRIS, DONALD WAYNE, economist, educator; b. Durango, Colo., June 29, 1941; s. William Henry and Vina May (Baird) M.; m. R. Elaine Williams, July 17, 1959; children: Dawn, Kelly, Chris. BS in Econs., N.Mex. State U., 1969, MS in Econs., 1971; postgrad., U. N.Mex., Los Alamos, 1983—. Dep. dir. human resources div. Gov's. Office, Santa Fe, N.Mex., 1971-75; with engring. cost estimates group Los Alamos (N.Mex.) Nat. Lab., 1976-78, prin. investigator environ. assessments group, with environ. assessments group, prin. investigator energy techs. group, adminstrv. mgr. econs. and energy policy group, 1984—; govs. appointee to N.Mex./Mex. Border Jan. Devel. Commn., 1979-83; mem. Los Alamos Econ. Devel. Bd., 1985—, 3d Congl. Dist. High-Tech Devel. Com., 1983-84; spl. asst. Congressman Bill Richardson, Washington, 1983; adj. prof. econs. U. N.Mex., Los Alamos, 1972-82. Contbr. numerous articles to profl. jours. Mem. Govs. Fuel Allocation Bd., N.Mex., 1971-75, N.Mex. Biotech. Co., 1985—; regent N.Mex. Inst. Mining and Tech., 1983—, pres. bd. regents, 1984, N.Mex. Dem. State Cen. Com. Recipient Spl. Service award Western Govs. Policy Office, 1981. Avocation: politics. Home: 1951 D North Rd Los Alamos NM 87544 Office: Los Alamos Nat Lab PO Box 1663 Group S-4 MS F611 Los Alamos NM 87545

MORRIS, ELIZABETH TREAT, phys. therapist; b. Hartford, Conn., Feb. 20, 1936; d. Charles Wells and Marion Louise (Case) Treat; B.S. in Phys. Therapy, U. Conn., 1960; m. David Breck Morris, July 10, 1961; children—Russell Charles, Jeffrey David. Phys. therapist Crippled Children's Clinic No. Va., Arlington, 1960-62, Shriners Hosp. Crippled Children, Salt Lake City, 1967-69, Holy Cross Hosp., Salt Lake City, 1970-74; pvt. practice phys. therapy, Salt Lake City, 1975—. Mem. Am. Phys. Therapy Assn., Friendship Force Utah, U.S. Figure Skating Assn. Home: 4177 Mathews Way Salt Lake City UT 84124 Office: 2178 So 900 East Suite 3 Salt Lake City UT 84106

MORRIS, GORDON THOMAS, newspaper writer; b. Montreal, Que., Can., Apr. 17, 1943; s. Gordon Thomas Sr. and Lillian May (Harvey) M.; m. Mary Kay Heitzman, Sept. 4, 1983; 1 child, Eric Gordon. BJ, Bowling Green State U., 1965. Communications coordinator Chrysler Corp., Detroit, 1966-70; writer Detroit News, 1970-80, Autoweek mag., Detroit, 1978-81, Daily News, Los Angeles, 1981-83; spl. writer Los Angeles Times, 1983—; asst. media dir. Long Beach (Calif.) Grand Prix, 1981-83. Columnist Score News Auto mag.; contbr. articles numerous nat. mags. and newspapers. Served with U.S. Army, 1966-68. Mem. Am. Auto Racing Writers and Broadcasters Assn. (1st Pl. award 1983, 2d Pl. award 1985), Soc. Automotive Historians. Avocations: writing, snow skiing, ice hockey, auto racing. Home: 1670 Santa Maria Glendale CA 91208 Office: Los Angeles Times Spl Events Dept Times Mirror Sq Los Angeles CA 90053

MORRIS, GREGORY PAUL, energy systems development consultant; b. Rochester, N.Y., Nov. 18, 1952; s. Robert Irving and Marion Helen (Bendix) M.; m. Brenda Ruth Laytner, July 17, 1977; children: Beth Amy, Valerie Eden. BA cum laude, U. Pa., 1974; MS, U. Toronto, 1977; PhD, U. Calif., 1982. Research assoc. U. Calif., Berkeley, 1977-82, affiliated faculty Energy and Resources Group, 1982—; cons. Oakland, Calif., 1980—. Mem. AAAS, Am. Chem. Soc. Democrat. Jewish. Avocations: sailing, running, family activities. Home: 1159 Glendora Ave Oakland CA 94602 Office: Future Resources Assocs Inc 2000 Ctr St Suite 418 Berkeley CA 94704

MORRIS, HAROLD CLIFFORD, physician; b. Louisville, June 22, 1921; s. James Leroy and Grace Ann (Woertz) M.; m. Carol L. Morris, Oct. 20, 1945; children: Susan Grace, Douglas L. BS in Pharmacy, U. Ky., 1943; MS, Northwestern U., 1946, MD, 1950. Cert. Am. Bd. Internal Medicine. Intern Ky. Bapt. Hosp., 1950; resident in internal mediicne Louisville Gen. Hosp., 1951, VA Hosp., Hines, Ill., 1952; assoc. prof. pharmacology U. Ky., Louisville, 1948-51; clin. assoc. prof. medicine U. Louisville, 1952-78; practice medicine specializing in internal medicine Louisville, 1952-78; with Yucaipa (Calif.) Family Med. Group, 1978-80; chief gen. med. sect. VA Hosp., Loma Linda, Calif., 1980—; asst. prof. medicine Loma Linda U., 1980—; sr. med. clin. coord. for ex-POW's Dist. 25 VA, 1982—. Contbr. articles to profl. jours. Sec.-treas. Kimberly Pl. Homeowners Assn., Redlands, Calif., 1985. Recipient Gratitude award U. Louisville, 1978, Gratitude award Ex-P.O.W. Assn., 1985. Fellow Am. Coll. Physicians; mem. Am. Soc. Internal Medicine, San Bernardino County Med. Soc. (communications com.), Calif. Med. Soc., Sigma Xi. Republican. Roman Catholic. Avocations: golf, collector antique weapons, fishing. Home: 1131 Kimberly Pl Redlands CA 92373 Office: VA Hosp 11201 Benton St Loma Linda CA 92357

MORRIS, HENRY MADISON, III, corporate administrator; b. El Paso, Tex., May 15, 1942; s. Henry Madison and Mary Louise (Beach) M.; B.A. summa cum laude, Christian Heritage Coll., 1976; M.Div., Luther Rice Sem., 1977, D.Min., 1978; m. Janet Deckman, July 25, 1964; children—Henry M., Scotta Marie. Regional mgr. Integon Ins. Co., Greenville, S.C., 1969-75; ordained to ministry Bapt. Ch., 1968; pastor Hallmark Bapt. Ch., Greenville, 1969-75; asso. prof. Bible, Christian Heritage Coll., El Cajon, Calif., 1977-78, adminstrv. v.p., 1978-80; pastor First Bapt. Ch., Canoga Park, Calif., 1980-86; chief adminstrv. officer Wismer Assocs., Inc., Canoga Park, 1986—; lectr. in field. Served with U.S. Army, 1959-66. Republican. Author: Baptism: What is It?, 1977; Explore the Word, 1978; Churches: History and Doctrine, 1980. Office: 22134 Sherman Way Canoga Park CA 91306

MORRIS, J. JEFFERY, financial executive; b. Orange, Calif., Apr. 29, 1949; s. Coalson C. and Jean (Crawford) M.; m. Diane K. Grimberg, Sept. 10, 1983; 1 child, Jessica. BS, U. So. Calif., 1972. V.p. Hamilton Equipment Leasing, Santa Ana, Calif., 1973-78; prin. Jefcol, Laguna Beach, Calif., 1978-80; pres. Perry Morris Corp., Newport Beach, Calif., 1980—. Bd. dirs. Orange County YMCA, South Coast YMCA. Mem. Young Pres.' Orgn., Children's Hosp. Padrinos, U. So. Calif. Assocs.. Republican. Clubs: Center, Lincoln (Newport Beach) (legis. com. 1986). Home: 411 Emerald Bay Laguna Beach CA 92651 Office: Perry Morris Corp 567 San Nicholas Newport Beach CA 92660

MORRIS, JACQUELYN MCCOY, university library administrator; b. Columbus, Ohio, June 14, 1942; d. Donald Richard and Jeanne (Clark) McCoy; m. Richard David Morris, Mar. 19, 1960; children: Patricia A., Michelle A. BA cum laude, Syracuse U., 1971, MS in Library Sci., 1972. Asst. librarian SUNY, Syracuse, 1972-79; head reference div. Albert Mann Library, Cornell U., Ithaca, N.Y., 1979-82; assoc. dean of library U. Pacific, Stockton, Calif., 1982-86; library dir. Occidental Coll., Los Angeles, 1986—; dir. N.Y. Libraries Instructional Clearinghouse, SUNY, Syracuse, 1974-79; cons. U.S. Presdl. Council Environ. Quality, 1980. Author: Library Searching—Research and Strategies, 1978, Teaching Library Skills for Academic Credit, 1985, ACRL College Library Standards, 1986. Bd. dirs Tierra del Oro council Girl Scouts N.Am., cen. Calif., 1985-86. Recipient Chancellors award, SUNY, 1978. Mem. Am. Library Assn. (chmn. com.), Calif. Library Assn., AAAS, 49/99 (mem. exec. council, bd. dirs. 1984-86), Phi Alpha Theta, Beta Phi Mu. Avocations: backpacking, gardening, bicycling. Office: Occidental Coll MN Clapp Library 1600 Campus Rd Los Angeles CA 90041

MORRIS, JOHN, writer; b. Portland, Oreg., Aug. 8, 1912; s. Frank Ellis and Edith Phelps (Vernor) M.; m. Jean Cotant, Aug. 17, 1946; children: John Lowell, June, Robert Vernor, Charles Alan. AB, Bowdoin Coll., 1934; postgrad., U. Minn., 1955-57. Cert. fire protection engr., Calif., safety engr., Calif. Supr. safety engr. Standard Accident Ins. Co., New Eng. and Chgo., 1948-54; safety supr. instr. U. Minn., Mpls., 1955-57; safety coordinator U. Ill., Champaign, 1957-70; loss control cons. Fred. S. James & Co., Berkeley, Calif., 1970-76; loss control cons., writer Walnut Creek, Calif., 1976—. Author: Managing the Library Fire Risk, 1975, 2d edit., 1979, History of the Campus Safety Association, 1978, Library Disaster Preparedness Handbook, 1986; contbr. articles in field to profl. jours. Served to lt. comdr. USN, 1941-46. Mem. ALA, Nat. Fire Protection Assn. (life), Bay Area Fire Protection Forum, Am. Soc. Safety Engrs (prof. emeritus), Ret. Officers Assn. (officer East Bay Chpt. 1982-85). Republican. Presbyterian. Avocations: senior hockey league, tennis. Home and Office: 3333 Nutmeg Ln Walnut Creek CA 94598

MORRIS, JOHN THEODORE, planning official; b. Denver, Jan. 18, 1929; s. Theodore Ora and Daisy Allison (McDonald) M.; B.F.A., Denver U., 1955; m. Dolores Irene Seaman, June 21, 1951; children—Holly Lee, Heather Ann, Heidi Jo, Douglas Fraser. Apprentice landscape architect S.R. DeBoer & Co., Denver, summer 1949, planning technician (part-time), 1954-55; sr. planner and assoc. Trafton Bean & Assocs., Boulder, Colo., 1955-62; prin. Land Planning Assocs., planning cons., Boulder, 1962-65; planning dir. and park coordinator Boulder County, 1965-67; sch. planner Boulder Valley Sch. Dist., 1967-84, also dir. planning and engring., 1967-84, supr. facility improvement program, 1969-84; pvt. sch. planning cons., 1984—; cons. U. Colo. Bur. Ednl. Field Services, 1974. Bd. dirs. Historic Boulder, 1974-76; mem. parks and recreation adv. com. Denver Regional Council Govts., 1975-84. Served with USCG, 1950-53. Mem. Am. Inst. Cert. Planners, Am. Planning Assn., Council of Ednl. Facility Planners Internat. Home: 7647 N 32d St Jamestown Star Route Boulder CO 80302 Office: 7647 N 32d St Jamestown Star Route Boulder CO 80302

MORRIS, KAY WETZEL, social worker; b. Salt Lake City, July 9, 1939; d. Nevin Frank Wetzel and Jane Rawlins Deakin; student U. Utah, 1957-59; BA with highest honors, U. Calif., San Jose, 1961; MSW summa cum laude, Ohio State U., 1963; 1 son, Michael David. social worker children's service Napa (Calif.) State Hosp., 1963-66; pupil personnel dir. Trinity County Supt. of Schs. Office, 1967-70; founder, social worker Trinity County Mental Health Services, 1970-76; pvt. practice psychotherapy and consultation, Redding, Calif., 1967—; dir. Victor Residential Center, Inc. (Stepping Stones), 1976-81; rural services com., cons. children's service com. Calif. Conf. Local Mental Health Dirs., 1972-77; mental health cons. plan devel. com. No. Calif. Health Systems Agy., 1976-81; mem. Arthritis Rehab. Team, Redding, 1982—; speaker in field, Calif., Seattle, Omaha; speaker Calif. Sch. Bds. Assn., 1984, A.M. Calif., 1984; cons. Task Force for Handicapped Children, Shasta County Supt. of Schs., 1971-74, Seattle Children's Home, 1982—, Redding Med. Ctr., 1980—; developer Trinity County Mental Health Service, 1970. Trustee Redding Elem. Sch. Dist., 1977-81; bd. dirs. Group Home Assn. Calif., 1979-80. vol. KIXE Pub. Broadcasting System; Trinity County chmn. McGovern for Pres., 1972. NIMH fellow, 1961-62. Mem. Nat. Assn. Social Workers, AAUW, Psi Chi.

MORRIS, KENN GLENN, computer company marketing executive; b. Murray, Utah, Mar. 24, 1935; s. Glenn and Bertha Charlotte (Hansen) M. BS in Advt. and Journalism, U. Utah, 1957; MBA in Internat. Mgmt. with honors, Am. Grad. Sch. Internat. Mgmt., 1973. Copywriter Ross Jurney & Assocs. Advt., Salt Lake City, 1957-59; mgmt. trainee Gen. Electric Co., N.Y.C., 1959-61; pub. relations specialist Litton Industries, Beverly Hills, Calif., 1961-68; mgr. graphics communications Whittaker Corp., Los Angeles, 1968-71; mgr. mktg. services Audiotronics Corp., North Hollywood, Calif., 1971-72; mgr. corp. communications Envirotech Corp., Menlo Park, Calif., 1973-74; pub. affairs officer Office Internat. Affairs NASA, Washington, 1974-78; mgr. mktg. communications Callan Data Systems, Westlake Village, Calif., 1982-84, Cordata Techs., Thousand Oaks, Calif., 1984—. Mem. Advt. Club Los Angeles, Am. Mgmt. Assn., Assn. MBA Execs., Bus. and Profl. Advt. Assn., Assn. Indsl. Advertisers, Meeting Planners Internat., Pub. Relations Soc. Am., Chevaliers des Tastevin. Republican. Mormon.

MORRIS, LOUISE B., interior designer; b. Hubbard, Ariz., Aug. 21, 1925; d. William Franklin and Mary Anne (Adams) Butler; m. Gilbert Lavoy Morris, June 3, 1943; children: David, Joanne, Karen Morris Grissom, Donald, Gena Morris Raban, Irene, Dwayne. Prin. Morris Draperies and Interiors, Yuma, Ariz., 1961—; lectr. in field. Rep. precinct committeeman Yuma County, 1961—; mem. relief soc. Ch. Jesus Christ Latter-day Saints, past. primary sec., past pres., past. Sunday sch. and primary tchr. Mem. Am. Soc. Interior Designers (assoc.), Internat. Drapery Assn. (area bd. dirs.). Republican. Contbr. articles on home decorating to local newspapers. Office: Morris Draperies and Interiors 888 5th Ave Yuma AZ 85364

MORRIS, RANDALL DARREN, computer scientist; b. China Lake, Calif., July 22, 1959; s. Randall Warren and Ann Irene (Eyre) M.; m. Cynthia Lynn Williams, Apr. 26, 1985; 1 child, Randall John. Student, Cerro Coso Community Coll., 1976-77; BS in Math. with honors, So. Utah State Coll., 1981. Facility systems mgr. Naval Weapons Ctr., China Lake, 1981—. Recipient 2 Spl. Act or Service awards Aircraft Weapons Integration Dept. Naval Weapons Ctr., 1985. Mem. Digital Equipment Computer Users Soc. Republican. Mormon. Home: 608 E Beth Ln Ridgecrest CA 93555 Office: Naval Weapons Ctr Code 3114 China Lake CA 93555-6001

MORRIS, RANDY JOSEPH, architectural developer; b. Santa Ana, Calif., July 5, 1948; s. Bertrand J. Jr. and E. Irene (Stanley) M.; m. Catherine R. Roberts, Dec. 18, 1971; 1 child, Richard Bertrand. BArch, U. So. Calif.,

1971. Lic. architect, Calif. Prin. Morris, Pritchard, Hutton Co., Los Angeles, 1969-71; archtl. project mgr. Hugh Gibbs & Donald Gibbs, AIA, Long Beach, Calif., 1971-74; prin., architect Phelps, Morris & Assocs., AIA, Long Beach, 1974-85, Morris, Group Architects, AIA, Long Beach, 1985—. Bd. dirs. Long Beach Mus. Art, 1979-81; vice-chmn. Long Beach Housing Task Force, 1983; commr. Long Beach Econ. Devel. Commn., 1984—. Mem. AIA (v.p., pres. Cabrillo chpt. 1987). Democrat. Episcopalian. Club: Long Beach Yacht (bd. dirs. 1979-86, Legion of Merit award, 1979, 80, 81, Bd. Govs. award 1981). Lodge: Kiwanis. Avocations: sailing, golfing, skiing, art collecting; winner of yacht races from Newport Beach to Cabo San Lucas, 1981 and Long Beach to La Paz, Mex., 1979. Home: 4120 Pacific Ave Long Beach CA 90804 Office: Morris Group Architects AIA 4404 E Pacific Coast Hwy Long Beach CA 90804

MORRISH, WILLIAM BRADFORD, insurance company executive; b. Berkeley, Calif., June 6, 1931; s. Kendric Bradford and Marian Lathrop (Thomas) M.; m. Eva-Marie von Arnim, Mar. 31, 1962; children: Bettina, Kendric. BA in Letters and Sci., U. Calif., Berkeley, 1954; MBA in Econs. and Mktg., Stanford U., 1959. From br. mgr. to asst. div. mgr. Transam. Title Ins. Co., Berkeley and San Francisco, 1963-67; pres., chief exec. officer First Am. Title Guaranty Co., Oakland, Calif., 1967—. Bd. dirs. Oakland-Alameda (Calif.) County Coliseum, 1978—, Oakland C. of C., 1978-82, vice-chmn. 1984—; mem. Oakland Boy's Club (bd. dirs. 1967—); trustee The Coll. Preparatory Sch., 1970-86, v.p. 1980-82; trustee The Nat. Outdoor Leadership Sch., Wyo., 1982—, vice-chmn. 1984-85, chmn. 1986—; bd. dirs. New Oakland Com., pres. 1976; mem. bd. regents Bishop O'Dowd High Sch., 1983-86; bd. dirs. Samuel Merrit Hosp., 1976-79; bd. dirs. Oakland Symphony Orch. Assn., 1975-76, Oakland Mus. Assn., 1976-77; trustee U. Calif. Alumni Found., 1976-78; pres. Oakland Citizen's Com. for Urban Renewal, 1969-71. Mem. Calif. Land Title Assn. (bd. govs. 1979—, chmn. pub. affairs com. 1981-86, 2d v.p. 1986), Mortgage Bankers Assn. No. Calif. (bd. dirs. 1972-74), Assoc. Bldg. Industry (bd. dirs. 1977-78), Real Estate Research Council (bd. dirs. 1985). Republican. Congregationalist. Clubs: Bohemian (San Francisco), 100, Lakeview. Avocations: canoeing, kayaking, hiking, flyfishing, photography. Home: 5950 McAndrew Dr Oakland CA 94611 Office: First Am Title Guaranty Co 1535 Harrison St Oakland CA 94612

MORRISON, ANDREW DAVID, materials scientist; b. Brockton, Mass., Feb. 22, 1939; s. Sidney Lawrence and Ruth Edith (Dvlinsky) M.; m. Sandra Gertrude Perlmutter, Nov. 30, 1963; children: Jennifer, Jay Albert. AB in Geology, Boston U., 1961, MA in Geology, 1967. Mem. tech. staff RCA Labs., Princeton, N.J., 1967-71; design and devel. engr. Raytheon Corp., Waltham, Mass., 1971-73; research engr. Tyco Labs., Waltham, 1973-77; mgr. silicon lab. Solarex Corp., Rockville, Md., 1977-79; tech. group supr. Jet Propulsion Lab., Pasadena, Calif., 1979—. Co-editor: Silicon Material Preparation and Economical Wafering Methods, 1985; contbr. tech. papers to profl. jours.; patentee in field. Mem. AIAA, Am. Assn. Crystal Growth (founder, 1st pres. New Engl. sect. 1972-73, pres., co-founder So. Calif. sect. 1986—), Materials Research Soc. (founder So. Calif. sect. 1986), Electrochem. Soc. Avocations: gardening, cactus. Home: 2197 N Allen Ave Altadena CA 91001 Office: Jet Propulsion Lab 4800 Oak Grove Dr Pasadena CA 91109

MORRISON, CAROLYN ANN, nursing educator; b. Saginaw, Mich., Sept. 2, 1935; d. James E. and Victoria (McMullen) M. A.A., Compton Jr. Coll., 1955; R.N., Queen Angels Sch. Nursing, 1958; B.S., Chapman Coll., 1981, M.S. candidate, 1981—. R.N., Calif.; cert. tchr., Calif. Staff nurse out-patient dept. Orthopedic Hosp., Los Angeles, 1958-61, hosp. staff nurse, 1961-62; nurse-extender Dr. N.E. Diess, Downey, Calif., 1981—; staff nurse, asst. head nurse surg. dept. St. Francis Med. Ctr., Lynwood, Calif., 1964-74, asst. head nurse, unit supr. orthopedic dept., 1974—; clin. instr. Compton Community Coll., 1981—. Mem. AAUW, Nat. Assn. Female Execs., Calif. Nurses Assn., Am. Nurses Assn., Nat. Assn. Orthopedic Nurses, Am. Pub. Health Assn., Assn. Rehab. Nurses.

MORRISON, EMILY KITTLE, leadership development trainer, conultant, writer; b. Indpls., Apr. 17, 1942; d. John Sloan and Elizabeth (Mills) Kittle; m. William C. Kimball, Aug. 25, 1966; children—Ann Eve, Mary Lynn; m. 2d, Charles Edward Morrison, Aug. 5, 1982. B.A., Denver U., 1964; M.A., U. Ariz., 1966. Founder, pres. Jordan Enterprises, Tucson, 1980—. Active Jr. League, Girl Scouts U.S.A., Voluntary Action Ctr. Mem. Am. Soc. Tng. and Devel., Nat. Speakers Assn., Internat. Platform Assn., Am. Cancer Soc., Assn. Volunteer Adminstrs. Delta Gamma. Author: How to Get the Most Out of Being a Volunteer, 1980; Skills for Leadership, 1983, TravelTime Fun Series fo Children, 1986.. Office: PO Box 31084 Tucson AZ 85751

MORRISON, FRANK BRENNER, JR., state justice; b. McCook, Nebr., Sept. 27, 1937; s. Frank Brenner and Maxine Elizabeth (Hepp) M.; m. Sharon Romaine McDonald, June 28, 1959; children: John Martin, Anne Elizabeth. B.S., U. Nebr., 1959; LL.B., J.D., U. Denver, 1962. Bar: Nebr., Mont. Assoc. firm McGinley, Lane, Mueller & Shaanahan, Ogallala, Nebr., 1962-64; partner firm Eisenstatt, Higgins, Miller, Kinnamon & Morrison, Omaha, 1964-69, Morrison & Hedman, Whitefish, Mont., 1969-78, Morrison, Jonkel, Kemmis & Rossback, Missoula, Mont., 1978-80; justice Mont. Supreme Ct., 1981—; mem. part-time faculty Flathead Valley Community Coll., Kalispell, U. Mont. Law Sch. Past pres. Whitefish Community Devel.; past del. Democratic Nat. Conv. Recipient Disting. Service award Student Bar Assn. U. Mont. Law Sch., Disting. Service award Flathead County Bar Assn.; Gold medal award Law Sci. Acad. Am. Fellow Internat. Soc. Barristers; mem. Order St. Ives, Sigma Chi. Democrat. Episcopalian. Clubs: Toastmasters (past club pres., past area gov.), Kiwanis, Mont, Green Meadow Country. Home: 630 Monroe St Helena MT 59601 Address: Supreme Ct Mont State Capitol Helena MT 59620

MORRISON, FREDERICK JAMES, psychologist; b. Toronto, Ont., Can., Jan. 16, 1944; s. Frederick James and Dorothy (Adamo) M.; m. Catherine Eileen Lord, May 5, 1973; children: Janina Lord, Anthony Hayden. BA, U. Toronto, 1966; PhD, Harvard U., 1971. Sr. psychologist WHO, Guatemala City, Guatemala, 1972-73; asst. prof. psychology Dartmouth Coll., Hanover, N.H., 1973-77; assoc. prof. U. Minn., Mpls., 1977-81; Clifford E. Lee prof. child devel. U. Alta., Edmonton, Can., 1981—, dir. Ctr. Research Child Devel., 1985—. Author: The Child: An Introduction to Developmental Psychology, 1979; editor: Applied Developmental Psychology, 1984-86, Cognitive Development in Atypical Children, 1985. Recipient Research Scientist Devel. award NIMH, 1979-81; research grantee Nat. Scis. Engring. Research Council, 1982—. Fellow Internat. Acad. Research in Learning Disabilities; mem. AAAS, Am. Psychol. Assn., Soc. Research in Child Devel., Psychonomic Soc. Avocation: running. Home: 3919 Aspen Dr W, Edmonton CA T6J 2B5 Office: U Alta, Dept Family Studies, Edmonton, AB Canada T6G 2H1

MORRISON, GORDON EDWARD, computer company executive; b. Iowa City, June 18, 1945; s. Gordon Siverly and Alberta (Sanders) M. B.S. in Math. and Computer Sci., Met. State Coll., Denver, 1975. Research and devel. technician Micro Communications Co., 1968-69; computer specialist Environ. Research Lab. and Wave Propagation Lab., NOAA, 1975-78, project leader, 1980-81; sr. systems engr. Data Gen. Corp., 1978-80; mgr. systems ops. and standards Lear Siegler, Inc., 1981-82; chief scientist, chmn. bd. Morrison Computer Corp., Aurora, Colo., 1982—. Patentee in field. Mem. IEEE, Assn. Computing Machinery. Home: 16212A E Rice Pl Aurora CO 80015 Office: Morrison Computer Corp 4725 Walnut St Boulder CO 80301

MORRISON, GUS (ANGUS HUGH), mayor, engineer; b. Buffalo, Sept. 13, 1935; s. John Weir and Mary (Norton) M.; m. Joy Rita Hallenbarter, Feb. 7, 1959; children: Frank, Gloria, Heather. Technician Bell Aircraft Corp., Niagara Falls, N.Y., 1956-58; technician Lockheed Missiles and Space Corp., Sunnyvale, Calif., 1958-63, test. engr., 1963-78, group engr., 1978-86, dept. mgr., 1986—. Mayor Fremont, Calif., 1985—, council mem., 1978-85, planning commr., 1977-78; bd. dirs. Tri City Ecology Ctr., 1976—. Served with USN, 1953-56. Democrat. Roman Catholic. Avocations: computers, photography, seriography. Office: Office of Mayor 39700 Civic Center Dr Fremont CA 94538

MORRISON, JOHN ALBERT, ecological consultant; b. Wichita, Kans., Dec. 1, 1924; s. Ernest and Mary Millar (Forbes) M.; m. Joyce Eileen McNutt, Aug. 27, 1950; children: John, James, Julie. BS in Wildlife Tech., U. Mont., 1955, MS in Wildlife Tech., 1957; PhD in Zoology, Wash. State U., 1965. Leader coop. wildlife research unit, Okla. State U. U.S. Fish and Wildlife Service, Stillwater, 1967-75; chief tech. services div. U.S. Fish and Wildlife Service, Ft. Collins, Colo., 1975-78, Anchorage, 1978-85; ecol. cons. Environ. Interpretation, Anchorage, 1985—. Exec. bd. dirs. Okla. Wildlife Fedn., Oklahoma City, 1968-70; mem. research council Oklahoma City Zoo, 1973-75; chmn. natural resource info. mgmt. com. Alaska Land Mgrs. Task Force, Anchorage, 1978-82. Served with U.S. Army, 1948-51. Recipient Supr. Service award U.S. Dept. Interior, 1986. Mem. Ecol. Soc. Am. (cert.), Wildlife Soc. (cert., Outstanding Achievement Wildlife Research award Okla. chpt. 1975), Sigma Xi, Phi Sigma. Presbyterian. Clubs: Alaska Flyfishers (pres. 1983), Alaskan Scottish (pres. 1986) (Anchorage). Lodge: Rotary (Disting. Conservationist award Stillwater chpt. 1974). Home and Office: Environ Interpretation 12651 Mariner Dr Anchorage AK 99515

MORRISON, JOHN HADDOW, JR., engineering company executive; b. Bozeman, Mont., Aug. 24, 1933; s. John Haddow Sr. and Rosalie (Lehrkind) M.; m. Shirley Easbey, Sept. 11, 1954; children: Robert, Richard. BS, Mont. State U., 1955. Registered profl. engr., Mont., Nev., Oreg.; registered land surveyor, Mont. Project engr. Morrison-Maierle, Inc., Helena, Mont., 1957-64, chief, airport design, 1967-73, chief exec. officer, 1973—; pres. cons. engrs. council State of Mont., 1986-87. Bd. dirs. Mont. State U. Alumni Endowment, 1983—, sec.-treas. Helena YMCA, 1977-80. Served with U.S. Army 1955-57. Mem. ASCE, NSPE (pres. Helena chpt. 1968-69, Outstanding Young Engr., Helena chpt. 1965), Cons. Engrs. Council Mont. (sec., v.p.). Methodist. Lodges: Optimists (pres. 1976); Masons. Avocations: golf, photography. Home: 201 N Hannaford Helena MT 59601 Office: Morrison Maierle Inc 910 Helena Ave PO Box 6147 Helena MT 59604

MORRISON, KENNETH JESS, agronomist; b. Rudy, Ark., Feb. 14, 1921; s. Leslie Francis and Lula Mary (Cluck) M.; widowed Mar. 1984; children: Elizabeth A. Steffan, Arianna Morrison Steffan. BS, Kans. State U., 1948; MS, Purdue U., 1950, PhD, 1967. Registered cert. profl. agronomist. Teaching asst. Purdue U., Lafayette, Ind., 1948-50, research asst., 1959-60; extension agronomist Wash. State U., Pullman, 1950—, agronomist, 1965—. Mem. editorial bd. Crops and Soils publ., 1972-74. Served to lt. U.S. Army, 1942-45. E.O. Holland Fund grantee, Wash. State U., 1979. Fellow Crop Sci. Soc. Am., Am. Soc. Agronomy; mem. Western Soc. Crop Sci. (pres. 1978), Wash. and No. Idaho Seed Council (sec. 1967—), Wash. State Crop Improvement Assn. (sec., also bd. dirs., exec. bd., 1969—). Baptist. Lodges: Elks, Rotary, Masons (Master 1970-71). Home: NW 1300 Orion Dr Pullman WA 99163

MORRISON, MURDO DONALD, architect; b. Detroit, Feb. 21, 1919; s. Alexander and Johanna (Macaulay) M.; B.Arch., Lawrence Inst. Tech., 1943; m. Judy D. Morrison; children from previous marriage—Paula L., Reed A., Anne H. Individual practice architecture, Detroit, 1949, Klamath Falls, Oreg., 1949-65, Oakland, Calif., 1965-78; partner Morrison Assocs., San Francisco, 1978-85, Burlingame, Calif., 1985—; v.p. Lakeridge Corp., 1968—; chmn. Oreg. Bd. Archtl. Examiners, 1961-65, chmn., 1964. Mem. Town Council Klamath Falls, 1955-57; co-chmn. Oakland Pride Com., 1968-77; mem. Redwood City (Calif.) Gen. Plan Com., 1986. Served with USN, 1943-46. Recipient Progressive Architecture award, 1955, Alumni of Yr. award Lawrence Inst., 1965. Mem. AIA (treas. East Bay, chmn. Oakland chpt.). Presbyterian. Clubs: Commonwealth, Bombay Bicycle Riding. Architect: Gilliam County Courthouse (Progressive Architecture design award), 1955, Chiloquin (Oreg.) Elem. Sch., 1963, Legaspi Plaza hotel, Burlingame, 1982, Lakeridge Office Bldg., Reno, 1984, Provident Cen. Credit Union Bldg., Monterey, Calif., 1986, The McCosker Corp. Office Bldg., Oakland, Calif., 1986, others. Home: 3645 Jefferson Ave Redwood City CA 94062 Office: 1110 Burlingame Ave Burlingame CA 94010

MORRISON, ROBERT FLOYD, psychology educator; b. Mpls., Oct. 30, 1930; s. Floyd William and Ruth Angeline (Foster) M.; m. Kathryn Helene Olson, Jan. 30, 1953; children: Scott Robert, Rebekah Kim, Spencer Kirk, Bennett Todd, Holly Faith; m. Anne Deneiko, Oct. 11, 1975. Student, Grinnell Coll., 1948-49; BS, Iowa State U., 1952, MS, 1956; PhD, Purdue U., 1961. Employee relations asst. Mobil Oil Co., Casper, Wyo., 1956-59; staff assoc. Mead Corp., Chillicothe, Ohio, 1961-62; mgmt. devel. specialist Martin Co., Balt., 1962-64; personnel research mgr. Sun Co., Phila., 1964-70; assoc. prof. organization behavior U. Toronto, Ont., Can., 1970-76; supervisory research psychologist Navy Personnel Research and Devel. Ctr., San Diego, 1976—; pres. R.F. Morrison Assocs., Phila., Toronto, 1966-76; adj. prof. U. So. Calif., Los Angeles, 1978—; cons. in field. Contbr. articles to profl. jours., chpts. to books. Served as cpl. Signal Corps, U.S. Army, 1952-54. Mem. Am. Psychol. Assn. (James McKeen Cattell research design award, 1982), Acad. Mgmt., Internat. Assn. Applied Psychology, Summit Group, Sigma Xi, Psi Chi. Republican. Home: 6137 Syracuse Way San Diego CA 92122 Office: Navy Personnel Research and Development Ctr San Diego CA 92152

MORRISON, ROGER BARRON, geologist; b. Madison, Wis., Mar. 26, 1914; s. Frank Barron and Elsie Rhea (Bullard) M.; B.A., Cornell U., 1933, M.S., 1934; postgrad. U. Calif.-Berkeley, 1934-35, Stanford U., 1935-38; Ph.D., U. Nev., 1964; m. Harriet Louise Williams, Apr. 7, 1941; children—John Christopher, Peter Hallock and Craig Brewster (twins). Geologist U.S. Geol. Survey, 1939-76; vis. adj. prof. dept. geoscis. U. Ariz., 1976-81, Mackay Sch. Mines, U. Nev., Reno, 1984—; cons. geologist Morrison and Assocs., 1978—; prin. investigator 2 Landsat-1 and 2 Skylab earth resources investigation projects NASA, 1972-75. Fellow Geol. Soc. Am.; mem. AAAS, Internat. Assn. Quaternary Research (past mem. Holocene and pedology commns.), Am. Soc. Photogrammetry, Am. Soc. Agronomy, Soil Sci. Soc. Am., Internat. Soil Sci. Soc., Am. Quaternary Assn., Sigma Xi. Club: Colorado Mountain. Author 2 books, co-author one book; editor 1 book; co-editor 2 books; also co-editor Catena, 1973—. Contbr. over 95 articles to profl. jours. Home and Office: 13150 W 9th Ave Golden CO 80401

MORRISON, SID, congressman, orchardist; b. Yakima, Wash., May 13, 1933; s. Charles Freeman and Anne Helen (Fornfeist) M.; m. Marcella Britton, June 19, 1955; children: Wally, Mary Anne, Linda, Doris. Student, Yakima Valley Coll., 1950-51; B.S. in Agr., Wash. State U., 1954. Orchardist Morrison Fruit Co., Inc., Wash., 1956—; mem. 97th-100th Congresses from 4th Dist. Wash., 1981—, whip for Republican freshmen, 1981-82, asst. regional whip, 1983—. Mem. Task Force Budget Process, 1983—; mem. Task Force on Energy and Natural Resources, 1983—, Wash. Ho. of Reps., 1967-74, Wash. State Senate, 1975-80. Served with U.S. Army, 1954-56. Mem. Wash. State Apple Commn. (chmn.), Wash. State Hort. Assn. (dir.), Dept. Agr. Research Adv. Com., Wash. State Peach Council (pres.), Grange. Lodge: Rotary. Office: 1434 Longworth House Office Bldg Washington DC 20515 *

MORRISON, WILLIAM FOSDICK, electrical company executive; b. Bridgeport, Conn., Mar. 14, 1935; s. Robert Louis and Helen Fosdick (Mulroney) M.; m. E. Drake Miller, Dec. 14, 1957 (div. Sept. 1972); children: Donna Drake, Deanne Fosdick, William Fosdick; m. Carol Ann Stover, Nov. 20, 1972. BA in Econs., Trinity Coll., Hartford, Conn., 1957. Mgr. purchasing dept. Westinghouse Electric Co., Lima, Ohio, 1960-68; mgr. mfg. Westinghouse Electric Co., Upper Sandusky, Ohio, 1969; gen. mgr. Westinghouse Electric Co., Gurabo, P.R., 1970-71; mgr. tng. Westinghouse Electric Co., Pitts., 1972-84; program mgr. Westinghouse Electric Co., Sunnyvale, Calif., 1984—. Author: The Pre-Negotiation Planning Book, 1985; contbr. articles to profl. jours. Bd. dirs. Valley Inst. of the Theatre Arts, Saratoga, Calif., 1986. Served to capt. USAFR, 1958-64. Named Man of the Yr. Midwest Lacrosse Coaches Assn., 1983, recipient Service award U.S. Lacrosse Assn., 1982. Mem. Nat. Assn. Purchasing Mgmt. (pres. Lima chpt. 1966-67, dir. nat. affairs 1967-68, dist. treas. 1968-70). Club: Sunnyvale Golf Assn. (vice-chmn. 1985, chmn. 1986). Lodge: Elks. Avocation: golf. Home: 3902 Duncan Pl Palo Alto CA 94306 Office: Westinghouse Electric Co 401 E Hendy Ave Sunnyvale CA 94088

MORRISS, DOROTHY HARDER, microbiologist, educator, researcher; b. Wetamka, Okla., Feb. 26, 1925; d. Isaac and Mary (Fiene) Harder; m. F.V. Morriss, Jan. 29, 1949 (dec. June 1982); children: Stephen V., Nancy J. Morriss Murrin, Mary Jo. RN, Bethany Hosp., Kansas City, Kans., 1946; AB in Biology, N.Mex. Highlands U., 1951; MS in Microbiology, U. Mo., Kansas City, 1966; PhD in Microbiology, U. Mo., 1978; BSN, Loretto Heights Coll., 1986. Instr. St. Luke's Nursing Sch., Kansas City, Mo., 1954-58, Kansas City U., 1958-59, Barstow Sch., Kansas City, 1967-69; faculty mem. Denver U., 1979-82, 1984—; v.p., sr. microbiologist Gen. Genetics Corp., Golden, Colo., 1982-84. Contbr. articles to profl. jours. Den mother Cub Scouts, Boy Scouts Am., Kansas City, 1959-61; Brownie leader Girl Scouts U.S., Kansas City, 1962-63, leader Girl Scouts U.S., Kansas City, 1963-65; grief counselor Mt. Evans Hospice, Evergreen, Co., 1985—. HEW nurse scientist fellow, 1966; recipient Order of Blue Key nursing honor, 1945. Mem. Am. Soc. Microbiology, AAAS, Assn. Women in Sci., Am. Nurses Found. (grantee 1976, Katherine Grenough scholar 1978), Sigma Delta Epsilon (pres. 1969-70, fellowship 1975), Sigma Theta Tau. Home: 1527 S Shooting Star Dr Golden CO 80401

MORRISSEY, JOHN CARROLL, lawyer; b. N.Y.C., Sept. 2, 1914; s. Edward Joseph and Estelle (Caine) M.; m. Eileen Colligan, Oct. 14, 1950; children: Jonathan Edward, Ellen, Katherine, John, Patricia, Richard, Brian, Peter. B.A. magna cum laude, Yale U., 1937, LL.B., 1940; J.S.D., N.Y. U., 1951; grad., Command and Gen. Staff Sch., 1944. Bar: N.Y. State 1940, D.C. 1953, Calif. 1954, U.S. Supreme Ct. 1944. Asso. firm Dorsey and Adams, 1940-41, Dorsey, Adams and Walker, 1946-50; counsel Office of Sec. of Def., Dept. Def., Washington, 1950-52; acting gen. counsel def. Electric Power Adminstrn., 1952-53; atty. Pacific Gas and Electric Co., San Francisco, 1953-70; asso. gen. counsel Pacific Gas and Electric Co., 1970-74, v.p., gen. counsel, 1975-80; individual practice law San Francisco, 1980—; dir. Gas Lines, Inc. Bd. dirs. Legal Aid Soc. San Francisco; chmn. Golden Gate dist. Boy Scouts Am., 1973-75; commr. Human Rights Commn. of San Francisco, 1976—, chmn., 1980-82; chmn. Cath. Social Service of San Francisco, 1966-68. Served to col. F.A. U.S. Army, 1941-46. Decorated Bronze star. Mem. Calif. Conf. Public Utility Counsel, Am. Bar Assn., San Francisco Bar Assn., Fed. Power Bar Assn., Pacific Coast Electric Assn., Pacific Coast Gas Assn., Econ. Round Table of San Francisco, World Affairs Council, San Francisco C. of C., Calif. State C. of C., Phi Beta Kappa. Roman Catholic. Clubs: Electric, Serra, Commonwealth, Yale of No. Calif, Pacific-Union. Home: 2030 Jackson St San Francisco CA 94109 Office: 215 Market St Suite 215 San Francisco CA 94106

MORRISSEY, JOHN EDWARD, III, insurance company executive; b. Rockville Centre, N.Y., June 15, 1951; s. John Edward Jr. and Elsie (Lackmand) M.; m. Deborah Anne McLean, Sept. 16, 1979. A in Loss Control Mgmt., Ins. Inst. Am., 1983; BA, Adelphi U., 1983. Sr. field loss control rep. Specialized Surveys Inc., Los Angeles, 1976-78; sr. loss control rep. United Pacific Ins. Co., Santa Ana, Calif., 1978-80; asst. mgr. loss control CIGNA Corp., Los Angeles, 1980-84; loss control supr. Indsl. Indemnity Ins. Co., Orange, Calif., 1984—. Mem. Am. Soc. Safety Engrs. Avocations: skiing, golf, furniture design, investment analysis. Home: 2643 W 176th St Torrance CA 90504 Office: Indsl Indemnity Ins Co 1 City Blvd Suite 1600 Orange CA 92668

MORROW, CHARLES TABOR, aerospace consulting engineer; b. Gloucester, Mass., May 3, 1917; s. Charles Harvey and Melissa Luella (Tabor) M.; m. Julia Buxton Brown, June 4, 1949; children: Hope Elizabeth, Anne Barbara. AB, Harvard U., 1937, SM, 1938, SD, 1946. Sr. project engr. Sperry Gyroscope Co., Great Neck, N.Y., 1946-51; research physicist Hughes Aircraft Co., Los Angeles, 1951-55; mgr. sci. and engring. relations Ramo Wooldridge Co., Los Angeles, 1955-60; mgr. tech. relations Aerospace Corp., Los Angeles, 1960-67; staff scientist LTV Research Ctr., Anaheim, Calif. and Dallas, 1967-76; cons. in field., Dallas and Encinitas (Calif.), 1977—. Author: Shock and Vibration Engineering, 1963; also numerous articles to profl. jours. Pres. Covey Aux. San Diego Mus. Natural History, 1983-85. Fellow Acoustical Soc. Am., Inst. Environ. Scis. (Vigness award 1971), AIAA (assoc.); mem. IEEE (life), Inst. Noise Control Engring. (founding), Am. Soc. Engring. Edn., Sigma Xi. Avocations: music, photography, natural history, travelling. Home and Office: 1345 Cherrytree Ct Encinitas CA 92024

MORROW, JAMES THOMAS, financial executive; b. Seattle, Apr. 24, 1941; s. James Elroy and Helen Margaret (Helzer) M.; B.S. in Elec. Engring. and B.S. in Gen. Sci., Oreg. State U., 1964; Ph.D., U. Santa Clara, 1973, M.B.A., 1966; 1 child, Shannon F. Engr., Gen. Electric Co., San Jose, Calif., 1964-66; engring. mgr. Beckman Instruments, Inc., Palo Alto, Calif., 1966-69; pres. MSA Cons., Inc., Portland, Oreg., 1969-75; asst. prof. U. Portland, 1969-75; mgr. A.T. Kearney, Inc., San Francisco, 1975-78; v.p. mktg. Pierce Pacific Mfg., Portland, 1978-79; chmn., chief exec. officer Lanco Internat., Inc., Clackamas, Oreg., 1979-81; regional mgr., v.p. Case & Co., Portland, 1981-82; chmn. bd., exec. v.p. Morley Fin. Services, Inc., 1982—; v.p., chmn. bd. Biojet, Inc., 1985—, also bd. dirs.; dir. Accucom Data Network, Inc., Pierce Pacific Mfg., Lanco Internat., Energy Guard, Inc., G&R Devel. Co., Inc., MSA Cons., Inc., Criticare of Am., Inc., Oreg. Seed Capital, Inc., Recycling Research Corp., Criticare, Inc. sec.-treas. Everybody's Record Co., Inc. Bd. dirs. U.S. Small Bus. Acad., Found. for Oreg. Research and Edn., Jr. Achievement. Mem. Am. Mktg. Assn., Nat. Soc. Profl. Engrs., IEEE, Am. Inst. Indsl. Engrs., Am. Production and Inventory Control Soc., Sales and Mkg. Execs. Internat. Republican. Congregationalist. Contbr. articles to profl. jours., chpts. to textbooks. Home: 8525 SW Bridletrail Ave Beaverton OR 97005 Office: 4000 Kruse Way Pl Suite 300 Lake Oswego OR 97034

MORROW, RICHARD TOWSON, lawyer; b. Glendale, Calif., Aug. 3, 1926; s. Ray Leslie and Marion Elizabeth (Towson) M.; m. Virginia Alice Kaspar, June 28, 1947; children—Kathleen Ann, Randall Ray, Nancy Lynn. Student, Occidental Coll., 1944-45; B.A., UCLA, 1947; LL.B., U. So. Calif., 1950. Assoc. Musick & Burrell, Los Angeles, 1950-53; lawyer Walt Disney Prodns., Burbank, Calif., 1953-64, v.p., 1964-69, v.p., gen. counsel, 1969-85, dir., 1971-84; ptnr. Hufstedler, Miller, Carlson & Beardsley, Los Angeles, 1985—; trustee Roy Disney Family Found., Burbank. Pres., bd. dirs. Glendale YMCA, Calif.; mem. adv. bd. Glendale Salvation Army. Served to lt. (j.g.) USNR, 1944-46. Mem. ABA (chmn. corp. law dept. com. 1982-84, council corp. banking and bus. law sect. 1984—Calif. Bar Assn., Los Angeles County Bar Assn. (trustee 1975-77, Outstanding Corp. Counsel award 1984-85), Glendale Bar Assn. Republican. Presbyterian. Clubs: Calif., Chancery (Los Angeles); Lakeside Golf (North Hollywood, Calif.). Avocation: golf. Home: 1422 N Central Ave Apt 6 Glendale CA 91202 Office: Hufstedler Miller Carlson & Beardsley 355 S Grand Ave 45th Floor Los Angeles CA 90071-3107

MORROW, WINSTON VAUGHAN, business executive; b. Grand Rapids, Mich., Mar. 22, 1924; s. Winston V. and Selma (von Egloffstein) M.; m. Margaret Ellen Staples, June 25, 1948; children: Thomas Christopher, Mark Staples. A.B. cum laude, Williams Coll., 1947; J.D., Harvard U., 1950. Bar: R.I. 1950. Assoc. atty. Edwards & Angell, Providence, 1950-57; exec. v.p., asst. treas., dir., gen. counsel Avis, Inc. (and subsidiaries), 1957-61; pres., dir. Avis, Inc., 1964-75; v.p., gen. mgr. Rent A Car div. Avis, Inc., 1962-64; chmn., chief exec. officer, dir. Avis, Inc., Avis Rent A Car System, Inc., 1965-77; dir., cons. Flowtrans Internat., 1977; chmn., pres., dir. Teleflorists Inc. (and subsidiaries), 1978-80; pres., dir. Ticor, Los Angeles, 1981—, chief exec. officer, 1984—; pres., dir., chief exec. officer New TC Holding Corp., 1983—; chmn., chief exec. officer, dir. Ticor Title Ins. Co., 1982—; chmn. and bd. dirs. Ticor Realty Tax Services. Mem. Pres.'s Industry-Govt. Spl. Travel Task Force, 1968, Calif. Roundtable, 1986—; travel adv. bd. U.S. Travel Service, 1968-76; bd. dirs. Police Found., Washington, 1983—, Seligman & Latz, N.Y.C., 1986—; mem. Los Angeles City-Wide Airport Adv. Com., 1983-85, Los Angeles Mayor's Bus. Council, 1983-86, Housing Roundtable, Washington, 1983-85; co-chmn. Los Angeles Transp. Coalition; mem. juvenile task force, Nat. Council Crime & Delinquency, 1985-86. Served as technician, M.C. AUS, 1943-46. Decorated Stella della Solidarieta Italy; Gold Tourism medal Austria). Mem. Fed., R.I. bar assns., Car and Truck Rental and Leasing Assn. (nat. pres. 1961-63), Los Angeles Area C. of C. (bd. dirs. 1983—), Calif. Bus. Roundtable, Phi Beta Kappa, Kappa Alpha. Clubs: Pacific Union (San Francisco), Bald Peak Colony (N.H.), Racquet and Tennis (N.Y.C.), Williams (N.Y.C.), Internat. (Washington); California, Los Angeles Tennis, Lincoln Los Angeles, Centre Santa Ana. Home: 3200 La Rotonda Dr Rancho Palos Verdes CA 90274 also: Cushing

Corners Rd Freedom NH 03836 Office: 6300 Wilshire Blvd Los Angeles CA 90048

MORSE, JACK CRAIG, lawyer; b. Evanston, Ill., Aug. 11, 1936; s. Leland Robert and Pauline (Pettibone) M.; children by former marriage—David Leland, Katherine Malia. B.A., Beloit Coll., 1958; J.D., Northwestern U., 1965. Bar: Hawaii 1967, U.S. Dist. Ct. Hawaii 1969, U.S. Ct. Appeals (9th cir.) 1977. Legal staff Bishop Estate, Honolulu, 1966-68; dep. atty. gen. State of Hawaii, Honolulu, 1968-71; ptnr. Saunders & Morse, Honolulu, 1971-73; assoc. Chuck & Wong, Honolulu, 1974-75; officer, dir. Morse, Nelson & Ross, Honolulu, 1976—; mem. Hawaii Med. Claim Conciliation Panel, Honolulu, 1977—, chmn., 1980—; mem. panel of arbitrators First Judicial Cir., Hawaii, 1986—. Served to lt. USN, 1959-62. Hardy scholar Northwestern U., 1962. Mem. Am. Judicature Soc., Assn. Trial Lawyers Am., Omicron Delta Kappa. Office: Morse Nelson & Ross 345 Queen St Suite 600 Honolulu HI 96813

MORSE, JOSEPH GRANT, chemistry educator; b. Colorado Springs, Colo., Oct. 16, 1939; s. Grant Addison and Faris Ellen (Winninger) M.; m. Karen Dale Williams, Apr. 6, 1963; children: Robert Grant, Geoffrey Easton. BS, S.D. State Coll., 1961; MS in Chemistry, U. Mich., 1963, PhD, 1967. Asst. prof. chemistry Utah State U., Logan, 1968-75, assoc. prof., 1975—, dir. univ. honors program, 1986—. Contbr. articles to profl. jours. Served to capt. U.S. Army, 1966-68. Named Advisor of Yr., Utah State U. Coll. Sci., 1986; coop. fellow NSF, 1963-65. Mem. Am. Chem. Soc. (sect. chmn. 1976, nat. councillor 1986—), AAAS, Sigma Xi (chpt. pres. 1983-84), Phi Beta Kappa, Phi Kappa Phi, Phi Lambda Upsilon. Presbyterian. Avocations: running, youth soccer coach and referee. Home: 30 N Cherry Providence UT 84332 Office: Dept Chem and Biochem Utah State U Logan UT 84322

MORSE, KENNETH GEORGE, architect; b. Cleve., May 15, 1929; s. George Frederick and Edna (Rohde) M.; children: Kenneth George Jr., Valerie. BArch, Ohio State U., 1952. Registered architect, U.S., New Zealand, United Kingdom. Ptnr. IBS, Auckland, New Zealand, 1971-75; pvt. practice architecture Tucson, Ariz., 1975—. Served to 1st lt. U.S. Army, 1952-54, Korea. Mem. Mensa (pres. Tucson chpt. 1985—), L-5 Soc. Club: Tucson Skeptics (chmn., v.p. 1984—). Home: 2508 E 23d St Tucson AZ 85713

MORSE, LOWELL WESLEY, real estate and banking exec.; b. West Palm Beach, Fla., May 1, 1937; s. Alton and Blanche (Yelverton) M.; B.S., U. Santa Clara, 1968; grad. Def. Lang. Inst., Monterey, Calif., 1959; m. Vera Giacalone, June 22, 1958; children—Lowell Wesley, Stephen D., Michael S. Russian linguist U.S. Army Security Agy., 1957-60; asst. city mgr. City of Pacific Grove (Calif.), 1961-66; city mgr. Town of Los Altos Hills (Calif.), 1967-69; chmn. Morse & Assos., Inc., San Jose, Calif., 1972—, pres., 1986—; founder, dir. Plaza Bank of Commerce, San Jose, 1979—. Served with U.S. Army, 1957-60. Club: Univ. (San Jose.). Home: PO Box 222980 Carmel CA 93922 Office: 26619 Carmel Center Place Suite 201 Carmel CA 93923

MORSE, WENDELL RAY, university administrator; b. Logan, Utah, July 22, 1943; s. Brigham Glen and Susie (Stuart) M.; m. LeeAnn Hansen, Apr. 3, 1970; children: Wendy, David. BS, Utah State U., 1967; postgrad., U. Ill., 1967-68. Planner Province of Alta., Can., 1967; landscape planner U. Ill., Urbana, 1967; tchr. Champaign (Ill.) High Sch., 1967; planner Utah State U., Logan, 1968—; cons., 1968—; owner Morse Tree Farm, Hyde Park, Utah, 1976—. Author: Landscape Plants for Northern Utah, 1980. Chmn. Bicentennial Com., Hyde Park, 1975-76; scoutmaster, coordinator Boy Scouts Am., Hyde Park, 1975—, asst. dist. scout commr. N. Cache Dist., 1986—; county, state del. Democratci Party. Mem. Soc. Coll. and Univ. Planning, Nat. Hist. Trust. Democrat. Mormon. Club: Old Main Soc., Big Blue (Logan). Avocations: tennis, golf, skiing, art, traveling. Home: Box 385 Hyde Park UT 84318 Office: Utah State U Campus Planning Office Logan UT 84322-4600

MORSE, WILLIAM FRANCIS, clergyman; b. Western Springs, Ill., Aug. 25, 1899; s. Francis William and Phoebe A. (Kelsey) M.; student Eugene Bible U., 1920-23; Lingield Coll., 1940-41; m. Mary Quintila Shirley, Feb. 22, 1929; children—William George, Patricia Anne. Farmer Harrisburg, Oreg., 1923-26; retail salesman Chase Gardens, Eugene, 1927; mgr. Sunnyside Greenhouses, Portland, Oreg., 1928; owner, operator florist bus. Newberg, Oreg., 1928-40; mgr. relief work east end Yamhill County, Newberg, 1932-33; opened ch. Mt. Top, Newberg, 1932-40; ordained to ministry Christian Ch., 1935; pastor Ch. of Christ, Amity, Oreg., 1940-44, 48-50, Seaside (Oreg.) Christian Ch., 1944-48; organizer Wi-Ne-Ma Christian Camp, Inc., Cloverdale, Oreg., 1944, pres., 1944-69, gen. mgr., 1950-67, trustee, 1944-70; pastor Wi-Ne-Ma Christian Ch., 1951-70; research and geneal. work, 1970—; pres. Morse Soc., 1973—. Trustee Turner Meml. Home, 1946-80, trustee emeritus, 1980—; chmn. bd. trustees Oretown Cemetery Assn., 1970-78, trustee, 1979—. Mem. Newberg Park Commn., 1933-40, Sch. Bd., 1936-40; chmn. Area Agy. on Aging, Dist. 1, Tillamook-Clatsop County, Oreg., 1976-79, mem. exec. bd., 1976-82; bd. dirs. Am. Indian Evangelism Assn., 1977-86 . Served with U.S. Army, World War I. Mem. Nescticca Ministers Fellowship (pres. 1966-67), Oretown Grange, Vets. World War I. Home and Office: 42880 Ocean View Dr Cloverdale OR 97112

MORTELL, BONNIE PATRICIA, international exchange administrator, educator; b. Vancouver, Wash., June 29, 1945; d. William Henry and Loretta Ellen (Ellis) Lennox; 1 son, William Robert. B.A. magna cum laude in Edn., Seattle U., 1970; postgrad. various univs., 1972—. Cert. tchr., Wash. Tchr. Lake Washington High Sch., Kirkland, Wash., 1970-84, chairperson fgn. lang. dept., 1975-84; prof. Seattle U., 1984—; Greater Seattle regional rep. Iberoamerican Cultural Exchange Program, 1972-77, asst. dir., 1977-78, internat. program dir., 1978-84, exec. dir., 1984—; pres. Internat. Exchange Network of Wash. State, 1985—, Council on Standards for Internat. Ednl. Travel. Mem. Wash. Assn. Fgn. Lang. Tchrs., Internat. Exchange Assn. (bd. dirs.), Nat. Assn. Tchrs. Spanish and Portuguese, Oreg. Student Exchange Fedn., Kappa Gamma Pi. Office: 13920 93d Ave NE Kirkland WA 98033

MORTON, CHARLES BRINKLEY, bishop, former state legislator; b. Meridian, Miss., Jan. 6, 1926; s. Albert Cole and Jean (Brinkley) M.; m. Virginia Roseborough, Aug. 26, 1948; children—Charles Brinkley, Mary Virginia. JD with distinction, U. Miss., 1949; MDiv optime merens, U. South, 1959, DD, 1982. Bar: Miss. 1949, Tenn.; ordained to ministry Protestant Episcopal Ch. as deacon and priest, 1959. Sole practice Senatobia, Miss., 1949-56; mem. Thomas & Morton, Senatobia, Miss., 1952-56, Miss. Ho. of Reps., 1948-52, Miss. Senate, 1952-56; priest-in-charge Ch. of Incarnation, West Point, Miss., 1959-62; rector Grace-St. Luke's Ch., Memphis, 1962-74; dean Cathedral of Advent, Birmingham, Ala., 1974-82; bishop Episcopal Diocese of San Diego, 1982—. Contbr. articles to law and hist. jours. Mem. Miss. Commn. Interstate Coop., 1952-56, Miss. State Hist. Commn., 1952-56; chmn. bd. Bishop's Sch., La Jolla, Calif., Episcopal Community Services, San Diego; trustee Berkeley Div. Sch., Yale U.; active numerous civic and cultural groups. Served with AUS, World War II, Korea; col., chaplain Res. ret. Decorated Silver Star, Bronze Star medal with cluster, Purple Heart, Combat Inf. Badge; recipient Freedoms Found. Honor medal, 1967, 68, 72. Mem. Mil. Order World Wars, Am. Legion (past post comdr.), Phi Delta Phi, Tau Kappa Alpha, Omicron Delta Kappa, Phi Delta Theta. Lodge: Rotary. Office: Episcopal Diocese of San Diego 2728 Sixth Ave San Diego CA 92103

MORTON, DAVID EMERY, physician; b. Pueblo, Colo., Jan. 25, 1925; s. Albert Emile and Rebecca (Emery) M.; m. Kayoko Nakamura, Oct. 6, 1971; children: Nancy S., Ann A., Sarah M., Susan M. BS, Yale U., 1945, MD, 1948. Diplomate Nat. Bd. Med. Examiners. Intern New Haven Hosp., 1949-50, asst. resident, 1952-53; sr. asst. resident in medicine Barnes Hosp., St. Louis, 1955-56; physician examiner Colo. Fuel and Iron Corp., Pueblo, 1956-59; gen. practice medicine Pueblo, 1956—; instr. anatomy Yale U., New Haven, 1950-52, asst. clin. prof. medicine U. Colo. Sch. Medicine, Denver, 1980-85; ptnr. Lake Med. Bldg. Ptnrship., Pueblo, 1980—; full staff membership St. Mary-Corwin Hosp., Pueblo, 1956—; courtesy staff Parkview Episcopal. Hosp., Pueblo; cons. Colo. State Hosp., 1958-64. Contbr. articles on anatomy to profl. jours. Mem. Rosemount Victorian Ho. Mus. Assn., Pueblo. Served to capt. M.C., U.S. Army, 1952-54. Recipient Keese prize Yale U., 1948. Mem. AAAS, Pueblo County Med. Soc., Colo. Med. Soc., Sigma Xi, Alpha Omega Alpha. Club: Pueblo Country. Avocations: hiking, travelling, philately, collecting Indian artifacts, coin collecting. Home: 2209 7th Ave Pueblo CO 81003 Office: 2001 Lake Ave Pueblo CO 81004

MORTON, DONALD LEE, surgery educator; b. Richwood, W.Va., Sept. 12, 1934; s. Howard Jennings and Mary Gertrude (Boggs) M.; m. Wilma Miley (dec. Aug. 1982); children: Diana Lynn, Laura Ann, Donald Jr., Christen Helene. BA, U. Calif., Berkeley, 1955; MD, U. Calif., San Francisco, 1958. Diplomate Am. Bd. Surgery, Am. Bd. Thoracic Surgery; lic. surgeon Calif. State Bd. Med. Examiners. Intern U. Calif. Med. Ctr., San Francisco, 1958-59, resident in surgery, 1959-60, resident, surg. fellow, 1962-66; clin. assoc. surgeon Nat. Cancer Inst., NIH, Bethesda, Md., 1960-62; sr. investigator Nat. Cancer Inst., NIH, Bethesda, 1966-69, sr. surgeon, head tumor immunology sect., 1969-71; chief surgery VA Hosp., Sepulveda, Calif., 1971-74, chief oncology sect., surg. services, 1974-81; prof. surgery, chief surg. oncology div. UCLA, 1971—, chief gen. surgery div., 1977-82; hon. med. staff surgery Cedars-Sinai Med. Ctr., Los Angeles, 1981—; mem. immunology adv. segment Nat. Cancer Inst., 1969-71, search com., 1974, bd. sci. counselors, 1974-78, surg. oncology research devel. subcom. 1979; mem. com. for objective 6 Nat. Cancer Plan, chmn. surg. onconolgy research program planning, 1974; sci. adv. council Cancer Research Inst. 1974, bd. sci. advisors, 1974-80; sci. adv. bd. Wash. U., St. Louis, 1974-80; exec. policy com. Jonsson Comprehensive Cancer Ctr., UCLA, 1981—, ad hoc peer rev. com. 1984—. Mem. editorial bd. Jour. Nat. Cancer Inst., Jour. Surg. Oncology, Seminars in Oncology, Jour. Surg. Research, Surgery, Cancer Immunology and Immunotherapy; editorial adv. bd. Cancer Research, Clin. Orthopaedics Related Research. Served with USPHS, 1960-69. Recipient Superior Service award HEW, 1970, Esther Langer award U. Chgo., 1978, Chancellor's Assocs. Recognition award, 1983, Golden Scalpel Teaching Excellence award, 1983-84. Mem. AAAS, ACS, AMA, Am. Assn. Cancer Edn., Am. Assn. Cancer Research, Am. Assn. Thoracic Surgery, Am. Assn. Immunologists, Am. Radium Soc., Am. Soc. Exptl. Pathology, Am. Soc. Clin. Oncology (chmn. nominating com. 1976-77), Am. Soc. Microbiology, Am. Surg. Assn., Assn. Acad. Surgery, Bay Surg. Soc., Los Angeles County Med. Assn., Los Angeles Surg. Soc., Naffziger Surg. Soc., Pacific Coast Surg. Assn., Pan-Pacific Surg. Assn., Physician's Aid Assn., Reticuloendothelial Soc., Societe Internationale de Chirurgie, Soc. Head and Neck Surgeons, Soc. Surg. Oncology (ad hoc com. clin. research 1976-81, chmn. govt. relations com. 1978-81, long range planning com. 1981—, exec. com. 1981-82, clin. research and govt. relations com. 1984-85), Soc. Univ. Surgeons, Transplantation Soc., Western Med. Research Assn., Western Thoracic Surg. Soc., Am. Coll. Chest Physicians. Office: UCLA Sch Medicine Div Surg Oncology Louis Factor Bldg Los Angeles CA 90024

MORTON, FRANK ROBERT, oil company executive; b. Carthage, Tex., Oct. 28, 1949; s. Aaron Cole and Doris June (Miller) M.; m. Sandra Lynn Laughlin, June 18, 1971; children: Timothy, Joshua, Peter. AA in Electronic Tech., Bakersfield Coll., 1970; BS in Indsl. Tech. cum laude, Calif. State U., Fresno, 1973. Mechanic technician Getty Oil, Bakersfield, Calif., 1973-83, sr. automation technician, 1983-84; sr. automation technician environ. monitoring and service group Texaco Inc. (merger Texaco Inc. and Getty Oil), Bakersfield, Calif., 1984—. Co-author/compilor: Quality Assurance Manual for the Kern River Air Monitoring System, 1978, rev. 1986. Den leader Boy Scouts Am., Bakersfield, 1983-85. Mem. Ch. Christ. Avocations: trout fishing, camping. Office: Texaco Inc Box 5197-X Bakersfield CA 93388

MORTON, GEORGE ASHMUN, laboratory consultant, retired electronics researcher; b. New Hartford, N.Y., Mar. 24, 1903; s. Walter Hedden and Laura Savage (Johnson) M.; m. Lucy Groat, Sept. 15, 1934; children: Walter, George, Grace, Lewis. BS, MIT, 1926, MS, 1928, PhD, 1932. Research trainee Gen. Electric Co., Schenectady, N.Y., 1926-27; research asst. and instr. MIT, Cambridge, 1927-33; with research dept. RCA, Camden and Princeton, N.J., 1933-68; cons. RCA, Princeton, 1968-70, Lawrence Berkeley (Calif.) Lab., 1970—. Co-author: (books) Television, 1940, 2d rev. edit., 1954, Electron Optics and Electron Microscope, 1945; editor: Instrumentation for Environmental Monitoring: Radiation, 1983; patentee in field. Recipient Overseas Premium award Inst. Elec. Engrs., Eng., 1937, V.K. Zworykin award Inst. Radio Engrs. (later became IEEE), 1962, David Richardson medal Am. Optical Soc., 1967. Fellow Am Phys. Soc., IEEE (Nuclear and Plasma Soc. award 1974); mem. Sigma Xi. Lodge: Kiwanis. Avocations: lapidary, painting, computers. Home: 1122 Skycrest Dr Apt 6 Walnut Creek CA 94595

MORTON, HUGHES GREGORY, real estate development executive; b. St. Joseph, Mo., Aug. 11, 1923; s. William Marmaduke and Jeanette (Hughes) M.; B.S., Wharton Sch. U. Pa., 1947; postgrad. UCLA, 1949-50; children—William Marmaduke II, Hughes Gregory, Mary Gladys. Divisional personnel dir. Carnation Co., Los Angeles, 1950-52; contractors rep. Calif. Portland Cement Co., Los Angeles, 1959-64; v.p. Western Fed. Savs. & Loan Assn., Los Angeles, 1964-70; owner Morton and Assos., Beverly Hills, Calif., 1970—; chmn. United Housing Group, Inc., Beverly Hills, 1970—. Served as lt. (j.g.) USNR, 1941-46. Mem. Internat. Assn. Real Estate Appraisers. Office: PO Box 69421 Los Angeles CA 90069

MORTON, LINDA, real estate broker; b. Dec. 7, 1944; married; 2 children. BE with honors, U. Nebr., 1966. Lic. real estate broker. Tchr. Sunnyvale (Calif.) Elem. Sch., 1967-69, Jefferson County (Colo.) Sch. Dist., 1966-67, 69-70; real estate agt. Crown Realty, Lakewood, Colo., 1979-82, Van Schaack & Co., Lakewood, 1982-83, Re-Max Profls., Lakewood, 1983—. Mem. town council City of Lakewood, 1981—; represents Lakewood on Bd. Denver Regional Council of Govts., 1981—, vice chmn., chmn. program com., 1984—; appointed by Gov. Colo. to Met. Air Quality Council, 1985—. address: 423 S Devinney St Lakewood CO 80228

MORTON, MORTIMER ERVING, physician, educator; b. Columbus, Ohio, July 24, 1919; s. Ernest and Beatrice Gertrude (Becher) M.; m. Helene Steinberg, June 12, 1965; 1 child, Julia Diane. AB in Chemistry, UCLA, 1940; MA, U. Calif., Berkeley, 1941, PhD, 1942; MD, U. So. Calif., 1945. Diplomate Am. Bd. Nuclear Medicine. Chief radioisotope unit VA Hosp., Van Nuys, Calif., 1948-50, Long Beach, Calif., 1950-55; practice medicine specializing in nuclear medicine Calif., 1955—; assoc. prof. nuclear medicine U. Calif., Irvine, 1970-79, prof., 1979—; dir. nuclear medicine Med. Ctr. Garden Grove, Calif., 1983—; assoc. prof. biophysics, UCLA, 1948-55. Contbr. articles to profl. jours. Fellow Am. Coll. Nuclear Medicine; mem. Sigma Xi. Jewish. Office: Med Ctr Garden Grove Dept Nuclear Medicine 12650 Garden Grove Blvd Garden Grove CA 92643

MORTON, RANDALL EUGENE, aerospace electronics research executive, fiber optic consultant; b. Portland, Oreg., May 4, 1950; s. Eugene Randall and Kathryn Hazel (Myers) M.; m. Lori Kay Turner, Mar. 23, 1979; children: Nicole Ashley, Colin Tyler. B.S. in Elec. Engring., U. Wash., Seattle, 1972; M.S. in Nuclear Engring., 1974; Ph.D., 1979. Registered nuclear engr., Wash. Exec. cons. Holloran & Assocs., Bellevue, Wash., 1977-81; corp. cons. AGA Cons., Bellevue, 1981-82; sr. mfg. systems analyst Eldec Corp., Lynnwood, Wash., 1982-83, sr. engr. research and devel. staff, 1983-85, engring. mgr. advanced product devel., 1985—; owner Innovative Concepts, Redmond, Wash., 1984—. Contbr. articles to profl. jours.; inventor. Mem. Soc. Automotive Engrs. (mem. aerospace avionics and integration standards com.), Soc. Photo-Optical Instrumentation Engrs., Am. Nuclear Soc. (vice. chmn. Puget Sound chpt. 1981-82, chmn. 1982-84), IEEE, Optical Soc. Am., Wash. State Soccer League (Over-30 All-Star Club). Home: 10320 181st St NE Redmond WA 98052 Office: Eldec Corp 1522-217th Pl SE Bothell WA 98041-3006

MORTON, WALTER BENSON, JR., electronics engineer, consultant; b. Birmingham, Ala., July 1, 1926; s. Walter Benson and Jessie Gertrude (Coe) M.; divorced; children: Eric, Rachel, Peter, Bruce. BSEE, BSBA, Lehigh U., 1950. Registered profl. engr., Pa., Calif. Asst. prof. U. Calif., Long Beach, 1962-65; cons. Lockheed Corp. and Xerox Corp., Los Angeles, 1960-76; sr. project engr. Transrex Gulton Industries, Carson, Calif., 1977-80; mgr. Cipher Data Products, San Diego, 1980-85; lectr. U. Calif., San Diego, 1985—; cons. engr. San Diego, 1985—; cons. Augat, 1986—. Contbr. articles to profl. jours. Served with USN, 1943-46, PTO. Carnegie Mellon Fellow, 1951. Mem. IEEE (sr.), Assn. Computer Machinery, N.Y. Acad. Sci., AAAS. Home and Office: 803 21st St San Diego CA 92102

MOSBY, DOROTHEA SUSAN, municipal official; b. Sacramento, Calif., May 13, 1948; d. William Laurence and Esther Ida (Lux) M. AA in Sociology, Bakersfield (Calif.) Coll., 1966-69; BS in Recreation, San Jose State U., 1969-72; MA in Pub. Adminstrn., Calif. State U. Dominguez Hills, Carson, 1980-82. Asst. dept. personnel officer San Jose Parks and Recreation Dept., 1972-73, neighborhood ctr. dir., 1973-74; sr. recreation leader Santa Monica Recreation and Parks Dept., 1974-76, recreation supr., 1976-83, bus. div. head, 1983—; bd. dirs, officer Santa Monica City Employees Fedn. Credit Union, 1980—; mem. citizens adv. com. Los Angeles Olympic Organizing Com., 1982-84. Mem. choir, flute soloist Pilgrim Luth. Ch., Santa Monica, 1974—, treas.Luth. ch. council, 1984—; vol. driver XXIII Olympiad, Los Angeles, 1984; contbr. local housing assistance U.S. Olympic Com., Los Angeles, 1984; mem. adv. com. Windsor Sq. Hancock Park Hist. Soc., Los Angeles, 1983, dir. Christmas carolling, 1980—, chmn. Olympic com., 1984, bd. trustees, 1984—, chmn. pub. programs, 1985, co-chmn. pub. programs, 1986. Mem. Calif. Park and Recreation Soc. (bd. dirs. 1979-82, 86), Nat. Recreation and Park Assn., Mgmt. Team Assocs. (sec., treas. 1978-83), Chi Kappa Rho (pres. 1986), Pi Alpha Alpha. Avocations: flute, piano, reading, bicycling, tennis. Home: 1134 Chelsea Ave Apt C Santa Monica CA 90403 Office: Santa Monica Recreation & Parks Dept 1685 Main St Santa Monica CA 90401

MOSBY, LELAND DARRELL, counselor; b. Kansas City, Mo., Dec. 18, 1947; s. Ralph Byron and Hettie Ermine (Everett) M.; children: Leland Darell, Crystal Rachelle. BA, SW Baptist U., 1969; MDiv, Southwestern Bapt. Theol. Sem., 1972; D of Min., Midwestern Bapt. Theol. Sem., 1978; EdD U. Sarasota, 1986. Ordained to ministry Bapt. Ch., 1969. Pastor Norfleet Bapt. Ch., Kansas City, Mo., 1972-75, Concord Bapt. Ch., St. Louis, 1975-79; sr. pastor Applewood Baptist Ch., Wheat Ridge, Colo., 1979-83; counselor, cons., tchr. seminars. Author: The Lonely Valley, A Journey through Bereavement, 1978. Mem. Am. Assn. for Counseling and Devel., Am. Assn. Profl. Hypnotherapists, Christian Assn. Psychol. Study, Fla. Psychological Practitioners Assn., Am. Mental Health Counselors Assn., Colo. Mental Health Counselors Assn., Nat. Bd. Cert. Counselors.

MOSCHETTA, ROBERT P., safety engineering administrator; b. Pitts., Dec. 10, 1955; s. Robert C. and Frances (Katich) M.; m. Cynthia J. McGuirk, Aug. 20, 1981. BA in Environ. Studies, Calif. U. of Pa., 1978; MS in Safety Studies, W. Va. U., 1980. Underground coal miner J & L Steel Corp., Waynesburg, Pa., 1977-82; safety supr. Beaver Creek Coal Co. div. ARCO, Price, Utah, 1982-85; safety mgr. West Elk Coal Co. div. ARCO, Somerset, Colo., 1985—. Vol. disaster action team ARC, Price chpt., 1983-85. Mem. Am. Soc. Safety Engrs., Nat. Safety Mgmt. Soc., Am. Mining Congress (ad hoc diesel com.), Nat. Fire Protection Assn., Colo. Mining Assn. (health and safety com.). Democrat. Roman Catholic. Lodges: Elks, KC. Avocations: scuba diving, swimming, running, camping, bicycling. Home: 4055 German Creek Dr Paonia CO 81428 Office: West Elk Coal Co div ARCO PO Box 591 Somerset CO 81434

MOSCICKI, JOHN MARTIN, management development consultant; b. Clinton, Ind., Nov. 9, 1951; s. Martin C. and Yvonne E. (Uhrin) M.; m. Anne Marie Teters, May 31, 1986. BS, Fla. State U., 1973, MS, 1977; PhD, Columbia U., 1982. Instructional systems design engr. Grumman Aerospace, Bethpage, N.Y., 1978-79; sr. research mgr. Xerox Learning Systems, Stamford, Conn., 1979-83; ptnr. Keilty, Goldsmith & Boone, La Jolla, Calif., 1984—. Designer, exec. producer Internactive Video Feedback System, 1984; co-inventor, patentee in field. Avocations: fly fishing, hiking, photography. Home: 945 Corbett Ave San Francisco CA 94131 Office: Keilty Goldsmith & Boone 1298 Prospect St La Jolla CA 92037

MOSELEY, FURMAN C., timber company executive; b. 1935. With Simpson Paper Co., 1960—, formerly exec. v.p., now chmn. bd., also dir.; pres. Simpson Investment Co. Served USMC, 1956-59. Office: Simpson Investment Co 900 4th Ave Seattle WA 98164 *

MOSELEY, ROBERT DAVID, JR., radiologist, retired educator; b. Minden, La., Feb. 29, 1924; s. Robert David and Lettie E. (Looney) M.; m. Janet C. Watson, Mar. 15, 1947; children: Robert David III, Richard Havard, Marianne Lee. M.D., La. State U., 1947. Diplomate Am. Bd. Radiology. Intern Highland Sanitarium and Clinic, Shreveport, La., 1947-48; asst. resident U. Chgo. Clinics, 1949-50; asst. resident Los Alamos spl. research project, dept. radiology U. Chgo., 1950-51; staff mem. U. Calif.-Los Alamos Sci. Lab., 1951-52, radiologist, assoc. chief staff med. ctr., 1951-52; mem. staff dept. radiology U. Chgo., 1954-71, prof., chmn. dept., 1958-71; prof., asst. chmn., dir. div. diagnostic radiology U. N.Mex. Sch. Medicine, Albuquerque, 1971-78; prof., chmn. dept. radiology U. N.Mex. Sch. Medicine, 1978-85, prof. emeritus, 1985—; chief of staff Bernalillo County Med. Center, 1971-72, 78, 79; bd. dirs. Nat. Council Radiation Protection, 1973-80; mem. radiation study sect. USPHS, NIH, 1971-75; mem. radiology tng. com. NIH, 1966-70; chmn., 1969-70; U.S. rep. UN Sci. Com. on Effects Atomic Radiation, 1976-86; chmn. adv. com. on biology and medicine U.S. AEC, 1967-73; chmn. U.S. delegation Internat. Congresses of Radiology, Rio de Janeiro, 1977, Brussels, 1981; pres. XVI Internat. Congress Radiology, Hawaii, 1985. Pres. bd. dirs. James Picker Found., 1972-86. Served as lt. (s.g.) USNR, 1952-54. Fellow Chgo. Roentgen Soc. (past sec.-treas. bd. trustees, pres. 1966-67), Am. Coll. Radiology (pres. 1973-74, Gold medal 1980), Royal Coll. Radiologists (Eng.) (hon.), Swedish Soc. Med. Radiology (hon.); mem. Internat. Soc. Radiology (pres. 1985—), N.Mex. Med. Soc., Assn. U. Radiologists (founding mem., past pres., Gold medal 1980), Am. Roentgen Ray Soc., Radiation Research Soc., Acad. Soc. Lund (Sweden) (corr.), Deutsche Röntgengesellshaft (corr.), Radiol. Soc. N.Am., Inter Am. Coll. Radiology, Royal Physiographic Soc. (fgn. mem., Lund, Sweden), N.Mex. Soc. Radiologists, Sigma Xi, Sigma Nu, Phi Chi. Club: Univ. (Chgo.). Home: 635 Running Water Circle SE Albuquerque NM 87123

MOSER, CHARLES ALLEN, sexologist, researcher, psychotherapist; b. Bklyn., Apr. 3, 1952; s. George Philip and Miriam June (Ostrinsky) M. BS, SUNY, Stony Brook, 1974; MSW, U. Wash., 1975; PhD, Inst. Advanced Human Sexuality, Calif., 1979. Cert. sex educator and therapist. Social worker Central Islip (N.Y.) Psychiat. Ctr., 1976, Kingsboro Psychiat. Ctr., Bklyn., 1977-78, Patton (Calif.) State Hosp., 1979-80; designee county mental health dir. Criminal Justice Health Services, Martinez, Calif., 1980-84; pvt. practice psychotherapy San Francisco, 1978—; assoc. prof., clin. dir. sexual health care Inst. Advanced Study Human Sexuality, San Francisco, 1980—; also expert witness in criminal and civil ct. cases, San Francisco, 1980—. Contbr. articles and book chpts. to profl. publs. Mem. Soc. For Sci. Study Sex (bd. dirs. 1985-88), Assn. Sexologists, Nat. Assn. Social Workers (cert.), Soc. Sex. Therapy and Research, Am. Assn. Sex Educators Counselors and Therapists (cert.), The Am. Coll. Sexologists. Avocation: scuba diving. Home: 2060 Sutter St #508 San Francisco CA 94115 Office: Inst Advanced Study Human Sexuality 1523 Franklin St San Francisco CA 94109

MOSER, DEAN JOSEPH, accountant; b. San Francisco, Apr. 5, 1942; s. Joseph Edward and Velma Ida (Cruz) M.; B.S., U. San Francisco, 1964, postgrad. Law Sch., 1964-66; postgrad. Golden Gate U., 1966-86; m. Michele Patrice Cicerone, June 16, 1963; children—Jay, Lynele, Todd. Cert. fin. planner; lic. real estate broker, Calif. Owner, acct. DJM Bookkeeping Service, 1962-65; asst. controller Dymo Industries, Internat., Berkeley, Calif., 1965-67; mgr. taxes Arthur Andersen & Co., San Francisco, 1967-76; owner, mgr. Contadora Ltd., Novato, Calif., 1981—, Esprit Realty Co., Novato, 1981—; Dean J. Moser Accountancy Corp., Novato, 1981—, Stellar Properties; gen. ptnr. Galli Sq.; founding dir., treas., chief fin. officer Novato Nat. Bank, NorthBay Bancorp. Asst. scout master Boy Scouts Am.; past bd. dirs. Novato Human Needs Center. C.P.A., Calif. Mem. Calif. Soc. CPA's. Republican. Roman Catholic. Club: Rotary (Paul Harris fellow). Office: 394 Bel Marin Keys Blvd Novato CA 94947

MOSES, EDWARD CROSBY, painter; b. Long Beach, Calif.; s. Alfonsus Lemuel and Olivia (Branco) M.; m. Avilda Peters, Aug. 11, 1959; children: Cedd, Andrew. B.A., U. Calif., Los Angeles, 1954; M.A., U. Calif., 1956. lectr. painting, drawing UCLA, 1961, 75-76, U. Calif., Irvine, 1969-72, Bakersfield Coll., Calif., 1977; guest lectr. Oberlin Coll., Wichita Art Mus.,

Cranbrook Inst. Numerous one-man shows, 1958—, latest include Andre Emmerich Gallery, N.Y.C., 1974-75, Los Angeles County Mus. Art, 1976, Smith-Anderson Gallery, Palo Alto, Calif., Tex. Gallery, Houston, 1979, High Mus. Art, Atlanta, 1980, Dorothy Rosenthal Gallery, Chgo., 1982, Janus Gallery, Los Angeles, 1982, Bernard Jacobson Gallery, Los Angeles, 1983, Dorthy Rosenthal Gallery, Chgo., 1982-83, L.A. Louver Gallery, 1985-87; exhibited numerous group shows, 1958—, latest include Corcoran Gallery Art, Washington, 1979, High Mus., 1980, San Francisco Mus., 1980, San Francisco Art Inst., 1981, Mus. Modern Art, Paris, 1982, Los Angeles Mcpl. Gallery, 1982, Mus. Contemporary Art, Los Angeles, 1983, 86, Nat. Gallery Art, Washington, 1984; represented in permanent collections U. Calif. Art Mus., Berkeley, Seattle Art Mus., San Francisco Art Mus., Mus. Modern Art, N.Y.C., San Francisco Art Inst., Chgo. Art Inst., Hirshhorn Mus., Phila., Akron Art Inst., Ohio, Harvard U., Cambridge, Mass., Yale U., New Haven, Walker Art Mus., Mpls., Corcoran Gallery Art, Whitney Mus. Am. Art, N.Y.C., Mus. Modern Art., N.Y.C., Los Angeles County Mus. Art, Nat. Mus. Am. Art at Smithsonian Inst., Washington, Phila. Mus. Art. Served with USN, 1944-46. Recipient Tamarind fellowship in lithography, 1968; NEA grantee, 1976; Guggenheim fellow, 1980. Office: LA Louver Gallery 50 N Venice Blvd Venice CA 90291

MOSES, ROBERT EVERETT, publisher books, periodicals, journals; b. Rochester, N.Y., Apr. 24, 1946; s. C. Everett and Margaret C. (Coleman) M.; m. Anne Joyce Hargon, Apr. 24, 1971 (div. 1976); 1 child, Joshua A. BA in Philosophy, Hamilton Coll., 1968; postgrad., Denver U., 1971-73. Pres., founder SEI Pub. Corp., Denver, 1974—; bd. dirs., mem. Seniors! Inc., Denver. Recipient Oustanding Contribution to Colo.'s Sr. Citizens award High Time Radio program, Denver, 1978, Outstanding Communicator award Mental Health Assn. Colo., 1979, Excellence in Communication award Ctr. Hearing, Speech and Lang., Denver, 1985, Pub. Service award Am. Coll Health Care Adminstrn., 1987. Democrat. Avocations: reading, music, writing. Office: SEI Pub Corp 1660 Lincoln St Suite 2240 Denver CO 80264

MOSGOVOY, PAUL VADIM, electrical engineer; b. Livermore, Calif., July 19, 1960; s. Walter Vadim and Marylee (Mohr) M.; m. Leah Dawn Stallings, June 8, 1985. BSEE, Tex. A&M U., 1984. Design engr. Motorola Inc., Scottsdale, Ariz., 1984-86; project engr. Sperry Aerospace and Marine Group, Glendale, Ariz., 1986—. Mem. Tau Beta Pi, Eta Kappa Nu. Avocation: Classic Mustangs. Office: Sperry Aerospace and Marine Group PO Box 2111 Phoenix AZ 85036

MOSHER, SALLY EKENBERG, lawyer; b. N.Y.C., July 26, 1934; d. Leslie Joseph and Frances Josephine (McArdle) Ekenberg; m. James Kimberly Mosher, Aug. 13, 1960 (dec. Aug. 1982). MusB, Manhattanville Coll., 1956; postgrad. Hofstra U., 1958-60, U. So. Calif., 1971-73; JD, U. So. Calif., 1981. Bar: Calif., 1982. Musician, pianist, tchr. N.Y., Los Angeles, 1957-74; music critic Pasadena Star-News, 1967-72; mgr. Contrasts Concerts, Pasadena Art Mus., 1971-72; rep. Occidental Life Ins. Co., Pasadena, 1975-78; v.p. James K. Mosher Co., Pasadena, 1961-82; pres., 1982—; pres. Oakhill Enterprises, Pasadena, 1984—; assoc. White-Howell, Inc., Pasadena, 1984—. Contbr. articles to various publs. Bd. dirs. Pasadena Arts Council, 1966-68, Jr. League Pasadena, 1966-67, Encounters Concerts, Pasadena, 1966-72, U. So. Calif. Friends of Music, Los Angeles, 1973-76, Pasadena Chamber Orch., 1986—, Pasadena Arts Council, 1986—; v.p. Pasadena Chamber Orchestra, 1986—. Manhattanville Coll. hon. scholar, 1952-56. Mem. ABA, Calif. Bar Assn., Los Angeles Bar Assn., Pasadena Bar Assn., Am. Assn. Realtors, Calif. Assn. Realtors, Pasadena Bd. Realtors, Assocs. of Calif. Inst. Tech., Kappa Gamma Pi, Mu Phi Epsilon, Phi Alpha Delta. Republican. Clubs: Pasadena Athletic; Athenaeum, Jr. League. Home: 1260 Rancheros Rd Pasadena CA 91103 Office: 711 E Walnut St Suite 407 Pasadena CA 91101

MOSHIER, T. C., school official; b. Stonewall, Okla., Nov. 23, 1931; s. Earnest Spencer and Winnie Mildrer (Whipple) M.; m. Carolyn Mae Just, Aug. 22, 1969; children—Carol Laureen, Thomas Charles, Julie Lynn, James Anthony, Kimberly Renee. B.A., E. Central Okla. Coll., 1952; M.A., Fresno State U., 1960. Tchr., Traver Sch. Dist., Calif., 1956-61, supt., 1961-66; supt. Kings River Sch. Dist., Kingsburg, Calif., 1966—. Dir. Kingsburg Rotary Basketball Tournament, 1970—, Kings River Jr. Golf Tournament, 1975—; mem. Tulare County Supts. Adv. Com., Visalia, Calif., 1976-84. Served with USNR, 1952-56. Mem. Assn. Calif. Sch. Adminstrs., Democrat. Mem. Ch. of Christ. Club: Kings River Country. Lodge: Rotary (charter, past. pres. Kinsburg chpt.). : CA 93631 Office: Kings River Union Sch Dist 3961 Ave 400 Kingsburg CA 93631

MOSIER, ARVIN RAY, chemist, researcher; b. Olney Springs, Colo., June 11, 1945; s. Isaac James Ellen Rena (Ross) M.; m. Susan Minnick, Dec. 30, 1965; children: Andrew, Katherine. BS, Colo. State U., 1967, MS, 1967-68, PhD, 1974. Chemist agr. research services USDA, Ft. Collins, 1967—; Contbr. papers and book chpt. to profl. publ. Mem. AAAS, Am. Soc. Agronomy, Soil Sci. Soc. Am., Internat. Soil Sci. Soc., Council Agrl. Sci. Tech., Phi Kappa Phi, Sigma XI, Gamma Sigma Delta. Republican. Methodist. Club: Aresnal Competitive Soccer. Avocations: tennis, soccer. Home: 1219 Springwood Dr Fort Collins CO 80525 Office: Agrl Research Service USDA PO Box E Fort Collins CO 80522

MOSK, STANLEY, state justice; b. San Antonio, Sept. 4, 1912; s. Paul and Minna (Perl) M.; m. Edna Mitchell, Sept. 27, 1937 (dec.); 1 child, Richard Mitchell.; m. Susan Hines, Aug. 27, 1982. Student, U. Tex., 1931; Ph.B., U. Chgo., 1933; postgrad., U. Chgo. Law Sch., 1935, Hague Acad. Internat. Law, 1970; LL.D., U. Pacific, 1970, U. San Diego, 1971, U. Santa Clara, 1976, Calif. Western U., 1984, Southwestern U., 1987. Bar: Calif. 1935, U.S. Supreme Ct. 1956. Practiced in Los Angeles until 1939; exec. sec. to gov. Calif., 1939-42; judge Superior Ct. Los Angeles County, 1943-58; pro tem justice Dist. Ct. Appeal, Calif., 1954; atty. gen. Calif, also head state dept., justice, 1959-64; justice Supreme Ct. Calif., 1964—; mem. Jud. Council Calif., 1973-75, Internat. Commn. Jurists. Chmn. San Francisco Internat. Film Festival, 1967; mem. Dem. Nat. Com., Calif., 1960-64; bd. regents U. Calif., 1940; pres. Vista Del Mar Child Care Service, 1954-58; bd. dirs. San Francisco Law Sch., 1971-73, San Francisco Regional Cancer Found., 1980-83. Served with AUS, World War II. Recipient Disting. Alumnus award U. Chgo., 1958. Mem. Nat. Assn. Attys. Gen. (exec. bd. 1964), Western Assn. Attys. Gen. (pres. 1963), ABA, Calif., Los Angeles, Santa Monica, San Francisco bar assns., Am. Legion, Manuscript Soc., Calif. Hist. Soc., Am. Judicature Soc., Inst. Jud. Administrn., U. Chgo. Alumni Assn. No. Calif. (pres. 1957-58, 67), Order of Coif, Phi Alpha Delta. Mem. B'nai B'rith. Clubs: Hillcrest Country (Los Angeles); Commonwealth, Golden Gateway Tennis (San Francisco); Beverly Hills Tennis. Office: State Bldg San Francisco CA 94102

MOSLEHI, BEHZAD MOHAMAD REZA, fiber optic engineer, researcher; b. Tehran, Iran, Aug. 11, 1956; came to U.S., 1978; s. Mohamad and Ashraf Moslehi. BSEE, Arya-Mehr U. Tech., Tehran, 1978; MSEE, Stanford U., 1980, MS in Applied Physics, 1984, PhDEE, 1984. Research asst. Stanford (Calif.) U., 1980-84; engring. specialist Litton Systems Inc., Chatsworth, Calif., 1984—; vis. research scholar Stanford (Calif.) U., 1984—; research intern Quantex Corp., Sunnyvale, Calif., 1979; research engr. Xerox Corp., Palo Alto, Calif., 1980-81. Contbr. articles to profl. jours.; patentee in field. Mem. IEEE, Optical Soc. Am., Sigma Xi. Avocations: volleyball, soccer, chess, music. Home: 7007 Royer Ave West Hills CA 91307 Office: Litton Guidance and Control Systems 9172 Eton Ave Chatsworth CA 91311 Mailing: PO Box 7429 Stanford CA 94305

MOSQUEIRA, CHARLOTTE MARIANNE, dietitian; b. Los Angeles, July 26, 1937; d. Leo and Magdalene Tollefson; B.S., St. Olaf Coll., 1959; postgrad. U. Oreg. Med. Sch., 1959-60; M.A., Central Mich. U., 1980; children—Mark, Michael. Chief clin. dietitian, asst. dir. food service Queen of Angels Hosp., Los Angeles, 1968-70; asst. dir. food service Presbyn. Hosp. Ctr., Albuquerque, 1970-73; dir. food service Holy Cross Hosp., Salt Lake City, 1973-77; dir. dietetics Riverside Meth. Hosp., Columbus, Ohio, 1977-79; dir. nutrition and food service Fresno (Calif.) Community Hosp. and Med. Ctr., 1980—. Mem. Am. Soc. for Hosp. Food Service Adminstrs. (regional dir.), Am. Dietetic Assn., Calif. Dietetic Assn., AAUW. Republican. Lutheran. Club: Community Vocal Chorale.

MOSS, CARLA ANN, sculptor; b. San Francisco, Nov. 26, 1947; d. Clayton Omer and Patricia Louise (Shanahan) Erickson; m. Maver Bruyer Moss, Jr., Oct. 12, 1971. B.A., Mont. State U., 1969. Curator, Glacier Gallery, Kalispell, Mont., 1969—; with Powell Bronze Foundry, 1973-78; tchr. sculpture classes, art tchr. Whitefish Jr. High Sch., Mont., 1974-75. Represented in permanent collections: U. N.D., Fargo; monumental statue Glacier Park Internat. Airport, 1983; commd. by Anchorage Alaska for life-size eagles for Eagle River, Ernest Gruening Jr. High Sch., 1985; guest artist Area Women in the Arts, 1979. Recipient Best of Show Bronze award Septemberfest Art Show and Auction, Havre, Mont., 1981; Conv. award Nev. Longhorn Assn., 1983.

MOSS, CHARLES NORMAN, physician; b. Los Angeles, June 13, 1914; s. Charles Francis and Lena (Rye) M.; A.B., Stanford U., 1940; M.D., Harvard U., 1944; cert. U. Vienna, 1947; M.P.H., U. Calif.-Berkeley, 1955; Dr.P.H., UCLA, 1970; m. Margaret Louise Stakias; children—Charles Eric, Gail Linda, and Lori Anne. Surg. intern Peter Bent Brigham Hosp., Boston, 1944-45, asst. in surgery, 1947; commd. 1st lt. USAF, M.C., USAAF, 1945, advanced through grades to lt. col., USAF, 1956; Long course for flight surgeon USAF Sch. Aviation Medicine, Randolph AFB, Tex., 1948-49, preventive medicine div. Office USAF Surgeon Gen., Washington, 1955-59; air observer, med., 1954, became sr. flight surgeon 1956; later med. dir., Los Angeles div. North Am. Rockwell Corp., Los Angeles; chief med. adv. unit Los Angeles County, now ret. Decorated Army Commendation medal (U.S.); Chinese Breast Order of Yun Hui. Recipient Physicians Recognition award AMA, 1969, 72, 76, 79, 82. Diplomate in aerospace medicine and occupational medicine Am. Bd. Preventive Medicine. Fellow Am. Pub. Health Assn., AAAS, Am. Coll. Preventive Medicine, Royal Soc. Health, Am. Acad. Occupational Medicine, Western Occupational Med. Assn., Am. Assn. Occupational Medicine; mem. AMA, Mil. Surgeons U.S., Soc. Air Force Flight Surgeons, Am. Conf. Govt. Hygienests, Calif. Acad. Preventive Medicine, (dir.), Aerospace Med. Assn., Calif., Los Angeles County med. assns., Assn. Oldetime Barbell and Strongmen. Research and publs. in field. Home: 7714 Cowan Ave Los Angeles CA 90045

MOSS, MORTON HERBERT (MOSS HERBERT), newspaper columnist, editor, poet; b. N.Y.C., Mar. 21, 1914; s. Carl and Rose (Schnur) M.; student Columbia U., 1930-32; m. Ruth Miller, Feb. 19, 1939; 1 son, Eric. Sports writer N.Y. Post, N.Y.C., 1932-37, Internat. News Service, N.Y.C., 1937-40; sports editor, columnist Los Angeles Examiner (now Herald Examiner), 1941-61, asst. sports editor, columnist, 1962-68, TV editor, columnist, 1969-77, news wire editor, 1978-79. Mem. Nat. Acad. TV Arts and Scis., Los Angeles World Affairs Council, Greater Los Angeles Press Club, Poetry Soc. Am., Internat. Poetry Soc. Represented in Best Sports Stories, E.P. Dutton & Co., Inc., 1952, 1960, 61, 62, 64, 65, 66, 67. Author: In Sight of the Invisible, 1987; contbr. articles to various mags.; contbr. poetry to mags. Lyric, Ariz. Quar., Coastlines, Am. Poet, Global Architecture, also anthologies The Golden Year, 1960, The Various Light, 1964, Ipso Facto, 1975. Creator Simplified Five, the boxing scoring system adopted by Calif. State Athletic Commn., 1960-70. Home: 1909 N Normandie Ave Los Angeles CA 90027

MOSS, RICHARD SPENCER, energy company executive; b. Portland, Oreg., May 26, 1949; s. Harry and Mary Louise (Ruckdeschel) M.; m. Marilyn Jean Best, June 2, 1973; children—Emily Anne, Paul Spencer, Kathryn Elizabeth, Brian Richard. A.A., Mount Hood Community Coll., 1975; B.A. in Communications, U. Portland, 1977. Publs. mgr. First Nat. Bank Oreg., Portland, 1977; mgr. employee communications Ga.-Pacific Corp., Portland, 1977-80; dir. alumni and community relations U. Portland, 1980-84; dir. employee communications No. Energy Resources Co., Portland, 1984—. Served with USN, 1969-73; Vietnam. Recipient Arnold's Admirables award The Ragan Report, 1982. Mem. Pub. Relations Soc. Am., Internat. Assn. Bus. Communicators (chpt. dir., chpt. pres. 1985-86, Gold Quill award 1979, 83), Council Advancement and Support of Edn., Portland Dahlia Soc. Republican. Episcopalian. Home: 10125 SW Arborcrest Way Portland OR 97225 Office: NERCO Inc 111 SW Columbia St Portland OR 97201

MOSS, STEVEN DAVID, police officer, consultant, educator; b. San Diego, Apr. 21, 1955; s. David Lee and Patricia Ann (Hizer) M.; m. Lesli Kay Lord, Oct. 24, 1981; children: Adam Christopher, Ryan Andrew. BS, Nat. U., San Diego, 1981, MBA, 1986. Police officer San Diego Police Dept., 1978—; instr. San Diego Community Colls., 1982—; gen. ptnr., chief exec. officer C&M Collision Analysis, San Diego, 1982—. Author: Basic Collision Analysis and Scene Documentation, 1983. Mem. Internat. AAAS, Southwestern Assn. Tech. Investigators, Inc., Mcpl. Motorcycle Officers of Calif. Avocations: computer modeling, gardening.

MOSSMAN, FRED MCKEE, construction contractor; b. Valentine, Nebr., Feb. 4, 1934; s. Frederick Andrew and Edna (McKee) M.; m. Janie Patricia Louder, June 16, 1956; children: Frederick Andrew, Clark Edward, Matthew Howard, David Grant, Sarah Kathryn. BBA, U. N.Mex., 1956. Lic. contractor, N.Mex. V.p. Mossman-Gladden, Inc., Albuquerque, 1956-83; pres. Mossman Enterprises, Albuquerque, 1984—; bd. dirs. Am. Bank, Rio Rancho, N.Mex., AmeriWest Fin. Corp., Albuquerque, Albuquerque Fed. Savs. & Loan; S.W. rep. Anthony Services Nat. Builders Council. chmn. adv. bd. Albuquerque Library, 1972-76; pres. bd. trustees Albuquerque Acad., 1971—. Recipient Nat. Swimming Pool Design award for Excellance Anthony Industries, 1978-81, 84, 86. Mem. Nat. Spa and Pool Inst., Nat. Homebuilders Assn., Nat. Spa and Pool Inst. N. Mex., N. Mex. Homebuilders Assn. (pres. 1966), Albuquerque Homebuilders Assn. (pres. 1966). Republican. Baptist. Office: Mossman Enterprises Inc 7410 Montgomery NE Albuquerque NM 87109

MOSSMAN, SANDRA LYNNE ALKIRE, educational administrator; b. Scotts Bluff, Nebr., Mar. 10, 1945; d. John F. and Virginia L. (Alkire); children by previous marriage: Beal Monroe IV. B.S., U. Oreg., 1967; M.S., Mont. State U., 1979. Tchr., Taft Sch., Billings, Mont., 1967-78; Women in Sch. Adminstrn. prin. intern Arrowhead Sch., Billings, 1978-79; prin. Ponderosa Sch., Billings, 1979-85; prin. Eagle Cliffs Elem. Sch., 1986—; cons. in field. Grantee in edn. Second v.p. PTA, 1979—. Mem. Nat. Assn. Elem. Sch. Prins., Internat. Reading Assn., Assn. for Supervision and Curriculum Devel., Sch. Adminstrs. of Mont., Mont. Assn. Elem. Sch. Prins., Mont. Reading Council, Midland Empire Reading Council, Billings Assn. Elem. Sch. Prins., Mont. Assn. Female Execs., Phi Delta Kappa. Home: 2108 Pine St Billings MT 59101

MOSSMAN, THOMAS MELLISH, JR., TV producer, director; b. Honolulu, Nov. 20, 1938; s. Thomas Mellish and Marian (Ledwith) M.; m. Leonore Jean Stapleton, Aug. 25, 1960; children: Thomas M. III, James Michael. Student, U. Hawaii, 1954-57; BA, U. Denver, 1958, MA, 1965. Producer, dir. Sta. KRMA-TV, Denver, 1960-64, Sta. KCET-TV, Los Angeles, 1964-72, Mosaic Films, Los Angeles, 1972-73; dir. prodns., ops. KLCS-TV, Los Angeles, 1973-78; sta. mgr. Sta. KLCS-TV, Los Angeles, 1978-87; TV cons. Los Angeles, 1987—; instr. TV prodn. Calif. State U., Northridge, 1981—. Mem. Acad. TV Arts and Scis., Dirs. Guild Am. Episcopal. Club: Greater Los Angeles Press. Home: 24043 Avenida Crescenta Valencia CA 91355 Office: 24043 Ave Crescente Valencia CA 91355

MOSSOTTI, VICTOR GIOVANI, research chemist; b. St. Louis, May 20, 1948; s. Victor Giovoni and Mildred Lee (Cannon) M. PhD, Iowa State U., 1974. Assoc. prof. chemistry U. Minn., Mpls., 1974-81; research chemist Stanford U., Palo Alto, Calif., 1981-86, U.S. Geol. Survey, Menlo Park, Calif., 1981—. Editor: Treatise on Analytic Chemistry, Spectrochimica Acta, 1973-81; contbr. articles to profl. jours. Alexander V. Humboldt fellow, 1974, Gilbert fellow Dept. of Interior, 1981. Mem. IEEE, Am. Chem. Soc., Soc. Applied Spectroscopy. Avocation: polo. Office: US Geol Survey MS-938 345 Middlefield Rd Menlo Park CA 94025

MOSTELLER, JAMES WILBUR, III, data processing exec.; b. Ft. Riley, Kans., June 21, 1940; s. James Wilbur, Jr., and Ruth Renfro (Thompson) M.; B.S. in Econs., Rensselaer Poly. Inst., 1962; M.B.A., Temple U., 1971; m. Sandra Josephine Stevenson, Oct. 13, 1962; children—Margaret, Steven, Michael. Data processing systems analyst, Philco-Ford, Ft. Washington, Pa., 1966-69; data processing analyst and supr., Merck Sharp & Dohme, West Point, Pa., 1969-75, dir. mgmt. info. systems KELCO div. Merck and Co., San Diego, 1975—. Bd. dirs. San Diego Hall Sci., 1985—, New Horizons Montessori Sch., Ft. Washington, Pa., 1974-75; leader youth programs North County YMCA, 1977—; mem. San Diego Research Park Com., 1978—. Served with USN, 1962-66; mem. Res. 1966—. Cert. in data processing. Mem. Data Processing Mgmt. Assn., Assn. Systems Mgmt., Naval Reserve Assn., Beta Gamma Sigma, Sigma Alpha Epsilon (chpt. pres. 1961-62). Office: Kelco Div Merck & Co Inc 8355 Aero Dr San Diego CA 92123

MOSTOFI, KHOSROW, political scientist, educator; b. Tehran, Iran, July 8, 1921; came to U.S., 1949; s. Mostafa and Nasrin (Djam) M.; m. Nesrin Imamverdi, Aug. 18, 1960; 1 dau., Simin S. (dec.). B.A., U. Tehran, 1944; M.A., U. Utah, 1957, Ph.D., 1958, grad. cert. in public adminstrn., 1965. Instr. langs. Ministry Edn., Tehran, 1944-49; asst. U. Utah Inst. Govt., Salt Lake City, 1956-58; mem. faculty U. Utah Dept. Polit. Sci., 1960—; prof. polit. sci. U. Utah Inst. Govt., 1970—, dir. Middle East Center, 1967-83; coordinator Arab Devel. Program, 1976-81; pres. Western Asian Trade and Investment Corp., 1983-87; dir. Am. Center Iranian Studies, Tehran, summer 1970; instr. polit. sci. Portland (Oreg.) State Coll., 1958-59, asst. prof., 1959-60; cons. div. of higher edn. U.S. Dept. Edn., 1968-70, 76; co-sponsor, organizer Internat. Conf. on Islam, Iran, and Pakistan, 1975, Internat. Conf. on Higher Edn. and Devel. in Arab World, 1978; sponsor, organizer Internat. Conf. on Comparative Law, 1977. Author: Parsee Nameh, rev. edit, 1969, Aspects of Nationalism: A Sociology of Colonial Revolt, 1964; contbr. to: Ency. Britannica, 1974, 83, 87, Studies in Art and Literature of the Near East, 1974. Trustee Internat. Visitors-Utah Council, 1984-87. Recipient disting. service award Utah Acad. Scis., Arts and Letters, 1983, Service award World Trade Assn. of Utah, 1981. Fulbright-Hayes fellow, 1965-66; mem. Am. Inst. Iranian Studies (trustee), AAUP, Western Polit. Sci. Assn., Middle East Inst., Middle East Studies Assn., Ctr. Arabic Studies Abroad (bd. dirs. 1970-83), Pi Sigma Alpha, Phi Kappa Phi. Moslem. Home: 2481 E 1300 S Salt Lake City UT 84108 Office: University of Utah Dept Polit Sci Salt Lake City UT 84112

MOTAMEDI, MANOUCHEHR ED, electrical engineer; b. Esfahan, Iran; came to U.S., 1963.; s. Mahmood and Batool (Shams) M.; m. Soraya Amiri, July 28, 1969; children: Linda Farnaz, Michael Farshad. BSEE, U. Tehran, Iran; MSEE, Northwestern U., PhDEE. Prof. Arya-Mehr U., Tehran, 1971-74; prof. Rensselaer Poly. Tech., Troy, N.Y., 1974-76, research scientist, 1976-80; program mgr. Rockwell Internat., Anaheim, Calif., 1980—. Recipient Murphy Award, 1966. Mem. IEEE, Am. Phys. Soc., Electro-Chem. Soc., Ultrasonic. Avocations: photography, swimming, traveling. Home: 2408 Northpark St Thousand Oaks CA 91362 Office: Rockwell Internat 3370 Miraloma Ave MA 30 Anaheim CA 92803

MOTE, CLAYTON DANIEL, JR., mechanical engineer, educator; b. San Francisco, Feb. 5, 1937; s. Clayton Daniel and Eugenia (Isnardi) M.; m. Patricia Jane Lewis, Aug. 18, 1962; children—Melissa Michelle, Adam Jonathan. B.Sc., U. Calif., Berkeley, 1959, M.S., 1960, Ph.D., 1963. Registered profl. engr., Calif. Asst. specialist U. Calif. Forest Products Labs., 1961-62; asst. mech. engr. 1962-63; lectr. mech. engring. U. Calif., Berkeley, 1962-63, asst. prof., 1967-69, asst. research engr., 1968-69, asso. prof., asso. research engr., 1969-73, prof., 1973—, vice chmn. mech. engring. dept., 1976-80, 83-86, chmn. mech. engring. dept., 1987—; research fellow U. Birmingham, Eng., 1963-64; asst. prof. Carnegie Inst. Tech., 1964-67; vis. prof. Norwegian Inst. Wood Tech., 1972-73, vis. sr. scientist, 1976, 78, 80, 84, 85; cons. in engring. design and analysis. Contbr. articles to profl. jours. NSF fellow, 1963-64; Recipient Blackall award ASME, 1975; Distinguished Teaching award U. Calif., 1971; Pi Tau Sigma Excellence in teaching award U. Calif., 1975. Fellow ASME (v.p. environ. and transp., nat. chmn. noise control and acoustics 1980-84, chmn. San Francisco sect. 1978-79; v.p. 1986—), Internat. Acad. Wood Sci., Am. Soc. Biomechanics, Forest Products Research Soc., AAAS, Internat. Soc. Skiing Safety (v.p., sec. 1977-85, bd. dirs. 1977—, chmn. sci. com. 1985—), AIAA, ASTM (vice chmn. com. on snow skiing F-27), Acoustical Soc. Am., Sigma Xi, Pi Tau Sigma, Tau Beta Pi. Patentee in field. Office: Dept Mech Engring U Calif Berkeley CA 94720

MOTIL, JOSEPH SYLVESTER, senior chemist, optometrist; b. Stockett, Mont., May 29, 1910; s. Josef and Veronica Motil; m. Margaret Elaine Colton, July 15, 1939; children: William J., Joseph A. Student, Carroll Coll., 1932; AA, Vallejo Coll., 1949; BS and OD, Chgo. Coll. Optometry, 1951. Registered Optometrist, Mont., Ariz. Carpenter Frank Robbins Constrn., Stockett, 1933-37; carpenter, mine electrician Great Northern Coal Co., Giffen, Mont., 1937-41; machinist supr. USN, Vellejo, Calif., 1941-48; sr. chemist Goodyear Aerospace, Litchfield Park, Ariz., 1951-75; cons. Bronstein Labs., Phoenix, 1967. Inventor in field. Recipient Invention award Goodyear Aerospace Co., Litchfield Park, 1967. Mem. Cen. Chem. Soc., Am. Chem. Soc., Ariz. Optometrists Assn., Am. Optometrists Soc., Bolotie Soc., Am. Electroplaters Soc. Democrat. Roman Catholic. Club: Tempe (Ariz.) Bus. and Profl. Men's. Lodge: KC. Avocation: astronomy. Home: 611 E Fairmont Tempe AZ 85282 Office: 4711 E Southern Phoenix AZ 85040

MOTT, JUNE MARJORIE, educator, consultant, elected official; b. Faribault, Minn., Mar. 8, 1920; d. David C. and Tillie W. (Nelson) Shifflett; B.S., U. Minn., 1943, M.A., 1948; m. Elwood Knight Mott, Oct. 18, 1958. Tchr. high schs. in Minn., 1943-46, 48-53, 54-57; script writer, Hollywood, Calif., 1953-54; tchr. English, creative writing and journalism Mt. Miguel High Sch., Spring Valley, Calif., 1957-86, chmn. English dept., 1964-71, chmn. Dist. English council, 1967-68; mem. Press Bur., Grossmont (Calif.) High Sch. Dist., 1958-86; elected to Grossmont Union High Sch. Gov. Bd., 1986—; scriptwriter TV prodn. Lamp Unto My Feet, Jam Dandy Corp.; free-lance writer, Cons. travel writer, photographer. Vice chmn. polit. action San Diego County Regional Resource Center, 1980-81. Writing project fellow U. Calif., San Diego, 1978; named Outstanding Journalism Tchr., State of Calif., Outstanding Humanities Tchr., San Diego County, Tchr. of Yr. for San Diego County, 1978. Mem. Nat. Council Tchrs. English, Nat. Journalism Assn., NEA, AAUW, Assn. Supervision and Curriculum Devel., Calif. Assn. Tchrs. English, Calif. Tchrs. Assn., So. Calif. Journalism Assn., Grossmont Edn. Assn. (pres. 1978-80), Greater San Diego Council Tchrs. English, Nat. Writers Club, Am. Guild Theatre Organists, Calif. Sch. Bd. Assn., Nat. Sch. Bds. Assn., Sigma Delta Chi. Democrat. Lutheran. Club: Order Eastern Star. Author, editor in field. Home and Office: 2883 New Jersey Ave Lemon Grove CA 92045

MOTT, LAWRIE, environmental scientist; b. N.Y.C., Sept. 14, 1956; d. Charles Harold and Anne (Wittmer) M.; m. Marc Peter Reisner, Apr. 6, 1985. BA, U. Calif., Santa Cruz, 1978; MS, Yale U., 1981. Sr. staff scientist Natural Resources Def. Council, San Francisco, 1982—; mem. EPA Pesticide Adv. Com., Washington, 1984-85; bd. dirs. Nat. Coalition Against Misuse of Pesticides, Washington, 1984—. Mem. Am. Pub. Health Assn. Office: Natural Resources Def Council 90 New Montgomery San Francisco CA 94105

MOTT, MICHAEL IRVINE, marine corps officer; b. Nashville, Oct. 1, 1949; s. Charles Ransom and Edith (Whitehead) M.; m. Kathy Sue McDonald, July 21, 1973; children—Michael Irvine, Ashley Miriam. B.Engring., Vanderbilt U., 1971; M.S., U. So. Calif., 1981; student U.S. Naval Test Pilot Sch., 1978-79. Commd. 2d lt. U.S. Marine Corps, 1971, advanced through grades to maj., 1981; assigned Marine Fighter/Attack squadrons, 1971-78; test naval flight officer, Strike Aircraft Test Directorate, 1979-82; spl. project officer for chief of Naval Ops., Washington, 1982-83; aviation devel. officer, Yuma, Ariz., 1983—. Decorated Meritorious Service medal, Legion of Merit; recipient Test Naval Flight Officer of Yr. award Naval Air Test Center, 1981. Mem. Marine Corps Aviation Assn., Marine Corps Assn., Tailhook Assn., Assn. of Naval Aviation, Assn. of Old Crows, Nat. Eagle Scout Assn., Nat. Rifle Assn., Alpha Phi Omega. Presbyterian. Contbr. articles to profl. publs. Home: 1355 41st Dr Yuma AZ 85364 Office: MAWTS-1 Yuma AZ 85369

MOTTEK, CARL T., hotel company executive; b. 1928. With Hilton Hotels Corp., 1951—, dir. food and beverage ops., from 1964, v.p., 1965-68, sr. v.p. food and beverage ops., 1968-73, sr. v.p. so. region, 1973-85, exec. v.p., also pres. div. Hilton Hotels, 1985—; also bd. dirs. Office: Hilton Hotels Corp 9336 Santa Monica Blvd Beverly Hills CA 90210 *

MOTTELER, ZANE CLINTON, computer science educator; b. Wenatchee, Wash., July 4, 1935; s. Roy Huling and Elizabeth Ann (Stanford) M.; m. Marilynn Rae Ginsbach, June 25, 1960; children: Clinton, Cara, Renee, Seth. BS, Stanford U., 1957, MS, 1962, PhD, 1964; MS, Mich. State U., 1981. Mem. staff Los Alamos (N.Mex.) Nat. Lab., 1957-65; from asst. prof. to prof. math. Gonzaga U., Spokane, Wash., 1965-72, chmn. dept., 1966-71; prof. math. Mich. Tech. U., Houghton, 1972-82, head dept., 1972-80; prof. computer sci. Calif. Poly. State U., San Luis Obispo, 1982—; vis. lectr. computer sci. Mich. State U., East Lansing, 1980-81; cons. Los Alamos Nat. Lab., 1965-69; cons., sr. analyst IBM Corp., San Jose, Calif. and Austin, Tex., 1983—; sr. analyst Livermore (Calif.) Nat. Lab., 1986—, Chevron Corp., San Francisco, 1983. Author: Introduction to Ordinary Differential Equations, 1972, Introduction to Complex Analysis, 1975; co-author: Assembler Language for Univac 1110, 1982; translator: Partial Differential Equations of Elliptic Type, 1970. Fellow NSF, U. Minn., 1957-58, NASA, Am. Soc. Engring. Edn., Langley, Va., 1982. Mem. IEEE, Assn. Computing Machinery, Sigma Xi, Phi Beta Kappa, Phi Kappa Phi. Democrat. Roman Catholic. Avocations: music, philately, gardening. Home: 1253 Eleventh St Los Osos CA 94302-1330 Office: Calif Poly State U Computer Sci Dept San Luis Obispo CA 93407

MOTTER, ROBERTA LEE, marketing consulting firm executive; b. Honolulu, Mar. 8, 1936; d. Donald D. and Florence B. (Downie) Reed; student Cornell U., summer 1956, various other courses George Washington U.; children—Edwin, Lori, Lisa. Dir. personnel Hawaiian Village Hotel, Honolulu, 1956-59; office mgr. Fisher Constrn. Co., Honolulu, 1960-61; paymaster, computer specialist Gate City Steel, Omaha, 1961-64; payroll supr., accounts receivable supr. Mayflower Hotel, Washington, 1966-67; computer specialist, dir. personnel Alan M. Voorhees & Assos., McLean, Va., 1968-71, adminstrv. mgr. PRC Computer Center subs., 1972-73; conversion specialist accounts payable system Medenco, Inc., Houston, 1973-74; personnel dir., office mgr. Summit Ins. Co. of N.Y., Houston, 1974-75; dir. adminstrv. services N.Y. State Ins. Dept. Liquidation Bur., N.Y.C., 1975-80; supervisory procurement analyst Office of Customer and Industry Relations, GSA, Arlington, Va., 1980-84; pres. Contacts Unltd., Roseville, Calif., 1985—. Vol. presdl. inaugural coms.; bd. dirs. Lincoln Community Ctr., N.Y., 1979, Fairfax (Va.) Symphony, Washington Light Opera, Friends of Kennedy Ctr. Named Top 100 Women in Washington, Washington Women's Mag., 1985; recipient Commendable Service award Fed. Govt., 1984, awards for Outstanding Performance, 1982, 83, 84. Mem. Women in Information Processing, Am. Soc. Personnel Mgrs., N.Y. Purchasing Mgmt. Assn., Adminstrv. Mgmt. Soc. (bd. dirs. 1980-82), Washington Purchasing Mgmt. Assn., Hawaii State Soc., N.Y. Internat. Personnel Mgmt. Assn., Internat. Platform Assn., Community Entrepreneurs Orgn., Nat. Assn. Profl. Saleswomen, Sacramento Women's Network, Sales and Mktg. Execs., Les Amis du Vin, Beta Sigma Phi (named Woman of Yr. Delta Kappa chpt. 1979, 81, Xi Gamma Beta chpt. 1985, Yi Gamma Alpha chpt. 1986). Republican. Featured in N.Y. Met. Mag., 1976. Home: 1110 Oakridge Dr Roseville CA 95661

MOTULSKY, ARNO GUNTHER, geneticist, physician, educator; b. Fischhausen, Fed. Republic Germany, July 5, 1923; came to U.S., 1941; s. Herman and Rena (Sass) Molton; m. Gretel C. Stern, Mar. 22, 1945; children: Judy, Harvey, Arlene. Student, Cen. YMCA Coll., Chgo., 1941-43, Yale U., 1943-44; BS, U. Ill., 1945, MD, 1947. Diplomate Am. Bd. Internal Medicine, Am. Bd. Med. Genetics. Intern, fellow, resident Michael Reese Hosp., Chgo., 1947-51; staff mem. charge clin. investigation dept. hematology Army Med. Service Grad. Sch., Walter Reed Army Med. Ctr., Washington, 1952-53; research assoc. internal medicine George Washington U. Sch. Medicine, 1952-53; from instr. to assoc. prof. dept. medicine U. Wash. Sch. Medicine, Seattle, 1953-61, prof. medicine, prof. genetics, 1961—; head div. med. genetics, dir. genetics clinic Univ. Hosp., Seattle, 1959—, Children's Med. Ctr., Seattle, 1966-72; dir. Ctr. for Inherited Diseases, Seattle, 1972—; attending physician Univ. Hosp., Seattle; cons. Pres.'s Commn. for Study of Ethical Problems in Medicine and Biomed. and Behavioral Research, 1979-83; cons. various coms. NRC, NIH, WHO, others. Editor Am. Jour. Human Genetics, 1969-75, Human Genetics, 1969—, Progress in Med. Genetics, 1974—. Commonwealth Fund fellow in human genetics Univ. Coll., London, 1957-58; John and Mary Markle scholar in med. sci., 1957-62; fellow Ctr. Advanced Study in Behavioral Scis., Stanford U., 1976-77. Fellow A.C.P.; mem. Internat. Soc. Hematology, Am. Fedn. Clin. Research, AAAS, Genetics Soc. Am., Western Soc. Clin. Research, Am. Soc. Human Genetics, Am. Soc. Clin. Investigation, Am. Assn. Physicians, Nat. Acad. Scis., Inst. of Medicine, Am. Acad. Arts and Scis. Home: 4347 53d Ave NE Seattle WA 98105 Office: U Wash Div Med Genetics Seattle WA 98195

MOTZKO, CHARLES ANTHONY, electronics co. exec.; b. Mason City, Wash., Oct. 4, 1939; s. Donald Hart and Marjorie Jean (Kinnune) M.; student Fla. State U., 1960-64, Calif. State U., Los Angeles, 1974-75; BA, U. Redlands, 1982; MBA, UCLA, 1984; m. Rose Marie Anderson, Dec. 8, 1962; 1 dau., Patricia Ann. Lab. supr. Nat. Astro. Labs., 1965-67; mgr. Electro Rent, Burbank, Calif., 1967-73, products and data group mgr., 1979-84, v.p., 1984—; v.p., tech. dir. Comtel-NAL, Burbank, Calif., 1973-77; mgr. U.S. Instrument Rentals, San Mateo, Calif., 1977-79. Mem. State of Calif. Measurement Systems Adv. Com., 1976-77. Served with USAF, 1957-65. Registered profl. engr., Calif. Mem. Am. Soc. Quality Control, Precision Measurement Assn., Soc. Logistics Engrs. Republican. Lutheran. Home: 8377 Vine Valley Dr Sun Valley CA 91352 Office: 4209 Vanowen Pl Burbank CA 91505

MOUCK, NORMAN GARRISON, JR., retired college president; b. Omaha, Sept. 9, 1928; s. Norman Garrison and Madge Arvilla (Bossoh) M.; m. Dorothy Margaret Davis, Jan. 3, 1949; children: Susan Gayle, Richard Forrest, Teresa Joann. BS, Edinboro (Pa.) State Coll., 1953; MEd, UCLA, 1956, postgrad., 1956-58, 65-67; MBS, U. Colo., 1960. Instr. math., then asst. prof. Santa Barbara (Calif.) City Coll., 1961-66, dir. research, 1966-68; instr. math. Coll. of the Canyons, Valencia, Calif., 1979-82, v.p., 1968-79, pres., 1979, 82-83; lectr. U. Calif., Santa Barbara, 1965-66; cons. Stanford U. Sch. Math. Study Group, 1963-64, Coll. of the Canyons, 1983. Co-author: (textbooks) Mathematics Through Science, 1964, Elementary Algebra for College Students, 1968. Active United Crusade, Canyon County, Calif., 1972-74. Served with U.S. Army, 1946-53, Korea. Mem. AAAS, Math. Assn. Am., U.S. Ski Assn. (chmn. Far West div., mem. Far West competition bd., chmn. Masters Series Ski Racing), Phi Delta Kappa. Democrat. Presbyterian. Lodges: Kiwanis (internat. life mem. 1973, disting. pres. local chpt. 1978-79). Home: PO Box 3648 Incline Village NV 89450

MOULTON, CHRISTINE JANE, audiologist; b. Vallejo, Calif., Dec. 24, 1950. BA, Calif. State U., Fullerton, 1974; MS, Portland State U., 1983. Audiologist VA Med. Ctr., Portland, Oreg., 1982-87, Hollywood Audiology Clinic, Portland, 1983—. Mem. Am. Speech-Lang.-Hearing Assn., Oreg. Speech and Hearing Assn., Oreg. Deafness and Rehab. Assn. Office: Hollywood Audiology Clinic PO Box 13787 4259 NE Broadway Portland OR 97213

MOUND, DIANE HARDWICK, academic administrator; b. Bridgeport, Conn., Nov. 4, 1937; d. William Roger and Harriet Louise (Hardwick) McNeil; m. Richard Eric Ameis (dec. Aug. 1978); children: Robin Ellen Stapley, Todd McNeil, Dawn Melissa, Erica Lynn; m. John James Mound (dec.). AS, Housatonic Community Coll., 1971; BA, Ariz. State U., 1981; postgrad., Santa Anita Ministerial Sch., 1986—. Cert. Real Estate Broker. Owner, operator A. Roger Mc Neil, Inc., Stratford, Conn., 1960-71; owner, broker Diane Ameis Realty, Albuquerque, 1972-76; office mgr., co-owner Hoffmantown Auto Body Shop, Albuquerque, 1973-83; personnel mgr. Advanced Semi-Conductor Materials of Am., Phoenix, 1980-82; adminstrv. asst. DeVry Inst. Tech., Phoenix, 1982-84; dir. admissions Am. Acad. Dramatic Arts, West Pasadena, Calif., 1984-86; adminstr. Santa Anita Ch., Arcadia, Calif., 1986—. Mem. Nat. Research Ctr. Coll. and Univs., Nat. Assn. Coll. Admission and Councilors, Am. Mgmt. Assn., Nat. Master's Degree Assn., Tournament of Roses Assn. (bd. dirs. 1986), Ariz. State U. Alumni Assn., Pasadena C. of C., Nat. Council of Admissions Dirs., Kappa Delta Pi, Phi Epsilon. Republican. Club: Kronenstadt Ski (Pasadena). Avocations: skiing, sailing, philosophy. Office: Santa Anita Ch Arcadia CA 91006

MOUNDS, LEONA MAE REED, educator; b. Crosby, Tex., Sept. 9, 1945; d. Elton Phillip and Ora Lee (Jones) Reed; m. Aaron B. Mounds Jr., Aug. 21, 1965; 1 dau., Lisa Nichelle. B.S. in Elem. Edn., Bridgewater State Coll., 1973; M.A. in Mental Retardation, U. Alaska, 1980. Cert. tchr. Alaska, Colo., Tex., Mass., cert. adminstrv. prin. 1985. Tchr., Sch. Dist. 11, Colorado Springs, Colo., 1973-75; tchr. Anchorage Sch. Dist., 1976-78, 80—, mem. math. curriculum com., reading contact tchr., mem. talent bank. Tchr. Del Valle (Tex.) Sch. Dist., 1979-80. Bd. dirs. Urban League, 1974; 1st v.p. PTA, Crosby, Tex.; del. Tex. Democratic Conv., 1980; tchr. religious edn., lay Eucharist minister St. Martin De Pores Roman Cath. Ch., St. Patrick's Ch. Served with USAF, 1964-66. Alaska State Tchr. Incentive grantee, 1981; Ivy Lutz scholar, 1972. Mem. NEA (human relations coordinator Alaska chpt.), Anchorage Edn. Assn. (minority chmn. 1982—, mem. Black Caucus polit. action com., v.p. programs 1986-87), Black Educators of Pikes Peak Region (pres. 1974), Anchorage Edn. Assn. (v.p. programs com. 1986-87, women's caucus), Assn. Supervision and Curriculum Devel., Alaska Women in Adminstrn., Council for Exception Children, NAACP.

MOUNT, JACK DOUGLAS, science information specialist, librarian; b. Los Angeles, Mar. 17, 1943; s. Woodrow Wilson and Helen June (Popp) M.; m. Susan Skjarstad, 1969 (div. 1978); 1 child, Aaron Daniel; m. Patricia Frye, July 23, 1979. BS in Geology, Calif. State U., Los Angeles, 1969; MS in Geology, UCLA, 1972; MLS, Rutgers U., 1982. Instr. Calif. State U., Los Angeles, 1970-71, East Los Angeles Coll., 1971-72; mus. scientist U. Calif., Riverside, 1972-81; sci. reference librarian Rutgers U., Camden, N.J., 1982-84, U. Ariz., Tucson, 1984—; cons. paleontologist County of Orange, Calif., 1978-81; adj. curator Riverside Mcpl. Mus., 1979-80; mem. sci. adv. bd. Natural History Found. Orange County, 1973-76, 79-81. Author: Late Paleozoic Biostratigraphy, 1972; editor: Paleontological Tour of the Mojave, 1980; contbr. articles to profl. jours. Bd. dirs. Scouting Mus. of So. Ariz., Tucson, 1986; dist. commr. Boy Scouts Am., Tucson, 1985; bd. dirs. Riverside Mus. Assocs., 1973-74; judge Delaware Valley Sci. Fair, Phila., 1983, 84. Recipient Best Paper award Calif. Fedn. Mineral. Socs., 1976. Mem. Geosci. Info. Soc., Geo-Lit. Soc. (co-editor 1985-86), Spl. Libraries Assn., Paleontol. Soc. So. Ariz. (editor 1986—), So. Calif. Paleontol. Soc. (pres. 1977-78, editor 1969-71, 73-81), Geneal. soc. N.J., Sierra Club (treas. 1980-81). Democrat. Unitarian. Avocations: stereo photography, backpacking. Home: 664 N Citadel Tucson AZ 85748 Office: U Ariz Sci-Engring Library Tucson AZ 85721

MOUNT, ROBERT ARL, microbiologist, medical laboratory executive; b. Niles, Calif., Dec. 31, 1943; s. James Merle and Norma Belle (Springfield) M.; m. Madeleine J. Ehrlich, June 19, 1966; children: Monica, Aaron, Kimberly. BA, U. Calif., Berkeley, 1966; MA, San Jose State U., 1970. Lab. mgr. Community Hosp., Santa Rosa, Calif., 1970-74; pres. Redwood Med. Lab., Santa Rosa, Calif., 1974—; asst. prof. Sonoma State U., Cotati, Calif., 1984. Mem. Am. Soc. Microbiology. Democrat. Avocations: gardening, sports. Home: 1377 Wikiup Dr Santa Rosa CA 95401 Office: Redwood Med Lab 1166 Montgomery Dr Santa Rosa CA 95405

MOWBRAY, JOHN CODE, judge; b. Bradford, Ill., Sept. 20, 1918; s. Thomas John and Ellen Driscoll (Code) M.; m. Kathlyn Ann Hammes, Oct. 15, 1949; children: John, Romy, Jerry, Terry. B.A., Western Ill. U., 1940, L.H.D. (hon.), 1976, LL.D. (hon.), 1977; LL.D. (hon.), Far Eastern Civil Affairs Tng. Sch., Northwestern U., 1945; D.J. cum laude, U. Notre Dame, 1949; LL.D. (hon.), U. Nev., 1978. Bar: Nev. 1949, Ill. 1950. Dep. dist. atty. Clark County, Las Vegas, Nev., 1949-53; U.S. referee Fed. Cts. in Nev., 1955-59; dist. judge for Nev. 1959-67; justice Nev. Supreme Ct., Carson City, 1967—, chief justice, 1986—; founder 1st pub. defender program in Nev., 1967; mem. faculty Nat. Coll. State Judiciary, 1967. V.P. Boulder Dam Area council Boy Scouts Am., 1960-70; bd. dirs. Nev. Area council, 1967—; pres. City of Hope, 1963-64, NCCJ, 1965-66; v.p. YMCA, 1964—; chmn. Nev. Commn. on Bicentennial U.S. Constitution, 1986. Served to maj. AUS, 1942-46, PTO. Recipient Outstanding Alumni award Western Ill. U., 1971, Equal Justice award Western regional dept. NAACP, 1970, Minuteman award SAR, 1982, Silver Antelope award Boy Scouts Am., 1983, Jurist of Yr. award Nev. Trial Lawyers Assn., 1986, Judicial Officer of Yr. award State Sheriff and Police Assn., 1986; Mowbray Hall, Western Ill. U. named in his honor, 1974. Mem. ABA, Nev. Trial Lawyers Assn. (Jurist of Yr. award 1986), Am. Judicature Soc., State Sheriff and Police Assn. (Jud. Officer of Yr. award 1986), SAR (pres. Nev. 1969-70, Nat. Gen. MacArthur medal 1971, nat. trustee 1971—), VFW. Clubs: Rotarian (hon.), Elk. also: 189 Lake Glen Dr Carson City NV 89701 Office: Supreme Ct Bldg Capitol Complex Carson City NV 89710

MOWILOS, HENDRIK ARNOLD, service executive; b. Manado, North Celebes, Indonesia, Dec. 16, 1944; s. Herman J. and Aaltje Marie (Wuwungan) M. BA, Nat. Hotel Instn., 1966; CFBE, Mich. State U., 1985. Mgr. food and beverage Amfac Resorts, Honolulu, 1973-76; gen. mgr. Aeropacific Hotels, Jakarta, Indonesia, 1976-78; dir. food and beverages Capt. Cook Hotel, Anchorage, 1978-81; gen. mgr. Westlake Inn., Westlake Village, Calif., 1981-84; dir. food and beverages Hilton Hotel, Sherman Oaks, Calif., 1984-86; gen. mgr. Sagebrush Cantina, Inc., Calabasas, Calif., 1986—; lectr. Nat. Hotel Sch., Bandung, Indonesia, 1976-77. Mem. Food Service Exec. Assn., Traders Club, Nat. Catering Execs. Republican. Lodge: Optimists, Lions (Lion Tamer San Fernando Valley club 1984—). Avocations: deep sea fishing, surfing, soccer, martial arts, stamp collecting. Office: Sagebrush Cantina Inc 23527 Calabasas Rd Calabasas CA 91302

MOWRER, DON EUGENE, professor; b. Wooster, Ohio, Aug. 4, 1929; s. Ralph L. and Pearl E. Mowrer; children: Jack, Christine, Alan, Pat, Sue. BA, Fla. State U., 1951, MA, 1953; PhD, Ariz. State U., 1964. Instr. Phoenix Coll., 1963-64; prof. Ariz. State U., Tempe, 1964—. Author: Modification of Speech Behaviors, 1982, Parent's Speech Guide, 1986; co-author: Clinical Speech Disorders, 1982. Fellow: Am. Speech Hearing Assn. Office: Dept Speech and Hearing Ariz State U Tempe AZ 85287

MOYA, RITA BETH, public affairs administrator; b. Hastings, Neb., Dec. 24, 1949; d. Paul David and Anna (Ulmer) Becker; m. Steven Oscar Moya. BA, U. Neb., 1972; postgrad., U. Vienna, Austria, 1971; MA in Urban Planning, Va. Poly. Inst., 1974. Project adminstr. State of Calif. Citizens Adv. Council, 1974-78; assoc. dir. United Way, Inc., Los Angeles, 1978-79; engr. GTE Corp., Santa Monica, Calif., 1979-80, market analyst, 1980-81, mgr. and dir. community relations, 1981-85; dir. pub. affairs systems GTE Corp., Thousand Oaks, Calif., 1985—; adj. faculty mem. U. Redlands, Calif., 1977-83. Author (guidebook) Citizen Participation Handbook for Mental Health Bds., 1975. Mem. Overseas Edn. Fund, 1985—, Calif. Chamber Edn. Consortium, 1985—; dir., v.p. Vol. Ctr. of Los Angeles, 1982-85, Calif. Acad. Decathlon, 1981—. Fellow Alpha Chi Omega, 1972-73. Mem. Issues Mgmt. Assn., So. Calif. Research Council, So. Calif. Assn. Philanthropy (bd. dirs. 1986), Los Angeles C. of C., Manhattan Beach C. of C. Avocations: cooking, traveling.

MOYE, RENE DONALD, city official; b. Salem, Oreg., June 29, 1938; s. William A. and Harriet (Fritz) M.; m. Pamela Freeman, June 20, 1964; children—Nicole, Caje. B.S., Oreg. State U., 1963; M.S., San Francisco State Coll., 1969; student Shasta Jr. Coll., 1957-58. Recreation supr. City of Oakland (Calif.), 1964-69; supt. parks and recreation Chehalem Park and Recreation Dist., Newberg, Oreg., 1969-71; dir. parks and recreation City of San Bernardino (Calif.), 1971-74, City of Corvallis (Oreg.), 1974—; instr. park adminstrn. Oreg. State U., 1975-76. Served with AUS, 1960-62. Mem. Nat. Park and Recreation Assn., Oreg. Park and Recreation Soc. (pres. 1982), Nat. Park and Recreation Assn. (council affiliated pres.). Republican. Roman Catholic. Club: Kiwanis (pres. 1982) (Corvallis). Office: 501 SW Madison St Corvallis OR 97330

MOYER, NANCY KAY, management consultant; b. Omaha, Aug. 3, 1942; d. Stewart Harlan and Dorothy Irene (Evans) M. BA in Sociology, Psychology, Northwestern Coll., Mpls., 1964; MA in Mgmt., Claremont Grad. Sch., 1983. Asst. to pres World Vision, Monrovia, Calif., 1969-82; pres. Nancy Moyer & Assocs., Monrovia, 1983-86; exec. asst., sr. pastor Hollywood (Calif.) Presbyn. Ch., 1986-87; assoc. cons. Visionary Mgmt. Group, 1987—. Home: 925 Cabrillo Duarte CA 91010 Office: Hollywood Presbyn Ch 1760 Gower Hollywood CA 90028

MOZENA, JOHN DANIEL, podiatrist; b. Salem, Oreg., June 9, 1956; s. Joseph Iner and Mary Teresa (Delaney) M.; m. Elizabeth Ann Hintz, June 2, 1979. Student, U. Oreg., 1974-79; B in Basic Med. Scis., Calif. Coll. Podiatric Medicine, D in Podiatric Medicine, 1983. Resident in surg. podiatry Hillside Hosp., San Diego, 1983-84; cons. podiatrist Beaverton, Oreg., 1984-85; pvt. practice podiatry Portland, Oreg., 1985—; dir. residency Med. Ctr. Hosp., Portland, 1985—. Contbr. articles to profl. jours.; patentee sports shoe cleat design, 1985. Leader Holy Trinity High Sch. Youth Group, Beaverton, 1984. Fellow Am. Coll. Ambulatory Foot Surgeons; mem. Am. Coll. Foot Surgeons (assoc.). Republican. Roman Catholic. Avocations: softball, basketball, jogging. Office: Town Ctr Foot Clinic 8305 SE Monterey #101 Portland OR 97266

MRACKY, RONALD SYDNEY, management consultant in marketing and communications; b. Sydney, Australia, Oct. 22, 1932; came to U.s., 1947, naturalized, 1957; s. Joseph and Anna (Janousek) M.; student English Inst., Prague, Czechoslovakia, 1943-47; grad. Parsons Sch. Design, N.Y.C., 1950-53; postgrad. NYU, 1952-53; m. Sylvia Frommer, Jan. 1, 1960; children: Enid Hillevi, Jason Adam. Designer D. Deskey Assocs., N.Y.C., 1953-54; art dir., designer ABC-TV, Hollywood, Calif., 1956-57; creative dir. Neal Advt. Assocs., Los Angeles, 1957-59; pres. Richter & Mracky Design Assocs., Los Angeles, 1959-68; pres., chief exec. officer Richter & Mracky-Bates div. Ted Bates & Co., Los Angeles, 1968-73, pres., chief exec. officer Regency Fin., Internat. Fin. Services, Beverly Hills, Calif., 1974-76; sr. ptnr. Sylron Internat., Los Angeles, 1973—; mgmt. dir. for N.Am. Standard Advt.-Tokyo, Los Angeles, 1978—; chief. exec. officer Standard/Worldwide Cons. Group, Los Angeles and Tokyo, 1981—; cons. in field; exec. dir. Inst. for Internat. Studies and Devel., Los Angeles, 1976-77. Bd. dirs. Dubnoff Ctr. for Child Devel. and Ednl. Therapy, Los Angeles, John Wayne Cancer Clinic/UCLA; bd. dirs., chmn. exec. com. Calif. Chamber Symphony Soc., Los Angeles. Served with U.S. Army, 1954-56. Mem. Am. Mktg. Assn., Los Angeles Publicity Club (com. mem.), Toluca Lake C. of C. Contbr. articles to profl. jours. Recipient nat. and internat. awards design and mktg.

MRAZ, SHARON JANEEN TOWNER, speech pathologist, educator; b. Colorado Springs, Colo., June 30, 1948; d. Charles A. and R. Jeanne (Wisdom) T.; m. John D. Mraz, Feb. 9, 1974. BA, Calif. Western U., 1971; MA, U. Colo., 1974, Western N.Mex. U., 1987. Tchr. spl. edn. and speech pathologist Gallup-McKinley County (N.Mex.) Pub. Schs., 1974—; mem. profl. adv. bd. N.Mex. Little People, 1985—. Vol. exec. dir. N.Mex. Spl. Olympics, 1977-79, also mem. bd. dirs. 1977-81, area coordinator, Gallup, N.Mex., 1975—. Named Spl. Olympics Vol. of Yr., Am. Legion, 1978; recipient Human Rights award Bahais, Gallup, 1977, Champion Medalist Gallup Women's Golf Assn., 1985. Mem. Council Exceptional Children, N.Mex. Speech-Lang.-Hearing Assn., Alpha Delta Kappa (treas. N.Mex. chpt. 1982-84). Avocations: golf, community theatre. Home: 1104 Piano Ave Gallup NM 87301

MRAZEK, DAVID ALLEN, pediatric psychiatrist; b. Ft. Riley, Kans., Oct. 1, 1947; s. Rudolph George and Hazel Ruth (Schayes) M.; m. Patricia Jean, Sept. 2, 1978; children: Nicola, Matthew, Michael. AB in Genetics, Cornell U., 1969; MD, Bowman Gray Sch. Medicine, 1973. Lic. psychiatrist, child psychiatrist, North Carolina, Ohio, Colo. Lectr. child psychiatry Inst. of Psychiatry, London, 1977-79; dir. pediatric psychiatry Nat. Jewish Ctr. for Immunology and Respiratory Medicine, Denver, 1979—. Contbr. articles and book chpts. on child devel. and asthma to profl. publs. Recipient Research Scientist Devel. award NIMH. Fellow Am. Acad. Child Psychiatry; mem. Royal Coll. Psychiatrists. Office: Nat Jewish Ctr Immunology Respiratory Medicine 1400 Jackson St Denver CO 80206

MRAZEK, ROBERT VERNON, educator; b. Chgo., Jan. 15, 1936; s. Vernon Elmer and Marjorie (Saxon) M.; m. Joyce Ann Freeman, June 6, 1959; children—Ellen Marie, Steven James, Karen Louise. B.S., Purdue U., 1957; Ph.D., Rensselaer Poly. Inst., 1960. Registered profl. engr., Oreg. Chem. engr. Knolls Atomic Power Lab., Schenectady, 1960; faculty dept. chem. engring. Oreg. State U., Corvallis, 1960—; prof. Oreg. State U., 1967—; Tech. adviser Omark Industries, Portland, Oreg., 1962, U.S. Bur. Mines, Albany, Oreg., 1963—; research asso. Rensselaer Poly. Inst., 1962. Contbr. articles to profl. jours. Recipient Carter award outstanding teaching Sch. Engring., 1965, 79, Mosser award for teaching excellence, 1966, Elizabeth P. Ritchie Disting. Prof. award, 1978; all Oreg. State U.); NSF fellow, 1957-60. Mem. Oreg. chpt. Am. Inst. Chem. Engrs. (chmn. 1974-75), Am. Inst. Chem. Engrs. (mem. profl. exams. adv. com.), Blue Key (hon. faculty), Sigma Xi, Phi Eta Sigma, Omega Chi Epsilon, Tau Beta Pi. Home: 1525 NW 14th Pl Corvallis OR 97330

MUCHMORE, DON MONCRIEF, museum administrator; b. Wichita, Kans., Dec. 26, 1922; s. Floyd Stephen and Ivy Fay (Campbell) M.; m. Virginia Gunn, June 18, 1949 (div. Dec. 1978); children—Melinda, Marcia. B.A., Occidental Coll., Los Angeles, 1945; postgrad., U. So. Calif. Law Sch., 1945; postgrad. polit. sci., UCLA. Intern Nat. Inst. Pub. Affairs, Washington, 1944; exec. asst. to congressman Washington, 1946-48; teaching asst. UCLA, 1949-52; mem. faculty San Diego State U., 1949-52; asst. prof., adminstr. Calif. State U.-Long Beach, 1952-56; spl. asst. to supt. pub. instrn. Calif. Dept. Edn., Sacramento, 1956-57; exec. mus. dir. Calif. Mus. Sci. and Industry, Los Angeles, 1957-62, 82—; exec. v.p. Calif. Mus. Found., Los Angeles, 1957-62, 82—; dep. dir. Calif. Dept. Fin., Sacramento, 1960; vice chancellor Calif. State Colls. and Univs. System, Long Beach, 1962-64; sr. v.p., exec. asst. to chmn. and chief exec. officer Calif. Fed. Savs. and Loan Assn., Los Angeles, 1964-82; chmn. bd. dirs., chief exec. officer Opinion Research of Calif., Opinion Surveyors, The State Poll & Market Surveys, Inc., Long Beach, 1948-71, also M-R Assocs. campaigns; cons. in pub. opinion and mus. mgmt.; cons. DMM & Assocs., Long Beach, 1981—; mem. Inst. Mus. Services, 1983—; bd. dirs. Sci. Mus. Film Collaborative, Fort Worth, 1982—. Chmn. bd. Campbell Found., Long Beach, 1956—; mem./chmn. 4 Presdl. commns., 1970-82. Elks nat. scholar. Mem. Am. Assn. Mus., Calif. Mus. Assn. (bd. dirs. 1982—), Assn. Sci. and Tech. Ctrs. (bd. dirs. 1982—), Am. Assn. Pub. Opinion Research, Am. Polit. Sci. Assn., AAAS. Clubs: Virginia Country (Long Beach); Jonathan (Los Angeles). Home: 4225 Virginia Vista Long Beach CA 90807 Office: Calif Mus Sci and Industry 700 State Dr Los Angeles CA 90037

MUCHMORE, ROBERT BOYER, engineering consultant; b. Augusta, Kans., July 8, 1917; s. Ray Boyer and Charlotte (Macpherron) M.; m. Betty Vaughan, Jan. 29, 1944; children: Andrew Vaughan, Douglas Boyer. BS, U. Calif., Berkeley, 1939; MEE, Stanford U., 1942. Project engr. Sperry Gyroscope Co., Garden City, N.Y., 1942-46; sr. mem. tech. staff Hughes Aircraft, Culver City, Calif., 1946-54; v.p., chief scientist TRW Systems, Redondo Beach, Calif., 1954-73; cons. TRW Systems, Sonoma, Calif., 1973—; lectr. in engring. UCLA, 1954-58. Author: Essentials of Microwaves, 1952. Fellow IEEE; mem. AAAS, Assn. Computing Machinery, Sierra Club. Home: 4311 Grove St Sonoma CA 95476

MUCHNIC, SUZANNE, art critic, educator, lectr.; b. Kearney, Nebr., May 16, 1940; d. Walter Marian Ely and Erva Nell Liston; m. Paul D. Muchnic, 1963; B.A., Scripps Coll., 1962; M.A., Claremont Grad. Sch., 1963. Art instr. Weber State Coll., Ogden, Utah, 1972-73; art history instr. Los Angeles City Coll., 1974-82; editor for So. Calif., Artweek, 1976-78; art critic Los Angeles Times, 1978—; art criticism instr. Claremont Grad. Sch., 1984—. Author: Tim Nordin retrospective catalogue, 1982, Martha Alf retrospective catalogue, 1984, Mark Lere Catalogue, 1986. Recipient Disting. Alumna award Claremont Grad. Sch., 1982, Disting. Alumna award Scripps Coll., 1987. Mem. Coll. Art Assn., Internat. Assn. Art Critics. Office: Los Angeles Times Times-Mirror Sq Los Angeles CA 90053

MUDD, JOHN O., lawyer, university dean; b. 1943. BA, Cath. U., 1965, MA, 1966; JD, U. Mont., 1973; LLM, Columbia U., 1986. Bar: Mont. 1973. Ptnr. Mulroney, Delaney, Dalby & Mudd, Missoula, Mont., 1973-79; lectr. U. Mont., Missoula, 1973-74, 75-76, prof. law, dean, 1979—; pres. Mid-Continent Assn. Law Schs., 1982-83. Mem. ABA, Am. Judicature Soc. (bd. dirs. 1985—), State Bar Mont. Editor Mont. Law Rev., 1972-73. Office: U Mont Sch of Law Missoula MT 59812

MUDICA, ALBERT LEE, mechanical engineer; b. Jackson, Mich., Mar. 13, 1932; s. Albert R. and Dorothy M. (Lee) M.; widowed Feb. 1986; children: Terri L. Ellis, Albert T. BME, Tri-State U., Angola, Ind., 1953. Dir.

engring. Weatherite, Los Angeles, 1978-81; gen. mgr. Climate Engring., Belmont, Calif., 1981-82; chief engr. A&A Facilities Systems, San Jose, Calif., 1982-83; mgr. ops. Advanced Mech. Engring., Menlo Park, Calif., 1983; project engr. Cal Air Conditioning, San Jose, 1984—. Served with USAR, 1953-55. Mem. ASHRAE. Republican. Home: 6159 Heathercreek Way San Jose CA 95123-4725 Office: Cal Air Conditioning Co 1775 S 1st St Suite 66 San Jose CA 95112

MUECKE, CHARLES ANDREW (CARL MUECKE), U.S. judge; b. N.Y.C., Feb. 20, 1918; s. Charles and Wally (Roeder) M.; m. Claire E. Vasse; children by previous marriage: Carl Marshall, Alfred Jackson, Catherine Calvert. B.A., Coll. William and Mary, 1941; LL.B., U. Ariz., 1953. Bar: Ariz. 1953. Rep. AFL, 1947-50; reporter Ariz. Times, Phoenix, 1947-48; since practiced in Phoenix; with firm Parker & Muecke, 1953-59, Muecke, Dushoff & Sacks, 1960-61; U.S. atty. Dist. Ariz., 1961-64, U.S. dist. judge, 1964—, now sr. judge. Mem. Phoenix Planning Commn., 1955-61, chmn., 1960; chmn. Maricopa County Democratic Party, 1961-62; trustee U. San Diego Coll. of Law. Served to 1st lt. USMCR, 1942-45; to maj. Res. 1945-60. Mem. Fed., Ariz., Maricopa bar assns., Am. Trial Lawyers Assn., Dist. Judges Assn. Ninth Circuit, St. Thomas More Soc. (pres. Phoenix 1958), Phi Beta Kappa, Phi Alpha Delta, Omicron Delta Kappa. Office: US Courthouse 230 N 1st St Room 7009 Phoenix AZ 85025

MUELLER, FOORMAN LLOYD, lawyer; b. Chgo., Aug. 5, 1904; s. George Edgar and Bessie Dorothy (Foorman) M.; m. Isabel McFarland, Oct. 25, 1930; children—Georgeana (Mrs. Thomas J. McColloch), Foorman Lloyd. A.B., U. Mich., 1927; J.D., Kent. Coll. Law, Chgo., 1932. Bar: Ill. 1932, D.C. Assoc., George E. Mueller, Chgo., 1932-35; practice, Chgo., 1935-75; sole practice, Phoenix, 1975—; patent counsel Motorola, Schaumberg, Ill., 1935—. Chmn. Hinsdale (Ill.) Community Caucus, 1948, 49, Hinsdale Planning Commn., 1949-57. Mem. ABA, Ill. Bar Assn., Chgo. Bar Assn., Chgo. Patent Law Assn. (pres. 1967), Am. Patent Law Assn. (pres. 1953-54), Phi Gamma Delta, Phi Delta Phi. Presbyterian. Clubs: Union League (Chgo.); Hinsdale Golf; Paradise Valley Country. Home: 6721 E Cheney Rd Paradise Valley AZ 85253 Office: 4250 E Camelback Rd Suite 390K Phoenix AZ 85018

MUELLER, JANIE SCHIEFFELIN, educator; b. Denver, Apr. 9, 1960; d. Joseph and Marilyn Joan (Preusse) Schieffelin; m. W. Dean Mueller, Aug. 9, 1986. BS, Colo. State U., 1982. Tchr. biology, chemistry Fountain Ft. Carson High Sch., Colo., 1982—. Sponsor Fellowship Christian Athletes, Fountain, 1978—. Republican. Avocations: bicycling, hiking, doll collecting, cooking, needlepoint.

MUELLER, JEAN ELAINE, observation laboratory researcher; b. Huntington Park, Calif., Mar. 5, 1950; d. Roy Harold and Dorothy Jean (Hansen) Mueller. BA, Calif. State U., Northridge, 1972; MLS, U. So. Calif., 1973. Chief librarian Gerontology Ctr., U. So. Calif., 1977-83; night asst., observer Mount Wilson and Las Campanas obs. Carnegie Instn. of Wash., Pasadena, Calif., 1983-85; night asst. Palomar Obs., Calif. Inst. Tech., Pasadena, 1985—. Author: (appendix) Aging and Life: an introduction to gerontology, 1984; contbr. bibliographies to profl. jours. U.S. Dept. Edn. grantee. Mem. So. Calif. Online Users Group, Mount Wilson Obs. Assn. (trustee 1982-83). Democrat. Methodist. Office: Calif Inst Tech Dept Astrophysics 105-24 Pasadena CA 91125

MUELLER, KENT CARL, computer industry executive; b. St. Louis, Aug. 12, 1940; s. Carl and Lillian Clara (Johnson) M.; m. Judith Ann Laudenslager, Jan. 12, 1962; children—Sally, Daniel, Victoria. B.A. in Math., Westminster Coll., Fulton, Mo., 1962. Regional mgr. Ampex Corp., Chgo., 1971-74; nat. sales mgr. Intel, Santa Clara, Calif., 1974-75, dir. field ops., 1975-78, dir. sales and mktg., 1978-80; v.p., gen. mgr. Capex Corp., Phoenix, 1980-83; founder, pres. Mastersoft, Inc., Phoenix, 1983-85; founder, chmn. Silver Bullet Systems, Paradise Valley, Ariz., 1985—; dir. Interactive Mktg. Software, Inc., Phoenix; lectr. Ariz. State U., 1984-86. Served to 1st lt. U.S. Army, 1963-65. Presbyterian. Office: 4621 N 16th St Phoenix AZ 85016

MUELLER, MARK JONATHAN, structural engineer; b. Madison, Wis., June 1, 1959; s. Raymond Walter and LaVonne (Jacobsen) M. BSCE, U. Wis., 1982. Asst. mgr. Weides Wine Cellar, Madison, 1978-82; project mgr. Colo. Welding, Pueblo, 1982-83; structural engr. Boyle Engring., Inc., Vail, Colo., 1983—; cons. various cos., Vail, 1985—. Creator (radio program, aired Sta. KRVV) Reggae Music, 1985. Coach Vail Jr. Hockey Club, 1983-86. Mem. ASCE (assoc.), Eagle County Home Builders Assn. Lutheran. Avocations: skiing, hockey, backpacking. Home: PO Box 2747 Vail CO 81658 Office: Boyle Engring Inc 143 E Meadow Dr Suite N 10 Vail CO 81658

MUELLER, MARVIN MARTIN, research physicist; b. Broken Arrow, Okla., Sept. 29, 1928; s. Martin John and Elsie Arlene (Peper) M.; m. Barbara Ann Holler, Oct. 22, 1966 (div. 1984). BS in Physics, U. Okla., 1951, MS in Physics, 1954, PhD in Physics, 1959. Mem. laser fusion research staff Los Alamos (N.Mex.) Nat. Lab., 1959—. Contbr. chpts. to books Inquest on the Shroud of Turin, 1983, Science Confronts the Paranormal, 1986; contbr. articles to profl. jours. Mem. AAAS, Am. Physics Soc., Am. Assn. Physics Tchrs., Phi Beta Kappa, Sigma Chi. Avocations: reading, hiking, science, music. Home: 409 Estante Way Los Alamos NM 87544 Office: Los Alamos Nat Lab Physics Div MS-E554 Los Alamos NM 87545

MUELLER, ROBERT ANDREW, computer science educator; b. Rockville Center, N.Y., July 29, 1952; s. Thomas F. and Anais J. (Baurle) M.; m. Eileen M. Kent, Mar. 17, 1986; 1 child, Jared T. BS in Computer Sci., Colo. State U., 1974, MSME, 1976; PhD in Computer Sci., U. Colo., 1980. Asst. prof. computer sci. Colo. State U., Ft. Collins, 1980-85, assoc. prof., 1985—, dir. research Abell Ctr. Computer-assisted engring., 1985—, dir. Firmware engring. research lab., 1986—. Author: Automated Microcode Synthesis, 1984. Mem. ACM, Computer Soc. of IEEE (guest editor jour. 1986—), Am. Assn. Artificial Intelligence, Sigma Xi. Avocations: audiophile, bicycling. Office: Colo State U Dept Computer Sci Fort Collins CO 80523

MUELLER, WILLIAM ALAN, dentist; b. Covington, Ky., Sept. 9, 1947; s. William Lawrence and Theresa Myrtle (Fielding) M.; m. Lucienne Jane Popp; 1 child, William Fielding. BA, U. Ky., 1972; DMD, U. Louisville, 1977. Gen. practice dentistry Ft. Mitchell, Ky., 1977-79; resident Cin. Children's Hosp., 1979-81; dir. pediatric dental residency program U. Fla., Gainesville, 1981-85; chief dentistry The Children's Hosp., Denver, 1985—. Contbr. articles to profl. jours. Grantee Am. Cancer Soc., 1981, NIH, 1982, Nellcor Corp., 1984. Mem. ADA, Am. Assn. Dental Schs. (chmn. sect. grad. and postgrad. edn. 1985—, chmn.-elect 1984-85, sec. 1983-84), Am. Acad. Pediatric Dentistry, Am. Cleft Palate Assn., Internat. Assn. Dentistry for Children, Internat. Anesthesia Research Soc. Office: The Children's Hosp 1056 E 19th Ave Denver CO 80218

MUFSON, DANIEL, pharmaceutical company executive; b. Bronx, N.Y., Dec. 24, 1942; s. Jacob and Viola (Shutz) M.; m. ellen Lee Stein, Aug. 22, 1964; children: Cheryl Lynn, David Eric. BS, Columbia U., 1963, MS, 1965; PhD, U. Mich., 1968. Registered profl. pharmacist. Research pharmacist Parke, Davis & Co., Detroit, 1968-71; sr. investigator Smith, Kline & French, Phila., 1971-74; mgr. biopharmaceutics USV Pharms., Tuckahoe, N.Y., 1974-76; dir. pharmacy research and devel. Health Care Research div. Revlon, Tuckahoe, 1976-86; v.p. research and devel. Liposome Tech., Inc., Menlo Park, Calif., 1985-86, v.p. corp. devel., 1986—; course dir. Ctr. Profl. Advancement, East Brunswick, N.J., 1984-85. Mem. editorial bd. Clin. Research Practices and Drug Regulatory Affairs, 1984-85. Mem. Am. Soc. Hosp. Pharmacists, Am. Assn. Pharm. Scis., Sigma Xi, Rho Chi, Phi Lambda Upsilon.

MUGELE, RAYMOND ALFRED, engineering consultant; b. San Francisco, Apr. 13, 1914; s. Philip Louis and Dora Wilhelmina (Schmieder) M.; m. Olga Risch Vohs, July 21, 1945; children: Mary Carolyn, Richard Raymond, Carl Philip. BA, U. Calif., Berkeley, 1934, MA, 1935. Registered profl. engr., Calif. Teaching asst. U. Calif., Berkeley, 1934-35; weather officer USAF, 1941-45; engr. Shell Devel. Co., Emeryville, Calif., 1945-60; sr. industry devel. analyst IBM Corp., 1960-75; pres. Improvement Universal, Inc., Los Altos, Calif., 1980—; engring. cons., Los Altos, 1975—; instr. U. Calif. Extension, Berkeley, 1949-52. Contbr. articles to profl. jours. Troop chmn. Boy Scouts Am., San Jose, Calif., 1963-65, Caracas, Venezuela, 1965-67. Served to 1st lt. USAAF, 1941-45; ATO; ETO. Fellow Am. Inst. Chem. Engrs.; mem. Instrument Soc. Am., Am. Instrument Soc. (sr.), Am. Chem. Soc., Am. Math. Soc., Am. Meteorol. Soc., Sigma Xi, Phi Beta Kappa. Republican. Clubs: Sierra, Camera. Lodge: Sons in Retirement. Home: 74 Los Altos Sq Los Altos CA 94022 Office: Improvement Universal Inc 74 Los Altos Sq Los Altos CA 94022

MUGLER, LARRY GEORGE, regional planner; b. Chgo., June 22, 1946; s. Warren Franklin and Elaine Mae (Mittag) M.; m. Judy Ann Allison, Aug. 3, 1968; children: Jonathan, Allison. BSCE, Northwestern U., 1968; postgrad., Evang. Theol. Sem., 1968-70; MS in Urban and Regional Planning, U. Wis., 1972. Planning analyst State of Wis., Madison, 1970-72; dir. community devel. Cen. Okla. Econ. Devel. Dist., Shawnee, 1972-74; planner Denver Regional Council of Govts., 1974-80, dir. environ. services, 1980-83, dir. devel. services, 1983—. Pres. bd. dirs. Leawood Met. Recreation and Park Dist., Littleton, Colo., 1978—. Lasker Found. fellow, 1971. Mem. Am. Planning Assn., ASCE (subcom. chmn. 1985-86). Republican. Methodist. Avocations: soccer coach, choir. Office: Denver Regional Council Govts 2480 W 26th Ave Suite 200B Denver CO 80211

MUHLNICKEL, ISABELLE, mental health counselor; b. Strong, Colo., May 11, 1931; d. Albert and Frances (Martinez) Quintana; m. Ludwig Albert Muhlnickel, Jan. 13, 1952; children—Ludwig Albert, Elizabeth, Mary Karolyn. B.A. in Sociology, Met. State Coll.-Denver, 1980. Lic. psychiat. technician, Colo. Ednl. loan officer Lowry Fed. Credit Union, Denver, 1972-76; mgr., dir. Teamsters Credit Union, Denver, 1980-81; psychiat. technician State of Colo., Wheatridge, 1981—; founder, exec. dir. Fathers Crisis Center, Denver, 1984—. Met. State Coll. Colo. Scholars award, 1977, 78, 79. Fellow ACLU, Nat. Assn. Female Execs. Democrat. Roman Catholic. Avocations: travel; photography; skiing; hiking; painting.

MUILENBURG, ROBERT HENRY, hospital administrator; b. Orange City, Iowa, Apr. 29, 1941; s. Henry W. and Anna (Vander Zwaag) M.; m. Judith Ann Gebauer, Jan. 1, 1959; children: Ronald, Eric, Matthew. B.A., U. Iowa, 1964, M.A., 1966. Adminstrv. asst. Ill. Masonic Med. Ctr., Chgo., Ill., 1966-67; asst. adminstr. Ill. Masonic Med. Ctr., Chgo., Ill, 1967-68; assoc. adminstr. Ill. Masonic Med. Ctr., Chgo., Ill., 1968-71; assoc. adminstr. U. Utah Hosp., Salt Lake City, 1971-75, adminstr., 1975-78; adminstr. U. Wash. Hosp., Seattle, 1978-84; exec. dir. hosps. U. Wash. Hosp., 1984—; clin. assoc. prof. health services adminstrn. and planning U. Wash., 1978—. USPHS trainee, 1966. Mem. Am. Coll. Hosp. Adminstrs., Am. Hosp. Assn. (del. 1984—, chmn. metro. hosp. sect. 1987), Wash. State Hosp. Assn. (bd. dirs. 1982-84), Seattle Area Hosp. Council (pres. 1983). Home: 16580-35th Ave NE Seattle WA 98155 Office: U Wash Hosp SC-61 1959 NE Pacific St Seattle WA 98195

MUIRHEAD, JAMES SEGNER, systems engineer; b. Mpls., Sept. 28, 1938; s. Donald Beith and Sybil Mae (Segner) M.; m. Patricia Lynne Webb, Jan. 31, 1959; children: Lawrence Paul, Beverly June, Janice Kay. BS, U. Ill., 1960; PhD, U. Calif., Berkeley, 1964. Sr. engr. Rocketdyne, Canoga Park, Calif., 1964-70; engr. Aerojet Electrosystems, Azusa, Calif., 1970-76; sr. engr. IBM, Westlake Village, Calif., 1976-85; sr. program mgr. System Devel. Corp., Camarillo, Calif., 1985-87; tech. dir. Stanford Telecommunications, Inc., Westlake Village, Calif., 1987—. NSF fellow, Berkeley, Calif., 1961. Mem. AAAS, AIAA, Sigma Xi. Home: 1054 Winston Ct Westlake Village CA 91361 Office: Stanford Telecommunications Inc 31255 Cedar Valley Dr Westlake Village CA 91362

MULARZ, THEODORE LEONARD, architect; b. Chgo., Nov. 6, 1933; s. Stanley A. and Frances (Baycar) M.; m. Ruth L. Larson, Nov. 9, 1963; children—Anne Catherine, Mark Andrew. B.Arch., U. Ill., 1959. Registered architect Colo., Calif., Utah, Ariz. Assoc., Fredric A. Benedict architect, Aspen, Colo., 1959-63; prin. Theodore L. Mularz, AIA Architects, Aspen, 1963-77; v.p. Benedict-Mularz Assocs. Inc., 1978-81; prin. Theodore L. Mularz & Assocs., Aspen, 1981—. Designer numerous archtl. projects including: Manor Vail, Lord Gore Club, Vail, Colo.; Cooper Bldg., Aspen; additions to Bank of Aspen, Telemark Apts., Mason & Morse Bldg., Aspen; numerous other comml., indsl. and residential projects. Active, Music Assocs. of Aspen Fund Drive, 1969-80; vice-chmn. Pitkin County Bd. Appeals, 1972—, City of Aspen Bd. Appeals, 1985—; del. Colo. Democratic Conv., 1972, Colo. Dem. Assembly, 1974; mem. Colo. Bd. Examiners of Architects, 1975-85, pres., 1976-80, v.p., 1978. Served with USCGR, 1953-55. Recipient Nat. Acad. Design award, 1956; Design award for U. Ill. Health Ctr., 1957. Mem. AIA (coll.fellows), Nat. Council Archtl. Registration Bds. (profl. conduct com. 1977-78, procedures and documents com. 1978-82, chmn. edn. com. 1982-83, chmn. procedures and documents com. 1983-84, dir. 1982-84, pres. 1985-86, mem. interprofl. council on registration 1984-85, pres., 1985), Colo. Soc. Architects (Community Service award 1975), Aspen Architects Collaborative (chmn. 1973-74), Aspen C. of C. (past dir., past pres., past v.p.), Aspen Hist. Soc. (com. chmn. 1963-64). Roman Catholic. Home: PO Box 166 Aspen CO 81612 Office: 406 H Pacific Ave Aspen CO 81611

MULCAY, MICHAEL, communications company executive; b. London, June 23, 1939; came to U.S., 1964; s. James Michael Robert and Amy Elizabeth (Buncher) M.; m. Grace Marion Field, Aug. 15, 1959. C.Eng., Enfield Poly., London, 1964. Applications engr. Sylvania Electric, Woburn, Mass., 1964-65; project engr. Microwave Assocs., Burlington, Mass., 1965-68; tech. mktg. mgr. Raytheon Co., Norwood, Mass., 1968-75; product mgr. TRW Vidar, Mountain View, Calif., 1975-80; v.p. mktg. Lural Microwave, San Diego, 1980-82; pres., chief exec. officer TXR, Inc., Sunnyvale, Calif., 1982—. Contbr. articles to profl. jours. Fellow Inst. Electronic and Radio Engrs. Home: 10081 United Pl Cupertino CA 95014 Office: TXR Inc 777 Palomar Ave Sunnyvale CA 94086

MULCOCK, JAMES B. (BUD), JR., state and federal agency administrator; b. Roswell, N.Mex.; m. Louise Mulcock; 2 children. Student, George Washington U.; JD, U. N.Mex., 1971. Bar: N.Mex.; ordained to ministry Presbyn. Ch. Adminstrv. asst. U.S. rep. E.S. Johnny Walker, 1966-68; asst. atty. gen. State N.Mex., 1971-72; sr. v.p. corp. affairs Pub. Service Co. N.Mex., Albuquerque, 1972—. State chmn. YMCA Youth in Govt. Program, 1979—. Mem. N.Mex. Bar Assn., Albuquerque C. of C. (pres. 1984). Club: U. N.Mex. Lobo (bd. dirs.). Avocations: racketball, softball, cooking. Office: Pub Service Co of N Mex 1650 University Blvd NE Albuquerque NM 87102

MULDER, CLEYON LEE, diversified food products company executive; b. Clear Lake, S.D., Feb. 7, 1936; s. Henry E. and Mae (Johnson) M.; children: Renae, Reed, Bradley; m. Kay Corlett, May 22, 1981; children: Matthew, Katherine and Kimberly (twins). BS in Agrl. Engring., S.D. State U., 1958; MBA, U. Denver, 1976. Prodn. mgmt. staff Ralston Purina Co., Mpls., 1959-63; prodn. mgr. Ralston Purina Co., Montgomery City, Mo., 1963-68; plant engr. Ralston Purina Co., Denver, 1968-72, plant mgr., 1972—. Mem. Colo. Pub. Expenditure Council, Denver, 1985; bd. dirs. Ctr. Hearing, Speech and Language, Denver, 1976—, pres. bd. dirs. 1985; bd. dirs. Jr. Achievement Met. Denver, 1985—. Served to sgt. U.S. Army, 1959-63. Mem. Mountain States Employers Council, U. Denver Exec. MBA Club, Colo. Assn. Commerce and Industry (mem. legis. policy com. 1985), Denver C. of C. (trustee Inst. Better Govt. 1984), Colo. Council Econ. Edn. Republican. Lodge: Rotary. Avocations: skiing, golfing, jogging. Office: Ralston Purina Co 4555 York St Denver CO 80216

MULFORD, ROBERT IRWIN, management consultant; b. Taft, Calif., Oct. 17, 1935; s. Donald Milton Mulford and Jean (Stevens) Mulford Albrecht; m. Nancy Colleen Spencer, Mar. 4, 1960 (div. 1979); m. Martha June Whiteley, Apr. 21, 1979; children—Jennifer Lynn, Stephanie Ann. B.B.A., Woodbury U., 1960; cert. indsl. relations UCLA, 1965. Dir. personnel Computer Sci. Corp., Washington, 1969-72; v.p. personnel and adminstrn. Unionamerica, Inc., Los Angeles, 1972-76; mgmt. cons. in pvt. practice, San Francisco, 1977-78; mgr. employment Intel Corp., Santa Clara, Calif., 1978-80; corp. mgr. employment and tng. Signetics Corp., Sunnyvale, Calif., 1980-83; exec. v.p. Robert S. Blake Assocs., Cupertino, Calif., 1983-84, pres., 1985-86; pres. Mulford and Assocs., Inc., Cupertino, 1986—. Pub. safety commr., Saratoga, Calif., 1984—, chmn. com., 1986—; bd. dirs. United Cerebral Palsy, Los Angeles, 1975-76; bd. dirs., v.p. Exceptional Children's Found., Los Angeles, 1974-76. Served with U.S. Army, 1955-58, Europe. Mem. Am. Soc. Personnel Adminstrn., Employment Mgmt. Assn. Republican. Office: Mulford & Assocs Inc 20300 Systems Creek Blvd Cupertino CA 95014-2272

MULGANNON, TERRY PATRICK, magazine editor; b. San Francisco, Dec. 29, 1951; s. James Howard Mulgannon and Mary Frances (Pinjuv) Mulgannon Griffin. BA in Polit. Sci., U. Calif., Davis, 1979. Bus. editor Century City News, Los Angeles, 1979-80; editor CitySports Monthly, Los Angeles, 1980-82; Cen. Am. researcher Rand Corp., Santa Monica, 1982-83; editor Triathlon Mag., Culver City, Calif., 1983—. Contbr. articles on mil. sci. to profl. jours. Served with U.S. Army, 1971-77. Office: Triathlete Mag 8461 Warner Dr Culver City CA 90291

MULLAN, JACK W., real estate developer; b. Ft. Dodge, Iowa, Sept. 17, 1924; s. Paul B. and Florence (Zeller) M.; B.S., U. So. Calif., 1950; postgrad. U. J.W. Goethe, Frankfurt, Germany, 1953-54; Ph.D., San Gabriel U., 1970; m. Beverly Fortner, Feb. 8, 1951; children: Lori Lee, Jill Ann. Co-Pilot, United Airlines, 1951-53; mgr. Aero Exploration, Frankfurt, Germany, 1954-55; pres. Mullan Real Estate, and other real estate devel. cos., 1955—. Founding chmn. Orange County Econ. and Indsl. Conf., 1959, chmn., 1960; co-chmn. Orange County Econ. Devel. Conf., 1963; bd. dirs., pres. 1986-87 Orange Coast Assn., Project "21"; mem. Orange County Met. Area Com., 1963; chmn. City Newport Beach (Calif.) Air Traffic Adv. Com., 1967-68; financial steering com. Orange County Boy Scouts Am., 1959; chmn. 1st Orange County Redevel. Com.; trustee So. Calif. Aviation Council, pres., 1979-81. Served to capt. USAAF, 1942-46; PTO. Mem. Calif. Real Estate Assn. (dir. 1957-65, state chmn. indsl. and comml. div. 1961, regional v.p. 1962), Newport Harbor Bd. Realtors (pres. 1960), Aircraft Owners and Pilots Assn., So. Calif. Aviation Council (chmn. air mus. com. 1974-75), Orange County Coast Assn. (pres. 1986—), Orange County Redevel. Commn. (1st chmn.), Delta Tau Delta. Co-developer 1st horizontal condominium devel. in Calif. Home: 2031 Mesa Dr Santa Ana Heights CA 92707 Office: 3400 Irvine Newport Beach CA 92660

MULLEN, JOHN JOSEPH, JR., management consultant; b. N.Y.C., July 10, 1947; s. John Joseph Sr. and Mary Elizabeth (Murphy) M.; m. Kathleen Patricia Carty, Sept. 1, 1973; 1 child, Karina Carty Mullen. BA in Psychology, Seton Hall U., 1969; MA in Orgn. Devel., Montclair State Coll., 1973. Dir. intake C.O.P.E., Inc., Newark, 1969-73; intern, urban ednl. corps Montclair (N.J.) State Coll., 1973-74; mgmt. cons. Ft. Collins, Colo., 1973-75; dir. youth services N.E.D.A.C., Inc., Verona, N.J., 1975-78; mgmt. developer Mountain States Employers Council, Denver, 1979-82; prin. J.J. Mullen & Assocs., Evergreen, Colo., 1982—; bd. dirs. C.M.G., Inc., Englewood, Colo. Contbr. articles to profl. jours. Bd. dirs. Colo. Philharm. Orch., Evergreen, 1981. Grantee Urban Edn. Corps, Montclair, 1982-83. Mem. Craigmeur Ski Club (competition chmn. 1977-78), Am. Soc. Tng. and Devel., Canada W. Ski Areas Assn., Pacific N.W. Ski Areas Assn. Democrat. Avocations: mountaineering, kayaking, theater, symphony, skiing. Home: 6321 Kinney Creek Rd Evergreen CO 80439 Office: PO Box 2066 Evergreen CO 80439

MULLER, BURTON HARLOWE, physics educator; b. N.Y.C., May 11, 1924; s. Henry and Dorothy (Perlstein) M.; m. Babette J. Russell, Feb. 24, 1952; children—Lisa, Greta. B.A., Wesleyan U., Middletown, Conn., 1944; M.S., Yale, 1945; Ph.D., U. Ill., 1954. Research asst. S.A.M. Labs., Manhattan Project, 1945-46; faculty U. Wyo., Laramie, 1953—; prof. physics U. Wyo., 1962—; Vis. faculty U B.C., 1959-60; professorial research fellow U. Nottingham, Eng., 1965-66; univ. vis. prof. physics U. Kent, Canterbury, Eng., 1971-72. Served with AUS, 1945-46. NSF faculty fellow, 1959-60, 65-66; research grantee Research Corp., 1955-59; research grantee Research Corp. NSF, 1959-64; Petroleum Research Fund, 1962-68. Fellow AAAS; mem. Am. Phys. Soc. (Congressional Sci. fellow 1981), ACLU, Phi Beta Kappa. Home: 508 S 19th St Laramie WY 82070

MULLER, DONALD FREDRICK, computer software executive; b. Valapariso, Fla., July 14, 1948; s. James LeRoy and Dorothy Claire (Bramlett) M. BA, Wash. State U., 1970. Acct. exec. Merrill Lynch and Co., Seattle, 1970-78, Paine Webber, Seattle, 1978-84; v.p. mktg. Felx-Screen, Inc., Seattle, 1984—. Publicist Klavder for Congress, Everett, Wash., 1984, Com. to Elect Ron Meyers, Tacoma, 1986. Mem. Lamda Chi Alpha. Republican. Clubs: Seattle Yacht, Seattle Athletic. Avocations: sailing, golfing, skiing. Office: Flex-Screen Inc 216 Queen Anne Ave N Seattle WA 98109

MULLER, JEROME KENNETH, art dealer, editor; b. Amityville, N.Y., July 18, 1934; s. Alphons and Helen (Haberl) m.; m. Nora Marie Nestor, Dec. 21, 1974. BS, Marquette U., 1961; postgrad., Calif. State U., Fullerton, 1985-86, Nat. U., San Diego, 1987—. Comml. and editorial photographer N.Y.C., 1952-55; mng. editor Country Beautiful mag., Milw., 1961-62, Reprodns. Rev. mag., N.Y.C., 1967-68; editor, art dir. Orange County (Calif.) Illustrated, Newport Beach, 1962-67, art editor, 1970-79, exec. editor, art dir., 1968-69; owner, chief exec. officer Creative Services Advt. Agy., Newport Beach, 1969-79; founder, chief exec. officer Mus. Graphics, Costa Mesa, Calif., 1978—; tchr. photography Lindenhurst (N.Y.) High Sch., 1952-54; tchr. comic art U. Calif., Irvine, 1979; guest curator 50th Anniversary Exhbn. Mickey Mouse, 1928-78, The Bowers Mus., Santa Ana, Calif., 1978; organized Moving Image Exhbn. Mus. Sci. and Industry, Chgo., Cooper-Hewitt Mus., N.Y.C., William Rockhill Nelson Gallery, Kansas City, 1981; collector original works of outstanding Am. cartoonists which are exhibited continually at major mus. One-man shows include Souk Gallery, Newport Beach, 1970; Author: Rex Brandt, 1972; contbr. photographs and articles to mags. Served with USAF, 1956-57. Recipient two silver medals 20th Ann. Exhbn. Advt. and Editorial Art in West, 1965. Mem. Soc. Publ. Designers, Profl. Photographers West, Newport Harbor Art Mus., Mus. Modern Art (N.Y.C.), Met. Mus. Art, Art Mus. Assn. Am., Laguna Beach Mus. Art, Newport Harbor C. of C., Alpha Sigma Nu. Clubs: Los Angeles Press, Orange County Press. Home: 2438 Bowdoin Pl Costa Mesa CA 92626 Office: PO Box 10743 Costa Mesa CA 92627

MULLER, ROLF HUGO, chemist; b. Aarau, Switzerland, Aug. 6, 1929; came to U.S., 1957, naturalized, 1967; s. Wilhelm and Alice Louise (Schmid) M.; m. Dorothy Leah Donaldson, July 18, 1962; children: Wilhelm Karl, Alice Barbara. MS in Natural Sci., Fed. Inst. Tech., Zurich, Switzerland, 1953, teaching cert., 1955, PhD in Natural Sci., 1957; postgrad., U. Calif., Berkeley, 1960-61. Asst. in phys. chemistry Fed. Inst. Tech., 1955-56; research and devel. chemist E.I. DuPont de Nemours, Parkersburg, W.Va., 1957-60; research assoc. dept. chem. engring. U. Calif., Berkeley, 1961-62; staff scientist Lawrence Berkeley Lab., 1962-66, prin. investigator, 1966—, asst. div. head., 1970—, staff sr. scientist, 1978—; lectr. univ. dept. chem. engring., 1966—; sec. Nat. Battery Adv. Com. to Dept. Energy adhoc, Planning Subcom. 1977-85. Editor several books; contbr. articles to profl. jours. Mem. AAAS, Electrochem. Soc. (sect. chmn. 1971, councilor 1976, sec., treas. phys. electrochemistry div. 1985—), Internat. Soc. Electrochemistry (div. co-chmn. 1973-77, plenary lectr. Zurich 1976, chmn. tech. program 1984), Swiss Chem. Soc., Optical Soc. Am., U. Calif. at Berkeley Faculty. Home: 36 Highgate Rd Berkeley CA 94707 Office: Lawrence Berkeley Lab U Calif Materials and Chem Scis Div. 62-203 Berkeley CA 94720

MULLIGAN, JOHN DICKSON, fire chief; b. Oakland, Calif., Oct. 8, 1943; s. Robert Philip and Anna Grace (Dickson) M.; m. Dianne Elliott Love, 1966 (div. 1971); 1 child, Bryon John; m. Kathryn Ann Stone, June 10, 1971; children—Jim Stone, Shawnie Ann. B.A., Calif. State U.-Fullerton, 1971, M.A., 1976; A.S., Allan Hancock Coll., 1971, Mt. San Antonio Coll., 1965. Fire fighter West Covina Fire Dept., Calif., 1967-69; firefighter Lompoc Fire Dept., Calif., 1969-72, chief, 1976-78; capt. Foothill Fire Dist., Alta Loma, Calif., 1972-74, bn. chief, 1974-76; chief Ft. Collins and Poudre Fire Authority, Colo., 1978—. Mcpl. chmn. United Way, 1979-80, bd. dirs., Lompoc, 1976; mem. exec. bd. Salvation Army, Lompoc. Mem. Internat. Fire Chiefs Assn. (chmn. hazardous materials com. 1983—), Colo. Fire Chiefs Assn. (pres. 1982), Phi Kappa Phi. Club: Civitan. Home: 2908 Brookwood Pl Fort Collins CO 80525 Office: Poudre Fire Authority 505 Peterson St Fort Collins CO 80524

MULLIGAN, JOHN MICHAEL, lawyer; b. Herkimer, N.Y., Sept. 18, 1950; s. Arthur Harold and Mary Fleming (Lyng) M. B.A., Ohio No. U., Ada, 1972; J.D., Western State U., Fullerton, Calif., 1978. Bar: Calif. 1979, U.S. Dist. Ct. (no. dist.) Calif. 1981, U.S. Dist. Ct. (ea. dist.) Calif. 1980. Sole practice, Santa Cruz, Calif., 1979—. Mem. Calif. Bar Assn., Santa Cruz County Bar Assn. Roman Catholic.

MULLIGAN, MARTIN FREDERICK, clothing executive, professional tennis player; b. Sydney, Australia, Oct. 18, 1940; s. Frederick William and Marie Louise (Tome) M.; m. Rossella Rita Labella, Sept. 19, 1969 (div. Mar. 1980); children: Monica, Martin Thomas. Winner Tennis Singles Championships of Australia, 1952, 53, 55, 56, 57, 58; mem. Davis Cup team Australia, 1959, 60; winner Australian Hard Court Singles and Doubles tournaments, 1960, 64; finalist Wimbledon Singles tournaments, 1962—; winner Italian Open Singles tournaments, 1963, 65, 67; co-organizer Italian Open tournament, Rome, 1972-73; winner German Open Singles tournament, 1963; winner singles and doubles titles Monte Carlo Championships, 1964; coach Italian Davis Cup team, 1966-76; winner, Davis Cup tournament, 1976; winner Spanish Open tournament, 1966, 67, Swedish Open tournament, 1966, 67, Austrian Open tournament, 1966, 67, Champion Cup tournament, 1966, 67; promotional cons. Alpina Australian Mfg. Co., 1973-74; cons. and internat. promotion mgr. Diadora Co., 1973-78; internat. promotion mgr. FILA-Italy Sportswear, 1976-1978, v.p. of internat. promotion and pub. relations, 1979—; negotiated contracts between FILA and various sports profls. and celebrities. Ranked number 3 in world in tennis, 1967; ranked 5 times in world's top 10 tennis players. Avocation: stamp collecting. Office: FILAsports Inc 821 Indstrial St San Carlos CA 94070

MULLIKIN, HARRY LAVERNE, hotel executive; b. Hot Springs, Ark., Apr. 27, 1927; s. Carlton and LeVerne (Harper) Mahone; m. Judith Ann Thomas, July 25, 1970; children: Michael, Patricia, Scott, Kelly. Student, Wash. State Coll., 1947, U. Wash., Seattle, 1949. Resident mgr. Davenport Hotel, Spokane, 1953-57; gen. mgr. Olympic Hotel, Seattle; with Westin Hotel Co., Seattle, 1961—, sr. v.p., then exec. v.p., 1970-73, pres., 1973—, chief exec. officer, 1977—, chmn., 1981—, also dir.; chmn. Hilton Internat. Co., N.Y.C., 1987—; dir. UAL, Inc., United Airlines, SeaFirst Corp., Seattle-First Nat. Bank. Bd. dirs. Virginia Mason Hosp. Served with USAAF, World War II. Recipient Golden Plate award Internat. Foodservice Mfrs. Assn., 1972; Man of Year award Pa. State U., 1975; Alumni Achievement award Wash. State U., 1976. Mem. Am. Hotel and Motel Assn. (past pres., past chmn.), Nat. Restaurant Assn. (past dir.). Republican. Roman Catholic. Clubs: Seattle Golf (Seattle), Seattle Yacht Bohemian, Rainier (Seattle). Office: Westin Hotel & Resorts Westin Bldg Seattle WA 98121

MULLIN, FRANK PATRICK, computer information specialist, consultant; b. Phila., Nov. 13, 1940; s. Francis P. and Florence (Eisenberg) M.; m. Virginia Speltz, Apr. 10, 1965 (div. June 1983); 1 child, Erin. BA, Loyola U., Los Angeles, 1962; MA, U. So. Calif., 1969, postgrad., 1972. Automated wiring designer Rockwell Internat., Downey, Calif., 1962-67; project dir. E.H. White & Co., San Francisco, 1974-79; generalist I.P. Sharp Assocs., Toronto, Ont., Can., 1981-82; APL adminstr. TransAmerica, Los Angeles, 1984—; pres. Big Name Sports, Santa Monica, Calif., 1985—; cons. Head Start, Washington, 1974-77, Tiger Air, Los Angeles, 1979-80, Led Zeppelin, London, 1972-73, Blackfeet Tribe, Browning, Mont., 1977. Inventor. Chmn. Cable Task Force of Santa Monica, 1983-84. Recipient Mayor's Commendation, City of Santa Monica, 1985. Mem. Assn. Computing Machinery (APL spl. interest group advanced programming lang.). Avocations: photography, guitar, football. Home: 3104 Fourth St #105 Santa Monica CA 90405

MULLIN, RONALD KEY, laywer; b. Santa Barbara, Calif., May 28, 1949; s. Wallace Key and Sixta T. (Gomez) M.; m. Catherine Theresa Persons, Aug. 8, 1970; children: Scott Key, Timothy Michael. BA, St. Mary's Coll., Moraga, Calif., 1971; JD, U. Pacific, 1978. Bar: Calif. 1978. Police officer City of Concord, Calif., 1972-78; sole practice Concord, 1979-86; ptnr. Moyal, Mullin & Sluis, Concord, 1986—; chmn. adminstrv. services policy com. League of Cities, 1984-86; mem. fin., adminstrv. inter-govtl. relations policy steering com. Nat. League of Cities, 1986; 2d v.p. mayor's and councilmember's dept. League of Calif. Cities, 1986—. Mayor City of Concord, 1985—; chmn. Contra Costa Mayors Conf., 1986—; pres. Arts: Contra Costa, 1986, Queen of all Sts. Sch. Bd., Concord, 1985-86. Recipient Recognition award Boy Scouts Am., 1984, United Bay Area Crusade, Contra Costa County, 1983, YMCA, Contra Costa County, 1985. Mem. Contra Costa Bar Assn., Calif. State Bar. Democrat. Roman Catholic. Lodges: Rotary, K.C. Avocations: photography, backpacking. Home: 3141 Esperanza Dr Concord CA 94519 Office: Moyal Mullin Sluis 1899 Clayton Rd Suite 100 Concord CA 94520

MULLINEX, TRAVIS, food company executive. Pres. Tri/Valley Growers, Inc., San Francisco. Office: Tri Valley Growers Inc 1255 Battery St San Francisco CA 94111 *

MULLINS, RUTH GLADYS, nurse; b. Westville, N.S., Can., Aug. 25, 1943; d. William G. and Gladys H.; came to U.S., 1949, naturalized, 1955; student Tex. Womans U., 1961-64; B.S. in Nursing, Calif. State U.-Long Beach, 1966; M.Nursing, UCLA, 1973; m. Leonard E. Mullins, Aug. 27, 1963; children—Deborah R., Catherine M., Leonard III. Pub. health nurse, Los Angeles County Health Dept., 1967-68; nurse Meml. Hosp. Med. Center, Long Beach, 1968-72; dir. pediatric nurse practitioner program Calif. State U., Long Beach, 1973—, asst. prof., 1975-80, asso. prof., 1980-85, prof., 1985—; health service credential coordinator Sch. Nursing, chmn., 1979-81, coordinator grad. programs, 1985—; mem. Calif. Maternal, Child and Adolescent Health Bd., 1977-84; vice chmn. Long Beach/Orange County Health Consortium, 1984—. Tng. grantee HHS, Calif. Dept. Health; cert. pediatric nurse practitioner. Fellow Nat. Assn. Pediatric Nurse Assos. and Practitioners (exec. bd.); mem. Am. Pub. Health Assn., Assn. Faculties Pediatric Nurse Practitioner Programs, Calif. Assn. Pediatric Nurse Practitioners and Assocs., Am. Assn. U. Faculty, Ambulatory Pediatric Assn. Democrat. Methodist. Author: (with B. Nelms) Growth and Development: A Primary Health Care Approach; contbg. author: Quick Reference to Pediatric Nursing, 1984; asst. editor Jour. Pediatric Health Care. Home: 6382 Heil Ave Huntington Beach CA 92647 Office: Dept Nursing 1250 Bellflower Blvd Long Beach CA 90802

MULLIS, KARY BANKS, biochemist; b. Lenoir, N.C., Dec. 28, 1944; s. Cecil Banks Mullis and Bernice Alberta (Barker) Fredericks; m. Richards Dorothy Train, June 15, 1964 (div. Feb. 1972); 1 child, Louis; m. Cynthia Ann Gibson, May 25, 1976 (div. Dec. 1985); children: Christopher, Jeremy. BS in Chemistry, Ga. Inst. Tech, 1966; PhD in Biochemistry, U. Calif., Berkeley, 1973. Lectr. biochemistry U. Calif., Berkeley, 1972; postdoctoral fellow U. Calif., San Francisco, 1977-79, U. Kans. Med. Sch., Kansas City, 1973-76; scientist Cetus Corp., Emeryville, Calif., 1979-86; dir. molecular biology Xytronyx, Inc., San Diego, 1986—. Contbr. articles to profl. jours. Mem. Am. Chem. Soc., Inst. for Further Study (pres. 1983—). Avocations: computers, gardening, windsurfing, skiing. Home: 6767 Neptune Pl Apt#4 La Jolla CA 92037 Office: Xytronyx Inc 6555 Nancy Ridge Dr Suite 200 San Diego CA 92121

MULVANEY, JAMES EDWARD, chemistry educator; b. N.Y.C., Aug. 4, 1929; s. John F. and Helen (Ogden) M.; m. Carolyn Scott Mulvaney, May 29, 1983; children: Elizabeth A., Jean L., Sheila A., Pamela L. BS in Chemistry, Poly. Inst. of N.Y., 1951, PhD in Chemistry, 1959. Research assoc. U. Ill., Urbana, 1959-61; asst. prof. chemistry U. Ariz., Tucson, 1961-65, assoc. prof., 1965-71, prof., 1971—; cons. Gen. Motors, Warren, Mich., 1965-76, ARCO, Glenolden, Pa., 1968-72, Am. Optical, Worchester, Mass., 1968-73, UOP, Des Plaines, Ill, 1980-82, IMI-Tech., Elk Grove Vill., Ill., 1983—. Contbr. articles to profl. jours. Served with U.S. Army, 1953-55. Grantee numerous orgns. Mem. AAAS, Am. Chem. Soc. Avocations: golf, tennis. Office: U Ariz Dept Chemistry Tucson AZ 85721

MUNETA, JAMES DENNISON, social work adminstrator; b. Ft. Defiance, Ariz., Feb. 5, 1957; s. Tom and Sarah (Becenti) M. BA, Ft. Lewis Coll., 1984; M in Social Welfare, U. Calif., Berkeley, 1985. Researcher Nat. Indian Youth Council, Albuquerque, 1977-78; social worker Inter-tribal Friendship House, Oakland, Calif., 1984-85; exemplary services coordinator Dine' Ctr. for Human Devel., Tsaile, Ariz., 1985—; intern social worker Berkeley Mental Health, 1984-85. Bd. dirs. Am. Indian Environ. Council, N.Mex., 1980—; com. mem. South Am. Indian Info. Ctr., Berkeley, 1985—. Avocations: oil painting, martial arts, poetry, writing. Home: Gen Delivery Tsaile AZ 86556 Office: Dine' Ctr for Human Devel Navajo Community Coll Tsaile AZ 86556

MUNETIC, ANNALIESE, library information educator; b. Berlin, May 30, 1922; came to U.S., 1949; d. Walter and Maria Josepha (Halbhuber) Grube; m. Tomislav Munetic, Feb. 28, 1959 (div. 1968). MLS, Nat. Library Sch., Berlin, 1944; PhD, U. Tex., 1964. Cert. tchr., Calif. Reference librarian Mus. Modern Art, N.Y.C., 1959-60; cataloger U. Puerto Rico, Rio Piedras, 1961; asst. to curator Harvard Theatre Coll., Cambridge, 1962-63; head index dept. G.V. Hall Pub., Boston, 1964-67; head dept. library tech. City Coll., San Francisco, 1968-86. Author: Christian Adolph Klotz, 1964; compiler (bibliography) Mark Rothko, 1960. Mem. Wagner Soc., Mus. Soc. San Francisco, Calif. Hist. Soc. Avocations: fine books, prints, music.

MUNN, WILLIAM CHARLES, II, psychiatrist; b. Flint, Mich., Aug. 9, 1938; s. Elton Albert and Rita May (Coykendall) M.; student Flint Jr. Coll., 1958-59, U. Detroit, 1959-61; M.D., Wayne State U., 1965; m. Deborah Lee Munn, 1983; children by previous marriage—Jude Michael, Rachel Marie, Alexander Winston. Intern David Grant USAF Med. Center, Travis AFB, Calif., 1965-66; resident in psychiatry Letterman Army Hosp., San Francisco, 1967-70; practice medicine, specializing in psychiatry, Fairfield, Calif., 1972—; chief in-patient psychiatry David Grant Med. Center, 1970-71, chmn. dept. mental health, 1971-72; psychiat. cons. Fairfield-Suisun Unified Sch. Dist., 1971—, Fairfield Hosp. and Clinic, 1971, Intercommunity Hosp., Fairfield, 1971—, Casey Family Program, 1980—, Solano County Coroner's Office, 1981; asst. clin. prof. psychiatry U. Calif., San Francisco, 1976—; cons. VA Hosp., San Francisco, 1976, David Grant USAF Hosp., 1976. Served to maj., M.C., USAF, 1964-72, flight surgeon, chief public health, chief phys. exam. center McGuire AFB, N.J., 1966-67. Diplomate Am. Bd. Psychiatry and Neurology (examiner). Mem. Am. Psychiat. Assn., No. Calif. Psychiat. Soc., E. Bay Psychiat. Assn. Home: 450 Ridgewood Dr Martinez CA 94553 Office: 1245 Travis Blvd Suite E Fairfield CA 94533

MUNNERLYN, CHARLES RAY, laser company executive; b. Waskom, Tex., Mar. 27, 1940; s. James O'Ree and Lucille (Woolen) M.; m. Judith Ann Geldert, Aug. 24, 1963; children: William, Audrey, Stewart, Charles. BS in Physics, Tex. A&M U., 1962; PhD in Optical Engring., U. Rochester, 1969. Dir. research and devel. Tropel Inc., Fairport, N.Y., 1969-75, Coherent Med. Div., Palo Alto, Calif., 1975-82; pres. Ical Inc., Sunnyvale, Calif., 1982-85, CooperVision Laser Div., Santa Clara, Calif., 1985—. Contbr. numerous articles to profl. jours.; patentee in field. Served to lst lt. USAF, 1962-65. Fellow Am. Soc. Laser Medicine and Surgery; mem. Internat. Soc. Ocular Fluorophotometry (charter), Optical Soc. Am., Soc. PhotoInstrumentation Engrs., Sigma Xi, Phi Kappa Phi, Phi Eta Sigma. Avocations: astronomy, golf. Home: 1360 Bedford Ave Sunnyvale CA 94087 Office: CooperVision Laser Div 3420 Central Expressway Santa Clara CA 95051-0793

MUNNINGER, MICHAEL JOSEPH, architect; b. Albany, N.Y., Aug. 24, 1948; s. Karl Otto and Margaret Josephine (Craugh) M.; m. Kathryn Denmark, Feb. 10, 1979; children: Lisa, John Karl, Michael, Suzanne, Paul, Mark. BArch, U. Tex., 1971; postgrad., Ariz. State U., Phoenix, 1976-77. Registered architect, Ariz; lic. real estate salesman, Ariz. Founder, ptnr. Archtl. Alliance, Phoenix, 1974—. Contbr. articles to mags., newspapers. Active Boys Club Met. Phoenix, Ariz. Hunter Safety Instr. Program, Nat. Trust Hist. Preservation; mem. City of Phoenix Visual Improvement Com. Recipient 2d prize Art by Architects, 1982, Most Beautiful Home award Phoeniz mag., 1982, Visual Improvement award, City of Phoenix, 1984. Mem. Phoenix C. of C., Ariz. Indsl. Devel. Assn. Home: 10001 N 132d St Scottsdale AZ 85259

MUÑOZ, MARY HELEN, bank executive; b. Fowler, Calif., May 10, 1948; d. Manuel and Carmen (Campos) M. AS, Calif. City Coll., 1970; BA, Calif. State U., Fresno, 1976. Various positions Bank of Am., 1969-73; credit asst. Bank of Am., San Francisco, 1974-76; asst. cashier Bank of Am., San Diego, 1976-81; internat. fin. officer Security Pacific Nat. Bank, San Francisco, 1981, asst. v.p. mktg., 1981-82; asst. v.p. internat. mktg. Security Pacific Nat. Bank, San Diego, 1982-83, asst. v.p., mgr., 1983, v.p., mgr., 1983-84; v.p. mktg. Latin Am. region Security Pacific Nat. Bank, Los Angeles, 1984-86; credit union cons. So. Calif. Security Pacific Nat. Bank, Los Angeles, 1986—. Vol. Florence Crittendon Home, San Francisco, 1973-75, Arriba Juntos Ctr., 1973-75, VITA, 1976-78, Jr. World Trade, 1973-76, Am. Inst. Banking. Recipient Most Outstanding Service and Profl. Contbn. award Am. Inst. Banking. Mem. Nat. Assn. Bank Women (exec. com.), Nat. Assn. Female Execs., Hispanic Bankers Assn. (Most Disting. Mem. 1984), Los Angeles Jaycees, Pan Am. Soc. Office: Security Pacific Nat Bank W26-50 333 S Beaudry Ave Los Angeles CA 90017

MUÑOZ, ROBERT R., library science educator; b. Corpus Christi, Tex., Nov. 20, 1942; s. Manuel S. and Juanita R. M. AA in Bus. Adminstrn., Rio Hondo Coll., 1970; BA in History, Whittier Coll., 1972; MLS, Calif. State U., Fullerton, 1973. Cert. elem. and community coll. tchr., Calif., elem. tchr., Nev. Athlete tutor, acad. coordinator Whittier (Calif.) Coll., 1970-72; educator, librarian Herlong (Calif.) Elem. Sch. Dist., 1973-84; educator Lassen Community Coll., Herlong, 1982-83; pres., bus. edn. cons. Robert R. Muñoz, Inc., Reno, 1984—; educator Washoe County Sch. Dist., Reno, 1986—; chief negotiator Herlong Tchrs. Assn., 1976,81; pres., 1982; basketball coach Herlong High Sch. Dist., 1976-82; home tchr. for the terminally ill, Herlong Elem. Sch. Dist., 1980; mgmt. trainee, bus. cons., educator USPS, Reno. EEO/AA activist, Calif., Nev., 1965—; v.p. Sierra Fed. Credit Union, Herlong, 1978; coach Jr. Olympics, Herlong, 1981. Served with USAF, 1961-67. Recipient Outstanding Student award, Rio Hondo Coll., 1970. Mem. Omega Delta Kappa. Roman Catholic. Avocations: fishing, archaeology, traveling. Home: 2406 Marjay Ct Reno NV 89512

MUNRO, RALPH DAVIES, state government official; b. Bainbridge Island, Wash., June 25, 1943; s. George Alexander and Elizabeth (Troll) M.; m. Karen Hansen, Feb. 17, 1973; 1 son, George Alexander. B.A. in Polit. Sci. and Edn. (scholar), Western Wash. U. Successively indsl. engr. Boeing Co.; sales mgr. Continental Host, Inc.; asst. dep. dir. ACTION Agy; spl. asst. to gov. of Wash.; gen. mgr. Tillicum Enterprises & Food Services Co.; dir. Found. for Handicapped; pres. Northwest Highlands Tree Farm; now sec. of state of Wash. Chmn. community service com. Seattle Rotary Club 4; founder 1st pres. Rotary Youth Job Employment Center, Seattle. Named Man of Yr. Assn. Retarded Citizens, Seattle, 1970. Mem. Nat. Assn. Secs. State, Nat. Assn. Retarded Children, Wash. Historic Mus. (dir.), Wash. Trust Historic Preservation (founder), Nature Conservancy. Republican. Lutheran. Home: 4325 Rhodes End Crystal Springs Farm Bainbridge Island WA 98110 Office: Legislative Bldg Olympia WA 98504

MUNRO, SANFORD STERLING, JR., investment banking company executive; b. Madison, Wis., Mar. 2, 1932; s. Sanford Sterling and Dorothea Irene (Spears) M.; m. Valerie Gene Halbert, Apr. 4, 1956; children—Sanford Sterling, Margaret, Mary, Elizabeth, Peter, Matthew, Andrew. B.A., George Washington U., 1957. Mem. profl. staff U.S. Senate, Washington, 1953-61; adminstrv. asst. U.S. Senator Henry M. Jackson, 1961-75; chief of staff Jackson for Pres. Com., 1975-76; govtl. affairs cons. Wenatchee, Wash., 1977; adminstr. Bonneville Power Adminstrn., U.S. Dept. Energy, Portland, Oreg., 1978-81; v.p., nat. dir. pub. power John Nuveen & Co., Inc., Seattle and Chgo., 1981—; bd. dirs. Cen. Wash. Bank, Wenatchee. Bd. dirs. U.S. nat. com. World Energy Conf.; chmn. U.S. Entity for Columbia River Treaty; mem. Pacific N.W. River Basins Commn., 1978-81; trustee Central Wash. U., 1977-85, 85—. Served with U.S. Army, 1952-53. Mem. Electric Power Research Inst. (vice chmn. bd. 1978-81), Electric Club Oreg. Democrat. Episcopalian. Clubs: Portland City, Wash. Athletic, Wenatchee Swim and Tennis. Home: 1202 South Hills Dr Wenatchee WA 98801

MUNROE, DONNA SCOTT, data processing professional, statistician; b. Cleve., Nov. 28, 1945; d. Glenn Everett and Louise Lenox (Parkhill) S.; m. Melvin James Ricketts, Dec. 23, 1968 (div. Aug. 1979); 1 child, Suzanne Michelle; m. Peter Carlton Munroe, Feb. 14, 1981. BS in Sociology, Portland State U., 1976, BS in Philosophy, 1978, MS in Sociology, 1983. Lectr. Portland (Oreg.) State U., 1977-79; writing, editorial cons. Worth Pubs., N.Y.C., 1978-79; statis. cons. Oreg. U. Sch. Health Sci. and Morrison Ctr. for Youth and Family Services, Portland, 1979-82; tech. writer Equitable Ins. Co., Portland, 1981-82; account ops. mgr. Electronic Data Systems, Portland, 1982-87; mgmt. cons. Computer Mgmt. Systems, Inc., Portland, 1987—. Mem. Am. Mgmt. Assn., Sigma Xi. Democrat. Episcopalian. Home: 1435 SW Harrison Portland OR 97201

MUNROE, LYDIA DARLENE, jeweler, travel industry executive; b. San Diego, July 9, 1933; d. Daniel O. and Bertha E. (Smith) Thayer; m. H. Flack Jr., July 29, 1949 (div. 1953); children: Debrha Flack Miller, Mona Lynn Flack Pietz; m. Don Evan Heath, Oct. 13, 1953 (dec. 1968); 1 child, Daniel Evan; m. Duskin M. Shears, July 24, 1969 (dec. 1982); m. Albert G. Munroe, Nov. 26, 1982. Student, Sweetwater Adult Edn. Coll. With accounts receivable, payroll Burtrum Yacht Co., Miami, Fla., 1954-56; gen. bookkeeper Stafford and Gardner, 1956-57; bookkepper, switch bd. operator William Creek Copper Mines, 1957-59; with Brisbane (Australia) and Wonderlick, 1959-60; small bus. owner Coober Pedy South Australia Opal Fields, 1960-72, Down Under Opal, Seattle, 1972-86; tour guide, itinerary planner to Australia, 1982—; lectr. on Opals. Author: Pricing Opal. Active Widowed Info. and Cons. Services. Mem. Maplewood Gem Club (rep. to regional gem show com.), North Seattle Gem. Club (treas., show dealer chmn.), West Seattle Gem Club (treas., show chmn.), N.W. Opal Assn. (v.p., pres. show dealer chmn.), Puyallup Valley Gem Club, OES Juanita Chpt., Am. Mineral Gem Suppliers Assn., Greater Seattle C. of C. Avocations: making and designing jewelry, carving opal. Home: 716 SW 179th Ct Seattle WA 98166

MUNSEN, RICHARD STANLEY, vitreoretinal surgeon, ophthalmologist; b. Ames, Iowa, Dec. 31, 1945; s. Richard S. and Katherine S. (Jacobson) M. BA, St. Olaf Coll., 1968; MD, U. Iowa, 1972, cert. retinal surgery, 1979; cert. ophthalmology, U. Mich., 1978. Diplomate Am. Bd. Ophthalmology. Practice medicine specializing in retinal and vitreous surgery Seattle, 1980—. Served to capt. USAF, 1973-75. Fellow Am. Acad. Ophthalmology, Wash. State Acad. Ophthalmology (treas. 1984); mem. AMA, The Vitreous Soc. (charter). Lutheran. Avocations: hiking, mountain climbing, music, skiing. Home: 10 E Roanoke #2 Seattle WA 98102 Office: Vitreoretinal Assocs 1221 Madison St #1002 Seattle WA 98104

MUNSON, ALEXANDER LEE, management consultant; b. Hempstead, N.Y., Aug. 22, 1931; s. Alexander Lawrence and Bertha Louise (Geer) M.; m. Betty Sue Shideler, Dec. 14, 1957 (div. June 1978); children: Eric Lawrence, Genevieve Sue, Anna Lee. B.A., Amherst Coll., 1953; M.B.A., Harvard, 1960. Mgmt. trainee, credit analyst Mellon Nat. Bank & Trust Co., Pitts., 1953-54; asso. Cresap, McCormick & Paget; mgmt. cons. Cresap, McCormick & Paget, N.Y.C., 1960-62; financial adv. internat. finance Mobil Oil Corp., N.Y.C., 1962-64, Melbourne, Australia, 1964-65; mgr. spl. projects Mobil Internat., N.Y.C., 1965-66, mgr. treasury reports and analysis, 1966-67; treas. Mobil Latin Am. Inc., N.Y.C., 1968-70; v.p.-treas. Fairchild Camera & Instrument Co., Mountain View, Calif., 1971-72, Crown Zellerbach Corp., San Francisco, 1972-82; pres. A.L. Munson & Co., San Francisco, 1982—; bd. dirs. Holden-Day, Inc. Mem. Mayor's Fiscal Adv. Com., 1976—, mem. exec. com., 1982—; v.p., bd. dirs. San Francisco Civil Service Commn., 1984—. Served to lt. USCGR, 1954-64. Recipient SBA Advocate of Yr. award, 1976. Mem. Harvard Bus. Sch. Assn. of No. Calif. (exec. v.p. 1977-81, founder, chmn. minority bus. cons. group 1971-75), Financial Execs. Inst., Phi Gamma Delta. Republican. Presbyterian. Club: University. Home and office: 3369 Jackson St San Francisco CA 94118

MUNSON, DEE ALLISON, food marketing executive, consultant; b. Geneva, Ill., Nov. 17, 1936; d. R. Wayne and S. Dorothy Allison; m. William Walfred Munson, Aug. 20, 1960 (dec. Jan. 1976); children: Daniel Stewart, Katherine Allison. BS, Purdue U., 1958. Asst. food editor Better Homes & Gardens mag., Des Moines, 1958-60; food editor Institutions mag., Chgo., 1961-62; dir. home econs. Wheat Flour Inst., Chgo., 1970-72; v.p. advt. consumer edn. Am. Egg Bd., Chgo., 1976-82; v.p. Cole & Weber Advt., Seattle, 1982-86; prin., cons. Food Profls., Vashon, Wash., 1986—. Author: Miracle Blender Cook Book, 1965, Culinary Arts Nutrition Cook Book, 1974, 1974, Crepes Cook Book, 1975, Consumer Guide Food Processor Cook Book, 1975. Mem. Am. Home Economists Assn., Home Economists in Bus. (program chmn. 1983, nat. chmn.-elect 1986-87, nat. chmn. 1987—). Baha'i. Home and Office: Food Profls PO Box 1326 Vashon WA 98070

MUNSON, ELIZABETH ANN, social worker; b. Lynn, Mass., Aug. 6, 1960; d. Philip James Jr. and Dorothy Ann (Young) Allfrey: m. Dana Lyle Munson, Aug. 18, 1984. BA in Psychology, St. Anselm Coll., 1982; MSW, Boston Coll., 1984. Med. social worker Lynn Union Hosp., 1982-83; substance abuse counselor Boston VA Hosp., Jamaica Plains, Mass., 1983-84; program coordinator Sunrise, Avon Park, Fla., 1984-85; residential social worker Alinda Youth Services, Carmichael, Calif., 1985; area mgr. Ican, Inc., Sacramento, 1985-86; sr. counselor Alta Calif. Regional Ctr., Sacramento, 1986—. Mem. Nat. Assn. Social Workers, Am. Assn. Mental Deficiencies, Pi Gamma Mu. Home: 6151 Shadow Ln 202 Citrus Heights CA 95621 Office: Alta Calif Regional Ctr 2031 Home Ave Suite 100 Sacramento CA 95825

MUNSON, LUCILLE MARGUERITE (MRS. ARTHUR E. MUNSON), real estate broker; b. Norwood, Ohio, Mar. 26, 1914; d. Frank and Fairy (Wicks) Wirick; R.N., Lafayette (Ind.) Home Hosp., 1937; A.B., San Diego State U., 1963, student Purdue U., Kans. Wesleyan U.; m. Arthur E. Munson, Dec. 24, 1937; children—Barbara Munson Papke, Judith Munson Andrews, Edmund Arthur. Staff and pvt. nurse Lafayette Home Hosp., 1937-41; indsl. nurse Lakey Foundry & Machine Co., Muskegon, Mich., 1950-51, Continental Motors Corp., Muskegon, 1951-52; nurse Girl Scout Camp, Grand Haven, Mich., 1948-49; owner Munson Realty, San Diego, 1964—. Mem. San Diego County Grand Jury, 1975-76, 80-81; charter mem. Calif. Grand Jurors Assn. Mem. San Diego Bd. Realtors. Presbyterian. Home: 5765 Friars Rd Apt 200 San Diego CA 92108 Office: 2999 Mission Blvd # 102 San Diego CA 92109

MUNSTERTEIGER, KAY DIANE, speech language pathologist; b. Newcastle, Wyo., June 2, 1956; d. Donald Francis and Janice Mathilda (Emerson) M. BS, U. Wyo., 1978; MS, U. Nev., Reno, 1980. Speech lang. pathologist No. Nev. Speech lang. Clinic, Reno, 1980-82, Washakie County Sch. Dist. 1, Worland, Wyo., 1982—; pvt. practice speech pathologist Worland, 1982—; speech lang. pathologist, cons. Washakie County Sch. Dist. 2, Tensleep, Wyo., 1984-85; speech lang. pathologist Spl. Touch Presch., Worland, 1985-86. Mem. NEA, State Edn. Assn., Am. Speech Lang. Hearing Assn., Wyo. Speech Lang. Hearing Assn., Nat. Stuttering Project, Pub. Sch. Caucus, Assn. Childhood Edn. Internat., Phi Kappa Phi. Democrat. Roman Catholic. Avocations: traveling, reading, crafts. Office: Washakie County Sch Dist 1 800 S 17th Worland WY 82401

MUNTER, PAMELA OSBORNE, clinical psychologist; b. Santa Monica, Calif., Mar. 27, 1943; d. Eric John and Frances Margo (Dellinger) Osborne; m. Leo J. Munter, Aug. 2, 1970 (div. Dec. 1979); one child, Aaron. AB in Journalism, U. Calif., Berkeley, 1964; MA in Polit. Sci., Calif. State U., Northridge, 1966; postgrad., UCLA, 1967; MA in Psychology, Calif. State U., Los Angeles, 1969; cert. in alcohol studies, U. Nebr., 1971, PhD in Clin. Psychology, 1972; cert., Reproductive Biology Research Found., St. Louis, 1975. Reporter, critic The Christian Sci. Monitor, Boston, 1964; research writer CBS Inc., Hollywood, Calif., 1965; asst. prof. polit. sci. U. Panama (via Peace Corps), 1966; speech writer McKinsey & Co. Inc., Los Angeles, 1966-67; instr. in polit. sci. Calif. State U., Northridge, 1967-69; instr. in psychology U. Nebr., Lincoln, 1970-71; staff psychologist Lincoln Regional Ctr., 1972; children's consultation intern Mendota (Calif.) State Hosp., 1972-73; pvt. practice psychology Beaverton, Oreg., 1973—; asst. prof. psychology Portland (Oreg.) State U., 1973-76, assoc. prof., 1976-80; staff Providence Med. Ctr., St. Vincent Hosp.; pres. Westgate Press, Beaverton, 1985—; founding parent Oreg. Grad. Sch. Profl. Psychology; cons. in field. Author: Almost Famous, 1985; also articles; founding editor Oreg. Psychologist 1976-78, Almost Famous, 1985, Westgate Letter, 1986—. Co-founder, bd. dirs. Oreg. Grad. Sch. Profl. Psychology, 1975-80; bd. dirs. Northwest Film Study Ctr., 1976-82; coach, mgr. Sylvan Little League, 1980; mem. social action com. Temple Beth Israel, 1980; active Jewish Fedn. Oreg., 1985—. Grantee

NSF. Mem. ACLU, Am. Psychol. Assn., Western Psychol. Assn. (chair com. status of women 1973-76), Oreg. Psychol. Assn. (chair legis. com. 1974-76), Oreg. Acad. Profl. Psychology, Am. Soc. Clin. Hypnosis. Democrat. Avocations: performing, stock market speculating, writing. Office: Munter and Castles PC 225 Westgate Sq 3800 SW Cedar Hills Blvd Beaverton OR 97005

MUNTZ, ANDREW JOHN, utility executive, magazine editor; b. Tacoma, Sept. 3, 1952; s. Robert William and Shirley Mae (Furseth) M.; m. Leslie Rena Anderson, July 26, 1975; children: Nathan, Aaron. BA in Communications, Wash. State U., 1974. Corp. editor Pay 'n Save Corp., Seattle, 1974-79, with employee devel. dept., 1981; dir. pub. relations Seafair, Inc., Seattle, 1979-80; cons. Edmonds, Wash., 1980-81; coordinator pub. info. Snohomish County Pub. Utilities Dist., Everett, Wash., 1981-86, mgr. pub. info., 1986-87, mgr. customer relations, 1987—; editor-in-chief Boatracing mag., Redmond, Wash., 1980—; chmn. bd. dirs. Muncey Prodns., Inc., Redmond. Author: Roostertails Unlimited, 1973; contbr. numerous articles to profl. pubs. Bd. dirs. Pilchuck Council Camp Fire, Inc., Everett, 1986—; vice chmn. pub. affairs com. Snohomish County celebrations of Wash. State Centennial, Everett, 1986—, publicity chmn. Squire Shop Unltd. Hydroplane Regatta, Seattle, 1978, Seafair Trophy Race, Seattle, 1977. Mem. Pub. Relations Soc. Am., Pub. Relations Roundtable, Boating Writers Internat, Am. Power Boat Assn. Lutheran. Clubs: Nat. Gray W., Seafair Boat (publicity chmn. 1977-79). Home: 14313 Beverly-Edmonds Rd Edmonds WA 98020 Office: Snohomish County Pub Utility Dist 2320 California St Everett WA 98201

MUNTZ, ERIC PHILLIP, aerospace engineering and radiology educator, consultant; b. Hamilton, Ont., Can., May 18, 1934; came to U.S., 1961, naturalized, 1985; s. Eric Percival and Marjorie Louise (Weller) M.; m. Janice Margaret Furey, Oct. 21, 1964; children: Sabrina Weller, Eric Phillip. B.A.Sc., U. Toronto, 1956, M.A.Sc., 1957, Ph.D., 1961. Halfback Toronto Argonauts, 1957-60; group leader Gen. Electric, Valley Forge, Pa., 1961-69; assoc. prof. aerospace engring. and radiology U. So. Calif., Los Angeles, 1969-71, prof., 1971-87, chmn. aerospace engring., 1987—; cons. to aerospace and med. device cos., 1967—; mem. rev. of physics (plasma and fluids) panel NRC, Washington, 1983-85. Contbr. numerous articles in gas dynamics and med. diagnostics to profl. publs., 1961—; patentee med. imaging, isotope separation, nondestructive testing. Mem. Citizens Environ. Adv. Council, Pasadena, Calif., 1972-76. U.S. Air Force grantee, 1961-74, 82—; NSF grantee, 1970-76; FDA grantee, 1980-86. Fellow AIAA (Aerospace Contbn. to Soc. award 1987); mem. Am. Assn. Physicists in Medicine. Episcopalian. Home: 1560 E California Blvd Pasadena CA 91106 Office: U So Calif University Park Los Angeles CA 90089

MUNZER, RUDOLPH JAMES, gas company executive; b. Mpls., Mar. 9, 1918; s. William Warren and Myrtle T. (Drysdale) M.; m. Daphne Donohue, June 29, 1946; children: Daniel, Anne, William. BA, Stanford U., 1940. V.p. Andrews Butane Co., Long Beach, Calif., 1946-54; with Petrolane Inc., Signal Hill, Calif., 1954—, exec. v.p., gen. mgr., 1955-57, pres., 1957-71, chmn. bd., 1971—; trustee Cash Mgmt. Trust Am.; bd. dirs. First Am. Title Ins. Co., Bond Fund Am., Inc., Tax-Exempt Bond Fund Am., Investment Co. Am., Los Angeles, Chubb Corp., N.Y.C. Bd. dirs. Long Beach Meml. Hosp., St. Anthony High Sch. Found., Jones Found. Served to lt. USNR, 1942-45. Mem. Nat. Liquefied Petroleum Gas Assn. (pres. 1960, hon. bd. dirs.). Clubs: Va. Country (Long Beach); Calif. (Los Angeles); Pauma Country (Pauma-San Diego County). Office: Petrolane Inc 1600 Hill St Long Beach CA 90806 *

MURAD, FERID, physician; b. Whiting, Ind., Sept. 14, 1936; s. John and Josephine (Bowman) M.; m. Carol Ann Leopold, June 21, 1958; children: Christine, Marianne, Carrie, Julie, Joseph. BA, De Paul U., 1958; MD, Case Western Reserve U., 1965, PhD, 1965. Diplomate Nat. Bd. Med. Examiners. Intern and resident Mass. Gen. Hosp., Boston, 1965-67; clin. assoc. NIH, Bethesda, Md., 1967-70; from assoc. prof. to prof. U. Va., Charlottesville, 1970-81, dir. clin. research ctr., 1971-81, dir. clin. pharmacology, 1973-81; prof. Stanford (Calif.) U., 1981—, assoc. chmn. dept. medicine, 1984—; chief of medicine VA Med. Ctr., Palo Alto, Calif., 1981—, chief. of medicine, 1981—. Assoc. editor Jour. Applied Cardiology, 1985—, co-editor The Pharmacological Basis of Therapeutics, 7th edit., 1985; patentee in field; contbr articles to profl. jours. Recipient numerous awards for accomplishments in field. Fellow ACP; mem. Am. Fedn. Clin. Research, Am. Soc. for Pharmacology and Exptl. Therapeutics, Albemarle Med. Soc., AAAS, Edocrine Soc., Va. Heart Assn. (research adv. com. 1971-75), Am. Coll. Clin. Pharmacology, So. Soc. Clin. Investigation, Assn. Clin. Research Ctr. Program Dirs., NIH Alumni Assn. (mem. task force Evaluation of Research Needs in Endocrinology and Metabolic Diseases 1978-79, ad hoc mem. Molecular Cytology study sect. 1979, Pathology study sect. 1979, Endocrinology Tng. Grant study sect. 1980, Pharmacology study sect. 1980, 84), Am. Cancer Soc. (ad hoc rev. and site vis. 1979), Am. Soc. Biol. Chemists, N.Y. Acad. Scis., Am. Soc. Clin. Investigation, Assn. Am. Physicians, Assn. VA Chiefs of Medicine, Western Assn. Physicians, NSF (ad hoc rev. 1982), Am. Heart Assn. (mem. Council on Basic Sci. 1984). Home: 27197 Black Mountain Rd Los Altos Hills CA 94022 Office: VA Med Ctr Dept Medicine Palo Alto CA 94304

MURAKAMI, HIDEO, comptroller, architect; b. Hilo, Hawaii, Oct. 17, 1930; s. Shozo and Shiho Murakami; m. Lillian Reiko Nakamoto, Dec. 18, 1953 (dec. 1977); children: Norman Ko, Peter Kan, Leo Shin; m. Teruko Ninagawa, Nov. 10, 1982. BS, Iowa State U., 1952; MS, Kans. State U., 1953. Registered architect, Hawaii, Kans., Washington. Archtl. apprentice, fellow Frank Lloyd Wright Found., Scottsdale, Ariz. and Spring Green, Wis., 1954; archtl. design draftsman V. Osipoff Architect, Honolulu, 1956, George Lee Architect, Honolulu, 1957-58; architect City and County of Honolulu, 1959; pvt. practice architecture Honolulu, 1959-74; state comptroller Hawaii, 1974—. Prin. works include Pagoda Hotel and Restaurant, Parker Elem. Sch., Moore Hall at the U. Hawaii, Nanakuli High Sch., Japan-Am. Inst. Mgmt. Sci., Hawaii Pavilion Expo 70, Osaka, Japan. Served with U.S. Army, 1954-56. Mem. ASTM, Am. Concrete Inst., Am. Specifications Inst., Nat. Assn. State Auditors, Comptrollers and Treasurers, Conf. State Gen. Service Officers. Democrat. Buddhist. Office: State Comptroller Dept Acctg and Gen Services 1151 Punchbowl St Honolulu HI 96813

MURANAGA, ALFRED SHIGEMI, electronics company executive; b. Stockton, Calif., Aug. 19, 1957; s. Yoshitaro and Mitsuye (Fujimoto) M. AA in Bus. Adminstrn. with honors, Coll. of San Mateo, 1978; postgrad., Calif. State U., San Francisco, 1978-80. Produce purchaser Lucky Stores, San Mateo, Calif., 1975-80; acct., asst. dir. Kmega Tech., Sunnyvale, Calif., 1980-81; v.p. KMEGA Tech., San Jose, Calif., 1981-83, pres., 1983—; founder Silicon Valley Bank, San Jose, 1982—. Mem. Propeller Club of the U.S., Delta Sigma Pi. Avocations: sports, computers, stereo equipment, finance. Home: 1230 Sierra Village Pl San Jose CA 95132 Office: Kmega Tech 2890 Zanker Rd Suite 201 San Jose CA 95134 Office: KMEGA GMBH, Villingen West Germany Office: KMEGA AG, Zurich Switzerland

MURARKA, ISHWAR PRASAD, research soil scientist; b. Nawalgarh, Rajasthan, India, Sept. 6, 1942; came to U.S., 1966; s. Misri Lall and Moni (Khemka) M.; m. Ragini S. Shah, May 19, 1972; children: Neel, Sameer. BA with honors, Calcutta (India) U., 1962, MA, 1964; MS, Oreg. State U., 1968, PhD, 1971; MBA, U. Chgo., 1979. Statistician Tex. Instruments, Verplank, N.Y., 1973-74; environ. scientist Argonne (Ill.) Nat. Lab., 1974-79; project mgr. Electric Power Research Inst., Palo Alto, Calif., 1979-83, sr. project mgr., 1983-85, subprogram mgr., 1985-86, program mgr., 1986—; adj. asst. prof. No. Ill. U., DeKalb, 1976-79. Author, editor: Solid Waste Disposal and Reuse in the U.S., 1987. Univ. Grants Commn. Jr. fellow Govt. India, Calcutta, 1965-66; NIH fellow, 9171-73. Mem. ASTM, Am. Geophys. Union, Am. Statis. Assn., Soil Sci. Soc. Am. (cert.), Am. Soc. Agronomy, Biometrics Soc., Council for Agrl. Scis. and Tech. (bd. dirs. 1987-89), Sigma Xi (life). Home: 6232 Via De Adrianna San Jose CA 95120 Office: Electric Power Research Inst 3412 Hillview Ave Palo Alto CA 94304

MURAWSKI, WILLIAM JOSEPH, art director; b. Chgo., Aug. 19, 1950; s. Joseph Edward and Vivian (Hansen) M.; m. Robin M. Bernstein, Aug. 17, 1980. BFA, Eastern Ill. U., 1973. Designer Rand McNally, Skokie, Ill., 1976-79; with Polar Communications Inc., Burbank, Calif., 1980—; art dir. Graphics Two div., Burbank, Calif., 1980—. Avocations: painting, golf, shopping. Office: Polar Communications Inc Graphics Two div. 819 S Main St Burbank CA 91506

MURDOCH, JOHN LAMONT, physician; b. Watford, Eng., Aug. 7, 1938; came to U.S., 1953; s. William Gordon and Ruth Mae (Rittenhouse) M.; m. Judith Ann Murdoch, Dec. 22, 1963 (dec. Sept. 1981); children: Julie, Linda, Patricia. BA, Columbia Union Coll., 1959; MD, Loma Linda U., 1963. Intern White Meml. Hosp., Los Angeles, 1963-64; resident Loma Linda (Calif.) U. Med. Ctr., 1964-66, fellow, 1966-67, mem. faculty, 1969—; fellow Johns Hopkins U., Balt., 1968-69. Named Clin. Tchr. of Yr., Macpherson Soc., 1975. Fellow ACP; mem. AMA, Endocrine Soc., Calif. Med. Assn., San Bernardino County Med. Assn., Alpha Omega Alpha. Republican. Adventist. Office: Loma Linda U Med Ctr Loma Linda CA 92350

MURDOCK, CAROL ANN, lawyer, nurse; b. New Albany, Ind., May 28, 1946; d. Ernest William Murdock and Charlotte Louise (King) Brown. BS in Nursing, Ind. U., 1968; MS in Nursing, UCLA, 1973; JD, Glendale U., 1983. Bar: Calif., 1984, D.C., 1984. Head nurse Cen. State Hosp., Indpls., 1968-69; staff nurse Mt. Sinai Hosp., Beverly Hills, Calif., 1970-71; asst. prof. nursing Pasadena (Calif.) City Coll., 1973-85; assoc. Law Office of John T. Tate Jr., Pasadena, 1983—; assoc. atty. Wills and Rifkin, A.P.C., South Pasadena, Calif., 1987—. Mem. ABA, Los Angeles County Bar Assn., Assn. Trial Lawyers Am. Home: 1933 Rodney Dr Apt 107 Los Angeles CA 90027

MURDOCK, DAVID H., diversified company executive; b. 1923; married. Chmn. Cannon Mills Co., Kannapolis, N.C., 1982-86, chief exec. officer, 1982-84; now sole proprietor, chmn. Pacific Holding Corp., Los Angeles, Calif.; also with Castle & Cooke, Inc., San Francisco, Calif., chmn., chief exec. officer, 1985—. Served with USAAF, 1941-45. Office: Pacific Holding Corp Murdock Plaza 10900 Wilshire Blvd N 1600 Los Angeles CA 90024 Office: Castle & Cooke Inc 50 California St San Francisco CA 94111 *

MURDOCK, PAMELA ERVILLA, wholesale travel company executive, retail travel company executive; b. Los Angeles, Dec. 3, 1940; d. John James and Chloe Conger (Keefe) M.; children—Cheryl, Kim. B.A., U. Colo., 1962. Pres., Dolphin Travel, Denver, 1972—, Mile Hi Tours, Denver, 1974—, MH Internat., 1987—. Named Wholesaler of Yr., Las Vegas Conv. and Visitors Authority, 1984. Mem. Am. Soc. Travel Agts., Colo. Assn. Commerce and Industry, Nat. Fedn. Independant Businessmen. Republican. Office: Mile Hi Tours Inc 2120 S Birch Denver CO 80222

MURDY, SUSAN M., public relations professional; b. Newport Beach, Calif., Sept. 19, 1955; d. John A. and Margie A. (Edmondson) M. BA in Broadcast Journalism, U. So. Calif., 1977. Acct. mgr. pub. relations Gloria Zigner & Assocs., Newport Beach, Calif., 1978-83; dir. pub. relations Carol Campbell & Co., Newport Beach, 1983-85; officer pub. relations Union Bank, Los Angeles, 1985—; bd. dirs. The Murdy Found. Inc., Freeway Indsl. Park. Contbr. articles to profl. jours. Mem. Newport Harbor Art Mus. Contbrs. Club, Newport Beach, 1984—, La Jolla Mus. Contemporary Art, 1985—, Los Angeles Conservancy, 1986—. Recipient MAME award Sales and Mktg. Council Bldg. Industry Assn. So. Calif., 1983, Protos awards Pub. Relations Soc. Am., 1981, 82. Mem. Pub. Relations Soc. Am., Publicity Club Los Angeles, Gamma Phi Beta. Club: Los Angeles Spinsters (v.p. 1984-85, publicity chmn. 1983-84). Avocations: travel, contemporary art, theater, music, dance. Office: Union Bank 445 S Figueroa St Los Angeles CA 92663

MURGEL, GEORGE ANTHONY, environmental engineer, consultant; b. Helena, Mont., Sept. 18, 1954; s. Anton G. and Irene Joyce (Petek) m.; m. Christine Ann Sadlowski, Nov. 25, 1978; 1 child, Joseph Anton Sadlowski. BSCE, Mont. State U., 1976, MSCE, 1978; postgrad., Cornell U., 1986—. Registered profl. engr., Mont. Environ. engr. Sverdrup & Parcel & Assocs., St. Louis, 1978-79, Edward C. Jordan Co., Inc., Portland, Maine, 1979-80, Stahly Engring. & Assocs., Kalispell, Mont., 1980-86. Mem. ASCE, Nat. Soc. Profl. Engrs., Am. Water Works Assn., Water Pollution Control Fedn. Roman Catholic. Avocations: stamp collecting, hiking, arts and crafts.

MURINE, GERALD EDWARD, software quality company executive; b. Struthers, Ohio, Feb. 24, 1934; s. John George and Agnus Marie (Majzun) M.; m. Carol Edna Jacque, Nov. 22, 1956; children: Kurt, Lynn, Brian, Eric. BS, Kent State U., 1956, MEd, 1959, MA, 1960; postgrad., U. Tex., Austin, 1961-62, Marquette U., 1963. Software engr. N.Am. Aviation, Downey, Calif., 1963-65; computer scientist Computer Scis. Corp., El Segundo, Calif., 1965-69; systems engr. Aerojet Electrosystems, Azusa, Calif., 1969-70; software mgr. McDonnell Douglas, Monrovia, Calif., 1970-79; mgr. dept. systems analysis Softech, Inc., San Diego, 1979-81; pres. Metriqs, Inc., Carlsbad, Calif., 1981—; asst. prof. math. John Caroll U., Cleve., 1961-63; asst. prof. U. So. Calif., Los Angeles, 1963-69; lectr. State-of-Art Seminars, Los Angeles, 1980-82, Nippon Electric Co., Tokyo, 1982, Mitsubishi Corp., 1983, Fusitsu Corp., 1984. Contbr. numerous tech. papers to profl. jours. Mem. IEEE, Assn. Unmanned Vehicles, Am. Soc. Quality Control, Soc. Software Quality. Avocations: music, reading, writing. Office: Metriqs Inc 390 Oak Ave Suite G Carlsbad CA 92008

MURKOWSKI, FRANK HUGHES, senator; b. Seattle, Mar. 28, 1933; s. Frank Michael and Helen (Hughes) M.; m. Nancy R. Gore, Aug. 28, 1954; children—Carol Victoria Murkowski Sturgulewski, Lisa Ann, Frank Michael, Eileen Marie Murkowski Van Wyke, Mary Catherine, Brian Patrick. Student, Santa Clara U., 1952-53; B.A. in Econs, Seattle U., 1955. With Pacific Nat. Bank of, Seattle, 1957-59; with Nat. Bank of Alaska, Anchorage, 1959-67; asst. v.p., mgr. Nat. Bank of Alaska (Wrangell br.), 1963-67; v.p. charge bus. devel. Nat. Bank of Alaska (Wrangell br.), Anchorage, 1965-67; commr. dept. econ. devel. State of Alaska, Juneau, 1967-70; pres. Alaska Nat. Bank of the North, Fairbanks, 1971-80; U.S. Senator from Alaska, 1981—; mem. Energy and Natural Resources Com., Vets. Affairs Com.; mem. Fairbanks adv. bd. Alaska Airlines. Vice pres. B.C. and Alaska Bd. Trade; Rep. nominee for U.S. Congress from Alaska, 1970. Served with USCGR, 1955-57. Mem. Am. Bankers Assn, Alaska Bankers Assn. (pres. 1973), Young Pres.'s Orgn. (Pacific NW chpt.), Alaska C of C (pres. 1977), Anchorage C of C (dir. 1966), B.C. C of C, Fairbanks C of C (dir. 1973-78). Clubs: Elks, Lions, Wash. Athletic. Office: 709 Hart Senate Bldg Washington DC 20510 *

MURPHEY, ROBERT WILLIAM, publishing company executive; b. Oakland, Calif., Oct. 30, 1933; s. John Patrick and Alice Julia (Knudsen) M.; m. Kay Louise Wandmaker, Apr. 13, 1957; children: Diane, Karen, Maureen, John. AA, Coll. San Mateo, 1954; BA, San Jose State U., 1956, MS, 1957; postgrad., Iowa State U., 1964. Mgmt. position Pacific Bell Co., Oakland and San Francisco, Calif., 1957-65; dist. mgr. Pacific Bell Co., San Diego, 1965-85; owner, pub. Fireside Pubs., San Diego, 1984—; instr. Chapman Coll., Orange and San Diego, Calif., 1986—, Grossmont Coll., El Cajon, Calif., 1986—, Southwestern Coll., Chula Vista, Calif., 1986—. Author: Methods and Procedures of Handling Employee Grieviences, 1957. Pres. Home of Guiding Hands, Lakeside, Calif., 1972-74, Home of Guiding Hands Found., 1975; 1st v.p. Cystic Fibrosis, San Diego, 1985. Mem. Navy League, Pi Kappa Alpha (pres. alumni 1957). Republican. Lutheran. Avocation: golf. Home and Office: 6490 Lake Shore Dr San Diego CA 92119

MURPHREE, A. LINN, pediatric ophthalmologist; b. Houston, Miss., June 6, 1945; d. John Alan and Maxine (Linn) M. BS, U. Miss., 1967; MD, Baylor Coll., 1972. Cert. Am. Bd. Ophthalmology. Resident affiliated hosps., 1973-76, chief resident ophthalmology, 1975-76; fellow ophthalmic genetics and pediatrics The Wilmer Inst., Johns Hopkins U. Hosp., 1976-77; asst. prof. ophthalmology and pediatrics U. So. Calif., Los Angeles, 1978-83, assoc. prof., 1983—, dir. pediatric and devel. ophthalmology, 1978—; head, div. ophthalmology Children's Hosp. Los Angeles, 1978—, dir. Clayton Found. Ctr. Ocular Oncology, 1978—; chief med. ops. Childrens Hosp. of Los Angeles, 1986—; profl. adv. com. Blind Children's Ctr., Los Angeles, 1980—; med. adv. bd. Nat. Assn. Visually Handicapped, 1980—. Contbr. numerous articles to profl. jours. Served to capt. med. corps., USAR, 1972-80. Dolly Green scholar Research to Prevent Blindness, 1984, Fulbright scholar U. Copenhagen, 1967-68; Medical Genetics fellow Baylor Coll. of Med. Affiliated Hosps., 1972-73. Mem. Calif. Assn. Ophthalmology, Calif. Med. Assn., Los Angeles County Med. Assn., Los Angeles Ophthalmol. Soc., Los Angeles Pediatric Soc., Ophthalmology Research Study Club Los Angeles, Pacific Coast Oto-Ophthalmol. Soc., Saleri Collegium, Am. Acad. Ophthalmology (honor award 1983), Am. Assn. Pediatric Ophthalmology and Strabismus, Am. Orthoptic Council, Assn. Research in Vision and Ophthalmology, Ophthalmic Genetics Study Club, Am. Bd. Ophthalmology (assoc. examiner), Internat. Soc. Genetic Eye Disease (sec. 1986—). Office: Childrens Hosp Los Angeles Div Ophthalmology 4650 Sunset Blvd Los Angeles CA 90027

MURPHY, BLANCHE MAXINE, speech pathologist; b. Shandon, Ohio, Oct. 22, 1916; d. Elmer P. and Margaret (Hayes) Heitfield; A.A. (Rotary scholar 1954), Ventura Coll., 1954; B.A. in Speech Therapy, Los Angeles State U., 1956; M.A. in Edn., U. Santo Tomas (Philippines), 1970; M.A. in Counseling Psychology, Ball State U., 1975; m. Harry Blaisdell Murphy, Aug. 24, 1952. Tchr., Santa Paula (Calif.) Sch. Dist., 1954-55, speech therapist, 1956-57; speech therapist Oxnard (Calif.) Sch. Dist., 1957-58, Ventura County (Calif.) Schs., 1958-61, Dept. Def. Dependent Schs., Clark Air Base, Republic of Philippines, 1961-70; speech pathologist Dept. Def. Dependent Schs., European Area, Sembach, Germany, 1970-77, Dept. Def. Dependent Schs., Okinawa, Japan, 1977—; speaker edn. seminars, in-service tng. Pacific Area Command Air Force, 1963-70; condr. workshops for Am. tchrs. Am. Sch., Saigon, Viet Nam, 1963. Recipient Ofcl. commendation for outstanding performance Dept. Army, 1976, Outstanding Service and Conduct award Dept. Def. Dependent Schs., Sembach, 1976; Outstanding Contbn. award as sec. of conf. European Council Parents and Students, 1977; lic. speech pathologist State of Calif. Mem. NEA, Am. Speech and Hearing Assn. (cert. clin. competence in speech pathology 1969), Calif. Speech and Hearing Assn., Am. Personnel and Guidance Assn., Overseas Edn. Assn., Council for Exceptional Children, Phi Delta Kappa, Pi Lambda Theta. Episcopalian. Author: Speech Improvement for First Grade Children, 1970; Speech Improvement of the Primary School Child Through Ear Training Techniques, 1975. Home: PO Box 833 FPO Seattle WA 98773 Home: 1804 Parkside Terr, Okinawa Japan

MURPHY, CAROL LEE, speech pathologist, consultant; b. Oakland, Calif., June 12, 1947; d. Robert Thomas and Mildred Nadine (Hill) Ouillett; m. William Francis Murphy, Aug. 22, 1970; children: Ryan Patrick, Kathryn Jeanine. BS, San Jose State U., 1970, MS, 1976. Itinerant speech pathologist Richmond (Calif.) Unified Schs., 1970-74; pvt. practice speech pathologist, cons. Santa Cruz (Calif.) County, 1974-76; tchr. severe lang. disorders Office of Edn., Santa Cruz, 1974-76, speech pathologist, 1976-78; resource specialist Mountain Sch. Dist., Soquel, Calif., 1978-83; owner, dir. Speech and Learning Services, Aptos, Calif., 1983—; cons. Santa Cruz Learing Ctr., 1983—. Mem. Am. Speech-Lang.-Hearing Assn. (cert. clin. competence), Calif. Speech-Lang.-Hearing Assn., Santa Cruz Speech-Lang.-Hearing Assn. (pres. 1977-78). Republican. Roman Catholic. Avocation: fitness dancing. Office: Speech and Learning Services PO Box 2257 Aptos CA 95001

MURPHY, DENNIS RAE, economics educator, administrator; b. Rocanville, Sask., Can., Oct. 23, 1941; came to U.S., 1956, naturalized, 1976; s. Ray J. and Dorothy E. (Woods) M.; m. Sandra L. Olson, June 15, 1962; 1 son, James Rush. B.A. in Econs., Western Wash. U., 1969, M.A. in Econs., 1970; Ph.D., Ind. U., 1974. Assoc. instr. Ind. U., Bloomington, 1972-73, lectr., 1973-74, asst. prof., 1975-76; asst. prof. Emory U., Atlanta, 1976-79; assoc. prof. Western Wash. U., Bellingham, 1979-84, prof., 1985—, M.B.A. program dir., 1982-83 , dean Coll. Bus. and Econs., 1983—; cons. in field. Contbr. articles to profl. jours. Book rev. editor Pub. Fin. Quar., 1981-83. NSF grantee, 1978-80; McMaster fellow, 1970-71; recipient Teaching award Ind. U., 1973. Mem. Am. Econ. Assn., Soc. Econs. Assn. Republican. Methodist. Home: 507 14th St Bellingham WA 98225 Office: Coll Bus and Econs Western Wash U Bellingham WA 98225

MURPHY, FRANCIS SEWARD, journalist; b. Portland, Oreg., Sept. 9, 1914; s. Francis H. and Blanche (Livesay) M.; B.A., Reed Coll., 1936; m. Clare Eastham Cooke, Sept. 20, 1974. With The Oregonian, Portland, 1936-79, TV editor, Behind the Mike columnist, 1952-79. Archeol. explorer Mayan ruins, Yucatan, Mex., 1950—, mem. Am. Quintana Roo Expdn., 1965, 66, 68. Served with AUS, 1942-46. Mem. Royal Asiatic Soc., Royal Hong Kong Jockey Club. Democrat. Congregationalist. Clubs: City (bd. govs. 1950, 64-66); Explorers, Am. Club of Hong Kong. Home: 4213 NE 32d Ave Portland OR 97211 Home: 1102 Tavistock,, 10 Tregunter Path,, Hong Kong Hong Kong

MURPHY, FRANKLIN DAVID, physician, educator, publisher; b. Kansas City, Mo., Jan. 29, 1916; s. Franklin E. and Cordelia (Brown) M.; m. Judith Joyce Harris, Dec. 28, 1940; children: Judith (Mrs. Walter Dickey), Martha (Mrs. Craig Crockwell), Carolyn Murphy Milner, Franklin. A.B., U. Kans., 1936; M.D., U. Pa., 1941. Diplomate: Am. Bd. Internal Medicine. Intern Hosp. U. Pa., 1941-42, instr., 1942-44; instr. medicine U. Kans., 1946-48, dean Sch. Medicine, assoc. prof. medicine, 1948-51, chancellor, 1951-60; chancellor UCLA, 1960-68; chmn. bd., chief exec. officer Times Mirror Co., 1968-81, chmn. exec. com., 1981-86; trustee J. Paul Getty Trust; dir. emeritus Times-Mirror Co. Chmn. Kress Found., Nat. Gallery of Art.; trustee Los Angeles County Mus. Art. Served to capt. AUS, 1944-46. Named One of Ten Outstanding Young Men U.S. Jr. C. of C., 1949; recipient Outstanding Civilian Service award U.S. Army, 1967. Fellow A.C.P.; mem. Phi Beta Kappa, Sigma Xi, Alpha Omega Alpha, Beta Theta Pi, Nu Sigma Nu. Episcopalian. Home: 419 Robert Ln Beverly Hills CA 90210 : Times Mirror Co Times Mirror Sq Los Angeles CA 90053

MURPHY, JOHN THOMAS, lawyer; b. Pierre, S.D., July 20, 1932; s. Bernard J. and Gertrude (Loner) M.; LL.B., U. S.D., 1957; m. Rose Marie Cogorno. Admitted to S.D. bar, 1957, Calif. bar, 1962; practiced Stockton, Calif., 1965-75, Modesto, Calif., 1975—; atty. Office Gen. Counsel Q.M. Gen. Dept. of Army, 1957-58; asst. chief counsel Sharpe Army Depot, 1958-63, gen. counsel, 1963-65; assoc. Short, Short, Scott & Murphy, and predecessor firm, 1965-68; partner Hulsey, Beus, Wilson, Scott & Murphy, Stockton, 1968-70. Sec. Golden Bear Assn. Beagle Clubs. Bd. dirs. Delta-Stockton Humane Soc., 1970-75; bd. govs. Calif. Trout Inc. Mem. State Bar Calif., Assn. Trial Lawyers Am., Calif. Trial Lawyers Assn., Beta Theta Pi, Phi Delta Phi. Republican. Episcopalian. Clubs: Commonwealth, Stockton Beagler's (sec., dir.), Am. Kennel (Beagle adv. com. 1984-86). Home: 2162 Parkridge Dr Modesto CA 95355 Office: 1104 12th St Modesto CA 95353

MURPHY, JOSEPH PATRICK, internist; b. Casper, Wyo., Aug. 5, 1927; s. Patrick Joseph and Hester Theresa (Sullivan) M.; B.S., Notre Dame U., 1945; M.D., Stritch Sch. Medicine, Chgo., 1949; m. Rita Frances Sullivan, Oct. 24, 1953; children—Patrick, Mary Ann, Donald, Kevin, Mark, Sheila, Michelle, Rita, Kathleen, Maureen, Robert, Anne. Intern, U. Colo. Med. Center, Denver, 1949-50, resident in internal medicine, 1950-51, 53-55; pvt. practice medicine, specializing in internal medicine, Denver, 1955-56, Casper, 1957—; chief of staff Natrona County Meml. Hosp., 1962-64; pres. Casper Clinic, 1976-77; coordinator continuing med. edn. U. Wyo.; mem. faculty medicine U. Colo. Med. Center, 1955-57; mem. sci. adv. bd. Colo.-Wyo. Arthritis and Rheumatism Found. Columnist Progress Notes, Casper Star-Tribune; mem. editorial bd. Patient Care Jour., Western Jour. Medicine. Bd. dirs. Central Wyo. Counseling Center, 1972-75; vol. physician for Vietnam, 1966, Mex., 1972. Served with M.C., AUS, 1951-53; Japan, Korea. Decorated Distinguished Service award; recipient Nat. Vol. Service citation Arthritis Found., 1978. Fellow A.C.P. (gov. 1979-84); mem. Wyo. Soc. Internal Medicine (pres. 1968-70), Wyo., Natrona County med. socs., AMA, U. Notre Dame Alumni Assn. (bd. dirs.), Am. Soc. Internal Medicine, Cath. Physicians Guild (nat. dir. 1976-78). Roman Catholic. Home: 3200 Hawthorne Ave Casper WY 82604 Office: The Medical Annex 3210 Hawthorne Ave Casper WY 82604

MURPHY, KEVIN CLIFFORD, psychologist; b. Mpls., May 19, 1944; s. Clifford Joseph and Helen (Eastum) M.; m. Judith Anne Light, June 23, 1968; children—Leah, Jozanna, Matthew, Darren. B.A., U. Minn., 1966, Ph.D., 1970. Lic. psychologist. Mont. Asst. prof. U. Western Ont., London, Can., 1970-76, dir. counseling, 1972-77; asst. prof. U. Minn., 1977-82; head psychology Missoula Community Hosp., Mont., 1982—, dir. pain program, 1983—. Contbr. articles to profl. jours. Mem. Am. Psychol. Assn., Mont. Psychol. Assn. Democrat. Home: 103 Takima Dr Missoula MT 59803 Office: Missoula Community Hosp 2827 Ft Missoula Rd Missoula MT 59801

MURPHY, KEVIN ROBERT, computer company executive; b. Albany, N.Y., Mar. 5, 1942; s. Arthur Joseph and Marjorie (Ward) M.; student Holy Cross Coll., 1959-60; B.S., U.S. Mil. Acad., 1964; postgrad. Bucknell U., 1969-70; m. Joanne Maloy Howell, Sept. 6, 1964; children—Arthur, Brendan, Brian. With IBM, various locations, 1970-81, adminstrv. asst., Atlanta, 1979-80, nat. sales mgr., 1980-81; v.p. field ops. Pt 4 Data Corp., Irvine, Calif., 1981-82; v.p. sales the TRW-Fujitsu Co., Los Angeles, 1982-84; sr. v.p. mktg. Fujitsu Systems Am., 1984—. Served to capt. U.S. Army, 1964-70; Vietnam. Decorated Air medal, Bronze Star. Mem. Assn. Grads. U.S. Mil. Acad., West Point Club So. Calif. Roman Catholic.

MURPHY, LEWIS CURTIS, mayor of Tucson; b. N.Y.C., Nov. 2, 1933; s. Henry Waldo and Elizabeth Wilcox (Curtis) M.; m. Carol Carney, Mar. 10, 1957; children—Grey, Timothy, Elizabeth. B.S. in Bus. Adminstrn, U. Ariz., 1955, LL.B., 1961. Bar: Ariz. bar 1961. Individual practice law Tucson, 1961-66; trust officer So. Ariz. Bank & Trust Co., 1966-70; atty. City of Tucson, 1970-71; mayor 1971—; mem. law firm Schroeder and Murphy, Tucson, 1978—; trustee U.S. Conf. Mayors, 1978—, chmn. transp. com., 1984—; mem. pub. safety steering com. Nat. League Cities, 1973—, mem. transp. steering com., 1973—; exec. bd. Ariz. League Cities and Towns; v.p. Central Ariz. Project Assn., 1978; exec. com. Orgn. U.S. Border Cities, 1977; mem. Region IX Intergovtl. Relations Com., 1977. Served with USAF, 1955-58. Mem. Ariz. Bar Assn., Pima County Bar Assn., Ariz. Acad. Republican. Presbyterian. Office: PO Box 27210 Tucson AZ 85726

MURPHY, LINDA SUE, city official; b. Lynchburg, Va., June 7, 1948; d. Carter P. and Dorothy L. (Clark) Tucker; m. Daniel K. Murphy, Mar. 25, 1972; 1 child, Krystal Grace. Student, Longwood Coll., 1966-68. Exec. sec. First Nat. Bank of Anchorage, Seward, Alaska, 1976-80; clk. of ct., asst. magistrate Alaska Ct. System, Seward, 1980-81; city clk., personnel officer City of Seward, 1981—. Sec., Seward Concert Assn., 1982; chmn. Seward Sch. Adv. Bd., 1983; v.p. bd. dirs. Seward Life Action Council, 1983-84, pres. bd. dirs., 1984—; chmn. Seward-Obihiro Sister City Com., 1984. Mem. Internat. Inst. Mcpl. Clks., Alaska Assn. Mcpl. Clerks (sec. 1984-85, v.p. 1985-87, pres. 1986—), Alaska Women in Govt. (v.p. 1985-86). Democrat. Home: NHN Salmon Creek Rd Seward AK 99664 Office: Seward City Hall PO Box 167 Seward AK 99664

MURPHY, MARTIN JAMES, astrophysicist; b. Washington, May 22, 1951; s. Francis Thomas and Frances Marie (Scott) M.; m. Kathleen Louise Marquess, Oct.1, 1977; 1 child, Lauren Alicia. BS, Brown U., 1973; PhD, U. Chgo., 1980. Research assoc. U. Calif., Berkeley, 1979-82; research faculty U. Wash., Seattle, 1982-85; research sci. Lockheed Research Lab., Palo Alto, Calif., 1985—. Contbr. articles to profl. jours. Mem. AAAS, Am. Phys. Soc., Sigma Xi (assoc.). Home: 1777 Walnut St San Carlos CA 94070 Office: Lockheed Research Lab 3251 Hanover St 9120/255 Palo Alto CA 94304

MURPHY, MICHAEL LEO, retail food products executive; b. Glendale, Calif., Sept. 21, 1948; s. Glenn Eugene and Ila May (Draper) M.; m. Lucy Ann Brown, May 27, 1971; children: Michael, Amanda, Erin, Aimee. BA, Brigham Young U., 1972. Mall mgr. E.W. Hahn, Inc., Billings (Mont.), San Jose (Calif.), Murray (Utah) and Newport (Va., 1972-78, L.B. Nelson Corp., Mountain View, Calif., 1978-79; real estate sales rep. Coldwell Banker Co., San Jose, 1979-80; sr. v.p. Mrs. Fields Cookies, Park City, Utah, 1980—, also bd. dirs.; lectr. Brigham Young U., Provo, 1984-85, U. Wash., Seattle, 1984-85; with property mgmt. dept. Alexian Bros. Hosp., San Jose, 1981-84. Coach Little League Baseball, Sandy, Utah, 1973, Am. Youth Soccer Orgn., San Jose, 1978-80; cubmaster San Jose council Boy Scouts Am., 1981-82, com. chmn. 1985-86. Recipient Key to City Mayor of City of Billings, 1975, Devoted Service award Mrs. Fields Cookies, 1981, Excellence in Achievement award, 1985. Mem. Internat. Council Shopping Ctrs. (moderator 1977, lectr. 1981, chmn. panel 1982-83). Republican. Mormon. Lodges: Rotary, Sons of Utah Pioneers. Avocations: sailing, tennis, percussion music. Office: Mrs Fields Cookies 333 Main St Park City UT 84060

MURPHY, MICHAEL PATRICK, analytical chemist, laboratory administrator; b. Williams AFB, Ariz., May 21, 1949; s. Roland R. and Doyce Ray (Manning) Kruse; m. Mary Ellen Sheston, May 19, 1980; children: Patrick, Ann, Daniel. AA, Phoenix Coll., 1974; BS, Ariz. State U., 1976, PhD, 1982. Sr. research chemist Dow Chemical, Pittsburg, Calif., 1982-85, project leader, 1985—; program chmn. Pacific Conf. on Chemistry and Spectroscopy, 1984; conf. chmn., 1985. Adv. Jr. Achievement, Antioch, Calif., 1983. Served to sgt. U.S. Army, 1967-71. Mem. Am. Chem. Soc., Soc. Applied Spectroscopy (officer No. Calif. chpt. 1985—), Phi Lambda Upsilon (treas.), Alpha Chi Sigma (master of ceremonies). Republican. Roman Catholic. Avocations: racquetball, camping, hiking. Office: Dow Chemical PO Box 1398 Pittsburg CA 94565

MURPHY, ROY EMERSON, computer scientist, economist; b. Indpls., Sept. 30, 1926; m. Joyce Harley, Sept. 21, 1951; children: Mark T., Kathleen H. BSEE, Purdue U., 1950; MSEE, U. Conn., 1956; PhD, Stanford U., 1962. Registered profl. engr., Calif. V.p. research and devel. Quantum Sci. Corp., Palo Alto, Calif., 1962-68; pres. Info. Telecommunications Corp., Sunnyvale, Calif., 1968-72; v.p. research and devel. Computer Usage Co., Palo Alto, 1972-73, Lex Computer Systems, Menlo Park, Calif., 1973-83, Azuray Inc., Scott's Valley, Calif., 1983—; mem. faculty U. Conn., Storrs, 1956-58, Stanford (Calif.) U., 1962-64. Author: Adaptive Processes, 1965; patentee in field. Served with USN, 1944-46. Varian fellow Varian Family, 1958-62. Mem. IEEE, Soc. Info. Display, Sigma Xi. Avocations: amateur radio, model railroading. Office: Azuray Inc 5 Victor Square Scott's Valley CA 95066

MURPHY, SUSAN LYNN, marketing company executive; b. Flint, Mich., Dec. 12, 1951; d. Edward Conrad and Joanne Loraine (Valentine) Arndt; children by previous marriage—Kerry Elizabeth, Kelly Michael. B.S., U. Mich.-Flint, 1974. Advt. dir. Ross Showrooms, Grand Blanc, Mich., 1971-73; asst. advt. dir. Sybra Inc., Grand Blanc, 1973-76; v.p. Marr Mktg., Grand Blanc, 1976-81; prin. Murphy Mktg. Inc., Salt Lake City, 1981-86; pres., owner The Gentry and The Lady, Salt Lake City. Mem. Utah Advt. Fedn., DAR (charter Grand Blanc chpt.); ruling elder Presbyterian Ch. Republican. Office: care The Gentry and the Lady Hilton Hotel 150 W 500 S Salt Lake City UT 84101

MURPHY, TERENCE MARTIN, botany educator; b. Seattle, July 1, 1942; s. Norman Walter and Dorothy Louise (Smith) M.; m Judith Baron, July 12, 1969; 1 child, Shannon Elaine. BS, Calif. Inst. Tech., 1964; PhD, U. Calif. San Diego, La Jolla, 1968. Sr. fellow dept. biochemistry U. Wash., Seattle, 1969-70; asst. prof. botany U. Calif., Davis, 1971-76, assoc. prof., 1976-82, prof., 1982—, chmn. dept. botany, 1986—. Contbr. articles to profl. jours. Mem. AAAS, Am. Soc. Plant Physiologists, Am. Soc. Photobiology, Internat. Soc. Plant Molecular Biology, Scandinavian Soc. Plant Physiology. Home: 725 N Campus Way Davis CA 95616 Office: U Calif Dept Botany Davis CA 95616

MURPHY, THOMAS JOSEPH, bishop; b. Chgo., Oct. 3, 1932; s. Barthomew Thomas and Nellie M. A.B., St. Mary of the Lake Sem., 1954, S.T.B., 1956, M.A., 1957, S.T.L., 1958, S.T.D., 1960. Ordained priest Roman Catholic Ch., 1958; various positions with Archdiocese of Chgo.; bishop of Great Falls-Billings Mont., 1978-87; coadjutor bishop of Seattle 1987—. Office: Archdiocese of Seattle 910 Marion St Seattle WA 98104

MURPHY, WILLIAM JOSEPH, business systems marketing professional; b. Lawrence, Mass., Sept. 12, 1945; s. Joseph William and Elsie (Boucher) M.; m. Brenda Claire LaChance, June 21, 1969; children: Cheryl, Kristin. BSEE, Tufts U., 1967; MBA, San Diego State U., 1973. Engr. electronics Gen. Electric Co., Pittsfield, Mass., 1967-69; mgr. product mktg. Hewlett Packard Co., San Diego, 1968-75; mktg. mgr. Hewlett Packard Co., Boise, Idaho, 1975-81, group mktg. mgr., 1981-83; personal computer field and group mktg. mgr. Hewlett Packard Co., Cupertino, Calif., 1983-86, bus. systems sector mktg. mgr., 1986—. Chmn. bd. dirs. Boise chpt. ARC, 1978-83, Santa Clara chpt., 1986—, also chmn. personnel com. and bd. dirs. San Jose (Calif.) chpt.; bd. dirs. Boise chpt. United Way, 1981-83, Bogos Basin Recreation Assn., Boise, 1982-83. Mem. Am. Mgmt. Assn., Mktg. Council of Am. Mgmt. Assn. Avocations: tennis, golf, skiing, fly fishing. Office: Hewlett-Packard Co 19091 Prune Ridge Ave Cupertino CA 95014

MURRAY, BARBARA OLIVIA, psychologist; b. Summit, N.J., July 8, 1947; d. Archibald and Anna Cutler (Mattison) M.; student Inst. d'Etudes Francaises Pour Etrangers, France, 1965, Universite de Grenoble, France, 1968; B.A. in Psychology, Lake Erie Coll., 1969; M.A. in Clin. Psychology, Cleve. State U., 1971; postgrad. Gestalt Inst. Cleve., 1971-73; Ph.D. in Clin. Psychology, Calif. Sch. Profl. Psychology, Fresno, 1976. Mental health worker Cleve. Clinic Hosp., 1970-71, assoc. psychologist, 1971-73; psychiat. intake worker Cleve. Free Clinic, 1971, group leader, 1972; cons. St. John's Coll., Cleve., 1972-73; psychology intern Fresno County Dept. Health, 1973-75, student profl. worker, 1974; mem. faculty Calif. Sch. Profl. Psychology, Fresno, 1974; psychology intern Calif. State U., Fresno, 1975, lectr., 1976-77; treatment program dir. E. Ross Clark Home for Children, Inc., Modesto, Calif., 1976-77; clin. psychologist Santa Cruz County (Calif.) Community Mental Health Services, 1977-79, dir. psychol. services, 1979-83; pvt. practice psychotherapy, Soquel, Calif., 1979—; mem. Dominican Hosp. med. staff, 1983—, Citizens Involvement Assocs., 1984—; vice chair dept. psychiatry/psychology, 1985—; adj. faculty Pacific Grad. Sch. Psychology, 1984—; cons. NOW, 1973-76, Community Hosp., Fresno, 1974; expert witness Santa Cruz and San Francisco counties, 1979—, law and ethics workshop, 1984, CPI-MMPI workshop, 1986, child sexual assault asst. workshop, 1986. Mem. Women's Studies Adv. Bd., Fresno, 1975-76. Recipient Disting. Psychologist award Calif. State Psychol. Assn., 1982. Hill scholar, 1968, Smith scholar, 1969, Fritz Perls scholar, 1970; lic. psychologist, Calif. Mem. Am. Psychol. Assn., Western Assn. Women Psychologists, Western Psychol. Assn., Calif. State Psychol. Assn. (bd. dirs. Observer 1981-83), Mid-Coast Psychol. Assn. (pres. 1981, forensic chmn. 1983—), Psychol. Inst., Forensic Mental Health Assn., No. Calif. Psychologists for Social Responsibility, Laurel Soc., Psi Chi (v.p. 1968-69), Kappa Alpha Sigma. Club: Cotuit Mosquito Yacht Contbr. articles to jours. in psychology. Home and Office: 4595 Fairway Dr Soquel CA 95073

MURRAY, BRIAN JOSEPH, retired data processing executive; b. Chgo., May 26, 1940; s. Harry F. and Ann M. (Kelly) M.; m. Carole J. VanLanen, Aug. 20, 1980; 1 child, Kellie A. B.S.I.E., Ill. Inst. Tech., 1962; M.B.A., U. Chgo., 1971. Systems engr. IBM, Chgo., 1966-68; mgr. data processing Canteen Corp., Chgo., 1968-69; asst. mgr. info. services Boise Cascade, Chgo., 1969-77, group mgr. data processing, Portland, Oreg., 1977-86. Served to lt. USN, 1962-66. Mem. Paper Industry Mgmt. Assn. (chmn. mgmt. info. systems com. 1984-82), Am. Paper Inst. (mgmt. info. systems com.). Republican. Home: 11190 SW Lynnvale Dr Portland OR 97225

MURRAY, EDWARD FRANCIS, III, lawyer; b. Cheyenne, Wyo., Mar. 28, 1958; s. Edward Francis Jr. and Barbara Ann (Bourne) M.; m. Catherine Martin McInerney, Aug. 30, 1986. BSBA, U. Ariz., 1980; JD, U. Wyo., 1983. Bar: Wyo. 1984, U.S. Dist. Ct. Wyo. 1984, U.S. Tax Ct. 1984; lic. in real estate. Atty. Dray, Madison & Thomson P.C., Cheyenne, Wyo., 1984—. Bd. dirs. Retired Citizens Vol. Project, Cheyenne, 1985—, Christian Counseling Service, Cheyenne, 1984-85. Mem. Wyoming Trial Lawyers Assn., Laramie County Bar Assn., Wyoming State Bar Assn., Assn. Trial Lawyers Am., Cheyenne C. of C. (bd. dirs. fin. planning sect.). Republican. Roman Catholic. Clubs: Cheyenne Country, Rocky Mountain (Cheyenne). Avocations: outdoor activities, religious activities, philosophy. Office: Dray Madison & Thomson PC 204 E 22d St Cheyenne WY 82001

MURRAY, JO BUMBARGER, public relations executive; b. Scotland County, N.C., Oct. 8, 1945; d. Paul William and Sara (Ward) B.; m. Cecil Lawrence Murray, July 12, 1967 (div. 1979); m. Harre Wilkins Demoro, Mar. 1, 1986. BA, Mich. State U., 1967. Writer Del. River Port Authority Log, Camden, N.J., 1968-69; assoc. editor Oakland (Calif.) Tribune, 1972-81; prin. Jo Murray Pub. Relations, Oakland, 1981—. Recipient writing award State Bar Calif., 1975, feature writing award Press Club San Francisco, 1975, Best Pub. Service Reporting In-State award Sigma Delta Chi N.J. chpt., 1968, Best News Writing Phila. area award Sigma Delta Chi Phila. chpt., 1968. Mem. Pub. Relations Soc. Am. (v.p. 1987, sec. East Bay chpt. 1986, chair profl. devel. com. 1985), Alameda/Contra Costa County Bench/Bar Com. (chmn. 1981), Bay Area Electric RR Assn. Democrat. Club: Lakeview (Oakland). Mem. expedition on Mt. McKinley, Alaska, 1975, completed 175-mile trek through Nepal on foot, 1981. Avocations: skiing, backpacking, contract bridge. Office: 4100 Redwood Rd Suite 200 Oakland CA 94619

MURRAY, JOHN FREDERIC, physician, educator; b. Mineola, N.Y., June 8, 1927; s. Frederic S. and Dorothy M.; m. Diane Lain, Nov. 30, 1968; children—James R., Douglas S., Elizabeth. A.B., Stanford, 1949, M.D., 1953; D.Sc. (hon.), U. Paris, 1983. From instr. to asso. prof. medicine U. Calif. at Los Angeles, 1957-66; mem. sr. staff Cardiovascular Research Inst., U. Calif., San Francisco, 1966—; asso. prof. medicine Cardiovascular Research Inst., U. Calif. (Sch. Medicine), 1966-69, prof., 1969—; chief chest service San Francisco Gen. Hosp., 1966—; Vis. prof. Brompton Inst. for Diseases of the Chest, London, 1972-73; Macy faculty scholar Inst. Nat. de la Santé et de la Recherche Medicale, Paris, 1979-80; mem. adv. council and pulmonary disease adv. com. Nat. Heart, Lung and Blood Inst.; mem. clin. studies panel NRC.; bd. govs. Am. Bd. Internal Medicine, bd. govs. Am. Bd. Emergency Medicine. Author: The Normal Lung; co-author: Diseases of the Chest, 4th edit; Editor: Am. Rev. Respiratory Disease, 1973-79; Contbr. articles to profl. jours. Bd. govs. Am. Bd. Emergency Medicine. Served with USNR, 1945-46. Mem. Assn. Am. Physicians, Am. Soc. Clin. Investigators, Am. Physiol. Soc., Western Soc. Clin. Research, Western Assn. Physicians, Am. Thoracic Soc. (pres. 1981-82). Home: 24 Edith Pl San Francisco CA 94133 Office: Chest Service SK1 San Francisco Gen Hosp San Francisco CA 94110

MURRAY, KATHLEEN ELLEN, editor; b. Chgo., Feb. 23, 1946; d. John Joseph and Marie Agnes (Stoltzman) M.; B.A., Calif. State U., Sacramento, 1973; A.A., Am. River Coll., 1968. File clk. Allstate Ins. Co., Sacramento, 1964-66; clk. typist Calif. Hwy. Patrol, Sacramento, 1968-69; copy editor Sacramento Bee, 1971—; instr. Calif. State U., Sacramento, 1975-76. Newspaper Fund intern, scholar, 1971. Club: Sacramento Press. Home: PO Box 606 Nevada City CA 95959

MURRAY, PATRICIA ANN, periodontist; b. Cambridge, Mass., Oct. 6, 1949; d. William John Jr. and Edna Lucille (Maguire) M.; m. Joseph David Thornton, Aug. 29, 1970 (div. July 1974). BA magna cum laude, Boston Coll., 1971; DMD, U. Conn., 1979; PhD, SUNY, Buffalo, 1984. Tchr. Scarborough (Maine) High Sch., 1971-74; postdoctoral fellow SUNY, 1979-83; asst. prof. U. Calif., San Francisco, 1983—; dental cons. Letterman Hosp., San Francisco, 1983—; grad. program dir. U. Calif., San Francisco, 1984—; continuing edn. dir. U. Calif., San Francisco, 1986. Co-author: Anaerobic Bacteria, 1983; contbr. articles to sci. jours. NIH postdoctoral fellow, 1979-83; grantee 1985—; recipient Young Scientist award 1983-86. Fellow Am. Acad. Periodontology; mem. ADA, Internat. Assn. Dental Research, Am. Soc. Microbiologists. Roman Catholic. Avocations: skiing, sailing, running, aerobics, dance. Home: 372 24th Ave San Francisco CA 94121 Office: U Calif HSW 661 Box 0512 San Francisco CA 94143

MURRAY, ROBERT GERALD, financial executive; b. Portland, Oreg., Mar. 4, 1937; s. Robert Byrd and Geraldine (Ley) M.; m. Janice L. Wheatley, Sept. 9, 1962; children—Kevin B., Stacie A. B.S., Portland State U., 1962; postgrad., U. Oreg., 1962-64, Harvard Bus. Sch., 1970. Chartered fin. analyst. Asst. v.p., dir. research trust div. First Interstate Bank, Portland, Oreg., 1964-69; sr. investment officer St. Paul Cos., 1969-75; asst. v.p., then v.p., sr. v.p., mgr. investment services First Interstate Bank, Portland, 1975-81, sr. v.p. trust fin. services, 1981-82, exec. v.p. trust fin. services, 1982—. Fin. chmn. pioneer dist. Boy Scouts Am.; trustee Med. Research Found., Waverley Children's Home; trustee, chmn. bd. trustees Marylhurst Coll. Served with U.S. Army, 1956-59. Mem. Inst. Chartered Fin. Analysts (council examiner 1974-78, research com. 1975-77), Am. Bankers Assn. (investment com.), Am. Inst. Banking, Portland C. of C. (bd. dirs.), Fin. Analysts Fedn., Portland Analyst Soc. (pres. 1968-69). Republican. Episcopalian. Clubs: Portland Golf, University, Arlington. Home: 939 SE Lakefront Rd Lake Oswego OR 97034 Office: First Interstate Bank of Oreg 1300 SE 5th Ave Portland OR 97201

MURRAY, SPENCER JACK, hospital administrator; b. Urbana, Ill., Feb. 4, 1936; s. Spencer J. and Agnes L. (Smith) M.; B.A., U. Wash., 1967, M.P.A., 1975; m. Peggy Patricia Gray, Aug. 18, 1962; children—Spencer, Derek, Brandon, Brenda. Asst. mgr. Capitol Music Co., 1963-65; graphic illustrator Boeing Co., 1965-67; employment interviewer, employment mgr., asst. to personnel dir., asst. hosp. adminstr. for personnel U. Wash. Hosp., Seattle, 1973-74, asst. hosp. adminstr. for patient care, 1975—; treas. Wash. State Hosp. Safety Council, 1979. Trustee Seattle Children's Home, Community Psychiatry Center, Seattle. Served with USNG, 1961-66. Mem. Am. Hosp. Assn. Roman Catholic. Club: Rotary. Home: 15840 37th St NE Seattle WA 98155 Office: 1959 NE Pacific St Seattle WA 98195

MURRAY, WILLIAM HOWARD, computer components marketing executive; b. Boston, July 16, 1952; s. Wallace Shordon and Eleanor Muriel (Grandy) M.; m. Linda Joan Kelly, Dec. 6, 1980; 1 child, Jennifer Lynn. BA in Psychology, BA in Anthropology, U. Calif., Santa Barbara, 1974. Sales adminstr. Okidata Corp., Santa Barbara, 1974-81; dir. mktg. and sales Info. Magnetics Corp., San Diego, 1981—. Choreographer (ballet) Reveries of an Afternoon, 1975. Bd. dirs. Goleta (Calif.) Civic Ballet, 1976-80. Mem. Newcomen Soc. Episcopalian. Avocation: classical ballet. Home: 13079 Treecrest St Poway CA 92064 Office: Info Magnetics Corp 9177 Skypark Ct San Diego CA 92123

MURREN, DOUGLAS EDWARD, pastor; b. Wenatchee, Wash., July 16, 1951; s. Virgil Edward and Gloria Mae (Humphres) M.; m. Debra Jean Landin, Mar. 27, 1971; children: Matthew Douglas, Raissa Anne. BA in Religion, Seattle Pacific U. Lic. pastor Internat. Ch. Foursquare Gospel. Asst. pastor Bethesda Christian Ctr., Wenatchee, 1974-79; founding pastor Eastside Christian Communion, Bellevue, Wash., 1979-80, Eastside Foursquare Ch., Kirkland, Wash., 1981—; conf. speaker, cons. various orgns., Poland, USSR, Norway, Fed. Republic Germany, Haiti, and U.S.; supt. div Foursquare Gospel Ch., N. King County, Wash., 1985—. Author: Iceman, 1986; editor Pastoral Resource, 1986—; host (radio show) Growing Together; contbr. articles to profl. jours. Office: Eastside Foursquare Ch PO Box 536 Kirkland WA 98083-0536

MURRO BOTERO, INGRID ELIZABETH, personnel consultant; b. Neuthard-Brushal, Fed. Republic Germany, July 13, 1946; came to. U.S., 1969; d. Edmund and Paula (Bond) Schaefer; m. Joseph Botero, May 11, 1985; 1 child, Jennifer Lynn. Diploma in English, U. Cambridge, Eng., 1966; grad. with honors, Comml. Coll., Fed. Republic Germany, 1964. Regional indsl. relations mgr. Robert Bosch Corp., Melville, N.Y., 1969-77; mgr. employee realtions Hazeltine Corp., Greenlawn, N.Y., 1978-80; personnel mgr. Transcontrol Corp., Melville, 1980-81; dir. personnel Siemens Corp., Scottsdale, Ariz., 1981-83; prin. Hay Career Cons., N.Y.C. and Boston, 1983-84; v.p. Hay Career Cons., Phoenix, 1984-86; founder, pres. Murro & Assocs. Inc., Phoenix, 1986—. V.p. bd. dirs. Ariz. Easter Seals. Mem. Personnel Dirs. Council Long Island Assn. (chairperson 1979-80), Am. Soc. Personnel Adminstrs., Personnel Soc. Long Island. Republican. Roman Catholic. Home: 8620 E San Ardo Dr Scottsdale AZ 85258 Office: Murro & Assocs Inc 3900 E Camelback Phoenix AZ 85018

MURTHY, KESHAVA SUBRAMANYAM, research chemist; b. Belur, India, Sept. 7, 1940; s. Subramanyam and Sharadamma M.; m. Prema Murthy, June 29, 1964; children: Narendra, Veena. BS in Physics, Chemistry and Math., U. Mysore, India, 1958; BSChemE, Indian Inst. of Chem. Engrs., Calcutta, 1966; MS in Environtl. Engring., U. Cin., 1974. Registered profl. engr., Ohio. Chemist air pollution sect. City of Alexandria, Va., 1969-70; environ. engr. Dept. Environ. Protectionergy, Montgomery County, Md., 1970-72; staff scientist, program mgr. Battelle Pacific Northwest Labs., Richland, Wash., 1973—. Author: The National Environmental Policy Act; contbr. articles to profl. jours. Mem. Am. Inst. Chem. Engrs., Am. Nuclear Soc. (div. program chmn. 1984—). Home: 2368 Easton Ave Richland WA 99352 Office: Battelle Northwest Labs Battelle Blvd Richland WA 99352

MUSACCHIO, THEODORE ALPHONSUS, international business consultant; b. Fresno, Calif., Aug. 11, 1934; s. Anthony and Constance (Ambrogio) M.; B.A., Fresno State Coll., 1956; postgrad. U. Calif. Sch. Law-San Francisco, 1959-61; m. Darlene June Mirigian, Mar. 20, 1955; 1 child, Kirk Anthony. Exec. trainee Bank of Am., NT & SA, Fresno, 1956-59; exec. Wells Fargo Bank, San Francisco, 1961-64; adminstrv. v.p. Columbus Savs. & Loan Assn., San Francisco, 1964-72; sr. v.p. Imperial Savs. and Loan Assn., San Francisco, 1972-76; dir., pres., chief exec. officer Columbus-Marin Savs. and Loan Assn., TAM Fin. Corp., Marcent Fin. Corp. and Columbus Fin. Corp., 1976-85; chmn. bd. and chief exec. officer KTM Corp., 1986—. Mem. exec. com. Boys' Towns of Italy, 1965—; pres. San Francisco Columbus Day Celebration, 1968. Mem. Fin. Instns. Mktg. Assn. (charter), Musicians' Union, Internat. Assn. Machinists, Am. Savs. and Loan Inst. (past pres. San Francisco chpt.), Il Cenacolo, Order Sons of Italy in Am., Italian Fedn. Calif. (past bd. dirs.), Sigma Pi. Clubs: Commonwealth of Calif., Family, Villa Taverna (San Francisco). Lodges: Masons (32 deg.), Shriners. Home: 130 El Dorado Ct San Bruno CA 94066 Office: 201 Spear St Suite 1010 San Francisco CA 94105

MUSGRAVE, JAMES EMERSON, physician, pediatrics educator; b. Mpls., July 14, 1939; s. Emerson Kidwell and Mable Virginia (Reynolds) M. AB, Westminster Coll., 1961; MD, Wash. U., St. Louis, 1965. Diplomate Am. Bd. Pediatrics, Pediatric Nephrology. Asst. prof. pediatrics U. Oreg., Portland, 1971-77; assoc. prof. U. Hawaii, Honolulu, 1979—. Served to capt. USAF, 1968-70. Fellow Am. Acad. Pediatrics. Office: Queens Physicians Office Bldg 1380 Lusitana St Suite 808 Honolulu HI 96813

MUSHEN, ROBERT LINTON, ophthalmologist; b. Klamath Falls, Oreg., Mar. 4, 1943; s. Samuel Albert and Beulah (Gore) M.; B.S. in Chemistry (Nat. Merit scholar), Stanford U., 1964; M.D., U. Oreg., 1968; m. Deborah Campbell, July 5, 1969; children—Melanie, Gregory, Timothy. Intern, Santa Clara Valley Med. Center, San Jose, Calif., 1968-69; resident in ophthalmology Brooke Army Med. Center, San Antonio, 1972-75; chief service Kerrville (Tex.) VA Hosp., 1975-76; mem. staff Madigan Army Med. Center, Tacoma, 1976-77; chief of staff and eye service Kadlec Hosp., Richland, Wash., 1977—; pres. Richland Eye Clinic, 1977—; cons. in field. Served with M.C., U.S. Army Res., 1969-75. Recipient award Oreg. Mus. Sci. and Industry, 1960; Nat. Eye Found. fellow, 1974-75. Mem. A.C.S., Am. Acad. Ophthalmology, Am. Intraocular Implant Soc., Soc. Eye Surgeons, AMA, Wash. Med. Assn., Wash. Acad. Ophthalmology, Benton-Franklin County Med. Soc., Alpha Omega Alpha. Republican. Co-author: Neuroanatomy Guide, 1967; contbr. articles to med. jours. Inventor bifocal trial lens. Home: 34 Vienna Ct Richland WA 99352 Office: 948 Stevens Dr Richland WA 99352

MUSICK, JAMES ROWLAND, biotechnology company executive; b. Mendota, Ill., Mar. 24, 1946; s. Rowland Harold and Virginia (Quinn) M. BA, Northwestern U., 1968, PhD, 1975. Instr. U. Utah, Salt Lake City, 1975-80, asst. prof., 1980-84; dir. research Ultra Pure Labs., Inc., Salt Lake City, 1983—, pres., 1984—, pres., dir. research, 1983-87; pres., chief operating officer Electr-med Internat., Inc., Salt Lake City, 1987—; dir. research N.Am. Labs., Stamford, Conn., 1983-85; bd. dirs. Tinder Block, Inc., Salt Lake City. Contbr. articles to profl. jours. Mem. Union Concerned Scientists, Cambridge, Mass., 1982. Postdoctoral fellow Muscular Dystrophy Assn., 1975-77. Mem. AAAS, N.Y. Acad. Scis., Sigma Xi. Avocations: skiing, biking. Home: 630 Fifth Ave Salt Lake City UT 84103 Office: Ultra Pure Labs Inc 2755 S 300 W Salt Lake City UT 84115

MUSIHIN, KONSTANTIN K., electrical engineer; b. Harbin, China, June 17, 1927; s. Konstantin N. and Alexandra A. (Lapitsky) M.; came to U.S., 1967, naturalized, 1973; ed. YMCA Inst., 1942, North Manchurian U., 1945, Harbin Poly. Inst., 1948; m. Natalia Krilova, Oct. 18, 1964; 1 son, Nicholas. Asst. prof. Harbin Poly. Inst., 1950-53; elec. engr. Moinho Santista, Sao Paulo, Brazil, 1955-60; constrn. project mgr. Caterpillar-Brazil, Santo Amaro, 1960-61; mech. engr. Matarazzo Industries, Sao Paulo, 1961-62; chief of works Vidrobras, St. Gobain, Brazil, 1962-64; project engr. Brown Boveri, Sao Paulo, 1965-67; sr. engr. Kaiser Engrs., Oakland, Calif., 1967-73; sr. engr. Bechtel Power Corp., San Francisco, 1973-75; supr. power and control San Francisco Bay Area Rapid Transit, Oakland, 1976-78; chief elec. engr. L.K. Comstock Engring. Co., San Francisco, 1978-79; prin. engr. Morrison

Knudsen Co., San Francisco, 1979-84; prin. engr. Brown and Caldwell, Cons. Engrs., Pleasant Hill, Calif., 1984-85; cons. engr. Pacific Gas and Electric Co., San Francisco, 1986—. Registered profl. engr., Calif., Colo., N.Y., N.J., Pa., Ill., Wash. Mem. IEEE (sr.), Instrument Soc. Am. (sr.), Am. Mgmt. Assn., Nat., Calif. socs. profl. engrs., Nat. Assn. Corrosion Engrs., Instituto de Engenharia de Sao Paulo. Mem. Christian Orthodox Ch. Clubs: Am.-Brazilian, Brit.-Am. Home: 320 Park View Terr Unit 207 Oakland CA 94610

MUSSELWHITE, EDWIN A., management consulting company executive; b. Miami, Fla., Jan. 21, 1940; s. Thomas A. and Edna B. W.; BS, Northwestern U., 1964; m. Linda Silvestrini, 1984; Kenneth, Thomas, Zachary. Mktg. rep. IBM, Chgo., 1964-68, exec. staff asst., 1968, br. sales mgr., Aurora, Ill., 1968-69; dir. profl. personnel Leasco Systems Corp., Oakbrook, Ill. 1969-70; exec. v.p. Deltak, Inc., Oakbrook, Ill., 1970-76; pres. Systems Growth Inst., Santa Cruz, Calif., 1976-82; v.p. Zenger-Miller, Inc., Cupertino, Calif., 1982—, also chmn. bd. dirs.; cons. mgmt. to IBM, Gen. Electric Co., Fireman's Fund Ins. Co., Stanford U., TRW, others; guest lectr. at univs.; mem. bd. advs., bd. chmn. Zenger-Miller., Inc., 1986—; Center for Orgn. and Mgmt. Devel., San Jose State U. Served as sgt. U.S. Army, 1964. Mem. Am. Soc. Tng. Devel., Orgn. Devel. Network. Co-author: Toward excellence, 1983; contbg. author: Everybody Wins, 1976; Interpersonal Dimensions, 1981; producer over 2000 hours of video-based instrn. in mgmt. devel, data processing and sales skills, 1973—. Office: Zenger-Miller Inc 10201 Torre Ave Cupertino CA 95014

MUSSER, C. WALTON, physical scientist, consultant; b. Mt. Joy, Pa., Apr. 5, 1909; s. Ezra Nissley and Cora Grace (Weidman) M.; m. Edna Mae Hoak, June 23, 1937; children—Lila Darle (Mrs. Richard Hackman), Yvonne Duane (Mrs. Harold Graham), Stanley Walton. Student, Chgo. Tech. Coll., 1926-28, Leavitt Sch. Psychology, 1928-29, Wharton Sch. Finance and Commerce, 1929-30, U. Pa., 1930-32, Mass. Inst. Tech., 1957. Chief engr. product devel. Indsl. Improvement Corp., Phila., 1936-41; research adviser Dept. Def., 1941-56; pres., dir. research Sci. Research, Inc., Glenside, Pa., 1945-52; pvt. practice cons., adviser in research and devel. 1936—. Holder of over 162 U.S. Patents in 32 different classes. Recipient Exceptional Civilian Service award for First Working Recoilless Weapon, Sec. of War, 1945; John C. Jones medal for Disting. Service, Am. Ordnance Assn., 1951; Machine Design award ASME, 1968; named to Ordnance Hall of Fame. Mem. Acad. Applied Scis., Am. Def. Preparedness Assn. (hon. life), Nat. Soc. Profl. Engrs., Sigma Xi. Address: 1206 Lela Ln Santa Maria CA 93454

MUSSLER, MICHAEL EUGENE, electronics engineer; b. Wooster, Ohio, July 6, 1956; s. Raymond Charles and Shirley Ladene (Stevens) M.; m. Janice Marie Bigler, May 23, 1981. BS, U.S. Merchant Marine Acad., 1978; BSEE, U. Akron, 1984. From 3d to 2d officer Mil. Sealift Command, Bayonne, N.J., 1978-80; co-op engring student Nat. Security Agy., Ft. Meade, Md., 1982-83; design engr. Ball Aerospace Systems Div., Boulder, Colo., 1984—. Contbr. articles to profl. jours. Info. rep. U.S. Merchant Marine Acad. Pub. Info Office, Kings Point, N.Y., 1986. Recipient Cargo Caire award, Cargo Caire Engring. Co., 1978, Astronaut See Honor award, Armed Forced Communications and Electronics Assn., 1978, NSA Spl. Performance award, Nat. Security Agy., 1982. Mem. IEEE, Antennas and Propagation Soc. Republican. Presbyterian. Lodge: Masons. Avocations: amateur radio, hunting, fishing, camping, swimming. Home: Bonanza Star Rt Nederland CO 80466 Office: Ball Aerospace Systems Div PO Box 1062 MS BE-6 Boulder CO 80306

MUSSMAN, WILLIAM EDWARD, III, lawyer; b. San Francisco, Jan. 31, 1951; s. William Edward and Janet Jonn (Skittone) M. B.S., Stanford U., 1973; J.D., U. Calif.-San Francisco, 1976. Bar: Calif. 1976, U.S. Dist. Ct. (no. dist.) Calif. 1976,, U.S. Dist. Ct. (cen. dist.) Calif. 1982, U.S. Supreme Ct., 1986. Assoc. Lasky, Haas, Cohler & Munter, San Francisco, 1980-82, Pillsbury, Madison & Sutro, San Francisco, 1982-84; assoc. Carr & Mussman, San Francisco, 1984—. Sustaining mem. Yosemite Area council Boy Scouts Am., 1981—; missionary Ch. Jesus Christ Latter Day Sts., Tokyo, 1977-78. Mem. ABA, San Francisco Bar Assn., Latter Day Saints Bus. Club (pres. 1982-84), Am. Horse Shows Assn., Brigham Young U. Mgmt. Soc. (bd. dirs., 1984-88, v.p. 1984-86, pres. 1986—), Stanford Alumni Assn. (life), Tau Beta Pi. Club: Commonwealth of Calif. Office: Carr & Mussman 3 Embarcadero Ctr Suite 1060 San Francisco CA 94111

MUSSO, JOHN DOMINIC, elementary principal; b. Pueblo, Colo., Mar. 2, 1954; s. Dominic John and Frances M. (Dazzio) M.; m. Anita K. Hicks, July 1, 1978; 1 child, Kristin K. BA, U. So. Colo., 1975; MA in Pub. Adminstrn., U. No. Colo., 1978; cert., Western State Coll., Gunnison, Colo., 1980. Cert. elem. tchr., Colo. Student tchr. Baxter Elem. Sch., Pueblo, Colo., 1975; studio supr., newscastor Pueblo Calbevision, 1973-75; counselor, clin. therapist Parkview Med. Ctr., Pueblo, 1975-86; tchr. Beulah (Colo.) Sch., 1976-81; prin. Rye (Colo.) Elem. Sch., 1976—; rev. committeeman Sch. Dist. 70, 1977-78; program committeeman Sch. Dist. 70, 1983-84; report card rev. committeeman Sch. Dist. 70, 1984-85; computer curriculum committeeman Sch. Dist. 70, 1984-85; dist. accountability committeeman Sch. Dist. 70, 1984—; kindergarten screening committeeman Sch. Dist. 70, 1985—; Colp. Dept. Edn. state accountability planning committeeman Sch. Dist. 70, 1985—. Committeeman Pueblo Clean Community Commn., Colo., 1977-79, Gifted and Talented Cluster Com., Pueblo, 1985—. Recipient Gov's. award, 1977,78,79, Chevron Chem. Nat. award, 1979; named Tchr. of the Yr., Beulah Sch., 1979, one of Outstanding Young Men of Am., 1982. Mem. Nat. Assn. of Elem. Sch. Prins., Assn. for Supervision and Curriculum Devel., Colo. Assn. of Sch. Execs., Pueblo County Assn. of Sch. Execs., Phi Delta Kappa. Democratic. Roman Catholic. Lodge: Eagles. Avocations: reading, fishing, bowling, sports. Home: 105 Kenwood Dr Pueblo CO 81004 Office: Rye Elem Sch PO Box 240 Rye CO 81069

MUSTACCHI, PIERO, physician, educator; b. Cairo, Egypt, May 29, 1920; came to U.S., 1947; naturalized, 1952; s. Gino and Gilda (Rieti) M.; m. Dora Lisa Ancona, Sept. 26, 1948; children—Roberto, Michael. B.S. in Humanities, U. Florence, Italy, 1938; postgrad. in anatomy, Eleve Interne, U. Lausanne, Switzerland, 1938-39; M.B., Ch.B., Fouad I U., Cairo, Egypt, 1944, grad. in Arabic lang. and lit., 1946; D Medicine and Surgery, U. Pisa, 1946. Lic. physician Egypt, 1946. Diplomate, Am. Bd. Internal Medicine. House officer English Hosp., Ch. Missionary Soc., Cairo, Egypt, 1945-47; clin. affiliate U. Calif., San Francisco, 1947-48; intern Franklin Hosp., San Francisco, 1948-49; resident in pathology U. Calif., San Francisco, 1949-51; resident in medicine Meml. Ctr. Cancer and Allied Diseases, N.Y.C., 1951-53; research epidemiologist Dept. HEW, Nat. Cancer Inst., Bethesda, Md., 1955-57; cons. allergy clinic U. Calif., San Francisco, 1957-70, clin. prof. medicine and preventive medicine, 1970—, head occupational epidemiology, 1975—, head div. internat. health edn. dept. epidemiology and internat. health, 1985—; med. cons., vis. prof. numerous ednl. and profl. instns. including U. Calif.-San Francisco, U. Marseille, 1981, 82, U. Pisa, Italy, 1983, U. Gabon, 1984, U. Siena, Italy, 1985, U. Calif.-San Francisco Ctr. for Rehab. and Occupational Health, 1984—, Work Clinic, 1975—; cons. numerous govtl. agys. throughout the world. Contbr. chpts. to books, articles to profl. jours. Editorial bd. Cancer Research, Medecine d'Afrique Noire, Ospedali d'Italia. Served with USN, USPHS, 1953-55. Decorated Order of Merit (Italy), Ordre de la Legion d'Honneur (France), Medal of St. John of Jerusalem, Sovereign Order of Malta, Order of the Republic (Egypt); Scroll, Leonard da Vinci Soc., San Francisco, 1965; award Internat. Inst. Oakland, 1964; Hon. Vice Consul. Italy, 1971—. Fellow Am. Soc. Occupational Medicine, ACP; mem. AAAS, Am. Soc. Environ. and Occupational Health, Am. Assn. Cancer Research, Calif. Soc. Allergy and Immunology, Calif. Med. Assn., San Francisco Med. Soc., West Coast Allergy Soc. (founding mem.), Mexican Congress on Hypertension (corr.), Assn. Internationale pour la Recherche Medicale et l'Edn. Continue (U.S. rep.). Democrat. Clubs: Villa Taverna (San Francisco), Accademia Italiana della Cucina. Avocations: Mathematics; music; languages. Home: 3344 Laguna St San Francisco CA 94123 Office: U Calif Parnassus Ave San Francisco CA 94143

MUSTAFA, MOHAMMAD GHULAM, biochemistry educator; b. Dhaka, Bangladesh, Mar. 1, 1940; came to U.S., 1963, naturalized, 1978; s. Mohammad and Quamerunnesa Yaseen; m. Sultana Begum Mustafa, Nov. 6, 1969; 1 child, George E. BS, Dhaka U., 1960, MS summa cum laude, 1962; MA, U. Calif., Berkeley, 1966; PhD, SUNY, Albany, 1969. Asst. research biochemist U. Calif., Davis, 1969-73, asst. adj. prof., 1973-75; adj. asst. prof. UCLA, 1975-78, assoc. prof. in residence, 1978-79, assoc. prof., 1979-84, prof. environ. and occupational health sci., 1984—. Co-editor: Biomedical Effects of Ozone, 1983; mem. editorial bd. Toxicology and Indsl. Health, Princeton, N.J., 1984—; contbr. articles to profl. jours. Recipient Research Career Devel. award NIH, 1976-81; grantee NIH, 1970—. Mem. Am. Chem. Soc., Am. Coll. Toxicology, Air Pollution Control Assn., AAAS, N.Y. Acad. Sci., Sigma Xi. Democrat. Muslim. Avocations: badminton, volleyball, swimming, bicycling. Home: 10534 Louisiana Ave Los Angeles CA 90025 Office: UCLA Sch Pub Health 405 Hilgard Ave Los Angeles CA 90024

MUTH, GILBERT JEROME, biology educator; b. Modesto, Calif., Mar. 1, 1938; s. Douglas Leland and Margaret Erma (Olander) M.; m. Betty Lavelle Krier, Aug. 23, 1959; children: Stephen Andrew, Jenny Adele. BA, Pacific Union Coll., 1961, MA, 1967; PhD, U. Calif., Davis, 1976. Tchr. sci. Napa (Calif.) Jr. Acad., 1961-66; tchr. sci. Pacific Union Coll., Angwin, Calif., 1966—, dept. chmn., 1982—; pres. bd. dirs. Howell Mountain Mut. Water Co., Angwin; chmn. State Calif. Rare Plant adv. com., Sacramento, 1979—. Author (computer software) Specimen Label Info. Directory, 1973—. Named one of Outstanding Young Men Am., 1968. Mem. Calif. Native Plant Soc., Calif. Bot. Soc., Sigma Xi. Republican. Adventist. Home: 305 Sky Oaks Dr Angwin CA 94508 Office: Pacific Union Coll Dept Biology Angwin CA 94508

MUTSCHLER, HERBERT FREDERICK, librarian; b. Eureka, S.D., Nov. 28, 1919; s. Frederick and Helena (Oster) M.; m. Lucille I. Gross, Aug. 18, 1945; 1 dau., Linda M. B.A., Jamestown Coll., 1947; M.A., Western Res. U., 1949, M.S., 1952. Tchr. history high sch. Lemmon, S.D., 1947-48; asst. librarian Royal Oak (Mich.) Library, 1952-55; head librarian Hamtramck (Mich.) Library, 1955-56; head public services Wayne County Library System, Wayne, Mich., 1956-59; asst. county librarian Wayne County Library System, 1960-62; dir. King County Library System, Seattle, 1963—; library bldg. cons. Wayne County Library, 1956-62, Wash. State Library, 1966—; cons. Salt Lake County Library, Pierce County Library, North Olympic Library; lectr. U. Wash. Sch. Librarianship, 1970-71; bldg. cons. Hoquiam (Wash.) Library, Olympic (Wash.) Regional Library. Contbr. articles profl. jours. Served with AUS, 1941-45; to capt. 1950-52. Decorated Silver Star, Bronze Star with cluster, Purple Heart. Mem. ALA (councilor at large 1965-69, chpt. councilor 1971-75, pres. library adminstrv. div. 1974-75), Pacific N.W. Library Assn., Wash. Library Assn. (exec. bd. 1964-65, 69-71, pres. 1967-69). Republican. Lutheran. Club: City, Municipal League. Lodge: Kiwanis. Home: 5300 128th Ave SE Bellevue WA 98006 Office: 300 8th Ave N Seattle WA 98109

MYER, PETER LIVINGSTON, artist, educator; b. Dzone Park, N.Y., Sept. 19, 1934; s. Percy Livingstone and Martha Angeline (MacPherson) M.; m. Ila Marie Lytle, June 4, 1955; children: Sara Danae, Marc Damon, Seth Jamison, Paul Darius, Aaron Lytle, Amie Rachel. BA, Brigham Young U., 1956, MFA, U. Utah, 1959. Tchr. Cen. Jr. High Sch., Parsippany, N.J., 1956-57; asst. prof. art Carbon Jr. Coll., Price, Utah, 1959-62; assoc. prof., chmn. art dept. U. Nev., Las Vegas, 1962-72; gallery dir. Brigham Young U., Provo, Utah, 1972-78, prof. art, 1978—; dir. Paris Ctr. Brigham Young U. semester abroad, Provo, 1978. One-man shows include Springville (Utah) Mus. Art 1979, Salt Lake Art Ctr. 1980 (purchase prize for self portrait sculpture 1975), Kimball Art Ctr., Park City, Utah, 1985; exhibitions include Nat. Art Roundup, 1965 (sweepstakes prize 1965), Art Roundup, 1966 (first prize 1966, best in show award 1965). Chmn. Allied Arts Council, Las Vegas, 1964-65; regional dir. Experiments in Art and Tech., Nev., 1968-72; bd. dirs. Las Vegas Symphony, 1971-72; judge Sterling Scholar awards, Utah, 1973-86. Served to sgt. U.S. Army, 1957-58. Republican. Mormon. Home: 1425 E Oakcliff Dr Provo UT 84604

MYERS, AL, realtor property mgmt., mayor; b. Oakland, Calif., Aug. 6, 1922; s. Alvi A. and Emma (Thoren) M.; student Oreg. Inst. Tech., 1940-41; m. Viola Doreen Wennermark, Sept. 11, 1954; children—Susan Faye, Pamela Ann, Jason Allen. Supt.'s asst. Aluminum Co. Am., Troutdale, Oreg., 1942-44; asst. mgr. Western Auto Supply Co., Portland, 1944-46; owner, operator Al Myers Auto & Electric, Gresham, Oreg., 1946-53; realtor, broker Al Myers Property Mgmt., 1954—; v.p., sec. Oreg. Country, Inc.; faculty Mt. Hood Community Coll. Chmn., Indsl. and Econ. Devel. Com. for Multonomah County, Oreg. Real Estate Ednl. Program, 1961. Mayor Gresham, Oreg., 1972—. Pres. East Multonomah County Dem. Forum, 1965—, mem. exec. com., 1958—. Served with AUS, 1943. Mem. Portland Realty Bd., Nat. Assn. Real Estate Bds., Christian Bus. Men's Com. Internat., Internat. Platform Assn., Rho Epsilon Kappa (pres. Oreg.). Mem. Evang. Ch. (trustee, treas.). Home: 935 NW Norman Ave Gresham OR 97030 Office: 995 NE Cleveland Ave Gresham OR 97030

MYERS, BARTON, architect; b. Norfolk, Va., Nov. 6, 1934; s. Barton and Meeta Hamilton (Burrage) M.; m. Victoria George, Mar. 7, 1959; 1 child, Suzanne Lewis. BS, U.S. Naval Acad., 1956; MArch with honors, U. Pa., 1964. Commd. 2d lt. USAF, 1956, resigned, 1961; architect Louis I. Kahn, Phila., 1964-65, Bower, Fradley, Phila., 1967-68; architect, prin. A.J. Diamond & Barton Myers, Toronto, Ont., Can., 1968-75; architect, prin. Barton Myers Assocs., Toronto, 1975—, Los Angeles, 1981—; disting. vis. prof. Ariz. State U., Tempe, 1986—; sr. prof. UCLA, 1981—; Thomas Jefferson Prof. U. Va., Charlottesville, 1982; vis. prof., lectr., Harvard U., U. Pa., other univs. U.S. and Can., 1968—. Prin. works inlcude Myers Residence, Toronto (Ont. Assn. Architects Toronto Chpt. Annual Design award, 1971, Can. Housing Design Council award, 1971), Wolf Residence, Toronto (Architectural Record: Record Houses of 1977, Twenty-Five Yrs. of Record Houses, 1981), Housing Union Bldg., Edmonton (Can. Housing Design Council award, 1974, Design in Steel award, 1975), Citadel Theatre, Edmonton (City of Edmonton Design award, 1978, Stelco Design award, 1978), Seagram Mus., Waterloo (Gov. Gen.'s Medal for Architecture, 1986), Phoenix Mcpl. Ctr., Phoenix (Winning Competition Entry, 1985), Portland Ctr. for the Performing Arts, Portland (Progressive Architecture Design award, 1984), others. Fellow Royal Archtl. Inst. Can.; mem. AIA, Soc. Archtl. Historians, Royal Can. Acad. Art, Tau Sigma Delta. Avocations: traveling, reading, tennis. Office: Barton Myers Assocs Inc 6834 Hollywood Blvd Los Angeles CA 90028 Office: 322 King St, West Toronto M5V1J2, CAN

MYERS, CATHERINE MERTENS, engineer; b. Spokane, Wash., Dec. 6, 1960; d. Joseph H. and M. Elaine (Vaughn) Mertens; m. Mark S. Myers, Sept. 17, 1983. BS in Engring. and Chemistry, U. Portland, 1983. Registered engr. in tng. Resource engr. Pacific N.W. Utilities Conf. Com., Portland, Oreg., 1983—. Mem. Am. Chem. Soc. (chmn. 1987), Soc. Women Engrs. Democrat. Roman Catholic. Avocations: pianist, outdoor sports, reading. Home: 7025 SW Burlingame Portland OR 97219 Office: Pacific NW Utilities Conf Com 520 SW 6th Suite 505 Portland OR 97204

MYERS, DOUGLASS NELSON, healthcare executive; b. Salem, Oreg., July 3, 1953; s. John Arthur and Marilyn Joan (Nelson) M.; m. Patricia Elaine Thompson, May 1, 1982; 1 child, Hadley Dean. BA, U. Redlands, 1974; M in Health Adminstrn., Duke U., 1976; MBA, Claremont Grad. Sch., 1982, MA in Mgmt., 1983; postgrad., U. Mich., 1986—. Adminstrv. fellow Hoag Meml. Hosp., Newport Beach, Calif., 1976-77, adminstrv. asst., 1977-80, dir. strategic planning, chief devel. officer, 1980-82; pres., chief exec. officer Irvine (Calif.) Med. Ctr., 1982—; v.p., bd. dirs. Sunriver (Oreg.) Inst., 1981—. Bd. dirs. bus. council Newport Harbor Art Mus., 1985—; bd. dirs., founder, chmn. The Found., Newport Beach, 1982—; bd. dirs. Orange County chpt. ARC, 1985—, chmn. health and safety com., 1986—; mem. fin. com. Community Congl. Ch., Corona del Mar, Calif., 1982-83; bd. dirs. Edn. for Bus. Inst., 1986—. USPHS grantee, Duke U., Durham, N.C., 1975-76; Pew fellow, 1986—. Mem. AAAS, Am. Coll. Healthcare Execs., Healthcare Execs. of So. Calif., Am. Hosp. Assn., Soc. Hosp. Planning and Mktg. Home: 9 Mill Creek Irvine CA 92715

MYERS, DWIGHT ANDREW, publishing company executive; b. Jamestown, N.Y., Nov. 24, 1931; s. Melvin Andrew and Fredrika Wilhelmina (Eichler) M.; m. Carol Ann McClary, Sept. 16, 1950; children—Robert Andrew, Debra Ann, James Allen. B.A. in Edn., U. N.Mex., 1959. Salesman Prentice-Hall Inc., N.Mex., 1959-60, nat. sales mgr. library div., Englewood Cliffs, N.J., 1963-70, asst. v.p. sales, N.Mex., 1965—; exec. dir. N.Mex. Book League, Albuquerque, 1972—; book reviewer Book Talk mag., Albuquerque, 1972—; mem. White House Conf. on Libraries, Washington, 1979. Author: (with others) In Celebration of the Book: Literary New Mexico, 1983 (S.W. Library award 1984). Contbr. articles to profl. jours. Bd. dirs. U. N.Mex. Library, N.Mex. State U. Library, St. Johns Library, N.Mex., 1981—. Served with USAF, 1950-54. Mem. N.Mex. Library Assn. (bd. dirs. 1982—). Republican. Baptist. Home: 8632 Horacio Pl NE Albuquerque NM 87111 Office: Prentice-Hall Inc Box 500 Englewood Cliffs NJ 07632

MYERS, ELMER, psychiatric social worker; b. Blackwell, Ark., Nov. 12, 1926; s. Chester Elmer Myers and Irene (Davenport) Lewis; widowed; children: Elmer Jr., Keith, Kevin. BA, U. Kans., 1951, MA, 1962; student, U. Calif., Santa Barbara, 1977-78. Psychiat. social worker Hastings (Nebr.) State Hosp., 1960-62; psychiat. social worker State of Calif., Sacramento, 1962-75; supr. psychiat. social worker, 1975-80; supr. psychiat. social worker Alta Calif. Regional Ctr., Sacramento, 1980-85; exec. dir. Tri-County Family Services, Yuba City, Calif., 1966-69; cons. to 3 convalescent Hosps., Marysville, Calif., 1969-71; lectr. Yuba Coll., Marysville, 1971-76; assoc. prof. Calif. State U., Chico, 1972-73; cons. in field, Marysville, 1985—. Juror Yuba County Grand Jury, Marysville, 1965; sec. Y's Men's Club, Yuba City, 1964-65; chmn. Tri-County Home Health Agy., Yuba City, 1974-76; vice-chmn. Gateway Projects, Inc., Yuba City, 1974-75; bd. dirs. Yuba County Truancy Bd., Marysville, 1964-67; bd. dirs. Golden Empire Health Systems Agy., Sacramento, 1972-76; bd. dirs. Youth Services Bur., Yuba City, 1967; bd. dirs. Bi County Mental Retardation Planning Bd., Yuba City, 1972; bd. dirs. Yuba County Juvenile Justice Commn., Marysville, 1982—; bd. dirs. Am. Cancer Soc., Marysville, 1985—; bd. dirs. Yuba County Rep. Cen. Com., 1983—. Recipient Cert. Spl. Recognition Calif. Rehab. Planning Project, 1969, Cert. Spl. Recognition State of Calif., 1967; Cert. Spl. Recognition Alta Calif. Regional Ctrs., 1985. Mem. Nat. Assn. Social Workers (cert.), Kern County Mental Health Assn. (chmn. 1978-79). Lodge: Rotary (bd. dirs. Marysville club 1975-76). Avocations: fgn. lang. study, gardening, reading, computers. Home and Office: 3920 Highway 20 Marysville CA 95901

MYERS, GENE JAY, trainer, adult educator; b. Springfield, Mass., Apr. 19, 1931; s. Elbryn Howard and Miriam Kraybill (Bard) M.; B.A., Pa. State U., 1952; m. Norma Lee Barrett, Sept. 23, 1972. Prin., sr. trainer N.W. Social Systems, Seattle, 1969-74; mgr. tng. Westinghouse Hanford Co., Richland, Wash., 1974-78; nat. seminar adminstr. Pacific Inst., Seattle, 1978-80; instructional design and implementation specialist corp. tng. Morrison-Knudsen Co., Inc., Boise, Idaho, 1980-83; pres. Gene Myers Seminars, 1983—; adj. faculty Western Wash. U.; vocat. instr. Columbia Basin Coll. (Pasco, Wash.). Active Boy Scouts Am., named Commr. of Year, Inland Empire council, 1967, mem. Order of Arrow, 1968. Mem. Am. Soc. Tng. and Devel., Internat. Platform Assn. Episcopalian. Author: Old Style Sioux Costumes, 1968. Office: 3910 Buckingham Pl Boise ID 83704

MYERS, GORDON JEROME, transportation executive; b. Seattle, Apr. 28, 1935; s. Julius Moscovici and Florence (Warshal) M.; 1 child, Edelle Laine. AS, Marion Mil. Inst., 1955; grad., U.S. Naval Acad., 1957; BA, U. Wash., 1958; MA, Kennedy Western U., 1985. Gen. mgr. Fin. Service Co., Vancouver, B.C., Can., 1962; pilot Zantop Air Transport, Detroit, 1965, PanAm. World Airways, 1965-86, United Airlines, 1986—; founder and pres. Air Bahia Airlines, San Diego, 1978-80; founder and chief exec. officer LA Helicopter Airline, Los Angeles, 1985—; faculty advisor Kennedy Western U. Sch. Bus., Airling Mgmt. Dept. Served to lt. USCG, 1958—. Mem. Regional Airline Assn., Air Courier Conf. Am., Los Angeles Air Cargo Assn., Profl. Helicopter Pilots Assn. (hon.), Assn. Aero. Internat. Office: Los Angeles Internat Airport LA Helicopter Inc PO Box 92934 Los Angeles CA 90009

MYERS, JOHN LESTER, mining executive; b. Columbus, Ind., Aug. 8, 1928; s. John Lester and Elna Clara (Schoessel) M.; m. Kathryn Louise Banta, Jan. 28, 1951 (div. July 1976); children: Deborah, Sandra, Les; m. Donna Jean Lewis, Sept. 4, 1976; 1 child, Kimberly. BSChemE, Purdue U., 1951. Tech. supr. Union Carbide Corp., Oak Ridge, Tenn. and Paducah, Ky., 1951-66; research engr. Union Carbide Corp., Niagra Falls, N.Y., 1966-67, mktg. mgr., 1970-81; tech. supt. Union Carbide Corp., King City, Calif., 1967-70, mgr. ops., 1981-85; pres. KCAC, Inc., King City, 1985—, also bd. dirs.; chmn. Asbestos Info. Assn. N.Am., 1981—. Patentee in field. Mem. Planning Commn. King City, 1984-86; elected Council mem. King City, 1986—; bd. trustees Mee Meml. Hosp., 1982—. Mem. Am. Chem. Soc., Am. Inst. Chem. Engrs. Republican. Lutheran. Lodge: Rotary. Avocations: golf, furniture refinishing. Office: KCAC Inc PO Box K King City CA 93930

MYERS, JOHN PHILIP, social work administrator; b. York, Pa., Sept. 10, 1936; s. Leroy Hildebrand and Pauline Susanna (Sinner) M.; m. Barbara Ann Yohe, Aug. 17, 1962; children: Keith Alan, Mark Leslie. B in Music, U. Miami, 1959; MSW, U. Pitts., 1964. Ednl. program cons. Council on Social Work Edn., N.Y.C., 1977-78; asst. prof. N.Mex. State U., Las Cruces, 1978-84; program mgr. behavioral health services N.Mex. Dept. Health and Environ., Santa Fe, 1985, exec. asst., 1985-86; dir. staff devel. and tng. Ft. Boynard (N.Mex.) Med. Ctr., 1987—; governing body mem. N.Mex. Health Systems Agy., Albuquerque. Contbr. articles to profl. jours. Bd. dirs. Emergency Med. Service, Las Cruces, A-95 Tech. Adv. Council, Las Cruces, N.Mex. Council on Crime and Deliquency, Albuquerque, Community Action Agy., Las Cruces, v.p. 1982; adv. bd. Community Devel. Priorities Com., Las Cruces, 1982-85, Comprehensive Planning Com., Las Cruces, 1983-85; sec. YMCA service club, York, Pa. 1960-62; bd. dirs. York Jr. C. of C. 1960-62. Named Social Worker of Yr. Dona Ann Programs Unit, 1982. Fellow Am. Orthopsychiat. Assn.; mem. Nat. Assn. Social Workers (bd. dirs., v.p. 1983), Dona Ann County Mental Health Assn. (bd. dirs.), N.Mex. Pub. Health Assn. (bd. dirs.). Democrat. Avocations: tennis, writing. Home: 1812 Ash Ave Las Cruces NM 88001

MYERS, NOVELLA VAUGHAN GREGG, counselor; b. Berthoud, Colo., Sept. 8, 1924; d. Leo S. and Christie (Bullock) Vaughan; m. Mark P. Gregg, Nov. 21, 1943 (dec. June 1954); children: Mark Vaughan, Kent Bradley, Gwendolyn Gregg Lowden; m. Lowell E. Myers, Dec. 27, 1958. BSW with honors, Colo. State U., 1981, MEd, 1984. Owner Lessor Farm Mgmt., Johnstown, Colo., 1954-74; real estate broker Loveland, Colo., 1958—; account exec. KLOV Radio, Loveland, 1966-67; counselor Meth. C.S. Inc., Loveland, 1983—. Chmn. Social Concerns Com., Meth. Ch., Loveland; mem. Human Relations Commn., City of Loveland, Interfaith Needs Task Force, Loveland, 1982, Needs Assessment Task Force, Loveland, 1983—, Loveland Residence Council, 1985. Mem. Nat. Assn. Social Workers, Colo. Assn. Continuing Adult Edn., Colo. State U. Alumni Assn., Phi Kappa Phi, Delta Delta Delta Alumni Club. Democrat. Methodist. Avocations: traveling, antiques, card playing, reading. Home: 2116 Abeyta Ct Loveland CO 80538 Office: Methodist Counseling Services Inc 6th at Grant Loveland CO 80537

MYERS, PHILLIP FENTON, business executive; b. Cleve., June 24, 1935; s. Max I. and Rebecca (Rosenbloom) M.; m. Hope Gail Strum, Aug. 13, 1961. B.I.E., Ohio State U., 1958, M.B.A., 1960; D.B.A., Harvard U., 1966. Staff indsl. engr. Procter & Gamble Co., Cin., 1958; sr. cons. Cresap, McCormack & Paget, N.Y.C., 1960-61; staff assoc. Mitre Corp., Bedford, Mass., 1961; cons. Systems Devel. Corp., Santa Monica, Calif., 1963-64; corp. asst. long range planning Electronic Specialty Co., Los Angeles, 1966-68; chmn. Atek Industries, 1968-72; pres. Myers Fin. Corp., 1973—, Steel Fuels Corp., 1976-77; chmn. Amvid Communication Services, Inc., 1975-79, Gen. Hydrogen Corp. Am., 1976-79, Omni Resources Devel. Corp., 1979-83; chmn., pres. Am. Internat. Mining Co., Inc., 1979-83; pres. Whitehall Internat. Mgmt. Co., Inc., 1982—, Synentek Internat. Corp., 1983-84; gen. ptnr. Pacific Internat. Devel. Co., 1985—; founding dir. Warner Ctr. Bank, 1980-83; lectr. bus. adminstrn. U. So. Calif., Los Angeles, 1967-74; prof. Pepperdine U. Grad. Sch. Bus. Adminstrn., 1974-81. Trustee, treas. Chamber Symphony Soc. Calif., 1971-78; pub. safety commr. City of Hidden Hills, Calif., 1977-83, chmn., 1982-83; co-chmn. budget adv. com. Las Virgenas Sch. Dist., 1983-86; mem. Mayor's Blue Ribbon Fin. Com., 1981-82; mem. dean's select adv. com. Coll. Engring., Ohio State U., 1984—. Served to capt. USAF, 1958-60. Ford Found. fellow, 1961-64. Mem. Harvard Bus. Sch. Assn., Ohio State Alumni Assn. Club: Harvard of So.

Calif. (bd. dirs. 1970-74, treas. 1971-73). Home and Office: 5819 Fitzpatrick Rd Suite 1000 Calabasas CA 91302

MYERS, ROBERT EUGENE, educator, writer; b. Los Angeles, Jan. 15, 1924; s. Harold Eugene and Margaret (Anawalt) M.; A.B., U. Calif., Berkeley, 1955; M.A. (Crown-Zellerbach fellow), Reed Coll., 1960; Ed.D., U. Ga., 1968; m. Patricia A. Tazer, Aug. 17, 1956; children—Edward E., Margaret A., Hal R., Karen I. Employed in phonograph record business, 1946-54; tchr. elem. sch., Calif., Oreg., Minn., 1954-61; research asst. U. Minn., 1961-62; asst. prof. Augsburg Coll., 1962-63, U. Oreg., 1963-66; elem. tchr., Eugene, Oreg., 1966-67; asso. prof. U. Victoria, 1968-70; asso. research prof. Oreg. System of Higher Edn., 1970-73; film maker, producer ednl. filmstrips, books and recs., 1973-77; with Oreg. Dept. Edn., Salem, 1977-81, learning resources specialist, 1977-81, with Linn-Benton Edn. Service Dist., Albany, Oreg., 1982—. Mem. exec. bd. Nat. Assn. for Gifted Children, 1974-77. Served with U.S. Mcht. Marine, 1944-45. Recipient CINE Golden Eagle award Council Internat. Non-theatrical Events, 1973. Mem. Internat. Reading Assn. Democrat. Lodge: Rotary. Author: (with E. Paul Torrance) Creative Learning and Teaching (Pi Lambda Theta award 1971), 1970, Can You Imagine?, 1965, Invitations to Thinking and Doing, 1964, Invitations to Speaking and Writing Creatively, 1965, Plots, Puzzles, and Ploys, 1966, For Those Who Wonder, 1966; Timberwood Tales, Vol. II, 1977; Wondering, 1984, Imagining, 1985. Home: 2846 NW Angelica Dr Corvallis OR 97330 Office: 905 4th Ave Albany OR 97321

MYERS, SHIRLEY STOFLE, interior designer, educational consultant; b. Seattle, Mar. 5, 1921; d. Sterling Leroy S. and Grace Evelyn (Lyden) Stofle; m. Edward A. Myers, Sept. 5, 1945; children: Sterling, Mindy Bingham, Marlyce. BA in Decorative Arts, U. Calif., Berkeley, 1944; MA, Calif. State U., Los Angeles, 1967. Cert. elem. and secondary tchr., Calif. Prin. and instr. math. Temple City, Calif., 1956; editor Calif. State Math. Jour., 1964-70; commr. Calif. Curriculum Commn., 1972-76; interior designer Betty Willis Interiors Co., Arcadia, Calif., 1981—; adj. prof. math methods and tchr. tng. Calif. State U. Los Angeles, 1964-78, Whittier (Calif.) Coll., 1974-82. Author: Sensory Learning Approach to Mathematics, 1976, The Laboratory Approach to Mathematics, 1970, Math. Framework for Calif. State Dept. Edn., 1974; contbr. articles to publs. Mem. PTA (life). Recipient Calif. Tchrs. Assn. Demonstration Tchr. award, 1965; Fellow Jamieson Found., 1965; NSF grantee, 1963, 67. Mem. Am. Soc. Interior Designers, Calif. Sch. Adminstrn., Found. for Edn., U. Calif. Alumni Assn. (life), Delta Kappa Gamma, Pi Lambda Theta, Alpha Delta Pi (fellow 1943). Republican. Methodist. Home and Office: 235 N Pacific Ave Solana Beach CA 92075

MYERS, THOMAS ARTHUR, accountant; b. Long Branch, N.J., Jan. 12, 1945; s. Arthur Louis and Gladys (Kampf) M.; m. Rose Torrez, June 19, 1976; children—Kirsten, Rhonda, Rhoda. B.S. in Math., N.Mex. Sch. Mines, 1966; B.S. in Acctg., U. No. Colo., 1977. Tax cons. Touche Ross & Co., Denver, 1977-82; producer surfing films, Honolulu, 1970-76; founding ptnr. T.A. Myers & Co., C.P.A.s, Denver, 1980—. lectr., cons. Fed. Home Loan Bank, profl. orgns.; chmn. Northwest Ctr. Mem. Am. Inst. C.P.A.s, Colo. Soc. C.P.A.s, Internat. Tax Group. Republican. Methodist. Club: Denver Athletic. Author: Tax Planning for Canadian Investment in the United States; Taxation of Foreign Investments in the United States, American Bankers Association Construction Policy and Lending Manual; contbr. articles to profl. jours. Home: 6256 W 86th Ave Arvada CO 80002

MYHREN, TRYGVE EDWARD, communications company executive; b. Palmerton, Pa., Jan. 3, 1937; s. Arne Johannes and Anita (Blatz) M.; m. Carol Jane Enman, Aug. 8, 1964; children: Erik, Kirsten, Tor; m. 2d Victoria Hamilton, Nov. 14, 1981; 1 stepdau., Paige. B.A. in Philosophy and Polit. Sci., Dartmouth Coll., 1958, M.B.A., 1959. Sales mgr., unit mgr. Procter and Gamble, Cin., 1963-65; sr. cons. Glendinning Cos., Westport, Conn., 1965-69; pres. Auberge Vintners, 1970-73; exec. v.p. Mktg. Continental, Westport, 1969-73; v.p., gen. mgr. CRM, Inc., Del Mar, Calif., 1973-75; v.p. mktg. Am. TV and Communications Corp., Englewood, Colo., 1975-78, sr. v.p. mktg. and programming, 1978-79, exec. v.p., 1980, pres., 1981, chmn. bd., chief exec. officer, 1982—; v.p. Time Inc., N.Y.C., 1981-86; treas., vice chmn., then chmn. bd., mem. exec com. Nat. Cable TV Assn., Washington, 1982—; bd. dirs. Home Box Office, N.Y.C., 1980-85, Temple-Eastex, Diboll, Tex., 1980-83. Vice chmn. Pub. Edn. Coalition. Served to lt. (j.g.) USN, 1959-62. Mem. Cable TV Adminstrn. and Mktg. Soc. (pres. 1978-79), Dartmouth Assn. Gt. Divide (trustee 1982-85). Episcopalian. Office: Am TV and Communications Corp 160 Inverness Dr West Englewood CO 80112

MYKLES, DONALD LEE, zoologist, crustacean biologist; b. Stockton, Calif., Oct. 23, 1950; s. Norman and Dorothy (Alldredge) M.; m. Vicki Fogel, Sept. 10, 1978. AB, U. Calif., Santa Barbara, 1973; PhD, U. Calif., Berkeley, 1979. Postdoctoral fellow Oak Ridge (Tenn.) Nat. Lab., 1979-85; asst. prof. zoology Colo. State U., Ft. Collins, 1985—. Contbr. articles to profl. jours. Grantee NIH, 1979-82, Muscular Dystrophy Assn., 1982-83, NSF, 1986—. Home: 321 Garfield St Fort Collins CO 80524 Office: Colo State U Dept Zoology Fort Collins CO 80523

MYLES, MARGARET JEAN, hospital supplies buyer, real property appraiser; b. Detroit, Oct. 26, 1952; d. William Thompson and Patricia (Maclean) M. Student, Western Mich. U., 1973, Oakland U., 1974; AA, Coast Line Coll., 1986. Unit sec. Hoag Meml. Hosp., Newport Beach, Calif., 1976-80, buyer, 1981-86; real estate appraiser P.M. Myles & Assocs., Irvine, Calif., 1980—. Mem. Nat. Assn. Purchasing Mgmt., Purchasing Mgmt. Assn. Orange County. Home: 120 A Carriage Dr Santa Ana CA 92707 Office: PM Myles & Assocs 17962 Sky Park Circle Suite B Irvine CA 92714

NACHMAN, JOSEPH FRANK, metallurgical consultant; b. Toledo, Jan. 22, 1918; s. Frank and Jane (Wujciak) N.; m. Rosemary Anderson, May 4, 1943; children: Richard Joseph, Ronald James. BS in Chemistry, U. Toledo, 1940; MS in Metallurgy, Ohio State U., 1947. Registered profl. engr., Calif., Colo., Md. Chief metallurgy branch U.S. Naval Ordnance Lab., Silver Spring, Md., 1948-56; mgr. alloy devel. U. Denver Research Inst., 1956-63; group leader Atomics Internat., Canoga Park, CA, 1963-66; chief applied scis. Solar Turbines, San Diego, 1966-77, research staff specialist, 1977-81; pres. Metall. Cons. Services, Inc., San Diego, 1981—. Editor: Rare Earth Research, 1961, Proceeding of 7th Conference on Rare-Earth Research vols. I & II., 1968; patentee in field; contbr. articles to profl. jours. Served to lt. commdr. USNR, 1943-46. Recipient Meritorious Civilian Service award, USN Ordnance Lab., 1953. Mem. Am. Soc. Metals (life), AAAS, Nat. Assn. Corrosion Engrs., Sigma Xi, Alpha Sigma Phi (v.p. 1939-40). Republican. Methodist. Avocations: travel, photography, geneal. research. Home and Office: Metall Cons Services Inc 7060 Murray Park Dr San Diego CA 92119

NACHMAN, RICHARD JOSEPH, management training company executive; b. Washington, Sept. 18, 1944; s. Joseph Frank and Rosemary (Anderson) N.; m. Nancy Ruth Hodgson, Feb. 4, 1966 (div. Oct. 1975); children: Russell J., Kirk L.; m. Christina Maria Schulz, Jan. 2, 1979; 1 child, C. Hoff. BA, U. Colo., 1968. Program dir. mgmt. edn. Grad. Sch. Bus. U. Mich., Ann Arbor, 1968-70; dir. Ctr. Mgmt. and Tech. Programs U. Colo., Boulder, 1970-74; pres. Mgmt. Research Corp., Boulder, 1974—, RJN and Assocs., Boulder, 1977—. Contbr. articles to profl. publs.; producer seminars The Art of Negotiating, The One Minute Manager, Japanese Manufacturing Techniques, World Class Manufacturing. Mem. Full Gospel Businessmen's Fellowship Internat. Republican. Avocations: travel, fishing, skiing, camping.

NACHMAN, RONALD JAMES, research chemist; b. Takoma Park, Md., Feb. 1, 1954; s. Joseph Frank and Rosemary (Anderson) N.; m. Lita Rose Wilson, Dec. 18, 1976. BS in Chemistry, U. Calif., San Diego, 1976; PhD in Organic Chemistry, Stanford U., 1981. Research asst. Scripps Inst. Oceanography, La Jolla, Calif., 1974-76; chemist Western Regional Research Ctr., USDA, Berkeley, Calif., 1981—; vis. scientist The Salk Inst., La Jolla, 1985. Contbr. sci. articles to profl. jours. Fellow Sci. and Humanities Symposia; mem. AAAS, Am. Chem. Soc., N.Y. Acad. Scis., Sigma Xi. Avocations: travel, photography, jogging, racketball. Home: 7 Peak Ct Hercules CA 94547 Office: USDA Western Regional Research Ctr 800 Buchanan St Berkeley CA 94710

NACHT, STEVE JERRY, geologist; b. Cleve., July 8, 1948; s. Max and Elfrida (Kamm) N.; m. Patricia Katherine Osicka, Aug. 3, 1976; 1 child, David Martin. BS in Geology, Kent State U., 1971, MS in Geology, 1973; Ms in Environ. Scis., Cleve. State U., 1979. Cert. profl. geologist, Ind. Geologist Cleve. Utilities Dept., 1974-78; geologist, hydrologist Dalton, Dalton & Newport, Cleve., 1979-82; prin. scientist Lockheed-Emsco, Las Vegas, Nev., 1983-86; sr. geologist, project mgr. Earth Tech. Inc., Long Beach, Calif., 1986—. Contbr. articles to profl. jours. Mem. AAAS, Am. Inst. Profl. Geologists (cert.), Assn. Ground Water Scientists and Engrs. (jour. reviewer), Assn. Engring. Geologists, Nat. Mgmt. Assn., ASTM (com. mem. groundwater, chmn. working group, chmn. ground water monitoring well abandonment standards).

NADELL, ANDREW THOMAS, psychiatrist; b. N.Y.C., Nov. 3, 1946; s. Samuel Tyler and Bertha Elaine (Trupine) N. MA, Columbia U., 1968; MSc, U. London, 1973; MD, Duke U., 1974. Diplomate Am. Bd. Psychiatry and Neurology. Resident in psychiatry U. Calif., Davis, 1974-77; clin. instr. psychiatry Stanford (Calif.) U. Sch. Medicine, 1979-84, clin. asst. prof. psychiatry, 1984—. Fellow Royal Soc. Medicine; mem. Am. Psychiat. Assn., Am. Assn. History of Medicine, Am. Osler Soc., Bay Area History Medicine Soc. (sec. 1984—), Soc. for Social History Medicine, Assn. Internat. de Bibliophilie, Soc. Internat. d'Histoire de la Médecine. Clubs: Grolier (N.Y.C.); Roxburghe, Colophon, Commonwealth, Book of Calif. (San Francisco). Avocation: book collecting. Office: 1828 El Camino Real Burlingame CA 94010

NADLER, GERALD, industrial engineering educator; b. Cin., Mar. 12, 1924; s. Samuel and Minnie (Krumbein) N.; m. Elaine Muriel Dubin, June 22, 1947; children: Burton Alan, Janice Susan, Robert Daniel. Student, U. Cin., 1942-43; B.S.M.E., Purdue U., 1945, M.S. in Indsl. Engring, 1946, Ph.D., 1949. Registered profl. engr., Mo., Wis. Instr. Purdue U., 1948-49; asst. prof. indsl. engring. Washington U., St. Louis, 1949-52; assoc. prof. Washington U., 1952-55, prof., head dept. indsl. engring., 1955-64; prof. U. Wis., Madison, 1964-84; chmn. dept. indsl. engring. U. Wis., 1964-67, 71-75; prof., chmn. dept. indsl. and systems engring. U. So. Calif., 1983—, IBM prof. engring. mgmt., 1986—; v.p. Artcraft Mfg. Co., St. Louis, 1956-57; dir. Intertherm Inc., St. Louis, 1969-85; pres. Planning, Design, and Improvement Methods Group, Los Angeles, 1980—; vis. prof. U. Birmingham, Eng., 1959, Waseda U., Tokyo, 1963, Ind. U., 1964, U. Louvain, Belgium, 1975, Technion-Israel Inst. Tech., Haifa, 1976; speaker in field. Author: Work Design: A Systems Concept, 1970, (with J. T. Johnston and J. E. Bailey) Design Concepts for Information Systems, 1975, (with M. Norton and W.C. Bozeman) Student Planned Acquisition of Required Knowledge, 1980, The Planning and Design Approach, 1981; contbr. numerous articles to profl. jours.; reviewer books, papers, proposals. Mem. Ladue Bd. Edn., St. Louis County, 1960-63; acting exec. dir. Higher Edn. Coordinating Council Met. St. Louis, 1962-63; chmn. planning com. Wis. Regional Med. Program, 1966-69, mem. steering com., 1969-73. Served with USN, 1943-45. Recipient Gilbreth medal Soc. Advancement Mgmt., 1961; Editorial award Hosp. Mgmt. Mag., 1966; Disting. Engring. Alumnus award Purdue U., 1975; Inst. Indsl. Engrs. Book of Yr. award, 1983. Fellow AAAS, Inst. Indsl. Engrs.; mem. Am. Soc. Engring. Edn., Inst. Mgmt. Scis., AAUP, Nat. Acad. Engring., World Future Soc., Japan Work Design Soc. (hon. adv. 1968—), Council Understanding of Tech. in Human Affairs (bd. dirs.), Sigma Xi, Alpha Pi Mu (nat. officer), Pi Tau Sigma, Omega Rho, Tau Beta Pi. Patentee ultrasonic measurement of body movements. Office: University Park GER 240 Los Angeles CA 90089-0193

NADY, JOHN, electronics company executive; b. Agfalva, Hungary, Feb. 13, 1945; came to U.S., 1951; s. John and Hermine Nady. BSEE, Calif. Inst. Tech., 1968; MSEE, U. Calif., Berkeley, 1968. Elec. engr. Lawrence Radiation Lab., Livermore, 1966-71, Westinghouse Corp., Oakland, Calif., 1971-72; owner, chief exec. officer Nady Systems, Inc., Oakland, Calif., 1976—, Club Omni, Inc., Oakland, Calif., 1985—. Patentee in field. Mem. Nat. Assn. Broadcasters, Audio Engring. Soc., Nat. Assn. Music Merchants. Avocations: electric guitar, skiing, tennis, golfing, softball. Office: Nady Systems Inc 1145 65th St Oakland CA 94608

NAEGELE, CARL JOSEPH, university academic administrator, educator; b. Newark, Jan. 1, 1939; s. Carl Joseph Sr. and Mabel (Flood) N.; n. Elizabeth C. McVey, June 19, 1971; children: Jennifer, Erin. BS, Kean Coll., 1965; MS, Syracuse U., 1969; PhD, Cornell U., 1974. Tchr. physics Summit (N.J.) High Sch., 1965-68; instr. physics Kean Coll., Union, N.J., 1968-70; research assoc. Cornell U., Ithaca, N.Y., 1973-75; prof. Mich. State U., East Lansing, 1975-79; program dir. NSF, Washington, 1979-81; dean coll. arts and scis. U. San Francisco, 1981—; computer cons. San Rafael, Calif., 1981—. Author: Physics for the Life and Health Sciences, 1974, Laboratory Experiment in General Physics, 1976, Electronic Mail and Communication Networks, 1984; contbr. articles to profl. jours. Served with U.S. Army, 1959-61, Korea. Recipient Leadership award U. San Francisco, 1985, Outstanding Teaching award Mich. State U., 1978; grantee NSF, 1968, 78, Council for Basic Edn., 1984-86. Mem. IEEE, Am. Phys. Soc., Am. Assn. Physics Tchrs., Am. Assn. Univ. Adminstrs., Assn. Computing Machinery. Avocations: flying, boating, skiing, tennis, running. Office: Univ of San Francisco Coll of Liberal Arts and Scis Ignatian Heights San Francisco CA 94117

NAEGELE, JOSEPH LOYOLA, lawyer; b. San Francisco, July 19, 1955; s. Charles Frederick and Rosemary Cecilia (Ledogar) N.; m. BeaLisa Elizabeth Sydlik, Feb. 21, 1981; children: Joseph Loyola Jr., Elizabeth Anne. B.A., U. Calif.-Davis, 1977; J.D., U. Calif.-San Francisco, 1981. Bar: Calif. 1982. Legal intern U.S. Congress, Washington, 1976; legal extern Calif. Ct. Appeals, San Francisco, 1980; law clk. U.S. Dist. Ct., San Francisco, 1981, Sacramento Dist. Atty.'s Office, Sacramento, 1982; tchr. St. Francis High Sch., Sacramento, 1982; atty. Law Offices of Jack Komar, San Jose, Calif., 1983-85; ptnr. Naegele & Naegele, San Jose, 1985—; prof. Lincoln Law Sch., San Jose, 1983-85. Mem. Santa Clara County Bar Assn., Calif. Trial Lawyers Assn., Santa Clara County Trial Lawyers Assn., St. Thomas Moore Soc., Barristers Club. Democrat. Roman Catholic. Home: 1105 Loupe Ave San Jose CA 95121 Office: 111 W St John St Suite 650 San Jose CA 95113-1105

NAEGLE, A. BRADLEY, business executive; b. Casper, Wyo., June 27, 1931; s. Owen A. and Gladys Josephine (Bradley) N.; B.S., U. Denver, 1953; m. Dorothy Elizabeth Bolstad, June 30, 1957. Supr. corp. planning and control Douglas Aircraft, Santa Monica, Calif., 1955-61, TRW, Inc., Redondo Beach, Calif., 1961-63; pres., founder Manpower, Inc. of Santa Barbara, 1963-84; founder, WORK, Inc., 1968, pres., 1971, mem. exec. com., 1968—; pres., founder Bus. Research Corp., 1984—. Served with U.S. Army, 1953-55. Mem. Assn. Manpower Franchise Owners (dir., corp. sec.), Beta Gamma Sigma. Republican. Presbyterian. Club: Kiwanis. Office: 1727 State St Santa Barbara CA 93101

NAFZIGER, RALPH HAMILTON, metallurgical chemist, researcher; b. Mpls., Aug. 9, 1937; s. Ralph Otto and Charlotte Monona (Hamilton) N. BS, U. Wis., 1960; PhD, Pa. State U., 1966. Registered geologist, Oreg. Field asst. U.S. Geol. Survey, Denver, 1963; research assoc. Pa. State U., University Park, 1966-67; research chemist U.S. Bur. Mines, Albany, Oreg., 1967-79, research supr., 1981—; research supr. U.S. Bur. Mines, Mpls., 1979-81; key reader Metall. Transactions, Pitts., 1980—. Contbr. articles to profl. jours. Member Albany Concert Band, 1970—, bd. dirs. 1975-76, pres. 1977; mem. Salem (Oreg.) Pops Orch., 1969-79, Salem Concert Band, 1981-83, West Oreg. State Coll. Summer Band, Monmouth, 1975—. Recipient Outstanding Performance award U.S. Bur. Mines, Albany, 1973, 77, 84-86. Mem. Am. Soc. Mining, Metall. and Petroleum Engrs. (phys. chemistry com. 1980—, nonferrous metals com. 1986—, Copper, Nickel, Cobalt, Precious Metals com. 1986—), Am. Soc. Metals, Am. Foundrymen's Soc. (fuels com. 1980—, charge materials com. 1984—), Mineral. Soc. Am. (abstractor 1977—), Geol. Soc. Am., Oreg. Acad. Sci., Geol. Soc. Oreg. County, Internat. Horn Soc., Sigma Xi (v.p. local chpt. 1972, pres. 1973). Clubs: Chemeketans (Salem) (v.p.-treas. 1975-78), Mazamas (Portland), Obsidians (Eugene). Avocations: photography, astronomy, sports, automobiles, music. Home: 1084 SW 33d Ave Albany OR 97321 Office: US Bur Mines 1450 SW Queen Ave Albany OR 97321

NAG, NABIN KRISHNA, fuels engineering educator; b. Laugram, India, Apr. 27, 1944; came to U.S., 1977; s. Joges C. and Lilavati (Ray) N.; m. Sahana Sinha, Mar. 8, 1967; children: Sridip, Nilanjan. BS, Calcutta U., India, 1963; MS, Patna U., India, 1966; PhD, IIT, Kharagpur, India, 1972. Postdoctoral fellow Twente U., Enschede, Holland, 1976-77, U. Del., Newark, 1977-79; vis. scientist Max-Planck Inst., West Berlin, Fed. Republic of Germany, 1979-80; scientist Regional Research Lab., Hyderabad, India, 1981-82; research prof. fuels engring. U. Utah, Salt Lake City, 1984-86; sr. research chemist Harshaw/Filtrol Partnership, Los Angeles, 1986—. Contbr. 30 sci. papers to profl. publs. Mem. Am. Chem. Soc., Western States Catalysis Club, Catalysis Soc. India. Avocations: reading history, chess, fishing. Home: 9150 Brookshire Ave #141 Downey CA 90240 Office: Harshaw/Filtrol Partnership 3250 E Washington Blvd Los Angeles CA 90023

NAGATA, KENNETH MASUHISA, botanist; b. Honolulu, June 26, 1945; s. Kanao and Kiyome Nagata; m. Linda Yamada, Sept. 10, 1977. BA, U. hawaii, Manoa, 1968; MA, U. hawaii, 1980. Research asst. Lyon Arboretum U. Hawaii, Manoa, 1969-74, research assoc. II, 1974—, instr. botany, 1972-74; instr. botany Chaminade U., Honolulu, 1977-78, Kapiolani Community Coll., 1978, 81, Leeward Community Coll., Pearl City, Hawaii, 1984; botanist Hawaiian Animal Species Adv. Commn., 1978-86, State of Hawaii Natural Areas Reserves Commn., Honolulu, 1986—; acad. advisor liberal arts, U. Hawaii, Honolulu, 1975—; assoc. judge Hawaiian Sci. Engring. Fair, Honolulu, 1982—. Co-author: Hawaii's Vanishing Flora, 1980; contbr. articles to profl. jours. Grantee U. Hawaii, 1978, Garden Club Honolulu, 1979. Mem. Soc. Econ. Botany, Hawaiian Bot. Soc., Tex. Acad. Sci., Lyon Arboretum Assn., Bishop Mus. Assn. (field botanist 1978—), Sierra Club, Sigma Xi. Avocations: hiking, fishing, sports. Office: Lyon Arboretum 3860 Manoa Rd Honolulu HI 96822

NAGATA, RAYMOND SHOGO, contractor; b. Honolulu, Jan. 5, 1924; s. Keizo and Tome N.; student U. Hawaii, 1941, 46, Chgo. Tech. Coll., 1946-48; m. Betty Sanaye Sakurada, June 5, 1949; children—Steven M., Russel S., Kathleen S., Noreen R. Pres., K. Nagata Ltd., Honolulu, 1948—, K. Nagata Constrn. Inc., 1951—. Mem. Contractors Licence Bd. Commn., 1969-77. Trustee, Hawaii Carpenters Pension Trust Fund, Hawaiian Carpenter Health and Welfare Trust Fund; treas. Gen. Contractor Assn. Hawaii. Served with M.I., U.S. Army, 1942-45. Mem. Gen. Contractor Assn. Hawaii (dir.). Address: 723C Umi St Honolulu HI 96819

NAGEL, GLENN MARSHALL, biochemistry educator; b. Blue Island, Ill., Apr. 16, 1944; s. Lewis A. and Annette (Jaedtke) N.; m. Greta Kallio, Sept. 3, 1966; children: Christina L., Paul W. BA, Knox Coll., 1966; PhD, U. Ill., Chgo., 1971; postgrad., U. Calif., Berkeley, 1972. Asst. prof. biochemistry Calif. State U., Fullerton, 1972-76, assoc. prof., 1976-80, prof., 1980—. Contbr. articles to profl. jours. Research grantee NSF, NIH, Calif. Heart Assn. Research Corp., 1972—. Mem. Am. Chem. Soc. Lutheran. Office: Calif State Univ Dept Biochemistry Fullerton CA 92634

NAGEL, JEROME KAUB, architect; b. Denver, Dec. 26, 1923; s. Fritz Andrew and Josephine (Gaylord) N.; m. Cynthia Fels, Sept. 1, 1951; children—Peter Barry, James Gaylord. B.Arch., Yale U., 1949. Registered architect, Colo. Prin. J.K. Nagel Architect, Denver, 1953-61, Rogers & Nagel, Denver, 1961-66, Rogers, Nagel, Langhart, Architects, 1966-77, Interplan Inc., 1969-77; pres. Nagel Investment Co.; dir. Bank Western, Denver, Field Devel. Corp., Denver. Mem. Colo. Hwy. Commn., chmn., 1982-83; bd. dirs. Planned Parenthood Fed. Am. Inc., N.Y.C., 1974-78, Rocky Mountain Planned Parenthood, Denver, 1972-76, Colo. chpt. ARC, 1957-60, 80-81; mem. panel arbitrators Am. Arbitration Assn., 1962—; chmn. Colo. Bicycle Adb. Bd. Served to 1st lt. AC U.S. Army, 1943-45. Decorated D.F.C., Air medal with 11 oak leaf clusters. Mem. AIA (nat. life; sec. chpt. 1960-61, pres. 1962-63). Republican. Episcopalian. Clubs: Denver Country (bd. dirs. 1983-86), University (bd. dirs. 1962-66)Mile High. Lodge: Rotary. Home: 67 Eudora St Denver CO 80220

NAGEL, PATRICIA JO, non-profit public policy administrator, lawyer; b. Billings, Mont., Sept. 24, 1942; d. Robert Mark and Evelyn Margaret (Lipsack) McKeown; m. Robert Wells Nagel, Aug. 18, 1963; children: Stacia, Susanna. BA in Polit. Sci., N.Mex. State U., 1965; JD, U. Wyo., 1983. Bar: Wyo. 1984. Interior designer Nassif's Interiors, Cedar Rapids, Iowa, 1965-67, Cedar Rapids Paint, 1973-74; law clk. to presiding justice 7th jud. dist., Casper, Wyo., 1983-84; sole practice Casper, 1984—; dir. Wyo. Futures Project, Casper, 1986—. Sr. editor Land and Water Law Rev., 1982-83. Mem. planning commn. City of Casper, 1980; pres., bd. dirs. Friends of Library, Casper, 1980; pres. Meadowlark Montessori Sch., Casper, 1979; sec. Casper Bicentennial Com., 1976; v.p. Nicolaysen Art Mus., Casper, 1985-86; sec., bd. dirs. Hospice Cancer Treatment Ctr., Casper, 1985-86. Mem. ABA, Natrona County Bar Assn., Wyo. State Bar Assn., Assn. Trial Lawyers Am. Republican. Lutheran. Avocations: writing, tennis. Home: 233 E 12th Casper WY 82601 Office: 300 S Wolcott Casper WY 82601

NAGHDI, PAUL MANSOUR, engineering educator; b. Tehran, Iran, Mar. 29, 1924; came to U.S., 1944, naturalized, 1948; s. G. H. and A. (Momtaz) N.; m. Patricia Spear, Sept. 6, 1947 (dec. Mar. 15, 1975); children: Stephen, Suzanne, Sondra. B.S., Cornell U., 1946; M.S., U. Mich., 1948, Ph.D., 1951. From instr. to prof. engring. mechanics U. Mich., 1949-58; prof. engring. sci. U. Calif., Berkeley, 1958—, chmn. div. applied mechanics, 1964-69; Miller prof. Miller Inst. Basic Sci., 1963-64, 71-72; cons. theoretical and applied mechanics 1953—; Mem. U.S. Nat. Com. on Theoretical and Applied Mechanics, 1972-84, chmn., 1979-80; mem. gen. assembly Internat. Union Theoretical and Applied Mechanics, 1978-84. Served with AUS, 1946-47. Recipient Disting. Faculty award U. Mich., 1956, George Westinghouse award Am. Soc. Engring. Edn., 1962; Guggenheim fellow, 1958. Fellow ASME (chmn. applied mechanics div. 1971-72, Timoshenko medal 1980, hon. mem. 1983), Acoustical Soc. Am., Soc. Engring. Sci. (dir. 1963-70, A.C. Eringen medal 1986); mem. Nat. Acad. Engring., Soc. Rheology, Sigma Xi. Home: 530 Vistamont Ave Berkeley CA 94708

NAGLE, ROBERT OWEN, lawyer; b. Watertown, S.D., Feb. 10, 1929; s. John Raymond and Kathleen Margaret (McQuillen) N.; m. Louise Emerson H'Doubler, Mar. 14, 1954; children—Robert Owen, Charles Francis, Margaret Louise. B.S. in Economics, U. Wis., 1951; LL.B., U. Calif., 1957. Bar: Calif. 1957. Asso. firm Morrison, Foerster, Holloway, Clinton and Clark, San Francisco, 1957-62; partner Morrison, Foerster, Holloway, Clinton and Clark, 1962-64; gen. atty. Spreckels Sugar div. Amstar Corp., San Francisco, 1964-66; v.p. Spreckels Sugar div. Amstar Corp., 1966-68, exec. v.p., 1968-71; v.p. parent co. Spreckels Sugar div. Amstar Corp., N.Y.C., 1971-76; exec. v.p. Am. Sugar div. Amstar Corp., N.Y.C., 1975-76; pres., chief exec. officer Calif. and Hawaiian Sugar Co., San Francisco, 1976-82; also dir. Calif. and Hawaiian Sugar Co.; ptnr. Brobeck, Phleger & Harrison, 1982-86; private investor Piedmont, Calif., 1986—; bd. dirs. Providence Hosp., Oakland, Calif. Bd. dirs. San Francisco Bay Area council Boy Scouts Am.; trustee U. Calif. Berkeley Found., Wis. Alumni Research Found., Pacific Vascular Research Found., San Francisco. Served to lt. j.g. USN, 1951-54, Korea. Decorated Air medal, Bronze Star. Mem. Am. Bar Assn., State Bar Calif., Bar Assn. San Francisco, U. Wis. Found. Clubs: Claremont Country, Pacific Union.

NAGLESTAD, FREDERIC ALLEN, legislative advocate; b. Sioux City, Iowa, Jan. 13, 1929; s. Ole T. and Evelyn Elizabeth (Erschen) N.; student (scholar) U. Chgo., 1947-49; m. Beverly Minnette Shellberg, Feb. 14, 1958; children—Patricia Minnette, Catherine Janette. Pub. affairs, pub. relations, newscaster, announcer KSCJ-radio, Sioux City, Iowa, 1949-51; producer, dir., newscaster, announcer WOW-TV, Omaha, 1953-57; program mgr. WCPO-TV, Cin., 1957-58; mgr. KNTV-TV, San Jose, Calif., 1958-61; owner Results Employment Agy., San Jose, 1961-75; legis. advocate Naglestad Assocs., Inc., Calif. Automotive Wholesalers Assn., Assn. News Distbrs., Air Quality Products, Calif. Auto Service Assn., Calif. Assn. Wholesalers-Distbrs., Quakemaster, many others, 1969—. Pres. Calif. Employment Assn., 1970-72. Asst. concertmaster Sioux City Symphony Orch., 1945-47. Served as sgt. AUS, 1951-53. Recognized for outstanding contbn. to better employment law, Resolution State Calif. Legislature, 1971. Office: 3991 Fair Oaks Blvd Sacramento CA 95864

NAGOSHI, CRAIG TETSUO, psychology researcher; b. Honolulu, Mar. 9, 1956; s. Kunio and Tokiko (Nonaga) N. BA in Psychology, U. Hawaii, 1978, MA in Psychology, 1980, PhD in Psychology, 1984. Researcher Inst.

Behavioral Genetics U. Colo., Boulder, 1984—; statis. cons., Honolulu, 1980-84. Contbr. articles to profl. jours. Mem. Colo. FREEZE Voter, 1985—. Drug Abuse Tng. grantee Nat. Inst. Drug Abuse, 1984-86. Mem. Behavior Genetics Assn., Internat. Soc. Biomed. Research on Alcoholism, Sigma Xi. Democrat. Avocations: guitar, songwriting, poetry, reading, bicycling. Home: 408 S Lashley Ln Boulder CO 80303 Office: U Colo Inst Behavioral Genetics Campus Box 447 Boulder CO 80309

NAGRANI, SHYAM KISHINCHAND, electrical engineer; b. Bombay, Sept. 9, 1948; s. K.H. and Ratna K. (Kshatriya) N.; m. Mira Shyam Kalanjee, Nov. 30, 1973; children: Manisha, Shefali. Student, Indian Inst. Tech., Bombay, 1966-69; BSEE, Ga. Tech., 1970; MSEE, U. So. Calif., 1972. Engr. Tata Electric Cos., Bombay, 1972-77, Burroughs Corp., Pasadena, Calif., 1977-78; sr. engr. Intersil, Inc., Cupertino, Calif., 1978-80; section mgr. Synertek, Inc., Santa Clara, Calif., 1980-84; proj. engr. mgr. Chips & Techs., Milpitas, Calif., 1985—; bd. dirs. Antech Inc., Atlanta, Calif., 1981—. Mem. Eta Kappa Nu, Tau Beta Pi. Office: Chips & Techs Inc 521 Cottonwood Ave Milpitas CA 95035

NAGURSKI, JAN STEPHEN, controller; b. Long Beach, Calif., Sept. 23, 1944; s. Stephen and Edna Mae (Hart) N.; m. Bernadette Esther Barrett, Apr. 23, 1976; children: Mark, Brian, Kevin. BA in English, Calif. State U., Long Beach, 1967; degree in civilian club mgmt. with honors, Air Force Inst. Tech., Wright-Patterson AFB, Ohio, 1971; MBA, Pepperdine U., 1983. Commd. 2d lt. USAF, 1967, advanced through grades to capt., 1970, resigned, 1975; acct. Sta. WBAP/KSCS, Ft. Worth, Tex., 1975-76; mgmt. acct. Adria Ltd., Strabane, Ireland, 1976-78; gen. mgr. Bundoran (Ireland) Holidays, 1978-81; corp. fin. planning mgr. Luxfer USA, Riverside, Calif., 1981-87; controller Superform USA, Inc., Riverside, 1987—; cons., controller Superform USA, Riverside, 1985—. Author/editor newsletter Smudgepot, 1984-86. Cubmaster Boy Scouts Am., Canyon Lake, Calif. Recipient Gold Medal Menu award Nat. Restaurant Assn., Ft. Worth, 1973. Mem. Nat. Assn. Accts. (pres. 1985-86), Data Processing Mgmt. Assn., Inst. Adminstrv. Acctg., U.K. Republican. Roman Catholic. Home: 23667 Brook Dr Canyon Lake CA 92380 Office: Superform USA Inc 6825 Jurupa Ave Riverside CA 92504

NAGY, BARTHOLOMEW STEPHEN, geochemist, educator; b. Budapest, Hungary, May 11, 1927; came to U.S., 1948, naturalized, 1955; s. Stephen and Mary (Mueller) N.; m. Marjorie Lois Bibey, Feb. 1, 1952; 1 dau., Erika Anne; m. Lois Anne Brach, Aug. 10, 1967; 1 child, Yvonne Maria. Student, Peter Pazmany U., Budapest, 1945-48; M.A., Columbia U., 1950; Ph.D., Pa. State U., 1953. With Stanolind Oil & Gas Co., Tulsa, 1953-55; supr. geophys. research Cities Service Research & Devel. Co., Tulsa, 1955-57; assoc. prof. Fordham U., 1957-65; vis. assoc. prof. U. Calif., San Diego, 1963-65, assoc. research geochemist, 1965-68; prof. geoscis. U. Ariz., Tucson, 1968—; Mem. adv. bd. Lunar Sci. Inst., 1972. Author 3 books, articles in field.; editor-in-chief Jour. Precambrian Research. Mem. N.Y. Acad. Scis. (chmn. geol. scis. sect. 1961-63), Geochem. Soc. (counselor 1961-64), Am. Chem. Soc., Internat. Soc. for Study of Origin of Life. Research petroleum and organic geochemistry, X-ray crystallography and analytical chemistry, carbonaceous meteorites; prin. investigator lunar samples, 1969-74. Home: 245 Greenock Dr Tucson AZ 85704 Office: U Ariz Lab Organic Geochemistry 522 Gould-Simpson Bldg Tucson AZ 85721

NAGY, KENNETH A(LEX), biology educator; b. Santa Monica, Calif., July 1, 1943; s. Alex J. and Phyllis F. Nagy; m. Patricia Vaughan, June 11, 1967; children: Mark S., Erik M. AB in Biology, U. Calif., Riverside, 1967, PhD in Biology, 1971. Asst. prof. biology UCLA, 1971-77, assoc. prof., 1977-83, prof., 1983—. Contbr. articles to profl. jours. Active Boy Scouts Am., Los Angeles, 1982—. Served with U.S. Navy, 1962-64. Grantee NSF, U.S. Dept. Energy. Mem. AAAS, Ecol. Soc. Am., Am. Soc. Ichthyologists and Herpetologists. Avocation: photography. Home: 11833 Allaseba Dr Los Angeles CA 90066 Office: Lab Biomed and Environ Scis UCLA 900 Veteran Ave Los Angeles CA 90024

NAGY, WILLIAM WALLACE, dentist, prosthodontist, army officer; b. Battle Creek, Mich., Aug. 31, 1944; s. Joseph Vincent and Dorothy Marion (Wallace) N. BS, U. Akron, 1966; DDS, Ohio State U., 1970. Diplomate Am. Bd. Prosthodontics. Commd. capt. U.S. Army, 1970, advanced through grades to col., 1984; dental surgeon 1st Cav. Div., Ft. Hood, Tex., 1970-73; assoc. prof. Baylor U., Acad. Health Scis. U.S. Army, Ft. Sam, Houston, 1973-76; dental hygiene course dir. Acad. Health Scis., U.S. Army, 1973-75, officer-in-charge, dental lab., 1975-76; dir. resident prosthodontics U.S. Army, Ft. Leonard Wood, Mo., 1978-79, asst. dir. of dental and gen. practice, residency, 1979-83; asst. chief clinician U.S. Army, Ft. Richardson, Alaska, 1983-84, chief clinician 1984-86, dep. comdr. of all Alaska dental activities, 1984-86; dir. resident instruction and fixed prosthodontics, U.S. Army, Ft. Ord, Calif., 1986—. Contbr. articles to profl. jours. Decorated Army Commendation medal, Meritorious Service medal with oak leaf cluster. Fellow Am. Coll. Prosthodontists; mem. ADA, Assn. Mil. Surgeons of U.S., Fedn. Prosthodontic Orgns., Order Mil. Med. Merit, Omicron Kappa Upsilon (hon.), Psi Omega. Republican. Episcopalian. Clubs: West Yellowstone Flyfishers; Driftskippers (pres. 1984-86) (Alaska)., Driftskippers (Alaska) (pres. 1984—). Home: 9936 Timothy Path Salinas CA 93907 Office: USA Dentac Burke Dental Clinic Fort Ord CA 93944-1034

NAHMAN, NORRIS STANLEY, electrical engineer; b. San Francisco, Nov. 9, 1925; s. Hyman Cohen and Rae (Levin) N.; m. Shirley D. Maxwell, July 20, 1968; children: Norris Stanley, Vicki L., Vance W., Scott T. B.S. in Electronics Engring, Calif. Poly. State U., 1951; M.S.E.E., Stanford U., 1952; Ph.D. in Elec. Engring, U. Kans., 1961. Registered profl. engr., Colo. Electronic scientist Nat. Security Agy., Washington, 1952-55; prof. elec. engring., dir. electronics research lab. U. Kans., Lawrence, 1955-66; sci. cons., chief pulse and time domain sect. Nat. Bur. Standards, Boulder, Colo., 1966-73; chief time domain metrology, sr. scientist Nat. Bur. Standards, 1975-83, group leader field characterization group, 1984-85; v.p. Picosecond Pulse Labs, Inc., Boulder, 1986—; prof., chmn. dept. elec. engring. U. Toledo,, 1973-75;; prof. elec. engring. U. Colo.., Boulder,, 1966—; disting. lectr., prin. prof. Centre Nat. d'Etude des Telecommunications Summer Sch., Lannion, France, 1978; disting. lectr. Harbin Inst. Tech., Peoples Republic China, summer 1982; mem. faculty NATO Advanced Study Inst., Castelvecchio, Italy, 1983, Internat. Radio Sci. Union/NRC; chmn. internat. intercommn. group Waveform measurements 1981—, chmn. Commn. A, 1985-86. Contbr. research articles to sci. publs.; patentee superconducting coaxial cable. Asst. scoutmaster Longs Peak council Boy Scouts Am., 1970-73, 75—. Served with U.S. Mcht. Marine, 1943-46; with U.S. Army, 1952-55. Ford Found. faculty fellow MIT, 1962; Nat. Bur. Standards sr. staff fellow, 1978-79; recipient commendation medal for research contbns. U.S. Army, 1954, Disting. Alumnus award Calif. State Poly. U., 1972, Order of Arrow Boy Scouts Am., 1976. Fellow IEEE (editorial bd. Trans. on Instrumentation and Measurement 1982-86, Andrew H. Chi award for best tech. paper 1984), Internat. Sci. Radio Union; mem. Am. Assn. Engring. Edn., Sigma Pi Sigma, Tau Beta Pi, Eta Kappa Nu, Sigma Tau. Club: Am. Radio Relay League (life). Office: PO Box 44 Boulder CO 80306

NAHMIAS, VICTOR JAY, architect; b. Woodside, N.Y., May 2, 1951; s. Leon and Judith (Haupt) N.; m. Michal Caspi, June 24, 1975; children: Ariel, Tamar. BA, U. Pa., 1973; BArch, U. B.C., Vancouver, 1977. Registered profl. architect. Carpenter's asst. Weir Constrn., Vancouver, 1973; designer, draftsman Kenn Butts, Northridge, Calif., 1977-78; project mgr. B. Robert Axton, Sherman Oaks, Calif., 1978-79, Howard R. Lane, Woodland Hills, Calif., 1979-81; project architect Rochlin & Baran Assocs., Los Angeles, 1981-84, Kaiser Permanente, Pasadena, 1984—. Democrat. Jewish. Avocations: photography, philately, reading, music, skiing. Home: 3643 Kalsman Dr #1 Los Angeles CA 90016 Office: Kaiser Found Health Plan 393 E Walnut St Pasadena CA 91188

NAIDU, MOTUPALLI VENKAMA, chemist; b. Velam Padu, Andra Pradesh, India, July 1, 1952; came to U.S., 1979; s. Motupalli Narasappa and Kanthamma (Kilari) N.; m. Prameela Velidi, Aug. 19, 1983; children: Vasu, Motupalli. BS, Sri Venkateswara U., Tirupati, India, 1973, MS, 1975; PhD, Indian Inst. of Sci., Bangalore, 1979. Research assoc. Rice U., Houston, 1979-83; radiosynthesis chemist Shell Agrl. Chem. Co., Modesto, Calif., 1983—. Contbr. articles to profl. jours. Recipient Prof. Neelakantam scholarship S.V. U., Tirupati, India, 1975, Prof. B.H. Iyer Gold medal Indian Inst. Sci., 1980. Mem. Am. Chem. Soc., Health Physics Soc., Bay Area Radiosynthesis Chemists Group. Hindu. Avocations: chess, gardening, racquetball. Home: 166 Fairhill Dr Wilmington DE 19898 Office: Shell Agrl Chem Co PO Box 4248 Modesto CA 95352

NAITO, VERNER RICHARD, management consultant; b. Portland, Oreg., May 13, 1955; s. Samuel T. and Mary (Kawanami) N. BA, Pomona Coll., 1977; MBA, Harvard U., 1982. CPA, Oreg. Cons. mgr. Arthur Andersen & Co., Portland, 1982—; bd. dirs. Norcrest China Co., Portland. Mem. Planning Execs. Inst. (pres. 1984-85), Oreg. Bankers Assn., The Planning Forum. Republican. Clubs: Univ., Harvard. Bus. Sch. (Portland). Office: Arthur Andersen & Co 111 SW Columbia Suite 1400 Portland OR 97201

NAKAGAKI, DAVID AKIRA, civil engineer; b. Berkeley, Calif., Oct. 14, 1954; s. George Yasuyoshi and Haruye (Yoshiwara) N; BSCE, MSCE, Stanford U., 1977; MBA, UCLA, 1985. Registered profl. engr., Calif., 1979. Project engr. Los Angeles County Sanitation Dists., Whittier, Calif., 1977—, solid waste mgmt. dept., 1982—. Recipient Student award ASTM, 1976. Mem. ASCE, Am. Water Works Assn., Water Pollution Control Fedn., Tau Beta Pi, Chi Epsilon. Democrat. Presbyterian. Home: 21302 Wavecrest Circle Huntington Beach CA 92646 Office: PO Box 4998 Whittier CA 90607

NAKAGAWA, ALLEN DONALD, radiologic technologist; b. N.Y.C., Mar. 14, 1955; s. Walter Tsunehiko and Alyce Tsuneko (Kinoshita) N. BS in Environ. Studies, St. John's U., Jamaica, N.Y., 1977; MS in Marine Biology, C.W. Post Coll., 1980. Cert. radiologic technologist, Calif. Research asst. environ. studies St. John's U., 1976-78; lab. asst. Bur. Water Surveillance, Nassau Co. of Health Dept., Wantaugh, N.Y., 1978; clin. endocrinology asst. U. Calif. VA Hosp., San Francisco, 1981-83; student technologist St. Mary's Hosp., San Francisco, 1985-86; radiologic technologist Mt. Zion Hosp., San Francisco, 1986—. Contbr. articles to profl. jours., chpts. to books. Recruiting chmn. hunger project C.W. Post Coll., 1979. Mem. Calif. Soc. Radiologic Technologists (San Francisco and state chpts.), Calif. Marine Mammal Ctr., AAAS, Am. Registry Radiol. Technologists (cert.), Calif. Acad. Scis., Sigma Xi. Democrat. Methodist. Avocations: assisting handicapped, photography, music, bowling, writing. Home: 1251-8 Ave Apt 7 San Francisco CA 94122 Office: Mt Zion Hosp Radiology Dept 1600 Divisadero San Francisco CA 94117

NAKAHATA, TADAKA, retired consulting engineer, land surveyor; b. Kauai, Hawaii, Nov. 24, 1924; s. Tadao and Yae (Ohta) N.; B.S. in Civil Engring., U. Hawaii, 1951; m. Clara S. Sakanashi, June 23, 1956; children—Leanne A. Nikaido, Holly E., Merry Y. Engr./surveyor B.H. McKeague & Assos., Honolulu, 1951-55, Harland Bartholomew & Assos., Honolulu, 1955-56, Paul Low Engring. Co., Honolulu, 1956-59, Nakahata, Kaneshige, Imata & Assos., 1959-63; owner T. Nakahata, Honolulu, 1964-83, ret., 1983; mem. Hawaii Bd. Registration of Architects, Engrs. and Land Surveyors, 1980-83. Served with AUS, 1946-47. Mem. ASCE, Am. Congress Surveying and Mapping, Nat. Soc. Profl. Engrs. Mem. Makiki Christian Ch.

NAKAI, GEORGE SUMIYA, physician; b. Los Angeles, Feb. 1, 1930; s. Kanesabura and Yoshiko (Iwatake) N.; m. Nadine Mitsuye Fukagawa, Feb. 27, 1959; children: Richard, Kenneth. BS, U. Utah, 1952, MD, 1956. Intern Kings County Hosp., Bklyn., 1956-57; resident VA Hosp., N.Y.C., 1957-59, Lenox Hill Hosp., N.Y.C., 1959-60; hematology fellow UCLA, 1960-62; spl. fellow Calif. Inst. Tech., Pasadena, 1965-67; asst. prof. U. N.Mex., Albuquerque, 1967-71; hematologist VA Hosp., Long Beach, Calif., 1971-80; med. dir. Atlantic Richfield Co., Los Angeles, 1980-85; physician Dept. Water and Power, Los Angeles, 1985-86, Internat. Tech. Corp., Torrance, Calif., 1986—; asst. prof. UCLA, 1964-71; assoc. adj. prof. U. Calif., Orange, 1972-81; clin. prof. U. Calif., Irvine, 1981—. Contbr. articles to profl. jours. Served with U.S. Army, 1948-49. Fellow ACP; mem. Am. Soc. Clin. Onocology, Am. Soc. Hematology, Am. Occupational Med. Assn., Am. Acad. Occupational Medicine, Los Angeles County Med. Assn., Am. Med. Joggers Assn. Democrat. Unitarian Universalist. Avocations: Western Americana books. Office: Internat Tech Corp 23456 Hawthorne Blvd Torrance CA 90505

NAKAKUKI, MASAFUMI, physician, psychiatry educator; b. Shimotsuma, Ibaragi, Japan, Mar. 1, 1930; came to U.S., 1969, naturalized 1975; s. Keisuke and Toi (Saito) N.; m. Ritsuko Oka, May 25, 1957; children—Mari, Emma. M.S., U. Ibaragi, 1949; M.D., U. Tokyo, 1953. Diplomate Am. Bd. Psychiatry and Neurology. Intern U. Tokyo Hosp., 1953-54, dir. psychiat. inpatient service, 1966-69; resident in psychiatry U. Tokyo, 1954-60, U. Colo.-Denver, 1962-66; asst. prof. psychiatry U. Colo. Med. Ctr., Denver, 1969-73; staff psychiatrist Ft. Logan Mental Health Ctr., Denver, 1973-74, Arapahoe Mental Health Ctr., Englewood, Colo., 1974-76; med. dir. Park East Mental Health Ctr. Denver, 1977-83; pres. Masafumi Nakakuki, M.D., P.C., Denver, 1977—; pres. med. staff Bethesda Hosp., Denver, 1982-83; psychiat. cons. Asian Pacific Devel. Ctr., Denver, 1983—. Author: Textbook of Psychiatry for the General Practitioner, 1968; New Parenting and Culture, 1982. Bd. dirs. Asian Human Service Assn., Denver, 1982. Fulbright scholar, 1961. Mem. Am. Psychiat. Assn., Colo. Med. Soc., AAAS, N.Y. Acad. Scis. Office: 4770 E Iliff Ave Denver CO 80222

NAKAMURA, HIROMU, psychologist; b. Los Angeles, Nov. 6, 1926; s. Genjiro and Misao (Kamura) N.; A.B., U. Redlands, 1948; M.A., UCLA, 1951; Ph.D., U. So. Calif., 1973; m. Tamaye Yumiba, Mar. 27, 1955; children—Glenn Vernon, Colleen Patricia. Clin. psychology intern Massillon (Ohio) State Hosp., 1951-52; clin. psychologist Patton (Calif.) State Hosp., 1952-58; clin. psychologist Lanterman State Hosp. and Developmental Center (formerly Pacific State Hosp.), Pomona, Calif., 1958—, program dir., 1971—. Mem. Am., Calif. psychol. assns., Am. Assn. Mental Deficiency, AAAS, Am. Pub. Health Assn., Nat. Geographic Soc., Town Hall Calif., Los Angeles World Affairs Council, World-wide Acad. Scholars, N.Y. Acad. Scis., Psi Chi. Presbyterian. Home: 3861 Shelter Grove Dr Claremont CA 91711 Office: PO Box 100 Pomona CA 91766

NAKAMURA, ROBERT MOTOHARU, pathologist; b. Montebello, Calif., June 10, 1927; s. Mosaburo and Haru (Suematsu) N.; m. Shigeyo Jane Hayashi, July 29, 1957; children: Mary, Nancy. AB, Whittier Coll., 1949; MD, Temple U., 1954. Cert. of spl. qualification in pathology immunopathology, Am. Bd. Pathology, Mich., 1983. Prof. pathology U. Calif., Irvine, 1971-74, adjunct prof. pathology, 1974-75; chmn. dept. pathology Scripps Clinic and Research Found., La Jolla, Calif., 1974—; with dept. molecular tech. Scripps Clinic and Research Found., La Jolla, 1980—; pres. Scripps Clinic Med. Group, La Jolla, 1981—; adjunct prof. of pathology U. Calif., San Diego, 1975—. Author, editor profl. publs. Fellow: Coll. Am. Pathologists, Am. Soc. Clin. Pathologists, Assn. Clin. Scientists, Am. Coll. Nutrition; mem. Internat. Acad. Pathology. Avocation: reading. Home: 8841 Nottingham Pl La Jolla CA 92037-2131

NAKANO, KENNETH K(ENJI), neurologist; b. Los Angeles, Jan. 29, 1942; s. Samuel T. and Kazuko K. (Nishimine) N.; B.A., Pomona Coll., 1963; M.D., Columbia U., 1967; M.P.H., Harvard U., 1971, S.M. in Epidemiology, 1972; m. Juanita Wynne, Feb. 14, 1968; children—Kenneth K., Kim K., Kam K., Kari K. Diplomate Am. Bd. Pschiatry and Neurology. Intern Queen's Hosp., Honolulu, 1967-68; resident fellow Harvard U. Med. Sch., 1968-71, fellow in neurology, 1968-71, asst. prof., 1973-75; resident in neurology Peter Bent Brigham Hosp., Boston, 1968-71, Children's Hosp., Boston, 1968-71, Beth Israel Hosp., Boston, 1968-71; research fellow in epidemiology Harvard U. Sch. Public Health, 1971-73; neurologist Straub Clinic, Honolulu, 1975—; med. dir. Straub Found.; cons. in field. Recipient George Thorn Teaching award Harvard U., 1974, Professional Activities award Honolulu, 1983. Fellow Royal Coll. Physicians (Can.); mem. Am. Assn. Electromyography and Electrodiagnosis, Royal Soc. Medicine, Am. Assn. Neurological and Orthopaedic Surgeons, (cert., v.p. 1982, pres.), AMA, Am. Acad. Neurology, Am. Public Health Assn., Am. EEG Soc., Am. Med. EEG Assn., World Fedn. Neurology, Hawaii Med. Assn., Mass. Med. Soc. Author: Pediatric Neurology, 1976, Neurology of Musculoskeletal and Rheumatic Disorders, 1979, Current Neurology, 1979, Textbook of Rheumatology, 1980, Back Pain: Is There a Cure?, 1983; editor Straub Proceedings. Home: 824A N Kalaheo Ave Kailua HI 96734 Office: 888 S King St Honolulu HI 96813

NAKANO, KENNETH RIKUJI, real estate and travel exec.; b. Hilo, Hawaii, Nov. 10, 1915; s. Genatro and Takiyo (Kawakami) N.; ed. Waseda Internat. Inst., Tokyo; polit.-economy certificate, Waseda U., 1938; Ph.D., H.H.D., St. John's Theol. Sem.; m. Ellen Nakatani, June 12, 1942; 1 dau., Judith. Chmn. Nakano Ken Realty (Tokyo) Inc.; sales coordinator, travel cons. Travel Booking, Inc.; v.p. Internat. Bus. Service Co. Ltd., Tokyo, Hawaii Jet Travel, Inc.; prin. broker Cen. Pacific Kosan, Inc., Honolulu; dir. Hawaiian Lanes Inc., Banpo Shoji Co. Tokyo Inc. Mem. Honolulu City Traffic Commn., 1953, Honolulu City Rent Control Commn., 1957; bd. govs. Goodwill Industries, Honolulu; mem. Honolulu chpt. Nat. Crime and Delinquency. Assn.; mem. rural dist. bd. mgrs. YMCA; exec. bd. Aloha council Boy Scouts Am. Recipient Lions Internat. Charter-Monarch 25 Yr. award, 1971, Humanitarian award Mountain Dist., 1984; cert. of distinguished service strengthening ties State of Calif. and Hawaii, County of Los Angeles, 1973; lic. minister Ho. of God Ch. and Bible Sch. Inst. Mem. Honolulu C. of C., Pacific Air Travel Assn., Am. Soc. Travel Agts., Honolulu Bd. Realtors, Smithsonian Assocs. Clubs: Lions, Masons, K.T., Shriners, Honolulu Press. Home and Office: PO Box 245 Waianae HI 96792

NAKARADO, GARY LEE, lawyer; b. Petosky, Mich., Aug. 30, 1949; s. Richard William and Helen Bedola (Campbell) N.; m. Christine M. Manchester, June 19, 1971; children: Kirtley Campbell, Christian Hart. AB with spl. honors, U. Chgo., 1971; JD, U. Mich., 1973. Bar: Ill. 1974, Colo. 1978. Ptnr. Head, Moye, Carver & Ray, Denver, 1981-83, Mineral Resources, Steamboat Springs, Colo., 1983-85; of counsel Moye, Giles, O'Keefe, Vermeire & Gorrell, Denver, 1985-86, ptnr., 1986—; bd. dirs. Loft House, Denver, 1984—. NSF grantee, 1970. Mem. ABA (com. on Nat. Resources), Colo. Bar Assn. (chmn. tax sect. 1984-85), Denver Bar Assn. Republican. Avocations: computers, skiing, kites. Home: 864 Aster Way Golden CO 80401 Office: Moye Giles O'Keefe Vermeire Gorrell 730 17th St #600 Denver CO 80202-3582

NAKASHIMA, YOSHIO, dentist; b. Salinas, Calif., June 19, 1935; s. Tsuyoshi and Ayako (Sato) N.; m. Jean S. Takahashi, June 18, 1961; children: Karen Y., Paula L., Steven S. AB, Fresno State Coll., 1957; DDS, Coll. Physicians and Surgeons, 1961. Intern USAF, Washington and Tripler Gen. Hosp., Honolulu, 1961-62; co-chmn. peer review com. San Francisco Dental Soc., 1976-80, pres., 1981-82; chmn. council dental health Calif. Dental Assn., Los Angeles, 1980-81; examining com. Calif. Bd. Dental Examiners, Sacramento, 1985—. Commr., v.p. San Francisco Planning Commn., 1977—; v.p. gen. ops. Nat. Japanese Am. Citizens League, 1984—, dist. gov., 1980-84. Served to capt. USAF, 1961-64. Fellow Am. Coll. Dentists, Internat. Coll. Dentists; mem. Calif. Dental Assn. (bd. trustees), San Francisco Dental Soc. Democrat. Methodist. Avocation: photography. Office: 3400 California St #302 San Francisco CA 94118-1881

NAKASHIMADA, BONNIE CHARLENE, minister; b. Regina, Sask., Can., Aug. 12, 1960; came to U.S., 1982; d. Andrew Joseph and Audrey Mildred (Schmuland) Gouinchuck; m. David Nakashimada, Aug. 31, 1985. BRE, Can. Bible Coll., Regina, 1982. Lic. to ministry Christian Ch., 1982. Intern youth ministry Salem (Oreg.) Alliance Ch., 1982-83; youth minister Portland (Oreg.) Alliance Ch., 1983—; mem. Christian edn. dist. com. Christian and Missionay Alliance, Canby, Oreg., 1983—. Avocations; running, athletic teams. Office: Portland Alliance Ch 1832 NE 39th Ave Portland OR 97212

NAKASONE, HIROTAKA, speech scientist; b. Okinawa, Japan, June 20, 1947; came to U.S., 1974; s. Kan-ei and Haruko N.; m. Aiko Takara, Aug. 15, 1972. BA, U. Ryukyus, Okinawa, Japan, 1972, U. S.C., 1976; MA, Mich. State U., 1979, PhD, 1984. Cert. voice examiner. Legal court interpreter Naha (Japan) Dist. Ct., 1972-74; asst. prof. Mich. State U., East Lansing, 1984-85; research dir. Nat. Forensic Voice and Acoustics Lab., Inc., East Lansing, 1985—; adj. asst. prof. Mich. State U., 1985—; research scientist Speaker Identification Project Los Angeles Sheriff's Dept., Whittier, Calif., 1985—; cons. U.S. Secret Service, Washington, 1984—. Mem. IEEE, Am. Speech-Lang. Hearing Assn., Internat. Assn. Identification. Avocations: computer programming, fishing. Home: 507 Raymond Dr Pasadena CA 91107 Office: Los Angeles County Sheriffs Dept STARS Ctr 11515 S Colima Rd E112 Whittier CA 90604

NAKATANI, ROY EIJI, biologist, educator; b. Seattle, June 8, 1918; s. Ushinosuke and Fuku N.; m. Harue Okihara, May 28, 1955; children—Ronald L., Dale E., Scott M., Mika L., Mark I. B.S. cum laude in Fisheries, U. Wash., 1947, Ph.D., 1960. Research asso. U. Wash., 1954-59; biol. scientist Gen. Electric Co., 1959-62; mgr. aquatic biology Hanford Labs., 1962-66; mgr. ecology Battelle-Northwest Labs., 1966-70; asso. prof. fisheries U. Wash., 1970-73, prof., 1973—; asst. dir. Fisheries Research Inst., 1970-73, asso. dir., 1973—; cons. in field. Contbr. articles in field to profl. jours. Served as sgt. U.S. Army, 1941-46. Fellow AAAS, Internat. Acad. Fish Sci., Am. Inst. Fish Research Biology; mem. Am. Fisheries Soc., Ecol. Soc. Am., Am. Soc. Limnology and Oceanography, Sigma Xi. Home: 6719 152d Ave NE Redmond WA 98052 Office: Fish Research Inst Univ Wash Seattle WA 98195

NAKHJIRI, KAREN SUE, environmental engineer; b. Albany, Oreg., Nov. 30, 1955; d. Neil Andrew and Lois Darlene (Troyer) Birky; m. Mehdi Nakhjiri, Dec. 9, 1977. BS in Biology, Portland State U., 1978; MSPH in Environ. Health and Engring., U. Wash., 1982. Environ. specialist EPA, Seattle, 1979-82; prin. Sciential Environ. Services, Seattle, 1982-83; water quality specialist Parametrix, Inc., Bellevue, Wash., 1983-84; spl. projects coordinator solid waste div. Snohomish County Dept. Pub. Works, Everett, Wash., 1984—; cons. Oreg. Environ. Council, Portland Audubon Soc. Mem. AAAS, ASCE, Am. Water Works Assn., Govtl. Refuse Collection and Disposal Assn. Avocations: reading, skiing, white water rafting, hiking. Office: Snohomish County Dept Pub Works 3000 Rockefeller Ave Everett WA 98201

NALIBOFF, ELLEN MARIE, speech language pathologist; b. St. Louis, June 1, 1929; d. Joseph Patrick Clark and Marie (Kelly) Flanagan; m. Stuart Naliboff, June 27, 1954; children: Gregory, Alec. BS, U. So. Calif., 1951; MA, San Jose State U., 1967. Clin. fellow John Font, PhD. Voice and Speech Disorders, San Jose, 1967-69; speech pathologist Community Home Health Service, 1970-71, Torrey Pines (Calif.) Convalescent Hosp., 1970-80; pvt. practice speech pathology San Diego, 1970—; speech pathologist Calif. Convalescent Hosp., 1971-82; dir. speech pathology Scripps Meml. Hosp., La Jolla, 1971-82; speech pathologist San Diego Home Patient Care, 1982—; dir. out-patient program for rehab. of adults after minor head injury Coll. Park Hosp., 1984—; speech pathologist Mission Bay Home Health Service, 1984—, Mercy Home Health Service, 1985—; instr. San Jose State U., 1967-68, San Diego Community Coll. Dist., 1986—; speech pathologist program developer Vis. Nurse Assn., Santa Clara County, Calif., 1967-68. Mem. Am. Speech-Lang.-Hearing Assn. (cert.), Calif. Speech-Lang.-Hearing Assn., Calif. Speech Pathologists and Audiologists in Pvt. Practice, Phi Beta, Kappa Delta. Democrat. Roman Catholic. Club: San Diego Ski. Home: 6114 Madra Ave San Diego CA 92120

NAMIAS, JEROME, meteorologist; b. Bridgeport, Conn., Mar. 19, 1910; s. Joseph and Saydie (Jacobs) N.; m. Edith Paipert, Sept. 15, 1938; 1 child, Judith Ellen. Student, MIT, 1932-34, M.S., 1941; M.S., U. Mich., 1934-35; Sc.D. (hon.), U. R.I., 1972, Clark U., 1984. Research asst. Blue Hill Meterol. Obs., Milton, Mass., 1933-35; research assoc. MIT, Boston, 1936-41, Woods Hole (Mass.) Oceanographic Inst.; mgr. extended forecast br. U.S. Weather Bur., Washington, 1941-64; assoc. dir. Nat. Meteorol. Ctr., 1964-66, chief extended forecast div., 1966-71; vis. scientist NYU, N.Y.C., 1966; research meteorologist Scripps Inst. Oceanography, La Jolla, Calif., 1968—; vis. scholar Rockefeller Study and Conf. Center, Bellagio, Italy, 1977; frequent cons. USAAF, USN. Author: An Introduction to the Study of Air Mass and Isentropic Analysis, 1936, Extended Forecasting by Mean Circulation Methods; monograph, 1947, Thirty-Day Forecasting, 1953; Short Period Climatic Variations, Collected Works of Jerome Namias, 1934-74, 1975-82, 83; also tech. articles to sci. jours.; Editorial bd.: Geofisica Internacional, Mexico. Recipient Meisinger award Am. Meteorol. Soc., 1938; citation for weather forecasts North African invasion Sec. of Navy, 1942; Dept. Commerce Meritorious Service award, 1950; Rockefeller Pub. Service award, 1955; award for extraordinary sci. accomplishment Am. Meteorol. Soc., 1955; Sverdrup Gold medal Am. Meteorol. Soc., 1981; Gold medal for distinguished achievement Dept. Commerce, 1965; Chancellor's Assocs. award excellence in research U. Calif.-San Diego; Compass award for research Marine Tech. Soc., 1984; Rossby fellow Woods Hole (Mass.) Oceanographic Instn., 1972. Fellow Am. Geophys. Union, Washington Acad. Scis., AAAS, Am. Meteorol. Soc. (councilor 1940-42, 50-53, 60-63, 70-73), Explorers Club, Am. Acad. Arts and Sci., Royal Meteorol. Soc. Great Britain., Nat. Acad. Sci. Developer of system for extending time range of gen. weather forecasts up to a season. Home: 240 Coast Blvd 2C La Jolla CA 92037 Office: Scripps Inst Oceanography Poss Bldg A-024 La Jolla CA 92093

NANCE, ROBERT DANIEL, health care executive, consultant; b. Redlands, Calif., May 16, 1942; s. William Franklin and Helen Frances (Ary) N.; m. Margaret Ruth Riggins, Dec. 81962 (div. 1974); children: Christa Darleen, Amy Rebecca; m. Sandra June Taddie, May 2, 1982. BS, U. Redlands, 1974. Sales rep. Upjohn Co., Kalamazoo, 1974-76; planning mgr. Beckman Instruments, Fullerton, Calif., 1976-81; v.p. sales and mktg. Am. Diagnostics, Newport Beach, Calif., 1981-82; chmn., chief exec. Diamedex Internat., Costa Mesa, Calif., 1983—, ANZA Pharm., Inc., San Pedro, Calif., 1986—; cons. Robert Nance & Assocs., San Pedro, 1981—; sr. cons. Lenders Fin., Santa Ana, 1985—. Republican. Baptist. Avocations: photography, skiing, cycling. Home: 1985 Mount Shasta Dr San Pedro CA 90732 Office: Diamedex Internat Inc 3941 B South Bristol Suite 93 Santa Ana CA 92704

NANEY, DAVID GLEN, corporate executive, lawyer, educator; b. Bakersfield, Calif., Apr. 21, 1952; s. Glen Tillman and Olivia Mae N.; children—David Tillman, Michael Christian. A.A., Bakersfield Coll., 1972; B.A., UCLA, 1974; J.D., Loyola U., 1977. Bar: Calif. 1977, U.S. Dist. Ct. (cent. dist.) Calif. 1981, U.S. Dist. Ct. (ea. dist.) Calif. 1980. Law clk. Engstrom and Lipscomb, Los Angeles, 1976, Roberts Farms Inc., Bakersfield, Calif., Greater Bakersfield Legal Assistance Inc., 1977; atty. firm Freeman, Freeman & Smiley, Los Angeles, 1978-80; sole practice, Bakersfield, 1980-86; v.p. Cemco Corp.; exec. v.p. Cemland Dev., 1986; v.p. Kem Valley Tank Lines, 1986—; former judge pro tempore West Kern Mcpl. Ct. Dist., other Kern County Justice Cts.; prof. law Bakersfield Coll.; legal adviser CAP; instr. in estate planning. Mem. scholarship com.; Bakersfield Coll.; pro-bono legal counsel TEAMM Resources Inc., also Parents with Spl. Children; active Sheets for Sheriff, Ferguson for Dist. Atty. campaigns, 1982. Mem. Kern County Bar Assn., Calif. State Bar Assn., Assn. Trial Lawyers Am., ABA, UCLA Alumni Assn., Bakersfield Coll. Alumni Assn., Phi Alpha Delta. Republican. Club: Lions (East Bakersfield). Author (with Douglas K. Freeman): How to Incorporate a Small Business, 1978. Office: 2308 Holden Way Bakersfield CA 93304

NANNINGA, ALAN RICHARD, vehicle sales and manufacturing executive; b. Manhattan, Kans., Mar. 30, 1932; s. Albert G. and Hilma P. (Nordgren) N.; m. Patricia A. Rupert, Aub. 31, 1952; children: P. Gayle, Mark A, Mary J., P. Anne. BS in Bus., U. Kans., 1953. Purchasing and contracting officer USAF, Randolph AFB, Tex., 1954-56; sales executive Nanninga Ford Sales, Whitewater, Kans., 1956-62, Winfield, Kans., 1962-64; gen. mgr. Bankers Motor Leasing Co., Colorado Springs, Colo., 1964—; chief exec. officer Layton Truck Equipment, Inc., Colorado Springs, 1978—; chmn. bd. dirs. Nat. Tour Div. Corp., Colorado Springs; chmn. Thrifty Rent A Car com., Tulsa, Okla., 1973-75; treas., bd. dirs. Petroleum Funding Corp., Colorado Springs, 1984—. Served as 1st lt. USAF, 1954-56. Mem. Car and Truck Rental and Leasing Assn. (pres. Colo. chpt. 1972-74). Republican. Methodist. Club: The Registry (Colorado Springs). Lodge: Rotary. Avocations: stock car racing, hunting, fishing, hot air ballooning. Home: 3017 Drakestone Dr Colorado Springs CO 80909 Office: Bankers Motor Leasing Inc 6314 E Platte Ave Colorado Springs CO 80915

NANUS, BURTON BENJAMIN, management educator, researcher; b. N.Y.C., Mar. 21, 1936; s. Max and Mollie (Rothstein) N.; m. Marlene Guttman, June 30, 1969; 1 child, Leora. BSME, Stevens Inst. Tech., 1957; MS in Indsl. Mgmt., MIT, 1959; DBA, U. So. Calif., 1967. Research asst. MIT, Cambridge, 1957-59; mgr. advanced edn. techniques Sperry Rand Univac, N.Y.C., 1959-61; tng. dir. Ops. Research Inc., Santa Monica, Calif., 1962; sr. tech. advisor to mgmt. System Devel. Group, Santa Monica, 1962-67; pres. Planning Tech., Inc., Los Angeles, 1967-69; prof. mgmt. U. So. Calif., Los Angeles, 1969—, dir. Ctr. for Futures Research,, 1971—; cons. Am. Inst. CPA's, N.Y.C., 1982-85, Nat. Gov's Conf., Nashville, 1984, AT&T, Continental Airlines, Honeywell, TRW, Monsanto, others. Co-author: Management Games: A New Technique of Executive Development, 1961, The Social Implications of the Use of Computers Across National Boundaries, 1973, The Emerging Network Marketplace, 1981, Leaders: The Strategies for Taking Charge, 1985; mem. editorial bd. Jour. Indsl. Engring., 1963-68, Jour. Systems Mgmt., 1967-75, New Mgmt., 1982—, Futures Research Quarterly, 1985; contbr. numerous articles to profl. jours. Cons. nat., state and local govt. adv. activities, 1972-82; bd. dirs. Los Angeles Pvt. industry Council, 1986. Recipient Disting. Contbns. to Planning award So. Calif. Corp. Planners Assn., 1980, Commerce Assocs. award U. So. Calif., 1980, Assn. Systems Mgmt. award, 1972, Am. Inst. Indsl. Engrs. award, 1968. Mem. World Future Soc., Tau Beta Pi. Avocations: tennis, swimming. Office: U So Calif University Park Los Angeles CA 90089

NAQVI, HIMAYAT HUSSAIN, botanist, ecologist; b. Peshawar, Pakistan, June 16, 1936; came to U.S., 1964, naturalized, 1982; s. Wilayat Hussain-Shah and Nawab Begum (Jafary) N.; m. Patricia Sandra Palmer, July 17, 1971; 1 child, Jamil Hussain. BS, U. Peshawar, 1958, MS, 1960; PhD, U. Calif., Santa Barbara, 1969. From asst. prof. to assoc. prof. U. Peshawar, 1969-76; sr. research assoc. Calif. Arboretum Found., Arcadia, 1977-82; assoc. research specialist new crops, dept. botany and plant scis. U. Calif., Riverside, 1982—; co-investigator guayule rubber plant genetics project U. Calif., Riverside, 1982—. Contbr. over 50 scientific articles to profl. jours. Research grantee Govt. Pakistan, NSF, USDA. Mem. AAAS, Soc. for Econ. Botany, Guayule Rubber Soc. (bd. dirs., founder/editor El Guayuleros pub. 1979—, Guayule Research Achievement award 1986), Am. Soc. Agronomy, Bot. Soc. Am., Ecol. Soc. Am., Am. Inst. Biol. Scis., Crop Sci. Soc. Am., Am. Soc. Horticultural Scis., Sigma Xi. Avocations: tennis, nature photography. Home: 1552 Shamrock Ave Upland CA 91786 Office: U Calif Dept Botany and Plant Scis Riverside CA 92521

NARCISIAN, ANN LAURA, public relations professional; b. Denver, July 4, 1959; d. Harry K. and Madge Carole (Evans) N. BA, Ariz. State U., 1981. Coordinator pub. relations Western Savs. and Loan, Phoenix, 1981-83; mgr. mktg. and pub. relations Bapt. Health System, Phoenix, 1983-84; pub. relations officer United Bank of Ariz., Phoenix, 1984—. Chmn. media com. Phoenix Urban League, 1985; reader Sun Sounds, Phoenix, 1980-82; mem. founding bd. dirs. Footlights theatre co. Recipient Cert. Excellence, Strathmore Graphics Gallery, 1984. Mem. Women in Communications Inc. (pres.-elect 1986—, bd. dirs. 1983—, pres. 1987—, Award of Merit, 1983), Pub. Relations Soc. Am. (bd. dirs. 1984—, editor newsletter 1982-83), Ariz. Bankers Assn. (pub. relations com. 1984—), Internat. Assn. Bus. Communicators. Republican. Avocations: skiing, sailing, tennis, art, travelling. Office: United Bank Ariz 3300 N Central Ave Phoenix AZ 85012-2908

NARITA, HIRO, cinematographer; b. Seoul, Republic of Korea, June 26, 1941; came to U.S., 1957; s. Masao Morikawa and Masako (Kojima) Morikawa ; m. Barbara Parker, Sept. 9, 1971. BFA in Design, San Francisco Art Inst., 1964. V.p. Pictures & Words, Berkeley, Calif., 1972—; lectr. Mill Valley Film Festival, 1984, Hawaii Internat. Film Festival, 1984. Dir. photography for films: Farewell to Manzanar, 1976 (Emmy award nomination 1976), Never Cry Wolf, 1983 (Best Cinematography, 1983), Solomon Northup's Odyssey, 1984, Go Tell It On The Mountain, 1985, Fire With Fire, 1985, Amerika, 1987. Served with U.S Army, 1964-66. Mem. Internat. Assn. Theatrical Stage Employees (cert.). Office: Pictures and Words 1807B Fourth St Berkeley CA 94710

NARODITSKY, VLADIMIR ALEXANDER, mathematics educator; b. Kiev, USSR, July 6, 1955; came to U.S., 1979; s. Alexander S. and Margarita G. (Gitman) N.; m. Polina Reznichenko, Jan. 29, 1982 (div. Jan. 1983). BS, Kiev State U., 1975, MS, 1976; PhD, U. Denver, 1982. Asst. prof. math. San Jose (Calif.) State U., 1982-85, assoc. prof., 1985—; vis. scholar U. Bielefeld, Fed. Republic Germany, summer 1985, U. Bohum, Fed. Republic Germany, summer 1986. Contbr. articles to profl. jours. Participant Com. Concerned Soviet Scientists, N.Y.C., 1985. Mem. Am. Math. Soc., Math. Assn. Am., N.Y. Acad. Scis., Smithsonian Research Soc., Sigma Xi. Republican. Jewish. Avocations: martial arts, chess. Office: San Jose State U Dept Math and Computer Sci San Jose CA 94132

NARULA, MOHAN LAL, realtor; b. Ferozepur, India, Feb. 2, 1939; came to U.S., 1962; s. Ram Dyal and Pemeshwari Narula; m. Sylvia Conway, Aug. 31, 1968; children: Rabinder, Rajinder. BS, Panjab U., India, 1960; BSME, Calif. Poly. State U., San Luis Obispo, 1965; MS in Engring., Calif. State U., Northridge, 1970. Engr. Abex Corp., Oxnard, Calif., 1965-69; salesman, realtor Walker & Lee, Oxnard, Calif., 1970-73; owner, realtor Narula Co. Realtors, Oxnard, Calif., 1973—. Mem. Cert. Comml. Investment Mem. (designate 1979), Oxnard Harbor Bd. Realtors (mem. profl. standard com. 1980—), Los Angeles Cert. Comml. Investment Mem. (bd. dirs., treas. 1985). Home: 2830 W Hill St Oxnard CA 93033 Office: Narula Co Realtor 3201 Samuel Ave Suite 7 Oxnard CA 93033

NASH, RICHARD EUGENE, aerospace engineer; b. San Diego, Feb. 18, 1954; s. Clifford Arthur Jr. and Dorothy Fay (Johnson) N.; m. Lynn Elora Martin, Aug. 5, 1978. BSCE, U. Ky., 1981; postgrad., U. So. Calif., 1983—. Registered profl. civil engr., Calif., 1985. Mem. tech. staff Rockwell Internat., Downey, Calif., 1982-86, lead engr. space shuttle propulsion systems, 1986—; pvt. practice civil engring., Buena Park, Calif., 1985—. Scoutmaster Boy Scouts Am., Covington, Ky., 1972-74, Williamstown, Ky., 1976-82, asst. scoutmaster, Ft. Hood, Tex., 1975-76. Recipient Eagle Scout award Boy Scouts Am., 1972; named to Hon. Order of Ky. Cols. 1985. Mem. NSPE, Nat. Eagle Scout Assn. (advisor 1983), Chi Epsilon. Republican. Avocations: backpacking, scouting. Office: Space Transp and Systems Div Rockwell Internat 12214 Lakewood Blvd Downey CA 90241

NASKY, H(AROLD) GREGORY, lawyer; b. Titusville, Pa., June 9, 1942; s. Harold G. and Majella Marie (Beck) N.; m. Rosanne Guson, July 22, 1967. AB, St. Bonaventure U., 1964; JD, U. Notre Dame, 1967. Assoc. Eaton & Hill, Warren, Pa., 1967-68, Vargas, Bartlett & Dixon, Reno, 1972-73; ptnr. Vargas & Bartlett, Las Vegas, Nev., 1974—, mng. ptnr., 1981—; corp. sec. Showboat, Inc. (NYSE-SBO), Las Vegas, 1978—, bd. dirs. 1983—. Legal advisor Nev. Dance Theatre, Las Vegas, 1977—; legal com. Nev. Resort Assn., Las Vegas, 1978-85; mem. Rep. Nat. Com., Washington, 1984—; exec. com. mem. Boulder Dam Council Boy Scouts Am., Las Vegas, 1986—; del. People to People Citizen Ambassador Program, People's Republic China, 1985. Served to capt. JAGC, U.S. Army, 1968-72, Vietnam. Decorated Bronze Star, 1970. Mem. ABA, Pa. Bar Assn., State Bar Nev. (mem. dispute com. 1983—), Notre Dame Alumni Assn. (pres. Las Vegas chpt. 1978-79). Roman Catholic. Office: Vargas & Bartlett 300 S 4th St # 500 Las Vegas NV 89101

NASO, VALERIE JOAN, automobile dealership executive, travel company operator, photographer, writer; b. Stockton, Calif., Aug. 19, 1941; d. Alan Robert and Natalie Grace (Gardner) McKittrick Naso; m. Peter Joralemon, May 31, 1971 (div.). Student pub. schs., Piedmont, Calif. Cert. graphoanalyst. Pres., Naso Motor Co. (formerly Broadway Cadillacs, Oakland, Calif.) Bishop, Calif., 1964—; owner, operator Wooden Horse Antiques, Bishop, 1970-82; editor, writer, photographer Sierra Life Mag., Bishop, 1980-83; freelance writer, photographer, 1975—; owner, operator Boredom Tours, Bishop, 1981—; owner, sole photographer, Renaissance Photography, N.Y.C. and Bishop, Calif., 1982—, Keyboard Colors, 1986; cons. graphoanalyst. Fiction, non-fiction work pub. in Horse and Horseman, Am. Horseman, Cameo Mag., Desert Mag., Sierra Life Mag. Mem. Authors Guild, Inc., Authors League Am., Am. Film Inst., Archives of Am. Art, Bishop C. of C., Victorian Soc. Am., Nat. Trust for Hist. Preservation, Nat. Rifle Assn., Beethoven Soc. Clubs: Cadillac LaSalle; Wagner Soc. (N.Y.C.). Home: 220 E 54th St Apt 9A New York NY 10022 Office: 783 N Main St Bishop CA 93514

NASON, GEORGE MALCOLM, computer systems and services co. exec.; b. Spokane, Wash., Feb. 17, 1933; s. George Malcolm and Ella (Buist) N.; B.S., Calif. State Coll. at Long Beach, 1958; m. Dolores Irene Lockinger, Oct. 7, 1951; children—George Malcolm III, Scott, Lance, Natalie. Data processor, project mgr. Gen. Motors Corp., Los Angeles, 1956-65; systems mgr. dairy div. Arden Mayfair, 1965-68; dir. systems Gallo Winery, Los Angeles, Modesto, Calif., 1968-73; dir. systems and data processing Familian Corp., 1973-74; v.p. Coldwell Banker & Co., Los Angeles, 1974-78; pres. Nason & Assos., Inc., Long Beach, Calif., 1978—, GEMCAD Corp., 1986—. Bd. dirs. Confrat. of Christian Doctrine High Sch., Long Beach, 1969-70. Served with USMCR, 1951-54. Mem. Data Processing Mgmt. Assn. Republican. Roman Catholic. Home: 4503 Pepperwood Ave Long Beach CA 90808

NASONI, DOROTHY IRENE, data processing executive; b. Chgo., July 12, 1935; d. Herbert Walter and Edith Martha (Rousar) Young; m. Richard Leon Nasoni, Oct. 20, 1962; 1 child, Mark Oliver. BA, Kalamazoo Coll., 1957; postgrad., U. Chgo., 1958-59; MA, U. Ariz., 1969. Math. tchr. U. Chgo. Lab. High Sch., 1958-59; systems engr. IBM Corp., Evanston, Ill., 1961-62; programmer Hughes Aircraft Co., Tucson, 1962-63; asst. dir. data processing Tucson Unified Sch. Dist., 1963-75, dir. data processing, 1976—; assoc. faculty Pima Community Coll., Tucson, 1971-72. Zone capt. Nat. Cancer Soc., Tucson, 1982. Mem. Assn. Ednl. Data Systems (bd. dirs. 1980-83), Nat. Council Adminstrv. Women in Edn. (program chairperson 1983—). Office: Tucson Unified Sch Dist 1010 E 10th St Tucson AZ 85719

NASONI, RICHARD LEON, research scientist; b. Scranton, Pa., Aug. 13, 1933; s. I. Edward and Ellen B. (Schlesinger) N.; m. Dorothy Irene Young, Oct. 20, 1962; 1 child, Mark Oliver. BS, Pa. State U., 1955; MS, U. Ariz., 1968, MBA, 1971, PhD, 1978. Staff physicist U. Chgo. Labs. for Applied Scis., 1957-61, Armour Research Found., Chgo., 1961-62; instr. U. Ariz., Tucson, 1963-73; research assoc. U. Ariz. Health Scis. Ctr., 1979-83; research scientist U. Ariz. Dept. Physics, 1983—; assoc. faculty Pima Community Coll., Tucson, 1974-78. Contbr. articles to profl. jours. Mem. Am. Phys. Soc., Am. Assn. Physicists in Medicine, Acoustical Soc. Am., IEEE, Sigma Pi Epsilon, Pi Mu Epsilon, Sigma Xi. Home: 4900 N Via Entrada Tucson AZ 85718 Office: U Ariz Dept Physics Tucson AZ 85721

NASSIF, GEORGE FREDERICK, tax lawyer; b. Los Angeles, Jan. 20, 1957; s. George A. and Nadia (Haddad) N. BA, UCLA, 1978; JD, Calif. Western Law Sch., 1982; LLM in Taxation, Boston U., 1983. Bar: Calif. 1982, Mass. 1983, U.S. Dist. Ct. (cen. dist.) Calif. 1985, U.S. Tax Ct. 1983. Gen. counsel First Fin. Home Loans, Inc., Van Nuys, Calif., 1984—, also bd. dirs.; dist. counsel atty. IRS, Los Angeles, 1985-86. Democrat. Eastern Orthodox.. Home: 2050 N Berendo St Los Angeles CA 90027 Office: First Fin Home Loans Inc 6454 Van Nuys Blvd Van Nuys CA 90027

NASSIR, NICHOLAS, chemical engineer, consultant; b. Bklyn., Dec. 19, 1911; s. Andrew F. and Frieda (Khoury) N.; m. Louise Marie Milan, July 31, 1938; children: Andrew M., William J., Carol J. Campbell. Registered profl. engr., Calif. Prin., engr. C.F. Braun & Co., Alhambra, Calif., 1943-76; pres. and owner Power Recovery Corp., La Jolla, Calif., 1977-87; v.p. and ptnr. La Jolla Funding co., 1983-87. Inventor, patentee power recovery in oil refineries. Office: Power Recovery Corp 5605 La Jolla Blvd La Jolla CA 92037

NATAF, ELIE, data processing professional; b. Tunis, Tunisia, Oct. 20, 1945; came to U.S., 1972; s. Jeshua and Marie Nataf; m. Lydia Nuret, May 17, 1972 (div. 1978); 1 child, Oren; m. Isiling Mack, Feb. 20, 1979. Grad., Ecole National des Beaux Arts, Paris, 1967-70, Control Data Inst., San Francisco, 1972-73. Computer instr. JST Communications, San Francisco, 1978-82; cons. Inspro Ins. Service, Walnut Creek, Calif., 1978-81; data processing mgr. Interstate Nat. Inc., San Rafael, Calif., 1980—; cons. Cargo Contintntal Airlines, San Francisco, 1984-85. Art exhbn. Mosiac Exhbn., 1976 (2d Place award). Served to sgt. Israeli Air Force, 1963-66. Avocations: chess, painting. Home: 715 Haight St #6 San Francisco CA 94117 Office: Interstate Nat Inc 2971 E Francisco Blvd San Rafael CA 94901

NATCHER, STEPHEN DARLINGTON, lawyer, business executive; b. San Francisco, Nov. 19, 1940; s. Stanlus Zoch and Robena Lenore Collie (Goldring) N.; m. Carolyn Anne Bowman, Aug. 23, 1969; children: Tanya Michelle, Stephanie Elizabeth. A.B. in Polit. Sci., Stanford U., 1962; J.D., U. Calif., San Francisco, 1965. Bar: Calif. 1966. Asso. firm Pillsbury, Madison & Sutro, San Francisco, 1966-68; counsel Douglas Aircraft div. McDonnell Douglas Corp., Long Beach, Calif., 1968-70; asst. gen. counsel Electronic Memories & Magnetics Corp., Los Angeles, 1970-71; asst. sec. Security Pacific Nat. Bank, Los Angeles, 1971-72; v.p., asst. sec. Security Pacific Nat. Bank, 1972-76, v.p., sec., 1976-79; asst. gen. counsel Security Pacific Corp., 1979-80; v.p., sec., gen. counsel Lear Siegler, Inc., Santa Monica, Calif., 1980—. Served with USCG, 1965-66. Republican. Club: St. Francis Yacht (San Francisco). Office: Lear Siegler Inc 2850 Ocean Park Blvd Santa Monica CA 90406

NATERA, MARIA, educational consultant; b. Artesia, N.Mex., June 3, 1941; d. Angel and Elisa (Fierro) N.; m. Irv Boyles, June 25, 1966 (div. Nov. 1973); 1 child, Arman Christoff. BA, Calif. State U., Fresno, 1964; MS, U. So. Calif., 1975, EdD, 1977. Cert. tchr., adminstr., Calif. Coordinator Los Angeles City Schs., 1973-76; prin. Santa Paula (Calif.) Sch. Dist., 1976-79, Soquel Sch. Dist., Santa Cruz, Calif., 1979-80; asst. supt. Alisal Sch. Dist., Salinas, Calif., 1980-83; pres. Natera & Assocs., Aptos, Calif., 1983—; trainer U. So. Calif., 1975-76; adj. prof. U. Santa Clara, Calif., 1981—; adj. prof., program coordinator U. San Francisco, 1982-85. Rep. Hispanic Legis. Caucus, 1984—; chair Santa Cruz County Women's Commn., 1986; bd. dirs. U. So. Calif. Educare, Los Angeles, chairperson, 1985. Mem. Assn. Calif. Adminstrs. (chair women's caucus 1984—), Calif. Futures Network (chair 1984-85), LWV (local bd. dirs., edn. advisor), Phi Delta Kappa. Republican. Roman Catholic. Avocations: aerobics, hiking, writing. Home: 818 Cathedral Dr Aptos CA 95003 Office: Natera & Assocs PO Box 127 Aptos CA 95001

NATHAN, GERALD DALE, psychologist, farmer; b. Norfolk, Nebr., Oct. 1, 1938; s. Raymond John and Esther Marie (Neuwerk) N.; m. Kathleen O'Neil Pugmire, Aug. 31, 1985. Student, Wayne State Coll., Nebr., 1956-57, Yale U., 1959-60; B.A., U. Nebr., 1966, M.A., 1968, Ph.D. (NDEA fellow), 1970. Lic. marriage counselor, Calif., 1972; cert. sex educator, 1973, sex therapist, 1975; lic. psychologist, Oreg., 1974. Cons. psychologist Calaveras County Edn. Dept., San Andreas, Calif., 1970-72; pvt. practice sex and marital therapy, lifestyle and stress mgmt., Salem, Oreg., 1972—; cons. psychologist Community Counseling Center, Salem, 1972-73; sex educator Oreg. Dept. Continuing Edn., Salem, 1972-74; cons. William Temple House, Portland, Oreg., 1974-77; vis. prof. Willamette U., Salem, 1981. Mem. Salem Community Chorus, 1978—, pres., 1980-81. Served with USAF, 1959-63. Mem. Am. Psychol. Assn., Am. Assn. Marriage and Family Therapy, Am. Assn. Sex Educators, Counselors and Therapists, Oreg. Assn. Marriage and Family Therapists (dir. 1976-77), Salem Psychol. Soc. (co-chmn. 1981-82), Common Cause, ACLU, Nature Conservancy, Union Concerned Scientists, Regenerative Agr. Assn., Am. Minor Breeds Conservancy, Sierra Club. Office: 635 Church NE Salem OR 97301

NATHAN, ROBERT, data processing executive; b. San Francisco, Sept. 6, 1927; s. Robert Sr. and Lucille (Almoslino) N.; m. Anita Levine, July 21, 1950; children: Sheila, Andrew. AB in Math. and Chemistry, U. Calif., 1951; PhD in Phys. Chemistry and Physiology, Calif. Inst. Tech., 1956. Staff scientist Jet Propulsion Lab., Calif. Inst. Tech., Pasadena, 1956—; pres. Nathan Computer Images, Pasadena, 1969—; v.p. research and devel. Synaptek, Pasadena, 1986—; cons. mil. agys., 1965—, NIH, Bethesda, Md., 1969—, U.S. Senate 1974-79, 86. Author: Computer Programming Handbook, 1960; editor Mechanisms of Aging and Devel. Jour, 1975; patentee silicon chip image processing, med. image ultrasound. Research grantee Indsl. Research 500, 1970, NASA, 1985. Mem. AAAS, Am. Crystallographic Assn., Electron Microscope Soc. Am., Soc. Exploration Geophysicists. Democrat. Avocations: searching for extraterrestial intelligence, research on aging and longevity. Home: 1125 Rexford Ave Pasadena CA 91107 Office: Jet Propulsion Lab Calif Tech 4800 Oak Grove Dr MS168-427 Pasadena CA 91107

NATHANSON, GERALD, Pres. Pay'N Save Corp., Seattle. Office: Pay'n Save Corp 1511 6th Ave Seattle WA 98101 *

NATHANSON, MARJORIE ANN, clinical psychologist; b. Boston, Sept. 3, 1942; d. George B. and Sylvia (Dane) N.; m. Theodore Edwin Keeler, Aug. 29, 1982; 1 child, Daniel Christopher. A.B., Vassar Coll., 1964; Ph.D., U. Calif.-Berkeley, 1974; candidate San Francisco Jung Inst., 1980-85, mem., 1985—. Lic. psychologist, Calif. Pvt. practice psychologist, Berkeley, Calif., 1976—; supr. Psychol. Inst., 1976-86. Margaret Floy Washburn fellow, 1964. Mem. Jungian Analysts No. Calif., Internat. Assn. Analytical Psychologists. Democrat. Office: 921 The Alameda Berkeley CA 94707

NATHANSON, THEODORE HERZL, aeronautical engineer; architect; b. Montreal, Que., Can., Apr. 20, 1923; came to U.S., 1949; naturalized, 1983; s. Henry and Minnie (Goldberg) N.; student McGill U., 1940-42; S.B. in Aero. Engring., M.I.T., 1944; M.Arch., Harvard U., 1955. Research engr. Noorduyn Aviation Ltd., Montreal, 1944-45; stress engr. Canadair Ltd., Montreal, 1945-46; structural engr. A.V. Roe (Can.) Ltd., Malton, Ont., 1946-47; with Mies van der Rohe, Chgo., summer 1949, R. Buckminster Fuller, Forest Hills, N.Y., summer 1951; cons. engr. and architect, Montreal, Boston, Los Angeles, 1955—; mem. tech. staff mission ops. and advanced concepts, Rockwell Internat., Space Sta. Systems Div. Downey, Calif., 1979—; lectr. architecture, McGill U., 1967-68. Fellow Brit. Interplanetary Soc.; mem. Order Engrs. Que., Order Architects Que., Soc. Am. Registered Architects, Nat. Soc. Profl. Engrs., AIAA, Royal Archtl. Inst. Can., Nat. Mgmt. Assn., Copley Soc. of Boston. Jewish. Clubs: M.I.T. of So. Calif. (bd. govs.); Can. Soc. (Los Angeles). Projects and models included in group shows: Mus. Fine Arts, Springfield, Mass., 1961, N.Y. World's Fair, 1965, Winterfest, Boston, 1966, Boston Artists' Project '70. Home: 123 S Figueroa St Apt 231A Los Angeles CA 90012 Office: 12214 Lakewood Blvd Downey CA 90241

NATHE, DENNIS GERHARDT, ranch exec.; b. Scobey, Mont., Dec. 12, 1938; s. Michael Henry and Saralda Sophia (Korf) N.; B.S., St. Benedicts Coll., Atchison, Kans., 1962; M.S., Creighton U., 1966; m. Della Mae Snyder, Dec. 28, 1970; children—Alycia, Michael. Pharm. detail man Lederle Labs., Am. Cyanamid Co., Omaha, 1962-64; clin. research coordinator Med. Products div. 3M Co., St. Paul, 1967; farming, ranching, Redstone, Mont., 1967—; pres. Nathe Ranch Inc., 1973-80 ; pres. Wanmdi Kinyan, Inc., 1981—. Vice-chmn. Mont. Environ. Quality Council, 1977-79, chmn., 1979-81 , public mem., 1981-83 ; Mont. State Rep., 1977-81, 85— ; chmn. Sheridan County Planning and Improvement Council, 1973-76; del. Economic Devel. Assn. Eastern Mont., 1973-76; chmn. Three Corners Boundary Assn., 1976-77; Democratic Precinct committeeman, 1968-76; vice chmn. Coal Tax Oversight Com., 1985—; mem. Mont. Rural Area Devel. Com., 1976—; alternate Mo. River Barge Transp. Com., 1980—; mem. Gov.'s Groundwater Task Force, 1983-85; bd. suprs. Sheridan County Conservation Dist., 1969-78; chmn. Eastern Mont. Range Improvement Com., 1973-78; chmn. Sheridan County Republican Central Com., 1980—; mem. Mont. Extension Adv. Council, 1980-82 , participant numerous other civic activities. Served with AUS, 1957-58. Mem. Soc. Range Mgmt., (chmn. Mont. Old West regional range program 1975-79), Durum Growers Assn., K.C. Republican. Roman Catholic. Address: Box 4 Redstone MT 59257

NATT, JOHN JULIAN, business economist; b. Portland, Oreg., June 8, 1942; s. Theodore Manfried and Martha Sue (McClelland) N.; m. Catherine Monroe, June 18, 1970; children: Andrew Harper, Megan Michele. BA in Chemistry, U. Oreg., 1964; MS in Phys. Chemistry, U. Wash., 1966; MBA in Applied Econs., U. Calif., Berkeley, 1969. Engr. Tex. Instruments Inc., Dallas, 1968; bus. economist Weyerhaeuser Co., Tacoma, 1969-74; corp. economist Crown Zellerbach Corp., San Francisco, 1974-81, group dir. planning and adminstr. for timber and wood products, 1981-85; mng. dir. Clear Vision Assocs., Larkspur, Calif., 1985—; bd. dirs. Westmedia Corp. Bd. dirs. Strawberry Area Community Council, Mill Valley, Calif., 1986. Mem. Am. Chem. Soc., Nat. Assn. Bus. Econs., Western Forest Economists (chmn. 1981). Republican. Episcopalian. Avocations: reading, running, skiing, swimming, volleyball. Home: 14 Sky Rd Mill Valley CA 94941 Office: Clear Vision Assocs 700 Larkspur Landing Circle #199 Larkspur CA 94939

NATT, THEODORE MCCLELLAND, newspaper editor, publisher; b. Portland, Oreg., Mar. 28, 1941; s. Theodore Manfred and Martha Sue

(McClelland) N.; B.S., U. Oreg., 1963; postgrad. Stanford, 1966-67; M. Diane Gail Shields, Dec. 27, 1962; children—Theodore McClelland, Lorena Sue, David Morris, Morgan Sadler. Reporter, Walla Walla (Wash.) Union-Bull., 1963-64, Oregonian, Portland, 1964-65; news editor St. Helens (Oreg.) Sentinel-Mist, 1965-66; asso. editor Daily News, Longview, Wash., 1968-71, mng. editor, 1971-74, editor, asst. to pub., 1974-77, publisher, 1977—; dir., sec., exec. v.p. Longview Pub. Co., 1971-86; pres., chief exec. officer Westmedia Corp., Longview, 1986—. Mem. adv. com. Wash. Dept. Social and Health Services, 1972-74; mem. Wash. Bench, Bar and Press Commn., 1977—. Bd. dirs., pres. Lower Columbia Mental Health Center, Longview, 1970-84. Stanford U. profl. journalism fellow, 1966-67; Pulitzer prize juror, 1977, 83, 84. Recipient Pulitzer prize, 1981. Mem. Wash. Asso. Press Assn. (pres. 1974-75), Soc. Profl. Journalists, Am. Soc. Newspaper Editors, Asso. Press. Mng. Editors Assn. (v.p. 1983, pres. 1984), Washington Athletic Club (Seattle), Kappa Sigma, Sigma Delta Chi (Disting. Service award 1981). Democrat. Episcopalian. Elk. Clubs: Rainier (Seattle); Longview Country; Nat. Press (Washington). Home: 2341 W Hills Dr Longview WA 98632 Office: 770 11th Ave Longview WA 98632

NATTENBERG, DAVID, communications common carrier co. exec.; b. Chgo., Aug. 4, 1937; s. Philip M. and Mildred P. (Pogrund) N.; student Fresno State U., 1955-57; BA, U. Calif., 1959; m. Judith Cohen, Jan. 25, 1945; children: Heidi, Scott, Jill. Area mgr. Common Carrier Sales Motorola, Inc., Sacramento, 1964-68; v.p. Nat. Communications Co., Sacramento, 1968-69; area mgr. Airsignal Internat., Inc., Sacramento, 1969-72; v.p., gen. mgr. Radiocall, Inc., Honolulu, 1972-79; pres. Aircall of Guam, Inc., 1979-85, Medi-Page, Inc., Honolulu, 1979-85, Tele-Page, Inc., Honolulu, 1979-85; exec. v.p. Aircall Internat., Honolulu, 1983-85; mng. dir. Tel-Net Joint Venture, Honolulu, 1985-87, pres. 1987—. Sec., trustee Temple Emanu El; trustee United Jewish Welfare Fund; bd. dirs. Am. Youth Soccer Orgn. Served to 2d lt. U.S. Army, 1959-61. Mem. Hawaii C. of C., Hawaii Telecommunications Assn. (pres.), Armed Forces Communications and Electronics Assn. Hawaii Execs. Assn. Home: 904 Iiwi St Honolulu HI 96816 Office: 737 Bishop St Suite 1470 Honolulu HI 96813

NAYAK, DEBI PROSAD, microbiology, immunology educator; b. Eadpore, India, Apr. 1, 1937; came to U.S., 1961; d. Sarat Chandra and Durga Rani (Mandal) N.; m. Abantika Datta Nayak, June 18, 1965; children: Prasun, Dipak. B in Vet. Sci., U. Calcutta, India, 1957; MS, U. Nebr., 1963, PhD, 1965. Acting asst. prof. UCLA Sch. Medicine, 1965-66, asst. research virologist, 1966-68, asst. prof., 1968-71, assoc. prof., 1971-77, prof., 1977—; mem. study sect. NIH, 1986—. Author, editor: The Molecular Biology of Animal Viruses Volumes I & II, 1977, Genetic Variation Among Influenza Viruses, 1981. NIH grantee, 1973—; Sr. Dernham fellow Am. Cancer Soc., 1969-74. Mem. AAAS, Am. Soc. Virologists, Am. Soc. Microbiology, NIH (study sect., research grantee 1973—). Office: UCLA Sch Medicine Dept Microbiology Immunology Los Angeles CA 90024

NAYMARK, SHERMAN, consulting engineer; b. Duluth, Minn., May 12, 1920; s. David N. and Lena (Naymark); children by previous marriage: Ronald L., Janet Naymark Stone. B.S. in Engring., U.S. Naval Acad., 1941; M.S. in Engring. and Constrn., MIT, 1946. Registred profl. engr., N.Y., Ill., Iowa, Wis., Minn., Pa. reigstered elec. and nuclear engr., Calif. Sr. scientist Argonne Nat. Lab., (Ill.), 1948-52; dir. reactor div. project, engring. mgr. Schenectady office AEC, 1952-56; with Gen. Electric Co., 1956-70; engring. mgr. nuclear turnkey plants AEC, San Jose, 1967-69; pres. Quadrex Corp., Campbell, Calif., 1970-86; chmn. Quadrex Corp., 1986; lectr. U. Va., MIT, U.S. Naval Res. Officer tng. Schs.; adviser to U.S. del. 3d Internat. Conf. on Peaceful Uses of Atomic Energy, Geneva, 1964; sr. examiner Profl. Engrs. State of Calif., 1960-70 ; mem. fusion power coordinating com. Dept. Energy. Contbr. numerous articles on nuclear research, devel., engring. to profl. jours. Served to capt. USN, 1941-54. Fellow Am. Nuclear Soc. (gen. chmn. ann. meeting, nat. treas. 1978-80), nat. treas. (mem. governing bd. Nuclear Tech. 1979-81); mem. AAAS, Am. Pub. Power Assn. (assoc.), U.S. Naval Inst. (hon. life). Democrat. Jewish. Home: 218 Forrester Rd Los Gatos CA 95030

NAZARIAN, HAGOP NUBAR, engineer; b. Aleppo, Syrian Arab Republic, Apr. 10, 1937; came to U.S., 1957; s. Kevork Habib and Vehanush (Der Khazarian) N.; m. Sylvia Diane Bent, 1963; children: Greg K., Ani Sonig. BSCE, Ind. Inst. TEch., 1959; MS in Structural Engring., U. Cin., 1962. Registered profl. engr., Calif.; cert. fallout shelter analyst, Calif. Structural engr. Whitman Atkinson Assocs., Pasadena, Calif., 1963-66; sr. engr. C.F. Braun Co., Alhambra, Calif., 1966-68; assoc. engr. Agbabian Assocs., El Segundo, Calif., 1968-69; engring. supr. Bechtel Power Corp., Norwalk, Calif., 1969-86; pres. Nazarian Engring., Rancho Palos Verdes, Calif., 1986—, also bd. dirs. Author (booklet) Fallout Shelter Analysis, 1971. Chmn. Tekeyan Armenian Cultural Assn., Los Angeles, 1971, 75; mem. Armenian Monument Council, Los Angeles, 1967-80; vice chmn. we. dist. com. Armenian Dem. Orgn., Los Angeles, 1978-79. Mem. ASCE, Structural Engrs. Assn. So. Calif. (seismology com.), Am. Inst. Steel Constrn., Am. Concrete Inst., Armenian Profl. Soc., Sigma Xi. Republican. Mem. Armenian Gregorian Ch. Club: Papazian (Los Angeles). Avocations: playing violin, classical music, sports.

NEAL, PHILIP MARK, JR., specialty chemical company financial executive; b. San Diego, Aug. 28, 1940; s. Philip Mark and Florence Elizabeth (Anderson) N.; m. Linda Reardon, Aug. 2, 1962; children: Brian, Kevin. B.A., Pomona Coll., 1962; M.B.A., Stanford U., 1964. Mgr. financial planning and analysis CBS, Hollywood, 1964-66; cons. McKinsey & Co., Los Angeles, 1966-73; v.p., controller Avery Internat. Corp., Los Angeles, 1974-78; sr. v.p. fin. Avery Internat. Corp., 1979—. Mem. Fin. Execs. Inst., University Club. Republican. Episcopalian. Home: 518 Pacific Ave Manhattan Beach CA 90266 Office: Avery Internat Corp 150 N Orange Grove Blvd Pasadena CA 91103

NEAL, ROBERT EUGENE, JR., financial and legal printing executive; b. Lebanon, Ind., Aug. 22, 1944; s. Robert Eugene and Ruth Winifred (Medsker) N.; A.B., Wabash Coll., 1966; postgrad. Butler U., 1967-68; m. Gretchen Ann Rolfe, June 21, 1975; children—Patricia Lee, Lisa Lyn, David Christopher. With R. R. Donnelley & Sons, Chgo., 1966-69, exec. salesman, 1968-69; with Arcata Corp., Menlo Park, Calif., 1970-76, mgr. corp. planning and devel., 1975-76; Bowne & Co., Inc., 1976-83; pres. Bowne of San Francisco, Inc., 1979-83; pres. Pandick, San Francisco, 1983-86; exec. v.p. Pandick Calif., Inc., 1986—; mng. ptnr. Corp. Fin. Assocs. of San Ramon, Calif. Mem. Am. Soc. Corp. Secs., Assn. Corp. Growth, Printing Industries No. Calif. Republican. Clubs: Kiwanis, Tennis (San Francisco); Round Hill Golf and Country (Alamo, Calif.); Commonwealth of Calif. Home: 28 Bushmint Pl Alamo CA 94507 Office: 18 Crow Canyon Ct Suite 206 San Ramon CA 94583

NEALY, CARSON LOUIS, chemist, consultant; b. Natchitoches, La., Dec. 24, 1938; s. Preston and May Bell (Gallion) N.; m. Sara E. Watford, Nov. 21, 1966; 1 child, Kimberly. BS in Chemistry, Northwestern State U., Natchitoches, 1960; MS in Chemistry, Fla. State U., 1963, PhD in Chemistry, 1965. Chemist Shell Devel. Co., Houston, 1965-70; research chemist Shell Oil Co., Houston, 1970-72; mgr. analytic chemistry Energy System Group of Rockwell, Canoga Park, Calif., 1972-84; sr. scientist Rocketdyne, Canoga Park, 1984—. Contbr. articles to sci. publs. Mem. AAAS, Am. Chem. Soc., Sigma Xi. Republican. Episcopalian. Home: 5912 Adler Ave Woodland Hills CA 91367 Office: Rocketdyne 6633 Canoga Ave Canoga Park CA 91303

NEDROW, FAY MARCELLE, optical dispensary professional, model; b. Breckenridge, Tex., July 30, 1946; d. Woodrow Benton and Georgia Fay (Huffman) Mason; m. James L. Nedrow, Sept. 23, 1967; children: Brooke T., Blake J. Student, Tex. Tech U., 1965-67. Artist, copywriter Dunlaps, Lubbock, Tex., 1967, Lipman-Wolfe, Portland, Oreg., 1968-69; sec. to pres. Pershing Coll., Beatrice, Nebr., 1970-73; copywriter Sta. KWBE Radio, Beatrice, 1973-74; owner, mgr. Reflections, Beatrice, 1977-80; buyer, mgr. The Optical Dispensary, Beatrice, 1980—, dress designer, 1986—; exec. dir. Miss S.E. Nebr./Am., Beatrice, 1986; model, actress, instr. Miller and Paine, Lincoln, Nebr., 1985-86; model, actress Nancy Bounds Agy., Lincoln and Omaha, 1986, Jackie Beavers Agy., Lincoln, 1986. Actress Lubbock Community Theatre, 1966 (Best Supporting actress award 1966); designer, creator Community players costumes, 1975-86. Pres., bd. dirs. YWCA, Beatrice, 1986, chmn. ann. fund raiser, 1985, chmn. teen programs, 1985; vol. United Way Campaign, Beatrice, 1985-86, Teen Pregnancy Program, 1985-86, March of Dimes Jail and Bail Fund Raiser, Beatrice, 1985, Reagan for Pres., Nebr., 1978, 85, Bob Kerry for Gov., Nebr., 1982, Charly Thone for Gov., Nebr., 1978; artist, vol. Gage County Reps., Beatrice, 1986; chmn. Community Players Ann. Fund Raiser, Beatrice, 1980-82; pres. Parent Tchr. League St. Paul's Sch., Beatrice, 1984-85; mem. exec. bd. Children's Library Guild, Beatrice, 1975-77, Beatrice Community Hosp. Guild, 1984-85; chmn., organizer Seymour Safely Program, Nebr., 1977; mem. Am. Charter Adv. Bd., 1986-87; state coordinator Mrs. Nebr. America Pageant, 1987; adv. bd. Salvation Army, 1987—. Named Mrs. Nebr., 1985. Mem. Nebr. Optometric Auxiliary (pres. 1978-79, sec., treas. 1977-78), Beatrice C. of C., Beta Sigma Phi. Lutheran.

NEELANS, BILL HOWARD, II, information systems manager; b. Oceanside, Calif., Dec. 3, 1952; s. Bill Howard Neelans and Wilma Bernadine (Hall) La Pete; m. Carolyn Anderson, May 24, 1975; children: Christopher Thomas, Jeffrey Adam, Erika Marie, Elyse Michelle. AA, Riverside City Coll., 1978; BA, U. Calif., Riverside, 1980. Fringe benefits adminstr. Jurupa Unified Sch. Dist., Riverside, 1976-79; adminstrv. analyst, mgmt. info. systems ops. supr. Bear Med. Systems Inc., Riverside, 1979-82; info. systems mgr. City of Baldwin Park, Calif., 1982—. Bd. dirs., coach, referee Am. Youth Soccer Orgn., 1981-87, Fontana and Riverside, Calif., 1981-86; scouting coordinator Boy Scouts Am., Bloomington, Calif., 1985-87; bishopric 1st counselor Ch. Jesus Christ of Latter Day Saints, Rialto, Calif., 1985-86; mem. Riverside County Underwater Search and Recovery. Served with USN, 1972-76. Mem. Data Processing Mgmt. Assn., Assn. Mcpl. Data Processin g Dirs. (v.p. 1986-87), Hewlett Packards Internat. Users Group. Republican. Club: Riverside County Underwater Search and Recovery. Avocations: baseball, genealogy, racquetball, photography, scuba diving. Home: 731 W Fontlee Ln Rialto CA 92376 Office: City Baldwin Park 14403 E Pacific Ave Baldwin Park CA 91706

NEELY, GAYLE, nurse practitioner; b. Stillwater, Okla., Oct. 29, 1950; d. William Fred and Mary Glynn (Munger) Cochran; m. Richard Kent Baldwin, Jan. 28, 1971; m. 2d, Gary Wayne Neely, Jan. 23, 1982. Student, Okla. Bapt. U., Shawnee, 1967-71; B.S.N., Central State U., Edmond, Okla., 1973; cert. U. Ariz., 1980. Staff nurse neonatal ICU, U. Okla. Health Scis. Center and Children's Hosp., Oklahoma City, 1973-75; nurse Presbyn. Hosp., Oklahoma City, 1975; pub. health nurse, newborn follow up program Ariz. Dept. Health Services, 1975-77; asst. dir. nursing Westside Community Hosp., Long Beach, Calif., 1977-78; nurse newborn nursery Desert Samaritan Hosp., Mesa, Ariz., 1978-80; neonatal nurse practitioner Good Samaritan Med. Center, Phoenix, 1980-83, neonatal nurse practitioner Air Evac, Phoenix, 1983-85; neonatal nurse practitioner Scottsdale (Ariz.) Meml. Hosp., 1985—; nurse practitioner Mead Johnson & Co. grantee, 1980. Mem. Neonatal Nurse Practitioners Assn. Ariz., Ariz. Perinatal Trust. Office: 1111 E McDowell Rd Good Samaritan Med Center Phoenix AZ 85062

NEELY, JERRY W., petroleum and mining equipment manufacturing company executive; b. Torrance, Calif., 1936; married. With Smith Internat., Inc., 1966—, asst. to pres., 1969-70, mgr. corp. devel., 1970-71, group v.p., 1971-74, exec. v.p., chief operating officer, 1974-76, chief exec. officer, 1976—, also chmn. bd., dir.; dir. Avery Internat. Co. Mem. Petroleum Equipment Suppliers Assn. (pres.). Office: Smith Internat Inc 4490 Von Karman Ave Newport Beach CA 92660 *

NEEPER, DONALD ANDREW, physicist; b. N.Y.C.. BA, Pomona Coll., 1958; MS, U. Wis., 1961, PhD, 1964. Research assoc. U. Chgo., 1966-68; staff, dep. group leader Los Alamos (N.Mex.) Nat. Lab., 1968-79, group leader, 1979-83, staff mem., 1983—. Contbr. articles on solar energy, low temperature physics to profl. jours. Chmn. Los Alamos chpt. N.Mex. Citizens for Clean Air and Water, 1972-77. Served to capt. U.S. Army, 1964-66. Mem. Internat. Solar Energy Soc. Avocation: hiking. Home: 2708 Walnut St Los Alamos NM 87544

NEES, HAROL (HAL) HUGH, II, law enforcement administrator, consultant; b. Champaign, Ill., Jan. 5, 1947; s. Harol Hugh and Katheryn L. (Wilson) N.; m. Sally L. Rhodes, June 1, 1974; 1 child, Devon. BS, N. Ariz. U., 1969, Met. State U., 1976; MA, U. No. Colo., 1977; M in Criminal Justice, U. Colo., 1981, Dr. Pub. Adminstrn., 1986. Officer Boulder Police Dept., Colo., 1970-75, sgt., 1975-79, lt., 1979-83, div. chief, 1983—; cons. Human Systems Inc., Boulder, 1981-82; assessor mgmt. practices Dept. Justice, 1985-86; mem. Govs. Child Abuse Com., Denver, 1984—; instr. U. No. Colo. Contbr. articles to profl jours. Pres. Attention Homes bd., Boulder, 1980-81; bd. dirs. Boulder County Ptnrs., 1985-86. Named Boulder County Officer of Yr., Jaycees, 1972. Mem. Internat. Assn. Chiefs of Police (instr.), Am. Soc. Pub. Adminstrn., Criminal Justice Adminstrn. sect. Am. Soc. Pub. Adminstrn. (rep. Washington, 1984—). Democrat. Avocations: reading, writing. Office: Boulder Police Dept 1777 6th St Boulder CO 80303

NEFF, EDWARD JOHN, accountant; b. North Hackensack, N.J., July 1, 1924; s. George Jacob and Anna Gladys (Sindle) N.; m. Francine Irving, July 7, 1948; children: Sindle Neff Tomforde, Edward Vann. BBA, U. N.Mex., 1947. CPA, N.Mex. Founding ptnr. Neff and Co. CPA's, Albuquerque, 1947—; pres. Clifford Corp. Mgmt., Albuquerque, 1986—. Bd. dirs. Albuquerque Community Council, 1962, Albuquerque Symphony Orchestra, 1969-72, N.Mex. Neurol. Found., 1968-73, Albuquerque Little Theatre, 1970-72, Friends of Indian Pueblo Cultural Ctr. Served to 2d lt. U.S. Army, ETO. Mem. N.Mex. Soc. CPA's (pres. 1958-59), N.Mex. Estate Planning Council (pres. 1962), Am. Inst. CPA's (council mem. at large 1974, com. taxation 1964-67, com. mng. acctg. practice 1971-74), Am. Mgmt. Assn., Phi Delta Theta (treas. 1946-48). Republican. Episcopalian. Club: 4 Hills Country (Albuquerque) (charter, bd. trustees 1958, v.p.). Home: 1509 Sagebrush SE Albuquerque NM 87123 Office: Neff & Co CPA's 7001 Prospect Pl NE Albuquerque NM 87110

NEFF, RAYMOND KENNETH, statistician, educator; b. N.Y.C., May 1, 1942; s. Francis Rudolph and Madge Alma (Pecora) N.; AB, Dartmouth Coll., 1964; SM, Harvard U., 1967, ScD, 1977; m. Mary Elizabeth Gordon, Aug. 9, 1969. Dir. Health Scis. Computing Facility Harvard U., Boston, 1971-82, lectr. biostats., 1974-78, 81-84, asst. prof., 1978-81; dir. sci. computing Dana Farber Cancer Inst., Boston, 1979-82; assoc. prof. biostats. Dartmouth Med. Sch., Hanover, N.H., 1982-84, assoc. prof. math. and computer sci. Dartmouth Coll., 1983-84, dir. computing services, 1984; staff statistician Norris Cotton Cancer Center, Hanover, 1982-83, dir. biostats., 1983-84, asst. vice-chancellor info. systems and tech. U. Calif., Berkeley, 1984—, assoc. prof. biostats., 1984—; trustee, acting pres., acting treas., pres. New England Regional Computing Program, Wellesley, 1973-76; regent Inst. for Info. Mgmt., Santa Clara, Ca., 1986—; trustee, treas. BITNET, Princeton, N.J., 1987—; cons. in field. Mem. exec. com. Dartmouth Alumni Assn. Eastern Mass., 1970-73. USPHS fellow 1966-71. Mem. Assn. Computing Machinery, Am. Public Health Assn., Biometric Soc., AAAS. Am. Statis. Assn. Author: (with Emanuel A. Friedman) Pregnancy Hypertension, 1977, Labor and Delivery: Impact on Offspring, 1987; contbr. articles to profl. jours. Home: 170 Tamalpais Rd Berkeley CA 94708 Office: U Calif Info Systems and Tech 209 Evans Hall Berkeley CA 94720

NEFF, SCOTT RICHARD, speech pathologist, counselor aide; b. Battle Creek, Mich., Oct. 1, 1958; s. J. Scott and Mary B. (Willis) N. BA, Mich. State U., 1981, MA, 1982. Speech lang. pathologist Roswell (N.Mex.) Ind. Sch. Dist., 1982—; counselor aide Roswell Assurance Home, Inc., 1986—. Mem. Am. Speech Lang. Hearing Assn. (cert. clin. competent), N.Mex. Speech Lang. Hearing Assn. Republican. Avocation: photography. Home: PO Box 1152 Roswell NM 88201 Office: Roswell Ind Sch Dist 300 N Kentucky Roswell NM 88201

NEHER, RAYMOND EDWIN, soil scientist; b. McCune, Kans., Feb. 5, 1925; s. Eli Edwin and Myra Sybil (Lange) N.; m. Marjorie Anne Roepke, Oct. 28, 1950; 1 dau., Elizabeth Anne. B.S., Kans. State U., 1950; student Cornell U., 1965, N.Mex. State U., 1966. Cert. soils scientist Southwest Engrs.; cert. soils specialist Dona Ana County, N.Mex. Student asst. Agronomy Dept., Kans. State U., 1946-50; soil scientist trainee U.S. Dept. Agr., Emporia, Kans., 1950, soil scientist, 1950-53; self-employed rancher, farmer, Manhattan, Kans., 1953-56; soil scientist, party leader, Mountainair, N.Mex., 1956-60, Lordsburg, N.Mex., 1960-63, Taos, N.Mex., 1963-66, Las Cruces, N.Mex., 1966-77, Truth or Consequences, N.Mex., 1977-79, area soil scientist Soil Conservation Service, U.S. Dept. Agr., Las Cruces, 1979-83; ret., 1983. Served with USNR, 1944-46. Registered Soil Scientist, soil classifier, soil specialist. Mem. Soil Conservation Soc. Am. (past pres.), Am. Soc. Agronomy, Soil Sci. Soc. Am., Soil Sci. Soc. N.Mex. (past pres.). Methodist (lay speaker). Clubs: Kiwanis, Mesilla Valley Radio, The Singing Men of Las Cruces. Contbr. articles to U.S. Dept. Agr. and univs. Home: 1930 E Madrid Ave Las Cruces NM 88001

NEHER, THOMAS BEERY, sales executive; b. Dayton, Ohio, Sept. 14, 1936; s. Robert Roy and Francis Lucille (Rudy) N.; m. Wendy Rae Woodward, Sept. 13, 1969 (div. Dec. 1975); 1 child, Kimberly Ann. AA, Phoenix Coll., 1958. Sr. buyer Del Mar Engring., Irving, Calif., 1971-75; sales person Woods Co., Burbank, Calif., 1975-76; buyer Bendix, Sylmar, Calif., 1976-79; sr. buyer CitiCorp/TTI, Santa Monica, Calif., 1979—. Served with U.S. Army, 1955-62. Republican. Methodist. Lodge: Eagles (pres. Lakewood, Calif., 1974-75). Avocations: gardening, musician, bowling. Home: PO Box 923 Los Alamitos CA 90701

NEHLSEN-CANNARELLA, SANDRA LEE, immunologist; b. Chgo., Dec. 31, 1940; s. Herbert O. and Cecelia C. Nehlsen; m. C.A. Cannarella, July 23, 1978. RN, Augustana Hosp. Sch. Nursing, 1961; BA in Biology, N.Y.U., 1968; PhD in Immunology, Nat. Inst. for Med. Research, 1971. Sect. head immunology Montefiore Med. Ctr., Bronx, N.Y., 1973-78, asst. dir. immunohematology, 1973-78, dir. transplantation immunology, 1978-85; dir. immunology ctr., histocompatibility lab. Loma Linda (Calif.) U. Med. Ctr., 1985—, prof. surgery, 1985—, research prof. pathology, 1985—; cons. in field, 1983—. Contbr. numerous articles to profl. jours. Grantee NIH, 1976-80. Mem. Am. Fedn. Clin. Research., Am. Assn. Immunologists, Am. Soc. Histocompatibility and Immunogenetics, Am. Transplant Physicians, Am. Council on Transplantation, Soc. for Analytical Cytology, Inst. Advancement of Health. Avocations: sculpturing, drawing, guitar. Office: Loma Linda U Med Ctr Immunology Ctr 11234 Anderson St Loma Linda CA 92354

NEIDLINGER, HERMANN HEINRICH, polymer chemist, educator; b. Bolanden, Federal Republic of Germany, Feb. 13, 1944; came to U.S., 1975; s. Heinrich and Lieselotte (Korrell) N.; m. Kathleen Louise Darwin, Mar. 27, 1973; children: Petra, Karen, Erik. BS, Gutenberg U., Mainz, Fed. Republic Germany, 1968, MS, 1971, PhD, 1975. Research chemist BASF, Ludwigshafen, Fed. Republic of Germany, 1970-71; NATO research fellow Stanford (Calif.) U., 1975-76; asst. prof. polymer sci. U. So. Miss., Hattiesburg, 1976-80, assoc. prof., 1980-82; sr. scientist Solar Energy Research Inst., Golden, Colo., 1982—; mem. adv. bd. Miss. Energy Research Ctr., 1979—. Contbr. articles to profl. jours. Deutscher Akademischer Austauschdienst fellow, 1972; NATO fellow, 1975-76; U.S. Dept. of Energy research grantee, 1977-83. Mem. Am. Chem. Soc., Gesellschaft Deutscher Chemiker, Miss. Acad. Scis. (chmn. 1980), Sigma Xi. Office: Solar Energy Research Inst 1617 Cole Blvd Golden CO 80401

NEIL, SUE, truck company official; b. Columbus, Ohio, Jan. 13, 1941; d. Edgar Gordon and Marian Ida (Scheuffler) Beckemeyer; m. James G. Neil, June 28, 1968; children—James G. II, Chadwick G. B.S., Ohio State U., 1962, postgrad., Antioch U., 1986—. Personnel supr. Bloomingdale's Dept. Store, N.Y.C., 1962-64; tng. supr. United Mchts. & Mfrs., N.Y.C., 1964-66; tng. dir. Accuray Corp., Columbus, 1966-71; asst. v.p., mgr. First Interstate Bank of Wash., Seattle, 1974-79; with Kenworth Truck Co., Seattle, 1979—, mgr. employee relations Seattle factory, 1981-87; corp. dir. tng. Paccar, Inc., Bellevue, Wash., 1987—; instr. City U., Seattle; cons. to bus. and govt.; lectrs. Mem. Am. Soc. Tng. Devel. (pres. Wash. State chpt. 1979, regional v.p. for West Coast, 1981-82, nat. dir. 1981-82, Nat. Torch award 1981), Futurist Soc. Am., Am. Soc. Personnel Adminstrn., Mortar Bd. Home: 21711 SE 259th St Maple Valley WA 98038 Office: Paccar Inc 777 106 NE Bellevue WA 98004

NEILL, H. RICHARD, structural engineer; b. Riverside, Calif., June 15, 1931; s. Harley Russell and Helen Virginia (Harper) N.; m. Marilyn O'Grady, 1957 (div. 1974); children: Darlene Mary, Michael Russell, Stephen James. BS in Math., Calif. Poly. State U., San Luis Obispo, 1956, BSArchE, 1957. Registered profl. civil and structural engr., Calif., Hawaii, Ariz. Structural designer Moffatt & Nichol Engrs., Long Beach, Calif., 1957-66, chief structural engr., 1966—. Prin. works include Gerald Desmond Bridge, Long Beach, 1966, Willamette River Bridge, Oregon City, 1970, Tippecanoe Bridge, 1985 (award City of San Bernardino, Calif. 1985). Mem. adv. commn. Santa Ana Fire Dept., 1976. Served with U.S. Army, 1950-52, Korea. Mem. ASCE, Am. Concrete Inst., Concrete Reinforcing Steel Inst., Earthquake Engring. Research Inst. Republican. Episcopalian. Avocations: fishing, woodworking, furniture restoration. Home: 1831 W Brewer Santa Ana CA 92704 Office: Moffatt & Nichol Engrs 250 W Wardlow Rd Long Beach CA 90807

NEILSON, JOHN WILBERT TENNANT, research company executive, consultant, educator; b. Oakland, Calif., May 9, 1944; s. Donald Wilbert Tennant and Mary Vera (Peart) N.; divorced; children—Sean Wilbert Tennant, Kimberly Mary. B.S. in Edn., So. Oreg. State Coll., 1969, M.S. in Gen. Studies, 1972. Registered sanitarian trainee Oreg. State Dept. Health, 1973. Dept. chmn. Days Creek (Oreg.) High Sch., 1969-70; chmn. biology dept. South Umpqua High Sch., Myrtle Creek, Oreg., 1970-75; microbiologist, chemist Umpqua Research Co., Myrtle Creek, Oreg., 1973-76, field rep., 1976-78; prof. sci. Lane Community Coll., Eugene, Oreg., 1976-78; salesman Jewett Office Supply, Medford, Oreg., 1978-80, Truscott Office Products, Medford, 1978-82, chief exec. officer pres. Neilson Research Medford, 1976—; lab. analyst, cons. drinking water; chief exec. officer, pres. Am. Service Group, Medford, 1986—; mktg. lab. services. Served with U.S. Army, 1962-65, USAR, 1976—. Mem. Am. Soc. Microbiology, Am. Water Works Assn., Assn. Ofcl. Analytical Chemists. Republican. Episcopalian. Club: Rotary. Author: Northwestern CB Log Book, 1976. Office: Neilson Research Corp 446 Highland Dr Medford OR 97504

NEITZEL, GEORGE PAUL, engineering educator; b. Atlanta, Nov. 28, 1947; s. George Paul Sr. and Bettymae Irene (Chapman) N.; m. Evelyn Kathleen Heaps, Nov. 29, 1974; children: Erik Paul, Jason Ward, Michael Brent, Timothy Jacob. BS, Rollins Coll., 1969; MS, Johns Hopkins U., 1974, PhD, 1979. Mathematician, engr. U.S. Army Ballistic Research Lab., Aberdeen Proving Ground, Md., 1969-79; asst. prof. engring. Ariz. State U., Tempe, 1979-83, assoc. prof., 1983—; cons. Monsanto Corp., St. Peters, Mo., 1984—; vis. prof. Universität Karlsruhe, Fed. Republic Germany, 1985-86, Imperial Coll., London, 1986. Contbr. articles to sci. jours. Repcipient Presdl. Young Investigator award NSF, 1984; Alexander Von Humboldt fellow, 1985. Mem. Am. Phys. Soc., Soc. Indsl. and Applied Math., AIAA, Am. Acad. Mechanics, Union of Concerned Scientists, Sigma Xi. Democrat. Mem. Unitarian Ch. Avocations: phys. fitness, camping, music. Home: 1035 E Wesleyan Dr Tempe AZ 85282 Office: Ariz State U Dept Mech Aerospace Engring Tempe AZ 85287

NEITZEL, JOHN MARK, advertising agency executive; b. LaCrosse, Wis., May 8, 1954; s. Gilbert Arthur and Marie Ardene (Eckelberg) N. BA in Journalism, U. Wis., 1976. Media planner, buyer Leo Burnett Co., Chgo., 1976-78, asst. account exec., 1978-79, account exec., 1979-81; account exec. Ketchum Advt., San Francisco, 1981-83; v.p., account supr. DDB Needham Worldwide, Inc., San Francisco, 1983—. Recipient EFFIE award Am. Mktg. Assn., 1986. Mem. San Francisco C. of C. (bus. vol. for arts 1986—), San Francisco Advt. Club. Democrat. Episcopalian. Avocations: sailing, skiing, piano, organ. Home: 66 Woodland Ave San Francisco CA 94117 Office: DDB Needham Worldwide Inc 530 Bush St San Francisco CA 94108

NELIPOVICH, SANDRA GRASSI, artist; b. Oak Park, Ill., Nov. 22, 1939; d. Alessandro and Lena Mary (Ascareggi) Grassi; m. John Nelipovich Jr., Aug. 19, 1973. BFA in Art Edn., U. Ill., 1961; postgrad., Northwestern U., 1963, Gonzaga U., Florence, Italy, 1966, Art Inst. Chgo., 1968; diploma, Accademia Universale Alessandro Magno, Prato, Italy, 1983. Tchr. art Edgewood Jr. High Sch., Highland Park, Ill., 1961-62, Emerson Sch. Jr. High Sch., Oak Park, 1962-77; batik artist Calif., 1977—; supr. student tchrs., Oak Park, 1970-75; adult edn. tchr. ESL, ceramics, Medinah, Ill., 1974; mem. curriculum action group on Human Dignity, EEO workshop demonstrator, Oak Park, 1975-76; guest lectr. Muckenthaler Ctr., Fullerton,

Calif., 1980. One-woman shows include Lawry's Calif. Ctr., Los Angeles, 1981-83, 1982, Whittier (Calif.) Mus., 1985-86, Anaheim (Calif.) Cultural Ctr., 1986; also gallery exhibits in Oak Brook, Ill., 1982, La Habra, Calif., 1983; represented in permanent collections McDonald Corp., Oak Brook, Ill., Glenkirk Sch., Deerfield, Ill. Recipient numerous awards, purchase prizes, 1979—. Mem. AAUW (hospitality chmn. 1984-85), Oak Park Art League, Orange Art Assn. (jury chairperson 1980), Anaheim Art Assn., Muckenthaler Ctr. Circle. Roman Catholic. Club: Anaheim Hills Women's. Avocations: cooking, swimming, tennis, travel. Homeand Office: 5922 Calle Cedro Anaheim CA 92807 Office: 5922Calle Cedro Anaheim CA 92807

NELLA, ALFRED LAWRENCE, accountant; b. Petaluma, Calif., July 6, 1928; s. Lawrence and Clelia Alice (Spolini) N.; B.S., U. San Francisco, 1951. Partner Samuel Mendelson & Co., C.P.A.'s, San Francisco, 1954-73, Nella & Getz, C.P.A.'s, San Francisco, 1973-76; propr. Alfred L. Nella, C.P.A.'s, San Francisco, 1976—; chief exec. officer Alan J. Blair Personnel Services, Inc.; dir. G-W Tank Lines, Inc., Pacific Blue, Inc., Berkeley Warehouse and Drayage Co., Inc., Berkeley Truck Leasing, Inc., Club Turkish, Inc., Groskopf-Weider Trucking Co., Dart Personnel Agy., Inc., F.J. Burns Draying, Inc., F.J. Burns Warehouse, Inc., Wilson Trucking Co., Inc. Bd. dirs., v.p. Fin. of Pride Found.; dir., treas. San Francisco Concert Opera Assn., Stop AIDS Project. C.P.A., Calif. Mem. Am. Inst. C.P.A.'s, Calif. Soc. C.P.A.'s, Golden Gate Bus. Assn. (dir., treas.). Republican. Roman Catholic. Home: 77 Fair Oaks St San Francisco CA 94110 Office: 425 Gough St San Francisco CA 94102

NELSON, ALBERT ALVIN, mechanical engineer; b. Billings, Mont., Mar. 22, 1949; s. Adolph Albert Nelson and Lorraine Ophelia (Skalsky) Shepard; m. Maura Eileen Berger, Feb. 12, 1972; children: Jeffry, Carol, Jeremy, Timothy. BS, Mont. State U., 1978; MA in Applied Behavioral Sci., Whitworth Coll., 1983; postgrad., Calif. Coast U., 1985—. Cert. stationary engr., Mont. Assignment supr. UNC Nuclear Industries, Richland, Wash., 1978-79, sr. engr., 1979-82, orgn. devel. cons., 1982-83, sr. job mgr., 1983—; cons. UNC Nat. Mgmt. Assn., 1983—, Nelson and Assocs., Kennewick, Wash., 1983—. coach Kennewick Grid Kids, 1983—; asst. scoutmaster Boy Scouts Am., Kennewick, 1984—; company commdr. Wash. Army N.G., Toppenish, Wash., 1983—. Served with USN, 1967-73, Vietnam. Mem. ASME (assoc.), U.S. Armor Assn., Assn. U.S. Army, Nat. Mgmt. Assn., Am. Legion. Roman Catholic. Lodge: KC. Avocations: snowskiing, backpacking, coaching youth athletics. Home: 2315 S Anderson Pl Kennewick WA 99337 Office: UNC Nuclear Industries PO Box 490 1100/104/R9/100N Richland WA 99352

NELSON, ALLEN F., investor relations co. exec.; b. Portland, Oreg., Oct. 17, 1943; s. Roy August and Mildred Mary (Jensen) N.; BS, U. Iowa, 1965, MA, 1968; m. Johanna Molenaar, Dec. 8, 1973. V.p. Shareholder Communications Corp., N.Y.C., 1970-72, Trafalgar Capital Corp., N.Y.C., 1973; pres. Nelson, Lasky & Co., Inc., N.Y.C., 1974-76; account exec. Corp. Communications Inc., Seattle, 1976-77; pres. Allen Nelson & Co., Inc., Seattle, 1977—. Mem. Fin. Analysts Fedn., Nat. Investor Relations Inst., Nat. Security Traders Assn., Practising Law Inst., Pub. Relations Soc. Am., Am. Soc. Corporate Secs. Clubs: Rainier, Washington Athletic. Home: 5702 SW Admiral Way Seattle WA 98116 Office: Allen Nelson & Co Inc 1906 California Ave SW Seattle WA 98116

NELSON, ANITA JOSETTE, educator; b. San Francisco, June 10, 1938; d. George Emanuel and Yvonne Louise (Borel) N. B.A., San Francisco State Coll., 1960; M.A., U. Denver, 1969. Dir. Community Ctr., Nurenberg, W.Ger., 1961-63; dir. program spl. services Community Ctr., Tokyo, 1964-66; resident counselor U. Denver, 1967-69; dir. student activities Maricopa (Ariz.) Tech. Coll., 1969-72, coach women's varsity tennis, coordinator campus activities, 1972-75; counselor, fgn. student advisor Scottsdale (Ariz.) Community Coll., 1975—. Named Phoenix Mgmt. Council Rehabilitator of Year, 1977. Mem. Nat. Assn. Women Deans, Adminstrs. and Counselors, Am. Personnel and Guidance Assn. Republican. Office: Scottsdale Community Coll 9000 E Chaparral Rd Scottsdale AZ 85253

NELSON, AUDREY IRENE, interior designer; b. Cleve., Apr. 11; d. Clyde Allen Davis; m. Robert A. Nelson (div. 1971); children: Bruce, Susan, Robin, Scot, Mark, Lori. Student, Cleve. Inst. Art, 1948, Ohio State U., 1952; AA, UCLA, 1960. Prin. Mediterrain Design Studio, Pacific Palisades, Calif., 1964-66; designer, store planner, buyer Breuners Furniture, Los Angeles, 1972-80; importer Mex. artifacts 1980-85; travel cons. Tradewinds Travel, Palm Desert, 1985—; freelance comml. set designer, Los Angeles, 1976—. Mem. Rep. Womens Group, Los Angeles, 1967; vol. UCLA Med. Ctr., 1967, Desert Hosp., Palm Springs, Calif., 1979. Mem. Nat. Soc. Interior Designers, Palm Springs C. of C., Palm Desert C. of C. Roman Catholic. Avocations: travelling, painting, aerobics. Home: 516 Sunset Way Palm Springs CA 92263

NELSON, BENJAMIN NORMAN, chemist; b. Bayonne, N.J., Oct. 31, 1921; s. Herman and Gertrude (Klitzman) N.; m. Miriam Nelson, July 4, 1948; children: Joel D., Ann G., Daniel E. BS in Chemistry, Polytech. Inst. Bklyn., 1943. Chemist Aluminum Research Lab., New Kensington, Pa., 1946-51; chemist, statistician Westinghouse Elec. Co., Pitts., Pa., 1951-61; statistician Youngstown (Ohio) Sheet and Tube, 1961-66; quality control engr. Wheeling (W.Va.) Steel Co., 1966-67; instr. reliabilty-stats. Lockheed Missiles and Space Corp., Sunnyvale, Calif., 1967-69, 1972-81, instr. profl. skills, space history, 1981—; cons. in field, 1961—; lectr. in field, 1975—. Contbr. articles to profl. jours. Served with U.S. Army, 1944-45. Recipient Van Der Hoof award, Lockheed Missile & Space Co., 1982. Mem. Nat. Speakers Assn. Democrat. Club: Toastmasters (Sunnyvale) (pres. 1973—, Disting. Toastmaster, 1980). Avocations: stress mgmt., self-awareness, imagery, biofeedback, profl. speaking. Home: 10151 Bonny Dr Cupertino CA 95014 Office: Lockheed Missiles & Space Co O/6679 B/595 PO Box 504 Sunnyvale CA 94086

NELSON, BONNIE KAY, educator; b. Paso Robles, Calif., Aug. 3, 1950; d. Vernon Carroll and Hilda Marie (Engelke) N. Degree in standard elem. edn., Calif. Poly. State U., San Luis Obispo, 1973, cert. early childhood edn., 1976. Tchr. kindergarten Paso Robles Union Elem. Sch. Dist., 1973—; sch. improvement project coordinator Paso Robles Union Elem. Sch. Dist., 1980-83, sch. site council chmn., 1981-82. Recipient service award, Paso Robles PTA, 1983; named Outstanding Young Educator for Paso Robles, Paso Robles Jaycees, 1985, Outstanding Young Educator for State Calif., Jaycees, 1986. Mem. Paso Robles Tchrs. Assn. (pres. 1980-82), Computer Using Educators, Cen. Coast Math Council, North County Athletic Assn., San Luis Obispo Antique Bottle Soc. (communications officer 1980—) Phi Delta Kappa, Delta Kappa Gamma (communications officer 1982-84). Republican. Baptist. Avocations: skiing, sailing, photography, sports, traveling. Home: 124 21st St Paso Robles CA 93446

NELSON, BRYAN H(ERBERT), retail executive; b. Yakima, Wash., July 3, 1956; s. Herbert B. and Marilyn A. (Cupper) N.; m. Linda K. Miller, June 16, 1979; children: Christofer A., Bryanne E. BEd, Ea. Wash. U., 1977, MS in Speech Pathology, 1978. Speech pathologist Ednl. Service Dist. 101, Spokane, Wash., 1978-83, coordinator speech pathology, 1983-84, coordinator inservice tng., 1985; processor fruit broker Herb Nelson Inc., Yakima, 1985—; guest lectr. Ea. Wash. U., Cheney, 1984-85; chmn. very spl. arts festival Ednl. Service Dist 101, 1985, on-site coordinator IDEAS conv., 1983. Mem. allocation panel United Way, Yakima, 1974. Lodge: Elks. Avocations: reading, golf, skiing, refinishing furniture. Home: 700 Mapleway Rd Selah WA 98942 Office: Herb Nelson Inc 3 W Yakima Ave Yakima WA 98902

NELSON, CHARLES ROBERT, financial planner; b. Philippines, Jan. 14, 1930; m. Beverly Ann Nelson, May 17, 1980. Vice pres., mgr. Paine Webber Jackson and Curtis, Newport Beach, Calif., 1972-73, Bache Halsey Stuart, Tucson, 1973-77; owner, mgr. King Of The North, Irvine, Calif., 1978-84; owner, mgr. Nelson Fin., Laguna Hills, Calif., 1983-84; gen. mgr. First Liberty Securities, Carlsbad, Calif., 1984-86; sr. ptnr. Nelson Fin. Assocs., Laguna Niguel, Calif., 1986—. Mem. planning adv. com. Orange County Hosp., 1979; bd. dirs., v.p. Palm Desert Resort Country Club Homeowner's Assn., 1982-83. Mem. Internat. Assn. Fin. Planners, Alpha Delta Phi. Club: Marbella Country (San Juan Capistrano, Calif.). Lodge: Rotary. Office: Nelson Fin Assocs 27782 El Lazo Suite B Laguna Niguel CA 92677

NELSON, DONALD ARVID (NELLIE), professional basketball coach; b. Muskegon, Mich., May 15, 1940. Student, U. Iowa. Player NBA teams, Chgo. Zephyrs, 1962-63, Los Angeles Lakers, 1963-65, Boston Celtics, 1965-76; from asst. to head coach Milw. Bucks NBA, 1976-87, also dir. player personnel; exec. v.p., part owner Golden State Warriors, NBA, Oakland, Calif., 1987—; mem. Nat. Basketball championship teams, 1966, 68, 69, 74, 76. Named Coach of Yr. NBA, 1983, 85. Office: care Golden State Warriors Oakland Coliseum Arena Oakland CA 94621 *

NELSON, DREW VERNON, mechanical engineering educator; b. Elizabeth, N.J., Oct. 11, 1947; s. Andrew K. and Myra G. (Kempson) N. BSME, Stanford U., 1968, MSME, 1970, PhDME, 1978. Research asst. Stanford U., Calif., 1971-74, asst. prof., 1978-83, assoc. prof., 1983—; engr. Gen. Electric Co., Sunnyvale, Calif., 1975-76, sr. engr., 1977-78; cons. in field. Editor: Fatigue Design Handbook, 1986; contbr. articles to profl. jours.; inventor Optical Stress Determination Systems. Recipient Spergel Meml. award for Most Outstanding Paper, 32nd Internat. Wire and Cable Symposium, 1984. Mem. ASTM, Soc. Automotive Engrs. Avocations: tennis, running, skiing, writing. Home: 840 Cabot Ct San Carlos CA 94070 Office: Stanford U Mech Engr Dept Stanford CA 94305

NELSON, ELDRED CARLYLE, computer technology consultant; b. Starbuck, Minn., Aug. 14, 1917; s. Carl Nicolae and Minnie Josephine (Olson) N.; m. Klaire Bertha Aicher, Jan. 19, 1946 (div. Oct. 1958); 1 child, Debra; m. Helen Grovene Bishop, Oct. 12, 1963. BA in Physics, St. Olaf Coll., 1938; PhD in Physics, U. Calif., Berkeley, 1942. Instr. physics U. Calif., Berkeley, 1942-43; group leader Los Alamos (N.Mex.) Lab., 1943-46; research assoc. Calif. Inst. Tech., Pasadena, 1946; asst. prof. U. Chgo., 1946-47; ptnr. Frankel & Nelson, Los Angeles, 1947-48; lab. head Hughes Aircraft Co., Culver City, Calif., 1948-53; tech. mgr. TRW Def. Systems, Redondo Beach, Calif., 1953-83; pvt. practice computer tech. cons. Los Angeles, 1983—. Author: Our Atomic World, 1946; contbr. tech. papers to profl. jours.; patentee in field. Named Disting. Alumnus, St. Olaf Coll., 1961. Mem. Assn. Computing Machinery, Sigma Xi. Republican. Lutheran. Avocation: music. Home and Office: 1808 Melhill Way Los Angeles CA 90049

NELSON, ERROL NELS, environmental analyst; b. Modesto, Calif., Feb. 11, 1939; s. Nels and Lillian Eleanor (Anderson) N.; m. Eva Lorraine Wisti, July 30, 1965; children: Eric, Erika. BS in Chemistry, Seattle Pacific Coll., 1962; MS in Forestry, U. Wash., 1968. Registered profl. engr., Wash. Chemist Weyerhaeuser Co., Seattle, 1964-66; air quality control specialist Northwest Air Pollution Authority, Mt. Vernon, Wash., 1968-72; air quality specialist Northwest Environments Tech. Labs., Bellevue, Wash., 1972-74; environ. analyst Wilsey & Ham, Bellevue, Wash., 1974-84, Nelson Environ. Products and Specialists, Issaquah, Wash., 1984—. Contbr. articles to profl. jours. Mem. Wash. State Winter Recreation Com., Olympia, 1983—, Tech. Adv. Com. Wash. State Environ. Policy Commn., Olympia, 1981-83; chmn. Issaquah Sch. Dist. Bd. Com., 1978. Mem. Air Pollution Control Assn., Xi Sigma Pi. Club: Mountaineers (Seattle) (pres. 1981-84). Avocations: skiing, soccer, stamp collecting. Home: 24304 SE 30th Issaquah WA 98027 Office: Nelson Environ Products and Services PO Box 114 Issaquah WA 98027

NELSON, GERALD EUGENE, geology educator; b. Missoula, Mont., Dec. 23, 1947; s. Harold G. and Marjorie (Millis) N.; m. Pamela Joan Boyd, Oct. 17, 1970; children: Inga Katrine, Birgitta Ann. BS, Mont. State U., 1973; PhD, U. Kans., 1983. Research asst. U. Kans., Lawrence, 1973-77; prof. geology Casper (Wyo) Coll., 1977—, dir. mus., 1979—; cons. Assocs. in Geology, Casper, 1977—. Editor: Cretaceous Geology of Wyoming, 1985; contbr. articles to profl. jours. Served with C.E., U.S. Army, 1970-77, Vietnam. Fulbright-Hays fellow, Uppsala, Sweden, 1975-76. Mem. Wyo. Geol. Soc. (edn. chmn. 1986—, editor guidebook 1985-86), Geol. Soc. Am., Quaternary Soc. Am., Wyo. Assn. Vietnam Vets. (organizer, treas. 1983-85), Mensa, VFW, Sigma Xi. Democrat. Avocations: photography, hunting, fishing, hiking. Home: 628 E 14th Casper WY 82601 Office: Casper Coll 125 College Dr Casper WY 82607

NELSON, HARRY, anthropologist, educator; b. Hazleton, Pa., Nov. 13, 1915; s. Abram and Anna (Rosenthal) N.; m. Donna Granger, June 28, 1956 (div. 1978); m. Sandra Quint, Sept. 23, 1985. BS, Bloomsburg (Pa.) U., 1939; MA, Columbia U., 1941; PhD, U. Calif., Berkeley, 1953. Instr. Santa Monica (Calif.) City Coll., 1956-65; prof. emeritus Foothill Coll., Los Altos, Calif., 1965-86. Author: (filmstrip) Fossil Man, 1969; co-author: (book) Atlas of Human Evolution, 1979, Introduction to Physical Anthropology, 1985, Understanding Physical Anthropology and Archeology, 1984. Served to capt. U.S. Army, 1942-46. Fellow Am. Anthrop. Assn., Am. Assn. Phys. Anthropology, N.Y. Acad. Sci., Calif. Acad. Scis., Southwest Anthrop. Assn. Democrat. Jewish. Avocation: rose cultivation, photography, swimming, tennis. Home: 535 Dewey Blvd San Francisco CA 94116 Office: Foothill Coll Los Altos CA 94022

NELSON, IRENE GIMSE, interior designer; b. Chgo., June 7, 1935; d. Ingvald and Ragnhild (Falck) Gimse; m. Jack Peter Nelson, June 14, 1955 (div. 1970); children: Steven Christopher, Kari Patricia, Lisa Diane, Cynthia Lee. Student, Miami U., Oxford, Ohio, 1954-57. Interior designer Serendipity Shop, Northfield, Ill., 1962-70, Irene Nelson Interiors, Steamboat Springs, Colo., 1972—; owner White Hart Gallery, Steamboat Springs, 1986—. Producer Southwestern Art Show, Steamboat Springs, 1981, Old Glory Art Festival, 1982, Randy Newman concert, 1986; orgnl. chmn. Kaleidoscope Winter Art Show, 1983; contbr. articles on architecture, skiing to mags. Instr. Steamboat Ski Sch., 1970—; chmn. Chgo. Maternity Ctr., Barrington, Ill., 1974-78, Northbrook (Ill.) Assn. for Arden Shore Sch., Lake Bluff, Ill., 1976-79; group leader Jr. Great Books, Barrington, 1975-79; trustee Whiteman Sch., 1982—. Republican. Congregationalist. Avocations: swimming, skiing, hunting, painting, golf. Home and Office: PO Box 880880 Steamboat Springs CO 80488

NELSON, JACK RUSSELL, university administrator; b. Portland, Oreg., Dec. 18, 1929; s. George Bahn and Elsa Margaret (Hamilton) N.; m. Bonita Casey, June 17, 1951; children: Richard Meredith, Ronald Gregory, Robert Geoffrey. B.A., Pacific Union Coll., 1952; M.B.A., UCLA, 1957, Ph.D., 1962. Chief accountant St. Helena Sanitarium and Hosp., 1951-53; mgr. Modesto City Hosp., 1954-55; assoc. prof. Andrews U., 1959-61; from asst. prof. to prof. U. Minn. Sch. Bus., 1961-70; asst. to pres. U. Oreg., 1966-67; vice provost, prof. U. Colo., Boulder, 1970-71; assoc. provost U. Colo., 1971-72, v.p., 1972-74, exec. v.p., 1974-78, acting chancellor, 1977, chancellor, 1978-81; pres. Ariz. State U., Tempe, 1981—. Contbr. articles to profl. jours. Bd. dirs. Del E. Webb Corp. Mem. Am. Econ. Assn. Office: Ariz State U Office of Pres Tempe AZ 85287

NELSON, JAMES F., judge, religious organization administrator. BS, U. Calif., LLB, Loyola U., Los Angeles. Bar: Calif. 1954. Judge, Los Angeles Mcpl. Ct. Chmn. Baha'i Faith Nat. Spiritual Assembly Bahais of the U.S., Wilmette, Ill. *

NELSON, JAMES MILTON, lawyer; b. Chgo., Apr. 29, 1957; s. Morris and Jeanne (Allenbach) N.; m. Marilyn Jean Giebelhausen, Aug. 18, 1979; children: Sara Rachael, Christopher Daniel. BA, U. Ariz., 1979; postgrad., Valparaiso U., 1979-80; JD, U. Ariz., 1981. Bar: Ariz. 1982, Calif. 1985, U.S. Dist. Ct. Ariz. 1982, U.S. Dist. Ct. (ea. dist.) Calif. 1985, U.S. Ct. Appeals (9th cir.) 1982, U.S. Ct. Appeals (D.C. cir.) 1985, U.S. Supreme Ct. 1985, U.S. Claims Ct. 1987. Staff asst. U.S. Senate Com. Judiciary, Subcom. Constitution, Washington, 1981; assoc. Shimmel, Hill, Bishop & Gruender, P.C., Phoenix, 1982-87, Diepenbrock, Wulff, Plant & Hannegan, Sacramento, 1987—. Active U. Ariz. Law Coll. Assn., Tucson, 1982—; sustaining mem. Rep. Nat. Com., Washington, 1982—; charter mem. Statue of Liberty Ellis Island Centennial Commn., 1984. Mem. Ariz. Bar Assn., Calif. Bar Assn., Maricopa County Bar Assn., Pima County Bar Assn., ABA, Def. Research Inst., Practicing Law Inst., Phoenix Metro C. of C., Phi Delta Theta. Home: 4524 Stonewall Fair Oaks CA 95628 Office: Diepenbrock Wulff et al 300 Capitol Mall 17th Floor Sacramento CA 95814

NELSON, JOHN HENRY, chemistry educator; b. Ogden, Utah, Mar. 25, 1940; s. Henry Everett and Reva Ann (Weddle) N.; m. Kathleen Louise Watkins, Mar. 19, 1964; children: Kirk, Brian, Kristine, Dominique. AS, Weber State Coll., 1961; BS, U. Utah, 1964, PhD, 1968. Postdoctoral fellow Tulane U., New Orleans, 1968-70; asst. prof. U. Nev., Reno, 1970-74, assoc. prof., 1974-79, prof., 1979—; vis. scientist China Lake (Calif.) Naval Weapons Ctr., 1972, Universite Louis Pasteur, Strasbourg, France, 1981-82; analytical chemist Farmers' Grain Coop, Ogden, 1961-64; vis. prof. Universite de Rennes (France), 1982. Author: Laboratory Experiments, 1977; editorial adv. bd. C&E News, 1981—; contbr. numerous articles to profl. jours. Active Ch. Basketball League, State of Nev. Fast Pitch Softball Team, local Cub Scout Pack; judge U. Nev. Intercollegiate Debate Tournament, local and regional Sci. Fair, Nev. State Forensic Tournament; coach Little League baseball, basketball and soccer teams. Served as sgt. USAF, 1962-68. Mem. Am. Chem. Soc. (chmn. Sierra Nev. sect. 1976-77, councilor 1980—, mem. com. on publs. 1981—, mem. ad Hoc com. on Sci. Data 1985). Republican. Mormon. Avocations: philately, active participation in sports. Office: U Nev Dept Chemistry Reno NV 89557

NELSON, JOHN I., government administrator; b. Berkeley, Calif., Nov. 15, 1932; s. John Henry and Helen Virginia (Hahn) N.; m. Jane Worthington, Apr. 27, 1956; children—John Andrew, Susan Howat. B.A. in History, U. Calif.-Berkeley, 1955; postgrad. Def. Intelligence Sch., Anacostia, Md., 1965-66. Notary Public, Wash. Mktg. rep. Hallmark Cards, Inc., Berkeley, 1957-60; commd. ensign U.S. Navy, 1955, advanced through grades to lt., 1963; intelligence officer, Vietnam, 1966-67; resigned, 1967; with HEW and successor HHS, Washington, 1967-70, staff asst., Seattle, 1970—; radio reader Wash. State Library for Blind and Physically Handicapped. Past pres. United Ch. Christ; ski chaperone jr. and sr. high ski sch., 1970-82, co-dir. ski sch., 1978; active in community opera, 1981-82; loaned exec. United Way King County, 1982; mem. Mercer Island Arts Council, 1983—, chmn., 1985—; mem. Mercer Island Community Fund, 1985. Served with USN, 1955-57. Recipient various profl. and community service commendations. Club: Mercer Island Country. Lodge: Rotary. Home: 7818 SE 76th St Mercer Island WA 98040 Office: HHS 2901 3d Ave Seattle WA 98121

NELSON, JOHN JOSEPH, JR., cabinet company executive; b. Phila., June 14, 1942; s. John Joseph and Kathleen T. (Conboy) N.; B.S. in Elec. Engring., Villanova U., 1965; M.B.A., Pepperdine U., 1975; m. Claire Brydahl, June 12, 1975; children—Kathleen Anne, John Joseph. Supr. subcontracts Ford Aerospace and Communications Co., Newport Beach, Calif., 1974-76, program mgr., 1976-81, dir. material Divad div., 1981-82, program dir., 1982-84; pres. Hoffman-Atchley Cabinets, Chatsworth, Calif., 1984—. Trustee So. Calif. Lumber Ind. Retirement Health and Welfare Funds., 1986—. Served to maj. USMC, 1965-74, col. Res. Decorated D.F.C., Air medal with 16 oak leaf clusters. Mem. Nat. Mgmt. Assn. (dir. chpt. 1980-83), Nat. Kitchen Cabinet Assn., (bd. dirs. 1986—). Republican. Roman Catholic. Home: 2039 Glastonbury Rd West Lake Village CA 91361 Office: Hoffman-Atchley Cabinets 20701 Plummer St Chatsworth CA 91313

NELSON, J(OHN) PHILLIP, orthopedic surgeon; b. Red Oak, Iowa, Dec. 23, 1936; s. Carroll C. and Marian E. (Amblad) N.; m. Charleen A. Nelson, Feb. 17, 1963; children: Christopher, Wendy, Andrew, Joel. BA, Grinnell Coll., 1958; MD, Northwestern U., 1962. Intern King County Hosp., Seattle, 1962-63; resident Mayo Clinic, Rochester, Minn., 1963-69; orthopedic surgeon Orthopedic Assocs., Denver, 1969-83, Cherry Creek Orthopedic Surgery P.C., Denver, 1983—. Editor: The Hip, 1982; contbr. articles to profl. jours. Served to lt. comdr. USN, 1966-68. Fellow Am. Acad. Orthopedic Surgeons (bd. dirs. 1978-79); mem. ACS, Am. Orthopedic Assn., The Hip Soc. (sec.-treas. 1984—), Assn. Bone and Joint Surgeons, Denver Med. Soc. (pres. 1980-81), Alpha Omega Alpha. Club: Cherry Hills Country. Avocation: breeding-tng. and showing of cutting horses. Home: 35878 E Mississippi Ave Watkins CO 80137 Office: Cherry Creek Orthopedic Surgery PC 3535 Cherry Creek N Dr Denver CO 80209

NELSON, JOHN THOMAS, civil engineer; b. Canton, Ill., July 3, 1942; s. Ralph Gilbert and Doris Ruth (Hammond) N. AA, Canton Jr. Coll., 1963; BS, Bradley U., 1967. Registered profl. engr., Wyo. Mining engr. Rocy Mtn. Energy, Rock Springs, Wyo., 1969-75; sr. mining engr. Cons. Engrs., Denver, 1975-83; county engr. Sweetwater County, Green River, Wyo., 1983—. Served with U.S. Army, 1967-69. Mem. Wyo. Soc. Profl. Engrs. (math counts 1983—, pres. 1985), Soc. Mining Engrs. (pres. 1974). Democrat. Presbyterian. Avocations: restoring antique cars. Home: 1229 Lowell Rock Springs WY 82901 Office: Sweetwater County Courthouse 80 W Flaming Gorge Green River WY 82935

NELSON, JOY HAUN, interior designer; b. Astoria, Oreg., Dec. 25, 1941; d. James J.D. and Sylvia (Pakes) Haun; m. Alfred Charles Nelson, Feb. 12, 1966; children: Kristin Anne, Erik Christopher. BS in Interior Design, U. Oreg., 1964. Interior designer Herman Miller Space Planning, San Francisco, 1964-66, Lubin Bus. Interiors, New Haven, 1969-72; tchr. Paire Sch. of Design, Hamden, Conn., 1969-72; interior designer R.L. Bryan Co., Columbia, S.C., 1973-76, Harry Wolf Assocs., Charlotte, N.C., 1976; pvt. practice interior design cons. Portland, Oreg., 1976-84; interior designer Yost Grube Hall, Portland, Oreg., 1984—; cons. Tektronix, Beaverton, Oreg., 1977-78, cons. U.S. Bankcorp, Portland, 1981-84. Mem. Profl. Inst. Bus. Designers (pres. 1981-82, founding bd. dirs. 1980-82, v.p. 1982-84), Nat. Creditation for Interior Design Qualification. Roman Catholic. Club: Multnomah Athletic. Avocations: sewing, skiing, cooking, swimming. Office: Yost Grube Hall 1211 SW 5th #2700 Portland OR 97204

NELSON, KATHERINE METCALF, art historian, art critic; b. San Francisco, Sept. 18, 1940; d. John Robert and Catherine Jane (Rolph) Metcalf; m. James Alonzo Nelson, July 16, 1966; children: John, Julie. BA in History, Stanford U., 1962; MA in Art History, U. Calif., Berkeley, 1965. Instr. art history Calif. Coll. Arts and Crafts, Oakland, 1966-67, 69-71; part time instr. Westminster Coll., Salt Lake City, 1975-85; Utah corr. Artweek, 1983—, Art News, 1986—. Contbg. editor Art News, San Francisco, 1966-67, Utah Holiday, Salt Lake City, 1981—; contbr. art revs. to various publs. Adv. panel for Visual Arts Utah Arts Council, Salt Lake City, 1983—; adv. bd. Salt Lake City Arts Council, 1985—. Recipient Kress fellowship in art history U. Calif., Berkeley, 1966. Avocations: skiing, fly fishing, gardening. Home: 1708 Forest Hills Dr Salt Lake City UT 84106 Office: Utah Holiday 419 E 100 South Salt Lake City UT 84111

NELSON, KAY LEROI, educator, chemist; b. Richmond, Utah, Apr. 4, 1926; s. Parley LeRoi and Margaret (Peterson) N.; m. Ina Shepherd, Sept. 4, 1947; children—Marlene, Alan LeRoi, Ronald Leslie, Harold Lynn, Karalee, David LeRoi. B.S., Utah State U., 1948; Ph.D., Purdue U., 1952. AEC thesis research fellow Purdue U., 1950-52, instr., 1953-54; postdoctoral research Office Naval Research fellow UCLA, 1952-53; asst. prof. Wayne State U., 1954-56; asso. prof. Brigham Young U., Provo, Utah, 1956-61; prof. Brigham Young U., 1961—, dept. chmn., 1968-71; vis. prof. Oreg. State U., 1971-72; vis. scientist Tex. A&M U., 1985. Author: Laboratory Projects in Organic Chemistry, 1966, Laboratory Excursions in Organic Chemistry, 1969, Correlated Organic Laboratory Experiences, 1972, rev. edit., 1975, Guided Organic Laboratory Experiences, 1983, 3d edit., 1986, ABC Nomograph, 1983; poem My Prayer, 1972. Served with AUS, 1944-45. Mem. Am. Chem. Soc., AAAS, Sigma Xi, Phi Kappa Phi, Phi Lambda Upsilon, Pi Kappa Alpha. Club: Kiwanian. Home: 2010 N Oak Ln Provo UT 84604

NELSON, LAWRENCE OLAF, educator; b. Hartford, Conn., Feb. 1, 1926; s. Lawrence Olaf and Gerda Amelia Elizabeth (Hanson) N.; m. Kathleen Alice Brito, Aug. 26, 1950; children: Scott Laurence, Adam Foster. B.S., Central Conn. State U., 1949; M.A., U. Conn., 1953; Ph.D., Mich. State U., 1960. Tchr. pub. schs. Stamford, Conn., 1949-52; asst. dir. U. Conn., 1952-55; asst. to pres. State Coll., Moorhead, Minn., 1956-57; dean of adminstrn. State Coll., 1957-58; cons. Office of Edn., HEW, Washington, 1960; mem. faculty Purdue U., Lafayette, Ind., 1960-74; adminstrv. dean Purdue U., 1967-74; dean Purdue U. (Ft. Wayne Campus), 1969-70, asst. to provost, 1974; prof. higher edn., dean continuing edn. U. Ariz., Tucson, 1974-81; prof. ednl. founds., adminstrn. and higher edn. U. Ariz., 1974—; cons. in field. Mem. planning com. Ind. Gov.'s Regional Correction Center, 1969-71; mem. adv. panel Ind. Higher Edn. Telecommunications System, 1971-74; adv. bd. Midwestern Center, Nat. Humanities Series, 1972-74; mem. Ind.

Com. for Humanities, 1972-74, Tucson Com. on Fgn. Relations, 1975—; bd. dirs. Continuing Edn. for Deaf, 1975-81, Ariz. Consortium for Edn. in Social Services, 1977-81. Author: Cooperative Projects Among Colleges and Universities, 1961. Mem. Am. Assn. Higher Edn., Assn. Continuing Higher Edn., Nat. Assn. Student Personnel Administrators, NEA, Nat. Univ. Continuing Edn. Assn., Nat. Univ. Extension Assn. (award 1971, dir. 1978-80), Phi Delta Kappa, Epsilon Pi Tau, Delta Chi. Clubs: Kiwanis of Greater Lafayette (pres. 1967), Kiwanis of Moorhead (dir. 1957-58), Rotary of Tucson (dir. 1979-80, pres. 1980-81). Home: 1330 Indian Wells Rd Tucson AZ 85718 Office: 629 Education Bldg U Ariz Tucson AZ 85721

NELSON, LINDA KATHERINE SUTTON, stagecraft company executive; b. Kankakee, Ill., Nov. 8, 1951; d. Milford E. and Dorothea A. Sutton; B.A., U. Md., 1974; m. John Morgan Nelson, Apr. 9, 1977; 1 son, Damon John. Lighting design cons. Alaska Stagecraft, Inc., Anchorage, 1976-83, corp. v.p., 1979-83, sec.-treas., 1983-84, pres., gen. mgr., 1984—; bus. agt. Internat. Alliance of Theatrical Stage Employees and Moving Picture Machine Operators of U.S. and Can., Local 770, Anchorage, 1978-83, founder, pres. Local 918, 1983-86; master electrician Anchorage Civic Opera, 1978-80, lighting designer, 1980-81; resident lighting designer Anchorage Community Theatre, 1980-84; partner SRO Productions, Anchorage, 1981-85. Vol. lighting designer Theatre Guild, Inc., Anchorage, 1976-81, tech. instr., 1976-81; trustee Alaska Theatre of Youth. Mem. Nat. Assn. Female Execs., Am. Mgmt. Assn., Am. Rental Assn. Democrat. Episcopalian. Office: PO Box 200506 Anchorage AK 99520

NELSON, MARTHA J., magazine editor; b. Pierre, S.D., Aug. 13, 1952; d. Bernard Anton and Pauline Isabel (Noren) N. BA, Columbia U., 1976. Mng. editor Signs: Jour. of Women in Culture, N.Y.C., 1976-80; editor Ms. Mag., N.Y.C., 1980-85; editor-in-chief Women's Sports and Fitness Mag., Palo Alto, Calif., 1985—. Editor: Women in the American City, 1980; contbr. articles to profl. jours. Bd. dirs. Painting Space 122, N.Y.C., 1982-85, Urban Athletic Assn. Mem. Am. Soc. Mag. Editors, Western Pubs. Assn. Office: Women's Sports Magazine 501 2d St San Francisco CA 94115 Other Address: Women's Sport & Fitness 310 Town & Country Village Palo Alto CA 94301 Other Address: Women's Sports Magazine 310 Town & Country Village Palo Alto CA 94301

NELSON, MARY CARROLL, artist, author; b. Bryan, Tex., Apr. 24, 1929; d. James Vincent and Mary Elizabeth (Langton) Carroll; B.A. in Fine Arts, Barnard Coll., 1950; M.A., U. N.Mex., 1963; m. Edwin Blakely Nelson, June 27, 1950; children—Patricia Ann, Edwin Blakely. Group shows include: Southwestern Watercolor Soc., Dallas, N.Mex. Watercolor Soc., Nat. League Am. Pen Women, N.Mex. State Fair; represented in pvt. collections in U.S., Germany, Eng., Australia; author: American Indian Biography Series, 1971-76; (with Robert E. Wood) Watercolor Workshop, 1974; (with Ramon Kelley) Ramon Kelley Paints Portraits and Figures, 1977; The Legendary Artists of Taos, 1980; (catalog) American Art in Peking, 1981; Masters of Western Art, 1982; Connecting, The Art of Beth Ames Swartz, 1984; (catalog) Layering, An Art of Time and Space, 1985; contbg. editor Am. Artist, 1976—. Mem. Soc. Layerists in Multi-Media (founder 1982), Albuquerque Mus. Found., Nat. Fedn. Press Women, N.Mex. Watercolor Soc., N.Mex. Press Women. Home: 1408 Georgia St NE Albuquerque NM 87110

NELSON, NANCY ELEANOR, pediatrician, educator; b. El Paso, Apr. 4, 1933; d. Harry Hamilton and Helen Maude (Murphy) N. B.A. magna cum laude, U. Colo., 1955, M.D., 1959. Intern, Case Western Res. U. Hosp., 1959-60, resident, 1960-63; practice medicine specializing in pediatrics, Denver, 1963—; assoc. clin. prof. U. Colo. Sch. Medicine, Denver, 1977—, asst. dean Sch. Medicine, 1982—. Mem. Am. Acad. Pediatrics, AMA, Denver Med. Soc. (pres. 1983-84), Colo. Med. Soc. (bd. dirs. 1985—). Home: 1265 Elizabeth Denver CO 80206 Office: 4200 E 9th Ave Denver CO 80262

NELSON, RANDALL ERLAND, surgeon; b. Hastings, Nebr., Dec. 28, 1948; s. Marvin Erland and Faith Constance (Morrison) N.; m. Carolyn Joy Kaufman, Feb. 28, 1976. BS in Chemistry cum laude, Bethany Nazarene Coll. (now So. Nazarene U.), 1971; MD, U. Nebr., 1975; MS in Surgery, U. Ill., Chgo., 1979. Diplomate Nat. Bd. Med. Examiners, Am. Bd. Surgery. Intern in gen. surgery Strong Meml. Hosp., Rochester, N.Y., 1975-76; resident in gen. surgery U. Rochester Affiliated Hosps., 1976-78, Rush-Presbyn.-St. Luke's Med. Ctr., Chgo., 1978-81; gen. surgeon Surg. Group San Jose, Calif., 1981—; instr. gen. surgery U. Rochester Sch. Medicine and Dentistry, 1975-78, Rush Med. Coll., Chgo., 1978-80; adj. attending surgeon Rush-Presbyn.-St. Luke's Med. Ctr., 1980-81. Mem. Rep. Nat. Com., Washington, 1984—. Fellow ACS; mem. AMA, Calif. Med. Assn., Santa Clara County Med. Soc., San Jose Surg. Soc., U.S. C. of C., Circle-K Club, Phi Delta Lambda. Republican. Lodge: Rotary (San Jose West). Avocations: photography, model rocketry, traveling, bicycling, collecting coins and stamps. Office: Surg Group of San Jose 2101 Forest Ave Suite #124 San Jose CA 95128-1489

NELSON, RANDY MARTIN, systems specialist; b. Holdredge, Nebr., Mar. 19, 1955; s. Dale Wayne Nelson and Marilyn Ann (Hultman) Jacobsen; m. Carla Ann Eldredge, Nov. 6, 1982 (div. Mar. 1986). AA in Computer Sci. with honors, Ariz. Tech., 1981. System mgr. Ariz. Tech., Phoenix, 1981-83, Hughes Aircraft, Tucson, 1983-84; CADD systems mgr. Anderson Debartolo Pan, Tucson, 1984-86; customer engr. Intergraph Corp., Scottsdale, Ariz., 1986—. Mem. Ariz. Intergraph Users Assn. (v.p. 1984-85, treas. 1985-86). Libertarian. Roman Catholic. Home: 8387 E Indian School Rd Scottsdale AZ 85251

NELSON, RICHARD HAYWARD, data processing executive; b. Provo, Utah, Apr. 26, 1932; s. Byron E. and Dorothy (Hayward) N.; m. Mary Frances Peterson, Sept. 25, 1952; children: Eric Jed, Kari. BS, Brigham Young U. Programmer Hercules Powder Co., Salt Lake City, 1961-64; systems rep. Burroughs Corp., Oakland, Calif., Denver, Salt Lake City, 1965-72; program analyst Amalgamated Sugar Co., Ogden, Utah, 1973-76, data processing mgr., 1976-81, mgr. software and long range planning, 1982—. Served as sgt. Signal Corps, U.S. Army, 1952-54. Mormon. Home: 3824 S 2000 W Roy UT 84067 Office: Amalgamated Sugar Co 801 1st Security Bank 24th and Washington Ogden UT 84402

NELSON, RITA MCDERMOTT, research biochemist; b. Waterby, Conn., Mar. 9, 1943; d. John Michael and Annastasa (Purcell) McDermott; m. John James Nelson, Aug. 14, 1965; children: Bridget, Kristin, Maura, Patrick, Meghan. BS, U. Portland, 1965; MS, U. Oreg., 1969. Research asst. U. Minn. Health Sci., Mpls., 1969-70; research assoc. St. Paul Ramsey Hosp., 1970-74; research assoc. Utah State U., Logan, 1976-84, sr. research tech., 1984—. Patroller Nat. Ski Patrol, Beaver, Mont., 1975. Mem. Am. Chem. Soc. Club: Cache Valley Soccer League (Logan) (bd. dirs. 1984—). Home: 1785 E 1500 N Logan UT 84321 Office: Utah State U 0300 Logan UT 94322

NELSON, ROBERT JOHN, manufacturing company executive, marketing professional; b. Portland, Oreg., Jan. 4, 1935; s. Eskil Mathias and Thelma Margaretha (Raz) N.; m. Emily Elizabeth Johnson, Mar. 16, 1956; children: Lisa, Jana, Kristina, Britta. BSChemE, Oreg. State U., 1957, MSChemE, 1961. Synthetic detergent mgr. Procter & Gamble, Long Beach, Calif., 1961-63; asst. chief chemist Pubs. Paper Co., Oregon City, Oreg., 1963-65; internat. mgr. Neptune Micro Floc Inc., Corvallis, Oreg., 1965-71; v.p., ptnr. Arthur Forsyth Co., Portland, 1971-81; mktg. dir. Sandwell Internat., Portland, 1981-84; v.p. sales and mktg. Rovang Inc., Portland, 1984—. Chmn. Duniway Sch. Citizens Adv. Com., Portland, 1975. Mem. Valve Mfrs. Assn. (rep.), Am. Inst. Chem. Engrs., Am. Mgmt. Assn., Tech. Assn. Pulp and Paper Industry, Instrument Soc. Am. (sect. pres. 1978-79). Republican. Clubs: Agenda (pres. 1975-76), Multnomah Athletic. Avocations: swimming, remodeling, golf, reading. Home: 3680 SE Glenwood Portland OR 97202 Office: Rovang Inc 1945 N Columbia Blvd Portland OR 97217

NELSON, ROBERT M., astronomer; b. Los Angeles; s. Steve and Margaret (Yeager) N.; m. Carolyn Valley (div.); children: Tom, Chet; m. Marguerite Renner. BS, CUNY, 1966; MA, Wesleyan U., Middletown, Conn., 1969; PhD, U. Pitts., 1977. Research assoc. Jet Propulsion Lab., Pasadena, Calif., 1978-80, sr. scientist, 1980—; producer weekly sci. radio show Sta. KPFK, 1980—. Vice chmn. Pasadena Dem. Club, 1984—; commr. Pasadena Pub. Utilities, 1984—. Mem. AAAS, Am. Astron. Soc. (press officer div. planetary scis. 1983—), Am. Geophys. Union, Internat. Astron. Union, So. Calif. Fedn. Scientists (co-chmn. 1981—). Home: 775 N Mentor Ave Pasadena CA 91104 Office: Jet Propulsion Lab 4800 Oak Grove Dr Pasadena CA 91103

NELSON, ROBERT MORRIS, management consultant; b. Spokane, Wash., Feb. 18, 1925; s. Walter Daniel and Doris (Morris) N.; m. Jane Randall Gray, Sept. 1, 1951; 1 dau., Deborah. B.A., Whitman Coll., 1950; M.A., U. Chgo., 1955. Personnel officer U.S. Navy Dept., Lawrence Berkeley Lab., Calif., 1951-67; personnel dir. Stanford Linear Accelerator Ctr. (Calif.), 1968-69; dir. personnel/employee relations Stanford U. (Calif.), 1970-71; personnel mgr. Lawrence Livermore Nat. Lab., Calif., 1972-73, Bechtel Group, San Francisco, 1973-77; pvt. practice mgmt. cons., San Francisco, 1978—; dir. Greater San Francisco Opportunities Industrialization Ctr., 1976-80. Treas. Democratic Central Com. Alameda County, 1964-68. Served to cpl. U.S. Army, 1943-46. Mem. Am. Soc. Personnel Adminstrs., Profl. Services Mgmt. Assn., Mechanics Inst. San Francisco. Club: Commonwealth (San Francisco).

NELSON, ROSEJANE MARKHAM, management recruitment executive; b. Erie, Pa., Jan. 14, 1923; d. Frank D. and Agnes T. Wiertel; m. Frank Houpt (dec.); children: David J., Diane L.; m. 2d Tom A. Markham, Aug. 6, 1949 (dec.); children: Tom A., Brad, Brooke, J. Brian; m. 3d Hugh C. Nelson, Sept. 1, 1974. Grad. in bus. Erie Bus. Coll., 1941; student Buffalo Law Sch., 1972. Columnist Gen. Electric News, Erie, Pa., 1946-49; prin. Rosejane Markham, real estate brokerage, Chautauqua County, N.Y., 1952-74; broker McCullough Real Estate Corp., Pa. and N.Y. State, 1972; ptnr., v.p., sec.-treas. Roth Young, Phoenix, 1977—. Town assessor Town of Mina (N.Y.), 1966-68, town justice, 1972. Republican. Avocations: artist, rare book collector, internat. traveler. Home: 514 W Townley Ave Phoenix AZ 85021 Office: 5150 N 16th St Suite 236B Phoenix AZ 85016

NELSON, RUSSELL MARION, surgeon, educator; b. Salt Lake City, Sept. 9, 1924; s. Marion C. and Edna (Anderson) N.; m. Dantzel White, Aug. 31, 1945; children: Marsha Nelson McKellar, Wendy Nelson Maxfield, Gloria Nelson Irion, Brenda Nelson Miles, Sylvia Nelson Webster, Emily Nelson Wittwer, Laurie Nelson Marsh, Rosalie Nelson Ringwood, Marjorie Nelson Helsten, Russell Marion, Jr. B.A., U. Utah, 1945, M.D., 1947; Ph.D. in Surgery, U. Minn., 1954; Sc.D. (hon.), Brigham Young U., 1970. Diplomate: Am. Bd. Surgery, Am. Bd. Thoracic Surgery (dir. 1972-78). Intern U. Minn. Hosps., Mpls., 1947; asst. resident surgery U. Minn. Hosps., 1948-51; first asst. resident surgery Mass. Gen. Hosp., Boston, 1953-54; sr. resident surgery U. Minn. Hosps., Mpls., 1954-55; practice medicine (specializing in cardiovascular and thoracic surgery), Salt Lake City, 1959-84; staff surgeon Latter-day Saints Hosp., Salt Lake City, 1959-84; dir. surg. research lab. Latter-day Saints Hosp., 1959-72, chief cardiovascular-thoracic surg. div., 1967-72, also bd. govs., 1970-84, vice chmn., 1979—; staff surgeon Primary Children's Hosp., Salt Lake City, 1960; attending in surgery VA Hosp., Salt Lake City, 1955-84, Univ. Hosp., Salt Lake City, 1955-84; asst. prof. surgery U. Utah Med. Sch., 1955-59, asst. clin. prof. surgery, 1959-66, asso. clin. prof. surgery, clin. prof., 1966-69, research prof. surgery, 1970—; staff services Utah Biomed. Test Lab., 1970-84; dir. tng. program cardiovascular and thoracic surgery at Univ. Utah affiliated hosps., 1967-84; mem. policyholders adv. com. New Eng. Mut. Life Ins. Co., Boston, 1976-80. Contbr. articles to profl. jours. Mem. White House Conf. on Youth and Children, 1960; Bd. dirs. Internat. Cardiology Found.; bd. govs. L.D.S. Hosp., 1970—, Deseret Gymnasium, 1971-75, Promised Valley Playhouse, 1970-79. Served from 1st lt. to capt. M.C. AUS, 1951-53. Markle scholar in med. scis., 1957-59; Fellowship of Medici Publici U. Utah Coll. Medicine, 1966; Distinguished Alumni award, 1967; Gold Medal of Merit, Argentina, 1974. Fellow A.C.S. (chmn. adv. council on thoracic surgery 1973-75), Am. Coll. Cardiology, Am. Coll. Chest Physicians; mem. Am. Assn. Thoracic Surgery, Am. Soc. Artificial Internal Organs, AMA, Dirs. Thoracic Residencies (pres. 1971-72), Utah Med. Assn. (pres. 1970-71), Salt Lake County Med. Soc., Am. Heart Assn. (exec. com. cardiovascular surgery 1972, dir. 1976-78, chmn. council cardiovascular surgery 1976-78), Utah Heart Assn. (pres. 1964-65), Soc. Thoracic Surgeons, Soc. Vascular Surgery (sec. 1968-72, pres. 1974), Utah Thoracic Soc., Salt Lake Surg. Soc., Samson Thoracic Surg. Soc., Western Soc. for Clin. Research, Soc. U. Surgeons, Am., Western, Pan-Pacific surg. assns., Inter. Am. Soc. Cardiology (bd. mgrs.), Phi Beta Kappa, Sigma Xi, Alpha Omega Alpha, Phi Kappa Phi, Sigma Chi. Mem. Ch. of Jesus Christ of Latter-day Saints (pres. Bonneville Stake 1964-71, gen. pres. Sunday sch. 1971-79, regional rep. 1979-84, Quorum of the Twelve Apostles 1984—). Home: 1347 Normandie Circle Salt Lake City UT 84105 Office: 47 E S Temple Salt Lake City UT 84150

NELSON, SARAH MILLEDGE, archaeology educator; b. Miami, Fla., Nov. 29, 1931; d. Stanley and Sarah Woodman (Franklin) M.; m. Harold Stanley Nelson, July 25, 1953; children: Erik Harold, Mark Milledge, Stanley Franklin. BA, Wellesley Coll., 1953; MA, U. Mich., 1969, PhD, 1973. Instr. archaeology U. Md., Seoul, Republic Korea, 1970-71; asst. prof. U. Denver, 1974-79, assoc. prof., 1979-85, prof. archaeology, 1985—, chair dept. anthropology, dir. women's studies program, 1985—; vis. asst. prof. U. Colo., Boulder, 1974. Grantee Southwestern Inst. Research on Women, 1981, Acad. Korean Studies, Seoul, 1983, Internat. Cultural Soc. Korea, Seoul, 1986. Fellow Am. Anthrop. Assn.; mem. Soc. Am. Archaeology, Assn. Asian Studies, Royal Asiatic Soc., Sigma Xi (sec.-treas. 1978-79). Democrat. Avocations: skiing, gardening, bridge. Home: 4970 S Fulton St Englewood CO 80111 Office: U Denver Dept Anthropology Denver CO 80208

NELSON, SCOTT DOUGLAS, political activist, government relations director; b. Watford City, N.D., Dec. 14, 1954; s. Thomas Oliver and Irene Lettie (Hoover) N.; m. Paula Sue Plamondon, Mar. 18, 1978; children: Erica Suzanne, Margret Irene. B.A., U. Puget Sound, 1978. Free-lance comml. photographer, 1974-77; staff asst. to U.S. Rep. Norman Dicks, Tacoma, Wash., 1978-80, dist. rep., Tacoma, 1980-81; western regional dir. Democratic Nat. Com., Issaquah, Wash., 1981-84; dir. govtl. relations The Wash. Natural Gas Co., 1985—; mem. polit. staff or cons. to numerous Dem. campaigns for Gov., U.S. Senate, U.S. Congress and state constl. offices. Bd. dirs. Puget Sound Older Workers Employment Agy., Tacoma, 1979-80, Ret. Sr. Vol. Program Pierce County, Tacoma, 1978-80; fin. chmn. Dist. 2 Boy Scouts Am., 1980. Recipient Eagle Scout award Boy Scouts Am., 1968, Pro Deo Et Patria, 1969; Nat. Merit scholar, 1973. Mem. Pub. Relations Soc. Am., The Pub. Affairs Council, Ctr. Study Dem. Instns., Am. Assn. Polit. Cons., (pub. affairs council), MENSA, Pi Kappa Delta, Sigma Nu. Lutheran. Author monographs: Juvenile Justice in Washington State, 1977; Computers in Politics—Legal and Moral Questions, 1980; others. Home: 4659 190th SE Issaquah WA 98027

NELSON, THOMAS ADAMS, electrical engineer, transportation consultant; b. Berkeley, Calif., Aug. 26, 1921; s. Thomas Fleming and Mabel Margaretta (Adams) N.; m. Mary Anne Mares, July 12, 1958. A.A., Los Angeles City Coll., 1942; B.S., U. So. Calif., 1949, M.S., 1953; cert. bus. mgmt. UCLA, 1970. Registered profl. engr., Calif. Design engr. Los Angeles Dept. Water and Power, 1950-53, quality assurance engr., U.S., Europe and Japan, 1953-65, asst. chief quality assurance engr., Los Angeles, 1965-68, chief quality assurance engr., 1968-72, mgr. communications, transmission lines, sta. maintenance and distbn. trouble, 1972-80; rail transp. cons., Ariz. and Nev., 1973-79, rep. to Calif. Power Pool, 1975-77; cons. engr., transp. cons., Los Angeles, 1980—; reviewer rail transit plans So. Calif. Rapid Transit Dist., Los Angeles County Transp. Commn., Orange County Transit Dist., Caltrans, San Diego Transp. Devel., 1978-87. Editor, major author Railroad Chronology Compendium, 1976, 50 Years of Railroading in Southern California, 1987; editor Jour. Pacific R.R. Soc., 1980-84, 87—. Contbr. articles to profl. jours. Mem. Citizens Adv. Commn. for Met. Rail, Hollywood, Calif., 1982-84, Met. Rail CORE Forum, 1987. Served to capt. USAAF, 1942-45, ETO. Mem. IEEE (sr.), Pacific R.R. Soc. (bd. dirs. 1977-80, 82-85, v.p. 1986—, pres. 1987—), Eta Kappa Nu, Tau Beta Pi, Phi Kappa Phi.

NELSON, WILLARD GREGORY, veterinarian, mayor; b. Lewiston, Idaho, Nov. 21, 1937; s. Donald William and Eve Mae (Boyer) N.; m. Mary Ann Eklund, Apr. 3, 1965 (div.); children—Elizabeth Ann, John Gregory. B.S. in Premedicine, Mont. State U., 1959; D.V.M., Wash. State U., 1961. Lic. veterinarian, Wash., Oreg., Idaho, Mont. Pvt. practice vet. medicine, Kuna, Idaho, 1963-66; asst. to dir. Idaho Dept. Agr., Boise, 1966-78; asst. chief Idaho Bur. Animal Health, 1978-80, chief, 1980-81; adminstr., state veterinarian Idaho Div. Animal Industries, 1981—; mayor City of Kuna (Idaho), 1984—; chmn. Idaho Gov.'s Human and Animal Health Consortium, 1983—. Kuna city councilman, 1964-68, pres. Planning and Zoning Commn., 1968-72; mem. bd. trustees Joint Sch. Dist. 3, 1970-71, pres., 1972-76; mem. adv. bd. Mercy Med. Hosp., Nampa, Idaho, 1986—; mem. adv. com. Wash., Oreg., Idaho Coll. Vet. Medicine, 1983—. Served as capt. U.S. Army Vet Corps, 1961-63; lt. col. Idaho Army N.G., 1979—. Mem. Idaho Vet. Med. Assn. (v.p. 1987), S.W. Idaho Vet. Med. Assn., U.S. Animal Health Assn. (chmn. anaplasmosis com. 1987—, v.p. nat. assembly), AVMA, Western States Livestock Assn., Am. Legion. Lutheran. Club: Lions (Kuna). Home: 2270 Old Penitentiary Rd Boise ID 83702

NELSON, WILLIAM BISCHOFF, business educator; b. St. Louis, Apr. 14, 1940; s. A.L., Jr. and M.M.H. (Bischoff) N.; student Washington U., St. Louis, 1958-60; B.S., U. Ariz., 1962, M.S. in Mktg., 1963; cert. bus. communicator; m. Julianne McDevitt, Dec. 1, 1972; children—Keli Anne, William Bischoff, Jr. Field advt. rep. Procter & Gamble Co., Cin., 1962; mem. mktg. staff Ford Motor Co., Dearborn, Mich., 1963-66; instr. mktg. U. Ariz., 1966-70; prof., head bus. div. Pima Community Coll., Tucson, 1970—. Active United Way, other civic and polit. orgns.; mem. fund raising com. St. Joseph's Hosp. Mem. Nat. Assn. Mgmt. Educators (v.p. 1973-77), Am. Mgmt. Assn., Am. Mktg. Assn. (emeritus), Point-of-Purchase Advt. Inst., Audit Bur. Circulations, Internat. Newspaper Advt. Execs., So. Mktg. Assn., Southwestern Mktg. Assn., Bus. and Profl. Advt. Assn. (life), Tucson Mus. Art, Ariz.-Sonora Desert Mus., Ariz. Hist. Soc., Nat. Trust Historic Preservation, Nat. Bus. Edn. Assn., Acad. Mktg. Sci., Direct Mktg. Assn. (research council) Am. Acad. Advt., Am. Film Inst., Internat. Platform Assn., NEA, AAUP, Ariz. Edn. Assn., Pima Community Coll. Edn. Assn. (bd. govs. 1972-74), Smithsonian Assos., Am. Mus. Natural History, Nat. Archives Trust, Delta Sigma Pi, Beta Gamma Sigma, Phi Kappa Phi. Club: Tucson Press. Office: PO Box 41630 Tucson AZ 85717

NELSON, WILLIAM ROY, nuclear engineer; b. Tacoma, Mar. 10, 1952; s. Ralph H. and Dorothy L. (Ilton) N.; m. Laurie Donner; children: Lindsay Renee, Marshall William. BS in Physics, Seattle Pacific Coll., 1974; MS in Nuclear Engring., U. Wash., 1980. Sr. engring. specialist Idaho Nat. Engring. Lab., Idaho Falls, 1976—. Contbr. articles to profl. jours. Mem. IEEE (standards com. Working Group Human Factors Standards, 1982-83), Am. Nuclear Soc. (tech. program com., exec. com. Human Factors div. 1982-83), Am. Assn. Artificial Intelligence, Instn. Diagnostic Engrs. Avocation: rowing. Home: 7260 Valco Dr Idaho Falls ID 83401 Office: EG&G Idaho Inc PO Box 1625 Idaho Falls ID 83401

NEMERE, ILKA MARIA, biochemist; b. Los Angeles, Jan. 1, 1953; d. Nick Frederick and Else Martha (Ickert) N.; m. Barry Alan Biehl, Aug. 5, 1978. BA, U. Calif. San Diego, La Jolla, 1974; PhD, UCLA, 1980. Postgrad. research biochemist U. Calif., Riverside, 1980-83, asst. research biochemist, 1984—; cell biologist, postdoctoral fellow U. Calif. San Diego, La Jolla, 1983-84; vis. asst. prof. UCLA, 1985. Contbr., reviewer articles to profl. jours. Summer research fellow Cedars-Sinai Hosp., Los Angeles, 1968-69; postdoctoral grantee NIH, 1983. Mem. Endocrine Soc., Am. Soc. Cell Biology, Am. Soc. Bone and Mineral Research., AAAS, Sigma Xi. Avocations: reading, horseback riding, camping. Office: U Calif Dept Biochemistry Riverside CA 92521

NEMETZ, NATHANIEL THEODORE, chief justice British Columbia; b. Winnipeg, Man., Can., Sept. 8, 1913; s. Samuel and Rebecca (Birch) N.; m. Bel Newman, Aug. 10, 1935; 1 son, Peter Newman. B.A. with 1st class honors, U. B.C., 1934, LL.D. (hon.), 1975; LL.D. (hon.), Simon Fraser U., 1975, U. Victoria, 1976. Bar: Created King's Counsel 1950. Spl. counsel Public Utilities Commn., 1958-61; spl. counsel to cities of Vancouver, Burnaby, New Westminster, B.C., Can., 1959-63; justice B.C. Supreme Ct., 1963-68, Ct. Appeal, 1968-73; chief justice B.C. Supreme Ct., 1973-78, B.C., 1979—; mem. Royal Commn. to investigate election irregularities, 1965; arbitrator fishing, lumber and hydro industries West Coast shipping dispute, 1966-73; chmn. Lehal Conf., Stanford U., 1986. Contbr. articles in field to profl. publs. Mem. senate, chmn. bd. govs. U. B.C., 1957-68, chancellor, 1972-75; chmn. Can. edn. del. to China, 1974; Chmn. Univ. Dist. Sch. Bd., 1957-59. Named hon. fellow Hebrew U., Jerusalem, 1976; recipient award Can. Council Christians and Jews, 1958; Great Trekker award U.B.C., 1969; Beth Emeth Brotherhood award, 1969; Canada medal, 1967; award of distinction U. B.C. Alumni, 1975; Queen Elizabeth medal, 1977. Mem. Can. Jud. Council (exec. 1973—), Can. Bar Assn., Faculty Assn. U. B.C. (hon.), Alumni Assn. U. B.C. (pres. 1957). Jewish. Clubs: Faculty (U. B.C.); Vancouver (Vancouver), University (Vancouver) (pres. 1961-62). Office: Law Courts, 800 Smithe St, Vancouver, BC Canada V6Z 2E1

NEMIR, DONALD PHILIP, lawyer; b. Oakland, Calif., Oct. 31, 1931; s. Philip F. and Mary (Shavor) N.; A.B., U. Calif. at Berkeley, 1957, J.D., 1960. Admitted to Calif. bar, 1961; sole practice San Francisco, 1961—; pres. Law Offices Donald Nemir. Mem. ABA (litigation com.), Calif. State Bar Assn. (litigation com.). Phi Delta Phi. Club: Univ. (San Francisco). Office: One Maritime Plaza San Francisco CA 94111

NEMIRO, BEVERLY MIRIUM ANDERSON, writer, educator; b. St. Paul, May 29, 1925; d. Martin and Anna Mae (Oshanyk) Anderson; m. Jerome Morton Nemiro, Feb. 10, 1951 (div. May 1975); children: Guy Samuel, Lee Anna, Dee Martin. Student Reed Coll., 1943-44; B.A., U. Colo., 1947; postgrad., U. Denver. Tchr., Seattle Pub. Schs., 1945-46; fashion coordinator, dir. Denver Dry Goods Co., 1948-51; fashion model, Denver, 1951-58, 78—; fashion dir. Denver Market Week Assn., 1952-53; free-lance writer, Denver, 1958—; moderator TV program Your Preschool Child, Denver, 1955-56; instr. writing and communications U. Colo. Denver Ctr., 1970—, U. Calif., San Diego, 1976-78; dir. pub. relations Fairmont Hotel, Denver, 1979-80; free lance fashion and TV model; author: The Complete Book of High Altitude Baking, 1961, Colorado a la Carte, 1963, Colorado a la Carte, Series II, 1966, (with Donna Hamilton) The High Altitude Cookbook, 1969, The Busy People's Cookbook, 1971 (Better Homes and Gardens Book Club selection 1971), Where to Eat in Colorado, 1967, Lunch Box Cookbook, 1965, Complete Book of High Altitude Baking, 1961, (under name Beverly Anderson) Single After 50, 1978, The New High Altitude Cookbook, 1980. Co-founder, pres. Jr. Symphony Guild, Denver, 1959-60; active Denver Art Mus., Colo. Opera Guild, Denver Symphony Group. Recipient Achievement Rewards for Coll. Scientists, Children's Hosp. Assn., Top Hand award Colo. Authors' League, 1969, 72, 79-82, 100 Best Best Books of Yr. award N.Y. Times, 1969, 71; named one of Colo.'s Women of Yr., Denver Post, 1964. Mem. Pub. Relations Soc. Am., Am. Soc. Journalists and Authors, Nat. Writers Club, Colo. Authors League (dir. 1969—), Authors Guild, Authors League Am., U. Denver Woman's Library Assn., Colo. Women's Coll. Library Assn., Sigma Delta Chi, Kappa Alpha Theta. Address: 420 S Marion Pkwy Apt 1003 Denver CO 80209

NEMIROFF, MAXINE CELIA, museum curator, director, educator; b. Chgo., Feb. 11, 1935; d. Oscar Bernard and Martha (Mann) Kessler; m. Paul Rubenstein, June 26, 1955 (div. 1974); children: Daniel, Peter, Anthony; m. Allan Nemiroff, Dec. 24, 1979. BA, U. So. Calif., 1955; MA, UCLA, 1974. Sr. instr. UCLA, 1974—; dir., curator art gallery Doolittle Theater, Los Angeles, 1985-86; leader of worldwide art tours; cons. L'Ermitage Hotel Group, Beverly Hills, Calif., 1982—, Broadway Dept. Stores, Southern Calif., 1979—, Security Pacific Bank, Calif., 1978—; art chmn. UCLA Thieves Market, Century City, 1960—, Los Angeles Music Ctr. Mercado, 1982—. Named Woman of Yr. UCLA Panhellenic Council, 1982, Instr. of Yr. UCLA Dept. Arts, 1984. Mem. Los Angeles County Mus. Art council art mus., UCLA Art Council, UCLA Art Council Docents, Alpha Epsilon Phi (alumnus of yr. 1983). Democrat. Jewish. Avocations: tennis, horseback riding, skiing, piano and guitar.

NEPTUNE, JOHN ADDISON, chemistry educator, consultant; b. Barnesville, Ohio, Nov. 27, 1919; s. George Addison and Lola Mae (Skinner) N.; m. Ruth Elizabeth Dorsey, Aug. 24, 1947; 1 child, Benjamin. B.S. summa cum laude, Muskingum Coll., 1942; M.S., U. Wis., 1949, Ph.D., 1952. Instr. chemistry Muskingum Coll., New Concord, Ohio, 1943-44, 45-48; foreman Tenn. Eastman Corp., Manhattan Project, 1944-45; asst. prof. chemistry Bowling Green State U., Ohio, 1949-50; instr. pharm. chemistry U. Wis.-

Madison, 1952-55; asst. prof. chemistry San Jose State U., Calif., 1955-58, assoc. prof., 1958-61, prof., 1961—, chmn. dept., 1973-86; cons. FMC Corp., Crown-Andersen Corp. Mem. Am. Chem. Soc., AAUP. Methodist. Home: 50 Cherokee Ln San Jose CA 95127 Office: San Jose State U Dept Chemistry San Jose CA 95192

NERI, BARBARA THORNHILL, contracts manager; b. St. Louis, June 23, 1941; d. Roy A. and Lillian (Oliver) Thornhill; m. Raimundo J. Neri, Sept. 16, 1967. Student Wayne State U., 1960-65; B.B.A. magna cum laude, Nat. U., San Diego, 1979, M.B.A., 1981. Adminstrv. asst. Mich. Blue Cross, 1967-70; adminstrv. asst. various firms, 1970-78; asst. contract adminstr. IRT Corp., San Diego, 1978-79; contract adminstr. JAYCOR, San Diego, 1979-83; contracts manager Computer Scis. Corp., San Diego, 1983—; Mem. Nat. Contract Mgmt. Assn.(chmn. hospitality com.), Nat. Assn. Female Execs., AAUW. Home: 836 W Pennsylvania Ave #117 San Diego CA 92103 Office: 9808 Scranton Rd San Diego CA 92121

NERO, PETER, pianist, conductor, composer, arranger; b. N.Y.C., May 22, 1934; s. Julius and Mary (Menasche) N.; m. Marcia Dunner, June 19, 1956; children—Beverly, Jedd; m. Peggy Altman, Aug. 31, 1977. Ed., Juilliard Sch., N.Y.C. Nat. tour with Paul Whiteman on TV and in concert, 1953-57, appearances concert halls, theatres, colls., TV and supper clubs throughout U.S., Eng., France, Holland, Italy, Scandinavia, 1962—; appeared at Grand Gala du Disque, Amsterdam, The Netherlands, 1964, five TV specials on, BBC-TV; arranged, appeared and, recorded with Boston Pops Orch.; music dir., Philly Pops Orch., 1979—; recording artist for, RCA Victor, Arista Records, Crystal Clear Records, Columbia; albums include Peter Nero Now; appeared in film Sunday in New York; composer: condr. more than 150 symphony orchs., 1971—. Honored by Internat. Soc. Performing Arts Adminstrs., 1986. Address: care Columbia Artists Mgmt Inc 4605 Lankershim Blvd Suite 421 North Hollywood CA 91602

NESBET, ROBERT KENYON, physicist; b. Cleve., Mar. 10, 1930; s. Clarence Kenyon and Elsie (Bowen) N.; m. Helen MacPherson, July 17, 1958; children: Anne, Susan, Barbara. AB summa cum laude, Harvard U., 1951; PhD, Cambridge U., Eng., 1954. Research assoc. Lincoln Lab., MIT, Boston, 1954-56; asst. prof. physics Boston U., 1956-62; mem. staff RIAS, Martin Co., Balt., summers 1958-59; NIH spl. research fellow Institut Pasteur, Paris, 1960-61; mem. staff Brookhaven Nat. Lab., summer 1962, IBM Research Lab. (now IBM Almaden Research Ctr.), San Jose, Calif., 1962—; vis. prof. chemistry U. Wis., 1967; vis. prof. physics U. Paris, 1973, U. Kaiserslautern (Fed. Republic Germany), 1979-80. Assoc. editor Jour. Computational Physics, 1969-74, Jour. Chem. Physics, 1971-73; co-editor Computational Methods for Large Molecules and Localized States in Solids, 1973; author: Variational Methods in Electron-Atom Scattering Theory, 1980; contbr. articles to profl. jours.; patentee high resolution electron energy device and method. Fellow Am. Phys. Soc.; mem. AAAS, Phi Beta Kappa, Sigma Xi. Home: 17268 Zena Ave Los Gatos CA 95030 Office: IBM Almaden Research Ctr San Jose CA 95120

NESBITT, PAUL EDWARD, state historian, author, educator; b. Balt., Dec. 25, 1943; s. William Ervin and Margaret Caroline (Shaw) N.; m. Donna Jean Coppock, Aug. 15, 1966 (dec. 1972); children—Erik-Paul A., Janelle M., m. Anita Louise Wood, Dec. 8, 1984. A.B., U. Wash., 1965; M.A., Wash. State U., 1968; Ph.D., U. Calgary, 1972. Instr., Tacoma Community Coll., Wash., 1968-69; grad. research-teaching U. Calgary, Alta., Can., 1969-71; exec. Hudson's Bay Co., Calgary, 1971; prof. Western Oreg. U., Monmouth, 1971-74; state historian State of Calif., Sacramento, 1974—; dir. Am. Sch. of Interior Design, San Francisco, 1974, HBC Bow Fort Research, Morley, Atla., 1970-71; instr. Am. River Coll., Sacramento, 1980—; exec. mgr. Calif. State Govt. United Way Campaign, 1986; cultural research cons. pvt. contracts western states. Contbr. articles to prof. jours. Fellow Am. Anthropl. Assn.; mem. Calif. Hist. Soc., Am. Inst. of Interior Designers (profl. 1974-77, bd. dirs. energy planning and devel. cos.), Am. Inst. Architecture (Central Valley chpt.). Office: Resources Agy Dept Pks & Rec PO Box 2390 Sacramento CA 95811

NESKO, THOMAS ANTON, retail store official; b. Garfield, N.J., Jan. 31, 1935; s. Milan Emil and Elizabeth (Havilir) N.; m. Mathilda L. Museler, Feb. 8, 1957; children—Linda A., Nancy E. B.A.B.A., Columbia (Mo.) Coll., 1978. Enlisted in USAF, 1954, served throughout world to 1975; support enforcement officer Seattle Dept. Social and Health Services, 1975-78; personnel mgr. Morrison Knudsen Saudi Arabia Consortium, Hafir Al-Batin, 1978-81; dir. human resources Klopfenstein's, Seattle, 1981-86; gen. mgr., 1986—. Trustee, Spokane Civic Theatre (Wash.), 1970-71; notary public. Mem. Personnel Execs. Seattle, Am. Mgmt. Assn., Pacific N.W. Personnel Mgmt. Assn. Republican. Lutheran. Home: 14124 126th Pl NE Kirkland WA 98034 Office: Klopfenstein's 600 Pine St Seattle WA 98101

NESLEN, H(OWARD) EDWARD, art educator; b. Grand Junction, Colo., Apr. 30, 1917; s. Uel Francis and Hazel Elizabeth (Barnes) N.; m. Florence LaRue Frandsen, June 23, 1948; 1 child, Howard E. B.A., U. Utah, 1938, M.A., 1946. Cert. secondary tchr., Utah. Tchr. art Garfield Sch. Dist., Granite Sch. Dist. and Tropic, Utah, 1938-83; tchr. art Granite High Sch., 1949-83, cons., Inventory Granite Sch. Art collections, 1983-86 , planner art curriculum, 1947-83; vocat. art curriculum planner Utah State Bd. Edn., Salt Lake City, 1975-80. Designer stage sets for many plays, musicals, 1945-83; archtl. renderings, 1945-85; one-man shows at Utah State Hist. Soc. Gallery, Salt Lake City, 1960, Sylvester's, Salt Lake City, 1976. Judge, Days of '47 Parade, Salt Lake City, 1950, 69; founder, chmn. Utah High Sch. Art Exhbn., Salt Lake City, 1959-72; chmn. hanging com. Assoc. Utah Artists, Salt Lake City, 1972—, Utah Bi-Centennial Art Exhbn., Salt Lake City, 1976. Creator horror posters for Zip Your Lip campaign, Ft. Ord, Calif., 1942-43. Served with U.S. Army, 1941-45. Recipient Edn. Service award Granite Edn. Assn., 1976; Utah Tchr. of Yr. award Utah State Bd. Edn., 1976; Spl. Service award Granite High Sch. Music Dept., 1977; Lime Light award Murray Eagle, 1983. Mem. Utah Art Educators (exec. bd. dirs. 1946-72, pres. 1950, Spl. award 1970-72), Utah Vocat. Graphics Assn. (pres. 1975-77, exec. bd. dirs. 1977-80), Granite Edn. Assn. (bldg. rep., exec. bd. dirs. 1947-50), NEA (life mem.).

NESTMAN, CHADWICK HENRY, engineer; b. Mobile, Ala., Sept. 4, 1945; s. William Frank and Edna Rogene (Langham) N.; divorced; children: Jodie Allison, Matthew Brandt; m. Elizabeth L. Jung, Dec. 14, 1984; Timothy and Jonathan (twins) (dec.). BS, U. Ala., 1968; MS in Indsl. Engring., U. Tex., Arlington, 1972; PhD, So. Ill. U., 1978. Mathematician Def. Intelligence Agy. Pentagon, Washington, 1968-69; programmer LTV Electrosystems, Dallas, 1969-71; systems analyst U. Tex. Med. Sch., Dallas, 1972; regional systems analyst Harris Data Communications, Boston, 1974-75; project mgr. software quality assurance NCR Data Communications, Columbia, S.C., 1975-76; asst.prof. info. systems Va. Commonwealth U., Richmond, 1979-82; prof. info systems N. Tex. State U., Denton, 1984-85; pres. Info. Decision & Support Systems Inc., Denton, 1983-85; sr. group engr., computer engring. and systems Martin Marietta Info. and Communications Systems, Denver, 1985—; prin. COM-AUDIT, 1980-82. Author: Introduction to Computers and Information Processing: An Instructor's Manual, 1981, A Systems Morphology for the Understanding of Decision Support Systems, 1981, Computers in Society: Instructor's Manual, 1982, Advanced Systems Analysis and Design, 1984, Effective Tools for Analysis and Design, 1985; contbr. articles to profl. jours. Assoc. commr. Little League, 1981-82; elder Reorganized Ch. Jesus Christ of Latter-day Saints. Fellow Postgrad. Acad. Higher Edn. (founder); mem. Assn. Systems Mgmt., Am. Inst. Indsl. Engrs.(sr., past dir. of computer and info. systmes div.), Richmond Joint Engrs. Council (past pres.), Am. Inst. Decision Scis., Assn. Computing Machines. Home: 7449 S Ivy Way Englewood CO 80112 Office: Box 1260 Denver CO 80201-1260

NESTOR, JAMES JOSEPH, physician, internist; b. Detroit, Mar. 22, 1939; s. Edward Mary and Kathleen (O'Brien) N.; m. Rebecca Nadine Adams. BSME, U. Detroit, 1962; MD, U. Pa., 1978. Diplomate Am. Bd. Internal Medicine; registered profl. engr., Mich. Test engr. Cadillac Motor Car, Detroit, 1962-66; design engr. Westinghouse Elec. Co., Balt., 1966-69; research engr. U. Calif., Berkeley, 1970-73; internist Kaiser Permanente Med. Clinic, San Jose, Calif., 1981—. Mem. AAAS, Soc. Med. Decision Making, Internat. Soc. Philos. Enquiry. Avocations: diagnostic imaging, decision analysis. Office: Kaiser Permanente Med Clinic 770 Calaveras Blvd Milpitas CA 95035

NETA, BENY, mathematics educator, researcher; b. Tripoli, Libya, Nov. 2, 1945; s. Shalom and Ahuva (Vittori) N.; m. Tamar Cerklevitz, Aug. 15, 1971; children: Itay, Leeor, Maital. BSc, Tel Aviv U., 1967, MSc, 1971; PhD, Carnegie-Mellon U., 1977. Asst. prof. math. No. Ill. U., De Kalb, 1977-80; asst. prof. numerical analysis Tex. Tech U., Lubbock, 1980-84; assoc. prof. Naval Postgrad. Sch., Monterey, Calif., 1985—. Contbr. articles to profl. jours. Pres. Lubbock chpt. PTA, 1983-84. Grantee Nat. Acad. Scis., 1984-85. Mem. Am. Math. Soc., Soc. Indsl. and Applied Math., AAAS, N.Y. Acad. Scis., Sigma Xi. Home: 1410 Augusta Pl Monterey CA 93940 Office: Naval Postgrad Sch Dept Math Code 53ND Monterey CA 93943

NETTING, FLORENCE ELLEN, social work educator, researcher, gerontologist; b. Kingsport, Tenn., July 3, 1949; d. Millege Howard and Ada (Quillin) Daniel; m. Karl Arthur Netting, Aug. 30, 1969. BA, Duke U., 1970; MSW, U. Tenn., 1975; PhD, U. Chgo., 1982. Dir. Loudon County (Tenn.) Office on Aging, Loudon, 1975-76, Foster Grandparent Program, Knoxville, Tenn., 1976-78; research and devel. E. Tenn. Human Resource Agy., Knoxville, Tenn., 1978-79, 1981-83; asst. prof. social work Ariz. State U., Tempe, 1983—; Mem. adv. council Area Agy. Aging, Phoenix, 1985—, Beatitudes Ctr. DOAR, Phoenix, 1984—, Christian Care, Phoenix, 1985—. Contbr. articles to profl. jours. Named one of Outstanding Young Women Am., 1980, tchr. of yr. Ariz. State U. Sch. Social Work, 1985, 86. Mem. Nat. Assn. Social Workers (Acad. Cert. Social Workers, Washington, 1977), Am. Soc. Aging (co-com. chmn. 1985-86), So. Gerontological Soc. (sec. 1983-84), Council Social Work Edn., Gerontological Soc. Am. Methodist. Avocation: watercolor art. Home: 3202 N 81st St Scottsdale AZ 85251 Office: Ariz State U Sch Social Work Tempe AZ 85287

NETTLER, GWYNNE, writer, retired educator; b. N.Y.C., July 7, 1913; s. Harry Lester and Dorothy (Wald) N. AB, UCLA, 1934; MA, Claremont Coll., 1936; PhD, Stanford U., 1946. Dir. child research project Community Council, Houston, 1957-59; assoc. psychologist Dando, S.A., Mexico City, 1959-61; sr. clin. psychologist Nev. Dept. Health, Reno, 1961-63; prof. emeritus U. Alta., Edmonton, Can., 1963-85. Author: Explanations, 1970, Explaining Crime, 1974, 78, 84, Social Concerns, 1976, Criminal Careers, 1982. Recipient Achievement award Govt. of Alta., 1982. Fellow Royal Soc. Can., Am. Soc. Criminology (E.H. Sutherland award 1982), Am. Sociol. Assn. Club: Swim and Tennis (Rancho Bernardo, Calif.). Home: 12862 Circulo Dardo San Diego CA 92128

NETTLES, WILLIAM BENJAMIN, computer co. exec.; b. Mt. Vernon, N.Y., Oct. 31, 1942; s. Alexander and Marjorie (Robinson) N.; m. Leonie Dolores March, Jan. 29, 1966; children—Lea Denise, Lesley Dahlia, William Benjamin. Student Pace Coll., 1960-61; B.A., L.I. U., 1969; M.A., Rutgers U., 1976. With IBM, 1967—, computer programmer, San Jose, Calif. 1976—. Mem. Am. Sociol. Assn., Assn. for Computing Machinery Rutgers U. Alumni Assn. No. Calif. Democrat. Home: 7226 Silver Lode Ln San Jose CA 95120

NETZEL, DANIEL ANTHONY, research chemist; b. Chgo., Feb. 16, 1934; s. Louis Al and Harriet (Folz) N.; m. Janet Cynthia Genua, June 14, 1958; children: Mark, Michael, Ronald. BS in Chemistry, U. Ill., 1957; MS in Chemistry, U. Mo., Kansas City, 1961; PhD in Chemistry, Northwestern U., 1975. Research asst., then assoc. research chemist Midwest Research Inst., Kansas City, 1958-67; nuclear magnetic resonance spectroscopist DeSoto Inc., Mt. Prospect, Ill., 1967-69; analysis lab. supr. Northwestern U., Evanston, Ill., 1969-75; spectroscopy lab. supr. Laramie (Wyo.) Energy Technologies, 1975-83; sr. research scientist Western Research Inst., Laramie, 1983—; lectr. chemistry U. Wyo., Laramie, 1978-80, adj. asst. prof., 1981-82, adj. assoc. prof, 1982—. Contbr. articles to profl. jours. Chmn. Homes Assn., Overland Pk., Kans., 1964, Sherman Hill, Wyo., 1978. Mem. Am. Chem. Soc. (Wyo. sect. sec. 1977-78, treas. 1983-85, chmn.-elect 1986-87, chmn. 1987—), Soc. Applied Spectroscopy (Chgo. sect. pres.-elect 1973-74, 1974-75). Republican. Roman Catholic. Avocation: hiking. Home: 2526 Sky View Ln Laramie WY 82070 Office: Western Research Inst PO Box 3395 Laramie WY 82071

NETZEL, PAUL ARTHUR, fund raising management exec., consultant; b. Tacoma, Sept. 11, 1941; s. Marden Arthur and Audrey Rose (Jones) N.; B.S. in Group Work Edn., George Williams Coll., 1963; m. Diane Viscount, Mar. 21, 1963; children—Paul M., Shari Ann. Program dir. S. Pasadena-San Marino (Calif.) YMCA, 1963-66; exec. dir. camp and youth programs Wenatchee (Wash.) YMCA, 1966-67; exec. dir. Culver-Palms Family YMCA, Culver City, Calif., 1967-73; v.p. met. fin. devel. YMCA Met. Los Angeles, 1973-78, sr. v.p., 1979-82, exec. v.p. devel., 1982-85; pres. bd. dirs. YMCA Employees Credit Union, 1977-80; chmn. N.Am. Fellowship of YMCA Devel. Officers, 1980-83; adj. faculty U. So. Calif. Coll. Continuing Edn., 1983-86, Loyola Marymount U., Los Angeles, 1986—; chairman, chief exec. officer Netzel/Steinhaus and Assocs., Inc., 1985—; pvt. practice cons., fund raiser. Pres. bd. Culver City Guidance Clinic, 1971-74; mem. Culver City Bd. Edn., 1975-79, pres., 1977-78; mem. Culver City Edn. Found., 1982—; bd. dirs. Los Angeles Psychiat. Service; mem. Culver City City Council, 1980—, vice-mayor, 1980-82, 84-85, mayor, 1982-83, 86-87; mem. Culver City Redevel. Agy., 1980—, chmn., 1983-84, 87—, vice chmn, 1985-86; bd. dirs. Los Angeles County Sanitation Dists., 1982-83, 85-87, Region IV United Way, 1986—; vice-chmn. bd. dirs. Calif. Youth Model Legislature, 1986—. Recipient Man of Year award Culver City C. of C., 1972. Mem. Nat. Soc. Fund Raising Execs. (vice-chmn. bd. dirs. Greater Los Angeles chpt. 1986—, Profl. of Yr. 1983). Roman Catholic. Clubs: Los Angeles Athletic, Rotary (Los Angeles). Address: 9696 Culver Blvd Suite 104 Culver City CA 90232

NEU, CARL HERBERT, JR., management consultant; b. Miami Beach, Fla., Sept. 4, 1937; s. Carl Herbert and Catherine Mary (Miller) N.; B.S., MIT, 1959; M.B.A., Harvard U., 1961; m. Carmen Mercedes Smith, Feb. 8, 1964; children—Carl Bartley, David Conrad. Indsl. liaison officer MIT, Cambridge, 1967-69; coordinator forward planning Gates Rubber Co., Denver, 1969-71; pres., co-founder Dyna-Com Resources, Lakewood, Colo., 1971-77; pres., founder Neu & Co., Lakewood, 1977—; mng. dir. Pro-Med Mgmt. Systems, Lakewood, 1981—; lectr. Grad. Sch. Pub. Affairs, U. Colo. Denver, 1982-84. Mem. exec. council Episcopal Diocese Colo., 1974; mem. Lakewood City Council, 1975-80, pres., 1976; chmn. Lakewood City Charter Commn., 1982, Lakewood Civic Found., Inc., 1986—; pres. Lakewood on Parade, 1978, bd. dirs., 1978-80; pres. Classic Chorale, Denver, 1979, bd. dirs., 1978-83; pres. Lakewood Pub. Bldg. Authority, 1983—. Served with Ordnance Corps, U.S. Army, 1961-67. Decorated Bronze Star medal, Army Commendation medal; recipient Arthur Page award AT&T, 1979; Kettering Found. grantee, 1979-80. Mem. World Future Soc., Internat. City Mgrs. Assn., Lakewood C. of C. (bd. dirs. 1983—, chmn. elect 1987, chmn. 1987-88). Republican. Episcopalian. Contbr. articles to profl. jours. Home: 8169 W Baker Ave Lakewood CO 80227

NEU, WILLIAM CARL, insurance company executive; b. Springfield, Ill., June 11, 1911; s. William Florian and Wilhelmina (Schniepp) N.; m. Shirleen Stevenson, June 7, 1963; children: Larry William, Shelly Rae Ainsworth. BA, Ill. Coll., 1932. Asst. actuary H.N. Bruce, Peoria, Ill., 1932-39, Alliance Life Ins. Co., Peoria, 1932-39; field mgr. Order Ry. Conductors, Cedar Rapids, Iowa, 1939-43; v.p., sec. Security Life of Denver, 1946-76, v.p. spl. projects, 1984—; exec. v.p. Internat. Arabian Horse Assn., Burbank, Calif. now Denver, 1976-82. Mem. Lakewood (Colo.) Park Bd. Served with USN, 1943-46, 50-51. Recipient Dirs. award Internat. Arabian Horse Assn., 1977; named Colo. Vocat. Man of Yr., Colo. Vocat. Edn. Assn., 1970. Mem. Adminstr. Mgmt. Soc. (pres., bd. dirs. 1951-70), Actuarial Club Pacific States. Republican. Methodist. Home: 9000 Squirrel Creek Rd Beulah CO 81023 Office: Security Life of Denver Ins Co 1290 Broadway Denver CO 80203

NEUBAUER, JAMES EMMANUEL, real estate developer; b. Sterling, Colo., Dec. 6, 1952; s. John and Patricia (Westland) N.; m. Pamela Dee Fisher, Nov. 27, 1976; children: Heather, Jonathan. Student, Stanford U., 1977, Northwestern U., 1977. V.p. Continental Bank, Phoenix, 1974-78; exec. v.p. P.F. West Inc., Tucson, 1978-85, pres., 1985—. Pres. Tucson Boys Chorus, 1984—; bd. dirs. Pima County (Ariz.) Research Council, 1984—. Mem. Southern Ariz. Home Builders Assn. Republican. Episcopalian. Club: Toastmasters (Phoenix), Presidents (U. Ariz. 1986—). Avocations: snow skiing, scuba diving, 4-wheeling, golfing. Home: 5941 N Via Verdoza Tucson AZ 85715 Office: PF West Inc 5995 E Grant Rd Tucson AZ 85712

NEUBAUER, LARRY ROBERT, engineer, weather forecaster; b. Fargo, N.D., Sept. 27, 1948; s. Lawrence and Helen (Moratis) N.; m. Bonnie Lea Becker, June 22, 1971 (div. June 1975); children: Tammy, Tessa; m. Florence Judy Butler, Aug. 9, 1980; children: Dvorah, Miriam, Pocahontas, Elizabeth. Student, N.C. State U., 1968-69; BSChemE, N.D. State U., 1971, postgrad., 1971-73; postgrad., Pa. State U., 1974-75, U. Wyo., 1975-76, U. Okla., 1977; MS, U. Utah, 1979; PhD, Brigham Young U., 1986. State solar officer Dept. of Energy, Bismarck, N.D., 1979; v.p. Energy Dakota, Bismarck, 1979-80; tech. dir. Domain Magnetics, Jerusalem, 1980-81; scientist NASA, Greenbelt, Md., 1983; phys. scientist U.S. Army, Dugway, Utah, 1985—; long range weather forecaster AccuWeather, Inc., State College, Pa., 1984—. Contbr. articles to profl. jours. Served with U.S. Army, 1966-69, Vietnam. Mem. AAAS, Astron. Soc. Pacific, Am. Geophys. Union, Am. Meteorol. Soc., Sigma Xi. Democrat. Mormon. Avocations: mountain climbing, photography, cross country skiing. Home: 52 South 300 West Springville UT 84663 Office: Brigham Young U 350 CB Provo UT 84602

NEUDECKER, STEPHEN KRAMER, environmental scientist, consultant; b. St. Louis, Sept. 25, 1953; s. Thomas Earl and JoAnn (Kramer) N.; m. Karen Denis Worley, Aug. 31, 1974; children: Austin Kyle, Stephanie Sierra. BS in Zoology, U. Ky., 1974; MS in Biology, U. Guam, Agana, 1978; PhD in Ecology, U. Calif., Davis, 1982. Cert. profl. ecologist. Sr. scientist Ecol. Analysts, Lafayette, Calif., 1979-84; sr. project mgr. Henwood Energy, Sacramento, 1985-86; pres. Environ. Cons. Services, Davis, 1984—; cons. Santa Fe Engring., Agana, 1977-78, Dames & Moore, San Francisco, 1983; chmn. 5th Internat. Coral Reef Congress, 1985. Contbr. articles to profl. jours., chpts. to books. Mem. AAAS, Ecol. Soc. Am., Sacramento C. of C. (environ. affairs com. 1983-85), Sigma Xi. Home: 1301 Union Dr Davis CA 95616

NEUFELD, NAOMI DAS, pediatric endocrinologist; b. Butte, Mont., June 13, 1947; d. Dilip Kumar and Maya (Chaliha) Das; m. Timothy Lee Neufeld, Nov. 27, 1971; children: Pamela Anne, Katherine Louise. AB, Pembroke Coll., 1969; M. in Med. Sci., Brown U., 1971; MD, Tufts U., 1973. Diplomate Am. Bd. Pediatrics, Am. Bd. Endocrinology. Intern R.I. Hosp., Providence, 1973-74, resident in pediatrics, 1974-75; fellow in pediatric endocrinology UCLA, 1975-78; staff endocrinologist Cedars-Sinai Med. Ctr., Los Angeles, 1978-79, chief pediatric endocrinology sect., 1979-85, dir. pediatric endocrinology, 1985—; asst. research pediatrician UCLA, 1978-79, asst. prof.-in-residence pediatrics, 1979-85, assoc. prof.-in-residence, 1985—. Contbr. articles to profl. jours. Named Clin. Investigator, NIH, 1978; grantee United Cerebral Palsy Soc., 1979, March of Dimes, 1981. Mem. Am. Diabetes Assn., Soc. Pediatric Research, Endocrine Soc., Juvenile Diabetes Found. (research grantee 1980). Presbyterian. Avocations: sailing, reading, sewing, cooking. Home: 16821 Charmel Ln Pacific Palisades CA 90272 Office: Cedars Sinai Med Ctr 8700 Beverly Blvd Los Angeles CA 90048

NEUMAN, THOMAS HERBERT, chemist; b. El Paso, Tex., June 27, 1955; s. Melvin Eugene and Delane (Rice) N.; m. Jody Seaman, Aug. 20, 1977; children: Colby Rice, Patricia Ann. BS in Chemistry, U. Utah, 1977, MS in Chemistry, 1979. Analytical chemist Reilly Tar & Chem., Indpls., 1980-81; plant chemist Texasgulf Soda Ash, Granger, Wyo., 1981-84; supr. prepregnancy testing Hercules, Inc., Magna, Utah, 1984—. Mem. Am. Chem. Soc. Home: 2104 Roosevelt Ave Salt Lake City UT 84108 Office: Hercules Inc PO Box 98 Magna UT 84044

NEUMAN, VICTOR ALLEN, mechanical engineer; b. Brawley, Calif., Dec. 5, 1955; s. Milton Ray and Marilyn Gay (Phillips) N.; m. Robin Stevenson, June 12, 1982. Cert., Cambridge (Eng.) U., 1980; BS in Engring. summa cum laude, U. Redlands, 1978. Registered profl. engr., Calif. Research engr. Naval Ocean Systems Ctr., San Diego, 1978-79, Cambridge U., 1979-81; mech. engr. Mitchell-Webb Assocs., San Diego, 1981-83, Earl-Walls Assocs., San Diego, 1984—. Nat. Merit scholar, 1974, Rotary scholar, Redlands, Calif., 1979. Mem. ASME, ASHRAE (sec. 1984-85, treas. 1985-86), Assn. Energy Engrs., Am. Soc. Plumbing Engrs. Democrat. Methodist. Avocations: bicycling, choral singing, sci. fiction. Home: 527 Splitrail Dr Encinitas CA 92024 Office: Earl Walls Assocs 5348 Carroll Canyon Rd San Diego CA 92121

NEUMANN, ALFRED KURT, medical educator; b. Milw., July 25, 1930; s. Alfred P. and Hannah A. (Lange) N.; B.A., U. Wis., 1952, M.A., 1955; M.D., NYU, 1958; M.P.H., Harvard U., 1960; m. Charlotte Grantz, Sept. 10, 1959; children—Frederick, Peter, Daniel. Diplomate Am. Bd. Preventive Medicine. Intern, Kings County Gen. Hosp., Bklyn., 1958-59; resident in preventive medicine Mass. Dept. Pub. Health-Harvard U., 1960-62; gen. practice medicine, Marathon, Wis., 1959; pub. health physician Mass. Dept. Pub. Health, 1960-61, asst. med. dir., 1961-65; instr. Tufts U. Sch. Medicine, Boston, 1963-65; dir. Health Dept. Brookline (Mass.), 1964-65; lectr. Johns Hopkins U., Balt., 1965-68; asst. prof. UCLA, 1968-71, assoc. prof., 1972-76, prof. Sch. Pub. Health, 1977—; vis. prof. People's Republic China, 1983, 85, 86; officer rural health project Narangwal, India, 1965-68; prin. investigator, co-dir. Danfa Comprehensive Rural Health Project, Ghana, 1970-79; cons. World Bank, WHO, UNFPA, Am. Pub. Health Assn.; chmn. Internat. Health Adv. Com., Project Concern Internat.; sec., bd. dirs. New Era Found. for Internat. Devel., Inc., Stanford, Conn. Fellow Soc. Applied Anthropology, Am. Pub. Health Assn.; mem. Wis. Acad. Sci., Arts and Letters, African Studies Assn., Internat. Health Soc. (pres. 1985-86), Delta Omega. Baha'i. Contbr. articles to profl. jours. Home: 520 20th St Santa Monica CA 90402 Office: Rm 21 245CHS Sch Pub Health UCLA Los Angeles CA 90024

NEUMANN, HARRY, philosophy educator; b. Dormoschel, Germany, Oct. 10, 1930; came to U.S., 1937, naturalized, 1948; s. Siegfried and Frieda (Lion) N.; m. Christina Sopher, Sept. 25, 1959. B.A., St. John's Coll., 1952; M.A., U. Chgo., 1954; Ph.D., Johns Hopkins U., 1962; postgrad., U. Heidelberg, Germany, 1956-58. Mem. faculty Mich. State U., 1962-63, Lake Forest Coll., 1963-65; prof. philosophy, and govt. Claremont Grad. Sch. Scripps Coll., Claremont, Calif., 1966—; research assoc. Rockefeller Inst., N.Y.C., 1963. Contbr. articles profl. jours. Mem. nat. adv. bd. Am. Security Council, U.S. Def. Com. Served with AUS, 1954-56. Classical Philosophy fellow Center Hellenic Studies, Dumbarton Oaks, Washington, 1965-66; research fellow Salvatori Center for the Study of Individual Freedom in the Modern World, 1970; research fellow Earhart Found., 1973-74, 78, 82, 86. Mem. Am. Security Coundil (U.S. Def. com.), N.Am. Nietzsche Soc., Univ. Centers Rational Alternatives, Univ. Profs. for Acad. Order, John Brown Cook Assn. for Freedom (advisor). Home: Scripps Coll Claremont CA 91711

NEUMAYER, ROBERT CHARLES, aerospace engineer; b. Carroll, Iowa, May 14, 1937; s. Charles A. and Anne (Ortner) N.; children—Deborah, John. B.S. in Chem. Engring., Iowa State U., 1959; M.S., U. Wash., 1969; M.Engring. Adminstrn., U. Utah, 1973. Devel. chem. engr. Union Carbide Chems. Co., South Charleston, W.Va., 1959-60; commd. 2d lt. U.S. Air Force, 1960, advanced through grades to lt. col., 1976; served in Phu Cat and Saigon, Vietnam, 1969-70, pilot, flying safety officer, airlift controller, engr., engring. mgr., ops. officer, staff officer, tech. dir., ret., 1980; mgr. test and evaluation Martin Marietta Aerospace, Wakefield, Mass., 1980-84, mgr. test ops. Martin Marietta Denver Aerospace, Littleton, Colo., 1984—. Decorated Meritorious Service medal, Air medal; Vietnam Gallantry Cross with palm, others. Mem. Phi Kappa Phi, Tau Beta Pi, Phi Lambda Epsilon. Roman Catholic. Lodge: Elks. Home: 8104 S Spruce Ct Englewood CO 80112 Office: PO Box 179 Denver CO 80201

NEUSTADT, MORRIS, physicist; b. San Francisco, Nov. 21, 1917; s. Julius and Frances (Nathan) N.; m. Joan Raphael, June. 2, 1946; children: Julie Neustadt Heifetz, John Robert. AB in Physics summa cum laude, U. Calif., Berkeley, 1939, MA in Physics, 1942, PhD in Physics, 1943. Prin. engr. Northrop Corp., Hawthorne, Calif., 1956-72; sr. engr. scientist McDonnell Douglas Astronautics Co., Huntington Beach, Calif., 1972—. Mem. Sigma

Xi, Phi Beta Kappa, Pi Mu Epsilon. Avocations: reading, walking, hiking. Home: 1840 Fairburn Ave #212 Los Angeles CA 90025 Office: McDonnell Douglas Astronautics Co 5301 Bolsa Ave Mail Station 12-M Huntington Beach CA 92647

NEVILLE, ROY GERALD, management engineering and pollution control consultant; b. Bournemouth, Eng.; came to U.S., 1951; naturalized, 1957; s. Percy Herbert and Georgina Lallie (Jenkins) N.; m. Jeanne Frances Russ, July 26, 1952; children: Laura Jean, Janet Marilyn. BS, U. London, 1951; MS, U. Oreg., 1952, PhD, 1954; FRIC, Royal Inst. Chemistry, London, 1963, DS (hon.), 1973. Research chemist Monsanto Chem. co., Seattle, 1955-57; sr. chem. engr. Boeing Co., Seattle, 1957-58, head dept. materials Scis. Lab., Boeing Sci. Research Labs., 1967-69; sr. research scientist Lockheed Missiles & Space Co., Palo Alto, Calif., 1958-61; sr. staff scientist Aerospace Corp., El Segundo, Calif., 1961-63; prin. scientist Rockwell Internat. Corp., Los Angeles, 1963-67; sr. engirng. specialist Bechtel Corp., San Francisco, 1969-73; pres. Engring. & Tech. Cons., Inc., Redwood City, Calif., 1973—. Contbr. numerous articles to profl. jours.; patentee in field. Fulbright scholar to U.S., 1951; USPHS fellowship, 1951-52, Research Corp. fellow, 1952-54; chartered chemist, London. Fellow Royal Soc. Chemistry (London), Am. Inst. Chemists, AAAS; mem. Am. Chem. Soc., Am. Inst. Chem. Engrs., History Sci. Soc., Soc. Study Early Chemistry, Royal Instn. Gt. Britain, Research Soc. Am., Soc. Mining Engrs. of AIME, Sigma Xi. Office: Box 912 San Carlos CA 94070

NEVILLES, JOHN ELLSWORTH, business machines company manager, consultant; b. Mpls., Jan. 24, 1940; s. Wilbur E. and Phillis A. N.; m. Amelia Carbajal, Feb. 2, 1959; children—John, Sonya. A.B.A., St. Philips Coll., 1974. Personnel specialist, resource planner U.S. Army, 1958-78; indsl. engr. IBM, Tucson, 1978-80, sr. recruiting specialist, 1981, mgr. quality services, 1982-86, mgr. quality tech. ops., 1986—; lectr. career planning, quality assurance, statis. quality control, continuous flow mfg. Adv. mem. Job Corps, Tucson Skills Ctr. Author: Processing Guide Quality Information, 1986, Decision Guide for Choosing Control Charts, 1985. Decorated Bronze Star. Mem. Am. Soc. Quality Control, Am. Statis. Assn., Am. Soc. Tng. and Devel., Nat. Assn. Trade Tech. Schs. (cert.), VFW, Am. Legion. Democrat. Roman Catholic. Home: 3225 S Eastview Tucson AZ 85730 Office: IBM GPD Dept 43F/060 Tucson AZ 85744

NEVIN, CROCKER, investment banker; b. Tulsa, Mar. 14, 1923; s. Ethelbert Paul and Jennie Crocker (Fassett) N.; m. Mary Elizabeth Sherwin, Apr. 24, 1952 (div. 1984); children: Anne, Paul, Elizabeth, Crocker; m. Marilyn Elizabeth English, Nov. 3, 1984. Grad. with high honors, St. Paul's Sch., 1942; A.B. with high honors, Princeton U., 1946. With Vick Chem. Co., 1949-50, John Roberts Powers Cosmetic Co., 1950-52; with Marine Midland Grace Trust Co. of N.Y., 1952—, exec. v.p., 1964-66, pres., 1966-70, chmn. bd., chief exec. officer, 1968-73; also dir.; vice chmn. bd. Evans Products Co., N.Y.C., 1974-76, Drexel Burnam Lambert Co., investment bankers, N.Y.C., 1976—; dir. Medco Containment Services Inc., Magnatck, Inc., BOC Group PLC. Chmn. exec. com. ACCION Internat.; Bd. dirs. Sta. WNET, public TV. Served to lt. (j.g.) AC USN, 1942-46. Clubs: Links (N.Y.C.), N.Y. Yacht (N.Y.C.); Blind Brook. Home: 62 E 91st St New York NY 10028 Office: Drexel Burnam Lambert Co 60 Broad St New York NY 10004

NEVIN, DAVID WRIGHT, real estate broker; b. Culver City, Calif., July 27, 1947; s. Wilbur D. and Anita J. (Hulderman) N.; m. Shirley Grimes, Nov. 12, 1977; children—Jenny, David Wright Jr. B.A., Calif. State Poly. U., 1974. Rural manpower asst. employment devel. State Calif., Riverside, 1970-74; personnel mgr. Lindsay Olive Growers, Calif., 1974-79; employee relations mgr. Morton Salt Co., Newark, Calif., 1979-80; real estate salesman Valley Realty, Fremont, Calif., 1980, The Property Professionals, Fremont, Calif., 1980-85; owner Nevin & Nevin, Inc., 1984—; owner CitiBrokers Real Estate, Inc., 1986—; co-owner Brokers Exchange, Inc., 1985-86. Sustaining mem. Republican Nat. Com., Washington, 1984; mem. Presdl. Task Force, Washington, 1984. Served with U.S. Army, 1967-69. Mem. Internat. Real Estate Fedn., So. Alameda County Bd. Realtors (local govt. relations com. 1983—). Mem. Assemblies of God. Home: 7461 Hansen Dr Dublin CA 94568 Office: CitiBrokers Real Estate Inc 39650 Liberty St Suite 100 Fremont CA 94538

NEW, ROSETTA HOLBROCK, home economics educator, nutrition consultant; b. Hamilton, Ohio, Aug. 26, 1921; d. Edward F. and Mabel (Kohler) Holbrock; m. John Lorton New, Sept. 3, 1943; 1 son, John Lorton Jr. BS, Miami U., Oxford, Ohio, 1943; MA, U. No. Colo., 1971; PhD, Ohio State U., 1974. Cert. tchr., Colo. Tchr. English and sci. Monahans (Tex.) High Sch., 1943-45; emergency war food asst. U.S. Dept. Agr., College Station, Tex., 1945-46; dept. chmn. home econs., adult edn. Hamilton (Ohio) Pub. Schs., 1946-47; tchr., dept. chmn. home econs. East High Sch., Denver, 1948-59, Thomas Jefferson High Sch., Denver, 1959—; mem. exec. bd. Denver Pub. Schs.; also lectr.; exec. dir. Ctr. Nutrition Info. U.S. Office of Edn. grantee, 1971-73. Mem. Am. Home Econs. Assn., Am. Vocat. Assn., Ohio State U. Assn., Ohio State Home Econs. Alumni Assn., Fairfield (Ohio) Hist. Soc., Republican Club of Denver, Internat. Platform Assn., Phi Upsilon Omicron. Presbyterian. Lodges: Daughters of the Nile, Order of Eastern Star, Order White Shrine of Jerusalem. Office: 1600 E Quincy Ave Englewood CO 80110

NEWBERG, DOROTHY BECK (MRS. WILLIAM C. NEWBERG), portrait artist; b. Detroit, May 30, 1919; d. Charles William and Mary (Labedz) Beck; student Detroit Conservatory Music, 1938; m. William C. Newberg, Nov. 3, 1939; children: Judith Anne Bookwalter, Robert Charles, James William, William Charles. Trustee Detroit Adventure, 1967-71, originator A Drop in Bucket Program for talented inner-city children. Bd. dirs. Bloomfield Art Assn., 1960-62, trustee 1965-67; bd. dirs. Your Heritage House, 1972-75, Franklin Wright Settlement, 1972-75, Meadowbrook Art Gallery, Oakland U., 1973-75; bd. dirs. Sierra Nevada Mus. Art, 1978-80; deacon Reno Presbyn. Ch. Recipient Heart of Gold award, 1969; Mich. vol. leadership award, 1969. Mem. Nat. League Am. Penwomen, Sierra Art Found., Birmingham Soc. Women Painters. Home: 2000 Dant Blvd Reno NV 89509

NEWBERG, ELLEN JOYCE, library administrator; b. Wellman, Iowa, Sept. 29, 1941; d. Carl Clarence and Elda Grace (White) Herr; m. Alan Keith Newberg, June 11, 1965. B.A., Sioux Falls Coll., 1962; M.L.S., U. Ill., 1963. Asst. dir. library Sioux Falls Coll., S.D., 1963-66; library cataloger U. Wyo., Laramie, 1966-67, U. Oreg., Eugene, 1967-69; asst. library dir. Rocky Mountain Coll., Billings, Mont., 1969-73; head tech. services library Parmly Billings Library, 1973-82, dir., 1982—; Western Library Network retrospective conversion trainer Mont. State Library, 1981-82; OCLC installation trainer Dowling Coll. Library, Oakdale, N.Y., 1978-79. Contbr. articles to profl. jours. Recipient Great Performance in the Library award Exxon, 1985. Mem. Mont. Assn. Female Execs., ALA, Mont. Library Assn. (various offices), Pacific Northwest Library Assn. (Mont. rep. 1980-82, joint planning team 1981-82). Avocations: gourmet cooking; gardening; hiking. Office: Parmly Billings Library 510 N Broadway Billings MT 59101 *

NEWBERG, WILLIAM CHARLES, stock broker, real estate broker, automotive engineer; b. Seattle, Dec. 17, 1910; s. Charles John and Anna Elizabeth (Anderson) N.; B.S. in Mech. Engring., U. Wash., 1933; M. in Mech. Engring., Chrysler Inst. Engring., 1935; LL.B. (hon.), Parsons Coll., 1958; m. Dorothy Beck, Nov. 3, 1939; children—Judith N. Newberg Bookwalter, Robert Charles, James William, William Charles. Salesman, Am. Auto Co., Seattle, 1932-33; student engr. Chrysler Corp., Detroit, 1933-35, exptl. engr., 1935-42, chief engr. Chgo. plant, 1942-45, mem. subs. ops. staff, Detroit, 1945-47, pres. airtemp. div., Dayton, Ohio, 1947-50, v.p., dir. Dodge div., Detroit, 1950-51, pres. Dodge div., 1951-56, group v.p., Detroit, 1956-58, exec. v.p., 1958-60, pres., 1960; corp. dir. Detroit Bank & Trust, Detroit, 1955-60; corp. cons., Detroit, 1960-76; realtor Myers Realty, Inc., Reno, 1976-79; owner Bill Newberg Realty, 1979—; account exec. Allied Capital Corp., Reno, 1980—; chmn. Newberg Corp., 1982. Elder, St. John's Presbyterian Ch., Reno, 1976—; exec. bd. Detroit Area council Boy Scouts Am., 1955-74, Nev. Area council Boy Scouts Am., 1976—; Mich. state chmn. March of Dimes, 1967-68. Mem. Soc. Automotive Engrs., Am. Def. Preparedness Assn. (life), Automotive Orgn. Team (life), U. Wash. Alumni Assn. (life), Newcomen Soc., Franklin Inst., Alpha Tau Omega. Clubs: Bluecoats of No. Nevada, Prospectors, Harley Owners Group, Goldwing Road Riders, Rider Motorcycle Touring, Internat. Retreads. Lodge: Elks. Home: 2000 Dant Blvd Reno NV 89509

NEWBERRY, CONRAD FLOYDE, aerospace engineering educator; b. Neodesha, Kans., Nov. 10, 1931; s. Ragan McGregor and Audra Anitia (Newmaster) N.; m. Sarah Louise Thonn, Jan. 26, 1958; children: Conrad Floyde Jr., Thomas Edwin, Susan Louise. A.A., Independence Jr. Coll., 1951; B.Engring. in Mech. Engring. (Aero. Sequence), U. So. Calif., 1957; M.S. in Mech. Engring., Calif. State U., Los Angeles, 1971, M.A. in Edn., 1974; D.Environ. Sci. and Engring., UCLA, 1985. Registered profl. engr., Calif., Kans., N.C., Tex. Mathematician Los Angeles div. N.Am. Aviation Inc., 1951-53, jr. engr., 1953-54, engr., 1954-57, sr. engr., 1957-64; asst. prof. Calif. State Poly. U., Pomona, 1964-70; assoc. prof. Calif. State Poly. U., 1970-75, prof. aerospace engring., 1975—; staff engr. EPA, 1980-82. Recipient John Leland Atwood award Am. Inst. Aeronautics and Astronautics/Am. Soc. Engring. Edn. Fellow Inst. Advancement Engring., Brit. Interplanetary Soc.; assoc. fellow AIAA (dep. dir. edn. region VI 1976-79, dep. dir. career enhancement 1982—); mem. Am. Soc. Engring. Edn. (chmn. aerospace div. 1979-80, div. exec. com. 1976-80, exec. com. ocean and marine engring. div. 1982-86), ASME, Am. Meteorol. Soc., Nat. Soc. Profl. Engrs., Soc. Naval Architects and Marine Engrs., Am. Helicopter Soc., Air Pollution Control Assn., Inst. Environ. Scis.,Tau Beta Pi, Sigma Gamma Tau, Kappa Delta Pi. Democrat. Mem. Christian Ch. (Disciples of Christ). Home: 861 Kenwood Street Upland CA 91786 Office: Calif State Poly U 3801 W Temple Ave Pomona CA 91768

NEWBIGGING, WILLIAM, publisher, journal executive; b. Toronto, Ont., Can., Feb. 3, 1939; s. William and Dorothy (Ridge) N.; children—William, Patricia, Scott, Dorothy, Ty. Jr. reporter Edmonton Jour., Alta., Can., 1957-65; city editor Edmonton Jour., 1965-67, news editor, 1967-71, asst. to pub., 1971-73, v.p., pub., 1982—; exec. to pub. Ottawa Citizen, Ont., 1973-74; bus. mgr. Ottawa Citizen, 1974-76, gen. mgr., 1976-78, v.p., pub., 1978-81; dir. Can. Press, Newspaper Mktg. Bur. Mem. Can. Daily Newspaper Pubs. Assn. (bd. dirs.). Anglican. Clubs: Edmonton, Centre. Home: 5503 175 St, Edmonton, AB Canada T6M 1C3 Office: Edmonton Jour, 10006 101 St, Edmonton, AB Canada T5J 2S6

NEWBILL, WILLIAM CURTIS, insurance broker; b. Sacramento, Calif., Nov. 25, 1943; s. George Curtis and Dorothy Elizabeth (Parks) N.; m. Sally N. Kornblite, Oct. 20, 1973 (div. Sept. 1982); 1 child, Harold Curtis. AA with honors, Sacramento City Coll., 1965; BA with honors, Calif. State U., Sacramento, 1967, MA with honors, 1968. Asst. presonnel mgr. Mercy Hosps., Sacramento, 1968-69; with mktg. dept. Standard Oil Co., Sacramento, 1969; pres. McClatchy Ins. Co., Sacramento, 1969—, W.C. Newbill Ins. Services, Sacramento, 1986—; bd. dirs. Involvement Corp. Mem. Ind. Ins. Agts. and Brokers, Profl. Ins. Agts., Western Assn. Ins. Brokers. Republican. Avocations: snow skiing, tennis, golf, sailing. Office: McClatchy Ins Agy 2410 Fair Oaks Blvd #140 Sacramento CA 95825

NEWBY, BARBARA ANNE, educator, tennis coach; b. Moberly, Mo., Aug. 28, 1933; d. James Edgar, Jr., and Anne V. (Roof) N. B.A. in Edn., U. Mo.-Columbia, 1955. Tchr., Arvada (Colo.) Jr. High Sch., 1955-56, Harrington Elem. Sch., 1957-60, Horace Mann Jr. High Sch., 1960-67; tchr. phys. edn., dept. chmn. Hill Middle Sch., Denver, 1967—; tennis coach Thomas Jefferson High Sch.; coach Olympics of the Mind; credit union rep.; vol. Leukemia Assn., Heart Assn. Named Outstanding Coach in Tennis, Denver Pub. Schs. Coaches Assn., 1981-82. Mem. AAHPER, Colo. Assn. Health, Phys. Edn. and Recreation, Coaches Assn., Nat. Assn. Female Execs., Colo. Tennis Assn., NEA, Colo. Edn. Assn., Mo. U. Alumni, Women's Internat. Bowling Congress, Denver Women's Bowling Assn., U.S. Tennis Assn. Republican. Mem. Christian Ch. Clubs: Bowling League. Home: 15810 E Ford Pl Aurora CO 80017 Office: Hill Middle School 451 Clermont St Denver CO 80220

NEWBY, FRANK CURTIS, JR., computer services company executive; b. Indpls., Jan. 15, 1928; s. Frank Curtis and Mary Louella (Watkins) N.; m. Gayle Terris Burton, Aug. 13, 1950; children—Mark Alan, Terry Curtis. B.S., Butler U., 1950, M.S., 1956. Tchr. pub. schs., Ind. and N.Mex., 1950-58; prin. elem. sch., Estes Park, Colo., 1958-61; sales rep. Random House, Inc., Denver, 1968-82; owner Tri-State Computer Services, Denver, 1982—. Served with USN, 1946-48. Mem. Colo.-Wyo. Bookmen (pres. 1977-78), Colo.-Wyo. Media Assn. (sec. 1982-83), Phi Beta Alpha. Democrat. Baptist. Lodges: Masons, Shriners, Order Eastern Star. Home: 920 Phillips Dr Denver CO 80233 Office: 11178 N Huron Unit #5 Northglenn CO 80234

NEWCOMB, DUANE GRAHAM, how-to and self-help writer, consultant; b. Oklahoma City, Okla., Feb. 12, 1929; s. Wilbur Kenneth and Grace (Graham) N.; m. Patricia Ann Luck, Aug. 26, 1954 (div. Oct. 1970); children: Kathy, Ronald Alan; m. Karen Lee Ball, Sept. 27, 1978; 1 child, Steven Duane. BS in Forestry, U. Wash., 1953; postgrad., U. Colo., 1955, U. Okla., 1956, Calif. State U., San Jose, 1965. Cartographer U.S. Geol. Survey, Sacramento, 1953-57; owner, mgr. West Valley Firestone, San Jose, 1957-62; author, lectr. Grass Valley, Calif., 1962—; instr. Am. River Coll., Sacramento, 1967-77; lectr. U.S. C. of C., Washington, 1975-76; cons., lectr. various other orgns.; founder Sierra Writing Camp, Sly Park, Calif., 1975—. Author: Mobile Home Gardening Guide, 1962, Trailer Owner's Driving Guide, 1965, Trailering in Canada, 1964, How to Make Big Money Freelance Writing, 1970, The Wonderful World of Houseboating, 1974, Spare Time Fortune Guide (Spanish Edition), 1974, Word Power Makes the Difference, 1974, A Complete Guide to Marketing Magazine Articles, 1975, The Postage Stamp Garden Book, 1975, The Poor Man's Guide to Riches, 1976, The Apartment Farmer, 1976, Georgie Clark, Thirty Years of River Running, 1977, The Parker Business Handbook, 1979, The Vegetable Gardener's Sourcebook, 1980, The Owner Built Adobe House, 1980, $10 Can Make You Rich, 1981, Growing Vegetables the Big Yield/Small Space Way, 1981, Rx for Vegetable Gardens, 1982, Fortune Building Secrets of the Rich, 1983. Mem. Am. Soc. Journalists and Authors (charter No. Calif. chpt.), Calif. Writers (v.p. Sacramento chpt. 1974), Phi Delta Kappa, Phi Sigma. Club: Toastmasters (Grass Valley). Avocations: skiing, hiking, Indian pottery. Home and Office: 18293 Crystal St Grass Valley CA 95949

NEWCOMBE, GERALD MASON, fire protection official; b. San Bernardino, Calif., Aug. 29, 1933; s. Francis Dudley and Nita Clementine (Craw) N.; m. Barbara Louise Eddins, Aug. 26, 1953; children—Elizabeth, Gerald Mason, Janet, Mary. A.A., San Bernardino Valley Coll., 1959; B.A., Calif. State U.-San Bernardino, 1976, M.P.A., 1982. With San Bernardino Fire Dept., 1960—, dep. chief, 1976-80, chief, 1980—; corp. mem. Arrow Head Health Care Systems. Mem. State Bd. Fire Services, 1984. Bd. dirs. Red Cross Service Ctr., 1980; chmn. bd. San Bernardino Community Against Drugs, Inc.; mem. bd. councillors Sch. Adminstrn., Calif. State U., San Bernardino, 1980—. Mem. Calif. Fire Chiefs Assn., Air Force Assn. (bd. dirs. local chpt., v.p.), Internat. Assn. Fire Chiefs, Nat. Fire Protection Assn., Am. Soc. Pub. Adminstrn. (bd. dirs. 1981-83), San Bernardino County Fire Chiefs (pres. 1982). Republican. Episcopalian. Lodges: Kiwanis (bd. dirs. 1979-81), Elks, Native Sons Golden West. Office: San Bernardino City Fire Dept 200 E 3d St San Bernardino CA 92410

NEWELL, GORDON WILFRED, health research administrator; b. Madison, Wis., Aug. 27, 1921; s. Wilfred R. and Gertrude M. (Odell) N.; m. Rosemary Kathleen Plummer, June 22, 1948; children: William, Allan, Nancy, Betsy. BA in Chemistry, U. Wis., 1943, MS Biochemistry, 1944, PhD in Biochemistry, 1948. Biochemist Wallace & Tiernan Co., Belleville, N.J., 1949-50; dir. toxicology dept. SRI Internat., Menlo Park, Calif., 1950-78; assoc. exec. dir. bd. on toxicology and environ. health hazards Nat. Acad. Scis., Washington, 1978-82; sr. program mgr. Electric Power Research Inst., Palo Alto, Calif., 1982—; chmn. chancellor's adv. com. on lab. animal care bd. U. Calif., Berkeley, 1983—, mem. pres.'s adminstrv. panel on lab. animal care bd. Stanford U., 1983—; cons. EPA, NIH, FDA 1962-85. Contbr. articles to profl. jours. Mem. San Mateo Industry-Edn. Council, 1961-63; bd. dirs. Palo Alto-Stanford Hosp. Ctr., 1963-68, Palo Alto C. of C., 1966-69, Community Blood Reserve, 1966-74. Wilson & Co. fellow, U. Wis., Madison, 1944-48, Novadel Agene fellow, U. Wis., 1948-49. Mem. Am. Coll. Toxicology (pres. 1986-87), Soc. Toxicology (chmn. animal in research com. 1982-83), Soc. Risk Analysis (treas. 1980-81), Environ. Mutagen Soc. (pres. 1982), Acad. Toxicol. Scis. (chmn. profl. standards bd. 1981-85, bd. dirs., diplomate), Nat. Swimming Pool Fedn., Phi Delta Kappa. Home: 4163 Hubbartt Dr Palo Alto CA 94306 Office: Electric Power Research Inst 3412 Hillview Ave Palo Alto CA 94303

NEWELL, LEONARD JACKSON, JR., university dean, educator; b. Dayton, Ohio, Oct. 11, 1938; s. Leonard J. and Henrietta (Wahlenmaier) N.; m. Linda King, June 15, 1963; children—Christine, Jennifer, Eric, Heather. Student Deep Springs Coll., Calif., 1956-59; B.A. in History, Ohio State U., 1961, Ph.D. in Higher Edn., 1972; M.A. in History, Duke U., 1964. Instr. history Deep Springs Coll., Calif., 1965-67, cons. to bd. trustees, 1979—; asst. dean Coll. Liberal Arts, U. N.H., 1967-70; assoc. dir. Univ. Council for Ednl. Adminstrn., Columbus, Ohio, 1970-74; successively asst. prof., assoc. prof., prof. higher edn., U. Utah, Salt Lake City, 1974—, dean student affairs 1974-78, dean liberal edn., 1974—; vis. prof. Anglican Mgmt. Ctr., Danbury, Essex, Eng., 1978; prin. investigator curricular devel. fund for improvement of post-secondary Nat. Inst. Edn., 1981-83; Co-author: A Study of Professors of Education Administration, 1973, A History of Thought and Practice in Educational Adminstrn., 1987. Contbr. numerous articles to profl. jours.; Editor Rev. of Higher Edn., 1986—; Co-editor: Dialogue: A Journal of Mormon Thought, 1982—; bd. editors Jour. Gen. Edn., 1983—. Bd. dirs. Utahns United Against Nuclear Arms Race, Salt Lake City, 1982—; voting dist. chmn. Democratic Orgn., Salt Lake City, 1975-77; scoutmaster Boy Scouts Am., Salt Lake City, 1984—. Thomas Holy fellow, Ohio State U., 1971. Mem. Assn. for Gen. and Liberal Studies (pres.-elect 1987—), Am. Ednl. Research Assn. (assoc. program chmn. 1986—), Assn. for Study of Higher Edn., Assn. Am. Colls. (instl. rep. 1983—), Phi Beta Kappa, Phi Kappa Phi (chpt. pres. 1985), Phi Alpha Theta, Phi Delta Kappa. Home: 1218 Harvard Ave Salt Lake City UT 84105 Office: U Utah 210 Park Bldg Salt Lake City UT 84112

NEWHART, ROBERT LINCOLN, II, business consulting executive; b. Washington, Dec. 29, 1948; s. Robert Lincoln Newhart and Doris Ruth Alexander McElroy; m. Joyce Anne Kessler, Aug. 5, 1967; children: Bleuberry, RainBow, Cordon. AA, Orange Coast Coll., 1969; BS in City and Regional Planning, Calif. Poly. State U., 1972; M in Community Planning, U. Cin., 1974. Asst. dir. S.E. Idaho Council of Govts., Pocatello, 1974-77; assoc. dir. Pacific N.W. Regional Commn., Vancouver, Wash., 1977; pres. The Evergreen Assocs., Coeur D'Alene, Idaho, 1978—; co-owner Bitterroot Dry Goods Co., Coeur D'Alene, 1979-86; asst. prof. U. Vt., Burlington, 1985—; project dir. Entrepreneurial Mgmt., Coeur D'Alene, 1985—, Be Your Own Boss Project, Coeur D'Alene, 1984; expert witness U.S. Senate Commn. on Aging, 1977; bd. dirs. Idaho Made, Inc. Author: Entrepreneurial Policy for Idaho, 1985, Small Business Workbook, 1985; co-author Grubstake, 1985; contbr. articles to profl. jours. Bd. dirs. Idaho Dept. Health and Welfare, Coeur D'Alene, 1984; v.p. Fort Grounds Assn., Coeur D'Alene, 1983. Mem. World Future Soc., Am. Planning Assn., Idaho Ind. Bus. Assn (acting pres. 1983—), Vt. C. of C. (com. on econ. devel. 1985—). Office: The Evergreen Assocs Ltd PO Box 1136 Coeur d' Alene ID 83814

NEWHOFF, STANLEY NEAL, advertising executive; b. Bronx, N.Y., Jan. 31, 1944; s. Norman and Daisy (Weiss) N.; m. Hayde Mathilde Stekkinger, June 16, 1969 (dec. Nov. 1984); children: Michelle Hayde, Angela Robin. BA in English, UCLA, 1967. Columnist UCLA Daily Bruin, 1963-64; tabulator, asst supr., asst. dir. corp. communications Audience Studies, Inc., Los Angeles, 1964-65; English tchr. Beit Safer Tichon Makief High Sch., Qiryat Gat, Israel, 1969-70; advt. copywriter Doyle Dane Bernbach; Foote, Cone & Belding and others, Los Angeles, 1970-74; v.p., creative dir. Basso Boatman, Inc., Newport Beach, Calif., 1976-79; prin., pres. Lerner-Newhoff Advt., Los Angeles, 1974-76, Stanley Newhoff & Assocs., Irvine, Calif., 1979-81, Newhoff & Prochnow, Inc., Costa Mesa, Calif., 1981-85; prin., chmn. Newhoff & Russakow, Inc., Newport Beach, 1985—. Contbr. articles on advt. to publs. Mem. Med. Mktg. Assn., Irvine Edn. Found. (founding, pres.), Nat. Energy Research Info. Inst. (mem. founding task force), Mensa. Republican. Jewish. Avocations: writing, golfing, racquetball, roller skating, snorkeling. Home: 21 Silkberry Irvine CA 92714 Office: Newhoff & Russakow Inc 4667 MacArthur Blvd #310 Newport Beach CA 92660

NEWKIRK, HERBERT WILLIAM, materials scientist; b. Jersey City, Nov. 23, 1928; s. Herbert William and Elsie Eugenia (Bertell) N.; m. Madeline Dorothy Smith, Sept. 6, 1952; children: Philip, Elicia, David. Bsc, Bklyn. Poly. Inst., 1952; PhD, Ohio State U., 1956. Research engr. Gen. Electric Co., Richland, Wash., 1956-59, RCA Labs., Princeton, N.J., 1959-60; staff scientist Lawrence Livermore (Calif.) Nat. Lab., 1960—. Pres. Interfaith Housing, Inc., Livermore, 1969; mem. housing commn. City of Livermore, 1974-76, chmn. energy commn., 1976—. Served as sgt. N.J. N.G., 1948-52. Fellow Socony Vacuum, Ohio State U., 1955. Mem. Am. Assn. Crystal Growth (sci. advisor, treas. 1986). Office: U Calif/Lawrence Livermore Nat Lab Livermore CA 94550

NEWLANDER, NANCY GAIL, industrial hygienist; b. Van Nuys, Calif., Feb. 19, 1954; d. Arthur Alexander and Lauretta Jane (Hallberg) Bain; m. Allen Newlander, Mar 7, 1970 (dec. Aug. 1972); 1 child, Jerrod J. BS in Environ. and Occupational Health, Calif. State U., Northridge, 1983, MS in Environ. and Occupational Health, 1985. Indsl. hygienist Bitter & Assocs., Sherman Oaks, Calif., 1982-83; West Coast supr. risk control edn. services IT Corp., Cerritos, Calif., 1983—; mem. adv. com. Fire Sci. Dept. Los Angeles Valley Community Coll., Van Nuys, Calif., 1983—; cons. Valley Fire Edn. Assn., Moor Park, Calif., 1985—, Mchts. and Mfrs. Assn., Los Angeles, 1986—; speaker Emergency Response Awareness, 1983—, Hazardous Materials Mgmt., 1984—, Hazard Communication Standard, 1986—. Mem. Am. Soc. Safety Engrs., Am. Indsl. Hygiene Assn., Nat. Environ. Tng. Assn. Democrat. Baptist. Avocations: sailing, horseback riding, aerobics, tennis.

NEWLIN, DOUGLAS RANDAL, marketing communications manager; b. Denver, Mar. 26, 1940; s. Loren Randall and Nola Berneice (Paris) N.; m. Sandra Temple, June 22, 1968; children: Jason Britt, Jeremy Owen. BS in Journalism, U. Colo., 1968. Advt. prodn. mgr. Am. Sheep Producers Council, Denver, 1968-70; promotion dir. Sta. KLZ-AM-FM, Denver, 1970-71; account mgr. Curran-Morton Advt., Denver, 1971-72; advt. and sales promotion specialist Gates Rubber Co., Denver, 1972-78; mktg. communications mgr. Hewlett Packard Co., Ft. Collins, Colo., 1978—; vis. lectr. U. Colo., Boulder, 1972-73, statis. quality control course George Washington U., Washington, 1984. Author hardware and software catalogs, 1984—; contbr. articles to profl. jours. Pres. Lake Sherwood Homeowners Assn., Ft. Collins, 1982; treas. Lake Sherwood Lake Com., Ft. Collins, 1983-85. Served with U.S. Army, 1959-61. Recipient Gold Key award Bus. and Profl. Advt. Assn., 1976. Democrat. Avocation: bicycling. Home: 4112 Mount Vernon Ct Fort Collins CO 80525 Office: Hewlett Packard Co 3404 E Harmony Rd Fort Collins CO 80525

NEWMAN, ALFRED S., entertainment executive, marketing professional; b. Bklyn., Nov. 16, 1940; s. Murray and Lee (Littman) N.; m. Gloria Gail Campbell, Jan. 13, 1979. BS, NYU, 1967. With pub. relations dept. Equitable Life Co., N.Y.C., 1967; dir. publicity Columbia Pictures, N.Y.C., 1968-72; v.p. MGM/United Artists Entertainment, Culver City, Calif., 1972-84, 20th Century Fox, Los Angeles, 1984-85; exec. v.p. Rogers & Cowan, Inc., Los Angeles, 1985—. Bd. dirs. Santa Monica (Calif.) Airport Assn. Mem. Acad. Motion Picture Arts and Scis., Acad. TV Arts and Scis., Los Angeles Film Info. Council, Am. Med. Support Flight Team. Avocations: flying, cooking, tennis. Office: Rogers & Cowan Inc 10000 Santa Monica Blvd Los Angeles CA 90067

NEWMAN, BARRY I., bank executive; b. N.Y.C., Mar. 19, 1932; s. M.A. and T.C. (Weitman) N.; B.A., Alfred U., 1952; J.D., N.Y. U., 1955; m. Jean Short, Mar. 6, 1965; children: Suzanne, Cathy, David. Admitted to N.Y. State Bar, 1957, Ohio bar, 1957, U.S. Supreme Ct. bar, 1967; practiced in N.Y.C., 1957; partner firm Shapiro Persky Marken & Newman, Cleve., 1957-63; asst. v.p. Meinhard & Co. (now Meinhard Comml. Corp.), N.Y.C., 1963-65; v.p. Amsterdam Overseas Corp., N.Y.C., 1966-68; pres. No. Fin. Corp., Los Angeles, 1968-72; sr. v.p. Aetna Bus. Credit, Inc., Hartford, Conn., 1972-78; exec. v.p. Security Pacific Fin. Corp., San Diego, 1978-81, chmn., pres., chief exec. officer, 1981-82; sr. exec. v.p. Gt. First Savs. Bank, 1982—; chmn. bd. dirs. San Diego County Capital Asset Leasing Corp. Served with U.S. Army, 1955-57. Recipient Distinguished Service award Cleve. Jr. C. of C., 1961. Mem. ABA, N.Y. State Bar Assn., Ohio Bar Assn.,

San Diego Bar Assn., San Diego Taxpayers Assn. (bd. dirs.). Republican. Club: Fairbanks Ranch Country. Lodge: Masons. Home: 3308 Avenida Sierra Escondido CA 92025 Office: 600 B St San Diego CA 92183

NEWMAN, CLARENCE WALTER, research agriculture educator; b. Lake Providence, La., Aug. 3, 1932; s. Clarence Earl and Dolly (Russell) N.; m. Lanier Kay Johnston, June 2, 1954 (div. Oct. 1980); children: Steven Earl, Craig Lanier; m. Rosemary Kramp, Mar. 21, 1982. BS, La. State U., 1954, PhD, 1965; MS, Tex. A&M U., 1958. Instr. animal nutrition La. Agrl. Exptl. Sta., Bossier City, 1958-60; lectr. La. State U., Baton Rouge, 1961-62, assoc. prof. animal sci., 1963-64; prof. Mont. State U., Bozeman, 1964—; adj. prof. Swedish U. Agrl. Scis., Uppsala, 1983. Contbr. numerous articles to profl. jours. Served as sgt. Med. Service Corps, U.S. Army, 1954-56. Grantee USAID, Bozeman, 1973-77, Yellowstone Internat. Inc., Bozeman, 1985, Mont. Wheat Commn., Bozeman, 1985-86, Ross Labs, 1986, 87. Mem. Am. Inst. Nutrition, Am. Soc. Animal Sci., Am. Registry Profl. Animial Scientists, Sigma Xi, Gamma Sigma Delta. Avocations: camping, hiking, photography, bird watching. Home: 304 E Lincoln Bozeman MT 59715 Office: Mont State U Bozeman MT 59717

NEWMAN, DARRELL FRANCIS, research and development manager, nuclear engineer; b. Ft. Knox, Ky., Mar. 22, 1940; s. Charles Carlisle Newman and Lillian Evelyn (Karmann) McDonald; m. Sue Carol Farley, June 18, 1966; 1 child, Donald Farley (dec.). BS in Nuclear Engring., Kans. State U., 1963; MS in Nuclear Engring., U. Wash., 1970. Registered profl. nuclear engr., Wash. Engr. Gen. Electric Co., Richland, Wash., 1963; ordnance lt. U.S. Army, Aberdeen Proving Grounds, Md., 1963-65; sr. research engr. Battelle Northwest Lab., Richland, 1966-80; tech. advisor U.S. Dept. of Energy, Washington, 1980-81; spent fuel program mgr. Battelle Pacific Northwest Lab., Richland, 1982-85, nuclear waste systems program mgr., 1985-86, mgr. tech. integration, 1987—; cons. U.S. State Dept., Washington, 1983-84. Author: Glossary of Terms in Nuclear Science and Technology, 1986; co-author: Radioactive Waste Technology, 1985. Served to 1st lt. U.S. Army, 1963-65. Recipient Lab. Dir. award Pacific Northwest Lab., 1968, excellence in sci. and tech. award Battelle Meml. Inst., 1968. Mem. Nat. Soc. Profl. Engrs. (named engr. of the yr. 1978-79), Am. Nuclear Soc. (standard chmn. 1977-84), Wash. Soc. Profl. Engrs. (chmn. energy com. 1978-80), N.Y. Acad. Scis., AAAS, Sand and Sage Sports Car Club, Eastern Wash. Sports Car Council. Republican. Home: 1100 McMurray Richland WA 99352 Office: Battelle Pacific Northwest Labs PO Box 999 Richland WA 99352

NEWMAN, EDGAR LEON, historian; b. New Orleans, Jan. 21, 1939; s. Isidore and Anna (Pfeifer) N.; B.A., Yale U., 1962; Ph.D., U. Chgo., 1969; children—Jonathan, Suzanne. Assoc. prof. N.Mex. State U., Las Cruces, 1969-75, assoc. prof. history, 1975—; lectr. U. Peking, 1985; bd. dirs. Am. Com. on Bicentennial of French Revolution of 1789. Fulbright fellow, 1965-66; Am. Philos. Soc. fellow, 1971; Nat. Endowment for Humanities fellow, 1975-76. Mem. Western Soc. for French History (pres. 1977-78), Sociètè d'histoire de la Révolution de 1848 (mem. comité directeur), Soc. Scis. History Assn., French Hist. Studies Assn., Am. Hist. Assn. Editor: Dictionary of French History 1815-1852. Office: Box 3-H New Mex State U Las Cruces NM 88003

NEWMAN, EUGENE WAYNE, comptroller; b. Wisconsin Rapids, Wis., June 28, 1940; s. Theodore Edward and Eva Margaret (Hurd); m. Sharon Woodard, Oct. 9, 1971. BA, U. Wash., 1968. CPA. Asst. controller Dept. Motor Vehicles, Olympia, Wash., 1971-76; fiscal mgmt. analyst Dept. Social and Health Services, Olympia, Wash., 1976-77; chief budget and fin. Parks and Recreation Commn., Olympia, Wash., 1977-79, asst. dir., 1979-81; chief state fin. policies Office of Fin. Mgmt., Olympia, Wash., 1981-84; comptroller of transp. Dept. Transp., Olympia, Wash., 1984—. Served to sgt. U.S. Army, 1963-65. Mem. Am. Inst. CPA's, Wash. Soc. CPA's, Assn. Govt. Accts. (pres. Olympia chpt. 1986—, registered agt. 1986—), Mensa. Lodge: Elks. Avocations: traveling, dancing, bicycling. Home: 2909 28th Ave SE Olympia WA 98501 Office: Dept Transp Transp Bldg Olympia WA 98504

NEWMAN, JOHN V., agriculturist, corporation executive; b. Pomona, Calif., Apr. 25, 1910; s. Carl V. and Florence (White) N.; m. Ruth Tantlinger, May 6, 1933; children: Peter V., Michael J. B.A., Pomona Coll., 1931. Citrus grower, rancher 1931—; dir. Utt Devel. Co., Oxnard, Calif., 1942—; pres. Utt Devel. Co., 1969-76, C.B.S.-Sony Calif., Inc., Oxnard, 1976—; chmn. bd. Irvine Co., Newport Beach, Calif., 1972-77; dir. SUnkist Growers, Inc., Sherman Oaks, Calif., 1959—; chmn. bd. Sunkist Growers, Inc., Sherman Oaks, Calif., 1972-77, 82-86; dir. So. Calif. Edison Co., 1957-83; Mem. Calif. Bd. Agr., 1947-62; Calif. rep., spl. farm adv. com. Dept. Labor, 1950-61; agrl. adviser Employer del. ILO, Geneva, 1952—. Commr. Calif. Horse Racing Bd., 1968-76, chmn., 1972-75; dir. Hollywood Park, 1977—; Bd. dirs. James Irvine Found., Pomona Coll. Mem. Council Calif. Growers (pres. 1960-61), Seaboard Lemon Assn. (dir. 1942-62, pres. 1962-72, chmn. bd. 1972-85), Saticoy Lemon Assn. (bd. dirs. 1986—), Ventura County Citrus Growers Com. (pres. 1962-68), U.S. C. of C. (agrl. com. 1952-57), Rancheros Vistadores (dir. 1957—, pres. 1967-69). Club: California. Home: 10175 Santa Ana Rd Ventura CA 93001 Office: Sunkist Growers Inc 4300 Etting Rd Oxnard CA 93033-5998

NEWMAN, MARC ALAN, electrical engineer; b. Jasper, Ind., Nov. 21, 1955; s.Leonard Jay and P. Louise (Shainberg) N.; m. Shelley Jane Martin, Aug. 13, 1977. BSEE, Purdue U., 1977, MSEE, 1979. Sr. elec. engr. Sperry Corp. Flight Systems, Phoenix, 1979-85; staff engr. Motorola Inc., Tempe, Ariz., 1985—; prolog expert Motorola Inc., Tempe, 1985—. Mem. IEEE, Ariz. Artifical Intelligence Assn. (founder), Phi Sigma Kappa, Eta Kappa Nu. Avocations: fine music, photography, astronomy, bicycling, traveling. Home: 18414 N 46th Dr Glendale AZ 85308 Office: Motorola Inc Govt Electronics Group 2100 E Elliot Rd Tempe AZ 85282

NEWMAN, MELVA JEWELL, social worker; b. Shreveport, La., Mar. 3, 1932; d. William and Minnie Lee (Burton) Collins; m. Joseph Newman, June 27, 1957; children: Sheri, Toni, Colette. BA in Psychology, UCLA, 1953, MSW, 1957. Asst. prof. Calif. State U., Northridge, 1969-70, Los Angeles, 1970-78; lectr. Calif. Poly. Inst., Pomona, 1978-79; prin. Family Actualization, Altadena, Calif., 1980—; cons. Frederick Douglas Child Devel. Ctr., Los Angeles, 1982—; vis. faculty Pacific Oaks Coll., Pasadena, Calif., 1982—. Mem. Adv. Council Child Abuse Prevention, Calif., 1978, Adv. Bd. Office Creative Connections, Pasadena, 1985-86. Named Woman of Yr. Zeta Phi Beta, 1983, one of Women of Distinction Soroptimists Internat., 1985; recipient 2d Century award Pasadena YWCA, 1985. Mem. Nat. Assn. Social Workers, Assn. Black Social Workers of Greater Los Angeles (life), Assn. Black Social Workers in Family Service, So. Calif. Group Psychotherapy Assn. Home and Office: 524 E Loma Alta Dr Altadena CA 91001

NEWMAN, MELVIN MICKLIN, surgeon; b. Chgo., Dec. 20, 1921; s. Morris and Cecilia (Micklin) N.; m. Joyce Kligerman, Sept. 11, 1949; children: Rebecca, Morris H. BS, U. Chgo., 1941, MD, 1944. Diplomate Am. Bd. Surgery, Am. Bd. Thoracic Surgery. Intern U. Chgo. Clinics, 1944-45, from resident to instr. gen. thoracic surgery, 1946-52; from asst. to assoc. prof. medicine SUNY, Bklyn., 1954-59; chief surgery Nat. Jewish Hosp., Denver, 1959-68; assoc. prof. and attending surgeon U. Colo., Denver, 1968-84; surgeon City of Hope Med. Ctr., Duarte, Calif., 1984-86, CIGNA Med. Group, 1986—; cons. VA Hosp. Ft. Hamilton, Bklyn., 1957-59; assoc. vis. surgeon Kings County Hosp., Bklyn., 1955-59; clin. assoc. prof. U. So. Calif. Contbr. chpts. to books, articles to profl. jours. Served to lt. USN, 1945-46, with Res. 1952-54. Grantee NIH, 1961-64, 64-66, 71-74. Fellow ACS, Am. Coll. Chest Physicians (gov. Colo. chpt. 1972-77); mem. Am. Soc. Artificial Internal Organs (pres. 1960-61), Am. Assn. Thoracic Surgery, Soc. Univ. Surgeons, Phi Beta Kappa, Alpha Omega Alpha. Democrat. Jewish. Avocations: violin and viola music, photography. Home: 1750 E Mountain St Pasadena CA 91104 Office: CIGNA Health Plans 1711 W Temple St Los Angeles CA 90026

NEWMAN, MICHAEL JOSEPH, finance executive; b. N.Y.C., Dec. 23, 1936; s. Ferdinand and Madelon (Silvert) N.; m. Suzette Juniper, May 7, 1967; 1 child, Kent. BS in Indsl. Engring., Lehigh U., 1958; MBA in Fin. and Acctg., Harvard U., 1963. Dir. cash mgmt., mgr. spl. fin. projects TransWorld Airlines, Inc., N.Y.C., 1963-68; treas. Capitol Industries, Los Angeles, 1968-71; v.p. fin., corp. sec. Midwestern Fin. Corp., Denver, 1971-74; controller internat. materials and control div. Tex. Instruments, Attleboro, Mass. and Nice, France, 1976-79; v.p. and controller transp. group ITEL Corp., San Francisco, 1979-80; v.p. fin. and adminstrn., sec.-treas. Graphics Tech. Corp., Boulder, Colo., 1980-83; v.p. fin. and adminstrn., treas. and corp. sec. Staodynamics, Inc., Longmont, Colo., 1983—. Served to 1st lt. U.S. Army, 1958-61. Avocations: tennis, skiing, biycling, reading. Home: 700 Cascade Ave Boulder CO 80302 Office: Staodynamics Inc 1225 Florida Ave Longmont CO 80501

NEWMAN, MICHELE MARIE, cartographer, graphic artist; b. Sheridan, Wyo., Dec. 15, 1954; d. Eric Carl and Harriet Ann (Wilder) N. BS in Geography, Ariz. State U., 1977. Map drafter ARCO, Denver, 1977, exploration drafter, 1977-79, lead drafter geology, 1980, exploration drafting specialist technician, 1981-85; with Petromerican, Denver, 1985—; exploration drafter Amerada Hess Corp., Denver, 1979; pres. treas. Petromer Cartographics, Inc., Denver. Mem. Assn. Desk and Derrick Clubs, Rocky Mountain Energy Drafters (dir. 1984, pres. 1985), Nat. Assn. Women Bus. Owners, Assn. Am. Geographers, Denver C. of C., Ariz. State U. Alumni Assn. Republican. Methodist. Club: Ariz. State U. Century. Contbg. author: Our Twentieth Century's Greatest Poems, 1982. Home: 1696 S Steele St Denver CO 80210

NEWMAN, SHELLEY JANE, mechanical engineer; b. Plymouth, Ind., Nov. 9, 1957; d. Hubert Lincoln and Alice Louise (Miller) Martin; m. Marc Alan Newman, Aug. 13, 1977. BSME, Purdue U., 1979. Sr. engr. Sperry Flight Systems, Phoenix, 1979-85; engring. project leader Motorola Govt. Electronics Group, Tempe, Ariz., 1985—. Named Hoosier scholar, Ind., 1975-79, Jaycees scholar, Plymouth, Ind., 1975-79. Mem. ASME. Avocations: classical piano, sewing, cake decorating, crossword puzzles. Office: Motorola Govt Elec Group 2100 E Elliot Rd Tempe AZ 85282

NEWPORT, EUGENE NORMAN, mayor; b. Rochester, N.Y., Apr. 5, 1935; s. Leon and Bertha (Richardson) N.; m. Claudine Smith, Feb. 1958; 1 child, Kyle; m. Maria Luisa Vigo, Nov. 9, 1974; 1 child, Maria Mercedes. B.A. in Bus. Adminstrn., Internat. Coll., Los Angeles, 1975. Specialist employment tng. U.S. Dept. Labor, 1971-74, 77-79; dir. youth employment services City of Berkeley, Calif., 1975-76, sr. adminstrv. analyst, 1976, mayor, from 1979; cons. Office of Research, Calif. Assembly; chmn. subcom. on edn. U.S. Conf. Mayors, mem. adv. bd., 1983-84; pres. Alameda County Mayors Conf.; co-chmn. U.S. Peace Council, v.p. World Peace Council; mem. regional planning commn., regional housing commn. Assn. Bay Area Govt. Bd. dirs. SANE, Nat. Alliance Against Racist and Political Repression. Served with U.S. Army, 1958-60. Mem. NAACP (life). Democrat. Office: 2180 Milvia St Berkeley CA 94704

NEWQUIST, WELDON DAVID, JR., communication company executive; b. Gt. Falls, Mont., Jan. 30, 1950; s. Weldon David and Patsy Juliene (Reaves) N.; m. Jane Ann Johnson, May 12, 1973; children: David Bryan, Jason John. BBA, Colo. State U., Ft. Collins, 1972. Mktg. rep. IBM, Birmingham, Ala., 1972-76; account exec. John H. Harland Co., Birmingham, 1976-79; tech. cons. So. Cen. Bell, Birmingham, 1979-80, account exec., 1980-81; account exec. Mountain Bell, Denver, 1981, tech. cons. I, 1981-83; tech. cons. II AT&T Info. Systems, Denver, 1983-84, systems mgr., 1984-87, br. systems mgr., 1987—. Pres. Wellshire Presch. Assn. Mem. Colo. State Alumni Bus. Assn. Republican. Home: 6992 S Niagara Ct Englewood CO 80112 Office: AT&T Info Systems 6200 S Syracuse Way Englewood CO 80111

NEWSTADT, DAVID ROLAND, food company executive; b. N.Y.C., Mar. 19, 1930; s. Herbert Morris and Evelyn (Bleckerman) N.; m. Millicent R. Brown, Nov. 23, 1952; children—A. Todd, Tracy Heather. A.B. magna cum laude, Syracuse U., 1951; M.B.A., NYU, 1957. With Johnson & Johnson, 1955-58, 61-73, various product mgmt. positions to dir. mktg., 1961-69, gen. mgr. dental div., domestic operating co., 1969-71, v.p., mem. mgmt. bd. domestic operating co., 1971-72; pres. Johnson & Johnson Dental Products Co., 1972-73; asst. account exec. Compton Advt., 1958-59, account exec., 1959-61; with CPC Internat. Inc., 1974-85; pres., chief exec. officer Sun-Diamond Growers Calif., Pleasanton, 1986—; chmn., pres., chief exec. officer S.B. Thomas, Inc. affiliate CPC N.Am., 1974-78; pres. Consumer Devel. unit CPC N.Am., 1978-81; v.p. CPC Internat. Inc., 1978-85; pres. Best Foods U.S. unit CPC N.Am., 1981-84; exec. v.p. Best Foods N.Am. div. CPC Internat. Inc., Englewood Cliffs, N.J., 1984-85; dir. GoodMark Foods Inc., Raleigh, N.C. Served to lt. (j.g.) USNR, 1951-55. Mem. Am. Mgmt. Assn. (pres. assn.), NYU Grad. Sch. Bus. Alumni Assn. (bd. dirs. 1977-86), Phi Beta Kappa, Psi Chi. Republican. Jewish. Office: Sun-Diamond Growers of Calif Pleasanton CA *

NEWSTEAD, ROBERT RICHARD, urologist; b. Detroit, Sept. 16, 1935; s. Oran Henry and Agnes Audery (Lewandowski) N.; m. Marie Carmela LiPuma, Aug. 5, 1961; children: Elizabeth Marie, Peter Joseph, Angela Agnes, Paul Michael. Student, Coll. Idaho, 1955-57, Quincy Coll., 1957-58; MD, Loyola U., Chgo., 1963. Intern Walter Reed Gen. Hosp., Washington, 1963-64; resident U. Iowa, Iowa City, 1967-71; urologist Urology Clinic Yakima, Wash., 1971-84, pres., 1984—; chief of surgery St. Elizabeth Med. Ctr., Yakima, 1980-81, Yakima Valley Hosp., 1978-79. Bd. dirs. St. Elizabeth Found., Yakima, 1983—, The Capital Theater, 1987—, Boy Scouts Am., Yakima, 1982-86. Served to capt. U.S. Army, 1962-67. Fellow Am. Cancer Soc., Iowa City, 1969-70, Am. Cancer Soc., 1961; named one of Outstanding Young Men Am., 1968. Fellow Am. Bd. Urology, ACS, Am. Urol. Assn., Wash. State Urol. Bd.; mem. AMA, Rubin Flocks Soc. (pres. 1985-86), Yakima Surgical Soc. (pres. 1982-83). Roman Catholic. Lodge: Rotary. Avocations: art, skiing, golf. Home: 814 Conestoga Blvd Yakima WA 98908 Office: Urology Clinic Yakima 206 S 11th Ave Yakima WA 98902

NEWTON, CHARLES ALLEN, computer systems engineer; b. Duluth, Minn., Apr. 11, 1938; s. Eldred Charles and Margaret Louise (Paulson) N.; m. Vera Ann Glose, Sept. 5, 1964; children: Teresa Yvonne, Catherine Leslie, Pamela Louise. AB in Math., San Diego State Coll., 1965; MS in Info. Sci., Ga. Inst. Tech., 1968. Engr. aide Convair Astronautics, San Diego, 1958-60; commd. 2d lt. USAF, 1961, advanced through grades to lt. col., 1977, navigator, 1960-71, sr. program mgr., 1971-74, command and control specialist, 1974-83, ret., 1983; systems engr. Ramtek Corp., Napa, Calif., 1983—. Pres. PTA Am. Sch., Oslo, 1982. Decorated DFC Air medal. Mem. Assn. Computing Machinery, Am. Mensa, Air Force Assn., Armed Force Communications and Electronics Assn., Retired Officers Club. Republican. Presbyterian. Lodge: Rotary. Home: 3591 Twin Oaks Dr Napa CA 94558

NEWTON, RAY CLYDE, university administrator; b. Denver, Colo., Sept. 26, 1935; s. Louis Weiss and Thelma (Sipe) N.; m. Patricia Rae (Boekhaus), Dec. 27, 1956; children: Sheri D., Lynn D., William L. Grad., Kans. State U., Ft. Hays, 1957; postgrad., S.D. State U., 1959-61, U. Tex., 1970-72. Tchr., chmn. English dept. LaCrosse (Kans.) High Sch., 1957-59; mem. faculty N.Mex. Highlands U., Las Vegas, 1961-73, instr., asst. dean students, 1961-63, dir. pub. info. and pubs., adminstrv. asst. to pres., 1965-73, asst. prof., then assoc. prof. journalism, 1965-73; mem. faculty No. Ariz. U., Flagstaff, 1973—, prof. journalism, asst. dean creative and communication arts, 1984-87, dean, 1987—; dir. bilingual mass media program N.Mex. Highlands U., 1972-73; corr. Sta. KGGM-TV, Albuquerque, 1966-71; cons. in field to newspapers and mcpl. govts. Author: (with Newsom and Wellert) Media Writing, 1984; contbr. articles and revs. to profl. jours. and popular mags. Mem. adminstrv. bd. Trinity Heights Meth. Ch.; mem. exec. council Grand Canyon council Boy Scouts Am.; bd. dirs. Flagstaff Festival of the Arts; ex-officio bd. dirs. Ariz. Alliance for Arts Edn. Grantee Rotary Found. 1968, Danforth Found., 1969-70; Walter fellow U. Tex., 1971-72; named Journalism Prof. of Yr., Ariz. Newspaper Assn., 1984, Disting. Faculty mem. No. Ariz. U., 1984; recipient Nat. Teaching award Poynter Inst. Media Studies, St. Petersburg, Fla., 1985. Mem. Assn. Edn. Journalism/Mass Communication, Am. Soc. Journalism Sch. Administrs., Am. Soc. Newspaper Editors (mem. minorities edn. com.), Ariz. Press Assn. (mem. bd. dirs., chmn. edn. com.), Western Social Scis. Assn. (v.p. 1979-80, mem. exec. council, editorial bd.), Am. Assn. Higher Edn., Inter-Am. Press Assn., 1st Amendment Coalition (mem. bd. dirs.), Coll. Sports Info. Dirs. Assn., Flagstaff C. of C., Phi Eta Sigma, Lambda Iota Tau, Sigma Delta Chi, Phi Delta Kappa, Pi Rho Sigma, Phi Kappa Phi, Kappa Tau Alpha. Lodge: Kiwanis. Home: 1520 Appalachian Flagstaff AZ 86001 Office: No Ariz U Coll Creative-Communications Arts Box 5755 Flagstaff AZ 86001

NEWTON, STANLEY BARCLAY, automobile executive; b. Worcester, Mass., Apr. 23, 1946; s. Stanley and Barbara Louise (Clark) N.; m. Karen Mary Rizzuto, Apr. 9, 1966; children: Lynette Marie, Kim Michelle. Assocs. in Acctg., New England Sch. Acctg., Worcester, 1966. Staff acct. Tupper Moore & Co. CPA, Worcester, 1966-69; office mgr. Muzi Ford, Needham, Mass., 1969-73; bus. mgr. Kelly Buick Co. Inc., Worcester, 1973-76, Al Ives Chevrolet, Worcester, 1976-80; treas. Holmes Tuttle Ford, Tucson, 1980—. Bd. dirs. Loshe Br. YMCA, Tucson, 1985—; cons. Jr. Achievement, Tucson, 1980-1983. Served with USAR, 1966-72. Republican. Club: Skyline (Tucson), Pueblo. Lodge: Kiwanis (pres. Worcester chpt. 1979). Avocations: golf, classic car collection. Office: Holmes Tuttle Ford 800 E Broadway PO Box 2552 Tucson AZ 85702

NEYENHUIS, HUGO, health, safety institute executive; b. Amsterdam, The Netherlands, Nov. 1, 1926; came to U.S., 1960; s. Hugo and Wilhelmima Josephina (Marchand) N.; m. Loes Th. Wijckelsma-Muller Bsse., June 18, 1953; children: Rudolf, Marijke, Yvonne. Cert. indsl. medicine, Inst. Medische Voorlichting, Amsterdam, 1957; D in Podiatry, Acad. voor Lichaamscultuur, Amsterdam, 1957. Cert. safety exec., hazard control mgr., occupational hearing conservationsist, product safety mgr., hazardous materials mgr. Safety dir. Fred Meyer, Inc., Portland, Oreg., 1960-82; pres. Intersafe Tng. Inst., Ltd., Portland, 1982—; bd. med. govs. Emergency Med. Planning, Eugene, Oreg., 1979—; v.p. Oreg. sect. Pacific Northwest Safety Ctr., 1982—. Contbr. articles to profl. jours. Active Boy Scouts Am., Portland, 1964-75. Served to sgt. maj. Army of The Netherlands, 1950-60. Mem. World Safety Orgn. (mem. cert. bd. 1985—, officer 1985), Am. Soc. Safety Engrs. (pres. 1986), Nat. Safety Mgmt. Soc., Vets. of Safety Internat. (pres. 1986), Field Fed. Safety Council (affiliate). Democrat. Home: 6019 NE Alton St Portland OR 97213 Office: Intersafe Tng Inst Ltd 8383 NE Sandy Blvd Suites 230-35 Portland OR 97220

NEYLON, MARTIN JOSEPH, clergyman; b. Buffalo, Feb. 13, 1920; s. Martin Francis and Delia (Breen) N. Ph.L., Woodstock Coll., 1944, Th.L., 1951; M.A., Fordham U., 1948. Ordained priest Roman Cath. Ch., 1950, bishop, 1970; mem. Soc. of Jesus; tchr. Regis High Sch., N.Y.C., 1952-54; master Jesuit novices Poughkeepsie, N.Y., 1955-67; chaplain Kwajalein Missile Range, Marshall Islands, 1967-68; superior Residence for Jesuit Students, Guam, 1968-70; coadjutor bishop Caroline and Marshall Islands, 1970-80; Vicar apostolic 1971—; residential bishop New Diocese of Carolines-Marshalls, 1980—. Address: Truk TT 96942

NG, LAWRENCE MING-LOY, physician; b. Hong Kong, Mar. 21, 1940; came to U.S., 1967, naturalized, 1977; s. John Iu-cheung and Mary Wing (Wong) N.; B.Med., U. Hong Kong, 1965, B.Surg., 1965; m. Bella May Ha Kan, June 25, 1971; children—Jennifer Wing-mui, Jessica Wing-yee. House physician Queen Elizabeth Hosp., Hong Kong, 1965-66, med. officer, 1966-67; resident physician Children's Hosp. of Los Angeles, 1967-68; resident physician Children's Hosp. Med. Center, Oakland, Calif., 1968-70, fellow in pediatric cardiology, 1970-72, now mem. teaching staff; practice medicine, specializing in pediatrics and pediatric cardiology, San Leandro, Calif., 1972—, Oakland, Calif., 1982—; chief of pediatrics Oakland Hosp., 1974-77; chief of pediatrics Vesper Meml. Hosp., 1977-79, sec. staff, 1984, v.p. staff, 1985; chief pediatrics Meml. Hosp., San Leandro, 1986—. Active Republican Party. Diplomate Am. Bd. Pediatrics. Fellow Am. Acad. Pediatrics; mem. AMA, Calif. Med. Assn., Am. Heart Assn., Los Angeles Pediatric Soc., East Bay Pediatric Soc., Smithsonian Assos., Nat. Geog. Soc., Orgn. Chinese Ams. (chpt. pres. 1984), Chinese-Am. Physicians Soc. (co-founder, sec. 1980, pres. 1983), Oakland Mus. Assns., Oakland Chinatown C. of C. (bd. dirs. 1986—). Buddhist. Club: Bay-O-Vista. Office: 345 9th St Suite 204-205 Oakland CA 94607 Other: 345 9th St Suite 204 Oakland CA 94607

NG, WANG CHEUNG, electrical engineer; b. Hong Kong, Oct. 15, 1956; came to U.S., 1975; s. Sze Hung and Chu Wan (Louie) N.; m. Linda S. Chu, Oct. 9, 1983; children: Ned, Bob. BSEE, U. Calif., Davis, 1979, MSEE, 1982, PhDEE, 1986. Registered licensedengr., Calif. Electronics engr. USAF, McClellan AFB, Calif., 1981-86; engr. Lawrence Livermore (Calif.) Nat. Lab., 1986—; instr. Calif. State U., Sacramento, 1981; research asst. U. Calif., Davis, 1979-86. Mem. IEEE. Avocations: sports, electronic projects, micro-computers. Office: Lawrence Livermore Nat Lab Microwave EMP Group PO Box 808/L-228 Livermore CA 94550

NGAI, ANTHONY KIN WA, architect, computer-aided design consultant; b. Hong Kong, Aug. 10, 1949; came to U.S., 1968; s. Richard K. and Monica S.T. (Wong) Nee; m. Margaret Jean McFall, Sept. 29, 1973. BA, U. Calif., Berkeley, 1972. Registered architect, Calif. Draftsman Thomas Lile, Architect, San Francisco, 1972-73, Oakland (Calif.) Pub. Schs., 1973-75; architect Leidenfrost, Architect, Los Angeles, 1975-77; pres. A.K. Ngai & Assocs., Los Angeles, 1977—. Mem. Chinatown Housing Com., Los Angeles, 1980-85. Recipient 1st place archtl. design Calif. State Senator, Hollywood, 1983, Award of Nat. Excellence, HUD, Washington, 1984. Mem. Assn. for Computers in Design, AIA, Asian Am. Architects and Engrs. Roman Catholic. Avocations: tennis, scuba diving, cycling, photography. Home: 4441 Ben Ave North Hollywood CA 91607 Office: 1833 Victory Blvd Glendale CA 91201

NGUYEN, ANN CAC KHUE, pharmaceutical and bioorganic chemist; b. Sontay, Vietnam; came to U.S., 1975; d. Soan Van and Hieu Thi (Luu) N. BS, U. Saigon, 1973; MS, San Francisco State U., 1978; PhD, U. Calif., San Francisco, 1983. Teaching and research asst. U. Calif., San Francisco, 1978-83, postdoctoral fellow, 1983-86; research scientist U. Calif., 1987—. Contbr. articles to profl. jours. Recipient Nat. Research Service award, NIH, 1981-83; Regents fellow U. Calif., San Francisco, 1978-81. Mem. Am. Chem. Soc., AAAS, Bay Area Enzyme Mechanism Group, Nat. Coop. Drug Discovery Group. Roman Catholic. Home: 122 Serrano Dr San Francisco CA 94132 Office: U Calif Dept Pharmaceutical Chemistry San Francisco CA 94143

NGUYEN, CAM VAN, electrical engineer, researcher; b. Quang Ngai, Vietnam, July 14, 1954; s. Suong Xuan and Huong (Le) N.; m. Diep Ngoc Tran, Sept. 1, 1979; children: An,Christine. BS in Physics, U. Saigon, Vietnam, 1975; BSEE, Calif. State Poly. U., Pomona, 1979; MSEE, Calif. State U., Northridge, 1982. Design engr. ITT Gilfillan, Van Nuys, Calif., 1979-82; mem. tech. staff Hughes Aircraft Co., Torrance, Calif., 1982-83, TRW, Redondo Beach, Calif., 1983—. Contbr. over 20 tech. papers to profl. jours., chpt. to book. Mem. IEEE, Sigma Xi. Home: 5019 E Fairfield St Anaheim CA 92807 Office: TRW M/S 138-4934 1 Space Park Redondo Beach CA 92708

NGUYEN, HIET LE, industrial engineer; b. Bien Hoa, Socialist Rep. of Vietnam, Mar. 10, 1959; came to U.S., 1975; s. Huan Le Nguyen and That Thi Tran. BS, U. Calif., Berkley, 1981. Cert. cert. prodn. and inventory mgmt. Indsl. engr. Perkins Elmer Corp., Hayward, Calif., 1981, Peerless Electric Co., Berkeley, Calif., 1981-82; sales mgr. Gen. Devel. Corp., Cornwell Heights, Pa., 1984-85; sr. indsl. engr. Hughes Aircraft Co., Irvine, Calif., 1982—; cons. Vietnamese Profl. Engrs., Irvine, 1984-86; pres. Internat. Trading Co., Cornwell Heights, Pa., 1986—. Writer reports, short stories for Vietnam Hai Ngoai, 1981. Recipient Mgr. Dinner award, Hughes Aircraft Co., El Segundo, Calif., 1982; named Outstanding Salesman Gen. Devel. Corp., Va., 1984. Mem. Am. Inst. Indsl. Engrs. Roman Catholic. Avocations: photography, reading, travel, music.

NGUYEN, HUNG DINH, meachanical engineer; b. Khanh Hoa, Socialist Republic of Vietnam, Feb. 14, 1957; came to U.S., 1975; s. Huu Dinh Nguyen and Lien Anh Tran; m. Myle Chau, Dec. 26, 1984. BSME, U. Ala. Plant engr. U. Ala., Tuscaloosa, 1978-79; sr. mechanical design engr. Cushman Electronics, San Jose, Calif., 1980—. Mem. ASME, Capstone Engring. Soc. Avocations: camping, hunting, auto mechanics. Office: Cushman Electronics Inc 1525 Atteberry Ln San Jose CA 95131

NGUYEN, PHUC VAN, electronic packaging engineer, consultant, educator; b. Hanam, Republic of Vietnam, Oct. 31, 1951; came to U.S., 1975; s. Truong Van Nguyen and Te (Thi) Dang. BA, Saigon U., Socialist Republic of Vietnam, 1974; postgrad., Vietnam Naval Acad., Nhatrang; AS, San Diego City Coll., 1978; postgrad., USN Pacific Fleet Tng. Sch., San Diego. Lapper tech. Spin Physics Inc., San Diego, 1976-79; printed circuit designer Mesa Design, San Diego, 1979-80; drafting supr. Interocean Systems Inc., San Diego, 1980-82; electronic designer Coopervision Diagnostics Inc., San Diego, 1982-85, Qualidyne Systems Inc., San Diego, 1985—; owner, pres. Truong Phuc Design, San Diego, 1981—; instr. electronics San Diego City Coll., 1986—. Editor mag. Dac San De II Bao Binh, 1984—. Served as an officer Vietnamese Army, 1970-75. Mem. Internat. Electronics Packaging Soc., Hoi Ai Huu De II Bao Binh (gen. sec. San Diego chpt.). Republican. Roman Catholic. Avocations: music writing and performance, reading, writing. Home: 10455 Londonderry Ave San Diego CA 92126 Office: Qualidyne Systems Inc 3055 Del Sol Blvd San Diego CA 92154

NGUYEN, UNG DUC, mechanical design engineer; b. Saigon, Vietnam, Feb. 5, 1949; came to U.S., 1981; s. Trung Duc and Mai Thi N.; m. Hong Thi Do, Feb. 23, 1974; children: Dan Ha, Tuyet Ha. BSME, Sch. Mech. Engring., Nat. Inst. Tech., Saigon, 1972. Registered profl. engr., Colo. Instr. Nat. Inst. Tech., Saigon, 1972-75; mech. engr. Mekong Pulp and Paper Mfg. Co., Thu Duc, Vietnam, 1974-75; assembler Valley Lb., Inc., Boulder, Colo., 1983, Storage Tech., Inc., Louisville, Colo., 1983-84; draftsman HTI Superior, Inc., Lakewood, Colo., 1984; mech. design engr. Ball Aerospace Systems div., Boulder, 1984—. Avocations: swimming, camping. Home: 906 Glenwood Dr Lafayette CO 80026

NIBLETT, CHARLES TILLMAN, former military officer, retired real estate broker; b. Birmingham, Ala., Oct. 26, 1920; s. Edgar Marvin and Emma Marie (Nuttall) N.; m. Norma Adrienne Booth, Nov. 4, 1943; children—Linda Anne Budge, Adrienne Wilson. B.F.A., U. Ga., 1942; postgrad. U. S.C., 1951-53, U. Md., 1954-56, U. Mass., 1957-59. With Stockham Valves & Fittings, Birmingham, 1947-50; recalled to active duty as capt. USAF, 1950, advanced through grades to col., 1968, ret., 1969; owner/broker Charles T. Niblett, Realtor, Tucson, 1970-85. Bd. dirs. Pima Air Mus., 1975—, pres., 1983-85; mem. Com. on Employer Support of Guard and Res., 1978—. Served with USAAF, 1942-46; CBI. Decorated D.F.C., Air medal with oak leaf cluster, Air Force Commendation medal. Mem. Air Force Assn., Ret. Officers Assn., Order Daedalians, Tucson Metro C. of C., Lambda Chi Alpha. Republican. Clubs: Westerners, Una Noche Plateada. Address: 5837 N Paseo Ventoso Tucson AZ 85715

NIBLEY, ROBERT RICKS, lawyer; b. Salt Lake City, Sept. 24, 1913; s. Joel and Teresa (Taylor) N.; m. Lee Allen, Jan. 31, 1945 (dec.); children—Jane, Annette. A.B., U. Utah, 1934; J.D., Loyola U., Los Angeles, 1942. Bar: Calif. bar 1943. Accountant Nat. Parks Airways, Salt Lake City, 1934-37, Western Air Lines, Los Angeles, 1937-40; asst. mgr. market research dept. Lockheed Aircraft Corp., Burbank, Calif., 1940-43; asso. firm Hill, Farrer and Burrill, Los Angeles, 1946-53; partner Hill, Farrer and Burrill, 1953-70, of counsel, 1971-78. Served from ensign to lt. comdr. USNR, 1943-46. Mem. Am., Los Angeles bar assns., Phi Delta Phi, Phi Kappa Phi, Phi Delta Theta. Club: California (Los Angeles). Home: 4860 Ambrose Ave Los Angeles CA 90027

NICARTHY, GINNY ANN, psychotherapist, writer; b. Palo Alto, Calif., Apr. 30, 1927; d. Paul Aloysius and Alice (Byrne) McCarthy. MSW, U. Wash., 1974. Tchr. Seattle pub. schs., 1968-72, 74-75; dir. Rape Relief, Seattle, 1972-73; co-dir., therapist Women's Counseling Group, Seattle, 1979—; profl. trainer Eng., Scotland, Norway, U.S., 1978—. Author Getting Free, 1982, 2d rev. edit., 1986 (Gov.'s award 1982), Talking it Out, 1984; contbr. articles to profl. jours. V.p. Wash. State chpt. ACLU, 1984. Mem. Nat. Assn. Social Workers, Nat. Coalition vs. Domestic Violence, King County Coalition vs. Domestic Violence (Innovator award 1983), Feminist Therapy Inst., Assn. Women in Social Work, Wash. State Shelter Network, Amnesty Internat., Women's Internat. League Peace and Freedom, Feminist Writers Guild, Internat. Network Against Violence Against Women (writer, editor 1986—). Home: 626 36th Ave Seattle WA 98122 Office: Womens Counseling Group 2811 E Madison #205 Seattle WA 98112

NICE, CARTER, conductor, music director; b. Jacksonville, Fla., Apr. 5, 1940; s. Clarence Carter and Elizabeth Jane (Hintermister) N.; m. Jennifer Charlotte Smith, Apr. 4, 1983; children: Danielle, Christian. MusB, Eastman Sch. Music, 1962; MusM, Manhattan Sch. Music. Asst. condr., concert master New Orleans Philharm., 1967-79; condr., music dir. Sacramento Symphony, 1979—; music dir., conductor Bear Valley Music Fest., 1985—. Office: Sacramento Symphony Orch 2848 Arden Way Suite 210 Sacramento CA 95825

NICHOLAS, DAVID RICHARD, lawyer, state senator; b. Gillette, Wyo., Mar. 2, 1941; s. Thomas Arthur and Mary Margaret (McKean) N.; B.A., Harvard Coll., 1963; J.D., U. Wyo., 1966; m. Karen Kay Brewer, Aug. 25, 1963; children—Kristin Kay, Alexander McKean. Admitted to Wyo. bar, 1967, U.S. Ct. Mil. Appeals, 1967; partner Corthell, King, McFadden, Nicholas & Prehoda, Attys., Laramie, Wyo., 1971—; instr. polit. sci. U. Wyo., Laramie, 1977-78, 83-84; mem. Wyo. Senate, Laramie, 1979-87, chmn. travel, recreation and wildlife com., mem. judiciary com. Justice of Peace, Albany County, Wyo., 1977-78; bd. dirs. Salvation Army, 1971-80, Cathedral Home for Children, 1975—, Sr. Ctr., 1975-81, Albany County Pub. Library, 1979-83; mem. Wyo. Council for Humanities, 1982—; civilian aide to Sec. of Army, 1984—. Served to capt. Judge Adv. Gen.'s Corps, U.S. Army, 1967-71. Mem. ABA, Albany County Bar Assn., Wyo. Bar Assn. Republican. Club: Rotary (past pres.). Office: PO Box 1147 Laramie WY 82070

NICHOLS, AMBROSE REUBEN, JR., chemistry professor, college president, retired; b. Corvallis, Oreg., June 21, 1914; s. Ambrose R. and Cecil (Matthews) N.; m. Barbara Seward; children: David S., Deborah Sue Poulos, Eleanor Joy. Student, San Jose State Coll., 1931-34; BS, U. Calif., Berkeley, 1935; PhD, U. Wis., 1939; LHD (hon.), Nat. U., San Diego, 1976. Research chemist U. Calif. Radiation Lab., Berkeley, 1943-45, Oak Ridge (Tenn.) Nat. Lab., 1951-52; from instr. to prof. chemistry San Diego State Coll., 1939-61; pres. Sonoma State Coll., Rohnert Park, Calif., 1961-70, prof. chemistry, 1970-76, prof. emeritus, 1976; pres. emeritus trustees Calif. State U., 1983. Bd. dirs. Santa Rosa (Calif.) Symphony Assn., 1963—, Sonoma County Arts Council, Santa Rosa, 1978-82, Sonoma County Community Found., Santa Rosa, 1984—, Santa Rosa Community Concerts, 1976—. Mem. Am. Chem. Soc. (sect. chmn. 1941), AAUP, Sigma Xi. Home: 2513 Creekside Rd Santa Rosa CA 95405

NICHOLS, BERNICE PAULINE, civic worker, artist; b. Delta, Colo., Jan. 13, 1932; d. John Obert and Pauline Gertrude (Hockett) Graybeal; m. Darrel Duaine Nichols, Sept. 3, 1950; children: Linda F. Nichols Baker, E. Marlene Nichols DeMarcus, Dennis D. Art student Whitworth Coll. Sales clk. J.C. Penny Co., Spokane, Wash., 1950-51; fashion show dir. Sarah Coventry Jewelry, Ephrata, Wash., 1958-59; welcome hostess Merchants of Ephrata, 1969-71; Artist "Fruit Basket" still life (hon. mention 1983), black and white drawing Fall Art Festival. Jurist Grant County Superior Ct., Ephrata, 1968, Spokane County Superior Ct., Wash., 1978; mem. Spokane County Library Assn., 1980—; pres. Am. Luth. Ch. Women, 1980-81; mem. parents council Pacific Luth. U., Spokane, 1982-85. Recipient 6th Flight Runner Up award Lakeview Golf and County Club, 1968. Republican. Club: Compass (Spokane). Lodges: Eagles, Narcisse Grange. Avocations: painting, golf, swimming, walking, singing. Home: 212 W Dawn Spokane WA 99218

NICHOLS, BETSY SHERMAN, computer professional; b. Cin., Feb. 5, 1951; d. Hugh L. and Doreen (Sherman) N.; m. Donald D. Young, May 21, 1977. BA, Barnard Coll., 1972; cert. in data processing, Inst. Cert. Computer Profls., 1982; MBA, U. N.Mex, 1984. Programmer TCC Ins. Servicea Inc., Austin, Tex., 1976-77; programmer/analyst Sci. Applications Inc., McLean, Va., 1978-80; systems analyst Applied Mgmt. Engring., Albuquerque, 1980-83; sr. programmer/analyst Planning Research Corp., Albuquerque, 1983-85; prin. computer systems designer Data Systems div. Martin Marietta Corp., Albuquerque, 1985—. Served with USAR. Recipient awards for chocolate fudge and crochet work, N.Mex. State Fair, 1984-85. Mem. Albuquerque Aerostatic Ascension Assn. Avocations: knitting and crocheting, hot air balloon chasing, gardening, wine and beer making. Home: Star Rt Box 401 Placitas NM 87043

NICHOLS, CHARLES FRED, state official; b. San Bernardino, Calif., Nov. 6, 1947; s. Charles Blackwell and Virginia Patricia Nichols; B.S.I.E., Calif. State Poly. U., 1970; M.B.A., So. Ill. U., 1975; m. Nancy Claire Parks, June 13, 1971; children—Charles Kyle, Brent Alan, Erik Brock. Analyst intern City of Hope Nat. Med. Ctr., 1969-70; productivity analyst, San Bernardino County (Calif.), 1972-84; prin. productivity analyst exec. dept. State of Oreg., 1984—. Chmn., Rialto (Calif.) Planning Commn., 1978-82; pres. Rialto Colt League, 1972-73; loaned exec. West End and Fontana United Way, 1982. Served with USN, 1971. Recipient Nat. Assn. Counties award for Productivity advancement, 1977. Mem. Am. Mgmt. Assn., Inst. Indsl. Engrs. (sr.), Am. Assn. Pub. Adminstrs, Productivity Council of S.W. Club: Kiwanis (pres. 1978-79). Office: State of Oreg 155 Cottage St NE Salem OR 97310

NICHOLS, CHESTER ENCELL, minerals exploration consultant, geochemist; b. Boston, Dec. 28, 1935; s. Herbert Bishop and Ruth (Christie) N.; m. Carolyn Louise Gregg, Nov. 11, 1962; children: Elizabeth Christie, Valerie Celeste. AB, Cornell U., 1960; MS, U. Iowa, 1965; PhD, U. Mo., Rolla, 1977. Cert. profl. chemist Nat. Commn. Chemistry. Exploration geologist Union Carbide Corp., Corpus Christie, Tex., 1968-72; sr. mines geologist Union Carbide Corp., Uravan, Colo., 1973-75; project geochemist Union Carbide Corp., Oak Ridge, Tenn., 1975-78; project geologist Union Carbide Corp., Grand Junction, Colo., 1978-80; sr. staff geologist Union Carbide Corp., Reno, 1981-82; pvt. practice minerals exploration cons. Reno, 1983—; environ. scientist individual mobilization augmentee U.S. Army Research Office, Research Triangle Park, N.C., 1984-87; lectr. mineral assessment workshop Bur. Land Mgmt., Reno, 1983; chief geologist Placer Mgmt. Group, Reno, 1985; sr. staff geologist Columbus Mines, Inc., 1987—. Contbr. articles to profl. jours. Chmn. bd. dirs. First Ch. Christ Scientist, Reno, 1984. Served to lt. col. USAR, 1984—. Fellow Am. Inst. Chemists (life); mem. AAAS, Geol. Soc. Am., Assn. Exploration Geochemists (councillor 1984—, editor jour. 1984-86), Geophysics and Hydrogeology divs. Geol. Soc. Am., Sigma Xi. Mem. Christian Sci. Ch. Lodge: Masons. Home: 1192 La Via Way Sparks NV 89431 Office: Nichols Assocs 680 Greenbrae Dr Suite 290 Sparks NV 89431

NICHOLS, COURTLAND GEOFFREY, plant scientist, horticulturist; b. Wilmington, Del., May 16, 1934; s. James Burton and Eleanor Cary (Hansen) N.; m. Sylvia Sherman Eccles, July 25, 1959; children: William, Elizabeth, Alice. BS, Pa. State U., 1956; MS, U. Wis., 1959, PhD, 1963. Plant geneticist Campbell Soup Co., Paris, Tex., 1963-65, St. Charles, Ill., 1966-67, Davis, Calif., 1968-69; plant breeder Ferry-Morse Seed Co., San Juan Bautista, Calif., 1969—. Contbr. articles on plant breeding to profl. jours. Served as sgt. USAR, 1957-63. Mem. Am. Phytopathol. Soc., Am. Soc. Hort. Sci., Tomato Genetics Coop., Sigma Xi. Republican. Lutheran. Home: 1241 Sunset Dr Hollister CA 95023 Office: Ferry-Morse Seed Co 2191 San Juan-Hollister Rd Box 1010 San Juan Bautista CA 95045

NICHOLS, FREDERICK CARL, personnel manager; b. Riverside, Calif., Mar. 16, 1949; s. Nota William Walter Frederick and Alice (Newby) N.; m. Sonia Mayella Mora, July 29, 1972; children: Adrian Aaron Mora, Ian Vincent Mora. AA in English, El Camino Coll., 1973; BBA, Pepperdine U., 1976; postgrad., Loyola Marymount U., Los Angeles, 1978-80. Cert. community coll. tchr. in bus. and indsl. mgmt. Supr. prodn. ops. electronics div. Xerox Corp., El Segundo, Calif., 1973-79, mgr. skills and tech. tng. electronics div., 1979-83, mgr. edn. and tng., printing systems div., 1983-85, mgr. employement, facilities, security, printing systems div., 1985, mgr. personnel field ops., systems group, 1985—. Bd. dirs. South Bay Mayors Com. for Employment of Handicapped, Torrance and El Segundo and Manhatten Beach Calif., 1986; mem. South Bay Union High Sch. Dist. Citizen's Com., 1985; advisor City of Los Angeles Mayor's Office of Handicapped Edn., 1983—. Served with USCG, 1967-71. Republican. Home: 118 Manhattan Ave Hermosa Beach CA 90254 Office: Xerox Corp 101 Continental Blvd El Segundo CA 90245

NICHOLS, JACQUELINE BRUCE, archeologist; b. Harlan, Ky., Oct. 14, 1941; d. Jack Corum and Martha Jayne (Miracle) Bruce; B.A., Wellesley Coll., 1963; M.A., SUNY, Albany, 1977; m. David Edward Nichols, Mar. 4, 1963; children—Corinna Elizabeth, David Andrew, Patrick Edward. Tchr., Bedford (Eng.) Schs., 1963-64; dir. Archeol. Field Labs., SUNY, Albany, 1976-77, Cath. U., 1978; v.p. Gt. Basin Found. for Archeol. Research, 1979; pres. Atechiston, Inc., Albuquerque, 1980—; co-founder, editor Flintknappers Exchange, 1977; founder, pub. Contract Abstracts & CRM Archeology, 1980—; pub. Am. Archeology. Wallace Stegner fellow, 1963-64. Mem. AAAS, Soc. Am. Archaeology, Nat. Assn. Women Bus. Owners, Soc. Archeol. Sci., Found. for Desert Archaeology (dir. 1980—). Republican. Office: 4426 Constitution NE Albuquerque NM 87110

NICHOLS, JOHN WELDON, advertising executive; b. Berkeley, Calif., Oct. 11, 1947; s. John Ellsworth Nichols and Faye (Beattie) Rinehart; m. Julianne Doreen Keith, June 21, 1970; children: Makenzie, John. Student, U. Oreg., 1969-72. Account supr. Gerber Advt., Portland, Oreg., 1978-81; regional advt. mgr. Taubman and Assocs., Detroit, 1981-83; v.p. Davis Johnson Mogul & Colombatto Advt., Portland, 1983—; co-owner Nichols & Assocs., Beaverton, Oreg., 1984—; cons. Pacific Oil Conf., Sacramento, 1985—. Author: Retail Advertising, 1985. Served with USMC, 1966-68, Vietnam. Mem. Advt. Golf Assn., Portland C. of C. (recreation resource com. 1983—). Republican. Presbyterian. Avocations: golf, photography, boating. Home: 17610 Outlook Ln Beaverton OR 97006 Office: Davis Johnson Moaul & Colombatto 101 SW Main Suite 1200 Portland OR 97204

NICHOLS, ROBERT EDMUND, communications consultant; journalist; b. Daytona Beach, Fla., Feb. 14, 1925; s. Joe D. and Edna A. (Casper) N.; m. Diana R. Grosso; children by previous marriage: Craig S., Kim S., Robin K. Student, San Diego State Coll., 1942-43, St. John's Coll., 1944-45, George Washington U., 1948-49. Reporter San Diego Union, 1942-44; corr. Washington bur. N.Y. Herald Tribune, 1945-48, CBS, 1948-51, Time, Inc., 1951-61; contbg. editor, asst. edn. dir. Life mag., N.Y.C., 1951-52; corr. representing Time, Life, Fortune, Sports Illus. mags., San Diego area, 1952-61; Sunday editor San Diego Union, 1952-61; fin. editor Los Angeles Times, 1961-68, mem. editorial bd., 1965-68; spl. asst. to bd. govs. Fed. Res. System, 1968-70; v.p., dir. editorial services and pub. info. Bank of Am., 1970-73, v.p., dir. pub. relations, 1973-78, v.p., dir. policy and program devel., 1978-85; prin. Robert E. Nichols Communications, San Francisco, 1985—. Writer, dir. film and radio documentaries. Recipient Loeb Newspaper Spl. Achievement award, 1963, Loeb award distinguished financial reporting, 1964. Fellow Royal Geog. Soc., Explorers Club; mem. Calif. Scholarship Fedn. (hon. life), Soc. Am. Bus. Writers (pres. 1967-68), Soc. Profl. Journalists. Clubs: South Polar Press (Little Am. Antarctic); S.Am. Explorers (Lima). Home and Office:: 38 Ord Ct San Francisco CA 94114

NICHOLSON, GEORGE, lawyer, agency administrator; b. Dallas, Feb. 15, 1941; s. George William and Delighon (Ross) N.; m. Brenda Hommel, Nov. 14, 1959; children: Peggy, Christopher. AA, Oakland City Coll., 1962; BA in Polit. Sci., Calif. State U., Hayward, 1964; JD, U. Calif., San Francisco, 1967. Bar: Calif., U.S. Ct. Appeals (9th cir.), U.S. Dist. Ct. (ea. and no. dists.) Calif., U.S. Supreme Ct. Sr. trial dep. dist. atty. Alameda County, Oakland, Calif., 1966-76; exec. dir. Calif. Dist. Atty.'s Assn., Sacramento, 1976-79; sr. asst. atty. gen. Calif. Dept. Justice, Sacramento, 1979-83; legal and edal. advisor Gov. Calif., Sacramento, 1983-84; dir. and chief counsel Nat. Sch. Safety Ctr., Sacramento, 1984-86; sole practice Sacramento, 1986—; adv. bds. Fed. Office Juvenile Justice and Delinquency Prevention-Nat. juvenile justice code project, Nat. restitution project; pres.'s adv. com. Victims of Crime, 1980-81; adj. prof. edn. Grad. Sch. Edn. Psychology, Pepperdine U., Malibu, Calif. Prin. author Proposition 8, California Victims' Bill Rights, 1982, California Constitutional Right to Safe Schools; (with others) Forgotten Victims: An Advocate's Anthology, 1977, Crime Victims' Handbook, 1981, School Crime and Violence: Victims' Rights, 1986; editor School Safety Legal Anthology, 1985; contbr. articles to profl. jours. Vol. legal counsel Parents of Murdered Children, Los Angeles, 1982; Laws at Work, Los Angeles, 1980-82; Calif. Rep. exec. com., 1983—; Rep. nominee Calif. Atty. Gen., 1982. Mem. Nat. Assn. Coll. and Univ. Attys., Victims' Assistance Legal Orgn. (bd. dirs.), ABA (com. Victims of Crime 1982-84), Nat. Sch. Bd. Assn. (mem. council sch. lawyers), Nat. Orgn. Legal Problems of Edn. Presbyterian. Avocations: legal edn. subjects, skiing, baseball. Home and Office: 6844 Havenside Dr Sacramento CA 95831

NICHOLSON, JAMES BRAYTON, marketing professional; b. Chgo., Sept. 13, 1930; s. Douglas Ingersoll Nicholson and Elinor (Brayton) Brown; m. Kay Carrole Ellis, Apr. 27, 1952; children: Brian James, Nancy C. BS in Physics and Math., Calif. State Poly. U., Pomona, 1960; MBA, Holy Names Coll., Oakland, Calif., 1986. Scientist Applied Research Labs., Sunland, Calif., 1960-74; area sales mgr. Tektronix, Los Gatos, Calif., 1974-76; v.p. mktg., sales Accelerators, Austin, Tex., 1976-77; asst. gen. mgr. Etec Corp., Hayward, Calif., 1977-80; dir. mktg. Perkin Elmer EBT, Hayward, 1980-83; sr. exec. mktg., sales UTI Instruments, Milpitas, Calif., 1983-87; pres. Mgmt. Recruiters, Milpitas, 1987—; mktg. cons. Quest Assocs., Hayward, 1980—; mem. Engrs. Architects Council. Contbr. articles to profl. jours.; co-investigator (invention) soft x-ray diffraction by gratings; prin. investigator (invention) soft x-ray tube. Served with USNR, 1951-56. Mem. Am. Vacuum Soc. Republican. Avocations: gardening, stamp and coin collecting. Home: 3218 Oakes Dr Hayward CA 94542 Office: MRM Co 830 Hillview Ct #260 Milpitas CA 95035-4599

NICHOLSON, MARGARET R., educational association administrator; b. Berkeley, Calif., July 1, 1915; d. Seth Barnes and Alma M. (Stotts) N. AB magna cum laude, Pomona Coll., 1936; postgrad., U. Calif., Berkeley, 1936-38. Cert. secondary tchr., Calif. Tchr. pub. schs. Angels Camp and Lafayette, Calif., 1938-81; chairperson dept. sci. Acalanes High Sch., Lafayette, 1950-81; asst. exec. dir. Calif. Sci. Tchrs. Assn., Berkeley, 1981-85, exec. dir., 1985—. Co-Author: Chemistry, A Modern Approach, 1963, rev. as Chemistry, Patterns and Properties, 1971; assoc. editor: CHEM Study Text, 1961. Recipient Outstanding Educator award Contra Costa County chpt. Calif. Tchrs. Assn., 1979; Chemistry Tchr. of Yr. award No. Calif. Chem. Industries Council, 1977, Award for Excellence in Chemistry Teaching Mfg. Chemists Assn., 1966. Mem. Calif. Sci. Tchrs. Assn. (pres. No. sect. 1954-55, pres. state assn. 1981-82, bd. dirs. 1972-85, Disting. Service award 1983), Delta Kappa Gamma (pres. Contra Zeta Zeta chpt. 1974-76). Democrat. Home: 3428 Shangri-la Rd Lafayette CA 94549 Office: Calif Sci Tchrs Assn U Calif Lawrence Hall Sci Berkeley CA 94720

NICHOLSON, SKIP (GEORGE), educator; b. Glendale, Calif., Apr. 21, 1942; s. George Jay Nicholson and Colleen Carol (Crist) Astrahantseff. BA, UCLA, 1964; postgrad., Calif. State U., Fullerton. Tchr. Burbank (Calif.) High Sch., 1967-84; tchr. English, French South Pasadena (Calif.) High Sch., 1984—; vis. assoc. U. Ill., Urbana, 1979-80; faculty tchr. Folger Shakespeare Library, Washington, 1985-86. Mem. Nat. Council Tchrs. English (chmn. task force on ctrs. of excellence, exec. com. 1981-85), Am. Assn. Tchrs. French, Assn. Supervision and Curriculum Devel., Internat. Reading Assn., Shakespeare Soc. Am. Home: 4500 Palmero Dr Los Angeles CA 90065 Office: South Pasadena High Sch 1401 Fremont Ave South Pasadena CA 91030

NICHOLSON, WILLIAM JOSEPH, forest products company executive; b. Tacoma, Aug. 24, 1938; s. Ferris Frank and Athyleen Myrtle (Fesenmaier) N.; m. Carland Elaine Crook, Oct. 10 1964; children: Courtney, Brian, Kay, Benjamin. SB in ChemE, MIT, 1960, SM in ChemE Practice, 1961; PhD in ChemE, Cornell U., 1965; MBA, Pacific Luth. U., 1969. Registered profl. chem. engr., Wash. Sr. devel. engr. Hooker Chem. Co., Tacoma, 1964-69, Battelle N.W., Richland, Wash., 1969-70; planning assoc. Potlatch Corp., San Francisco, 1970-75, mgr. corp. energy service, 1976—. Mem. Am. Chem. Soc., Am. Inst. Chem. Engrs. (assoc.), Tech. Assn. Pulp and Paper Industry, AAAS, Sigma Xi. Republican. Club: Commonwealth (San Francisco). Avocation: industrial history. Home: PO Box 1114 Ross CA 94957 Office: Potlatch Corp PO Box 3591 San Francisco CA 94119

NICK, FRED JOSEPH, social science director; b. Price, Utah, May 26, 1951; s. Frank John and Shirley Maybell (Lampshire) N.; m. Ruth Marie Ross, Sept. 3, 1982. BS in Math., U. Wash., 1975, BA in Philosophy, 1975. Sci. programmer ctr. quanititative studies U. Wash, Seattle, 1975-79, acting dir. ctr. quantitative studies, 1979-81; asst. dir. ctr. soc. sci. computation and research U. Wash., Seattle, 1981-82, acting dir., 1982-83; dir. ctr. soc. sci. computation and research U. Wash., 1983—; head Macintosh Users Group, U. Wash., Seattle, 1984—. Software devel. grantee U. Wash., 1984; equipment grantee U. Wash., 1986. Mem. Assn. Computing Machinery, Internat. Assn. Soc. Sci. Info. Service and Tech. Avocations: photography, microcomputing. Home: 2749 NE 98th Seattle WA 98115 Office: U Wash Ctr Soc Sci Computation Research 149 Savery Hall DK-45 Seattle WA 98195

NICKEL, JOHN HOWARD, chemist; b. Big Timber, Mont., Dec. 31, 1957; s. Howard John and Margaret (Stewart) N.; m. Marilyn Jean Reed, Dec. 27, 1980. BS in Chemistry, Oreg. State U., 1980; PhD in Analytical Chemistry, U. Houston, 1984. Student technician Teledyne Wah-Chang, Albany, Oreg., 1979-80, Analytical Consulting Services, Houston, 1980-81; software engr., chemist Nelson Analytical Inc., Cupertino, Calif., 1984-85; software engr. Brownlee Labs., Inc., Santa Clara, Calif., 1985—; programing cons. Tech. Inc. Life Sci. Div., Houston, 1984. Contbr. articles to profl. jours. Mem. Am. Chem. Soc. (analytical div.), Phi Kappa Phi. Avocations: camping, reading. Home: 3965 Hamilton Park Dr San Jose CA 95130 Office: Brownlee Labs Inc 2045 Martin Suite 204 Santa Clara CA 95050

NICKERSON, ROBERT FLETCHER, software company executive; b. Winchester, Mass., Mar. 25, 1930; s. Herbert Henry and Nedra Eloise (Fletcher) N.; 1 child, Jeffrey Fletcher. BS, Tufts U., 1952, MS, 1953; PhD, U. Calif., Berkeley, 1958. Chemist Lawrence Livermore (Calif.) Nat. Lab., 1958-71; computing analyst Calif. Inst. Tech., Pasadena, 1972-81; mgr. Sierra Geophysics, Inc., Redmond, Wash., 1981-83, dir., 1983—. Fellow Sigma Xi; mem. Am. Mgmt. Assn. Home: 6479 137th Ave NE #374 Redmond WA 98052 Office: Sierra Geophysics Inc PO Box 3886 Seattle WA 98124

NICODEMUS, FRED(ERICK) E(DWIN), writer, editor, consultant on optical radiometry; b. Osaka, Japan, July 25, 1911; (parents Am. citizens); s. Frederick Bowman and Ella Cora (Neubauer) N.; m. Margaret Ethel Shaw, July 13, 1935. AB in Physics, Reed Coll., 1934; postgrad., Boston U., 1956. Tech. adminstrv. asst., physicist USAF Cambridge (Mass.) Research Labs., 1946-55; engring. optics specialist Sylvania Electronic Def. Labs., Mountain View, Calif., 1955-69; sr. physics cons. U.S. Naval Weapons Ctr., China Lake, Calif., 1969-74; physicist Nat. Bur. Standards, Gaithersburg, Md., 1974-81, Cath. U. Am., Washington, 1981-85; editor, writer, cons. Los Altos and Mountain View, 1985—; cons. InfraRed Info. and Analysis Ctr., U. Mich., Willow Run Labs, Ann Arbor, 1957-69, Internat. Commn. on Illumination, Paris, 1972—; mem. evaluation panel to Nat. Bur. Standards heat div. Nat. Acad. Sci., Nat. Acad. Engring., NRC, Washington, 1970-74. Editor, author: NBS Self-Study Manual on Optical Radiation Measurements, 1967—; contbr. numerous articles to profl. jours. Fellow Optical Soc. Am. (No. and So. Calif. chpts.), Soc. Photo-Optical Instrumentation Engrs.; mem. Sigma Xi. Avocations: photography, classical and chamber music. Home: 720 Brentwood Pl Los Altos CA 94022 Office: GTE Govt Systems Corp 100 Ferguson Dr Mountain View CA 94039

NICOL, MICHAEL JON, electrical engineer; b. Holland, Mich., Mar. 11, 1954; s. Roy Elmer and Gretchen (Holkaboer) N.; m. Linda Claire Tyink, Mar. 15, 1974 (div. April 1976); m. Nguyethgn Thi Nguyen, May 31, 1984. BS in Physics, Mich. State U., 1981, postgrad., 1981-82. Elec. engr. Hughes Aircraft Co., El Segundo, Calif., 1983—; owner, mgr. U.E. Computer Cons., Redondo Beach, Calif., 1985—. Served with U.S. Army, 1974-77. Mem. Santa Barbara (Calif.) Planetary Soc. Avocations: camping, hiking, philosophy, astrophysics. Home: 1239 Amethyst St #C Redondo Beach CA 90277 Office: HAC-EDSG BLDG El/MIS B131 PO Box 902 El Segundo CA 90245

NICOL, WILLIAM JAMES, health care management executive; b. Peoria, Ill., Sept. 2, 1943; s. William Charles and Marjorie Jean (O'Dea) N.; m. Sarah Ann Sparkman, May 16, 1970; children—William James, Darcey Meghan, John Charles. B.A., Bradley U., 1969. With Comprehensive Care Corp., Newport Beach, Calif., 1970-87, v.p. fin. and adminstrn., 1978-82, sr. v.p. fin. and adminstrn., 1982-83, exec. v.p., sec., 1983-85, vice chmn., 1985-87. also bd. dirs.; pres., chief exec. officer Rehab Care Corp., Chesterfield,

Mo., 1987—, also bd. dirs.; bd. dirs. Total Phram. Care, Inc. Mem.Sheriff's Adv. Council, Orange County, Calif., 1982—. Served with U.S. Army, 1964-67. Fellow Am Acad. Med. Adminstrn.; mem. Fin. Execs. Inst. Republican. Presbyterian. Clubs: Big Canyon Country, Old Ranch Tennis. Home: 10391 Lassen St Los Alamitos CA 90720 Office: Rehab Care Corp 1795 Clarkson Rd Suite 301 Chesterfield MO 63017

NICOLAI, EUGENE RALPH, investments consultant; b. Renton, Wash., June 26, 1911; s. Eugene George and Josephine (Heidinger) N.; student U. Wash., 1929, Whitman Coll., 1929-30; B.A., U. Wash., 1934; postgrad. Am. U., 1942; M.A., George Washington U., 1965; m. Helen Margaret Manogue, June 5, 1935; 1 son, Paul Eugene. Editor, U. Wash. Daily, Seattle, 1934; asst. city editor, writer, nat. def. editor Seattle Times, 1934-41; writer Sta. KJR, Seattle, 1937-39; writer, editor, safety edn. officer Bur. Mines, Washington, 1941-45; news dir. Grand Coulee Dam and Columbia Basin Project, Washington, 1945-50; regional info. dir. Bur. Mines, Denver and Pitts., 1950-55, asst. chief mineral reports, Washington, 1955-61, news dir. office of oil and gas, 1956-57; sr. info. officer, later sr. public info. officer Office Sec. Interior, Washington, 1961-71, staff White House Nat. Conf. on Natural Beauty, spl. detail to White House, 1971, ret.; now public relations cons., tech. editor, writer. Formerly safety policy adviser Interior Dept.; com. mem. Internat. Cooperation Year, State Dept., 1971. With George Washington U. Alumni Found.; founder, mng. dir. Josephine Nature Preserve; pres. Media Assocs. Bd. dirs. Wash. State Council on Alcoholism; adviser Pierce Transit Authority, Pierce County Growth Mgmt., Pierce County Ethics Commn. Named Disting. Alumnus, recipient Penrose award, both Whitman Coll., 1979. Mem. Nature Conservancy, Wash. Environ. Council, Nat. Audubon Soc. (Am. Belgian Tervuren dist. rep.), Crook County (Oreg.) Hist. Soc., Washington State Hist. Soc., Emerald Shores Assn, Sigma Delta Chi, Pi Kappa Alpha. Presbyn. Clubs: George Washington U., Purdy (pres.). Lodge: Masons. Author: The Middle East Emergency Committee; editor: Fed. Conservation Yearbooks. Home: Box 573 Wauna WA 98395

NICOLLS, KEN E., anatomist, consultant; b. Albuquerque, Nov. 28, 1935; s. Secretes Berdet and Opal Irene (Brandenburg) N.; m. Ruth Elvira Vaiciulenas, Dec. 19, 1964; children: John Berdet, James Byron, Jason Barret. BS, Colo. State U., 1959, MS, 1961, PhD, 1969; postgrad., U. Iowa, 1978. Nat. Inst. Dental Research trainee Colo. State U., Ft. Collins, 1965-69; asst. prof. anatomy U. N.D., Grand Forks, 1969-76; NIH fellow U. Iowa, Iowa City, 1976-78; asst. prof. No. Ariz. U., Flagstaff, 1978-80, assoc. prof., 1980—; ind. cons. human clin. anatomy, Flagstaff, 1978—. Contbr. articles to profl. jours. Mem. Am. Assn. Anatomists, Ariz.-Nev. Acad. of Sci., Soc. of Sigma Xi, Xi Sigma Pi, Phi Kappa Phi. Republican. Methodist. Avocations: gardening, shooting, hunting. Home: 1095 W Basalt Ln Flagstaff AZ 86001

NICOLSON, MARY CLAIRE, technical services librarian; b. Billings, Mont., Nov. 16, 1949; d. John Stuart and Elizabeth Claire (Briggs) N. BA in German, Colo. State U., 1972; MLS, Ind. U., 1974; MA in German, U. Idaho, 1977. Catalog librarian U. Idaho, Moscow, 1974-77; acquisitions librarian N.D. State U., Fargo, 1977-79; tech. services librarian Hobart & William Smith Coll., Geneva, 1979-82, U. Alaska, Juneau, 1982—; mem. Alaska statewide coop. collection devel. steering com., 1982—. Mem. ALA (profl. devel. grant 1976), Pacific Northwest Library Assn., Alaska Library Assn., Assn. Coll. Research Libraries. Home: 2188 B Lawson Creek Rd Douglas AK 99824 Office: U Alaska 11120 Glacier Hwy Juneau AK 99801

NIDA, JEANNINE JENSEN, artist, educator; b. Los Angeles, Feb. 15, 1941; d. Gene M. and Genevieve Zenobia (Stimson) Jensen; m. Robert Hale Nida, June 20, 1964; children: Kathryn Beth, James Hale. BS, U. Calif., Santa Barbara, 1963; teaching credential, UCLA, 1964; postgrad., U. Tenn., 1986. Cert. gen. secondary tchr., Calif. Tchr. Los Angeles City Schs., 1964-65; substitute tchr. Monrovia (Calif.) Adult Edn. Schs., 1976—, Tri-County Adult Edn. Schs., Covina, Calif., 1978—; free-lance weaver San Marino, Calif., 1976—. Designer woven fashions, 1986 (Arrowmont award 1986). Vol. officer Huntington Meml. Hosp. Clinic Aux., Pasadena Calif., 1979—, Am. Field Serve, San Marino and Sacramento, 1971-74, 84—; leader San Marino council Girl Scouts of U.S., 1976—. Mem. Handweavers Guild Am., So. Calif. Handweavers Guild, Bobbinwinders Guild, Pi Beta Phi (corr. and recording sec. 1974—, scholar 1986). Republican. Avocations: crafts, reading, sewing, weaving, tennis. Home and Studio: 1495 Mirasol Dr San Marino CA 91108

NIDEVER, EVA LASKIN, clinical psychologist; b. Berlin, Oct. 25, 1929; came to U.S., 1936; d. Ernst Moritz and Ilse (Chotzen) R.; m. Franklin Theodore Laskin, Oct. 17, 1954 (div. Dec. 1983); Jack Nidever, Jan. 8, 1984; children: Welcome Dean, Nathaniel Seth. BA, Bryn Mawr Coll., 1950; MA, Columbia U., 1952; PhD, Yale U., 1955. Postdoctoral research NIMH, Stanford (Calif.) U., 1955-56; postdoctoral intern VA Hosp., Palo Alto, Calif., 1956-57; staff psychologist Adult and Child Guidance Clinic, San Jose, Calif., 1957-59; mem. tng. com. Family Project Mental Research Inst., Palo Alto, Calif., 1960-69; adminstr. Assoc. Psychotherapists, Santa Clara, Calif., 1958-83; pvt. practice psychology San Jose, Calif., 1959-83, Arnold, Calif., 1983—; Bd. dirs. Mental Health Advisory Bd., Calaveras County, Calif. Mem. editorial bd. Psychotherapy Jour.; contbr. articles to profl. jours. Recipient Silver Psi award Calif. State Psychol. Assn., 1975. Fellow Am. Psychol. Assn. (fin. com. 1979-82, Ins. Trust 1974-79, bd. profl. affairs 1972-75, others); mem. Calif. State Psychol. Assn. (pres. div. I 1972-73, sec. bd. 1968-71, ethics com. 1970), South Bay Soc. Profl. Psychologists (pres. 1966-69), Santa Clara County Psychol. Assn. (sec. 1964-66), CHAMPUS (nat. peer rev. com.), Sigma Xi. Avocations: skiing, hiking, tennis, dance, music. Home: PO Box 526 Arnold CA 95223 Office: 2293 E Hwy 4 PO Box 526 Arnold CA 95223

NIEBOER-TURPIN, NANCY ANN SCHWARZ, behavioral scientist, educator; b. Kingston, N.Y., May 22, 1942; d. Ernst Joseph and Margaret Virginia (Marklin) Schwarz; m. Kourtney C. Nieboer, Feb. 1963 (div. July 1974); m. Patrick A. Turpin, Jan. 1984. A.B., Hope Coll., 1964; M.Ed., Springfield Coll., 1969; Ph.D., U.S. Internat. U., 1975. Asst. editor Quinn Pub. Co., Kingston, N.Y., 1964; tchr. French, Chicopee (Mass.) Pub. Schs., 1965-69; counselor, instr. psychology Chapman Coll. Ctr., George AFB, Calif., 1970-71; edn. counselor, Edwards AFB, Calif., 1971; cons. USAF Social Actions Programs, Soesterberg AB, Netherlands, 1972-73; edn. coordinator U.S. Army Dist. Recruiting Commands, Cleve. and Columbus, 1976-79; program mgr. high sch. testing program U.S. Army Recruiting Command Hdqrs., Fort Sheridan, Ill., 1979-82; adj. research prof. psychology Naval Postgrad. Sch., Monterey, Calif., 1982-86; research psychologist Def. Personnel Security Research and Edn. Ctr., Monterey, Calif., 1986—. Recipient Outstanding Performance award U.S. Army, 1977-81. Mem. Am. Personnel and Guidance Assn., Assn. Measurement and Evaluation in Guidance, Mil. Educators and Counselors Assn. (founding; chmn. bylaws com.), Am. Vocat. Assn. (chmn. Armed Services interest sect. of guidance div. 1980-81), Mil. Testing Assn., Ohio Personnel and Guidance Assn., Mensa. Author: Army Recruiter's Guide to the High School ASVAB, 1979, 82; offering Commercial Aptitude Tests in the Defense Student Testing Program, 1984, 85; Feasibility of Screening for Unsuitability through Background Investigation, 1987, Profiles of "Square Pegs", 1987. Office: PERSEREC 99 Pacific St Bldg 455 Suite E Monterey CA 93940-2481

NIEDERAUER, GEORGE FREDERICK, computer software engineer, diversified engineering company executive; b. Long Beach, Calif., Nov. 24, 1942; s. George Wilson and Bernita Belle (Rombough) N.; m. Rose Marie Ufen, Aug. 18, 1963; children: Mark Quinn, George Michael. BS in Math., S.D. Sch. Mines and Tech., 1964, BS in Nuclear Engring., 1966; PhD in Nuclear Engring., Iowa State U., 1967. Sr. scientist Lewis Research Ctr., NASA, Cleve., 1968-73; prin. scientist Aerojet Nuclear Co., Idaho Falls, Idaho, 1973-74; prin. scientist Energy Inc., Idaho Falls, 1974-79, dir. analysis and software, 1979-81, v.p. software and cons. group, 1981—; cons. Nuclear Regulatory Commn., Washington, 1973-74; mem. engring. adv. bd. U. Idaho, Moscow, 1985—. Contbr. articles to profl. jours.; developer computer software programs. Chmn. bd. edn. Willowtree Sch., Idaho Falls, 1975-78. Served to capt. C.E., U.S. Army, 1968-70. Mem. Am. Nuclear Soc., Am. Mgmt. Assn., Am. Youth Soccer Orgn. (local club coach, 1978-82). Lodge: Lions. Avocations: flying, woodworking. Home: 3785 Brookfield Ln Idaho Falls ID 83401 Office: Energy Inc One Energy Dr Idaho Falls ID 83401

NIEDERBERGER, MAURICE GUSTAVE, banker; b. Ely, Nev., July 7, 1926; s. Gustave Ernest and Mary Grace (Delosio) N.; m. Phyllis Nevada Alger, July 14, 1946; 1 child, Randy James. Assoc. Applied Sci., Western Nev. Community Coll., 1977; student banking, U. Wis., 1977-80; student auditing U. Notre Dame, 1980. Mgr. Nev. Bank of Commerce, Reno, 1957-66; v.p., mgr. Pioneer Citizens Bank of Nev., Reno, 1966-70, v.p. real estate, 1970-73, v.p., auditor, 1974—. Mem. Am. Inst. Banking, Am. Legion. Republican. Roman Catholic. Office: Pioneer Citizens Bank of Nev 10 State St Reno NV 89505

NIEDERHOFFER, ERIC CARY, bioinorganic chemist, consultant; b. Glen Oaks, N.Y., Feb. 27, 1957; s. Alfred and Lorayne Naomi (Gootenberg) N. BA in History, BS in Chemistry, U. Rochester, 1979; PhD in Inorganic Chemistry, Tex. A&M U., 1983. Postdoctoral assoc. MIT, Cambridge, Mass., 1983-85, Los Alamos (N.Mex.) Nat. Lab., 1985—; cons. MIT, Cambridge, 1985. Author: Bioinorganic Chemistry of Ni, 1986; also articles. Rochester Nat. scholar, 1975-79, Welch Postdoctoral fellow Tex. A&M U., 1979-83. Mem. Am. Chem. Soc., Phi Lambda Upsilon (Sharon Dabney award 1983). Avocations: music, cooking, volleyball, soccer, philosophy. Home: 1717 Medio Santa Fe NM 87501 Office: Los Alamos Nat Lab Inc 4 MS C345 Los Alamos NM 87545

NIEFFENEGGER, RANDOLPH CALKINS, biotechnology laboratory executive; b. Wendell, Idaho, Dec. 19, 1947; s. Daniel Jones and Doris Evelyn (Calkins) N.; m. Janice Nebeker, Mar. 20, 1970; children: Melissa Ann, Trent Randolph, Karin Sue, Spencer Randolph. BS in Biochemistry, U. Calif., Davis, 1973. Cert. med. technologist, Calif. Med. technician Woodland (Calif.) Clinic, 1973-74; clin. chemist Sacramento Clin. Lab., 1974-77; v.p. Valley Toxicology Lab., Davis, Calif., 1977-79; pres. J.R. Sci., Woodland, 1979—; bd. dirs. Porton Products, Ltd., Encino, Calif. Mem. Calif. Assn. Med. Technologists, Tissue Culture Assn., AAAS, Am. Microbiol. Soc., Nat. Filtration Soc. Republican. Mormon. Lodge: Rotary. Avocations: gold panning, hunting, fishing. Office: J R Sci PO Box 1862 1 Harter Ave Suite B Woodland CA 95695

NIEHAUS, MERLE H., agricultural educator, international agriculture consultant; b. Enid, Okla., Mar. 25, 1933; s. Roy H. and Hazel (Ferris) N.; m. Allene Rollier, Aug. 20, 1954; children: Lisa, Mark. BS, Okla. State U., 1955, MS, 1957; PhD, Purdue U., 1964. From asst. prof. to prof. agr. Ohio Agrl. Research and Devel. Ctr., Wooster, 1964-75, assoc. chmn. dept. agr., 1975-78; head dept. agr. N.Mex. State U., Las Cruces, 1978-83, dir. agrl. exptl. sta., 1983-84; dean coll. agrl. sci. Colo. State U., Ft. Collins, 1984—; cons. Food and Agrl. Orgn./United Nations, Rome, 1982. Contbr. articles to profl. jours. Mem. sch. bd. City of Wooster, 1976-77. Mem. AAAS, Agronomy Soc. Am., Crop Sci. Soc. Am. Office: Colo State U Coll Agriculture Fort Collins CO 80523

NIELSEN, BOJE TURIN, landscape architect; b. Copenhagen, Oct. 9, 1944; came to U.S., 1946; d. Poul and Grete Turin; m. Carol Nielsen, 1981; 1 child, Kelsey. AS, Hudson Valley Community Coll., 1964; BS, U. Mass., 1975, M Landscape Architecture, 1978. Engr. Vappi & Co., Cambridge, Mass., 1965-68; interior designer Scandinavia House, Manchester, Vt., 1968-74; landscape architect Rio Grande Nat. Forest, Monte Vista, Colo., 1977, Tonto Nat. Forest, Phoenix, 1978-80, Deerlodge Nat. Forest, Butte, Mont., 1980—. Prin. works include Sheepshead Camp for Handicapped, 1982 (several awards). Recipient Green Leaf award Internat. Arborculture Soc., 1983. Mem. Am. Soc. Landscape Architects (chpt. bd. dirs. 1982—), Vintage D'Fenders (sec. 1985—), Butte C. of C. (com. chmn. 1982-84, cons. 1982, Arborculture Soc. award 1983). Lodge: Masons. Avocations: drawing, photography, skiing, arboriculture, gardening. Home: 1102 Waukesha Box 107 Butte MT 59703-0107 Office: Deerlodge Nat Forest 400 Main St Box 400 Butte MT 59073-0400

NIELSEN, DAVID CHRISTOPHER, research agronomist; b. Ft. Dodge, Iowa, May 9, 1955; s. Lawrence Marius and Mary Verna (Gleim) N.; m. Bonnie Ann Jones, Nov. 19, 1983; children: Amy, Gordon. BS, Iowa State U., 1977, MS, 1979; PhD, U. Nebr., 1983. Research technologist U. Nebr., Lincoln, 1980-83; research agronomist Agrl. Research Service USDA, Akron, Colo., 1983—. Contbr. articles to profl. jours. Research grantee BASF Wyandette Corp. 1984, Standard Oil Co. Ohio 1985. Mem. Am. Soc. Agronomy, Crop Sci. Soc. Am., Sigma Xi (student travel grantee 1981), Phi Kappa Phi, Gamma Sigma Delta. Republican. Morman. Office: USDA Agrl Research Service Cen Great Plains Research Station PO Box K Akron CO 80720

NIELSEN, DONALD RODNEY, soil and water science educator; b. Phoenix, Oct. 10, 1931; s. Irven Roy and Irma Evelyn (Chase) N.; m. Joanne Joyce Locke, Sept. 26, 1953; children: Cynthia, Pamela, Barbara, Wayne, David. BS, U. Ariz., 1953, MS, 1954; PhD, Iowa State U., 1958; DSc (hon.), Ghent (Belgium) State U., 1986. Asst. prof. soil and water sci. U. Calif., Davis, 1958-63, assoc. prof., 1963-68, prof., 1968, dir. Kearney Found. of Soil Sci., 1970-75, assoc. dean, 1970-80, dir. Food Protection and Toxicology Ctr., 1974-75, chmn. dept. land, air and water resources, 1975-77, prof., 1968—, exec. assoc. dean Coll. Agrl. Environ. Scis., 1986—; cons. corps. and govtl. agys. Editor Nitrogen in the Environment; co-editor Water Resources Research, 1985—; mem. editorial bd. Irrigation Sci., Jour. Soil Sci., Soil Sci., Outlook In Agrl., Soil and Tillage Research, contbr. articles to profl. jours. NSF fellow, 1965-66. Fellow Am. Geophys. Union, Soil Sci. Soc. Am. (pres. 1983-84), Am. Soc. Agronomy; mem. Sigma Xi, Phi Kappa Phi, Gamma Sigma Delta, Phi Lambda Upsilon, Alpha Zeta. Democrat. Home: 1004 Pine Ln Davis CA 95616 Office: U Calif LAWR-Veihmeyer Hall Davis CA 95616

NIELSEN, JAMES WILEY, state senator; b. Fresno, Calif., July 31, 1944; s. Woodrow E. and Geraldine P. (Hudson) N.; B.S. in Agribus., Fresno State Coll.; m. Brenda Wahl, July 30, 1983; children—Prima, Brandi, Kelly, Chris. Farm mgr.; farmer; mem. Calif. Senate, now minority leader; involved in library funding, edn. and welfare reform, econ. devel., rural aid, coll. support throughout Calif., 1983—. Chmn. Sacramento Valley Water Task Force. Named Agrl. Spokesman of Year, 1976; Legislator of Yr., Calif. Rifle and Pistol Assn., 1982, Calif. Bus. Edn. Assn., 1982, Calif. Ind. Producers Assn., 1983; Leadership Program fellow, 1975-76. Mem. Council State Legislators, Farm Bur., Calif. Welfare Fraud Investigators Assn. (life mem.), Native Sons Golden West. Republican. Lutheran. Home: 4990 Country Club Dr Rohnert Park CA 94928 Office: State Capitol Sacramento CA 95814

NIELSEN, JORGEN SVEND, import company executive; b. Aarhus, Denmark, Aug. 10, 1932; came to U.S., 1977; s. Svend Aage and Henny (Pedersen) N.; m. Brenda de Silva, Feb. 20, 1960; children: Jens, Paul. Diploma, Sch. Commerce, Copenhagen, 1953. Clk. East Asiatic Co., Copenhagen, 1950-55; asst. dept. mgr. East Asiatic Co., Kuala Lumpur, Malaysia, 1955-60; dept. mgr. East Asiatic Co., Copenhagen, 1966-77, R.T. Briscoe, Accra, Ghana, 1960-66; v.p. Eskofot Am. Inc., San Carlos, Calif., 1977-81, Douglas Homs Corp., Belmont, Calif., 1981—. Served as sgt. Danish Army, 1953-55. Lodge: Rotary (local sec. 1985—). Home: 2541 Poppy Dr Burlingame CA 94010 Office: Douglas Homs Corp 1538 Industrial Way Belmont CA 94002

NIELSEN, MARTIN SENIUS, energy cons.; b. Cody, Wyo., Nov. 29, 1940; s. Senius and Mary Elizabeth (Jensen) N.; student N.W. Community Coll., 1961-62; B.S., U. Wyo., 1965; m. Judy Lee Deardorff, Dec. 27, 1975; children—Tim, Greg, Chris, Marette. Owner, mgr. N & P Supply, Cody, Wyo., 1962-67; fish culturist Wyo. Game and Fish, 1965-70; owner, operator ranch, farm, Cody, 1970—; pres. Al-Agri Renewable Resources, Inc., Cody, 1980—; bd. dirs. Shoshone River Power. Mem. North Big Horn Basin Malt Barley Growers Assn. (co-founder), Wyo. Gasohol Assn., Nat. Cattlemen's Assn., Wyo. Stockgrowers Assn., Am. Quarter Horse Assn., U. Wyo. Alumni Assn. Republican. Presbyterian. Clubs: Lions, Elks. Home: PO Box 1613 Cody WY 82414 Office: PO Box 1085 Cody WY 82414

NIELSEN, RICHARD A. (RICK), broadcasting actor; b. Los Angeles, Jan. 26, 1952; s. Frederick Andrew and Sally Ann (Anderson) N. MusB, U. So. Calif., 1974. Broadcaster Sta. KFAC, Los Angeles, 1974-85; freelance announcer and actor 1985—. Author: Magical Cats of the Hil-giledh; writer numerous poems. Mem. AFTRA, AAAS, The Planetary Soc. Democrat. Avocations: astrophysics, particle physics. Home and Office: 6300 Lankershim Blvd #101 North Hollywood CA 91606

NIELSEN, STUART DEE, chemist; b. Green River, Wyo., Oct. 26, 1932; s. Julian Woodruff and Reva May (Stewart) N.; m. Lila Ellen Larett, June 10, 1954; children: Laura May, Martha Ellen, Karl Allen, Jennifer Marie, Isabelle Anne. BS, U. Wyo., 1954; PhD, U. Wash., 1962. Research chemist Rohm & Haas Co., Phila., 1962-66; research scientist Gen. Tire & Rubber Co., Akron, Ohio, 1966-78; chemist Los Alamos (N.Mex.) Nat. Lab., 1978—. Patentee in field. Scoutmaster Boy Scouts Am., Akron, 1970-78. Served with U.S. Army, 1954-56. Allied Chem. Co. fellow, 1960. Mem. Am. Chem. Soc., Soc. Applied Spectroscopy, Am. Indsl. Hygiene Assn., Sigma Xi. Mormon. Avocations: music, photography. Home: 114 Sherwood Blvd Los Alamos NM 87544 Office: Los Alamos Nat Lab Group HSE-9 MS K484 Los Alamos NM 87545

NIELSON, ELDON DENZEL, biochemist, consultant; b. Salt Lake City, Dec. 4, 1920; s. Hiram D. and Rachel Augusta (Ek) N.; m. Geraldine Rasmussen, Dec. 13, 1942; children: Dennis L., Karen G. Bridges, Karla S. AB in Chemistry, U. Utah, 1946; PhD in Biochemistry, U. Ill., 1948. Instr. biochemistry U. So. Calif., Los Angeles, 1948-49; research biochemist The Upjohn Co., Kalamazoo, 1949-56; head biochem. dept. Armour Pharm. Co., Kankakee, Ill., 1956-58, Sterling-Winthrop Research Inst., Rensselaer, N.Y., 1958-61; mgr. biologic research R.J. Reynolds Industry, Winston-Salem, N.C., 1961-70; dir. licensing Bristol-Myers and Co., Evansville, Ind., 1970-83; pres. PharmaSci Internat., Sandy, Utah, 1983—. Mem. exec. com. Citizens United Reform Effort, Albany, N.Y., 1961-62; Rep. chmn. Forsyth County, Winston-Salem, 1963-66; mem. Rep. exec. com., N.C., 1964-66; alternate del. at large Rep. Nat. Conv., San Francisco, 1964; candidate for Congress Rep. primary election, 5th dist., N.C., 1968. Mem. AAAS, Am. Chem. Soc., Licensing Execs. Soc. Avocations: music, travel. Home and Office: 11790 S Nicklaus Rd Sandy UT 84092

NIELSON, HARRIET RAE, speech-language pathologist; b. Milford, Utah, June 8, 1940; d. Harold and Loretta (Murdock) Cline; m. James Russell Nielson, Aug. 18, 1962; children: Eric Cline, Jay Russell, Colleen Rae. BS, U. Utah, 1962; MA, DePaul U., 1964; PhD, U. Utah, 1983. Speech pathologist Murray (Utah) Sch. Dist., 1970-76; supr. speech pathology U. Utah, Salt Lake City, 1980-83, adj. faculty, 1983-85, adj. asst. prof., 1983—; dir. advanced tech. clinic. Utah Easter Seal Soc., Salt Lake City, 1986—; licensure bd. dirs. State Dept. Occupational and Profl. Licensure, Utah, 1977-85. Author, creator computer programs. Mem. Am. Speech-Lang.-Hearing Assn. (cert., Ethical Practices com. 1985—, Continuing Edn. award, 1984, 86), Utah Speech and Hearing Assn (pres. 1986-87, 1st pres. elect 1985-86, 2d pres. Profl. Matters Com. 1984-85). Avocations: skiing, hiking, sewing, running. Home: 2759 Commonwealth Ave Salt Lake City UT 84109 Office: Utah Easter Seal Soc 331 S Rio Grand St Salt Lake City UT 84101

NIELSON, HOWARD CURTIS, congressman, statistics educator; b. Richfield, Utah, Sept. 12, 1924; s. Herman Taylor and Zula May (Curtis) N.; m. Julia Adams, June 18, 1948; children: Noreen (Mrs. Stephen Astin), Elaine (Mrs. Stanley Taylor), John, Mary Lee (Mrs. Paul Jackson), James, Jean (Mrs. Clay Cundick), Howard Curtis. B.S. in Math, U. Utah, 1947; M.S. in Math, U. Oreg., 1949; M.B.A., Stanford U., 1956, Ph.D. in Bus. Adminstrn. and Statistics, 1958. Statistician C & H Sugar Refining Corp., 1949-51; research economist and statistician Stanford Research Inst., 1951-57; mem. faculty Brigham Young U., Provo, Utah, 1957-82; prof. statistics Brigham Young U., 1961-82, chmn. dept., 1960-63; dir. Center for Bus. and Econ. Research, 1971-72; sr. statistician, acting field mgr. C-E-I-R, Inc., 1963-64, mgr., cons., 1964-65; prin. scientist GCA Corp., 1965-67; dir. econ. research Eyring Research Inst., 1974-75; asso. commr. higher edn. State of Utah, 1976-79; mem. 98th, 99th and 100th Congresses from 3d dist. Utah; econ. adviser Kingdom of Jordan, Ford Found., 1970-71; prof. Am. U., Beirut, 1970; adj. prof. U. Utah, 1972-76. Author: The Efficiency of Certain Truncated Order Statistics in Estimating the Mean of Various Distributions, 1949, Population Trends in the United States Through 1975, 1955, The Hows and Whys of Statistics, 1963, Experimental Designs Used in industry, 1965, Membership Growth of the Church of Jesus Christ of Latter Day Saints, 1957, 67, 71, 75, 78, Evaluation of the Seven Year Plan for Economic Development in Jordan, 1971, Economic Analysis of Fiji, Tonga, Western and Am. Samoa, 1972; co-author: The Newsprint Situation in the Western Region of North America, 1952, America's Demand for Wood, 1954, also reports. Mem. Utah Gov.'s Econ. Research Adv. Council, 1967-72; Dir. bur. ch. studies Ch. of Jesus Christ of Latter-day Saints, 1958-63; research dir. Utah Republican Party, 1967-68; mem. Utah Ho. Reps., 1967-75, majority leader, 1969-71, speaker, 1973-75, mem. legis. budget-audit com., 1967-73, chmn., 1971-73, chmn. legis. council, 1973-75; mem. Utah Council Sci. and Tech., 1974-76; chmn. Utah County Rep. Com., 1979-81. Mem. Am. Statis. Assn. (pres. Utah 1964-65, nat. council 1967-70), Sci. Research Soc. Am., Order of Artus, Phi Beta Kappa, Sigma Xi, Pi Mu Epsilon, Sigma Pi Sigma, Phi Kappa Phi. Office: 1229 Longworth Washington DC 20515

NIELSON, JONATHAN MACAULEY, historian; b. Ann Arbor, Mich., Apr. 25, 1946; s. Marvin Lowell Bodeen and Estelle Macauley; m. Joyce Johnson, Apr. 1, 1966 (div. June 1968); 1 child, Jeff Macauley; m. Susan McMahon, Aug. 21, 1973; 1 child, Evan Andrew. BA, U. Calif., Irvine, 1969; MA, U. Alaska, 1974; PhD, U. Calif., Santa Barbara, 1976. Instr. history U. Md., Wurtzburg, Fed. Republic Germany, 1976; instr. history U. Alaska, Fairbanks, 1977-79, asst. prof., 1983—; instr. history Tanana Valley Community Coll., Fairbanks, 1978-80, 83-84; teaching asst. in history U. Calif., Santa Barbara, 1981-83; historian, cons. North Slope Borough, Barrow, Alaska, 1977-80; historian Bur. Land Mgmt., Fairbanks, 1978; prin., historian Hist. Research and Cons., Fairbanks, 1978-84; lectr., 1983—; curriculum specialist Alaska Permanent Fund Corp., 1986. Author: Beaufort Sea Study, 1977, Focus on Interior History, 1980, Alaska's Military Heritage, 1980, American Historians at the Versailles Peace Conference 1919, 1987; hist. cons. Alaska at War, Documentary, 1986; contbr. articles to profl. jours. Disting. scholar U. Calif., Santa Barbara, 1982, 83; Alaska Humanities Forum grantee, 1979; Regents fellow U. Calif., Santa Barbara, 1984; Barmath Dissertation award, 1986. Mem. Alaska Hist. Soc., Tanoma Yukon Hist. Soc., Orgn. Am. Historians, Soc. Historians Am. Fgn. Relations, Am. Hist. Assn., Am. Assn. Univ. Profs., Phi Alpha Theta. Democrat. Episcopalian. Home: PO Box 80443 College AK 99708 Office: U Alaska Dept of History Fairbanks AK 99701

NIELSON, LESLIE LUTHER, chemical company sales representative; b. Yankton, S.D., Dec. 7, 1958; s. Luther Olaf and Joan (Madison) N. BS, S.D. State U., 1982. Salesman Moorman Mfg., Grand Island, Nebr., 1982-84; sales rep. Chevron Chem. Co., Sioux Falls, S.D., 1984—; industry rep. S.D. No-Till Assn., Ipswich, 1985—. Recipient Personal Contribution award Soil Conservation Service, 1986. Democrat. Lutheran. Avocations: competitive rifle shooting, hunting, fishing, skiing, golf. Home: 2912 S Louise Apt 207 Sioux Falls SD 57106 Office: Chevron Chem Co PO Box 5458 Fresno CA 93755

NIELSON, MARK GILBERT, management educator, consultant; b. Racine, Wis., Feb. 13, 1950; s. Carl Gilbert and Irene Louise (Mantle) N.; m. Norma Lee, Nov. 20, 1982; 1 child, Eric Gordon. BA, Calif. Poly. State U., San Luis Obispo; BS, Calif. State U., San Diego; postgrad., U. So. Calif. Advt. mgr. Carrows Restaurants, Santa Barbara, Calif., 1974-76; prin. Nielson, Alexander and Barron, Santa Barbara, 1976-79; mktg. mgr. U. So. Calif., Los Angeles, 1981-85; adj. prof. Oreg. State U., Corvallis, 1985—, cons., 1985—; cons. Calif. Preferred Providers Inc., Santa Barbara, 1985, Pacific Crest Software, Corvallis, 1985-86. Served to lt. (j.g.) USN, 1969-72, Vietnam. Fellow Acad. Mktg. Sci.; mem. Am. Mktg. Assn. (cert.). Democrat. Avocations: sailing, skiing. Office: Oreg State U Bexell Hall 325 Corvallis OR 97331

NIEM, ALAN RANDOLPH, geology professor; b. N.Y.C., Mar. 7, 1944; s. Alan A. and Mary Niem; m. Wendy Adams, June 10, 1967. Student, Leeds (Eng.) U., 1964-65; BS in Geology, Antioch Coll., 1966; MS in Geology, U. Wis., 1968, PhD in Geology, 1971. Registered geologist, Oreg. Grad. research and teaching asst. U. Wis., Madison, 1966-70; asst. prof. geology Oreg. State U., Corvallis, 1970-76, assoc. prof., 1976—; vis. prof. Colo. Coll., Colorado Springs, 1970, 73; geologist George H. Otto Cons. Geologist, Chgo., 1966, U.S. Geol. Survey, Menlo Park, Calif., 1972-85; sedimentologist

U.N. Sponsored Com. for Coordination of Joint Prospecting for Mineral Resources in South Pacific Offshore Areas Cruise, Solomon Islands, 1984, Deep Sea Drilling Project, La Jolla, Calif., 1978. Mem. Geol. Soc. Am., Am. Assn. Petroleum Geologists, Soc. Econ. Paleontologists and Mineralogists, N.W. Petroleum Assn., Oreg. Acad. Sci. Home: 1550 NW Circle Blvd Corvallis OR 97330 Office: Oreg State U Dept Geology Corvallis OR 97331-5506

NIEMAN, DAVID ARNOLD, psychologist; b. Gulfport, Miss., Apr. 1, 1948; s. Arlo DeVere and Emma Jeanette (Tullos) N.; m. Veronique Michelle Ramirez, Oct. 12, 1970; 1 child, David Scott. BA in Psychology, Miss. Coll., 1970; MSW, Tulane U., 1971; PhD in Psychology, Internat. U., 1982. Lic. psychologist. Psychiat. social worker M.I. Pickens Hosp., Greenville, S.C., 1972-73; psychiat. social worker Meml. Hosp. Med. Ctr., Long Beach, Calif., 1974-75, dir. dept. clin. social work, 1975-80; dir. social services Greenville Gen. Hosp., 1973-74; pvt. practice psychology Santa Ana, Calif., 1980—; radio guest Sta. KBRT, Sta. KWVE-FM, KPRZ-AM; TV show guest Mid Morning, Los Angeles, Off Hand, Joy, 1984-86. Concept developer (film) A Chain to be Broken, 1978. Co-founder, past chmn. Long Beach Area Child Trauma Council, Med. Social Workers Orgn.; co-founder, past pres. Calif. Consortium Child Abuse Councils; past mem. Ops. Com. Los Angeles County Inter-Agy. Child Abuse and Neglect Council. Recipient Recognition award Soc. Hosp. Social Work Dirs., So. Calif. chpt., 1979, Outstanding Services to Youth award Long Beach Coordinating Council, 1979, Leadership award Los Angeles County Bd. Suprs., 1985. Mem. Am. Psychol. Assn., Am. Orthopsychiatric Assn., Am. Group Psychotherapy Assn., Los Angeles Group Psychotherapy Assn., Calif. State Psychol. Assn., Orange County Psychol. Assn., So. Calif. Soc. Hosp. Social Work Dirs. (past pres.). Office: The Nieman Ctrs 3620 S Bristol #203 Santa Ana CA 92704

NIEMEYER, DANIEL CHARLES, university media director, consultant; b. Breese, Ill., Sept. 29, 1939; s. Charles D. and Agnes (Schmitz) N.; m. Rita Ann Berndsen, Nov. 23, 1967; children: Jerry C., Robert D. BS in Journalism, U. Ill., 1961; MA in Communication, Temple U., 1963; PhD in Edn., U. Colo., 1985. TV dir. Temple U., Phila., 1961-63, Sta. WSIU-TV, Carbondale, Ill., 1963-66; TV dir. U. Colo. TV, Boulder, 1966-75, prodn. mgr., 1975-85; media dir. U. Colo., Boulder, 1985—; cons. Nat. Audio Visual Assn., Bloominton, Ind., 1978, Boise Cascade, Louisville, Colo., 1979, N. Cen. Assn., Boulder, 1983, Adams County Schs., Westminster, Colo., 1986. Author: TV Production Workbook, 1980; creator (video tapes) Basic TV Prodn., 1984. Served with U.S. Army, 1960-61. Mem. Nat. Inst. TV Council (v.p. 1985-86, pres. 1986—), Mountain Plains Media Leadership, Nat. Assn. Edn. Communication and Tech. Avocations: railroad travel, watersports. Home: 1390 Oak Ct Boulder CO 80302 Office: U Colo Media Ctr Campus Box 379 Boulder CO 80309-0379

NIEMI, KAROL TONI, interior design; b. Longview, Wash., Feb. 16, 1949; d. Albert Howard and Toini Kathryn (Vahala) N.; m. Dennis Eugene Batke, Oct. 19, 1973. B in Interior Architecture, U. Oreg., 1971. Sr. designer Zimmer, Gunsul, Frasca Architects, Portland, Oreg., 1971-76, Yakeley Assocs., Architects, Cambridge, Eng., 1977-78; owner, prin. Karol Niemi Assoc. Interior Planning and Design, Portland, 1978—. Prin. works include Providence Med. Ctr., Pacific NW Bell Lincoln Bldg., VNA Corp. Hdqrs., Wanke Cascade Hdqrs., St. Vincent's Med. Ctr.; contbr. articles to profl. jours. Bd. dirs. Pacific Ballet Theatre, Portland, Oreg., 1984-85; bd. dirs. Oreg. Sch. Design, Portland, 1984-87; mem. design adv. bd. Wash. State U., bd. visitors U. Oreg. Recipient Am. Cermaic Tile Inst. award, 1982. Mem. Inst. Bus. Designers (corp. mem.), Found. for Interior Design Edn. Research (mem. nat. bd. vis. 1985-88). Avocation: traveling. Home: 1122 NW Summit Portland OR 97210 Office: Karol Niemi Assocs 1020 SW Taylor Suite 880 Portland OR 97205

NIERENBERG, WILLIAM AARON, oceanography educator; b. N.Y.C., Feb. 13, 1919; s. Joseph and Minnie (Drucker) N.; m. Edith Meyerson, Nov. 21, 1941; children—Victoria Jean (Mrs. Tschinkel), Nicolas Clarke Eugene. Aaron Naumberg scholar, U. Paris, 1937-38; B.S., CCNY, 1939; M.A., Columbia U., 1942, Ph.D. (NRC predoctoral fellow), 1947. Tutor CCNY, 1939-42; sect. leader Manhattan Project, 1942-45; instr. physics Columbia U., 1946-48; asst. prof. physics U. Mich., 1948-50; assoc. prof. physics U. Calif. at Berkeley, 1950-53, prof., 1954-65; dir. Scripps Instn. Oceanography, 1965-86, dir. emeritus, 1986—; vice chancellor for marine scis. U. Calif. at San Diego, 1969-86; dir. Hudson Labs., Columbia, 1953-54; assoc. prof. U. Paris, 1960-62; asst. sec. gen. NATO for sci. affairs, 1960-62; spl. cons. Exec. Office Pres., 1958-60; sr. cons. White House Office Sci. and Tech. Policy, 1976-78. Contbr. papers to profl. jours. E.O. Lawrence lectr. Nat. Acad. Sci., 1958, Miller Found. fellow, 1957-59, Sloan Found. fellow, 1958, Fulbright fellow, 1960-61; mem. U.S. Nat. Commn. UNESCO, 1964-68, Calif. Adv. Com. on Marine and Coastal Resources, 1967-71; adviser-at-large U.S. Dept. State, 1968—; mem. Nat. Sci. Bd., 1972-78, 82—; mem. Nat. Adv. Com. on Oceans and Atmosphere, 1971-77, chmn., 1971-75; mem. sci. and tech. adv. council Calif. Assembly; mem. adv. council NASA, 1978-83, chmn. adv. council, 1978-82; mem. council Nat. Acad. Scis., 1979—. NATO Sr. Sci. fellow, 1969; Decorated officer Nat. Order of Merit France; recipient Golden Dolphin award Assn. Artistico Letteraria Internazionale, Disting. Pub. Service medal NASA, 1982, Delmer S. Fahrney medal The Franklin Inst., 1987, Compass award Marine Tech. Soc., 1975. Fellow Am. Phys. Soc. (council, sec. Pacific Coast sect. 1955-64); mem. Am. Acad. Arts and Scis., Nat. Acad. Engring., Nat. Acad. Scis., Am. Philos. Soc., Am. Assn. Naval Architects, Navy League, Fgn. Policy Assn. (mem. nat. council), Sigma Xi (pres. 1981—, Proctor prize, 1977). Club: Cosmos. Home: PO Box 8949 La Jolla CA 92038-8949 Office: Scripps Instn Oceanography U Calif A-021 La Jolla CA 92093

NIES, ALAN SHEFFER, pharmacology educator; b. Orange, Calif., Sept. 30, 1937; s. Arthur J. and Mary Dora (Sheffer) N.; m. Sally K. Goode; children: Lorrie Kathyrn, Craig Alan. BS, Stanford U., 1959; MD, Harvard Med. Sch., 1963. Intern King County Hosp., Seattle, 1963-64; resident U. Wash. Hosp., Seattle, 1964-66; fellow in clin. pharmacology Cardiovascular Research Inst. U. Calif., San Francisco, 1966-68; chief. clin. pharmacology Walter Reed Army Inst. Research, Washington, 1968-70; asst. prof. medicine and pharmacology Vanderbilt U. Sch. Medicine, Nashville, 1970-72, assoc. prof. medicine and pharmacology, 1972-76, prof. medicine and pharmacology, 1976-77; prof. medicine and pharmacology, head div. clin. pharmacology U. Colo., Denver, 1977—. Contbr. articles to numerous profl. jours. Served to major U.S. Army, 1968-70. Recipient Clin. Pharmacology award Burroughs Wellcome Fund, 1975. Mem. ACP, Am. Soc. Clin. Investigation, Assn. Am. Physicians, Am. Soc. Pharmacology and Exptl. Therapeutics, Western Assn. Physicians (sec., treas. 1983-86), Am. Soc. Clin. Pharmacology and Therapeutics (Rawls-Palmer Progress in Medicine award 1985). Avocations: photography. Home: 6146 S Fulton St Englewood CO 80111 Office: Univ of Colo Health Scis Ctr Sch of Medicine Dept of Medicine Denver CO 80262

NIETO, JUAN MANUEL, physician; b. Alpine, Tex., Sept. 24, 1949; s. Edmundo Miguel and Socorro (Herrera) N.; BS, U. Notre Dame, 1970; MD, U. Colo., 1974; children: Ana Raquel, Cristina Marie. Intern, Los Angeles County, U. So. Calif. Med. Ctr., 1974-75; physician Community Health Found., Los Angeles, 1975-77, Emergency Dept. Physicians Med. Group, Marina Del Ray, Calif., 1977-78; resident in emergency medicine Denver Gen.-St. Anthony Hosp. Systems, 1978-80; mem. staff North Colo. Med. Center, Greeley, Colo., 1980-83; emergency physician, med. dir. emergency dept. Brackenridge Hosp., Austin, Tex., 1984-85, physician, 1983—; mem. planning com. Starflight Helicopter Air Transport, 1985; instr. advanced cardiac life support, 1977; bd. dirs. Nat. Chicano Health Orgn., 1971-74; adv. E. Los Angeles Hypertension Screening Program, 1978; med. adv. Weld County Ambulance Service, 1980-83; med. dir. Air Life, 1980-83. del. Colo. Med. Soc., 1983. Fellow Am. Coll. Emergency Physicians; mem. Am. Coll. Emergency Physicians, Am. Public Health Assn., Tex. Med. Assn., Travis County Med. Soc., Acad. Polit. Sci.

NIGHTINGALE, RICHARD EDWIN, chemical company research and development executive; b. Walla Walla, Wash., June 3, 1926; s. Edwin Simnitt and Helen Carpenter (Coston) N.; m. Joyce Helen Neel, June 11, 1944; children: Katherine, Susan, Laura. BA in Chemistry, Whitman Coll., 1949; PhD in Phys. Chemistry, Wash. State U., 1953. Post-doctoral fellow U. Minn., Mpls., 1952-54; scientist Gen. Elec. Co., Richland, Wash., 1954-59, mgr. materials research, 1959-64; mgr. metallurgy and ceramics Battelle Northwest, Richland, 1965-69, mgr. chem. technology, 1969-84, program mgr., 1984—; instr. phys. chemistry Joint Ctr. for Grad. Study, Richland, 1959-63; del. Geneva Conf. Peaceful Uses of Atomic Energy, 1958, 62; mem., leader numerous sci. delegations to Europe, 1957-85. Author, editor: Nuclear Graphite, 1962; contbr. articles on materials and chemistry to profl. jours. Bd. dirs. Benton-Franklin Chpt. ARC, Kennewick, Wash., 1970-75. Served with U.S. Army air corps, 1944-45. Fellow Am. Nuclear Soc. (cert. of merit 1968); mem. Am. Carbon Soc. (exec. com. 1964-68), Am. Chem. Soc., Sigma Xi, Phi Beta Kappa, Phi Lambda Upsilon. Republican. Methodist. Avocations: fishing, computers. Home: 2711 Canal Dr Kennewick WA 99336 Office: Battelle Northwest PO Box 999 Richland WA 99352

NIGL, ALFRED JAMES, psychologist, cons., researcher, author; b. Oshkosh, Wis., July 30, 1949; s. Alfred Joseph and Marion Jane (Roberts) N.; m. Marie E. Mauritz, Mar. 2, 1968; m. Terri S. Abbott, Feb. 19, 1982; children: William Scott, Geoffrey Alan, Brandon Abbott. BA in Psychology, U. Wis., 1971; MA in Clin. Psychology, U. Cin., 1973, PhD in Clin. Psychology, 1975. Lic. psychologist, Wis., Calif. Clin. intern or grad. trainee Cin. Gen. Hosp., 1971, Rollman Psychiat. Clinic, Cin., 1971, U. Cin. Univ. Counseling Ctr., 1971, 73, U. Cin. Med. Ctr. Cen. Psychiat. Clinic, 1972, Cin. Ctr. Developmental Disorders, 1973-75, U. Cin. Crises Intervention Clinic, 1973-75, U. Cin. mental health program, 1974-75; acting dir. tng. and research, mental health program U. Cin. Student Health Program, 1974-75; cons. staff psychologist Psychol. and Mgmt. Cons. Services, S.C., Milw., 1975-76; pres. Milw. Devel. Ctr., 1975-78; chief psychologist Jackson Psychiat. Ctr., Milw., 1978-80; dir. child and adolescent services Oxnard (Calif.) Mental Health Ctr., 1980-81; cons., dir. biofeedback Kaiser-Permanente Healthwise, 1982-83; dir. rehab. psychology Grossmont Dist. Hosp., 1983-85; pvt. practice psychology, 1985—; cons. Calif. Regional Ctrs. for Developmentally Disabled; staff psychologist Luth. Hosp. Milw., 1978-70, dept. psychiatry Waukesha Meml. Hosp., 1978-80; dir. biofeedback, family practice residency program Waukesha Meml. Hosp. affiliated with Med. Coll. Wis., 1980; adj. clin. prof. Grad. Sch. Pub. Health, San Diego State U., 1983—; pres. Biofeedback Soc. Wis., 1979-80. Bd. dirs. Big Bros./Big Sisters, Ventura County, Calif., 1981-82, Ventura County Rape Crisis Ctr., 1982. U. Cin. Gradn. sch. Council research grantee, 1974; Am. Psychol. Assn. Overseas travel grantee, 1982. Mem. Am. Acad. Behavioral Medicine, AAAS, Am. Psychol. Assn., N.Y. Acad. Scis., Acad. Psychosomatic Medicine, Biofeedback Soc. Am. (rep. to Council State Biofeedback Socs. 1980), Ventura County Psychol. Assn. (dir. 1982-83). Author: (with Fischer-Williams and Sovine) A Textbook of Biological Feedback, 1981, The Development of Children's Understanding of Spatial Relations, vol. 62 of European Univ. Studies-Psychology, 1981, Biofeedback and Behavioral Strategies in Pain Treatment, 1984; research, publs. in field. Office: 1662 E Main St Suite 216 El Cajon CA 92021

NIKAS, ARISTIDES JAMES, III, geologist; b. San Francisco, Dec. 10, 1956; s. A. James and Theresa Dorothy (Steilberg) N. B.A., San Francisco State U., 1979; postgrad. Golden Gate U., 1982—. Instr. Calif. Acad. Scis., San Francisco, 1972-73; lab. technician Brit. Petroleum, San Francisco, 1974-80; geologist Standard Oil of Ohio, San Francisco, 1980-84; dir., pres. New World Expressions, San Rafael, Calif., 1983—, Video Properties King County, Inc., Bellevue, Wash., 1984-85; pres. GeoMarketing, San Francisco, 1984—; venture analyst Internat. Tech. Consortium Corp., San Jose, Calif.; fin. cons., San Francisco. Mem. Am. Assn. Petroleum Geologists, Soc. Econ. Paleontologists and Mineralogists, Coast Geol. Soc., No. Calif. Geol. Soc. Republican. Greek Orthodox.

NIKU, SALAR DAVID, consulting engineer; b. Tehran, Iran, Nov. 20, 1947; came to U.S., 1974; s. Saleh S. and Sara Niku; m. Hannah Souferian, July 4, 1984. BS, MS, Polytech. U., Tehran, 1969; MS, Stanford U., 1975, Degree Engr., 1976; PhD, U. Calif., Davis, 1979. Registered profl. engr., Calif. Research asst. Stanford (Calif.) U., 1975-76; research engr. U. Calif., Davis, 1976-79; sr. engr. Brown & Caldwell, Pasadena, Calif., 1979-84; supervising engr. BCEI, Santa Monica, Calif., 1984-86, Honeywell Tetra Tech. Inc., 1986—; instr. U. So. Calif., Los Angeles, 1985—. Author books; contbr. articles to profl. jours. Bd. dirs. Iranian-Jewish Fedn., Los Angeles, 1984—. Mem. ASCE, Water Pollution Control Fedn., Calif. Water Pollution Control Assn. Lodge: Toastmasters (pres., v.p. 1982-83). Avocations: orgn. devel., books, music. Home and Office: 5344 Zelzah Ave Encino CA 91316

NILSSON, NILS JOHN, computer science educator, researcher; b. Saginaw, Mich., Feb. 6, 1933; s. Walter A. and Pauline (Glerum) N.; m. Karen Braucht, July 19, 1958; children: Kristen, Lars. MS, Stanford U., 1956, PhD, 1958. Sr. scientist SRI, Menlo Park, Calif., 1961-84; chmn. computer sci. dept. Stanford U., Palo Alto, Calif., 1985—; founder Tioga Pub. Co., 1979—; bd. dirs. Morgan Kaufmann Pub. Served to lt. USAF, 1958-61. Avocations: hiking, skiing. Home: 150 Coquito Way Portola Valley CA 94025 Office: Stanford U Stanford CA 94305

NIMITZ, JONATHAN SHELLEY, chemistry educator; b. Loma Linda, Calif., May 27, 1955; s. Jack and Mildred Lucille (Donnelly) N. BS in Chemistry, UCLA, 1976; PhD in Organic Chemistry, Stanford U., 1981. Asst. prof. U. N.Mex., Albuquerque, 1982—. Contbr. articles to profl. jours. Hertz fellow, Stanford U., 1977-81. Mem. Am. Chem. Soc., Phi Beta Kappa. Taoist. Office: U N Mex Chemistry Dept Albuquerque NM 87131

NIMNI, MARCEL EPHRAIM, biochemistry educator; b. Buenos Aires, Feb. 1, 1931; came to U.S., 1955; s. Sam and Sarah Dora (Freedman) N.; m. Berta Silber, Jan. 15, 1962 (div. Jan. 1983); children: Elizabeth, Brian Sam; m. Judith Taylor, Oct. 7, 1983; children: Mark, Christina. BS in Pharmacy, U. Buenos Aires, 1954, PhD, 1960; MS, U. So. Calif., 1957. Research fellow U. So. Calif., Los Angeles, 1960-61, asst. prof. biochemistry, 1963-66, assoc. prof., 1966-72, prof., 1972—; dir. biology Don Baxter Labs., Glendale, Calif., 1962; cons. Hancock Labs., Anaheim, Calif., 1970-78, Dow Corning Wright, Memphis, 1985—, pathobiochemistry study sect. NIH, 1980-85, orthopaedics and biomechanics study sect., 1987—; dir. biochemistry research Orthopaedic Hosp., Los Angeles, 1980—. Editor: Collagen: Biochemistry, Biotechnology and Molecular Biology, 1987; (jours.) Collagen and Research Research, 1980—, Connective Tissue Research, 1973—. Research grantee NIH Arthritis Inst., 1966—, NIH Aging Inst., 1982—. Fellow AAAS; mem. Am. Inst. Nutrition, Am. Assn. Biol. Chemists, Am. Rheumatism Assn., Soc. Biomaterials (Founders award 1986). Home: 2800 Neilson Way #908 Santa Monica CA 90405 Office: Orthopaedic Hosp 2400 S Flower Los Angeles CA 90007

NING, ROBERT YEFONG, chemical development scientist; b. Shanghai, Rep. of China, Mar. 12, 1939; came to U.S., 1958; BS in Chemistry, Rochester Inst. Tech., 1963; PhD in Bioorganic Chemistry, U. Ill., 1966; MBA, Fairleigh Dickinson U., 1978. Sr. chemist Hoffman-LaRoche Inc., Nutley, N.J., 1967-72, chem. research fellow, 1972-78, group leader, devel., 1978-81, head interferon pilot plant, 1981-85; sr. investigator, head therapeutics pilot plant Hybritech Inc., San Diego, 1985—. Mem. Essex County, N.J. Dem. Com., 1969; vestry St. Peter's Episc. Ch., Essex Fells, N.J., 1979-85. Contbr. articles to profl jours.; holder of 17 patents novel drugs and processes. Mem. Am. Chem. Soc. Republican. Avocations: gardening, tennis, Christian service. Office: Hybritech Inc 9850 Distribution Ave PO Box 269006 San Diego CA 92126

NISH, ALBERT RAYMOND, JR., writing consultant, retired newspaper editor; b. San Bernardino, Calif., Mar. 16, 1922; s. Albert Raymond and Mabel Clair (Shay) N.; m. Lois Maxine Ringgenberg, June 21, 1942; children—Steven Raymond, Richard Henry, Kathleen Lorie Jenner. Student San Bernardino Valley Jr. Coll., 1939-41, U. Calif., Berkeley, 1941-42, Wash. State Coll., 1943; Am. Press Inst., 1977. Pony wire editor AP, San Francisco, 1941-42; reporter Chico Record, Calif., 1945-46, Berkeley Daily Gazette, Calif., 1946-48; valley editor Modesto Bee, Calif., 1948-60, asst. mng. editor, 1960-62, mng. editor, 1962-85. Served as fighter pilot USAAC, 1942-45, PTO. Decorated DFC. Mem. Soc. Profl. Journalists, Calif. Soc. Newspaper Editors. Episcopalian.

NISHI, GREGORY HIDEO, energy management representative, consultant; b. Toppenish, Wash., May 30, 1953; s. Goro and Sumako (Hide) N. BS in Indsl. Tech., Calif. Poly. State U., 1979. Energy mgmt. rep. Pacific Gas & Electric Co., San Luis Obispo, Calif., 1979—; chief cons. San Luis (Obispo) Solar Co., 1979—. Mem. Assn. Profl. Energy Mgrs., Am. Chemical Soc. (v.p. San Luis Obispo chpt., 1975-76). Republican.

NISHI, HARVEY GLENN, designer, architect; b. Ft. Lipton, Colo., Feb. 9, 1943; s. Harry Kazuo Nishi and Evelyn Etsko (Koshio) Carter. BArch, Ariz. State U., 1975. Designer Johnson, Fermelia and Crank, Kemmerer, Wyo., 1975-85; designer, treas. Crank Cos., Inc., Kemmerer, 1985—. Chmn. Kemmerer Zoning Bd., 1982-85; mayor Kemmerer, 1985—; vice chmn. Lincoln-Hinta Assn. Govt., Kemmerer, 1986—. Served with USAF, 1963-67. Mem. Wyo. Engring. Soc. Avocations: fishing, hunting, photography, travel. Office: Crank Cos Inc 722 Cedar Ave Kemmerer WY 83101 Home: PO Box 13 408 Upper Sunset Dr Kemmerer WY 83101

NISHIMURA, HOWARD ISAMU, accountant; b. Seattle, Aug. 31, 1936; s. Toshimi and Marumi (Hamada) N.; student Los Angeles City Coll., 1955-57; B.S., U. Calif. at Los Angeles, 1961; m. Hideko Omura, Aug. 11, 1963; children—Derek Isamu, Julia Miyuki. Mgr., Kenneth Leventhal & Co., C.P.A.s, Los Angeles, 1961-67; partner Furuta & Nishimura, C.P.A.s, Los Angeles, 1967-76; pres. Nishimura, Kojima & Sy, Los Angeles, 1978-79; commr. City of Los Angeles Community Redevel. Agy., 1978-84, treas., 1979-81, chmn., 1982-84; mem. community unit for participation in housing and urban devel. City Los Angeles, 1976-82; dir. Skid Row Devel. Corp., 1979—, SRO Housing Inc., 1984. Chmn., Little Tokyo Community Devel. Adv. Com., 1975-78; pres. So. Calif. Nisei Golf, 1974-78; mem. Nisei Week Festival Com., 1977—, chmn., 1980. C.P.A., Calif. Mem. Am. Inst. C.P.A.s, Calif. Soc. C.P.A.s, Los Angeles-Nagoya Sister City Affiliation (bd. dirs. 1981—, chmn. 1982), Japan-Am. Soc. So. Calif. Home: 3307 Landa St Los Angeles CA 90039 Office: 120 S San Pedro St Suite 523A Angeles CA 90012

NISKANEN, PAUL MCCORD, travel company executive; b. Bend, Oreg., July 6, 1943; s. William Arthur and Nina Elizabeth (McCord) N.; m. Christine Campbell; 1 son, Tapio. Student U. Freiburg, W. Ger., 1963-64; B.A., Stanford U., 1965; M.B.A., U. Chgo., 1966. Fin. analyst Kimberly-Clark Corp., Neenah, Wis., 1966-68; bus. mgr. Avent Inc. subs. Kimberley-Clark Corp., Tucson, 1968-70; v.p., gen. mgr. Pacific Trailways Bus. Line, Portland, Oreg., 1970-81; chmn. bd., owner Niskanen & Jones, Inc., Moab, Utah, 1982—, Perspectives, Inc., Portland. Appointed counsel for Finland, 1980—; Mem. Gov.'s Travel Adv. Com., Salem, Oreg., 1976-81; 1st pres. Oreg. Hospitality and Visitors Assn., Portland, 1977-78; bd. dirs. Suomi Coll., Hancock, Mich., 1981—; nat. co-chmn. Dole for Pres. Com., 1987. Mem. Travel Industry Assn. Am., Am. Assn. Travel Agts., Pacific Northwest Travel Assn. (chmn. 1978-79), Scandinavian Heritage Found. (bd. dirs. 1984). Republican. Home: 4366 SW Hewett Blvd Portland OR 97221 Office: Niskanen & Jones Inc 452 N Main St Moab UT 84532

NITZ, FREDERIC WILLIAM, electronic engineer; b. St. Louis, June 22, 1943; s. Arthur Carl Paul and Dorothy Louise (Kahm) N.; m. Kathleen Sue Rapp, June 8, 1968; children: Frederic Theodore, Anna Louise. AS, Coll. Marin, 1970; BS in Electronics, Calif. Poly. State U., San Luis Obispo, 1972. Electronic engr. Sierra Electronics, Menlo Park, Calif., 1973-77, RCA, Somerville, N.J., 1977-79; engring. mgr. EGG-Geometrics, Sunnyvale, Calif., 1979-83; v.p. engring. Basic Measuring Insts., Foster City, Calif., 1983—; cons. in field, Boulder Creek, Calif., 1978—. Bd. dirs. San Lorenzo Valley Water com., Boulder Creek, 1983—, Water Policy Task Force, Santa Cruz County, Calif., 1983-84. Served with U.S. Army, 1965-67. Democrat. Lutheran. Home: 12711 East St Boulder Creek CA 95006 Office: BMI 402 Lincoln Centre Dr Foster City CA 94404

NIXON, ALAN CHARLES, chemist; b. Workington, Eng., Oct. 10, 1908; married; 2 children. B.Sc., U. Saskatchewan, 1929, M.Sc., 1931; Ph.D. in Chemistry, U. Calif.-Berkeley, 1934. Instr. chemistry U. Calif., 1934-36, research asso., 1936-37, 72—; research chemist Shell Devel. Co., Emeryville, Calif., 1937-54; research supr. Shell Devel. Co., 1954-70, cons., 1970—; sec. Calsec Cons., Inc., 1979-83, pres., 1982—; dir. Teck Research, Inc., Moli Energy Ltd. Moderator, Arlington Community Ch., 1980; dir. No. Calif. conf. United Ch. of Christ; chmn. Council Sci. Soc. Pres., 1973-74. Recipient awards in field. Fellow AAAS, Am. Inst. Chemists; mem. Am. Chem. Soc. (pres. 1973, bd. dirs. 1972-74, Henry A Hill award 1984), AIAA, Combustion Inst., Catalysis Soc., Sierra Club, Sigma Xi, Alpha Chi Sigma. Address: care Wells Fargo Bldg Suite 511 2140 Shattuck Ave Berkeley CA 94704 : 2727 Marin Ave Berkeley CA 94708

NIXON, EDWARD CALVERT, trade executive, consultant; b. Whittier, Calif., May 3, 1930; s. Francis Anthony and Hannah (Milhous) N.; m. Gay Lynne Woods, June 1, 1957; children—Amelie, Elizabeth. B.S., Duke U., 1952; M.S., N.C. State U., 1954. Lic. real estate broker, Wash. With comml. dept. Pacific N.W. Bell, Seattle, 1962-63, 67-68; tech. personnel supr. Bellcomm, Inc., Washington, 1964-67; cons., trustee Richard Nixon Found., Los Angeles, 1969-74; assoc. broker Harmon & Assocs., Seattle, 1975-77; exec. v.p. DNA Corp., Newport Beach, Calif., and Cairo, 1977-79; pres. Nixon World Enterprises, Inc., Lynnwood, Wash., 1980—; chmn. Great Circle Resources, Inc., 1986—. Mem. Wash. Republican Central Com., Olympia, 1968; co-chmn. Com. for Reelection of Pres., Washington, 1972; mem. sea grant adv. panel U. So. Calif., 1971. Served to capt. USNR, 1955-62. Mem. Am. Wind Energy Assn., Nat. Assn. Realtors, Am. Soc. Oceanography (bd. dirs. 1969-71), AIME. Mem. Soc. Friends. Clubs: Rainier, Wash. Athletic (Seattle); Pisces (Washington). Home: 1609 175th St SW Lynnwood WA 98037 Office: Great Circle Resources Inc 4418 176th St SW A-2 Lynnwood WA 98037

NOBE, KENNETH CHARLES, agricultural economist, educator; b. Venedy, Ill., Oct. 26, 1930; s. Elmer F. and Alvina (Froekhe) N.; m. Hazel Leona McCullough, Oct. 22, 1949; children—Sandra, Jeffrey, Michael. B.S., So. Ill. U., 1953; M.S., Cornell U., 1954, Ph.D., 1959. Mktg. agt. Dept. Agr., Ithaca, N.Y., 1954-55; instr. Cornell U., 1955-56; economist Dept. Agr., Washington, 1958-61, USPHS, Denver, 1961-63, Dept. Interior, Washington, 1963-64; econ. cons. Harza Engring. Co. Internat., Lahore, West Pakistan, 1964-65; assoc. prof. econs. Colo. State U., Ft. Collins, 1966-69, prof. econs., chmn. econs. dept. Colo. State U., 1969-83, prof. agrl. econs., chmn. dept. agr., natural resources and econs., 1984—; chmn. exec. council Environ. Resources Center, 1970-71; dir. Internat. Sch. Econ. Devel. Studies, 1980-83; exec. dir. Internat. Sch. Agr. and Resource Devel., 1983-85; econ. adviser to dir. Water and Power Devel. Authority West Pakistan, 1964-65; cons. U.S. State Dept., AID, 1966, 76-84, Ford Found./India, 1980, World Bank, 1984-85; chmn. Western Agrl. Econs. Council, 1976-78; cons. Dept. Agr., Republic of Philippines, 1977. Served with USAF, 1948-50. Recipient Ill. State Farmer award Future Farmers Am., 1947, Disting. Service award Colo. State U., 1979. Mem. Am. Econs. Assn., Am. Agrl. Econs. Assn., Western Agrl. Econs. Assn., Soil Conservation Soc. Am., Internat. Assn. Agrl. Econs., Omicron Delta Epsilon. Home: 3510 Terry Ridge Rd Fort Collins CO 80524

NOBEL, PARK S., biology educator; b. Chgo., Nov. 4, 1938; s. James Dodman and Ruth (Uetz) N.; m. Eiko Mizuguchi, Feb. 7, 1965; children: Cathrine, Elizabeth. B in Enging Physics, Cornell U., 1961; M in Physics, Calif. Inst. Tech., 1963; PhD in Biophysics, U. Calif., Berkeley, 1965. NSF postdoctoral fellow Tokyo, Japan, 1965-66; from asst. prof. to assoc. prof. biology U. Calif., Los Angeles, 1967-75, prof., 1975—; prof. London, 1966-67; vis. sci. Guggenheim Found., Canberra, Australia, 1973-74. Author: Plant Cell Physiology, 1970, Plant Physiology, 1974, Biophysical Ecology, 1983, The Cactus Primer, 1986. Office: U Calif Dept Biology 405 Hilgard Ave Los Angeles CA 90024

NOBLE, CHARLES NORMAN, electronics company executive, consultant; b. Englewood, N.J., Aug. 22, 1935; s. Charles Lawrence Atherton and Dorothy Marie (Noble) Smith; m. Mina Jean Nichols, Jan. 28, 1958; children—Deborah Lynn (Mrs. D. Knox), Jean Marie, Cynthia Louise. B.A., Colgate U., 1957. Sr. mktg. rep. Honeywell, Mpls., 1960-66; mgr. market research Sundstrand Corp., Redmond, Wash., 1966-69; mktg. dir. Western Marine Electronics, Seattle, 1969-73; v.p. AIRMARC Corp., Bellevue, Wash., 1973-76; pres. Noble Internat. Bellevue, 1976-80; mktg. mgr. Butler Controls, Kirkland, Wash., 1980-84, mktg. mgr. Avtech Corp., Seattle,

1984—; lectr. Am. Mgmt. Assn., Seattle City Coll. Author: The Power & The Story, 1982, In Search of Green Pastures, 1985, Full Sales Ahead, 1985, The Marketing of Jesus, 1986. Creator advt. series for Overlake Christian Ch. Contbr. numerous mktg. articles to profl. jours. Bd. dirs. Wash. State Internat. Trade Fair, Seattle, 1970—. Served as cpl. U.S. Army, 1955-57. Recipient Presidential E award Pres. Gerald Ford, 1975; 1st place award for ads Wash. State Newspaper Assn., 1976, 77, 78, 79. Mem. Am. Mktg. Assn., Soc. Preservation and Encouragement of Barbershop Quartet Singing in Am. (chpt. pres. 1960-62). Republican. Club: World Trade. Home: 12920 NE 25th Pl Bellevue WA 98005

NOBLE, ERNEST PASCAL, physician, biochemist, educator; b. Baghdad, Iraq, Apr. 2, 1929; came to U.S., 1946; s. Noble Babik and Barkev Grace (Kasparian) Babikian; m. Inga Birgitta Kilstromer, May 19, 1956; children—Lorna, Katharine, Erik. B.S. in Chemistry, U. Calif.-Berkeley, 1951; Ph.D. in Biochemistry, Oreg. State U., 1955; M.D., Case Western Res. U., 1962. Diplomate Nat. Bd. Med. Examiners. Sr. instr. biochemistry Western Res. U., Cleve., 1957-62; intern Stanford Med. Ctr., Calif., 1962-63, resident in psychiatry, 1963-66, research assoc., asst. prof., 1965-69; assoc. prof. psychiatry, psychobiology and pharmacology U. Calif.-Irvine, 1969-71, prof., chief neurochemistry, 1971-76, 79-81; dir. Nat. Inst. Alcohol Abuse and Alcoholism HEW, 1976-78, assoc. adminstr. sci., alcohol, drug abuse and mental health, 1978-79; Pike prof. alcohol studies, dir. Alcohol Research Ctr. UCLA Sch. of Medicine, 1981—. Mem. various med./sci. jour. editorial bds.; contbr. numerous articles to profl. jours., chpts. to books. Fulbright scholar, 1955-56; Guggenheim fellow, 1974-75; Sr. Fulbright scholar, 1984-85; recipient Career Devel. award NIMH, HEW, 1966-69. Fellow Am. Coll. Neuropsychopharmacology; mem. Internat. Soc. Neurochemistry, Am. Soc. Pharmacology and Exptl. Therapeutics, Research Soc. on Alcoholism. Office: UCLA 760 Westwood Plaza Los Angeles CA 90024

NOBLE, ORSON BATES, food service executive; b. Sandpoint, Idaho, Aug. 15, 1937; s. Monroe Clarence and Nelle Alnora (Mills) N.; m. Anna Fay Mortensen, June 10, 1957 (dec. Jan. 1976); m. Dorothy Lee Borges, Nov. 20, 1976. BS in Bus. Edn., U. Oreg., 1966. V.p., gen. mgr. Jac Mar Sales Co., Alhambra, Calif., 1979-82, Chasin & Co., Los Angeles, 1982-84; cons. commodities Interstate Restaurant Supply Co., Los Angeles, 1984-85, S.E. Rykoff, Los Angeles, 1985—. Served with U.S. Army, 1959-61. Mormon. Avocations: reading, hiking, bowling, tennis. Office: SE Rykoff 761 Terminal St Los Angeles CA 90021

NOBLE, RICHARD LLOYD, lawyer; b. Oklahoma City, Oct. 11, 1939; s. Samuel Lloyd and Eloise Joyce (Millard) N. A.B. with distinction, Stanford, 1961, LL.B. (Benjamin Harrison fellow), 1964. Bar: Calif. 1964. Assoc. firm Cooper, White & Cooper, San Francisco, 1965-67; assoc., ptnr. firm Voegelin, Barton, Harris & Callister, Los Angeles, 1967-70; ptnr. firm Noble, Campbell & Uhler, Los Angeles, San Francisco, 1970—; dir. Langdale Corp., Los Angeles, Gt. Pacific Fin. Co., Sacramento; lectr. Tax Inst. U. So. Calif., 1970; Treas. Young Republicans Calif., 1960-62; Bd. govs. St. Thomas Aquinas Coll.; mem. Colo. River Bd. of Calif. Contbr. articles to legal jours. Recipient Hilmer Oehlman Jr. award Stanford Law Sch., 1962. Mem. Am., Los Angeles, San Francisco bar assns., State Bar Calif., Pi Sigma Alpha, Delta Sigma Rho. Republican. Clubs: Commercial (San Francisco), Commonwealth (San Francisco); Stock Exchange (Los Angeles), Jonathan (Los Angeles); Beach Tennis (Pebble Beach, Calif.); Capitol Hill (Washington). Home: 2222 Ave of Stars Los Angeles CA 90067 Office: Noble Campbell Uhler 888 W 6th St Los Angeles CA 90017

NOBLE, ROBERT LAING, medical researcher; b. Toronto, Ont., Can., Feb. 3, 1910; s. Robert Thomas and Susanah (Hodgetts) N.; m. Mary Aimee Eileen Dillon, Aug. 20, 1935; children: Michael Courtney, John James, Robert Thomas, Richard Dillon. MD, U. Toronto; PhD, U. London, DSc; DSc (hon.), U. Western Ont. Med. researcher dept. cancer endocrinology Cancer Control Agy., Vancouver, B.C., Can. Home: 4746 W 2d Ave, Vancouver Can V6T 1B9 Office: Cancer Control Agy, Dept Cancer Endocrinology, Vancouver Can

NOBLE, THOMAS CARL, safety engineer; b. Kingman, Ariz., June 6, 1948; s. Thomas Carl and Opal Cathrine (Thomas) N.; m. Karen A. Phelps, Nov. 8, 1968 (div. June 6, 1975); 1 child, Kimberly T.; m. Cathryn Anne Sibley, Aug. 23, 1980. BS, SUNY, Albany, 1980; MS, U. So. Calif., 1982. Cert. safety profl. Asst. IH officer USN, Pearl Harbor, Hawaii, 1978-80; safety and health dir. Safety Specialists Inc., Santa Clara, Calif., 1980-82; safety engr. Lockheed Missiles and Space Co., Sunnyvale, Calif., 1982-85; safety mgr. Physics Internat., San Leandro, Calif., 1985—; indsl. hygienist Kairos Corp., Mountain View, Calif., 1980-85; chmn. 7th Internat. System Safety Conf., San Jose, Calif., 1985. Contbr. articles to profl. jours. Served with USNR, 1965—. Mem. System Safety Soc. (pres. No. Calif.), Am. Soc. Safety Engrs., Am. Pub. Health Assn., Nat. Safety Mgmt. Soc. Republican. Home: 4686 Phebe Ave Fremont CA 94536-7584 Office: 2700 Merced St San Leandro CA 94577

NOE, GUY, social services administrator; b. Brussels, Jan. 28, 1934; came to U.S., 1955, naturalized, 1961; s. Marinus Cornelis and Johana Dorothea (Beijne) N.; 1 dau., Jeanette Sue. B.S., Regional Agrl. Sch., Loiret, France, 1954. Social worker State of Wyo., Casper, 1962-66; dir. Natrona County (Wyo.) Dept. Public Assistance, Casper, 1966-79, Wyo. Div. Mental Health, Cheyenne, 1979—; former mgr. Platte County Office Pub. Assistance and Social Services, Wheatland, Wyo.; cons. family and childrens services program Juvenile Community Alternative and Children's Shelter Programs, Wheatland, Wyo.; lectr. in field. Vice pres. Wyo. chpt. Big Bros., 1976-77; chmn. adv. council social services State of Wyo., 1969-79; bd. dirs. Casper United Way, 1970—, Casper Salvation Army, 1970—, Casper chpt. ARC, 1977—. Named Outstanding Adminstr. State of Wyo., 1976. Mem. Am. Public Welfare Assn. (Wyo. membership chmn.), Am. Soc. Public Adminstrn. Democrat. Club: Toastmasters. Home: 2731 Deming Blvd Cheyenne WY 82001 Office: Platte County Office Pub Assistance and 975 Gilchrist Wheatland WY 82201

NOE, SALLY (SARA) WOODWORTH, educator, local history researcher; b. Kansas City, Mo., Mar. 18, 1926; s. Hugh Johnson and Katharine (McAntire) Woodworth; m. Robert Clark Noe, Aug. 14, 1945; children: Katharine Merry, Thomas Clark, William Dean. BA, U. N.Mex., 1969, MA, 1984. Cert. tchr., N.Mex. Elem. tchr. Morenci Pub. Schs., Ariz., 1946-47; elem. tchr. Gallup-McKinley County Sch. Dist., N.Mex., 1955-56, tchr. Office Navajo Edn. Opportunity, Concentrated Employment Practice, 1968-69, tchr. secondary social studies, 1969—, chmn. dept. social studies, 1977—; social studies evaluator, N.Mex. schs., 1975—; instr. N.Mex. history U. N.Mex., Gallup, 1986—. Author N.Mex. Council for Social Studies and State N.Mex. Dept. Edn. unit for Native Am. history, 1979; author Gallup centennial calendar, 1981. Head rug clk. InterTribal Indian Ceremonial, Gallup, 1976—; bd. dirs. N.Mex. Law Related Edn.; regional dir. N.Mex. History Day; mem. com. Ft. Wingate Preservation Task Force, 1984, Com. on Status of History in N.Mex. Pub. Schs., 1984. Recipient 3d Place award High Sch. div. econs. Kazanjian Found., 1970, Tchr.'s medal Freedom Found. at Valley Forge, 1973, Inst. for Am. Indian History award Newberry Library, 1978; Ethnic Am. Coe fellow Stanford U., Calif., 1979; S.W. Inst. Research on Women fellow U. Ariz., 1983; Spl. Programs in Citizenship Edn. fellow Wake Forest U. Sch. Law, 1985. Mem. N.Mex. Council for Social Studies (pres. 1980-81), N.Mex. Hist. Soc. (presenter), Nat. Council Social Studies, N.Mex. Archeol. Soc. (cert. crew mem., presenter state meeting 1986), N.Mex. Soc. for Preservation History, Gallup Hist. Soc., Delta Kappa Gamma (pres. Gallup chpt. 1979-80), Alpha Delta Pi. Democrat. Episcopalian. Lodges: Order Eastern Star, PEO. Home: PO Box 502 1911 Mark St Gallup NM 87301 Office: Gallup High Sch PO Box 39 Gallup NM 87301

NOECKER, CARL BLUE, lawyer; b. Lancaster, Ohio, Apr. 17, 1912; s. G.O. and Maude (Hedges) N.; J.D., Ohio State U., 1936; m. Ada Margaret Coon. Nov. 30, 1934 (dec. June 1962); children—Nadine, Daniel B., Karen, Scott; m. 2d, Virginia O. Simpson, Oct. 26, 1962 (dec. Mar. 1973); m. 3d, Eleanore M. Benson, Jan. 5, 1974. Admitted to Ohio bar, 1936, Calif. bar, 1949; practiced law, Columbus, Ohio, 1936-43, Walnut Creek, Calif., 1950—; real estate rep. Texaco, Inc., San Francisco, 1947-50. Mem. Calif. City, County, State People to People Delegation to Eng., Germany, Russia, Poland, Hungary, France, 1967. City atty., Walnut Creek, 1959-65. Bd. govs. Shriners Hosps. for Crippled Children, San Francisco. Served to lt. comdr. USNR, 1943-47. Mem. State Bar Calif., Am., Ohio, Contra Costa, Central Contra Costa (past pres.) bar assns., Walnut Creek Area C. of C. (past pres., dir.), Am. Arbitration Assn., Royal Order Jesters. Mason (Shriner). Clubs: Elks (Walnut Creek); Commonwealth of Calif. (San Francisco). Home: 3915 S Pearldale Dr Lafayette CA 94549 Office: 2363 Blvd Circle Highland Bldg Suite #3 Walnut Creek CA 94595

NOEL, DONNA MARIE, chemist, assayer; b. Phila., Oct. 7, 1959; d. Donald Edward Noel and Darla Rae (Bradley) Johnson. BS in Chemistry, U. Idaho, 1982, BS in Microbiology, 1984. Chief assayer, chemist Superior Mining Co., Boise, Idaho, 1982-85; chief assayer CoCa Mines, Inc., Rosamond, Calif., 1985—. Mem. Am. Chem. Soc. Republican. Episcopalian. Avocations: skiing, swimming, motorcycle riding, rollerskating. Home: 333 Dennison Rd #36 Tehachapi CA 93561 Office: Cactus Gold Mines Co Rt #1 Box 253 Rosamond CA 93560

NOEL, HOWARD GEORGE, public relations executive; b. Cedar City, Utah, Nov. 27, 1948; s. Floyd Clark and Dorothy (Clark) N.; m. Mary Lynne Germer, Apr. 7, 1971; children: McKay, Carole Ann, David, Kristine, Elisa, Richard. BA, Weber State Coll., 1974. News dir. Sta. KANN Radio, Ogden, Utah, 1974-75, Sta. KLO Radio, Ogden, 1975-76; news corr. Sta. KSL TV, Salt Lake City, 1976-79; dir. pub. relations Weber State Coll., Ogden, 1979—; owner, pres. Howard Communications Cons., Ogden, 1984—. Writer, producer (TV program) Off Campus, 1986, several radio programs and media shows, 1974—. Pres. Lincoln PTA, Ogden, 1977; bd. dirs. Am. Cancer Soc., Weber County, Utah, 1979-80; del. Rep. State Conv., Utah, 1978-84; chmn. Weber Vocat. Workshop Trustees, Ogden, 1986. Mem. Internat. Assn. Bus. Communicators. Republican. Mormon. Avocations: magician, sports announcer, musician. Office: Weber State Coll 3750 Harrison Blvd Ogden UT 84408-1010

NOERDLINGER, PETER DAVID, astrophysicist, educator; b. N.Y.C., May 3, 1935; s. Julius Peter and Helen Caroline (Jacobs) N.; m. Carol Anne White, June 1957 (div. 1962); 1 dau., Lucy Anne; m. Judy Anne Nau, Nov. 4, 1964 (dec. 1986); children: Henry Clifford, Frederick Nicholas, Rachel Holly, Victor David. A.B. magna cum laude (Harvard Coll. Hon. fellow), Harvard Coll., 1956; Ph.D. (U.S. Steel Found. fellow 1958-59, Howard Hughes fellow 1959-60, NSF fellow 1959), Calif. Inst. Tech., 1960. Instr. U. Chgo., 1960-63, asst. prof., 1963-66; assoc. prof. U. Iowa, 1966-68; asso. prof. N.Mex. Inst. Mining and Tech., 1968-69, prof., 1969-71; vis. prof. U. Calif., Santa Cruz, 1971; prof. astronomy and astrophysics Mich. State U., 1971—, acting chmn. dept. astronomy and astrophysics, 1974-75; NSF sr. resident research assoc. NASA, Ames Research Center, Moffett Field, Calif., summers 1974-75; NRC sr. resident research assoc. NASA, Ames Research Center, 1979-80; prin. research analyst Solar Energy Research Inst., 1981-82; staff mem. Los Alamos Nat. Lab., 1982—; NASA-Stanford U. summer fellow, 1969-70, NRC sr. postdoctoral research assoc., summer 1971; vis. scientist Smithsonian Astrophys. Obs., Harvard U., summer 1973, High Altitude Obs., Boulder, Colo., 1977-78; sr. research assoc. Astron. Inst., U. Amsterdam, summer 1976; vis. research assoc. U. Colo., 1977-78; disting. lectr. U. N.Mex., 1978. Contbr. articles to sci. jours. Active Council for a Livable World, 1963-66; campus rep. Fedn. Am. Scientists, 1973-77; mem. adv. bd. Am. Friends Service Com., Chgo., 1963-66, Lansing, Mich., 1972-75. Recipient hon. mention Gravity Research Found., 1971; NSF research grantee, 1977-79. Fellow Am. Phys. Soc., Royal Astron. Soc.; mem. Am. Astron. Soc., AAAS, Am. Assn. Physics Tchrs., Fedn. Am. Scientists, Internat. Astron. Union, Am. Geophys. Union, Phi Beta Kappa, Sigma Xi (award for meritorious research 1974). Quaker. Home: 4702 Hayman Ave La Canada CA 91011 Office: Jet Propulsion Lab Calif Inst Tech Mail Stop 238-322 4800 Oak Grove Dr Pasadena CA 91109

NOETH, LOUISE ANN, journalist; b. Evergreen Park, Ill., Nov. 17, 1954; s. Cy John and Alice Rose (Bobrovich) N. Editor Petersen Pub. Co., Inc., Calif., 1980; assoc. pub., editor Autoscene Mag., Westlake Village, Calif., 1981; investigative editor Four Wheeler Mag., Canoga Park, Calif., 1982—; cons. Stehrenberger/Clénet, Inc., Pontiac Motor Div., others; mem. Green Mamba Racing Team (Spirit of Am. World Speed Racing Record), Reseda, Calif., 1978—; graphic art comms. for Ferro Corp., Crown Oldsmobile, Glendale Porsche-Audi, others. Editor Hot Rod Performance and Custom, 1979; contbr. articles to numerous automotive mags. Recipient Moto award in investigative news category, 1983-84, 86. Mem. Internat. Motor Press Assn. (sec. 1986—), Specialty Equipment Market Assn. (pub. relations com. 1983, suspension and tire com. 1984-85), Am. Auto Racing Writers and Broadcasters Assn. Office: Landspeed Prodns 3645 Saviers Rd Suite 14 Oxnard CA 93033

NOGES, ENDRIK, engineering educator, consultant; b. Moisakula, Estonia, Apr. 5, 1927; s. Jaan and Alice (Kont) N.; m. Evelyn C. Case, Nov. 23, 1951; children: Paul Endrik, Robert Jaan, Linda Alice. BSEE, Northwestern U., 1954, MSEE, 1956, PhD, 1959. Registered profl. engr., Wash. Asst., then assoc. prof. elec. engring. U. Wash., Seattle, 1958-69, asst. dean Coll. Engring., 1966-71, prof., 1969-83, dir. televised instrn. in engring., 1983-86, assoc. chmn. elec. engring., 1986—; fellow Deutsche Forschungsgemeinschaft, Karlsruhe, Fed. Republic Germany, 1972-73; vis. prof. U. Karlsruhe, 1972-73. Co-author: Pulsefrequenzmodulierte Regelungs-systeme, 1975; contbr. articles to profl. jours. Mem. Nat. Ski Patrol, Crystal Mountain, Wash., 1964—, patrol leader, 1966-71; first aid instr. ARC, Seattle, 1966—. Walter D. Murphy fellow Northwestern U., 1957-58, Fulbright lectr., Helsinki, Finland, 1963-64. Sr. mem. IEEE (chmn. Seattle sect. 1966-67); mem. Am. Soc. Engring. Educators, Sigma Xi. Club: Billiken Ski (Crystal Mountain, Wash.) (pres. 1966-67). Office: U Wash Dept Elec Engring FT-10 Seattle WA 98195

NOGUCHI, HIDEO, insurance agency executive; b. Kyoto, Japan, Jan. 17, 1945; s. Tasao and Ishiko (Tsujii) N.; m. Eleanor Kazuko Horii, May 7, 1970; children—Mark H.Y., Mitchell H.Y. B.B.A., U. Hawaii, 1969. Buyer RCA Purchasing Co., Tokyo, 1969-73; ins. specialist Continental Ins. Agy., Honolulu, 1973-82; pres. Noguchi & Assocs., Inc., Honolulu, 1983—; cons. Recipient Nat. New Agt. Leadership award CNA Corp., 1974, Agt. of Yr. award Continental Ins. Agy., annually 1973-81, Key Club award CNA Co., 1975, 79-81. Mem. Nat. Assn. Life Underwriters, Honolulu Assn. Life Underwriters, Million Dollar Round Table. Lodge: Rotary (dir. Ala Moana, Honolulu club). Home: 3678 Woodlawn Terrace Pl Honolulu HI 96822 Office: 1600 Kapiolani Blvd Suite 1040 Honolulu HI 96814

NOLAN, CHARLES E. JR., architect; b. Midland, Tex., Mar. 6, 1930; s. Charles Edward and Alice Bernice (Davis) N.; m. Dolores Ann Howell, Dec. 22, 1953 (div. Jan. 1981); children: Paige, Laurel (dec.), Elaine (dec.), Ellen; m. Martha Louise McMurry, Jan. 30, 1981; children: Carolyn, Candice, Cynthia, Robert. BArch, Tex. Tech. U., 1953. Registered architect, Tex., N.Mex., Miss., Ariz. Draftsman Haynes & Kirby, Architects, Lubbock, Tex., 1953-54; from. draftsman to chief draftsman McMurtry & Craig, Architects, Lubbock, Tex., 1957-60; draftsman Landry & Matthes, Architects, Hattiesburg, Miss., 1960-61, Charlie & Nolan, Architects, Lubbock, 1961-63; ptnr. Voll, Buffington & Nolan, Roswell and Alamogordo, N.Mex., 1963-69; pres. Charles E. Nolan Jr. & Assocs., Alamogordo and Albuquerque, 1969—. Chmn. Planning Commn. City of Alamogordo, 1973; pres. Amigos de los Ninos, Inc., Alamogordo, 1980; active N.Mex. delegation White House Conf. on Small Bus., Washington, 1980, 86. Mem. Am. Inst. Architects (lectr. 1st microcomputer seminar at nat. conv. 1981, N.Mex. so. chpt. pres. 1966, 76, 83), N.Mex. Soc. Architects (pres. 1971), Alamogordo C. of C. (pres. 1970). Home: 9812 Coda Pl NE Albuquerque NM 87111 Office: Charles & Nolan Jr & Assocs PO Box 1788 Almogordo NM 88310

NOLAN, DENNIS PAUL VINCENT, engineer; b. Detroit, Dec. 8, 1954; s. James Vincent and Anastasia Theresa (Kulick) N. BS in Fire Protection Engring., U. Md., 1977; MS in Systems Mgmt., Fla. Inst. Tech., 1979; cert. sch. offshore, U. Tex., 1981. Registered profl. engr., Calif. Assoc. engr. Boeing Aerospace Co., Kennedy Space Ctr., Fla., 1977-80; engr. Marathon Oil Co., Findlay, Ohio, 1980-83; sr. engr. Lockheed Missiles and Space Co., Vandenburg AFB, Calif., 1984-87; fire protection engr. Occidental Petroleum Corp., Los Angeles, 1987—. Mem. NSPE, Nat. Mgmt. Assn., Mil. Vehicle Collectors Club. Avocation: restoration of antique mil. automotive vehicles, skiing, white water rafting, golf. Home: 473 Hartnell Rd Santa Maria CA 93455 Office: Occidental Petroleum Corp 10889 Wilshire Blvd Los Angeles CA 90024

NOLAN, JAMES MARTIN, structural engineer, consultant; b. Joliet, Ill., Feb. 25, 1950; s. Aloysius Edward and Marjorie Cecelia (Drauden) N.; m. Denise Dorothy Lavoie, Jan. 17, 1972; children: Tanya Marie, Shannon Kathleen. BS in Engring., U. Colo., 1973; postgrad., U. Colo., Denver, 1975-79, Calif. State U., Fullerton, 1974. Profl. engr., Colo., Kans., Mo., Iowa, Wyo., Okla., N.Mex., Calif., Ariz. Bridge engr. Colo. Dept. Hwys., Denver, 1975-78; structural engr. E.W. Peterson, Cons., Lakewood, Colo., 1978-80, HDR, Denver, 1980-82; v.p. KTN and Assocs., Lakewood, Colo., 1982-84; chief structural engr. CRS Sirrine, Inc., Denver, 1984—; engring. cons. Englewood, Colo., 1984. Bd. dirs. Havana Water and Sanitation Dist., Denver, 1982—, Cherry Creek Vista Met. Recreation and Park Dist., Englewood, Colo., 1979-84; del. Rep. Caucus, Arapahoe County, 1984. Mem. ASCE, Am. Concrete Inst., Am. Cons. Engrs. Council. Avocations: basketball, tennis, skiing, reading. Home: 10806 E Maplewood Pl Englewood CO 80111 Office: CRS Sirrine Inc 216 16th St Suite 1700 Denver CO 80202

NOLAN, PAUL T., telephone company executive. Pres. Gen. Telephone Co. of the Northwest. Office: Gen Telephone Co of the NW Office of the Pres 1800 41st St Everett WA 98206 *

NOLAN, THOMAS FRANCIS, nursing educator; b. Bemidji, Minn., June 30, 1938; s. Francis Albert and Catherine Marie (Retzlaff) N.; m. Mary Alice Miller, May 28, 1983. BA, St. John's U., Collegeville, Minn., 1961, M Divinity, 1965; BS, Cornell U., 1972; MA, NYU, 1974, PhD, 1980. Registered nurse, Calif., N.Y., Minn. Clin. instr. Sloan-Kettering Cancer Ctr., N.Y.C., 1972-74; lectr. Columbia Tchr's Coll., N.Y.C., 1974-75; asst. prof. CCNY, N.Y.C., 1975-77, Coll. Mt. St. Vincent, Riverdale, N.Y., 1977-80, U. Calif., San Francisco, 1980-83; prof. nursing Sonoma State U., Rohnert Park, Calif., 1983—; pvt. practice family therapist N.Y.C., 1974-80, San Francisco, 1980-83, Novato, Calif., 1983—. Mem. adv. bd. Marin County (Calif.) Mental Health Assn., 1984-85. Mem. Am. Nurses Assn., Calif. Nurses Assn., Sigma Theta Tau. Democrat. Roman Catholic. Avocation: gourmet cooking. Home: 194 Drakewood Pl Novato CA 94947 Office: Sonoma State U 1801 E Cotati Ave Rohnert Park CA 94928

NOLTE, CHARLES WINFIELD, publisher; b. Lewistown, Mont., June 23, 1945; s. Glen Ormandy and Hilda margaret (Lohof) N.; m. Janet René Richards, Aug. 24, 1976; children: Michele, Melinda, Lynne, James. Grad. high sch., Billings, Mont. Mgr. sales Rimrock Lodge, Billings, 1967-70; owner, mgr. Alpine Lodge, Bozeman, Mont., 1970-72; v.p., dir. ops. Am. Inns, Billings, 1972-76; pres. Winfield Import Co., Seattle, 1976-79; pres., pub. Innkeeping World, Seattle, 1979—. Author: 500 Guest Service Ideas, 1985, Creative Packages-100 Ideas for Increasing Business, 1986. Chmn. Bozeman Convention and Vis. Bur., 1971. Office: Innkeeping World Box 84108 Seattle WA 98124

NOLTON, GARY WAYNE, photographer; b. Los Angeles, Jan. 6, 1958; s. Richard Wayne and Betty Rae (Bonner) N.; m. Julie Ann Lillegard, Jan. 23, 1982. Student, Pasadena City Coll., 1976-78, Art Ctr. Coll. Design, 1978-79. Asst. cameraman Sunn Classic Prodns., Park City, Utah, 1979-80; prin. Noltonstudio, Portland, Oreg., 1982—; tchr. Mt. Hood Community Coll., Gresham, Oreg., 1986—. Recipient Art Dirs. Merit award N.Y. Art Dir.'s Club, 1985, Rosey award Excellence APortland Advt. Fedn., 1985, Gold Medal award Council Advancement of Edn., 1985, N.Y. Art Dir.'s award N.Y. Art Dir.'s Club, 1986. Mem. Am. Soc. Mag. Photographers. Avocations: fly fishing, skiing, cycling. Office: Noltonstudio 107 NW 5th Ave Portland OR 97209

NOMURA, MASAYASU, scientist, educator; b. Hyogo-Ken, Japan, Apr. 27, 1927; s. Hiromichi and Yaeko N.; m. Junko Hamashima, Feb. 10, 1957; children—Keiko, Toshiyasu. Ph.D., U. Tokyo, 1957. Asst. prof. Inst. Protein Research, Osaka (Japan) U., 1960-63; asso. prof. genetics U. Wis., Madison, 1963-66; prof. U. Wis., 1966-70, prof. genetics and biochemistry, 1970-84; co-dir. U. Wis. (Inst. for Enzyme Research), 1970-84; prof. biol. chemistry, Grace Bell chair U. Calif., Irvine, 1984—. Recipient U.S. Steel award in molecular biology Nat. Acad. Scis., 1971; recipient Acad. award Japanese Acad. Arts and Sci., 1972. Mem. Am. Acad. Arts and Scis., Nat. Acad. Scis., Royal Danish Acad. Scis. and Letters. Home: 26 Starlight Irvine CA 92715 Office: U Calif Dept Biol Chemistry Med Sci I D240 Irvine CA 92717

NONG, artist; b. Seoul, Korea, Oct. 10, 1930; came to U.S., 1952, naturalized, 1958; m. Helen Whang. Propr., chmn. Nong Gallery, Inc., San Francisco, 1966—; commr. Asian Art Commn., City and County San Francisco, 1981—. One-man exhbns. paintings and/or sculpture include, Fort Lauderdale (Fla.) Mus. Arts, 1965, Santa Barbara (Calif.) Mus. Art, 1965, E.B. Crocker Art Gallery, Sacramento, 1965, One-man shows of paintings and/or sculpture include, Ga. Mus. Art, Athens, 1967, El Paso Mus. Art, 1967, Galerie Vallombreuse, Biarritz, France, 1970, Nat. Mus. History, Taiwan, 1971, Nihonbashi Gallery, Tokyo, Japan, 1971, Shinsegye Gallery, Seoul, Korea, 1975, Nat. Mus. Modern Art, Seoul, 1975, San Francisco Zool. Garden, 1975, Tongin Art Gallery, Seoul, 1978, Consulate Gen. Republic of Korea, Los Angeles, 1982, Choon Chu Gallery, Seoul, 1982, Hartman Rare Art, Dallas, Consulate Gen. Republic of Korea, N.Y.C., 1983, Korean Cultural Service, N.Y.C., 1983, numerous group shows, 1961—, latest being, Salon de Artistes Francais, Paris, France, 1971, Salon d'Automne, Paris, 1969-71, Salon Grands et Jeunes d'Aujourd'hui, Paris, 1971-77; represented in numerous permanent collections including, Santa Barbara Mus. Art, Anchorage (Alaska) Hist. and Fine Art Mus., Museo de Arte, Lima, Peru, Govt. Peru, Nat. Mus. History, Govt. of Republic of China, Oakland (Calif.) Art Mus., Ga. Mus. Art, Athens, Korean Embassy, Lima, Peru, Nat. Mus. of Modern Art, Govt. of Republic of Korea, Seoul, Kook Min U., Seoul, City of Beijing (China), U.S. Nat. Bank, Portland, Oreg., City of Shanghai (China), Nat. Gallery of Modern Art, New Delhi, India, Asian Art Mus. San Francisco, Govt. of People's Republic China, others.; author: Nong Questions, 1982. Chmn. San Francisco-Seoul Sister City Com., City and County San Francisco, 1980—. Served with U.S. Army, 1956-59; Served with USAF, 1959-62. Recipient numerous awards including citations from Republic of Korea., numerous awards including citations from Cert. Disting. Achievement State of Calif., cert. disting. achievement State of Calif., proclamation City and County of San Francisco. Mem. Art Soc. Republic of China (hon.). Home: 999 Green St No 2701 San Francisco CA 94133 Office: Nong Gallery Hyatt on Union Square San Francisco CA 94108

NONOMURA, ARTHUR MICHIO, biotechnology company executive; b. Washington, Dec. 15, 1950; s. Yuko N. BA, U. Calif., Santa Cruz, 1973; MA, U. Calif., Berkeley, 1977, PhD, 1980. Microgardener U. Calif., Berkeley, 1975-77; dir. phytoproducts Internat. Plant Research Inst., San Carlos, Calif., 1980-83; dir. research Microbio Resources, Inc., San Francisco, 1983-84, dir. research and devel., 1985—; assoc. to exec. dir. Nat. Health Screening Council for Vol. Orgns. Health Fair, San Francisco, 1982-83; chief tech. advisor Brine Biotech. Project, UN Devel. Program, 1986—. Author: Yakup; contbr. articles to profl. jours., chpts. to books; patentee composition for treatment of Herpes Simplex Virus, 1985. Vol. ARC; bd. govs. Japanese-Am. Citizens League, San Francisco, 1982-84. Recipient Mutsumi Nobe award Japanese-Am. Citizens League, 1976, Mutsumi Nobe scholar, 1977; recipient Star award, Sci. and Tech. Advisor Research award UN Devel. Programme, N.Y.C., 1985, 10-yr. Vol. Service award ARC, 1965; Mombusho scholar Japanese Ministry Edn., Tokyo, 1975, State Calif. scholar, 1970, Sakamoto Koso Cultural Exchange scholar, 1970; fellow U. Calif. San Francisco Dept. Lab. Medicine, 1983. Mem. Phycol. Soc. Am., Internat. Phycol. Soc., Am. Chem. Soc., Am. Inst. Biol. Scis., Native Plant Soc., Sigma Xi. Mem. Ch. Shingon-shu. Club: Halberstadt Fencer's (San Francisco) (Maitre d'Arms 1982). Avocation: fencing, classical guitar. Home: 242 Dolphin Cove Ct Del Mar CA 92014

NOODLEMAN, LOUIS, research chemist; b. Dayton, Ohio, Jan. 3, 1950; s. Samuel and Doris (Udisky) N. BS in Physics, MIT, 1971, MS, 1972, PhD in Materials Sci., 1975. Research fellow U. B.C., Vancouver, 1975-77; sci. collaborator Theoretical Chemistry Free U., Amsterdam, The Netherlands, 1980-82; research assoc. dept. chemistry U. Wash., Seattle, 1977-80, vis. scientist, 1983-84, postdoctoral fellow, 1984-85, faculty research assoc. Ctr.

for Bioengring., 1985—. Reviewer Inorganic Chemistry, 1986—, Jour. Chem. Physics, 1979-82; contbr. articles to profl. jours. Del. Dem. Dist. Caucus, Seattle, 1984. Killam fellow U. B.C., 1976-77; recipient John Wulff award for Excellence in Teaching MIT, 1971-72. Mem. AAAS, Biophys. Soc., Am. Chem. Soc. (jour. reviewer 1981—). Office: U Wash Ctr for Bioengring WD-12 Seattle WA 98195

NOONAN, BRUCE DOUGLAS, ophthalmologist, surgeon; b. West Point, N.Y., Aug. 2, 1945; s. Clayton Thomas and Sherleen Marie (Denney) N.; m. Nancy Jean Parda, June 28, 1969 (div. Dec. 1978); children: Deeanna, Daniel; m. Deanna Jean Read, Aug. 20, 1983. AB, Dartmouth Coll., 1967, MB, 1969; MD, U. Wash., 1971. Diplomate Am. Bd. Ophthalmology. Intern Hennepin County Gen. Hosp., Mpls., 1971-72; resident ophthalmology U. Calif., Davis, 1975-78; pvt. practice specializing in ophthalmology Edmonds, Wash., 1978—; attending physician, surgeon Children's Orthopedic Hosp., U. Wash., 1980—. Served with USN, 1972-75, capt. USNR. Fellow Am. Acad. Ophthalmology; mem. Assn. Mil. Surgeons U.S. Home: 14508 55th Pl W Edmonds WA 98020 Office: 21700 76th Ave W Edmonds WA 98020

NOONAN-DRACHKOVITCH, STEPHANIE ANN, television producer; b. Ft. Lewis, Wash., June 26, 1957; d. Richard Burke and Sandra Marie (Faroe) Noonan; m. Rasha Drachkovitch, Apr. 27, 1985; 1 child, Michael Ryan. Student, U. Nebr., Lewis and Clark Coll.; BA, U. Oreg., 1980. Assoc. producer Sta. KATU-TV, Portland, Oreg., 1979-81, Sta. WPVI-TV, Phila., 1981-82; exec. producer Sta. WCAU-TV, Phila., 1982-83; producer Telepictures Corp., Sherman Oaks, Calif., 1983-84; ptnr. 44 Blue Prodns., San Francisco, 1984—; producer Bay City Limits TG14 Sta. KRON-TV, San Francisco, 1985-86. Recipient Gold Medal Boradcast Promotion and Mktg. Execs., 1985; nominated for local Emmy award NATAS Phila. chpt., 1983. Mem. Women in Film, Am. Women in Radio and TV, Women in Communications. Avocations: writing, running, aerobics, travel, equestrian activities. Office: 44 Blue Prodns 3352 B Sacramento St San Francisco CA 94118

NORA, JAMES JACKSON, physician, author; b. Chgo., June 26, 1928; s. Joseph James and May Henrietta (Jackson) N.; m. Barbara June Fluhrer, Sept. 7, 1949 (div. 1963); children: Wendy Alison, Penelope Welbon, Marianne Leslie; m. Audrey Faye Hart, Apr. 9, 1966; children: James Jackson Jr., Elizabeth Hart Nora. AB, Harvard U., 1950; MD, Yale U., 1954; MPH, U. Calif., Berkeley, 1978. Assoc. prof. pediatrics Baylor Coll. Medicine, Houston, 1965-71; prof. genetics, preventive medicine and pediatrics U. Colo. Sch. Medicine, Denver, 1971—; dir. preventive cariology U. Colo. Sch. Medicine, 1978—; dir. genetics rose Med. Ctr., Denver, 1980—; dir. pediatric cardiology and cardiovascular tng. U. Colo. Sch. Medicine, 1971-78; mem. task force Nat. Heart and Lung Program, Bethesda, Md., 1973; cons. WHO, Geneva, 1983—; mem. U.S.-U.S.S.R. Exchange Program on Heart Disease, Moscow and Leningrad, 1975. Author: The Whole Heart Book, 1980; (with F.C. Fraser) Medical Genetics, 1981, Genetics of Man, 1986. Com. mem. March of Dimes, Am. Heart Assn., Boy Scouts Am. Served to lt. USAAC, 1945-47. Grantee Nat. Heart, Lung and Blood Inst., Nat. Inst. Child Health and Human Devel., Am. Heart Assn., NIH; recipient Virginia Apgar Meml. award. Fellow Am. Coll. Cardiology, Am. Acad. Pediatrics; mem. Am. Pediatric Soc., Soc. Pediatric Research, Am. Heart Assn., Teratology Soc., Transplantation Soc., Am. Soc. Human Genetics, Authors Guild, Authors League, Acad. Am. Poets. Democrat. Presbyterian. Club: Rocky Mountain Harvard (Denver). Avocations: writing fiction, poetry. Home: 6135 E 6th Ave Denver CO 80220 Office: U Colo Sch Medicine A-007 4200 E 9th Ave Denver CO 80262

NORBERG, GUNNAR, travel agency executive; b. Kenora, Ont., Can., Feb. 4, 1907; s. Nils Albert and Thilda (Osterberg) N.; brought to U.S., 1908, naturalized, 1944; m. Barbara Drew Collins, Sept. 5, 1936 (dec. Aug. 1972); children—Eric Gunnar, Karin Collins; m. Wies H. Christianson, June 24, 1973. Student Stanford U., intermittently 1926-31. Office boy, cashier, chief clk. operating dept. Coast div. S.P. Co., 1925-35; creator, editor College Forum mag., 1931; columnist Hearst morning papers, Pacific Coast, 1931; contbg. editor Penguin mag., 1932; asst. mng. editor Fawcett Publs., 1935-36; asso. editor Screen Guide, 1936; asst., asso., mng. editor Radio Guide, 1936-37; 1st editor Click, 1937; assoc. editor Electrical Week, 1938, Outdoor Life, 1939, Vocational Trends, 1940; owner, operator Norberg Travel Service, agy., from 1941. Sec., Carmel (Calif.) Taxpayers Assn., 1957-58; councilman City of Carmel, 1958-62, 64-68, 72-80, vice mayor, 1972-76, mayor, 1976-80; chmn. Monterey County (Calif.) Conf. Mayors, 1976-79; dir. Carmel Town Hall, 1950-52; founder chmn. Main St. League, 1961—, Monterey County Coop. Council, 1959-61; gen. chmn. Carmel 50th Anniversary Celebration Year, 1966; pres. Monterey Peninsula Republican Men's Club, 1961, 64-65; producer Shakespeare plays Carmel's Forest Theater, 1971-73; pres. Forest Theater Guild, 1972-73; v.p. Carmel Area Coalition, 1971-78. Served from pvt. to cpl. AUS, 1943-45; radio news writer Office Inter-Am. Affairs during formation of UN, 1945. Republican. Clubs: Commonwealth (San Francisco); Rotary (treas. 1954-59). Author: The Norberg Plan for a Heritage City, 1971; The Would-be Soldier Who Tried and Tried, 1984; contbr. short stories and articles to popular mags.; columnist Carmel Pine Cone, 1970-75, 82-87. Home: 8th and Dolores Sts PO Box 1147 Carmel CA 93921

NORD, PAUL ELLIOTT, accountant; b. Carona, N.Y., Mar. 22, 1936; s. Abe and Rose (Guss) N.; m. Marcia B. Gross, June 13, 1965; children—Howard, Aimee, Samuel. Student U. Utah, 1952-56; B.A., LaSalle Extension Inst., 1966. C.P.A., Calif. Staff acct. Robinson, Nowell & Co. (merged with Muncy McPherson & Co., Muncy McPherson McCune Dieckman 1967), 1966-73, ptnr., 1973-81, mng. ptnr., 1981—. Bd. dirs. Congregation Beth Sholom, San Francisco, 1969—, pres., 1979-81; mem. budget and allocations com. Jewish Fedn., East Bay, 1981-84. Served with U.S. Army, 1957-58, 61-62. Mem. Am. Inst. C.P.A.s (acctg. standards exec. com. 1979-81), Calif. Soc. C.P.A.s (chmn. sub-com. acctg. principles 1981-83), C.P.A. Assocs. (bd. dirs. 1986—), Mensa. Jewish. Home: 931 Walnut Ave Walnut Creek CA 94598 Office: 44 Montgomery St Suite 2800 San Francisco CA 94104

NORDBY, GENE MILO, college administrator; b. Anoka, Minn., May 7, 1926; s. Bert J. and Nina Grace N.; m. Arlene Delores Anderson, Aug. 27, 1949 (dec. Nov. 1974); children: Susan Pamela, Brett Gene, Lisa Lea; m. Dusilla Anne Rycroft, July 8, 1975. B.S. in Civil Engring., Oreg. State U., 1948; M.S. in Civil Engring., U. Minn., 1949, Ph.D. in Civil Engring., 1955. Registered profl. engr., Colo. Ariz., Okla. Grad. asst. U. Minn., 1948-50; structural designer Pfeiffer and Shultz (engrs.), Mpls., summer 1950; instr., then asst. prof. civil engring. U. Colo., 1950-56; asso. prof. civil engring., research engr. Joint Hwy. Research Project, Purdue U., 1956; engr. program dir. engring. scis. NSF, 1956-58; lectr. civil engring. George Washington U., 1956-58; prof. civil engring., head dept. U. Ariz., 1958-62; dir., then chmn. adv. com. Ariz. Transp. and Traffic Inst. at univ., 1959-62; prof. engring. U. Okla., 1962-77; dean U. Okla. (Coll. Engring.), 1962-70, v.p. for adminstrn. and fin., 1969-77; v.p. for bus. and fin., prof. civil engring. Ga. Inst. Tech., 1977-80; chancellor U. Colo., Denver, 1980-85; prof. civil engring. U. Colo., Denver and Boulder, 1985-86; prof. agrl. engring., head dept. U. Ariz., Tucson, 1986—; mem. Reinforced Concrete Research Council Engring. Found., 1954-60; trustee Frontiers of Science Found., 1963-70; pres. Tetracon Assos., Inc., 1968-86; cons. structural engring., research financing and programming, ednl. facilities planning and constrn., reinforced concrete, also higher edn. adminstrn., engring. program accreditation, NSF, 1984-87, panel engring. ctrs. of excellence, 1983-87; bd. dirs. Higher Edn. and the Handicapped, Am. Council on Edn., 1980-83; pres. Accreditation Bd. for Engring. and Tech., 1985-86; gen. chmn. Nat. Congress on Engring. Edn., Washington, 1986. Co-author: Introduction to Structural Mechanics, 1960; Cons. editor, MacMillan Co., 1962-70. Bd. visitors Air Force Inst. Tech., 1985—Served with AUS, 1943-46. Recipient Citation for Service to State Okla. Ho. of Reps., 1977; recipient Linton E. Grinter Disting. Service award Accreditation Bd. for Engring. and Tech., 1982. Fellow ASCE (com. on engring edn., 1964-68, com. on research needs, 1965-70, com. on ednl. research, 1976-79, Edmund Friedman Profl. Devel. award 1982); mem. Am. Soc. Engring. Edn. (projects bd. 1969-70, chmn. Curtis W. McGraw award com. 1968, Dean's Inst. Com. 1966-69, Accreditation Process Com. 1979-81), Nat. Soc. Profl. Engrs., Am. Arbitration Assn., Am. Soc. Agrl. Engrs., Engrs. Council for Profl. Devel. (chmn. engring. edn. and accreditation com. 1970, dir. 1976-79, 83-87), Ariz. Soc. Profl. Engrs., Okla. Soc. Profl. Engrs. (dir. 1966-69), Nat. Assn. State Univs. and Land Grant Colls. (commn. edn. engring. profession 1966, 70-73), Engring. Colls. Adminstrv. Council (mem. exec. bd. 1966), Ga. Soc. Profl. Engrs. (bd. dirs. Atlanta chpt. 1978-79), Nat. Assn. Coll. and Univ. Bus. Officers (chmn. personnel com. 1977-79), Sigma Tau, Omicron Delta Pi, Tau Beta Pi, Chi Epsilon. Club: Mason. Office: U Ariz 507 Shantz Bldg #38 Tucson AZ 85718

NORDBY, PAULA JUNE, social worker, consultant; b. Mobridge, S.D., May 29, 1940; d. Clifford A. and June H. (Martin) N.; children: Kari, Jason, Verda. Student, U. Alaska, 1958-60; BSW, Richmond Profl. Inst., 1962; postgrad., Claremont Grad. Sch., 1963; MSW, U. Calif., Berkeley, 1966. Child welfare worker Alameda County, Oakland, Calif., 1966-69; adoption caseworker State of Calif., Santa Rosa, 1969-74, adoption supr., 1974-79; dir. social service WACAP, Port Angeles, Wash., 1979-85; adoption worker Hope Services, Port Angeles, 1985—; patient advocate Olympic Meml. Hosp., Port Angeles, 1985-86; mem. profl. adv. bd. Northwest Home Health Care, Port Angeles, 1985—; social work cons., grief counselor and tng. coordinator Hospice Clallam County, Port Angeles, 1985—; v.p., bd. dirs. Hospice Clallam County, Port Angeles, 1986—, pres. 1987—. Contbr. articles on adoption to various profl. jours. Mem. Nat. Assn. Social Workers (cert.), Women into Scandinavian Heritage. Democrat. Lutheran. Avocations: sewing, needle crafts, dulcimer. Home: 1105 South H St Port Angeles WA 98362

NORDBY, R. DOUGLAS, film industry executive. Pres., chief ops. officer Lucasfilm, Ltd., San Rafael, Calif. Office: Lucasfilm Ltd PO Box 2009 San Rafael CA 94912 *

NORDIN, THOMAS ALLEN, civil engineer; b. Tacoma, Aug. 6, 1949; s. Arnold Lawrence and Marian Lucille (Lyvere) N.; m. Shirley Ann King, Aug. 2, 1968; children—Tracy A., Christine R., Anthony C., Jeremy T. B.S.C.E., U. Wash., 1971. Registered profl. engr., Wash. Drafter, technician Boeing Co., Seattle, 1968-70; assessor's aide King County, Seattle, 1970; engr. technician Wash. Dept. Hwys., Issaquah, 1971; staff engr. Enplan Corp., Kirkland, Wash., 1972-73; office engr. Olympic Engring. Co., Seattle, 1973; project mgr. City of Bellevue, Wash., 1973—. Contbr. to Wash. Fishin' Holes mag., 1978—. Mem. Am. Pub. Works Assn., Inst. Traffic Engrs. Mormon. Club: Eastside Steelheaders (Kirkland) (bd. dirs. 1976—, v.p. 1978-80). Home: 12714 NE 135th St Kirkland WA 98034 Office: City of Bellevue PO Box 90012 Bellevue WA 98009

NORDMEYER, MARY BETSY, vocational specialist educator; b. New Haven, May 19, 1939; d. George and Barbara Stedman (Thompson) N. ABPhil, Wheaton Coll., Norton, Mass., 1960; MEd, San Jose State U., 1968; AS in Computer Sci., West Valley Coll., 1985. Cert. tchr. spl. edn., Calif.; cert. secondary tchr., Calif. Instr. English Santa Clara (Calif.) Unified Sch. Dist., 1965-77, vocat. specialist, 1977—, dir. project work ability, 1984—. Author poetry, 1960, Career and Vocat. Edn. for Students With Spl. Needs, 1986; author/designer Career English, 1974, Career Information, 1975. Facilitator Project Work-Ability Region 5, 1985—; mem. community adv. com. Santa Clara Unified Sch. Dist. Recipient Outstanding Secondary Educator award, 1975, Award of Excellence, Nat. Assn. Vocat. Edn., 1984; named Tchr. of Yr. in Spl. Edn., Santa Clara Unified Sch. Dist., 1984-85. Mem. Calif. Assn. Work Experience Educators, Sierra Club, Epsilon Eta Sigma. Democrat. Avocations: backpacking, skiing, mountain climbing, computers, gardening. Home: 14920 Sobey Rd Saratoga CA 95070 Office: Santa Clara Unified Sch Dist 1889 Lawrence Rd Santa Clara CA 95052

NORDQUIST, JOAN MARIE, bibliographer, indexer, researcher; b. San Jose, Calif., Nov. 23, 1937; d. Kenneth James and Evelyn C. (Wood) Beam; m. Gilbert Nelson Nordquist, Aug. 10, 1963; 1 child, Diana Artemis. BA, San Jose State U., 1959, MLS, 1976. Library researcher Encyclopaedia Britannica, Chgo., 1962-74; librarian Santa Cruz (Calif.) Pub. Library, 1975-78; indexer, bibliographer, cons. Reference and Research Services, Santa Cruz, 1982—; research specialist U. Calif., Santa Cruz, 1980—. Editor, indexer: Audiovisuals for Women, 1980 (Choice Best Acad. Books of Yr. 1980-81), The Left Index, 1982—, Social Theory: A Bibliographic Series, 1986—, Contemporary Social Issues: A Bibliographic Series, 1986—, City on a Hill Index, 1986—. Avocation: reading. Office: Reference and Research Services 511 Lincoln St Santa Cruz CA 95060

NORDSTROM, BRUCE A., department store executive; b. 1933; married. BA, U. Wash., 1956. With Nordstrom, Inc., Seattle, 1956—, v.p., 1964-70, pres., 1970-75, chmn., 1975-77, co-chmn., 1977—, dir. Office: Nordstrom Inc 1501 5th Ave Seattle WA 98101 *

NORDSTROM, DARRELL KIRK, geochemist, consultant; b. San Francisco, Nov. 14, 1946; s. Maurice Oliver Jr. and Margene (Johnson) N.; m. Karen Lynn Greenwood, Sept. 15, 1973; children: Margaret Sophia, Lars Erik. BA, So. Ill. U., 1969; MS, U. Colo., 1971; PhD, Stanford U., 1977. Asst. prof. U. Va., Charlottesville, 1976-80; hydrogeochemist U.S. Geol. Survey, Menlo Park, Calif., 1980—; chmn. hydrogeochem. adv. group Internat. Stripa Project, Stockholm, 1980—; cons. Swedish Nuclear Waste Co., Stockholm, 1980—, EPA, 1983—. Author: Geochemical Thermodynamics, 1985. NSF fellow, 1970; research grantee NSF, 1980, cons. grantee Swedish Nuclear Fuel and Waste Mgmt. Co., Stockholm, 1983. Mem. AAAS, Geochem. Soc., Mineral. Soc. Am., Geol. Soc. Am., Sigma Xi. Democrat. Avocations: swimming, tennis, camping, biking, stamp collecting. Office: US Geol Survey 345 Middlefield Rd Menlo Park CA 94025

NORDSTROM, JAMES F., apparel company executive; b. 1940; married. BBA, U. Wash., 1962. Various positions Nordstrom, Inc., Seattle, 1960—, exec. v.p. 1975-78, pres., 1978—, also bd. dirs. Office: Nordstrom Inc 1501 5th Ave Seattle WA 98101 *

NORDSTROM, JOHN N., department store executive; b. 1937; married. BA, U. Wash., 1958. With Nordstrom, Inc., Seattle, 1958—, v.p., 1965-70, exec. v.p., 1970-75, pres., 1975-77, co-chmn., 1977—, dir.; bd. dirs. Puget Sound Power and Light Co., SeaFirst Corp., Seattle First Nat. Bank. Office: Nordstrom Inc 1501 5th Ave Seattle WA 98101 *

NORDYKE, JAMES WALTER, economist, educator; b. Rock Springs, Wyo., June 21, 1930; s. Ray Beatty and Gracia Marie (Perry) N. B.A. with gt. distinction, Stanford U., 1952; M.A. (Sanxay fellow 1952-53, univ. fellow 1955-56), Princeton U., 1957, Ph.D., 1959. Research asst. Princeton U., 1956-58; instr., then asst. prof. econs. Kenyon Coll., Gambier, Ohio, 1958-64; mem. faculty N.Mex. State U., Las Cruces, 1964—; prof. econs. N.Mex. State U., 1969—, chmn. dept., 1974—. Author: International Finance and New York, 1976; co-author: Comparative Economic Systems, 3d edit, 1983. Served with AUS, 1953-55. Recipient Westhafer award excellence in teaching N.Mex. State U., 1973. Mem. Phi Beta Kappa, Phi Kappa Phi, Delta Sigma Pi. Home: 2035 Rentfrow Ave Las Cruces NM 88001 Office: Dept Econs New Mex State Univ Box 3511 University Park Las Cruces NM 88003

NOREEN, TERRY GENE, health and safety consultant; b. Walla Walla, Wash., May 21, 1946; s. Arthur Sanford and Norma Jean (Slater) N.; A.S., Grossmont Coll., 1974; B.A., San Diego State U., 1976; M.S., Portland State U., 1980; m. Linda Lou Mays, May 2, 1965 (div. 1982); children: Holly, Tina, Terry Gene; m. Cindra L. Starmer, Dec. 9, 1983; children: Jennifer, Ryan, Erin, Jenice. Dir. data communications equipment Naval Communications Sta., San Diego, 1972-76; health and safety specialist Tidewater Barge Lines, Vancouver, Wash., 1976-82; health and safety cons. to marine and gen. industry, 1982—. Contbg. author trade jours. Mem. Clark County Sheriff Res., 1981; leader Boy Scouts Am., 1981-86. Served with USN, 1963-71. Cert. hazard control mgr.; lic. tankerman U.S. Mcht. Marine. Mem. Oil Chem. and Atomic Workers Union (shop steward 1978-80, health and safety steward 1979-82), Columbia River Boatman's Union (sec. 1977-78), Portland Shipyard Safety Council, Am. Soc. Safety Engrs., Auto Body Craftsmen's Soc. (co-dir. chpt. 1984-86, program dir. 1983-85, program dir. SW Wash. chpt. 1983-84, Wash. State health and Safety dir. 1984-86), Nat. Fire Protection Assn., Am. Pub. Health Assn., Nat. Safety Mgmt. Soc., C. of C. U.S.A. Mormon. Lodge: Lions (bd. dirs. 1985). Home: 25604 NE Manley Rd Battle Ground WA 98604 Office: 7622 NE 47th Ave Vancouver WA 98661

NORFLEET, MARY ANN, psychologist, educational administrator; b. Wichita, Kans.; d. D.L. and Fern C. Warburton. B.S., U. Kans., 1964, M.S., 1965; Ph.D., U. Oreg., 1969. Staff psychologist Agnew State Hosp., San Jose, Calif., 1969-72; clin. psychologist, dir. biofeedback North County Community Mental Health Clinic, Palo Alto, Calif., 1972-80; mem. health team study group Stanford U., 1974-76; dir. clin. evaluation and research Bay Area Pain Center, O'Connor Group, San Jose, 1979-81; v.p. acad. affairs Western Grad. Sch. Psychology, 1978—; clin. faculty dept. psychiatry and behavioral scis., Stanford U. Med. Sch., 1983—. Fellow Am. Orthopsychiat. Assn.; mem. Internat. Assn. for Study of Pain, Psychosomatic Medicine Soc., Am. Psychol. Assn., Santa Clara County Psychol. Assn. (past pres.), Sigma Xi, Psi Chi. Club: 99's. Office: 555 Middlefield Rd Palo Alto CA 94301

NORIAN, ROGER W., glass manufacturing company executive; b. Chgo., Apr. 16, 1943; s. Richard and Eunice (Sandusky) N.; m. Patricia Adelaar, Feb. 24, 1967; children: Jennifer, Michelle, Kristina. B.S. in Bus. Adminstrn, Northwestern U., 1965, M.B.A., 1966. Asso. corp. fin. dept. A.G. Becker & Co., 1966-68; asst. to chmn., chief fin. officer Duplan Corp., N.Y.C., 1968-75; chief fin. officer Kerr Glass Co., Los Angeles, from 1975; now pres., chmn. bd., chief exec. officer Kerr Glass Co. Address: Kerr Glass Mfg Co 501 S Shatto Pl Los Angeles CA 90020

NORLING, BRIAN LEE, mechanical engineer; b. Mpls., Sept. 29, 1954; s. Ralph E. and Phylis M. (Benson) N.; m. Lori K. Nelsen; 1 child, Amber L. BSME, U. Wash., 1977; MBA with honors, Seattle U., 1987. Registered profl. engr., Wash. Design engr. Paccar, Renton, Wash., 1977-80, sr. design engr., 1980-82; sr. design engr. Sundstrand Data Control, Redmond, Wash., 1981-82, project engr., 1982-84, prin. engr., 1984-86, engring. supr. advanced tech., 1986—; cons. various instrumentation projects, Wash. Patentee in field; inventor in field; contbr. articles to profl. jours. Active Mill Creek (Wash.) Community Assn. Roman Catholic. Avocations: skiing, backpacking, softball, tennis, basketball. Office: Sundstrand Data Control Overlake Indsl Park MS-R21 Redmond WA 98052

NORMAN, DONALD MORRIS, environmental chemist; b. New Orleans, June 26, 1953; s. Edward Cobb and June Marie (Morris) N. Student, U. N.C., 1971-72; BS in Biology, Tulane U., 1976; BS in Oceanography, U. Wash., 1980; postgrad., Western Wash. U., 1986—. Lab technician La. State U. Med. Ctr., New Orleans, 1973-74; waiter Yellowstone Nat. Park, Wyo., summers, 1976, 1977; lab technician dept. envrion. health U. Wash., Seattle, 1978-81, research technologist dept. envrion. Health, 1981-86. Precinct committeeman King County Dems., Mae Precinct 1st legis. dist., Seattle, 1980—; mem. dist. 1 Citizens Water Quality Adv. Com., Seattle King County METRO, 1981-83; co-founder Citizens United for Food Safety, Seattle, 1985—; bd. dirs. Wash. Pub. Interest Research Group, 1978-79, Puget Consumers Coop., Seattle, 1985-86, mem. product info. com. Mem. AAAS, Seattle Audubon Soc., N. Plains Resource Council, Ctr. Sci. Pub. Interest, Friends of the Earth. Democrat. Club: Richmond Beach Revelers (Duke 1980-86). Home: 2112 NW 199th St Seattle WA 98177

NORMAN, JOE G., chemistry educator; b. Brevard, N.C., Aug. 8, 1947; s. Josephus Gaston and Nelle Livingston (Bookout) N. BA in Chemistry, Rice U., 1969; PhD in Chemistry, MIT, 1972. Asst. prof. U. Wash., Seattle, 1972-77, assoc. prof., 1977-82, prof., 1982—, assoc. dean, 1980—; cons. Monsanto Co., Gen. Motors, Bell Labs., Boeing, 1976-82; proposal reviewer NSF, Am. Chem. Soc., Research Corp., 1974—; invited lectr. various universities and socs., 1976-80. Editorial bd. Jour. Computational Chemistry, 1980—. Mem. Seattle-King County Leadership Tomorrow, 1985-86, Seattle-King County Mcpl.League, 1985—, Wash. Environ. Council, Seattle, 1974—. Alfred P. Sloan Found. fellow, 1978-80; NSF research grantee, 1976-83, Am. Chem. Soc. research grantee, 1972-83. Avocations: photography, internat. natural history, performing arts.

NORMAN, JOHN BARSTOW, JR., designer, educator; b. Paloa, Kans., Feb. 5, 1940; s. John B. and Ruby Maxine (Johnson) N.; B.F.A., U. Kans., 1962, M.F.A., 1966; m. Roberta Jeanne Martin, June 6, 1967; children—John Barstow III, Elizabeth Jeanne. Designer and illustrator Advt. Design, Kansas City, Mo., 1962-64; asst. instr. U. Kans., Lawrence, 1964-66; art dir. Hallmark Cards, Inc., Kansas City, Mo., 1966-69; instr. dept. art U. Denver, 1969-73, asst. prof., 1973-78, assoc. prof., 1978—, Disting. prof., 1980, chmn. design dept.; design cons. Mo. Council Arts and Humanities, 1966-67; cons. designer Rocky Mountain Bank Note Corp., Denver, 1971—, Signage Identity System, U. Dever; bd. dirs. communications U. Denver; dir. Internat. Design Conf. in Aspen Seminar Group; tech. cons. Denver Art Mus., 1974—, designed exhbns., 1974-75; adv., cons. Jefferson County (Colo.) Sch., System, 1976—; chmn. Design and Sculpture Exhbn., Colo. Celebration of the Arts, 1975-76; chmn. arts and scis adv. com., Career Edn. Adv. Bd., Denver Pub. Sch. System, 1976-77. One man shows include: Gallery Cortina, Aspen, Colo., 1983; commd. works include: Jedda, Saudi Arabia, Synegistics Corp., Denver, Gillette (Wyo.) Pub. Library; represented in permanent collections Pasadena Ctr. for the Arts, N.Y. Art Dirs. Club, Midland Art Council/Fiber Collection, Pasadena (Calif.) Ctr. for the Arts, 1984, N.Y. Art Dirs. Club, 1985 Midland Art Council/Fiber Collection, 1985; represented in traveling exhbns. Los Angeles Art Dirs. Show and N.Y. Art Dirs. Show, U.S., Europe, Japan, 1985; featured in Denver Post, 1984, Post Electric City Mag., 1984, Rocky Mt. News, 1984, Douglas County Press, 1984, Mile High Cabel Vision, 1985, Sta. KWGN-TV, 1985; work represented in film collection Mus. Modern Art, N.Y.C. Recipient Silver Medal award N.Y. Internat. Film and Video Competition, 1976, Design awards Council Advancement and Support of Edn., 1969, 71, 73, 76, Honor Mention award Los Angeles Art Dirs. Club, 1984, Honor Mention award N.Y. Art Dirs. Club, 1984, 1st place Nat. Native Am. Wearable Art Competition, 1985, 5th place Nat. Wind Sail: Am. Banners Competition, Midland, Mich., 1985, also awards for surface designs in Colo. Ctr. for the Arts Wearable Art Competition, 1984-85, Foothills Art Gallery Nat. Wearable Art Competition, 1984-85, Fashion Group of Denver Competition, 1984-85. Mem. Art Dirs. Club Denver (ednl. liaison, 6 Gold medals 1974-82, Best of Show Gold medal 1983, Honor Mention award, 1984), Univ. Art Dirs. Assn. Home: PO Box 302 751 Willow Lake Dr Franktown CO 80116 Office: U Denver Sch Art 2121 E Asbury St Denver CO 80208

NORMAN, JOHN EDWARD, independent petroleum landman; b. Denver, May 22, 1922; s. John Edward and Ella (Warren) N.; m. Hope Sabin, Sept. 5, 1946; children—J. Thomas, Gerould W., Nancy E., Susan G., Douglas E. B.S.B.A., U. Denver, 1949, M.B.A., 1972. Clk., bookkeeper Capitol Life Ins. Co., Denver, 1945-46; salesman Security Life and Accident Co., Denver, 1947; bookkeeper Central Bank and Trust Co., Denver, 1947-50; automobile salesman H.A. Hennies, Denver, 1950; petroleum landman Continental Oil Co. (name changed to Conoco Inc. 1979), Denver, 1950-85; ind. petroleum landman, 1985—. Lectr. pub. lands Colo. Sch. Mines, 1968-85; lectr. mineral titles and landmen's role in oil industry Casper Coll., 1969-71. Mem. Casper Mcpl. Band Commn., 1965-71, mem. band, 1961-71, mgr., 1968-71; former musician, bd. dirs. Casper Civic Symphony; former bd. dirs. Jefferson Symphony, performing mem., 1972-75. Served with AUS, World War II. Mem. Am. Assn. Petroleum Landmen (dir. at large, chmn. publs. for regional dir.), Wyo. Assn. Petroleum Landmen (pres.), Denver Assn. Petroleum Landmen, Rocky Mountain Oil and Gas Assn. (pub. lands com. 1981—), Rocky Mountain Petroleum Pioneers. Episcopalian (mem. choir, vestryman, past dir. acolytes). Club: Elks. Home and Office: 2710 S Jay St Denver CO 80227

NORMAN, WILLIAM LESTER, photography equipment manufacturing executive; b. South Gate, Calif., Feb. 10, 1941; s. Lovell Burch and Margaret Estelle (Reese) N.; m. Elaine Frances, May 12, 1963 (div. Dec. 1983); children: Thomas Kevin, Stacey Lynn.; m. H. Faye Norman, May 17, 1985; 1 child, Janelle. AS, Western States Coll. Engring., 1962; MS in Photography (hon.), Brooks Inst., 1983. Pres., founder Norman Enterprises, Burbank, Calif., 1963—; pres. Bardwell & McAlister, Hollywood, Calif., 1985—; bd. dirs. Photo-Control Corp., Mpls. Author: The Bank Book, 1985; contbr. articles on photography to profl. jours. Recipient Photographic Craftsman award Profl. Photographers Am., 1974, Appreciation for Achievement award Profl. Photographers of Mex., 1978. Mem. Mech. Bank Collectors of Am. (v.p. 1985—). Republican. Avocation: collecting old mech. banks. Office: Norman Enterprises Inc 2601 Empire Ave Burbank CA 91504

NORMANDY, GEORGE MITCHELL, JR., electrical engineer; b. Decatur, Ga., Oct. 23, 1935; s. George Mitchell and Martha Randolph (Jones) M.; m. Marcia Del Farris, May 23, 1955 (div. Sept. 1969); children: Penny, Patricia, George III, Pamela, Paulette; m. Jean Edna Stolberg, Jan. 15, 1971; children: Jo Ann, John, Penny. AA in Phys. Sci, AA in Math., San Diego State U., 1977, BSEE, 1981; AA in Psychology, AS in Mfg. Tech., San Diego City Coll., 1984; postgrad., West Coast U., 1984-86. Enlisted USN, 1954-69, resigned, 1969; with customer service Motor Machine Co., San Diego, 1969-80; engr. Gen. Atomic Co., San Diego, 1980-82; sr. engr. GA Techs. Inc., San Diego, 1982—. Mem. IEEE, Assn. Computing Machinery, Am. Nuclear Soc., Mensa. Republican. Lutheran. Avocation: home computer. Home: 3935 Centraloma Dr San Diego CA 92107 Office: GA Techs Inc Box 85608 San Diego CA 92138

NORRIS, ANDREW EDWARD, chemist; b. Santa Rosa, Calif., Jan. 13, 1937; s. Andrew Taylor and Nelle Vienna (Carter) N.; m. Mary Susan Millard, Mar. 17, 1979; 1 child, Celeste Joy. SB, U. Chgo., 1958; PhD, Washington U., St. Louis, 1963. Research assoc. Brookhaven Nat. Lab., Upton, N.Y., 1964-66; mem. staff Los Alamos (N.Mex.) Nat. Lab., 1966—; prin. investigator for geochem. testing Nev. Nuclear Waste Storage Investigations, Las Vegas, 1985—. Contbr. articles to Phys. Rev. Deacon Christian and Missionary Alliance Ch., 1984-85. Mem. AAAS, Am. Chem. Soc. (sec. cen. N.Mex. sect. 1973, 75), Am. Phys. Soc., Sigma Xi. Republican. Office: Los Alamos Nat Lab MS J514 Los Alamos NM 87545

NORRIS, GARY ARTHUR, traffic engr.; b. Bellingham, Wash., Mar. 7, 1950; s. James Carol and Joy Loraine (Elerding) N.; m. Dariel Lynn Brady, Aug. 12, 1973; children—James, Rebeccah, Jeffrey, Christian. Student Western Wash. U., Bellingham, 1968-70; B.C.E., U. Wash., 1973, M.C.E., 1977. Registered profl. engr., Wash. Transp. planner enging. dept. City of Seattle, 1973-74; transp. engr. City of Bellevue (Wash.), 1975-80; traffic engr. City of Renton (Wash.), 1980—. Active Boy Scouts Am., Preston, Wash.; organist, elder Rose Hill Presbyn. Ch. U.S.; mem. King County Snoqualmie Plan Adv. Com. Dept. Transp., Fed. Hwy. Adminstrn. Hwy. Safety scholar, 1974-75. Mem. Inst. Transp. Engrs. (former sec.-treas. Wash. sect., pres. 1984-85, mktg. expo. 1986).

NORRIS, JERRY BROWNING, land use planner; b. San Francisco, Sept. 29, 1942; s. Jerry Freuler and Dorothy (Browning) N.; m. Maureen Elise Pendergast, Feb. 6, 1971; children: John, Tom. AA, City Coll., San Francisco, 1970; BA, Calif. State U., San Francisco, 1970; postgrad., Golden Gate U., 1977. University archivist U. Calif., San Francisco, 1964-70; asst. dir. Council of State Govts., San Francisco, 1970-75, dir., 1975-80; exec. dir. Pacific Basin Devel. Council, Honolulu, 1980—. Co-contbr. U. Calif. Pictorial History, 1968; contbr. numerous articles on govt. and devel. to profl. jours. Served as cpl. USMC, 1960-66. Mem. Am. Soc. Pub. Adminstrn. (pres. 1981—). Democrat. Roman Catholic. Avocations: reading, writing, traveling. Home: 94092 Puanane Loop Mililani HI 96789 Office: Pacific Basin Devel Council 567 S King #320 Honolulu HI 96813

NORRIS, MARCIA MATHESON, speech pathologist; b. Visalia, Calif., May 20, 1939; d. Stanley Theodore and Anna Newell (Machlachlan) Matheson; m. Edward J. Norris, Sept. 5, 1959 (div. 1980); children: Geoffrey, Mary Ann. AA, Monterey Peninsula Coll., 1959; student, Duke U., 1960-61; BA, U. Ala., 1972; MA, San Jose State U., 1976. Speech lang. specialist Monterey (Calif.) Peninsula Coll., 1975-79, 81-84, instructional specialist High Tech. Ctr. for Disabled, 1984-86; coordinator High Tech Ctr. for Diabled 1986—; speech lang. specialist Carmel (Calif.) Schs., 1979-80. Pres. Carmel Music Soc., 1986. Mem. Am. Speech Lang. Hearing Assn. (cert.), Calif. Speech Lang. Hearing Assn., Calif. Assn. Postsecondary Educators of Disabled, Phi Kappa Phi. Democrat. Episcopalian. Home: PO Box 2823 Carmel CA 93921 Office: Monterey Peninsula Coll 980 Fremont Monterey CA 93921

NORRIS, PHILIP, brokerage executive; b. N.Y.C., Oct. 16, 1928; s. Claude Basil and Fannie Inez (Bell) N.; m. Rose Martin, Aug. 24, 1957 (div.); children: Laura Ashley Coats, Susan Martin, Philip Blair; m. Rebecca Snider, Oct. 1, 1977. BA, Claremont McKenna Coll., 1953. Account exec. Dean Witter & Co., Honolulu, 1960-66; Hawaii area mgr. E.F. Hutton & Co., Honolulu, 1966—; mem. bus. conduct com. Nat. Assn. Securities Dealers, San Francisco, 1972-74. Bd. dirs. Downtown Improvement Assn., Honolulu, 1983—; vice chmn. Met. YMCA, Honolulu, 1985—; mem. bd. trustees Seabury Hall, Maui, Hawaii. Served to maj. USMC, 1954-60. Mem. Securities Industry Assn. (govt. relations com. 1980—), Hawaii C. of C. (bd. dirs. 1985—). Republican. Mem United Ch. Christ. Lodge: Rotary (pres. Honolulu club 1986—, pres. Waikiki club 1966-67). Home: 3721 Kanaina Ave Apt 122 Honolulu HI 96813 Office: EF Hutton & Co Inc 1001 Bishop St Suite 2500 Honolulu HI 96822

NORRIS, ROBERT MATHESON, geologist; b. Los Angeles, Apr. 24, 1921; s. Robert DeWitt and Jessie (Matheson) N.; m. Virginia Grace Oakley, Jan. 5, 1952; children—Donald Oakley, James Matheson, Elizabeth Anne. A.B., UCLA, 1943, M.A., 1949; Ph.D. Scripps Inst. Oceanography, U. Calif., San Diego, 1951. Teaching asst. UCLA, 1946-49; asso. marine geology Scripps Inst. Oceanography, 1951-52; mem. faculty U. Calif., Santa Barbara, 1952—; prof. geology U. Calif., 1968—; also dir. Channel Islands Field Sta., 1970-75. Contbr. articles profl. jours. Served with USNR, 1944-46. Fulbright scholar, 1961-62. Mem. Geol. Soc. Am., Geol. Soc. N.Z., Nat. Assn. Geology Tchrs., Am. Assn. Petroleum Geologists, Soc. Econ. Paleontologists and Mineralogists, AAUP, Sigma Xi, Phi Kappa Sigma, Phi Delta Kappa. Congregationalist. Address: 4424 Nueces Dr Santa Barbara CA 93110

NORSELL, PAUL ERNEST, service executive; b. Salt Lake City, Jan. 28, 1933; s. Alf Raae and Florence Emily (Freer) N.; m. Mary Elizabeth Rynd, Sept. 2, 1958; children: Stuart, Daryl, Paula. BSEE, Purdue U., 1954; MSEE, UCLA, 1956. Program mgr. applications tech. satellite Hughes Aircraft Co., Culver City, Calif., 1954-64; v.p. engring., ops. Litton Data Systems Div., Van Nuys, Calif., 1964-69; pres. Litton LITCOM Div., Melville, N.Y., 1969-73; v.p. Litton Indsl. Profl. Services and Equipment Group, Beverly Hills, Calif., 1973; pres. EXECUDEX West Los Angeles, Inc., 1974—. Contbr. articles to profl. jours. Mem. econ. devel. council Los Angeles Area C. of C., 1985, mem. transp. and pub. works council, 1985; mem. exec. com., chmn. exploring div. Boy Scouts Am., Suffolk County, N.Y, 1971-73; mem. exec. com., bd. mgrs. YMCA, Huntington, L.I., N.Y., 1972-73; bd. dirs. exec. com. L.I. Assn. Commerce and Industry, 1970-73. Hughes Masters Engring. fellow Hughes Aircraft Co., 1954-56; Purdue Alumni scholar Purdue Alumni Assn., 1952-54. Mem. IEEE, AAAS, Ctr. Entrepreneurial Mgmt., Nat. Assn. Accts., Chem. Engring. Soc., Calif. Exec. Recruiters Assn., U.S. Yacht Racing Union, Eta Kappa Nu. Clubs: Long Beach Yacht (Long Beach, Calif.); Transpacific Yacht (Honolulu). Office: EXECUDEX West Los Angeles Inc PO Box 4113 Woodland Hills CA 91365

NORSTADT, FRED A., soil scientist; b. Sidney, Iowa, Mar. 15, 1926; s. James and Clara Bell (Carman) N.; m. Rozellen Ballard, June 1, 1950; children: Bethan, Lynn. Student, Mont. Sch. Mines, 1946-48; BS, Peru State Tchrs. Coll., 1950; MS in Agronomy, U. Nebr., 1958, PhD in Agronomy, 1966. Tchr., prin. Nebr. Pub. Schs., various locations, 1949-55; instr. extension div. U. Nebr., Lincoln, 1955-64; chemist soil and water conservation research div. USDA, Lincoln, 1964-66; soil scientist Agrl. Research Service, USDA, Grand Junction, Colo., 1966-69, Ft. Collins, Colo., 1969—; affiliate faculty Colo. State U., 1969—, mem. grad. student coms., assoc. mem. grad. faculty. Contbr. articles to profl. jours. Served with USN, 1944-46. Regents Tuition fellow U. Nebr., 1956-64, Franklin E. and Orlinda M. Johnson fellow U. Nebr., 1957-58. Fellow Soil Conservation Soc. Am. (mem. Colo. chpt., Commendation award 1976, Chpt. Pres. award 1974, 76, 77); mem. Am. Soc. Agronomy, Crop Sci. Soc. Am., Soil Sci. Soc. Am., Internat. Soil Sci. Soc. Am., Western Soil Sci. Soc., Orgn. Profl. Employees USDA, Colo. Assn. Soil Conservation Dists., Sigma Xi, Gamma Sigma Delta, Kappa Delta Pi. Republican. Presbyterian. Avocations: gardening, reading, home fruit orchard, canning and freezing fruits and vegetables. Home: 1933 Yorktown Ct Fort Collins CO 80526 Office: USDA Agrl Research Service 301 S Howes Fort Collins CO 80522

NORTH, DANIEL WARNER, consulting analyst; b. N.Y.C., Mar. 12, 1941; s. James Dennis and Margaret P. North; m. Diane M. Tarantino, Nov. 26, 1978; 1 child, Evan Armstrong. BS, Yale U., 1962; MS, Stanford U., 1964, PhD, 1970. Analyst SRI Internat., Menlo Park, Calif., 1967-74, asst. dir. decision analysis dept., 1974-77; prin., v.p. Decision Focus Inc., Los Altos, Calif., 1977—; mem. sci. adv. bd. EPA, Washington, 1978—. Mem. Soc. Risk Analysis, Inst. Mgmt. Sci., Ops. Research Soc. Am., Sigma Xi. Office: Decision Focus Inc 4984 El Camino Real #200 Los Altos CA 94022

NORTH, KATHRYN E. KEESEY (MRS. EUGENE C. NORTH), ret. educator; b. Columbia, Pa., Jan. 25, 1916; d. Issac and Elizabeth (French) Keesey; B.S., Ithaca Coll., 1938; M.A., N.Y. U., 1950; m. Eugene C. North, Aug. 18, 1938. Dir. music Cairo (N.Y.) Central Sch. Dist., 1938; music edn. cons. Argyle (N.Y.) Central Sch. Dist., 1939; dir. gen. music curriculum Hartford (N.Y.) Central Sch. Dist., 1939; mem. staff Del. Dept. Pub. Instrn., Dover, 1943; dir. music edn. Herricks (N.Y.) Pub. Schs., 1944-71; ret., 1971. Vis. lectr. Ithaca Coll., summers 1959, 60, 62-65, Fairleigh-Dickinson U., Rutherford, N.J., summer 1966, Albertus Magnus Coll., New Haven, summer 1968; instr. Adelphi Coll., 1954-55, Sch.. Edn., N.Y.U., 1964-65. Mem. Music Educators Nat. Conf., N.E.A., N.Y. State Sch. Music Assn., N.Y. State Tchrs. Assn., Nassau Music Educators Assn. (exec. bd. 1947-58), N.Y. State Council Adminstrs. Music Edn. (chpt. v.p. 1967-68), Herricks Tchrs. Assn. (pres. 1948), Sigma Alpha Iota. Mem. Order Eastern Star. Home: 1645 Calle Camille La Jolla CA 92037

NORTHCUTT, HELENE LOUISE BERKING (MRS. CHARLES PHILLIP NORTHCUTT), artist, educator; b. Hannibal, Mo., July 6, 1916; d. Robert Stanley and Alice Lee (Adkisson) Berking; student Christian Coll., Columbia, Mo., 1932-33; B.S., U. Mo., 1939, A.M., 1940, Ed.D., 1959; m. Charles Phillip Northcutt, June 4, 1938 (dec.); children—John Berking, Francois Lee Northcutt Hedeen. Art tchr., supr. Oakwood High Sch. and Elem. Sch., 1937-39; tchr. jr. high sch. U. Mo. Lab. Sch., 1939-40; tchr. elem. art, Memphis, Mo., 1941; county fine arts supr., Ralls County, Mo., 1941-42; tchr. art high sch., Columbia, 1943-44; tchr. art jr. high sch., Hannibal, Mo., 1951-54; supr. art Ralls County Reorganized Sch. Dist. VI, New London, 1954-56; vis prof. U. Upper Iowa, 1956; instr. U. Mo., 1956-57; prof. art Eastern Mont. Coll. unit U. Mont., Billings, from 1957, now prof. emeritus, mem. grad. faculty; vis. prof. art U. B.C., Vancouver, 1965; cons. in curriculum in art edn.; cons. environ. edn., cons. on Indian edn., early childhood; exhibits fibers and paintings; state dir. Am. Art Week, Am. Artists Profl. League, 1963-65; exhibit chmn. E.M.C. Gallery Fine Arts; program chmn. Becky Thatcher council Girl Scouts U.S.A., 1946-48; bd. dirs., treas. United Christian Campus Ministry; bd. dirs. Growth Through Art. Recipient scholarship Delta Kappa Gamma, 1956-57; Nat. Press award Gen. Fedn. Women's Clubs, 1951; named Outstanding Honor Grad. U. Mo., 1968; citations for distinctive service Eastern Mont. Coll., Helene B. Northcutt Gallery named in her honor. Mem. Nat. Soc. Coll. Profs., AAUP, Mont. Edn. Assn. (past pres. Eastern Faculty unit; v.p. dept. higher edn. 1966-68, dept. pres. 1968-70) Nat., Mont. (sec. 1967-69) art edn. assns., AAUW (past chpt. pres.), Mont. Early Childhood Edn. Assn., Gen. Fedn. Women's Clubs (local past pres.), Delta Kappa Gamma (past chpt. pres., chmn. com., chmn. state world fellowship), Delta Phi Delta, Kappa Delta Epsilon. Methodist (mem. commn. higher edn. ministries, trustee Yellowstone Conf.). Club: Eastern Montana College Faculty (Billings, Mont.). Author: Creative Expression, 1964; Competency base Module-Methods and Materials, 1974; contbr. to publs. in field; reviewer, editor manuscripts on art and art edn. Home: M-3 Timbers Townhomes 3224 Granger Ave E Billings MT 59102

NORTHEN, HELEN ESTHER, social work educator; b. Butte, Mont.; d. John Alfred and Amelia Sigred (Anderson) N. AB, U. Wash., 1939; MS, U. Pitts., 1944; PhD, Bryn Mawr Coll., 1953. Program dir. YWCA, Pitts., 1945-49; field instr. U. Pitts., 1945-49; research asst. Bryn Mawr (Pa.) Coll., 1949-51; assoc. prof. U. Hawaii, Honolulu, 1951-53; assoc. prof. U. So. Calif., Los Angeles, 1953-59, prof., 1959-82, prof. emeritus, 1982—; vis. prof. U. Alabama, Tuscaloosa, 1982-83; cons. Huntington Meml. Hosp., Pasadena, Calif. 1983—. Author: Social Work with Groups, 1969, Clinical Social Work, 1982, (with others) Child Family Neighborhood, 1982; co-editor Theories of Social Work with Groups, 1976, mem. editorial bd. Social Work with Groups, 1976—, Small Group Behavior, 1968—. Nat. bd. dirs. Camp Fire Girls, Inc., N.Y.C. 1961-69, hon. mem. 1969—; mem. Friends of the London School of Econs. and Polit. Sci., Washington, 1976—. Named Disting. Practitioner Nat. Acads. of Practice, 1982, Disting. Faculty Mem. U. So. Calif. Sch. of Social Work, 1979. Mem. Nat. Assn. Social Workers (mem. various coms. 1953—), Council on Social Work Edn. (mem. various coms.), Soc. Hosp. Social Work Dirs. (bd. dirs. 1984—), Group for the Advancement of Social Work (mem. exec. com. 1984—), Phi Kappa Phi (bd. dirs. 1983—). Democrat. Avocations: traveling, writing. Home: 1707 Micheltorena St #304 Los Angeles CA 90026 Office: U So Calif Sch Social Work Univ Park Los Angeles CA 90089-0411

NORTHEY, LORI MARIE, mechanical engineer; b. Helena, Mont., Oct. 29, 1958; d. Ronald Henry and Darlene Mae (Campbell) Martinson; m. Michael David Northey, Apr. 9, 1983. BSME, Mont. State U., 1982. Student engr. Crown Zellerbach, Camas, Wash., 1980; engr. Alcoa Aluminum Co., Wenatchee, Wash., 1981; assoc. engr. Westinghouse Hanford Co., Richland, Wash., 1982-84, engr., 1984—, also quality circle facilitator, 1985—. Mem. Explorer post Boy Scouts Am., Richland, 1985-86. Mem. ASME, Nat. Mgmt. Assn., Soc. Mfg. Engrs. Robotics Internat., Am. Nuclear Soc., Alpha Gamma Delta. Republican. Avocations: water and snow skiing, bowling, jogging, cooking, fishing. Home: 415 Scot Richland WA 99352 Office: Westinghouse Hanford Co Remote Handling Engring PO Box 1970 Richland WA 99352

NORTHROP, JOHN HOWARD, scientist; b. Yonkers, N.Y., July 5, 1891; s. John I. and Alice Belle (Rich) N.; m. Louise Walker, June 1918; children—Alice Havemeyer, John. W.B. B.S., Columbia U., 1912, M.A., 1913, Ph.D., 1915, D.Sc., 1937; D.Sc., Harvard U., 1936, Yale U., 1937, Princeton U., 1940, Rutgers U., 1941; LL.D., U. Calif., 1939. Cutting traveling fellow Columbia U., 1915; apptd. asst. Rockefeller Inst. for Med. Research, 1916, asso. mem., 1922, member of Inst., 1924-62, prof. of Inst. emeritus, 1962—; Hitchcock prof. U. Calif., 1939; Thayer lectr. Johns Hopkins U., 1940, De Lamar lectr., 1937; Jesup lectr. Columbia, 1938; prof. bacteriology, biophysics, research biophysicist Donner Lab., U. Calif., 1958-59, prof. emeritus, 1959—; mem. com. on proteins NRC cons. and official investigator to NDRC, 1942. Author: Crystalline Enzymes; Hon. editor, contbr.: Jour. Gen. Physiology; contbg. editor: Funk & Wagnalls Ency. Trustee Marine Biol. Lab., Woods Hole, Mass. Capt. C.W.S. U.S. Army, 1918-19. Recipient Stevens prize Coll. Phys. and Surg., Columbia, 1930; Chandler medal Columbia, 1937; Giraud medal Nat. Acad. Sci., 1944; shared Nobel prize in chemistry, 1946; certificate of merit, 1948; Columbia Lion Award Alumni Club of Essex County, 1949; Alexander Hamilton medal Columbia U., 1961; Hon. fellow Chem. Soc., London. Mem. Nat. Acad. Sci., S.A.R., Am. Soc. Biol. Chemistry, Soc. Gen. Physiologists, Soc. Philomathique (Paris), Am. Philos. Soc., Sigma Xi (research fellowship com.), Phi Lambda Upsilon, Kais. Deutch. Akad. der Naturforscher, Delta Kappa Epsilon. Club: Century Assn. Home: PO Box 1387 Wickenberg AZ 85358

NORTHWAY, ROBERT BRUCE, veterinarian; b. Modesto, Calif., Feb. 6, 1935; s. Harry Calvin and Lucille (Peterson) N.; m. Mary Ann Baars, Apr. 24, 1959 (div. Nov. 1985); 1 child, Mark Eric. BS, U. Calif., Davis, 1958, DVM, 1960; postgrad student, U. So. Calif., Catalina, 1980. Lic. veterinarian, Calif.; cert. jr. coll. tchr., Calif. Pvt. practice Northway Vet. Hosp., Merced, Calif., 1960-78, Catheys Valley, 1970—; prin. Pacific Sci. Research, Catheys Valley, Calif., 1965—, chmn. bd. dirs.; prin. Northway Land and Investment, Catheys Valley, 1966—; chmn. bd. dirs. Pacific Research, Cathys Valley, 1972—; owner Specialized Surgery, Catheys Valley, 1978—. Author: Baja Pirates, 1978; contbr. articles to profl. jours. Recipient Cert. Merit award Nat. Small Bus. Adminstrn., 1977. Fellow (founding) Acad. Surg. Research; mem. AVMA, AAAS, Calif. Vet. Med. Assn., Sierra Club (chmn. 1954—), Merced Aquanauts (pres. 1969-76). Avocations: flying, mountain climbing, photography, skiing, diving. Home: Star Rt Hwy 140 Catheys Valley CA 95306 Office: Pacific Sci Research 4343 Hwy 140 Catheys Valley CA 95306

NORTON, FRANK TRACY, sports organization executive, electrical engineer; b. San Francisco, Jan. 21, 1936; s. Tracy Murray and Loretta Gladas (Buchel) N.; m. Loretta Yvonne Tally, June 25, 1955; children: Lynn Dora Norton, Lori Ann Kober, Lisa Marie Ligouri. Degree in elec. engring., Internat. Corresponence Sch., 1957; degree in modern bus., Alexander Hamilton Inst., 1967; degree in Am. law and procedure, La Salle Extension U., 1970; degree in microcomputers, Nat. Radio Inst., 1985. Cert. profl. tennis tchr. Design engr. Pacific Gas & Electric Co., San Francisco, 1954—; pres. Tennis Outings, Inc., San Francisco, 1976—, also bd. dirs.; exec. dir. Club Tennis, San Francisco; profl. tennis teaching pro Blue Lake Springs, Arnold, Calif., 1984—. Contbr. articles to sports mags. Bd. dirs. Recreation and Park Dept. Ind. div., San Francisco, 1972-78, v.p. bd. dirs. 1977-78. Mem. U.S. Profl. Tennis Assn., U.S. Profl. Tennis Registry, Profl. Stringers Assn., U.S. Racquet Stringers Assn. Christian Scientist. Home: 126 Madrone Ave San Francisco CA 94127 Office: Tennis Outings Inc PO Box 915 Arnold CA 95223

NORTON, JACK RICHARD, chemistry educator; b. Dallas, May 5, 1945; s. Milton Kennedy and Agatha Mae (Duff) N. AB, Harvard U., 1967; PhD, Stanford U., 1972. Postdoctoral fellow Cambridge (Eng.) U., 1972; asst. prof. chemistry Princeton (N.J.) U., 1973-79; assoc. prof. Colo. State U., Ft. Collins, 1979-81, prof., 1981—; cons. FMC Copr., Princeton, 1976-79, Tenn. Eastman, Kingsport, 1979—. Contbr. articles to profl. jours. Fellow NSF, Washington, 1967-72, Alfred P. Sloan Found., N.Y.C., 1977; Dreyfus Found. Tchr. scholar, N.Y.C., 1976. Mem. Am. Chem. Soc., Royal Soc. Chemistry. Democrat. Home: 1325 Birch #18 Fort Collins CO 80521 Office: Colo State U Dept Chemistry Fort Collins CO 80523

NORTON, KAREN ANN, accounting executive; b. Paynesville, Minn., Nov. 1, 1950; d. Dale Francis and Ruby Grace (Gehlhar) N. B.A., U. Minn., 1972; postgrad. U. Md., 1978; cert. acctg. U.S. Dept. Agr. Grad. Sch., 1978; postgrad. Calif. State Poly. U.-Pomona, 1984—. C.P.A., Md. Securities transactions analyst Bur. of Pub. Debt., Washington, 1972-79, internal auditor, 1979-81; internal auditor IRS, Washington, 1981; sr. acct. World Vision Internat., Monrovia, Calif., 1981-83, acctg. supr., 1983—; cons. (vol.) info. systems John M. Perkins Found., Pasadena, Calif., 1985-86. Author (poetry): Ode to Joyce, 1985 (Golden Poet award 1985). Second v.p. chpt. Nat. Treasury Employees Union, Washington, 1978, editor chpt. newsletter; mem. M-2 Prisoners Sponsorship Program, Chino, Calif., 1984-86. Recipient Spl. Achievement award Dept. Treasury, 1976, Superior Performance award, 1977-78; Charles and Ellora Alliss scholar, 1968. Mem. Christian Ministries Mgmt. Assn., Nat. Assn. Accts. Mem. Covenant Ch. Avocations: chess; racquetball; mountain climbing; whitewater rafting; sky diving.

NORTON, ROBERT ALLEN, plant biochemist; b. Pleasant Hill, Mo., July 25, 1942; s. Frank Samuel and Willard Josephine (Brain) N.; m. Koralia Stefanidis, Sept. 25, 1982. BA, U. Mo., Kansas City, 1970, Ms, 1977; PhD, U. B.C., Vancouver, Can., 1985. Postdoctoral researcher U. Calif., Irvine, 1984—. Contbr. articles to profl. jours. Mem. AAAS, Guayule Rubber Soc., Internat. Assn. Plant Tissue Culture, Phytochem. Soc. N.Am. Democrat. Avocation: plant photography. Home: 14906 Newport Ave Apt F Tustin CA 92680 Office: U Calif Dept Ecology & Evolutionary Biology Irvine CA 92717

NORTON, RORY DEAN, marketing professional; b. Riverside, Calif., May 3, 1946; s. Cecil Abby and Barbara Jean (Bronner) N.; m. Patricia Ann Green, June 25, 1966; children: Kyle Christopher, Kristin Michelle. BS in Mktg., Calif. State U., Northridge, 1968; BA in Police Sci., Los Angeles Police Acad., 1972. Account exec. Pacific Telephone Co., Los Angeles, 1968-77; account exec. Nev. Bell Co., Reno, 1977-80, multi-media mgr., 1980-82; nat. account mgr. AT&T, Los Angeles, 1982-84; br. mgr. Rolm/IBM Corp., Los Angeles, 1984—; security cons. Carson City, Nev., 1980-82. Res. officer Los Angeles Police Dept., 1972; res. sheriff Carson City Sheriff's Office, 1980; pres. Pop Warner Football, Carson City. Recipient Felony Arrest Commendation award Carson City Sheriff's Office, 1979, 80; named #1 Sales Rep. AT&T, 1984. Mem. Am. Mktg. Assn., Calif. State U. Alumni Assn., Los Angeles Jaycees (sec. 1977-80), Phi Kappa Psi (pres. 1965-66). Republican. Baptist. Avocations: model railroading, softball, tennis. Office: Rolm/IBM Corp 23801 Calabasas Rd Calabasas CA 91302

NORVELL, WILLIAM WOODSON, small business owner; b. Tulsa, Mar. 18, 1948; s. George Eldon and Opal Margarite (Cluck) N.; m. Stephanie Marie Toth, Apr. 11, 1981; 1 child, Juliana Marie. BS in Mgmt., Okla. State U., 1970; MBA, U. Okla., 1971. Mgr. Silvernail Magnavox, Tulsa, 1972-75; adminstrv. asst. Price Internat., Manama, Bahrain, 1975-76; mgr. Remco Enterprises, Mesa, Ariz., 1976-78; prin. TeleSound Rentals and Tele-Vid Rentals Inc., Tempe, Ariz., 1978—. Mem. Better Bus. Bur., Phoenix, 1978; exec. mem. Citizens for An Environmentally Sound Park Devel. in Phoenix. Named One of Outstanding Mgrs., Remco Enterprises, 1977. Mem. Assn. Progressive Rental Orgns. (charter mem.), Video Software Dealers Assn., Small Bus. Assn. (assoc.), Phoenix C. of C., Ahwatukee, Ariz. Jaycees, Phi Delta Theta. Republican. Roman Catholic. Lodge: Rotary. Avocations: jogging, swimming, tennis.

NORWOOD, GEOFFREY ALEXANDER, hospital administrator; b. Erwin, N.C., Feb. 26, 1950; s. George McIntosh and Zabelle (Corwin) N.; m. Christine Cramer, July 12, 1975; children: Bryan Teague, Kathryn Blakely. BA in English, U. N.C., 1972; M in Hosp. Adminstrn., George Washington U., 1978. Fin. planner Meridian Engring., Phila., 1972-75; adminstrv. resident St. Luke's Med. Ctr., Phoenix, 1977-78; with planning dept. Scottsdale (Ariz.) Meml. Hosp., 1978-80, mgr. Family Health Unit, 1980-82; asst. adminstr. United Gen. Hosp., Sedro Woolley, Wash., 1982-84, chief exec. officer, 1984—. Pres. Babe Ruth Baseball League, Skagit County, Wash.; bd. dirs. United Way, Skagit County. Mem. Am. Coll. Health Care Execs., Wash. State Hosp. Assn. (mem. planning com. 1985), Hosp. Shared Services Assn. Presbyterian. Lodge: Rotary (bd. dirs. local chpt.). Avocations: baseball, fishing, traveling. Office: United Gen Hosp 1971 Hwy 20 Sedro Woolley WA 98284

NORWOOD, TOM W., social worker; b. Morriliton, Ark., Sept. 12, 1944; s. J.C. and Mary Louise (Eubanks) N.; 1 child, Martin; m. Sharon Ray, Aug. 16, 1986. BA in Psychology, U. Ark., 1967; MSW, U. Ga., 1969. Lic. clin. social worker, Calif. Area dir. Apalachee Community Mental Health Ctr., Tallahassee, 1971-79; clin. social worker Pacifica Hosp., Huntington Beach, Calif., 1979-82, St. Jude Rehab. Ctr., Fullerton, Calif., 1982—; cons. in field, 1970—. Mem. League Religious Sci. Practitioners. Served with U.S. Army, 1969-71. Mem. Nat. Assn. Social. Workers (Diplomate), Assn. Social Workers in Rehab. (v.p., pres. 1985-86). Democrat. Avocations: tennis, nature walks, social groups. Home: 218 S Marigold Ave Fullerton CA 92631 Office: St Jude Hosp and Rehab Ctr 101 E Valencia Mesa Dr Fullerton CA 92634

NOSSAMAN, NICHOLAS JUDD, general physician, homeopathist; b. Denver, Dec. 20, 1942; s. Carl Allen and Helen Lola (Doran) N.; m. Karen Frieda Kaiser, Sept. 10, 1966; children: Gwendolyn, Aason. BSin Applied Math., U. Colo., 1964; MD, U. Colo., Denver, 1968, MS in Health Adminstrn., 1973. Diplomate Am. Bd. Family Practice. Intern Hennepin County Gen. Hosp., Mpls., 1968-69; contract physician Denver Dept. Health & Hosps. Neighborhood Health Program, 1971, staff physician Adult & Family Practice Unit, La Mariposa Health Sta., 1973-82; staff physician USPHS, div. Indian Health Hosp., Crownpoint, N.Mex., 1969-71, med. dir., 1970-71; contract physician Metro. State Coll. Student Health Service, Denver, 1971-73, Plan de Salud del Valle (Valley Health Plan), Migrant Health Program, Ft. Lupton, Colo., 1972-73; pvt. practice specializing in family medicine and homeopathy Denver, 1976—; mem. profl. adv. bd. for planning health care devel. programs, Ft. Lewis Coll., Durango, Colo., 1971; USPHS coordinator Navajo Tribal Community Health Rep. Program, Crownpoint, 1969; profl. adv. com. Plan de Salud del Valle, Ft. Lupton, 1972-73; staff mem. Denver Gen. Hosp., 1974—, Mercy Hosp., Denver, 1977—; bd. dirs. Nat. Ctr. for Homeopathy, 1977-81, pres., 1980-81. Contbr. articles to profl jours. Boettcher scholar, U. Colo., 1960-64; recipient Mosby Book award for proficiency in ob-gyn, U. Colo., 1968. Mem. Am. Inst. Homeopathy (pres. elect 1984). Avocations: photography, music. Home: 1585 Glencoe Denver CO 80220 Office: 1750 High St Denver CO 80218

NOTESTINE, SANDRA DARLENE, engineering technician; b. St. Louis, Oct. 18, 1950; d. Elvis Mansfield McLain and Freda M. (Morgan) Bailey; m. Les Emmet Notestine, Nov. 27, 1971; children: Alan Ross, Jonathan Robert. Student, St. Louis Jr. Coll., 1970-71, Anchorage Community Coll., 1975-85. Acctg. clk. Amoco Oil Co., Anchorage, 1974-79; engring. sec. Municipality of Anchorage Water and Wastewater Utility, Anchorage, 1979-80, engring. techncian, 1980—, mem. task force, 1982-83. Acctg. asst. Parents United, Anchorage, 1983; career devel. trainer Municipality Anchorage, 1984-85. Mem. Nat. Assn. Female Execs. Avocations: landscape painting, fishing, camping. Office: Anchorage Water/Wastewater Utility 401 W International Anchorage AK 99518

NOTH, ROBERT HENRY, physician, educator, endocrinologist; b. Detroit, May 10, 1940; s. Paul Henry and Dorothy-Ann (Erehart) N.; m. Mary-Jo Cone, June 8, 1968; children: Robert Joseph, Elizabeth Marianne. BS, Stanford U., 1963; MD, Yale U., 1967. Intern Temple U. Hosp., Phila., 1967-68; resident in medicine Yale U.-New Haven Hosp., 1970-72; fellow in endocrinology Yale U., New Haven, 1972-74, asst. prof. medicine, 1974-80; chief endocrinology VA Med. Ctr., West Haven, Conn., 1977-80; assoc. prof. medicine U. Calif., Davis, 1980—; chief endocrinology unit VA Med. Ctr., Martinez, Calif., 1980—. Contbr. articles to profl. jours. Served with USPHS, 1968-70. Fellow ACP; mem. AAAS, Am. Fedn. Clin. Research. Avocations: photography, skiing, cellist. Office: VA Med Ctr Dept Medicine 150 Muir Rd Martinez CA 94533

NOTHMANN, RUDOLF S., legal researcher; b. Hamburg, W.Ger., Feb. 4, 1907; came to U.S., 1941, naturalized, 1943; s. Nathan and Henrietta G. (Heymann) N. Referendar, U. Hamburg, 1929, Ph.D. in Law, 1932; postgrad. U. Liverpool Law Sch. (Eng.), 1931-32. Export, legal adviser, adviser ocean marine ins. various firms, Ger., Eng., Sweden, Calif., 1933-43, 46-47; instr. fgn. exchange, fgn. trade Extension div. UCLA, 1947-48, vis. assoc. prof., 1951; asst. prof. econs. Whittier Coll., 1948-50, assoc. prof., 1950-51; contract work U.S. Air Force, U.S. Navy, 1953-59; contract negotiator space projects, space and missile systems orgn. U.S. Air Force, Los Angeles, 1959-77; pvt. researcher in internat. comml. law, Pacific Palisades, Calif., 1977—. Served with U.S. Army, 1943-45; ETO. Recipient Gold Tape award Air Force Systems Command, 1970. Mem. Internat. Bar Assn. (vice chmn. internat. sales and related comml. trans. com. 1977-82), Am. Econ. Assn., Am. Soc. Internat. Law. Author: The Insurance Certificate in International Ocean Marine Insurance and Foreign Trade, 1932; The Oldest Corporation in the World: Six Hundred Years of Economic Evolution, 1949. Club: Uebersee (Hamburg). Home: PO Box 32 Pacific Palisades CA 90272

NOTLEY, NORMAN THOMAS, chemist, research consultant, photographic and polymer researcher; b. Bristol, Eng., Apr. 10, 1928; came to U.S. 1952; s. Thomas and Hilda (Buckland) N.; m. Gretchen Denmon Carichner, June 28, 1958; children—Margaret Lee, James Lee. B.Sc., U. Bristol, 1949, Ph.D., 1952. Postdoctoral asst. Cornell U., Ithaca, N.Y., 1952-54; research chemist E.I. du Pont, Parlin, N.J., 1954-59; dir. phys. chem. Metal Box Co., London, Eng., 1959-62; dir. research and devel. Kalvar Corp., New Orleans, 1962-66; dir. chem. research B.E.G. Bell & Howell, Chgo., 1966-69; research cons., Pasadena, Calif., 1969—. Contbr. articles to profl. jours. Patentee in field. Mem. Am. Chem. Soc., Soc. Photog. Sci. and Engring., Sigma Xi. Home: 1895 E Orange Grove Pasadena CA 91104 Office: Novamedia Box 80818 San Marino CA 91108

NOTRICA, WILLIAM LEE, stockbroker; b. Los Angeles, Nov. 26, 1948; s. Solomon and Kerry Elaine (McInnes) N.; m. Lynn Roice, July 26, 1980; children: Blaire Roice, Nicole Lynn. BA, Calif. State U., Long Beach, 1972. V.p. Bateman Eichler, Long Beach, Calif., 1981-86, 1st v.p., 1986—; cert. fin. planner U. So. Calif., Los Angeles, 1984—. Mem. Long Beach Bond Club (pres. 1980), Bateman Eichler Hill Richards Millionaires Club (pres.'s council 1985—). Republican. Office: Bateman Eichler PO Box 97 6621 E Pacific Coastway Long Beach CA 90801

NOTT, EDWARD CLIFFORD, JR., military officer; b. Abilene, Tex., Mar. 4, 1932; s. Edward Clifford and Althea Mendel (Drennen) N.; m. Patsy Ruth Davies, July 21, 1954; children: Deborah, Jerold, Judith, Monte. BBA, U. Tex., 1954; MS in Mgmt., Naval Postgrad. Sch., 1965. Commd. ensign USN, 1954, advanced through grades to commdr., 1966, ret., 1977; exec. recruiter Mgmt. Recruiters, Colorado Springs, Colo., 1977-85; owner, recruiter OMNI, Colorado Springs, Colo., 1985—. Pres. Teen Club, Keflavick, Iceland Naval Station, 1971, Cabin Owners Assn., Cuchara, Colo., 1976-77; bd. dirs. Sch. Dist. Budget. Rev. Com., Colorado Springs, 1982. Mem. Soc. Mining Engrs., Colo. Mining Assn., Navy League, Ret. Officers Assn. Republican. Club: Blazer Ski (Colorado Springs, v.p., pres. 1984-85). Avocations: skiing, woodworking, outdoors. Home: 2511 Holiday Pl Colorado Springs CO 80909 Office: OMNI 559 E Pikes Peak 320 Colorado Springs CO 80903

NOVACK, GARY DEAN, research pharmacologist; b. Oakland, Calif., Nov. 21, 1953; s. Robert Lloyd and Dorothy Louise (Scheibner) N.; m. Dona Ann Greb, Aug. 28, 1977; children: Rebecca, Philip. AB, U. Calif., Santa Cruz, 1973; PhD, U. Calif., Davis, 1977. Postdoctoral fellow UCLA Brain Research Inst., 1977-79; sr. research pharmacologist Merrell Dow, Cin., 1979-82; clin. coordinator Allergan, Irvine, Calif., 1982-84, mgr. clin. research, 1984—; asst. research neurobiologist U. Calif., Irvine, 1984—. Contbr. articles to profl. jours. Anthony fellow U. Calif., Davis, 1977. Mem. Am. Soc. Clin. Pharmacology and Therapeutics. Avocation: photography. Office: Allergan 2525 DuPont Dr Irvine CA 92715

NOVAK, JULIE, nursing educator; b. Peoria, Ill., Oct. 2, 1950. BS in Nursing, U. Iowa, 1972, MA in Nursing, 1976; postgrad., U. San Diego, 1985. RN. Instr. med. sur. nursing St. Luke's Sch. Nursing, Cedar Rapids, Iowa, 1973-74; instr. familiy and community health U. Iowa Coll. of Nursing, 1974-75; perinatal nurse clinician U. Iowa Hosps., 1976-77; pediatric nurse practitioner Chicano Community Health Ctr., 1978-80; lectr., asst. prof. nursing San Diego State U., 1977-79; nurse, pediatric coordinator U. Calif., San Diego, 1978-82; pediatric nurse San Diego City Schs., 1980-82; coordinator infant spl. care ctr. U. Calif., San Diego, 1982-83, asst. clin. prof. intercampus grad. studies, 1983—; cons. child health San Diego State U. Child Study Ctr.; mem. accident prevention com. Am. Acad. Pediatrics; lectr. in field. Contbr. articles to profl. jours. Chairperson Annual Refugee Clothing Dr., E. San Diego, Car Seat Roundup, San Diego, 1983-85; mem. telethon March of Dimes, Indochinese clothing dr. Fletcher Hills Presbyn. Ch.; chmn. ways and means com. Benchley-Weinberger Elem. Sch. PTA, 1985-87; educator presch. health San Carlos Meth. Ch. Mem. Am. Nurses Assn., Nat. Assn. Pediatric Nurse Practitioners (assocs. program com., coordinator legis. field). Calif. Nurses Assn., Pi Lambda Theta, Sigma Theta Tau, Healthy Mothers/Healthy Babies (steering com.). Home: 7497 Gorge View Terr San Diego CA 92120

NOVAK, ROBERT E., audiology educator; b. Spring Valley, Ill., Apr. 30, 1949; s. Chester John Novak and Elnore (Anna) Roberts; m. Julia K. Novak, Aug. 12, 1972; children: Andrew, Nicholas and Christopher (twins. BA, U. Iowa, 1971, MA, 1974, PhD, 1977. Lic. audiologist. Audiology trainee VA Hosp., Iowa City, 1976-77; audiologist St. Luke's Hosp., Cedar Rapids, Iowa, 1973-74; assoc. prof. audiology San Diego State U., 1977—, acting chmn. dept., 1984-85; forensic audiologist San Diego Lawyers, 1983—; cons. community noise, San Diego, 1984—; cons. univ. hearing conservation program San Diego State U., 1986—. Co-author chpts. to books; contbr. articles to profl. jours. Bd. dirs. Crusaders Soccer League, San Diego, San Diego Sr. Community Ctrs., 1982-84, San Diego Noise Bd., 1986—; chmn. sch. site council, pres. PTA Benchley-Weinberger Elem. Sch., San Diego. Fellow U.S. Dept. Edn., 1974-77, San Diego State U., 1981; recipient Meritorious Performance and Profl. Promise award San Diego State U., 1985; univ. tng. grantee U.S. Dept. Edn., 1984-85. Mem. Am. speech Lang. Hearing Assn., Calif. Speech Lang. Hearing Assn. (bd. dirs. dist. 9 1980, 86), Tau Kappa Epsilon (sec. 1968-71, alumni advisor 1972-77), Sigma Xi. Republican. Avocations: piano, art, tennis, swimming, coaching. Home: 7497 Gorgeview Terr San Diego CA 92120

NOVEY, HAROLD SIDNEY, physician, educator; b. Balt., Sept. 20, 1926; s. Allen and Ree (Snyder) N.; m. Lindsay Mercedes Chance, A.B., Johns Hopkins U., 1946; M.D., U. So. Calif., 1951. Diplomate Am. Bd. Internal Medicine, Am. Bd. Allergy and Immunology. Resident, U.S. VA Hosp., Long Beach, Calif., 1951-52, acting chief allergy, 1957-58; resident U.S. VA Hosp., Los Angeles, 1952-53; fellow Mass. Gen. Hosp., Boston, 1955-56; clin. instr. UCLA, 1958-65, asst. clin. prof., 1965-71; chief allergy U. Calif.-Irvine, 1971-82, assoc. clin. prof., 1972-80, prof. medicine, 1980—. Contbr. articles to med. jours. Served as 1st lt. M.C., USAF, 1953-55. Fellow ACP, Am. Acad. Allergy; mem. Western Soc. Allergy-Immunology (bd. dirs. 1983—), Calif. Soc. Allergy (pres. 1972), Los Angeles Soc. Allergy (pres. 1967). Office: Dept of Medicine U Calif-Irvine 101 City Dr S Orange CA 92668

NOVICK, LAURENCE MARTIN, obstetrician-gynecologist; b. Chgo., June 8, 1941; s. Rudolph G. and Judith (Topin) N.; m. Marilyn Sagett, June 26, 1964 (div. Sept. 1978); children: Steven Paul (dec.), Sharon Gail, Susan Rachel, Sarah Beth; m. Linda Lott, Feb. 3, 1969. BA, U. Ill., 1962; MD, Northwestern U., 1966. Diplomate Am. Bd. Ob-Gyn. Intern Evanston (Ill.) Hosp., 1966-67, resident in ob-gyn, 1967-71; mem. staff John C. Lincoln Hosp., Phoenix, 1973—; mem. courtesy staff Phoenix Bapt. Hosp., 1973—, St. Joseph's Hosp., Phoenix, 1973—; practice medicine specializing in ob-gyn Phoenix, 1986—; ob-gyn North Phoenix Ob-Gyne, Phoenix, 1973-75, Bethany Ob-Gyne, Phoenix, 1975-86. Served to maj. USAF, 1971-73. Fellow Am. Coll. Obstetricians and Gynecologists; mem. Phoenix Ob-gyn Soc., S.W. Ob-gyn Soc., Am. Assn. Gynecologic Laparoscopists, Maricopa Med. Soc., Ariz. Med. Soc. Office: 1728 W Glendale Ave Phoenix AZ 85021

NOVIE, MARY KELTZ, manufacturing company executive; b. Lawrence, Kans., Mar. 23, 1949; d. Harold L. and Dorothy C. (Cohen) Keltz; m. Jan Novie, July 7, 1972 (div. Feb. 1983). BA, Colo. Coll., 1971. Sales rep. Livingston's, San Francisco, 1971, buyer, 1972-80, mdse. mgr., 1981-84; v.p. Circa Corp., San Francisco, 1985—. Grantee Ford Found., 1971. Mem. Fashion Group (past treas., past program chmn.), Friends of Ethnic Art, Women's Profl. Network. Democrat. Club: Commonwealth (San Francisco). Avocations: jogging, collecting primitive art, traveling, cultural anthropology. Office: Circa Corp 2300 Harrison St San Francisco CA 94110

NOVIN, DONALD, psychology educator; b. N.Y.C., Apr. 13, 1936; s. Edward Isadore and Mary (Solow) N.; m. Carolyn Smith, June 19, 1964; children: Wade, Eli. BA, U. Minn., 1956; MS, Yale U., 1958, PhD, 1960. Postdoctoral fellow Royal Vet. Coll., Stockholm, 1960-62; research anatomist U. Bristol, Eng., 1968; asst. prof. UCLA, 1962-67, assoc. prof., 1968-74, prof. psychology, 1974—; mem. staff Brain Research Inst., UCLA; allied investigator Ctr. for Ulcer Research and Edn., Wadsworth VA Hosp., Los Angeles, 1980—. Editor: Hunger: Basic Mechanisms and Clinical Implications, 1976, Neural Basis of Feeding and Reward, 1982; mem. editorial bd. Am. Jour. Physiology, 1982—, Appetite, 1981—, Internat. Jour. of Obesity, 1980—. Asst. scoutmaster Boy Scouts Am., Encino, Calif., 1985—. Recipient Roche Found. award Hoffman La Roche Inc., Switzerland; grantee NIH 1964-84, NIMH, 1964—. Mem. AAAS, Soc. for Neuroscis., Acad. Behavioral Medicine Research, Sierra Club. Avocations: skiing, fishing, backpacking, reading history. Office: U of Calif Los Angeles Psychology Dept 1283 Franz Hall Los Angeles CA 90024

NOVKOV, DONALD JAMES, aerospace engineer; b. Phoenix, Mar. 20, 1961; s. Milton Arthur and Shirley Lauraine (Zeug) N. BSME, Ariz. State U., 1983. Devel. engr. Garrett Pneumatic Systems Co. subs. Garrett Corp., Tempe, Ariz., 1984—. Home: 747 E Granada Dr Tempe AZ 85281 Office: Garrett Pneumatic Systems PO Box 22200 Box 427 Tempe AZ 85284

NOVOTNY, EDWARD JOHN, child neurologist, researcher; b. White Plains, N.Y., Nov. 18, 1953; s. Edward John Sr. and Michelle Marie (Elliffe) N. BS in Biology, BA in Chemistry, U. Calif., Irvine, 1975; MD, St. Louis U., 1979. Intern, then resident U. Calif. Davis, Sacramento, 1979-81; resident Stanford (Calif.) U., 1981-84, fellow in Epilepsy and EEG, 1984-86, acting asst. prof. neurology, 1986—. Mem. Am. Acad Neurology (S. Weir Mitchell award 1985), Am. Epilepsy Soc., Am. Acad. Pediatrics, Child Neurology Soc. Democrat. Roman Catholic. Avocations: pilot, bicycling. Office: Stanford U Med Ctr Dept Neurology Rm C-338 Stanford CA 94305

NOWAK, MARY JANE, social worker, educator; b. Milw., May 30, 1926; d. George Henry and Irma Angeline (Schuh) N. PhB, Marquette U., 1949; MSSW, U. Wis., 1955; PhD, Cath. U., 1972. Lic. social worker, Ky.; cert. clin. and adminstrv. mgmt. Case worker, supr. Milw. County Dept. Pub. Welfare, 1949-61; prof., asst. to dean U. Wis., Milw., 1961-67, Cath. U., Washington, 1967-73; prof., asst. dean student affairs U. Ky., Lexington, 1973-76; assoc. prof. Ariz. State U., Tempe, 1976-83; prof., evaluator U. Phoenix, 1984—; cons. in field, Milw., Washington, Ky., N.C., Ariz., 1955—; program specialist Council On Social Work Edn., N.Y.C., 1971-72. Co-author: Foster Family Parent Education, 1970; contbr. articles to profl. jours. Reviewer Child Welfare Resource Info. Exchange, N.Y.C., 1978-85; mem. Foster Parent Rev. Bd., Supreme Ct. Ariz., Phoenix, 1979-83; vol. Tempe Library, 1984-85, Tempe Family and Children's Services, 1984-85. Grantee U. Wis., 1954; Cath. U., 1972; HEW and Pakistani Govt., 1978. Mem. Nat. Assn. Social Work, Council on Social Work Edn. Democrat. Roman Catholic. Home: 5253 S Monaco Dr Tempe AZ 85283 Office: U Phoenix Phoenix AZ 85004

NOWELL, ELIZABETH CAMERON CLEMONS, author; b. Berkeley, Calif.; d. Alfred George and Edith (Catton) Cameron; A.B. San Jose State Coll., 1928; M.A., Stanford U., 1937; m. Wood Clemons, Dec. 22, 1946 (div. Dec. 1958); m. Arthur G. Robinson, May 27, 1961 (dec. Jan. 1967); m. Nelson T. Nowell, Feb. 15, 1969 (dec. Sept. 1973). With edn. dept. San Jose State Coll., 1928-39, in service tng. U. Calif. Extension Div., 1939-42; elem. editor The John C. Winston Co., 1942-43, Silver Burdett Co., 1943-44, D.C. Heath, 1944-46; instr. English dept. U. Minn., 1947; writing, editing publs. services Gen. Mills, 1947-50; freelance writer, 1950—; mem. faculty Monterey Peninsula Coll., Monterey, Calif., 1978-83; reading cons. Monterey City Sch., 1959-62, asso. editor Calif. edit. Am. Home Mag., 1965-70; mem. seminar faculty Embroiderers Guild, 1980, Monterey Peninsula Coll., 1978-82; judge needle-work Good Samaritan Hosp., Los Angeles, 1977, 79, 83, 87, Montalvo Center for Arts, Saratoga, Calif., 1980, 82, Status Needle Art Show, Burlingame, Calif., 1982, Altrusa Needlework Exhbn., Santa Maria, Calif., 1982, Scripps Meml. Hosp., La Jolla, Calif., 1980, 86, others. Bd. dirs. Community Hosp. Aux.; bd. dirs. Harrison Meml. Library, 1971-76, Monterey Symphony Assn., 1974-75; vestryman St. Dunstan's Episcopal Ch., 1974-77. Mem. Nat. League Am. Pen Women, Authors Guild, LWV, Nat. Embroidery Tchrs. Assn. (nat. dir. 1978-81), Embroiderers Guild Am. (nat. dir. 1978-81, nat. fin. com. 1984—; nat. fin. guidelines chmn. 1986—; nat. judges cert. com. 1984—, chmn. 1986; pres. chpt. 1977-78; judge needlework exhbns. 1977—), Kappa Alpha Theta, Pi Lambda Theta, Delta Phi Upsilon, Kappa Delta Pi, Delta Kappa Gamma. Republican. Clubs: Casa Abrego (historian 1979-83), Monterey Peninsula Country, Soroptimist. Author: The Pixie Dictionary, 1953; the Catholic Child's First Dictionary, 1954; The Winston Dictionary for Canadian School Children, 1955; Away I Go, 1956; All About Baby, 1956; I Live on A Farm, 1956; A Wish for Billy, 1956; Wings, Wheels, and Motors, 1957; The Big Book of Real Fire Engines, 1958; The Big Book of Real Trains, 1958; The Big Book of Real Trucks, 1958; Rodeo Days, 1960; Shells Are Where You Find Them, 1960; Rocks and The World Around You, 1960; Big and Little, 1961; Tide Pools and Beaches, 1964; Tides, Waves, and Currents, 1967; Here and There Stories; Now and Then Stories; Near and Far Stories; A Source Book for the Teaching of Literature for Children (all 1967); The Seven Seas, 1971; The Friendly Frog, 1971; What I Like, 1971; also feature articles in nat. mags. Address: PO Box 686 Carmel CA 93921

NOWICKI, NORBERT JOHN, fiduciary and management services executive; b. Hamtramck, Mich., June 23, 1935; s. Adam Lubicz and Clara Jane (Siwanowicz) N.; B.B.A. magna cum laude; M.P.A.; m. Sara Joseph, Nov. 1, 1957; children—Renee Jaunty, Richard Ethan. Enlisted U.S. Marine Corps, 1953, advanced through grades to capt., 1968; service in Middle East, Vietnam, Japan, Morocco as adj. personnel officer, ret., 1973; engaged in estate planning and real estate investing, 1974-75; exec. dir. Engrs. and Gen. Contractors Assn., San Diego, 1975-77; adminstr. San Diego County Constrn. Laborers Benefit Funds, San Diego, 1977-85; founder, pres. Beneco Inc., 1985—; mem. Constrn. Industry Coordinating Council, 1975-76; instr. employee benefits compensation and social ins. Nat. U. San Diego, 1978-86; cons., writer, speaker in field, trust adminstr., fiduciary. Chmn. energy task force San Diego Overall Econ. Devel. Program, 1975-79; mem. council Boy Scouts Am., 1975—. Decorated Bronze Star, Navy Commendation medal. Mem. Internat. Found. Employee Benefit Funds, Am. Soc. Personnel Adminstrn., Western Pension Conf., Ret. Officers Assn. Home: PO Box 83248 San Diego CA 92138 Office: 344 Kalmia St San Diego CA 92101

NOWIK, DOROTHY ADAM, medical equipment company executive; b. Chgo., July 25, 1944; d. Adam Harry and Helen (Kichkaylo) Wanaski; m. Eugene Nicholas Nowik, Aug. 9, 1978; children—George Eugene, Helen Eugene. A.A., Columbia Coll., 1980. Sec., adminstrv. asst. to pres. Zenco Engring Corp., Chgo., 1970-71; sales rep. Medizenco USA Ltd., Chgo., 1971-73; ptnr. Pacific Med. Systems, Inc., Bellevue, Wash., 1973-76, pres., 1976—. Mem. Nat. Assn. Female Execs. Mem. Orthodox Ch. Am. Home: 10249 SE 7th St Bellevue WA 98004 Office: 15055 NE Bel-Red Rd Bellevue WA 98007

NOWINSKI, STUART ALAN, chemist, educator; b. Colorado Springs, Colo., Oct. 28, 1953; s. Stanley Anthony and Beatrice Ellen (Merefield) N. BS in Chemistry, Calif. State U., Long Beach, 1975. Cert. secondary phys. sci. tchr. Analytical chemist U.S. Borax and Chemical, Wilmington, Calif., 1976-78; tchr. chemistry and advanced placement chemistry San Marino (Calif.) High Sch., 1978-85; tchr. chemistry Pasadena (Calif.) City Coll., 1985; tchr. chemistry and advanced placement chemistry Los Alamitos (Calif.) High Sch., 1985—. Recipient PTSA Service award, San Marino, Calif., 1983; DOE research grantee, 1985. Mem. Am. Chem. Soc. (exec. com. So. Calif. sect. 1982-85, chmn. ednl. affairs com. So. Calif. sect. 1983-85, Chemistry Tchr. of Yr. award So. Calif. sect. 1984, Western Regional Teaching award 1984), Calif. Assn. Chemistry Tchrs. (treas. So. sect. 1983-86), Nat. Sci. Tchrs. Assn., State of Calif. Single Subject Credential Review Bd., Calif. State U. Long Beach Secondary Edn. Adv. Com., Phi Lambda Upsilon. Republican. Roman Catholic. Avocations: hiking, travel, bicycling, photography. Home: 7890 E Spring 7C Long Beach CA 90815

NOWLIN, JANET, utilities company manager; b. Buffalo, July 16, 1953; d. Sam Angelo and Josephine (Sciolino) Conti; m. Harry Wayne Nowlin, Nov. 30, 1973; 1 child, Wesley Wayne. Student, Phoenix Coll., 1972-73; cert., IBM Tech., 1986. Cert. data processor and programmer. Supr. data processing Levitz Furniture, Phoenix, 1970-74; mgr. data processing dept. Ariz. Water Co., Phoenix, 1974—, cons., 1984. Mem. Data Processing Mgmt. Assn., Postal Customer Council, Beta Sigma Phi (sec. 1985-86). Republican. Roman Catholic. Avocations: reading, camping, music. Home: 4008 W Danbury Glendale AZ 85308 Office: Ariz Water Co 2612 N 16th St Phoenix AZ 85006

NOYCE, ROBERT NORTON, electronics company executive; b. Burlington, Iowa, Dec. 12, 1927; s. Ralph B. and Harriet (Norton) N.; m. Ann S. Bowers, Nov. 27, 1975; children: William B., Pendred, Priscilla, Margaret. BA, Grinnell Coll., 1949; PhD, MIT, 1953. Research engr. Philco Corp., Phila., 1953-56; research engr. Shockley Semicondr. Lab., Mountain View, Calif., 1956-57; founder, dir. research Fairchild Semicondr., Mountain View, 1957-59; v.p., gen. mgr. Fairchild Semicondr., 1959-65; group v.p. Fairchild Camera & Instrument, Mountain View, 1965-68; founder, pres. Intel Corp., Santa Clara, Calif., 1968-75; chmn. Intel Corp., 1968-75; vice chmn. 1979—; dir. Diasonics Inc., Milpitas, Calif. Trustee Grinnell Coll., 1962—; regent U. Calif., 1982—. Recipient Stuart Ballentine award Franklin Inst., 1967, Harry Goode award AFIPS, 1978; Nat. Medal of Sci. Pres. of U.S., 1979; I.E.E. Faraday medal, 1979; Harold Pender award U. Pa., 1980. Fellow IEEE (Cledo Brunetti award 1978, medal of honor 1978); mem. Nat. Acad. Engring., AAAS, Nat. Acad. Sci. Patentee in field. Office: 3200 Lakeside Dr Santa Clara CA 95051

NOYES, H(ENRY) PIERRE, physicist; b. Paris, Dec. 10, 1923; s. William Albert and Katharine Haworth (Macy) N.; m. Mary Wilson, Dec. 20, 1947; children—David Brian, Alan Guinn, Katharine Hope. B.A., Harvard U., 1943; Ph.D., U. Calif., Berkeley, 1950. Physicist MIT, 1943-44, U. Calif., Berkeley, 1949-50; Fulbright fellow U. Birmingham, Eng., 1950-51; asst. prof. U. Rochester, N.Y., 1951-55; group leader Lawrence Livermore Lab., 1955-62; Leverhulme lectr. U. Liverpool, Eng., 1957-58; adminstrv. head theory sect. Stanford Linear Accelerator Center, 1962-69; asso. prof. Stanford U., 1962-67, prof., 1967—; vis. scholar Center Advanced Study Behavioral Scis., Stanford, 1968-69; cons. in field. Author papers in field. Chmn. Com. for Direct Attack on Legality of Vietnam War, 1969-72; mem. steering com. Faculty Political Action Group, Stanford U., 1970-72; mem. policy com. U.S. People's Com. on Iran, 1977-79. Served with USNR, 1944-46. Fellow NSF, 1962; Fellow Nat. Humanities Faculty, 1970; recipient Alexander von Humboldt U.S. Sr. Scientist award, 1979. Mem. Alternative Natural Philosophy Assn. (pres. 1979-87), Am. Phys. Soc., AAAS, Sigma Xi. Home: 823 Lathrop Dr Stanford CA 94305 Office: SLAC Bin 81 PO Box 4349 Stanford CA 94305

NOYES, RICHARD MACY, physical chemist, educator; b. Champaign, Ill., Apr. 6, 1919; s. William Albert and Katharine Haworth (Macy) N.; m. Winninette Arnold, July 12, 1946 (dec. Mar. 1972); m. Patricia Jean Harris, Jan. 26, 1973. A.B. summa cum laude, Harvard U., 1939; Ph.D., Calif. Inst. Tech., 1942. Research assoc. rocket propellants Calif. Inst. Tech., 1942-46; mem. faculty Columbia U., 1946-58, assoc. prof., 1954-58; Guggenheim fellow, vis. prof. U. Leeds, Eng., 1955-56; prof. chemistry U. Oreg., 1958—, head dept., 1963-68, 75-78. Editorial adv. com.: Chem. Revs, 1967-69; editorial adv. com.: Jour. Phys. Chemistry, 1973-80; assoc. editor: Internat. Jour. Chem. Kinetics, 1972-82, Jour. Phys. Chemistry, 1980-82; Contbr. to profl. jours. Fulbright fellow; Victoria U. Wellington, New Zealand, 1964; NSF sr. postdoctoral fellow Max Planck Inst. für Physikalische Chemie, Göttingen, Germany, 1965; sr. Am. scientist awardee Alexander von Humboldt Found., 1978-79. Fellow Am. Phys. Soc.; mem. Nat. Acad. Scis., Am. Chem. Soc. (chmn. div. phys. chemistry 1961-62, exec. com. div. 1960-75, mem. council 1960-75, chmn. Oreg. sect. 1967-68, com. on nominations and elections 1962-68, com. on publs. 1969-72), Chem. Soc. (London), Wilderness Soc., ACLU, Phi Beta Kappa, Sigma Xi. Club: Sierra (past chmn. Atlantic and Pacific N.W. chpts., N.W. regional v.p. 1973-74). Research mechanisms chem. reactions, developing gen. theories, intrepretation phys. properties chemicals. Home: 2014 Elk Dr Eugene OR 97403

NOZIGLIA, CARLA MILLER, crime lab director, forensic scientist; b. Erie, Pa., Oct. 11, 1941; d. Earnest Carl and Eileen (Murphy) Miller; m. Keith William Noziglia, Nov. 21, 1969; children: Pama, Kathryn. BS, Villa Maria Coll., 1963; MS, Lindenwood Coll., 1984. Pathologist's assoc. Galion (Ohio) Comm. Hosp., 1969-75; crime lab. dir. Mansfield (Ohio) Police Dept., Richland County Crime Lab., 1978-81; crime lab. supr. St. Louis County Police, Clayton, Mo., 1981-84; crime lab. dir. Las Vegas Met. Police, 1984—. Tech. abstracts editor Jour. Police Sci. and Adminstrn., 1983—. Recipient Ohio award Ohio House of Reps., 1971. Fellow Am. Acad. Forensic Sci. and Criminalistics (sect. sec. 1986—, sect. chmn. 1987); mem. Am. Soc. Crime Lab. Dirs. (bd. dirs. 1980-87, treas. 1981-82, pres. 1986-87), Am. Soc. Pub. Adminstrn., Am. Legion Aux. Home: 1025 Pagosa Way Las Vegas NV 89128 Office: Crime Lab Las Vegas Met Police 601 E Fremont Las Vegas NV 89101

NTESO, TŠEPO OBED, computer scientist; b. Leribe, Lesotho, Oct. 1, 1944; came to U.S., 1971; s. Lekokoto Elliot and Mamoahloli (Flora) N.; m. Jane Mookho Manyeli, Aug. 31, 1968; children: Teboho Derek, Thato Yevette. BSEE, U. Alta., Can., 1968; MSEE, Carleton U., Ottawa, Can., 1972. Jr. programmer Computer Machinery Corp., Santa Monica, Calif., 1972-74; sr. programmer Transaction Tech. Inc., Los Angeles, 1974-77, Data Gen., Anaheim, Calif., 1977-80; computer scientist McDonnel Douglas Astronautics, Monrovia, Calif., 1980-82; software engr. Tylan Corp., Carson, Calif., 1982—. Mem. AAAS, N.Y. Acad. Sci., Planetary Soc.

NUDELMAN, BURTON MORRIS, consultant, retailer; b. Seattle, Aug. 9, 1928; s. Edward P. and Sara (Herns) N.; m. Jacquelyn E. Woron, Aug. 18, 1957; children: Joel, James. Student UCLA, 1948; BA in Econs., U. Wash., 1949, BA in Bus., 1950. Cert. mgmt. cons. Pres. Lloyd Ctr. Mchts., Portland, 1964, 67-69, J. Burton Inc., Portland, 1972-83, Large Fashion Forum of U.S., 1977-80; sec., dir. Bio-Fiber, Eugene, 1983-84; bd. dirs. Mail Order Products Bur., Kinetic Neon. Mem. Assn. Mgmt. Cons., Inst. Mgmt. Cons. Republican. Jewish. Lodge: Shriners. Office: 6443 SW Beaverton Hwy Suite 406 Portland OR 97221

NUNES, LOUISE DEE, real estate executive; b. Tulsa, Feb. 25, 1932; d. Wayne Shurlock and Erma Marie (Holmquist) Underwood; m. Russell Anthony Nunes, Sept. 2, 1955; children: Russell Anthony Jr., Theresa Louise, Margaret Jennifer, Louise Marie, Constance. BS, Tex. Woman's U., 1953. Cert. med. technologist, lab. technologist, Calif. Med. technologist Seward (Alaska) Hosp., 1954-56, St. Mary Corwin Hosp., Pueblo, Colo., 1958-59, 62-63, Gen. Hosp. of Everett, Wash., 1963-66, Drs. Huber and Hahn, Arlington, Wash., 1966-72, Cascade Valley Hosp., Arlington, 1972-75, Skagit Valley Lab., Mt. Vernon, Wash., 1975-79; mfg. planner Boeing Co., Everett, 1979-86; realtor Centry 21, Heart Realty, Modesto, Calif., 1987—. Leader Campfire Girls, Stanwood, Wash., 1969-70. Avocations: reading, dancing, golfing, gardening, sewing.

NUNEZ, ERNEST VINCENT, social worker; b. Rock Springs, Wyo.. AS, Utah Tech. Coll., 1978; BS, Weber State Coll., 1983; MSW, U. Utah, 1985. Adolescent counselor Esperanza Para Mañana, Salt Lake City, 1983-84; therapist Human Affairs Internat., Salt Lake City, 1984-85; adolescent counselor Decker Lake Youth Ctr., Salt Lake City, 1985; mental health specialist Dept. Mental Health, Salt Lake City, 1984-85; child welfare worker Dept. Adoptions, Los Angeles, 1985-86; psychiat. social worker Dept. Mental Health, Los Angeles, 1986—. Com. chmn. Cub Scouts, Ogden, Utah, 1982; mem. Chicano Scholarship Com., Salt Lake City, 1985; com. mem. Community Improvement Council, Ogden, 1982; v.p. Spanish Speaking Community Orgn., Ogden, 1981. Gov.'s Vocat. scholar, Utah Tech. Coll., Salt Lake City, 1976, Ethnic Minority scholar Weber State Coll., Ogden, 1982, 83, Chicano scholar, Salt Lake City, 1984, Nat. Hispanic scholar, San Francisco, 1985. Mem. Nat. Assn. Social Workers, East Los Angeles Jaycees. Roman Catholic. Avocations: basketball, tennis, softball, weightlifting, poetry writing.

NUNIS, RICHARD ARLEN, amusement parks executive; b. Cedartown, Ga., May 30, 1932; s. Doyce Blackman and Winnie E. (Morris) N.; m. June Elaine Kirk, June 13, 1954; children—Lisa Lea (dec.), Richard Dean. B.S. in Edn, U. So. Calif., 1954. With Walt Disney Prodns., 1955—; mem. supervisory and mgmt. staff Disneyland, Calif., 1955-61; dir. ops. Disneyland, 1961-68, chmn. park ops. com., 1968-74; corp. v.p. Disneyland ops., 1968—, Walt Disney World, Orlando, Fla., 1971—; exec. v.p., then pres. Disneyland and Walt Disney World and Disneyland Internat., 1972—; mem. exec. com. Walt Disney Co.; dir. Pacific Nat. Bank Fin. Group. Mem. exec. com. Pres.'s Council for Internat. Youth Exchange. Republican. Methodist. First academic All-American, U. So. Calif., 1952. Office: 1313 Harbor Blvd Anaheim CA 92803

NUWER, MARC ROMAN, neuroscientist, physician; b. Buffalo, July 8, 1948; s. Donald Charles and Arlene Ruth (Ebert) N.; m. Beverly Ann Jones, Oct. 12, 1978; children: Jamie Marie, Charles Marc. BA, Stanford U., 1970, MSEE, 1972, PhD, 1975, MD, 1975. Diplomate Am. Bd. Psychiatry and Neurology. Asst. prof. neurology UCLA, 1979, chief evoked potential lab., 1979, chief EEG lab., 1986; chmn. UCLA Neurology Profl. Group, 1985—. Author: Evoked Potential Monitoring in the Operating Room, 1986. Med. research grantee NIH, 1980-85. Fellow Am. Acad. Neurology, Am. EEG Soc. (chmn. 1985), Am. Epilepsy Soc.; mem. Am. Soc. Neurol. Investigation (pres. 1984-85). Home: 711 Haverford Ave Los Angeles CA 90272 Office: UCLA Dept Neurology 710 Westwood Plaza Los Angeles CA 90024

NYAIESH, ALI REZA, phycisist; b. Isfahan, Iran, Jan. 21, 1948; came to U.S., 1984; s. Mohamad Hassan and Ezat (Ghalamkari) N.; m. Lena Carina Lehto, Aug. 14, 1982; children: Syrus Sebastian Reza, Etienne-Nicholas Reza. B.Sc. in Physics, Isfahan U., 1970; M.Sc. in Physics, Sussex U., U.K., 1976, PhD in plasma processing, 1983. Lectr. Isfahan Nuclear Tech., 1976-78; asst dean Sch. Nautical Studies, Chah Bahar, Iran, 1978-79; cons. Norrfrys, Haparanda, Sweden, 1983; research assoc. SLAC Stanford U., Calif., 1984—. Contbr. articles to profl. jours.; patentee in field of magnetron and thin film physics. Served with Iranian Army, 1970-72. Mem. Inst. Physics, Am. Vacuum Soc. Islam. Avocations: running, squash, swimming, hiking. Office: Stanford U Bin 72 SLAC PO Box 4349 Stanford CA 94301

NYBAKKEN, JAMES WILLARD, marine biology educator; b. Warren, Minn., Sept. 16, 1936; s. Clarence G. and Effie Pearl (Knutson) N.; m. Bette Halvorsen, Aug. 20, 1960; children: Kent Edward, Scott Jordan. B.A. summa cum laude, St. Olaf Coll., Northfield, Minn., 1958; M.S., U. Wis., 1961, Ph.D., 1965. Curator zool. museum U. Wis., 1961-62, 64-65; mem. faculty Calif. State U., Hayward, 1965—; prof. marine ecology and invertebrate zoology Calif. State U., 1972—; mem. staff Moss Landing (Calif.) Marine Lab., 1966—; environ. cons., 1972—. Author: Readings in Marine Ecology, 1971, 2d edit., 1986, Elements of Zoology, 4th edit, 1977, General Zoology, 6th edit, 1978, Guide to the Nudibranchs of California, 1980, Marine Biology: An Ecological Approach, 1982. Fellow Calif. Acad. Scis.; mem. AAAS, Am. Soc. Zoologists, Am. Malacological Union (pres. 1985-86), Ecol. Soc. Am., Malacological Soc. London, Western Soc. Malacologists (pres. 1974-75), Western Soc. Naturalists (pres.-elect 1985, pres, 1986), Sigma Xi. Address: PO Box 450 Moss Landing CA 95039

NYE, BRIAN A., accountant, real estate developer; b. Boise, Idaho, Nov. 4, 1956; s. William A. and Mary Loa (Layne) N.; married. BBA, Idaho State U., 1979. CPA, Idaho. Acct. Coopers & Lybrand, Boise, 1979-83; controller Chandler Corp., Boise, 1983-84; ptnr. Brian Nye & Assocs. P.A., Boise, 1984—; pres. NICOM Properties, Boise, 1984—; v.p., bd. dirs. Margenes, Inc., Boise, 1985—. Supporter LeRoy for Gov., Boise, 1986; v.p. Idaho Shakespeare Festival, 1984-85. Named one of Outstanding Young Men, 1984; Buttrey Food Stores fellow, 1979-80. Mem. Am. Inst. CPA's. Idaho Soc. CPA's, Sales and Mktg. Execs., Boise C. of C. (vice chmn. 1984-85). Republican. Methodist. Lodge: Rotary (local pres. 1985-86). Avocations: tennis, golf, cooking, wine collecting. Home: 7552 Thunder Mountain Dr Boise ID 83709

NYE, (ROBERT) KIM, advertising executive; b. Hessel, Mich., Aug. 17, 1934; d. Fred and Florence (Volker) N.; divorced; children: Sherry Lynn, Scarlett Louise. Student, Mich. State U., 1952-53. Spl. events coordinator SEMA, Los Angeles, 1976-80; nat. advt. dir. Promotions Inc., Detroit, 1980-83; advt. dir. Off Road mag., Los Angeles, 1983-86; v.p. mktg. & advt. Challenge Publs. Inc., Canoga Park, Calif., 1986—; mem. adv. bd. Off Road Com., Los Angeles, 1985-86. Served to sgt. USMC, 1953-55. Avocations: old cars, basketball. Home: 1247 Amhearst #3 Brentwood CA 90025 Office: Challenge Publs Inc 7950 Deering Ave Canoga Park CA 91304

NYHAN, WILLIAM LEO, pediatrician, educator; b. Boston, Mar. 13, 1926; s. W. Leo and Mary (Cleary) N.; m. Christine Murphy, Nov. 20, 1948; children: Christopher, Abigail. Student, Harvard U., 1943-45; M.D., Columbia U., 1949; M.S., U. Ill., 1956, Ph.D., 1958; hon. doctorate, Tokushima U., Japan, 1981. Intern Yale U.-Grace-New Haven Hosp., 1949-50, resident, 1950-51, 53-55; asst. prof. pediatrics Johns Hopkins U., 1958-61, assoc. prof., 1961-63; prof. pediatrics, biochemistry U. Miami, 1963-69, chmn. dept. pediatrics, 1963-69; prof. U. Calif., San Diego, 1969—; chmn. dept. pediatrics U. Calif., 1969-86; mem. FDA adv. com. on Teratogenic Effects of Certain Drugs, 1964-70; mem. pediatric panel AMA Council on Drugs, 1964-70; mem. Nat. Adv. Child Health and Human Devel. Council, 1967-71; mem. research adv. com. Calif. Dept. Mental Hygiene, 1969-72; mem. med. and sci. adv. com. Leukemia Soc. Am., Inc., 1968-72; mem. basic adv. com. Nat. Found. March of Dimes, 1973-81; mem. Basil O'Connor Starter grants com., 1973—; mem. clin. cancer program project rev. com. Nat. Cancer Inst., 1977-81; vis. prof. U. del Salvador (Argentina), 1982. Author: (with E. Edelson) The Heredity Factor, Genes, Chromosomes and You, 1976,Genetic & Malformation Syndromes in Clinical Medicine, 1976, Abnormalities in Amino Acid Metabolism in Clinical Medicine, 1984, Diagnostic Recognition of Genetic Disease, 1986; editor: Amino Acid Metabolism and Genetic Variation, 1967, Heritable Disorders of Amino Acid Metabolism, 1974; mem. editorial bd. Jour. Pediatrics, 1964-78, King Faisal Hosp. Med. Jour., 1981-85, Western Jour. Medicine, 1974-86, Annals of Saudi Medicine, 1985—; mem. editorial com. Ann. Rev. Nutrition, 1982-86; mem. editorial staff Med. and Pediatric Oncology, 1975-83. Served with U.S. Navy, 1944-46; U.S. Army, 1951-53. Nat. Found. Infantile Paralysis fellow, 1955-58; recipient Commemorative medallion Columbia U. Coll. Physicians and Surgeons, 1967. Mem. AAAS, Am. Fedn. Clin. Research, Am. Chem. Soc., Soc. Pediatric Research (pres. 1970-71), Am. Assn. Cancer Research, Am. Soc. Pharmacology and Exptl. Therapeutics, Western Soc. Pediatric Research (pres. 1976-77), N.Y. Acad. Sci., Am. Acad. Pediatrics (Borden award 1980), Am. Pediatric Soc., Am. Inst. Biol. Scis., Soc. Exptl. Biology and Medicine, Am. Soc. Clin. Investigation, Am. Soc. Human Genetics (dir. 1978-81), Inst. Investigaciones Citologicas (Spain; corr.), Biochem. Soc., Socié té Franç aise de Pediatrie (corr.), Sigma Xi, Alpha Omega Alpha. Office: Dept Pediatrics U Calif San Diego CA La Jolla CA 92093

NYHOLM, CAROL JOYCE, training consultant, association executive, social worker; b. Wenatchee, Wash., Mar. 12, 1932; d. Edward and Flora Agnes (Bray) Nyholm. B.A. in Sociology, Wash. State U., 1954; M.S.W., U. Mich., 1967. Cert. social worker. Program dir. YWCA, Long Beach, Calif., 1954-60; teenage dir. YWCA, San Diego, 1960-61; youth program YWCA Mid-Peninsula, Palo Alto, Calif., 1961-65; city wide youth program YWCA, Pitts., 1967-69, assoc. exec., 1969-72, exec. dir., 1972-77; exec. dir. YWCA, Long Beach, Calif., 1977-84; tng. cons. YWCA of USA Leadership Devel. Ctr., Phoenix, 1984-85; exec. dir. YWCA of Maricopa County, Phoenix, 1985—. Bd. dirs. South Coast Ecumenical Council, 1980-82, chmn. community action com., 1980-82; bd. dirs. Bouggess-White Scholarship Found., 1979-80; steering com. Shalom Ctr., 1979-81; mem. United Way Campaign Cabinet, 1980, council of execs., 1977-84; mem. equitable salaries com. Pacific S.W. Conf. United Meth. Chs., 1981-84. Grace H. Dodge Merit fellow YWCA, 1965-66, Florence Allen Roblee scholar YWCA 1966-67. Named Boss of Yr. Jubilee chpt. Am. Bus. Women's Assn., 1978, Susan B. Anthony Woman of Yr., Long Beach chpt. NOW. Mem. Nat. Assn. Social Workers, Nat. Assn. Female Execs., Nat. Conf. Social Welfare. Methodist. Home: 5043 W Sweet Water Ave Glendale AZ 85304 Office: 755 E Willetta St Phoenix AZ 85006

NYMAN, CARL JOHN, JR., university dean and official; b. New Orleans, Oct. 21, 1924; s. Carl John and Dorothy (Kraft) N.; m. Betty Spiegelberg, July 15, 1950; children: Gail Katherine, John Victor, Nancy Kraft. B.S., Tulane U., 1944, M.S., 1945; Ph.D., U. Ill., 1948. Jr. technologist Shell Oil Co., Wilmington, Cal., 1944; instr. chemistry U. Ill., 1948, Wash. State U., Pullman, 1948-50; asst. prof. Wash. State U., 1950-55, assoc. prof., 1955-61, prof., 1961—, acting dean Grad. Sch., 1968-70, dean Grad. Sch., 1970—, now also vice provost for research; vis. asst. prof. Tulane U., summer 1950; vis. fellow Cornell U., 1959-60, Imperial Coll. Sci. and Tech., 1966-67; Chmn. acad. council Center Grad. Study, Richland, Wash., 1968-70, N.W. Assn. Colls. and Univs. for Sci., 1969; mem. Gov.'s Adv. Council on Nuclear Energy. Author: (with G.B. King and J.A. Weyh) Problems for General Chemistry and Qualitative Analysis, 4th edit, 1980, (with R.E. Homm) Chemical Equilibrium, 1967, (with W.E. Newton) Procs. of the 1st Internat. Conf. Nitrogen Fixation; Contbr. articles to profl. jours. Mem. Am. Chem. Soc. (chmn. Wash.-Idaho border sect. 1961-62), AAAS, Sigma Xi, Phi Lambda Upsilon, Alpha Chi Sigma, Omicron Delta Kappa. Home: NW 1320 Orion Dr Pullman WA 99163

NYMAN, DAVID HAROLD, nuclear engineer; b. Aberdeen, Wash., May 21, 1938; s. Carl Victor and Elsie Ingagord (Laaksonen) N.; m. Lawana Flora Rice, July 19, 1939. Assoc., Grays Harbor Coll., 1958; BSMetE, U. Wash., 1961, MSMetE, 1963. Engr. Gen. Electric Co., Richland, Wash., 1963-68; engring. specialist United Nuclear Corp., New Haven, 1968-73; mgr. Westinghouse Hanford subs. Westinghouse Corp., Richland, 1973—. Contbr. articles to profl jours. Mem. ASTM (chmn. membership com. 1986-87), Robotics Internat. of Soc. Mfg. Engrs. (div. chmn. 1985-86, tech. v.p. 1986—), Robots West Conf. (adv. com. 1984, vice-chmn. 1986), Am. Nuclear Soc. (vice-chmn. tech. program com. 1986-87), Am. Soc. Metals., Columbia Basin Dog Tng. Club (pres. 1982-84), Richland Kennel Club, West Highland White Terrier Club of Puget Sound. Republican. Lutheran. Office: Westinghouse Hanford Co PO Box 1970 Richland WA 99352

NYPAN, LESTER JENS, engineering educator; b. Mpls., Oct. 30, 1929; s. Jens Lars and Lillian Louise (Martinson) N.; m. Yoko Aoki, Dec. 15, 1955 (dec. Jan. 1982); m. Dorothy Lih-Meeh Koe, Nov. 1982; 1 child, Jade. BS, U. Minn., 1951, MS in Mech. Engring., 1952, PhD, 1960. Registered profl. engr., Calif. Instr. U. Minn., Mpls., 1954; sr. engr. Gen. Mills, Inc., Mpls., 1956-60, Lockheed, Calif., Co., Burbank, 1960-62; prof. engring. Calif. State U., Northridge, 1962—; mem. tech. staff Litton Industries, Woodland Hills, Calif., 1983-85. Contbr. articles to profl. jours. Served to maj. USAF, 1952-54. Mem. Am. Soc. Mech. Engrs., Am. Soc. Engring. Edn., Am. Soc. Lubrication Engrs., Calif. Soc. Profl. Engrs., Tau Beta Pi, Pi Tau Sigma. Avocations: bearings research, photography. Home: 9515 Gladbeck Ave Northridge CA 91324 Office: Calif State U Sch Engring 18111 Nordoff St Northridge CA 91324

NYQUIST, MAURICE OTTO, federal parks agency manager; b. Fairmont, Minn., May 30, 1944; s. Carl Arther and Wilda Yvette (Freitag) N.; m. Mary Maud Magee, Aug. 8, 1977; children: Gretchen, Beth. BS in Biology, Hamline U., 1966; MA in Biology, Mankato State U., 1968; PhD in Zoology, Wash. State U., 1973. Asst. prof. zoology Wash. State U., Pullman, 1973-74; scientist Nat. Park Service, Lakewood, Colo., 1974-76, mgr., 1979—; cons. Ch2M-Hill, Seattle, 1972-73. Contbr. sci. articles to profl. jours. Bd. dirs. Nat. Park Service Equal Employment Opportunity Com., Denver, 1981, chmn., 1982. Recipient Mgrs. award Nat. Park Service, Lakewood, 1981; research grantee Nat. Rifle Assn., 1972. Mem. Am. Soc. Photogrammetry and Remote Sensing (bd. dirs. 1987—, asst. dir. remote sensing applications div. 1985-87, dir. 1987—), The Wildlife Soc., ELAS Users Group (co-chair 1985-86, chmn. 1986-87), Sigma Xi. Avocations: tennis, skiing. Office: Nat Park Service WASO-GISFU PO Box 25287 Denver CO 80225-0287

OAKES, BILL, computer infosystem executive; b. Columbus, Ga., Aug. 19, 1959; s. Bill Oakes and Kay (Frederick) Cape. AA in Bus., AA in Data Processing, Tidewater Coll., 1980; BS in Bus., Old Dominion U., 1981. Materials analyst Cambridge Plan Internat., Monterey, Calif., 1981-83; materials mgr. Genesis Internat., Los Angeles, 1982-84; mgr. data processing Postal Instant Press, Los Angeles, 1984—. Mem. Am. Prodn. and Inventory Control Soc., Data Processing Mgmt. Assn., Los Angeles Computer Users Group, Delta Nu Alpha. Avocations: scuba, tennis, bicycle racing, astronomy, photography. Home: 840 Larrabee #1-309 Los Angeles CA 90069 Office: Postal Instant Press 8201 Beverly Blvd Los Angeles CA 90048

OAKS, DALLIN HARRIS, clergyman; b. Provo, Utah, Aug. 12, 1932; s. Lloyd E. and Stella (Harris) O.; m. June Dixon, June 24, 1952; children: Sharmon, Cheri Lyn, Lloyd D., Dallin D., TruAnn, Jenny June. B.A. with high honors, Brigham Young U., 1954, LL.D., 1980; J.D. cum laude, U. Chgo., 1957; LL.D. (hon.), Pepperdine U., 1982. Bar: Ill. 1957, Utah 1971. Law clk. to Supreme Ct. chief justice Earl Warren, 1957-58; with firm Kirkland, Ellis, Hodson, Chaffetz & Masters, Chgo., 1958-61; mem. faculty U. Chgo. Law Sch., 1961-71, assoc. dean and acting dean, 1962, prof., 1964-71, mem. vis. com., 1971-74; pres. Brigham Young U., Provo, Utah, 1971-80; also prof. law J. Reuben Clark Law Sch., 1974-80; justice Utah Supreme Ct., 1981-84; mem. Council of Twelve Apostles Ch. Jesus Christ of Latter-day Saints, 1984—; asst. states atty. Cook County, Ill., summer 1964; legal counsel Bill of Rights com. Ill. Constl. Conv., 1970. Author: (with G.G. Bogert) Cases on Trusts, 1967, 78, (with W. Lehman) A Criminal Justice System and The Indigent, 1968, The Criminal Justice Act in the Federal District Courts, 1969, (with M. Hill) Carthage Conspiracy, 1975, Trust Doctrines in Church Controversies, 1984; editor: The Wall Between Church and State, 1963. Mem. Wilson council Woodrow Wilson Internat. Center for Scholars, 1973-80; trustee Intermountain Health Care Inc., 1975-80; mem. adv. com. Nat. Inst. Law Enforcement and Criminal Justice, 1974-76; bd. dirs. Rockford Inst., 1980—, Notre Dame Center for Constl. Studies, 1977-80; bd. dirs. Pub. Broadcasting Service, 1977-84, chmn., 1980-84. Fellow Am. Bar Found. (exec. dir. 1970-71); mem. Am. Law Inst., ABA (mem. com. to survey legal needs 1971-78, mem. cons. panel on advanced legal and jud. edn. 1978-80), Am. Assn. Presidents Ind. Colls. and Univs. (pres. 1975-78, dir. 1971-78), Nat. Assn. Ind. Colls. and Univs. (dir. 1977-79), Order Coif. Mem. Ch. of Jesus Christ of Latter-day Saints (regional rep. 1974-80; past 1st counselor Chgo. South Stake). Address: 47 East South Temple St Salt Lake City UT 84150

OBENCHAIN, THEODORE GUY, neurosurgeon; b. Boise, Idaho, Jan. 4, 1937; s. Artie Lorraine and Violet Josephine (Isaacson) O.; A.A., Boise State U., 1957; grad. Coll. of Idaho, 1958; M.D., U. Utah, 1962; m. Jean Arline Martinovich, Jan. 8, 1968; children—Kristin Marie, Monica Lynn, Theodore John. Intern, Bellevue Hosp., N.Y.C., 1962-63; med. fellow dept. neurology U. Minn. Med. Sch., 1966-67; resident in surgery Highland Gen. Hosp., Oakland, Calif., 1967-68; resident in neurosurgery UCLA Sch. Medicine, 1968-73; asst. prof. U. Calif., San Diego Sch. Medicine, 1973-75; practice medicine, specializing in neurosurgery, Boise, 1975-77, Escondido, Calif., 1977—; mem. staff Palomar Hosp., Pomerado Hosp., Sharp Hosp. Served with U.S. Navy, 1963-66. Mem. Am. Assn. Neurol. Surgeons, Congress of Neurol. Surgeons, Fedn. Western Socs. Neurol. Sci., San Diego Acad. Neurol. Surgeons. Contbr. articles to med. jours. Office: 355 N Grand Ave Escondido CA 92025

OBERING, ROLAND GENE, civil engineer, consultant, land surveyor; b. Minden, Nebr., July 30, 1948; s. Edwin Frederick Herman and Meta (Fruhling) O.; m. Kathy Lynn McGee, June 3, 1972; children: Aspen Lynn, Shannon Gene. BSCE, U. Nebr., 1971. Registered profl. civil engr., Colo., profl. land surveryor, Colo. Civil engr., cons. Leigh Whitehead & Assocs., Colorado Springs, Colo., 1971-86; pres. Obering, Wurth & Assocs., Colorado Springs, 1986—. Author drainage study, 1982 (Pub. Works award 1983); designer Velodrome U.S. Olympic Com. Mem. ASCE, Home Builders Assn. Met. Colorado Springs. Republican. Lutheran. Lodge: Sertoma (pres. Sunset chpt. 1982-83). Avocations: skiing, hiking, fishing, snowmobiling, trailbike riding. Office: Obering Wurth & Assocs 1015 Elkton Dr Colorado Springs CO 80907

OBERST, BRUCE HENRY, psychologist; b. Coos Bay, Oreg., Feb. 27, 1934; s. Henry William and Hazel Isabel (Duvall) O.; m. Bonnie Lou Bowder, June 26, 1955; children: Gail, Bruce Jr., Douglas, Paul. B in Theology, Northwest Coll. of the Bible, 1958; BS in Psychology, U. Oreg., 1970; MEd in Counseling, West Oreg. State Coll., 1971; PhD in Counseling Psychology, Laurence U., 1984. Ordained to ministry, 1957. Minister Ch. of Christ, Portland, Oreg., 1958-63, Anchorage, 1964-66, Eugene, Oreg., 1968-70; counselor Umpqua Community Coll., Roseburg, Oreg., 1971—, chmn. dept. social scis., 1982-86. Author: Letters from Peter, 1962, Deuteronomy, 1968. Mem. Oreg. Coll. Counseling Assn. (pres. 1986—), Phi Delta Kappa. Republican. Avocations: jogging, fishing, backpacking. Home: 828 Echo Dr Roseburg OR 97470 Office: Umpqua Community Coll Dept Social Sci PO Box 967 Roseburg OR 97470

OBERTI, SYLVIA MARIE ANTOINETTE, rehabilitation counselor and administrator, career advisor, textile consultant; b. Fresno, Calif., Dec. 29, 1952; d. Silvio Lawrence and Sarah Carmen (Policarpo) O. B.A. in Communicative Disorders, Calif. State U.-Fresno, 1976, M.A. in Rehab. Counseling, 1977. Lic. vocat. cons., Calif.; cert. rehab. counselor Commn. Rehab. Counselors; cert. life tchr. community coll. Rehab. counselor intern Calif. Dept. Rehab., Fresno, 1977; vol. counselor Fresno Commn. Aging, 1976-77; rehab. counselor trainee traumatic injury ward, Fresno Community Hosp., 1976-77; sr. rehab. cons. Crawford Rehab. Services, Inc., Emeryville, Calif., 1978-80; vocat. rehab. counselor Rehab. Assocs., Inc., San Leandro, Calif., 1980-81; owner, textile cons. Rugs and Carpets of the Orient, Oakland, Calif., 1979—; adminstr., counselor Oberti & Lohr, Oakland and San Jose, Calif., 1981-83; exec. dir. Oberti Co., Oakland, San Francisco and San Jose, 1983—; cons. to industry, ins. cos., disabled; tchr. job seeking skills to the disabled. Bd. dirs., treas. Pacific Basin Sch. Textile Arts, 1982-86; active Calif. Assn. Physically Handicapped, Inc., 1976—, Bay Area Profl. Women's Network, 1979—. HEW grantee, 1976-77. Mem. Am. Personnel and Guidance Assn., Am. Rehab. Counseling Assn., Calif. Assn. Rehab. Profls., Indsl. Claims Assn., Internat. Round Table Advancement of Counseling, Nat. Rehab. Assn., Nat. Rehab. Counseling Assn., Nat. Vocat. Guidance Assn., LWV, Women Entrepreneurs. Office: 2169 Union St San Francisco CA 94123 Office: 3629 Grand Ave Suite 101 Oakland CA 94610

OBIE, BRIAN, city official. Mayor City of Eugene, Oreg. Office: Office of Mayor 777 Pearl St Eugene OR 97401 *

OBLAD, ALEXANDER GOLDEN, chemist, chemical engineer, educator; b. Salt Lake City, Nov. 26, 1909; s. Alexander H. and Louie May (Brewster) O.; m. Bessie Elizabeth Baker, Feb. 23, 1933; children: Alex Edward, Elizabeth (Mrs. D. Sonne), Virginia Oblad Christensen, John R.B., Hayward B., Jean Rio B.(Mrs. S. Calder). B.A. in Chemistry, U. Utah, 1933, M.A. in Phys. Chemistry, 1934, D.Sc. (hon.), 1980; Ph.D. in Phys. Chemistry, Purdue U., 1937, D.Sc. (hon.), 1959. Research chemist Standard Oil Co., Whiting, Ind., 1937-42, Magnolia Petroleum Co., Dallas, 1942-43; sect. leader Magnolia Petroleum Co., 1943-46, chief chem. research, 1946; head indsl. research Tex. Research Found., Dallas, 1947; dir. chem. research Houdry Process Corp., Marcus Hook, Pa., 1947-52; assoc. mgr. research and devel. Houdry Process Corp., 1952-55, mgr., 1955, v.p., dir., 1955-57; v.p. research and devel. M.W. Kellogg Co., N.Y.C., 1957-66, v.p. research and engring. devel., 1966-69; v.p. IRECO Chems., Salt Lake City, 1969-70; prof. metallurgical and fuels engring. U. Utah, 1969-75, disting. prof. metallurgical and fuels engring., 1975—, prof. chemistry, 1975—; assoc. dean U. Utah Coll. of Mines, 1970-72, acting dean, 1972-75; co-founder, dir. Ireco Chemicals Co., Salt Lake City, 1958-72, 74-75; mem. Sec. of Interior's Saline Water Conversion Adv. Com., Office of Saline Water, Washington, 1959-61; mem. fossil energy research working group Dept. Energy, 1980-82. Mem. editorial bd.: Catalysis Revs., Fuel Processing Tech, 1976; mem. internat. adv. bd.: Ency. of Chem. Processing and Design, 1973—; Contbr. numerous articles on phys. chemistry, catalysis, petroleum chemistry and chem. engring. to tech. and sci. jours. Mem. alumni research council Purdue Research Found., Lafayette, Ind., 1960-63; chmn. sustaining membership campaign Orange Mountain council Boy Scouts Am., 1966-67; mem. adv. council Brigham Young U., Provo, Utah, 1962-81; mem. nat. adv. council U. Utah, 1962-77, Dixie Coll.; bd. dirs. Internat. Congress on Catalysis, 1956-65. Recipient First Purdue Chemist's award, 1959, Distinguished Alumni award U. Utah, 1962. Mem. Am. Chem. Soc. (mng. editor publs. div. petroleum chemistry 1857-69, sec. treas. div. petroleum chemistry 1952-54, div. petroleum chem. 1956 , E.V. Murphree award 1969), Am. Inst. Chem. Engrs., AAAS, Calif. Catalysis Soc., Western States Catalysis Soc., Rocky Mountain Fuel Soc., Nat. Acad. Engring., Am. Inst. Chemists (Chem. pioneer award 1972), Sigma Xi, Phi Lambda Upsilon, Sigma Pi Sigma, Phi Kappa Phi, Tau Beta Pi. Mormon. Lodge: Rotary. Patentee in field. Home: 1415 Roxbury Rd Salt Lake City UT 84108 Office: 302 Browning Mineral Science Bldg Univ of Utah Salt Lake City UT

OBLESKI, BERT MICHAEL, aerospace engineer; b. Niagara Falls, N.Y., Oct. 31, 1954; s. Bert Mickey and Gloria Maria (Pino) O.; m. Maxine Kay Spangler, Aug. 13, 1977. BS in Aerospace Engring., U. Pitts., 1976, MSME, 1979. Aerospace engr. Martin Marietta, Denver, 1984—. Contbr. articles to profl. jours. Served to capt. USAF, 1978-84. Mem. AIAA, ASME, Tau Beta Pi, Pi Tau Sigma (pres. 1975-76). Avocations: sports, softball, ice hockey, running, reading.

OBNINSKY, VICTOR PETER, lawyer, real estate developer; b. San Rafael, Calif., Oct. 12, 1944; s. Peter Victor and Anne Bartholdi (Donston) O.; m. Clara Alice Bechtel, June 8, 1969; children: Mari, Warren. B.A., Columbia U., 1966; J.D., U. Calif., Hastings Coll. Law, 1969. Bar: Calif. 1970. Sole practice, Novato, Calif., 1970—; arbitrator Marin County Superior Ct., San Rafael, 1979—; lectr. real estate and ptnrshp. law; dir. several corps. Bd. dirs. Calif. Young Reps., 1968-69, Richardson Bay San. Dist., 1974-75, Marin County Legal Aid Soc., 1976-78; baseball coach Little League, Babe Ruth League, 1970-84; mem. nat. panel consumer arbitrators Better Bus. Bur., 1974—; leader Boy Scouts Am., 1970-84. Mem. State Bar Calif., ABA, Marin County Bar Assn. (bd. dirs. 1985-87, treas. 1987), Phi Delta Phi, Phi Gamma Delta. Russian Orthodox. Club: Commonwealth (San Francisco). Author: The Russians in Early California, 1966. Home: PO Box 5068 Novato CA 94948-5068 Office: 2 Commercial Blvd Suite 103 Novato CA 94948-5068

OBREMSKI, ARLENE JOYCE, special education teacher; b. Bklyn., Mar. 13, 1944; s. Richard Edgar and Antonia Agnes (Bonsignore) B.; m. Robert John Obremski, Aug. 29, 1964; children: Christine Michelle, Robin Joyce. BS in History, Calif. State U., Fullerton, 1974, MS in Reading, 1977, cert. spl. edn., 1979, MS in Counseling, 1985. Gen. teaching credential; reading specialist credential, learning disabilities credential, severely handicapped credential. Tchr. Holy Redeemer Sch., College Park, Md., 1964-66, Sch. of Our Lady, Santa Ana, Calif., 1974-75; 2d grade tchr., vice prin. St. Angela's Sch., Brea, Calif., 1975-79; spl. edn. tchr. Commonwealth Sch., Fullerton, 1979-83, Orangethorpe Sch., Fullerton, 1983—. Author: ABC of

Ocean, 1984, Special Education in Hong Kong, Storytelling Orange Thorpe Style, Storytelling and the Arts for the Handicapped Child. Named Tchr. of Yr. Fullerton Dist., Orange County, 1987. Mem. Internat. Reading Assn., Reading Educators Guild (v.p., sec. 1978-82), Orange County Reading Assn., Children and Adult Handicapped Council, Spl. Arts Orange County (adv. bd.). Avocations: skiing, storytelling, tennis, golf, reading, swimming. Home: 19792 La Tierra Ln Yorba Linda CA 92686

O'BRIEN, DANIEL KEVIN, safety engineer; b. Fresno, Calif., Apr. 18, 1956; s. Robert Aloyisuis and Margie Jean (Dandois) O'B. BA in Geography, BS in Health Sci., Calif. State U., Fresno, 1979. Engr. Indsl. Risk Ins. Co., Anaheim, Calif., 1979-80; tech. rep. Hartford Ins. Co., Fresno, 1980-85; mgr. product services Citation Ins. Co., Fresno, 1985—. Instr. first aid, CPR, ARC, Fresno, 1982—; chmn. United Way of Fresno County, 1981-82. Mem. Am. Soc. Safety Engrs. (pres. 1983-84), Soc. Fire Protection Engrs. Lodge: Blue Goose. Home: 3964 N Drexel Fresno CA 93726 Office: Citation Ins Co 83 E Shaw Ave Fresno CA 93710

O'BRIEN, DEANA MICHAEL, semiconductor manufacturing executive; b. Mt. Shasta, Calif., Dec. 14, 1951; d. Arthur Junior and Lola Dell (Weiss) Michael; m. Forrest James O'Brien, Feb. 7, 1971; children—Shannon Renee, Michael James. A.A., Bryant & Stratton Coll. Commerce, San Jose, Calif., 1972. Mktg. sec. Am. Microsystems, Inc., Santa Clara, Calif., 1973-74, adminstrv. asst., 1974-76, program adminstr., 1976-80; mktg. adminstr. Calif. Devices, Inc., San Jose, 1981-83, product mktg. mgr., 1983-85; tactical mktg. mgr. Monolithic Memories, Inc., Santa Clara, 1985—; ptnr. Forrest O'Brien Engring., Inc., automotive repair and after market turbocharging, Santa Clara, 1976—. Mem. Nat. Assn. for Female Execs. Avocations: traveling; boating; camping; jeeping; antiques. Office: Monolithic Memories Inc 2175 Mission College Blvd MS Bldg 10 Santa Clara CA 95054

O'BRIEN, HELEN VICTORIA, nurse, epidemiologist; b. Holyoke, Mass., Aug. 18, 1934; d. Joseph Stephen and Rose Katherine (Dolat) Kornacki; m. John Francis O'Brien, Sept. 24, 1955; 1 child, Steven Michael. Diploma, Cooley Dickinson Hosp., 1955; BSN, Villa Maria Coll., 1969; MS, Calif. State U., Northridge, 1984. Cert. infection control. Med. surg. supr. Hamot Hosp., Erie, Pa., 1964-69; staff nurse VA Med. Ctr., Buffalo, 1969-70; staff nurse VA Med. Ctr., Los Angeles, 1970, head nurse, 1970-71, nurse epidemiologist, 1971-75; nurse epidemiologist VA Med. Ctr., Sepulveda, Calif., 1975—. Author, editor: Infection Control Manual, 1972, 76, 81, 86. Mem. Assn. Practitioners in Infection Control, Los Angeles Chpt. Assn. Practitioners in Infection Control (coordinator San Fernando Valley 1977, com. mem. Am. Nurses Assn. Position Paper 1977, pres.-elect 1978, chmn. edn. com. 1978, Calif. statewide steering com. 1978, pres. 1979, bd. dirs. 1980), Sigma Theta Tau. Republican. Roman Catholic. Avocations: gardening, baking, computers. Home: 18637 Vintage St Northridge CA 91324 Office: VA Med Ctr 16111 Plummer St Sepulveda CA 91343

O'BRIEN, JOHN WILLIAM, JR., investment management company executive; b. Bronx, N.Y., Jan. 1, 1937; s. John William and Ruth Catherine (Timon) O'B.; B.S., MIT, 1958; M.S., UCLA, 1964; m. Jane Bower Nippert, Feb. 2, 1963; children—Christine, Andrea, Michael, John William III, Kevin Robert. Sr. asso. Planning Research Corp., Los Angeles, 1962-67; dir. fin. systems group Synergetic Scis., Inc., Tarzana, Calif., 1967-70; dir. analytical services div. James H. Oliphant & Co., Los Angeles, 1970-72; chmn. bd., chief exec. officer, pres. O'Brien Assos., Inc., Santa Monica, Calif., 1972-77; v.p. A.G. Becker Inc., 1977-81; chmn., chief exec. officer Leland O'Brien Rubinstein Assos., 1981—. Served to 1st lt. USAF, 1958-62. Recipient Graham and Dodd award Fin. Analysts Fedn., 1970. Mem. Delta Upsilon. Home: 231 Surfview Dr Pacific Palisades CA 90272 Office: 707 Wilshire Blvd 13th Floor Los Angeles CA 90017

O'BRIEN, KEVIN CHARLES, research engineer; b. Pitts., Dec. 30, 1957; s. Charles James and Minerva A. (Mars) O'B.; m. Ann Marie Poydock, Oct. 9, 1982. BS in Polymer Engring., Case Western Res. U., 1979, MS in Macromolecular Engring., 1981, PhD in Macromolecular Engring., 1984. Grad. fellow Case Western Res. U., Cleve., 1979-82, staff technician I, 1982-84; postdoctoral research assoc. dept. chem. engring. U. Tex., Austin, 1984-85; sr. research engr. Dow Chem. USA, Walnut Creek, Calif., 1985—. Contbr. articles to profl. jours. Instr. religious edn. Newman Cath. Ctr. U. Tex., Austin, 1985. B.F. Goodrich fellow, 1981. Mem. Am. Phys. Soc., Am. Chem. Soc., Materials Research Soc., N.Am. Membrane Soc., Sigma Alpha Epsilon. Avocations: sports, photography, calligraphy. Office: Dow Chem USA 2800 Mitchell Dr Walnut Creek CA 94598

O'BRIEN, RAYMOND FRANCIS, transportation executive; b. Atchison, Kans., May 31, 1922; s. James C. and Anna M. (Wagner) O'B.; m. Mary Ann Baugher, Sept. 3, 1947; children: James B., William T., Kathleen A., Christopher R. B.S. in Bus. Adminstrn, U. Mo., 1948; grad., Advanced Mgmt. Program, Harvard, 1966. Accountant-auditor Peat, Marwick, Mitchell & Co., Kansas City, Mo., 1948-52; controller-treas. Riss & Co., Kansas City, Mo., 1952-58; regional controller Consol. Freightways Corp. of Del., Indpls., also, Akron, Ohio, 1958-61; with Consol. Freightways, Inc., San Francisco, 1961—; controller-treas. Consol. Freightways, Inc., 1962-63, v.p., treas., 1963-67, v.p. finance, 1967-69, exec. v.p., 1969-75, pres., 1975—, chief exec., 1977, chmn., chief exec. officer, 1979, also dir., pres. motor carrier subs., 1973-75; dir. Consol. Freightways Corp. of Del., CF Data Services, Inc., CF Land Services, Inc., Canadian Freightways Ltd., Canadian Freightways Eastern Ltd., CF Air Freight Inc., Transam. Corp., Union Bank, Watkins-Johnson, Inc., CF Ocean Services; past chmn., now dir. Western Hwy. Inst. Former mem. bus. adv. bd. Northwestern U., U. Calif., Berkeley; chmn. bd. trustees St. Mary's Coll.; bd. dirs. Charles Armstrong Sch. Served to 1st lt. USAAF, 1942-45. Mem. Am. Trucking Assn. Clubs: Pacific Union, World Trade, Commonwealth (San Francisco); Palo Alto Hills Golf and Country, Burning Tree Country, Menlo Country, Congressional Country, Firestone Country. Home: 26347 Esperanza Dr Los Altos Hills CA 94022 Office: Consol Freightways Inc PO Box 10340 Palo Alto CA 94303

O'BRIEN, RICHARD BATCHELDER, aerospace company executive; b. Council Bluffs, Iowa, Jan. 29, 1929; s. Robert Roland and Linda (Batchelder) O'B.; m. Diane Tucker, Apr. 20, 1958; children: Richard Kirk, Kellee Diane. BSME, U. Colo., 1952. Supr. health and safety Gen. Electric, Idaho Falls, Idaho, 1954-61, prin. engr. nuclear safety, 1961-69; mgr. nuclear and operational safety Aerojet Nuclear Co., Idaho Falls, 1969-76; dir. security, health and safety EG&G Idaho, Inc., Idaho Falls, 1976-80; dir. environ. affairs and safety Aerojet Gen., La Jolla, Calif., 1980—; mem. govs. com. Atomic Energy, Idaho, 1956-60. Mem. Calif. Mfrs. Assn. (environ. com. 1980—), Health Physics Soc., System Safety Soc., Assn. Profl. Energy Mgrs., Calif. C. of C. (safety and waste coms.). Republican. Home: 13957 Ipava Dr Poway CA 92064 Office: Aerojet Gen 10300 N Torrey Pines Rd La Jolla CA 92037

O'BRIEN, ROBERT S., state official; b. Seattle, Sept. 14, 1918; s. Edward R. and Maude (Ransom) O'B.; m. Kathryn E. Arvan, Oct. 18, 1941 (dec. June 1984). Student public schs. With Kaiser Co., 1938-46; restaurant owner 1946-50; treas. Grant County, Wash., 1950-65, State of Wash., 1965—; chmn. Wash. Fin. Com., 1965—, Wash. Public Deposit Protection Commn., 1969—, Wash. Public Employees Retirement Bd., 1969-77, Law Enforcement Officers and Firefighters Retirement System, 1971-77, Wash. State Investment Bd., 1981—; mem. Wash. Data Processing Adv. Bd., 1967-73, Gov.'s Exec. Mgmt. and Fiscal Affairs Com., 1978-80, Gov.'s Cabinet Com. on Tax Alternatives, 1978-80; trustee Wash. Tchr.'s Retirement System, 1965—. Recipient Leadership award Joint Council County and City Employees-Fedn. State Employees, 1970, Eagles Leadership award, 1967. Mem. Nat. Assn. State Auditors, Comptrollers and Treasurers (pres. 1977), Nat. Assn. Mcpl. Fin. Officers, Nat. Assn. State Treasurers, Western State Treasurers Assn. (pres. 1970), Wash. County Treas. Assn. (pres. 1955-56), Wash. Assn. Elected County Ofcls. (pres. 1955-58), Olympia Area C. of C., Soap Lake C. of C. (pres. 1948). Democrat. Clubs: Elks (hon. life); Moose, Eagles, Lions, Olympia Yacht, Olympia Country and Golf; Empire (Spokane); Wash. Athletic (Seattle). Address: Legislative Bldg Olympia WA 98504

O'BRIEN, ROBERT THOMAS, microbiologist, educator, consultant; b. Bismarck, N.D., Dec. 20, 1925; s. Ernest Peter and Etta W. (Webster) O'B.; m. Beverly Ruth Asbridge, Dec. 22, 1948; children—Shawnne M., Timothy E., Barbara R., Phillip T., Mary B. B.S., U. N.D., 1950, M.S., 1952; Ph.D., Wash. State U., 1956. Biol. scientist Gen. Electric Co., Richland, Wash., 1956-63, sr. scientist, 1963-64, co. cons., Syracuse, N.Y., 1964-66; prof. biology N. Mex. State U., Las Cruces, 1966, chmn. dept. biology, 1978-84; cons. in field. Contbr. articles, abstracts to profl. publs. Served to sgt. USAAF, 1943-46, ETO. Grantee NSF, NIH, Dept. Energy, U.S. Army. Fellow AAAS; mem. Am. Soc. Microbiology, Soc. Gen. Microbiology. Roman Catholic. Home: 2901 Karon Dr Las Cruces NM 88001 Office: N Mex State U Dept Biology Las Cruces NM 88003

O'BRIEN, SUE, journalist, state official; b. Waukon, Iowa, Mar. 6, 1939; d. John Gordon and Jean (Schadel) O'B.; children—Peter, Sarah, Andrew. B.A., Grinnell Coll., 1959; M.P.A., JFK Sch. Govt., Harvard U., 1985. Reporter, KTLN/KTLK, radio, Denver, 1968-70; anchor, reporter KBTR-AM, Denver, 1970-73; anchor, reporter, commentator KOA-AM/TV, Denver, 1973-75; corr. NBC Radio, N.Y.C., 1975-76; news dir., exec. editor KOA AM/FM/TV, Denver, 1976-80; press sec. Gov. Colo., Denver, 1980-85; campaign mgr. Roy Romer 1985-86; asst. city editor The Denver Post, 1987—. Chmn., Christian Social Relations div. Episcopal Diocese Colo., 1964-68; chmn., editor Colo. Journalism Rev., 1974-75; press sec. Coloradans for Lamm/Dick, 1982. Recipient Headliner award Women in Communications Colo., 1972, Big Hat award U. Colo. Soc. Profl. Journalists, 1973, Alumni award Grinnell Coll., 1974. Mem. Soc. Profl. Journalists (v.p. 1977-78), Radio and TV News Dirs. Assn., Mortar Bd., Phi Beta Kappa. Democrat. Episcopalian. Club: Denver Press. Home: 17 Ogden St Denver CO 80218 Office: The Denver Post City Desk 650 15th St Denver CO 80202

O'BRIEN, THOMAS JOSEPH, bishop; b. Indpls., Nov. 29, 1935. Grad., St. Meinrad Coll. Sem. Ordained priest Roman Catholic Ch., 1961. Bishop of Phoenix 1982—. Office: 400 E Monroe Phoenix AZ 85004 *

O'BYRNE, PAUL J., bishop; b. Calgary, Alta., Can., Dec. 21, 1922. Ordained priest Roman Catholic Ch., 1948; bishop of Calgary 1968—. Office: Catholic Pastoral Care Ctr, 1916 2d Ave SW Room 205, Calgary, AB Canada T2S 1S3 *

O'CALLAGHAN, J. PATRICK, newspaper publisher; b. Mallow, Ireland, Oct. 8, 1925; imigrated to Can., 1959, naturalized, 1964; s. Michael Joseph and Marguerita (Hayes) O'C.; m. Lorna E. Nattriss, June 28, 1947; children: Patrick, Michael, Sean, Brendan, Fiona. Student, Christian Brothers Sch., Limerick, Ireland, 1931-32, Cotton Coll., Eng. Reporter, deskman English newspapers 1947-53; asst. editor Liverpool (Eng.) Echo, 1953-59; mng. editor, asst. pub. Red Deer Advocate, Alta., 1959-68; asst. to pub. Edmonton Jour. (Alta.), 1968, pub., 1976-82; exec. editor Southam News Services, Ottawa, Ont., Can., 1969-71; exec. asst. to mng. dir. Southam Press Ltd., 1971-72; v.p., pub. Windsor Star (Ont.), 1972-76; pub. Calgary (Alta.) Herald, 1982—. Served with RAF, 1943-47. Mem. Can. Daily Newspaper Pubs. Assn. (past pres.), Canadian Press (chmn.), Am. Press Inst. (dir.), Commonwealth Press Union, Internat. Press Inst. Roman Catholic. Home: 1416 Chardie Pl SW, Calgary, AB Canada Office: Calgary Herald, Calgary, AB Canada T2P 0W8

OCCELLI, MARIO LORENZO, chemical engineer, researcher; b. Luino, Italy, Dec. 16, 1942; came to U.S. 1963; s. Lorenzo and Maria B. (Borri) O.; m. Susan C. Bush, Aug. 10, 1970; children: Maria, Teresa, Lucia, Matthew. BS ChemE., Iowa State U., 1967, PhD in Phys. Chem., 1972. System analyst Air Products, Allentown, Pa., 1972-76; project mgr. PQ Corp., Phila., 1976-77; sr. research chemist Davison Corp., Columbia, Md., 1977-79, Gulf Oil Corp., Pitts., 1979-85; research assoc. Unocal Corp., Brea, Calif., 1985—. Contbr articles to profl. jours.; patentee in field. Fulbright scholar, 1963-67; Merit scholar Iowa State U., 1964-67. Mem. Am. Chem. Soc. (petroleum chem. div.), The Clay Mineral Soc., Internat. Zeolite Assn., Tau Beta Phi. Office: Unocal Corp 376 S Valencia Brea CA 92621

OCCHIATO, MICHAEL ANTHONY, city official; b. Pueblo, Colo.; s. Joseph Michael and Joan Occhiato; m. Peggy Ann Stefonowicz, June 27, 1964 (div. Sept. 1983); children: Michael, James, Jennifer; m. Patsy Gay Payne, June 2, 1984; children: Kim Carr, Jerry Don Webb. BBA, U. Denver, 1961; MBA, U. Colo., 1984; postgrad., U. So. Colo. Sales mgr. Tivoli Brewing co., Denver, 1965-67, acting brewmaster, prodn. control mgr., 1967-68, plant mgr., 1968-69; adminstrv. mgr. King Resources Co., Denver, 1969-70; ops. mgr. Canners Inc., Pepsi-Cola Bottling Co., Pueblo, 1970-76; pres. Pepsi-Cola Bottling Co., Pueblo, 1978-82; gen. mgr. Pepsi-Cola Bottling Group div. PepsiCo., Pueblo, 1982, area v.p., 1982-83; ind. cons. Pueblo, 1983—. mem. council City of Pueblo, 1978—, pres. 1986—; mem. bd. health, 1978-80, regional planning commn., 1980-81, Pueblo Action Inc., 1978-80, Pueblo Planning and Zoning Commn., 1985; chmn. Pueblo Area council Govts., 1980-82; mem. Pueblo Econ. Devel. Corp., 1983-85; chmn. fundraising Pueblo chpt. Am. Heart Assn.; bd. dirs. El Pueblo Boys Ranch, 1971-73. Served to lt. USN, 1961-65. Mem. So. Colo. Emergency Med. Technicians Assn. (pres. 1975), Pueblo C. of C. Lodge: Rotary. Home: 11 Harrogate Terr Pueblo CO 81001 Office: City of Pueblo 1 City Hall Pl Pueblo CO 81003

OCHS, GARY LEE, chemical research consultant; b. Escondido, Calif., Nov. 4, 1949; s. Clarence Conrad and Darlene Raye (Dyckman) O.; m. Elizabeth Woodard Otto, Dec. 23, 1971. AA, Palomar Community Coll., 1969; BS, U. Calif., Riverside, 1971. Chemist Twin City Testing and Engring., St. Paul, 1972-76; dir. field services Corning Labs., Cedar Falls, Iowa, 1976-79; project mgr. York Research Cons., Denver, 1979-83, program mgr., 1983-85, v.p., 1985-86; mgr. Ochs Oil Co., San Marcos, Calif., 1986—. Sec. Cedar Falls (Iowa) Community Theater Bd. Dirs., 1977-79. Recipient Order of the Arrow award Boy Scouts Am., 1966; named Scout of Yr. troop 729 Boy Scouts Am., 1963, 66. Mem. Am. Chem. Soc., Air Pollution Control Assn., Assn. Energy Engrs., Air Pollution Control Assn. Micro-computer Users Group (sec. 1984-85). Roman Catholic. Avocations: hiking, carpentry, acting, creative writing. Office: Ochs Oil Co 145 Via Vera Cruz San Marcos CA 92069

OCHS, GERARD RAHN, physicist; b. St. Louis, Jan. 2, 1928; s. Oscar A. and Laura Ann (Rahn) O.; m. S. Alice Jenkins, Sept. 6, 1959; children: Letha, Travis. BSEE, Washington U., St. Louis, 1950; BS in Engring. Physics, U. Colo., 1956. Electronic scientist Nat. Bur. Standards, Boulder, Colo., 1956-65; physicist NOAA, Boulder, 1965—. Contbr. articles to profl. jours. Served to lt. USN, 1950-55. Fellow Optical Soc. Am.; mem. AAAS, Am. Geophys. Union, Soc. Photo-Optical Instrumentation Engrs., Commn. F Internat. Union of Radio Sci. Avocations: ind. ranching, raising horses. Home: 4885 Oxford Rd Longmont CO 80501 Office: NOAA/ERL R/E/WP1 325 Broadway Boulder CO 80303

OCKANDER, DONALD LEE, retail company official; b. Wahoo, Nebr., May 5, 1930; s. Vedor and Leona (Robinson) O.; m. Naomi J. Raish, June 7, 1953; children—Steven E., Gregory J. B.S.B.A., U. Nebr., 1952. Mgmt. trainee F.W. Woolworth Co., 1954-58, store mgr., 1958-68, dist. mgr., Seattle, 1968-72, dir. manpower devel., Burlingame, Calif., 1972-83, regional dir. personnel, 1982-84, regional dir. mgmt. devel., 1984—. Hon. mem. adv. bd. Salvation Army Harbor Light, San Francisco, 1976—. Served to lt. USN, 1952-55. Mem. Am. Soc. Tng. and Devel., Republican. Presbyterian. Home: PO Box 530 Gualala CA 95445 Office: FW Woolworth 1733 California Dr Burlingame CA 94010

OCKNER, ROBERT KEITH, gastroenterology educator; b. New Kensington, Pa., July 30, 1936; s. Lee and Sara E. (Weis) O.; m. Patricia L. Gammon, June 17, 1960; children—James, Matthew, Peter. B.A., Pomona Coll., 1957; M.D., Harvard U., 1961. Diplomate Am. Bd. Internal Medicine, Am. Bd. Gastroenterology. Intern, then resident Boston City Hosp., 1961-63, 65-66; clin. assoc. NIH, Bethesda, Md., 1963-65; fellow in gastroenterology Mass. Gen. Hosp., Boston, 1966-68; asst. then assoc. prof. medicine U. Calif.-San Francisco, 1968-72, 72-76, prof., 1976—, chief of gastroenterology, 1983—, dir. Liver Ctr., 1983—. Assoc. editor Jour. Lipid Research, 1972-76; editor Gastroenterology, 1981-86. Trustee, Reed Union Sch. Dist., Tiburon, Calif., 1973-77, pres., 1975-76. NIH grantee, 1969—; recipient Western Gastroenterology Research prize, 1980. Fellow ACP; mem. Am. Gastroent. Assn., Am. Assn. Study of Liver Diseases (pres. 1983-84), Am. Soc. Clin. Investigation, Assn. Am. Physicians, Phi Beta Kappa, Alpha Omega Alpha. Office: U Calif San Francisco Sch Medicine Room 1120 HSW San Francisco CA 94143

OCKO, FELIX HUGH, psychoanalyst, psychiatrist; b. Bklyn., Oct. 18, 1912; s. Samuel E. and Annie (Richman) O.; m. Ida Blank, Aug. 4, 1941 (dec. Mar. 1986); children: JoEllen Ocko Lezotte, Jonathan K. BS, CCNY, 1932; MS, Emory U., 1933; MD, U. Chgo., 1937. Diplomate Am. Bd. Psychiatry; cert. psychoanalyst. Commd. USN, 1937, advanced through grades to capt., med. officer; chief. psychiat. services USN Hosps., Great Lakes Naval Air Station, Glenview, Ill. and St. Albans, Oakland,, Calif., 1937-61; ret. USN Hosps., 1961; assoc. clin. prof. psychiatry U. Calif. Med. Ctr., San Francisco, 1959-82; dir. psychiat. tng. Herrick Hosp., Berkeley, Calif., 1961-72; chief. psychiat. services Herrick Hosp., Berkeley, 1968-72; cons. Alameda County Probation Dept., Oakland, Calif., 1967-71, Laguna Honda Hosp., San Francisco, 1981—. Active Alameda County Mental health Adv. Bd., Oakland, 1971-76. Fellow Am. Psychiat. Assn.; mem. ACP (life), Am. Psychoanalytic Assn. (life), S.E. Psychoanalytic Inst. (pres. 1976-77). Club: Commonwealth (San Francisco). Home: 642 Blair Ave Piedmont CA 94611 Office: Profl Offices 2006 Dwight Way Room 301 Berkeley CA 94704

O'CONNELL, KEVIN, lawyer; b. Boston, Sept. 4, 1933; s. Michael Frederick and Kathryn Agnes (Kelley) O'C.; m. Sarah Miller, Oct. 7, 1978; children—Tiffany W., Elizabeth H. A.B., Harvard, 1955, J.D., 1960. Bar: Calif. bar 1961. Asso. firm O'Melveny & Myers, Los Angeles, 1960-63; asst. U.S. atty. criminal div. Central Dist. Calif., Los Angeles, 1963-65; staff counsel Gov. Calif. Commn. to Investigate Watts Riot, Los Angeles, 1965-66; partner firm Tuttle & Taylor, Los Angeles, 1966-70, Coleman & O'Connell, Los Angeles, 1971-75; individual practice law Los Angeles, 1975-78; of counsel firm Simon & Sheridan, Los Angeles, 1978—. Bd. editors: Harvard Law Rev, 1958-60. Mem. Los Angeles County (Calif.) Democratic Central Com., 1973-74. Served to lt. USMCR, 1955-57. Home: 8913 Wonderland Park Suite 400 Los Angeles CA 90046 Office: Simon & Sheridan 2404 Wilshire Blvd Los Angeles CA 90057

O'CONNELL, MARY ANN, state senator; b. Albuquerque, Aug. 3, 1934; d. James Aubrey and Dorothy Nell (Batsel) Gray; m. Robert Emmett O'Connell, Feb. 21, 1977; children: Ervin Jeffery, Aubrey Gray. Grad. high sch. Albuquerque. Exec. dir. Blvd. Shopping Ctr., Las Vegas, Nev., 1968-76, Citizen Pvt. Enterprise, Las Vegas, 1976; media supr. Southwest Advt., Las Vegas, 1977—; owner, operator Confort Inn, Las Vegas, 1985—; mem. Nev. Senate, 1984—; state senator 1987—; chmn. gov. affairs; vice chmn. commerce and labor; mem. taxation com.; rep. Nat. Conf. State Legislators. P-res. explorer div. Boulder Dam Area council Boy Scouts Am., Las Vegas 1979-80; pres. Citizen Pvt. Enterprise, Las Vegas, 1982-84, Secret Witness, Las Vegas, 1981-82; vice chmn. Gov.'s Mental Health-Mental Retardation, Nev., 1983—; community adv. bd Care Unit Hosp., Las Vegas; adv. bd. Kidney Found. Recipient Silver Beaver award Boy Scouts Am., 1980, Outstanding Citizenship award Bd. Realtors, 1975, Commendation award Mayor O. Grayson, Las Vegas, 1975. Republican. Mem. Christian Ch. Home: 7225 Montecito Circle Las Vegas NV 89120 Office: 525 Bonanza Rd Las Vegas NV 89120

O'CONNOR, GEORGE ALBERT, research soil chemistry educator; b. Mar. 30, 1944. BS, U. Mass., Amherst, 1966; MS, Colo. State U., 1968, PhD, 1970. Asst. prof. soil chemistry N.Mex. State U., Las Cruces, 1970-75, assoc. prof., 1975-81, prof., 1981—, univ. fellow acad. adminstrn., 1984-85; acting dir. N.Mex. Water Resources Research Inst., Las Cruces, 1982-83. Co-author: Soil Chemistry, 1985; contbr. articles to profl. jours. Mem. Am. Soc. Agronomy, Soil Sci. Soc. Am., Western Soil Sci. Soc. Am., Council Agrl. Sci. and Tech. Home: 1130 Sharon Circle Las Cruces NM 88001 Office: NMex State U Dept Agronomy and Horticulture Box 3Q Las Cruces NM 88003

O'CONNOR, G(EORGE) RICHARD, ophthalmologist; b. Cin., Oct. 8, 1928; s. George Leo and Sylvia Johanna (Voss) O'C. A.B., Harvard U., 1950; M.D., Columbia U., 1954. Resident in ophthalmology Columbia-Presbyn. Med. Center, N.Y.C., 1957-60; research fellow Inst. Biochemistry, U. Uppsala, Sweden, 1960-61, State Serum Inst., Copenhagen, 1961-62; asst. prof. ophthalmology U. Calif., San Francisco, 1962-68; prof. U. Calif., 1972-84; dir. Francis I. Proctor Found. for Research in Ophthalmology, 1970-84; mem. Nat. Adv. Eye Council NIH, 1974-78. Author: (with G. Smolin) Ocular Immunology, 1981; asso. editor: Am. Jour. Ophthalmology, 1976-81. Served with USPHS, 1955-57. Recipient Janeway prize Coll. of Physicians and Surgeons, Columbia U., 1954; Doyne medal Oxford U., 1984; NIH grantee, 1962-84. Mem. Am. Bd. Ophthalmology (examiner), Assn. for Research in Vision and Ophthalmology (trustee 1979-83), AMA, Am. Ophthal. Soc., Calif. Med. Assn., Frederic C. Cordes Eye Soc., Pan Am. Ophthal. Assn. Republican. Presbyterian. Club: Faculty. Home: 22 Wray Ave Sausalito CA 94965 Office: 315-S University of California Med Center San Francisco CA 94143

O'CONNOR, HUBERT PATRICK, bishop; b. Huntingdon, Que., Can., Feb. 17, 1928; s. Patrick Joseph and Mary Stella (Walsh) O'C. B.A., St. Patrick's Coll., Ottawa, 1952; L.S.T., Holy Rosary Scholasticate, Ottawa, 1956. Joined Congregation Missionary Oblates Mary Immaculate, 1948; ordained priest Roman Cath. Ch., 1955; mem. staff Holy Rosary Scholasticate, 1956-61; pastor St. John's Parish, Lillooet, B.C., 1967-68; prin. Cariboo Indian Residential Sch., Williams Lake, B.C., 1961-67; sec.-treas. Order Oblates Mary Immaculate in B.C., Vancouver, 1968-71; dir. St. Paul's Provincial House, 1968-71, Western region Oblate Fathers Indian-Eskimo Commn., 1968-71; bishop Diocese of Whitehouse, Y.T., Can., 1971-86, Diocese of Prince George, B.C., Can., 1986—; nat. dir. Cath. Women's League Can., 1973-78; chmn. Missions Commn., Can. Conf. Cath. Bishops. Club: K.C. (state chaplain B.C. and Yukon).

O'CONNOR, JUNE ELIZABETH, religious studies educator; b. Chgo., June 3, 1941; s. Philip Kevin and Eva Marie (Ennis) O'C.; m. Harry Hood, Aug. 11, 1973; 1 child, Meagan Hood. BA in English Lit., Mundelein Coll., 1964; MA, Marquette U., 1966, Temple U., 1972; PhD, Temple U., 1973. Instr. theology Mundelein Coll., Chgo., 1965-69, Temple U., Phila., 1970-73; asst. prof. religion U. Calif., Riverside, 1973-79, assoc. prof., 1979—, chmn. program in religious studies, 1985—; instr. theology Rosary Coll., River Forest, Ill., 1971; cons. William H. Sadlier Pubs., N.Y., 1971-81. Author: The Quest for Political and Spiritual Liberation: A Study in the Thought of Sri Aurobindo Ghose, 1977; assoc. editor Jour. Religious Ethics, 1978-82, mem. editorial bd. 1982-85; contbr. articles to profl. jours. Grantee U. Calif., Riverside, 1975—. Mem. Am. Acad. Religion (pres. Western region 1984-85, v.p., program chmn. 1983-84, mem. nat. com. on edn. study of religion), Soc. Christian Ethics (bd. dir. 1979-83, chmn. Pacific sect. 1977-78, vice chmn., program chmn. 1976-77), Coll. Theology Soc., Danforth Found. (assoc.), Pacific Coast Theol. Soc., Soc. Values in Higher Edn. Office: U Calif Program Religious Studies Riverside CA 92521

O'CONNOR, MARY J(ANE), accountant; b. Flint, Mich., Sept. 2, 1942; d. Gain Miller and Jane Elizabeth (Hulswit) Stinson; m. Wayne C. Parlberg (div.); 1 child, John C.; m. B.J. O'Connor, Aug. 20, 1977. BBA, U. Alaska, 1984. Corp. sec. Ch. Builders, Grand Rapids, Mich., 1969-73; bookkeeper Seidman & Seidman, Grand Rapids, 1973-77; internal auditor Hickel Investments, Anchorage, 1977-80; ptnr. O'Connor and Assocs., Anchorage, 1980—. Mem. Am. Soc. Women Accts. (nat. dir. 1981-84), Nat. Assn. Accts. (local chpt. pres. 1986—), Anchorage Philatelic Soc. (treas.), Anchorage C. of C. Republican. Club: Toastmasters (local sec., treas. 1985, Treas. of Yr. 1985). Avocations: needlework, stained glass, reading. Home: 6981 Laser Dr Anchorage AK 99504 Office: PO Box 92935 Anchorage AK 99509

O'CONNOR, MAUREEN, mayor; b. San Diego, July 14, 1946; m. Robert O. Peterson, 1977. B in Psychology and Sociology, San Diego State U., 1970. Council mem. City of San Diego, 1971, 75, dep. mayor, 1976, mayor, 1986—; with Calif. Housing Fin. Agy., 1977-79; port commr. San Diego, 1980-85; mem. Rules, Legis., and Intergovtl. Relations com.; chmn. pub. services and safety com. 1974-75; mem. League Calif. Cities' Com. on Human Resources Devel., Natl League Cities' Manpower and Income Support com.; chmn. mayor's crime commn. Office: Office of the Mayor 202 C St San Diego CA 92129

O'CONNOR, NANCY CAROLYN, space and technology company executive; b. Nurnberg, W. Ger., Dec. 31, 1948; came to U.S., 1949; d. Charles John and Sylvia Carolyn (Tint) O'C. Student U. Fla., 1965-69; B.A. in Bus. and Mgmt., Calif. State U.-Dominguez Hills, 1981, M.B.A., 1982; postgrad. Loyola Law Sch.; J.D. magna cum laude, Georgetown U., 1986. Mgr., Dub's Nightclub and Lounge, Gainesville, Fla., 1973-74; mgr. pub. relations advt. Gt. So. Music Hall, Gainesville, 1975-76; bus. analyst Iran Project Office, Systems Engring. and Integration Div. TRW, Tehran, 1976-77, Redondo Beach, Calif.; bus. adminstr. FLTSATCOM Project Office, Space and Tech. Group, TRW E&D, Redondo Beach, 1978-79, sr. bus. adminstr. Internat. Polar Solar Mission, 1980-81, mgr. fin. planning Def. Support Program, 1981-83; TRW rep. to Conf. Bd.'s Congl. Asst. Program, 1984; legis. asst. to Senator John H. Chafee, 1985—; mgr. project fin. TRW Command Support Div., Fed. Systems Group, 1985—; tutor TRW Adopt-A-Sch. Program. Mem. Nat. Contract Mgmt. Assn., ABA, Phi Alpha Delta. Office: TRW FSG 2701 Prosperity Ave Fairfax VA 22031

O'CONNOR, PATRICIA JOAN, social work administrator; b. Bethune, Sask., Can., Mar. 17, 1933; came to U.S., 1959; d. Malcolm Oliver and Rita Kathleen (MacDonald) Moffatt; m. Robert Emmerson O'Connor, Feb. 19, 1955 (dec.); children: Danny, Erin, Sean. BA with honors, Mo. So. State Coll., 1978; MSW, U. Okla., 1980. Social worker Oreg. Dept. Children's Services, The Dalles, Oreg., 1981-83; dir. Mt. Hood Treatment Ctr., Sandy, Oreg., 1984—; cons. social worker Mt. Hood Hospice, Sandy, 1984—. Chmn. Friends of Hospice, Sandy, 1985—. Served to sgt. RCAF, 1951-58. Mem. Nat. Assn. Social Workers (cert.), Phi Theta Kappa, Pi Gamma Mu, Alpha Gamma Sigma. Episcopalian. Avocation: collecting and restoring antique furniture. Home: 975 SE Spruce Ct Gresham OR 97030 Office: Mt Hood Treatment Ctr 39400 SE Dubarko Sandy OR 97055

O'CONNOR, ROBERT JEROME, power company executive; b. Uniontown, Wash., Aug. 23, 1927; s. Eugene Joseph and Kathryn (Lunders) O'C.; m. Margaret Jean Carter, Aug. 27, 1950; children: Mary Sue, John. B.S. in Elec. Engring., U. Idaho, 1951. Vice pres., asst. to pres. Idaho Power Co., Boise, 1970-72, sr. v.p. adminstrn., 1972-76, exec. v.p. ops., 1976-81, pres., chief operating officer, 1980-86, pres., chief exec. officer, 1985—, also dir.; dir. Idaho Power Co., Idaho Bank & Trust Co. bd. dirs. St. Lukes's Regional Med. Ctr.; exec. com. Idaho Council on Econ. Edn., 1983—. Served with U.S. Army, 1946-48. Mem. Idaho Assn. Commerce and Industry (chmn. bus. week 1979), Boise C. of C. (exec. com.). Republican. Roman Catholic. Lodge: Rotary. Home: 710 Ranch Rd Boise ID 83702 Office: Idaho Power Co 1220 Idaho St PO Box 70 Boise ID 83707 *

ODA, MARGARET YURIKO, educational administrator; b. Hakalau, Hawaii, Mar. 26, 1925; d. Satoru and Satoyo Kurisu; m. Glenn K. Oda (dec.); 1 child, Marjorie. B.Ed., U. Hawaii, 1947; M.A., Mich. State U., 1950; Ed.D., U. Hawaii, 1977. Tchr. Hilo Intermediate Sch., Hawaii, 1951, counselor, 1951-52, 53-56, vice prin., 1956-63; prin. Hakalau-Honomu-Pepeekeo, Hilo, 1963-64; dir. gen. edn. State Dept. Edn., Honolulu, 1965-75; prin. Kaiser High Sch., Honolulu, 1978-82; supt. Honolulu Sch. Dist., Honolulu, 1982-84; state dep. supt. Hawaii State Dept. Edn., Honolulu, 1984-87, dist. supt., 1987—; mem. Western Regional Adv. Panel Coll. Bd., 1984-86, Northwest Regional Ednl. Lab. Adv. Bd., Portland, Oreg., 1984-85, exec. bd. Chief State Sch. Officers Study Commn., 1985-87; coordinator State Edn. Policy Seminars, 1985-87. Bd. dirs. Hawaii Heart Assn., Honolulu, 1979-84, Honolulu Community Theatre, 1972-75, Honpa Hongwanji Buddhist Orgn., 1984—, Pan Pacific Found., 1982—, Jr. Achievement, 1986—. Fellow Ctr. for Study Edn. Yale U., 1973. Mem. Am. Assn. Sch. Adminstrs., Nat. Assn. Secondary Sch. Prins., Pi Lambda Theta. Club: Japanese Women's Soc. (pres. 1983-85). Avocations: swimming; horticulture. Office: State Dept Edn Honolulu Dist 4967 Kilauea Ave Honolulu HI 96816

ODA, YOSHIO, physician; b. Papaaloa, Hawaii, Jan. 14, 1933; s. Hakuai and Usako (Yamamoto) O.; A.B., Cornell U., 1955; M.D., U. Chgo., 1959. Intern U. Chgo. Clinics, 1959-60; resident in pathology U. Chgo., 1960-62, Queen's Hosp., Hawaii, 1962-63, Long Beach (Calif.) VA Hosp., 1963-65; resident in allergy, immunology U. Colo. Med. Center, 1966-67; practice internal medicine, Los Angeles, 1965-66; practice internal medicine, allergy and immunology, Honolulu, 1970—; asst. clin. prof. medicine U. Hawaii, Honolulu, 1970—. Served to maj. M.C., AUS, 1968-70. Diplomate Am. Bd. Internal Medicine. Mem. A.C.P., Am. Acad. Allergy. Office: Piikoi Med Bldg 1024 Piikoi St Honolulu HI 96814

ODDO, THOMAS CHARLES, university president, clergyman; b. Jamaica, N.Y., June 12, 1944; s. Dominick Charles and Catherine Anna (Arthen) O. AB, U. Notre Dame, 1965, MTh, 1969; PhD, Harvard U., 1979. Ordained priest Roman Catholic Ch., 1970. Joined Congregation of Holy Cross, 1965; asst. prof. religious studies Stonehill Coll., North Easton, Mass., 1974-82; pres. U. Portland, (Oreg.), 1982—. Bd. dirs. United Way of Columbia-Williamette, 1983—; bd. dirs. DePaul Alcoholism Treatment Ctr., Portland, 1982—, Ecumenical Ministries of Oreg., 1982—. Recipient Pres.' Medallion U. Notre dame, 1965; fellow Harvard Div. Sch., 1970-71, Harvard U., 1971-73. Mem. Am. Acad. Religion, Coll. Theology Soc. Club: City (Portland). Office: U Portland 5000 N Willamette Blvd Portland OR 97203

O'DELL, PETER LEON, computer infosystems executive; b. Poughkeepsie, N.Y., Jan. 11, 1956; s. William H. and Viola (Peterson) O'D.; m. Lisa Sorensen, Dec. 29, 1984. BSBA, U. Colo., 1982. Programmer System Devel. Corp., Colorado Springs, Colo., 1980-81; sr. systems analyst Digital Equipment Corp., Colorado Springs, Colo., 1981-83; database adminstr. Microsoft, Bellevue, Wash., 1983—; dir. tech. services Criton Techs., Bellevue, Wash., 1984—. Contbr. articles to profl. jours. Served as sgt. U.S. Army, 1975-79. Mem. Mensa. Avocations: personal computers, running, reading, traveling, skiing. Home: 6260 139th Ave NE #86 Redmond WA 98052 Office: Criton Techs 10800 NE 8th St Bellevue WA 98004

ODELL, SHARON CASEY, marketing researcher, consultant; b. San Francisco, May 16, 1953; d. Donald Edward and Ernestine (Aichele) Casey; m. Timothy William Odell, June 15, 1980; children: Ian Douglas, Katherine Janet. BS in Chemistry, Stanford U., 1975; MBA, U. Santa Clara, 1979. Market research analyst SRI Internat., Menlo Park, Calif., 1979, Merck & Co., Inc., San Diego, 1981-85; pvt. practice market research cons. Lafayette, Calif., 1985—. Mem. Am. Chem. Soc., Chem. Mktg. Research Assn., Walnut Creek (Calif.) Masters Swim Team. Avocations: masters swimming. Home and Office: 5 Del Rio Ct Lafayette CA 94549

ODELL, STEPHANIE DAVIS, chemist; b. Rochester, Minn., Aug. 23, 1953; d. Windon Hewitt and Betsy Louise (Faber) Davis; m. William Jeff Odell, Sept. 3, 1983; children: Megan Elizabeth, Casey Ann Odell. BA, U. No. Colo., 1980. Lab. technician City of Loveland, Colo., 1983-84, lab. chemist, 1984-86; lab chemist, pretreatment coordinator City of Loveland, 1986—. Asst. chair Trinity Episc. Antique Show, Greeley, Colo., 1983—; active fundraising drive Home for Battered Women, Greeley, 1985—. Mem. Am. Chem. Soc., Water Pollution Control Fedn., Rocky Mtn. Water Quality Analysts. Republican. Avocations: softball, downhill skiing, running. Home: 5909 West C St Greeley CO 80634 Office: City of Loveland 410 E 5th Loveland CO 80537

ODELL, WILLIAM LUCIEN, labor relations consultant; b. Oakland, Calif., May 1, 1940; s. William Rockhold and Mildred (Griffee) O.; m. Diane Lee Codding, June 29, 1963 (div. Aug. 1979); children: Scott D., Linda K.; m. Elizabeth Louise Smith, Sept. 29, 1979; children: Donald H., Ronald L., Susan L. BA, Stanford U., 1962; MA, Syracuse U., 1963. Asst. personnel dir. San Mateo (Calif.) High Sch. Dist., 1965-72; personnel dir. Santa Cruz (Calif.) Sch. Dist., 1972-74; pvt. practice labor relations cons. Redding, Calif., 1974—. Bd. dirs. Shasta County YMCA, Redding, 1980—. Mem. Assn. Calif. Sch. Adminstrs., Internat. Pub. Personnel Mgmt. Assn.

ODERMATT, ROBERT ALLEN, architect; b. Oakland, Calif., Jan. 3, 1938; s. Clifford Allen and Margaret Louise (Budge) O.; m. Diana Birtwistle, June 9, 1960; children: Kristin Ann, Kyle David. B.Arch., U. Calif.-Berkeley, 1960. Registered architect, Calif., Oreg., Nev., Colo. cert. Nat. Council Archtl. Registration Bds. Draftsman Anderson Simonds Dusel Campini, Oakland, 1960-61; architect James R. Lucas, Orinda, Calif., 1961-62, ROMA Architects, San Francisco, 1962-76; architect, pres. ROMA Architects, 1976-84; prin. ROMA Design Group, San Francisco, 1962—. Prin. designer (comprehensive plan), Grand Canyon Nat. Park, 1977, Yosmite Nat. Park, 1987, prin. planner (devel. plan); prin.-in-charge: Hotel Complex, Westin Hotel, Vail, Colo., 1982, U.S. Embassy, Manama, Bahrain, Kaanapali Resort Master-Plan, 1987. Mem. Oakland Mayors Com. on High Density Housing, 1982; prin. charge U.S. Embassy, Bahrain. Fellow AIA (dir. East Bay chpt. 1969-71, pres. 1980-81, dir. Calif. council 1979-81, nat. dir. 1983-86, nat. v.p. 1986-87). Office: ROMA Design Group 1420 Sutter St San Francisco CA 94109

ODIER, PIERRE ANDRE, educator, writer, photographer, artist; b. Lausanne, Switzerland, May 24, 1940; came to U.S., 1959; s. Leon Odier and Gretha (Vesper) Hough; m. Mary Ellen Patton, Apr. 2, 1967 (div. Apr. 1984); children—Yvette, Debbi. B.A., U. Puget Sound, 1967; M.F.A., Calif. State U., Los Angeles, 1974; postgrad., UCLA, 1976-83. Cert. tchr., Calif. Owner restaurant The End, Tacoma, Wash., 1961-64; owner gallery Place des Arts, Tacoma, 1964-65; interpeter Weyerhauser Corp., Tacoma, 1964; chairperson dept. fine arts Hoover High Sch., Glendale, Calif., 1967—. Author: The Rock, A History of Alcatraz, 1983; Lummis Inside his Habitat, 1977 (State Hist. Soc. award 1981). Editor: Nat. Photographers Assn. quar., 1980-84. Served with U.S. Army, 1959-62. Recipient Tchr. of Yr. award Parent Tchrs. Student Assn., Glendale, Calif., 1979; Tchr. of Yr. award Glendale C. of C., 1983. Mem. Glendale Tchrs. Assn. (contract negotiator 1977), Nat. Photography Instrs. Assn. (chmn. election com., pres. 1980-85, chairperson conv. 1982), NEA. Democrat. Lutheran. Home: 1255 Hill Dr Eagle Rock CA 90041 Office: Hoover High Sch 651 Glenwood Rd Glendale CA 91202

O'DONNELL, MICHAEL LAWRENCE, international business executive, consultant; b. San Diego, Oct. 27, 1949; s. Michael Daniel and Cherry Joy (Pratt) O'D.; m. Jan Lesna Ansel, Oct. 3, 1970; children—Arish, Tennyson, Katie, Michael, Mandy, Jeremy. A.A., Cypress Coll., 1969; B.A., Calif. Western U., 1982, M.B.A., 1984. Cert. purchasing mgr.; lic. pvt. pilot. Gen. mgr. Utah Parks Co., Cedar City, 1969-71; mgr. K.S.I., Inc., Cedar City, 1971-74; purchasing mgr. Brigham Young U. and Polynesian Cultural Ctr., Honolulu, 1974-77; purchasing mgr. Latter Day Saints Ch., Honolulu, 1977-80, materials mgmt. mgr., 1980-83, regional mgr., APIA, Western Samoa, 1983-86; dir. procurement Sheraton Corp., of Hawaii-Japan, Honolulu, 1986—, also bd. dirs.; trustee Enterprise Trust Co., Independence, Mo., 1981—; bd. dirs. Watanabe Floral, Inc., Honolulu; chmn. bd. Bus. Specialists Internat. Inc., Honolulu, 1981—, Internat. Mgmt. Specialists Inc., Honolulu, 1976—. Author articles in field. Dist. commr. Aloha Council Boy Scouts Am., Honolulu, 1977-83; chmn. Deseret Mut. Benefit, Western Samoa, 1983-85. Recipient King Kamehameha award, Polynesian Cultural Ctr., Honolulu, 1977, David O. McKay award, Brigham Young U., Laie, Hawaii, 1979, R. Billings award, Billings Energy Corp. (Mo.), 1982. Mem. Nat. Assn. Ednl. Buyers, Nat. Assn. Purchasing Mgmt. (v.p. 1980-81, dir. 1981-83, award 1983). Purchasing Mgmt. Assn. Hawaii (pres. 1978-79, Cliff C. Dalen award 1980). Internat. Fedn. Purchasing and Material Mgmt. (rep. 1976-83). C. of C. APIA Western Samoa. Mormon. Home: 91-951 Kalapu St Ewa Beach HI 96706 Office: Sheraton Corp PO Box 8559 Honolulu HI 96830

O'DONNELL, WILLIAM THOMAS, radar systems mktg. exec.; b. Latrobe, Pa., Feb. 22, 1939; s. William Regis and Kathryn Ann (Coneff) O'D.; student Eastern N.Mex. U., 1958-61; student in mktg. John Carroll U., 1961-65, Ill. Inst. Tech., 1965-66; B.S.B.A., U. Phoenix, 1982, M.B.A. with distinction, 1984; m. Judith Koetke, Oct. 1, 1965; children—William Thomas and William Patrick (twins), Allison Rose, Kevin Raymond. Various sales positions Hickok Elec. Instrument Co., Cleve., 1961-65, Fairchild Semicondr., Mpls., 1965-67; Transitron Semicondr., Mpls., 1967-69; Burroughs Corp., Plainfield, N.J., 1967-71; mktg. mgr. Owens-Ill. Co., 1972-73, v.p. mktg. Pantek Co., subs. Owens-Ill. Co., Lewistown, Pa., 1973-75, v.p. mktg., nat. sales mgr., Toledo, 1975-76; mktg. mgr., nat. sales mgr. Govt. Electronics div. group Motorola Co., Scottsdale, Ariz., 1976-80, U.S. mktg. mgr. radar positioning systems Motorola Govt. Electronics Group, 1981—; gen. mgr. J. K. Internat., Scottsdale, 1980-81; cons. mktg., mgmt; adj. prof. Union Grad. Sch.; guest lectr. U. Mich. Grad. Sch. Bus. Adminstrn.; instr. U. Phoenix, Scottsdale Community Coll.; adj. prof. Union grad. sch. Maricopa Community Coll. Chmn., Rep. Precinct, Burnsville, Minn., 1968-70; city fin. chmn., Burnsville; dir. community devel. U.S. Jaycees, Mpls., 1968-69; mem. Scottsdale 2000 Com. Served with USAF, 1957-61. Recipient Outstanding Achievement award Govt. Electronics div. Motorola Co., 1976, also Mktg. Mgmt. award Motorola Co., 1983, Marketing Orgn. award Motorola Co., 1985, Citation for Faciliation Ability U. Phoenix, 1986, Excellence in Orgn. award Motorola, 1986; named to Million Dollar Club, Burroughs Co., 1969-71; hon. citizen, Donaldsville, La., 1978; others. Mem. Phoenix Execs. Club, Am. Mktg. Assn., U. Phoenix Faculty Club (officer). Roman Catholic. Clubs: North Cape Yacht, Scottsdale Racquet, Toftness Country. Home: 8432 E Belgian Trail Scottsdale AZ 85258 Office: 2100 E Elliot Rd Tempe AZ 85282

O'DOWD, DONALD DAVY, university president; b. Manchester, N.H., Jan. 23, 1927; s. Hugh Davy and Laura (Morin) O'D.; m. Janet Louise Fithian, Aug. 23, 1953; children: Daniel D., Diane K., James E., John M. B.A. summa cum laude, Dartmouth Coll., 1951; postgrad. (Fulbright fellow), U. Edinburgh, Scotland, 1951-52; M.A., Harvard U., 1955, Ph.D., 1957. Instr., asst. prof. psychology, dean freshmen Wesleyan U., Middletown, Conn., 1955-60; assoc. prof., prof. Wesleyan U., 1960, dean Univ., 1960-65, provost, 1965-70; pres. Oakland U., Rochester, Mich., 1970-80; exec. vice chancellor SUNY, Albany, 1980-84; pres. U. of Alaska Statewide Syst., 1984-. Bd. dirs. Research Found. SUNY, State Univ. Constrn. Fund, N.Y. Sea Grant Inst., Albany Symphony Orch.; pres. Capital Repertory Theatre Co. Served with AUS, 1945-47. Carnegie Corp. fellow, 1965-66. Mem. Am. Psychol. Assn., AAAS, AAUP, Am. Assn. Univ. Adminstrs., Phi Beta Kappa, Sigma Xi. Office: U of Alaska Statewide System Office of the President Fairbanks AK 99775 *

OECHEL, WALTER CLARENCE, professor ecology, researcher; b. San Diego, Jan. 15, 1945; s. Walter Clarence and Gloria Dawn (Gordon) O.; m. Judith Lynne Riley, June 25, 1967. AB, San Diego State U., 1966; postgrad., Duke U., 1969-70; PhD, U. Calif., Riverside, 1970. Fellow dept. life scis. U. Calif., Riverside, 1967-70; from asst. prof. to prof. ecology McGill U., Montreal, Can., 1970-79; prof. San Diego State U., 1979—, dir. Systems Ecology Research Group, 1982—, prin. scientist U.S. Dept. Energy, 1982—; mem. watershed research adv. com. Calif. Dept. Forestry, U. Calif., 1982-85, watershed mgmt. task force County of San Diego Dept. Agr., 1982-85; vis. research prof. Systems Ecology Research Group, 1978-82; cons. USDA So. Plains Research Sta., Woodward, Okla., 1982-85. Contbr. numerous articles to profl. jours. Grantee NSF, 1972—, U.S. Dept. Energy grantee, 1981—, grantee U.S. Forestry Service, 1978-86. Mem. AAAS, Ecol. Soc. Am. (chmn. physiol. ecology sect., 1982-83), Calif. Native Plant Soc., Internat. Assn. Bryologists, Internat. Assn. Ecology, N.Y. Acad. Scis., Western Soc. Naturalists, Sigma Xi. Office: San Diego State U Systems Ecology Research Group San Diego CA 92182

OEH, GEORGE RICHARD, electrical engineer; b. Tacoma, Aug. 29, 1936; s. George Kenneth and Elsie Linnea (Ness) O.; BEE, U. Wash., 1958, MS (teaching fellow 1960), 1962; m. Diane Manley, Aug. 18, 1962; children: Karen Michelle, Jason Robert. Instr., U. Wash., 1961-62; advanced devel. engr., Philco-Ford Co., 1963-64; mgr. electromagnetics dept. GTE-Sylvania Co., 1964-72; mgr. sales Watkins Johnson Co., Palo Alto, Calif., 1972-82; v.p. Dalmo Victor Singer, Belmont, Calif., 1982—. Mem. Sunnyvale Park and Recreation Bd., 1968-69; bd. dirs. Sunnyvale Little League, 1977-78. Served with USAF, 1958-60. Mem. IEEE (chmn. San Francisco chpt. 1970-71), Armed Forces Communications Electronics Assn., Assn. Old Crows (past officer and dir.), Assn. Former Intelligence Officers, Res. Officers Assn. Democrat. Clubs: Western World Trade, Elks. Author papers in field. Home: 1056 Firth Ct Sunnyvale CA 94087 Office: 1515 Industrial Way Belmont CA 94002

OELRICH, MARGARET HAZEL, counseling educator, consultant; b. Chgo., Jan. 28, 1927; d. Paul A. and Myrtle C. (Matson) Malmborg; m. Carl Oelrich, Oct. 22, 1949; 1 son, Paul Raymond. B.S., Western Mich. U., 1949; M.A., Central Mich. U., 1984. Registered occupational therapist; cert. trainer Nat. Inst. Drug Abuse. Asst. dir. occupational therapy N. Shore Health Resort, Winnetka, Ill., 1949; coordinator vol. services Latterman State Hosp., Pomona, Calif., 1953-60; dir. rehab. City of Hope Med. Ctr., Duarte, Calif., 1960-79; program coordinator, vocat. specialist II Network, Honolulu, 1979-81; lectr. Leeward Community Coll., Pearl City, Hawaii, 1981—; cons., tng. specialist, career-life counselor, 1981—; guidance counselor Army Edn. Ctr. Schofield Barracks and Tripler Army Med. Center, Hawaii, 1982-87, sr. guidance counselor tng. and devel., 1987—; presenter numerous lectures, workshops, seminars at various hosps., U. So. Calif., Los Angeles City Coll., Calif. Nursing Sch., Inc.; lectr. profl. groups. Bd. dirs., 2d v.p., mem. program and evaluation coms. Recreation and Edn. for Adults, Children with Handicaps; staff instr., leader family support group Ptnrs. in Health, Honolulu. Mem. Am. Assn. for Counseling and Devel., Am. Arbitration Assn. (nat. panel mem.), Am. Soc. Tng. and Devel. (mem. exec. bd., chmn. chpt. devel., mem. program com. Hawaii chpt.), Nat. Rehab. Assn., Nat. Assn. Female Execs., Hawaii Assn. Parks and Recreation, Joy of Learning. Named Outstanding Health Care Adminstr. So. Calif. Occupational Therapy Assn., 1975; Counselor of Yr. award Hawaii Personnel and Guidance Assn., 1983. Contbr. articles to profl. jours. chpts. to books. Home: 469 Ena Rd #2803 Honolulu HI 96815 Office: Army Edn Ctr Schofield Barracks HI 96857-5000

OFSOWITZ, PAULA JOYCE, computer pogramming executive; b. Detroit, Nov. 21, 1942; d. Samuel and Pearl (Bernstein) Ofsowitz. Student, Dade County (Fla.) Jr. Coll., 1961-62; programming cert. Control Data Instr., 1971, Inst. Advanced Tech., 1982. Programmer, Fla. Comml. Banks, Inc., Miami, Fla., 1972-73, First Fed. Savs. and Loan, Miami, 1973-77; contract programmer, Computer Dynamics, Inc., Southfield, Mich., 1977-79; tech. team leader, sr. systems programmer, tech. instr., systems engr. Four Phaze Systems, Inc., Southfield, 1979-80, Cupertino Calif., 1981—. Mem. Smithsonian Inst. Assocs. Democrat. Home: 485 Northlake Dr Apt 102 San Jose CA 95117 Office: Tandem Computers 2860 San Tomas Santa Clara CA 95051

O'GARA, BARTHOLOMEW WILLIS, wildlife biologist, zoologist; b. Laurel, Nebr., Mar. 21, 1923; s. Edward William and Hilda Juliet (Windquist) O'G.; m. Lucille Lillian Rogers, Oct. 15, 1947 (dec. Jan. 1987). BS, Mont. State U., 1964; PhD, U. Mont., 1968. Enlisted USN, 1940, advanced through grades to master chief aviation machinists mate, ret., 1960; asst. leader Mont. Coop Wildlife Research Unit, Missoula, 1968-77, leader, 1978—; leader Northern Rocky Mountain Wolf Recovery Team, 1983—. Mem. The Wildlife Soc., Am. Soc. Mammalogists, Northwest Bird Mammal Soc. Roman Catholic. Home: 1224 Lincoln Rd Missoula MT 59802 Office: US Fish and Wildlife Service Mont Coop Wildlife Research Unit U Mont Missoula MT 59812

OGBURN, HUGH BELL, manufacturing company executive; b. Lexington, Va., July 13, 1923; s. Sihon Cicero Jr. and Bettie Mae (Bell) O.; m. Anne Wotherspoon, Mar. 2, 1946 (div.); children: Margaret Mathews Berenson, Scott A.; m. Nancy Wrenn Petersen, Sept. 5, 1974. B.S., Princeton U., 1944, M.S., 1947, Ph.D., 1954. Sect. dir. research and devel. dept. Atlantic Refining Co., Phila., 1950-61; mgr. process engring. M.W. Kellogg Co., N.Y.C., London, 1961-67; dir. research and engring. Union Carbide Corp., N.Y.C., 1967-69; dir. new bus. devel. Weyerhaeuser Co., Tacoma, 1969-72; pres. H.B. Ogburn Assoc., Greenwich, Conn. and Honolulu, 1971—; v.p., dir. Incontrade Inc., Stamford, Conn., 1973-78; v.p. Pacific Resources Inc., Honolulu, 1978-83; chmn. Pacific Oasis, Los Angeles, 1983-85; dir. Danmore Corp., Planning Research Corp.; cons. AEC; prof. chem. engring. Drexel U., Phila., 1951-61. Contbr. articles to profl. jours.; patentee in field. Pres. bd. trustees Woman's Hosp., Phila., 1954-62, Kapiolani Women's and Children's Med. Ctr., 1980—; mem. adv. bd. Princeton U., 1960-70. Served to lt. j.g. USNR, 1942-46, PTO. Mem. Am. Inst. Chem. Engrs., Am. Chem. Soc., Research Engrs. Soc., Am. Inst. Chem. Engrs. London, Phi Beta Kappa, Sigma Xi, Tau Beta Pi. Republican. Presbyterian. Clubs: Pacific (Honolulu); Greenwich Field (Conn.); Merion Cricket (Haverford, Pa.); Princeton (N.Y.C.). Home and Office: 4340 Pahoa Ave 16 A Honolulu HI 96816

OGDEN, DANIEL MILLER, JR., government official, educator; b. Clarksburg, W.Va., Apr. 28, 1922; s. Daniel Miller and Mary (Maphis) O.; m. Valeria Juan Munson, Dec. 28, 1946; children: Janeth Lee Martin, Patricia Jo Hunter, Daniel Munson. BA in Polit. Sci., Wash. State U., 1944; MA, U. Chgo., 1947, PhD, 1949. From instr. to assoc. prof. Wash. State U., Pullman, 1949-61; staff asst. resources program Wash. Dept. Interior, 1961-64; asst. dir. Wash. Bur. Outdoor Recreation, 1964-67; dir. budget U.S. Dept. Interior, Washington, 1967-68; dean Coll. Humanities and Social Scis. Colo. State U., Ft. Collins, 1968-76; disting. vis. prof. Lewis and Clark Coll. and Portland (Oreg.) State U., 1977-78; dir. Office of Power Mktg. Coordination Wash. Dept. Energy, 1978-84; mgr. Pub. Power Council, Portland, Oreg., 1984—; mem. profl. staff com. Interstate and Fgn. Commerce, U.S. Senate, 1956-57; spl. asst. to chmn. Dem. Nat. Com., 1960-61; lectr. Exec. Seminar Ctrs., U.S. Office Personnel Mgmt., 1966—. Co-author: Electing the President, rev. edit., 1968, American National Government, 7th edit., 1970, American State and Local Government, 5th edit., 1972, Washington Politics, 1960. Committeeman Wash. Dem. Cen. Com., 1952-56; chmn. Whitman County Dem. Cen. Com., 1958-60. Served with inf. U.S. Army, 1943-46. Mem. Phi Beta Kappa, Phi Kappa Phi, Pi Sigma Alpha, Sigma Delta Chi. Mem. Unitarian Ch. Home: 3118 NE Royal Oaks Dr Vancouver WA 98662 Office: Pub Power Council 500 W 8th St Vancouver WA 98660

OGDEN, JAMES RUSSELL, professor; b. Paris, Ill., Nov. 4, 1954; s. Russell Lee and Marianne (Johnson) O.; m. Margaret Anne Berg, Aug. 27, 1977; children: David James, Anne Marie. B in Bus., Eastern Mich. U., 1978; MS, Colo. State U., 1981; PhD, U. No. Colo., 1986. Grad. fellow Colo. State U., Ft. Collins, 1979-81, asst. mgr. family housing, 1979-81; placement counselor U. No. Colo., Greeley, 1981-83, mktg. instr., 1982-83; assoc. prof. mktg. Adams State Coll., Alamosa, Colo., 1983—, also grad. counselor; bd. dirs. City of Alamosa Personnel Bd., Downtown Alamosa Devel. Dist. contbr. articles to profl. jours.; pub. speaker. Treas. Com. to Elect Jorge Amaya County Commr., Colo., 1985; treas. Bob Pastore for Senate Com.; senator Assoc. Student and Faculty Senate, Adams State Coll., Alamosa, 1984-85; faculty adv. Alpha Kappa Psi Profl. Bus. Frat. Named Outstanding Educator Adams State Coll., Alamosa, 1984-85, Outstanding Young Men of Am. Adams State Coll., Alamosa, 1983, 84, 85. Mem. Nat. Assn. Student Personnel Adminstrs., Am. Mktg. Assn., Western Mktg. Educators Assn. (paper reviewer), Acad. Mktg. Sci., Pueblo Advt. and Mktg. Assn., Phi Delta Kappa, Phi Beta Lambda. Club: Dist. Edn. Clubs of Am. Lodges: Masons, Elks. Avocation: Scuba. Home: 5597 Rd 9.6 S Alamosa CO 81101 Office: Adams State Coll Div Bus and Econs Alamosa CO 81102

OGDEN, MYRON WALDO, former ednl. adminstr.; b. Cambridge, Mass., July 8, 1917; s. Waldo M. and Florence (Newton) O.; B.S. in Edn., Boston U., 1949; M.S. in Spl. Edn., U. Wash., Seattle, 1966; children—David M., Darren R. Instr. history Peninsula Coll., Port Angeles, Wash., 1967-70; dir. adult edn. Neah Bay (Wash.) Schs., 1969-70, dir. spl. edn., 1973-76, ret., 1976. Rep. Sch. Community Council, 1970-76. Mem. NEA, Wash., Clallam County (past pres.) edn. assns., Pi Gamma Mu, Phi Delta Kappa. Home: Belvedere 702 35th Ave Seattle WA 98122

OGG, WILSON REID, poet, lawyer, educator; b. Alhambra, Calif., Feb. 26, 1928; s. James Brooks and Mary (Wilson) O. Student Pasadena Jr. Coll., 1946; A.B., U. Calif. at Berkeley, 1949, J.D., 1952; Cultural D in Philosophy of Law, World Univ. Roundtable, 1983. Assoc. trust Dept. Wells Fargo Bank, San Francisco, 1954-55; admitted to Calif. bar; pvt. practice law, Berkeley, 1955-78; real estate broker, cons., 1974-78; curator-in-residence Pinebrook, 1964—; research atty., legal editor dept. of continuing edn. of bar U. Calif. Extension, 1958-63; psychology instr. 25th Sta. Hosp., Taegu, Korea, 1954; English instr. Taegu English Lang. Inst., Taegu, 1954. Trustee World U., 1976-80; dir. admissions Internat. Soc. for Phil. Enquiry, 1981-84; dep. dir. gen. Internat. Biographical Centre, Eng., 1986—; dep. gov. Am. Biographical Inst. Research Assn., 1986—. Served with AUS, 1952-54. Cert. community coll. instr. Fellow Internat. Acad. Law and Sci.; mem. ABA, State Bar Calif., San Francisco Bar Assn., Am. Arbitration Assn. (nat. panel arbitrators), World Univ. Round Table (cult. D. in Philosophy of Law 1983), World Future Soc. (profl. mem.), AAAS, Am. Assn. Fin. Profls., Am. Soc. Psychical Research, Calif. Soc. Psychical Study (pres., chmn. bd. 1963-65), Suomi Soc., Soc. for Phys. Research (London), Parapsychol. Assn. (asso.), 999 Soc., Internat. Soc. Unified Sci., Worldwide Acad. Scholars, Am. Acad. Polit. and Social Sci., Internat. Platform Assn., Intertel, Ina Coolbrith Circle, Am. Legion, VFW, Am. Mensa, Lawyers in Mensa, Psychic Sci. Spl. Interest Group, Am. Legion, VFW. Unitarian. Mason, Elk. Clubs: Faculty (U. Calif.), City Commons (Berkeley); Press (San Francisco); Commonwealth of Calif.; Town Hall Calif. Editor: Legal Aspects of Doing Business under Government Contracts and Subcontracts, 1958, Basic California Practice Handbook, 1959; contbr. numerous articles profl. jours; contbr. poetry to various mags. including American Poetry Anthology Vol. VI Number 5, New Voices in American Poetry, 1987. Home: 1104 Keith Ave Berkeley CA 94708-1607 Office: Eight Bret Harte Way Berkeley CA 94708-1611

OGILBY, PETER REMSEN, chemistry educator; b. Manila, Apr. 9, 1955; came to U.S., 1967; s. Lyman Cunningham and Ruth (Dale) O. BA, U. Wis., 1977; PhD, UCLA, 1981. Postdoctoral assoc. U. Calif., Berkeley, 1981-83; asst. prof. chemistry U. N.Mex., Albuquerque, 1983—. Mem. Am. Chem. Soc., Am. Phys. Soc., Sigma Xi. Office: U N Mex Dept Chemistry Albuquerque NM 87131

OGILVIE, ANDREW DAVID, electrical engineer; b. Warrington, England, Nov. 8, 1951; came to U.S., 1952; s. Terry Leslie and Joyce Vivienne (Taylor) O.; m. Rachel Ann Martinez, Feb. 23, 1980. BSEE, San Jose State U., 1984. Microwave test engr. Avantek, Inc., Santa Clara, Calif., 1977-84; systems engr. Lockheed Missiles and Space Co., Sunnyvale, Calif., 1984—. Served to staff sgt. USAF, 1972-76. Republican. Mem. Ch. England. Avocation: collecting and flying antique and classic aircraft. Home: 15075 Big Basin Hwy Boulder Creek CA 95006 Office: Lockheed Missiles and Space Co 1111 Lockheed Way Sunnyvale CA 94089

OGLESBY, CLARKSON HILL, civil engineering educator, writer; b. Clarksville, Mo., Nov. 9, 1908; s. Edwin Bright Oglesby and Frances Lewis Thomas; m. Ardis May Hansen, June 8, 1938; children: Virginia Lee Hancock, Judith Lynne Donaghey, Marjorie Kay Zellner. AB in Engring., Stanford U., 1932, degree in civil engring., 1936. Registered civil engr., Calif. Draftsman to engr. State of Ariz. Dept. Transportation, Phoenix, 1928-41; constrn. engr. Vinson and Pringle, Phoenix, 1941-43; acting asst. prof. civil engring. Stanford (Calif.) U., 1943-46, asst. prof., 1946-48, assoc. prof., 1947-52, prof., 1952-74; cons. Calif. Toll Bridge Author, San Francisco, 1948; prof., cons. in constrn. mgmt. Cath. U., Chile, U. New South Wales, Australia and U. Cape Town, South Africa. Author: Highway Engineering, 1952, 4th rev. edit., 1982, Methods Improvement, 1972; also articles. Mem. ASCE (hon.), NSPE (Outstanding Constrn. Educator 1984), Phi Beta Kappa, Sigma Xi, Tau Beta Pi. Democrat. Congregationalist. Home: 850 Webster St #923 Palo Alto CA 94301 Office: Stanford U Dept Civil Engring Stanford CA 94305

OGLESBY, MYRNA LEE, lawyer; b. Ukiah, Calif., Sept. 29, 1935; d. Earl Victor and Ruby Alice (Phillips) Snook; m. Neal Vernon Oglesby, June 13, 1964; children: Keith, Deborah, Gerald, Donald, Linda. Bar: Calif. 1983. Assoc. Rawles, Hinkle, Carter, Brigham, Gaustad and Behnke, Ukiah, Calif., 1983-85, ptnr., 1985—; asst. prof. Sonoma State Coll. extension, Rohnert Park, Calif., 1986-87. Treas. Ukiah Bus. and Profl. Women, 1986-87; hearing officer Mendocino County Dept. Mental Health. Mem. Mendocino County Bar Assn. (bd. dirs. lawyer referral service com. 1985—), State Bar Calif., Calif. Women Lawyers, ABA. Democrat. Baptist. Avocation: travel. Office: Rawles Hinkle Carter et al 169 Mason St Suite 300 PO Box 720 Ukiah CA 95482

O'GRADY, JAMES BRADLEY, director of public works; b. Grand Forks, N.D., June 24, 1949; s. Lowell Alexander and Mary Virginia (Conners) O'G.; m. Jean Margaret Ferry, June 3, 1972; children: Michael, Kristin. BS, U. N.D., 1971; MS, U. Ariz., 1973. Registered profl. engr., Colo. Transp. planner City of Arvada, Colo., 1972-74, dir. traffic, 1974-80, dir. transp., 1980-84; dir. pub. works City of La Mesa, Calif., 1984—; active transp. adv. com. Denver Regional Council Govts., 1974-84, chmn., 1979; nat. com. on uniform traffic control devices Grade Crossing Subcom., Washington, 1978-84; spl. asst. to city mgr., City of Arvada, 1983. Contbr. articles to profl. publs. Activity leader Boy Scouts Am., San Diego, 1986; bd. dirs. La Mesa Beautiful, 1985—. Mem. Inst. Transp. Engrs., Am. Pub. Works Assn. (bd. dirs. 1984—), Transp. Research Bd., World Future Soc., Fed. Aid Urban Com. Democrat. Roman Catholic. Avocations: golf, bridge, running, woodworking. Home: 6202 Lambda Dr San Diego CA 92120 Office: City of La Mesa 8130 Allison Ave La Mesa CA 92041

O'GREEN, FREDERICK WILBERT, multi-industry company executive; b. Mason City, Iowa, Mar. 25, 1921; s. Oscar A. and Anna (Heikkinen) O'G.; m. Mildred G. Ludlow, Mar. 21, 1943; children: Susan Renee, Jane Lynn O'Green Koenig, John Frederick, Eric Stephen. Student, Mason City Jr. Coll., 1939-40; B.S. in Elec. Engring, Iowa State U., 1943; M.S. in Elec. Engring, U. Md., 1949; LL.D. (hon.), Pepperdine U., 1977. Project engr. Naval Ordnance Lab., White Oak, Md., 1943-55; dir. Agena D project Lockheed Aircraft Co., Sunnyvale, Calif., 1955-62; v.p. Litton Industries, Inc., Beverly Hills, Calif., 1962-66, sr. v.p., 1966-67, exec. v.p., 1967-72, pres., 1972-81, chmn., chief exec. officer, 1981—, also dir. Served with USNR, 1945. Recipient Meritorious Civilian Service award U.S. Navy, 1954; Outstanding Achievement award Air Forces Systems Command, 1964; Disting. Achievement citation Iowa State U., 1973; Energy Exec. of Yr. award Third World Energy Engring. Congress, 1980. Mem. AIM, AIAA, U.S. C. of C., Assn. U.S. Army, Phi Kappa Psi, Phi Mu Alpha. Republican. Lutheran. Office: Litton Industries Inc 360 N Crescent Dr Beverly Hills CA 90210 *

OGREN, JOHN ROGER, industrial scientist; b. Calumet, Mich., Sept. 29, 1933; s. George John and Linda Marie (Honkanen) O.; m. Irene Elizabeth Mannisto, Apr. 10, 1954 (dec. Jan. 1982); children: Jean Elizabeth, Ann-Marie, John Matthew, Patricia Lynn, Cynthia Kaye, Paavo Arne. BS, No. Mich. U., 1955; MS in Physics, Iowa State U., 1957, PhD in Metallurgy, 1964. Asst. prof. physics No. Mich. U., Marquette, 1957-60, Calif. Poly. State U., San Luis Obispo, 1960-62; from mem. tech. staff to chief materials scientist TRW Space Systems, Redondo Beach, Calif., 1965—; mem. tech. staff Rockwell Internat., Ltd., Anaheim, Calif., 1968; investigator moon rock from 1st lunar trip, 1969. Patentee in field; editor Jour. Materials for Energy Systems, 1978—; contbr. articles to profl. jours. Grantee NSF, 1957-65; recipient Outstanding Alumni award No. Mich. U., 1986. Fellow Am. Soc. Metals (chmn. energy div. 1976-80); mem. Am. Nuclear Soc., Am. Inst. Physics, Am. Inst. Mining, Metall. and Petroleum Engrs. Home: 11973 S Ramona Hawthorne CA 90250 Office: TRW 01-2040 1 Space Park Redondo Beach CA 90278

OGREN, KEITH ALAN, marketing professional; b. Hayward, Wis., Apr. 6, 1952; s. Warren Alfred and Vivian Kate (Pfister) O.; m. Shawn M. Gibbs, May 27, 1957. BS, U. Wis., LaCrosse, 1974. Recruiter data processing Dennis Newell & Assocs., Mpls., 1974-77; nat. account exec. Wang Labs., Mpls., 1977-84; br. mktg. mgr. Wang Labs., Denver, 1984-85; pres. Direct Source, Inc., Denver, 1985—. Mem. Sports Car Club Am. Republican. Lutheran. Avocations: sports cars, skiing, shooting. Office: Direct Source Inc 12585 E 39th Ave Denver CO 80239

O'HAIR, SUSAN ELINOR, educator; b. San Francisco, July 13, 1939; d. Donald Leigh O'Hair and Jane Elinor (Larsen) Hudkins. BA, Calif. State U., Sacramento, 1961. Cert. gen. edn. tchr. (life). Tchr. Redondo Beach (Calif.) City Schs., 1961-65; tchr. San Ramon (Calif.) Valley Unified Sch. Dist., 1965-67, librarian, 1967-69, tchr., 1969-77, tchr. English and World History, 1977—. Author: Best Loved Contemporary Poem, 1979. Vice chmn. San Ramon Valley Arts Council, Danville, 1978-81; bd. dirs. San Ramon Library Found., 1985. Named Mentor Tchr. San Ramon Valley Unified Sch. Dist., Danville, 1985, Tchr. of Month Pine Valley PTA, San Ramon, 1985. Mem. AAUW (pres. local br. 1970—), NEA (life), Calif. Tchrs. Assn. (legis. chmn. 1985-86, pres. Contra Costa County chpt. 1971-72, state council rep. 1972-75, We Honor Ours award 1975), Calif. Tchrs. English, Nat. Assn. Tchrs. English (del.), Delta Kappa Gamma. Democrat. Methodist. Clubs: Red Barn (San Ramon); Tao House (Danville). Avocations: pub. speaking, travel, theater arts, reading. Home: 2563 Marsh Dr San Ramon CA 94583

O'HALLORAN, (LAVERNE M.) KATHLEEN (MRS. JOHN R. O'HALLORAN, JR.), real estate broker; b. Laurium, Mich., Nov. 15, 1921; d. Joseph Wilfred and Della K. (Gervais) Shaffer; student Fond Du Lac Comml. Coll., 1938-40, Fresno City Coll., 1965-66; m. John Richard O'Halloran, Jr., July 15, 1942; children: Sheila Ann O'Halloran Stoll, Gregory, Michael, Maureen O'Halloran Benelli, Sean, Margaret. Co-owner Hamlin Hotel, San Francisco, 1946-48, Lazy F Guest Ranch, Ellensburg, Wash., 1948-50; owner, broker Kathy O'Halloran Realty, Fresno, 1980—; pres. C & R Investments, 1974-75; broker Settlers Real Estate, Inc., Fresno, 1975-80. Charter mem. Infant of Prague Adoption Agy. Aux., 1954—, sec., 1955; mem. Mayor's Com. for Community Devel., 1963-64; pres. Sacred Heart Mothers Club, 1959; pres. Calif. Citizens for Decent Lit., 1961-63, Central Calif. Citizens for Decent Lit., 1959-64; precinct chmn. Goldwater campaign, 1964; chmn. Fresno County United Republicans Calif., 1962; area coordinator Clean Campaign Ballot Initiative, 1966; candidate Fresno City Council, 1961; mem. Women's League of Fresno Arts Center, 1976—, St. Agnes Service Guild, 1983—, Fresno Fiber Guild, 1985—. Mem. Fresno Bd. Realtors, Nat. Assn. Real Estate Bds. Roman Catholic. Home: 3503 N Bond St Fresno CA 93726 Office: 3503 N Bond St Fresno CA 93726

O'HARA, MICHAEL LOUIS, chemical process engineer; b. Hobart, Ind., Jan. 22, 1961; s. John Joseph and Nedra Jean (Ross) O. BSChemE, U. Calif., Santa Barbara, 1986. Prodn. technologist D and F Industries, Orange, Calif., 1983; fin. analyst Burroughs Corp., Camarillo, Calif., 1985-86; chem. engr. Interlink Electronics, Santa Barbara, 1986—; cons. Robert Bleuitt and Assocs., Santa Barbara, 1984; speaker New Products Devel. Sensors Exposition, Chgo., 1986. mem. AAAS, Am. Chem. Soc. (student affiliate 1984-86). Republican. Roman Catholic. Club: A (Antioch, Ill.) (pres. 1978-79). Avocations: running, swimming, hiking, motorcycle riding. Home: 220 Ladera Apt 306 Santa Barbara CA 93101 Office: Interlink Electronics 535 E Montecito St Santa Barbara CA 93103

O'HARA, PATRICK DONOVAN, electronics company executive; b. Arlington, Calif., Mar. 2, 1938; s. Ralph Elsworth O'Hara and Leona Fern Parnell; m. Elizabeth Annie O'Hara, Nov. 27, 1958; 1 child, William Robert. BS in Mgmt., La Salle U., 1963; BSEE, Loyolla U., Paris, 1965; BBA, PhD in Bus. Adminstrn., Columbia Pacific U., 1983. Field engr. Honeywell Corp., San Francisco, 1966-69; engr. writer Hewlett-Packard, Palo Alto, Calif., 1969-71, internat. support engr., 1971-75; internat. service mgr. Osborne Computer Corp., Hayward, Calif., 1980-82; tech. field ops. mgr. Bull Peripherals Corp., Sunnyvale, Calif., 1985—; mem. faculty Columbia Pacific U., San Rafael, Calif., 1984—; chmn. bd. dirs. Vets. Resource Council, Fremont, Calif., pres. O-TEK Enterprises, Fremont, 1984—. Served with USN, 1961-65. Mem. Assn. Field Service Mgrs. Republican. Club: Toastmasters (area gov.). Lodge: Masons. Avocations: travelling, fishing, camping, house building. Home: 43425 Jerome Ave Fremont CA 94539

OHM, ROBERT LEE, II, architect; b. Portsmouth, Va., Oct. 31, 1953; s. Robert Lee and Frances Virginia (Freeman) O.; m. Sharon June Leslie, March 8, 1980; 1 child, Lindsay Adrian. BArch, U. Kans., 1977. Lic. architect, Wash., Mo. Draftsman Prickett, Onek Architects, Topeka, 1976-77, Midgley, Shaughnessy, Fickel and Scott, Kansas City, Mo., 1977-78; project mgr. Patty Berkebile Nelson Assocs., Kansas City, Mo., 1978-81; project architect Charles Kober Assocs., Seattle, 1981-82, The Richardson Assocs. Co., Seattle, 1982—. Republican. Lutheran. Club: Blue Ridge (Seattle) (bd. dirs. 1985—). Avocations: tennis, golf, camping, fishing. Home: 1312 NW Woodbine Way Seattle WA 98177 Office: TRA 215 Columbia Seattle WA 98104

OHMAN, JOHN MICHAEL, lawyer; b. Dec. 22, 1948; s. John W. and D. Jeanne (Forster) O.; m. Susan M. Samson; children: Brittany Michelle, Andrea Michaela. BSBA, Creighton U., 1971, JD, 1972. Bar: Idaho 1973, Nebr. 1973, U.S. Dist. Ct. Idaho 1973, U.S. Dist. Ct. Nebr. 1973, U.S. Ct. Appeals (9th cir.) 1978, U.S. Interstate Commerce Commn. 1975, U.S. Supreme Ct. 1978. Atty. Cox & Ohman, Idaho Falls, Idaho, 1978—; lectr. various locations. Contbr. articles to profl. jours. Bd. dirs. Idaho Transp. Dept.; chmn. Bonneville County Hist. Soc.; exec. bd. Assn. Humanities in Idaho, legal advisor; active United Way, YMCA; past pres. Am. Cancer Soc.; judge advocate Intermountain dist. Civitan Internat., also past pres. Idaho Falls chpt.; legal adv. Mayor's Com. for Handicapped, Mayor's Com. for Swimming Pool, Community Concert Assn., Idaho Falls Symphony Soc., Eastern Idaho Spl. Services Agy.; dir. Group Homes, Inc.; campaign coordinator Gov. Idaho; mem. State Dem. Cen. Com.; precinct committeeman. Served to capt. U.S. Army. Recipient Outstanding Pres. award Civitian Internat., Century Club mem. YMCA, Idaho Safe Pilot award; named del. to Hong Kong, to People's Republic of China and Japan by Idaho Bus. Leaders. Mem. ABA (litigation sect., family law sect., tort and ins. practice sect., div. law and procedures com.), Am. Soc. Law and Medicine, Am. Judicature Soc., Idaho State Bar Assn. (adv. council continuing legal edn.), Nebr. State Bar. Assn., Seventh Judicial Dist. Bar Assn., Am. Trial Lawyers Assn., Idaho Trial Lawyers Assn., Assn. Interstate Commerce Practitioners, Idaho Law Found., Unauthorized Practice Law Com., Western Assn. State Hwy. and Transp. Officials, Am. Assn. State Hwy. and Transp. Officials, Smithsonian Inst. (assoc.), Internat. Platform Assn., Am. Mus. Natural History, Airplane Owners and Pilots Assn., Nat. Arbor's Day Found., C. of C. (chmn. legis. com.), Phi Alpha Delta, Omicron Delta Epsilon, Phi Kappa Psi. Democrat. Roman Catholic. Club: Toastmasters. Lodge: Elks (legal advisor). Avocations: aquatic sports, numismatics, reading, aviation, racquetball. Office: Cox and Ohman PO Box 621 Idaho Falls ID 83402

OHMAN, MARK DAVID, research oceanographer; b. San Francisco, Dec. 6, 1951; s. Carl David and Audre Marie (Marcus) O.; m. Cynthia Lois Claxton, June 2, 1984. BA, U. Calif., Santa Cruz, 1974; MA, Calif. State U., San Francisco, 1977; PhD, U. Wash., 1983. Postdoctoral research assoc. Friday Harbor (Wash.) Labs., 1983-84; NSF postdoctoral research assoc. New Zealand Oceanographic Inst. and Portobello Marine Lab., Wellington and Dunedin, 1984-85; asst. research oceanographer Scripps Inst. Oceanography, La Jolla, Calif., 1985—. Contbr. articles to profl jours. William Evans fellow U. Otago, Dunedin, 1985. Mem. New Zealand Marine Scis. Soc., AAAS, Am. Soc. Limnology and Oceanography, Ecol. Soc. Am., Sigma Xi. Office: Scripps Inst Oceanography Marine Life Research Group A-027 La Jolla CA 92093

OHMAN, ROBERT BAIRD, university chaplain, minister; b. Marietta, Okla., Nov. 19, 1934; s. Raymond Norman and Marion Margaret (Baird) O.; m. Carol Anne Bartel, June 21, 1958; children: Julie Amelia, Christopher Baird, Jonathan Robert. BS in History, Wheaton Coll., 1957; ThM, Dallas Theological Sem., 1962; D in Ministry, Fuller Theological Sem., 1976. Ordained to ministry Presbyn. Ch., 1968. Asst. minister Calvary Ch., Pacific Palisades, Calif., 1962-64, Westminster Presbyn. Ch., San Jose, Calif., 1964-68; assoc. minister Trinity United Presbyn. Ch., Santa Ana, Calif., 1968-75; chaplain Westmont Coll., Santa Barbara, Calif., 1977—. Republican. Avocations: skiing, photography. Home: 3938 State St Santa Barbara CA 93105

OHMS, STEPHEN EARL, architect; b. Boise, Idaho, 1957; S. Richard and Mavis Ohms; m. Angelika A. Ohms, Aug. 22, 1986. BArch, U. Idaho, 1980. Heavy equipment operator McIntosh & Sons, Lewiston, Idaho, 1980-81; project mgr. U.S. Coast Guard, N.Y.C., 1981-84; chief. support br. U.S. Coast Guard, Petaluma, Calif., 1984-85, facilities architect, 1985—. Author: Facilities Master Planning, 1985. Internat. Architect group leader N.Y. Arts Group, N.Y.C., 1983. Mem. AIA (assoc.), Internat. Facilities Mgmt. Assn. Lodge: Toastmasters (sec. Petaluma chpt. 1985—).

OJAKANGAS, DENNIS ROGER, infosystems specialist, geologist; b. Moose Lake, Minn., Jan. 18, 1936; s. Waino Jacob Ojakangas and Grace Marie (Maki) Wold; m. Eileen Ruth Taylor, June 21, 1958; children: Kara Lynn, Scott Charles, Lea Ann. BA, U. Minn., Duluth, 1957; MA, U. Mo., 1958; PhD, Stanford U., 1967. Instr. U. Omaha, 1959-62; systems analyst Standard Oil Co. Calif., San Francisco, 1962-67; geologist Chevron Standard Ltd., Calgary, Alta., Can., 1967-69; pres. Info. and Computing Ctrs. Can. Ltd., Calgary, Alta., Can., 1969-70; mgr. data ctr. U. Calgary, 1970-71; dir. computing and lectr. of geology U. Calif., Davis, 1971—. Mgr. Little League Baseball, Davis, 1971-74; Acitve Davis Luth. Ch., 1971—. Served to 1st lt. USAF, 1958-62. Mem. Am. Assn. Petroleum Geologists, Internat. Assn. Math. Geologists, Assn. Computing Machinery (instl. rep.), Sigma Xi. Democrat. Clubs: Optimists (Davis) (editor, v.p. 1971-75), Faculty (Davis) (pres., house com. 1978—). Avocations: bldg. houses, painting, gardening, running, hunting. Home: 755 Sycamore Ln Davis CA 95616 Office: U Calif Davis CA 95616

O'KEEFE, THOMAS BRIAN, real estate investor, consultant, lecturer; b. San Pedro, Calif., Dec. 29, 1945; s. John Joseph and Wilma (Gessner) O.; m. Carol Ann Ranson, Aug. 28, 1970; children—Peter John, Elizabeth Ann. Student U. Md., Munich, W.Ger., 1964-65; B.S.F.S., Georgetown U. Sch. Fgn. Service, 1968; B.I.M., Am. Grad. Sch. Internat. Mgmt., 1970, M.I.M., 1971. Lic. real estate broker, Calif. Cons. Grubbs & Ellis Co., Newport Beach, Calif., 1971-75; staff rep. to Africa Los Angeles Olympic Com., 1984; owner Thomas B. O'Keefe Co., Newport Beach, Calif., 1975—, founder Corp. Nat. Bank, Santa Ana, Calif., 1982—; lectr. internat. mktg. and econs. Chapman Coll., Orange, Calif., 1973—; chmn. admissions com. Orange County Georgetown U., 1983—. Dir. Opera Pacific, 1983-87; staff organizer Grand Prix for Retinitus Pigmentosa, 1984; active Textile Mus., 1979—; chmn. Los Angeles-Bordeaux Sister Cities Affiliation, 1985—. Recipient Ariz. Republic most outstanding advt. campaign 1971; Inst. Real Estate Mgmt. cert. appreciation 1978. Mem. Newport Harbor-Costa Mesa Bd. Realtors, Orange County Assn. Real Estate Investment Brokers. Republican. Clubs: Aston Martin Owners (West Coast rep.) (London), Pasadena Wine and Food Soc., Les Amis du Vin (Newport Beach); Alliance Francaise (Laguna Beach, Calif.). Contbr. articles to jours. in field.

OKUBO, RUBY SUMIKO, hospital consultant; b. Los Angeles, May 2, 1926; d. Ben Toshimune and Susan Shizue Okubo. BS, UCLA, 1965, M.P.H., 1966. Chief med. records librarian U.S. Air Force Hosp., Lowry AFB, Denver, 1951-54; asst. dir. med. records St. Vincent's Hosp., Los Angeles, 1954-55, dir. med. records, 1955-64; systems analyst hosp. data processing UCLA Hosp. and Clinics, Los Angeles, 1966-69, sr. systems analyst, 1969-74, prin. ADP systems analyst, 1974-78, mgr. med.-adminstrv. applications hosp. data processing, 1978-84, mgr. med. info. systems liaison, 1984-85, staff asst. to dir., 1986. Mem. Am. Med. Records Assn., Calif. Med. Record Assn., So. Calif. Med. Record Assn. (chmn. public relations com. 1962), Am. Public Health Assn., Health Info. Soc., Internat. Fedn. Med. Record Orgns. (chmn. U.S. subcom. 1968-70), Electronic Computing Health Oriented Orgn., So. Calif. Pub. Health Assn., UCLA Sch. Pub. Health Alumni Assn. (dean's council). Office: 10833 Le Conte Ave Los Angeles CA 90024

OKUMA, ALBERT AKIRA, JR., architect; b. Cleve., Feb. 10, 1946; s. Albert Akira Sr. and Reiko (Suwa) O.; m. Janice Shirley Bono, July 17, 1971; children: Reiko Dawn, Benjamin Scott. BS in Archtl. Engring, Calif. Poly. State U., San Luis Obispo, 1970, BArch, 1975. Lic. architect, Calif. Architect USN, Point Mugu, Calif., 1975-76; designer Wilson Stroh Wilson Architects, Santa Paula, Calif., 1976-79; architect, project mgr. W.J. Kulwiec AIA & Assocs., Camarillo, Calif., 1979-83, Wilson & Conrad Architects, Ojai, Calif., 1983-84, Dziak, Immel & Lauterbach Services Inc., Oxnard, Calif., 1984-85; ptnr. Conrad & Okuma Architects, Oxnard, 1985—. Treas. Spiritual Assembly of Baha'is of Ventura, Calif., 1978-79, 84, 86—; treas.'s rep. Nat. Spiritual Assembly of Bahai's of U.S., Wilmette, Ill., 1981—. Served to 1st lt. U.S. Army, 1971-73. Mem. AIA (chpt. bd. dirs. 1976-79, 81—, chpt. sec. 1981, v.p. 1982, pres. 1983.), Constrn. Specifications Inst., Design Methods Group. Office: Conrad & Okuma Architects 183 Montgomery Ave Oxnard CA 93030

OLAFSON, JON HERMANN, chemist; b. Winnipeg, Manitoba, Can., Nov. 4, 1916; came to U.S., 1916; s. John K. and Kirstin (Hermann) O.; m. Josephine Lawless, Oct. 14, 1950; children: Eric Jon, Theodore Joseph, Christopher Paul. BS in Chemistry, U. N.D., 1942; MS in Biochemistry, U. Minn., 1950; postgrad. in botanical sci., UCLA, 1953-56. Chemist UCLA, 1950-62; research scientist Northrop Corp., Hawthorne, Calif., 1962-67; sr. research scientist Battelle Northwest, Richland, Wash., 1967-70; sr. chemist Eberline Instruments, West Chgo., Ill., 1970-73; project chemist Dames and Moore, Seattle, 1974-77; data communications specialist Systems Analysis, Bellevue, Wash., 1978-86; ret. 1986. Contbr. articles to profl. jours. Served to sgt. U.S. Army, 1942-45. Mem. Gamma Alpha, Alpha Zeta, Sigma Xi (assoc.). Republican. Lutheran. Avocations: wine making, sports. Home: 11722 NE 149th St Kirkland WA 98034

O'LAGUE, KELLY MELINDA, social worker; b. Berkeley, Calif., Mar. 14, 1958; d. John Harris and Mary O'Malley (Tynan) O'L.; m. Matthew Joseph Dulka, June 21, 1986. BA, U. Calif., 1982, MSW, 1984. Clin. social worker Children's Health Council, Palo Alto, Calif., 1984-86; cons. and vol. counselor Cath. Charities Office for Prisoner and Community Justice, Oakland, Calif., 1984-86. Mem. Nat. Assn. Social Workers, Child Welfare League Am. Democrat. Roman Catholic. Home: 26622 Jamaica Ln Hayward CA 94545 Office: Childrens Health Council 700 Sand Hill Rd Palo Alto CA 94304

OLAH, GEORGE ANDREW, educator, chemist; b. Budapest, Hungary, May 22, 1927; came to U.S., 1964, naturalized, 1970; s. Julius and Magda (rasznai) O.; m. Judith Agnes Lengyel, July 9, 1949; children: George John, Ronald Peter. Ph.D., Tech. U. Budapest, 1949. Mem. faculty Tech. U. Budapest, 1949-54; assoc. dir. Cen. Chem. Research Inst., Hungarian Acad. Scis., 1954-56; research scientist Dow Chem. Can. Ltd., 1957-64, Dow Chem. Co., Framingham, Mass., 1964-65; prof. chemistry Case-Western Res. U., Cleve., 1965-69; C.F. Mabery prof. research Case-Western Res. U., 1969-77; Donald P. and Katherine B. Loker disting. prof. chemistry, dir. Hydrocarbon Research Inst., U. So. Calif., Los Angeles, 1977—; vis. prof. chemistry Ohio State U., 1963, U. Heidelberg, Germany, 1965, U. Colo., 1969, Swiss Fed. Inst. Tech., 1972, U. Munich, 1973, U. London, 1973-79, L. Pasteur U., Strasbourg, 1974, U. Paris, 1981; hon. vis. lectr. U. London, 1981; cons. to industry. Author: Friedel-Crafts Reactions, Vols. I-IV, 1963-64, (with P. Schleyer) Carbonium Ions, Vols. I-V, 1969-76, Friedel-Crafts Chemistry, 1973, Carbocations and Electrophilic Reactions, 1973, Halonium Ions, 1975, (with G.K.S. Prakash and J. Somer) Superacids, 1984; (with G.K.S. Prakash, R.E. Williams, L.D. Field and K. Wade) Hypercarbon Chemistry, 1987; also chpts. in books, numerous papers in field. Recipient Leo Hendrik Baekeland award N.J. sect. Am. Chem. Soc., 1966, Morley medal Cleve. sect., 1970; Alexander von Humboldt sr. U.S. scientist award, 1979; Guggenheim fellow, 1972. Fellow Chem. Inst. Can., AAAS; mem. Nat. Acad. Scis., Italian Nat. Acad. Scis., Am. Chem. Soc. (award petroleum chemistry 1964, award synthetic organic chemistry 1979), German Chem. Soc., Brit. Chem. Soc. (Centenary lectr. 1978), Swiss Chem. Soc., Sigma Xi. Patentee in field. Home: 2252 Gloaming Way Beverly Hills CA 90210 Office: Univ So Calif Dept Chemistry Los Angeles CA 90007

OLAH, SUSAN ROSE, artist; b. Budapest, Hungary, June 14, 1947; d. Joseph and Emma (Hupcsak) Olah; came to Can., 1957, naturalized, 1962; student Art Instrn. Sch. Mpls., 1966-69, grad. 1969. One woman shows Gallery of Roof, Regina, Sask., 1973, Galerie Mouffe, Paris, 1977, Galerie Vallombreuse, Biarritz, France, 1977; exhibited in group shows Gallery of Roof, Galerie Mouffe; tchr. art Wascana Hosp., Regina, 1969-72, art cons., 1970-72. Recipient award for painting, Mpls., 1967, Gold medal Accademia Italia delle Arti e del Lavoro, 1979, Golden Centour award Accademia Italia, 1982, Gold medal Internat. Parliament for Peace and Safety, U.S.A., 1982, European Banner of Arts, Gold medal Accademia Europea, 1985, Oscar d' Italia, 1985, Fiamma d'Oro World Parliament award Accademia Italia, U.S.A., 1986. Mem. Internat. Order of Vols. for Peace. Home: 37 Haultain Crescent, Regina, SK Canada S4S 4B4

OLANDER, DONALD EDGAR, chemist, engineering executive; b. Chgo., Aug. 12, 1929; s. Albert Edgar and Abbie (Snyder) O.; m. Dayle Neva Roberts, June 22, 1950 (div. Jan. 1973); children: Mark, Eric, Lauren, Paul, Lisa; m. Geraldine June Frere, Feb. 25, 1975; children: Russell, Basilio, Kimberly, Bebe. BS in Chemistry, Northwestern U., 1951; MS in Chemistry, St. Louis U., 1955; PhD in Engring., Calif. Coast U., 1980. Chemist Mallinckrodt Co., St. Louis, 1951-53; project engr. Universal Match Corp., Ferguson, Mo., 1959-67; engr., quality control mgr. Aerojet-Gen. Co., Nimbus, Calif., 1959-67; staff scientist Explosive Tech., Fairfield, Calif., 1967-69; v.p. Networks Electronic Corp., Chatsworth, Calif., 1969-72; staff scientist Hi-Shear Tech. Corp., Torrance, Calif., 1979—. Patentee in field; contbr. articles to profl. jours. Asst. scoutmaster Boy Scouts Am., Fair Oaks, Calif., 1959-65; active Fair Oaks Presbyn. Ch., 1959-71. Mem. ASTM, Am. Chem. Soc., Am. Def. Preparedness Assn. Avocations: photography, music. Home: 16432 Mark Ln Huntington Beach CA 92647 Office: Hi-Shear Tech Corp 2830 Lomita Blvd Torrance CA 90505

O'LAUGHLIN, THOMAS WILLIAM, publisher; b. Evanston, Ill., Feb. 28, 1930; s. Thomas William and Caroline Maud (Clinkenbroomer) O'L.; m. Mary Ellen Warner, Oct. 22, 1983. BS in Biochemistry, U. Ill., 1956; grad. pub. course, Stanford U. Pres. Golfax, Ltd., San Diego, 1976—; v.p., dir. JT&T Inc., San Diego, 1978—; pub. Resort and Hotel Mgmt. mag., San Diego, 1982-85. Contbr. articles to profl. jours. Vol. Big Bros., San Diego, 1978-83. Mem. San Diego Press Club, Hotel Sales and Mgmt. Assn. Republican. Episcopalian. Club: Toastmasters. Lodge: Rotary (v.p. San Diego 1982-86). Avocations: reading, running, econ. systems. Office: Golfax Ltd 2437 Morena Blvd San Diego CA 92117

OLBRECHTS, GUY ROBERT, electrical engineer, consultant; b. Mechelen, Belgium, May 22, 1935; came to U.S., 1967, naturalized, 1978; s. Alphonse and Blanche (Van Coolput) O.; m. Andree Julia Van Nes, Oct. 19, 1961; children: Philippe, Ingrid, Dominique. Ingenieur civil electricien Catholic U. Leuven, Belgium, 1960; M.B.A., Seattle U., 1976. Lead engr. Ctr. D'Etudes Nucleaires, Mol, Belgium, 1962-65; quality control mgr., chief engr. for magnetics Sprague Electromag., Ronse, Belgium, 1965-67; sr. engr. Boeing Co., Seattle, 1967-79; sect. mgr. data systems engring. and product support Sundstrand Data Control Corp., Redmond, Wash., 1979—; propr., cons., designer Gentronics, Bellevue, Wash., 1970—. Patentee gyro wheel speed modulator, 1981, integrated strapdown/airdata sensor system, 1981, slow-acting phase-locked loop, 1983. Served as cpl. Belgian Army, 1961-62. Recipient inventor award Boeing Co., 1978. Republican. Roman Catholic. Home: 4809 116th Ave SE Bellevue WA 98006 Office: Sundstrand Data Control Corp Overlake Indsl Park Redmond WA 98052

OLCOTT, JOANNE ELIZABETH, naval officer; b. Portland, Oreg., May 12, 1958; d. Richard Hutton and Eleanor (Looker) O. BS, Oreg. State U., 1980; postgrad. in sci., Naval Postgrad. Sch., 1987—. Commd. ensign U.S. Navy, 1980, advanced through grades to lt., 1985; oceanographic watch officer, Guam, 1981-82, Antigua, W.I., 1982-84; adminstrv. officer, Antigua, 1983-84; ops. officer, 1984-85, chief testing mgmt. sect., 1985-87, Salt Lake City. Mem. Nat. Assn. Female Execs., Kappa Delta. Republican. Episcopalian. Avocations: athletics, reading. Home: Portland OR 97208 Office: NPS Monterey CA 94939

OLD, CARL ANGELO, nutritionist; b. Livermore, Calif., July 29, 1954; s. Carl Coonce and Regina Rose (Antonini) O.; m. Marie Ann Banach, Mar. 21, 1981; 1 child, Brian Angelo. BS, U. Calif., Davis, 1976, PhD, 1982; MS, Colo. State U., 1978. Tech. rep. Loomix Inc., Arroyo Grande, Calif., 1982-83; nutritionist MacGowan-Smith Ltd., Exeter, Calif., 1983—; vis. staff scientist Los Alamos (N.Mex.) Nat. Lab., 1978; cons. Tenneco Inc., Houston, 1984-85. Rosenberg fellow U. Calif., Davis, 1981. Mem. Am. Animal Sci. Assn., Am. Dairy Sci. Assn., Am. Registry Profl. Animal Scientists, Sigma Xi. Republican. Roman Catholic. Avocations: skiing, softball, backpacking. Home: 42232 S Fork Dr Three Rivers CA 93271 Office: MacGowan-Smith Ltd PO Box 817 Exeter CA 93221

OLDENDORPH, JAMES EDWARD, advertising executive; b. St. Louis, July 25, 1945; s. Edward Roy and Viola S. O.; children—James Jr., Jessica Sara. B.A., U. Mo., 1967. Regional advt. mgr. Seven Up Co., 1968-70, N.Y. area mktg. mgr., 1970-71, Los Angeles area mktg. mgr., 1971-73; dir. mktg. Seven Up Bottling Cos. So. Calif., Los Angeles, 1973-78; mktg. mgr. Plus Products, Irvine, Calif., 1978-79; v.p. account services Seideman & Moiselle Advt., Encino, Calif., 1979-83; v.p., account supr. Louis & Saul Advt., Santa Monica, Calif., 1983-85; sr. vp., ptnr. Devlofev, Wilson, Oldendorph Advt., Culver City, Calif., 1985—. Recipient Am. Mktg. Assn. So. Calif. Marsy award, 1982, Effie award, 1983, Sandi award, 1983, Off Premise Merit award 1985. Mem. Sales and Mktg. Execs. Club Los Angeles, Am. Mktg. Assn., Los Angeles Advt. Club, U. Mo. Alumni Assn., Sigma Alpha Epsilon. Office: 8630 Hayden Pl Culver City CA 90230

OLDERMAN, GERALD MYRON, medical device company executive; b. N.Y.C., July 16, 1933; s. Cass and Hilda (Klein) O.; m. Myrna Ruth Schwartz, Aug. 3, 1958; children: Sharon, Neil, Lisa. BS in Chemistry, Rensselaer Poly Inst., 1958; MS Phys. Chemistry, Seton Hall U., 1971, PhD, 1972. Research chemist Nat. Cash Register, Dayton, Ohio, 1958-61; tech. mgmt. positions Johnson & Johnson, New Brunswick, N.J., 1961-75, v.p. research and devel. Surgikos div., 1975-78; v.p. research and devel. Am. Convertors div. Am. Hosp. Supply Corp., Evanston, Ill., 1978-85, Am. Pharmaseal div. Am. Hosp. Supply Corp., Valencia, Calif., 1985—; bd. dirs. Am. Convertors. Served with USMC, 1954-56. Recipient Robert Wood Johnson medal, Johnson & Johnson, 1969. Mem. Assn. Advancement Med. Instrumentation, Assn. Nonwovens Industry (bd. dirs., corp. rep. 1986, 87), Nat. Fire Protection Assn. (industry rep.), Am. Chem. Soc., Am. Soc. Artificial Internal Organs. Home: 17300 Citronia St Northridge CA 91325 Office: Am Pharmaseal 27200 N Tourney Rd Valencia CA 91355

OLDFIELD, JAMES EDMUND, nutrition educator; b. Victoria, B.C., Can., Aug. 30, 1921; came to U.S., 1949; s. Henry Clarence and Doris O. Oldfield; m. Mildred E. Atkinson, Sept. 4, 1942; children: Nancy E. Oldfield McLaren, Kathleen E. Oldfield Sansone, David J., Jane E. Oldfield Imper, Richard A. BSA, U. B.C., 1941, MSA, 1949; PhD, Oreg. State U., 1951. Faculty Oreg. State U., Corvallis, 1951—, dir. Nutrition Research Inst., 1986—; mem. nat. tech. adv. com. on water supply U.S. Dept. Interior, Washington, 1967-68; bd. dirs. Council for Agrl. Sci. and Tech., Ames, Iowa, 1978-84; mem. nutrition study section NIH, Bethesda, Md., 1975-80, 85—. Editor: Selenium in Biomedicine, 1967, Sulphur in Nutrition, 1970, Selenium in Biology and Medicine, 1987; author: Selenium in Nutrition, 1971. Served to maj. Can. Army, 1942-46, ETO. Fulbright research scholar U.S. Dept. State, 1974. Fellow Am. Soc. Animal Sci. (pres. 1966-67, Morrison award 1972); mem. Am. Chem. Soc., Am. Inst. Nutrition. Republican. Episcopalian. Lodge: Kiwanis (pres. 1964, lt. gov. 1986). Home: 1325 NW 15th St Corvallis OR 97330 Office: Oreg State U Nutrition Research Inst Corvallis OR 97331

OLDHAM, GARY LEWIS, fire communications manager; b. Los Angeles, Aug. 1, 1957; s. Ralph M. and Rose (Brakovich) O. Grad. in exec. devel. Nat. Fire Acad., Emmitsburg, Md., 1984.. Lic. Fed. Communications Commn. Police officer San Marino Police dept., San Marino, Calif., 1975-77; sr. dispatcher Pasadena Police, Fire Dept., Calif., 1977-80, lead dispatcher Glendale Fire Dept., Calif., 1980-83; communications mgr. Orange County Fire Dept., Calif., 1983-87; communications facility mgr. Heartland Communications Facility Authority, El Cajon, Calif. 1987—; instr. fire services; cons. Orange County, 1982—; lectr. orgns., 1983—; chmn. FIRESCOPE Communications Specialist Group, 1985-86. Opinion editor Pasadena Chronicle, 1973-75; also contbr. feature articles Pasadena Union, 1974. Advisor Pasadena Police Explorer Post, 1972-77; Youth Safety Run, So. Calif., 1974-77; reservist Pasadena Paramedic Dept., 1982-83. Recipient Campaigner award United Way, Orange County, 1983, 84, 85, 86. Mem. Associated Pub. Safety Communications Officers, Orange County Fire Chief's Assn., So. Calif. Assn. Foresters and Fire Wardens, Orange County Fire Communications Mgrs. Assn. (pres. 1984-85, 87). Republican. Office: 180 E Lexington Ave El Cajon CA 92020

OLDHAM, MARK FRANK, social worker; b. Eugene, Oreg., Sept. 10, 1948; s. Guy James and Leta Lena (Dieckgraeff) O.; m. Valerie Lynn Spence, May 24, 1971; children: Katelyn Starr, Henry Thomas. BA, U. Oreg., 1970; postgrad., U. Ams., Mexico City, 1967-68; MSSW, U. Louisville, 1973. Instr. community service and pub. affairs U. Oreg., Eugene, 1970-72; social worker Met. Social Services Dept., Louisville, 1973-74, Children's Services Div., Eugene, 1974-82, Sacred Heart Gen. Hosp. Dept. Psychiatry and Behavioral Medicine, Eugene, 1982—; adj. asst. prof. human services U. Oreg., 1974—; cons. Inst. Social Evaluation, Eugene, 1976—. Bd. dirs. Planned Parenthood Lane County, Eugene, 1969-72; mem. Lane County Adv. Com. Adult Corrections, Eugene, 1979—, chmn. 1981-82; softball coach Eugene Sports Program, 1985-86. Mem. Nat. Assn. Social Workers (treas. 1986—, cert.), Am. Orthopsychiat. Assn. Democrat. Avocations: softball, tennis, reading. Home: 1842 Riverview St Eugene OR 97403 Office: Sacred Heart Gen Hosp 1255 Hilyard St Eugene OR 97401

OLDHAM, MAXINE JERNIGAN, real estate broker; b. Whittier, Calif., Oct. 13, 1923; d. John K. and Lela Hessie (Mears) Jernigan; m. Laurance Montgomery Oldham, Oct. 28, 1941; 1 child, John Laurence. A.A., San Diego City Coll., 1973; student Western State U. Law, San Diego, 1976-77, LaSalle U., 1977-78; grad. Realtors Inst., Sacramento, 1978. Mgr. Edin Harig Realty, LaMesa, Calif., 1966-70; tchr. Bd. Edn., San Diego, 1959-66; mgr. Julia Cave Real Estate, San Diego, 1970-73; salesman Computer Realty, San Diego, 1973-74; owner Shelter Island Realty, San Diego, 1974—; internat. platform speaker Fedn. Internationale des Professions Immobilieres; Author: Jernigan History, 1982, Mears Geneology, 1985. Mem. Civil Service Commn., San Diego, 1957-58. Mem. Nat. Assn. Realtors, Calif. Assn. Realtors, San Diego Bd. Realtors, San Diego Apt. Assn., Federation Internationale des Professions Immobilieres, DAR, Colonial Dames 17th Century, Internat. Fedn. Univ. Women. Republican. Roman Catholic. Avocations: music; theater; painting; geneology; continuing edn. Home: 3348 Lowell St San Diego CA 92106 Office: Shelter Island Realty 2810 Lytton St San Diego CA 92110

OLDHAM, WILLIAM GEORGE, electrical engineering and computer science educator; b. Detroit, May 5, 1938; s. William D. and Freada (Howes) O.; m. Nancy Dereich; children: Katherine Ann, William James. B.S., Carnegie Mellon Inst., 1960, M.S., 1961, Ph.D., 1963. Staff scientist Siemens-Schuckert, Erlangen, W.Ger., 1963-64; mem. faculty elec. engring. and computer scis. dept. U. Calif.-Berkeley, 1964—, prof., 1972—, dir. Electronics Research Lab., 1985—; project mgr. Intel Corp., Santa Clara, Calif., 1974-75, cons., 1975—; cons. Monsanto Corp., St. Louis, 1981—, Xerox Corp., Palo Alto, Calif., 1981-86. Author: An Introduction to Electronics, 1972, Electrical Engineering, An Introduction, 1984. NSF fellow, 1970; Guggenheim fellow, 1985-86. Fellow IEEE; mem. Nat. Acad. Engring. Office: U Calif-Berkeley Dept EECS Berkeley CA 94720

OLDSHUE, MARY HOLL, mining/natural resource company executive; b. Utica, N.Y., Oct. 15, 1951; d. Oscar and Rosemary (Goetz) Holl; m. Paul F. Oldshue, July 12, 1975; children: Emily, Andrew. AB, Vassar Coll., 1973; postgrad., NYU, 1977. Asst. sec. Chem. Bank, N.Y.C., 1973-78; asst. v.p. 1st Interstate Bank, Portland, Oreg., 1978-79; dir. fin. adminstrn. NERCO, Inc. sub. PacifiCorp, Portland, 1980-81, mgr. fin. adminstrn., 1981-82, treas., 1982—. Mem. Fin. Execs. Inst., Met. Mus. Art, Oreg. Mus. Sci. & Industry. Clubs: Vassar of N.Y. and Oreg. Office: NERCO Inc 111 SW Columbia Suite 800 Portland OR 97201

OLDSHUE, PAUL FREDERICK, banker; b. Chgo., Nov. 4, 1949; s. James Young and Betty Ann (Wiersema) O.; m. Mary Elizabeth Holl, July 12, 1975; children: Emily Jane, Andrew Armstrong. B.A., Williams Coll., Williamstown, Mass., 1971; M.B.A., N.Y.U., 1978. With Chem. Bank, N.Y.C., 1973-78, asst. sec., 1976-78; with Orbanco Fin. Services Corp., 1978-84, v.p., treas., 1980-83; v.p., treas. Oreg. Bank, Portland, 1984—, exec. v.p., 1985—. Mem. Fin. Execs. Inst., Robert Morris Assocs. Republican. Club: Univ. (Portland).

O'LEARY, CHARLOTTE MAE, retail computer executive; b. Ontario, Oreg., Dec. 18, 1942; s. Harold A. and Mabel (Marcum) Warren; m. James Ernest O'Leary, Aug. 16, 1962; children: James II, Shelley Renée, Shawna Lenée. AS, Treasure Valley Community Coll., 1980. Head draftsman Interstate Engring. Co., Ontario, 1978-80; owner, operator House of Computers, Ontario, 1980—, Hudco Engring., Ontario, 1980-84; agt. Western Union, Ontario, 1983—; instr. computers, small bus. adminstrn., Treasure Valley Community Coll., Ontario, 1986. Pres. Ontario Downtown Merchants Assn., 1986. Named Nat. Top Dealer Datasphere, Inc., 1984. Mem. Phi Theta Kappa. Avocations: photography, travel, art, sewing. Office: House of Computers 249 S Oregon St Ontario OR 97914

O'LEARY, STEPHEN EDWARD, advertising executive; b. Santa Monica, Dec. 1, 1947; s. Mark E. and Ann H. (Reese) O.; m. Patricia Ruth Hearn, Apr. 12, 1969; children: Mark Edward, Ryan Patrick, Kathryn Ann. BS, U. Oreg., 1969. Account exec. J. Walter Thompson, N.Y.C., 1969-72, Nov. Group, N.Y.C., 1972; sr. v.p., mgr. supr. Marschalk Co., N.Y.C., 1972-81; sr. v.p. Wells, Rich, Greene, Townsend, Newport Beach, Calif., 1981-82; gen. mgr., v.p. Wells, Rich, Greene, Los Angeles, Calif., 1982-83; pres. Townsend & O'Leary, Costa Mesa, Calif., 1983—; speaker Am. Mgmt. Assn., N.Y.C., 1975. Bd. dirs. Del Obispo Youth Baseball, Dan Point, Calif., 1985—, Sch. Journalism U. Oreg., Eugene, 1985—. Mem. Internat. Franchise Assn., U.S. C. of C., U. Oreg. Alumni Bd. Republican. Avocations: coaching sports for children, scouting. Home: 25591 Rocky Beach Ln Dana Point CA 92629 Office: Townsend & O'Leary Inc 3151 Airway Ave F-205 Costa Mesa CA 92626

OLES, STUART GREGORY, lawyer; b. Seattle, Dec. 15, 1924; s. Floyd and Helen Louise (La Violette) O.; B.S. magna cum laude, U. Wash., 1947, J.D., 1948; m. Ilse Hanewald, Feb. 12, 1954; children—Douglas, Karl, Stephen. Admitted to Wash. bar, 1949, U.S. Supreme Ct. bar, 1960; dep. pros. atty. King County (Wash.), 1949, chief civil dept., 1949-50; gen. practice law, Seattle, 1950—; sr. partner firm Oles, Morrison, Rinker, Stanislaw & Ashbaugh, and predecessor, 1955—. Chmn. Seattle Community Concert Assn., 1955; pres. Friends Seattle Pub. Library, 1956; mem. Wash. Pub. Disclosure Commn., 1973-75; trustee Ch. Div. Sch. of Pacific, Berkeley, Calif., 1974-75; mem. bd. curators Wash. State Hist. Soc., 1983; mem. Seattle Symphony Bd.; pres. King County Ct. House Rep. Club, 1950, U. Wash. Young Rep. Club, 1947; Wash. conv. floor leader Taft, 1952, Goldwater, 1964; Wash. chmn. Citizens for Goldwater, 1964; chmn. King County Rep. convs., 1966, 68, 76, 84, 86, Wash. State Rep. Conv., 1980. Served with USMCR, 1943-45. Mem. Seattle, King County, Wash., Am. (past regional vice chmn. pub. contract law sect.) bar assns., Order of Coif, Scabbard and Blade, Am. Legion, Phi Beta Kappa, Phi Alpha Delta. Episcopalian (vestryman, lay-leader). Clubs: Rainier, Seattle Yacht, Beavers. Home: 5051 50th Ave NE #40 Seattle WA 98105 Office: Columbia Seafirst Ctr Seattle WA 98054

OLGEIRSON, ERIK ROBERT, ecologist, consultant; b. Bismarck, N.D., Dec. 11, 1946; s. Robert Hagen and Evelyn (Nack) O.; m. Kathleen Leroux, June 4, 1966 (div. Apr. 1984); children: Christopher, Ian Joseph; m. Jane Vonderahe, Oct. 25, 1986. BA, U. Colo., 1969, PhD, 1972. Instr. Kent Country Day, Englewood, Colo., 1972-73; sr. ecologist Colo. Div. Hwys., Denver, 1973-74, Atlantic-Richfield Co., Denver, 1974-76, Shell Oil Co., Denver, 1976-77; pres. ERO Resources Corp., Golden, Colo., 1977-87; cons. ecologist Denver, 1986—; mem. Colo. Water Congress, Denver, 1985—, Colo. Assn. Commerce, Denver, 1985—, Rocky Mountain Oil and Gas, Denver, 1973-75, Adv. Com. on Improved Plant Materials for Reveg. of High Altitiudes, Ft. Collins, Colo., 1927-73; adj. prof. grad. faculty U. Colo., Denver, 1986—. Contbr. tech. reports to profl. publs. Treas. Evergreen (Colo.) Soccer Assn., 1978-84; bd. dirs. Nat. Repertory Orch., Evergreen, 1985—. Mem. Brit. Ecol. Soc., Ecol. Soc. Am., Wildlife Soc., Soc. Range Mgmt., Calif. Bot. Soc., Assn. Wetland Mgrs. Avocations: skiing, water sports, interior design, cooking, woodworking. Office: 1700 Humboldt St Suite 102 Denver CO 80218

OLHAUSEN, DALE DEAN, civil engineer, consultant; b. Hartley, Iowa, Jan. 24, 1935; s. Edward Henry and Leona Matilda (Kruse) O.; m. Lynn Ruth Schroeder, June 14, 1958; children: Jill, Jeff, Judy. BSCE, S.D. State U., 1957; postgrad., U. So. Calif., 1959-61. Registered profl. engr., land surveyor in 14 states. Engr. Los Angeles County Engrs., 1957-62; project engr. Parker & Underwood, Greeley, Colo., 1962-67; owner, engr. Rocky Mountain Engring., Greeley, 1967-69; sec., mgr. Cen. Weld County Water Dist., Greeley, 1968—; ptnr., engr. Hogan & Olhausen, Inc., Loveland, Colo., 1969-82; mgr. Larimer County Sanitation Dist., Loveland, 1980-86; pres., owner Landmark Engring. Ltd., Loveland, 1982—, Landmark Labs. Ltd., Loveland, 1982—. Mem. Loveland Water and Sewer Bd., Colo. Water Congress, U.S. Com. on Irrigation and Drainage. Mem. NSPE, Am. Cons. Engring. Council, Am. Water Works Assn., Water Pollution Control Fedn., Loveland C. of C. Republican. Lutheran. Lodge: Rotary. Home: 1804 Ponderosa Pl Loveland CO 80537 Office: Landmark Engring Ltd 2300 W Eisenhower Blvd Loveland CO 80537

OLHOEFT, GARY ROY, research geophysicist; b. Akron, Ohio, Feb. 15, 1949; s. Roy Carl and Helen Frances (Landefeld) O.; m. Jean Carolyn Kane, Sept. 2, 1972. BSEE, MSEE, MIT, 1972; PhD, U. Toronto, Ont., Can., 1975. Registered profl. engr., Ont. Research technician MIT, Cambridge, 1967-72; electrical engr. NASA MSC, Houston, 1971; scientist Lockheed Electronics Co. div. Lockheed Corp., Houston, 1972-73; research engr. U. Toronto, 1973-75; research geophysicist U.S. Geol. Survey, Denver, 1975—; cons. Keneccott Copper, Lexington, Mass., 1970-72; mem. chief geologist's sci. adv. com. U.S. Geol. Survey, 1984—, nat. com. rock mechanics NRC/NAS, 1983-86, other sci. adv. coms. Mem. editorial bd. Internat. Jour. Thermophysics, 1979-85; contbr. articles to profl. jours. Nat. Merit scholar 1967; co-recipient Lunar Sci. Group Achievent award 1975. Mem. AAAS, IEEE, ASTM, Am. Geophys. Union (Best Rev. award 1984), Soc. Exploration Geophysics (assoc. editor Geophysics 1985—, Best Presentation award 1972), Royal Soc. Chemistry, Soc. Profl. Well Log Analysts. Avocation: skiing. Home: PO Box 10870 Edgemont Golden CO 80401-4498 Office: US Geol Survey PO Box 25046 DFC MS964 Denver CO 80225

OLIPHANT, CHARLES ROMIG, physician; b. Waukegan, Ill., Sept. 10, 1917; s. Charles L. and Mary (Goss) R.; student St. Louis U., 1936-40; M.D., 1943; postgrad. Naval Med. Sch., 1946; m. Claire E. Canavan, Nov. 7, 1942; children: James R., Cathy Rose, Mary G., William D. Intern, Nat. Naval Med. Ctr., Bethesda, Md., 1943; pvt. practice medicine and surgery, San Diego, 1947—; pres., chief exec. officer Midway Med. Enterprises; former chief staff Balboa Hosp., Doctors Hosp., Cabrillo Med. Ctr.; chief staff emeritus Sharp Cabrillo Hosp.; mem. staff Mercy Hosp., Children's Hosp., Paradise Valley Hosp., Sharp Meml. Hosp.; sec. Sharp Sr. Health Care, S.D.; mem. exec. bd., past. comdr. San Diego Power Squadron. Charter mem. Am. Bd. Family Practice. Served with M.C., USN, 1943-47. Fellow Am. Geriatrics Soc., Am. Acad. Family Practice, Am. Assn. Abdominal Surgeons; mem. AMA, Calif. Med. Assn., Am. Acad. Family Physicians (past pres. San Diego chpt., del. Calif. chpt.), San Diego Med. Soc., Public Health League, Navy League, San Diego Power Squadron (past comdr.), SAR. Clubs: San Diego Yacht, Cameron Highlanders. Home: 4310 Trias San Diego CA 92103

OLIPHANT, ERNIE L., safety educator, public relations executive, consultant; b. Richmond, Ind., Oct. 25, 1934; d. Ernest E. and Beulah A. (Jones) Reid; m. George B. Oliphant, Sept. 25, 1955; children—David, Wendell, Rebecca. Student, Earlham Coll., 1953-55, Ariz. State U., 1974, Phoenix Coll., 1974-78. Planner, organizer, moderator confs., programs for various women's clubs, safety assns., 1971-86; nat. field coordinator Operation Lifesaver, Inc., 1986—; assoc. dir. Operation Lifesaver Nat. Safety Council, Phoenix, 1978—; cons. Fed. R.R. Adminstrn.; lectr. in field.; adviser Am. Ry. Engring. Assn., Calif. Assn. Women Hwy. Safety Leaders, numerous others. Mem. R.R./Hwy. grade crossing com. Ariz. Corp. Commn.; mem. transp. and system com. Ariz. Gov.'s Commn. on Environment; mem. Ariz. Gov.'s Council Women for Hwy. Safety; mem. motor vehicle traffic safety at hwy.-r.r. grade crossings com., roadway environment com., women's div. com. Nat. Safety Council; mem. Phoenix Traffic Accident Reduction Program; task force mem. U.S. Dept. Transp. on Grade Crossing Safety. Recipient Safety award SW Safety Congress, 1973; citation of Merit Adv. Commn. on Ariz. Environment, 1974; Gov.'s award for hwy. safety, 1978; Gov.'s Merit of Recognition Outstanding Service in Hwy. Safety, 1980. Mem. Assn. R.R. Editors, Nat. Assn. Female Execs., Inc., Pub. Relations Soc. Am., R.R. Pub. Relations Assn., Nat. Acad. Scis. (dir. transp. research, planning, adminstrn. of transp. safety com., r.r.-hwy. grade crossing safety com.), Women's Transp. Seminar, Ariz. Fedn. Women's Clubs (named pres. of yr. 1968), Ariz. Safety Assn. (safety recognition award 1975), Gen. Fedn. Women's Clubs (internat. bd. dirs.), Nat. Assn. Women Hwy. Safety Leaders, Phi Theta Kappa. Republican. Quaker. Author of tech. publs.

OLIVA, STEPHEN EDWARD, resource conservationist; b. San Rafael, Calif., Jan. 31, 1946; s. George Verdelli Jr. and Dorothy Margaret (Austin) O.; m. Susan Rebecca Ellis, May 5, 1984; 1 child, Stephanie Rebecca. BA, U. Calif., Santa Barbara, 1972. Planner Calif. Energy Commn., Sacramento, 1976, Calif. Air Resources Bd., Sacramento, 1976-79; spl. asst. to sec. The Resources Agy., Sacramento, 1979-80; spl. asst. Calif. Dept. Conservation, Sacramento, 1980, mgr. land conservation, 1981—; spl. asst. Calif. Dept. Forestry, Sacramento, 1980-81; mem. governing bd. Calif. Tahoe Regional Planning Agy., South Lake Tahoe, 1979-81; mgr. Land Conservation Unit, Calif. Dept. Conservation, chief, 1987—. Served with U.S. Army, 1966-68, Vietnam. Democrat. Avocations: snorkeling, skiing, photography, film studies. Office: Calif Dept Conservation 1516 Ninth St Room 400 Sacramento CA 95819

OLIVE, GRAHAM, research physicist; b. Hinckley, Eng., Feb. 8, 1942; s. Stanley and Ivy Louise (Starbuck) O.; m. Noriko Miwa, Feb. 23, 1967; children: Andrew, Lisa. BSc with honors, Brunel U., Uxbridge, Eng., 1965; MA in Sci., U. B.C., Vancouver, Can., 1969, PhD, 1973. Research officer B.C. Research, Vancouver, 1973-76; instr. physics B.C. Inst. Tech., Burnaby, 1976-81; vis. scientist IBM Research Lab., San Jose, Calif., 1981-82, research staff mem., 1983—; vis. scientist IBM Research Lab., Yorktown Heights, N.Y., 1982-83; cons. displays B.C. Research, 1976; bd. dirs. Avanti Industries, Vancouver. Contbr. articles to profl. jours.; patentee in field. Mem. Am. Vacuum Soc. (exec. mem. No Calif. chpt., sec. 1984—), Electrochem. Soc. Avocations: hiking, sailing, photography, classical music. Office: IBM Almaden Research Ctr K41-803 650 Harry Rd San Jose CA 95120

OLIVE, JOSEPH MANUEL, insurance executive; b. N.Y.C., June 26, 1945; s. Francis Gerard and Carmen Josefa (Guma) O.; B.A., St. Alphonsus Coll., Suffield, Conn., 1967; M.A., Mt. St. Alphonsus, Esopus, N.Y., 1970, M.R.E., 1971, M.Div., 1971, Ph.D., 1973; m. Linda Fern Clark, Apr. 18, 1976. Missionary, Roman Cath. Ch., Brazil, 1970-75; sales mgr., asst. treas. James E. Clark II Corp., Santa Paula, Calif., 1975-78; fin. cons., spl. agt. Cal Farm Ins. Co., 1978-83; owner, operator ins. agy. Farmers Ins., Ventura, 1983—. Bd. dirs. Ojai Independence Day Com., 1985-86; head Emergency Med. Disaster Team for Ojai Valley, 1984—. Mem. Calif. Farm Bur., Calif. Christmas Tree Growers Assn., Nat. Assn. Life Underwriters, Ventura Assn. Life Underwriters, Jaycees. Democrat. Club: Optimists of Ojai (bd. dirs. 1981—, pres. 1983-84). Home: 10990 Creek Rd Ojai CA 93023 Office: 2149 Portola Ventura CA 93003

OLIVE, ROBERT EDWARD, public relations executive; b. Cambridge, Mass., Jan. 20, 1943; s. Charles Whitney Sr. and Edith Emma (Thivierge) O.; m. Susan Elizabeth Dolan, Feb. 19, 1976 (div. 1981); 1 child, Carrie. BMus, New Eng. Conservatory, 1964, MMus, 1966. Solo classical musician Boston, 1966-69; dir. music Dover-Sherborn Schs., Mass., 1968-78; personal press rep. for Wolfman Jack Los Angeles, 1979-80; acct. exec. Age, Stevens & Acree, Los Angeles, 1980-81, ptnr., 1981-82; prin. The Olive Co., Los Angeles, 1982—; mem. event com., cons. Los Angeles Garlic Week, 1983—; cons. Music Bus. Symposium, 1986—. Episcopalian. Home and Office: 6472 Colgate Ave Los Angeles CA 90048

OLIVER, EDDY GLENN, communications director; b. Jackson, Mich., Nov. 9, 1957; s. Vincent Glenn and S. Elaine (McPherson) O. BS, Cen. Mich. U., 1979. Asst. dir. community relations Foote Meml. Hosp., Jackson, Mich., 1979-82; dir. pub. relations Rushmore Nat. Health System, Rapid City, S.D., 1982-85; dir. communications Golden Gate Bapt. Sem., Mill Valley, Calif., 1985—. Chmn. bd. dirs. Golden Gate Choral Soc., Mill Valley, 1986—; mem. Mid-Day Jaycees, Rapid City, 1984; Bd. dirs. Black Hills Voices in Concert, Rapid City, 1983-85; deacon Tiburon (Calif.) Bapt. Ch., 1986—. Recipient Pres.'s award S.D. Assn. Hosp. Pub. Relations, 1984, 1st pl. award S.D. Advt. Fedn., 1984; named one of Outstanding Young Men of Am., 1986. Mem. Pub. Relations Soc. Am. Democrat. Baptist. Avocations: choral, piano and organ music, tennis, bicycling. Home: 1441 Casa Buena Dr #205 Corte Madera CA 94925 Office: Golden Gate Bapt Sem Strawberry Point Mill Valley CA 94941

OLIVER, KENNETH CHARLES, software engineer; b. Teaneck, N.J., Feb. 21, 1961; s. Wallace and Annette Rose (Edge) O.; m. Ann Elizabeth Van Winkle, Aug. 7, 1982. BS in Systems Sci., U. Calif., San Diego, 1982. Registered profl. engr. Software engr. Wiltron Co., Mortan Hill, Calif., 1982—. Coach Morgan Hill Youth Recreation, 1984-85. Mem. IEEE. Democrat. Methodist. Avocations: soccer, rugby, woodworking, gardening, home computers. Home: 17435 Carriage Lamp Way Morgan Hill CA 95037 Office: Wiltron Co 490 Jarvis Dr Morgan Hill CA 95037

OLIVER, LANCE BRIAN, insurance executive; b. Tillamook, Oreg., Oct. 10, 1938; s. Harold W. and Martha V. (Straub) O.; m. Bonnie C. McGary, July 4, 1974; children: Brock, Billie, Brenda. Student, U. Oreg., 1960-64. Dist. mgr. Am. Nat. Ins., Eugene, Oreg., 1963-68; gen. agt. Am. Nat. Ins., Boise, Idaho, 1968-74; pres., owner SunCo Ltd., Tempe, Ariz., 1974—. Chmn. Bus. div. United Fund, Ada County, Idaho, 1973-74. Served with USN, 1956-59. Mem. Assn. Life Underwriters (pres. 1972-73). Republican. Lodge: Elks. Office: SunCo Ltd 600 E Basline Suite B-10 Tempe AZ 85283

OLIVER, MICHAEL THOMAS, financial advisor; b. Honolulu, Apr. 2, 1943; s. Thomas and Edna Louise (Johnson) O.; m. Barbara Susan Smith, Mar. 19, 1967; children: Michael Jr., Katherine, Kimberly. BA, Colgate U., 1965; MBA, U. Va., 1967. Asst. v.p. Morgan Guaranty Trust Co., N.Y.C., 1967-72; v.p. Alex Brown Realty Advisors, Balt., 1972-83, JMB Realty, Chgo., 1983-85, Kennedy Assocs. Real Estate Council, Seattle, 1985-87; v.p. real estate securities fund Pension Realty Advisors, San Francisco, 1987—; bd. dirs. Home Free Village Resorts. Mem. N.Y. Soc. Security Analysts, Fin. Analysts Fedn., Mcpl. Treas. Assn., Internat. Found. of Employee Benefit Plans, Nat. Assn. Retirement Adminstrs. Lutheran. Avocations: reading, fishing. Home: 14261 157th Pl NE Woodinville WA 98072 Office: Pension Realty Advisors 100 Spear St Suite 930 San Francisco CA 94105

OLIVER, PAT PHILLIPS, publisher, editor, writer; b. Crown Point, Ind.; d. John Adam and Anna (Kindness) Patterson; student U. Chgo., 1941, Ind. U., 1938-40; m. Charles Everett Phillips, Jr., Sept. 17, 1941 (div.); children: Anne, Jill, Candace, Pamela; m. 2d, Eddie Oliver, Feb. 2, 1963 (dec.). Columnist, feature writer Ind. newspapers, nat. mags., 1935-40; women's editor, feature writer Burbank (Calif.) Daily Rev., 1953-57, Hollywood (Calif.) Citizen-News, 1957-63; mng. editor, exec. editor Palm Springs Life mag., 1964-79, Palm Springs Pub. Relations, 1980-85; lifestyle editor Indio (Calif.) Daily News, 1985—; owner, pub. Palm Springs Personages, 1982—. Mem. Theta Sigma Phi. Clubs: Desert Press, Hollywood Women's Press, Palm Springs Women's Press (founding, Lifetime Achievement in Journalism award 1986). Office: PO Box 1004 Palm Springs CA 92263

OLIVER, ROBERT WARNER, economics educator; b. Los Angeles, Oct. 26, 1922; s. Ernest Warner and Elnore May (McConnell) O.; m. Darlene Hubbard, July 1, 1946; children: Lesley Joanne, Stewart Warner. A.B., U. So. Calif., 1943, A.M., 1948; A.M., Princeton U., 1950, Ph.D., 1958. Teaching asst. U. So. Calif., 1946-47; instr. Princeton U., 1947-50, Pomona Coll., Claremont, Calif., 1950-52; asst. prof. U. So. Calif., Los Angeles, 1952-56; economist Stanford Research Inst., South Pasadena, Calif., 1956-59; mem. faculty dept. econs. Calif. Inst. Tech., 1959—, prof. econs., 1973—; urban economist World Bank, Washington, 1970-71; cons. Brookings Instn., 1961, OECD, Paris, 1979; vis. prof. U. So. Calif., 1985. Author: An Economic Survey of Pasadena, 1959, International Economic Cooperation and the World Bank, 1975, Bretton Woods, A Retrospective Essay, 1985, Oral History Project The World Bank, 1986; contbg. author: Encyclopedia of Economics, 1981. Mem. Human Relations Com., City of Pasadena, 1964-65; mem. Planning Commn., 1972-75; bd. dirs. Pasadena City Council, 1965-69, mem. Utilities Adv. Commn., 1984—, Strategic Planning Com., 1985; bd. dirs. Pasadena Minority History Found., 1984—. Served to lt. (j.g.) USN, 1942-46. Social Sci. research fellow London Sch. Econs., 1954-55; Rockefeller Found. fellow, 1974; Danforth assoc., 1981; recipient Outstanding Teaching award, 1982. Mem. Internat. Inst. Strategic Studies, Calif. Seminar on Internat. Security and Fgn. Policy, Am. Econs. Assn., Royal Econs. Assn., Com. on Fgn. Relations, Western Econs. Assn., Phi Beta Kappa, Phi Kappa Phi, Delta Tau Delta. Democrat. Methodist. Club: Athenaeum. Home: 3197 San Pasqual Pasadena CA 91107 Office: 1201 California Blvd Pasadena CA 91125

OLIVER, RUTH RAYMONDA, social worker; b. West Point, N.Y., June 30, 1952; d. Nelson Raymond and Anna (Allen) O.; m. Charles Henry Holly, June 30, 1979 (div. Feb. 1982). BA in Sociology, Wagner Coll., 1974; MA, U. Chgo., 1976. Coordinator Maricopa Tech. Community Coll., Phoenix, 1977-78; family counselor Behavioral Health Agy. Cen. Ariz., Casa Grande, 1978-79; clk. Pacific Motor Trucking, Phoenix, 1979-80; social worker II Dept. Econ. Security, Phoenix, 1980-81; counselor II Superior Ct. Conciliation, Phoenix, 1981-85; caseworker City of Glendale, Ariz., 1985—; mem. Behavioral Health Task Force, Phoenix, 1984—. Vol. ARC, Phoenix, 1986, Planned Parenthood, Phoenix, 1980-81. Mem. AAUW, Nat. Assn. Social Workers (cert.), Acad. Family Mediators, Assn. Sch.-Age Parenting, Phoenix Black Social Workers (pres. 1984-86). Avocations: jazz dancing, music, playing piano, reading. Home: 1001 N 43 Ave Space A 231 Phoenix AZ 85009

OLIVERIA, LARRY LELAND, science educator; b. San Jose, Calif., Jan. 17, 1957; Ernest Edwin and Beverly Ann (Cleveland) O.; m. Melinda Lee Hall, Nov. 24, 1981. Cert., U. Santa Clara, 1981, BS in Biology, 1979; postgrad. in paleontology, San Jose State U., 1985—. Cert. secondary tchr., Calif. Sci. tchr. Mitty High Sch., San Jose, Calif., 1981—, chmn. sci. dept., 1983—. Brown fellow Santa Clara U., 1980-81. Mem. Mid-Am. Paleontol. Soc., Am. Assn. Physics Tchrs., Geol. Soc. Am., Nat. Sci. Tchrs. Assn. Democrat. Avocations: paleontology, natural history. Office: Mitty High Sch 5000 Mitty Ave San Jose CA 95129

OLLIPHANT, JO ANN, language professional, educator; b. Kalispell, Mont., Mar. 1, 1944; d. Glenn Elmer and Dorothy Alice (Moore) Manning; m. Webb Buckley Olliphant Jr., Dec. 15, 1970. BA, U. Mont., 1966; MA, Pacific Luth. U., 1982. Tchr. French U.S. Mil. Schs., Fed. Republic of Germany, 1968-73, The Annie Wright Sch., Tacoma, Wash., 1974-80, Epiphany Sch., Seattle, 1982—; methods instr. The Lang. Sch., Seattle, 1982—; cons. in field, 1984—; instr. Western Wash. U., Whitworth Coll.; dir. curriculum and tchr. tng. Pacific Luth. U., 1983—. Recipient Creative Innovation to the Profession award Wash. Assn. Fgn. Lang. Tchrs., 1986. Mem. Am. Council on Teaching Fgn. Langs., Tchrs. of English to Speakers of Other Langs., New Horizons for Learning, Am. Assn. Tchrs. of French, Pacific N.W. Council on Fgn. Langs, (mem. exec. council 1985—). Office: Epiphany Sch 3710 E Howell Seattle WA 98122

OLLSON, DOROTHY GORE, county official; b. Knox City, Tex., Jan. 15, 1924; d. Roy and Lydia Edna (Moss) Gore; m. George B. Ollson, June 7, 1961 (dec.); children: Lynnette Brandon, Andrew Rogers, Georgann Hackenbracht, Greg, Marjori. Student Ariz. State U., 1940-41. With Gila County Engr.'s Office, Globe (Ariz.) Justice Ct., 1958—, research analyst, 1980—. Mem. Gila County Dem. Women's Club, mem. Globe City Council, mem. minerals extraction task force com.; elected Office of Justice of Peace Globe Precinct, Gila County, 1986-90; appointed Globe City Magistrate, 1986—. Mem. VFW Aux. Club: Emblem 235. Home: 257 N 2d St Globe AZ 85502 Office: Gila County Engrs Office 1400 E Ash St Globe AZ 85501

OLMSTEAD, MARILYN MORGAN, x-ray crystallographer; b. Glendale, Calif., Dec. 8, 1943; d. Morgan Paul and Naomi (Gotwals) Morgan; m. Alan Lester Olmstead, Aug. 20, 1966; children: Janis May, Nathan Lester. BA, Reed Coll., 1965; PhD, U. Wis., 1969. Lectr. U. Calif., Davis, 1969-75, research assoc., 1975—. Contbr. numerous article to sci. publs. Woodrow Wilson fellow, 1965-66. Mem. Am. Chem. Soc., Am. Crystallographic Assn. Avocation: tennis. Office: U Calif Dept Chemistry Davis CA 95616

OLMSTED, MAXINE BLAKEMORE, writer; b. Seattle, Dec. 18, 1907; d. John Flick and Cassa Geneva (Illsley) Blakemore; B.A. in Drama, U. Wash., Seattle, 1931; m. Joel Burleson Olmsted, Sept. 5, 1931; children—Cassa Blakemore, Spalding Maxine. Pub. relations dir. United Cerebral Palsy Assn. Central Ariz., 1957-59, Maricopa County and Ariz. assns. mental health, 1959-61, Ariz. Assn. Crippled Children and Adults, 1962-64, Phoenix Jewish Community Center, 1965-68, Ariz. Commn. Arts and Humanities, 1969-70; Maricopa County coordinator Ariz. Commn. Arts and Humanities for dance/movement in elementary schs., 1970-79; author histories of Phoenix and Scottsdale for photography book Phoenix: 1870-1970, 1970; also articles, stories; editor Ariz. Dance Guild News, 1974-79; leading actor in documentary film The Desert Speaks (Golden Eagle award 1978). Recipient various service citations. Mem. Screen Actors Guild, AFTRA, Nat. League Am. Pen Women, Ariz. Dance Arts Alliance (a founder), Artes Bellas (a founder), Phoenix Art Mus., Scottsdale Center for Arts, Ariz. Humane Soc. Republican. Episcopalian. Address: 8531 N 11th Ave Phoenix AZ 85021

OLNEY, KATHRYN LOUISE, magazine research director; b. Upperdarby, Pa., Dec. 9, 1955; d. Edward Stuart and Marilyn (Patterson) O.; m. Clifford Jay Bell, June 17, 1979; 1 child, Lindsay Olney-Bell. BA, Purdue U., 1978. Library assoc. DePaul U., Chgo., 1978-79, U. of Pacific, Stockton, Calif., 1979-81; cons. Mother Jones mag., San Francisco, 1982-83, research dir., 1984—; researcher California mag., San Francisco, 1983-84. Home: 454 Jersey St San Francisco CA 94112 Office: Mother Jones Mag 1663 Mission St San Francisco CA 94103

OLPIN, ROBERT SPENCER, art history educator; b. Palo Alto, Calif., Aug. 30, 1940; s. Ralph Smith and Ethel Lucille (Harman) O.; m. Mary Florence Catharine Reynolds, Aug. 24, 1963; children: Mary Courtney, Cristin Lee, Catharine Elizabeth, Carrie Jean. BS, U. Utah, 1963; AM, Boston U., 1965, PhD, 1971. Lectr. art history Boston U., 1965-67; asst. prof. U. Utah, Salt Lake City, 1967-72, assoc. prof., 1972-76, prof., 1976—, chmn. dept., 1975-82, dir. art history program, 1968-76, 83—, assoc. dean Coll. Fine Arts, 1987—; cons. curator Am. and English art Utah Mus. Fine Arts, 1973—. Grantee U. Utah, 1972, 85, Utah Mus. Fine Arts, 1975, Utah Bicentennial Commn., 1975, Ford Found., 1975; trustee Salt Lake Art Ctr., 1979, Utah Endowment for Humanities, 1985-86. Mem. Archives Am. Art Smithsonian Instn., Coll. Art Assn. Am., Mid-Am. Coll. Art Assn., Utah Acad. Scis. Arts Letters, Utah Art History Assn., Assn. Historians Am. Art, Utah Heritage Found., Phi Kappa Phi, Sigma Nu. Republican. Mormon. Author: Alexander Helwig Wyant, 1836-92, 1968, Mainstreams of American Architecture, 1973, American Painting Around 1850, 1976, Art-Life of Utah, 1977, Dictionary of Utah Art, 1980, A Retrospective of Utah Art, 1981, Waldo Midgley: Birds, Animals, People, Things, 1984, A Basket of Chips, 1985, The Works of Alexander Helwig Wyant, 1986. Home: 887 Woodshire Ave Murray UT 84107 Office: U Utah Dept Art Salt Lake City UT 84112

OLSEN, ALFRED JON, lawyer; b. Phoenix, Oct. 5, 1940; s. William Hans and Vera (Bearden) O.; m. Susan K. Smith, Apr. 15, 1979. B.A. in History, U. Ariz., 1962; M.S. in Acctg, Ariz. State U., 1964; J.D., Northwestern U., 1966. Bar: Ariz. 1966, Ill. 1966; C.P.A., Ariz., Ill. cert. tax specialist. Acct. Arthur Young & Co., C.P.A.s, Chgo., 1966-68; dir. firm Ehmann, Olsen & Lane (P.C.), Phoenix, 1969-76; dir. Streich, Lang, Weeks & Cardon (P.C.), Phoenix, 1977-78; v.p. Olsen-Smith, Ltd., Phoenix, 1978—. Bd. editors: Jour. Agrl. Law and Taxation, 1978—, Practical Real Estate Lawyer, 1983—. Mem. Phoenix adv. bd. Salvation Army., 1973-81. Fellow Am. Coll. Probate Counsel, Am. Coll. Tax Counsel; Mem. Central Ariz. Estate Planning Council (pres. 1972-73), State Bar Ariz. (chmn. tax sect. 1977-78), ABA (chmn. com. on agr., sect. taxation 1976-78, chmn. CLE com. sect. taxation 1982-84), Am. Law Inst. (chmn. tax planning for agr. 1973—), Nat. Cattlemen's Assn. (tax com. 1979—), Internat. Acad. Estate and Trust Law (academician), Sigma Nu Internat. (pres. 1986—). Office: 3300 Liberty Bank Plaza 301 E Virginia Ave Phoenix AZ 85004

OLSEN, ARTHUR ROBERT, economist, educator, author; b. Bklyn., Dec. 1, 1910; s. Martin and Clara Anita (Hansen) O.; m. Helen Marie Fehleisen, June 25, 1938; 1 dau., Karen Marie Steadman. B.S., NYU, 1939, A.M., 1940, Ed D., 1942. Prin. Elwood School, L.I., N.Y., 1935-37; asst. prin., instr. No. Merrick School, L.I., 1937-43; instr. Pratt Inst., N.Y.C., 1943-44; statistician Rayonier Inc., N.Y.C., 1944-47; prof. Western Ill. U., 1947-70, now emeritus; disting. adj. prof. econs. Ariz. State U., 1981-82; economist, author Southwestern Publ. Co., Cin., 1957—; del. U.S. Nat. Commn. UNESCO, economist S.W. Mo. Council on Econ. Edn.; bd. dirs. Ill. Council Econ. Edn.; bd. dirs. Community Edn. project, Macomb, Ill., 1957-59; past dir. and moderator WKAI Round Table of the Air. Mem. Republican Presdl. Task Force, 1982; v.p. Sun City Agrl. Club, 1982. Served with USNG, 1930-33. Recipient Alumnus of Yr. award SUNY, 1978; Joint Council Econ. Edn. fellow, 1960. Mem. NEA (life), Am. Econ. Assn., Ill. Council Social Studies (past pres.), Smithsonian Assocs., Nat. Geog. Soc., Phi Delta Kappa, Kappa Delta Pi, Omicron Delta Epsilon. Republican. Protestant. Clubs: N.Y.U., Sun City Country. Lodge: Masons (33d degree). Author: (with T.J. Hailstones), Economics, 10th edit., 1985; Economic Institutions, 1958; Readings on Marriage and Family Relations, 1953; Economics Transparancies, 1973; Beat the Market, 1973; contbr. articles to profl. jours. Home and Office: 9232 107th Ave Sun City AZ 85351

OLSEN, BRUCE LLOYD, church organization administrator, educator; b. Price, Utah, Apr. 30, 1939; s. George Linwood and Jane Aleen (Cox) O.; m. Christine Payne, May 26, 1966; children: Cherilyn, David Bruce, Nad William, Robert Burke. AS, Coll. Eastern Utah, 1959; BS, Brigham Young U., 1963, MA in Communication, 1965. Dir. sch. relations Brigham Young U., Provo, Utah, 1966-68, dir. admission adv. program, 1966-71, asst. dean admissions and records, 1970-73, asst. to pres. univ. relations, 1973-82, instr. communications, 1975-82, assoc. prof., 1985—; sr. assoc. Coltrin and Associates, N.Y.C., 1983-87; pres. Pub. Relations Cons., Inc., 1987—; pres. Mass. Boston mission The Ch. Jesus Christ of Latter-day Saints, Cambridge, Mass., 1982-85. Co-founder Utah County Heritage Found.; trustee Utah Heritage Found.; bd. dirs. Utah Citizens League Nursing, Utah Lung Assn.; bishop Orem (Utah) 77th Ward and Brigham Young U. 4th Ward, also counselor, stake pres. Brigham Young U. 4th stake, Ch. Jesus Christ Latter-day Saints. Utah Parents and Tchrs. scholar; Sigma Delta Chi scholar. Mem. Pub. Relations Soc. Am. (accredited), Am. Assn. Higher Edn., Internat. Pub. Relations Assn. Republican. Home: 535 W 750 S Orem UT 84057 Office: Brigham Young U F527 Harris Fine Arts Ctr Provo UT 84602

OLSEN, CURTIS WAYNE, systems engineer; b. Milw., Sept. 5, 1954; s. Vernie James and Gertrude Francis (Capello) O.; m. Teri C. Bennett, June 21, 1979 (div. May 1985); 1 child, Autumn Marie; m. Carol D. Knight, Oct. 25, 1986. AAS in ABCET, Milw. Sch. Engring., 1976, BS in Archtl. Bldg. Constrn. Engring. Tech., 1976, MSin Engring. Mgmt., 1984. Cert. instr., Calif.; registered profl. engr., Calif., Wis. Design engr. Akerlow Industries, Grafton, Wis., 1976-78; structural mech. engr. Modern Equipment Co., Port Washington, Wis., 1978-81; systems engr. Job Shopping Inc., Milw., 1981-83, San Diego, 1983-85; civil engr. Integrated Systems Service div. Amex/Allied Signal Corp., Chula Vista, Calif., 1985, project engr., 1985-87; adj. instr. Milw. Sch. Engring., 1981-82; pres. C.W. Cons., Milw. 1982—, San Diego, 1983—, Terminal Networks Inc., San Diego, 1986. Contbr. articles to profl. jours. V.p. Menomenee Falls (Wis.) Judo Assn., 1974; soccer and basketball coach Milw. YMCA, 1981. Mem. ASHRPE, Cons. Engrs., Plumbing Engrs., Wis. Soc. Profl. Engrs., AISC. Mem. ASHRAE, Am. Soc. Cons. Engrs., Am. Soc. Plumbing Engrs., Am. Inst. Steel Constrn., Calif. Soc. Profl. Engrs., Wis. Soc. Profl. Engrs., Am. Judo Fedn. Avocations: stamp collecting, snow skiing, scuba diving, judo, sky diving. Home: 208 Countryhaven Rd Encinitas CA 92024-3105 Office: CWO Inc Engring 208 Countryhaven Rd Encinitas CA 92024-3105

OLSEN, DANIEL PAUL, computer systems professional; b. Butte, Mont., May 31, 1952; s. Paul B. and Rose Patrica (Roe) O.; m. Barbara Diane Nelson, May 28, 1983; children: Lisa Lynn, Christina Danielle, Ashley Dyan. Student, Mont. State U., 1970-72; BS in Computer Sci., U. Mont., 1975; postgrad., Mont. Coll. Mineral Sci. and Tech., 1977—. Cert. data processor. Programmer Mont. Power Co., Butte, 1976-77, systems programmer, 1977-78, sr. systems programmer, 1978-83, sr. system support analyst, 1983, supr. Prime services, 1983—; adj. instr. Mont. Coll. of Mineral Sci. and Tech., butte, 1977-79. Pres. Echo Lake (Mont.) Homeowners Assn., 1981—. Mem. Assn. Cert. of Computer Profls. Avocations: skiing, water sports, hunting, carpentry, bicycling. Home: PO Box 524 Butte MT 59703-0524 Office: Mont Power Co 40 E Broadway Butte MT 59701

OLSEN, DAVID MAGNOR, science educator; b. Deadwood, S.D., July 23, 1941; s. Russell Alvin and Dorothy M. Olson; m. Muriel Jean Bigler, Aug. 24, 1963; children: Merritt, Chad. BS, Luther Coll., 1963; MS in Nat. Sci., U. S.D., 1967. Instr. sci., math. Augustana Acad., Canton, S.D., 1963-66; instr. chemistry Iowa Lakes Community Coll., Estherville, Iowa, 1967-69; instr. chemistry Merced (Calif.) Coll., 1969—, instr. astronomy, 1975—, div. chmn., 1978—. Bd. trustees Merced Union High Sch. Dist., 1983—, pres. 1986-87. Mem. Am. Chem. Soc., Astron. Soc. of the Pacific, NEA, Calif. Tchrs. Assn., Merced Coll. Faculty Assn. (pres. 1975, treas. 1980—). Democrat. Lutheran. Club: Track (Merced) (mem. exec. bd. 1981—). Lodges: M Star (pres. Merced club 1981), Sons of Norway (v.p. 1983). Home: 973 Idaho Dr Merced CA 95340 Office: Merced Coll 3600 M St Merced CA 95340

OLSEN, DIANA LE, social worker; b. Levi, Ky., June 22, 1944; d. Clarence Leroy and Dorthea (Thoms) Burton; m. Earl G. Olsen, Aug. 24, 1965; children: Cathy Ann, Tammy Lynn. B in Social Welfare, Brigham Young U., Laie, Hawaii, 1981; M in Social Welfare, U. Hawaii, 1983. Social worker Hawaii Dept. Health, Honolulu, 1983-84; social worker child protective services Hawaii Dept. Social Services, Honolulu, 1984—. Mem. Nat. Assn. Social Workers (ELAN com. 1981—), Assn. Cert. Social Workers (cert.). Republican. Baptist. Home: 1015 Aoloa Pl #451 Kailua HI 96734

OLSEN, DONALD RICHARD, management consultant; b. Butte, Mont., June 20, 1941. Student, Mont. Tech. U., Montana State U.; BA in Math., U. Mont., 1964, MS in Organic Chemistry, 1966, postgrad. in Chemistry and Environment, 1971-72; postgrad. in Chemistry and Bus. Adminstrn., U. Idaho, 1967-69. Cert. safety profl., cert. indsl. hygienist. Analytical chemist Dow Chem. Co., Rocky Flats, Colo., 1966-67, U.S. AEC Health Services Lab., 1967-71; indsl. hygienist U.S. Dept. Labor, Occupational Safety and Health Adminstrn., Billings, Mont., 1972-74; sr. indsl. hygienist U.S. Dept. Labor Occupational Safety and Health Adminstrn., Anchorage, 1974-75, Portland, Oreg., 1975-77; regional safety mgr. U.S. Fish and Wildlife Service, Portland, 1977-79; accident prevention mgr. Ga.-Pacific Corp., Portland, 1979-81, corp. mgr. indsl. hygiene, 1981-82, safety and workers' compensation mgr., 1982-83; mgr. loss control Boise Cascade Corp., Portland, 1983-85; owner, cons. Olsen Cons., Kent, Wash., 1985—. Contbr. articles to profl. jours. Mem. tech. adv. group mem. Washington Dept. Labor and Industries, 1982-85; active Oreg. Occupational Safety and Health Conf., 1985; rep. Oreg. Fire Standards and Accreditation Bd. Industry, 1983-85. Mem. Am. Acad. Indsl. Hygiene, Am. Indsl. Hygiene Assn., Am. Soc. Safety Engrs., Am. Conf. Govtl. Indsl. Hygienists, Am. Indsl. Hygiene Assn. (pres. Pacific Northwest sect. 1986-87, pres. elect 1985-86, bd. dirs. 1982-83), Portland Field Fed. Safety and Health Council (chmn. 1977-78), Nat. Safety Council (forest industries sect. com. mem. 1979-85, gen. chmn. 1984, vice chmn. and program chmn. 1983, newsletter editor 1982, sec. 1981), Forest Products Safety Conf. (exec. com. 1979-85, statistician 1985, treas. 1982-84), Am. Paper Inst., Nat. Forest Products Assn. (workplace chem. com. 1979-85), Am. Plywood Assn. (chmn. safety and health com. 1983, chmn. formaldeyde task force 1982-83, wood dust task group 1979-85), Forest Products Indsl. Hygiene Forum (chmn. 1980, 85), Wash. Gov.'s. Indsl. Safety and Health Conf. Pulp and Paper Standards, Wash. Labor/Mgmt. Adv. Com. Pulp and Paper Standards, Vets. of Safety. Office: 25825 104th Ave SE Suite 393 Kent WA 98031

OLSEN, GEORGE DUANE, pharmacology educator; b. DeKalb, Ill., Jan. 5, 1940; s. George Meyer and Ida Mae (Hahn) O.; m. Deborah Jane Morgan, June 24, 1965; children: Derrick Meyer, Sonja Julia. AB, Dartmouth Coll., 1962, B Med. Sci., 1964; MD, Harvard U., Boston, 1966. Intern Univ. Hosp., Cleve., 1966-67; med. dir. Indian Health Ctr., USPHS, Tucson, 1967-69; post-doctoral fellow Oreg. Health Scis. U., Portland, 1969-70, asst. prof. pharmacology, 1970-78, assoc. prof., 1978—; invited speaker Norwegian Pharmacology Soc., Beito, Norway, 1982. Contbr. articles to profl. jours. Active Tigard (Oreg.) Sch. Dist., 1983, officer high sch. band booster orgn., 1984—. Served as med. dir. USPHS, 1967-69. Fellow NIH, NATO; grantee Nat. Inst. Drug Abuse. Mem. Am. Soc. Pharmacological and Exptl. Therapeutics (exec. com. devel. sect. 1985—), Am. Soc. Clin. Pharmacological Therapeutics (med. edn. com. 1978—, editorial bd. jour. 1986—), Internat. Narcotic Research Conf., Perinatal Research Soc., AAAS. Avocations: classical piano, skiing, hiking. Office: Oreg Health Scis U Dept Pharmacology L221 3181 SW Sam Jackson Pk Rd Portland OR 97201

OLSEN, JOHN WILFRED, archaeology educator; b. Concord, Mass., Dec. 4, 1955; s. Stanley J. and Eleanor L. (Vinez) O. Student, Fla. State U., 1973; BA with honors, U. Ariz., 1976; MA, PhD, U. Calif., Berkeley, 1980. Postdoctoral research assoc. U. London, 1982-84; vis. asst. prof. U. Ariz., Tucson, 1980-82, asst. prof., 1984—. Co-editor: Palaeoanthropology and Palaeolithic Archaeology in the People's Republic of China, 1985; contbr. articles to profl. jours. Mem. Soc. Am. Archaeology, Am. Anthropol. Assn., Soc. Vertebrate Palaeontology, Assn. Asian Studies, Am. Oriental Soc., Phi Beta Kappa, Sigma Xi, Phi Kappa Phi. Avocations: photography, hiking. Office: U Ariz Dept Anthropology Tucson AZ 85721

OLSEN, JUDY WINN-BELL, English educator; b. Bozeman, Mont., Dec. 20, 1944; d. Howard Jay Winn and Jean Eleanor (Wallace) Bell; m. Rober E. W-B Olsen, July 29, 1972. Student, Jochi U., Tokyo, 1962-63, U. Hawaii, 1963-64; BA in English Linguistics, San Jose State U., 1967; MA in English, Cert. Teaching ESL, UCLA, 1970; MA in Adult Edn., San Franisco State U., 1985. Cert. secondary tchr., Calif. Instr. ESL Alemany Community Coll. Ctr., San Francisco, 1970—; lectr. Oreg. State U. Teaching English to Speakers of Other Langs. summer Inst., 1984, Methods and Materials in Teaching ESL, U. Calif.,Berkeley, 1982; cons. staff devel. Oakland (Calif.) Unified Sch. Dist., 1986; cons., lectr. in Japan, Thailand, Indonesia, Yemen. Author: Communication-Starters, 1977, Look Again Pictures, 1984; co-author: Back and Forth, 1985; dir., producer video tchr. tng. series Communicative Classroom Routines, 1982. Mem. Assn. Suprs. and Curriculum Developers, Am. Assn. Applied Linguistics, Am. Soc. Tng. and Devel., Tchrs. of English to Speakers of Other Langs., Calif. Tchrs. of English to Speakers of Other Langs., Japan Assn. Lang. Tchrs. Avocations: snorkeling, computer graphics. Home: 1282 29th Ave San Francisco CA 94122 Office: Alemany Community Coll Ctr 750 Eddy St San Francisco CA 94109

OLSEN, KENNETH MICHAEL, manufacturing and distributing company executive; b. Coeur D'Alene, Idaho, Apr. 15, 1948; s. Howard George and Irma Dean (Harris) O.; m. Dixie Kathleen McCowan, Dec. 28, 1968; children—Glenn Michael, Kerri Michelle. B.A. in Bus. Adminstrn. with high honors, U. Wash., 1970, M.B.A., 1971. C.P.A., Wash., Idaho. Staff auditor Arthur Andersen & Co., Seattle, 1971-73, sr. auditor, Boise, Idaho, 1973-75, audit mgr., 1975-80; treas., chief fin. officer Futura Corp., Boise, 1980-83, v.p., 1981-83; controller Southwest Forest Industries, Inc., Phoenix, 1983-86; v.p., chief fin. officer ISC Systems, Inc., Spokane, Wash., 1986—; spl. lectr. acctg. Boise State U., 1976. Mem. Am. Inst. C.P.A.s, Idaho Soc. C.P.A.s, Am. Acctg. Assn., Inst. Internal Auditors, Fin. Execs. Inst., Am. Mgmt. Assn. Republican. Home: 10621 E 46th Spokane WA 99201 Office: ISC Systems Inc PO Box TAF-C8 Spokane WA 99220

OLSEN, MELVIN EUGENE, computer systems manager; b. Baker, Oreg., July 16, 1938; s. Clifford Eugene and Zelpha Lucille (Carnes) O.; m. Mary Ellen Ottesen, May 10, 1963; children: Jeanine, Janette, Steven Mel, Michael Eugene. Student, Brigham Young U., 1956-58, 60-63. Forklift and truck driver Smith Canning Co., Pendleton, Oreg., 1962-63; sect. head geneal. dept. Jesus Christ of Latter Day Saints Ch., Salt Lake City, 1965-68, systems mgr., 1968-80, mgr. names processing systems, 1980—; corr. mem. Internat. Council Archives Automation com., Paris, 1977—; mem. program com. 1969 World Conf. on Records, Salt Lake City, registration com. 1981 World Conf. on Records, Salt Lake City. Author Introducing Automation Into Archives, 1981. Vol. firefighter U.S. Forest Service, Pendleton, 1957-58; chmn. Planning and Zoning com., South Salt Lake, Utah, 1978-86, Mayor and City Council Re-election Commn., South Salt Lake, Utah, 1985, councilman City of South Salt Lake, 1986—; dist. vice chmn. Boy Scouts Am., Great Salt Lake Council, 1973. Served with USAR, 1955-63. Recipient Silver Beehive award Boy Scouts Am., 1971, Silver Ox award Boy Scouts Am., 1970, Flood Service award South Salt Lake Police Dept. Mem. SAR (state registrar 1965-66). Republican. Mormon. Home: 30 E Sunset Ave South Salt Lake UT 84115 Office: Geneal Dept 50 E North Temple Salt Lake City UT 84150

OLSEN, PAUL JOSEPH, fire chief; b. Spokane, Wash., May 23, 1928; s. Herbert Leonard and Marguerite Marie (Devlin) O.; m. Vivian Nadine Kellmer, Nov. 17, 1951; 1 child, Kathleen. Student Eastern Wash. U., 1948, Spokane Community Coll., 1960—. Firefighter, Spokane Fire Dept., 1951-58, lt., 1958-63, capt., 1963-65, bn. chief, 1965-72, asst. chief, 1972-81, chief, 1981—. Mem. adv. bd. dirs. Salvation Army, Spokane, 1981; mem. adv. bd. Spokane Community Coll., 1969. Mem. Nat. Fire Protection Assn., Internat. Fire Chiefs Assn., Western Fire Chiefs Assn., Wash. State Fire Chiefs Assn., Inland Empire Fire Chiefs Assn., Spokane Area C. of C. Club: Spokane.

Lodge: Rotary. Office: Spokane Fire Dept W 44 Riverside Ave Spokane WA 99201 *

OLSEN, ROBERT ARTHUR, finance educator; b. Pittsfield, Mass., June 30, 1943; s. Arthur Anton and Virginia O.; B.B.A., U. Mass., 1966, M.B.A., 1967; Ph.D., U. Oreg., 1974; m. Maureen . Joan Carmell, Aug. 21, 1965. Security analyst Am. Inst. Counselors, 1967-68; research assoc. Center for Capital Market Research, U. Oreg., 1972-74; asst. prof. fin. U. Mass., 1974-75; prof. fin. Calif. State U., Chico, 1975—; cons. research mktg. Calif. State U., Chico, Endowment Fund, U.S. Forest Service. Stonier Banking fellow, 1971-72; Nat. Assn. Mut. Savs. Banks fellow, 1975-76; scholar Stanford U., Decision Research, Inc., 1986. Recipient Research award Calif. State U.-Chico, 1983, 86, Profl. Achievement award, 1985. Mem. Am. Fin. Assn., Fin. Execs. Inst., Western Fin. Assn. (Trefftzs award 1974), Southwestern Fin. Assn., Fin. Mgmt. Assn., Eastern Fin. Assn., Sierra Club. Contbr. articles to profl. jours. Office: Calif State U Sch Bus Chico CA 95929

OLSHER, LESLEY RUTH, social worker, consultant; b. Cleve., Aug. 13, 1948; d. Sandford and Natalie Anne (Pollak) Lepene Finkle; m. Richard Henry Olsher, Dec. 22, 1968; children—Daniel Joseph, Dahlia Debra. A.A., Santa Fe Community Coll., 1969; B.A., U. Ala.-Huntsville, 1972; M.S.W., U. Md., 1974. Social worker Md. Dept. Juvenile Services, Balt., 1974-76; founder, pres., legis. activist Md. Alliance Nonsmokers, Inc., Severna Park, 1972-78, N.Mex. Nonsmoker Protection Projects, Los Alamos, 1978—; cons. Nonsmoker Consultancy, Los Alamos, 1982—; pres. Stereo House, Los Alamos, 1982—; profl. singer, N.Mex., 1986—. Founder, coordinator Los Alamos Cesarian Support Group, 1978—; Los Alamos County 1st Offenders Program; publicity coordinator Support Group for Parents of Gifted Children, Los Alamos, 1982-83; lead soprano Coll. of Santa Fe Chorus, N.Mex., 1983-85, Santa Fe Community Coll., 1983—. Coordinator first offender program Dept. Juvenile Services, Los Alamos County, N.Mex., 1986—. Mem. Nat. Assn. Social Workers, Internat. Platform Soc., People Advocating Gifted Edn. Democrat. Club: Hadassah (publicity chair 1978-82). Office: N Mex Nonsmoker Protection Projects and Nonsmoker Cons ultancy 86 Joya Loop Los Alamos NM 87544

OLSON, ARNOLD MARVIN, airline pilot; b. Vancouver, B.C., Can., July 6, 1951; s. Elmer Adolf and Elva Julia (Smiley) O.; m. Lucy Jean Wardle, June 16, 1973; children: Joshua Paul, Jesse David, Joel Scott. AA, Trinity Western Coll., 1971; BSc, Simon Fraser U., Vancouver, 1973. Unit mgr. Mfrs. Life Ins. Co., Vancouver, 1975-78; instr., charter pilot Skyway Air Services, Langley, B.C., 1978-79; pilot Air Can., Vancouver, 1979—; chmn. aviation div. Trinity Western U., Langley, 1982—; pres. Avcon Aviation Cons., Surrey, B.C., 1982—. Area mgr. B.C. Social Credit, 1974, Progressive Conservative Party of Can., 1984. Mem. Christian Ch. Home: 2684 137 St, Surrey Can V4A 4G5 Office: Trinity Western U, 7600 Glover Rd, Langley Can V3A 4R9

OLSON, BONNIE WAGGONER-BRETERNITZ (MRS. O. DONALD OLSON), civic worker; b. North Platte, Nebr., May 30, 1916; d. Floyd Emil and Edith (Waggoner) Breternitz; A.B., U. Chgo., 1947; m. O. Donald Olson, May 17, 1944; children—Pamela Lynne, Douglas Donald. Dep. clk. Dist. Ct., Lincoln County, Nebr., 1940-42; advt. researcher Burke & Assos., Chgo., 1942; contbg. newspaper columnist Chgo. Herald-Am., 1943; social worker A.R.C., Chgo., 1942-44, Sacramento, Calif., 1944, Amarillo, Tex., 1945; exec. sec. Econometrica, Cowles Commn. for Research in Econs., Chgo., 1945-47; interior designer, antique dealer. Col.; participant Chgo. Maternity Ctr. Fund Drive, 1953, Chgo. Council on Fgn. Relations, 1948-54; mem. Colo. Springs Community Council, 1956-58, chmn. children's div., 1956-58, mem. exec. bd., 1956-58, mem. budget com., 1957-58; mem. Colorado Springs Charter Assn., 1956-60, mem. exec. bd., 1957-59, sec., 1958; chmn. El Paso County PTA, Protective Services for Children, 1959-61; chmn. women's div. fund drive ARC, 1961; mem. League Women Voters, 1957—, mem. state children's law com., 1961-63, chmn. ad hoc com. El Paso County Citizens' Com. for Nat. Probation and Parole Survey, Juvenile Ct. Procedures and Detention, 1957-61; mem. children's adv. com. Colo. Child Welfare Dept., 1959-63, chmn., 1961; del. White House Conf. on Children and Youth, 1960, 70; sec. Citizens Ad Hoc Com. for Comprehensive Mental Health Clinic for Pikes Peak Region, 1966—; mem. Colorado Springs Human Relations Commn., 1968-71; sustaining mem. Symphony Guild, 1970-72, Fine Arts Ctr., 1957—; mem. Pikes Peak Mental Health Ctr., 1964-67; Colo. del. White House Conf. on Aging, Colo. Gov.'s Conf. on Aging, 1981, Dist. Atty.'s Child Abuse Task Force, 1986. Recipient Lane Bryant Ann. Nat. Awards citation, 1971; alumni citation for pub. service U. Chgo., 1961. Mem. Am. Acad. Polit. and Social Sci., Nat. Trust Historic Preservation, Women's Ednl. Soc. Colo. Coll. (life), Council on Religion and Internat. Affairs. Episcopalian. Clubs: Quadrangular, University (Chgo.); Broadmoor Golf, Garden of the Gods (Colorado Springs). Home: 2110 Hercules Dr Colorado Springs CO 80906

OLSON, BRIAN CHARLES, fire protection engineer; b. Los Angeles, Nov. 1, 1947; s. Kenneth Alexander and Josephine Helen (Compton) O.; m. Jamie Ann Matt, Aug. 1, 1970; children: Robert, Jennifer, Matthew. BS in Engring., Calif. State U., 1970. Cert. safety profl. in comprehensive practice; profl. fire protection engr., Colo., Calif., Wyo., Oreg., Va., Tenn. Fire protection specialist M&M Protection Cons., Los Angeles, 1977-78; fire protection engr. Argonne Nat. Lab., Idaho Falls, Idaho, 1978-80, U.S. Dept. Energy, Denver, 1980-82, Rockwell Internat. Co., Denver, 1982-85; pres. FireMeasure, Inc., Westminster, Colo., 1985—. Served with U.S. Army, 1971-74. Mem. Nat. Fire Protection Assn., Soc. Fire Protection Engrs., Rocky Mountain chpt. Soc. Fire Protection Engrs. (founding pres. 1983-85), Internat. Conf. Bldg. Ofcls., Am. Soc. Safety Engrs. Republican. Presbyterian. Avocation: fly fishing. Home and Office: 9525 Flower St Westminster CO 80020-4364

OLSON, BURNEY LEE, interior designer, hotel administrator; b. Tacoma, Apr. 5, 1932; s. Ralph Greger and DeLoris E. (Bourdon) O.; m. Sally J. Potter, Aug. 24, 1956; children: Jeffrey, Greger, Liane. Student, Tacoma Vocat. Sch., 1950-51, U. Wash., 1957-59. Design engr. B.P. John Furniture Co., Portland, Oreg., 1958-70; gen. mgr. M&M Fixtures, Portland, 1970-73; project coordinator Red Lion Motor Inns, Vancouver, Wash., 1973-83; prodn. coordinator Alexander Mfg. Co., Portland, 1983-84; dir. design Raffles Hotels & Inns, Vancouver, 1985—. Served with USAF, 1952-56. Republican. Methodist. Avocation: golf. Office: Raffles Hotels & Inns 610 Esther St Vancouver WA 98660

OLSON, DAVID PETER, veterinarian, educator; b. Mpls., Sept. 28, 1935; s. John W. and Gladys Regina) Olson; m. Jane Marie Nieters, June 20, 1959; children: Dree Ann, Steven William, Alane Marie. BS, U. Minn., 1958, DVM, 1960; MS, Mich. State U., 1972, PhD, 1975. Gen. practice vet. medicine Worthington, Minn., 1960-69; instr. Mich. State U., East Lansing, 1969-75; assoc. prof. vet. medicine U. Idaho, Moscow, 1975-81, prof., 1981—; adj. grad. faculty Wash. State U., Pullman, 1980—; chmn. Coop. Western Region Research Commn., 1983; affiliate faculty U. Wash. Sch. Medicine, Seattle, 1984; vis. scientist U.S. NAS, Czechoslovakia, 1985. Host family Am. Field Service Exchange program, Moscow, 1981, 84. Mem. AAAS, N.Y. Acad. Sci., Am. Vet. Med. Assn., Sigma Xi, Gamma Sigma Delta. Home: 1402 Borah Ave Moscow ID 83843 Office: U Idaho Dept Vet Sci Moscow ID 83843

OLSON, DWIGHT CLARANCE, computer infosystems executive; b. Los Angeles, Apr. 18, 1943; s. Melvin F. and Mildred I. (Lund) O.; m. Lois E. Monson, May 29, 1965; children: Spencer, Jonathan. BS, Augsburg U., 1965, teaching cert., 1966. Programmer Sperry-Univac, St. Paul, Minn., 1966-68; product line mgr. Control Data Corp., Mpls. and San Diego, 1968-78; mgr. System Sci. Software, San Diego, 1968-79; dir. MAE Cons., San Diego, 1979-80; mgr. template Megatek, San Diego, 1980-83; v.p. Data Securities Internat., San Diego, 1983—; also bd. dirs. Patentee in field. Mem. Assn. Data Processing Service Orgns., Gamma Phi Omega. Lutheran. Avocations: stamps, woodworking, reading. Office: Data Securities Internat Inc 5703 Oberlin Dr San Diego CA 92121

OLSON, ENID CLARA THALMAN, former state official, educator; b. Richfield, Utah, Mar. 10, 1923; d. John Earl and Ida Arelia (Hansen) Thalman; m. Arnold Olson, Apr. 23, 1942 (div.); 1 son, Steven Arnold. B.S. in Psychology, U. Ariz., 1971, M.S. in Child Devel. and Family Relations, 1972. Cert. community coll. instr., Ariz.; cert. educator, counselor, supr., adminstrv. officer Calif. Extension agt. Coop. Extension Service, Tucson, 1975-76; health services surveyor II Ariz. Dept. Health Services, Phoenix, 1977-79; supr. counselling and case mgmt. City of Phoenix, 1980-82; state coordinator Expanded Food and Nutrition Edn. Program, Coop. Extension Service, U. Hawaii, 1982-84; social services supt. Dept. Social Services and Housing West Hawaii, 1984—. Chmn. grant rev. Santa Cruz County (Ariz.) Comprehensive Health Planning Council, 1972-74; co-chmn. Ariz. Human Resource Commn., 1977. Mem. Hawaii Nutrition Council, Hawaii UN Assn. (exec. bd.), Hawaii Home Econs. Assn., Psi Chi, Phi Theta Kappa, Kappa Delta Pi. Democrat. Unitarian Universalist. Club: Altrusa (pres., dir. Ambos Nogales, pres. Phoenix 1981-82, pres. Honolulu 1984-85).

OLSON, FERRON ALLRED, metallurgist, educator; b. Tooele, Utah, July 2, 1921; s. John Ernest and Harriet Cynthia (Allred) O.; m. Donna Lee Jefferies, Feb. 1, 1944; children: Kandace, Randall, Paul, Jeffery, Richard. BS, U. Utah, 1953, PhD, 1956. Consecrated Bishop Mormon Ch., 1962. Research chemist Shell Devel. Co., Salt Lake City, 1956-61; assoc. research prof. U. Utah, Salt Lake City, 1961-63, assoc. prof., 1963-68, chmn. dept mining, metall. and fuels engring., 1966-74, prof. dept. metallurgy and metall. engring., 1968—; cons. U.S. Bur. Mines, Salt Lake City, 1973-77, Ctr. for Investigation Mining and Metallurgy, Santiago, Chile, 1973-77, Aetna Life and Casualty Farmers Ins. Group, Salt Lake City; dir. U. Utah Minerals Inst., 1980—. Author: Collection of Short Stories, 1985; contbr. articles to profl. jours. Del. State Rep. Conv., Salt Lake City, 1964. Served with U.S. Army, 1943-46, PTO. Named Fulbright-Hayes lectr., Yugoslavia, 1974-75, Disting. prof. Fulbright-Hayes, Yugoslavia, 1980, Outstanding Metallurgy Instr. U. Utah, 1979-80, Disting. Speaker U. Belgrade-Bor, Yugoslavia, 1974. Mem. Am. Inst. Mining, Metall. and Petroleum Engrs. (chmn. Utah chpt. 1978-79), Am. Soc. Engring. Edn. (chmn. Minerals div. 1972-73), Am. Soc. Metals, Am. Bd. Engring. and Tech. (bd. dirs. 1975-82), Fulbright Alumni Assn. Republican. Club: Ensign Dinner (Salt Lake City) (pres. 1973-74). Avocations: cabin building, fiction writing, skiing, hunting. Home: 1862 Herbert Ave Salt Lake City UT 84108 Office: U Utah Dept Metallurgy 412 Browning Bldg Salt Lake City UT 84112

OLSON, GERALD THEODORE, ednl. cons.; b. Rockford, Ill., Mar. 10, 1928; s. Ernest Hjalmer and Irma Lena (Widgren) O.; B.S., U. San Francisco, 1953; M.A., San Francisco State U., 1960; M.Ed., U. So. Calif., 1964; Ph.D., U. Calif., Berkeley, 1974; m. Jean Vujovich, Aug. 28, 1949; children—Gerald Theodore, Kathleen Elaina Olson Groves, John Ernest, Carol Frances Olson Love. Counselor, tchr., dir. student activities Canyon High Sch., Castro Valley, Calif., 1964-70, also lectr. Calif. State U., Hayward, 1971-72 and instr. Chabot Coll., Hayward, 1964-73; cons. counseling and guidance Colo. Dept. Edn., Denver, 1973; cons. career, vocat. counseling and guidance, ednl. services group Los Angeles County Office of Supt. Schs., 1973—. Served with USMC, 1946-49, with Army Res. and Calif. Army N.G., 1950-81. Cert. secondary sch. teaching, secondary sch. adminstrn., gen. pupil personnel services, community coll., marriage, family and child counseling, Calif. Contbr. articles to profl. jours. NDEA scholar, 1963-64; NIMH trainee, 1971-72; decorated Meritorious Service medal USAR, 1981. Mem. Am. Psychol. Assn., Western Psychol. Assn., Calif. Career Edn. Assn. (pres. 1986-87), Calif. Assn. for Counseling and Devel. (editor Compass newsletter 1982-83, 86-87, pres. 1984-85), Calif. Assn. Measurement and Evaluation in Guidance (pres. 1981-82). Democrat. Home: 3366 Tempe Dr Huntington Beach CA 92649 Office: 9300 E Imperial Hwy Downey CA 90242-2890

OLSON, GLEN ROBERT, lawyer, researcher; b. Berkeley, Calif., Jan. 15, 1956; s. Elmer Henry and Pauline Elizabeth (Spiersch) Homo; m. Diane Frances Lake, Apr. 8, 1983. AB with distinction, U. Calif., Berkeley, 1978; JD cum laude, U. Calif., San Francisco, 1983. Bar: Calif. 1983, U.S. Dist. Ct. (no. Calif.) 1983, (ea. Calif.) 1984. Research atty. Supr. Ct. of Sonoma County, Santa Rosa, Calif., 1983-84; assoc. Kornblum, Kelly & Herlihy, San Francisco, 1984—. Asst. mng. editor Hastings Law Jour., U. Calif. San Francisco, 1982-83; contbr. articles to law jours. and profl. pubs. Recipient Am. Jurisprudence award Bancroft-Whitney, 1981. Mem. Calif. Young Lawyers' Assn., Barrister's Club, Calif. Bar Assn., San Francisco Bar Assn. Democrat. Episcopalian. Home: 3433 Guido St Oakland CA 94602 Office: Kornblum Kelly & Herlihy 445 Bush St 6th Fl San Francisco CA 94108

OLSON, JAMES WILLIAM PARK, architect; b. St. Louis, Oct. 6, 1940; s. Louis Garfield and Gladys Helen (Schuh) O.; m. Katherine Fovargue, June 11, 1971. BArch, U. Wash. Registered architect, Wash., Oreg., Calif. Ptnr. Olson/Sundberg Architects, Seattle; assoc. architect New Seattle Art Mus., 1986. Prin. works include Pike and Virginia Bldg. (AIA honor 1980), Fryberger Boat Bldg. (AIA citation 1981), Stewart Coffee Bldg. (AIA honor 1984), South Arcade Bldg. (AIA honor 1985). Bd. dirs. Ctr. Contemporary Art, Seattle, 1982—, Artist Trust, Seattle, 1986—, Henry Art Gallery, Seattle, 1986—; founding mem. Gang of 5 Urban Study Group, Seattle, 1983. Recipient Seattle Art award Seattle Arts Commn., 1983, Best Architect award Seattle Mag., 1985. Mem. AIA, Seattle Art Mus., Allied Arts, Mus. Modern Art (N.Y.C.). Avocation: art. Office: Olson/Sundberg Architects 101 Yesler #202 Seattle WA 98104

OLSON, KRISTEN ANNE, marketing executive; b. San Francisco, Aug. 21, 1949; d. Austin Carlen and Judith Anne (Zemer) O.; m. Mark Fowle, Apr. 22, 1984. BA in English, Stanford U., 1971, MBA, 1981; MAT in English, Harvard U., 1972. Cert. elem. and secondary tchr., Calif. Tchr. Fremont (Calif.) Unified Sch. Dist., 1973-78; market research adminstr. Synertek, Santa Clara, Calif., 1978-81; product mgr. Apple Computer, Cupertino, Calif., 1981-84; dir. mktg. Ansa Software, Belmont, Calif., 1984—. Mem. Stanford Bus. Sch. Alumni Assn. (past chmn. new enterprise forum com.). Democrat. Office: Ansa Software 1301 Shoreway Rd Belmont CA 94002

OLSON, MARK EDWARD, engineer; b. Salt Lake City, Aug. 13, 1957; s. Norman A. and Marilyn Ann (Mathis) O. B.S. in Material Sci. and Engring., U. Utah, 1980; M.B.A., Brigham Young U., 1982. Research asst. U. Utah, Salt Lake City, 1979-80; engr. Aerospace div. Hercules, Inc., Magna, Utah, 1981, proposal adminstr., 1982-84, cost contract negotiator and lead proposal adminstr. for Trident II program, 1983-84, implementation mgr. composite structures, 1984-85, quality circle leader, 1984, bus. mgr. Small ICBM, 1985-86; sr. bus. research analyst Hercules Aerospace Products Group, 1986—. Missionary rep. Mormon Ch., Brisbane, Australia, 1976-78, young adult chmn., Salt Lake City, 1978, 79, missionary preparation coordinator, 1979, 80, pres. elders quorom, 1983-84, bishophric, 1985. Dean's scholar U. Utah Coll. Engring., 1979. Mem. Assn. M.B.A. Execs., Tau Beta Pi. Republican. Home: 1140 E 4420 S Salt Lake City UT 84124 Office: Hercules Aerospace Products Group PO Box 30181 Salt Lake City UT 84130

OLSON, RICHARD DEAN, pharmacology educator; b. Rupert, Idaho, June 22, 1949; s. Emerson J. and Thelma Maxine (Short) O.; m. Carol Ann Dyba, Jan. 5, 1974; children: Stephan Jay, David Richard, Jonathan Philip. BS, Coll. Idaho, 1971; postgrad., Idaho State U., 1972-74; PhD, Vanderbilt U., 1978. Instr. Vanderbilt U., Nashville, 1980-81, asst. prof., 1982, head pediatric clin. pharmacology unit, 1982—; asst. prof. U. S. Ala., Mobile, 1982-83; acting asst. prof. U. Wash., Seattle, 1984-85, research assoc. prof., 1985—; chief cardiovascular pharmacology research VA Med. Ctr., Boise, Idaho, 1984—; hon. dir. cardiovascular research lab. Capital Inst. Medicine, Beijing, Peoples Republic of China, 1986; investigator Am. Heart Assn., Nashville, 1981, NIH, Mobile, 1982. Contbr. articles to profl. jours. Pres. Fellowship Crusade for Christ, Inc., Nampa, Idaho, 1986. Grantee Am. Heart Assn., 1981, 83, 84, 86, Am. Fedn. Aging Research, Inc., Boise, 1985; VA Merit Review grantee, 1985; NIH trainee, 1975-78; NIH fellow, Am. Fedn. Aging Research, Inc. 1985—, U. Colo., Denver, 1978-80. Mem. AAAS, N.Y. Acad. Scis., Am. Soc. Pharmacology and Exptl. Therapeutics, Am. Heart Assn., Am. Fedn. for Clin. Research, Sigma Xi. Avocations: camping, radio-controlled model airplanes. Home: 425 N Benewah Nampa ID 83651 Office: VA Med Ctr #151 500 W Fort St Boise ID 83702

OLSON, ROBERT HOWARD, lawyer; b. Indpls., July 6, 1944; s. Robert Howard and Jacquline (Wells) O.; m. Diane Carol Thorsen, Aug. 13, 1966; children—Jeffrey, Christopher. BA in Govt. summa cum laude, Ind. U., 1966; JD cum laude, Harvard U., 1969. Bar: Ohio 1969, Fla. 1980, U.S. Dist. Ct. (no. dist.) Ohio 1970, U.S. Dist. Ct. (no. Dist.) Ind. 1970, U.S. Dist. Ct. (so. Dist.) Ohio 1971, U.S. Supreme Ct. 1973, Ariz. 1985. Assoc. Squire, Sanders & Dempsey, Cleve., 1969, 70-71, 76-81, ptnr., 1981—, ptnr., Phoenix, 1985—; sr. law clk. U.S. Dist. Ct., No. Dist. Ind. 1969-70; chief civil rights div. Ohio Atty. Gen.'s Office, Columbus, 1971-73, chief consumer protection, 1973-75, chief counsel, 1975, 1st asst. (chief of staff), 1975-76; instr. Law Sch., Ohio State U., Columbus, 1974. Author monograph on financing infrastructure, 1983; also law rev. articles on civil rights, consumer protection. Treas. Alfred for Mayor Campaign, Shaker Heights, Ohio, 1983; bd. dirs. 1st Unitarian Ch. Phoenix. Mem. Greater Cleve. Bar Assn. (sec. health law sect. 1984), Am. Acad. Hosp. Attys., Ariz. State Bar Assn., Phi Beta Kappa. Democrat. Home: 5201 E Paradise Dr Scottsdale AZ 85254 Office: 201 N Central Ave Suite 2200 Phoenix AZ 85073

OLSON, THOMAS EDWARD, wildlife biologist; b. Santa Monica, Calif., Dec. 11, 1954; s. Carl Peter and Kathryn Evelyn (Guerin) O.; m. Susan Celeste Tolerton, Dec. 18, 1976 (div. 1981); m. Grace Marie Geer, Feb. 21, 1987. BS in Natural Resources Mgmt., Calif. Poly. State U., San Luis Obispo, 1977; MS in Wildlife Biology, Colo. State U., 1980. Cert. wildlife biologist. Wildlife technician Colo. Div. Wildlife, Ft. Collins, 1980-81, 82-83; research assoc. Colo. State U., Ft. Collins, 1981-82, 83-84; biol. technician. U.S. Fish and Wildlife Service, Ft. Collins, 1982-84; environ. scientist Dames and Moore Cons., Santa Barbara, Calif., 1985—. Contbr. articles to profl. jours.; referee Jour. Wildlife Mgmt., Fort Collins, 1980-82. U.S. Fish and Wildlife Service grantee, 1978-80. Mem. Am. Ornithologists Union, Wilson Ornithol. Soc., The Wildlife Soc. (cert. wildlife biologist), Nature Conservancy, Colo. Wildlife Fedn., Sigma Xi, Phi Kappa Phi. Democrat. Avocations: birdwatching, hiking, writing, basketball. Office: Dames and Moore 222 East Anapamu St Santa Barbara CA 93101-2074

OLSON, WILLIAM HERBERT, physician, administrator; b. Sioux City, Dec. 3, 1925; s. Victor L. and Leona (Hewitt) O.; m. LuEtta Brunn, Sept. 4, 1949; children—Daniel John, Susan Louise. B.A., Sioux Falls Coll., 1949; M.D., State U. Iowa, 1953. Diplomate Am. Bd. Internal Medicine, Am. Bd. Nuclear Medicine. Resident in internal medicine Seaside Meml. Hosp., Long Beach, Calif., 1954-55, Long Beach VA Hosp., 1955-57; practice medicine specializing in internal medicine, Long Beach, 1958-67; dir. dept. nuclear medicine Long Beach Community Hosp., 1967—, chief of staff, 1985-87; cons. nuclear medicine Long Beach VA Hosp., 1958-72; clin. instr. medicine U. Calif.-Irvine, 1962—. Contbr. articles to profl. jours. Ruling elder Covenant Presbyn. Ch., Orange, Calif., 1981. Served with USAF, 1944-46. Fellow ACP.; mem. Long Beach Soc. Internal Medicine (pres. 1967). Republican. Home: 4609-8 Via La Paloma Orange CA 92669 Office: Long Beach Community Hosp 1720 Termino Ave Long Beach CA 90804

OLSON, WILLIAM THOMAS, educator; b. Coeur d'Alene, Idaho, May 1, 1940; s. William Anthony and Julia Glenn (Hunter) O.; B.A., U. N.Mex., 1968; postgrad. U. Va., 1968-72; m. Diana Jean Dodds, Aug. 22, 1962; children—Kristin Ann (dec.), Kira Lynn. Intelligence agt. U.S. Army, 1962-65; asso. editor Newspaper Printing Corp., Albuquerque, 1965-66; news and pub. affairs dir. KUNM-FM, U. N.M., 1966-68; news person KOAT-TV, Albuquerque, 1968; news dir. WCHV Radio, Charlottesville, Va., 1968-69; moderator, producer Radio-TV Center, U. Va., 1969-73; columnist The Jefferson Jour., Charlottesville, Va., 1972; instr. history U. Va., 1971-73; information specialist Wash. State U. Cooperative Ext. Service, Pullman, 1973-77, instr. Sch. Communications, 1976-77, asst. program dir., info. officer Wash. Energy Ext. Service, 1977-79; dir. Spokane County Head Start, 1979-84; adminstr. Community Colls. of Spokane, 1984—; cons. United Indians of All Tribes Found., 1980—. Dir., Ryegrass Sch., Spokane, 1978—. Bd. dirs. Charlottesville-Albemarle Mental Health Assn., 1969-72; bd. dirs. Charlottesville-Albemarle chpt. ACLU, 1969-71, Spokane chpt., 1983—; mem. adv. bd. Spokane Pub. Radio, 1983—; pres. Charlottesville-Albemarle Human Relations Council, 1970-71; chairperson Pullman area chpt. ACLU, 1976-79, chmn., 1976-78; dir. Connoisseur Concerts Assn., 1983-86, pres. 1985-86; dir. West Cen. Community Devel. Assn., pres., 1985-86; dir. Spokane Community Ctrs. Found., 1986—. Served with AUS, 1962-65. Mem. Nat. Council for Resource Devel., Nat. Head Start Dirs. Assn. (region V steering com. chmn. 1981-82, regional sec. 1980). Author TV documentary (with Ken Fielding): The Golden Years?, 1973; film (with B. Dale Harrison and Lorraine Kingdon) New Directions Out of the Culture of Poverty, 1974. Home: E 2018 14th Ave Spokane WA 99202 Office: Inst for Extended Learning W 3305 Ft George Wright Dr MS 3090 Spokane WA 99204

OLSTAD, ROGER GALE, educator; b. Mpls., Jan. 16, 1934; s. Arnold William and Myra (Stroschein) O.; m. Constance Elizabeth Jackson, Aug. 20, 1955; children: Karen Louise, Kenneth Bradley. B.S., U. Minn., 1955, M.A., 1959, Ph.D., 1963. Instr., U. Minn., Mpls., 1956-63; asst. prof. U. Ill., Urbana, 1963-64; mem. faculty U. Wash., Seattle, 1964—; asso. prof. sci. edn. U. Wash., 1967-71, prof., 1971—, asso. dean grad. studies Coll. Edn., 1969-81. Fellow AAAS; mem. Nat. Sci. Tchrs. Assn. (dir.), Wash. Sci. Tchrs. Assn. (pres. 1973-74), Nat. Assn. Research Sci. Teaching (pres. 1977-78, dir.), N.W. Sci. Assn. (chmn. 1966-68), Assn. Edn. Tchrs. in Sci. (regional pres. 1966-68), Nat. Assn. Biology Tchrs., Phi Delta Kappa. Club: U. Wash. Faculty. Home: 20143 53d Ave NE Seattle WA 98155 Office: U Wash Coll of Edn Seattle WA 98195

OLUM, PAUL, mathematician, univ. pres.; b. Binghamton, N.Y., Aug. 16, 1918; s. Jacob and Rose (Citlen) O.; m. Vivian Goldstein, June 8, 1942; children—Judith Ann, Joyce Margaret, Kenneth Daniel. A.B. summa cum laude, Harvard, 1940, Ph.D. (NRC predoctoral fellow 1946-47), 1947; M.A., Princeton, 1942. Theoretical physicist Manhattan Project, Princeton, 1941-42, Los Alamos Sci. Lab., 1943-45; Frank B. Jewett postdoctoral fellow Harvard, 1947-48, Inst. Advanced Study, 1948-49; mem. faculty Cornell U., Ithaca, N.Y., 1949-74; prof. math. Cornell U., 1957-74, chmn. dept., 1963-66, trustee, 1971-75; prof. math., dean Coll. Natural Scis. U. Tex. at Austin, 1974-76; prof. math., v.p. for acad. affairs, provost U. Oreg., Eugene, 1976-80; acting pres. U. Oreg., 1980-81, pres., 1981—; mem. Inst. Advanced Study, 1955-56; on leave at U. Paris (France) and Hebrew U., Jerusalem, 1962-63; vis. prof. U. Wash., 1970-71. Author monograph, research articles on algebraic topology. Mem. adv. com. Office Ordnance Research, NRC, 1958-61. NSF fellow Stanford, 1966-67. Mem. Am. Math. Soc., AAUP, Math Assn. Am., Phi Beta Kappa, Sigma Xi. Office: Office of Pres U Oreg Eugene OR 97403

O'MALLEY, PETER, professional baseball club executive; b. N.Y.C., Dec. 12, 1937; s. Walter F. and Kay (Hanson) O'M.; m. Annette Zacho, July 10, 1971; children—Katherine, Kevin, Brian. B.S. in Econs, U. Pa., 1960. Dir. Dodgertown, Vero Beach, Fla., 1962-64; pres., gen. mgr. Spokane Baseball Club, 1965-66; v.p. Los Angeles Dodgers Baseball Club, 1967-68, exec. v.p., from 1968; pres. Los Angeles Dodgers, Inc., 1970—. Bd. dirs. Los Angeles Police Meml. Found.; vice chmn. bd. govs. Los Angeles Music Center Performing Arts Council; trustee Little League Found., Washington, Knudsen Found., Los Angeles. Address: Los Angeles Dodgers 1000 Elysian Park Ave Los Angeles CA 90012 Office: Dodger Stadium Los Angeles CA 90012

O'MALLEY, TIMOTHY JOHN, broadcasting executive; b. Berkeley, Calif., Jan. 29, 1951; s. John Thomas and Mary (Madigan) O'M. Pres. OMPC Prodn. Co., Richmond, Calif., 1968-73, news dir., 1973; pres. Corp. Community Radio, Richmond, 1969-73, OMPC Wireless Broadcast Co., Inc., Richmond, 1979-81; founder, news anchor, producer NGN Radio Network, 1981-86; chief exec. officer, news anchor, producer, dir. Am. Cities Radio Network, 1986—; lectr. mass communications, cons., sr. systems analyst Bank of Am., Blue Cross of Calif., Firemans Fund Ins. Co. Irish tenor; (albums) What Have I, Searching, Love is the Thing; producer 2 gold records; producer, singing host The Radio Village Broadcasts. Mem. Nat. Assn. Broadcasters (plaque), NorCal Radio/TV News Dirs. Assn. Democrat. Roman Catholic. Home: 2422 Branchwood Ct Richmond CA 94806 Office: PO Box 29341 Oakland CA 94604

O'MEARA, MARCIAN THOMAS, priest; b. Denison, Iowa, Mar. 4, 1929; s. Clarence Joseph and Elizabeth Ruth (Hassett) O'M. B.A., Conception Sem., 1954, M.A., 1959. Ordained priest, Roman Cath. Ch., 1959; prior St. Pius X Priory, Pevely, Mo., 1969, abbot, 1972-77; chaplain dir. St. Anthony Hosp., Denver, 1977-83; dir. Permanent Diaconate, Archdiocese of Denver, 1981-86, dir. Formation for Seminarians, dir. vocations, 1983-85. Vicar for

Religious 1985—, vicar for Ppermanent Deacons, 1986—; liaison for Cursillo Movement, 1986—. Democrat. Address: 200 Josephine St Denver CO 80206

OMHOLT, BRUCE DONALD, product designer, mechanical engineer, consultant; b. Salem, Oreg., Mar. 27, 1943; s. Donald Carl and Violet Mae (Buck) O.; m. Mavis Aronow, Aug. 18, 1963 (div. July 1972); children—Madison, Natalie; m. 2d, Darla Kay Faber, Oct. 27, 1972; 1 son, Cassidy. B.S.M.E., Heald Coll. Engring., San Francisco, 1964. Real estate salesman R. Lea Ward and Assocs., San Francisco, 1962-64; sales engr. Repco Engring., Montebello, Calif., 1964; in various mfg. engring. and mgmt. positions Ford Motor Co., Rawsonville, Saline, Owosso and Ypsilanti, Mich., 1964-75; chief engr. E. F. Hauserman Co., Cleve., 1975-77; dir. design and engring. Am. Seating Co., Grand Rapids, Mich., 1977-80; pres. Trinity Engring., Grand Rapids, Mich., 1980-81, Rohnert Park, Calif., 1981—; 1986 U.S. Patent For Vertical Mitre Machine; cons. mfg. U.S., fgn. patentee carrier rack apparatus, motorcycle improvements, panels.

OMURA, JIMMY KAZUHIRO, electrical engineer; b. San Jose, Calif., Sept. 8, 1940; s. Shomatsu and Shizuko Dorothy (Takesaka) O. B.S., MIT, 1963, M.S., 1963; Ph.D. (NSF fellow 1963-66), Stanford U., 1966. Research engr. Stanford Research Inst., 1966-69; mem. faculty UCLA, 1969—, prof. elec. engring., 1977-83; founder, chmn. bd. Cylink Corp., Sunnyvale, Calif., 1983—; cons. to industry and govt.; founder CYLINK, 1984. Co-author: Principles of Digital Communication and Coding, 1979, Spread Spectrum Communications, Vols. I, II, III, 1985; contbr. articles profl. jours. NSF grantee, 1970-78. Fellow IEEE (info. theory group). Office: Cylink Corp 920 W Fremont Ave Sunnyvale CA 94087

ONDREJKA, ARTHUR RICHARD, electrical engineer; b. N.Y.C., Mar. 20, 1934; s. Joseph and Mary (Malik) O.; student Manhattan Coll., 1952-54; B.A., U. Colo., 1962, M.S. in E.E., 1973; m. Delores Ione Anderson, June 17, 1959; children—Therese Marie, Richard Joseph, Juli Ann. With Nat. Bur. Standards, Boulder, Colo., 1959—, project leader power sect., 1966-74, project leader time domain metrology sect., electromagnetic interference group, 1983-86. Served with USAF, 1955-59. Mem. Sigma Xi. Roman Catholic. Patentee standard for measurement of short duration microwave power. Research in temporal characteristics of high speed laser phenomena, precision measurement of EM interference. Home: 67 Anemone Dr Boulder CO 80302 Office: 325 Broadway Boulder CO 80302

O'NEAL, GARY STUART, federal agency administrator; b. Los Angeles, Sept. 14, 1938; s. Rudy L. Schlank and Ruth Lilian (Parker) O'Neal; m. Kathleen Ann McClary, June 14, 1966; children: Jennifer, Brian, Seth, Olga. BSBA, U. Calif., Berkeley, 1960; MA in Internat. Studies, U. Oreg., 1967. Mgmt. intern U.S. Dept. Commerce, Washington, 1967-68; field rep. OEO, Washington, 1968-70; sr. field rep. OEO, Seattle, 1970-71; coordinator VISTA ACTION, Seattle, 1971-74; dir. Peace Corps ACTION, San José, Costa Rica, 1974-77; state dir. ACTION, Salt Lake City, 1977—; pres. real estate co. O'Neal & Schlank Assocs., Salt Lake City, 1984—. Co-author; The United Nations, 1966. Pres. Utah Issues Governing Bd., Salt Lake City, 1985; v.p. Greater Salt Lake YMCA, 1983-86; mem. Gov.'s Adv. Council on Aging, 1983-85. Served to lt. USMCR, 1960-62. Recipient Dedication and Commitment award Greater Salt Lake YMCA, 1985. Mem. Fed. Execs. Assn., Utah Area Assn. Dirs. of Vols., Amnesty Internat., Sierra Club. Democrat. Avocations: fishing, river running, soccer referee, designing solar water heaters. Home: 768 2d Ave Salt Lake City UT 84103 Office: Utah State Office ACTION 350 S Main St Suite 484 Salt Lake City UT 84101

O'NEIL, JAMES JOSEPH, oil company executive; b. Youngstown, Ohio, Oct. 1, 1938; s. James Joseph and Alice (Duckett) O'N.; m. Marie Smith, 1960; children: Shaune, Gareth. BS, SUNY, Albany, 1986. Cert. class IV water/wastewater ops., Alaska. Chief operator U.S. Civil Service, Eielser AFB, 1973-76; mgr. wastewater dept. City of Fairbanks, Alaska, 1976-80; environ. cons. Fairbanks, 1980—; water utilities supr. Standard Alaska Petroleum Co., Prudhoe Bay, Alaska, 1980—. Mem. Water Pollution Control Fedn. (bd. dirs. 1978-81), Am. Water Works Assn., Alaska Water Mgmt. Assn. (pres. 1975-76), AAAS. Avocations: photography, hunting, fishing, computer programming. Home: PO Box 55591 North Pole AK 99705

O'NEIL, MICHAEL JOSEPH, opinion survey executive; b. Springfield, Mass., June 22, 1951; s. James Francis and Mary Helen (Apolis) O'N.; m. Catherine Mary Zirkel, Sept. 10, 1983; 1 child, Heather Rose. BA, Brown U., 1974, MA, 1975; PhD, Northwestern U., 1977. Mem. faculty U. Ill., Chgo., 1977; mem. faculty U. Mich., Ann Arbor, 1977-79, postdoctoral fellow Inst. Social Research, 1977-79; dir. Pub. Opinion Research Ctr., Ariz. State U., Tempe, 1979-81; pres. O'Neil Assocs., Tempe, 1981—; reviewer grant proposals NSF, Washington, 1977—. Manuscript reviewer Social Problems, 1977—, Pub. Opinion Quarterly, 1977—, Urban Affairs Quarterly, 1977—; contbr. articles to profl. jours. Chmn. Tempe Union High Sch. Dist. Bus. Edn. adv. com., 1986; mem. mktg. com. Mesa Assn. Retarded Citizens, 1985—; bd. dirs. Tri-City Community Behavioral Health Ctr., Mesa, 1985—. Mem. Am. Mktg. Assn., Am. Assn. Pub. Opinion Research, Alumni Assn. Brown U. (bd. dirs. 1985—), Phi Beta Kappa. Democrat. Club: Brown U. of Phoenix (pres. 1984—), Phoenix City (bd. dirs.). Avocation: tennis. Home: 418 E Erie Dr Tempe AZ 85282 Office: O'Neil Assocs 412 E Southern Tempe AZ 85282

O'NEILL, DAVID EDWARD, university infosystems administrator; b. Missoula, Mont., Oct. 28, 1950; s. Robert Winston and Audrey (Fialka) O'Neill; m. Barbara Bruce, Dec. 25, 1972; children: Sami, Andrew. BS in Forest Mgmt., Wash. State U., 1973, MA in Agrl. Econs., 1983; MBA, U. Mont., 1979. Forester Weyerhaeuser, Tacoma, 1972; research asst. Agrl. Econs. Dept., Pullman, Wash., 1979-81; acct. Coop Extension, Pullman, 1981; procedures analyst Wash. State U., Pullman, 1981-83, univ. adminstr., 1983—, mgmt. infosystem coordinator, v.p., 1983—; resource cons., Palouse, Wash., 1979—. Contbr. articles to profl. jours. Scout leader Boy Scouts Am., Palouse, 1979—; mem. city counsel, Palouse, 1983—; chmn. Palouse Community Float Royalty, 1985—. Served to 1st lt. USMC, 1972-76. Recipient Order of the Arrow, Boy Scouts Am., Spokane, 1964; named Eagle Scout, 1965. Republican. Home: PO Box 293 Palouse WA 99164-0293 Office: Wash State U Pullman WA 99164

O'NEILL, DENNIS VINCENT, architect, computer software consultant; b. Newark, Dec. 21, 1942; s. Raymond V. and Grace O'N.; B.Arch., N.D. State U., 1967; M.Arch., U. Calif.-Berkeley, 1968. Partner, Ishimaru & O'Neill, Architects, Oakland, Calif., 1972-80; owner, mgr. O'Neill Software, San Francisco, 1980—; computer software cons. Mem. Assn. Computing Machinery, IEEE Computer Soc., Mensa. Office: 440 Davis Ct Suite 1822 San Francisco CA 94111

O'NEILL, MICHAEL FOY, business educator; b. Milw., Apr. 16, 1943; s. Edward James and Marcellian (Wesley) O'N.; m. Karen Lynn Shoots, June 13, 1968; children: Kristine, Brenna. BBA, Ohio State U., 1966; PhD in Bus. Adminstrn., U. Oreg., 1978. Cons. Robert E. Miller and Assocs., San Francisco, 1969-73; mem. faculty Calif. State U., Chico, 1971-73, 1980—, U. Oreg., Eugene, 1974-77, U. Ariz., Tucson, 1977-79; pres. Mktg. Research Data Inc., Chico, Decision Sci. Inst., Atlanta, 1986—, v.p., 1985-86. Contbr. articles to profl. jours. Served with U.S. Army, 1962-68. Recipient Dean's Research award Calif. State U., Chico, 1981. Avocations: golf, fly fishing. Home: 2819 North Ave Chico CA 95926 Office: Calif State U Dept Fin and Mktg Chico CA 95926

O'NEILL, NORAH ELLEN, airline pilot; b. Seattle, Aug. 23, 1949; d. John Wilson and Bertha Ellen (Moore) O'N.; m. Scott Reynolds, Jan. 31, 1970 (div. Apr. 1973); m. Scott Edward Byerley, Jan. 29, 1983; children: Cameron, Bren Maxey. Student, U. Calif., Santa Barbara, 1967-68, San Diego State U., 1868-70; BS in Profl. Aeros., Embry-Riddle Aero. U. Lic. airline transport pilot (comml., instrument instr.). Flight instr. Reynolds Aviation, Anchorage, 1973; flight instr. Alaska Cen. Air, Fairbanks, 1973-74, mail, commuter, medivac pilot, 1974-76; DC-8 pilot Flying Tigers, Los Angeles, Seattle, N.Y.C., 1976-80; 747 pilot Flying Tigers, Los Angeles, 1980—. Mem. Airline Pilots Assn., Women Airline Pilots Soc. (co-founder 1978, v.p. 1979-80), The 99's (hon.). Avocations: writing, skiing, racquetball. First woman to commercially fly the DC-8, 1977, the 747, 1980. Home: PO Box 1504 Walla Walla WA 99362 Office: Flying Tigers 7401 World Way West Los Angeles CA 90009

O'NEILL, SALLIE BOYD, educator, business owner; b. Ft. Lauderdale, Fla., Feb. 17, 1926; d. Howard Prindle and Sarah Frances (Clark) Boyd; A.A., Stephens Coll., 1945; m. Roger H. Noden, July 8, 1945; children—Stephanie Ann Ballard, Ross Hopkins Noden; m. 2d, Russell R. O'Neill, June 30, 1967. Course coordinator UCLA Extension, 1960-72, specialist continuing edn. dept. human devel., 1972-83; pres. Learning Adventures, a Calif. Corp., 1983-85; v.p., chief fin. officer The Learning Network, Inc., 1985-86; ptnr. The Prin. Investment Group, 1986—; ednl. cons. HEW Women's Edn. Equity grantee, 1976-77. Mem. Nat. Univ. Extension Assn. UCLA Assn. Acad. Women, NOW, Learning Resources Network. Home: 15430 Longbow Dr Sherman Oaks CA 91403 Office: 520 S Sepulveda Los Angeles CA 90024

O'NEILL, TIMOTHY HUGH, sales professional; b. Portland, Oreg., Feb. 15, 1948; s. Hugh Collins and Jo Ann (Smith) O'N.; m. Joyce Ann Boehm, Oct. 4, 1980; 1 child, Jeffrey Collins. Student, U. Calif., Santa Barbara, 1966-68; B in Engring., UCLA, 1970, postgrad., 1970. Sales rep. Johnson & JOhnson Co., Denver, 1971-72, San Diego, 1972-76; sales rep. Baxter Travenol Labs., Inc., San Diego, 1976-83, dist. sales mgr., 1983—. Mem. Am. Soc. Hosp. Pharmacists, San Diego Forum (pres. 1979-80). Republican. Episcopalian. Avocations: skiing, golfing, camping, readinng.

ONG, JAMES MON, insurance company executive; b. San Francisco, June 9, 1934; s. Chester and Lee Ong; children: Jonathan, Jeffery. BA, Occidental Coll., 1956. Prin. Ong Assocs., Oakland, Calif., 1958—. Contbr. articles to profl. jours. Treas. Oakland Chinese Presbyn. Ch., 1959—. Served with USN, 1956-58. Recipient Silver Beaver award Boy Scouts Am., 1975. Mem. Nat. Soc. Pub. Accts., East Bay San Francisco Assn. Enrolled Agts. (past pres. 1981), Nat. Assn. Enrolled Agts. (bd. dirs. 1983-85), Calif. Soc. Enrolled Agts. (Sacramento bd. dirs. 1979), Ind. Ins. Agts. and Brokers Assn. Calif. (bd. dirs. 1975-78), Oakland Chinatown C. of C. (founding dir. 1985). Republican. Lodge: Kiwanis (pres. Oakland chpt. 1971). Avocations: fishing, camping. Office: Ong Assocs 701 Franklin St Oakland CA 94607

ONGARO, MARIO PETER, priest; b. Verona, Italy, Apr. 7, 1926; came to U.S., 1947; s. Giuseppe and Giulia (Bonfante) O. BA, Athenaeum of Ohio, 1951; MA, Xavier U., 1961; MLS, U. Mich., 1964. Ordained priest Roman Cath. Ch., 1951; lic. psychologist, Ohio. Pastoral ministry Pala Indians, San Diego, 1956-58; instr. classics Sacred Heart Sem., Monroe, Mich., 1952-56, instr. philosophy classics, 1961-64; instr. classics Sacred Heart Sem., Cin., 1958-61, sch. counselor, 1964-68; adminstr. Comboni Mission Ctr., Cin., 1968-83; psychologist, educator Casa Comboni, Los Angeles, 1983—; mem. com. re-writing constitutions Comboni Missionaries, Rome, 1976-79, provincial counselor, 1979-84. Mem. Am. Psychol. Assn., Ohio Psychol. Assn., Am. Orthopsychiat. Assn., Soc. Personality Assessment. Home and Office: 1301 W 41st Pl Los Angeles CA 90037

ONISHI, YASUO, hydraulic researcher; b. Osaka, Japan, Jan. 25, 1943; came to U.S., 1969; s. Osamu and Tokiko (Domukai) O.; m. Esther Anna Stronczek, Jan 22, 1972; children: Anna Tokiko and Lisa Michiyo. BS, U. Osaka Prefecture, 1967, MS, 1969; PhD, U. Iowa, 1972. Research engr. U. Iowa, Iowa City, 1972-74; sr. research engr. Battelle Meml. Inst., Richland, Wash., 1974-77, staff engr., 1977—, mgr. research program office, 1984—. Co-author: Principles of Health Risk Assessment, 1985; contbr. articles to profl. jours. Recipient Best Platform Presentation award ASTM, 1979. Mem. ASCE (chmn. task com. 1986—), Internat. Assn. Hydraulic Research, Nat. Council Radiation Protection and Measurements (task com. 1983—), Sigma Xi. Lutheran. Avocations: camping, skiing. Home: 144 Spengler Rd Richland WA 99352 Office: Battelle Pacific NW Labs Batelle Blvd Richland WA 99352

ONO, BRYAN KEITH, product design engineer; b. San Francisco, Sept. 1, 1956; s. Dan Den and Misako (Maruyama) O. BSME, UCLA, 1980. Product engr. Teledyne Laars, North Hollywood, Calif., 1981-84; sr. design engr. Mattel Toys, Hawthorne, Calif., 1984-86; project engr. Wham-O, San Gabriel, Calif., 1986—. Patentee in field. Buddhist. Avocations: sports, magic, audiophile stereos, automobiles. Home: 1733 Centinela Ave #2 Santa Monica CA 90404 Office: Wham-O Inc 835 E El Monte St San Gabriel CA 91778

ONO, KENNETH TAKAO, hospital administrator; b. Hilo, Hawaii, May 3, 1950; s. Takeo and Sueko Ono; m. Delta H., May 16, 1976; children: Michelle, Julie. BBA, U. Hawaii, 1972; MHA, Duke U., 1976. Exec. dir. South Bay Hosp., Redondo Beach, Calif. Active Redondo Beach Bus. Roundtable, 1985—. Named Young Man of Yr. Redondo Beach Jaycees, 1985. Mem. Am. Coll. Healthcare Execs., Healthcare Fin. Mgmt., Calif. Hosp. Assn. (membership com.), Hosp. Assn. of Hawaii (bd. dirs. 1980-81). Home: 30129 Via Victoria Rancho Palos Verdes CA 90274 Office: South Bay Hosp 514 N Prospect Redondo Beach CA 90277

ONO, YOSHIHIKO, computer software company executive; b. Okayama, Japan, May 6, 1955; came to U.S., 1980; s. Norihiko and Teruko (Hosokawa) O. Diploma in Computer Sci., Fujitsu Inst., Tokyo, 1978. Sr. systems programmer NEC Corp., Tokyo, 1976-79; cons. Sumisho Computer, Tokyo, 1979-80; sr. programmer, analyst PennCorp., Santa Monica, Calif., 1981-82; cons. Todd Pacific Ship, San Pedro, Calif., 1983-84, Redken Labs., Canoga Park, Calif., 1984; ltd. ptnr. Meadows Cellular Communications, Tucson, 1983—; assoc. Marina Info. Systems, Marina del Ray, Calif., 1983-85; owner, pres. Celembest Internat. Mgmt., Los Angeles, 1982—, Celembest Publ., Los Angeles, 1984—. Republican. Buddhist. Office: Celembest Internat Mgmt PO Box 25309 Los Angeles CA 90025

ONSKT, NANCY RAE, systems engineer; b. Findlay, Ohio, Apr. 17, 1939; d. Raymond E. and Bonita M. (Leary) O. Student U. Toledo, 1966, Owens Tech. Coll., 1972. Order entry supr. Four-Phase, Cupertino, Calif., 1974-76; mgr. mktg. systems, Fairchild, San Jose, Calif., 1976-81; sr. product mgr. Savin, Sunnyvale, Calif., 1981-82; MIS mgr. Inmac Corp., Santa Clara, Calif., 1982-85; system engr. Hewlett-Packard, Santa Clara, 1985—; systems cons. System Application Computer Services, Santa Clara, 1976—. Mem. NOW, Assn. System Mgmt., Summit Orgn., Women's Found., Women's Entrepreneur Assn. Democrat. Roman Catholic. Home: 2404 Golf Links Circle Santa Clara CA 95050

ONSTOTT, EDWARD IRVIN, research chemist; b. Moreland, Ky., Nov. 12, 1922; s. Carl Ervin and Jennie Lee (Foley) O.; m. Mary Margaret Smith, Feb. 6, 1945; children—Jenifer, Peggy Sue, Nicholas, Joseph. B.S. in Chem. Engring., U. Ill., 1944, M.S. in Chemistry, 1948, Ph.D. in Inorganic Chemistry, 1950. Chem. engr. Firestone Tire & Rubber Co., Paterson, N.J., 1944, 46; research chemist Los Alamos Nat. Lab., 1950—. Patentee in field. Served with C.E., AUS, 1944-46. Fellow AAAS, Am. Inst. Chemists; mem. Am. Chem. Soc., Electrochem. Soc., N.Y. Acad. Scis., Internat. Assn. Hydrogen Energy, Rare Earth Research Confs., Izaak Walton League. Republican. Methodist. Home: 225 Rio Bravo Los Alamos NM 87544 Office: Los Alamos Nat Lab MS G738 Los Alamos NM 87545

OONK, RODNEY LEE, aerospace engineer; b. Sheboygan, Wis., June 10, 1951. BS in Mech. Engring., U. Wis., 1973, MS in mech engring., 1975. Registered profl. engr., Colo. Devel. engr. Solaron Corp., Denver, 1975-79; sr. engr. Beech Aircraft Corp., Boulder, Colo., 1979-83, Ball Aerospace Systems Div., Boulder, 1983—. Author tech. papers and reports. Avocations: skiing, racquetball, softball. Office: Ball Aerospace Systems Div PO Box 1062 Commerce & Arapahoe Boulder CO 80306

OPFELL, JOHN BURTON, chemical engineer, educator; b. Cushing, Okla., July 24, 1924; s. Edward Uriah and Carrie Evelyn (Walker) O.; m. Olga Anna Strandvold, Sept. 10, 1954; children: Christopher Kaj, Thane Fredrick, Jon Guido. BS, U. Wis., 1945; MS, Calif. Inst. Tech., 1947, PhD, 1954; MBA, Stanford U., 1951. Registered profl. engr., Calif. Engr. Cutter Labs., Berkeley, Calif., 1955-61, Dynamic Sci. Corp., South Pasadena, Calif., 1961-64, Philco-Ford Corp., Newport Beach, Calif., 1964-69; asst. mgr. corp. planning Sunkist Growers, Sherman Oaks, Calif., 1970-73; asst. to exec. v.p. Henningson, Durham and Richardson, Santa Barbara, Calif., 1980-83; engr. AiResearch Mfg. Co., Torrance, Calif., 1973-80, 1983—; lectr. Calif. Inst. Tech., Pasadena, 1954, U. Calif., Santa Barbara, 1973, 82, Calif. State U., Northridge, 1986; cons. Vitaminerals Corp., Glendale, Calif., 1973-78, Meditech Pharmaceuticals Corp., Beverly Hills, Calif., 1983—. Author: (with others) Momentum Transfer in Fluids, 1956, Equations of State for Hydrocarbons, 1959; contbr. articles to profl. jours. Served as lt. (j.g.) USN, 1944-54. Fellow AAAS, Royal Soc. for Health (London); mem. Am. Inst. Chem. Engrs., Ops. Research Soc. Am., Sigma Xi. Democrat. Lodge: Masons. Avocation: foreign languages. Home: 1007 Park Circle Dr Torrance CA 90502 Office: AiResearch Mfg Co 2525 W 190th Torrance CA 90509

OPITZ, JOHN MARIUS, pediatrician, clinical geneticist; b. Hamburg, Germany, Aug. 15, 1935; came to U.S., 1950, naturalized, 1957; s. Friedrich and Erica Maria (Quadt) O.; children—Elisabeth, Gabriella, John, Chrisanthi, Felix. B.A., State U. Iowa, 1956, M.D., 1959; D.Sc. (hon.), Mont. State U., 1983; MD (hon.), U. Kiel, Fed. Republic of Germany, 1986. Diplomate Am. Bd. Pediatrics, Am. Bd. Med. Genetics. Intern, State U. Iowa Hosp., 1959-60, resident in pediatrics, 1960-61; resident and chief resident in pediatrics U. Wis. Hosp., Madison, 1961-62; fellow in pediatrics and med. genetics U. Wis., 1962-64, asst. prof. med. genetics and pediatrics, 1964-69, assoc. prof., 1969-72, prof., 1972-79; dir. Wis. Clin. Genetics Ctr., 1974-79; clin. prof. med. genetics and pediatrics U. Wash., Seattle, 1979—; adj. prof. medicine, biology, history and philosophy of sci., vet. research and vet. sci. Mont. State U., Bozeman, 1979—; coordinator Shodair Mont. Regional Genetic Services Program, Helena, 1979-82; chmn. dept. med. genetics Shodair Children's Hosp., Helena, 1983—. Editor: X-Linked Mental Retardation, 1984; founder, editor-in-chief Am. Jour. Med. Genetics, 1977—; mng. editor European Jour. Pediatrics, 1977-85. Mem. German Acad. Scientists Leopoldina, Am. Soc. Human Genetics, Am. Pediatric Soc., Soc. Pediatric Research, Am. Bd. Med. Genetics, Birth Defects Clin. Genetic Soc., Am. Inst. Biol. Scis., Am. Soc. Zoologists, AAAS, Teratology Soc., Genetic Soc. Am., European Soc. Human Genetics, Soc. Study Social Biology, Am. Acad. Pediatrics, German Soc. Pediatrics (corr.), Western Soc. Pediatrics Research, Sigma Xi. Democrat. Roman Catholic. Home: 579 2d St Helena MT 59601 Office: Shodair Children's Hosp 840 Helena Ave Helena MT 59601

OPLER, PAUL ALEXANDER, biologist, government official; b. Ann Arbor, Mich., Aug. 3, 1938; s. Ascher Weinstein and Pauline Elizabeth (Schneirla) O.; m. Sandra Sue Segler, Oct. 21, 1961; children: Timothy, Christian, Laura. BS, U. Calif., Berkekey, 1960; PhD, U. Calif., Berkekey, 1970; MA, Calif. State U., San Jose, 1965. Research assoc. Orgn. Tropical Studies, San Jose, Costa Rica, 1970-74; br. chief U.S. Fish and Wildlife Service, Washington, 1974-83; research and devel. sect. chief U.S. Fish and Wildlife Service, Ft. Collins, Colo., 1983-86; adj. faculty Colo. State U., Ft. Collins, 1984—. Author: Oak Lepidoptera Ecology, 1975, Butterflies East of Plains, 1984; contbr. articles to profl. jours. Served with U.S. Army, 1961-63. Alt. fellow NSF; recipient Spl. Achievement award U.S. Fish and Wildlife Service, 1986. Mem. Assn. Tropical Biology (exec. dir. 1984—), Am. Inst. Biol. Scis. (sec.-treas. 1985—), Xerces Soc. (v.p. 1985—), Entomol. Soc. Am. (sect. chmn. 1978), Lepidopterists' Soc. (council 1986—). Democrat. Avocations: gardening, hiking, photography. Home: 5100 Greenview Ct Fort Collins CO 80525 Office: US Fish and Wildlife Service 1025 Pennock Suite 212 Fort Collins CO 80524

OPPEDAHL, PHILLIP EDWARD, computer company executive; b. Renwick, Iowa, Sept. 17, 1935; s. Edward and Isadore Hannah (Gangstead) O.; B.S. in Naval Sci., Navy Postgrad. Sch., 1963, M.S. in Nuclear Physics, 1971; M.S. in Systems Mgmt., U. S.C., 1978; m. Sharon Elaine Ree, Aug. 3, 1957; children—Gary Lynn, Tamra Sue, Sue Ann, Lisa Kay. Commd. ensign U.S. Navy, 1956, advanced through grades to capt., 1977; with Airborne Early Warning Squadron, 1957-59, Anti-Submarine Squadron, 1959-65; asst. navigator USS Coral Sea, 1965-67; basic jet flight instr., 1967-69; student Armed Forces Staff Coll., 1971; test group dir. Def. Nuclear Agy., 1972-74; weapons officer USS Oriskany, 1974-76; program mgr. for armament Naval Air Systems Command, Washington, 1977-79; test dir. Def. Nuclear Agy., Kirtland AFB, N.Mex., 1979-82, dep. comdr. Def. Nuclear Agy., 1982-83; pres., chief exec. officer Computer Horizons Corp., Albuquerque, 1983—. Decorated Meritorious Service medal. Mem. Naval Inst., Am. Nuclear Soc., Aircraft Owners and Pilots Assn., Assn. Naval Aviation Navy League. Lutheran. Author: Energy Loss of High Energy Electrons in Beryllium, 1971; Understanding Contractor Motivation and Incentive Contracts, 1977. Home: 13305 Desert Flower Pl NE Albuquerque NM 87111 Office: Computer Land of Albuquerque 2226A Wyoming NE Albuquerque NM 87112

OPPENHEIM, ELLEN, public administrator; b. N.Y.C., Feb. 18, 1951; d. Don Bruce and Irene (Gartner) O.; m. Steven William Davidson, June 8, 1974; 1 child, Anne Oppenheim. BA, U. Wis., 1972, MBA, 1977. Dir. minicourse U. Wis., Madison, 1974-75, mgr. ops., 1975-77; asst. dir. Tresidder Union Stanford (Calif.) U., 1977-80, dir. Tresidder Union, 1980-83, assoc. dean students, 1983-87; asst. dir. City of San Jose (Calif.) Parks and Recreation Dept., 1987—. Bd. dirs. Stanford Fed. Credit Union, 1984—. Mem. Am. Mgmt. Assn., Wis. Meml. Union Bldg. Assn. (voting mem. 1985—), Assn. Coll. Univs. (chairperson internat. conf. com. 1983-85). Avocation: skiing. Home: 304 Tioga Ct Palo Alto CA 94306 Office: Parks and Recreation Dept City of San Jose 151 West Mission St San Jose CA 95110

OPPENHEIM, PAUL ANDREW, composite structures engineer; b. Rochester, N.Y., Dec. 13, 1955; s. Everett Philip and Mary Jacqueline (Prevost) O. AA, Mesa Community Coll., 1981; BSME, Ariz. State U., 1984. Mech. technician Motorola Corp., Mesa, Ariz., 1974-79; engring. aid Motorola Corp., Chandler, Ariz., 1979-81; process engr. Hercules Bacchus Works, Magna, Utah, 1984—; Fortran cons. Ariz. State U., Tempe, 1982-83. Mem. Phi Theta Kappa. Avocations: skiing, rock climbing, backpacking, sky diving. Home: 4595 S 2930 W #116 West Valley UT 84119 Office: Hercules Bacchus Works PO Box 98 Magna UT 84044-0098

OPPENHEIMER, STEVEN BERNARD, biology educator; b. Bklyn., Mar. 23, 1944; s. Hugo and Irma (Schellenberg) O.; m. Carolyn Roberta Weisenberg, May 23, 1971; 1 child, Mark. BS magna cum laude, Bklyn. Coll., 1965; PhD, Johns Hopkins U., 1969. Am. Cancer Soc. postdoctoral fellow U. Calif., San Diego, 1969-71; asst. prof. biology Calif. State U., Northridge, 1971-74, assoc. prof., 1974-77, prof., 1977—, dir. Sch. Sci. and Math. Ctr. for Cancer and Devel. Biology; speaker in field; panel mem. NSF, Washington, 1985; prin. investigator NIH, Northridge, 1972-84, 1986—; NSF, Northridge, 1981—; cons. Northridge Hosp., 1984—. Author: Introduction to Embryonic Development, 1980, 2d rev. edition 1984, Cancer, Biological and Clinical Introduction, 1982, 2d rev. edition 1985, Cancer Prevention Guidebook, 1984; editor Cancer, Longevity Letter, 1984—; writer (film) Cancer Prevention, A Way of Life, 1986; contbr. articles to profl. jours. Grantee NSF, 1981—, Nat. Cancer Inst., 1972-84, Am. Cancer Soc., 1977—, Nat. Inst. Child Health and Human Devel., 1986—; fellow Exxon 1982, Thomas Eckstrom Trust, 1982—; recipient Disting. Prof. award, Calif. State U., 1977, Statewide Outstanding Prof. award Bd. Trustees of 19 Campuses, 1984. Fellow N.Y. Acad. Scis.; mem. AAAS, Am. Soc. Zoologists (nat. program chmn., devel. biology and nat. membership chmn. 1983-85), Am. Soc. Cell Biology, Soc. Devel. Biology, Am. Cancer Soc. (bd. dirs. San Fernando Valley chpt. 1985—, Pub. Edn. award 1985), Sigma Xi (Disting. Research award 1984), Phi Kappa Phi. Home: 8933 Darby Ave Northridge CA 91325 Office: Calif State U Dept Biology 18111 Nordhoff St Northridge CA 91330

OPPERMANN, EDWARD BELZ, academic administrator; b. St. Louis, Jan. 19, 1930; s. Theodore William and Marie Isabel (Belz) O.; m. JoAnn Jean Ruehrup, Aug. 1, 1953; children: Kimberly R., Kurt E. BS in Engring., U.S. Naval Acad., 1953; MBA, Air Force Inst. Tech., 1958; PhD in Econs., Ind. U., 1965. Commd. 2d lt. USAF, 1953, advanced through grades to lt. col., retired, 1973; asst. prof. USAF Acad., Colorado Springs, Colo., 1960-62, prof., 1965-73; prof. U. Colo., Colorado Springs, 1973-84, acting resident dean, coll. bus., 1984-86. Author: Business and Economic Statistics, 3d rev. ed., 1986. Vestryman Ch. St. Michael the Archangel, Colorado Springs, 1985—. Mem. Decisions Scis. Inst., Ops. Research Am. Republican. Episcopalian. Avocation: numismatics. Home: 6535 Arequa Ridge Ln Colorado Springs CO 80919 Office: U Colo Dept Bus PO Box 7150 Colorado Springs CO 80933

ORBACH, NEVENA LONIC, marketing consultant, journalist; b. Kukljica, Zadar, Yugoslavia, May 21, 1955; came to U.S., 1961, naturalized, 1967; d. Ante and Ljubica (Gobic) Lonic; m. Stuart Joseph Orbach, Aug. 27, 1982. B.A. summa cum laude in Journalism, L.I.U., 1977. Lic. real estate salesperson, Calif. Editor-in-chief N.Y. News Service, 1974-76; editor NBC Network Radio, WRC-NBC, Washington, 1975-77; account exec. Burson-Marsteller, Pub. Relations, N.Y.C., 1977-78; news editor Burbank (Calif.) Daily Rev., 1978-80; dir. sales PIC Audio-Visual Communications, Burbank, 1980-82; co-owner Foto-Com, Multi-Media Communications, Beverly Hills, Calif., 1982—. Bd. dirs. Burbank Community Hosp. Health Care Found., 1981-82, Burbank Landlord Tenant Vol. Rev., 1981-82. Univ. scholar, 1973-77; N.Y. Deadline Club scholar, 1977; recipient N.Y. State C. of C. First prize, 1973; Friends of Earth Nat. Writing Competition award, 1973. Mem. Women in Communications (pres. chpt.), Optimates, Burbank C. of C., Sigma Delta Chi, Kappa Tau Alpha. Club: Advt. of Los Angeles.

ORD, DON GRANT, electrical engineer; b. Los Angeles, Nov. 4, 1923; s. Grant Leland and Nanna Christina (Shettle) O.; B.S. in Engring., U. Calif. at Los Angeles, 1951; M.S. in Elec. Engring., Calif. State U., Northridge, 1971; m. Lucille Elaine Wuster, Apr. 5, 1952; children—David Kent, Scott Christopher, Craig Neil, Kimberly Ann. Engr., Northrup Aircraft Co., 1951-55; supr. Arnoux Corp., 1955-58, 61-63; lead engr. Marquardt Aircraft Co., 1958-61; with Rockwell Internat. Co., 1963—, engr., supr. autonetics div., 1965—; tchr. engring. Calif. State U., Northridge, 1964. Active local Boy Scouts Am., 1962—, merit badge counselor, 1972—, instnl. rep., 1962-63, 72, com. chmn., 1968-72. Served with USAAF, 1942-46. Mem. IEEE. Republican. Mem. Ch. of Jesus Christ of Latter-day Saints (mem. Bishopric 1962-63, stake Sunday sch. supt. 1965-66, high priest group leader 1966, financial clk. 1973, ch. Sunday Sch. pres. 1974—). Author: Techniques and Trade-offs in Digital Design, 1971. Home: 5412 Willowick Circle Anaheim CA 92807 Office: Rockwell Internat 3370 Miraloma St Anaheim CA 92803

ORD, ROBERT PAUL, controller; b. Nephi, Utah, May 23, 1936; s. Russell Vincent and Margie (Berger) O.; m. Virginia Wilson, Dec. 21, 1955; children: Cherryl, Terri, Lisa, Aimee. BA in Fin., Acctg., Weber State Coll., 1979; MBA, Utah State U., 1985. Programmer Mountain Fuel Supply, Salt Lake City, 1958-65, supr. data processing, 1965-69, sr. systems analyst, 1969-78; mgr. acctg. Mountain Fuel Resources, Salt Lake City, 1978-82, controller, 1982—. Mem. Nat. Assn. Accts. (v.p. adminstrn. 1985-86, pres. 1986-87). Home: 1022 S 1650 E Bountiful UT 84010 Office: Mountain Fuel Resources Box 11450 79 S State Salt Lake City UT 84147

ORÉ, FERNANDO, chemical engineer; b. Trujillo, Peru, Apr. 26, 1926; s. Jose S. and Maria Julia (Cedamanos) O.; m. Carole Frances Botelho, Jan. 19, 1957; children: Fernando Jose, Michelle. BAChemE, San Marcos U., Lima, Peru, 1949; MSChemE, U. Wash., 1954, PhD, 1959. Sr. research engr. Am. Potash Co., Trona, Calif., 1959-64; project research engr. Am. Potash/Kerr McGee, Whittier, Calif., 1965-67; sect. head Kerr McGee Corp., Whittier, 1968-69; mgr. process devel. Occidental Research Corp., LaVerne, Calif., 1970-74; dir. research Occidental Research Corp., LaVerne, Irvine, Calif., 1975-83; v.p. Occidental Devel. Co. sub. Occidental Petroleum Corp., Los Angeles, 1984—. Contbr. articles to profl. jours.; patentee in field. Recipient Kirkpatrick award Am. Potash Co., 1963, Personal Achievement award Chem. Engring. mag., 1978, Pres.'s Outstanding Achievement award Hooker Chem. Co., 1978. Office: Occidental Devel Co 4500 Campus Dr Suite 488 Newport Beach CA 92660

O'REILLY, JOHN GERARD, computer company executive; b. Waterbury, Conn., Nov. 12, 1953; s. John James and Marjorie Veronica (Touponse) O'R.; student Worcester Poly. Inst., 1971-74; M.S., Case Western Res. U., 1978; Ph.D., Stanford U., 1981; m. Cindy Andrea Hollasch, Aug. 28, 1982. Research assoc. Stanford U. (Calif.), 1976-79; engr. decision systems dept. Systems Control, Inc., Palo Alto, Calif., 1979-82; sr. engr. Ford Aerospace and Communications Corp., Palo Alto, 1982-83; pres. VIDCO Inc., Belmont, Calif., 1983—. Mem. IEEE (Computer Soc.), Am. Phys. Soc., AAAS, Mensa. Republican. Author: Distributed Control, 1982; Distributed Systems: Concepts and Implementations, 1983; also numerous tech. articles. Home: 766 La Prenda Rd Los Altos CA 94022

O'REILLY, WENDA BREWSTER, writer, researcher, management consultant; b. Frankfurt, Fed. Republic of Germany, Mar. 29, 1948; d. William Russell Brewster and Harriet Stimson Bullitt; m. James Patrick Brewster O'Reilly, July 18, 1981; children: Andrea Mariele Brewster O'Reilly, Noelle Christine Brewster O'Reilly. BA in Psychology, U. Wash., 1975; MEd, Harvard U., 1977; MA, Stanford U., 1977, PhD in Edn., 1983. Gen. asst. King Broadcasting Co., Seattle, 1965-66; media buyer Benton & Bowles Advt. Agy., N.Y.C, 1967-68; acct. exec. Young & Rubicam Advt. Agy., Milan, 1969-70; advt. producer McCann-Erickson Advt. Agy., Milan, 1971-73; researcher, scholar Inst. for Research on Women and Gender Stanford (Calif.) U., 1983—; exec. dir. The Birth Place, Menlo Park, Calif., 1985-87; guest lectr., seminar leader in women in mgmt., communications and childbirth isssues, 1979—; statis. analyst and research asst., Stanford U., 1978-81. Author: The Beautiful Body Book, 1984; contbr. chpts. to books, articles to profl. jours. V.p., bd. dirs. Calif. Assn. Free-standing Birth Ctrs., 1986—. Grantee William H. Donner Found. Mem. Am. Psychol. Assn., Mid-peninsula Access Corp. (founding bd. dirs. Calif. chpt.). Democrat. Episcopalian.

ORLEANS, PATRICIA LORENA, psychiatric social worker; b. Twin Falls, Idaho, Feb. 6, 1955; d. Roy Chris and Lorena (Nicholson) Wiedenman; m. Lawrence Orleans, June 28, 1980. BA, Colo. State U., 1977; MSW, U. Denver, 1978. Lic. social worker, Colo. Child and family counselor Southeastern Colo. Family Guidance and Mental Health, LaJunta, Colo., 1978-80; sr. therapist and program dir. Weld Mental Health Ctr., Inc., Greeley, Colo., 1980—; med. social worker N.E. Home Health Care, Greeley, 1985-86. Mem. Nat. Assn. Social Workers. Avocations: pianist, downhill skiing, tennis, bike riding, hiking. Home: PO Box 7 214 E Union Ave LaSalle CO 80645 Office: Weld Mental Health Ctr Inc 1306 11th Ave Greeley CO 80631

ORMAND, DONALD REAGAN, manufacturing company manager; b. St. Thomas, Ont., Can., Mar. 21, 1941 (parents Am. citizens); s. Reagan Durwood and Dorothy Junita (Boren) O.; BS in Physics, U. Tex., Arlington, 1964; MS in Mgmt. Sci., West Coast U., 1974; m. Barbara Ann Spoon, Nov. 24, 1960; children: Donald Scott, John Reagan. With Hughes Aircraft Co., Fullerton, Calif., 1966—, mgr. advanced projects staff, 1977-80, mgr. Ukadge project dept., 1980-82, mgr. FAA AAS project dept., 1982-84, chief scientist Software Tech. Lab., 1984-87, mktg. mgr. software engring. div. 1987—; treas. Octug, Inc. Youth counselor, then chmn. outreach commn. United Meth. Ch., 1965-68. Mem. Tech. Mktg. Assn. Am., Hactug Computer Club, West End Gun Club (bd. dirs.). Republican. Office: 1901 W Malvern St Fullerton CA 92634

ORME, CHERYL L., speech and language pathologist; b. Idaho Falls, Idaho, Apr. 22, 1953; d. H.J. and Beth (Terry) O. BS, Utah State U., 1975, MS, 1976. Window glazier Orme Co., St. Anthony, Idaho, 1968-74; speech pathologist Soda Springs (Idaho) Schs., 1976-77; specialist communicative disorders Davis County (Utah), Farmington, 1977—; pvt. practice speech pathology Ogden, Utah, 1981—; conducted numerous presentation on communication disorders various local edn. orgns.; guest lectr. Weber State Coll., Utah; various com. memberships with state agys. and assns. related to communication disorders. Mem. Am. Speech Lang. Hearing Assn. (cert. clin. competence), Utah Speech and Hearing Assn., NEA, Utah Edn. Assn., Davis County Edn. Assn., Utah State U. Alumni Assn. (membership com.), Phi Kappa Phi. Mormon. Avocations: gardening, traveling, reading, sports, handcrafts. Home: 1379 31st St Ogden UT 84403

ORME, MAYNARD EVAN, broadcasting executive; b. Fresno, Calif., Dec. 7, 1936; s. Otis Lowe and Lila (Morton) O.; m. Joan Frances King, Apr. 2, 1966; children: Jennifer Ariana, Juliana Alaire. MusB, U. Calif., Berkeley, 1961; MA in Theatre Arts, UCLA, 1967, PhD in Edn., 1978. Cert. community coll. tchr., Calif. Research asst. Instructional Media Ctr. Dept. Edn. UCLA, 1965-66; producer-dir., instructional TV coordinator, news dir. Sta. KVCR-TV San Bernardino (Calif.) Valley Coll., 1966-68; learning resources coordinator, dir. Sta. KCET-TV, Los Angeles, 1968-73; gen. mgr., dir. media services, exec. dir. Sta. KTEH-TV, San Jose, Calif., 1973-86; exec. dir. Oreg. Pub. Broadcasting, Portland, 1986—; mem. TV adv. com. Calif. State Instructional TV, 1977-82, chmn. 1979-80. Vice chmn. San Jose Police Activities League, 1982-83, chmn., bd. dirs. 1983-85. Served to 1st lt. U.S. Army, 1961-66. Mem. Assn. Calif. Pub. TV Stas. (pres. 1982—), Calif. Media and Library Educators Assn., Nat. Acad. TV Arts and Scis., Pacific Mountain Network (bd. dirs. 1981—, v.p. 1984—), Calif. Pub. Broadcasting Commn. (chmn. TV adv. com. 1978-79), Pub. Broadcasting Service (bd. dirs. 1984—, chmn. membership com.), UCLA Doctoral Alumni Assn., Big C Soc., Los Gatos Athletic Assn. (v.p. 1975, pres. 1976, bd. dirs.), Los Gatos Elem. Ednl. Found. (bd. dirs. 1982-84), West Valley Joggers and Striders, Order of Golden Bear, Phi Delta Kappa, Alpha Epsilon Rho. Home: 16360 Belmont Ave Monte Sereno CA 95030 Office: Oreg Pub Broadcasting 2828 SW Front Ave Portland OR 97201-4899

ORMSBY, LIONEL, advertising agency executive; b. Oakland, Calif., Jan. 16, 1909; s. Edgar L. and Georgia (Council) O.; A.B., U. Calif.-Berkeley, 1934; m. Myrtez Boehmer Rush, Apr. 22, 1941 (dec.); children—John Rush, Jean; m. 2d, Lola B. Ensminger, Sept. 11, 1982. Advt. prodn. San Francisco News, 1936-40; asst. account exec. McCann-Erickson, Los Angeles, 1940-42; account exec. Shaw Advt. Agy., Los Angeles, 1942-46, 56-60; account exec. Dozier-Eastman & Co., Los Angeles, 1946-56; owner Hammer & Ormsby Advt., 1960—; pub. Sales Talk, syndicated newsletter; editor Rexall Reporter, Rexall Drug Co., Trade Secrets, Bank Americard Corp.; tchr. journalism Alameda (Calif.) High Sch., 1934-36; tchr. copywriting Los Angeles City Coll., 1950-53. Contbr. articles to jours., mags., and newspapers. Chmn. publicity com. Los Angeles County Tb and Health Assn., 1955-61; vice chmn. Beverly Hills council Boy Scouts Am. Bd. dirs. Los Angeles Beautiful, Inc. Mem. Assn. Indsl. Advertisers, Sales and Mktg. Execs. Assn., Los Angeles Advt. Club (1st v.p.), No. Calif. Golf Assn. Club: Sirs. (Oakmont br.). Home: 476 Hillsdale Dr Santa Rosa CA 95405

ORONA, ERNEST JOSEPH, real estate and constrn. co. exec.; b. Belen, N.Mex., Oct. 5, 1942; s. Joseph B. and Melinda (Sanchez) O.; B.A. in Latin Am. Affairs and Spanish, U. N.Mex., 1968; m. Margaret M. Guinan, Aug. 22, 1964; children—Mary Melinda, Marie-Jeanne. Vol. community devel. Peace Corps, Colombia, S. Am., 1962-64; instr. Peace Corps tng. U. Mo., Kansas City, summer 1964, Baylor U., Waco, Tex., summer 1965, also U. Ariz., N.Mex. State U., Las Cruces, 1966, U. N.Mex., Albuquerque, 1966; exec. dir. Mid-Rio Grande Community Action Project, Los Lunas, N.Mex., 1965-66; community devel. cons. Center for Community Action Services, Albuquerque, 1967-68; project dir. Peace Corps Tng. Center, San Diego State U., Escondido, Calif., 1968-70; propr., developer GO Realty and Constrn. Co., Albuquerque, 1970—. Mem. Albuquerque Sister Cities. Mem. Nat. Bd. Realtors, Albuquerque Bd. Realtors, Albuquerque C. of C., Albuquerque Com. on Fgn. Relations. Roman Catholic. Home: 908 Sierra Dr SE Albuquerque NM 87108 Office: 10601 Lomas NE Suite 112 Albuquerque NM 87112

O'ROURKE, EUGENE LAWRENCE, public utility executive; b. San Antonio, Aug. 12, 1929; s. Lawrence F. and Rose (Lackey) O'R.; m. Marilyn Jean Rickert, June 25, 1955; children—Ronald E., Kenneth R., Craig A. B.S. in Mech. Engring., UCLA, 1955. Sales engr. indsl. div. Am. Standard Corp., Los Angeles, 1955-60; exec. Coswel Corp., Newport Beach, Calif., 1961-62; gen. mgr. Coastal Publs. Corp., Fullerton, Calif., 1962-64; v.p. So. Calif. Gas Co., Los Angeles, 1964—. Pres., Orange County Young Reps., 1961, Newport Harbor Union High Sch. Dist., 1964. Served with U.S. Army, 1952-54. Mem. Am. Gas Assn. (vice chmn. ops. sect.), Pacific Coast Gas Assn., Town Hall, Orange County World Affairs Council. Republican. Presbyterian. Clubs: Balboa Bay (Newport Beach), Los Angeles (pres. 1986). Lodge: Masons. Home: 1039 Tiller Way Corona Del Mar CA 92625 Office: So Calif Gas Co 810 S Flower St Los Angeles CA 90017

O'ROURKE, PATRICK J., university administrator. Chancellor U. Alaska, Fairbanks, 1983—. Office: U Alaska Office of Chancellor Fairbanks AK 99701 *

O'ROURKE, THOMAS WALTER, instrument company executive; b. Chicago Heights, Ill., Feb. 2, 1937; s. John Thomas and Minnie (Meyer) O'R.; m. Glenda Carol Weigum, July 24, 1964; children: John Edward, Alix Carey. Student, Purdue U., 1959; BS in Chem. Engring., Northwestern U., 1960; LLB, George Washington U., 1962. Bar: U.S. Patent Office, Colo., N.Y. Patent lawyer Eastman Kodak Co., Rochester, N.Y., 1960-68; sr. patent lawyer Ball Corp., Boulder, Colo., 1965-72; sole practice Boulder, 1972-74; ptnr. O'Rourke & Harris, Boulder, 1974-81; pres. Scientech, Inc., Boulder, 1981—, also bd. dirs.; bd. dirs. Ingalls Engring., Longmont, Colo. Patentee in field. Mem. ABA, Am. Patent Law Assn. Inter-region racing champion Sports Car Club Am., Denver, 1975. Home: 7212 Old Post Rd Boulder CO 80301 Office: Scientech Inc 5649 Arapahoe Boulder CO 80303

OROZCO, JOHN HERMAN, computer company executive; b. Alameda, Calif., May 7, 1950; s. Jess and Ruth (Puentes) O.; m. Claudia Jean Corchero, July 15, 1972; children: Aaron John, Andrea Jean. AA, Chabot Coll., 1970; BS, Calif. State U., Hayward, 1972; MA, Stanford U., 1973. Cert. secondary sch. instr., Calif.; cert. jr. coll. instr., Calif. Tchr. New Haven Unified Sch. Dist., Union City, Calif., 1972-78; account rep. Xerox Corp., San Francisco, 1978-83; computer sales exec. Hewlett Packard Co., Pleasanton, Calif., 1984—. Mem. Pleasanton C. of C., Stanford Alumni Assn. Democrat. Roman Catholic. Lodge: Rotary. Home: 1193 Vintner Way Pleasanton CA 94566 Office: Hewlett-Packard 5725 Las Positas Rd Pleasanton CA 94566

ORPHAL, DENNIS L., physicist, researcher; b. Columbia, S.C., Aug. 28, 1942; s. John J. and Helen Virginia (Heil) O.; m. Viki J. Gojack, Apr. 25, 1964; children: Jonathan, David. Student, Case Inst. Tech., 1960-62; BA in Physics, Ohio Wesleyan U., 1964; postgrad., U. Nev., 1970-72. Registered geophysicist, Calif. adv. panel Def. Nuclear Agy., Washington, NASA, Washington, 1979-84, Def. Advanced Research Projects Agy., Washington, Office of Undersec. Def. (Research and Engring.), 1980-81. Contbr. articles to profl. jours.; patentee in field. Mem. Am. Phys. Soc., Am. Geophys. Union, AAAS, AIAA, Seismol. Soc. Am., Am. Def. Preparedness Assn. Avocation: racquetball. Office: Calif Research and Tech Inc 5117 Johnson Dr Pleasanton CA 94566

ORQUIOLA, REYNALDO GUEVARA, chemist; b. Nasugbu, Batangas, Philippines, Sept. 6, 1936; came to U.S., 1967; s. Juan Seneres and Leoncia Ignacio (Guevara) O.; m. Linda Dumago, Sept. 18, 1966 (div. Aug. 1982); children: Janet, Ray Jr., John, Melissa. BS in Chemistry, U. Philippines, 1965; MS in Chemistry, Adamson U., Manila, 1967. Registered chemist, Philippines. Chem. analyst Reynolds Aluminum, Longview, Wash., 1967-68; chemist dept. ecology Wash. State U., Olympia, 1968-75; city chemist Santa Barbara (Calif.) Pub. Works, 1975-82; chemist, owner Water Testing and Cons.Lab., Santa Barbara, 1979-85, Water Testing and Cons., Carpinteria, Calif., 1985—. Mem. Am. Chem. Soc., Am. Works Assn., Smithsonian Inst. Republican. Roman Catholic. Club: Filipino Community (Santa Barbara). Avocation: research and devel. of pollution control. Office: Water Testing and Cons Lab 3825 Santa Claus Ln Carpinteria CA 93013

ORR, DENNIS MARK, real estate developer; b. Winamac, Ind., Jan. 12, 1940; s. Mark Ulysses and Clara Belle (Riley) O.; AB, Ind. U., 1962; m. Edna Ann Winckelbach, Aug. 18, 1962 (div. 1983); 1 child, Colin Patrick; m. Judyth Troup Smith, May 11, 1985. V.p., Investments in Real Estate, Denver, 1968-72; sr. v.p. The Lincoln Cos., Denver, 1972-74; pres. Cotter-Orr Devel. Co., Littleton, Colo., 1974-76, Duffy Storage & Moving, Denver, 1976-78; chmn. bd., chief exec. officer Poor Richards Ltd., 1978-83; exec. v.p. Gibraltar Devel. Co., 1983-86; pres. The Sycamore Group, Ltd., 1986—; dir. Interiors by Heloise; chmn. Rocky Mountain Communications, 1987; chmn. bd. Bayaud Industries. Chmn. Littleton City Planning Commn., 1975-84; chmn. leadership Denver, 1975; mem. Gov.'s I-470 Ad Hoc Commn., 1975-76; bd. dirs. Inst. for Internat. Edn., Inc.; bd. dirs. Support Systems Consol. Rep. precinct committeeman. Served to capt. USAF, 1962-67. Named Outstanding Young Republican Male of Colo., Young Rep. League, 1971. Mem. Denver C. of C. (dir. 1975-79), Am. Mgmt. Assn., S. Suburban Bd. Realtors, Assn. Indsl. and Office Parks (chmn. bd.), Am. Trucking Assn., Nat. Assn. Indsl. and Office Parks, Crane and Rigging Assn. (bd. govs. 1977), Nat. Fedn. Ind. Bus. (Colo. adv. council), Phi Sigma Kappa. Republican. Clubs: Univ., Arapahoe Men's (pres. 1968-73). Home: 721 Ballantine Road Golden CO 80401 Office: 5340 S Quebec Suite 350 Englewood CO 80111

ORR, FRANKLIN MATTES, JR., petroleum engineering educator; b. Baytown, Tex., Dec. 27, 1946; s. Franklin Mattes and Selwyn Sage (Huddleston) O.; m. Susan Packard, Aug. 30, 1970; children: David, Katherine. BSChemE, Stanford U., 1969; PhDChemE, U. Minn., 1976. Sanitary engr. EPA, Washington, 1970-72; research engr. Shell Devel. Co., Houston, 1976-78; sr. engr. N.Mex. Petroleum Recovery Research Ctr., Socorro, 1978-84; assoc. prof. petroleum engring. Stanford (Calif.) U., 1985—. Contbr. articles to profl. jours. Served with USPHS, 1970-72. Mem. Soc. Petroleum Engrs., Am. Inst. Chem. Engrs., AAAS, Soc. Indsl. and Applied Math. Home: 927 Cottrell Way Stanford CA 94305

ORR, JEAN MARY, state agency official; b. Los Angeles, Sept. 23, 1923; d. Theodore Leverne and Regina Margaret (Riley) Wallace; children—Linda Lei Cox, Terri Regina Gomes. Student Porterville, Coll., 1942. Lic. real estate salesman, Calif. Co-owner White Oaks Realty, San Carlos, Calif., 1948-58; mgr. Career Counselors, San Mateo, Calif., 1960-64; owner, mgr. Merle Norman Studio, San Carlos, 1964-67; mgr., v.p. Flight Records, San Carlos, 1973-75; owner, mgr. Flight of Fantasy, San Carlos, 1973-78; adminstrv. asst. Rucker Fuller, San Francisco, 1978-82; data base mgr. Computer Connection, San Francisco, 1983; chief Bur. Personnel Services, State of Calif., Sacramento, 1983—. Pres. State of Calif. Rep. Assembly, 1981-82, conv. site chmn., 1972-80; mem. exec. com. Rep. party State of Calif., 1981-82, 85-86; past pres. San Mateo County Fedn. Rep. Women; speaker Coll. Notre Dame Women's Re-entry Program; chmn., coordinator Heritage Faire '76, San Mateo County; vice-chmn. San Mateo County Heritage '76; chmn. San Carlos Bicentennial, 1975-76; past nat. bd. dirs. Psoriasis Research Assn.; past pres. San Carlos Community Ch. Jr. Matrons; chmn. of San Carlos Mothers' March of Dimes; chmn. small bus. United Crusade, San Carlos; active Girl Scouts U.S.A. Named Outstanding Citizen, San Carlos, 1976. Mem. Bus. Profl. Women (Redwood City Outstanding Woman 1974). Lodges: Soroptimists (Woman of Achievement 1975), Order of Eastern Star (San Carlos). Home: 133 Garnet Ave San Carlos CA 94070 Office: 1426 Howe Ave Sacramento CA 95825

ORRAS, GEORGE L., social worker; b. Chincoteeque, Va., Mar. 4, 1952; s. George and Elsie (Hill) O. BA in Sociology, U. S. Fla., 1974; MSW, Ariz. State U., 1976; PhD in Social Work, U. So. Calif., 1983. Psychotherapist Tri City Mental Health, Mesa, Ariz., 1976-78; social worker for handicapped Phoenix High Sch., 1978-80; instr. U. So. Calif., Los Angeles, 1981-82; emergency room social worker Long Beach (Calif.) Meml. Hosp., 1982-84; pvt. practice in psychotherapy Long Beach, 1983—; clin. program dir. outstretch services Coll. Hosp., Cerritos, Calif., 1983—; cons., stress reduction Cen. Ariz., Phoenix, 1978-80; cons. tng., Phoenix, 1978-80; cons., developer Crisis Response Unit, Cerritos; cons. Orange County Hotline, Los Alamitos, Calif., 1985—; practitioner hypnosis, Los Angeles, 1985—. Bd. dirs. Long Beach Drug Prevention, 1986—; bd. dirs. Turn Est, Venice, Calif., 1986—. Fellow Soc. Clin. Social Workers; Mem. Nat. Assn. Social Workers, Omicron Delta Kappa. Democrat. Roman Catholic. Avocations: skiing, surfing, golf, tennis, raquetball. Office: Coll Hosp 10802 College Pl Cerritos CA 90701

ORRICK, WILLIAM HORSLEY, JR., judge; b. San Francisco, Oct. 10, 1915; s. William Horsley and Mary (Downey) O.; m. Marion Naffziger, Dec. 5, 1947; children: Mary-Louise, Marion, William Horsley III. Grad., Hotchkiss Sch., 1933; B.A., Yale, 1937; LL.B., U. Calif.-Berkeley, 1941. Bar: Calif. 1941. Partner Orrick, Dahlquist, Herrington & Sutcliffe, San Francisco, 1941-61; asst. atty. gen. civil div. Dept Justice, 1961-62, antitrust div., 1963-65; dep. under sec. state for adminstrn. Dept. State, 1962-63; practice law San Francisco, 1965-74; former partner firm Orrick, Herrington, Rowley & Sutcliffe; U.S. dist. judge No. Dist. Calif., 1974—. Past pres. San Francisco Opera Assn., Trustee, World Affairs Council; former trustee San Francisco Law Library, San Francisco Found., Children's Hosp. San Francisco, Grace Cathedral Corp. Served to capt. M.I. AUS, 1942-46. Fellow Am. Bar Found.; mem. Bar Assn. San Francisco (past trustee, treas.). Office: US Courthouse PO BOx 36060 San Francisco CA 94102

ORRISON, RICHARD CARL, food industry executive; b. Cheyenne, Wyo., Mar. 27, 1951; s. Carrol Payton and Barbara Colleen (Kiehm) O.; m. Janet Sue Eversull, Sept. 11, 1983; children: Richard, Angela, Rachael. BS in Bus., U. Wyo., 1979. Prof. musician Boyles Bros., 1969-74; br. mgr. Orrison Distbg., Laramie, Wyo., 1974-79; sales mgr. Orrison Distbg., Cheyenne, 1979-82; v.p., gen. mgr. Orrison Distbg., Wyo. and Colo., 1982—, pres., 1987—; bd. dirs. Western Bank, Cheyenne, 1984—, Rocky Mountain Conf. Beer Distbrs., 1986; bd. dirs. Wyo. Beer Wholesalers, 1982—, treas. 1985—. Legis. action coordinator Anheuser Busch, Inc., Wyo., 1984—; bd. dirs. Mil. Affairs Com., Warren AFB, Wyo., 1986—. Mem. Air Force Assn., Quarterback Club, Cheyenne C. of C. (bd. dirs. 1986, Outstanding Community Service award 1985). Republican. Mormon. Club: Cheyenne Country (bd. dirs. 1986—). Lodges: Kiwanis, Elks, Moose. Avocations: golfing, skiing. Home: 3500 Sunrise Cheyenne WY 82001 Office: Orrison Distbg Inc 1111 Dunn Ave Cheyenne WY 82001

ORSINO, DONALD EUGENE, marketing researcher; b. Plainfield, N.J., Feb. 10, 1941; s. Joseph Anthony and Mary Louise (Carson) O.; m. Lynn Deanne Hall, Feb. 25, 1966; m. Mary Jane Wayment, Apr. 10, 1982. B.S.J., Northwestern U., 1962, M.S.J., 1963. Survey supr. Field Research Corp., San Francisco, 1965-66; sr. project dir. Communications Research Ctr., San Francisco, 1966-69; account mgr. Drossler Research Corp., San Francisco, 1969-71, v.p., 1972-74; assoc. Haug Assocs., San Francisco, 1971-72; ptnr. Mktg. Research Assocs., San Francisco, 1974-78; pres. Consumer Research Assocs., San Francisco, 1978—; asst. prof. mktg. San Francisco State U., 1969-70. Served in USCGR, 1963-70. Mem. Am. Mktg. Assn., Photog. Mktg. Assn., San Francisco Advt. Club. Republican. Club: Loch Lomond Yacht (San Rafael, Calif.). Home: 401 Fairway Dr Novato CA 94947 Office: 1738 Union St Suite 100 San Francisco CA 94123

ORTEGA, RUBEN BAPTISTA, police chief; b. Glendale, Ariz., July 17, 1939; s. Epifanio Dominguez and Clara (Baptista) O.; B.S. in Criminal Justice and Police Adminstrn., No. Ariz. U., 1980; m. Nellie Ann Alvarado, Nov. 23, 1958; children—Karen Ann, Jeffrey Randal. With Phoenix Police Dept., 1960—, police chief, 1980—; instr. Phoenix Police Regional Tng. Acad., 1969-73; cons. Juvenile Crime Prevention Task Force, Phoenix, 1975-79. Bd. dirs. NCCJ, 1979-81. Recipient Outstanding Community Service awards Am. Legion, 1979, also others. Mem. Ariz. Organized Crime Prevention Council, Ariz. Law Enforcement Office Adv. Council, Internat. Assn. Chiefs of Police. Roman Catholic. Office: City of Phoenix Police Dept 620 W Washington St Phoenix AZ 85003 *

ORTH, CHARLES JOSEPH, nuclear, geochemist; b. Fontana, Calif., Aug. 13, 1930; s. Joseph C. and Rose M. (Oeser) O.; m. Marjorie A. Pernick, June 30, 1959; 1 child, Stephen M. BA, San Diego State U., 1954; PhD, U. N.Mex., 1969. Staff mem. Los Alamos (N.Mex.) Nat. Lab., 1956-83, fellow, 1983—. Contbr. articles to sci. jours. Served as cpl. with U.S. Army, 1954-56. Mem. AAAS, Am. Phys. Soc., Am. Chem. Soc. (recipient John Dustin Clark medal 1984), Geol. Soc. Am., Paleontol. Soc. Republican. Roman Catholic. Avocations: philately, volleyball, tennis. Home: 281 Chamisa Los Alamos NM 87544 Office: Los Alamos Nat Lab Mail Stop J514 Los Alamos NM 87545

ORTH, JAMES NEAL, financial executive; b. Kearney, Nebr., Mar. 24, 1947; s. Melvin Fae and Geneva Lucille (Gillespie) O.; m. Susan Covington Sayles, Aug. 23, 1975. B.S., U. Wyo., 1969. Mktg. rep. IBM Corp., Denver, 1969-76; mktg. rep. ENI Corp., Denver, 1976-78, v.p., br. mgr., Los Angeles, 1978-80; pres. dir. Shuman, Orth & Co., Newport Beach, Calif., 1980—, Am. Vending Co., 1985—, Venture Cons. Group, Inc., 1984—; v.p., sec., dir. N.B. Equities, Inc., Newport Beach, 1981—, Prism Real Estate, Inc., 1982—; pres., dir. Energy Ventures, Inc., Newport Beach, 1980-83. Mem. Hoag Hosp. Found., 1980—. Mem. Orange County C. of C., Romance Lang. Honor Soc., Econ. Honor Soc., U. Wyo. Alumni Assn., Sigma Nu. Republican. Clubs: Balboa Bay, Univ. Athletic. Office: Shuman Orth & Co 2500 Michelson Suite 300 Irvine CA 92715

ORTIZ, ELIZABETH THOMPSON, college educator, consultant; b. Woodstock, Vt., Nov. 13, 1941; d. Albert Francis and Sarah Symmes (Fletcher) Thompson; m. Edward George Ortiz, June, 1966 (div.1975); 1 child, Cecilia Francis. BA, Barnard Coll., 1963; MSW, Columbia U., 1969, DSW, 1981. Dir. social services St. Mary Hosp., Hoboken, N.J., 1972-75; lectr. and asst. dean in social work San Diego State U., 1977-82; asst. prof. social work Calif. State U., Long Beach, 1983—; cons. USCG Hdqrs. Family Program Office; editorial cons. Allyn & Bacon Inc., Springfield, 1986; nat. del.Council on Social Work Edn., 1985—. Contbr. articles to profl. jours. Mem. Orange County (Calif.) Adv. Bd., 1982-85, San Diego Social Welfare Adv. Bd., 1981-83, Hudson County (N.J.) Health Systems Adv. Com., 1973-75. Carnegie Found. grantee, 1963; Fulbright lectr. to India, 1965-66. Mem. Nat. Assn. Social Workers (cert., editorial cons. Dictionary 1986), Am. Pub. Health Assn., Authors Guild. Office: Calif State U Dept Social Work Long Beach CA 90840

ORTIZ, VICTOR RICARDO, management consultant; b. N.Y.C., Dec. 3, 1951; s. Hector Ortiz-Garzón and Signe Sophie (Midelfart) O. BA, MA, Rosebridge Inst., 1983. Program dir. Freedom House Found., Stockton, Calif., 1973-78; contract coordinator A.H. Tng. and Devel., Oakland, Calif., 1978-81; mgr. Ortiz Tng. Services, Oakland, 1981-83; assoc. Serafini Assocs., Cupertino, Calif., 1983; sr. assoc. Interaction Assocs., San Francisco, 1983—; lead cons. Calif. Dept. Alcohol and Drug Abuse, Sacramento, 1980-83. Mem. plenary task force 1969 Wis. Gov.'s Conf. Children and Youth, Madison; mem. White House Conf. Youth, Washington, 1970. Mem. Am. Soc. Tng. and Devel., Bay Area Orgn. Devel. Network, Profl. Ski Instrs. Am. (assoc. cert. 1981). Democrat. Mem. Soc. Friends. Avocations: skiing, scuba diving, tennis, travel, classical guitar. Home: 3508 Seminary Ave Oakland CA 94605 Office: Interaction Assocs 185 Berry St Suite 150 San Francisco CA 94107

ORULLIAN, B. LARAE, banker; b. Salt Lake City, May 15, 1933; d. Alma and Bessie (Bacon) O.; cert. Am. Inst. Banking, 1961, 63, 67; grad. Nat. Real Estate Banking Sch., Ohio State U., 1969-71. With Tracy Collins Trust Co., Salt Lake City, 1951-54; sec. to exec. sec. Union Nat. Bank, Denver, 1954-57; exec. sec. Guaranty Bank, Denver, 1957-64, asst. cashier, 1964-67, asst. v.p., 1967-70, v.p., 1970-75, exec. v.p., 1975-77, also dir.; pres., chief exec. officer, dir. The Women's Bank N.A., Denver, 1977—, Equitable Bankshares of Colo., 1980—; vice chmn. Equitable Bank Littleton; vice chmn. bd., dir. Colo. Blue Cross/Blue Shield, lectr. Nat. treas. Girl Scouts U.S.A., 1981. Mem. Bus. and Profl. Women Colo. (3d Century award 1977), Denver C. of C. (chair govtl. relations), Am. Inst. Banking, Nat. Assn. Bank Women, Women in Bus. Assn., Women's Forum, Com. of 200, Denver Partnership, Colo. Bankers Assn. (bd. dirs.). Republican. Mormon. Clubs: Zonta, Soroptimist, Denver. Home: 10 S Ammons St Lakewood CO 80226

ORUMCHIAN, JANET HUNTER, French and English as second language educator; b. Bottineau, N.D., Dec. 15, 1938; d. Frank Samuel and Marion Agnes (McBain) Hunter; m. Abbas Ali Orumchian, Jan. 28, 1962; children: Kim Abbas, Soraya. BA, U. N.D., 1960; licentiate diploma in teaching ESL, Trinity Coll., London, 1976; MA in Counseling and Guidance, U. Ala., 1977; EdD, Seattle U., 1984. Cert. secondary tchr., Calif., Wash. Tchr. French, German Fullerton (Calif.) Union High Sch. Dist., 1960-61; tchr. French Campbell (Calif.) Union High Sch., 1962-63; tchr. adult edn. Palo Alto (Calif.) Adult Edn., 1967-68; instr. Eng. lang. and lit. Pars U., Teheran, Iran, 1973-78; tchr. French, ESL Lake Wash. Sch. Dist., Kirkland, 1979-86. Author: A Study of Cognitive Style Among Recent Indochinese Immigrant Students, 1984; co-author (manual) ESL Manual for Classroom Teachers, 1981; translator Le Djinn Eskandar, The Bible in Islam, 1985-86. Sponsor China Experience, Redmond, Wash., 1985-86; bd. trustees Youth Eastside Service, Bellevue, Wash., 1985—; area canvasser Heart Fund Campaign, Issaquah, Wash., 1983, Beth Bland Com., Issaquah, 1984-85; coordinator fund raising United Way, Redmond, 1983-84. Arneberg scholar U. N.D., 1960. Mem. NEA, Assn. Supervision and Curriculum Devel., Internat. Reading Assn., Nat. Council Tchrs. English, Mortar Bd., Phi Beta Kappa, Phi Delta Kappa. Democrat. Home: 2510 Bombadil Ln Davis CA 95616 Office: Redmond High Sch 17272 NE 104th Redmond WA 98052

ORUND, VALDEK JAAN, mech. engr.; b. Estonia, USSR, July 4, 1922; s. Jaan and Johanna O.; M.S.M.E., Tallinna Politehniline Instituut, 1941; came to U.S., 1950, naturalized, 1963; m. Katharina Baumstark, Aug. 13, 1966. Engr., Shaffer Tool Works, Brea, Calif., 1952-69; product engring. mgr. Rucker Co., Brea, 1969-77; chief engr. research and devel. N.L. Shaffer, N. L. Industries, Inc., Brea, 1977-82, engring. specialist, 1982—. Mem. ASME, Computer Soc. of IEEE (affiliate mem.), Soc. Exptl. Stress Analysis, Am. Soc. Metals, AIME, Soc. Mfg. Engrs., Robotics Internat. Republican. Lutheran. Patentee in field. Office: 200 N Berry St Brea CA 92621

OSBORN, PAUL GORDON, civil engineer; b. San Antonio, Oct. 30, 1943; s. Roy Osborn and Helen O. (Gilbertson) Enloe; m. Cynthia D. Koshelek, Aug. 7, 1963; children: Michael, Paula. BSCE, U. Ariz., 1967. Registered profl. engr., Ariz.; registered land surveyor, Ariz. Petroleum engr. Amoco Oil Corp., Ft. Worth, 1967-69; project engr. Cella Barr & Assocs., Tucson, 1969-74; div. mgr. Pima County Dept. Transp., Tucson, 1974-77; prin. Osborn, Petterson, Walbert & Assocs., Tucson, 1977—. Mem. NSPE, ASCE, Ariz. Soc. Profl. Engrs., So. Ariz. Home Builders Assn. (assoc., co-chmn. tech. com. 1984-85, 87). Republican. Lutheran. Club: La Paloma, Plaza (Tucson). Avocations: auto restoration, camping, golf. Office: Osborn Petterson Walbert & Assocs 6383 E Grant PO Box 31330 Tucson AZ 85751-1330

OSBORN, TERRELL JAN, systems safety engineer, management educator, retired air force officer; b. Anthony, Kans., Oct. 19, 1941; s. Ralph Pike and LouVelma (Pearl) O.; 1 dau., Kristin. B.A., U. Kans., 1963; M.B.A., U. Utah, 1977; Dr.Bus.Adminstrn., U.S. Internat. U., 1980. Maj., U.S. Air Force, 1965; F-4C Phantom fighter pilot, 1965-67, F-4 instr. pilot, Davis-Monthan AFB, Ariz., 1967-70, flight examiner, Homestead AFB, Fla., 1970-72, pilot in Korea, 1973, chief safety Luke AFB, Ariz., 1974-78, chief Flight Mishap Final Eval. Br., Inspection Safety Center, Norton AFB, Calif., 1978-83, ret., 1983; assoc. prof. mgmt. Embry-Riddle Aero. U., Prescott, Ariz., 1983-86; system safety engr. Northrop Aircraft div. Northrop Corp., 1986—. Vol., United Way. Decorated D.F.C., Air medals (13); cert. safety profl.; USAF Chief of Staff Individual Safety award, 1977. Mem. Am. Soc. Safety Engrs., Internat. Soc. Air Safety Investigators, System Safety Soc., Air Force Assn., Beta Gamma Sigma. Clubs: Daedalians, Red River Fighter Pilots Assn. Club: Kiwanis (past pres.). Contbr. articles to profl. jours. Home: 1707 Pacific Coast Hwy #215 Hermosa Beach CA 90254

OSBORNE, KENT LEIGH, lawyer; b. Tokyo, Japan, Nov. 15, 1947; s. Monta Lee and Helen (Weaver) O. B.A., U. Calif.-Berkeley, 1970; J.D., U. Calif.-Davis, 1973. Bar: Ill., 1973. Assoc. Bloom, Denberg & Vanasco, Chgo., 1976-78; tax counsel Stone & Webster Appraisal Corp., Woodland Hills, Calif., 1978-80; v.p. Arthur D. Little Valuation, Inc., Woodland Hills, Calif., 1980—. Served to capt. U.S. Army, 1973-76. Decorated Army Commendation medal. Mem. Ill. State Bar. Office: 21900 Burbank Blvd Woodland Hills CA 91367

O'SCANNLAIN, DIARMUID FIONNTAIN, circuit judge; b. N.Y.C., Mar. 28, 1937; s. Sean Leo and Moira (Hegarty) O'S.; m. Maura Nolan, Sept. 7, 1963; children: Sean, Jane, Brendan, Kevin, Megan, Christopher, Anne, Kate. AB, St. John's U., 1957; JD, Harvard U., 1963. Bar: Oreg. 1965, N.Y. 1964. Tax atty. Standard Oil Co. (N.J.), N.Y.C., 1963-65; assoc. Davies, Biggs, Strayer, Stoel & Boley, Portland, Oreg., 1965-69; dep. atty. gen. Oreg., 1969-71; public utility commr. of Oreg., 1971-73; dir. Oreg. Dept. Environ. Quality, 1973-74; sr. ptnr. Ragen, Roberts, O'Scannlain, Robertson & Neill, Portland, 1978-86; judge, U.S. Ct. Appeals (9th cir.), San Francisco, 1986—; cons. Office of Pres.-Elect and mem. Dept. Energy Transition Team (Reagan transition), Washington, 1980-81; chmn. com. adminstrv. law Oreg. State Bar, 1980-81. Mem. council of legal advisers Republican Nat. Com., 1981-83; mem. Rep. Nat. Com., 1983-86, chmn. Oreg. Rep. Party, 1983-86; del. Rep. Nat. Convs., 1976, 80, chmn. Oreg. del., 1984; Rep. nominee U.S. Ho. of Reps., First Congl. Dist., 1974; team leader Energy Task Force, Pres.'s Pvt. Sector Survey on Cost Control, 1982-83. Served to maj. USAR, 1955-78. Mem. Fed. Energy Bar Assn., ABA. Roman Catholic. Club: Multnomah (Portland), Nat. Lawyers (Washington). Home: 2421 SW Arden Rd Portland OR 97201 Office: U S Ct Appeals Pioneer Courthouse 555 SW Yamhill St Portland OR 97204-1396

OSGOOD, FRANK WILLIAM, urban and economic planner; b. Williamston, Mich., Sept. 3, 1931; s. Earle Victor and Blanche Mae (Eberly) O.; children: Ann Marie, Frank William Jr. BS, Mich. State U., 1953; M in City Planning, Ga. Inst. Tech., 1960. Prin. planner Tulsa Met. Area Plnning Commn., 1958-60; sr. assoc. Hammer & Co. Assocs., Washington, 1960-64; econ. cons. Marvin Springer & Assocs., Dallas, 1964-65; sr. assoc. Gladstone Assocs., Washington, 1965-67; prof. urban planning Iowa State U., Ames, 1967-73; pres. Frank Osgood Assoc./Osgood Urban Research, Dallas, 1973-84; dir. mktg. studies MPSI Americas Inc., Tulsa, 1984-85, Comare Systems/Roulac & Co., San Francisco, 1985-86; pres. Osgood Urban Research, Millbrae, Calif., 1986—; adj. prof. U. Tulsa, 1974-76; lectr. U. Tex., Dallas, 1979, 83. Author: Control Land Uses Near Airports, 1960, Planning Small Business, 1967, Continuous Renewal Cities, 1970; contbr. articles to profl. jours. Chmn. awards Cub Scouts Am., Ames, 1971-73; deacon Calvary Presbyn. Ch., San Francisco, 1987. Served to 1st lt. USAF, 1954-56. Recipient Community Leaders and Noteworthy Americans award 1976. Mem. Am. Planning Assn. (mem. Calif. and N.Cen. Tex. chpts.), Am. Inst. Planners (v.p. Okla. chpt. 1975-77), Okla. Soc. Planning Cons. (sec.-treas. 1976-79), Urban Land Inst. Republican. Presbyterian. Club: Le Club. Home and Office: 12 Elder Ave Millbrae CA 94030

OSGUTHORPE, RUSSELL TRENT, instructional science educator, consultant; b. Salt Lake City, Dec. 4, 1946; s. Wesley Trenton and Iva LaRue (Russell) O; m. Lola Amelia Sedgwick, Aug. 7, 1969; children: Russell, Richard, Aaron, Emily, Lisa. BS in Psychology, Brigham Young U., 1971, MS in Sch. Psychology, 1973, PhD in Instructional Psychology, 1975. Research assoc., asst. prof. Nat. Tech. Inst. for Deaf, Rochester, N.Y., 1975-78; assoc. prof. to prof. instructional sci. Brigham Young U., Provo, Utah, 1978—; cons. Utah Office Edn., 1978—, U.S. Dept. Edn., Washington, 1980—. Named Outstanding Researcher Brigham Young U. Coll. Edn., 1986; U.S. Dept. Edn. research grantee, 1982-86. Mem. Am. Ednl. Research Assn., Council for Exceptional Children (chpt. pres. 1983-85). Mormon. Avocations: music, skiing, biking. Home: 476 W 1000 S Orem UT 84058 Office: Brigham Young U 201-C MCKB Provo UT 84602

OSGUTHORPE, SUSAN GALE LIKINS, nurse adminstrator, consultant; b. Salt Lake City, July 8, 1948; d. Corwin Hale and Virginia Louise (Snyder) Likins; m. Steven Garn Osguthorpe, Jan. 29, 1983. B.S. in Nursing cum laude, U. Utah, 1971, M.S. in Nursing, 1981. Staff nurse Holy Cross Hosp., Salt Lake City, 1971-73, Sisters of Mercy Hosp., Buffalo, 1973, St. Joseph's Hosp., Syracuse, N.Y., 1973-74; staff nurse Holy Cross Hosp., Salt Lake City, 1974-75, supr., 1975-81, critical care nurse clinician, 1981-82, clin. dir. critical care services, 1982-84; clin. dir. cardiovascular nursing Virginia Mason Hosp., Seattle, 1984—; mem. clin. faculty Weber State Coll., 1980-84, U. Utah, 1982-84, u. Wash., 1986—; Mem. healthside com. Wash. Heart Assn., 1984—. Named Outstanding Young Woman of Am., 1981. Mem. Am. Heart Assn., Am. Assn. for Critical Care Nurses (Puget Sound chpt.), Am. Assn. for Critical Care Nurses, Am. Nurses Assn., Sigma Theta Tau (Gamma Rho chpt., ann. research award 1982), Alpha Lambda Delta. Republican. Congregationalist. Home: 5808 E Mercer Way Mercer Island WA 98040 Office: Virginia Mason Hosp 925 Seneca St Seattle WA 98111

O'SHEA, MARTIN LESTER, investment banker, real estate investor; b. San Francisco, Dec. 6, 1938; s. Adolph Martin and Maria Carola (Bergmann) O'S.; B.A., Stanford, 1959; postgrad. (Fulbright scholar), Oxford (Eng.) U., 1959-61; M.B.A., Harvard, 1963; m. Barbara Ann Behn, Aug. 2, 1969 (div. July 1984); children—Laura Elizabeth, Amy Susanna, Amanda Catherine, m. Camille de Campos, July 28, 1984. Asso., Dean Witter & Co., N.Y.C., 1963-66; v.p. First Calif. Co., Inc., San Francisco, 1966-69; pres. O'Shea & Co., Inc., San Francisco, 1970-84; trustee First Eastern Realty Trust Boston, 1963-67; partner Gen. Western Co., San Francisco, 1967—;dir. Savs. Financial, Guarantee Savs. & Loan Assn. Livermore Valley. Pres., St. Francis Republican Assembly, 1972-74, 76-78, dir., 1973-80; dir. San Francisco County Coordinating Rep. Assembly, 1970-80; mem. San Francisco County Rep. Central Com., 1972-74, 76-86, chmn., 1979-83; treas. Rep. County Chairmen's Assn. Calif., 1979-81, v.p., 1981-83; mem. Nat. Adv. Council on Adult Edn., 1983-86; Commr. Commn. on Calif. State Govt. Orgn. and Economy, 1984—, bd. dirs. Cow Hollow Improvement Assn., 1975-85. Clubs: Harvard (N.Y.C.); Commonwealth (chmn. sect. on law enforcement 1971-75, bd. govs. 1975-78), Harvard (sec. 1972-74), Harvard Business School (San Francisco). Author: Tampering with the Machinery: Roots of Economic and Political Malaise, 1980. Home: 2863 Pacific Ave San Francisco CA 94115 Office: 235 Montgomery St San Francisco CA 94104

OSHMAN, M(ALIN) KENNETH, electrical engineer; b. Kansas City, Mo., July 9, 1940. AB, Rice U., 1962, BSc, 1963; MSc, Stanford U., 1965, PhD, 1967. Mem. tech. staff Sylvania Elec. Products, 1963-69; formerly pres. Rolm Corp., Santa Clara, Calif. Mem. IEEE, Nat. Acad. Engring. Address: 3000 Sand Hill Rd Menlo Park CA 94025 *

OSKAMP, STUART, psychology educator; b. Oak Park, Ill., May 31, 1930; s. Alfred Stuart and Catharine Roberts (Willard) O; m. Barbara F. Harvey, Dec. 26, 1955 (div. Mar. 1972); m. Catherine Cameron, Dec. 18, 1973; children: David Bryan, Karen Elisabeth. BA with honors, Grinnell Coll., 1951; PhD, Stanford U., 1960. Asst. prof. psychology Claremont (Calif.) Grad. Sch., 1960-64, assoc. prof. psychology, 1964-70, chmn. grad. faculty psychology, 1967-68, prof. psychology, 1970—; field assessment officer U.S. Peace Corps, Hilo, Hawaii, 1963; psychologist Tri-City Mental Health Authority, Pomona, Calif., 1964-66; research assoc. Inst. Social Research U. Mich., 1966-67, dept. psychology U. Bristol (Eng.), 1971; acad. vis. dept. social psychology London Sch. Econs., 1978; vis. prof. Sch. Psychology, U. New South Wales, Australia, 1985. Author: (with R.M. Suinn) Predictive Validity of Projective Measures, 1969, Attitudes and Opinions, 1977, Applied Social Psychology, 1984; adv. editor Jour. Cons. and Clin. Psychology, 1969-73, Jour. Population, 1978—; editor Applied Social Psychology Ann., 1984-87, Jour. Social Issues, 1987—. Pres. Claremont Chorale, 1974-75; coach Am. Youth Soccer Assn., 1970-78. Served with USNR, 1951-55. USPHS predoctoral fellow, 1956-57, VA clin. psychology intern, 1957-60, Am. Psychol. Assn. vis. scientist, 1967-68, NIMH grantee, 1965-66, 70-71, Marshall Fund grantee, 1966-67, coll. Entrance Exam. Bd. grantee, 1969-70, Nat. Inst. Child Health and Human Devel. grantee, 1973-78. Fellow Am. Psychol. Assn. (pres. div. population and environ. psychology 1980-81, council reps. 1982-85); mem. Soc. Psychol. Study Social Issues (mem. exec. council 1977-82, 85—), Soc. Exptl. Social Psychology, AAUP, Western Psychol. Assn. Office: Claremont Grad Sch Claremont CA 91711

OSKIN, ROBERT EUGENE, ceramic artist, educator; b. Detroit, Jan. 12, 1944; s. Jacob McC. Oskin and Pearl H. (Peltier) Thompson; m. Marilyn L. Gregory, Jan. 20, 1968; children: Michael, Mark, Peter. BA, Calif. State U.-Fullerton, 1967, MA, 1969. Cert. jr. coll. tchr., Calif. Ceramics instr. Orange Coast Coll., Costa Mesa, Calif., 1969-77, Norwalk-La Mirada Unified Sch. Dist., La Mirada, Calif., 1969—. Recipient Art Achievement award Artists' Soc. Internat., 1987. Group shows include: Design West, Los Angeles, 1965-67, Santa Ana Jr. Coll., 1968-69, Syracuse Nat. Ceramic Show, N.Y., 1969, La Mirada Fiesta de Artes, 1971-72, Brand Library, 1974, 80, Calif. Poly. State U., 1974, Calif. State U.-Los Angeles, 1976, U. Kans., 1977, Riverside Art Ctr. and Mus., Calif., Ilona and Gallery, Detroit, 1981-82, Irvine Fine Arts Ctr. (2d prize), 1983, Downey Mus. Art, 1983, Olympic Arts Festival, Los Angeles, 1984, Calif. show Elaine Potter Gallery, San Francisco, 1986, Asi Art Competition, San Francisco, 1987, Silverwood Gallery, Costa Mesa, 1987. Address: 9402 Harcourt Circle Huntington Beach CA 92646

OSNER, GEORGE THOMAS, urban planner; b. Oakland, Calif., Aug. 4, 1947; s. Henry Joseph and and Myrtle Marie (Madding) O.; m. Elise Marie Kawin, June 21, 1968; children: Jeremy Henry, Gabriel Peter, Blythe Marie, Miriam Elizabeth. AB in Ecology, U. Calif., Berkeley, 1970; secondary teaching credential, Calif. State U.-Humboldt, Arcata, 1971; AM, Washington U., St. Louis, 1975. Tchr. pub. sch. Scattergood Sch., West Branch, Iowa, 1971-73; research and teaching assoc. Washington U., 1973-75; prin. planner City of Modesto, Calif., 1976—; cons. Viewdata Corp., Miami Beach, Fla., 1985-86. Author: (document) Noise and Conservation Elements, City of Modesto General Plan; editor Disk Network, 1986—. Cubmaster Cub Scout Pack 177, Modesto, Calif., 1980-83. Mem. Am. Planning Assn., AAAS, World Future Soc., Stanislaus Apple Group (software librarian 1980—). Mem. United Ch. of Christ. Club: Modesto Engrs. Avocations: computer programming, backpacking, philately. Home: 1124 Brady Modesto CA 95350 Office: City of Modesto PO Box 642 Modesto CA 95353

OSORNO, BRUNO, electrical engineering educator; b. Mexico City, July 31, 1947; came to U.S., 1976; s. Marcelo Osorno and Guadalupe Escareño; m. Patricia Nava. BSEE, Poly. Inst. Tech., Mexico City, 1970; MSEE, U. Colo., 1978. Design engr. Monsanto (IRSA), Mexico City, 1971-73, supr. services, 1974-75; teaching asst. N.Mex. State U., Las Cruces, 1979-82; asst. prof. No. Ariz. U., Flagstaff, 1984—. Mem. IEEE, Eta Kappa Nu. Home: 3415 Foxlair Flagstaff AZ 86004 Office: No Ariz U PO Box 15600 Flagstaff AZ 86011

OSSE, TIMOTHY JAMES, ocean engineer; b. Louisville, Ky., Oct. 25, 1957; s. Albert and Dorothy (Donohue) O. BS in Engring., U. Wash., 1979, MS in Engring., 1981. Ocean engr. Applied Physics Lab. U. Wash., Seattle, 1981—; owner Oceanus Marine, Kirkland, Wash., 1985—. Author: (papers) Fishing Vessel Stability, 1982, Thermal Characteristics of Li Batteries, 1983, Fixed Weapon Target, 1984. Mem. Soc. Naval Architects and Marine Engrs (assoc.). Avocations: mountaineering, backpacking, skiing, scuba diving, sailing. Home: 109 6th St Kirkland WA 98033 Office: Applied Physics Lab 1013 NE 40th St Seattle WA 98105

OSSERMAN, ROBERT, mathematician, educator; b. N.Y.C., Dec. 19, 1926; s. Herman Aaron and Charlotte (Adler) O.; m. Maria Anderson, June 15, 1952; 1 son, Paul; m. Janet Adelman, July 21, 1976; children—Brian, Stephen. B.A., NYU, 1946; postgrad., U. Zurich, U. Paris; M.A., Harvard U., 1948, Ph.D., 1955. Teaching fellow Harvard U., 1949-52, vis. lectr., research assoc., 1961-62; instr. U. Colo., 1952-53; mem. faculty Stanford U., 1955—, prof. math., 1966—, chmn. dept. math., 1973-79, Mellon Prof. Interdisciplinary Studies, 1987—; mem. NYU Inst. Math. Scis., 1957-58, Math. Scis. Research Inst., Berkeley, Calif., 1983-84 head math. br. Office Naval Research, 1960-61. Author: Two-Dimensional Calculus, 1968, A Survey of Minimal Surfaces, 1969, 2d edit., 1986. Fulbright lectr. U. Paris, 1965-66; Guggenheim fellow, 1976-77; vis. fellow U. Warwick, Imperial Coll., U. London. Mem. Math. Assn. Am., Am. Math. Soc. Research, publs. on differential geometry, complex variables, differential equations, especially minimal surfaces, Laplace operator, isoperimetric inequalities, ergodic theory. Office: Math Dept Stanford U Stanford CA 94305

OSSINGER, RICHARD WARD, marketing executive; b. Seattle, July 24, 1932; s. Elmo Hudgins and June Feltz Ossinger-Bunce; m. Dorothy Ann Moll, Aug. 3, 1963; children: Michelle Lynn Schlott, Richard Scott, Shaun Alan. BA in Radio and TV, U. Wash., 1955, BA in Sociology, 1966, postgrad., 1957-60. Lab. technician Dept. of Comml. Fisheries, Seattle, 1958-62; owner Economy Cleaners, 1962-65; prin. Richard Ossinger & Assocs. Network Mktg. Co., Edmonds, Wash., 1965—. Avocations: ham radio, beachcombing, reading, pub. speaking, investing. Home and Office: 928 9th Ave N Edmonds WA 98020

OSTERMAN, CONSTANCE E., Canadian provincial government minister; b. Acme, Alta., Can· June 23, 1936; m. Joe Osterman, Oct. 30, 1954; children: Theo, Kurt, Kim, Kelly, Joe Jr. MLA representing Three Hills constituency Alta. Legis. Assembly, 1979-82, 82-85, 86—, party whip, mem. edn. caucus and agr. caucus coms., 1979-82, Minister of Consumer and Corp. Affairs, mem. social planning com. of cabinet, cabinet/caucus com. on legis. rev., agr. caucus com., 1982-85, Minister of Social Services and Community Health, 1986—, mem. social planning, energy, met. affairs and mgmt. policy coms. of cabinet, 1986—; served select legis. com. to rev. surface rights issue, lead role in passing of Surface Rights Act, 1983. Active exec. bds. local ch., home and sch. assns., Carstairs, Alta., 1958—, surface rights area; commr., charter mem. Alta. Human Rights Commn., 1973-78; pres. Can. Assn. Statutory Human Rights Agys. Office: Office Minister Social Services, 424 Legislature Bldg, Edmonton, AB Canada T5K 2B6

OSTERMAN, ERIC FLOYD, shipyeard manager, industrial engineer; b. Seattle, Nov. 18, 1942; s. Floyd Eugene and Helen Wilma (Munson) O.; m. Margaret Sydney Immel, Aug. 3, 1973; 1 child, Heidi Yoko. AS, Olympic Coll., 1962; BSME, U. Wash., 1968, MBA, 1976. Registered profl. engr., Wash. Process engr. The Boeing Co., Seattle, 1972-75; from asst. mgr. to gen. mgr. Todd Shipyards Corp., Seattle, 1976-77, asst. plant engr., 1977-78, asst. program mgr., 1978—. Served with U.S. Army, 1962-65, Korea. Mem. Inst. Indsl. Engrs. (sr.). Republican. Buddhist. Avocations: tennis, chess, reading. Home: 5915 S Cooper St Seattle WA 98118 Office: Todd Shipyards Corp 1801 16th Ave SW Seattle WA 98124

OSTERMILLER, JOHN VICTOR, real estate company executive; b. Lincoln, Nebr., Nov. 4, 1910; s. John and Louise (Bernhardt) O.; m. Margaret Ellen Kerr, June 17, 1934; children: Karen Rea, John Kerr. Student, U. Nebr., 1927-28; BS, Colo. State U., 1932. Tchr. vocat. agr., pub. sch. Colo., 1934-42; agrl. fieldman Gt. Western Sugar Co., Brush, Colo., 1942-49; asst. mgr. Brush and Ft. Morgan, 1949-57; mgr. Longmont, Colo., 1957-63; agrl. mgr. Ft. Morgan, 1963-70, N.E. Colo. asst. dist. agrl. mgr., 1970-73; v.p. Gt. Western Sugar Export Co., 1973-75; mgr. farm and ranch dept. Crown Realty Co., Denver, 1975-78, Carriage House Realtors, Ft. Morgan, 1978-83, Realty Assocs., Ft. Morgan, 1984—. Contbr. articles to profl. jours. Instr. Adult Edn., Yuma, Colo., 1935-38, Brush, 1938-42. Rep. precinct committeeman, Morgan County, 1950-57, 64-74, Boulder County, 958-63; mem. St. Vrain Valley Sch. Bd., Longmont, 1961-63; bd. dirs. Brush Civic Club, 1944-50, Ft. Morgan Heritage Found., pres. 196-75; bd. dirs., pres. Colo. State U. Found., 1973-86. Mem. Ft. Morgan C. of C. (dir. 1965-69, pres. 1968), Colo. State U. Alumni (dir. 1971-82, pres. 1975-76), Am. Sugar Beet Soc. Technologists, Alpha Tau Alpha, Lamda Gamma Delta, Sigma Phi Epsilon. Presbyterian. Lodges: Masons, Lions. Home: 4 Yates Terr Fort Morgan CO 80701 Office: Realty Assocs 209 State St Fort Morgan CO 80701

OSTHEIMER, JOHN MAURICE, political science educator, dean; b. West Chester, Pa., Nov. 22, 1938; s. Alfred James and Ruth Eloise (Magargle) O.; m. Nancy Jane Cushing, June 8, 1963; children: Ellen Shaw, J. Gibson, William Allen. BA, Yale U., 1960, MA, 1964, PhD, 1967. Asst. prof. polit. sci. No. Ariz. U., Flagstaff, 1967-71, assoc. prof., 1971-81, prof., 1981-85, dept. chmn., 1981-85; prof. U. Colo., Denver, 1985—, dean Coll. Liberal Arts and Scis., 1985—. Author: Politics of the Western Indian Ocean Islands, 1975, Nigerian Politics, 1973; contbr. chpts. to books, articles to profl. jours. Fellow Eisenhower Consortium for Western Environ. Forestry Research, 1974-76, Fulbright-Hayes Sr. Research fellow, 1973. Mem. Council of Colls. of Arts and Scis., Conf. for Urban Colls. of Arts Letters and Scis., Flagstaff Youth Hockey Club (pres. 1981-82), No. Ariz. Flycasters (pres. 1984-85). Democrat. Episcopalian. Club: City (Denver). Avocation: flyfishing. Home: 200 Kearney St Denver CO 80220 Office: U Colo Coll Liberal Arts and Scis 1100 14th St Denver CO 80202

OSTLIE, DALE ALLAN, physics educator, astrophysics researcher; b. Northfield, Minn., Sept. 18, 1955; s. Dean Arthur and Dorothy Marie (Carlson) O. BS in Physics, Math., St. Olaf Coll., 1977; PhD in Astrophysics, Iowa State U., 1982. Asst. prof. physics Bates Coll., Lewiston, Maine, 1982-84, Weber State Coll., Ogden, Utah, 1984—; cons. Space Telescope Sci. Inst., Balt., 1983; collaborator Los Alamos (N.Mex.) Nat. Lab., 1985—. dir. choir Ascension Luth. Ch., Ogden. Recipient Richard G. Patrick award physics dept., Iowa State U., 1981. Mem. Am. Astron. Soc., Astron. Soc. Pacific, Am. Assn. Variable Star Observers, Pitt Band, Sigma Pi Sigma. Avocations: skiing, tennis, sailing, choral and instrumental music, photography. Home: 3253 Harrison Blvd Apt #12C Ogden UT 84403 Office: Weber State Coll Dept Physics MS2508 Ogden UT 84408

OSTRANDER, WILLIAM SCOTT, research and development engineer; b. East Lansing, Mich., Mar. 4, 1956; s. Lester Vernon and Lorna Kay (Carlson) O. BSME cum laude, U. Mich., 1978, MSME, 1979. Process engr. Stanford Park div. Hewlett Packard Corp., Palo Alto, Calif., 1979-81, sect. mgr. Stanford Park div., 1981-84, research and devel. engr. printed circuit div., 1986—; process engr. Signal Analysis Network Measurement div. Hewlett Packard Corp., Rohnert Park, Calif., 1984-85; cons. Tandem Computers, Cupertino, Calif., 1980. Whirlpool fellow, 1978-79. Mem. Pi Tau Sigma, Tau Beta Pi. Republican. Avocations: skiing, windsurfing, bicycling. Office: Hewlett Packard Corp 3500 Deer Creek 26U Palo Alto CA 94304

OSTROWSKI, SCOTT WILLIAM, safety engineer; b. Grosse Pointe, Mich., Aug. 8, 1961; s. John Walter and JoAnn Elizabeth (Scammell) O.; m. Rayanne Elaine Baring, June 2, 1984. BS in Safety Engring., Tex. A&M U., 1983; MS in Safety, U. So. Calif., 1986. Cert. safety profl. (assoc.). System safety engr. Lockheed Missiles & Space Co., Sunnyvale, Calif., 1984—. Marathol Oil Co. scholar, 1982-83. Fellow System Safety Soc.; mem. Am. Soc. Safety engrs. (v.p. student chpt. 1982-83, scholar 1982), Tau Beta Pi. Lutheran. Office: Lockheed Missiles & Space Co 111 Lockheed Way Sunnyvale CA 94088

OTCHIS, JOHN IRVING, controller; b. Los Angeles, June 14, 1946; s. Allan and Florence (Bender) O.; m. Donna Lee, Apr. 8, 1965; children: Lucinda, Julie, Susie, Shira, Joshua. BS in Math., U. Calif., Santa Barbara, 1973. Controller GSM Inc, Santa Barbara, 1972-78, Black Ice Inc., Napa, Calif., 1978-83; asst. controller Charles Krug Winery, St. Helena, Calif., 1983-86; controller, chief fin. officer Cuvalson Winery, Napa, Calif., 1986—. Democrat. Jewish. Avocation: sailing. Home: 1039 Mount George Ave Napa CA 94558 Office: Cuvalson Winery Inc PO Box 384 Calistoga CA 94515

OTELSBERG, BARRY LEWIS, real estate finance executive; b. Bklyn., Aug. 7, 1950; s. Martin and Lila (Chayt) O.; m. Joan Marlene Silverman, Sept. 18, 1976; children: Jamie, Sandi, Jennifer. BA, Calif. State U., Northridge, 1972. With sales, fin. dept. Nat. Acceptance Co., Beverly Hills, Calif., 1972-76; pres. Foothill Real Estate Lending, Agoura, Calif., 1976—; exec. v.p. Foothill Thrift and Loan, Agoura, Calif., 1985—; also bd. dirs. Foothill Thrift and Loan. Mem. Nat. Assn. Rev. Appraisers and Mortgage Underwriters, Mortgage Bankers Assn. Office: Foothill Thrift and Loan 30343 Canwood St #104 Agoura CA 91301

O'TOOLE, BRIAN JOSEPH, risk management consultant; b. Sunnyvale, Calif., Sept. 14, 1955; s. Joseph Clinton and Louise (Sinn) O'T. BA, Stanford U., 1978. Ins. broker O'Toole Ins., Los Altos, Calif., 1978-84, Flamer & Co., Los Altos, 1984-85; risk mgr. Abag Plan, Cupertino, Calif., 1985—. Rep. asst. treas. Calif., 1983—; pres. Peninsula div. League of Calif. Cities, 1985—; elector 1985 Electoral Coll., mem. Santa Clara (Calif.) County Traffic Authority, 1985—; Mayor of Sunnyvale, 1985-86. Mem. Christian Sci. Ch. Avocations: tennis, racquetball. Home: 969 D Mesa Terr Sunnyvale CA 94086

O'TOOLE, MARGUERITE MARY, marketing professional; b. Worcester, Mass., May 5, 1953; d. Austin Francis and Marie Pauline Marguerite (Daigneault) O'T. BS, Boston U., 1975; MBA, U. Phoenix, 1986. Mktg. rep. Blue Cross of Mass., Worcester, 1976-80; sr. rep. Blue Cross of Mass., Boston, 1980-82; account exec. FHP, Inc., Salt Lake City, 1982-83, mktg. mgr., 1983-85; dir. mktg., Ariz. region Family Health Program, Inc., Tempe, 1985—; lectr. Clark U., Worcester, 1978-80, Assumption Coll., Worcester, 1979-80, Weber State Coll., Ogden, Utah, 1983-85, U. Utah, Salt Lake City, 1983-85. Conductor mktg. seminars March of Dimes Salt Lake City chpt., 1985. Mem. Ariz. Ins. Council (lic. agt. 1985—). Democrat. Avocations: travel, music, sports. Office: Family Health Program Inc 1600 W Broadway Suite 245 Tempe AZ 85282

OTOSHI, TOM YASUO, elec. engr.; b. Seattle, Sept. 4, 1931; s. Jitsuo and Shina Otoshi; B.S.E.E., U. Wash., 1954, M.S.E.E., 1957; m. Haruko Shirley Yumiba, Oct. 13, 1963; children—John, Kathryn. With Hughes Aircraft Co., Culver City, Calif., 1956-61; mem. tech. staff Jet Propulsion Lab., Calif. Inst. Tech., Pasadena, 1961—; cons. Recipient NASA New Tech. awards. Mem. IEEE (sr.), Sigma Xi. Contbr. articles to profl. jours. Patentee in field. Home: 3551 Henrietta St La Crescenta CA 91214 Office: Jet Propulsion Lab 4800 Oak Grove Dr Pasadena CA 91109

OTSMAA, MATI TOOMAS, advertising exeuctive; b. Los Angeles, July 26, 1951; s. Herman and Maie (Zirnask) O. Cert. in lit. and arts, U. Salzburg, Austria, 1970; BA in Psychology, Biology, U. So. Calif., 1973, MBA in Multinat. Mktg., 1975. Account exec. Ogily & Mather, N.Y.C., 1975-78; account dir. Ogily & Mather, San Francisco, 1985-86; brand mgr. Johnson & Johnson, Piscataway, N.J., 1978-80; account supr. Chiat Day, San Francisco, 1980-82; mgmt. supr. J. Walter Thompson, San Francisco, 1982-85; prin. The Invicta Group, San Francisco, 1986; gen. mgr. Dancer Fitzgerald Sample Dorland Direct, San Francisco, 1986—. Contbr. articles to Newport Life mag., 1973-75. Bd. dirs. Los Angeles County Rep. Heritage Council, 1973-75. Mem. San Francisco Advt. Club. Lutheran. Home: 2694 Sacramento #2 San Francisco CA 94115 Office: Invicta Group 2694 Sacramento Suite 2 San Francisco CA 94115

OTT, DONALD G(EORGE), organic chemist, researcher; b. Kinsley, Kans., Aug. 13, 1926; s. George Henry and Sadie Flora (Norman) O.; m. Mary Jane Curtis, Aug. 8, 1948; children: Pamela Sue, Kevin Curtis. BS in Chemistry, Colo. State U., 1950; PhD in Chemistry, Wash. State U., 1953; postgrad., Cambridge U., England, 1960-61. Mem. research staff Dow Chem. Co, Midland, Mich., 1953-54; mem. research staff Los Alamos (N.Mex.) Nat. Lab., 1954-63, dep. group leader biomed. research, 1963-72, group leader organic and biochem. synthesis, 1972-76; mgr. Los Alamos div. Stohler Isotope Chems., 1976, mem. research staff, 1976—. Author: Syntheses with Stable Isotopes, 1980; also approximately 100 articles in profl. jours.; patentee in field. Served with USNR, 1944-46, PTO. Recipient Spl. Fellowship, NIH, 1960-61. Fellow AAAS, The Chem. Soc. (London); mem. Am. Chem. Soc., Sigma Xi. Republican. Clubs: Soaring Soc. Am.; N.Mex. Soaring Club (gov. 1979—). Avocations: soaring, fly fishing, backpacking. Home: 2423 Club Rd Los Alamos NM 87544 Office: Los Alamos Nat Lab Explosives Tech Los Alamos NM 87545

OTT, JONATHAN EDWARD, chemist; b. New Haven, June 1, 1949; s. David George and Ann Marie (Cox) O. BS, The Evergreen State Coll., 1975. Free-lance writer Vashon, Wash., 1976-83; pres. Natural Products Co., Vashon, Wash., 1984—. Author: Hallucinogenic Plants of North America, 1976, The Cacahuatl Eater, 1985; editor Teonanacatl: Hallucinogenic Mushrooms of North America, 1978; translator LSD: My Problem Child, 1980. Fellow The Linnean Soc.; mem. AAAS, Soc. Econ. Botany, Ethnobiology Soc. Home and Office: Natural Products Co PO Box 273 Vashon WA 98070

OTT, WENDELL LORENZ, art museum director, artist; b. McCloud, Calif., Sept. 17, 1942; s. Wendell and Rose (Jacob) O. Student, San Francisco Art Inst., 1960-61, 62-63; B.A., Trinity U., San Antonio, 1968; M.F.A., U. Ariz., 1970; postgrad., Mus. Mgmt. Inst., U. Calif., 1984. Asst. dir. Roswell (N.Mex.) Mus. and Art Center, 1970-71, dir., 1971-86; dir. Tacoma Art Mus., 1986—; chmn. Roswell Humanities Series, 1972-73; instr. N.Mex. Mil. Inst., Roswell; mem. visual arts adv. com. Coll. of Santa Fe, 1985; grant reviewer Inst. Mus. Services, Washington, 1983. One man exhbns. include, Trinity U., 1967, 68, Men of Art Guild, San Antonio, 1967, 68, David Orr's Gallery, Roswell, 1976, G.W.V. Smith Art Mus., Springfield, Mass.; group exhbns. include Tex. Painting and Sculpture, Dallas Mus. Fine Arts, 1966, Witte Meml. Mus., San Antonio, 1967, 68, 1st ann. S.W. Arts Festival, Tucson, 1969, Graphics 69, Western N.Mex. U., 1969, 11th Ariz. ann. Phoenix Art Mus., 1969 (purchase awards), 9th ann., Security, Colo., 1969, 5th invitational Yuman Art Center, Yuma, Ariz., 1970, Juarez (Mexico) Mus. Art and History, 1973. Served with AUS, 1964-66. Mem. N.Mex. Assn. Museums (chmn. 1973-75), Am. Assn. Museums (MAP surveyor mus. assessment program 1984). Home: 7425 Ruby Dr SW Tacoma WA 98498 Office: 12th and Pacific Tacoma WA 98402

OTTER, CLEMENT LEROY, lieutenant governor; b. Caldwell, Idaho, May 3, 1942; s. Joseph Bernard and Regina Mary (Buser) O.; m. Gay Corinne Simplot, Dec. 28, 1964; children: John Simplot, Carolyn Lee, Kimberly Dawn, Corinne Marie. BA in Polit. Sci., Coll. Idaho, 1967; PhD, Mindanao State U., 1980. Mgr. J.R. Simplot Co., Caldwell, Idaho, 1971-76, asst. to v.p. adminstrn., 1976-78, v.p. adminstrn., 1978-82, internat. pres., 1982—; lt. gov. State of Idaho, Boise, 1987—. Mem. Presdl. Task Force-AID, Washington, 1982-84; com. mem. invest tech. devel. State Adv. Council, Washington, 1983-84; mem. exec. council Bretton Woods Com., 1984—; mem. U.S. C. of C., Washington, 1983-84. Mem. Young Pres.' Orgn., Sales and Mktg. Execs., Idaho Assn. Commerce and Industry, Idaho Agrl. Leadership Council, Idaho Ctr. for Arts, Idaho Internat. Trade Council, Pacific N.W. Waterways Assn., N.W. Food Producers, Ducks Unltd. Republican. Roman Catholic. Clubs: Arid, Hillcrest Country. Lodge: Moose, Elks. Avocations: jogging, music, art collecting, horse training, fishing. Office: Office of the Lt Gov State House Rm 225 Boise ID 83702

OTTING, EDWARD ALBERT, information systems specialist; b. Indpls., Apr. 6, 1931; s. Albert Henry and Kathryn Lucille (Hutchison) O.; m. Mary Lou Beck, July 12, 1953; 1 child, Angela. BS, Ind. U., 1953, MBA, 1957. Dir. computer ops. Eli Lilly and Co., Indpls., 1971-72, dir. corp. materials planning, 1972-74, dir. info. systems, 1974-82, dir. info. systems and planning, 1982-83, dir. infor. systems ops., 1983—; mem. adv. bd. State Ind. Dept. Mental Health, Indpls., 1968-71. Mem. MBA Adv. Council Ind. U. Grad. Sch. Bus., Bloomington, 1978—, Industry Adv. Council Purdue U. Computer Tech.Dept., West Lafayette, Ind., 1979-84, Science and Engring. Council U. Evansville, Ind., 1984—; mem. bd. info. services City and County Govt., Indpls., 1984—; mem. adv. council Nat. Communications Forum, Chgo., 1985—. Served with U.S. Army, 1954-56. Recipient Outstanding Citizen award Am. Legion, Indpls., 1979. Mem. Assn. Retarded Citizens (pres. 1978-80), Edn. Found. Data Processing Mgmt. Assn. (pres. 1982—). Republican. Avocations: boating, hiking, reading, spectator sports. Home: 1775 Glencary Crest Indianapolis IN 46208 Office: Eli Lilly and Co Lilly Corp Ctr Indianapolis IN 46285

OTTLEY, JEROLD DON, choral conductor, educator; b. Salt Lake City, Apr. 7, 1934; s. Sidney James and Alice (Warren) O.; m. JoAnn South, June 22, 1956; children: Brent Kay, Allison. B.A., Brigham Young U., Provo, Utah, 1961; M.Mus., U. Utah, 1967; Fulbright study grantee, Fed. Republic Germany, 1968-69; D.M.A. (grad. teaching fellow), U. Oreg., 1972. Tchr. public schs. Salt Lake City area, 1961-65; mem. faculty U. Utah, 1967—, asst. prof. music, 1971-78, adj. assoc. prof. music, 1978-81, adj. prof. music, 1981—; assoc. conductor Salt Lake Mormon Tabernacle Choir, 1974-75, conductor, 1975—; also guest conductor throughout U.S. Rec. artist, CBS Masterworks. Past mem. gen. music coms. Mormon Ch., cultural arts com. Salt Lake City C. of C., past bd. advs. Barlow Endowment Music Composition. Served with U.S. Army, 1957-59. Faculty Study grantee U. Utah, 1972. Mem. Am. Choral Dirs. Assn., Am. Choral Found., Music Educators Nat. Conf., Master Tchr. Inst. Arts. (past trustee). Office: Mormon Tabernacle Choir 50 E North Temple Salt Lake City UT 84150

OTTO, JEFFERY LEE, pharmaceutical company executive; b. Colorado Springs, Colo., Aug. 4, 1955; s. Carlyle Leonard and Lelia Irene (Carr) O. BA in Chemistry, U. Colo., 1977, PhD in Analytical Chemistry, 1981. Sr. research analyst Cord Labs., Broomfield, Colo., 1982-85, mgr. analytical research and devel., 1985—. Named Eagle Scout Boy Scouts Am., 1969. Mem. Am. Chem. Soc.; Rocky Mountain Chromatography Discussion Group. Republican. Lutheran. Avocation: photography. Home: 790 Newland Ct Boulder CO 80303 Office: Cord Labs 2555 W Midway Boulder CO 80020

OTTO, STEPHEN DOUGLAS, store planner, designer, consultant; b. Hyannis, Mass., Aug. 16, 1944; s. Clarence Edmund and Helen Mary (Holyst) O. AA in Bus., Coll. San Mateo, 1965; BBA, San Jose State U., 1971. Sales mgr. Internat. Agy., San Jose, Calif., 1971-74; sales engr. The Trane Co., San Jose, 1974-75; mfrs. rep. Streater Store Fixtures, Albert Lea, Minn., 1975-77; store planner Calif. Retail Hardware Assn., San Francisco, 1977-83; store planning cons. San Francisco Distbn. Ctr. Ace Hardware Corp., Benicia, Calif., 1983—. Served with USNR, 1966-68, Vietnam. Recipient Home Ctr. of Yr. award Home Ctr. mag., 1979, 82. Mem. Inst. Store Planners (v.p. 1986—), Soc. Advancement Mgmt. (dir. fin. San Jose chpt. 1970-71). Republican. Roman Catholic. Avocations: breeding exotic African tropical fish, tennis, sailing, horseback riding. Home: 131 Chilpancingo Pkwy Pleasant Hills CA 94523 Office: Ace Hardware Corp San Francisco Distbn Ctr 433 Industrial Way PO Box 826 Benicia CA 94510

OTTO, WALTER DAVIS, educational adminstrator; b. Los Angeles, Apr. 8, 1936; s. James E. and Francis L. (Thrall) O.; m. Christine Linda Murray, June 20, 1962; m. 2d, Pamela Steel Huie, May 15, 1948; children—Matthew Logan, James Bradford. A.A., Pasadena City Coll., 1958; student U. Houston, 1958-59; B.A., Los Angeles State Coll., 1961, postgrad, 1962; M.S., Calif. State U.-Fullerton, 1969. Tchr., athletic dir., sports commr. Pago Pago, Am. Samoa, 1962-64; tchr. Sycamore Jr. High Sch., 1965-66; tchr., coach Westminster High Sch., 1966-69; vice-prin. Madrone Intermediate Sch., 1969-70; counselor, tchr. Hawaii Prep. Acad., 1970-71; sch./community coordinator Marina High Sch., 1971-73; tchr., coach Laguna Beach (Calif.) High Sch., 1973-79; real estate salesman, Laguna Beach, Calif., 1979-80; vice-prin. Perris Valley Jr. High Sch., Perris, Calif., 1980-81, prin., 1981-87. Sch. power mem. Laguna Beach Schs., 1979-85; active Perris Valley Swimming Pool Orgn., 1980-85. NDEA grantee Los Angeles State Coll., 1961-62; named Tchr. of Yr., Laguna Beach High Sch., 1975. Mem. Assn. Supervision and Curriculum Devel., Nat. Assn. Secondary Sch. Prins., Calif. Leadership Acad. Trainer, Nat. Swim and Waterpolo Coaches Assn., Friends of Library, Assn. Calif. Sch. Adminstrs., Calif. Tchrs. Assn., Western Riverside Adminstrs. Assn., Phi Delta Kappa. Lodge: Rotary Internat.

OURADA, GERALD LYNN, electrical engineer; b. Boise, Idaho, Sept. 11, 1959; s. Earl Stanley and Kathleen Mary (Loucks) O. BSEE, U. Idaho, 1982. Officer Moscow (Idaho) Police Dept., 1979-81; engr. power distbn. Idaho Power Co., Boise, 1980-81; enlisted USAF, 1981, advanced through grades to capt., 1986; engr. missile systems USAF, Vancenberg AFB, Calif., 1982-86; engr. space projects USAF, Los Angeles AFS, 1986—. Coordinator young adult group Cath. Ch., Santa Maria and Torrance, Calif. Mem. Nat. Rifle Assn., Smithsonian Inst., Air Force Assn. Avocations: backpacking, rock climbing, shooting, hunting, racquetball. Home: PO Box 34 Hawthorne CA 90251

OUTCALT, DAVID LEWIS, mathematician, university administrator; b. Los Angeles, Jan. 30, 1935; s. Earl Kinyon and Alberta Estes Ferguson O.; m. Marcia Lee Beach, July 1, 1956; children—Jeffrey David, Kevin Douglas, Gregory Mark, Eric Matthew. B.A. in Math., Pomona Coll., 1956; M.A. in Math., Claremont Grad. Sch., 1958; Ph.D. in Math., Ohio State U., 1963; D.Pub. Adminstrn. (hon.), Kyung Hee U., Korea, 1984. Asst. prof. math. Claremont McKenna Coll., 1962-64; asst. prof. to prof. math. U. Calif.-Santa Barbara, 1964-80, chmn. dept. math., 1969-72, dean instrnl. devel., 1977-80; vice chancellor acad. affairs U. Alaska, Anchorage, 1980-81, prof. math., 1980-86, chancellor, 1981-86; prof. sci., environ. change, math. U. Wis., Green Bay, 1986—, chancellor, 1986—. Contbr. articles on math. and higher edn. to profl. jours. Moderator bd. trustees Humana Hosp. Anchorage, 1982-83; mem. exec. bd. Western Alaska council Boy Scouts Am., 1982-86; mem. Anchorage Symphony Bd., 1986. Grantee USAF Office Sci. Research, 1964-71, U. Calif., 1975-78, NSF, 1976-79. Mem. Math. Assn. Am., Sigma Xi. Lodge: Rotary. Office: U Wis Office of Chancellor 2420 Nicolet Dr Green Bay WI 54301-7001

OUTLAND, GEORGE FAULKNER, educator, cons.; b. Cambridge, Mass., May 8, 1929; s. George Elmer and Virginia Margaret (Stevenson) O.; B.A., U. Calif. at Santa Barbara, 1952; M.A., San Francisco State Coll., 1957; Ed.D., U. Calif. at Berkeley, 1971; m. Carolyn Wolfe, July 12, 1953; 1 dau., Marilyn Merry. Apprentice printer, Calif., Va., 1943-52; journeyman compositor, proofreader various firms Calif., D.C., 1952-65; printing tchr. Oakland (Calif.) High Sch., 1956-63, social sci. tchr., debate coach, 1961-64; vocat. coordinator Oakland Public Schs., 1964-65; dir. research and resources San Mateo (Calif.) Union High Sch. Dist., 1965-75, 84-86, vocat. adviser Adult Sch., 1975-76; tchr. social sci., adminstrv. asst. Burlingame (Calif.) High Sch., 1976-77; dir. Tech. Tng. Inst., for GTE Sylvania, Tehran, Iran, 1977-78; head compensatory edn. dept. San Mateo High Sch., 1978—, Aragon High Sch., 1981-84; tchr. vocat. edn. U. Calif. at Berkeley, 1966-72; tchr. program planning and budgeting systems Coll. Notre Dame, 1971-72; tchr. indsl. edn. Calif. State U., San Francisco, 1972-73; vocat. researcher U.S. Office Edn., Washington, 1962, 67, Calif. State Dept. Edn., 1963-64; ednl. cons. to U.S. Office Edn., various state depts. edn., also county and local sch. systems; cons. and lectr. various colls. and univs.; chmn. vis. coms. accrediting commn. Western Assn. Schs. and Colls. Co-chmn. Adv. Com. on Calif. Assembly ACR 127, 1970-72. Served with USN, 1952-54; capt. Res. Recipient Honor Key, U. Calif. at Santa Barbara, 1952, Letter of Commendation Sec. of Navy, 1969, Navy Commendation medal, 1978. Mem. Am. Vocat. Assn. (life), U. Calif. at Santa Barbara Alumni Assn. (life), Am. Vocat. Edn. Research Assn. (membership sec. 1968-71), Calif. Indsl. Edn. Assn. (life), U.S. Naval Inst. (life), Naval Order U.S. (life), U.S. Navy League (life), U.S. Capitol Hist. Soc. (life), Navy-Marine Corps-Coast Guard Mus., San Mateo County Hist. Assn., Naval Res. Assn. (life), Blue Jackets Assn. (life), Res. Officers Assn. (life), Phi Delta Kappa (life). Republican. Club: Commonwealth (San Francisco). Home: PO Box 214 Burlingame CA 94011

OVERALL, JAMES CARNEY, JR., professor; b. Nashville, Sept. 27, 1937; s. James Carney and Evelyn Byrd (Duncan) O.; m. Marie Kathryn Pauli, Aug. 14, 1965; children: David, Paul. BS, Davidson Coll., 1959; MD, Vanderbilt U., 1963. Cert. pediatrics. Intern Vanderbilt U. Hosp., Nashville, 1963-64; resident Columbia Presbyn. Med. Ctr., N.Y.C., 1964-66; research assoc. Nat. Inst. Child Health, Bethesda, Md., 1966-68; instr. pediatrics Rochester, N.Y., 1968-70; asst. prof. pediatrics, microbiology U. Utah Sch. Med., Salt Lake City, 1970-74, assoc. prof. pediatrics, microbiology, 1974-79, prof. pediatrics, 1979—, prof. pathology, 1981—; chief pediatrics infectious diseases Univ. Utah Sch. Med., 1970—; bd. govs. Primary Children's Med. Ctr., Salt Lake City, 1976-78; dir. virology course U. Utah Sch. Med., 1980—; vice chmn. pediatrics dept. U. Utah Sch. Med., 1982—; assoc. dir. diagnostic virology lab., 1981—. Contbr. chpts. to textbooks, articles to profl. jours. vice moderator Holladay United Ch. Christ, Salt Lake City, 1982-85. Served to lt. comdr. USPHS, 1966-68. Recipient Investigator award Howard Hughes Med. Inst., 1974-80. Mem. Am. Pediatric Soc., Soc. Pediatric Research, Am. Soc. Virology. United Ch. of Christ. Home: 382 L St Salt Lake City UT 84103 Office: Univ Utah Coll Med Dept Pediatrics Salt Lake City UT 84132

OVERBY, JOHN CHARLES, electronic company executive; b. Wallace, Idaho, Sept. 10, 1946; s. James Milton and Teresa (Sack) O.; m. Susan Weeks, Sept. 2, 1967; children—Michael, Nicholas. B.S.E.E. cum laude, U. Idaho, 1969. Mktg. mgr. Clare Penar, Post Falls, Idaho, 1969-74; internat. mktg. mgr. Keytronic, Spokane, 1974-77; product mgr. Gen. Instrument, Post Falls, 1977-79; pres., founder Advanced Input Devices, Coeur d'Alene, Idaho, 1979—; dir. 1st Nat. Bank of North Idaho, Coeur d'Alene; mem. Kootenai County Devel. Corp., Coeur d'Alene, 1981—; bd. dirs. Output Tech. Corp., Spokane, Wash., Idaho Research Found., Old Mission Assocs., Wallace, Advanced Input Devices, Coeur d' Alene. Contbr. articles to profl. jours. Mem. adv. bd. Coll. Bus. and Econs. U. Idaho, Boise. Mem. Am. Mktg. Assn., Am. Mgmt. Assn., Coeur d'Alene C. of C. (bd. dirs.). Clubs: Spokane, Hayden Lake Country.

OVERBY, LACY RASCO, biotechnology company executive; b. Model, Tenn., July 27, 1920; s. Alious William and Oma Catherine (Thomas) O.; m. Elizabeth Mae Hulette, Oct. 1, 1948; children—Megan Stewart, Ross Vincent, Alison Brooke, Alexander Scott. B.A., Vanderbilt U., 1941, M.S., 1948, Ph.D., 1951. Prodn. supr. DuPont Corp., Barksdale, Wis., 1941-43; teaching asst. Vanderbilt U., Nashville, 1946-49; div. v.p. Abbott Labs., North Chicago, Ill., 1949-83, cons., 1983-84; v.p. Chiron Corp., Emeryville, Calif., 1983—; cons. Children's Meml. Hosp., Chgo., 1970-73; lectr. in molecular biology Northwestern U., Evanston, Ill., 1968-81. Editor: Viral Hepatitis, 1979, rev. edit., 1983; assoc. editor Jour. Med. Virology, 1977—, Asian Jour. Clin. Scis., 1980-84; contbr. articles to profl. jours.; patentee in field. Chmn. bd. dirs. Am. Cancer Soc., Lake County, Ill., 1978-82. Served to comdr. USNR, 1943-46; ETO, PTO. DuPont fellow Vanderbilt U., 1948; vis. scholar U. Ill., Urbana, 1962. Mem. Am. Soc. Biol. Chemists, Am. Soc. Study Liver Diseases, Am. Soc. Microbiology (Pasteur award 1986), Am. Chem. Soc., Sigma Xi. Republican. Episcopalian. Club: Round Hill Country (Alamo, Calif.). Avocations: sports; travel; antique furniture. Home: 28 Cherry Hills Ct Alamo CA 94507 Office: Chiron Corp 4560 Horton St Emeryville CA 94608

OVERFIELD, THERESA, nursing educator, researcher; b. Buffalo, July 22, 1935; d. Norbert J. and Mary (Waver) O.; m. David B. Morris. Diploma in Nursing, Sisters of Charity Sch. Nursing, 1956; BS in Nursing, D'Youville Coll., 1958; MPH, Columbia U., 1962; PhD in Phys. Anthropology, U. Colo., 1975. Registered nurse. Instr. nursing Canisius Coll., Buffalo, 1957-58; itinerant pub. health nurse Alaska Dept. Health, Bethel, 1959-61; nurse epidemiologist Arctic Health Research Ctr., USPHS, Anchorage, 1962-65; cons. nursing Colo. Dept. Pub. Health, Denver, 1966-69; research asst. prof. U. Utah, Salt Lake City, 1975-76, asst. prof. nursing, 1976-78; assoc. prof. nursing Brigham Young U., Salt Lake City, 1978-84, dir. research Coll. Nursing, 1979-86, prof. nursing, 1984—; clin. instr. U. Colo., Denver, 1967-68; adj. prof. anthropology U. Utah, 1976-85, research prof. 1985—; cons. in field; mem. adv. bd. Western Jour. Nursing Research, 1978-82; mem. research steering com. Western Commn. Higher Edn. in Nursing, 1978-82; mem. peer rev. group Div. Nursing USPHS, 1979. Contbr. articles, revs. on nursing, phys. anthropology, plant toxicology, and genetics to profl. jours. Bd. dirs. Salt Lake Indian Health Ctr., 1981-82, also mem. adv. com.; mem. nursing research com. VA Med. Ctr., Salt Lake City, 1982—, sci. rev. com. Recipient Excellence in Writing award Am. Jour. Nursing, 1981; grantee USPHS, NSF, Am. Nurses Found., U. Utah. Mem. Am. Nurses Assn., Utah Nurses Assn. (chairperson transcultural nursing conf. group 1978-80, mem. newsletter research com. 1985—), Am. Assn. of Phys. Anthropologists, Soc. Med. Anthropologists, Human Biology Council, AAAS, Western Soc. Research in Nursing, Council Nursing and Anthropology, Soc. Study Human Biology, Utah Pub. Health Assn. (bd. dirs. 1983-86), Am. Pub. Health Assn. Avocations: mountain climbing, backpacking, cross-country skiing.

OVERHOLT, MILES HARVARD, cable TV consultant; b. Glendale, Calif., Sept. 30, 1921; s. Miles Harvard and Alma Overholt; A.B., Harvard Coll., 1943; m. Jessie Foster, Sept. 18, 1947; children—Miles Harvard, Keith Foster. Mktg. analyst Dun & Bradstreet, Phila., 1947-48; collection mgr. Standard Oil of Calif., Los Angeles, 1948-53; br. mgr. RCA Service Co., Phila., 1953-63, ops. mgr. Classified Aerospace project RCA, Riverton, N.J., 1963; pres. CPS, Inc., Paoli, Pa., 1964-67; mem. pres.'s exec. com. Gen. Time Corp., Mesa, Ariz., 1970-78; gen. mgr., dir. service Talley Industries, Mesa, 1967-78; v.p., gen. mgr. Northwest Entertainment Network, Inc., Seattle, 1979-81; mcpl. cable cons., 1981—. Served with USMCR, 1943-46. Decorated Bronze Star, Purple Heart (two). Mem. Assn. Home Appliance Mfrs., Nat. Assn. Microwave Distbn. Service Cos. Editor, publisher Mcpl. Cable Regulation Newsletter. Club: Harvard (N.Y.C.). Home: 8320 Frederick Pl Edmonds WA 98020 Office: 4517 California Ave SW Suite B Seattle WA 98116

OVERLEY, JACK CASTLE, physics educator; b. Kalamazoo, Aug. 23, 1932; s. Christopher H. and Ida Maureen (Castleton) O.; m. Madgil Adelaide Fox, July 6, 1959. SB, MIT, 1954; PhD, Calif. Inst. Tech., 1961. Research fellow Calif. Inst. Tech., Pasadena, 1960-61, vis. assoc., 1975-76; research fellow U. Wis., Madison, 1961-63; asst. prof. physics Yale U., New Haven, 1963-68, asst. dir. Wright Nuclear Structure Lab., 1966-68; assoc. prof. U. Oreg., Eugene, 1968-83, asst. dean sci. services, 1973-75, prof., 1983—, assoc. chmn. dept. physics, dir. grad. studies, 1984—. Contbr. articles to profl. jours. Mem. AAAS, Am. Phys. Soc., Am. Assn. Physics Tchrs., Sigma Xi. Home: 285 E 38th Ave Eugene OR 97405 Office: U Oreg Dept Physics Eugene OR 97403

OVERSBY, VIRGINIA MCCONN, geochemist; b. Leominster, Mass., Nov. 2, 1943; d. Raymond Allen and Grace May (Havey) McConn; m. Brian Sedgwick Oversby, Sept. 9, 1967 (div. 1978). AB in Chemistry, Wellesley Coll., 1965; MA in Geology, Columbia U., 1967, PhD in Geology, 1969. Research fellow Australian Nat. U., Canberra, 1969-75, 79-81; tchr. Cath. Girls High Sch., Canberra, 1976-79; research scientist, mgr. Lawrence Livermore (Calif.) Nat. Lab., 1981—. Author: Chemical Equilibria in the Earth, 1971; contbr. articles to profl. jours. Fellow The Meteoritical Soc.; mem. AAAS, Sigma Xi. Home: 1647 Vancouver Way Livermore CA 94550 Office: Lawrence Livermore Nat Lab Livermore CA 94550

OVERSON, BRENT C., municipal official, former state senator; b. Nephi, Utah, Apr. 18, 1950; s. Fay Dean and Elda Rae (Huntsman) O.; m. Joanne Robison, Nov. 18, 1971; 3 children. A.A., U. Md., 1978; B.S. in Fin., U. Utah, 1982. Lic. real estate broker. Sales agt., office mgr. Envirowest Realty, Inc., Salt Lake City, 1978-82, 85-87; v.p. real estate and devel. Trailside Gen. Stores, Bountiful, Utah, 1982-85; mem. Utah Senate, 1983-86; chief dep. assessor, Salt Lake County, 1987—. Served with USN, 1972-78. Mem. Nat. Assn. Realtors. Republican. Mormon. Office: N2300 2001 S State Salt Lake City UT 84190-1300

OVERTON, EDWIN DEAN, campus minister, educator; b. Beaver, Okla., Dec. 2, 1939; s. William Edward and Georgia Beryl (Fronk) O. B.Th., Midwest Christian Coll., 1963; M.A. in Religion, Eastern N.Mex. U., 1969, Ed.S., 1978; postgrad. Fuller Theol. Sem., 1980. Ordained to ministry Christian Ch., 1978. Minister, Christian Ch., Englewood, Kans., 1962-63; youth minister First Christian Ch., Beaver, Okla., 1963-67; campus minister Central Christian Ch., Portales, N.Mex., 1967-68, Christian Campus House, Portales, N.Mex., 1968—; tchr. religion, philosophy, counseling Eastern N.Mex. Univ., Portales, 1970—, campus minister, Christian Campus House, 1968—, dir., 1980—; farm and ranch partner, Beaver, Okla., 1963—. State dir. Beaver Jr. C. of C., 1964-65; pres. Beaver High Sch. Alumni Assn., 1964-65; edler Cen. Christian Ch., Portales, N.Mex., 1985—; chmn. Beaver County March of Dimes, 1966; pres. Portales Tennis Assn., 1977-78. Mem. AAUP, Internat. Platform Assn., U.S. Tennis Assn. Republican. Club: Lions. Home: 1129 Libra St Portales NM 88130 Office: 223 S Ave K Portales NM 88130

OVESON, W. VAL, state lieutenant governor, accountant; b. Provo, Utah, Feb. 11, 1952; s. Wilford W. and LaVon Oveson; m. Emilee Nebeker, Sept. 1, 1973; children: Polly, Libby, Peter, Benjamin. Student U. Utah, 1973-74; BS in Acctg., Brigham Young U., 1976. CPA, Utah. Acct. Squire and Co., Orem, Utah, 1975-79; pvt. practice acctg., Orem, 1979-80; state auditor State of Utah, Salt Lake City, 1981-84, lt. gov., 1985—; mem. dist. export council U.S. Dept. Commerce, 1985—; bd. examiners, 1981-84; chmn. State Records Com., 1981-84. Bd. dirs., unit campaign dir. United Way of Greater Salt Lake, 1985-86; trustee Travis Found., 1985—; treas. Utah County Rep. Party; mem. State Platform Com., 1982, 84; exec. com. Utah State Rep. Party, 1981—. Mem. Nat. Conf. Lt. Govs., Am. Inst. CPA's (mem. governing council 1986), Utah Assn. CPA's (Pub. Service award 1984). Republican. Mormon. Avocations: personal finance, computers, house plants, fishing. Home: 2125 S 900 E Bountiful UT 84010 Office: Lt Govs Office 203 State Capitol Salt Lake City UT 84114

OWADES, JOSEPH LAWRENCE, chemist, consultant; b. N.Y.C., July 9, 1919; s. Samuel and Gussie (Horn) O.; m. Ruth Markowitz, Sept. 7, 1969. BS, CCNY, 1939; MS, Poly. Inst. Bklyn., 1944, PhD, 1950. Research chemist Fleischman Labs., N.Y.C., 1948-51; v.p., tech. dir. Rheingold Breweries, N.Y.C., 1951-69; tech. coordinator Anheuser-Busch, St. Louis, 1969-72; v.p. brewing Carling-O'Keefe, Waltham, Mass., 1972-75; dir. Ctr. for Brewing Studies, San Francisco, 1975—. Contbr. articles on beer and brewing to profl. jours. Fellow Inst. of Brewing, London; mem. N.Y. Acad. Scis., AAAS, Master Brewers Assn. Am., Am. Soc. Brewing Chemists. Avocation: gardening. Home: 2164 Hyde St San Francisco CA 94109 Office: Ctr Brewing Studies 3097 Wood Valley Rd Sonoma CA 95476

OWADES, RUTH MARKOWITZ, marketing company executive; b. Los Angeles, Sept. 2, 1944; d. David and Yonina (Graf) Markowitz; m. Joseph L. Owades, Sept. 7, 1969. B.A. with honors, Scripps Coll., Claremont, Calif., 1966; M.B.A., Harvard U., 1975; postgrad. U. Strasbourg (France), 1966-67. Exec. asst. Los Angeles Econ. Devel. Bd., N.Y.C., 1968-69; copywriter D'Arcy Advt. Co., St. Louis, 1970-71; asst. program dir. KMOX-AM Radio, St. Louis, 1971-72; assoc. producer WCVB-TV, Boston, 1972-73; mktg. project mgr. United Brands Co., Boston, 1975; mktg. dir. CML Group Inc., Concord, Mass., 1975-78; founder, pres. Gardener's Eden Inc., Boston, 1978-82; pres. Gardener's Eden, div. Williams-Sonoma Inc., Emeryville, Calif., 1982—; dir. Hellenic Breweries S.A., Athens, Greece. Recipient Bausch & Lomb award, 1962; Fulbright scholar, 1966; named student Goodwill Ambassador to Nagoya, Japan, 1960. Mem. Direct Mktg. Assn., Phi Beta Kappa. Club: Harvard (N.Y.C.), Women's Forum West (treas.). Home: 2164 Hyde St San Francisco CA 94109 Office: 100 Northpoint St San Francisco CA 94133

OWEN, CHARLES THEODORE, journalist, association executive; b. Beech Grove, Ind., June 14, 1941; s. James Robert and Helen Maurine (Sayre) O.; m. Kathleen Rose Dellaria, Apr. 29, 1967. A.S. in Journalism, Vincennes U., 1972; B.A. in Social Sci., Chapman Coll., 1976; M.B.A., Nat. U. San Diego, 1984. Served as enlisted man U.S. Marine Corps, 1959-72, commd. 2d lt., 1973, advanced through grades to capt., 1979; combat journalist/photographer, Vietnam, 1967-68; dep. dir. Joint Pub. Affairs Office, Camp Pendleton, 1976-79; dir. Pub. Affairs Office, Marine Corps Recruit Depot, San Diego, 1980-81; dir. communications and mil. affairs div. Greater San Diego C. of C., 1981-82, v.p., bd. dirs. 1982—; v.p. mktg. Marcoa Pub. Co.; adj. prof. Nat. U., San Diego. Mem. San Diego County Cable TV Commn. Decorated Cross of Gallantry, medal of Honor 2d class (Vietnam); recipient Thomas Jefferson award, 1981. Mem. Marine Corps Combat Corrs. Assn., Pub. Relations Soc. Am., Pub. Relations Club San Diego (dir.), Press Club San Diego, Vietnam Vets. Leadership (dir.), Am. C. of C. Execs., Sigma Delta Chi. Republican. Pub.: Newswriting Program Instruction, 1972. Office: Greater San Diego C of C 110 W C St Suite 1600 San Diego CA 92101

OWEN, HERBERT RODNEY, data processing executive; b. Bremerton, Wash., Oct. 10, 1935; s. Herbert Harry Owen and Maude Winona (Byington) Garner; children: Jeffrey Rod, Perry Jay. BSCE, Walla Walla Coll., 1962; BS in Phys. Scis., Wash. State U., 1973; M in Internat. Mgmt., Am. Grad. Sch. Internat. Mgmt., 1974. ADP intern Mgmt. Engring. Tng. Agy., Rock Island, Ill., 1963-64; ADP dir. Naval Sta., Keflavik, Iceland, 1968-70; ADP project mgr. Naval Ships System Command, Bremerton, 1970-74; supr. systems analyst Naval Supply Depot, Subic Bay, Philippines, 1975-79; ADP coordinator Far East Engring. Dist., Seoul, Republic of Korea, 1981-83; ADP security officer Trident Tng. Facility, Bangor, Wash., 1979-81, 83-85; ADP dir. Commdr. Fleet Activities, Okinawa, Japan, 1985—. Bus. mgr. Northwest Chess Mag. Mem. U.S. Chess Fedn. (sr. tournament dir.), Wash. Chess Fedn. (bd. dirs.), Am. Bowling Assn. (regional pres.). Republican. Clubs: Flying (Keflavik), Toastmasters. Avocations: chess, microcomputers, international travel, sports. Office: Navy Air Facility Kadena ADP Commdr Fleet Activities Okinawa Seattle WA 98770-1150

OWEN, JOHN WADE, aerospace company professional; b. Norfolk, Va., Feb. 18, 1952; s. Clarence Benjamin and Helen Jacqueline (Davis) O.; m. Catherine Ann Mench, July 6, 1985. Student, Youngstown State U., 1971-72, Pikes Peak Community Coll., 1982-83. Commd. U.S. Army, 1974, advanced through grades to sgt., 1977, resigned, 1984; helicopter inspector McDonnell Douglas Helicopter Co., Mesa, Ariz., 1984-86, quality control supr., 1986—. Mem. Rep. Nat. Com., Mesa, 1986. Mem. Am. Mgmt. Assn., U.S. Army Res. Episcoplian. Avocations: sailing, golf. Home: 622 N Saint Paul St Mesa AZ 85205 Office: McDonnell Douglas Helicopter Co 5000 E McDowell Rd Mesa AZ 85205

OWEN, JOYCE LAURIE, molecular biologist; b. Cambridge, Mass., Mar. 31, 1937; s. Augustus and Mae Louise (Laurie) Haffer; m. Robert Louis Emrich (divorced); 1 child Glen David; m. Harold John Owen, Aug. 20, 1970; children: Russell Eric, Laura Ellen. AB, U. Chgo., 1956; PhD, U. Oreg., 1971. Research assoc. U. Oreg. Inst. Molecular Biology, Eugene, 1963-79; pvt. computer tchr. Eugene, 1983-85; asst. prof. biology U. Oreg., Eugene, 1984-86; writer and editor EBI, San Francisco, 1985—. Bd. dirs. Am. Lung Assn. of Oreg., Eugene, 1981-84, chmn. pub. policy com., 1982—; trail guide Mt. Pisqah Arboretum, Eugene, 1983—. Recipient Community Service award, Am. Lung Assn. of Oreg., 1979-80, Wendell Van Loan award, Am. Lung Assn. of Oreg., 1985; named Trailblazer of Yr., Willamette Valley Observer, 1980, Councillor of Yr., Lane County Council Am. Lung Assn. of Oreg., 1981, 86, One of Outstanding Vols. of Yr., Voluntary Action Ctr., 1987. Mem. AAAS. Avocations: gardening, music. Home and Office: 2830 Emerald St Eugene OR 97403

OWEN, PAUL HOWARD, manufacturing executive; b. South Gate, Calif., June 6, 1944; s. Perry Paul and Ruby Irene (Wolpers) O.; m. Diane Carol Gifford, Nov. 20, 1970; 1 child, Garrick Christopher. AA, East Los Angeles Coll., 1965; BA, Calif. State U., Long Beach, 1967, MA, 1972. Research engr. Environics Inc., Huntington Beach, Calif., 1971-76; lab. mgr. USD Corp., Santa Ana, Calif., 1976—. Cubmaster Boy Scouts Am., Orange, Calif., 1984-85, Webelos leader, 1985-86. Mem. Instrument Soc. Am. (sr.). Democrat. Lutheran. Avocations: camping, fishing, photography, travel. Home: 1934 W Beverly Dr Orange CA 92668 Office: USD Corp 3323 W Warner Box 25018 Santa Ana CA 92799-5018

OWEN, STANLEY PAUL, biochemist, pharmaceutical company executive; b. Earlie, Alta., Can., Mar. 30, 1924; s. Paul and Bertha Margaret (Davidson) O.; m. D. Evelyn McCaig, July 5, 1946; children—Donna Marie, James Douglas. B.Sc. in Agr., U. Alta., Edmonton, 1950, M.Sc. in Biochemistry, 1952; Ph.D. in Biochemistry, U. Wis., 1955, postgrad., 1963. Scientist The Upjohn Co., Kalamazoo, Mich., 1955-62, research scientist, 1962-67, head, 1967-69, mgr., 1969-76, group mgr., 1976-81, dir., 1981-85, exec. dir., 1985-86; mem. com. of revision U.S. Pharmacopiae, Rockville, Md., 1977-80, mem. exec. com. drug standards div., 1985—, mem. gen. com. of revision, 1985. Served with RCAF, 1942-45. U. Alta. research scholar, 1950-51; recipient Wis. Alumni Research Found. award, 1952-55. Mem. Internat. Assn. Biol. Standardization, Fedn. Internat. Pharmaceutique, Am. Soc. Microbiology, AAAS, Am. Pharm. Assn., Sigma Xi, Phi Lambda Upsilon. Presbyterian. Avocations: history of American Indians.

OWEN, STEVEN EARL, educator, consultant; b. San Luis Obispo, Calif., July 29, 1947; s. Leland Earl and Lucille Nancy Ann (Varda) O.; m. Janet Gail Smith, Oct. 22, 1976; children: Richard Earl, Shawn Marie. B.S., Calif. State Poly. U., 1969, postgrad., 1969-70; postgrad. Calif. State U.-Stanislaus, 1970-72; M.A.Ed., Fresno Pacific Coll., 1983. Cert. tchr., Calif. Faculty Rivera Jr. High Sch., Merced (Calif.) Sch. Dist., 1970—, tchr., 1970-79, resource tchr. curriculum devel., 1979—, mem. dist. curriculum council, 1970-85, dist. sci. cons., 1983—; instr. sci., math. and computers Fresno Pacific Coll., 1983—; founder Merced/Mariposa Counties Math. Conf., 1979, chmn., 1979-84; mem. program rev. teams Calif. Dept. Edn., 1979-82, 84—; partipant Project AIMS, NSF. Fellow Calif. Sch. Leadership Acad. Mem. Calif. Tchrs. Assn., Assn. Supervision and Curriculum Devel., Calif. Math. Council (affiliate council Central sect.), Nat. Sci. Tchrs. Assn., Nat. Biology Tchrs. Assn. Democrat. Baptist. Clubs: Breakfast, Kiwanis (Merced). Co-author: From Head to Toe, I, 1982; co-author Key to Balancing Equations, 1983; editor: Handbook of State and Local Government, Merced County, 1984; Am. editor/contbn. editor Delto Pubs. Internat. div. Delto Verlag; author profl. publs., choral readings. Office: 945 Buena Vista Ave Merced CA 95340

OWEN, THOMAS LON, physiology educator; b. Oakland, Calif., Oct. 1, 1945; s. Thomas Langdon and Eleanor Louise (Keehner) O.; m. Cecilia Joan Gould, June 22, 1968; children: Lisa, Julie, Thomas. AA, Sierra Coll., 1965; student, U. Calif., Berkeley, 1965-66; BA, U. Calif., Davis, 1967, PhD, 1972; MA, Calif. State U., Sacramento, 1969. Postdoctoral fellow Mich. State U., East Lansing, 1972-74; asst. prof. physiology No. Ariz. U., Flagstaff, 1974-80, assoc. prof., 1980—; vis. assoc. prof. U. Ariz., Tucson, 1984-85; mem. research com. Am. Heart Assn., Ariz., 1978—, chmn. research com., 1982-83, chmn. research com. S.W. region, 1983-85, mem. nat. research com. 1983-85, bd. dirs. Contbr. articles to profl. jours. Bd. dirs. Big Bros. of No. Ariz., Flagstaff, 1980—. Fellow NIH U. Calif., 1970-72, NIH Mich. State U., 1972-74; grantee NIH No. Ariz. U., 1980-83, 86—. Mem. AAAS, Am. Physiol. Soc., Sigma Xi. Republican. Roman Catholic. Avocations: racquetball, swimming, jogging, hiking, soccer. Home: 1932 N Crescent Dr Flagstaff AZ 86001 Office: No Ariz U Dept Biol Scis Flagstaff AZ 86011

OWEN, WILLIAM FREDERICK, engineering and management consultant; b. Pontiac, Mich., July 27, 1947; s. Webster Jennings and Elizabeth (Hayes) W.; m. Delores T. Owen, Mar. 30, 1974 (div. Dec. 1978); m. Janice L. Pierce, July 29, 1983. BS, Mich. Tech. U., 1972; MS, U. Mich., 1973; PhD, Stanford U., 1978. Research engr. Neptune Microfloc, Corvallis, Oreg., 1973-75, process applications engr., 1975-76; process applications engr. Dr. Perry McCarty, Stanford, Calif., 1976-78; sr. engr. Culp/Wesner/Culp, Cameron Park, Calif., 1978-82; pres. Owen Engring. and Mgmt. Cos., Denver, 1982—. Author: Energy in Wastewater Treatment, 1982. Del. People-to-People, People's Republic China, 1986. Served with USN, 1965-68. Recipient Local Govt. Innovations award Denver Regional Council Govt., 1983, Boettcher Innovations award Denver Regional Council Govt., 1984, Energy Innovations award Colo. Council Energy Ofcls., 1983. Club: Pinehurst Country (Denver). Avocations: tennis, golf, downhill skiing. Home: 3829 S Chase St Denver CO 80235 Office: Owen Engring and Mgmt Cons Inc 5353 W Dartmouth Ave Denver CO 80227

OWENS, BILL MAX, advertising executive; b. Oneanta, Ala., Apr. 23, 1934; s. Cecil S. and Mary Elizabeth (Jones) O.; m. Marta L. Olson, May 29, 1953; children—Mark, Matt. B.A., Woodbury U., 1955. Advt. dir. Los Angeles Daily Jour., 1954; asst. advt. dir. Wright Mfg., Ariz., 1955; advt. dir. John S. Turner, Ariz., 1956-59; account supr. Carl Lawson Advt., Ariz., 1959; pres., chief exec. officer Owens & Assocs. Advt., Phoenix, 1960—; mem. adv. bd. Phoenix Bus. Jour. Pres. bd. trustees Kyrene Sch. Bd., Tempe, Ariz., 1970-77; chmn., pub. relations dir. Internat. Arabian Horse Assn., Denver, 1978-84; bd. dirs. Better Bus. Bur., Phoenix, 1982, Maricopa County Fair, Phoenix, 1977-83, Woodbury U. Named Advt. Man of Yr., Phoenix AD-2, 1982. Mem. Am. Assn. Advt. Agys. (chmn. Sun Country council 1970-71, 82-83, bd. govs. western region 1982-83), Advt. Mktg. Internat. Network, Am. Advt. Fedn., Phoenix Advt. Club (pres. 1982-83). Clubs: Phoenix Country, Plaza, Arizona (Phoenix). Episcopalian. Home: 9211 S Terrace St Tempe AZ 85284 Office: Owens & Assocs Advt Inc 2600 N Central Suite 1700 Phoenix AZ 85004

OWENS, GARY, radio-TV performer, author; b. Mitchell, S.D., May 10; s. Bernard Joseph and Vennetta Florence (Clark); m. Arleta Lee Markell, June 26; children: Scott Michael, Christopher Dana. Student (Speech scholar), Dakota Wesleyan U., Mitchell; student, Mpls. Art Inst. With KMPC, Los Angeles, 1962-82; with KPRZ, Los Angeles, 1982—, KKGO, Los Angeles, 1985—; With KFI, Los Angeles, 1986—; pres. The Foonman & Sons, Inc.; v.p., nat. creative dir. Gannett Broadcasting, 1985—. Radio performer, 1955—; nat. creative dir., Golden West Broadcasters, 1981-82; syndicated radio show The G.O. Spl. Report, 1969—; host: world-wide syndicated show Soundtrack of the 60's, 1981—, Biff Owens Sports Exclusive, 1981—; USA Today, Mut. Broadcasting System, 1982—; performer, writer: world-wide syndicated show Sesame St, 1969—, Electric Co, 1969—; numerous animated cartoons including Dyno-Mutt, ABC-TV, 1975—, Roger Ramjet, 1965—, Space Ghost, 1968, also over 1400 animated cartoons including Godzilla's Power Hour, 1979, Space Heroes, 1981, Mighty Orbots, 1984, World's Greatest Adventures, 1986; appeared: in films The Love Bug, 1968, Prisoner of Second Ave., 1975, Hysterical, 1982, Nat. Lampoon's European Vacation, 1985, others; performer: Rowan and Martin's Laugh-in, 1968-73; TV host: Gong Show, ABC-TV, 1976—, Monty Pythons Flying Circus, 1975—; regular performer: TV Games People Play, 1980-81, Breakaway, 1983—; author: Elephants, Grapes and Pickles, 1963; 12 printings The Gary Owens What To Do While Your're Holding the Phone Book, rev, 1973, A Gary Owens Chrestomathy, 1980; author: (screenplay) Three Caraway Seeds and an Agent's Heart, 1979; columnist: (screenplay) Radio and Records newspaper, 1978—, Hollywood Citizen-News, 1965-67, Hollywood mag., 1983—, The Daily News, 1981—; rec. artist (screenplay), MGM, ABC, Epic, Warner Bros., RCA, Reprise, Decca. Chmn. Multiple Sclerosis dr. Los Angeles, 1972; chmn., grand marshall So. Calif. Diabetes Dr., 1974—; mayor City of Encino, Calif., 1972—; bd. govs. Grammy awards, 1968—, Emmy awards, 1972; adv. bd. Pasadena (Calif.) City Coll., 1969—, Sugar Ray Robinson Youth Found., 1971—; mem. nat. miracle com. Juvenile Diabetes Found., 1981—, nat. com. for Carousel Ball Children's Diabetes Found. Denver; radio adv. bd. U. So. Calif., 1980—; hon. chmn. Goodwill Industries Sporting Goods Dr., 1986, chmn. 1986 campaign.; bd. dirs. D-Fly (anti-drug org.), D.A.R.E. (drug education program) Los Angeles Police Dept., 1986. Named outstanding radio personality in U.S., 1965-79, top Radio Personality in World, Internat. Radio Forum, Toronto, 1977, Man of Yr. All-Cities Employees Assn., City of Los Angeles, 1968, Top Radio Broadcaster, Nat. Assn. Broadcasters, 1986, Radio Man of Yr. Nat. Assn. Broadcasters, 1986; recipient Distinguished Service award Hollywood Jaycees, 1966, David award, 1978, Hollywood Hall of Fame award, 1980, Am. award Cypress Coll., 1981, 5 Grammy nominations, Emmy award for More Dinosaurs, 1986; Star on Hollywood Walk of Fame, 1981; honored by U.S. Dept. Treasury, 1985. Hon. mem. No. Calif. Cartoonists Assn.; mem. Cartoonists and Artists Profl. Soc. Office: 610 S Ardmore Los Angeles CA 90005

OWENS, ROBERT PHILLIP, police official; b. Stamford, Conn., Sept. 12, 1931; s. Robert Evan and Ann (Humphreys) O.; m. Linda Lee Kittredge, Sept. 6, 1969; children—Steven, Olga. B.S. Police Adminstrn., Calif. State U.-Los Angeles, 1968; M.B.A., Pepperdine U., 1973. With Los Angeles County Sheriff's Dept., Los Angeles, 1954-67; chief police San Fernando City, Calif., 1967-70, Oxnard Police Dept., Calif., from 1970, now pub. safety dir.; cons. U.S. Dept. Justice, 1977-81, Office Criminal Justice Planning Calif., 1977—, Ind. U., 1974-78. Served with USMC, 1949-53. Named Outstanding Law Enforcement Officer, Calif. Trial Lawyers Assn., 1984; recipient Oxnard trophy Greater Oxnard C. of C, 1983. Mem. Nat. Orgn. Victim Assistance (bd. dirs. 1981—). Republican. Unitarian. Lodge: Rotary (pres. 1975-76). Office: Oxnard Police Dept 251 So C St Oxnard CA 93030 *

OWENS, RONALD STEPHEN (RONN), radio talk show host; b. N.Y.C., Oct. 17, 1945; s. Stanley S. Lowenstein and Monica (Frank) Owens; m. Elizabeth Naylor Owens, Mar. 22, 1986. BA with honors, Temple U., 1967, MA, 1969. Talk show host Sta. WCAU, Phila., 1968-70, Sta. WKAT, Miami Beach, Fla., 1970-71, Sta. WERE, Cleve., 1971-74, Sta. WRNG, Altanta, 1974-75, KGO/ABC, San Francisco, 1975—. Hosted live radio call-in from S. Africa, 1985. Bd. dirs. Am. Lung Assn., San Francisco. Named Top Radio Personality in San Francisco Bay Area, Oakland Tribune, 1986, One of top three Radio Talk Show Hosts in USA Radio and Records, 1985. Club: Concordia-Argonaut (San Francisco). Avocation: thoroughbred racing. Office: Sta KGO/ABC Radio 900 Front St San Francisco CA 94111-1450

OWENS, THERESA R., lawyer; b. Phila., Oct. 31, 1951; d. George Augustus and Catherine Elizabeth (Egan) O. BA with honors, U. Calif., Santa Cruz, 1981; JD, U. Calif., Davis, 1984. Bar: Calif. 1984, U.S. Dist Ct. (no. and ea. dists.) Calif. 1984, U.S. Ct. Appeals (9th cir.) 1984. Legisltv. asst. Re. Leon E. Panetta, Washington, 1979-81; assoc. Adams, Duque & Hazeltine, San Francisco, 1984-87, Seltzer, Ewell & Cravet, San Francisco, 1987—. editor articles U. Calif. Davis Law Review, 1983-84. Named Nat. Quarter Finalist Nat. Trial Competition, Houston, 1984, Regional Champion Nat. Trial Competition, San Francisco, 1984. Mem. ABA, Bar Assn. San Francisco (vol. legal services program), Queens Bench, Calif. Women Lawyers. Democrat. Home: 814 Cole St San Francisco CA 94117 Office: Seltzer Ewell & Cravat 260 California St 11 Floor San Francisco CA 94111

OWENS, THOMAS, music educator; b. Torrance, Calif., July 24, 1938; s. Huntley Thomas and Edith Sarah (Little) O.; m. Karen Ann Gilbertson, Jan. 29, 1967; children: Holly, Scott, Steven. AA, El Camino Coll., 1959; BA, UCLA, 1961, MA, 1965, PhD, 1974. Free lance musician Calif., 1954-66; instr. music El Camino Coll., Torrance, 1966—. Recipient Atwater-Kent award in Musicology UCLA, 1964; NEH summer stipend, 1980. Mem. Soc. Ethnomusicology, Nat. Assn. Jazz Educators, Jazz Heritage Found. Office: El Camino Coll Dept Music 16007 Crenshaw Blvd Torrance CA 90506

OWENS, WARREN SPENCER, librarian; b. Massena, N.Y., Dec. 28, 1921; s. Spencer Bacon and Charlotte (Eaton) O.; m. Pauli Hartung, Jan. 20, 1946; children: Christie, Patrick, Martha, Andrew. B.A., Kalamazoo Coll., 1943; M.A., U. Chgo., 1947; A.M. in L.S, U. Mich., 1953. Lectr. English Ind. U. Calumet Center, East Chicago, 1947-49; instr. English U. N.D., 1950-52; mem. staff U. Mich. Library, 1952-61, supr. divisional libraries, 1959-61; dir. libraries Temple U., 1961-68, U. Idaho, Moscow, 1968-70; dean library services U. Idaho, 1970-87. Chmn. Moscow United Fund, 1972-73; sec. Ballet Folk of Moscow, Inc., 1974-75, chmn., 1977-78; pres. Friends of KUID, Inc., 1981-84; bd. dirs. Wash.-Idaho Symphony Assn., 1985—, Latah County Hist. Soc., 1985—. Served with AUS, 1943-45. Mem. ALA, Idaho Library Assn., Pacific N.W. Library Assn. (pres. 1973-75), Assn. Coll. and Research Libraries, Phi Kappa Phi (pres. chpt. 1980—). Home: PO Box 8487 Moscow ID 83843 Office: Univ Library U Idaho Moscow ID 83843 *

OWENS, WAYNE, congressman. Mem. 100th Congress from 2d Utah dist., mem. interior and insular affairs, fgn. affairs coms. Office: Offices of House Mems care The Postmaster Washington DC 20515 *

OWINGS, BENJAMIN FRANKLIN, JR., oil company executive, geophysicist; b. Little Rock, July 1, 1919; s. Benjamin Franklin and Mary Lou (Brewster) O.; m. Mary Ann Mugford, Feb. 20, 1943; children—Diann Owings Warren, Mike, Steve. B.S. in Physics, U. Tex., 1941. Seismic field party chief Nat. Geophys. Co., Dallas, 1943-50; staff geophysicist Honolulu Oil Co., 1950-54; supr. Continental Geophys. Co., Midland, Tex., 1954-56; div. geophysicist Forest Oil Corp., Midland, 1956-72; cons. geophysicist, 1972-76; mgr. Anschutz Corp., Denver, 1976-81; gen. ptnr. Banner Oil and Gas Co., Denver, 1981—. Home: 3400 Kipling Dr Wheat Ridge CO 80033 Office: Banner Oil and Gas Co 555 17th St Suite 3565 Denver CO 80202

OWINGS, MARGARET WENTWORTH, conservationist, artist; b. Berkeley, Calif., Apr. 29, 1913; d. Frank W. and Jean (Pond) Wentworth; m. Nathaniel Alexander Owings, Dec. 30, 1953; 1 dau., Wendy Millard Osorno. A.B., Mills Coll., 1934; postgrad., Radcliffe Coll., 1935. One-woman shows include, Santa Barbara (Calif.) Mus. Art, 1940, Stanford Art Gallery, 1951, stitchery exhbns. at, M.H. De Young Mus., San Francisco, 1963, Internat. Folk Art Mus., Santa Fe, 1965. Commr. Calif. Parks, 1963-69, mem., Nat. Parks Found. Bd, 1968-69; bd. dirs. African Wildlife Leadership Found., 1968-80, Defenders of Wildlife, 1969-74; founder, pres. Friends of the Sea Otter, 1969—; trustee Environmental Def. Fund, 1972-83; Regional trustee Mills Coll., 1962-68. Recipient gold medal, Conservation Service award Dept. Interior, 1975, Conservation award Calif. Acad. Scis., 1979, Am. Motors Conservation award, 1980, Joseph Wood Krutch medal Humane Soc. U.S., 1980, Nat. Audubon Soc. medal, 1983, A. Starker Leopold award Calif. Nature Conservancy, 1986. Home: Big Sur CA 93920

OWINGS, RAYMOND MARK, pathologist; b. Atlanta, May 5, 1950; s. Raymond Hays and Letty Frieda (Ahmann) O.; m. Christine Lee Dreher, Aug. 22, 1970; children: Luke, Anne. BA, Lewis and Clark Coll., 1971; PhD, Portland State U., 1976; MD, Emory U., 1979. Pathologist St. Vincent Hosp., Portland, Oreg., 1983—. Contbr. articles to med. jours. Fellow Coll. Am. Pathologists, Am. Soc. Clin. Pathologists; mem. Oreg. Pathologists Assn., Am. Chem. Soc., Internat. Acad. Pathology, Portland Acad. Medicine, Gastrointestinal Pathology Soc. Avocations: sports, model railroading, baking bread. Office: St Vincent Hosp Dept Pathology 9205 SW Barnes Rd Portland OR 97225

OWNBEY, JAMES LINUS, anatomic pathologist, photomicrographer; b. Alton, Ill., Feb. 15, 1948; s. Robert James and Jenna V. (Stephenson) O.; m. Marianne Rebecca Harrison, Aug. 8, 1981; 1 child, Edwin Harrison. BS in Chemistry with honors, U. Tex., Austin, 1970; MD, U. Tex., San Antonio, 1974. Diplomate Am. Bd. Pathology. Commd. officer U.S. Army, 1974, advanced through grades to lt. col.; intern Fitzsimons Army Med. Ctr., Aurora, Colo., 1974-75, resident, 1975-78, med. dir. blood bank, 1980-83, chief anatomic pathology, 1983—; pathologist 121st Evacuation Hosp., Seoul, Korea, 1978-79, Ft. Carson, Colorado Springs, Colo., 1979-80. Fellow Coll. Am. Pathologists. Republican. Methodist. Home: 11461 E Adriatic Pl Aurora CO 80014 Office: Pathology Dept FAMC 12101 E Colfax St Aurora CO 80045

OXELSON, ERIC CARL, mental health program manager, psychotherapist.; b. Vallejo, Calif., June 3, 1942; s. Carl Edward and Ruth Lamina (Cox) O.; m. Maureen Teresa Reilly, Jun 11, 1966; children: Eva Maria, Canh Eric, Meghan Teresa. BA cum laude, Harvard U., 1966; MSW, U. Minn., 1968. Vol. U.S. Peace Corps, Peru, 1964-66; social worker St. Paul Ramsey County Mental Health Ctr., 1968-70, social work supr., 1971-72; program mgr. Kingsview Community Services, Reedley, Calif., 1973-77; chief of community counseling ctrs. County Dept. Mental Health, 1977-86; dep. dir. clin. services Maderd (Calif.) County Mental Health Ctr., 1986—. Active Mental Health Adv. Bd., Madera County, 1986—, Boy Scouts Am. Troop Com., Madera, 1983—; Affirmative Action Com., Madera Unified Sch. Dist., 1983—; pres. Calif. Mental Health Advocates for Children and Youth, Sacramento, 1983—;. Fellow NIMH, 1967-68. Mem. Nat. Assn.

Social Workers (cert., Calif. chpt. regional dir. 1982-84, chmn., Social Worker of Yr., 1984—), Am. Group Psychotherapy Assn. Democrat. Roman Catholic. Avocations: wood carving, reading, camping. Office: Merced County Dept Mental Health 480 E 13th St Merced CA 95340

OYAMA, SHIGEO TED, research chemical engineer; b. Tokyo, Feb. 16, 1955; came to U.S., 1972; s. Tsunaaki and Yoshiko (Aoki) Ohyama; m. Hideko Tamaru, May 29, 1982. BS in Chemistry, Yale U., 1976; MSChemE, Stanford U., 1978, PhDChemE, 1981. Registered profl. engr., Calif. Research engr. Catalytica Assocs., Mountain View, Calif., 1981—; vis. scholar U. Calif., Berkeley, 1986. Mem. AAAS, Am. Inst. Chem. Engrs., Am. Chem. Soc. Home: 1891 Newcastle Dr Los Altos CA 94022 Office: Catalytica Assocs 430 Ferguson Bldg 3 Mountain View CA 94043

OZAKI, CYNTHIA KAY, interior designer; b. Bend, Oreg., Jan. 5, 1958; d. Richard Wayne and Beverley Ann (Esselstrom) Patterson; m. Calvin Brent Ozaki, Jan. 26, 1980. Student, Cen. Oreg. Community Coll., 1975-76; BS, Oreg. State U., 1979. Designer Dick's Interiors, Bend, 1973-80, Duke Interiors, Livermore, Calif., 1980; prin. Interiors by Cynthia, Livermore, 1980-85; designer Copperfield's, Albuquerque, 1985—; mem. design rev. com. Livermore, 1984-85. Mem. ASID (assoc.), Beta Sigma Phi. Republican. Lutheran. Lodge: Soroptimists. Avocations: reading, travel, music, sports. Home: 13307 Nube Blanca NE Albuquerque NM 87111 Office: 5420 Academy Rd NE Albuquerque NM 87109

OZANICH, CHARLES GEORGE, real estate broker; b. Fayette County, Pa. Aug. 11, 1933; s. Paul Anthony and Alma Bertha (Sablotne) O.; student Am. River Coll., Sierra Coll.; m. Betty Sue Carman, Feb. 20, 1955; children—Viki Lynn, Terri Sue, Charles Anthony, Nicole Lee. Owner, broker Terrace Realty, Basic Realty, Grass Valley, Calif., 1971—. Mem. Grass Valley Vol. Fire Dept., 1965-85. Served with USAF, 1951-55; Korea. Decorated Bronze Star with three oak leaf clusters, Korean Presdl. citation, UN citation. Mem. Neveda County Bd. Realtors (dir. 1973-74). Lodges: Masons, Shriners. Nat. champion Truck Drivers Roadeo class 5 semi-trailer 18 wheeler div., 1954. Home: 15053 Chinook Ln Grass Valley CA 95945 Office: 10113 Alta Sierra Dr Suite 100 Grass Valley CA 95945

OZOLS, SANDRA LEE, lawyer; b. Casper, Wyo., June 24, 1957; s. Virgil Carr and Doris Louise (Conklin) McC.; m. Ojars Herberts Ozols, Sept. 2, 1978; children: Michael Ojars, Sara Ann, Brian Christopher. BA with distinction, U. Colo., 1978; JD magna cum laude, Boston U., 1982. Bar: Colo. 1982, U.S. Dist. Ct. Colo. 1985. Assoc. Cohen, Brame and Smith, Denver, 1983-84, Parcel, Meyer, Schwartz, Ruttum and Mauro, Denver, 1984-85, Mayer, Brown and Platt, Denver, 1985—. Mem. ABA, Denver Bar Assn., Colo. Bar Assn., Am. Bus. Women's Assn., Phi Beta Kappa, Phi Delta Phi. Republican. Mem. Ch. of Christ. Avocations: tennis, photography. Home: 793 Dexter Dr Broomfield CO 80020 Office: Mayer Brown and Platt 600 17th St #2800 S Denver CO 80202

PAASCH, WAYNE CHARLES, bank executive; b. Abington, Pa., July 26, 1951; s. Robert Henry and Ruth Ann (Rosell) P.; m. Wanda Joy Tackett, Apr. 14, 1984; 1 child, Christopher. BSBA in Mgmt., U. Fla., 1973, MBA in Quantitative Mgmt., 1974. Systems analyst Procter & Gamble Co., Cin., 1974-78, Firemans Fund Ins. Co., San Rafael, Calif., 1978; mgr. profit ctr. Informatics Inc., San Francisco, 1978-82; pres. Mgmt. Systems Group, San Francisco, 1982-84; mgr. Wells Fargo Bank, San Francisco, 1984-85; group product mgr. Bank of Am., San Francisco, 1985—; cons. in field, 1978-84. Author, producer, The IBM PC-A Comprehensive View, 1983. Democrat. Roman Catholic. Avocations: water sports, snow sports. Office: Bank of Am PO Box 37000 Dept 5532 San Francisco CA 94137

PAAVOLA, LEE THOMAS, university adminstrator; b. Flint, Mich., July 26, 1948; s. Carroll Oswald and Martha Elizabeth (Klingbeil) P.; m. Christine Marie Trombley, Aug. 16, 1968; children—Dana, Sarah, Andrew, David. B.S. in Edn., M.A., Central Mich. U., Community sch. coordinator Salem Pub. Schs., Oreg., 1971-72; community sch. coordinator Portland Pub. Sch., Oreg., 1972-74, area coordinator, 1974-78; mfg. supr. A.C. Spark Plug, Flint, Mich., 1978-80; dir. continuing edn. U. Alaska-Juneau, 1980—; chmn. Juneau Interagy. Tng. Council, 1983—; co-facilitator Alaska Community Edn. Adv. Council, Juneau, 1983—; bd. dirs. Alaska Ctr. for Community Edn., Juneau, 1983—. Facilitator Process Facilitation Manual for Community Educators, 1976. Mem. Juneau-Douglas Sch. Dist. Adv. Com., 1983; mem. Fed. Employee of the Yr. Com., Juneau, 1982-83; group facilitator Lemon Creek Prison, Juneau, 1984—. Named Oreg. Community Educator of Yr., Oreg. Community Edn. Assn., 1978, Outstanding Young Man of Yr., Juneau Jaycees, 1983; Mott Found. fellow, 1970-71. Mem. Nat. Council on Community Services, Alaska Assn. Community Edn. (exec. sec. 1982—, award 1983, life mem. award 1984), Phi Delta Kappa. Home: 8212 Birch Ln Juneau AK 99801 Office: U Alaska 11120 Glacier Hwy Juneau AK 99801

PAAVONEN, JORMA ANTERO, physician, educator; b. Helsinki, Finland, Apr. 10, 1947; came to U.S., 1981; s. Aarne V. and Elsa E. (Elomaa) P.; m. Marjoriitta U.I. Heinonen, May 22, 1972; children: Kristian J.A., Karri J.A. MD, U. Helsinki, 1973, PhD, 1979. Cert. Bd. Ob-gyn., Finland, 1979. Resident in ob-gyn U. Helsinki, 1974-80; assoc. prof. U. Tampere, Finland, 1983-84; asst. prof. U. Wash., Seattle, 1984—; vis. scientist U. Wash., Seattle, 1981-82; cons. Harborview Med. Ctr., Seattle, 1984—; researcher Acad. Finland, 1986—. Contbr. numerous articles to profl. jours.; chpts. to books. Mem. Am. Soc. Microbiology, Scandinavian Soc. Sexually Transmitted Diseases, Am. Venereal Disease Assn., Infectious Disease Soc. of Ob-gyn. Lutheran. Home: 9039 E Shorewood Dr Mercer Island WA 98040 Office: Harborview Med Ctr 325 9th Ave Seattle WA 98104

PACE, NATHAN LEON, anesthesiologist, educator; b. San Diego, Feb. 28, 1943; s. Joseph Leon and pauline (Clyde) P.; m. Jennifer Anna Geertsen, Jan. 13, 1973; children: Garrett, Ramsey, Andalyn, Marielle, Evany. BS, U. Calif., Berkeley, 1967; MD, U. Calif., San Francisco, 1970. Diplomate Am. Bd. Anesthesiology. Intern Santa Clara Valley Med. Ctr., San Jose, Calif., 1970-71; resident in asesthesiology U. Wash., Seattle, 1971-74; staff anesthesiologist U.S. Army, Ft. Sam Houston, Tex., 1974-76; prof. anesthesiology U. Utah, Salt Lake City, 1976—; vis. prof. various med. schs. Contbr. articles to profl. jours. 1st tenor Utah Symphony Chorus, Salt Lake City, 1977—. Served to maj. USAR, 1974-76, with hosp., Ft. Douglas, Utah, 1979—. Mem. Am. Soc. Anesthesiologists, AMA, Soc. Critical Care Medicine, Am. Thoracic Soc., Assn. Univ. Anesthetists, Phi Beta Kappa. Republican. Mormon. Avocations: travel, singing, reading. Home: 2211 S Scenic Dr Salt Lake City UT 84109 Office: U Utah Sch Medicine Dept Anesthesiology Salt Lake City UT 84132

PACHA, SANDRA JEAN, speech-language pathologist; b. Fairfield, Iowa, Mar. 13; d. Cletus Eugene and Dolores Ann (Conrad) P. BSE, Northeast Mo. State U., 1980; MA, Northeast Miss. State U., 1981. Speech-lang. pathologist So. Prairie Area Edn. Agy., Oskaloosa, Iowa, 1981-85, Ottumwa (Iowa) Regional Hosp., 1983-85, Lincoln-Uinta Child Devel. Assn., Evanston, Wyo., 1985—. Active Evanston Civic Chorale, 1985—. Mem. Am. Speech Lang. Hearing Assn. (cert.). Democrat. Club: Evanston Christian Singles. Avocations: music, tennis, biking, wildlife study. Home: PO Box 385 SPBC Bible College MN 55375 Office: LUCDA Box 697 440 Elm Evanston WY 82930

PACIFIC, JOSEPH NICHOLAS, JR., educator; b. Honolulu, Oct. 27, 1950; s. Joseph Nicholas Sr. and Christine Mary (Mondelli) P.; m. Paulette Kay Miller, July 7, 1975. BA in Math., BS in Biology, BSEE, Gonzaga U., 1974; MMSc in Clin. Microbiology, Emory U., 1978. Cert. tchr., Hawaii, Wash. Research specialist Ctr. Disease Control, Atlanta, 1978-82; supr. Joe Pacific Shoe Repair, Honolulu, 1983; lab. technician Mont. State U., Bozeman, 1984; sci. tchr. Hawaii Preparatory Acad., Kamuela, 1985-87; research assoc. U. Hawaii, Honolulu, 1987—. Mem. Nat. Registry Microbiologists, Sigma Xi, Pi Mu Epsilon, Phi Sigma, Kappa Delta Pi, Alpha Sigma Nu. Avocations: microscopy, bicycling. Home: 2013 Kaola Way Honolulu HI 96813 Office: U Hawaii Dept Microbiology RM 306 2538 The Mall Honolulu HI 96822

PACIOREK, KAZIMIERA JOLA LILIANA, chemist; b. Krakow, Poland, Feb. 18, 1931; came to U.S., 1956; d. Henryk Josef and Maria Ada (Haberfeld) Thieberg; m. Thaddeus Anthony Paciorek, Jan. 12, 1957; 1 child, Henryk Adam. BSc, U. Western Australia, Perth, 1952, BSc with honors, 1954, PhD, 1956. Postdoctoral fellow Wayne State U., Detroit, 1956-57; research chemist Wyandotte (Mich.) Chem. Corp., 1957-61, U.S. Naval Ordnance Lab., Corona, Calif., 1961-64; sr. research scientist MHD Research Inc., Newport Beach, Calif., 1964-66; mem. advanced tech. staff Marquardt Corp., Newport Beach, 1966-70; sr. scientist Dynamic Sci., Irvine, Calif., 1970-72, Ultrasystems, Inc., Irvine, 1972—. Patentee in field; contbr. articles to profl jours. Mem. Am. Chem. Soc. (mem. exec. com. Fluorine Div. 1982-84), Royal Australian Chem. Inst., N.Y. Acad. Scis. Home: 1425 Seacrest Dr Corona del Mar CA 92625 Office: Ultrasystems Inc 16845 Von Karman Ave Irvine CA 92714

PACK, PHOEBE KATHERINE FINLEY, civic worker; b. Portland, Oreg., Feb. 2, 1907; d. William Lovell and Irene (Barnhart) Finley; student U. Calif., Berkeley, 1926-27; B.A., U. Oreg., 1930; m. Arthur Newton Pack, June 11, 1936; children: Charles Lathrop, Phoebe Irene. Layman referee Pima County Juvenile Ct., Tucson, 1958-71; patron Menninger Found., Topeka; mem. Alcoholism Council So. Ariz., 1960—; bd. dirs. Kress Nursing Sch., Tucson, 1957-67, Pima County Assn. for Mental Health, 1958—, Ariz. Assn. for Mental Health, Phoenix, 1963—, U. Ariz. Found., Casa de los Niños Crisis Nursery; co-founder Ariz.-Sonora Desert Mus., Tucson, 1975—, Ghost Ranch Found., N.Mex.; bd. dirs. St. Mary's Hosp., Tucson, Tucson Urban League, Tucson YMCA Youth Found. Mem. Mt. Vernon Ladies Assn. Union (state vice regent, 1962-84),Mt. Vernon One Hundred (founder), Nature Conservancy (life), Alpha Phi. Home: Villa Compana Apt 415K 6651 E Carondelet Tucson AZ 85710

PACKARD, DAVID, manufacturing company executive, electrical engineer, former deputy secretary of defense; b. Pueblo, Colo., Sept. 7, 1912; s. Sperry Sidney and Ella Lorna (Graber) P.; m. Lucile Salter, Apr. 8, 1938 (dec., 1987); children: David Woodley, Nancy Ann Packard Burnett, Susan Packard Orr, Julie Elizabeth Stephens. B.A., Stanford U., 1934, M.E.E., 1939; LL.D. (hon.), U. Calif., Santa Cruz, 1966, Catholic U., 1970, Pepperdine U., 1972; D.Sc. (hon.), Colorado Coll., 1964; Litt.D. (hon.), So. Colo. State Coll., 1973; D.Eng. (hon.), U. Notre Dame, 1974. With vacuum tube engrng. dept. Gen. Electric Co., Schenectady, 1936-38; co-founder, ptnr. Hewlett-Packard Co., Palo Alto, Calif., 1939-47, pres., 1947-64, chief exec. officer, 1964-68, chmn. bd., 1964-68, 72—; U.S. dep. sec. defense Washington, 1969-71; dir. Genetech Inc., 1981—; bd. dirs. Genetech, Inc., The Boeing Co., Caterpillar Tractor Co., 1972-83, Chevron, 1972-85; co-chmn. Presdl. Commn. on Def. Mgmt., 1985-86; mem. White House Sci. Council. Mem. President's Commn. Personnel Interchange, 1972-74, Trilateral Commn., 1973-81; pres. bd. regents Uniformed Services U. of Health Scis., 1975-82; mem. U.S.-USSR Trade and Econ. Council, 1975-82; trustee The Ronald Reagan Presdl. Found., 1986—; mem. bd. overseers Hoover Instn., 1972—; bd. dirs. Nat. Merit Scholarship Corp., 1963-69; dir. Found. for Study of Presdl. and Congl. Terms, 1978—, Alliance to Save Energy, 1977—, Atlantic Council, 1972-83, (vice chmn. 1972-80), Am. Enterprise Inst. for Public Policy Research, 1978—, Nat. Fish and Wildlife Found., 1985—, Hitachi Found. Adv. Council, 1986—; trustee Herbert Hoover Found., 1974—, Wolf Trap Found.; vice chmn., trustee The Calif. Nature Conservancy, 1983—; trustee Stanford U., 1954-69, (pres. bd. trustees 1958-60), The Hoover Instn., The Herbert Hoover Found., 1972—. Decorated Grand Cross of Merit Fed. Republic of Germany, 1972; recipient numerous awards including Medal of Honor Electronic Industries Assn., 1974, Silver Helmet Defense award AMVETS, 1973, Washington award Western Soc. Engrs., 1975, Hoover medal ASME, 1975, Gold Medal award Nat. Football Found. and Hall of Fame, 1975, Good Scout award Boy Scouts Am., 1975, Vermilye medal Franklin Inst., 1976, Internat. Achievement award World Trade Club of San Francisco, 1976, Merit award Am. Consulting Engrs. Council Fellows, 1977, Achievement in Life award Ency. Britannica, 1977, Engring. Award of Distinction San Jose State U., 1980, Thomas D. White Nat. Def. award U.S. Air Force Acad., 1981, Disting. Info. Scis. award Data Processing Mgmt. Assn., 1981, Sylvanus Thayer award U.S. Mil. Acad., 1982, Environ. Leadership award Natural Resources Def. Council, 1983, Dollar award Nat. Fgn. Trade Council, 1985. Fellow IEEE (Founders medal 1973); mem. Nat. Acad. Engring. (Founders award 1979), Instrument Soc. Am. (hon. lifetime mem.), Wilson Council, The Bus. Roundtable Advt. Council, Bus. Council, Am. Ordnance Assn. (Crozier Gold medal 1970), Sigma Xi, Phi Beta Kappa, Tau Beta Pi, Alpha Delta Phi (named Disting. Alumnus of Yr. 1970). Clubs: Bohemian, Commonwealth, Pacific Union, World Trade, Engrs. (San Francisco); The Links (N.Y.C.); Alfalfa, Capitol Hill (Washington); California (Los Angeles). Office: Hewlett-Packard Co 1501 Page Mill Rd Palo Alto CA 94304

PACKARD, DOUGLAS RANDALL, senior engineer, nuclear materials researcher, program manager; b. Madison, S.D., Oct. 27, 1936; s. Sidney Douglas and Anna (Dehaan) P.; m. Carol Jean Jacobson, July 10, 1958; children: Vernon Randall, Sidney Thomas. BS in Engring. Physics, S.D. State U., 1964; MS in Physics, Iowa State U., 1967. Scientist Battelle N.W., Richland, Wash., 1967-69; scientist, engr. Gen. Electric Vallecitos Nuclear Ctr., Sunol, Calif., 1969-77; sr. engr. Gen. Electric Fuels Mfg., Wilmington, N.C., 1977-78, Advanced Nuclear Fuels Corp. (formerly Exxon Nuclear Co.), Richland, 1979—. Patentee in field. Served with U.S. Army, 1956-60. Mem. Am. Nuclear Soc. (5.3. working group, 1985-86), ASTM (G1.08 task force 1985), Sigma Tau. Lodge: Masons. Avocations: sailing, backpacking, motorcross riding. Home: 30003 Caballo Pl Kennewick WA 99337 Office: Advanced Nuclear Fuels Corp 2101 Horn Rapids Rd Richland WA 99336

PACKARD, ROBERT GOODALE, III, planner; b. Denver, Apr. 12, 1951; s. Robert and Mary Ann (Woodward) P.; m. Jane Ann Collins, Aug. 25, 1973; children—Jessica Nelson, Robert Gregg. B.A., Willamette U., 1973; M.Urban and Regional Planning/Community Devel., U. Colo., 1976. Project mgr. Environ. Disiciplines, Inc., Portland, Oreg., 1973-75; asst. dir. planning Portland Pub. Schs., 1976-78; dir. planning Bur. of Parks, Portland, 1978-79; dir. planning and urban design Zimmer Gunsul Frasca, Portland, 1979-81, dir. project devel., 1981-84, mng. ptnr., 1984—. Co-author: The Baker Neighborhood/Denver, 1976. Contbr. articles to profl. jours. Mem. City of Portland Waterfront Commn., 1982-83; mem. Mayor's Task Force for Joint Use of Schs., Portland, 1979-80; mem. Washington Park Master Plan Steering com., Portland, 1980-81; bd. dirs. Washington Park Zoo, 1983-86, pres. Arts Celebration Inc./Artquake, 1986—. New Rose Theatre, 1981-83; dir., pres. Grant Park Neighborhood Assn., Portland, 1981-83. Recipient Spl. Citation, Nat. Sch. Bds. Assn., 1978; Meritorious Planning Project award Am. Planning Assn., 1980, Nat. Am. Planning Assn., 1981; Meritorious Design award Am. Soc. Landscape Architects, 1981; Honor award Progressive Arch., 1983. Mem. AIA (assoc.), Am. Planning Assn., Soc. Mktg. Profls. Clubs: Oreg. Road Runners, City. Home: 3313 SW Fairmount Blvd Portland OR 97201 Office: Zimmer Gunsul Frasca Ptnrship 320 SW Oak Suite 500 Portland OR 97204

PACKARD, RONALD, congressman; b. Meridian, Idaho, Jan. 19, 1931; m. Jean Sorenson; children: Chris, Debbie, Jeff, Vicki, Scott, Lisa, Theresa. Student, Brigham Young U., 1948-50, Portland State U., 1952-53; D.M.D., U. Oreg., Portland, 1953-57. Gen. practice dentistry Carlsbad, Calif., 1957—; mem. 98th-100th Congresses from 43d Dist. Calif. Mem. Carlsbad Sch. Dist. Bd., 1960-72; bd. dirs. Carlsbad C. of C., 1972-76; mem. Carlsbad Planning Commn., 1974-76, Carlsbad City Council, 1976-78; Carlsbad chmn. Boy Scouts Am., 1977-79; mayor City of Carlsbad, 1978-82; mem. North County Armed Services YMCA, North County Transit Dist., San Diego Assn. Govts., Coastal Policy Com., Transp. Policy Com.; pres. San Diego div. Calif. League of Cities. Served with Dental Corps USN, 1957-59. Republican. Mormon. Office: 316 Cannon House Office Bldg Washington DC 20515

PACKEE, EDMOND CHARLES, forester, researcher; b. Milw., Sept. 8, 1940; s. Harry G. and Blanche (Verlinden) P.; m. Judith Anne Larson, Aug. 27, 1966; children: Edmond C., Anne C., Jessica B., Elise M. BS in Forestry, U. Mont., 1962; M in Forestry, Yale U., 1963; PhD, U. Minn., 1976. Cert. profl. soil scientist. Forester USDA Forest Service, Hayward, Wis., 1966-67; silviculturist MacMillan Bloedel Ltd., Nanaimo, B.C., Can., 1967-82; asst. prof. forest mgmt. U. Alaska, Fairbanks, 1983—; cons. Alaska Timber Task Force, Juneau, 1984-86. Mem. group com. Boy Scouts Am., Fairbanks, 1984—, Boy Scouts Can., Nanaimo, 1976-83. Mem. Internat. Union Forest Orgns. (chmn. working party), Soc. Am. Foresters, Soil Sci. Soc. Am., AAAS, Northwest Forest Soils Assn. Avocations: fishing, travel, birds, western history and art, forest industry. Office: U Alaska Agrl and Forestry Expt Station Fairbanks AK 99775-0080

PACKER, MARK BARRY, lawyer, financial consultant; b. Phila., Sept. 18, 1944; s. Samuel and Eve (Devine) P.; A.B. magna cum laude, Harvard U., 1965, LL.B., 1968; m. Donna Elizabeth Ferguson, July 2, 1967; children—Daniel Joshua, Benjamin Dov, David Johannes. Admitted to Wash. bar, 1969, Mass. bar, 1971; assoc. Ziontz, Pirtle & Fulle, Seattle, 1968-70; ptnr. Millhouse Nelle & Packer, Bellingham, Wash., 1972-82, sole practice, Bellingham, 1982—; bd. dirs., corp. sec. No. Sales Co., Inc. Mem. Bellingham Planning and Devel. Commn., 1975-84, chmn., 1977-81, mem. shoreline subcom., 1976-82; pres. Congregation Beth Israel, Bellingham, 1980-82, chmn. rabbi search com., 1986-87; mem. Bellingham Mcpl. Arts Commn., 1986—, landmark rev. bd., 1987—; treas. World Affairs Council N.W. Wash., 1985—; chmn. Bellingham campaign United Jewish Appeal, 1979—. Mem. ABA (sec. urban, state and local govt. law, commn. land use, planning and zoning, sec. real property probate and trust), Wash. State Bar Assn. (sec. environ. and land use law). Republican. Home: 208 S Forest St Bellingham WA 98225 Office: 1501 Eldridge Ave Bellingham WA 98225

PACKWOOD, BOB, senator; b. Portland, Oreg., Sept. 11, 1932; s. Frederick William and Gladys (Taft) P.; m. Georgie Ann Oberteuffer, Nov. 25, 1964; children: William Henderson, Shyla. A.B., Willamette U., 1954; LL.B., NYU, 1957; LL.B. (hon.), Yeshiva U., 1982, Gallaudet Coll., 1983. Chmn. Multnomah County Rep. Cen. Com., 1960-62; mem. Oreg. Legislature, 1963-69; U.S. senator from Oreg. 1969—, chmn. fin. com., mem. commerce com. sci. com., transp. com., com. on small bus., 1969—. Mem. Internat. Working Group of Parliamentarians on Population and Devel., 1977; mem. Pres.'s Commn. on Population Growth and the Am. Future, 1972; chmn. Nat. Rep. Senatorial Com., 1977-78, 81-82; bd. dirs. NYU; bd. overseers Lewis and Clark Coll., Portland. Named One of Three Outstanding Young Men of Oreg., 1967; Portland's Jr. 1st Citizen, 1967; Oreg. Speaker of Yr., 1968; recipient Arthur T. Vanderbilt award NYU Sch. Law, 1970; Anti-Defamation League Brotherhood award, 1970; Torch of Liberty award B'nai B'rith, 1971; Richard L. Neuberger award Oreg. Environ. Council, 1972; Conservation award Omaha Woodmen Life Ins. Soc., 1974; Monongahela Forestry Leadership award, 1976; Solar Man of Yr., Solar Energy Industries Assn., 1980; Guardian of Small Bus. award Nat. Fedn. Ind. Bus., 1980; Forester of Yr., Western Forest Industries Assn., 1980; Am. Israel Friendship award B'nai Zion, 1982; Grover C. Cobb award Nat. Assn. Broadcasters, 1982; Religious Freedom award Religious Coalition for Abortion Rights, 1983; 22d Ann. Conv. award Oreg. State Bldg. and Constrn. Trade Council, 1983. Mem. Oreg., D.C. bar assns., Beta Theta Pi. Office: 259 Russell Senate Bldg Washington DC 20510 *

PADIAN, KEVIN, biology, paleontology educator; b. 1951. BA, Colgate U., 1972, MAT, 1973; M.Phil., Yale U., 1978, PhD, 1980. Assoc. prof. U. Calif., Berkeley, 1980—; cons. Smithsonian Instn. Author, editor: The Beginning of the Age of Dinosaurs, 1986; contbr. articles to profl. jours. Grantee NSF, 1978, 85, Nat. Geographic Soc., 1981-82, Am. Chem. Soc., 1981-82, DAAD, 1986. Fellow Calif. Acad. Scis.; mem. Soc. Vertebrate Paleontology, Soc. for the Study of Evolution, Soc. for Systematic Zoology, Bay Area Com. of Correspondence for Sci., Sigma Xi. Office: U Calif Dept Paleontology Berkeley CA 94720

PADILLA, MATTHEW DANIEL, university administrator; b. Tomé, N.Mex., Jan. 3, 1947; s. Placido F. and Crisanta C. (Baca) P.; m. Lillian J. Roybal, Aug. 9, 1969; children—Roderigo, Raquel. B.A., N.Mex. Highlands U., 1969, M.A. in Phys. Edn. with honors, 1972, M.A. in Counseling with honors, 1973, M.A. in Ednl. Adminstrn. with honors, 1975; Ph.D. in Counseling and Adminstrn., U. N.Mex., 1981. Cert. tchr., counselor, adminstr., N.Mex. Tchr. and coach Los Lunas Schs., N.Mex., 1969-70, Belen Schs., N.Mex., 1970-72; dir. student services El Rito Vocat. Sch., N.Mex., 1973-74; Native Am. counselor, recruiter N.Mex. Highlands U., Las Vegas, 1974-77, dir. Yemen and Argentine projects, 1977-78, v.p. student affairs, 1980-84; dir. N.Mex. Career Info. System and Vocat. Guidance Project, U. N.Mex., Albuquerque, 1984—. Gen. Electric Educators-in-Industry fellow, 1982, Title IV Bilingual fellow, 1979-80. Mem. Nat. Assn. Student Personnel Adminstrs., Pi Gamma Mu, Phi Kappa Phi. Roman Catholic. Home: 5818 Delbert NW Albuquerque NM 87114 Office: Univ New Mexico Albuquerque NM 87131

PAETZEL, DAVID RICHARD, interior designer; b. Valdosta, Ga., Nov. 8, 1956; s. Harold Roger and Barbara Jean (Dorfer) P. AA, Temple Jr. Coll., 1978; student, Tex. A&M U., 1978-80; BS, Tex. Tech U., 1983. Interior designer J.D. Kazar, Las Vegas, Nev., 1983-84, Design Ctr., Las Vegas, 1985—. Recipient Outstanding Achievement award Nat. Observer, 1977. Mem. Am. Soc. Interior Designers (assoc.). Republican. Lutheran. Avocations: painting, paper sculptures, rug design.

PAGANI, ALBERT LOUIS, aerospace system engineer; b. Jersey City, Feb. 19, 1936; s. Alexander C. and Anne (Salvati) P.; m. Beverly Cameron, Feb. 23, 1971; children: Penelope, Deborah, Michael. BSEE, U.S. Naval Acad., 1957; MBA, So. Ill. U., 1971. Commd. 2d lt. USAF, 1957, advanced through grades to col., 1978; navigator USAF, Lake Charles, La., 1957-63; pilot USAF, McGuire AFB, N.J., 1963-65; command pilot USAF, Anchorage, Alaska, 1965-68; mgr. airlift USAF, Saigon, Socialist Republic of Vietnam, 1968-69; chief spl. missions USAF, Scott AFB, Ill., 1969-74; commd. tactical airlift group USAF Europe, Mildenhall, Eng., 1974-76; dep. comdr. Rhein Main Air Base USAF Europe, Frankfurt, Fed. Republic Germany, 1976-78; chief airlift mgmt. USAF Military Airlift Command, Scott AFB, Ill., 1978-81, dir. tech. plans and concepts, 1981, dir. command and control, 1982-85; ret. 1985; mem. sr. staff C3I systems Lockheed Missile and Space Co., Sunnyvale, Calif., 1985—. V.p. Cath. Ch. Council, Mildenhall, 1974, pres., 1975. Decorated Legion of Merit, Bronze Star, Air medal, Vietnam Cross of Gallantry. Mem. Nat. Def. Transp. Assn., Soc. Logistics Engrs., Air Force Assn., Armed Forces Communication and Electronics Assn., Air Lift Assn., Daedalions, Mensa. Avocation: snow skiing. Home: 41090 Driscoll Terr Fremont CA 94539 Office: Lockheed Missile and Space Co Advanced Programs 69-90 1111 Lockheed Way Sunnyvale CA 94539

PAGE, CURTIS MATTHEWSON, minister; b. Columbus, Ohio, Oct. 24, 1946; s. Charles N. and Alice Matthewson P.; m. Martha Poitevin, Feb. 12, 1977; children: Allison, Charles, Abigail. BS, Ariz. State U., 1968; M in Div., San Francisco Theol. Sem., 1971, D in Ministry, 1985. Ordained to ministry, 1971. Pastor Ketchum (Idaho) Presbyn. Ch., 1972-80, Kirk O'The Valley Presbyn. Ch., Reseda, Calif., 1980—; bd. dirs. Express Pub., Ketchum, 1977—, Mary Magdalene Home, Reseda, 1987—; moderator Kendall Presbytery, 1978. Chmn. Ketchum City Zoning Commn., 1979-80; Dem. precinct committeeman, Ketchum, 1978; mem. Ketchum Master Planning Commn., 1974. Avocations: amateur radio, tennis, snow skiing. Home: 19955 Lanark Canoga Park CA 91306 Office: Kirk O' The Valley Presbyn 19620 Vanowen Reseda CA 91335

PAGE, DENNIS B(RETT), electronic engineer; b. Glendale, Calif., Nov. 16, 1949; s. Brett and Annabelle Saunders Page; m. Marcia Ryan, July 19, 1986; 1 child, Jodi Renee. Student, West Coast U., 1984—. Electronic technician Hughes Aircraft Co., Los Angeles, 1968-74; research asst. Hughes Aircraft Co., Culver City, Calif., 1974-78, sr. assoc. engr., 1978-80; sr. mem. tech. staff Hughes Aircraft Co., El Segundo, Calif., 1980-85, sect. head, 1985—. Contbr. articles to profl. jours.; patentee in field. Mem. Inst. Environ. Scis. (sr. co-chmn. personal computer users group 1985—, tech. com. 1984—, editorial adv. bd. 1985—, bd. dirs 1984—), Inst. Soc. Am. (sr.), So. Calif. Meter Assn. Republican. Club: Hughes Ski. Avocations: surfing, outdoors. Office: Hughes Aircraft Co R1/C319 PO Box 92426 Los Angeles CA 90009

PAGE, RICHARD MAX, insurance company executive; b. Salem, Oreg., June 14, 1926; s. Everill Maxwell and May Day (Tate) P.; m. Evelyn Johnson, June 19, 1954; 1 child, Martha Ann. Student, Willamette U., 1946-47; A.B., Stanford U., 1949, M.B.A., 1951. C.P.A., Calif. Staff acct. Haskins & Sells, C.P.A., San Francisco, 1951-57; controller Standard Ins. Co., Portland, Oreg., 1957-59, asst. v.p., controller, 1960-64, v.p., controller, 1965—, v.p., sec. subs. cos.; mem. Portland adv. council Region X, SBA; dir. Oreg. Tax Research, pres., 1977-79. Bd. dirs. Portland area council Camp

Fire, 1972—, nat. treas., Kansas City; com. mem. United Way, Portland; treas. State Treas. Clay Myers Re-Election Com., 1976-80. Served with USN, 1944-45. Recipient Boss of Yr. award Timberline chpt. Am. Bus. Women's Assn., 1963. Fellow Life Office Mgmt. Assn.; mem. Oreg. Soc. C.P.A.s, Calif. Soc. C.P.A.s, Am. Inst. C.P.A.s, Assn. for Systems Mgmt. (pres. Portland chpt. 1967-68), Assoc. Oreg. Industries (taxation com.), Oreg. Taxpayers Assn. (bd. dirs. 1969—, pres. 1977-79), Oreg. Tax Found. (trustee), Portland C. of C. Republican. Presbyterian. Clubs: Multnomah Athletic, Toastmasters. Home: 6727 SW 13th St Portland OR 97219 Office: Standard Ins Co 1100 SW 6th St Portland OR 97204

PAGE, THOMAS ALEXANDER, utility executive; b. Niagara Falls, N.Y., Mar. 24, 1933; m. Evelyn Rainnie, July 16, 1960; children: Christopher, Catherine. B.S. in Civil Engring, Purdue U., 1955, M.S. in Indsl. Adminstrn, 1963. Registered profl. engr., N.Y. C.P.A., Wis., Tex. Comptroller, treas. Wis. Power & Light Co., Madison, 1970-73; treas. Gulf States Utilities Co., Beaumont, Tex., 1973-75, sr. v.p. fin., 1975, exec. v.p., 1975-78, also bd. dirs.; exec. v.p., chief operating officer San Diego Gas & Electric Co., 1978-81, pres., chief exec. officer, 1981—, chmn., 1983—, also bd. dirs., 1979—. Mem. Dane County Bd. Suprs., Wis., 1968-72. Served to capt. USAF, 1955-57. Home: 1904 Hidden Crest Dr El Cajon CA 92020 Office: San Diego Gas & Electric Co 101 Ash St San Diego CA 92112 *

PAGE, THOMAS LEE, ecological scientist, research administrator; b. Lima, Ohio, Mar. 5, 1941; s. Harold Alan and Chloe Hazel (Harris) P.; m. Wilma Louise Pfister, Aug. 24, 1963; children: Alan, Stephanie. BA, Ohio No. U., 1963; MA, Kent State U., 1966, PhD, 1971. Postdoctoral fellow Washington U., St. Louis, 1970-72; sr. research scientist Battelle- N.W., Richland, Wash., 1972-79, mgr. freshwater scis., 1979-82, mgr. applied ecology, 1982-86, mgr. environ. pathways and assessment, 1986—. Contbr. numerous tech. reports and articles to profl. jours. and pubs. Mem. Am. Inst. Fisheries Research Biologists, Am. Fisheries Soc., Ecol. Soc. Am., Internat. Soc. Theoretical and Applied Limnology, Am. Soc. Limnology and Oceanography, Ohio Acad. Sci. (life), N.W. Sci. Assn. Home: 1725 Birch Richland WA 99352 Office: Battelle NW Lab PO Box 949 Richland WA 99352

PAGELLA, MAURICE VONDY, oil company financial executive; b. London, July 22, 1946; came to U.S., 1979; s. Clovis Eugene and Ethel Mary (Johnson) P.; m. Gillian Mary Tanfield, Jan. 5, 1974; children: Amanda, Desmond, Samantha. BA in Econs., Cambridge U., Eng., 1967, MA in Econs., 1969. CPA. Auditor, mgr. Arthur Andersen & Co., London, 1967-79; v.p. controller Solus Ocean Systems, Houston, 1979-82; v.p. fin. planning Pacific Resources Inc., Honolulu, 1982—. City councillor London Borough of Sutton, 1974-78; mem. fin. com. Episcopal Diocese of Hawaii, Honolulu, 1985—. Fellow Inst. of Chartered Accts. in Eng. and Wales; mem. Hawaii Soc. CPA's, Hawaii Soc. Corp. Planners. Avocations: sailing, theatre, music, traveling. Home: 22 Kailua Rd Kailua HI 96734 Office: Pacific Resources Inc Box 3379 Honolulu HI 96734

PAGET, JOHN ARTHUR, mech. engr.; b. Ft. Frances, Ont., Can., Sept. 15, 1922; s. John and Ethel (Bishop) P.; B.Applied Sci., Toronto, 1946; m. Vicenta Herrera Nunez, Dec. 16, 1963; children—Cynthia Ellen, Kevin Arthur, Keith William. Chief draftsman Gutta Percha & Rubber, Ltd., Toronto, Ont., 1946-49; chief draftsman Viceroy Mfg. Co., Toronto, 1949-52; supr., design engr. C.D. Howe Co. Ltd., Montreal, Que., Can., 1952-58, sr. design engr. Combustion Engring., Montreal, 1958-59; sr. staff engr. Gen. Atomic, Inc., La Jolla, 1959-81. Mem. ASME, Am. Inst. Plant Engrs., Soc. Mfg. Engrs., Profl. Engrs. Ont., Soc. for History Tech., Inst. Mech. Engrs., Soc. Am. Mil. Engrs., Newcomen Soc., Brit. Nuclear Energy Soc. Patentee in field. Home: 3183 Magellan St San Diego CA 92154 Office: PO Box 427 Nestor CA 92053

PAIGE, EDWARD JAY, communications corporation executive; b. Los Angeles, Apr. 15, 1956; s. Morton Lewis and Ruth May (Pura) P. Communications cons. various orgns., Los Alamitos, Calif., 1979-80; pres., chief exec. officer Paige Communications, Corp., Tustin, Calif., 1982—, also bd. dirs.; pres., chief exec. officer Fast Eddie Enterprises, Tustin, 1984—, FEE Fin. Services, Inc., 1985—, Entrepreneurial Mgmt., Inc. Author: The Benefits of Ownership. Contbr. articles to mags. Mem. Statue of Liberty-Ellis Island Centennial Commn. Served to petty officer USN, 1974-79. Recipient Good Conduct award, 1978. Mem. So. Calif. Tech. Exec. Network, C. of C. Club: Rotary Internat. Office: Paige Communications Corp 2620 Walnut Ave Tustin CA 92680

PAILLE, RICHARD LEE, marketing professional; b. Reno, May 9, 1949; m. Julie Ann Paille, July 31, 1976; children: Remy Alexis, Matthew Alain. Student, U. Nev., Las Vegas, 1968-69; BS in Speech Communications, U. Nev., Reno, 1970-73. Lic. real estate agt., Nev., Calif. Pres. Design Corp., Incline Village, Nev.; real estate broker Design Realy/Realty 500; v.p. I.T.D. Corp., Lake Tahoe, Nev.; owner Washoe County Pant Co., Lakeside Tennis Club Pro Shoppe; assoc. fin. cons. McDuff Scott and Assocs. Past pres. bd. realtors Incline Village, 1980, past chmn. pub. relations com., budget com., grievance com. Served with Nev. N.G., 1968-71, USAF, 1971-74. Mem. Nat. Assn. Realtors (trustee, treas., polit. action com.), Realtor's Inst., Nat. Assn. Real Estate Appraisers, Nat. Assn. Rev. Appraisers & Mortgage Underwriters, Nat. Assn. Security Dealers, Nat. Assn. Realtors, Nev. Assn. Realtors (past bd. dirs.), Incline Village Bd. Realtors, Sierra Reno Exchangers, Calif. Assn. Realtors, Co-op Investment Bankers, Realty 500, Gideons Internat. Home: 115 Tramway Rd Incline Village NV 89450 Office: Design Corp 885 Tahoe Blvd Incline Village NV 89450

PAILLET, FREDERICK LAWRENCE, geophysical research chemist; b. New Haven, Conn., Sept. 5, 1946; s. George Lawrence and Zenaide (Ferron) P.; m. Margaret Sandra Davies, Sept. 6, 1969 (div. Aug. 1985); children: Jennifer Suzanne, Aimee Elizabeth. BS, U. Rochester, N.Y., 1968, MS, 1969, PhD, 1974. Base civil engr. USAF, Great Falls, Mont., 1969-72; fluid dynamacist, Flight Dynamics Lab. USAF, Dayton, Ohio, 1974-76; asst. prof. Wright State U., Fairborn, Ohio, 1976-78; geophysicist U.S. Geol. Survey, Denver, 1978-83, research project chief, 1983—. Contbr. more than 20 articles to profl. jours. Served to capt. USAF, 1969-76. Mem. Soc. Exploration Geophysicists, Am. Geophys. Union, Am. Meteorol. Soc., Soc. Profl. Well Log Analysts (technol. com. 1983-85). Roman Catholic. Avocations: pen and ink drawing, botanical studies, distance running. Home: 6549 S Allison Ct Littleton CO 80123 Office: US Geol Survey Denver Fed Ctr MS403 Lakewood CO 80225

PAINE, ROBERT TREAT, chemistry educator; b. Colorado Springs, Colo., Dec. 15, 1944; Robert T. and Marietta H. Paine; m. Bonnie P. Paine, June 20, 1967; children: Andrew S., Matthew H., Joanna M. BS, U. Calif., Berkeley, 1966; PhD, U. Mich., 1970. Postdoctoral work Northwestern U., Evanston, Ill., 1970-72; postdoctoral work Los Alamos (N.Mex.) Nat. Lab., 1972-74, cons., 1974—; asst. prof. U. New Mex., Albuquerque, 1974-78, assoc. prof., 1978-82, prof., 1982—. Contbr. articles to profl. jours. Trainee NASA, 1966-69. Mem. AAAS, Am. Chem. Soc., Materials Research Soc. Office: U NMex Dept Chemistry Albuquerque NM 87131

PAINE, THOMAS OTTEN, government official; b. Berkeley, Calif., Nov. 9, 1921; s. George Thomas and Ada Louise (Otten) P.; m. Barbara Helen Taunton Pearse, Oct. 1, 1946; children: Marguerite Ada, George Thomas, Judith Janet, Frank Taunton. A.B. in Engring, Brown U., 1942; M.S. in Phys. Metallurgy, Stanford, 1947; Ph.D., Stanford U., 1949. Research asso. Stanford, 1947-49; with Gen. Electric Co., 1949-68, 70-76, GE Research Lab., Schenectady; mgr. center advanced studies Santa Barbara, Calif., 1963-68; v.p., group exec. power generation 1970-73; sr. v.p. sci. and tech. GE Research Lab., 1973-76; pres., dir. Northrop Corp., Los Angeles, 1976-82; chmn. Thomas Paine Assocs., Los Angeles, 1982—, Nat. Commn. on Space, 1984-86; dep. adminstr., then adminstr. NASA, 1968-70; dir. NIKE, Quotron Systems, Orbital Scis. Contbr. articles to tech. publs. Bd. dirs. Pacific Forum, Honolulu. Served to lt. USNR, World War II. Decorated Submarine Combat insignia with stars, USN Commendation medal; grand ufficiale della Ordine al Merito Italy; recipient Distinguished Service medal NASA, 1970, 86, Apollo Achievement award, Disting. Service Medal, Washington award Western Soc. Engrs., 1972; John Fritz medal United Engring. Socs., 1976; Faraday medal Inst. Elec. Engrs., London, 1976; Humanitarian award NCCJ; John F. Kennedy award Am. Astronautical Soc., 1987. Fellow AIAA; mem. Nat. Acad. Engring., N.Y. Acad. Scis., Am. Phys. Soc., IEEE, U.S. Naval Inst., Am. Astronautical Soc. (John F. Kennedy Astronautics award 1987), Sigma Xi. Clubs: Explorers (N.Y.C.), Lotos (N.Y.C.), Sky (N.Y.C.); Cosmos (Washington), Army and Navy (Washington); Calif., Regency (Los Angeles). Co-inventor lodex R magnets. Home: 765 Bonhill Rd Los Angeles CA 90049 Office: Thomas Paine Assocs 2401 Colorado Ave #178 Santa Monica CA 90404

PAINTER, REESE BLAIR, controller; b. Payson, Utah, Aug. 23, 1943; s. Leslie Reese and Maxine (Sperry) P.; m. Susan Harper, Feb. 10, 1973; children: Ryan, Nicholas, Natalie, Cameron. AS in Bus., Snow Coll., 1964; BS in Acctg., Utah State U., 1966. Acct. Signetics Corp., Orem, Utah, 1969-70, Gates Rubber Co., Nephi, Utah, 1971-73; controller NRP Corp., Nephi, 1973-83; v.p., treas. G.H. Industries, Nephi, 1983-85; sr. acct. Utah Tech. Coll., Provo, 1985-86; controller Nephi Rubber Products, 1985—; pvt. practice tax preparer, Nephi, 1970—. Dem. city chmn., Nephi, 1984-86; active Nephi Jaycees, 1972-77, state officer Utah, 1975-76. Served with U.S. Army, 1966-68, Vietnam. Mormon. Avocations: boating, bowling, fishing. Office: Nephi Rubber Products 255 W 1100 N Nephi UT 84648

PALANISWAMY, VENKATAPURAM A(NGAPPA), chemist; b. Venkatapuram, India, July 14, 1945; came to U.S., 1977; s. Kalianna and Valliammal Angappa Gounder; m. Punithavathi Palaniswamy, Feb. 27, 1974; children: Guhapriya, Kiruthiga. BSc, U. Madras, T.Nadu, India, 1968, MSc, 1970; PhD, Okla. State U., 1981. Asst. prof. chemistry Gobi (India) Arts Coll. and U. Madras, 1971-77; asst. Okla. State U., Stillwater, 1978-81; research assoc. U. Conn., Storrs, 1982, Oreg. State U., Corvallis, 1982—. Mem. Am. Chem. Soc., Phi Lambda Upsilon. Avocations: basketball, reading. Home: 3930 NW Witham Hill Dr #158 Corvallis OR 97330 Office: Oreg State U Dept Chemistry Corvallis OR 97331

PALAU, LUIS, religious organization administrator; b. Buenos Aires, Nov. 27, 1934; came to U.S., 1960; s. Luis Sr. and Matilde (Balfour) P.; m. Patricia Marilyn Scofield, Aug. 5, 1961; children; Kevin and Keith (twins), Andrew, Stephen. BA, St. Alban's Coll., Buenos Aires, 1954; grad. cert. in Bible, Multnomah Sch. of Bible, 1961; DD (hon.), Talbot Theol. Sem., 1977, Wheaton Coll., 1985. Missionary Overseas Crusades, Inc., Santa Clara, Calif., 1961-71, field dir. Latin Am. sect., 1967-71; pres. Luis Palau Evangelistic Assn., Portland, Oreg., 1971—. Author: Walk on Water, Pete, 1974, Sex and Youth, 1974, Whom Shall I Marry, 1976, The Schemer and the Dreamer, 1976, The Moment to Shout, 1977, Heart After God, 1978, Our God Reigns, 1981, Tough Questions, 1984, Time to Stop Pretending, 1985, So You Want to Grow, 1986; co-author: Scottish Fires of Revival, 1980, Luis Palau: Calling the Nations to Christ, 1983; author/editor numerous tracts, articles and booklets on current socio-religious topics. Office: Luis Palau Evangelistic Assn PO Box 1173 Portland OR 97207-1173

PALERMO, DONALD ANTHONY, electronics company executive; b. North East, Pa., Sept. 14, 1933; s. Anthony and Mary (Muscarella) P.; m. Josephine Budenz, Aug. 4, 1962; children: Damien Joseph, Christopher James, Tomàs Adrian. BE, U. Detroit, 1956; BS, Stanford U., 1959. Engr., mgr. Lockheed Missiles & Space Co., Sunnyvale, Calif., 1956-74, program mgr., 1974-82; exec. v.p. Tiburon Systems, Inc., San Jose, 1982—. Contbr. articles to profl. jours. Pres. parish council St. Nicholas Cath. Ch., Los Altos, Calif., 1984-85, also pres. sch. bd., 1978-79. Mem. Armed Forces Communications and Electronics Assn. (co. rep.), Pi Tau Sigma, Tau Beta Pi. Republican. Roman Catholic. Avocations: writing, collecting rare books, golf, Roman history. Office: Tiburon Systems Inc 2085 Hamilton Ave San Jose CA 95125

PALKE, KENNETH ALAN, newspaper editor; b. Inglewood, Calif., Sept. 30, 1948; s. Byron Park and Shirley Mae (Allen) P.; m. Susan B. Peterson, Mar. 27, 1982. B.J., Calif. State U.-Long Beach, 1975. Reporter, editor Palos Verdes (Calif.) Peninsula News, 1974-77; reporter, columnist Daily Southeast News, Downey, Calif., 1977-79; editor Polk County Itemizer, Dallas, Oreg., 1979, Salem (Oreg.) Capital Press, 1979—. Served with USN, 1967-71; mem. Oreg. N.G., 1982-83, 1st lt. Oreg. N.G.R., 1985—. Decorated Vietnam Service medal. Mem. Sigma Delta Chi, U.S. Ski Writers Assn. Democrat. Baptist. Lodge: Kiwanis. Office: PO Box 2048 Salem OR 97308

PALLADINO, GERALD MICHAEL, meeting planner; b. Fresno, Calif., June 6, 1944; s. Arthur Joseph and Angelina Lena (Mongelli) P.; children: Michael Arthur, Gabrielle Nicolette. B.S. in Journalism, Calif. State U.-Fresno, 1966; M.S., U. So. Calif., 1969; M.B.A., Stanford U., 1974. Account exec. McCann-Erickson, Inc., Los Angeles, 1967-70; advt., mktg. mgr. Memorex Corp., Santa Clara, Calif., 1970-74; sr. v.p., dir. spl. events Bank of Am., San Francisco, 1974—; mem. meeting planner adv. bd. Sonesta Internat. Hotels Corp., 1984—; speaker, seminar leader, panelist meeting confs., 1979—; Mem. planning bd. Good Samaritan Hosp., San Jose, Calif., 1983—; bd. dirs. San Francisco Child Abuse Council, 1985—. Named Mktg. Mgr. of Yr., Memorex Corp., 1973; recipient Recognition award Bank of Am., 1982. Mem. Meeting Planners Internat. (pres. 1984-85), Internat. Exhibitors Assn. (bd. dirs. 1981-83). Republican. Roman Catholic. Home: 5569 Copeland Place San Jose CA 95124 Office: Advt Dept Bank of Am 315 Montgomery St San Francisco CA 94104

PALLAS, ROBERT MERRILL, advertising executive; b. Detroit, Feb. 4, 1947; s. Harold Edward and Rebecca (Merrill) P.; m. Kristine Kay Pugh, Jan. 1, 1982; 1 child, Erin Merrill. BBA, Western Mich. U., 1969. With Kalamazoo (Mich.) Container Co., 1969-71, J. Walter Thompson Co., N.Y.C., then San Francisco, 1971-75, 75-79; v.p. San Francisco office J. Walter Thompson Co., 1979; dir. acct. mgmt. Gardner Communications, Calif., 1979-85; prin. Pallas Advt., Inc., San Francisco, 1985—. Office: 55 Green St San Francisco CA 94111

PALM, NANCY CLEONE, medical center administrator, radiography technologist; b. Portland, Oreg., July 8, 1939; d. Oscar Emanuel and Hallie Vernice (Thurber) Palm. Student U. Oreg. Sch. Radiology, 1957; grad. Hosp. Corpswave, Hosp. Corps Sch., Great Lakes (Ill. Naval Base, 1958; grad. X-ray Tech., Sch. Radiology, Bremerton, Wash. Naval Base, 1961. Lic. radiography technologist, Oreg. Chief radiography technologist New Lincoln Hosp., Toledo, Oreg., 1961-63; sr. radiography technologist Gresham (Oreg.) Gen. Hosp., 1963-65; chief radiography technologist Neurol. Clinic, Portland, Oreg., 1965-79; head bookkeeper Rinehart Clinic, Wheeler, Oreg., 1979-80; owner, gen. mgr. San Dune Motel, Marzanita, Oreg., 1971-83; bus. agt. Rinehart Found., Inc., Manzanita, 1983—; owner Sears & Roebuck Catalog Store, Nehalem, Oreg., 1979-81; adminstrn. mgr. Rinehart Found., Inc. (Nehalem Bay Med. Ctr.), Manzanita and Garibaldi, Oreg., 1980—. Sponsor Willamette council Campfire Girls, Inc., 1982-84. Served with USN, 1958-61. Fellow Nat. Coll. Radiography Technologists; mem. Oreg. Med. Group Mgmt. Assn., Nat. Assn. Female Execs., Am. Registry Clin. Radiography Technologists (nat. dir. 1970-76, trustee 1972-74, sec. 71-72, pres. 72-74; Citation award 1970, Disting. Service award 1971, 73, Order of Golden Ray 1974, founder Margaret Harris Award Competition 1973). Republican. Presbyterian. Home: 423 Dorcas Lane PO Box 262 Manzanita OR 97130 Office: PO Box 580 Manzanita OR 97130

PALMBY, DONALD HENRY, aeronautics engineer; b. Vernon Center, Minn., Apr. 9, 1931; s. Henry J. and Lillien (Leseman) P.; m. W. Fay De Wall, June 18, 1951; children: Dawn Palmby Meyer, Keith. BS in Gen. Sci., Mankato State U., 1953. Tchr. sci. Bertha (Minn.) High Sch., 1953-56; mass properties engr. Lockheed Missiles & Space Co., Sunnyvale, Calif., 1957-80, cost analyst, 1980-82, mgr., 1982—. Mem. Soc. Allied Weight Engrs. (sr., bd. dirs. 1979-80), Inst. Cost Analysts, Internat. Soc. Parametric Analysts, Space Systems Cost Analysis Group, AIAA. Republican. Methodist. Avocations: gardening, camping. Office: Lockheed Missiles & Space Co PO Box 3504 Dept 67-42/MS 559 Sunnyvale CA 94088

PALMER, ARTHUR ARVIN, educational administrator; b. Winslow, Ariz., Aug. 8, 1940; s. LeRoy Arthur and Lucille (Thomas) P.; m. Jean Smith, Sept. 6, 1963; children—Lani Kay, Jeanette Arvanne, Bryce Arvin. Student Brigham Young U.-Hawaii, 1959-61; B.A., Ariz. State U., 1965, M.A., 1966; Ph.D., Claremont Grad. Sch., 1969. Lectr. polit. sci. Whittier Coll. (Calif.), 1967-69, asst. prof., 1969-75, dean co-curricular affairs, 1972-75; county sch. supt. Navajo County, Holbrook, Ariz., 1976; dean gen. edn. and extension Northland Pioneer Coll., Holbrook, 1977-78, dean instrn., 1978-82, v.p., dean instrn., 1982—; cons. and evaluator N. Cen. Assn., 1984—. Author: Buddhist Politics: Japan's Clean Government Party, 1971; Elijah Was a Valiant Man, 1982; co-author: Taylor, Arizona: A Historical Review, 1978; contbr. articles to profl. jours. Pres. UN Assn., Whittier, 1969; charter mem. Nat. Human Services Consortium; Washington, 1981; mem. Sixco Pvt. Industry Council, Flagstaff, Ariz., 1983; chmn. Ariz. Community Colls. Council Acad. Administrs., 1985-86; v.p. Ariz. Community Coll. Adminstrs. Assn., 1986-87. Named Pioneer Educator, Northland Pioneer Coll., 1982; acad. adminstrn. intern Am. Council on Edn., 1971-72; Haynes Found. fellow, 1970. Mem. Western Polit. Sci. Assn., Phi Theta Kappa, Omicron Delta Kappa (advisor 1973-74), Pi Sigma Alpha (v.p. 1965-66). Democrat. Mem. Ch. of Jesus Christ of Latter-day Saints. Home: 349 Casa Linda Dr PO Box 205 Taylor AZ 85939 Office: Northland Pioneer Coll 1200 E Hermosa Dr Holbrook AZ 86025

PALMER, BEVERLY BLAZEY, psychologist, educator; b. Cleve., Nov. 22, 1945; d. Lawrence E. and Mildred M. Blazey; m. Richard C. Palmer, June 24, 1967; 1 child, Ryan Richard. PhD in Counseling Psychology, Ohio State U., 1972. Lic. clinical psychologist, Calif. Adminstrv. assoc. Ohio State U., Columbus, 1969-70; research psychologist Health Services Research Ctr. UCLA, 1971-77; commr. pub. health Los Angeles County, 1978-81; pvt. practice clin. psychology Torrance, Calif., 1985—; prof. psychology Calif. State U., Carson, 1973—. Reviewer manuscripts for numerous textbook pubs; contbr. numerous articles to profl. jours. Recipient Proclamation County of Los Angeles, 1972, Proclamation County of Los Angeles, 1981. Mem. Am. Psychol. Assn. Office: Calif State U Dominquez Hills Dept Psychology Carson CA 90747

PALMER, CURTIS HOWARD, diversified company executive, lawyer; b. Oakland, Calif., 1908; s. Howard H. and Catherine May (Larkin) P.; m. Helen Hayes, Apr. 8, 1936. LL.B., U. Calif., 1932. Sole practice 1932-35; tax counsel Calif. Bd. of Equalization, 1935-43; gen. counsel Alfred Hart, Los Angeles, 1943-60; exec. officer City Nat. Bank, Beverly Hills, Calif., 1960-75, chmn. bd., 1975; chmn. bd. Arden Group, Inc., Beverly Hills, 1976—; dir. Internat. Aluminum Corp.; chmn. bd. dirs. Arden Group Inc. Office: 9595 Wilshire Blvd Suite 212 Beverly Hills CA 90012

PALMER, DOUGLAS ARTHUR, physicist; b. Oceanside, Calif., Jan. 26, 1950; s. Arthur Ernest and Leona Marie (McLarty) P. BS in Physics, U. Calif. San Diego, La Jolla, 1972; MPhil. in Physics, Yale U., 1975, PhD in Physics, 1978. Staff physicist Yale U., New Haven, 1978-80, U. Calif. San Diego, 1980-83; systems engr., mgr. M/A-Com, San Diego, 1983-85; sr. supr. scientist Western Research Corp., San Diego, 1986—. Author: Quijin, 1986. Mem. Soc. of Friends. Avocation: writing. Home: 3967 LaCresta Dr San Diego CA 92107

PALMER, JAMES RUSSWORTH, theoretical physicist, high energy laser optics researcher; b. Madera, Calif., Oct. 12, 1936; s. James Russworth Palmer and Georgella (Bartmann) Palmer Irelan; m. Norma Elizabeth Boyer (div. 1974); children—Susan Lynn, Debra Ann, Martin Daniel; m. Bonnie Elizabeth Shields, Aug. 7, 1977 (div. 1986). B.S.Ch.E., Calif. State U., 1963, M.S.Ch.E., 1966; Ph.D., UCLA, 1973. Project scientist Aerospace Controls, Los Angeles, 1963-66; project engr. Electroptical Systems, Pasadena, Calif., 1966-70; pres.-cons. Doc Jim Enterprises, Orange, Calif., 1970—; chief scientist Comarco, Inc., Ridgecrest, Calif., 1983—; cons. Seven Engring., Santa Monica, Calif., 1980—. Author: Laser Damage in Optical Thin Films, 1985; also numerous articles, 1963—. Served to lt. (j.g.) USN, 1955-59. Mem. Optical Soc. Am., Am. Inst. Physics, N.Y. Acad. Scis., Internat. Soc. Optical Engring. (Rudolf Kingslake Silver medal 1984), Sigma Xi.

PALMER, JOEL, sales manager; b. Winchester, Mass., May 11, 1946; s. Edwin Joseph and Marjorie Bernice (Batchelder) P.; m. Marilyn Sarina Fils, Mar. 23, 1975; children: Eric, Lindsay. BS in Mgmt., Boston U., 1971; MBA, UCLA, 1972. Nat. sales mgr. Diablo Systems Xerox, Los Angeles, 1982—; bd. dirs. Tarzana Property Owners Assn. Served to cpl. USMC, 1966-68. Office: Diablo Systems Xerox 2029 Century Park E Los Angeles CA 90067

PALMER, JOHN LEWIS, retired lawyer, plumbing mfr.; b. Milw., Nov. 22, 1921; s. John Lewis and Florence Margaret (Schneider) P.; B.A., Beloit (Wis.) Coll., 1947; J.D., U. Wis., 1949; m. Virginia Frances Smith, July 15, 1944; children—Michael John, Steven Peter. Admitted to Wis. bar, 1949; partner firm Whyte & Hirschboeck, Milw., 1949-71; exec. v.p., gen. counsel, sec., dir. Bradley Corp. and subsidiaries, Menomonee Falls, Wis., 1971-79, pres., dir., 1979-80, chmn. bd., chief exec. officer, dir., 1980-85; bd. dirs. Kieckhefer Assos., Inc., Eilcar Corp., Alpha Cellulose Corp. Alumni trustee Beloit Coll., 1972-75. Served to capt. USMCR, 1943-46. Mem. Am., Wis., Milw. bar assns., Order of Coif, Phi Beta Kappa. Republican. Congregationalist. Clubs: Milw. Country, Tucson Nat. Golf., Garden of Gods, Mountain Oyster. Contbr. articles to profl. jours. Home: 7939 N Tuscany Dr Tucson AZ 85741

PALMER, LOUIS THOMAS, pathologist; b. Omaha, Dec. 12, 1937; s. Harry Calvin and Helen Irene (Hansen) P.; m. Rosario Garcia, Dec. 28, 1977; children: Ria Charrise, Ryan Christopher. BS, Wash. State U., 1960; MS, Kans. State U., 1965; PhD, U. Minn., 1968. Plant pathologist Rockefeller Found., Mex. and India, 1968-71; extension plant pathologist U. Nebr., Lincoln, 1971-75; plant pathologist Internat. Rice Research Inst., Sukamandi, Indonesia, 1975-79; dir. United Fruit Co., La Lima, Honduras, 1979-81; field devel. biologist E.I. duPont de Nemours, Campinas, Brazil, 1982-85; mgr. E.I. duPont de Nemours, Madera, Calif., 1985—. Contbr. articles to profl. jours. Advisor Boy Scouts Am., Campinas, 1983-85, councilor, Madera, 1985—. Served to capt. U.S. Army, 1961-64, Res. 1965-66. Recipient Eagle Scout award Boy Scouts Am., 1955; Carl Raymond Grey scholar Union Pacific R.R., 1955, Carl J. Erickson scholar Benton County, Washington, 1956. Mem. Am. Phytopathol. Soc., N.Y. Acad. Sci., Indian Phytopathol. Soc., Sigma Xi. Roman Catholic. Lodge: Kiwanis. Avocations: photography, swimming, tennis. Home: 2612 Pinewood Dr Madera CA 93637 Office: DuPont Field Sta 19 13130 Madera CA 93637

PALMER, PATRICIA ANN TEXTER, English language educator; b. Detroit, June 10, 1932; d. Elmer Clinton and Helen (Rotchford) Texter; m. David Jean Palmer, June 4, 1955. B.A., U. Mich., 1953; M.Ed., Nat. Coll. Edn., 1958; M.A., Calif. State U.-San Francisco, 1966; postgrad. Stanford U., 1968, Calif. State Coll.-Hayward, 1968-69. Chmn. speech dept. Grosse Pointe Univ. Sch. (Mich.), 1953-55; tchr. South Margerita Sch., Panama, 1955-56, Kipling Sch., Deerfield, Ill., 1955-56; grade level chmn. Rio San Gabriel Sch., Downey, Calif., 1957-59; tchr. newswriting and devel. reading Roosevelt High Sch., Honolulu, 1959-62; tchr. English, speech and newswriting El Camino High Sch., South San Francisco, 1962-68; chmn. English as 2d lang. dept. South San Francisco Unified Sch. Dist., 1968-81; dir. English as 2d lang. Inst., Millbrae, Calif., 1978—; adj. faculty New Coll. Calif., 1981—; Calif. master tchr. English as 2d lang. Calif. Council Adult Edn., 1979-82; cons. in field. Recipient Concours de Francais Prix, 1947; Jeanette M. Liggett Meml. award for excellence in history, 1949. Mem. Internat. Platform Assn., Calif. Assn. Tchrs. English to Speakers Other Langs., TESOL, Nat. Assn. for Fgn. Student Affairs, Computer Using Educators, AAUW, U. Mich. Alumnae Assn., Nat. Coll. Edn. Alumnae Assn., Ninety Nines (chmn. Golden West chpt.), Chi Omega, Zeta Phi Eta. Club: Peninsula Lioness (pres.). Home: 2917 Franciscan Ct San Carlos CA 94070 Office: 450 Chadbourne Ave Millbrae CA 94030

PALMER, PAUL E., communications executive; b. York, Pa., Nov. 18, 1942; s. Daniel Isaih Palmer and Eleanor (Beard) Wolff; m. Margaret Ann Strong, Oct. 2, 1965; children: Paul Joseph, Wendy Suzanne, Caroline Marie. BA in Speech Radio/TV, U. Md. With Sta. WBAL Radio, Balt., 1964-65; account exec. Sta. KDKA Radio, Pitts., 1965-68, RAR, Chgo., 1968-70; sales mgr. Sta. WIND Radio, Chgo., 1970-72; v.p., gen. mgr. Sta. KFMB AM-FM, San Diego, 1972—; pres. Sun Mountain Broadcasting, Inc., San Diego, 1985—. Mem. Assn. Ind. Met. Stas. Home: 2915 Woodford Dr La Jolla CA 92037 Office: Station KFMB AM-FM 7677 Engineer Rd San Diego CA 92111

PALMER, SAMUEL DREW, geological engineer; b. Goldsboro, N.C., Nov. 10, 1960; s. William Franklin and Delores Arlene (Dean) P. Student, U. Nev., Las Vegas, 1978-80; BS in Geol. Engring., U. Nev., Reno, 1983. Geol. engr. CER Corp., Las Vegas, 1983, asst. mgr. field testing, 1983-85; sr. staff engr. Converse Cons. SW, Inc., Las Vegas, 1985—. AMEX scholar, 1982, 83. Mem. Assn. Engring. Geologists, AIME. Republican. Presbyterian. Club: Pilot's (Rifle, Colo.). Home: 2840 S Mann St Las Vegas NV 89102 Office: Converse Cons SW Inc 4055 S Spencer St Suite 120 Las Vegas NV 89119

PALMER, STEVEN WAYNE, real estate management consultant, executive; b. Pasadena, Calif., Sept. 13, 1944; s. Joseph Jerome and Ella Lorraine (Balliet) P.; m. Angelia Jeanette Stewart, Dec. 4, 1981 (div. 1987); 1 son, Joseph Christian. B.A. in History, Long Beach State U., 1970. Central transit mgr. Security Pacific Nat. Bank, Los Angeles, 1964-65; with advt. and promotions Zellerbach Paper Co., Los Angeles, 1966-68; v.p. Christopher Robin Designs, Long Beach, Calif., 1970-74; pres. AMMC, Rodeo, Calif., 1974—. Patentee marine signal device. Mem. Oakland Tribune Citizens Adv. Com., 1984, 85, 86; pres. bd. trustees John Swett Unified Sch. Dist., Rodeo, Crockett and Port Costa, Calif., 1985; chmn. Rodeo Hometown Parade Commn., 1983-85; past bd. dirs. Carquinez Coalition. Mem. Rodeo C. of C. (v.p. 1983, 85, pres. 1986). Republican. Roman Catholic. Lodge: Lions (pres. 1984-85). Office: AMMC 520 2d St Rodeo CA 94572

PALMER, THEODORE WINDLE, mathematician, educator; b. Boston, Oct. 19, 1935; s. Ernest Jesse and Elizabeth (McDougall) P.; m. Laramie Phillips, Aug. 11, 1961; children: Jesse David, Abraham Amos, Ruth Elizabeth. BS, MS in Biochemistry, Johns Hopkins U., 1958; AM, Harvard U., 1959, PhD in Math., 1966. Vis. asst. prof. Math. Research Ctr., Madison, Wis., 1966-67; asst. prof. math. U. Kans., Lawrence, 1967-69, assoc. prof., 1969-70; assoc. prof. U. Oreg., Eugene, 1970-75, prof. math., 1975—, head dept. math., 1980-83; assoc. dean for personnel Coll. Arts and Scis. U. Oreg., 1986—. Contbr. articles to profl. jours. Pres. Friends of Mount Pisgah Arboretum, Eugene, 1982-83, bd. dirs., 1974—; bd. dirs. Friends of Library, Eugene. Named Hon. fellow Woodrow Wilson Found., 1958. Mem. AAAS, AAUP, Am. Math. Soc., Math. Assn. Am., Oreg. Hist. Soc., Hauluys Societs, Soc. Hist. of Disciples, Inst. Soc. Hist. Cartography, Western Hist. Assn., Lewis and Clark Heritage Found., Jedediah Smith Soc., Oreg. Trail Assn., Calif. Trail Assn., Colo. R.R. Hist. Soc., Phi Beta Kappa, Sigma Xi. Avocations: collecting rare books, hiking. Home: 259 W 23d Ave Eugene OR 97405 Office: U Oreg Dept Math Eugene OR 97403

PALMER, THOMAS ADOLPH, chemist; b. Salt Lake City, Oct. 12, 1935; s. Robert Everett Allen and M. Josephine Palmer. BS cum laude, U. Santa Clara, 1957; PhD, Iowa State U., 1961. Sr. research analyst Olin Matheson Chem., New Haven, 1961-62; sr. chemist Lockheed Propulsion Co., Redlands, Calif., 1962-66; sr. staff research chemist Kaiser Aluminum and Chem. Corp., Pleasanton, Calif., 1966—. Mem. Am. Chem. Soc., Internat. Union Pure and Applied Chemistry. Avocations: bicycling, gardening, square dancing. Office: Kaiser Aluminum PO Box 877 Pleasanton CA 94566

PALMER, VINCENT ALLAN, constrn. cons.; b. Wausa, Nebr., Feb. 18, 1913; s. Victor E. and Amy (Lindquist) P.; AA, Modesto Jr. Coll., 1933; BSCE, U. Calif., Berkeley, 1936; m. Louise V. Cramer, Mar. 12, 1938 (dec. June 1979); children: Margaret, Georgia, Vincent Allan; m. 2d, Hope Parker, Jan. 23, 1982. Constrn. engr. Kaiser Engrs., 1938-63, constrn. mgr., 1963-69, mgr. constrn., 1970-75, project mgr., 1975-76; project mgr. reef runway Universal Dredging Corp., Honolulu, 1975-76; pvt. practice constrn. cons., Walnut Creek, Calif., 1976—. Mem. ASCE (life), Project Mgmt. Inst., Monterey Bay Aquarium, Sierra Club. Clubs: San Francisco Press; Tattersall's (Sydney, Australia). Home and Office: 1356 Corte Loma Walnut Creek CA 94598

PALMER, WENDELL PHILLIPS, engineering company executive; b. Washington, Apr. 21, 1943; s. Wendell Phillips and Ann (Sibert) P.; m. Ann Louise Rothlisberger, June 26, 1966; children: Phillip, Nicole, Bryan, Jennifer. B in Archtl. Engring., Pa. State U., 1966. Design engr. E.I. DuPont Corp., Newark, 1966-69; mktg. mgr. Peter F. Loftus Corp., Pitts., 1969-73; v.p. Matrix Engrs., Pitts., 1973-76; dir. bus. devel. Greenhorne & O'mara, Riverdale, Md., 1976-82; v.p. Baker Engrs., Beaver, Pa., 1982; exec. v.p. Greiner Engring., Denver, 1982—; seminar leader Mktg. for Prins., 1983, 85, 86, 87. Mem. adv. bd. Archtl. Engring. Mktg. Jour., 1983, seminar leader, 1980—. Mem. Soc. Mktg. Profl. Services, Am. Pub. Works Assn. (sec. Colo. chpt. 1985—, pres.-elect 1987), Cons. Engrs. Council Colo. (com. chmn.). Roman Catholic. Avocation: computer software development. Home: 7026 S Miller Ct Littleton CO 80127 Office: Greiner Engring 570 W 44th Ave Denver CO 80216

PALMER, WILLIAM WARE, engineering company proprietor; b. Opelika, Ala., May 14, 1919; s. William Ware and Margaret Lee (Boswell) P.; m. Ada Belle Bowman, July 15, 1945; children: William, Pamela Palmer. BEE, U. Tenn., 1948. Registered profl. elec. engr., Calif. Engr. Gen. Electric Co., Schenectady, N.Y., 1948-53, San Francisco, 1953-67, San Jose, Calif., 1968-82; engr., propr. Palmer Enterprises, Los Altos, Calif., 1982—; cons. Roy & Assocs., Los Gatos, Calif., 1984, Southwall Techs., Palo Alto, Calif., 1985, S. Levy Inc., Campbell, Calif., 1985—, Nat. Nuclear Corp., Mountain View, Calif., 1986-87. Author: Motors for Centrifugal Pumps, 1972; contbr. articles to profl. jours.; developed battery switching-type speed control for electric vehicles. Sr. warden Christ Episcopal Ch., Los Altos, 1960, 68. Served to lt. comdr. USNR, 1941-46, ETO and PTO. Mem. IEEE (sr.), Electric Auto Assn. (founder, pres. 1971,74,78, treas. 1980—). Republican. Avocations: photography, backpacking. Home: 44 Dior Terr Los Altos CA 94022

PALUCHOWSKI, CAROL ANNE, child and family therapist, program manager; b. Buffalo, July 28, 1953; d. Theodore and Clara (Jakusz) P.; m. Bruce Gary Borsak, May 17, 1980; 1 child, Ethan Joshua. BSW, SUNY, Brockport, 1975; MA summa cum laude, Wash. State U., 1981; MSW, U. Wash., 1983. Trainer, advo. Pullman (Wash.) Crisis Line, 1978-81; child therapist psychology dept. Wash. State U., Pullman, 1978-79; counselor, trainer Whitman County Alcohol Ctr., Pullman, 1979-81; child therapist Skagit Mental Health, Mt. Vernon, Wash., 1981-82; clin. social worker Naval Air Sta. Whidbey Family Service Ctr., Oak Harbor, Wash., 1982; therapist, program mgr. Luth. Social Services, Bremerton, Wash., 1983-86; psychotherapist Group Health Coop., Redmond, Wash., 1986—; trainer Koinonia House, Pullman, 1981. Mem. Nat. Assn. of Social Workers, Wash. Assn. Child Abuse Councils, Assn. of Women Social Workers, Educators for Social Responsibility, Families for Peace, Phi Kappa Phi. Democrat. Avocations: running, cross country skiing, gardening, martial arts. Home: 5014 48th Ave NE Seattle WA 98105 Office: Group Health Coop Eastside Mental Health Services 2700 152d Ave NE Redmond WA 98052

PAMPLIN, ROBERT BOISSEAU, JR., agricultural company executive, minister, writer; b. Augusta, Ga., Sept. 3, 1941; s. Robert Boisseau and Mary Katherine (Reese) P.; m. Marilyn Joan Hooper; children: Amy Louise, Anne Boisseau. Student in bus. adminstrn. Va. Poly. Inst., 1960-62; BSBA, Lewis and Clark Coll., 1964, BS in Acctg., 1965, BS in Econs., 1966; MBA, U. Portland, 1968, MEd, 1975, LLD (hon.), 1972; MCL, Western Conservative Bapt. Sem., 1978, DMin, 1982; PhD, Calif. Coast U.; cert. in wholesale mgmt. Ohio State U., 1970; cert. in labor mgmt., U. Portland, 1972; cert. in advanced mgmt., U. Hawaii, 1975; DD (hon.), Judson Baptist Coll., 1984; DBA (hon.), Marquis Giuseppe Scicluna Internat. U. Found., 1986. Pres. R. B. Pamplin Corp., Portland, Oreg., 1964—; chmn. bd. Columbia Empire Farms, Inc., Lake Oswego, Oreg., 1976—; pres. Twelve Oaks Farms, Inc., Lake Oswego, 1977—; dir. Mt. Vernon Mill Inc.; lectr. bus. adminstrn. Lewis and Clark Coll., 1968-69; adj. asst. prof. bus. adminstrn., U. Portland, 1973-76; pastor Christ Community Ch., Lake Oswego, Oreg. lectr. in bus. adminstrn. and economics, U. Costa Rica, 1968, Va. Tech. Found., 1986, dir. R.B. Pamplin Corp., Ross Island Sand & Gravel Co. Author: Everything is Just Great, 1985, The Gift, 1986, Another Virginian: A Study of the Life and Beliefs of Robert Boisseau Pamplin, 1986, (with others): A Portrait of Colorado, 1976, Three in One, 1974, The Storybook Primer on Managing, 1974; editor: Oreg. Mus. Sci. and Industry Press, 1973, trustee, 1971, 74—; editor: Portrait of Oregon, 1973, (with others): Oregon Underfoot, 1975. Mem. Nat. Adv. Council on Vocat. Edn., 1975—; mem. Western Interstate Comm. for Higher Edn., 1981-84; co-chmn. Va. Tech. $50 million Campaign for Excellence, 1984-87, Va. Tech. Found., 1986—, Albert Einstein Acad. Bronze medal, 1986, Va. 0 Oreg. State Scholarship Commn., 1974—, chmn., 1976-78; mem. Portland dist. adv. council SBA, 1973-77; mem. Rewards Review Com., City Portland, 1973-78, chmn., 1973-78; mem. bd. regents U. Portland, 1971-79, chmn. bd., 1975-79, regent emeritus, 1979—; trustee Lewis and Clark Coll., 1980-84, 85, Oreg. Epis. Schs., 1979. Named disting. alumnus, Lewis and Clark Coll., 1974; recipient Air Force ROTC Disting. Service award, USAF, 1974, Albert Einstein Acad. Bronze medal, 1986; Va. Tech Coll. of Bus. Adminstrn. renamed R.B. Pamplin Coll. of Bus. Adminstrn. in his honor. Mem. Acad. Mgmt., Delta Epsilon Sigma, Beta Gamma Sigma, Sigma Phi Epsilon. Republican. Episcopalian. Clubs: Waverley Country, Arlington, Multnomah Athletic, Capitol Hill. Lodge: Rotary. Address: 3131 West View Ct Lake Oswego OR 97034

PAN, HERMES, choreographer; b. Memphis, Dec. 10, 1910; s. Pantelis and Mary (Huston) Panagiotopulos. Ed., pvt. sch., Nashville. Dancer: Broadway musicals, 1927-30; choreographer musical films including: Flying Down to Rio, 1933; The Gay Divorcee, 1934; Top Hat, 1935; I Dream Too Much, 1935; Swing Time, 1936; Shall We Dance, 1937; Damsel in Distress (Oscar), 1937; Carefree, 1938; The Story of Vernon and Irene Castle, 1939; That Night in Rio, 1941; Moon Over Miami, 1941; Rise and Shine, 1941; Song of the Islands, 1942; My Gal Sal, 1942; Sweet Rosie O'Grady, 1943; Pin-Up Girl, 1944; Irish Eyes Are Smiling, 1944; Blue Skies, 1946; The Shocking Miss Pilgrim, 1947; I Wonder Who's Kissing Her Now, 1947; The Barkleys of Broadway, 1949; Let's Dance, 1950; Excuse My Dust, 1951; Lovely to Look At, 1952; Kiss Me Kate, 1953; The Student Prince, 1954; Jupiter's Darling, 1955; Hit the Deck, 1955; Meet Me in Las Vegas, 1956; Silk Stockings, 1956; Pal Joey, 1957; Porgy and Bess, 1959; Can-Can, 1960; Flower Drum Song, 1961; My Fair Lady, 1964; Finian's Rainbow, 1968; Darling Lili, 1969; Lost Horizon, 1973; choreographer An Evening With Fred Astaire (Emmy award), 1961. Recipient Nat. Film award for Achievement in Cinema, 1980. Roman Catholic. Home: 9550 Cherokee Ln Beverly Hills CA 90210

PAN, YUNG HSIN, clinical chemist, researcher; b. Tainan, Taiwan, Dec. 22, 1937; came to U.S., 1962; s. Kuan and Sueh-chi (Lin) P.; m. Chiou Chwen Kang, Oct. 22, 1967; children: Patrick Tienbin, Vivian Yuenchi. BS, Nat. Taiwan U., Taipei, 1960; MS, U. Utah, 1967, PhD, 1969. Postdoctoral fellow Syntex Research Ctr., Palo Alto, Calif., 1969-71, vis. scientist, 1971-72; chemist, research projects McGaw Lab. div. Am. Hosp. Supply Corp., Glendale, Calif., 1972-74; adj. vis. assoc. prof., vis. research fellow Nat. Taiwan U., 1974-75; mgr. product devel. and sr. research scientist ICL Sci. Co. (affiliated Böehringer Mannheim), Fountain Valley, Calif., 1976-84; dir. and v.p. research and devel. P.I.E. Co., Fountain Valley, 1984—; vis. research fellow Inst. Biol. Chemistry, Academia Sinica; advisor and cons. China Chem. and Pharm. Co., Ltd., Taipei, Taiwan and Burbank, Calif., 1974-76. Contbr. articles to profl. jours.; patentee in field. Served to 2d lt. ROTC Armor Corp., 1960-61. Mem. Am. Assn. Clin. Chemistry (clin. chemist's recognition award 1986), Am. Chem. Soc., N.Am. Chinese Clin. Chem. Assn. (bd. dirs. 1983-84, founding com. 1980). Clubs: Toastmasters Internat. (Huntington Beach, Calif.), Los Caballeros Sports (Fountain Valley). Avocations: music appreciation, sports events, reading. Office: PIE Co 17200 Newhope St #29 Fountain Valley CA 92708

PANASCI, NANCY ERVIN, speech pathologist, cookbook writer, communications consultant; b. Fairborn, Ohio, Mar. 24, 1954; d. Lindsay James and Frances E. (Erickson) Ervin; m. Ernest James Panasci, Aug. 7, 1976; 1 child, Caitlin Alba, Adele Frances. BS, Colo. State U., 1976; MA, Cath. U., Washington, 1979. Tchr. Montessori Sch., Rome, N.Y., 1971-72, Fairfax (Va.) Sch. Dist., 1976-77; speech pathologist Littleton (Colo.) Pub. Schs., 1979—; communication cons. speech pathology Trial Attys., Denver, 1986—. Com. chairperson Jr. League Denver, 1982-86. Named Best Cook in West, Rocky Mountain Newspaper, Denver, 1982. Mem. Am. Speech Hearing Lang. Assn. (cert. clin. competence 1980), Colo. Speech Hearing Assn. (com. chairperson 1982-86). Roman Catholic. Clubs: Valley (Aurora, Colo.), Racquet World (Englewood, Colo.). Avocations: skiing, tennis, golf, sewing, gardening. Home: 5610 S Kingston Way Englewood CO 80111 Office: Littleton Pub Schs Littleton CO 80120

PANCK, KENNETH EUGENE, electronic company executive; b. Plymouth, Ind., Apr. 20, 1942; s. James Eugene and Winifred Ruby (Chadderdon) P.; m. Ruth Ann Miller, Aug. 28, 1971; children: Mary Elizabeth, Michael Kenneth. A.S. in Elec. Engring., Colo. Tech. Inst., 1962; B.S. in Elec. Engring., U. Denver, 1974; M.B.A., U. Portland, 1978. Research technician Denver Research Inst., 1963-71; computer engr. Computer Image Corp., Denver, 1971-72; electronic design engr. Tektronix Inc., Beaverton, Oreg., 1974-78, engring. group mgr., 1978-82, engring. mgr. Gen. Purpose Instruments, 1982-83, div. engring. mgr. Instrument Systems Integration, 1983-85, with lab. instruments div. mktg. dept., 1985—. Past mem. allocation panel United Way of the Columbia, Portland, Oreg., 1982-84; mem. adv. bd. Wash. State U. Coll. Engring., 1985—. Mem. Eta Kappa Nu. Republican. Methodist. Home: 20366 SW Carlin Blvd Aloha OR 97007 Office: Tektronix Inc Howard Vollum Park Beaverton OR 97077

PANDIT, THAKOR JOE, municipal administrator; b. Gana, India, Apr. 22, 1937; came to U.S., 1966; s. Bhikhabhai D. and Chachal B. Pandya; m. Vanleela Pandit, May 23, 1957; children: Parimal, Punita, Priti. BSCE, S.V. U., Vidyanagar, India, 1958; MSc, Poona (India) U., 1962; MS, U. Iowa, 1967. Registered profl. civil engr. Sr. engr. Wilsey and Ham, Foster City, Calif., 1983-85; dir. Santa Clara Valley Water Dist., San Jose, Calif., 1983—; cons. Pandit & Assocs., San Jose, 1985—. Mem. Greenbelt Task Force, San Jose, Intergovtl. Council, San Jose. Fellow Govt. India, 1960-63; scholar U. Iowa, 1966-67. Mem. ASCE, Am. Pub. Works Assn., Nat. Assn. Realtors, ACWA Water Mgmt. Assn., Indian Cultural Assn. (trustee 1985—). Republican. Hindu. Avocations: camping, traveling, community service. Home: 6929 Azalea Dr San Jose CA 95120 Office: Santa Clara Valley Water Dist 5750 Almaden Expressway San Jose CA 95118

PANECALDO, LORETO ANTONIO (TONY), III, business executive, consultant, political worker; b. Yuba City, Calif., June 19, 1948; s. Loreto Antonio and Marjorie Isabelle Sarmento Thayer; A.A., Yuba Coll., 1969. Floral designer and decorator, owner, gen. mgr. Tony Panecaldo III, Florist, Gridley, Calif., 1977-86; councilman City of Gridley, 1976-80, mayor, 1978-80. Chmn., Butte County Republican Central Com., 1974-78; mem. Calif. Rep. Central Com., also mem. exec. com., platform com., 1978; mem. Calif. Rep. Assembly, alt. del. Rep. Nat. Conv., 1976; bd. dirs. Gridley Hospice of Love. Mem. Butte County Hist. Soc. (dir.), Bidwell Mansion Restoration Assn., Bidwell Mansion Cooperating Assn., Gridley Art League. Christian Scientist. Clubs: Commonwealth (San Francisco), Order of DeMolay (life), Masons. Home: 1800 Hazel St Gridley CA 95948

PANELLI, EDWARD ALEXANDER, associate justice; b. Santa Clara, Calif., Nov. 23, 1931; s. Pilade and Natalina (Della Maggiora) P.; m. Lorna Christine Mondora, Oct. 27, 1956; children: Thomas E., Jeffrey J., Michael P. BA cum laude, Santa Clara U., 1953, JD cum laude, 1955, LLD (hon.), 1986. Bar: Calif. 1955. Ptnr. Pasquinelli and Panelli, San Jose, Calif., 1955-72; judge Santa Clara County Superior Ct., 1972-83; assoc. justice 1st Dist. Ct. of Appeals, San Francisco, 1983-84; presiding justice 6th Dist. Ct. of Appeals, San Jose, 1984-85; assoc. justice Calif. Supreme Ct., San Francisco, 1985—; instr. Continuing Legal Edn., Santa Clara, 1976-78. Trustee West Valley Community Coll., 1963-72; trustee Santa Clara U., 1963—, chmn. bd. trustees, 1984—. Recipient Citation, Am. Com. Italian Migration, 1969, Community Legal Services award, 1979, 84, Edwin J. Owens Lawyer of Yr. award Santa Clara Law Sch. Alumni, 1982, Merit award Republic of Italy, 1984. Mem. Nat. Italian ABA (inspiration award 1986), Calif. Trial Lawyers Assn. (Trial Judge of Yr. award Santa Clara County chpt. 1981), Calif. Judges Assn. (bd. dirs. 1982). Republican. Roman Catholic. Avocations: jogging, sailing. Office: Supreme Ct Calif 350 McAllister St San Francisco CA 94102

PANERAL, ALLEN JEROME, human resources executive; b. Chgo., Feb. 20, 1930; s. Albert James Paneral and Sophia Marie Toppen; m. Pauline Marie Madler, July 30, 1955; children: Allen, Mary, Mike, Paul. BSBA, De Paul U., 1952; MS in Indsl. Relations, Loyola U., Chgo., 1958. Supr. personnel Internat. Minerals and Chems., Skokie, Ill., 1960-63; mgr. personnel Internat. Minerals and Chems., Carlsbad, N.Mex., 1963-67, mgr. employee relations, 1968—; mgr. personnel Internat. Minerals and Chems., Bartow, Fla., 1967-68; instr. personnel N.Mex. State U., Carlsbad, 1983—. Bd. dirs. Carlsbad City Spirit Arts Assn., 1983—, Carlsbad C. of C., 1984—. Served as cpl. U.S. Army, 1952-54. Mem. Am. Soc. Personnel Adminstrs., Indls. Relations Research Assn., N.Mex. Mining Assn. (bd. dirs.), N.Mex. Assn. Commerce and Industry. Lodges: Elks, K.C. Avocations: golf, swimming, bridge. Home: 1007 S Country Club Carlsbad NM 88220 Office: Internat Minerals Chems-Carlsbad PO Box 71 Carlsbad NM 88220

PANETTA, LEON EDWARD, congressman; b. Monterey, Calif., June 28, 1938; s. Carmelo Frank and Carmelina Maria (Prochilo) P.; m. Sylvia Marie Varni, July 14, 1962; children: Christopher, Carmelo, James. B.A. magna cum laude, U. Santa Clara, Calif., 1960, LL.B., J.D., 1963. Bar: Calif. bar 1965, U.S. Supreme Ct. 1965, Fed. Dist. Dist. No. Dist. Calif 1965, U.S. Ct. Appeals 1965. Legis. asst. to U.S. Sen. Thomas Kuchel, Washington, 1966-69; dir. U.S. Office Civil Rights, HEW, Washington, 1969-70; exec. asst. to Mayor of N.Y.C., 1970-71; partner firm Panetta, Thompson & Panetta, Monterey, 1971-76; mem. 95th-100th Congresses from 16th Calif. Dist., mem. agr. com., chmn. subcom. on domestic mktg., consumer relations, and nutrition; others, mem. House adminstrn. com., chmn. subcom. on personnel and police, dep. majority whip, mem. Select com. on hunger; chmn. Task Force on domestic hunger. Author: Bring Us Together, 1971. Counsel Monterey Regional Park Dists.; counsel NAACP, 1971-76; Bd. trustees U. Santa Clara Law Sch.; founder Monterey Coll. Law; mem. Monterey County Democratic Central Com., 1972-74; v.p. Carmel Valley Little League, 1974-75. Served with AUS, 1964-66. Decorated Army Commendation medal.; recipient Lincoln award NEA, 1970, Disting. Service award NAACP, 1972; named Lawyer of Yr., U. Santa Clara Law Sch., 1970; Bread for World award, 1978; Nat. Hospice Orgn. award, 1984. Mem. Calif. Bar Assn. Roman Catholic. Office: Room 339 Cannon House Office Bldg Washington DC 20515

PANG, HERBERT GEORGE, ophthalmologist; b. Honolulu, Dec. 23, 1922; s. See Hung and Hong Jim (Chuu) P.; student St. Louis Coll., 1941; B.S., Northwestern U., 1944, M.D., 1947; m. Dorothea Lopez, Dec. 27, 1953. Intern Queen's Hosp., Honolulu, 1947-48; postgraduate course ophthalmology N.Y.U., Med. Sch., 1948-49; resident ophthalmology Jersey City Med. Center, 1949-50, Manhattan Eye, Ear, & Throat Hosp., N.Y.C., 1950-52; practice medicine specializing in ophthalmology, Honolulu, 1952-54, 56—; mem. staffs Kuakini Hosp., Children's Hosp., Castle Meml. Hosp., Queen's Hosp., St. Francis Hosp.; asst. clin. prof. ophthalmology U. Hawaii Sch. Medicine, 1966-73, now asso. clin. prof. Cons. Bur. Crippled Children, 1952-73, Kapiolani Maternity Hosp., 1952-73, Leahi Tb. Hosp., 1952-62. Served to capt. M.C., AUS, 1954-56, Diplomate Am. Bd. Ophthalmology. Mem. AMA, Am. Acad. Ophthalmology and Otolaryngology, Assn. for Research Ophthalmology, ACS, Hawaii Med. Soc. (gov. med. practice com. 1958-62, chmn. med. speakers com. 1957-58), Hawaii Eye, Ear, Nose and Throat Soc. (pres. 1960), Pacific Coast Oto-Ophthalmological Soc., Pan Am. Assn. Ophthalmology. Mason (Shriner). Clubs: Eye Study Club (pres. 1972—)(N.Y.C.). Home: 346 Lewers Rd Honolulu HI 96815 Office: Pang Eye Ear Nose Throat Clinic 1374 Nuuanu Ave Honolulu HI 96817

PANG, KAM-YEE YU, biophysicist; b. Canton, Peoples Republic of China, Mar. 14, 1943; came to U.S., 1967; d. Wah-Sek and Sui-Fa (Ng) Yu; m. Sing chin Pang, Apr. 3, 1974; 1 child, Caspar Jing-Wei. BSc, The Chinese U. of Hong Kong, 1966; PhD, U. Pitts., 1972. Research fellow Harvard Med. Sch., Boston, 1976-78, instr., 1982-83, asst. prof., 1983-84; asst. biophysicist Mass. Gen. Hosp., Boston, 1978-83, assoc. biophysicist, 1983-84; asst. prof. UCLA, 1984—. Contbr. articles to profl. jours. Mem. South Bay Chinese Lang. Sch., Palos Verdes Estates, 1985—. Andrew Mellon Found fellow, 1968-71. Mem. AAAS, Am. Soc. Cell Biology, Gastroenterology Research Group, Am. Gastroenterology Assn. Avocations: reading, hiking. Office: Research & Edn Inst Inc UCLA Med Ctr 1024 W Carson St Torrance CA 90502

PANISH, BRIAN JOSEPH, lawyer; b. Waco, Tex., Apr. 19, 1958; s. Howard Raymond and Mary Patricia (Murphy) P. Student, Calif. State U., 1980. Bar: Calif. 1984, U.S. Dist. Ct. (no., ea. and cen. dists.) Tex. 1984. Assoc. Engstrom, Lipscomb & Lack, Los Angeles, 1984-86, Greene, O'Reilly, Broillet, Paul, Simon, McMillan, Wheeler & Rosenberg, Los Angeles, 1986—. Mem. Los Angeles County Bar Assn., Assn. Trial Lawyers Am., Calif. Trial Lawyers Assn., Los Angeles Trial Lawyers Assn., Hollywood Bar Assn. Home: 2527 3d St Santa Monica CA 90405 Office: Greene O'Reilly Broillet Paul 816 S Figueroa Los Angeles CA 90010

PANKOVE, JACQUES ISAAC, physicist; b. Chernigov, Russia, Nov. 23, 1922; came to U.S., 1942, naturalized, 1944; s. Evsey Leib and Miriam (Simkine) Pantchechnikoff; m. Ethel Wasserman, Nov. 24, 1950; children: Martin, Simon. B.S.E.E., U. Calif., Berkeley, 1944, M.S.E.E., 1948; Ph.D. in Physics, U. Paris, 1960. Mem. tech. staff RCA Labs., Princeton, N.J., 1948-70; physicist, fellow RCA Labs., 1970-85; prof. U. Colo., Boulder, 1985—; disting. research fellow Solar Energy Research Inst., 1985—; vis. McKay lectr. U. Calif., Berkeley, 1968-69; vis. prof. U. Campinas, Brazil, 1975; participant NAS sci. exchange program with: Romania, 1970, Hungary, 1972, Yugoslavia, 1976. Mem. hon. editorial bd. Solid State Electronics, 1970—, Solar Energy Materials, 1984—, Optoelectronics, 1986—; regional editor Crystal Lattice Defects and Amorphous Materials, 1984—; author: Optical Processes in Semiconductors, 1971, 75; editor: Electroluminescence, 1977, Display Devices, 1980, Hydrogenated Amorphous Silicon, 1984; author: (ednl. film) Energy Gap and Recombination Radiation, 1962; laser sculpture, Bklyn. Mus., 1968; contbr. articles to sci. jours.; organizer sci. confs. Trustee Princeton Art Assn., 1970-82; mem. Experiment-in-Arts-and-Tech., Berkeley, 1968-69. Served with U.S. Army, 1944-46. Recipient RCA achievement awards, 1952, 53, 63; David Sarnoff scholar, 1956. Fellow IEEE (J.J. Ebers award 1975, assoc. editor Jour. Quantum Electronics 1968-77), Am. Phys. Soc.; mem. Nat. Acad. Engring. (hon.), Electrochem. Soc., Sigma Xi. Patentee. Home: 2386 Vassar Dr Boulder CO 80303 Office: Univ Colo Dept Electrical Engring Boulder CO 80309-0425 also: Solar Energy Research Inst 1617 Cole Blvd Golden CO 80401

PANOSSIAN, HAGOP VARTEVAR, aerospace engineer; b. Anjar, Lebanon, June 8, 1946; came to U.S., 1973; s. Vartevar Sarkis and Satenig B. (Injeyan) P.; m. Ani Kochakjian, Aug. 31, 1975; children: Lorig, Baruir, Armen. BSc, Am. U. Beirut, 1969; MSc, U. S.C., 1974; Engr. degree, UCLA, 1979, PhD, 1981. Dept. head C. Gulbenkian Coll., Anjar, 1969-73; grad. teaching asst. U. S.C., Columbia, 1973-74; post grad. research engr. UCLA, 1975-80; sr. engr. HR Textron, Valencia, Calif., 1980-85, engring. supr., 1986-87; sr. specialist Rockwell Internat., Rocketdyne div., Canoga Park, Calif., 1987—. Contbr. articles to profl. jours.; inventor in field. Mem. IEEE (sr.), Soc. Indsl. and Applied Math., Armenian Engrs. and Scientists of Am. (pres., founder). Republican. Orthodox. Avocations: camping, indoor games. Home: 18106 Miranda St Tarzana CA 91356 Office: Rockwell Internat Rocketdyne div 6633 Canoga Ave AC-13 Canoga Park CA 91303

PANOWSKI, EILEEN JANET THOMPSON, writer, anthropologist; b. Lincoln, Nebr., Mar. 17, 1920; d. Hugh and Nelle J. (Masters) Thompson; m. John Bruce Panowski, Sept. 5, 1942; children: Thomas Michael, Bruce Philip, Daryl Anne and Lynn Eileen (twins). BA, Miami U., Oxford, Ohio, 1941; cert., Famous Writers Sch., Westport, Conn., 1963; MA in Anthropology, U. N.Mex., 1971, PhD in Anthropology, 1985. Radiochemistry technician Los Alamos (N.Mex.) Nat. Lab., 1956-64, sci. mus. guide, 1969-77; writer, researcher Albuquerque, 1978—. Author: The Blue-Stone Mystery, 1963, The Spanish Deed Mystery, 1964, The Apache Gold Mystery, 1965, The Dog Show Mystery, 1966, The Golden Coyote, 1971 (Jr. Literary Guild selection), White Falcon, 1977; short stories. Mem. Phi Beta Kappa. Republican. Methodist. Avocations: birdwatching, genealogy, custom clothing design and sewing, photography. Home and Office: 722 Solar Rd NW Albuquerque NM 87107

PANSKY, STANLEY HOWARD, architect; b. N.Y.C., Dec. 29, 1923; s. Jack H. and Rose (Hirsch) P.; m. Hazel May Borne, Apr. 8, 1944 (dec. 1955); m. Iris Albrecht Barron, Apr. 7, 1957; children—Thomas E., Jane Emilia. B.Engring., NYU, 1944; postgrad. Ill. Inst. Tech., 1944; M.Arch., Harvard U., 1950. Registered architect, N.Y., Oreg., Ariz.; registered profl.

engr, N.Y., Oreg. Assoc. Skidmore Owings & Merrill, N.Y.C., 1950-64, Portland, Oreg., 1964-73; cons. St. Francis Med. Ctr., San Francisco, 1974; architect Daniel, Mann, Johnson, Mendenhall, Portland, 1975-80; pvt. practice architecture, Portland, 1981-82, 86—; sr. architect Battelle Pacific N.W. Labs., Richland, Wash., 1982-86; adj. prof. Oreg. Sch. Design, Portland, 1981-82. Contbr. articles to profl. jours. Bd. dirs., pres. Portland Civic Theatre, 1970-74; health care adviser Gov. Tom McCall, 1980-81; tchr. Office Econ. Opportunity, 1980. Served to lt. (j.g.), USN. 1945. Fellow Am. Acad. in Rome; mem. AIA (chpt. treas. 1978). Jewish. Club: Multnomah Athletic. Home and Office: 2647 SW Vista Ave Portland OR 97201

PANTER, KIP EUGENE, research animal scientist; b. Idaho Falls, Idaho, Nov. 27, 1951; s. Donald Cahoon and Florence (Corbett) P.; m. Jenifer Lee Hill, Sept. 8, 1972; children: Jeremy, Joseph, Brady, Aimee. BS, Utah State U., 1975, MS, 1978; PhD, U. Ill., 1983. Research animal caretaker USDA, Logan, Utah, 1973-81, research postdoctoral fellow, 1983-84, research animal scientist, 1984—; research asst. U. Ill., Champaign, 1981-83; cons. plant poisoning cons. Animal Poison Control Ctr., Champaign, 1981-82; lectr. in field. Contbr. articles to profl. jours. Youth Coach Cache Valley Little League Baseball, Richmond, Utah, 1983, Cache Valley Soccer League, 1983-86; com. chmn. Richmond City, 1984. Mem. AAAS, Mountain West Chpt. Soc. of Toxicology. Republican. Mormon. Avocations: horseback riding, gardening, family activities. Home: 247 E 100 N Richmond UT 84333 Office: USDA Agrl Research Service Poisonous Plant Research Lab 1150 E 1400 N Logan UT 84321

PANTUSO, JOHN GERARD, electro-mechanical designer; b. Chester, Pa., Jan. 2, 1958; s. John Joseph and Gloria Lenore (Young) P. AS in Applied Sci., Mercer County Community Coll., 1977. Mech. designer Eidal Internat. Corp., Albuquerque, 1980-81; structural steel designer Rio Grande Steel Co., Albuquerque, 1981-82; electro/mech. designer Albuquerque, 1982-84; structural designer Mega Corp., Albuquerque, 1984, Sandia Nat. Labs., Albuquerque, 1984—. Republican. Roman Catholic. Home: 771 Lisbon Ave SE Rio Rancho NM 87124 Office: Sandia Nat Labs PO Box 5800 Albuquerque NM 87185

PAO, BRUCE, architectural designer, educator; b. Honolulu, Feb. 24, 1948; s. Nicholas Rodrigues and Mabel (Sylvester) P.; m. Paula Young, June 20, 1970 (div. July 1983); 1 child, Adrienne. BFA in Architecture, U. Hawaii, 1970. With Kaiser Engrs., Oakland, Calif., 1970-72; designer Conversano & Assocs., Oakland, 1972-73; project mgr. Max Garcia Assocs., San Francisco, 1974-76; v.p. environ. planning and research Caudill, Rowlett, Scott & Sirrine, San Francisco, 1976-85; instr. Fashion Inst. Design Merchandising, San Francisco, 1982—; pres. IPA Design, Inc., Berkeley, Calif., 1985—. Prin. works include design for dept. stores Carson Pirie Scott, 1982 (Inst. Store Planners-Nat. Assn. Store Fixture Mfrs. Outstanding Merit award 1982), Bullock's Fashion Island, 1982 (Inst. Store Planners-Nat. Assn. Store Fixture Mfrs. First Place New Store award 1982), Bullock's Oakridge, 1980 (Inst. Store Planners-Nat. Assn. Store Fixture Mfrs. Outstanding Merit award 1980), Robinson's Horton Plaza, 1985, Robinson's Santa Monica, 1982. Music com. chmn. Unitarian Ch., Berkeley, Calif., 1979-82. Mem. Inst. Store Planners (profl.), AIA (assoc.). Democrat. Roman Catholic. Avocations: photography, music, swimming. Office: IPA Design Inc 2550 9th St Suite 112 Berkeley CA 94710

PAOLINI, SHIRLEY JOAN, university dean, humanities educator; b. Cleve.; d. James Francis and Ann Dorothy (Jurist) Burke; m. Maurizio Paolini; children—Kenneth, Marco, Angela, Laura. B.A., Mt. St. Mary's Coll., 1954; postgrad. U. Lausanne, Switzerland, 1954-55; M.A., Calif. State U.-Fullerton, 1966; Ph.D., U. Calif.-Irvine, 1973. Asst. dir. edn. Nat. Systems Corp., Newport Beach, Calif., 1971-73; asst. prof. English, asst. specialist U. Hawaii, Manoa, 1977-78; dir. planning Chaminade U., Honolulu, 1975-78; art reach dir. Anchorage Arts Council, Anchorage, 1978-79; asst. dean acad. affairs Alaska Pacific U., Anchorage, 1979-80, dean continuing edn., 1980-82, dean univ. affairs, 1982-83, dean spl. programs, 1983-85; cons. Hawaii State Govts., Honolulu, 1977-78, Alaska Ednl. Agys., 1979—. Author: Confessions of Sin and Love, 1982. Editor: North American School of Conservation, 1971-73, Studies in Interdisciplinarity, 1987—. Contbr. articles to various publs. Recipient French Govt. award, Los Angeles Consulate, 1954; Swiss Govt. fellow U. Lausanne, 1954-55. Mem. Am. Comparative Lit. Assn., MLA, Internat. Comparative Lit. Assn., Council for Adult and Exptl. Learning (co-mgr. Alaska region, 1985—), Philol. Assn. Pacific Coast, Am. Assn. Italian Studies and Australian Studies. Democrat. Roman Catholic. Clubs: La Mirada Womens (v.p. 1965-66) (Calif.). Home: 1242 St Gotthard Ave Anchorage AK 99508 Office: Alaska Pacific Univ 4101 University Dr Anchorage AK 99508

PAPEN, FRANK O'BRIEN, banker, state senator; b. Dec. 2, 1909; m. Julia Stvenson; 1 dau., Michele Papen-Daniel. Dir., exec. v.p. First Nat. Bank Dona Ana County, Las Cruces, N.Mex., 1957-60, pres., 1960-71, chmn. bd. dirs., chief exec. officer, 1971—, pres., chmn. bd., 1982—; mem. Ho. of reps. State of N.Mex., 1957-58, senator, 1969-84; vice-chmn. 12 regional adv. com. on banking practices and policies, 1965-66; mem. adv. com. on fed. legis., 1966; mem. N.Mex. State Investment Council, 1963-67; mem. N.Mex. Dept. Devel. Adv. Council, 1967-68; mem. steering com. Edn. Commn. States; mem. Albuquerque dist. adv. council SBA; pres. N.Mex. State U. Pres. Assocs. Recipient Citizen of Yr. award N.Mex. Assn. Realtors, 1966, Branding Iron award N.Mex. State U., 1977, The Pres.'s award for Service N.Mex. State U., 1983, Regent's medal N.Mex. State U., 1985. Mem. Am. Bankers Assn. (savs. bond chmn. N.Mex. 1964-66), N.Mex. Bankers Assn. (pres., mem. exec. com. 1965-66), Las Cruces C. of C., Alpha Kappa Lambda. Democrat. Lodges: Kiwanis, KC. Office: PO Box FNB Las Cruces NM 88004

PAPPAGIANIS, DEMOSTHENES, microbiology educator; b. San Diego, Mar. 31, 1928; s. George John and Mary (Terzakis) P.; m. Alice Ertel, Jan. 28, 1956; children: Michele, Marika. A.B., U. Calif.-Berkeley, 1949, M.A., 1951, Ph.D., 1956; M.D., Stanford U., 1962. Diplomate Am. Bd. Microbiology. Rotating intern Walter Reed Gen. Hosp., Washington, 1962-63; asso. prof. Sch. Public Health, U. Calif., Berkeley, 1963-67; prof. med. microbiology Sch. Medicine, U. Calif., Davis, 1967—; chmn. dept. med. microbiology Sch. Medicine, U. Calif., 1968-85; asso. mem. Armed Forces Epidemiol. Bd. Contbr. to profl. jours. and books. Served from 1st lt. to capt. M.C. U.S. Army, 1962-63. Fellow Infectious Disease Soc. Am.; mem. Am. Soc. for Microbiology, Am., Calif. thoracic socs., Internat. Soc. for Human and Animal Mycology, Sigma Xi, Alpha Omega Alpha (asso.). Home: 1523 Orange Ln Davis CA 95616 Office: U Calif Sch Medicine Dept Med Microbiology Davis CA 95616

PAPPAS, MARGARET, infosystems consultant; b. Newark, Mar. 25, 1949; d. Steven William and Theresa (Cebulesky) Pappas. BA, Seton Hall U., 1971; MLS, Rutgers U., 1972. Cert. N.J. sch. media specialist, N.J. profl. librarian. Profl. librarian W.O. Pub. Library, West Orange, N.J., 1972-73; sch. media specialist Jersey City Pub. Schs., 1973-75, Secaucus (N.J.) Pub. Schs., 1975-77, Livingston (N.J.) Pub. Schs., 1977-81; dir. learning resource ctr. Calif. Family Studies Ctr., Burbank, 1981-85; systems cons. The Organizers, Monrovia, Calif., 1986—; cons. St. Jane Francis, North Hollywood, 1982-84, Immaculate Conception, Monrovia, 1984-85. Treas. Com. to Elect. Roger Chandler, Arcadia, Calif., 1986. N.J. Library Assn. scholar, 1971; West Orange Pub. Library grantee, 1971. Mem. NSPE, Nat. Assn. Profl. Organizers, Beta Phi Mu. Club: Quota. Avocations: dancing, reading, computers, handicrafts. Home: 742 Oakdale Ave Monrovia CA 91016 Office: The Organizers 742 Oakdale Ave Monrovia CA 91016

PAPPAS, THETIS HERO, real estate broker; b. Astoria, N.Y., Sept. 9, 1920; d. Thomas John and Andromahe (Krahtis) Hero; m. Costas Ernest, June 9, 1940; children: Alceste T., Conrad T.E. BA in Chemistry with honors, Hofstra U., 1943; diploma, N.Y. Sch. Interior Design, 1954; MS in Counseling, L.I. U., 1967; cert. real estate broker, Coll. San Mateo, 1982. Cert. secondary tchr. Pvt. practice investments, developments, interior design Huntington, N.Y., 1950-63; tchr. chemistry Half Hollow Hills High Sch., Huntington, 1963-68; cons. Pappas Assocs., Palo Alto and Emeryville, Calif., 1968-79; pvt. practice real estate broker San Mateo, Calif., 1979—; bd. dirs. San Mateo/Burlingame Bd. Realtors, San Mateo, 1985—, chmn. membership com., 1985—, chmn. edn. com., 1982-84; mem. real estate adv. com. Coll. San Mateo, 1985—. Life mem. archives com. Redwood City Pub. Library, 1985. Hofstra U. scholar, Hempstead, N.Y., 1941-42; recipient George A. Thuss Meml. award Real Estate Cert. Inst., San Mateo, 1984. Mem. Am. Chem. Soc., Calif. Real Estate Edn. Assn., Hofstra U. Alumni Assn., Lawrenceville (N.J.) Sch. Women's Auc. Avocations: reading, writing, painting, travelling, music. Home and Office: PO Box 5633 San Mateo CA 94402

PARADY, JOHN EDWARD, information systems executive, consultant; b. Inglewood, Calif., Sept. 26, 1939; s. Raymond Oliver and Ella Louise (Timm) P.; m. Barbara Lyn Pettit, Aug. 13, 1966; chidlren: John, Renee, Stacy. BS, Calif. State U., Los Angeles, 1966; MS, U. So. Calif., 1969. Cert. data processing. Dir. info. systems Weyerhauser Co., Tacoma, Wash., 1975-82; exec. dir. McKenna, Conner & Cuneo, Los Angeles, 1982-83; sr. v.p. Bank of Am., San Francisco, 1983-85, Ticor, Los Angeles, 1985—; pvt. practice cons., Los Angeles, 1986—; mem. The Research Bd., N.Y.C., 1983-86; bd. dirs. The Ctr. for Info. Systems Research, Cambridge, Mass., 1977-85. Served to 2d lt., U.S. Army, 1959-64. Republican. Mormon. Avocations: fishing, camping, woodworking. Home: 1004 Vista Del Valle La Canada CA 91011 Office: 1004 Vista Del Valle La Canada CA 91011

PARASHAR, OM DATT, business management consultant, researcher, educator; b. Delhi, India, Sept. 15, 1939; came to U.S., 1971, naturalized, 1980; s. Ram Sawrup and Ram Davi (Vashistha) P.; m. Usha Joshi, Oct. 21, 1979; children—Amish, Amita. M.A. in Philosophy, Punjab U., India, 1960; M.A. in Psychology, U. Delhi, 1965; ednl. psychology cert. Oxford (Eng.) U., 1969; M.Ed., U. Toronto (Ont., Can.), 1971; Ed.D. in Spl. Edn. (HEW fellow), U. Cin., 1973. Tchr., Mcpl. Corp. of Delhi Schs., 1957-62; research fellow Nat. Council Ednl. Research and Tng. (with HEW), New Delhi, 1963-67; spl. edn. tchr. Bucks County Sch., High Wycombe, Eng. and lectr. Wycombe Coll., High Wycombe, 1967-70; instr. U. Cin., 1971-73; asst. prof. spl. edn. Va. Commonwealth U., 1973-79; dir., cons. psychology of mgmt. Parashar Entrepreneurs, Los Alamitos, Calif., 1979—; pres. Mktg. Research Assocs., Los Alamitos, 1979—; mem. exec. com. Race Relations Commn., Eng., 1967-70; Brit. Commonwealth Edn. and Travel scholar, Can., 1970. Mem. Am. Psychol. Assn. (past), Brit. Psychol. Soc. (asso.), Soc. Prevention of Delinquency and Other Problems in Children and Youth (pres. 1979—). Author books, most recent being: Psycho-educational Diagnosis: Identifying Learning and Behavior Problems, 1976; Parashar Behavior Rating Scale, 1976; Dictionary of Special Education, 1977; contbr. articles to profl. jours.

PARBURY, CHARLES ALAN, investment company executive, consultant; b. Palo Alto, Calif., Aug. 13, 1947; s. Charles Byron and Ethel (Noakes) P.; m. Heidi Thometz, June 15, 1970 (div. June 1975); m. Sandra Wanderer, June 10, 1978; children: Cynthia, Holly. BS in Commerce, U. Santa Clara, 1970; postgrad., Coll. San Mateo, 1971-72, Columbia Pacific U., 1985. Sales and ops. mgr. GranTree Corp., Portland, Calif., 1970-75; gen. mgr. Alameda (Calif.) Joe's, Inc., 1979-81; sr. cons. Gustafson Williams, Walnut Creek, Calif., 1981-82; v.p. TWA Mgmt. Corp., Walnut Creek, 1982—, Cypress Capital Corp., Walnut Creek, 1983—, Fortune Planning Services, Danville, Calif., 1984—. Author: Sales Management, 1984. Vol. Spl. Olympics and Little League of Am., Big Brothers. Mem. Internat. Assn. Fin. Planning (bd. dirs.), Contra Costa Devel. Assn., Walnut Creek C. of C. Republican. Roman Catholic. Club: Crow Canyon Country (Danville). Lodges: Kiwanis (pres. local club), Elks. Avocations: sports including baseball, golf. Home: PO Box 534 Alamo CA 94507 Office: Cypress Capital Corp 1515 Oakland Blvd Suite 204 Walnut Creek CA 94596

PARCELL, RAYMOND EUNICE, JR., aerospace company manager; b. Fredericksburg, Va., Sept. 22, 1930; s. Raymond Eunice and Irene (Smith) P.; B.S. in Elec. Engring., Va. Poly. Inst. and State U., 1951; M.B.A. (Harriman scholar), Columbia U., 1958; exec. course UCLA, 1984-85; m. Winifred Patricia Slaght, Nov. 8, 1974. With Hughes Aircraft Co., Culver City, Calif., 1954-59, program mgr. Japan Hughes Internat., 1959-62, mgr. Hughes Washington Internat. office, 1962-65, mgr. Advanced Programs for Air Def., Hughes Aero. Systems Div., 1965-68, mktg. mgr. Roland Program, 1968, spl. projects mgr. Hughes Aerospace Groups, 1974-75, corp. mgr. spl. programs Hughes Aircraft Co., Culver City, 1975—; dir. Perry D. Edson, Inc., Los Angeles, Raybilron, Inc., Staunton Va. Served with U.S. Army, 1951-53; to col. Res. Tau Beta Pi, Pi Delta Epsilon, Eta Kappa Nu, Alpha Kappa Psi. Methodist. Clubs: Calif. Yacht, Interstellar, Icarian Flying, Masons. Office: PO Box 2999 242/1 Torrance CA 90509

PARDINI, SHARON KAY BROWN, architectural and interior designer; b. Grand Junction, Iowa, Apr. 15, 1938; s. Loyal Melvin Blanshan and Frances Mildred (Brown) Manen; m. Frederick Brown, Oct. 19, 1957 (div. Apr. 1963); 1 child Randal Alan; m. Joseph Leslie Pardini, Nov. 11, 1975; 1 child, Tiana Margaret. BA in Cosmetology, Lee Ann Acad., 1957. Owner Sharon's Hair Fashions Salons, Oakland, Calif., 1958-80; v.p., sec., treas. Western Container Transp. Inc.i, 1978—; pres. Par-West Inc. Design Firm, 1983—; adv. bd. mem. Bd. Cosmetology, Oakland., 1965-69. Task force mem. Republicans, Washington, 1981—; mem. service league Santa catalina Sch., Monterey, Calif., 1986. Mem. Calif. Cosmetologist Assn. (v.p. 1973-75, bd. dirs. 1970-77). Club: Mission Hills Country. Avocations: studying architecture and designing, horticulture, navigational boating. Office: Par-West Designs Inc 3190 Old Tunnel Rd Lafayette CA 94549

PARDON, DONNA MARIE, audiologist; b. Lansing, Mich., Mar. 29, 1956; d. Myrle B. and Marian Ruth (Moss) Leisenring; m. Scott Timothy Pardon, Aug. 12, 1978 (div.). BSEd in Edn., Cen. Mich. U., 1979, MA in Audiology, 1981. Audiologist San Mateo (Calif.) Med. Clinic, 1982, Silas B. Hays Army Community Hosp., Ft. Ord, Calif., 1982—. Mem. Am. Speech-Lang.-Hearing Assn. (cert. audiologist). Avocations: bible study, hiking, swimming. Office: Silas B Hays Army Community Hosp Gigling Rd Fort Ord CA 93941

PAREDES, ALFONSO, psychiatrist; b. Mexico City, Sept. 19, 1926; came to U.S., 1951, naturalized, 1960; s. Cipriano and Dolores (Fernandez) P.; m. Lois E. Foster, Sept. 24, 1954; children—Alfonso Jr., John M., Nancy M., Susan M. M.D., U. Mex., 1951. Intern St. Joseph Hosp., Kansas City, Mo., 1951-52; fellow in psychiatry Herrick Meml. Hosp., Berkeley, Ga., 1952-53; resident in psychiatry U. Kans., Kansas City, Kans., 1953-55; sr. asst. resident in psychiatry U. Md. Psychiat. Inst., Balt., 1955-56; asst. prof. psychiatry U. Okla., Oklahoma City, 1960-64; prof. U. Okla., 1969-79; prof. psychiatry U. So. Calif. and; dep. dir. mental health Los Angeles County, 1979-81; prof. psychiatry U. Calif., Los Angeles, 1981—; asso. prof. psychiatry Jefferson Med. Coll., Phila., 1964-69. Pres. Oklahoma City Council on Alcoholism, 1970-75, Okla. Partners of Ams., 1972-74. Fellow Am. Psychiat. Assn., Am. Coll. Psychiatrists; mem. AAAS, Am. Psychopathol. Assn., N.Y. Acad. Scis., AMA, Sigma Xi. Roman Catholic. Home: 524 Bonita Ave San Marino CA 91108 Office: West Los Angeles VA Med Ctr 11301 Willshire Blvd Los Angeles CA 90073

PAREDES, (NOR)BERT, computer systems engineer; b. Frankfurt, Fed. Republic Germany, Dec. 27, 1947; s. George and Elfriede (Kleebach) P.; m. Linda L. Stubblefield, July 5, 1968 (div. 1986). BS in Computer Sci., SUNY, Albany, 1970; postgrad., U. Colo., 1977-78. Enlisted U.S. Army, 1970, programmer/analyst, 1970-79, resigned, 1979; staff engr. Martin Marietta Denver Aerospace div., 1979-81; sr. staff engr. Martin Marietta of Denver Aerospace div., 1984—; regional analyst, mgr. Gould Computer Systems, Denver, 1981-84; mgr. tech. analysis and support Denelcor, Inc., Aurora, Colo., 1984; Pres., chief exec. officer A.C.T., Inc., Denver, 1982-84. Contbr. articles to profl. jours. Vol. cons. Opera Colo., Denver, 1982—. Nat. Merit scholar, 1966. Mem. Assn. Computing Machinery, Armed Forces Communications and Electronics Assn., Am. Rose Soc., Mensa, Denver Mus. Natural History, Denver Bot. Gardens. Libertarian. Lutheran. Home: PO Box 4060 Highlands Ranch CO 80126 Office: Martin Marietta Denver Aerospace MS-L0421 PO Box 179 Denver CO 80201

PARENT, DENISE CLAIRE, research chemist; b. Sherbrooke, Que., Can., June 1, 1954; came to U.S., 1961; d. Gilbert Paul and Rita (Turgeon) P. BA in Chemistry, U. Calif., Santa Barbara, 1977, PhD in Phys. Chemistry, 1983. NATO postdoctoral fellow Université de Paris-Sud, Orsay, France, 1983-84; research assoc. Centre National de la Recherche Scientifique, Orsay, 1984-85; postdoctoral fellow Los Alamos (N.Mex.) Nat. Lab., 1985—. Contbr. articles to profl. jours. Nat. Merit scholar, 1973, Regents scholar U. Calif., 1973, Pacific Gas and Electric scholar, 1973; grantee Sigma Xi, 1981, U. Calif. Santa Barbara, 1980, 81. Mem. Am. Chem. Soc., Am. Soc. Mass Spectrometry, Optical Soc. Am., Phi Beta Kappa. Avocations: photography, needlework, music, travel. Office: Los Alamos Nat Lab MS G738 Los Alamos NM 87545

PARENTE, ROBERT BRUCE, electrical engineer; b. N.Y.C., Sept. 10, 1936; s. Almerico Elmer and Royda (Boyd) P.; B.S. in Elec. Engring., MIT, 1959, M.S. in Engring., 1959, E.E., 1961, Ph.D., 1966; m. Rozalinda Thelma Saturnio, May 28, 1977; children—Jennifer Dee, Jessica Dale, Jacquelyn Dawn. Instr. elec. engring. Mass. Inst. Tech., Cambridge, 1959-65; asst. prof. engring. UCLA, 1965-70; mgr. electric power systems System Devel. Corp., Santa Monica, Calif., 1970-72, dir. planning, 1973-75, dep. dir. energy devel., 1975-76; sr. cons. Theodore Barry & Assos., Los Angeles, 1976-78; propr. Parente & Assocs., mgmt. cons., 1978—; expert witness before utility commns. Res. lt. sheriff Los Angeles County Sheriff's Dept., 1970—. Registered profl. engr., Calif. Mem. IEEE, Inst. Mgmt. Scis., Ops. Research Soc. Am., Sigma Xi, Tau Beta Pi, Eta Kappa Nu, Hex-Alpha, Theta Chi. Author: Electric Power Pools, 1983; contbr. articles to profl. jours. Patentee in field. Office: PO Box 241987 Los Angeles CA 90024

PARENTI, KATHY ANN, interior designer, hotel executive; b. Gary, Ind., Sept. 24, 1957; d. Lee Everett Huddleston and Barbara Elizabeth (Daves) Tilley; m. Michael A. Parenti, Mar. 31, 1979. Student, Ind. U., Gary, 1977; cert., U. Nev., Las Vegas, 1978; diploma, Interior Design Inst., Las Vegas, 1984. Office mgr. Realty Execs., Las Vegas, 1977-78, Jet Set Internat., Las Vegas, 1978-79; bookkeeper Las Vegas Water Dist., 1979-80; supr. Circus Circus Hotel, Las Vegas, 1980—; owner Interior Views, Las Vegas, 1984-87; sales rep. Win-Glo Window Coverings. Mem. Las Vegas C. of C., Women's Council (membership com.), Internat. Brotherhood of Teamsters, Chauffeurs, Warehousemen, and Helpers of Am. Republican. Avocations: songwriting, racquetball, swimming.

PARK, EDWARD CAHILL, JR., physicist; b. Wollaston, Mass., Nov. 26, 1923; s. Edward Cahill and Fentress (Kerlin) P.; m. Helen Therese O'Boyle, July 28, 1951. AB, Harvard U., 1947; postgrad., Amherst Coll., 1947-49; PhD, U. Birmingham, Eng., 1956. Instr. Amherst (Mass.) Coll., 1954-55; mem. staff Lincoln Lab., Lexington, Mass., 1955-57, Arthur D. Little, Inc., Cambridge, Mass., 1957-60; group leader electronic systems Arthur D. Little, Inc., Santa Monica, Calif., 1960-64; sr. staff engr., head laser system sect. Hughes Aircraft Co., Culver City, Calif., 1964-68; sr. scientist Hughes Aircraft Co., El Segundo, Calif., 1986—; mgr. electric optical systems sect. Litton Guidance and Control Systems, Woodland Hills, Calif., 1968-70; sr. phys. scientist The Rand Corp., Santa Monica, 1970-72; sr. scientist R&D Assocs., Marina Del Rey, Calif., 1972-1986, cons., 1986—. Contbr. articles to profl. jours.; patentee in field. Served to 1st lt. USAAF, 1943-46. Grantee Dept. Indsl. and Sci. Research, 1953. Fellow Explorers Club (sec. So. Calif. chpt. 1978-79); mem. IEEE, Optical Soc. Am., Armed Forces Communications and Electronics Assn., Assn. Old Crows, Sigma Xi. Democrat. Clubs: 20-Ghost (Eng.), Harvard (So. Calif.). Avocations: music, art, architecture, body surfing, gardening. Home: 932 Ocean Front Santa Monica CA 90403 Office: Hughes Aircraft Co PO Box 902 E55/G216 El Segundo CA 90245

PARK, ELEANOR LOUISE, clinical social worker; b. Portland, Oreg., Oct. 5, 1929; d. William Edward and Lucille Eleanor (Bowman) Hunt; m. Benjamin Wallace Park, June 14, 1964 (div. Aug. 1967). BA, Lewis and Clark Coll., 1953; teaching credential, Fresno State Coll., 1958; MSW, U. Calif., Berkeley, 1960. Psychiat. social worker Napa State Hosp., Imola, Calif., 1960-62; sr. psychiat. social worker Alameda County Mental Health Agy., Oakland, Calif., 1962-80; advanced clin. social worker Met. Family Service, Portland, Oreg., 1980—; pvt. practice Acadian Counseling Services, Tualatin, Oreg., 1982—. Participant The New Left, Berkeley, 1964-66, Berkeley Citizen Action, 1977-80. Mem. Nat. Assn. Social Workers (cert.), Acad. Cert. Social Workers, Internat. Orgn. Social Workers, Oreg. Psychoanalytical Found. Democrat. Avocations: skiing, dancing, hiking, walking, reading. Home: 12717 SW Barberry Dr Beaverton OR 97005 Office: Acadian Counseling PO Box 931 Tualatin OR 97062 Office: Met Family Service 1049 SW Baseline Hillsboro OR 97123

PARK, JOHN Y., research chemist; b. Chonju, Korea, Feb. 28, 1938; came to U.S., 1963, naturalized, 1976; s. Suh J. and Hong Sup (Kim) P.; B.S., Yon Sei U., 1961; M.S., La. Poly. Inst., 1966; Ph.D., U. Houston, 1971; m. Hija Lee, Dec. 4, 1971; children—Eleanor M., Linus Y. Postdoctoral fellow Calif. Inst. Tech., Pasadena, 1972-73; sr. chemist Beckman Instruments Inc., Irvine, Calif., 1973-75; research scientist McGaw Labs., Irvine, 1976-77, sr. research scientist, 1978-80; sr. research scientist Allergan Pharm. Inc., Irvine, Calif., 1981—; cons. Jet Propulsion Lab., Calif. Inst. Tech., 1971. Served with Med. Bn., Army Republic of Korea, 1961-62. Welch Found. research fellow, 1970-71; AEC research fellow, 1968-69. Mem. Am. Chem. Soc., Soc. Applied Spectroscopy, Alpha Chi Sigma. Presbyterian. Contbr. sci. papers to publs.; patentee in field. Home: 13122 Shasta Way Santa Ana CA 92705 Office: Allergan Pharm Inc 2525 DuPont Dr Irvine CA 92713

PARK, ROBERT LYNN, animal scientist, educator; b. Idaho Falls, Idaho, Sept. 1, 1932; s. William Densell and Ardella (Laird) P. m. Elaine Burke, May 24, 1962; children: Richard, Rhonda, Rita, Roxanne, Raquel, Elizabeth. Student, U. Idaho, 1950-53; BS, Brigham Young U., 1956; MS, Cornell U., 1958, PhD, 1962. 4-H county agt. U. Ariz., Tucson, 1959; agrl. and livestock husbandman ARS-USDA, St. Croix, Virgin Islands, 1961-65; from asst. to full prof. animal sci. Brigham Young U., Provo, Utah, 1965—; U.S. Virgin Islands rep. Caribbean Com. Agr., 1962-64; vis. prof. N.C. State U., Raleigh, 1971-72, Cornell U., Ithaca, N.Y., 1978; cons. U.S. Virgin Islands Dept. Agr., St. Croix, 1973. Author: Agriculture: Food and Man, 1975; contbr. articles to profl. jours. Adult unit, dist. and council leadership positions Boy Scouts Am., 1958—; county del. Rep. Party, Provo, 1985. Served to cpl. U.S. Army, 1953-54. Recipient Cert. Appreciation, Animal Disease Eradication div. USDA, 1964. Mem. Am. Soc. Animal Sci., Am. Dairy Sci. Assn., Sigma Xi, Phi Kappa Phi, Alpha Zeta (advisor). Mormon. Lodge: Kiwanis (pres. 1987—, Provo Youth Services chmn.). Avocations: reading, camping, hiking, golfing,. Home: 1218 N 1160 W Provo UT 84604 Office: Brigham Young U 387 WIDB Provo UT 84602

PARK, ROY HAMPTON, communications company executive; b. Dobson, N.C., Sept. 15, 1910; s. I.A. and Laura Frances (Stone) P.; m. Dorothy Goodwin Dent, Oct. 3, 1936; children—Roy Hampton, Adelaide Hampton Park Gomer. BBA, N.C. State U., Raleigh, 1931; LHD (hon.), Keuka Coll., 1967; HHD (hon.), N.C. State U., 1978; LLD (hon.), Ithaca Coll., 1985, Wake Forest U., 1985. Dir. pub. relations Farmers Coop. Exchange, N.C. Cotton Growers Coop. Assn., Raleigh, 1931-42; founder, editor, pub. Coop. Digest, Farm Power, 1939-66; sr. editor Rural Electrification Adminstrn., 1936-37; pres., also bd. dirs. RHP Ind., Ithaca, 1945—; pres. Hines-Park Foods, Inc., Ithaca, N.Y., Hines-Park Foods, Ltd., Can. and Duncan Hines Inst., Inc., 1949-56, v.p., 1956-63; pres., also bd. dirs. Avalon Citrus Assocs., Inc., Orlando, Fla., 1962—, Roy H. Park Broadcasting Inc., Greenville, N.C., 1962—, Sta. WDEF-TV-AM-FM, Chattanooga, Tenn., 1963—, Sta. WJHL-TV, Johnson City, Tenn., 1964—, Sta. WTVR-TV-AM-FM, Richmond, Va., 1965—, Sta. WNAX-AM, Yankton, S.D., 1968—, Sta. WUTR-TV, Utica-Rome, 1969—, Sta. WSLS-TV, Roanoke, 1969—, CobbHouse of Rock Hill (S.C.) Inc., 1968, Sta. WBMG-TV, Birmingham, 1973—, KWJJ Radio and Contemporary FM Inc., Sta. KJIB-FM, Portland, Oreg., 1973—, Sta. KJJO-FM, The Lake Country, 1974, Sta. KEZX-TV, Seattle, 1975, Sta. WHEN-AM, Syracuse, N.Y., 1976—, Sta. WRRB-FM, Syracuse, 1977—; pres. Park Outdoor Advt. and Park Displays, Ithaca, 1964-84, chmn. bd., 1984—, also bd. dirs.; pres. Park Outdoor Advt., Inc., Scranton, Pa., 1969-84; pres., also bd. dirs. Warner Robins Ga. Inc., 1972, Park Newspapers, Inc., Ithaca, 1972—; and Ga., 1972—, Manassas, Va., 1972—, Nebraska City, Nebr., 1975—, Brooksville, Fla., 1975—, Ogdensburg, N.Y., 1975—, Plymouth, Ind., 1977—, Norwich, N.Y., 1977—, McAlester, Okla., 1978, Macomb, Ill., 1979, Newton, Morganton and Statesville, N.C., 1979, Perry, Ga., 1980, Mich., 1980, Ark., 1981, Moore County, Lumberton, Marion and Devils Lake, N.C., 1982, Waynesboro, Va., 1983, Medina, N.Y., 1984, Clark County, Ind., 1984, Hudson, N.Y., 1985, Ky., 1985, Pa., 1986, Iowa, 1986; pres., also bd. dirs. RHP Newspapers Inc., Ithaca, 1973—, Lockport (N.Y.) Pubs. Inc., 1973—, Kannapolis (N.C.) Pub. Co., 1978—, State and Aurora Inc., Broken Arrow, Okla., 1979, WND Inc.,

Sapulpa, Okla., 1979; bd. dirs. Molinos de P.R., Tompkins County Area Devel. Corp., Ithaca, First Research Devel. Corp., Ithaca; pres. Upstate Small Bus. Investment Co., Ithaca, 1960-66; assoc. chmn. laymen's nat. Bible com. Nat. Bible Week, 1972; chmn. pub. relations com. N.C. State U. Devel. Council, 1963-72, vice chmn. council, 1964-72, chmn., 1972—; trustee Endowment Funds N.C. State U. Found., Ithaca Coll., 1973—, mgr. exec. com., 1977—, chmn. exec. com., 1981—. Asso. chmn. laymen's nat. Bible com. Nat. Bible Week, 1972; chmn. pub. relations com. N.C. State U. Devel. Council, 1963-72, vice chmn. council, 1964-72, chmn., 1972—; trustee N.C. State U., 1977-85; bd. dirs. N.C. State U. Found., 1962-66, trustee endowment funds; trustee, chmn. exec. com. Ithaca Coll., 1973—. Recipient spl. citation Am. Inst. Coops., 1947; Disting. Service award Tompkins County United Fund, 1961; Meritorious Service award N.C. State U. Alumni Assn., 1970; Abe Lincoln award So. Bapt. Radio-TV Commn., 1971, Gold Plate award Am. Acad. Achievement, 1984; named Country Squire by Gov. N.C., 1953, hon. citizen New Orleans, 1958, hon. citizen Tenn., 1961, Ky. col., 1963, adm. in Gt. Navy Neb., 1961, Soc. Prodigal Son by Gov. N.C., 1964. Mem. N.C. State U. Alumni Assn. (pres. 1960-61, gen. fund chmn. 1962), Pub. Relations Soc. Am., Am. Agrl. Editors Assn., Am. Assn. Agrl. Coll. Editors, Agrl. Relations Council, Sales Execs. Club N.Y.C., Friends Ithaca Coll., Lucullus Circle, Les Amis D'Escoffier Soc., Confrerie de la Chaines des Rotisseurs, Antique Automobile Club Am., Va., N.C., Nat. assns. broadcasters, Am., So. newspaper pubs. assns., N.Y. State Pubs. Assn. (pres. 1981), Ga. Pr Assn. (dir.), Phi Kappa Phi, Pi Sigma Epsilon, Alpha Phi Gamma, Pi Phi Pi. Presbyn. (ruling elder 1969—). Clubs: Nat. Press, Capitol (Washington); Sales Execs. (dir. 1980, v.p. 1981-82), N.Y. Athletic, Cornell, Marco Polo (N.Y.C.); Union League (N.Y.C.); City, Capital City, Sphinx (Raleigh); Ithaca Country; Statler (Cornell U.); Commonwealth (Richmond); Shenandoah (Roanoke). Home: 205 Devon Rd Ithaca NY 14850 Office: Terrace Hill Box 550 Ithaca NY 14851

PARK, U. YOUNG, nuclear engineer; b. Seoul; s. M.W. and D.C. (Chang) P.; B.S., Seoul Nat. U., 1963; M.S., U. Cin., 1970; m. Linda Rugh; children—Tara, Thomas. Nuclear engr. State of Ohio, to 1978, Battelle Meml. Inst., Columbus, Ohio, 1978-81; power plant system engr. Bechtel Power Corp., San Francisco, 1981—. Author: Power Engineering, 1977, 79. Lic. profl. engr. Mem. Am. Nuclear Soc. Office: PO Box 3965 San Francisco CA 94119

PARK, WILLIAM LAIRD, agricultural economics educator, consultant; b. Idaho Falls, Idaho, Mar. 29, 1931; s. William D. and Ardella (Laird) P.; m. Ann Payne, Aug. 7, 1953; children—Leslie, David W., Wayne I., Andrea, John L. B.S., Utah State U., 1957, M.S., 1958; Ph.D., Cornell U., 1963. Dep. chief coop. relations N.Y./N.J. Milk Marketing Adminstrn., N.Y.C., 1958-65; assoc. prof. agrl. econs. Rutgers U., New Brunswick, N.J., 1965-68, chmn. dept. agrl. econs. and mktg., 1970-77; sr. agrl. economist Devel. and Resources Corp., Sacramento, 1969-70; chmn. dept. agrl. econs. Brigham Young U., Provo, 1977-83, prof., 1983—; pres. Ag-Econ Research Assocs., Orem, Utah, 1978—; bd. dirs. N.E. Agrl. Econs. Council, 1972-77; cons. agr., agribus. Author: Estimating Demand and Price Structures by Residual Analysis 1970; author numerous bulls., reports on dairy econs., feasibility analysis, internat. econ. devel.; contbr. articles to profl. jours. Served to cpl. U.S. Army, 1953-55. Mem. Western Agrl. Econs. Assn., Am. Agrl. Econs. Assn., Sigma Xi, Phi Kappa Phi. Republican. Mormon. Home: 1051 E 600 N Orem UT 84057 Office: Brigham Young U Dept Agrl Econs 471 WIDB Provo UT 84602

PARK, WON-HONG WALTER, realtor; b. Seoul, Republic of Korea, June 11, 1942; came to U.S., 1967; s. Tae-Arm and Sungryong (Sohn) P.; m. Young-Hee Chung, May 8, 1967; children: John Hee-Jong, Wendy Hee-Won. BA, Korea U., Seoul, 1965; MA in Polit. Sci., U. Hawaii, 1969; postgrad, UCLA, 1985—. Fgn. and polit. reporter Korea Times and Orient Press, Seoul, 1964-73; bur. chief Orient Press of Korea, Washington, 1973-74; chief editor Dong-A Daily News, Los Angeles, 1974-77; pres. Walter Park & Co., Realtors, Los Angeles, 1977—; owner, instr. Wilshire Real Estate Sch., Los Angeles, 1978—. Author: Language of American Real Estate, 1981, American Real Estate Practice, 1985. Served as cpl. Republic of Korea Army, 1961-63. Mem. Nat. Assn. Realtors (cert.), Real Estate Educators Assn. Office: Walter Park & Co Realtors 2520 W 8th St Suite 205 Los Angeles CA 90057

PARKER, ANNE WHITNEY, speech pathologist; b. Kansas City, Mo., Oct. 13, 1947; d. Jack Howe and Martha Kathryn (Adair) Whitney; children: Alison Beth, Casey Lynn. BS, Colo. State U., 1969, MS, 1984; postgrad., U. No. Colo., 1985—. Speech-lang. specialist Thompson R2-J Schs., Loveland, Colo., 1984—; guest speaker U. Colo., Boulder, 1986, Boulder Valley Schs., 1986. Residential co-chmn. Am. Cancer Soc., Ft. Collins, Colo., 1983, chmn. golf tournament, 1981; vol. Spl. Olympics, Loveland, 1986. Colo. State U. fellow, 1983. Am. Speech-Lang. and Hearing Assn. (cert.), Colo. Speech-Lang. and Hearing Assn. (chmn. supervision forum 1984, mem. adv. council 1986), Pub. Sch. Affairs Com. Avocations: bicycle touring, racquetball, golfing.

PARKER, BRIAN PRESCOTT, forensic scientist; b. Norfolk, Va., Aug. 31, 1929; s. Milton Ellsworth and Louise Randall (Smith) P.; B.S. in Quantitative Biology, M.I.T., 1953; J.D., Northwestern U., 1957; M.Criminology, U. Calif., Berkeley, 1961, D.Criminology, 1967; m. Sonia Garcia Rosario, Dec. 23, 1960; children—Robin Marie, Augustin Keith. Research asst. U. P.R. Med. Sch., 1961; cons. P.R. Justice Dept., 1961-63; spl. asst. FDA, Washington, 1964; lectr., then asst. prof. criminology U. Calif., Berkeley, 1964-70; sr. criminalist, then sr. forensic scientist Stanford Research Inst., Menlo Park, Calif., 1971-73; prof. forensic sci. and criminal justice Calif. State U., Sacramento, 1973—; project dir. phys. evidence Dept. Justice, 1969-70; vis. fellow Nat. Police Research Unit, Australia, 1985; vis. prof. Elton Mayo Sch. Mgmt., South Australia Inst. Tech., 1985. Fellow Am. Acad. Forensic Scis.; mem. Am. Acad. Polit. and Social Sci., Am. Chem. Soc., Acad. Criminal Justice Scis., Calif. Assn. Criminalists, Forensic Sci. Soc. London. Co-author: Physical Evidence in the Administration of Criminal Justice, 1970, The Role of Criminalistics in the World of the Future, 1972; asso. editor Law, Medicine, Science—and Justice, 1964; contbr. to Ency. Crime and Justice, 1983. Home: 5117 Ridgegate Way Fair Oaks CA 95628 Office: 6000 J St Sacramento CA 95819

PARKER, CATHERINE SUSANNE, psychotherapist; b. Norwood, Mass., Nov. 4, 1934; d. George Leonard and Hazel Olga (Remmer) P. BA, Bates Coll., 1956; MSW, U. Denver, 1961. Lic. social worker, Colo. Social worker Taunton (Mass.) State Hosp., 1956-59; social worker Ft. Logan Mental Health Ctr., Denver, 1961-66, clin. team leader, 1966-72; dir. adult services Western Inst. Human Resources, Denver, 1973-74; pvt. practice psychotherapy Denver, 1974—; instr. U. Denver, 1977-79; workshop facilitator Arapahoe Community Coll., 1986—. Mem. Nat. Assn. Social Workers, Acad. Cert. Social Workers, Internat. Transactional Analysis Assn. Avocations: tennis, skiing, fishing, antiques, gardening. Home: 6453 S Downing St Littleton CO 80121 Office: Denver Mental Health 165 Cook St Suite 100 Denver CO 80206

PARKER, CHARLES EDWARD, lawyer; b. Santa Ana, Calif., Sept. 9, 1927; s. George Ainsworth and Dorothy P.; m. Marilyn Esther Perrin, June 23, 1956; children—Mary, Catherine, Helen, George. Student, Santa Ana Coll., U. So. Calif.; J.D., S.W. U.-La. Bar: Calif. 1958, U.S. Dist. Ct. (cen. dist.) Calif. 1958, U.S. Supreme Ct. 1969, D.C. 1971, U.S. Dist. Ct. (no. and so. dists.) Calif. 1981. Prof. law Western State U., Fullerton, Calif., 1973-81; spl. counsel Tidelands, First Am. Title Co., 1980-82; dir. First Am. Fin. Corp., 1981-82. Served to sgt. U.S. Army, 1951-53. Mem. ABA (com. improvement land records, sect. real property), Orange County Bar Assn., Calif. Bar Assn., D.C. Bar Assn. Club: Santa Ana Kiwanis, Lodge: Elks (Santa Ana). Contbr. articles in field to profl. jours. Office: 18101 Charter Rd Villa Park CA 92667

PARKER, COLLEEN MARY, municipal agency administrator; b. Pitts., Jan. 28, 1955; d. Robert John and Lila Jean (Shcarer) Moran; m. Jeffrey D. Parker, June 25, 1977. BA, Mt. Union Coll., 1977; MA, Kent State U., 1979. Office coordinator Summit County (Ohio) Prosecutor, Akron, 1978-79; instr. Wilkes Community Coll., Wilkesboro, N.C., 1979-81; mgr. dept., police planner Chandler (Ariz.) Police Dept., 1981—; mem. traffic safety com., Chandler, 1983—, Maricopa County Criminal Justice Adv. com., 1985—. FChmn. fire master plan com., Chandler, 1984; mem. Maricopa County Needs Assessment Commn., Phoenix, 1983. Recipient Spl. Merit award City of Chandler, 1983. Mem. Nat. Mgmt. Assn. (com. chmn., Service award 1985), Nat. Assn. Police Planners, Ariz. Criminal Justice Planner's Assn. (sec./treas. 1986—). Avocations: racquetball, swimming, hiking, biking, reading. Home: 3811 E Ahwatukee Dr Phoenix AZ 85044 Office: Chandler Police Dept 250 E Commonwealth Chandler AZ 85225

PARKER, FRANK, dermatologist; b. Seattle, Aug. 13, 1932; s. Joseph Frank and Martha (Kurus) P.; m. Karen M. Robertson, Mar. 19, 1955; children: Tyler, Garth, Kirk, Paige. Student, U. Wash., 1950-54, MD, 1958. Diplomate Am. Bd. Dermatology. Intern Columbia-Presbyn. Hosp., N.Y.C., 1958-60; resident U. Wash., Seattle, 1960-62, fellow in dermatology, 1962-64, instr. dermatology, 1962-64, asst. prof., 1964-68, assoc. prof., 1968-72, prof., 1974-78; clin. prof. Virginia Mason Clinic, Seattle, 1972-74; prof. dermatology Oreg. Health Science, Portland, 1978—, chmn. dept., 1978—. Served to 1st lt. USAR. Fellow Am. Acad. Dermatology, Am. Coll. Dermatology; mem. Am. Soc. Clin. Investigation, Western Soc. Clin. Research, Am. Dermatology Assn. Home: 2288 SW Humphrey Park Rd Portland OR 97221 Office: Oreg Health Scis U Dept Derm 3181 Sam Jackson Park Rd Portland OR 97220

PARKER, FRANKLIN, educator, writer; b. N.Y.C., June 2, 1921; m. Betty June Parker, June 12, 1950. BA, Berea Coll., 1949; MS, U. Ill., 1950; EdD, Vanderbilt U., 1956. Librarian, speech tchr. Ferrum (Va.) Coll., 1950-52; librarian Belmont Coll., Nashville, 1952-54, George Peabody Coll. Tchrs. of Vanderbilt U., Nashville, 1955-56; assoc. prof. edn. SUNY, New Paltz, 1956-57, U. Tex., Austin, 1957-64; prof. edn. U. Okla., Norman, 1964-68; Benedum prof. edn. W. Va. U., Morgantown, 1968-86; disting. vis. prof. Ctr. for Excellence in Edn. No. Ariz. U., 1986—; research fellow U. Coll. Rhodesia, Africa, 1957-58, Rhodes-Livingstone Inst. Social Research, Africa, 1961-62; vis. prof. edn. U. Calgary, Alta., Can., summer 1969, U. Alta., Edmonton, summer 1970, No. Ariz. U., Flagstaff, summer 1971, U. Lethbridge, Can., (summers) 1971-73, Meml. U., Nfld., summer 1974; mem. Internat. Conf. African Adminstrn., Cambridge, (Eng.) U., 1957, European Bur. Adult Edn., Finland and Fed. Republic of Germany, 1966, nat. conf. White House Conf. on Edn., 1965, Nat. Fgn. Policy Conf. of Educators Dept. State, 1966; cons. Office Edn. HEW, 1970-75, NSF, 1980-86. Author: African Development and Education in Southern Rhodesia, 1960, 74, Africa South of the Sahara, 1966, George Peabody, A Biography, 1971, The Battle of the Books: Kanawha Country, 1975, What Can We Learn from the Schools of China?, 1977, British Schools and Ours, 1979; co-author: John Dewey: Master Educator, 2d rev. edit., 1961, Government Policy and International Education, 1965, Church and State in Education, 1966, Strategies for Curriculum Change: Cases from 13 Nations, 1968, Dimensions of Physical Education, 1969, International Education: Understandings and Misunderstandings, 1969, Understanding the American Public High School, 1969, Education in Southern Africa, 1970, Curriculum for Man in an International World, 1971, Administrative Dimensions of Health and Physical Education Programs, Including Athletics, 1971, Education and the Many Faces of the Disadvantaged, 1972, The Saber-Tooth Curriculum, meml. edit., 1972, Accelerated Development in Southern Africa, 1974, Myth and Reality: A Reader in Education, 1975, Six Questions: Controversy and Conflict in Education, 1975, Crucial Issues in Education, 6th rev. edit., 1977, Censorship and Education, 1981; series compiler and editor American Dissertations on Foreign Education, A Bibliography with Abstracts, vol. I Can., 1971, vol. II India, 1972, vol III Japan, 1972, vol. IV Africa, 1973, vol. V Scandinavia, 1974, vol. VI China, 1975, vol. VII Korea, 1976, vol. VIII Mex., 1976, vol. IX South Am., 1977, vol. X Cen. Am., 1978, vol. XI Pakistan, Bangladesh, 1979, Vol. XII Iran and Iraq, 1980, vol. XIII Israel, 1980, vol. XIV Middle East, 1981, vol. XV Thailand, 1983, vol. XVI Asia, 1985, vol. XVII Pacific, 1986; (with Betty June Parker) Education in Puerto Rico and of Puerto Ricans in the U.S.A., vol. I, 1978, vol. II, 1984; Women's Education--A World View: Annotated Bibliography of Doctoral Dissertations, 1979; U.S. Higher Education: A Guide to Information Sources, 1980; Women's Education--A World View: Annotated Bibliography of Books and Reports, 1981, Education in the People's Republic of China, Past and Present: Annotated Bibliography, 1986; cons. editor Jour. of Thought, 1965-80, Western Carolina U. Jour. Edn., 1969-76, W. Va. U. Mag., 1969-78, Ednl. Studies, 1975-77, Rev. Edn., 1977-86, Core (Collected Original Resources in Edn.), 1977—, Internat. Jour African Hist. Studies, 1977-86 Edn. Digest, 1976-80, U.S.A. Today, 1981—, Americana Ann., 1961—, Collier's Yearbook, 1965-72, Compton's Yearbook, 1965-66, Dictionary of Am. Biography, supplement 5, 1951-55, 77, Dictionary of Scientific Biography, vol. 8, 1973, vol. 10, 1974, vol. 14, 1976, McGraw-Hill Ency. of World Biography, 1973, Acad. Am. Ency., 1979, Reader's Digest Almanac and Yearbook, 1968-73, others. Served with USAAF, 1942-46. Sr. Fulbright research scholar, 1961-62. Mem. African Studies Assn., Philosophy Edn. Soc. (pres. 1960), Am. Acad. Polit. and Social Sci., Am. Ednl. Research Assn., US Comparative and Internat. Edn. Soc. (feature writer 1963-68, v.p. 1963-64, internat. sec. 1965-68), Can. Comparative and Internat. Edn. Soc., Comparative Edn. Soc. Europe, History Edn. Soc. (pres. 1963-64), Appalachian Writers Assn., Kappa Delta Pi (life mem., Harold R.W. Benjamin fellow internat. edn. 1957-58, sec. commn. on internat. edn. 1968-70), Phi Delta Kappa (life, research award chmn. commn. on internat. relations in edn. 1963-67), Phi Gamma Mu, Phi Kappa Phi (life). Office: No Ariz U Ctr Excellence in Edn Box 5774 Flagstaff AZ 86011-0004

PARKER, HAROLD M(ARION), JR., history educator; b. Oklahoma City, Feb. 9, 1923; s. Harold Marion and Fredonia Angie (Nash) P.; m. Constance Eleanor Christensen, May 16, 1946 (div. 1967); 1 child, Howard Mikel; m. Barbara Ann Malin, May 31, 1967; 1 child, Harold Malin. AB, Park Coll., 1944; BD, Louisville Presbyn. Theol. Seminary, 1946, ThM, 1952; ThD, Iliff Sch. of Theology, 1966. Pastor First Presbyn. Ch., Winfield, Kans., 1957-61; instr. Southwestern Coll., Winfield, 1961-66, Friends U., Wichita, Kans., 1966-67; prof. history Western State Coll., Gunnison, Colo., 1967—; with Community Presbyn. Ch., Lake City, Colo., 1968—. Author: Sermons on the Minor Prophets, 1979, Studies in Southern Presbyterian History, 1979; Bibliography of Published Articles on American Presbyterianism, 1901-1980, 1985; contbr. articles to profl. jours. Chmn. Inskip Recreation Commn., Knoxville, Tenn., 1955-57; mem. Bd. Adjustment and Appeals, Gunnison, past chmn. Named Tchr. Yr. Southwestern Coll., 1964, Citizen Yr. Hinsdale County C. of C., 1979; recipient James H. Thornwell award Presbyn. Hist. Found., 1972, 78. Mem. Presbyn. Hist. Soc., Am. Soc. Ch. History., Am. Schs. Oriental Research, Soc. Bibl. Lit., Winfield Oratorio Soc. (chmn. 1960-61), Phi Alpha Theta. Republican. Avocation: stamp collecting. Home: 500 E Virginia Gunnison CO 81230 Office: Western State Coll Dept Social Studies Gunnison CO 81230

PARKER, JIMMY DEAN, wholesale distribution company executive; b. Checotah, Okla., July 6, 1942; s. Horace Delton and Myrtle Elizabeth (Terry) P.; m. Mary Ruth Davidson, Dec. 14, 1961; children—Carl Dean, Craig James, Keith David. Grad., high sch., Bakersfield, Calif. Warehouseman, truck driver Glaser Bros. subs. Core-Mark Distbrs., Inc., Bakersfield, 1962-66, warehouse mgr., 1966-69, salesman, 1969-76; asst. mgr. Glaser Bros. subs. Core-Mark Distbrs., Inc., Carpinteria, Calif., 1976-77, distbn. ctr. mgr., 1977-79; distbn. ctr. mgr. Glaser Bros. subs. Core-Mark Distbrs., Inc., Los Angeles, 1979-83, sr. v.p. ops., 1983-84; sr. v.p. ops. Core-Mark Distbrs., Inc., Hollywood, Calif., 1984-85, pres., 1985—. Com. chmn. local council Boy Scouts Am., Bakersfield, 1975-76; v.p. boy's baseball Ojai Baseball Assn., Calif., 1977-78. Honoree, Los Angeles Candy Brokers Club, 1979. Republican. Mem. Pentecostal Holiness Ch. Avocations: golf; bowling; hunting; fishing; billiards. Office: Core-Mark Distbrs Inc 1800 N Vine St Hollywood CA 90028

PARKER, JOHN HAVELOCK, Canadian provincial official; b. Didsbury, Alta., Can., Feb. 2, 1929; s. Bruce T. and Rose H. P.; m. Helen A. Panabaker, 1955; children: Sharon, Gordon. B.Sc. in Engring. Geology, U. Alta., Edmonton, 1951. Mng. engr. Norman W. Byrne, Ltd., Uranium City and Yellowknife, N.W.T., Can., 1951-63; pres. Precambrian Mining Services Ltd., 1964-67; councillor Town of Yellowknife, 1959-63, mayor, 1964-67; councillor N.W.T., 1967-74; dep. commr. 1967-79, commr., 1979—. Mem., vice chmn. Duke of Edinburgh's Award in Can.; mem. senate Univ. Alb.; patron Tree of Peace, Yellowknife; vice-prior St. John Ambulance for the Northwest Ters. Decorated knight Order of St. John; named to Order of Can. Fellow Arctic Inst. N.Am.; mem. Can. Inst. Mining and Metallurgy, Assn. Profl. Engrs. Alta.

PARKER, JOHN WILLIAM, pathology educator, investigator; b. Clifton, Ariz., Jan. 5, 1931; s. Vilas William and Helen E. (Coughlin) P.; m. Barbara Ann Atkinson, June 7, 1957; children: Ann Elizabeth, Joy Noelle, John David, Heidi Susan. BS, U. Ariz., 1953; MD, Harvard U., 1957. Diplomate Am. Bd. Pathology. Clin. instr. pathology U. Calif. Sch. Medicine, San Francisco, 1962-64; asst. prof. U. So. Calif. Sch. Medicine, Los Angeles, 1964-68, assoc. prof., 1968-75, prof., 1975—, co-chmn. dept. Pathology, 1985—; dir. U. So. Calif. clin. labs., 1975—; co-chmn. 15th Internat. Leucocyte Culture Conf., Asilomar Calif., 1982; chmn. 2nd Internat. Lymphoma Conf., Athens, Greece, 1981. Founding editor Jour. Hematological Oncology, 1982—; assoc. editor Jour. Clin. Lab. Analysis, 1985—; co-editor: Intercellular Communication in Leucocyte Function, 1983; contbr. articles to profl. jours. Named sr. oncology fellow Am. Cancer Soc., U. So. Calif. Sch. Medicine, 1964-69, Nat. Cancer Inst. vis. fellow Walter and Eliza Hall Inst. for Med. Research, Melbourne, Australia, 1972-73. Fellow Coll. Am. Pathologists, Am. Soc. Clin. Pathologists; mem. Am. Assn. Pathologists, Am. Soc. Hematology, Internat. Acad. Pathology, Phi Beta Kappa, Phi Kappa Phi. Republican. Roman Catholic. Avocations: making stained glass windows, fishing, hiking. Office: U So Calif Sch Medicine HMR 315 Dept Pathology 2025 Zonal Ave Los Angeles CA 90033

PARKER, JOSEPH RICHARD, engineering physicist; b. Grand Island, Nebr., May 8, 1916; s. Pearl Edith and William Henry Parker; m. Mary Stuart Webster, June 26, 1948; children—Mary S., Kate L., Eric W., John W. B.Sc., U. Nebr., 1943; grad. Oak Ridge Inst. Nuclear Studies, 1948; M.Sc., U. Pa., 1952. Registered profl. engr., N.J. Student engr. RCA, Camden, N.J., 1943-44, engr. communications div., 1944-49, engring. physicist sci. instruments, 1949-57, engring. physicist applied physics, 1958-61; staff mem. RCA Systems Engring. & Research, 1961-63; staff mem., cons. Los Alamos Nat. Lab., N. Mex., 1963—; pres. Parker Enterprises, 1981—; cons. in electro-optics. Patentee in field. Contbr. articles to profl. jours. Mem. IEEE (pres. 1985-86), Internat. Soc. Optical Enging., Laser Inst. Am. (pres. 1982-83, 85-86), Optical Soc. (sec. 1983-86), Pajarito Astronomers (pres. 1972-80). Republican. Presbyterian. Home: 333 Potrillo Dr Los Alamos NM 87544 Office: Los Alamos Nat Lab Box 1663 MS E523 Los Alamos NM 87545

PARKER, JOYCE HOPE, clinical social worker; b. Neptune, N.J., Dec. 11, 1946; d. Milton Donald and Lillian Sonia (Fishbein) Steinfeld; m. Lawrence Neil Parker, July 11, 1970; children: Jill Monica, Gregory Robert. MEd, Boston U., 1969; MSW, UCLA, 1976, postgrad., 1983—. Lic. clin. social worker, Calif. Clin. social worker Orange County Mental Health, Westminster, Calif., 1976-80; pvt. practice social work Redondo Beach, Calif., 1980—; psychology intern Airport Marina Counseling Service, Westchester, 1986—; trainer Ctr. for Improvement of Child Caring, Studio City, Calif., 1985—. Fellow Nat. Assn. Social Workers, Soc. For Clin. Social Work. Democrat. Jewish. Avocations: jogging, gourmet cooking.

PARKER, KATHERINE LEE, electronic publishing systems consultant; b. San Francisco, Jan. 3, 1950; d. René Conrad and Betty Lee (Putnam) P. Student, San Francisco State Coll., 1967-68, Schaeffer Sch. Design, San Francisco, 1968-71, Coll. of Marin, Greenbrae, Calif., 1981-82. Mgr. prodn. Pacific Sun Pub. Co., Mill Valley, Calif., 1975-78; mgr. composition Type by Design, San Rafael, Calif., 1978-79; typesetter George Lithograph, San Francisco, 1979-80; prin. Katherine Parker and Assocs., Sausalito, Calif., 1980-82; sr. application engr. Atex, Inc., South San Francisco, 1982-84; sr. product support engr. ViewTech, Inc., Mountain View, Calif., 1984-86; cons. in field, 1986—. Mem. Media Alliance, Soc. for Tech. Communication. Democrat. Avocations: photography, skiing, reading, travel, oeneological studies. Home and Office: 621 Fairmount Ave Oakland CA 94611

PARKER, KEITH KROM, neuropharmacologist; b. Billings, Mont., Jan. 24, 1950; s. Barbara Louise (Krom) P.; m. Julie Ann Anders, Sept. 7, 1985; children: Jenny, Jackie, Cory. BS, Mont. State U., 1972; PhD, U. Calif., 1977. Postdoctoral fellow U. Colo. Health Sci. Ctr., Denver, 1977-79; research assoc. U. Denver, 1979-81; asst. prof. Western Mont. Coll., Dillon, 1981-86, assoc. prof., 1987—; dir. Western Mont. Coll. Found., Dillon, 1986; cons. in field, 1981—, pres. faculty assoc., 1983—. Author book chpts.; contbr. articles to profl. jours. Mem. AAAS, Am. Chem. Soc., Am. Soc. Pharmacology, Sci. Research Soc., Western Pharmacol. Soc., Mont. Acad. Scis. Democrat. Avocations: reading, Mont. history and geography. Home: 933 S Washington Dillon MT 59725 Office: Western Mont Coll 710 S Atlantic Dillon MT 59725

PARKER, M. J., executive assistant; b. Bay City, Mich., Nov. 3, 1950; d. Guy R. and Virginia M. (Switala) P.; m. Daniel A. Gielda, May 9, 1970 (div.). Student Delta Coll., Golden Gate Coll., San Francisco. Lic. real estate sales rep., Mich. Relocation worker for HUD, City of Bay City, 1975-79; exec. asst. to sr. v.p. and chief fin. officer Shaklee Corp., San Francisco, 1980—; bd. dirs. Shaklee Employees Fed. Credit Union Chmn. Youth in Law Day. Mem. San Francisco Jr. Assn. Commerce and Industry (mem. of yr. 1982, dir. quarter 1983), Nat. Assn. Female Execs., San Francisco Mus. Soc., San Francisco Mus. Vol. Council, Mill Valley Ctr. Performing Arts, Cal Drama Assn. Republican. Club: Commonwealth.

PARKER, MICHAEL DAVID, computer scientist, consultant; b. Ft. Wayne, Ind., Feb. 27, 1954; s. Milton Duane and Katherine Elizabeth (Sours) P. BS in Systems Engring., U. Ariz., 1976, MS in Computer Science, 1977. Systems programmer Grumman Data Systems, Oxnard, Calif., 1978-80; project mgr. Omnidata, Thousand Oaks, Calif., 1980-82; test specialist Raytheon Data Systems, Thousand Oaks, 1982-83; lead designer Logicon, San Diego, 1983-85; computer security mgr. Gen. Dynamics, San Diego, 1985-86; pres. MDPC, San Diego, 1986—. Avocation: photography. Office: MDPC PO Box 261369 San Diego CA 92126-0993

PARKER, PATRICK WARREN, library director; b. Decatur, Ar., Mar. 10, 1950; s. Paul Webster and Grace Inex (Cox) P. BSEd, Pittsburg State U., Kans., 1971, MSEd, 1976. Asst. mgr. Foodtown Stores, Inc., Pittsburg, 1974-77; librarian Westark Community Coll., Ft. Smith, Ark., 1977-84; dir. learing resource ctr. Cen. Ariz. Coll., Coolidge, 1984—. Active Vaquero Found., Casa Grande, Ariz., 1986—, Cen. Ariz. Coll. Found. Mem. Ariz. Community Coll. Library Adminstrs. Council (pres. elect). Democrat. Avocations: canoeing, hiking, photography. Home: 772 E Pepper Dr Casa Grande AZ 85222 Office: Cen Ariz Coll Woodruff at Overfield Rd Coolidge AZ 85228

PARKER, PIERCE DOW, geologist, exploration company executive; b. Portland, Oreg., Sept. 26, 1927; s. Ralph Dow and Vada Margaret (Pierce) P.; m. Lucille Rosilyn Clausen, Sept. 12, 1953; children—Janis, Nancy. B.S. in Geology, Mont. Sch. Mines, 1951; M.S., U. Wis., 1955, Ph.D., 1960; postgrad. U. Utah., 1958-59; hon. diploma geol. engring., Mont. Tech., 1981. Registered profl. geologist, Ariz. Project geologist AMAX Inc., Salem, Mo., 1963-65, regional geologist, Webb City, Mo., 1966-67, regional mgr., Tucson, 1967-68, chief geologist AMAX Exploration, Inc., Denver, 1972-78, sr. v.p., Denver, 1978-82, pres., Golden, Colo., 1982-86; pres. Parker Cons. Services, Englewood, Colo., 1986—; mem. rev. com. for research proposals for NSF. Contbr. articles to profl. jours. Mem. com. Dent County Hosp., Salem, Mo., 1965. Served to capt. USAF, 1951-53. Mem. Soc. Econ. Geologists, Soc. Exploration Geochemists, Internat. Soc. Mining and Metallurgy, Ariz. Geol. Soc., Can. Inst. Mining and Metallurgy, AIME, Phi Beta Kappa, Sigma Xi, Theta Tau. Lodges: Kiwanis (past pres.), Rotary (past pres.). Home: 13041 N Travois Trail Parker CO 80134 Office: Parker Consulting Services 6474 S Quebec Englewood CO 80155

PARKER, RICHARD BENNETT, microbiology educator and researcher; b. Ontario, Oreg., Sept. 19, 1925; s. William T. and May Belle (Bennett) P.; m. Jeanette Steege, June 27, 1945; children—Dawn Parker Forrest, Marsha Parker Sundquist, Barbara Parker Weaver, Heidi. Student, Wis. State Coll., 1943-44, Boise Jr. Coll., 1947-48; M.S., Oreg. State Coll., 1952, Ph.D., 1956; postgrad., U. Wis., 1954-55, UCLA, 1958-59. Project asst. Oreg. State Coll., 1949-50, instr., 1952-54; sr. scientist Carnation Research Center, Van Nuys, Calif., 1955-59; asst. prof. bacteriology U. Oreg. Dental Sch., Portland, 1959-61, assoc. prof., 1961-64, prof. microbiology, 1964—, dir. div. oral biology, 1968-77, prof. bacteriology, 1968, chmn. dept. microbiology, 1969-77; v.p. research and devel. microbial genetics div. Pioneer Hi-Bred Internat., Portland, 1977-86; pres. Xeroferm Microbial Genetics and Products, Portland,

1986—; researcher on benificial uses of microorganisms; bd. dirs. Oreg. Found. Dental Research, Portland, Cascade Coll., Portland. Author four sci. texts.; Contbr. articles to profl. jours. Served with USAAF, 1943-46. Mem. A.A.A.S., Am. Inst. Biol. Scis., Am. Soc. Microbiology, Internat. Assn. Dental Research, Soc. Exptl. Biology and Medicine, Sigma Xi, Omicron Kappa Upsilon, Alpha Zeta. Home: 296 S Birdshill Loop Portland OR 97219

PARKER, ROBERT JOSEPH, physiology educator; b. N.Y.C., Apr. 1, 1936. BA in Math., Marist Coll., 1958; MS in Math., Notre Dame U., 1964, PhD in Physics, 1970; postdoctoral student, Albert Einstein Coll. Medicine, 1971-74, Roche Inst. Molecular Biology, 1974-76. Cert. high sch. tchr., Calif., N.Y. Postdoctoral researcher Albert Einstein Coll. Medicine, N.Y.C., 1971-74; research assoc. Roche Inst. Molecular Biology, Nutley, N.J., 1974-76; ESAA tchr. edn. N.Y.C. Bd. Edn., 1977-78; dir., founder Hands Research Inst., San Francisco, 1978-85; tchr. Abraham Lincoln High Sch., San Francisco, 1985-86; prof. U. Calif., Berkeley, 1985—, Vista (Calif.) Community Coll., 1985—; cons. on nutrition and aging, San Francisco, 1983-85; dir. extensive research physiol. aging effects. Author: Aging and Nutrition, 1974; contbr. articles to profl. jours. NIH postdoctoral award, Albert Einstein Coll. Medicine, 1971-74; ESAA fellow, 1977-78. Mem. Gerontol. Soc. Am., Orthomolecular Med. Soc. Club: Baglis (San Francisco) (co-founder 1984-86). Avocation: backpacking. Home and Office: 1335 Clay St #2 San Francisco CA 94109

PARKER, ROBERT MICHAEL, teratologist, anatomy educator; b. San Diego, Aug. 31, 1946; s. Thomas Jackson Parker and Sue Ellen (Randall) Muka; stepson Joseph Abbott Muka, Jr.; m. Karen May Green, Jan. 29, 1972; children—Jenifer May, Alexis Diane. B.S., San Diego State Coll., 1970; M.S., U. Calif.-Davis, 1975, Ph.D., 1980. Staff research assoc. Calif. Primate Research Ctr., Davis, 1976-80, postgrad. researcher, 1980-81; lectr. in biol. sci., Calif. State U., Sacramento, 1978; guest lectr. in embryology, Sch. Medicine U. Calif., Davis, 1980; lectr. in biology, Calif. State Coll., San Bernardino, 1982-84; asst. prof. anatomy Coll. Osteo. Medicine of the Pacific, Pomona, Calif., 1981-85; perinatal biologist, Pathology Assocs., Inc., Nat. Ctr. for Toxicol. Research, Jefferson, Ark., 1985—. Contbr. articles to profl. jours. Mem. Republican Presdl. Task Force, Washington, 1983-86, U.S. Senatorial Club, 1983-86, Jefferson County Rep. Cen. Com., 1985-86; mem. sci. com. Southeast Ark. Arts and Sci. Ctr., 1985-86. Mem. Teratology Soc., Am. Assn. Anatomists, AAAS, Sigma Phi Epsilon (alumni bd. 1975-78). Roman Catholic. Club: Toastmasters. Lodge: Lions. Office: Pathology Assocs Inc Nat Ctr Toxicol Research PO Box 26 Jefferson AR 72079

PARKER, ROY ALFRED, transportation planner, engineer; b. Conway, Ark., Apr. 6, 1930; s. Walter Lane and Harriett Mae (Diffee) P.; m. Dixie Anna Dean, June 9, 1953; children: Walter Lane II, David Dean, Shauna Amyr. BS, U. Idaho, 1953; cert. in hwy. traffic, Yale U., 1958. Registered profl. traffic engr., Calif. Asst. planning programming engr. Bur. Pub. Roads (now Fed. Hwy. Adminstrn.), Sacramento, 1958-59; asst. traffic engr. City of Phoenix, 1959-62; traffic engr. Palo Alto, Calif., 1962-66; sr. transp. engr. Wilbur Smith & Assocs., London, 1966-68; project mgr. Wilbur Smith & Assocs., Sacramento, 1980; sr. transp. engr. F.R. Harris Engring. Corp., São Paulo, Brazil, 1968-69; prin. assoc. R.W. Crommelin & Assocs., Los Angeles, 1969-70; dep. transp. dir. City and County of Honolulu, 1970-75, dir. dept. transp. services, 1981-83; exec. dir. Oahu Met. Planning Orgn., Honolulu, 1975-79; sr. traffic engr. Lyon Assocs., Inc., Damascus, Syrian Arab Republic, 1979; pres. Roy A. Parker and Assocs., La Jolla, Calif., 1980; transp. engr. City of Concord, Calif., 1983-84, dep. pub. works dir., 1984—; lectr. dept. civil engring., Coll. Engring. U. Hawaii, 1971-75; lectr. Inst. Transp. Studies, U. Calif., Berkeley, 1983—. Served with USAF, 1953-57. Fellow Inst. Transp. Engrs. (pres. western dist. 1975-76); mem. Soc. Preservation and Encouragement of Barbershop Quartet Singing in Am., Phi Eta Sigma, Sigma Tau. Democrat. Home: 1160 Sunrise Hill Concord CA 94518 Office: City of Concord Pub Works Dept 1950 Parkside Dr Concord CA 94519

PARKER, SARA ANN, state librarian; b. Cassville, Mo., Feb. 19, 1939; d. Howard Frankline and Vera Irene (Thomas) P. B.A., Okla. State U., 1961; M.L.S., Emporia State U., Kans., 1968. Adult services librarian Springfield Pub. Library, Mo., 1972-75, bookmobile dir., 1975-76; coordinator Southwest Mo. Library Network, Springfield, 1976-78; library developer Colo. State Library, Denver, 1978-82; state librarian Mont. State Library, Helena, 1982—; cons. and lectr. in field. Author, editor, compiler in field; contbr. articles to profl. jours. Sec., Western Council State Libraries, Reno, Nev., 1984-86, mem. Mont. State Data Adv. Council, 1983—, Mont. Telecommunications Council, 1985, WLN Network Council, vice chmn., 1984-87, Kellogg ICLIS Project Mgmt. Bd., 1986—. Inst. Ednl. Leadership Ednl. fellow, 1982. Mem. ALA, Chief Officers State Library Agys., Mont. Library Assn. (bd. dirs. 1982—), Mountain Plains Library Assn. (sect. chmn. 1980, v.p. 1986—). Club: Montana (Helena). Home: 135 Seventh Ave Helena MT 59601 Office: Mont State Library 1515 E Sixth Ave Helena MT 59620

PARKER, SYDNEY RICHARD, electrical engineering educator; b. N.Y.C., Apr. 18, 1923; s. Morris and Rose (DuGoff) P.; m. Dorothy Begg, Jan. 25, 1947; children: Stephen Bruce, Susan Margaret. BS, CUNY, 1944; MS, Stevens Inst. Tech., 1948, ScD, 1964. Registered profl. engr., N.Y., N.J., Pa., Calif. Project mgr. RCA, 1951-56; assoc. prof. elec. engring. CCNY, 1956-65; prof. U. Houston, 1965-66; prof. Naval Postgrad. Sch., Monterey, Calif., 1966-75, 76-87, chmn. dept. elec. engring., 1969-75; prof. elec. engring., computer sci. Rutgers U., New Brunswick, N.J., 1975-76, dean, 1975-76; vis. prof. elec. engring. Stanford (Calif.) U., 1983—; cons. Lawrence Livermore Lab., U. Calif., 1978—; mem. engring. edn. accreditation com. Engrs. Council for Profl. Devel., 1975-80; cons. to industry. Author: Principles of Control Systems Engineering, 1960; co-editor: Internat. Jour. on Circuits, Systems and Signal Processing, 1981—; contbr. numerous articles to profl. jours. Served to 1st lt. AUS, 1944-46. fellow IEEE (dir. Asilomar conr. Sircuits and systems 1966-74, mem. tech. activities bd. 1973-77, v.p. Circuits and Systems Soc. 1973, pres. 1973, assoc. editor Trans. on Circuits and Systems, 1975-77, co-editor Spl. Issue on Adaptive Signal Processing, 1981, Harry Diamond Meml. award 1984); mem. AAAS, Am. Soc. Elec. Engrs. (bd. dirs. Pacific region 1974-75, editor Trans. on Computers in Engring. Edn., 1975), N.Y. Acad. Scis., Sigma Xi, Tau Beta Pi, Eta Kappa Nu (bd. dirs. 1977-78, v.p. 1979, pres. 1980). Office: Naval Postgrad Sch Dept Elec and Computer Engring Monterey CA 93943

PARKER, THEODORE CLIFFORD, electronics engineer; b. Dallas, Oreg., Sept. 25, 1929; s. Theodore Clifford and Virginia Bernice (Rumsey) P.; B.S.E.E. magna cum laude, U. So. Calif., 1960; m. Jannet Ruby Barnes, Nov. 28, 1970; children—Sally Odette, Peggy Claudette. Vice pres. engring. Telemetrics, Inc., Gardena, Calif., 1963-65; chief info. systems Northrop-Nortronics, Anaheim, Calif., 1966-70; pres. AVTEL Corp., Covina, Calif., 1970-74, Aragon, Inc., Sunnyvale, Calif., 1975-78; v.p. Teledyne McCormick Selph, Hollister, Calif., 1978-82; sr. staff engr. FMC Corp., San Jose, Calif., 1982-85; pres. Power One Switching Products, Camarillo, Calif., 1985-86; pres. Condor D.C. Power Supplies, Inc., 1987—. Mem. IEEE (chmn. autotestcon '87), Assn. Computing Machinery, Am. Prodn. and Inventory Control Soc., Am. Def. Preparedness Assn., Armed Forces Communications and Electronics Assn., Nat. Rifle Assn. (life), Tau Beta Pi, Eta Kappa Nu. Home: 1290 Saturn Ave Camarillo CA 93010 Office: 2311 Statham Pkwy Oxnard CA 93033

PARKER, WILLIAM ELBRIDGE, consulting civil engineer; b. Seattle, Mar. 18, 1913; s. Charles Elbridge and Florence E. (Plumb) P.; m. Dorris Laurie Freeman, June 15, 1935; children—Dorris Laurie, Jane Elizabeth. B.S., U.S. Naval Acad., 1935. Party chief King County Engrs., 1935-39; exec. sec., cons. engr. State Wash., 1946-49; city engr., chmn. Bd. Pub. Works, City of Seattle, 1953-57; cons. City of San Diego, 1957; ptnr. Parker-Fisher & Assocs., 1958-66; cons. engr. Minish & Webb Engrs., Seattle, 1966-70; city engr. City of Bremerton (Wash.), 1970-76; owner Parker & Assocs., Seattle, 1976—. Served to capt. C.E.C., USNR, 1939-45, 51-53. Named to Broadway Hall of Fame. Registered profl. engr., Wash. Mem. Am. Pub. Works Assn., U.S. Naval Inst., Pioneers of State Wash. (pres.), U.S. Naval Acad. Alumni Assn., Club: College (Seattle). Lodges: Masons, Shriners.

PARKER, WILLIS LAMONT, publishing cons.; b. nr. Keokuk, Iowa, Oct. 14, 1904; s. Early Spring and Charlotte Jane (Robinson) P.; student Columbia, 1922-26; m. Grace Eleanor Evans, June 23, 1930 (dec. Sept. 1976); children—Sarah Martha, Daniel Evans (dec.). With Guaranty Trust Co., N.Y.C., 1927-30; free-lance editor, N.Y.C., 1930-44; mem. editorial staff U.S. Armed Forces Inst., Washington, 1944-45; with Pitman Pub. Co., N.Y.C., 1945-51, W. W. Norton and Co., N.Y.C., 1951-59; mng. editor Chandler Pub. Co., San Francisco, 1960-71; now pub. cons. Mem. Phi Gamma Delta. Home and Office: 454 Pope St San Francisco CA 94112

PARKS, DONALD ALFRED, geologist; b. N.Y.C., June 9, 1930; s. Arthur and Marie (Irene) P.; m. Barbara Anne Lawson, Aug. 25, 1979. B.A., Hofstra U., 1955; M.S., U. Mass, 1957; Ph.D., NYU, 1973. Cert. petroleum geologist. Prof. geology U. Mass., Amherst, 1955-57; exploration geologist Mobil Oil, Tripoli, Libya, 1957-61; exploration mgr. Pure Oil, Tripoli, 1961-67; staff geologist Newmont Mining, N.Y.C., 1967-72; sr. oil analyst Lehman Bros., N.Y.C., 1972-74; v.p. Bankers Trust Co., N.Y.C., 1974-78; exec. v.p. Catawba Corp., N.Y.C., 1978-79; pres. Taconic Petroleum Corp., N.Y.C., 1978-79, Parks Petroleum Co., N.Y.C. and Carefree, Ariz., 1979—; lectr. in field. Contbr. articles to profl. publs. Mem. Hoover Medal Bd., N.Y.C., 1979—, mem. deans council of 100 Ariz. State U.; bd. dirs. 187th Airborne Regiment Combat Team, 1984—. Served with U.S. Army, 1946-52, Korea, Japan. U. Mass. fellow, 1955-57. Fellow Geol. Soc. Am.; mem. Am. Assn. Petroleum Geologists (past pres. N.Y. chpt.), AIME, Soc. Petroleum Engrs., Am. Inst. Profl. Geologists, Assn. Profl. Geol. Scis., Ind. Petroleum Assn. Am. Republican. Presbyterian. Clubs: Mining, Union League (N.Y.C.). Home and office: PO Box 1406 Carefree Ranch Carefree AZ 85377

PARKS, DONALD LEE, human factors engineer, mechanical engineer; b. Delphos, Kans., Feb. 23, 1931; s. George Delbert and Erma Josephine (Boucek) P.; student Kans. Wesleyan U., 1948-50; B.S.M.E., Kans. State U., 1957, B.S. in Bus. Adminstrn., 1957, M.S. in Psychology, 1959; m. Bessie Lou Schur, Dec. 24, 1952; children—Elizabeth Parks Anderson, Patricia, Donna, Charles, Sandra. Elem. tchr., 1950-51; with Kans. State U. Placement Service, 1957-59; human factors engr., systems engr. Boeing Co., Seattle, 1959—, sr. specialist engr., 1972-74, sr. engring. supr., 1974—; cons., lectr. in field; participant workshops on guidelines in profl. areas, NATO, NSF, Nat. Acad. Sci., NRC. Mem. Derby (Kans.) Planning Commn., 1961-62, chmn., 1962; del. King County (Wash.) Republican Conv., 1972; mem. sci. com. Internat. Transp. Ctr. Served with AUS, 1952-54. Mem. Human Factors Soc. (Puget Sound Pres.'s award 1969), Assn. Aviation Psychologists, ASME, Am. Psychol. Assn., Midwestern Psychol. Assn. Presbyterian. Club: Elks. Contbr. numerous articles to tech. jours., chpts. to books. Home: 6232 127th Ave SE Bellevue WA 98006

PARKS, FLOYD MASON, accounting firm consultant; b. Phila., Dec. 9, 1952; s. Kenneth Earl and Twila Elene (Tomlin) P.; m. Melanie Ann Leonard, Feb. 17, 1979. AAS in Data Processing with distinction, U. So. Colo., 1976, BBA with distinction, 1978; MBA, U. Utah, 1982. Cert. systems profl.; cert. info. systems auditor. Dir. residence hall U. So. Colo., Pueblo, 1978; dir. student family housing U. Utah, Salt Lake City, 1978-79, staff specialist, 1979-82; sr. cons. Deloitte Haskins & Sells, Denver, 1982—. Rep. precinct chmn., Salt Lake City, 1981-82. Served with USNR, 1971-79, USAR, 1979-82, Vietnam. Mem. Am. Mgmt. Assn., Assn. MBA Execs., Mensa. Baptist. Office: Deloitte Haskins & Sells 1560 Broadway Suite 1800 Denver CO 80202

PARKS, GERALD THOMAS, JR., lawyer, business executive; b. Tacoma, Wash., Feb. 25, 1944; s. Gerald Thomas and Elizabeth (Bell) P.; m. Susan Simenstad, July 22, 1967; children—Julie, Christopher; m. 2d, Bonny Kay O'Connor, Jan. 15, 1979, 1 child, Garrett. B.A. in Polit. Sci., U. Wash., 1966; J.D., U. Oreg., 1969. Bar: Wash. 1969. Assoc. Graham & Dunn, 1972-77, ptnr., 1977-82; sole practice, 1982—; sec., treas. Holaday-Parks Fabricators, Inc., 1972-78, v.p., gen. mgr. (named changed to Holaday-Parks, Inc.), 1978-84; pres., chief exec. officer, 1984—. Served to lt. with USN, 1969-72. Mem. Wash. State Bar Assn., ABA. Clubs: Seattle Yacht, Broadmoor Golf, Seattle Tennis. Office: 6th Floor Lowman & Hanford Bldg 616 1st Ave Seattle WA 98104

PARKS, RICHARD DEE, theatre director; b. Omaha, Aug. 29, 1938; s. Charles and Josephine Marie-Rose P. B.A., San Jose State U., 1961; M.A., U. Wash., 1963; postgrad. Stanford U. Tchr. San Jose State U., 1964-65; tchr. oral interpretation Stanford U., 1965-66; tchr. San Jose State U., 1966-71, B.F.A. program U. Wash., 1971-72; dir. theatre San Jose State U., 1972-79, coordinator performance area, 1979—, coordinator auditions, 1975—, chmn. performance area, coordinator M.F.A. performance degree program, 1983—; exchange prof. Ventura Coll., spring 1982; exec. dir. Actors Symposium of Hollywood; actor, dir., producer; sr. producer Star Weekend projects NBC, 1978—; cons. profl. and community theatre orgns.; interim coordinator theatre arts grad. program, 1977-78; dialects coach, voice and diction tutor; research cons. Ednl. Films of Hollywood; cons. Monterey Peninsula's 4th St. Playhouse; cons., dir. Gen. Electric Sales Conf., Pajaro Dunes, 1983. Winner New Play Directing award Am. Coll. Theatre Festival Region I, 1975. Mem. Calif. Ednl. Theatre Assn. (exec. sec.-treas. 1978-80), Am. Theatre Assn., AAUP, Calif. Assn. Am. Conservatory Theatre, Am. Coll. Theatre Festival, Am. Film Inst., Dramatists Guild, Authors League Am. Episcopalian. Clubs: Brit. Am., San Jose Players. Author: How to Overcome Stage Fright, 1978; American Drama Anthology, 1979; (plays) Charley Parkhurst Rides Again!, 1978, Wild West Women, 1980, Ken Kesey's Further Inquiry, 1980; (book) Career Preparation for the TV-Film Actor, 1981; (play) stage adaptation of Tandem Prodns. Facts of Life, 1982; (teaching supplement) Calendar of American Theatre History, 1982; The Role of Myth in Understanding Amber in the Ancient World, 1983; How to Overcome Stage Fright, 1984; (textbook) Oral Expression, 1985, 2d. rev. edit., 1986. Office: Theatre Arts Dept San Jose State University San Jose CA 95192

PARKS, THOMAS RICHARD, food scientist; b. Melrose Park, Ill., Mar. 26, 1931; s. Clarence Thomas Parks and Goldie May Sheets; m. Althea Sayward, July 9, 1960; children: Richard, Alison. BS, U. Mass, 1953, MS, 1958. Process engr. Gerber Products Co., Oakland, Calif., 1959-62; mgr. product engring. research StarKist Food, Terminal Island, Calif., 1962-69; mgr. process engring. research Stanford Research Inst., Menlo Park, Calif., 1969-79; pres., chmn. bd. Food and AgroSystems Inc., Sunnyvale, Calif., 1979—; bd. dirs. Mitchell-Lane, Ind., Spokane, Wash.; cons in field. Inventor in field. Served to lt (j.g.) USNR, 1953-57. Mem. Inst. Food Technologists, Food Processing Machine and Supplies Assn. Republican. Methodist. Avocations: woodcarving, inventing, naval architecture. Home: 1289 Mandarin Dr Sunnyvale CA 94087 Office: Food and AgroSystems Inc PO Box 62185 Sunnyvale CA 94088

PARMA, FLORENCE VIRGINIA, magazine editor; b. Kenilworth, N.J., Aug. 30, 1940; d. Howard Frank and Mildred Faye (Lister) von Finkel; m. Wilson Henry Parma, June 15, 1973 (div. Aug. 1986). Studies with pvt. tutor, Chaumont, France, 1961-62; student, NYU, 1962-63. Copywriter Schless & Co., N.Y.C., 1963-65; editor, researcher Barchas Lab., Stanford, Calif., 1969-73; adminstrv. exec. Crater Inc., Honolulu, 1974-79; mgr., editor Off Duty mag., Honolulu, 1979—. Editor: Welcome to Hawaii Guide, 1985-86; co-editor: Serotonin and Behavior, 1972; freelance columnist. Republican. Episcopalian. Avocations: scuba diving, stained glass, hiking. Home: 3138 Waialae Ave #720 Honolulu HI 96816

PARMENTER, ROBERT HALEY, physics educator; b. Portland, Maine, Sept. 19, 1925; s. LeClare Fall and Esther (Haley) P.; m. Elizabeth Kinnecom, Oct. 27, 1951; children: David Alan, Douglas Ian. B.S., U. Maine, 1947; Ph.D., Mass. Inst. Tech., 1952. Mem. staff solid state and molecular theory group Mass. Inst. Tech., 1951-54; guest scientist Brookhaven Nat. Lab., 1951-52; mem. staff Lincoln Lab., 1952-54, RCA Labs., 1954-66; vis. scientists RCA Labs., Zurich, Switzerland, 1958; acting head solid state research group RCA Labs., 1962-65; prof. physics U. Ariz., 1966—, chmn. dept., 1977-83; mem. NASA research adv. com. electrophysics, 1964-68, chmn., 1966-68; mem. NASA research and tech. adv. com. basic research, 1966-68. Served with USNR, 1944-46. Fellow AAAS, Am. Phys. Soc.; mem. Sigma Xi, Tau Beta Pi. Home: 1440 E Ina Rd Tucson AZ 85718

PARMERLEE-GREINER, GLORIA ROSALIE, educator, coordinator; b. Pueblo, Colo., Sept. 4, 1940; d. Thomas Henry Whalen and Gladys Pearl (Parker) W.; m. Roscoe Hale Parmerlee, III, July 12, 1969 (dec.); m. Floyd Dale Greiner, July 31, 1982; children—Tannya Lynn Lane, Scott Gale Lane. B.A. with honors, U. So. Colo., 1968; M.A., U. Colo., 1973; postgrad. Colo. State U., U. No. Colo., U. Colo., Colo. Sch. Mines. Tchr., Boulder, 1969-80, coordinator and tchr. teen parenting program, 1980—. Mem. Colo. Ednl. Assn., Boulder Valley Schs. Ednl. Assn., NEA, Am. Home Econs. Assn., Colo. Home Economics Assn., Am. Vocat. Assn., Colo. Vocat. Assn., Phi Beta Kappa, Delta Kappa Gamma. Presbyterian. Contbr. articles to profl. jours. and popular mags. Home: 1755 Foothills Dr S Golden CO 80401

PARONI, GENEVIEVE MARIE SWICK, educator; b. Eureka, Nev., July 27, 1926; d. William Jackson and Myrtle Rose (Smith) S.; m. Walter Andrew Paroni, Dec. 26, 1954; 1 child, Andrea Marie. BA, U. Nev., Reno, 1948; MEd, U. Idaho, 1978; postgrad., MIT, Oreg. State U., U. Oreg., U. Wash., Ft. Wright Coll., U. Portland. Cert. elem. and secondary sect., Nev. Tchr., vice prin. Eureka County High Sch., 1948-66; assayer Eureka Corp. Mine, 1958; coast geodetic U.S. Govt., Eureka, 1950's; tchr., facilitator Dist. #393, Wallace, Idaho, 1968—; gov. library bd. State of Nev., Carson City, 1950; regional dir. NSTA, Idaho, Panhandle, 1982—; chmn. in service adv. State Dept. Edn., Boise, Idaho, 1980-83; commr. State Sci. Commn., State Dept. Edn., Boise, 1981-82. Contbr. history articles to profl. jours. Active Wallace City Council, 1970-80; library bd. mem. Wallace Pub. Library, 1983—; precinct chmn. Republicans, Wallace, 1970-80; bd. dirs. Greater Wallace, 1980—. Grantee Idaho Power, 1985; named Outstanding Tchr., Dist. #393, 1975. Mem. NEA, Idaho Edn. Assn., Wallace Edn. Assn. (sec. 1970's), AAUW (pres. 1970's), Bus. and Profl. Women Assn. (v.p. Nev. chpt. 1953-55), Delta Kappa Gamma (pres. 1980-82), Phi Delta Kappa. Episcopalian. Lodge: Pythian Sisters (Grand Guard, 1950), Order of Eastern Star (matron Nev. chpt.). Avocations: ch. organist, oil and water color painting, silversmithing. Office: Sch Dist #393 River St PO Box 500 Wallace ID 83873

PARONI, WALTER ANDREW, mining engineer; b. Berkeley, Calif., Dec. 5, 1921; s. Walter Andrew and Dorthea (Roust) P.; m. Genevieve Marie Swick, Dec. 26, 1954; 1 child, Andrea Marie. BS, U. Calif., Berkeley, 1950. Registered profl. engr., Nev. Mining engr. Kennecott Copper, Bingham, Utah, 1950; civil engr. Richmond/San Rafael br., Richmond, Calif., 1951-52; chief engr. Eureka (Nev.) Corp., Ltd., 1952-63; mining engr. Ruby Hill project Hecla Mining Co., Eureka, 1963-66; sr. mining engr. Hecla Mining Co., Wallace, Idaho, 1968—; v.p. engring. A.C. LoPrest Co., San Francisco, 1966-67. Mem. regional planning commn. State of Nev., Eureka, 1960s; trustee Eureka County Schs., 1954; warden St. James Episcopal Ch., Eureka, 1960s; bd. dirs. N.E. Nev. council Boy Scouts. Am., Ely, 1950s. Mem. AIME. Lodges: Lions, Masons (master, treas. Eureka chpt. 1950s-60s, Outstanding Service 1966), Elks, Shriners.

PARQUE, RICHARD ANTHONY, education and training consultant; b. Los Angeles, Aug. 10, 1935; s. Joe and Helen Margaret (Muto) P.; m. Vo Thi Lan, May 1, 1975; children—Kenneth, Phat, James. B.A., Calif. State U.-Los Angeles, 1958, M.A., 1966; postgrad. U. Redlands, 1966. Cert. life state teaching credential, Calif. Tchr. Yucaipa (Calif.) High School, 1961-66; sci. edn. adv. Calif. State U. System, 1966-68; profl. devel. adminstr. McDonnell Douglas Astronautics Co., 1968-71; prin. Parque Cons. Assocs., 1971-77, 79—; corp. dir. edn. and tng. Ralph M. Parsons Co., 1977-78; adj. faculty Calif. State U.-San Diego, 1966-68, U. Calif.-Irvine, 1972-73, Calif. State U.-Los Angeles, 1980, UCLA, 1982. Served with USMC, 1958-61. Recipient NASA Sci. Teaching award, 1966, numerous athletic awards. Mem. Am. Soc. Tng. and Devel., Organizational Devel. Network, Nat. Mgmt. Assn., Nat. Sci. Tchrs. Assn., Calif. Tchrs. Assn., Nat. Audubon Soc., Cons. Network, Internat. Trumpet Guild. Republican. Author: Sweet Vietnam, 1984; Hellbound, 1985, Firefight, 1986, Flight of the Phantom, 1987. Contbr. numerous articles to profl. jours., poetry to anthologies. Office: PO Box 327 Verdugo City CA 91046

PARRICK, GERALD HATHAWAY, communication and marketing executive; b. Cushing, Okla., Oct. 27, 1924; s. Gerald H. and Phyllis A. (Sheppard) P.: B.J., U. Mo., 1948; m. Gail V. Straney, Dec. 5, 1984; children: Gerald Hathaway III, Candace Anne. Creative account exec. George Knox & Assoc., Oklahoma City, 1948-51; account exec. Batten, Barton, Durstine & Osborn, San Francisco, 1952-60; account dir. McCann-Erickson, Los Angeles, 1960-67, v.p., Portland, Oreg., 1967-72; dir. communications Pacific Power Co., Portland, 1972-77, spl. asst. to chmn. bd., 1977-79; pres. Entreepublic Communications, West Linn, Oreg., 1979—, Bailey/Parrick, Inc., Portland, 1981-84, Parrick/Milpacher, Inc., Portland, 1984-85; The Laugh Clinic, Inc., Portland, 1984—. Author: A 20th Century Miracle, 1981. Mem. Oreg. Advt. Rev. Bd., 1974-75. Served to capt. AUS, 1943-45, 51-52, ETO. Named Oreg. Advt. Man of Yr., Oreg. Advt. Club, 1971. Mem. Am. Advt. Fedn. (chmn. edn. western region 1973-74), Portland Advt. Fedn. (pres. 1974-75), Kappa Tau Alpha. Club: Toastmasters (pres. 1966-67) (Encino, Calif.). Home: 3950 Elmran Dr West Linn OR 97068

PARRISH, GEORGE R(ODERICK), architectural specifications writer; b. Litchfield, Minn., Apr. 19, 1943; s. Clarence Lestor and Georgia Jane (Fitze) P.; m. Donna Jean Sjogren, June 11, 1966; children: Catherine Jeneen, Robert Thomas, Michelle Marie. Student, U. Minn., 1962-63, Winona State Coll., 1964-66, Roosevelt U., 1982. Cert. constrn. specifier. Archtl. draftsman Setter Leach & Lindstrom, Inc., Mpls., 1966-68, Armstrong, Schlichting, Torseth & Skold, Inc., Mpls., 1968-72; chief specifications writer and archtl. draftsman Chapman Desai Sakata, Inc., Honolulu, 1972—, sr. assoc., 1983—; prin. specifications cons. G. Parrish Services, Kailua, Hawaii, 1981—; guest speaker U. Hawaii Sch. Architecture; guest instr. Earle M. Alexander, Ltd. Author/editor (computer program package) Office Cost Control System, 1982, 4th rev. edit., 1984. Mem. Constrn. Specifications Inst. (v.p. Honolulu chpt. 1985-86, pres. 1986-87, Certificate of Appreciation for Ednl. Service 1979, Certificate of Appreciation 1980, 1981). Roman Catholic. Home: 647 N Kainalu Dr Kailua HI 96734 Office: Chapman Desai Sakata Inc 1001 Bishop St Pauahi Tower Suite 400 Honolulu HI 96813-3499

PARRISH, MICHAEL UDY, editor; b. Salt Lake City, Nov. 13, 1945; s. LaMar Steed and Lona (Udy) P.; m. Judie Lewellen, May 22, 1981; 1 child, Suzanne Lewellen. BA, Reed Coll., 1970. Editorial asst. I.F. Stone's Biweekly, 1970; mng. editor San Francisco Fault, 1971; editorial prodn. mgr. L.A. newspaper, 1972; mng. editor San Francisco mag., 1973-75; editor City Mag., San Francisco, 1975, Los Angeles Free Press, 1976; asst. editor opinion sect., editorial page Los Angeles Times, 1977-79; assoc. editor news and features Los Angeles Times mag., 1985, editor, 1985—. Contbr. articles to profl. pubs., includingLife, Smithsonian, Calif. mags. Office: Los Angeles Times Mag Times Mirror Sq Los Angeles CA 90053

PARRON, RONALD LEE, account executive; b. Orlando, Fla., Mar. 29, 1958; s. Ronald Leon and Annette (Harper) P. Grad. high sch., Orlando. Regional energy dir. McDonald's Corp., St. Petersburg, Fla., 1979, regional drive-thru coordinator, 1980-81; equipment purchasing mgr. Sigmacon div. Gen. Mills, Orlando, 1981-82; area maintenance engr. Sambo's Restaurants, Carpinteria, Calif., 1982-83; N.W. zone Constrn. coordinator Foodmaker, Inc., San Diego, 1983-84; West coast field engr. Vicorp Restaurants, Denver, 1985; account exec. Raygal Design Assocs., Irvine, Calif., 1985—. Debate mem. Nat. Forensics League, Orlando, 1976; mem. Future Scientists Am., Miami, Fla., 1973. Recipient Gold medal Am. Legion, Orlando, 1976, 1st Place plaque Am. Legion, Orlando, 1976. Republican. Presbyterian. Avocations: computers, stereos.

PARROTT, DENNIS BEECHER, employee benefit cons.; b. St. Louis, June 13, 1929; s. Maurice Ray and Mai Ledgerwood (Beecher) P.; B.S. in Econs., Fla. State U., Tallahassee, 1954; postgrad. Princeton U., 1964; M.B.A., Pepperdine U., 1982; m. Vivian Cleveland Miller, Mar. 24, 1952; children—Constance Beecher, Dennis Beecher, Anne Cleveland. With Prudential Ins. Co. Am., 1954-74, v.p. group ins. mktg., Los Angeles, 1971-74; sr. v.p. Frank B. Hall Cons. Co., Los Angeles, 1974-83; v.p. Johnson & Higgins, Los Angeles, 1983—; speaker in field. Chmn. Weekend with the Stars Telethon, 1976-80; chmn. bd. dirs. United Cerebral Palsy/Spastic Children's Found. Los Angeles County, 1979-82, chmn. bd. govs., 1982-83; bd. dirs. Nat. United Cerebral Palsy Assn., 1977-82, pres., 1977-79; mem. community adv. council Birmingham High Sch., Van Nuys, Calif., 1982-85 ;

sect. chmn. United Way, Los Angeles, 1983-84; bd. dirs. The Betty Clooney Found. for Brain Injured, 1986—; mem. com. to fund an endowed chair in cardiology at Cedars-Sinai Med. Ctr., 1986—; adv. council Family Health Program Inc., 1986—. Served to 1st lt. AUS, 1951-53. C.L.U. Mem. Am. Soc. C.L.U.s, Internat. Found. Employee Benefits, Merchants and Mfrs. Assns. 44th Annual Mgmt. Conf. (chmn. 1986), Employee Benefits Planning Assn. So. Calif. Republican. Presbyterian. Clubs: Los Angeles, Woodland Hills Country, Jonathan (Los Angeles). Office: One Century Plaza 2029 Century Park E Los Angeles CA 90067

PARROTT, DENNIS LLOYD, lawyer; b. Des Moines, May 13, 1944; s. Alva Dennis and Myra Harriet (Larson) P.; m. Jeanne Kathleen Felix, Nov. 10, 1972; children: Stanley Edward, Lloyd Christopher. BA, U. Ariz., 1966, JD, 1970. Bar: Ariz. 1971, U.S. Dist. Ct. Ariz. 1973. Asst. researcher Max Planck Inst., Hamburg, Fed. Republic Germany, 1971; researcher Metra Divo, Frankfurt-Niederrad, Fed. Republic Germany, 1971; staff atty. Office of Prosecutor, City of Phoenix, 1971-72; sole practice, Tucson, 1972—. Office: 6812 N Oracle Rd Suite 114 Tucson AZ 85704

PARRY, ATWELL, JR., state senator, retailer; b. Ogden, Utah, June 14, 1925; s. John Atwell and Nina Virginia (McEntire) P.; m. Elaine Hughes, Feb. 6, 1946; children—Bonnie, Michael, Jay, Donald, David, Delbert, Kent. Student pub. schs., Nampa, Idaho. Salesman, King's Packing Co., Nampa, 1947-54, credit mgr., 1954-55; plant mgr. Stone Poultry Co., Nampa, 1955-56; salesman Nestle Chocolate Co., 1956-64; owner, mgr. Melba Foods, Idaho, 1964-82; mem. Idaho Senate, 1981—. Bd dirs. Alcohol Treatment Ctr., Nampa, 1978-82; mem. adv. bd. Mercy Med. Ctr., Nampa, 1976—; mem. Melba City Council, 1971-74. Recipient Silver Beaver award Boy Scouts Am., 1959, Service award Mercy Med. Ctr. Republican. Mormon.

PARRY, ROBERT TROUTT, economist; b. Harrisburg, Pa., May 16, 1939; s. Anthony C. and Margaret R. (Troutt) P.; m. Brenda Louise Grumbine, Dec. 27, 1956; children: Robert Richard, Lisa Louise. BA magna cum laude, Gettysburg (Pa.) Coll., 1960; MA in Econs, U. Pa., 1961, PhD, 1967. Asst. prof. econs. Phila. Coll. Textiles and Sci., 1963-65; economist Fed. Res. Bd., Washington, 1965-70; v.p., chief economist Security Pacific Nat. Bank, Los Angeles, 1970-76, sr. v.p., chief economist, 1976-81, exec. v.p., chief economist, 1981-86; pres., chief exec. officer Fed. Res. Bank San Francisco, 1986—; former dir. exec. com. Bunker Hill Income Securities Inc.; dir. Nat. Bur. Econ. Research; mem. adv. bd. Pacific Rim Bankers Program; adv. bd. Ctr. for Fin. and Real Estate; dir. San Francisco Bay Area Council; lectr. Pacific Coast Banking Sch., 1976-78. Contbr. articles to profl. jours. NDEA fellow, 1960-63. Mem. Nat. Assn. Bus. Economists (pres. 1979-80), Am. Bankers Assn. (chmn. econ. adv. com.), Calif. Bankers Assn. (bd. dirs. 1982-83), Am. Econs. Assn., Western Econs. Assn. Home: 90 Overhill Rd Orinda CA 94563 Office: Fed Res Bank San Francisco PO Box 7702 San Francisco CA 94120

PARSONS, ERIC KEITH, research scientist; b. Lewistown, Mont., Oct. 9, 1951; s. Kenneth Robert Parsons and Dorothy Helen (Upham) Dewit; m. Cathryn Jean Tait, Feb. 14, 1986. B Applied Sci., U. Toronto, 1974; MS, Stanford U., 1976, PhD, 1982. Research asst. U. Toronto, Ont., Can., 1973-74, Stanford (Calif.) U., 1974-80; assoc. research scientist Lockheed Corp. research and devel. div., Palo Alto, Calif., 1980-85, research scientist, 1985—; cons. NASA Ames Research Ctr., Mountain View, Calif., 1979-80. Recipient Canadian Bechtel Bursary award, 1974. Mem. AIAA, Sigma Xi. Republican. Avocations: ball room dancing, hiking, camping, skiing. Home: 780 Las Lomas Dr Milpitas CA 95035 Office: Lockheed Palo Alto Research Lab Dept 92-30 Bldg 205 3251 Hanover St Palo Alto CA 94304

PARSONS, LEONARD LELAND, electrical and optical engineer; b. Portland, Oreg., Oct. 5, 1945; s. Ernest Bert and Marjorie (Shaw) P.; m. Sylvia F.M. LeSage, June 20, 1970; children: Mark Allen, JoAnne Frances. Enlisted USN, 1963, chief electronics technician, 1963-83, retired, 1983; mfg. engr. Tektronix Inc., Redmond, Oreg., 1983-85, mgr. optics lab., 1984-85, mgr. test and staff engrs., 1986—; tchr. USN, San Francisco, 1969-72; tech. rep., cons. USN, Pearl Harbor, Hawaii, 1976-80; logistics coordinator USN, Indian Ocean, 1980-82; electronics advisor Vietnam Navy, Quin Yon, 1966-67. Leader 4-H Club Electronics, Madras, Oreg., 1984. Mem. Soc. Reliability Engrs. Democrat. Avocations: computer programming, gentleman farmer. Home: 590 SE Dover Ln Madras OR 97741 Office: Tektronix Inc 635 SE Salmon Redmond OR 97756

PARSONS, PHILIP TABER, health science professional; b. Oakland, Calif., May 5, 1927; s. Augustus Taber and Emma (Sawyer) P.; m. Margaret Hastings, Dec. 11, 1965; 1 child, Carol Emma. BS in Chemistry, Stanford U., 1948; AA in Indsl. Mgmt., Coll. San Mateo, 1964. Registered sanitarian, Calif. Owner Bay Pest Control Co., San Mateo, Calif., 1948-57; chemist Yosemite Chem. Co., San Francisco, 1957; research asst. Stanford (Calif.) U., 1958-65; sanitarian County of San Mateo, Redwood, Calif., 1965—. Mem. Water Pollution Control Fedn. Republican. Episcopalian. Clubs: Emerald Lake Country (Redwood City) (bd. dirs. 1977-79), Met. Yacht (Oakland), Commonwealth (San Francisco). Home: 62 W Summit Dr Redwood City CA 94062 Office: San Mateo Office Environ Health 590 Hamilton St Redwood City CA 94063

PARSONS, ROBERT (JACK), filmmaker, photographer; b. N.Y.C., Apr. 30, 1939; s. Henry McIlvaine and Renee (Oakman) P.; m. Joan Rebecca Mason, Sept. 1, 1961; children—Alexander McIlvaine, Christopher William. B.A., U. Colo., 1962; M.A., 1965; diploma London Sch. Film Technique, 1967. Ptnr., Blue Sky Prodns., Santa Fe, 1975-81; ptnr., v.p. Pub. Media, Inc., Santa Fe, 1981-84. Cinematographer: Weave of Time, 1986 (Earthwatch award Margaret Mead Film Festival); Gembaku Shi (Killed by the Atomic Bomb), 1984; producer: La Musica de los Viejos, 1983; cinematographer, project dir.: Slim Green (Merit award Western Heritage awards, Cowboy Hall of Fame), 1981; co-producer, cinematographer: Pancho Villa's Columbus Raid (Am. Film Festival), 1983; producer, cinematographer: Luisa Torres (Silver medal MLA), 1981; cinematographer: Rio Grande (N.Mex. Bicentennial film, Bronze medal N.Y. Internat. Film and TV Festival, Am. Film Festival), 1976; author, stills photographer: (with Michael Earney) Land and Cattle, 1978; contbr. photog.: Cowboy, 1984; Santa Fe, The City in Photographs, 1984k, Santa Fe Style, 1986. Mem. Santa Fe Ctr. for Photography, Sierra Club, Nature Conservancy. Home: 1281 Cerro Gordo Santa Fe NM 87501 Office: 355 E Palace Ave Santa Fe NM 87501

PARSONS, THOMAS SAMUEL, university administrator; b. Niles, Mich., Mar. 24, 1924; s. Cecil Bernard and Dorothy May (Elder) P.; m. Sara Bedell Perry, Dec. 18, 1968; children: Timothy Dion, Pamela Lynn. AB, U. Mich., 1950, MS, 1952, PhC, 1962. Registered psychologist, Ill. Research dir. Charles S. Mott Found., Flint, Mich., 1952-63; lectr., research assoc. U. Mich., Ann Arbor, 1953-63; research dir. Joint Youth Devel. Commn., Chgo., 1963-64; owner, cons. Community Edn. Assocs., Park Forest, Ill., 1964-67; assoc. dean Pub. Services, dir. Ctr. Community Devel. Calif. State U., Humboldt, 1967—. Editor: The Tolowa Language, 1984, Handbook of Community Development and Services, 1984; contbr. articles to profl. jours.; producer Again A Person I've Become, 1982. Bd. dirs. The Am. Lung Assn. Calif., Oakland, 1985—, pres. 1982-83; pres. United Way of Humboldt, Eureka, Calif., 1983-84. Served to staff sgt. USAAF, 1942-45, ETO. Decorated D.F.C. Air medal with three oak leaf clusters; recipient Innovation award Nat. U. Extension Assn., Am. Coll. Testing Program, 1973, Community Devel. Achievement award Community Devel. Soc., 1984. Mem. Am. Sociol. Assn., Am. Psychol. Assn., Internat. Soc. Polit. Psychology, Nat. U. Continuing Edn. Assn. (chmn. community devel. div. 1979-80, Innovation in Community Devel. award 1980, Spl. Program award 1983, Philip E. Frandson award 1986), 8th Air Force Hist. Soc. (life), 2d Air Div. Assn., Phi Delta Kappa (life), Phi Kappa Phi (life). Democrat. Episcopalian. Avocations: downhill and cross country skiing, sailing, fishing. Home: 1589 Stewart Ct Arcata CA 95521 Office: Calif State U Humboldt Ctr for Community Devel Arcata CA 95521

PARTAIN, LARRY DEAN, solar research engineer; b. McKinney, Tex., Apr. 27, 1942; s. Archie Leon and Vergie Ann (Young) P.; m. Deborah Patton, July 1986. B.S.E.E., U. Tenn., 1965; Ph.D., Johns Hopkins U., 1971. Assoc. prof. elec. engring. U. Del., Newark, 1971-78; engr. Engring. Research div. Lawrence Livermore Nat. Lab., Calif., 1978-80; sr. research engr. Chevron Research Co., Richmond, Calif., 1980-87; sr. scientist Varian Research Ctr., Palo Alto, Calif., 1987—. Contbr. articles to tech. jours.; patentee microwave sensor, solar cell. Grantee Solar Energy Research Inst., 1978-79, 84-86; duPont research grantee, 1974-75; grantee U.S. Air Force Wright Aeronautical Lab., 1984-85, Sandia Nat. Labs., 1985-86. Mem. IEEE, Sigma Xi. Office: Varian Research Ctr 611 Hansen Way Palo Alto CA 94303

PARTEE, DONNA MARKLE, psychiatric social worker, nurse; b. Danville, Pa., May 5, 1946; d. George Bushar IV and Donna (Umstead) M.; m. Morriss Henry Partee, Aug. 26, 1972; children: Donna Faith, Marian Dewar; stepchildren: Morriss Mark, David Matthew, Joel Timothy. BA, Smith Coll., 1968; MS in Nursing, N.Y. Med. Coll., 1970; MSW, U. Utah, 1984. RN; cert. social worker; lic. clin. social worker. Psychiat. nurse Roosevelt Hosp., N.Y.C., 1970-71, Neuropsychiat. Inst., Los Angeles, 1971-72, Murray (Utah) Jordan Mental Health, 1973; social worker, psychiat. nurse Valley West Mental Health, Kearns, Utah, 1984—. Mem. League Women Voters, Salt Lake City, 1977-86; deacon First Presbyn. Ch., Salt Lake City, 1981-84; choir mem. First Presbyn./Mt. Olympus Presbyn., Salt Lake City, 1974—. Mem. Nat. Assn. Social Workers, Phi Beta Kappa, Phi Kappa Phi. Avocations: choral singing, Spanish, travel.

PARTIN, RICHARD ALLEN, account operations manager, data processor; b. Eugene, Oreg., Oct. 20, 1941; s. Donald Sinclair and Wanda Glen (Loughary) P.; m. Lecta Faye Waddell, Sept. 26, 1971. BBA, Oreg. State U., 1964; MBA, Golden Gate U., 1980. Systems engr. trainee Electronic Data Systems, San Francisco, 1971; asst. data entry mgr. Electronic Data Systems, Los Angeles, 1972; data entry mgr. Electronic Data Systems, Santa Barbara, Calif., 1972-80, account ops. mgr., 1980—; project mgr., cons. United Airlines, Chgo., 1976-77; transition mgr., cons. Tex. Blue Cross, Dallas, 1979. Author, editor: (tng. book) EDS Managers Guide for Managers of Production Employees, 1978, Meeting the Challenge of the Union Organizer, 1972, (tng. course) Supervisor Training Course, 1973. Sec. bd. dirs. Work Inc. (handicapped workshop), Santa Barbara, 1984. Served to capt. USMC, 1964-71. Decorated D.F.C. with one bronze oak leaf cluster; Air medal. Republican. Methodist. Lodge: Kiwanis (local pres. 1977-78, treas. 1984-86, div. sec. 1981-82). Avocations: pvt. aviation, raising collies. Home: 411 E Figueroa St Santa Barbara CA 93101 Office: Electronic Data Systems Corp 735 State St Suite 100 Santa Barbara CA 93101

PARTINGTON, CYRUS WILLIAM, radiologist; b. Denver, July 10, 1925; s. Cyrus Brown and Margaret (Crotty) P.; B.S., La. Poly. U., 1949; M.D., U. Colo., 1949, M.S. in Radiology, 1955; m. Nancy Clair Farrell, Aug. 6, 1955; children—Anne Elizabeth, Mary Margaret, Nancy Jane, Ellen Catherine, Cyrus William Walmsley. Intern, U. Hosp., Madison, Wis., 1949-50; resident VA Hosp., U. Colo., 1952-55; practice medicine, specializing in radiology, Colorado Springs, Colo., 1955—; radiologist St. Francis Hosp., Colorado Springs, 1955-75, dir. radiology, 1975—, vice chief staff, 1964, chief staff, 1971-72; staff radiologist Evans Army Hosp., Ft. Carson, Colo.; cons. radiologist USAF Clinic, Peterson Field, Colo., USAF Hosp., Colorado Springs. Bd. dirs. Regis Coll., Denver. Served with M.C., USNR, 1950-52. Cert. Am. Bd. Radiology in radiology and nuclear radiology; diplomate Nat Bd. Med. Examiners. Fellow Am. Coll. Radiology; mem. AMA, Colo., El Paso County med. socs., Radiol. Soc. N.Am., Rocky Mountain, Colo. (treas. 1960-63) radiol. socs., U. Wis. Med. Alumni Assn., Soc. Nuclear Medicine, Am. Coll. Nuclear Medicine (charter), Am. Coll. Nuclear Physicians, U. Colo. Med. Alumni Assn., Catholic Physicians Guild, Phi Kappa Phi, Nu Sigma Nu. Republican. Roman Catholic. Clubs: Rotaryan (pres. Colorado Springs 1970-71); Broadmoor Golf. Home: 30 Tanglewood Dr Broadmoor Colorado Springs CO 80906 Office: St Francis Hosp Colorado Springs CO 80903

PARTOVI, PARVIZ, physician; b. Bojnoord, Iran, Nov. 9, 1936; came to U.S., 1961; s. Ziaollah and Maryam (Jahanbani) P. MD, U. Tehran, 1960. Diplomate Am. Bd. Surgery. Intern St. Margaret Meml. Hosp., Pitts., 1961-62, resident in pathology, 1962-63; resident in surgery U. Louisville Hosps., 1963-67; surgeon Muehlenburg Hosp., Greenville, Ky., 1970-71, VA Hosp. Livermore (Calif.), 1971-72; pvt. practice specializing in surgery Spokane, Wash., 1972—. Fellow ACS, Internat. Coll. Surgeons; mem. AMA, World Med. Assn. Home: PO Box 28104 Spokane WA 99218-8104 Office: N 5901 Lidgerwood Suite 219 Spokane WA 99207

PARVIN, ROSE A., marriage and family counselor; b. Iran, Feb. 8, 1950; naturalized, 1985; d. Ebraheim and Hamdam (Mostashar) Assier; m. Ben. A. Parvin, Aug. 22, 1971 (div.); children: Ellie, Shaun. BA in Psychology, Calif. State U., Long Beach, 1976; MA in Marriage and Family Counseling, Chapman Coll., 1981. Lic. marriage, family and child counseling, Calif. Counseling coordinator, clin. supr. Free Clinic fo Orange County, Anaheim, Calif., 1982-85; clin. supr. Laguna Beach (Calif.) Free Clinic, 1984-85; family counselor, exec. dir., founder Parvin Ctr. Devel. Health, Newport Beach and Beverly, Calif., 1985—; lectr., seminar leader, researcher in field. Mem. adv. bd. YWCA, 1985—. Mem. Calif. Assn. Marriage and Family Counselors, Am. Personnel and Guidance Assn., Am. Assn. Counseling and Devel., Orange County Assn. Marriage and Family Therapists. Republican. Moslem. Home: 3135 Breakers Dr Corona Del Mar CA 92683 Office: 1501 Westcliff Dr Suite 318 Newport Beach CA 92660 Office: 414 Camden Dr Suite 905 Beverly Hills CA 90210

PARZANESE, ANTHONY JOSEPH, SR., photographer; b. Hazleton, Pa., Feb. 19, 1939; s. Tony Fortunato and Helen Margaret (Demyon) P.; m. Anna Victoria Radosky, Nov. 4, 1961; children—Anthony Joseph, Teresa M. Eastman, Vincent G., Angela A. Grad. Central Bucks High Sch., 1957. Photographic chief U.S. Marine Corps, 1956-77; owner, operator Parzanese Photography, Escondido, Calif., 1978—. Decorated Vietnamese Cross of Gallantry. Mem. Profl. Photographers Am., Profl. Photographers Calif., Fleet Res. Assn. Republican. Roman Catholic. Clubs: Escondido East Rotary (pres. 1982-83, Paul Harris fellow 1984).

PASCHKE, DONALD VERNON, music educator; b. Menominee, Mich., Oct. 22, 1929; s. Leo Carl Ferdinand and Augusta O. (Fritz) P.; m. Helen Inez Burton, Feb. 17, 1951; children: David Vernon, Celeste Eileen. MusB, BS in Choral Music Edn., U. Ill., 1957, MusM in Voice, 1958; D Mus. Arts, U. Colo., 1972. Instr. music Berea (Ky.) Coll., 1958-62; asst. prof. music Eastern N.Mex. U., Portales, 1962-71, assoc. prof., 1971-76, prof., 1976—. Translator, editor: A Complete Treatise on the Art of Singing, Part Two, 1975; Part One, 1984. Songleader Portales Men's Breakfast, 1976—, pres. 1974-76. Served with U.S. Army, 1951-53. Mem. NEA, Music Educators Nat. Conf., N.Mex. Music Educators Assn., Nat. Assn. Tchrs. Singing (lt. gov. N.Mex. 1968-72, v.p. Gt. Plains chpt. 1972-74, chpt. pres. 1974-78), Pi Kappa Lambda, Phi Kappa Phi. Republican. Presbyterian. Avocations: photography, do-it-yourself projects. Home: 228 Kansas Dr Portales NM 88130 Office: Eastern NMex U Sch Music Portales NM 88130

PASCOA, ORLANDO SANTOS, school counselor; b. Oakland, Calif., Dec. 27, 1942; s. Joao dos Santos and Leonilda Viera (Norte) P.; B.A., San Francisco State U., 1970; M.S. in Counseling, Calif. State U., Hayward, 1978. Technician, Xerox Corp., 1967-69; tchr. indsl. edn. Oakland pub. schs., 1971-77, counselor secondary sch., 1977—. Standard secondary teaching credential, pupil personnel services credential, community coll. counselor and instr. credentials, Calif. Mem. Am. Assn. for Counseling and Devel., Calif. Assn. for Counseling and Devel., NEA, Calif. Tchrs. Assn., Oakland Edn. Assn., Calif. Secondary Counselor Assn. Democrat. Roman Catholic. Office: 12250 Skyline Blvd Oakland CA 94619

PASCOE, GARY ALAN, research toxicologist; b. Phila., Nov. 28, 1952; s. Lucien Arthur and Mary Helen (Rottinghaus) P. BA, U. Calif., San Diego, 1976; PhD, U. Calif., San Francisco, 1983. Research assoc. Oreg. State U., Corvallis, 1983-86; owner Toxicology Info. Services, Seattle, 1986—. Contbr. articles biochem. jour.; editor newsletter Quilting and Computers, 1986. Predoctoral traineeship NIH, 1980; postdoctoral fellow Nat. Inst. Environ. Health Scis., 1983, fellow U. Wash. Dept. Medicinal Chemistry, 1986—. Mem. AAAS, ACS, Pacific N.W. Assn. Toxicologists, Sierra Club (info. dissemination, San Francisco 1982, voter registration drive Corvallis 1984). Avocations: backpacking, skiing. Home: 14311 19H Ave NE Seattle WA 98125 Office: U Wash Dept Medicinal Chemistry Seattle WA 98195

PASELK, RICHARD ALAN, chemist, educator; b. Inglewood, Calif., July 20, 1945; s. Robert Arthur and Doris Mae (Miller) P.; m. Gail Annette Gulliver, Mar. 18, 1967; children: Laura Ann, Deborah Ailene. BS in Biophysics, Calif. State U., Los Angeles, 1968; PhD in Biochemistry, U. So. Calif., 1975. Research tech. U. So. Calif. Sch. Medicine, Los Angeles, 1968-69; lectr. Calif. State U., Long Beach, 1974-76; asst. prof. Humboldt State U., Arcata, Calif., 1976-81; assoc. prof. Humboldt State U., Arcata, 1981-86, prof., chmn. dept. chemistry, 1986—. Tech. editor Zymed Corp., S. San Francisco, 1984-85; contbr. articles to profl. jours. Bd. dirs. Sierra-Cascade Girl Scouts U.S., Eureka, Calif., 1977-80; docent Clark Meml. Mus., Eureka, 1980-86. Avocations: wood and metal working, history, reproducing ancient sci. instruments. Home: 3201 Zelia Ct Arcata CA 95521 Office: Humboldt State U Chemistry Dept Arcata CA 95521

PASHAYAN, CHARLES, JR., congressman; b. Fresno, Calif., Mar. 27, 1941; s. Charles and Lillie P.; m. Sallie Jean Christian, Aug. 17, 1985. B.A., Pomona Coll., 1963; J.D., U. Calif., 1968; M.Litt., Oxford U., 1977. Bar: Calif. 1969, D.C. 1972, U.S. Supreme Ct. 1977. Spl. asst. to gen. counsel HEW, Washington, 1973-75; mem. 96th-100th congresses from 17th Calif. Dist. Capt. Strategic Intelligence U.S. Army, 1969-70. Mem. Fresno County Bar Assn., Royal Inst. Internat. Affairs, Internat. Inst. Strategic Studies. Republican. Office: 129 Cannon House Office Bldg Washington DC 20515 *

PASKERIAN, CHARLES KAY, JR., plastics co. exec.; b. Medford, Mass., Mar. 18, 1933; s. Charles Kay and Gertrude (Russian) P.; B.A. in Econs., Tufts U., 1954; M.B.A., Stanford, 1959; m. Susan Eileen Poland, Jan. 4, 1958; children—Michael Charles, Matthew Wayne. Salesman kordite div. Mobil Chem. Co., Los Angeles, 1959-60; dist. sales mgr., 1960-64; Western sales mgr. Webster Ind. div. Chelsea Ind., Los Angeles, 1964-66; pres. Flexi-Pac, Inc., Santa Ana, Calif., 1966—, also dir. Pub. mem. speech pathology and audiology examining com. Calif. Bd. Med. Examiners, 1973—. Mem. bd. edn. Santa Ana Unified Sch., 1969-74, pres., 1971-72. Trustee Holy Family Adoption Service, Rancho Santiago Coll. Served to capt. USAF, 1954-58. Mem. Indsl. Devel. Assn. (dir.), Soc. Plastics Engrs., Inc., Santa Ana C. of C. (dir. 1971-74), Zeta Psi. Republican. Conglist. (chmn. bd. trustees). Mason. Office: 2020 S Hathaway St Santa Ana CA 92706

PASQUALETTI, MARTIN JOSEPH, educator, energy consultant; b. San Francisco, Feb. 5, 1945; s. Phyllis Laverne (Johnson) P.; m. Jennifer Smith, Sept. 5, 1967 (dec. July 1970); m. Mari Anne Williams, May 27, 1972; 1 child, Erika Britt. BA, U. Calif., Berkeley, 1967; MA, La. State U., 1969; PhD, U. Calif., Riverside, 1977. Asst. prof. Ariz. State U., Tempe, 1977-82, assoc. prof., 1983—; prin. Energy Planning Assocs., Tempe, 1986—; hons. research prof. Ariz. State U., 1983, U. London, 1984-85. Editor: Nuclear Energy, 1984; contbr. articles on energy to jours. Served with U.S. Army, 1968-74. Research grantee Ariz. State U., 1983, NSF, Dept. Energy, Ariz. Energy Office. Mem. Assn. Am. Geographers (sec., treas. energy splty. group 1979-82, chmn. 1982-84), AAAS, Geothermal Resources Council, Sierra Club. Democrat. Presbyterian. Avocations: tennis, racquetball, photography. Office: Ariz State U Dept of Geography Tempe AZ 85282

PASQUALUCCI, FAUSTO, aerospace company executive, consultant; b. Rome, Italy, May 9, 1943; came to U.S., 1977; s. Francesco and Luigia (Renzi) P.; m. Virginia L. Norlund, May 10, 1986. MSc in Electronics Engring., U. of the Witwatersrand, Johannesburg, Republic of South Africa, 1972, PhD in Electronics Engring., 1977. Registered profl. engr., Calif., Fla., Colo. Chief research officer Council Sci. and Indsl. Research Nat. Inst. Telecommunications Research, Johannesburg, 1967-77; vis. scientist Rosenstiel Sch. Marine and Atmospheric Sci. U. Miami, Coral Gables, Fla., 1973-74; postdoctoral research assoc. NRC, Washington, D.C., 1978; research assoc. Coop. Inst. Research in Environ. Scis. U. Colo., Boulder, 1978-80; project mgr. radar meteorology dept. Environ. Research and Wave Propagation labs., divs. of NOAA, Boulder, 1980-84; also cons. Environ. Research and Wave Propogation labs., divs. of NOAA, Boulder; dept. mgr. microwave products div. Hughes Aircraft Co., Torrance, Calif., 1984—; session leader polarization techniques workshop, Miami, Fla., 1980. Contbr. sci. articles to profl. jours. Kans. Fgn. Student scholar Inst. Internat. Edn., 1965. Mem. Am. Meteorol. Soc., IEEE, Am. Geophys. Union, AAAS, N.Y. Acad. Scis., Amici d'Italia (pres. 1983-84). Avocations: skiing, tennis, scuba diving, swimming. Home: 6407 Ridgebyrne Ct Rancho Palos Verdes CA 90274 Office: Hughes Aircraft Co 3100 Fujita St 245/1420 Torrance CA 90505

PASSALACQUA, KRISTINE GAY, interior designer; b. Phoenix, July 30, 1955; d. Richard Elmer and Doris Helen (Emerick) Anderson; m. Glenn Allen Frank, Aug. 7, 1976 (dec. Apr. 1980), m. David Passalacqua, July 7, 1984. AA with honors, Mountain San Antonio Coll., 1976. Design asst. Debby's Interiors, Upland, Calif., 1979-80; prin. Kristine Gay Interiors, Ontario, Calif., 1980-84, Benicia, Calif., 1981—; prin. Kristine Passalacqua Studio of Interior Design, Benicia, 1984—. Republican. Clubs: Dona Benicia Lioness, Welcome Wagon (2d v.p.). Lodge: Soroptimists. Avocations: snow and water skiing, parisailing, camping, gardening, cooking. Home and Office: 1453 Sherman Dr Benicia CA 94510

PASSERI, KENNETH JOSEPH, podiatrist; b. Burlingame, Calif., Nov. 30, 1957; s. Louis R. and Delores L. (Naciamento) P. Student, Coll. San Mateo, 1976; BA, San Francisco State U., 1980; D in Podiatric Medicine, Calif. Coll. Podiatric Medicine, 1984. Resident in podiatric medicine and surgery VA Hosp., Seattle, 1985-86; pvt. practice podiatry Foster City, Calif., 1986—. Mem. Am. Podiatric Med. Assn., Calif. Podiatric Med. Assn. Republican. Roman Catholic. Avocations: sailing, soccer, string musician. Home: 1180 Rickover Ln Foster City CA 94404

PASSMORE, JAN WILLIAM, insurance company executive; b. Winchester, Ind., Nov. 5, 1940; s. Gale Orth and Helen Louise (Hoskinson) P.; student Nebr. State U., 1959-61; B.S., Ball State U., 1963; m. Pamela Boa, Feb. 14, 1964. With Aetna Life & Casualty, 1964-75, Western region dir., San Jose, Calif., 1972-75; broker, Sanders & Sullivan, San Jose, 1975-78, partner, 1978-80, pres., 1980-81; pres., chief exec. officer Corroon & Black, San Jose, 1981—; chmn. nat. adv. council INA Marketdyne, 1980-82; chmn. Nat. Producer's Council Cigna Corp., 1983-86; chmn. Aetna Life & Casualty Regional Adv. Council, 1982-83. Chmn. bd. Goodwill Industries, 1978-80, 86—; pres. Boy Scouts Am., 1981-83; bd. dirs. Music and Arts Found., 1980-85, Alexian Bros. Hosp. Found., 1978-85; chmn. bd. Hope Rehab., 1985-87; chmn. bd. dirs. Santa Clara County United Way; mem. San Jose Trolley Commn.; chmn. bd. trustees Alum Rock Meth. Ch. Named Citizen of Yr., Aetna Life & Casualty Co., 1975, Disting. Citizen of Yr. Santa Clara County, 1985; INA-Marketdyne Golden Circle, 1977-82. Mem. Western Assn. Ins. Brokers (trustee 1987-89), Nat. Assn. Ind. Ins. Agts. Republican. Methodist. Clubs: San Jose Country (treas., bd. dirs.), Sainte Claire, Spartan Found., Pres.'s Council San Jose State U., Aetna Life and Casualty Gt. Performers. Lodges: Masons, Shriners, Kiwanis (pres. San Jose 1986). Home: 10952 Prieta Ct San Jose CA 95127 Home: 1385 Woodland Way Tahoe City CA 95730 Office: 1530 The Alameda St San Jose CA 95126

PASTERNACK, IRWIN G(ENE), architect; b. Cheyenne, Wyo., Aug. 20, 1949; s. Jack and Bess (Weinstein) P. BArch, U. Ariz., 1972; postgrad., Ariz. State U., Phoenix. Registered architect, Wyo., Ariz., Iowa. With Varney, Sexton, Sydnor, Phoenix, 1972-73; architect Peter A. Lendrum Assocs., Phoenix, 1973-75; pres. Irwin G. Pasternack, AIA, Architecture and Planning, Phoenix, 1975—, Irwin G. Pasternick, AIA, & Assoc., P.C., Phoenix, 1977—. Prin. works include Southwest Interior Design Ctr., 1983 (Visual Improvement award City of Phoenix, 1984), Trammell Crow Indsl. Complex, 1986 (City of Tempe award of Distinction 1986), Trammell Crow Comml. Ctr., 1986. Recipient Merit award City of Tempe, Ariz., 1977, Beautification award City of Tempe, 1980, Excellence award Ariz. Rock Products Assn., 1983, Visual Improvement award City of Phoenix, 1984. Mem. Nat. Council Archtl. Registration Bds., AIA (ethics com. cen. Ariz. chpt. 1977), Nat. Assn. Indsl. and Office Parks, Phoenix Art Mus., Phoenix Zoo Assn. (Men's Aux.). Avocations: watercolor painting, skiing, Persian cats, photography, travel. Office: 745 E Maryland Suite 100 Phoenix AZ 85014

PASTERNAK, DERICK PETER, physician, medical executive, internist; b. Budapest, Hungary, Apr. 21, 1941; s. Leslie Laszlo and Hedvig Eva (Hecht) P.; came to U.S., 1956, naturalized, 1962; B.A., Harvard U., 1963, M.D. cum laude, 1967; MBA, U. N.Mex., 1985; m. Nancy Jean Clark, June 6, 1969; children—Kenneth Zoltan, Katherine Renee, Sarah Marie. Intern, jr. resident Bronx Municipal Hosp., N.Y.C., 1967-69; resident in internal medicine U. Calif. Hosps., San Francisco, 1971-73; mem. staff Lovelace Med. Center, Albuquerque, 1973—, med. dir. quality assurance program, 1976-80; med. dir. Lovelace Med. Found., 1980-86, pres., chief exec. officer, 1986—; pres. N.Mex. PSRO, Inc., 1980-82; clin. assoc. prof. medicine U. N.Mex. Referee U.S. Soccer Fedn. Served to capt. M.C., AUS, 1969-71. Decorated Bronze Star, Army Commendation Medal. Diplomate Am. Bd. Internal Medicine. Fellow ACP; mem. ABA, Am. Coll Physician Execs., N.Mex. Med. Soc. (councillor), Greater Albuquerque Med. Assn., Am. Diabetes Assn. Office: 5400 Gibson Blvd SE Albuquerque NM 87108

PASTORE, MICHAEL ANTHONY, college administrator; b. Fresno, Calif., Aug. 31, 1932; s. Michele Constantino and Rosa Maria (Damiani) P.; A.A., Coll. of Sequoias, Visalia, Calif., 1952; B.S., U. San Francisco, 1954; M.A., Fresno State Coll., 1969; Ph.D., U. Wash., 1976; m. Elizabeth Anne York, Dec. 23, 1955; children—Michael Anthony, Christi Anna, Maria Delisa. Agt., M.A. Pastore Ins. Co., Fresno, 1963-69; instr., coordinator, div. chmn. Edmonds Community Coll., Lynwood, Wash., 1969-73; founder, pres. City Univ. Seattle, 1973—. Served with U.S. Army, 1956-57. Democrat. Roman Catholic. Clubs: Wash. Athletic, Rainier (Seattle); Glendale Country (Bellevue, Wash.). Home: 618 175th Pl NE Bellevue WA 98008 Office: 16661 Northrup Way Bellevue WA 98008

PASTREICH, PETER, orchestra manager; b. Bklyn., Sept. 13, 1938; s. Ben and Hortense (Davis) P.; children: Anna, Milena; children by previous marriage: Emanuel, Michael. A.B. magna cum laude, Yale Coll., 1959; postgrad., N.Y. U. Sch. Medicine, 1959-60. Asst. mgr. Denver Symphony, Balt. Symphony; Mgr. Greenwich Village Symphony, N.Y.C., 1960-63; gen. mgr. Nashville Symphony, 1963-65, Kansas City Philharmonic, 1965-66; asst. mgr., mgr. St. Louis Symphony, 1966-78, exec. dir., 1966-78; exec. dir. San Francisco Symphony, 1979—; instr. orch. mgmt. Am. Symphony Orch. League; bd. dirs. Nat. Com. for Symphony Orch. Support; founder San Francisco Youth Orch.; rep. planning and constrn. Davies Symphony Hall, San Francisco Symphony, 1980. Author: TV comml., 1969 (CLIO award); contbr. articles to various newspapers. Mem. recommendation bd. of the Avery Fisher Artist Program, Yale U. Council com. on music; past mem. adv. panel Nat. Endowment for the Arts, co-chmn. music panel, 1985; founding mem. bd. dirs. St. Louis Conservatory, mem. policy com. Maj. Orch. Mgrs. Conf., chmn., 1980; bd. dirs. Laumeier Sculpture Park, St. Louis, Stern Grove Festival, San Francisco Conv. and Visitors Bur.; chmn. fund campaign French-Am. Internat. Sch., San Francisco. Served with U.S. Army, 1960. Recipient First Disting. Alumnus award Yale U. Band, 1977, cert. Merit Yale Sch. Music, 1984. Mem. Am. Symphony Orch. League (dir., chmn., former chmn. task force on mgmt. tng.; mem. exec. and long-range planning com., chmn. standing com. on adminstrv. policy), Assn. Calif. Symphony Orchs. (dir.), Bankers Club of San Francisco. Club: Yale (N.Y.C.). Office: Davies Symphony Hall San Francisco CA 94102

PATACSIL, PETER ESPEJO, science administrator; b. Honolulu, Sept. 25, 1937; s. A.N. Patacsil and Donatela Ayson (Espejo) Enrado; m. Julia Lizama Leon-Guerrero, Apr. 16, 1966; children: Peter Kenneth, Matthew Raymond, Catherine Elizabeth. BSCE, U. Hawaii, 1960; MS in Ops. Research, U.S. Naval Postgrad. Sch., 1966; diploma, Air Command and Staff Coll., 1971. Commd. ensign USN, Newport, R.I., 1961; advanced through grades to comdr. USN, Honolulu, 1976; retired USN, San Diego, 1983; sr. analyst Sci. Applications Internat. Corp., San Diego, 1983—. Contbr. reports to tech. pubs. Ex-officio mem. Guam Territorial Bd. Edn., Agana, 1976-78; chmn. Chamorro Dist. Aloha Council Boy Scouts Am., Agana, 1977-78, exec. bd. dirs. 1977-78; chmn. Role Com. Kamahameha Dist. Aloha Council Boy Scouts Am., Aiea, Hawaii, 1975-76; bd. dirs. Jr. Achievement, Agana, 1976-78; mem. Guam Adv. Council on Vocat. Edn., Agana, 1977-78, exec. com. 1st and 2d annual Spl. Olympics, Agana, 1977-78, Guam State Adv. Council for Handicapped, Agana, 1977-78; mem. Guam Eagles chpt. Pop Warner Football Assn. 1977-78; treas. Mira Mesa High Sch. chpt., San Diego, 1983-84, Mira Mesa High Sch. class of '88 Parent Booster Club, 1985—; vice-chmn. Agueda Johnston Jr. High Sch. PTA, Chalan Pago, Guam, 1977-78. Named to Ancient Order of the Chamorri, Gov. of Guam, Agana, 1978. Mem. Armed Forces Communications and Electronics Assn. Republican. Roman Catholic. Avocation: numismatics. Office: Sci Applications Internat Corp 1200 Prospect St La Jolla CA 92030

PATANO, PATRICIA ANN, health and fitness professional, marketing and public relations specialist; b. Chgo., June 14, 1950; d. Thomas Vincent and Gladys Estelle (Olejniczak) P. Student, Los Angeles Pierce Coll., 1968-70, UCLA, 1974-84. Pub. relations mgr. Motel 6, Inc., Century City, Calif., 1974-77; mgr. corp. communications 1st Travel Corp., Van Nuys, Calif., 1977-79; mktg. pub. relations mgr. Unitours, Inc., Los Angeles, 1979-81; asst. v.p. pub. relations Los Angeles Olympic Com., 1981-84; pres., co-owner PaVage Fitness Innovations, Playa del Rey, Calif., 1984—; trustee Nat. Injury Prevention Found., San Diego, 1983—; cons. Dick Clark Productions, Burbank, Calif., 1985, Reebok USA Ltd., Boston, 1983—. Co-author: MuscleAerobics, 1985; contbr. articles to profl. jours. Vol. Motion Picture Hosp., Woodland Hills, Calif., 1968-70; bd. dirs. Los Angeles Boys and Girls Club, 1984—. Recipient Corp. award Pres.'s Council Phys. Fitness, 1983. Mem. Los Angeles Advt. Club. Republican. Presbyterian. Clubs: Mid Valley Athletic (Reseda, Calif.); Marina City (Marina del Rey, Calif.). Office: PaVage Fitness Innovations 200 E Culver Blvd Playa del Rey CA 90291

PATEL, MARILYN HALL, judge; b. Amsterdam, N.Y., Sept. 2, 1938; d. Lloyd Manning and Nina J. (Thorpe) Hall; m. Magan C. Patel, Sept. 2, 1966; children: Brian, Gian. B.A., Wheaton Coll., 1959; J.D., Fordham U., 1963. Mng. atty. Benson & Morris, N.Y.C., 1963-65; sole practice N.Y.C., 1965-67, San Francisco, 1971-76; atty. Dept. Justice, San Francisco, 1967-71; judge Alameda County Mcpl. Ct., Oakland, Calif., 1976-80, U.S. Dist. Ct. (no. dist.) Calif., San Francisco, 1980—; adj. prof. law Hastings Coll. of Law, San Francisco, 1974-76. Author: Immigration and Nationality Law, 1974; also numerous articles. Mem. bd. of visitors Fordham U. Sch. of Law. Mem. ABA (litigation sect., jud. adminstrn. sect.), ACLU (former bd. dirs.), NOW (former bd. dirs.), Am. Law Inst., Am. Judicature Soc. (bd. dirs.), Calif. Conf. Judges, Nat. Assn. Women Judges (founding mem.), Internat. Inst. (bd. dirs.), Advs. for Women (co-founder). Democrat. Avocations: piano playing; travel. Office: US District Court 450 Golden Gate Ave PO Box 36060 San Francisco CA 94102

PATENT, DOROTHY HINSHAW, author, photographer; b. Rochester, Minn., Apr. 30, 1940; d. Horton Corwin and Dorothy Kate (Youmans) Hinshaw; m. Gregory Joseph Patent, Mar. 21, 1964; children: David Gregory, Jason Daniel. BS, Stanford U., 1962; MA, U. Calif., Berkeley, 1965, PhD, 1968; postgrad., U. Wash., 1965-67. Postdoctoral fellow Sinai Hosp., Detroit, 1968-69, Stazione Zoologica, Naples, Italy, 1969-70; acting asst. prof. U. Mont., Missoula, 1977. Author: The Way of the Grizzly, 1987, The Quest for Artificial Intelligence, 1986, Draft Horses, 1986, Maggie-A Sheep Dog, 1986 (Jr. Lit. Guild Selection award 1986), Buffalo: The American Bison Today, 1986, A Picture Book of Cows, 1982, Spider Magic, 1982 (Am. Library Assn. Notable Book award), The Lives of Spiders, 1980 (Golden Kite Nonfiction award 1980), Evolution Goes on Every Day, 1977 (Golden Kite Honor Book award 1977), Weasels, Otters, Skunks and Their Family, 1973, others. Mem. AAAS, Am. Inst. Biol. Scis., Soc. Children's Book Writers, Am. Soc. Zoologists, Authors Guild. Avocations: gardening, racquetball, soccer.

PATEY, PAMELA ARDELLE, business educator; b. San Diego, June 28, 1947; d. Paul Allen and Ardelle Pauline (Dykstra) Willis; m. Alan Kent Patey, Sept. 3, 1967; children: Nicolette Joanné, Shane Patrick. AA in Stenography, La Sierra Coll., 1967; BS in Office Adminstrn., Loma Linda U., 1970, MA in Bus. Edn., 1973. Supr. teaching U.S. Govt. Bur. Indian Affairs-Sherman Indian High Sch., Riverside, Calif., 1970-76; assoc. prof. bus. and office adminstrn. Riverside Community Coll., 1976—; cons. Word Star, Corona/Norco (Calif.) Sch. Dist., 1985—, bus. English, Fleetwood Enterprises, Inc., Riverside, 1986—. Author: Wordstar Made Easy, 1983, 2d rev. edit., 1985. Mem. adv. bd. Loma Linda U., Riverside, 1982—. Recipient Outstanding Performance award U.S. Govt.-Sherman Indian High Sch., 1972, 75, Honored Tchr. Disabled Students award Riverside Community Coll., 1986. Mem. Assn. Info. Systems Profls., Calif. Bus. Edn. Assn. Republican. Adventist. Avocations: aerobics, horseback riding, running, writing, reading. Office: Riverside Community Circle 4800 Magnolia Ave Riverside CA 92506

PATIENCE, GEORGE ED, civil engineer; b. Murray, Utah, Oct. 25, 1938; s. George L. and Ellen Jane (Champion) P.; divorced; children: Debra, Georgia. BSCE, U. Utah, 1971. Registered profl. engr., Utah, Nev., Idaho, Wyo., Colo., land surveyor, Utah, Wyo., Ariz. Design engr. Call Engring., Salt Lake City, 1971-73; project engr. Gibbons & Reed Co., Salt Lake City, 1973-76; pres. P/S Assocs., Inc., Salt Lake City, 1976-81; asst. div. mgr. DMJM, Salt Lake City, 1981—. Mem. ASCE, Nat. Soc. Profl. Engrs., Inst. Transp. Engrs., Utah Council of Land Surveyors (pres. 1981). Avocations: running, fishing, hunting, hiking, photography. Home: 5767 S 920 East Salt Lake City UT 84121 Office: DMJM 5330 S 900 East Salt Lake City UT 84117

PATIK, CAROL ANN, publishing company executive; b. Riverton, Wyo., Dec. 12, 1958; d. Harvey Francis and Violette Marie (Ward) Woolery; m. Steve Adam Patik, Apr. 10, 1982. Grad. high sch., Kinnear, Wyo.; student, Cen. Wyo. Coll., U. Wyo. Ranch hand Woolery Ranch, Kinnear, 1979; driller Bur. Reclamation, Riverton, 1980; bank teller United Savs. of Wyo., Riverton, 1980-83; circulation coordinator Internat. Aviation Pub., Riverton, 1983—. Republican. Episcopalian. Avocations: horseback riding, snowmobiling, skiing, dog sledding. Home: Fremont County Fairgrounds Riverton WY 82501 Office: Internat Aviation Pubs Inc 1000 College View Dr Riverton WY 82501

PATIL, PRAKASH RACHAPPA, food products executive; b. Gokak, India, June 28, 1948; s. Rachappa Mallappa and Bhagirathi R. (Pattanshetty) P.; m. Sarala Prakash David, Sept. 7, 1980; 1 child, Sneha Prakash. MS, Karnatak U., Dharwar, India, 1971; PhD, Indian Inst. Tech., Bombay, 1978. Postdoctoral fellow U. Iowa, Iowa City, 1982-83, U. Mich., Ann Arbor, 1983; dir. quality assurance Delano (Calif.) Growers Grape Products, 1985—; quality control chemist Lankro Chems. (India) Ltd., Bombay, 1978-80; research chemist Lever Bros., (India) Ltd., Bombay, 1981-82. Contbr. articles to profl. jours. Fellow Inst. Food Tech.; mem. Am. Chem. Soc., Am. Inst. Chemists. Avocations: photography, reading. Office: Delano Growers Grape Products Rte 1 PO Box 283 Delano CA 93215

PATRASCU, ANGHEL, engineer; b. Romania, July 28, 1930; came to U.S., 1964, naturalized, 1969; s. Ion and Elena (Mihalache) P.; m. Clara A. Troubitzine, June 8, 1963; children—Daniel, Helene. Diploma in Engring., Can. Inst. Sci. and Tech., Toronto, Ont., Can., 1969; B.A. in Econs., Rutgers U., 1974; M.B.A. in Project Mgmt., Golden Gate U., 1984. Estimator Can. Vickers, Montreal, 1955-60; sr. estimator Liquid Air, Montreal, Can., 1960-64; mgr. Airco Inc., Murray Hill, N.J., 1964-74, R.M. Huffington Inc., Jakarta, Indonesia, 1974-76, Sohio, San Francisco, 1976-81; specialist project controls Chevron Corp., San Francisco, 1981-86; mgr. cost engring. Liquid Air Engring. Corp., Walnut Creek, Calif., 1986—; adj. prof. Golden Gate U., San Francisco. Author: Construction Cost Engineering, 1978. Contbr. articles to profl. publs. Fellow Am. Assn. Cost Engring. (past pres. N.J. and San Francisco sects.); mem. ASME, Project Mgmt. Inst. Republican. Greek Orthodox. Home: 44 Elda Dr San Rafael CA 94903 Office: Liquid Air Engring Corp 2121 N California Blvd Walnut Creek CA 94596

PATRICK, LESLIE DAYLE, hydrologist; b. Grand Island, Nebr., Nov. 20, 1951; d. Robert Norman and Charlotte Ruth (Thomas) Mayfield; m. Jeffrey Rogan Patrick, July 1, 1972. BA in Geology, U. Alaska, Anchorage, 1975. Hydrologist water resources div. U.S. Geol. Survey, Anchorage, 1975—. Mem. Alaska Groundwater Assn. (sec./treas. 1980). Office: US Geol Survey Water Resources Div 4230 University Dr Suite 201 Anchorage AK 99508-4664

PATRIDGE, WILLIAM EARL, construction company executive, consultant; b. Lostant, Ill., Feb. 18, 1918; s. William Thomas and Lela Mae (Hiltabrand) P.; m. Maxine Doris Hembree, Nov. 14, 1942; 1 child, Patricia Ann. Student, U. Calif., San Francisco, 1946-47. Project mgr. Ralph E. Murphy & Sons, San Rafael, Calif., 1946-58, Swinerton & Walberg Co., San Francisco, 1959-63; v.p. Walbert & Co., Honolulu, 1963-70, 1970-75; pres. and chief exec. officer W.E. Patridge, Inc., Honolulu, 1975—, Pacific Constrn. Co., Ltd., Honolulu, 1983-86. Bd. dirs. Oahu Devel. Conf., Honolulu, 1970—; mem. bd. regents Chaminade U., Honolulu, 1985—. Served to sgt. USAF, 1941-45. Mem. Gen. Contractors Assn. (bd. dirs. 1984), Honolulu C. of C. Republican. Presbyterian. Clubs: Plaza (bd. dirs. 1984—), Outrigger Canoe, Oahu Country (Honolulu). Lodge: Rotary. Home: 999 Wilder Ave Honolulu HI 96822 Office: Pacific Constrn Co Ltd 828 Fort St Honolulu HI 96813

PATRIQUIN, JOANIE HALL, interior designer; b. Charlottesville, Va., Jan. 26, 1944; d. Hanford Bourne and Sallie Elizabeth (Jones) Hall; divorced; 1 adopted child, Scott Duval Corbin; m. Daniel Keith Patriquin, July 16, 1983. Student, U. Va., 1965, 68, 72, Liberty U., 1982-83. Exec. sec. to v.p. CENTEL, Charlottesville, 1964-65; interior designer Sherwin Williams Co., Charlottesville, 1965-68, STUDIO B, Charlottesville, 1968-75; prin. Designs by R.T.P. Ltd., Charlottesville, 1975-79; designer, office mgr. Creative Kitchens, Charlottesville, 1979-82; designer, sales rep. Patriquin's, Kingman, Ariz., 1985—. Author poetry; contbr. articles to profl. jours. Family counselor Personal Mission, Kingman, 1983—; founder Concerned Friends of the Hotel Beale, Kingman, 1986; chmn. area drive Am. Heart Assn., Charlottesville, 1972-79; vol. U. Va. Rehab. Ctr., Charlottesville, 1975-79; dir. Manzanita Bapt. Children's Choir, Kingman, 1985—; chmn. Stonecroft Ministries, Kingman, 1984-87, project advisor, 1987—. Republican. Baptist. Avocations: handpainted eggs, crewel, embroidery, arts and crafts. Home and Office: 2940-2950 Butler Ave Kingman AZ 86401

PATT, YALE NANCE, computer science educator; b. Medford, Mass., June 29, 1939; s. Abraham Walter and Sarah Clara (Tankel) P. BSEE, Northeastern U., 1962; MS, Stanford U., 1963, PhD, 1966. Asst. prof. elec. engring. Cornell U., Ithaca, N.Y., 1966-67; assoc. prof. computer sci., elec. engring/N.C. State U., Raleigh, 1969-76; prof. San Francisco State U., 1976—; vis. prof. U. Calif., Berkeley, 1979—; co-dir. Aquarius High Performance Computer Research Group, Berkeley; cons. numerous cos., orgns. including Digital Equipment Corp., Frankford Arsenal, 1973-77, EPA, 1975-76, NCR Corp.; frequent lectr.; seminar and conf. coordinator numerous computer sci. orgns. Contbr. articles to profl. jours. Served to capt. U.S. Army, 1967-69. Mem. IEEE (chmn. curriculum assistance com. of computer soc. 1978-81, jour. and conf. reviewer), Assn. for Computing Machinery (5 time nat. lectr. 1975-87), Sigma Xi, Tau Beta Pi, Eta Kappa Nu. Home: PO Box 27531 San Francisco CA 94127 Office: San Francisco State Univ 1600 Holloway Ave San Francisco CA 94132

PATTABHIRAMAN, TAMMANUR RAMACHANDRA, research chemist; b. Kanchipuram, Madras, India, Nov. 3, 1934; s. Ramachandra and Janaki Iyer; m. Rangamani Krishnaswami, Sept. 21, 1973. MA in Chemistry, U. Madras, 1957; PhD in Chemistry, U. Hawaii, 1965. Lectr. Vivekananda Coll., Madras, 1958-61; scientist Cen. Food Inst., Mysore, India, 1965-68; research assoc. U. Okla., Norman, 1968-71, U. So. Calif., Los Angeles, 1971-81; sci. dir. Allergy and Immunology Lab., Pasadena, Calif., 1981—. Contbr. articles to profl. jours. Mem. Am. Chem. Soc., Internat. Soc. Toxicology, Sigma Xi. Avocations: gardening, real estate. Office: Allergy & Immunology Cons Lab 100 N Madison Ave Pasadena CA 91101 Home: 3805 Fairmeade Rd Pasadena CA 91107

PATTEN, ASHER HOWARD, materials handling equipment executive; b. Paonia, Colo., Mar. 5, 1904; s. Frank Howard and Annie (Parker) P.; m. Jean Davy, Dec. 28, 1929 (dec. May 1955); children: Jack Davy, Robert Wendall; m. Myrtle Lang, July 4, 1956. BSEE, U. Denver, 1925. Registered profl. engr., Colo. Elec. engr. Moffat Tunnel, Tolland, Colo., 1925-28, Traylor Vibrator, Denver, 1929-32; chief engr. Denver Equipment Co., 1932-46; pres. Patten Engring., Denver, 1946—. Author: The Welding of Vibrating Equipment, 1927, Thrytron Tubes for Creating Vibration, 1928, The First Commercial Florescent Lighting in Building, 1936; patentee safety matchbox, 1929. Treas. Colo. chpt. Lukemia Soc., 1974-86, bd. trustees, 1974—. Mem. Colo. Sch. Mines Alumni Assn., Colo. Mining Assn. (sustaining, pres. 1978). Republican. Congregationalist. Lodges: Masons, Shriners, Jesters. Avocations: swimming, bowling. Office: 1740 W 13th Ave Denver CO 80204

PATTEN, BENTON PENROD, artist, educator; b. Elberta, Utah, Jan. 3, 1934; s. Carl Alva and Vera (Penrod) P.; m. Karol June Payne, Jan. 15, 1959; children—Craig Payne, Lori Michelle, Kendal David. B.S., Brigham Young U., 1960, M.A., 1963; postgrad. Bklyn. Mus. Art Sch., 1963-65; Ed.D., Ill. State U., 1974. Asst. prof. Tex. Women's U., Denton, 1974-75, Pan Am. U., Edinburg, Tex., 1977, N.Mex. Highlands U., Las Vegas, 1977-78; instr. art dept. U. Utah, Salt Lake City, 1979-82; prof. graphic design Utah Tech. Coll., Salt Lake City, 1981-86; vis. artist Bountiful-Davis Artcenter, Utah, 1984—; artist-in-residence Utah Arts Council, Salt Lake City, 1981-82. One man shows include Weber State Coll., Ogden, Utah, 1967, Ill. State U., Normal, 1972, 73, Tex. Women's U., Denton, 1974, Ricks Coll., Rexburg, Idaho, 1979; exhibited in group shows at Utah Rotunda, Salt Lake City, 1969, North Shore Art League, Winnetka, Ill., 1974, Mail Art Exhibit, Utrecht, Holland, 1977, Bountiful Art Ctr., Utah, 1984, Springville Salon, 1986, Nat. Acad. Art and Design, 1986, Utah Portraiture Christmas exhibit Springville Mus., 1986; represented in permanent collections Brigham Young U., Ill. State U., N.Mex. Highlands U., also pvt. collections. Max Beckmann Meml. scholar Bklyn. Mus. Art Sch., 1963-65, Monitor scholar Pratt Graphic Art Ctr., N.Y.C., 1964; Springville Salon, 1986; Nat. Acad. Art and Design, 1986, recipient Storefront Renewal Program award McClean County Assn. Commerce and Industry, Normal, Ill., 1972-73. Mem. Coll. Art. Assn., NEA. Republican. Mormon. Address: 246 E 2200 S Bountiful UT 84010

PATTEN, DUNCAN THEUNISSEN, ecologist educator; b. Detroit, Oct. 13, 1934; s. Marc T. and Doris (Miller) P.; m. Eva Chittenden, July 27, 1957; children: Michael, Marc, Robin, Scott. BA, Amherst Coll., 1956; MS, U. Mass., Amherst, 1959; PhD, Duke U., 1962. Asst. prof. ecology Va. Poly. Inst., Blacksburg, 1962-65; asst. prof. ecology Ariz. State U., Tempe, 1965-67, assoc. prof., 1967-73, prof., 1973—, dir. ctr. environ. studies, 1980—. Contbr. articles to profl. jours. Fellow AAAS, Ariz.-Nev. Acad. Sci.; mem. Ecol. Soc. Am. (bus. mgr. 1979—), Brit. Ecol. Soc., Soc. Range Mgmt., Am. Inst. Biol. Scis., Sigma Xi. Office: Ariz State U Ctr for Environ Studies Tempe AZ 85287

PATTEN, PRISCILLA CARLA, college president, religion educator; b. Berkeley, Calif., Jan. 30, 1950; s. Carl Thomas and Bebe (Harrison) P. B.S., Patten Bible Coll., 1969; B.A., Coll. Holy Names, Oakland, 1971; M.A., Wheaton Coll. (Ill.), 1972; Ph.D., Drew U., 1976. Ordaine dto ministry Christian Evang. Chs. Am., 1963, v.p., 1964—; co pastor Christian Cathedral, Oakland, 1964—; assoc. prof. N.T. Patten Coll., Oakland, 1975-82, prof., 1982—, pres., 1983—, chmn. div. Bibl. studies, 1977-83, dir. cathedral choirs, 1975—; founder dir. choir Patten Christian Schs., 1976—. Author: Before the Times, 1980; The World of the Early Church, 1984. Mem. Am. Acad. Religion, Soc. Bibl. Lit., Religion and Ethics Inst., Am. Assn. Univ. Profs., Am. Assn. of Ind. Colls. and Univs, Assn. Pres.'s Ind. Coll. and Univs., AAUP, Inst. Bibl. Research, Bar Assn. Greater Bay Area, Oakland C. of C., Phi Delta Kappa. Office: Patten Coll 2433 Coolidge Ave Oakland CA 94601

PATTEN, THOMAS HENRY, JR., educator; b. Cambridge, Mass., Mar. 24, 1929; s. Thomas Henry and Lydia Mildred (Lindgren) P.; m. Jule Ann Miller, Aug. 27, 1972; children—Laurie Kathryn, Rhonda Josephine, Jenny Lydia. A.B., Brown U., 1953; M.S., Cornell U., 1955, Ph.D., 1959. Dir. program planning Ford Motor Co., Dearborn, Mich., 1957-65; prof. mgmt. and sociology U. Detroit, 1965-67; prof. orgnl. behavior and personnel mgmt. Sch. Labor and Indsl. Relations, Mich. State U., E. Lansing, 1967-84; prof. mgmt. and human resources Calif. State Poly. U., Pomona, 1984—; cons. in field. Author: The Foreman: The Forgotten Man of Management, 1968, Manpower Planning and the Development of Human Resources, 1971, OD-Emerging Dimensions and Concepts, 1973, A Bibliography of Compensation Planning and Administration, 1960-1974, 2d rev. edit., 1981, 3d rev. edit., 1987, Pay: Employee Compensation and Incentive Plans, 1977, Classics of Personnel Management, 1979, Organizational Development Through Teambuilding, 1981, A Manager's Guide to Performance Appraisal, 1982. Served with USMC, 1946-48. Mem. Indsl. Relations Research Assn. (chpt. pres. 1970-71), Am. Soc. Tng. and Devel. (chmn. orgn. devel. div. 1972), Am. Sociol. Assn., Internat. Personnel Mgmt. Assn., Internat. Indsl. Relations Assn., Orgnl. Behavior Teaching Soc., Pacific Basin Found., Inst. Applied Behavioral Sci., Acad. Mgmt., Am. Compensation Assn. Home: 1538 Beloit Ave Claremont CA 91711 Office: Dept Mgmt and Human Resources Calif State Poly U Pomona CA 91768

PATTERSON, CAROL JEAN, self-help services coordinator, counselor; b. San Francisco, June 28, 1954; d. Donald Lloyd and Virginia Anne (Neall) P. BA, U. Calif., Hayward, 1982; MSW, San Francisco State U., 1986. Counselor Bay Area Community Services, Oakland, Calif., 1981-83; intern case mgmt. Regional Ctr. East Bay, Oakland, 1982-83; intern play therapy St. Vincent's Sch. for Boys, San Rafael, Calif., 1983-84; coordinator San Francisco Network of Mental Health Clients, 1985; BUILD project coordinator Ind. Living Resource Ctr., San Francisco, 1985—; bd. dirs., treas. Patients' Rights Advocacy Services, San Francisco; conf. coordinator Calif. Network Mental Health Clients, San Francisco, 1985; cons. Hospitality House, San Francisco, 1986—. Mem. Nat. Assn. Social Workers, Mental Health Assn. (self-help com. 1985—), Sierra Club. Office: Ind Living Resource Ctr 4429 Cabrillo St San Francisco CA 94121

PATTERSON, DAWN MARIE, educator, consultant; b. Gloversville, N.Y., July 30; d. Robert Morris and Dora Margaret (Perham) P.; m. Robert Henry Hollenbeck, Aug. 3, 1958 (div. 1976); children—Adrienne Lyn, Nathaniel Conrad. B.S. in Edn., SUNY-Geneseo, 1962; M.A., Mich. State U., 1973, Ph.D., 1977; postdoctoral U. So. Calif. and Inst. Ednl. Leadership. Librarian, Brighton (N.Y.) Central Schs., 1962-67; asst. to regional dir. Mich. State U. Ctr., Bloomfield Hills, 1973-74; grad. asst. Mich. State U., 1975-77; cons. Mich. Efficiency Task Force, 1977; asst. dean Coll. Continuing Edn., U. So. Calif., Los Angeles, 1978-84; dean continuing edn. Calif. State U., Los Angeles, 1984—; pres. Co-Pro Assocs. Mem. Air Univ. Bd. Visitors, 1986—, Calif. Hist. Soc., Los Angeles Town Hall, Los Angeles World Affairs Council; Dora Louden scholar, 1958-61; Langworthy fellow, 1961-62; Edn. Professions Devel. fellow, 1974-75; Ednl. Leadership Policy fellow, 1982-83. Mem. AAUW (pres. Pasadena br. 1985-86), Am. Assn. Adult and Continuing Edn. (charter), Nat. Univ. Continuing Edn. Assn., Calif. Coll. and Mil. Educators Assn. (pres.), Los Angeles Airport Area Edn. Industry Assn. (pres. 1984), Kappa Delta Pi, Phi Delta Kappa. Republican. Unitarian. Club: Fine Arts of Pasadena. Lodge: Zonta. Office: 5151 State University Dr Los Angeles CA 90032

PATTERSON, IAN DAVID, consulting chemical engineer; b. Eckford, Mich., Apr. 6, 1897; s. Louis Kosuth and Eva Josephine (Blair) P.; m. Phoebe Frances Marsh, June 10, 1922; children—Marilyn, Joanne. A.B., Albion Coll., 1919; B.S. in Chem. Engring., U. Mich., 1920. Registered profl. engr., Ohio. Chem. engr. Goodyear Tire & Rubber, Akron, Ohio, 1920, Chem. Warfare, Edgewood, Md., 1921; tire compounder Goodyear Tire & Rubber, Akron, 1921-27, chief chemist, Wolverhampton, Eng., 1927-36, devel. mgr., 1936-39, plant mgr., St. Mary's, Ohio, 1939-42; cons. chem. engr., Sun City, Ariz., 1964—. Patentee in field. Served with U.S. Army, 1918. Fellow Plastics and Rubber Inst.; mem. Am. Chem. Soc., Am. Inst. Chem. Engrs. Republican. Presbyterian. Lodge: Kiwanis. Summer Home: 75 N Portage Path Apt 705 Akron OH 44303

PATTERSON, JOHN NEWTON, lawyer; b. Taylor, Tex., Oct. 13, 1943; s. Herbert Newton and Helga Antoinetta (Engstrom) P.; m. Janet Charlene Taylor, Sept. 12, 1970 (dec. July 1980); m. Janice M. Ahern, June 18, 1983. BA in English, U. Va., 1967; JD, U. Tex., 1970. Bar: N.Mex. 1971, U.S. Ct. Claims 1973, U.S. Ct. Appeals (10th cir.) 1971. Ptnr. Standley, Quinn & Patterson, Santa Fe, 1971-76, Byrd, Connelly & Patterson, Santa Fe, 1976-80; shareholder White, Koch, Kelly & McCarthy, Santa Fe, 1980—; lectr. N.Mex. State Bar, Albuquerque, 1982—. Mem. ABA, Community Assns. Inst. Democrat. Office: White Koch Kelly & McCarthy 433 Paseo de Peralta Santa Fe NM 87501

PATTERSON, LISA ADAMS, music educator, arranger, choreographer; b. Walnut Creek, Calif., Oct. 10, 1954; d. Chambers Daniel and Cornelia Hilda (Hulst) Adams; m. Richard North Patterson, Apr. 10, 1982. Student Reid Sch. Music, U. Edinburgh, Scotland, 1975-76; B.A. in Music, U. Calif.-Davis, 1977. Orff cert. levels 1, 2. Dir. music lower sch. Hamlin Sch., San Francisco, 1978-83, head fine arts dept., 1983—. Adapter, arranger, choreographer mus. prodns. Give My Regards to Broadway, 1979, Around-the-World in Movie Daze, 1980, The Frog Prince, 1981, You're A Good Man, Charlie Brown, 1981, 84, 86, Alice in Wonderland, 1982, 86, OZ!, 1983, Joseph and the Amazing Technicolor Dreamcoat, 1982, 87, Peter Pan, 1984, The Velveteen Rabbit, 1985, A Christmas Carol, 1986. Active San Francisco Children's Opera, 1982—. Recipient achievement award fine arts Bank Am., 1972. Mem. No. Calif. Orff-Schulwerk Assn. Office: Hamlin Sch 2129 Vallejo San Francisco CA 94123

PATTERSON, NORWOOD JAMES, JR., broadcasting station executive, consulting engineer, advertising agent; b. San Mateo, Calif., Feb. 18, 1948; s. Norwood James and Gloria Dawn (Peterson) P.; m. Sharon Anne LeTourneau, June 17, 1967; children: Brian James, Jason James. AA, Coll. of San Mateo, 1966; BS, San Francisco Coll. of Electronics, 1968; postgrad. Stanford U. Registered profl. engr., Calif.; cert. radio engr. 1st class FCC. Prodn. assoc. Family Radio Network, San Francisco, 1966-68; sta. mgr. Sierra Broadcast Co., Fresno, Calif., 1968-74; pres. New Life Communications, Fresno, 1974—; pres. Radio Reps., Santa Ynez, Calif., 1980—; pres. Radio Engring. Co., Santa Barbara, Calif., 1980—. Exec. producer TV spl. From Fresno to Kenya with Love, 1981. Bd. dirs. Evangel Home, 1980—, Youth for Christ, 1982—; mem. Fresno City Human Relations Commn., 1985—; active Young Reps. of Fresno County; chmn. Fresno Evang. Polit. Action Council, 1983. Recipient Partnership in Ministry award World Vision Internat., 1978, Outstanding Service award Fresno City and County C. of C., 1986; named An Outstanding Young Man of Am., Jr. C. of C., 1983. Mem. Christian Broadcasters Am. (founder, pres. 1978—), Nat. Religious Broadcasters Assn. (bd. dirs., excellence awards, 1981, 82, 83, Merit award 1986), Nat. Assn. Evangelicals (pres. Fresno chpt. 1983). Mem. Evangelical Free Ch. Lodge: Rotary. Home: 7256 N Teilman St Fresno CA 93711 Office: New Life Communications 3636 N 1st St Suite 142 Fresno CA 93726

PATTERSON, PEGGY PRACHT, science laboratory financial administrator; b. Oakland, Calif., Dec. 23, 1947; d. Loren Eugene and Frankie Ethelene (DuPree) Pracht; m. Michael William Patterson, Dec. 10, 1983 (div. July 1985); 1 child, John Thomas Yeandle. BA in Music, Calif. State U., Hayward, 1970, postgrad. in Bus., 1979-81. Computer operator Haskins & Sells CPA, San Francisco, 1974-75; staff asst. to dir. Lawrence Berkeley (Calif.) Lab., 1976-86; fin. adminstr. for directorate Lawrence Berkeley Lab., 1986—. Mem. Nat. Notary Assn. Republican. Baptist. Home: 15267 Central Ave San Leandro CA 94578 Office: Lawrence Berkeley Lab 1 Cyclotron Rd Berkeley CA 94720

PATTISON, GORDON LEE, periodontist, medical educator; b. Boulder City, Nev., Sept. 22, 1945; s. Gordon Lee and Betty Yoland (Major) P.; m. Anna Michiko Matsuishi, July 3, 1970; 1 child, Geoffrey Kazuo. BA, U. So. Calif., 1967, DDS, 1971; postgrad., Boston U., 1975. Practice dentistry specializing in periodontics Los Angeles, 1975—; asst. prof. U. So. Calif., Los Angeles, 1975-81, U. Calif., Los Angeles, 1981-83; adj. asst. prof. UCLA, 1983—. Author: Periodontal Instrumentation, 1979, Clinical Periodontology, 1985; contbr. articles to profl. jours. Mem. ADA, Calif. Dental Assn., Western Dental Soc., Am. Acad. Periodontology, Western Soc. Periodontology, Omicron Kappa Upsilon. Democrat. Home: 10519 Clarkson Rd Los Angeles CA 90064

PATTISON, PATRICK DAVIE, marketing executive; b. Balboa, Calif., Dec. 9, 1953; s. Raylinn and Lillian Harriet (Davie) P.; m. Amy Elizabeth Bjorklund, Nov. 29, 1975 (div. Aug. 1985); 1 child, Jessamyn Lynn. Student, Orange Coast Coll., 1971-73, U. Redlands, 1974. V.p. adtg. Sta. KTTV-TV, Los Angeles, 1978-80; v.p. advt. Sta. WTTG-TV, Washington, 1980-82; v.p. mktg. Metromedia Inc., Hollywood, Calif., 1982-85; v.p. creative services Walt Disney Co., Burbank, Calif., 1985—. Author: History of Sci-Fi, 1979; producer (TV programs) Disney Magic I, 1986, Dynasty Marketing, 1985, Wonderful World of Disney. Recipient Silver award Internat. Advt. Festival, N.Y.C., 1985, Silver award Hollywood Key Art, 1985. Mem. Sci. Fi Acad. (assoc.), Broadcast Promotors (assoc., bd. dirs.), Broadcast Promotion and Mktg. Execs. Avocations: kayaking, surfing. Office: Walt Disney Co 500 S Buena Vista Burbank CA 91521

PATTON, AUDLEY EVERETT, retired business executive; b. Eve, Mo., Nov. 9, 1898; s. Charles Audley and Letitia Virginia (Earhart) P.; B.S. in Indsl. Adminstrn., U. Ill., 1921, M.S. in Bus. Orgn. and Operation, 1922, Ph.D. in Econs., 1924; m. Mabel Dickie Gunnison, Aug. 5, 1930 (dec. Feb. 1976); 1 dau., Julie Ann Patton Watson; m. 2d, Mary Ritchie Key, June 24, 1977. Auditor, Mfg. Dealers Corp., Cambridge, Mass., 1921; instr. econs. public utilities U. Ill., Champaign-Urbana, 1924-25, asst. prof. econs. Coll. Commerce and Bus. Adminstrn., 1925-26; asst. to pres. Chgo. Rapid Transit Co., Chgo. South Shore & South Bend R.R. Co., Chgo. North Shore & Milw. R.R. Co., Chgo. Aurora & Elgin R.R. Co., 1926; asst. to pres. Public Service Co. No. Ill., Chgo., 1926-43, sec., 1928-52, asst. treas., 1928-44, v.p., 1943-53; v.p., dir. No. Ill. Gas Co., Aurora, 1953-54; v.p. Commonwealth Edison Co., Chgo., 1952-63, ret., 1963; asst. to pres. Presbyn-St. Luke's Hosp., Chgo., 1963-65; former v.p., dir. Big Muddy Coal Co.; past dir. Gt. Lakes Broadcasting Co., Chgo., Chgo. & Ill. Midland Ry. Co., Allied Mills, Inc., Chgo., Am. Gage & Machine Co., Elgin, Ill., HMW Industries, Inc., Stamford, Conn. Treas., Katherine Kreigh Meml. Home for Children, Libertyville, Ill., 1929-36; mem. adv. com. on pub. utilities U. Ill., 1937-40, mem. gen. adv. com., 1943-46. Bd. dirs. Am. Cancer Soc. Ill. div., 1948-76, pres., 1957-59, chmn. bd., 1959-62, mem. fin. com., 1970-76; bd. dirs. Civic Fedn. Chgo., 1945-63, v.p., 1954-63; bd. dirs. South Side Planning Bd. Chgo., 1950-58; bd. dirs., mem. exec. com. Ill. C. of C., 1957-61; trustee Kemper Hall Sch. for Girls, Kenosha, Wis., 1929-37, Highland Park (Ill.) Hosp., 1946-51, Christine and Alfred Sonntag Found. for Cancer Research, 1965-81. Recipient Am. Cancer Soc. medal, 1951. Mem. U. Ill. Found., U.S. Men's (dir. 1958-62, v.p. 1960-65), Midwest (dir. 1956-60) curling assns., OX5 Aviation Pioneers (life mem.), Beta Gamma Sigma, Phi Eta, Delta Sigma Pi, Phi Kappa Phi, Delta Chi. Episcopalian. Clubs: Univ. (dir. 1944-46, treas. 1945-46), Tower (Chgo.); Chgo. Curling (pres. 1956-57) (Northbrook, Ill.). Contbr. articles to profl. jours. Home and office: 14782 Canterbury Tustin CA 92680

PATTON, CHARLES DWIGHT, architect; b. St. Louis, Sept. 29, 1920; s. Harry Claude and Lotta Anna (Schafer) P.; m. Nancy Williams Downes, June 21, 1943; children—Richard Wade, Susan Ann. B.Arch., Cath. U., 1949; student Washington U., St. Louis, Mo. Sch. Mines, U. Wis.-Madison, U. N.Mex. Registered architect Va., D.C., N.Mex., Colo., Md. Ptnr., Bailey & Patton, Arlington, Va., 1951-59; prin. Charles D. Patton, Architect, Bethesda, Md., 1950-67; dir., exec. v.p. Louis C. Kingscott Assocs., Kalamazoo, Mich., 1967-71; prin. Charles D. Patton, Architect, Angel Fire, N.Mex., 1971-81, Ft. Collins, Colo., 1983—; cons., 1983-84. Served with USNR, 1942-45. Mem. AIA. Democrat. Home: 1229 Teakwood Dr Fort Collins CO 80525

PATTON, DAVID WAYNE, hospital administrator; b. Utica, N.Y., June 15, 1942; s. Dale Willard and Eleanor (Miller) P.; B.S., Ariz. State U., 1964; M.H.A., U. Minn., 1966; m. Karmen Louise Rames, June 12, 1965; children—Jodi Lynn, Steven Wayne. Asst. adminstr. Maricopa County Gen. Hosp., Phoenix, 1969-71; adminstr. Holy Rosary Hosp., Miles City, Mont., 1971-74; exec. dir. St. Luke's Hosp., Aberdeen, S.D., 1974-79; pres., chief exec. officer Parkview Episcopal Med. Ctr., Pueblo, Colo., 1979-84; pres. Community Health Corp. and Riverside (Calif.) Community Hosp., 1984—. Bd. dirs. San Louis Valley Health Maintenance Orgn., 1982-84. Served to capt. USAF, 1966-69. Fellow Am. Coll. Healthcare Execs. (regent 1976-79); mem. Am. Acad. Med. Adminstrs. Am. Hosp. Assn., Calif. Hosp. Assn., Young Pres.' Orgn. (Inland Empire chpt.), Riverside C. of C. (bd. dirs. 1986—). Republican. Presbyterian. Clubs: Victoria, Monday Morning. Home: 2596 Raeburn Dr Riverside CA 92506 Office: 4445 Magnolia Riverside CA 92501

PATTON, JOCK, lawyer; b. Elizabeth, N.J., Dec. 11, 1945; s. Robert Ainsworth and Mary Louise (Bergstrom) P.; m. Katherine Jean Stone, Dec. 23, 1968 (div. Nov. 1984); children: Matthew, Morgan; m. Sonchen Carr, Sept. 26, 1986. AB, U. Calif., Berkeley, 1967; JD, U. Calif., Hastings, 1972. Bar: Ariz. 1972, U.S. Dist. Ct. Ariz. 1972, U.S. Ct. Appeals (9th cir.) 1972. Assoc. Streich, Lang, Weeks & Cardon, Phoenix, Ariz., 1972-76; ptnr. Streich, Lang, Weeks & Cardon, Phoenix, 1976—; Bd. dirs. Am. West Airlines, Inc. Contbr. articles on securities law to profl. jours. Served to 1st lt. U.S. Army, 1968-70, Vietnam. Republican. Office: Streich Lang Weeks & Cardon PO Box 471 Phoenix AZ 85001

PATTON, RICHARD WESTON, mortgage banking company executive; b. Evanston, Ill., Sept. 26, 1931; s. Robert Ferry and Sue Buckley P.; m. Lynda A. Kruse, Feb. 2, 1971; 1 child, Robert Weston. B.A., Amherst Coll., 1954. Sales engr. Thermo Fax Sales Corp., Chgo., 1958-60; account exec. Nat. Mortgage Investors, Inc., Chgo. and Pasadena, Calif., 1960-66; asst. v.p. Nat. Mortgage Investors, Inc., 1966-67, v.p., 1967-69, exec. v.p., 1969-73, pres., chief exec. officer, dir., 1973-84, vice-chmn. bd., 1984—, pres.; chmn. exec. com., dir. Ocean Park Restaurant Corp., Santa Monica, Calif., 1977—; dir. Century Fed. Savs. and Loan Assn., Cenfed Corp. Bd. dirs. Pasadena Boys' Club, 1963-66; mem. steering com. Amherst Coll. Capital Fund Drive, 1963-66; bd. dirs. Opera Assocs., 1984—. Served with USMCR, 1955-58. Mem. Calif. Savs. and Loan Assn. League, U.S. League Savs. Assns., Amherst Coll. Alumni Assn. (bd. dirs. 1963—, pres. 1977-79, 86—. Clubs: Overland (sec., dir.), Kronenstadt Ski (past pres.). Office: 87 N Raymond Ave Pasadena CA 91103

PAUL, CAROLYN RHAYE, data processing executive; b. Indpls., July 8, 1956; d. Anthony and Barbara Ellen (Moore) P. Student in ops. mgmt., Computer Learning Ctr. Los Angeles, 1978. Computer operator Herald Examiner, Los Angeles, 1978-81, ops. supr., 1981-84, ops. mgr., 1984-86; ops. analyst Santa Barbara Research Ctr. div. Hughes Aircraft Co., Goleta, Calif., 1986—. Served with USNG, 1978-81. Mem. Assn. Computer Ops. Mgrs., Assn. Contingency Planners. Republican. Roman Catholic. Avocations: writing sci. fiction and poetry, drawing, crossword puzzle creation and solving.

PAUL, DAVID LEO, state banking official; b. Kansas City, Kans., Aug. 11, 1949; s. Lyell David and Ruth Helen (Hartnett) P.; m. Carol Christine Pedersen, Oct. 2, 1971; children—Krista, Evan. B.A. in Econs., U. Kans., 1971; postgrad. U. Conn., 1974, Mich. State U., 1976. Savs. and loan examiner Fed. Home Loan Bank Bd., Des Moines and N.Y.C., 1971-78; savs. and loan commr. Dept. Regulatory Agys., State of Colo., Denver, 1978—; mem. state liaison com. Fed. Fin. Instns. Examination Council, Washington, 1981-85; cons. Ill. Savs. and Loan Dept., Springfield, 1981, Ohio div. Savs. and Loan Assns., Columbus, 1982; mem. fed. savs. and loan adv. council Fed. Home Loan Bank Bd., Washington, 1984. Contbr. articles to profl. jours. Recipient letter of commendation SBA, 1972; Outstanding Service award Fed. Home Loan Bank Bd., 1973; letter of commendation Gov. Richard D. Lamm, Colo., 1978; Boss of Yr. award Am. Bus. Women's Assn., 1982. Mem. Nat. Assn. State Savs. and Loan Suprs. (bd. dirs. 1981—, treas., chmn. fin. com. 1981-82, v.p., chmn. legis. and legal com. 1982-83, pres. 1983-84). Club: Pinery Country. Office: Div Savs and Loan State of Colo 1560 Broadway Suite 705 Denver CO 80202

PAUL, JEFF HERBERT, library administrator; b. Woodland, Calif., Mar. 15, 1952; s. Herbert Joseph and Shirley Gladys (Wayrynen) P.; m. Chris Sue Hampton, June 7, 1972; children: Peter Hampton, Andrew Nicholas. BA in Spanish and Psychology, Chico State U., 1974; MLS, San Jose State U., 1976, MEd, 1978. Cert. tchr. community coll., Calif. Librarian Chico (Calif.) State U., 1977; reference librarian San Jose (Calif.) State U., 1978-79, media dept. head, 1979-84, 87—; reference dept. head Lamson Library, Plymouth, N.H., 1984-85; coordinator Chicano Library Research Ctr., San Jose, 1981—; acting asst. dir. San Jose State U. Library, 1985-87; cons. Calif. Postsecondary Edn., Sacramento, 1978. Contbr. articles to profl. jours. Mem. ALA, Bibliotecas Para la Gente, Calif. State Coll. Librarians (sec., treas. 1979-80, editor newsletter 1979-82), Calif. Acad. and Research Librarians (co-editor newsletter 1983-84). Democrat. Home: 5588 Sunny Oaks San Jose CA 95123 Office: San Jose State U Library 1 Washington Sq San Jose CA 95192-0028

PAUL, JEFFREY WILLIAM, apparel company executive; b. Los Angeles, Sept. 11, 1946; s. Jerome Otto and Doris Sidney (Jacobson) P.; B.S. in Bus. Adminstrn., U. Calif., Berkeley, 1968; M.S. in Fin., UCLA, 1970; m. Nancy J. Sockett, Oct. 14, 1979. Mgmt. trainee Security Pacific Nat. Bank, Los Angeles, 1968-69; fin. analyst Citibank N.A., N.Y.C., 1970-71; asst. treas. Cyprus Mines Corp., Los Angeles, 1971-79, mgr. planning and project evaluations, 1979-80; v.p. fin. The Olga Co., Van Nuys, Calif., 1980-81, v.p. ops., chief fin. officer, 1981-84, pres. and chief exec. officer, 1984—. Served with U.S. Army, 1971. Mem. Am. Apparel Mfrs. Assn. (chmn. western region), Fin. Execs. Inst. (chmn. acad. relations com.), UCLA Grad. Sch. Mgmt. (annual fund com.), Concern Found. (grants com.), Calif. Alumni Assn. Republican. Jewish. Club: Hillcrest Country. Home: 2541 Pesquera Dr Los Angeles CA 90049 Office: The Olga Co 7900 Haskell Ave Van Nuys CA 91409

PAULEY, RICHARD HEIM, real estate counselor; b. Cleve., Dec. 14, 1932; s. Kenneth H. and Romaine (Heim) P.; m. Jan E. Minnick, Oct. 26, 1957; children—Tyler Kent, Elysa Pauley Del Guercio. B.A. in Polit. Sci., Stanford U., 1954; postgrad. U. So. Calif. Sch. Law, 1956-57. Lic. pvt. pilot. Sr. cons. Coldwell Banker & Co., Newport Beach, Calif., 1963-77; owner Richard H. Pauley Co., Investment Realtors, Newport Beach, Beverly Hills and Tustin, Calif., 1977—; sr. mktg. exec. The Seeley Co., Irvine, Calif., 1986—; ins. rep. Quint-Ingham, Coates & Payne, Pasadena, Calif., 1980—; registered prin. First Dominion Fin. Services, Inc., Newport Beach, 1982—. Bd. dirs. Orange Coast YMCA, 1973-78. Served to capt. USAFR, 1965. Recipient cert. of appreciation City of Newport Beach, 1975-76; Disting. Service award Rehab. Inst. Orange County, 1973. Mem. Am. Soc. Real Estate Counselors, Internat. Real Estate Fedn., Calif. Assn. Realtors, Nat. Assn. Realtors, SAR, Beta Theta Pi, Phi Delta Phi. Club: Center (Costa Mesa); Stanford of Orange County (past pres.). Republican. Club: Center (Costa Mesa, Calif.). Home: 1437 Antigua Way Newport Beach CA 92660 Office: 100 Pauley Bldg 17371 Irvine Blvd Tustin CA 92680 Office: One Park Plaza Suite 100 Irvine CA 92714-5910

PAULIN, HARRY WALTER, German language educator; b. Chgo., June 17, 1928; s. William and Gertrude Emily (Schmidt) P.; m. Jean Gertrude Stewart, June 12, 1954; children: Kerry Ann, Kathryn Joy. BA in English, German, N. Cen. Coll., 1950; MA in German, U. Ill., 1955, PhD in German, 1959. Tchr. German and English Downers Grove (Ill.) High Sch., 1955-57; instr. German Northwestern U., Evanston, Ill., 1959-62; asst. prof. San Diego State U., 1962-66, assoc. prof., 1966-70, prof. German, 1970—; exchange tchr. Gisela Gymnasium, Munich, 1966-67. Editor: (textbook) Hier Spukt es, 1979; contbr. articles to profl. jours. Served as sgt. U.S. Army, 1951-53. Mem. Am. Assn. Tchrs. of German, MLA, Philol. Assn. Pacific Coast, Am. Assn. University Profs. Democrat. Christian Scientist. Avocations: swimming, sailing, photography, reading. Office: San Diego State U Dept German and Russian San Diego CA 92182-0439

PAULING, LINUS CARL, chemistry educator; b. Portland, Oreg., Feb. 28, 1901; s. Herman Henry William and Lucy Isabelle (Darling) P.; m. Ava Helen Miller, June 17, 1923 (dec. Dec. 7, 1981); children: Linus Carl, Peter Jeffress, Linda Helen, Edward Crellin. B.S., Oreg. State Coll., Corvallis, 1922, Sc.D. (hon.), 1933; Ph.D., Calif. Inst. Tech., 1925; Sc.D. (hon.), U. Chgo., 1941, Princeton, 1946, U. Cambridge, U. London, Yale, 1947, Oxford, 1948, Bklyn. Poly. Inst., 1955, Humboldt U., 1959, U. Melbourne, 1964, U. Delhi, Adelphi U., 1967, Marquette U. Sch. Medicine, 1969; L.H.D., Tampa, 1950; U.J.D., U. N.B., 1950; LL.D., Reed Coll., 1959; Dr. h.c., Jagiellonian U., Montpellier (France), 1964; D.F.A., Chouinard Art Inst., 1958; also others. Teaching fellow Calif. Inst. Tech., 1922-25, research fellow, 1925-27, asst. prof., 1927-29; assoc. prof., 1929-31, prof. chemistry, 1931-64; chmn. div. chem. and chem. engring., dir. Calif. Inst. Tech. (Gates and Crellin Labs. of Chemistry), 1936-58, mem. exec. com., bd. trustees, 1945-48; research prof. (Center for Study Dem. Instns.), 1963-67; prof. chemistry U. Calif. at San Diego, 1967-69, Stanford, 1969-74; pres. Linus Pauling Inst. Sci. and Medicine, 1973-75, 78—, research prof., 1973—; George Eastman prof. Oxford U., 1948; lectr. chemistry several univs. Author several books, 1930—, including How to Live Longer and Feel Better, 1986. Contbr. articles to profl. jours. Fellow Balliol Coll., 1948; Fellow NRC, 1925-26; Fellow John S. Guggenheim Meml. Found., 1926-27; Recipient numerous awards in field of chemistry, including; U.S. Presdl. Medal for Merit, 1948, Nobel prize in chemistry, 1954, Nobel Peace prize, 1962, Internat. Lenin Peace prize, 1972, U.S. Nat. Medal of Sci., 1974, Fermat medal, Paul Sabatier medal, Pasteur medal, medal with laurel wreath of Internat. Grotius Found., 1957, Lomonosov medal, 1978, U.S. Nat. Acad. Sci. medal in Chem. Scis., 1979, Priestley medal Am. Chem. Soc., 1984, award for chemistry Arthur M. Sackler Found., 1984, Chem. Edn. award Am. Chem. Soc., 1987. Hon., corr., fgn. mem. numerous assns. and orgns. Home: Salmon Creek Big Sur CA 93920 Office: Linus Pauling Inst Sci and Medicine 440 Page Mill Rd Palo Alto CA 94306

PAULOS, JOHN ROBERT (BOB), communications company executive; b. Wood River, Ill., Aug. 21, 1924; s. Peter John and Lola Myrtle (Springer) P.; m. Virginia Louraine Deeter, Sept. 13, 1945; 1 child, Patricia Ann. Grad., Wood River (Ill.) High Sch. Mem. editorial staff Alton (Ill.) Evening Telegraph, 1940-43, 1945-48; gen. mgr. Sta. WOKZ, Alton, 1948; editor Wood River Jour., 1949; mem. editorial staff Idaho State Jour., Pocatello, 1950-53; editor Daily Inter Lake, Kalispell, Mont., 1953-58; pub. The Dalles Chronicle, The Dalles, Oreg., 1958-61, Enterprise-Courier, Oregon City, Oreg., 1961-63, Waikiki Beach Press, Honolulu, 1963-66; v.p. Hagadone Corp., Coeur d'Alene, Idaho, 1966—. Served to lt. USAF, 1943-45. Named Newspaper Man of Yr. Advt. Assn. of Hawaii, Honolulu, 1964, 65. Mem. Internat. Newspaper Promotion Assn. (bd. dirs. 1976, pres. western region, 1980, Silver Strand 1982), Honolulu Advt. Club (pres. 1965),. Republican. Club: Hayden Lake (Idaho) Country. Lodges: Lions (dist. gov. 1956-57), Shriners. Avocation: golf. Home: 100 Military Dr Coeur d'Alene ID 83814 Office: Hagadone Corp PO Box 1178 Coeur d'Alene ID 83814

PAULSEN, BORGE REGNAR, agricultural cooperative executive; b. San Francisco, July 26, 1915; s. Anton and Christa (Regnar) P.; m. Beverly Ann Gephart, July 3, 1942; children: Lee Ann Paulsen Hanna, R. Anthony, Eric Dana, Carol Louise Paulsen Thomsen. Student Stanford, 1933-35; BS, U. Calif., Berkeley, 1937. Sec., Agrl. Adjustment Adminstrn., Yolo County, Calif., 1937-41; owner, operator Sunset Rice Dryer, Inc., Woodland, Calif., 1946—; pres. Demeter Corp. Woodland, Agrivest Corp., Woodland; pres. Crane & Cross Books, Inc., Sacramento; dir. emeritus Wells Fargo Bank, 1986—; dir. Wells Fargo & Co.; farmer, rice grower, 1937—; mem. rice research and mktg. com. U.S. Dept. Agr., others; chmn. adv. bd. Berkeley Bank for Coops., 1976. Bd. dirs., v.p. Calif. Rice Research Found., Yuba City, Woodland Meml. Hosp., also former pres.; former pres. Sutter (Calif.) Mut. Water Co.; bd. dirs. Robert Louis Stevenson Sch., Pebble Beach, Calif., Agrl. Council Calif.; adv. bd. Calif. State U., Sacramento. Served with U.S. Army, 1941-46. Recipient Distinguished Service award Calif. Farm Bur., 1974, Outstanding Service award Woodland Meml. Hosp., 1976, Calif. Rice Industry Man of Year award, 1978; named Agribus. Man of Yr., Yolo County Calif. Mem. Rice Research and Mktg. Bd. Calif. (v.p.), Rice Growers Assn. Calif. (pres., chmn. bd. 1968-70), Bean Growers Assn. Calif. (past pres.), Delta Kappa Epsilon. Republican. Episcopalian. Clubs: Commonwealth, Bankers (San Francisco); Rotary Woodland (former pres.); Sutter, Yolo Fliers Country, El Macero Country; Alderbrook Golf and Yacht (Union, Wash.). Home: 202 Rancho Way St Woodland CA 95695 Office: 1021 Lincoln Ave Woodland CA 95695

PAULSEN, CRAIG ARTHUR, mechanical engineer; b. San Mateo, Calif., May 21, 1952; s. Fred Arthur and Dorothy Mae (Fesler) P.; m. Ginger Kay Bevilacqua, Aug. 7, 1977; 1 dau., Sabrina. AS in Engring. Design Tech., BS in Indsl. Mechs., U. Nev., 1975. Mech. engr. Filper Corp., Reno, 1977-81; project engr. Internat. Game Tech. U. Nev., Reno, 1981—. Democrat. Episcopalian. Club: Nat. Assn. for Stock Car Auto Racing. Office: Internat Game Tech 520 S Rock Blvd Reno NV 89502

PAULSEN, GEORGE ARTHUR, physician; b. Cascade, N.H., Apr. 17, 1922; s. Levi and Benny-Marie (Nelson) P.; B.S., U. N.H., 1943; M.D., Tufts U., 1946; m. Vera Towner; children—Theodore Alan, Thomas Craig, Donald Scott. Intern, Mass. Meml. Hosp., Boston, 1946-47, resident in surgery, 1946-48, 50-52; thoracic surgery tng., Los Angeles, 1952-55; asst. med. dir. LaVina Sanitorium and Hosp., Altadena, Calif., 1952-55; pvt. practice thoracic surgery, Bakersfield, Calif., 1955—; chief surgery Kern County Gen. Hosp., 1960-63, chmn. staff, 1964. Pres. Kern County Tb Assn., 1959; pres. Kern County unit Am. Cancer Soc., 1962-63; exec. com. Kern County council Boy Scouts Am., 1963—, pres. So. Sierra council, 1970-72; adv. bd. Salvation Army, 1962—; pres. Kern County Heart Assn., 1966; bd. dirs. Kern County United Fund, 1972. Served from 1st lt. to capt., USAF, 1948-50. Recipient Silver Beaver award Boy Scouts Am., 1968, Silver Antelope award, 1972. Diplomate Am. Bd. Surgery. Fellow Am. Coll. Chest Physicians; mem. Am. Thoracic Soc., Bakersfield Surg. Soc. (pres. 1965), So. Calif. Tennis-Assn. (dir.), Soc. Thoracic Surgeons (a founder), Am. Acad. Tb Physicians, Pan Am. Med. Assn. (diplomate mem.), Kern County Med. Soc. (sec.-treas. 1976), Bakersfield Tennis Patrons Assn. (pres. 1964-65). Club: Bakersfield Racquet (pres. 1961-62). Contbr. articles to profl. publs. Home: Star Route 1 Box 2960 Tehachapi CA 93561 Office: Calif Correctional Instn PO Box 1031 Tehachapi CA 93561

PAULSEN, JOANN RUTH, fashion accessory business executive; b. San Francisco, Aug. 13, 1941; d. James Steven and Ruth Elizabeth (Harmon) Paulsen; m. Armando Ernesto Damy, July 28, 1966 (div. 1970). AA, Santa Rosa Jr. Coll., 1961; BFA, Inst. Allende, San Miguel de Allende, Mex., 1975. Freelance artist and photographer, Mexico City, 1963-73; owner, designer Frajo, San Miguel Allende, 1975—; pres. Frajo, Ltd., La Mesa, Calif., 1982—; co-owner Pizazz Accessories, San Diego, 1986—. Exhibited paintings and photography in one-woman shows, Mexico City, 1961-80. Recipient Grand Cross of Colors, Rainbow Girls, 1959; Excelsior trophy Excelsior Newspaper, 1969. Mem. Nat. Assn. Women Bus. Owners, Nat. Art Dealers Assn., La Mesa C. of C., U.S. C. of C., Grow. Address: PO Box 3839 La Mesa CA 92041 Office: Frajo Ltd PO Box 3839 La Mesa CA 92041

PAULSEN, THOMAS DEAN, naval officer; b. Watford City, N.D., Apr. 14, 1936; s. H. Arthur and Agnes Lillian (Quale) P.; m. Marbeth Hirsch, Dec. 18, 1960; children—Kari Anne, Kendel Ames, Katherine, Avery F. B.S. in Elec. Engring., U.S. Naval Acad., 1960; M.S. in Computer Sci., U.S. Naval Postgrad. Sch., Monterey, Calif., 1970. Commd. ensign U.S. Navy, 1960, advanced through grades to capt., 1980; weapons and communications officer USS Corporal, Charleston, S.C., 1960-63; navigation and ops. officer USS Theodore Roosevelt, Groton, Conn., 1963-68; exec. officer USS Sailfish, Pearl Harbor, Hawaii, 1970-72, USS Reeves, Pearl Harbor, 1973-75; comdg. officer USS Whipple, Pearl Harbor, 1975-77; fleet ASW readiness officer staff, comdr. 7th Fleet, Yokosuka, Japan, 1977-80; dir. profl. devel. div. U.S. Naval Acad., Annapolis, Md., 1980-83; comdg. officer USS Blue Ridge, Yokosuka, 1984—. Co-author: Naval Officer's Guide, 1983. Recipient Meritorious Service medal Sec. Dept. Navy, 1980, Navy Commendation medal, 1977, Navy Achievement medal, 1972. Mem. Naval Inst., U.S. Naval Acad. Alumni Assn. Office: Comdg Officer USS Blue Ridge (LCC-19) FPO San Francisco CA 96628

PAULSON, ALAN CHARLES, editor; b. Milw., Dec. 1, 1947; s. Robert C. and Dorothy (Lohneis) P.; B.S., U. Wis., 1970; M.S., U. Alaska, 1973. Instr. biology Kodiak Community Coll., Alaska, 1974-75; fisheries biologist Alaska Dept. Fish and Game, Kodiak, 1973-75; instr. biology U. Alaska, Fairbanks, 1975, research biologist Inst. Marine Sci., 1975-76; editor Inst. Water Resources, 1978-86, Inst. No. Engring., 1986—; freelance writer Fairbanks, 1977-78; 1978-86, editor Inst. Northern Engring., 1986—; comml. hot air balloon pilot, Fairbanks, 1981—, profl. diver, 1964—, freelance photographer, 1974—. Contbr. articles photographs on natural history, biology, art, panoramic photography, no. engineering silenced and automatic weapons, aviation to profl. jours. and popular mags. Recipient Fejes book writing award, journalism dept. U. Alaska, 1984; named Alaska Writer of Yr. in Natural Resources, Alaska N.W. Publ. Co., 1977; grantee Internat. Assn. Panoramic Photographers, 1972, AEC. Mem. Internat. Assn. Panoramic Photographers, Nat. Press Photographers Assn., AAAS, Am. Soc. Ichthyologists and Herpetologists, Balloon Fedn. Am. Home: 1349 Chena Ridge Rd Fairbanks AK 99709 Office: U Alaska Inst No Engring Fairbanks AK 99775-1760

PAULSON, CINDY PATRICE, occupational therapist; b. San Jose, Calif., Apr. 16, 1949; d. Gordon Delmar and Necia Rose (Rhodes) P. BA in Cultural Anthropology, U. Calif.-San Diego, La Jolla, 1971; MA in Occupational Therapy, U. So. Calif., 1975; ThM, Fuller Theol. Sem., 1979. Program dir. Calif. Youth Home, Inglewood, 1973-76; pvt. practice occupational therapy Pasadena, Calif., 1979-80, Phoenix, 1982-85, Tempe, Ariz., 1986—; adminstr., pres. bd. dirs. SMARTS 4 U, Covina, Calif., 1980-82; exec. dir. Found. Blind Children, Scottsdale, Ariz., 1985-86; clin. instr. occupational therapy U. So. Calif., 1976-79; co-chmn. legis. network Occupational Therapy Assn. Calif., 1976. Vol. McCain for Congress campaign, Tempe, 1982, Maricopa County Health Dept., Phoenix, 1985; agy. relations vol. Valley of Sun United Way, Phoenix, 1985—; bd. dirs. Covina (Calif.) Presbyn. Ch., 1981-82. pol. Am. Occupational Therapy Assn. (cert., mem. editorial bd. Am. Jour. Occupational Therapy 1982-84), Ariz. Occupational Therapy Assn. (chmn. phys. disability com. 1984-85). Republican. Lodge: Soroptomists (bd. dirs. 1985-86). Avocations: writing, weaving, watercolor, outdoor activities.

PAULSON, DONALD ROBERT, chemistry educator; b. Oak Park, Ill., Sept. 6, 1943; s. Robert Smith and Florence Teresa (Beese) P.; m. Elizabeth Anne Goodwin, Aug. 20, 1966; children: Matthew, Andrew. BA, Monmouth Coll., 1965; PhD, Ind. U., 1968. Asst. prof. chemistry Calif. State U., Los Angeles, 1970-74, assoc. prof., 1974-78, prof., 1979—, chmn. dept., 1982—; vis. prof. U. B.C., Vancouver, Can., 1977-78, U. Sussex, Brighton, Eng., 1984-85. Author: Alicyclic Chemistry, 1976; contbr. articles to profl. jours. Named Outstanding Prof., Calif. State U., Los Angeles, 1978. Mem. Am. Chem. Soc., Chem. Soc. (London), InterAm. Photochem. Soc., Nat. Assn. Sci. Tchrs., Sigma Xi. Democrat. Episcopalian. Avocations: photography, hiking, soccer. Home: 1627 Laurel St South Pasadena CA 91030 Office: Calif State U Dept Chemistry 5151 State University Dr Los Angeles CA 90032

PAULSON, FRANCIS JAMES, lawyer; b. Denver, Feb. 10, 1922; s. Joseph Z. and Helen Agatha (Murphy) P.; m. Annabelle McIntire, Jan. 18, 1947; 1 son, Gregory Francis. J.D. summa cum laude, U. Notre Dame, 1946. Bar: Ill. 1947, U.S. Supreme Ct. 1959, Colo. 1974. Assoc. Pope & Ballard, Chgo., 1948-56, Braun, Johnson & Ryan, Chgo., 1948-56; ptnr. Haring & Paulson, Chgo., 1956-59, Paulson & Ketchum, Chgo., 1959-74; gen. counsel High Country Corp., Denver, 1978—; pros. atty. Village of Riverdale (Ill.), 1970-74. Recipient Good Citizenship award Mut. Trust Life Ins. Co., 1970. Mem. Colo. Bar Assn., ABA; former mem. Chgo. Trial Lawyers Assn. (pres. 1956), Chgo. Soc. Trial Lawyers, Chgo. Bar Assn., Am. Arbitration Assn. (accident claims adv. council, Chgo.). Roman Catholic. Club: Chgo. Athletic Assn. Co-author Ill. Jury Instructions, 1954. Home: 255 Monaco Pkwy Denver CO 80220 Office: 1860 Lincoln Suite 100 Denver CO 80295

PAULSON, JOAN MERRYANN, development and property manager, consultant; b. Tacoma, Oct. 30, 1951; d. Arthur Gilbert and Billie Bernice (Butler) P. BA in Urban Planning, U. Wash., 1983. Lic. real estate salesperson, Wash. Coordinator, liaison Pike Place Project, City of Seattle, 1972-79; constrn. and devel. coordinator Pike Place Market Preservation and Devel. Authority, 1979-82; property mgr., assoc. William J. Charles Assocs., Seattle, 1983—; resident apt. mgr. Fairmount Apts., 1979—; mem. Mayor's Task Force on 1982-84 Downtown Plan. Pres. Denny Regrade Community Council, 1982-85; mem. LWV, 1983—, Seattle Mcpl. League, 1981—; trustee Allied Arts of Seattle, 1982—; mem. Seattle Shorelines Coalition, 1981—; bd. dirs. Downtown Human Service Council, 1983, sec.-treas. 1984—, chmn. housing com. Recipient award for preservation of affordable housing Seattle Tenants Union, 1980; recipient 1st award for Denny Regrade Firm Alternative, Wash. chpt. Am. Planning Assn., 1981-82. Mem. Seattle-King County Bd. Realtors. Democrat. Contbr. articles to profl. jours. Office: William J Charles Assocs 2208 Market St NW Suite 100 Seattle WA 98107

PAULSON, RICHARD, management consultant; b. Erie, Pa., Feb. 10, 1920. 1 dau., Kathy. Field test engr. Convair-Astronautics, San Diego, 1953-63; sr. cons. Bruce Payne Assocs., Los Angeles, 1963-65; self employed mgmt. cons., Beverly Hills, Calif., 1965-72; founder, pres. O.N. Eno Co., Fresno, Calif., 1972—. Served to 1st lt. USAAF, 1943-45; ret. USAFR, 1963. Author, pub.: The ABC's of Time Study, 1978; contbr. articles on mgmt. to bus. jours., tech. articles to engring. jours., travel articles, miscl. material to mags.; songwriter; designer, inventor toys, games, restaurants, artistic, comml. projects. Office: PO Box 11032 Fresno CA 93771

PAULSON-EHRHARDT, PATRICIA HELEN, laboratory administrator; b. Moses Lake, Wash., June 10, 1956; s. Luther Roanoke and Helen Jane (Baird) Paulson; m. Terry Lee Ehrhardt, Mar. 12, 1983. Student, Pacific Luth. U., 1974-76; BS in Med. Tech., U. Wash., 1976; BS in Biology, MS in Biology, Eastern Wash. U., 1982. Med. technologist Samaritan Hosp., Moses Lake, 1979-81; lab. supr. Moses Lake Clinic br. Wenatchee Valley Clinic, 1983-87; with Kalispell (Mont.) Regional Hosp., 1987—; mem. med. lab. tech. adv. com. Wenatchee (Wash.) Valley Coll., 1984-85, chmn., 1985-86. Mem. Flathead Valley Community Band, 1987—. Mem. Am. Soc. Med. Technologists (hematology judge 1986 Wash. State Student Bowl), Wash. State Soc. Med. Techologists (coordinator sci. assembly small lab. 1986), Wash. Assn. Diabetic Educators, Am. Soc. Clin. Pathologists (cert.), Pan Players Flute Soc., AAUW, Flathead Tennis Assn., Sigma Xi, Kappa Delta (pledge class pres. 1976). Republican. Lutheran. Club: Moses Lake Volleyball Assn. (pres. 1985-86). Lodge: Rotary (active wive's br. Moses Lake, 1985). Avocations: tennis, volleyball, flying, fishing, playing flute. Home: 3270 Airport Rd Kalispell MT 59901

PAUSTENBACH, DENNIS JAMES, environmental toxicologist; b. Pitts., Oct. 29, 1952; s. Albert Paustenbach and Patricia Jean (Iseman) Murray; m. Louise Dunning, Feb. 23, 1985; 1 child, Mark Douglas. BSChemE, Rose-Hulman Inst. Tech., 1974; MS in Indsl. Hygiene, U. Mich., 1977; MS in Indsl. Psychology, Ind. State U., 1978; PhD in Environ. Toxicology, Purdue U., 1982. Diplomate Am. Bd. Toxicology; cert. indsl. hygienist, safety profl. Chem. process engr. Eli Lilly & Co., Clinton, Ind., 1974-76; indsl. hygiene engr. Eli Lilly & Co., Lafayette, Ind., 1977-80; instr. toxicology and indsl. hygiene Purdue U., West Lafayette, Ind., 1978-82; risk assessment scientist Stauffer Chem. Co., Westport, Conn., 1982-84; mgr. indsl. and environ. toxicology Syntex Corp., Palo Alto, Calif., 1984—; cons. Eli Lilly & Co., Indpls., 1980-82, Gen. Electric Co., Ft. Wayne, Ind., 1980-82, Hewlett-Packard, San Diego, 1984-86, Semiconductor Indsl. Assn., San Jose, Calif., 1984-86. Contbr. chpts. to books, articles to profl. jours. Mem. Am. Inst. Chem. Engring., Am. Indsl. Hygiene Assn., Soc. Toxicology, Internat. Soc. Chronobiology, Bd. Cert. Safety Profls., Soc. Environ. Toxicology and Chemistry. Roman Catholic. Avocations: antique furniture, jogging, golf, tennis. Home: 1537 Belleville Way Sunnyvale CA 94087 Office: Syntex Corp 3401 Hillview Ave Palo Alto CA 94303

PAVANASASIVAM, GOWSALA, chemist; b. Uduvil, Jaffna, Sri Lanka, Jan. 30, 1945; came to U.S., 1976; s. Chellappah and Valiammai Subramaniam; m. Velupillai Pavanasasivam, Mar. 31, 1973; 1 child, Dhileepan. BS in Chemistry, U. Srilanka, Peradeniya, 1967, MS in Organic Chemistry, 1973; PhD in Organic Chemistry, U. Md., 1980. Asst. lectr. U. Srilanka, Peradeniya, 1967-70, research asst., 1970-76; teaching asst. U. Md., College Park, 1976-80, post-doctoral fellow, 1980-83; Fogarty fellow Nat. Cancer Inst., Md., 1983-84; scientist Neo Rx, Seattle, 1984—, sect. head, 1985—; Contbr. articles on cancer to profl. jours. Patentee in field of cancer research. Mem. Am. Chem. Soc. Avocations: gardening, cooking. Home: 23504 97th Pl W Edmonds WA 98020 Office: Neo Rx 410 W Harrison Seattle WA 98119

PAVLONNIS, THERESA CASSIDY, school adminstrator; b. West Orange, N.J., Feb. 27, 1951; d. Patrick Raymond and Carmine (Patuto) Cassidy; m. Richard Alan Pavlonnis, Aug. 24, 1974; children: Dawn Rose, Cassidy Anne. BA, William Paterson Coll., 1973; MEd, Rutgers U., 1975; EdD, Mont. State U., 1985. Tchr. Sayreville (N.J.) Schs., 1973-76; tchr. Great Falls (Mont.) Schs., 1976-78, adminstr., 1978—; mem. adv. council for edn. Mont. State U., accreditation team for on-site evaluation Office Pub. Instruction, Mont. Coordinator United Way. Mem. Council Exceptional Children, Mont. Assn. Sch. Pricipals, AAUW (chmn. house tour, scholarship commn.), Nat. Assn. Secondary Sch. Principals, Assn. Supervison and Curriculum Devel., Phi Delta Kappa (election, research and membership coms.). Avocations: reading, sewing. Home: 82 Woodland Estates Rd Great Falls MT 59401 Office: Great Falls Pub Schs PO Box 2428 Great Falls MT 59403

PAWULA, KENNETH JOHN, artist, educator; b. Chgo., Feb. 4, 1935; s. John and Clara (Brzezinski) P.; student Northwestern U., 1956, Art Inst. Chgo., 1956; B.F.A., U. Ill., 1959; M.A. in Painting, U. Calif., Berkeley, 1962. Graphic designer Motorola, Inc., Chgo., 1959-60; grad. asst. printmaking U. Calif., Berkeley, 1961-62, asso. in art, 1962-63; archaeol. delineator for Islamic excavation Am. Research Center, Egypt, 1964-65; instr. Sch. of Art, U. Wash., Seattle, 1965-67, asst. prof., 1967-73, asso. prof., 1974—; participant artist-in-residence program of Ecole Superieure Des Beaux-Arts D'Athenes at Rhodos Art Center, Greece, 1978; cons. to Wydawnictwo Interpress, Warsaw, Poland, 1978; mem. art jury ann. painting, drawing and sculpture show Art Mus. of Greater Victoria, Can., 1971, Unitarian Art Gallery, Seattle, 1968, Cellar Gallery, Kirkland, Wash., 1968, Lakewood Artist's Outdoor Exhibit, Tacoma, Wash., 1968; participant Painting Symposium, Janow Podlaski, Poland, 1977. One-man shows of paintings include: Univ. Unitarian Fine Arts Gallery, Seattle, 1970, Polly Friedlander Gallery, Seattle, 1970, Lynn Kottler Galleries, N.Y.C., 1971, U. Minn. Art Gallery, Mpls., 1971, Art Mus. of Greater Victoria, Can., 1972, Second Story Gallery, Seattle, 1972; group shows include: Worth Ryder Gallery, U. Calif., Berkeley, 1962, Seattle Art Mus., 1964, 70, 65, 66, Frye Art Mus., Seattle, 1966, San Francisco Art Ins., 1966, Henry Gallery, U. Wash., Seattle, 1966, 67, 70, State Capitol Mus., Olympia, Wash., 1967, Attica Gallery, Seattle, 1967, 69, Sec. of State's Office, Olympia, 1968, Eastern Mich. U., Ypsilanti, 1968, Rogue Gallery, Medford, Oreg., 1968, Marylhurst Coll., Oreg., 1968, Spokane Art Mus., 1968, Cheney Cowles Mus., Spokane, 1969, Jade Gallery, Richland, Wash., 1969, Alaska U., 1970, Polly Friedlander Gallery, Mpls., 1971, Anchorage Art Mus., 1972, U. Nev. Art Gallery, 1972, Juneau (Alaska) Art Mus., 1972, Springfield (Mo.) Art Mus., 1973, U. N.D., Grand Forks, 1974, Washington and Jefferson Coll., Washington, Pa., 1975, MacMurray Coll., Jacksonville, Ill., 1976, Gallery of Fine Arts, Eastern Mont. Coll., 1976, Inst. of Culture, Janow Podlaski, Poland, 1977, Seattle Arts Commn., 1978, Polish Cultural Center, Buffalo, 1979, Cabo Frio Internat. Print Biennial, Brazil, 1983, Sunderland (Eng.) Poly. U. Faculty Exchange Exhbn., 1984, Internat Art Biennial Mus. Hosio Capranica-Viterbo, Italy, 1985; represented in permanent collections: San Francisco Art Mus., Seattle Art Mus., Henry Gallery, U. Wash., Seattle, Highline Coll., Midway, Wash., Marylhurst Coll., Art Mus., Janow Podlaski, Poland, Tacoma Nat. Bank, Fine Arts Gallery of San Diego. Mem. Coll. Art Assn., AAUP. Home: 10037 NE 115th Ln Kirkland WA 98033 Office: School of Art Coll Arts and Scis U Wash Seattle WA 98195

PAXTON, DAVID OLAF, office manager, pilot, retired army officer; b. Socorro, N.Mex., Nov. 2, 1927; s. Emery Foster and Ruth Mildred (Bursum) P.; m. Nancy Lee Shulthiess, Nov. 23, 1950; children—Mark Emery, Deborah Chandler Antonucci, Matthew Radford; m. 2d, Nancy Nordhaus Minces, Nov. 5, 1976. Student N.Mex. Mil. Inst., 1943-45, U. N.Mex., 1946, N.Mex. A&M U., 1947-48, U.S. Armed Forces Inst., 1964-66. Lic. airline transport and comml. helicopter pilot. Cattle rancher, Socorro County N.Mex., 1943-50; commd. 2d lt. Army N.G. 1950; advanced through grades to col., 1970; served as helicopter pilot, intelligence analyst Philippines, Okinawa, Japan, Korea, Germany, Panama, Viet Nam, and Washington, 1950-70; spl. investigator state's atty. gen. and sheriff's dept., Bernillio County, N.Mex., 1970-72; pres., owner Paxton Enterprises, Inc., Albuquerque, 1972-76; br. mgr. Health and Human Services, Social Security Adminstrn., Hobbs, N.Mex., 1974—. Co-chmn. Lea County United Way; search mission pilot, CAP. Decorated Legion of Merit with oak leaf cluster, Bronze star with 2 oak leaf clusters, Air medal with 5 oak leaf clusters, Joint Service Commendation medal, Army Commendation medal with two oak leaf clusters, Navy medal for valor, Purple Heart; recipient outstanding service citation Social Security Adminstrn., 1980. Mem. Social Security Mgmt. Assn., Aircraft Owners and Pilots Assn., N.Mex. Cattle Grower's Assn., Ret. Officer's Assn., Assn. Ret. Intelligence Officers, N.Mex. Mil Inst. Alumni Assn. (bd. govs.), Am. Legion, VFW, Am. Contract Bridge League, Dalmatian Club Am. Republican. Clubs: Elks, Lea County Bridge League. Author: Owning Your First Dalmatian, 1957. Home: 1318 W Taos St Hobbs NM 88240

PAXTON, JAY RENFRO, banking consultant; b. Santa Barbara, Calif., Nov. 3, 1924; s. Joe D. and Helen M. (Jacobson) P.; m. Elizabeth Murdoch, Feb. 4, 1961; children: Jan E., John C. BA, U. Calif., Santa Barbara, 1950. Mgmt. trainee Union Bank, Los Angeles, 1950-54; with credit dept. County Nat. Bank, Santa Barbara, Calif., 1955-56; credit mgr., asst. v.p. Bank of Encino, Calif., 1957-60; mgr. Bank of A. Levy, Simi Valley, Calif., 1960-83, v.p., regional adminstr., 1983—. Served with USAAC, 1943-46. Mem. Lambda Chi Alpha. Republican. Lodges: Masons, Rotary. Home: 1082 Hacienda Dr Simi Valley CA 93065

PAYEN, LOUIS ARTHUR, archaeologist; b. Sacramento, Jan. 30, 1940. BA in Anthropology, Calif. State U., Sacramento, 1962, MA in Anthropology, 1966; PhD in Anthropology, U. Calif., Riverside, 1982. Archaeologist I Calif. State Dept. Parks and Recreation, 1966-70; research asst. Radiocarbon Lab. U. Calif., Riverside, 1978-82, postgrad. research anthropologist Radiocarbon Lab., 1982—, instr. anthropology, 1982, 83; participant in numerous short term and seasonal archaeol. projects, 1957-83. Contbr. numerous articles to profl. jours. Mem. Soc. Am. Archaeology, Soc. Hist. Archaeology, Soc. Archaeol. Scis., Am. Quaternary Assn., Cen. Calif. Archaeol. Found., Cave Research Assocs., Southwestern Anthropol. Assn., Sigma Xi. Home: PO Box 152 Loyalton CA 96118 Office: U Calif Radiocarbon Lab Dept Anthropology Riverside CA 92521

PAYNE, ALBERT FRANKLIN, architectural photographer; b. Phoenix, Jan. 3, 1946; s. Dale Franklin and Lela June (Marks) P.; m. Patricia Dorothy Sparkes, Aug. 8, 1967 (div. 1971); m. Judith Coralynn Gibson, June 21, 1979; children: Mark A., Whitney L. BS, Ariz. State U., 1968, BA, 1971. Mgr. car sales Tercar Sales and Leasing, Concord, Calif., 1968-69; mgmt. trainee DelMonte Corp., San Francisco, 1968-69; computer sales rep. SCM Corp., Phoenix, 1969-71; psychol. youth counselor Maricopa County Youth Services Bur., Phoenix, 1970-71; pvt. practice archtl. photography Phoenix, 1971—; guest speaker AIA, Phoenix, 1984, Inst. Bus. Designers, Phoenix, 1984, Mpls. Indsl./Comml. Photog. Assn., Mpls., 1985, No. Ariz. U., Flagstaff, 1985-86. Photographer: (books) A Guide to the Architecture of Phoenix, 1983, Corporate Design, 1983; (mags.) Interior Design, 1984, Interiors, 1984-85. Corp. donor Ariz. State U. Century Club, Tempe, 1985—, Phoenix Children's Theatre, Phoenix, 1985—, The Breakthrough Found., San Francisco, 1979—, The Hunger Project, San Francisco, 1979—. Mem. Ariz. Profl. Photographers (past pres., Apple award 1985, Al Buehman Meml. award 1984, 85, Sweepstakes award 1983), Am. Soc. Mag. Photographers (bd. dirs.), Profl. Photographers Am., Phoenix Profl. Photoographers Assn., Ariz. Bus. Alliance. Democrat. Presbyterian. Avocation: sports car enthusiast. Home and Office: 830 N 4th Ave Phoenix AZ 85003

PAYNE, DANIEL FRANKLIN, entrepreneur; b. Los Angeles, Aug. 7, 1945; s. William Franklin and Patricia Jean (Gordon) P. Student U. Mont., 1962, Calif. Western U., 1963, U. Ga., 1964, U. Denver, 1965, George Washington U., 1966, UCLA, 1967, Loyola Law School, 1968; M.B.A. Calif. Western U., 1976, Ph.D. in Bus., 1978. Pres., owner Design Trust and World in Water Corp., 1969-73; west coast mgr. Arbitron/Control Data, 1973-76; mktg. mgr. Dickinson Communications, Huntington Beach, Fountain Valley and Westminster, Calif., 1976-78; dir. franchising, gen. mgr. Six Star Cablevision Co., Los Angeles, N.Y.C. and Chgo., 1978-81; pres., chief exec. officer Internat. Cablesystems, Inc., Beverly Hills, Calif., 1981-83; founder, gen. ptnr. Am. TV Network, owners TV channels in Anchorage, Alaska, Durango, Colo. Coos Bay, Oreg., Maui, Hawaii, Cheyenne, Wyo., 1979-86; owner, founder Discount Travel of Los Angeles and Glendale; owner Priceless Places, Paige One Designs; owner, architect, builder Rivendell Retreat Compound. Mem. Calif. Rare Fruit Growers Assn., Mensa. Libertarian. Home: Rivendell Retreat 1870 Burnell Dr Los Angeles CA 90065 Office: PO Box 1211 Glendale CA 91209

PAYNE, GEORGE SANDERSON, orthodontist; b. Jerome, Ariz., Apr. 16, 1930; s. Maude Emily (Sanderson) P.; m. Marilyn Jean Heinbockel, Aug. 28, 1955; children: Warren, Janice, John, Brian. BS, U. Calif., Berkeley, 1951; DDS, U. Calif., San Francisco, 1959. Diplomate Am. Bd. Orthodontics. Asst. prof. dentistry U. Calif., San Francisco, 1959-70, lectr., 1978—; v.p., chmn. underwriting and communications The Dentists Insurance Co., Sacramento, Calif., 1983—. Planning commn. City of Santa Rosa, Calif., 1965-72. Served to 1st lt. U.S. Army, 1953-55, Korea. Mem. Edward H Angle Soc. N. Calif. (pres. 1977-78), Calif. State Soc. Orthodontics (pres. 1982-84), Redwood Empire Dental Soc. (pres. 1978), Calif. Dental Assn. (v.p. 1985-86). Lodges: Rotary (pres. Santa Rosa chpt. 1974-75), Masons. Avocations: skiing, backpacking, tennis. Office: 3850 Montgomery Dr Santa Rosa CA 95405

PAYNE, MAGGI D., composer, recording engineer; b. Temple, Tex., Dec. 23, 1945; d. Ralph B. and Pauline Elizabeth (Wilson) P. MusB, Northwestern U., 1968; postgrad., Yale U., 1968-69; MusM, U. Ill., 1970; MFA, Mills Coll., 1972. Faculty Mills Coll., Oakland, Calif., 1972—, San Francisco Art Inst., 1982-83; artist-in-residence Exploratorium, San Francisco, 1983-85; prodn. engr. King Broadcasting, San Francisco, 1983—; faculty Mills Coll., Oakland, Calif., 1972—. Composer: (record album) Crystal, 1986, (songs) Ling, 1982, White Night, 1984, Subterranean Network, 1985, Shimmer, 1985, Airwaves, 1987. Video grantee Rocky Mountain Film Ctr., 1983-84, Mellon Found., 1983; composer grantee Nat. Endowment for the Arts, 1979-80. Mem. Audio Engring. Soc., Composers' Forum, Bay Area Video Coalition, New Langton Arts Assn., Am. Fedn. Musicians. Office: Mills Coll Box 9830 Oakland CA 94613

PAYNE, RAYMOND LEE, JR., lawyer; b. Kansas City, Mo., Nov. 7, 1927; s. Raymond Lee and Erma Elizabeth (Whitaker) P.; m. Betty Joyce Billingsley, 1948; children—Raymond Lee, Janifer H. Payne Joel, Gregory M.; m. Kathleen Marie Wood, Dec. 14, 1957; m. Patricia Paschall Chancellor, June 17, 1977. B.S., U. Denver, 1959, J.D., 1960. Bar: Colo. 1960; cert. hotel/motel adminstr. Assoc. Harding & Herman, Denver, 1960-62; assoc. Tilly & Skelton, Denver, 1962-66; sole practice, Denver, 1966-67; ptnr. Safran & Payne and predecessors, Denver, 1968-78; sole practice, Denver, 1978—; sec., dir. Commerce Motor Hotel Corp., Adventure Travel Corp., ptnr. Cameron Assocs.; Chmn. bd. S.W. Denver Community Mental Health Services, 1960-74; bd. dirs. Denver Bar Assn. Credit Union, 1979—, chmn. loan com., 1982, pres., 1983-84; chmn. Downtown Dem. Forum. Served with AUS, 1946-47. Mem. Colo. Bar Assn., Denver Bar Assn., Colo.-Wyo. Hotel/Motel Assn. (bd. dirs.). Democrat. Clubs: Over the Hill Gang Ski Team, City of Denver; Toastmasters (Lakewood, Colo.); Masons. Home: 9200 Cherry Creek South Dr Denver CO 80231 Office: 8000 E Girard Ave South Tower Suite 415 Denver CO 80231

PAYNE, THOMAS A., mayor, city of Bakersfield, Calif., 1985—. Office: Office of Mayor 1501 Truxtun Ave Bakersfield CA 93301 *

PAYZANT, THOMAS, school superintendent. Supt. schs. City of San Diego. Office: San Diego Unified Sch Dist Office of the Supt 4100 Normal St San Diego CA 92103 *

PAZ, LAWRENCE RAYMOND, social worker; b. Las Cruces, N.Mex., July 6, 1951; s. Raymond Marcello and Caroline (Benavidez) P.; m. Barbara Alvarez, Aug. 14, 1981; 1 child, Daniel Lawrence. BSW, N.Mex. State U., 1982; MSW, N.Mex. Highlands U., 1983. Relief counselor Southwest Community Mental Health Ctr., Las Cruces, 1980-82; planner N.Mex. State Housing Authority, Santa Fe, 1982-83; therapist drug treatment program Aliviane, Inc., El Paso, Tex., 1983-84; foster care coordinator Human Service Dept., Las Cruces, 1984—; planner, cons. Dona Ana County, La Union, N.Mex., 1984—. Editor newsletter Vivienda, 1982; author Jour. Holistic Health Resources, 1982, (slide show) Intro. to Social Work, 1980. Mem. adv. bd. Santa Teresa chpt. Hosp., 1986—; mem. fin. bd. Las Cruces Family YMCA; trustee City of La Union, 1986; vol. Las Cruces Dems., 1978. Served with U.S. Army, 1971-78. Mem. Nat. Assn. Social Workers (vice chmn. 1984-85), Good Life Found., Inc., (bd. dirs. 1985—), Dona Ana County Mental Health Assn., Dona Ana Human Services Consortium. Methodist. Avocations: fishing, outdoor sports. Office: NMex Human Services Dept PO Box 16227 Las Cruces NM 88004-6227

PAZ SOLDÁN, MIGUEL MATEO, process engineer, financial/tax planner; b. Lima, Peru, Feb. 11, 1945; came to U.S., 1968; s. Fernando and Elsa Ricardina (Estrada) P.; m. Harriet Sue Skousen; children: Michelle, Monica, Miguel Jr., Manuel, Marcy, Marc, Marcella, Melinda, Melissa, Myra. BS in Chemistry and Microbiology, Ariz. State U., 1980; M of Internat. Mgmt., Am. Grad. Sch. Internat. Mgmt., Glendale, Ariz., 1982. Chemist Motorola Inc., Phoenix, 1980-82; fin. planning, adminstrv. mgr. Motorola Inc., Mesa, Ariz., 1984-85; process engineer Motorola Inc., Mesa, 1983-84, 85-86; mgr. fin. and tax planning M.P.S. Acctg. and Tax Services, Chandler, Ariz., 1986—. Cubmaster Boy Scouts Am., Chandler, Ariz., 1980—. Mem. Electrochem. Soc. Republican. Mormon. Home: 22231 S 118th St Chandler AZ 85249 Office: MPS Acctg and Tax Services 22231 S 118th St Chandler AZ 85249

PEACHES, DANIEL, college regent, former state legislator; b. Kayenta, Ariz., Sept. 2, 1940; s. Henry and Adelaide (Donald) P.; B.S., No. Ariz. U., 1967. Mem. Nat. Adv. Council Indian Edn., Washington, 1972; bd. regents Haskell Indian Jr. Coll., 1975-83; exec. staff Office of Chmn. Navajo Nation, Window Rock, Ariz., 1971-83; mem. Ariz. Ho. of Reps., 1975-85; pres. Navajo Mountain Soil and Water Conservation Dist., 1984—; regent Northland Pioneer Coll., Holbrook, Ariz., 1985—. Republican. Home: PO Box 1801 Kayenta AZ 86033 Office: Northland Pioneer Coll Holbrook AZ 86025

PEAKMAN, DAVID CHARLES, cytogeneticist, consultant; b. Birmingham, Warwickshire, Eng., Apr. 30, 1938; came to U.S., 1963, permanent resident; s. Charles and Mary Ellen (Farmer) P.; m. Maradee Lyn Verburg, Apr. 5, 1968; children—Lindsay Anne, Jonathan Mark. Assoc., Inst. Med. Lab. Tech., U. Birmingham Med. Sch. and Matthew Boulton Coll., 1962. Research technologist Birmingham Med. Sch., Eng., 1956-63, Henry Ford Hosp., Detroit, 1963-64; cytogenetics lab supr. U. Colo. Med. Ctr., Denver, 1964-72; asst. dir. cytogenetics Nat. Jewish Hosp., Denver, 1972-78; assoc. dir. cytogenetics Genetics Ctr., Tempe, Ariz., 1978-80; dir. cytogenetics lab. Reproductive Genetics Ctr., Denver, 1980—; pres. Peakman & Assocs., Denver, 1983—. Co-author book chpt. Contbr. articles to profl. jours. Mem. Assn. Cytogenetics Technologists, Am. Soc. Human Genetics. Office: Reproductive Genetics Ctr 455 S Hudson Denver CO 80222

PEARCE, LAER, advertising executive; b. Oakland, Calif., Dec. 26, 1950; s. John Edward and Jean P.; m. Melissa Kay Farlow, Dec. 30, 1978 (div. Jan. 1980); m. Beth Eileen Trochman, Oct. 30, 1982; 1 child, Lauren Ashley. BA in Journalism, Ind. U., 1974. Reporter The Sentinel-News, Shelbyville, Ky., 1974-76; pub. relations acct. mgr. The Wenz-Neely Co., Louisville, 1976-80; nat. sales mgr. Indsl. Liaison, Inc., Costa Mesa, Calif., 1980-82; pres. Wordsmith, Lake Forest, Calif., 1982-83, Corp. Creativity Group, Lake Forest, 1983—; mem. curriculum adv. com. Mktg. Communications Program, U. Calif., Irvine. Named to Hon. Order Ky. Cols., 1980. Mem. Pub. Relations Soc. Am. (accredited), Orange County Pub. Relations Soc. (bd. dirs. 1985, pres. 1987, 3 Protos awards 1986, Order of Orange 1985), Saddleback Regional C. of C. (bd. dirs. 1983-85), Western and English Mfrs. Assn. (bd. dirs. 1981-82). Avocations: bicycling, weight tng. Office: Corp Creativity Group 22471 Aspan St #206 Lake Forest CA 92630

PEARCE-PERCY, HENRY THOMAS, physicist, electronics executive; b. Melbourne, Victoria, Australia, Sept. 7, 1947; came to U.S., 1970; s. Thomas Walker Pearce-Percy and Valda Marion (Mills) Woinarski; m. Virginia Kathleen Shattuck, Apr. 18, 1975; children—Patrick Walker, Nicole Kathleen. B.S., U. Melbourne, 1968, M.S., 1970; Ph.D., Ariz. State U., 1975. Guest scientist Inst. für Elektronenmikroskopie, Max-Planck-Gesellschaft, West Berlin, Fed. Republic Germany, 1974-76; mem. tech. staff Tex. Instruments, Inc., Dallas, 1977-84; mgr. KLA Instruments, Inc., Santa Clara, Calif., 1984-86; pvt. practice cons., Los Gatos, Calif., 1986—. Author numerous research articles. Pres. Richardson Noon Toastmasters, Tex., 1983. Mem. AAAS, Am. Phys. Soc., Electron Microscopy Soc. Am., N.Y. Acad. Sci., Toastmasters Internat., Jaycees.

PEARL, BONNIE P., speech pathologist; b. Lafayette, Ind., Mar. 19, 1942; d. Joseph Klein and Madonna Mae (Mahoney) Pottlitzer; m. Philip Raymond Pearl, Aug. 16, 1968 (div. Dec. 1985); children: David, Deborah, Douglas. BS, Purdue U., 1964; MA, Calif. State U., Long Beach, 1980. Lic.

speech pathologist, Calif.; cert. tchr., Calif.; cert. spl. edn. tchr., Calif. Itinerant speech specialist pub. schs. Los Angeles, 1964-69; speech pathologist G. Kohn Schs. for Multiply Handicapped, Long Beach, Huntington Beach and Garden Grove, Calif., 1975-79, Craig & Ford Inc., Anaheim, Calif., 1979—; pvt. practice speech pathology H.B. Speech-Language-Hearing Ctr., Huntington Beach, 1982—; lectr. Coastline Regional Occupational Program, Fountain Valley, Calif., 1986—. Lectr. St. Vincent de Paul Ch., Huntington Beach, 1979—, eucharistic minister to sick, 1981—. Mem. Am. Speech Lang. and Hearing Assn. (cert.), Calif. Speech Lang. and Hearing Assn., Calif. Speech Pathologists and Pvt. Practitioners Assn., Internat. Orofacial Myology, Nat. Stuttering Project. Democrat. Roman Catholic. Home: 8849 Swordfish Ave Fountain Valley CA 92708 Office: H B Speech Lang Hearing Ctr 17692 Beach Blvd Suite 305 Huntington Beach CA 92646

PEARLMAN, DANIEL LAWRENCE, advertising executive; b. N.Y.C., Aug. 13, 1946; s. Benedict and Muriel (Halpern) P.; m. Lynn Lubin, Oct. 10, 1970 (div. 1973). AB, UCLA, 1968, MBA, 1970. Account exec. Young and Rubicam, N.Y.C., 1970-73; account supr. Ogilvy and Mather, N.Y.C. and Los Angeles, 1973-77; v.p. Admktg. Inc., Los Angeles, 1977-79; sr. v.p. Carl Terian Assoc., Los Angeles, 1979-83; pres., CEO Pearlman Wohl Inc., Los Angeles, 1983—. Bd. dirs. Scopus Soc., Beverly Hills, Calif., Los Angeles Inst. Contemporary Art, Pres. Adv. Council City of Hope, Los Angeles. Recipient Andy award Denver Advt. Club, 1975, Lulu award Los Angeles Advt. Women Am., 1981. Mem. Los Angeles Advt. Club (Clio award 1979), Advt. Agy. Assn. Am. Avocations: golf, tennis, skiing. Home: 8787 Shorcham Dr Los Angeles CA 90069 Office: Pearlman/Wohl/Olshever/Marchese 1901 Ave of Stars Los Angeles CA 90067

PEARLMAN, MARION OLA, educational administrator, actress, consultant; b. Mechanicsville, N.Y., Dec. 24, 1920; d. Charles Forrest and Minnie (Mayhew) McBride; m. Albert M. Pearlman, June 9, 1963 (dec. Jan. 1985); 1 son, Michael Edward. B.S., SUNY-Buffalo, 1951; M.Ed., U. Ariz., 1959. Tchr., Pierce Creek Sch., Binghamton, N.Y., 1940-42; tchr. Skaneateles, N.Y., 1942-43; vacation relief agt., reservation clk., ticket agt., auditor, supr. sales control Am. Airlines, Buffalo, 1943-48; ins. analyst Aetna Casualty and Surety Co., Buffalo, 1948-49; tchr., Lancaster, N.Y., 1949-51, University Heights, Tucson, Ariz., 1951-59; Livingston, Calif., 1959-60; cons. elem. edn. County Office Edn., Napa, Calif., supr. Alum Rock Sch. Dist., San Jose, Calif., 1961-62; supr. schs. Nogales, Ariz., 1962-63; tch. Gump Sch. for retarded, blind, emotionally handicapped, deaf, trainable and educable retarded, 1964-78; prin. Valencia Sch., Sunnyside Unified Sch. Dist. #12, Tucson, 1978-83; pvt. cons., 1983—; actress Sunset Years, Access TV, 1984—; lectr. Kans. State Tchrs. Coll., Emporia. Mem. exec. com. Tucson House for Retarded; bd. dirs. Beacon Found. for Mentally Retarded; active PTA, PTO; del. to Ariz. State Assembly. Cert. elem. tchr. Democrat. Jewish. Mem. NEA, Ariz. Edn. Assn., Tucson Edn. Assn., Sunnyside Adminstrs. Assn., AAUW (membership com., del. to nat. conv.), Phi Delta Kappa, Pi Lambda Theta.

PEARLMAN, SAMUEL JAMES, medical educator; b. Fort Wayne, Ind., Apr. 8, 1893; s. Samuel James and Ida Pearlman; m. Della Zekman, Mar. 5, 1925; children: Irene Pearlman Breckler, Jerome T. SB, U. Chgo., 1915, SM, 1916; MD, Rush Med. Coll., 1917. Intern Cook County Hosp., Chgo., 1917-19; assoc. prof. emeritus Northwestern U. Med. Sch., Evanston, Ill., 1942-60; attending surgeon Cook County Hosp., Chgo., 1926-60, past chmn.; lectr. UCLA Sch. Medicine, 1960—, Samuel J. and Della Z. Pearlman chair div. head and neck surgery, 1985. Served to capt. U.S. Army, 1918-19, Allied Expeditionary Force. Mem. Sigma Xi. Republican. Jewish. Club: Standard (Chgo.).

PEARLSTEIN, ARNE JACOB, engineering educator; b. Los Angeles, Mar. 18, 1952; s. Benjamin Jacob and Fanny (Lilienthal) P. BS, MS, UCLA, 1977, Engineer, 1979, PhD, 1983. Asst. prof. mechanical engring. U. Ariz., Tucson, 1983—. Contbr. articles to profl. jours. Recipient Presdl. Young Investigator award NSF, 1985. Mem. ASME, Am. Inst. Chem. Engrs. Office: U Ariz Dept Aerospace and Mech Engring Tucson AZ 85721

PEARSALL, DUANE DARWIN, financial executive, venture capitalist; b. Pontiac, Mich., Mar. 3, 1922; s. Sheldon Lansing and Margery (Kincheloe) P.; m. Marjorie Lee Fewel, July 22, 1944; children—Mark S., Craig A., MaryAnn K., Cynthia L. B.S. in Bus. Adminstrn., U. Denver, 1947; diploma Gen. Motors Inst., 1942. Region constrn. mgr. Honeywell Corp., Denver, 1948-55; pres. Pearsall Co., Denver, 1955-67, Statitrol Corp., Lakewood, Colo., 1963-78; Small Bus. Devel. Corp., Golden, Colo., 1978-83; gen. ptnr. Columbine Venture Fund, Ltd., Englewood, Colo., 1983—; dir. Clin. Diagnostics, Inc., 1986—. Developer first home smoke detector, 1970. Mem. nominating commn. Colo. Supreme Ct., Denver, 1981—. Served to lt. USNR, 1942-45. Named Nat. Small Bus. Person of Yr., SBA, 1976, Citizen of Yr., Sertoma of Denver, 1978, Fire Protection Man of Yr., Soc. Fire Protection Engrs., Boston, 1980. Mem. Denver C. of C. (exec. com., bd. dirs. 1976-79), Colo. Assn. Commerce and Industry (vice chmn. 1984—). Republican. Lutheran. Office: Columbine Venture Fund Ltd 5613 DTC Pkwy Suite 510 Englewood CO 80111

PEARSON, ANNE MOREL, dietitian, consultant; b. Queens Ville, N.Y., Nov. 29, 1947; d. Alfred Frances Morel and Charlotte Adelaide (Ward) Hauck; m. John Howard Pearson, June 27, 1981. AA, So. Sem., 1967; BS, U. Mass., 1969, MS, 1975. Registered dietitian; cert. math. tchr., Mass. Math. tchr. Highland Falls (N.Y.) High Schs., 1969-71; clin. dietitian Aspen (Colo.) Valley Hosp., 1974-75; dir. food services Colo. Rocky Mountain Sch., Carbondale, 1975-76; asst. adminstrv. dietitian Cabell Huntington (Va.) Hosp., 1977-78; head clin. dietitian St. Mary's Hops. and Med. Ctr., Grand Junction, Colo., 1978-82; pvt. practice specializing in nutrition Grand Junction, 1983-85; clin. dietitian Valley View Hosp., Glenwood Springs, Colo., 1985-87; nutrition software trainer Practorcare, Inc., Denver, 1987—; nutrition instr. Colo. Mountain Coll., Aspen, 1975; author, dir., instr. Weight Loss Program, 1983; nursing home cons. Beverly Manor, Grand Junction, 1984, 86. Community speaker representing St. Mary's Hosp., Grand Junction area, 1978-82, Western Colo. Dietetic Assn., 1978-84. Mem. Western Colo. Dietic Assn. (pres. 1980-81, health fair nutrition counselor 1983-86), W.Va. Dietetic Assn., Am. Dietetic Assn. Club: Mesa Monument Striders. Avocations: pen and ink art, running, biking, hiking, down-hill and cross-country skiing.

PEARSON, CALVIN HOLBROOK, agronomy educator, agricultural researcher; b. Ogden, UT, Jan. 25, 1954; s. Carmen Perry and Beth (Holbrook) P.; m. Heidi Williams, May 17, 1979; children: Kirk, Tyler, Candice. AS, Ricks Coll., 1976; BS, Brigham Young U., 1978; MS, Okla. State U., 1978-79; PhD, Oreg. State U., 1983. Research assoc. Oreg. State U., Corvallis, 1983-84; asst. prof. agronomy Colo. State U., Ft. Collins, 1984—; western mgr. Colo. State U. Found. Seed, Grand Junction, 1984—. Contbr. articles to sci. jours., other profl. pubs. Coordinator Western Colo. Council troop 365 Boy Scouts Am., 1986—. Recipient Wimberly Small Grains award Okla. State U., 1979; faculty research grantee Colo. State U., Ft. Collins, 1984; DuPont Teaching fellow Oreg. State U., 1980, 81. Mem. Am. Soc. Agronomy, Crop Sci. Soc. Am., Grand Junction C. of C. (Agri-Bus. group 1985-86), Sigma Xi, Gamma Sigma Delta, Alpha Zeta. Republican. Mormon. Avocations: fishing, photography, gardening. Office: Fruita Research Ctr PO Box 786 Grand Junction CO 81502

PEARSON, CHARLES JAMES, financial analyst, software designer; b. Los Angeles, July 4, 1936; s. Charles Alpha and Sarah Marianna (Fay) P.; m. Ann O'Brien Jones, June 24, 1965; children: Charles Joseph, James Beckett, Cathryn Alexandra. AB in Physics, Occidental Coll., 1958; MA in Physics, U. So. Calif., 1961; PhD in theoretical physics, U. Calif., Riverside, 1965. Tech. supr. Hughes Aircraft Ground Systems, Fullerton, Calif., 1966-68; chief scientist Sycom Inc., Orange, Calif., 1968-74; sr. v.p., dir. research Gifford Fong Assocs., Los Angeles, 1974—. Fellow NSF, 1958. Mem. The Inst. Mgmt. Scis., Ops. Research Soc. Am., Phi Beta Kappa, Sigma Pi Sigma, Sigma Xi. Republican. Presbyterian. Avocation: music. Home: 17427 Rockrose Circle Yorba Linda CA 92686 Office: Gifford Fong Assocs 1052 W Sixth St Los Angeles CA 90017

PEARSON, JACK WILLARD, obstetrics and gynecology educator; b. Joliet, Ill., Jan. 16, 1929; s. John Willard and Ida Mae (Bailey) P.; m. Marilyn Nordin, 1951 (dec. Jan 1958); 1 child, Deborah Lee; m. E. Hope Tillman, June 6, 1958; children: Joan Elizabeth, Jack William, Hope Anne. BS, U. Ill., MD. Diplomate Am. Bd. Ob-Gyn (dir. pro tem 1973—). Commd. 1st lt. U.S. Army, 1953, advanced through grades to col., 1967, ret., 1973; prof. ob-gyn Ind. U., Indpls., 1973-83, U. Ariz., Tucson, 1983—; cons. to Surgeon Gen. U.S. Army, 1968-73. Contbr. articles to profl. jours., chpts. to books. Decorated Legion of Merit. Fellow Am. Coll. Obstetricians and Gynecologists; mem. AMA, Cen. Assn. Obstetricians and Gynecologists, Assn. Profs. of Ob-Gyn, Soc. Med. Cons. to Armed Forces. Republican. Club: Cañada Hills Country. Avocations: golf, swimming, investments. Home: 5161 Circulo Sobrio Tucson AZ 85718 Office: U Ariz Ariz Health Scis Ctr 1501 N Campbell Ave Tucson AZ 85724

PEARSON, JOHN, mechanical engineer; b. Leyburn, Yorkshire, U.K., Apr. 24, 1923; came to U.S., 1930, naturalized, 1944; s. William and Nellie Pearson; m. Ruth Ann Billhardt, July 10, 1944; children—John, Armin, Roger. B.S.M.E., Northwestern U., 1949, M.S., 1951. Registered profl. engr., Calif. Research engr. Naval Ordnance Test Sta., China Lake, Calif., 1951-55, head warhead research br., 1955-58, head solid dynamics bd., 1958-59, head detonation physics group, 1959-67; head detonation physics div. Naval Weapons Ctr., China Lake, Calif., 1967-83, sr. research scientist, 1983—; cons., lectr. in field; founding mem. adv. bd. Ctr. for High Energy Forming, U. Denver; mem. bd. examiners Sambalpur U., India, 1982-83. Author: Explosive Working of Metals, 1963; Behavior of Metals Under Impulsive Loads, 1954. Contbr. articles to profl. publs. Patentee impulsive loading, explosives applications. Charter mem. Sr. Exec. Service U.S., 1979. Served with C.E., U.S. Army, 1943-46. Recipient L.T.E. Thompson medal, 1965, William B. McLean medal, 1979, Superior Civilian Service medal U.S. Navy, 1984, Haskell G. Wilson award, 1985, cert. of recognition Sec. Navy, 1975, Merit award Dept. Navy, 1979, cert. of commendation Sec. Navy, 1981. Fellow ASME; mem. Am. Soc. Metals, Am. Phys. Soc., N.Y. Acad. Scis., AIME, NSPE, Fed. Exec. League, Sigma Xi, Tau Beta Pi, Pi Tau Sigma, Triangle. Home: 858 N Primavera Rd PO Box 1390 Ridgecrest CA 93555 Office: PO Box 1390 Ridgecrest CA 93555

PEARSON, MICHAEL JOHN, research chemist; b. Manchester, England, Sept. 25, 1938; came to U.S., 1962; s. Norman Dudley and Dorothy Alice (Hughes) P.; m. Christine Glover, Sept. 29, 1962 (div. Aug. 1984); children: Fiona, Deborah. BS in Chemistry with honors, U. Leeds, England, 1959; PhD in Chemistry, U. Leeds, 1962; postdoctoral fellow, U. Washington, 1964. Chemist Chevron Chem. Co., Richmond, Calif., 1964-67; staff research chemist Kaiser Aluminum and Chem. Corp., Pleasanton, Calif., 1967—. Contbr. articles to profl. jours; patentee in field. Mem. Am. Chem. Soc., Calif. Catalysis Soc. Republican. Congregationalist. Home: 5991 Skyfarm Dr Castro Valley CA 94552 Office: Kaiser Aluminum and Chem Corp PO Box 877 Pleasanton CA 94566

PEARSON, RICHARD JARVIS, business executive; b. Chgo., June 3, 1925; s. Andrall E. and Dorothy M. (MacDonald) P.; m. Janice Lee Pope, Mar. 2, 1951; 1 child, Douglas R. BA, U. So. Calif., 1946; MBA, Harvard U., 1947. Dir. mktg. Bireley's, Hollywood, Calif., 1947-55; dir. mktg. Forest Lawn Meml. Park, Glendale, Calif., 1955-57, Revell, Inc., Venice, Calif., 1957-60; dir. mktg. Avery Label Co., Monrovia, Calif., 1960-64, v.p., gen. mgr., 1964-70; group v.p. Avery Internat., San Marino, Calif., 1970-76, exec. v.p., 1976-81; exec. v.p., chief operating officer Avery Internat., Pasadena, Calif., 1981-83, pres., chief operating officer, 1983—; dir. Ameron, Inc., Monterey Park, Calif., Ducommun, Inc., Los Angeles. Chmn. United Way, 1982-83; bd. dirs. Boy Scouts Am., 1983-84. Served to lt. (j.g.) USN, 1946. Mem. Merchants and Mfrs. Assn. (bd. dirs. 1986—). Republican. Presbyterian. Club: Annandale. Avocation: golf. Home: 1046 Oak Grove Pl San Marino CA 91108 Office: Avery Internat 150 N Orange Grove Blvd Box 7090 Pasadena CA 91103

PEARSON, VERNON R., state supreme court justice; b. 1923. B.A., Jamestown Coll. (S.D.), 1947; LL.B., U. Mich., 1950. Instr. legal research and writing U. Wash.; atty. OPS; ptnr. Davies, Pearson, Anderson & Pearson, Tacoma; judge Ct. Appeals, 1969-82; assoc. justice Wash. Supreme Ct., 1982-87, chief justice, 1987—. Mem. Tacoma-Pierce County Bar Assn. (past pres.), Wash. State Bar Assn. (past gov.). Office: Supreme Court Wash Temple of Justice Olympia WA 98504

PEARSON, WALTER HOWARD, marine biologist, researcher; b. Troy, N.Y., Mar. 25, 1946; s. Howard Stevenson and Mazel Mott (Brownhill) P.; m. Cynthia-Ruth Egan, June 17, 1972; children: Kristin Turnbull, Jeffrey Mott. BS in Biology, Bates Coll., 1967; MS in Biology, U. Alaska, 1970; PhD in Oceanography, Oreg. State U., 1977. Fishery biologist, researcher Nat. Marine Fisheries Service, Sandy Hook Lab., Highlands, N.J., 1975-78; sr. research scientist Battelle Marine Research Lab., Sequim, Wash., 1978—. Contbr. articles on behavior of marine organisms to jours. Served to sgt. U.S. Army, 1969-71. NSF grantee, 1967-69. Mem. Assn. Chemoreception Scis. (charter), AAAS, N.Y. Acad. Sci., Animal Behavior Soc., Crustacean Soc., Western Soc. Naturalists. Episcopalian. Avocations: scuba diving, aikido. Home: PO Box 1858 Sequim WA 98382 Office: Battelle Marine Research Lab 439 W Sequim Bay Rd Sequim WA 98382

PEASE, CAROL HELENE, oceanographer; b. Bay City, Mich., Dec. 29, 1949; d. George Olson and Mernabelle Hattie (Laabs) P.; m. Alexander Jeffrey Chester, June 16, 1974 (div. May, 1978). Student, U. Mich., 1968-71; BS in Math., U. Miami, Coral Gables, Fla., 1972; MS in Phys. Oceanography, U. Wash., Seattle, 1975, MS in Meteorology, 1981, postgrad., 1985. Research asst. Arctic Ice Dynamics Joint Experiment, U. Wash., Seattle, 1972-75; oceanographer Pacific Marine Environ. Lab., NOAA, Seattle, 1975-78, sea ice project leader, 1978—. Contbr. articles to profl. jours. Mem. Arboretum Found., Seattle, 1975—, Seattle Art Mus., 1978—, Nat. Women's Polit. Cacus, Seattle, 1984—; sustaining mem. Friends of KUOW, KCTS Found., Seattle, 1978, 82. Recipient numerous performance awards NOAA, 1977, 82, 85. Mem. AAAS, Assn. Women in Sci., Am. Geophys. Union, Am. Meteorol. Soc. (standing com. polar meteorology and oceanography 1985—, chmn. 1987—, session chmn. symposium meteorology and oceanography of North Am. High Latitudes 1984). Clubs: Corinthian Yacht (Seattle). Lodges: Valkyrien (sec. 1978-81), Daughters of Norway. Avocations: racing keelboats, gardening. Office: Pacific Marine Environ Lab 7600 Sand Point Way NE Seattle WA 98115

PEASE, MARC, cable TV administrator; b. Seattle, Dec. 5, 1950; s. Larry Merton and Margaret Marie (Bratcher) P. Student, U. Wash., 1973. Program mgr. TelePrompter Cable, Burien, Wash., 1973-76; instr. TV Inst. Media, Seattle, 1976-78; rep. Mktg. Masters, Issaquah, Wash., 1978-80; cable adminstr. City of Tacoma, 1980—; cons. in field. Producer (videos) Government Speaks, 1985, CrimeStoppers, 1985, Municipal Programming, 1985. Mem. Tacoma Art Mus., 1985-86; bd. dirs. CrimeStoppers Tacoma Pierce County, 1981-86, Allied Arts of Pierce County, Tacoma, 1985-86. Mem. Nat. Assn. Telecommunication Officers and Advisors (state chmn.). Club: Howards Softball. Home: 1518 N Steele Tacoma WA 98402 Office: City of Tacoma Mcpl TV 747 Market St 220 Municipal Tacoma WA 98402

PEASE, ROBERT ALLEN, electrical engineer; b. Rockville, Conn., Aug. 22, 1940; s. Mahlon Harold and Beulah May (Kammer) P.; m. Nancy Jean Baker, Aug. 12, 1961; children: Benjamin, Jonathan. BSEE, MIT, 1961. Chief engr. Teledyne PhilBrick, Dedham, Mass., 1961-75; staff scientist Nat. Semiconductor Corp., Santa Clara, Calif., 1976—; cons. editor EDN CAHNERS, Newton, Mass., 1978—. Contbr. articles to profl. jours.; patentee in field. Mem. IEEE, Com. Concerned Elec. Engrs. Episcopalian. Avocations: ferroequinologist, indsl. archeology. Home: 682 Miramar Ave San Francisco CA 94112-1232 Office: Nat Semiconductor MSC 2500 PO Box 58090 Santa Clara CA 95052-8090

PEAVY, GEORGE MERRILL, veterinarian; b. Bakersfield, Calif., Dec. 19, 1949; s. Merrill A. and Nancy Peavy; m. Lynn B. Peavy, May 8, 1982. BS, U. Calif., Davis, 1972, DVM, 1974. Diplomate Am. Bd. Vet. Practitioners. Staff vet. Rialto (Calif.) Animal Hosp., 1974-75, Macy & Thomas Vet. Hosp., Whittier, Calif., 1975-80, San Clemente (Calif.) Vet. Hosp., 1980—; mem. health adv. com. U.S. Sen. S.I. Hayakawa, 1977-84. Contbr. numerous articles to vet. jours. Mem. Orange County (Calif.) Rep. Cen. Com., 1983-84; mem. fundraising com. Richard M. Nixon Presdl. Library Found., 1985. Mem. Am. Animal Hosp. Assn. (Outstanding Service award 1983), AVMA (policy bd. of polit. action com. 1982—), Calif. Vet. Med. Assn. (Merit award 1979), So. Calif. Vet. Med. Assn., Sigma Xi, Theta Xi. Lodge: Rotary. Office: San Clemente Vet Hosp 1833 S El Camino Real San Clemente CA 92672

PECCORINI, FRANCISCO LETONA, retired philosopher, educator; b. San Miguel, El Salvador, Nov. 27, 1915; came to U.S., 1962, naturalized, 1976; s. Miguel Vinerta and Julia (Letona) P.; m. Teresa Samayoa; 1 stepdau., Teresa Moran Enneman. Ph. Licentiate, Colegio de San Francisco Javier, Burgos, Spain, 1943; Ph.D., Pontifical U. Comillas, Santender, Spain, 1958. Tchr. San Jose High Sch., San Salvador, 1943-47; writer Estudios Centro Americanos, San Salvador, 1947-52; editor mag. Estudios Centro Americanos, 1952-55; prof. philosophy U. Deusto, Bilbao, Spain, 1956-58, Nat. U., San Salvador, 1959-62; asst. prof. U. San Diego, 1963-66; mem. faculty Calif. State U., Long Beach, 1966—, prof. philosophy, 1972-86, prof. emeritus, 1986. Author: A Method of Self-Orientation to Thinking, 1970, La Voluntad del Pueblo en la Emancipación de El Salvador, 1972, From Gentile's "Actualism" to Sciacca's "Idea," 1981, On to the World of Freedom. A Kantian Meditation on Finite Selfhood, 1982, Selfhood as Thinking Thought in The Work of Gabriel Marcel, 1987; also articles. Mem. Nat. Acad. Historia of San Salvador, Acad. Lang. El Salvador (corr.), Medieval Acad. Am., Medieval Assn. Pacific, Am. Philos. Assn., Inst. for Ency. of Ultimate Reality and Meaning (Toronto). Office: Dept Philosophy Calif State Univ Long Beach CA 90840

PECHERER, MICHAEL SAUL, construction company executive; b. Montclair, N.J., Dec. 16, 1942; s. Benjamin and Miriam (Kroll) P.; m. Karen K. Pecherer, Dec. 29, 1969 (dec. Aug. 1973). BS, U. Mich., 1964; MBA, JD, Columbia U., 1968. Bar: N.Y. 1968, Calif. 1970. Law clk. U.S. Ct. Appeals, N.Y.C., 1968-69; sole practice San Francisco, 1969-82; pres. Solaris Development Co., San Francisco, 1982—; instr. Golden Gate U., San Francisco, 1984—. Mem. San Francisco Bar Assn. Home and Office: 2310 Divisadero San Francisco CA 94115

PECHMANN, JAMES (WILLIAM) CHRISTOPHER, seismologist; b. Binghamton, N.Y., July 22, 1954; s. Karl and Helen (Guley) P.; m. Judith Burt, Aug. 26, 1978; children: George Karl, Jessica Mary. BA in Geology, Hamilton Coll., 1976; MS in Geophysics, Calif. Inst. Tech., 1979, PhD in Geophysics, 1983. Research assoc. U. Utah, Salt Lake City, 1983-84, research asst. prof., 1984—. Contbr. articles to profl. jours. Mem. Am. Geophys. Union, Seismol. Soc. Am., Sigma Xi.

PECHTER, STEVEN JEROME, merchandising company executive; b. Bklyn., May 26, 1958; s. Lawrence Stanley and Harriet Shirley (Silverman) P. BS in Biol. Scis., U. Calif., Irvine, 1980, MBA, 1983. Ops. mgr. United Merchandising, Hawthorne, Calif., 1975—; cons. Micro Computers-Software & Hardware Systems; lectr. U. Calif., Irvine, 1982-84. Asst. scoutmaster Orange County (Calif.) Boy Scouts Am., 1979-83. Mem. Nat. Eagle Scout Assn. Democrat. Club: Snowbounders (Anaheim, Calif.). Avocations: snow skiing, sail boarding, computing. Home: 2513 Voorhees Ave #2 Redondo Beach CA 90278 Office: United Merchandising Corp 14440 Ocean Gate Ave Hawthorne CA 90278

PECK, JAMES MASON, JR., industrial hygienist, consultant; b. Vallejo, Calif., May 5, 1945; s. James Mason Sr. and Virginia Lee (Grant) P.; m. Brenda Kay Bell, Sept. 3, 1977; children: James Mason III, Lindsey Marie. BS in Zoology, George Washington U., Washington, 1968; MS in Pub. Health, U. Hawaii, 1975, MBA in Mgmt., 1978. Lab technician Hazeltine Labs., Vienna, Va., 1969-72; marine biologist Hawaiian Electric Co., Honolulu, 1972-80, environ. scientist, 1980-86, indsl. hygienist, 1986—. Mem. Hawaiian Pub. Health Assn., Hawaii sect. of Am. Indsl. Hygiene Assn. Avocations: fin. planning, photography, softball, scuba. Home: 119 Aikahi Loop Kailua HI 96734 Office: Hawaiian Electric Co Inc Safety div PO Box 2750 Honolulu HI 96840

PECK, KENNETH ELDON, lawyer; b. Carson City, Nev., June 20, 1950; s. Donald Leon and Thelma Louise (Robinson) P.; m. Katherine Louise Weeks, Oct. 20, 1973; children: Jason Z., Jennifer D., Joy H., Jessica K. BA in Polit. Sci. cum laude, U. Colo., 1971; MA in Pub. Adminstrn., U. Va., 1975; JD, Georgetown U., 1979. Bar: Colo. 1979, U.S. Dist. Ct. Colo. 1979, U.S. Ct. Appeals (10th cir.) 1980, U.S. Supreme Ct. 1983. Research analyst Va. Hwy. Research Council, Charlottesville, 1972-73; budget and mgmt. analyst Prince Georges County Schs., Upper Marlboro, Md., 1974-76; chief legis. asst. U.S. Rep. Paul Trible, Washington, 1977-79; atty. Holland & Hart, Denver, 1979-83, Hopper & Kanouff, Denver, 1983-85, Phelps, Hall, Singer & Dunn, Denver, 1985—; mem. nat., regional and state adv. councils SBA, 1981—; mem. bd. appeals U.S. Dept. Edn., Washington, 1982-84; profl. lobbyist Colo. Legis., Denver, 1983-84; nat. commr. of econ. policy White House Conf. on Small Bus., Denver, 1986. Asst. campaign mgr. Jim Tate for Congress, Fairfax, Va., 1976; bd. dirs. Jefferson County Srs.' Resource Ctr., Wheatridge, Colo., 1982—; pres. Arvada Rep. Club, Colo., 1982; mem. bd. mgrs. Northwest YMCA, Arvada, 1982—. William McIntyre fellow U. Va., 1971-72; law fellow Georgetown U. Law Ctr., 1976-77. Mem. ABA (litigation sect., real property and bus. sect., various coms.), Assn. Trial Lawyers Am., Colo. Bar Assn. (various coms.), Colo. Assn. Comml. Industry (chmn. small bus. legis. com. 1983-85), Denver Bar Assn. (various coms.). Republican. Mem. Ch. of Christ. Avocations: golf, hiking, coaching youth sports. Home: 10935 W 68th Ave Arvada CO 80004 Office: Hopper Kanougg Smith et al 1610 Wynkop St Suite 200 Denver CO 80202

PECK, MICHAEL ALAN, real estate executive; b. Grand Rapids, Mich., Jan. 17, 1949; s. Freeling William and Ruth Jean (De Vries) P.; m. Marilyn Jean Groters, June 15, 1968; children: Michelle Joy, Michael Freeling, Mindy Jean. AA, Grand Rapids Jr. Coll., 1969; BS, Western Mich. U., 1972, MA, 1973. Printing foreman Kalamazoo Bd. Realtors, 1970-74; exec. v.p. Holland (Mich.) Bd. Realtors, 1975-78; asst. exec. v.p. Grand Rapids Real Estate Bd., 1979-83; exec. v.p. Mesa-Chandler-Tempe Bd. Realtors, Ariz., 1983—; real estate coordinator Grand Valley State Colls., Allendale, Mich., 1978-83. Editor newsletter Grand Rapids Real Estate Bd., 1980-83. Mem. Ariz. Rep. Caucus, Mesa. Mem. Am. Inst. Parliamentarians, Nat. Assn. Parliamentarians, Ariz. State Assn. Parliamentarians (2d v.p. alpha chpt. 1986), Am. Soc. Assn. Execs. (cert.), Omea Tau Rho. Lodge: Rotary. Home: 4233 E Covina St Mesa AZ 85205 Office: Mesa-Chandler-Tempe Bd Realtors 435 W Holmes Ave PO Box 5509 Mesa AZ 85201

PECK, RAYMOND CHARLES, SR., driver and traffic safety research specialist; b. Sacramento, Nov. 18, 1937; s. Emory Earl and Margaret Helen (Fiebiger) P.; m. Ella Ruth Enriquez, Sept. 5, 1957; children—Teresa M. Peck Montijo, Linda M. Peck Heisler, Margaret H. Peck Ryzak, Raymond C., Christina M. B.A. in Exptl. Psychology, Calif. State U.-Sacramento, 1961, M.A. in Exptl. Psychology, 1968. Jr. research tech. Calif. Dept. Motor Vehicles, Sacramento, 1962-63, asst. social research analyst, 1963-64, staff research analyst, 1967-71, sr. research analyst, program mgr., 1971-80, research program specialist II, 1980, acting, chief research, 1980-81, research program specialist II, 1981-84, chief of research, 1984—; cons. to Computing and Software, Inc., Mentoris Co., Sims & Assocs., Pub. Systems, Inc., Planning Research Corp., Nat. Pub. Services Research Inst., Dunlap & Assocs., Sacramento Safety Council, Nat. Safety Council, Boston U., Sch. Pub. Health. Chmn. com. on operator regulation Transportation Research Bd., Nat. Acad. Scis., 1976-82. Recipient Met. Life award of Hon., Nat. Safety Council, 1970, Met. Life Cert. of Commendation, 1972; A.R. Lauer award Human Factor Soc., 1981; award of Hon., award of Merit Traffic Safety Evaluation Research Rev., 1983. Mem. Am. Statis. Assn., Western Psychol. Assn. Democrat. Contbr. articles to profl. jours.; editorial adv. bd. Jour. Safety Research, Accident Analysis and Prevention, Traffic Safety Evaluation Research Rev., Abstracts and Revs. in Alcohol and Driving. Home: 2667 Coleman Way Sacramento CA 95818 Office: Calif Dept Motor Vehicles 2415 First Ave Sacramento CA 95818

PECK, ROBERT SHANNON, II, video dir. and producer, real estate investment and appraising co. exec.; b. Balt., July 10, 1946; s. Clemmer Marcus and Ruth Davies P.; B.S., Menlo Sch. Bus. Adminstrn., 1972; m. Julia Ann Spaich, Dec. 14, 1974; children—Robert Shannon, Heather Jeanine, Britton Cecelia, Connor Nedjo. Foreman, Spaich Bros. Ranch; expeditor Simi Winery; in mgmt. Tandy Corp.; cons. Assoc. Mgmt. Systems, Palo Alto, Calif.; pres. The White Co., Saratoga, Calif., 1979—; pres. J.P.

Video Prodn. Co., 1986—, BOD Gateway Prodns., 1987. Served with U.S. Army, 1967-70. Mem. Calif. Real Estate Assn., Nat. Assn. Realtors, San Jose Real Estate Bd., Saratoga-Los Gatos Real Estate Bd., Santa Cruz Real Estate Bd., Santa Clara County Appraisers Assn. Republican.

PECKA, DUSAN CHARLES, infosystems specialist, consultant; b. Prague, Czechoslovakia, July 31, 1940; came to U.S., 1957; s. Charles and Anna (Mahler) P. BA in Physics and Math., Lewis and Clark Coll., 1962; MS in Physics, U. Wis., 1963; PhD in Physics, Wash. State U., 1967. Mgr. tech. sect. advanced concepts office The Aerospace corp., El Segundo, Calif., 1967-73; dir. elec. scis. lab. Lockheed Missile and Space Co., Palo Alto, Calif., 1973-84; v.p. ops. and mktg. Systems Control Tech., Inc., Palo Alto, 1985—; cons. Litton Data Systems, Van Nuys, Calif., 1984-85, Titan Corp., San Diego, 1984-85. Contbr. articles to profl. jours. Fellow U. Wis. Alumni Research Found, 1962-63; grantee NDEA, 1965-67. Mem. Am. Phys. Soc., AIAA, Sigma Xi, Phi Kappa Phi. Republican. Avocations: private pilot, running. Home: 1105 Royal Ln San Carlos CA 94070 Office: Systems Control Tech Inc 1801 Page Mill Rd Palo Alto CA 94304

PECKHAM, ROBERT FRANCIS, chief U.S. district judge; b. San Francisco, Nov. 3, 1920; s. Robert F. and Evelyn (Crowe) P.; m. Harriet M. Behring, Aug. 15, 1953 (dec. Apr. 1970); children: Ann Evelyn, Sara Esther; m. Carol Potter, June 9, 1974. A.B., Stanford U., 1941, LL.B., 1945; postgrad. in law, Yale U., 1941-42; LL.D., U. Santa Clara, 1973. Bar: Calif. 1945. Adminstrv. asst. to regional enforcement atty. OPA, 1942-43; pvt. practice in Palo Alto and Sunnyvale, 1946-48; asst. U.S. atty., 1948-53, chief asst. criminal div., 1952-53; mem. firm Darwin, Peckham & Warren, San Francisco, Palo Alto and Sunnyvale, 1953-59; judge Superior Ct., Santa Clara County, Calif., 1959-66; presiding judge Superior Ct., 1961-63, 65-66; U.S. dist. judge No. Dist. Calif., 1966-76, chief judge, 1976—; trustee Foothill Coll. Dist., 1957-59, pres., 1959; mem. bd. visitors Stanford Law Sch., 1969-75, chmn., 1971-72. State chmn. Adv. Bd. Friends Outside; council mem. Friends of Bancroft Library, 1981—. Recipient Brotherhood award Nat. Conf. Christians and Jews, 1968; recipient award for alt. dispute resolution leadership Ctr. for Pub. Resources, 1984, scholar, 1985. Fellow Am. Bar Found.; mem. ABA (chmn. Nat. Conf. Fed. Trial Judges 1983-84, ho. of dels. 1984—), Fed., San Francisco, Santa Clara County bar assns., Am. Law Inst., Am. Judicature Soc., Soc. Calif. Pioneers (bd. govs. 1984—) Calif. Hist. Soc. (trustee 1974-78), Council Stanford Law Socs. (chmn. 1974-75), U.S. Dist. Ct. for No. Dist. Calif. Hist. Soc. (chmn. 1979—), World Affairs Council (trustee 1979—), Asia Found. (sr. mem. Am.-Asia law del. 1984-85), Phi Beta Kappa, Phi Delta Phi. Office: US Courthouse San Francisco CA 94102

PECSAR, RAYMOND E., engineering executive; b. Cleve., Nov. 29, 1937; s. Ernest F. and Irma (Horvath) P.; m. Cora G. Wallace, Aug. 30, 1958; children: Wendy Thomas, Jeffrey, Gregory, Cheryl. BSChemE, U. Calif., Berkeley, 1959; MSChemE, U. Mich., 1960, MS in Math., 1963, ScD in Chem. Engring., 1964. Engr. Beckman Instruments, Fullerton, Calif., 1960-61; mem. adv. tech. staff Marquardt Corp., Van Nuys, Calif., 1965-67; mgr. engring. Varian Aerograph, Walnut Creek, Calif., 1967-73; mgr. mktg. Varian, Palo Alto, Calif., 1973-78; mgr. instrumentation Bio-Rad Labs., Richmond, Calif., 1978-82; dir. engring. and devel. UTI Instruments, Milpitas, Calif., 1982—; instr. extension courses U. Calif., Berkeley, 1969-75, Cogswell Coll., San Francisco, 1975-79. Co-author: Preparative Gas Chromatography, 1973; contbr. articles to profl. jours.; patentee in field. Scout leader Boy Scouts Am., Walnut Creek, Sunnyvale, Calif., 1970-76; asst. minister Resurrection Ch., Sunnyvale, 1974-78, St. Lawrence Ch., Santa Clara, Calif., 1985—. Fellow Standard Oil of Calif., 1962, Allied Chem. Corp., 1963, Horace H. Rackham, U. Mich., 1964. Fellow Instrument Soc. Am.; mem. Am. Chem. Soc., ASTM (chmn. 1972-73), SEMI (mem. standards com. 1983—), Electronics Assn. Calif. (adv. bd. 1985—), PACE, U. Mich. Alumni Assn., Phi Lambda Upsilon. Avocations: hiking, camping, square dancing. Home: 1088 Castleton Way Sunnyvale CA 94087 Office: UTI Instruments 497 S Hillview Dr Milpitas CA 95035

PEDEN, CHARLES HILTON FERGUSON, research chemist; b. Honolulu, Apr. 4, 1953; s. John Bole and Lorena Arlene (Fishel) P.; m. Marilyn Jean Bostwick, Aug. 11, 1974 (div. Oct. 1979); children: Sean Michael, Brandon March; m. Martha Marie Anderson, Oct. 11, 1980; 1 child, Amanda Marie Anderson. BA with distinction, Calif. State U., Chico, 1978; MA, Calif. State U., Santa Barbara, 1981, PhD, 1983. Temp. doctoral appointee Sandia Nat. Labs., Albuquerque, 1983-85, mem. tech. staff, 1985—. Contbr. articles to profl. jours. U. Calif. predoctoral fellow, 1978. Mem. Am. Chem. Soc., Am. Vacuum Soc., Calif. Scholastic Fedn., Phi Kappa Phi. Democrat. Unitarian. Office: Sandia Nat Labs 1846 PO Box 5800 Albuquerque NM 87185

PEDERSEN, CHARLES EDWARD, banking executive; b. Guide Rock, Nebr., Feb. 8, 1930; s. Henry and Doris May (Sims) P.; m. Wanda L. Browning, July 22, 1952; children: Marsha, Mark, Merle, Eric, Kirsten. BS, Oreg. State U., 1957; postgrad., U. Wash., 1970. Loan officer First Interstate Bank of Oreg., Portland, 1948-63, br. mgr., 1963-71, regional v.p., 1971-74; pres., chief exec. officer First Interstate Bank Gt. Falls, Mont., 1974-85, First Interstate Bank Casper, Wyo., 1985—. Bd. dirs. No. Rocky Mountain Easter Seal Soc., Casper Coll. Found., Casper Symphony Orch. Served with USAF, 1949-53. Presbyterian. Lodges: Rotary, Masons, Shriners. Office: First Interstate Bank Casper 104 S Wolcott Casper WY 82601

PEDERSEN, DARHL MAX, psychology educator; b. Orem, Utah, Oct. 12, 1935; s. Max Barlow and Edith (Aiken) P.; m. Elizabeth Allen, Aug. 11, 1971; one child, Clark. BS, Brigham Young U., 1957, MS, 1958; PhD, U. Ill., 1962. Asst. prof. psychology Brigham Young U., Provo, Utah, 1962-65, assoc. prof., 1966-70, prof., 1971—; postdoctoral assoc. Ames Research Ctr., NASA, Moffett Field, Calif., 1969-70. Author: Psychological Tests and Measurements, 1965, Essentials for Understanding Statistics, 1978, Environmental Psychology, 1978. Commr. Provo council Boy Scouts Am., 1978—. NSF fellow, 1962. Mem. Sigma Xi (ann. lecture 1973), Phi Kappa Phi, Psi Chi. Republican. Mormon. Avocations: outdoor activities. Home: 1815 N 1550 E Provo UT 84604 Office: Psychology Dept Brigham Young U Provo UT 84602

PEDERSEN, JOHN DAVID, dentist, dental group administrator; b. Lawrence, Kans., Aug. 1, 1946; s. Peter and Carol Anita (Fowler) P.; m. Mary Lee Mullen, Apr. 18, 1970; children—David Erik, Kimberlee Lund; m. 2d, Shirlee Ann Lund, Oct. 14, 1979. A.A., Glendale Coll., 1968; D.D.S., U. So. Calif., 1973. Instr. fixed prosthodontics Sch. Dentistry U. So. Calif., 1973-74; pvt. practice dentistry, Newport Beach, Calif., 1974-80, owner San Bernardino Dental Group, San Bernardino, Calif., 1980—, Inland Family Dental Group, Riverside, Calif., So. Calif. Ceramics, Inc., Riverside; lectr. in field of gnathology. Mem. ADA, Tri-County Dental Soc., San Bernardino C. of C. Republican. Lutheran. Contbr. article to profl. jour.

PEDERSEN, JOHN MARTIN, consultant, former educational adminstrator; b. Racine, Wis., Sept. 29, 1932; s. Ralph Ceasar and Goldie Florence (Johnson) P.; m. Jacqueline Marie Williams, Dec. 27, 1952; children—Scott, Chris, Debra Albahrani, Susan. B.A. with distinction, U. N.Mex., 1976, M.A., 1979. Cert. tchr., guidance counselor, Ariz. Evaluator, Whiteriver Unified Sch. Dist., 1979-80, Title I coordinator, 1980-81, dir. Chpt. I, 1981-84; title IV coordinator Alamajo Navajo Sch., Albuquerque, 1985—; cons. computer assisted instrn. Served to maj. USAF, 1952-72. Mem. Assn. Supervision and Curriculum Devel., Phi Kappa Phi. Republican. Presbyterian (elder). HomeandOffice: 220 Solano Dr SE Albuquerque NM 87108

PEDERSEN, MARTIN ALBERT, consulting engineer, surveyor; b. Rawlins, Wyo., Dec. 2, 1946; s. Rasmus and Ella (Rasmussen) P.; m. Karen Louise Bond, Aug. 26, 1967 (div. 1978); children: David Frank, Jennifer Louise; m. Patricia Ann Smith, Mar. 1, 1980; 1 child, Hans Rasmus. Student, U. Wyo., 1965. Registered land surveyor, Wyo., Mont., Idaho, Nev., Ariz., N.Mex., N.D., S.D., Colo. Surveyor Robert Jack Smith & Assocs., Rawlins, 1966-75, prin., 1975—. Scoutmaster Boy Scouts of Am., Rawlins, 1969-75, dist. chmn., 1975-81; head Rawlins Search and Rescue Dive Team, 1984—; mem., past chmn. Rawlins Carbon County Airport Bd.; elder Christ Luth. Ch., Rawlins, 1985—. Mem. Wyo. Assn. Cons. Engrs. and Surveyors (pres. 1978), Profl. Land Surveyors Wyo. (pres. 1980-81), Am. Congress Surveying and Mapping, Ducks Untld. (chmn. Rawlins chpt.). Lodge: Elks. Avocations: scuba diving, photography, hunting, fishing, flying. Home: 207 E Heath Rawlins WY 82301 Office: Robert Jack Smith Assocs Inc 1015 Harshman Box 1104 Rawlins WY 82301

PEDERSEN, PALLE WURM, manufacturing company executive; b. Copenhagen, Sept. 19, 1944; came to U.S., 1967; s. John Laurits Wurm and Lissie Edith (Andersen) P.; m. Toril Pettersen, Dec. 27, 1969 (div. May 1982); 1 child, John Wurm; m. Jacalyn Bates, July 9, 1982; 1 child, Erika Nicole. MBA, Merchants Acad., Copenhagen, 1964. Gen. mgr. The East Asiatic Co., N.Y.C., Kuala Lumpur, Malaysia, Houston and Chgo., 1967-77; pres. Internat. Wood Products Inc., Memphis, 1977-82, Swedish Match Industries, Laguna Hills, Calif., 1982-85, PWP Internat. Inc., Laguna Niguel, Calif., 1985—; chmn. Far Eastern Timber Exporters Assn., Kuala Lumpur, 1970-72. Served to lt. The Royal Danish Guard, 1964-66. Republican. Avocations: flying, tennis, swimming, reading. Home: 29802 Andrea Way Laguna Niguel CA 92677 Office: PWP Internat Inc PO Box 7708 Laguna Niguel CA 92677

PEDERSEN, THELMA JEAN JORGENSON, mathematician; m. Kent A. Pedersen. B.S., Brigham Young U., 1955. M.S. in Math., U. Utah, 1958. Cert. secondary tchr., Utah. Tchr. math., public jr. and sr. high schs., Utah, 1958-59; instr. math. U. Utah, 1959-65; asst. prof. U. Santa Clara, 1965-72, lectr., 1972-85; sr. lectr. 1985—; lectr. NSF Vis. Scientist Program, 1963-65, and active various other NSF programs, 1959-79; dir. Bay Area Women and Math. Lectureship Program, 1975-80. Mem. Am. Math. Soc., Math. Assn. Am. (lectr. women and math. lectureship program mem. panel vis. lectrs., gov. No. Calif. sect. 1981-84), Calif. Math. Council, Nat. Council Tchrs. Math, Santa Clara Valley Math. Assn. (pres. 1976-77). Author: (with E. Allan Davis) Essentials of Trigonometry, 1969, 2d edit., 1973, 74; (with Kent A. Pedersen) Geometric Playthings, 1973, 3rd edit., 1986; (with Allan Davis) Essentials of Trigonometry, 1975; (with Franz O. Armbruster) A New Twist (To Arithmetic Drill Through Problem Solving), 1979; (with Peter J. Hilton) Fear No More, An Adult Approach to Mathematics, 1983; contbr. numerous articles to profl. publs.; assoc. editor Math. Mag. Home: PO Box 26 New Almaden CA 95042

PEDERSON, CURTIS ROGER, information services executive; b. Everett, Wash., July 1, 1946; s. Palmer Henry and Mildred (Rice) P.; m. Patricia Ann Aubin, Jan. 26, 1965; children: Jeffrey, Jill. BA in Pub. Adminstrn. cum laude, U. Puget Sound, 1975; M in Pub. Adminstrn., Seattle U., 1986; cert. in tech. edn., Wash. State community coll. Mgr. office services Snohomish County Pud 1, Everett, Wash., 1980-84, mgr. materials mgmt., 1984-85, dir. info. services, 1985—. Mem. World Future Soc., Mem. Am. Soc. Pub. Adminstrn. Roman Catholic. Office: Snohomish County Pud 1 2320 California Everett WA 98206

PEDERSON, JORDAN CRANDALL, wildlife biologist; b. Chgo., July 11, 1939; s. Jordan Jr. and Louise (Crandall) P.; m. Aurelia Lambert, Aug. 26, 1960; children: Linda Louise, Mary Ann. BS, Brigham Young U., 1964, PhD, 1985; MS, U. Utah, 1970. Conservation officer Utah Wildlife Resources, Blanding, 1965-66; wildlife biologist Utah Wildlife Resources, Salt Lake City, 1966-70, Monticello, 1970-75; wildlife biologist Utah Wildlife Resources, Springville, 1975-78, mgr. game, 1978—. Contbr. articles to profl. jours. Firefighter Monticello Vol. Fire Dept., 1971-74, fire chief, 1974-75; councilman Boy Scouts Am., Monticello, 1971-75, advisor, Provo, Utah, 1984-86. Mem. The Wildlife Soc., Soc. Range Mgmt., Audubon Soc., Internat. Bear Biology Assn., Sigma Xi, Phi Kappa Phi, Beta Beta Beta. Mormon. Avocations: fishing, hunting, photography, travel. Home: 1381 East 700 South Provo UT 84601 Office: Utah Div Wildlife Resources 1115 N Main Springville UT 84663

PEDERSON, PETER ORLO, fire chief; b. Los Angeles, July 2, 1934; s. Orlo G. and Idia (Wilson) P.; m. Betty Lou Pederson, Nov. 27, 1954; children—David, Chris. B.A., Calif. State U.-Long Beach, 1957; M.S., Pepperdine U., 1978. Bn. chief Los Angeles County Fire Dept., 1973-80, asst. fire chief, 1980-81; fire chief Salt Lake City Fire Dept., 1981—. Served with USN, 1952-54. Mem. Nat. Fire Protection Assn., Internat. Assn. Fire Chiefs, Western Fire Chiefs Assn., Metro Fire Chiefs Assn. Lodge: Rotary. Office: Salt Lake City Fire Dept 159 E 1st St S Salt Lake City UT 84111 *

PEEPLES, MAIJA WOOF, artist; b. Riga, Latvia, Nov. 21, 1942; d. Herberts Amandus and Biruta (Slavcitajs) Gegeris; came to U.S., 1950, naturalized, 1955; student San Francisco Art Inst., 1963; B.A., U. Calif. at Davis, 1964, M.A., 1965; m. Earl Peeples, July 29, 1972, Artist; one-woman shows at Candy Store Gallery, Calif., annually 1965-86, Nelson Gallery, U. Calif. at Davis, 1972, Crocker Art Mus., Sacramento, 1980, Meml. Union Gallery, 1976, Solano Community Coll., 1972, Matthews Art Center, Tempe, Ariz., 1971, "World of Woof" toured Ariz., 1971-72, Sigi Krauss Gallery, London, Eng., 1970, Hansen-Fuller Gallery, San Francisco, 1969, LaJolla (Calif.) Mus. Art, 1967, Works Gallery, San Jose, Calif., 1984, Rubicon Gallery, Los Altos, Calif., 1983, J'Nette Gardens Gallery, Oakland, Calif., 1986-87; exhibited in group shows: Sea of Japan 1973-74, San Francisco Mus., 1973, Sacramento Sampler-Crocker Art Gallery, Sacramento and Sau Paulo, Brazil, 1972, Am. River Coll., 1976, Calif. Sec. State's Office, 1976, De Saisset Art Gallery, U. Santa Clara (Calif.), 1980, Susan Whitney Gallery, Regina, Sask., Can., 1980, Crocker Art Mus., Sacramento, 1982, Gallery Imago, San Francisco, 1986; represented in permanent collections at LaJolla Mus., Crocker Art Gallery, Sacramento, Matthews Art Center, Tempe, Candy Store Gallery, Folsom. Teaching, Laney Coll., Oakland, 1968-69, Sierra Coll., Rocklin, Calif., 1970-72, U. Calif. at Davis Extension, 1972; lectr. Calif. Art Assn., 1983. Recipient Ceramics Excellence Prize Calif. State Fair Art Show, 1974, others. Mem. Artists Stable of Candy Store Gallery. Home: 2586 King Richard Dr El Dorado Hills CA 95630 Office: 8770 Greenback Ln Orangevale CA 95662

PEERS, MICHAEL GEOFFREY, archbishop; b. Vancouver, B.C., Can., July 31, 1934; s. Geoffrey Hugh and Dorothy Enid (Mantle) P.; m. Dorothy Elizabeth Bradley, June 29, 1963; children: Valerie Anne Leslie, Richard Christopher Andre, Geoffrey Stephen Arthur. B.A., U. B.C., Vancouver, 1956; L.Th., Trinity Coll., Toronto, Ont., 1959, D.D. (hon.), 1978; D.D. (hon.), St. John's Coll., Winnipeg, Man., 1981. Ordained to ministry Anglican Ch.; asst. curate St. Thomas Ch., Ottawa, 1959-61; chaplain U. Ottawa, 1961-66; rector St. Bede's Ch., Winnipeg, 1966-72, St. Martin's Ch., Winnipeg, 1972-74; dean of Qu'Appelle, Regina, Sask., 1974-77; bishop Qu'Appelle, 1977-82, archbishop, 1982-86; primate The Anglican Ch. Can., 1986—; instr. Ottawa Tchrs. Coll., 1962-66, St. Paul's High Sch., Winnipeg, 1967-69. Office: Anglican Ch Canada, Church House 600 Jarvis St, Toronto, ON Canada M4Y 2J6

PEERY, J. CRAIG, developmental psychologist; b. Salt Lake City, Apr. 21, 1945; s. Joseph Smith and Phyllis (Evans) P.; m. Irene Weiss, June 21, 1969; children: Joseph, Christie, Samuel. BA, Columbia U., 1970, MA, 1973, PhD, 1973. Research scientist N.Y. Psychiat. Inst. and Research Found. for Mental Hygiene, N.Y.C., 1970-73; asst. prof. family and human devel. Utah State U., Logan, 1973-80, assoc. prof., 1980; assoc. prof. family scis. Brigham Young U., Provo, Utah, 1980-85, prof., 1985—, dir. Program for Optimal Devel., 1985—; spl. asst. to chmn. U.S. Senate Labor and Human Resources Com., Washington, 1980-82; staff assoc. U.S. Senate Subcom. for Family and Human Services, 1983-84; mem. several nat. adv. panels on children, adolescents, families. Editor: Music and Child Development, 1987. Com. mem. Utah Symphony. Mem. AAAS, Soc. Research in Child Devel., Am. Psychol. Assn., Nat. Council on Family Relations, Southwestern Soc. for Research in Child Devel., Utah Acad. Scis. Arts & Letters, Am. Orthopsychiat. Assn., Sigma Xi, Phi Kappa Phi. Mem. Ch. Jesus Christ of Latter Day Saints. Cons. editor and contbr. articles to profl. jours; contbr. chpts. to books. Office: Brigham Young U 1000 SWKT Provo UT 84602

PEERY, WENDELL WALLACE, banker, lawyer; b. Higbee, Mo., Nov. 15, 1931; s. Wallace B. and Hazel V. (Harbert) P.; m. Dolores Jean Williams, Feb. 3, 1952; children—Stan, Steven. B.S. in Agr., U. Mo., 1953, J.D., 1959. Bar: Mo., 1959. Spl. agt. FBI, Mpls., 1961-63; trust officer U.S. Nat. Bank, Portland, Oreg., 1963-70; v.p., sr. trust officer Oreg. Bank, Portland, 1970-74; v.p., trust officer Seattle 1st Nat. Bank, 1974-76; exec. v.p. Baker Boyer Bank, Walla Walla, Wash., 1976-86, exec. v.p., treas., 1986—; dir., 1980-86; dir. Bank of Commerce, Milton Freewater, Oreg., 1987. Trustee Blue Mountain Area Found., Walla Walla, 1984—. Served to capt. U.S. Army, 1953-55. Mem. Mo. Bar Assn., Oreg. Bar Assn., Walla Walla Valley Estate Planning (pres. 1978-79), Corp. Trustees Wash. (bd. dirs. 1980-83, pres. 1982-83), Walla Walla C. of C. (pres. 1984-85), Wash. Banker Assn. (bd. dirs. 1980-83). Republican. Methodist. Lodge: Rotary. Office: Baker Boyer Bank PO Box 1796 Walla Walla WA 99362

PEET, WILLIAM CREIGHTON, III, marketing executive, author, inventor; b. San Francisco, May 21, 1957; s. William Creighton Jr. and Helen Talcott (Hope) P. BA in Internat. Relations, Stanford U., 1979. Asst. dir. George Bush for Pres. Calif. Campaign, San Francisco, 1980-81; account mgr. Benton and Bowle Advt., N.Y.C., 1981-82, Foote, Cone and Belding, San Francisco, 1982-84; pvt. practice mktg. cons. San Francisco, 1984—. Exec. com. mem. U.S. Ski Team Ball, San Francisco, 1985; mem. campaign for St. Mark's Sch., Southboro, Mass., 1985—. Clubs: Calif. Tennis, Bay (San Francisco). Avocations: skiing, tennis.

PEETERS, RANDALL LOUIS, engineering manager; b. San Bernardino, Calif., Dec. 9, 1945; s. Louis Charles and Suzanne (Dinning) P.; m. Doris Marguerite Berry, Dec. 10, 1965; children: Shawn R., Todd L. BS in Aerospace Engring., Calif. State Poly. U., 1967; MS in Aeros. and Astronautics, U. Wash., 1969, PhC in Aeros. and Astronautics, 1971, PhD in Solid Mechanics, 1973. Assoc. engr. The Boeing Co., Seattle, 1967-68; materials engr. Air Force Rocket Propulsion Lab., Edwards, Calif., 1972-76; mem. staff Los Alamos (N.Mex.) Nat. Lab., 1976-80; mgr. tech. Xerox Corp., Webster, N.Y., 1980-81; research assoc. Eastman Kodak Co., Rochester, N.Y., 1981-82; engring. mgr. Aerojet Strategic Propulsion Co., Sacramento, 1982—; guest speaker Portland (Oreg.) State U., 1976, Sacramento State U., 1982; guest lectr. Univ. Coll., Cork City, Ireland, 1979; seminar speaker U. Wash., Seattle, 1985. Contbr. numerous articles to profl. jours. Adult leader Boy Scouts Am., Roseville, Calif., 1969—. Solar scholar, Solar Aircraft Co., Pomona, Calif., 1966; NDEA IV fellow, Seattle, 1969; NASA trainee, Seattle, 1971. Mem. ASME, Soc. Exptl. Mechanics, Am. Inst. Aeronautics and Astronautics, Soc. Natural Philosophy, Joint Army-Navy-Air Force Structural and Mech. Behavior Subcom. Republican. Avocations: surfing, kayaking, rafting, rock and ice climbing, skiing. Home: 1600 Presidio Way Roseville CA 95661 Office: Aerojet Strategic Propulsion Co PO Box 15699C Sacramento CA 95852-1699

PEIFER, KENNETH ROBERT, transportation company executive; b. Staten Island, N.Y., Jan. 3, 1944; m. Susan Roe; 4 children. B, CUNY, 1968, M in Pub. Adminstrn., 1975; cert. labor mgmt., U. San Francisco. Banker 1st Nat. City Bank, N.Y.C., 1961-63; various positions dept. ops. C&O-B&O R.R.'s (now CSX Corp.), N.Y., Balt., 1965-71; with labor relations dept. Rock Island R.R., Chgo., 1972; mgr. labor relations Western Pacific R.R. (parent co. Union Pacific System), Calif., 1973-77; mgr. spl. projects So. Pacific Transp. Co., San Francisco, 1977-83, asst. v.p. labor relations, 1983—; mem. coalition bargaining group Nat. Railway Labor Conf., various ad hoc coms. for labor negotiations, industry problems, grievance investigations, arbitration proceedings; conductor seminars arbitrations, negotiations, merger plannings in transp. industry. Mem. No. Calif. Human Resources Council, Am. Soc. Pub. Adminstrn. Office: So Pacific Transp Co 1 Market Plaza Room 304 San Francisco CA 94105

PEIL, KELLY MAC, environmental engineer; b. Watonga, Okla., Dec. 14, 1944; s. Raymond Peil and E. Jean (Testerman) Janssen; m. Sharon Lynn Robinson, Dec. 22, 1967; children: Ryan K., Andrea S. BA, Okla. State U., 1967, MS, 1969, PhD, 1972. Registered profl. sanitary engr., Pa., Tex., N.Mex. Engr. Roy F. Weston, Inc., West Chester, Pa., 1975-76, Houston, 1976-82; engr. Roy F. Weston, Inc., Albuquerque, 1982-86, office mgr., 1986—. Contbr. articles to profl. jours. Served to capt. Med. Service Corps, U.S. Army, 1972-75. Mem. ASCE, Water Pollution Control Fedn., Sigma Xi. Republican. Avocations: racquetball, golf, softball. Home: 14201 Vista Ct NE Albuquerque NM 87123 Office: Roy F Weston Inc 5301 Central Ave Albuquerque NM 87108

PEIRANO, LAWRENCE EDWARD, civil engineer; b. Stockton, Calif., May 13, 1929; s. Frank Lloyd and Esther Marie (Carigiet) P.; m. Mary Ellen Alabaster, July 26, 1952; children: Thomas Lawrence, Ellen Marie. BSCE, U. Calif., Berkeley, 1951, MSCE, 1952. Registered profl. engr., Calif., Nev.; diplomate Am. Acad. Environ. Engrs. Assoc. civil engr. Calif. Div. Water Resources, 1952-53; with Kennedy/Jenks/Chilton, Inc. (formerly Kennedy Engrs. Inc.), San Francisco, 1955—, project mgr., 1960—, v.p., chief environ. engr., 1974—, dir. ops., 1979—, sr. v.p., regional mgr., 1986—, also bd. dirs.; spl. lectr. san. engring. U. Calif., Berkeley, 1976. Served with U.S. Army, 1953-55, Korea. James Monroe McDonald scholar, 1950-51. Fellow ASCE; mem. Water Pollution Control Fedn., Am. Water Works Assn., Cons. Engrs. Assn. Calif., Internat. Assn. on Water Pollution Research and Control, Sierra Club, Far West Ski Assn., U. Calif. Alumni Assn., Tau Beta Pi, Chi Epsilon. Republican. Roman Catholic. Home: 3435 Black Hawk Rd Lafayette CA 94549 Office: Kennedy Jenks Chilton 657 Howard St San Francisco CA 94105

PEIRCE, JOHN WENTWORTH, geophysicist; b. Boston, Oct. 17, 1946; came to Can., 1976; s. John Wentworth and Grace Wentworth (Minot) P.; m. Dorcas Davenpost Sheldon, Sept. 1, 1969 (div. 1975); 1 child, Webster; m. Nancy Jane Netherington, Sept. 10, 1977; children: Jennifer, Alexander. AB, Dartmouth Coll., 1968; PhD, MIT and Woods Hole Oceanographic Instn., 1977. Registered profl. physicist, Alta. Asst. prof. Dalhouse U., Halifax, N.S., 1976-78; mgr. gravity and magnetics Petro Can., Calgary, Alta., 1978-86, supr. regional exploration internat., 1986—; Can. rep. site survey panel Ocean Drilling Project, 1983—. Contbr. articles to profl. jours. Chmn. Nose Hill Park Comminities Bd., Calgary, 1980—; bd. dirs. Cambrian Heights Community Assn., Calgary, 1979—. Served to lt. USN, 1968-72. Fellow Geol. Soc. Am., Geol. Assn. Can.; mem. Am. Geophys. Union, Can. Geophys. Union, Soc. Exploration Geophysicists, Can. Soc. Exploration Geophysicists. Office: Petrocanada, PO Box 2844, Calgary, AB Canada T2P 3E3

PEJZA, JOHN PHILIP, priest, school principal; b. Neshkoro, Wis., Aug. 5, 1934; s. Philip Peter and Regina Rosalie (Dombrowski) P. Student, Order of St. Augustine, 1952; BA, Villanova U., 1957, MA, 1961, MSSS, 1964; MA, U. San Francisco, 1981; postgrad., U. San Diego, 1982, EdD, 1987. Cert. tchr., Calif., adminstr., Calif.; ordained priest Cath. Ch., 1961. Tchr. Malvern (Pa.) Prep Sch., 1961-63; tchr. St. Augustine High Sch., San Diego, 1963-64, 70-75, prin., 1983—; tchr., asst. prin. Villanova Prep Sch., Ojai, Calif., 1964-70; prin. Cen. Cath. High Sch., Modesto, Calif., 1975-80, Marian High Sch., San Diego, 1981-83; secondary cons. Diocese of Stockton, Calif., 1977-80; exec. sec. province planning commn. Province of St. Augustine, Los Angeles, 1974-75; counselor Province of St. Augustine, Order of St. Augustine, Los Angeles, 1975-79. Contbr. articles to profl. jours. Mem. Nat. Cath. Ednl. Assn. (regional assoc. secondary div. 1987—), Augustinian Secondary Ednl. Assn., Assn. Calif. Sch. Adminstrs., Nat. Assn. Secondary Sch. Prins., Internat. Radio Club Am. (pres. 1977-79), Phi Delta Kappa. Avocations: backpacking, reading, photography, shortwave radio. Home and Office: St Augustine High Sch 3266 Nutmeg St San Diego CA 92104-5799

PEKARY, ALBERT EUGENE, research endocrinologist; b. Santa Monica, Calif., Aug. 13, 1943; s. Raymond Henry and Thelma Wray (Yeager) P.; m. Jean Aurelio Nicolas, Mar. 29, 1969; children: Dianne Nicolas, Leslie Ann. BS, Stanford U., 1965; PhD, U. Calif., Berkeley, 1970. Research assoc. Calif. Inst. Tech., Pasadena, 1970-72; postdoctoral fellow U. So. Calif. Med. Sch., Los Angeles, 1972-73; supervisory research chemist VA Wadsworth Med. Ctr., Los Angeles, 1973—; adj. asst. prof. UCLA Dept. Medicine, 1976-82, adj. assoc. prof., 1982—; computer cons. Hormone Research Lab., Torrance, Calif., 1980; cons. Arnel Products, N.Y.C., 1984—. Calif. State scholar 1961-65; fellow NIH, 1966-70, Rockefeller Found., N.Y.C., 1970-72; recipient Outstanding Performance award VA, Los Angeles, 1979, 84. Mem. AAAS, Endocrine Soc., Am. Fedn. Clin. Research, Pacific Coast Fertility Soc., Am. Thryoid Assn. Democrat. Presbyterian. Avocations: running, swimming, reading. Office: VA Wadsworth Med Ctr Bldg 114 Room 200 Los Angeles CA 90073

PEKMEZIAN, RICHARD THOMAS, sales executive; b. N.Y.C., June 7, 1962. BA, Rutgers U., 1984. Pub. Targum Pub. Co., New Brunswick, N.J., 1983-84; sales exec., advertising Hearst Bus. Pubs., Santa Clara, Calif., 1984—. Mem. Bus./Profl. Advt. Assn., Am. Mktg. Assn., Phi Gamma Delta.

PELISSON, GILLES CHRISTIAN, restaurant chain executive; b. Lyons, France, May 26, 1957; came to U.S., 1980; s. Henry Abel and Suzanne (Colomban) P.; m. Sylvie Veronique Poulet, Sept. 27, 1980. BBA, Ecole Superieure Des Scis. Econs. et Commls., Paris, 1979; MBA, Harvard U., 1983. Credit analyst Societe Generale Bank, N.Y.C., 1980-81; asst. v.p. devel. Accor N. Am., Scarsdale, N.Y., 1983-85; v.p. mktg. Seafood Broiler Restaurants, Lakewood, Calif., 1985—; cons. Booz, Allen & Hamilton, London, summer 1982. Mem. French-Am. C. of C. Club: Harvard (N.Y.C.). Avocations: tennis, downhill skiing, photography. Office: Seafood Broiler Inc 5150 Candlewood St Suite 4 Lakewood CA 90714

PELL, ROGER MARTIN, sales and marketing executive; b. Camp White, Oreg., Oct. 3, 1943; s. Roger Martin and Constance Margaret (Santanello) P.; B.S., Fairleigh Dickinson U., 1965; m. Rose-Marie L. Jonasson, Feb. 19, 1976; 1 dau., Kristina Ann. Pres., Century Am. Corp., Los Angeles, 1972-74; dir. mktg. Pacific Fidelity Life, 1974-77; chmn. Romarc, Los Angeles, 1977-84; co-founder, pres., chmn. bd. Ins. Agys. Systems Corp., 1981-85, Romarc Rating Systems, Romarc Fin. Systems, 1982-85; founder, pres., chmn. bd. The Pell Group, Inc., 1981—. Mem. Rep. Presdl. Task Force. Mem. Internat. Assn. Fin. Planners, Smithsonian Assos., Nat. Audubon Soc., Am. Mgmt. Assn. Author: Navigating the Computer Services Maze, 1979, Field Support System Manual, 1980, Financial Counseling Workshop, 1982, Client Centered Selling, 1986, Sales Leadership for Bankers, 1986. Office: 5530 Corbin Ave Suite 370 Tarzana CA 91356

PELLAM, JOHN LONERGAN, advertising agency executive, publisher; b. Washington, May 7, 1951; s. John Rudolph and Ruth Ellen (Lonergan) P.; m. Myrian René Cirilli, Mar. 21, 1981; step children: Marie-Dominque, Christoph. BA, U. Calif., Irvine, 1978. Pub. Design Mag., Laguna Beach, Calif., 1978-83; pvt. practice advt. Laguna Beach, 1978—; pub. Ann. Resource Directory, Laguna Beach, 1984—; mem. adv. com. extension program in mktg. communications U. Calif., Irvine, 1985—. Author: Cost-Effective Advertising for the Competitive Business, 1984; (manual) Direct Mail/Direct Response: from a Manager's Perspective, 1986. Recipient MAGGIE finalist award Western Pubs. Assn., 1982, Golden Oranges Finalist award Orange County Advt. Fedn., 1983, MAGGIE award Western Pubs. Assn., 1986. Office: 696 Playa Station Laguna Beach CA 92652

PELLEGRINI, RONALD, telecommunications consultant; b. Beaver Falls, Pa., Feb. 9, 1941; s. Elvidio and Armandina (Piroli) P.; m. Catherine Hitomi Pickhover, Feb. 17, 1985; children—Damon, Kent. B.A., Calif. State U.-Los Angeles, 1964. Communications cons. Pacific Telephone, Los Angeles, 1965-70, market mgr., San Francisco, 1975-77; regional mgr. AT&T, Los Angeles, 1970-75; sales mgr. SP Communications, San Francisco, 1977-79; br. mgr. MCI, San Francisco, 1979-80; mgr. telecommunications cons. Coopers & Lybrand, San Francisco, 1980-82; sr. mgr. telecommunications cons. Price Waterhouse, San Francisco, 1982-86; sr. mgr. info. systems cons. Peat, Marwick, Mitchell and Co., San Francisco, 1986—; mem. faculty Golden Gate U., San Francisco, 1982-83, mem. faculty adv. com. on telecommunications, 1982—. Mem. N.Am. Telephone Assn., Internat. Info. and Telecommunications Policy Com. Republican. Roman Catholic. Office: Peat Marwick Mitchell and Co 3 Embarcadero Ctr San Francisco CA 94111

PELLONE, DAVID THOMAS, controller; b. Ashtabula, Ohio, Mar. 15, 1944; s. Frank Joseph and Shirley Edna (Foster) P.; m. Sunny Jewel Unfug, May 28, 1977; children: Todd Gary, Michelle Christine. BBA in Indsl. Mgmt., Kent (Ohio) State U., 1967; MBA in Acctg. and Fin., U. Santa Clara, Calif., 1973. Product supr., indsl. engr. Owens Corning Fiberglass, Santa Clara, 1970-72; line controller Fairchild Semiconductor, Mountain View, Calif., 1973-74; corp. controller Cermetec, Inc., Mountain View, 1974-76; various mgmt. Minn. Mining and Mfg., Ventura, Calif., 1976-83; cons. J&P Assoc, Menlo Park, Calif., 1983-84; area fin. mgr. GenRad, Inc., Milpitas, Calif., 1984-86; corp. controller Genus, Inc., Mountain View, 1986—. Served with U.S. Army, 1967-69. Mem. Am. Acctg. Assn., Inst. Internal Auditors, Inst. Indsl. Engrs. (sr.), AMA. Republican. Episcopalian. Office: Genus Inc 515 Ellis St Mountain View CA 94043

PELOQUIN, JOHN JOSEPH, entomologist, molecular biologist; b. Escanaba, Mich., Dec. 11, 1952; s. Wilfred Alexander and Patricia Catherine (Houle) P. BS in Biology, Notre Dame U., 1975, MS in Biology, 1980; PhD in Entomology, Texas A&M U., 1984. Postgrad. entomology research U. Calif., Berkeley, 1984-85; staff research assoc. U. Calif., Riverside, 1985—. Mem. AAAS, Sigma Xi, Phi Sigma. Republican. Roman Catholic. Avocations: soccer, music, movies, literature, auto rally. Home: 200 W Big Springs #13 Riverside CA 92507 Office: U Calif Dept Nematology Riverside CA 92507

PELOSI, NANCY, congresswoman. Formerly chmn. Calif. State Dem. Com.; committeewoman Dem. Nat. Com.; elec. to U.S. Congress from 5th dist. Calif. 1987. Office: Offices of House Members care The Postmaster Washington DC 20515 *

PELOTTE, DONALD E., bishop; b. Waterville, Maine, Apr. 13, 1945. Student, Eymard Sem. and Jr. Coll., Hyde Park, N.Y., John Carroll U., Fordham U. Ordained priest Roman Cath. Ch., 1972. Ordained coadjutor biship Diocese of Gallup, N.Mex., 1986—. 1st Native Am. bishop. Address: Coadjutor Bishop of Gallup PO Box 1338 Gallup NM 87301 *

PELPHREY, MICHAEL WAYNE, management consultant; b. Huntington Park, Calif., Dec. 12, 1946; s. Arthur D. and Anne (Chimick) P.; m. Teresa A. DeBorde, May 2, 1970; children: Mark A. BBA, Calif. State U., Fullerton, 1973; MS in Fin., West Coast U., 1975. Dir. mfg. services Elconics, Inc., Newport Beach, Calif., 1975-77; prin. Master Achievements, Santa Ana, Calif., 1978-80; dir. profl. services Comserv Corp., Eagan, Minn., 1980-85; prin. Pelphrey, Gilson and Assocs., Westminster, Calif., 1985—; former chmn. bd., chief exec. officer, pres. Keck's Drapery Mfg., Garden Grove, Calif.; mem. steering com. Aerospace and Defense, Los Angeles, 1985—; conf. dir. APICS Aerospace and Def. Integrated Planning and Control Symposium. Contbr. articles to profl. jours. Served to sgt. USAF, 1965-68, Vietnam. Mem. Am. Prodn. and Inventory Control Soc. (cert.). Republican. Avocations: racquetball, swimming. Home: 1505 W Surrey Ln Santa Ana CA 92704 Office: Pelphrey Gilson and Assocs 5455 Garden Grove Blvd 3d floor Westminster CA 92683

PELTASON, JACK WALTER, university chancellor; b. St. Louis, Aug. 29, 1923; s. Walter B. and Emma (Hartman) P.; m. Suzanne Toll, Dec. 21, 1946; children: Nancy Hartman, Timothy Walter H., Jill K. B.A., U. Mo., 1943, M.A., 1944, LL.D. (hon.), 1978; A.M., Princeton U., 1946, Ph.D., 1947; LL.D. (hon.), U. Md., 1979, Ill. Coll., 1979, Gannon U., 1980, U. Maine, 1980, Union Coll., 1981, Moorehead (N.D.) State U., 1980; L.H.D. (hon.), 1980, Ohio State U., 1980, Mont. Coll. Mineral Scis. and Tech., 1982, Buena Vista Coll., 1982, Assumption Coll., 1983, Chapman Coll., 1986. Asst. prof. Smith Coll., Mass., 1947-51; asst. prof. polit. sci. U. Ill., Urbana, 1951-52, assoc. prof., 1953-59, dean Coll. Liberal Arts and Scis., 1960-64, chancellor, 1967-77; vice chancellor acad. affairs U. Calif., Irvine, 1964-67, chancellor, 1984—; pres. Am. Council Edn., Washington, 1977-84; Cons. Mass. Little Hoover Commn., 1950. Author: The Missouri Plan for the Selection of Judges, 1947, Understanding the Constitution, 10th edit, 1985, Federal Courts in the Political Process, 1957, (with James M. Burns) Government by the People, 13th edit, 1987, Fifty-eight Lonely Men, 1961, also articles, revs. Recipient James Madison medal Princeton U., 1982. Fellow Am. Acad. Arts and Scis.; mem. Am. Polit. Sci. Assn. (council 1952-54), Phi Beta Kappa, Phi Kappa Phi, Omicron Delta Kappa, Alpha Phi Omega, Beta Gamma Sigma. Home: 6 Gibbs Ct Irvine CA 92715

PEÑA, DANIEL STEVEN, oil company executive; b. Jacksonville, Fla., Aug. 10, 1945; s. Manual Solterro and Amy (Tinoco) P.; m. Linda Elaine Sewall, July 13, 1973; children: Daniel Steven Jr., Derreck Stewart. BS, Calif. State U., Northridge, 1971. Dir. corp. services Hornblower, Weeks, Hemphill, Noyes, Los Angeles, 1972-74; dir. fin. planning Paine, Webber, Jackson & Curtis, Los Angeles, 1974-77; v.p. Bear Stearns & Co., Los Angeles, 1977-78; chief exec. officer JPK Industries, Los Angeles, 1978-82, also chmn. bd. dirs.; pres., chief exec. officer Great Western Resources Inc., Houston, 1982—, also chmn. bd. dirs. Served to 1st lt. U.S. Army, 1966-69. Recipient Merit award Sports Illus., 1976, Latin Businessman of Yr. Latin Businessman's Assn., 1981, Outstanding Bus. Owner award Hispanic mag., 1981. Democrat. Roman Catholic. Club: Jonathon (Los Angeles). Avocations: golf, racquetball, shooting.

PENA, FEDERICO FABIAN, mayor of Denver, lawyer; b. Laredo, Tex., Mar. 15, 1947; s. Gustavo J. and Lucille P. B.A., U. Tex.-Austin, 1969, J.D., 1972. Bar: Colo. 1973. Ptnr. firm Pena & Pena, Denver, 1973-83; mayor City and County of Denver, 1983—; mem. Colo. Gen. Assembly, 1979-83, ho. Dem. leader, 1981; mem. Colo. Bd. Law Examiners, Denver; assoc. Harvard Ctr. for Law and Edn., Cambridge, Mass. Named Outstanding House Dem. Legislator Colo. Gen. Assembly, 1981. Roman Catholic. Home: 3214 W 26th Ave Denver CO 80211 Office: City and County of Denver 350 City and County Bldg Denver CO 80202

PENA, MANUEL, JR., state senator; b. Cashion, Ariz., Nov. 17, 1924; s. Manuel and Elvira (Gomez) P.; student public schs.; m. Aurora Cruz, June 13, 1945; children: Yolanda, Mary, Henry, Steve, Patricia, Geraldine, Manuel III. Owner Pena Realty & Ins. Agy., Phoenix, 1951—; pres. Penasco, Inc.; mem. Ariz. state adv. com. U.S. Commn. Civil Rights, 1981—, Ariz. Ho. of Reps., Phoenix, 1967-72, Ariz. Senate, Phoenix, 1973—. Exec. sec. Ariz. Athletic Commn., 1964-66; commr. human relations City of Phoenix, 1967-71. Served with U.S. Army, 1945-46. Mem. Am. Legion (comdr.). Democrat. Roman Catholic. Office: PO Box 6482 Phoenix AZ 85005

PENALUNA, JAMES ELLIOT, manufacturing processing educator; b. Grass Valley, Calif., Mar. 3, 1957; s. William Stanley and Doris Mae (Wilder) P.; m. Betty Lorraine Fuller, May, 12, 1984. AA, Sierra Community Coll., Rocklin, Calif., 1978; BA, Calif. State U., Chico, 1980; MA, Calif. State U., Sacramento, 1984. Welder 17th Dist. Agrl. Assn., Grass Valley, 1974-76; machinist, welder Precision Machine Works, Grass Valley, 1976-77, 80-82, Fieldon Mfg. Co., Chico, 1978, Calif. State U., Chico, 1979-80; instr. metals tech. Sierra Community Coll., Rocklin, Calif., 1980—; lectr. mfg. processes Calif. State U., Sacramento, 1985—. Mem. Calif. Tchrs. Assn., Am. Soc. Metals, Calif. Blacksmiths Assn. Lodge: Masons. Avocations: hunting, fishing, camping, ornamental iron work. Office: Calif State U Dept Mech Engr 6000 J St Sacramento CA 95819

PENDER, DOUGLAS HOWARD, social service administrator; b. Auburn, N.Y., Jan. 1, 1934; s. Howard Douglas and Mary Elizabeth (Schetrompf) P.; m. Crystle Fayne Klein, Feb. 12, 1956; children: Helen Elizabeth Wood, Judith Fayne Walker. BA, Idaho State U., 1961; DD (hon.), Universal Life Ch., 1979. Dir. Mohave Co. Community Action Agy., Kingman, Ariz., 1970-71, Hualapai Com. Action Agy., Peach Springe, Ariz., 1971-76; career counselor Ariz. Army N.G., Kingman, 1976-80; human service worker Ariz. Dept. Econ. Security, Lake Havasu City, 1980-86; pres. Concepts Beyond, Lake Havasu City, 1986—; bd. dirs. Graphoanalytics, Lake Havasu, 1986—. Pub. Hualapai Times, 1973. Served with Ariz. N.G., 1971-80. Mem. Am. Assn. Counseling and Devel., Nat. Career Devel. Assn., Am. Rehab. Counselors Assn. Republican. Presbyterian. Lodges: Shriners (sec. treas. Lake Havasu City club 1982-84), Masons. Developed a system of analysis for hands and handwriting. Home: 457 Sunfield Dr Lake Havasu City AZ 86407 Office: GraphoAnalytics Inc 1990D McCulloch Blvd Suite 265 Lake Havasu City AZ 86403

PENDERGHAST, THOMAS FREDERICK, educator; b. Cin., Apr. 23, 1936; s. Elmer T. and Dolores C. (Huber) P.; BS, Marquette U., 1958; MBA, Calif. State U., Long Beach, 1967; D in Bus. Adminstrn. Nova U., 1987; m. Marjorie Craig, Aug. 12, 1983; children: Brian, Shawna, Steven, Dean, Maria. Sci. programmer Autonetics, Inc., Anaheim, Calif., 1960-64; bus. programmer Douglas Missile & Space Ctr., Huntington Beach, Calif., 1964-66; computer specialist N.Am. Rockwell Co., 1966-69; asst. prof. Calif. State U., Long Beach, 1969-72; assoc. prof. Sch. Bus. and Mgmt., Pepperdine U., Los Angeles, 1972—; spl. adviser Commn. on Engring. Edn., 1968; v.p. Visual Computing Co., 1969-71; founder, pres. Scoreboard Animation Systems, 1971-77; exec. v.p. Microfilm Identification Systems, 1977-79; pres. Data Processing Auditors, Inc., 1981—; data processing cons. designing computer system for fin. health and mfg. orgns., 1972—. Mem. Orange County Blue Ribbon Com. on Data Processing, 1973; mem. Orange County TEC Policy Bd., 1982—. Served to lt. USNR, 1958-60. Cert. in data processing. Mem. Users of Automatic Info. Display Equipment (pres. 1966). Home: 17867 Bay St Fountain Valley CA 92708

PENDLETON, JAMES ABERCROMBIE, engring. geologist; b. Reading, Pa., Nov. 6, 1946; s. Joseph Saxton and Mary Driscoll (Vernon) P.; A.B. magna cum laude, Princeton U., 1969; M.S. (NDEA fellow), U. Colo., 1973, Ph.D., 1978; m. Nancy Marie Haffey, Aug. 2, 1969. Geol. aide Gilbert-Commonwealth, Inc., Reading, summer 1967, geologist, summer 1969; engring. geologist City of Boulder (Colo.), 1970-78, city engr., 1978-79; supervising geologist Colo. Div. Mined Land Reclamation, Denver, 1980—; cons. geology, 1970-79; dir. Bristlecone Investments, Inc. Recipient John Wesley Powell award U.S. Geol. Survey, 1979. Mem. Geol. Soc. Am., Assn. Engring. Geologists, Am. Inst. Profl. Geologists, Nat. Water Well Assn., Colo. Engring. Council (pres.), Sigma Xi. Home: 174 Anemone Dr Sunshine Canyon Boulder CO 80302 Office: Colo Div Mined Land Reclamation 1313 Sherman St Room 423 Denver CO 80203

PENDLETON, LANE ROBERTS, aerospace company executive; b. Thayne, Wyo., Nov. 17, 1931; s. Calvin George and Espesa (Roberts) P.; m. Yovonne Archibald, Sept. 6, 1956; children: Jannette, Judith, Michael, Jolene. BSCE, Utah State U., 1956; MS in Aerospace Engring., U. So. Calif., 1958; postgrad., Stanford U., 1958-60. Assoc. engr. Lockheed Missiles and Aircraft Corp., Burbank, Calif., 1958—; mem. advanced studies staff Lockheed Missiles and Aircraft Corp., Sunnyvale, Calif., 1958-61, research engr., 1961-65, research specialist, 1965-82, staff engr., 1982-84, engring. supr., 1984—; shock and vibration specialist, joint U.S. and U.K. missile programs, 1976-79, 83—. Contbr. articles to tech. jours. Mem. AIAA (pyro-shock com.), Sigma Tau, Phi Kappa Phi. Mormon. Avocations: flying, skiing, computer programming. Office: Lockheed Missiles & Space Co 1111 Lockheed Way Sunnyvale CA 94088

PENDLETON, OTHNIEL ALSOP, fund raiser, clergyman; b. Washington, Aug. 22, 1911; s. Othniel Alsop and Ingeborg (Berg) P.; m. Flordora Mellquist, May 15, 1935; children: John, James (dec.), Thomas, Ann, Susan. AB, Union Coll., Schenectady, N.Y., 1933; BD, Eastern Bapt. Theol. Sem., 1936; MA, U. Pa., 1936, PhD, 1945; postgrad., Columbia U., 1937-38. Ordained to ministry Bapt. Ch., 1936. Pastor chs. Jersey City, 1935-39, Phila., 1939-43; dean Sioux Falls Coll., S.D., 1943-45; fund raiser Am. Bapt. Ch., N.Y.C., 1945-47, Mass. Bapt. Ch., Boston, 1947-54; fund raiser Seattle, Chgo., Boston, Washington and N.Y.C., 1955-64, Westwood, Mass., 1971-84; staff mem. Marts & Lundy, Inc., N.Y.C., 1964-71; lectr. Andover-Newton Sem., Newton, Mass., 1958, Boston U. Sch. Theology, 1958, Harvard U., Cambridge, Mass., 1977-84. Author: New Techniques for Church Fund Raising, 1955, Fund Raising: A Guide to Non-Profit Organizations, 1981; contbr. articles in field to profl. jours. Address: 529 Berkeley Ave Claremont CA 91711

PENDOLA, LUCILLE JOAN, educational administrator; b. Boston, Sept. 14, 1947; d. Joseph John and Lucille Amilda (Griffin) P. A.B., Manhattanville Coll., 1969; student Andover-Newton Theol. Inst., Newton Coll. Sacred Heart, Fordham U., 1971, Oakland U., 1973; M.S., U. Notre Dame, 1977; student Inst. Christian Initiation of Adults, Holy Names Coll., Oakland, 1980, Jesuit Sch. Theology, Berkley, 1981. Tchr., Convent of Sacred Heart, Greenwich, Conn., 1969-70; acting head middle sch. Newton (Mass.) Country Day Sch., 1970-71; asst. head middle sch. Acad. Sacred Heart, Bloomfield Hills, Mich., 1971-74, head middle sch., 1974-78; directress Kenwood Summer Day Camp, Albany, N.Y., summer 1973; instr. religious edn. U. Detroit, 1977-78; mem. religious edn. curriculum revision com. Archdiocese of Detroit, 1978-80; dir. religious edn. Our Lady of the Lakes Parish, Waterford, Mich., 1978-80, also trustee Our Lady of the Lakes Scholarship and Ednl. Excellence Found.; dir. religious edn. St. Paschal's Parish, Oakland, Calif., 1980-83, prin. St. Paschal's Sch., 1981—; master catechist Diocese of Calif., also mem. 1st diocesan pastoral council. Mem. Assn. for Supervision and Curriculum Devel., Nat. Cath. Edn. Assn. Democrat. Roman Catholic. Office: 3710 Dorisa Ave Oakland CA 94605

PENG, YENG KAUNG, electrical engineer; b. Shanghai, Republic of China, Dec. 14, 1948; came to U.S., 1977; s. Shaw Chang and Wei Lun (Lin) P. B in Engring., Coll. Maritime Tech., Taiwan, Republic of China, 1971; MSME, U. Nebr., 1978, PhD in Materials Sci., 1980. Marine engr. Oriental Navigation Co., Hong Kong, 1972-76; from research asst. to research assoc. U. Nebr., Lincoln, 1977-80, postdoctoral researcher, 1981; mem. tech. staff Nitron Corp., Cupertino, Calif., 1981-83; yeild enhancement engr., device engr. Monolithic Memories Inc., Santa Clara, Calif., 1983—. Contbr. articles to sci. jours. Mem. IEEE, Sigma Xi. Home: 460 Auburn Way #6 San Jose CA 95129 Office: Monolithic Memories Inc 2175 Mission Coll Blvd MS 07-30 Santa Clara CA 95054-1592

PENIKETT, ANTONY DAVID JOHN, politician; b. Nov. 14, 1945; s. Erik John Keith and Sarah Ann (Colwell) P.; m. Lula Mary Johns, 1974; children—John Tahmoh, Sarah Lahlil, Stephanie Yahsan. Nat. exec. asst. to leader New Dem. Party, Ottawa, Ont., Canada, 1975-76, nat. pres., 1981-85, fed. councillor, 1973—; leader New Dem. Party, Yukon Whitehorse, Y.T., Canada, 1980—; campaign mgr. New Dem. Party, N.W.T., Canada, 1972; city councillor City of Whitehouse, Y.T., Canada, 1977-79; mem. legis. assembly Yukon Legis. Assembly, 1978—; opposition leader Yukon Legis. Assembly, Y.T., Canada, 1982-85, elected govt. leader Y.T., 1985—. Author (film): The Mad Trapper, 1972; La Patrouille Perdu, 1974. Mem. Christian Socialist Ch. Home: PO Box 4584, Whitehorse, YT Canada Y1A 2R8 Office: Yukon Territorial Govt, PO Box 2703, Whitehorse, YT Canada Y1A 2C6

PENLEY, LARRY EDWARD, management educator; b. Bristol, Va., Feb. 9, 1949; s. William Edward and June (Caudill) P.; m. Yolanda Elva Sanchez, Nov. 25, 1977; children: Jonathan Andrew, Josephine Anna. BA, Wake Forest U., 1971, MA, 1972; PhD, U. Ga., 1976. Assoc. dean U. Tex., San Antonio, 1980-85; vis. prof. ITESM, Monterey, Mex., 1977, Universidad de Carobobo, Valencia, Venezuela, 1978; prof., chmn. dept. Ariz. State U., Tempe, 1985—. Contbr. articles to profl. jours.; mem. editorial rev. bd. Borderlands Jour., 1985—. Mem. Acad. Mgmt. (chmn. div. program 1986), Southwestern Council Latin Am. Studies, Internat. Communication Assn., Am. Soc. Personnel Adminstrn., Acad. Internat. Bus. Democrat. Roman Catholic. Home: 2209 W Keating Mesa AZ 85202 Office: Ariz State U Dept Mgmt Tempe AZ 85287

PENN, JANICE, nurse, educator; b. Bronx, N.Y., May 2, 1941; d. Leonard and Eva Willis (Chandler) Penn; B.S., SUNY Downstate Med. Center, 1973; M.A., NYU, 1975; Ph.D., Tex. Women's U., Denton, 1982; 1 son, Jose Gonzalez. Nurse, Albert Einstein Coll. Hosp., Bronx, 1973, Bronx Montefiore Morrisania Hosp., 1973-74, Bronx VA Hosp., 1974; mem. faculty U. Albuquerque, 1975-76; supr. Bernalillo County Med. Ctr., Albuquerque, 1975-76; mem. faculty, mem. advanced psychiat. council U. N.Mex., Albuquerque, 1976—; mem. faculty U. Tex.-Arlington, 1980-83, U. Colo., 1983-84; head nurse, mem. faculty Mental Health-Hosp. Div., U. N.Mex, 1984-86; dir. Found. for Health Guidance, Rio Rancho, N.Mex., 1986—. Mem. Am., N.Mex. nurses Assns., Sigma Theta Tau. Democrat. Home: 305 Coronado Ct SE Rio Rancho NM 87124 Office: Found for Health Guidance 1117 Rio Rancho Dr SE Suite 2 Rio Rancho NM 87124

PENNING, JOHN RUSSELL, JR., research engineer; b. Spokane, Wash., Dec. 13, 1922; s. John Russell Sr. and Mildred Evelyn (Clark) P.; m. Dorothy June Benn, Dec. 20, 1960 (dec. Jan. 1975); m. Hak Sun Kim, June 7, 1975; 1 child, Flora Meehwa. BS, U. Wash., 1948, PhD, 1956. Research scientist Space Tech. Labs., Los Angeles, 1956-59; research engr. Northrop Corp., Newbury Park, Calif., 1963-65; research scientist Boeing Co., Seattle, 1959-63, 65—. Contbr. articles to profl. jours. Served as sgt. USAF, 1942-45, ETO. Mem. Am. Phys. Soc., Phi Beta Kappa, Sigma Xi. Home: 32554 36th Ave SW Federal Way WA 98023 Office: Boeing Co PO Box 3707 Seattle WA 98124

PENNINGTON, GARY NOEL, accountant; b. Portland, Oreg., June 22, 1947; s. Lloyd Drew and Hazel Pauline (Franke) P.; m. Carolyn Diane Wolfe, Sept. 1, 1968; children: Cheryl, Lisa, Janice, Bryan. BSBA, U. Calif., Berkeley, 1969; M in Profl. Acctg., U. Tex., 1971. CPA, Oreg. Staff acct. PMM & Co., Houston, 1971-73; tax acct. PMM & Co., Portland, Oreg., 1973-77; tax mgr. Bohemia, Inc., Eugene, Oreg., 1977-84, controller, 1984—. Treas. Univ. Children's Choir Assn., Eugene, 1985—. Served to capt. USAR, 1971-78. Mem. Am. Inst. CPA's, Oreg. Soc. CPA's. Republican. Methodist. Avocations: photography, camping, fishing. Home: 490 Dartmoor Dr Eugene OR 97401 Office: Bohemia Inc 2280 Oakmont Way Eugene OR 97401

PENNINGTON, JOHN DAVID, optometrist, educator; b. Puyallup, Wash., Sept. 17, 1924; s. David Franklin and Kathleen Marie (Rakestraw) P.; m. Gloria Penoyer, 1943 (div.); m. 2d, Gennie A. Gottberg, Nov. 25, 1949; children—David, James, Nancy, John. B.S., Pacific U., 1953, O.D., 1954, M.S., 1966. Lic. optometrist. Practice optometry, Enumclaw, Wash., 1954-59; Pueblo, Colo., 1959-65; teaching fellow Pacific U., Forest Grove, Oreg., 1965-66; faculty mem. Pa. Coll. Optometry, Phila., 1966-70; staff mem. Group Health Co-op. of Puget Sound, Seattle, 1970—; instr. Seattle Central Community Coll., 1972-75; council mem. Clin. Council Optometric Care, 1977-85; cons. Interstudy, Mpls.; speaker profl. meetings. Served with USN, 1943-46. Fellow Am. Acad. Optometry; mem. Wash. Optometric Assn., Am. Optometric Assn. (multidisciplinary practice sect., cons. inter-assn./interprofl. affairs adv. com.). Republican. Contbr. articles to profl. jours. Home: 205 NW 177th St Seattle WA 98177 Office: Group Health Co-op of Puget Sound 20200 W 54th St Lynnwood WA 98036

PENNINGTON, WILLIAM ROY, art consultant; b. Greeley, Colo., July 27, 1925; s. Roy Richard and Vivian Eileen (Weiss) P.; m. Elizabeth LaVern Genge; children: Donald William, Kathleen Jean. BSBA, U. Denver, 1951. Asst. buyer May Co., Denver; order service rep. Explosives div. E.I. DuPont de Nemours Co., Denver, 1952-70; various sales positions Denver, 1970-73; adminstrv. officer State of Colo., Denver, 1973-86; art cons. Shelby Fine Arts, Denver, 1986—. Author Dept. Natural Resources Grant Mgrs. Fiscal Tng. Manual, 1984. Ruling elder Faith United Presbyn. Ch., Aurora, 1968-70; mem. City of Aurora Planning and Zoning Commn., 1969-70, Bd. of Adjustment and Appeals, 1966-69; Arapahoe County Rep. Precinct committeeman, Aurora, 1966-70; organizational rep. Boy Scouts Am. Aurora council, 1964-66; active YMCA Indian Guides, Indian Princesses, Aurora, 1966-67. Mem. Nat. Assistance Mgmt. Assn., Acacia (pres. Denver chpt. 1949). Republican. Lodge: Masons. Home: 428 S Wheeling Way Aurora CO 80012

PENWELL, JONES CLARK, real estate appraiser and consultant; b. Crisp, Tex., Dec. 19, 1921; s. Clark Moses and Sarah Lucille (Jones) P.; B.S., Colo. State U., 1949; m. A. Jerry Jones, July 1, 1967; children—Dale Maria, Alan Lee, John Steven, Laurel Anne, Tracy Lynn. Farm mgmt. supr. Farmers Home Adminstrn., Dept. Agr., 1949-58; rancher 1958-61; real estate appraiser/realty officer Dept. Interior, Tex., Calif., Ariz., Colo., Washington, 1961-78, chief appraiser Bur. Reclamation, Lakewood, Colo., 1978-80; ind. fee appraiser, cons., 1980—. Served with USN, 1940-46. Accredited rural appraiser; cert. review appraiser; recipient Outstanding Performance awards U.S. Bur. Reclamation, 1964, 75, 80. Mem. Am. Soc. Farm Mgrs. and Rural Appraisers, Internat. Right-of-Way Assn., Nat. Assn. Rev. Appraisers (regional v.p. 1978-79), Soc. Real Estate Appraisers (asso.), Jefferson County Bd. Realtors. Democrat. Presbyterian. Clubs: Elks, Rotary, Mt. Vernon Country. Author: Reviewing Condemnation Appraisal Reports, 1980; The Valuation of Easements, 1980. Home and office: 10100 W 21st Place Lakewood CO 80215

PEPITONE ARREOLA ROCKWELL, FRANCES MARIE, psychologist; b. San Mateo, Calif., June 3, 1941; d. Joseph Pepitone and Hope Norma (Arreola) Gunn; m. Don Arthur Rockwell, Dec. 23, 1965; children: Grant Arthur, Chad Arthur. RN, Highland Sch. Nursing, 1961; BA, Calif. State

U., San Francisco, 1966; MA, Calif. State U., Sacramento, 1971; PhD, Calif. Sch. Profl. Psychology, 1974. Asst. prof. psychology U. Calif., Davis, 1974-82, dir. women's resources and research ctr., 1978-82, assoc. prof., 1982-84, asst. dean acad. affairs, 1982-84; assoc. prof. Drew Med. Sch., Los Angeles, 1985-87; asst. dir. devel. programs Undergrad. Admissions and Relations with Schs., UCLA, Los Angeles, 1987—. Editor: Dual Career Couples, 1980; style editor (jour.) Psychotherapy, 1980-84; contbr. articles to profl. jours. Founding mem. Yolo County (Calif.) Sex Assault Ctr., 1976-78; mem. sexual assault adv. com. State of Calif., 1982-83; com. mem. rape adv. panel Office of Criminal Justice, Sacramento, 1977; com. mem. Yolo County Health Assn., Davis, 1971-72. Mem. AAAS, Assn. Med. Colls. (women's liaison officer 1981-84), council Nat. Register of Health Service Providers, Psychology of Women and Psychotherapy div. of Am. Psychol. Assn. (program reviewer 1985-86), Sigma Xi. Avocations: spectator car racing, tennis. Office: UCLA Undergrad Admissions and Relations with Schs Los Angeles CA 90024

PEPKA, KATHLEEN MARY, sales and marketing executive; b. Niagara Falls, N.Y., Feb. 2, 1949; d. Edmund Francis and Casmera Josephine (Nowak) Olszowka; m. Leon Michael Pepka, Aug. 16, 1968 (div. Aug. 1986); children: Cheri, Deanna. AA, Saddleback Coll., 1982; BS, U. La Verne, 1985. Dir. merchandising W.R. Grace Properties, Newport Beach, Calif., 1975-79; mgr. mktg. Campeau Corp., Newport Beach, 1979-82; dir. sales and mktg. Mission Viejo (Calif.) Co., 1982—. Mem. Inst. Residential Mktg., Nat. Sales and Mktg. Council, Home Builders Council, So. Calif. Sales and Mktg. Council, Bldg. Industry Assn. (treas. Sales and Mktg. council 1982, v.p. 1983, pres. 1984; Pres.'s Achievement award 1981, 83, Major Achievement in Merchandising Excellence 1984-86, Mktg. Dir. of Yr. 1986). Republican. Roman Catholic. Avocations: crafts, jogging, cooking. Home: 27981 Sheffield Mission Viejo CA 92692 Office: Mission Viejo Co 26137 La Paz Rd Mission Viejo CA 92691

PEPPER, DAVID M., physicist, educator, author; b. Los Angeles, Mar. 9, 1949; s. Harold and Edith (Kleinplatz) P. BS in Physics summa cum laude, UCLA, 1971; MS in Applied Physics, Calif. Inst. Tech., 1974, PhD in Applied Physics, 1980. Mem. tech. staff Hughes Research Labs., Malibu, Calif., 1973—; adj. prof. math. and physics Pepperdine U., Malibu, 1981—. Co-author: Optical Phase Conjugation, 1983, Laser Handbook Vol. 4, 1985; guest editor Soc. Photo-Optical Engring. Instrumentation Jour. 1982 (Rudolf Kingslake award 1982); contbr. numerous articles to profl. tech. jours.; patentee in field. Mem. Sons and Daughters of 1939 Club, 2d Generation of Martyrs Meml., Mus. Holocaust. NSF trainee Calif. Inst. Tech., 1971; Howard Hughes fellow Hughes Aircraft Co., 1973-80. Mem. Am. Phys. Soc., Optical Soc. Am., IEEE, Sigma Xi (v.p. 1986—), Sigma Pi Sigma. Jewish. Avocations: classical music, travel, sports, astronomy, nature. Office: Hughes Research Labs RL 65 3011 Malibu Canyon Rd Malibu CA 90265

PEPPER, JOHN ROY, oil and gas executive; b. Denver, Feb. 24, 1937; s. Wesley Wayne and Lucille (Stith) P.; m. Sallie K. Force, Dec. 13, 1958 (div. July 1970); m. Judithea Lawrence, Sept. 24, 1977; stepchildren: Sarah Douglas, Kenneth R. Douglas. BSBA, U. Denver, 1961; postgrad., UCLA, 1962, U. Denver, 1965. Analyst Texaco, Inc., Los Angeles, 1962-63; landman Texaco, Inc., Bakersfield, Calif., 1963-65; prin. John Pepper, Landman, Denver, 1965-75; owner, operator John R. Pepper Oil & Gas Co., Denver, 1975—; bd. dirs. Trans-Telecom, Miami, Fla.; cons. Organizer Friends of Bob Crider campaign, Denver, 1985. Mem. Ind. Petroleum Assn. Mountain States, Ind. Petroleum Assn. of Ams. (pub. lands com. 1968-74), Denver Assn. Petroleum Landmen. Republican. Lutheran. Clubs: Kenosha Trout (Park County, Colo.) (chmn. first aid and fish procurement coms. 1974-82); Denver, Rump (Denver). Avocations: sailing, fishing, bird hunting. Home: 6161 S Forest Ct Littleton CO 80121 Office: John R Pepper Oil & Gas Co 1800 Glenarm Pl Denver CO 80202

PERA, IRIS CAMPODONICO, financial analyst; b. San Francisco, Sept. 13, 1936; d. Rudolph Louis and Siria Elda (Baldocchi) Campodonico; m. Richard Ignatius Pera, May 14, 1960 (div. 1983); Richard, Angelo, Carol. B.A., Dominican Coll., 1958. Dir. of community and legis. affairs New Century Beverage Co., San Francisco; fin. analyst Newkirk-Sloane, San Rafael, Calif.; founder, owner The Bottom Line, San Rafael, Calif.; dir., chief fin. officer New Horizons Savs. & Loan Assn. Bd. dirs., treas. Dominican Coll. Alumni Assn.; mem. citizens adv. com. Dominican Coll.; aux. vol. Bur. of Marin. Club: Cristoforo Colombo. Home: 101 Lombard St San Francisco CA 94111 Office: 938 B St San Rafael CA 94901

PERA, LAUREN CANNON, chemist; b. San Francisco, Sept. 7, 1958; d. William Thomas and Jayne (Kettler) Cannon. BA in Biophysics, U. Calif., Berkeley, 1981. Applications chemist Varian Co., Palo Alto, Calif., 1981-82; applications chemist Bio-Rad Labs., Richmond, Calif., 1982-84, sr. applications chemist, 1984-85, product mgr., 1985-86, group product mgr., 1986—. Contbr. articles to profl. jours. Avocations: sailing, hiking, gardening, reading. Office: Bio-Rad Labs 1414 Harbour Way S Richmond CA 94804

PERALTA-RAMOS, LEE GAMBLE, architectural and interior designer; b. St. Louis, Aug. 5, 1952; d. James Carr and Dorothy Lee (Wharton) Gamble; m. Arturo Huddleston Peralta-Ramos, May 31, 1975; children: Lindsey Elise, Ashley Elizabeth. BS, Skidmore Coll., 1974; degree in Interior Design, N.Y. Sch. Interior Design, 1976. Asst. buyer Abraham & Strauss, Bklyn., 1974-75; mgr. Trevi Co., Pitts., 1975; buyer Saks Fifth Ave., N.Y.C., 1975-77; prin. West Wind Designs, Cody, Wyo., 1977—; cons. design Wyo. Waterfowl Trust, Cody, 1984-86. Mem. Zoo Mont. (bd. dirs. 1985—). Republican. Presbyterian. Avocations: snow skiing, gardening. Office: West Wind Designs 1501 Stampede Ave PO Box 2930 Cody WY 82414

PERATE, HANNAH MARY, educator; b. Phila., Oct. 3, 1946; d. Frank Leo and Hannah Mary (Arnold) P. B.A., Russell Coll., 1969; M.A., Calif. State Coll., 1981. Standard tchr. credential, reading specialist tchr. credential, Calif. Tchr. St. Athanasius Sch., Mountain View, Calif., 1968, Holy Name Sch., San Francisco, 1969-72, Our Lady of Angels Sch., Burlingame, Calif., 1972-75, St. Pius X Sch., Santa Fe Springs, Calif., 1975-78, Sacred Heart Sch., Redlands, Calif., 1978-79, Wrightwood (Calif.) Elem. Sch., 1979—, sec. Sch. Site Council, journalism moderator. Mem. Republican Presdl. Task Force; mem. Nat. Right to Life Com. Mem. Internat. Reading Assn., Assn. Supervision and Curriculum Devel., Calif. State Coll. Alumni Assn., Edn. Chpt. Calif. State Coll., Nat. Rifle Assn., Phi Kappa Phi. Roman Catholic. Contbr. short stories to Purpose, Venture; contbr. poems to various publs. Office: Wrightwood Elem Sch Box 368 Wrightwood CA 92397

PERCELAY, DAVID, broadcast executive; b. Providence, July 21, 1952; s. Alvan Merrill and Sheela (Mittelman) P.; m. Sylvia Salzberg, Sept. 2, 1974. AB, Brown U., 1974; MBA with honors, Harvard U., 1976. Asst. to pres., v.p. CBS News, N.Y.C., 1982-83, v.p. adminstrn., 1983-84; v.p. CBS News/Broadcast Group, N.Y.C., 1984-85; v.p., sta. mgr. Sta. KCBS-TV, Hollywood, Calif., 1985—. Clubs: Harvard, Harvard Bus. Sch.

PERCHOROWICZ, JOHN THOMAS, biochemist; b. Joliet, Ill., July 1, 1948; s. John and Josephine Irene (Ballun) P. AA, Coll. of the Desert, 1968; BA, U. Calif., Riverside, 1971, MA, 1973; PhD, Brandeis U., 1979. Adj. asst. prof. U. Ariz., Tucson, 1979-82; mng. prin. scientist Calgene, Inc., Davis, Calif., 1982-86, mng. scientist, 1986—. Contbr. articles to profl. jours. Grantee USPHS, 1970-71, 74-77. Mem. Am. Soc. Plant Physiology. Avocations: photography, swimming, softball. Office: Calgene, Inc. 1920 5th St Davis CA 95616

PERDUE, JAMES RICHARD (JIM), communications company administrator; b. Cheshire, Ohio, Dec. 8, 1945; s. Dennis C. and Olivene M. (Lambert) P.; m. Michelle Y. Ament, Oct. 4, 1969; children: Nicholas Alexander, Monique Marie. ASEE magna cum laude, Victor Valley Coll., 1976; BSBA suma cum laude, U. Redlands, 1986, postgrad. Cert. tchr., Calif. With dept. communications tech. Contel, Barstow, Calif., 1965-68; with dept. def. communications Contel, Delta, Utah, 1968-72; with dept. research and devel. Contel, Victorville, Calif., 1973-84, network support superintendent dept. info. resources, 1984—; cons. Contel, San Jose, Calif., 1974-76. Pres. Parent-Tchrs. Group, Apple Valley, Calif., 1984; provider Child Abuse task force, Victorville, 1984—. Served as sgt. U.S. Army, 1966-68, Vietnam. Recipient Outstanding Contbns. to Data Processing award Victor Valley Coll., Victorville, Calif., 1976. Mem. Am. Mgmt. Assn., UCLA Alumni Assn., U. Redlands Alumni Assn., VFW, Am. Legion. Avocations: swimming, camping, walking, software development. Home: 18361 Chapae Ln Apple Valley CA 92307-4553 Office: Contel 16461 Mojave Dr Victorville CA 92392-3699

PEREGRINE, PAUL KENT, photographer; b. Denver, May 16, 1951; s. William Phillip and Margaret Ann (Kountz) P. BFA, Colo. State U. Owner, pres. Peregrine Studios, Denver, 1973—, Lightware, Denver, 1983—; tchr. Colo. Inst. Art, 1978-80, Arapaho Community Coll., Littleton, Colo., 1976-77, Metro State Coll., Denver, 1975-76; cons. photography Chimera Copr., Boulder, Colo., 1981-85. Recipient ALFIE awards Denver Ad Fedn., 1980-87, Award of Excellence Mead Paper Co., 1981, 84. Mem. Am. Soc. Mag. Photographers (treas. 1980-82, pres. 1982-84, bd. dirs. 1983-84). Club: Art Dir.'s of Denver (awards of Excellence 1980-86). Avocations: skiing, fly-fishing, traveling, target and trap shooting, bicycling. Office: Peregrine Studios 1541 Platte St Denver CO 80202

PEREIRA, TERESINKA, language educator, writer; b. Belo Horizonte, Brazil, Nov. 1, 1934; came to U.S., 1960; d. Pindaro de Paula and Maria Albertina (Alves) P.; m. Heitor Martins, Nov. 1, 1958 (div. 1976); children: Luzia Martins, Emilia Martins; m. Pedro Segundo Melendez, Mar. 2, 1978; 1 child, Pedrinho. B Faculdade Filosofia, U. Minas Gerais, Brazil, 1956; MA, U. N.Mex., 1962, PhD in Spanish, 1972; diploma, Accademy Universale, Rome, 1982, Ateneu Angrense Letras, Rio de Janeiro, 1972. Instr. Portuguese Tulane U., New Orleans, 1962-68; vis. prof. Georgetown U., Washington, 1973-74; asst. prof. U. Colo., Boulder, 1975-80, assoc. prof., 1980—; lectr. Portuguese Stanford (Calif.) U., 1968. Author: Torre de Mitos, 1973, Peligro los Angeles Se Caen, 1973; editor mag.: Poema Convidado, 1970-74; translator numerous books. Recipient Nat. Prize, Servico Nacional de Teatro, 1972, The Am. Poet award Exposicion Monumental Poesia, 1979; named Personality of Yr., Jornal A. Mensagem, 1979, Poet of Yr., Can. Soc. Poets, 1977. Fellow Internat. Poet Soc. (pres. 1975—, yrbook. editor 1985—); mem. Academia Universale (Rome), Academia Brasileira de Literatura, Associaçao Mexicana de Escritores. Clubs: Internat. de Vol Libre, dos Trovadores Brasileiros. Office: U Colo Dept Spanish Portuguese Box 278 Boulder CO 80309

PERELSON, ALAN STUART, theoretical biologist; b. Bklyn., Apr. 11, 1947; s. Morris L. and Ruth D. (Ferst) P.; m. Janet Arlene Gerard, June 23, 1968; children: Elissa Danielle, Andrew Jacob. BS, MIT, 1967; BSEE, U. Calif., Berkeley, 1967, PhD, 1972. Acting asst. prof. med. physics U. Calif., Berkeley, 1973; NIH postgrad. research assoc. in chem. engring. U. Minn., Mpls., 1973-74; asst. prof. med. scis. Brown U., Providence, 1978-80; mem. staff theoretical div. Los Alamos (N.Mex.) Nat. Lab. and U. Calif., 1974—. Editor: Theoretical Immunology, 1978, Cell Surface Dynamics, 1984; adv. editor Jour. of Theoretical Biology, Jour. Math. Biology, lecture Notes in Biomathematics; assoc. editor Jour. Math. Applied in Medicine and Biology; mem. editorial bd. Springer-Verley Textbooks in Biomath.; book rev. editor Math. Bioscis.; contbr. numerous articles to profl. jours. Recipient Research Career Devel. award NIH, 1979-84. Mem. IEEE, Soc. Math. Biology (bd. dirs. 1982-86), Am. Assn. Immunology, Soc. Indsl. and Applied Math. Democrat. Home: 820 Los Arboles Ln Sante Fe NM 87501 Office: Los Alamos Nat Lab Group T-10 Mail Stop K710 Los Alamos NM 87545

PEREZ, ARAM, design engineer; b. Gary, Ind., Dec. 2, 1954; s. Rafael and Nereida (Hernandez) P.; m. Cynthia Ann Phillips, June 18, 1978; children: Eric, Marcus, Chantel. Student, Antillian Coll., Mayaguez, P.R., 1972-73; BS in Engring., Walla Walla Coll., 1978; student, Calif. State U., Sacramento, 1982-85. Cert. engr. in tng. Software engr. Teletek Enterprises Inc., Sacramento, 1978-82, Wismer & Becker, Sacramento, 1982; sr. systems design engr. Jones Futurex Inc., Rancho Cordova, Calif., 1983—. Mem. IEEE. Seventh-day Adventist. Avocations: music, art, guitar, radio-controlled cars, family. Office: Jones Futurex Inc 3079 Kilgore Rd Rancho Cordova CA 95670

PEREZ, BEATRICE, agency administrator; b. Salinas, Calif., Oct. 18, 1938; d. Ralph Mora and Conchita (Arroyo) Rueda; m. Raymond B. Perez, Apr. 19, 1958; children: Jeanine, Kelly, Kathy, Michael, Timothy. Student, Hartnell Jr. Coll., 1956-57. Cert. occupancy specialist Nat. Ctr. Housing Mgmt. Med. sec. Jose Perez MD, Salinas, 1956-57, F.A. Gonzales MD, Salinas, 1957-59; cashier, loan officer Pacific Fin. Corp., Salinas, 1963-67, Assocs. Fin., Salinas, 1968-69; ops. mgr. Investors Thrift, Salinas, 1970-74; eligibility supr. Housing Authority, Salinas, 1974—; cons. Developers/Tax-exempt Bond Project, Monterey County, Calif., 1982—; instr. cert. apartment mgmt. Nat. Apartment Assn., Dept. Real Estate, Sacramento, Calif., 1985; mediator City of Salinas Rent Mediation Bd., 1982—; panel mem. New Horizons Housing Task Force, Monterey, 1983—. Bd. dirs. Alcoholism Adv. Bd., Monterey County, 1982-85, Housing Task Force, Seaside, Calif., 1985, Consumer Adv. Panel Pacific Gas & Electric Co., Salinas, 1985—, Mil. Housing Liason, Ft. Ord, Calif., 1983—. Named Woman of Yr., K.C., 1978, Mediator of Yr., City of Salinas, 1982; recipient Silver Achievement award 4-H Council, Salinas, 1982. Democrat. Roman Catholic. Avocations: crocheting, knitting. Office: Housing Authority 134 E Rossi St Salinas CA 93901

PEREZ, FIDEL JUSTO ADELICIO, journeyman machinist; b. Albuquerque, Oct. 27, 1944; s. Frank Martinez Perez and Flora Gutierrez; m. Shirleen Evelyn Baca, Dec. 5, 1964; children—Christine Eileen, Fidel Steven. Student U. N.M., 1962-63, 74-76. Apprentice machinist Sandia Labs., Albuquerque, 1968-72, journeyman machinist, 1972—. Loan exec. campaign drive United Way, Albuquerque, 1984—; Democratic candidate for state rep., Albuquerque, 1980. Recipient 3000 Vol. Hours award Com. Pol. Edn., 1983; Dem. ward chmn., 1983—. Mem. Metal Trades Council (sec.-treas. 1979—), Internat. Assn. Machinists and Aerospace Workers (pres. N.Mex. council 1984—, chmn. non-partisan pol. league 1981—), Bernalillo County Central Labor Council (v.p. 1982—), Union Label Dept. (pres. 1982—). Democrat. Roman Catholic. Home: 9820 Guadalupe Trail NW Albuquerque NM 87114 Office: Metal Trades Council 1030 San Pedro NE Albuquerque NM 87110

PERI, PATRICIA JEAN, public relations consultant; b. Denver, May 2, 1954; d. James Eugene and Dorothy Virginia (Rylander) P. B.A. in Journalism and Pub. Relations, U. No. Colo., 1976. Pub. relations intern Del Calzo & Assocs., Inc., Denver, 1976, client services coordinator, 1977, jr. account exec., 1977-78, account exec., 1978-80, exec. asst., asst. to pres., 1980-81, asst. v.p., 1981-82; pub. relations cons., Denver, 1982; media and communications dir. Copper Mountain Resort, Colo., 1982-83; pres. Perfect Promotions Plus, Denver, 1983-85; mgr. retail mktg. Am. Express Travel Related Services, Inc., Denver, 1985-86; dir. pub. relations, Henry-Gill, Inc., Denver, 1987—; pub. affairs mgr. Tabor Ctr., Denver, 1984-85. Mem. Pub. Relations Soc. Am. (Silver Anvil 1980, Gold Pick award Colo. chpt. 1980, 1985, Grand Pick award, 1985), Denver Advt. Fedn., U. No. Colo. Alumni Assn. (bd. dirs.), Rocky Mountain Ski Writers Assn., Sigma Delta Chi. Roman Catholic. Home: 1818 S Quebec Way #5-8 Denver CO 80231

PERITO, JOSEPH GERALD, JR., educator, counselor, consultant; b. Denver, Feb. 9, 1927; s. Joseph and Rose (Comillo) P.; B.A. in Music Edn., Denver U., 1950, M.A., 1955; Ed.D., U. No. Colo., 1967. Tchr. music Jefferson County (Colo.) Pub. Schs., Lakewood, 1950-57, supr. music, 1957-64, research specialist, 1964-65; prin. Carmody Jr. High Sch., Lakewood, 1965-78, adminstrv. asst. in central adminstrn., 1978-81; ednl. cons. in adminstrn., 1983—. Mem. Am. Ednl. Research Assn., Am. Acad. Polit. and Social Scis., Nat., Colo. assns. secondary sch. prins., Music Edn. Nat. Conf., Am. Choral Dirs. Assn., Am. String Tchrs. Assn., NEA, Colo. Edn. Assn., Kappa Delta Pi, Phi Delta Kappa. Home: 430 N Garrison St Denver CO 80226 Office: 430 N Garrison St Lakewood CO 80226

PERKIN, RONALD MURRAY, pediatritian; b. Denver, July 31, 1948; s. Robert Murray and Marion Kathryn (Thompson) P.; m. Cynthia Louise Waters, Oct. 4, 1980; 1 child, Matthew Murray. BS in Engring., U. Colo., 1970; postgrad., Johns Hopkins U., 1970-71; MD, U. South Fla., 1976. Diplomate Am. Bd. Pediatrics. Resident in pediatrics Children's Med. Ctr., Dallas, 1976-79, fellow in pediatric intensive care, 1979-81, asst. dir. pediatric intensive care, 1981; clins. asst. prof. pediatrics U. Tex. Health Sci. Ctr. Southwestern Med. Sch., Dallas, 1981; asst. adj. prof. pediatrics U. Calif. Sch. Medicine, San Diego, 1982-84, co-dir. pediatric intensive care, 1982-84; dir. pediatric ICU attending physician Childrens Hosp. Orange (Calif.) County Hosp., 1984—; attending physician newborn ICU St. Joseph's Hosp., Orange, 1984—; cons. Naval Hosp., San Diego, 1983-84; asst. adj. prof. pediatrics U. Calif., Irvine, 1984—; dir. pediatric intensive care fellowship program U. Calif. Irvine and Children's Hosp. Orange County, 1984—; mem. critical care adv. com., critical care council, Extra Corporeal Membrane Oxygenation found. So. Calif., emergency dept. com., ethics com., infection control com., pharmacy and therapeutics com., resident evaluation sub-com., respiratory care com., risk mgmt. adv. com; lectr. in field. Editor: (with others) Brain Insults in Infants and Children: Pathophysiology and Management; Emergency Management of the Critically Ill Child; reviewer Capistrano Press, Ltd., 1982-84, Jour. Pediatrics, 1982—; contbr. numerous articles and to profl. jours. Served with USN, 1971-73. Recipient student awards U. South Fla. Coll. Medicine, faculty awards U. Calif., Irvine, Lange Ann. award Lange Book Co., 1974; Mosby scholar Mosby Book Co., 1975-76. Fellow Am. Acad. Pediatrics; mem. Soc. Critical Care Medicine, So. Claif. Pediatric Intensive Care Network (treas. 1986), Calif. Children Services (adv. com. rev. pediatric ICU's 1986—). Office: Children's Hosp Orange County 455 S Main St Orange CA 92668

PERKINS, DAVID GARRISON, social worker; b. Oakland, Calif., May 11, 1923; s. Hugh McVieh and E. Louise (MacPherson) P.; m. Mary Amelia Harberd, Aug. 10, 1950; children: James David, Susan Louise Kane. MSW, U. Wash., 1967. Casework, supr. Wash. State Dept. Social Health Services, Wenatchee, 1964-75; vol. coordinator Wash. State Dept. Social Health Services, Olympia, 1975-77; regional licensing specialist Wash. State Dept. Social Health Services, Spokane, 1977. Pres. Wash. Assn. Social Welfare, 1965-66. Mem. Nat. Assn. Social Workers, Am. Soc. Pub. Adminstrn., Am. Pub. Welfare Assn. Home: 1428 Terrace Ct East Wenatchee WA 98801 Office: Wash State Dept Health Services Div Family Child Services N 1425 Washington Spokane WA 99201

PERKINS, DOROTHY A., association executive; b. Weiser, Idaho, Aug. 13, 1926; d. Ross William and Josephine Stanford (Gwilliam) Anderson; m. Leonard Taylor Perkins, Nov. 16, 1948; children: Larry Taylor, Michael A., Drew A., Nancy. Grad. high sch., Boise, Idaho. Sec. Meadow Gold Dairies, Boise, 1944-46; sec. to supt. Idaho State Police, Boise, 1946-48, Idaho State Dept. Edn., Boise, 1952-56; sec. to maintenance engr. Idaho State Dept. Hwys., Boise, 1956-58; adminstrv. sec., asst. mgr. Casper (Wyo.) C. of C., 1962-72, exec. v.p., 1972—. Mem. Wyo. Ho. Reps., 1982—; pianist, organist, choir dir. Casper Ch. Jesus Christ Latter Day Sts. Mem. Wyo. C. of C. Execs. (sec.-treas. 1978—, past pres.), Mountain States Assn. (bd. dirs. 1979—, past pres.), Wyo. Heritage Soc. (steering com. 1984—), Wyo. Hwy. Users Found. (bd. dirs. 1978—). Republican. Avocations: reading, walking, sewing, music. Home: 1014 Surrey Ct Casper WY 82609 Office: Casper Area Chamber of Commerce PO Box 399 500 North Ctr Casper WY 82602 Other Address: 1581 Nottingham Dr Casper WY 82609

PERKINS, FLOYD JERRY, theology educator; b. Bertha, Minn., May 9, 1924; s. Ray Lester and Nancy Emily (Kelley) P.; m. Mary Elizabeth Owen, Sept. 21, 1947 (dec. June 1982); children: Douglas Jerry, David Floyd, Sheryl Pauline; m. Phyllis Geneva Hartley, July 14, 1984. AB, BTh, N.W. Nazarene Coll., 1949; MA, U. Mo., 1952; MDiv, Nazarene Theol. Sem., 1952; PhD, U. Witwatersrand, Johannesburg, South Africa, 1974. Ordained to Christian ministry, 1951. Pres. South African Nazarene Theol. Sem., Florida Transvaal, Africa, 1955-67; pres. Nazarene Bible Sem., Lourenzo Marques, Mozambique, 1967-73, Campinas, Brazil, 1974-76; prof. missions N.W. Nazarene Coll., Nampa, Idaho, 1976; prof. theology Nazarene Bible Coll., Colorado Springs, Colo., 1976—; chmn., founder com. higher theol. edn. Ch. of Nazarene in Africa, 1967-74; sec. All African Nazarene Mission Exec., 1967-74; ofcl. Christian Council Mozambique, 1952-74. Author: A History of the Christian Church in Swaziland, 1974. Served with USN, 1944-46. Mem. Am. Schs. Oriental Research, Am. Soc. Missiology, Assn. Evan. Missions Profs. Republican. Avocation: golf. Home: 1529 Lyle Dr Colorado Springs CO 80915 Office: Nazarene Bible Coll 122 Chapman Dr Colorado Springs CO 80935

PERKINS, HENRY CRAWFORD, engineer, educator; b. Miami, Fla., Nov. 23, 1935; s. Henry Crawford and Dorothy Du Bois (Israel) P.; m. Barbara Joan Parvin; children: Jennifer Anne, William Bruce, Susan Elizabeth, David Parvin. B.S., Stanford U., 1957, M.S., 1960, Ph.D., 1963. Research assoc. Stanford U., 1962-63, acting asst. prof., 1963-64; asso. prof. aerospace and mech. engring. U. Ariz., 1964-67, prof., 1967—; vis. prof. Danish Tech. U., 1971-72, U.S. Mil. Acad., 1978-79, Stanford U., 1981-82. Author: (with W.C. Reynolds) Engineering Thermodynamics, 1970, 2d edit., 1977, (with W.M. Kays); chpt. in Handbook of Heat Transfer, 1973, 2d edit., 1984; Air Pollution, 1974. Recipient Teetor award Soc. Automotive Engrs., 1975, Creative Teaching award U. Ariz., 1982; AEC fellow, 1960-61. Fellow ASME; mem. Phi Beta Kappa, Tau Beta Pi. Home: 6758 E Rosewood Circle Tucson AZ 85710

PERKINS, JAN MARCIA, software engineer; b. Bklyn., July 8, 1956; d. Arthur and Sheila (Traub) Marmor; m. Emerson Joseph Perkins, Jan. 5, 1985. AS in Physics, Suffolk County Community Coll., 1978; BS in Computer Sci., SUNY, Stony Brook, 1980; student, Ithaca Coll., 1974-76. Asst. mgr. Susie's Casuals, Lake Grove, N.Y., 1978-79; software engr. McDonnell Douglas Astronautics Co., Huntington Beach, Calif., 1980-83; software engr. Rockwell Internat., Anaheim, Calif., 1983—, responsible engr., 1983—. Mem. Mensa, Pi Alpha Sigma. Avocations: skiing, scuba diving, travelling, music, electronics. Home: 1758 Concerto Dr Anaheim Hills CA 92807 Office: Rockwell Internat 3370 Mira Loma D/268 Bldg 85 MS OB38 Anaheim CA 92803

PERKINS, KENNETH LEE, physicist; b. St. Charles, Mo., Sept. 7, 1924; s. John William and Hallie Harrison (Cope) P.; B.E.E. magna cum laude, St. Louis U., 1950, M.S. in Physics, 1952, Ph.D. in Physics (teaching fellow), 1956; m. Margaret Ann Kendall, Feb. 14, 1948; children—Kenneth, Michael, Mark, Thomas. Instr. elec. engring. St. Louis U., 1956; with Rockwell Internat. Co., and predecessors, Anaheim, Calif., 1956—, specialist electromech. engring., 1966-68, mem. tech. staff, 1968—. Active Cub Scout group Boy Scouts Am., 1965-76; asso. mem. Orange County Democratic Com., Calif. Dem. Com., 1975-76; Dem. candidate Ho. of Reps., 1974. Served with USAAF, 1943-46; PTO. Decorated Air medal with 2 Bronze Stars. Mem. Sigma Xi, Pi Mu Epsilon, Eta Kappa Nu. Contbr. articles to profl. jours. Patentee in field. Home: 5162 Wendover Rd Yorba Linda CA 92686 Office: 3370 Miraloma Ave Anaheim CA 92803

PERKINS, LEONARD (LEN) WESLEY, small business owner; b. St. Joseph, Mo., June 16, 1937; s. John Leonard Perkins and Ruby Pearl (Cole) Wells; divorced; children: Kimra, Jeff, Mark. Student, Ripon Coll., 1955-57; BA in History, U Mo., 1959. Mgmt. trainee Home Ins. Co., N.Y.C., 1960; v.p. Encinal Terminals subs. Warehousing div. DelMonte Corp., San Francisco, 1961-73; sr. product mgr. Ore-Ida Foods, div. H.J. Heinz, Boise, Idaho, 1974-75; regional dir., owner SOS Emergency Response Techs., Boise, 1976—. Served to tech. sgt. USAFR, 1969—. Mem. Am. Mktg. Assn. (Boise chpt. pres. 1975). Republican. Presbyterian. Club: Mountain West (Boise). Avocations: backpacking, hiking, fishing, cross-country skiing. Home: 1605 N 21st Boise ID 83702 Office: SOS Emergency Response Techs PO Box 9272 Boise ID 83707

PERKINS, PATRICIA MAUREEN, author, public speaker, business consultant; b. Oakland, Calif., Apr. 21, 1932; d. Melvin Francis and Florence Edith Fitzgerald; div.; children—Donald, Thomas, Teresa. B.S., La Jolla U., 1980. Dir. sales and on-site logistics, coordinator Cole Assocs., La Jolla, Calif., 1978-81; co-dir. New Wave Cons., La Jolla, 1981—; public speaker on success, promotion and motivation, 1980—; commodities broker Internat. Trading Group, 1985—; author: Making The Break, 1982; How To Forgive Your Ex-Husband, 1982; Change Your Life in 7 Days, 1984; facilitator U. West Fla. and U. Ariz., 1980-81. Bd. dirs. San Diego chpt. Nat. Council Alcohol Problems, also mem. Pres.'s Council. Mem. G.R.O.W., Career Women's Network, Women in Mgmt., Winners Circle Breakfast Clubs (nat. dir. 1979-80), So. Calif. Publicists. Club: Soroptomists.

PERKINS, PHILLIP ORVILLE, architect; b. Twin Falls, Idaho, Feb. 21, 1950; s. Charles Alva and Margaret J. (Chevalier) P. B in Interior Architecture, U. Oreg., 1986. Real estate broker Chuck Perkins Realty, Twin Falls, 1976-80; archtl. designer Bates & Sun Architects, Ketchum, Idaho, 1983, Genser & Assocs. Architects, San Francisco, 1984—. Recipient 1st place award Inst. Bus. Designers, 1984. Avocations: psychology, skiing, tennis, windsurfing, golfing. Home: 3780 20th St San Franicsco CA 94110

PERKINS, STERRETT THEODORE, physicist; b. Oakland, Calif., July 25, 1932; s. Frank Bernard and Mary Elizabeth (Scott) P.; children: Charles, Pamela, Jill, Terri, Lisa, Sheila. BS, U. Calif., Berkeley, 1956, MS, 1957, PhD, 1965. Registered nuclear and mech. engr., Calif. Sr. nuclear engr. Aerojet-Gen., San Ramon, Calif., 1957-59, prin. nuclear engr., 1960-65; physicist Lawrence Livermore Nat. Lab., Livermore, Calif., 1959-60, sr. physicist, 1965—; cons. Aerojet-Gen., San Ramon, 1959-60. Contbr. articles to profl. jours. Bd. dirs. Livermore Heritage Guild, 1955-59. Mem. Am. Phys. Soc., Am. Nuclear Soc., Sigma Xi. Office: Lawrence Livermore Nat Lab PO Box 808 L-298 Livermore CA 94550

PERKINS, THOMAS JAMES, venture capital company executive; b. Oak Park, Ill., Jan. 7, 1932; s. Harry H. and Elizabeth P.; m. Gerd Thune-Ellefsen, Dec. 9, 1961; children: Tor Kristian, Elizabeth Siri. B.S.E.E., M.I.T., 1953; M.B.A., Harvard U., 1957. Gen. mgr. computer div. Hewlett Packard Co., Cupertino, Calif., 1965-70, dir. corp. devel., 1970-72; gen. partner Kleiner & Perkins, San Francisco, 1972-80; sr. partner Kleiner Perkins Caufield & Byers, San Francisco, from 1980; chmn. bd. Tandem Computers, Genentech; dir. Spectra Physics., Corning Glass Works, Collagen Corp., LSI Logic Corp., Hybritech Inc., Econics Corp., Vitalink Communications Corp. Author: Classic Supercharged Sports Cars, 1984. Trustee San Francisco Ballet, 1980—. Mem. Nat. Venture Capital Assn. (chmn. 1981-82, pres. 1980-81). Clubs: N.Y. Yacht, Links, Am. Bugatti (pres. 1983—). Office: Tandem Computers Inc 19333 Vallco Pkwy Cupertino CA 95914 Office: Genentech Inc 460 Point San Bruno San Francisco CA 94080

PERKINS, WILLIS DRUMMOND, chemical physicist; b. Porterville, Calif., Dec. 20, 1926; s. Willis D. and Amelia Marie (Hanson) P.; m. Georgia Joy Harrington, Aug. 22, 1954. BS, MIT, 1948; MA, Harvard U., 1950, PhD, 1952. Research technologist Shell Oil Co., Martinez, Calif., 1952-60; product specialist Perkin-Elmer Corp., Norwalk, Conn., 1960-69, asst. product mgr., 1969-82; scientist Perkin-Elmer Corp., Mountain View, Calif., 1982—; lectr. ARiz. State U., 1975—. Contbr. articles to profl. jours. Served to col. USAR, 1944—. Mem. Am. Chem. Soc., Am. Phys. soc., Optical Soc. Am., Soc. Applied Spectroscopy. Republican. Roman Catholic. Avocation: advanced amateur photogrpahy. Home: 4081 Petulla Ct San Jose CA 95124 Office: The Perkin-Elmer Corp 411 Clyde Ave Mountain View CA 94043

PERKINSON, GREGORY MARTIN, military officer; b. Hunnington, N.Y., Dec. 23, 1960; s. Edward Myron Perkinson and Vivian Jean (Smith) Faircloth. BS in Architecture magnu cum laude, Kent State U., 1983, BArch magna cum laude, 1984. Mem. archtl. design staff Carter Lumber Co., Tallmadge, Ohio, 1984, W.P Ross & Assocs. Architects, Cuyahoga Falls, Ohio, 1984; commd. 2d lt. USAF, 1984, advanced through grades to 1st lt., 1986. Designer Ohio Edison Energy Competition (1st Place 1983). Tutor Dire Kelly Sch., Sacramento, 1985-86. Superior scholar Kent State U., 1983-84, George and Edith Abott Bryant scholar Kent State U., 1983. Mem. AIA (assoc.), Soc. Am. Mil. Engrs., Air Force Assn., Co. Grade Officers Council (publicity chmn. 1984—), Tau Sigma Delta. Episcopalian. Clubs: Raquetball (pres. 1981-82), Outdoors. Avocations: backpacking, fishing, skiing, photography, softball. Home: 3658 #37 Kings Way Sacramento CA 95821 Office: 2852 CES McClellan AFB Sacramento CA 95652

PERKS, BARBARA ANN MARCUS, psychologist; b. Wilson, Pa., July 1, 1937; d. Alfred M. and Lillian (Reibman) Marcus; B.S., Pa. State U., 1959; M.A., Columbia U., 1963; cert. in ednl. psychology Oxford (Eng.) U., 1965; postgrad. U. Oreg., U.S. Internat. U.; Ed.D., U. B.C., 1984; m. Anthony Manning Perks, Sept. 9, 1963. Tchr. gifted Hamden (Conn.) Sch. Dist., 1959-62; reading cons. Oxfordshire County, Littlemore, Eng., 1964-65; sch. psychologist Vancouver (B.C., Can.) Sch. Bd., 1972-76; supr. student tchrs. U. B.C., Vancouver, 1977-78, cons. Research Center, 1978-79, ednl. psychologist, child and family unit child psychiatry Health Scis. Centre Hosp., 1979-81, lectr., 1977—; instr. psychology Langara Coll., 1985; pvt. practice counseling and teaching, Vancouver, 1984-87, counseling and sch. psychology, Burnaby, B.C., 1985—. Recipient Can. Daus. League award; Provincial Council of B.C. award, 1981, U. B.C. awards, 1980; Jonathan Rogers award, 1984; Univ. fellow, Dr. MacKenzie Am. Alumni scholar U. B.C., 1976; U. B.C. summer scholar, 1982; cert. psychologist, B.C. Mem. Am. Psychol. Assn., B.C. Psychol. Assn., Assn. Humanistic Psychology, Nat. Assn. Sch. Psychology, Am. Ednl. Research, N.Am. Soc. Adlerian Psychology, Am. Orthopsychiat. Assn., Mortar Bd., Pi Sigma Alpha, Pi Lambda Theta, Kappa Delta Pi. Clubs: Figure Skating (Vancouver, B.C., New Haven, Conn., Allentown, Pa.). Author research papers. Home: 4570 Glenwood Ave, North Vancouver, BC Canada V7R 4G5

PERL, MARTIN LEWIS, physicist, educator; b. N.Y.C., June 24, 1927; s. Oscar and Fay (Rosenthal) P.; m. Teri Hoch, June 19, 1948; children: Jed, Anne, Matthew, Joseph. B.Chem. Engring., Poly. Inst. Bklyn., 1948; Ph.D., Columbia U., 1955. Chem. engr. Gen. Electric Co., 1948-50; asst. prof. physics U. Mich., 1955-58, asso. prof., 1958-63; prof. Stanford, 1963—. Author: High Energy Hadron Physics, 1975; contbr. articles on high energy physics and on relation of sci. to soc. to profl. jours. Served with U.S. Mcht. Marine, 1944-45; Served with AUS, 1945-46. Recipient Wolf prize in physics, 1982. Fellow Am. Phys. Soc.; mem. Nat. Acad. Scis., AAAS. Home: 3737 El Centro Ave Palo Alto CA 94306 Office: Stanford Linear Accelerator Center Stanford U Stanford CA 94305

PERLMAN, GERALD M., technical systems specialist; b. N.Y.C., May 25, 1937; s. Nathan and Anna (Fessel) P.; m. Janet Horowitz, Jan. 21, 1962; children—Eric S., Joshua N. B.A. in Biology City U. N.Y., 1961; postgrad. NYU, 1966-68. Pharm. testing Revlon, Bronx, N.Y., 1964-67; programmer Airborne Instruments, Melville, N.Y., 1967-68; programmer, analyst SSI, N.Y, 1969; systems programmer Am. Express, N.Y.C., 1969-72, Phoenix, 1972-74; tech. systems analysis, programmer City of Phoenix, 1974—; mem. Phoenix City Mgr.'s Microcomputer Task Force, 1981; cons. Phoenix, 1981—; instr. Maricopa Community Coll., Phoenix, 1980-83; instr. Rio Salado Community Coll., Phoenix, 1983-87; instr. Golden Gate U., Phoenix, 1987—. Pres. City of Hope Phoenix chpt. 1976-78; v.p. Grandview Jr. High Sch. PTO, Phoenix, 1979-80. Served with USAR, 1960-66. Mem. Assn. Systems Mgrs., Profl. and Tech. Employees Assn. City of Phoenix. Office: City of Phoenix Police Computer Services Bureau 620 W Washington Phoenix AZ 85003

PERLMAN, ROBERT HOWARD, electronics company executive, accountant, lawyer; b. N.Y.C., Apr. 6, 1944; s. George Joseph and Libby (Cooper) P.; m. Lynn Roberta Karlin, Dec. 1, 1968; 1 child, Barry Ross. BA, Alfred U., 1964; MBA, Cornell U., 1967, JD, 1968; LLM, NYU, 1976. CPA, N.Y. Sr. tax staff mem. Touche Ross & Co., N.Y.C., 1968-69, 71-73; tax mgr. Norton Simon Inc., N.Y.C., 1973-76, Memorex Corp., Santa Clara, Calif., 1976-78; dir. tax and customs, asst. treas. Intel Corp., Santa Clara, 1978—. Served to capt. U.S. Army, 1969-70. Mem. Tax Execs. Inst. (v.p., com. chmn.), Am. Electronics Assn. (tax com.), Machinery and Allied Products Inst. (tax council II), U.S. C. of C. (tax com.), Semiconductor Industry Assn. (tax com.), ABA, Am. Inst. CPA's, N.Y. Bar Assn., N.Y. Soc. CPA's, Blue Key Honor Soc., Pi Gamma Mu. Jewish. Home: 7055 Anjou Creek Circle San Jose CA 95120 Office: Intel Corp 3065 Bowers Ave Santa Clara CA 95051

PERLMUTTER, LEONARD MICHAEL, concrete construction company executive; b. Denver, Oct. 16, 1925; s. Philip Permutter and Belle (Perlmutter); m. Alice Love Bristow, Nov. 17, 1951; children: Edwin George, Joseph Kent, Cassandra Love. B.A., U. Colo., 1948, postgrad., 1948-50. Ptnr. Perlmutter & Sons, Denver, 1947-58; v.p. Prestressed Concrete of Colo., Denver, 1952-60; pres. Stanley Structures, Inc., Denver, 1960-83; chmn. bd. Stanley Structures, Inc., 1983—; dir. Colo. Nat. Bankshares, Inc.; chief exec. officer Econ. Devel. Gov.'s Office State of Colo., 1987—. Chmn. bd. U. Colo. Found., Boulder, 1979-81; dir. Santa Fe Opera Assn., N.Mex., 1976-85; v.p. Santa Fe Fedn., 1979—; chmn. bd. Nat. Jewish Hosp.-Nat. Asthma Ctr., Denver, 1983-86; pres. Denver Symphony Assn., 1983-84, chmn. bd., 1985—. Recipient Humanitarian Am. Jewish Com., 1981. Mem. Am. Concrete Inst., Prestressed Concrete Inst. (pres. 1977, dir. 1973-74). Club: Rolling Hills Country (Golden) (pres. 1966-68). Home: 15125 Foothill Rd Golden CO 80401 Office: Stanley Structures Inc 7000 N Broadway Bldg 3 Denver CO 80221

PERLOFF, JEAN MARCOSSON, lawyer; b. Lakewood, Ohio, June 25, 1942; d. John Solomon and Marcella Catherine (Borngen) Marcosson; m. William Harry Perloff, Dec. 26, 1968. B.A. magna cum laude, Lake Erie Coll., 1965; M.A. in Italian, UCLA, 1967; J.D. magna cum laude, Ventura Coll. Law, 1976. Bar: Calif. 1976. Assoc. in Italian U. Calif.-Santa Barbara, 1967-70; law clk., paralegal Ventura County Pub. Defender's Office, Ventura, Calif., 1975; sole practice, Ventura, 1976-78; co-prin. Clabaugh & Perloff, A Profl. Corp., Ventura, 1979-82; sr. jud. atty. to presiding justice 6th div. 2d Dist. Ct. Appeals, Los Angeles, 1982—; instr. Ventura Coll. Law, 1976-79. Bd. dirs. Santa Barbara Zool. Gardens. Mem. ABA, Calif. State Bar, Ventura County Bar Assn., Calif. Women Lawyers, Women Lawyers Ventura County, Ventura County Criminal Def. Bar Assn. (pres. 1979), Mar Vista Bus. and Profl. Women, Kappa Alpha Sigma. Democrat. Home: 1384 Plaza Pacifica Santa Barbara CA 93108 Office: 2d Dist Ct of Appeals 1280 S Victoria Ventura CA 93003

PERLSTEIN, GARY ROBERT, criminology educator; b. N.Y.C., Feb. 7, 1940; s. Maurice and Eva (Abramowitz) P.; m. Judith Ann Wilkinson, June 15, 1968 (div. Dec. 1980); m. Carol Jane Flato, Feb. 22, 1981. BA, Cen. Coll., 1961; MA, U. Mo., 1965; PhD, Fla. State U., 1971. Child welfare worker State Mo. Div. Welfare, Kansas City, 1961-63; instr. S.W. Mo. State Coll., Springfield, 1965-68; corrections planner Inter-Agy. Law Enforcement Planning Council, Tallahassee, 1969-71; asst. prof. justice adminstrn. Portland (Oreg.) State U., 1971-73, assoc. prof., 1973-79, prof., 1979—; cons. numerous criminal def. attys., Portland, 1980—. Editor: Alternatives to Prison, 1975; contbr. articles to profl. jours. Bd. dirs. Indigent Def. Bd. State Oreg., Salem, 1986. Mem. Acad. Criminal Justice Scis., Am. Soc. Criminology, Am. Corrections Assn., Western Soc. Criminology. Avocation: hiking. Home: 5555 SW Childs Rd Lake Oswego OR 97035 Office: Portland State U Dept Justice Adminstrn PO Box 751 Portland OR 97207

PERRELLA, ANTHONY JOSEPH, electronics engineer; b. Boulder, Colo., Sept. 16, 1942; s. Anthony Vincent and Mary Domenica (Forte) P.; B.S., U. Wyo., 1964, postgrad., 1965; postgrad. U. Calif. at San Diego, 1966-67, U. Calif. at Irvine, 1968-70; m. Pamela Smith, July 19, 1980. Flight engr. U.S. Naval Tng. Devices Center, San Diego, 1965-67; research engr. Collins div. Rockwell Internat. (formerly Collins Radio Co.), Newport Beach, Calif., 1967-69, electromagnetic interference and TEMPEST group head, 1969-74, supr., 1974-75, mgr., 1975-77, mgr. systems integration, 1977, mgr. space communication systems, 1977-78; sr. mem. tech. staff ARGOSystems Inc., Sunnyvale, Calif., 1978—, program mgr., 1978-81, dep. dept. mgr. EW Systems, 1980-83, div. EW staff engr., 1983-84, dept. mgr., 1984—; v.p. research and devel. Things Unlimited, Inc., Laramie, Wyo., 1965-72, pres., 1972-75. Mem. Am. Mgmt. Assn., IEEE, AAAS, N.Y. Acad. Scis., Assn. Old Crows, Tau Kappa Epsilon. Roman Catholic. Home: 931 Brookgrove Ln Cupertino CA 95014 Office: 884 Hermosa Ct Sunnyvale CA 94086

PERRENOD, DOUGLAS ARTHUR, aerospace engineer; b. Weehawken, N.J., Sept. 13, 1947; s. George Edward and Eunice Lillian (Cohn) P. Student, Fla. Inst. Tech., 1968-72; B.A. in Astronomy, U. South Fla., 1973; postgrad. Calif. State U., 1982—; grad. engring. mgmt. program Calif. Inst. Tech., 1987. Cert. glider flight instr. FAA. Engr. trainee NASA Kennedy Space Ctr., Fla., 1969-73; quality control engr. Pelletech Corp., Fontana, Calif., 1976-77; electronics specialist Gen. Telephone Co., San Bernardino, Calif., 1977-79; aerospace and project engr. Rockwell Internat., Downey, Calif., 1979-85, Lockheed Corp., Ontario, Calif., 1986—; aviation cons., owner-founder Flight Unltd., Long Beach, Calif.; mission pilot, project engr. Flight Level 500 High Altitude Soaring Project. Vol. mem. Orange County Human Services Agy., 1981—; active Big Bros. of Am., 1978. Served to maj. USAF, 1973-75. Recipient Amelia Earhart award CAP, 1968, Manned Flight Apollo 11 medallion NASA, 1971, 1st Shuttle Flight award NASA, 1981, Aerospace Maintenance Officer of Yr. award USAFR, 1979; named to Engr. Honor Roll, Rockwell Internat., 1982. Mem. AIAA, Res. Officers Assn., Air Force Assn., Soaring Soc. Am., Toastmasters Internat., Speakers Bur. (Rockwell Internat.), Assoc. Glider Club of So. Calif., Long Beach Navy Aero. Club. Designer telescope mount for 1st astronomy obs. Fla. Inst. Tech., 1969; mission pilot and project engr. for FL500 high altitude soaring project. Home: PO Box 3522 Ontario CA 91761-0953

PERRIN, CHARLES LEE, chemist; b. Pitts., July 22, 1938; s. Samuel Robert and Ethel (Katz) P.; m. Marilyn B. Heller, June 14, 1964; children: David M., Edward J. AB summa cum laude, Harvard U., 1959, PhD, 1963. NSF postdoctoral fellow U. Calif., Berkeley, 1963; asst. prof. chemistry U. Calif. San Diego, La Jolla, 1964-71, assoc. prof., 1971-80, prof., 1980—; cons. in field; NIH spl. research prof. Gothenburg U., Sweden, 1972-73; NATO prof. U. Padua, Italy, 1986. Author: Mathematics for Chemistry, 1969, Organic Polarography, 1970; contbr. articles to profl. jours.; patentee in field. NSF grantee. Fellow AAAS; mem. Am. Chem. Soc. (grantee), Phi Beta Kappa, Sigma Xi. Home: 8844 Robinhood Ln La Jolla CA 92037 Office: U Calif San Diego Dept Chemistry D-006 La Jolla CA 92093

PERRIN, EDWARD BURTON, biostatistician, health services researcher, public health educator; b Greensboro, Vt., Sept. 19, 1931; s. Justus N. and Dorothy E. (Willey) P.; m. Carol Anne Hendricks, Aug. 18, 1956; children—Jenifer, Scott. B.A., Middlebury Coll., 1953; postgrad. (Fulbright scholar) in stats, Edinburgh (Scotland) U., 1953-54; M.A. in Math. Stats, Columbia U., 1956; Ph.D., Stanford U., 1960. Asst. prof. dept. biostats. U. Pitts., 1959-62; asst. prof. dept. preventive medicine U. Wash., Seattle, 1962-65; asso. prof. U. Wash., 1965-69, prof., 1969-70, prof., chmn. dept. biostats., 1970-72, prof. dept. health services, 1975—, chmn. dept., 1983—; clin. prof. dept. community medicine and internat. health Sch. Medicine, Georgetown U., Washington, 1972-75; dep. dir. Nat. Center for Health Stats., HEW, 1972-73, dir., 1973-75; research scientist Health Care Study Center, Battelle Human Affairs Research Centers, Seattle, 1975-76, dir., 1976-78; dir. Health and Population Study Center Battelle Human Affairs Research Centers, Seattle, 1978-83; sr. cons. biostats. Wash./Alaska regional med. programs, 1967 -72; biometrician VA Co-op Study on Treatment of Esophageal Varices, 1961-73; mem. panel on health services research NRC, 1981. Contbr. articles on biostats., health services and population studies to profl. publs.; mem. editorial bd.: Jour. Family Practice, 1978—. Mem. tech. bd. Milbank Meml. Fund, 1974-76. Recipient Outstanding Service citation HEW, 1975. Fellow AAAS, Am. Public Health Assn. (Spiegelman Health Stats. award 1970, program devel. bd. 1971, chmn. stats. sect. 1978-80, governing council 1983-85), Am. Statis. Assn. (mem. adv. com. to div. statis. policy 1975-77); mem. Inst. Medicine of Nat. Acad. Sci. (chmn. membership com. 1984-86), Population Assn. Am., Biometrics Soc. (pres. Western N.Am. Region 1971), Inst. Math. Stats., Internat. Epidemiologic Assn., Sigma Xi, Phi Beta Kappa. Home: 4900 NE 39th St Seattle WA 98105 Office: U Wash Dept Health Services SC-37 Seattle WA 98195

PERRIN, HELEN JOYCE, semi-retired public relations administrator, consultant; b. Oskaloosa, Iowa, Mar. 23, 1915; d. Leslie R. and May (Hendrix) P. BS, Iowa Wesleyan Coll., 1935; MD, U. Iowa, 1941; MPH, UCLA, 1975. Diplomate Am. Bd. Neurology and Psychiatry. Intern Santa Barbara, Calif., 1941-42; resident St. Elizabeth's Hosp., Washington, 1942-44, N.Y. Neurol. Inst., N.Y.C., 1944-45; practice medicine specializing in Neurology and Psychiatry Des Moines, 1945-54, cons. to various orgns., 1945-54; practice medicine specializing in neurology and psychiatry Long Beach, Calif., 1954-64; also cons. to various orgns. Long Beach, 1954-64; cons. mental and pub. health Los Angeles Pub. Schs., VA Hosp., U. Calif., Irvine, 1964-70; cons. mental health State of Calif., Los Angeles, 1970-75; prin. Joyce Perrin, M.D. Pub. Relations, Seal Beach, Calif., 1979—. Author: Portraits, 1964, Happiness Doctor, 1965; writer numerous poems and short stories. Served with USNR, 1948-75. Fellow Am. Psychiat. Assn. (life); mem. AMA (life), Pub. Relations Soc. Am. Congregationalist. Avocations: duplicate bridge, writing, cooking, travel, reading. Home and Office: PO Box 3669 Seal Beach CA 90740

PERRINE, RICHARD LEROY, environmental engineering educator; b. Mountain View, Calif., May 15, 1924; s. George Alexander and Marie (Axelson) P.; m. Barbara Jean Gale, Apr. 12, 1945; children: Cynthia Gale, Jeffrey Richard. A.B., San Jose State Coll., 1949; M.S., Stanford U., 1950, Ph.D. in Chemistry, 1953. Research chemist Calif. Research Corp., La Habra, 1953-59; asso. prof. UCLA, 1959-63, prof. engring. and applied sci., 1963—, chmn. environ. sci. and engring., 1971-82; cons. environ. sci. and engring., energy resources, flow in porous media; mem. Los Angeles County Energy Commn., 1973-81; mem. adv. council South Coast Air Quality Mgmt. Dist., 1977-82; mem. air conservation com. Los Angeles County Lung Assn., 1970-84. Editor-in-chief The Environ. Profl., 1985—. Served with AUS, 1943-46. Recipient Outstanding Engr. Merit award in environ. engring. Inst. Advancement Engring., 1975; ACT-SO award in field of chemistry West Coast region NAACP. Mem. Am. Chem. Soc., Soc. Petroleum Engrs., Am. Inst. Chem. Engrs., Can. Inst. Mining and Metallurgy, Nat. Assn. Environ. Edn., Nat. Assn. Environ. Profls., Air Pollution Control Assn., Am. Water Resources Assn., AAAS, N.Y. Acad. Scis., Western Regional Sci. Assn., Soc. Environ. Toxicology and Chemistry, Internat. Assn. Impact Assessment, Internat. Assn. for Great Lakes Research, Assn. Environ. Engring. Profs., Sierra Club, Wilderness Soc., Audubon Soc., Sigma Xi, Tau Beta Pi, Phi Lambda Upsilon. Home: 22611 Kittridge St Canoga Park CA 91307 Office: U Calif Engring I Room 2066 Los Angeles CA 90024-1600

PERROTT, ELAINE VIRGINIA, compliance engineer; b. Cambridge, Mass., Oct. 5, 1947; d. Peter Laird and Marie Alyce (Robertson) Schneider; m. Bernard John Perrott, Sept. 17, 1983. B.A. in English, St. Mary's Coll., 1983. Policyholder service rep. Liberty Mut. Ins., Natick, Mass., 1969-72; personnel asst. Ludlow Corp., Needham Heights, Mass., 1972-77; tng. program developer Balt. Gas & Electric, 1980-83; nuclear tng. auditor Ariz. Pub. Service Co., Phoenix, 1983-85, compliance engr., 1985—; status bd. keeper APS-Emergency Response Team, 1984—. Author self-paced instrn. tng. plan workbook. Served with USNR, 1977-80. Mem. Nat. Assn. Female Execs. (affiliate), Naval Enlisted Reserve Assn. (v.p. local chpt.), St. Mary's Community Theater, Am. Soc. Tng. and Devel. Republican. Roman Catholic. Club: Chesapeake Country. Home: 10611 W Avenida Glenrosa St Phoenix AZ 92022 Office: Ariz Pub Service Co PO Box 21666 Sta 6088 Phoenix AZ 85036

PERRY, BONNE LU, social service agency administrator; b. Miles City, Mont., Mar. 26, 1929; d. Daniel Glen and Mabel Jane (Scriven) Harris; adopted d. Albert Hartford and Bertha Gertrude (Erickson) P. Student, No. Mont. Coll., 1947-49; BA, U. Mont., 1951, postgrad., 1953-56; postgrad., Queens Coll., 1966. Cert. social worker, Mont. Tchr. English Whitefish (Mont.) High Sch., 1951-53; tchr. English and drama Great Falls (Mont.) High Sch., 1953-58; tchr. English Northport (N.Y.) High Sch., 1958-67; social worker Roosevelt County Dept. Pub. Welfare, Wolf Point, Mont., 1969-74; social worker supr. I Roosevelt, Sheridan, and Daniels Counties Dept. Pub. Welfare, Wolf Point, Mont., 1974-78; county dir. II Richland County Dept. Pub. Welfare, Sidney, Mont., 1978—. Author: (poetry) Winter, 1978. Mem. Mont. Pub. Welfare Assn., Am. Pub. Welfare Assn., Mont. County Dirs., Eastern Mont. Mental Health Assn., Community Health Mtg., U. Mont. Alumni Assn., Alpha Phi. Mem. Mont. Pub. Welfare Assn., Am. Pub. Welfare Assn., Mont. County Dirs., Eastern Mont. Mental Health Assn., Community Health Mtg., U. Mont. Alumni Assn., Whitefish Edn. Assn. (pres. 1952-53), Alpha Phi. Democrat. Congregationalist. Lodges: Order of Eastern Star, PEO (recording sec. 1984-85. Avocations: reading, writing, community concerts, public tv. Home: 120 7th St SW Lot 25 Sidney MT 59270 Office: Richland County Dept Pub Welfare 221 5th St SW Sidney MT 59270

PERRY, BRUCE WILLIAM, risk analyst; b. Los Angeles, June 7, 1955; s. Thomas Leon and Margaret (Pryor) P.; m. Susan Conan, June 21, 1980; 1 child, Scott Thomas. BS, U. Calif., Irvine, 1977; MSPH, UCLA, 1980. Staff analyst IWG Corp., San Diego, 1980—. Author: Oil Shale Risk Analysis, 1984; contbr. articles to profl. jours. Pres. Scripps Ranch Community Theater, 1985-86. Mem. Soc. Epidemiologic Research. Republican. Presbyterian. Avocation: community theater. Office: IWG Corp 3065 Rosecrans Pl #210 San Diego CA 92110

PERRY, DALE LYNN, chemist; b. Greenville, Tex., May 12, 1947; s. Francis Leon and Violet (Inabinette) P. B.S., Midwestern U., 1969; M.S., Lamar U., 1972; Ph.D., U. Houston, 1974. NSF fellow dept. chemistry Rice U., Houston, 1976-77; Miller Research fellow dept. chemistry U. Calif.-Berkeley, 1977-79; prin. investigator inorganic and surface chemistry Lawrence Berkeley Lab. U. Calif., 1979—, sr. scientist, 1987—. Contbr. articles to profl. jours. Recipient Sigma Xi Nat. Research award U. Houston, 1974; NSF Postdoctoral fellow, 1976-77. Mem. Am. Chem. Soc., Soc. Applied Spectroscopy, Coblentz Soc., Materials Research Soc. Sigma Xi. Office: Lawrence Berkeley Lab U Calif Mail Stop 70A-115 Berkeley CA 94720

PERRY, DAN LORING, safety engineer; b. Whittier, Calif., July 14, 1958; s. Adrian Franklin and Mary Gladys (Gill) P.; m. Rebecca Ann Reimschissel, Sept. 19, 1980; children: Brooke Marie, Jordan Franklin, Nicole. Freelance topgraphical draftsman Dezign, Inc., Richfield, Utah, 1977, 79-81; plant draftsman Martin Marietta Cement, Nephi, Utah, 1981-82; asst. safety coordinator, fire marshall Weber State Coll., Ogden, Utah, 1982-83; safety engr. Hercules Aerospace, Inc., Magna, Utah, 1983-85, Intermountain Power Service Corp., Delta, Utah, 1985—; instr. ARC First Aid, Utah, 1984—; cons. in field, Utah, 1986—. Co-author (functional program) Weber State College Emergency Disaster Program, 1983. Lt. Hinckley (Utah) City Fire Dept., 1986. Mem. Am. Soc. Mfg. Engrs., Am. Soc. Safety Engrs. Mormon.

PERRY, DAPHNE, social worker; b. Salt Lake City, June 13, 1926; d. Edwin Samuel and Eunice Naomi (Crosby) Bliss; m. Clarence Kettle, Sept. 6, 1943 (dec. 1947); m. John Calvin Perry, Dec. 20, 1949; children: Don Richard, John David, Scott Edwin, Brian Calvin, Douglas Todd. BA, Calif. State U., Long Beach, 1969; MSW, Portland (Oreg.) State U., 1985. Caseworker Washington County C.S.D., Hillsboro, Oreg., 1969-80; acting dir. Beaverton (Oreg.) Community Youth Services, 1980; pvt. social work practice Beaverton; co-owner, sec. Electro-Static Refinishers, Beaverton, 1983—; vol. cons. Fir Grove Sch., Beaverton, 1980; cons. Ctr. Prevention Child Abuse, Portland; tchr. Parenting Dynamics classes, Beaverton, 1980-85. Founder Beaverton Community Youth Service Ctr., 1980, bd. dirs., 1986—; sponsor Parents Anonymous, Beaverton. Mem. Nat. Assn. Social Workers, Social Workers for Peace and Disarmament, World Beyond War. Republican. Avocations: cabin building, fishing, hiking, camping, reading. Home: 2380 NW 154th Pl Beaverton OR 97006

PERRY, DAVID NILES, public relations comapny executive; b. Utica, N.Y., Mar. 7, 1940; s. Francis N. and Marion H. P.; B.S., Utica Coll. Syracuse U., 1962; m. Jacqueline J. Adams, Dec. 21, 1962. Pub. affairs rep. Allstate Ins. Co., Pasadena, Calif., 1966-67; dir. press relations Los Angeles C. of C., 1968; rep. pub. relations Lockheed Propulsion Co., Redlands, Calif., 1968-70; mgr. pub. relations Bozell & Jacobs Inc., Los Angeles, 1970-73, Phoenix, 1971-74; pres. David Perry Pub. Relations Inc., Scottsdale, Ariz., 1974—; cons. in field. Bd. dirs. Ariz. Gov.'s Commn. Ariz. environment, 1972—, Ariz. chpt. ARC. Served with USNR, 1962-65. Mem. Pub. Relations Soc. Am. (accredited) (dir. Phoenix chpt. 1975-82, pres. 1978). Office: 6819 E Diamond St Scottsdale AZ 85257

PERRY, JACK RICHARD, treasurer; b. Canton, Ohio, July 15, 1945; s. Genessee Jack and Audrey Z. (Hupp) P.; m. Rebecca Susan Koval, May 20, 1972; children: Danielle Briana, Caitlin Elise. BBA, Ohio U., 1974, MBA, 1976. CPA, Ill. Design engr. NCR, Cambridge, Ohio, 1967-74; sr. cons. AA & Co., Chgo., 1976-78; audit mgr. GTE Service Corp., Chgo., 1978-80; controller GTE EDP, Hampton, Va., 1980-81; treas. GTE Communicatons Systems Corp., Phoenix, 1981—. Served with USN, 1963-65. Mem. Am. Inst. CPA's, Ill. Soc. CPA's, Am. Prodn. and Inventory Control (cert.), Nat. Assn. Accts. Office: GTE CSC 2500 W Utopia Rd Phoenix AZ 85027

PERRY, JOHN VAN BUREN, historian, educator; b. Aberdeen, S.D., Feb. 7, 1928; s. Van Buren and Elise (Andersen) P.; B.Sc., No. State Coll., S.D., 1954; postgrad. Law Sch., N.Y. U., 1954-55; M.A., U. Calif., Berkeley, 1959; postgrad. U. So. Calif., 1965-66. Instr. history Calif. State Univ. Fresno and

Sonoma, 1963-65; asst. prof. Kern Community Coll. Dist., Bakersfield and Porterville, Calif., 1969-71; prof. social scis. and humanities Central Wyo. Coll., Riverton, 1971-75; prof. history, humanities and social scis. Lake Tahoe Community Coll., South Lake Tahoe, Calif., 1975—, pres. faculty senate, 1979-80, senate sec., 1983-84, advisor Truman Scholarship, 1979—, chmn. student com., 1986—, founder/advisor Lambda Tau chpt. Alpha Gamma Sigma Soc.. Pres., Lake Tahoe Community Concert Assn., 1977-79, 81—, bd. dirs., 1975—, campaign mgr., 1979-81; pres. Arts in Action, 1973-75; del. Wyo. Council on Arts, 1972-75, Wyo. Council for Humanities, 1973-75; bd. dirs. Riverton Community Concert Assn., 1972-75, Assn. to Restore Tallac Sites, 1981-83; bd. dirs. Lake Tahoe Cultural Arts Alliance, 1981—, treas., 1982-84, 86—, co-pres., 1984-86. Served with USN, 1946-50. Root-Tilden fellow, 1954-55. Mem. Am. Hist. Assn., Community Coll. Humanities Assn., Mus. Soc. San Francisco, Los Angeles County Mus. Art, Met. Mus. N.Y.C., Am. Philatelic Soc., Smithsonian Instn. Club: Scottish Rite. Home: PO Box 14266 South Lake Tahoe CA 95702 Office: PO Box 14445 South Lake Tahoe CA 95702

PERRY, JOSEPH JOHN, fashion merchandising educator; b. Chgo., Apr. 3, 1931; s. John F. and Anne (Hoffmann) P.; m. Eve R. Buffardi, Feb. 1, 1958; 1 child, Margot Eve. Diploma, Crane Tech. Inst., 1948; BS, Northwestern U., 1955. Asst. buyer Wieboldt's, Chgo., 1954-55, buyer, 1956-59; asst. buyer Coulter's, Los Angeles, 1959-60; buyer Montgomery Wards, Los Angeles, 1960-62, Bullock's, Los Angeles, 1962-68; sales mgr. Burt Stanley Co., Los Angeles, 1968-72; chmn. dept. fashion merchandising Brook Coll., Long Beach, Calif., 1972—. Center mgr. Cerebral Palsy Telethon, Long Beach., 1979—. Served as sgt. U.S. Army, 1951-53, Korea. Decorated Bronze Star. Mem. Alpha Beta Gamma (advisor, 1978—, nat. chmn. 1980-82). Avocations: tennis, handball, swimming, theatre arts, modeling. Home: 900 Village Dr Monterey Park CA 91754

PERRY, JUDITH ADAMS, psychiatrist; b. Zimbabwe, July 20, 1947; d. George O. and Ruth Ena (Barrett) Adams; m. James Albert Perry, Aug. 22, 1967; 2 children. BS, Walla Walla Coll., 1967; MD, Loma Linda U., 1972, MS, 1975. Diplomate Am. Bd. Psychiatry and Neurology. Resident in psychiatry Loma Linda (Calif.) U., 1972-75, asst. prof. psychiatry, 1975-78; dir. resident tng. Harding Hosp., Worthington, Ohio, 1978-83; practice medicine specializing in psychiatry Worthington, 1983-85, Yakima, Wash., 1985—; cons. Continuing Community Care, Riverside, Calif., 1972-78, Columbus Area Community Mental Health Ctr., 1981-83, Indian Health Services, Toppenish, Wash., 1985—; asst. clin. prof. psychiatry Ohio State U., Columbus, 1978-82, assoc. clin. prof., 1982-85. Mem. AMA, Am. Psychiat. Assn., Am. Med. Women's Assn. Home: 4706 Snowmountain Rd Yakima WA 98902 Office: Yakima Med Ctr 1111 W Spruce St Suite 22 Yakima WA 98902

PERRY, LEE ROWAN, lawyer; b. Chgo., Sept. 23, 1933; s. Watson Bishop and Helen (Rowan) P.; m. Barbara Ashcraft Mitchell, July 2, 1955; children: Christopher, Constance, Geoffrey. B.A., U. Ariz., 1955, LL.B., 1961. Bar: Ariz. 1961. Since practiced in Phoenix; clk. Udall & Udall, Tucson, 1960-61; mem. firm Carson, Messinger, Elliott, Laughlin & Ragan, 1961—. Mem. law rev. staff, U. Ariz., 1959-61. Mem. bd. edn. Paradise Valley Elementary and High Sch. Dists., Phoenix, 1964-68, pres., 1968; treas. troop Boy Scouts Am., 1970-72; mem. Ariz. adv. bd. Girl Scouts U.S.A., 1972-74, mem. nominating bd., 1978-79; bd. dirs. Florence Crittenton Services Ariz., 1967-72, pres., 1970-72; bd. dirs. U. Ariz. Alumni, Phoenix, 1968-72, pres., 1969-70; bd. dirs. Family Service Phoenix, 1974-75; bd. dirs. Travelers Aid Assn. Am., 1985—; bd. dirs. Vol. Bur. Maricopa County, 1975-81, 83-86, pres., 1984-85; bd. dirs. Ariz. div. Am. Cancer Soc., 1978-80, Florence Crittenton div. Child Welfare League Am., 1976-81; bd. dirs. Crisis Nursery for Prevention of Child Abuse, 1978-81, pres., 1978-80. Served to 1st lt. USAF, 1955-58. Mem. State Bar Ariz. (conv. chmn. 1972), Am., Maricopa County bar assns., Phi Delta Phi, Phi Delta Theta (pres. 1954). Republican (precinct capt. 1970, chmn. Reps. for Senator De Concini 1976, 82, 88, precinct committeeman 1983-84). Episcopalian (sr. warden 1968-72). Clubs: Rotary (dir. 1971-77, pres. 1975-76), Plaza, Ariz. Office: United Bank Tower PO Box 33907 Phoenix AZ 85067

PERRY, LOIS JEANNE, research biochemist; b. Tacoma, Oct. 23, 1952; d. James Allen and Shirley Masaye (Shiroma) P. BS in Chemistry, San Jose State U., 1978, MA in Biology, 1982. Research assoc. Genentech Inc., South San Francisco, Calif., 1982-85, sr. research assoc., 1985—. Contbr. articles to profl. jours. Mem. AAAS, Am. Chem. Soc. Democrat. Avocations: philately, running. Office: Genentech Inc 460 Point San Bruno Blvd South San Francisco CA 94080

PERRY, MICHAEL LAWRENCE, museum director; b. Nampa, Idaho, Jan. 6, 1946; s. Lowell Delmar and Lucy Dora (Lemon) P.; m. Sandra Lynne Miles, Dec. 13, 1968; children: Allyson, Justin, Adrienne. BS, U. Utah, 1971, MS, 1973. Animal care handler U. Utah, Salt Lake City, 1965-73, asst. curator, 1968-73, teaching fellow, 1969-73; dir. Dinosaur Natural History Mus., Vernal, Utah, 1973-81, Idaho Mus. Natural History, Pocatello, 1981-84, Mus. Western Colo., 1984—; cons. Idaho Assn. for Humanities, Pocatello, 1981-84; bd. dirs. Canyonlands Field Inst., Moab, Utah, 1985—. Co-author: Utah Birds, 1975; contbr. articles to profl. jours. Bd. dirs. Grand Junction (Colo.) Visitors and Conv. Bur., 1986, Grand Junction Downtown Assn., 1985. Recipient Leadership Achievement award Grand Junction Downtown Assn., 1985, Outstanding Employee award Utah Div. Parks and Recreation, 1979, Outstanding Pub. Service award Vernal C. of C., 1978, Outstanding Achievement award Salt Lake Tribune, 1980. Mem. Am. Assn. Mus., Mountain Plains Mus. Assn., Colo.-Wyo. Assn. Mus., Grand Junction C. of C., Sigma Xi. Republican. Mormon. Lodge: Lions. Avocations: photography, camping, outdoor sports. Home: 1909 Monument Canyon Dr Grand Junction CO 81503 Office: Mus of Western Colo 248 S 4th St Grand Junction CO 81501

PERRY, PHYLLIS JEAN, school administrator; b. Nevada City, Calif., Oct. 23, 1933; d. William Henry and Winifred (Elliott) Penaluna; m. David Louis Perry, Feb. 8, 1953; children: Janet Marie Miller, Jill Louise Fernandez. AB, U. Calif., Berkeley, 1955; MA, San Francisco State U., 1960; EdD, U. Colo., 1980. Instructional design specialist Boulder (Colo.) Valley Schs., 1976-80, curriculum and instrn. specialist, 1980-82, ednl. programs specialist, 1982-84, prin. Martin Park Sch., 1984—, dir. talented and gifted, 1980—. Author: Full Flowering: A Parent/Teacher Guide to Programs for the Gifted, 1985, A Look At Colorado, 1986; contbr. articles to profl. jours. Mem. Colo. Council Internat. Reading Assn., Nat. Assn. for Gifted Children, Assn. for Curriculum Devel., State Colo. Adv. Com. on Gifted Student Programming, Colo. Coordinators Council. Office: Martin Park Sch 3740 Martin Dr Boulder CO 80303

PERRY, RONALD DENNIS, administrative analyst; b. Spokane, Wash., Sept. 27, 1946; s. Ross Joseph and Carolyne (Arancio) P; m. Linda Strang. BA, Seattle U., 1968; MA, U. Wash., 1971, PhD, 1975. Research analyst Wash. Ho. Reps., Olympia, 1975; prin. mgmt. analyst Legis. Budget Com., Olympia, 1976—; mem. honors program adv. bd. Seattle U., 1985; cons. Ctr. for Support of Children, Seattle, 1985—. Trustee Villa Acad., Seattle, 1986—. Mem. Am. Hist. Assn. Roman Catholic. Clubs: Wash. Athletic, View Ridge Community (Seattle). Avocations: music, cooking, photography. Office: Legis Budget Com 506 E 16th Olympia WA 98504

PERRY, RONALD WILLIAM, public affairs educator; b. Phoenix, Nov. 13, 1949; s. Hugh and Katherine Elizabeth (Ham) P.; m. Paula Piper, Mar. 3, 1972; 1 child, Elizabeth. BS, Ariz. State U., 1971, MA, 1973; PhD, U. Wash., 1975. Lectr. sociology Pacific Luth. U., Tacoma, 1973-75; asst. prof. sociology U. Hartford, Conn., 1975-77; sr. research scientist Battelle Inst., Seattle, 1977-83; prof. pub. affairs Ariz. State U., Tempe, 1983—; mem. com. U.S. emergency preparedness Nat. Acad. Scis., Washington, 1978-81, com. emergency mgmt., 1981-83. Author: Minority Citizens in Disaster, 1986, Comprehensive Emergency Management, 1985, Disaster Management, 1984. Human Adjustment to Volcanoes grantee NSF, 1980—, Flood Response Mgmt. grantee NSF, 1978-80. Mem. Am. Sociol. Assn., Internat. Sociol. Assn., Pacific Sociol. Assn., Ariz. Emergency Services Assn. Office: Ariz State U Sch Pub Affairs Tempe AZ 85287

PERRY, STEVE CARL, freelance writer; b. Baton Rouge; s. George H. and Willa M. (Dean) P.; m. C. Dianne Waller, Nov. 19, 1966; children: Dal R., Stephani D. Student, La. State U., 1965-67; Cert. as Lic. Practical Nurse, Baton Rouge Vocat. Tech. Sch., 1974. Pvt. practice as pvt. investigator Baton Rouge, 1970-75; physician's asst. Hill Med. Clinic, Baton Rouge, 1975-78; freelance writer Portland, Oreg., 1978—. Author: (with Michael Reaves) Hellstar, 1984, The Matador Trilogy, 1985, The Omega Cage, 1986; author (TV scripts) Centurions, 1986. Bd. dirs. Beaverton (Oreg.) Library Bd., 1985—. Mem. Sci. Fiction Writers Am. Avocations: martial arts, bodybuilding.

PERRY, THOMAS WILBUR, computer security consultant; b. Jacksonville, Fla., Dec. 16, 1955; s. Julius Cesear Perry and Magdlene (Carrol) Arnold; m. Dinah Lynn Gaines, July 11, 1981; 1 child, Sheldon. AA, Fla. Jr. Coll., 1975; BS, U. West Fla., 1977; postgrad., Golden Gate U., 1978-81. Assoc. programmer Control Data Corp., Sunnyvale, Calif., 1977-78; data system programmer Lockheed Corp., Sunnyvale, 1978-80; analyst/programmer Applied Tech., Sunnyvale, 1980-82; cons. EDP Audit Controls, Oakland, Calif., 1982-84; mng. ptnr. Ozier, Perry & Assoc., San Francisco, 1984—. Mem. Info. Systems Security Assn., Computer Security Inst., Data Processing Mgmt. Assn., EDP Auditors Assn., Classified Info. Processing Spl. Interest Group. Democrat. Baptist. Avocations: tennis, fishing, hiking, basketball, baseball. Home: 620 Iris Ave Sunnyvale CA 94086 Office: Ozier Perry & Assocs 870 Market St Suite 1001 San Francisco CA 94102

PERRY, TIMOTHY RANDOLPH, military officer, aviator; b. Zebulon, N.C., May 21, 1952; s. Sonny Maxwell and Rosa (Tempie) P.; m. Karen Marie Price, Jan. 2, 1975. BS in Zoology and Biochem. with honors, N.C. State U., 1975. Mgr. prodn. Corning Electronics, Raleigh, N.C., 1975-76; commd. ensign USN, 1976, advanced through grades to lt. comdr., 1986; jet student naval aviator USN, Beeville, Tex., 1976-78; replacement pilot USN, San Diego, 1978-79; carrier based pilot USN, FPO, N.Y.C., 1979-82, officer software systems, 1979-81, systems analyst, 1980-82; jet instr. pilot USN, Beeville, 1982-85; recalled to active duty USN, Calif., 1986; mgr. systems tests Litton Data Systems, Colorado Springs, Colo., 1985-86. Mem. Young Reps. for Reagan, San Antonio, 1984. Air Force ROTC scholar N.C. State U., 1971; recipient USAF Acad. appointment U.S. Senate, 1971, Meritorious Unit citation USN, 1982, 84, Naval Aviator award USN, 1978, Naval Battle E award, 1981. Mem. Aircraft Owner's and Pilots Assn., Future Airline Pilots Assn. Roman Catholic. Club: Management (Colorado Springs). Avocations: jogging, weightlifting, squash, backpacking, microcomputers. Home: 2465 Shoreline Dr Apt 101 Alameda CA 94501-5030

PERRY, VANN, data processing executive; b. Muskogee, Okla., Oct. 13, 1947; s. Ted and Virginia Perry; m. Sue Perry, (div. Aug. 1975); children: Dana, Seth; m. Rhonda Perry, Jan. 28, 1975; 1 child, Teddy. BS in Math., U. Colo., 1969; MS in Computer Sci., Tex. A&M, 1970. Statis. cons. Inst. Behavioral Scis., Boulder, Colo., 1971-78; researcher, programmer Ctr. Health Services Research, Denver, 1978-81; mgr. systems and programming Colo. State Judicial Dept., Denver, 1981—. Mem. Am. Mgmt. Assn., Data Processing Mgmt. Assn. Democrat. Avocations: gardening, camping, hiking, softball. Home: 5472 Pueblo Pl Boulder CO 80303 Office: Colo State Judicial Dept 2 E 14th Ave Denver CO 80203

PERRY, WILLIAM JAMES, mathematical scientist; b. Vandergrift, Pa., Oct. 11, 1927; s. Edward Martin and Mabelle Estelle (Dunlap) P.; m. Leonilla Mary Green, Dec. 29, 1947; children: David Carter, William Wick, Rebecca Lynn, Robin Lee, Mark Lloyd. B.S. in Math, Stanford U., 1949, M.S., 1950; Ph.D., Pa. State U., 1957. Instr. math. Pa. State U., 1951-54; sr. mathematician HRB-Singer Co., State College, Pa., 1952-54; dir. electronic def. labs. GTE Sylvania Co., Mountain View, Calif., 1954-64; pres. ESL, Inc., Sunnyvale, Calif., 1964-77; tech. cons. Dept. Def., Washington, 1967-77; under sec. def. for research and engring. Dept. Def., 1977-81; mng. dir. Hambrecht & Quist (investment bankers), San Francisco, 1981-85; pres. H&Q Tech. Ptnrs., Inc., San Francisco, 1985—. Served with U.S. Army, 1946-47. Recipient Outstanding Civilian Service medal U.S. Army, 1962; Outstanding Civilian Service medal Def. Intelligence Agency, 1977; Disting. Public Service medal Dept. Def., 1980, 81; Medal of Achievement Am. Electronic Assn., 1980; Disting. Service medal NASA, 1981; decorated Knight Comdr.'s Cross of Fed. Republic of Germany, grand officier de l'Ordre National du Merite (France). Mem. Am. Math. Soc., Nat. Acad. Engring., Sigma Xi. Home: 10701 Mora Dr Los Altos CA 94022 Office: 3000 Sand Hill Rd Menlo Park CA 94025

PERSKY, GEORGE, electrical engineer; b. Bklyn., Apr. 26, 1938; s. Nathan and Lillian R. (Robinson) P.; m. Sandra Schechter, Aug. 16, 1964; children: Cheryl Renee, Judith Gail. BSEE, Rensselaer Poly. Inst., Troy, 1959; MSEE, Poly. Inst. Bklyn., 1961, PhD in Physics, 1968. Mem. tech. staff Bell Labs., Murray Hill, N.J., 1967-78; from sr. project engr. to dept. mgr. Hughes Aircraft Co., Newport Beach, Calif., 1978-83; dept. mgr. Hughes Aircraft Co., Carlsbad, Calif., 1983—. Patentee in field; contbr. articles to profl. jours. Mem. Planning Bd., North Plainfield, N.J., 1972-78. Mem. IEEE (sr.), Am. Phys. Soc., Sigma Xi. Avocations: gardening, traveling, investments. Home: 24751 Doria Way Mission Viejo CA 92691 Office: Hughes Aircraft Co 6155 El Camino Real Carlsbad CA 92008

PERSOFF, RICHARD ELIHU, insurance company executive; b. Los Angeles, Oct. 7, 1928; s. Albert Morton and Ada Persoff; m. Jessica Matilda Bowling, 1959. BA, Pomona Coll., 1949. Cert. indsl. hygienist. Freelance photographer San Francisco, 1959-67; mgr. Lifelite div. Radiant Color, Richmond, Calif., 1967-69; sr. tech. cons. Hartford Ins. Co., San Francisco, 1969—. Served with U.S. Army, 1953-55. Mem. AAAS, Am. Indsl. Hygiene Assn. (bd. dirs. no. Calif. sect. 1984-87, sec. 1982-84), Media Tech. Info. Ctr. (vice-chmn. 1985—), Am. Chem. Soc. Lodge: Elks. Office: Hartford Ins Group 650 California St San Francisco CA 94119

PESCE, GABRIEL VINCENT, research civil engineering consultant; b. Staten Island, N.Y., Apr. 21, 1924; s. Vincent S. and Mary (Paratore) P.; m. Lois Jean Ballintine, June 30, 1950; children: Vincent, Mary Anne (dec.), David, Laurie, Barbara. BCE, Cornell U., 1949, MCE, 1951; ScB, Brown U., 1945; PhD in Archaeology, UCLA, 1986. Registered profl. engr., Calif. Hydraulic research engr. TVA, Knoxville, 1949-50; instr. Cornell U., Ithaca, N.Y., 1948-49, 50-53; prin. research engr. Republic Aviation Corp., Farmingdale, N.Y., 1953-56, Lockheed Aircraft, Marietta, Ga., 1956-57; v.p. Abex Aerospace, Oxnard, Calif., 1957-72; pres. G.V. Pesce & Assocs. Inc., Camarillo, Calif., 1972—; instr. Ventura (Calif.) Coll., 1974—; bd. dirs. Santa Anita Mut. Water Co., Gaviota, Calif. Patentee in field. Bd. dirs., v.p., Hollister Ranch Coop., Gaviota, 1982—, Hollister Ranch Owners Assn., Gaviota, 1978. Served with USN, 1942-47; to lt. col. USAFR, 1949-76; ret. col. Mem. ASCE, Soc. Am. Mil. Engrs., Earthquake Engring. and Research Inst., Am. Geophys. Union, Calif. Land Surveyors Assn., Council Cons. Engrs., Ventura County Archaelogical Soc., Am. Water Works Assn., Navy League, Air Force Assn., Chi Epsilon. Republican. Roman Catholic. Home: 24 La Crescenta Dr Camarillo CA 93010 Office: GV Pesce & Assocs Inc 541 Calle San Pablo Camarillo CA 93010

PETCHEL, JOHN JOSEPH, computer services company executive; b. Milw., Oct. 15, 1942; s. Leo John and June Bernice (Adams) P.; m. Anne Roxie Bau, July 16, 1965 (div. Feb. 1972); children: Roxanne Marie, John Joseph II; m. Sandra Theresa Weaver, June 21, 1974; children: Anthony Scott, Jennifer Marie. Student, Ariz. Western U.; AA, Glendale (Ariz.) Coll., 1971; student, Ariz. State U. Lic. gen. contractor, Calif. Enlisted USMC, 1961, advanced to staff sgt., resigned, 1970; engr. OSP Mountain Bell Telephone, Phoenix, 1970-74; v.p. Tesinc, Phoenix, 1974-81; pres. Saztec USA, Rolling Hills Estates, Calif., 1981—; bd. dirs. Saztec Internat., Rolling Hills Estates, Saztec Europe, London. Bd. dirs. Rancho Palos Verdes chpt. Multiple Sclerosis Soc., 1985-86; mem. Rancho Palos Verdes Sch. Bd., 1985; donor South Bay Edn. Fund, Rolling Hills Estates, 1985-86. Republican. Roman Catholic. Avocations: tennis, racquetball, golf, tournament chess. Home: 5622 Sunmist Dr Rancho Palos Verdes CA 90274 Office: Saztec Internat 27250 Hawthorne Hills Blvd #170 Rolling Hills Estates CA 90274

PETENBRINK, NANCY ANN, employee assistance program director; b. Cin., Jan. 8, 1950; d. Ray Geiger and Anna Mae (DeWalt) P. BEd, Ohio U., 1972, MEd, 1976; postgrad., Ohio State U., 1977-79. Developer, dir. altnative to impaired driving program Regional Alcoholism Ctr., Columbus, Ohio, 1976-78; spl. health services coordinator Buckeye Union Ins. Co., Columbus, 1977-78; clinic coordinator The Nisonger Ctr. Ohio State U., Columbus, 1978-83; employee assistance program counselor Gerlach, Lear and Assocs., Columbus, 1981-83; employee assistance program coordinator Kernview Hosp. and Mental Health Ctr., Bakersfield, Calif., 1983-84; West coast regional employee assistance program coordinator Anheuser-Busch Cos., Van Nuys, Calif., 1984-87; owner, prin. Profl. Employee Assistance Cons., Van Nuys, 1987—; guest lectr. employee assistance program Mission Coll., North Hollywood, Calif., 1986. Trustee Southeast Mental Health Ctr., Columbus, 1982-83; hon. life mem. Citizens' Coalition for Rational Traffic Laws. Recipient Community Service in the Area of Humanitarian Achievement award Columbus Dispatch, 1983. Mem. Nat. Assn. Female Execs., Assn. Labor Mgmt. Adminstrs. and Cons. on Alcoholism (sec. 1983-86). Democrat. Mem. Ch. of Christ. Avocations: photography, sports car racing. Office: Profl Employee Assistance Cons 16360 Roscoe Blvd Suite 101 Van Nuys CA 91402

PETERS, B. JEANNE, management consultant; b. Chgo., May 26, 1940; d. James William and Evelyn (Short) Hill; children—Lisa L., Krylyn G. B.A., No. Ill. U., 1962; postgrad. U. Ill., Northwestern U. Tchr., ednl. writer suburban sch. dists. Ill., 1962-74; pres. Affirmative Action Cons., Wheeling, Ill., 1974-77; employee relations adminstr. Motorla, Inc., 1977-78, corp. mgr. compliance programs, 1978-79, corp. dir. affirmative action and compliance, 1979-83, dir. tng., 1984-85; v.p. Phoenix Assocs., Inc., 1986—; tech. adv. mem. U.S. Employer Del. ILO, 1981-83, 86. Bd. dirs. Minority Econ. Resources Corp., Des Plaines, Ill., 1979-81, Operation Uplift, Maywood, Ill., 1978-83; mem. mgmt. devel. bd. Ariz. Dept. Adminstrn., 1984—; mem. Ariz. Forum for Pub. Edn., 1984—. Recipient award YWCA, 1978. Phoenix C. of C. (edn. com. 1984—). Unitarian. Home: 7811 E Beryl Dr Scottsdale AZ 85258 Office: 500 E Thomas Rd Phoenix AZ 85012

PETERS, BARBARA ANN, counselor, interior designer; b. LaSalle, Ill., Sept. 26, 1938; d. Lewis H. and Virginia L. (Dare) Livengood; m. Harold O. Nuss, June 26, 1960 (div. Jan. 1967); children—Kim Kristy, Douglas Alan; m. 2d, Barry J. Peters, June 2, 1968 (div. Nov. 1981). A.A., Scottsdale Community Coll., 1981; B.S., Ariz. State U., 1982, M.C., 1984; diploma interior design LaSalle U., 1967. Membership sec. Assn. Ednl. Data Systems, Washington, 1972; adminstrv. asst. pres. D.C. Transit Co., Washington, 1971-73; dist. sec. Congressman Robert H. Michel, Peoria, Ill., 1975; bus. mgr. Robinson Enterprises, Peoria, Ill., 1976-78; sec. to chmn. counselor edn. Ariz. State U., Tempe, 1982-83; crisis counselor Communications Info., Phoenix, 1983—; counselor Northwest Community Coll., Powell, Wyo., 1984-85; job placement counselor Goodwill Industries, Phoenix, 1985—; pvt. practice counseling Hugs Counseling, 1985—; psychotherapist Westside Mental Health, Glendale, Ariz., 1986—. Designer Hug Bear Watch, 1986. Bd. dirs. Women in Transition, 1982. Mem. Am. Assn. Counseling and Devel., Am. Bus. Women's Assn., Ariz. Assn. U. Women. Republican. Roman Catholic. Home: 8738 E Whitton Ave Scottsdale AZ 85251

PETERS, DOUGLAS CAMERON, mining engineer, geologist; b. Pitts., June 19, 1955; s. Donald Cameron and Twila (Bingel) P. B.S. in Earth and Planetary Sci., U. Pitts., 1977; M.S. in Geology, Colo. Sch. Mines, 1981, M.S. in Mining Engring., 1983. Technician, inspector Engring. Mechanics, Inc., Pitts., 1973-77. Research asst. Potential Gas Agy., Golden, Colo., 1977-78; geologist U.S. Geol. Survey, Denver, 1978-80; cons. Climax Molybdenum Co., Golden, 1981-82; cons., Golden, 1982-84; mining engr., prin. investigator U.S. Bur. Mines, Denver, 1984—; bur. rep. to Geosat Com., 1984—; program chmn. Geotech '84, '85, '86, 87 Conf., Denver, 1984-87. Author: Physical Modeling of Draw of Broken Rock in Caving, 1984; editor COGS Computer Contbns., 1986—. Contbr. articles to profl. jours. Mem. Computer Oriented Geol. Soc. (charter) (com. chmn. 1983—, pres. 1985, dir. 1986), Geol. Soc. Am., Rocky Mountain Assn. Geologists, AIME (jr. mem., Soc. Mining Engrs., Am. Assn. Petroleum Geologists (com. mem. 1984—), Am. Soc. Photogrammetry and Remote Sensing, Pitts. Geol. Soc. Republican. Office: US Bur Mines Box 25086 Bldg 20 Denver Fed Ctr Denver CO 80225

PETERS, LINDA ELLEN, interior designer, educator, real estate agent; b. Oak Park, Ill., July 9, 1946; s. Russell C. and Vilma (Janik) Lowry; m. Roger W. Peters, June 24, 1967 (div. Jan. 1982). BS in Nursing with honors, U. Ill., Chgo., 1968; MA, Memphis State U., 1976; PhD, U. Ga., 1983. RN; cert. tchr., Mo., Calif.; lic. real estate agt., Calif. Tchr. Augusta (Ga.) Coll., 1978-80; designer J.T. Interiors, Athens, Ga., 1984, Hallmark Interiors, Los Angeles, 1985; tchr. Woodbury U., Los Angeles, 1985—; prin. Intraspace Design, Los Angeles, 1986—. V.p. Friends of Hollyhock (Frank Lloyd Wright) Ho., Los Angeles, 1986—. Mem. Am. Soc. Interior Designers, Soc. Archtl. Historians (treas. 1986—), Coll. Art Assn., Alpha Lambda Delta, Sigma Theta Tau. Avocations: growing orchids, jogging, camping. Office: Stevenson-Dilbeck Residential Inc 740 E Green St Pasadena CA 91101

PETERS, LINDA LAW, lawyer; b. Nashua, N.H., Sept. 27, 1951; d. Arthur E. and Sophie T. (Stanulis) Law; m. William A. Peters. Bar: Calif., U.S. Dist Ct. (no., ea., so. dists.) Calif. Atty. Calif. Dept. Indsl. Relations, San Francisco, 1984—. Office: Calif Dept Indsl Relations 525 Golden Gate Room 614 San Francisco CA 94102

PETERS, RAYMOND ROBERT, banker; b. Concord, Calif., Sept. 14, 1942; s. Robert V. and Pegi M. (Carr) P.; m. Nancy Choy; children: Angel, Ray, Matthew. BBA, U. Oreg., 1964. Head customer securities Bank of Am., San Francisco, 1969-71, Eurocurrency and fgn. exchange mgr., London, 1971-72, San Francisco, 1972-76, sr. v.p., head offshore funds, 1976-85, sr. v.p. head treasury, 1985—; mem. fgn. exchange com. N.Y. Fed. Res. Bank, 1978-87, chmn., 1984-85; mem. Chgo. Merc. Exchange, 1987—; mem. Chgo. Bd. Trade, 1987—; cons. on fgn. currency, offshore banking matters U.S. Fed. Res., fgn. central banks. Served to lt. USN, 1964-68. Office: Bank of Am Treasury Div 555 California St Suite 3170 San Francisco CA 94104

PETERS, ROXANNE LEIGH, nurse practitioner, consultant; b. Gillette, Wyo., Sept. 11, 1954; d. Leonard Andrew and Margaret Rose (DeGering) McCullough; m. Michael James Thiry, Dec. 27, 1975 (div. Aug. 1978); m. John Peters, Oct. 28, 1978; 1 child, Mandi. B.A. in Nursing, Augustana Coll., Sioux Falls, S.D., 1976; cert. nurse practitioner U. N.D., 1978. R.N., Wyo.; cert. physicians asst. Nurse, Crook County Meml. Hosp., Sundance, Wyo., 1976-77; nurse practitioner So. Nev. Meml. Hosp., Las Vegas, 1978, Advanced Health Systems, Sundance, 1978-82; v.p., cons. Med. Emergency Rescue Cons., Sundance, 1981—; bus. mgr., patient edn. coordinator N.W. Wyo. Med. Ctr., Sundance, 1986—; cons. Parachute Med. Ruscue Service, Kalamazoo, Mich., 1981, Refugee Relief Internat., Boulder, Colo., 1983—. Treas., trustee Crook County Sch. Dist., Sundance, 1982-85; chmn. Crook County unit Am. Cancer Soc., Cheyenne, Wyo., 1983—; trustee Bd. Coop. Ednl. Services, Gillette, 1982-85, vice chmn., 1984-85; bd. dirs. Crook County Family Violence and Sexual Assault Services, 1985—, vice chmn., vol. trainer. Kellogg Found. grantee, 1977. Fellow Wyo. Assn. Physician Assts. (bd. dirs. 1978); mem. Am. Acad. Physicians Assts., Am. Pub. Health Assn. Republican. Home: PO Box 1070 Sundance WY 82729 Office: NE Wyo Med Ctr 301 Main St Sundance WY 82729

PETERSCHMIDT, JAMES JOHN, air force officer, lawyer; b. Tulsa, July 29, 1941; s. John Edward and Romilda G. (Tenoever) P.; m. Drenda Lea Stout, May 30, 1969 (dec.). BA cum laude, U. Notre Dame, 1963; MBA summa cum laude, Okla. State U., 1970; LLD, U. Tulsa, 1979. Bar: Okla. 1979, U.S. Ct. Appeals (10th cir.) 1979. Commd. USAF, 1963, advanced through grades to col., 1986; asst. to pres. Pepsico Trans/NTC, Tulsa, 1970-75; pres. Sterling Ventures, Inc., Tulsa, 1978—; sole practice law Okla., and Colo., 1979—. Mem. Presdl. Task Force, Washington, 1980-86. Mem. Okla. Bar Assn., Tulsa Bar Assn., Air Force Assn., Res. Officer Assn. (nat. staff 1981-85). Republican. Roman Catholic. Home: 5755 S Kittredge Ct Aurora CO 80015 Office: ARPC/XP Denver CO 80280-5000

PETERSELL, JEFFREY CURTIS, chemist; b. Pueblo, Colo., Jan. 7, 1958; s. John Petersell. BS, U. So. Colo., 1979. Engring. and sci. asst. I Sandia Nat. Labs., Albuquerque, 1980; analytical chemist Rockwell Internat., Golden, Colo., 1980-83, sr. research engr., 1983—. scouting coordinator Boy Scouts Am. explorers post in engring., Westminster, Colo., 1984-85. Mem. Colo. Water Quality Analysts Assn., Am. Chem. Soc. (assoc.), Div. Environ. Chemistry of Am. Chem. Soc., Ion Chromatography Users Group. Avocations: karate, skiing, racquetball, photography, hiking. Home: 9246 Pierce St

Westminster CO 80020 Office: Rockwell Internat Rocky Flats Plant PO Box 460 Bldg 881 Golden CO 80402-0464

PETERSEN, A. LEE, lawyer; b. Murray, Utah, June 6, 1930; s. Franklin H. and Myrtle (Jensen) P.; m. Cynthia Z. Dalley, Mar. 4, 1961 (div. Sept. 1974); children—Kirsten Marie, Jared Franklin, Eric John, Adam Lewis, Mark Haydn, Amanda Simone. A.B., Brigham Young U., 1955; J.D., NYU, 1959. Bar: Utah 1960. Law clk., assoc. Monroe J. Paxman, Provo, Utah 1959-60; assoc. Thacher, Proffit, Priser, Crawley & Wood, N.Y.C., 1960-62; sole practice, Fillmore, Utah, 1962-68; asst. U.S. atty. Dist. Alaska, 1968-75; mem. Gregg, Fraties, Petersen, Page & Baxter, 1975-77, Fraties & Petersen, 1977-78; sole practice, Anchorage, 1978-84, ptnr. Law Offices of A. Lee Petersen, P.C., 1987—; of counsel Cummings & Routh, P.C., 1984-86; atty. fin. center br. 1st Nat. Bank, Ketchikan, Alaska, 1976-78; atty. Flowell Electric Assn., 1962-68; city atty. Fillmore, 1964-68, Whittier, Alaska, 1976-77; pres., dir. INI Builders, Inc., 1984—. Republican party legis. dist. chmn., 1965-68, voting dist. chmn., 1966-68; bd. dirs. Fillmore Indsl. Found., 1966-68. Mem. So. Utah Bar Assn. (pres. elect 1967), Fed. Bar Assn., Utah Bar Assn., Assn. Trial Lawyers Am., Alaska Bar Assn., ABA, N.Y. State Bar, Fillmore C. of C. (past dir., sec.). Office: 1113 W Fireweed Ln Suite 204 Anchorage AK 99503

PETERSEN, BENT EDVARD, mathematician, educator; b. Copenhagen, July 31, 1942; came to U.S., 1964; s. Edvard Valdemar and Grethe Julie (Larsen) P.; m. Marguerite Kathleen Anne McCrindle, Aug. 21, 1965; children: Erik, Poul, Kirsten. BS, U. B.C., Vancouver, Can., 1964; PhD, MIT, 1968. Asst. prof. math. Oreg. State U., Corvallis, 1968-74, assoc. prof. math., 1974-80, prof. math., 1980—; vis. mem. Inst. Advanced Study, Princeton, N.J., 1973-74; guest scientist Internat. Atomic Energy Agy., Trieste, Italy, 1975. Author: Introduction to the Fourier Transform and Pseudo-differential Equations, 1983. Mem. Am. Math. Soc., Math. Assn. Am., Sigma Xi. Office: Oreg State U Dept Math Corvallis OR 97331-4605

PETERSEN, DANIEL CARL, management consultant; b. Omaha, Mar. 4, 1931; s. John Peter and Ebba Julianna (Sorensen) P.; B.S., Iowa State U., 1952; M.S. in Psychology, U. Nebr., 1972; Ed.D. in Organizational Behavior, U. No. Colo., 1980; m. Nadyne Alley, Sept. 14, 1951; children—Susan, Patricia, Thomas. Cons., Employers Ins. of Wausau, 1954-62, tng. dir., 1962-66, mgr., 1966-67; asst. v.p. Indsl. Indemnity Co., 1967-69; dir. loss control Allstate Ins. Co., 1969-70, cons., 1970-72; dir. loss control Nationwide Ins. Co., 1972-75; dir. grad. program U. Ariz., Tucson, 1975-77; asso. prof. indsl. scis. and microbiology Colo. State U., Ft. Collins, 1977-80; mgmt. cons. in safety and organizational behavior, Tucson, 1980—; tchr. various univs. Served to 1st lt. C.E., U.S. Army, 1952-54. Registered profl. engr., Calif.; cert. safety profl., Bd. Cert./Profl. Safety Profls. Mem. Am. Soc. Safety Engrs. (v.p., dir.), Nat. Safety Mgmt. Soc. (internat. pres., dir.). Republican. Lutheran. Author: Techniques of Safety Management, 1971, rev. edit., 1978; The OSHA Compliance Manual, 1975, rev. edit., 1978; Safety Management, 1975; Safety Supervision, 1976, rev. edit., 1984; Safety by Objectives, 1978; Industrial Accident Prevention, 1980; Readings in Industrial Accident Prevention, 1980; Behavioral Safety Mgmt., 1985, Analyzing Safety Performance, 1980, rev. edit., 1984; Human Error Reduction, 1981, rev. edit., 1984; cons. editor Safety Management series, 1980—. Home and Office: 3431 N Camino Suerte Tucson AZ 85715

PETERSEN, FINN BO, oncology researcher; b. Copenhagen, Mar. 26, 1951; came to U.S., 1983; s. Jorgen and Ebba Gjeding (Jorgensen) P.; m. Merete Secher Lund, Mar. 7, 1979; children: Lars Secher, Thomas Secher, Andreas Secher. BA, Niels Steensen, Copenhagen, 1971; MD, U. Copenhagen, 1978. Intern in internal medicine Copenhagen, 1978-79, resident in hematology, 1980-83; fellow oncology Fred Hutchinson Cancer Research Ctr. U. Wash., Seattle, 1983-85, assoc. researcher oncology, 1985-87, asst. mem. in clin. research, 1987—. Author: Hematology, 1977; contbr. articles to profl. jours. Mem. AMA, AAAS, Danish Med. Assn., Assn. Gnotobiology, Exptl. Soc. Hematology. Office: U Wash Fred Hutchinson Cancer Research Ctr 1124 Columbia St Seattle WA 98104

PETERSEN, JAMES NIELS, chemical engineering educator; b. Great Falls, Mont., July 26, 1954; s. Theodore Peter and Mary Elenor (Murphy) P.; m. Renee Karla Barnes, June 9, 1975; children: Matthew Nathan, Jonathan James, Johanna Danielle. BSChemE, Mont. State U., 1976; PhDChemE, Iowa State U., 1979. Asst. prof. Wash. State U., Pullman, 1979-85, assoc. prof., 1985—; vis. prof. chem. engring. Weyerhaeuser Co., Tacoma, 1980, Chevron Research Co., Richmond, Calif., 1981; cons. Chevron Chem., Richmond, 1982. Contbr. articles to profl. jours. Deacon Grace Baptist Ch., Moscow, Idaho, 1981—. Named Prof. of Yr., Wash. State U., 1985, 87. Mem. Am. Soc. Engring. Educators (Dow Outstanding Young Faculty 1985, activity coordinator), Instrument Soc. Am., Am. Inst. Chem. Engrs., Sigma Xi. Avocations: reading, photography, gardening. Home: 836 N Eisenhower Moscow ID 83843 Office: Wash State U Chem Engr Dept Pullman WA 99164-2710

PETERSEN, JOSEPH CLAINE, chemist; b. Fielding, Utah, Feb. 14, 1925; s. Claudius Neils and Jane Elma (Christensen) P.; Erma Irene Boam, May 25, 1949; children: Brent Claine, Claudia, Warren Lee, Anne. BS, U. Utah, 1952, PhD, 1956. Chemist Am. Gilsonite Co., Salt Lake City, 1956-61; sr. research chemist E.I. duPont de Nemours, Wilmington, Del., 1961-64; project leader U.S. Bur. Mines Laramie (Wyo.) Energy Tech. Ctr. Dept. Energy, 1964—, sect. supr. asphalt research program, 1974-85, disting. scientist, 1985—; mem. adv. com. Nat. Acad. Scis./NRC, chmn. Transp. Research Bd. Coms. Contbr. articles to profl. jours.; patentee nonwoven bonded sheets, pavement antistrip agts. Served with USN, 1943-46. Mem. Am. Chem. Soc. (chmn. Wyo. sect.), Assn. Asphalt Paving Technologists, Sigma Xi, Phi Beta Kappa, Phi Kappa Phi. Home: 1072 Colina Dr Laramie WY 82070 Office: Western Research Inst PO Box 3395 Laramie WY 82070

PETERSEN, KARL ARTHUR, product development engineer; b. Washington, Nov. 15, 1942; s. Perry Harold and Barbara Anne (Pierce) P.; m. Robin Lee Worth, June 2, 1973; 1 child, Eric Lee. BS in Bldg. Scis., Rensselaer Poly. Inst., 1964, BArch, 1965. Product devel. engr. Integrated Ceilings Inc., West Los Angeles, 1966-67; packaging design engr. Kett Avionics, Santa Monica, Calif., 1967; sr. human factors engr. Lockheed Calif. Co., Burbank, Calif., 1967, 71-74; research engr. Santa Ana, Calif., 1967-74; product devel. engr., mgr. Preco Inc. Santa Clara Plastics Div., Boise, Idaho, 1975—. Editor/pub. (newsletter) Classic Jaguar Assn. News and Tech. Bull., 1968-71 (pres.'s award 1968). Pres. PTA Campus Sch., Boise, 1984-86; mem. Snake River Alliance, Boise, 1983—. Mem. Semiconductor Equipment and Materials Inst. (assoc.), Steam Auto Club Am. (bd. dirs. 1968-86; editor/pub./author quarterly mag. 1977-84), Citroen Car Club (bd. dirs. 1968, editor/pub./author monthly mag. 1984—, Golden Quill award 1985). Home: 350 Hulbe Rd Boise ID 83705 Office: Preco Inc Santa Clara Plastics Div 400 Benjamin Ln Boise ID 83704

PETERSEN, NORMAN WILLIAM, naval officer, engineer; b. Highland Park, Ill., Aug. 26, 1933; s. Jens Edlef and Marie (Wenderling) P.; m. Ann Nevin, Aug. 24, 1956; children: Richard Nevin, Robert William, Thomas Marshall, Anita, David Arthur. BEE, U. N.Mex., 1956; MEE with distinction, Naval Postgrad. Sch., Monterey, Calif., 1962; postgrad., Harvard Bus. Sch., 1982. Registered profl. engr., Mass., Calif. Shops engr. Naval Station, Key West, Fla., 1956-59; personnel dir. Bur. Yards and Docks, Washington, 1959-60; pub. works officer Fleet Anti-Air Warfare Ctr., Dam Neck, Va., 1962-64; engring. coordinator Southwest div. Naval Facilities Engring. Command, San Diego, 1964-66; exec. officer Amphibious Constrn. Battalion 1, San Diego, 1966-67; force civil engr. Comdr. Naval Air Force Pacific, San Diego, 1967-70; pub. works officer Naval Air Sta. Miramar, San Diego, 1970-73; exec. officer Pub. Works Ctr., Great Lakes, Ill., 1973-75; comdg. officer Navy Civil Engring. Research Lab., Port Hueneme, Calif., 1975-78, Pub. Works Ctr. San Francisco Bay Area, Oakland, Calif., 1978-80; comptroller, programs dir. Naval Facilities Engring. Command, Washington, 1980-84; pub. works officer Pacific Missile Test Ctr., Point Mugu, Calif., 1984-86; deputy assoc. dir. for plant engring. Lawrence Livermore (Calif.) Nat. Lab., 1986—. Contbr. articles to profl. jours. Bd. dirs. CBC Fed. Credit Union, Port Hueneme, 1984-86, Ventura County United Way, Oxnard, Calif., 1976-78, strategic planning com., Camarillo, Calif., 1984-86; guest mem. Ventura County Assn. Govts., 1984-86. Decorated Legion of Merit; Gallantry Cross (Republic Vietnam). Mem. Am. Soc. Mil. Comptrollers, Soc. Am. Mil. Engrs., Assn. Phys. Plant Adminstrs. (affiliate), Navy League, Oxnard Gem and Mineral Soc. (2d v.p.), Sigma Xi, Lambda Chi Alpha. Avocations: stamp collecting, astronomy, rock hounding. Office: Lawrence Livermore Nat Lab PO Box 5506 L-657 Livermore CA 94550

PETERSEN, VERNON LEROY, communications and engineering corporation executive; b. Mason, Nev., Nov. 3, 1926; s. Vernon and Lenora Eloise (Dickson) P.; certificate Naval Architecture, U. Calif., 1944, cert. in plant engring., adminstrn. and supervision UCLA, 1977; cert. in real estate exchanging Orange Coast Coll., 1978; children—Anne C., Ruth F. Chief, Philippines Real Estate Office, U.S. C.E., 1950-55; pres., gen. mgr. Mason Merc. Co., 1956-62; pres., gen. mgr. Mason Water Co., 1956-62; pres. Petersen Enterprises, Cons. Engrs., Nev. and Calif., Downey, 1962-79, Vernon L. Petersen, Inc., 1980—; pres., chief exec. officer Castle Communications Co. Inc., 1985—; Sta. KCCD-TV, 1985—; installation mgr. Pacific Architects & Engrs., Los Angeles and Vietnam, 1969-72, facilities engr., ops. supr., acting contract mgr. Los Angeles and Saudi Arabia, 1979-82; bldg. engr. Purex Co., Inc., Lakewood, Calif., 1975-79; lectr. plant engring., various colls. in Calif., 1975—. Candidate for U.S. Congress, 1956, del. Republican state conv., 1960-64. Served with AUS, 1944-47. Fellow Soc. Am. Mil. Engrs. (life mem.; named Orange County Post's Engr. of Year 1977, founder Da Nang Post 1969, Orange County Post 1977, pres. 1978-79, Red Sea Post, Jeddah, Saudi Arabia 1980), Internat. Platform Assn., Orange County Engr. Council (pres. 1978-79), Am. Inst. Plant Engrs. (chpt. 38 Engring. Merit award 1977-78), Soc. Women Engrs. (assoc.), AIAA. Mormon. Home: PO Box 787 Temecula CA 92390 Office: Castle Communications PO Box 3669 Tonopah NV 89049

PETERSON, BARBARA JO, public relations director; b. San Diego, Aug. 21, 1943; d. Warner Ernest and Opal Oneida (Weeks) P. Student, U. Houston, 1966, U. Ghana, West Africa, 1970-71; BA, UCLA, 1972, MA, 1975, postgrad., 1977. Jr. publicist Maslansky/Koenigsberg Pub. Relations, Los Angeles, 1980; publicist Mahoney/Wasserman Pub. Relations, Los Angeles, 1980; account exec. Scanlon, Skalsky, Menken Pub. Relations, Los Angeles, 1981; assoc. Henri Bollinger Pub. Relations, Los Angeles, 1982-85; ptnr. Alexander/O'Sullivan/Peterson Pub. Relations, Los Angeles, 1986; sr. account exec. Cooper Communications, Inc., Los Angeles, 1987—. Editor: (mag.) World Series of Poker, 1984—. Chancellor's fellow, UCLA, 1972. Mem. Women In Film, Publicists Guild of Am., Phi Beta Kappa, Phi Alpha Theta, Pi Gamma Mu. Republican. Greek Orthodox. Avocations: music, art, horse back riding. Office: Cooper Communications Inc 16250 Ventura Blvd Suite 335 Encino CA 91436

PETERSON, BROOKE ALAN, lawyer; b. Omaha, Dec. 6, 1949; s. Lloyd Earl and Priscilla Anne (Bailey) P.; m. Linda Jane Harlem, June 30, 1979 (div. 1980). B.A., Brown U., 1972; J.D., U. Denver, 1975. Bar: Colo. 1975, U.S. Dist. Ct. Colo. 1975. Assoc. Garfield & Hecht, Aspen, Colo., 1975-77, Robert P. Grueter, Aspen, 1977-78; ptnr. Wendt, Grueter & Peterson, Aspen, 1978-79; prin. Brooke A. Peterson, P.C., Aspen, 1979—; mcpl. judge, Aspen, 1980—. Chmn. election commn., Pitkin County, 1979—. Mem. ABA, Colo. Bar Assn. (bd. govs. 1984-86, exec. council 1986—), Pitkin County Bar Assn. (pres. 1981-83), Am. Trial Laywers Assn., Colo. Trial Lawyers Assn. Avocations: skiing, surfing, softball, squash, music. Home: 0222 Roaring Fork Dr Aspen CO 81611 Office: 315 E Hyman Aspen CO 81611

PETERSON, CHARLES ERIC, senator, automotive executive; b. Ogden, Utah, June 4, 1914; s. Charles Eric and Dora Ann (Brown) P.; m. Harriet Robison, Oct. 4, 1935; children: Charlese, Joan P. Fisher, Kent D., Steven V. Student, Weber Coll., 1931-33; BA, U. Chgo., 1935; AA, Utah Tech. Coll., 1985. Personnel supr. Kimberly-Clark, Neenah, Wis., 1935-42, U.S. Steel Co., Provo, Utah, 1942-46; mgr. Barbizon Co., Provo, 1946-49; ptnr. Utah Office Supply, Provo, 1949-59; owner, mgr. Chuck Peterson Motors, Provo, 1959-84; senator State of Utah, Provo, 1984—; pres. Utah Auto Dealers, Salt Lake City, 1965. Speaker Utah Ho. of Reps., 1951-55; vice chmn. Utah Bd. Regents, 1969-79; pres. Utah C. of C., 1959, Utah Jaycees, 1957, Chgo. Mission Mormon Ch., 1980-83. Recipient Pub. Service award Brigham Young U., 1978, Presdl. citation Weber Coll., 1980, Quality Dealer award Time Mag., 1973; named Hon. Alumnus Brigham Young U., 1975, Citizen of Yr., Utah County, 1978. Republican. Clubs: Riverside Country, Brigham Young U. Cougar. Lodge: Kiwanis. Avocations: sports, golf, travel. Home: 2737 Edgewood Provo UT 84604

PETERSON, CHASE N., university president; b. Logan, Utah, Dec. 27, 1929; s. E.G. and Phebe (Nebeker) P.; m. Grethe Ballif, 1956; children: Erika Elizabeth, Stuart Ballif, Edward Chase. A.B., Harvard U., 1952, M.D., 1956. Diplomate: Am. Bd. Internal Medicine. Asst. prof. medicine U. Utah Med. Sch., 1965-67; assoc. Salt Lake Clinic; dean admissions and fin. aids to students Harvard U., 1967-72, v.p. univ., 1972-78; v.p. health scis. U. Utah, Salt Lake City, 1978-83, pres., 1983—. Home: 1532 Arlington Dr Salt Lake City UT 84103 Office: Univ of Utah Office of the President Salt Lake City UT 84112

PETERSON, CONRAD ALYN, banker; b. Ong, Nebr., Aug. 17, 1934; s. Kenneth L. and Dorothea (Erickson) P.; m. Mary Beth Hanson, Aug. 5, 1956; children: Julie S., Pamela J., Richard S. BA, Hastings Coll., 1958; postgrad., So. Meth. U., 1970-71. Asst. v.p. Security Pacific Nat. Bank, Los Angeles, 1962-70, v.p., 1970-79, sr. v.p., 1979—. Served with U.S. Army, 1954-56. Republican. Club: Jonathan. Avocation: sports. Office: Security Pacific Nat Bank 333 S Hope St Los Angeles CA 90071

PETERSON, CRAIG MENZIES, psychologist; b. Pocatello, Idaho, March 20, 1941; s. Earl Thormod and Dorothy Elizabeth (Menzies) P.; m. Carol Ann Augustus, Mar. 20, 1980; 1 son, Craig Christopher. Student, Oreg. State U., Corvallis, 1959-62; B.S., U. Oreg., Eugene, 1964, M.S., 1968, Ph.D., 1971. Lic. psychologist, Oreg., 1977. Instr., Idaho State U., Pocatello, 1967-1971; psychology intern VA Hosp., Palo Alto, Calif., 1969-71; clin. child psychologist Lane County Mental Health Clinic, Eugene, Oreg., 1972-73; clin. psychologist Fairview Hosp., Salem, Oreg., 1973-74; sch. psychologist. Vancouver (Wash.) Sch. Dist., 1975—; cons. Wyo. Game and Fish Dept, summers 1985, 87; chmn. symposium Project Normalcy: Programming the Mentally Retarded for Social Integration, Western Psychol. Assn. Conv., 1974, annual conf. Oreg. Assn. Learning Disabilities, 1983-85. U.S. Govt. Rehab. Services Adminstrn. fellow, 1964-66. Mem. Am. Psychol. Assn., NEA. Club: Mazamas Mountaineering (Portland, Oreg.). Democrat. Methodist. Home: 8901 NE 59th St Vancouver WA 98662 Office: 605 N Devine Rd Vancouver WA 98661

PETERSON, DEAN EVERETT, chemist; b. Aledo, Ill., Apr. 14, 1941; s. Edward Lawrence and Marie Elizabeth (Anderson) P.; m. Suzanne Blance Watters, Dec. 27, 1966 (div. June 1984); children: Ann, Mark. BA, Monmouth Coll., 1964; PhD, U. Kans., 1972. Chemist Argonne (Ill.) Nat. Lab., 1963-64, Savannah River Nat. Lab., Aiken, S.C., 1966-67; chemist Los Alamos (N.Mex.) Nat. Lab., 1972—, dep. group leader, 1985—. Category editor Bull. Alloy Phase Diagrams, 1984—; contbr. articles to profl. jours. Named Outstanding Chemist, Am. Inst. Chemists, 1964. Mem. Am. Chem. Soc., Sigma Xi. Republican. Lutheran. Avocation: skiing. Home: 505 Oppenheimer @310 Los Alamos NM 87544 Office: Los Alamos Nat Lab MS-G730 Los Alamos NM 87545

PETERSON, DONALD BRUCE, chemistry educator; b. Erie, Pa., Dec. 16, 1931; s. Dean Potter and Gladys (Lehmann) P. BA, Pa. State U., 1954; MS, Carnegie Inst. Tech., 1957, PhD, 1958. Vis. scientist Argonne (Ill.) Nat. Lab., 1960; sessional asst. prof. McMaster U., Hamilton, Ont., Can., 1960-61; research scientist U. Notre Dame, Ind., 1961-64; acting dean U. San Diego, 1976-77, 83, prof. chemistry, 1964—; tech. advisor U.S. House of Reps., Washington, 1984-85, Calif. State Energy Commn., Sacramento, 1977-78. Contbr. articles to profl. jours. Mem. Energy Adv. Bd., San Diego, 1983-84, Citizen's Adv. Bd. Project SANDER, San Diego County, 1981-82, Task Force 2000, San Diego, 1980-81; bd. dirs. San Diego Conservation Soc., San Diego, 1976-78. NSF fellow, NSF faculty fellow, 1958-60, Am. Soc. Environ. Edn. fellow. Mem. Am. Chem. Soc., Am. Inst. Chemists. Democrat. Avocations: bike riding, weight lifting, music, gastronomy, reading. Home: 1663 Guy St San Diego CA 92103 Office: U San Diego Alcala Park San Diego CA 92110

PETERSON, EDWIN CUTHBERT, counselor, educational administrator, adult educator; b. Sault Ste. Marie, Mich., Feb. 11, 1936; s. Edwin B. and Gladys M. (Cuthbert) P. B.S., No. Mich. U., 1958, M.A. in Sch. Adminstrn., 1965; M.S. in Guidance, U. Wis., 1962; cert. in guidance, U. Mass., 1967; cert. in urban affairs, U. So. Calif., 1972, Ed.D. in Supervision Adminstrn., 1977; cert. in resource mgmt., Indsl. Coll. Armed Forces, 1979; cert. edn. Harvard U., 1985; nat. cert. counselor, 1983. Edn. adviser 507th Fighter Wing, Aerospace Def. Command, Kincheloe AFB, Mich., 1958-60, 327th Fighter Wing, Truax Field, Wis., 1961-62; edn. services officer, 410th Bombardment Wing, SAC, K. I. Sawyer AFB, Mich., 1963-65; chief edn. br. 8th AF Hdqrs, Westover AFB, Mass., 1965-67; chief of edn. and tng. div. Aerospace Def. Command Hdqrs., Colorado Springs, Colo., 1967-72; chief of edn. services div., Hdqrs., Pacific Air Forces, Hickam AFB, Hawaii, 1972—. Co-chmn. 1st Community Coll. of the Air Force Adv. Panel, 1977-78, 83-84, chmn. 1984-85; mem. Veteran's Edn. Adv. Council, Chaminade U., Hawaii, 1972-74. Recipient Disting. Alumni award, No. Mich. U., 1981; Outstanding Service award, Community Coll. of the Air Force, 1979, 85; Career Edn. award U.S. Civil Service Commn., 1971; Outstanding Achievement in Aerospace Edn. award, SAC, 1967, Disting Edn. Achievement award, 1966, Ednl. Achievement award, 1965; award for Meritorious Civilian Service Dept. of Air Force, 1983, Outstanding Individual award Nat. Continuing Edn. Assn. 1986. Mem. Am. Assn. for Adult and Continuing Edn. (v.p. for programs, 1978-79, Hawaii del. 1975-77, Meritorious Service award 1979, Tilton Davis Jr. Mil. Educator of Yr. 1986), Am. Assn. for Counseling and Devel., Assn., Hawaii Personnel and Guidance Assn., Nat. Univ. Continuing Edn. Assn., Phi Delta Kappa. Home: PO Box 592 Honolulu HI 96809-0592 Office: HQ PACAF/DPAE Hickam AFB HI 96853-5001

PETERSON, EDWIN J., state supreme court justice; b. Gilmanton, Wis., Mar. 30, 1930; s. Edwin A. and Leora Grace (Kitelinger) P.; m. Anna Chadwick, Feb. 7, 1971; children: Patricia, Andrew, Sherry. B.S., U. Oreg., 1951, LL.B., 1957. Bar: Oreg. 1957. Asso. firm Tooze, Kerr, Peterson, Marshall & Shenker, Portland, 1957-61; mem. firm Tooze, Kerr, Peterson, Marshall & Shenker, 1961-79; assoc. justice Supreme Ct. Oreg., Salem, 1979—, chief justice, 1983—; bd. dirs. Conf. Chief Justices, 1985—. Chmn. Portland Citizens Sch. Com., 1968-70; vice chmn. Young Republican Fedn. Orgn., 1951; bd. visitors U. Oreg. Law Sch., 1978-83, chmn. bd. visitors, 1981-83. Served to 1st lt. USAF, 1952-54. Mem. ABA, Am. Judicature Soc., Internat. Assn. Ins. Counsel, Council State Bar Presidents, Oreg. State Bar (bd. examiners 1963-66, gov. 1973-76, vice chmn. profl. liability fund 1977-78), Multnomah County Bar Assn. (pres. 1972-73), Phi Alpha Delta, Lambda Chi Alpha. Episcopalian. Home: 3365 Sunridge Dr S Salem OR 97302 Office: Supreme Ct Bldg Salem OR 97310

PETERSON, ELLEN LENORE, accountant, supervisor; b. Elmira, N.Y., Dec. 31, 1949; d. Wilbur Laverne and Elsie Elizabeth (Jensen) P. BA in Chemistry, Whitman Coll., 1971; MBA with honors, MPub. Acctg., U. Wash., 1985. CPA, Wash. Chemist U.S. Testing, Richland, Wash., 1975-79, tech. supr., 1980-81; acct. Quelo, Seattle, 1983-85; mgmt. analyst Metro Transit, Seattle, 1985; accting. supr. United Adminstrs., Seattle, 1986—; bd. dirs. Cases Inc., Seattle, Durabilt Cases Ltd., Burnaby B.C., Can., 1986. Mem. fin. com. Nat. Abortion Rights Action League, Seattle, 1983—; del. Benton County Dem. Conv., Richland, 1980; acct. The Dorian Group, Seattle, 1985-86. Recipient Charles F. Frankland Fund scholarship, U. Wash., Seattle, 1983-84, Arthur H. Carter scholarship, 1983. Mem. Wash. Soc. CPA's, Am. Chem. Soc. (various offices 1977-81), U. Wash. MBA Alumni Assn., Beta Alpha Psi.

PETERSON, FRANK LYNN, geology educator, hydrogeology consultant; b. Klamath Falls, Oreg., May 8, 1941; s. Burton Henry and Elizabeth (Ritsch) P.; m. Barbara Bennett, July 1, 1967. B.A., Cornell U., 1963; M.S., Stanford U., 1965, Ph.D., 1967. Field geologist Climax Molydenum, Nev., 1963; teaching/research asst. Stanford U., Calif., 1963-67; asst. prof. geology U. Hawaii, Honolulu, 1967-71, assoc. prof., 1971-76, prof., 1976—; acting prof. Chapman Coll., 1973, U. Oreg., 1973, U. Colo., 1978; cons. on hydrogeology, 1967—. Co-author: Groundwater in Hawaii, 1981; Hawaii Geography, 1983; Volcanoes in the Sea, 1983; also numerous articles. Fellow Geol. Soc. Am; mem. Am. Geophys. Union, Nat. Water Well Assn., Am. Water Resources Assn., Assn. Engring. Geologists, Hawaiian Acad. Scis. Home: 1341 Laukahi St Honolulu HI 96821 Office: Dept Geology and Geophysics U Hawaii Honolulu HI 96822

PETERSON, GARY ANDREW, agronomics researcher; b. Holdrege, Nebr., Apr. 30, 1940; s. Walter Andrew and Evelyn Christine (Johnson) P.; m. Jacquelyn Charlene Flick, June 18, 1965; children: Kerstin, Ingrid. BS, U. Nebr., 1963, MS, 1965; PhD, Iowa State U., 1967. Research assoc. agronomy Iowa State U., Ames, 1964-67; prof. U. Nebr., Lincoln, 1967-84; prof. agronomy Colo. State U., Ft. Collins, 1984—. Assoc. editor Agronomy Jour., 1979-81, tech. editor, 1981-83, editor, 1984—; contbr. articles to profl. jours. and popular mags. Fellow Am. Soc. Agronomy (Ciba-Geigy Agr. Achievement award 1974), Soil Sci. Soc. Am.; mem. Soil Conservation Soc. Am. Republican. Avocations: reading, hiking, skiing. Office: Colo State U Dept Agronomy Fort Collins CO 80523

PETERSON, GARY JON, engineer, educator; b. Morris, Ill., Oct. 7, 1939; s. Grant Elwood and Gladys Juliet (Pierson) P.; m. Sharon Ann Cazan, Dec. 18, 1965; children—Matthew, Jessica. B.S. in Mech. Engring., U. Ariz., 1968, M.S. in Mech. Engring., 1970. Registered profl. engr., Calif.; cert. mfg. engr., Mich. Grad. research assoc. U. Ariz., Tucson, 1968-70; research and devel. research engr. Hewlett-Packard Co., Loveland, Colo., 1970-78, prodn. engring. mgr., 1978-81, mfg. engring. mgr., 1981-84, sect. mgr., 1984-85, fabricating ops. engring. mgr., 1985—; campus team mem. Accreditation Bd. for Engring. and Tech., N.Y.C., 1975-77; proposal evaluator Mfg. Engring. Edn. Found. of Soc. Mfg. Engrs., 1983—. Author tech. papers and articles. Adv. bd. Met. State Coll., Denver, 1978-82; adv. com. Colo. State U., Ft. Collins, 1981-84, faculty affiliate, 1982-84. Recipient Disting. Service award, Colo. State U., 1983. Mem. Soc. Mfg. Engrs. (sr., nat. dir. 1981—, nat. sec.-treas. 1986—, v.p. 1987—, citation for profl. achievement 1976, Presdl. award 1975), ASME. Republican. Lutheran. Club: Sertoma. Home: 2000 Valley Forge Ave Fort Collins CO 80526 Office: Hewlett-Packard Co 815 14th St SW Loveland CO 80537

PETERSON, GARY LEE, geology educator; b. Fargo, N.D., June 24, 1936; s. Arnold K. and Elsa M. (Wohl) P. BA in Geology, U. Colo., 1959; MS in Geology, U. Wash., 1961, PhD in Geology, 1963. Asst. prof. geology San Diego State U., 1963-66, assoc. prof., 1966-69, prof., 1969—, chmn. dept. geology, 1973-76. Contbr. articles to profl. jours. Mem. AAAS, Geol. Soc. Am., Am. Assn. Petroleum Geologists, Soc. Econ. Paleontologists and Mineralogists, Mensa, Sigma Xi. Republican. Club: San Diego Track. Avocations: running, music, investments. Home: 7605 Jennite Dr San Diego CA 92119 Office: San Diego State U San Diego CA 92182

PETERSON, GEORGE ELLSWORTH, JR., financial executive; b. Bklyn., Apr. 15, 1937; s. George Ellsworth and Marjorie (Day) P.; A.B., San Francisco State Coll., 1960. Internal auditor, plant controller Crown Zellerbach Corp., San Francisco, Miami, Fla. and Newark, Del., 1963-72; internal auditor, controller, corp. center Planning Research Corp., Los Angeles, 1972-76; controller Casa Blanca Convalescent Homes, San Diego, 1976-78, Medevac Inc., emergency med. services, San Diego, 1978-79; pvt. practice fin. cons., 1979-80; dir. internat. acctg. Welton Becket Assocs., Santa Monica, Calif., 1981-83; bus. mgr. Buss, Silvers Hughes & Assocs., San Diego, 1984-85; controller Jerde Ptnrship. Inc., Los Angeles, 1985—. Served with U.S. Army, 1960-62. Mem. Newark C. of C. Episcopalian.

PETERSON, HAROLD ALBERT, electrical engineer, educator; b. Essex, Iowa, Dec. 28, 1908; s. John Albert and Augusta Matilda (Hultman) P.; m. Marion Frances Pray, Apr. 7, 1934; children: Joye Frances (dec.), David West, Gilbert Moseley. B.S.E.E., U. Iowa, 1932, M.S.E.E., 1933. Registered profl. engr. Elec. engr. Gen Electric Co., 1943-46; prof. elec. engring. U. Wis., 1946-75, Wis. Utilities prof. elec. power engring., 1967-75, Edward Bennett prof. emeritus, 1975—, chmn. dept. elec. engring., 1947-67; cons. on elec. power systems analysis and edn. to industry, colls.; sr. Fulbright lectr., W. Ger., 1961; chmn. industry adv. com. on underground power transmission FPC, 1965-66. Author: Transients in Power Systems, 1951; contbr. numerous articles to profl. jours.; patentee in field. Recipient Benjamin Smith Reynolds award for outstanding teaching, 1957. Fellow IEEE (life,

Edn. Gold medal 1978; Centennial medal 1984); mem. Am. Soc. Engring. Edn. (life), NSPE (life), ASME (life), Congress Internat. Grande Reseaux Elec., Nat. Acad. Engring. Presbyterian. Lodge: Rotary. Office: 121 W Montana Jack Green Valley AZ 85614

PETERSON, HOWARD COOPER, tax lawyer, accountant, financial planner; b. Decatur, Ill., Oct. 12, 1939; s. Howard and Lorraine (Cooper) P.; B.S. in Elec. Engring., U. Ill., 1963; M.S., San Diego State Coll., 1967; M.B.A., Columbia U., 1969; J.D., Calif. Western Sch. Law, 1983; LLM in Taxation NYU, 1985. Bar: Calif., cert. fin. planner.; CPA, Tex.; registered profl. Engr., Calif.; cert. neuro-linguistic profl. Elec. engr. Convair div. Gen. Dynamics Corp., San Diego, 1963-67, sr. electronics engr., 1967-68; gen. partner Costumes Characters & Classics Co., San Diego, 1979-86; v.p., dir. Equity Programs Corp., San Diego, 1973-83; pres., dir. Coastal Properties Trust, San Diego, 1979—; chief fin. officer and dir. Imperial Screens of San Diego, 1977—, A.S.A.P. Ins. Services Inc., 1983-85, Juno Securities, Inc., 1983—, Juno Real Estate, Inc., 1983—. Mem. ABA, Interamerican Bar Assn., Nat. Soc. Public Accts., Internat. Assn. Fin. Planning, Assn. Enrolled Agts. Office: 1769 San Diego Ave Suite B San Diego CA 92110

PETERSON, HOWARD GEORGE FINNEMORE, sports executive; b. Presque Isle, Maine, Mar. 23, 1951; s. George Conrad and Valeda (Finnemore) P. Student New Eng. Conservatory of Music, 1967-68, Andrews U., 1968-71, Orson Welles Film Sch., 1971-72, Loma Linda U., 1972-75. Pres., Nat. Ski Touring Operators Assn., 1977-79; exec. v.p. mktg. U.S. Ski Assn., 1979-81, exec. dir., Colorado Springs, Colo., 1981-85, sec. gen. 1985—; dir. Mountain Rescue Service, Inc. Mem. U.S. Ski Coaches Assn. (dir.), Nat. Ski Touring Operators Assn. (dir.), Internat. Ski Fedn. (eligibility com., TV and sponsorship freestyle com.), U.S. Olympic Com. (nat. governing bodies council), U.S. Skiing Found. (exec. dir., trustee). Author: Cross Country Citizen Racing, 1980; I Hope I Get a Purple Ribbon, 1980; Cross Country Ski Trails, 1979; Cannon: A Climber's Guide, 1972. Office: US Ski Assn US Olympic Complex 1750 E Boulder St Colorado Springs CO 80909

PETERSON, JAMES DOUGLAS, telecommunications equipment manufacturing executive; b. St. Louis, May 19, 1948; s. James Algert and Gladys Marie (Pearson) P.; m. Kay Louise Hiniker, Aug. 31, 1974; children: Brian Jerome, Daniel Lloyd. Student, U. Mont., 1965-66; MusB, U. Chgo., 1971, PhD in Biochemistry, 1974. Postdoctoral fellow UCLA, 1974-75, U. Del., Newark, 1975-77; research assoc., adj. asst. prof. Kans. U. Med. Ctr., Kansas City, 1977-79; planner, systems engr. AT&T Bell Labs., Naperville, Ill., 1979-85; project mgr. GTE Communications Systems, Phoenix, 1985—; vice chmn. TIXI-2 Telecommunications Standards Group, 1986—. Contbr. papers to profl. jours. NIH postdoctoral fellow, 1976. Mem. Am. Chem. Soc. Democrat. Mem. Unitarian Ch. Avocations: jazz guitar, folk music. Home: 4909 E Emile Zola Ave Scottsdale AZ 85254 Office: GTE Communication Systems 2500 W Utopia Rd Phoenix AZ 85027

PETERSON, JOHN ALBERT, investment counselor; b. Spokane, Wash., May 26, 1931; s. Albert C. and Dorothy Dee (Moore) P.; m. Janet Fuller, Apr. 27, 1957; children—Claire, John, Robb. A.B., Whitman Coll., 1954; M.B.A., Harvard U., 1956. Vice-pres. Kidder, Peabody & Co., San Francisco, 1959-67, 70-77; v.p., dir. William Hutchinson & Co., San Francisco, 1967-70; pres. Peterson Investment Mgmt., Inc., Spokane, Wash., 1977—. Bd. overseers Whitman Coll., 1968; trustee Joel E. Ferris Found., Spokane, 1981. Served to 1st lt. U.S. Army, 1956-59. Fellow Fin. Analysts Fedn.; mem. San Francisco Analysts Soc. Republican. Office: 1266 Paulsen Bldg Spokane WA 99201

PETERSON, JUDYTH DIANE, accountant; b. Tacoma, Wash., Sept. 16, 1942; d. Roger W. and Edna M. (Alexander) Van Buskirk; m. Norman C. Peterson, June 5, 1965; children—Brandon Eric, Lori Anne. B.S., U. Wyo., 1965. C.P.A., Wyo., Colo., Calif. Staff acct. Bob Kinnison, C.P.A., 1964-65, John Cowan, C.P.A., 1965-67; acct., office mgr. food services U. Wyo., 1967-69; acct. Auxiliary Enterprises U. Wyo., 1969-73; exec. sec. Wyo. Soc. C.P.A.s, 1974-77; pvt. practice acctg., Laramie, Wyo., 1973-79, Niwot, Colo., 1979-81; mng. ptnr. Brolyer, Peterson and Assocs., Laramie, 1978-79; tax acct. Tostevin Accountancy Corp., Monterey, Calif., 1981-82; sr. staff acct. Falge Vance & Wilsey; C.P.A.s, Carmel, Calif., 1982-84; controller Community Pacific Broadcasting Corp., Salinas, 1984—. Co-founder, v.p. Laramie Estate Planning Council; chmn. Niwot Fund Days races; treas. Harvest Baptist Women's Fellowship. Mem. Am. Inst. C.P.A.s, Wyo. Soc. C.P.A.s, Am. Women's Soc. C.P.A.s. Clubs: Zonta, PEO, Soroptomists (treas.), Bus. and Profl. Women. Home: 23 Caribou Ct Monterey CA 93940 Office: PO Box 80011 Salinas CA 93912

PETERSON, KATHERINE NANCY, women's private club executive; b. Weslaco, Tex., Feb. 19, 1929; d. Mumpford P. and Maurice Ione (Erwin) Wilson; m. Clifford Don Peterson, July 4, 1953; children—Rici Lynne, Austin Laine. B.A., U. Tex., 1953. Dir. Colo. refugee program Colo. Div. Employment, Denver, 1980-81, employee relations coordinator, 1981; prin. Conv. coordinator West, Denver, 1981-83; pres. Arrangement Brokers, Denver, 1983; prin. Penrose Mgmt Co., Denver, 1983—; founder, exec. dir., chmn. bd.Holy Spirit Hospice, Denver, 1982—; chmn. bd. dirs. Colo. Dept. Employment Employees Adv. Council, Denver, 1980-82. County clk. Los Alamos, 1964; mem. adv. bd. women's ctr. U. Colo.-Denver, bd. dirs. Colo. Women's Hall of Fame, also chmn. facilities com. 1986—, Woman Sch. Network, also chair, Tribute to Women media event, 1986. Mem. Meeting Planners Internat. (publicity chmn. 1982-83), Travel and Tourism Research Assn., Colo. Soc. Assn. Execs., Exec. and Profl. Women's Council, Women Bus. Owners Assn. Club: Penrose Exec. (pres., chmn. bd., exec. dir. 1984—). Lodge: Daus. of King. Office: Penrose Exec Club 1313 S Clarkson St Denver CO 80210

PETERSON, KEVIN BRUCE, newspaper editor and assistant publisher; b. Kitchener, Ont., Can., Feb. 11, 1948; s. Bruce Russell and Marguerite Elizabeth (Hammond) P.; m. Constance Maureen Bailey, Feb. 11, 1975 (dec. May 1975); m. Sheila Helen O'Brien, Jan. 9, 1981. B.A., U. Calgary, Alta., Can., 1968. Chief bur. Calgary Herald, 1972-75, city editor, 1976-77, news editor, 1977-78, bus. editor, 1978, mng. editor, 1978-86, editor, asst. pub., 1986-87, gen. mgr., 1987—; pres. Canadian U. Press, Ottawa, Ont., Can., 1968-69. Harry Brittain Meml. fellow Commonwealth Press Union, London, 1979. Mem. Can. Mng. Editors (bd. dirs. 1983-87), Am. Soc. Newspaper Editors, Horsemen's Benevolent and Protective Assn., Alta. Legis. Press Gallery Assn. (v.p. 1971-76). Clubs: Calgary Petroleum, Ranchmen's, 100-to-1 (Arcadia, Calif.). Avocations: thoroughbred horse racing; art collecting. Office: Calgary Herald, 215 16th St SE, Calgary, AB Canada T2P 0W8 *

PETERSON, LOREN ROLF, nuclear, electronics engineer; b. Phoenix, Apr. 17, 1937; s. Loren R. and Beatrice (Riggins) P.; m. Susan Nourse, Dec. 22, 1959 (div. Jan. 1983); children: Sharon Lynn, Steven Rolf, Linda Ellen; m. Jan Preston, Jan. 14, 1984. BSEE, Stanford U., 1960; MS in Nuclear Engring., U. Ariz., 1964. Registered profl. engr., Calif. Reactor engr., supr. Lawrence Livermore Nat. Lab., Mercury, Nev., 1964-70, reactor project physicist, 1970-79, prompt diagnostics physicist, 1972-78, reactor safety and human factors project engr., 1979-83; reactor safety and human factors engr. Lawrence Livermore Nat. Lab., Livermore, Calif., 1983-85, electronics field test project engr., 1985—; reactor safety cons. U.S. Nuclear Regulatory Commn. Region V, Walnut Creek, Calif., 1984—; mem. reactor safety com. U.S. Army Combat Systems Test Activity, Aberdeen Proving Ground, Md., 1971—. Author U.S. Nuclear Regulatory Commn. Human Factors Guidance and Human Factors Control Room Revs., 1980-85; editor Dept. of Energy Human Factors Guidance and Human Factors Rev. Plan, 1984-85. Served to lt. (j.g.) USN, 1959-62. Mem. Am. Nuclear Soc., Human Factors Soc., Nat. Assn. Flight Instrs. Avocations: flying, skiing, hiking, fishing. Home: 5193 Diane Ct Livermore CA 94550 Office: Lawrence Livermore Nat Lab PO Box 808 Livermore CA 94550

PETERSON, LOWELL, motion picture camera operator; b. Los Angeles, Feb. 1, 1950; s. Lowell Stanley and Catherine Linda (Hess) P.; m. Deanna Rae Terry, Aug. 2, 1981. Student, Yale U., 1968-69; BA in Theater Arts, UCLA, 1973. Motion picture camera asst. CBS Studio Ctr., Hollywood, Calif., 1977-84; freelance camera operator Hollywood, 1977—; motion picture camera operator Warner Bros., Hollywood, 1984—. Career credits include Blind Ambition, Something About Amelia, Lou Grant, Hawaii Five-O, Scarecrow and Mrs. King (Emmy nomination for best series photography 1985). Mem. Soc. Motion Picture and TV Engrs., Internat. Photographers Guild. Home: 750 S Spaulding Ave Los Angeles CA 90036

PETERSON, LOWELL S., former state senator, rancher; b. Ogden, Utah, July 20, 1937; s. Rulon P. and Naomi (Skeen) P.; m. Kathleen Shurtleff, 1959; children—Dale Lowell, Laurie, Lisa, Lorna, Douglas Shurtleff, Mary Ann, Emily. B.S., Utah State U., 1961. Pres., Bar 70 Ranches, 1966-69; mng. ptnr. Peterson Bros. Herefords, 1971, mng. gen. ptnr., 1971—; mng. gen. ptnr. The Hayloft Restaurant, 1982—; mem. Utah Ho. of Reps. from Dist. 50, 1979-80, Utah State Senate, from Dist. 20, 1981-86. Commr. Weber County (Utah), 1987—; past pres. Utah State U. Young Republicans, Golden Spike Nat. Livestock Show. Mem. Utah Hereford Assn. (past pres., v.p.) Phi Kappa Phi. Republican. Mormon. Home: 4538 S 1725 W Roy UT 84067 Office: Utah State Senate Salt Lake City UT 84067

PETERSON, MARTHA ANGELL, bank executive; b. Nebr., Mar. 28, 1945; d. Robert Geyer and Barbara Patricia (Bartlett) Angell; m. Carroll Floyd Peterson, Feb. 5, 1972; children: Andrew Lars, Wyatt Angell. BS in Acctg. magna cum laude, U. So. Calif., 1967. CPA, Calif. Supr. Ernst & Whinney, Los Angeles, 1967-72; sr. mgr. Ernst & Whinney, San Francisco, 1972-84; v.p., mgr. fin. reporting and acctg. Crocker Nat. Bank, San Francisco, 1985, 1st v.p., mgr. fin. planning and analysis, 1985-86; sr. v.p., chief fin. officer, treas. Midland Am. Corp., San Francisco, 1986—. Chmn. Graphic Arts Council, San Francisco, 1985—; bd. dirs. Jr. League, San Francisco, 1985-86; v.p., treas. Hearing and Speech Ctr., San Francisco, 1975-81. Named Outstanding Career Woman, Bus. and Profl. Women, 1974. Mem. Fin. Execs. Inst., Am. Inst. CPA's (mem. task force 1983-84), Calif. Soc. CPA's, St. Vincent de Paul Soc. (treas., bd. dirs. 1984—, Price Waterhouse & Co. scholar 1967), Beta Alpha Psi, Phi Kappa Phi, Beta Gamma Sigma. Club: St. Francis Yacht (San Francisco). Office: Midland Am Corp 1 Montgomery St West Tower 25th San Francisco CA 94104

PETERSON, MELVIN NORMAN ADOLPH, marine geologist, academic administrator, educator, researcher; b. Evanston, Ill., May 27, 1929; s. Frederick Gothard Walter and Norma Alberta (Johnson) P.; m. Margaret Stewart Forbes, June 14, 1958; children—Katrina Elizabeth, John Frederick Forbes, Bruce Norman Adolph, Valerie Anne. B.S., Northwestern U., 1951, M.S., 1956; Ph.D., Harvard U., 1960. Registered profl. geologist, Calif. Asst. research geologist U. Calif.-San Diego, Scripps Instn. Oceanography, La Jolla, 1960-63, asst. prof., 1963-66, assoc. prof., 1966-71, acad. adminstr. V-VII marine geology program, 1971—, chief scientist deep sea drilling project, 1967-72, program dir. deep sea drilling project, 1973—. Program dir. series: Initial Reports of the Deep Sea Drilling Project, 1969—. Mem. sch. bd. Del Mar Union Elem. Schs., Calif., 1965-77, pres., 1975-77. Served to lt. (j.g.) USN, 1951-54, Korea. Recipient Blue Pencil award Fed. Editors Assn., 1969, spl. commendation Marine tech. Soc., 1970. Fellow Geol. Soc. Am.; mem. Pacific Research Found. (founder, pres. bd. dirs.). Republican. Presbyterian. Home: 1221 Umatilla Rd Del Mar CA 92014 Office: U Calif-San Diego Code A-031 Deep Sea Drilling Project La Jolla CA 92093

PETERSON, NANCY CAROL, music teacher, clarinetist; b. Berwyn, Ill., Jan. 6, 1949; d. Charles William and Emily Frances (Fagulec) Attaway; m. Edward Myron Peterson, June 15, 1969. BA, Calif. State U., Long Beach, 1970, MA, 1972. Cert. tchr., Calif. Dir. music Bert M. Lynn Middle Sch., Torrance, Calif., 1971-79, McGarvin Intermediate Sch., Garden Grove, Calif., 1979-85, Serrano Intermediate Sch., El Toro, Calif., 1985—; prin. clarinetist So. Calif. Philharmonia, Long Beach, 1971-81, Coterie Symphonique, Long Beach, 1980-85, Garden Grove Symphony, 1984—, Capistrano Symphony, Mission Viejo, Calif., 1984—. Mem. So. Calif. Sch. Band and Orch. Assn., Calif. Tchrs. Assn., Am. Fedn. Musicians, Internat. Clarinet Soc. Republican. Avocations: crafts, travel, camping. Home: 25711 Orchard Rim Ln El Toro CA 92630 Office: Serrano Intermediate Sch 24642 Jeronimo El Toro CA 92630

PETERSON, NORMAN CHARLES, electronics company executive; b. Sioux City, Iowa, Sept. 17, 1922; s. John Carroll and Ella Leah (Glasgow) P.; m. Donna June Bleekman, Apr. 1, 1944; children: Nancy Carroll, Sandra Leah. BS, U. Mich., 1943; MS, Calif. Inst. Tech., 1947, PhD, 1949. Scientist Rand Corp., Santa Monica, Calif., 1949-59; dir. program devel. Hughes Aircraft Corp., Culver City, Calif., 1959-69; sr. v.p. ops. I.M.S., Inc., Los Angeles, 1969-70; pres. Communication Terminals-Rapifax Co., Santa Monica, 1971-73, exec. v.p., 1973-77; dir. bus. planning electronics ops. Rockwell Internat., 1977-80; dir. devel. TRW, Inc., 1980-85; cons., author, Santa Monica, 1985—; founder Los Angeles Corp. Planners, 1968, mem., 1968—. Contbr. articles to profl. jours. Trustee Santa Monica Hosp.; ruling elder Presbyn. Ch., Santa Monica, 1955—. Served to lt. (j.g.) USNR, 1943-46. Mem. IEEE, Sigma Xi, Phi Kappa Phi, Phi Eta Sigma. Home: 350 16th St Santa Monica CA 90402

PETERSON, OTIS GRANVILLE, physicist; b. Galesburg, Ill., Nov. 17, 1936; s. Paul Gustav and Elizabeth (Granville) P.; m. Sandra Lou Duke, June 30, 1960 (div. 1973); children: Scott G., Trevor A.; m. Kathleen Gail Moore, Aug. 2, 1975; children: Heather A., Kristopher D., Kirsten C. BS in Engring. Physics, U. Ill., 1958, MS in Physics, 1960, PhD in Solid State Physics, 1965. Sr. mem. staff, group leader Eastman Kodak Co., Rochester, N.Y., 1965-73; staff physicist Lawrence Livermore (Calif.) Nat. Lab., 1973-75; research assoc., mgr. Allied Chem. Co., Morristown, N.J., 1975-79; staff physicist, group leader Los Alamos (N.Mex) Nat. Lab., 1979—. Patentee in field; contbr. articles to profl. jours. Mem. Redesign pub. sch. curriculum com., Rochester, 1972. Mem. IEEE, Am. Phys. Soc., Optical Soc. Am. Presbyterian. Club: Mariners (Rochester) (commodore 1968). Avocations: biking, skiing, sailing. Home: 220 Kimberly Los Alamos NM 87544 Office: Los Alamos Nat Lab MS J564 Los Alamos NM 87545

PETERSON, PAMELA JOANNE, counselor; b. Lake City, Minn., June 22, 1946; d. D.L. and Sherry Paulene (Murphy) Mills. B.A. in Sociology, U. Minn., 1972; M.S. in Rehab. Counseling, San Diego State U., 1980. Established Women's Action Service, program for low income young women in San Diego County, San Diego, 1973; established ctr. for low income minority young women, San Diego, 1974; program adminstr. Youth for Progress, San Diego, 1981, exec. dir., 1982—; instr. rehab. counseling San Diego State U.; substance abuse cons.; pvt. practice counseling. Mem. Am. Personnel and Guidance Assn., Am. Rehab. Counselor Assn. Home: 1230 23d St San Diego CA 92102 Office: Youth for Progress 348 W Market St San Diego CA 92101

PETERSON, RICHARD ARVID, architect; b. Chgo., Jan. 3, 1929; s. Arvid F. and Nellie Peterson; m. Jean Louise MacDonald, Feb. 22, 1958; children: Lisa Jean, Erik MacDonald. Student, Ind. U., 1946-48, Ill. Inst. Tech., 1958-59; BArch, U. Mich., 1952; M in City Planning, MIT, 1961. Project mgr. Wurster, Bernardi & Emmons, San Francisco, 1958; research asst. MIT, Cambridge, 1959-60; assoc. planner Adams Howard and Greeley, Cambridge, 1960; lectr. U. Calif., Berkeley, 1961-63; assoc. prof. Sch. Architecture U. Minn., Mpls., 1963-65; univ. and community planner U. Calif., Santa Cruz, 1966-70; dir. planning and research Ernest J. Kump Assocs., Palo Alto, Calif., 1970-71; prin. Richard Peterson Assocs., Aptos, Calif., 1971—; practitioner in residence, lectr. Sch. Architecture and Environ. Design, Calif. Poly. State U., San Luis Obispo, 1983—. Pres. Camp Fire Girls Council, Monterey Bay, Calif., 1973-74. Served to lt. (j.g.) USN, 1952-55. Grantee Dept. State to South Am., 1960, NSF, 1964. Mem. AIA, Am. Inst. Cert. Planners, Am. Planning Assn., Soc. Archtl. Historians, Urban Land Inst. Office: 8048 Soquel Dr Aptos CA 95003

PETERSON, RICHARD WILLIAM, JR., banker; b. Menominee, Mich., Mar. 30, 1924; s. Richard William and Lillian (Floodstrand) P.; m. Frances Parsons, July 3, 1947 (div. Jan. 1972); children—Richard William III, Mark; m. Beverly Jean Hendler, June 30, 1984. B.S., Ariz. State U., 1949; M.B.A., 1970. Vice pres. First Interstate of Ariz., Phoenix, 1965-77, First Interstate Bank of Nev., Las Vegas, 1977-82; vice chmn. bd. dirs. Continental Nat. Bank, Las Vegas, 1982—; mem. adv. bd. Coll. Bus. Econ. Research, U. Nev.-Las Vegas, 1978-86, Community Bankers ABA Adv. Council, 1984-87. Served with U.S. Army, 1943-45, ETO. Decorated Bronze Star. Mem. Beta Gamma Sigma. Democrat.

PETERSON, ROLAND OSCAR, electronics company executive; b. Bklyn., Jan. 18, 1932; s. Oscar Gustaf and Klara Ingegerd (Lindau) P.; m. Agnes Frances Walsh, Sept. 12, 1953; children: Joan, Lauren, Paul, Michael. BEE, Poly. Inst. N.Y., 1953, MEE, 1954. Registered profl. engr., N.Y. Research fellow Microwave Research Inst., Bklyn., 1953-54; sr. engr. Sperry Gyroscope Co., Great Neck, N.Y., 1956-60; with Litton Industries Inc., Woodland Hills, Calif., 1961—; v.p. advanced systems engring. Guidance and Control Systems div., Litton Industries Inc., Woodland Hills, Calif., v.p. bus. devel., pres.; v.p. Litton Industries Inc.; sr. v.p., group exec. Litton Industries Inc., Beverly Hills, Calif. Regional chmn. Los Angeles United Way campaign , 1985-86. Served to 1st lt. U.S. Army, 1954-56. Recipient Disting. Alumni award Poly. Inst. N.Y., 1986. Mem. Am. Electronics Assn., Inst. Navigation (western regional v.p. 1975-76, Hays award 1982). Roman Catholic. Avocations: skiing, tennis.

PETERSON, RONALD ARTHUR, emeritus business law educator; b. Valley, Nebr., June 21, 1920; s. Arthur Lawrence and Hazel McClellan (Foster) P.; m. Patricia Marguerite North, Aug. 29, 1942; children—Ronald, Kathleen, Patrick, James, John, Thomas, Mary, Joseph. B.A. in Poly. Sci., U. Omaha, 1943; J.D. in Law, Creighton U., 1948; postgrad. U. Wash., 1963-64. Bar: Nebr. 1948, Wash. 1949. Asst. prof. Seattle U., 1963-76, dir. legal studies, 1973-83, assoc. prof., 1976-84, prof. emeritus dept. bus. law, 1984—; dir., resident agt. Lesan Corp., Seattle. Mem. editorial bd. Introduction to Law and the Legal Process, 1980. Mem. Spl. Task Force on Legislation for Wash. system of pub. libraries, 1971-73; founding mem. Seattle Archdiocese Sch. Bd., Western Wash., 1969; mem. St. Vincent DePaul Soc., Seattle, 1984. Served to lt. USNR, 1943-46. Recipient Exemplary Tchr. award Alpha Kappa Psi, 1964. Mem. Am. Bus. Law Assn. (del. 1980), Pacific Northwest Bus. Law Assn. (pres. 1984-85), Beta Gamma Sigma. Roman Catholic. Home: 1625 McGilvra Blvd E Seattle WA 98112

PETERSON, STEPHEN EDWARD, data processing executive; b. Los Angeles, Nov. 28, 1946; s. Duane and Ruth (Sands) P.; m. Carol Ann Slupski, July 20, 1968; children: Christina Marie, Matthew Tyler. B.S.E.E., Calif. State U.-Fullerton, 1976. Programmer/analyst Hunt Foods, Fullerton, Calif., 1974-75; lead programmer Baker Oil Tool, Los Angeles, 1975-76; product mgr. ADP, Arcadia, Calif., 1976-78; systems mgr. Carter Hawley Hale, Anaheim, Calif., 1979-81; v.p. mgmt. info. services Global Services, Anaheim, Calif., 1981-84; regional mgr. info. services Hewlett Packard, North Hollywood, Calif., 1984—. Cubmaster Boy Scouts Am., Anaheim, 1983-86, asst. scoutmaster, 1986—. Mem. Assn. Computing Machinery, Data Processing Mgmt. Assn., IEEE Computer Soc. Democrat. Roman Catholic. Office: Hewlett Packard Co 5161 Lankershim Blvd North Hollywood CA 91601

PETERSON, SUSAN JEANNE, underwriter, educator; b. Sacramento, Aug. 23, 1948; d. Michael Bryte Peterson and Elizabeth Claire (Murray) Berenson. B.A. in English, Dominican Coll. San Rafael, 1972. C.P.C.U. Underwriter trainee Fireman's Fund Ins. Cos., San Rafael, Calif., 1977, underwriter, 1977-79, sr. underwriter, 1979, underwriting program mgmt. analyst, 1979-82, underwriting tech. specialist, 1982—; dir. Line of Bus. Tng., 1983—; tchr. evening adult classes Ins. Ednl. Assn.; leader seminars in career evaluation for employees. Mem. adv. com. Dominican Coll. Citizens Ednl. Bd., San Rafael, 1982-83. Recipient Meml. award Sister Catherine Marie, 1972; named Marin Ins. Assoc. of Yr., 1984. Mem. Soc. C.P.C.U.s (v.p. no. Calif.), AAUW, Nat. Assn. Ins. Women (Merritt Co. Essay award 1981; Region VIII Speak-Off winner 1982; Rookie of Yr. 1982), Ins. Women Marin (pres. 1983-84). Republican. Roman Catholic. Home: 8140 Sunflower Dr Cotati CA 94928 Office: Fireman's Fund Ins Cos PO Box 777 Novato CA 94998

PETERSON, THERISIA LEE, commercial real estate broker; b. Pasadena, Calif., Oct. 19, 1941; d. Nathan Davis and Bonny May (Williams) Whitman; m. Harold Kenneth Peterson, Oct. 14, 1973 (div. Mar. 1980); 1 dau. Lauren Elizabeth. BS in Econs., U. Nev., 1964. Lic. corp. broker, Nev. Purchaser Nev. Dept. Motor Vehicles, Carson City, 1960-67; job devel. and placement specialist Nev. Dept. Human Resources, Carson City, 1967-70; bus. mgr. Nev. League Cities, Carson City, 1970-73; office mgr. econs. dept. U. Nev., Reno, 1973-75; owner T&P Investments, Reno, 1975—; from sales assoc. to ptnr. Lucini & Assocs., Reno, 1977-83, cons. real estate investments, 1978—; comml. div. mgr., cons. Keystone Realty, Reno, 1983-85; comml. real estate broker, cons., 1985—; instr. Realty 500, Reno, 1980-83. Chmn. Nev. affiliate Am. Heart Assn., 1982-84, pres. No. Div., 1980-82, sec. No. Div., 1979-80, SW region rep. Nev. affiliate, 1984—; subcom. chmn. Easter Seals, 1981—, Am. Lung Assn., 1985—; bd. dirs. Community Runaway and Youth Services. Recipient Devoted Service award Am. Heart Assn., 1983, Ann. Million Dollar Club awards, 1978—. Mem. Realtors Nat. Mktg. Inst. (cert. Comml. Investment Mem. 1981, grader, mem. other coms.), Nat. Assn. Realtors, Nev. Assn. Realtors (grad. realtors inst., 1979, Omega Tau Rho award 1984), Real Estate Securities and Syndications, Internat. Real Estate Fedn., Reno Bd. Realtors. Republican. Lutheran. Lodge: Soroptomist (dir. 1979-81). Avocations: skiing, water skiing, hiking and camping, reading, piano. Home: 959 Nixon Ave Reno NV 89509 Office: 401 Ryland St Suite #300 Reno NV 89502

PETERSON, TOMMER JOSEPH, graphic designer; b. Tacoma, Wash., June 19, 1949; s. Sidney Axel and Edna Genevive (Bernier) P.; m. Mimi Sang. Student, Seattle U., 1967, U. Wash., 1968-71. Instr. art. Highline Community Coll., Midway, Wash., 1971-72; graphic designer 405 Cedar Street Studios, Seattle, 1971-72; preparator, exhibition designer Henry Art Gallery U. Wash., Seattle, 1972-74; graphic designer, ptnr. What It Is: Studio, Seattle, 1976-78; curator 1% for Art Program, Seattle, 1975-78; exhibit designer Gideon Kramer Assocs., Seattle, 1975-76; graphic designer, ptnr. Wilkins & Peterson Graphic Design and Mktg., Seattle, 1978—; instr. design The New Sch. Visual Concepts, Seattle, 1982—. One-man shows include N&N Gallery, Seattle, 1975, Traver Sutton Gallery, Seattle, 1983, The Nordic Heritage Mus., Seattle, 1984-85; exhibited in group shows at N.Y. Art Dirs. Club 60th Annual Exhibition, 1981 (Merit award 1981), 1982 (Merit awards), CA-82 The Twenty-third Annual Exhibition, 1982 (award of Excellence), Print Regional Design Annual, 1985, Creativity '85, Lahti VI Poster Biennale, 1985 (award); represented in permanent collections and/or Gallery, Henry Art Gallery, 1% for Art Collection, The Seattle Art Mus. Commr. Seattle Arts Commn., 1978, City of Seattle Bumbershoot Festival Commn., 1987; mem. exec. com. Target Seattle, 1982-83; advt. art program adv. com. Seattle Cen. Community Coll., 1982-83; bd. dirs. and/or Gallery, Seattle, 1978-80; trustee The Artist Trust of Wash., 1987. Mem. Seattle Design Assn. (bd. dirs. 1981-82). Office: Wilkins & Peterson 206 3d South Seattle WA 98104

PETERSON, WAVERLY JANE, chemical engineer; b. Nampa, Idaho, Jan. 4, 1958; d. James Whittaker and Waverly Joan (Williams) H.; m. Ricky Lee Peterson, Oct. 3, 1981. BS in Chem. Engring., U. Idaho. Cert. engr. in tng. Design engr. Exxon USA, Inc., Baton Rouge, 1980-81; plant engr. Chevron Chem. Corp., Kennewick, Wash., 1981-84, process engr., 1984-86, supr. quality control, 1986—. Mem. NSPE, Idaho Soc. Profl. Engrs., Delta Delta Delta. Club: Tri City Alumni (Kennewick, Wash.) (pres. 1984—). Lodges: Order Eastern Star, Job's Daughters (guardian sec., 1984—, guardian treas. 1983-84). Avocations: golfing, sewing, reading. Office: Chevron Chem Co PO Box 6148 Kennewick WA 99336

PETERSON-FALZONE, SALLY JEAN, research speech pathologist, educator; b. Paxton, Ill., Feb. 22, 1942; d. Clarence Eugene and Dorothy Lucille (Stine) Peterson; m. Nicholas R. Falzone, May 17, 1975. BS, U. Ill., 1964, MA, 1965; PhD, U. Iowa, 1971. Research assoc. U. Ill., Chgo., 1965-67, asst. prof., 1971-78, assoc. prof., 1978—; chief speech pathology Inst. Phys. Medicine and Rehab., Peoria, Ill., 1970-71; assoc. prof. med. ctr. U. Calif., San Francisco, 1985—; cons. Rancho Los Amigos Hosp., Downey, Calif., 1985—. Assoc. editor Jour. Speech and Hearing Research, 1984—. Research grantee NIH, 1983. Fellow Soc. Ear, Nose and Throat Advances in Children, Am. Speech, Lang. and Hearing Assn. (cert. clin. competence); mem. AAAS, Am. Cleft Palate Assn. (pres. 1985-86), , Internat. Assn. Logopedics and Phoniatrics, Sigma Xi, Phi Beta Kappa, Phi Kappa Phi, Zeta Phi Eta. Office: U Calif Ctr Craniofacial Anomalies 747 S Medical Sciences San Francisco CA 94143

PETRAKIS, LEONIDAS, petroleum company scientist, educator; b. Sparta, Greece, July 23, 1935; came to U.S., 1951; s. Ismene (Lempesis) Petrakis; m. Lina Contos, June 21, 1959; children: Ismene L., Alexis L. BS, Northeastern U., 1958; PhD, U. Calif., Berkeley, 1961. Faculty research grantee Nat. Research Council, Can., 1961-62; prof. chemistry U. Md., College Park, 1962-63; researcher DuPont Co., Wilmington, Del., 1963-65; sr. scientist Chevron Research Co., Richmond, Calif., 1965-86; sr. vis. lectr. Carnegie-Mellon U., Pitts., 1972-73; vis. prof. U. Paris, 1985; adj. prof. U. Pitts., 1981—. Author: Free Radicals in Syn Fuels, 1983, NMR for Liquid Fuels, 1986; editor and author three books on chemistry for fossil engineering, 1978, 1980, 1984; contbr. articles to profl. jours. Research grantee Dept. Energy, Washington, 1979-83. Mem. Am. Chem. Soc. (adv. bd. 1979-83, officer 1974-78, Pitts. award 1984), Am. Phys. Soc. (officer 1961-85, also symposium organizer), AAAS, NSF (grantee, Washington 1981-85, also symposium organizer), ASI (dir. sci. affairs div. Crete, Greece chpt., 1983), Sigma Xi, Research Honor Soc. of Sigma Xi. Office: Chevron Research Co PO Box 1627 Richmond CA 94802

PETRIE, ALLAN KENDRICK, insurance company executive; b. Buffalo, Mar. 14, 1928; s. William Alexander and Hazel Victoria (Ball) P.; student U. Idaho, 1948-50; M.S. in Program Mgmt., West Coast U., 1978. Vice pres. Western Internat. Ins. Brokers, Newport Beach, Calif., 1979-83; pres. Petrie Ins. Offices, Redondo Beach, Calif., 1983—. Served to capt. U.S. Army, 1945-48. Mem. Am. Soc. Safety Engrs., Wine and Food Soc. So. Calif., Lambda Chi Alpha. Contbr. articles to mags. and newspapers. Home: 27808 Palos Verdes Dr E Rancho Palos Verdes CA 90274

PETRIE, PHILIP JOST, advertising designer; b. Torrance, Calif., Feb. 11, 1955; s. Jost Gordon and Doris Elizabeth (Robertson) P. Student, Santa Monica Coll., 1984-85. Ptnr. Petrie Music, Newhall, Calif., 1968-79; circulation acct. Evening Outlook News, Santa Monica, Calif., 1979-82; designer, cons. Sign Exchange, North Hollywood, Calif., 1982-84; advt. designer, artist Armstrong, Inc., Santa Monica, 1984—. Mem. Marina Del Rey C. of C., Culver City C. of C. Republican. Avocations: classical flute, modern jazz dancing, biographies and autobiographies. Home: 2028 14th St #P Santa Monica CA 90405

PETROV, FERDINAND, fine art restorer, art conservation cons.; b. Tapiosuly, Hungary, July 16, 1930; came to Can., 1965, naturalized, 1976; s. Ferdinand and Maria (Dvorak) P.; student interior design U. of Fine Arts, Hungary, 1951-52, U. Winnipeg, Man., Can., 1969-71; Arts D. in Art Restoration History, Acad. of Sci. of Man, Eng., 1978; m. Szilvia Szody, July 4, 1969; children—Ferdinand, Aniko, Zsuzsi. Apprentice cabinet maker, Hungary, 1945-49; various positions in fine furniture mfg., Budapest, Hungary, 1949-52; asst. interior designer Hungarian Govt., 1952-55; draftsman, cabinet maker and free lance restorer, Switzerland, 1957-65; chief conservator restoration dept. Winnipeg (Man.) Art Gallery, Can., 1966-71; free lance restorer dept. public works Province of Man., 1971-73, Winnipeg, 1971-74, Montreal, Que., Can., 1974-75, Ottawa, Ont., Can., 1976-79; fine and decorative arts conservator Canadian Conservation Inst., Ottawa, 1975-76; pres. Petrov Restoration Gallery Ltd., Vancouver, B.C., Can., 1979—; restored numerous murals and panel paintings; guest lectr. on restoration techniques Chem. Inst. Can., 1973, U. Man., 1973, Winnipeg Art Gallery. Mem. Internat. Inst. Conservation, Can. Assn. Profl. Art Conservators, Arbeitsgemeinschaft des Technischen Museumpersonals. Designer, developer various tools and techniques for art restoration; contbr. articles to profl. jours. Home: 2909 Marine Dr, West Vancouver, BC Canada V7V 1M3 Office: 2448 Marine Dr W, Vancouver, BC Canada V7V 1L1

PETRUCCI, STEPHEN GERARD, lawyer; b. Kalamazoo, Mich., Dec. 2, 1951; s. Gerard S. and Mary (Stouck) P.; m. A. Nannette Nugent, May 28, 1973; children: Angela, Anthony, Matthew. BBA, U. Notre Dame, 1973; MS, Western Mich. U., 1977; JD, U. Denver, 1980. Bar: Colo. 1981, U.S. Dist. Ct. Colo. 1981, U.S. Ct. Appeals (10th cir.) 1983. Strategic and mktg. planning staff Upjohn Co., Kalamazoo, 1973-78; asst. to vice chancellor legal affairs U. Colo. Health Sci. Ctr., Denver, 1979-80; contracts staff Martin-Marietta, Denver, 1981-82; dir. legal affairs, gen. counsel Lear-Siegler, Inc., Denver, 1982-83; shareholder Burg, Aspinwall & Petrucci, P.C., Denver, 1983-85; ptnr. Petrucci & Burk, Denver, 1985—; pres. Pro-Phase, Inc., Denver, 1985—. Mem. ABA, Colo. Bar Assn., Denver Bar Assn., Assn. Trial Lawyers of Am., Colo. Trial Lawyers Assn., Sports Lawyers Assn., Am. Soc. Law and Medicine, Beta Gamma Sigma. Roman Catholic. Home: 6227 E Long Pl Englewood CO 80112 Office: Petrucci & Burk Plaza Tower One Suite 1700 6400 S Fiddlers Green Circle Englewood CO 80111

PETSCHEK, ALBERT GEORGE, physics educator; b. Prague, Czechoslovakia, Jan. 31, 1928; came to U.S., 1938; s. Hans and Eva (Epler) P.; m. Marilyn Adiene Poth, June 25, 1949; children: Evelyn A., Rolfe G., Elaine L., Mark A. BS, MIT, 1947; MS, U. Mich., 1948; PhD, U. Rochester, 1953. Jr. research physicist Carter Oil Co., Tulsa, 1948-49; staff mem. Los Alamos (N.Mex.) Nat. Lab., 1953-68, 1980-81; sr. research scientist Systems, Sci. and Software, San Diego, 1968-71; prof. physics N.Mex. Inst. Tech., Socorro, 1966-68, 1971—; fellow Los Alamos (N.Mex.) Nat. Lab., 1981—; cons. in field. Contbr. articles to profl. jours. Fellow AAAS; mem. AAUP, Am. Phys. Soc., Am. Astron. Soc. Republican. Mem. Unitarian Ch. Home: 122 Piedra Loop Los Alamos NM 87544 Office: NMex Inst Tech Dept Physics Socorro NM 87801

PETTENGILL, MICHAEL KENT, fund-raising executive, market research consultant; b. Barre, Vt.; s. Hardy William and Ruth Urbana (Anderson) P.; m. Constance Judith Swift; children—Michelle, Catherine, Kimberly, John. Student, Mansfield Coll., Washington U.; B.S. in Bus. Adminstrn., U. Central Calif., 1979, M.S. in Health Care Adminstrn., 1981, Ph.D. in Pub. Adminstrn., 1982; Cert. in real estate brokerage, Lee Inst., 1966. Exec. dir. Pa.-N.Y. Chpts. Nat. Found. March of Dimes, 1969-72, adminstr. Central N.Y., 1971-72, regional dir. N.Y.-N.J., 1972-73, exec. dir. No. Calif., 1973-75; v.p. ind. cons. and chief exec. officer American Fund Raising Services, Sacramento, 1975—; v.p. Ask America Mktg. Research, Sacramento, 1980—; exec. dir., instr. market research U. Calif.-Davis, 1984—; dir. Groupe Health Service Plan, Inc., 1977-84. Col. Calif. State Mil. Res., 1979—; Spl. Recognition, Calif. Senate, 1975. Mem. Am. Mktg. Assn., Am. Assn. Polit. Consultants, Direct Mail Fund Raising Assn., Nat. Soc. Fund Raising Execs., Sacramento Valley Mktg. Assn., Nat. Guard Assn. Calif., Sacramento Metropolitan C. of C. Home: 3365 Ridgeview Dr El Dorado Hills CA 95630 Office: 1932 Stockton Blvd Sacramento CA 95816

PETTES, DAVID MOON, social science educator; b. Atlanta, Dec. 20, 1944; s. Thompson Porter and Dorothy (Moon) P.; m. Irma Encinas, Aug. 11, 1973; children: Anthony Moon, Michael Thompson. BA in History, Duke U., 1967; MA in Teaching, Emory U., 1968; postgrad., U. Ariz. Cert. community coll. tchr., Ariz. Social sci. instr. DeKalb County Sch. System, Decatur, Ga., 1968; chmn. sci., math., social sci., adminstrn. justice, health, phys. edn., recreation div. Cochise Coll., Douglas, Ariz., 1968—; mem. Ariz. State Articulation Task Force, Ariz. Bd. Regents, Phoenix, 1985—, Task Force on Community Coll. Instr. Cert., Ariz. Bd. Regents, 1983; researcher, mem. Southwestern Border Coll. Consortium, 1980—. Author articles and monographs on Hispanic students and Mathematics. Dem. cons. for Cochise County, Bisbee, Ariz., 1985-86. Fulbright fellow, U.S. Dept. Edn., 1984, Innovative summer fellow Cochise Coll., 1984, 86; curriculum grantee Southwest Consortium for Internat. Studies, 1986. Mem. Southwest Border Coll. Consortium (research grantee 1981, 83, 84). Episcopalian. Lodge: Kiwanis (bd. dirs. 1985-86, sec. 1986-87). Avocations: fishing, backpacking, running, gardening. Home: 2319 15th St Douglas AZ 85607 Office: Cochise Coll Dept Math and Sci Douglas AZ 85607

PETTIS, SHIRLEY MCCUMBER, former congresswoman; b. Mountain View, Calif.; d. Harold Oliver and Dorothy Susan (O'Neil) McCumber; m. John J. McNulty (dec.); m. Jerry L. Pettis (dec. Feb. 1975); children: Peter Dwight, Deborah Neil Pettis Moyer. Student, Andrews U., U. Calif., Berkeley. Mgr. Magnetic Tape Diplicators, Hollywood, Calif., Audio-Digest Co., Los Angeles; sec.-treas. Pettis, Inc., Hollywood, 1958-68; mem. 94th-95th Congresses from 37th Calif. Dist., mem. interior com., internat. relations com. and edn. and labor com.; bd. dirs. Kemper Group; pres. Women's Research and Edn. Inst., 1979-81. Mem. Pres.'s Commn. on Arms Control and Disarament, 1980-83. Mem. Nat. Women's Econ. Alliance Found. Clubs: Capitol Hill (Washington); Pauma Valley Country.

PETTIT, GHERY DEWITT, veterinarian; b. Oakland, Calif., Sept. 6, 1926; s. Hermon DeWitt Pettit and Marion Esther (St. John) Menzies; m. Frances Marie Seitz, July 5, 1948; children: Ghery St. John, Paul Michael. BS in Animal Sci., U. Calif., Davis, 1948, BS in Vet. Sci., 1951, DVM, 1953. Diplomate Am. Coll. Vet. Surgeons (recorder 1970-77, pres., chmn. bd. dirs. 1978-80). Asst. prof. vet. surgery U. Calif., Davis, 1953-61; prof. vet. surgery Wash. State U., Pullman, 1961—; vis. fellow Sydney (Australia) U., 1977. Author/editor: Intervertebral Disc Protrusion in the Dog, 1966; cons. editoral bd. Jour. Small Animal Practice, Eng., 1970—; mem. editoral bd. Compendium on C.E., Lawrenceville, N.J., 1983-86, editoral rev. bd. Jour. Vet. Surgery, Phila., 1984-86, editor 1987—; contbr. articles to profl. jours., chpts. to books. Elder Presbyn. Ch., Pullman, 1967—. Served with USN, 1944-46. Recipient Norden Disting. Tchr. award Wash. State U. Class 1971, Faculty of Yr. award Wash. State U. Student Com., 1985. Mem. Am. Vet. Med. Assn., Wash. State Vet. Med. Assn., Wash. State Vet. Bd. Govs., Sigma Xi, Phi Zeta, Phi Kappa Sigma (chpt. advisor 1981—). Republican. Avocations: camping, small boat sailing. Office: Wash State U Vet Hosp Pullman WA 99164-6610

PETTIT, HENRY JEWETT, JR., editor, emeritus English language educator; b. Olean, N.Y., Dec. 8, 1906; s. Henry Jewett and Anne Benson (Edwards) P.; student Bucknell U., 1924-25; B.A., Cornell U., 1932, Ph.D., 1938; M.A., U. Oreg., 1934; m. Mary Madelyn Mack, July 18, 1927 (dec.); 1 dau., Judith Walsh; m. 2d, Gertrude Stockton Eckhardt, Apr. 9, 1977. Instr. English, U. Tulsa, 1934-36, Cornell U., Ithaca, N.Y., 1936-38, Yale, 1938-39; asst. prof. English, Beloit (Wis.) Coll., 1939-40; from assoc. prof. to prof. English, U. Colo., Boulder, 1940-72, prof. emeritus, 1972—, hon. keeper of rare books Norlim Library, 1950-62; vis. prof. U. Vt., summer 1958. Served with USNR, 1942-45. Recipient U. Colo. Faculty fellowships, 1948, 54, 60, 66, 69; Am. Philos. Soc. grantee, 1960, 66, 69; Am. Council Learned Socs. grantee, 1963. Mem. Modern Humanities Research Assn. (nat. sec. 1958-63), MLA (exec. sec. Rocky Mountain chpt. 1966-70), AAAS, Naval Res. Assn. Democrat. Clubs: Town and Gown (Boulder); Univ. (Denver). Author: A Bibliography of Young's Night-Thoughts, 1954; A Collection of English Prose, 1660-1800, 1962; The Correspondence of Edward Young 1683-1765, 1971; Annual Bibliography of English Language and Literature, 1942-52; A Dictionary of Literary Terms, 1951; The Authentic Mother Goose, 1960. Editorial bd. Western Humanities Rev., 1950—, Colo. Quar., 1957-77; English Language Notes, 1963-74. Home: 1333 King Ave Boulder CO 80302

PETTIT, PETER ACKER, research library director, minister; b. Bethlehem, Pa., Mar. 9, 1955; s. Alfred Wells and Betty Adelaide (Acker) P.; m. Lynn Freund, Aug. 8, 1976; children: Jennifer Leigh, Sarah Freund. AB with honors, Princeton U., 1975; MDiv, Luth. Theol. Sem., Phila., 1980; postgrad., Claremont Grad. Sch., 1981—. Staff asst. Luth. Ch. in Am., N.Y.C., 1975-76; seminarian asst. New Hanover Luth. Ch., Gilbertsville, Pa., 1979-80; text analyst Inst. for Antiquity and Christianity, Claremont, Calif., 1982-83; cataloguer, interim dir. Ancient Bibl. Manuscript Ctr., Claremont, 1983-84, dir., 1985—; theol. cons. Nat. Conf. Christians and Jews, Inc., N.Y.C. and Los Angeles, 1984-86; instr. Sch. Theology, Claremont, 1986—. Co-author: An Inventory of Race Relations: The Lutheran Church in America, 1976; translation editor: Am. Bible Soc., N.Y.C., 1983-84. Named One of Outstanding Young Men of Am., U.S. Jaycees, 1979; Nat. Merit scholar, 1972-75; Timken-Sturgis fellow Claremont Grad. Sch., 1982-83, teaching fellow Luth. Theol. Sem., 1980-81. Mem. Soc. Bibl. Lit., Am. Schs. Oriental Research, Sigma Xi (assoc.). Democrat. Lodge: Rotary (Found. Grad. scholar 1984-85). Avocation: golf. Office: Ancient Bibl Manuscript Ctr PO Box 670 Claremont CA 91711

PETTITE, WILLIAM CLINTON, pub. affairs cons.; b. Reno, Nev.; s. Sidney Clinton and Wilma (Stibal) P.; m. Charlotte Denise Fryer; children—Patrick Keane, William Ellis, Joseph Clinton. Owner, Market Lake Citizen & Clark County Enterprise Newspapers, Roberts, Idaho, 1959-70, pub., 1959-61; publicity dir. Golden Days World Boxing Champs, Reno, 1970; public affairs cons., Fair Oaks, Calif., 1966—. County probate judge, Idaho, 1959-61; acting County coroner, 1960-61; sec., trustee Fair Oaks Cemetery Dist., 1963-72; dir. Fair Oaks Water Dist., 1964-72, v.p., 1967-68, pres., 1968-70; dir., v.p. San Juan Community Services Dist., 1962-66, 68-72; exec. sec. Calif. Bd. Landscape Architects, 1976-77. Cons. Senate-Assembly Joint Audit Com. Calif. Legislature, 1971-73; exec. officer Occupational Safety and Health Appeals Bd., 1981-82; mem. regulatory rev. commn. Calif. FabricCare Bd., 1981-82; mem. Sacramento County Grand Jury, 1981-82, cons. bd. supvs. Sacramento County, 1985-86. Election campaign coordinator for E.S. Wright, majority leader Idaho Senate, 1968, Henry Dworshak, U.S. Senator, 1960, Hamer Budge, U.S. Rep., 1960, Charles C. Gossett, former Gov. Idaho, 1959-74; asst. sgt. at arms Rep. Nat. Conv., 1956; chmn. Rep. County Central Com., 1959-61; del. Rep. State Conv., 1960. Chmn. Idaho County Centennial Commn., 1959-61. Recipient Idaho Centennial award, 1968, 69. Mem. Assn. Sacramento County Water Dists. (dir. 1967-72, pres. 1970-72), Nat. Council Juvenile Ct. Judges (com. 1959-61). Author: Memories of Market Lake, Vol. I, 1965; A History of Southeastern Idaho, Vol. II, 1977, Vol. III, 1983; contbr. articles to newspapers, profl. jours. Home: PO Box 2127 Fair Oaks CA 95628 Office: 2631 K St Sacramento CA 95816

PETTY, DONALD GRIFFIN, information executive, educator; b. Montgomery, Ala., Nov. 4, 1949; s. William Henry and Ellen Marie (Ford) P.; m. Patricia Marie Sanchez, Sept. 1, 1984. BS in Chemistry, Colo. State U., 1972; MA in Tech. Journalism, U. Colo., 1976; postgrad., Regis Coll., 1987. Geochemist Hazen Research Inc., Golden, Colo., 1973-75; mktg. specialist Tech. Dynamics Corp., Denver, 1976-77; publ. specialist Community Coll. Denver, 1977-78; mktg. coordinator Micro Motion Inc., Boulder, Colo., 1978; info. mgr. Solar Energy Research Inst., Golden, 1978—; instr. Community Coll. Denver, 1977—. County coordinator Colo. Literacy Action, Denver, 1985—; Rep. precinct capt., Denver, 1984—. Named one of Outstanding Young Men Am., Jaycees, 1981. Mem. AAAS, Soc. Tech. Communication (sr.), Am. Chem. Soc., Am. Inst. Chemists. Republican. Office: Solar Energy Research Inst 1617 Cole Blvd Golden CO 80401

PETTY, GUY JAMES, designer, scenic engineer, theatrical consultant; b. Pueblo, Colo., Sept. 8, 1951; s. Walter Lee and Anna Elizabeth (Kilsay) P.; m. Carla Rene Hord, Oct. 6, 1972. BS, U. So. Colo., 1973; postgrad., U. Wyo., 1973-75. Art dir., theater mgr. Lincoln Plaza, Oklahoma City, 1975-76; art dir. Design Concepts, Las Vegas, Nev., 1976-79; freelance art dir. the Design Table, Las Vegas, 1979-83, freelance art dir., producer, 1985—; art dir. Las Vegas Scenery Studios, 1983-85; cons. design Safari's, Las Vegas, Mitsui Greenland, Fukuoka, Japan, Maritz Communications, St. Louis; art dir. Englebert Humperdinck, Hollywood, Calif. Prin. works include: (concert tour) stage design Michael Jackson World Tour, 1979; (stage show) scenic design Mikado 20th anniversary, Tokyo, 1984; (ice stage show) scenic design New Fujiya Grand Opening, Atami, Japan, 1986; (trade show) exhibit design Shell Oil Co., 1986; scenic design local chpt. Muscular Dystrophy Assn., Las Vegas, 1983-85, United Cerebral Palsy, 1984. Recipient scholarship U. So. Colo., 1970-73, Best Show Design award Am. Water Exhibit, Las Vegas, 1984. Mem. Internat. Assn. Theatrical Stage Employees (Local 720). Home and Office: The Design Table 241 N Crestline Dr Las Vegas NV 89107

PETTY, SHARON ELAINE, accountant, hotel/casino executive; Wichita, Kans., Nov. 13, 1943; d. Eldo Beard and Darleen Fay (Reed) Jardon; m. Douglas LaVell Petty, May 27, 1960; children—Scott, Eric. Student U. Nev.-Las Vegas, 1972. Chief acct. Community Chevrolet, Las Vegas, 1962-64; corp. acct. auto sales and leasing firms, Las Vegas, 1964-73; controller Aladdin Hotel Corp., Las Vegas, 1973-80, Maxim Hotel/Casino, Las Vegas, 1980-86, Palace Sta. Hotel/Casino, Las Vegas, 1986—; guest lectr. hotel adminstrn. U. Nev.-Las Vegas. Mem. 2d Amendment Found.; mem. Christ Episcopal Ch., Las Vegas; bd. dirs. Statewide Credit Union, Las Vegas. Recipient Cert. of Achievement, Chrysler Inst., 1969; acctg. honor award, Chrysler Leasing System, 1970, 71, 72. Mem. Internat. Assn. Hospitality Accts. (pres. Las Vegas chpt. 1980), Nat. Com. on Gaming. Republican. Home: 4725 S Pearl St Las Vegas NV 89121

PETYAK, FRANK MICHAEL, sales executive; b. Gallitzin, Pa., June 20, 1945; s. Michael J. and Stella E. (Zonts) P. BSBA, George Mason U., 1972. Project mgr. Dept. Def., Washington, 1972-77; mktg. mgr. GMS/IBS, Phoenix, 1978-82, ATV Systems, Santa Ana, Calif., 1982-83; western regional mgr. Secom Gen., Santa Ana, Calif., 1983-84; dir. worldwide sales Pick Systems, Irvine, Calif., 1984—. Contbr. numerous articles on mktg. to profl. jours. Mem. World Trade Assn. Office: Pick Systems 1691 Browning Irvine CA 92714

PETZEL, FLORENCE ELOISE, educator; b. Crosbyton, Tex., Apr. 1, 1911; d. William D. and A. Eloise (Punchard) P.; Ph.B., U. Chgo., 1931, A.M., 1934; Ph.D., U. Minn., 1954. Instr., Judson Coll., 1936-38; vis. instr. Tex. State Coll. for Women, 1937; asst. prof. textiles Ohio State U., 1938-48; asso. prof. U. Ala., 1950-54; prof. Oreg. State U., 1954-61, 67-75, 77, prof. emeritus, 1975—, dept. head, 1954-61, 67-75; prof., div. head U. Tex., 1961-63; prof. Tex. Tech U., 1963-67; vis. prof. Wash. State U., 1967. Effie I. Raitt fellow, 1949-50. Mem. Seattle Art Mus., Oreg. Art Mus., Textile Mus., Met. Opera Guild, San Francisco Opera Assn., Portland Opera Assn. Sigma Xi, Phi Kappa Phi, Omicron Nu, Iota Sigma Pi, Sigma Delta Epsilon. Author articles in field. Home: 730 NW 35th St Corvallis OR 97330

PETZOLD, HORST WILLY, aviation research executive; b. Leipzig, German Dem. Republic, Feb. 21, 1923; came to U.S., 1962; m. Margarete Gertrud Reher, Jan. 20, 1948; 1 child, Gunnar Horst. Student, numerous flying schs., German Dem. Republic, Indsl. Engring. Sch., German Dem. Republic. Pres. World Import, Canada, 1955-60; cons. Canada, U.S., 1962—, writer, 1955—; gen. mgr. Kasper Aircraft, Seattle, 1971-81; pres. Aviation Research, Seattle, 1962—. Contbr. articles to profl. jours. Adv. mem. Rep. Party, Washington. Served with German Air Force, 1939-45. Mem. Am. Security Council, German Am. Nat. Congress, Aviation Space Writers Assn. Avocations: writing, reading, flying, polit. and hist. research. Home and Office: 3935 SW Elmgrove Seattle WA 98136

PEURA, ROBIN ELAYNE, speech-language pathologist; b. Bowling Green, Ohio, Sept. 21, 1960; d. Robert Edward and Eleanore (Fuller) P. EdB, Bowling Green State U., 1982, MA, 1983. Speech-lang. pathologist Albuquerque Pub. Schs., 1983—, Inspeech Inc., Albuquerque, 1985; head swimming coach Albuquerque Pub. Schs., 1983—. Mem. Am. Speech Lang. and Hearing Assns. (cert.). Home: 337 Garcia NE Albuquerque NM 87123 Office: Albuquerque Pub Schs General Somervell NE Albuquerque NM 87123

PEVAR, ALAN MARK, counselor, psychotherapist, educator, consultant; b. Bklyn., Nov. 1, 1950; s. Irving and Florence (Roff) P.; m. Cindy, Jan. 17, 1976. B.A. in Psychology, Richmond Coll., CUNY, 1975; M.A. in Psychology, New Sch. Social Research, 1977. Lic. marriage, family and child counselor; registered hypnotherapist. Counselor, Transitional Services N.Y., Inc., Queens Village, 1977-79; team supr. Builders for Family and Youth, Community Support System, Rockaway, N.Y., 1979-80; client program coordinator, counselor Kern Regional Ctr., Bakersfield, Calif., 1980—; practice marriage, family and child counseling and therapy, Bakersfield, 1981—; instr. psychology Bakersfield Coll., 1981—; cons. and therapist Arthritis Assn. Kern County; expert examiner Bd. Behavioral Sci. Examiners. Mem. Calif. Assn. Marriage and Family Therapists, Am. Personnel and Guidance Assn. Contbr. articles to profl. jours. Home: 3904 Casey Ct Bakersfield CA 93309 Office: 2104 24th St Suite 3 Bakersfield CA 93301

PEVEY, TAMI LEE, stockbroker, small business executive; b. Englewood, Colo., Nov. 19, 1959; d. James Louis and Mona Lee (Higgins) Guilliams; m. Jackie Dean Pevey Jr., Mar. 2, 1985; 1 child, Jackie Dean III. AS, Arapahoe Community Coll., 1979. Fin. sec. 1st Affiliated Securities, San Diego, 1982-83; sales asst. Gattini & Co. and Wall St. West, Englewood, 1983; adminstrv. asst. Atlantis Securities, Aurora, Colo., 1984; corp. sec. Allied Capital Group, Englewood, 1984-85; rep. Royce Park Investments, Denver, 1985; pres. Forget-Me-Knot Greetings, Aurora, 1985—; cons. J.B. Power Securities, Denver, 1984-85. Mem. Nat. Assn. Female Execs., Am. Soc. Clin. Pathologists. Republican. Avocations: books, horses, dancing. Office: Forget-Me-Knot Greetings 3124 S Parker Rd #C314 Aurora CO 80014

PEWITT, NELSON DOUGLAS, physicist; b. Winter Haven, Fla., Dec. 31, 1940; s. Kenton T. and Edith M. (Norwood) P.; m. Bettie Sue Woods, Oct. 20, 1962; children: Leslie Paige, Douglas Woods. BS, U. W. Fla., 1969; PhD, Fla. State U., 1974. Chief sci. and space OMB, Washington, 1976-79; dep. dir. Office of Energy Research DOE, Washington, 1979-81; asst. dir. Sci. Office The White House, Washington, 1981-84; v.p. Western Research, San Diego, 1984-85, Sci. Applications Internat. Corp., San Diego, 1985—. Served to capt. USNR, 1961-85, Vietnam. Recipient Meritorious Exec. medal, Pres. of U.S., 1980, Outstanding Service award Sec. of Energy, Washington, 1981. Mem. U.S. Naval Inst., Am. Phys. Soc., AAAS. Republican. Office: Sci Applications Internat Corp Campus Point Dr San Diego CA 92121

PEXTON, LARRY HARDING, JR., electronics company executive, designer; b. Boston, Sept. 23, 1946; s. Larry H. and Margaret (Mugrage) P.; m. Margaret McCasland, June 20, 1968 (div. 1977); one child, Anne; m. Janice A. Kuranz, Sept. 5, 1980; children: Christopher, Nicole. BA, Cornell U., 1964; postgrad., U. Stockholm, 1969; MA, U. Pitts., 1971. Owner Midline Bar, Ithaca, N.Y., 1972-76; gen. mgr. Aspen (Colo.) Audio Clinic, 1977-78; pres. Aspen Recreational Products (Triad Design), Carbondale, Colo., 1979-86; bd. dirs. Carbondale Econ. Devel. Corp., 1984—. Mem. Audio Engring. Soc., Electronic Industries Assn. (Design and Engring. Showcase award 1982, 84, 85, 86). Avocations: music, skiing, flying, motorcycling. Office: Triad Design Inc 302 NE 2d Troutdale OR 97060

PEXTON, PATRICIA DEBRY, marketing executive; b. Salt Lake City, Mar. 19, 1942; d. James John and Ruby (Robison) DeBry; m. Robert Milton Pexton, Aug. 16, 1963; children: Stacey, Allison, Jonathan Robert, Jamison Bryan. BA in Psychology cum laude, U. Utah, 1986. TV model, fashion coordinator, spl. events dir. Z.C.M.I., Salt Lake City, 1960-67; sales rep., model True Earth Cosmetics, N.Y.C., 1974; v.p. DeBry-Pexton Inc., Salt Lake City, 1977-86, pres., 1986—, also bd. dirs.; pres. Chambre d'Ami div. DeBry-Pexton, Salt Lake City, 1986—. Author: The Three Ingredient Cookbook, 1982; co-author: Factory Outlet Shopping Guide for New York, New Jersey and New England, 1971. Active Cache Valley Sheltered Workshop, Logan, Utah, 1977—. Mem. Psi Chi. Republican. Mormon. Avocations: reading, yoga, cooking, collage. Office: DeBry-Pexton Inc 2949 S 300 West Salt Lake City UT 84115

PFAELZER, MARIANA R., fed. judge; b. 1926. A.B., U. Calif.; LL.B., UCLA Sch. Law. Bar: bar 1958. Judge U.S. Dist. Ct. for Dist. Central Calif. Mem. Am. Bar Assn. Office: US Dist Ct 312 N Spring St Los Angeles CA 90012

PFANSTIEL, SCOTT DANIEL, graphics engineer; b. Feb. 8, 1959; s. Rudolph D. and Marie T. (Angelillo) P. AAS, Rochester Inst. Tech., 1980, BS, 1981. Graphics engr. info. products div. Xerox Corp., Fremont, Calif., 1981—. Roman Catholic. Avocations: flying, photography. Home: 29 Lone Tree Ct Milpitas CA 95035 Office: Xerox Corp Info Products div 901 Page Ave Box 5030 Fremont CA 94537

PFEIFFER, ROBERT JOHN, business executive; b. Suva, Fiji Islands, Mar. 7, 1920; came to U.S., 1921, naturalized, 1927; s. William Albert and Nina (MacDonald) P.; m. Mary Elizabeth Worts, Nov. 29, 1945; children—Elizabeth Pfeiffer Tumbas, Margaret Pfeiffer Colbrandt, George, Kathleen. Grad. high sch., Honolulu, 1937; DSc (hon.), Maine Maritime Acad.; HumD (hon.), U. Hawaii. With Inter-Island Steam Navigation Co., Ltd., Honolulu, (re-organized to Overseas Terminal Ltd. 1950); With (merged into Oahu Ry. & Land Co. 1954), 1937-55, v.p., gen. mgr., 1950-54, mgr. ship agy. dept., 1954-55; v.p., gen. mgr. Pacific Cut Stone & Granite Co., Inc., Alhambra, Calif., 1955-56, Matcinal Corp., Alameda, Calif., 1956-58; mgr. div. Pacific Far East Line, Inc., San Francisco, 1958-60; with Matson Nav. Co., San Francisco, 1960—; v.p. Matson Nav. Co., 1966-70, sr. v.p., 1970-71, exec. v.p., 1971-73, pres., 1973-79, chmn. bd., chief exec. officer, 1979-84, 85—, chmn. bd., pres., chief exec. officer, 1984; v.p. The Matson Co., San Francisco, 1968-70; pres. The Matson Co., 1970-82; v.p., gen. mgr. Matson Terminals, Inc., San Francisco, 1960-62; pres. Matson Terminals, Inc., 1962-70, chmn. bd., 1970-79; chmn. bd. Matson Services Co., 1973-79, Matson Agys., Inc., 1973-78; sr. v.p. Alexander & Baldwin, Inc., Honolulu, 1973-77; exec. v.p. Alexander & Baldwin, Inc., 1977-79, pres., 1979-80, chmn., pres., chief exec. officer, 1980-84, chmn., chief exec.

officer, 1985—, also dir.; bd. dirs. A&B Devel. Co. (Calif.), A&B Properties, Inc., McBryde Sugar Co. Ltd., First Hawaiian Inc., First Hawaiian Bank, Pacific Resources, Inc., Calif. and Hawaiian Sugar Co., Wailea Devel. Co. Inc., also pres. Past chmn. maritime transp. research bd. Nat. Acad. Sci.; former mem. select com. for Am. Mcht. Marine Seamanship Trophy Award, commn. sociotech. systems NRC.; Mem. adv. com. Joint Maritime Congress; trustee Pacific Tropical Bot. Garden, Bishop Mus., U. Hawaii Found., Pacific Aerospace Mus., also bd. dirs.; mem. Japan-Hawaii Econ. Council, Army Civilian Adv. Group; vice-chmn. Hawaii Maritime Ctr.; mem. adv. council Girl Scouts U.S. Council of the Pacific. Served to lt. USNR, World War II; comdr. Res. ret. Mem. Nat. Assn. Stevedores (past pres.), Internat. Cargo Handling Coordination Assn. (past pres. U.S. nat. com.), Propeller Club U.S. (past pres. Honolulu), Nat. Def. Transp. Assn., Conf. Bd., 200 Club, Long Beach C. of C., Portland C. of C., Oakland C. of C., Richmond (Calif.) C. of C., Seattle C. of C., Kauai C. of C., Los Angeles C. of C., San Francisco C. of C., Hawaii Island C. of C., Hawaii C. of C., Maui C. of C., Am. Bur. Shipping (bd. mgrs.), Aircraft Owners and Pilots Assn., Hawaiian Sugar Planters' Assn. (bd. dirs., mem. exec. com.). Republican. Clubs: Pacific, Outrigger, Oahu Country (Honolulu); Maui (Hawaii) Country, U. Hawaii, Pacific Union, Bohemian, World Trade (San Francisco). Lodges: Masons, Shriners. Home: 535 Miner Rd Orinda CA 94563 Office: 822 Bishop St Honolulu HI 96813

PFLUEGER, JOHN MILTON, architect; b. San Francisco, Aug. 23, 1937; s. Milton Theodore and Genevive (Wendgard) P.; B.S., Stanford, 1959, B.Arch., 1960; m. Lynne Williams, Jan. 23, 1963; children—Peter, John Thomas, Christopher Timothy. Partner-in-charge Pflueger Architects, San Francisco, 1976; lectr. Urban Life Inst., U. San Francisco, U. Colo., 1978; campus architect U. San Francisco, Coll. of Holy Names, City Coll. San Francisco; ptnr., exec. v.p. Warfield Co., 1984—, Smart Office Co., 1984—. Mem. planning com. San Francisco Downtown Assn., 1971-83. Lic. architect, Calif., Nev., Hawaii. Mem. AIA (pub. edn. com. No. Calif. chpt. 1970-79), NCARB, Constrn. Specifications Inst., Soc. Coll. and Univ. Planning, San Francisco Planning and Urban Renewal, Sierra Club, U.S.C. of C., Audubon Soc., Smithsonian Instn., Calif. Acad. Scis., Soc. Am. Mil. Engrs., Delta Tau Delta. Clubs: Olympic (bldg. com. 1973-78, properties commn. 1979-81), Family (San Francisco). Major works include: Cowell Hall, Calif. Acad. Scis. (Prestress Concrete Inst. award 1969), Creative Arts Extension, City Coll. San Francisco (AIA design excellence award 1974), Fish Roundabout, Calif. Acad. Scis., 1976, Natural Energy Office Bldg., 1977 (Honor award State of Calif.), Batmale Hall, City Coll. San Francisco, 1978, Calif. Farm Bur. Fedn., Sacramento, 1980 (Owens Corning, Dept. Energy and ASHRAE awards), San Jose State U. Library, 1982, Nev. Nat. Bank Hdqrs., Reno, 1982 (ASHRAE award), Performing Arts Ctr. and Fine Arts Mus., Sierra Arts Found., Reno; 8 major bldgs. at Stanford U., including Environ. Safety Facility, 1986; Co-Generation facility and Health and Recreation Ctr., U. San Francisco, 1987; rehabilitation Santa Rosa Ferry Boat, James Licks Bathhouse, 1981, Warfield Office Bldg. and Theater, 1985; major hosps. include Shriners Hosp. for Crippled Children, Walter Reed Army Med. Ctr. (Pre-Stressed Concrete Inst., Dept. Def. design awards 1980). Home: 29 Redwood Dr Ross CA 94957 Office: 165 10th St San Francisco CA 94103

PFORZHEIMER, HARRY, III, computer company executive; b. Cleve., June 6, 1954; s. Harry and Jean (Barnard) P.; m. Barbara Jean Flaig, June 7, 1975; children—Harry IV, Lucas Chase. B.S., St. Johns U., 1973. Vice pres. corp./pub. affairs and adminstrn. Paraho Devel. Corp., Denver, 1977-82; cons. pub., fin. and govt. relations, Denver, 1982-83; mgr. media/pub. relations United Banks Colo., Inc., Denver, 1983-86; dir. corp. communications Storage Tech. Corp., Denver, 1986—. Mem. Pub. Relations Soc. Am., Colo. Press Assn., Colo. Broadcasters Assn. Republican. Roman Catholic. Club: Denver Press. Home: 2704 W 118th Ave Westminister CO 80234 Office: Storage Tech Corp 2270 S 88th St Louisville CO 80028

PFORZHEIMER, HARRY, JR., oil consultant; b. Manila, Nov. 19, 1915; s. Harry and Mary Ann (Horan) P.; B.S. in Chem. Engring., Purdue U., 1938; postgrad. Case Inst. Tech., Law Sch., George Washington U., Case Western Res. U.; m. Jean Lois Barnard, June 2, 1945; children—Harry, Thomas. Mem. Petroleum Adminstrn. for War, Washington, 1942-45; with Standard Oil Co. (Ohio), various locations, 1938-80, pres. White River Shale Oil Corp., 1974-76, v.p. Sohio Natural Resources Co., 1971-80, program dir. Paraho oil shale demonstration, Grand Junction, 1974-80; pres., chmn. bd., chief exec. officer Paraho Devel. Corp., 1980-82; pres. Harry Pforzheimer Jr. and Assocs., 1983—; dir. IntraWest Bank Grand Junction; adj. prof. chem. engring. Cleve. State U. Contbr. articles to tech. and trade jours. Mem. planning adv. bd. St. Mary's Hosp. and Med. Ctr.; bd. dirs. Colo. Sch. Mines Research Inst.; chmn. Wayne N. Aspinall Found. Mem. Am. Inst. Chem. Engrs. (chmn. Cleve. 1955, gen. chmn. internat. meeting, Cleve. 1961), Am. Petroleum Inst., Am. Mining Congress, Colo. Mining Assn., Rocky Mountain Oil and Gas Assn., Denver Petroleum Club, Purdue Alumni Assn., Sigma Alpha Epsilon. Clubs: Army and Navy (Washington), Bookcliff Country, Rio Verde Country. ours. Home: 2700 G Rd #1-C Grand Junction CO 81506 Office: 743 Horizon Ct Grand Junction CO 81506

PFOST, DALE ROBERT, industrial engineering executive; b. Palo Alto, Calif., Apr. 22, 1957; s. Robert Fred and JoAnn (Burr) P. BS, U. Calif., Santa Barbara, 1980; MS, Brown U., 1982, PhD, 1985. Pres. Infinitek, Inc., Sunnyvale, Calif., 1983-85; robotics mgr. Beckman Instruments, Palo Alto, Calif., 1985—. Contbr. papers to sci. jour.; creator laser tape, 1984; inventor automated multi purpose analytical chemistry processing work station. Mem. AAAS, IEEE, Am. Physical Soc. Office: Beckman Instruments 1050 Pagemill Rd Palo Alto CA 94304

PFUND, EDWARD THEODORE, JR., electronics co. exec.; b. Methuen, Mass., Dec. 10, 1923; s. Edwrd Theodore and Mary Elizabeth (Banning) P.; B.S. magna cum laude, Tufts Coll., 1950; postgrad U. So. Calif., 1950, Columbia U., 1953, U. Calif., Los Angeles, 1956, 58; m. Marga Emmi Andre, Nov. 10, 1954; children—Angela M., Gloria I., Edward Theodore III. Radio engr., WLAW, Lawrence-Boston, 1942-50; fgn. service staff officer Voice of Am., Tangier, Munich, 1950-54; project. engr. Crusade for Freedom, Munich, Ger., 1955; project mgr., materials specialist United Electrodynamics Inc., Pasadena, Calif., 1956-59; cons. H.I. Thompson Fiber Glass Co., Los Angeles, Andrew Corp., Chgo., 1959, Satellite Broadcast Assocs., Encino, Calif., 1982; teaching staff Pasadena City Coll. (Calif.), 1959; dir. engring., chief engr. Electronics Specialty Co., Los Angeles and Thomaston, Conn., 1959-61; with Hughes Aircraft Co., various locations, 1955, 61—, mgr. Middle East programs, also Far East, Latin Am. and African market devel., Los Angeles, 1971—, dir. internat. programs devel., Hughes Communications Internat., 1985—. Served with AUS, 1942-46. Mem. Phi Beta Kappa, Am. Inst. Aeros. and Astronautics, Sigma Pi Sigma. Contbr. articles to profl. jours. Home: 25 Silver Saddle Ln Rolling Hills Estates CA 90274 Office: PO Box 92919 Airport Station Los Angeles CA 90009

PFUNTNER, ALLAN ROBERT, medical entomologist; b. Buffalo, May 19, 1946; s. Robert James and Verna May (Colton) P.; m. Sri Hartini Hartono, Aug. 23, 1970; children: Nicolis Dean, Erin Tristina. BA in Biology, San Jose State U., 1969, MA in Biology, 1977. Sanitarian Monterey County Health Dept., Salinas, Calif., 1972-73; vector control asst. Santa Clara County Health Dept., San Jose, Calif., 1973-75; entomologist Northwest Mosquito Abatement Dist., Riverside, Calif., 1975-84; asst. mgr. West Valley Vector Control Dist., Chino, Calif., 1984—; cons., bd. dirs. Consol. Labs., Corona, Calif., 1984—. Contbr. articles to jours. Served with U.S. Army, 1969-72. Mem. Entomol. Soc. Am., Am. Mosquito Control Assn., Am. Registry Profl. Entomologists (cert.), Soc. Vector Ecologists. Democrat. Avocations: sailing, skiing, photography. Office: West Valley Vector Control Dist 5050 Schaefer Ave Chino CA 91710

PHAM, KINH DINH, electrical engineer; b. Saigon, Republic of Vietnam, Oct. 6, 1956; came to U.S., 1974; s. Nhuong D. and Phuong T. (Tran) P.; m. Ngan-Lien T. Nguyen, May 27, 1985. BS with honors, Portland State U., 1979; MSEE, U. Portland, 1982. Registered profl. engr., Oreg. Elec. engr. Irvington-Moore, Tigard, Oreg., 1979-80, Elcon Assocs., Inc., Beaverton, Oreg., 1980—; adj. prof. Portland (Oreg.) Community Coll., 1982—. Mem. IEEE. Buddhist. Avocations: reading, teaching. Home: 10650 SW 33d Portland OR 97219 Office: Elcon Assocs Inc 10550 SW Allen Blvd Beaverton OR 97005

PHANNENSTIEL, RUDOLPH, Chief of police city of Denver. Office: City of Denver Police Dept 1331 Cherokee St Denver CO 80204 *

PHELPS, E. JACK (EUGENE JOHN), financial service executive; b. Royal Oak, Mich., Dec. 15, 1936; s. Marion Eugene Phelps and Rosemary Jean Burger; m. Sharon Lyn Bailey, Apr. 20, 1958 (div. Aug. 1973); m. Mary Joy Phelps, Aug. 12, 1974; adopted children: Gregory Allen, Stacey Marie. BSBA, San Diego State U., 1964. CLU, Chartered fin. cons. Agt. Northwestern Mut. Life Ins. Co., San Diego, 1964-68; ptnr. Phelps & Jessen Assocs., San Diego, 1968-72; pres. E.J. Phelps & Co., San Diego, 1972—. Trustee La Jolla (Calif.) Mus. Contemporary Art, 1983—; bd. dirs. Mission Valley YMCA, San Diego, 1984—; mem. adv. bd. U. Calif.-San Diego, La Jolla, 1983—. Served as cpl. USMC, 1956-58. Mem. Nat. Assn. Accts., Nat. Assn. Life Underwriters, CLU's of San Diego, San Diego Employee Benefit Council, Western Pension Council, San Diego Estate Planning Council. Republican. Lutheran. Clubs: Variety (v.p. 1978-80), 20-30 Internat. (pres. 1972) (San Diego). Avocations: snow skiing, racquetball. Office: 233 A St Suite 1111 San Diego CA 92101

PHELPS, HARVEY WILLIAM, physician, former state senator; b. Pueblo, Colo., June 27, 1922; s. Harvey Jay and Honor Twinet (Wright) P.; B.S., Idaho State Coll., 1946; M.D., St. Louis U., 1949; m. Adah Lucile Godbold, Sept. 1, 1948; children—Castle Wright, Stuart Harvey, Martha Gail. Intern, Brooke Gen. Hosp., Fort Sam Houston, Tex., 1949-50; resident in internal medicine Fitzsimmons Gen. Hosp., Denver, 1951-54; practice medicine specializing in internal medicine, 1954—; commd. 1st lt. U.S. Army, 1949, advanced through grades to lt. col., 1961; chief med. service U.S. Army Hosp., Ft. MacArthur, Calif., 1955-57; asst. chief pulmonary disease service Fitzsimmons Gen. Hosp., Denver, 1958-59; chief dept. medicine U.S. Army Med. Center, Japan, 1959-62; cons. internal medicine to Surgeon, U.S. Army, Japan, 1959-62; cons. pulmonary disease Tri-Service, Japan, 1959-62; chief dept. medicine DeWitt Army Hosp., Fort Belvoir, Va., 1963-65; chief pulmonary disease service Valley Forge Gen. Hosp., Phoenixville, Pa., 1965-66, ret., 1966; dir. inhalation therapy St. Mary-Corwin Hosp. and Parkview Episcopal Hosp., Pueblo, Colo., 1966-78; Pueblo County coroner, 1967-76; cons. disease of the chest Colo. State Hosp., 1966-76; dir. So. Colo. State Coll. asso. degree program in respiratory therapy, 1971—; mem. Colo. State Senate, 1976-85. Mem. Colo. State Air Pollution Variance Bd., 1967-76. Recipient James J. Waring award Am. Lung Assn., 1972. Fellow ACP, Am. Coll. Chest Physicians; mem. Colo. State Med. Soc. (del. 1970—, Community Service award 1980), Pueblo County Med. Soc., AMA. Democrat. Methodist. Clubs: Masons, Shriners, Vintage Motor of Am. Contbr. articles on respiratory disease to profl. jours. Home: 2424 N Greenwood St Pueblo CO 81003 Office: 517 Colorado Ave Pueblo CO 81004

PHELPS, JOSEPH ALFRED, social services administrator, small business owner; b. Detroit, May 4, 1927; s. Alfred Henry and Laura Etta (Flynn) P.; m. Alberta Johnigan, May 1, 1948 (div. Aug. 1971); children: Wanda M., Linda J., Joey A., David J., Shawn E. AA, Solano Community Coll., 1968; BA, Sonoma State U., 1974; MA, San Francisco State U., 1978. Cert. community coll. instr. (life). Enlisted USAF, 1945, advanced through grades to master sgt., 1965; served at various AFBs Calif., Alaska, Colo., also Fed. Republic Germany, 1946-67; retired USAF, 1967; adminstrv. services officer HHS Marin County, San Rafael, Calif., 1968—; instr. drama Solano Community Coll., Fairfield, Calif., 1978, 84-85; owner JAMV Pub. Co., Novato, Calif., 1985—. Author: On Being Black in America, 1978, Breaking Out--On Becoming More Than I Was, 1985; writer numerous poems; dir., producer local prodns. (plays) A Medal for Willie, The Amen Corner, A Raisin in the Sun. Active Concerned Parents of Novato, 1986. Recipient Non-fiction Writer's award Santa Barbara (Calif.) Writer's Conf., 1984, Poetry Achievement award Santa Barbara Writer's Conf., 1985, Outstanding Achievement in Writing award Santa Barbara Writer's Conf., 1986. Democrat. Congregationalist. Avocations: tennis organizer of agy. tournaments. Home: 199 Posada del Sol #19 Novato CA 94947

PHELPS, MARK STEVEN, psychiatric treatment facility administrator; b. San Francisco, Aug. 13, 1947; s. Rodney Earl and Patricia Jean (Anderson) P.; m. Susan Loebig, Nov. 11, 1980. BA, Ft. Lewis State Coll., 1970; MA, U. No. Colo., 1980. With Peace Corps (Vista), 1966-68; state probation counselor Colo. Jud. Dept., Durango, 1970-78; psychotherapist Mental Health Ctr., Crescent City, Calif., 1978-80; supt. Kans. Correctional Facility, Atchison, 1980-85; chief exec. officer Children's Home of Stockton, Calif., 1985—; cons. juvenile justice to pub., pvt. agys., 1973—. Named Kans. Pub. Adminstr. of Yr. Am. Soc. Pub. Adminstrn., 1985. Mem. Am. Correctional Assn., Calif. Assn. Services for Children. Lodge: Rotary. Home: 2115 Cedar Ridge Dr Stockton CA 95207 Office: Childrens Home of Stockton PO Drawer R Stockton CA 95201

PHIBBS, HARRY ALBERT, interior designer, professional speaker, lecturer; b. Denver, Jan. 9, 1933; s. Harry Andrew and Mary May (Perriam) P.; m. Alice Conners Glynn, Oct. 23, 1957; children: Kathleen Ann, Paul Robert, Mary Alice, Michael John, Peter James, Daniel Edward. B.A., U. Colo., 1954, B.F.A., 1957. Interior designer Howard Lorton, Inc., Denver, 1957-68; interior designer, v.p. Ronald Ansay Inc., Wheatridge, Colo., 1969-71; interior designer, pres. Phibbs Design Assos., Inc., Denver, 1972-78; interior designer, mgr. Howard Lorton, Inc., Colorado Springs, Colo., 1979—; pres. Interior Designers Housing Devel. Corp., 1969-72. Vice pres. Arvada (Colo.) Hist. Soc., 1973; bd. dirs. Colo. Opera Festival, also pres., 1986; bd. dirs. Downtown Colorado Springs, Inc., also pres., 1984. Served with U.S. Army, 1954-56. Fellow Am. Soc. Interior Designers (nat. pres. 1977); mem. Am. Arbitration Assn., Theta Xi (pres. Denver Area alumni club 1958-64). Democrat. Roman Catholic. Club: Plaza. Home: 3430 Clubheights Dr Colorado Springs CO 80906 Office: 27 S Tejon St Colorado Springs CO 80903

PHILBRICK, RALPH N., botanist; b. San Francisco, Jan. 1, 1934; s. Howard R. and Elizabeth (Jauckens) P.; children—Lauren P. Lester, Winston H., Edward W. B.A., Pomona Coll., 1956; M.A., UCLA, 1958; Ph.D., Cornell U., 1963. Research assoc. Cornell U., 1957-63; assoc. in botany U. Calif., Santa Barbara, 1963-64; biosystematist Santa Barbara Botanic Garden, 1964-73, dir., 1974—; research assoc. U. Calif., Santa Barbara, 1964-82. Mem. Santa Barbara County Planning Commn., 1981-85. Mem. Sigma Xi, Phi Kappa Phi. Office: 29 San Marcos Trout Club Santa Barbara CA 93105

PHILIPPART DE FOY, MICHEL PAUL, medical researcher, neurology and pediatrics educator; b. Ixelles, Belgium, Aug. 1, 1935; came to U.S., 1962; s. Paul and Denise (Wodon) P. de F.; m. Corinne Dratz, Oct. 14, 1958; children: Henry, Claire-Aimee. BS, Free U. Brussels, 1956, MD, 1960. Diplomate Am. Bd. Neurology. Head neurochemistry lab. C. Inst. Bunge, Antwerp, Belgium, 1965-66; head lab. development neurology Born-Bunge Found. Research, Antwerp, 1966-67; mem. Brain Research Inst., UCLA Sch. Medicine, 1968—; asst. prof. UCLA, 1967-69, assoc. prof., 1969-75, prof., 1975—; mem. profl. adv. bd. Internat. Rett Syndrome Assn.; mem. internat. com. Glycolipid Nomenclature; mem. med. adv. bd. United Leukodystrophy Found.; mem. admission com., human subject protection com. UCLA, pharmacy and therapeutics com.; dir. med. edn. Lanterman State Hosp.; grant reviewer Nat. Found. March Dimes and NIH Spl. Study Sect.; cons. pediatric neurology Olive View Hosp., Harbor-UCLA Med. Ctr., Lanterman State Hosp. Contbr. articles to profl. jours. Recipient Travel award Laureate of Belgian Govt., 1963, Sr. Fellowship award Parkinson Disease Found., 1965-66, Ordre de la Couronne award, Belgium, 1977, award Inst. Pediatrico Giannina Gaslini of Genoa, 1977. Mem. AAAS, Soc. Neurosci., Soc. Pediatric Research, Soc. Exptl. Biology and Medicine, Am. Acad. Neurology, Belgian Soc. Neurology, Internat. Soc. Neurochemistry, Am. Soc. Neurochemistry, Internat. Child Neurology Assn., N.Y. Acad. Scis., Child Neurology Soc., Japanese Soc. Child Neurology, Am. soc. human Genetics. Democrat. Home: 12218 Sarazen Pl Granada Hills CA 91344 Office: UCLA 760 Westwood Plaza Los Angeles CA 90024

PHILLIPPI, MARTIN ALLEN, chemist; b. Chgo., Jan. 31, 1955; s. Edward Louis and Genevieve (Matteucci) P.; m. Leslie Lynn Nickels, June 12, 1976; children: Daniel Edward, Amber Nicole. BA, Carthage Coll., 1976; PhD, U. Iowa, 1980. Postdoctoral research Los Alamos Nat. Lab., 1980-81; research assoc. Clorox Co., Pleasanton, Calif., 1981—. Contbr. articles to profl. jours. 3M fellow, 1979; Iowa Acad. Sci. grantee, 1979. Mem. Am. Chem. Soc., Soc. Applied Spectroscopy, Internat. Soc. Magnetic Resonance, Nat. Rifle Assn., Phi Beta Kappa, Alpha Phi Omega. Republican. Roman Catholic. Clubs: Nat. Rifle Assn., Clorox Trap and Skeet (pleasanton), Rod and Gun (Livermore, Calif.). Home: 3641 Dunsmuir Circle Pleasanton CA 94566 Office: The Clorox Co PO Box 493 Pleasanton CA 94566

PHILLIPS, ADRAN ABNER, oil company executive, geologist; b. Sugden, Okla., Feb. 6, 1924; s. James M. and Jennie Elizabeth (Norman) P.; m. Carmel Darlene Pesterfield, Aug. 20, 1949; 1 son, John David. B.S. in Geology, U. Okla., 1949. With Exxon Corp. and affiliates, 1949-76, dist. geologist, Chico, Calif., 1959-64, ops. geologist, Sydney, Australia, 1964-67, exploration coordinator North Slope Alaska, Houston, 1968-70, div. geologist, Denver, 1970-71, exploration mgr. P.T. Inc., Stanvac, Jakarta, Indonesia, 1971-73, exploration mgr. ESSO exploration, Singapore, 1973-76; div. mgr. Exxon U.S.A., Denver, 1976-79; v.p. Coors Energy div., Golden, Colo., 1979-80, pres., 1980—. Mem. Am. Assn. Petroleum Geologists, Ind. Petroleum Assn. Mountain States (past pres.), Ind. Petroleum Assn. Am. (dir.). Office: Coors Energy Co PO Box 467 Golden CO 80401

PHILLIPS, ARLENE MARIE, educator; b. Lindsborg, Kans., May 14, 1936; d. Herbert Jeremiah and Florence Eleanor (Swenson) Watts; children: Kirk, Scott. BS, McPherson Coll., 1959; postgrad. Colo. State U., 1966-67. Tchr. home econs. Alexander ((Kans.) High Sch., 1959-61; adult edn. tchr., Oberlin, Kans., 1964-65; tchr. home econs. Lincoln Jr. High Sch., Ft. Collins, Colo., 1967-68, Blevins Jr. High Sch., Ft. Collins, 1968—. Mem. Poudre Edn. Assn., Colo. Edn. Assn., NEA, Am. Vocat. Assn., Colo. Vocat. Assn., Nat. Assn. Vocat. Home Econs. Tchrs., Colo. Assn. Vocat. Home Econs. Tchrs. (sec. 1984-86), Alpha Delta Kappa (pres. 1986—). Mem. Christian Ch. Home: 1933 Oakwood Dr Fort Collins CO 80521 Office: 2101 S Taft Hill Fort Collins CO 80521

PHILLIPS, BARBARA FLORENCE, real estate broker, educator; b. Santa Monica, Calif., Aug. 12, 1921; d. Hans Terkel and Eleanor Margurite (Stratton) Hansen; m. James L. Phillips, Aug. 27, 1949 (dec. June 1958); 1 son by previous marriage, Carl Antony Smith; 1 dau., Andrea Ynez. Student Pasadena Jr. Coll., 1938-39; tchr. tng. course UCLA; grad. Realtors Inst., 1974. Real estate broker, Temple City, Calif., 1962-64, Incline Village, Nev., 1964-75; real estate broker, co. trainer Baldwin Realty, Arcadia, Calif., 1975-83; sales mgr. Sunset Realtors, Inc., Santa Maria, Calif., 1983-84; v.p. Resort Mgmt, Inc., 1984—, Resort Mgmt. Inc., Calif. Desert Rentals, Palm Desert, 1986—; tchr. real estate Pasadena City Coll., Rio Hondo Coll., Coll. of Desert, Palm Desert. Vol. Pasadena Hospice; mem. adv. com. Pasadena City Coll., 1976—, pres., 1981. Named Real Estate Tchr. of Yr., 1981. Mem. Calif. Assn. Realtors, Nat. Assn. Realtors, Real Estate Educators Assn., Calif. Assn. Real Estate Tchrs. (trustee). Republican. Contbr. to Handbook of Real Estate, 1984. Office: Calif Desert Rentals 73-160 El Paseo Palm Desert CA 92260

PHILLIPS, CARLTON VERNON, banker; b. Dartmouth, Mass., July 19, 1924; s. Robert Henry and Helen Estelle P.; A.B. in Econs., Brown U., 1957; grad. U.S. Army Command and Staff Coll., 1972, U.S. Air Force War Coll., 1976; M.A. in Mgmt., St. Mary's Coll. of Calif., 1979; m. Gladys Marie Lynch, Apr. 23, 1949; children—Carlton Vernon, John, Maura, Sally, Sheila, Regina, Nathan. Resident mgr. Mitchum Jones & Templeton, Phoenix, 1966-70, Quinn and Co., Phoenix, 1970-71; sr. v.p., pres. Continental Am. Securities, Inc., 1971—; chmn. and chief exec. officer Century Pacific Corp., 1984-86; dir. Ad Tech Microwave, U.S. Aircraft, Miller Technology. Served with U.S. Army, 1942-54, served to col. USAR. Decorated D.F.C., Air Medal with 3 oak leaf clusters. Mem. Pacific Coast Stock Exchange, Nat. Security Traders Assn. Republican. Roman Catholic. Clubs: Brown U. (Ariz. chpt., Phoenix), Res. Officers Assn. (Scottsdale), KC (Scottsdale). Home: 5112 N Wilkinson Rd Paradise Valley AZ 85253 Office: 2747 E Camelback Phoenix AZ 85016

PHILLIPS, DAVID ATLEE JR., archaeological research administrator, consultant; b. Santiago, Chile, Jan. 14, 1952; came to U.S., 1967; s. David Atlee and Helen (Haasch) P.; m. Deni Joanne Seymour (div. 1985) m. Linda Lou Swann, June 15, 1985. BA in Anthropology with honors, Prescott Coll., 1973; MA in Anthropology, U. Ariz., 1976, PhD in Anthropology, 1979. Research asst. Ariz. State Mus., Tucson, 1973-74; NSF fellow U. Ariz, Tucson, 1974-77; co-supr. Nat. Park Service, Tucson, 1978; vis. lectr. U. Calif., Santa Cruz, Calif., 1979-81; dir. western div. New World Research, Inc., Tucson, 1981-85; dir. research sect. Mus. N.Mex., Santa Fe, 1985—; prin. investigator Galisteo Dam and Reservoir Survey, Santa Fe County, 1982, Two Rivers Dam and Reservoir Project, Roswell, N.Mex., 1981; cons. Proyecto Basura, Centro de Ecodesarrollo, Mex. City, 1982. Co-author La Basura: Consumo y Desperdicio en el Distrito Federal, 1982; contbr. articles to profl. jours. Wenner-Gren Found. grantee, 1979. Mem. AAAS, Am. Anthropol. Assn., Soc. Am. Archaeology, Am. Assns. Mus., N.Mex. Assn. Mus., Ariz. Archaeol. Soc., Ariz. Archaeol. Council, Sigma Xi. Democrat. Roman Catholic. Avocations: hiking, cross-country and downhill skiing. Home: 2331 Calle Luminoso Santa Fe NM 87505 Office: Mus NMex Research Sect PO Box 2087 Santa Fe NM 87505

PHILLIPS, DAVID TURNER, physicist, consultant; b. Charles City, Iowa, Oct. 9, 1938; s. Richard Malcolm and Catherine Vernon (Turner) P.; m. Linda Jean Kanner, Sept.1, 1963; children: Daniel Alan, Glen Richard. BS in Physics, Iowa State U., 1960; PhD in Physics, U. Calif., Berkeley, 1966. Asst. prof. physics U. Calif., Santa Barbara, 1966-70; chief scientist Sci. Spectrum, Santa Barbara, 1970-79; prin. Glendan Co., Santa Barbara, 1971—; sr. staff scientist Renco Corp., Goleta, Calif., 1980-86; v.p. research and devel. Wyatt Tech., Santa Barbara, 1986-87; mem. tech. staff Gen. Research Corp., Santa Barbara, 1987—. Contbr. articles to profl. publs.; patentee in field. Fellow NSF, 1961-66. Mem. IEEE, Am. Phys. Soc., Parapsychology Assn. (assoc.). Home: 5107 Calle Asilo Santa Barbara CA 93111 Office: Gen Research Corp 5383 Hollister Ave Santa Barbara CA 93160

PHILLIPS, GENEVA FICKER, editor; b. Staunton, Ill., Aug. 1, 1920; d. Arthur Edwin and Lillian Agnes (Woods) Ficker; m. James Emerson Phillips, Jr., June 6, 1955 (dec. 1979). B.S. in Journalism, U. Ill., 1942; M.A. in English Lit., UCLA, 1953. Copy desk Chgo. Jour. Commerce, 1942-43; editorial asst. patents Radio Research Lab., Harvard U., Cambridge, Mass., 1943-45; asst. editor adminstrv. publs. U. Ill., Urbana, 1946-47; editorial asst. Quar. of Film, Radio and TV, UCLA, 1952-53; mng. editor The Works of John Dryden, Dept. English, UCLA, 1964—. Bd. dirs. Univ. Religious Conf., Los Angeles, 1979—. UCLA teaching fellow, 1950-53, grad. fellow 1954-55. Mem. Assn. Acad. Women UCLA, Friends of Huntington Library, Friends of UCLA Library, Renaissance Soc. So. Calif., Conf. Christianity and Lit., Soc. Mayflower Descs. Lutheran. Home: 213 First Anita Dr Los Angeles CA 90049 Office: Dept English UCLA 2225 Rolfe Hall Los Angeles CA 90024

PHILLIPS, JOHN HOWELL, microbiology consultant; b. Fresno, Calif., Dec. 19, 1925; s. John Howell and Daisy Isabel (Trott) P.; m. Arlene Louise Warren, July 30, 1954 (dec. Apr. 1974); children: John III, Melissa, Charles; m. Mary Metteer, July 11, 1984. AB in Bacteriology, U. Calif., Berkeley, 1949, MA in Bacteriology, 1953, PhD in Bacteriology, 1954. Prof. microbiology U. Calif., Berkeley, 1956-62, Stanford (Calif.) U., 1962-80; cons. Hawaiian Abalone Farms, Kailua-Kona, 1980—; instr. Monterey (Calif.) Peninsula Coll., 1968-69, 76-84; mem. exec. com. Monterey Bay Ocean Scis. Council, 1967-69, coordinating com. Council Higher Edn., Calif., 1968, adv. com. Monterey Basin Pilot Monitoring Program, Calif., 1972-73, pesticide adv. com. Dir. Agrl., Calif., 1969—, exec. com. Lyceum of the Monterey Peninsula, 1968-73, scholarship com. Monterey Inst. Fgn. Studies, 1968; rep. Assn. Ind. Colls. and Univs., 1968; cons. marine pollution NSF, 1970. Bd. dirs. Del Monte Forest Property Owners Assn., 1970-75. Served with USN, 1944-46, with Res. 1950-55. Mem. AAAS, Am. Assn. Immunologists, N.Y. Acad. Scis., Sierra Club (exec. com. Ventana chpt. 1972-74), Pacific Grove Mus. natural History Assn. (bd. dirs. 1971—), Sigma Xi. Home: 78-6842 Alii Dr Kailua-Kona HI 96740 Office: Hawaiian Abalone Farms PO Box A Kailua-Kona HI 96745

PHILLIPS, JOHN P(AUL), physician; b. Danville, Ark., Oct. 14, 1932; s. Brewer William Ashley and Wave Audrey (Page) P.; A.B. cum laude, Hendrix Coll., 1953; M.D., U. Tenn., 1956; m. June Helen Dunbar, Dec. 14, 1963; children—Todd Eustace, Timothy John Colin, Tyler William Ashley. Intern, Charity Hosp. La., New Orleans, 1957; resident in surgery U. Tenn. Hosps., 1958; resident in neurol. surgery U. Tenn. Med. Units, 1958-62; practice medicine, specializing in neurol. surgery, Salinas, Calif., 1962—; chief of staff, chief of surgery Salinas Valley Meml. Hosp.; mem. staffs Community Hosp. Monterey Peninsula, U. Calif. Hosp., San Francisco; asst. clin. prof. U. Calif., 1962-—. Commd. Ky. col. Diplomate Am. Bd. Neurol. Surgeons. Mem. ACS, Internat. Coll. Surgery, Harvey Cushing Soc., Congress Neurol. Surgery, Western Neurosurg. Assn., AMA, San Francisco Neurol. Soc., Pan Pacific Surg. Assn., Alpha Omega Alpha, Phi Chi, Alpha Chi. Home: 6 Mesa del Sol Salinas CA 93901 Office: 220 San Jose St Salinas CA 93901

PHILLIPS, KENNETH EUGENE, environmental engineer; b. Balt., Sept. 27, 1949; s. Samuel Nixon and Gloria Ann (Minor) P.; m. Kathy Charmaine Sanders, Dec. 30, 1977; children: Korey Scott, Cameron Sanders. BS in Physics, N.C. Agrl. and Tech. State U., 1971; MS in Environ. Engring., U. Wis., 1972; PhD in Environ. Engring., Johns Hopkins U., 1976. Environ. engr. Greiner Engring., Balt., 1973-76; assoc. engr. The Rand Corp., Santa Monica, Calif., 1976—; mem. synthetic fuels facilites safety com. NRC. Contbr. articles to profl. jours. Mem. Los Angeles Energy Mgmt. Com. Office of Mayor, 1979-82. Scholar U. Wis., Madison, 1971-72; fellow Johns Hopkins U., 1973-76. Avocations: bicycling, sailing, O-scale model railroads, stained glass window. Office: Rand Corp 1700 Main St Santa Monica CA 90406

PHILLIPS, LEROY DANIEL, management consultant; b. Texarkana, Tex., July 10, 1935; s. Leroy and Jessie Mae (Sharp) P.; m. Mary A. Scott, July 10, 1955; 1 child, Kevin V. AA, Los Angeles City Coll., 1967; BA, Calif. State U., Los Angeles, 1972; MBA, Century U., 1979. Chief supply and transp. div. Los Angeles County Mech. Dept., 1967-74, bldg. crafts mgr., 1974-85; mgmt. cons. Harbor City, Calif., 1985—; instr. psychology Los Angeles County Mech. Dept., 1979; mem. interview bd. Los Angeles County Personnel Dept., 1977-83, Los Angeles City Personnel Dept., 1979-81. Chmn. subcom. on tng. and devel. Los Angeles County, 1979, Coastal Mental Health Governing Bd., Los Angeles, 1980-83; mem. resources and devel. com. Los Angeles County Health Services, 1981. Recipient United Way award Los Angeles, 1985, Leadership award Brotherhood Crusade, 1986, Leadership award United Negro Coll. Fund, 1986, Spl. Citation, AFL-CIO Service Employees Union, 1985. Mem. Los Angeles County Employees Assn., Diane Watson Semi-Profl. Sports Assn. (pres. 1986). Democrat. Avocations: fishing, photography. Home and Office: 914 Oakmere Dr Harbor City CA 90710

PHILLIPS, LOIS GAIL, exotic bird breeder; b. Detroit, June 21, 1939; d. John Patrick and Leona Victoria (Wagner) P.; B.S. in Chemistry, Fresno (Calif.) State Coll., 1962. Radiol. chemist Nat. Canners Assn., Berkeley, Calif., 1963-64; tchr. Progress Sch., Long Beach, Calif., 1966-67; vol. Peace Corps tchr., Nepal, 1967-69; univ. extension tchr. Nepal tng. programs, Davis, Calif., 1969-71; nursery employee Valley Gardens, Woodland, Calif., 1971-74, Farrell's Garden Center, Sonoma, Calif., 1974-75; mgr. 7-Eleven Store, Petaluma, Calif., 1977-85; chemist, Chem. Waste Mgmt. ENRAC div.; owner Bodega Birds, Petaluma. Bd. dirs. Sonoma County People Econ. Opportunity, 1978-83, sec. to bd., 1978-79. Mem. ACLU, Am. Fedn. Aviculture, Nat. Audubon Soc., Sierra Club. Home: 1821 Lakeville St Apt 55 Petaluma CA 94952 Office: 3400 Standist Ave Santa Rosa CA 95407

PHILLIPS, NANCY GILBERT, entrepreneur; b. N.Y.C., Apr. 13, 1931; d. Reuben and Claire (Heller) G.; m. Robert Solomon, May 25, 1952 (div. Mar. 1980); children: Michael Neil, Tricia Ann; m. George Phillips, Sept. 14, 1986. BA in Psychology, BA in Theatre Arts, Adelphi U., 1951; MSW, U. So. Calif., 1967; postgrad., Ariz. State U., 1977—. Lic. clin. social worker, Calif.; lic. marriage counselor, Calif. Counselor Los Angeles County (Calif.) Dept. Adoptions, 1962-71; practice social work specializing in marriage counseling Los Angeles, 1967-71; Ariz. dir. Vietnamese-Ams. Resettlement Effort, Phoenix, 1975-76; child welfare worker Jewish Family Service, Phoenix, 1977-79; pres. The Pet Pad Ltd., Phoenix, 1979-85, Transitions, Phoenix, 1985—; cons. Family Service of Palmdale, Calif., 1970-71; pres. Thomas Mall Mchts. Assn., Phoenix, 1981-85. Mem. Ariz. Retailers Assn., Acad. Cert. Social Workers (assoc.), Alpha Psi Omega, Psi Chi. Home: 6141 E Calle Del Norte Scottsdale AZ 85251

PHILLIPS, OREN BURTON, JR., mechanical engineer; b. Wilmington, Del., June 12, 1945; s. Oren Burton and Elizabeth Jane (Hackman) P.; B.M.E., U. Del., 1968; m. Judith Ann Norman, Nov. 30, 1968. Asst. program mgr. Thiokol Corp., Elkton, Md., 1967-69, program chief, 1969-74, mgr. space systems, 1974-82, sr. mgr. space systems depts., 1982-85; gen. mgr. Morton Thiokol La. Div., 1985-86; v.p. aerospace group Morton Thiokol, Inc., 1986—. Mem. Republican Election Dist. Com., 1979-81. Mem. AIAA (past chpt. pres. 1968—), U. Del. Engring. Alumni Assn. (v.p., dir. 1974-85), Am. Def. Preparedness Assn., Soc. Automotive Engrs., AIA, Shreveport Mfrs. Mgr. Council, Shreveport, Minden and Bossier City C. of C., Ogden C. of C., Delaware City Hist. Soc., U.S. Jaycees, Kappa Alpha. Club: Lions (past dir.). Home: 2788 Shamrock Dr Ogden UT 84403 Office: Morton Thickol Inc Aerospace Group Hdqrs 3340 Airport Rd Ogden UT 84405

PHILLIPS, RICHARD LEE, lawyer; b. Fresno, Calif., Apr. 3, 1948; s. Floyd Gilbert and Emma Beatrice (Rivas) P.; m. Sandra Kay Evans, Feb. 2, 1969 (div. Nov. 1984); children: Lisa Marie, Laurel Jane. BA in Polit. Sci., U. Ill., Urbana, 1970; JD, U. Puget Sound, 1975. Dep. pros. atty. office of King County Prosecutor, Seattle, 1975-77; assoc. Hutchins, Plumb & Wheeler, Tacoma, 1977-79; assoc. Moriarty and Mikkelborg, Seattle, 1979-83, ptnr., 1984-85; ptnr. Mikkelborg, Broz, Wells, Fryer & Yates, Seattle, 1985—. Mem. ABA (litigation sect. bus. com.), Maritime Law Assn. of U.S., Nat. Assn. Criminal Def. Lawyers, U. Ill. Alumni Assn., U. Puget Sound Alumni Assn. Democrat. Avocations: softball, golf, photography, sci. and space tech., woodworking. Office: Mikkelborg Broz Wells et al 1001 4th Ave Plaze Suite 3300 Seattle WA 98154

PHILLIPS, RUSSELL COLE, business consultant; b. Bad Axe, Mich., Apr. 28, 1923; s. Douglas Evans and Laura (Cole) P.; m. Marilynn Winona Ott, Aug. 3, 1946; children: Jeffrey D., Deborah A. BSChemE, Mich. State U., 1944; MS ChemE, Poly. Inst. N.Y., 1947. Registered chem. engr., Calif. Chem. engr. Gen. Foods Corp., Hoboken, N.J., 1945-47, Huron Milling Co., Harbor Beach, Mich., 1947-49, Blaw-Knox Co., Ann Arbor, Mich., 1949-51; sr. chem. engr. Stanford Research Inst. Internat., Menlo Park, Calif., 1951-59, mgr. research services, phys. and life scis. div., 1959-60, mgr. research and facilities service, 1961-64, dir. chem. engring. lab., 1964-83, sr. cons., 1987—; gen. mgr. Coal-Tec, Menlo Park, Calif., 1983-87. Contbr. articles to profl. jours.; patentee in field. Publicker fellow N.Y. Polytech. Inst., 1944. Republican. Congregationalist. Home: 861 Garland Dr Palo Alto CA 94303

PHILLIPS, TED RAY, advertising agency executive; b. American Falls, Idaho, Oct. 27, 1948; s. Virn E. and Jessie N. (Aldous) P.; m. Dianne Jacqulynne Walker, May 28, 1971; children—Scott, Russell, Stephen, Michael. B.A., Brigham Young U., 1972, M.A., 1974. Account exec. David W. Evans, Inc., Salt Lake City, 1972-75; dir. advt. Div. Continuing Edn., U. Utah, Salt Lake City, 1975-78; sr. v.p. Evans/Lowe & Stevens, Inc., Atlanta, 1978, exec. v.p., 1979; pres., chief exec. officer David W. Evans/Atlanta, Inc., 1979-80; dir. advt. O.C. Tanner Co., Salt Lake City, 1980-82; pres. Thomas/Phillips/Clawson Advt., Inc., Salt Lake City, 1982-86; pres. Hurst, Jarrard, Phillips, Salt Lake City, 1987—; advt. instr. div. continuing edn. Brigham Young U., 1983. Dir. publicity, promotion Western States Republican Con., 1976. Mem. Am. Advt. Fedn. (8 Best-in-West awards, 2 nat. Addy awards, Clio finalist 1984), Utah Advt. Fedn. (bd. dirs. 1976-78, 80-87, pres. 1984-85). Mormon. Home: 1094 E Gravel Hills Dr Sandy UT 84070 Office: 342 W 200 S Salt Lake City UT 84101

PHILLIPS, TEDDY STEVE, conductor, saxaphone player, prodn. co. exec.; b. Chgo., June 15, 1917; s. Steve and Kaliope P.; student U. Ill., 1935-39; children—Jody, Teddy. Saxaphone player with big bands, across country, 1940-45; staff musician Radio Sta. CBS, Chgo., 1944-45; condr. Teddy Phillips Orch., across country, 1945-55, 1957-62; prin. Teddy Phillips Show, Sta. WBKB-TV-ABC, Chgo., 1956-57; condr. Tedd Phillips and Orch., Ambassador Hotel, Los Angeles and Flamingo Hotel, Las Vegas, Nev., 1962-80, Statler Hotels, Aragon Ballroom, Chgo., Hilton Hotels, Chgo.; dir. Guy Lombardo Orch. and Royal Conadians, 1980—; pres. P&M Prodns., Woodland Hills, Calif., 1976—; TV producer Great Concert in the Sky; record producer; writer Do the Camel Hump?, Wishin, Do the Camel Hump; writer, arranger, conductor on tour Great Concert in the Sky, 1986—. Served with U.S. Army, 1940-41. Recipient Gould Tech. Achievement award. Mem. Musicians Union. Greek Orthodox. Club: Masons. Rec. artist. Home and Office: 6252 1/2 Nita Ave Woodland Hills CA 91367

PHILLIPS, TINA BOYD, banking executive; b. Phoenix, July 14, 1953; d. James Boyd and Evelyn (Wasem) P. BBA, So. Meth. U., 1975; student, U. Colo., 1986—. Project leader research info. ctr. Greyhound Corp., Phoenix, 1975-76; mgmt. trainee United Bank Ariz., Phoenix, 1976-77, asst. cashier, mgr., 1977-81, asst. v.p., mgr., 1981-85, v.p., mgr., 1985—. Fin. advisor Kappa Kappa Gamma, Ariz. State U., Tempe, 1981-83, personal advisor, 1983—; active in funds allocation for Western states to re-elect Reagan and Bush, 1984; bd. dirs. CODMA Drug Rehab. Program for Youth, Phoenix, 1980-81. Recipient Cert. Appreciation Ariz. Alliance Bus., Phoenix, 1982-83. Mem. Nat. Assn. Bus. Women in Banking, Council Fin. Competition (adv. bd. dirs.), Jr. League Ariz. Avocations: all sports, travel. Home: 7950 E Starlight Way Apt 147 Scottsdale AZ 85253 Office: United Bank Ariz PO Box 2908 Phoenix AZ 85016

PHILLIPS, WILLIAM HENRY, English educator; b. Indpls., Mar. 16, 1940; s. Howard Dare and Catherine Elizabeth (Lostetter) P.; m. Eva L. Santos; 1 child, Rey Arnaldo. BA, Purdue U., 1962; MA, Rutgers U., 1966; PhD, Ind. U., 1972. Instr. U. Toledo, 1965-69; asst. prof. film criticism, scriptwriting, expository writing Calif. State U. Stanislaus, Turlock, 1974-77, assoc. prof., 1977-82, prof., 1982—; vis. lectr. U. Ill., Urbana, 1973-74; vis. prof. English, Ind. U., South Bend, 1984-85. Author: St. John Hankin, 1979, Analyzing Films, 1985. Mem. Soc. Cinema Studies, Univ. Film and Video Assn. Home: 1045 Frago Ct Turlock CA 95380 Office: Calif State U Stanislaus 801 Monte Vista Ave Turlock CA 95380

PHILLIPS, WILLIAM TERHUNE, real estate investor, advisor; b. Phila., Jan. 30, 1941; s. Rutherford Terhune and Alba (Amati) P.; m. Karen Hoyer, Aug. 27, 1960 (div. Aug. 1985); children: Robert Rutherford, Jill; m. Rebecca Trevino, Dec. 14, 1985. BS, U. Colo., 1962; MBA, U. Calif., 1964. Lic. real estate broker, Calif. Project mgr. Draper Cos., San Francisco, 1964-65; assoc. Harman, O'Donnel & Henninger, Denver, 1965-68; project dir. Dillingham Corp., San Francisco, 1968-69; sr. v.p. Pacific Gen. Devel. Co., San Francisco, 1969-85; v.p. Pacific Realty Advisors, San Francisco, 1979—, also bd. dirs.; ptnr. Pacific Gen. Ptnrs., San Francisco, 1985—; bd. dirs. Real Property West Inc., San Francisco. Recipient commendation Calif. Hist. Resources Commn., 1982. Mem. Urban Land Inst. (nat. policy council 1975—). Democrat. Roman Catholic. Avocations: skiing, distance running. Office: Pacific Gen Ptnrs 44 Montgomery St #4230 San Francisco CA 94104

PHITAKSPHRAIWAN, PHUANGNOI, child neurologist; b. Trang, Thailand, Sept. 19, 1927; d. Phra and Amphorn P.; came to U.S., 1962; M.D., Siriraj Med. Sch., Bangkok, Thailand, 1951; m. Wisutr Yontwises, Dec. 27, 1966. Intern, Siriraj Hosp., Bangkok, 1951-52; resident in pediatrics St. Louis Children's Hosp., 1955-56, Driscoll Found. Children's Hosp., Corpus Christi, Tex., 1962-63; mem. pediatric staff Children's Hosp., Bangkok, Thailand, 1956-62; fellow in neonatology Baylor U. Med. Coll., Houston, 1963-64, in pediatric neurology U. Okla. Med. Center, Oklahoma City, 1964-65; resident in neurology U. Miss. Med. Center, Jackson, 1967-68; staff physician, cons. neurologist Denton (Tex.) State Sch., 1969-74; instr. pediatrics U. Tex. Health Scis. Center, Dallas, 1975-76, asst. prof., 1976-80 pediatric dir. univ. affiliated facility, 1976-80; staff Lanterman State Hosp., Pomona, Calif., 1980—, cons. pediatric neurology, 1981—; cons. pediatric neurologist Ft. Worth State Sch., 1978-79. Fulbright scholar, 1954-55. Mem. Am. Acad. Neurology (asso.), Am. Assn. Mental Deficiency. Home: 23819 Country View Dr Diamond Bar CA 91765 Office: 3530 W Pomona Blvd Pomona CA 91786

PHOENIX, DAVID ALLEN, research hydrologist, consultant; b. Lompoc, Calif., June 25, 1916; s. Allen Mead and Dorothy (Webb) P.; m. Roberta Dell Selover, Feb. 14, 1938; children: David Allen II, Roberta Ann Phoenix Saunders. AA, Santa Ana Coll., 1938; BA, U. Calif., Berkeley, 1941; MS, Stanford U., 1954. Registered geologist, Calif. Recorder, U.S. Geol. Survey, Oreg., 1941, jr. geologist, Nev., Utah, Wash., 1941-45, asst. geologist, Nev., Colo., 1945-49, assoc. geologist, Colo., 1949-55, geologist, Colo., Utah and Washington, 1955-62, sr. geologist, Nigeria and Washington, 1962-67, research hydrologist, Washington and Calif., 1967-72; cons. Boyle Engring. Corp., also others, Calif., 1972—; vis. lectr. Chapman Coll., 1973-74, U. Calif.-Fullerton, 1981; vol. exec. Internat. Exec. Service Corps, Stamford, Conn., 1974, 76, 79, 83, field assoc., 1983—; chmn. Laguna Beach Seismic and Safety Com., 1977-78; chmn. bd. dirs. Laguna Niguel Bot. Preserve, 1984—. Contbr. articles to profl. jours. Mem. Calif. Rep. Assembly. Recipient Service awards U.S. Geol. Survey, Internat. Exec. Service Corps; Internat. Exec. Service Corps and Perca, Ltda. grantee. Fellow Geol. Soc. Am.; mem. Soc. Econ. Geologists, Am. Geophys. Union, AAAS, South Coast Geol. Soc., Geol. Soc. Washington, Am. Inst. Hydrology, Sigma Xi. Episcopalian. Lodge: Rotary. Home and office: 450 Ruby St Laguna Beach CA 92651

PI, WEN-YI SHIH, aircraft company engineer, researcher; b. Peiping, People's Republic of China, Feb. 28, 1935; came to U.S., 1959; d. Chih-Chuan and Hsiu-Yun (Yang) Shih; m. William Shu-Jong Pi, July 2, 1961; 1 child, Wilfred. BS, Nat. Taiwan U., Taipei, Republic of China, 1956; MS, Stanford U., 1961, PhD, 1963. Research assoc. Stanford (Calif.) U., 1963-64; engring. specialist Northrop Corp., Hawthorne, Calif., 1965-83, sr. tech. specialist, 1983—. Contbr. articles to profl. jours. Recipient Silver Achievement award Los Angeles YMCA, 1983; Amelia Earhart Scholar Zonta Internat., 1961-62. Fellow: AIAA (assoc.); mem. Sigma Xi. Office: Northrop Corp Aircraft Div One Northrop Ave Dept 3854/82 Hawthorne CA 90250-3277

PIANTANIDA, LILLIAN GIOVANNA, industrial hygienist; b. Pitts., Sept. 2, 1948; d. John Louis and Lillian Catherine (Zanotti) P.; m. Thomas Jerome Walker, Aug. 31, 1985. BS in Microbiology, U. Pitts., 1966-69. Cert. indsl. hygienist. Asst. mgr. environ. health ILZRO, N.Y.C., 1974-80; corp. indsl. hygienist Celanese Corp., N.Y.C., 1980-81; assoc. indsl. hygienist Calif. div. Occupational Safety and Health Adminstrn., San Francisco, 1981-83; v.p. Thomas J. Walker, Inc., Piedmont, Calif., 1983-86; sr. indsl. hygiene cons. The FPE Group, Lafayette, Calif., 1986—. Editor: (with others) Environmental Lead, 1981. Diplomate Am. Acad. Indsl. Hygienists; mem. Am Indsl. Hygienic Assn. (chairperson N.Y.C. 1980-81), Am. Soc. Safety Engrs., Nat. Safety Mgmt. Soc. (sec. Golden Gate chpt. 1985-86), Am. Conference Govtl. and Med Hygienists. Avocations: violin, chess, travel, golf. Office: The FPE Group 3687 Mt Diablo Blvd Lafayette CA 94549

PIATT, DAVID MEYER, research psychologist, systems analyst, consultant; b. Columbus, Ohio, Oct. 22, 1917; s. Morris and Charlotte (Weiss) P.; m. Yvonne Audry Simmonson, Dec. 1, 1947 (dec.); m. Maria Weitzel, Sept. 11, 1982. BA in Physiology, U. So. Calif., 1947, MA in Psychometrics, 1951, postgrad., 1953. Lic. psychologist, Calif. Sect. head Radio/Plane div. Northrop Aircraft Corp., Van Nuys, Calif., 1954-56; from dept. mgr., dir. life scis. to tech. mgr. Litton Space Sci. Lab., Beverly Hills, Calif., 1957-67; asst. gen. mgr. Dallons Instruments div. Internat. Rectifier Corp., El Segundo, Calif., 1967-69; sr. staff scientist Litton Industries, Van Nuys, 1969-83; pres. David M. Piatt Cons. Services, Inc., Woodland Hills, Calif., 1883—. Patentee in field. Served as cpl. USAAF, 1943-46. Mem. Psi Chi. Home and Office: 5918 Elba Pl Woodland Hills CA 91367

PIAZZA, DUANE EUGENE, biomedical researcher; b. San Jose, Calif., June 5, 1954; s. Salvador Richard and Mary Bernice (Mirassou) P. BS in Biology, U. San Francisco, 1976; MA in Biology, San Francisco State U., 1986. Staff research assoc. I U. Calif., San Francisco, 1975-81; sr. research technician XOMA Corp., San Francisco, 1981-82; biologist II Syntex USA Inc., Palo Alto, Calif., 1982-85; pres., cons. Ryte For You, Oakland, Calif., 1985—; research assoc. I Cetus Corp., Emeryville, Calif., 1986—. Instr. CPR ARC, San Francisco, 1985-86; instr., First Aid sta. vol., Santa Cruz, Calif., 1985-86; First Aid sta. vol. disaster action team ARC, Oakland, 1986—. Mem. AAAS, N.Y. Acad. Scis., Astron. Soc. Pacific. Republican. Roman Catholic. Avocations: scuba diving, swimming, backpacking, photography, astronomy. Home: 3755 Emerson Way Apt E Oakland CA 94610 Office: Cetus Corp 1400 53d St Emeryville CA 94608

PIAZZOLA, DANIEL JOSEPH, geophysicist; b. Whitehall, Mont., Aug. 2, 1946; s. Lawrence John and Nora Dell (Paddock) P.; m. Dianne Marie Bettison, June 6, 1969; children: Marcus, Christopher, Sara. BS in Geophys. Engring., Mont. Coll. Mineral Sci. and Tech., 1969. Geophysicist Shell Oil Co., Midland, Tex., 1969-73, Mobil Oil Corp., Denver, 1973-75; cons. Pexcon Corp., Denver, 1975-78; sr. geophysicist Patrick Petroleum Co., Billings, Mont., 1978-82; geophysicist E.N.I., Billings, 1982-83; regional geophysicist Meridian Oil Co., Billings, 1983—; lectr. Rocky Mountain Coll., Billings, 1982, Mont. Coll. Mineral Sci. and Tech., Butte, 1986. Bd. dirs. Magic City Soccer Club, Billings, 1984-86; treas. campaign Schneider for Pub. Service Commn., Mont., 1980, 84. Mem. Soc. Exploration Geophysicists (profl. affairs com. 1981-86), Am. Assn. Petroleum Geologists, Denver Geophys. Soc., Mont. Geol. Soc., Billings Geophys. Soc. (pres. 1982). Club: Billings Petroleum. Avocations: coaching, youth soccer, art, gardening, sports. Home: 1033 Evergreen Dr Billings MT 59105 Office: Meridian Oil Norwest Bank Bldg Billings MT 59103-1855

PICARD, DONNA JEFFRIES, community college administrator; b. Lancaster, Mo., Feb. 2, 1939; d. Woodrow Walter and Betty Jane (Fraser) Jeffries; divorced; 1 child, James Jeffries Kinkead; m. Raymond Picard, April 8, 1986. B.S. in Edn., Ark. State U.-Jonesboro, 1966, M.S. in Edn., 1967; Ed.D., U. So. Calif., 1982. Cert. community coll. adminstr., Calif. Instr. Brevard Community Coll., Fla., 1967-70; dept. chmn., instr. secretarial sci. Santa Ana Coll., Calif., 1970-73, dean instructional services, 1973-78, dean occupational edn., 1978-80, dean applied arts and scis., 1980—; cons. in field. Mem. adv. com. YWCA, Santa Ana, 1976-78, Orange County Manpower Com., Santa Ana, 1978-80; bd. dirs. Orange County March of Dimes, Costa Mesa, Calif., 1983—. Mem. Assn. Calif. Community Coll. Adminstrs. (bd. dirs. 1978—), Orange County Industry Edn. (bd. dirs. 1978-80), Calif. Community Coll. Assn. Occupational Edn. (bd. dirs. 1978-80). Democrat. Office: Rancho Santiago Coll 17th St at Bristol St Santa Ana CA 92706

PICARD, JAMES CASTLEBERRY, real estate executive; b. Menominee, Mich., Sept. 1, 1946; s. George W. and Juanita Picard; m. Gayle Cummings, June 1, 1968 (div. June 1975); m. Anne M. Bayer, Oct. 1, 1977; children: Ann, Jessica, Heather. BS in Bus. Mgmt., Old Dominion U., 1973. V.p. real estate lending Alaska USA Fed. Credit Union, Anchorage, 1975—. Served with USN, 1965-69. Mem. Alaska Mortgage Bankers Assn. (bd. dirs. 1986—). Lodge: Elks. Avocations: 3 wheeling, hunting, reading. Home: 4840 Talus Dr Anchorage AK 99516

PICK, ARTHUR JOSEPH, JR., chamber of commerce executive; b. Louisville, Mar. 22, 1931. BS, U. Calif., Riverside, 1959; MA in Urban Studies, Occidental Coll., 1969. Mem. Riverside County Rep. Cen. Com., 1962-63; founding dir. Riverside Civic League, 1963, pres., 1964; resident mgr. J. Henry Helser & Co., Investment Mgrs., Riverside, 1965-72; exec. v.p. Greater Riverside C. of C., 1972—. Pres. Young Life of Riverside, 1966-68; deacon, Sunday sch. tchr. Calvary Presbyn. Ch., 1966-68; v.p., pres. Riverside Symphony Orch. Soc. 1966; founding pres. Riverside Cultural Arts Council, 1969; elected Riverside City Council, 1967, re-elected, 1971; chmn. City Council Fin. com., Cable TV com., Civic Ctr. com.; candidate assembly State of Calif. Legis., 1972; mem. adv. bd. Riverside Jr. League, 1975-79, LWV, 1976-80; v.p The Friends of the Mission Inn, 1977-79; bd. dirs., exec. com., treas. Citizens Goals Greater Riverside Area, 1982—; founding mem. exec. com. adv. bd., treas. Calif. Citrus Heritage Park, 1969—. Served with U.S. Army, 1953-55. Named Outstanding Young Man of Am., Riverside Jaycees, 1966; recipient Disting. Service award Riverside Jaycees, 1966, Patron of Arts award Cultural Arts Council, 1977. Mem. Mayors and Councilmen Assn. Riverside County (pres. 1968-69), Inland Area Urban League (founder, bd. dirs., Pacesetter award 1982), U. Calif. Alumni Assn. Riverside (bd. dirs. 1981-87), Riverside Jaycees (life). Office: Greater Riverside C of C 4261 Main St Riverside CA 92501

PICK, JAMES BLOCK, university administrator; b. Chgo., July 29, 1943; s. Grant Julius and Helen (Block) P.; B.A., Northwestern U., 1966; M.S. in Edn., No. Ill. U., 1969; Ph.D., U. Calif., Irvine, 1974, C.D.P., 1980. C.S.P., 1985, C.C.P., 1986. Asst. research statistician, lectr. Grad. Sch. Mgmt. U. Calif., Riverside, 1975-84, dir. computing, adj. lectr., 1984—, mem. Univ. Commons Bd., 1982-86; cons. U.S. Census Bur. Internat. Div., 1978. Trustee Newport Harbor Art Mus., 1980—, treas. acquisitions council, 1979-81, chmn., 1982-83. Mem. Assn. Computing Machinery, Assn. Systems Mgmt. (profl., pres. Orange County chpt. 1978-79, sec.-treas. Div. 22 regional council 1979-80, vice chmn. 1980-81, chmn. 1981-82), AAAS, Am. Statis. Assn., Population Assn. Am., Internat. Union for Sci. Study of Population, Soc. Info. Mgmt. Clubs: Balboa Bay (Newport Beach); Standard (Chgo.). Author: Computer Systems in Business, 1986; co-author: (with Edgar W. Butler) Geothermal Energy Development: Problems and Prospects in the Imperial Valley, California, 1982; condr. research in info. systems, environ. studies; contbr. sci. articles to publs. in field. Home: 1833 Galatea Terr Corona del Mar CA 92625 Office: Grad Sch Mgmt U Calif Riverside CA 92521

PICK, MALCOLM JOHN, computer systems consultant; b. Wakefield, Eng., Jan. 24, 1945; came to U.S., 1984; s. Leslie and Olive (Hoyland) P.; m. Aylin Yurdakurban, July 6, 1968. BS in Math., Physics with honors, Birmingham (Eng.) U., 1966; MS in Ops. Research, London U., 1967. Cons. Coopers & Lybrand CPA's, London, 1967-70; analyst NCR, Utrecht, The Netherlands, 1970-71; mgr. Levi Strauss, Brussels, Belgium, 1971-74; head data processing Reed Internat., Eng., 1975-77; ptnr. SGV Group (now Arthur Anderson) CPA's, Philippines and Malaysia, 1977-84; exec. dir. De Faro Software Systems, 1984—; mng. dir. Inst. Advanced Computer Tech., Philippines and Malaysia, 1978-84, ASCE Ltd., Eng., 1975-77. Contbr. articles to profl. jours. Recipient award Malaysian Inst. Personnel Mgrs. 1982, Malaysian Inst. Accts. 1983, Philippine Computer Soc. 1980, 81, 82. Fellow Brit. Inst. Mgmt.; mem. Brit. Computer Soc. (full), Bus. Grads. Assn. AVocations: boating, property investments. Office: De Faro Software PO Box 928 Redondo Beach CA 90277

PICKARD, BRIAN ALAN, lawyer; b. London, Ont., Can., June 10, 1952; came to U.S., 1975; s. Harold Alan and Pearl Victoria (Pudney) P. BA, U. Western Ont., 1974; MAM, Embry-Riddle Aero. U., 1977; JD, Western State U., 1980. Bar: Calif. 1981. With Pearpic Mgmt. Corp., London, Ont., 1973-75, mgmt. cons., 1977—; sole practice Fullerton, Calif., 1981—. Contbr. articles to profl. jours. Recipient Nat. Pilots Assn. Flight award, 1979, Am. Jurisprudence award, 1979, Best Advocate in Trial Practice award West Pub. Co., 1980. Mem. Calif. Trial Lawyers Assn., Orange County Trial Lawyers Assn., Assn. Trial Lawyers Am., Internat. Platform Assn., Alpha Eta Rho (v.p.). Republican. Club: Aviation Facilities Flying. Home: 1907 Deer Park Dr Fullerton CA 92631 Office: 12377 Lewis St Suite 206 Garden Grove CA 92640

PICKARD, DAVID JANARD, endowment fund exec.; b. Colorado Springs, Colo., Nov. 23, 1933; s. Kenneth Leonard and Ann Ruth (Wemyss) P.; A.B., U. Nebr., 1956; student Berkeley Div. Sch., Yale, 1956-58; children—Laurel Jane, John Mark. Exec. v.p. Tri State Supply, Inc., Scottsbluff, Nebr., 1958-73, Tri State Supply of Sidney, Inc. (Nebr.), 1959-73, v.p. Tri State of Alliance, Inc. (Nebr.), 1965-73, pres. Tri State of Wyoming, Inc., Torrington, 1967-73, exec. v.p. Tri State Warehousing, Inc., Scottsbluff, 1965-73; commr., asst. treas. Kappa Sigma Endowment Fund, Denver, 1973—, also dir. devel. Named Adm., Nebr. State Navy. Mem. SAR, Colo. Yale Assn. Republican. Episcopalian. Club: Univ. (Lincoln, Nebr.). Lodge: Masons. Home: 2675 Fairway Dr Colorado Springs CO 80909 Office: PO Box 7715 Colorado Springs CO 80933

PICKARD, MICHAEL JAMES, architect; b. Tempe, Ariz., Aug. 24, 1954; s. Thomas Nelson and Elizebeth (Dickman) P.; m. Karyn Ann Parks, July 8, 1978 (div. Feb. 1986); m. Sally Anne Fitzpatrick, Apr. 4, 1987. BArch magna cum laude, Ariz. State U., 1978. Registered architect, Ariz. Project designer J. Barry Moffitt and Assocs., Phoenix, 1978-80; assoc. Dwayne G.

Lewis Architects, Inc., Phoenix, 1980-85; regional dir., project mgr. BSHA Architects, Phoenix, 1985—. Mem. AIA, Phi Kappa Phi. Republican. Avocations: photography, travel. Office: BSHA Architects 2929 N 44th St 400 Phoenix AZ 85018

PICKENS, ALEXANDER LEGRAND, educator; b. Waco, Tex., Aug. 31, 1921; s. Alex LeGrand and Elma L. (Johnson) P.; m. Frances M. Jenkins, Aug. 20, 1955. B.A., So. Methodist U., 1950; M.A., North Tex. State U., Denton, 1952; Ed.D., Columbia U., 1959. Tchr. art public schs. Dallas, 1950-53, Elizabeth, N.J., 1953-54; mem. faculty U. Mich. Coll. Architecture and Design, 1954-59, U. Ga., Athens, 1959-62, U. Hawaii Coll. Edn., Honolulu, 1962—; prof. edn. U. Hawaii Coll. Edn., 1968—, dir. coll. devel., 1984—, chmn. doctoral studies curriculum instrn., 1984—; dir. children's classes Ft. Worth Children's Museum, 1951-53; head art Nat. Music Camp, Interlochen, Mich., summers 1957-58, U. Oreg., Portland, summers 1959-60, 62; cons. youth art activities Foremost Dairies, 1964-74; cons. art films United World Films, 1970-75; art edn. cons. Honolulu Paper Co., 1970-76, Kamehameha Sch., Bishop Estate, 1978—. Exhibited ceramics, Wichita Internat. Exhbn., Syracuse (N.Y.) Nat. Exhbn., St. Louis Mus., Dallas Mus., San Antonio Mus., Detroit Art Inst., Hawaii Craftsmen, also others; editorial bd.: Arts and Activities mag, 1955-82; editor: U. Hawaii Ednl. Perspectives, 1964—; contbr. articles to profl. jours. Mem. adult com. Dallas County chpt. Jr. ARC, 1951-53; exec. com. Dallas Crafts Guild, 1950-53; v.p., publicity chmn. U. Ga. Community Concert Assn., 1960-62. Served with USAAF, 1942-44. Recipient award merit Tex. State Fair, 1957; All Am. award Ednl. Press Assn. Am., 1968, 70, 72, 75, 79. Mem. Internat. Soc. Edn., NEA, Nat. Art Edn. Assn., AAUP, Phi Delta Kappa, Kappa Delta Pi. Address: 1471 Kalaepohaku St Honolulu HI 96816

PICKENS, ALLEN ARTHUR, accountant; b. Des Moines, Iowa, Nov. 29, 1940; s. Leo Arthur and Odessa Leona (Sly) P.; m. Dianne Patricia Guelff, Feb. 15, 1969; children—Shawn, Courtney, Megan. B.S. in Bus. Adminstrn., Drake U., 1965. C.P.A., Hawaii, Guam. Acct. Peat Marwick Main & Co., Agana, Guam, 1965—, ptnr. in charge Guam office, Agana, 1975—; instr. U. Guam, Am. Inst. Banking. Chmn. Territorial Bd. Pub. Accountancy, 1970-78; pres. Guam Growth Council, 1978-83; pres. USO, 1976-77; pres. Guam Soc. Cultural Exchange, 1979-80, Jr. Achievement of Guam Inc., 1984-86. Served with USAF, 1958-62. Named Guam Person of Yr. 1979, Rotary Club of Tumon Bay. Mem. Am. Inst. C.P.A.s, Guam Soc. C.P.A.s (founder, pres. 1973-75), Assn. Govt. Accts., Am. Acctg. Assn., Navy League U.S. (pres. Guam 1978-79), Air Force Assn. (pres. Guam chpt. 1982-83), Guam C. of C. (chmn. 1982-84). Roman Catholic. Clubs: Rotary (Guam) (pres. 1975-76, 80-81).

PICKENS, ANNE THOMSON, marketing professional; b. Mountain View, Calif., Aug. 22, 1962; d. Charles Thomson and Ethel Ira (Shope) Hoppe; m. William Gregory Pickens, Jan. 4, 1986. BS, U. Santa Clara, 1984. Tech. support asst. Convergent Techs., San Jose, Calif., 1982-84, mktg. product mgr., 1984—. Avocations: reading, outdoor sports. Office: Convergent Techs 2310 N 1st St San Jose CA 95131

PICKERING, AVAJANE, specialized education facility executive; b. New Castle, Ind., Nov. 5, 1951; d. George Willard and Elsie Jean (Wicker) P. BA, Purdue U., 1974; MS in Spl. Edn., U. Utah, 1983, postgrad., 1985—. Tchr. Granite Community Edn., Salt Lake City, 1974-79; tchr. coordinator Salt Lake City Schs., 1975-85; co-dir., owner Specialized Ednl. Programming Service, Inc., Salt Lake City, 1976—; adj. instr. U. Utah, Salt Lake City, 1985—. Rep. del. Utah State Conv., also county conv.; vol. tour guide, hostess Temple Square, Ch. Jesus Christ of Latter-Day Saints, 1983—. Mem. Council for Exceptional Children, Assn. Children and Adults with Learning Disabilities, Delta Kappa Gamma. Home: 1595 S 2100 E Salt Lake City UT 84108 Office: 2022 S 2100 E Suite 201 Salt Lake City UT 84108

PICKERING, TERRY ALLEN, infosystems specialist; b. Adrian, Mich., July 15, 1952; s. Benjamin Jacob and Blanche Loring (Skinner) P.; m. Rhonda Jo Hancock, Aug. 15, 1970 (div. Apr. 1982); children: Theresa, Brian; m. Peggy Rhonda Fleming, Dec. 14, 1985; one child, Tricia. AA in Computer Programming, Lane Community Coll., 1977, AA in Computer Ops., 1977; BS in Bus. Mgmt., Linfield Coll., 1984. Computer operator Weyerhauser Co., Springfield, Oreg., 1977-78; info. systems supr. Springfield Utility Bd., 1978-84; mgmt. info. systems dir. Consol. Supply Co., Portland, Oreg., 1984-85; pres. Mgmt. Cons. Services, Portland, 1986—. Bd. dirs. Willamalane Park and Rec. Dist., Springfield, 1980-84, chmn. bd. dirs. 1984. Served with USAF, 1972-75. Mem. Data Processing Mgmt. Assn. (edn. chmn. 1983-84), Oreg. Regional Users Group. Democrat. Clubs: Toastmasters (local pres. 1983-84). Avocations: bicycling, photography, volleyball. Home: 10235 SW 59th Pl Portland OR 97219 Office: Mgmt Cons Services 10235 SW 59th Pl Portland OR 97219

PICKETT, MARGARET ANNE, educational adminstrator; b. Banning, Calif., May 9, 1924; d. Charles Sheldon and Mary Edith (Mack) Hill; m. Ralph D. Pickett, Dec. 25, 1952; children—Mary Anne, Margaret E. B.A., U. Redlands, 1947, M.A., 1969. Dir. Head Start, Banning, Calif., 1966-68; tchr. kindergarten Beaumont (Calif.) Unified Sch. Dist., 1968-70, dir. spl. projects/elem. prin., 1973-80, dir. spl. projects, curriculum, spl. edn., 1980-83, dir. instr., 1983-86, supt. 1986—; adviser Beaumont Presch., Am. Field Service, 1978—. Mem. Assn. Supervision and Curriculum Devel., Assn. Woman Mgrs., Nat. Assn. Adminstrs. State and Federally Funded Edn. Programs, Assn. Calif. Sch. Adminstrs., Delta Kappa Gamma. Republican. Religious Scientist. Office: PO Box 187 Beaumont CA 92223

PICKLE, JOSEPH WESLEY, JR., educator, clergyman; b. Denver, Apr. 8, 1935; s. Joseph Wesley and Wilhelmina (Blacketor) P.; m. Judith Ann Siebert, June 28, 1958; children—David E., Kathryn E., Steven J. B.A., Carleton Coll., Minn., 1957; B.D., Chgo. Theol. Sem., 1961; M.A., U. Chgo., 1962, Ph.D., 1969. Ordained to ministry Am. Baptist Conv., 1962. Asst. pastor Judson Meml. Ch., N.Y.C., 1959-60; from asst. prof. to prof. religion Colo. Coll., Colorado Springs, 1964—, acting dean summer session, 1969-70, chair dept. religion, 1972-84; cons. Colo. Humanities Program, Denver, 1975-82. Co-editor: Papers of the 19th Century Theology Group, 1978. Bd. dirs., pres. Pikes Peak Mental Health Ctr., Colorado Springs, 1975; mem. Colo. Health Facilities Rev. Council, Denver, 1976-84, chmn., 1979-84; mem. Colo. Bd. Health, Denver, 1986-87. Am. Baptist Conv. scholar, 1953-57; Fulbright-Hays fellow U. Tübingen, Ger., 1963-64; Danforth fellow, 1957-63; Malone Faculty fellow, Cairo, 1987. Fellow Soc. Values in Higher Edn.; mem. Am. Theol. Soc., Am. Acad. Religion, (region pres. 1983-84), Phi Beta Kappa. Democrat. Home: 20 W Caramillo Colorado Springs CO 80907 Office: Colo Coll Colorado Springs CO 80903

PICKRELL, JACK EVON, accountant; b. Ottumwa, Iowa, Apr. 15, 1933; s. Robert Lee, Jr., and Emily Margaret (Merrill) P.; student Georgetown U., 1955-56, State U. Iowa, 1956, U. Md., 1957-58; BS in Acctg., Met. State Coll., Denver, 1980; m. Reiko Washizu, Feb. 6, 1959; 1 dau., Linda Reiko. Enlisted in U.S. Navy, 1950; served with USN, 1950-54, USAR, 1954-56, USNR, 1956-57, USAF, 1957-73, master sgt., 1968-73; ret., 1973; ops. mgr. Diamond Gas & Fuel Co., Englewood, Colo., 1973-76; gen. mgr. Alpine Pipe & Supply Co., Denver; pvt. practice pub. acct., Denver, 1977—. Decorated Bronze Star, Air Force Commendation medal with oak leaf clusters (3). Mem. U.S. Naval Cryptologic Vets. Assn., Better Bus. Bur. Greater Denver (arbitration judge). Republican. Home: 3065 Olive St Denver CO 80207 Office: 3390 Brighton Blvd Denver CO 80216

PIELE, PHILIP KERN, infosystems educator; b. Portland, Oreg., May 14, 1935; s. Theodore R. and Helen D. (Hanson) P.; m. Sandra Jean Wright, Aug. 10, 1963; children: Melissa, Kathryn. BA, Wash. State U., 1957; student, U. Wash., 1960, San Jose State U., 1964; MS, U. Oreg., 1963, PhD, 1968. Asst. prof. dept. ednl. adminstrn. U. Oreg., Eugene, 1968-72, assoc. prof. dept. ednl. adminstrn., 1972-79, prof. dept. ednl. policy and mgmt., 1979—, dir. ERIC Clearinghouse on Ednl. Mgmt., 1969—; dir. numerous ednl. orgns. and coms., U. Oreg. Coll. Edn., Eugene, 1968—; vis. scholar Stanford U., 1984; exec. sec. Oreg. Sch. Study Council, 1980—; dir. Ctr. for Advanced Tech. in Edn., 1984—. Author numerous books, chpts., monographs; editor numerous books; contbr. articles to profl. jours. Active Oreg. Tax Relief Com., Eugene, 1978; bd. dirs. Oreg. Bach Festival, Eugene, 1980-83. Served to 1st lt. U.S. Army, 1958-60. Mem. Nat. Orgn. on Legal Problems in Edn. (pres. 1977-78), Nat. Sch. Devel. COuncil (pres. 1985-86). Home: 455 Lochmoor Pl Eugene OR 97405 Office: ERIC Clearinghouse on Exec Mgmt 1787 Agatea St Eugene OR 97403

PIEPER, ORVILLE ELDEN, agri-business coordinator, farmer; b. Yuma, Colo., July 12, 1930; s. Ervin William and May Caroline (Imhof) P.; m. Bernice Ethel Bryant, July 24, 1955; children—Kathleen Kim Pieper Trum, Todd Bryant. B.S., U. Denver, 1959, M.A., 1963. Cert. in vocat. agr. State Bd. Community Colls. and Occupational Edn. Wheat, millet farmer, 1948-51, 54—; ins. agt. Farmers Union, 1954-63; tchr. bus. edn. Englewood (Colo.) High Sch., 1959-61; instr. bus. Northeastern Jr. Coll., Sterling, Colo., 1963-66; agri-bus. coordinator, 1966-86, coordinator community-based occupational programs, 1986—. Mem. local Luth. Laymen's League. Served with U.S. Army, 1952-53. Mem. Colo. Vocat. Agr. Tchrs. Assn., Nat. Vocat. Agr. Tchrs. Assn., Colo. Vocat. Assn., Nat. Vocat. Assn., Colo. Edn. Assn., NEA, Nat. Assn. Colls. and Tchrs. Agr. Contbr. articles to profl. jours. Home: Route 4 Sterling CO 80751 Office: Northeastern Jr College Sterling CO 80751

PIEPER, REX DELANE, range ecologist; b. Idaho Falls, Idaho, Jan. 18, 1934; s. Gustave H. and Maud E. (Beam) P.; m. Susan J. Tuyeffort, June 11, 1965; children: Julie, Loren, Tracy. BS, U. Idaho, 1956; MS, Utah State U., 1958; PhD, U. Calif., Berkeley, 1963. Asst. prof. animal and range sci. N.Mex. State U., Las Cruces, 1963-69, assoc. prof., 1969-75, prof., 1975—. Contbr. numerous articles to profl. jours. Recipient Disting. Tchr. award N.Mex. State U. Coll. Agr., 1972, Disting. Research award N.Mex. U. Coll. Agr., 1979. Fellow AAAS, Soc. Range Mgmt.; mem. S.W. Assn. Nature, Am. Soc. Animal Sci. Home: 4825 Senita Rd Las Cruces NM 88001 Office: U New Mex Dept Animal and Range Scis Box 3i Las Cruces NM 88003

PIEPGRASS, DON HOLMAN, muncipal agency administrator; b. Raymond, Alta., Can., Jan. 13, 1947; came to U.S., 1978; s. Ellys D. and Hellen (Holman) P.; m. Debra Ray Mecham, June 16, 1979; children: David, Brian. BSCE, U. Alta., 1973; MSCE, Brigham Young U., 1983. Registered profl. engr., Utah. Jr. engr. Associated Engring. Services Ltd., Edmonton, Alta., 1973-75; project engr. City of Calgary (Alta) Engring., 1975-78; engr. Kennecott Copper Corp., Salt Lake City, 1979-83; asst. street supt. Salt Lake City Corp., 1983-87; cons. engr. 1987—. Served to lt. Can. Mil., 1972-78. Mem. ASCE, Am. Pub. Works Assn., Govt. Refuse Collection and Disposal Assn. Republican. Mormon. Club: Deseret Gym (Salt Lake City). Avocations: writing, reading, hunting, flying, scuba diving.

PIEPMEIER, EDWARD HARMAN, chemistry educator; b. St. Louis, June 6, 1937; s. Francis Harman and Mildred Elizabeth (Branom) P.; m. Karen Sue Swanson, Feb. 11, 1961; children: Edward Jr., Eric, Kristen. BS in Sci. Engring., Northwestern U., 1960; PhD in Chemistry, U. Ill., 1966. Teaching asst. U. Ill., Urbana, 1962-66; asst. prof. Oreg. State U., Corvallis, 1966-73, assoc. prof., 1973-79, prof., 1979—. Editor: Analytical Applications of Lasers, 1986; contbr. articles to profl. jours.; inventor multi-electrode plasma source, 1985. Served to lt. USN, 1960-62. Fellow Delft U. of Tech., The Netherlands, 1973, NASA, 1979; grantee NSF, 1969-86. Mem. AAUP, Am. Chem. Soc. (local pres. 1979), Analytical Chem. Div. Am. Chem. Soc., Soc. Applied Spectroscopy. Office: Oreg State U Dept Chemistry Corvallis OR 97331

PIERCE, GEORGE ADAMS, university official; b. Carlsbad, N.Mex., May 21, 1943; s. Jack Colwell and Shirley (Adams) P.; m. Margaret Mary Brakel, Feb. 10, 1980; children: Christopher, Catherine Rose. BA in Polit. Sci., Fairleigh Dickinson U.; MA in Polit. Sci., New Sch. Social Research; PhD in Higher Edn., Claremont Grad. Sch. Asst. dir. promotion Afco, N.Y.C., 1969-71; dir. spl. programs U. Calif., Riverside, 1971-73; asst. to pres. Claremont (Calif.) Grad. Sch., 1973-75; asst. to pres. Seattle U., 1975-78, dir. planning, 1978-83, v.p. adminstrn., 1983—; chmn. regional review panel Truman Scholarship Found., 1977—. Chmn. Seattle Ctr. Adv. Commn., 1977-83; bd. dirs. N.W. Kidney Found., Seattle, 1986—. Served with USAF, 1963-65. Recipient Cert. Merit Riverside County Comprehensive Health Planning, 1972, Cert. Appreciation Office Mayor City of Seattle, 1983, Nat. Truman Scholarship Found., 1986. Mem. Am. Assn. Higher Edn., Assn. Instnl. Research (regional pres. 1977—), Soc. Coll. and Planning, Cause. Democrat. Roman Catholic. Club: City (Seattle). Avocations: backpacking, canoeing, swimming, tennis. Home: 6510 129th Ave SE Bellevue WA 98006 Office: Seattle U Broadway and Madison Sts Seattle WA 98122

PIERCE, JAMES FRANKLIN, data systems consultant; b. Seaford, N.Y., Aug. 24, 1950; s. James Franklin and Marion April (Augustine) P.; m. Kit Lan Lee, July 4, 1980; 1 child, James Franklin. AAS, Olympic Coll., 1970; BSBA, U. Phoenix, 1984; BS, SUNY, 1984; MBA, U. Phoenix, 1986. Cert. systems profl. Cons. GTE-Informatics Co., N.Y.C., 1974-75, Frito-Lay Co., Dallas, 1976-77, Occidental Petroleum Co., Houston, 1977-78, Lockheed Missiles & Space Co., Sunnyvale, Calif., 1978-79; cons., owner Intel Corp., San Jose, Calif., 1979—. Mem. Republican Task Force. Mem. Assn. Systems Mgmt., ACM. Home and Office: 831 W Pampa Ave Mesa AZ 85202

PIERCE, JON PAGE, aluminum and chemical company executive, personnel administrator; b. Mobile, Ala., Oct. 26, 1940; s. Edwin Patterson and Teva (Jordan) P.; m. Sherry Kaye Hammack, July 18, 1964; children: Lesley, Julie, Brad. BS in Labor and Personnel Mgmt., U. Ala., 1963. Plant employee relations mgr. Kaiser Aluminum and Chem. Corp., Baton Rouge and Spokane, Wash., 1969-77; mgr. employee relations div. Kaiser Aluminum and Chem. Corp., Oakland, Calif., 1977-82, dir. compensation and benefits, 1982-85, personnel director, 1985—; instr. Dale Carnegie, Walnut Creek, Calif., 1979-80; adv. group Sr. Human Resources, San Francisco Bay, 1985—. Bd. dirs., exec. com. United Crusade, Spokane, 1970-73, Baton Rouge, 1976; bd. dirs., mem. exec. com. Spokane C. of C., 1970-73, Jr. Achievement, 1970-73. Served to 1st lt. U.S. Army, 1963-65. Recipient Outstanding Alumnus award dept. mgmt. U. Ala., 1985. Mem. Western Pension Conf., Am. Mgmt. Assn., Am. Compensation Assn., Council on Employee Benefits, Sigma Chi (pres. 1962, Outstanding Mem. award 1963). Republican. Lutheran. Clubs: Sherwood Forest Country; Spokane; Lakeview (Oakland). Avocations: art, golf, fishing, boating, tennis. Home: 8 Golden Hill Ct Walnut Creek CA 94596 Office: Kaiser Aluminum and Chem Corp 300 Lakeside Dr Oakland CA 94643

PIERCE, KIM MARIE, oceanographic institute administrator; b. Pasadena, Calif., July 19, 1946; d. Lawrence Kenneth and Esther Charlotte (Wood) Beavers; m. Thomas Wayne Reese, Sept. 14, 1968 (div. May, 1974); children: Brian, Shannon; m. David Lee Pierce Aug. 1, 1979. Student, San Diego State U., 1964-67. Sr. clk. U. Calif. San Diego, La Jolla, 1967-70; administrv. asst. Scripps Inst. Oceanography, La Jolla, 1970-78, administrv. analyst, 1978-81, sr. administrv. analyst, 1981-83, mgmt. service officer, 1983—; Propr. Video Renter Stores, San Diego, 1984—; lectr. Dress for Success, San Diego, 1982-84. Del. citizens adv. com. to Japan and People's Republic of China, Spokane, Wash., 1986. Mem. W. Assn. Coll. Univ. Bus. Officers, Digital Equipment Corp. User Soc., Soc. Research Administrs., Acad. Bus. Officers Group, U. Calif. San Diego Women's Caucus, San Diego, Nat. Assn. Coll. and U. Research Adminstrs. Republican. Home: 3234 N Star Dr San Diego CA 92117 Office: Scripps Inst Oceanography 8605 La Jolla Shores Dr La Jolla CA 92117

PIERCE, RICHARD SCOTT, mathematics educator; b. Long Beach, Calif., Feb. 26, 1927; s. Robert Scott and Dorothea Stinson (Bloomfield) P.; m. Mary Elizabeth Ray, June 26, 1953 (div.); 1 child, Eric; m. Marilyn Louise Neher, Nov. 23, 1971. BS, Calif. Inst. Tech., 1950, PhD, 1952. From asst. prof. to prof. math. U. Wash., Seattle, 1955-70; prof. U. Hawaii, Honolulu, 1970-75, U. Ariz., Tucson, 1975—. Author: Algebraic Foundations of Math, 1963, Introduction to Abstract Algebras, 1968, Associative Algebras, 1983; contbr. articles to profl. jours. Served with U.S. Army, 1945-46. Fellow Yale U., 1952-53, Harvard U., 1953-55, NSF postdoctoral fellow, 1961-62. Mem. AAAS, Assn. Symbolic Logic, Math. Assn. Am., Am. Math. Soc. (assoc. sec. 1958-74), Sigma Xi. Home: 4525 Placita Del Bac Tucson AZ 85718 Office: U Ariz Dept Math Tucson AZ 85721

PIERCE, SHANCY, casting director; b. Los Angeles, Sept. 30, 1942; d. Warren Alfred and Loraine Rice (Potter) P. A.A., Valley Jr. Coll., 1973; B.A. in Anthropology, Calif. State U.-Northridge, 1979. Animation camerаperson Walt Disney Studios, Burbank, Calif., 1961-63; prodn. asst. Dick Clark Prodns., Los Angeles, 1972-73; talent coordinator Solowitz Orgn., Hollywood, Calif., 1975-77; casting dir. Spungbuggy Works Inc., Los Angeles, 1977-83; owner, operator Slate Please, Los Angeles, 1983—. Pres., Van Nuys (Calif.) chpt. Young Republicans, 1974. Recipient CLIO award, 1980, 81, 84, Telly award 1983, 84, Internat. Film and TV Festival award of N.Y., 1982. Mem. Nat. Assn. Female Execs., Calif. State U. Northridge Alumni Assn. (pres.), Comml. Casting Dirs. Assn. Christian Scientist. Office: 3917 Riverside Dr #9109 Burbank CA 91505

PIERCE, WAYNE STANLEY, botany educator; b. Atascadero, Calif., Mar. 8, 1942; s. Charles Robert and Frances Teresa (Peterson) P.; m. Donna Martine Breidenthal, Aug. 29, 1964; 1 child, Amy. AB in Botany, Humboldt State U., 1964; MS in Botany, Wash. State U., 1967, PhD in Botany, 1971. Research asst. Wash. State U., Pullman, 1971; asst. prof. Calif. State U. Stanislaus, Turlock, 1971-76, prof. botany, 1981—; vis. faculty U. Houston, 1978; vis. prof. U. Md., 1986—. Contbr. articles to profl. jours. Mem. Am. Soc. Plant Physiologists, Japanese Soc. Plant Physiologists, Sigma Xi. Democrat. Avocations: golf, fishing. Office: Calif State U Stanislaus Dept Biol Scis Turlock CA 95380

PIERCY, GORDON CLAYTON, banker; b. Takoma Park, Md., Nov. 23, 1944; s. Gordon Clayton and Dorothy Florence (Brummer) P.; B.S., Syracuse U., 1966; M.B.A., Pace U., 1973; m. Roberta Margaret Walton, 1985; children: Elizabeth Anne, Kenneth Charles. Mgmt. trainee Suburban Bank, Bethesda, Md., 1962-66; mktg. planning asso. Chem. Bank, N.Y.C., 1966-70; sr. market devel. officer Seattle-First Nat. Bank, 1970-74; product expansion adminstr., mktg. planning mgr. Nat. BankAmericard, Inc., San Francisco, 1974-76; v.p., dir. mktg. Wash. Mut. Savs. Bank, Seattle, 1976-82; v.p., mktg. dir. First Interstate Bank of Wash. N.A., 1983-86; v.p. mktg., dir. Puget Sound Nat. Bank, Tacoma, 1986—. Mem. Am. Mktg. Assn., Bank Mktg. Assn., Mktg. Communications Execs. Internat., Seattle Advt. Fedn., Tacoma Ad Club, Am. Bankers Assn. (retail electronic services and bank card div., exec. com.), Sigma Nu, Alpha Kappa Psi, Delta Mu Delta. Episcopalian. Home: 23632 SE 225th St Maple Valley WA 98038 Office: PO Box 2076 Tacoma WA 98401

PIERUCCI, MAURO, aerospace engineer, educator; b. Lucca, Italy, Jan. 5, 1942; came to U.S., 1955, naturalized, 1961; s. Albert and Mary (Moschini) P.; B.S., Poly. Inst. N.Y., 1963, M.S., 1964, Ph.D., 1968; m. Mary Di-Massi, May 29, 1965; children—Marc, Claudia. Research asso. Poly. Inst. N.Y., 1965-68; prin. engr. electric boat div. General Dynamics Corp., Groton, Conn., 1968-79; lectr. (part-time) U. New Haven, Conn., 1974-75; prof. aerospace engring. and engring. mechanics dept. San Diego (Calif.) State U., 1979—; cons. acoustics and aerodynamics, 1972—. Mem. Ledyard (Conn.) Town Com., 1977-79. ONR Summer Faculty fellow, 1986, 87, NSF fellow, 1964-66. Fellow Acoustical Soc. Am. (chmn. engring. acoustics com. 1981-85); assoc. fellow AIAA (mem. exec. com. Conn. sect. 1978-79, treas. Conn. sect. 1979), Acoustical Soc. Am. (engring. acoustics com. 1978—, chmn. com. spl. tutorial sessions 1984—, medals and awards com. 1986—), Sigma Xi, Sigma Gamma Tau, Tau Beta Pi. Contbr. articles on acoustics and fluid mechanics to profl. publs. Home: 2701 Summit Dr Escondido CA 92025 Office: Dept Aerospace Engring San Diego State Univ San Diego CA 92182

PIES, RONALD E., city official; b. Rochester, N.Y., Mar. 21, 1940; s. Herman S. and Sylvia P.; m. Bernita Orloff, Aug. 27, 1964; children—Cara Jean, David Paul; B.S., Ariz. State U., 1963; Recreation leader City of Phoenix, Ariz., 1962-64; head recreation div. City of Scottsdale (Ariz.) Parks and Recreation Dept., 1964-69; dir. parks and recreation, City of Tempe, Ariz., 1969-84, community services dir., 1984—; guest lectr. Ariz. State U. Mem., pres. Kyrene Sch. Dist. Governing Bd., 1979-82. Chmn., bd. regents Pacific Revenue Sources Mgmt. Sch. NRPA; gen. chmn. Fiesta Bowl Soccer Classic, 1982—; founding mem. Tempe YMCA bd. mgrs.; appointed mem. Ariz. State Parks Bd., 1987—. Named Outstanding Young Man, Jaycees. Mem. Tempe C. of C., Ariz. Parks and Recreation Assn. (bd. dirs. 1986—, pres. adminstrs., Disting. Fellow award 1983), Nat. Recreation and Parks Assn., Sigma Alpha Epsilon. Club: Tempe Diablos. Office: 3500 S Rural Rd Tempe AZ 85282

PIETRZAK, LAWRENCE MICHAEL, research engineer; b. Detroit, June 27, 1942; s. Eugene Anothony and Stella (Majchrzak) P.; m. Betty Jane Sandora, June 19, 1965; children: Jeffrey, Michelle, Elizabeth. Student, Villanova U., 1960-62; BS summa cum laude, U. Detroit, 1965; MS summa cum laude, MIT, 1966, profl. engring. degree, 1967. Research engr. Gen. Research Corp., Santa Barbara, Calif., and Washington, 1967-74; dir. protection tech. systems group Mission Research Corp., Santa Barbara, 1974—; mem. com. on fire modeling Nat. Bur. Standards, Gathersburg, Md., 1978—, mem. com. on fire suppression equipment Nat. Fire Protection Association, Boston, 1979—. Contbr. articles to profl. jours. Mem. youth group YMCA, Santa Barbara, 1978-80. Recipient Outstanding Fire Service award County of Santa Barbara, 1979; fellow NSF, 1965-66, Am. Inst. Steel Constrn., 1966-67. Mem. AAAS, ASCE, Am. Soc. Indsl. Security, Soc. Computer Simulation, Sigma Xi, Tau Beta Pi, Chi Epsilon, Phi Sigma Tau, Theta Tau. Roman Catholic. Lodge: KC. Avocations: mountain backpacking, fishing, biking, reading. Home: 6541 Camino Caseta Goleta CA 93117 Office: Mission Research Corp PO Drawer 719 735 State St Santa Barbara CA 93102

PIETTE, LAWRENCE HECTOR, educator, biophysicist, university dean and official; b. Chgo., Jan. 4, 1932; s. Gerald John and Lillian (Bumgardner) P.; m. Mary Irene Harris, Aug. 15, 1957; children—Jeffrey, Martin. B.S., Northwestern U., 1953, M.S., 1954; Ph.D., Stanford U., 1957. Mgr. research biochemistry and biophysics Varian Assos., 1956-65; prof. biophysics U. Hawaii, 1965—, chmn. dept., 1968—, dir. Cancer Research Lab., 1970-84; exec. dir. Cancer Center Hawaii, 1974; Chmn. cancer adv. com., regional med. program, research com. Hawaii div. Am. Cancer Soc.; dean. Sch. Grad. Studies Utah State U., Logan, 1984—; assoc. v.p. research Utah State U., 1984—, prof. biochemistry, 1984—. Contbr. articles to profl. jours.; Asso. editor: Jour. Organic Magnetic Resonance. Mem. Am. Chem. Soc., Biophys. Soc., A.A.U.P. Home: 363 Boulevard Logan UT 84321

PIGNATARO, AUGUSTUS, physicist; b. N.Y.C., Aug. 12, 1943; s. Frank and Amelia (Teneriello) P.; m. Lynn M. Kline, Oct. 16, 1965; children; Lisa M., Julie M., Jeffrey D. BS, Calif. State U., Los Angeles, 1965; MBA, Calif. Luth. U., 1975. Engr. Atlantic Research Corp., Costa Mesa, Calif., 1965-67; electro-optical physicist Pacific Missile Test Ctr., USN, Point Mugu, Calif., 1967—. Mem. Naval Aviation Exec. Inst., Infrared Info. Symposium. Republican. Roman Catholic. Home: 1094 Harris Ave Camarillo CA 93010 Office: USN Code 4033 Pacific Missile Test Ctr Point Mugu CA 93042

PIGOTT, CHARLES MCGEE, transportation equipment manufacturer; b. Seattle, Apr. 21, 1929; s. Paul and Theiline (McGee) P.; m. Yvonne Flood, Apr. 18, 1953. B.S., Stanford U., 1951. With PACCAR Inc, Seattle, 1959—; exec. v.p. PACCAR Inc, 1962-65, pres., 1965—, chief exec. officer, chmn. bd. dirs.; dir. Boeing Co., Citibank/Citicorp, Chevron Corp. Pres. Nat. Boy Scouts Am., 1986-87, mem. exec. bd. Mem. Bus. Council. Office: PACCAR Inc Business Center Bldg 777 106th Ave NE PO Box 1518 Bellevue WA 98004 *

PIGOTT, GEORGE MORRIS, food engineering educator; b. Vancouver, Wash., Oct. 25, 1928; s. Alexander William and Moreita (Howard) P.; m. Joyce Burroughs (div. 1980); 5 children; m. Barbee W. Tucker; 5 children. BS in Chem. Engring., U. Wash., 1950, MS in Chem. Engring., 1955, PhD in Food Sci. and Chemistry, 1962. Prof. food engring. U. Wash., 1962—; cons. engr. Sea Resources Engring., Inc., Bellevue, Wash., 1958—. Author: Pathway to a Healthy Heart, 1983, Fish and Shellfish in Human Nutrition, 1987; over 200 tech. papers; patentee in field. Served to lt. U.S. Army, 1950-53. Mem. Am. Inst. Chem. Engrs., Am. Inst. Nutrition, Am. Chem. Soc., Inst. Food Technologists, Am. Assn. Agrl. Engrs., ASPE. Avocations: scuba diving, skiing, beekeeping. Office: Inst for Food Sci and Tech U Wash HF-10 Seattle WA 98195

PIIRTO, DOUGLAS DONALD, forester, educator; b. Reno, Nev., Sept. 25, 1948; s. Rueben Arvid and Martha Hilma (Giebel) P.; BS, U. Nev., 1970;

MS, Colo. State U., 1971; PhD, U. Calif., Berkeley, 1977; m. Mary Louise Cruz, Oct. 28, 1978. Research asst. Colo. State U., 1970-71, U. Calif., Berkeley, 1972-77; forester, silviculturist U.S. Dept. Agr., Forest Service, Sierra Nat. Forest, Trimmer and Shaver Lake, Calif., 1977-85; assoc. prof. natural resources mgmt. dept. Calif. Poly. State U., San Luis Obispo, 1985—; instr. part-time Kings River Community Coll., Reedley, Calif. Registered profl. forester, Calif.; cert. silviculturist U.S. Forest Service. Mem. Soc. Am. Foresters, Am. Forestry Assn., Forest Products Research Soc., Soc. Wood Sci. and Tech., Alpha Zeta, Xi Sigma Pi, Sigma Xi, Beta Beta Beta, Phi Sigma Kappa. Lutheran. Contbr. articles to sci. and forestry jours. Home: 3032 E Paul Ave Fresno CA 93710 Office: Calif Poly State U Dept Natural Resource Mgmt San Luis Obispo CA 93710

PIKE, DOUGLAS EUGENE, political scientist; b. Cass Lake, Minn., July 27, 1924; s. Clarence Eugene and Esther (Jensen) P.; m. Myrna Louise Johnson, Sept. 15, 1956; children: Andrew Jefferson, Victoria Louise, Ethan Edward. BA, U. Calif., 1953; MA, Am. U., 1961; postgrad., MIT, 1963-64. Writer UN, Korea, 1950-52; fgn. service officer U.S. Govt. State Dept., Washington, Saigon, Hong Kong, Tokyo, and Taipei, Taiwan., 1958-82; dir. Indochina Studies Program, U. Calif., Berkeley, 1982—. Author: Viet Cong: The Organizational Techniques of the National Liberation Front of South Vietnam, 1965, War, Peace and the Viet Cong, 1969, History of Vietnamese Communism, 1978, PAVN: People's Army of Vietnam, 1986, Vietnam and the USSR: Anatomy of an Alliance, 1987; editor: Indochina Chronology, 1983—; contbr. numerous articles to profl. jours. Bd. dir. Vietnam Refugee Assn., Washington, 1975-82. Recipient Surperior Honor award, U.S. Info. Agy., 1976, Sec. Def. medal, U.S. Dept. Def., 1981. Mem. Author's Guild, Army-Navy Club (Washington), Fgn. Service Club, Faculty Club U. Calif. Methodist. Avocation: philately. Home: 2265 Alva Ave El Cerrito CA 94530 Office: U Calif 6701 San Pablo Ave Berkeley CA 94720

PIKE, GEORGE RUSSELL, lawyer, financial executive, investor; b. Reno, Jan. 2, 1938; s. Miles Nelson and Marchand Elise (Newman) P.; m. Eunice Heidi Pike, June 6, 1963 (dec.); m. Mirjana Klaich, Mar. 30, 1974; children: Miles N., Mirjana Elise. BSBA, U. Nev., Reno, 1961; JD, Georgetown U., 1965. Bar: Nev. 1965. U.S. commr. Dist. Nev., Reno, 1968-71, U.S. magistrate, 1971-75; sr. v.p., gen. counsel, exec. asst. to pres. First Fed. Savs. of Nev., Reno, 1970-79; pres. Russell Investment Co., Reno, 1970—, First Fin. Service Corp., Reno, 1976-81, Triad Fin. Corp., San Francisco, 1982-84; v.p. GRZ & A, Walnut Creek, Calif., 1985-86. Bd. dirs. ARC, Reno, 1978-79. Served to capt. U.S. Army, 1965-67. Mem. ABA, State Bar Nev., Washoe County Bar Assn., Calif. Savs. and Loan League. Republican. Episcopalian. Home: 2680 Spinnaker Dr Reno NV 89509 Office: 121 California Ave Reno NV 89509

PILATTI, BARBARA DRAKE, banker; b. Louisville, Ky., Apr. 29, 1945; d. Robert Drake Stevens and Della Katherine (Beebee) Jones; m. Michael Phillip Boggioni, Aug. 20, 1963 (div. Aug. 1966); m. Lloyd Leslie Pilatti, Apr. 22, 1980; children: Marci, Mike, Gina, Robert, Robin, Jonathan. Student, Riverside City Coll., 1963-69, Coll. Guam, Coll. of the Desert. Planning dir. City of Indio, Calif., 1969-72; adminstrv. asst. Odlum Properties, Indio, 1972-74, S.W. Calif. Prodn. Credit Assn., Riverside, Calif., 1974-79; v.p. Fed. Land Bank So. Calif., Indio, 1979—; co-owner Lloyd Produce Express, Cherry Valley, Calif., 1983—; v.p., br. mgr. Fed. Land Bank of So. Calif. and So. Calif. Prodn. Credit Assn., 1986—; advisor FFA, Riverside, 1984; bd. dirs. F. Bolger Transp. Inc., El Paso, Tex. Mem. Am. Agri-Women, Calif. Women for Agriculture, Good Sports Internat. (dist. pres. 1978-80). Republican. Methodist. Lodges: Order Eastern Star, Soroptimists (treas. Indio club 1983-84). Office: Fed Land Bank So Calif 83-057 Requa Indio CA 92201

PILGERAM, LAURENCE OSCAR, biochemist; b. Great Falls, Mont., June 23, 1924; s. John Rudolph and Bertha Roslyn (Phillips) P.; m. Marilyn June Heinrich, Feb. 11, 1951; children: Karl Erich, Kurt John. AA, U. Calif., Berkeley, 1948, BA, 1949, PhD, 1953. Instr. dept. physiology U. Ill. Profl. Coll., Chgo., 1954-55; asst. prof. dept. biochemistry Stanford (Calif.) U. Sch. Medicine, 1955-57; dir. arteriosclerosis research lab. U. Minn. Sch. Medicine, Mpls., 1957-65, Santa Barbara, Calif., 1965-71; dir. coagulation lab., assoc. dir. Cerebrovascular Research Ctr., Baylor Coll. Medicine, Tex. Med. Ctr., Houston, 1971-75; dir. Thrombosis Control Labs., Palo Alto, Calif., 1975-79, Santa Barbara, 1979—; cons. NIH, Bio-Sci. Labs., FDA; del. Council on Thrombosis and Council on Strokes, Am. Heart Assn. Assembly. Co-editor: Nutrition and Thrombosis for the Nat. Dairy Council, 1973; contbr. sci. articles to profl. jours. Recipient CIBA award, London, 1958, Karl Thomae award, Germany, 1973; NIH grantee, 1954-75; LIfe Ins. Med. Research Fund fellow, 1952-54. Mem. Am. Soc. Biol. Chemists. Office: PO Box 1583 Goleta PO Santa Barbara CA 93116

PILKINGTON-MIKSA, ROBERT MAREK, film and TV executive; b. London, Oct. 17, 1948; came to U.S., 1985; s. Wlodimiercz Janush and Angela Marion (Pilkington) Pilkington-Miksa; m. Charlotte Susan Yorke-Long, May 24, 1980; 1 child, Lara Louise. Diploma in French, English, Aiglon Coll., Vaud, Switzerland, 1966; grad. SLX officer, Britannia Royal Naval Coll., Dartmouth, Eng., 1967. Diplomate psychotheraphy, London. Pvt. practice psychotherapy London, 1976-81; assoc. Graphic Films Ltd., London, 1983-84; sr. exec. Boyds Film co., London, 1984-85; exec. v.p. Whitefeather Prodns., Los Angeles, 1985-87, pres., 1987—. Recipient Yachmaster cert. Dept. Trade, London, 1980. Mem. Hollywood Radio and TV Soc., Acad. TV Arts and Scis. Club: Annabels (London). Avocations: sailing, music. Home: 2526 Thames St Los Angeles CA 90046 Office: Whitefeather Prodns 8455 Beverly Blvd #406 Los Angeles CA 90048

PILL, JEFFREY MACLIN, television and film producer; b. Le Mars, Iowa, Oct. 12, 1942; s. Edward and Dorothy (Kushner) P. BA, U. Iowa, 1964, MA, 1969. Producer/writer CBS News, Chgo., 1969-71; producer/dir./writer Sports Action Profile, Chgo., 1971-73, David Wolper Prodns., Los Angeles, 1974-78; series producer Alan Landsburg Prodns. "In Search of...", Los Angeles, 1978-80; sr. producer ABC News 20/20, N.Y.C., 1980-81; pres. Pill Enterprises, Inc., Los Angeles, 1981—. Author/editor: Larry Mahan's Rodeo, 1972. Served to lt. USNR, 1964-67. Mem. Nat. Acad. TV Arts and Scis., Writers Guild of Am. Avocations: sailing, fly fishing. Home: 117 S Doheny Dr #209 Los Angeles CA 90048

PILLAI, PARAMESWARAN, educator; b. Trivandrum, India, Oct. 29, 1927; came to U.S., 1960; s. Padmanabha and Bhageerathi (Amma) P.; m. Becky B. Grieve, Mar. 2, 1967; 1 child, Shanti. BSc, Univ. Coll., Trivandrum, 1947; MS, U. Kerala, Trivandrum, 1953; PhD, U. Colo, 1964. Entomologist Cashewnut Assn., Quilon and Kerala, India, 1953-60; pest control researcher Food Tech. Inst., Mysore, India, 1965-67; project assoc. U. Wis., Madison, 1967-68; sci. pool officer U. Kerala, 1968-70; sci. tchr. Santa Monica (Calif.) Montessori Sch., 1970—, sci. dir., 1980—; instr. sci. Community Sch., Los Angeles, 1978-80. Author: Pests of Stored Fish, 1957; also articles. Active Univ. Elem. Sch. Family-Sch. Alliance, UCLA, 1973-79, Santa Monica-Malibu Unified Sch. Dist. PTA, 1979-85. Fulbright grantee, 1960; fellow Indian Council Agrl. Research, 1949-52. Mem. East-West Culture Ctr., Stanford Parents' Club, Sigma Xi (assoc.). Avocations: vegetarian cooking, yoga, consciousness research. Home: 1139 16th St Santa Monica CA 90403 Office: Santa Monica Montessori Sch 1619 20th St Santa Monica CA 90404

PILLAR, CHARLES LITTLEFIELD, mining consultant; b. Denver, May 25, 1911; s. Charles and Alice May (Littlefield) P.; m. Elizabeth Reed Broadhead, Sept. 10, 1932 (div. May 1939); m. 2d Gwendola Elizabeth Lotz, Sept. 16, 1939; children—Ann, Catherine, Pamela. Engr. mines, Colo. Sch. Mines, 1935. Registered profl. engr., B.C., Ariz. Various positions in field, 1935-75; mine cons. Pillar, Lowell & Assocs., Tucson, Ariz., 1976-83; cons. Bechtel Corp., San Francisco, 1976-79, Fluor Corp., Redwood City, Calif., 1979—; mem. Colo. Sch. Mines Research Inst., Golden, 1975—; dir. Internat. Geosystems Corp., Vancouver, B.C. Contbr. articles to profl. jours. Served to capt. USAF, 1942-45. Mem. AIME William Saunders Gold Medal award), Can. Inst. Mining and Metallurgy, Profl. Engrs. B.C. Republican. Episcopalian. Club: Vancouver, Tucson Nat. Country. Home: 9460 N Camino Del Plata Tucson AZ 85741 Office: Mining Cons 5115 N Oracle Rd Tucson AZ 85704

PILLAY, SIVASANKARA K.K., research scientist; b. Puliyoor, India, Jan. 28, 1935; came to U.S., 1960; s. Raman T.N. and Janaki Amma Pillay; m. Revathi Krishnamurthy, Mar. 22, 1964; 1 child, Gautam. BS with honors, U. Mysore, Bangalore, India, 1955, MS, 1956; PhD, Pa. State U., 1965. Lectr. U. Mysore, 1956-60; teaching asst. Pa. State U., University Park, 1960-65, assoc. prof. nuclear engring., 1971-81; research assoc. Argonne (Ill.) Nat. Lab., 1965-66; sr. research scientist Western N.Y. Nuclear Research Ctr., Buffalo, 1966-71; scientist Los Alamos (N.Mex.) Nat. Lab., 1981—; cons. Pa. State Police, Harrisburg, 1971-75, Brookhaven Nat. Lab., Upton, N.Y., 1976-80, U.S. Dept. Energy, Washington, 1977-80, Radiation Mgmt. Corp., Phila., 1978-81. Author: Laboratory Experiments in Applied Nuclear and Radiochemistry, 1979, Nuclear Technology Laboratory Experiments, 1979; editor Pa. State Cosmopolitan, 1962-63; contbr. articles to profl. jours. Sec. Boy Scouts Am., Chitradurga, India, 1957-50, treas., University Park, 1975-76; warden Silver Jubilee Orphanage, Chitradurga, 1958-60. Fellow Kopper Chem. Co., 1962-63, ERDA, 1976. Fellow Am. Inst. Chemists (cert. chemist); mem. AAAS, Am. Nuclear Soc. (asst. tech. program 1982, chmn. program isotopes and radiation div. 1984—), Inst. Nuclear Materials Mgmt., Am. Chem. Soc., Health Physics Soc., N.Y. Acad. Scis., Sigma Xi. Home: 369 Cheryl Ave Los Alamos NM 87544 Office: Los Alamos Nat Lab Group N-4 Mail Stop E541 Los Alamos NM 87545

PIMENTEL, GEORGE CLAUDE, chemist; b. Rolinda, Calif., May 2, 1922; s. Emile J. and Lorraine Alice (Reid) P.; m.; children: Anne Christine, Tess Loren, Janice Amy. AB, UCLA, 1943; PhD in Chemistry, U. Calif., Berkeley, 1949. From instr. to assoc. prof. chemistry U. Calif., Berkeley, 1949-59, prof., 1959—; dep. dir. NSF, Washington, 1977-80; dir. Lab. Chem. Biodynamics, U. Calif., Berkeley, 1981—; participant U.S.-Japan Eminent Scientists Exchange Program, 1973-74. Editor: Chemistry-An Experimental Science, 1963; co-author: Understanding Chemistry, 1971, Introductory Quantitative Chemistry, 1956; editor: Chem. Study, 1960; contbr. papers to profl. jours. Served with USNR, 1944-46. Guggenheim fellow, 1955; recipient Campus Teaching award U. Calif., Berkeley, 1968, Coll. Chemistry Teaching award Mfg. Chemists Assn., 1971, Joseph Priestley Meml. award Dickinson Coll., 1972, Spectroscopy Soc. Pitts., 1974, Alexander von Humboldt Sr. Scientist award, 1974, Pauling medal, 1982, Wolf prize, 1982, Debye award, 1983, Madison Marshall award, 1983, Nat. Medal of Sci. award, 1985, Gesselleschaft Deutscher Chemiker medal, August-Wilhelm-von Hofmann-Denkumnze, 1985, William Proctor prize, 1985, Robert A. Welch award in Chemistry, 1986. Fellow Am. Acad. Arts and Sci.; mem. Nat. Acad. Scis., Am. Chem. Soc. (pres. 1986—, Precision Sci. award 1959, award Calif. sect. 1957), Am. Phys. Soc. (Earle K. Plyer prize 1979, Lippencott medal 1980), Optical Soc. Am., Phi Beta Kappa, Sigma Xi., Phi Eta Sigma, Phi Lambda Epsilon, Alpha Chi Sigma. Home: 754 Coventry Rd Kensington CA 94707 Office: Univ of Calif Lab Chem Biodynamics Berkeley CA 94720

PINAR, ELIZABETH SMITH, nutrition educator, dietitian; b. Mt. Vernon, Ohio, Mar. 13, 1918; d. Wiley and Susan Ada (McCormick) Smith; m. Robert E. Pinar, Aug. 17, 1946 (div.); children—Robert W., John F., Jeffrey K. B.S., Ohio State U., 1940, B.A., 1941, M.S., 1948; postgrad. Colo. State U., 1972—. Tchr. home econs. and English, LaGrange and Shelby, Ohio, 1941-43; asst., then head dietitian Marshall Coll., Huntington, W.Va., 1943-44, 45-46; asst. mgr. Pomerene Refectory, Ohio State U., Columbus, 1946-48, 61-62, lab. instr. quantity foods Pomerene Refectory, 1961-62; head dietitian Otterbein Coll., Westerville, Ohio, 1950-52; tchr. Tecumseh High Sch., New Carlisle, Ohio, 1963-70; clin. dietitian Porter Meml. Hosp., Denver, 1971-75; instr. nutrition, program dir. dietetic tech. Front Range Community Coll., Westminster, Colo., 1971—. Active numerous civic and ch. groups. Mem. Am. Dietetic Assn. (registered dietitian), Colo. Dietetic Assn., Denver Dietetic Assn., Nutrition Today Soc. (charter). Home: 8706 W 86th Dr Arvada CO 80005 Office: Front Range Community Coll Sci and Health 3645 W 112th Ave Westminster CO 80030

PINBOROUGH, JUDITH ANN, speech and language pathologist; b. Salt Lake City, Oct. 15, 1952; d. Walter Hebern and Madeline Jane (Snowball) P. BS magna cum laude, U. Utah, 1974, MS magna cum laude, 1976, postgrad., 1984—. Cert. clin. competence. Speech pathologist Granite Sch. Dist., Salt Lake City, 1976-78, Utah Dept. Health, Salt Lake City, 1978—; aux. faculty U. Utah, Salt Lake City, 1979—, instr. 1985; licensing examiner Utah Speech and Hearing, Salt Lake City, 1982; cons. Primary Children's Med. Ctr., Salt Lake City, 1984—. Del. Rep. Party, 1979. Mem. Utah Speech and Hearing Assn. (sec., treas. 1978-80), Am. Speech and Hearing Assn. Mormon. Office: Utah Dept Health 44 Medical Dr Salt Lake City UT 84106

PINCUS, IRWIN JACK, retired medical educator; b. Braddock, Pa., Dec. 2, 1912; s. Jacob M. and Ethel (Brioda) P.; m. Lena Magaziner, Sept. 24, 1939; children: David F., Robert F., Carol J. Pincus Fiacco. BA, U. Pa., 1934; MD, Thomas Jefferson U., 1937; MS, U. Pa., 1949, DSc, 1951. Diplomate Am. Bd. Internal Medicine, Am. Bd. Gastroenterology. Intern Los Angeles County Gen. Hosp., 1937-39; resident in medicine U. Pa. Grad. Hosp., Phila., 1940-41; fellow in physiology and gastroenterology Thomas Jefferson U., Phila., 1941-42, asst. prof. physiology, 1946-50, assoc. prof., 1950-56; assoc. prof. medicine U. Pa., Phila., 1948-60; dir. medicine Cedars of Lebanon Hosp. (name now Cedars-Sinai Med. Ctr.), Los Angeles, 1960-64; lectr. physiology U. So. Calif., Los Angeles, 1962-69, clin. prof. medicine, 1970—. Contbr. articles to profl. jours. Fellow ACP; mem. AMA, Am. Physiol. Soc., Am. Gastroent. Assn. Home: 610 N Roxbury Dr Beverly Hills CA 90210

PINE, CHARLES JOSEPH, clinical psychologist, health services administrator; b. Excelsior Springs, Mo., July 13, 1951; s. Charles E. and LaVern (Upton) P.; m. Mary Day, Dec. 30, 1979; children: Charles Andrew, Joseph Scott, Carolyn Marie. BA in Psychology, U. Redlands, 1973; MA, Calif. State U.-Los Angeles, 1975; PhD, U. Wash., 1979; postdoctoral UCLA, 1980-81. Lic. psychologist, Calif. Psychology technician Seattle Indian Health Bd., USPHS Hosp., 1977-78; psychology intern VA Outpatient Clinic, Los Angeles, 1978-79; instr. psychology Okla. State U., 1979-80, asst. prof., 1980; asst. prof. psychology and native Am. studies program Wash. State U., 1981-82; dir. behavioral health services Riverside-San Bernardino County Indian Health Inc., Banning, Calif., 1982-84; clin. psychologist, clin. co-dir. Inland Empire Behavioral Assocs., Colton, Calif., 1982-84 ; clin. psychologist VA Med. Ctr., Long Beach, Calif., 1984-85; clin. psychologist VA Med. Ctr., Sepulveda, Calif., 1985—; clin. dir. Traumatic Stress Treatment Ctr., Thousand Oaks, Calif., 1985—; asst. clin. prof. UCLA Sch. Medicine, 1985—; editorial cons. White Cloud Jour., 1982-85; cons. Dept. Health and Human Services, USPHS, NIMH, 1980. Vol. worker Variety Boys Clubs Am., 1973-75; coach Rialto Jr. All-Am. Football League, 1974, Conejo Youth Flag Football Assn. U. Wash. Inst. Indian Studies grantee, 1975-76, UCLA Inst. Am. Cultures grantee, 1981-82; fellow Menninger Found. Mem. Am. Psychol. Assn., Nat. Indian Counselors Assn., Soc. Indian Psychologists (pres. 1981-83), Western Psychol. Assn., AAAS, Calif. State Psychol. Assn., Internat. Council Psychologists, Sigma Alpha Epsilon. Republican. Baptist. Contbr. psychol. articles to profl. lit. Home: 2379 Sirius St Thousand Oaks CA 91360 Office: VA Med Ctr Psychology Service 116B 16111 Plummer St Sepulveda CA 91343

PINE, LOIS ANN HASENKAMP, nurse; b. Cheyenne, Wyo., Feb. 21, 1950; d. Clifford Norbert and Julie Adda (Younglund) Hasenkamp; m. Julius William Pine Jr., Feb. 16, 1974; children: Margaret Ann, Julius William III, Lawrence Michael. BS, U. Wyo., 1976. RN. From staff nurse to charge nurse Ivinson Meml. Hosp., Laramie, Wyo., 1976—. Mem. St. Lawrence Council of Cath. Women, Laramie, 1980—, St. Cecilia's Group, Laramie, 1980—, Albany County PTA, Laramie, 1985—, Crisis Pregnancy Program; asst. den header Cub Scouts. Mem. Nurses Assn. Am. Coll. of Ob-Gyns. (sect. vice chmn. 1980-86), Am. Acad. Pediatrics (perinatal pediatrics dist. VIII sect.), Nat. Assn. Neonatal Nurses (charter), Rebel Bowling Leauge, Sigma Theta Tau. Democrat. Avocations: reading, knitting, crocheting, bowling, basketball. Home: 1614 Whitman Laramie WY 82070

PINEDA, ANSELMO, neurosurgery educator; b. Lima, Peru, Apr. 3, 1923; s. Anselmo Vicente and Juana (Munayco)P.; m. Monique Yvonne Martin, Mar. 15, 1955; children: Patricia M., Richard A., Gilbert V., Katherine A. MD, San Marcos U., Lima, 1951; MS, Northwestern U., 1962. Diplomate Am. Bd. Neurol. Surgery. Rotating intern Loayza Hosp., Lima, 1950-51; head histology sect. Leprosy dept. Ministry Pub. Health, Lima, 1951; asst. pathologist Nat. Inst. Neoplastic Diseases, 1952; vol. asst. lab. normal and path. histology nervous system San Marcos U. Sch. Medicine, 1953; rotating intern Augustana Hosp., Chgo., 1954, resident in gen. surgery, 1955; jr. asst. resident in neurosurgery U. Chgo., 1955-56, sr. asst. resident in neurosurgery, 1956-57, chief resident in neurosurgery, 1957-58; assoc. instr. neurosurgery U. Tex., 1958-61; assoc. neurosurgeon John Sealy Hosp., Galveston, Tex., 1960-61, attending neurosurgeon, 1961; acting chief neurosurgery VA Hosp., Long Beach, Calif., 1962-63; assoc. clin. prof., mem. Brain Research Inst. UCLA, 1962—; cons. VA Hosp., Long Beach, 1966-67. NIH spl. fellow in Neuroanatomy Northwestern U., 1961-62. Fellow ACS, Am. Coll. Angiology, Royal Soc. Medicine; mem. AAUP, AAAS, AMA, Contress of Neurol. Surgeons, Harvey Cushing Soc., World Med. Assn., Calif. Med. Assn., Los Angeles County Med. Assn., Am. Acad. Neurology, Am. Assn. Neuropathologists, Internat. Coll. Surgeons, Am. Assn. Anatomists, Am. Assn. Trauma, Am.Soc. Stereotaxic and Functional Neurosurgery, N.Y. Acad. Scis., Internat. Assn. Study Pain, Sigma Xi. Home: 16571 Carousel Ln Huntington Beach CA 92649 Office: 2880 Atlantic Ave Suite 160 Long Beach CA 90806

PINES, ALEXANDER, chemistry educator, researcher; b. Tel Aviv, June 22, 1945; came to U.S., 1968.; s. Michael and Neima (Ratner) P.; m. Ayala Malach, Aug. 31, 1967 (div. 1983); children: Itai, Shani; m. Ditsa Kafry, May 5, 1983; children: Noami, Jonathan, Talia. BS, Hebrew U., Jerusalem, 1967; PhD, MIT, 1972. Asst. prof. chemistry U. Calif., Berkeley, 1972-75, assoc. prof., 1975-80, prof., 1980—; faculty sr. scientist materials and molecular research div. Lawrence Berkeley Lab., 1975—; cons. Mobil Oil Co., Princeton, N.J., 1980-84, Shell Oil Co., Houston, 1981—; chmn. Bytel Corp., Berkeley, Calif., 1981-85; adv. prof. East China Normal U., Shanghai, People's Rep. of China, 1985; scientific dir. Nalorac, Martinez, Calif., 1986—. Mem. bd. editors Chem. Physics, Spectrochimica Acta, Chem. Physics Letters, Nuir: Basic Principles and Progress; contbr. articles to profl. jours.; patentee in field. Recipient Strait award North Calif. Spectroscopy Soc., Outstanding Achievement award Dept. of Energy, Disting. Teaching award U. Calif. Fellow Am. Phys. Soc., Inst. of Physics; mem. Am. Chem. Soc. (Signature Award, Baekeland Medal), Royal Soc. Chemistry. Office: U Calif Chem Dept Berkeley CA 94720

PING, WENDY LEE, chemical account executive; b. Rochester, N.Y., Apr. 16, 1954; d. Clifford Charles and Ruth May (Matthies) Stewart; m. Steven Wayne Ping, Nov. 24, 1978; children: Shawna Marie, Eric Wayne. BS in Ceramic Engring., BA in French, Alfred U., 1976; MS in Material Sci. and Engring., U. Calif., Davis, 1985. Sr. research engr. Kaiser Refractories, Pleasanton, Calif., 1976-79; research engr. Lawrence Livermore (Calif.) Nat. Lab., 1979-81; staff research engr. Kaiser Chems., Pleasanton, Calif., 1981-86; acct. mgr. Kaiser Chems., Pleasonton, Calif., 1986—. Mem. Am. Ceramic Soc. (treas., sec., vice-chair No. Calif. sect., 1981-83, chmn. 1984), Nat. Inst. Ceramic Engrs., Karamos, Calif. Catalysis Soc. Avocations: skiing, backpacking, scuba diving, soccer. Home: 3349 Muscat Ct Pleasanton CA 94566 Office: Kaiser Chems PO Box 877 Pleasanton CA 94566

PINGS, ANTHONY CLAUDE, architect; b. Fresno, Calif., Dec. 16, 1951; s. Clarence Hubert and Mary (Murray) P.; m. Carole Clements, June 25, 1983. AA, Fresno City Coll., 1972; BArch, Calif. Poly. State U., San Luis Obispo, 1976. Lic. architect, Calif.; cert. Nat. Council Archtl. Registration Bds. Architect Aubrey Moore Jr., Fresno, 1976-81; architect, prin. Anthony C. Pings, AIA, Fresno, 1981-83, 86—, Pings-Taylor Assocs., Fresno, 1983-85. Prin. works include Gollaher Profl. Office (Masonry Merit award 1985, Best Office Bldg. award 1986), Fresno Imaging Ctr. (Best Institutional Project award 1986, Nat. Healthcare award Modern Health Care mag. 1986). Mem. Calif. Indsl. Tech. Edn. Consortium Calif. State Dept. Edn., 1983, 84. Mem. AIA (bd. dirs. Calif. chpt. 1983-84, v.p. San Joaquin chpt. 1982, pres. 1983). Democrat. Home: 4350 N Safford Ave Fresno CA 93704 Office: 1640 W Shaw Suite 107 Fresno CA 93711

PINKEL, BENJAMIN, retired research engineer, civic activist; b. Gloversville, N.Y., Mar. 31, 1909; s. Herman and Ethel (Turower) P.; m. Anne Abel, Jan. 28, 1940; children: Sheila Mae, Joseph Charles. BSEE, U. Pa., 1930. Registered profl. engr., Ohio, Calif. Engr. Nat. Adv. Commn. Aeros., Langley Field, Va., 1931-38; sect. head Nat. Adv. Commn. Aeros., Cleve., 1938-42; chief div. Nat. Adv. Commn. Aeronautics, Cleve., 1942-56; assoc. dept. head Rand Corp., Santa Monica, Calif., 1956-68, sr. staff engr., 1968-72; adv. com. numerous govtl. agys. and tech. socs. Author: The Existential Adventure, 1976; contbr. articles to profl. jours. and reference books; patentee in field. Bd. dirs. NCCJ, Santa Monica, 1960—; treas. Westside Ecumenical Conf., Santa Monica, 1980—. Recipient Brotherhood award NCCJ, 1984, Disting. Merit citation, NCCJ, 1986. Fellow: AIAA; mem. ASME, AAAS, Am. Nuclear Soc., The Planetary Soc., Jewish Fedn. Council (budget com. Western region, 1981—), Tau Beta Pi. Avocations: writing philos. books, essays. Home: 726 Adelaide Pl Santa Monica CA 90402

PINKHAM, JEFFREY DAVID, biology educator; b. Mpls., Sept. 5, 1952; s. Marjorie Adoris (Dahl) Hennessy; m. Kathleen Mary Ethen, Apr. 28, 1984. BS, Gustavus Adolphus Coll., 1974; MS, N.D. State U., 1980, PhD, 1984. Jr. scientist Mayo Meml. Hosp., Mpls., 1974-76; asst. prof. Calif. Polytech. State U., San Luis Obispo, 1984—; crop cons., San Luis Obispo, Calif., 1985—. Co-author (lab. manual) Pest Management, 1985; contbr. articles to profl. jours. Fund raiser San Luis Obispo Hospice Orgn., 1986, Cen. Coast Symphony, San Luis Obispo, 1986; judge Future Farmers of Am. State Competition, San Luis Obispo, 1985—; advisor Calif. Poly. 4H Club, 1984-85. Beatty-Monro scholar, N.D. State U., 1978; recipient Innovative Tchg. Techniques award North Cen. Br. Entomol. Soc. Am., 1986. Mem. Cen. States Entomol. Soc., Can. Entomol. Soc., Entomol. Soc. Am., Sigma Xi. Avocations: cross country skiing, photography, hiking. Office: Calif. Polytech State U Crop Sci Dept San Luis Obispo CA 93407

PINNELL, BETTY LOU, school superintendent; b. Siloam Springs, Ark., Feb. 7, 1931; d. Evert L. and Loueva (Mathis) Smith; m. Loris A. Pinnell, Dec. 31, 1954; children: Patricia Prince, Robert, Donna Gardner, John. AA, Phoenix Coll., 1968; BS, Grand Canyon Coll., 1970; MEd, U. Ariz., 1977. Cert. elem. tchr., secondary tchr., secondary supr., elem. supr., secondary prin., elem. prin., supt., Ariz. Tchr. Safford (Ariz.) Pub. Schs., 1970-72, Bowie (Ariz.) Pub. Schs., 1972-74, Lordsburg (N.Mex.) Pub. Schs., 1974-75; tchr., supr. Patagonia (Ariz.) Union High Sch., 1975-81; prin., adminstr. Santa Cruz Elem. Sch., Nogales, Ariz., 1981-85, supt., 1985—. Mayor Town of Patagonia, 1981-82, mem. council, 1978-82; mem. Manpower Planning Council, Santa Cruz County, Ariz., 1978-82; bd. dirs. Pvt. Industry Council, Santa Cruz County, 1983—. Mem. NEA, Ariz. Edn. Assn., Internat. Reading Assn., So. Ariz. Sch. Adminstrs., Ariz. Sch. Adminstrs. Office: Santa Cruz Elem Sch Dist 28 HCR Box 50 Nogales AZ 85621

PINNELL, ROBERT PEYTON, chemistry educator; b. Fresno, Calif., Dec. 5, 1938; s. Paul Peyton and Iris Ione (Shepherd) P.; m. Sharron Lyne Gregory, Aug. 18, 1962; children: Jason Peyton, Sabrina Lyne. BS, Calif. State U., Fresno, 1960; PhD, U. Kansas, 1964. Postdoctoral fellow U. Tex., Austin, 1964-66; asst. prof. chemistry Claremont (Calif.) McKenna Coll., Scripps Coll. and Pitzer Coll., 1966-72, assoc. prof., 1972-78, prof., 1978—, chmn. joint sci. dept., 1974-77; vis. assoc. prof. chemistry Calif. Inst. Tech., 1973-74. Postdoctoral fellow U. Calif. at Santa Barbara, 1980-81. Mem. Am. Chem. Soc., Calif. Assn. Chemistry Tchrs., Sigma Xi. Democrat. Avocation: reading. Office: Claremont McKenna Scripps and Pitzer Colls Joint Sci Dept Claremont CA 91711

PINNELL-STEPHENS, JUNE ALICIA, information broker, consultant; b. Dayton, Ohio, June 11, 1948; d. Earl Emery and Helen Marie (Fedash) Pinnell; m. Dennis James Stephens, Jan. 3, 1982. BA, Pomona Coll., 1971; MLS, U. Wash., 1972. Cert. librarian, Wash., cert. tchr., Alaska. Children's librarian King County Library System, Seattle, 1972-76; coordinator children's services Bellingham (Wash.) Pub. Library, 1976-80; librarian Mat-Su Community Coll., Palmer, Alaska, 1980-82; newsroom librarian Daily News-Miner, Fairbanks, Alaska, 1982-83; prin. Borealis Research, Fairbanks, 1983-85; sr. research assoc. ASK* Info. Search, Fairbanks, 1985-87; prin. Profl. Info. Resources, Fairbanks, 1987—; adj. faculty Western Wash. U., Bellingham, 1978-79; instr. U. Alaska, Palmer, Kodiak, Fairbanks, 1980-81, 84; chmn. Alaska We the People Project, Fairbanks, 1984—; cons. Northwest Arctic Sch. Dist., Kotzebue, Alaska, 1985—. Contbr. articles to profl.

jours.; editor: AkLA Intellectual Freedom Manual, 1985. Mem. library com. Mayor's Transition Task Force, Fairbanks, 1985; del. Dem. Dist. Conv., Fairbanks, 1986; mem. gov.'s celebration commn. U.S. Constitutional Bicentennial, 1986—; bd. dirs. Fairbanks Symphony Assn. Mem. Alaska Library Assn. (chmn. IFC 1984-85, v.p., pres. 1985-87), Wash. Library Assn. (chmn. Children's and Young Adults Service Interest Group 1976-78, 2d v.p. 1979-80), ALA (chmn. Wash. membership com. 1979-80), Pacific Northwest Library Assn. (chmn. Intellectual Freedom Interest Group 1986—), Alaska Civil Liberties Union (bd. dirs. 1987—). Avocations: Scottish highland dance and music, gardening, boating, hunting. Home and Office: 3140 Roden Ln Fairbanks AK 99709

PINO, ALBERT, telecommunications executive; b. Salt Lake City, Dec. 15, 1948; s. Ross S. and Ann (Bernardi) P.; m. Linda Huber, Nov. 30, 1974; children: Bryan, Troy, Sara. BS in Computer Sci., U. Utah, 1972. System analyst First Security Service Co., Salt Lake City, 1976-77, program team mgr., 1977-81, asst. ops. mgr., 1980-81, asst. v.p. network mgr., 1981-85, v.p. corp. telecommunications mgr., 1985—. Mem. West Jordan (Utah) Community Counsel, 1984-86, Jordan Sch. Dist. Audit Adv. Com., Sandy, Utah, 1986; coach West Jordan Babe Ruth Baseball Assn., 1983-86, elected v.p., 1986—. Served to capt. U.S. Army, 1972. Mem. Telecommunication Assn. Democrat. Roman Catholic. Avocations: golf, tennis, swimming, skiing. Home: 6853 S Clover Circle West Jordan UT 84084 Office: First Security Service Co 260 N Charles Lindbergh Dr Salt Lake City UT 84126

PINOLA, JOSEPH JOHN, banker; b. Pittston, Pa., May 13, 1925; m. Doris Jean Walker; children: Mary, James. B.A. in Econs, Bucknell U., 1949; postgrad., Dartmouth Coll., 1960; A.M.P., Harvard Grad. Sch. Bus. Adminstrn., 1971; H.L.D., Wilkes Coll., 1978. With Bank of Am., 1953-76, sr. v.p., 1970-74, exec. v.p. N.Am. div., 1974-76; pres., dir. United Calif. Bank, 1976-77; dir. First Interstate Bancorp. (formerly Western Bancorp.), Los Angeles, 1977—; chmn., chief exec. officer First Interstate Bancorp. (formerly Western Bancorp.), 1978—; dir. First Interstate Bank Wash., First Interstate Bank Calif., Lockheed Corp., So. Calif. Edison Co. Mem. adv. bd. Salvation Army, Los Angeles; campaign chmn. Los Angeles Area United Way, 1981-82; chmn. Music Ctr. Unified Campaign, 1986. Served with USNR. Mem. Assn. Res. City Bankers. (bd. dirs.). Clubs: California, Los Angeles Country. Office: First Interstate Bancorp 707 Wilshire Blvd Los Angeles CA 90017

PINTA, WANDA BOHAN (MRS. R. JACK PINTA), home economist; b. Greenfield, Ia., Sept. 11, 1918; d. Edward Philip and Stella (Plymesser) Bohan; B.S., Ia. State U., 1943; postgrad. Los Angeles State Coll., 1956-59; m. R. Jack Pinta, Apr. 17, 1948 (dec. Sept. 1982). Tech. writer, editor Gen. Motors Corp., Milford, Mich., 1943-45; sr. home economist Los Angeles Dept. Water and Power, 1956-61, dir. home econs., 1961—, dir. ednl. services, 1981-86, ret., 1986. Sec. Assn. for UN, Des Moines, 1953-55. Mem. mayor's Community Adv. Com. Recipient Laura McCall Home Service Achievement award, 1960; acceptor Aham's Alma award, 1970-72. Mem. Am. (consumer interests com. 1968-70), Cal. (exec. council, pres. Los Angeles dist. 1966-67) home econs. assns., Los Angeles Home Economists in Bus., Elec. Women's Round Table (dir. 1974, nat. pres. 1978-80), Soc. Consumer Affairs Profls. in Bus. (sec. So. Calif. chpt. 1978-79), Los Angeles City/County Energy Edn. Council (communications chmn. 1981-83, pres. 1983-84), Calif. Energy Edn. Forum, LWV (exec. bd. Des Moines 1953-55), Los Angeles World Affairs Council, Town Hall, Ia. State U. Alumni Assn. Episcopalian. Mem. Order Eastern Star. Club: Pilot (pres. Van Nuys 1962-63). Home: 5744 Vantage Av North Hollywood CA 91607 Office: PO Box 111 Los Angeles CA 90051

PINTO, JOHN VINCENT, real estate broker; b. Bklyn., Oct. 17, 1951; s. Francesco and Nancy (Barone) P.; m. Ellen Serino, Oct. 27, 1973. BA, Hunter Coll., 1973. Salesman Realty House, Inc., Sunnyvale, Calif., 1974-77; v.p. Golden Gate Properties, Sunnyvale, 1977-79; pres. Pinto Enterprises, Inc., Campbell, Calif., 1979—. Contbr. articles to profl. jours.; producer TV show Pinto on Real Estate Results, 1984. Bd. dirs. Project Match United Way Agy., San Jose, 1985—. Mem. San Jose Real Estate Bd. (bd. dirs. 1986—), Calif. Assn. Realtors (bd. dirs. 1984—, trustee pension and investment com. 1986—), Fedn. Internationale des Professions Immobilieres (bd. dirs. 1986—), Italian-Am. Heritage Found. Republican. Roman Catholic. Avocations: internat. traveling, handball, weight tng.

PIPAL, GEORGE HENRY, journalist; b. Lafayette, Ind., Oct. 14, 1916; s. Francis John and Belle (Kadavy) P.; m. Caroline Dunsmore, Aug. 17, 1946; children—John, Susan, Philip, Frank. B.A., U. Nebr., 1937; M.S., Columbia, 1939. Corr. various bureaus UPI, 1937-41; bur. mgr. UPI, Prague, 1946; mgr. for UPI, Eastern Europe, 1947, Germany, 1948; dir. Computer Services, 1949-51; gen. European bus. mgr. European Services, Europe, Middle East, Africa, 1952-65; gen. sales exec. European Services, N.Y.C., 1966-68; gen. mgr. fgn. internat. div. 1968-78; mng. dir. UPI (U.K.), Ltd., 1964-65; v.p. United Features Syndicate, 1978-84, United Media Enterprises, 1985—. Served as lt. USNR, 1942-46. Mem. Sigma Delta Chi, Chi Phi. Club: Sonoma County Press (pres. 1986). Office: United Media 1 Snoopy Pl Santa Rosa CA 95401

PIPER, DAVID ZINK, geologist; b. Lexington, Ky., Mar. 12, 1935; s. Lewis A. and Anna (Zink) P.; children: Judith, Lewis, Lucy, Gregory; me. Gail Elizabeth Piper. BS, U. Ky., 1960; MS, Syracuse U., 1962; PhD, Scripps Inst., 1968. Asst. prof. geology U. Wash., Seattle, 1968-75; geologist U.S. Geol. Survey, Menlo Park, Calif., 1975—. Contbr. articles to profl. jours. Office: US Geol Survey MS 902 345 Middlefield Menlo Park CA 94025

PIPER, KATHRYN THOMAS, public relations and advertising writer; b. Denver; d. Ernest and Thelma Sue (Wall) Thomas; divorced; children: James B., Jerrold Scott, Sue Shakespeare. BA, Loretto Heights Coll., 1973. Owner, pres. Piper and Assocs., Denver, 1965—; editor Denver Social Register, 1967—; v.p. Yuan Chinese Restaurant, Denver, 1978—, Pacific Internat., Denver, Hong Kong, 1981—. Recipient 1st Pl. 30 Second comml. Colo. Broadcasters, 1971. Mem. Nat. Fedn. Press Women (Woman of Achievement 1978, numerous writing awards 1970—), Denver Press Women, Colo. Press Women. (Colo. Woman of Achievement 1977). Clubs: Garden of the Gods (Colo. Springs), Met. (Denver). Avocations: backgammon, dancing, travel. Home: 120 S Marion Pkwy Denver CO 80209 Office: Piper and Assocs 1805 S Bellaire # 215 Denver CO 80222

PIPES, KENNETH WAYNE, human resources administrator, former marine corps officer; b. Bakersfield, Calif., Oct. 19, 1937; s. Roy Jackson and Neva Opel (Wilcher) P.; m. Sharon Lee Hussey, Dec. 9, 1961; children: Daniel Grady, Timothy Shannon. AA, Fresno City Coll., 1958, BA, Fresno State Coll., 1961; MA, U. Va., 1976; grad. Marine Corps Amphibious Warfare Sch., 1976, Marine Corps Command and Staff Coll., 1972. Commd. 2d lt., U.S. Marine Corps, 1961, advanced through grades to lt. col., 1977—, dep. asst. chief of staff, personnel services, Marine Corps Base, Camp Pendelton, Calif., 1981-82; instr. Marine Corps Amphibious Warfare Sch., 1972-76; inspector/instr. Marine Corps Res., 1968-71, recuriting officer, 1977-79, ret., 1982; human resource adminstr. security div. San Onofre Nuclear Generating Sta., San Clemente, Calif., 1982—. Bd. dirs. Oxnard Salvation Army, 1968-71, Oceanside (Calif.) YMCA, 1981-82. Decorated Silver Star, Bronze Star medals, Meritorious Service medal; Vietnam Cross of Gallantry with Bronze and Silver Star, Purple Heart; recipient USN League Disting. Service award, 1971; Salvation Army Service award, 1971; cert. of appreciation Combined Fed. Campaign, 1981, 82; cert. of commendation Boy Scouts Am., 1982; Regional Finalist, White House fellow, 1969; others; McMahan's scholar, 1959-60. Mem. Marine Corps Assn., Navy League, Sigma Alpha Epsilon. Republican. Baptist. Club: Rotary.

PIPES, MARILYN ANNE SCHMARDER, speech-language pathologist; b. Corning, N.Y., Sept. 5, 1954; d. Francis Raymond and Rita Anne (Sloan) Haradon. AS, Corning Community Coll., 1977; BS, Northeastern U., 1981; MS, U. Ariz., 1983. Speech-lang. pathologist San Juan Regional Med. Ctr., Farmington, N.Mex., 1983-86; tutor, clin. supr. Am. Indian profl. tng. in speech-lang. pathology, audiology U. Ariz. Dept. Speech and Hearing Scis., Tucson, 1986—. Choreographer San Juan Stage Co., Farmington, 1984-86, dancer, crew worker. Mem. Am. Speech-Lang.-Hearing Assn. (cert., Continuing Edn. award 1986), N.Mex. Speech-Lang.-Hearing Assn. (mem. govtl. affairs com. and pub. info. com. 1984-86). Avocations: dance of all types, hiking, cross-country skiing. Home: 1325 A E Allen Rd Tucson AZ 85719 Office: Am Indian Profl Tng U Ariz Dept Speech Hearing Scis Tucson AZ 85721

PIPKIN, YVONNE MAE, industrial research administrator; b. Dodgeville, Wis., Sept. 11, 1949; d. Homer Dale and Marcia Mae (Collentine) Jackson; m. Gary Clyde Pipkin, June 9, 1972; children: Ryan Allyn, Shad Leigh. BA in Secondary Edn., Boise (Idaho) State U., 1971; postgrad., City U., Bellevue, Wash., 1985—. Cert. tchr., Idaho. Tchr. Spanish Vallivue Jr.-Sr. High Sch., Caldwell, Idaho, 1971-72; dept. sec. Southland Corp., Seattle, 1978-80; adminstrv. asst. Spectron Devel. Labs., Seattle, 1981-84; with contracts and adminstrn. dept. Sigma Research, Inc., Seattle, 1984—. Mem. Wash. State PTA, Renton, 1982-87. Mem. Nat. Contracts Mgmt. Assn, U.S. Power Squadron, Bellevue, (aux. exec. bd. 1984-85). Republican. Avocations: sailing, ceramics, poetry writing. Home: 1120 N 38th St Renton WA 98056 Office: Sigma Research Inc 8710 148th Ave NE Redmond WA 98052

PIRASTEHFAR, HASSAN, electrical company executive; b. Shiraz, Iran, Jan. 7, 1947; came to U.S., 1969; s. Mohammad and Shams (Kazemy) P.; m. Lisa Ann Lohmeyer, Apr. 23, 1983; 1 child, Amelia. BSEE, Kans. State U., 1974; MSEE, Ariz. State U., 1976, PhD, 1981. Device engr. Small Signal Motorola Inc., Phoenix, 1974-76, sect. mgr., 1977-78; device engrng. mgr. Small Signal and Opto Orgn., Phoenix, 1978-79, system mgr., 1980-84, dir. new product development optoelectronics, 1984—. Contbr. articles to profl. jours.; patentee in field. Mem. Optical Soc. Am. Home: 1454 E Grandview Mesa AZ 85203 Office: Motorola Inc 5005 E McDowell Rd MD B322 Phoenix AZ 85008

PIRBAZARI, MASSOUD, environmental engineering professor, consultant; b. Shiraz, Iran, Aug. 2, 1941; came to U.S., 1967; s. Keyghobad and Sherafat (Ghoorkhanian) P. BS MechE, Tehran Poly. U., Iran, 1964; MS MechE, Mich. State U., 1969; MSCE, Wayne State U., 1973; PhD in Environ. Engrng., U. Mich., 1980. Project engr. Smith, Hinghman & Grylls, Detroit, 1969-73; research scholar U. Ill., Urbana, 1980-81; asst. prof. civil and environ. engrng. U. So. Calif., Los Angeles, 1981-86, assoc. prof., 1986—. Mem. ASCE (vice chmn. environ. engrng. session programs com. 1986—), Am. Waterworks Assn. (chmn. subcom. taste and odor treatment 1983—), Am. Chem. Soc., Water Pollution Control Fedn., Am. Soc. Microbiology. Home: 11634 Gorham #101 Los Angeles CA 90049 Office: U So Calif 213 H Los Angeles CA 90089-0231

PIRCHER, LEO JOSEPH, lawyer; b. Berkeley, Calif., Jan. 4, 1933; s. Leo Charles and Christine (Moore) P.; m. Phyllis McConnell, Aug. 4, 1956 (div. April 1981); children—Christopher, David, Eric. B.S., U. Calif.-Berkeley, 1954, J.D., 1957. Bar: Calif. 1958, N.Y. 1985; cert. specialist taxation law Calif. Bd. Legal Specialization. Assoc. Lawler, Felix & Hall, Los Angeles, 1957-62, ptnr., 1962-65, sr. ptnr., 1965-83; sr. ptnr. Pircher, Nichols & Meeks, Los Angeles, 1983—; adj. prof. Loyola U. Law Sch., Los Angeles, 1959-61; corp. sec. Am. Metal Bearing Co., Gardena, Calif., 1975—, dir. Varco Internat. Inc., Orange, Calif., Amex Systems Inc., Los Angeles, 1982—; speaker various law schs. and bar assns. edn. programs. Author: (with others) Definition and Utility of Leases, 1968. Chmn. pub. fin. and taxation sect. Town Hall, Los Angeles, 1970-71. Mem. Calif. State Bar, N.Y. State Bar, Los Angeles County Bar Assn. (exec. com. comml. law secton), ABA, Nat. Assn. Real Estate Investment Trusts Inc. (cert. specialist taxation law). Republican. Club: California (Los Angeles). Office: Pircher Nichols & Meeks 10100 Santa Monica Blvd Los Angeles CA 90067

PISCHEL, KEN DONALD, research physician, educator; b. Glendale, Calif., Aug. 11, 1950; m. Katherine M. Ozanich, Mar. 15, 1980. BS in Biology, Calif. Inst. Tech., 1972; MD, PhD, Washington U., St. Louis, 1979. Diplomate Am. Bd. Internal Medicine, Am. Bd. Rheumatology; lic. physician, Calif. Intern, resident Jewish Hosp. St. Louis, 1979-82; fellow in rheumatology U. Calif.-San Diego, La Jolla, 1982-85, asst. prof. medicine, 1985—. Mem. Am. Assn. Immunologists, Am. Fedn. Clin. Research, Am. Rheumatism Assn. (Western Regions fellow award 1984, Arthritis Investigator award 1985), AAAS, ACP. Office: U Calif Med Ctr 7H-811 G 225 W Dickinson St San Diego CA 92103

PISCHKE, GARY MICHAEL, petroleum geologist; b. San Francisco, Sept. 21, 1953; s. Henry James and Esther Adeline P. B.S. in Earth Sci., U. Calif.-Santa Cruz, 1975; M.S. in Geology, San Diego State U., 1979. Registered geologist, Calif. Environ. mgmt. specialist County of San Diego, 1979-80; geologist Texaco U.S.A., Los Angeles, 1980-82, petroleum geologist, 1982—. Contbr. articles to profl. jours. Recipient Sr. Sci. award Sci. Council, Santa Clara, 1971. Mem. Geol. Soc. Am., Am. Assn. Petroleum Geologists, Planetary Soc., Los Angeles Basin Geol. Soc. Democrat. Roman Catholic. Office: Texaco USA 10 Universal City Plaza Universal City CA 91608

PISCIOTTA, SAMUEL JAMES, small business owner; b. Pueblo, Colo., Dec. 10, 1938; s. Sam Jr. and Eva May (Padula) P.; m. Cynthia Diane Garrett, Aug. 8, 1961; children: Samuel, Pamela, Richard, Michael. BA, Western State Coll., 1967. Pres., mgr. Family Athletic Club, Inc., Pueblo, Colo., 1961—. Named one of Outstanding Young Men of Am., 1970. Mem. Nat. Swim and Recreation Assn. (pres. 1976-77), Greater Pueblo Sports Assn., Pueblo Hall of Fame (co-founder 1972), Jaycees (state dir. 1973-75), Pueblo Bus. Exchange (co-founder 1982, pres. 1984), So. Colo. Better Bus. Bur. (co-organizer Pueblo office 1985—, bd. dirs. 1986—), Tau Kappa Epsilon. Republican. Lodge: Kiwanis (bd. dirs. 1986), Elks, Masons, Knight Templar, Royal Order of Jesters, Shriners, So. Colo. Consistory Ritualistic Team. Avocations: golfing, swimming, fishing, fast walking, tennis. Composer, profl. pianist. Home: 27 Pedregal Ln Pueblo CO 81005 Office: Family Athletic Club Inc 1500 W 4th St Pueblo CO 81004

PISTEK, MIROSLAV JOHN, chemical company executive; b. Moravia, Czechoslovakia, Nov. 11, 1923; came to U.S., 1930; s. John and Anna (Kubis) P.; m. Claudia Ninesling, July 6, 1952; children: Michael John, Melissa Jeanne, Marianna Josephine. B in Chem. Engrng., CCNY, 1951. Registered profl. engr. Ill., Pa., Del.; registered profl. safety engr., Calif. Process engr. Stauffer Chem. Co., Monongahela, Pa., 1951-55; process engr., area prodn. supr. Imperial Color and Chem. div. Hercules, Inc., Glens Falls, N.Y., 1955-63; safety supr., fire chief Monsanto, Inc., Sauget, Ill., 1963-67; asst. corp. mgr., safety and loss prevention ICI Americas, Inc., Wilmington, Del., 1967-74; div. and regional mgr. safety and loss prevention Allied Corp., Morristown (N.J.) and Pittsburg (Calif.), 1974-82; corp. mgr. environmental affairs Romic Chem. Corp., Palo Alto, Calif., 1983—. Asst. scoutmaster Boy Scouts Am., Webster Groves, Mo., 1963-67; instr., counselor Girl Scouts U.S., Wilmington, 1969-73. Served to sgt. U.S. Army, 1943-46, PTO. Mem. Am. Soc. Safety Engrs. (chpt. pres. 1973-74), Am. Inst. Chem. Engrs., Bd. Cert. Safety Profls., Del. Soc. Profl. Engrs. (auditor 1972-74), Calif. Trucking Assn. (bd. dirs. 1986—. chmn. hazardous waste haulers conf. 1986). Avocations: photography, golf, travel.

PISTONE, DANTE CHARLES, public relations executive; b. Yerington, Nev., Sept. 9, 1950; s. Dante John and Charlotte (Borghi) P.; m. Katherine Mary Lipe, June 8, 1974; 1 child, Allison Marie. BA in Journalism, U. Nev., 1973. Pub. info. rep. State of Nev., Carson City, 1974-76; legis. press aide U.S. Rep. Jim Santini, Washington, 1976-77, press sec., 1977-79; dist. office mgr. U.S. Rep. Jim Santini, Reno, 1979-81; pub. info. officer Sierra Pacific Power Co., Reno, 1981-84; dir. communications SW Gas Corp., Phoenix, 1984-87; mgr. pub. communications SW Gas Corp., Las Vegas, 1987—. Author: Nevada Bicentennial, 1976. Campaign vol. numerous candidates, Nev., 1974-84; v.p. Nev. State Soc., Washington, 1978; bd. dirs. Am. Cancer Soc. of Washoe County, Reno, 1984. Mem. Pub. Relations Soc. Am., Pacific Coast Gas Assn., Nev. Press. Assn., Nev. Broadcasters Assn., Ariz. Newspaper and Broadcasters Assns., Assn. Ho. Dem. Press Assts. Republican. Roman Catholic. Lodge: Rotary (chmn. bd. dirs. Sparks, Nev. chpt. 1981-84). Avocations: golf, fishing, hunting, traveling. Home: 2835 Mann St Las Vegas NV 89102 Office: SW Gas Corp 5241 Spring Mountain Rd Las Vegas AZ 89114

PITCHER, HELEN IONE, advertising executive; b. Colorado Springs, Colo., Aug. 6, 1931; d. William Forest Medlock and Frankie La Vone (Hamilton) Tweed; m. Richard Edwin Pitcher, Sept. 16, 1949; children: Dushka Myers, Suzanne, Marc. Student, U. Colo., 1962-64, Ariz. State U., 1966, Maricopa Tech. Coll., 1967, Scottsdale Community Coll., 1979-81. Design draftsman Sundstrand Aviation, Denver, 1962-65; tech. illustrator Sperry, Phoenix, 1966-68; art dir. Integrated Circuit Engring., Scottsdale, Ariz., 1968-71, dir. advt., 1981—; advt. artist Motorola Inc., Phoenix, 1971-74; pres. Pitcher Tech. Pubs., Scottsdale, 1974-81. Profl. advisor Paradise Valley Sch. Dist., Phoenix, 1984-85. mem. Nat. Audio Visual Assn., Bus. Profl. Advt. Assn. (treas. 1982-86), Direct Mktg. Club. Democrat. Mem. Ch. Christ. Avocations: raising and showing Am. Saddlebred horses and Hackney ponies. Home: 13681 N Pima Rd PO Box 2313 Scottsdale AZ 85252 Office: Integrated Circuit Engring Corp 15022 N 75th St Scottsdale AZ 85260

PITCHER, WAYNE HAROLD, JR., biotechnology company executive; b. St. Louis, Jan. 5, 1944; s. Wayne Harold Sr. and Ethel Pauline (Gehrke) P.; m. Julia Frances Liberace, Aug. 22, 1970; children: Wayne Harold III, Maria Beatrice. BS in Chem. Engring., Calif. Inst. Tech., 1966; SM in Chem. Engring., MIT, 1968, ScD in Chem. Engring., 1972. Sr. chem. engr. Corning (N.Y.) Glass Works, 1972-74, sr. research chem. engr., 1974-76, engring. supr., 1976-81, mgr. biotech. portfolio, 1981-83; v.p. devel. Genencor, South San Francisco, 1983—. Editor: Immobilized Enzymes for Food Processing, 1980; editorial bd. (jour.) Applied Biochemistry and Biotech.; contbr. articles to profl. jours.; contbr. chpts. to books; patentee in field. Mem. AAAS, Am. Inst. Chem. Engrs., N.Y. Acad. Sci., Am. Chem. Soc., Sigma Xi. Office: Genencor 180 Kimball Way South San Francisco CA 94080

PITCHER-MAURIÉR, KELLY JO, interior designer; b. Mpls., Apr. 2, 1959; d. Donald Eugene and Bettye Pitcher; m. Timothy Laurence Mauriér, Apr. 20, 1985. BS in Environ. and Interior Design, Colo. State U., 1981. Asst. designer Urban Design Group, Denver, 1982-83; designer Corona Pacific, Irvine, Calif., 1983-84; project designer Reel Grobman and Assocs., Santa Ana, Calif., 1984-86; project designer, planner Hill Pinckert Architects, Irvine, 1986—. Mem. Am. Soc. Interior Designers, Interior Bus. Designers.

PITELKA, LOUIS FRANK, ecologist; b. Berkeley, Calif., Mar. 28, 1947; s. Frank Alois and Dorothy (Riggs) P.; m. Sandra Lea Sanders, Sept. 20, 1969; children: Erik Loren, Jessica Kristine. BS in Zoology, U. Calif., Davis, 1969; PhD in Biol. Scis., Stanford U., 1974. Asst. prof. biology Bates Coll., Lewiston, Maine, 1974-81, assoc. prof., 1981-84, chmn. dept. biology, 1982-84; program dir. NSF Population Biology & Physiol. Ecology Program, Washington, 1983-84; project mgr. Electric Power Research Inst., Palo Alto, Calif., 1984—; mem. various coms. NSF, Nat. Acid Precipitation Assessment Program, other programs. Contbr. numerous articles to profl. jours. Predoctoral fellow NSF, 1969-72; research grantee NSF, 1980-85. Mem. AAAS, Am. Inst. Biol. Scis., Brit. Ecol. Soc., Ecol. Soc. Am., Bot. Soc. Am. (chmn. ecol. sect. 1982-83), Phi Kappa Phi, Phi Beta Kappa. Home: 838 Richardson Ct Palo Alto CA 94303 Office: Electric Power Research Inst PO Box 10412 Palo Alto CA 94303

PITT, DONALD, professional basketball team executive. Pres. Phoenix Suns, Nat. Basketball Assn. Office: care Phoenix Suns 2910 N Central Phoenix AZ 85012 *

PITT, WILLIAM ALEXANDER, cardiologist; b. Vancouver, B.C., Can., July 17, 1942; came to U.S., 1970; s. Reginald William and Una Sylvia (Alexander) P.; m. Judith Mae Wilson, May 21, 1965; children: William Matthew, Joanne Katharine. MD, U. B.C., Vancouver, 1967. Diplomate Royal Coll. Physicians Can. Intern, Mercy Hosp., San Diego, 1967-68, resident, 1970-71; resident Vancouver Gen. Hosp., 1968-70, U. Calif., San Diego, 1971-72; assoc. dir. cardiology Mercy Hosp., San Diego, 1972—; bd. trustees San Diego Found. for Med. Care, 1983—, pres., chmn. bd. trustees, 1986—; bd. dirs. Mut. Assn. for Profl. Services, Phila., 1984—. Fellow Royal Coll. Physicians Can., Am. Coll. Cardiology (assoc.); mem. AMA, Am. Heart Assn., Calif. Med. Assn., San Diego County Med. Soc. (councillor), San Diego County Heart Assn. (bd. dirs. 1982—). Episcopalian. Office: Mercy Cardiology Med Group 4077 5th Ave San Diego CA 92103

PITTER, RICHARD LEON, meteorology educator; b. Whittier, Calif., Apr. 4, 1947; s. Jack F. and Eva L. (Ketchum) P.; m. Keiko M. Murata, Nov. 21, 1971; children: Gregory, Jacqueline. AB in Meteorology, UCLA, 1969, MS in Meteorology, 1970, postgrad., p972, PhD in Meteorolgy, 1973. From instr. to asst. prof. Oreg. Grad. Ctr., Beaverton, 1973-77; asst. prof. U. Md., College Park, 1977-81; assoc. research prof. Desert Research Inst., Reno, 1981—. Author: Using Microcomputers, 1985. Mem. AAAS, Am. Meterol. Soc., Royal Meteorol. Soc., Meteorol. Soc. Japan, Am. Geophys. Union. Avocations: jogging, computers. Office: Desert Research Inst PO Box 60220 Reno NV 89506

PITTMAN, JAMES EUGENE, JR., entrepreneur; b. Long Beach, Calif., May 28, 1948; s. James E. and Lenora Fern (Hunsaker) P.; student in vermiculture and soil husbandry; m. Brenda June Petker, Nov. 12, 1977; children—Kerri Lynn, Michelle N., Olivia Marie. Earthworm grower, owner Templeton (Calif.) Worm Ranch, 1975—; mktg. dir. Invivo Inc., Iowa City, 1977—, Bio-Eco-Systems Inc., Indpls., 1976—; pres. Am. Eco Systems Inc., Oceanside, Calif., 1977—; owner, operator Calif. Smog. Inspection Ctrs.; mktg. dir. other corps; mem. Calif. Farm Bur., 1975—. Charter mem. Republican Presl. Task Force. RecipientSpl. Presdl. Commn., Community Leaders Am. award 1979-80, Community Leaders World award 1985-86, award of appreciation Rotary Internat., 1977, Kiwanis, 1977, Lions, 1976, C. of C. of Atascadero, Calif., 1976, Calif. U.-Calif. Poly. Inst., 1976, Madera Unified Sch. Dist., 1977; cert. Los Angeles County Health Dept.; Presdl. Medal of Merit Mem. Vermiculturists Trade Assn., Western Organic Growers Assn., Calif. Water Pollution Control Assn. (San Diego sect.), Nat. Fedn. Ind. Bus., Nat. SBA, Internat. Platform Assn. Clubs: Elks, Masons, Rotary (dir. local club 1977-78, chmn. world community services local club 1978-79). Home: 190 McKinley St Oceanside CA 92056

PITTMAN, MELINDA ELIZABETH, theatre director, administrative director; b. Washington, June 21, 1953; d. Edgar Ansel and Mary Elizabeth (White) P. B.A., Va. Poly. Inst., 1975; postgrad. Tulane U., 1977. Stage mgr. Oregon Shakespearean Festival, Ashland, 1976-78; prodn. asst. Arena Stage, Washington, 1979; stage mgr. Portland Opera Assn., Oreg., 1979-86; artistic program coordinator Artquake, Portland, 1980-81; artistic dir., songwriter, composer, performer Portland Labor Players II, 1980-83; bus. mgr. Storefront theatre, Portland, 1981-83; bus. mgr., grantwriter Do Jump! Dance Theatre, Portland, 1983-85; adminstrv. and devel. dir. Oreg. Fair Share, Portland, 1983-85; mng. dir. Artists Repertory Theatre, Portland, 1985—; promoter, producer Artspot, Portland, 1981; com. mem. Met. Arts Commn., Portland, 1983. Dir. plays most recent being 1934 Blood and Roses (best dir. 1981), Hot L Baltimore (outstanding dir. 1983), Passion, 1986; author, composer, dir., producer play Atlantis, 1984; performer, singer The Fallen Angel Choir, 1986. Contbr. poetry to Telephone and Poetry Venture. Adminstr. Fair Share Non-partisan Action Com., Portland, 1983-85. recipient Theatre Project award Met. Arts Commn., Portland, 1983. Mem. Am. Theatre Assn., Citizen Action Coalition, NOW, Phi Kappa Phi, Omnicron Delta Kappa. Democrat. Episcopalian. Home: 2217 NW Johnson Portland OR 97210 Office: Artists Repertory Theatre 1111 SW 10th Ave Portland OR 97205

PITTS, MALCOLM JOHN, oil consulting firm executive; b. Paris; s. Malcolm Everett and Kathryne (Accola) P.; m. Janice Kathleen Kopec, Jan. 3, 1976. BA in Chemistry, U. Colo., 1972; MS in Biochemistry, Purdue U., 1974; PhD in Chemistry, Georgetown U., 1979. Grad. research assoc. Purdue U., West Lafayette, Ind., 1972-74; chemist Hazen Research, Golden, Colo., 1974-75; grad. research assoc. Georgetown U., Washington, 1975-79; predoctoral fellow Am. Heart Assn., Washington, 1977-79; postdoctoral research assoc. Nat. Jewish Hosp. and Research Ctr., Denver, 1979-80; dir. petroleum tech. Sartek, Inc., Golden, 1980—. Treas. North Fork Council, Denver, Colo., 1985—. Mem. AAAS, Am. Chem. Soc. (cert.), N.Y. Acad. Sci., Soc. Petroleum Engrs. (chmn. enhanced oil recovery study group Denver sect. 1984-86, tech. info. correspondence and publicity officer Denver sect. 1986—). Home: 12401 E LaSalle Pl Aurora CO 80014 Office: Surtek Inc 1511 Washington Ave Golden CO 80401

PITTS, WILLIAM HENRY, cable television manager; b. Portland, Oreg., July 5, 1937; s. Gregory Angelo Pitts and Rose Margarete (Ryan) Bellmore; m. Barbara Jean Manning, Mar. 3, 1968; children: Tom, Shawn, Rosa, Scott, Bill. BA, U. Portland, 1959; MSA, Pepperdine U., 1976. Cert. tchr., Calif., Oreg.; lic. real estate agt., Md. Commd. 2d lt. USAF, 1959, advanced through grades to maj., 1970, ret., 1980; v.p. Vacations Unltd., Annapolis, Md., 1980-81; tchr. math. and sci. Oreg. Pub. Schs., Florence, Mapleton and Reedsport, 1981-83; office mgr. McCaw Cablevision, Florence, 1983—. Pres. City Council, Dunes City, Oreg., 1984-85; bd. dirs. Lane County Council Govts., Oreg., Neighborhood Watch, Dunes City, 1985, pres., 1983-84. Decorated Air medal with 6 oak leaf clusters, Vietnam Service medal with 8 devices, Rep. of Vietnam Gallantry Cross with 1 device. Democrat. Roman Catholic. Lodges: Kiwanis, Elks (Appreciation award 1984-85). Avocations: fishing, mushrooming, agate hunting, beachcombing, reading. Home: 05346 Buckskin Bob Ln Florence OR 97439 Office: McCaw Cablevision 630 Hwy 101 Florence OR 97439

PITUCH, ANNETTE CYNTHIA, marketing professional; b. Union City, Pa., Sept. 24, 1959; d. Walter Charles and Estelle (Lewandowski) P. BA in Pub. Relations, Purdue U., 1981; MA in Advt., Mich. State U., 1983. Advt. sales rep. The Purdue Exponent, West Lafayette, Ind., 1978-80, The Erie (Pa.) Times News, 1978; radio advt. copywriter Sta. WRIE Radio, Erie, 1979-80; advt. agy. intern Engel & Tirak, Erie, 1981; mktg. coordinator Am. Water Works Assn., Denver, 1983-84; mktg. mgr. Nat. Conf. State Legislatures, Denver, 1984—. Mem. Big Sisters, Denver, 1986—; mem. crime prevention com. Capitol Hill United Neighborhoods, Inc., Denver, 1985—. Mem. Polish Nat. Alliance, Purdue Club of Denver (dir. 1986—). Roman Catholic. Club: Women Make Cents Investment (Denver). Avocations: reading, cooking, cinema. Home: 1058 Pearl St #3 Denver CO 80203 Office: Nat Conf State Legislatures 1050 17th St #2100 Denver CO 80265

PIVA, LILLY BELLE, former county and city labor union official; b. Gatesville, Tex., Aug. 11, 1918; d. William Wesley and Lillie Emaline (Lawrence) Payne; m. Francis Peter Piva, Jan. 21, 1937; children—Francis Anthony, Robert Lewis, Nicholas Dean. Student Tacoma Community Coll., 1968. Riveter Boeing Aircraft, Tacoma, 1942-43; cook mgr. Tacoma Sch. Dist., 1950-59; staff rep. Am. Fedn. State, County and Mcpl. Employees Council II, Seattle, 1962-78, staff rep. local 120, 1962-78; v.p. Central Labor Council, Tacoma, 1976-78. Bd. dirs. United Way Pierce County, Tacoma, 1967-72; commr. Tacoma Housing Authority, 1978-82; union counsellor Community Services AFL-CIO, Tacoma, 1967; committeeperson Democratic party, Tacoma, 1985; mem. adv. bd. Vocat. Tech. Inst., Tacoma, 1986; sec. Tacoma/Pierce County Nat. Council Sr. Citizens, 1986. Recipient Certs. of Appreciation, Supt. Pub. Instrn., State Wash., 1985, Dem. Nat. Com., Washington, 1982. Democrat. Methodist. Clubs: 1918 Club, Candidates Forum (vice-chmn.) (Tacoma). Avocations: bowling. Home: 2410 N Stevens St Tacoma WA 98406

PIZZICA, STEPHEN VIROY, engineer; b. Chgo., Aug. 6, 1939; s. Viro M. and Irene M. (Peterson) P. BS in Engring., Northwestern U., 1962; MS in Engring., UCLA, 1969; MBA, U. So. Calif., 1980. Registered profl. elec. engr., Calif. Mem. tech. staff Hughes Aircraft Co., Culver City, Calif., 1962-70, group head, 1970-78; sr. staff engr. Hughes Aircraft Co., El Segundo, Calif., 1978-86, scientist, engr., 1986—; mem. engring. dean's council UCLA, 1981—. Mem. NSPE, Calif. Soc. Profl. Engrs., IEEE, Soc. Info. Display, Beta Gamma Sigma, Hughes Mgmt. Club. Home: Box J 152 Manhattan Beach CA 90266 Office: Hughes Aircraft Co PO Box 92426 Los Angeles CA 90009

PIZZULLI, FRANCIS COSMO JOSEPH, lawyer, bioethicist; b. Bklyn., May 16, 1950; s. Dominick Lawrence and Rose Nancy (Ieracitano) P. B.A. in Math. with high honors, U. Calif.-Santa Barbara, 1971; J.D., U. So. Calif., 1974. Bar: Calif. 1975. NEH postdoctoral fellow Inst. of Soc., Ethics and the Life Scis., Hastings Ctr., Hastings-on-Hudson, N.Y., 1974-75; law clk. U.S. Ct. Appeals (9th cir.), 1975-76; assoc. Tuttle & Taylor, Los Angeles, 1977-79, Weissburg & Aronson, Los Angeles, 1979-80, Engel & Engel, Beverly Hills, Calif., 1980-81; sole practice, Santa Monica, Calif., 1981—; speaker, lectr., panelist in bioethics field; bd. dirs. MILA Import Export, Inc., 1985—; pres., dir. Geotermica, Ltd., 1986—. Editor So. Calif. Law Rev., 1973-74. Contbr. articles to profl. publs. Spl. cons. Nat. Commn. for Protection Human Subjects of Biomed. and Behavioral Research, Washington, 1976-77; big brother Cath. Big Bros., Los Angeles, 1979-82. Mem. Los Angeles County Bar Assn. (chmn. and founder biol. and behavioral tech. com. 1977-78, co-chmn. bioethics com. 1981-82), Italian-Am. Lawyers Assn., Order of Coif. Roman Catholic. Lodge: KC. Office: 1337 Ocean Ave Santa Monica CA 90401

PLAGMAN, KEVIN GEORGE, communications company executive; b. Lakewood, Ohio, Sept. 18, 1950; s. George Earl and Kathryn Eloise (Malone) P.; m. Mary Margaret Madden, Feb. 8, 1975; 1 child, Kerry Marie. BS in Journalism, Ohio U., 1973. Account supr. Lowry, Russom & Leeper, San Francisco, 1973-81; dir. pub. relations Scroggin & Fischer, San Francisco, 1981-83; prin. Communications West, San Francisco, 1983—. Recipient Publication award San Francisco Ad Council, 1976. Mem. Assn. Multi-Image (Best of Show award 1980), Pub. Relations Soc. Am. (winner Mktg. Support 1976, Mktg. Communications 1986). Democrat. Office: Communications West 1426 18th St San Francisco CA 94107

PLAKOSH, PAUL, JR., psychologist; b. Pitts., May 17, 1949; s. Paul and Leonora (Durso) P.; B.S. summa cum laude, U. Pitts., 1973; M.A., U. Iowa, 1976; Ph.D., Palo Alto Sch. Profl. Psychology, 1978. Research psychologist Langley Porter Inst., U. Calif., San Francisco, 1978-81; exec. dir. Franklin Clinic, San Francisco, 1981—. Mem. Am. Psychol. Assn., Internat. Neuropsychol. Soc., AAAS. Address: 291 Broderick St San Francisco CA 94117

PLANAS, RODOLFO E., planning consultant; b. Bremen, Germany, Apr. 1, 1915; s. Juan J.J. and Elsa H.C. (Koechert) Planas y Calvet (parents Spanish citizens); m. Herta Boeninger-Armstrong. B.A., U. Barcelona (Spain); B.Sc. equivalent, Fed. Inst. Tech., Zurich; Ph.D. in Econs., U. Zurich. Jr. exec. Hoffmann-La Roche, Inc., Nutley, N.J., 1942-46; dir. internat. ops Forstner, Inc., Irvington, N.J., 1946-61, cons. internat. ops., East Orange, N.J., 1961-64; pres. Quickbonner Team, Inc., planning cons., Millburn, N.J., 1965-76; cons., lectr. on office facilities and systems planning, 1976—; mem. speakers panel bi-ann. Office Landscape Symposium. Bd. editorial advs. McGraw Hill Handbook of Modern Office Management and Administrative Services, 1972; contbg. author: Am. Mgmt. Assn. Handbook, 2d edit., 1984. Mem. adv. council to F.E. Seidman Coll. Bus. Adminstrn., Grand Valley State U., Allendale, Mich. Mem. Am. Soc. Interior Designers (hon.), Orgn. Facility Mgrs. and Planners (hon.). Introduced office landscape planning concept and methods, U.S and Can. Address: Apt 316 1640 Ufton Ct, Kelowna, BC Canada V1Y 8L5

PLATNICO, EDMUND ROY, systems analyst; b. Mpls., Jan. 6, 1930; s. Raymond Platnico; m. Alice Mae Johnson, Jan. 7, 1950; children—Valerie Lynn Platnico Foster, John Edmund. Student U. Calif.-Berkeley. Research analyst Bank of Am., San Francisco, 1957-71; cons., Dublin, Calif., 1971-73; instr. City of San Lorenzo, Calif., 1973-78; instr. Ray Ctr., U. Alaska-Juneau, 1979—; systems analyst Alaska Div. Vocat. Rehab., Juneau, 1978—. Served with USMC, 1948-57, Korea. Mem. Data Processing Mgmt. Assn. Jewish. Home: 8601 Marilyn Ave Juneau AK 99801 Office: Alaska Div Vocat Rehab Dept Correcitons MS 2000 Juneau AK 99801

PLATT, ALLISON MICHAEL, nuclear engineer, consultant; b. Schenectady, N.Y.; m. Marinel Dean Platt, Sept. 2, 1945; children: Terri Linda, Victoria Gail. BS, Carnegie Mellon U., 1943; MS, Tex. A&M U., 1950. Sr. engr. Gen. Electric Co., Richland, Wash., 1951-58; mgr. chem. devel. and waste calcination dept. Battelle Pacific Northwest Lab., Richland, 1958-64, mgr. chem. tech. dept., 1965-72, mgr. nuclear tech., 1972—; mem. Adv. Com. on Reactor Safeguards cons. Nuclear Waste Mgmt., 1981—; mem. 1st delegation to USSR on radioactive waste purification and disposal, 1964; advisor IAEA Regional Nuclear Fuel Cycle Ctr. Project, 1976, IAEA tech. com. on High Level and Alpha Bearing Waste, 1972-80, IAEA Internat. Nuclear Fuel Cycle Evaluation Waste Mgmt. 1978-81. Editor-in-chief Internat. Jour., 1980—; contbr. Encyclopedia of Energy. Fellow Am. Nuclear Soc. (chmn. nuclear fuel cycle div. 1974, Outstanding Achievement in Nuclear Waste Isolation Tech. award 1982). Home: 2401 Alexander Richland WA 99352 Office: Battelle Pacific Northwest Lab PO Box 999 Richland WA 99352

PLATT, JOSEPH BEAVEN, former college president; b. Portland, Oreg., Aug. 12, 1915; s. William Bradbury and Mary (Beaven) P.; m. Jean Ferguson Rusk, Feb. 9, 1946; children—Ann Ferguson Walker, Elizabeth Beaven Garrow. B.A., U. Rochester, 1937; Ph.D., Cornell U., 1942; LL.D., U. So. Calif., 1969, Claremont McKenna Coll., 1982; D.Sc., Harvey Mudd Coll., 1981. Instr. physics U. Rochester, 1941-43, successively asst. prof. to prof. physics, 1946-56, assoc. chmn. dept., 1954-56; staff mem. radiation lab. Mass. Inst. Tech., 1943-46; pres. Harvey Mudd Coll., 1956-76, Claremont U. Center, Calif., 1976-81; now sr. prof. physics part-time Harvey Mudd Coll.; dir. Bell & Howell, Am. Mut. Fund, DeVry, Inc., Sigma Research, Inc.; chmn., dir. Automobile Club So. Calif.; chmn., trustee Analytic Services, Inc.; trustee Aerospace Corp., 1972-85, Office Field Service, NDRC, 1944-46, Consortium Advancement of Private Higher Edn., 1985—; chief physics br. AEC, 1949-51; cons. NSF, U.S. Office Ordnance Research, 1953-56; bd. dirs. Lincoln Found., 1979-85, now cons.; mem. com. on sci. in UNESCO, Nat. Acad. Scis.-NRC, 1960-62, com. on internat. orgns. and programs, 1962-64; chmn. subcom. on Sino-Am. Sci. Cooperation, 1965-79; sci. adviser U.S. del. UNESCO Gen. Conf., Paris, 1960; mem. panel on internat. sci. Pres.'s Sci. Adv. Com., 1961; alt. del. U.S. delegation UNESCO Gen. Conf., Paris, 1962; chmn. select com. Master Plan for Higher Edn. Calif., 1971-73; mem. NSF Adv. Com. Sci. Edn., 1973—, chmn., 1974. sr. prof. physics (part-time) Harvey Mudd Coll. Trustee China Found. for Promotion of Edn. and Culture; trustee Carnegie Found. for Advancement Teaching, 1970-78; mem. Carnegie Council for Policy Studies in Higher Edn.; bd. dirs. Los Angeles World Affairs Council, 1973-79; Governing bd. Am. Inst. Physics, 1957-60. Fellow Am. Phys. Soc.; mem. IEEE, Automobile Club So. Calif. (chmn.), Phi Beta Kappa, Sigma Xi, Phi Kappa Phi. Clubs: California (Los Angeles), Sunset (Los Angeles), Town Hall (Los Angeles); Twilight (Pasadena); Cosmos (Washington); Bohemian (San Francisco). Home: 452 W 11th St Claremont CA 91711

PLEMING, LAURA CHALKER, educator; b. Sheridan, Wyo., May 25, 1913; d. Sidney Thomas and Florence Theresa (Woodbury) Chalker; B.A., Long Beach State Coll. (now Calif. State U., Long Beach), 1953, M.A. in Speech and Drama, 1954; postgrad. U. So. Calif., 1960-63; Rel.D., Sch. Theology, Claremont, Calif., 1968; m. Edward Kibbler Pleming, Aug. 25, 1938; children—Edward Kibbler, Rowena Pleming Chamberlin, Sidney Thomas. Profl. Bible tchr., 1953—; lectr. Calif. State U., Long Beach, 1960-66, U. So. Calif., 1963-65; Bible scholar for teaching Scriptures Program, First Ch. of Christ Scientist, Boston, 1970-75; free-lance Bible lectr., tchr., resource person for adult seminars, 1954—; active in summer teaching for young people, 1963-68, 86-87; tchr. adult edn. Principia Coll., summers 1969-71; tour lectr. to Middle East, yearly, 1974—; mem. archaeol. team, Negev, Israel. Mem. Am. Acad. Religion, AAUP, Soc. Biblical Lit. and Exegesis, Am. Schs. Oriental Research, Inst. Mediterranean Studies, Religious Edn. Assn., Internat. Congress Septuagint and Cognate Studies, Internat. Platform Assn., Phi Beta, Zeta Tau Alpha, Gamma Theta Upsilon. Republican. Christian Scientist. Author: Triumph of Job, 1979; editor Bibleletter Rev., 1968, 76, 81, 8-84. Home: 2999 E Ocean Blvd Apt 2020 Long Beach CA 90803

PLENERT, GERHARD JOHANNES, educator, management consultant; b. Backnang, Fed. Republic Germany, Dec. 2, 1948; came to U.S., 1953; s. George Johannes and Ida (Reisner) P.; m. Kathleen Mary Ensminger, 1970 (div. 1979); children: Heidi, Dawn, Gregory; m. Renee Sangray, Mar. 24, 1980; children: Gerick, Joshua, Natasha. BA in Math., Calif. State U., Sacramento, 1970, MBA, 1983, MA in Internat. Studies; PhD in Mineral Econs., Colo. Sch. Mines. V.p. Profit Controls, Portland, Oreg., 1976-78; indsl. systems specialist NCR, Dayton, Ohio, 1978-80; mgr. corp. systems TREMEC, Queretaro, Mex., 1980-81; indsl. cons. Calif. and Oreg., 1982-84; prof. mgmt. info. systems, prodns., ops. Brigham Young U., Provo, Utah, 1984-85; prof. U. Colo., Denver, 1985-86, Calif. State U., Chico, 1986—; cons. GMS, Thompson Diggs, Moody, Sacramento, 1982-84. Author: In Search of Ex Around World, 1986; contbr. articles to profl. jours. Mem. Am. Prodn. and Inventory Control Soc. (cert.), Soc. Mfg. Engrs.

PLESKO, LESLIE, editor, writer; b. Budapest, Hungary, Jan. 8, 1954; came to U.S., 1961; s. George and Susan (Mikes) P. Student, UCLA. Asst. editor Creative Age Pub., Los Angeles, 1978-79; editor Citrus House Pub., Los Angeles, 1979-83; mng. editor Cahners Pub., Los Angeles, 1983-85, Brentwood Pub., Los Angeles, 1985—; editor Tradeshow and Exhibit Manager mag., 1985-86, also author. Mem. Internat. Exhibitors Assn., Nat. Assn. Expn. Mgrs. Avocations: reading, internat. affairs. Office: Brentwood Pub 1640 5th St Santa Monica CA 90401

PLESSNER, GERALD MAURICE, fund raising management executive; b. St. Louis, Oct. 10, 1934; s. Herman and Ida Rose (Goldstein) P.; m. Carole Renee Spirtas, May 25, 1959; children—Mitchell Scott, Janice Aurelia, Ellen Beth. B.A. in Human Relations, Mo. Valley Coll., 1957. Cert. fund raising exec. Exec. Boy Scouts of Am., St. Joseph, Mo., St. Louis, Pitts., Miami, Fla., Chgo. and Pasadena, Calif., 1957-75; mng. editor Consumer Newsletter, Los Angeles, 1975-76; pres. Fund Raisers, Inc., Arcadia Calif., 1976—; pub. VIP1000 Los Angeles, 1984; pres. Non-Profit Network, 1986—; adj. faculty U. So. Calif., Loyola Marymount U., Los Angeles. Served as sgt. CIC, U.S. Army, 1959-62. Recipient Disting. Alumni award Mo Valley Coll. 1979; named Pro of Yr., 1983. Mem. Nat. Soc. Fund Raising Execs. (pres. Los Angeles chpt., pres.' award 1982), San Fernando Valley Pub. Relations Round Table (exec. bd.). Clubs: Publicity of Los Angeles, Am. Humanics (Kansas City). Republican. Jewish. Author: Charity Auction Management Manual, 1980; Golf Tournament Management Manual, 1981; Testimonial Dinner and Luncheon Management Manual, 1981; Vip 1000 Los Angeles, 1984. Contbr. articles to profl. jours. Office: 524 South First Avenue Arcadia CA 91006

PLĒSUMS, GUNTIS, architecture educator; b. Riga, Latvia, Dec. 17, 1933; came to U.S., 1950, naturalized 1954; s. Valdemārs and Velta (Braslis) P.; m. Māra Mazutis, Aug. 28, 1965; children: Jāna, Kārla. BArch, U. Minn., 1961; MArch, MIT, 1964. Registered architect, N.Y., Oreg. Architect Affleck, Desbarats, Dimakopoulos, Lebensold & Sise, Montreal, Que., Can., 1964-66; instr. R.I. Sch. Design, Providence, 1967-69; prof. architecture U. Oreg., Eugene, 1969—; pvt. practice architecture Eugene, 1980—; vis. assoc. prof. Kans. State U., Manhattan, 1976; adj. assoc. prof. Oreg. Sch. Design, Portland, 1983; lectr. U.S., Eng., Japan. Author: Townframe: Environments for Adaptive Housing, 1978; contbr. articles to profl.; prin. works include: theme pavilion Man the Producer for Expo 67, Montreal, 1964-66. Served as sgt. U.S. Army, 1953-56. Fellow Fulbright, 1966-67, NEA, 1982, Graham Found. Advanced Studies in Fine Arts, 1974; recipient Hon. Mention award Helios Design Competition, 1980. Home: 1410 E 20th Ave Eugene OR 97403 Office: U Oreg Sch Architecture and Allied Arts Eugene OR 97403

PLIES, DENNIS BRYON, music professor; b. Monterey Park, Calif., Mar. 15, 1942; s. Raymond Amos and Dorcas (Hansen) P.; m. Barbara Ann Duddleston, Sept. 12, 1964; children: Matt, Daniel, Melanie, Rachel. BA, Biola U., 1966; BM, Am. Conservatory of Music, 1971, MM, 1972; DA, Western Colo. U., 1983. Writer, announcer Far East Broadcasting Co., Naha, Japan, 1967-69; instr. percussion Harper Coll., Palatine, Ill., 1971-72; pvt. tchr. music Portland, Oreg., 1972-79; prof. music Warner Pacific Coll., Portland, 1979—; adj. instr. Marylhurst (Oreg.) Coll., 1976—. Named one of Outstanding Young Men of Am., 1979. Mem. Jazz Soc. Oreg., Nat. Assn. Jazz Educators, Nat. Keyboard Arts Assocs., Oreg. Music Tchrs. Assn., Percussion Arts Soc. Mem. Evang. Covenant Ch. Am. Avocations: racquetball, hiking, biking, traveling. Home: 5336 SW Hamilton St Portland OR 97221 Office: Warner Pacific Coll 2219 SE 68th Ave Portland OR 97215

PLISETSKAYA, ERIKA MICHAEL, biologist, physiologist; b. Leningrad, USSR, Dec. 8, 1929; came to U.S., 1980; d. Michael Israel and Amalia Zachary (Utevskaya) P. BS in Biology, State U., Leningrad, 1952, PhD in Physiology, 1958; DSc, Pavlov's Inst. Physiology Acad. Sci., USSR, 1972. Research scientist Inst. Evolutionary Physiology Acad. Sci., Leningrad, 1958-79; research assoc. dept. zoology U. Wash., Seattle, 1980-84, research scientist III dept. zoology, 1984—. Author: Hormonal Regulation of Carbohydrate Metabolism in Lower Vertebrates, 1975; editor Evolution of Pancreatic Islets, 1977; contbr. articles to profl. jours. Research grantee NSF, 1985-87. Mem. AAAS, Am. Soc. Zoologists, N.Y. Acad. Sci. Avocations: travel, music, flowers, animals. Office: U Wash Dept Zoology NJ-15 Seattle WA 98195

PLOCK, RICHARD JAMES, physicist; b. Mineola, N.Y., Apr. 22, 1931; s. Henry John and Evelyn Charlotte (Scheu) P. BS in Chemistry, Poly. Inst. Bklyn., 1952; MS, Yale U., 1954, PhD, 1957. Theoretical physicist U. Calif. Radiation Lab., Livermore, 1956-62; aerospace scientist NASA Goddard Space Flight Ctr., Greenbelt, Md., 1962-64; asst. prof. U. Redlands, Calif., 1964-68; cons. specialist Systems Cons. Inc., Ridgecrest and San Diego, Calif., 1979-81; sr. scientist Sci. Applications Internat. Corp., San Diego, 1981—; cons. in field, Redlands, 1966-78. Mem. AAAS, Am. Phys. Soc., Am. Chem. Soc., Am. Inst. Chemists., Sigma Xi. Avocations: chess, wargames, painting, herpetology, photography. Office: Sci Applications Internat Corp 10260 Campus Point Dr San Diego CA 92121

PLORDE, JAMES JOSEPH, physician, educator; b. Brewster, Minn., Feb. 16, 1934; s. James Arthur and Mary Jeanette (Lutz) P.; m. Diane Sylvia Koenigs, Aug. 28, 1964 (div. July 1974); children: Lisa Marie, Michele Louise, James Joshua. BA, U. Minn., 1956, BS, 1957, MD, 1959. Diplomate Am. Bd. Internal Medicine, Am. Bd. Pathology. Vol. leader Peace Corps, Gondar, Ethiopia, 1964-66; intern King County Hosp., Seattle, 1959-60; resident U. Wash., Seattle, 1960-62, asst. prof. medicine, 1967-69, assoc. prof., 1971-78, prof. medicine, lab. medicine, 1978—; head clin. investigation U.S. Naval Med. Research, Addis Ababa, Ethiopia, 1968-71; chief infectious diseases, microbiology VA Hosp., Seattle, 1973—; cons. WHO, 1975, Suez Canal U. Faculty of Medicine, Ismailia, Arab Republic of Egypt, 1981-85. Contbr. numerous articles to profl. jours., chpts. to books. Fellow Infectious Disease Soc., ACP; mem. AAAS, Am. Soc. Microbiology, Acad. Clin. Lab. Physicians and Scientists. Home: 3164 W Laurelhurst Dr NE Seattle WA 98105 Office: Vets Med Ctr 1660 S Columbian Way Seattle WA 98108

PLOSKI, CYNTHIA BERRESSE, artist; b. Stroudsburg, Pa., Feb. 21, 1932; d. Joseph Ray and Anne Elizabeth (Dreher) Feindel; m. William G. Berresse, Oct. 12, 1957 (div. 1979); children: Melanie, James, Alissa, Michael; m. 2d, Thaddeus E. Ploski, Nov. 24, 1982. AA, Joliet Jr. Coll., 1977; BA, Middlebury Coll., 1954; postgrad. Ill. State U., 1978; Governor's State U., 1979-80. Cartographer, demographer Burns Data Maps, Middlebury, Vt., 1954-55; gen. asst. pub. relations Allied Chem. Co., N.Y.C., 1955-57; gen. mgr., pres. Pep Mfg. Co. Tanite Co., Stroudsburg, Pa., 1967-82; community resource coordinator Joliet Twp. High Sch., Ill., 1978-80; mgr. vocat. assessment ctr., 1980-82; owner Art by Cynthia, Rio Rancho, N.Mex., 1982—. Various local, regional and nat. shows (artwork awards), 1975—; internationally rep. in Art Expo, N.Y.C., 1984. Sponsor, cons. Welcome Wagon, Internat., Memphis, 1982—; com. chmn. Community Leadership Sch., Joliet, 1979-82; bd. dirs. Drug Coordinating and Info. Council, Joliet, 1979-82. Recipient Outstanding Service award CETA, Joliet, 1982; Outstanding Service award Community Leadership Sch., Joliet, 1981; Oscar Joliet Jr. Coll., 1977. Mem. N.Mex. Watercolor Soc., Internat. Soc. of Artists, Nat. Soc. Layerists in Multi-media. Office: 1460 Brierwood Ct Rio Rancho NM 87124

PLOTNICK, ROBERT DAVID, educator, economic consultant; b. Washington, Aug. 3, 1949; s. Theodore and Jean (Hirshfeld) P.; m. Gay Lee Jensen, Dec. 22, 1972. BA, Princeton U., 1971; MA, U. Calif., Berkeley, 1973, PhD, 1976. Research assoc. Inst. Research on Poverty, Madison, Wis., 1973-75; asst. prof. Bates Coll., Lewiston, Maine, 1975-77, Dartmouth Coll., Hanover, N.H., 1977-84; assoc. prof. U. Wash., Seattle, 1984—; cons. Wash. Dept. Social and Health Services, Olympia, 1984—. Author: Progress Against Poverty, 1975; also numerous articles. Recipient Teaching Excellence award U. Wash., 1985. Mem. Am. Econ. Assn., Assn. Policy Analysis and Mgmt. Avocations: tennis, hiking, bird watching. Office: U Wash Grad Sch Pub Affairs DP-30 Seattle WA 98195

PLOWMAN, PAUL DEARBORNE, state agency administrator; b. Sheboygan, Wis., Nov. 29, 1924; s. Paul Dearborn and Florence (Scmitt) P.; m. Jeanne Marie Bondbrake, June 6, 1949 (div. Mar. 1979); children: Glenn Mark, Bruce Warren; m. Helen Marie Peterson, June 3, 1983; stepchildren: Erik, Ingrid, Daniel, Nels. BA in Polit. Sci., Carleton Coll., 1949; MA in Polit. Sci., U. Wis., 1951; EdD in Sch. Adminstrn., Stanford U., 1958. Cert. gen. sch. adminstr.; cert. secondary tchr. Tchr. Kamehameha Schs., Honolulu, 1951-53; counselor, tchr. San Jose (Calif.) Unified Sch. Dist., 1954-56; dean boys San Juan Unified Sch. Dist., Sacramento, 1957-58; secondary cons. Washington Unified Sch. Dist., West Sacramento, 1959-61; cons. state edn. Calif. State Dept., Sacramento, 1962—; summer faculty U. Alta., Edmonton, Can., 1964; cons. commr. U.S. Office Edn., Washington, 1968-69; bd. dirs. Council State Dirs. Programs for the Gifted, 1986, pres., 1963; grant writing cons. speaker Calif. State Dept. Edn., Sacramento, 1962—. Author book and curriculum guides, 1968-71; contbr. articles to profl. jours. Initiator, organizer Am. Field Service, San Jose, 1955; chmn. seccion Presbyn. Ch., West Sacramento, 1960; christian edn. commn. Meth. Ch., Sacramento, 1963. Grantee U.S. Office Edn., Washington, 1963-81; recipient Cert. Recognition, U.S. Office Edn., 1976. Mem. Calif. Assn. Supervision and Curriculum Devel. (pres. No. Sect. 1960), Nat. Assn. Gifted and Talented, Calif. Assn. Gifted and Talented (council excptl. children 1979-82; named Educator of Yr., 1981), Council State Dirs. Programs for Gifted (pres. 1963, bd. dirs. 1986—), Phi Delta Kappa. Avocations: hiking, bicycling, swimming, reading. Home: 6357 Seastone Way Sacramento CA 95814

PLUMMER, LEAVELLE, correctional educator; b. Sulligent, Ala., Sept. 5, 1941; d. Marvin G. and Azelle (Weaver) Duncan; m. John R. Plummer, June 14, 1959 (div.); children—Vicki Sue, Karen Kay Plummer. B.S., U. So. Colo., 1971; postgrad. U. No. Colo., Adams State Coll., Colo. State U. Teaching cert., Colo. Legal sec. J. Harrison Hawthorne, Canon City, Colo., 1965-67; adult edn. instr. Colo. State Penitentiary, Canon City, 1971-82; vocat. educator Pueblo Community Coll., Canon City, 1983—; presentor in English adult basic edn. div. State of Colo. Dept. Edn. Nominated Outstanding Correctional Educator, Colo., 1982. Mem. AAUW, Nat. Correctional Edn. Assn. (program chmn. region IV 1985, Tchr. of Yr. 1985, 86), Nat. Correctional Assn., Colo. Correctional Assn., Colo. Assn. Continuing Adult Edn. (pres. elect), Colo. Edn. Assn. (editor constitution and by-laws), Am. Vocat. Assn., Colo. Vocat. Assn., Colo. Edn. for and about Bus. Republican. Methodist. Club: Rebakah's Foresters. Home: 320 Autumn Ridge Circle Colorado Springs CO 80906 Office: PO Box 500 Canon City CO 81212

PLUNKETT, JOSEPH CHARLES, electrical engineering educator; b. Centerville, Tenn., Dec. 3, 1933; s. Harold D. and Lorraine (Lewis) P. B.S., Middle Tenn. State U., 1964; B.S.E.E., U. Tenn., 1966; M.S.E.E., Ga. Inst. Tech., 1973; Ph.D., Tex. A&M U., 1978. Registered profl. engr., Mass. Devel. engr. Martin Marietta Co., Orlando, Fla., 1966-69; research engr. Raytheon Co., Wayland, Mass., 1969-71, IIT Research Inst., Annapolis, Md., 1971-72, Tex. A&M U., College Station, 1974-77; assoc. prof. elec. engring. Calif. State U.-Fresno, 1977-80, prof., chmn. dept., 1980-84; cons. Author numerous articles in field. Served to capt. Ordnance Corps, U.S. Army, 1958-66. Mem. IEEE, Nat. Soc. Profl. Engrs., N.Y. Acad. Scis., Sigma Xi, Eta Kappa Nu. Republican. Mem. Ch. of Christ. Office: Calif State U Fresno CA 93740

PLUSKAT, THOMAS JOHN, real estate property manager; b. Sheboygan, Wis., Aug. 17, 1951; s. Edwin C. and Virginia B. Pluskat; m. Rosemary T. Vessels, Apr. 8, 1978; children: David, Suzanne. BS in Nuclear Engring., U. Wis., 1973; cert. in real estate, Fullerton (Calif.) Coll.; D Bus. Adminstrn., Pacific Western U., 1987. Registered profl. mech. engr., Calif.; lic. real estate salesman, Calif.; lic. gen. contractor, Calif. Cons. Bechtel Corp., Norwalk, Calif., 1973-79; prin., chief exec. officer Innovative Dynamics, Lakewood, Calif., 1975—. Author: Real Estate to a Better Future and Financial Independence, 1986. Mem. NSPE, Tau Beta Pi, Phi Eta Sigma. Republican. Avocations: woodworking, hiking, biking. Office: Innovative Dynamics Co PO Box 4474 Lakewood CA 90711

PO, HENRY NG, chemistry educator; b. San Fernando, The Philippines, Oct. 4, 1937; came to U.S. 1960; s. Son Tiat and Bon Tin (Ng) P.; m. Josephine C. Marbella, June 12, 1966; children: Stephanie, Janet. BSChemE, Mapua Inst. Tech., Manila, 1960; MSChemE, U. Wis., 1962; PhD in

Chemistry, U. Calif., Davis, 1967. Research asst. U. Wis., Madison, 1961-62, U. Calif., Davis, 1966-67; research engr. Allis Chalmers Mfg. Co., Milw., 1962-63; research assoc. Brookhaven Nat. Lab., Upton, Long Island, N.Y., 1967-68; prof. chemistry Calif. State U., Long Beach, 1968—; grad. coordinator Calif. State U., Long Beach, 1976—. Author: Experiments in Introductory Inorganic Chemistry, 1981; contbr. numerous articles to profl. jours. Recipient Disting. Service award Long Beach Heart Assn., 1973, Award of Merit, Long Beach Heart Assn., 1974, Exceptional Merit Service award Calif. State U., 1984, Meritorious Performance award Calif. State U., 1986. Mem. Am. Chem. Soc., So. Calif. Acad. Scis., Sigma Xi. Office: Calif State U 1250 Bellflower Blvd Long Beach CA 90840

POCKLINGTON, PETER H., business executive; b. Regina, Sask., Can., Nov. 18, 1941; s. Basil B. and Eileen (Dempsey) P.; m. Eva McAvoy, June 2, 1974; 4 children. Pres. Westown Ford, Tilbury, Ont., Can., 1967-69, Chatham, Ont., 1969-71, Edmonton, Alta., from 1971; now chmn. Pocklington Fin. Corp. Ltd., Edmonton; owner, gov. Edmonton Oiler Hockey Club, 1976—. Office: Pocklington Fin Corp Ltd, 2500 Sun Life Pl, 10123-99 St, Edmonton, AB Canada T5J 3H1 *

POCRASS, RICHARD DALE, management consultant; b. Meadville, Pa., Mar. 7, 1940; s. Irving F. and Roslyn (Sperber) P.; m. Rena Levy, Feb. 3, 1968; children—Michael B., S. Douglas. B.S. in Math., U. Pitts., 1962; M.B.A. in Fin., 1964. EDP sales mgr. NCR Corp., Pitts., 1962-67, retail mktg. mgr., Los Angeles, 1972-74; v.p., dir. Nanoseconds Systems, Fairfield, Conn., 1967-69, dir. 1968-72; v.p. gen. mgr. Hart Jewelry Co., Warren, Ohio, 1969-71, dir. 1981—; mktg. mgr. Data Source Corp subs. Hercules, Inc., El Segundo, 1974-75; pres. Webster-Pocrass & O'Neil (name changed to Pocrass Assocs. 1981), Los Angeles, 1976—, Health Tech. Inc. Pub., author: The Recruitment Letter; author (with Maronde) Drug Abuse Study for Hoffman LaRoche, 1980. Bd. dirs. West Valley Little League. Mem. Los Angeles Speakers Bur., Am. Soc. Personnel Adminstrs., Woodland Hills C. of C., Am. Mktg. Assn., Bank Mktg. Assn., Retail Controllers Assn., Calif. Exec. Recruiters Assn., Republican. Jewish. Lodge: Rotary. Home: 18815 Paseo Nuevo Dr Tarzana CA 91356 Office: 16133 Ventura Blvd Suite 625 Encino CA 91436

PODBOY, JOHN WATTS, clinical psychologist; b. York, Pa., Sept. 27, 1943; s. August John and Harriett Virginia (Watts) P.; m. Carolyn Sue Baughman, Feb. 6, 1972; 1 son, Matthew John. B.A., Dickinson Coll., 1966; M.S., San Diego State Coll., 1971; Ph.D., U. Ariz., 1973. Dir., Vets. Counseling Center, U. Ariz., Tucson, 1972-73; project dir. San Mateo County (Calif.) Human Relations Dept., Redwood City, 1974; staff psychologist Sonoma State Hosp., Eldridge, Calif., 1975-81; cons. clin. psychologist Comprehensive Care Corp., Newport Beach, Calif., 1974-75, Sonoma County (Calif.) Probation Dept., 1976—; asst. prof. Sonoma State U., 1977-81; dir. Sonoma Diagnostic and Remedial Center, 1979-82. Chmn. San Mateo County Diabetes Assn., 1975. Served to lt. USNR, 1966-69. Fellow Am. Coll. Forensic Psychology, Am. Bd. Med. Psychotherapists (fellow); mem. Am. Psychol. Assn., Western Psychol. Assn., Redwood Psychol. Assn. (pres. 1983), Nat. Council Alcoholism, Nat. Rehab. Assn. Home: PO Box 488 Kenwood CA 95452

PODENSKI, FRANCINE P., communications educator; b. El Paso, Tex., Jan. 24, 1948; d. Francis E. and Mary Ethel (Lambert) P.; m. Daniel Roembach, Mar. 20, 1984. Student, Clarke Coll., 1966-68, U. Wis., Platteville, 1968-70; BA, San Francisco State U., 1978, MA, 1982. Asst. mgr. Roxie Theater, San Francisco, 1977-80; instr. Coll. San Mateo, Calif., 1979-81; instr. communications arts City Coll. San Francisco, 1978-81, prof., 1982—; lectr. San Francisco State U., 1981-82; facilitator, exec. asst. Transformative Arts Inst., Albany, Calif., 1985—; promotion and mktg. cons. Ctr. for Investigation and Tng. Intuition, Berkeley, Calif., 1980-83, Healing Tao Ctr., San Francisco, 1985. Performing arts rep. Sunset Tunnel Park Com., San Francisco, 1975-80. Mem. Inst. Noetic Sci. (assoc.), Western Speech Communication. Democrat. Avocations: gardening, camping, hiking, martial arts, cultural anthropology. Office: City Coll San Francisco 50 Phelan Ave San Francisco CA 94117

PODESTO, ANTOINETTE LINDA, school system administrator; b. Stockton, Calif., May 13, 1947; d. Antonio and Georgia M. (Tons) P.; m. Anthony L. Pessino. BA, Calif. State U., Sacramento, 1969. Cert. elem. and secondary tchr., Calif.; cert. ednl. adminstr., Calif. Tchr. Stockton Unified Sch. Dist., 1970-84, staff devel. specialist, 1984—; mem. math. adv. com. Calif. Assessment Program, Sacramento, 1982—; assoc. EQUALS, Berkeley, Calif., 1985—; bd. dirs. Stockton Ednl. Enrichment Found., 1985—; Calif. Math. Staff Developer; mem. Calif. Math. Initiative. Recipient NEWMAST award, NASA, 1984; named Outstanding Math Educator, Stockton Unified Sch. Dist., 1985. Mem. Nat. Council Math. Tchrs., Calif. Math Council (Outstanding Math Educator 1984), AAUW, Assn. for Supervision and Curriculum Devel., NASA Ednl. Workshop for Math. and Sci. Tchrs., Nat. Council Suprs. Math, Nat. Sci. Tchr. Assn., Delta Kappa Gamma. Democrat. Roman Catholic. Club: AAUW (Stockton). Avocations: travel, shopping, gardening, reading. Office: Stockton Unified Sch Dist 701 N Madison Stockton CA 95202

PODGORNY, LESTER ANDREW, electronics company executive; b. Phoenix, Jan. 3, 1932; s. Leo J. and Cecilia Helen (Balchezki) P.; m. Shigeko Kojima, Apr. 29, 1957; children: Brian L., Hope C. BS, Bradley U., 1954; MA, Naganuma, Tokyo, 1959; B in Fgn. Trade, Grad. Sch. Internat. Mgmt., 1960. CLU. Mgr. Emery Air Freight, Tokyo, 1961-63; dir. Internat. Metallurgical, Ltd., Tokyo, 1963-65; pvt. practice ins. and securities Seattle, 1966-75; acct. exec. Merrill Lynch Ins. Service, Seattle, 1976-79; v.p. Pletronics, Inc., Seattle, 1979—. Served to sgt. U.S. Army, 1954-57. Roman Catholic. Avocations: reading history, basketball, gardening, cooking. Office: Pletronics Inc 9026 Roosevelt Way NE Seattle WA 98115

PODLEY, KRISTIN ZELARNEY, medical social worker; b. Los Angeles, June 14, 1959; d. Frank Rudolph and Joan Beverly (Myers) Zelarney; m. Phillip Eric Podley, July 10, 1982; 1 child, Anthony Rocco. BA in Psychology, Loyola Marymount U., 1981; MSW, San Diego State U., 1983. Cert. alcohol studies; lic. clin. social worker. Alcoholism counselor intern Viewpark Community Hosp., Los Angeles, 1980; substance abuse counselor intern Via Avanti, Pacoima, Calif., 1981; social worker intern Naval Regional Med. Ctr., Camp Pendelton, Calif., 1982; med. social worker Hilhaven Convalescent, Anaheim, Calif., 1983-84, Circle City Hosp., Corona, Calif., 1984—. Leader Girls Scouts U.S., Los Angeles, 1981-82; Rep. vol., Phila., 1976. Mem. Nat. Assn. Social Workers, Psi Chi. Roman Catholic. Avocations: camping, crafts. Office: Circle City Hosp 710 Old Magnolia Ave Corona CA 91720

POE, JONATHAN KEITH, electrical engineer; b. Honolulu, Mar. 11, 1960; s. Richard V. and Barbara W. Poe. BSEE, Cornell U., 1982; MSEE, Air Force Inst. Tech., 1983. Commd. USAF, 1983, advanced through grades to capt., 1986; elec. engr. USAF, Dayton, Ohio, 1982-83; systems design engr. USAF, Sunnyvale, Calif., 1983-84, satellite computer systems engr., 1984-86, mgr. advanced space systems, 1986—. Author: Measuring InP Coefficients, 1983, (pamphlet) USAF Computer Security, 1984, DSM Software UpGrades, 1984, AFSCF Master Plan, 1986; inventor in field. Mem. IEEE (engring. mgmt. soc., communications soc., computer soc., aerospace soc.), Air Force Assn., Cornell Univ. Alumni., Aerospace Club. Republican. Episcopalian. Avocations: sailboating, soccer, snow skiing, volleyball, antique autos. Home: 2474 Poett Ln Santa Clara CA 95051-1240 Office: AFSCF/DVA PO Box 3430 Sunnyvale CA 94088-3430

POGGENBURG, JOHN KENNETH, JR., biotechnologist; b. N.Y.C., Jan. 18, 1935; s. J. Kenneth and Elizabeth M. (Nicolais) P.; m. R. Sheila Clarke, Aug. 3, 1963; children: Clare, Joseph, Laura, Carola, David. BS in Chemistry, Holy Cross Coll., Worcester, Mass., 1956; PhD in Nuclear Chemistry, U. Calif., Berkeley, 1966. Mem. staff Oak Ridge (Tenn.) Nat. Lab., 1965-73, group leader, 1973-77, sect. head, 1977-78; mgr. nuclear products Med. Products div. Union Carbide, Tuxedo, N.Y., 1978-81; dir. research and devel. Analytab Products Inc., Plainview, N.Y., 1981-84; dir. radiopharms. Hybritech, Inc., San Diego, 1984—; instr. chemistry U. Tenn. extension, Oak Ridge, 1968-70. Served to lt. USN, 1956-61. Mem. AAAS, Am. Chem. Soc. (chmn. East Tenn. sect. 1978), Soc. Nuclear Medicine, N.Y. Acad. Scis., Sigma Xi. Democrat. Roman Catholic. Home: 1526 Linda Sue Ln Encinitas CA 92024 Office: Hybritech Inc PO Box 269006 San Diego CA 92126

POGGENDORF, JOHN HUSS, advertising agency executive; b. Toledo, Ohio, Dec. 6, 1947; s. John Frederick and Patricia Josephine (Dalton) P.; m. Donna Lynn Mohan, Sept. 20, 1974 (div. Feb. 1985). BJ in Advt. cum laude, Ohio U., 1970. Account supr. Stanford Agy. (subs. Southland Corp.), Dallas, 1976-80, D'Arcy, MacManus and Masius, St. Louis, 1980-82; regional mktg. mgr. Pizza Hut Inc. subs. PepsiCo Inc., Los Angeles, 1982-83; mktg. dir. Loves BBQ Restaurants, Los Angeles, 1983-84; account supr. Dancer Fitzgerald Sample Advt., Los Angeles, 1984-85, Winters, Franceschi and Callahan Advt., Inc., Phoenix, 1986—. Republican. Avocations: snooker, cribbage, camping, fine arts, active and spectator sports. Office: WFC Advt 2020 N Central Ave 6th Floor Phoenix AZ 85004

POGGIO, ANDREW JOHN, electronic engineer; b. N.Y.C., Nov. 3, 1941; s. Elno Joseph and Frances (Oddone) P.; m. Margaret Ellen Locher, Dec. 23, 1982 (div. 1978); 1 child, Natalie Louise. BEE, Cooper Union U., 1963; MSEE, U. Ill., 1964, PhdEE, 1969. Research engr. MBAssocs., San Ramon, Calif., 1969-71; research assoc. Cornell Aeronautical Lab., Buffalo, 1971-73; engr. group leader Lawrence Livermore (Calif.) Nat. Lab., 1973-78, program leader for safeguards, 1978-83, project engr., group leader, 1983—. Patentee in field; contbr. articles to profl. jours. Mem. IEEE, Antennas and Propagation Soc. of IEEE, Microwave Theory and Techniques Soc. of IEEE, Internat. Union Radio Sci., Sigma Xi. Avocations: sailing, cycling. Home: 1438 Hudson Way Livermore CA 94550 Office: Lawrence Livermore Nat Lab PO 808 Livermore CA 94550

POGGIOLI, ROBERT STEPHEN, computer scientist, hydrologist; b. N.Y.C., Feb. 15, 1944; s. Henry Joseph and Julia Marie (Carpaneto) P. BS, Yale U., 1965; PhD, SUNY, Stony Brook, 1974. Software engr. Ford Aerospace Corp., Palo Alto, Calif., 1979-80; research scientist CGS, Inc., Urbana, Ill., 1980-81, Mission Research Corp., Alexandria, Va., 1981-82; risk assessment analyst U.S. Nuclear Regulatory Commn., Washington, 1982-83; sr. computer scientist Computer Scis. Corp., Falls Church, Va., 1983-85; sr. systems engr. Hughes Aircraft Co., El Segundo, Calif., 1985—. Contbr. articles to profl. jours. Recipient DeForest Pioneers Prize Yale U.; Leeds and Northrup Found. fellow; Charles Grosvenor Osgood fellow Princeton U., NSF. Mem. AAAS, Assn. Computing Machinery, Yale U. Sci. and Engring. Assn., Phi Beta Kappa. Democrat. Avocation: performing arts. Home: 467 S Arnaz Dr Apt 205 Los Angeles CA 90048 Office: Hughes Aircraft Co Radar Systems Group El Segundo CA 90245

POGLAYEN, IVO, zoo director; b. Berlin, Germany, Jan. 16, 1921; came to U.S., 1954; s. Stefan and Gabriella (Brüll) Poglayen-Neuwall; m. Ingeborg Maria Poglayen, Aug. 9, 1950. PhD in Zoology. Dir. Rio Grande Zoo, Albuquerque, 1955-63, Louisville Zool. Garden, 1963-74, Reid Park Zoo, Tucson, 1975—; research assoc. U. Ariz., Tucson, 1975—; adj. prof. biology U. Louisville, 1965-76; cons. Sedgwick County Zool. Soc., Wichita, Kans., 1965, Buffalo Park, Flagstaff, Ariz., 1962, Theran Zoo, Teheran, Iran, 1977-78. Served to 2d lt. Italian Army/German Army, 1941-45. Named to Hon. Order Ky. Cols., 1973. Mem. Am. Assn. Zool. Parks and Aquariums, Am. Soc. Mammalogists, Deutsche Ges. Saugetierkunde. Avocations: photography, hiking, climbing, swimming, fossil hunting. Home: 1765 N Indigo Dr Tucson AZ 85745 Office: Gene Reid Zool Park 900 S Randolph Way Tucson AZ 85716

POGUE, ANNALEE, chemist; b. Visalia, Calif., June 30, 1945; d. Richard Lee and Anna Vivan (Palm) P. BA, San Jose State U., 1967. Chemist Monolithic Dielectrics, Burbank, Calif., 1966-68; mgr. materials U.S. Capacitor Corp., Burbank, 1968-71; emgr. tech. sales Sel-Rex Corp., Santa Ana, Calif., 1971-72; mgr. materials div. Cladan Inc., San Marcos, Calif., 1972-73; pres. Ann Pogue & Assoc. Inc., Solana Beach, Calif., 1972—. Bd. dirs. Solana Beach Town Council, 1974-81; sec. San Dieguito Citizens Planning Group, Solana Beach, 1975-76; chmn. local coastal plan com. City of Solana Beach. Mem. Cons. Chemist Assn. (treas. 1982-87—), Women in Bus. (support group 1986, bd. dirs. 1987-89), Am. Ceramic Soc., Am. Chem. Soc., Internat. Soc. Hybrid Microelectronics, Sierra Club (SCCOPE treas. 1986, Susan B. Miller award 1985), San Diego Land Conservancy (bd. dirs. 1986—), Sierra Club (nat. com. chmn., regional vice chmn. for conservation, San Diego chpt. treas.). Republican. Presbyterian. Avocation: fgn. adventure travel. Home and Office: 258 Barbara St Solana Beach CA 92075-1232

POINDEXTER, CANDACE COMMONS, education educator; b. Racine, Wis., Sept. 13, 1945; d. Joe Morris and Frances (Lindsay) Commons; m. Larry Lee Poindexter, Nov. 20, 1970; 1 child, Tracy. BA, UCLA, 1967, EdD, 1985; MEd, Loyola Marymount U., 1977. Tchr. Inglewood (Calif.) Unified Schs., 1968-75, cons., 1975-77, 84—, coordinator, 1977-84; prof. edn. Loyola Marymount U., Los Angeles, 1985—, dir. reading ctr., 1984—; cons. Archdiocese Schs., Los Angeles, 1984—. Author: A Technique for Teaching Students to Draw Inferences from Text, 1986; co-author: Schools in Crisis: Why our Children Still Can't Read, 1986. Mem. Assn. Supervision and Curriculum Devel., Los Angeles Reading Assn., Calif. Reading Assn., Internat. Reading Assn., Delta Kappa Gamma. Home: 336 29th St Hermosa Beach CA 90254 Office: Loyola Marymount U Loyola Blvd at W 80th St Los Angeles CA 90045

POIZNER, HOWARD, psychologist; b. Lake Charles, La., June 5, 1949; s. Erwin Jacob and Pearl (Greenberg) P.; m. Bridget Ann Casey, Aug. 12, 1973; children: Alan, Jeffrey. Student, Harvey Mudd Coll., 1967-69; BA, U. Tex., 1973; PhD, Northeastern U., 1977. Lectr. psychology Northeastern U., Boston, 1975-76; research assoc. Salk Inst., San Diego, 1978-81, staff scientist, 1981—, assoc. dir. lab. for lang. and cognitive studies, 1985—; asst. adj. prof. U. Calif., San Diego, 1983—. Author: (with others) What the Hands Reveal About the Brain, 1987; ad hoc reviewer NSF jours., 1981—; contbr. articles to profl. jours. NIMH fellowship, 1976-77. Mem. AAAS, Internat. Neuropsychol. Assn., Acad. Aphasia, Psychonomics Soc., Linguistics Soc. Am., Nat. Acad. Scis. (working groups on lang. and lang. processing 1985). Avocation: sports. Office: The Salk Inst PO Box 85800 San Diego CA 92138

POLAKOFF, KEITH IAN, historian, university administrator; b. N.Y.C., Dec. 12, 1941; s. Irwin L. and Edna (Sopkin) P.; B.A. magna cum laude, Clark U., 1963; M.A., Northwestern U., 1966, Ph.D., 1968; m. Carol J. Gershuny, June 21, 1964; children—Amy Ellen, Adam Matthew. Lectr., Herbert H. Lehman Coll., CUNY, 1967-69; asst. prof. history Calif. State U., Long Beach, 1969-73, assoc. prof. 1973-78, prof., 1978—; editor The History Tchr., 1972-77, prodn. mgr., 1977-80; assoc. dean instrnl. support Sch. Social and Behavioral Scis., Calif. State U., Long Beach, 1980-81, asst. dean ednl. policy, 1981-84, dean Sch. Fine Arts, 1984-85, dean Sch. Social and Behavioral Scis., 1985-86, assoc. v.p. academic affairs and dean grad. studies, 1986—; mem. council Pacific Coast Athletic Assn., 1982—, Western Collegiate Athletic Assn., 1982-85 . Mem., clk. bd. trustees Los Alamitos Sch. Dist., 1980-81; bd. dirs. Long Beach Opera Assn., 1981—, pres. 1982-83. Mem. Orgn. Am. Historians (exec. bd. 1977-80), So. Hist. Assn., Phi Beta Kappa. Democrat. Jewish. Author: The Politics of Inertia, 1973; (with others) Generations of Americans, 1976; Political Parties in American History, 1981; contbg. author: The Presidents: A Reference History, 1984. Home: 2971 Druid Ln Los Alamitos CA 90720 Office: Calif State U Long Beach CA 90840

POLAN, DAVID JAY, television company executive, lawyer; b. Chgo., Feb. 16, 1951; s. Julius and Jeanne Warsaw (Fox) P.; m. Terri Susan Lapin, Aug. 3, 1980; children—Adam Michael, Daniel Jacob. B.A., U. Ill., 1972; J.D., John Marshall Law Sch., Chgo., 1975. Bar: Ill. 1975, U.S. Dist. Ct. (no. dist.) Ill. 1975, U.S. Ct. Appeals (7th cir.) 1976. Atty., Pritzker & Glass, Ltd., Chgo., 1975-78, Barnett, Ettinger, Glass, Berkson & Braverman, Chgo., 1978-79; gen. mgr. Y.P. Aurora, Ltd., Ill., 1979-83; counsel, corp. sec. JP Communications Co., Tucson, 1981—; sta. mgr. KPOL-TV, Tucson, 1983-86, gen. mgr., 1986—; gen. counsel Northtown Bus Service, Ltd., Lincolnwood, Ill., 1975—; gen. ptnr. THC Ptnrs., Chgo., 1980—; co-owner LV Pictures, Las Vegas, 1984—. Active Orchard Village Assn. for Handicapped, Skokie, Ill., 1981; mem. Soviet Jewry commn. and young leadership commn. Jewish Fedn. So. Ariz., Tucson, 1984, chmn. young leadership commn., 1985, leadership devel. program, 1984—, chmn., 1985—, bd. dirs., 1985—, active various coms.; mem. bd. Congregation Bet Shalom, 1984; assoc. mem. Hadassah, Tucson, 1984; mem. nat. com. for leadership devel. Council Jewish Fedn., 1986—; bd. dirs. Jewish Family Services, 1986—, Tucsonans Say No to Drugs, 1986—, 88-Crime, 1986—. Recipient Community Service Award Jewish Fedn. So. Ariz., 1987. Mem. ABA, Davis-Mountain AFB Council of 50, 1987—. Clubs: Volk Jewish Community Ctr., Diehard Cubs Fan. Office: KPOL-TV Channel 40 2475 N Jack Rabbit Ave Tucson AZ 85745

POLHILL, DENNIS LEE, engineer; b. Freeport, Ill., Sept. 12, 1946; s. Robert Lee Polhill and Darlene (Lenora) Hering; m. Deborah Ann Reque, Nov. 23, 1982; children: Elizabeth, Kimberly, Christa. BS in Math, BS in Engring., U. Ill., 1970; MSCE, MS in Mgmt., U. Pitts., 1978. Registered profl. engr., Md., Wash., Pa., Colo., Ariz., Nev., Wyo., Utah, N.Mex., Tex. Asst. city engr. City of Urbana, Ill., 1970-72; pub. works engr. City of Cumberland, Md., 1972-77, dir. pub. works, 1977-79; city engr. City of Lakewood, Colo., 1979-81; v.p. Pavement Mgmt. Systems, Lakewood, 1981—. Contbr. articles to profl. jours. Mem. ASCE, Am. Pub. Works Assn. (pres. 1984, Outstanding Engr. 1984, Meritorious Service award 1986), Profl. Engrs. of Colo. (pres. 1983-84), Transp. Research Bd., Cons. Engrs. Council (com. chmn. 1982-84), Lakewood Jaycees. Club: Applewood Athletic (Lakewood). Avocations: skiing, racquetball, volleyball, hiking, mountain climbing. Home: 690 Cody Ct Lakewood CO 80215 Office: Pavement Mgmt Systems Inc 245 S Benton St Suite 230 Denver CO 80226

POLIS, SAMUEL, chemical company executive; b. Phila., Feb. 15, 1926; s. Abraham and Reba (Shalita) P.; m. Bette Jane Oaks, Dec. 27, 1950; children: Stephen Guy, Diane Gayle. BSChemE, U. Pa., 1950; MBA, U. Conn., 1980. Plastics engr. Naval Air Exptl. Sta., Phila., 1952-56; tech. service rep. flexible urethane foam Mobay Chem. Co., Pitts., 1956-60; mgr. urethane research and devel. Olin Corp., New Haven, 1960-82; tech. dir. western region Crain Industries, Compton, Calif., 1982—. Contbr. articles to profl. jours.; patentee in field. Served to capt. U.S. Army, 1944-45, ETO, 1950-52, Korea. Decorated Bronze Star medal with oak leaf cluster; recipient Superior Accomplishment award Naval Air Exptl. Sta. 1956. Mem. Soc. Plastics Industry (asst. chmn. flexible foam tech. com. 1968-69, chmn. 1970-71, 78-80), Am. Legion (vice comdr. Wilton, Conn. chpt. 1981-82). Avocations: boating, swimming, fishing, target shooting. Home: 170 Grumman Hill Rd Wilton CA 06897 Office: Crain Industries PO Box 4606 19201 S Reyes Compton CA 90803

POLITE, CORNELIUS, advertising executive; b. Phila., May 14, 1950; s. Henry David and Harweda (Levy) P. AA, Los Angeles City Coll., 1972; BA in Speech Communication and Advt., Calif. State U. Northridge, Los Angeles, 1976. Pres. Polite Advt. and Mktg. Co., Los Angeles, 1969—. Contbr. articles to auto racing mags. Staff asst. senator John Glenn, Los Angeles, 1984. Recipient Award of Merit, Hollywood (Calif.) C. of C., 1969. Office: Polite Advt & Mktg 5404 Corning Ave Los Angeles CA 90056

POLITICO, JOVENCIO LACERNA, anesthesiologist; b. Manila, Philippines, May 5, 1939; came to U.S., 1969, naturalized, 1977; s. Inocencio M. and Esperanza Y. (Lacerna) P.; A.A., Manila Central U., 1957; M.D., U. Santo Tomas, 1963; m. Zenona P. Maghuyop, May 4, 1968; children—Jeanette, Josephine, Joan, Karen, Carl, Jeffrey, Shirley, Jennifer. Intern, St. Joseph Hosp., St. John, N.B., Can., 1967-69; resident Boston City Hosp., 1971-73, N.Eng. Med. Center, Boston, 1973-74; anesthesiologist VA Hosp., Altoona, Pa., 1975-77, Phoenix, 1977—. Diplomate Am. Bd. Anesthesiology. Fellow Am. Coll. Anesthesiologist; mem. Am. Soc. Anesthesiologists, Assn. Philippine Practicing Physicians Ariz., Ariz. Soc. Anesthesiologists. Republican. Roman Catholic. Club: Filipino Am. of Ariz. Home: 1937 E Caroline Ln Tempe AZ 85284 Office: 7th St and Indian School Rd Phoenix AZ 85012

POLITZER, PETER A., physicist; b. Reigate, Surrey, Eng., Feb. 23, 1943; came to U.S., 1946; s. Alan A. and Valerie T. (Diamant) P.; m. Lisa N. Izenberg, June 16, 1966; children: Benjamin E., Rebecca S. BS, MIT, 1964; PhD, Princeton U., 1969. Mem. research staff MIT, Cambridge, 1969-73, asst. prof. nuclear engring., 1973-76, assoc. prof., 1976-79, prin. scientist plasma fusion ctr., 1979-84; sr. staff scientist GA Technologies Inc., San Diego, 1984—. Contbr. articles to profl. jours. Mem. AAAS, Am. Phys. Soc., Sigma Xi. Office: GA Technologies Inc PO Box 85608 San Diego CA 92138

POLIZZI, ANTHONY JAMES, electrical engineer; b. Detroit, June 21, 1955; s. James Anthony and Mary Ann (D'Alessandro) P.; m. Michele Marie Roberge, July 18, 1981. BS in Indsl. Tech., Ea. Mich. U., 1979; BSEE, Wayne State U., 1982. Engr. McDonnell Douglas Astronautics Co., Huntington Beach, Calif., 1982—; instr. electronics Golden West Coll., Huntington Beach, 1986—. Mem. Soc. Automotive Engrs. Avocations: auto repair, woodworking. Office: McDonnell Douglas 5301 Bolsa MS 10-3 Huntington Beach CA 92647

POLL, ROBERT ALLEN, physicist; b. Scranton, Pa., Nov. 2, 1935; s. Nathan and Bertha (Rubin) P.; m. Ellen Kathryn Briggs, Dec. 30, 1970 (div. Dec. 1986); children: Jeri, Karyn. AB, UCLA, 1957; MS, Calif. State U., San Diego, 1965. Dir. corp. devel. S-Cubed, San Diego, 1967-72; sr. staff mem. R&D Assocs., Santa Monica, Calif., 1972-75, Marina del Rey, Calif., 1977-80; asst. dep. dir. Def. Nuclear Agy., Washington, 1975-77; v.p. JAYCOR, Santa Monica, 1980—. Mem. IEEE, AAAS. Home: 1309 Georgina Ave Santa Monica CA 90402 Office: JAYCOR 2811 Wilshire Blvd Suite 690 Santa Monica CA 90403

POLLACK, BETTY GILLESPIE, health care executive; b. Oak Park, Ill., Apr. 4, 1940; d. Leon H. and Elta F. Gillespie; B.A., Whittier coll., 1962; M.S., Columbia U., 1964; m. David Pollack, Dec. 18, 1971; 1 son, Michael Alan. Community organizer, Boston, 1964-66; faculty mem. Grad. Sch. Social Welfare, U. Calif., Berkeley, 1967-71; exec. dir. Calif. chpt. Nat. Assn. Social Workers, Millbrae, 1971-81; pres., chief exec. officer Vis. Nurse Assn., Santa Clara County, Calif., 1981—; mem. exec. com. Assn. United Way Agencies, 1982-85, chmn. Cert. Assn. Execs. Study Course, 1981. Mem. No. Calif. Soc. Assn. Execs. (sec.-treas. 1980-82, pres.-elect 1982-83, pres. 1983-84, program chmn. 1984-85, chmn. nominating com. 1985-86), Peninsula Profl. Women's Network (sec. 1981-82, chmn. networking conf. 1981, pres. ednl. fund 1981-82), No. Calif. Coalition Vis. Nurse Assns. (v.p. 1983-85, pres. 1985), Bay Area Profl. Women's Network (mem. newsletter com. 1980-81), Am. Soc. Assn. Execs., LWV. Democrat. Home: 316 Sycamore St San Carlos CA 94070 Office: 2216 The Alameda Santa Clara CA 95050

POLLACK, DANIEL, pianist, educator; b. Los Angeles, Jan. 23, 1935. BS in Music, Juilliard Sch., 1955; MS, Acad. Musik, Vienna, 1957. Asst. prof. U. Hartford, Conn., 1966-70; from assoc. prof. to prof. piano U. So. Calif., 1971—. Performances include Daniel Pollack Recital, Artia-MK (Russia), 1958, 61, Columbia Spl. Prodn., 1973, The Competition (Prokofiev) MCA, 1981; concert performances include People's Republic of China, 1980. Grantee Fulbright, 1957-58, Martha Baird Rockefeller, 1963. Mem. Am. Fedn. Musicians, Kosciuszko Found., Music Tchrs. Nat. Assn. Office: U So Calif Dept Music Los Angeles CA 90089 *

POLLAK, MARTHA, dentist; b. Mercedes, Uruguay, Apr. 4, 1939; came to U.S., 1968; d. Abraham and Kreindla (Fuss) Rechelzon; m. Erich W. Pollak, Feb. 5, 1961; children: Adriana Ethel, Elizabeth Susana. BA, U. Calif., Davis, 1976; DDS, U. Mo., 1982. Asst. prof. U. Mo. Sch. Dentistry, 1982-83; lectr. U. Calif. Sch. Dentistry, Los Angeles, 1984—. Home: 2542 Westwood Blvd Los Angeles CA 90064 Office: Mancy Med Dental Ctr 14100 Francisquito Ave #14 Baldwin Park CA 91706

POLLAK, RICHARD BERNARD, research chemist; b. Chgo., Dec. 8, 1911; s. Victor and Amy Barbara (Silverman) P.; m. Ruth Avseev, Dec. 29, 1944 (dec. Aug. 1978). BS in Chemistry, U. Chgo., 1934; postgrad., U. So. Calif., 1938-39. Cons. chemist ABC Chemists, Los Angeles, 1947; research chemist Polycraft Corp., Inglewood, Calif., 1947-48; gen. mgr. Advance Finishes, Inc., El Segundo, Calif., 1948-69; chemist Amberitone Corp., Compton, Calif., 1969-72, Trail Chem. Corp., El Monte, Calif., 1972; research chemist Lee Pharms., South El Monte, Calif., 1973—; instr. U. So. Calif., Los Angeles, 1943-45; pres. Better Value, Inc., Los Angeles, 1980—. Patentee in field. Warden air raids Los Angeles Police Dept., 1943-45. Recipient 2d Pl. award Nat. Contest N.Y. Times 1931, 2d Pl. award Chgo.

Tribune 1933. Mem. Am. Chem. Soc., Los Angeles Soc. for Coating Tech. (chmn. tech. com. 1942-46, Nat. First Prize Paper, 1942, 46), Sierra Club. Avocation: hiking. Home: 4315 Inglewood Ave Los Angeles CA 90066 Office: Lee Pharms 1444 Santa Anita Ave South El Monte CA 91733

POLLARD, FRANKLIN DAWES, clergyman, seminary president; b. Olney, Tex., Feb. 25, 1934; s. Daniel Spurgeon and Ova Roena (Boone) P.; m. Jane Shepard, Sept. 1, 1955; children—Brent, Suzanne. B.D., Southwestern Bapt. Theol. Sem., Fort Worth, 1959; D.Min., New Orleans Bapt. Theol. Sem., 1983; D.D. (hon.), Miss. Coll., Clinton, 1977; L.H.D., Calif. Bapt. Coll., Riverside, 1983. Ordained to ministry So. Bapt. Conv., 1956. Pastor First Bapt. Ch., Seagraves, Tex., 1961-64; pastor First Bapt. Ch., Dimmitt, Tex., 1964-66, Tulia, Tex., 1966-70; pastor Shiloh Terr. Bapt. Ch., Dallas, 1970-74; pastor First Bapt. Ch., Jackson, Miss., 1974-80, San Antonio, 1980-83; pres. Golden Gate Bapt. Theol. Sem., Mill Valley, Calif., 1983-86; preacher The Bapt. Hour radio show, Fort Worth, 1976-86; pastor 1st Bapt. Ch., Jackson, Miss., 1986—; host, Bible tchr. At Home with the Bible, radio and TV show, 1978-83; v.p., exec. bd. Bapt. Gen. Conv., Tex., 1973; exec. bd. Miss. Bapt. Conv., 1977-80. Author: How to Know When You're a Success, 1973; The Bible In Your Life, 1978; After You've Said I'm Sorry, 1982; Keeping Free, 1983. Recipient Disting. Service award Jaycees, 1966, Valley Forge Freedom Found. award, 1982; named one of Seven Outstanding Preachers, Time mag., 1979. Lodge: Rotary. Home: 10 Chapel Dr Mill Valley CA 94941

POLLARD, LOUISE, systems librarian; b. Ft. Worth, Oct. 26, 1937; d. Sam Albert and Annie Bill (Prestridge) Kelley; m. Melvin E. Pollard, Apr. 2, 1961; children—Kelley Jean, Raymond Douglas. B.A. in English, N. Tex. State Coll., Denton, 1959; M.L.S., U. Md.-College Park, 1977. Interlibrary loan specialist Morgan, Lewis & Bockius, Washington, 1977-78; librarian U.S. Ct. Customs & Patent Apls., Washington, 1978-79; librarian Kennecott Minerals Co., Salt Lake City, 1979-82; systems librarian Am. Express Co., Salt Lake City, 1982—. Mem. Utah Library Assn., Spl. Libraries Assn., Assn. Info. Mgrs., Beta Phi Mu. Presbyterian. Office: 4315 S 2700 W Salt Lake City UT 84184

POLLARD, WILLIAM SHERMAN, JR., consulting engineer, educator; b. Oak Grove, La., Jan. 1, 1925; s. William Sherman and Carrie Lois (Hornor) P.; m. Gloria Louise Ponder, June 29, 1946; children: William Sherman, III, Katherine Lynn. B.S. in Civil Engring, Purdue U., 1946, M.S., 1948. Instr. civil engring. Purdue U., 1948-49; instr. U. Ill., 1949-51, assoc. prof., 1951-55; with Harland Bartholomew & Assos., St. Louis, 1955-71; assoc. partner, chief civil engr. Harland Bartholomew & Assos., 1956-58; partner Harland Bartholomew & Assos., Memphis, 1958-71; head ops. Harland Bartholomew & Assos., 1958-60; head Harland Bartholomew & Assos. (Memphis office), 1960-71; pres. William S. Pollard Cons. (Ins.), Memphis, 1971-81; prof. civil engring. U. Colo., Denver, 1981—; adj. prof. urban planning Memphis State U., 1973-81; dir. Ctr. Urban Transp. Studies, U. Colo.; chmn. WKNO-TV, Memphis. Served with USMC, 1942-46. Named Distinguished Engring. Alumnus Purdue U., 1969. Fellow Am. Cons. Engrs. Council, ASCE (state of the art award 1970), Inst. Transp. Engrs.; mem. Am. Rd. Builders Assn., Cons. Engrs. Memphis, Nat. Assn. Environ. Profls., Nat. Soc. Profl. Engrs., Soc. Am. Mil. Engrs., Urban Land Inst., Transp. Research Bd., Navy League, Lambda Alpha. Presbyterian. Clubs: Engrs, Summit. Lodge: Rotary (pres. 1979-80). Office: 1100 14th St Denver CO 80202

POLLCHIK, ALLAN LEE, psychologist; b. Denver, Sept. 18, 1949; s. Morris and Helen Ruth (Perlmutter) P.; B.A., UCLA, 1971; M.A., Vanderbilt U., 1973, Ph.D., 1975; m. Linda Lee Brown, Oct. 31, 1970 (div. 1985); 1 child, Scott David McNaughton; m. Victoria Susan Profitt. Intern, Langley Porter Neuropsychiat. Inst., U. Calif. Med. Sch., San Francisco, 1975-76; instr. San Diego State U., 1977—; clin., cons. psychologist El Camino Psychology Center, Oceanside, Calif., 1976-78; pres. Allan L. Pollchik, Ph.D., P.C., Oceanside, 1978—. Pres., Seawind/Oceanside Homeowners Assn., 1980. Nat. Merit scholar, 1967-71; NSF fellow, 1972-73; NIMH fellow, 1973-75. Mem. North County Psychol. Assn. (pres. 1980-81). Mem. Am. Psychol. Assn., Calif. Psychol. Assn., Interam. Soc. Psychology, Soc. Psychol. Study Social Issues, Zeta Beta Tau. Club: Oceanside Health. Home: 1138 Arden Dr Encinitas CA 92024 Office: 2101 El Camino Real Suite 203A Oceanside CA 92054

POLLEY, TERRY LEE, lawyer; b. Long Beach, Calif., June 2, 1947; s. Frederick F. and Geraldine E. (Davis) P.; m. Patricia Yamanoha, Aug. 4, 1973; children: Todd, Matthew. AB, UCLA, 1970; JD, Coll. William and Mary, 1973. Bar: Calif. 1973. Assoc. Loeb & Loeb, Los Angeles, 1973-78; ptnr. Ajalat & Polley, Los Angeles, 1978—; lectr. taxation law U. So. Calif. Mem. editorial bd. William and Mary Law Rev. Elder Grace Brethren Ch., Long Beach. Mem. Calif. Bar Assn. (steering com., property, sales and local tax com. taxation sect.), Los Angeles County Bar Assn. (chmn. and exec. com. taxation sect., chmn. state and local tax com. taxation sect.), Omicron Delta Epsilon. Democrat. Office: Ajalat & Polley 643 S Olive St Suite 200 Los Angeles CA 90014

POLLOCK, GERALD ARTHUR, toxicologist; b. St. Louis, Jan. 12, 1950; s. Glenn E. and Paula (Waldes) P.; children: Rachel Christine, Nathan Jeremy, Sarah Elizabeth. BS, U. Calif., Davis, 1972, PhD, 1977. Asst. prof. Wash.-Oreg.-Idaho Regional Program Vet. Medicine, U. Idaho, Moscow, 1977-82; research supr. Diamond Shamrock Corp., Painesville, Ohio, 1982-84; staff toxicologist Calif. Dept. Health Services, Sacramento, 1984—. Mem. Soc. Toxicology, Am. Chem. Soc. Democrat. Presbyterian. Home: 2644 Blackburn Dr Davis CA 95616 Office: Calif Dept Health Services 714 P St Room 1392 Sacramento CA 95814

POLLOCK, JOHN JOSEPH, English language educator; b. Mt. Vernon, N.Y., Jan. 14, 1945; s. John Birch and Thelma Alice (Madden) P.; m. Penny Louise Hazelton, July 19, 1969; 1 child, Jeremy DeWitt. BA, U. Calif., Davis, 1967, MA, 1969, PhD, 1971. Assoc. prof. English San Jose (Calif.) State U., 1973-77, prof. English, 1978—, coordinator grad. English program, 1986—. Author: The Magic Coat, 1985; editor: We Lie Down In Hope, 1976, The Black Feet of the Peacock, 1985; contbr. articles and poems to mags. NDEA fellow, 1968. Mem. MLA, Renaissance Soc. Am., No. Calif. Renaissance Conf., Philol. Assn. Pacific Coast, Phi Beta Kappa, Phi Kappa Phi. Office: San Jose State U Dept English One Washington Sq San Jose CA 95192

POLLOCK, JOHN PHLEGER, lawyer; b. Sacramento, Apr. 28, 1920; s. George Gordon and Irma (Phleger) P.; m. Juanita Irene Gossman, Oct. 26, 1945; children: Linda Pollock Harrison, Madeline Pollock Chiotti, John, Gordon. A.B., Stanford U., 1942; J.D., Harvard U., 1948. Bar: Calif. 1949, U.S. Supreme Ct. 1954. Partner Musick, Peeler & Garrett, Los Angeles, 1953-60, Pollock, Williams & Berwanger, Los Angeles, 1960-80, Rodi, Pollock, Pettker, Galbraith & Phillips, Los Angeles, 1980—. Contbr. articles to profl. publs. Active Boy Scouts Am.; former trustee Pitzer Coll., Claremont, Calif., 1968-76; trustee Jones Found., Good Hope Med. Found., Pacific Legal Found. Served with AUS, 1942-45. Fellow Am. Coll. Trial Lawyers; mem. ABA, Los Angeles County Bar Assn. (trustee 1964-66), Am. Judicature Soc. Home: 30602 Paseo del Valle Laguna Niguel CA 92677 Office: 611 W 6th St Los Angeles CA 90017

POLLOCK, RICHARD EDWIN, former county adminstrator; b. Phila., Aug. 27, 1928; s. Ernest Edwin and Evelyn Marie (Scarlett) P.; student Armstrong Coll., 1947, U. Calif., Berkeley, 1949-51, 55; B.A. in Recreation, San Jose State U., 1961; postgrad. San Fernando Valley State U., 1969-70, U. Calif., Davis, 1963-77, UCLA, 1964, U. Calif., Santa Barbara, 1970, U. Redlands, 1979; m. Yvonne May Graves, Oct. 11, 1952; children—Colleen May, Karen Marie, Richard Irvin, Annette Yvonne, Mary Ann. Swim pool mgr. and instr. Berkley Tennis Club, 1955-56; police officer City of Berkeley, 1956; recreation and aquatic supr. Pleasant Hill (Calif.) Recreation and Park Dist., 1956-62; gen. mgr. Pleasant Valley Recreation and Park Dist., Camarillo, Calif., 1962-68; bldg. insp. Ventura County (Calif.), 1969-71; adminstr. Sacramento County-Carmichael Recreation and Park Dist., 1971-73; dir. parks and recreation Imperial County (Calif.), 1973-81; ret., 1981; 73; dir. parks and recreation Imperial County (Calif.), 1974-85, others; aquatic cons., mem. faculty Imperial Valley Jr. Coll., 1974-85, others; aquatic cons., 1957—; real estate investor, 1984—; chmn. San Francisco Bay Area Conf. for Cooperation in Aquatics, 1958-59. Adviser/scoutmaster Desert Trails council Boy Scouts Am.; bd. dirs., instr. ARC; work with devel. disabled and handicapped children and adults. Served from pvt. to lt. U.S. Army, 1951-55; Korea. Recipient recognition for 41 years vol. service ARC, 1978; registered recreator and park mgr.; cert. elem., secondary and community coll. tchr., Calif. Mem. Nat. Recreation and Park Assn., AAHPER, Calif. Park and Recreation Soc., Calif. County Dirs. Parks and Recreation Assn., Calif. Boating Safety Officers Assn., Aircraft Owners and Pilots Assn., Nat. Assn. Emergency Med. Technicians. Democrat. Mormon. Author: Bibliography: A Pool of Aquatic Sources, 1960. Home: PO Box 3100 El Centro CA 92244-3011

POLLOCK, VICKI EILEEN, psychologist; b. Portland, Oreg., Apr. 24, 1956; d. Richard Edward and Margorie Helen (Smith) P. AB summa cum laude, Washington U., St. Louis, 1977; MA, U. So. Calif., 1982, PhD, 1985. Sr. research asst. Mo. Inst. Psychiatry, St. Louis, 1977-79; psychophysiol. lab. chief Psykologisk Institut, Copenhagen, 1979-80; data analyst Ctr. for Longitudinal Research, Los Angeles, 1980-83, data coordinator, 1983-85; psychology intern Neuropsychiatric Inst., Los Angeles, 1984-85; asst. prof. psychiatry (psychology) U. So. Calif., 1985—. Contbr. articles to profl. jours. Fellow Nat. Inst. Alcohol Abuse and Alcoholism, Washington, Grass Found. fellow, 1976. Soc. for Psychophysiol. Research, AAAS, Behavior Genetics Assn., Sigma Xi. Avocations: classical music, swimming. Office: U So Calif Med Ctr Psychiat Hosp 1934 Hosp Pl Los Angeles CA 90033

POLON, LINDA BETH, educator, writer, illustrator; b. Balt., Oct. 7, 1943; d. Harold Bernard and Edith Judith Wolff; m. Marty I. Polon, Dec. 18, 1966 (div. Aug. 1983); m. Robert Dorsey, Apr. 13, 1986. B.A. in History, UCLA, 1966. Elem. tchr. Los Angeles Bd. Edn., 1967—; writer-illustrator Scott Foresman Pub. Co., Glenview, Ill., 1979—, Frank Schaffer Pub. Co., Torrance, Calif., 1981-82, Learning Works, Santa Barbara, Calif., 1981-82; editorial reviewer Prentice Hall Pub. Co., Santa Monica, Calif., 1982-83. Author: (juvenile books) Creative Teaching Games, 1974; Teaching Games for Fun, 1976; Making Kids Click, 1979; Write up a Storm, 1979; Stir Up a Story, 1981; Paragraph Production, 1981; Using Words Correctly, 3d-4th grades, 1981, 5th-6th grades, 1981; Whole Earth Holiday Book, 1983; Writing Whirlwind, 1986; Magic Story Starters, 1986. Mem. Soc. Children's Book Writers. Democrat. Home: 1515 Manning Ave Apt 3 Los Angeles CA 90024 Office: Los Angeles Bd of Edn 900 S Hobart Blvd Los Angeles CA 90006

POLSKIN, LOUIS JULIAN, physician; b. N.Y.C., July 3, 1914; s. Frank and Ida Polskin; m. Frances Golub, June 5, 1943. AB, NYU, 1935; MS in Biochemistry, Rutgers U., 1937, PhD, 1940; MD, Chgo. Med. Sch., 1943. Rotating intern St. Peter's Gen. Hosp., New Brunswick, N.J., 1946-47; surg. resident S. Highlands Infirmary, Birmingham, Ala.; gen. practice medicine Lakeland, Fla., 1949-75; civilian staff physician Tripler Army Med. Ctr., Honolulu, 1975—. Contbr. articles to med. jours. Served to capt. M.C., AUS, 1951-53, Korea. Recipient Community Service award Fla. Sect. Am. Chem. Soc., 1970. Fellow Am. Acad. Family Practice; mem. IEEE (sr., Appreciation award Fla. W. Coast Sect. 1968), AMA, Hawaii Med. Assn. Democrat. Jewish. Lodges: Shriners, Nat. Sojourners. Home: PO Box 15966 Honolulu HI 96830-5966 Office: Tripler Army Med Ctr Honolulu HI 96859

POLSKY, ABE, writer, consultant; b. Phila., Aug. 13, 1935; s. Max and Helen (Matkes) P.; m. Merrily Evelyn Dixon, May 5, 1974; 1 child, Matthew Brian. BA, UCLA, 1956. Freelance plawright and screenwriter 1958-86, freelance writer, workshop dir., 1986—; pres. Worldwide Film Projects, Los Angeles, 1965-80; dir. Unified Writers Workshop, Santa Barbara, Calif., 1980—. Producer, screenwriter The Baby, 1970; scriptwriter Decline and Fall of A Very Nice Lady, 1975; playwright of stageplay Devour the Snow, 1978-80. Grantee Nat. Endowment of Arts, 1981, Los Angeles Drama Critics Circle, 1978. Mem. Writers Guild of Am., Dramatists Guild of lam., Screenwriters Assoc. Santa Barbara, Writers Consortium, Spiritual Scis. Inst., Internat. Soc. Dramatists, Montecito Y.M.C.A. Avocations: photography, traveling, snorkeling, chess, spiritual scis. Home and Office: 4848 Sawyer Ave Carpinteria CA 93013

POLSKY, MICHAEL, neurologist; b. Bklyn., July 26, 1938; s. Edward and Sarah (Rabinowitz) P.; m. Rita Klaitman, Aug. 17, 1968; children: Yarom, Ronen, Sarit, Avital. BA, Bklyn. Coll., 1960; MD, Faculté de Medecine Lariboisiere-St. Louis, Paris, 1969. Diplomate Am. Bd. Neurology. Intern Jeffrey Hales's Hosp., Quebec City, Can., 1969-71; resident in internal medicine Bronx VA Hosp., N.Y., 1970-71; commed. 2d lt. U.S. Army, 1971, advanced through grades to lt. col., resigned, 1980; neurologist Walter Reed Army Med. Ctr., Washington, 1971-74; from asst. chief to acting chief Neurology Service Brooke Army Med. Ctr., San Antonio, 1974-80; practice medicine specializing in neurology Las Cruces, N.Mex., 1980—. Mem. AMA, Am. Acad. Neurology, N.Y. Acad. Scis., Wilderness Med. Soc. Republican. Jewish. Avocations: backpacking, paleontology, mil. history. Office: 2467 Telshor Blvd Las Cruces NM 88001

POLSON, DONALD ALLAN, surgeon; b. Gallup, N.Mex., May 12, 1911; s. Thomas Cress and Carrie Fern (Cantrall) P.; student Stanford U.; M.D., Northwestern U., 1936, M.Sc., 1947; m. Cecily, Lady Avebury, Nov. 9, 1946; 1 dau., Carolyn Kathleen. Intern, then resident in surgery St. Luke's Hosp., Chgo., 1936-38; practice medicine specializing in gen. surgery, Phoenix, 1947-83; formerly chmn. Drs. Polson, Berens & Petelin, Ltd.; chief staff Maricopa County Hosp., 1952-53, St. Joseph's Hosp., 1961; bd. dirs. Ariz. Blue Shield, 1950-55, pres., 1956. Served to col. M.C., AUS, World War II. Diplomate Am. Bd. Surgery. Mem. AMA, A.C.S., Ariz. Med. Assn. (dir. 1955-60), Maricopa County Med. Soc. (pres. 1954), Phoenix Surg. Soc. (pres. 1959). Republican. Episcopalian. Clubs: Paradise Valley Country, White Mountain Country. Home: 7619 N Tatum Blvd Paradise Valley AZ 85253 Office: 550 W Thomas Rd Phoenix AZ 85013

POLSTER, SUSAN ATWOOD, public relations executive; b. Price, Utah, Sept. 17, 1952; d. Charles Russell and Gayle Rhea (Brotherson) Atwood; m. Richard Stephen Polster, July 3, 1976; 1 child, Trenton James. AS, Coll. Eastern Utah, 1972; Bs, U. Utah, 1974; postgrad., Brigham Young U., 1986—. Media buyer Nicholson-Bainbridge, Provo, Utah, 1974; advt. layout artist Sears Co., Salt Lake City, 1975-76, Phone Directories, Price, 1976-77; pub. relations coordinator, tchr. Coll. Eastern Utah, Price, 1977—; guest lectr. on self esteem and dressing for success to women's groups, 1978—. Editor coll. mags., 1982—; contbr. articles to profl. publs. Bd. dirs. Miss Coll. Eastern Utah Pageant, 1978—; bd. govs. Women's Resource Group, 1980—, pres. 1986; senate rep., chmn. mothers-daughters weekend Coll. Eastern U.; rep. Utah Consortium of Women in Higher Edn; pub. relations consortium rep. Utah Community Coll.; instr. communications Price Council Boy Scouts Am., 1983—; dir. Cheerleading Clinic, Price. Univ. Utah Faculty scholar 1972-74, Coll. Eastern Utah, 1972; named one of Outstanding Young Women in Am., 1983, 84. Mem. U. Utah Young Alumni, Nat. Newspaper Advisors, Nat. Cheerleader Advisors, AAUW, Utah Profl. Bus. Women, Phi Beta Kappa, Kappa Tau Alpha. Democrat. Mormon. Home: RFD 1 Box 2253 Price UT 84501 Office: 451 E 4th St N Price UT 84501

POMERANTZ, CLIFFORD MATTHEW, civil engineer; b. N.Y.C.; s. Leonard Henry and Elaine Marion (Rosenstein) P.; m. Elaine Marie Kulczyk; children Sarah Marie, Carrie Elizabeth. AA, SUNY, Farmingdale, 1972; BS, Cornell U., 1974, M in Engring., 1975—. Registered profl. engr. Assoc. engr. Greeley & Hansen, Phoenix, 1975-85, 1985—. Fellow ASCE; mem. Water Pollution Control Fedn., Ariz. Water and Wastewater Assn. Democrat. Jewish. Office: Greeley & Hansen 426 N 44th St Phoenix AZ 85008

POMEROY, HARRY FRANCIS, JR., science educator; b. Bklyn., Feb. 19, 1934; s. Harry F. and Margaret A. (Paskowitz) P.; m. Mona C. Howe, June 8, 1957; children: Marsha M. Pomeroy-Huff, Linda Susan Pomeroy Brown. BS, U. N.Mex., 1957; MEd, Eastern N.Mex. U., 1965. cert. sci. tchr., N.Mex. Tchr. Hatch (N.Mex.) Mcpl. Sch., 1960-62, Clovis (N.Mex.) Mcpl. Sch., 1962—; lab. instr. N.Mex. Inst. Mining and Tech., Socorro, 1965, 66, 68; adj. faculty Eastern N.Mex. U., Clovis, 1978—. Contbr. articles to profl. jours. Elder Westminster Presbyn. Ch., Clovis, 1966—; merit badge counselor Boy Scouts Am., Clovis, 1975-84. Fellow AAAS, N.Mex. Acad. Sci. (pres. 1977-78, Outstanding Sci. Tchr. 1981); mem. Nat. Assn. Geology Tchrs. (pres. S.W. sect. 1972), N.Mex. Sci. Tchrs. Assn., Nat. Sci. Tchrs. Assn. (finalist Presdl. Awards for Excellence, 1985), U. N.Mex. Alumni Assn. (v.p. 1984), Phi Delta Kappa. Republican. Lodge: Masons. Avocations: model railroading, computers, gardening. Home: 1512 Kingston Pl Clovis NM 88101 Office: Clovis Mcpl Schs 8th at Pile St Clovis NM 88101-6681

POMEROY, LEASON FREDERICK, III, architect; b. Orange, Calif., May 9, 1937; s. Leason Fredrick Pomeroy Jr. and Dorothy (Finley) Kidd; m. Marlene Egerer, June 18, 1960; children: Joselyn Miller, Leason Pomeroy IV. AA, Orange Coast Coll., 1958; BS, Ariz. State U., 1961; BArch, U. So. Calif., 1965. Registered architect, Calif. Oreg., Wash., Nev., Utah., Mont., Ariz., Tex., Colo., Hawaii, Pa., N.J., Va., Ind., S.C., Fla., Md., Idaho. Architect Schwager-Desatof, Costa Mesa, Calif., 1961-65; pres. Leason Pomeroy and Assocs. Inc., Orange, 1965—. Bd. dirs. Orange County Devel. Corp., Newport Beach, Calif., 1985; trustee Orange YMCA, 1985. Served with U.S. Army, 1960-66. Recipient numerous design awards. Fellow AIA (design com. 1985-86, bd. dirs. Calif. council 1984-85; appreciation award 1982-85); mem. Orange County AIA (bd. dirs. 1982-83), Soc. Am. Regular Architects (spl. service award 1985-86), Internat. Council Shopping Ctrs., Urban Land Inst., Phi Delta Theta. Republican. Lodge: DeMolay. Avocations: fly fishing, art collecting. Office: Leason Pomeroy Assocs Inc 44 Plaza Sq Orange CA 92666

POMEROY, STEVEN HAMBLIN, public accounting executive; b. Phoenix, Aug. 27, 1949; s. Benjamin Kent and Laverne (Hamblin) P; m. Patricia Ann Daily, Dec. 27, 1972; children—Elizabeth Ann, Amanda Suzanne, Rebecca Loree, Joseph Steven, Adam Daily. B.S. in Acctg., Brigham Young U., 1973; M.S. in Acctg., Ariz. State U., 1975. C.P.A. Various positions with Pomeroy & Co., Phoenix, 1973—, sec., dir., 1975-79, pres., bd. chmn. 1979-85; ptnr. Eide Helmeke & Co. CPAs, Phoenix, 1985—. Scoutmaster, troop com. chmn, Explorer advisor Boy Scouts Am., 1973-84. Recipient Boy Scouts Duty to God award, 1967. Mem. Am. Inst. C.P.A.s, Ariz. Soc. C.P.A.s (past pres. central chpt., bd. dirs.). Republican. Mem. Ch. of Jesus Christ of Latter-day Saints. Home: 13857 N 67 St Scottsdale AZ 85254-3307

POMRANING, GERALD CARLTON, nuclear engineer; b. Oshkosh, Wis., Feb. 23, 1936; s. Carlton Chester and Lorraine Helen (Volkman) P.; m. Gayle Ann Burkitt, May 27, 1961 (div. 1983); children—Linda Marie, Sandra Lee. B.S., U. Wis., 1957; cert., Technische Hogeschool, Delft, Holland, 1958; Ph.D. (NSF fellow), MIT, 1962. Mgr. Gen. Electric Co., Pleasanton, Calif., 1962-64; group leader Gen. Atomic Co., La Jolla, Calif., 1964-69; v.p. Sci. Applications, La Jolla, 1969-76; prof. nuclear engring. UCLA, 1976—; cons. to govt. and industry. Author: Radiation Hydrodynamics, 1973; editor: Reactor Physics, 1966; contbr. articles to profl. jours. Fulbright fellow, 1957-58. Fellow AAAS, Am. Nuclear Soc. (Mark Mills award 1963), Am. Phys. Soc.; mem. Math. Assn. Am., Soc. Indsl. Applied Math., Soc. Engring. Sci., N.Y. Acad. Scis., Sigma Xi, Alpha Xi Sigma, Phi Eta Sigma, Phi Kappa Phi, Tau Beta Pi, Phi Lambda Upsilon.

PONT, ROSENDO JAIME, energy company executive; b. Bogota, Colombia, Dec. 13, 1947; came to U.S., 1966; s. Rosendo and Dolores (Rosell) P.; m. Leslie Oga, Mar. 25, 1972. BSE, Stanford U., 1968, PhD, 1976; MBA, Columbia U., 1970. Systems engr. Lockheed Corp., Sunnyvale, Calif., 1976-80; dir. bus. devel. Dravo Corp., San Jose, Calif., 1980-84; v.p. fin. Centennial Energy, Inc., San Francisco, 1984—. Chmn. Imperial Valley Transmission Study Group, San Francisco, 1985—. Mem. Geothermal Resources Council, Internat. Cogeneration Soc. Avocations: history, music, travel. Home: 1184 Laureles Dr Los Altos CA 94022 Office: Centennial Energy Inc 650 California St San Francisco CA 94108

POOL, ROBERT ALFRED FRANK, research viticulture educator; b. San Francisco, June 17, 1937; s. Robert William and Marie Mildred (Luce) P.; m. Linda Elaine Shook, June 23, 1962; children: Eric, Suzan. BA in Zoology, U. Calif., Berkeley, 1961; MA in Biology, Sacramento State Coll., 1965; PhD in Botany, Mont. State U., 1967. Cert. jr. coll. instr., Calif.; cert. vocat. coll. instr., Wash. Radiation chemist Atomic Energy Commn., Davis, Calif., 1961-63; research specialist Geigy Chem. Corp., Ardsley, N.Y., 1967-68; sr. scientist, supr. Calif. Dept. Food and Agrl., Sacramento, 1968-80; instr. Am. River Coll., Sacramento, 1980-81; instr. viticulture, chmn. dept. Spokane (Wash.) Community Coll., 1981—; cons. crop injury, Sacramento, 1971-81; adjustor crop ins. Grange Ins. Co., Spokane, 1982—. Contbr. articles to profl. jours. Chmn. judging Spokane C. of C. Wine Festival, 1985-86. Served as comdr. USNR. NSF grantee, Bozeman, Mont., 1964; Nat. Def. Edn. Act fellow, Bozeman, 1965-66. Home: PO Box 181 Newman Lake WA 99025 Office: Spokane Community Coll N 1810 Greene St Spokane WA 99207

POOLE, CECIL F., judge; b. Birmingham, Ala.; children: Gayle, Patricia. LL.B., U. Mich.; LL.M., Harvard U., 1939. Practice of law San Francisco, former asst. dist. atty., 1951-58; clemency sec. to Gov. Brown of Calif., 1958-61; U.S. atty. No. Dist. Calif., 1961-70; Regents prof. Law U. Calif., Berkeley, 1970; counsel firm Jacobs, Sills & Coblentz, San Francisco, 1970-76; judge U.S. Dist. Ct., No. Dist. Calif., 1976-79, U.S. Ct. of Appeals for 9th Circuit, 1979—; adj. prof. Golden Gate U. Sch. Law, 1953-58; mem. adv. com. Nat. Commn. for Reform Fed. Criminal Laws, 1968-70. Served to 2d lt. AUS, World War II. Mem. ABA (chmn. sect. individual rights 1971-72, ho. of dels. 1972-74), San Francisco Bar Assn. (dir. 1975-76). Office: PO Box 547 US Ct Appeals and Post Office Bldg San Francisco CA 94101

POOLE, H. SUSAN, manufacturing executive; b. Phila., Feb. 4, 1942; d. Roy Charles and Grace (Lucas) Fitzgerald; m. Fred Carpenter, June 10, 1966 (div. 1976); children: Paul Joseph, Patricia Janette, Fred Thomas; m. Bruce Birdus Poole, June 16, 1984. BS, Ohio State U., 1963; MBA, U. Calif., Berkeley, 1965. Adminstrv. specialist Ohio State U., Columbus, 1965-70; mng. ptnr. Profitmakers, Inc., Oakland, Calif., 1970-78; v.p. ops. Pierce Cons. Internat., Richmond, Calif., 1978-82; ops. mgr. ATA Industries, Oakland, 1982—; founder Expatriate Mgmt. Cons., Inc., 1980-82. Mem. Am. Mgmt. Assn., Nat. Bus. Profl. Women's Clubs Am. (pres. 1982-84), Nat. Negro Bus. Profl. Women's Clubs, Nat. Council Negro Am. Avocations: tennis, racquetball, violinist. Home: 2046 Placer Dr San Leandro CA 94578 Office: ATA Industries Inc 4901 E 12th St Oakland CA 94601

POOLE, JAY MARTIN, editor, librarian; b. Clinton, Okla., Aug. 6, 1934; s. Cleo Lloyd and Arlie (Martin) P. B.A., U. Tulsa, 1957, postgrad., 1958-60; M.L.S., U. Okla., 1970. Reference librarian, spl. programs librarian U. Wash., 1970-73; head reference dept. SUNY, Buffalo, 1973-74; head librarian undergrad. library U. Tex., Austin, 1974-79; editor Choice mag., Middletown, Conn., 1979-82; asst. dir. collection devel. Tex. A&M U., College Station, 1982-85; asst. univ. librarian pub. service U. Calif., Irvine, 1985—. Recipient Outstanding service to librarianship citation U. Okla., 1979. Mem. ALA, Pacific Northwest Library Assn., Wash. Library Assn., Tex. Library Assn., Southwestern Library Assn., Calif. Library Assn., Nat. Book Critics Circle, Soc. Scholarly Pubs., Kappa Alpha, Phi Mu Alpha, Theta Alpha Phi. Democrat. Episcopalian. Office: Univ Library U Calif-Irvine PO Box 19557 Irvine CA 92713

POOLE, JOHN W., development corporation executive; b. 1923. Engr. BC Homes, Ltd., 1946-64; chmn. bd. dirs. BCE Devel. Corp. (formerly Daon Devel. Corp.), Vancouver, B.C., Can. Office: BCE Devel Corp, 999 W Hastings St, Vancouver, BC Canada V6C 2W7 *

POOLE, KEITH E., service company executive; b. Rangely, Colo., Nov. 17, 1950; s. Julius Morgan and Martha Lomell (Croom) P.; m. Colleen Rose Caldwell, Nov. 5, 1975; children: Mariah Courtney, Dalton Keith. BS, Adams State Coll., 1973. Crew hand, operator, supr. Colo. Well Service, Rangely, 1973-77, v.p., 1977-84; pres. CRC Colo. Well, 1984—; bd. dirs. Rio Blanco State Bank, Rangely. Republican. Avocations: skiing, camping, hunting, trapshooting. Office: CRC Colo Well Inc 2602 E Main Rangely CO 81648

POOLEY, JOEL BRANNAN, airline pilot, real estate broker; b. San Diego, May 20, 1938; s. Carl Brannan and Lorena (Jones) P.; m. Lynda Lou Myers, Nov. 16, 1958; children: John Myers, Julia Jean. AA, Skagit Valley Coll. Charter pilot, flight instr. Anacortes, Wash., 1959-66; flight engr. Western

Airlines, Los Angeles, 1966-67, co-pilot, 1st officer, 1967-75, capt., 1975—; real estate salesman Century-21, Huntington Beach, 1972-76, broker, 1976—. Mem. com. Boy Scouts Am., Huntington Beach, 1971, scoutmaster, 1973-75; pres. swimming team Am. Athletic Union, Huntington Beach, 1975. Recipient Wood badge award Boy Scouts Am., 1974, Letter of Merit BSA, 1975. Mem. Airline Pilots Assn., Huntington Beach-Fountain Valley Bd. Realtors, Quiet Birdmen. Republican. Methodist. Lodge: Masons. Avocations: tennis, fishing, running.

POON, RAYMOND S., biotechnology consultant; b. Hong Kong, Feb. 21, 1944; s. Cho Fun and Rose (Woo) P.; m. Susie Y. Chan; May 15, 1971; 1 child, Michael. BS, U. Ill., 1966, MS, 1968; PhD, UCLA, 1974; MBA, Golden Gate U., 1981. Research assoc. Harvard Med. Sch., Boston, 1974-76; research biochemist U. Calif., San Francisco, 1976-79; applications chemist Beckman Instruments, Palo Alto, Calif., 1983; cons. SRI Internat., Menlo Park, Calif., 1983—. Contbr. articles to profl. jours. Fellow Anna Fuller Fund Cancer Research, New Haven, 1974-76. Mem. AAAS. Office: SRI Internat 333 Ravenswood Ave Menlo Park CA 94025

POONJA, MOHAMED, business management consultant; b. Mombasa, Kenya, Nov. 8, 1948; came to U.S., 1984; s. Abdulrasul and Maleksultan (Dharsee) P.; m. Zaitun Virji, Feb. 24, 1979. Student, Inst. Chartered Accts., Dublin, Ireland, Chartered Assn. Cert. Accts., London; MS in Mgmt. and Organizational Behavior, U.S. Internat. U. CPA. Audit supr. Ernst & Whinney, Dublin, Ireland, 1966-72, Coopers & Lybrand, Dublin, 1973-76; group controller Diamond Trust of Kenya, Nairobi, 1976-78; gen. mgr. Kenya Uniforms, Ltd., Nairobi, 1978-81; sr. mgr. Coopers & Lybrand, Calgary, Alta., Can., 1981-84; regional mgr. Coopers & Lybrand, San Jose, Calif., 1984—. Mem. ABA, Brit. Inst. Mgmt., Am. Bankruptcy Inst., Assn. Insolvency Accts., Brit. Inst. Bankers, Can. Insolvency Assn. Avocations: music, art. Home: 630 Milverton Rd Los Altos CA 94022 Office: Coopers & Lybrand One Almaden Blvd Suite 500 San Jose CA 95113

POOR, CLARENCE ALEXANDER, physician; b. Ashland, Oreg., Oct. 29, 1911; s. Lester Clarence and Matilda Ellen (Doty) P.; A.B., Willamette U., 1932; M.D., U. Oreg., 1936. Intern U. Wis., Madison, 1936-37, resident in internal medicine, 1937-40, instr. dept. pathology Med. Sch., 1940-41, clin. instr., clin. asst. dept. internal medicine, 1942-44; practice medicine specializing in internal medicine, Oakland, Calif., 1944—; mem. attending staff Highland Alameda County Hosp., Oakland, 1949—; mem. staff Providence Hosp., Oakland, 1947—, pres. staff, 1968-69; assoc. staff mem. Samuel Meritt Hosp., Oakland, 1958—, also Peralta Hosp., 1968—. Mem. Nat. Council on Alcoholism, 1974—, bd. dirs. Bay Area, 1977—. Diplomate Am. Bd. Internal Medicine. Mem. Am., Calif., Alameda-Contra Costa med. assns., Alameda County Heart Assn. (trustee 1955-62, 72-82, pres. 1960-61), Calif. Heart Assn. (dir. 1962-72), Soc. for Clin. and Exptl. Hypnosis, Am. Soc. Clin. Hypnosis, San Francisco Acad. Hypnosis (dir. 1966—, pres. 1973). Home: 1241 West View Dr Berkeley CA 94705 Office: 400 29th St Oakland CA 94609

POPE, HENRY ORSON, museum director; b. St. Louis, Sept. 3, 1914; s. Joseph Frances and Anna Mae (Davidson) P.; student pub. schs., Canon City, Colo.; m. Evelyn Victoria Parker, Sept. 1, 1939; children—Henry Orson II, Larry Alan. Truck driver, buyer John Jacobs Co., Canon City, 1933; salesman Nash Finch Co., Cedar Rapids, Iowa, 1934-38, Great Falls, Mont., 1939-44; owner, operator Loma Mercantile Co. (Mont.), 1944-76; owner, operator Earth Sci. Mus., Loma, 1976—. Recipient Disting. Service awards U.S. Dept. Commerce Bur. Census, 1957, 58, 59, 60, 61, 62. Mem. N.W. Fedn. Mineral. Socs. (pres. 1966), Mont. Council Rock and Mineral Clubs (pres. 1963-64), Mus. Assn. Mont. (v.p. 1981-82, pres. 1983-85, editor newsletter 1986-87), Whoop-Up Trail Rockhounds Club. Home: 108 Main St Loma MT 59460 Office: 106 Main St Loma MT 59460

POPE, MAX LYNDELL, pub. utility ofcl.; b. Clinton, N.C., Nov. 5, 1932; s. William Walter and Maggie (Honeycutt) P.; B.A., Idaho State Coll., 1962; grad. U.S. Army Command and Gen. Staff Coll., 1977, Security Manpower Program, Indsl. Coll. Armed Forces, 1980; m. Sarah Jane Norris, Dec. 10, 1954. City mgr. City of Rangely (Colo.), 1963-66, City of Seaside (Oreg.), 1966-69, City of Pasco (Wash.), 1969-70; city adminstr. City of Coeur d'Alene (Idaho), 1971-72; planner State of Idaho, Boise, 1972-75; city adminstr. City of Woodburn (Oreg.), 1975-85; gen. mgr. Woodinville Water Dist., Wash., 1986—. Ordained elder Presbyn. Ch., 1958, elder, Woodburn, 1976—. Served with U.S. Army, 1953-56, 70-71. Recipient Distinguished Service award Rangely Jaycees, 1964. Mem. Internat. City Mgmt. Assn., Am. Soc. Public Adminstrn., Am. Public Works Assn., Internat. Union Local Authorities, Civil Affairs Assn., Res. Officers Assn., Woodburn C. of C. Clubs: Rotary, Gowen Field Officers, Elks. Home: 14206 NE 181st Pl Suite L203 Woodinville WA 98072 Office: 17238 Woodinville-Duvall Rd Woodinville WA 98072

POPE, PETER T., forest products company executive; b. 1934; married. B.A., Stanford U., 1957, M.B.A., 1959. With Pope & Talbot Inc., Portland, Oreg., 1960—, asst. sec., 1964-68, v.p., 1968-69, v.p., gen. mgr., 1969-71, chmn. bd., chief exec. officer, 1971—, also dir. Served with USAR, 1957-58. Office: Pope & Talbot Inc 1500 SW 1st Ave PO Box 8171 Portland OR 97201

POPEJOY, WILLIAM J., savings and loan association executive; b. 1938; married. B.A., Calif. State U., 1961, M.A., 1962. Pres. Fed. Home Loan Mortgage Corp., 1971-74; pres. Am. Savs. & Loan Assn., Los Angeles, 1974-80, chmn., pres., chief exec. officer, 1984—; pres. Far West Savs. & Loan Assn., 1980-81; pres., chief fin. officer Fin. Fedn. Inc., Culver City, Calif., from 1981; chmn., pres., chief exec. officer Fin. Corp. Am., Irvine, Calif., 1984—. Office: Fin Corp of Am 18401 Von Karman Ave Irvine CA 92715 *

POPJÁK, GEORGE JOSEPH, biochemist, educator; b. Kiskundorozsma, Hungary, May 5, 1914; came to U.S., 1968; s. George and Maria (Mayer) P.; m. Hasel Marjorie Hammond, Apr. 9, 1941. M.D., Royal Francis Joseph U., Szeged, Hungary, 1938; D.Sc., U. London, 1961. Intern U. Szeged Clinics, 1937-38; postdoctoral Brit. Council scholar Postgrad. Med. Sch., U. London, 1939-41; lectr. pathology St. Thomas's Hosp., London, 1941-47; mem. sci. staff Nat. Inst. Med. Research, London, 1947-53; dir. M.R.C. Exptl. Radiopathology Research Unit, Hammersmith Hosp., London, 1953-62; joint dir. chem. enzymology lab. Shell Research Ltd., Sittingbourne, Eng., 1962-68; prof. biochemistry and psychiatry U. Calif. at Los Angeles Med. Sch., 1968-84, prof. emeritus, 1984—; vis. scientist Nat. Heart Inst., Bethesda, Md., 1960-61; hon. sr. lectr. biochemistry Royal Postgrad. Med. Sch., U. London, 1953-68; prof. molecular scis. U. Warwick (Eng.), 1965-68. Contbr. profl. jours. Hon. mem. med. adv. com. Nat. Heart Found., 1968. Recipient Ciba medal Brit. Biochem. Soc., 1965, Davy medal Royal Soc., London, 1968, Stouffer prize Stouffer Found., 1967, Lipid Biochem. award Am. Oil Chemists Soc., 1977; Vanderbilt Centenary medal Vanderbilt U., 1978; Disting. Sci. Achievement award Los Angeles affiliate Am. Heart Assn., 1979; Beit Meml. fellow med. research, 1943-47; Harvey lectr., 1970. Fellow Royal Soc. Chemistry, Royal Soc. London; mem. Am. Acad. Arts and Scis., Royal Flemish Acad. Scis. and Fine Arts (fgn.), Am. Soc. Biol. Chemists (hon.), N.Y. Acad. Scis., Alpha Omega Alpha (hon.). Home: 511 Cashmere Terr Los Angeles CA 90049

POPKO, STEVEN MARK, lawyer; b. Elizabeth, N.J., May 31, 1956; s. John Thomas and Marianne (Mesgleski) P. BA, U. Calif.-San Diego, La Jolla, 1978; JD, U. San Diego, 1982. Bar: Calif. 1983, U.S. Dist. Ct. (so. dist., no. dist.) Calif. 1984, U.S. Dist. Ct. (ea. dist.) Calif. 1985, U.S. Ct. Appeals (9th cir.) 1984, U.S. Ct. Appeals (fed. cir.) 1984, U.S. Ct. Appeals (10th cir.) 1985, U.S. Ct. Appeals (5th and 11th cirs.) 1986, U.S. Ct. Claims 1984, U.S. Ct. Internat. Trade. 1984, U.S. Tax Ct. 1984, U.S. Ct. Mil. Appeals 1984, Temporary Emergency Ct. Appeals for U.S. 1984, U.S. Supreme Ct. 1987. Assoc. Popko, Cornblum & McLean, San Diego, 1983-85; atty. Popko & Popko, San Diego, 1985—. Mem. ABA, Internat. Bar Assn., Assn. Trial Lawyers Am., Calif. Trial Lawyers Assn., San Diego Trial Lawyers Assn. Jehovah's Witness. Office: Popko and Popko 8775 Aero Dr Suite 232 San Diego CA 92123-1778

POPPA, RYAL ROBERT, manufacturing company executive; b. Wahpeton, N.D., Nov. 7, 1933; s. Ray Edward and Annabelle (Phillips) P.; m. Ruth Ann Curry, June 21, 1952; children: Sheryl Lynn, Kimberly Marie. BBA, Claremont Men's Coll., 1957. Sales trainee IBM, Los Angeles, 1957-59, sales rep., 1959-62, product mktg. rep., 1963, sales mgr., 1964-66; v.p., gen. mgr. Comml. Computers Inc., Los Angeles, 1966-67; v.p. Greyhound Computer Corp., Chgo., 1967-68, pres., chief exec. officer, bd. dirs., 1969-70; pres., chief exec. officer, bd. dirs., mem. exec. com. Data Processing Fin. & Gen., Hartsdale, N.Y., 1970-72; exec. v.p., chief fin. officer, bd. dirs., mem. exec. com. Mohawk Data Sci. Corp., Utica, N.Y., 1972-73; chmn., pres., chief exec. officer Pertec Computer Corp., Los Angeles, 1973-81, BMC Industries, Inc., St. Paul, 1982-85; chmn., chief exec. officer Storage Tech. Corp., Louisville, Colo., 1985—; dir. Western Digital Corp., Irvine, Calif.; founder Charles Babbage Inst.; past dir. Spacelabs, Inc. Trustee Claremont Men's Coll., Colo. Music Festival; chmn. fin. com., mem. Chmn.'s Circle Colo. Reps.; past mem. Pres. Com. Nat. Medal of Sci. Recipient Exec. of Yr. award U. Colo. MBA Alum Assn., 1986, Community Service award Inst. Human Relations Am. Jewish Com., 1980. Mem. World Bus. Council, Chief Exec. Orgn., World Bus. Council, Computer and Communications Industry Assn. (past bd. dirs., chmn., mem. exec. com.), Am. Electronics Assn. (past bd. dirs., mem. exec. com. Colo. chpt.). Club: Boulder (Colo.) Country. Office: Storage Tech Corp 2270 S 88th St Louisville CO 80028-4315

POPPE, CARL HUGO, research physicist; b. Chgo., Nov. 23, 1936; s. Carl Hermann and Emilie W. (Herrmann) P.; married; children: Catherine Jean, Rebecca Jane, Susan Irene, Carl James. BA, DePauw U., 1957; MS, U. Wis., 1959, PhD, 1962. Asst. prof. physics U. Minn., Mpls., 1962-65, assoc. prof., 1965-76; cons. Lawrence Livermore (Calif.) Nat. Lab., 1974-76, sr. physicist, 1976—, leader exptl. physics div., 1983-84, leader L-div. prompt diagnostics program, 1984-86, leader nuclear chemistry div., 1986—. Contbr. articles to profl. jours. Fellow Am. Phys. Soc., Phi Beta Kappa, Sigma Xi. Republican. Office: Lawrence Livermore Nat Lab PO Box 808 L-231 Livermore CA 94550

POPPINO, ROLLIE EDWARD, history educator, academic administrator; b. Milwaukie, Oreg., Oct. 4, 1922; s. Rollie Burnal and Greta Esther (McFeron) P.; m. Lois Lamberson, June 17, 1950; children: Richard Rollie, Margaret Lois, Stephen Lamberson. AB in Internat. Relations, Stanford U., 1948, MA in History, 1949, PhD in History, 1953. Instr. Stanford (Calif.) U., 1953-54; intelligence research specialist Dept. of State, Washington, 1954-61; lectr. U. Calif., Davis, 1961-67, prof. history, 1967—, chmn. dept. history, 1967—; vis. lect. Am. U., Washington, 1959-61. Author: International Communism in Latin America, 1964, Feira de Santana, 1968, Brazil: The Land and People, 1968, 2d rev. edit., 1973; also articles. Recipient Colar Don Pedro I award Instituto Histórico e Geográfico de São Paulo, 1972. Mem. Am. Hist. Assn., Instituto Histó e Geográfico Brasileiro, Conf. on Latin Am. History. Office: U Calif Dept History Davis CA 95616

PORCELLO, LEONARD JOSEPH, engineering research and development executive; b. N.Y.C., Mar. 1, 1934; s. Savior James and Mary Josephine (Bacchi) P.; m. Patricia Lucille Berger, July 7, 1962; children—John Joseph, Thomas Gregory. B.A. in Physics, Cornell U., 1955; M.S. in Physics, U. Mich., 1957, M.S. in Elec. Engring, 1959, Ph.D. in Elec. Engring, 1963. Research asst. U. Mich., Ann Arbor, 1955-58; instr. elec. engring. U. Mich., 1958-61; research engr. Radar & Optics Lab., 1968-72; asso. dir. Willow Run Labs., 1970-72, asso. prof., 1969-72, prof., 1972—, adj. prof., 1973-75; dir. radar and optics div. Environ. Research Inst. of Mich., Ann Arbor, 1973-76, v.p., 1973-76, trustee, 1975; asst. v.p., mgr. sensor systems operation Sci. Applications Internat. Corp., Tucson, 1976-79, v.p., 1979-85, corp. v.p., 1985—, mgr. def. systems group, 1986—. Bd. dirs. Tucson Jr. Strings, 1977-79, chmn., 1978-79. Fellow IEEE; mem. Optical Soc. Am., AAAS, Sigma Xi, Eta Kappa Nu. Roman Catholic. Research on imaging radar, synthetic aperture radar systems and radar remote sensing. Home: 3925 N Pantano Rd Tucson AZ 85715 Office: Willow Run Lbas 5151 E Broadway St Suite 1100 Tucson AZ 85711

PORT, MIKE, professional baseball team executive; b. Los Angeles, Calif., July 24, 1945; m. Thaylea Port; children: Brian, Adam. B.B.A., Calif. Western U. Minor league infielder San Diego Padres, 1969; gen. mgr. Key West team, Fla. State League, 1969-79, Lodi team, Calif. league, 1970-71; dir. promotions San Diego Padres, 1972, minor league dir., 1973-77; dir. player personnel Calif. Angels, Anaheim, 1977-80, v.p., chief adminstrv. officer, 1980-84, sr. v.p., gen. mgr., 1984—. Office: Calif Angels PO Box 2000 Anaheim CA 92803 *

PORTER, ARTHUR WOODS, lawyer; b. Darien, Conn., Nov. 6, 1955; s. Arthur Leaholme and Margaret Jane (Woods) Porter. AB in Econs. magna cum laude, Boston U., 1979; JD, Am. U., 1982. Bar: Colo. 1983, U.S. Dist. Ct. Colo. 1983, U.S. Ct. Appeals (10th cir.) 1983. Assoc. Holland and Hart, P.C., Colorado Springs, Colo., 1982-85; sr. assoc. Spurgeon, Haney & Howbert (now Holland & Hart), Colorado Springs, Colo., 1986—. Active Colo. Young Reps., Colorado Springs, 1985—; cons. to Jr. Achievement project bus., Colorado Springs, 1984—. Recipient B V rating Martindale-Hubbell, 1985, Vigil Hon. Order of Arrow Boy Scouts Am., Bronze Palm; named Eagle Scout Boy Scouts Am.; research grantee Am. U., 1980. Mem. Assn. Trial Lawyers Am., Colo. Bar Assn., El Paso County Bar Assn., Colo. Trial Lawyers Assn., Nat. Inst. Trial Advocacy, Mortar Board. Methodist. Club: Plaza (Colorado Springs). Avocations: photography, horses, automobiles, camping. Home: 29 Cragmor Village Rd Colorado Springs CO 80907 Office: Holland and Hart 1400 Holly Sugar Bldg PO Box 2340 Colorado Springs CO 80901

PORTER, BLAINE ROBERT MILTON, educator; b. Morgan, Utah, Feb. 24, 1922; s. Brigham Ernest and Edna (Brough) P.; m. Elizabeth Taylor, Sept 27, 1943 (dec.); children—Claudia Black, Roger B., David T., Patricia A. Hintze, Corinna. Student, Utah State U., 1940-41; B.S., Brigham Young U., 1947, M.A., 1949; Ph.D. (Grant Found. fellow family life edn. 1951-52), Cornell U., 1952. Instr. sociology Iowa State Coll., 1949-51; asst. prof. sociology and child devel. Iowa State U., 1952-55; prof., chmn. dept. human devel. and family relationships Brigham Young U., 1955-65; dean Brigham Young U. (Coll. Family Living), 1966-80, Univ. prof., 1980—; vis. prof., Fulbright research scholar U. London, 1965-66. Editor: The Latter-day Saint Family, 1963, rev. edit., 1966; editor quar. jour.: Family Perspective, 1966-82; contbr. articles to profl. jours. Pres. elect Iowa Council Family Relations, 1954-55; pres. Utah Council Family Relations, 1957-58; chmn. sect. marriage counseling Nat. Council Family Relations, 1958-59, bd. dirs., 1957-60, exec. com., 1958-72, pres., 1963-64; bd. dirs. Am. Family Soc., 1975—. Served as pilot USAAF, 1942-45. Recipient Prof. of Year award Brigham Young U., 1964. Mem. Am. Home Econs. Assn. (vice chmn. sect. family relations and child devel. 1955-56), Am. Sociol. Assn. (sec. sect. on family 1964-67), Am. Assn. Marriage and Family Therapists, Am. Psychol. Assn., Soc. Research in Child Devel., Sigma Xi, Phi Kappa Phi (chpt. pres. 1969-71). Home: 1675 Pine Ln Provo UT 84604 Office: Brigham Young U 2240 SFLC Provo UT 84602

PORTER, CHRISTOPHER JOHN, communications and media researcher; b. Milw., July 1, 1952; s. John Hamlin and Helen Meak (Smith) P.; m. Margaret Elizabeth Evans, Oct. 6, 1984. BA, Lawrence U., 1974; MA, U. Ga., 1983. Staff announcer Sta. WITI-TV, Milw., 1974; staff announcer, program dir. Sta. WIVI-FM, St. Croix, V.I., 1974-76; mgr. Custom Hi-Fi, Oklahoma City, 1977-78; staff announcer Sta. WKTM-FM, Charleston, S.C., 1978-81; grad. asst. U. Ga., Athens, 1981-83; sr. research dir. Surrey Research (formerly Surrey Cons. and Research), Denver, 1983—. George Peabody fellow U. Ga., 1982. Mem. Am. Mktg. Assn., Nat. Assn. Broadcasters (corp., Harold Fellows scholar 1982), Broadcast Edn. Assn., Colo. Assn. Broadcasters, Lawrence U. Alumni Assn. (recruiting fund raising coms. 1985—). Avocations: numismatics, golf, swimming, photography. Home: 5742 S Pierson St Littleton CO 80127 Office: Surrey Research 165 S Union #606 Denver CO 80228

PORTER, DIXIE LEE, insurance executive, consultant; b. Bountiful, Utah, June 7, 1931; d. John Lloyd and Ida May (Robinson) Mathis. B.S., U. Calif. at Berkeley, 1956, M.B.A., 1957. Personnel aide City of Berkeley (Calif.), 1957-59; employment supr. Kaiser Health Found., Los Angeles, 1959-60; personnel analyst U. Calif. at Los Angeles, 1961-63; personnel mgr. Reuben H. Donnelley, Santa Monica, Calif., 1963-64; personnel officer Good Samaritan Hosp., San Jose, Calif., 1965-67; fgn. service officer AID, Saigon, Vietnam, 1967-71; gen. agt. Charter Life Ins. Co., Los Angeles, 1972-77, Kennesaw Life Ins. Co., Atlanta, from 1978, Phila. Life Ins. Co., San Francisco, from 1978; now pres. Women's Ins. Enterprises, Ltd.; cons. in field. Co-chairperson Comprehensive Health Planning Commn. Santa Clara County, Calif., 1973-76; bd. dirs. Family Care, 1978-80, Aegis Health Corp., 1977—, U. Calif. Sch. Bus. Adminstrn., Berkeley, 1974-76; mem. task force on equal access to econ. power U.S. Nat. Women's Agenda, 1977—. Served with USMC, 1950-52. C.L.U. Mem. C.L.U. Soc., U. Calif. Alumni Assn., U. Calif. Sch. Bus. Adminstrn. Alumni Assn., AAUW, Bus. and Profl. Women, Prytanean Alumni, The Animal Soc. Los Gatos/Saratoga (pres. 1987—), Beta Gamma Sigma, Phi Chi Theta. Republican. Episcopalian. Home and Office: PO Box 64 Los Gatos CA 95031

PORTER, FREDERICK CHARLES, aerospace engineer; b. New Orleans, Jan. 10, 1937; s. Frederick Charles Porter and Jane (Currens) Fitz-Randolph; m. Gayle Mae Johnson, June 7, 1959; children: Steve, Linda. BSME, U. Colo., 1959; cert. exec. tng. (hon.), Alexander Hamilton Inst., 1965. Registered profl. engr., Calif. Structures engr. Rockwell Internat., Los Angeles, 1959-60; sr. project engr. Gen. Dynamics Corp., San Diego, 1960—. Contbr. articles to profl. jours. Fellow AIAA (assoc., treas. 1970-71, Outstanding Contbr. award 1969); mem. Nat. Mgmt. Assn., Am. Security Council. Republican. Club: U.S. Senatorial (Washington). Home: 1950 Woodglen Way El Cajon CA 92020 Office: Gen Dynamics/Convair PO Box 85357 San Diego CA 92138

PORTER, JACK WILLIAM, engineering recruitment company executive; b. Belvidere, Ill., July 23, 1937; s. William R. and Edna M. (Carpenter) P. m. Beverly J. Siverson, June 2, 1962; children—Keith, Joan, Jacquelyn, Robert, Steven. B.B.A., U. Wis., 1959. Cert. personnel cons. With Am. Can Co., 1959-79, salesman, Dallas, 1976-78, sales mgr., San Francisco, 1978-79; pres. Jack Porter Assocs. Inc., Issaquah, Wash., 1979—. Coach Little League Baseball, 1962-78; active Boy Scouts Am., 1964-78; organizer Spl. Olympics, 1979. Mem. Issaquah C. of C. (chmn. Salmon Days parade 1980—, bd. dirs., pres. 1987), Delta Tau Delta, Phi Mu Alpha. Republican. Lutheran. Lodge: Issaquah Valley Kiwanis (pres. 1983-84). Home: 24119 SW 18th Pl Issaquah WA 98027 Office: Jack Porter Assocs Inc 385 Front St N Issaquah WA 98027

PORTER, JANET KAY, language arts educator; b. Charleston, W.Va., June 29, 1945; d. Arthur Russell and Nellie Arlene (Higginbotham) Smith; m. Charles Franklin Hayes, May 8, 1967 (div. Sept. 1978); children: Michael Kevin, Jim Kenneth; m. Michael Pell Porter, Feb. 13, 1983. BA in Edn., W.Va. U., 1967; MA in English, U. Hawaii, 1974. Tchr. Highlands Intermediate Sch., Pearl City, Hawaii, 1967-69, King Intermediate Sch., Kaneohe, Hawaii, 1972-73, Hawaii Bapt. Acad., Honolulu, 1974-76; instr. U. Hawaii, Honolulu, 1976-79; tchr. Punahou Sch., Honolulu, 1978-79; instr. lang. arts Leeward Community Coll., Pearl City, 1978—, faculty advisor. Vol. Bishop Mus. Service League, Honolulu, 1984—; host family Friends of East-West Ctr., Honolulu, 1984—; newsletter editor St. Andrew's Cathedral, Honolulu, 1984. Mem. Hawaii Council of Tchrs. of English (second v.p. 1985—, newsletter editor 1985—), Hawaii Alliance for Arts in Edn., Hawaii Literary Arts Council (membership chair 1979-80), Storytelling Assn. Hawaii; writer Hawaii Alliance Arts in Edn., Honolulu, 1984. Episcopalian. Home: 972 Kealaolu Ave Honolulu HI 96816 Office: Leeward Community Coll Lang Arts 96-045 Ala Ike Pearl City HI 96782

PORTER, KATHERYNE ADELADE, postmaster; b. Springerville, Ariz., May 13, 1934; d. Manning Lee Sr. and Rena Belle (Sudduth) Lewis; m. Walter Clyde Porter, July 28, 1950; children: Lynnda, Larry, Chris, Sandra, Sharon, Carla. Grad. high sch., Fence Lake, N.Mex., 1951. Postmaster U.S. Postal Service, Alpine, Ariz., 1984—. Republican. Avocations: fishing, gardening, house plants. Home: Box 404 Alpine AZ 85920-0404 Office: US Postal Service Alpine AZ 85920-9998

PORTER, MARLEY E., architect; b. Mesa, Ariz., June 13, 1954; s. Bernard Clyde and Emily Winona (Brimhall) P.; m. Alyce Schneider, Aug. 21, 1975; children: Marlyce, Dana, Erin Donn and Kami Jo (twins). BArch, Ariz. State U., 1979. Prin. Design Assocs., Tempe, Ariz., 1979-81, PPB Architects, Tempe, 1981-84, PPDW Architects, Tempe, 1984—; instr. architecture Ariz. State U., Tempe, 1980—. Contbr. articles to design mag. Leader Boy Scouts Am., 1980-84, explorer post advisor, 1985—; facilitator Mesa Mus. for Youth, Mesa, 1985. Mem. AIA (sec. 1982, pres. Rio Salado chpt. 1985—). Republican. Mormon. Avocations: hangliding, scuba diving, motorcycle racing, designing. Home: 18 N La Arboleta Gilbert AZ 85234 Office: Porter Pang & Baldinger 1921S Alma Sch Rd 106 Mesa AZ 85202

PORTER, MICHAEL PELL, lawyer; b. Indpls., Mar. 31, 1940; s. Harold Troxel and Mildred Maxine (Pell) P.; m. Alliene Laura Jenkins, Sept. 23, 1967 (div.); 1 child, Genevieve Natalie; m. Janet Kay Smith Hayes, Feb. 13, 1983. Student, DePauw U., 1957-58; BA, Tulane U., 1961, JD, 1963. Bar: La. 1963, U.S. Ct. Mil. Appeals 1964, N.Y. 1969, Hawaii 1971. Clk., U.S. Ct. Appeals (5th cir.), New Orleans, 1963; assoc. Sullivan & Cromwell, N.Y.C., 1968-71; assoc. Cades Schutte Fleming & Wright, Honolulu, 1971-74, ptnr., 1975—; mem. deans council Tulane Law Sch., 1981—; dep. vice chancellor Episcopal Diocese Hawaii, 1980—. Bd. dirs. Jr. Achievement Hawaii, Inc., 1974-84, Inst. Human Services, Inc., 1980—, Hoa Kokua Hospice Vols., Inc., 1984-85. Served with JAGC, U.S. Army, 1963-66, Vietnam. Tulane U. fellow, 1981. Mem. ABA, Assn. Bar City N.Y., Hawaii State Bar Assn. Republican. Episcopalian. Club: Pacific (Honolulu). Office: Cades Schutte Fleming & Wright 1000 Bishop St Honolulu HI 96813

PORTER, STEPHEN CUMMINGS, research geology educator; b. Santa Barbara, Calif., Apr. 18, 1934; s. Lawrence Johnson Porter Jr. and Frances (Cummings) Seger; m. Anne Mary Higgins, Apr. 2, 1959; children: John, Maria, Susannah. BS, Yale U., 1955, MS, 1958, PhD, 1962. Asst. prof. geology U. Wash., Seattle, 1962-66, assoc. prof., 1966-71, prof., 1971—, dir. Quaternary Research Ctr., 1982—; mem. bd. earth scis. Nat. Acad. Sci., Washington, 1983-85; mem. advisory com., div. polar programs NSF, Washington, 1983-84; vis. fellow Clare Hall Cambridge (Eng.) U., 1980-81. Co-author: Physical Geology, 1986; editor: Late Quaternary Environments of the United States, 1983, (jour.) Quaternary Research, 1976—; assoc. editor (jour.) Radiocarbon, 1982—. Served to lt. USNR, 1955-57. Recipient Benjamin Silliman prize Yale U., New Haven, 1962, Willis M. Tate Lectr., So. Meth. U., Dallas, 1984; Fulbright-Hays Sr. Research fellow New Zealand, 1973-74. Fellow Geol. Soc. Am., Arctic Inst. N.Am. (bd. govs); mem. AAAS, Internat. Glaciol. Soc., Am. Quaternary Assn (council), Sigma Xi. Club: Am. Alpine (N.Y.C.). Avocations: photography, mountaineering. Home: 18034 15th Ave NW Seattle WA 98177 Office: U Wash Quaternary Research Ctr Seattle WA 98195

PORTER, THOMAS JENKS, physician; b. Pasadena, Calif., Oct. 12, 1934; s. Francis McKibbon and Sara Elizabeth (Jenks) P.; m. Mary Noelie Driscoll, Aug. 12, 1961 (div.); children: Michele, Heidi, Jennifer, Daniel. BS, San Diego State Coll., 1957, MS, 1960; MD, U. Md., 1964. Diplomate Am. Bd. Pediatrics, Am. Bd. Med. Examiners. Rotating intern USPHS Hosp., Balt., 1964-65; resident USPHS Hosp., Norfolk, Va., 1965-67; chief med. officer USPHS Out Patient Clinic, Portland, Oreg., 1967-69; resident in pediatrics U. Oreg., Portland, 1969-71, fellow in perinaeology, 1971-72; sr. pediatrician Alaska Native Med. Ctr., Anchorage, 1972—; instr. preventive medicine, pub. health U. Oreg. Med. Sch., Portland, 1967-69, instr. pediatrics, 1972—, Uniformed Services Health Scis. U., Washington, 1982—; assoc. clin. dir. Alaska Newborn Care Project, 1972—. Co-author: Transport Manual-Alaska, 1975. Recipient Guardsman award Oreg. N.G., 1972; fellow U. Oreg., 1971-72. Fellow Am. Acad. Pediatrics (sec., treas. 1976-82, alt. chpt. chmn. 1982—); mem. North Pacific Pediatric Soc., Commr. Officers Assn. USPHS, Am. Soc. Limnology and Oceanography. Office: Alaska Native Med Ctr 255 Gambell PO Box 7-741 Anchorage AK 99510

PORTER, WALTER THOMAS, JR., banker; b. Corning, N.Y., Jan. 8, 1934; s. Walter Thomas and Mary Rebecca (Brookes) P.; m. Dixie Jo Thompson, Apr. 3, 1959; children—Kimberlee Paige, Douglas Thompson, Jane-Amy Elizabeth. B.S., Rutgers U., 1954; M.B.A., U. Wash., 1959; Ph.D., Columbia U., 1964. C.P.A., Wash., N.Y. Staff cons. Touche Ross & Co., Seattle, 1959-61; NDEA fellow Columbia U., 1961-64; dir. edn. Touche Ross & Co., N.Y.C., 1964-66; assoc. prof. U. Wash., 1966-70, prof., 1970-74; vis. prof. N. European Mgmt. Inst., Oslo, Norway, 1974-75; nat. dir. planning Touche Ross & Co., Seattle, 1975-78, dir. exec. fin. counseling, 1978-84, exec.

v.p., mgr. pvt. banking, Rainier Nat. Bank, 1984-87, exec. v.p., mgr. capital mgmt. and pvt. banking, 1987—; vis. lectr. taxation U. Wash., 1978—. Mem. Seattle adv. bd. Salvation Army, 1975-83; trustee Ryther Child Ctr., 1975-85 , pres., 1979-81; trustee Lakeside Sch., 1977-87, treas., 1970-81, 1st v.p. 1982-84, pres. 1984-86; trustee Virginia Mason Research Ctr., 1982—; trustee Mus. History and Industry, 1982-83 . Served with U.S. Army, 1955-57. Author: Auditing Electronic System, 1966; (with William Perry) EDP: Controls and Auditing, 1970, 5th edit., 1987; (with John Burton) Auditing A Conceptual Approach, 1974; (with D. Alkire) Wealth: How to Achieve It, 1976; Touche Ross Guide to Personal Financial Management, 1983, 3d edit., 1987; (with D. Porter) The Personal Financial Planner's Practice Sourcebook, 1986. Mem. Am. Inst. CPA's. Congregationalist. Club: Wash. Athletic, Sand Point Country. Office: Rainier Bank PO Box 3966 Seattle WA 98124

PORTERFIELD, RALPH IRA, health care executive, consultant; b. Cheverly, Md., Oct. 31, 1946; s. Ralph Alton and Audrey Marie (Gilmore) P.; m. Susan Elizabeth Smart, Mar. 15, 1969; children: Tera Ann, Laura Ellen. BS in Chemistry, Capital U., 1968; PhD in Pharm. Analytical Chemistry, Ohio State U., 1972. Quality control supr. Pfizer Pharms., Groton, Conn., 1972-77; qualtiy assurance mgr. Baxter Travenol, Chgo., 1977-80; ops. mgr. Cobe Labs., Denver, 1980-84; pres. Porterfield Enterprises, Golden, Colo., 1984—; founder Porterfield Enterprises, Golden, 1984—; v.p. Dialysis Mgmt., Golden, 1984—; treas., officer Early Diagnostics, Littleton, Colo., 1985—; regional dir. TFE, Inc., Augusta, 1984—; ptnr. The Colo. Consortium, Golden, 1985—. Contbr. over 15 articles in health care and tech. mgmt.; mem. editorial adv. bd. Medical Device & Diagnostics Industry, 1984—. Chmn. bd. Mountain Christian Fellowship Ch., Arvada, Colo., 1983-84, co-chmn. 1986; treas. Genesee Swim Team, Golden, 1983, vice chmn. 1986. Mem. Am. Chem. Soc., Biotech. Roundtable, Am. Soc. Quality Control, Nat. Com. Clin. Lab. Standards, Rho Chi. Republican. Home: 1079 Genesee Vista Rd Golden CO 80401 Office: Porterfield Enterprises 1079 Genesee Vista Rd Golden CO 80401

PORTHAN, EDWARD RICHARD, school system administrator; b. Ely, Minn., Oct. 6, 1939; s. Edward Emil and Mary Ann (Seme) P.; m. Kathleen Ann Luhman, Aug. 11, 1962 (div. 1978); children: Teresa, Tammy, Todd; m. Nancy Williams, Dec. 21, 1979. BA, Hamline U., 1967; MA, St. Thomas Coll., 1968; EdD, U. No. Colo., 1978. Tchr. St. Paul Pub. Sch., 1962-67, Mounts View Pub. Sch., New Brighton, Minn., 1967-79; dir. Fremont County Sch., Lander, Wyo., 1980—; cons. Maximizing Potential, Inc., Lander, Wyo., 1980—. Originator Apple Festival Triathlon, Lander, 1983; vol. Spl. Olympics, Lander, 1986. Mem. Assn. Supervision and Curriculum Devel. (pres. 1983-84), Wyo. Curriculum Coordinators. (pres. 1984-85), Phi Delta Kappa. Republican. Lutheran. Avocations: running, photography, triathlon athletics, reading. Home: PO Box 473 Lander WY 82520 Office: Fremont County Sch Dist 1 Balwin Creek Rd Lander WY 82520

PORTIS, ALAN MARK, physicist, educator; b. Chgo., July 17, 1926; s. Lyon and Ruth (Libman) P.; m. Beverly Aline Levin, Sept. 5, 1948; children: Jonathan Marc, Stephen Robert, Lori Ann, Frederick Sean. Ph.B., U. Chgo., 1948; A.B., U. Calif., Berkeley, 1949, Ph.D., 1953. Mem. faculty U. Pitts., 1953-56; mem. faculty U. Calif.-Berkeley, 1956—, prof. physics, 1964—, asst. to chancellor for research, 1966-67, asso. dean grad. div., 1967-68, dir. Lawrence Hall Sci., 1969-72, univ. ombudsman, 1981-83, assoc. dean Coll. Engring., 1983-87. Contbg. author: Berkeley Physics Laboratory, 1964, 65, 66, 71; author: Electromagnetic Fields/Sources and Media, 1978. Fulbright fellow, 1961, 67; Guggenheim fellow, 1965. Fellow Am. Phys. Soc., AAAS; mem. Am. Assn. Physics Tchrs. (Robert Andrews Millikan award 1966), Sigma Xi.

PORTWAY, PATRICK STEPHEN, telecommunications consulting company executive, telecommunications educator; b. June 18, 1939; s. Christopher Leo and Ceciala (King) P.; m. Patricia May Devers, Sept. 13, 1980; children by previous marriage—Shawn, Pam, Vicki. BA, U. Cin., 1963; MA, U. Md., 1973; postgrad., Columbia U. Regional ADP coordinator GSA, Washington, 1963-68; mgr. strategic mkt. planning Xerox Corp., 1969-74; mgr. plans and programs System Devel. Corp., 1974-78; fin. indsl. mktg. exec. Satellite Bus. Systems, 1978-80; western regional mgr. Am. Satellite Co., 1980-81; pres. Applied Bus. Telecommunications, San Ramon, Calif., 1981—; adj. prof. Golden Gate U. Grad. Sch., San Francisco, 1983—; pub. mag. Teleconference, 1981—. Author: (with others) Teleconferencing. Presdl. elector Electoral Coll., Va., 1976; candidate Va. State Legislature from 19th Dist., 1971. Served to 1st lt. U.S. Army, 1963-65. Mem. Internat. Teleconferencing Assn. (founder, bd. dirs. 1983—), Nat. Univ. Teleconferencing Networdk (mem. adv. bd., bd. dirs. 1986—), Electronic Funds Transfer Assn. (founder, bd. dirs. 1980), Satellite Profls., Jaycees charter pres. Chantilly, VA., Disting. Service award Dale City, VA. Club: Commonwealth. Home: 4024 Greenwich Dr San Ramon CA 94583 Office: Applied Bus Telecommunications 2500 Old Crow Canyon Rd San Ramon CA 94583

POSIN, JONATHAN PHILIP, diagnostic radiologist; b. Boston, Jan. 18, 1954; s. Herbert Israel Posin and Ruth (Lipper) Lappin; m. Catherine Marie Mills, June 25, 1983. BA in Engring. and Applied Physics cum laude, Harvard U., 1975; MD cum laude, Tufts U., 1979. Diplomate Am. Bd. Radiology in Diagnostic Radiology. Intern in surgery Tufts New England Med. Ctr. Hosp., Boston, 1979-80, resident in surgery, 1980-81, resident in radiology, 1981-82; resident in radiology U. Calif., San Francisco, 1982-84, instr. radiology, research fellow in magnetic resonance imaging Radiologic Imaging Lab, 1984-85, asst. clin. prof. radiology Sch. Medicine, 1985—; diagnostic radiologist Pinole (Calif.) Radiology Group, 1985—; dir. North Bay MRI Ctr., Pinole, 1986—; cons., lectr., reviewer in field., 1984—. Author: (with C.M. Mills, J. de Groot) Magnetic Resonance Imaging Atlas of the Head, Neck and Spine, 1987; contbr. chpts. to books and numerous articles to profl. jours. Mem. AMA, Radiol. Soc. N.Am., Am. Coll. Radiology, Soc. Magnetic Resonance in Medicine, San Francisco Radiol. Soc., Calif. Radiol. Soc., East Bay Radiol. Soc., Bay Area Magnetic Resonance Soc., Alameda-Contra Costa Med. Assn., Alpha Omega Alpha. Home: 2414 Gough St San Francisco CA 94123 Office: Pinole Radiology 2150 Appian Way Suite 101 Pinole CA 94564

POSKANZER, ALAN MICHAEL, chemist electronics industry, executive; b. Albany, N.Y., June 1, 1947; s. Alfred Thomas Poskanzer and Beatrice (Sacherson) Martin; m. Carol Ann Huska, Aug. 24, 1968 (div. Oct. 1982); children: Alison Michele, Jessica Leigh. BS in Chemistry, Clarkson Coll. Tech., 1969, MS in Chemistry, 1971, PhD in Chemistry, 1974. Sr. research chemist Shipley Co., Inc., Newton, Mass., 1974-76; tech. dir. Morton/Thiokol Corp., Tustin, Calif., 1976-84; regional sales mgr. Enthone, Inc., Long Beach, Calif., 1984-86; cons. ChemProTech Enterprises, Dana Point, Calif., 1985—; pres. LinMar Tech., Inc., Dana Point, 1986—. Contbr. articles to profl. jours. Served to capt. USAR, 1970-83. Mem. Am. Chem. Soc., Am. Electroplaters Soc., Calif. Citrus Assn. (program chmn. 1986—, newsletter editor 1986—). Republican. Office: care ChemProTech 34184-B Coast Hwy 176 Dana Point CA 92629

POSNICK, MARK KENNETH, mortgage banking executive; b. Bklyn., June 26, 1939; s. Harry and Pearl (Kastin) P.; m. Frances Sheridan, July 21, 1962; children: Jill Ellen, David Franklin. B.S. in Econs., U. Pa., Phila., 1961; postgrad. NYU Sch. Bus., 1964-65, Sch. Mortgage Banking, 1978. Cert. mortgage banker. Pres., Interior Enterprises, Inc., N.Y.C., 1966-73; vice chmn., chief operating officer Margaretten & Co., Inc. div. Am. Can Co., Inc., Perth Amboy, N.J., 1974-82; pres. and chief exec. officer Criterion Fin. Corp. div. Criterion Mortgage Holding Corp., City Investing Cos., Dallas, 1982-85, chmn., chief exec. officer , 1985—; faculty mem. Sch. Mortgage Banking; mem. bd. govs. Mortgage Bankers Assn. Am.; mem. Nat. adv. council, adv. bd. Southwestern region Fed. Nat. Mortgage Assn.; dir. Dallas Symphony Bd. of Govs.; mem. pres.'s council U. Pa.; bd. dirs. Found. for Craniofacial Disorders. Served to lt. (j.g.) USN, 1962-65. Willis Bryant scholar, 1978. Home: 3831 Turtle Creek Blvd Suite 10-C Dallas TX 75219 Office: Criterion Fin Corp 5055 Keller Springs Rd Dallas TX 75248

POST, ALAN, economist, artist; b. Alhambra, Calif., Sept. 17, 1914; s. Edwin R. and Edna (Stickney) P.; m. Helen E. Wills, Nov. 21, 1940; 1 son, David Wills. A.B., Occidental Coll., 1938; student Chouinard Inst. Art, 1938; M.A., Princeton, 1940; LL.D., Golden Gate U., 1972, Occidental Coll., 1974, Claremont Grad. Sch., 1978. In banking bus., 1933-36; instr. econs. Occidental Coll., 1940-42; asst. prof. Am. U., 1943; economist Dept. State, 1944-45; research dir. Utah Found., 1945-46; chief economist, adminstrv. analyst State of Calif., 1946-50, state legis. analyst, 1950-77; cons. to commn. studying higher edn. Wells Commn., N.Y.; cons. Milton Eisenhower Com. Higher Edn. and State, 1964; mem. Nat. Com. Support of Public Schs., 1967; mem. nat. adv. panel Nat. Center Higher Edn. Mgmt. Systems, 1971-72; chmn. Calif. Gov.'s Commn. on Govt. Reform, 1978—; mem. faculty U. So. Calif. Grad. Sch. Public Adminstrn., 1978—; Regents' prof. U. Calif., Davis, 1983, vis. prof., 1984; spl. cons. Touche Ross and Co., 1977-87; cons., interim exec. dir. Calif. Commn. for Rev. of Master Plan for Higher Edn., 1985, vis. prof. U. Calif., Davis, 1984-85.; mem. adv. bd. Cali. Tomorrow nat. shows and one-man shows; dir. Crocker Art Gallery Assn., pres., 1966-67; dir. IMMUDX Inc. Bd. dirs. People to People Council, U. Calif. Art Mus., 1984—; mem. adv. com. on future ops. Council State Govts., 1965; bd. mgrs., pres. YMCA; bd. dirs. Sacramento Civic Ballet Assn.; trustee Calif. Coll. Arts and Crafts, 1982—; chmn. Calif. State Task Force on Water Future, 1981-82, Sacramento Regional Found.; bd. dirs. Calif. Mus., pres., 1976-77, mem adv. bd. Calif. Tomorrow, 1984—, Policy Analysis for Calif. Edn., 1985—, Senate Adv. Commn. on Control of Cost of State Govt., 1986—. Served with USNR, 1943-44. Mem. Council State Govts. (research adv. com. 1966—), Nat. Legis. Service Conf. (exec. com. 1956-57), Nat. Acad. Public Adminstrn., Phi Beta Kappa, Kappa Sigma. Home: 1900 Rockwood Dr Sacramento CA 95864

POST, GEORGE, consulting wildlife pathologist; b. Rapid City, S.D., May 12, 1918; s. Marion A. and Louise (Mill) P.; m. Charlotte M. Shafer, Apr. 19, 1943; children: George Phillip, Charles Arthur. BS, U. Wyo., 1947, MS, 1948; PhD, Utah State U., 1963. Dir. wildlife disease research lab. Wyo. Game and Fish Dept., Laramie, 1948-60; fish pathologist Utah Fish and Game Dept., Logan, 1960-64; asst. unit leader U.S. Fish & Wildlife Service, Fort Collins, Colo., 1964-66; asst. prof. wildlife and fish disease, fish nutrition, water quality Colo. State U., Fort Collins, 1964-66, assoc. prof., 1966-76, prof., 1976-84; cons. Ft. Collins and Rio Rico, Ariz., 1967—. Author: Textbook of Fish Health, 1983. Bd. dirs. Rio Rico Property Owners Assn., 1986. Served with U.S. Army, 1941-46. Fellow Assn. Fishery Research Biologists; mem. Am. Fishery Soc. (cert. pathologist, fish health sec., pres. Colo.-Wyo. chpt. 1975), Wildlife Disease Assn., Sigma Xi, Phi Kappa Phi. Democrat. Avocations: lapidary, leather carving. Home and Office: 1803 Paseo Venado Estates #13 Rio Rico AZ 85621

POST, JONATHAN VOS, publishing company executive, aerospace computer consultant; b. N.Y.C., Sept. 3, 1951; s. Samuel H. and Patricia Francis (Vos) P.; m. Christine Mary Carmichael, Feb. 14, 1986. BS in Math., BS in Poetry, Calif. Inst. Tech., 1973; MS in Computer and Info. Sci., U. Mass., 1975, postgrad., 1975-77. Freelance computer author, cons. N.Y., N.J., Mass., 1967-79; with computer systems design and analysis Boeing Aerospace Co., Seattle, 1979-83; software engr. Jet Propulsion Lab. of NASA, Pasadena, Calif., 1983-85, Voyager mission planning engr., 1984-85; aerospace computer cons. FAA, Fullerton, Calif., 1985-86; chief exec. officer Computer Futures Inc., Los Angeles, 1984—; cons., pub. Computer Futures Inc., Pasadena, 1986—; chief exec. officer Emerald City Pub., Seattle, 1979—; speaker in field. Contbr. numerous articles to profl. jours. Elected mem. Town Meeting, Amherst, Mass., 1977. Fellow Brit. Interplanetary Soc.; mem. Beverly Hills Mgmt. Assn. (sec. 1974—), Sci. Fiction Writers Am., Mystery Writers Am., Assn. Computing Machinery, Poets and Writers Inc. Avocations: poetry, songwriting, speaking, screenwriting. Home: 385 S Catalina #231 Pasadena CA 91106-3353

POST, RODNEY EMMET, JR., manufacturing executive; b. Nyack, N.Y., May 9, 1929; s. Rodney Emmet and Helen Anna (Falkenstern) P.; m. Gerda Minna Bock, May 30, 1953; children: Paul, Mark, Timothy, Erich, Rachel. B in Mech. Engring., Stevens Inst. Tech., 1951, MS in Elec. Engring. with honors, 1954; MBA with honors, U. Rochester, 1969. Engr. Sperry Gyroscope Co., Gt. Neck, N.Y., 1951-54; project engr. The Hays Corp., Michigan City, Ind., 1957-61; mgr. engring. Bausch & Lomb, Inc., Rochester, N.Y., 1961-70; program mgr., dir. mfg. Hamilton Watch Co., Lancaster, Pa., 1970-71; pres. W.O. Hickok Mfg. Co., Harrisburg, Pa., 1971-76, Herron Optical Co., Wilmington, Calif., 1976-80; mgr. mfg. engring. Aeronutronic div. Ford Aerospace and Communications Corp., Newport Beach, Calif., 1980—. Dist. dir. YMCA Fund Drive, 1968-69; counselor truant boys County Detention Home, Lancaster, 1973-74. Served to lt. USNR, 1954-57. Mem. Soc. Mfg. Engring., Tau Beta Pi, Beta Gamma Sigma. Republican. Presbyterian. Club: Huntington Valley Tennis (Fountain Valley, Calif.). Avocations: tennis, running, swimming, biking, camping. Office: Ford Aerospace & Communications Corp Aeronutronic Div Ford Rd Newport Beach CA 92660

POST, ROY GRAYSON, nuclear engineering educator; b. Asherton, Tex., June 24, 1923; s. Albert K. and Ruth (Grisham) P.; m. Kate Jordan, Mar. 31, 1946; children: Ruth Jean, Jack K., Carol B., Martha A. BSChemE, U. Tex., 1944, PhD in Chemistry, 1952. Registered profl. nuclear engr., Ariz. Sr. engr. Manhattan Project U. Chgo., 1944-49; sr. engr. Gen. Electric Co., Richland, Wash., 1952-58; sect. head Tex. Instruments, Dallas, 1958-61; prof. nuclear engring. U. Ariz., Tucson, 1961—. Mem. Am. Nuclear Soc. (editor newsletter 1969—, sect. chmn. 1986—), Electrochem. Soc. (chmn. Tex. sect. 1960), Am. Inst. Chem. Engrs., AAAS, Sigma Xi. Democrat. Home: Box 17690 Tucson AZ 85731 Office: U Ariz Dept Nuclear and Energy Engring Tucson AZ 85721

POSTEL, MITCHELL PAUL, association administrator; b. Chgo., May 27, 1952; s. Bernard and Rosalin P.; B.A., U. Calif.-Berkeley, 1974; M.A., U. Calif.-Santa Barbara, 1977; m. Kristie McCune, Mar. 29, 1981. Devel. officer San Mateo County Hist. Mus., San Mateo, Calif., 1977-81; exec. dir. Fort Point and Army Mus. Assn., San Francisco, 1981-84, San Mateo County Hist. Assn., 1984—; faculty Coll. of San Mateo. Bd. dirs. Ano Nuevo Interpretive Assn., 1981—. Author: History of the Burlingame Country Club, 1982; Seventy-five Years in San Francisco, History of Rotary Club No. 2. Home: 1931 Santiago St San Francisco CA 94116 Office: San Mateo County Hist Assn 1700 W Hillside Blvd San Mateo CA 94402

POSTIER, ROBERT ALLEN, manufacturing executive; b. Norman, Okla., Dec. 7, 1953; s. Norman Joseph and Anita June (Potts) P.; m. Bonnie Susanne Pimental, June 24, 1978 (div. May 1982); 1 child, Robert Brandon; m. Karla Jean Searles, May 29, 1982; 1 stepchild, Marcia Allison Piekaar. Student, N.E. La. U., 1973-74, El Camino Coll., Torrance, Calif., 1976-77. Indsl. engr. Northrop Corp., Hawthorne, Calif., 1977-80; internat. mktg. dir. aerospace div. GGT, Inc., Tolland, Conn., 1980-85; account exec. CCF, Inc. div. BASF, Charlotte, N.C., 1985—; cons. Hexstar, Plecentia, Calif., 1983—, Huck Mfg., Wilmington, Calif., 1985. Patentee in field. Mem. Soc. Mfg. Engrs., Soc. Advancement of Mfg. and Prodn. Engrs. Republican. Avocations: archaeology, photography, off-road travel, hiking, fishing. Office: CCF Inc 200 E Sandpointe S 741 Santa Ana CA 92707

POSTLER, PAUL ROBERT, JR., educator; b. San Francisco, Nov. 30, 1921; s. Paul Robert and Charlotte (Kane) P.; student City Coll. San Francisco, 1940-41; A.B., Fresno State Coll., 1954; m. Mildred Katheryn Upshaw, June 6, 1948; children—Paul Albert, Katheryn Ruth, Suzanne Marie, Lawrence Gerard, Marcella Jan, Keith David, Robert Paul. Employed as asst. purchasing agt. vessel materials Western Pipe & Steel Co. of Calif., 1941-44; dist. adminstrv. prin. Fort Washington-Lincoln Sch. Dist., Fresno County, Calif., 1947-59; adminstrv. dist. prin. Figarden Elem. Sch. Dist., Fresno, 1959-63; social sci. instr., student adviser, now ednl. guidance cons. Washington U. High Sch., Fresno; past prin. Washington Union Continuation High Sch.; instr. adult edn. evening high sch., Fresno; pupil personnel student welfare and attendance dean, dir. evening adult high sch., Easton, Calif.; evening lectr./instr. psychology West Hills Coll. Adult extension div., Coalinga, Calif., 1972-82; dist. cons. State Center Regional Adult and Vocat. Ednl. Council. Dist. commr. No. Fresno dist. Boy Scouts Am.; adv. CAP San Joaquin Valley. Served from pvt. to sgt. maj. U.S. Army, 1944-46. Mem. Calif. Tchrs. Assn. (pres. Clovis, 1955-57, local pres. 1966-67), Internat. Assn. Pupil Personnel Adminstrs., Calif. Elem. Sch. Adminstrs. Assn., Assn. Secondary Sch. Adminstrs., NEA (life), Am. Legion (adj. officer 1948), Calif. Council Adult Edn., Am. Edn. Research Assn., Calif. Guidance and Counseling Assn. (charter), DAV (life), Non-Commd. Officers Assn., Fresno State U. Bulldog Found., Fresno State U. Alumni Assn., Sierra Club, Phi Delta Kappa (chpt. pres.), Delta Xi, Epsilon Delta Chi. Democrat. Roman Catholic. Clubs: Commercial, Commonwealth of Calif. (San Francisco); Lions, Y Men's (Fresno); Elks. Address: 5531 Columbia Dr N Fresno CA 93727

POSTMA, JAMES MICHAEL, chemist, educator; b. Long Beach, Calif., Nov. 5, 1953; s. William Franklin and Laura Corrine (Van Sloten) P.; m. Beverly Lynn Lofgren, Jan. 25, 1975; children: Sarah Rose, Annalisa. BA, Calif. State U., Chico, 1974; PhD, U. Calif., Davis, 1982. Prof. chemistry Calif. State U., Chico, 1982—. Author: General Chemistry in the Laboratory, 1984, 2d edit., 1987. Treas. Evang. Free Ch. of Chico, 1985, chmn. 1986—. Mem. AAAS, Am. Chem. Soc., Nat. Sci. Tchrs. Assn. Office: Calif State Univ Chemistry Dept Chico CA 95929

POSTON, WILLIAM KENNETH, JR., superintendent schools; b. Sioux City, Iowa, Nov. 11, 1938; s. William Kenneth and Wilma Beatrice (Schultz) P.; m. Marcia Sue Bottorff, Aug. 19, 1961; children—Heather Mikaleen, Holly Janelle. B.A., Iowa State Tchrs. Coll., 1961; Ed.S., Ariz. State U.-Tempe, 1966, Ed.D., 1969. Tchr. sci.-math., San Bernardino, Calif., 1961-63; tchr. sci. Tempe (Ariz.) High Sch., 1963-64; research asst. Ariz. State U., Tempe, 1964-65; research coordinator, asst. prin., prin. Jr.-Sr. High Sch., asst. supt. ednl. services Mesa (Ariz.) Pub. Schs., 1965-74; supt. Flowing Wells Schs., Tucson, 1974-83, Billings (Mont.) Pub. Schs., 1983—. Tucson chmn. United Way, 1982; mem. adv. panel Gallup Edn. Poll; active YMCA, Freedoms Found., Community Effort Council, Tucson. Served to capt. USMCR, 1958-61 N.G., 1963-71. Recipient Disting. Service award Ariz. State U., 1978; award Young Ednl. Leaders Am., 1980; Alumni Achievement award U. No. Iowa, 1981, award citation Freedoms Found., 1983. Mem. Am. Assn. Sch. Adminstrs., Assn. Supervision and Curriculum Devel., Phi Delta Kappa (past internat. pres.), Sierra Club, Sigma Phi Epsilon. Democrat. Methodist. Lodges: Rotary, Masons, Shriners. Contbr. articles to profl. jours.

POTASH, STEPHEN JON, international public relations counselor; b. Houston, Feb. 25, 1945; s. Melvin L. and Petrice (Edelstein) P.; m. Jeremy Warner, Oct. 19, 1969; 1 son, Aaron Warner. B.A. in Internat. Relations, Pomona Coll., 1967. Account exec. Charles von Loewenfeldt, Inc., San Francisco, 1969-74, v.p., 1974-80; founder, pres. Potash & Co., Pub. Relations, Oakland, Calif., 1980—; cons. Am. Pres. Lines, 1979—; exec. dir. Calif. Council Internat. Trade, 1970—, editor newsletter, 1969-86; mem. adv. council U.S.-China Bus. Inst., San Francisco, 1985—. Columnist Pacific Shipper, 1982—. Bd. dirs. Temple Sinai, Oakland, 1979-81; mem. Citizens adv. council, Dominican Coll., San Rafael, Calif., 1985—. Mem. Pub. Relations Soc. Am. (counselors acad.), Japanese C. of C., Korea-Am. C. of C. Clubs: Lakeview (Oakland); Commonwealth of Calif. Office: Potash & Co 77 Jack London Sq Suite L Oakland CA 94607

POTE, HUGH LENOIR, biology educator; b. St. Louis, July 3, 1927; s. Horace Wiley and Louise (Thomas) P.; m. Charlotte Green, June, 6, 1953; children: Randall Thomas, Lawrence Webster, Cynthia Louella, Lorraine Leanne. BA, U. Denver, 1950; MS, Colo. State U., 1955; PhD, U. Ill., 1958. Prof. biology Temple Buell Coll., Denver, 1965-69; research biologist Martin Marietta Corp., Denver, 1969-72, cons., 1969; research biologist Denver Research Inst., 1972-74; prof. Metro State Coll., Denver, 1974-80, Columbia Coll., Aurora, Colo., 1980—. Contbr. articles to profl. jours. Chmn. United Fund Drive, Temple Buell Coll., 1967-68; vestry St. Thomas Episcopal Ch., Denver, 1973-75. Served with U.S. Army, 1945-47. UpJohn Pharm. Co. fellow, 1955-58; named Prof. of Yr. Temple Buell Coll., 1969; recipient NSF Coll. Tchr. Participation award, 1966-67. Fellow AAAS; mem. Sigma Xi, Lambda Chi Alpha. Avocations: mountain climbing, photography, gardening, water sports. Home: 4801 E Florida Ave Denver CO 80222 Office: Columbia Coll 2600 S Parker Rd Aurora CO 80014

POTICHA, GERALD SANDER, physician; b. Chgo., Mar. 30, 1938; s. Joseph S. and Helen (Edwards) P.; m. Myrna S. Spilky, July 2, 1967; children: David, Helene, Adam. BA, U. Mich., 1959; MD, Northwestern U., 1963. Diplomate Am. Bd. Internal Medicine, Am. Bd. Endocrinology and Metabolism. Intern Los Angeles County Gen. Hosp., 1964; resident Northwestern VA Research Hosp., Chgo., 1964-67; endocrinology fellow Cook County Hosp., Chgo., 1967-68; private practice internal medicine, endocrinology Denver, 1970—; assoc. clin. prof. U Colo., Denver, 1972—. Tchr. diabetes class Porter Meml. Hosp., Denver, 1974-86. Served to maj. M.C., U.S. Army, 1968-70. Mem. Am. Diabetes Assn., Endocrine Soc., Arapahoe Med. Soc., Colo. Soc. Endocrinology and Metabolism, Colo. Med. Assn. Democrat. Jewish. Club: Valley Country (Aurora, Colo.). Avocations: reading, golf, tennis, skiing. Home: 5405 S Niagara Ct Englewood CO 80111 Office: 8120 S Holly St Littleton CO 80122

POTOCKI, JOSEPH EDMUND, marketing company executive; b. Jersey City, Jan. 31, 1936; s. Joseph and Estelle (Bielski) P.; m. Margaret Mary Shine, May 21, 1960; children: Joseph, Meg, David. BS, Seton Hall U., 1957. Asst. regional sales mgr. Gen. Mills Inc., Valley Stream, N.Y., 1960-67; group mgr. merchandising Warner Lambert Co., Morris Plains, N.J., 1967-84; dir. merchandise services Beatrice Hunt/Wesson, Fullerton, Calif., 1974-83; pres., chief exec. officer Joseph Potocki & Assocs., Newport Beach, Calif., 1983—; pres. Mktg. Fulfillment Services, Tustin, Calif., 1985—; chief exec. officer Clarke Hooper U.S.A., Newport Beach, 1987—; dir. Clarke Hooper PLC, London; sec. Nat. Premium Sales Exec., Union, N.J., 1982-87. Served to lst lt. U.S. Army, 1957-59. Recipient Mktg. Motivator award Los Angeles Mktg. Exhibition, 1981. Mem. Promotion Mktg. Assn. (chmn. bd. dirs. 1977-79, v.p. West sect. 1980—, Reggie award 1984, 85, 87), Promotion Mktg. Assn. Am. (dir. exec. com. 1978—, recipient Chmn. Bowl, 1979), Nat. Premium Sales Execs. (dir. exec. com. 1980-87, Pres. award 1985). Republican. Roman Catholic. Avocations: sailing, golf, woodworking, travel. Home: 26952 Pueblo Nuevo Mission Viejo CA 92691 Office: Joseph Potocki & Assocs 5015 Birch St Newport Beach CA 92660

POTTENGER, FRANCIS MARION, III, education educator; b. Pasadena, Calif., July 19, 1928; s. Francis Marion Jr. and Elizabeth (Saxour) P.; m. Larma Jean McGuire, Dec. 24, 1950; children: Francis Jeffery, Malcolm Tyler, Mary Yvonne Pottenger Hockaday, Marcus Samuel. BS, Otterbein, 1950; MEd, Xavier U., 1957; MS, N.Mex. Highlands U., 1964; PhD, Claremont Grad. Sch., 1969. Cert. tchr. (life), Calif. Sci. tchr. Goshen (Ohio) Sch. Dist., 1955-56, Bethel (Ohio)-Tate Sch. Dist., 1956-57, Whittier (Calif.) Union High Sch. Dist., 1957-65; chemistry instr. Citrus Community Coll., Glendora, Calif., 1963-65; instr. Claremont (Calif.) Grad. Sch., 1965-66; asst. prof. edn. U. Hawaii, Honolulu, 1966-70, assoc. prof. edn., 1970-74, prof. edn., 1974—, chmn. sci. sect. curriculum research and devel. group, 1966-83, dir. foundational approaches in sci. teaching curriculum research and devel. group, 1967-83, dir. summer sci. enrichment project curriculum research and devel. group, 1970—, project mgr. individualized math. title IV project curriculum research and devel. group, 1972-73, dir. high sch. marine sci. study project curriculum research and devel. group, 1974—, co-dir. marine social studies project curriculum research and devel. group, 1975-76, dir. coastal zone mgmt. project curriculum research and devel. group, 1976—, dir. Hawaii nutrition edn. project curriculum research and devel. group, 1979—, dir. exploratory computer literacy elem. project curriculum research and devel. group, 1982-83, co-dir. SCOPE math.-sci. project curriculum research and devel. group, 1982-83, dir. sci. projects curriculum research and devel. group, 1983—, co-dir. exploratory secondary project computer literacy curriculum research and devel. group, 1983-84, co-dir. FAST project curriculum research and devel. group, 1983—, dir. YAP-Kosrae health project curriculum research and devel. group, 1983—, dir. Hawaii exploratory A-1 tech. project curriculum research and devel. group, 1984—. Author, co-author numerous curriculum manuals; co-author: Fundamentals of Chemistry, 1976; contbr. articles to profl. jours. Active Panel for Devel. of Bishop Mus. Sci. Ctr., Honolulu, 1969, Gov's. Marine Edn. Com., Honolulu, 1978-79, Higher Edn. Com. Meth. Ch., Honolulu, 1980—; organizer Gov's. Conf. on Environ. Edn., Honolulu, 1972, participant; organizer Gov's. Pacific Basin Conf., Kahuku, Hawaii, 1980, participant; organizer Gov's. Conf. on Coastal Zone Mgmt., Honolulu, 1983, participant; co-chmn. Focus on Excellence Lecture Series, Honolulu, 1985. Served as sgt. U.S. Signal Corp, 1953-55. Fellow NSF, 1960-64; numerous grants including Hawaii State Dept. Edn.,1973, U. Hawaii, 1974, U.S.-Israel Binat. Sci. Found., 1975-77, March of Dimes, 1985; recipient Merit award U. Hawaii, 1986. Mem. AAUP, Am. Chem. Soc. (mem. Hawaii br.), Hawaii Acad. Sci., Hawaii Nutrition Edn. Assn., Hawaii State Tchrs. Assn., Hawaii Sci. Tchrs. Assn. (bd. dirs. 1973-76, pres. elect 1983-84, pres. 1984-85),

NEA, Nat. Assn. of Lab. Schs., Nat. Assn. Research in Sci. Teaching, Nat. Assn. Sci. Tchrs., Pacific Circle Consortium (commendation 1985), U. Hawaii Profl. Assembly, Phi Kappa Delta. Democrat. Avocations: painting, hiking, fishing. Home: 426 Portlock Rd Honolulu HI 96825 Office: U Hawaii 1776 University Ave Honolulu HI 96825

POTTER, CHARLES ARTHUR, JR., trust company executive; b. St. Charles, Ill., July 25, 1925; s. Charles Arthur and Althea Mae (Whitney) P.; m. Joan Patricia Johnson, June 12, 1948; 1 child, Charles Arthur. Student, Western Mich. Coll., 1943, Officers Candidate Sch., U.S. Marine Corps, Quantico, Va., 1945; B.S., U. Ill., 1948, J.D., 1949; postgrad., Northwestern U., 1956. Bar: Ill. 1949. Mem. firm Gately & Burns, Chgo., 1949-50; spl. agt. FBI, Washington, Boston, N.Y.C. and Chgo., 1951-54; asst. trust officer Elmhurst Nat. Bank, Ill., 1955-59, United Calif. Bank, Los Angeles, 1959-61; v.p. trust officer First Am. Title and Trust Co., Santa Ana, Calif., 1961-68, also dir.; pres. First Am. Trust Co., Santa Ana, Calif., 1968—; dir. Eldorado Bank, Tustin, Calif., First Am. Title Co. of Nev.; chmn. Nat. Def. Univ. Found., Washington, 1985-87; treas., dir. Mansfield Ctr. Pacific Affairs, Helena, Mont., 1984-87, Orange County Estate Planning Council, 1966-69. Bd. dirs. Orange County Sports Celebrities, 1971-80, Providence Speech and Hearing Ctr., Orange County chpt. Multiple Sclerosis Soc., 1978—, Orange County area AMC Cancer Research Ctr., 1985—, Children's Hosp. Orange County Found., 1980—; mem. adv. bd. Salvation Army, Santa Ana, 1980—; trustee Calif. Med. Coll., U. Calif., Irvine, 1985—. Served with USMC, 1943-45. Recipient County of Los Angeles Cert. Commendation for pub. service, 1975. Mem. Soc. Former Spl. Agts. FBI (Western regional v.p. 1976-77), Calif. Bankers Assn. (chmn. trust div. 1982-83, dir. 1982-83), So. Calif. Trust Officers Assn. (pres. 1973-74), ABA, Ill. Bar Assn., Orange County Bar Assn., Def. Orientation Conf. Assn. (pres. 1982-84, dir., 1975—, chmn. 1985-86), Phi Delta Phi, Alpha Delta Phi. Clubs: Big Canyon Country (Newport Beach, Calif.); Indian Wells Country (Calif.), The Center (Costa Mesa, Calif.). Home: 47 Pinewood St Irvine CA 92714 Office: 421 N Main St Santa Ana CA 92701

POTTER, DAVID SAMUEL, former automotive company executive; b. Seattle, Jan. 16, 1925; children: Diana (Mrs. Paul Bankston), Janice (Mrs. Robert Meadows), Tom, Bill; m. Nancy Shaar, Dec. 1979. B.S., Yale U., 1945; Ph.D., U. Wash., 1951. Mem. staff Applied Physics Lab., U. Wash., 1946-60, asst. dir., 1955-60; with Gen. Motors Corp., 1960-73; chief engr. Milw. ops. GM Delco Electronics div., 1970-73; dir. research and devel. Detroit Diesel Allison div., 1973; asst. sec. for research and devel. Dept. Navy, 1973-74, under sec., 1974-76; v.p. environ. activities staff Gen. Motors Corp., Detroit, 1976-78; v.p. and group exec. public affairs group Gen. Motors Corp., 1978-83, v.p. in charge power products and def. ops. group, 1983-85; ret. 1985; Mem. Gov. Calif. Adv. Commn. Ocean Resources, 1964-68; mem. adv. panel Nat. Sea Grant Program, 1966; adv. bd. Naval Postgrad. Sch., Dept. Energy; bd. dirs. Sanders Assocs. Inc., Sci. Appplications Internat. Co., John Fluke Mfg. Co. Served to ensign USNR, 1943-46. Mem. Nat. Acad. Engring., NSF, Marine Tech. Soc., Am. Phys. Soc., AIAA, Am. Acoustical Soc., Nat. Oceanographic Assn. (v.p. 1966), Soc. Automotive Engrs. (chmn. tech. bd. 1978-79, dir. 1981-83). Club: Cosmos (Washington); Detroit, Birmingham Athletic (Mich.); Birnam Wood Country (Montecito, Calif.). Research cosmic rays, magnetics, underwater acoustics. Home: 877 Lilac Dr Santa Barbara CA 93108

POTTER, EARL WYLIE, lawyer; b. Los Angeles, Aug. 14, 1943; s. Henry Codman and Lucilla (Wylie) P.; B.A. cum laude, Yale U., 1965; J.D., Stanford U., 1968; m. Deborah Dozier; children—Wyle, Cody, Henry C. Admitted to N.Mex. bar, 1969, Calif. bar, 1970; atty. VISTA, 1968-69; dir. Santa Fe Legal Aid, 1969-70; mem. firm Sutin, Thayer & Browne, Santa Fe, 1972-77; county atty. Santa Fe County (N.Mex.), 1977-81; sr. ptnr. Potter & Kelly, Santa Fe, 1983—. Mem. Dem. Cen. Com., N.Mex., 1987—, treas. Santa Fe County Dem. Party, 1987—; bd. dirs. Santa Fe Vis. Nurse Services, 1971—, No. N.Mex. Legal Services, 1970-73; pres. bd. trustees Old Santa Fe Assn., 1978-79; mem. Santa Fe Devel. Code Rev. Com. Author Santa Fe County Land Devel. Code, 1980. Home: 690 Gonzales Rd Santa Fe NM 87501 Office: 126 E De Vargas St Santa Fe NM 87501

POTTER, GEORGE KENNETH, artist; b. Bakersfield, Calif., Feb. 26, 1926; s. Howard Eugene and Edythe (Keast) P.; m. Heliodora Carneiro de Mendonca, July 30, 1954 (div. July 1956); 1 dau., Helen Marcia; m. Ruth Mary Griffen, Aug. 4, 1962; children: Katherine Werle, Claire Lorraine, Cynthia Ann. Student, Acad. Art, San Francisco, 1947-48, Academie Frochot, Paris, 1950-52, Instituto Statale dei Belli Arti, Florence, Italy, 1951, Jean Metzinger, Paris; BA magna cum laude, San Francisco State U., 1974. tchr. pvt. art classes; lectr. San Francisco State U.; judge Marin County Ann., 1963, Calif. State Fair Art Exhbn., 1968. One-man shows include U. Calif.-Berkeley, 1959, U. Santa Clara, Calif., 1958, Coll. Marin, Calif.,1958, Rosacrucian Mus., San Jose, Calif., 1959, Brazilian-Am. Inst., Rio de Janeiro, 1955, Frances Young Gallery, Ross, Calif., 1952, John A. Muir Gallery, Modesto, Calif., 1958, Gallerie 8, Paris, 1952, Maxwell Galleries, San Francisco, 1958, 62, Gallery 5, Santa Fe, 1960, Rotunda Gallery, San Francisco, 1949, 52, Marquoit Galleries, San Francisco, 1973, Palo Alto (Calif.) Cultural Ctr., 1977, Art Ovations Gallery, San Francisco, 1980, Kaiser Art Ctr. Gallery, Oakland, Calif., 1980, Marin County Civic Ctr., San Rafael, Calif., 1985, Northwond Gallery, Mill Valley, Calif., 1987, Nuttree Gallery, Vacaville, Calif., 1987, numerous others; exhibited in group shows at Am. Watercolor Soc., 1961, 74, 76, 79, Phelan awards competition San Francisco Mus. Art, 1949, San Francisco Art Festival (Purchase award), 1958, Palace Legion Honor, San Francisco, 1958, 60, 63, 75 (Art Festival Exhbn. award 1975), Springville (Utah) Invitational, 1963, Jack London Invitational (award 1958), Oakland, Calif., 1957-65, Calif. State Fair (awards 1958, 72) Sacramento, 1957-58, 61-68, 70-74, 76, 79, Oakland Watercolor Ann., 1948, 52, Mother Lode Ann., Sonora, Calif., 1957-58, 63, 65, Kingsley Ann., E.B. Crocker Art Gallery (award), Sacramento, 1958, 61, 62, 64, 65, Marin Soc. Artists Ann., 1948-49, 58, 61, 65-73, 75, 77, Marin County Ann. (awards 1966, 67), 1962, 65-67, 70, 71, 76, Western Assn. Mus. Shows, 1964, 67, 74, No. Calif. Arts Ann., Fukuoka (Japan) Invitational Exchange Show with Oakland, 1964, Soc. Western Artists Ann., 1956-64, Statewide Watercolor Show (award), Santa Cruz, 1958, Watercolor U.S.A., Springfield, Mo., 1973, 74, Royal Watercolor Soc. Invitational Exhbn., London, 1975; executed murals Moore Bus. Forms, Inc., Oakland, Town Hall, Corte Maera, Calif., Mfacy's of Calif., Sacramento, San Mateo, Stockton, stained glass dome for Hale Meml., Soc. Calif. Pioneers, San Francisco, 1974, Calif. Dept. Motor Vehicles, Oakland, 1975; stained glass and resin triptych U. Calif. at San Francisco Moffitt Hosp., 1976; represented in permanent collections including HUD San Francisco regional officers, San Francisco Art Commn.,; art dir. McCann-Erickson Advt. Inc., Rio de Janeiro, 1954-55, Johnson and Lewis Advt., San Francisco, 1957, Michelson Advt., Palo Alto, Calif., 1959-60; contbr. The Calif. Style-Watercolor Artists 1925-55 (McClelland and Last), 1985. Served with USMCR, 1944-46, PTO. Recipient Macy's Art award, San Francisco, 1958, 1st award Watercolor Delta Ann., Antioch, Calif., 1969, 1st award Alameda County Fair, 1974, 79, 85, Santa Rosa 12th Ann., 1975, numerous other awards. Mem. West Coast Water Color Soc. (pres. 1968-69), Marin Soc. Artists. Address: 7000 Fair Oaks Blvd #35 Carmichael CA 95608

POTTER, JACK MICHAEL, anthropology educator; b. Oakdale, Tenn., Oct. 13, 1936; s. Gordon B. and Frances E. (Phillips) P.; m. Sulamith Heins; children: Elizabeth, Noah. AB, U. Calif., Berkeley, 1958, PhD, 1964. Asst. prof. anthropology U. Calif., Berkeley, 1963-68, assoc. prof., 1968-71, prof., 1971—. Author: Capitalism and the Chinese Peasant, 1968, Thai Peasant Social Structure, 1976; editor: Peasant Society, 1967. Fellow Woodrow Wilson Found., U. Chgo., 1958, Wang Inst., 1985; Fulbright Found. scholar, Thailand, 1971-72. Mem. Am. Anthropol. Assn., Assn. Asian Studies. Office: U Calif Dept Anthropology Berkeley CA 94720

POTTER, MARY JOAN, management consultant; b. Indpls., July 23, 1947; d. Donald A. and Marian H. (Loughery) P. BA in Sociology, Siena Heights Coll., Adrian, Mich., 1971; MA in Personnel and Counseling, Northwestern U., 1973. V.p. store ops. Betty's Winnetka, Ill., 1972-74; dir. product mktg. Tratec Inc., Los Angeles, 1974-78, so-founder, 1979; sr. ptnr. Occidental Cons. Group Inc., Lafayette, Calif., 1979—; bd. dirs. McCord Group, Inc., Casper Mktg., Inc. Ill. State scholar, 1965. Mem. Sales and Mktg. Execs., Personnel Testing Council, Jr. League San Francisco. Republican. Roman Catholic. Club: San Francisco Tennis. Home: 9 Hawks Hill Ct Oakland CA 94618 Office: 3685 Mt Diablo Blvd Suite 291 Lafayette CA 94549

POTTER, RODNEY DALE, lawyer, accountant; b. Chamberlain, S.D., May 2, 1948; s. Richard Dewayne and Velma Marie (Koch) P.; m. Julie Ann Davis, Aug. 30, 1968; children—Michelle Maree, Michael Dale, Melissa Mae. B.A., U. Utah, 1970, M.B.A., 1971, J.D., 1978. Bar: Utah 1978, U.S. Dist. Ct. Utah 1978. Sr. acct. Arthur Andersen & Co., Los Angeles, 1971-75; instr. U. Utah, Salt Lake City, 1975-80; sole practice and pres., Salt Lake City, 1979—. Contbr. articles to profl. jours. Mng. editor Utah Law Rev., 1977-78. Mem. ABA, Assn. Trial Lawyers Am., Utah Bar Assn., Am. Inst. C.P.A.'s, Utah Assn. C.P.A.'s, Phi Kappa Phi, Beta Gamma Sigma. Mormon. Home: 2197 E Claybourne Salt Lake City UT 84109 Office: 466 West Lawndale Dr Salt Lake City UT 84115

POTTERFIELD, PETER LOUNSBURY, editor; b. Jacksonville, Fla., Oct. 3, 1949; s. Jack Maxwell and Peggy (Lounsbury) P. Student, Washington & Lee U., 1967-69; BA in English, U. Fla., 1971. Writer Atlanta Constitution, 1971-72; editor Santa Fe Reporter, 1975-77, N.W. Skier, Seattle, 1977-79, Pacific N.W. Mag., Seattle, 1979—. Mem. Wash. State Centennial Commn., 1986. Finalist Nat. Mag. award for Gen. Excellence, 1983, Maggie-Most Improved Publ. award Western Pub. Assn., 1981. Mem. Am. Soc. Mag. Editors, Soc. Profl. Journalists (Excellence in Journalism award 1980-86). Democrat. Club: City (Seattle). Avocations: mountain climbing, travel. Home: PO Box 9114 Seattle WA 98119 Office: Pacific NW Mag 222 Dexter Ave N Seattle WA 98119

POTTORFF, GEORGE BYRON, public relations executive; b. Moyers, Okla., Sept. 13, 1918; s. George Byron and Jettie (Henderson) P.; m. Mary Virginia Rhodes, Feb. 14, 1957; children—James Harvey, Robert Edward. B.S., U. Ariz., Tucson, 1943. Dir. pub. relations Pacific PanAm, Honolulu, 1944-50, dir. pub. affairs Pacific, San Francisco, 1951-61; pres. Pottorff & Assocs., Redwood City, Calif., 1961-82; chmn. Pottorff, Macfarlane & Assocs., Palo Alto, Calif., 1982—. Mem. San Mateo Mounted Patrol, Woodside, Calif., 1954; treas. Shack Riders, Woodside, 1954; bd. dirs. San Mateo County Fair, Calif., 1957; foreman pro-tem San Mateo County Grand Jury, 1985. Mem. Pub. Relations Soc. Am. (accredited), Sigma Chi (life). Clubs: San Francisco Press; Peninsula Press (San Mateo). Home: 485 Cervantes St Portola Valley CA 94025 Office: Pottorff MacFarlane & Assocs 480 California Ave Palo Alto CA 94306

POTTS, DONALD CAMERON, biologist, educator; b. Edinburgh, Scotland, Apr. 4, 1942; came to U.S., 1978; s. Edward Dickinson and Jean Julia Mairi (Cameron) P.; m. Laurel Ruth Fox, Dec. 20, 1970; children: Stephen Edward, Shaina Sophie. BSc, U. Queensland, Brisbane, Australia, 1963, BSc with honors, 1965; PhD, U. Calif., Santa Barbara, 1972. Research asst. U.S. Antarctic research program, 1966; lectr. Bishops U., Lennoxville, Que., Can., 1971-72, Flinders U., Adelaide, Australia, 1972-73; research fellow Australian Nat. U., Canberra, 1973-78; asst. prof. U. Calif., Santa Cruz, 1978-85, assoc. prof., 1985—; vis. scientist Australian Inst. Marine Sci., Townsville, 1984—. Contbr. articles to profl. jours. Commonwealth scholar Australia, 1960-62; Ford Found. fellow Santa Barbara, 1968-71; vis. fellow Australian Nat. U., Canberra, 1976-85; vis. scholar SUNY Stony Brook, 1985-86. Mem. Australian Coral Reef Soc. (Great Barrier Reef Com., councillor 1974-77), Australian Marine Sci. Assn. (councillor 1975-77), Am. Soc. Limnology an Oceanography, Ecol. Soc. Am., British Ecol. Soc., Soc. Study Evolution, Internat. Soc. Reef Studies, Internat. Assn. Biol. Oceanographers (Coral reef com. 1986—). Office: U Calif Dept Biology and Inst Marine Scis 273 Applied Scis Bldg Santa Cruz CA 95064

POTTS, DONALD HARRY, math educator; b. Seattle, Dec. 15, 1921; s. Harry Samuel and Gladys Selma (Hammer) P.; m. Betty Loreen McFarland, Feb. 22, 1946 (div. Nov. 1953); children: Robert Lindley, Pauline Elizabeth Yonts; m. Jennifer Jean Christiansen, July 1, 1962; children: Jennifer Victoria, Valerie Kathleen. BS, Calif. Inst. Tech., 1943, PHD, 1947. Teaching asst. Calif. Inst. Tech., Pasadena, 1943-46; instr., asst. prof. math. Northwestern U., Evanston, Ill., 1946-51; supervisory mathematician U.S. Navy Electronics Lab., San Diego, 1951-58; assoc. prof. Calif. State U., Long Beach, 1958-61; lectr. math. U. Calif., Santa Barbara, 1961-64; prof. math. Calif. State U., Northridge, 1965—. Contbr. articles to profl. publs. Sci. Faculty fellow NSF, 1964-65. Fellow AAAS; mem. Am. Math. Soc., Math. Assn. Am. (sect. chmn., sec.), Assn. Symbolic Logic, Assn. Track and Field Statisticians (exec. com., pres. 1972-76). Republican. Episcopalian. Home: 7017 Armstrong Rd Goleta CA 93117 Office: Calif State U 18111 Nordhoff St Northridge CA 91330

POTTS, KEVIN JOSEPH, medical education company executive; b. Rock Springs, Wyo., July 8, 1958; s. William Milan and Elizabeth (Hodge) P. Student Weber State Coll., 1984. Adminstr., Emergicenter, Salt Lake City, 1981-83; mktg. dir. Now Care, Inc., Ogden, Utah, 1983-84; pres. ESI Medical Salt Lake City, 1984—; chief fin. officer Lone Peak Food & Beverage, Inc., Salt Lake City, 1984-87 ; pres., dir. Dist II-A EMT, Inc., Ogden, 1978-86. Recipient book review awards Wyo. Library System, 1972. Mem. Utah Assn. Emergency Med. Technicians (cert.), Nat. Assn. Freestanding Emergency Ctrs., Ogden Area C. of C., Salt Lake Area C. of C. Republican. Roman Catholic. Club: Weber (Ogden), Wasatch Mountain Food & Wine Soc. (Salt Lake City). Office: PO Box 151411 Salt Lake City UT 84115

POTTS, ROBERT WILLIAM LATELLE, entomologist; b. Denver, June 22, 1911; s. Harry Latelle and Agnes (Richardson) P.; student Colo. Agrl. Coll., 1929-31; B.A., U. Denver, 1934; M.Sc., U. Calif., Berkeley, 1943; m. Geraldine Ratliff, May 20, 1937; 1 son, Michael Robert; m. 2d, Elizabeth Randall, May 30, 1969. Acting curator entomology Colo. Mus. Natural History, Denver, 1936-38; head curator Cheyenne Mountain Mus., Colorado Springs, Colo., 1938-41; teaching asst. U. Calif., Berkeley, 1942-45; systematic entomologist Calif. Dept. Agr., San Francisco, 1945-49, 50-67; research asso. entomology NRC, Truk, Caroline Islands, 1949; plant quarantine specialist in entomology Agri. Research Service, Dept. Agr., San Francisco, 1967-72; asso. in entomology Calif. Acad. Scis., 1972—. Fellow Photog. Soc. Am., Explorers Club; mem. Am. Inst. Biol. Scis., Entomol. Soc. Am., Western Soc. Naturalists, Calif. Acad. Sci., Photochrome Soc. San Francisco, Camera Expressionists, Sigma Xi, Alpha Tau Omega, Pi Kappa Delta, Beta Beta Beta, Gamma Alpha, Phi Sigma. Democrat. Episcopalian (lay reader 1954-67). Author: Lab Manual of Medical Entomology, 1943. Home: PO Box 336 Coarsegold CA 93614

POTTS, ROY EARL, lawyer; b. Vincennes, Ind., Dec. 24, 1918; s. Roy F. and Elizabeth (Klein) P.; B.S. in Mech. Engring., Purdue U., 1940; LL.B., Yale U., 1951; m. Dorthy Birdeen Ragle, Aug. 16, 1940. Mgmt. trainee Santa Fe R.R., Albuquerque, 1940-42; instr. mech. engring. U. Tex., Austin, 1946-47; engr. Standard Oil Co. Inc., Whiting, Ind., 1947-49; admitted to Calif. bar, 1952; atty. O'Melveny & Myers, Los Angeles, 1951-62; atty. Kindel & Anderson, Los Angeles, 1962, ptnr., 1963-82; ptnr. firm Overton, Lyman & Prince, Los Angeles, 1982—. Mem. Town Hall, Los Angeles. Served to maj. AUS, 1942-46. Mem. Los Angeles County Bar Assn., Mchts. and Mfrs. Assn. Republican. Congregationalist. Clubs: Jonathan, Wilshire Country, Mens Garden (Los Angeles). Home: 645 Landor Ln Pasadena CA 91106 Office: 550 Flower St Los Angeles CA 90071

POULOS, CLARA JEAN, nutritionist, biologist; b. Los Angeles, Jan. 1, 1941; d. James P. and Clara Georgie (Creighton) Hill; Ph.D. in Biology, Fla. State Christian U., 1974; Ph.D. in Nutrition, Donsbach U., 1979; D in Nutritional Medicine, John F. Kennedy U., 1986; m. Themis Poulos, Jan. 31, 1960. Dir. research Leapou Lab., Aptos, Calif., 1973-76, Monterey Bay Research Inst., Santa Cruz, Calif., 1976—; nutrition specialist, Santa Cruz, 1975—; dir. nutritional services, health enhancement, lifestyle planning, Santa Cruz, 1983—; instr. Santa Cruz Extention U. Calif. and Stoddard Assocs. Seminars; cons. Biol-Med. Lab., Chgo., Nutra-Med Research Corp., N.Y., Akorn-Miller Pharmacal, Chgo., Monterey Bay Aquaculture Farms, Threshhold Lab., Calif., Resurrection Lab., Calif. Recipient Najulander Internat. Research award, 1971, Wainwright Found. award., 1979, various state and local awards. Fellow Internat. Coll. Applied Nutrition, Am. Nutritionist Assn., Internat. Acad. Nutritional Consultants; mem. Am. Diabetes Assn. (profl., pres. Santa Cruz chpt., sec. No. Calif. chpt.), AAAS, Internat. Platform Soc., Am. Public Health Assn., Calif. Acad. Sci., Internat. Fishery Assn. (health asct.), Clubs: Toastmistress, Quota. Author: Alcoholism—Stress - Hypoglycemia, 1976; The Relationship of Stress to Alcoholism and Hypoglycemia, 1979; assoc. editor Internat. Jour. Bio-social Research, Health Promotion Features; contbr. articles to profl. jours. Office: 1595 Soquel Dr Suite 222 Santa Cruz CA 95065

POULSON, RICHARD EDWIN, environmental scientist, researcher; b. Detroit, Sept. 26, 1928; s. Otto Henry Poulson and Corinne Augusta (Matteson) Hendricks; m. Alyce Jean Thompson, Aug. 28, 1954; children: Jean, Sharon, Mary, David. BS in Chemistry, Mich. State U., 1953; PhD in Phys. Chemistry, Mich State U., 1959; MS in Phys. Chemistry, U. Calif., Berkeley, 1957. Research chemist Beckman Instruments, Fullerton, Calif., 1959-63, U.S. Bur. Mines, U.S. Energy Research and Devel. Adminstrn., U.S. Dept. Energy, Laramie, Wyo., 1963-76; mgr. environ. sci. U.S. Dept. Energy, Laramie, 1976-83; sr. research scientist Western Research Inst., Laramie, 1983—. Served with USN, 1946-49. Mem. Am. Chem. Soc., ASTM (chromatography com. chmn. 1984—). Republican. Methodist. Avocations: hiking, photography, electronics design. Home: PO Box 3136 Laramie WY 82071 Office: Western Research Inst PO Box 3395 Laramie WY 82071

POUNDS, ELTON WILLIAM, priest, religion/health care administrator; b. Smith Ctr., Kans., June 27, 1935; s. Elton Lee and Thelma (Wookey) P.; children from previous marriages: Jan, Mark, Kimberly, Andrew, christopher, Kyra, Chandra. AB, Hastings Coll., 1957; MDiv, Seabury-Western Theol. Sem., 1960. Rector Grace Ch., Columbus, Nebr., 1965-69, Holy Trinity Parish, Gillette, Wyo., 1969-72; dir. Trinity Ranch Diocese of Colo., Wetmore, 1972-77; curate Grace Ch., Colorado Springs, Colo., 1977-85; dir. pastoral care AMI-St. Luke's Hosp., Denver, 1985—; chmn. bd. examining Chaplains, Diocese of Colo., 1968—. Editor: Large Print Book of Common Prayer, 1982. Judge Campbell County, Wyo., 1970-72; pres. Chaplaincy Corps Colorado Springs Police Dept., 1980-81; mem. Civil Rights Commn., 1965-67; del. Gov.'s Conf. on Aging, Colo., 1980. Fellow Seabury, 1971, 78, Citizens' Goals, 1981. Mem. AAAS, Am. Assn. Clin. Pastoral Edn., Gerontol. Soc. Am., Western Gerontol. Soc. Am. (presenter model program on aging 1981), Amnesty Internat., Episcopal Soc. Ministry on Aging (bd. dirs. 1980-82). Republican. Episcopalian. Avocations: tennis, skiing. Home: 2657 S University E Denver CO 80210 Office: St Lukes Hosp 601 E 19th Ave Denver CO 80203

POURNELLE, JERRY EUGENE, author; b. Shreveport, La., Aug. 7, 1933; s. P. Eugene and Ruth (Lewis) P.: M. Roberta Jane Isdell, July 17, 1959; children: Alexander, Francis Russell, Phillip Eugene, Richard Steffan. BS, U. Wash., 1954, MS, 1957, PhD, 1964. Instr. U. Wash., Seattle, 1956-57; research engr., aviation psychologist Boeing Co., Seattle, 1958-64; mgr. spl. studies Aerospace Corp., San Bernardino, Calif., 1964; prof., dir. research inst. Pepperdine U., Los Angeles, 1965-69; exec. asst. to mayor City Los Angeles, 1969; author, lectr., cons. Studio City, Calif., 1970—; cons. Directorate of Plans USAF, 1968; chief cons. Profl. Educators Los Angeles, 1970; cons. to chancellor Calif. State Colls., 1970—. Author: Human Temperature Tolerance in Astronautic Environments, 1959, Stability and National Security, 1968, Congress Debates Viet Nam, 1971, The Right to Read, 1971, Red Heroin, Red Dragon, 1971, West of Honor, 1976, The Mercenary, 1977, High Justice, 1977, Janissaries, 1979, King David's Spaceship, 1980, (with Stefan Possony) The Strategy of Technology, 1970, (with Larry Niven) The Mote in God's Eye, 1974, Inferno, 1976, Lucifer's Hammer, 1977, Oath of Fealty, 1981, Footfall, 1985, (with Roland Green) Janissaries: Clan and Crown, 1982, (with Dean Ing) Mutual Assured Survival, 1984; editor: 2020 Vision; sci. editor, columnist Galaxy Sci. Fiction, 1975-78, Byte mag., 1978—, InfoWorld, 1986—. Scoutmaster Boy Scouts Am., 1958; chmn. bd. dirs. Seattle Civic Playhouse Assn., 1960-63; asst. chmn. San Bernardino County Rep. Com., 1964; assoc. dir. Sam Yorty for Mayor Campaign, 1969; bd. dirs. Pepperdine Research Inst., 1966-69. Served with AUS, 1950-52; mem. Rep. Bd. Govs., 1962-63. Decorated Bronze medal; recipient Excellence award Am. Security Council, 1969, John W. Campbell award 1973. Fellow AAAS; mem. Inst. Strategic Studies, AIAA, Ops. Research Soc. Am., Univ. Prof. for Acad. Order (bd. dirs. 1971), Sci. Fiction Writers Am. (pres. 1973-74). Episcopalian. Home and Office: 12051 Laurel Terr Studio City CA 91604

POWELL, AMARYLLIS LILLES, music educator; b. Portland, Oreg., Nov. 12, 1931; d. Thomas Peter and Mary Jean (Manos) Lilles; m. George Chris Drougas, Jan. 1, 1956; m. 2d, Richard Lee Powell, June 7, 1962; children: Leslie, Christian, Donald, David, Mary. B.M.E., Willamette U., 1953, M.M.E., 1966. Mem. Honolulu Symphony, 1954-55; tchr. vocal/band Iolani Episcopal Sch. for Boys, Honolulu, 1954-55; tchr. vocal music Beaverton (Oreg.) Schs., 1962-63, 63-64; tchr. elem./jr. high band, dist. music coordinator Tigard (Oreg.) Schs., 1976—, mem. talented and gifted com., 1977—; mem. music textbook com. State Oreg. Dept. Edn., 1980—. Mem. alumni bd. Willamette U.; mem. troop com. Century Club, Boy Scouts Am.; mem. ednl. com. Oreg. Symphony Orch.; active Oreg. Episcopal Schs. Rodney Soc., also alumni bd.; active Portland Rose Festival, Interlochen Nat. Music Camp. Mem. Music Educator's Nat. Conf., Oreg. Music Educators Assn. (bd. dirs.), NEA, Assn. Supervision and Curriculum Devel., Assn. Sch. Suprs., N.W. Women in Ednl. Adminstrn., Oreg. Advocates for the Arts, Oreg. Assn. Sch. Suprs. (chmn. art and music 1986—), Oreg. Edn. Assn., Conf. Oreg. Sch. Adminstrs., Oreg. Alliance for the Arts (edn. bd.), Mid-Willamette Valley Music Suprs. (chmn.), 13th Coast Guard Dist. Retiree Council, Pi Beta Phi, Mu Phi Epsilon. Republican. Episcopalian. Club: West Hills Raquet (Portland, Oreg.). Home: 7455 SW Newton Pl Portland OR 97225 Office: 14650 SW 97th St Twality Jr High Sch Tigard OR 97223

POWELL, BETTIE BLANCHE, librarian; b. Galena, Mo., May 17, 1935; s. Charlie Lester and Blanche G. (Carney) Evans; m. Lavon I. Powell, Aug. 16, 1963; children—Phillip, Susan, Elizabeth. B.A., Kansas City Bible Coll., 1960; M.A. in Librarianship, U. Denver, 1963. Cataloguer, U. No. Colo., Greeley, 1963-64; acquisitions librarian, curriculum lab. dir. Ft. Hays State U., Hays, Kans., 1979-82; library dir. Page Pub. Library, Ariz., 1982—. Vice pres. Page Band Parents, 1984—. Mem. Kans. Library Assn. (sec.-treas. coll. and univ. library sect. 1979-80), Ariz. Library Assn. Republican. Baptist. Home: PO Box 3165 34 Bonita Rd S Page AZ 86040 Office: Page Pub Library PO Box 1776 Page AZ 86040

POWELL, DONALD ALLAN, advertising executive; b. Edmonton, Alta., Can., May 8, 1935; s. Harry Leonard and Joan Myrna (Smith) P.; m. Peggy Jean LaViolette, Sept. 14, 1957; children—Anthony, Alison. B.A. in Journalism, U. Calif.-Berkeley, 1957. Internat. creative dir. MacManus, John & Adams, London, 1967-72; dir. advt. The Irvine Co. (Calif.), 1972-75; pres. Don Powell Advt., Irvine, 1976—. Recipient 1st prize award Columbus Film Festival, 1962; Best Read Ad By Men award Gallup-Robinson London, 1969. Unitarian. Home: 4971 Paseo de Vega Irvine CA 92715

POWELL, MEL DANIEL, educational administrator, lawyer; b. N.Y.C., July 7, 1935; children—Anthony, Vanessa. B.S., N.J. State U., 1957; M.A., George Washington U., 1963; J.D., U. Balt., 1966; Ph.D., U. Md., 1968. Bar: Md. 1966. Atty., City of Greenbelt, Md., 1966-67; dir. contract research Nat. Assn. Counties, 1967-71; assoc. prof. urban affairs U. No. Colo., Greeley, 1971-72; dir. Office of Research Mgmt., Appalachian Region Com., Washington, 1972-73; dean Grad. Ctr. Pub. Policy and Adminstrn., Calif. State U.-Long Beach, 1973—; cons. in field. Author: Education for the Future Public Service, 1981; Achieving Closer Ties, 1984. Contbr. articles to profl. jours. Mem. Mayor's Task Force City of Long Beach, 1978, mem. charter comm., 1979, bd. dirs. poverty program, 1980. Served to lt. (j.g.), U.S. Navy, 1959-63. Mem. Western Govt. Research Assn. (pres. 1980-82, exec. sec. 1982—), Urban Affairs Assn. (chmn. 1986-87, program chmn. Nat. Conf. 1984). Am. Soc. Pub. Adminstrn. (pres. Los Angeles Metro chpt. 1976-77, Dykstra award 1977, Will Baughman award 1982). Democrat. Roman Catholic. Home: 16491 Tropez Ln Huntington Beach CA 92649 Office: Calif State Univ Grad Ctr for Pub Policy and Adminstrn Long Beach CA 90840

POWELL, PEGGY JEAN, public relations executive; b. La Grande, Oreg., June 29, 1933; d. Kenneth Gladstone and Clara Gertrude (Hercher) LaViolette; m. Donald Allan Powell, Sept. 14, 1957; children: Anthony Forrest, Alison Carol. BA, U. Calif., Berkeley, 1956; postgrad, Wayne State U., 1967. Writer Mademoiselle Mag., N.Y.C., 1955-56; reporter Berkeley Daily Gazette, 1956-57, Vancouver (B.C., Can.) Sun, 1957-59; freelance writer

Calif., 1960-75; pvt. practice pub. relations cons. Irvine, 1975-85; ptnr. Investor Communication Systems, Irvine, 1985—. Contbr. numerous articles to profl. and entertainment jours. Mem., docent, patron Newport Harbor Art Mus., Newport Beach, Calif., 1972-84; bd. dirs. Campus View Homeowners Assn., Irvine, 1976. Recipient Golden Orange award Orange County (Calif.) Advt. Fedn., 1981. Mem. Pub. Relations Soc. Am., Orange County Chpt. Pub. Relations Soc. Am. (3 Excellence awards 1984, 2 Excellence awards 1985), Publicity Club Am., U. Calif. Berkeley Alumni Assn., Prytanean Alumni Assn., Alpha Gamma Delta. Democrat. Unitarian. Office: Investigator Communication Systems 4400 MacArthur #930 Newport Beach CA 92660

POWELL, ROBERTA ANN, social worker; b. Eugene, Oreg., Aug. 9, 1952; d. Robert Anthony and Ruthann Blanche (Cartier) Saul; m. Robert Burns Powell, Apr. 12, 1980. BA, U. Oreg., 1974; MSW, Portland State U., 1978. Registered clin. social worker, Oreg. Psychiat. technician St. John's Hosp., Longview, Wash., 1974-76; counselor Portland (Oreg.) Mil. and Vets. Counseling Ctr., 1976-79; mental health counselor adult rehab. services Ind. Living Service, Portland, 1979-84; social worker, case coordinator Rio Outpatient Program, Portland, 1983—; Mem. adv. bd. region I Oreg. Vocat. Rehab. Div., 1983—. Vol. Brooklyn Action Corps, Portland, 1984-86; mem. Holy Trinity Parish, Beaverton, Oreg. Mem. Nat. Assn. Social Workers (cert.), Sierra Club, Alpha Lambda Delta. Democrat. Roman Catholic. Avocations: running, aerobics, hiking, skiing, weightraining. Office: Rio Outpatient Program 1040 NW 22d Suite 500 Portland OR 97210

POWELL, SCOTT WADE, ethanol fuel company consultant; b. Nampa, Idaho, Oct. 15, 1954; s. Hyrum Shields and Clover Mae (Ormond) P.; m. Debra Rasmussen, Aug. 10, 1976; children: Nicole, Bruce. Student, Ricks Coll., 1972-73; BS in Chemistry cum laude and Gen. Studies, Eastern Oreg. State Coll., 1980. With Oreg. Alcohol Fuels Clearing House Eastern Oreg. State Coll., LaGrande, 1979-80; project developer Wolff Devel., San Diego, 1980-81; pres. Genetic Engring. Mgmt., Inc., Jerome, Idaho, 1981-84; with ethanol fuels prodn. and foods devel. dept. Mountain Devel. Corp., Portales, N.Mex., 1984-86; prin. Ethanol Fuels Cons., Portales, 1986—; cons. Albuquerque N.Mex. Food Show, 1985, Coor's Food Products Co., 1986—, Arrowhead Mills, Hereford, Tex., 1986—. Mem. tng. com. Boy Scouts Am., LaGrande, 1976-84; bd. dirs. Union County Health Systems Agy., LaGrande, 1980-82; media rep. Rep. Cen. Com., LaGrande, 1982; missionary for The Ch. of Jesus Christ of Latter-day Sts., Belfast, Ireland, 1974-76. Named one of Outstanding Young Men of Am., U.S. Jaycees, 1982. Mem. Am. Chem. Soc., Sigma Pi Sigma. Avocations: hunting, gardening, family.

POWELL, TED FERRELL, micrographics specialist; b. Rexburg, Idaho, Feb. 2, 1935; s. Edward Lewis and Thelma Mae (Arnold) P.; m. Nedra Scoresby, Jan. 15, 1954; children: Janeal, Julia, Greg F., Megan, Kara, N. Elizabeth. BS in Acctg., U. Utah, 1962. Supr. geneal. library Ch. Jesus Christ Latter-day Saints, Salt Lake City, 1967-70, supr. granite mountain records vault, 1970-71, dir. microfilming field ops., 1971-85, ops. analyst geneal. dept., 1985—; mem. com. preservation hist. records Nat. Research Council, Washington, 1984—. Co-author: A Guide to Micrographics, 1984; also articles. Mem. Assn. Info. and Image Mgmt. (chpt. pres. 1976-77, bd. dirs. 1977-80, Disting. award 1978), Inst. Internal Auditors (cert.), Internat. Council Archives (com. reprography 1976—). Republican. Home: 3144 S 160 W Bountiful UT 84010 Office: Ch Jesus Christ Latter-day Saints 50 East North Temple Salt Lake City UT 84150

POWELL, WILLIAM HOUSTON, plant scientist; b. Lakeview, Oreg., Sept. 5, 1926; s. Ralph and Elvira (Houston) P.; m. Donna Correen Rutkowski, Apr. 9, 1966; 1 child, Kay Marie. Student, U. Calif., Davis, 1946-48; BS, Calif. Poly. State U., San Luis Obispo, 1960, U. Ariz., 1962; PhD, U. Wyo., 1965. Sr. agronomist Kern County Land Co., Bakersfield, Calif., 1965-70; supervising agronomist Belridge Land Co., Bakersfield, 1970-71; v.p. R-L-C-s Internat., Crookston, Minn., 1971-73; agronomic officer Devel. and Resources Corp. div. World Bank, Andimeshk, Iran, 1974-76; sr. research officer Near East Found. U.S. AID, Maseru, Lesotho, 1977-79; agronomist Nat. Cottonseed Prodn., Memphis, 1980-83; agrl. cons. Tempe, Ariz., 1983—; cons. in field, Collierville, Tenn., 1983-84, IECO, Dacca, Bangladesh, 1979-80; instr. Ariz. State U., Tempe, 1973-74. Contbr. articles to profl. jours. Pres. Shalimar East, Tempe, 1984-85. Served with USN, 1944-46, PTO. U.S. Health Dept. grantee, Laramie, Wyo., 1962-65. Mem. Am. Soc. Agronomy (cert.), Crop Sci. Soc. Am. (cert.), Sigma Xi. Republican. Lutheran. Clubs: Prescott Country (Ariz); 20-30 (Tulelake, Calif.). Lodges: Rotary, Elks, Masons. Avocations: reading, swimming, hunting, travelling. Home and Office: 3147 S Fairfield Dr Tempe AZ 85282

POWER, BARBARA JOYCE, architect; b. Mesa, Ariz., July 22, 1953; d. Kent J. and Joyce (Hicks) P. B.Arch., Arizona State U., 1975. Registered architect, Ariz. Draftsman Trico Internat., Tempe, Ariz., 1974-75; Stuart Siefer, Tempe, 1976, Ferguson, Morris, Simpson, Phoenix, 1976; designer Sherrow Constrn., Phoenix, 1975-76; staff architect in tng. Shill, Judd, Richards & Johnson, Mesa, Ariz, 1976-77; staff architect Leo J. Miller & Assocs. Inc., Phoenix, 1977—. Mem. AIA. Democrat. Mormon. Office: Leo J Miller & Assocs Inc 2929 N 44th St Suite 230 Phoenix AZ 85018

POWER, CORNELIUS MICHAEL, archbishop; b. Seattle, Dec. 18, 1913; s. William and Kate (Dougherty) P. Student, St. Patrick Sem., 1933-35, St. Edward Sem., 1935-39; J.C.D., Cath. U. Am., 1943. Ordained priest Roman Catholic Ch., 1939; asst. pastor St. James Cathedral, Seattle, 1939-40; resident chaplain Holy Names Acad., Seattle, 1943-52; adminstr. Parish of Our Lady of Lake, Seattle, 1955-56; pastor Parish of Our Lady of Lake, 1956-69; vice chancellor Archdiocese of Seattle, 1943-51, chancellor, 1951-69; apptd. domestic prelate 1963, 2d bishop of Yakima, 1969, bishop of Yakima, 1969-74; archbishop Portland, Oreg., 1974-86; ret. 1986. Address: Archdiocese of Portland 2838 E Burnside Portland OR 97214

POWER, DENNIS MICHAEL, museum director; b. Pasadena, Calif., Feb. 18, 1941; s. John Dennis Power and Ruth Augusta (Mott) Zwicky; m. Kristine Moneva Fisher, Feb. 13, 1965 (div. Aug. 1984); children: Michael Lawrence, Matthew David; m. Leslie Gabrielle Baldwin, July 6, 1985; 1 stepchild, Katherine G. Petrosky. B.A., Occidental Coll., 1962, M.A., 1964; Ph.D. (NSF fellow), U. Kans., 1967. Asst. curator ornithology Royal Ont. Mus.; also asst. prof. zoology U. Toronto, 1967-71; asso. curator Royal Ont. Mus., Toronto, 1971-72; dir. Santa Barbara (Calif.) Mus. Natural History, 1972—; biol. researcher; cons. ecology. Editor: The California Islands: Proceedings of a Multidisciplinary Symposium, 1980; contbr. articles sci. jours. Grantee NRC Can., 1968-72; Grantee NSF, 1974-78. Mem. Cooper Ornithol. Soc. (dir. 1976-79, pres. 1979-81), Am. Ornithologists Union (sec. 1981-83), Am. Assn. Mus. (council 1980-83), Calif. Assn. Mus. (dir. 1980—), Western Mus. Conf. (dir. 1977-83, pres. 1981-83), AAAS, Am. Soc. Naturalists, Assn. Sci. Mus. Dirs., Ecol. Soc. Am., Soc. Study of Evolution, Soc. Systematic Zoology, Sigma Xi. Office: 2559 Puesta del Sol Rd Santa Barbara CA 93105

POWERS, CHERYL ANN, science educator; b. Geneva, N.Y., June 8, 1944; s. William Selleck Heit and Eleanor (Ringer) Butler; m. Stephen Edward Powers, Sept. 4, 1965 (div. Nov. 1977); children: Christopher Kevin, Timothy Stephen. BS, Cornell U., 1966. Cert. tchr., N.Y., Tex. Lab. technician Upstate Med. Ctr., Syracuse, N.Y., 1966-68; sci. tchr. Jamesville (N.Y.)-Dewitts Sch. Dist., 1968-70, Union-Endicott (N.Y.) Sch. Dist., 1970-71, Rosary Acad., Sparkill, N.Y., 1973-76; biology tchr. Alief I Sch. Dist., Houston, 1976-82; chmn. sci. dept. Cate Sch., Carpinteria, Calif., 1982—. Author: (with others) Critical Thinking in a Nuclear Age, 1984-85, Exeter II Report, 1985-86. Fellow GTE, 1986-87. Mem. Nat. Sci. Tchrs. Assn., Nat. Biology Tchrs. Assn., Calif. Assn. Ind. Schs. (head sci. dept. acad. services com. 1986—), Assn. Computing Tchrs., Calif. Sci. Tchrs. Assn. Home: 1930 Cate Mesa Rd PO Box 68 Carpinteria CA 93013 Office: Cate Sch PO Box 68 Carpinteria CA 93013

POWERS, EDWIN MALVIN, consulting engineer; b. Denver, July 20, 1915; s. Emmett and Bertha Malvina (Guido) P.; m. Dorothy Lavane Debler, Jan. 18, 1941; children: Dennis M., Kenneth E., James M., Steven R. B.S. in Chem. Engring., U. Denver, 1939, M.S., 1940. Registered profl. engr., N.J., Colo., Fall Out Analysts Engr., U.S. Fed. Emergency Mgmt. Agency. P-rodn. supr. Nat. Aniline Div., Buffalo, 1940-45; engr., project supr. Merck & Co., Rahway, N.J., 1945-67, chief project coordinator, 1967-72, purchasing engr., 1972-82; ret., 1982; cons. engr., Conifer, Colo., 1982—. Mem., del. Conifer Home Owners Assns. Protect Our Single Homes, 1984-86, Regional Environ. Assn. Concerned Home Owners, 1985-86, task force area devel. Hwy. 285/Conifer Area County Planning Bd. Community, 1986-87. Mem. Am. Chem. Soc., NSPE, Am. Inst. Chem. Engrs. (treas. N.J. 1960, exec. com. 1961-63). Home and office: 26106 Amy Circle Dr Conifer CO 80433

POWERS, GAIL MARGUERITE, social worker; b. San Francisco; d. Norman Thomas and Eleanor Catherine (Krabach) Allen; m. William Joseph Reynolds, Nov. 26, 1958 (div.); children: Rick Joseph, Joseph Scott, Rebecca Gail; m. Stephen Powers, Dec. 28, 1968. BEd, U. Ariz., 1981; postgrad., Ariz. State U., 1987. Cert. elem. tchr., Ariz. Eligibility worker Sacramento County Welfare, 1968; tchr. Amphitheater and Tucson Unified Sch. Dists., 1980-84; social worker Child Protective Services Dept. Econ. Security, Tucson, 1985; in-home therapist Ariz. Children's Home, Tucson, 1986—; Mem. steering com. Children's Hospice and Chronic Care Ctr., Tucson, 1984-86. Mem. Nat. Assn. Social Workers, Ariz. Chpt. Nat. Assn. Social Workers, Ariz. Assn. Marriage and Family Therapy (in process). Baha'i. Home: 2235 N Madelyn Ave Tucson AZ 85712

POWERS, KENNETH LAWRENCE, civil engr., assn. exec.; b. Kalispell, Mont., July 30, 1912; s. William Allan and Anna Dorcus (Harrington) P.; B.S., U. Puget Sound, 1935; postgrad. U. Wash., 1937; m. Gladys Marie Neff, June 5, 1940 (dec. July 1969); 1 dau., Sharron Marie (Mrs. Joseph Dennis Delaney); m. Catherine Elaine Coughenour, Dec. 26, 1970. Assayer, Alaska div. Kennecott Copper Corp., 1935-38; insp. gen. constrn. Grand Coulee, Altus project U.S. Bur. Reclamation, Altus, Okla., 1938-41, engr. Altus project, Denver, 1942-48, field engr. Bonny Dam, Republican River Valley, Sargent project, Farwell project, St. Paul, Nebr., 1948-61, constr. engr., 1961-65, chief constrn. coordination and estimates br., region 7, Denver, 1965-67, regional engr., region 4, Salt Lake City, 1967-73; cons. engr., Denver, 1973-74; exec. sec. Profl. Engrs. of Colo., 1974-81; ret., 1981. Registered profl. engr., Colo. Fellow ASCE, Nat. Soc. Profl. Engrs. (chpt. v.p. 1972-73), U.S. Com. on Large Dams, U.S. Com. on Irrigation and Flood Control. K.C. (4 deg.), Elk, Lion (dist. govt. 1964-65). Address: 12938 W Virginia Ave Lakewood CO 80228

POWERS, NANCY L(OUISA), neuroscience nurse specialist; b. Bethlehem, Pa., May 16, 1948; 1 child, Seth B. Shikora. Diploma, Abington Meml. Hosp., 1971; BS in Nursing, Moravian Coll., 1971; MS, U. Pa., 1976; D in Nursing Sci., The Cath. U. Am., 1980. Staff nurse Hahnehmann Med. Coll. and Hosp., Phila., 1971-72, asst. adminstrv. supr., 1972-73; instr. Abington Meml. Hosp. and others, Phila., 1973-77; asst. prof. U. Calif., San Francisco, 1980-83; pres., practitioner Healing Resources, Inc., Walnut Creek, Calif., 1984—; bd. dirs. Diablo Valley Bus. Forum, Walnut Creek. Contbr. articles to profl. jours. Mem. AAAS, Internat. Assn. Study of Pain, Calif. Nurses Assn. Office: Healing Resources Inc 1615 N Broadway Walnut Creek CA 94596

POWERS, STEPHEN, educational researcher, consultant; b. Bakersfield, Calif., June 10, 1936; s. Robert Boyd and Mildred (Irwin) P.; m. Gail Marguerite Allen, Dec. 28, 1968; children—Rick, Joseph, Rebecca. B.S in Edn., No. Ariz. U., 1959; M.A., U. Ariz., Tucson, 1970, M.Ed., 1972, Ph.D., 1978. Cert. tchr., Calif.; cert. tchr., adminstr., jr. coll. tchr., Ariz. Policeman, City of Bakersfield, 1967-69; tchr. Marana (Ariz.) Pub. Schs., 1969-72; dir. Am. Sch. Belo Horizonte, Brazil, 1972-73; tchr. Nogales (Ariz.) Pub. Schs., 1973-75; research specialist Tucson Unified Sch. Dist., 1975—; adj. prof. ednl. psychology, U. Ariz.; assoc. faculty mem. in computer sci. Pima Coll. Nat. Inst. Edn. grantee, 1980; Ariz. State Reading Council, 1982. Mem. Am. Ednl. Research Assn., Psychometric Soc., Am. Psychol. Assn., Am. Sociol. Assn., Am. Statis. Assn. Bahai. Contbr. articles to profl. jours. Office: 1010 E 10th St Tucson AZ 85719

POWLEY, EDWARD HARRISON, musicology educator; b. Orange, N.J., Jan. 10, 1943; s. Edward H. Powley and Elizabeth Francis Malinowski; m. Ellen Mildred Lockwood, June 12, 1967; children: William, Barrett, Martha, Edward, Philip, Julianne, Sarah. BMus, Eastman Sch. Mus., 1965, MA, 1968, PhD, 1974. Asst. prof. mus. Brigham Young U., Provo, 1969-74, assoc. prof., 1974-82, prof., 1982—, head area musicology, 1986—. Editor: Symphonies of Druschetzky, 1985, Il Trionfo di Dori, 1987; contbr. articles to profl. jours. Grantee NDEA, 1966, Fulbright, Vienna, Austria, 1965-66, Brigham Young U., 1983. Mme. Am. Musicol. Soc. (chmn. local chpt. 1986-87, nat. council 1985-87), Percussive Arts Soc. (chmn. research com. 1977-87), Internat. Musicol. Soc,Sonneck Musicol. Soc., Coll. Mus. Soc., Am Mus Instrument Soc. Mormon. Home: 2220 N 1400 E Provo UT 84604 Office: Brigham Young U Dept Mus E-579 HFAC Provo UT 84604

PRACHT, PEGGY, scientific laboratory administrator; b. Oakland, Calif., Dec. 23, 1947; d. Loren Eugene and Frankie Ethelene (Dupree) Pracht; 1 son, John Thomas Yeandle. B.A. in Music, Calif. State U., Hayward, 1970, student in Bus. Adminstrn. Computer operator Haskins & Sells, C.P.A.s, San Francisco, 1974-75; staff asst. to dir. Lawrence Berkeley Lab., 1976—. Mem. Nat. Notary Assn., Nat. Assn. Female Execs. Home: 15267 Central Ave San Leandro CA 94578 Office: Lawrence Berkeley Lab Calif 1 Cyclotron Rd Berkeley CA 94720

PRAKASH, SURYA G.K., chemistry educator; b. Bangalore, India, Oct. 7, 1953; came to U.S., 1974; s. Krishnamurthy Gubbi and Anasuya Hebbur; m. Rama S. Prakash, Dec. 20, 1981; 1 child, Archana. BSc with honors, Bangalore U., 1972; MSc, Indian Inst. Tech., Madras, 1974; PhD, U. So. Calif., 1978. Jr. fellow U. So. Calif., Los Angeles, 1978-81, asst. prof. research, 1981-84, assoc. prof. research, 1984—; cons. corps. in Calif., 1984—. Author: Superacids, 1985; also articles. Recipient Research Excellence award Hydrocarbon Inst. U. So. Calif, 1984, Phi Kappa Phi Faculty Recognition award, 1986. Mem. Am. Chem. Soc., Internat. Soc. Magnetic Resonance. Avocations: music, reading. Home: 1946 Deerpeak Dr Hacienda Heights CA 91745 Office: U So Calif Hydrocarbon Research Inst University Park Los Angeles CA 90089-1661

PRATER, CHARLES DWIGHT, scientist, engineer; b. Sylacauga, Ala., Jan. 2, 1917; s. Rubin Walker and Mary Hunt (Corley) P.; m. Willie Lee Miller, May 28, 1938; children: Anne Marie, Linda Lee, Susan Lynn. B.S., Auburn U., 1940; postgrad., U. Chgo., 1940-41; Ph.D., U. Pa., 1951. Physicist Bartol Research Found., Franklin Inst., 1941-46; research assoc. Johnson Found. of Med. Physics, U. Pa., 1946-51; sr. research physicist research dept. Mobil Oil Corp., 1951-57, research assoc., 1957-62, sr. research assoc., 1962-67, mgr. process research and devel., 1967-77, sr. scientist, research advisor, 1977-82, cons., 1982—; mem. faculty Calif. Inst. Tech., 1982—. Recipient Alpha Chi Sigma in Chem. Engring. research Am. Inst. Chem. Engrs., 1972. Fellow Am. Inst. Chem. Engrs.; mem. AAAS, Am. Chem. Soc., Nat. Acad. Engring., Sigma Xi. Home: 7160 Gilespie Street Las Vegas NV 89119

PRATER, JAMES FRANKLIN, auditor; b. San Francisco, May 16, 1943; s. Walter Rufus and Edith (Griffin) P. BS, San Jose State U., 1965. Sr. auditor Allstate Ins. Co., Menlo Park, Calif., 1970-72; instr. Hartnell Coll., Salinas, Calif., 1976-79; audit dir. 20th Century Ins. Co., Woodland Hills, Calif., 1982—. Mem. People for Am. Way, Washington, 1982-86. Served to sgt. U.S. Army, 1968-70. Mem. Inst. Internal Auditors (bd. mem., bd. govs., San Fernando Valley chpt. 1984-86, author, editor monthly newsletter), Calif. Real Estate Tchrs. Assn., Real Estate Cert. Inst. Democratic. Avocations: artistry, desert hiking. Home: 11901 Laurelwood Dr #3C Studio City CA 91604 Office: 20th Century Ins Co 6301 Owensmouth Ave Woodland Hills CA 91367

PRATER, JAMES SCOTT, electrical engineer; b. Pueblo, Colo., Aug. 29, 1961; s. Joseph C. and Edith M. (Holly) P. BSEE, Colo. State U., 1984. Design engr. NCR Microelectronics, Ft. Collins, Colo., 1984—. Mem. IEEE (treas. centennial subsect. 1986—), soc. Motion Picture and TV Engrs. Democrat. Baptist. Avocations: reading, hiking, fishing. Home: 221 Mathews #21 Fort Collins CO 80524 Office: NCR Microelectronics 2001 Danfield Ct Fort Collins CO 80525

PRATER, JOHN DINGLE, metallurgical engineer; b. Dalroy, Alta., Can., June 24, 1917; Came to U.S., 1923; s. Lewis and Eliza Allen (MacKelvie) P.; widowed 1984; children: Gerald W., Donald L., Kenneth R., Elaine F. BSMetE, Mont. Sch. Mines, 1939; MSMetE, U. Idaho, 1940. Chemist Anaconda (Mont.) Co., 1940-42; research metallurgist U.S. Bur. Mines, Salt Lake City, 1942-52; research scientist Kennecott Co., Salt Lake City, 1942-83, retired, 1983. Contbr. numerous articles to profl. jours.; patentee in field. Mem. AIME (sr.). Republican. Methodist. Lodge: Masons (master local chpt. 1985-86). Home and office: 2860 E 3185 S Salt Lake City UT 84109

PRATER, JOHN L., minister, educator; b. Granite City, Ill., Feb. 28, 1939; s. Roy J. and Doris Marie (Hensley) P.; m. Eloise Grace Crum, Apr. 6, 1963; children: Timothy Lee, James Robert. BA, Los Angeles Pacific, 1963; MDiv, Asbury Theol. Sem., 1967. Lic. psychologist counselor, Mo. Educator Free Meth. Ch., Winona Lake, Ind., 1959-74; supr. adminstrn. Pacific Telephone and Telegraph, Los Angeles, 1963-64, Sorenson Engring., Yucaipa, Calif., 1974-75; minister Pentocostal Ch. of God, Joplin, Mo., 1976; educator, adminstr. Assemblies of God, Springfield, Mo., 1976—; chaplain, cons. City of Duarte, Calif., 1967-69, City of Barstow, Calif., 1973-74; psychol. counselor San Bernadino County, Barstow, 1973-74; chaplain, counselor Sheriff's Dept., Mohave County, Ariz., 1981-85. Recipient Cert. Appreciation Duarte City Council, 1969, Barstow City Council, 1974. Mem. Assn. Christian Schs. Internat., Christian Camping Internat., Ch. Bus. Adminstrs. Republican. Club: Bullhead City (treas. 1981-84) Lodge: Lions. Avocations: electronics, aviation. Home and Office: Assembly of God Campground 1840 Iron Springs Rd Prescott AZ 86301

PRATER, WALTER LLOYD, mechanical engineer; b. Tulsa, Apr. 11, 1955; s. Samuel Lewis and Patricia (Gaylor) P.; m. Shari Lynn Loeffler, July 28, 1985. BSME, U. Kans., 1978; MSME, San Jose State U., 1985. Registered mechanical engr., registered mfg. engr. Mfg. engr. IBM, San Jose, Calif., 1978-80, test engr., 1980-83; adv. prodn. devel. engr. IBM, San Jose, 1983—. Contbr. some articles to profl. jours. Scholar Amoco, 1977-78; recipient First Pl. award in Zoology Long's Peak Sci. Fair, 1973. Mem. ASME, Soc. Mfg. Engrs., Tau. Beta Pi, Pi Tau Sigma. Democrat. Avocations: bicycle frame bldg., bicycle touring, illustrator, perfumer. Home: 679 S 11th St Apt #3 San Jose CA 95112 Office: IBM G62/70B 5600 Cottle Rd San Jose CA 95193

PRATHER, CALVIN WHEELER, social worker, psychotherapist; b. China Lake, Calif., July 24, 1950; s. Wheeler and Betty Jane (Coddington) P.; m. Loretta Cherie Moore, Feb. 12, 1972; children: Cristen Livette Paris, Chandra Danielle Elizabeth. AA, Grossmont Community Coll., 1968-70; BA, San Diego State U., 1977, MSW, 1979. Lic. clin. social worker, Calif. Counselor Effective Problem Intervention Ctr., San Diego, 1975-76; psychiat. aide Vista Hill Hosp., Chula Vista, Calif., 1976-78; clin. social worker Ctr. on Aging, San Diego, 1978, San Diego VA Med. Ctr., 1978; program dir. Adult Protective Services, San Diego, 1979-81; asst. dir. Coll. Ave. Counseling Ctr., San Diego, 1981-86; psychotherapist Rancho Bernardo Counseling Assocs., San Diego, 1985-86; dir. Mission Valley Counseling Assocs., San Diego, 1986—. Served to sgt. USAF, 1971-75. Mem. Nat. Assn. Social Workers, Christian Assn. Psychol. Studies. Republican. Baptist. Avocations: tennis, stained glass. Office: Mission Valley Counseling Assocs 3638 Camino del Rio North San Diego CA 92108

PRATT, CHARLES DUDLEY, JR., utility executive; b. Honolulu, Sept. 30, 1927; s. Charles Dudley and Dora (Broadbent) P.; m. Dale Logan, July 2, 1978; children by previous marriage—Charles Dudley, Timothy G., Sarah E., Melinda L. B.C.E. with honors, Yale U., 1950, M.Structural Engring., 1951; M.B.A., U. Hawaii, 1971. Registered profl. engr., Hawaii. With Hawaiian Electric Co., Inc., 1953—, v.p. planning, 1971, then exec. v.p., 1980, pres., from 1981, also dir., chmn., chief exec. officer; chmn. bd. Maui Electric Co., Ltd., Hawaii Electric Light Co., Inc. Bd. dirs. Aloha United Way; v.p. Aloha council Boy Scouts Am. Served with AUS, 1946-48, 51-53. Mem. ASCE (past pres. Hawaii sect.), Hawaii Soc. Corp. Planners, Hawaii C. of C. (dir.), U. Hawaii M.B.A. Alumni Group, USCG Aux., Beta Gamma Sigma, Tau Beta Pi. Clubs: Pacific, Kaneohe Yacht. Home: 276 N Kalaheo Ave Kailua HI 96734 Office: Hawaiian Elec Co Inc 900 Richards St Honolulu HI 96813 *

PRATT, GEORGE JANES, JR., psychologist, consultant; b. Mpls., May 3, 1948; s. George Janes and Sally Elvina (Hanson) P.; BA cum laude, U. Minn., 1970, MA, 1973; PhD with spl. commendation for overall excellence, Calif. Sch. Profl. Psychology, San Diego, 1976; 1 dau., Whitney Beth. Psychology trainee Ctr. for Behavior Modification, Mpls., 1971-72, U. Minn. Student Counseling Bur., 1972-73; predoctoral clin. psychology intern San Bernardino County (Calif.) Mental Health Services, 1973-74, San Diego County Mental Health Services, 1974-76; affiliate staff San Luis Rey Hosp., 1977-78; postdoctoral clin. psychology intern Mesa Vista Hosp., San Diego, Calif., 1976; clin. psychologist, dir. Psychology and Cons. Assocs. of San Diego, 1976—; chmn. Psychology and Cons. Assocs. Press, 1977—; bd. dirs. Optimax, Inc., 1985—; pres. George Pratt Ph.D., Psychol. Corp., 1979—; chmn. Pratt, Korn & Assocs., Inc., 1984—; founder La Jolla Profl. Workshops, 1977; clin. psychologist El Camino Psychology Ctr., San Clemente, Calif., 1977-78; grad. teaching asst. U. Minn. Psychology and Family Studies div., 1971; teaching assoc. U. Minn. Psychology and Family Studies div., Mpls., 1972-73; instr. U. Minn. Extension div., Mpls., 1971-73; faculty Calif. Sch. Profl. Psychology, 1974-83, San Diego Evening Coll., 1975-77, Nat. U., 1978-79, Chapman Coll., 1978, San Diego State U., 1979-80; vis. prof. Pepperdine U., Los Angeles, 1976-80; cons. U. Calif. at San Diego Med. Sch., 1976—, also instr. univ., 1978—, Facial Pain Clinic at U. Calif. San Diego Med. Ctr., 1983—; psychology chmn. Workshops in Clin. Hypnosis, 1980-84; cons. Calif. Health Dept., 1974, Naval Regional Med. Ctr., 1978-82, ABC-TV; also speaker. Mem. South Bay Youth Services Com., San Diego, 1976-80. Served with USAR, 1970-76. Licensed and cert. psychologist, Calif. Fellow Am. Soc. Clin. Hypnosis; mem. Am. Psychol. Assn., Calif. Psychol. Assn., Internat. Soc. Hypnosis, San Diego Psychology Law Soc. (exec. com.), Am. Assn. Sex Educators, Counselors and Therapists (cert.), San Diego Soc. Sex Therapy and Edn. (past pres.), San Diego Soc. Clin. Hypnosis (past pres.), Acad. San Diego Psychologists, Soc. Clin. and Exptl. Hypnosis., U. Minn. Alumni Assn., Nat. Speakers Assn., Beta Theta Pi. Republican. Lutheran. Author: HyperPerformance; A Clinical Hypnosis Primer; Sensory/Progressive Relaxation; Effective Stress Management; Clinical Hypnosis: Techniques and Applications; contbr. chpts. to various books. Office: Scripps Hosp Med Bldg 9834 Genesee Ave Suite 321 La Jolla CA 92037

PRATT, JOHN ROBERT, JR., city official, aviation services executive; b. St. Joseph, Mich., June 15, 1942; s. John Robert Sr. and Helen Dorothy (Long) P.; m. Elaine C. Hartman, Apr. 26, 1968. B.S., Purdue U., 1965; student USAF Air War Coll., 1983-84. Cert. comml. pilot, mechanic FAA. Commd. 2d lt. U.S. Air Force, 1965, advanced through grades to lt. col., 1986, active service, 1965-77, Res., 1977—; prin. Pratt Aviation Services, Anchorage, 1975-86, Aero Forensics, Anchorage, 1986—;mgr. Elmendorf Aero Club, 1977-80; maintenance mgr. Dept. Transit, Municipality of Anchorage, 1980-86; field dir. for Alaska, Seaplane Pilots Assn., 1980—; mem. navigability project adv. com. Alaska Dept. Natural Resources, 1981-86; mem. adv. com. Upper Cook Inlet Airport system study Alaska Dept. Transp. and Pub. Facilities, 1979-82, mem. industry task force Alaska aviation system plan Dept. Transp. and Pub. Facilities; mem. Mcpl. Airports Adv. Commn., Anchorage, 1979-80, planner Merrill Field Air Shows, 1980-84; bd. govs. Elmendorf Aero Club, 1974-75, mgr., 1977-80; mem. Merrill Field Master Plan Adv. Com., 1977-78; mem. air traffic control adv. com. Anchorage Community Coll., 1984—; mem. master plan update and FAA noise study coms. Juneau and Anchorage Internat. Airports, Dept. Trans. and Pub. Facilities, State of Alaska, 1985—; mem. trans. com. Anchorage C. of C., 1986—. Contbr. articles to profl. jours. Decorated Bronze Star, Air Force Commendation medal, Viet Nam Service medal, Viet Nam Gallantry Cross, others. Mem. Quiet Birdmen, Alaska Airmen's Assn. (life, controller 1983—, dir. 1984—), Seaplane Pilots Assn., Exptl. Aircraft Assn., Aircraft Owners and Pilots Assn., Air Force Assn. (life), Nat. Rifle Assn. (life). Republican. Lutheran. Office: 2520 E 16th Anchorage AK 99508

PRATT, PAUL WILLIAM, publisher, editor; b. New Castle, Pa., Oct. 9, 1946; s. Paul N. and Ann D. (Morella) P. BS, Pa. State U., 1968; DVM, U. Pa., 1973. Lic. med. vet., Pa., Del. Assoc. vet. Soc. Hill Vet. Hosp., Phila., 1973-75, Kirkwood Animal Hosp., Newark, Del., 1975-77; vet. med. officer Food and Drug Adminstrn., Rockville, Md., 1977-78; pub., editor Am. Vet. Publs., Inc., Santa Barbara, Calif., 1978—; editorial cons. Audio Vet.

Medicine, Monrovia, Calif., 1978—. Author, editor: Veterinary Practice Management, 1979; editor: Lab Profiles of Small Animal Diseases, 1980, Equine Medicine and Surgery, 1982, Feline Medicine, 1983, Lab Procedures for Animal Health Technicians, 1985, Medical Nursing for Animal Health Technicians, 1985, Modern Vet. Practice Jour., 1978—, Vet. Computing, 1982—. Am. Vet. Med. Assn. (local sec. 1980). Avocations: running, backpacking, skiing, writing. Office: Am Vet Publs Inc 5782 Thornwood Dr Goleta CA 93117

PRATT, ROSALIE REBOLLO, harpist, educator; b. N.Y.C., Dec. 4, 1933; d. Antonio Ernesto and Eleanor Gertrude (Gibney) Rebollo; Mus.B., Manhattanville Coll., 1954; Mus.M., Pius XII Inst. Fine Arts, Florence, Italy, 1955; Ed.D., Columbia U., 1976; m. Samuel Orson Pratt, Aug. 11, 1964; children—Francesca Christina Pratt Ferguson, Alessandra Maria Pratt Jones. Prin. harpist N.J. Symphony Orch., 1963-65; soloist Mozart Haydn Festival, Avery Fisher Hall, N.Y.C., 1968; tchr. music public schs., Bloomfield and Montclair, N.J., 1962-73; mem. faculty Montclair State Coll., 1973-79; prof. Brigham Young U., Provo, Utah, 1979—, coordinator grad. studies dept. music. Fulbright grantee, 1979; Myron Taylor scholar, 1954. Mem. Am. Harp Soc. (Outstanding Service award 1973), AAUP (co-chmn. legis. relations com. N.J. 1978-79), Music Edn. for Handicapped (co-founder, co-chmn., exec. dir., editor MEH Bulletin), Coll. Music Soc., Music Educators Nat. Conf., Phi Kappa Phi, Sigma Alpha Iota. Co-author: Elementary Music for All Learners, 1980; contbr. articles to Music Educators Jour., Am. Harp Jour., others. Editor procs. 2d, 3d and 4th Internat. Symposia Music Edn. for Handicapped, 1981, 83, 85. Office: Harris Fine Arts Center Brigham Young U Provo UT 84602

PRATT, VAUGHAN RONALD, computer engineering educator; b. Melbourne, Australia, Apr. 12, 1944; s. Ronald Victor and Marjorie (Mirams) P.; m. Margot Frances Koster, Feb. 2, 1969; children: Jennifer Katherine, Jacqueline Andrea. BSc with honors, Sydney U., Australia, 1967, MSc, 1970; PhD, Stanford U., 1972. From asst. to assoc. prof. MIT, Cambridge, 1972-82; head of research Sun Microsystems Inc., Mountain View, Calif., 1983-85; prof. Stanford (Calif.) U., 1981—. Author: Shellsort and Sorting Networks, 1979. Mem. Assn. for Computing Machinery, Assn. for Symbolic Logic. Office: Stanford U Stanford CA 94305

PRAUSNITZ, JOHN MICHAEL, chemical engineer, educator; b. Berlin, Germany, Jan. 7, 1928; came to U.S., 1937, naturalized, 1944; s. Paul Georg and Susi Prausnitz; m. Susan Frieda Prausnitz, June 10, 1956; children: Stephanie, Mark Robert. B.Chem. Engring., Cornell U., 1950; M.S., U. Rochester, 1951; Ph.D., Princeton, 1955; Dr. Ing., U. L'Aquila, 1983. Mem. faculty U. Calif., Berkeley, 1955—, prof. chem. engring., 1963—; cons. to cryogenic, polymer, petroleum and petrochem. industries. Author: (with others) Computer Calculations for Multicomponent Vapor-Liquid Equilibria, 1967, (with P.L. Chueh) Computer Calculations for High-Pressure Vapor-Liquid Equilibria, 1968, Molecular Thermodynamics of Fluid-Phase Equilibria, 1969, (with others) Regular and Related Solutions, 1970, Properties of Gases and Liquids, 1977, 2d edit., 1987, Computer Calculations for Multicomponent Vapor-Liquid and Liquid-Liquid Equilibria, 1980; contbr. to profl. jours. Guggenheim fellow, 1962, 73; Miller research prof., 1966, 78; Recipient Alexander V. Humboldt Sr. Scientist award, 1976; fellow Inst. Advanced Study, Berlin, 1985. Mem. Am. Inst. Chem. Engrs. (Colburn award 1962, Walker award 1967), Am. Chem. Soc. (E.V. Murphree award 1979), Nat. Acad. Engring., Nat. Acad. Scis. Home: 52 The Crescent Berkeley CA 94708

PRAY, RALPH EMERSON, metallurgical engineer; b. Troy, N.Y., May 12, 1926; s. George Emerson and Jansje Cornelius (Owejan) P.; student N.Mex. Inst. of Mining and Tech., 1953-56, U. N.Mex., 1956; BSMetE, U. Alaska, 1961; DScMetE. (Ideal Cement fellowship, Research grant), Colo. Sch. of Mines, 1966; m. Beverley Margaret Ramsey, May 10, 1959; children: Maxwell, Ross, Leslie, Marlene. Engr.-in-charge Dept. Mines and Minerals, Ketchikan, Alaska, 1957-61; asst. mgr. mfg. research Universal Atlas Cement div. U.S. Steel Corp., Gary, Ind., 1965-66; research metallurgist Inland Steel Co., Hammond, Ind., 1966-67; owner, dir. Mineral Research Lab., Monrovia, Calif., 1968—; pres., Keystone Canyon Mining Co., Inc., Pasadena, Calif., 1972-79, U.S. Western Mines, 1973—, Silveroil Research Inc., 1980-85; v.p. Mineral Drill Inc., 1981—; owner Precision Plastics, 1973-82; ptnr. Mineral Research and Devel. Co., 1981-86; lectr., Purdue U., Hammond, Ind., 1966-67, Nat. Mining Seminar, Barstow (Calif.) Coll., 1969-70; guest lectr. Calif. State Poly U., 1977-81, Western Placer Mining Conf., Reno, Nev., 1983, Dredging and Placer Mining Conf., Reno, 1985, others; v.p., dir. Wilbur Foote Plastics, Pasadena, 1968-72; strategic minerals del. People to People, Republic of S. Africa, 1983. Served with U.S. Army, 1950-52. Fellow Geol. Mining and Metall. Soc. India (life), Am. Inst. Chemists, South African Inst. Mining and Metallurgy; mem. Soc. Mining Engrs., Am. Chem. Soc., Am. Inst. Mining, Metall. and Petroleum Engrs., NSPE, Can. Inst. Mining and Metallurgy, Geol. Soc. South Africa, Sigma Xi, Sigma Mu. Contbr. articles to sci. jours.; guest editor Calif. Mining Jour., 1978—; patentee chem. processing and steel manufacture. Home: 212 W Sierra Madre Blvd Arcadia CA 91006 Office: 805 S Shamrock Ave Monrovia CA 91016

PRAZAK, PAUL RONALD, electronic engineer, consultant; b. Richmond, Calif., Feb. 11, 1949; s. Waldemar J. and Bernardine Rose (Beck) P.; m. Eva Linda Oliveira, Apr. 3, 1971. A.S. in Electronics, Contra Costa Coll., 1968; B.S. in Elec. Engring., Calif. State U.-Sacramento, 1971; M.S. in Elec. Engring., U. Ariz., 1973. Electronic design engr. Burr-Brown Research Corp., Tucson, 1973-78, group leader, 1978-80, mgr. high-resolution data conversion, data acquisition design, 1980-82, product design mgr., 1982-83, mgr. data conversion product design, 1983-85, gen. mgr. Data Products Div., 1985—; cons. active filter design. Active Special Olympics. Mem. IEEE (sr.), Internat. Soc. Hybrid Microelectronics, Nat. Soc. Profl. Engrs., So. Ariz. Roadrunning Club, Clique Camera Club. Patentee digital-to-analog, analog-to-digital conversion methods; contbr. numerous articles to profl. jours. Home: 502 N Chalet Ave Tucson AZ 85710 Office: Burr-Brown Research Corp 6730 S Tucson Blvd Tucson AZ 85734

PREECE, TIMOTHY FRANCIS, real estate executive, manufacturing executive; b. Waterloo, Iowa, July 13, 1927; s. Wade Owen and Mary Agnes (Molumby) P.; m. Maryanne Elizabeth Dunn, June 27, 1953; children—Catherine Mary, Sarah Montgomery, Thomas Wade. B.S., Georgetown U., 1951; M.B.A., Harvard U., 1953. Asst. mgr. banking Ford Internat., N.Y.C., 1953-55; mgr. internat. office Carborundum Co., N.Y.C., 1955-58; sr. asst. treas. Mobil Internat., N.Y.C., 1953-67; treas. internat. Kaiser Aluminum and Chem., Oakland, Calif., 1967-71, v.p. adminstrn. and systems, 1972-75, v.p. planning and control, 1975-82; chmn., pres. Kaiser Devel. Co., Oakland, 1982—. Vice chmn. no. Calif. NAACP Legal Def. Fund, San Francisco, 1977-85; v.p. Oakland Police Activities League, 1977-85; bd. dirs. Bay Area Sports Hall of Fame, San Francisco, 1981-85, Oakland Conv. Ctr., 1981-83. Served with USN, 1945-47. Roman Catholic. Office: Kaiser Devel Co 300 Lakeside Dr Oakland CA 94643

PREGERSON, HARRY, U.S. circuit judge; b. Los Angeles, Oct. 13, 1923; s. Abraham and Bessie (Rubin) P.; m. Bernardine Seyma Chapkis, June 28, 1947; children: Dean Douglas, Kathryn Ann. B.A., UCLA, 1947; LL.B., U. Calif.-Berkeley, 1950. Bar: Calif. 1951. Assoc. Morris D. Coppersmith, 1952; ptnr. William M. Costley, Van Nuys, 1953-65; judge Los Angeles Municipal Ct., 1965-66, Los Angeles Superior Ct., 1966-67, U.S. Dist. Ct. Central Dist. Calif., 1967-79, U.S. Ct. Appeals for 9th Circuit, 1979—; faculty mem., seminar for newly appointed distr. Judges Fed. Jud. Center, Washington, 1970-72; mem. faculty Am. Soc. Pub. Adminstrn., Inst. for Ct. Mgmt., Denver, 1973—. Served to 1st lt. USMCR, 1944-46. Decorated Purple Heart. Mem. ABA (vice-chmn., com. on fed. rules of criminal procedure and evidence sect. of criminal 1972—), Los Angeles County Bar Assn., San Fernando Valley Bar Assn., State Bar Calif., Marines Corps Res. Officers Assn. (pres. San Fernando Valley 1966—). Office: US Ct Appeals US Courthouse 312 N Spring St Los Angeles CA 90012

PREGLIASCO, JANICE LYNN, architect; b. San Jose, Calif., Jan. 13, 1956; d. Alfred Paul and Ruth Nadine (Perry) P.; m. Scott E. Smith, Oct. 21, 1984. BS in Design, U. Calif., Davis, 1978. Lic. architect, Calif. Designer Seth Curlin Assocs., San Francisco, 1978-81; project designer Yerba Buena Ctr., San Francisco, 1981-82; staff architect EPR, San Francisco, 1982-83; pvt. practice San Francisco, 1983-86; guest lectr. U. Calif., Davis, 1983, guest critic, 1985-86, Calif. Main St. Architect, Sacramento, 1986—. Guest editor Bay Architects Rev., 1986. Mem. AIA, People for Open Space, Nat. Trust Historic Preservation. Democrat. Avocations: writing, folk art, photography, travel. Home: 156 Sycamore Ave Mill Valley CA 94941

PREKEGES, DEMITRIOS PETER (JIM), mathematics consultant; b. Cheyenne, Wyo., June 28, 1930; s. Peter George and Paraskeri (Agglezi) P.; m. Marilyn Gertrude Daugherty, Aug. 11, 1953; children: Peter Allen, David James, Donald Lee, Paul Scott. BA in Edn., Eastern Wash. U., 1951; MA in Math. Teaching, U. Mont., 1963; EdD in Math. Edn., U. B.C., Vancouver, Can., 1974. Cert. tchr., prin., Wash. Tchr. Warden (Wash.) Pub. Schs., 1951-53, Wishram (Wash.) Pub. Schs., 1953-56, CleElum (Wash.) Pub. Schs., 1956-58, Mead (Wash.) Sch. Dist., 1958-62; prof. math. Eastern Wash. U., Cheney, 1963-83, Gonzaga U., Spokane, Wash., 1983-85; cons. Merrill Pub. Co., Columbus, Ohio, 1985—; speaker many math. confs. throughout U.S., 1963—; dir. NSF summer workshops, Wash., 1974, 75, 76. Author: Teaching Elementary School Math; author, presenter (TV series) Teaching Intermediate Algebra, Teaching College Algebra; contbr. numerous articles to profl. jours. Advisor Warden council Boy Scouts Am., 1951-53; pres. Cheney Little League, 1968-71; bd. dirs. City of Cheney Park Bd., 1970-74; mem. Cheney Sch. Bd., 1974-78. Served as cpl. U.S. Army, 1948-49. NSF fellow, Ohio State U., 1962-63. Mem. Nat. Council Tchrs. Math. (conf. and conv. com. 1974-78, regional services sect. 1978-81), Sch. Sci. and Math., Calif. Math. Council, Wash. State Math. Council (v.p. 1971-73), Phi Delta Kappa. Home: 20508 Chaparral Circle Penn Valley CA 95946

PRENDERGAST, THOMAS JOHN, JR., physician, epidemiologist; b. St. Louis, June 17, 1940; s. Thomas John Sr. and Virginia (Hyatt) P.; m. Mary Lou Fairfield, Mar. 7, 1965 (div. Apr. 1981); children: Thomas John III, Allen David, Brian Lee. BA, Washington U., St. Louis, 1962, MD, 1966; MPH, U. N.C., 1972. Lic. physician, Mo., N.C., Calif.; Diplomate Am. Bd. Preventive Medicine. Intern St. Luke's Hosp., St. Louis, 1966-67, resident, 1967; assoc. Duke U. Med. Ctr., Durham, N.C., 1971-72; asst. prof. U. Mo., Columbia, 1972-77; dir. epidemiology and disease control Health Care Agy., Orange County, Calif., 1977—; assoc. clin. prof. U. Calif. Med. Ctr., Irvine, 1977—; cons. Disease Control Com. Calif. Conf. Local Health Officials, Sacramento, 1977—; lectr. in field. Editor: Orange County Physician's Bull., 1977; contbr. articles to profl. jours. Bd. dirs. ARC, Am. Lung Assn.; pres. Am. Cancer Soc., Orange County, 1985—. Served to maj. USAR, 1968-71. Recipient Community Service award Vietnamese Cultural Soc., Orange County, 1980, Disting. Service award, AIDS Response Program, Orange County, 1986, Vol. Service Recognition award, Am. Cancer Soc., 1981. Mem. Am. Pub. Health Assn., Soc. Tchrs. Preventive Medicine, Assn. Practitioners in Infection Control, So. Calif. Pub. Health Assn. (chmn. epidemiology sect. 1979—, Best Section 1982, pres. 1983-84), Sigma Xi, Delta Omega, Pi Tau Epsilon Pi. Avocations: jogging, tennis, golf. Home: 4902 Rochelle Ave Irvine CA 92714 Office: Orange County Health Care Agy 511 N Sycamore Box 355 Santa Ana CA 92702

PRENTISS, CHARLES GARY, museum director; b. Astoria, Oreg., June 29, 1942; s. Donald Crane and Marian Caroline (Gary) P.; m. Dianne Ritner, June 18, 1966 (div. 1980); children: Carlos, Katherine; m. Nikki Silva, July 3, 1982; 1 child, Molly. BS in Zoology, U. Calif., 1966. Curator, dir. Santa Cruz (Calif.) City Mus., 1969—. Editor: Fossils of Santa Cruz County, 1977. Served with USAR, 1963-69. Recipient Civic Improvement award SCOPE, 1982, Craftsman Exhibit award Santa Cruz Hist. Soc., 1983. Mem. Am. Assn. Mus. (catalogue editor 1974). Home: 89 D Spring Valley Rd Watsonville CA 95076 Office: Santa Cruz City Mus 1305 E Cliff Dr Santa Cruz CA 94062

PRESANT, CARY ARNET, oncologist, hematologist; b. Buffalo, Dec. 16, 1942; s. Allen and Reeta (Coplon) P.; m. Sheila Lassman, June 11, 1966; children: Seth, Sean, Jaron, Jaclyn. Student, U. Buffalo, 1960-62; MD, SUNY, Buffalo, 1966. Diplomate Am. Bd. Internal Medicine. Intern. Columbia Presby. Med. ctr., N.Y.C.; resident Barnes Hosp., St. Louis; staff assoc. Nat. Cancer Inst., Bethesda, Md., 1967-69; asst. prof. medicine Wash. U., St. Louis, 1973-79; dir. med. oncology City of Hope, Durate, Calif., 1979-82; prof. medicine U. So. Calif., Los Angeles, 1982—; staff physician Wilshire Oncology Med. Group, Los Angeles, 1982—; chmn. Melanoma Sarcoma com. Southeastern Cancer Study Group, Birmingham, Ala., 1974-82; sci. adv. bd. Vestar Research Co., Pasadena, Calif., 1982—; Sklarow Meml. lectr. Maimonedes Soc., 1981. Contbr. numerous articles to sci. jours. Fellow ACP; mem. Am. Cancer Soc. (bd. dirs.), Am. Soc. Clin. Oncology (chmn. tech. assessment subcom.), Am. Soc. Hematology, Am. Assn. Cancer Research, Internat. Soc. Hematology, Los Angeles Oncologic Inst. (bd. dirs.), Phi Beta Kappa, Alpha Omega Alpha. Jewish. Office: Wilshire Oncology Med Group 935 S Sunset Ave West Covina CA 91790

PRESCOTT, GAIL HELENE, librarian; b. Lawrence, Kans., Sept. 27, 1942; d. William C. and Phyllis M. (Burgert) Kupfer; m. G. Garrett Prescott, April 1, 1967. BA in Social Sci., San Jose State U., 1968, MLS, 1973. Librarian Hewlett Packard Co., Boise, Idaho, 1980—. Mem. Treasure Valley Library Assn. (pres. 1983-84), Idaho Library Assn. Avocations: running, areobics, cooking, knitting. Home: 1835 E Paradise Ln Meridian ID 83642 Office: Hewlett Packard Co 11413 Chinden Blvd M Stop 0354 Boise ID 83707

PRESCOTT, GERALD H(EBER), hospital program administrator; b. Wendell, Idaho, June 16, 1937; s. Heber L. and Thelma (Williams) P.; children: Jeff, Jerilyn, Jennifer. BS, Coll. Idaho, 1959; postgrad., Wash. State U., 1960; DMD, Washington U., St. Louis, 1964; MS, Ind. U., 1966. Diplomate Am. Bd. Med. Genetics. Asst. prof. med. genetics U. Oreg. Sch. Medicine, Portland, 1968-74, assoc. prof., 1974-81, prof., 1981; dir. Prenatal Diagnosis Clinic Emanuel Hosp., Portland, 1981—; cons. NIH, Bethesda, Md., 1979-86, March of Dimes, Portland, States of Idaho, Wash. Named Swanman Lectr., 1978, 82, 84, 86, 87. Fellow Am. Acad. Pathology; mem. AAAS, Am. Soc. Human Genetics, Oreg. Soc. Ob-gyn, Am. Soc. Craniofacial Genetics (pres. 1979). Avocations: tennis, backpacking. Home: 48 Eagle Crest Dr #1A Lake Oswego OR 97034 Office: Emanuel Hosp 2801 N Gantenbein Portland OR 97227

PRESCOTT, LAWRENCE MALCOLM, medical and health writer; b. Boston, July 31, 1934; s. Benjamin and Lillian (Stein) P.; B.A., Harvard U., 1957; M.Sc., George Washington U., 1959, Ph.D., 1966; m. Ellen Gay Kober, Feb. 19, 1961 (dec. Sept. 1981); children—Jennifer Maya, Adam Barrett; m. 2d, Sharon Lynn Kirshen, May 16, 1982; children—Gary Leon Kirshen, Marc Paul Kirshen. Nat. Acad. Scis. postdoctoral fellow U.S. Army Research, Ft. Detrick, Md., 1965-66; microbiologist/scientist WHO, India, 1967-70, Indonesia, 1970-72, Thailand, 1972-78; cons. health to internat. orgns., San Diego, 1978—; author mans. and contbr. articles in diarrheal diseases and lab. scis. to profl. jours., 1965-81; contbr. numerous articles, stories, poems to mags., newspapers, including Living in Thailand, Jack and Jill, Strawberry, Bangkok Times, Sprint, 1977-81; mng. editor Caduceus, 1981-82; pub., editor Teenage Scene, 1982-83; pres. Prescott Pub. Co., 1982-83; med. writer Anesthesiology News, Cardio, Jour. AMA, Med. Post, Health, Health and Care, Genetic Engring. News, Diagnostic Imaging, Med. Tribune, others, 1982—; author: Curry Every Sunday, 1984. Home and Office: 11307 Florindo Rd San Diego CA 92127

PRESKILL, JOHN PHILLIP, physics educator; b. Highland Park, Ill., Jan. 19, 1953; m. Roberta M. Gross, June 22, 1975; 1 child, Carina Lou. AB in Physics, Princeton U., 1975; AM in Physics, Harvard U., 1976, PhD in Physics, 1980. Jr. fellow Harvard Soc. Fellows, 1980-81; asst. prof. physics Harvard U., Cambridge, Mass., 1981-82, assoc. prof., 1982-83; assoc. prof. theoretical physics Calif. Inst. Tech., Pasadena, 1983—. Recipient Presdl. Young Investigator award NSF, 1984—; fellow NSF, 1975-78, Alfred P. Sloan Found., 1982—. Home: 2110 Canyon Rd Arcadia CA 91006 Office: Calif Inst of Tech Div Physics Math & Astronomy Pasadena CA 91125

PRESLEY, ROBERT BUEL, state senator; b. Tahlequah, Okla., Dec. 4, 1924; s. Doyle and Annie (Townsend) P.; grad. FBI Nat. Acad., Washington, 1962; student Riverside City Coll., 1960; A.A., UCLA, m. Ahni Ratliff, Aug. 20, 1944; children—Donna Thurber, Marilyn Raphael, Robert Buel. Various positions Riverside County Sheriff's Dept. (Calif.), 1950-62, undersheriff, 1962-74; mem. Calif. Senate, 36th Dist., 1974—; lectr. ethics. Served with U.S. Army, 1943-46. Decorated Bronze Star. Mem. FBI Nat. Acad. Assn. (pres. Calif. chpt. 1974). Baptist. Clubs: Lions, Elks, Am. Legion, V.F.W., Moose, Riverside County Democratic Century (pres. 1972-73). Home: 5508 Grassy Trail Dr Riverside CA 92504 Office: State Capitol Room 4048 Sacramento CA 95814

PRESS, PHILIP SAMSON, TV executive; b. Bklyn., July 10, 1944; s. Manny and Florence (Denkwood) P.; m. Susan Ann Weiner, Nov 9, 1969 (div. July 1986). Student, Boston U.; BS in Speech, Emerson Coll. Account exec. CBS Nat. Sales, N.Y.C., 1973-76; gen. sales mgr. WCAU-TV CBS Inc., N.Y.C., 1976-78; dir. sales WCAU-TV CBS Inc., Phila., 1978-82, WCBS-TV CBS Inc., N.Y.C., 1982-85; v.p., gen. mgr. Sta. KTVU-TV San Francisco/Oakland, 1985—; exec. producer, dir. WGAN-TV, Portland, Maine, 1968-69; producer Nat. Edn. TV, Portland, 1969; head editorial bd. KTVU-TV, Oakland, Calif., 1985-86. Co-producer: Christmas is Just Another Day, 1964; producer: The Willy Pen Achievements, 1978. Mem. Oakland Com. Bus. Caucus, 1985-86, Oakland Symposium Com., 1985-86; tchr. Eagle scouts Boy Scouts Am., Salinas, Monterey, Calif., 1969-70. Recipient Addy award Am. Advt. Fed., 1968. Mem. STAR, Oakland C. of C., Alpha Pi Theta (pres. 1964-65). Jewish. Clubs: Havre De Grace Yacht (Md.); TV Radio Advt. (Phila.). Avocations: sailing, photography, music. Home: 54 Wildwood Gardens Piedmont CA 94623 Office: KTVU TV 2 Jack London Sq Oakland/San Francisco CA 94623

PRESSLEY, JAMES RAY, electrical engineer; b. Ft. Worth, July 14, 1946; s. Loy Dale and Dorothy Helen (Foust) P.; m. Barbara Kay McMillin, Oct. 9, 1968; children—James Foust Pressley, Kreg Milam Pressley; m. Susan Marie Straw, Apr. 27, 1985; children: Shaye Eugene Straw, Rebecca Alycen Straw, Rachel Leilani Straw. B.S.E.E., U. Tex., Arlington, 1970. Registered profl. engr., Alaska, Hawaii, Oreg., Wash. Designer/draftsman Romine & Slaughter, Ft. Worth, 1967-71; engr. Crews MacInnes & Hoffman, Anchorage, 1971-73, O'Kelly & Schoenlank, Anchorage, 1973-75, Theodore G. Creedon, Anchorage, 1975-77; v.p. Fryer, Pressley Elliott, Anchorage, 1977-80, Fryer/Pressley Engring., 1980—; mem. elec. constrn. and maintenance industry evaluation panel, 1982-83, 83-84. Mem. Illuminating Engring. Soc., Internat. Assn. Elec. Inspectors, Alaska Profl. Design Council. Office: 560 E 34th St Suite 300 Anchorage AK 99503

PRESTON, FREDERICK WILLARD, surgeon; b. Chgo., June 27, 1912; s. Frederick Augustus and Margaret (Atwater) P.; m. Gertrude Eldred Bradford, June 23, 1942 (div. 1961); children: Frederick Willard Jr., David E., William B. Preston; m. Barbara Gay Hess, July 30, 1961. B.A., Yale U., 1935; M.D., Northwestern U., 1940, M.S., 1942; M.S., U. Minn., 1947. Intern Presbyn. Hosp., Chgo., 1940-41; fellow surgery Mayo Clinic, Rochester, Minn., 1941-42, 46-48; practice surgery Chgo., 1950-75; instr. surgery Northwestern U. Med. Sch., 1950-51, assoc. surgery, 1951-53, asst. prof., 1953-58, assoc. prof., 1958-60, prof. surgery, 1960-75; assoc. attending surgeon Northwestern Meml. Hosp., 1950-75; attending surgeon Skokie Valley Community Hosp., 1964-75, Henrotin Hosp., 1950-75; chief surg. service VA Research Hosp., Chgo., 1953-68; chmn. dept. Surgery Santa Barbara Gen. Hosp., 1975-78; dir. surg. edn. Santa Barbara Cottage Hosp., 1975-83. Author, editor: Basic Surgical Physiology; Loose-Leaf Practice of Surgery, Manual of Ambulatory Surgery; contbr. 128 articles to profl. jours. Bd. dirs. Schweppe Found., Love Med. Research; gov. mem., mem. planning com. Shedd Aquarium, 1968-75. Served to maj. M.C., AUS, 1942-46. Fellow ACS (chpt. pres. 1965-66); mem. AMA, Chgo. Surg. Soc. (sec. 1961-64, pres. 1968-69), Chgo. Acad. Scis. (sec. 1963-67), Am. Assn. Cancer Research (pres. Chgo. sec. 1963-64), Am. Geriatrics Soc., Am. Fedn. Clin. Research, AAAS, Am. Surg. Assn., Central Surg. Assn., Western Surg. Assn., Pacific Coast Surg. Assn., Pan Pacific Surg. Assn., Société Internationale de Chirurgie, Soc. Surgery Alimentary Tract. Clubs: Santa Barbara, La Cumbre Golf and Country; Chgo. Literary, University (Chgo.). Home: 755 Via Airosa Santa Barbara CA 93110 Office: Santa Barbara Cottage Hosp Pueblo and Bath Sts Santa Barbara CA 93102

PRESTON, JOHN DAVID, clinical psychologist; b. Midland, Tex., July 13, 1950; s. Conrad Smith and Betty Jeanne (Stark) P.; m. Bonnie Lynn Johnson, Aug. 19, 1978; children—Matthew, David. B.A., Southwestern U., Georgetown, Tex., 1972; M.S., Trinity U., San Antonio, 1973; PsychologyD., Baylor U., 1979. Lic. psychologist, Calif.; cert. Am. Bd. Profl. Neuropsychology. Program dir. outpatient clinic Nueces County Mental Health Ctr., Corpus Christi, 1979-80, dir. adult mental health services, 1980-81; clin. psychologist, psychiatry dept. Permanente Med. Group, Sacramento, 1981—, chief psychologist, 1986—; pvt. practice neuropsychology, 1981—; faculty Profl. Sch. Psychology, San Francisco, 1981—. Author: (profl. cassette tape series) Differential Diagnosis of Psychoses, 1979, How to Conduct a Neuropsychological Examination, 1981, Neuropsychological Screening Examination, 1982; Medication Consult: Psychopharmacology, 1983, others, (book) Quick Reference to Exner's Rorschach, Comprehensive System; contbr. articles to profl. jours. Mem. Am. Psychol. Assn. Office: 6600 Bruceville Rd Permanente Med Group Sacramento CA 95823

PRETTO, FRANKLIN DAVID, priest; b. Colon, Panama, Jan. 27, 1946; came to U.S., 1966; s. David Elias Pretto and Hilda Louise (Ferro) De Pretto. BA, St. Thomas Theol., Denver, 1969; MDiv, St. Patrick Theol., Menlo Park, Calif., 1971. Ordained priest Roman Catholic Ch., 1972. Assoc. dir. Aquinas Newman Ctr., Albuquerque, 1970-75; dir. St. Paul Newman Ctr., Las Vegas, Nev., 1975-77; assoc. pastor Our Lady of Guadalupe Ch., Santa Fe, 1980-82; pastor San Isidro Ch., Santa Fe, 1982—. Entertainer various restaurants; record album Tamboritos Panamenos, 1981. Bd. mem. 375th Anniversary of Santa Fe, 1986; mem. Congressman Bill Richardson's Com. Hispanic Artists, Santa Fe, 1986. Named Young Citizen of Yr., Santa Fe C. of C., 1981; Frank Pretto Day proclaimed by City of Santa Fe, 1981. Avocations: swimming, acting, movie poster collecting, travel. Office: San Isidro Cath Ch Rt 6 Box 11 Santa Fe NM 87501

PREUSS, PAUL FREDERICK, writer; b. Albany, Ga., Mar. 7, 1942; s. Paul Theodore and Mona Elizabeth (McDonald) P.; m. Marsha Pettit, Mar. 10, 1963 (div. Nov. 1968); 1 child, Mona Helen; m. Karen Reiser, Mar. 3, 1973. BA, Yale U., 1966. Writer mktg. projects BBDO Advt., N.Y.C., 1966-67; floor dir. King TV, Seattle, 1967-68; creative dir. King Screen Prodns., Seattle, 1968-72; staff cons., author, producer Biol. Scis. Curriculum Study, Boulder, Colo., 1972-74, San Francisco, 1974—. Author: Broken Symmetries, 1983, Human Error, 1985; contbr. articles to nat. mags., revs. to newspapers. Recipient Gold Medal Spl. award N.Y. Film & TV Festival, 1972. Mem. AAAS, Nat. Book Critics Circle, No. Calif. Sci. Writers Assn. (coordinator memberships), Bay Area Book Reviewers Assn. Democrat. Lutheran. Avocations: hiking, camping. Home and Office: PO Box 590773 San Francisco CA 94159

PREVIN, ANDRE, composer, conductor; b. Berlin, Germany, Apr. 6, 1929; came to U.S., 1938, naturalized, 1943; s. Jack and Charlotte (Epstein) P.; m. Mia Farrow, Sept. 10, 1970 (div. 1979); children: Matthew and Sascha (twins), Fletcher, Lark, Daisy, Soon-Yi.; m. Heather Hales, Jan. 1982; 1 son, Lukas. Student, Berlin Conservatory, Paris Conservatory; privately with, Pierre Monteux, Mario Castelnuovo-Tedesco. mem. faculty Guildhall Sch., London, Royal Acad. Music., Berkshire Music Ctr. Rec. artist classical music, for RCA, EMI, Phillips, Telarc, 1946—; composer chamber music, Cello Concerto, Guitar Concerto, piano music, serenades for violin, brass quintet, song cycle on poems by Philip Larkin Every Good Boy Deserves Favour, Principals, Reflections, Piano Concerto, 2d Cello Concerto, Triplet for Brass Ensemble, film scores, 1950-59; condr.-in-chief Houston Symphony, 1967-69; prin. condr. London Symphony Orch., 1968-79, Royal Philharmonic Orch., Eng., 1985—; guest condr. maj. symphon orchs. and festivals in U.S. and Europe including: Covent Garden Opera, festivals in Salzburg, Edinburgh, Flanders, Vienna, Osaka, Prague, Berlin, Bergen; music director South Bank Music Festival, London, 1972-74, Pitts. Symphony, 1976-84, Los Angeles Philharmonic, 1984—; author: Music Face to Face, 1971, Orchestra, 1979. Served with AUS, 1950-51. awards Nat. Gramophone Soc. Mem. Acad. Motion Picture Arts and Scis., Dramatists Guild, Brit. Composers Guild, Nat. Composers and Condrs. League. Club: Garrick. Office: care Los Angeles Philharmonic 135 North Grand Los Angeles CA 90012 also: London Symphony Orch,, 1 Mortage St,, London WC1 England *

PREZANT, BRADLEY DENNIS, industrial hygienist; b. N.Y.C., Dec. 29, 1953; s. Leo and Adele (Eisenstein) P. BA cum laude, Brandeis U., 1975; MPH, U. Wash., 1982. Diplomate Am. Bd. Indsl. Hygiene; cert. secondary sch. tchr., Mass. Indsl. hygienist Todd Shipyards, Seattle, 1981-82; sr. indsl. hygienits U. Wash. Sch. Pub. Health and Community Medicine, Seattle, 1982-87; prin. Prezant & Assocs., Seattle, 1983—. Nat. Inst. Occupational Safety and Health fellow, 1979-82. Mem. Human Factors Soc., Am. Soc. Heating, Refrigeration and Air Conditioning Engrs., Am. Conf. Govtl. Indsl. Hygienists. Jewish. Avocations: sea kayaking, bird watching. Home: 421 N 40 Seattle WA 98103

PRICE, ARTHUR R., Pres. Husky Oil Ltd., Calgary, Alta. Office: Husky Oil Ltd, 707 8th Ave SW, Calgary, AB Canada T2P 1H5 *

PRICE, CHRISTOPHER ELDREGE, aerospace engineer; b. Ottumwa, Iowa, Sept. 18, 1944; s. Warren Eldrege and Muriel Maxine (Jones) P.; m. Francis Paul, Nov. 15, 1970 (div. Mar. 1974); m. Gail Joyce Goodman, Aug. 4, 1984; 1 child, Gregory. BSEE, U. Neb., 1967; MS in Computer Sci., West Coast U., 1977. Engr., scientist McDonnell Douglas, Long Beach, Calif., 1967-73; tech. staff Rockwell Internat., Downey, Calif., 1973—; bd. dirs. Bd. Realtors, Sacramento, 1981—. Mem. Mensa. Avocations: real estate, auto racing, sports cars. Home: 1310 Wyeth Circle Orange CA 92667 Office: Rockwell Internat 12214 Lakewood Blvd Downey CA 90241

PRICE, EARL J., infosystems specialist; b. Hailey, Idaho, Sept. 8, 1953; s. David Lorin Price and Sarah Louise (Anderson) Davenport; m. Kathleen B. Houtchens, Aug. 19, 1977; children: Julia, Jason, Brian, Stacy. AA, Ricks Coll., 1975; BS cum laude, Brigham Young U., 1978; MBA, U. Oreg., 1979. Seismologist U.S. Geol. Survey, Idaho Falls, Idaho, 1977; fin. analyst Burroughs Corp., West Lake Village, Calif., 1979-80; mgr. infosystems, controller Artco Corp., Rexburg, Idaho, 1979—. Mem. Data Processing Mgmt. Assn., Am. Prodn. and Inventory Control Soc. Republican. Mormon. Avocations: skiing, hiking, photography. Home: 2938 S 2810 W Rexburg ID 83440 Office: 1 Stationary Pl Rexburg ID 83441

PRICE, EDWARD DEAN, U.S. District Court judge; b. Sanger, Calif., Feb. 12, 1919; s. Earl Trousdale and Daisy Shaw (Biggs) P.; m. Katherine S. Merritt, July 18, 1943; children—Katherine Price O'Brien, Edward M., Jane E. B.A., U. Calif., Berkeley, 1947, LL.B., 1949. Bar: Calif. 1949. Assoc. Cleary & Zeff, Modesto, Calif., 1949-51; assoc. Zeff & Halley, Modesto, Calif., 1951-54; ptnr. Zeff, Halley & Price, Modesto, Calif., 1954-63, Zeff & Price, Modesto, Calif., 1963-65, Price & Martin, Modesto, Calif., 1965-69, Price, Martin & Crabtree, Modesto, Calif., 1969-79; judge U.S. Dist. Ct., Fresno, Calif., 1980—; mem. adv. bd. governing com. Continuing Edn. of Bar, San Francisco, 1963-71, governing bd. Calif. State Bar, 1973-76; v.p. Jud. Council, Calif., 1978-79. Contbr. articles to profl. jours. Served with U.S. Army, 1943-46. Mem. ABA, Am. Coll. Trial Lawyers, Am. Bd. Trial Advocates. Democrat. Methodist. Home: 1012 Wellesley Modesto CA 95350 Office: US Dist Ct 1130 O St Fresno CA 93721

PRICE, FREDERICK KENNETH CERCIE, minister; b. Santa Monica, Calif., Jan. 3, 1932; s. Fred Cercie and Winifred Bernice (Ammons) P.; m. Betty Ruth Scott, Mar. 29, 1953; children: Angela Marie Price Evans, Cheryl Ann Price Crabbe, Stephanie Pauline, Frederick Kenneth. Diploma (hon.), Rhema Bible Tng. Ctr., Tulsa, 1976; DD (hon.), Oral Roberts U., 1982. Ordained to ministry Bapt. Ch., 1955, African Meth. Episcopal Ch., 1957, Kenneth Hagin Ministries, 1975. Asst. pastor Mt. Sinai Bapt. Ch., Los Angeles, 1955-57; pastor African Meth. Episcopal Ch., Val Verde, Calif., 1957-59; pastor, Christian Missionary Alliance W. Washington Community Ch., Los Angeles, 1965-73; pastor Crenshaw Christian Ctr., Los Angeles, 1973—; founding mem. bd. trustees Internat. Conv. Faith Ministers, Inc., Tulsa, 1979—. Author numerous books including How Faith Works, 1976, Explanation to Receiving Your Healing by the Laying on of Hands, 1980, High Finance, God's Financial Plan, Tithes and Offerings, 1984. Democrat. Avocation: scuba diving. Office: Crenshaw Christian Ctr Attention Angela Evans Mailing PO Box 90000 Los Angeles CA 90009

PRICE, GUY ROBERT, lawyer; b. Pocatello, Idaho, Oct. 13, 1954; s. Horace L. and Clarice (Thomas) P.; m. Julie Ann Henry, Sept. 1, 1978; children: Emily, Casey, Morgan, Abigail. BS magna cum laude, Brigham Young U., 1980; JD, U. Utah, 1983. Bar: Idaho 1983, U.S. Dist. Ct. Idaho 1983, U.S. Ct. Appeals (9th cir.) 1983. Ptnr. Green, Service, Gasser & Kerl, Pocatello, 1983—. William Leary scholar U. Utah Law Sch., 1983-85. Mem. ABA (tort and ins. practice sect., vice chmn. alternate dispute resolution com.), Am. Trial Lawyers Assn., Idaho Trial Lawyers Assn. Republican. Mormon. Office: Green Service Gasser & Kerl PO Box 4883 Suite C-1 Center Plaza Pocatello ID 83205

PRICE, JACK STANLEY, school district administrator, consultant; b. Hamilton, Ont., Can., Feb. 28, 1931; came to U.S., 1935; s. Jasper and Edythe Marie (McCourt) P.; m. Barbara Ann Mangum, Jan. 8, 1981; children by previous marriage—Michael, Robert; adopted children—Sally Price, Susan Strehlow, Sherry, Stephanie Hickethier. B.A., Eastern Mich. U., Ypsilanti, 1952; M.Ed., Wayne State U., 1957; postgrad. Yale U., 1959-60; Ed.D., Wayne State U., 1965. Tchr. math., sci. Detroit Pub. Schs., 1953-65; mathematics and sci. cons. San Diego County Office Edn., 1965-68, dir. curriculum, 1968-71; asst. supt. programs San Diego City Schs., 1971-76; supt. schs. Vista Unified Sch. Dist., Calif., 1976-83, Palos Verdes Peninsula Sch. Dist., Palos Verdes Estates, Calif., 1983—. Author 6 textbooks in field of sci., math. Editor: Changing School Mathematics, 1982. Named Disting. Alumnus, Wayne State U. Coll. Edn., 1976. Fellow AAAS; mem. Nat. Council Tchrs. Math. (bd. dirs. 1972-74, mat., sci. edn. bd.), Am. Assn. Sch. Adminstrs. Democrat. Lodge: Rotary. Home: 805 Gatos Pl Palos Verdes Estates CA 90274 Office: Palos Verdes Peninsula Unifed Sch Dist 3801 Via La Selva Palos Verdes Estates CA 90274

PRICE, JAMES NEWTON, engineer; b. Dinuba, Calif., Nov. 2, 1947; s. W.N. and Jean (Asquith) P.; m. Joan C. Sieber, Feb. 18, 1978. BSEE, U. Calif., Santa Barbara, 1969, MSEE, 1971. Electronics engr. Naval Ocean Systems Ctr., San Diego, 1971-82, engring. supr. and head, system devel. br., 1982—. Editor jour.; contbr. articles to prof. jours. Recipient Superior Performance award Naval Ocean Systems Ctr., 1978, Performance Exceeding Expectations awards Naval Ocean Systems Ctr., 1981-86. Mem. Soc. for Info. Display (mem. various coms., bd. dirs., editor jour., symposium chmn. 1985), Packards Internat. (pres. San Diego chpt. 1976-78), Mission Trail Network (pres. Calif. chpt. 1973-75), Classic Chevys of San Diego (editor). Democrat. Avocations: antique autos, ghost towns, photography, ham radio, jukeboxes. Office: Naval Ocean Systems Ctr Code 713 San Diego CA 92152

PRICE, JAY BERRY, city ofcl.; b. Los Angeles, Mar. 9, 1915; s. John Berry and Nancy Alice (Gipson) P.; A.A., Compton Coll., 1957; m. Gertrude Margaret Lydon, Apr. 19, 1941; children—William Berry, John Jay, Nancy Alice. Insp., U.S. Internal Revenue Service, Los Angeles, 1939-76. Mayor, councilman, Bell, Calif., 1958—; dist. dir. So. Calif. Rapid Transit Dist., Los Angeles, 1971—. Dir. Los Angeles County Sanitation Dists. 1 and 2; mem. revenue and taxation com. Los Angeles County div., also mem. state revenue and taxation com. League Calif. Cities; trustee, pres. S.E. Mosquito-Abatement Dist., South Gate; alt. trustee rep. So. Calif. to trustee corporate bd. Calif. Mosquito Control Assn.; mem. adv. council 4th West County region Los Angeles County Library; City of Bell rep. of gen. assembly So. Calif. Assn. Govts. Mem. Christian Ch. (deacon, trustee, treas.). Home: 6900 Crafton Ave Bell CA 90201 Office: 6330 Pine Ave Bell CA 90201

PRICE, JEANNINE ALLEENICA, clinical psychologist; b. Cleve., Oct. 29, 1949; d. Q. Q. and Lisa Denise (Wilson) Ewing; m. T. R. Price, Sept. 2, 1976. B.S., Western Res. U., 1969; M.S., Vanderbilt U., 1974. Cert. alcoholism counselor, Calif. Health Service coordinator Am. Profile, Nashville, 1970-72; exec. dir. Awareness Concept, San Jose, Calif., 1977-80; mgr. employee assistance program Nat. Semiconductor, Santa Clara, Calif., 1980-81; mgmt. cons. employee assistant programs. Mem. Gov.'s Adv. Council Child Devel. Programs. Mem. Am. Bus. Women's Assn., Nat. Assn. Female Execs., AAUW, Coalition Labor Women, Calif. Assn. Alcohol counselors, Almaca. Author: Smile a Little, Cry a Lot; Gifts of Love; Reflection in the Mirror. Office: 728 N 1st St San Jose CA 95112

PRICE, JOE, artist, educator; b. Ferriday, La., Feb. 6, 1935; s. Edward Neill and Margaret (Hester) P. B.S., Northwestern U., 1957; postgrad. Art Ctr. Coll., Los Angeles, 1967-68; M.A., Stanford U., 1970. Free-lance actor, artist, N.Y.C., 1957-60; free-lance illustrator, actor, Los Angeles, 1960-68; free-lance comml. artist, San Carlos, Calif., 1968-69; package designer Container Corp. Am., Santa Clara, Calif., 1969; prof. studio art Coll. San Mateo, Calif., 1970—. One man shows include Richard Sumner Gallery, Palo Alto, Calif., 1975, San Mateo County Cultural Ctr., 1976, 82, Tahir Galleries, New Orleans, 1977, 82, Kerwin Galleries, Burlingame, Calif., 1977, Edits. Gallery, Melbourne, Australia, 1977, Ankrum Gallery, Los Angeles, 1978, 84, Edits. Ltd. West Gallery, San Francisco, 1981, Miriam Perlman Gallery, Chgo., 1982, San Mateo County Arts Council Gallery, 1982, Candy Stick Gallery, Ferndale, Calif., 1984, Assoc. Am. Artists, N.Y.C. and Phila., 1984, Gallery 30, San Mateo, 1984, Triton Mus. Art, Santa Clara, Calif., 1986, Huntsville (Ala.) Mus. Art, 1987; exhibited in groups shows at Berkeley Art Ctr., Calif., 1976, Burlingame Civic Art Gallery, 1976, Syntex Gallery, Palo Alto, Calif., 1977, Gump's Gallery, San Francisco, 1976, 77, Nat. Gallery of Australia, 1978, Sonoma County Gallery, 1979, Gov. Dummer Acad. Art, Byfield, Mass., 1979, Miss. Mus. Art, 1982, C.A.A. Galleries, Chautauqua, N.Y., 1982, Huntsville Mus. Art, 1983, Tahir Gallery, New Orleans, 1983, Hunterdon Art Ctr., N.J., 1984; represented in permanent collections San Francisco Mus. Modern Art, Achenbach Found. Graphic Arts, San Francisco, Phila. Mus. Art, New Orleans Mus. Art, Portland Mus. Art, Maine, The Library of Congress, Washington. Huntsville Mus. Art, Midwest Mus. Am. Art, Ind., Cracow Nat. Mus., Poland, Cabo Frio Mus., Brazil. Recipient Kempshall Clark award Peoria Art Guild, 1981; Paul Lindsay Sample Meml. award 25th Chautauqua Nat. Exhbn. of Am. Art, 1982. Mem. Am. Color Print Soc., Audubon Artists (assoc. mem., Louis Lozowick Meml. award 1978), Boston Printmakers (Ture Bengtz Meml. award 1987), Calif. Soc. Printmakers (mem. council 1979-81), Los Angeles Printmaking Soc., Phila. Print Club (Lessing J. Rosenwald prize 1979), Arts Council of San Mateo County. Democrat. Home: 2031 Belle Monti Belmont CA 94002 Office: Coll San Mateo 1700 W Hillside Blvd San Mateo CA 94402

PRICE, JOHN DOUGLAS, social worker; b. Waynesboro, Pa., Sept. 5, 1952; s. John Clayton Price and Lois Olive (Pensinger) Fetters; m. Lois Gail Myslinski, June 9, 1973 (div. June 1978); children: Mark Clayton, Sean David; m. Cynthia Ann Ruppel, Sept. 1, 1986. BA, U. Pa., 1974; MSW, Temple U., 1976. Dir. br. office Luth. Family and Social Service of Nebr., Ogallala, 1976-78; dir. area agy. on aging program Northeastern Colo. Assn. of Local Govts., Ft. Morgan, 1978-86, exec. dir., 1981-86; community devel. grants officer Adams County, Brighton, Colo., 1986—; clin. social worker Northeast Home Health Care, Ft. Morgan, 1984-86. Adv. council mem. Morgan Community Coll., Ft. Morgan, 1986—; br. pres. Aid Assn. for Luths., Ft. Morgan, 1986—. Recipient Recognition award Gov.'s Conf. on Aging, 1980; named Outstanding Young Man of Am. U.S. Jaycees, 1982. Mem. Nat. Assn. Social Workers (cert., bd. dirs. 1981-83), Colo. Gerontol. Soc., Nat. Assn. Area Agys. on Aging (state pres. 1980-81), Ft. Morgan C. of C. Republican. Lodge: Rotary. Avocations: swimming, golf, tennis. Home: 309 N 15th Ave Brighton CO 80601 Office: Adams County Office Community Outreach and Technical Assistance 450 S 4th Ave Brighton CO 80601

PRICE, JUDITH HOLM, educational psychologist; b. Milw., Nov. 6, 1937; d. Paul James and Dorothy Ruth (Munton) Holm; m. Thomas Munro Price, Aug. 8, 1959; children: Scott Michael, Andrea Lynn. BA, Carroll Coll., 1959; MA, U. Iowa, 1973; PhD, U. Wyo., 1980. Cert. sch. psychologist, Wyo. Tchr. Waukesha (Wis.) Pub. Schs., 1959, Madison (Wis.) Pub. Schs., 1959-63; presch. assessment specialist Grant Wood Area Edn. Agy. 10, Cedar Rapids, Iowa, 1976-78; Ednl. Resource Ctr. facilitator Albany County Sch. Dist. 1, Laramie, Wyo., 1980—; substitute tchr. Melbourne (Australia) Schs., 1978; temporary prof. U. Wyo., Laramie, 1981, 84; mem. computer conf. com. Wyo. Dept. Edn., Casper, 1984-85; speaker Wyo. Fedn. CEC, Riverton, 1986; conf. mem. Council for Exceptional Children Software Conf., Washington, 1986. Mem. Nat. Assn. Sch. Psychologists (alt. del. 1983), Wyo. Sch. Psychoednl. Assn. (membership chmn. 1986), Council for Exceptional Children, Phi Kappa Phi, Phi Delta Kappa. Avocations: computers, skiing, camping, traveling. Office: Albany County ERC 309 S 9th Laramie WY 82070

PRICE, MAUREEN GAIL, research scientist; b. Rochester, N.Y., June 26, 1951; d. James Robert and Dorothy Elizabeth (Wentworth) P. BA, Goucher Coll., Towson, Md., 1973; PhD, U. Pa., 1980. Reseach fellow Calif. Inst. Tech., Pasadena, 1980-82; asst. research physiologist UCLA, 1982-85; research assoc. Scripps Clinic, La Jolla, Calif., 1985—; v.p. Soc. Fellows, La Jolla, 1985—; reviewer NSF, 1984—, In Vitro (jour.), 1984-85, Am. Heart Assn., 1985—. Contbr. articles to profl. jours. Vol. Am. Heart Assn., San Diego, 1986. Recipient Nat. Research Service award NIH, 1980-83, New Investigator award NIH, 1985—, Sr. Investigator award Am. Heart Assn., 1983-84, Laubisch award UCLA Med. Sch., 1984-85. Mem. AAAS, AAUW, Am. Assn. Anatomists, Am. Soc. Cell Biology, Sigma Xi. Democrat. Avocations: reading, music, walking. Office: Scripps Clinic and Research 10666 N Torrey Pines Rd La Jolla CA 92037

PRICE, PAUL ARTHUR, lawyer; b. Williston, N.D., Sept. 18, 1951; s. Winston E. and Jeanette (Trumbo) P.; m. Kathryn Ann Kruzick, Dec. 22, 1973; 1 child, Andrew. BS, U. N.D., 1974; JD, Western State U., 1978. Bar: Calif. 1983, Utah 1984. Instr. Internat. U., London, 1979-81; trust counsel 1st Security Bank Utah, Salt Lake City, 1981-83; gen. counsel MountainWest Savs., Salt Lake City, 1983—. Mem. Calif. Bar Assn., Utah Bar Assn., ABA (sect. corp., banking and bus., sect. taxation, subcom. savings insts.).

PRICE, PAUL BUFORD, physicist, educator; b. Memphis, Nov. 8, 1932; s. Paul Buford and Eva (Dupuy) P.; m. JoAnn Margaret Baum, June 28, 1958; children—Paul Buford III, Heather Alynn, Pamela Margaret, Alison Gaynor. B.S. summa cum laude, Davidson Coll., 1954, D.Sc., 1973; M.S., U. Va., 1956, Ph.D., 1958. Fulbright scholar U. (Eng.) Bristol, 1958-59; NSF postdoctoral fellow Cambridge (Eng.) U., 1959-60; physicist Gen. Elec. Research & Devel. Center, Schenectady, 1960-69; vis. prof. Tata Inst. Fundamental Research, Bombay, India, 1965-66; adj. prof. physics Rensselaer Poly. Inst., 1967-68; prof. physics U. Calif. at Berkeley, 1969—, chmn. dept. physics, 1987—; dir. U. Calif. at Berkeley (Space Scis. Lab.), 1979-85; dir. Terradex Corp., Walnut Creek, Calif., 1978-86; cons. for NASA (on Lunar Sample Analysis Planning Team); mem. space sci. bd. Nat. Acad. Scis.; vis. prof. U. Rome, 1983; sci. assoc. CERN, 1984; Miller research prof. U. Calif.-Berkeley, 1972-73. Author: (with others) Nuclear Tracks in Solids; Contbr. (with others) articles to profl. jours. Recipient Distinguished Service award Am. Nuclear Soc., 1964, Indsl. Research awards, 1964, 65, E.O. Lawrence Meml. award AEC, 1971, medal exceptional sci. achievement NASA, 1973; John Simon Guggenheim fellow, 1976-77. Fellow Am. Phys. Soc., Am. Geophys. Union; mem. Nat. Acad. Scis. (chmn. geophysics sect. 1981-84, sec. phys. scis. 1985—), Am. Astron. Soc. Research on space and astrophysics, nuclear physics, particularly devel. solid state track detectors and their applications to geophysics, space and nuclear physics problems Research on space and astrophysics, nuclear physics, particularly devel. solid state track detectors and their applications to geophysics, space and nuclear physics problems.

PRICE, PETER WILFRID, ecology educator, researcher; b. London, Apr. 17, 1938; came to U.S., 1971; BSc with honors, U. Wales, Bangor, 1958-62; MSc, U. New Brunswick, Fredericton, 1964; PhD, Cornell U., 1970. Asst. prof. U. Ill., Urbana, 1971-75, assoc. prof., 1975-79; research ecologist Mus. No. Ariz., Flagstaff, 1979-80; assoc. prof. No. Ariz. U., Flagstaff, 1980-85, prof. ecology, 1985—. Author: Insect Ecology 2d edition, 1984, Evolutionary Biology of Parasites, 1980; editor A New Ecology, 1984, Evolutionary Strategies of Parasitic Insects, 1975. Guggenheim fellow, 1977-78. Fellow AAAS, NSF (panel mem. 1978-81), Am. Soc. Naturalists, Ecol. Soc. Am. (bd. editors 1973-76), Brit. Ecol. Soc., Am. Soc. Parasitologists. Home: 3003 Cooper Dr Flagstaff AZ 86001 Office: No Ariz U Box 5640 Flagstaff AZ 86011

PRICE, RAYMOND F., industrial engineer, manufacturing engineer; b. San Diego, Feb. 8, 1937; s. Earl Willard and Neoma Luella (Burke) P.; m. Joan Karlyn Lawson, Apr. 23, 1954 (div. 1961); children—Guy Warren, Ray Steven; m. 2d, Polly Louise Metts, Nov. 6, 1961; children—Thomas Howard, Kirsten Alys, Audra Paget. Tech. cert. indsl. engring. East Central Jr. Coll., Decatur, Miss., 1970; cert. mgmt. theory Brown U., 1972. Warehouseman Gen. Mills., San Diego, 1955-56, asst. foreman, 1956-64; erection supr. Taylor Machine Works, Louisville, Miss., 1964-69; indsl. engr., machining gen. foreman, 1969-71; indsl. mfg. engr. Allis Chalmers, Boston, 1972-73, mfg. engr., Jackson, Miss., 1973-75, assembly supr., 1975; sr. project mgr. computer aided mfg. systems Mgmt. Sci. Inc., Carson City, Nev., 1975-86; v.p. client tng. Computer Aided Mfg. Systems Karma, Inc., Carson City, 1986—. Served to sgt. Army N.G., 1954-63. Mem. Soc. Mfg. Engrs. Republican. Baptist. Author manuals. Office: 400 Hot Springs Rd Suite 7 Carson City NV 89701

PRICE, R(ICHARD) MARCUS, physics educator, academic administrator; b. Colorado Springs, Colo., Jan. 18, 1940; s. George Marcus and Letha Belle (Smith) Price; m. Elaine Beverley Haley, Sept. 13, 1968. BS in Physics, Colo. State U., 1961; PhD in Astronomy, Australian Nat. U., Canberra, A.C.T., 1966. From asst. prof. to assoc. prof. physics MIT, Cambridge, Mass., 1967-75; from frequency mgr. to astronomy sect. head NSF, Washington, 1975-79; prof. and chmn. physics and astronomy dept. U. N.Mex., Albuquerque, 1979-85, grad. dean, 1985—; cons. AID, NSF, Dept. Commerce, Washington, 1970—; frequency mgmt. adv. com. Dept. Commerce, 1979—. Contbr. articles to profl. jours. Served to capt. U.S. Army, 1965-67. Fulbright fellow, 1961-62; grantee NSF, 1962-65, 68—, DOD, 1968—, industry, 1979—. Mem. Am. Astron. Soc. (chmn. various coms. 1967—), N.Mex. Acad. Sci. (pres., exec. com.). Avocations: camping, hiking, music. Office: U N Mex Dept Physics and Astronomy Albuquerque NM 87131

PRICE, ROBERT O., police official; b. Abilene, Kans., Jan. 4, 1932; s. Iru Paul Price and Irene Isabel (Parrish) Price Brown; m. Dorothy Faye McCoy, Jan. 26, 1951; children—Fred Dennis, Donald Eugene. A.A., Bakersfield Coll., 1962; B.A., U. Redlands, 1978. With Bakersfield Police Dept., Calif., 1956—, capt., 1970-73, chief police, 1973—; pres. Secret Witness Bd., 1980-83. Recipient John W. Doubenmier award Am. Soc. Pub. Adminstrs., 1978, Boss of Yr. award Am. Bus. Women Assn., 1979, Cliff Morris award Calif. Probation, Parole and Corrections Officers Assn., 1982. Mem. Kern County Law Enforcement Adminstrs. Assn. (pres. 1974), Kern County Police Chiefs Assn. (pres. 1979), Calif Council Criminal Justice, Internat. Assn. Chiefs Police, Calif. Police Chiefs Assn., Calif. Peace Officers Assn., FBI Nat. Acad. Assts. Republican. Office: Bakersfield Police Dept 1601 Truxtun Ave Bakersfield CA 93301

PRICE, WALTER ERNEST, assurative sciences engineer; b. N.Y.C., Aug. 11, 1948; s. Obie and Marguerite (Smith) P.; m. R. Jean Hodge, July 28, 1972 (div. 1985). AA in Math., Bronx Community Coll., 1967; BEE, U. Dar Es Salaam, Tanzania, 1973; postgrad., Ga. Inst. Tech., 1980. Engring. assoc. Bell Labs., Atlanta, 1975-77; prin. engr. Computer Scis. Corp., Falls Church, Va., 1977-83; sr. engr. McDonnell Douglas Astronautics Co., St. Louis, 1980-81; assurance engr. Daniel, Mann, Johnson and Mendenhall, Los Angeles, 1983—; prin. Donaldson-Price Assocs., Ltd., Atlanta, 1981—. Mem. Audio Engring. Soc., Am. Soc. Quality Control (cert.), Sons Am. Legion. Avocation: yachting. Office: Metro Rail Transit Cons 548 S Spring St Los Angeles CA 90013

PRICE, WARREN, III, state attorney general; b. Washington, June 19, 1943; s. Warren and Frances (Davis) P.; m. Johna Kanoho, Mar. 21, 1967 (div. Mar. 1987); children: Warren Price IV, Brandon Phillip Price. BA in Econs., U. N.C., 1965; JD, U. Calif., San Francisco, 1972. Ptnr. Goodsill, Anderson, Quinn and Stifel, Honolulu, 1972-87; atty. gen. State of Hawaii, Honolulu, 1987—; mem. Jud. Selection Commn., Honolulu, 1985-87. Served to lt. USNR, 1965-69. Mem. Nat. Inst. of Trial Advocacy (faculty 1984-87), Pacific Law Inst. (bd. dirs., faculty 1985—), Order of the Coif, Am. Inns of Ct. Democrat. Episcopalian. Avocations: surfing, tennis. Office: Attorney General's Office 415 S Beretania St RM 405 Honolulu HI 96813

PRICKETT, DAVID CLINTON, physician; b. Fairmont, W.Va., Nov. 26, 1918; s. Clinton Evert and Mary Anna (Gottschalk) P.; m. Mary Ellen Holt, June 29, 1940; children—David C., Rebecca Ellen, William Radcliffe, Mary Anne, James Thomas, Sara Elizabeth. A.B., W.Va. U., 1944; M.D., U. Louisville, 1946; M.P.H., U. Pitts., 1955. Intern, Louisville Gen. Hosp., 1947; surg. resident St. Joseph's Hosp., Parkersburg, W.Va., 1948-49; gen. practice, 1949-50, 55-61; physician USAF, N.Mex., 1961-62, U.S. Army, Calif., 1963-64, San Luis Obispo County Hosp., 1965-66, So. Calif. Edison Co., 1981-84; assoc. physician indsl. and gen. practice Los Angeles County, Calif., 1967—; med. dir. S. Gate plant Gen. Motors Corp., 1969-71; physician staff City of Los Angeles, 1971-76. Med. officer USPHS, 1953-55, surgeon, res. officer, 1957-59; pres. W.Va. Pub. Health Assn., 1951-52; sec. indsl. and pub. health sect. W.Va. Med. Assn., 1956. Contbr. articles to profl. jours. Served to 2d lt. AUS, 1943-46. Named to Hon. Order Ky. Cols. Mem. Am., Western occupational med. assns., Am., Calif., Los Angeles County med. assns., Am. Acad. Family Physicians, Phi Chi. Contbr. articles to profl. jours. Address: PO Box 4032 Whittier CA 90607

PRICKETT, MICHAEL J., electrical engineer; b. Santa Monica, Calif., Sept. 4, 1944; s. James Monroe and Afton (Leavitt) P.; m. M. Kathryn Ingrum, Sept. 5, 1965; children—Jennifer, Jeremy, Stephen; B.E.E., Calif. State Poly. U., 1966; M.E.E., San Diego State U., 1969; M.S., U. So. Calif., 1974. Registered profl. engr., Calif. Product design engr. Convair div. Gen. Dynamics, San Diego, 1966-68; with Naval Ocean Systems Center, San Diego, 1968—, microwave systems design engr. satellite communications, 1968-79, program mgr. radar devel., 1979—; adj. prof. elec. and computer engring. San Diego State U., 1980—; cons. engring. mem. adv. com. San Diego Unified Sch. Dist., 1978-79. Recipient Superior Achievement award Naval Electronics Lab., 1975; Outstanding Engring. award Naval Ocean Systems Center, 1979. Fellow AIAA (assoc.); mem. IEEE (sr.). Republican. Contbr. articles to sci. and engring. jours. Patentee radar, electronic control, signal processing.

PRICOLO, EDITH MARIE, integrated circuit mask design engineer; b. Merced, Calif., Nov. 8, 1936; d. Tony and Edith Cecelia (Silva) Azevedo; m. Danny Ralph Pricolo, Feb. 19, 1955; children: Dennis, Dina, Danette, Damien. Student San Jose State U., 1953-54. Sales clk. J.J. Newberry store, San Jose, 1967; integrated circuit fabrication worker Fairchild Semicondr., Mountain View, Calif., 1967-68, integrated circuit mask designer, 1969-73; integrated circuit mask designer Advanced Microdevices, Sunnyvale, Calif., 1973-84, integrated circuit mask design engr., 1984—. Designer bipolar microprocessor AM 2901, 1975. Steering com. mem. Fleming Ave Homeowners Assn., San Jose, 1979-81; funding chmn., counselor Contact 24 hour crisis hotline, San Jose, 1985; tchr. Confrat. of Christian Doctrine, 1973-74. Mem. Nat. Assn. Female Execs. Avocations: refinishing furniture, dancing, photography, sewing. Home: 168 Clareview Ave San Jose CA 95127 Office: Advanced MicroDevices (Semicondr) 901 Thompson Pl Sunnyvale CA 94088

PRIDE, KENNETH RODNEY, lawyer, consultant; b. Los Angeles, Dec. 31, 1953; s. James Allen and Mable Louise (Jones) P.; divorced; children: Kenneth Rodney II, Jason Alexander. AA, Los Angeles Harbor Coll., 1975; BA, U. So. Calif., 1977; JD, Loyola U., Los Angeles, 1982; postgrad., Pepperdine U., 1985—. House counsel Mark Industries, Long Beach, Calif., 1982—; bd. dirs. Am. Equipment Ins. Ltd., Cayman Islands, Mark Credit Corp, Powered Mobile Platforms Corp, Mark Comml. Fin. Corp, Mark Industries Corp.; cons. Golden West Risk Mgmt. Inc., Los Angeles, 1986—. Author: The Cook Book for Men, 1986. Active Los Angeles County Cen. Com., 1974-79, State Cen. Com., Calif., 1975-78. Served with USAF, 1971-73. Mem. Farm and Indsl. Equipment Inst. (legal and legis. com. 1983—). Home: 6520 Selma Ave Hollywood CA 90028 Office: 11724 S Cimarron Ave Los Angeles CA 90047

PRIES, RICHARD ALLAN, mechanical engineer, utility researcher; b. Portland, Oreg., Mar. 1, 1940; s. Fred and Sigrid Violet (Kuja) P.; m. Sheila Hanson, Jan. 22, 1966; children: Dawna, Kurt, Kandace, Désirée. BS in Applied Sci., Portland State U., 1970; MME, U. Portland, 1975. Registered mech. engr., Oreg. Head estimating unit Transmission Engring. br. Bonneville Power Adminstrn., Portland, 1974-78, chief tech. staff Transmission

Engring. div., 1978-81, chief devel. and analysis unit, Geog. Engring. Resources sect., 1981—. Served with U.S. Army, 1961-64. Recipient Sustained Superior Performance award Bonneville Power Adminstrn., 1984, 85, Spl. Achievement Award Bonneville Power Adminstrn., 1973, 77. Mem. ASCE (assoc.), Am. Soc. Photogrammetry and Remote Sensing. Democrat. Avocations: hiking, old cars. Home: 4605 NE Royal Ct Portland OR 97213 Office: Bonneville Power Adminstrn Mail Stop-ETRM 1002 NE Holladay Portland OR 97232

PRIEUR, DAVID JOHN, veterinary pathologist, educator; b. Flint, Mich., June 18, 1942; s. Elmer Alfred and Cecilia (Amman) P.; m. Marilyn Kathleen Jordan, Nov. 23, 1966; children: Randolph, Sheila. BS, Mich. State U., 1964, DVM, 1966, MS, 1967; PhD, Wash. State U., 1971. Sr. staff fellow NIH, Bethesda, Md., 1971-74; NIH fellow Wash. State U., Pullman, 1967-71, from asst. prof. to prof. vet. microbiology, pathology, 1974—. Editor animal models sect. Am. Jour. Med. Genetics, 1983—; contbr. articles to sci. jours. Recipient Small Animal Research award Ralston-Purina Co., 1986; Upjohn fellow Mich. State U., 1966-67. Mem. AAAS, Internat. Acad. Pathology, Am. Assn. Pathologists, Am. Assn. Geneticists, Am. Soc. Human Genetics. Home: SE 1010 Kamiaken Pullman WA 99163 Office: Wash State U Dept Vet Microbiology Pathology Pullman WA 99164-7040

PRIGMORE, ALMA LOUISE, real estate broker; b. Ft. Worth, Apr. 17, 1921; d. Arthur Cornelius and Helen (Dwiggins) Bjork; m. James S. Prigmore, Jan. 28, 1944. Student pub. schs., Ft. Worth. Adminstrv. sec. Farmers Ins. Group, Los Angeles, 1952-71; realtor assoc. Ken Fujiyama Realty Inc., Hilo, Hawaii, 1976-79, broker, 1979-82; owner, prin. broker Tapa Realty, Inc., Hilo, 1982—. Named Realtor of Yr., Hawaii Island Bd. Realtors, 1980. Pres. Hawaii Exchangors; mem. Nat. Million Dollar Real Estate Club, Acad. Real Estate of Sarasota, Tigr Real Estate Exchange Club, Nat. Real Estate Bd., Hawaii Assn. Realtors, Hawaii Island Real Estate Bd., Hawaii C. of C. Baptist. Clubs: Hilo Women's, Paradise Hui Hanalike. Office: PO Box 4656 Hilo HI 96720

PRIGMORE, DONALD GENE, utility company executive; b. Leon, Kans., Sept. 26, 1932; s. Harry Edward and Mary Julia (Doyle) P.; m. June Mary O'Connell, May 15, 1970; children: Marc, Elizabeth Ann, Mary Kathryn, Christine. BSCE, Kans. State Coll., 1955; MBA, U. Mich., 1958. Registered profl. engr., Mich., Ind., Tex. Spl. studies engr. Gen. Telephone Co. of Mich., Muskegon, 1958-62; div. mgr. Gen. Telephone Co. of Mich., Three Rivers, 1962-69; pres. Gen. Telephone Co. of Mich., Muskegon, 1979-81; plant dir., service dir. GTE Service Corp., N.Y.C., 1969-72; regional v.p. mktg. and customer services GTE Service Corp., Irving, Tex., 1978-79; v.p. ops. Gen. Telephone Co. of Ind., Ft. Wayne, 1972-76, Gen. Telephone Co. S.W., San Angelo, Tex., 1976-77; v.p. mktg. and customer services Gen. Telephone Co. S.W., 1977-78; pres. Gen. Telephone Co. of S.E./Ky., Durham, N.C., 1981-84, GTE Sprint Communications Corp., Burlingame, Calif., 1984-86. Mem. adv. bd. Ft. Wayne United Way, 1972-75; gen. chmn. Tom Green County (Tex.) United Way, 1978; bd. visitors Sch. Engring., Duke U., 1983—; bd. dirs. Mfrs. and Employers, Muskegon, Mich., 1980, West Shore Symphony, 1980, Muskegon County United Way, 1979-80, United Way Durham/Durham County, 1981-84, N.C. Citizens for Bus. and Industry Bay Area Council, 1981-84; trustee Durham Acad., 1982-84; dir.-at-large Mich. State C. of C., 1980; dir. Durham C. of C., 1983-84; exec. com. ARC, 1980; trustee Greater Muskegon Indsl. Fund, 1980. Mem. Am. Mktg. Assn. (dir. Dallas chpt. 1978), Nat. Soc. Profl. Engrs., Phi Delta Theta. Clubs: Blackhawk Country. Office: GTE Sprint PO Box 974 Burlingame CA 94010

PRINCE, JOHN LUTHER, III, engineering educator; b. Austin, Tex., Nov. 13, 1941; s. John Luther and Glynda (Chollett) P.; m. Martha Ann Hight, Mar. 4, 1960; children: Cynthia Kay, John Luther IV, Alan Douglas, David William. BSEE, So. Meth. U., 1965; MEE, N.C. State U., 1968, PhD, 1969. Research engr. RTI, Res. Tri. Park, N.C., 1968-70; mgmt. infosystems Tex. Instruments, Dallas, 1970-75; from assoc. prof. to prof. Clemson (S.C.) U., 1975-80; dir. R.A. Intermedics, Inc., Freeport, Tex., 1980-83; prof. U. Ariz., Tucson, 1983—; cons. Inst. Def. Analyses, Washington, 1986, Jet Propulsion Lab., Pasadena, Calif., 1983-85, Battelle Labs., Res. Tri. Park, N.C., 1983—. Contbr. articles to profl. jours. Fellow NSF, 1965-68. Mem. IEEE, Am. Philatelic Soc. Lutheran. Avocations: stamp collecting, classic cars. Home: 7542 N San Lorenzo Tucson AZ 85704 Office: U Ariz Tucson AZ 85721

PRINDLE, ROBERT WILLIAM, geotechnical engineer; b. Los Angeles, Nov. 19, 1950; s. Robert Edward and Margaret Elizabeth (Johnson) P.; m. Nancy K. Hayden, Apr. 5, 1986. Student St. John's Coll., Camarillo, Calif., 1968-70; B.S.C.E. summa cum laude, Loyola U., Los Angeles, 1974; M.S., Calif. Inst. Tech., 1975. Engring. aide Los Angeles County Sanitation Dists., 1973-74; student engr. Los Angeles Dept. Water and Power, 1974, 75; staff engr. Fugro, Inc., Long Beach, Calif., 1976-78; sr. staff engr. Woodward-Clyde Consultants, Orange, Calif., 1978-79; mem. tech. staff Sandia Nat. Labs., Albuquerque, 1980—. Mem. N. Mex. Symphony Orch. Chorus, 1981-84. Registered profl. civil engr., Calif.; Calif. State Grad. fellow, 1974-75, Calif. Inst. Tech. Inst. fellow, 1974-75. Mem. ASCE, NSPE, Internat. Soc. for Soil Mechanics and Found. Engring., Tau Beta Pi. Republican. Roman Catholic. Contbr. articles to profl. jours. Office: Sandia Nat Labs Div 6312 Albuquerque NM 87185

PRINGLE, PETER LEE, systems engineer; b. Santa Monica, Calif., May 10, 1936; s. Gayland Paul and Helen (Schmidt) P.; m. Evamaria Rother, May 3, 1958; children: Ronald Lee, Karen Diane, Lynn Denise. BSChemE, Seattle U., 1958; MBA, Boise State U., 1973. With prodn. dept. Boise Cascade, Salem, Oreg., 1958-65; ops. research Boise (Idaho) Cascade, 1966-73, Kaiser Aluminum, Oakland, Calif., 1973-78; indsl. engring. Kaiser Aluminum, Trentwood, Wash., 1978-83, with automated systems, 1983—. Mem. The Inst. Mgmt. Sci., Jaycees. Clubs: Lake Merritt Sailing (Oakland) (commodore 1978); Lake Pend Oreille Yacht (Spokane, Wash.). Avocations: sailing,skiing, kayaking. Home: N 5011 Vista View Circle Spokane WA 99212 Office: Kaiser Aluminum E 15000 Euclid Spokane WA 99215

PRINTUP, ROBERT HALE, environmental services executive, consultant; b. Lincoln, Nebr., June 9, 1929; s. John Monroe and Grace A. (Ganschow) P.; m. Lanore Jean Coppens, Oct. 22, 1967; children—Robert H. Jr., Gregory, John, Tresa. Student, Tex. Christian U., 1948-50, U. Calif.-Riverside, 1971-72. Owner, operator Miracle Maintenance, Baldwin Park, Calif., 1957-64; pres. Miracle Investments, Baldwin Park, 1960-64; exec. housekeeper, dir. environ. services Pomona (Calif.) Valley Community Hosp., 1965-75, U. Chgo. Hosps., 1975-80, Brotman Med. Ctr., Culver City, Calif., 1980-81, St. John's Hosp. & Health Ctr., Santa Monica, Calif., 1981—; owner Am. Environ. Systems, Torrance, Calif., 1983—; tchr., lectr., cons. in ednl. instns. Pres. Baldwin Park Service Council, 1962; Contbr. (newsletter) Hospital Hazardous Waste, 1985—; active REACT Radio Club. Served with USAF, 1947-50. Recipient Merit award Los Angeles County, 1960; Grand award Nat. Soap and Detergent Assn., 1971. Mem. Nat. Exec. Housekeepers Assn. (numerous offices, awards), Assn. Practitioners Infection Control, Aircraft Owners and Pilots Assn., Baldwin Park Democratic Club, Western Hosps. Assn. (past chmn. housekeeping div.), Opportunity Investments Inc., Am. Hosp. Assn. (bd. dirs. Am. Soc. Health Care Environ. Services div. 1986—). Lutheran. Clubs: Rotary Internat, Optimists (Baldwin Park). Author: Housekeeping Management for Health Care Units, 1970; contbr. Management Handbook for Plant Engineers, 1980; mem. tech. adv. com. Executive Housekeeper Today mag.; contbr. articles to profl. jours.

PRISCU, JOHN CHARLES, ecologist, educator; b. Las Vegas, Sept. 20, 1952; s. John Charles and Dorothy Ann (Kirk) P.; m. Linda Rae Loetterle, June 25, 1979. BS, U. Nevada, Las Vegas, 1975, MS, 1978; PhD, U. Calif., Davis, 1981. Research assoc. U. Nev., Las Vegas, 1977-78; research asst. U. Calif., Davis, 1978-81; research scientist Dept. Scientific and Indsl. Research, Taupo, New Zealand, 1981-84; asst. prof. zoology Mont. State U., Bozeman, 1984—; cons. Chem-Pro Cons., Las Vegas, 1981—; research scientist Antarctic Research, Govt. of New Zealand, Taupo, 1984-85; U. So. Calif., Los Angeles, 1985-86. Contbr. articles to profl. jours. Grantee Antarctic aquatic ecology NSF, 1984-85, Antarctic oceanography, 1985-87, bacterial/agrl. interactions, 1985—; toxic algae blooms Mont. Water Research, 1985—. Mem. AAAS, Am. Soc. Liminology and Oceanography, Sigma Xi. Avocations: sports, music. Office: Mont State Univ Dept Biology Bozeman MT 59717

PRITCHARD, PAUL DAVID, educator, consultant; b. Seattle, Mar. 9, 1948; s. Elgin Elmer and Louise Lynette (Juzeler) P.; m. Kayleen Rae Scott, Aug. 24, 1968; children—Nathan, Nolle. B.A. in Edn., Western Wash. State Coll., 1970, M.Ed., 1973. Cert. tchr., prin., Wash. Tchr. social studies, curriculum specialist, sch. counselor Pub. Schs. Everett (Wash.), 1970—; tchr. social studies N Middle Sch., 1980-86; tchr. social studies Cascade High Sch., Everett, 1986—; speaker local and regional history. Vice pres. Port Gardner Assn., 1981-82; mem. hist. adv. com. City of Everett, 1983—. Recipient Letter of Commendation, Everett Pub. Library, 1982. Mem. NEA, Wash. Edn. Assn. Home: 1101 Grandview St Everett WA 98203

PRITCHETT, DAVID MARTIN, school system business manager, accountant; b. Idaho Falls, Idaho, Nov. 17, 1944; s. John and Flora (Sax) P.; children: Glen, Kris. BS, No. Ariz. U., 1969. Staff acct. Security Traveler, Boise, Idaho, 1971-72; fiscal acct. Boise Pub. Schs., 1972-77; owner Tax and Bookkeeping, Boise, 1977-79; fin. cons. State Dept. Edn., Boise, 1979-81; bus. mgr. Moscow (Idaho) Sch. Dist., 1981—. Served with U.S. Army, 1969-71. Mem. Idaho Assn. of Sch. Bus. Ofcls. (pres. 1984-85, regional bd. dirs. 1985-86), Assn. of Sch. Bus. Ofcls. Lodge: Rotary (treas. Moscow chpt. 1983-85). Avocations: fishing, hunting, chess, boating, hiking. Office: Moscow Sch Dist #281 410 E 3d St Moscow ID 83843

PRITCHETT, PHILIP LENTNER, physicist, educator; b. Chgo., Jan. 29, 1944; s. Charles Herman and Marguerite Almira (Lentner) P. AB, Oberlin Coll., 1965; MS, Stanford U., 1966, PhD, 1970. Postdoctoral fellow NATO/DESY, Hamburg, Fed. Republic of Germany, 1970-71; research assoc. Northwestern U., Evanston, Ill., 1971-73, vis. asst. prof. physics, 1973-75; NSF Energy fellow UCLA, 1975-76, asst. research physicist, 1976-81, assoc. research physicist, 1981-86, research physicist, 1986—. Contbr. articles to profl. jours. Grantee NSF, 1965-69, 1975-76, Woodrow Wilson Found., 1965-66. Mem. Am. Phys. Soc., Am. Geophys. Union, Sigma Xi. Office: UCLA Physics Dept 405 Hilgard Ave Los Angeles CA 90024

PRITZ, MICHAEL BURTON, neurological surgeon; b. New Brunswick, N.J., Oct. 8, 1947; s. John Ernest and Helen Violet (Rockoff) P.; m. Edmay Marie Gregorcy, Feb. 18, 1973; children: Edmond Louis, Benjamin David. BS, U. Ill., 1969; PhD, Case Western Res. U., 1973, MD, 1975. Diplomate Am. Bd. Neurol. Surgery. Asst. prof. neurol. surgery U. Calif. Irvine Med. Ctr., Orange, 1981-85, assoc. prof., 1985—. Contbr. articles to profl. jours. Recipient Herbert S. Steuer award Case Western Res. U., Cleve., 1975; NSF fellow, 1968; Edmund J. James scholar U. Ill., Champaign, 1968-69. Mem. Soc. Neurosci., Am. Assn. Anatomists, Am. Assn. Neurol. Surgeons, Congress Neurol. Surgeons, Soc. Neurol. Surgeons of Orange County (pres. 1985-86, sec.-treas. 1984-85). Office: U Calif Irvine Med Ctr 101 City Dr S Orange CA 92668

PRITZKER, BURTON STEVEN, photographer; b. Chgo., June 28, 1941; s. Harry and Adele (Simons) P.; m. Renée Christina Walker, Nov. 22, 1969. BArch, U. Calif., 1965. Free-lance photographer various states, 1976-86; ind. architect Calif., 1969-76; architect various firms in Europe and U.S., 1965-69. Contbr. photographs to mags. Recipient Excellence award Mead Ann. Report Show, N.Y., 1985, Excellence award Communication Arts Mag., Calif., 1985, Merit award New York Art Dirs. Club, N.Y., 1985, 86; Cert. of Excellence, Am. Inst. Graphic Art., N.Y., 1985. Home and Office: 456 Denton Way Santa Rosa CA 95401

PROBST, C.E., JR., orthopaedic surgeon; b. Hartford, Conn., Feb. 8, 1942; s. Charles Edwin Probst and Anne Howard; m. Jacqueline Kurokawa, Dec. 14, 1970; 1 child: Nicole Anne Jenine. BA, Williams Coll., 1964; MD, Jefferson Med. Coll., 1968. Intern. Phila. Gen. Hosp., Phila.; resident in orthopaedics Thomas Jefferson U. Hosp., Phila.; practice medicine specializing in orthopaedics Kahului, Hawaii, 1975—; cons. Kula (Hawaii) Gen. Hosp., 1975—, Shriners Hosp., Honolulu, 1981—. Contbr. articles to profl. jours. Team physician Maui High Sch. Football Team, Kahului, 1975—. Served to maj. U.S. Army, 1968-71, Vietnam, maj. USAR, 1983—. Fellow Am. Acad. Orthopaedic Surgery; mem. Western Orthopaedic Assn., Pan Pacific Surg. Assn., Am. Coll. Sports Medicine, AMA, Hawaii Orthopaedic Assn. Republican. Avocations: tennis, scuba diving, jogging, hunting, bicycling. Office: 53 Puunene Ave Kahului HI 96732

PROEBSTING, EDWARD LOUIS, JR., research horticulturist; b. Woodland, Calif., Mar. 2, 1926; s. Edward Louis and Dorothy (Critzer) P.; m. Patricia Jean Connolly, June 28, 1947; children: William Martin, Patricia Louise, Thomas Alan. BS, U. Calif., Davis, 1948; PhD, Mich. State U., 1951. Asst. horticulturist Wash. State U., Prosser, 1951-52, assoc. horticulturist, 1963—; vis. prof. Cornell U., Ithaca, N.Y., 1966; vis. scientiat Hokkardo U., Sapporo, Japan, 1978, Victoria Dept Agriculture, Tatura, Australia, 1986—. Contbr. numerous articles to profl. jours. Scoutmaster Boy Scouts Am., Prosser, 1963-76, dist. chmn., 1976-78. Served to lt. USNR, 1943-46, 52-54. Recipient Silver Beaver award Boy Scouts Am.; fellow Japan Soc. Promotion Sci., Sapporo, 1978, Res. Bank. Australia, 1986. Fellow AAAS, Am. Soc. Horticultural Sci. (pres. 1983-84). Methodist. Avocations: backpacking, native plants. Home: 1929 Miller Ave Prosser WA 99350 Office: Wash State U Irrigation Agrl Research Extension Ctr PO Box 30 Prosser WA 99350

PROESCHER, WARD HORNBLOWER, securities company executive, public speaker; b. Cary, N.C., Aug. 31, 1935; s. Andrew Jay and Gladys Elaine (Jones) P.; m. Susan Gamble Dittmar, May 1, 1971; children; Tobin Dittmar, Morgan Boehm. BS in Indsl. Relations, U. N.C., 1958. Personnel supr. Campbell Soup Co., Modesto, Calif., 1960-62; sales mgr. U.S. Audio & Copy Corp., San Francisco, 1962-65; stockbroker Hornblower & Weeks-Hemphill, Noyes, San Francisco, 1966-73; owner, pres. Hornblower Yachts, Inc., Berkeley, Calif., 1973-80; prin., chmn. Hornblower, Upson, Monfils & Proeschcer, Pleasant Hill, Calif., 1985; pres. Sea Ventures, Inc., 1975—; prin. Commodore Cruises, Oakland, Calif., 1986—. Author: Secrets of Success-Techniques for Building Greater Personal Effectiveness; founder, host (TV show) How Now Mr. Dow?, 1968-72; founder, pub. Montgomery Street Opinion, 1968-70; creator seminars Secrets of Success; pub. speaker, lectr. Served with USN, 1958-60. Mem. Nat. Speakers Assn., Bay Area Speakers Service (v.p. 1986—). Clubs: Little Venice Yacht (Stockton, Calif.) (fleet capt. 1984); Campbell Soup Mgmt. (Modesto) (pres. 1961-62). Avocations: walking, biking, chess, piano, horse riding. Home: 3266 Elvia St Lafayette CA 94549 Office: 91 Gregory Ln Suite 7 Pleasant Hill CA 94523

PROFFITT, RICHARD THOMAS, research biochemist; b. Toledo, May 13, 1944; s. Raymond Thomas and Dorothy Louise (Reingruber) P.; m. Barbara Ruth Siechert, June 27, 1969; children: Pamela Ruth, Sarah Louise, Roger Thomas. BA, Occidental Coll., 1966; MS, San Diego State U., 1970; PhD, U. Calif., Davis, 1973. Lectr. Calif. Poly. State U., San Luis Obispo, 1973; research asst. St. Louis U. Med. Sch., 1974-76; research assoc. Washington U. Sch. Medicine, St. Louis, 1977-79; asst. research scientist City of Hope Med. Ctr., Duarte, Calif., 1979-82; sr. research scientist Vestar Research Inc., Pasadena, Calif., 1982—, dir. pharmacology, 1984—. Contbr. articles to profl. jours., chpts. to books. NIH fellow, 1976-77. Mem. AAAS, Am. Chem. Soc., Soc. Nuclear Medicine. Home: 11 N Altura Rd Arcadia CA 91006 Office: Vestar Research Inc 939 E Walnut St Pasadena CA 91106

PROFIO, AMEDEUS EDWARD, engineering educator; b. New Castle, Pa.; s. A. Edward and Helen Agnes (Pearce) P.; m. Janet Lee Lazaran, Sept. 29, 1954; children: Christopher, Claudia, Susan. BS, MIT, 1953, PhD, 1963. Scientist Bettis Lab. Westinghouse Corp., Pitts., 1953-55; research assoc., asst. prof. MIT, Cambridge, 1957-64; scientist General Atomic, San Diego, 1964-69; prof. engring. U. Calif., Santa Barbara, 1969—; bd. dirs. Western Laser Inst., Santa Barbara; cons. EG&G, Inc., Goleta, Calif., 1969—. Author: Experimental Reactor Physics, 1976, Radiation Shielding and Dosimetry, 1979; contbr. articles to profl. jours. Served to 1st lt. U.S. Army, 1955-57. Mem. Am. Soc. Photobiology, Am. Nuclear Soc. (recipient Tech. Achievement award 1977), Tau Beta Pi, Sigma Xi. Avocations: breed and show Welsh ponies. Office: U Calif Santa Barbara CA 93106

PROHOSKY, DON ELBERT, social worker; b. Omaha, Feb. 25, 1930; s. Joseph Prohosky and Anna Mae (Drost) Taylor; m. Holly Idelle Ringsby, Aug. 28, 1964 (dec. May 1973); 1 child, Kathleen Kay Feeken. BS, Regis Coll., 1952; MSW, Ariz. State U., 1985. Chem. dependency therapist Camelback Hosp. Inc., Phoenix, 1983—; social worker VA Med. Ctr., Phoenix, 1984—; counselor, educator City of Phoenix DWI Ctr., 1984-85; mem. Research Soc. Process-Oriented Psychology, Zurich. Mem. Nat. Assn. Social Workers, Ariz. Bd. Cert. Alcoholism Counselors, Nat. Assn. Alcoholism and Drug Abuse Counselors, Soc. for Process Psychology, Phoenix Friends Carl Jung. Democrat. Roman Catholic. Avocations: watercolor and oil painting, tennis, art collecting. Home: PO Box 15072 Phoenix AZ 85060 Office: VA Med Ctr 7th St and Indian Sch Rd Phoenix AZ 85012

PROPHET, MATTHEW WALLER, JR., school superintendent; b. Okolona, Miss., Apr. 4, 1930; s. Matthew Waller and Elzira Elise (Walker) P.; m. Freddye Maxine Adams, Jan. 17, 1954; children—Michael, Matthew, Tony Michelle. B.Gen. Edn., U. Omaha, 1960; M.A. in Ednl. Supervision and Adminstrn., Roosevelt U., 1970; Ph.D., Northwestern U., 1972. Enlisted U.S. Army, 1951; commd. 2d lt., 1952; advanced through grades to comdr.; various assignments in Germany, Korea, other countries; advisor to Ohio N.G., 1964-65; personnel mgmt. advisor, Vietnam, 1965-66; chief ind. tng. 5th U.S. Army, Fort Sheridan, Ill., 1967-71; dep. supt. Lansing Sch. Dist., Mich., 1972-1978, supt., 1978-82; supt. Portland Pub. Schs., Oreg., 1982—; adj. prof. Coll. Edn. Mich. State U., East Lansing, Mich., 1974-82; coordinator Edn. Policy Fellowship Program, Mich., 1975-82; dir. Inst. Ednl. Leadership, Inc., Washington. Active United Way, Jr. Achievement, Mich. Soc. to Prevent Blindness, others. Decorated Bronze Star, Air medal, Legion of Merit, others. Mem. Mich. Assn. Sch. Adminstrs. (former nat. del.), Am. Assn. Sch. Adminstrs., Nat. Program for Ednl. Leadership, Mich. Middle Cities Edn. Assn., Area Educators Committed to Cooperation (former chmn.), Roundtable (Ingham County), Edn. Policy Fellowship Program, Adv. Council for Equal Ednl. Opportunity, Ret. Officers Assn. (U.S. Army), Alpha Chi, Phi Delta Kappa. Office: Portland Pub Schs 501 N Dixon Portland OR 97227 *

PROPST, MICHAEL TRUMAN, pathologist; b. Lebanon, Oreg., July 3, 1940; s. Lynn Edward and Vera Ruth (Forbes) P.; m. Susan Jean Joesting, Dec. 26, 1974; children: Christopher M., Andrew J., Matthew A., Michael Jonathan, Edwin Cam. BS, Oreg. State U., 1962; MD, U. Oreg., 1966. Diplomate Am. Bd. Pathology. Pathologist Humana Hosp., Anchorage, 1974-84; med. examiner State of Alaska, Anchorage, 1975—; med. dir. Physicians Med. Lab., Anchorage, 1984—. Served to maj. USAF, 1971-74. Fellow Coll. Am. Pathologists, Am. Soc. Clin. Pathologists, Am. Acad. Forensic Scientists; mem. Nat. Assn. Med. Examiners, Alaska State Med. Assn. Episcopalian. Office: Physicians Med Lab 4335 Laurel Anchorage AK 99508

PROSISE, ROBERT EDWARD, business educator; b. Napa, Calif., Oct. 28, 1929; s. Harry Theodore and Lena Olive (Attebery) P.; A.A., Napa Jr. Coll., 1949; B.S., U. Calif., Berkeley, 1951; M.B.A. (Univ. scholar 1956-57), Stanford U., 1957; m. Betty Rose Simmons, May 27, 1952; children—Kathleen, Harry, Pamela, Bonnie, Theodore. Sales rep. Adolph Blaich, Inc., Burlingame, Calif., 1957-59, div. mgr., 1960-62; with Browning Arms Co., Morgan, Utah, 1962-74, sales mgr. nat. accounts, 1968-70, mdse. mgr., 1970-74; mktg. mgr. Gerber Legendary Blades Co., Portland, Oreg., 1974-75; pres., dir. Jarman Co., Milw., 1976-83; assoc. prof. bus. So. Oreg. State Coll., Ashland, 1984—; mem. part-time faculty Portland State U., 1978-83. Served to lt. USNR, 1952-55. Republican. Home: 571 Henley Way Ashland OR 97520 Office: So Oreg State Coll Ashland OR 97520

PROSSER, JOHN MARTIN, architect, architectural educator, university dean, urban design consultant; b. Wichita, Kans., Dec. 28, 1932; s. Francis Ware and Harriet Corinne (Osborne) P.; m. Judith Adams, Aug. 28, 1954 (dec. 1982); children—Thomas, Anne, Edward; m. Karen Ann Cleary, Dec. 30, 1983; children—Timothy, Jennifer. B.Arch., U. Kans., 1955; M.Arch., Carnegie Mellon U., 1961. Registered architect, Kans., Colo. Architect, Robinson and Hissem, Wichita, 1954-56, Guirey, Srnka, and Arnold, Phoenix, 1961-62, James Sudler Assocs., Denver, 1962-68; ptnr., architect Nuzum, Prosser and Vetter, Boulder, 1969-73; from asst. prof. to prof. U. Colo., Boulder, U. Colo.-Denver, 1968—, acting dean, 1980-84, dean, 1984; dir. urban design U. Colo.-Denver, 1972-85; cons. John M. Prosser Assoc. Design Office, Boulder and Denver, 1974—; vis. prof. urban design Oxford Poly. U., Eng., 1979; vis. Critic Carnegie Mellon U., U. N.Mex., U. Ariz., Colo. Coll., Ft. Lewis Coll. Author, narrator PBS TV documentary Cities Are For Kids Too, 1984. Prin. works include (with others) hist. redesign Mus. Western Art, Denver (design honor 1984), Villa Italia, Lakewood, Colo., Mt. Carbon Community Ctr., Lakewood, Republic Bldg. parking facility, Denver, Auraria Higher Edn. Ctr., Colo., Fiddler's Green Amphitheater, Greenwood Village, Colo. Bd. dirs. Balarat Outdoor Edn. Assn., Denver, 1978-86, Cranmer Park Hilltop Assn., Denver, 1974—, Cherry Creek Found., Denver, 1981—; chmn. design rev. bd. Univs. Colo., Boulder, Denver and Colorado Springs, 1980—; mem. archtl. control com. Denver Tech. Ctr., 1984—; planning cons. Denver Trans Global Airport Expansion Project. Served to capt., as pilot USAF, 1956-59. Co-recipient 2d place nat. award Am. Soc. Interior Designers, 1984, honor award Colo. Soc. Architects, 1984. Mem. AIA (v.p. Denver chpt. 1979-80, pres. 1983, v.p. Colo. chpt. 1972-73, treas. 1974-75, sec. Western Mountain region 1984-86, treas. Colo. Central chpt. 1977-78). Republican. Club: Denver Country (bd. dirs. 1984—, pres. 1986-87). Lodge: Rotary. Home: 324 Ash St Denver CO 80220 Office: U Colo 1100 14th St Denver CO 80202

PROUDFOOT, EDWARD ALLEN, testing engineer; b. Youngstown, Ohio, Jan. 31, 1929; s. Byron K. and Martha (Arkwright) P.; m. Marthe Ann Watson; children: Harry, Andrew, Wendy, Edward Jr., Mary, David. BS in Edn., Slippery Rock State Coll., 1951; BSMetE, Carnegie Mellon U., 1960. Technician Westinghouse Bettis, McKeesport, Pa., 1951-56; technologist U.S. Steel Research Labs., Monroeville, Pa., 1956-61; supr. quality analysis Stone & Webster Engrs., Boston, 1970-74; mgr. nondestructive testing applications Avco Missile Space Div., Lowell, Mass., 1961-70, Westinghouse Hanford Co., Richland, Wash., 1974—. Contbr. tech. articles to jours. Fellow Am. Soc. Nondestructive Testing (local chmn. 1978-79); mem. ASME, Am. Soc. Metals. Avocations: woodworking, hunting. Office: Westinghouse Hanford Co PO Box 1970 Richland WA 99352

PROUT, CARL WESLEY, history educator; b. Bakersfield, Calif., Apr. 19, 1941; s. George Hecla and Ruth (King) P. B.A., U. Calif., Santa Barbara, 1964, M.A., 1965; postgrad. U. Tenn., Knoxville, 1968-71, Am. U. Cairo (Egypt), 1974, U. So. Calif., 1981, Ain Shams U., Cairo, 1981. Instr. history Santa Barbara Coll., 1965-66, U. Tenn., Knoxville, 1968-71; instr. history Orange Coast Coll., Costa Mesa, 1966-68, asst. prof., 1971-73, assoc. prof., 1973-75, prof., 1975—; treas. Willmore Corp., 1980-81, sec., 1984-85, v.p., 1985-86 , also dir; group facilitator Coastview Meml. Hosp., Long Beach, 1986—. Mem. Long Beach Beautification Assn.; pres., chmn. bd. Alamitos Heights Improvement Assn., 1979-80, bd. dirs., 1980-82; co-chmn. Ban Ugly Light Bulbs, 1978; mem. East Long Beach Joint Council, 1979-80, Local Coastal Planning Adv. Com., 1979-80. Recipient Salgo outstanding tchr. award, 1974, 75, 76. Mem. Am. Hist. Assn., Brit. Hist. Soc., Sigma Nu. Research and publs. in field. Clubs: Atlantic Alano, Meml. West Alumni. Office: Orange Coast Coll 2701 Fairview Rd Costa Mesa CA 92626

PROUT, RALPH EUGENE, physician; b. Los Angeles, Feb. 27, 1933; s. Ralph Byron and Fern (Taylor) P.; m. Joanne Morris, Sept. 17, 1980; children: Michael, Michelle. B.A., La Sierra Coll., 1953; M.D., Loma Linda U., 1957. Diplomate: Nat. Bd. Med. Examiners. Intern Los Angeles County Hosp., 1957-58; resident internal medicine White Meml. Hosp., Los Angeles, 1958-60; resident psychiatry Harding Hosp., Worthington, Ohio, 1960-61; practice medicine specializing in internal medicine Napa, Calif., 1961-63; staff internist Calif. Med. Facility, Vacaville, 1963-68, chief med. officer, 1968-84; chief med. cons. Calif. Dept. Corrections, 1977-86, chief med. services, 1983; med. cons. Wellness Cons., Placerville, Calif., 1986—; pres. Total Living Inc., 1984—; instr. Sch. Medicine, Loma Linda U., 1965-66; clin. asso. U. Calif. at Davis Sch. Medicine, 1978-84; med. cons. Substance Abuse Pine Grove Camp, 1985—. Treas. Vacaville Republican Assembly, 1972-75; del. Republican Central Com. Solano County, 1975-78; Bd. dirs. Napa-Solano County United Crusade, Vallejo, Calif., 1969-71, v.p., 1970-71; bd. dirs. Project Clinic, Vacaville, 1974-77, Home Health Com. Inter-Community

Hosp., Fairfield, 1978-80; pres. MotherLode Citizens for Drug-Free Youth, Amador County, 1985—. Named One of Outstanding Young Men of Am., 1968. Mem. Calif. Soc. Treatment of Alcoholism and other Drug Dependencies, Am. Nutritional Med. Assn., Am. Assn. Nutritional Cons., Nat. Fedn. Parents Drug-Free Youth, Mother Lode Citizens for Drug-Free Youth, Amador C. of C., Native Sons of Golden West, Alpha Omega Alpha. Republican. Home and Office: 24405 Shake Ridge Volcano CA 95689

PROUTY, DAVID FLETCHER, athletic organization executive; b. Sacramento, Nov. 28, 1945; s. Leroy Fletcher and Elizabeth Faye (Ballenger) P. BA, Vanderbilt U., 1967. Social worker Dept. Social Services, Fairfax, Va., 1967-69; tchr., counselor Dept. Corrections, Va., 1969-72, prison supt., 1972-74; exec. dir. Bikecentennial, Inc., Missoula, Mont., 1976-82, U.S. Cycling Fedn., Colorado Springs, Colo., 1983—; bd. dirs. 1986 World Championships, Inc., Colorado Springs, 1985—. Avocations: chess, reading, running, travel.

PROVOST, LINDA LOUISE, systems analyst; b. San Francisco, May 27, 1953; s. Louise Arthur-Marie and Helen Francis (Gray) P. B.A. in Psychology, U. Wash., 1975; postgrad. Edmonds Community Coll., 1980; cert. alcoholism studies Seattle U., 1975. Sales mgr. Seattle Art Galleries, 1977; counter/delivery person Standard AutoBody, Seattle, 1978-79; group clk. Boeing Co., Seattle, 1979-81, tool order writer, 1981-83, systems analyst, 1983-86, lead systems analyst, 1987—. Vol. phoneworker, asst. Supr. Crisis Clinic, Inc., Seattle, 1972-84; alcohol youth counselor Seattle King County Council on Alcoholism, Seattle, 1975. Home: 4122 212th St SW Apt A-106 Mountlake Terrace WA 98043

PROWELL, ROY WALTERS, JR., orthodontist; b. Pitts., Oct. 6, 1945; s. Roy Walters and Dorothy Jane (Forney) P.; student U. Calif., Davis, 1963-65, D.D.S. in Orthodontics (Regents scholar), U. Calif., San Francisco, 1969; m. Evelyn Joyce Morgan, Aug. 1, 1971 (div. June 1985); children—Roy Walters III, Ian Morgan. Assoc., Gordon Osser, D.D.S., Castro Valley, Calif., 1970-71, Willard Collins, D.D.S., Stockton, Calif., 1971-72; practice dentistry specializing in orthodontics, Pittsburg and Antioch, Calif., 1969-76; pres. R. Walt Prowell, D.D.S., Inc., Pittsburg and Antioch, 1976—; mem. staff Mt. Diablo Rehab. Center, Pleasant Hill, Calif.; mem. East Bay (Calif.) Cleft Palate Panel, East Bay Facial Surgery Panel. Pres., U. Calif. Orthodontic Alumni Found., 1978-81, treas., 1981-84. Republican. Presbyterian. Lodge: Masons, Rotary. Office: 3107 Lone Tree Way Suite D Antioch CA 94509

PRUDHOMME, HARRY P., utility executive; b. San Jose, Calif., Feb. 11, 1924; s. George A. and Margaret C. (Del Porte) P.; B.E.E., U. Santa Clara (Calif.), 1948; m. Virginia Myer, Dec. 27, 1947; children: Paul, James, Marilyn, Thomas, Karen, Jeffrey, Janice, Stephen. With Pacific Gas & Electric Corp., 1954-78, mgr. pipeline ops., also mgr. Standard Pacific Gasline, Inc., 1968-78; pres., dir. Pacific Gas Transmission Co., San Francisco, 1978-87, Pacific Transmission Supply Co., San Francisco, 1979—. Served to 1st lt. C.E., AUS, 1943-45, Mem. Am. Gas Assn., Gas Research Inst., Interstate Natural Gas Assn. Am. (dir.), Pacific Gas Assn. (Leadership award 1977), Can. Am. Soc. San Francisco, World Affairs Council No. Calif., Tau Beta Pi. Roman Catholic. Clubs: Commonwealth, Electric Engrs., World Trade (San Francisco). Office: Pacific Gas Transmission Co 160 Spear St San Francisco CA 94105

PRUGH, DANE GASKILL, child psychiatrist, pediatrician; b. Phila., June 3, 1918; s. Wallace Eby and Esther Ann (Gaskill) P.; m. Anne Davison, Feb. 27, 1943 (dec. 1983); children: Joan Elizabeth, Wallace Dane; m. Elisabeth Stiles, 1984. B.A., Miami U., Oxford, Ohio, 1940; M.D., Harvard U., 1943. Intern Children's Hosp., Boston, 1943; resident in pediatrics Children's Hosp., 1944; gen. practice medicine Dayton, Ohio, 1946-47; Commonwealth Fund fellow in psychiatry Strong Meml. Hosp., Rochester, N.Y., 1947-48; in pediatric psychiatry N.Y. Hosp., N.Y.C., 1948-49; instr. Harvard U. Med. Sch., Boston, 1949-51; asst. prof. pediatrics, psychiatry and public health Harvard U. Med. Sch., 1951-55; dir. psychiat. div. med. service Children's Hosp., Boston, 1949-55; assoc. prof. Rochester Sch. Medicine and chief child psychiatry div. Strong Meml. Hosp., 1955-63; prof., chief child psychiatry U. Colo. Med. Center, 1963-70; prof. psychiatry and pediatrics, dir. tng., child psychiatry and pediatric-psychiat. liaison U. Colo. Health Scis. Center, 1970-85, prof. emeritus, 1986—; lectr. Sch. Social Work, Denver U.; cons. in field; various vis. professorships including vis. prof. child health U. Otago Sch. Medicine, Dunedin, N.Z., 1969; various meml. lectureships; mem. Colo. Gov.'s Commn. on Children, Denver, 1977-80; mem. Task Panel on Pres.'s Commn. on Mental Health, 1977-78. Author: The Psychosocial Aspects of Pediatrics, 1983; contbr. numerous articles, chpt. to profl. publs.; editor: (with H. Stuart) The Healthy Child: Physical, Psychological and Social Development, 1960. Mem. subcom. Denver Mayor's Com. on Urban Renewal, 1967-69; chmn. East Arapahoe Human Relations Council, Denver, 1968-70. Served with M.C., U.S. Army, 1944-46. Recipient Whitehead award ACLU, 1970, Hannah Solomon award Nat. Council Jewish Women, 1970. Fellow Am. Orthopsychiat. Assn. (life; pres. 1968-69), Am. Acad. Pediatrics (chmn. sect. child devel. 1967-68), Am. Acad. Child Psychiatry (life; chmn. com. on liaison, primary care), Am. Psychiat. Assn. (life, chmn. com. on standards for children's facilities 1969-72), Am. Psychosomatic Soc. (council 1954-57); mem. Boston Psychoanalytic Soc., Western N.Y. Psychoanalytic Soc., Denver Psychoanalytic Soc., Group Advancement of Psychiatry (chmn. com. child psychiatry 1962-66), Soc. Pediatric Research, Am. Pediatric Soc., N.Y. Acad. Scis., Boylston Med. Soc., Phi Beta Kappa, Sigma Xi. Home: 9444 E Orchard Dr Englewood CO 80111

PRUSS, JOHN JOSEPH, architect; b. Butte, Mont., Dec. 29, 1935; s. John Francis Pruss and Cecilia Catherine (Zugel) Burns; m. Mary Joan Kelly, Dec. 28, 1957; children: Catherine, Jeffrey, Kelly, Curtis, Marya. BArch, U. Notre Dame, 1958. Registered architect, Wash., Alaska, Wis. Architect Leo A. Daly & Assoc., Seattle, 1962-63, 68-73, John Graham Co., Seattle, 1963-64, Woodman & Assoc., Bellevue, Wash., 1964-68, The Baylis Architects, Bellevue, 1973-75; architect, project mgr. CH2M Hill, Bellevue, 1975—; instr. U. Wash., Seattle, 1982. Mem. Planning Commn., Houghton, Wash., 1964-68, Kirkland, Wash., 68-77; mayor City of Houghton, 1968. Served to capt. USAF, 1958-62. Mem. Constrn. Specifications Inst. (Puget Sound chpt., dir. 1982-84, pres. 1984-85). Club: Bellevue Athletic. Avocations: model railroading, skiing, tennis. Home: 545 Fifth Ave West Kirkland WA 98033 Office: CH2M Hill 777 108 Ave NE PO Box 91500 Bellevue WA 98009-2050

PRUSSIA, LELAND SPENCER, banker; b. San Jose, Calif., 1929; s. Leland Spencer and Doris E. (Fowler) P.; m. Vivian Blom; children: Leslie, Alan L., Gregory. BA in Econs., Stanford U., 1951, MA in Econs., 1956; grad. Advanced Mgmt. Program, Harvard U., 1970; D in Econ. (hon.), U. San Francsico, 1984. Research economist Bank of Am. Nat. Trust & Savs. Assn., San Francisco, 1956-62, with bank investments securities div., 1962-65, v.p. investment portfolio activities, 1965-71, sr. v.p. investment securities div., 1971-74; exec. v.p., chief fin. officer Bank of Am. Nat. Trust & Savs. Assn., BankAm. Corp., San Francisco, 1974-78, 84-86, exec. officer World Banking dv., 1979-81; chmn. bd. BankAm. Corp., San Francisco, 1981-87; adv. dir. Gen. Motors-Hughes Electronics Corp.; bd. dirs. Calif. Econ. Devel. Corp., chmn. Pacific Rim Task Force; bd. dirs. Dimensional Corp. Fin., Inc.; prin. Diversified Corp. Loans, Inc.; mem. Calif. Senate Commn. on Corp. Governance, Shareholders Rights, Securities Transactions; lectr. in econs., U. San Francsico, 1957-65. Author: The Changing World of Banking: Bank Investment Portfolio Management. Trustee U. San Diego, Neighborhood Housing Services Am.; bd. dirs. Council for Basic Edn., U. San Francisco, U. Calif. Santa Barbara Found., Com. For Responsible Fed. Budget, St. Francis Found. of St. Francis Meml. Hosp.; adv. council J.L. Kellogg Grad. Sch. Mgmt. Northwestern U., San Francisco State U. Sch. Bus.; chmn. bd. Calif. Nature Conservancy, gov. nat. orgn.; mem. San Francisco Bay Area Leadership Task Force, Bus. Com. for Arts; adv. bd. Holy Family Day Home. Mem. Am. Econ. Assn., Western Econ. Assn., Am. Fin. Assn., Securities Industry Assn. (former Calif. region chmn., former dir. gov. bd.), Security Analysts of San Francisco, Stanford Assocs., Am. Polit. Found. (bd. dirs.). Clubs: Commonwealth of Calif., San Francisco Bond, Bankers San Francisco, Merchants Exchange, Pacific-Union, Bohemian. Office: Bank of Am Ctr Suite 4740 PO Box 37000 San Francisco CA 94137

PRYOR, KAREN WYLIE, biologist, writer; b. N.Y.C., May 14, 1932; d. Philip Gordon Wylie and Sally Ondeck; m. Taylor A. Pryor, June 25, 1954 (div. 1973); children: Tedmund, Michael, Gale; m. Jon M. Lindbergh, May 14, 1983. BA in English, Cornell U., 1954; postgrad., U. Hawaii, 1957-59, NYU, 1977-79, Rutgers U., 1979-82. Founder, curator Sea Life Park Oceanarium, Honolulu, 1960-71; copywriter Fawcett-McDermott, Honolulu, 1973-76; drama critic Honolulu Advertiser, 1971-75; free lance writer 1963—, marine mammal cons., 1970—; sci. advisor U.S. Tuna Found., Washington, 1976-82; cons. NSF, NASA, Nat. Geographic Soc., 1976—; commr. Marine Mammal Commn., Washington, 1984—. Author: Nursing Your Baby, 1963, 73, Lads Before the Wind: Adventures in Porpoise Training, 1975, Don't Shoot the Dog! The New Art of Teaching and Training, 1984 (Excellence in Media award Am. Psychol. Assn. 1984), How to Teach Your Dog to Play Frisbee, 1985; contbr. articles to profl. jours. Mem. Internat. Marine Amimal Trainers Assn., Animal Behavior Soc., Authors Guild. Avocations: gardening, bird watching. Home: 44811 SE 166 St North Bend WA 98045

PUCK, THEODORE THOMAS, geneticist, biophysicist, educator; b. Chgo., Sept. 24, 1916; s. Joseph and Bessie (Shapiro) Puckowitz; m. Mary Hill, Apr. 17, 1946; children: Stirling, Jennifer, Laurel. B.S., U. Chgo., 1937, Ph.D., 1940. Mem. commn. airborne infections Office Surgeon Gen., Army Epidemiol. Bd., 1944-46; asst. prof. depts. medicine and biochemistry U. Chgo., 1945-47; sr. fellow Am. Cancer Soc., Calif. Inst. Tech., Pasadena, 1947-48; prof. biophysics U. Colo. Med. Sch., 1948—, chmn. dept., 1948-67, disting. prof., 1986—; dir. Eleanor Roosevelt Inst. Cancer Research, 1962—; Disting. research prof. Am. Cancer Soc., 1966—; nat. lectr. Sigma Xi, 1975-76. Author: The Mammalian Cell as a Microorganism: Genetic and Biochemical Studies in Vitro, 1972. Mem. Commn. on Physicians for the Future. Recipient Albert Lasker award, 1958; Borden award med. research, 1959; Louisa Gross Horwitz prize, 1973; Gordon Wilson medal Am. Clin. and Climatol. Assn., 1977; award Environ. Mutagen Soc., 1981; Heritage Found. scholar, 1983; E.B. Wilson medal Am. Soc. Cell Biology, 1984; Bonfils-Stanton award in sci., 1984; Phi Beta Kappa scholar, 1985. Fellow Am. Acad. Arts and Scis.; mem. Am. Chem. Soc., Soc. Exptl. Biology and Medicine, AAAS (Phi Beta Kappa award and lectr. 1983), Am. Assn. Immunologists, Radiation Research Soc., Biophys. Soc., Genetics Soc. Am., Nat. Acad. Sci., Inst. Medicine, Paideia Group, Phi Beta Kappa, Sigma Xi. Address: Eleanor Roosevelt Inst Cancer Research 1899 Gaylord St Denver CO 80206

PUCKETT, ALLEN EMERSON, aeronautical engineer; b. Springfield, Ohio, July 25, 1919; s. Roswell C. and Catherine C. (Morrill) P.; m. Betty J. Howlett; children—Allen W., Nancy L., Susan E.; m. Marilyn I. McFarland; children—Margaret A., James R. B.S., Harvard, 1939, M.S., 1941; Ph.D., Calif. Inst. Tech., 1949. Lectr. aeros., chief wind tunnel sect. Jet Propulsion Lab., Calif. Inst. Tech., 1945-49; tech. cons. U.S. Army Ordnance, Aberdeen Proving Ground, Md., 1945-60; mem. sci. adv. com. Ballistic Research Labs., 1958-65; with Hughes Aircraft Co., Culver City, Calif., 1949—, exec. v.p., 1965-77, pres., 1977-78, chmn. bd., chief exec. officer, 1978—; dir. Am. Mut. Fund, Lone Star Industries; mem. steering group OASD adv. panel on aeros.; cons. Pres.'s Sci. Adv. Com.; chmn. research adv. com. control, guidance and navigation NASA, 1959-64; vice chmn. Def. Sci. Bd., 1962-66; mem. Army Sci. Adv. Panel, 1965-69, NASA tech. and research adv. com., 1968-72, space program adv. council, 1974-78; Wilbur and Orville Meml. lectr. Royal Aero. Soc., London, 1981. Author: (with Hans W. Liepmann) Introduction to Aerodynamics of a Compressible Fluid, 1947; editor: (with Simon Ramo) Guided Missile Engineering, 1959; contbr. tech. papers on high-speed aerodynamics. Trustee U. So. Calif. Recipient Lawrence Sperry award Inst. Aero. Scis., 1949, Lloyd V. Berkner award Am. Astronautical Soc., 1974; named Calif. Mfr. of Yr., 1980. Fellow AIAA (pres. 1972); mem. Aerospace Industries Assn. (chmn. 1979), Los Angeles World Affairs Council (pres.), Nat. Acad. Scis., Nat. Acad. Engring., A.A.A.S., Sigma Xi, Phi Beta Kappa. Office: Hughes Aircraft Co PO Box 45066 Los Angeles CA 90045 *

PUCKETT, ALLEN WEARE, industrial supplies distribution company executive; b. Pasadena, Calif., Mar. 17, 1942; s. Allen Emerson Puckett and Betty Jane (Howlett) Ward; m. Joan Adrienne Roth, Apr. 10, 1965 (div. 1980); children: Glenn A., Tod A.; m. M. Suzanne Reber, Dec. 20, 1982. BS, U. Calif., Berkeley, 1963; JD, Harvard U., 1966. Bar: Calif. 1966. Prin. McKinsey & Co., San Francisco, 1966-78; pres. Atman Corp., San Francisco, 1979-83; v.p. VWR Sci., San Francisco, 1980-83, Univar Corp., Seattle, 1984-85; sr. v.p. fin. VWR Corp., Seattle, 1986—; bd. dirs. SeaMed Corp., Redmond, Wash. Bd. dirs. Seattle Family Services, 1984—. Recipient Nathan Burkan prize ASCAP, 1966. Mem. Am. Statis. Assn. Democrat. Club: Rainier (Seattle). Avocations: skiing, squash, music. Home: 10550 Riviera Pl NE Seattle WA 98125 Office: VWR Corp Kell Ctr 1900 Bellevue WA 98004

PUDNEY, GARY LAURENCE, television exec.; b. Mpls., July 20, 1934; s. Lawrence D. and Agnes (Hansen) P. B.A., UCLA, 1956. Vice pres. ABC, Inc., N.Y.C., 1968—; v.p., sr. exec. in charge of spls. and talent ABC Entertainment, 1979—. Exec. producer for United Cerebral Palsy Aspen and Lake Tahoe Pro-Celebrity Tennis Festivals, 4 yrs., AIDS Project Los Angeles Dinner, 1985. Bd. dirs. Nat. Cerebral Palsy Found. Served to capt. USAF, 1957-60. Recipient Helena T. Deveraux Meml. award, 1985, Humanitarian award Nat. Jewish Ctr. for Immunology and Respiratory Medicine, 1986. Mem. Hollywood Radio and TV Soc. (bd. dirs.), Acad. TV Arts and Scis. (exec. com.), Met. Mus. Art, Mus. Modern Art. Democrat. Lutheran. Office: ABC Entertainment 2040 Ave of the Stars Century City CA 90067

PUENTE, JOSE GARZA, safety coordinator; b. Cuero, Tex., Mar. 19, 1949; s. Roque Leos and Juanita Vela (Garza) P.; m. Francisca Rodriguez Estrada, Sept. 7, 1969; 1 son, Anthony Burk. B.A., W. Tex. State U., Canyon, 1972; postgrad. U. Ariz.-Tucson, 1980; grad. U.S. Army transp. courses, 1972, 78; student U.S. Army Command and Gen. Staff Coll., 1981—. Cert. U.S. Council Accreditation in Occupational Hearing; cert. Audiometric Technicians of Am. Indsl. Hygiene Assn. Asst. gen. mgr. Am. Transit Corp., Tucson, 1972-75; pub. transp. supt. City of Tucson, 1975-77; asst. safety coordinator, Tucson, 1977-81; safety coordinator Mesa, Ariz., 1981—; owner La Paz Gospel Supplies & Gift shop, Tucson, 1979-80. Mem. Tucson Child Care Assn., 1973-74; mem. Citizen Task Force, Sunnyside sch. bd., 1977; co-founder Ray Morales Aid Fund, 1980. Serving as maj. USAR, 1971—. Fellow Advanced Mgmt. Seminar Urban Mass Transp. Adminstrn., Northeastern U., Boston, 1976-77; recipient Excellence award Ariz-Safety Assn., 1984. Mem. Am. Soc. Safety Engrs. (Safety Profl. of Yr. 1984), Mexican Am. Govtl. Employees (charter mem. Tucson), Res. Officers Assn., Ariz. Safety Engrs. Assn. Democrat. Baptist. Clubs: Internat. Order DeMolay (charter), Dobson Ranch Lions, Mesa Bowling League. Home: 2341 W Del Campo Mesa AZ 85202 Office: 648 N Mesa Dr Mesa AZ 85201

PUESCHEL, ROY MYRON, electrical engineer, consultant; b. Gardner, Kans., Aug. 9, 1954; s. William Robert and Sylvia Marie (Barker) P. BSEE, Calif. State U., Long Beach, 1976; MDiv., Biola U., 1982. Design engr. Griffin Tech., Rancho Dominguez, Calif., 1980-83; ptnr. Telion Software, San Pedro, Calif., 1983-85; staff engr. Hughes Aircraft, Los Angeles, 1985-86; cons. Q-Com, Santa Ana, Calif., 1984-85. Author: (software) Instant Access, 1985, Memory, 1985. Deacon First Baptist Ch., San Pedro, Calif., 1976-82. Republican. Avocation: amateur radio operator. Home: 927 W 30th St San Pedro CA 90731 Office: Hughes Aircraft PO Box 92919 Los Angeles CA 90009

PUETTER, RICHARD CHARLES, research astrophysicist; b. Chgo., June 5, 1952; s. Fritz and Trudee (Jeeninga) P.; m. Rosalinda Salazar, June 23, 1974. BA in Physics, U. Chgo., 1974; MS in Physics, U. Calif.-San Diego, La Jolla, 1977, PhD in Physics, 1980. Asst. research physicist U. Calif.-San Diego, La Jolla, 1980—; adj. lectr. physics U. Calif., San Deigo. Contbr. articles to profl. jours. Grantee NASA, NSF. Mem. AAAS, Am. Astron. Soc., Astron. Soc. Pacific. Office: U Calif San Diego Ctr Astrophysics & Space Scis C-011 La Jolla CA 92093

PUGAR, ELOISE ANN, research chemist; b. Pitts., May 4, 1957; d. Mark Louis and Olga Rose (Klasnick) P. Student, Carnegie-Mellon U., 1974-76; BS summa cum laude, U. Pitts., 1978; postgrad., U. Calif., Santa Barbara. Inorganic chemist Rockwell Internat., Thousand Oaks, Calif., 1982—. Contbr. articles to profl. jours. Mem. AAAS, Am. Chem. Soc., Internat. Union of Pure and Applied Chemistry, Am. Ceramic Soc. (1st Place Ceramographic award 1984), N.Y. Acad. Arts and Scis. Republican. Avocation: oil painting.

PUGAY, JEFFREY IBANEZ, mechancial engineer; b. San Francisco, June 26, 1958; s. Herminio Salazar and Petronila (Ibanez) P. BSME, U. Calif., Berkeley, 1981, MSME, 1982; MBA, Pepperdine U., 1986. Registered profl. engr., Calif. Assoc. tech. staff Aerospace Corp., Los Angeles, 1981; project engr. Hughes Aircraft Co., Los Angeles, 1982—. Mem. SME, Pi Tau Sigma. Republican. Roman Catholic. Avocations: racquetball, scuba diving, sailing, backpacking. Home: 8180 Manitoba St 120 Playa del Rey CA 90293 Office: Hughes Aircraft Co. PO Box 92919 MS S21/E349 Los Angeles CA 90009

PUGEL, ROBERT JOSEPH, publisher, English educator; b. Pueblo, Colo., Aug. 15, 1941; s. Joseph E. and Margaret E. (Jachetta) P.; A.A., U. So. Colo., 1959; B.A., Western State Coll. Colo., 1961, M.A., 1965; postgrad. (Univ. internat. fellow) U. London, 1968, U. Denver, 1967-69; m. E. Elke Williamson, June 29, 1968. Asst prof. English, U. So. Colo., 1965-67; teaching fellow U. Denver, 1967-69; prof. English, Met. State Coll., 1969-86; pres., owner Pugel Ranch, Pueblo, Colo., 1986—; founder, pub. Scribes mag., Denver, 1975—; poetry judge; Can./U.S.A. grantee McMaster U., Hamilton, Ont., Can., 1975; Rocky Mountain advisor Brit. Univs., 1970—; owner, operator Pugel Ranch, Pueblo, Colo. Mem. Colo. Dem. Central Com., 1970-81; chmn. Colo. Dem. House Dist. 39, 1974-80; del. Colo. Gov.'s Conf. on Aging, 1980. Recipient award for outstanding community service Public Relations Soc. Am., 1978; named Outstanding Contbr. to Colo. Sr. Community, 1978, 79, 80. Mem. Nat. Council Tchrs. English, Internat. Assn. Bus. Communicators, Pub. Relations Soc. Am., Congress Colo. Communicators, Am. Poetry Soc., NEA, AAUP, English-Speaking Union (internat. bd. govs. 1970-81, 1st v.p. 1974—, chmn. scholarship com. 1975—, organizer, condr. Conoco (Colo.) speech forum), Nat. Writers Club (featured poet 1978 Conf.), St. Andrew's Soc., Denver Zoo, Denver Art Mus., Denver Mus. Natural History, PEN, Colo. Poetry Soc., Poetry Soc. Am., Inst. Internat. Edn., Greenpeace, Sierra Club, Nat. Wildlife Fedn., Fund for Animals. Roman Catholic. Club: Racquet World. Editor, pub.: (poems) Chrysalis Seed, 1986; lit. mags. Paradigm Shift, Reality and Other Illusions, Turquoise Windows; founder, pub. Metrosphere, 1983—. Contbr. fiction, articles and poetry to various nat., region and local mags. and newspapers. Home: 7239 E Euclid Dr Englewood CO 80111 Office: Pugel Ranch 125 S Pugel Dr Pueblo CO 80204

PUGH, HELEN PEDERSEN, realtor; b. San Francisco, Feb. 17, 1934; d. Christian Edward and Gladys Phoebe Zumwalt Pedersen; m. Howard Brooks Pugh, Sr., Oct. 11, 1974; children—Catherine Collier, Stephen Leach, Matthew Leach, Virginia Schmitt. A.A., U. Calif.-Berkeley, 1953. Pvt. sec. to exec. dir. Republican party, Phoenix, 1972, Henderson Realty, Phoenix, 1973; sta. mgr. Mobil Oil Co., Phoenix, 1973-74; realtor, Russ Lyon Realty, Scottsdale, Ariz., 1978—. Vol. coordinator William Baker for Congress, Phoenix, 1972; vol. Phoenix Meml. Hosp., Scottsdale Hosp. North Devel. Com.; master tchr. Presbyterian Ch., youth leader; troop leader Cactus-Pine council Girl Scouts U.S.A., 1960-74; asst. den leader Roosevelt Council Boy Scouts Am.; instr. Jr. Achievement; v.p. Planned Parenthood Aux., Family Service Agy. Aux.;bd. dirs. Phoenix Symphony Aux., Phoenix Art Mus.; deacon Presbyn. Ch. Mem. Scottsdale Bd. Realtors, Scottsdale Comml. Bd., Phoenix Comml. Bd. (Multiple Listing Service Forms Com. award 1981), Internat. Real Estate Fedn. (Ariz. chpt. bd. dirs.), Farm and Land Inst., Valley of Sun Real Estate Exchangers, LWV, Scottsdale C. of C. (ambassador), U. Calif. Alumni Assn. (Ariz. chpt. pres., internat. tour dir.), Scottsdale Rep. Forum, Cactus Wren Rep. Women, Palo Verde Rep. Women, Delta Zeta. Clubs: Toastmasters (past pres., youth leader, gov. area 7, dist-ing.), Camelback. Lodge: Soroptimists. Home: 7463 E Raintree Ct Scottsdale AZ 85258 Office: 7150 E Lincoln Dr Scottsdale AZ 85253

PUGH, WARREN EDWARD, engine company executive; b. Salt Lake City, Dec. 21, 1909; s. William Edward and Eva May (Murphy) P.; m. Leta Vivian Curtis, Sept. 1, 1933; children: Carol Matheson, Lorin K., Donald E. Student, Latter-day Sts. Bus. Coll., Stevens Hennager Coll., U. Utah. Mgr. Cummins Intermountain Diesel Sales Co., Salt Lake City, 1943-75, chmn. exec. com., 1975—; also chmn. bd. dirs. Cummins Intermountain Idaho Inc., Boise; pres. Indsl. Devel. and Sales Co., Salt Lake City, 1945—. Chmn. transp. and pub. safety standing com., 1967-72, edn. subcom. Joint Appropriations Com., 1971-72, senate appropriations com. 1973—, Utah Hwy. Users Conf.; chmn., trustee Latter-day St. Hosp., Utah Found.; mem. Utah Ho. of Reps., 1959-60, Utah State Senate, 1967—, U. Utah Nat. Adv. Council, Latter-day St. Ch. Gen. Ch. Audit Com.; majority leader Utah Senate, 1969-70, pres. 1973-74; co-chmn. Senate and Ho. Exec. Appropriation Com., 1973—; trustee U. Utah Research Inst.; pres. Salt Lake Area C. of C. 1972-73; past mem. Latter-day St. Ch. Gen. Sunday Sch. Bd., High Council Salt Lake Holladay South Stake Latter-day St. Ch.; past bishop Halladay 8th Ward Latter-day St. Ch.; past pres. No. Calif. Latter-day St. Ch. Mission; patriarch Salt Lake Holladay South Stake Latter-day St. Ch. Clubs: Ft. Douglas Hidden Valley Country, Alta (Salt Lake City). Home: 5124 Cottonwood Ln Salt Lake City UT 84117 Office: Cummins Intermountain Diesel Sales Co 1030 Gale St Salt Lake City UT 84125

PUGH, WILLIAM OWEN, retired museum director; b. Terry, Mont., Feb. 7, 1918; s. Arthur Job and Opal Kerns P.; A.B., Whitman Coll., 1939; M.A., U. Pacific, 1947; postgrad. U. Iowa, 1939, 40; m. Sydney Houtz, Sept. 12, 1943; children—Michael W., Randall K., Julie L., Christopher L. Instr., then asst. prof. Whitman Coll., 1946-49; vice-chmn. English dept. Am. U., Beirut, Lebanon, 1949-52; exec. Yakima (Wash.) C. of C., 1953-56; personnel and community services mgr. Republic Pub. Co., Yakima, 1957-58; regional blood services adminstr. Columbia River Region, Yakima, 1958-76; dir. Yakima Valley Mus. and Hist. Assn., Yakima, 1976-84; Field reviewer Inst. Mus. Services, 1984-85. Mem. Wash. State Adv. Council on Archaeol. and Historic Preservation. Served to maj. Adj. Gen. Corps, AUS, 1941-46. Lanham scholar Z.A. Lanham Found., 1936-40. Mem. Am. Assn. State and Local History, Res. Officers Assn., Wash. Congress Parents and Tchrs. (life). Republican. Methodist. Clubs: Ice Skating, Lions.

PUGSLEY, JOHN ALLEN, entrepreneur, economist; b. Mpls., Jan. 5, 1934; s. Lawrence Eugene and Cleota Rae (Johnson) P.; m. Gloria Terry, Jan. 11, 1958 (div. Feb. 1981); children: Joseph, Hollis, Tamara. Student, El Camino Jr. Coll., 1951-52, U. Fla., 1952-53; BA, UCLA, 1960; postgrad., San Diego State Coll., 1960-61. V.p., then pres. Sky Camp Stores Inc., Downey, Calif., 1958-59, Porta Shop Systems Inc., Livonia, Mich., 1961-67; pres. Club Caribbean Inc., Newport Beach, Calif., 1967-69; investment counselor John Dye, Assocs., Newport Beach, 1969-73; pres. The Common Sense Press Inc., Costa Mesa, Calif., 1974-85, The Comparison Shopper Inc., Newport Beach, 1985—. Author: Common Sense Economics, 1974, The Alpha Stategy, 1980, The Bank Book, 1982; editor Common Sense Viewpoint, 1975-85. Served with U.S. Army, 1954-56. Avocations: skiing, scuba diving, sailing, woodworking. Home: PO Box 471 Corona Del Mar CA 92625 Office: The Comparison Shopper Inc 4121 Westerly Pl #112 Newport Beach CA 92660

PULLEN, KENT EDWARD, state legislator, chemist; b. El Paso, Tex., May 4, 1942; s. Eugene Hoyt and Maris Morie (Glover) P.; m. Fay Lynnette Endres, June 13, 1964; children—Katherine Ann, Walter David. B.S., U. N.Mex., 1963; Ph.D., U. Wash., 1967. Asst. prof. chemistry U. Idaho, Moscow, 1967-68; engr. Boeing Co., Seattle, 1968—; mem. Wash. Ho. Reps., Olympia, 1973-75, Wash. Senate, 1975—. Bd. dirs. Citizen Taxpayers Assn., Kent, Wash., 1979-85; chmn. Citizens Against Crime, 1975; co-chmn. Com. for Honest Elections, Kent, 1977. Mem. Seattle Profl. Engring. Employees Assn. (council). Club: Mountaineers. Wash. State Chess Champion, 1985. Office: Wash State Senate Legislative Bldg Olympia WA 98504

PULLEY, GEORGE GRAFTON, software company executive, data processing consultant; b. Amarillo, Texas, Jan. 10, 1947; s. George Henry and Mary Katherine (McInnish) P. AS, Amarillo Coll., 1970; BSBA, Texas Tech U., 1971; postgrad. in bus. administrn. West Texas State U., 1972. Systems and program mgr. Sunwest Bank, Albuquerque, 1972-79; pres. G. G. Pulley & Assoc., Inc., Albuquerque, 1979—; data processing cons. for banking ops. Mem. Data Processing Mgmt. Assn. (bd. dirs. 1981-82), Spl. Interest Group in Bus. Data Processing (v.p. 1980), Assn. Computing Machinery, Assn. Inst. Cert. Computer Profls. Republican. Methodist. Office: G G Pulley & Assocs Inc 5700 Harper Dr NE Suite 340 Albuquerque NM 87109

PULLIAM, EUGENE S., newspaper publisher; b. Atchison, Kans., Sept. 7, 1914; s. Eugene Collins and Myrta (Smith) P.; m. Jane Bleecker, May 29, 1943; children—Myrta, Russell, Deborah. A.B., DePauw U., 1935, LL.D., 1973. Reporter, UP, Chgo., Detroit, Buffalo, 1935-36; news editor Radio Sta. WIRE, Indpls., 1936-41; city editor Indpls. Star, 1947-48; mng. editor Indpls. News, 1948-62; publisher Indpls. Star and News, 1962-76; pres. Phoenix Newspapers, 1979—; exec. v.p. Central Newspapers, Indpls., 1979—. Mem. Am. Soc. Newspaper Editors, Am. Newspaper Pubs. Assn. Found. (past pres.), Hoosier State Press Assn. (treas.), Soc. Profl. Journalists, Delta Kappa Epsilon. Club: Paradise Valley Country. Office: The Indpls Star Indpls Newspapers Inc 307 N Pennsylvania St Indianapolis IN 46204

PULLIAM, PAUL EDISON, electrical engineer; b. Nickerson, Kans., June 6, 1912; s. George Washington and Hattie Lucy (Vandeventer) P.; B.S. in E.E., U. Mo., 1951; m. Ila M. Catrett, Feb. 3, 1945; children—Carol Ann Pulliam Rolls, Paula Ann Pulliam Bermingham. Elec. engr. Ozark Dam Constructors, Powerhouse, Bull Shoals Dam, Baxter County, Ark., 1951-52; commd. 2d lt. U.S. Army Res., 1937, advanced through grades to maj., 1961; field engr. RCA, Fighter Wing Tactical Air Command, 1952-53; elec. engr. Goodyear Atomic Corp., 1957-60; missiles engr. Chrysler Corp., Redstone Arsenal, Ala., 1957-60; ret., 1972 constrn. insp. Sacramento County Dept. Pub. Works, Sacramento, Calif., 1977-80. Registered profl. engr., Mo., Nev., Calif. Mem. Soc. Am. Mil. Engrs., IEEE (life), Res. Officers Assn. (life), SAR (pres. Sacramento chpt.), VFW (life). Democrat. Baptist. Club: Toastmasters. Initiated VHF Radio Balun antenna assemblies devel. by USAF personnel, 1986, provided concept for electric-drive torpedoes for USN, USCG. Home: 7916 Grandstaff Dr Sacramento CA 95823 Office: Med Emergency Response 7916 Grandstaff Dr Sacramento CA 95823

PURCELL, ALEXANDER HOLMES, entomologist, educator; b. Summit, Miss., Oct. 12, 1942; s. Alexander H. and Dorothy (Adams) P.; m. Rita Hall, Oct. 14, 1946. BS, USAF Acad., 1964; PhD, U. Calif., Davis, 1974. Commd. capt. USAF, 1964, officer, pilot, 1964-70, resigned, 1970; grad. research asst. U. Calif., Davis, 1971-74; entomologist, assoc. prof. U. Calif., Berkeley, 1974—; cons. FAO (UN), 1981. Contbr. articles to profl. jours. Mem. AAAS, Entomological Soc. Am., Am. Phytopath. Soc. Avocations: flying, camping. Office: U Calif Dept Entomological Scis 201 Wellman Hall Berkeley CA 94720

PURCELL, JENNIFER ESTELLE, oceanographer, educator; b. Kansas City, Mo., Oct. 25, 1954; d. Hoyt and Genevieve Marie (Heiman) P. BS, MS, Stanford U., 1976; PhD, U. Calif., Santa Barbara, 1981. Postdoctoral scientist Woods Hole (Mass.) Oceanographic Inst., 1981-83, U. Victoria, B.C., Can., 1983-84; asst. prof. oceanography Oreg. State U., Corvallis, 1984-86, Horn Point Environ. Labs. U. Md., Cambridge, 1987—; speaker Sea Grant Extension, Coos Bay and Astoria, Oreg.; NSF vis. prof. U. Wash. Friday Harbor Labs., 1986-87. Reviewer NSF Biol. Oceanography; contbr. articles to profl. jours. Recipient Seagrant, NOAA, 1982; NATO/NSF fellow, 1985. Mem. Am. Soc. Limnology and Oceanography, Western Soc. Naturalists, Assn. Women in Sci., Sigma Xi. Avocations: swimming, country dancing, skiing, hiking. Office: U Md Horn Point Environ Labs PO Box 775 Cambridge MD 21613

PURDIE, ROGER KENT, fire chief; b. San Diego, July 31, 1942; s. Alden A. and Elsie (Brizendine) P.; m. Heather Lynn; children—Roger, Christa. A.S., Chaffey Coll., 1968. B.S., Calif. State U., 1980; With City of Rialto (Calif.) Fire Dept., 1964—, battalion chief, 1974-77, fire chief, 1977—; fire sci. instr. San Bernardino Valley Coll., 1973-77, Crafton Hills Coll., 1981—; fire, rescue coordinator San Bernardino County operational area; interim city adminstr. City of Rialto. Field service rep. Rialto Salvation Army; mem. Am. Heart Assn. Bd. dirs., pres. Lung Assn. San Bernardino County, Inyo-Mono Counties. Mem. Rialto Firemen's Benefit Assn., Rialto Fire Police Protective League (past pres.), San Bernardino County Tng. Officers Assn. (v.p. San Bernardino County), San Bernardino County Fire Prevention Officers, Calif. Fire Chief-Fire Prevention Officers Assn., San Bernardino County Fire Chiefs Assn. (pres. 1979), (bd. dirs., rescue and paramedic com. chmn.), Citrus Belt Fire Chief Assn. (pres. 1980). Republican. Lutheran (v.p. council). Home: PO Box 1104 Rialto CA 92376 Office: 131 S Willow Ave Rialto CA 92376

PURE, MELINDA ALICE, business manager; b. San Bernardino, Calif., Sept. 17, 1960; d. Kenneth Walter and Marian Lucille (Bown) P. BA in Mgmt., cert. computers and programming, Calif. State U., San Bernadino, 1983. Bus. mgr. Bruggeman, Smith & Peckham, Attys., San Bernadino and Rancho Cucamonga, Calif., 1983—. Mem. Employer's Adv. Council, San Bernadino, 1984—. Mem. ABA (assoc.), Assn. Legal Administrators, Alumni Assn. Calif. State U. San Bernadino (life), Nat. Assn. Female Execs. Republican. Baptist. Avocations: scuba diving, swimming, home improvement, collecting stamps, spoons, antiques. Office: Bruggeman Smith & Peckham 524 N Mountain View Ave San Bernadino CA 92401-1295

PURIFOY, CECIL ERNEST, JR., retired educator; b. Houston, Sept. 22, 1927; s. Cecil Ernest Sr. and Ruth Agnes (Dupre) P. BEd, U. Tex., 1949; MA, Mich. State U., 1952, PhD, 1970. Cert. tchr., Tex. Tchr. Panama Canal Co., Canal Zone, Republic of Panama, 1962-63, 66-67; asst. prof. U. Tenn., Knoxville, 1966-67, 69-71; assoc. prof. Ball State U., Muncie, Ind., 1971-85. Teaching fellow Mich. State U., 1950-52, 53-54, 64-66. Mem. Nat. Council Tchrs. English, Maui Ret. Tchrs. Assn., Hawaii Ret. Tchrs. Assn., Am. Assn. Retired Persons, Phi Delta Kappa. Republican. Mem. Christian Sci. Ch. Home: 2792 Aina Lani Dr Pukalani HI 96768-8404

PURISCH, ELLEN CAROL, clinical social worker; b. Washington, June 29, 1953; d. Albert Phillip and Adelaide Sylvia (Yarus) Maslow; m. Arnold David Purisch, Aug. 10, 1975; 1 child, Daniel Zachary. Lic. clin. social worker, marriage, family and child counselor. Psychiat. social worker United Family and Children's Soc., Plainfield, N.J., 1979-83; clin. social worker Child Guidance of Orange County, Huntington Beach, Calif., 1983-85; dir. Health Directions, Fountain Valley, Calif., 1985—; cons. Johnson & Johson, New Brunswick, N.J., 1981-83; mem. extended faculty UCLA, 1985. Mem. Nat. Assn. Social Workers, Acad. Cert. Social Workers, Phi Kappa Phi. Democrat. Office: Health Directions 8840 Warner Ave Suite 301 Fountain Valley CA 92708

PURNELL, WILLARD DALE, geotechnical engineer, engineering geologist; b. Seattle, Dec. 27, 1931; s. Harry Francis and Eleanor Dagmar (Olson) P.; m. Helen Georgina Coates, Aug. 24, 1957; children: Angela Gail, Marcus Girard. AAS, Everett Community Coll., 1956; BS in Geology and Engring., U. Wash., 1959. Registered geologist, Calif., Idaho; cert. engring. geologist, Calif. Staff geologist Dames & Moore, Seattle, 1958-69; chief soils engr., engring. geologist The Sanwick Corp., Seattle, 1969-72; prin. W.D. Purnell & Assocs., Seattle and Bellingham, Wash., 1972—; v.p. Sun Mark Property Devel., Bellevue, Wash., 1972-73; gen. ptnr. The Glen Co., Bellingham, 1973—. Chmn. bd. dirs. Lower Snoqualmie Valley Sch. Dist., Carnation, Wash., 1964-69. Served with USN, 1952-53. Mem. Wash. State Assn. Engring. Geologists (chmn. 1970-71), N.W. Wash. Engrs. Club, Am. Legion. Republican. Club: Bellingham Yacht. Avocations: camping, big game hunting, fishing, mountaineering. Home: 1392 Chuckanut Dr Bellingham WA 98226 Office: W D Purnell & Assocs 4200 Meridian Suite 200 Bellingham WA 98226

PURSEL, HAROLD MAX, SR., mining engr.; b. Fruita, Colo., Sept. 15, 1921; s. Harold Maurice and Viola Pearl (Wagner) P.; B.S. in Civil Engring., U. Wyo., 1950; m. Virginia Anna Brady, May 6, 1950; children—Harold Max, Leo William, Dawn Allen, Helen Virginia, Viola Ruth. Asst. univ. architect U. Wyo., 1948-50; with Sharrock & Pursel, Contractors, 1951-55; owner Max Pursel, Earthwork Constrn., 1955-59; project engr. Farson (Wyo.) Irrigation Project, 1960-61; owner Wyo. Builders Service, Casper, 1962-66; head dept. home improvement Gamble Stores, Rawlins, Wyo., 1967; resident work instr. Casper (Wyo.) Job Corps Conservation Center, 1968; P.M. coordinator Lucky Mc Uranium Mine, Riverton, Wyo., 1969-80; constrn. insp. U.S. Bur. Reclamation, 1983—; cons. freelance heavy and light constrn., 1984—. Served with U.S. Army, 1942-45. Mem. Nat. Rifle Assn., Internat. Platform Assn., Mensa. Clubs: Eagles, Masons, Shriners. Exptl. research with log, timber and frame constrn. in conjunction with residential applications. Home: PO Box 572 Riverton WY 82501

PURSELL, CARROLL WIRTH, history educator; b. Visalia, Calif., Sept. 4, 1932; s. Carroll Wirth and Ruth Irene (Crowell) P.; m. Joan Young, Jan. 28, 1956 (dec. 1985); children: Rebecca Elizabeth, Matthew Carroll; m. Angela Woollacott, Dec. 20, 1986. B.A., U. Calif., Berkeley, 1956, Ph.D., 1962; M.A., U. Del., 1958. Asst. prof. history Case Inst. Tech., Cleve., 1963-65; asst. prof. U. Calif., Santa Barbara, 1965-69; asso. prof. U. Calif., 1969-76, prof., 1976—; Mellon prof. Lehigh U., Bethlehem, Pa., 1974-76; vis. research scholar Smithsonian Instn., 1970. Author: Early Stationary Steam Engines in America, 1969, The Military Industrial Complex, 1972, From Conservation to Ecology. Fellow AAAS; Mem. Soc. History of Tech. (former sec.), History of Sci. Soc., Orgn. Am. Historians, Am. Hist. Assn., Phi Beta Kappa. Democrat. Home: 624 Chelham Way Santa Barbara CA 93108 Office: Dept History U Calif Santa Barbara CA 93106

PURSER, LEE WASHBURN, sales and management consultant, author; b. N.Y.C., Dec. 7, 1945; d. Carr Robinson and Grace (Pelzer) P.; m. Russell Lawrence Nichols, Oct. 1976 (div.); 1 child, Sky. Student Vassar Coll., 1963-66, Inst. Des Professeurs de Francais à L'Etrangé, 1967; BA, U. N.C., 1969; PhD in Philosophy, Internat. Coll., 1978. Lic. real estate agt., Calif. Asst. editor Macmillan Pubs., N.Y.C., 1968-69; assoc. editor Med. Aspects of Human Sexuality, N.Y.C., 1969-70; chmn. French dept., student counselor Barlow Sch., Amenia, N.Y., 1970-72; cons., tchr. San Diego Inst. Transactional Analysis, 1978-82; nat. seminar leader, individual and group cons., La Jolla, Calif., 1974-87, to groups and bus., 1974-84; sales mgr. Country View Condominiums, San Diego, 1984-85; bus. cons. Terry Cole/Whittaker Ministries, Brehm Communities, 1983-85; sales, floor supr. Hanson Art Galleries, 1986-87; media personality; guest lectr. Brandeis U., U. San Diego, Internat. Coll., others; keynote speaker to KFMB, Gen. Atomic, Fin. Exec. Inst., Women in Mgmt., Nat. Accts. Assn., others. Named Outstanding Young Woman of Am. Fuller & Dees, Washington, 1975. Mem. Internat. Transactional Analysis Assn. (clin. mem.). Author: Help Your Self, 1982. Home: 2098 Sea Village Circle Cardiff By The Sea CA 92007

PURVES, WILLIAM KIRKWOOD, scientist; b. Sacramento, Oct. 28, 1934; s. William Kirkwood and Dorothy (Brandenburger) P.; m. Jean McCauley, June 9, 1959; 1 son, David William. B.S., Calif. Inst. Tech., 1956; M.S., Yale U., 1957, Ph.D., 1959. NSF postdoctoral fellow U. Tubingen, Ger., 1959-60; Nat. Cancer Inst. postdoctoral fellow UCLA, 1960-61; asst. prof. botany U. Calif., Santa Barbara, 1961-65; assoc. prof. biochemistry U. Calif., 1965-70, prof. biology, 1970-73, chmn. dept. biol. scis., 1972-73; prof. biology, head biol. sci. group U. Conn., Storrs, 1973-77; Stuart Mudd prof. biology Harvey Mudd Coll., Claremont, Calif., 1977—; chmn. depts. biol. and computer sci. Harvey Mudd Coll., 1985—; adj. prof. plant physiology U. Calif., Riverside, 1979-85; vis. fellow computer sci. Yale U., 1983-84. Author: Life, the Science of Biology, 1983, 2d ed., 1987. NSF sr. postdoctoral fellow U. London, 1967; NSF sr. postdoctoral fellow Harvard U., 1968; NSF research grantee, 1962—. Fellow AAAS; mem. Am. Soc. Plant Physiologists, Am. Inst. Biol. Scis., Am. Assn. Artificial Intelligence, Cognitive Sci. Soc., Sigma Xi. Democrat. Home: 2817 N Mountain Ave Claremont CA 91711 Office: Harvey Mudd Coll Claremont CA 91711

PURVIS, JOHN ANDERSON, lawyer; b. Greeley, Colo., Aug. 31, 1942; s. Virgil J. and Emma Lou (Anderson) P.; m. Charlotte Johnson, Apr. 3, 1976; 1 child, Whitney; children by previous marriage—Jennifer, Matt. B.A. cum laude, Harvard U., 1965; J.D., U. Colo., 1968. Bar: Colo. 1968, U.S. Dist. Ct. Colo. 1968, U.S. Ct. Appeals (10th cir.) 1978, U.S. Ct. Claims, 1980. Dep. dist. atty. Boulder, Colo., 1968-69; asst. dir. and dir. legal aid U. Colo. Sch. Law, 1969; assoc. Williams, Taussig & Trine, Boulder, 1969; head Boulder office Colo. Pub. Defender System, 1970-72; assoc. and ptnr. Hutchinson, Black, Hill, Buchanan & Cook, Boulder, 1972-85; ptnr. Buchanan, Gray, Purvis and Schuetze, 1985—; acting Colo. State Pub. Defender, 1978; adj. prof. law U. Colo., 1981, 84—, others; lectr. in field. Chmn., Colo. Pub. Defender Commn., 1979—; mem. nominating commn. Colo. Supreme Ct., 1984—; chmn. Boulder County Criminal Justice Com., 1975-81, Boulder County Manpower Council, 1977-78. Recipient Ames award Harvard U., 1964; Outstanding Young Lawyer award Colo. Bar Assn., 1978. Mem. Internat. Soc. Barristers, Colo. Bar Assn., Boulder County Bar Assn., Colo. Trial Lawyers Assn., Am. Trial Lawyers Assn., Trial Lawyers for Pub. Justice. Democrat. Address: 1050 Walnut St Suite 501 Boulder CO 80302

PUSTIS, STEPHEN JOHN, textile and forest products executive; b. Ancon, Canal Zone, Panama, June 19, 1955; came to U.S., 1970; s. Joseph John and Louise Constance (Kalakowsky) P.; m. Nancy Nadine Carlson, Oct. 18, 1980; children: Robert Joseph, Brenna Louise, Lyssa Marie. AA, St. Petersburg Jr. Coll., Clearwater, Fla., 1975; BS in Conservation and Forest Resources, U. Fla., 1978; A in Computer Info. Systems with honors, Cen. Oreg. Community Coll., 1986. Timber mgmt. forester Willamette Nat. Forest Orgn., Detroit, Oreg., 1978-80, Malheur Nat. Forest Orgn., Burns, Oreg., 1980-81; tree improvement and reforestation forester Ochoco Nat. Forest Orgn., Prineville, Oreg., 1981-84; office mgr. Diamond Internat. Corp., Bend, Oreg., 1984—; Mem. bus. computer adv. com. Cen. Oreg. Community Coll., Bend, 1986—. Panel mem. computer standardization com. City of Bend, 1986—; Bend C. of C. Wood Products Task Force; scoutmaster Boy Scouts Am., Detroit, Oreg., 1979-80; emergency fire med. technician Detroit-Idanha Ambulance Service, 1978-80, Burns Fire Dept., 1980-81; U.S. Forest Service Fire Med. Technician, 1979-81; vol. Deschutes Forest Plan Citizens' Group, Bend, 1986. Mem. Soc. Am. Foresters (sec., treas. 1986—), Alpha Zeta, Phi Theta Kappa. Republican. Roman Catholic. Club: U. Fla. Alumni. Avocations: scuba diving, woodworking, sailing. Home: 61606 Summershade Dr Bend OR 97702 Office: Diamond Internat Corp 1627 NE 3d Bend OR 97701-4028

PUTMAN, CAROL JEAN, poet, writer; b. San Francisco, Jan. 1, 1943; d. Joe Alfred and Jessie Jane (Harris) P. AA, Diablo Valley Coll., 1965; student, Sacramento State Coll., 1966; BA, Calif. State U., Hayward, 1968. Freelance photographer Clayton, Calif., 1975-80; exec. sec. Bank of Am., San Francisco, 1980; group sec. physics dept. U. Calif., Berkeley, 1974-75, sec. civil engring. dept., 1981-84, faculty sec. journalism dept., 1984-85, adminstrv. asst. math. dept., 1985-86; writer, poet Walnut Creek, Calif., 1986—. Avocations: sailing, bicycling.

PYE, DAVID THOMAS, life sciences company executive; b. Darby, Pa., June 12, 1942; s. David and Grace Marie (Dale) P. B.S., Widener U., 1964. C.P.A., Pa., Calif. Tax cons. Price Waterhouse & Co., Phila., 1964-70; dir. taxes AID, Inc., Phila., 1970-75; dir. tax adminstrn. Syntex Corp., Palo Alto, Calif., 1975—. Mem. Am. Inst. C.P.A.s, Calif. C.P.A. Soc., Pa. Inst. C.P.A.s, Tax Execs. Inst. Home: 9 Crags Ct San Francisco CA 94131 Office: Syntex Corp 3401 Hillview Ave Palo Alto CA 94304

PYE, DORI, association executive; b. Atlanta; d. Irving Joseph and Grayce Edna (Dobbins) Nowak; div.; children: Joshua, Kenneth. M.A., Columbia U. Sch. Journalism, 1948; postgrad. advanced acad. program mgmt. Notre Dame U., 1978, exec. mgmt. UCLA, 1981. Cert. C. of C. exec., Calif. Motion picture, TV actress, 1950-60; pres., chief exec. officer Los Angeles W. C. of C., 1969—; apptd. mem. Calif. Conf. Small Bus., 1980; mem. adv. com. bus. ins. Calif. State Senate, 1984—; founder-organizer, Westwood Thrift & Loan Assn., 1982—; mem. Nat. Women's Forum, 1986. Bd. dirs. Century City Hosp.; vice chmn. Los Angeles City Housing Commn., 1984—. Recipient nat., state and city awards. Club: Regency (Los Angeles). Office: 10880 Wilshire Blvd Suite 1103 Los Angeles CA 90024

PYKE, RONALD, mathematics educator; b. Hamilton, Ont., Can., Nov. 24, 1931; s. Harold and Grace Carter (Digby) P.; m. Gladys Mary Davey, Dec. 19, 1953; children: Darlene, Brian, Ronald. BA (hon.), McMaster U., 1953; MS, U. Wash., 1955, PhD, 1956. Asst. prof. Stanford U., Calif., 1956-58; prof. Columbia U., N.Y.C., 1958-60; prof. math. U. Wash., Seattle, 1960—; vis. prof. U. Cambridge, Eng., 1964-65, Imperial Coll., London, 1970-71; pres. Inst. Math. Stats., 1986—; cons. Boeing Co. Editor Ann. Prob., 1972-75; contbr. articles to profl. jours. NSF grantee, 1961—. Fellow Internat. Statis. Inst., Am. Statis. Assn., Inst. Math. Stats. (pres. 1986-87); mem. Am. Math. Soc., Math. Assn. Am. Home: 15804 NE 116 St Redmond WA 98052 Office: U Wash Dept Math Seattle WA 98195

PYLE, NORMAN, bank executive; b. Jersey City, July 9, 1925; s. Louis Apgar and Elizabeth (Healy) P.; m. Marjorie Wohlfahrt; children: James N., Susan, Douglas N., David N., Jeffrey N. Student, Cornell U., 1943-45, Rutgers U., 1946-47; BA with honors, Wesleyan U., 1949, postgrad., 1949-50. Cert. data processor, infosystems auditor, quality analyst. Auditor First Nat. Bank Oreg., Portland, 1950-54, EDP auditor, 1957-75, gen. auditor, 1975-76, quality assurance officer, 1976-80; auditor Peoples Trust Co. Bergen County, Hackensack, N.J., 1955-56; mgr. EDP audit dept. First Interstate Bank Oreg., Portland, 1981—. Active Portland Chamber Orch. Assn. Served with USN, 1943-46. Mem. EDP Auditors Assn., Data Processing Mgmt. Assn., Computer Security Inst. Republican. Avocations: tennis, golf, swimming, weight lifting. Office: First Interstate Bank Oreg PO Box 3131 Portland OR 97208

PYPER, JAMES WILLIAM, chemist; b. Wells, Nev., Sept. 5, 1934; s. William Jones and Wilma (Bjelke) P.; m. Phyllis Diane Henry, Aug. 30, 1957; children: Scott, Mark, Gregory, Tara, Tammy, Wendy, Michael, Tanya, David. BS, Brigham Young U., 1958, MS, 1960; PhD, Cornell U., 1964. Ordained to ministry Ch. Jesus Christ of Latter-day Saints as bishop, 1973. Research chemist Lawrence Livermore (Calif.) Nat. Lab., 1963-84, mass spectrometry group leader, 1973-75, tritium tech. group leader, 1977-78, applied phys. chemistry group leader, 1979-80, sect. leader for analytical chemistry, 1980-83, dep. sect. leader for analytical chemistry, 1983-87, assoc. div. leader condensed matter and analytical scis. div., 1987—. Contbr. articles to sci. jours. Presided over local congregation, 1973-75; mem. stake high council, 1976—. Republican. Office: U Calif Lawrence Livermore Nat Lab Livermore CA 94550

PYZDEK, THOMAS, management consultant; b. Omaha, July 13, 1948; s. Charles Joseph and Margaret (Cosgriff) P.; m. Carol Lynn Krajicek, Aug. 23, 1969; children: Angela, Amy. BS in Econs., U. Nebr.; MS in Indsl. Engring., U. Ariz. Cert. coll. instr., Ariz. Quality, reliability engr. Valmont Industries, Omaha, 1973-75, supr. quality, reliabiligy engring., 1977-79; sr. product assurance engr. Hughes Aircraft Co., Tucson, 1979-82, head total quality assurance, 1982-83; pres., chief exec. officer Quality Am. Inc., Tucson, 1983—. Author: An SPC Primer, 1984, (software) SPC-PC, 1986, Certified Quality Engineer Exam Study Guide, 1984, What Every Engineer Should Know About Quality 1987; editor: Quality Engineering HBK, 1986; contbr. articles to profl. jours. Mem. Am. Soc. Quality Control (sr., cert.), Mensa. Office: Quality Am Inc 5430 S 12th Ave #C Tucson AZ 85706

QUAAS, LEROY M., city engineer; b. Maple Plain, Minn., Feb. 24, 1942; s. Carl F. and Dorothy (Leiter) Q.; m. Patricia De La Cruz, Apr. 10, 1965; children—Thad, Theron, Tara, Travis; B.C.E., Valparaiso U., 1964; student U. So. Calif., 1965-66, Ariz. State U., 1975. Registered Profl. Engr., Calif., Ariz. Asst. bridge engr., resident engr. State of Calif., 1964-70; asst. county engr. Imperial County (Calif.), 1970-72; asst. city engr. City of Tempe (Ariz.), 1972-78, city engr., 1978—. Mem. Am. Pub. Works Assn., Tau Beta Pi. Office: City of Tempe 31 E 5th St Tempe AZ 85281

QUAY, STEVEN CARL, pharmaceutical company executive; b. Coldwater, Mich., Nov. 7, 1950; s. LaGene Madsen and Roberta Jean (Yarrington) Q.; m. Judy Ellen Newitt, Aug. 14, 1971; 1 child, Stephanie. BA cum laude, Western Mich. U., 1971; MS, U. Mich., 1974, PhD Biol. Chemistry, 1975, MD, 1977. Diplomate Am. Bd. Anat. Pathology. Instr. pathology Harvard U. Med. Sch., Boston, 1977-80; asst. prof. pathology Stanford (Calif.) U. Sch. Medicine, 1980-86; pres., chief exec. officer Salutar, Inc., Sunnyvale, Calif., 1986—, also chmn. bd. dirs.; chmn. bd. dirs. Vital Devices Inc., Los Altos, Calif. Contbr. articles to profl. jours. Named Disting. Alumnus Western Mich. U., Kalamazoo, 1981. Mem. Am. Assn. Pathologists, Am. Soc. Biol. Chemists, Soc. Nuclear Medicine, Internat. Acad. Pathology, Biophys. Soc. Presbyterian. Clubs: University (Palo Alto), Stanford U. Faculty.

QUEVEDO, ERMEL B., engineering consultant; b. Guayaquil, Ecuador, Sept. 21, 1947; came to U.S., Sept. 1966, naturalized, 1981; s. Ermel G. and Evelina (Bejarano) Q.; m. Mary Christine Breitenbach, Aug. 26, 1972; children: Michelle, Christy, Katherine. BCE, Gonzaga U., 1970; MCE, U. Idaho, 1972; MBA, U. Portland, Oreg., 1986. Registered profl. engr., Oreg., Wash. Staff engr. Mirza Engring., Chgo., 1972-74; prin. engr. Shannon & Wilson, Portland, 1974-84; asst. mgr. Cornforth Cons., Portland, 1984—. Coach Cedar Splinters Soccer Club, Beaverton, Oreg., 1983-86. Mem. ASCE (mem. task force on City of Portland spl inspection program 1984), Geotech. Engring. Group (chmn. Portland br. 1982-83), Internat. Soc. Soil, Mechanics. and Found. Engrs. Cons. Engring. Council Oreg. Roman Catholic. Avocations: soccer, volleyball. Home: 15220 NW Acorn Pl Beaverton OR 97006

QUICK-RUBEN, STEVEN, lawyer; b. Los Angeles, Aug. 27, 1955; s. Merton and Jeanne C. (Thompson) Ruben. BA, U. Wis., Madison, 1981; JD, U. Puget Sound, 1983. Bar: Wash. 1984, U.S. Dist. Ct. (we. dist.) Wash. 1984, U.S. Ct. Appeals (9th cir.) 1984. Newsman Sta. KRAM, Las Vegas, Nev., 1973-75, Sta. WZEE-FM, Madison, 1975-78; legal editor Dewitt Sundby et al, Madison, 1978-80; assoc. Tuell, Anderson & Fisher, Tacoma, 1981-87; pres. Safecard, Inc., Seattle, 1987—. Editor: Public Assistance in Wisconsin, 1980; Mcpl. Law Bull., 1978-80. Pres., bd. dirs. Camerata Singers, Tacoma, 1984-85; bd. dirs., v.p. Tacoma Unit Bridge Assn., 1983-86; bd. dirs. Tacoma Philharm., 1981-84. Max C. Fleischman Found. grantee, 1973. Mem. Assn. Trial Lawyers Am., Wash. State Trial Lawyers Assn., Am. Contract Bridge League. Democrat. Home: 1514 N Fife St Tacoma WA 98406 Office: Tuell Anderson & Fisher 3790 3d Ave NE Seattle WA 98115

QUIGLEY, DANIEL PATRICK, lawyer; b. Chgo., May 21, 1959; s. John Michael and Esther Therese (Duffy) Q.; m. Ane Marie Tierney, June 5, 1982; children: Brigid Anne, Maura Colleen. BA with highest distinction, U. Ariz., 1981; JD magna cum laude, Georgetown U., 1984. Bar: Ariz. 1984, U.S. Dist. Ct. Ariz., 1984. Assoc. Brown & Bain, P.A., Phoenix, 1984—. Pres. Silvertree Homeowners' Assn., Phoenix, 1986—. Mem. ABA, Assn. Trial Lawyers Am., Maricopa County Bar Assn. Democrat. Roman Catholic. Avocations: sports, reading. Home: 3813 E Betty Elyse Ln Phoenix AZ 85032 Office: Brown & Bain PA 222 N Central Ave PO Box 400 Phoenix AZ 85001

QUIGLEY, JOHN MICHAEL, economist, educator; b. N.Y.C., Feb. 12, 1942. B.S. with distinction, U.S. Air Force Acad., 1964; M.Sc. with honors, U. Stockholm, Sweden, 1965; A.M., Harvard U., 1971, Ph.D., 1972. Commd. 2d lt. U.S. Air Force, 1964, advanced through grades to capt., 1968; asst. prof. econs. Yale U., 1972-74, assoc. prof., 1974-81; prof. pub. policy U. Calif., Berkeley, 1979—; prof. econs. U. Calif., 1981—; vis. prof. econs. and stats. U. Gothenberg, 1978; cons. numerous govt. agys. and pvt. firms; econometrician Hdqrs. U.S. Air Force, Pentagon, 1965-68; research assoc. Nat. Bur. Econ. Research, N.Y.C., 1968-78; mem. com. on nat. urban policy Nat. Acad. Sci., 1985—. Author, editor, contbr. articles to profl. jours.; mem. editorial bd. Land Econs., 1974-81, Jour. Urban Econs., 1978—, Council on Pub. Policy and Mgmt., 1979—, AREVE Jour., 1985—. Fulbright scholar, 1964-65; fellow NSF, 1968-69, Woodrow Wilson, 1968-71, Harvard IBM, 1969-71, NDEA, 1969-71, Thord-Gray Am. Scandinavian Found. 1971-72, Social Sci. Research Council, 1971-72. Mem. Am. Econ. Assn., Econometric Soc., Regional Sci. Assn. (bd. dirs. 1986—), Nat. Tax Assn., Assn. for Pub. Policy and Mgmt. (bd. dirs. 1986—). Home: 875 Hilldale Ave Berkeley CA 94708 Office: U Calif 2607 Hearst Ave Berkeley CA 94720

QUILLIGAN, EDWARD JAMES, educator; b. Cleve., June 18, 1925; s. James Joseph and Maude Elvira (Ryan) Q.; m. Betty Jane Cleaton, Dec. 14, 1946; children—Bruce, Jay, Carol, Christopher, Linda, Ted. B.A., Ohio State U., 1951, M.D., 1951; M.A. (hon.), Yale, 1967. Intern Ohio State U. Hosp., 1951-52, resident, 1952-54; resident Western Res. U. Hosps., 1954-56; asst. prof. obstetrics and gynecology Western Res. U., 1957-63, prof., 1963-65; prof. obstetrics and gynecology UCLA, 1965-66; prof., chmn. dept. Ob-

Gyn Yale U., 1966-69; prof., chmn. dept. Ob-Gyn U. So. Calif., 1969-78, asso. v.p. med. affairs, 1978-79; prof. Ob-Gyn. U. Calif., Irvine, 1980-83, U. Wis., 1983-85; prof., chmn. Ob-Gyn U. Calif.-Davis Med. Ctr., Sacramento, 1985—. Contbr. articles to med. jours.; Editor: Am. Jour. Obstetrics and Gynecology. Served to 2d lt. AUS, 1944-46. Recipient Centennial award Ohio State U., 1970. Mem. Soc. Gynecologic Investigation, Am. Gynecol. Soc., Am. Coll. Obstetics and Gynecology, Sigma Xi. Home: 4281 Cameron Rd Cameron Park CA 95682 Office: U Calif 1621 Alhambra Blvd Suite 2500 Sacramento CA 95816

QUILLIN, RICHARD LEE, infosystems specialist, municipal official; b. Las Vegas, May 27, 1939; s. Carl A. and Ruth Lucille (Twohig) Q.; m. Carol June Thompson, Jan. 12, 1962; children: Susan Maree, Kara Leigh. BS, N.Mex. State U., 1963. Western regional mgr. Call-A-Computer, Mpls., 1966-70; v.p. Bio-Med. Communications Systems, Mpls., 1971-76; cons. Mpls., 1976; various mgmt. positions City of Albuquerque, 1976-82, group mgr. user services, 1982-84, info. systems officer, 1984—. Advisor Am. Heart Assn., Albuquerque, 1982; mem. computer adv. com. Albuquerque Pub. Schs., 1984—. Mem. IEEE, Computer Soc. of IEEE. Democrat. Episcopalian. Avocations: bicycling, fishing, camping, cross-country skiing. Home: PO Box 1029 Corrales NM 87048

QUINLAN, MARVIN WALTER, JR., lawyer; b. Billings, Mont., May 16, 1956; s. Marvin Walter Sr. and Leona Marie (Mickell) Q. BA in Agrl. Edn., Mont. State U., 1979, MS in Agrl. Edn., Pub. Adminstrn., 1980; JD, U. Puget Sound, 1984. Bar: Mont. 1984, U.S. Dist. Ct. Mont. 1985. Atty., legal intern Graves, Staurset & Mauritz, Tacoma, 1982-84; sole practice Forsyth and Bozeman, Mont., 1984—; atty. Rosebud County, Forsyth, Mont., 1987—; agrl. law research cons. Mont. State U., Bozeman, 1984—; owner Western Agrl. Mgmt. and Analysis, Inc., Bozeman, 1985—; advisor Mont. Ceres, Inc., Bozeman, 1984—, Mont. Farmhouse Assn. Inc., Bozeman, 1978—; adj. asst. prof. agrl. law Mont. State U., 1986—. Author: Montana Agricultural Law Handbook, 1986—. Leadership fellow Nat. Ctr. for Food and Agrl. Policy, 1986. Mem. Mont. Bar Assn., ABA, Am. Trial Lawyers Assn., Am. Agrl. Law Assn., Agrl. Council Am., Alpha Zeta, Phi Kappa Phi, Phi Eta Sigma. Democrat. Lutheran. Avocations: photography, backpacking, traveling, sailing, horseback riding. Home: Drawer 109 Forsyth MT 59327 Office: Rosebud County Atty Drawer 69 Forsyth MT 59327

QUINN, DAVID HAROLD, JR., airline pilot; b. Evanston, Ill., July 1, 1931; s. David Harold and Hope Duncan (Naylor) Q.; A.B., Stanford U., 1953; m. Jo Ann Elizabeth Gregory, Aug. 20, 1955; children—Laura Elizabeth (Mrs. B. Bueermann), Paul Gregory. With Pan Am. World Airways, 1956-86; with United Airlines, 1986—; 1st officer, 1966-76, capt. Boeing 707, 1976-77, check capt. 707, 1977-80, capt. Boeing 747, San Francisco, 1980—. Served to lt. col. U.S. Air Force Res. Decorated Air Force Commendation medal. Mem. Air Line Pilots Assn., Res. Officers Assn., Stanford Alumni Assn., Sigma Nu. Republican. Mormon. Clubs: Olympic (San Francisco); Outrigger Canoe (Honolulu). Home: 112 Lyford Dr Tiburon CA 94920 Office: San Francisco Internat Airport San Francisco CA 94128

QUINN, DAVID PHILLIP, electrical engineer; b. Pennsville, N.J., Dec. 26, 1956; s. Gorman Leonard and Helen (Stone) Q. SBEE, MIT, 1979; MBA, Ariz. State U., 1986. Circuit designer H.G. Fischer, Chgo., 1979; engr. Litton Inc., Woodland Hills, Calif., 1980-81, Martin Marietta Corp., Orlando, Fla., 1981-84; sr. software engr. Motorola Inc., Scottsdale, Ariz., 1984—; cons. in field. Mem. IEEE, MIT Enterprise Network (charter), Leadership Tng. and Devel., Beta Gamma Sigma. Club: Toastmasters (Orlando sgt. at arms 1982-83). Home: 1740 Leisure World Mesa AZ 85206

QUINN, FRANCIS A., bishop; b. Los Angeles, Sept. 11, 1921. Ed., St. Joseph's Coll., Mountain View, Calif., St. Patrick's Sem., Menlo Park, Calif., Cath. U., Washington, U. Calif., Berkeley. Ordained priest Roman Cath. Ch., 1946; ordained titular bishop of Numana and aux. bishop of San Francisco 1978, apptd. bishop of Sacramento, 1979. Office: 1119 K St PO Box 1706 Sacramento CA 95808

QUINN, JOHN BRIAN PATRICK (PAT QUINN), professional hockey coach; b. Hamilton, Ont., Can., Jan. 29, 1943; came to U.S., 1960; s. John Ernest and Jean (Ireland) Q.; m. Sandra Georgia Baker, May 1, 1963; children—Valerie, Kathleen. BA in Econs., York U., 1972; JD, Del. Law Sch., 1987. Player Toronto Maple Leafs, Ont., 1968-70; player Vancouver Canucks, B.C., Can., 1970-72, Atlanta Flames, 1972-77; coach Phila. Flyers, 1977-82, Los Angeles Kings, 1984-86; gen. mgr. Vancouver Canucks, 1987—; player rep. NHL, Atlanta, 1973-77. Named Def. Man of Yr., Vancouver Canucks, 1971; named Coach of Yr. NHL, 1979-80; Coach of Yr., Sporting News, 1980, Hockey News, 1980. Roman Catholic. Office: care Vancouver Canucks, Pacific Coliseum, 100 N Renfrew St, Vancouver, BC Canada V5K 3N7 *

QUINN, JOHN R., archbishop; b. Riverside, Calif., Mar. 28, 1929; s. Ralph J. and Elizabeth (Carroll) Q. Ph.B., Gregorian U., Rome, 1950, S.T.B., 1952, S.T.L., 1954. Ordained priest Roman Catholic Ch., 1953; asst. priest St. George Ch., Ontario, Calif., 1954-55; prof. theology Immaculate Heart Sem., San Diego, 1955-62, vice rector, 1960-62; rector St. Francis Coll. Sem., El Cajon, Calif., 1962-64, Immaculate Heart Sem., 1964-68; aux. bishop, vicar gen. San Diego, 1967-72; bishop Oklahoma City, 1972-73, archbishop, 1973-77; archbishop San Francisco, 1977—; provost U. San Diego, 1968-72; pres. Nat. Conf. Cath. Bishops, 1977-80; apptd. pontifical del. for religious in U.S., 1983. Mem. Cath. Theol. Soc. Am., Canon Law Soc. Am., Am. Cath. Hist. Soc., Calif. Cath. Conf. (pres. 1985—). Address: 445 Church St San Francisco CA 94114 *

QUINN, JOSEPH R., state supreme court judge; b. Elizabeth, N.J., Nov. 18, 1932; s. Patrick F. and Claire E. Q.; m. Olga B. Taylor, July 28, 1962; children: Theresa, Lisa, Rita, James, Maria. A.B., St. Peter's Coll., 1957; LL.B., Rutgers U., 1961. Apptd. judge Colo. Dist. Ct., Dist. 2, 1973-80; justice Supreme Ct. of Colo., Denver, 1980—. Office: Supreme Ct of Colo State Capitol Denver CO 80203 *

QUINN, KAREN TAKLE, infosystem management consultant; b. Madison, Wis., May 22, 1937; d. Carl Knutsen and Gunvor Takle; m. Francis Thomas Quinn, May 24, 1969. BS, U. Wis., 1958; cert., Oslo U., Norway, 1958; MSLS, Rutgers U., 1959. Engring. librarian Princeton (N.J.) U., 1959-63; asst. prof. Drexel U., Phila., 1963-65; sr. librarian IBM Corp., San Jose, Calif., 1965-74; info. ctr. specialist IBM Corp. STL, Palo Alto and San Jose, Calif., 1965-74; engr. specialist IBM Corp. E/S, Palo Alto, 1983-84; product cons. IBM Corp. IEBC, San Jose, 1984—; cons. Ford Found., Singapore; lectr. San Jose State U., 1971—; advisor online conf. Knowledge Mgmt., Los Angeles, 1986—. Editor: Advances in Office Automation, 1985, Info. Hotline jour., 1967-82; contbr. articles to profl. jours.; inventor. NSF grantee, 1963; U. Oslo scholar, 1958. Fellow Inst. Info. Scientists; mem. Am. Soc. Engring. (div. chairperson 1965-68), Soc. Women Engrs., Internat. Fed. Documentation (affiliate), Am. Soc. Info. Sci. (chairperson 1983-85), Spl. Libraries Assn. (dir. San Francisco Bay Chpt. 1966-68), German Shepherd Dog Fanciers No. Calif. (bd. dirs. 1985—). Lodge: Order of Eastern Star. Office: IBM Corp Internat Exec Briefing Ctr 555 Bailey Ave San Jose CA 95150

QUINN, KENNETH WELLINGTON, food company executive; b. Edmonton, Alta., Can., July 17, 1926; s. Charles Eugene and Ethel Evelyn (Morris) Q.; m. Blanche Voila Moir, Sept. 4, 1948; children: Carol Ann, Douglas Charles, William James. Acct., McCannel, Gee & Quinn, 1951-57; fin. cons. IGA Distbrs. of Can. Ltd., 1957-59; sec.-treas. Horne & Pitfield Foods Ltd, Edmonton, Alta., 1959-62; v.p., gen. mgr. Horne & Pitfield Foods Ltd, 1962-66, pres., 1966-76; pres., chief exec. officer Horne & Pitfield Foods Ltd., 1976—; chmn. Alta. Motor Assn. Ins. Co. Ltd.; dir. Market Wholesale Grocery Co., Santa Rosa, Calif., IGA Can. Ltd.; dir. Hong Kong Bank of Can., R. Angus Alberta Ltd., Consumers Distbg. Co. Ltd.; bd. govs. Alta. Motor Assn. Hon. bd. dirs. Jr. Achievement. Served in Can. Army, 1944-46. Mem. Inst. Chartered Accountants Alta. Clubs: Edmonton Country, Edmonton Petroleum. Home: 17412 53d Ave, Edmonton, AB Canada T6M 1C4 Office: Horne and Pitfield Foods Ltd, PO Box 10, Edmonton, AB Canada T5J 2G9 *

QUINN, PAT See QUINN, JOHN BRIAN PATRICK

QUINN, ROD KING, laboratory administrator; b. Sherman, Tex., Oct. 2, 1938; s. Earl Yarborough and Rachel (MacDonald) Q.; m. Carolyn Leggett, Aug. 3, 1960; children: Cynthia, Joel. BS in Chemistry, So. Meth. U., 1961, MS in Phys. Chemistry, 1963; PhD in Phys. Inorganic Chemistry, U. Tex., 1967. Engr. Tex. Instruments Inc., Dallas, 1961-62; instr. chemistry So. Meth. U., Dallas, 1962-63; mem. tech. staff Sandia Nat. Labs., Albuquerque, 1967-78, div. supr., 1978-85; assoc. div. leader Los Alamos (N.Mex.) Nat. Lab., 1985—. Contbr. articles to profl. jours. Fellow Am. Inst. Chemists; mem. Materials Research Soc. (program chmn. 1984—, nat. mtg. chmn. 1986), Am. Chem. Soc., Electrochem. Soc. (symposia chmn. 1967—), Sigma Xi, Phi Lambda Upsilon. Republican. Methodist. Avocations: running, skiing, fishing, biking. Office: Los Alamos Nat Lab Chemistry Div PO Box 1663 Los Alamos NM 87545

QUINN, TOM, communications executive; b. Los Angeles, Mar. 14, 1944; s. Joseph Martin and Grace (Cooper) Q.; m. Amy Lynn Friedman, Nov. 24, 1982; children—Douglas, Lori. B.S., Northwestern U., 1965. Reporter, newswriter ABC Radio, Chgo. and Los Angeles, 1965; reporter, producer Sta. KXTV, Sacramento, 1966; day editor City News Service, Los Angeles, 1966-68, chmn., 1980-85; pres. Americom, Inc., Los Angeles, 1985—; pres. Radio News West, Los Angeles, 1968-70; campaign mgr. Jerry Brown for Sec. State, Los Angeles, 1970; dep. sec. state Calif., Sacramento, 1971-74; campaign mgr. Brown for Gov., Los Angeles, 1974; sec. Calif. Dept. Environ. Affairs, Sacramento, 1975-79; pres. Sta. KFSO Radio, Fresno, 1985—; pres. K-HITS Radio, Reno, Nev.; dir. Parallel Communications Co. Chmn. Tom Bradley Mayoral Campaign, 1985. Recipient Headliner of Yr. award Greater Los Angeles Press Club, 1978; Environ. Protection award Calif. Trial Lawyers Assn., 1979. Democrat. Office: 6255 Sunset Blvd Suite 1901 Los Angeles CA 90028

QUINT, DAVID WARREN, electrical engineer; b. Barron, Wis., Dec. 4, 1945; s. Warren Austin and Johanna (Vick) Q.; m. Penny Ann Younge, June 30, 1973; children: Matthew, Patrick, McKenzie. BSEE, U. Wis., 1972, MSEE, 1976; PhDEE, MIT, 1980. Mem. tech. staff Bettis Atomic Power Lab., West Mifflin, Pa., 1972-73; mgr. plant Siren (Wis.) Telephone Co., 1973-75; mem. tech. staff Hewlett Packard Co., Ft. Collins, Colo., 1980—. Patentee in field. Home: 2842 Claremont Dr Fort Collins CO 80526 Office: Hewlett Packard Corp 3404 E Harmony Rd Fort Collins CO 80525

QUINTANA, JUAN FELIPE, chemical engineer; b. Irapuato, Mexico, May 11, 1957; s. Ricardo and Josefina (Merino) Q.; m. Martha Elena Franco, July 19, 1985; 1 child, Samantha Grace. BSChemE, N.Mex. State U., 1982. Student trainee in chem. engring. D.W.T. Naval Ship Research and Devel. Ctr., Bethesda, Md., 1977-82; materials engr. Naval Air Rework Facility, San Diego, 1982—. Named Eagle Scout Boy Scouts Am., 1974; coop. edn. scholar Naval Material Command, 1977. Mem. Soc. Hispanic Am. Profl. Engrs., North Island Profl. Engrs. Assn. Democrat. Roman Catholic. Avocations: soccer, camping. Home: 1516 Village Pine Way San Deigo CA 92073 Office: Code 34126 Naval Air Rework Facility NAS North Island San Diego CA 92135

QUIROLLO, EDNA STARR, medical technologist; b. Ft. Benning, Ga., Aug. 9, 1946; d. Ernest Edward and Dorothy Lula (Pittman) Starr; m. Lawrence Forrest Quirollo, Aug. 9, 1968; 1 son, Troy Alan. Student, U. Hawaii, 1965; B.S. in Med. Tech., Incarnate Word Coll., San Antonio, 1968. Lic. med. technologist, Calif. Lab. asst. Santa Rose Med. Ctr., San Antonio, 1967-68; staff technologist Gen. Hosp., Eureka, Calif., 1969—, evening supr., 1977-81, asst. dir. lab. services, 1981—. Mem. Am. Soc. Clin. Pathologists (lic. 1968), Am. Soc. Med. Technologists, Calif. Assn. Med. Lab. Technologists. Democrat. Methodist. Home: 1745 East Ave Eureka CA 95501

QUISENBERRY, ROBERT MAX, architect, researcher; b. Eugene, Oreg., Nov. 18, 1956; s. Clifford Hale and Annemaria Gertrude (Frank) Q.; m. Dawnese Elaine Tarr, Sept. 18, 1982. BArch, U. Oreg., 1982. Registered architect, Wash. Intern R. Merriman Assocs., Tacoma, 1978-81; owner Solar Design Assocs., Tacoma, 1981-83; job capt. Robert Jones, AIA, Tacoma, 1983; project architect Merritt & Pardini, Tacoma, 1984-87, Lorimer-Case, San Diego, 1987—. Recipient Washington State Passive Solar Design and Building award Western Solar Utilization Network, 1981. Mem. AIA, Am. Sect. of Internat. Solar Energy Soc., Earthquake Engring. Research Inst. Republican. Home: 7275 Charmant Dr #324 San Diego CA 92122 Office: Architects Lorimer-Case 1747 Hancock St San Diego CA 92101

QUISTAD, GARY BENNET, biochemist; b. Riverside, Calif., Jan. 17, 1947; s. Bennet Carol and Elna Pearl (Russell) Q.; m. Virgina Adams, Sept. 18, 1982; children: Kelly, Kerry. BS, U. Calif., Riverside, 1969; PhD, UCLA, 1972. Sr. scientist Zoecon Corp., Palo Alto, Calif., 1973-80, group leader, 1980-81, sr. sectional head, 1981—. Contbr. articles to profl. jours. Mem. Am. Chem. Soc., AAAS, Phi Beta Kappa. Home: 2442 Benjamin Dr Mountain View CA 94043 Office: Zoecon Research Inst 975 California Ave Palo Alto CA 94304

QUITER, JAMES ROBERT, consulting engineer; b. Rochester, Minn., July 29, 1953; s. Joseph James and Helen Patricia (O'Neill) Q.; m. Karen Helen Younes, June 14, 1981; one child, Jeffrey Collin. BS with honors, Ill. Inst. Tech., 1975. Registered profl. engr., Calif., Ariz., Hawaii, Nev., Wash., Ill., Utah. Engring. rep. Ins. Services Office, Boston, 1975-77; with Rolf Jensen & Assocs., Springfield, Va., 1977-81, mktg. mgr., 1981-82; engring. mgr. Rolf Jensen & Assocs., Pleasant Hill, Calif., 1982-85, v.p., 1985—. Mem. Concord (Calif.) Bd. Appeals, 1984—. Mem. Soc. Fire Protection Engrs., Nat. Fire Protection Assn. (mem. safety to life com.), Internat. Conf. Bldg. Officials (non-voting mem. fire and life safety com.). Roman Catholic. Avocations: tennis, travel. Office: Rolf Jensen & Assocs 300 Ellinwood Way Pleasant Hill CA 94523

QURESHEY, SAFI U., electronics manufacturing company executive; b. Karachi, Pakistan, Feb. 15, 1951; s. Razi and Ishrat (Temuri) Q.; m. Anita Sue Savory, Sept. 19, 1976; children: Uns, Zeshan. BS in Physics, U. Karachi, 1971; BSEE, U. Tex., 1975. Test specialist Documentor div. A.M. Internat., Santa Ana, Calif., 1975-77; test engr. Computer Automation, Irvine, Calif., 1977-78; design engr. Telefile Computer Products, Irvine, 1978-80; founder, pres. AST Research, Inc., Irvine, 1980—. Mem. So. Calif. Tech. Execs. Network (bd. dirs.). Islamic. Avocations: bicycling, golf. Office: AST Research Inc 2121 Alton Ave Irvine CA 92714

QURESHI, MOHAMMED JAMIL, college official, consultant; b. Jagadhri, Panjab, India, Mar. 29, 1939; came to U.S., 1971; s. Mohammad Ibrahim and Fatima (Bibi) Q.; m. Saeeda Farhat, Apr. 13, 1975; children—Khalid Jamil, Naz Jamil. B.S. U. Panjab, 1962, D.L.S., 1964; M.A., U. Karachi, Pakistan, 1966; M.L.S., U. Toronto, Ont., Can., 1968; Ed.D., U. No. Colo., 1978. Audit clerk, fin. advisor, chief accounts officer Pakistan Western Rys., Lahore, 1960-63; lectr. Forward Coll., Lahore, 1963-65; librarian Panjab U. Library, 1964-65; bookmobile librarian Cape Breton Regional Library, Sydney, N.S., Can., 1966-67; adult services librarian North York Pub. Libraries, Toronto, 1968-69; asst. librarian, asst. dir. learning resources ctr. Red River Community Coll., Winnipeg., Man., Can., 1969-72; dir. learning resources ctr. State Community Coll., East St. Louis, Ill., 1971-72, dean learning resource services, 1972-73; dir. learning resources ctr. Pikes Peak Community Coll., Colorado Springs, Colo., 1974-80, assoc. dean, 1980-83, v.p. student services, 1981—; mem. library formula com. State of Colo., 1976-82; mem. instrn./instructional support/student services subcom., centralization/decentralization com. Colo. Bd. Community Colls. and Occupational Edn., 1982-83, chmn. instructional support com., mem. student services com., mem. credential rev. com. for vocat. guidance specialist and job devel. specialist, 1982-84, chmn. state adv. com. for student personnel services, 1983-85; vice chmn. ednl. accountability com., chmn. vocat. edn. sub-com. Sch. Dist. 11, Colorado Springs, 1982—. Author: Book Selection Aids for the Community College Staff, 1970; Cataloging and Classification Use and Trends in Canadian Community College Libraries (survey), 1971; compiler (with Master Rasheeduddin) bibliography on 1st prime minister of Pakistan, Nawabzada Liaqat Ali Khan, 1966; mem. Urban League Colorado Springs, 1974—; mem. planning com. Plains and Peaks Regional Library System, Colorado Springs, 1975-76, pres. governing bd., 1977-78; chmn. edn. com. Colorado Springs br. NAACP, 1979-83, bd. dirs., 1979-85. Grad. library fellow U. Toronto, 1967-68; grad. acad. scholar U. No. Colo., 1971-72. Mem. ALA, Assn. Ednl Communications and Tech., Community Coll. Assn. Instrn. and Tech., Colo. Library Assn. (chmn. coll. and univ. action subcom. 1976-77, mem. legis. com. 1977-78, budget com. 1978-79), Assn. Colo. Community Coll. Learning Resources Ctrs. (v.p. 1977-78, pres. 1978-79), Colo. Ednl. Media Assn., Nat. Assn. Student Personnel Adminstrs., Kappa Delta Pi. Home: 2855 Villa Loma Dr Colorado Springs CO 80917 Office: Pikes Peak Community Coll 5675 S Academy Blvd Colorado Springs CO 80906

RAAB, GREGORY ALAN, mineralogist; b. Long Beach, Calif., May 30, 1948; s. Jack Fisher and Ardeane (Mar) R.; m. Sandra Ruth Ganley, Nov. 27, 1976; children—Laura C., Kimberly M. A.A., Cypress Coll., 1968; B.A., Humboldt State U., 1972; Diplom Mineralogie, U. Heidelberg, W. Ger., 1974. Mineralogist, assayer Cyprus Mines Corp., Los Angeles, 1975-78; staff geologist II, Occidental Research Corp., Irvine, Calif., 1978-83; chief assayer U.S. Energy Corp., Riverton, Wyo., 1983-84, sr. scientist Lockheed Engring. & Mgmt. Services Co., Las Vegas, 1984—. Contbr. articles to profl. jours. Mem. Soc. Mining Engrs. of AIME, Soc. Econ. Paleontologists and Mineralogists. Republican. Roman Catholic. Home: 5250 Pinetree St Las Vegas NV 89122 Office: Lockheed Engring & Mgmt Services Co 944 E Harmon Ave Las Vegas NV 89114

RAABE, OTTO GEORGE, research biophysicist, toxicologist, educator; b. Passaic, N.J., Oct. 3, 1936; s. Otto George and Elsie Ann (Egatz) R.; m. Evelyn Eugenia Kircher, Aug. 20, 1960; children: Diana E., Otto G., Bruce J., Liane M., Ruth A. BS in Physics with distinction, U. N.Mex., 1958; PhD, U. Rochester, 1967. Diplomate Am. Coll. Health Physics. Head dept. Inhalation Toxicology Research Inst., Albuquerque, 1966-76, asst. dir., 1975-76; prof. U. Calif., Davis, 1976—; bd. dirs. Lab. for Energy-Related Health Research. Contbr. articles to profl. jours. Served to lt. (j.g.) USN, 1958-61. Recipient Frank R. Blood award Soc. Toxicology, 1980. Mem. Health Physics Soc., Am. Coll. Toxicology, AAAS, Am. Indsl. Hygiene Assn., Brit. Occupational Hygiene Soc., Air Pollution Control Assn., Am. Assn. Aerosol Research, Am. Chem. Soc., Gesellshaft Aerosolforshung, The Gideons Internat. (pres. of Woodland Camp 1985-86). Republican. Episcopalian. Avocation: canary breeding. Home: 652 Buchanan St Davis CA 95616 Office: U Calif Lab Energy-Related Health Research Davis CA 95616

RABENOLD, KATHRYN TUTTLE, missionary, pianist, public accountant; b. Burlington Boro, Pa., Apr. 21, 1907; d. Clay F. and Mae Elsie (Beach) Tuttle; student public schs., Sayre, Pa., courses Internat. Accts. Soc., Pa. State U.; m. LeRoy M. Cook, Dec. 26, 1929 (dec. June 1953); children—Doris Anne (Mrs. Thomas P. Knapp), William LeRoy; m. 2d, Clarence R. Rabenold, Sept. 19, 1959 (dec. June 1971). Bookkeeper, Merritt Plumbing Shop, Waverly, N.Y., 1923-26; clk.-stenographer Ingersoll-Rand Co., Athens, Pa., 1926-29; payroll clk. Perfection Laundry, Sayre, 1930; partner with husband in acctg. office, Athens, 1937-53; owner, operator Cook Acctg. Service, Athens, 1953-69; public acct. with H. E. Weller, Athens, 1969-77; pianist with Patsy Prescott, gospel singer, 1977—. Telephone counselor Trinity Broadcasting Assn., Phoenix; mem. Glendale Women Aglow Fellowship, Enrolled to practice before IRS. Mem. Nat., Pa. socs. public accts., Nat. Soc. Tax Cons. (life). Mem. Assembly of God Ch. Home: 6500 W Glendale Ave Sp 49 Glendale AZ 85301

RABENSTEIN, DALLAS LEROY, chemistry educator; b. Portland, Oreg., June 13, 1942; s. Melvin Leroy and Rose Marie (Nelson) R.; m. Gloria CArolyn Duncan, Aug. 30, 1964; children: Mark, Lisa. BS, U. Wash., 1964; PhD, U. Wis., 1968. Lectr. U. Wis., Madison, 1967-68; research chemist Chevron Research Co., Richmond, Calif., 1968-69; from asst. prof. to prof. chemistry U. Alta., Edmonton, Can., 1969-85; prof. U. Calif., Riverside, 1985—. Contbr. articles to profl. jours. Fellow Chem. Inst. Can. (Fisher Sci. Lecture award 1984); mem. Am. Chem. Soc. Avocations: reading, gardening, music. Home: 5162 Palisade Circle Riverside CA 92506 Office: U Calif. Dept Chemistry Riverside CA 92521

RABINOWITZ, JAY ANDREW, justice Alaska Supreme Ct.; b. Phila., Feb. 25, 1927; s. Milton and Rose (Rittenberg) R.; m. Anne Marie Nesbit, June 14, 1957; children: Judith, Mara, Max, Sara. B.A., Syracuse U., 1949; LL.B., Harvard, 1952. Bar: N.Y. State bar 1952, Alaska bar 1958. Practiced in N.Y.C., 1952-57; law clk. U.S. Dist. Ct. judge, Fairbanks, Alaska, 1957-58; asst. U.S. atty. Fairbanks, 1958-59; dep. atty. gen.; chief civil div. State of Alaska, 1959-60; judge Superior Ct. Alaska, 1960-65; justice Alaska Supreme Ct., Juneau, 1965—; chief justice Alaska Supreme Ct., 1972-75, 78—; lectr. U. Alaska. Served with AUS, 1945-46. Mem. N.Y., Alaska bar assns. Club: Harvard (N.Y.C.). *

RABORG, FREDERICK ASHTON, JR., journalist, author; b. Richmond, Va., Apr. 10, 1934; s. Frederick Ashton and Marguerette (Smith) R.; A.A., Bakersfield Coll., 1970; B.A. in English Lit., Calif. State Coll., Bakersfield, 1973, postgrad., 1973-75; m. Eileen Mary Bradshaw, Oct. 19, 1957; children—Frederick Ashton, Donald Wayne, Marguerette Jeannette, Wayne Patrick, Jayne Alyson, Kevin Douglas. Freelance writer, 1956—; columnist Bakersfield News Bull., 1972-74; editor Oildale News, 1968-70; drama and book reviewer Bakersfield Californian, 1974—; editor Amelia, lit. mag., 1983—; instr. journalism Bakersfield Coll., 1970-75; nat. judge Nat. League Am. Pen Women poetry contest, Phoenix br.; nat. judge Kans. Poetry Contest; sponsor Richard Hugo award for Poetry Soc. Tex. ann. contest; sponsor for Amelia awards in Poetry, 1983—; local judge Kern County Drama Festival, Kern County Shakespearean Festival; mem. PACT local drama prodn. co.; active Bakersfield Community Theatre. Writer med. needs progress reports for Kern Health Manpower Consortium; instr. creative writing for out-patients Kern View Hosp. Served to sgt. maj., F.A., U.S. Army, 1952-55. Decorated Am. Spirit Honor medal for leadership Citizens Com. of Army, Navy and Air Force, 1953, certificate of achievement Maj. Gen. Leslie D. Carter, comdr. 25th Inf. Div. in Korea, 1954; recipient 1st prizes Class Internat. Intercollegiate Creative Writing Competition, 1969-70, Guideposts mag. Writing Workshop Competition, 1973, Writers Digest Non-Fiction award, 1972, East Side Herald award in poetry New York Poetry Forum, 1974, Netherlands-U.S.A. 200 Found. award, 1982, various other poetry awards. Mem. Authors League Am., Authors Guild, Dramatists Guild, Poetry Soc. Am., Acad. Am. Poets, Modern Poetry Assn., Internat. Platform Assn. Democrat. Roman Catholic. Author 17 novels; poetry vol. Why Should the Devil Have All the Good Tunes, 1972, Tule, 1986; (plays) The Other Side of the Island, 1972; Making It!, 1973; Ramon and the Artist, 1974. Contbr. short stories, articles and poetry to mags. and ednl. jours. Home: 329 E St Bakersfield CA 93304 Office: PO Box 2385 Bakersfield CA 93303

RACE, BRUCE ALAN, architect; b. Ann Arbor, Mich., Aug. 31, 1955; s. R. Douglas and Thressa R. (Switous) R.; m. Linda S. Champion, Aug. 20, 1983. AA, Jackson Community Coll., 1975; BS in Urban Regional Studies, BArch, Ball State U., 1980. Registered architect, Calif. Planner City of Indpls., 1980; designer Danadjieva & Keonig Assocs., Tiburon, Calif., 1980-81, Hansen & Assocs., Tiburon, 1981-82; pvt. practice architecture San Francisco, 1982-83; sr. designer Kaplan, McLaughlin, Diaz, San Francisco, 1983—. Prin. works include Sacramento Urban Design Plan, 1986, Little Tokyo Urban Design Plan, Los Angeles, 1985, Marin Gen. Hosp., Green Brea, Calif., 1985, Sunnyvale, Calif., Downtown Plan, 1986. Co-chmn. planning and devel. com. San Francisco Planning and Urban Research Assn., 1985-86. Mem. AIA, Alpha Rho Chi. Office: Kaplan McLaughlin Diaz 222 Vallejo San Francisco CA 94111

RACHELSON, JOYCE ANN, computer marketing corporation executive, consultant; b. Phila., Sept. 8, 1946; d. Abraham Rachelson and Mary (Gordon) Rachelson Levy; m. Harry Steven Lichter, Aug. 8, 1971 (div. June 1976). B.A. in History, Temple U., 1968. Jr. project dir. Herbert Epstein, Inc., N.Y.C., 1967-70, Data Probe, Inc., N.Y.C., 1970-73; dir. research service Grey Advt., Inc., N.Y.C., 1973-81; dir. Eng. and support Data Tab, Inc., N.Y.C., 1982-83; eastern regional dir. Computers for Mktg., Corp., San Francisco. 1983—. Vol., Phila. Assn. for Retarded Children, 1960-67, Vol. of

Yr., 1964. Mem. Am. Mktg. Assn. Club: Temple Har Zion Young Adults (pres. 1968-69). Avocations: European and Far Eastern travel, ancient history, foreign culture studies. Office: Computers for Mktg Corp 547 Howard St San Francisco CA 94105

RACINA, THOM (THOMAS FRANK RAUCINA), writer, editor; b. Kenosha, Wis., June 4, 1946; s. Frank G. and Esther May (Benko) Raucina; B.F.A., Goodman Sch. Drama, Art Inst., Chgo., 1970, M.F.A. in Theatre Arts and Directing with honors, 1971. TV writer Hanna-Barbera Co., Hollywood, Calif., 1973-74, MTM Enterprises, Inc., Hollywood, 1974-76, ABC-TV, Hollywood, 1978-80; assoc. head writer Gen. Hosp. daytime series ABC-TV, 1981-84; co-head writer Days of Our Lives daytime series NBC-TV, 1984-86, head writer NBC-TV series Another World, 1986—; author novels: Lifeguard, 1976, The Great Los Angeles Blizzard, 1977, Quincy, M.E., 2 vols., 1977, Kojak in San Francisco, 1977, FM, 1978, Sweet Revenge, 1978, The Gannon Girls, 1979, Nine to Five, 1980, Tomcat, 1981; Secret Sex: Male Erotic Fantasies (as Tom Anicar), 1976; Magda (as Lisa Wells), 1981; ghost writer non-fiction: The Happy Hustler (Grant Tracy Saxon), 1976, Marilyn Chambers: My Story (Marilyn Chambers), 1976, Making Love (Grant Tracy Saxon), 1977, Xaviera Meets Marilyn Chambers (Xaviera Hollander and Marilyn Chambers), 1977; musical plays: A Midsummer Night's Dream, music and lyrics, 1968, Allison Wonderland, music and lyrics, 1970, The Marvelous Misadventure of Sherlock Holmes, book, music and lyrics, 1971; TV scripts: Sleeping Over segment of Family, ABC, 1978, Russian Pianist segment of Family, ABC, 1979, Child of the Owl, NBC After-sch. Spl., 1979; contbr. articles to Playboy, Cosmopolitan, Penthouse, Oui, Los Angeles, Gentlemen's Quar., Westways; West Coast editor Grosset & Dunlap, Inc., N.Y.C., 1978—; theatre dir.; pianist; organist; composer. Recipient Juvenile Diabetes Found. Internat. Awareness award, 1985; U.S. Nat. Student Assn. grantee, 1965. Mem. Authors Guild Am., Writers Guild Am.—West, Nat. Acad TV Arts and Scis. (Emmy nominee 1983, 84). Democrat. Roman Catholic. Home and Office: 3449 Waverly Dr Los Angeles CA 90027

RACUYA, GUY PATRICK, art broker; b. Honolulu, Nov. 2, 1948; s. Carlito Michael and Aniana (Alfiche) R. Student, U. Calif., Davis; BFA, U. Calif., Berkeley, 1971. Devel. technician U. Calif., Berkeley, 1977-81; project mgr. Ann Sandifur & Co., Spokane, Wash., 1981-83; designer, drafting mgr. Synemed, Inc., Berkeley, 1983-84; mechanical product designer Motorola, Inc., Albuquerque, 1985; design cons. Santa Fe, 1985-86; art broker La Puebla, N.Mex., 1986—. Mem. Santa Fe C. of C. Democrat. Avocations: motorcycle road racing. Home and Office: Rt 3 Box 181 Espanola NM 87532

RADA, ALEXANDER, university official; b. Kvasy, Czechoslovakia, Mar. 28, 1923; s. Frantisek and Anna (Tonnkova) R.; came to U.S., 1954, naturalized, 1959; M.S., U. Tech. Coll. of Prague, 1948; postgrad. Va. Poly. Inst., 1956-59, St. Clara U., 1966-67; Ed.D., U. Pacific, 1975; m. Ingeborg Solveig Blakstad, Aug. 8, 1953; children: Alexander Sverre, Frank Thore, David Harald. Head prodn. planning dept. Mine & Iron Corp., Kolin, Czechoslovakia, 1941-42; mgr. experimenting and testing dept. Avia Aircraft, Prague, 1943-45; sec.-gen. Central Bldg. Office, Prague, 1948; head metal courses dept. Internat. Tech. Sch. of UN, Grafenaschau, W.Ger., 1949-50; works mgr. Igref A/S, Oslo, 1950-51; cons. engr., chief sect. machines Steel Products Ltd., Oslo, 1951-54; chief engr., plant supr. Nelson J. Pepin & Co., Lowell, Mass., 1954-55; sr. project engr., mfg. supt. Celanese Corp. Am., Narrows, Va., 1955-60; mgr. mfg., facilities and maint. FMC Corp., San Jose, Calif., 1960-62; mgr. adminstrn. Sylvania Electronic Systems, Santa Cruz, Calif., 1962-72; asst. to pres., devel. officer Napa (Calif.) Coll., 1972—; chief exec. officer NAVCO Pacific Devel. Corp., Napa, 1984—; prof. indsl. mgmt. Cabrillo Coll., Aptos, Calif., 1963-72; mgmt. and engring. cons., 1972—. Pres. ARC, Santa Cruz, 1965-72, bd. dirs., pres., Napa, 1977—; mem. Nat. Def. Exec. Res., U.S. Dept. Commerce, Washington, 1966—, chmn. No. Calif. region 9, 1981—; mem. President's Export Council-DEC, San Francisco, 1982—. Recipient Meritorious Service citation ARC, 1972, Etoile Civique l'Ordre de l'Etoile Civique, French Acad., 1985; registered profl. engr., Calif. Mem. Nat., Calif. socs. profl. engrs., Am. Def. Preparedness Assn., Assn. Calif. Community Coll. Adminstrs., World Affairs Council No. Calif., Phi Delta Kappa. Editor-in-chief Our Youth, 1945-48; co-editor (with P. Boulden) Innovative Management Concepts, 1967. Home: 1019 Ross Circle Napa CA 94558 Office: 2277 Napa Vallejo Hwy Napa CA 94558

RADER, RALPH WILSON, humanities educator; b. Muskegon, Mich., May 18, 1930; s. Ralph McCoy and Nelle Emily (Fargo) R.; m. June Willadean Warring, Sept. 3, 1950; children—Lois Jean, Eric Conrad, Michael William, Nancy Anne, Emily Rose. B.S., Purdue U., 1952; Ph.D., Ind. U., 1958. Instr. dept. English U. Calif., Berkeley, 1956-58; asst. prof. U. Calif., 1958-63, assoc. prof., 1963-67, prof., 1967—, chmn. dept., 1976-80; F.I. Carpenter vis. prof. English, U. Chgo., 1970; dir. seminar Nat. Endowment for Humanities, summer 1975, 83, 85; editorial com. U. Calif. Press, 1963-72, co-chmn., 1968-72; mem. exec. com. Assn. Depts. English, 1978-80. Author: Tennyson's Maud: The Biographical Genesis, 1963, reprinted, 1978. Co-author: Essays in Eighteenth Century Biography, 1968; New Approaches to Eighteenth Century Literature, 1974. Editor: (with Sheldon Sacks) Essays: An Analytic Reader, 1964; adv. bd. Yale edit. Private Papers of James Boswell; editorial bd. Critical Inquiry; The 18th Century: Theory and Interpretation; Prose Studies. Am. Council Learned Socs. grantee, 1959; Guggenheim fellow, 1972-73; recipient Disting. Teaching award U. Calif.-Berkeley, 1975-76. Mem. MLA, Phi Beta Kappa. Democrat. Home: 465 Vassar Ave Berkeley CA 94708

RADER, WILLIAM ERNEST, microbiologist, retired; b. Ellensburg, Wash., Aug. 21, 1916; s. Ben F. and Hilda Gutrude (Brunn) R.; m. Bernice Arlene Rubin, Sept. 2, 1938; children: William Ernest Jr., Evelyn Adell Rader Bentley. BS, Wash. State U., 1939; MS, Utah State U., 1942; PhD, Cornell U., 1946. Cert. tchr. community colls., Calif. Plant pathologist Shell Devel. Co., Modesto, Calif., 1946-67, nematologist, 1967-72, microbiologist, 1972-81; tchr. Modesto Jr. Coll., 1972-77. Contbr. articles to profl. jours. Organizing pres. Modesto Affiliated Ch. Housing Corp., 1967—, Modesto Community Concerts Assn., 1949; trustee Calif. Christian Home, Rosemead, 1974—; trustee, v.p. Retirement Housing Found., Long Beach, Calif., 1970—. Mem. Calif. Acad. Sci., Nat. Audubon Soc., Smithsonian Inst., Sierra Club, Sigma Xi. Republican. Home: 4901 Dale Rd Modesto CA 95356

RADIN, NONA SHARON, audiologist; b. Albany, N.Y., May 26, 1953; s. Norman Arthur and Pearl Claire (Goldstein) R. BS cum laude, Syracuse U., 1975; MS in Audiology, U. Wash., 1976. Audiologist Jonathan Chinn MD, Seattle, 1977-86, Charles Caplan MD, Renton, Wash., 1977-87; northwestern regional sales mgr. Rexton, Inc., 1987—. Bd. dirs. Concord Hill Condominiums, Bellevue, Wash., 1985—. Mem. U.S. Recreational Ski Assn. (NW sales coordinator 1986—), Am. Speech and Hearing Assn. (cert.), Wash. Speech and Hearing Assn., Wash. Soc. Audiology. Club: S'no Joke Ski (Seattle). Avocations: skiing, sailboat racing, bicycling, hiking, fishing. Home: 12366 SE 41st Ln Bellevue WA 98006 Office: Rexton Inc 768 Foster Ave Bensenville IL 60106

RADLO, MARJORIE RUTH, software company executive; b. Boston, Aug. 16, 1956; d. Jason Lester and Irene (Frank) Radlo; m. Behrouz S. Zandi, Sept. 1, 1985. B.A., U. Vt., 1978; M.B.A., Northeastern U., 1983. Sales rep. Metromedia, N.Y.C., 1980-81; internat. sales rep. Data Gen., Westboro, Mass., 1983-84; sales, computer staff A.B. Dick Co., Santa Clara, Calif., 1984-85; regional sales mgr. Marc Software Internat., Palo Alto, Calif., 1985—. Contbr. article to profl. jour. Mem. Assn. Exec. Saleswomen, Am. Mktg. Assn., Assn. M.B.A. Execs., Am. Mgmt. Assn., Sunnyvale C. of C., Sunnyvale Women in Bus. Jewish. Club: Sales Strategy and Mgmt. Group (San Jose). Avocations: Swimming; sailing; reading; films; travel. Home: 7439 Stanford Pl Cupertino CA 95014 Office: Marc Software Internat 260 Sheridan Ave Palo Alto CA 94306

RADOCHIA, JAMES PAUL, computer analysis company executive; b. Melrose, Mass., Dec. 10, 1954; s. Walter J. and Florence M. (Garbarino) R.; m. Ludmilla V. Ostrorog, July 14, 1978. BS in Ocean Engring., MIT, 1977, MS in Ocean Engring., 1977. Engr. NUSC, New London, Conn., 1975-77; devel. engr. Honeywell Corp., Seattle, Wash., 1977-80; structural cons. UCC, Bellevue, Wash., 1980-81; pres. JLR Computer Analysis, Seattle, 1981—. Mem. ASME, Soc. Naval Architects and Marine Engrs., Structural Engr. Assn. of Wash., Marine Tech. Soc. Club: MIT (Puget Sound, Wash.). Home: 19207 51st Ave NE Seattle WA 98155 Office: JLR Computer Analysis Inc 19207 51st Ave NE Seattle WA 98155

RADOVICH, JOHN MICHAEL, research chemical engineer; b. Phila., Aug. 12, 1948; s. John Joseph and Mildred May (Schmidt) R.; m. Ann Hill Goehausen, Sept. 11, 1970; children: Camille Ann, Amy Christine, Julie Ann. BS, U. Notre Dame, 1970; MS, Stanford U., 1971; DSci., Washington U., St. Louis, 1976. Process engr. Sun Oil Co., Marcus Hook, Pa., 1971-73; assoc. prof. U. Okla., Norman, 1976-85; sr. research engr. Bend (Oreg.) Research Inc., 1985—; cons. in field, 1973-85. Served with USAR, 1971-77. Named one of Oustanding Young Men Am., U.S. Jaycees, 1980, 83; recipient J.P. Baldwin award U. Okla. Alumni Assn., 1980, U. Okla. Regents' award, 1981, Delos award Am. Soc. Engring. Edn., 1982. Mem. Am. Inst. Chem. Engrs., Am. Chem. Soc., Tau Beta Pi. Republican. Roman Catholic. Avocations: reading, hiking, sports. Office: Bend Research Inc 64550 Research Rd Bend OR 97701

RADOVSKY, FRANK JAY, medical zoologist; b. Fall River, Mass., Jan. 5, 1929; s. David Reuben and Minnie Esther (Simon) R. AB, U. Colo., 1951; MS, U. Calif., Berkeley, 1959, PhD, 1964. Research parasitologist U. Calif., San Francisco, 1963-69; acarologist Bishop Mus., Honolulu, 1969-85, chmn. dept. entomology, 1972-85, asst. dir., 1977-85, disting. chair of zoology, 1984-86; research assoc. Calif. Acad. Scis., San Francisco, 1986; vis. prof. entomology Oreg. State U., Corvallis, 1986—; bd. dirs. Wau (New Guinea) Ecology Inst., 1972-86; sci. com. on entomology Pacific Sci. Assn., 1982—. Editor: Jour. Med. Entomology, 1969—, (assoc.) Annual Rev. Entomology, 1978—, (book) Pacific Tropical Biogeography, 1984; contbr. articles to profl. jours. Entomology mem. Nat. Area Reserves Commn., Hawaii, 1985. Served to lt. USNR, 1952-55. Fellow NIH, USPHS, 1959-62; grantee NIH, 1964-76, NSF, 1970-85. Mem. Entomol. Soc. Am., Internat. Congress Acarology (exec. sec. 1971-78), Soc. Vector Ecologists, Am. Soc. Tropical Medicine and Hygiene, Sigma Xi. Jewish. Office: Dept Entomology Oreg State U Corvallis OR 97331

RADZIEMSKI, LEON JOSEPH, physicist; b. Worcester, Mass., June 18, 1937; s. Leon Joseph and Josephine Elizabeth (Janczukowicz) R.; married; children: Michael Leon, Timothy Joseph. BA, Coll. Holy Cross, 1958; MS, Purdue U., 1961, PhD, 1964. Staff physicist Los Alamos (N.Mex.) Nat. Lab., 1967-83; head dept. physics N.Mex. State U., Las Cruces, 1983—; vis. scientist Laboratoire Aime Cotton, Orsay, France, 1974-75; vis. assoc. prof. dept. nuclear engring, U. Fla., Gainesville, 1978-79. Editor Marcel Dekker Series: Laser Advances; contbr. articles to profl. jours.; patentee in field. Served with USAF, 1964-67. Mem. Am. Phys. Soc., Optical Soc. Am., Soc. Applied Spectroscopy, Laser Inst. Am. (bd. dirs.). Home: 4709 Falcon Dr Las Cruces NM 88001 Office: NMex State U Dept of Physics Box 3D Las Cruces NM 88003

RAE, J. ALAN, university finance administrator; b. Lethbridge, Alta., Can., Dec. 25, 1934; s. John and Mercy Mabel (Jones) R.; m. Martha Christina Smith, June 11, 1955; children—Randy George, David John, Sheri Jill. Grad. Soc. Mgmt. Accts., 1977. Acct. St. Mary and Milk River Devel., Lethbridge, Alta., 1963-67; with U. Lethbridge, 1967—, asst. controller, 1970-73, controller, 1973-80, v.p. fin., 1980—. Bd. dirs. Can. Mental Health Assn., Edmonton, Alta., 1978, Alta. Heart Fund, Lethbridge, 1980, Univ. Academic Pension Plan Bd., Edmonton, 1980—, Can. Paraplegic Assn., Calgary, Alta., 1984. Mem. Soc. Mgmt. Accts. (provincial dir., provincial rep. 1983—), Can. Assn. Univ. Bus. Officers, Soc. Coll. and Univ. Planning, Nat. Assn. Coll. Aux. Services, Lethbridge C. of C. Club: Alpine of Can. (Banff, Alta.). Home: 921-21 Berkeley Pl, Lethbridge, AB Canada T1K 5N1 Office: Univ Lethbridge, 4401 University Dr, Lethbridge, AB Canada T1K 3M4

RAE, MATTHEW SANDERSON, JR., lawyer; b. Pitts., Sept. 12, 1922; s. Matthew Sanderson and Olive (Waite) R.; m. Janet Hettman, May 2, 1953; children: Mary-Anna, Margaret, Janet. A.B., Duke, 1946, LL.B., 1947; postgrad., Stanford U., 1951. Bar: Md. 1948, Calif. 1951. Asst. to dean Duke Sch. Law, Durham, N.C., 1947-48; assoc. Karl F. Steinmann, Balt., 1948-49; asso. Guthrie, Darling & Shattuck, Los Angeles, 1953-54; nat. field rep. Phi Alpha Delta Frat., Los Angeles, 1949-51; research atty. Calif. Supreme Ct., San Francisco, 1951-52; ptnr. Darling, Hall & Rae and predecessor firms, Los Angeles, 1955—; mem. Calif. Commn. Uniform State Laws, 1985—. Vice pres. Los Angeles County Republican Assembly, 1959-64; mem. Los Angeles County Rep. Central Com., 1960-64, 77—, exec. com., 1977—; vice chmn. 17th Congressional Dist., 1960-62, 28th Congl. Dist., 1962-64; chmn. 46th Assembly Dist., 1962-64, 27th Senatorial Dist., 1977—; mem. Calif. Rep. State Cen. Com., 1966—, exec. com., 1966-67; pres. Calif. Rep. League, 1966-67; trustee Republican Assocs., 1979—, pres., 1983-85, chmn. bd. dirs., 1985—. Served to 2d lt. USAAF, World War II. Fellow Am. Coll. Probate Counsel; academician Internat. Acad. Estate and Trust Law (exec. council 1974-78); mem. ABA, Los Angeles County Bar Assn. (chmn. probate and trust law com. 1964-66, chmn. legislation com. 1980-86, chmn. program com. 1981-82, chmn. membership retention com. 1982-83, trustee 1983-85), South Bay Bar Assn., State Bar Calif. (chmn. state bar jour. com. 1970-71, chmn. probate com. 1974-75, exec. com. estate planning trust and probate law sect. 1977-83, chmn. legislation com. 1977—, probate law cons. group Calif. Bd. Legal Specialization 1977—, chmn. conf. dels. resolutions com. 1987), Lawyers Club of Los Angeles (bd. govs. 1981—, 1st v.p. 1982-83), Am. Legion (comdr. Allied post 1969-70), Legion Lex (dir. 1964—, pres. 1969-71), Air Force Assn., Aircraft Owners and Pilots Assn., Town Hall (gov. 1970-78, pres. 1975), World Affairs Council, Rotary Internat., Internat. Platform Assn., Los Angeles Com. on Fgn. Relations, Phi Beta Kappa (councilor Alpha Assn. 1983—, v.p. 1984-86), Omicron Delta Kappa, Phi Alpha Delta (supreme justice 1972-74, elected to Disting. Service chpt. 1978), Sigma Nu. Presbyterian. Clubs: Commonwealth (San Francisco); Chancery, Stock Exchange (Los Angeles). Home: 600 John St Manhattan Beach CA 90266 Office: 606 S Olive St Suite 1900 Los Angeles CA 90014

RAEL, HENRY SYLVESTER, helth administrator; b. Pueblo, Colo., Oct. 2, 1928; s. Daniel and Grace (Abyeta) R.; A.B., U. So. Colo., 1955; B.A. in Bus Adminstrn., U. Denver, 1957, M.B.A., 1958; m. Helen Warner Loring Brace, June 30, 1956 (dec. Aug. 1980); children—Henry Sylvester, Loring Victoria Bush. Sr. boys counselor Denver Juvenile Hall, 1955-58; adminstrv. asst. to pres. Stanley Aviation Corp., Denver, 1958-61; Titan III budget and fin. control supr. Martin Marietta Corp., Denver, 1961-65; mgmt. adv. services officer U. Colo. Med. Center, Denver, 1965-72; v.p. fin., treas. Loretto Heights Coll., Denver, 1972-73; dir. fin. and adminstrn. Colo. Found. for Med. Care, 1973-86, Tri-County Health Dept., Denver, 1986—; instr. fin. mgmt., mem. fin. com. Am. Assn. Profl. Standards Rev. Orgn., 1980-85; speaker systems devel., design assns., univs., 1967-71. Mem. budget lay adv. com. Park Hill Elem. Sch., Denver, 1967-68, chmn., 1968-69; vol. worker Boy and Girl Scouts, 1967-73; bd. dirs. Community Arts Symphony, 1981-83, 85-87; controller St. John's Episcopal Cathedral, 1982-83; charter mem. Pueblo (Colo.) Coll. Young Democrats, 1954-55; block worker Republican party, Denver, 1965-68, precinct committeeman, 1978-84; trustee Van Nattan Scholarship Fund, 1974—; bd. dirs. Vis. Nurse Assn., 1977-84, treas., 1982-84. Served with USAF, 1947-53. Recipient Disting. Service award Denver Astron. Soc., 1968, Citation Chamberlin Obs., 1985; Stanley Aviation masters scholar, 1957; Ballard scholar, 1956. Mem. Assn. Systems Mgmt. (pres. 1971-72), Hosp. Systems Mgmt. Soc., Budget Execs Inst. (v.p. chpt. 1964-65, sec. 1963-64), Denver Astron. Soc. (pres. 1965-66), Am. Assn. Founds. for Med. Care (fin. com. 1981-82), Nat. Astronomers Assn. (exec. bd. 1965—). Epsilon Xi, Delta Psi Omega. Episcopalian. Home: 70 S Albion Denver CO 80222

RAFAEL, RUTH KELSON, archivist, librarian, consultant; b. Wilmington, N.C., Oct. 28, 1929; d. Benjamin and Jeanette (Spicer) Kelson; m. Richard Vernon Rafael, Aug. 26, 1951; children—Barbara Jeanette Rafael Martinez, Brenda Elaine. B.A., San Francisco State U., 1953, M.A., 1954; M.L.S., U. Calif.-Berkeley, 1968. Tchr. San Francisco Unified Sch. Dist., 1956-57; librarian Congregation Beth Sholom, San Francisco, 1965-83; asst. archivist Western Jewish History Ctr. of Judah L. Magnes Mus., Berkeley, Calif., 1968, head archivist, librarian, 1969—; cons. Inst. Righteous Acts, Berkeley, 1982-83, NEH, Washington, Congregation Sherith Israel, San Francisco, Mount Zion Hosp., San Francisco, Benjamin Swig archives project, San Francisco, Camp Swig, Saratoga, Calif. Author: Continuum, 1976, rev. edit., 1977; (with Davies and Woogmaster) (poems) Relatively Speaking, 1981; Western Jewish History Ctr.: Archival and Oral History Collections, Judah L. Magnes Meml. Mus., Second Hand, Maybe, Ghetto, No, The Californians, 1986; contbg. editor Western States Jewish Hist. Quar., 1979—. Mem. exec. bd. Bay Area Library Info. Network, 1986—. Bur. Jewish Edn. scholar, San Francisco, 1983; NEH grantee, 1985. Mem. Soc. Am. Archivists, ALA, Soc. Calif. Archivists, Calif. Library Assn., No. Calif. Assn. Jewish Librarians (pres. 1975-76), Jewish Arts Council of the Bay (bd. dirs. 1981-83). Office: Western Jewish History Ctr Judah L Magnes Mus 2911 Russell St Berkeley CA 94705

RAFATI, HAMID REZA, mechanical engineer; b. Tehran, Iran, Dec. 30, 1958; came to U.S., 1977; s. Lotfollah and Jaleh (Zolfaghari) R. BSME, U. Calif., Berkeley, 1983; MSME, MIT, 1985. Control and software engr. Measurex, Cupertino, Calif., 1985-86; project leader Advanced Rotorcraft Techs., Mt. View, Calif., 1986—. Mem. IEEE, Sigma Xi, Tau Beta Pi. Avocations: swimming, soccer. Home: 3698 Magellan Ave Santa Clara CA 95051 Office: Advanced Rotorcraft Techs 1804 Stierlin Rd Mountain View CA 94043

RAFEEDIE, EDWARD, federal judge; b. Orange, N.J., Jan. 6, 1929; s. Fred and Nabeeha (Hishmeh) R.; m. Ruth Ann Horton, Oct. 8, 1961; children: Fredrick Alexander, Jennifer Ann. BS in Law, U. So. Calif., 1957, JD, 1959; LLD, Pepperdine U., 1978. Bar: Calif. 1960. Sole practice law Santa Monica, Calif., 1960-69; mcpl. ct. judge Santa Monica Jud. Dist., Santa Monica, 1969-71; judge Superior Ct. State of Calif., Los Angeles, 1971-82; dist. judge U.S. Dist. Court for Central Dist. Calif., Los Angeles, 1982—. Trustee Santa Monica Hosp. Med. Ctr., 1979—; bd. dirs. Luth. Hosp. Soc. Corp., Los Angeles, 1985; mem. adv. bd. Greater Western council Boy Scouts Am., Los Angeles, 1980—. Served with U.S. Army, 1950-52, Korea. Office: US Dist Court 312 N Spring St Los Angeles CA 90012

RAFF, DOUGLASS ALAN, lawyer; b. Butte, Mont., Oct. 27, 1938; s. Colin W. and Ruth H. (Brinck) R.; m. Katherine L. Jones, Aug. 19, 1961; children—Colin, Katherine. A.B., Harvard U., 1961, J.D., 1964. Bar: Wash. 1964. Ptnr., Riddell, Williams, Bullitt & Walkinshaw, Seattle, 1964—; chmn. bd., dir. Sasquatch Pub., Inc.; dir. Harbor Properties, Inc., Independent Ale Brewery, Inc. Chmn. Seattle 2000 Commn., 1972-73; trustee World Without War Council; trustee Pilchuck Glass Sch.; mem. bd. visitors U. Wash. Coll. Architecture. Mem. ABA, Wash. State Bar Assn., Seattle-King County Bar Assn. Office: Seattle First Nat Bank Bldg Suite 4400 Seattle WA 98154

RAFFALOW, JANET TERRY, law librarian; b. Burbank, Calif., Oct. 11, 1947; d. Melvin and Honey (Sobel) Whitney; m. Richard Elliott Raffalow, June 9, 1984. BA, UCLA, 1968, MLS, 1969, cert. in pub. adminstrn., 1980. Cert. community coll. tchr., Calif. Young adult librarian Los Angeles Pub. Library, 1969-70; librarian Calif. Atty. Gen.'s Library, Los Angeles, 1970-78, supervising librarian, 1978—. Vol. Pub. TV-KCET, Los Angeles, 1973—; vice chmn. Los Angeles Jr. C. of C., 1979-81; vol. citizens commn. Los Angeles Olympic Organizing Com., 1982-84. Mem. Los Angeles Law Librarians Assn. (long range planning com.), Am. Assn. Law Libraries (cert.), So. Calif. Assn. Law Libraries, UCLA Library Sch. Alumni Assn. Democrat. Jewish. Club: Sunshines of Cedars Sinai, (v.p. 1971-73). Avocations: tennis, photography, travel. Office: Calif Atty Gen's Library 3580 Wilshire Blvd Room 701 Los Angeles CA 90010

RAFFI, CAROL ANN, sales professional; b. Newark, July 23, 1944; s. Joseph Williams and Marie Edwina (Messer) Smith; m. Giovanni Raffi, Sept. 15, 1973. AA, Newark Sch. Fine and Indsl. Arts, 1965. Textile designer Arcadia Fabrics, N.Y.C., 1966-70, M. Lowenstein & Sons, N.Y.C., 1970-73; sales assoc. Leonards Luggage, Scottsdale, Ariz., 1974-76, Hanny's Clothing, Scottsdale, 1977-79, Plaza Botique, Scottsdale, 1980-82; sales mgr. Lillie Rubin, Scottsdale, 1982-85; sales assoc. Broadway Southwest, Scottsdale, 1985—. Active PTA, Scottsdale, 1984-85. Republican. Roman Catholic. Avocations: painting, reading, swimming, walking, embroidery design. Office: Broadway Southwest 7333 E McDowell Rd Scottsdale AZ 85251

RAFFIN, STEVEN BENNETT, physician, educator; b. San Francisco, Aug. 22, 1942; s. Bennett Lyon and Caroline Meyer; m. Sherry Matlof, Dec. 23, 1967; children: Eric Daniel, Alec Cary, Michael Ian. AB, Stanford U., 1964; MD, Washington U., St. Louis, 1968. Intern then resident in internal medicine Jewish Hosp., Washington U., St. Louis, 1968-71; fellow in gastroenterology U. Calif., San Francisco, 1971-73, instr. medicine, 1973-74; tng. officer and staff gastroenterologist Navy Regional Med. Ctr., Oakland, Calif., 1974-76; practice medicine specializing in gastroenterology San Bruno, Calif., 1976—; from asst. clin. prof. to assoc. clin. prof. medicine U. Calif., San Francisco, 1976—; mem. staff Peninsula Hosp. and Med. Ctr., Burlingame, Calif., U. Calif. Hosps., various locations. Contbr. articles to profl. jours. Fellow ACP; mem. AMA, Calif. Med. Assn., Am. Gastroenterol. Assn., Am. Soc. Gastrointestinal Endoscopy, No. Calif. Soc. Clin. Gastroenterology, San Mateo County Med. Soc. Club: Discovery Bay Yacht. Avocations: boating, fly fishing. Office: 1001 Sneath Ln San Bruno CA 94066

RAGAINI, RICHARD CHARLES, environmental protection executive; b. Danbury, Conn., Feb. 7, 1942; s. David Joseph and Nellie Mary (Storoni) R.; divorced; children: Karen Ann, Christine Lynn. BA cum laude, Clark U., 1963; PhD, MIT, 1967. Research assoc. Los Alamos (N.Mex.) Nat. Lab., 1967-69, Brookhaven Nat. Lab., Upton, N.Y., 1969-70; asst. prof. Wash. State U., Pullman, 1970-71; assoc. div. leader Lawrence Livermore (Calif.) Nat. Lab., 1971—; dir. coms. atomic and nuclear chemistry and research, environ. research. Contbr. articles to profl. jours. Mem. Am. Men and Women of Sci., Am. Nuclear Soc., Am. Chem. Soc., Sigma Xi, Phi Beta Kappa, Sigma Pi Sigma. Home: 2107 Darby Ct Walnut Creek CA 94596 Office: Lawrence Livermore Nat Lab PO Box 808 Livermore CA 94596

RAGAN, RICHARD RYAN, management consultant, author; b. Cleve., Oct. 27, 1936; s. Fred Hathaway and Julia (Ryan) R.; m. Jeanne Remington, Sept. 3, 1958 (div.); children—Timothy Ryan, Corey Cristina; m. 2d, Elna Herring, Dec. 28, 1978. B.B.A., U. Hawaii, 1961; M.S., U. Colo., 1963. Cert. coll. instr., Calif. Asst. mgr. Waikikian Hotel, Honolulu, 1958-62; mgr. corp. tng. Wells Fargo Bank, San Francisco, 1963-76; prin. RRR & Assocs., Concord, Calif., 1976—; cons., lectr. Served with USAFR, 1958-64. Mem. Am. Soc. Tng. and Devel. (Torch award 1974), Golden Gate Assocs. Republican. Methodist. Contbr. articles to profl. jours.

RAGLAND, KATHRYN MARIE, dancer, educator; b. Lakewood, Ohio, Nov. 22, 1948; d. Earl Albert and Alice Maxine (Outzs) R.; m. Donald Glen Rubright, Sept. 1, 1973 (div. 1977); m. Jack Victor Rutberg, Mar. 9, 1980; 1 dau., Jessica Erin. A.A., Los Angeles Valley Coll., 1971; B.F.A. cum laude, U. Utah, 1973, M.F.A. in Dance, 1975. With Momentum Dance Co., Los Angeles, 1975-77; dance specialist pub. schs., Los Angeles, 1975-76; instr. Scripps Coll., Claremont, Calif., 1976-77; dir. of dance Cypress (Calif.) Coll., 1978-85; owner, operator Gymboree, 1985—; instr. dance Cypress Coll., 1986—, Hollywood (Calif.) Little Red Sch. House, 1985—; mem. arts assistance team Los Angeles supt. schs., curriculum council Los Angeles High Sch. Performing Arts, adv. bd., 1986—. Author/choreographer Kitty Kats, 1986; choreography work includes Man of La Mancha, 1976-80, Pippin, 1981, Fiddler on the Roof, 1982, Music Man, 1983, Spanish Suite, 1983, A Funny Thing Happened on the Way to the Forum, 1984, Skaters Edge, 1984, Cartoon, 1984, Urban Primitive, 1985, Cabaret, 1985. Mem. So. Calif. steering com. Legis. Action Coalition for Arts Edn. Mem. Calif. Dance Educators Assn. (v.p. 1980-82, legis. rep. 1982-86), Calif. Music Educators (legis. com. 1982-86), Los Angeles Area Dance Alliance, Faculty Assn. of Community Colls., Calif. Assn. Health, Phys. Edn., Recreation and Dance, AAHPERD, Calif. Ednl. Theatre Assn., So. Calif. Assn. for Edn. Young Children (bd. dirs. South Bay chpt.), ACLU, Calif. Confedn. of Arts. Democrat.

RAGLAND, SAMUEL CONNELLY, industrial engineer; b. Nashville, July 12, 1946; s. Julian Potter and Stella (Thompson) R.; m. Marilyn Margaret Oppelt, July 15, 1967; children—Sherry Anne, David Michael. B.S. in Bus.

Adminstrn., Ariz. State U., 1974. Indsl. engr. First Interstate Bank, Phoenix, 1966-76, Beckman Instruments, Scottsdale, Ariz., 1976-78; mgmt. analyst Ariz. Legislative Budget Com., Phoenix, 1978; indsl. engr. mgmt. systems ITT Courier Terminal Systems, Tempe, Ariz., 1978-81; project control adminstr. Gen. Host Corp., Phoenix, 1981; sr. cons. Arthur Young & Co., Phoenix, 1981-82; ops. analyst City of Phoenix, 1982-84; project leader Garrett Turbine Engine Co., Phoenix, 1984—; dir. Mary Moppets of Highland Inc., 1977-81. Mem. Inst. Indsl. Engrs. (v.p. cen. Ariz. chpt. 1986—, dir. community relations 1983-85, dir. chpt. devel. 1985-86, chpt. v.p. and pres.-elect 1986-87, pres. 1987—), Assn. Systems Mgmt., Phoenix Philatelic Assn. Contbr. articles to profl. pubis. Address: 11319 E Jenan Dr Scottsdale AZ 85259

RAGULSKY, FRANK ANDREW, academic administrator; b. Pueblo, Colo., Oct. 25, 1946; s. Frank Andrew and Helen (Gorshe) R.; m. Jane Dasnee Webb, July 21, 1969; children: Christine, Timothy. BS, U. So. Colo., 1968; MA, Adams State Coll., 1969; EdD, Okla. State U., 1969. Prof. St. Bonaventure U., Olean, N.Y., 1969-72; assoc. publisher univ. newspaper Okla. State U., Stillwater, 1972-75; dir. student pubs. So. Meth. U., Dallas, 1975-82; dir. student media Oreg. State U., Corvallis, 1982—. Bd. dirs. Boy Scouts Am., Corvallis, 1983. Mem. Assn. Edn. Journalism, Western Assn. Univ. Publ. Mgrs. (pres. 1981-82). Roman Catholic. Lodge: Rotary (bd. dirs. Corvallis 1985). Avocations: fishing, gardening. Home: 3661 NW Oleander Pl Corvallis OR 97330 Office: Oreg State U Meml Union East Corvallis OR 97331

RAIBLE, PETER SPILMAN, minister; b. Peterborough, N.H., Nov. 22, 1929; s. Robert Jules and Mildred (Galt) R.; m. Dee Dee Rainbow, June 18, 1950 (div. 1968); children: Stephen M., Robin S., Robert R., Deborah R. PhB, U. Chgo., 1949; BA, U. Calif., Berkeley, 1952; ThM, Starr King Sch. Ministry, 1953, D in Sacred Theology (hon.), 1974. Ordained to ministry Unitarian Ch. Asst. minister First Unitarian Ch., Providence, 1953-55; minister Unitarian Ch., Lincoln, Nebr., 1955-61, Univ. Unitarian Ch., Seattle, 1961—; bd. pres. Starr King Sch., Berkeley, 1967-68; mem. exec. com. Council Chs., Seattle, 1982—. Author: How to Case a Church, 1982; editor Jour. Liberal Ministry, 1965-71. Bd. dirs. Council Planning Affiliates, Seattle, 1969-73, Wash. State chpt. ACLU, Seattle, 1963-67; chmn. ministerial adv. com. Planned Parenthood Ctr., Seattle, 1963-68; pres. United Nations Assn., Lincoln, 1959-61. Served as cpl. USAF, 1948-49. Merrill fellow Harvard U., Cambridge, Mass., 1972. Mem. Unitarian Universalist Ministers Assn. (pres. 1973-75, Pacific N.W. dist. exec. 1962-64, mem. commn. on appraisal 1977-81). Office: Univ Unitarian Ch 6556 35th Ave NE Seattle WA 98115

RAICHLE, ROBERT WILLIAM, manufacturing executive; b. Rahway, N.J., Feb. 11, 1943; s. Herman Charles and Mildred Lois (Meyer) R.; m. Martha Ann Bass, Dec. 28, 1966; children: Brendon, Brittany. BS, Purdue U., 1965; MBA, Ind. U., 1970. Treas. Samsonite Corp., Denver, 1975-77, v.p. fin., 1977-81, v.p. mktg., 1981-83; exec. v.p. Spruce Engring., Boulder, Colo., 1983-84; pres., chief exec. officer Car Doctor U.S.A., Inc., Denver, 1984-85; v.p. fin. Beatrice Window Coverings, Inc., Westminster, Calif., 1985—; pres. R.W. Assocs., Laguna Niguel, Calif., 1983—. Served to 1st lt. U.S. Army, 1966-68. Mem. Indsl. League of Orange County, Fin. Execs. Inst., Planning Execs. Inst. Republican. Avocations: outdoor activities. Office: Beatrice Window Coverings Inc 7150 Fenwick Ln Westminster CA 92683

RAINEY, PAUL EUGENE, engineering technology educator; b. Marston, Mo., Jan. 13, 1944; s. Walter Herbert and Opal (McTernan) R.; m. Abbey Gay Ericson, June 25, 1966; children: Priscilla Marie, W. Eric. BSME, BSMetE, Purdue U., 1967; MSMetE, MIT, 1968; PhD, Tex. A&M U., 1981. Mech. engr. Cabot Corp.-Stellite, Kokomo, Ind., 1967; research asst. MIT, Cambridge, 1967-68; materials engr. U.S. Army Research Ctr., Watertown, Mass., 1968-71; asst. br. chief U.S. Army Research Lab., Champaign, Ill., 1971-72; instr. Laramie County CC, Cheyenne, Wyo., 1973-74; project engr. Texaco, Inc., Houston, 1974-75; asst. prof. U. Houston Coll. Tech., 1975-79; asst. prof. engring. tech. dept. Tex. A&M U., College Station, 1979-83; assoc. prof., dir. Western Wash. U., Bellingham, 1984—; cons. Johnston-Schlumberger, Sugarland, Tex., 1975-77, NASA, Johnson Space, Clear Lake, Tex., 1976, ARCO Oil and Gas Co., Dallas, 1982-83; bd. dirs. Wash. Tech. Ctr., Seattle, 1985—. Contbr. articles to profl. jours. Mem. ASME, Am. Soc. Engring. Edn., Am. Soc. Metals, Soc. Mfg. Engrs., Nat. Assn. Corrosion Engrs. Avocations: reading, motorcycling, hiking. Home: 1022 Beecher Ave Bellingham WA 98226 Office: Western Wash U Dept of Tech 516 High St Bellingham WA 98225

RAINEY, THOMAS EARLE, engineer, adminstrator; b. Clinton, Ill., June 18, 1947; s. Earle Emerson and Barbara (Ijams) R.; m. Judith Blevins, Feb. 23, 1974; children: Christina C., Michael E. BS in Aeron. and Astronautical Engring., U. Ill., 1970. Mech. process engr. Western Electric Co., Richmond, Va., 1970-76; test engr. Cen. Ill. Pub. Service, Coffeen, 1976-81; sr. engr., reactor engring. UNC Nuclear Industries, Richland, Wash., 1981-83, mgr. mech. restoration engring., 1983-85, mgr. mech. modification engring., 1985-86; mgr. project engring. Westinghouse Hanford Co., Richland, 1986—. Mem. Nat. Mgmt. Assn. (UNC chpt. booster), U. Ill. Alumni Assn. Home: 2502 W Grand Ronde Ave Kennewick WA 99336 Office: UNC Nuclear Industries PO Box 490 Richland WA 99352

RAINS, CAROLYN MARIE, health technician; b. Denver, Jan. 27, 1939; d. Joseph Webber and Catharine Elizabeth (Feuerstein) Beidler; m. Maurice Wayne Rains, Feb. 8, 1958 (div.); children: Richard Allan, Mark Edward, Jeffrey Joseph; m. Valtyr Omar Gudjonsson, Feb. 16, 1985 (div.). AA in Emergency Med. Tech., Pikes Peak Community Coll., 1979; student Pueblo Community Coll., 1952-56. Lic. practical nurse Colo.; cert. emergency medical technician, Colo. Nurse's aide Meml. Hosp. and Garden of the Gods Nursing Home, Colorado Springs, Colo., 1960-66; lic. practical nurse Norton's Nursing Home, Cheyenne, Colo., 1968-70; emergency med. technician U.S. Civil Service, Fort Carson, Colo., 1970-76, emergency medical technician motor vehicle operator, 1976-84; sec., trustee, exec. v.p. Am. Fedn. Govt. Employees Local 1345, 1971-78, pres., 1978—, gen. editor monthly publ., 1982-83, dist. nat. women's adv. com. rep., 1976-82, 84—, mem. women's adv. com., 1984-86, mem. Colo.-Wyo. Councio, 1985—, v.p. So. Dist.; v.p. Colo. Springs Area Labor Council, 1981—; sr. health technician U.S. Civil Service, Ft. Carson, Colo., 1984—; instr. emergency medicine Pikes Peak Community Coll., 1978-79, Utah State Fed. Woman's Program Conf., 1980, Dist. Tng. on Govtl. Issues, 1979-86; asst. instr. 13th. dist. tng. seminars, 1979-82. V.p. Colo.-Wyo. Labor Council, 1981-86. Served with USN, 1956-57. Mem. Federally Employed Women, Coalition Labor Union Women, NOW. Democrat. Buddhist. Home: 7479 Fortman St Fountain CO 80817

RAINS, HORACE, physician; b. Atlanta, Jan. 13, 1912; s. Igolius and Elizabeth (Ketchins) R.; B.S., Wilberforce U., 1937; M.A., Ohio State U., 1938; M.D., Meharry Med. Coll., 1953; m. Frances Mary McHie, May 1, 1951; children—Anthony John, Kimberly Ann. Intern, Los Angeles County Gen. Hosp., 1953-54; ins. salesman, Atlanta Life Ins. Co., 1938-40; instr. health and phys. edn. Lincoln U., Jefferson City, Mo., 1940; recreation dir. Nat. Youth Adminstrn., Wilberforce, Ohio, 1941; asst. prof. mil. sci. and tactics Wilberforce U., 1941-44; practice medicine, Long Beach, Calif., 1954-73, 77—, Los Angeles, 1973-77; mem. staff St. Mary Med. Center, 1977—, trustee, 1971—; chmn. med. edn. subcom. Calif. Research and Med. Edn. Fund, 1970-71. Chmn., Long Beach Human Relations Commn., 1972-75; chmn. United Civil Rights Com., 1963-65; mem. Long Beach City Planning Commn., 1980—; bd. dirs. Family Service Long Beach, 1966-72, Fair Housing Found., 1965-75. Served with AUS, 1944-45; ETO, PTO. Recipient Man of Year award Bernard and Milton Sahl post Am. Legion, 1965. Fellow Am. Acad. Family Practice; mem. Am. Lung Assn. (state dir. 1980—), Calif. Lung Assn. (dir. 1966-71; pres. Long Beach chpt. 1964-65), Wilberforce U. Alumni Assn. (pres. So. Calif. chpt. 1969-74, nat. dir.), Internat. platform Assn., N.A.A.C.P. (life mem., pres. Long Beach chpt. 1961-62). Methodist. Club: Lions (pres. 1979-80). Home: 5621 El Jardin St Long Beach CA 90815 Office: 1045 Atlantic Ave Suite 808 Long Beach CA 90813

RAINS, PATRICIA JANE, learning handicapped educator; b. Portland, Oreg., Mar. 26, 1934; d. Lawrence Marion and Mary Leticia (Roberts) R. A.B. in Edn., Cascade Coll., 1960; BS in Elem. Edn., Portland State U., 1962. Cert. tchr. Tchr. Lynch Sch. Dist. 28, Portland, Oreg., 1960-70; tchr. high sch. learning ctr. Tillamook Edn. Service Dist., Oreg., 1970-79, Nehalem Learning Ctr., 1979—, teaching asst. physically handicapped breathing exercises sch. dist. 56, Nehalem, 1983-86; vol. adult tutor Portland Community Coll., 1969-70. Author: Land Series Program, 1957-86. Active Sweet Adelines; pres. Wesleyan Fellowship, Tillamook. Summer sch. scholar, Tillamook Ednl. Service and Oreg. State Dept., 1971. Mem. NEA, Tillamook Edn. Tchrs. Assn. (del., pres. 1970-86), Oreg. Ednl. Assn. (del. 1960-86), Council of Exceptional Children, Nat. Assn. Female Execs., Oreg. Sheriff's Assn. (hon.). Republican. Club: Internat. Tng. in Communication (pres. council 2, 1979). Avocations: travel; bowling; handicrafts; singing; teaching Sunday Sch. kindergarten. Home: PO Box 122 Netarts OR 97143 Office: Nehalem Lower Elementary Sch PO Box 190 Nehalem OR 97131

RAINWATER, JAMES CARLTON, physicist, researcher; b. N.Y.C., Jan. 9, 1946; s. Leo James and Emma Louise (Smith) R.; m. Sylvia White, Dec. 15, 1974. B.A., U. Colo., 1967, Ph.D., 1974. Lectr. U. Colo., Denver, 1974; research assoc. U. B.C. (Can.), Vancouver, 1975-76; research assoc. Nat. Bur. Standards, Boulder, Colo., 1976-78, physicist, 1978—; vis. physicist Nat. Bur. Standards, Washington, 1979; assoc. adj. prof. dept. physics U. Colo., 1985—. Contbr. articles to profl. jours. Recipient Cert. of Recognition, Nat. Bur. Standards, 1979, 81, 83, 84. Mem. Am. Assn. Physics Tchrs. Home: 2558 Franklin Ave Louisville CO 80027 Office: Nat Bur Standards 325 Broadway Boulder CO 80303

RAISBECK, JAMES DAVID, aircraft design executive; b. Milw., Sept. 29, 1936; s. Clifford Clinton and Minnie (Hommersand) R.; B.S., Purdue U., M.S. in Aero. Engring., 1961; 1 dau., Jennifer Lee Raisbeck Hunter. Aero. research engr. Boeing Co., Seattle, 1961-65, liaison to U.S. Air Force, 1966-68, program mgr. comml. STOL programs, 1968-69; chmn. bd., chief exec. officer Robertson Aircraft Corp., Renton, Wash., 1969-73; v.p. tech. Am. Jet Industries, Los Angeles, 1973-74; chmn. bd., chief exec. officer, founder Raisbeck Group, Los Angeles, 1974-80; founder, chmn. bd., chief exec. officer Raisbeck Engring., Inc., 1981—; cons. Served with SAC, USAF, 1955-58. Recipient Disting. Engring. Alumnus in Aeronautics, Purdue U., 1979. Mem. Soc. Automotive Engrs., AIAA, Tau Beta Pi, Sigma Gamma Tau, Phi Eta Sigma. Patentee in field of wing design. Address: 7536 Seward Park Ave S Seattle WA 98118

RAJAGOPAL, VIJAYAKUMAR, environmental scientist; b. Madras, India, Jan. 8, 1950; came to U.S., 1975; s. A.V. and Bhama (Rajan) R; m. Sarojini Sockalingam, June 21, 1972; children: Vinod, Gayathri, Savithri. BME, Coll. Engring. U. Madras, 1971; MSME, U. Minn., 1977, PhD, 1982. Mgmt. trainee Easun Group, Madras, 1971-73; works engr. Torrance and Sons, Madras, 1973-75; grad. asst. U. Minn., Mpls., 1976-82; program mgr., scientist EMSI, Camarillo, Calif., 1982—. Mem. ASME, Air Pollution Control Assn., Am. Assn. Aerosol Research. Home: 2116 W Silvertree Ln Edmond OK 73013 Office: EMSI 4765 Calle Quetzal Camarillo CA 93010

RAJAN, MAHESH, engineering educator; b. Poona, India, May 25, 1951; came to U.S., 1975; s. Muthuswamy and Parvatham Rajan; m. Sandhya Pennathur, Aug. 1, 1982; children: Pravin Sunder, Nisha Meghara. BSME, Bangalore (India) U., 1974; MSME, Howard U., Washington, 1977; PhD in Engring. Mechanics, Va. Poly. Inst. and State U., 1981. Asst. prof. Ariz. State U., Tempe, 1981-84, 1985—; sr. engr. Garrett Turbine Engr., Phoenix, 1984-85; faculty fellow NASA Lewis, Cleve., 1983; cons. K-Flow, Scottsdale, 1985—. Contbr. articles to profl. jours. Recipient H.H. Jeffcot award ASME, 1985. Mem. AIAA, Smithsonian Air and Space Soc., Sigma Xi. Avocations: tennis, racquetball. Office: Ariz State U Mech Aero Engring Dept Tempe AZ 85287

RAKOCHEVICH, WOOLAY, public mediator, psychologist; b. Belgrade, Yugoslavia, Jan. 10, 1939; came to U.S., 1969; s. Milinko and Zivana (Zujovich) R.; married; 1 child, Beck. PhD in Behavioral Sci., Lublana U., Yugaslavia, 1964; postgrad., Columbia U., 1976; PhD, NYU, 1976. Pvt. practice psychology Paradise Valley, Ariz., 1977—; founder Pub. Mediator Office, Inc., Scottsdale, Ariz., 1980—. Author: How to Become a Public Mediator, 1985. Republican. Russian Orthodox.

RAKUTIS, RUTA, chemical economist; b. Marijampole, Lithuania, Aug. 16, 1939; came to U.S., 1949; s. Juozas Rakutis and Natalia Pavilcius. BS cum laude, U. Ill., 1961; PhD, U. Iowa, 1968; MBA, Northeastern U., 1974. Sr. scientist Jet Propulsion Lab, Pasadena, Calif., 1968-70; scientist color lab. Polaroid Corp., Cambridge, Mass., 1970-74; sales mgr. Am. Cyanamid Co., Wayne, N.J., 1974-79; mktg. mgr. Lignin Chems., Am. Can. Co., Greenwich, Conn., 1979-81; indsl. economist SRI Internat., Menlo Park, Calif., 1981—. Contbr. articles to profl. jours. Dunlop fellow, 1967-68. Mem. Soc. Petroleum Engrs., Chem. Mktg. Research Assn. of Am. Chem. Soc., Peninsula Profl. Women's Network, Sigma Xi. Avocations: horseback riding, skiing, tennis.

RALEIGH, KAREN SANDERS, banking administrator; b. St. Louis, June 17, 1950; d. Orin Lee and Arlene (Woods) Sanders; m. Donald Joseph Raleigh, Dec. 31, 1971. BA in Edn., Knox Coll., 1972; MS in Personnel Adminstrn., Ind. U., 1974. Sr. conf. coordinator Ind. U., Bloomington, 1975-77; postdoctoral research grant adminstr. Nat. Acad. Scis., Washington, 1977-79; v.p. corp. acct. officer Bank of Hawaii, Honolulu, 1979—. Mem. Mortar Board. Office: Bank Hawaii PO Box 2900 Honolulu HI 96846

RALEY, DAVID EARL, credit union executive; b. Middletown, N.Y., Jan. 17, 1934; s. Foster E. and Mary L. (Goodwin) R.; m. Diane Brannon Knowles, Sept. 3, 1956; children: Margaret, Mark, Michael. BS, U. Md., 1966; MBA, Ariz. State U., 1972. Enlisted USAF, 1954, advanced through grades to col., 1975, ret., 1980; v.p. Bierly Assn., South Pasadena, Calif., 1980-84; mgr. The Norton Credit Union, Norton AFB, Calif., 1984—; bd. dirs. Calif. Credit Union League, Pomona, Calif. Editor (manual) Aircraft Accident Investigation, 1986. Mem. Am. Soc. Safety Engrs. (profl. mem., pres. Arrowhead chpt. 1977-78, mem. membership com., 1979-80), Phi Kappa Phi, Lambda Phi Alpha. Avocation: computers. Home: 1350 E Highland Ave Redlands CA 92374 Office: The Norton Credit Union Bldg S-21 Norton AFB CA 92409

RALEY, JOHN PATTERSON, sales and marketing executive; b. Oakland, Calif., July 28, 1947; s. John Howard and Patricia (Patterson) R.; m. Peggi Tabor, July 1, 1979; children—Elizabeth, Clifford. B.A., Stanford U., 1969; postgrad. in Bus. Adminstrn., San Jose State U., 1971. Tchr. jr. high sch. Heritage Ranch Sch., Calistoga, Calif., 1969-70; store mgr. Hedding's Bldg. Supply, San Ramon, Calif., 1970-71; order control, sales supr., region mgr., nat. sales mgr., nat. accounts mgr. The Flecto Co., Inc., Oakland, Calif., 1972-84; v.p. sales Logo Paris, Inc., Novato, Calif., 1984—; adv. com. Calif. Air Resources Bd., Los Angeles, 1976-78. Pres. Nobel Jr. High Sch. Parent Adv. Com., Northridge, Calif., 1980; cub master Boy Scouts Am., Albany, Calif., 1974-75; dir. Found. for Calif. Dance, Los Angeles, 1979-82. Mem. Am. Mgmt. Assn., Cardinal Club (Stanford U.). Democrat. Episcopalian.

RALEY, THOMAS P., grocery company executive; b. 1904. Founder, owner Raley's, Broderick, Calif., 1935—, now chmn. bd., dir. Served with U.S. Army, 1925-31. Lodges: Masons, Shriners. Office: Raley's 500 W Capital Ave Broderick CA 95605 *

RALPH, ROY D., oil refinery engineer; b. Sop's Arm, Nfld., Can., Mar. 22, 1947; s. Harvey M. and Aramanda (Elliott) R.; m. Olive May Hunt, July 17, 1968; children—Iris Lee, Ira Dee, Ian Roy. B.Engring., Meml. U. Nfld., 1975. Registered profl. engr., B.C. Project engr. Gulf Can. Products Co., N.S., 1975-79, maintenance coordinator, Ont., 1979-81, refinery engr., Port Moody, B.C., 1981-86; mech. design specialist, Calgary, Alta., 1986—. Organizer Liberal Party Nfld., 1970, Liberal Party Can., 1972. H.J. Crowe scholar, 1964; Electro Dist. scholar, 1963, 64. Mem. Assn. Profl. Engrs. B.C., B.C. Baseball Assn. (treas. 1981—), N.S. Football Assn. (v.p. 1974-79). Mem. Pentecostal Assemblies Can. Home: 21 Midpark Crescent SE, Calgary, AB Canada T2X 1S7

RALSTON, BARBARA JO, bank executive; b. Youngstown, Ohio, Apr. 11, 1940; d. Fred Kenneth and Juanita Ruth (Welch) Roof; m. Donald Gene Ralston, Jan. 9, 1960; children: Mark David, Lori Sue. Cert., Pacific Coast Banking Sch., Seattle, 1981. Sec. Bank of Scottsdale, Ariz., 1962-66; adminstrv. asst. Talley Industries, Mesa, Ariz., 1966-73; asst. mgr. Continental Bank, Phoenix, 1973-77; exec. v.p. Continental Bank Service Corp., Phoenix, 1977-85, pres., dir., 1985—; bd. dirs. Continental Bank Service Corp., Phoenix. Bd. dirs. Valley Big Bros.-Big Sisters, Phoenix, 1986; mem. Ariz. Acad., Phoenix, 1984; treas. Phoenix Together Town Hall, 1986. Recipient You Too Can Make A Difference award Valley Christian Ctrs., Phoenix, 1985. Mem. Nat. Assn. Bank Women (state pres. 1981-82), Am. Inst. Banking (state edn. chmn. Ariz. chpt. 1984—), Tumbleweed (pres. 1983). Republican. Methodist. Lodge: Soroptimists (pres. 1982, Women Helping Women award 1984). Avocations: reading, travel, sewing. Home: 3025 W Lupine Phoenix AZ 85029 Office: Continental Bank Service Corp 1302 W Indian School Rd Phoenix AZ 85013

RALSTON, GILBERT ALEXANDER, author, educator; b. Los Angeles, Jan. 5, 1912; s. Alexander Gilbert and Jeanette (Johnston) R.; grad. Pasadena Coll., 1929-32; grad. Am. Acad. Dramatic Arts, 1935; B.C.A., Sierra Nev. Coll., 1972; M.A., Fielding Inst., 1983; PhD, Columbia Pacific U., 1986; m. Mary K. Hart, Dec. 20, 1938; children—Michael, David. Actor, stage mgr. theatre prodns. N.Y.C., 1931-35; writer, dir. radio shows NBC, N.Y.C., 1936-38; prodn. supr. Compton Advt., Inc., N.Y.C., West Coast, 1939-42; organizer, mgr. radio dept. Proctor & Gamble, Cin., 1943-47, exec. producer inc. TV div., 1947-50; free lance producer TV films, 1950-55; exec. producer in charge TV drama CBS, 1955, dir. network programs originating in N.Y.C., 1956; producer High Adventure documentaries with Lowell Thomas, 1957; chmn. sch. communication arts Tahoe (Cal.) Paradise Coll., 1968; dean sch. communicative arts Sierra Nevada Coll., Incline Village, Nev., 1960-73, pres., 1973-83, pres. emeritus, 1983—; pres. Ralston Sch. Communicative Arts, Genoa, Nev., 1971—; v.p. Rule of Three Prodns., Los Angeles, 1973—; lectr. Fordham U., City Coll. City U. N.Y., Loyola U. of Los Angeles, St. Mary's Coll. of Calif. Mem. Authors Guild, ASCAP, Western Writers Am., Writers Guild Am., Am. Massage and Therapy Assn. Author: Ben, 1972; (with Richard Newhafer) The Frightful Sin of Cisco Newman, 1972; Dakota Warpath, 1973; Dakota: Red Revenge, 1973; Dakota Cat Trap, 1974; Dakota Murder's Money, 1974; Dakota: Chain Reaction, The Deadly Art, 1975, The Third Circle, 1976, The Tao of Touch, 1983, others. Author screenplays: No Strings Attached, 1962; A Gallery of Six, 1963; A Feast of Jackals, 1963; Cockatrice, 1965; Kona Coast, 1967; Night of the Locust, 1969; Ben, 1971, Third Circle, 1975, Sure, 1975. Author screen adaptations: Willard (by Stephen Gilbert), 1970; Bluebonnet (by Boris Sobelman and Jack H. Robinson), 1971; Dakota Red, 1987. Author scripts for TV sometime under pseudonym Gil Alexander: High Adventure, Naked City, Route 66, Follow the Sun, Bus Stop, The Untouchables, Alcoa Theatre, Ben Casey, Richard Boone Show, 12 O'Clock High, The Name of the Game, Daktari, Laredo, Combat, Big Valley, Gunsmoke, Amos Burke, Slattery's People, Alfred Hitchcock, Star Trek, It Takes a Thief, O'Hara, Cannon, numerous others. Address: PO Box 350 Genoa NV 89411

RALSTON, JERRY WILSON, management consulting company executive, educator; b. Seattle, Oct. 13, 1932; s. Jess Wilson and Agnes Beatrice (Creevey) R.; m. Attitha Brigitta Köhn, Feb. 17, 1967; children: Jess Wilson III, Kim Arthur, Tonia Lee, Kris Michelle, Yvonne Marie. BA, Whitman Coll., 1953; MS in Social Sci., U. Stockholm, 1961, MS in Econ., 1962; PhD, U. Geneva, 1969. European bus. advisor The Boeing Co., Geneva, 1962-66; internat. bus. advisor The Boeing Co., Seattle, 1966-69; internat. economist Rainier Bank, Seattle, 1969-73; pres., gen. mgr. Mgmt. Services Internat., Inc., Seattle, 1973-84; pres. MSI United, Ltd., Seattle, 1984—, also bd. dirs.; Faculty, U. Wash. Economist Seattle/King County Econ. Devel. Council, 1972. Served to maj. U.S. Army, 1953-57. Mem. Am. Econ. Assn., Nat. Assn. Bus. Economists, Internat. Inst. Strategic Studies, Assn. MBA Execs., Am. Acad. Polit. and Social Sci., Wash. Export Council. Republican. Avocations: skiing, windsurfing, hiking, reading, music. Home: 9828 62d Ave S Seattle WA 98118 Office: MSI United Ltd PO Box 78013 Seattle WA 98178

RALSTON, ROBERT ORVILLE, II, molecular biologist, researcher; b. Omaha, Nov. 20, 1951; s. Robert Orville and Dorothy Jane (Gill) R.; m. Anne Marie Stommes, Apr. 5, 1975. BA in English and Journalism cum laude, U. Nebr., 1974, postgrad., 1974-76, PhD in Chemistry, 1980. Grad. research asst. dept. chemistry U. Nebr., Lincoln, 1976-80, research assoc., 1977-80; postdoctoral fellow dept. microbiology and immunology U. Calif., San Francisco, 1981-85, staff research scientist George W. Hooper Research Found., 1985-86; prin. scientist dept. virology Chiron Corp., Emeryville, Calif., 1987—. Contbr. articles to profl. jours. Recipient Research Service award Nat. Cancer Inst., 1982-85, W.R. Hearst nat. journalism award, 1974; fellow Leukemia Soc. Am., 1981-82, F.O. Johnson, 1979-80, M.H. Fling, 1978-79; R. Bremer Journalism scholar, 1973-74. Mem. Am. Soc. Microbiology, Am. Chem. Soc., AAAS. Republican. Episcopalian. Avocations: hiking, climbing, skiing. Office: U Calif Hooper Research Found 1542 Health Scis W San Francisco CA 94143

RAMACHANDRAN, VILAYANUR SUBRAMANIAN, neuropsychology researcher, educator; b. Madras, India, Aug. 10, 1951; came to U.S., 1979; s. Vilayanur Mahadevan and Meenakshi (Alladi) Subramanian. MD, Stanley Med. Sch., Madras, 1974; PhD, Cambridge U., Eng., 1978. Postdoctoral fellow Oxford U., Eng., 1977-79; research fellow Calif. Inst. Tech., Pasadena, 1979-81; prof. U. Calif.-San Diego, La Jolla, 1983—; vis. assoc. in biology, Calif. Inst. Tech., 1983—. Editor: Consciousness and the Physical World, 1979; contbr. articles to profl. jours. Sr. Rouse Ball scholar Trinity Coll., Cambridge, Eng., 1977-78. Mem. Assn. Research on Vision and Ophthalmology, Soc. Neurosci., Helmholtz Club Southern Calif. (sec. 1980—). Avocations: hiking, travel, Indian music. Office: U Calif-San Diego Dept Psychology-C009 La Jolla CA 92093

RAMALEY, WILLIAM CHARLES, mathematics educator; b. Columbus, Ohio, Aug. 31, 1939; s. Edward Jackson and Pauline Frances (Folk) R.; m. Annette Joyce Waters, Mar. 18, 1967; 1 child, Julia Elizabeth. BS cum laude, Ohio State U., 1961; MA, PhD, U. Colo., 1969. Asst. prof. Carleton Coll., Northfield, Minn., 1966-71, Colo. Coll., Colo. Springs, 1971-73; mem. faculty Ft. Lewis Coll., Durango, Colo., 1973—, prof. math., 1982—; chmn. math. dept. Ft. Lewis Coll., Durango, Colo., 1983—. Author: Trails and Trailbuilders of the Rocky Mountain National Park, 1975; mem. editorial bd., Jour. Undergrad. Math., 1971—; contbr. articles to profl. jours. and pubs. Chmn. City of Durango Water Commn., 1984—. NSF summer fellow, U. Colo., 1973. Mem. Math. Assn. Am. (chmn. Rocky Mountain sect. 1979), Sigma Xi, Phi Beta Kappa, Pi Mu Epsilon, Kappa Mu Epsilon. Republican. Unitarian. Avocations: hiking, flower identification, Western hist., theater, photography. Home: 7 Animas Pl Durango CO 81301 Office: Fort Lewis Coll Dept Math Durango CO 81301

RAMANATHAN, KAVASSERI VAIDIANATHA, accounting educator, researcher, consultant; b. Trichur, Kerala, India, Nov. 26, 1932; came to U.S., 1966; s. Kavasseri Viswanatha and Saraswathy (Apathira) Vaidianathan; m. Rajalakshmi Ramanathan, Apr. 22, 1959; 1 dau., Saraswathy. B.Com., Calcutta U., India, 1954; M.B.A., Northwestern U., 1962, Ph.D., 1970. Systems mgr. Philips India Ltd., Calcutta, 1955-59; prof. acctg. Indian Inst. Mgmt., Ahmedabad, 1963-66; assoc. prof. acctg. U. Wash., Seattle, 1969-79, prof. acctg., 1979—, chmn. exec. M.B.A. program, 1982-86; vis. scientist Battelle Meml. Inst., Seattle, 1974-77; vis. prof. Harvard U., Cambridge, Mass., 1979-80; vis. fellow Australian Nat. LU., Canberra, 1983, Monash U., Australia, 1983; vis. prof. NYU, N.Y.C., 1986-87. Author: Management Control in Nonprofit Organizations, 1982; editor: Accounting for Managerial Decision Making, 1974, Readings in Management Control in Nonprofit Organizations, 1982. Adviser Sandeepany West, Piercy, Calif., 1981-82; bd. dirs. Arsha Vidya Pitam, Los Gatos, Calif., 1982—; pres. Ragamala, Seattle. Fulbright scholar Calcutta, 1960-63. Fellow Indian Inst. of Cost and Works Accts.; mem. Am. Acctg. Assn. (chmn. 3 coms. 1982-83), Am. Mgmt. Assn., Fin. Execs. Inst., Can. Comprehensive Auditing Found. Home: 10020 31st Ave NE Seattle WA 98125 Office: U Wash DJ 10 Dept Acctg Seattle WA 98195

RAMASWAMY, PADMANABHAN, materials scientist; b. Ambattur, India, Mar. 5, 1953; came to U.S., 1977; s. Ramaswamy Iyer and Bhagavathy (Narayanan) Padmanabhan; m. Nongluck Pankurddee, Jan. 8, 1986. BSc in Physics, Loyola Coll., Madras, India, 1972; B of Engring. in Metallurgy, Indian Inst. Sci., Bangalore, 1975; PhD in Materials Sci., Oreg.

Grad. Ctr., 1982. Research and devel. engr. Bharat Electronics, Ltd., Bangalore, 1975-77; research scientist Oreg. Grad. Ctr., Beaverton, 1982-83; sr. staff engr. Motorola, Inc., Phoenix, 1984—. Contbr. articles to profl. jours. Mem. Am. Vacuum Soc., Am. Inst. Mining, Metall. and Petroleum Engrs. Avocations: flying, photography, music. Home: 4530 E McDowell #228 Phoenix AZ 85008 Office: Motorola Inc B-136 5005 E McDowell Phoenix AZ 85026

RAMER, BRUCE M., lawyer; b. Teaneck, N.J., Aug. 2, 1933; s. Sidney and Anne S. (Strassman) R.; m. Ann G. Ramer, Feb. 15, 1965; children—Gregg B., Marc K., Neal I. A.B., Princeton U., 1955; J.D., Harvard U., 1958. Bar: Calif. 1963, N.J. 1958. Assoc., Morrison, Lloyd & Griggs, Hackensack, N.J., 1959-60; ptnr. Gang, Tyre, Ramer & Brown, Inc., Los Angeles, 1963—. Exec. dir. Entertainment Law Inst.; bd. of councilors Law Ctr. U. So. Calif.; past pres. Los Angeles chpt., nat. v.p., bd. govs.; chmn. Nat. Affairs Commn. Am. Jewish Com.; trustee Loyola Marymount U.; mem. corp. bd., mem. agy. task force, discretionary fund distribution United Way; bd. of trustees Los Angeles Children's Mus.; v.p. Fraternity of Friends of Los Angeles Music Ctr. Mem. Los Angeles County Bar Assn., ABA, Calif. Bar Assn., Beverly Hills Bar Assn., Los Angeles Copyright Soc. (pres. 1974-75), Calif. Copyright Conf. (pres. 1973-74). Office: 6400 Sunset Blvd Los Angeles CA 90028

RAMEY, CHERI DOLORES, advt. agy. exec.; b. Montreal, Que., Can., Apr. 17, 1944; d. Harold Edward and Bette Evlyn (Cameron) R.; came to U.S., 1951, naturalized, 1961; grad. Sch. Visual Arts, N.Y.C., 1961-64. Asst. art dir./designer Composing Room, N.Y.C., 1964-65, Katz Jacobs & Zlotnick, N.Y.C., 1965-66; art dir. Young & Rubicam, N.Y.C., 1966-69, sr. art dir., Los Angeles, 1969-71; creative dir. Ramey Communications Co., Los Angeles, 1971—, now pres., creative dir. Adv. bd. Los Angeles Trade Tech. Recipient awards Cannes Film Festival, 1969, N.Y. Art Dirs. Club, 1966, 68, 73, 76; Best in West award, 1980, others. Mem. Western States Advt. Agys. Assn. (dir.), Los Angeles Creative Club (dir.), Am. Assn. Advt. Agys. Democrat. Office: 3008 Wilshire Blvd Los Angeles CA 90010

RAMIREZ, DIANE NORTHROP, educational administrator, consultant; b. Columbus, Ohio, Dec. 22, 1945; d. James Abraham and Sharma Ann (Swank) Chamberlin; m. Richard Moreno Ramirez, Feb. 10, 1973; children—Ronan Northrop, Roderic Northrop. BFA, Ohio State U., 1967; student Columbus Coll. Art & Design, 1964-65; M in Spl. Edn., Calif. State Coll.-Los Angeles, 1971; EdD, U. So. Calif., 1987. Cert. elem., secondary tchr., community coll. instr., adminstr., Calif. Tchr. arts, crafts Recreation Dept., Columbus, Ohio, 1966-67; cons. Family Effectiveness, Coachella Valley, Calif., 1968-79; cons. trainable mentally retarded, Riverside County, Calif., 1968-70; tchr. secondary trainable mentally retarded Riverside County (Calif.) Supt. Schs., 1968-69, tchr. elem. trainable mentally retarded, 1969-70; tchr. bilingual lang. devel. Desert Sands Unified Sch. Dist., Indio, Calif., 1970; tchr. secondary remedial reading Coachella Valley High Sch., Thermal, Calif., 1971-72, tchr., developer secondary educationally handicapped, 1972-74; counselor, instr. for handicapped, Coll. of the Desert, Palm Desert, Calif., 1974-75; dir. handicapped programs and services, assoc. prof. spl. edn., 1975—; facilitator Region 9/Calif. Community Colls. Handicap Programs & Services, 1980—; field reader Disadvantaged Programs, HEW, 1979. Named Outstanding Tchr., Found. Exceptional Children, 1968-69. Mem. NEA, Calif. Tchrs. Assn., Educare Profl. Edn. Found., Assn. Supervision and Curriculum Devel., Calif. Personnel and Guidance Assn., Phi Delta Kappa. Republican. Author: Guide: Education of Handicapped Adults, 1978; developer curriculum guides for trainable mentally retarded. Home: 75-289 Desert Park Dr Indian Wells CA 92210 Office: 43-500 Monterey Ave Palm Desert CA 92260

RAMIREZ, MARTHA, computer firm executive, consultant; b. Washington, Mar. 26, 1942; d. Gilberto Velasco and Louise (Franklin) R.; m. Arthur W. Luehrmann, Sept. 15, 1961; children—Mia Kerstin, Nils Gordon. Student Smith Coll., 1959-60, George Washington U., 1960-61; B.S., Ill. Inst. Tech., 1965; M.B.A., Amos Tuck Sch. Bus. Adminstrn., Dartmouth Coll., 1977. Asst. to pres. The Zischke Orgn., San Francisco, 1977-80; mgr. adminstrv. group The Wyatt Co., San Francisco, 1980-81; pres. Computer Literacy, Berkeley, Calif., 1981—. Mem. Council on Ednl. Tech., State Bd. Edn., Calif. Recipient Lebovitz Prize, Amos Tuck Sch. Bus. Adminstrn., 1976; Amos Tuck scholar, 1977. Mem. Tuck Alumni Assn. No. Calif. Office: Computer Literacy 1466 Grizzly Peak Blvd Berkeley CA 94708

RAMIREZ, RICARDO, bishop; b. Bay City, Tex., Sept. 12, 1936; s. Natividad and Maria (Espinosa) R. B.A., U. St. Thomas, Houston, 1959; M.A., U. Detroit, 1968; Diploma in Pastoral Studies, East Asian Pastoral Inst., Manila, 1973-74. Ordained priest Roman Catholic Ch., 1966; missionary Basilian Fathers, Mex., 1968-76; exec. v.p. Mexican Am. Cultural Ctr., San Antonio, 1976-81; aux. bishop Archdiocese of San Antonio, 1981-82; bishop Diocese of Las Cruces, N.M., 1982—; cons. U.S. Bishop's Com. on Liturgy, 1981—; advisor U.S. Bishop's Com. on Hispanic Affairs, 1981—. Author: Fiesta, Worship and Family, 1981. Mem. N.Am. Acad. on Liturgy, Hispanic Liturgical Inst., Padres Asociada Derechos Religiosos Educativos y Sociales. Lodges: K.C; Holy Order Knights of Holy Sepulcher. Office: Diocese of Las Cruces 1280 Med Park Las Cruces NM 88004 *

RAMIREZ, WILLIAM EARL, clothing company executive; b. Dalhart, Tex., July 15, 1951; s. Manuel and Isabella Mary (Lindsay) R.; BBA in Acctg., Tex. Tech U., 1973; JD, U. Iowa, 1976; LLM in Taxation, DePaul U., 1980. Bar: Iowa 1976, Ill. 1976. Tax. acct. Price Waterhouse & Co., Chgo., 1976-77; tax research analyst Sunbeam Corp., Chgo., 1977-80; tax atty. Hughes Tool Co., Houston, 1980-85; tax mgr. Levi Strauss & Co., San Francisco, 1985—; speaker Internat. Joint Ventures, 1984. Bd. dirs., treas. Bellerive Homeowners, Houston, 1984-85; vol. Big Bros.-Big Sisters, Houston, 1983-85. Named an Outstanding Young Man, U.S. Jaycees, 1984. Mem. ABA, , Internat. Bar Assn., World Affairs Council. Mensa. Democrat. Methodist. Home: 350 Vernon St #2 Oakland CA 94610 Office: Levi Strauss & Co 1155 Battery LS 3 San Francisco CA 94120

RAMLER, WARREN JOSEPH, radiation equipment consultant; b. Joliet, Ill., Jan. 1, 1921; s. John George and Anna Louise (Kohlmeyer) R.; m. Ruth E. Wilder, Sept. 4, 1943; children: John W., Richard W., Barbara Anne. BSEE, Ill. Inst. Tech., 1943, MSEE, 1953; postgrad. Carnegie-Mellon U., 1943-46, U. Pitts., 1943-46. Instr. elec. engring. and physics Carnegie Inst. Tech., 1943, 44, 46; elec. engr. Tenn. Eastman Corp., Oak Ridge, 1944-46; sr. scientist, project dir. low energy accelerators Argonne (Ill.) Nat. Lab., 1946-73, cons., 1973—; gen. mgr. Radiation Polymer Co. div. PPG Industries, Plainfield, Ill., 1973-80; sr. v.p. RPC Industries, Plainfield and Hayward, Calif., 1980-86; pres. WJR Cons., Grand Lake, Colo.; cons. to industry on use of radiation, 1986, pres. WJR cons. Asso. chmn. Boy Scouts Am., Elmhurst, Ill., 1956-60; mem. sci. adv. com. York High Sch., 1962. Mem. IEEE, Am. Phys. Soc., Am. Mgmt. Assn., AAAS, N.Y. Acad. Scis., U.S. Power Squadron, Eta Kappa Nu, Tau Beta Pi, Rho Epsilon. Home: 155 Canyon Diablo Dr Sedona AZ 86336

RAMMING, DAVID WILBUR, research horticulturist; b. Oklahoma City, Oct. 31, 1946; s. Clarence and Adeline Ramming; m. Helen Ramming, May 31, 1975; children: Glenn, Michelle, Daniel. BA, Okla. State U., 1968, MA, 1972; PhD, Rutgers U., 1976. Research horticulturist USDA, Fresno, Calif., 1975—. Served with U.S. Army, 1969-70, Vietnam. Mem. Am. Soc. Hort. Sci., Am. Hort. Soc., Am. Pomol. Soc. Lutheran. Office: USDA/ARS 2021 S Peach Ave Fresno CA 93727

RAMO, SIMON, engineering executive; b. Salt Lake City, May 7, 1913; s. Benjamin and Clara (Trestman) R.; m. Virginia Smith, July 25, 1937; children: James Brian, Alan Martin. B.S., U. Utah, 1933, D.Sc. (hon.), 1961; Ph.D., Calif. Inst. Tech., 1936; D.Eng. (hon.), Case Inst. Tech., 1960, U. Mich., 1966, Poly. Inst. N.Y., 1971; D.Sc. (hon.), Union Coll., 1963, Worcester Poly. Inst., 1968, U. Akron, 1969, Cleve. State U., 1976; LL.D. (hon.), Carnegie-Mellon U., 1970, U. So. Calif., 1972, Gonzaga U., 1983, Occidental Coll., 1984, Gonzaga U., 1983, Occidental Coll., 1984. With Gen. Electric Co., 1936-46; v.p. ops. Hughes Aircraft Co., 1946-53; with Ramo-Woolridge Corp., 1953-58; sci. dir. U.S. intercontinental guided missile program 1954-58; dir. TRW Inc., 1954—, vice chmn. bd., 1961-78, chmn. exec. com., 1969-78; chmn. bd. TRW-Fujitsu Co., 1980-83; pres. The Bunker-Ramo Corp., 1964-66; vis. prof. mgmt. sci. Calif. Inst. Tech., 1978—; Regents lectr. UCLA, 1981-82, U. Calif. at Santa Cruz, 1978-79; chmn. Center for Study Am. Experience, U. So. Calif., 1978-80; Faculty fellow John F. Kennedy Sch. Govt., Harvard U., 1980—; dir. Union Bank, 1965—, Atlantic Richfield Co., 1984-86; past dir. Times Mirror Co., 1968-83; Mem. White House Energy Research and Devel. Adv. Council, 1973-75; mem. adv. com. on sci. and fgn. affairs U.S. State Dept., 1973-75; chmn. Pres.'s Com. on Sci. and Tech., 1976-77; mem. adv. council to Sec. Commerce, 1976-77; co-chmn. Transitition Task Force on Sci. and Tech. for Pres.-elect Reagan; mem. roster consultants to adminstr. ERDA, 1976-77; bd. advisors for sci. and tech. Republic of China, 1981—. Author sci., engring. and mgmt. books. Bd. dirs. Los Angeles World Affairs Council; bd. dirs. Music Center Found., Los Angeles, Los Angeles Philharm. Assn.; trustee Calif. Inst. Tech., Nat. Symphony Orch. Assn., 1973-83; trustee emeritus Calif. State Univs.; bd. visitors UCLA Sch. Medicine, 1980—; bd. dirs. W. M. Keck Found., 1983—; bd. govs. Performing Arts Council of Music Ctr. Los Angeles, pres., 1976-77. Recipient award IAS, 1956; award Am. Inst. Elec. Engrs., 1959; award Arnold Air Soc., 1960; Am. Acad. Achievement award, 1964; award Am. Iron and Steel Inst., 1968; Distinguished Service medal Armed Forces Communication and Electronics Assn., 1970; medal of achievement WEMA, 1970; awards U. So. Calif., 1971, 79; Kayan medal Columbia U., 1972; award Am. Cons. Engrs. Council, 1974; medal Franklin Inst., 1978; award Harvard Bus. Sch. Assn., 1979; award Nat. Medal Sci., 1979; Disting. Alumnus award U. Utah, 1981; UCLA medal, 1982; Presdl. Medal of Freedom, 1983; Jr. Achievement Bus. Hall of Fame award, 1984; others. Fellow IEEE (Electronic Achievement award 1953, Golden Omega award 1975, Founders medal 1980), Am. Acad. Arts and Scis.; mem. Nat. Acad. Engring. (founder, council mem. Bueche award), Nat. Acad. Scis., Am. Phys. Soc., Am. Philos. Soc., Inst. Advancement Engring., Internat. Acad. Astronautics, Eta Kappa Nu (eminent mem. award 1966). Office: T R W Office of the Chmn One Space Park Redondo Beach CA 90278

RAMON, CEON, bioengineer, researcher; b. Lucknow, India, Dec. 2, 1945; s. Ram A. and Ram. K. (Devi) Srivastava, m. Sneh K. Varma, Aug. 15, 1972 (div. May 1981). BS, Agra (India) U., 1963; BE with honors, Indian Inst. Sci., Bangalore, 1966; PhD, U. Utah, 1973. Postdoctoral fellow U. Utah, Salt Lake City, 1973-76, U. Wash., Seattle, 1977-78; asst. prof. SUNY, Stony Brook, 1978-79; research bioengr. Children's Orthopedic Hosp., Seattle, 1979-80; asst. prof. Seattle U., 1981-82; sr. scientist Inst. Applied Physicians and Medicine, Seattle, 1980—, research assoc., 1983. Mem. IEEE, Bioelectromagnetic Soc., Etta Kappa Nu, Sigma Xi. Buddhist, Hindu. Office: Inst Applied Physiology/Medicine 701 16th Ave Seattle WA 98122

RAMOS, ALBERT A., electrical engineer; b. Los Angeles, Feb. 28, 1927; s. Jesus D. and Carmen F. (Fontes) R.; B.S. in Elec. Engring., U. So. Calif., 1950, M.S. in Systems Mgmt., 1972; Ph.D., U.S. Internat. U., 1975; m. Joan C. Pailing, Sept. 23, 1950; children—Albert A., Richard R., James J., Katherine. With guided missile test group Hughes Aircraft Co., 1950-60; with TRW DSG, 1960—, sr. staff engr. Norton AFB, San Bernardino, Calif., 1969—. Served with USNR, 1945-46. Registered profl. engr., Calif. Mem. IEEE, Nat. Soc. Profl. Engrs., Air Force Assn., Mexican-Am. Engring. Soc., Mexican Am. Profl. Mgmt. Assn. (mem. adminstering commn. dept. community services), Sigma Phi Delta, Eta Kappa Nu, Tau Beta Pi. Home: 1457 W Cypress Ave Redlands CA 92373 Office: PO Box 1310 San Bernardino CA 92402

RAMOS, JACK MARKUS, dentist; b. Fresno, Cal., June 15, 1925; s. Joseph Markus and Gladys (Leonardo) R.; A.B., Fresno State U., 1950; D.D.S., U. Pacific, 1954; postgrad. in Edn., U. Calif.-San Francisco, 1958; m. Marie J. Rojas, June 11, 1950; children—Loretta Marie, Laura Ann. Gen practice dentistry, Fresno, 1954—. Mem. planning com. Adult Activity Center for Mentally Retarded, 1969-71; mem. mental retardation com. Fresno Community Council, 1965-67; mem. exec. com. Central Calif. Regional Center for Retarded, 1971-72; mem. nominating com. Calif. Assn. for Retarded, 1972-73, vice pres., 1973-76, chmn. fiscal affairs com., 1976-79, pres., 1977-79; mem. Atty. Gen.'s Vol. Adv. Council, 1972-78; chmn. adv. bd. Porterville State Hosp., also Fresno County Mental Health Adv. Bd., 1973—; active PTA; pres. Fresno Assn. Mentally Retarded, recipient Ann. Golden Circle award, 1975, 82; mem. Parents of Gifted, Fresno County Coordinating Council Developmentally Disabled; mem. long-range planning com. Valley Med. Center, 1980-83; pres. Valley Dental Care 1980-83. Found., 1980-83. Bd. dirs. Fresno Found. Mental Retardation; mem. Central Valley citizen adv. council U. Calif. Served with USNR, 1943-46; PTO. Fellow Acad. Gen. Dentistry, Acad. Dentistry Internat.; mem. Am. Dental Assn., Federation Dentaire Internationale, AAAS, V.F.W. (life), Fresno-Madera Dental Soc. (treas. 1976-77, sec., 1977-78, pres. 1980-82, chmn. legis. com., chmn. ins. com., chmn. peer rev. com. 1984—), Acad. Dentistry for Handicapped, Calif. Dental Assn. (by-laws reference com. 1980-81), Am. Soc. Preventative Dentistry, Pub. Health League, Calif. State Sheriff's Assn., Xi Psi Phi. Democrat. Roman Catholic. Clubs: Cabrillo, Rotary (vocat. services chmn., dir., Paul Harris fellow). Home: 1163 W Morris Ave Fresno CA 93705 Office: 946 N Van Ness Ave Fresno CA 93728

RAMOS-WRIGHT, JILL, recreation specialist, educator, consultant; b. Indpls., June 21, 1942; d. William Robert and Harriett Vivian (Howell) White; m. Ronald Jordan Ramos, Aug. 20, 1966 (div. 1981); children—Matthew William, Ryan Jordan; m. 2d, Steven Richard Wright, Dec. 2, 1983. B.S. in Edn., Ind. U., 1964, M.S. in Recreation Adminstrn., 1966. Nat. field counselor Alpha Xi Delta Soc., Indpls., 1965-66; dir. recreational therapy Mesa Vista Psychiat. Hosp., San Diego, 1966-68; pres. Recreation Assocs., La Jolla, Calif., 1968-70; cons. in recreation, San Diego, 1973-74; asst. prof. recreational therapy San Diego State U., 1974-80; v.p. Wright & Assocs., bus. systems, San Diego, 1983—; pres. JRW Exec. Services, 1983—. Bd. dirs. PTA, Painted Rock Sch., Poway, Calif., 1976-79; mem. gifted and talented edn. steering com. Twin Peaks Sch., Poway, Calif., 1981—; mem. Marion Ross drama scholarship steering com. San Diego State U., 1982-83. Jill Ramos Scholarship established at San Diego State U., 1979. Mem. Calif. Park and Recreation Soc. (cert. supervision 1968, cert. achievement 1980, coll. rep. Dist. XII 1975-76, v.p. dist. XII 1977-78), Los Amados Childrens Home Soc., Nat. Assn. for Female Execs. Republican. Methodist. Club: Home of Guiding Hands Aux. (San Diego). Home: 14343 Trailwind Rd Poway CA 92064

RAMSAY, JOHN BARADA, research scientist, educator; b. Phoenix, Dec. 28, 1929; s. John A. and Helen G. Ramsay; m. Barbara Ann Hilsenhoff, Apr. 18, 1953; children—Bryan J., Kathleen L., Carol A., David A. B.S. in Chemistry, Tex. Western U., 1950; Ph.D. in Analytical Chemistry, U. Wis., 1954. Mem. staff Los Alamos Nat. Lab., 1954-70, 73—; assoc. prof. Coll. Petroleum and Minerals, Dhahran, Saudi Arabia, 1970-73; cons. U.S. Navy, USAF, 1980—; adj. prof. U.Nex., Los Alamos, 1986—. Author sci. articles. Recipient award of excellence U.S. Dept. Energy, 1984. Mem. AAAS, N.Mex. Acad. Sci. (pres.-elect 1987), Am. Archeol. Soc. (chpt. pres. 1979), Sigma Xi. Democrat. Home: 6 Erie Ln Los Alamos NM 87544 Office: PO Box 1663 Los Alamos NM 87545

RAMSBY, MARK DELIVAN, small business owner; b. Portland, Oreg., Nov. 20, 1947; s. Marshall Delivan and Verna Pansy (Culver) R.; m. Carla Delores Hortsch, June 13, 1971; children: Aaron Delivan, Venessa Mercedes. Student, Portland (Oreg.) State U., 1966-67. With C.E.D., Portland, 1970-75; minority ptnr. The Light Source, Portland, 1975-78, pres., 1978-87; prin. Illume Lighting Design, Portland, 1987—; pvt. practice cons. Portland, 1979—. Recipient Top Ten Outstanding Achievement award Metalux Corp., 1981-85, 100% award, Gardco Lighting, 1985. Mem. Illuminating Engring. Soc. (sec.-treas. Oreg. sect. 1978-79). Republican. Lutheran. Avocations: lighting design, hist. restorations, flyfishing. Office: Illume Lighting Design 205 SE Grand Ave Portland OR 97214

RAMSEY, CLAUDE, foundation executive; b. Ramsey, W.Va., May 25, 1918; s. Melvin G. and Maude (Hawkins) R.; B.S., Morris Harvey Coll., 1938; B.J., U. Mo., 1939; m. Lilien Ernst, June 9, 1945; children—Patrick (dec.), Terry, Perry. Writer, United Press, Kansas City and Denver, 1940-42, bur. chief Houston and Lower Rio Grande Valley, 1945-52; pub. relations counsellor Kostka & Assos., Denver, 1953-55; founder, pres. Pub. Relations Inc., Denver, 1956-64; exec. dir. Morris Animal Found., Denver, 1964—; guest lectr. pub. relations Colo. State U., 1972-79. Mem. City Council, City of Greenwood Village (Colo.), 1973-75; mem. Arapahoe County Republican Exec. Com., 1976-80, 84-85; chmn. Rep. 6th Congl. Dist., 1982—; chmn. Colo. div. Am. Cancer Soc., 1979-81. Served to capt. Signal Corps, U.S. Army, 1941-45. Decorated Bronze Star; recipient award of Excellence, Colo. div. Am. Cancer Soc., 1976; Award of Merit, Am. Animal Hosp. Assn. Mem. Pub. Relations Soc. Am. (past pres. Colo. chpt., mem. nat. bd. 1962-63, Silver Anvil award 1959), Council on Founds., Sigma Delta Chi. Lutheran. Home: 5690 S Locust St Englewood CO 80111 Office: 45 Inverness Dr E Englewood CO 80112

RAMSEY, GEORGE LUTHER, engineer; b. Colorado Springs, Jan. 19, 1931; s. Willard Lawrence Ramsey and Lillian Margaret (Winget) Sandoval; m. Jeannine Anne Light, Dec. 14, 1952 (div. 1976); children: Christopher Michael, George Bruce; m. Shirley Jean Troxell, May 11, 1977. Student, Mesa Coll., 1949-50, 53-54. Sr. engr. Martin Marietta Corp., Denver, 1958-68, group engr., 1981—; test conductor Lockheed Corp., White Sands, N.Mex., 1977-79; mem. tech. staff Rockwell Inc., White Sands, 1979-81; test technician Chrysler Corp., Highland Park, Mich., 1953-58. Editor: Titan II Training Manual, 1964, Orbital Maneuvering System Familiarizations Manual, 1978. Bd. dirs. Santa Barbara (Calif.) County Alcohol Adv. Bd. Mem. Am. Assn. Aerosol Research, Inst. Environ. Scis., St. Crispian Soc. Republican. Avocations: shooting, skiing, diving. Home: 311 F Lolita Ln Santa Maria CA 93454 Office: Martin Marietta Corp PO Box 1681 375PR Vandenberg AFB CA 93437

RAND, PATRICIA JUNE, environmental consultant; b. Saint Paul, June 6, 1926; d. Frank Lee and Flavia Clara (Otto) R. BS, U. Minn., 1947, MS, 1953; PhD, Duke U., 1965. Instr. Hamline U., St. Paul, 1953-58; asst. prof. U. Ark., Fayetteville, 1962-66; asst. prof., then assoc. prof. U. Nebr., Lincoln, 1966-73; sr. sci. advisor Atlantic Richfield Co., Los Angeles, 1973-85; pres. SARA Assocs., Pasadena, Calif., 1985—; ranger, naturalist U.S. Nat. Park Service, Grand Canyon, Ariz., 1955-60, cons., Grand Canyon and Death Valley, Calif., 1960-73; cons. EPA, Washington, 1975-77. Author: Land and Water Issues, 1982; contbr. articles to profl. jours. Active SE Nebr. Pub. Health Council, Lincoln, 1969-72; v.p. Citizens for Environ. Improvement, Lincoln, 1971-72; nat. v.p. Grad. Women in Sci., 1972-73. Recipient Merit award N.Y. Art Dirs. Club 1983; named Outstanding Tchr., U. Ark., 1963; grantee in field. Fellow AAAS; mem. Ecol. Soc. Am., Bot. Soc. Am., Am. Inst. Biol. Sci., Sigma Delta Epsilon (chpt. pres. 1971). Democrat. Clubs: Los Angeles Athletic. Lodge: Order Eastern Star. Avocations: camping, hiking. Office: SARA Assocs PO Box 2139 Pasadena CA 91102

RANDALL, MICHAEL WILLIAM, building and energy systems designer, consultant; b. Athens, Greece, Feb. 6, 1957; s. Rodger and Victoria (Leonsteni) R. BS in Architecture, U. So. Calif., 1979; diploma, Internat. Progressive Montessori Assn., 1977. Tchr. Internat. Montessori Acad., Sierra Madre, Calif., 1977-82; assoc. architect R.M. Parsons Corp., Pasadena, Calif., 1979-81; bldg. designer King St. Luke, South Pasadena, Calif., 1984-85, Kazazian, Adrian, Glendale, Calif., 1985-86, O'Leary, Terasawa, Los Angeles, 1986—; cons. solar energy mktg. research and analysis Market Research Internat., Sierra Madre, 1982—. Mem. Internat. Hydrogen Assn., Internat. Montessori Assn., Ekistics: The Problems and Sci. Human Settlements, Phi Kappa Psi. Greek Orthodox. Office: PO Box 1028 Sierra Madre CA 91024

RANDALL, QUEEN FRANKLIN, college president; b. Pine Bluff, Ark., Jan. 28, 1935; d. Samuel and Ollie (Boykins) Franklin; 1 dau., Barbara Joyce. B.S. in Edn., Lincoln U., 1956; A.M., Ind. U., 1961; Ed.D., Nova U., 1975. Instr. math. Lincoln U., 1956-58; instr. math. Am. River Coll., Sacramento, 1962-70, chmn. math. and engring. div., 1970-72, assoc. dean instrn., 1972-76, dean instrnl. systems and student devel., 1976-78; pres. Pioneer Community Coll., Kansas City, Mo., 1978-80; asst. to chancellor Met. Community Coll. Dist., Kansas City, 1980-81; pres. El Centro Coll., Dallas, 1981-84; pres. Am. River Coll., Sacramento, 1984—; dir. Indsl. Devel. Corp. Dallas. Mem. Contact Dallas Advt. Bd., Treescape Dallas Adv. Bd. Fellow John Hay Whitney Found., 1961; trustee Am. River Hosp. Mem. Am. Assn. Women in Community and Jr. Colls., Crocker Art Mus. Assn. (bd. dirs.), Assn. Calif. Community Coll. Adminstrs., Delta Kappa Gamma. Club: Soroptimists. Home: 7123 Murdock Way Carmichael CA 95608 Office: Am River Coll 4700 College Oak Dr Sacramento CA 95841

RANDISI, ELAINE MARIE, apparel manufacturing executive; b. Racine, Wis., Dec 19, 1926; d. John Dewey and Alveta Irene (Raffety) Fehd; A.A., Pasadena Jr. Coll., 1946; B.S. cum laude (Giannini scholar), Golden Gate U., 1978; m. John Paul Randisi, Oct. 12, 1946 (div. July 1972); children—Jeanine Randisi Manson, Martha Randisi Cheney, Joseph, Paula Randisi Small, Catherine Randisi Tateo, George, Anthony. With Raymond Kaiser Engrs., Inc., Oakland, Calif., 1969-75, 77—, corp. acct., 1978-79, sr. corp. acct., 1979-82, sr. payroll acct., 1983-86, acctg. mgr., Lilli Ann Corp., San Francisco, 1986—; corp. buyer Kaiser Industries Corp., Oakland, 1975-77; lectr. on astrology Theosophical Soc., San Francisco, 1979—; mem. faculty Am. Fedn. Astrologers Internat. Conv., Chgo., 1982, 84. Mem. Speakers Bur., Calif. Assn. for Neurologically Handicapped Children, 1964-70, v.p. 1969; bd. dirs. Ravenwood Homeowners Assn., 1979-82, v.p., 1979-80, sec., 1980-81; mem. organizing com. Minority Bus. Fair, San Francisco, 1976; pres., bd. dirs. Lakewood Condominium Assn., 1984—. Mem. Am. Fedn. Astrologers, Calif. Scholarship Fedn. (life), Alpha Gamma Sigma (life). Mem. Ch. of Religious Science. Initiated Minority Vendor Purchasing Program for Kaiser Engrs., Inc., 1975-76. Home: 742 Wesley Way Apt 1-C Oakland CA 94610 Office: Lilli Ann Corp 2701 16th St San Francisco CA 94103

RANDOLPH, CARL LOWELL, corporate executive; b. Pasadena, Calif., May 30, 1922; s. Carl L. and Lulu (McBride) R.; m. Jane Taber, June 25, 1943; children—Margaret, Stephen. B.A., Whittier Coll., 1943; M.S., U. So. Calif., 1947, Ph.D., 1949; LL.D. (hon.), Whittier Coll., 1982; D. Pub. Service (hon.), U. Alaska, 1983. Licensed shipmaster. Prin. chemist Aerojet-Gen. Corp., 1949-57; v.p. U.S. Borax Research Corp., Anaheim, Calif., 1957-63; asst. to pres. U.S. Borax & Chem. Corp., Los Angeles, 1963-66; v.p. U.S. Borax & Chem. Corp., 1966-68, exec. v.p., 1968-69, pres., 1969-86, vice chmn., 1983—, also dir. Contbr. articles to profl. jours. Trustee, chmn. bd. Whittier Coll.; trustee Hollywood Presbyn. Hosp.; bd. dirs. Orange County Philharm. Soc., Ind. Colls. So. Calif. Served from ensign to lt. (j.g.) USNR, 1944-46. Mem. Am. Chem. Soc., Phi Beta Kappa, Sigma Xi. Patentee in field. Home: 16812 Baruna Ln Huntington Beach CA 92649

RANDOLPH, JAMES EUGENE, aerospace executive; b. Los Angeles, Jan. 19, 1940; s. Wallace L. and Katherine L. (Kane) R.; m. Gail Randolph; children: John, Julie, Jane. BSME, Calif. State U., 1964; MSME, U. So. Calif., 1967. Aerospace mgr. Jet Propulsion Lab, Pasadena, Calif., 1964-78; aerospace group supr., mgr. starprobe and Mars rover Jet Propulsion Lab, Pasadena, 1978—, aerospace studies mgr., 1985—. Contbr. papers and reports to profl. jour. Fellow AIAA (assoc.); mem. Am. Astron. Soc., Am. Geog. Union. Avocations: sailing, skiing.

RANEY, EILEEN FEIN, insurance brokerage executive; b. Los Angeles, Apr. 23, 1949; d. Samuel and Adlynn (McKnight) Yarvitz. Student Los Angeles Valley Jr. Coll., 1966-67, Pierce Jr. Coll., 1968-69. Cert. continuing edn. profl. designation; cert. employee benefit specialist. Adminstrv. aide Los Angeles County Employees Assn., 1970-72; program specialist Econ. & Youth Opportunities Agy., 1972-74; adminstrv. asst. Ins. Planning Assocs., 1974; account exec. Gannon Mgmt. Assocs., 1974-75; agt. Ind. Group Ins., Santa Ana, Calif., 1975-76; adminstr. Airport Med. Group, Irvine, Calif., 1975-76; mktg. rep. The Doctors Co., Santa Monica, Calif., 1977; adminstr. Tepper Med. Group, Alhambra, Calif., 1978; ind. group ins. specialist, Mendocino, Calif., 1978-79; dir. ins. services Hosp. Council So. Calif., Los Angeles, 1979-81; v.p. employee benefits BMF Mktg. Ins. Services, Inc., Los Angeles, 1981-83; sr. v.p. employee benefits Keenan & Assocs., Torrance, Calif., 1983—. Recipient Econ. and Youth Opportunities Assn. Community Activity award, 1971. Mem. Employee Benefit Planning Assn. (bd. dirs.), Nat. Health Lawyers Assn., Internat. Soc. Employee Benefit Specialists. Democrat. Jewish. Originator: Creative Health Plan Design, Calif., 1981. Office: Keenan & Assocs 2355 Crenshaw Blvd Suite 200 Torrance CA 90510

RANFTL, ROBERT MATTHEW, management consulting company executive; b. Milw., May 31, 1925; s. Joseph Sebastian and Leona Elaine (Goetz) R.; m. Marion Smith Goodman, Oct. 12, 1946. BSEE, U. Mich., 1946;

postgrad. UCLA, 1953-55. Product engr. Russell Electric Co., Chgo., 1946-47; head engring. dept. Radio Inst. Chgo., 1947-50; sr. project engr. Webster Chgo. Corp., 1950-51, product design engr., 1951-53, head equipment design group, 1953-54, head electronic equipment sect., 1954-55, mgr. product engring. dept., 1955-58, mgr. reliability and quality control, 1958-59, mgr. adminstrn. 1959-61, mgr. product effectiveness lab., 1961-74; corp. dir. engring./design mgmt., 1974-84, corp. dir. managerial productivity Hughes Aircraft Co., Los Angeles, 1984-86; pres. Ranftl Enterprises Inc., Mgmt. Cons., Los Angeles, 1981—; guest lectr. Calif. Inst. Tech., Cornell U., U. Calif.; mem. White House Conf. on Productivity, 1983; mem. human resources productivity task force Dept. of Def., 1985-86. Author: R&D Productivity, 1974, 78; (with others) Productivity: Prospects for Growth, 1981; contbr. articles to profl. jours. Mem. AAAS, AIAA, Am. Soc. Engring. Edn., Am. Soc. Tng. and Devel., IEEE, Inst. Mgmt. Scis., Acad. Mgmt., N.Y. Acad. Scis., U. Mich. Alumni Assn., UCLA Alumni Assn. Office: PO Box 49892 Los Angeles CA 90049

RANGILA, NANCY ARNEVNA, savings and loan executive, investment consultant; b. Petrozavodsk, Russia, Mar. 23, 1936; (mother Am. citizen); d. Henry Hjalmar and Myrtle Marie (Jacobson) Rangila. B.A. in Am. History, U. S.C., 1958, M.A. in Am. History, 1964; M.B.A. in Finance, U. So. Calif., 1973. Chartered fin. analyst; cert. employee benefit specialist. Fin. analyst Capital Research Co., Los Angeles, 1964-73; v.p., portfolio mgr., fin. analyst Capital Cons., Inc., Portland, Oreg., 1973-82; sr. v.p., Franklin Fin. Services (subs. Benj. Franklin Fed. Savings & Loan Assn.), Portland, 1982—; lectr. investments, retirement plans. Chmn. City of Portland Hosp. Facilities Authority. Mem. Portland Soc. Fin. Analysts, Fin. Analysts Fedn., Los Angeles Soc. Fin. Analysts, Western Pension Conf. (Portland chpt.). Republican. Clubs: City, Multnomah Athletic (Portland). Home: 2221 SW 1st Ave Apt 1625 Portland OR 97201 Office: Benjamin Franklin Fin Services 1 SW Columbia St Suite 900 Portland OR 97258

RANGWALA, ZOAIB ZAINUDDIN, electronics executive; b. Karachi, Pakistan, Aug. 22, 1951; came to U.S., 1973; s. Zainuddin Asgherally and Fizza (Abbasbhoy) R.; m. Jumana Zoaib Ebrahim, Aug. 14, 1977; 1 child, Fatema. BEE, Ned Engring. U., 1972; MSEE, U. Calif., Berkeley, 1975; MBA, U. Santa Clara, 1979. Design engr. Signetics Corp., Sunnyvale, Calif., 1976-78; design mgr. Data Gen., Sunnyvale, Calif., 1978-81; computer-aided design and applications mgr. Raytheon, Mountain View, Calif., 1981-85, product line mgr., 1985—. Contbr. tech. articles to profl. jours. Named Outstanding Tchg. Assoc. U. Calif., Berkeley, 1976. Mem. Beta Gamma Sigma. Islamic. Avocations: photography, racquetball, finance, lit., jogging. Home: 1232 Shadowfax Dr San Jose CA 95121 Office: Raytheon 350 Ellis St Mountain View CA 94043

RANKAITIS, SUSAN, artist; b. Cambridge, Mass., Sept. 10, 1949; d. Alfred Edward and Isabel (Shimkus) Rankaitis; m. Robbert Flick, June 5, 1976. B.F.A. in Painting, U. Ill., 1971; M.F.A. in Visual Arts, U. So. Calif., 1977. One person shows Los Angeles County Mus. Art, 1983; one person shows Internat. Mus. Photography, George Eastman House, 1983, Min Gallery of Tokyo, 1987; represented in permanent collections U. Ill., Santa Monica Coll., Ctr. for Creative Photography, UCLA, Mus. Modern Art, Santa Barbara Mus. Art, Los Angeles County Mus. Art, Mpls. Inst. Arts, San Francisco Mus. Modern Art, Security Pacific Bank, Mus. Modern Art, Lodz, Poland; assoc. prof. art Chapman Coll.; overview panelist visual arts Nat. Endowment for Arts, 1983, 84; mem. steering com. U. So. Calif. Friends of Fine Arts, 1983-84. Bd. dirs. Friends of Photography, 1985-87, mem. adv. bd. trustees. Nat. Endowment for Arts fellow, 1980; Chapman research fellow 1984-86; Graves award in the humanities, 1985. Mem. Soc. Photographic Edn., Los Angeles Inst. Contemporary Art, Los Angeles County Mus. Art, Friends of Photography, Center Creative Photography, Calif. Council Fine Arts Deans. Studio: 707 E Hyde Park Blvd Inglewood CA 90302

RANKIN, HELEN CROSS, cattle rancher, guest ranch executive; b. Mojave, Calif; d. John Whisman and Cleo Rebecca (Tilley) Cross; m. Leroy Rankin, Jan. 4, 1936 (dec. 1954); children—Julia Jane King Sharr, Patricia Helen Denvir, William John. A.B., Calif. State U.-Fresno, 1935. Owner, operator Rankin Cattle Ranch, Caliente, Calif., 1954—; founder, pres. Rank Ranch, Inc., Guest Ranch, 1965—; mem. sect. 15, U.S. Bur. Land Mgmt.; mem. U.S. Food and Agrl. Leaders Tour China, 1983, Australia and N.Z., 1985; dir. U.S. Bur. Land Mgmt. sect. 15. Pres., Children's Home Soc. Calif., 1945. Recipient award Calif. Hist. Soc., 1983, Kern River Valley Hist. Soc., 1983. Mem. Am. Nat. Cattlemen's Assn., Calif. Cattlemen's Assn., Kern County Cattlemen's Assn., Kern County Cowbelles (pres. 1949), Calif. Cowbelles, Nat. CowbellesRepublican. Baptist. Club: Bakersfield Country. Lodge: Bakersfield Raquet. Office: Rankin Ranch Caliente CA 93518

RANKIN, RICHARD ALLEN, technical manager; b. Ladysmith, Wis., July 4, 1954; s. Allen and Betty Jane (Crawford) R.; m. Janice Marie Cotterell, Nov. 7, 1980; children: Joshua James, Christopher John, Lindsay Ann. BS, U. Wis., Eau Claire, 1976; MS, U. Idaho, 1978. Chemist Allied Chem. Co., Idaho Falls, Idaho, 1978-79; sr. chemist Exxon Nuclear Idaho, Idaho Falls, 1979-82, scientist, 1982, supr., 1982-84; mgr. mass spectrometry Westinghouse Idaho, Idaho Falls, 1984—; assoc. faculty mem. U. Idaho, Idaho Falls, 1982—. Author (invention disclosure) Microprocessor Controlled Computer Interface, 1986, Mass Spectrometer Control, 1986; contbr. articles to profl. jours. Mem. Am. Chem. Soc. (chmn. exhibits 1985). Mormon. Avocations: computers, electronics, motorcycles. Home: 4015 S Ross Ammon ID 83401 Office: Westinghouse Idaho Nuclear Co PO Box 4000 Idaho Falls ID 83403

RANKIN, WILLIAM PARKMAN, educator, former publishing company executive, consultant; b. Boston, Feb. 6, 1917; s. George William and Bertha W. (Clowe) R.; m. Ruth E. Gerard, Sept. 12, 1942; children—Douglas W., Joan W. B.S., Syracuse U., 1941; M.B.A., NYU, 1949, Ph.D., 1979. Sales exec. Redbook mag., N.Y.C., 1945-49; sales exec. This Week mag., N.Y.C., 1949-55, adminstrv. exec., 1955-60, v.p., 1957-60, v.p., dir. advt. sales, sales devel. dir., 1960-63, exec. v.p., 1963-69; gen. exec. newspaper div. Time Inc., N.Y.C., 1969-70; gen. mgr. feature service Newsweek, Inc., N.Y.C., 1970-74, fin. and ins. advt. mgr., 1974-81; vis. prof. Walter Cronkite Sch. Journalism and Tellecommunicatiton, Ariz. State U., Tempe, 1981—; lectr. Syracuse U., NYU, Berkeley Sch.; mem. adv. council Sch. Journalism, Syracuse U. Mem. Soc. Profl. Journalists/Sigma Delta Chi, Alpha Delta Sigma. Clubs: N.Y. Dutch Treat, Met. Adv. Golf Assn.; Mesa Country. Author: Selling Retail Advertising, 1944; The Technique of Selling Magazine Advertising, 1949; Business Management of Consumer Magazines, 1980, 2 ed. 1984, The Practice of Newspaper Mgmt., 1986. Home: 1220 E Krista Way Tempe AZ 85284 Home: Bridge Rd Bomoseen VT 05732 Office: Ariz State U Walter Cronkite Sch Journalism/ Telecommunication Tempe AZ 85287

RANNEY, HELEN MARGARET, physician, educator; b. Summer Hill, N.Y., Apr. 12, 1920; d. Arthur C. and Alesia (Toolan) R. A.B., Barnard Coll., 1941; M.D., Columbia, 1947; Sc.D., U. S.C., 1979. Diplomate: Am. Bd. Internal Medicine. Intern Presbyn. Hosp., N.Y.C., 1947-48; resident Presbyn. Hosp., 1948-50; practice medicine specializing in internal medicine, hematology N.Y.C., 1954-70; asst. physician Presbyn. Hosp., 1954-60; instr. Coll. Phys. and Surg. Columbia, 1954-60; asso. prof. medicine Albert Einstein Coll. Medicine, 1960-64, prof. medicine, 1965-70; prof. medicine SUNY-Buffalo, 1970-73; prof. medicine U. Calif.-San Diego, 1973—, chmn. dept. medicine, 1973-86. Fellow AAAS, A.C.P.; mem. Am. Soc. for Clin. Investigation, Am. Soc. Hematology, Harvey Soc., Am. Assn. Physicians, Nat. Acad. Sci., Inst. Medicine, Am. Acad. Arts and Scis., Phi Beta Kappa, Sigma Xi, Alpha Omega Alpha. Home: 6229 La Jolla Mesa Dr La Jolla CA 92037 *

RANSOM, GRAYCE ANNABLE, emeritus educator; b. La Porte, Ind.; d. Irving H. and Louisa Sabra (Sawin) Annable; B.R.E., McCormick Theol. Sem., 1937; M.A., Lewis and Clark Coll., 1954; B.A., Kalamazoo Coll., 1965; Ph.D., U. So. Calif., 1967; m. John T. Seeley, Mar. 20, 1970; children—Judith Ransom Burney, Kenneth C., Janet. Asst. camp dir., Portland, Oreg., 1947-55; tchr. religious edn., tchr. tng. Portland Council of Chs., 1949-54; tchr. elementary sch., Portland, Los Angeles, 1955-62; asst. prof. Calif. State U., Long Beach, 1963-65; faculty U. So. Calif., Los Angeles, from 1965, prof. curriculum and reading instrn., from 1974, now emeritus, chmn. dept. curriculum and instruction, dir. Campus and NCL Reading Centers, 1967—; cons. Calif. State Dept. Edn., 1966—, various sch. dists. in Calif., 1965—; reading test cons. Ednl. Testing Service, Princeton, N.J., 1971-72; interim dir. parish program Westminster Presbyn. Ch., Portland, 1984-86. Bd. dirs. Footlighters Child Guidance Clinic. Recipient Merit award Calif. State Bd. Edn., 1981. Mem. Internat. (dir.), Calif. (pres. 1976-77, Marcus Foster award for outstanding contbns. to reading 1979), Los Angeles (pres. 1973-74) reading assns., AAUP, Am. Ednl. Research Assn., NEA, Nat. Council Tchrs. English, LWV (pres. Portland 1947-48), Pi Lambda Theta, Phi Delta Kappa (award for research 1982). Presbyterian (elder 1971—). Author: Crackerjacks, 1969; Evaluating Teacher Education Programs in Reading, 1972; Teacher's Guide for Electronic Card-Reading Machines, 1974; The Ransom Reading Program, 1974; Multi Media Kits-Reading, Researching, Reporting in Social Studies, 1975, Science, 1977, Health, 1977; Preparing to Teach Reading, 1978; California Framework for Reading, 1980. Research in computers in early childhood edn. Home: 13775 Old Scholl's Ferry Rd Beaverton OR 97006

RANSON, MARILYN JEANNE, communications, public relations executive; b. Palo Alto, Calif., Feb. 10, 1951; d. Earl C. and Evelyn Nancy (Sequist) Dietz; m. Steven Robert Ranson, Feb. 2, 1974 (div. Nov. 1980). BA in Journalism, U. Nev., 1973. Lic. emergency med. technician. Tv. traffic mgr. Sta. KYCU-TV, Cheyenne, Wyo., 1974-75, Sta. KOLO-TV, Reno, 1975-76; publicity dir. Media Cons., Reno, 1977; mng. editor Wells (Nev.) Progress, 1978-83; TV traffic mgr. Sta. KVIE-TV, Sacramento, 1983-84; dir. communications Calif. Grocers Assn., Sacramento, 1984—, editor newsletter, mag. Active Wells Vol. Ambulance Service, 1980-83. Recipient Golden Excellence awards Food Industry Assn., 1984, 85, Best Overall Editorial Content award Food Industry Assn., 1986. Mem. Nev. State Press. Assn., Sigma Delta Chi, Pi Beta Phi. Republican. Avocation: horseback riding. Home: 4502 Mary Lynn Ln #139C Carmichael CA 95608 Office: Calif Grocers Assn 1400 K St Suite 208 Sacramento CA 95814

RANU, RAJINDER SINGH, molecular biologist, veterinarian; b. Jallan, India, July 26, 1940; came to U.S., 1963; s. Jodh S. and Harnam Kaur (Chahal) R.; m. Phyllis E. Blatt, June 6, 1970; children: Manjeety, Emarit. DVM, Panjab (India) U., 1961; MS, U. Pa., 1966, PhD, 1971. Spl. postdoctoral fellow U. Chgo., 1971-73; from research assoc. to sr. research assoc. MIT, Cambridge, 1974-78; assoc. prof. microbiology Colo. State U., Ft. Collins, 1979—. Contbr. articles on protein biosynthesis and protein synthesis to profl. jours. Recipient Young and Talented Investigator award Am. Cancer Soc., 1973; NIH spl. fellow, 1972. Mem. Am. Soc. Microbiology, Am. Soc. Genetics, N.Y. Acad. Scis., Am. Soc. Biol. Chemists, AAAS. Office: Colo State U Dept Microbiology Fort Collins CO 80523

RAPHAEL, BERTRAM, computer research and development professional; b. N.Y.C., Nov. 16, 1936; s. Morris and Adella (Leav) R.; m. Anne Mildred Wagner, May 27, 1962; children: Glen Francis, Katherine Liuba. BS in Physics, Renssalaer Poly. Inst., 1957; MS in Applied Math., Brown U., 1959; PhD in Math., MIT, 1964. Dir. artificial intelligence ctr. SRI Internat., Menlo Park, Calif., 1971-76, exec. dir. computer resources, 1978-81; dir. computer sci. lab. Hewlett-Packard Labs, Palo Alto, Calif., 1981-83; dir. research and devel. info. resources Hewlett-Packard Co., Palo Alto, 1983-86; mgr. tech. analysis Hewlett-Packard Co., Cupertino, Calif., 1986—; lectr. computer sci. U. Calif. Berkeley, Stanford (Calif.) U., U. Mont., UCLA, 1965-86; Fulbright-Hayes Sr. lectr. Tech. U. Vienna, Austria, 1973-74; cons. artificial intelligence various orgns. and govts. including Republic of China, Australia and Holland; co-owner, automation system developer Compass Point Travel, Inc., Mountain View, Calif., 1981—. Author: The Thinking Computer, 1976; contbr. articles to profl. publs. Sr. patroller Nat. Ski Patrol System, Homewood, Calif., 1970—; first aid instr. ARC, Palo Alto. Mem. Am. Assn. Artificial Intelligence, Assn. Computing Machinery (nat. lectr., jour. editor 1984—), Sigma Xi. Democrat. Jewish. Avocations: skiing, software devel., travel. Home: 12820 Viscaino Rd Los Altos Hills CA 94022 Office: Hewlett Packard Co ITG 19111 Pruneridge Ave Bldg 44UD Cupertino CA 95014-9974

RAPHAEL, MARTIN GEORGE, research wildlife biologist; b. Denver, Oct. 5, 1946; s. Jerome Maurice and Ayce (Salmonson) R.; m. Susan Williams, August 4, 1967; 1 child, Samantha Marie. BA, Sacramento State U., 1968; BS, U. Calif., Berkeley, 1972, MS, 1976, PhD, 1980. Staff research assoc. U. Calif., Berkeley, 1974-80, assoc. specialist, 1980-84; project leader USDA Forest Service, Laramie, 1984—; adj. prof. U. Wyo., Laramie, 1986—; cons. ecologist Pacific Gas and Electric Co., San Ramon, Calif., 1981-84. Contbr. articles to sci. jours. Mem. AAAS, Am. Soc. Mammologists (recipient Best Poster award 1984), Am. Ornithologists' Union, Cooper Ornithol. Soc. (chmn. membership com. 1985—), The Wildlife Soc. (local pres. publs. com. 1983-84), Phi Beta Kappa, Sigma Xi, Xi Sigma Pi. Avocations: sailing, skiing, photography. Home: 2205 Skyview Ln Laramie WY 82070 Office: Rocky Mountain Forest and Range Experiment Sta 222 S 22nd St Laramie WY 82070

RAPIER, PASCAL MORAN, chemical engineer, physicist; b. Atlanta, Jan. 11, 1914; s. Paul Edward and Mary Claire (Moran) R.; m. Martha Elizabeth Doyle, May 19, 1945; children: Caroline Elizabeth, Paul Doyle, Mollie Claire, John Lawrence, James Andrew. BSChemE, Ga. Inst. Tech., 1939; MS in Theoretical Physics, U. Nev., 1959; postgrad., U. Calif., Berkeley, 1961. Registered profl. engr., Calif., N.J. Plant engr. Archer-Daniels-Midland, Pensacola, Fla., 1940-42; group supr. Dicalite div. Grefco, Los Angeles, 1943-54; process engr. Celatom div. Eagle Picher, Reno, Nev., 1955-57; project mgr., assoc. research engr. U. Calif. Field Sta., Richmond, 1959-62; project mgr. sea water conversion Bechtel Corp., San Francisco, 1962-66; sr. supervising chem. engr. Burnes & Roe, Oradell, N.J., 1966-74; cons. engr. Kenite Corp., Scarsdale, N.Y., Rees Blowpipe, Berkeley, 1960-66; sr. cons. engr. Sanderson & Porter, N.Y.C., 1975-77; staff scientist III Lawrence Berkeley Lab., 1977-84; bd. dirs. Newtonian Sci. Found.; v.p. Calif. Rep. Assembly, 1964-65. Contbr. articles to profl jours.; patentee agts. to render non-polar solvents electrically conductive, direct-contact geothermal energy recovery devices. Mem. Am. Inst. Chem. Engrs. Presbyterian. Discoverer bodies moving faster than light, origin of cosmic rays and galactic red shifts. Home: 3154 Deseret Dr Richmond CA 94803 Office: Lawrence Berkeley Lab 1 Cyclotron Rd Bldg 90 Berkeley CA 94550

RAPLEY, SUZANNE ELOISE, psychotherapist, dancer, educator; b. Hot Springs, Ark., July 27, 1951; d. John Howard and Jimmie Lee (Penny) R. BA in Psychology with honors, U. Calif., Berkeley, 1973; MS in Counseling Psychology, George Peabody Coll., 1976, EdS in Counseling Psychology, 1978; PhD in Clin. Psychology, Fielding Inst., 1987. Cert. marriage and family therapist, Calif.; secondary sch. counselor, Tenn. Recreational therapist asst. Napa State Hosp., Calif., 1972-73; dance and recreational therapist City of Berkeley, Calif., 1973; dance tchr., co-dir. Dancers' Workshop of Jackson Hole, Wyo., 1973-74; full time substitute elem. sch. tchr. Teton County Sch. Dist., Jackson, 1973-74; recreational therapist Community Hosp. of North Hollywood, Calif., 1975; child caseworker Hathaway Children's Village, Lake View Terrace, Calif., 1975; group therapist Ednl. Devel. Ctr., Nashville, 1976; group facilitator Sexual Attitude Reassessment Nat. Sex Forum, Nashville, 1977-78; program dir. Rap House, E.S., Inc., Nashville, 1977-78; staff counselor Empathy House, Boulder, Colo., 1979; psychotherapist, predoctoral intern Ctr. for Family Living San Fernando Valley Community Mental Health Ctr., Van Nuys, Calif., 1980-81; stress cons., speaker, group facilitator Voice in Communication Assocs., Santa Monica, Calif., 1981—; pvt. practice psychotherapy, Malibu, Calif., 1982-85; dir., psychotherapist Camarillo Psychotherapy Assocs., Calif., 1983—; mem. faculty U. LaVerne, Antioch U. Santa Barbara, Calif., 1983—; counselor alcohol detoxification unit Dept. Health, Boulder, 1979; intervention specialist Ventura County Ctr. for Drug Problems, 1985; dir. Zona Seca Alcohol Treatment Ctr., Lompoc, Calif., 1985-87; clin. dir. Klein Bottle Social Advocates For Youth, Santa Barbara, 1987—; cons., writer Corp. Fitness and Recreation mag.; lectr. various community service orgns., Los Angeles; facilitator workshops in field; speaker profl. groups. Contbr. sect. to publ. in field. Active Santa Monica Hosp. Aux., Nat. Abortion Rights Action League, Greater Los Angeles Council on Deafness; chmn. Nashville Drug Coalition, 1977-78; program coordinator, bd. dirs. Malibu Women's Resource Ctr., Calif. Recipient Brotherhood award NCCJ, 1965; grantee Nat. Endowment for Arts, 1973-74. Mem. Am. Psychol. Assn., Calif. Psychol. Assn., Assn. for Women in Psychology, Am. Assn. Sex Educators, Counselors and Therapists. Office: 542 La Marina Dr Santa Barbara CA 93109

RAPOPORT, BASIL, medicine educator; b. Port Elizabeth, Republic South Africa, May 13, 1943; came to U.S., 1967; s. Solomon and Rachiel (Bennun) R.; m. Frances Rosemary Coll, May 28, 1968; children: Lisa N., Ruth G. BSc, U. Witwatersrand, Johannesburg, Republic S. Africa, 1964; MB, ChB, U. Edinburgh, Scotland, 1967. Diplomate Am. Bd. Internal Medicine, Am. Bd. Endocrinology and Metabolism. Intern in medicine Highland Hosp., Rochester, N.Y., 1967-68; resident in internal medicine Northwestern U., Chgo., 1968-70; fellow in endocrinology U. Chgo., 1970-72; instr. medicine U. Calif., San Francisco, 1972-74, asst. prof., 1974-79, assoc. prof., 1979-85, prof., 1985—, assoc. dir. Thyroid Outpatient Clinic Med. Ctr., 1978—; chief Endocrinology-Metabolism Outpatient Clinic VA Hosp., San Francisco, 1976-85. Mem. editorial bd. Jour. Clin. Endocrinology and Metabolism, 1982-85, Am. Jour. Physiology: Endocrinology and Metabolism, 1982—; assoc. editor Jour. Clin. Investigation, 1987—; contbr. articles to profl. jours. Damon Runyon Found. fellow, 1970-72; recipient Research Assoc. award VA, 1975-78, Research Career Devel. award NIH, 1978-83, Armour-Van Meter award Am. Thyroid Assn., 1982. Mem. Am. Soc. Clin. Investigation, Am. Assn. Physicians. Jewish. Avocations: classical piano, swimming, skiing. Home: 115 Vista Grande Greenbrae CA 94906 Office: VA Hosp Bldg 2 Room 28 4150 Clement St San Francisco CA 94121

RAPPAPORT, HENRY, pathologist, educator; b. Lemberg, Austria, Mar. 12, 1913; came to U.S., 1940, naturalized, 1943; s. Leo and Amelia (Bak) R.; m. Dina Braude, May 24, 1939; children: Elizabeth, Edward, Katherine, Stephen. MD, U. Vienna, Austria, 1937. Asst. prof. pathology George Washington U., Washington, 1946-47, lectr. pathology, 1947-54; pathologist VA Hosp., Washington, 1947-49; sr. pathologist, chief sect. reticuloendothelial pathology and hematology Armed Forces Inst. Pathology, Washington, 1949-54; from assoc. prof. pathology to prof. oncology U Chgo. Med. Sch., 1954-65, prof. pathology, 1965-75, prof. emeritus, 1975—; chmn. dept. anatomic pathology City of Hope Nat. Med. Ctr., Duarte, Calif., 1975-87, disting. physician, 1986—; cons. Nat. Cancer Inst., Walter Reed Army Inst. Research; mem. WHO Internat. Reference Ctr. for Nomenclature and Histopathologic Classification of Leukemias and other Neoplastic Diseases of Hematopoietic System. Author: Tumors of the Hematopoietic System, 1966; also articles to profl. jours. Served to maj. AUS, 1943-46. Mem. ACP, Am. Soc. Cancer Research, Am. Soc. Cell Biology, Am. Hematology Soc., Internat. Hematology Soc., Am. Soc. Exptl. Pathology, Am. Assn. Pathologists and Bacteriologists. Home: 230 W Orange Grove Ave Arcadia CA 91006 Office: City of Hope Nat Med Ctr Duarte CA 91010

RASBAND, JUDITH ANN, home economist, educator, author, lecturer; b. Longview, Wash., Oct. 7, 1942; d. Archie Lisle and Maxine E. (Klingaman) Packard; m. Shirley Neil Rasband, Sept. 12, 1963; children—Nanette, Matthew, Daniel. B.S., U. Utah, 1964; M.S., Brigham Young U., 1978. Home econs. tchr. secondary schs. Salt Lake City, 1965-68; instr. U. Utah, 1969; adult edn. instr., N.J., La., Utah, 1969-70; instr. Brigham Young U., Provo, Utah, 1973-82; home economist in bus., Provo, 1980—; co-founder, v.p., product devel. dir. Personal/Profl. Image Cons., specializing in edn. relating to image awareness and improvement; cons. wardrobe and personal appearance, 1976—; contbr. weekly newspaper column: Let's Face It, 1980—; newspaper columnist Desert News, Stars and Stripes; lectr., condr. workshops, seminars in field. Bd. dirs. Utah Valley Symphony Guild. Recipient Leah D. Widstoe award as outstanding home economist, Home Economist Grad. award, 1964; named Utah's Outstanding Young Home Economist, 1983; featured in Top Ten Image Cons., Glamour mag., 1984; Outstanding Home Economist in Bus., Utah, 1985. Mem. Am. Home Econs. Assn., Utah Home Econs. Assn., Home Economists in Bus., Assn. Coll. Profs. of Textiles and Clothing, AAUW, Omicron Nu, Phi Kappa Phi. Republican. Mormon. Clubs: Brigham Young U. Women. Author: Alternative Methods of Pattern Alteration, 1978; How to Clothe Your Family, 1981; Color Crazed: A Report to Consumers, 1983; Pregnant and Beautiful, 1985; Fitting and Pattern Alteration: A Multi-Method Approach, 1985; contbr. articles to profl. and popular mags. Office: PO Box 7052 University Station Provo UT 84602

RASCO, CORNELIA N., architectural designer; b. Sarata Nova, Romania, Dec. 24, 1932; came to U.S. 1970, naturalized 1982; d. Stefan and Ecaterina (Agafonov) Ivanov; m. Victor Allen Rasco, July 1, 1961. degree in architecture, U. Bucharest, Romania, 1959. Registered architect. Field supt. Construction Co. No. 1, Bucharest, 1959-61; prin. architect Design Inst. Bucharest, 1961-69; draftsperson C.F. Murphy Assocs., Chgo., 1970-75; engring. aid, technician County of Orange, Santa Ana, Calif., 1975-77; architectural designer Gen. Services Agy., 1978—. Mem. Romanian Architects Assn., AIA (assoc.). Republican. Romanian Orthodox.

RASKOWITZ, ROBERT PHILIP, marketing executive; b. Bklyn., May 19, 1936; s. Harry and Betty (Horowitz) R.; B.S.E.E., Bridgeport Engring. Inst., 1966; M.S., U. Bridgeport, 1972; m. Hazel Myra Friedlander, June 16, 1963; children—Sheri Elena, Debra Helene. Project engr. Kollsman Instrument Corp., Elmhurst, N.Y., 1960-62, Perkin Elmer Corp., Wilton, Conn., 1962-63; sr. engr. Remington Office Machines div. Sperry Rand Corp., Norwalk, Conn., 1963-66; group leader Norden div. United Technologies, Norwalk, 1966-73; sales mgr. Panasonic Co., Div. Matsushita, Secaucus, N.J., 1973-77; dir. market and devel. Microelectronics Tech. Corp., Palo Alto, Calif., 1977—; instr., vis. lectr. U. New Haven, 1973, U. Bridgeport (Conn.), 1973, Rutgers U., New Brunswick, N.J., 1976. Mem. IEEE, Soc. Automotive Engrs. Jewish. Contbr. articles to profl. jours.; editor: ZNR Manuel, 1979. Home: 12642 Fredericksburg Dr Saratoga CA 95070 Office: 1072 East Meadow Circle Palo Alto CA 94303

RASMUSON, ELMER EDWIN, banker, mayor Anchorage; b. Yakutat, Alaska, Feb. 15, 1909; s. Edward Anton and Jenny (Olson) R.; m. Lile Vivian Bernard, Oct. 27, 1939 (dec. 1960); children: Edward Bernard, Lile Muchmore (Mrs. John Gibbons, Jr.), Judy Ann; m. Col. Mary Louise Milligan, Nov. 4, 1961. B.S. magna cum laude, Harvard U., 1930, A.M., 1935; student, U. Grenoble, 1930; LL.D., U. Alaska, 1970. C.P.A., N.Y., Tex., Alaska. Chief accountant Nat. Investors Corp., N.Y.C., 1933-35; prin. Arthur Andersen & Co., N.Y.C., 1935-43; pres. Nat. Bank of Alaska, 1943-65, chmn. bd., 1966-74, chmn. exec. com., 1975-82, now dir.; mayor City of Anchorage, 1964-67; civilian aide from Alaska to sec. army 1959-67; Swedish consul Alaska, 1955-77; Chmn. Rasmuson Found.; Rep. nominee U.S. Senate from Alaska, 1968; U.S. commr. Internat. N. Pacific Fisheries Commn., 1969-84; mem. Nat. Marine Fisheries Adv. Com., 1974-77, North Pacific Fishery Mgmt. Council, 1976-77, U.S. Arctic Research Commn., 1984—. Mem. City Council Anchorage, 1945, chmn. city planning commn., 1950-53; pres. Alaska council Boy Scouts Am., 1953; sec.-treas. Loussac Found.; regent U. Alaska, 1950-69; trustee King's Lake Camp, Inc., 1944—, Alaska Permanent Fund Corp., 1980-82; bd. dirs. Coast Guard Acad. Found. Decorated knight first class Order of Vasa, comdr. Sweden; recipient silver Antelope award Boy Scouts Am.; outstanding civilian service medal U.S. Army; Alaskan of Year award, 1976. Mem. Pioneers Alaska, Alaska Bankers Assn. (past pres.), Defense Orientation Conf. Assn., NAACP, Alaska Native Brotherhood, Explorers Club, Phi Beta Kappa. Republican. Presbyn. Clubs: Masons, Elks, Anchorage Rotary (past pres.); Harvard (N.Y.C.; Boston); Wash. Athletic (Seattle), Seattle Yacht (Seattle), Rainier (Seattle); Thunderbird Country (Palm Desert, Calif.); Bohemian (San Francisco); Eldorado Country (Indian Wells, Calif.). Address: PO Box 600 Anchorage AK 99510

RASMUSSEN, CATHERINE ANN, speech pathologist; b. Portland, Oreg., Oct. 13, 1953; d. Harold Reinhart and Josephine L. (Phillips) R. AA, Glendale (Ariz.) Community Coll., 1983; BS, U. Oreg., 1975; MS, Utah State U., 1977. Speech pathologist Roswell (N.Mex.) Ind. Sch. Dist., 1976-79; speech pathology mgr. Valley View Community Hosp., Youngtown, Ariz., 1979-82; speech pathology coordinator Phoenix Gen. Hosp., 1982-85; speech pathologist Paradise Valley Sch. Dist., Phoenix, 1985—, Phoenix Meml. Hosp., 1986—; cons. Phoenix Bapt. Hosp., 1984-85, Vis. Nurse Services, Phoenix, 1981; mem. adv. bd. Nursefinders, Phoenix, 1984-85. CPR Instr. and trainer Am. Heart Assn., Phoenix, 1981—. Mem. Ariz. Speech and Hearing Assn., Am. Speech and Hearing Assn. (cert. clin. competence), Canyon State Cloggers (treas. 1985-86), Chi Omega (alumni assn.). Republican. Lutheran. Home: 2222 W Michelle Dr Phoenix AZ 85023

RASMUSSEN, DONALD LINDEN, geologist; b. Lewistown, Mont., Apr. 13, 1941; s. Edward Linden and Frances Marie (Collins) R.; m. Geraldine Julé Dougherty, June 14, 1961; children: Stanley Linden, Dalton Lawrence. BA in Geology, U. Mont., 1963, MA in Geology, 1969; PhD in Geology, U. Kans., 1977. Geologist Pan Am. Petroleum Corp., New Orleans, 1966-70, Amoco Prodn. Co., Denver, 1974-79, Davis Oil Co., Denver, 1979-85; geologist, cons. Intermontane Research, Pine, Colo., 1985-86; geologist, pres. Rocky Mountain Geol. Databases, Denver, 1987—. Contbr. articles on geology and paleontology of Western U.S. to profl. jours. Mem. AAAS, Am. Assn. Petroleum Geologists, Am. Soc. Mammalogists, U. Kans. Mus. Natural History (assoc.), Computer Oriented Geol. Soc., Geol. Soc. Am., Mont. Geol. Soc., Rocky Mountain Assn. Geologists, Soc. Econ. Paleontologists and Mineralogists (Rocky Mountain sect.), Soc. Vertebrate Paleontology, Tobacco Root Geol. Soc., Western Interior Paleontol. Soc., Wyo. Geol. Assn. Republican. Methodist. Home: 1795 Mt Evans Blvd Pine CO 80470 Office: Rocky Mountain Geol Databases 2000 W 120th Denver CO 80234

RASMUSSEN, GARY STEVEN, engineering geologist; b. Ida Grove, Iowa, Aug. 30, 1944; s. Carol C. and Jeannette L. (Winslow) R.; m. Betty Joanne Amos, July 4, 1971 (div. Aug. 1978); children—Travis S., Tiana K. B.S., U. Ariz., 1967. Registered engrng. geologist, Calif., Oreg. V.p. Rasmussen Well Co., Inc., Ida Grove, 1965-70; staff engr. Pacific Found. Engrs., Bloomington, Calif., 1967-70; engrng. geologist, Rialto, Calif., 1970-71; br. mgr. Leighton & Assocs., Inc., La Habra, Calif., 1971-72; pres. Gary S. Rasmussen Assocs., Inc., San Bernardino, Calif., 1972—; mem. Calif. Bldg. and Safety Bd., 1981—; vis. lectr. various univs.; owner GCOMP, San Bernardino, 1983—. Contbr. articles to tech. jours. Mem. Assn. Engrng. Geologists (sect. chmn. 1981, chmn. legis. com. 1984, chmn. registration com. 1986-87), Seismol. Soc. Am., Geol. Soc. Am., Earthquake Engrng. Research Inst., Inland Geol. Soc. (founder), South Coast Geol. Soc. Lodge: Rotary. Home: PO Box 5488 San Bernardino CA 92412 Office: 1811 Commercenter W San Bernardino CA 92408

RASMUSSEN, IRENE KAY, public relations consultant, educator; b. Ajo, Ariz., Sept. 2, 1942; d. Charles William and Ruth Irene (Roberts) R.; m. John D. Lyons, Jr., June 19, 1965 (div. June 1978); 1 child, Rachel Roberts Lyons. Attended, U. Pacific, 1960-61; BA, U. Ariz., 1964, MEd, 1965. Cert. secondary edn. tchr., Ariz. Asst. to Gov. Ariz. Gov. Council Children, Youth and Families, Phoenix, 1977-79; exec. asst. to dir. Dept. Econ. Security, Phoenix, 1979-82; dir. volunteerism Community Council of Phoenix, 1982-84; dir. pub. relations Sandy Cowen Agy., Phoenix, 1984-85; pres. Irene Rasmussen & Assocs., Phoenix, 1984-86; cons. Ariz. Dept. Edn., Phoenix, 1978, TRANSLEX, Lima, Peru and La Paz, Bolivia, 1986. Coauthor English textbooks for Ethiopian Schs., 1969; book editor Women in Alternative Careers, 1977, STEREO, 1978. Bd. dirs. Jewish Family and Children's Services, Phoenix, 1980-84, Sojourner Ctr., Phoenix, 1977-81; inauguration chmn. Phoenix Mayor and City Council, 1984; Dem. precinct comitteeman, Phoenix, 1978—. Mem. Communicating Arts Group Ariz., Pub. Relations Soc. Am. (accredited). Presbyterian. Club: Phoenix City (charter mem.). Avocation: rancher in partnership with parents. Office: 903 E Colter St Phoenix AZ 85013

RASMUSSEN, JOHN EDWARD, research institute director; b. Denver, May 28, 1925; s. Harry Edward and Louise Marie (Cunningham) R.; m. Dorothy Jean Eggeling, Mar. 22, 1949; children—Anne Louise, James Edward. B.S., Northwestern U., 1947, M.A., 1949; Ph.D., Am. U., 1961. Served as enlisted man U.S. Navy, 1943-44, commd. ensign, 1945; advanced through grades to capt. Med. Service Corps, 1966; head clin., psychology sect. Bur. Medicine and Surgery, Dept. Navy, Washington, 1956-58; dir. dept behavioral sci. Naval Med. Research Inst., Bethesda, Md., 1959-64; liaison psychologist Office of Naval Research, London, 1964-67; asst. for med. and allied scis. Chief Naval Devel., Washington, 1967-69; ret. 1969; cons. to dir. Battelle-NW, Richland, Wash., 1969-71; dir. Battelle Human Affairs Research Ctrs., Seattle, 1971-82, Virginia Mason Research Ctr., Seattle, 1982—; mem. Pres.'s com. U. Wash., 1982—. Editor: (with Frederic O'R. Hayes) Centers for Innovation in the Cities and States, 1973; editor, contbg. author: Human Behavior in Isolation and Confinement, 1973. Decorated Meritorious Service medal; recipient John Shaw Billings award Assn. Mil. Surgeons U.S., 1962; VA fellow, 1948-50. Fellow Am. Psychol. Assn., AAAS, Royal Soc. Medicine. Republican. Clubs: Army and Navy (Washington); Seattle Yacht (trustee 1979-83); Rainier. Lodge: Rotary. Home: 71 Cascade Key Bellevue WA 98006 Office: Virginia Mason Research Ctr 1000 Seneca St Seattle WA 98101

RASMUSSEN, JOHN OSCAR, JR., chemistry educator, scientist; b. St. Petersburg, Fla., Aug. 8, 1926; s. John Oscar and Hazel (Ormsby) R.; m. Louise Brooks, Aug. 27, 1950; children—Nancy, Jane, David, Stephen. B.S., Calif. Inst. Tech., 1948; Ph.D., U. Calif. at Berkeley, 1952; M.A. (hon.), Yale U., 1969. Mem. chemistry faculty U. Calif. at Berkeley, 1952-68, 73—, prof. chemistry, 1973—; mem. research staff Radiation Lab., 1952-68; sr. research asso. Lawrence Berkeley Lab., 1972—; prof. chemistry Yale U. 1969-73; asso. dir. Yale Heavy Ion Accelerator Lab., 1970-73; vis. research prof. Nobel Inst. Physics, Stockholm, 1953; vis. prof. Inst. Nuclear Sci. U. Tokyo, 1974, Fudan U., Shanghai, 1979, hon. prof., 1984. Contbr. articles on radioactivity, nuclear models, heavy ion reactions. Served with USN, 1944-46. NSF sr. post-doctoral fellow Niels Bohr Inst., Copenhagen, Denmark, 1961-62; NORDITA fellow, 1979; recipient E.O. Lawrence Meml. award AEC, 1967; J.S. Guggenheim Meml. fellow, 1973. Fellow Am. Phys. Soc., AAAS; mem. Am. Chem. Soc. (Nuclear Applications in Chemistry award 1976), Fedn. Am. Scientists (chmn. 1969, mem. council 1967-73). Office: U Calif Dept Chemistry Berkeley CA 94720

RASMUSSEN, STUART RICARD, newspaper librarian; b. San Francisco, Nov. 7, 1906; s. Emil Jorgen and Christine (Johnsen) R.; student U. Calif. Extension; m. Nairn Margaret Abbott, June 1, 1940; children—Nairn Christine, Mark Abbott. In library San Francisco Examiner, 1929-37; head librarian San Francisco Call Bull., 1937-59, San Francisco News Call Bulletin, 1959-66; library staff San Francisco Examiner, 1966—, asst. head librarian, 1966-75, acting head librarian, 1975-78; engaged in spl. research for Metro-Goldwyn-Mayer movies, San Francisco Bay area, 1935—; actor Maxwell Burke Stock Co., Oakland and Berkeley, Calif., 1927-28, Blake, Turner Stock Co., San Francisco area, 1928; dir. children and adult plays San Geronimo Valley Community Centers; sometimes dir. Ross Valley Players Barn Theatre. Pres. Lagunitas Dist. Sch. Bd., 1955-58, San Geronimo Valley Little League, 1961. Mem. Spl. Libraries Assn., Am. Newspaper Guild (charter mem. San Francisco/Oakland chpt.). Democrat. Club: San Francisco Press (life mem.). Author drama revs. for The Peninsulan, 1936; several plays for children, 1955-60. Home: Alta Rd Lagunitas CA 94938 Office: 110 5th St San Francisco CA 94118

RASMUSSEN, VICTOR PHILIP, JR., soil science educator, computer scientist, consultant; b. Logan, Utah, Apr. 3, 1950; s. Victor Philip and Mary Velda (Peterson) R.; m. Linda Kay Schamber, Sept. 6, 1973; children—Angela Kay, Bryan Philip, Jenniffer Lynn, Neal Robert, Kathleen Marie. B.S., Utah State U., 1974, M.S., 1976; Ph.D., Kans. State U., 1979. Research technician 411 modelling group Agrl. Expt. Sta., Utah State U., 1974-76, asst. prof. soil sci. and biometeorology, state soils/computer extension specialist, 1981—; research assoc. NASA Wheat Modelling Group, Evapotranspiration Lab., Kans. State U., Manhattan, 1976-78; dir. microcomputer agrl. mgmt. lab., div. agr. Ricks Coll., Rexburg, Idaho, 1979-81; cons. agrl. microcomputer applications; mem., Utah State U. rep. Utah State Soil Conservation Commn., Utah Dept. Agr., Salt Lake City, 1981—; mem. Kellogg Found. Extension Computer Feasability Task Force for 13 Western States, 1982-83; apptd. to regional com. in charge of monitoring salinity control projects on Colo. River, 1982—; lead speaker Nat. Farm Computer Conf., Mpls., 1983. Mem. Am. Soc. Agronomy, Soil Sci. Soc. Am., Western Soil Sci. Soc., Internat. Soil Sci. Soc., Soil Conservation Soc. Am., N.W. Plant Food Assn. (sec. to Utah soil improvement com. 1981-83), Sigma Xi, Alpha Zeta, Phi Kappa Phi. Author Utah State U. Extension publs.; contbr. articles to profl. publs.

RASMUSSEN, WILLIAM OTTO, computer company executive; b. Burley, Idaho, Jan. 29, 1942; s. Otto M. and Eleanor M. (Kinney) R.; m. Bonnie K. Branson, Sept. 5, 1964; children: Robert, Christopher. BS in Physics, U. Idaho, 1964, MS in Physics, 1966; PhD, U. Ariz., 1973. Exploration geophysicist Heinrichs Geoexploration Co., Tucson, Ariz., 1968-70; assoc. prof. agrl. engrng and geol. engrng. U. Ariz., Tucson, 1973—; dir. Western Computer Consortium, Tucson, 1983—; cons. Bell Tech. Ops., Tucson, 1981-83. Author: Computer Applications in Agriculture, 1985. W.K. Kellogg Found. grantee, 1983—. Mem. AAAS, Am. Water Resources Assn., Assn. Computing Machinery. Home: 1325 N Goebel Tucson AZ 85715 Office: Western Computer Consortium 1132 E Mabel Tucson AZ 85719

RASOR, JACQUELIN HERMLING, educator; b. Danville, Ill., Aug. 9, 1946; d. Harold Otha and Elizabeth Matilda (Kendall) H.; m. Joseph James Rasor, June 1, 1968; children: Joseph II, Michelle Elizabeth. BA, Eureka Coll., 1968; MA, No. Ariz. U., 1976. Tchr. 2d grade La Rose Pub. Sch., Washburn, Ill., 1968-70, Bur. Indian Affairs Cottonwood Day Sch., Chinle, Ariz., 1970-74; tchr. kindergarten Bur. Indian Affairs Tuba City (Ariz.) Boarding Sch., 1974-76; substitute tchr. Tuba City Pub. Sch., 1976-77; tchr. kindergarten and 3d grade Bloomfield (N.Mex.) Pub. Schs., 1977—; owner, instr. Human Growth and Devel. Ctr., Bloomfield, 1978-79. Deacon Tuba City Presbyn. Ch., 1975-77; choir mem. Bloomfield Meth. Ch., 1984—, mem. adminstrv. bd., 1985—, sponsor youth group, 1986—; scout leader Girl Scouts U.S., 1982-84. Recipient Cert. of Merit Cottonwood Day Sch., Chinle, 1972. Mem. NEA (sch. rep. 1977-79), United Meth. Women Orgn., Epsilon Sigma Xi, Phi Kappa Phi. Republican. Methodist. Home: 1206 Lupine Rd Bloomfield NM 87413 Office: Naaba Ani Elem Sch PO box 3100 Bloomfield NM 87413

RASPONE, FAYE JUANITA, city official; b. Whitman County, Wash., Sept. 1, 1929; d. Fred Garfield and Iona (Nation) Heaton; m. John Alfred P. Prahinski, Apr. 15, 1949; 1 child, Stephen Kip; m. Raymond Aue, Nov. 1, 1957; m. Paul John Raspone, Aug. 5, 1972. Student pub. schs., Pullman. Telephone operator Gen. Telephone, Pullman, Wash., 1955-57; staff toll billing sect. Gen. Telephone, Spokane, 1957-58; telephone operator Wash. State U., Pullman, 1962-63; police dispatcher City of Pullman, 1963-68, chief dispatcher, 1968-73, supr. support services Dept. Pub. Safety, 1973—; pub. speaker. Mem. Assn. Pub. Communications Officers, Law Enforcement and Records Assn. Wash. (charter). Office: SE 260 Kamiaken St Pullman WA 99163

RASSAM, HORMUZD YOUSUF, architectural and engineering company executive; b. Mosul, Iraq, June 21, 1931; came to U.S., 1958; s. Yousuf Nimrud and Najma Towfiq (Bunney) R.; m. Cynthia K. Tribelhorn, Mar. 21, 1969; children—Najma Christine, Yousuf J. Hormuzd. Diploma in Civil Engring., Coll. Engring., Baghdad, Iraq, 1953; M.S.E., U. Mich., 1960; Ph.D., Colo. State U., 1969. Registered profl. engr., Calif., Colo., N.Mex.; registered land surveyor, Colo., N.Mex.; lic. gen. contractor, N.Mex. Civil engr. Iraq Petroleum Co., Iraq and U.K., 1953-58; mem. engring. faculty Ft. Lewis Coll., Durango, Colo., 1962-66; engring. cons., Durango, 1963-68; mem. faculty Colo. Sch. Mines, Golden, 1968-72; pres. TECH, Farmington, N.Mex., 1972—. Contbr. articles to profl. jours. Mem. panel of arbitrators Am. Arbitration Assn. Mem. ASCE, Nat. Soc. Profl. Engrs., ASTM, Council Ednl. Facility Planners Internat., Am. Plannign Assn., Internat. Council for Ednl. Planning, Am. Concil Ind. Labs., Am. Soc. Engring. Edn., Sigma Xi, Chi Epsilon. Democrat. Chaldean Catholic. Lodge: Elks. Home: 1100 Zuni Dr Farmington NM 87401 Office: TECH 333 E Main St Farmington NM 87401

RATCLIFFE, ALLEN THOMPSON, JR., financial consultant, lawyer; b. Beloit, Wis., Jan. 11, 1947; s. Allen T. Ratcliffe and Phyllis (Woellner) Weigand; m. Leslie Garland, Aug. 23, 1979. B.A., U. Cin., 1969; J.D., U. Denver, 1972; L.L.M., U. Miami, 1978. Bar: Colo. Assoc. Nicholas & Magill, Steamboat Springs, Colo., 1972-73; ptnr. Ratcliffe & Chamberlin, Steamboat Springs, 1974-83; of counsel, dir. devel. Robert J. Pope & Assocs., Palo Alto, Calif., 1983-84; chief ops. officer gaither & Fitzgerald, Menlo Park, Calif., 1984-85; equities coordinator, advanced underwriter David White and Assocs., Walnut Creek, Calif., 1986—; town atty. Yampa, Colo., 1972-74; city atty. Steamboat Springs, 1973-77; prof. Colo. Mountain Coll., Steamboat Springs, 1978-83; ptnr. Steamboat Cablevision, 1981-85. Lectr. Steamboat Springs Chamber Resort Assn., 1981, 82; pres. Tree Haus Homeowners Assn., 1981-82; v.p. Tree Haus Water and Sanitation District, 1982. Mem. Colo. Bar Assn., N.W. Colo. Bar Assn., Colo. Criminal Justice Planning Council (chmn. exec. com. 1976-76). Episcopalian. Lodge: Rotary. Home: 1155 Turtle Rock Ln Concord CA 94521 Office: David White and Assocs 309 Lennon Ln Walnut Creek CA 94598

RATHANA-NAKINTARA, THAWORN, physician; b. Nakornstrithamaraj, Thailand, June 5, 1933; came to U.S., 1959, naturalized, 1975; s. Tawan and Joan (Leelabandhu) Rathana-N. M.D., Chulalongkorn U., 1957; M.S.P., UCLA, 1971; postgrad. U. Mich., 1962-63. Resident in psychiatry Henry Ford Hosp., Detroit, 1960-61; med. dir. Mohave Mental Health Clinic, Inc., Kingman, Ariz., 1971-72; regional dir. psychiat. services, Sask., Can., 1967-68; dep. chief services Bklyn. State Hosp., 1972-74; acting dist. dir. North County Mental Health, Los Angeles, 1980-81; exec. dir. Internat. Inst. Preventive Psychiatry, Studio City, Calif., 1981—; pres. Center for the Advancement of Ability to Love, North Hollywood, Calif., 19—. Served to capt. Royal Thai Army, 1957-59. NIMH fellow, 1969-71. Mem. AMA, Am. Psychiat. Assn., World Med. Assn. Author: An Introduction to Priciples of True Love, 1976; Understanding love: The Key to Growth and Fulfillment, 1981. Home: 11445 Dona Dolores St Studio City CA 91604

RATHCKE, DOROTHY ANNE, nursing administrator; consultant; b. Napa, Calif., Mar. 19, 1922; d. Clifford Clark Harris and Florence Emily (Baldwin) Goodman; B.S. in Nursing, U. Calif., Berkeley, 1944; m. George L. Rathcke, Nov. 12, 1955; children—Karen Anne Boren, Clark Harold Kujawka, Karl Lewis. Staff nurse Napa State Hosp., Imola, Calif., 1951-52, psychiat. nursing edn., 1952-63, supt. nursing, 1963-71, nursing cons. office of program rev., 1971-77, coordinator nursing services, 1977-83; mem. task force to develop staffing standards for state hosps. Calif. Dept. Health, 1972-74. Mem. adv. bd. psychiat. technician and asso. degree nursing programs, Napa Coll.; mem. adv. bd. Regional Occupational Program, Napa Unified Sch. Dist.; mem. Com. on Continuing Edn. for Health Occupations, Napa County, 1975-83; bd. dirs. Napa chpt. Am. Heart Assn., 1975-81, v.p., 1976; mem. manpower adv. panel Dept. Mental Health State of Calif., 1981-83. Mem. adv. bd. Vintage House, 1985—, Foster Grandparents, 1985—. NIMH grantee, 1964-72. Mem. Nat. League Nursing, Calif. League Nursing-Adminstrn., Napa County Mental Health Assn. Democrat. Office: 1912 Sierra Ave Napa CA 94558

RATHSWOHL, M EUGENE JOSEPH, infosystems specialist, educator; b. Los Angeles, Nov. 8, 1942; s. Eugene Louis and Gertrude Sophia (Adams) R.; m. Sheila Anthony Horne, June 25, 1966; children: Eugene E., Anthony J., Mercedes, Weston L., Diana, Erin. BA, San Diego State U., 1964; MS, U. Dayton, 1970; PhD, U. Pitts., 1973. Human performance engr. Wright-Patterson AFB, Ohio, 1966-70; research assoc. U. Dayton Research Inst., 1970; asst. prof. info. sci. U. Tex., Austin, 1974-79; assoc. prof. U. San Diego, 1979—; cons. San Diego, 1979—. Contbr. articles on info. sci. to profl. jours. Served to capt. USAF, 1966-70. Grantee U. Tex., Austin, 1974-79, U. San Diego, 1979—. Mem. Soc. Info. Mgmt., Am. Soc. Info. Sci. Republican. Roman Catholic. Avocation: backpacking. Home: 12758 Roberto Way Poway CA 92064 Office: U San Diego Alcala Park San Diego CA 92110

RATLIFF, LEIGH ANN, pharmacist; b. Long Beach, Calif., May 20, 1961; d. Harry Warren and Verna Lee (Zwink) R. D in Pharmacy, U. Pacific, 1984. Registered pharmacist, Calif., Nev. Pharmacist intern Green Bros. Inc., Stockton, Calif., 1982-84, staff pharmacist Thrifty Corp., Long Beach, Calif., 1984-85, head pharmacist, 1986-87, pharm. buyer, 1987—. Mem. Nat. Assn. Female Execs., Am. Pharm. Assn., Am. Inst. History Pharmacy, Calif. Pharmacist Assn., Lambda Kappa Sigma. Republican. Methodist. Avocations: creative writing, horseback riding, fishing, house plants, painting. Home: 8100 Park Plaza Apt 224 Stanton CA 90680 Office: Thrifty Corp 3424 Wilshire Blvd Los Angeles CA 90010

RATNER, DAVID LOUIS, legal educator; b. London, Sept. 2, 1931. AB magna cum laude, Harvard U., 1952, LLB magna cum laude, 1955. Bar: N.Y. 1955. Assoc. Sullivan & Cromwell, N.Y.C., 1955-64; assoc. prof. Cornell Law Sch., Ithaca, N.Y., 1964-68, prof., 1968-82; dean, prof. law U. San Francisco Law Sch., 1982—; exec. asst. to chmn. SEC, Washington, 1966-68; chief counsel Securities Industry Study, Senate Banking Com., Washington, 1971-73; vis. prof. Stanford (Calif.) U., 1974, Ariz. State U., Tempe, 1974, U. San Francisco, 1980; Fulbright scholar Monash U., Australia, 1981. Author: Securities Regulation; Materials for a Basic Course, 3d edit., 1986; Securities Regulation in a Nutshell, 2d edit., 1982; Institutional Investors: Teaching Materials, 1978. Home: 84 Polhemus Way Larkspur CA 94939 Office: Univ San Francisco Law Sch Kendrick Hall 2130 Fulton St San Francisco CA 94117

RATZLAFF, STANLEY ABE, diversified holding company executive; b. Bakersfield, Calif., June 22, 1935; s. Abe S. and Verna A. (Heinrichs) R.; m. Bette Anne Riley, July 14, 1957; children: Deborah Ratzlaff Huff, Stephen, Diane. A.A. in Acctg., Bakersfield Coll., 1955; B.A. in Acctg. with distinction, San Jose State U., 1957; grad. mgmt. program, Harvard U., 1987. C.P.A., Calif. Sr. acct. Shell Oil Co., Los Angeles, 1957-61; audit mgr. Ernst & Ernst, Los Angeles, 1961-69; treas., controller Shareholders Capital Programs, Inc., Los Angeles, 1969-72; asst. controller Atlantic Richfield Co., Los Angeles, 1972-79; controller Standard Oil Co., Cleve., 1979-81; v.p., controller Occidental Petroleum Corp., Los Angeles, 1981-84, Pacific Lighting Corp., Los Angeles, 1984—. Mem. bd. advisors U. So. Calif. Sch. Acctg., 1982—; bd. dirs. Union Rescue Mission, Los Angeles, 1984—. Mem. Am. Inst. CPA's, Calif. Soc. CPA's, Fin. Execs. Inst. (dir., officer Los Angeles chpt. 1984—), Nat. Assn. Accts. (v.p. local chpt. 1968-69, named Most Valuable Mem. 1964), Am. Petroleum Inst., Pacific Coast Gas Assn., Am. Gas Assn. Republican. Office: Pacific Lighting Corp 810 S Flower St Los Angeles CA 90017

RAUCCI, JUDITH LYNN, speech pathology educator; b. New Haven, July 1, 1948; d. John Frank and Christine Raucci. BS, So. Conn. State Coll., 1970; MS, Syracuse U., 1972. Speech lang. specialist Los Angeles County, Downey, Calif., 1972-74, teaming specialist, 1974-75; coordinator speech and lang. Lowell Joint Sch. Dist., La Habra, Calif., 1976-80; program specialist Whittier (Calif.) Area Coop. Spl. Edn. Program, 1980—; speech pathologist Presbyn. Hosp., Whittier, 1976-78, Naomi Heller and Assocs., Los Angeles, 1980-82; clinic supr. Whittier Coll., 1985—, instr. 1986—. Mem. Am. Speech Lang. Hearing Assn., Calif. Speech and Hearing Assn., Council for Exceptional Children, Aviation Pilots and Owners Club, Pacific Dive Club, Delta Kappa Gamma (sec. 1982). Roman Catholic. Club: 99's Internat. (Fullerton, Calif.). Avocations: scuba diving, racquetball, travel, reading, flying. Office: Whittier Area Coop Spl Edn Program 8036 S Ocean View Whittier CA 90602

RAUCH, HERBERT EMIL, electrical engineer; b. St. Louis, Oct. 6, 1935; s. Herbert Leopold and Vera Hilda (Sieloff) R.; m. Marjorie Ann Beyer, June 18, 1961; children: Marta, Erik, Evan, Loren. BSEE, Calif. Inst. Tech., 1957; MSEE, Stanford U., 1958, PhDEE, 1962. Mem. tech. staff Hughes Space Systems Div., Los Angeles, 1957-62, Lockheed Palo Alto Research Lab., Calif., 1962—; gen. co-chmn. Astrodynamics Conf., 1975; gen. chmn. Asilomar Conf. Circuits, Systems and Computers, 1983, Am. Control Conf., 1984; part time tchr. San Jose (Calif.) State U., 1968-70. Editor-in-chief Jour. Astron. Scis., 1980-86; contbr. articles to profl. jours. Mem. Peninsula Sch. Bd., Menlo Park, Calif., 1973-82, Selective Service Bd., Santa Clara County, 1972-75; trustee Los Altos Sch. Dist., 1974-75; chmn. People for Los Altos Now (PLAN), 1974-75. Fellow Am. Astronautical Soc. (v.p. publs. 1980-82, v.p. tech. 1982-84); mem. IEEE (sr. mem., chmn. San Francisco chpt. Control Systems Soc. 1976-77, 1980-82, editor Control Systems mag. 1985—; community service award region 6, 1977, centennial award 1984), AIAA, Soc. Indsl. and Applied Mechanics, Internat. Fedn. Automatic Control (chmn. math. control com. 1984-87, organizing chmn. working group control applications nonlinear programming 1978-84). Office: Lockheed 92-20/254E 3251 Hanover St Palo Alto CA 94304

RAUCH, IRMENGARD, linguist, educator; b. Dayton, Ohio, Apr. 17, 1933; d. Konrad and Elsa (Knott) R.; m. Gerald F. Carr, June 12, 1965; children: Christopher, Gregory. Student, Nat. U. Mex., summer 1954; B.S. with honors, U. Dayton, 1955; M.A., Ohio State U., 1957; postgrad. (Fulbright fellow), U. Munich, Fed. Republic Germany, 1957-58; Ph.D., U. Mich., 1962. Instr., German and linguistics U. Wis.-Madison, 1962-63, asst. prof., 1963-66; assoc. prof. German U. Pitts., 1966-68; assoc. prof. German and linguistics U. Ill., Urbana, 1968-72; prof. U. Ill., 1972-79, U. Calif.-Berkeley, 1979—. Author: The Old High German Diphthongization: A Description of a Phonemic Change, 1967; editor: (with others) Approaches in Linguistic Methodology, 1967, Spanish edit., 1974, Der Heliand, 1974, Linguistic Method: Essays in Honor of Herbert Penzl, 1979, The Signifying Animal: The Grammar of Language and Experience, 1980, Language Change, 1983; contbr. articles to profl. jours. Named outstanding woman on campus U. Ill. sta. WILL, 1975; recipient Disting. Alumnus award U. Dayton, 1985; research grantee U. Wis., summer 1966, U. Ill., 1975-79, Eastern Ill. U., 1976, Nat. Endowment Humanities, 1978, U. Calif., Berkeley, 1979—; travel grantee NSF, Linguistics Soc. Am., 1972; IBM Distributed Acad. Computing Environment; Guggenheim fellow, 1982-83; IBM grant, 1986. Mem. Linguistics Soc. Am., MLA, Am. Assn. Tchrs. German, Societas Linguistica Europaea, Internat. Linguistic Assn., AAAS, AAUP, Phonetics Assn., Semiotic Soc. Am. (pres. 1982-83), Semiotic Circle of Calif., Alpha Sigma Tau, Delta Phi Alpha. Home: 2282 Clear View Circle Benicia CA 94510 Office: Dept German U Calif Berkeley CA 94720

RAUE, JORG EMIL, electrical engineer; b. Stettin, Federal Republic of Germany, June 13, 1936; came to U.S., 1952; s. Ludwig and Liselotte (Barth) R.; m. Anke Volkmann, June 29, 1957; children: Monika Kay, Jennifer Faye. BSEE, Milw. Sch. Engring., 1961; MSEE, Marquette U., 1965, PhDEE, 1968. Mem. faculty Milw. Sch. Engring., 1961-68, chmn. dept., 1968-69; research engr. TRW Systems, Redondo Beach, Calif., 1969-76; mgr. dept. TRW Systems, Redondo Beach, 1976-79; sr. research scientist TRW Electronic Systems, Rendondo Beach, Calif., advanced systems mgr., 1980—; chmn. dept. elec. engring. Calif. Polytech State U., San Luis Opispo, 1979-80; mem. faculty Marquette U., Milw., 1968-69, Loyola U., Los Angeles, 1970-72, U. So. Calif., Los Angeles, 1983—. Contbr. articles to profl. jours. Served with U.S. Army, 1955-58. Recipient Disting. Tchr. award Milw. Sch. Engring., 1968; named Outstanding Alumnus Milw. Sch. Engring., 1985. Fellow IEEE; mem. Microwave Soc. of IEEE (sec. adminstrn. com. 1985—), Sigma Xi. Avocations: tennis, bicycling, flying. Home: 28813 Rothrock Dr Rancho Palos Verdes CA 90274

RAUGHTON, JIMMIE LEONARD, urban planner, ednl. adminstr.; b. Knoxville, Tenn., Oct. 9, 1943; s. George L. and Ann (Simotes) R.; B.A. in Urban and Regional Planning, U. No. Colo., 1974, M.A., 1976, D of Pub. Adminstrn., U. Colo., 1986. Mgr., Flexitran div. Gathers, De Vilbliss Architects and Planners, Denver, 1966-68; asst. dir. planning City of Aurora, Colo., 1970-71, asst. dir., operational planner, 1973-74; planner City of Lakewood, Colo., 1971-73; planner City of Boulder, Colo., 1973-74, acting asst. dir. community devel., 1973-74; instr. urban planning Community Coll. of Denver, 1974-76, div. dir. Human Resources and Services, 1976-81, div. dir. sci. and tech., 1981-85; dir. program ops. State of Colo. Community Colls., 1985—; coordinator community coll. devel. Rocky Mountain Energy and Environ. Tech. Center, 1980. cons. Denver Regional Council of Govts. for Model Sign Code, 1973, City of Boulder Transp. Dept., 1975—; chmn. profl. advisory com. to Colo. Gov.'s Land Use Adviser, 1973; also public speaker. Mem. exec. bd. Civic Center Assn., Denver, 1973-75; supervisory com. Colo. State Employees Credit Union, 1986—;mem. bd. Support Systems Consol., 1984, Bridge Industry, 1984-85; Democratic candidate for Denver City Council, 1975; bd. dirs. Plan Metro Denver, 1975-76, Four Corner Art Coalition, 1973—. Recipient Citizen Award of Honor, Assn. of Beautiful Colo. Roads, 1972. Mem. Am. Inst. of Planners (mem. exec. bd. Colo. 1970-75, treas. 1972-73), Colo. City Mgrs. Assn., Am. Soc. Planning Ofcls., Am. Vocat. Assn., Am. Soc. for Tng. and Devel. Methodist. Contbr. articles to local newspapers. Home: 2501 High St Denver CO 80205 Office: State of Colo Community Colls 1313 Sherman Denver CO 80202

RAUH, ROBERT BRUCE, advertising executive; b. San Francisco, July 24, 1942; s. Rudoulph L. and Virginia I. (Vincelli) R.; m. Darlene A. Colose, Apr. 3, 1971; children—Joshua Edward, Joanna Teresa. B.A., San Jose State U., 1964. Prodn. mgr., asst. account exec., market research analyst Allen & Dorward Advt., San Francisco, 1963-66; account supr. ATD Advt., Palo Alto, Calif., 1966-68; v.p., creative dir. Markman Inc., Los Gatos, Calif., 1968-69; owner Robert B. Rauh Advt., San Jose, Calif., 1969-74; founder, pres. Rauh, Good, Darlo & Barnes Advt. Assocs. Inc., Los Gatos, 1974—; adj. prof. advt. San Jose State U. Trustee Loma Prieta Joint Union Sch. Dist. Served with USN, A.C., 1964-70. Mem. Am. Advt. Fedn. (Best in West award 1982), Am. Assn. Advt. Agys., San Jose Advt. Club (bd. dirs., past pres., AAF Silver medal 1982), Monterey Advt. Club, Santa Clara Valley Advt. Agys. Assn. (founder, past pres.). Democrat. Roman Catholic. Club: Democratic Century of Santa Clara County. Office: 15425 Los Gatos Blvd Los Gatos CA 95030

RAUM, WILLIAM JOSEPH, endocrinology educator; b. Cleve., July 6, 1947; s. George William and Helen Margaret (Phillips) R.; m. Sandra Kathleen Cartwright, Aug. 1, 1970; children: Kelly, Judy, Jennifer, James, Jody, Kristen. BS, Bowling Green State U., 1969, MA, 1970, PhD, 1974; MD, Med. Coll. Ohio, 1973. Diplomate Nat. Bd. Med. Examiners. Intern Med Coll. Ohio, Toledo, 1973-74; resident Kaiser Found. Hosp., Los Angeles, 1974-75; asst. prof. medicine UCLA, 1979-86, assoc. prof., 1986—; assoc. chief div. endocrinology Harbor-UCLA Med. Ctr., 1984—, dir. endocrine clinic, 1982—, assoc. dir. endocrine research labs., 1982—; acad. assoc. Nichols INst., San Juan Capistrano, Calif., 1980—; co-dir. Harbor Ctr. for Health Enhancement, Redondo Beach, Calif., 1983—. Contbr. articles to profl. jours.; inventor med. process., 1977. Bd. dirs. Palos Verdes (Calif.) Little League, 1986—. NIH Pub. Health Service fellow, 1976-78; grantee NIH, Am. Heart Assn. Mem. Am. Fedn. Clin. Research, Am. Physiol.Soc., Endocrine Soc., Nat. Rifle Assn. (life), Sigma Xi, Beta Beta Beta. Republican. Avocations: collecting antique mil. arms, softball coach. Office: Harbor-UCLA Med Ctr A-17 1000 W Carson St Torrance CA 90509

RAUTMAN, CHRISTOPHER ARTHUR, geologist; b. Albuquerque, Aug. 19, 1950; s. Arthur Louis and (Florence) Emily (Ward) R.; m. Jennifer Lynn Bingham, Apr. 6, 1974; 1 child, Anna Louise. AA, St. Petersburg Jr. Coll., 1970; BA, Carleton Coll., 1972; MS, U. Wis., 1974, PhD, 1976. Econ. geologist N.Mex. Bur. Mines, Socorro, 1976-78; research geologist Shell Devel. Co., Houston, 1978-80; project geologist Amoco Minerals Co., Englewood, Colo., 1980-85; mem. tech. staff Sandia Nat. Labs., Albuquerque, 1985—. Editor: Geology and Technology of Grants Uranium Region II, 1979; contbr. numerous articles to profl. jours. Grantee NSF, 1973-76. Mem. Geol. Soc. Am. (Penrose Research grantee 1974-75), Am. Assn. Petroleum Geologists, Sigma Xi (research grantee 1974-75), Phi Beta Kappa. Republican. Presbyterian. Home: 418 Tahoe NE Albuquerque NM 87107 Office: Sandia Nat Lab PO Box 5800 Albuquerque NM 87185

RAVELING, DENNIS GRAFF, biology educator; b. Devil's Lake, N.D., Feb. 28, 1939; s. Ralph Gordon and Martha Irene (Graff); R. m. Olga Catherine Masnyk, Mar. 3, 1962. BA, So. Ill. U., 1960, PhD, 1967; MA, U. Minn., 1963. Research scientist Can. Wildlife Service, Winnipeg, Man., Can., 1967-71; asst. prof. dept. wildlife-fisheries biology U. Calif., Davis, 1971-74, assoc. prof., 1974-80, prof., 1980—. Contbr. articles to profl. jours. NSF grantee, 1963, 73, 75, 77, 78. Fellow AAAS; mem. Am. Ornithologists Union (elective mem.), Am. Soc. Naturalists, Brit. Ornithologists Union, Cooper Ornithol. Soc., Wildlife Soc., Wilson Ornithol. Soc., Calif. Wetlands Fedn. (trustee), Sigma Xi. Home: 504 Del Oro Davis CA 95616 Office: U Calif Div Wildlife and Fisheries Biology Davis CA 95616

RAVEN, MERRILL LEE GALLO, magazine editor; b. Ft. Belvoir, Va., Nov. 1, 1950; d. Barbara Josephine (Gallo) Hutchison; m. Michael S. Raven, May 4, 1980. BA, U. Tex.; pvt. studies with Alden Amos, spinning wheelwright, 1980-82. Tech., acquisitions and copy editor Spin-Off mag. Interweave Press, Loveland, Colo., 1981—; instr. and demonstrator Renaissance Pleasure Faire, Novato, Calif., 1981-83; nationwide workshop instr. in Colo. and Calif., 1984—; juror Sonoma County Fair, 1984, conf. No. Calif. Handweavers, 1984, workshop co-chmn., 1985; textile specialist Lowie Mus. Anthropology U. Calif., Berkeley, 1984—; founding mem. Spinners Textile Study Group, 1981—. Author: Hands-On Spinning, 1987. Home: 1227 Monterey Ave Berkeley CA 94707 Office: Interweave Press 306 N Washington Loveland CO 80537

RAVIN, SHELDON JAY, physician; b. Detroit, Mar. 4, 1947; s. Sidney and Sylvia (Dorn) R.; m. Gail Frances Spiering, Aug. 3, 1974; children: Demian, Rachel. BS in Psychology, Wayne State U., 1969; DO, Chgo.'s Coll. Osteopathy, 1973. Diplomate Am. Bd. Family Practitice; cert. Am. Coll. Gen. Practice. Intern Chgo. Osteo. Hosp., 1973-74; physician Community Health Ctr., Colorado Springs, Colo., 1974-75, Skyway Family Practice, Colorado Springs, 1974—; med. dir. Adult and Adolescent Substance Abuse, Eisenhower Med. Ctr., Colorado Springs, 1983-86, vice chief staff, 1985-86, sec.-treas., 1984-85; lectr. Diabetes Assn., 1978—, Alcohol and Drug Workshop, Colorado Springs, 1978—; chief of staff Eisenhower Med. Ctr. Bd. dirs. Arthritis Assn., Colorado Springs, 1977-78, Colorado Springs Montessouri Sch., 1976-78; sec.-treas. CareNet, Colorado Springs, 1985—. Recipient physician recognition award St. Frances Hosp. Brown Emergency Ctr., Woodland Park, Colo., 1979. Mem. Am. Osteo. Assn., Colo. Soc. Osteo. Physicians (program com. 1983-84), Colo. Med. Soc., El Paso County Med. Soc., El Paso County Osteo. Assn., Colorado Springs Osteo. Assn. Jewish. Avocations: sports, painting, sculpting. Home: 6 Heather Circle Colorado Springs CO 80956 Office: Skyway Family Practice 1301 S 8th St Suite 300 Colorado Springs CO 80906

RAWLAND, ALLAN GORDON, county mental health administrator; b. Toronto, Ont., Can., Apr. 3, 1942; came to U.S., 1946, naturalized, 1950; s. Arthur Gordon and Dorothy Jane (Fillion) R.; A.A., Am. River Coll., 1965; B.A., Calif. State U.-Sacramento, 1967, M.S.W., 1971. Cert. mental health adminstr.; cert. social worker. Social worker Orange County Dept. Social Services, Calif., 1967-69; social service practitioner Orange County Community Services Project, Calif., 1971-73, sr. social rehab. dir., 1973-74; dep. dir. Orange County Dept. Mental Health, Calif., 1974-79; dep. dir. mental health Los Angeles County Dept. Mental Health, Calif., 1979-86; asst. dir. Los Angeles County Dept. Mental Health, 1986—; instr. social work Chapman Coll., Orange, 1972-75, Santa Ana Coll., Calif., 1974-78; lectr. U. Calif.-Irvine, 1975-76; bd. dirs., chmn. planning council Region II United Way, 1980—, Vols. of Am., Greater Los Angeles County, 1982-84; Chmn. Orange County Fair Housing Council, 1973-74. Mem. Nat. Assn. Social Workers, Nat. Assn. Mental Health Adminstrs., Calif. Assn. County Drug Program Coordinators (chmn. 1976-77). Home: 1825 Peaceful Hills Rd Walnut CA 91789 Office: 2415 W 6th St Los Angeles CA 90057

RAWLINGS, MARY, escrow company executive; b. Lansing, Mich., Nov. 17, 1936; d. Frederick Thomas and Anna (Bondy) Belbeck; m. Richard M. Rawlings, Feb. 11, 1967 (div. 1985); children—Bonita Rawlings Walker, Mary Rawlings Rios, R. Patrick. Student, So. Calif. Sch. Escrows, Los Angeles, 1956-57, Pierce Coll., Woodland Hills, Calif., 1959-60. Vice pres., gen. mgr. Manhattan Mortgage Co., North Hollywood, Calif., 1962-66; mgr. San Fernando Valley Escrow Co., Calif., 1966-67; v.p., mgr. Golden West Escrow Co., Panorama City, Calif., 1967-77; pres. The Escrow Office, Inc., Woodland Hills, 1977—; chmn. bd. Escrow Agt.'s Fidelity Corp., Newport Beach, Calif., 1983—; instr. Pierce Coll., 1978-80. Mem. 99's Inc. (Women Pilot of Yr. 1984), Calif. Escrow Assn. (bd. dirs. 1977—), San Fernando Valley Escrow Assn. (pres. 1977). Avocations: flying; air racing. Office: The Escrow Office Inc 21228 Ventura Woodland Hills CA 91364

RAWLINGS, ROBERT HOAG, newspaper publiser; b. Pueblo, Colo., Aug. 3, 1924; s. John W. and Dorothy (Hoag) R.; student Colo. U., 1944-45; B.A., Colo. Coll., 1947; m. Mary Alexandra Graham, Oct. 18, 1947; children—Jane Louise, John Graham, Carolyn Anne, Robert Hoag II. Reporter Pueblo Chieftain and Pueblo Star-Jour., 1947-51, advt. rep. 1951-62, gen. mgr., 1962-79, pub. and editor, 1980—; sec. Star-Jour. Pub. Corp., 1962-84, pres., 1984—; dir. Colo. Nat. Bank-Pueblo. Served with USNR, 1942-46. Mem. Colo. Press Assn., (dir. 1963-66, 76-78, v.p. and pres.-elect 1984, pres. 1985, chmn. bd. dirs. 1986), Rocky Mountain Ad Mgrs. (past pres.), Colo. AP (past pres.). Presbyn. Elk, Rotarian. Home: 3100 Country Club Dr Pueblo CO 81008 Office: 825 W 6th St Pueblo CO 81003 also: PO Box 36 Pueblo CO 81002

RAWLINSON, STUART ELBERT, geologist; b. Oakland, Calif., Dec. 2, 1950; s. Bradford Stevon and Margaret Edna (Lisman) R.; m. Carol Ann Baran, Jan. 6, 1979; 1 child, Karen Lynn. AA, Los Angeles Harbor Coll., 1972; BS, Calif. State U., Long Beach, 1974; MS, U. Alaska, 1979, postgrad., 1979—. Field asst. Holmes and Narver, Inc., McMurdo Sta., Antarctica, 1970-71; supply and logistics coordinator Holmes and Narver, Inc., South Pole Sta., Antarctica, 1974-75; instr. geology Tanana Valley Community Coll., Fairbanks, Alaska, 1977; diver, technician U. Alaska, Fairbanks, 1978-79, research asst., 1977-80; geologist State Alaska Dept. Natural Resources, Fairbanks, 1980—; mem. Permafrost com. NRC, Washington, 1984—, U.S. Permafrost delegate to People's Republic of China, 1984; leader field trip to Prudhoe Bay Oilfield 4th Internat. Conf. on Permafrost, 1983. Contbr. articles to profl. jours. Recipient U.S. Antarctic Service medal NSF, 1975. Mem. Am. Assn. Petroleum Geologists, Soc. Econ. Paleontologists and Mineralogists, Phi Kappa Phi. Republican. Methodist. Office: Alaska Dept Natural Resources Div Geol and Geophys Surveys 794 University Ave Basement Fairbanks AK 99709

RAWSON, RAYMOND D., dentist; b. Sandy, Utah, Nov. 2, 1940; s. James D. and Mable (Beckstead) R.; B.S., U. Nev. at Las Vegas, 1964; D.D.S., Loma Linda U., 1968; M.A., U. Nev., 1978; m. Linda Downey, July 23, 1959; children—Raymond Blaine, Mark Daniel, Pamela Ann, David James, Kristi Lynn, Kenneth Glenn, Richard Allen. Gen. practice dentistry, Las Vegas, 1968—; instr. dental hygiene, dental dir. Clark County Community Coll., 1977—, dep. coroner, chief dental examiner, 1977—; adj. prof. U. Nev., 1977—, adj. assoc. prof. oral diagnosis and forensic dentistry Northwestern U., Chgo., 1985—. Contbr. articles to profl. jours. Active Boy Scouts Am., 1968—; bishop Ch. Jesus Christ Latter-day Saints, 1978—; asst. majority leader Nev. State senator. Diplomate Am. Bd. Forensic Odontology (sec. 1984). Fellow Am. Acad. Forensic Scis. (pres., chmn.), ADA (editorial rev. bd. jour.), Federation Dentaire International, Omicron Kappa Upsilon. Republican. Office: 4121 Sahara Ave W Las Vegas NV 89102

RAY, BENJAMIN LOUIS, budget analyst; b. Sedalia, Mo., Mar. 12, 1949; s. Benjamin Jacob and Mary Ruth (Booth) R.; m. Penny Lee Peterson; 1 child, Rachael Lynne. BA in History, U. Colo., 1978. Enlisted USN, 1963, resigned, 1973; budget analyst Dunn & Bradstreet, Boulder, Colo., 1974—. Avocations: reading, running, cross-country skiing. Home: 584 Juniper Ct Louisville CO 80027 Office: Neo Data Services 3300 Walnut Boulder CO 80203

RAY, GEORGINE HAINES, audiologist; b. Johnstown, Pa., June 14, 1957; d. James Lynn and Sarah Ann (Baker) Haines; m. Patrick Pearce Ray, Nov. 28, 1981; 1 child, Elizabeth Marie. BS, Ariz. State U., 1979, MS, 1982. Cert. clin. competence in audiology; hearing aid dispensing lic., Ariz. Audiologist Meth. Hosp., Houston, 1981; Pvt. practice specializing in audiology Mesa, Ariz., 1982-83; pediatric audiologist Phoenix Children's Hosp., 1983—; mem. Com. on Early Identification of Hearing Loss, Ariz., 1985—. Mem. Am. Speech-Lang. Hearing Assn., Am. Auditory Soc., Ariz. Speech-Lang. Hearing Assn. Roman Catholic. Home: 10817 N 55th St Scottsdale AZ 85254 Office: Phoenix Childrens Hosp 909 E Brill St Phoenix AZ 85006

RAY, LEO ELDON, fish prodn. and mktg. co. exec.; b. Logan County, Okla., Dec. 9, 1937; s. Wilbur Houston and Florence Ivy (Doggett) R.; B.S. in Zoology, U. Okla., 1963; m. Judith Kay Croddy, Aug. 29, 1959; children—Tana Kim, Tod Kent, Kacy Kay. Research asst. U. Okla., 1961-63; tchr. public schs., Dumas, Tex., 1963-64, Grants, N.Mex., 1964-65, Anaheim, Calif., 1965-69; co-owner Fish Breeders, Niland, Calif., 1969—; pres. Fish Breeders of Idaho, Inc., Buhl, 1971—; pres. Big Bend Trout, Inc., 1977—. Served with U.S. Army, 1957-60. Mem. Calif. Catfish Farmers Am. (past pres.), Catfish Farmers Am. (past pres., dir.), U.S. Trout Farmers Assn. (past pres., dir.). Address: Route 3 Box 234 Buhl ID 83316

RAY, LEOPOLD AUGUSTUS, architect; b. Port Antonio, Jamaica, Oct. 30, 1951; came to U.S., 1959, naturalized, 1961; s. Robert, Jr. and Doris Beatrice (Byrd) R.; B.Arch. (AIA scholar Ariz. chpt. 1971, Sun Angel Found. archtl. scholar 1974, Dubois Found. scholar 1975, Dougherty scholar 1975), Ariz. State U., 1976; M.A. in Urban Planning (grad. fellow 1979), UCLA, 1980. Architect-in-tng. firms in Las Vegas, Nev., 1976-78; asst. economist Los Angeles Office Econ. Devel., 1980; assoc. A.K. Ngai & Assocs., architects/planners, Los Angeles, 1980-82; urban design cons. Vitalize Van Nuys, Inc., 1980; coordinator Sat. scholar program UCLA, 1979-80; architect/rehab. specialist Mark Briggs & Assocs., 1982; ptnr. The AEP Partnership, Architects and Engrs.; prin. works include DeMille Dr. Residence, Spreading Oak Residence (both Los Angeles), others. Mem. AIA, Am. Inst. Cert. Planners. Democrat. Roman Catholic. Co-author: Earth-Integrated Architecture, 1975. Office: 2221 Neilson Way Santa Monica CA 90405

RAY, ROBERT D., physician, educator; b. Cleve., Sept. 21, 1914; s. Clifford A. and Edna (Durant) R.; m. Genevieve Triau, Dec. 19, 1953; children—Frances Carol, Robert Triau, Esten Bernard, Gisele Antoinette, Charles Alexander. B.A. cum laude, U. Calif., 1936, M.A., 1938, Ph.D., 1948; M.D., Harvard U., 1943; Hon. H.D. (Docent), Umeö, Sweden. Diplomate Am. Bd. Surgery. Teaching asst. in anatomy U. Calif. Med. Sch., 1937-38, Carnegie research fellow, 1938-40, instr. anatomy, 1947-48; postgrad. tng. U. Calif. Hosp., San Francisco, 1949; intern Peter Bent Brigham Hosp., Boston, 1943; resident orthopaedic surgery Children's Hosp., Boston, 1944-45; asst. orthopaedic surgery Harvard U. Med. Sch., 1944-45; asst. prof. surgery, head orthopaedic surgery U. Wash. Sch. Medicine, 1948-51, asso. prof. surgery, 1954-56; prof., chmn. dept. orthopaedic surgery Presbyn.-St. Luke's Hosp., 1956-70; also U. Ill. Med. Sch., Chgo., 1956-85; ret. 1985; chief surgery 61st Sta. Hosp.; theatre cons. orthopaedic surgery MTOUSA, 1945-47. Contbr. articles to profl. publs. Recipient ann. award for outstanding orthopaedic research Kappa Delta, Chgo., 1954. Mem. Am. Orthopaedic Assn., Orthopaedic Research Soc., Soc. Nuclear Medicine, Internat. Assn. Orthopaedics and Traumatology, AAAS, Am. Assn. Anatomists, Am. Acad. Orthopaedic Surgery, A.C.S., Sigma Xi, Phi Sigma. Home: 2200 Laguna Vista Dr Novato CA 94947

RAY, ROBERT GLENN, advertising agency executive; b. Santa Monica, Calif., Jan. 13, 1950; s. Ben Gorchakoff and Kathryn (Coger) R.; m. Elizabeth Mary Adler, Jan. 12, 1971; 1 dau., Kelly Anne; m. 2d, Christine May Cheney, Apr. 30, 1976. A.A. in Telecommunications, Los Angeles City Coll., 1969; student U. So. Calif., UCLA, Occidental U., Calif. State U.-Los Angeles. TV producer Dating Game, 1966; nat. radio program dir., 1970-71; pres., chief exec. officer Bob Ray Creative Services, Inc., Santa Clara, Calif., 1975—; radio personality, 1967-79; host, producer TV show; syndicated voice radio sta. chains; radio/TV voice-over talent; guest lectr. advt. and telecommunications industry San Jose Unified Sch. Dist., San Jose State U. Grand Marshall Diabetes, Mar., 1977, San Jose March of Dimes, 1979, 80. Recipient 1st place best radio comml. Cable Car Competition, 1980; Murphy Advt. awards in radio and TV, 1980-83, for best radio campaign and best radio comml., 1984; San Jose Women in Advt. for best radio comml., and best TV comml., 1984, best radio spot, best radio campaign, best of show awards No. Calif. Addy, 1986. Mem. AFTRA, Internat. Brotherhood Elec. Workers, San Jose Ad Club, San Jose Women in Advt. Office: Bob Ray Creative Services Inc 14573 Big Basin Way Bldg C Saratoga CA 95070-6013

RAY, RODERICK JACK, JR., engineering executive; b. Portland, Oreg., Apr. 15, 1956; s. Roderick Jack Ray and Nancy Lee (Halsey) Zahl. BS, Oreg. State U., 1979; MS, U. Colo., 1981, PhD, 1983. Registered profl. engr., Colo. Dir. separations div. Bend (Oreg.) Research, Inc., 1983—. Mem. editorial bd. Jour. Membrane Separation Engring. Mem. adv. bd. Deschutes County Mental Health Clinic, Cen. Oreg. Community Coll. of Engring. Named Oreg. Scholar, 1974. Mem. AAAS, Am. Chem. Soc., Am. Inst. Chem. Engring., Sigma Xi, Tau Beta Pi. Republican. Episcopalian. Home: 19635 Ridgewood Dr Bend OR 97701 Office: Bend Research Inc 64550 Research Rd Bend OR 97701

RAY, WILLIAM CARROL, insurance company executive; b. Mobile, Ala., Nov. 10, 1939; s. James Carrol and Helene Marie (Hesselink) R.; m. Bernardina Roos, July 31, 1962; children: Tine B., Michael V., James J. BSCE, U. Wyo., 1968; MS in Engring., U. Calif., Berkeley, 1971. Enlisted USAF, 1958, advanced through grades to capt., 1970, ret., 1978; supr. indsl. hygiene Ariz. State Compensation Fund, Phoenix, 1978-83, mgr. loss prevention, 1983—. Mem. Ariz. Gov's. Task Force of Asbestos in Sch., Phoenix, 1980-83. Fellow Am. Acad. Indsl. Hygiene; mem. Am. Indsl. Hygiene Assn. (pres. Ariz. chpt. 1982-83), Am. Soc. Safety Engrs.(pres. Ariz. chpt. 1986-87, profl.), Bd. cert. Safety Profls., Am. Conf. Govtl. Indsl. Hygienists, S.W. Safety Congress (exec. bd. dirs. 1980—). Republican. Avocations: tennis, jogging. Home: 15809 N 31st Ave Phoenix AZ 85023 Office: Ariz State Compensation Fund 1616 W Adams Phoenix AZ 85007

RAYFIELD, ROBERT EMMETT, acadmic educator; b. Fayetteville, N.C., May 27, 1929; s. Amos Martin and Ruth Evelyn (Bodiford) R.; m. Ann Michael Bergin, Dec. 18, 1953; children: Ellen, Loretta, Robin, Thomas, Margaret, Pamela, Elizabeth. BA, U. Fla., 1950, MA, 1951; PhD, U. Tex., 1977. Commd. USAF, 1951, advanced through grades to col.; dep. dir. info. Strategic Air Command, Offutt AFB, Nebr., 1975-77, dir. pub. affairs, 1982-83, asst. col., 1977-78; dir. info. 15 airforce Strategic Air Command, March AFB, Calif., 1978-79; dir. pub. affairs U.S. Forces, Yokota AFB, Japan, 1979-82; ret. USAF, 1983; assoc. prof. Calif. State U., Fullerton, 1983—; mem. editorial bd. Pacific Stars and Stripes, Pacific Command, Tokyo, 1979-82; mem. program bd. Armed Forces Radio and TV Service, Pacific Air Force, Yokota AFB, 1979-82. Co-author: A brief History of The Anderson Grove Church, 1978; editor: Line Backer II: A view From The Rock, 1979; contbr. articles and papers to profl. jour. Escort internat. disting. visitors Orange County (Calif.) Office Protocol, 1986; Orangewood Pub. Relation Bd., Orange, Calif., 1986. Mem. Pub. Relations Soc. Am. (v.p. 1975, bd. dirs., chmn.-elect nat. educators sect.), Soc. Profl. Journalists, Air Force Assn., 15th Air Force Assn. Democrat. Roman Catholic. Avocations: light plane flying, writing, computer programming. Office: Dept Communications Calif State U Fullerton CA 92634

RAYMOND, EUGENE THOMAS, aircraft engineer; b. Seattle, Apr. 17, 1923; s. Evan James and Katheryn Dorothy (Kranick) R.; m. Bette Mae Bergeson, Mar. 1, 1948; children—Joan Kay Hibbs, Patricia Lynn, Robin Louise. B.S.M.E., U. Wash., 1944; postgrad., 1953-55; registered profl. engr., Tex. Research engr. The Boeing Co., Seattle, 1946-59, sr. group engr., 1959-63, 66-71, sr. specialist engr., 1971-81, prin. engr. flight control tech., 1982—; project design engr. Gen. Dynamics, Ft. Worth, 1963-66. Served to lt., USNR, 1943-46, 49-52; PTO. Recipient prize Hydraulics and Pneumatics mag., 1958. Mem. Soc. Automotive Engrs. (cert. of appreciation, chmn. adv. bd.com. A-6 nat. com. for aerospace fluid power and control tech. 1983—, vice-chmn. com. 1986—), Fluid Power Soc., Puget Sound Fluid Power Assn., AIAA, Beta Theta Pi. Lutheran. Clubs: Meridian Valley Country, Masons, Shriners. Aircraft editorial adv. bd. Hydraulics and Pneumatics mag., 1960-70; contbr. articles profl. jours. Patentee in field. Home: 25301 144 Ave SE Kent WA 98042 Office: PO Box 3707 Seattle WA 98124

RAYMOND, GENE, actor, producer, director, composer; b. N.Y.C., Aug. 13, 1908; s. LeRoy D. and Mary (Smith) Guion; m. Jeanette MacDonald, June 16, 1937 (dec. Jan. 14, 1965); m. former Mrs. Nel Bentley Hees, Sept. 8, 1974. Student, Profl. Children's Sch., N.Y.C. Broadway debut in: The Piper, 1920; other Broadway appearances include Eyvind of the Hills, 1921, Why Not?, 1922, The Potters, 1923, Cradle Snatchers, 1925, Take My Advice, 1927, Mirrors, 1928, Sherlock Holmes, 1928, Say When, 1928, The War Song, 1928, Jonesy, 1929, Young Sinners, 1929, A Shadow of My Enemy, 1957; other theater ppearances include The Man in Possession, Dennis, Mass., 1946; other theater appearances include The Guardsman, 1951, The Voice of the Turtle, 1952, Angel Street, Richmond, Va., 1952, Petrified Forest, 1952, Call Me Madam, 1952, Private Lives, 1953, The Moon is Blue, 1953, Be Quiet, 1953, My Love, 1953, Detective Story, 1954, The Devil's Disciple, 1954, The Fifth Season, 1955, Will Success Spoil Rock Hunter, Los Angeles, San Francisco, 1956, Los Angeles, San Francisco, 1956, Romeo and Juliet, 1956, The Seven Year Itch, 1958, Holiday for Lovers, Chgo., 1959; appeared as Joseph Cantwell in nat. touring co.: The Best Man, 1960; other theater appearances include Majority of One, 1962, Write Me A Murder, 1962, Mr. Roberts, 1962, Kiss Me Kate, 1962; other roles include Candida, 1961, The Moon is Blue, 1963, Madly in Love, 1963; film appearances include Personal Maid, 1931, Stolen Heaven, 1931, Ladies of the Big House, 1932, The Night of June 13th, 1932, Forgotten Commandments, 1932, If I Had a Million, 1932, Red Dust, 1932, Ex-Lady, 1933, The House on 56th Street, 1933, Zoo in Budapest, 1933, Brief Moment, 1933, Ann Carver's Profession, 1933, Flying Down to Rio, 1933, Sadie McKee, 1934, I Am Suzanne, 1934, Coming Out Party, 1934, Transatlantic Merry-Go-Round, 1934, Behold My Wife, 1935, The Woman in Red, 1935, Seven Keys to Baldpate, 1935, Hooray for Love, 1935, Love on a Bet, 1936, Walking on Air, 1936, The Bride Walks Out, 1936, The Smartest Girl in Town, Transient Lady, 1936, There Goes My Girl, 1937, Life of the Party, 1937, That Girl From Paris, 1939, Mr. and Mrs. Smith, 1939; film appearances include: Cross-Country Romance, 1940, Smilin' Thru', 1941; film appearances include The Locket, 1946, Assigned to Danger, 1948, Million-Dollar Weekend, 1948, Sofia, 1948, Hit the Deck, 1955, Plunder Road, 1957, The Best Man, 1964, I'd Rather Be Rich, 1964; TV appearances include: U.S. Steel Hour, 1920, The Defenders, 1920, Playhouse 90, 1920, Ironside, 1920, Name of the Game, 1920, Judd for the Defense, 1920, Bold Ones, 1920; TV appearances include Mannix, others; author: teleplay Prima Donna; composer: songs Release, Will You'9 , Le Me Always Sing. Past v.p. Arthritis Found. So. Calif.; pres. Motion Picture and TV Fund, 1980. Served with USAAF, 1942-45, ETO; served to col. USAFR, 1945-68. Decorated Legion of Merit and others.; Recipient Disting. Service award Arthritis Found.; Humanitarian award Air Force Assn.; Better World award VFW; Bronze Halo award So. Calif. Motion Picture Council. Mem. Screen Actors Guild (dir.), Acad. TV Arts and Scis. (bd. dirs.), Air Force Assn. (pres. Los Angeles chpt.). Clubs: Players (N.Y.C.); N.Y. Athletic; Bel Air Country (Los Angeles); Army and Navy (Washington); Order of Daedalians. Address: 9570 Wilshire Blvd Beverly Hills CA 90212

RAYMOND, GREGORY JACK, research biochemist, molecular geneticist; b. Brockton, Mass., Aug. 18, 1951; s. Jack Darrell and Alice Josephine (Baker) R.; m. Kathleen Campbell, Dec. 24, 1984. BA with honors, U. Wyo., 1973, BS in Chemistry/Biology Edn., 1987. Research assoc. U. Wyo., Laramie, 1979—; rep. staff council, U. Wyo., 1981-85, chmn., 1983-84, mem. budget com., 1983-84, mem. instl. biosafety com., 1985—. Contbr. articles to profl. jours. Named Eagle Scout Boy Scouts Am., 1967. Mem. AAAS, Phi Kappa Phi, Delta Sigma Phi. Avocations: backpacking, hunting, fly fishing, photography, gardening. Home: 356 N Buchanan St Laramie WY 82070 Office: U Wyo Dept Molecular Biology Box 3944 Univ Station Laramie WY 82071

RAYMOND, LAWRENCE PAUL, natural research company executive; b. Pasadena, Calif., Nov. 3, 1944; s. Stanley Walter Raymond and Pauline (Scherer) Johnson. BS, San Diego State Coll., 1968; PhD, U. Calif., Santa Cruz, 1979; MBA, U. Colo., 1986. Research asst. U.S. Bur. Comml. Fisheries, La Jolla, Calif., 1964-69; head environ. analysis and planning Oceanic Found., Waimanalo, Hawaii, 1971-75; cons. biomass prodn. State Dept. Planning and Econ. Devel., Honolulu, 1975-79; research scientist food and agriculture Battelle N.W. Inc., Richland, Wash., 1977-78; mgr. biomass program Solar Energy Research Inst., Golden, Colo., 1979-84; chief exec. officer Internat. Bio-Resources, Lakewood, Colo., 1983—; pres., chief exec. officer Inland Mariculture Co., Lakewood, Colo., 1986—; advisor marine biomass program Gas Research Inst., Chgo., 1980-83; advisor hyacinth project Disney World, Orlando, Fla., 1981-83; advisor Gov.'s Office Marine Affairs, Honolulu, 1975-79; co-chmn. biotech. 1st U.S.-China Tech. Exchange, Beijing, Peoples Republic of China, 1982. Contbr. articles to profl. jours.; patentee in field. Mem. Joint-Interagy. Subcom. on Aquaculture, Washington, 1981-82, Interagy. Subcom. Resource Recovery, Washington, 1979-80. Recipient Letter of Commendation, Garrison Study Commn., Denver, 1985. Mem. Phycol. Soc. Am. Republican. Roman Catholic. Avocations: sailing, swimming, hiking, scuba diving. Home: 14409 W Ellsworth Ave Golden CO 80401 Office: Internat Bio-Resources Inc 274 Union Blvd Suite 220 Lakewood CO 80228

RAYNDON, DARRA LYNN, lawyer; b. Andalusia, Ala., May 25, 1950; d. Loren Sibley and Mary Lou (Hardee) Campbell. BA in English, Birmingham So. Coll., 1972; JD, U. Wis., 1972-74; LLM in Tax, Georgetown U., 1981. Bar: Wis. 1975, N.Mex. 1977, Miss. 1979, Ariz. 1980, Md. 1981. Sole practice Madison, Wis., 1975-76, Albuquerque, 1977-80; in-house counsel Dixie Pine Chems., Hattiesburg, Miss., 1978-84; sole practice Washington, 1980-82; assoc. Killian, Legg, Nicholas, Fischer, Wirken, Cook & Pew, Mesa, Ariz., 1982-87; sole practice Mesa, 1987—; instr. grad. tax program Golden Gate U., Phoenix, 1983-85; legal counsel Children of the Earth Found., Tempe, Ariz., 1983—; bd. dirs. Lumberton Tech. Labs., Portfolio Dynamics Inc. Contbr. articles to profl. jours. Bd. dirs. Mesa

Symphony Orch., 1986—; co-chmn. 1984 Gov.'s Arts Awards Dinner, Mesa, 1983-84. Mem. Ariz. State Bar Assn., Maricopa County Bar Assn., East Valley Bar Assn. (sec. 1985-86, pres. elect 1986, pres. 1987), Ariz. Women Lawyer's Assn., Arts in Mesa Awards Com. Avocations: hiking, tennis, travel, music. Home: 8632 S Terrace Rd Tempe AZ 85284

RAYNER, ANTHONY GEORGE, bakery manager; b. Caterham, Surrey, Eng., July 11, 1944; came to U.S., 1974; s. George Victor and Nora Helen (Braker) R.; m. Ann Marie Louis Brush, Apr. 2, 1966 (div. Apr. 1983); children: Michelle Christine, Nicola Anne; m. Margaret Jean Davidson, June 29, 1985. City and guilds baking degrees, Croydon Tech. Coll., London, 1963. Mgr. bakery Sun Valley (Idaho) Co., 1974-76; v.p., gen. mgr. Anthony's Continental Bakery, Boise, Idaho, 1976-78; asst. gen. mgr. Mammas Restaurant and Old World Catering, Boise, 1978-83; bakery mgr. Smiths Mgmt. Corp., Boise, 1983-84; v.p. mfg.. Le Chatel Corp., Seattle, 1984—. Fellow City and Guilds Baking Inst.; mem. Idaho State Chef's Assn. (v.p. 1977-80), Royal Scottish Dance Soc. Presbyterian. Avocations: painting, dancing, cycling, fishing, indoor plants. Office: Le Chatel Corp 12735 28th Ave NE Suite A Seattle WA 98025

RAYNES, MARYBETH, psychotherapist; b. Provo, Utah, Apr. 16, 1945; s. Lincoln Francis and Beth (Milner) R.; m. Edward Partridge Black, Feb. 27, 1969 (div. May 1977); children: Teriesa, Nathan Jeffrey, Sara; m. Alan Thayer Parsons, July 29, 1983. BS in Psychology, Brigham Young U., 1965, MS in Marriage and Family Relationships, 1969; MSW, U. Utah, 1979. Licensed clin. social worker, Utah; licensed marriage and family therapist, Utah. Asst. dir. Manzanita Hall, Ariz State U., Tempe, 1969-70; spl. faculty Brigham Young U. Extension Ctr., Salt Lake City, Utah, 1972-79; assoc. instr. family and consumer studies dept., U. Utah, Salt Lake City, 1972-79; clin. social worker Salt Lake County Mental Health, 1979-86; pvt. practice psychotherapy Salt Lake City, 1981—; bd. dirs. Utah Council on Family Relations, 1979-82; clin. faculty Grad. Sch. of Social Work, U. Utah, 1981—, curriculum adv. com., 1984-85. Bd. editors Jour. Assn. Mormon Counselors and Psycholtherapists; columnist Sunstone mag., 1982—; contbr. articles to profl. jours. Mem. Gov.s' Commn. on Status of Women, Salt Lake City, 1978-80; mem. adv. bd. B.H. Roberts Soc., Salt Lake City, 1985—; speaker schs., church, women's orgns. Named Clin. Faculty of Yr., Grad. Sch. of Social Work, U. Utah, 1983-84. Mem. Am. Assn. of Marriage and Family Therapy (clin. mem.), Acad. of Cert. Social Workers (diplomate), Nat. Assn. of Social Workers, Assn. for Transpersonal Psychology. Mormon. Home: 225 6th Ave Salt Lake City UT 84103 Office: 24 M St 2 Salt Lake City UT 84103

RAZ, SHERYL WILEY, data processing specialist; b. Spokane, Wash., Sept. 4, 1945; s. Ernest Raymond and Lova Lorine (Sullivan) Wiley; m. William Larry Raz, Feb. 15, 1969; children: John Michael, Ernest William. Student, Lewis and Clark Coll., 1963-65; BM, Westminster Choir Coll., 1969; postgrad., Portland Community Coll., 1977-79; MBA, U. Portland, 1986. Minister music Hillsdale Community Ch., Portland, Oreg., 1969-76, Lake Oswego (Oreg.) United Ch. Christ, 1976-85; programmer Clackamas County Edn. Service Dist., Marylhurst, Oreg., 1979-81, systems analyst, 1981-83; systems and programming mgr. Oreg. Mutual Ins. Co., McMinnville, 1983—. Contbr. articles to profl. jours. Active Parent Tchr. Coop., Portland, 1979—. Mem. Acad. Mgmt., Inst. Profl. Women, Am. Bus. Women's Assn. Republican. Avocations: flying, organ, guitar. Home: 7640 SW 71st St Portland OR 97223 Office: Oreg Mutual Ins PO Box 808 McMinnville OR 97128

RAZRAN, GILBERT BRUCE, research co. exec., indsl. engr.; b. Walsenburg, Colo., Sept. 25, 1926; s. Bernard A. and Carolina I. (De Mallieu) R.; A.B., U. Miami (Fla.), 1949, M.S., 1950; Ph.D. in Indsl. Bioengring., Purdue U., 1953; m. Charlotte D. Bellant, Nov. 8, 1969; children—Rita Lynn, Steven Barry. Project engr. Gen. Electric Co., Ithaca, N.Y., 1953-59; systems analyst Burroughs Corp. Research Center, Paoli, Pa., 1959-63; dir. ops. research office Command & Control Systems, Washington, 1963-65; pres. Sci. Operational Systems, San Diego, 1965—; chmn., chief exec. officer Kingrexx, Inc., 1983—; prof. Grad. Sch., U.S. Internat. U., Calif., 1969-73; mem. U.S. Sci. Study Rev. Group, UN, Geneva, 1971. Mem. Library Bd., Upper Merion Twp., Pa., 1960-63. Bd. dirs. SOS-Disc, Inc., Las Vegas, Nev., chmn., 1972-75. Served with USNR, 1944-46; PTO; to capt. USAF, 1950-52. Recipient Inventor of Yr. award Patent Law Assn., 1980; registered profl. engr., N.Y., Pa., Calif. Mem. Nat. Security Indsl. Assn., Assn. for Advancement Med. Instrumentation, Mil. Ops. Research Soc., Am. Psychol. Assn., IEEE, Psi Chi, Sigma Xi. Author: Programmed Instruction Book in Electronics, 1966; CAI in Vocational Training, 1967. Contbr. articles to sci. jours. Inventor of oculometer. Office: SOS Inc 4380 Viewridge Rd San Diego CA 92123 Office: ILR Med Clinics Ltd, 9 Tooting High St, London SW17, England

REA, DONALD GEORGE, space research and exploration executive; b. Portage la Prairie, Man., Can., Sept. 21, 1929; came to U.S., 1951, naturalized, 1962; s. Hugh Charles and Jessie Mae (Miners) R.; m. Therese Hillman, Nov. 11, 1967; children: Michael Hugh, Steven Martin. BS, U. Man., Winnipeg, Can., 1950, MS, 1952, DSc, 1980; PhD, MIT, 1954. Postdoctoral research fellow Oxford (Eng.) U., 1954-55; dep. dir. planetary program office NASA, Washington, 1968-70; asst. lab. dir. for sci. Jet Propulsion Lab., Pasadena, Calif., 1970-76, dep. asst. lab. dir. for tech. and space program devel., 1979-80, asst lab dir. for tech. and space program devel., 1980—; research fellow J.F. Kennedy Sch. Govt. Harvard U., Cambridge, Mass., 1979-80. Assoc. editor ICARUS, 1968-76, Jour. of Geophys. Research, 1968-70; tech. editor IEEE Trans. Geosci. Electronics, 1976—; contbr. articles to profl. jours. Recipient Exceptional Sci. Achievement medal NASA, 1969, Exceptional Service medal NASA, 1985. Mem. AIAA, AAAS, Am. Astron. Soc., Am. Chem. Soc., Am. Inst. Physics, Am. Geophys. Union, Linda Vista Annandale Assn. (pres. bd. dirs. 1981-82). Democrat. Home: 1605 Pegfair Estates Dr Pasadena CA 91103 Office: Jet Propulsion Lab MS 180-704 4800 Oak Grove Dr Pasadena CA 91109

READ, ELEANOR MAY, financial analyst; b. Arcadia, N.Y., July 4, 1942; d. Henry and Lena May (Fagner) Van Koevering; 1 child, Robin Jo. Typist, clk., sec., credit corr. Sarah Coventry, Inc., Newark, N.Y., 1957-61; exec. sec. Mobil Chem. Co., Macedon, N.Y., 1961-68; bus. mgr. Henry's Hardware, Newark, 1968-72; with Xerox Corp., Fremont, Calif., 1973—, internat. clk. analyst, personnel adminstrv. asst., employment coordinator, exec. sec., cycle count analyst., tax preparer H&R Block, 1985—. Mem. Xerox/Diablo Mgmt. Assn., Am. Mgmt. Assn., Profl. Businesswomen's Assn. Office: 910 Page Ave FM-239 Fremont CA 94538

READ, ROBERT RICHARD, mathematical statistics educator; b. Columbus, Ohio, Oct. 5, 1929; s. Ira Jay and Pearl V. (Scott) R.; m. Dagmar Ann Ruud, Dec. 19, 1963 (div. Sept. 1974); children: Christopher, Steven, Darren. BSc, Ohio State U., 1951; PhD, U. Calif., Berkeley, 1958. Lectr., research statistician U. Calif., Berkeley, 1957-60; asst. prof. U. Chgo., 1961; prof. USN Postgrad. Sch., Monterey, Calif., 1961—; cons. Maritime Cargo Transp. Conf., San Francisco, 1959, United Tech. Ctr., Sunnyvale, Calif., 1962-65. Contbr. research articles to profl. jours. Coach Carmel (Calif.) Youth Baseball, 1972-85; parent supr. Safe Rides, Carmel, 1983-86. Mem. Inst. Math. Statistics, Sigma Xi. Home: PO Box 6191 Carmel CA 93921 Office: USN Postgrad Sch Monterey CA 93942

READE, ROBERT MELLOR, advertising executive; b. Elmhurst, Ill., Jan. 9, 1940; s. M.G. and Virginia A. (Mellor) R.; m. Carol Jean Coon, May 26, 1962; children—Christopher, Gregory. B.A. in Liberal Arts, U. Ariz., 1962. Charting mgr. Eller Outdoor Advt., Phoenix, 1964-69; sales mgr. Mullins Neon, Denver, 1969-70; pres. Gannett Outdoor Co. Ariz., Phoenix, 1970-84; sr. v.p. Gannett Outdoor Group, N.Y.C., 1984-85; sr. v.p. real estate and devel. Circle K Corp., Phoenix, 1985-86; pres., chief operating officer Circle K Internat., Phoenix, 1986—; bd. dirs. Western Savs. and Loan. Chmn. Phoenix chpt. Am. Humanics, 1983, Valley Youth Coalition, 1981, Phoenix City Bond Election, 1984; active Thunderbirds, 1978-83, Theodore council Boy Scouts Am., Community Council, Phoenix United Way, Camelback Mental Health Found. Served with USAR, 1963-69. Recipient U. Ariz. Alumni Appreciation award, 1975, 77, Slouaker award, 1977; Anti Defamation League Torch of Liberty award, 1981. Mem. Ariz. Safety Assn. (pres. 1981), Young Pres. Orgn., Outdoor Assn. Am., Inst. Outdoor Advt., Phoenix Advt. Club (pres. 1974). Club: Rotary (pres. 1982). Office: Circle K Convinience Stores Inc PO Box 52084 Phoenix AZ 85072

READER, AUGUST LAFAYETTE, III, neurophthalmologist; b. Ft. Worth, Feb. 24, 1949; s. August Lafayette and Charlotte Ann (Perkins) R.; children; Adrienne Marie, Elizabeth Ann; m. Nanette Marie Starke, May 11, 1984. B.S. in Biology, U. Tex., 1970, M.D., 1974. Diplomate Nat. Bd. Med. Examiners, Am. Bd. Ophthalmology. Intern in neurology Nat. Naval Med. Ctr., Bethesda, Md., 1974-75, resident in ophthalmology, 1975-76; fellow in neuroophthal E.S. Harkness Eye Inst., N.Y.C., 1978-79; neuroophthalmologist dept. ophthalmology Naval Hosp., San Diego, 1979-83, asst. chmn., 1983; neuroophthalmologist, ptnr. Beverly Hills Eye Med. Group, Los Angeles, 1983—; staff ophthalmologist Children's Hosp., Los Angeles, 1983—, Midway Hosp., Los Angeles, 1983—, Cedars-Sinai Med. Ctr., Los Angeles, 1984—; asst. clin. prof. U. So. Calif., Los Angeles, 1983—. Contbr. articles to med. jours. Served to lt. comdr. USN, 1973-83. Recipient cert. of appreciation from Alfred Atherton, U.S. Ambassador to Egypt, 1982. Fellow Am. Acad. Ophthalmology; mem. AMA, Calif. Med. Assn., Los Angeles County Med. Assn., Frank Walsh Soc. Democrat.

READER, PAUL DOUGLAS, manufacturing company executive; b. Cleve., Mar. 13, 1937; s. Austin Frederick and Geraldine Melrose (Bellinger) R.; m. Alice Marie Krupla, Sept. 13, 1958 (div. Feb. 1983); m. Gail Kathryn Baker, June 29, 1985; children: Timothy P., Amy M. BSE, Cleve. State U., 1960. Mem. tech. staff and sect. head NASA, Cleve., 1960-66, br. chief, 1969-72; asst. exec. sec. office adminstr. NASA, Washington, 1967; with Jet Propulsion Lab. NASA, Pasadena, Calif., 1968; with Electro Optical Div. Hughes, Culver City, Calif., 1973; pres. Ion Tech. Inc., Ft. Collins, Colo., 1974—. Contbr. articles to profl. jours.; patentee in field. Mem. Soc. Vacuum Coaters. Avocations: flying, soaring, sailing. Office: Ion Tech Inc 2330 E Prospect St Fort Collins CO 80525

READING, JAMES EDWARD, urban transportation executive; b. Milw., June 26, 1924; s. James Edward and Helen Marie (Boehm) R.; m. Ada Irene Kelly, May 24, 1944; children—Wendy Irene, James David, Christopher Kelly, Mary Katherine, Kevin Sinclair. Student, San Diego State U., 1942, Ga. Inst. Tech., 1944. With Union-Tribune Pub. Co., San Diego, 1942-59; dist. mgr. Union-Tribune Pub. Co., 1953-58, circulation promotion mgr., 1958-59; adminstrv. asst. to v.p. Copley Newspapers, La Jolla, Calif., 1959-60; dir. advt. and public relations San Diego Transit System, 1960-67; dir. mktg. Calif. Motor Express, 1967-68; asst. to exec. v.p. Am. Transit Assn., Washington, 1968; v.p. Nat. City Mgmt. Co.; resident mgr. Regional Transit Service, Rochester, N.Y., 1968-74; asst. gen. mgr. ops. regional transit dist. Denver, 1974-77; gen. mgr. Central Ohio Transit Authority, Columbus, 1977-85; dir. Santa Clara County Transp. Agy., San Jose, Calif., 1985—; guest lectr. numerous univs. Served with U.S. Army, 1943-46, ETO. Named Public Relations Man of Yr. Public Relations Club, San Diego, 1962; recipient Mass Transp. Adminstrs. award for outstanding pub. service, 1980, 82. Mem. Public Relations Soc. Am., Am. Public Transit Assn. (v.p. mktg.) Transp. Research Bd., Am. Soc. Pub. Adminstrs., Am. Legion, Tau Kappa Epsilon. Republican. Roman Catholic. Club: Rotary. Home: 887 Del Rio Ct Milpitas CA 95035 Office: 1555 Berger Dr San Jose CA 95112

READY, KENNETH LLOYD, forester; b. Willis, Tex., Sept. 16, 1934; s. Henry Bryant Ready and Grace Leon (Steed) Johnson; m. Annita Grace Draper, June 6, 1955; children: Dennis Edward, Clinton Crawford. B in Forestry, Stephen F. Austin State U., 1962. Lic. profl. forester, Calif. Forestry technician USDA Forest Service, Mammoth Lakes, Calif., 1961, 62-63; timber mgr. USDA Forest Service, Cleveland, Tex., 1963-64; watershed mgr. USDA Forest Service, Ashland, Miss., 1965; land mgr. USDA Forest Service, Saugus and Lake Almanor, Calif., 1966-78; silviculture forester USDA Forest Service, Ogden, Utah, 1978-81; genetics forester USDA Forest Service, Albuquerque, 1981—. Author: (with others) Silvicultural Systems For The Major Forest Types Of The United States, 1983. Served to sgt. USMC, 1954-58. Mem. Soc. Am. Foresters, Am. Forestry. Assn. Avocations: artist, cartooning, petrography. Home: 4609 Los Reyes Rd SE Rio Rancho NM 87124 Office: USDA Forest Service 517 Gold Ave SW Albuquerque NM 87102

REAGAN, GARY DON, lawyer; b. Amarillo, Tex., Aug. 23, 1941; s. Hester and Lois Irene (Marcum) R.; m. Nedra Ann Nash, Sept. 12, 1964; children—Marc, Kristi, Kari, Brent. A.B., Stanford U., 1963, J.D., 1965. Bar: N.Mex. 1965, U.S. Dist. Ct. N.Mex., 1965. Assoc. Smith & Ransom, Albuquerque, 1965-67; ptnr. Smith, Ransom, Deaton & Reagan, Albuquerque, 1967-68, Williams, Johnson, Houston, Reagan & Porter, Hobbs, N.Mex., 1968-77, Williams, Johnson, Reagan, Porter & Love, Hobbs, 1977-82; sole practice, Hobbs, 1982—; city atty. City of Hobbs, 1978-80; City of Eunice, N.M., 1980—; instr. N.Mex. Jr. Coll. and Coll. of S.W., Hobbs, 1978-84. Mayor, City of Hobbs, 1972-73, 76-77, city commr., 1970-78; pres., dir. Jr. Achievement of Hobbs, 1974-85; pres., trustee Landsun Homes, Inc., Carlsbad, N.Mex., 1972-84; trustee Lydia Patterson Inst., El Paso, Tex., 1972-84, N.Mex. Conf. United Meth. Ch., 1984—; chmn. County Democratic Com., 1983-85. Mem. ABA, State Bar N.Mex. (coms.), Lea County Bar Assn. (pres. 1976-77), Hobbs C. of C. (v.p. 1986-87). Lodge: Rotary (pres. Hobbs 1985-86), Hobbs Tennis (pres. 1974-75). Home: 200 Eagle Dr Hobbs NM 88240 Office: 501 N Linam Hobbs NM 88240

REAGAN, JANET THOMPSON, psychologist, educator; b. Monticello, Ken., Sept. 15, 1945; d. Virgil Joe and Carrie Mae (Alexander) Thompson; m. Robert Barry Reagan, Jr., Aug. 7, 1977; children—Natalia Alexandria, Robert Barry. B.A. in Psychology, Berea Coll., 1967; Ph.D. in Psychology, Vanderbilt U., 1972. Mgr. research and eval. Nashville Mental Health Center, 1971-72; mgr. eval. Family Health Found., New Orleans, 1973-74; asst. prof. dept. health systems mgmt. Tulane U., New Orleans, 1974-77; dir. eval. Project Heavy West, Los Angeles, 1977-78; lectr. dept. pub. adminstrn. U. So. Calif., 1979-82; asst. prof. health adminstrn. Calif. State U.-Northridge, 1978-83, assoc. prof., director health adminstrn., 1983—; cons. in field. Mem. Am. Pub. Health Assn., Assn. Health Services Research, Western Psychol. Assn., Eval. Research Soc., Psi Chi, Phi Kappa Phi. Mem. editorial adv. bd. Jour. of Long Term Care Administrn.; contbr. articles to profl. jours., papers to profl. assns. Home: 9354 Encino Ave Northridge CA 91325 Office: Calif State U Dept Health Sci Northridge CA 91330

REAL, JACK GARRET, helicopter company executive; b. Baraga, Mich., May 31, 1916; s. Edward Ignatius and Elizabeth Irene (Leary) R.; m. Janeth May Paden, Nov. 20, 1941; children: Daniel, Patricia. BSME, Mich. Tech. U., 1937, D in Engring. (hon.), 1968; D in Engring. (hon.), Selma Coll., 1984, Northrop U., 1985. Registered profl. engr., Calif. Jr. engr. to chief devel. engr. Lockheed Aircraft, Burbank, Calif., 1939-65, v.p. rotary wing, 1965-71; v.p. aviation Hughes Tool Co., Encino, Calif., 1971-76; sr. v.p. aviation Summa Corp., Los Vegas, 1977—; pres. Hughes Helicopter Co., Culver City, Calif., 1979; bd. dirs. Midway Airline, Chgo., Evergreen Internat., McMinnville, Oreg., Davey Industries, Cin. Contbr. articles to profl. jours. Bd. dirs. Great Western council Boy Scouts Am., Los Angeles, 1965—; bd. overseers U. Pa. Sch. Engring. and Applied Sci., Phila., 1975-81. Served to 1st lt. C.E., U.S. Army, 1937-42. Recipient Americanism award Boy Scouts Am., 1983. Fellow AIAA; mem. Am. Helicopter Soc., Am. Assn. Army Aviation. Democrat. Roman Catholic. Club: Calif. Yacht. Office: McDonnell Douglas Helicopter Co Centinela and Teale Sts Culver City CA 90230

REAL, MANUEL LAWRENCE, U.S. district judge; b. San Pedro, Calif., Jan. 27, 1924; s. Francisco Jose and Maria (Mansano) R.; m. Stella Emilia Michalik, Oct. 15, 1955; children: Michael, Melanie Marie, Timothy, John Robert. B.S., U. So. Calif., 1944, student fgn. trade, 1946-48; LL.B., Loyola Sch. Law, Los Angeles, 1951. Bar: Calif. 1952. Asst. U.S. Atty.'s Office, Los Angeles, 1952-55; pvt. practice law San Pedro, Calif., 1955-64; U.S. atty. So. Dist. Calif., 1964-66; U.S. dist. judge 1966—, now chief judge. Served to ensign USNR, 1943-46. Mem. Am., Fed., Los Angeles County bar assns., State Bar Calif., Am. Judicature Soc., Chief Spl. Agts. Assn., Phi Delta Phi, Sigma Chi. Democrat. Roman Catholic. Club: Anchor (Los Angeles). Office: US Courthouse 312 N Spring St Los Angeles CA 90012 *

REAM, ALLEN K., anesthesiologist, educator; b. Oakland, Calif., May 30, 1938. SB in Indsl. Mgmt., MIT, 1962, SB in Elec. Engring., 1962; MS in Elec. Engring., Stanford U., 1965; MS in Physiology, Northwestern U., 1967, MD, 1967. Intern Stanford (Calif.) U., 1967-68, asst. prof., 1973-79, cardiovascular anesthesiologist, 1973—, assoc. prof., 1979—; dir. med. sci. and clin. evaluation Inst. Engring. Design in Medicine, Stanford (Calif.) U., 1976—; resident in anesthesia U. Calif., San Francisco, 1971-73; vis. scholar U. Leiden, The Netherlands, 1980; bd. dirs. Anesthesia Patient Safety Found. Editor Jour. Clin. Monitoring, 1984—; bd. editors Internat. Jour. Clin. Monitoring and Computing, 1984-85; contbr. numerous articles to profl. jours. Recipient Borden Research award Pi Kappa Epsilon. Fellow Am. Coll. Anesthesiologists, Biomed. Engring. Soc. (bd. dirs.), Royal Soc. Medicine; mem. AAAS, Am. Heart Assn., Am. Soc. Anesthesiologists (various coms. 1982—), Assn. Advancement Med. Instrumentation (co-chmn. annual meeting 1984), Assn. Computing Machinery, Assn. Cardiac Anesthesiologists, Assn. U. Anesthetists, Calif. Soc. Anesthesiologists, IEEE, Internat. Soc. Artificial Organs, Soc. Critical Care Medicine, Soc. Cardiovascular Anesthesiologists, Soc. Neurosurg. Anesthesia, Nat. Com. Anesthesiology Rev. (editorial bd. 1979—), Biannual conf. patient monitoring (steering com. 1977—), Hosp. Instrumentation Com. (chmn. 1974—), Tau Beta Pi, Sigma Xi. Office: Stanford U Dept Anesthesia S-280 Stanford CA 94305

REAMS, LEE THOMAS, business executive, tax accountant, mechanical engineer; b. El Centro, Calif., Sept. 11, 1934; s. Lee B. and Sarah E. R.; m. Anne M. Morton, Sept. 18, 1965; children—Cheryll, Susan, Lee, Robert. B.S. in Mech. Engring., Calif. State U.-San Luis Obispo, 1957. Enrolled agt. IRS. Mech. engr. Rocketdyne div. Rockwell Internat., Canoga Park, Calif., 1957-75; pvt. practice tax acctg., Woodland Hills, Calif., 1972—; founder, pres. Ind. Preparer Services, Inc., Glendale, Calif., 1977—; gen. ptnr. Realty Investment Fund, Los Angeles, 1981—; lectr. tax law. Served with USN, 1952-60. Republican. Presbyterian. Author: Tax Implications of Divorce, 1981; Tax Implications of Real Estate Transactions, 1980, Tax Implications of Rental Property, 1981; Building A Successful Tax Practice, 1980. Office: Ind Preparer Services Inc 5115 Douglas Fir Suite H Calabasas CA 91302

REARDEN, CAROLE ANN, clinical pathologist, educator; b. Belleville, Ont., Can., June 11, 1946; d. Joseph Brady and Honora Patricia (O'Halloran) R. BSc, McGill U., 1969, MSc, MDCM, 1971. Diplomate Am. Bd. Pathology, Am. Bd. Immunohematology and Blood Banking. Resident and fellow Children's Meml. Hosp., Chgo., 1971-73; resident in pediatrics U. Calif., San Diego, 1974, resident then fellow, 1975-79, dir. histocompatability and clin. immunology lab., asst. prof. pathology, 1979-86, assoc. prof., 1986—; prin. investigator devel. monoclonal antibodies to erythroid antigens. Contbr. articles to profl. jours. Mem. Mayor's Task Force on Acquired Immune Deficiency Syndrome, San Diego, 1983. Recipient Young Investigator Research award NIH, 1979; grantee U. Calif. Cancer research Coordinating Com., 1982, NIH, 1983. Mem. Am. Assn. Pathologists, Am. Fed. Clin. Research, Am. Soc. Hematology, Am. Assn. Blood Banks (com. organ transplantation and issue typing 1982—), Am. Assn. Clin. Histocompatibility Testing, Am. Soc. Transplant Physicians. Office: U Calif Med Ctr Dept Pathology H-720 225 Dickinson St San Diego CA 92103

REARICK, DAVID EUGENE, research chemist; b. Mitchell, S.D., Nov. 12, 1943; s. David Edwin and Caryl Lorraine (Forell) R.; m. Pamela Jean Van Pelt, June 13, 1965; children: Elizabeth, Carol, David, John. BA, U. Oreg., 1966; PhD, U. Rochester, 1971. Postdoctoral fellow Ind. U., 1970-71, U. Louisville, 1971-73; instr. chemistry U. Va., Charlottesville, 1973-74; research chemist Amalgamated Sugar Co., Twin Falls, Idaho, 1974—; mem. exec. com. U.S. Nat. Com. Sugar Analysis, 1985—. Patentee in field; contbr. articles in field. Mem. Am. Chem. Soc., Assn. Official Analytical Chemists, Am. Soc. Sugar Beet Technologists. Lodge: Masons. Office: Amalgamated Sugar Co PO Box 127 Twin Falls ID 83303

REBER, TERILYN, marketing consultant; b. Salt Lake City, Feb. 18, 1955; d. Calvin Arther Reber and Shirley Ramona (Anderson) Ross. BS in Mktg., U. Cin., 1980. Quality control auditor Procter and Gamble Co., Cin., 1977-80; pres. Tiel Cons., Inc., Spokane, Wash., 1980—. Mgr. data collection Charterite Party, Cin., 1978; corp. recruiter United Appeal Campaign, Cin., 1978-80; mgr. data collection and reports Women's Fine Art Fair, Spokane, 1981, Cath. Charities, Spokane, 1982. Mem. NOW, Mktg. Research Assn., Am. Mktg. Assn., Nat. Assn. Female Execs. Democrat. Avocations: photography, prose. Home: E 543 Sanson Pl Spokane WA 99207 Office: Tiel Cons Inc N 1404 Thor Ct Spokane WA 99202

RECCA, LINDA ANDREWS LEE, public relations official, consultant, lecturer; b. Wichita, Kans., July 17, 1951; d. Harry Morton and Phyllis Lee (Stephenson) Crandell; m. John Anthony Recca, Aug. 27, 1983. B.S. in Journalism, U. Kans., 1973. Accredited bus. communicator. Media specialist Epilepsy Found. Am., Los Angeles, 1977-79; asst. mgr. pub. affairs div. Sunkist Growers, Los Angeles, 1979-82; pub. relations mgr. Allstate Savs., Glendale, Calif., 1982-84, Am. Savs., Stockton, Calif., 1984-85; pres. Recca communications, Golden, Colo., 1985—; guest lectr. UCLA, U. So. Calif. Recipient award of excellence Nat. Council Farmer Coops, 1982, photography award Coop. Editors Assn., 1982. Mem. Internat. Assn. Bus. Communicators (John Cartwright Meml. award Los Angeles chpt. 1983), Pub. Relations Soc. Am. Author: Sunkist Growers annual report, 1981, 82.

RECHARD, OTTIS WILLIAM, mathematics and computer science educator; b. Laramie, Wyo., Nov. 13, 1924; s. Ottis H. and Mary (Bird) R.; m. Dorothy Lee Duble, Nov. 19, 1943; children—Katherine L. (Mrs. Larry V. Baxter), Carol G. (Mrs. David P. Reiter), Nancy L. (Mrs. William Moore), Elizabeth A. B.A., U. Wyo., 1943; postgrad., U. Calif., Los Angeles, 1943; M.A., U. Wis., 1946, Ph.D., 1948. Instr. U. Wis., 1948; instr., asst. prof. Ohio State U., 1948-51; staff mem. Los Alamos (N.Mex.) Nat. Lab., 1951-56; prof., dir. computing ctr. Wash. State U., Pullman, 1956-68; prof., chmn. dept. computer sci. Wash. State U., 1963-76, prof., dir. systems and computing, 1968-70; prof. math. and computer scis. U. Denver, 1976—, dir. computing services, 1976-79; vis. prof., chmn. dept. computer sci. U. Wyo.; cons. NSF, Idaho Nuclear Corp., Los Alamos Nat. Lab.; program dir. computer sci. program NSF, 1964-65, chmn. adv. panel on instl. computing facilities, 1969-70. Mem. Los Alamos Sch. Bd., 1954-56; mem. Pullman Sch. Bd., 1967-74; Trustee, past pres. Westminster Found., Synod Wash.-Alaska. Served to 1st lt. USAAF, 1943-45. Decorated Order of Leopold II Belgium). Fellow AAAS; mem. Assn. for Computing Machinery, Am. Math. Soc., Math. Assn. Am., Soc. Indsl. and Applied Math., AAUP, Phi Beta Kappa, Sigma Xi, Phi Kappa Phi. Presbyn. (elder). Club: Rotarian. Home: 6980 E Girard Ave #405 Denver CO 80224

RECHARD, ROBERT PAUL, civil engineer; b. Cheyenne, Wyo., Oct. 8, 1955; s. Paul Albert and Mary Lou (Roper) R.; m. Patricia Louise Walker, July 14, 1984; 1 child, Kyle Lance. BS with honors, U. Wyo., 1978, MS, 1979. Registered profl. engr., N.Mex. Mem. tech. staff Sandia Nat. Labs., Albuquerque, 1980—. Dancer N.Mex. Ballet Co., Albuquerque. 1980—; actor/singer Albuquerque Civic Light Opera Assn., 1980—; counselor Sky High Hope Cancer Camp, Denver, 1983—. Mem. ASCE, Am. Geophys. Union, Sigma Xi, Phi Kappa Phi, Tau Beta Pi (chpt. pres. 1977-78). Republican. Presbyterian. Avocations: cross-country and downhill skiing, backpacking, fly fishing, leatherwork. Home: 12721 Chandelle Ct NE Albuquerque NM 87112 Office: Sandia Nat Labs PO Box 5800 Albuquerque NM 87185

RECKMEYER, WILLIAM JOHN, educator, systems scientist/cybernetician, consultant; b. Riverside, Calif., June 17, 1948; s. William John and Elizabeth Louise (Armstrong) R.; m. Joan Elizabeth Pasco, Dec. 27, 1969; children: Lorien Rhiannon, Jeremy Bronwyn, Devon Gwynedd. Student, Hobart Coll., 1966-68; BA, Randolph-Macon Coll., 1970; MA, Am. U., 1973, PhD, 1982. Research fellow INRI, McLean, Va., 1971-77; adj. prof. San Jose (Calif.) State U., 1977-83, assoc. prof., 1983—; disting. adj. prof. informatics and systems sci. Stockholm U. & Royal Inst. of Tech., 1984—; cons. in field, 1984—. Editor Gen. Systems Yearbook, 1986—, 2 other books; contbr. articles to profl. jours. Mem. Am. Soc. Cybernetics (pres. 1983-85, chmn. 20th Anniversary Meeting 1983), Soc. Gen. Systems Research (chmn. 25th Anniversary Meeting 1981). Avocations: middle earth, basketball, cabinetmaking. Home: 1785 El Codo Way San Jose CA 95124 Office: San Jose State U Cybernetic Systems Program San Jose CA 95192-0113

RECTOR, WILLIAM MICHAEL, marketing professional, electronics engineer; b. Berkeley, Calif., Nov. 4, 1944; s. Leon Elmer and Georgia (Ashton) R.; m. Janet Lynn Stromberg, Apr. 9, 1965; children: David Michael, Caryn Jean, Christina Lynn. AA, Peralta Coll., 1965. Sr. technician Watkins Johnson, Palo Alto, Calif., 1965-67, engr., 1968-76, mem. tech. staff internat. sales dept., 1976-82; mgr. maintenance facility Watkins Johnson, Munich, 1973-76; mgr. office Watkins Johnson, Bonn, Fed. Republic Germany, 1980-82; staff scientist Watkins Johnson, San Jose, Calif., 1982-84; mgr. product mktg. West div. GTE Govt. Systems Corp., Mountain View, Calif., 1984—. Project leader San Carlos 4-H Club. Mem. Assn. Old Crows. Republican. Presbyterian. Home: 730 Hillcrest Way Redwood City CA 94062 Office: GTE Govt Systems Corp West div 100 Ferguson Dr PO Box 7188 Mountain View CA 94039

REDDEN, JAMES ANTHONY, federal judge; b. Springfield, Mass., Mar. 13, 1929; s. James A. and Alma (Cheek) R.; m. Joan Ida Johnson, July 13, 1950; children: James A., William F. Student, Boston U., 1951; LL.B., Boston Coll., 1954. Bar: Oreg. bar 1955. Since practiced in Medford; mem. firm Collins, Redden, Ferris & Velure, 1957-73; dist. judge pro-tem 1958; treas. State of Oreg., 1973-77; atty. gen. 1977-80, U.S. dist. judge, 1980—. Chmn. Oreg. Pub. Employee Relations Bd.; mem. Oreg. Automobile Ins. Adv. Com.; Mem. Oreg. Ho. of Reps., 1963-69, minority leader, 1967-69. Served with AUS, 1946-48. Mem. Am., Mass. bar assns., Oreg. State Bar, Oreg. Assn. Def. Counsel. Democrat. Lodge: KC. Office: 612 US Courthouse 620 SW Main St Portland OR 97205

REDDIEN, CHARLES HENRY, JR., lawyer, business executive, securities financial consultant; b. San Diego, Aug. 27, 1944; s. Charles Henry and Betty Jane (McCormick) R.; m. 2d, Paula Gayle, June 16, 1974; 1 son, Tyler Charles. B.S.E.E., U. Colo.-Boulder, 1966; M.S.E.E., U. So. Calif., 1968; J.D., Loyola U., Los Angeles, 1972. Bar: Calif. 1972, Colo. 1981, U.S. Dist. Ct. 1981. Mgr., Hughes Aircraft Co., 1966-81; sole practice law, 1972—; owner, broker, real estate brokerage firm, 1978—; mem. spl. staff, co-dir. tax advantage group OTC Net Inc., 1981-82; pres., chmn. Heritage Group Inc., investment banking holding co., 1982-84, Plans and Assistance Inc., mgmt. cons., 1982-83, Orchard Group Ltd., investment banking holding co., 1982-84, J.W. Gant & Assocs., Inc., investment bankers, 1983-84; mng. ptnr., chief exec. officer J.W. Gant & Assocs., Ltd., 1984-85; chmn. bd. Kalamath Group Ltd., 1985-86, Heritage group Ltd. Investment Bankers, 1985—; dir. Virtusonics Corp., 1985—; v.p., dir. Heritage Fin. Planners Inc., 1982-83; pres., chmn. PDN Western Region Inc., 1987—; Recipient Teaching Internship award, 1964. Mem. Calif. Bar Assn., Nat. Assn. Securities Dealers, IEEE (chmn. U. Colo. chpt. 1965), Am. Inst. Aero. and Astronautical Engrs., Phi Alpha Delta, Tau Beta Pi, Eta Kappa Nu. Contbr. articles to profl. jours. Office: Harlequin Plaza S 7600 E Orchard Rd Suite 160 Englewood CO 80111

REDDIX, JOSEPH WILLIAM, computer company consultant; b. Gary, Ind., June 26, 1949; s. James David and Ophelia (Valentine) R.; m. Cynthia Ann Ramseur, June 11, 1977; 1 child, Bryan Joseph. Student, Purdue U., 1973-76. Coil feeder Gary Sheet & Tin Co., Ind., 1972-73; programmer/analyst Gary Nat. Bank, 1973-77, United Airlines, Elk Grove Village, Ill., 1978-79; systems analyst Allied Van Lines, Broadview, Ill., 1977-78; project mgr. Am. Express Co., Phoenix, 1979-83; dist. systems cons./telecommunications Wang Labs., Phoenix, 1983-87; sr. telecommunications cons., Computer Task Group, Phoenix, 1987—; prin. systems cons. Mem. NAACP (Maricopa County Br.), Phoenix Urban League. Served with USN, 1968-72. Democrat. Baptist. Home: 17434 N 36th Dr Glendale AZ 85308

REDDY, GUNUKULA SUDHAKAR, research chemist; b. Hyderabad, India, Mar. 20, 1952; came to U.S., 1981; s. G. Somi and G. Rukmini R.; m. Vanita G. Reddy, Sept. 14, 1984; 1 child, Suraj. BS, Osmania U., Hyderabad, 1973, MS in Chemistry, 1975; PhD in Chemistry, Pune (India) U., 1981. Research fellow Nat. Chem. Lab., Pune, 1976-80; postdoctoral fellow Utah State U., Logan, 1981-83, research chemist, 1985—; research assoc. U. Ariz., Tucson, 1984; Contbr. articles to profl. jours. Mem. Am. Chem. Soc., Am. Soc. for Mass Spectrometry. Office: Utah State U Dept Chemistry and Biochemistry Logan UT 84322-0300

REDDY, LAKSHMA ARRAM, research cancer biologist, immunologist; b. Hyderabad, Andhra Pradesh, India, June 24, 1942; came to U.S., 1967; s. Narisimha A. and Ahalaya (Madipeddi) R.; m. Usha A. Ramasayam, May 21, 1964; children: Mamatha, Rajeeth. MS, Osmania U., Hyderabad, 1964; PhD, U. Pitts., 1972. Research immunologist UCLA, 1972-75; research asst. prof. U. Wash., Seattle, 1976-84, research assoc. prof., 1984—. Contbr. articles to profl. jours. Bd. dirs. Ragamala, Seattle, 1985-86. Research grantee Am. Cancer Soc., 1972, NIH, 1983—. Mem. Internat. Soc. Devel. and Comparative Immunology. Club: Toastmasters (Seattle) (v.p. 1983-84). Avocations: painting, hiking, camping, tennis. Home: 5490 Highland Dr Bellevue WA 98006 Office: U Wash Dept Medicine RG-25 Seattle WA 98195

REDDY, NAGENDRANATH K., biochemist, researcher; b. Bangalore, India, Nov. 18, 1937; came to U.S., 1968; s. K. Rami and K. (Gnanamma) R.; m. Saraswati K., May 11, 1967; children: Kalpana, Sandip. BS, SRI Venkatesujara U., Andhra, India, 1957; MS, U. Saugor, Madhya Pradesh, India, 1959; PhD, Indian Inst. Sci., Bangalore, 1971. Jr. research asst. Nat. Dairy Research Inst., Bangalore, 1959-60; sr. research asst. Indian Inst. Sci., Bangalore, 1965-68; research assoc. Roswell Park Meml. Inst., Buffalo, 1968-73; asst. prof. U. Cin., 1975-80; asst. prof. research biochemistry U. So. Calif., Los Angeles, 1980—. Editor: Fibrinolysis, 1980; contbr. articles to profl. jours. Recipient Research Career Devel. award NIH, 1978. Mem. AAAS, Am. Chem. Soc., Am. Soc. Biol. Chemists, N.Y. Acad. Scis., Internat. Soc. Thrombosis and Haemostasis. Avocation: stamp collecting. Home: 3402 Punta Del Este Hacienda Heights CA 91745 Office: U So Calif 1303 N Mission Rd Los Angeles CA 90033

REDELSPERGER, ANNE ELIZABETH, real estate broker and land developer; b. Los Angeles, Mar. 13, 1943; d. James Kelleam and Annie Mae (James) Perkins; m. Kenneth Karl Redelsperger, Nov. 27, 1971; 1 child, Megan Elizabeth. BA, U. Calif., Berkeley, 1965. Cert. real estate broker Nev. Mgmt. trainee Broadway Dept. Stores, Los Angeles, 1967-72; real estate developer Country Place Inc., Pahrump, Nev., 1975—; real estate broker Pahrump Land Co., 1979—. Campaign mgr. Ken Redelsperger, 1980, 82, 84; pres. Pahrump Valley Rep. Women, 1983—; state del. Nev. Rep. Conv., 1982, 84; alt. del. Nat. Rep. Conv., Dallas, 1984; del. Nat. Rep. Women's Conv., Phoenix, 1985; trustee Pahrump Valley United Meth. Ch., 1984—. Mem. Fedn. Rep. Women Nev. (del. 1981, 83). Office: Pahrump Land Co PO Box 1059 Pahrump NV 89041

REDEMANN, ERIC JOHN, systems engineer; b. Calif., 1952; s. Carl T. and Phyllis S. Redemann. B.A. in Math., Revelle Coll., U. Calif.-San Diego, 1975. With Scripps Inst. Oceanography, La Jolla, Calif., 1972-75, Los Alamos Nat. Lab., 1975-77; project engr. Identronix Inc., Santa Cruz, Calif., 1977-78, Calif. R and D, Culver City, 1979-80; cons., Marina del Rey, Calif., 1980-84; mgr. mfg. engring. Cyberdisk Inc., Anaheim, Calif., 1984—. Mem. IEEE, NSPE, Internat. Platform Assn., Audio Engring. Soc., Assn. Computing Machinery, Soc. Info. Display. Office: Cyberdisk Inc 1531 S Sinclair St Anaheim CA 92806

REDENBAUGH, KEITH, biotechnology researcher; b. Indpls., July 6, 1951; s. Robert Leroy Redenbaugh and Mary Ruth (Magnus) Caress; m. Janet Marie Weichert, Mar. 23, 1974; children: Susan Jeanne, Neal Keith. BA in Biology with honors, U. Calif., Santa Cruz, 1975; PhD in Forest Genetics, SUNY, Syracuse, 1979. Postdoctoral research assoc. Dept. Chem. Biodynamics U. Calif., Berkeley, 1980-81; research scientist Plant Genetics, Inc., Davis, Calif., 1982-83, sr. research scientist, 1983-84, research group leader, 1984-86, sr. research group leader, 1986—; adj. prof., agrl. experiment station assoc. U. Calif., Davis, 1986—; lectr. Calif. Plant and Soil Conf., Fresno, 1985, 6th Internat. Congress Plant Tissue Culture, Mpls., 1986; speaker Gordon Conf. on Plant Cell and Tissue Culture; numerous other engagements. Patentee in field; contbr. articles in field to profl. jours. Elder First Baptist Ch. Davis, 1985—. Grantee USDA, 1985-88; recipient Coll. award SUNY, Syracuse, 1977, R.P. White Research Grant, 1978. Mem. AAAS, Soc. Am. Foresters, Tissue Culture Assn. (program chmn. plant div. 1983-85, vice chmn. 1984-86, chmn. council 1986—, exec. bd. 1986-88), Int. Assn. for Plant Tissue Culture, Int. Soc. for Plant Molecular Biology. Home: 802 Christie Ct Davis CA 95616 Office: Plant Genetics Inc 1930 5th St Davis CA 95616

REDEWILL, JOYCE CAROL, cosmetic manufacturing executive, consultant, lecturer; b. Bklyn., Oct. 7, 1945; d. Harold Arthur and Alice (Newton) Fliegner; m. Leslie Turner Redewell, May 21, 1977; children: Justin, Andrea; 1 son by previous marriage, Theodore K. Green; 1 stepson, Leslie T. Redewill. BS, Calif. State U., Long Beach, 1968; MBA, Pepperdine U., 1978. Interplanetary quarantine microbiologist Jet Propulsion Lab., Pasadena, Calif., 1968-69; staff research assoc. UCLA, 1969-75; pres. Caresse, Inc., Santa Monica, Calif., 1972-75, Au Naturel, Inc., Monterey Park, Calif., 1976-84; owner Au Naturel Cosmetics, Venice Beach, Calif., 1984—, De Nouveau Cos., The Nail Polish Factory, Los Angeles, 1985—; founder Cosmetic Research Inst., Los Angeles, 1986—; owner Joyce Carol Cosmetics, 1986—, cosmetic and fragrance warehouse, 1986. Dir. make-up Group W Cable; inventor nail enamel without formaldehyde resins, nail care natural skin care products. Mem. Friends of Whittier Library. Mem. Fedn. Coatings Tech., Cosmetic Chemist Soc., Beauty and Barber Supply Inst., Nat. Health Food Assn., Nat. Assn. Female Execs. Republican. Club: Women's (Whittier). Lodge: Soroptomists. Avocations: painting, sculpture, horeback riding. Office: Nail Polish Factory 8231 Allport Ave Santa Fe Springs CA 90670

REDFIELD, DAVID, research scientist, consultant; b. N.Y.C., Sept. 20, 1925; children: Andrew C., Steven D. BA, UCLA, 1948; MS, U. Md., 1953; PhD, U. Pa., 1956. Research physicist Union Carbide Corp., Parma, Ohio and Tarrytown, N.Y., 1955-64; assoc. prof. Columbia U., N.Y.C., 1964-67; mem. tech. staff RCA Labs, Princeton, N.J., 1967-85; cons. prof. Stanford (Calif.) U., 1985—; mem. photovoltaic adv. com. U.S. Dept. Energy, 1980-81. Editorial bd. mem. Semiconductors and Insulators, 1973—, Crystal Lettice Defects and Amorphous Materials, 1983—; contbr. articles to profl. jours. Served to 2d lt. USAF, 1943-45. Fellow Mobil Oil Co., 1953-54; recipient Outstanding Achievement award RCA Corp., 1973. Fellow Am. Phys. Soc. (mem. exec. com. div. solid state physics 1971-73); mem. IEEE (sr., mem. solar energy subcom. 1976-78), Fedn. Am. Scientists (chmn. chpt. 1972-73). Home: 4010 Villa Vera Palo Alto CA 94306 Office: Stanford U Dept Material Sci and Engring Stanford CA 94305

REDFIELD, ELAINE M., writer, critic, interior designer; b. N.Y.C., Dec. 9, 1917; d. Oscar L. and Gertrude (Hauser) Graf; m. Edward Mittelman, Apr. 11, 1943 (dec. Oct. 1960); m. William D. Redfield, Dec. 28, 1967. Student, Wellesley Coll., 1934-37; AB, UCLA, 1943. Book reviewer San Francisco Chronicle, 1943-45; sales asst. Associated Am. Artists, Beverly Hills, Calif., 1947-48; free-lance editorial asst. W.H. Freeman Co., San Francisco, 1953-54; publicity dir. Orange County Philharm. Soc., 1954-57, dir., 1957-70, mem. adv. bd., 1970—; interior design Elaine Mittelman Interiors, 1960—; Mem. Fullerton Cultural and Fine Arts Commn., 1965-77; bd. dirs. Friends of Library of U. Calif. at Irvine, 1964-71; bd. dirs. Music Assocs. Calif. State U., Fullerton, pres., 1970-73; trustee South Coast Repertory, 1976-85; mem. pres.'s assocs. Calif. State U., Fullerton, emeritus dir. 1986—; bd. dirs. Fullerton Civic Light Opera, 1979-83, Pacific Symphony Orch., 1979-85; bd. dirs. Orange County Performing Arts Ctr., 1974—, pres. 1979-80, chmn. bd. dirs. 1980-81; mem. Disneyland Community Service awards com., 1978—. Recipient Woman of Achievement award Fullerton Bus. and Profl. Women's Club, 1966, Woman of Yr. award Fullerton C. of C., 1971, 1st Patron of Arts award Orange County, 1979, Vol. Activist award Broadway Dept. Stores and Germaine Monteil, 1980, Today's Woman award Bullock's Dept. Stores, 1980, Silver Medallion award YWCA, 1981, Vol. Service to Arts award City of Newport Beach Arts Commn., 1982, CHampion of Yr. March of Dimes, 1984, Humanitarian of Yr award Nat. Conf. Christians and Jews, 1986, YWCA of So. Orange County award of Excellance, 1987; named Orange County Hon. Angel Saddleback Found., 1981. Mem. Am. Soc. Interior Designers (comml. design award Orange County chpt. 1976, Community Service award 1980), AAUW, LWV. Clubs: Center; South Coast Wellesley (pres. 1962-64). Lodge: Rotary (Community Service award Fullerton chpt. 1985). Home: 1403 Sunny Crest Dr Fullerton CA 92635

REDFORD, GARY WILLIAM, management consultant; b. Ogden, Utah, Jan. 13, 1951; s. James William and Lillian (Schmidt) R.; m. Marsha Adams, Sept. 9, 1978; 1 child, Joshua Weir. AAS, Utah Tech. Coll., 1974; BS, Weber State Coll., 1977; MBA, U. Utah, 1979. Programmer, analyst Surety Life Ins. Co., Salt Lake City, 1974-77, Skaggs Cos., Inc., Salt Lake City, 1977-78; sr. programmer, analyst dept. data processing U. Utah, Salt Lake City, 1978-80; prin., cons. G&M Cons., Salt Lake City, 1980-85, Lexus Group, Inc., Salt Lake City, 1984-85; v.p. Carter, Whitlock, Redford & Byrd, Inc., Salt Lake City, 1985-87; pres. G.W. Redford and Assocs., Salt Lake City, 1987—; prin. Tarrance Software, 1986—; instr. U. Utah, Salt Lake City, Weber State Coll., Ogden, 1980—. Republican. Mormon. Home: 1211 E 300 N Layton UT 84041 Office: GW Redford and Assocs 50 W Broadway Suite 1000 Salt Lake City UT 84101

REDMAN, SHERYL GUZMÁN, publications art director; b. Marlborough, Mass., July 21, 1946; d. Raoul and Annette Loraine (Kennard) G.; m. William Robert Redman II, June 14, 1986. Student, Calif. State Poly. U., Pomona, 1969-71. Art dir. Mainstream mag., San Diego, 1981-83, Ostomy Quarterly mag., Los Angeles, 1983—. Office: United Ostomy Assn 2001 W Beverly Los Angeles CA 90057

REDMON, EDWARD JOHN, aerospace company executive; b. Freeport, Ill., Sept. 25, 1914; s. Alexander E. and Mary Mabel (Hines) R.; A.B., UCLA, 1937; M.A., U. So. Calif., 1939; m. Helen Louise Brown, June 1, 1944. Sr. job analyst Lockheed Aircraft, Burbank, Calif., 1940-51, wage and salary adminstr., Marietta, Calif., 1951-53, with Missile Systems Div., 1953-57, mgr. wage and salary adminstrn., head mgmt. compensation, Sunnyvale, Calif., 1957-80; dir. spl. compensation projects Lockheed Corp., 1982-84, cons. in exec. compensation, Burbank, Calif., 1984-86; cons. and lectr. in field. Mem. Western Mgmt. Assn., Calif. Personnel Assn., Electronics Salary and Wage Assn., Electronics Industries Assn., Calif. Salary Adminstrs. Assn., Am. Mgmt. Assn. Republican. Methodist. Contbr. articles in field to profl. jours. Home: 1471 Fallen Leaf Lane Los Altos CA 94022

REDMOND, SHEILA GAIL, social worker; b. Salt Lake City, Mar. 4, 1946; d. George Vermont Redmond and Pearl LeNola (Dale) Hansen. BS, U. Utah, 1971, MSW, 1980. Cert. social worker, Utah. Intern Childrens Service Soc., Salt Lake City, 1978-79, VA Med. Ctr., Salt Lake City, 1979-80; dir. Odyssey House, Salt Lake City, 1980-82, 86—; sr. clinician Childrens Psychiat. Ctr., Red Bank, N.J., 1983-85; pvt. practice social work Salt Lake City, 1986; lectr. on social issues. Served with U.S. Army, 1974-77. Mem. Acad. Cert. Social Workers, Nat. Assn. Social Workers. Mormon. Avocations: reading, arts and crafts. Home: 4130 S 3115 W Salt Lake City UT 84119 Office: 68 S 600 E Salt Lake City UT 84102

REEB, RICHARD HOWELL, JR., political science educator; b. San Jose, Calif., Dec. 30, 1942; s. Richard Howell and Mildred Flora (Heckman) R.; m. Patricia Anne Stevens, Feb. 22, 1968; children: Robert, Richard, Andrea. BA in Journalism, San Jose State U., 1965, MA in Polit. Sci., 1970; PhD in Govt., Claremont Grad. Sch., 1974. Tchr. polit. sci. Barstow (Calif.) Coll., 1970—, asst dean, 1979-80; lectr. Calif. State U., San Bernardino, 1981-82; lectr. Claremont (Calif.) Inst., 1985-87. Author,editor Statesmanship and Utopianism, 1983; also articles. V.p. publicity Am. Field Service, Barstow, 1984—, pres., 1986—; chmn. campaign Allen for U.S. Senate, Barstow, 1986, Reagan for Pres., Barstow, 1976, 80; pres. Greater Barstow Rep. Assembly, 1977-78; mem. Accuracy in Media Inc., Washington, 1985—. Served with U.S. Army N.G., 1960-64. NEH fellow, 1975; recipient Great Tchr. Seminar award Am. Assn. Jr. and Community Coll., Montecito, Calif., 1979. Mem. Am. Polit. Sci. Assn., Community Coll. Humanities Assn. (treas. CCC assn. adminstrs. Liberal Arts 1979-80). Republican. Episcopalian. Avocations: mass media, fgn. policy, polit. parties.

REEBURGH, WILLIAM SCOTT, educator; b. Port Arthur, Tex., Feb. 25, 1940; s. Scott Leverett and Helen Hamilton (Focht) R.; m. Carelyn Elizabeth Yerkes, June 22, 1963; children: Scott Louis, Nancy Elizabeth, Peter William. BS, U. Okla., 1961; MA, Johns Hopkins U., 1964, PhD, 1967. Research staff asst. Johns Hopkins U., Balt., 1967-68; asst. prof. marine geochemistry U. Alaska, Fairbanks, 1968-72, assoc. prof., 1972-77, prof., 1977—, dir. grad. programs, 1983-86; adj. prof SUNY, Stony Brook, 1977—. Active Boy Scouts Am. Mem. AAAS, Am. Soc. Limnology and Oceanography, Am. Geophys. Union, Am. Soc. Microbiology, Geochemical Soc., Am. Chem. Soc., Phi Kappa Phi, Sigma Xi, Phi Lambda Upsilon. Home: PO Box 81628 Fairbanks AK 99708 Office: Inst of Marine Sci U Alaska Fairbanks AK 99775-1080

REED, CLAIRE HARRISON, public relations and advertising executive; b. N.Y.C., Apr. 18, 1934; d. Jack Carl and Arion (Nadler) Levine; B.A., Conn. Coll., 1955; postgrad. in Internat. Relations, U. Calif., Berkeley, 1956, in Clin. Psychology, Calif. State U., San Francisco, 1963; m. Edward G. Reed, Mar. 2, 1969; children by previous marriage—Stephen James Harrison, Martha Harrison Shocron. Exec. sec. San Francisco Jr. C. of C., 1955-56; exec. dir. No. Calif. div. UNA, San Francisco, 1959-61; asst. in research Langley Porter Neuropsychiat. Inst., U. Calif., San Francisco, 1963-64; chief, pub. relations and advt. San Francisco Theatre Div. United Artists, 1965-67; founder CHA/Claire Harrison Assocs., San Francisco, 1967-70, pres. Claire Harrison Assocs., Inc., 1970—; vis. lectr., speaker profl. groups, univs. Bd. dirs. San Francisco Contemporary Music Players, San Francisco Rock 'n' Roll Mus.; mem. Guarantor's Council San Francisco Symphony Orchestra; patron San Francisco Opera Assn. Recipient One Hundred Best award San Francisco Soc. Communicating Arts, 1979, also merit award, 1980; merit award Art Dir. Mag., 1984, award of excellence Communications Arts Mag., 1984, Creativity Cert. Distinction Art Direction mag., 1984, Lulu Award of Excellence for Pub. Relations program Los Angeles Women's Advt. Club, 1985, Silver Microphone award Wordsmith Radio Award program, 1986; named Murphy Gold award winner San Jose Ad Club, 1986. Mem. Public Relations Soc. Am. (chmn. counselors' sect. San Francisco chpt. 1984, medallion award for best community relations program 1980, merit award 1982, cert. merit 1985, Western Art Dir.'s Club award 1985), Am. Assn. Advt. Agys, Conn. Coll. Class of '55 Alumnae Assn. (pres.). Clubs: Metropolitan, Commonwealth. Office: 54 Mint St San Francisco CA 94103

REED, D. ROGER, lawyer; b. Portland, Oreg., Feb. 10, 1939; s. Donald Blackhall and Geraldine (Sumner) R.; B.Sci. and Polit. Sci., Wash. State U., 1961; J.D., U. Wash., 1967; m. Marilyn S. McConaghy, Sept. 16, 1961; children—Tara Lynn, Susan, Scott, Jonathan, William. Ford Found. legis. intern Wash. Legislature's Joint Com. Hwys. and Legis. Budget Com., 1962-64; admitted to Wash. bar, 1967; dep. pros. atty. County of Spokane (Wash.), 1967-69; sr. asst. atty. gen., chief Spokane office Wash. State Atty. Gen., 1969-76; sr. partner firm Reed & Giesa, P.S., Spokane, 1976—; adj. prof. law Gonzaga U., 1972-76. Trustee Spokane YMCA, 1972-78, United Way Spokane, 1974-77; chmn. juvenile justice project Spokane County, 1975-77. Mem. Wash. State Bar Assn. (chmn. trial sect. 1985-86), Spokane County Bar Assn. Republican. Mormon. Office: 410 Gt NW Bldg 222 N Wall St Spokane WA 99201

REED, DIANE MARY, advertising executive; b. Santa Monica, Calif., May 30, 1941; d. Floyd Leonard and Suzanne Lucille (Bryant) Creson; m. George Edward Calkin, Feb. 3, 1957 (div. Feb. 1967); children: George, Christopher, Holly; m. William Gerald Reed, Feb. 16, 1968 (div. Dec. 1975); stepchildren: Joseph, Susan, Nancy, Steven. Student, Fullerton Jr. Coll., U. Calif., Irvine; BA in Communications with honors, Calif. Christian U. Mng. editor Huntington Beach (Calif.) Ind., 1964-71, 73-77; dir. advt. Far West Savs., Newport Beach, Calif., 1978-81, United Savs., Culver City, Calif., 1981-83; pres. United Mktg., Long Beach, Calif., 1983-85; talk show hostess Sta. KPRO, Riverside, Calif, 1985; sr. v.p. mktg. and advt. Am. Savs., Irvine, 1985—. Author: The Underground Wedding Book (Best Adult Book award 1973), The Holy Terror, 1978, The Real Thing, 1978, The Oh, What a Wonderful Wedding Book, 1984; ghost writer 6 books; contbr. numerous articles to newspapers, mags. Polit. cons. to 8 Orange County campaigns, 1978-84. Appointed Lady of the Equestrian Order of the Knights of the Holy Sepulcher by Pope John Paul II, 1987. Mem. Orange County Advt. Fedn., Calif. Savs. and Loan League, Nat. Fedn. Press Women (bd. dirs., 1971, 73), Nat. Sch. Pub. Relations Assn. Democrat. Clubs: Orange County Press Women (pres. 1971, 73), Orange County Press (sec. 1969, 70). Avocations: cabaret vocalist, watercolorist, photographer, lectr., writer. Office: Am Savs and Loan Assn 18401 Von Karman Irvine CA 92713

REED, EDWARD CORNELIUS, JR., federal judge; b. Mason, Nev., July 8, 1924; s. Edward Cornelius Sr. and Evelyn (Walker) R.; m. Sally Torrance, July 14, 1952; children: Edward T., William W., John A., Mary E. BA, U. Nev.; JD, Harvard U. Atty. Arthur Andersen & Co., 1952-53; spl. dep. atty. gen. State of Nev., 1967-69; judge U.S. Dist. Ct. Nev., Reno, 1979—. Former vol. atty. Girl Scouts Am., Sierra Nevada Council, U. Nev., Nev. Agrl. Found., Nev. State Sch. Adminstrs. Assn., Nev. Congress of Parents and Teachers; mem. Washoe County Sch. Bd., 1956-72, pres. 1959, 63, 69; chmn. Gov.'s Sch. Survey Com., 1958-61; mem. Washoe County Bd. Tax Equalization, 1957-58, Washoe County Annexation Commn., 1968-72, Washoe County Personnel Com., 1973-77, chmn. 1973; mem. citizens adv. com. Washoe County Sch. Bond Issue, 1977-78, Sun Valley, Nev., Swimming Pool Com., 1978, Washoe County Blue Ribbon Task Force Com. on Growth, Nev. PTA (life); chmn. profl. div. United Way, 1978; bd. dirs. Reno Siver Sox, 1962-65. Served as staff sgt. U.S. Army, 1943-46, ETO, PTO. Mem. ABA (jud. adminstrn. sect.), Nev. State Bar Assn. (adminstrv. com. dist. 5, 1967-79, lien law com. 1965-78, chmn. 1965-72, probate law com. 1963-66, tax law com. 1962-65), Am. Judicature Soc. Democrat. Baptist. Office: US Dist Ct 5147 Federal Bldg 300 Booth St Reno NV 89509

REED, ELIZABETH ANN, nurse; b. Phila., July 14, 1943; d. Thomas B. and Ann B. (Kuzmann) R. Diploma, Thomas Jefferson U. Hosp. Sch. Nursing, Phila., 1961-64; student Temple U., 1964-68. R.N., Pa. Various nursing positions Thomas Jefferson U. Hosp., Phila., 1964-68, head nurse cardiac surgery, 1972; head nurse cardiovascular surgery Cooper Hosp., Camden, N.J., 1968-72, clin. coordinator cardiac surgery, 1972-75; head nurse clin. perfusion U. Calif.-San Francisco, 1975-76, quality assurance coordinator, 1976-78, adminstrv. nurse IV, 1978-86; operating room supr. Pacific Presbyn. Med. Ctr., San Francisco, 1986—, dir., 1985—; speaker numerous profl. meetings. Mem. Am. Nurses Assn., Calif. Nurses Assn., Assn. Operating Room Nurses (dir. 1977-81, dir. San Francisco chpt. 1980-84), Nurse's Alumnae Assn. Thomas Jefferson U. Hosp. Sch. Nursing, Assn. Advancement Med. Instrumentation (dir. 1981-84). Contbg. author Alexander's Care of the Patient in Surgery, 1978, 7th edit., 1983; contbr. articles to profl. jours. Home: 252-B Esperanza St Tiburon CA 94920 Office: Pacific Presbyn Med Ctr PO Box 7999 (P3101) San Francisco CA 94123

REED, ELIZABETH BUTTLER, physician, biochemist; b. Friedrichshafen, Fed. Republic of Germany, May 19, 1923; came to U.S., 1923; d. Karl and Grace Elizabeth (Buttler) Schmidt; m. Robert Guion Reed, May 23, 1941 (div. 1946); m. Kurt Josef Bendit, Dec. 29, 1960. AB, U. Calif., Berkeley, 1949; student, Washington U., St. Louis, 1949-51; MD, U. Calif., San Francisco, 1953, PhD, 1967. Intern U. Calif., San Francisco, 1953-54, trainee/fellow in biochemistry, 1961-67, research assoc. biochemistry, 1969-74, research physician in medicine, 1973-78, assoc. physician student health service, 1974—; resident, fellow Stanford (Calif.) U., 1954-56; resident in internal medicine VA, San Francisco, 1956-58, clin. investigator, 1959-60. Contbr. articles to profl. jours. Mem. AAAS, N.Y. Acad. Scis., Physicians for Social Responsibility, San Francisco Med. Soc., Phi Beta Kappa. Avocation: painting. Office: U Calif 380-U San Francisco CA 94143

REED, FRANK FREMONT, II, lawyer; b. Chgo., June 15, 1928; s. Allen Martin and Frances (Faurot) R.; student Chgo. Latin Sch.; grad. St. Paul's Sch., 1946; A.B., U. Mich., 1952, J.D., 1957; m. Jaquelin Silverthorne Cox, April 27, 1963; children—Elizabeth Matthiessen Mason, Laurie Matthiessen Stern, Mark Matthiessen, Jeffrey, Nancy, Sarah. Admitted to Ill. bar, 1958; asso. Byron, Hume, Groen & Clement, 1958-61, Marks & Clerk, 1961-63; individual practice, Chgo., 1963-78; dir. Western Acadia (Western Felt Works), 1960-75, chmn. exec. com., 1969-71. Republican precinct capt. 1972-78; candidate for 43d ward alderman, 1975; bd. dirs., sec. Chgo. Found. Theater Arts, 1959-64; vestryman St. Chrysostom's Ch., 1975-79, mem. ushers guild, 1964-79, chmn., 1976-78; bd. dirs. North State, Astor, Lake Shore Dr. Assn., 1975-78, pres. 1977-78; bd. dirs. Community Arts Music Assn. of Santa Barbara, 1984—. Served to cpl. AUS, 1952-54. Mem. ABA, Ill. Bar Assn., Phi Alpha Delta. Republican. Episcopalian. Clubs: Racquet, Wausaukee (sec., dir. 1968-71) (Chgo.); Birnam Wood Golf (Santa

Barbara, Calif.). Author: History of the Silverthorn Family, 3 vols., 1982, also ann. supplements. Contbr. articles to The Am. Genealogist, 1972-73, 76-77. Home: 1944 E Valley Rd Santa Barbara CA 93108

REED, FRANK METCALF, banker; b. Seattle, Dec. 22, 1912; s. Frank Ivan and Pauline B. (Hovey) R.; student U. Alaska, 1931-32; B.A., U. Wash., 1937; m. Maxine Vivian McGary, June 11, 1937; children—Pauline Reed Mackay), Frank Metcalf. Vice pres. Anchorage Light & Power Co., 1937-42; pres. Alaska Electric & Equipment Co., Anchorage, 1946-50; sec., mgr. Turnagain, Inc., Anchorage, 1950-56; mgr. Gen. Credit Corp., Anchorage, 1957; br. mgr. Alaska SBA, Anchorage, 1958-60; sr. v.p. First Interstate Bank of Alaska, Anchorage, 1960—, also dir., corp. sec.; dir. First Interstate Corp. of Alaska, pres., dir. Anchorage Broadcasters, Inc.; past pres., chmn. Microfast Software Corp.; ptnr. R.M.R. Co.; dir. Anchorage Light & Power Co., Turnagain, Inc., Alaska Fish and Farm, Inc., Life Ins. Co. Alaska, Alaska Hotel Properties, Spa Inc. Pres., Anchorage Federated Charities, Inc., 1953-54; mem. advisory bd. Salvation Army, 1948-58; mem. City of Anchorage Planning Commn., 1956; mem. City of Anchorage Council, 1956-57; police commr. Ter. of Alaska, 1957-58; chmn. City Charter Commn., 1958; mem. exec. com. Greater Anchorage, Inc., 1955-65; pres. Sch. Bd., 1961-64; mem. Gov.'s Investment adv. com., 1970-72; mem. Alaska State Bd. Edn.; mem. citizens adv. com. Alaska Meth. U.; chmn. Anchorage Charter Commn., 1975; chmn. bldg. fund dr. Community YMCA, 1976—; bd. dirs., mem. exec. com. Arts Alaska, 1976-78; sec.-treas. Breakthrough, 1976-78; bd. dirs. Anchorage Civic Opera, 1978, Rural Venture Alaska, Inc.; bd. dirs Alaska Treatment Ctr., pres. 1985-86; trustee Marston Found., Inc. Served as lt. USNR, 1942-46. Elected to Hall Fame, Alaska Press Club, 1969; named Outstanding Alaskan of Year Alaska C. of C., 1976; recipient Community Service award YMCA, 1975-78. Mem. Am. Inst. Banking, Am. (exec. council 1971-72) Alaska (pres. 1970-71) bankers assns., Nat. Assn. State Bds. Edn. (sec.-treas. 1969-70), C. of C. U.S. (Western region legislative com.), Anchorage C. of C. (pres. 1966-67, dir.), Pioneers of Alaska, Navy League (pres. Anchorage council 1961-62). Clubs: Tower (life), San Francisco Tennis. Lodges: Lions (sec. Anchorage, 1953-54, pres., 1962-63), Elks. Home: 1361 W 12th Ave Anchorage AK 99501

REED, GEORGE FORD, JR., investment exec.; b. Hollywood, Calif., Dec. 26, 1946; s. George Ford and Mary Anita Reed; B.A. in Econs. with honors, U. So. Calif., 1969, M.A., 1971; m. Kathryn Nixon, 1981. Analyst planning and research Larwin Group, Beverly Hills, Calif., 1971-72; with Automobile Club So. Calif., Los Angeles, 1972—, supr. mgmt. info., research and devel., 1973-74, mgr. fin. and market analysis, 1975-81, group mgr. fin. analysis and forecasting, 1981-86; pres. Reed Asset Mgmt. Co., Inc., Los Angeles, 1986—; instr. bus. and econs. Los Angeles Community Coll. Mem. population task force Los Angeles C. of C., 1974—; mem. Gov. Calif. Statewide Econ. Summit Conf., 1974. Served with U.S. Army, 1969. Mem. Assn. Corp. Real Estate Execs., Nat. Assn. Bus. Economists, Western Regional Sci. Assn., Am. Mgmt. Assn., Am. Fin. Assn., So. Calif. Planners Assn., Omicron Delta Epsilon. Home: 1001 S Westgate Ave Los Angeles CA 90049 Office: 1901 Ave of Stars Suite 1774 Los Angeles CA 90067

REED, JEAN SALAS, educational administrator; b. Torreon, N.Mex., Aug. 30, 1940; d. Ross Ray and Cora (Lopez) Salas; m. Cliff A. Reed, July 19, 1974. B.A. in Social Scis., Siena Heights Coll., 1969; M.A. in Ednl. Adminstrn., U. N.Mex., 1972, Edn. Specialist in Ednl. Adminstrn., 1974. Counselor Jobs for Progress, Albuquerque, 1971-72; tchr. Los Lunas Pub. Sch., N.Mex., 1972; edn. specialist N.Mex. State Dept. Edn., Santa Fe, 1973-75; prin. Harrington Jr. High Sch., Santa Fe, 1975-78, Capshaw Jr. High Sch., Santa Fe, 1978-86; asst. supt. elem. edn. Santa Fe Pub. Schs. 1986— ; resident advisor Job Corp Ctr. for Women, Albuquerque, 1971-72; prin. Holy Rosary Sch., Albuquerque, 1970-71; tchr. Co. of Mary Schs., Los Angeles, 1965-70. Bd. dirs. Cancer Soc., Santa Fe, N.Mex., 1982-85. Mem. Nat. Assn. Secondary Sch. Prins., N.Mex. Sch. Adminstrs. (mem. bd. 1981-85, pres. 1986—), N.Mex. Assn. Secondary Sch. Prins. (pres. 1981-82, honors for excellence program 1984), Phi Delta Kappa, Delta Kappa Gamma (pres. 1982-84, edn. scholar 1980). Democrat. Roman Catholic. Home: 1915 Camino Lumbre Santa Fe NM 87501 Office: Santa Fe Pub Schs 610 Alta Vista Santa Fe NM 87501

REED, MARGUERITE DIEUDONNE, social worker; b. Baker, Oreg., Oct. 25, 1918; d. Gaston and Elizabeth (Chary) Dieudonne; m. Preston B. Reed, Jan. 16, 1943; children: Gregory J., Terri M. Stillway, Timothy M., Veronica M. B, San Francisco Coll. for Women, 1940; MSW, Cath. U. Am., 1942. Cert. clin. social worker, Oreg. Caseworker Cath. Charities, San Francisco, 1942-43; welfare officer Palo Alto (Calif.) Police Dept., 1945-46; coordinator Mental Health Clinic, Baker, 1968-70; sch. social worker Baker Sch. Dist., 1972-83; adoption worker Cath. Services for Children, Baker, 1963—. Hospice vol. St. Elizabeth Hosp., Baker, 1985—, trustee, 1975—; dir. migrationa nd refugee services Diocese of Baker, 1975—. Mem. Nat. Assn. Social Workers (cert.), Delta Kappa Gamma. Republican. Roman Catholic. Club: St. Francis Altar (Baker) (past pres., sec.). Avocations: reading, knitting, visiting nursing homes, ch. choir. Home: 2605 2d St PO Box 68 Baker OR 97814 Office: Cath Services for Children PO Box 563 Baker OR 97814

REED, NANCY, business communicator; b. Denver, Jan. 6, 1954; d. Jerry Edward and Betty Jayne (Vaughan) R. BA in English and German summa cum laude, U. Denver, 1975, MA in Info. Mgmt., 1977. Accredited bus. communicator, pub. relations profl. Communication specialist, tng. rep. Coors Porcelain Co., Golden, Colo., 1977-79, communication supr., 1979-82, employee communication and pub. relations supr., 1982-84; dir. communications Geol. Soc. Am., Boulder, 1984—; speaker, cons. pub. relations U. Denver, 1978-79; cons. radiation/oncology dept., Presbyn. Hosp., Denver, 1980-81; task force mem. Futurism in Communications Conf., 1982, 83. Vol. editor local publs. Am. Cancer Soc.; del. Pres.'s White House Conf. on Youth, 1971; girl pres. ARC Youth All-City Council, Denver, 1970-71. Lucille R. Brown Found. scholar, 1973-77; Harriet E. Howe Alumni scholar, 1976-77; Fulbright-Hayes scholar U. Heidelberg (Ger.), 1976; recipient Bronze Quill award YWCA Met. Denver Women in Achievement award, 1982, Gold Key award, 1985, Gold Pick award, 1986. Mem. Internat. Assn. Bus. Communicators, Pub. Relations Soc. Am. (Colo. chpt. membership chmn. 1986, program chmn. 1987), Fulbright Alumni Assn. (mem. nat. bd. dirs., 1987—), ALA (David H. Clift scholar 1976-77), Phi Beta Kappa, Alpha Lambda Delta (Disting. scholar 1972-73). Republican. Presbyterian. Office: PO Box 9140 3300 Penrose Pl Boulder CO 80301

REED, PATRICIA ANN, nurse; b. Wenatchee, Wash., Sept. 11, 1938; d. Clare H. and Irene Marie (Diksen) Nordby. RN, Highland Sch. Nursing, 1956; BS, U. Calif., San Francisco, 1966, MS, 1968. cert. sch. nurse, pub. health nurse. Staff nurse Permanete Med. Assn., Oakland, Calif., 1960-64, Peralta Hosp., Oakland, 1960; vis. nurse Sonoma County, Santa Rosa, Calif., 1963-66; nurse Santa Rosa City Schs., 1968—; rep. Nat. Assn. Securities Dealers (cert.), Tchr. Mgmt. and Ivestment Inc., 1985—. Avocations: endurance racing, competitive horseback riding. Office: Santa Rosa City Schs PO Box 940 Santa Rosa CA 95402

REED, ROBERT GEORGE, III, petroleum company executive; b. Cambridge, Mass., Aug. 9, 1927; s. Robert George and Marjorie B. Reed; m. Maggie L. Fisher, Mar. 22, 1974; children: Sandra McNickle, Valerie Sloan, Jonathan J., John-Paul. BA in Econs., Dartmouth Coll., 1949; AMP, Harvard U., 1970. Mktg. mgr. Tidewater Oil subs. Getty Oil Co., Los Angeles, 1957-64; v.p. mktg. Cities Service Oil Co., Tulsa, 1964-72; exec. v.p. Tesoro Petroleum Corp., San Antonio, 1972-79; chmn. bd., chief exec. officer Clark Oil & Refining Corp., Milw., 1979-81, pres., chief exec. officer div. Apex Oil Co., St. Louis, 1981-85; chmn. bd., chief exec. officer Energy Sources Exchange, Inc., Houston, 1981—; chmn., pres., chief exec. officer Pacific Resources, Inc., Honolulu, 1985—; bd. dirs. Alexander and Baldwin, Inc., Honolulu, First Hawaiian Bank. Active Aloha United Way. Served with USN, 1945-46. Mem. Am. Petroleum Inst., Nat. Petroleum Refiners Assn. (bd. dirs.), Nat. Petroleum Council, Hawaii C. of C. Clubs: Pacific, Plaza, Waialae Country, Plaza. Office: Pacific Resources Inc 733 Bishop St PO Box 3379 Honolulu HI 96842

REED, VICKI ANNE, speech language pathologist, educator; b. Ute, Iowa, May 19, 1946; d. Roland Robert and Mariana (Sharp) R. BS, Northwestern U., 1968; MA, U. Denver, 1969; EdD, U. No. Colo., 1978. Cert. clin. speech lang. pathologist. Speech lang. pathologist Des Moines Pub. Schs., 1968; dept. head, speech lang. pathologist Sewall Rehab. Ctr., Denver, 1969-70; instr. Armstrong State Coll., Savannah, 1970-72; assoc. prof. U. No. Colo., Greeley, 1972—; grant field reader Office Spl. Edn., U.S. Dept. Edn., 1984—. Author: Basic Anatomy and Physiology of Speech and Hearing, 1982, An Introduction to Children with Language Disorders, 1986. Bd. dirs. Child Abuse Resource and Edn., Weld County, Colo. 1983—, pres., 1985-86. U. No. Colo. scholar, 1985; U.S. Dept. Edn. grantee, 1986. Mem. Am. Speech Lang Hearing Assn., Colo. speech Lang. Hearing Assn. Office: Dept Communication Disorders U No Colo Greeley CO 80639

REEDER, F. ROBERT, lawyer; b. Brigham City, Utah, Jan. 23, 1943; s. Frank O. and Helen H. (Heninger) R.; m. Joannie Anderson, May 4, 1974; children—David, Kristina, Adam. J.D., U. Utah, 1967. Bar: Utah 1967, U.S. Ct. Appeals (10th cir.) 1967, U.S. Ct. Mil. Appeals 1968, U.S. Supreme Ct. 1972, U.S. Ct. Appeals (D.C. and 5th cirs.) 1979. Shareholder, dir. Parsons, Behle & Latimer, Salt Lake City, 1968—. Bd. dirs., officer Holy Cross Hosp. Found. Served with U.S. Army, 1967-68. Mem. ABA, Utah State Bar, Salt Lake County Bar. Clubs: University (Salt Lake City), Cottonwood (past pres., bd. dirs.). Office: Parsons Behle & Latimer PO Box 11898 Salt Lake City UT 84147

REEDER, JOHN WILLIAM, geologist, explorer; b. Palmer, Alaska, Jan. 5, 1950; s. Albert William and Lavon (Nelson) R. B.S. in Geol. Engring., U. Idaho, 1972; M.S. in Geology, Stanford U., 1974, Ph.D. in Geology, 1981, M.S. in Geophysics, 1983. With water resources div. U.S. Geol. Survey, 1969-76, Nat. Ctr. Earthquake Research, 1976-79; teaching asst. dept. geology Stanford U., Calif., 1972-76; geologist div. geology and geophysics surveys State of Alaska, Anchorage, 1979—; mem. Idaho Bd. Engring. Examiners. Contbr. numerous articles to profl. jours. and mags. Explorations of Aleutians appeared in Nat. Geog. mag., 1983. Active Anchorage Fine Arts Mus. Assn., 1980—. Am. Smelting and Refining Co. scholar, 1969; geology fellow Stanford U., 1972-76. Mem. Am. Geophys. Union, Geol. Soc. Am., Seismol. Soc. Am., Am. Assn. Petroleum Geologists, Internat. Assn. Volcanology and Chemistry of Earth's Interior, Am. Soc. Photogrammetry, Archeol. Inst. Am., Internat. Glaciological Soc., Nat. Assn. Underwater Instrs., Am. Inst. Profl. Geologists (cert.), Alaska Geol. Soc., Alaska Anthropol. Assn., Sigma Xi. Geol. feature named in his honor, Makushin Volcano geothermal field of Aleutian Islands named Reeder Geothermal Field. Home: 5604 E 40th Unit A-103 Anchorage AK 99504 Office: Div Geological and Geophysical Surveys State of Alaska Pouch 7-028 Anchorage AK 99510

REEDER, VIRGINIA LEE, educator; b. Tuskahoma, Okla., Jan. 25, 1929; d. Clarence William and Alice (King) Foster; m. Walter Lee Reeder, July 24, 1950; children: Ralph Wesley, Alice Jean. BA, U. Redlands, 1974; MS, Pepperdine U., 1976. Elem. tchr. Harbor City Pub. Schs., 1960-61, First Bapt. Sch., Compton, Calif., 1961-64, Compton Unified Sch., 1980—; head start tchr. Compton Community Youth Ctr., Compton, 1964-76, Charles R. Drew Sch., Compton, 1976-80; tchr. early childhood edn. Compton Coll., 1974—. Democrat. Baptist. Home: 11919 E 161st St Norwalk CA 90650

REEDY, ROBERT CHALLENGER, nuclear scientist; b. Summit, N.J., Mar. 5, 1942; s. William A. and Esther (Challenger) R.; m. Maria Mercedes Homs, Aug. 23, 1969; children: Anne, John. BA, Colgate U., 1964; PhD, Columbia U., 1969. Postdoctoral research chemist U. Calif., San Diego, 1969-72; staff mem. Los Alamos (N.Mex.) Nat. Lab., 1972—; cons. NASA, Washington, 1975—. Contbr. articles to profl. jours. Recipient Achievement awards NASA, 1975-79. Fellow Meteoritical Soc.; mem. Am. Phys. Soc., AAAS, Phi Beta Kappa, Sigma Xi, Phi Lamda Upsilon. Avocations: running, skiing. Home: 152 Monte Rey Dr Los Alamos NM 87544 Office: Los Alamos Nat Lab Space Plasma Physics Group ESS-8 Mail Stop D438 Los Alamos NM 87545

REES, FORREST DARRYL, engineering company executive; b. Toledo, Apr. 28, 1936; s. Forrest R. and Elsie B. (Nicely) R.; m. Jane M. Heaney, Sept. 15, 1965 (div. Sept. 1976); children: Stacey J., Timothy F., Kimberly J. AA in TV Engring., DeVry Tech. Inst., 1956; AAEE, U. Toledo, 1958; BS in Bus. Mgmt., U. Calif., San Jose, 1975. Salesman, applications engr. Tektronix, Santa Clara, Calif., 1973-80; pres. Calif. Bus. Computers, Campbell, 1981-85; v.p. Merlin Engring. Works Inc., Palo Alto, Calif., 1982—. Author: Television Studio Timing, 1978; contbr. articles to profl. jours. Served with U.S. Army, 1961-63. Mem. Soc. Motion Picture and TV Engrs., Nat. Assn. Broadcasters (assoc.). Democrat. Avocations: snow skiing, hiking, tennis. Office: Merlin Engring Works Inc 2458 Embarcadero Way Palo Alto CA 94303

REES, GROVER JOSEPH, III, judge; b. New Orleans, Oct. 11, 1951; s. Grover Joseph and Patricia (Byrne) R.; 1 child, Grover Joseph. B.A., Yale U., New Haven, 1975; J.D., La. State U., Baton Rouge, 1978. Bar: La. 1978, U.S. Supreme Ct. 1982. Asst. prof. law U. Tex., Austin, 1979-86; spl. asst. to Atty. Gen. U.S. Dept. Justice, Washington, 1985, spl. counsel judicial selection, 1985-86; chief justice High Ct. Am. Samoa, Pago Pago, 1986—. Editor-in-Chief: La. Law Rev., 1977-78. Justice of Peace, New Haven, 1973-75. Mem. Order of Coif. Republican. Roman Catholic. Home: Tafuna Tutuila AS Office: High Ct Am Samoa Office of the Chief Justice Pago Pago AS 96799 also: Dept Justice Rm 4239 10th Constitution Ave NW Washington DC 20530 *

REES, WILLIAM SMITH, JR., chemistry educator; b. Quitaque, Tex., Nov. 2, 1959; s. William Smith Sr. and Gertrude (Lunsford) R.; m. Phyllis Ann Waite, June 14, 1986. BS, Tex. Tech U., 1980; PhD, UCLA, 1986. Research chemist Cosden Chem. Co., Big Spring, Tex., 1981; grad. fellow UCLA, 1981-86; postdoctoral fellow MIT, Cambridge, 1986—; vis. instr. UCLA, 1983; teaching asst. cons. office instructional devel., UCLA, 1982-83. Co-author: Synthetic Methods in Inorganic Chemistry, 1986; contbr. articles to profl. jours. Vol. Big Bros. Greater Los Angeles, 1981—. Grantee NRC, 1985, UCLA Grad. div., 1984. Mem. Am. Chem. Soc., N.Y. Acad. Scis., Am. Inst. Chemists, Internat. Union Pure and Applied Chemistry, AAAS, Sigma Xi. Republican. Avocations: backpacking, outdoor activities. Home: 9 Damon Pkwy 2d Floor Arlington MA 02174 Office: 9 Damon Park Arlington MA 02174

REESE, ANDREW JOEL, lawyer video producer-director; b. Los Angeles, May 5, 1945; s. John Henry and Margaret (Smith) R.; student U. So. Calif., 1963-64; B.S. with honors in Econs., Calif. State Poly. U., 1972; J.D., Harvard U., 1975; A.A. in Bus. and Real Estate, Mendocino Coll., 1979; postgrad. Santa Rosa Jr. Coll., 1985-86; m. Karon K. Wolf, Sept. 1, 1967 (div. 1981); 1 dau., Elisabeth K.; m. Beatriz P. Coleman, 1981 (div. 1986). Admitted to Calif. bar, 1975; asso. firm Pacht, Ross, Warne, Bernhard & Sears, Inc., Los Angeles, 1975-76; dep. dist. atty. Mendocino County Dist. Atty.'s Office, Ukiah, Calif., 1976-79; partner firm Adams, Henderson & Reese, Ukiah, 1980; sole practitioner Law Office of Andrew J. Reese, Ukiah, 1979, 81-83; dep. dist. atty. Sonoma County (Calif.), Santa Rosa, 1984—; contract public defender, Mendocino County, 1979-82; news cameraman, Sta. KFTU-TV, Santa Rosa, Calif., 1986—; instr. law and real estate Mendocino Coll., Ukiah, 1978-80; teaching asst. video prodn., Santa Rosa Jr. Coll., 1986. Sec.-treas., dir. Mendocino County Employees Credit Union, 1979; owner Uncommon Prodns., 1986—. Assoc. producer Knowledge Rich Video, Petaluma, Calif. Pres., Alcohol Rehab. Corp., 1980-82; chmn. interim policy adv. council Mendocino Alcohol Project, 1980. Served with USAF, 1964-68. Mem. Calif. Bar Assn. Republican. Home: 178 Jack London Dr Santa Rosa CA 95405 Office: Hall of Justice 600 Administration Dr Santa Rosa CA 95401 Office: Knowledge Rich Video 921 Transport Way Suite 20 Petaluma CA 94952

REESE, GAYLEN LESTER, audiologist; b. Logan, Utah, July 2, 1944; s. Lowell Sern and Helen Eunice (Pitcher) R.; m. Hallie Joye Sherman, Feb. 11, 1969; children: Nila Gaylene, Bret Gaylen. BA, Utah State U., 1966, MS, 1968. Audiologist VA Med. Ctr., Little Rock, Ark., 1972-78, Phoenix, 1978—; adj. instr. U. Ark. Med. Ctr., U. Ark., Little Rock, 1974-78. Served to capt. USAF, 1968-72. Mem. Am. Speech-Language-Hearing Assn. (cert., Continuing Edn. award 1983, 86), Ariz. Speech and Hearing Assn. Republican. Mormon. Club: Toastmasters (Phoenix)(ednl. v.p. 1985, pres. 1986). Avocations: music, movies, making audio and video recordings. Home: 4937 W Larkspur Dr Phoenix AZ 85304 Office: VA Med Ctr 7th St & Indian Sch Rd Phoenix AZ 85012

REESE, GILBERT, cellist; b. Long Beach, Calif., May 26, 1925; s. Robert and Mae (Gilbert) R.; m. Marianne Marshall, Apr. 11, 1964. Lic. Ecole Normale Musique, Paris, 1951; pvt. studies with Pablo Casals, France, 1949-52; B.A. in French Lit., Calif. State U.-Long Beach, 1968. Prin. cellist Indpls. Symphony, 1952-63; cellist Jordan String Quartet, 1954-63; founder, participant Spring Chamber Music Festival, Indpls., 1957-63; dir. SYMF, Los Angeles, 1968-77; concert cellist, soloist with maj. orchs., recitalist throughout Europe and Asia, 1950—; mem. Concert A Tre, 1981—; recs. include: Musique de l'Amerique, 1972; Sonata by Grieg and Fantasy Pieces by Schumann, 1974; Scandinavian Cello Music, 1976; French Scenarios, 1980. Served with USAAF, 1943-45. Mem. Am. String Tchrs. Assn. (dir. 1970-73), Chamber Music Am., Am. Fedn. Musicians (life). Home: 34 66th Pl Long Beach CA 90803

REESE, KERRY PAUL, educator; b. Hempstead, N.Y., Feb. 11, 1951; s. Dudley Paul and Leda Arlene (Collins) R.; m. Nancy Jean Starosielec, Aug. 11, 1973; children: Andrea, David. BS in Biology, Ind. U. of Pa., 1973; MS in Wildlife Sci., Clemson U., 1976; PhD in Wildlife Sci., Utah State U., 1982. Instr. avian ecology Utah State U., Logan, 1982-83; vis. asst. prof. U. Idaho, Moscow, 1983-84, asst. prof., 1984—. Contbr. articles to profl. jours. Recipient Alumni award for Faculty Excellence U. Idaho Alumni Assn., 1984. Mem. The Wildlife Soc. (cert. wildlife biologist), AAAS, Cooper Ornithol. Soc., Am. Ornithologists' Union, Nongame Wildlife Assn. of N.Am., Wilson Ornthol. Soc., Northwest Sci. Assn., Soc. Wetland Scientists, Western Bird Banding Assn. (bd. dirs.), Sigma Xi, Xi Sigma Pi. Democrat. Episcopalian. Lodge: Kiwanis. Avocations: hunting, hiking, reading. Home: 512 N Grant Moscow ID 83843 Office: U Idaho Coll Forestry Wildlife Range Scis Moscow ID 83843

REESE, ROBERT JENKINS, senator, lawyer; b. Green River, Wyo., June 2, 1947; s. William David and Elsa Edith (Bluhm) R.; m. Karen Lee Thompson, Nov. 27, 1971 (div. Dec. 1984); 1 child, William Derek; m. Mary Lynn Cockriel, Dec. 24, 1986. BA, Harvard U., 1969; JD, U. Wyo., 1978. Bar: Wyo. 1978, U.S. Dist. Ct. Wyo. 1978, U.S. Ct. Appeals (10th cir.) 1984. Tchr. Stratford Jr. High Sch., Arlington, Va., 1971-75; dep. county atty. Sweetwater County, Green River, Wyo., 1978-82; sole practice Green River, 1983-86; ptnr. Reese & Mathey, Green River, 1986—. Dem. chmn. Sweetwater County, Green River, 1983-85; senator Wyo. State, Cheyenne, Wyo., 1985—. Mem. Wyo. Trial Lawyers Assn. (bd. dirs. 1985-86), Green River C. of C. (bd. dirs. 1984-86), Sweetwater County Bar (pres. 1985-86).

REESER, DAVID MERL, environmental engineer; b. Kansas City, Kans., Feb. 2, 1930; s. Raymond M. and J. Marie (Surbaugh) R.; m. Ruby I. Blanchard, May 31, 1952; children—Deborah, Kathy, Warren. B.S. in Civil Engring., U. Kans., 1952; postgrad. U. Calif.-Berkeley, 1955. Diplomate Am. Acad. Environ. Engrs. Registered profl. civil engr., Wash., Oreg., Calif. Water Prodn. engr. City of Santa Cruz, Calif., 1960-65; supt. water treatment plants City of San Francisco, 1965-68; project mgr. Brown and Caldwell, San Francisco, Eugene, Oreg., 1968-73; v.p. heavy constrn. div. Teeples and Thatcher, Portland, Oreg., 1974; v.p., Northwest div. mgr. Barrett and Assocs., Portland, 1975; environ. process mgr. Rust Internat. Co., Portland, 1978—; lectr. in field. Nation chief YMCA Indian Guides, Sunnyvale, Calif., 1968. Served to lt. USPHS Res., 1955-65. Mem. Am. Water Works Assn. (chmn. operator's cert. com., Calif. sect. 1967-70, vice chmn. program com. chmn. purification div. Calif. sect. Water Polution Control Fedn., TAPPI (sec. water quarterly com. 1983-85, vice chmn. 1985-87, chmn. 1987—). Office: Rust Internat Corp PO Box 25374 Portland OR 97225

REESMAN, WILLIAM RICHARD, insurance marketing executive, financial planner; b. Wooster, Ohio, Dec. 21, 1940; s. John Kingsley and Esther Mae (Tanner) R.; m. Patricia Louise Greenawald, June 11, 1960; children: Jacqwyn, Suzanne. BSBA, Ohio State U., 1963; MBA, Pacific Western U., 1987. Airline pilot Northwest Orient, Mpls., 1969-70; sales dir. No. Nat. Life Ins. Co., Mpls., 1970-76; chief pilot Air N.G., Sioux City, Iowa, 1976-79; instr. pilot United Airlines, Denver, 1979-80; pres. Brokers Mktg. Group, Inc., Denver, 1980—, Fin. Profiles Group, Inc., Denver, 1987—. Author: How to Earn $360,000 a Year by Mass-Marketing Insurance, 1984. Served to capt. USAF, 1963-69, lt. col. N.G., 1984—. Decorated D.F.C., Air medals (11). Republican. Avocations: flying, photography, writing, reading, exercise. Home: 11803 E Yale Way Aurora CO 80014 Office: Brokers Mktg Group 2600 S Parker Rd #3-233 Aurora CO 80014

REEVES, DANIEL EDWARD, professional football coach; b. Rome, Ga., Jan. 19, 1944; m. Pam Reeves; children: Dana, Laura, Lee. Grad., U. S.C. Running back Dallas Cowboys, NFL, 1965-72; player-coach Dalls Cowboys, NFL, 1970-71; asst. coach Dallas Cowboys, NFL, 1972, 74-80; head coach Denver Broncos, NFL, 1981—. Player NFL Championship Game, 1966, 67, 70, 71. Mem. S.C. Hall of Fame. Office: care Denver Broncos 5700 Logan St Denver CO 80216 *

REEVES, JOHN FREDERICK, career development specialist, educator, writer; b. Morristown, N.J., June 11, 1954; s. John F. and Harriet P. Reeves; student U. Alaska, 1973-74, 80-83; M.A. in Human Resource Devel., Norwich U., 1984. Dir., career devel. trainer Adult Learning Programs of Alaska, CETA Tng., Tech. Assistance Project, Fairbanks, Alaska, 1977-80; dir., founder, career cons. Alaska Life/Work Planning Ctr., Fairbanks, 1980-86; cons., trainer, writer, Reeves Assocs., Fairfield, Iowa and Fairbanks, 1986-87; dir. membership devel. Nat. Assn. Entrepreneurs, Denver, 1987—. Pres. adv. bd. North Star Borough Sch. Dist. Community Edn., Fairbanks, 1982-83. Mem. Am. Soc. Tng. and Devel. (bd. dirs., communications chmn. Fairbanks chpt. 1982-86), Nat. Career Devel. Project, Profl. Devel. League, Internat. Meditation Soc. Author: Integrating Career Development with Human Resource Information Systems, 1983; Stalking the Great Alaskan Job, 1984. Home: PO Box 441 Fairfield IA 52556 Office: 7837 Sheridan Westminster CO 80003

REEVES, MICHAELYN MARIE, communications technician; b. S.I., N.Y., Nov. 3, 1956; d. Clyde James and Dorothy Grace (Brown) Tuggle; m. Robert Owen Reeves, Sept. 24, 1976 (div. Apr. 1978). Cashier I. Magnin, Pasadena, Calif., 1979-80; communication technician AT&T Communications, Los Angeles, 1980—. Served with USAF, 1974-79. Roman Catholic. Home: 14634 Vose St Van Nuys CA 91405

REFSLAND, GARY ARLAN, gerontology center administrator, sociology educator; b. Big Timber, Mont., May 5, 1944; s. William Anton and Agnes Eline (Freeberg) R.; m. Judith Estelle Hall, Aug. 20, 1969 (div. Aug. 1974). BS in Sociology, Mont. State U., 1970, MS in Sociology, 1971; postgrad., Internat. Grad. Sch., Stockholm, 1970; AA in funeral directing, Calif. Coll. Mortuary Sci., 1973. Cert. funeral dir., mortician. Instr. sociology Mont. State U., Bozeman, 1971-72, lectr., 1976—, coordinator of aging services Coll. Letters and Sci., 1976-77, acting dir. Ctr. Gerontology, 1977-79, dir. Mont. Ctr. Gerontology, 1979—; mortician Dokken Nelson Funeral Service, Bozeman, 1974-76; cons. State Agy. Aging, 1979—; mem. adv. bd. Sr. Community Services Employment program, Mont., 1983—, Regional Edn. and Tng. program Fed. Region VIII, 1980-82; state coordinator White Ho. Conf. on Aging, 1981-82. Writer, producer (TV show) Mont.'s Priorities for Aging, 1981; contbr. articles to profl. jours. Pres. Gallatin County Housing Authority Bd., Bozeman, 1981-82, sec. 1978-81; pres. Sourdough Ridge Property Owners Assn., Bozeman, 1982-84, Gallatin County Council on Aging, 1978-80. Served with USN, 1962-66. Recipient Cert. Appreciation U.S. Dept. Health and Human Services, Denver, 1982; named one of Outstanding Young Men Am., U.S. Jaycees, 1981. Mem. Am. Soc. Aging, Mont. Gerontology Soc. (charter officer 1982-83), Nat. Council on Aging (del. council 1982-83), Am. Legion, Alpha Kappa Delta. Avocations: motorcycling, hunting, tennis, carpentry. Home: 212 Ridge Trail Rd Bozeman MT 59715 Office: Mont State U Ctr Gerontology Bozeman MT 59717

REGALADO, RAUL L., airport executive; b. Los Angeles, Jan. 31, 1945; s. Raul and Antonia (Estavillo) R.; m. Christa Kohler, Mar. 16, 1971; children: Horst, Stephanie, Jennifer. BS, Embry-Riddle Aerospace U., 1972. Mgr.

airport City of Klamath Falls, Oreg., 1972-74, City of Fresno, Calif., 1974-79, Orange County, Santa Ana, Calif., 1979-80; dir. aviation San Jose (Calif.) Airport, 1980—. Served to capt. U.S. Army, 1966-71, lt. col. res. Decorated Bronze Star, D.F.C., Air medal with 49 oak leaf clusters. Mem. Am. Assn. Airport Execs., Calif. Assn. Airport Execs. (pres. 1980-81), Res. Officers Assn., Assn. U.S. Army, Calif., Airport Operators Council Internat. (bd. dirs. 1986—), Aerospace Club No. Calif. (bd. dirs. 1982—, pres. 1987—), Quiet Birdmen. Lodge: Rotary. Office: San Jose Internat Airport 1661 Airport Blvd Suite 205 San Jose CA 95110-1285

REGAN, MARTIN DANIEL, geologist, consultant; b. Butte, Mont., Aug. 19, 1933; s. Martin Michael and Mary Elizabeth (Broksle) R.; m. Marjorie C. McQuiston, Aug. 18, 1956 (div. 1974); children—Daniel W., Michael R., Timothy S., Alesia L. B.S. in Geol. Engring., Mont. Coll. Mineral, Sci. and Tech., 1957; M.S. in Mgmt., MIT, 1971. Cert. profl. geologist. Miner, sampler The Anaconda Co., Butte, 1952-56; resident geologist, engr. The Taylor Knapp Co., Philipsburg, Mont., 1956-59; exploration geologist Bear Creek Mining Co., N.Mex., Colo., Utah, 1960-64, sr. geologist, staff sr. geologist, Salt Lake City, 1965-70; exploration-acquisition mgr. Kennecott, Spokane, Wash., Salt Lake City, 1971-83; cons. geol. mgmt., Spokane, 1983-84; pres. M.D. Regan & Assocs., Spokane, 1985— . Student counselor MIT Ednl. Council, Spokane, 1972-75. Sloan fellow, MIT, 1970-71. Mem. Am. Inst. Profl. Geologists (cert.), Soc. Econ. Geologists, Soc. Mining Engrs.-Am. Inst. Mining Engrs., N.W. Mining Assn. (trustee 1974-77), Intermountain Assn. Geologists (sec., treas. 1965-66), Mont. Tech. Alumni Assn., MIT Alumni Assn., Theta Tau. Office: Suite P-1 MD Regan Cons PO Box 14663 E 9209 Mission Spokane WA 99214

REGAN, MICHAEL PATRICK, motion picture producer; b. Oyster Bay, N.Y., Aug. 29, 1948; s. John Thomas Patrick Joseph and Marcella Bridget (McCourt) R.; m. Suzan Gene Lavery, June 24, 1972; children: Gregory Michael, Timothy Daniel. Student, C.W. Post Coll., L.I. U., 1969-70. Dealer Amerada Hess Corp., Oceanside, N.Y., 1966-78; prin. Micky P's Restaurant, Hicksville, N.Y., 1978-80; assoc. dir. NCCJ, N.Y.C., 1979-80; movie producer GTR Productions, Reseda, Calif., 1980—. Author: (screenplay) The Grunt, 1981. Served to cpl. USMC, 1967-69, Vietnam. Democrat. Roman Catholic. Avocations: golf, guitar, swimming, perpetual motion. Home and Office: 18325 Vanowen St #121 Reseda CA 91335

REGAN, RICHARD WILLIAM, bank executive; b. Englewood, N.J., Oct. 10, 1949; s. Donald Thomas and Ann Gordon (Buchanan) R. BA, Washington and Lee U., 1971; MBA, Am. U., 1976. Comml. officer 1st Nat. Bank of Atlanta, 1976-78; asst. v.p. Univ. Nat. Bank, Denver, 1979-81; exec. asst. Dept. Commerce, Washington, 1981; sr. v.p. Denver Nat. Bank, 1981-86; v.p. 1st Interstate Bank of Denver, N.A., 1986—. Mem. fin. com. Colo. Reps., Denver, 1982-84. Mem. Colo. Bankers Assn., Robert Morris Assn. Office: 1st Interstate Bank 633 17th St 3N007 Denver CO 80270

REGAS, JENNINE, medical electronics company executive; b. Alamosa, Colo., Feb. 17, 1929; d. Max Tygart and Helene (Hanpeter) Chelf; m. Stelios Regas, June 19, 1955; children: Paul, Marie, Diane, Philip, Peter. AB, U. Colo., 1950; MS, U. Ill., 1955. Sci. cataloguer Brandeis U., Waltham, Mass., 1956-57; mktg. mgr. MX Internat., Inc., Aurora, Colo., 1973-76; tech. dir. Animark, Inc., Aurora, 1975-84; dir. communications and info. Zetek, Inc., Aurora, 1984—. Editor: (bibliography) Ultrasound in Medical Diagnosis, 1961. Fellow Internat. Council of Sex Edn. and Parenthood; mem. The Am. Fertility Soc.Royal Soc. of Medicine (assoc.), Am. Pub. Health Assn. Republican. Episcopalian. Office: Zetek Inc 794 Ventura St Aurora CO 80011

REGENSBURG, ANTHONY SHEPARD, wholesale distribution company executive; b. N.Y.C., July 31, 1928; s. Edward J. and Josephine (Copeland) R.; m. Patricia Hentz, Sept. 6, 1949; children: Victoria Regensburg Kahn, Paul Patric. B.S., Yale U., 1948; postgrad., Harvard U., 1966. Leaf tobacco trainee Gen. Cigar Co., N.Y.C., 1948-49; tobacco buyer, asst. factory supt., v.p. sales Admiration Cigar Co., N.Y.C., 1949-57, exec. v.p., 1958-64; with Bayuk Cigars Inc., Phila., 1964-78, sr. v.p., 1970-73, exec. v.p., 1973-78; sr. v.p. mktg. Gen. Cigar & Tobacco div. Culbro Corp., N.Y.C., 1978-79; pres. Glaser Bros., Los Angeles, 1979—, also dir.; dep. chmn. Core Marks Internat. Served to capt. arty. U.S. Army, 1952-54. Named Man of Yr. N.Y. Tobacco Table, 1970, Anti-Defamation League Man of Yr., 1982; recipient Brotherhood award NCCJ, 1985. Dir. Cigar Assn. Am., Nat. Assn. Tobacco Distbrs. (Young Exec. Achievement award 1968). Republican. Home: Beverly Hills CA 90210 Office: Core-Mark Distbrs Inc 1800 N Vine St Hollywood CA 90028 *

REGINATO, ROBERT JOSEPH, soil scientist; b. Palo Alto, Calif., Apr. 13, 1935; s. Guiseppi Primo and Carolina Theresa (Boccignone) R.; m. Donna Marie LeStum, Aug. 26, 1956; children—Richard Lynn, David Lewis, Christopher Michael, Michael Jeffrey. B.S., U. Calif.-Davis, 1957; M.S., U. Ill., 1959; Ph.D., U. Calif.-Riverside, 1973. Research asst. U. Calif., Davis, 1956-57, U. Ill., Urbana, 1957-59; soil scientist U.S. Water Conservation Lab., U.S. Dept. Agr.-Agrl. Research Service, Phoenix, 1959—, research leader, 1980—; vis. scientist U. Calif.-Davis, 1977-78; U.S. Dept. Agr. collaborator U. Ariz., Tucson, 1959—. Contbr. over 160 articles to tech. jours. Active Roosevelt council Boy Scouts Am., 1960-76. Fellow Am. Soc. Agronomy, Soil Sci. Soc. Am.; mem. Internat. Soil Sci. Soc., Western Soil Sci. Soc., Sigma Xi, Alpha Zeta, Kappa Sigma. Roman Catholic. Home: 525 Bishop Dr Tempe AZ 85282 Office: US Water Conservation Lab US Dept Agr-Agrl Research 4331 E Broadway Rd Phoenix AZ 85040

REGISTER, ULMA DOYLE, nutrition educator; b. West Monroe, La., Feb. 4, 1920; s. John William and Lillian (Reagan) R.; m. Helen Louise Hite, June 15, 1942; children: Rebecca, Dorothy, Deborah. BS, Madison Coll., 1942; MS, Vanderbilt U., 1944; PhD, U. Wis., 1950. Postdoctoral fellow Tulane Sch. Med., New Orleans, 1950-51; instr. biochemistry Loma Linda (Calif.) U., 1951-53, asst. prof., 1953-58, assoc. prof., 1959-67, prof. biochemistry, 1967—, chmn. dept. nutrition, 1967-84; pres. Calif. Nutrition Council, 1973. Co-author: Food for Us All, 1981, It's Your World Cookbook, 1981; contbr. numerous articles to sci. jours. Served to 1st lt. U.S. Army, 1944-47. Mem. Am. Inst. Nutrition, Am. Dietetic Assn., Soc. Nutrition Edn., Calif. Nutrition Council (pres. 1973), Delta Omega. Republican. Adventist. Home: 11448 Benton St Loma Linda CA 92354 Office: Loma Linda U Nutrition Sch Health Loma Linda CA 92350

REGNART, CLAUDIA SWANNACK, educator; b. Spokane, Wash., Aug. 11, 1937; d. John William and Leone Estelle (Roth) Swannack; B.A., U. Puget Sound, 1959; postgrad. E. Wash. Coll. Edn., summers 1958, 60, U. Wash., summer 1966, Alaska Pacific U., 1968-69, 84, U. Alaska, summers 1972, 74, 82; m. Ronald I. Regnart, Nov. 21, 1962; children—Jeffrey, Patrick. Tchr., Anchorage Sch. Dist., 1959-63, 64-65, 67, Nome (Alaska) Sch. Dist., 1963-64; tchr., owner Rabbit Creek Pre-Sch., Anchorage, 1972—. Chmn. PTA, Anchorage, 1970—; den mother Boy Scouts Am., 1973-79; vol. worker Cancer Fund, Heart Fund, FISH, Little League. Mem. Alaska Edn. Assn., NEA, Am. Assn. for Edn. of Young Children. Methodist. Club: Order Eastern Star. Home and Office: 4900 Rabbit Creek Rd SRA Book 476A Anchorage AK 99516

REGOLI, NICHOLAS ANTHONY, electrical engineer; b. New Kensington, Pa., Mar. 20, 1951; s. Bruno Batista and Louise Mary (Rivi) R.; m. Sandra Renee Baca, Apr. 11, 1986. BS in Engring. Sci. magna cum laude, U. Steubenville, 1973; MS, Westinghouse Nuclear Plant Engring. Sch., 1977. Registered profl. engr., Calif., Ohio. Field engr., supr. Ohio Power Co., Canton, 1973-77; field engr., cons. Westinghouse Electric Co., Pitts. and Mare Island, Calif., 1977-81; instrument and control supr. Pacific Gas and Electric Co., Avila Beach, Calif., 1981-86; dir. bus. devel. Spectrum RMS Inc., San Diego, 1986—. Lodge: Elks. Avocations: karate, snorkeling, aerobics. Home: 6465 Electric Ave La Jolla CA 92037 Office: Spectrum RMS Inc 12760 HIgh Bluff Dr Suite 340 San Diego CA 92130

REGOLI, ROBERT MICHAEL, sociologist, researcher; b. Pitts., Aug. 25, 1950; s. Arthur Adolph and Meta Hellen (Callan) R.; m. Deborah Kay White, June 10, 1972; children: Andrea Kay, Adam Michael. AA, Diablo Valley Coll., Concord, Calif., 1970; BS, Wash. State U., 1971, MA, 1972, PhD, 1975. Asst. prof. Ind. State U., Terre Haute, 1975-77, Tex. Christian U., Ft. Worth, 1977-81; assoc. prof. U. Colo., Boulder, 1981—; cons. Arvada (Colo.) Police Dept., 1985—, Nat. Inst. Justice, Washington, 1986—; pres. Acad. Criminal Justice Scis. Mem. Western Social Sci. Assn. (editor 1985-87), Acad. Criminal Justice Scis. (bd. trustees 1982-84, 2d v.p. 1984-85, 1st v.p. 1985-86, pres. 1986-87), Phi Beta Kappa. Democrat. Avocations: music video, jogging. Home: 1265 Scorpios Circle Lafayette CO 80026 Office: U Colo Dept Sociology CB 327 Boulder CO 80309

REGRAVE, MARTYN ROBERT, food service executive; b. Neenah, Wis., June 11, 1952; s. John Robert and Nancy Jean (Rosendale) R.; m. Lynn Akelman, July 16, 1977; children: John, Kristina. AB, Princeton U., 1974; MBA, NYU, 1976. CPA, N.Y. Staff acct. Arthur Andersen & Co., N.Y.C., 1974-76, audit sr., 1976-78, audit mgr., 1978-80; asst. corp. controller PepsiCo Inc., Purchase, N.Y., 1980-82; v.p. fin., chief fin. officer PepsiCo Food Service Internat., Purchase, 1982-84; sr. v.p. fin., chief. fin. officer Taco Bell Corp., Irvine, Calif., 1984—, also bd. dirs. Mem. fin. com. Orange County Performing Arts Ctr., Costa Mesa, Calif., 1985—. Mem. Am. Inst. CPA's, N.Y. State Soc. CPA's. Republican. Episcopalian. Clubs: Center (Costa Mesa); Nellie Gail Tennis (Laguna Hills, Calif.). Avocations: tennis, golf, skiing, racquetball, jogging, swimming. Home: 25882 Nellie Gail Rd Laguna Hills CA 92653 Office: Taco Bell Corp 17901 Von karman Ave Irvine CA 92714

REHFELD, THOMAS ARTHUR, marketing researcher; b. Phoenix, Nov. 26, 1955; s. Robert William and Jean (Lentz) R. Student, Hampshire Coll., 1973; BA, Grinnell Coll., 1978; MS, Northwestern U., 1979. Account exec. Foote, Cone and Belding, Phoenix, 1979-80, Patton Agy., Phoenix, 1980-81; research dir. Mithoff Advt., El Paso, Tex., 1981-82; dir. comsumer research Leach Research, Santa Fe, 1983-84; pres. Zia Research Assocs., Albuquerque, 1984—. Mem. Am. Mktg. Assn. (treas. 1986—, speaker 1986), Mktg. Research Assn., Am. Advt. Fedn., El Paso Jaycees, Albuquerque C. of C. Episcopalian. Avocations: trout fishing, tennis. Office: Zia Research Assocs 5907 Alice NE Suite A Albuquerque NM 87110

REICH, CHARLES WILLIAM, nuclear physicist; b. Oklahoma City, Sept. 12, 1930; s. Fred William And Gertrude Evelyn (Veal) R.; m. Juana Sue Woods, June 8, 1952; children: Paul William, Jane Kristen, Donna Karen. BS in Physics, U. Okla., 1952; MA in Physics, Rice U., 1954, PhD in Physics, 1956. Physicist, group leader Atomic Energy Div. Phillips Petroleum Co., Idaho Falls, Idaho, 1956-66; group leader, sect. chief Idaho Nuclear Corp., Idaho Falls, 1966-71; sect. chief Aerojet Nuclear Corp., Idaho Falls, 1971-76; prin. scientist, sect. chief EG&G Idaho, Inc., Idaho Falls, 1976—, sci., engring. fellow, 1982—; guest scientist Niels Bohr Inst., Copenhagen, 1964-65; U.S. rep., coordinator Internat. Atomic Energy Agy. coordinated research program, 1977—; com. mem. U.S. Dept. Energy Transplutonium Program com., 1978—; chmn. Decay Data subcom. Cross Sects. Evaluation Working Group, 1974—. Contbr. articles to profl. jours. NSF Predoctoral fellow, 1954-55; recipient H.A. Wilson research award Rice Inst., Houston, 1956. Fellow Am. Phys. Soc. (editorial bd. Phys. Rev. 1978, 1982-84); mem. AAAS, N.Y. Acad. Scis., Sigma Xi, Phi Beta Kappa. Mem. Ch. Nazarene. Office: Idaho Nat Engring Lab EG&G Inc PO Box 1625 Idaho Falls ID 83415

REICHARTZ, DAN, pres., Caesar's Palace Hotel. Office: Caesar's Palace Hotel Office of the Pres 3570 Las Vegas Blvd S Las Vegas NV 89109 *

REICHE, MARVIN GARY, restaurant executive; b. Sacramento, Sept. 2, 1949; s. Robert A. and Kate Kathleen (Groo) R.; m. Kathleen Louise Price, Feb. 10, 1968; children—Bradford, Renee, Darren, Michelle, Ryan, Brandon. With Harman Mgmt. Corp., 1967-79, cook and pie shell operator, Lodi, Calif., 1967, cook, Carmichael, Calif., 1967-68, store mgr., Sacramento, 1968-72, Fair Oaks, Calif., 1972-77, dist. mgr. Central Sacramento, 1977-79; owner, investor Kentucky Fried Chicken, Covina, West Covina, Long Beach, Lakewood, Bellflower, Los Angeles County, Garden Grove and Anaheim, Calif., 1979—; sole owner Kasmar Enterprises; dir. So. Calif. Kentucky Fried Chicken Advt. Assn. Judge Bank Am. Achievement Awards Program, 1983. Republican. Mormon.

REICHEK, JESSE, artist; b. Bklyn., Aug. 16, 1916; s. Morris and Celia (Bernstein) R.; m. Laure Guyot, May 16, 1950; children—Jonathan, Joshua. Student, Inst. Design, Chgo., 1941-42; diploma, Academie Julian, Paris, 1951. instr. dept. architecture U. Mich., 1946-47; prof. Inst. Design Ill. Inst. Tech., 1951-53; prof. dept. architecture U. Calif. at Berkeley, 1953—; Cons. Nat. Design Inst. Ford Found. project, Ahmedabad, India, 1963, San Francisco Redevel. Agy. Embarcadero Center, 1966—; lectr. Nat. Inst. Architects, Rome, 1960, U. Florence, 1960, U. Naples, 1960, Israel Inst. Tech., 1960, Greek Architects Soc., Athens, 1960, U. Belgrade, 1960, MIT, 1965, U. N.Mex., 1964, Am. Cultural Center, Paris, 1960, 64, Gujarat Inst. Engrs. and Architects, 1963, U. Colo., 1961, Harvard, 1962, U. Minn., 1962, U. Coll. London, 1967, Inst. Contemporary Arts, London, 1967, Ecole Nationale des Beaux-Ats, 1967; artist in residence Tamarind Lithography Workshop, 1966, Am. Acad. in Rome, 1971-72; research prof. Creative Arts Inst. U. Calif., 1966-67; artist in residence IBM Los Angeles Sci. Center, 1970-71. Exhibited one man shows at, Galerie Cahiers d'Art Paris, 1951, 59, 68, U. Calif. at Berkeley, 1954, Betty Parsons Gallery, N.Y.C., 1958, 59, 63, 65, 67, 69, 70, Molton Gallery, London, 1962, Am. Culture Center, Florence, Italy, 1962, Bennington Coll., 1963, U. N.Mex., 1966, U. So. Calif., 1967, Axiom Gallery, London, 1968, Yoseido Gallery, Tokyo, 1968, Los Angeles County Mus. Art, 1971; exhibited in group shows, Bklyn. Mus., 1959, Mus. Modern Art, N.Y.C., 1962, 65, 69, Knox-Albright Art Gallery, 1962, Art Inst. Chgo., 1963, Cin. Art Mus., 1966, Balt. Art Mus., 1966, Yale Art Gallery, 1967, Grand Palais, Paris, 1970, Nat. Mus. Art, Santiago, Chile, 1970, art and tech. exhibit, Los Angeles County Mus. Art, 1971, Maeght Found., St. Paul de Vence, France, 1971, Mus. Modern Art, Paris, 1971; represented in permanent collections, Mus. Modern Art, Art Inst. Chgo., Bibliotheque Nationale, Paris, Victoria & Albert Mus., London, Los Angeles County Art Mus., Grunwald Graphic Arts Found., U. Calif. at Los Angeles, San Diego Mus. Art, Amon Carter Mus., Fort Worth; Author: Jesse Reichek-Dessins, 1960, La Monte de la Nuit, 1961, Fontis, 1961, Etcetera, 1965, Le Bulletin Des Baux, 1972; e.g., 1976. Served to capt. C.E. AUS, 1942-46. Home: 5925 Red Hill Rd Petaluma CA 94953

REICHENBACH, DENNIS DALE, physician, pathology educator; b. Billings, Mont., Sept. 14, 1933; s. Ernest A. and Lilli (Stockland) R.; m. Jean Karen Hickey, Feb. 27, 1960; children: Stephen, Laura. BS in Basic Med. Sci., U. Wash., 1955, MD, 1958. Intern King County (Wash.) Hosp., Seattle, 1958-59; resident in pathology U. Wash., Seattle, 1959-63, asst. prof. pathology, 1966-70, assoc. prof., 1970-75, prof., 1975—; dir. pathology residency program, U. Wash., 1981—; pathologist in chief Harvorview Med. Ctr., Seattle, 1982—. Contbr. articles to profl. jours. Served with USPHS, 1963-65. Mem. Am. Assn. Pathologists (cert.), Soc. Cardiovascular Pathologists, King County Med. Assn. Home: 6548 49th NE Seattle WA 98115 Office: Harborview Med Ctr 325 9th Ave Seattle WA 98104

REICHER, ROBERT NATHAN, consulting firm executive; b. N.Y.C., June 9, 1944; s. Arthur M. and Eleanor G. R.; m. Suzanne P. Carter, Sept. 7, 1969; children—R. Michael, S. Christina. B.S., UCLA, 1966; M.B.A., U. So. Calif., 1967. Account exec. Foote, Cone & Belding, Newport Beach, Calif., 1967-69; mktg. dir. Litton Industries, Newport Beach, 1969-70; mktg. research dir. Leadership Homes, Newport Beach, 1970-73; pres. Reicher Corp., Newport Beach, 1973-83; dir. Orange County ops. The Goodkin Group, Newport Beach, 1983-85; mgr. Deloitte, Haskins & Sells, Costa Mesa, Calif., 1985—. Mem. Hoag Meml. Hosp. 552 Club, Urban Land Inst.; v.p. Newport Beach Improvement Assn., 1980; bd. dirs. Newport Mesa Schs. Found. Mem. Nat. Assn. Realtors, Urban Land Inst., Bldg. Industry Assn., Calif. Assn. Realtors. Club: Balboa Bay (Newport Beach). Office: Deloitte Haskins & Sells 695 Town Center Dr Costa Mesa CA 92626

REICHERT, RUSSELL RAYMOND, retail computer executive, consultant; b. Milw., Mar. 18, 1941; s. Harry J. and Marguerite A. (Doesburg) R.; m. Carol A. Schuppner, Jan. 7, 1961; children: Robert Scott, Holly J. BME, U. Wis., 1965. V.p. and regional mgr. Radio Shack div. Tandy Corp., Ft. Worth, 1966-77; pres. Millenium Corp., Sunnyvale, Calif., 1978-80; v.p. mktg. Abacus II, Santa Clara, Calif., 1980-83; dir. Velo-Bind, Sunnyvale, 1983-85; sr. v.p. Software Galeria, Sunnyvale, 1985—; cons. Memorex, Commodore and many other corps. Active Boy Scouts Am., Wis., Fla., and Ill., 1954-80. Served with USN, 1958-62. Lodge: Lions. Office: Software Galeria 1111 W El Camino Real Suite 213 Sunnyvale CA 94087

REICHMAN, SANDOR, chemistry educator; b. Budapest, Hungary, Nov. 24, 1941; came to U.S., 1956, naturalized, 1962; s. Ignac and Margit (Schwartz) R.; m. Edith Klein, June 21, 1966; children: Adrienne, Aaron, Abraham Z. BS, CCNY, 1963; PhD, NYU, 1967. Post-doctoral research U. Minn., Mpls., 1966-68; prof. chemistry Calif. State U., Northridge, 1968—. Mem. Am. Phys. Soc. Office: Calif State U-Northridge Dept Chemistry Northridge CA 91330

REICK, DONALD THOMAS, health science facilities consultant; b. New Brunswick, N.J., July 25, 1947; s. Edward Claire and Dora Jeanne (Straw) R.; m. Diane Marie Walsh, Nov. 18, 1967 (div. May 1972); 1 child: Danielle Rene; m. Connie Rae Gillespie, May 27, 1977. Student, Utah State U., 1966-67; BS in Psychology, Weber State Coll., 1971. Asst. dir. Utah Emergency Food and Med. Services, Salt Lake City, 1971-73; cons. Westinghouse Learning, Palo Alto, Calif., 1971-73; dir. meals on wheels and nutrition programs Salt Lake County Div. on Aging, 1973-75; admistrv. data mgr. Salt Lake County Div. of Mental Health, 1975-83; sr. systems analyst IMS Salt Lake City Corp., 1983-85; pres. Reick Cons. Inc., Salt Lake City, 1984—; cons. Norton Christensen Corp., Salt Lake City, 1985, Utah State Dept. Social Services, 1982-85, Internat. Airport Operators Assn., Norfolk Va., 1985, Salt Lake County Drug Referral, 1981, Eimco Jarvis Clark, 1986, Marriott Hotels, 1987. Contbr. articles to profl. jours. Co-chmn. Community Orgn. for Polit. Action, Ogden, Utah, 1972; mem. Utah Mental Health Program Evaluation Com., 1975-85, chmn. 1981-83. Mem. Nat. Home Delivered Meals Assn. (regional chmn. 1973-75). Roman Catholic. Avocation: reading. Office: Reick Cons 1817 S Main #16 Salt Lake City UT 84115

REID, ALBERT RAYMOND, public administrator, mechanical engineer; b. Braddock, Pa., Feb. 28, 1939; s. Albert John and Barbara Elizabeth (Rudy) R. m. Kathleen Louise Mauk, Nov. 9, 1963; children—David Albert, Anne Kathleen, Amy Louise, Daniel Raymond. B.S.M.E., Carnegie Inst. Tech., 1961; postgrad. U. So. Calif., 1962, U. Santa Clara, 1966. Systems analyst Lockheed Propulsion Co., Redlands, Calif., 1967-73; sr. adminstrv. services officer, spl. dists. coordinator County of San Bernardino (Calif.), 1974; asst. exec. officer Local Agy. Formation Commn., San Bernardino, 1974; dir. spl. dists., 1974-80; asst. county adminstr. County of San Bernardino, 1980-83, gen. services adminstr., 1983—; lectr., speaker local univs., community groups. Cubmaster Graybback dist. council Boy Scouts Am., 1974-76, dist. vice chmn., 1981, chmn., 1981-82, exec. bd. dirs. Inland Empire Council, 1975-80, v.p., 1983-84, council commr. 1985—; mem. parish council Sacred Heart Ch., 1977; mem. community diabetes council San Bernardino County Diabetes Demonstration Project, 1983-84; bd. dirs. Arrowhead United Way, 1983-85, Inland Empire chpt. Am. Diabetes Assn., also treas. Served to capt. USAF, 1962-67. Recipient Achievement award Nat. Assn. Counties, 1982, Silver Beaver award Boy Scouts Am., 1984. Mem. Am. Soc. Pub. Adminstrs., ASME. Republican.

REID, BELMONT MERVYN, brokerage house executive; b. San Jose, Calif., May 17, 1927; s. C. Belmont and Mary Irene (Kilfoyl) R.; B.S. in Engring., San Jose State U., 1950, postgrad.; m. Evangeline Joan Rogers, June 1, 1952. Pres., Lifetime Realty Corp., San Jose, 1969-77, Lifetime Fin. Planning Corp., San Jose, 1967-77; founder, chmn. bd. Belmont Reid & Co., Inc., San Jose, 1960-77; gen. ptnr., registered investment adv. JOBEL Fin. Inc., Carson City, Nev., 1980—; pres., chmn. bd. Data-West Systems, Inc., 1984—. County chmn. Carson City Rep. Cen. Com., treas., 1979-81; mem. Brewery Arts Ctr., Carson City Gen. Obligation Bond Commn., 1986—; rural county chmn. Nev. Rep. Cen. Com., 1984—; vice chmn. Carson City Charter Rev. Com., 1986—. Served with USN, 1945-46, 51-55. Decorated Air medals. Mem. Nat. Assn. Securities Dealers (mcpl. securities rulemaking bd.), Carson City Pilots Assn., Bush Pilots Internat., Nat. Futures Assn., Carson City C. of C. (pres., dir. 1986-87). Clubs: Capital of Carson City, Reno Executive. Lodge: Rotary (chpt. sec., pres.-elect). Home: 610 Bonanza Dr Carson City NV 89701 Office: 711 E Washington St Carson City NV 89701

REID, BILL, poet, psychotherapist, educator; b. Joplin, Mo., Mar. 8, 1936; s. James L. and Josephine (Kelley) R.; Ph.D., Brantridge Forest Sch., 1972; Litt.D. (hon.), U. Ryukyus, 1962; M.D., Ont. Med. Centre, 1978; m. Gwen Lewis; children—Cathy, James, Naida, Johanna, Elizabeth. Pvt. practice psychotherapy, Louisville, Ky., Jeffersonville, Ind., Reseda and Whittier, Calif., 1974—; nat. tech. tng. mgr. Epson Am., Inc., Torrance, Calif., 1983-86, prof. Pasadena Coll. of Chiropractic, Pico Rivera, Calif., 1986—; data processing educator Cert. Grocers of Calif., Ltd., 1981—1981-82; tchr. Spencerian Coll., Louisville, 1969-77, Van Nuys Coll. Bus., 1979-81; editor, pub. Internat. Violin and Guitar Makers jour., 1967—; v.p. Spectro-Chem., Inc., 1970-77. Diplomate Am. Bd. Examiners in Psychotherapy, Am. Bd. Cert. Psychoanalysts. Mem. Internat. Transactional Analysis Assn., Interam. Soc. Psychology, AAAS, AAUP, Nat. Assn. Sch. Psychologists, Internat. Rorshach Soc., Data Processing Mgmt. Assn., Assn. Humanistic Psychologists. Buddhist. Author: Just A Girl and A Night, 1969; Calling All Really Obscure Lovers, 1976; Do What Works, 1977; Thence A River, 1978; Who Was When, 1979; originator Causative Agency method of psychotherapy. Home and Office: 4459 Olive Ave Long Beach CA 90807

REID, (WILLIAM EARL) BILL, federal agency administrator; b. Nelson, B.C., Can., Aug. 13, 1934; s. William Earl and Dolly (Renwick) R.; m. Marion Joan Reid, June 21, 1957; children: Cathy Darlene, Laurie Joan, Gail Patricia, Sheila Marie. Alderman Delta, B.C., 1973-78; chmn. bd. dirs. Metro Transit Authority, 1978-79; charter mem. Urban Transit Authority, 1978-79; mem. B.C. Legis., 1983, cheif govt. whip, 1985, minister of tourism, 1986-. Candidate Progressive Conservative gen. election, 1972. Anglican. Club: Kinsman. Lodge Rotary. Office: Parliament Bldg, Victoria Can V8V 1X4

REID, EDWARD BROWN, chemical marketing executive; b. Houston, Jan. 15, 1943; s. William M. Reid and Nancy Jane (Pratt) Tucker; m. Connie Jean Goldston, May 25, 1974 (div. July 1980); 1 child, Lauren Cyd. BS, MS in Chemistry, Rice U., 1974; PhD in Chemistry, U. Houston, 1967. Tech. sales rep. Exxon Chem. Co., Houston, 1974-77; sales mgr. Cities Service Co., Houston, 1977-78; v.p. Dewitt and Co., Houston, 1978-80; proprietor Reid & Assocs., Houston, 1980-85, 86—; dir. pub. affairs Western States Art Found., Santa Fe, 1985-86. Pres. Native Houstonian Club, Houston, 1982. Mem. Chem. Market Research Assn., Am. Chem. Soc. Office: 508 Alto St Santa Fe NM 87501

REID, HARRY, U.S. senator; b. Searchlight, Nev., Dec. 2, 1939; s. Harry and Inez Reid; m. Landra Joy Gould; children—Lana, Rory, Leif, Josh, Key. AA in Sci., So. Utah State Coll., 1959; LLD (hon.), U. So. Utah, 1984; BS, Utah State U., 1961; JD, George Washington U., 1964. Bar: Nev. 1963, U.S. Supreme Ct. City atty. Henderson, Nev., 1964-66; trustee So. Nev. Meml. Hosp. Bd., 1967-69, chmn. bd. trustees, 1968-69; mem. Nev. Assembly, 1969-70; lt. gov. Nev., 1970-74; chmn. Nev. Gaming Commn., 1977-81; mem. 98th-99th Congresses, Washington, 1983—; U.S. senator from Nev. 1987—; mem. com. on sci. and tech., U.S. House of Reps., com. on fgn. affairs, select com. on aging; mem. com on appropriations, com. on environ., com. on pub. works, com. on aging U.S. Senate, 1985—; sec. treas. Calif. Dem. Congl. Del. Bd. dirs. Am. Cancer Soc., Legal Aid Soc., YMCA, Operation Life; judge Nev. State Athletic Commn.; pres. PTA; mem. exec. res. U.S. Office Emergency Planning. Named Nev. Jaycees Outstanding Young Man of Yr., 1970, Man of Yr., City of Hope; recipient Nat. Jewish Hosp.-Nat. Asthma Ctr. Humanitarian award, 1984. mem. Nev. Bar Assn., Am. Bd. Trial Advocates, Phi Kappa Phi. Office: US Senate Office of Senate Members Washington DC 20510

REID, JOSEPH LEE, physical oceanographer, educator; b. Franklin, Tex., Feb. 7, 1923; s. Joseph Lee and Ruby (Cranford) R.; m. Freda Mary Hunt, Apr. 7, 1953; children: Ian Joseph, Julian Richard. BA in Math., U. Tex., 1942; MS, Scripps Instn. Oceanography, 1950. Asst. research oceanographer Scripps Instn. Oceanography, La Jolla, Calif., 1957-61, assoc. research oceanographer, 1961-66, research oceanographer, 1966-74, assoc. dir. Inst. Marine Resources, 1975-82, prof. oceanography, dir. Marine Life Research

Group, 1974—; cons. Sandia Nat. Labs., Albuquerque, 1980—. Author: Intermediate Waters of the Pacific Ocean, 1965; contbr. articles to profl. jours. Served to lt. USNR, 1942-46, ETO, PTO. Recipient Nat. Oceanographic Data Ctr. award, Washington, 1984. Fellow AAAS, Am. Geophys. Union (pres. Ocean Scis. sec. 1972-74, 1984-86, pres.-elect 1982-84); mem. Am. Soc. Limnology and Oceanography. Home: 1105 Cuchara Dr Del Mar CA 92014 Office: Scripps Instn Oceanography Marine Life Research Group A-030 La Jolla CA 92093

REID, WILLIAM EARL See REID, (WILLIAM EARL) BILL

REIDER, RICHARD GARY, geographer, educator; b. Denver, Feb. 7, 1941; s. Alexander and Natalie Alice (Frick) R. BA, Colo. State Coll., 1963, MA, 1965; PhD, U. Nebr., 1971. Instr. geography Indiana U. of Pa., 1965-66; instr. geography U. Wyo., Laramie, 1969-71, asst. prof. geography, 1971-77, assoc. prof. geography, 1977-83, prof. geography, 1983—; cons. Smithsonian Inst., Washington, 1975-77, Office Wyo. Archaeologist, Laramie, 1975—, dept. anthropology U. Wyo., Laramie, 1975—, various firms, Wyo., 1977—. Contbg. author: The Agate Basin Site, 1982; contbr. articles to profl. jours. NSF grantee, 1975-76, Smithsonian grantee, 1975-77, 79. Mem. Assn. Am. Geographers, Geol. Soc. Am., Am. Quaternary Assn., Plains Anthrop. Soc., Sigma Xi. Office: U Wyo Dept Geography Laramie WY 82071

REIDY, RICHARD ROBERT, publishing company executive; b. Patchogue, N.Y., May 9, 1947; s. Joseph Robert and Irene (Jennings) R.; m. Carolyn Alyce Armstrong, Mar. 21, 1970; children: Dawn Patricia, Shawn Patrick, Christopher Keith. Student, Suffolk County Community Coll., 1966-68, L.I. Tech. Sch., 1969-70, Scottsdale Community Coll., 1983-84, 85-86. Lic. real estate agt., Ariz. Restaurant owner Reidy's, Patchogue, 1973-77; design draftsman Sverdrop & Parcel, Tempe, Ariz., 1978-79, Sullivan & Masson, Phoenix, 1979-81; pres. Success Pub. Co., Scottsdale, Ariz., 1983—, Am. Real Estate and Devel. Co., Scottsdale, 1986—; with U.S. Postal Dept., 1980—. Editor: Who's Who's in Ariz., 1984-85. Chief Scottsdale YMCA, 1983-84; eucharistic minister St. Daniel the Prophet Cath. Ch., Scottsdale, 1985—; World Wide Marriage Encounter, 1986—. Mem. Scottsdale C. of C., Phoenix Better Bus. Bur.

REIF, (FRANK) DAVID, artist, educator; b. Cin., Dec. 14, 1941; s. Carl A. and Rachael L. (Clifton) R.; m. Ilona Jekabsons, July 30, 1966; 1 child, Megan Elisabeth. BFA, Art Inst. Chgo., 1968; MFA, Yale U., 1970. Asst. prof. art U. Wyo., Laramie, 1970-74, assoc. prof., 1974-81, prof., 1981—; assoc. prof. U. Mich., Ann Arbor, 1980-81; head dept. art U. Wyo., Laramie, 1986—; selection cons. Ucross Found. Residency Program, Wyo., 1983—; exhibit juror Artwest Nat., Jackson, Wyo., 1986; panelist Colo. State U., Ft. Collins, 1981; lectr. U. Mich., 1980. One man shows include Dorsky Galleries N.Y.C., 1980, Colo. State U., 1978, No. Ariz. U., 1977; exhibited in group shows at First Wyo. Biennial Tour, 1984-85, U.S. Olympics Art Exhibition, Los Angeles, 1984, Miss. Mus. Art and NEA Tour., 1981-83. Served with U.S. Army, 1963-69. Recipient F.D. Pardee award Yale U., 1970; Best Sculpture award Joslyn Art Mus. Omaha, 1978; Nat. Endowment Arts grantee, 1978-79, Wyo. Basic Research grantee, 1983-84. Mem. Coll. Art Assn., Internat. Sculpture Ctr. Democrat. Home: 1117 Curtis St Laramie WY 82070 Office: U Wyo Dept Art Box 3138 Univ Sta Laramie WY 82071

REILLY, DOROTHY FRANCES, data processing executive; b. Chgo., Aug. 1, 1936; d. Daniel Kyoo and Naomi Frances (Kim) Hur; m. David Earl Reilly, May 16, 1958; children: Mark Cameron, Christopher Elliott. BA summa cum laude, Lawrence Coll., 1958; MS, U. Wis., 1960. Research asst. Midwestern U. Research Assoc., Madison, Wis., 1958-60; computer programmer and mgr. System Devel. Corp., Santa Monica, Calif., 1960-70; mgr. Xerox Corp., El Segundo, Calif., 1970—. Mem. Assn. Computing Machinery, Phi Beta Kappa. Avocations: gardening, personal computing, cooking, sewing. Office: Xerox Corp 701 S Aviation El Segundo CA 90245

REILLY, EUGENE HENRY, sales executive; b. N.J., Dec. 2, 1938; s. William Harry and Laura Eve (Startzar) R.; divorced; children: Kathleen, Karen, Maragaret, John; m. Ardithe Youngster, May 17, 1975. BS, Rutgers U., 1962; grad. advanced mgmt. program, UCLA, 1980. Registered SEC. Ops. analyst Sears Roebuck and Co., Chgo., 1962-65; mgmt. cons. Port of N.Y. Authority, N.Y.C., 1965-66; sales and mktg. mgr. Johnson & Johnson, New Brunswick, N.J., 1966-76; account exec. Merrill, Lynch, Pierce, Fenner & Smith, Beverly Hills, Calif., 1976-77; dir. sales, promotion, adminstrn. Max Factor and Co., Hollywood, Calif., 1977-78; v.p. U.S. Sales Corp., Los Angeles, 1978—; ptnr. Clocktower Mill, Hartford, Conn., 1986—, Capital Area Housing Program, Montgomery, Md., 1986—. Assoc. mem. Nat. Rep. Congl. Com., Washington, 1980—. Mem. Am. Assn. Individual Investors, So. Calif. Rutgers U. Alumni Club, Delta Sigma Pi (life). Republican. Methodist. Club: Village Bay (Lake Arrowhead, Calif.). Avocations: investments, photography, skiing, boating. Office: U S Sales Corp Los Angeles CA 91331

REILLY, PATRICK JOHN, engineering-construction company executive; b. Nutley, N.J., Oct. 10, 1925; s. Philip and Anna (Cox) O'Reilly; m. Marcia Garcia Vazquez, July 27, 1957; children: Anne Maria, Patrick John, Thomas J., Frank P. BSCE, NYU, 1950; cert. practical constrn. law, U. Santa Clara, 1977. Lin. gen. engring. contractor, Calif. Shaft engr. Lincoln Tunnel third tube Walsh Constrn. Co., N.Y.C., 1950-54; asst. equipment mgr. Brown-Raymond-Walsh, Madrid, 1954-55, project engr., 1955-57; v.p., project mgr. wastewater treatment plants Shanley Constrn. Co., San Francisco, 1957-65; constrn. mgr. W.W. Kimmins and Sons, Buffalo, 1965-70, gen. supt. hwy., utilities and underground constrn., 1970; dir. mcpl. waste projects, constrn. mgr. Monsanto Environ. Chem. Co., Chgo., 1970-74; v.p., project mgr., dir. constrn. and regional constrn. mgr. solid waste facilities BSP div. Envirotech Corp., Menlo Park, Calif., 1974-84, v.p. project mgmt., 1984—. Served with USAAF, 1943-45. Decorated D.F.C., Air medal with 5 oak leaf clusters. Mem. ASCE, Am. Arbitration Assn. (panel arbitrators). Roman Catholic. Home: 20719 Woodward Ct Saratoga CA 95070 Office: 3000 Sand Hill Rd Menlo Park CA 94025

REIMER, LARRY GENE, physician, pathology educator; b. Greeley, Colo., Jan. 24, 1949; s. Isaac R. and Opal M. (Nikkel) R.; m. Becky Lou Chesnut, Aug. 3, 1969; 1 child, Brendon Hollis. BA, Harvard U., 1971; MD, U. Colo., 1975. Asst. prof. medicine and pathology, dir. clin. microbiology W.Va. U., Morgantown, 1981-84, U. Utah, Salt Lake City, 1984—; bd. dirs. postgrad. tng. program clin. microbiology U. Utah VA Med. Ctr., Salt Lake City, 1984—. Contbr. articles to profl. jours. Mem. AAAS, ACP, Am. Soc. Microbiology, Infectious Diseases Soc. Am. Avocation: marathon running. Office: VA Med Ctr Dept Pathology 113 Salt Lake City UT 84148

REIN, BURTON MAXWELL, chemical company executive, consultant; b. N.Y.C., June 25, 1938; s. Ralph Philip and Etta (Slutsky) R.; m. Susan Kroll, Aug. 27, 1960; children: Tracy Lee, Pamela Sharon, Todd. BA, Alfred U., 1960; PhD, Syracuse U., 1964; postgrad., NYU, 1968. Group leader research and devel. Mobil Chem. Co., Edison, N.J., 1964-70; mgr. chem. research and tech. planning Chem Systems, Tarrytown, N.Y., 1970-72; asst. to pres. and chmn. GAF Corp., N.Y.C., 1972-75; v.p. mktg. and sales J.T. Baker Chem. Co., Phillipsburg, N.J., 1976-84, v.p. splty. chem. div., 1982-84; product ops. mgr. Motorola Inc., Albuquerque, N.Mex., 1984-86; cons. Albuquerque, 1986—. Patentee in field. Research grantee NIH, 1961-64. Mem. Chem. Mfrs. Assn., Am. Chem. Soc., Pharm. Mfrs. Assn., Fire Retardant Chem. Mfg. Assn. (founder, program chmn., 1973-75, editor newsletter), Drug Chem. Allied Trade Assn., Sigma Xi, Phi Lambda Upsilon. Avocations: skiing, tennis. Home and Office: 1143 Marigold Dr NE Albuquerque NM 87122

REINECKE, JEAN OTIS, industrial designer; b. Ft. Scott, Kans., July 9, 1909; s. Henry Hamon and Mary Estella (Knight) R.; 1 child, Barbra. Ptnr. Gen. Displays, Barnes & Reinecke, 1933-47; pres. Reinecke Assocs., Flintridge, Calif., 1947—; cons. MITI, Japan; instr. New Bauhaus; lectr. Northwestern U., Ill. Inst. Tech., Calif. Inst. Tech., UCLA, MIT, others. designer for firms including 3M, McGraw-Edison, Caterpillar, ITT, Hewlett-Packard Contbr. articles to profl. jours.; design editor Bus. Screen. Bd. dirs. Color Research Inst., Humanics Found.; adv. bd. Art Ctr. Coll. Design. Recipient Design awards Am. Designers Inst., Modern Plastics, Art Dirs. Club, Koppers Steel Packaging. Fellow Indsl. Designers Soc. Am. (chmn. bd., pres.); mem. Soc. Plastics Engrs. (bd. dirs.),. Clubs: Fin 'n' Feather, Riverside. Office: Reinecke Assocs 3780 Berwick Dr Flintridge CA 91011

REINER, ERIC ALAN, business consultant, author, lecturer, medical instrument company executive; b. N.Y.C., Feb. 3, 1944; s. Maury and Alice Jan (Berman) R. B.A. magna cum laude, Amherst Coll., 1966; postgrad. Oxford U., 1966-68, Grad. Inst. Film and TV, N.Y.U., 1969-70. Asst. buyer Gimbel Bros., 1966; asst. to pres. Fremantle Internat., 1968; free-lance motion picture cameraman, 1968-74; exec. dir. Celebrity Centre, N.Y.C., 1970-71, Narconon, N.Y.C., 1974-75; founder, pres. Eric Reiner Co., mgmt. cons., Los Angeles, 1974—; pres. Surg. Systems, Inc., Los Angeles, 1980—; lectr. on personal fin., inter-personal relationships, mgmt. skills. Bd. dirs. Hollywood Chorale; bd. dirs. Union Pacific Credit Union, 1979-80, Pres., 1980-81. Mem. Nat. Assn. Broadcast Engrs. in TV, Am. Arbitration Assn. (mem. bd. arbitrators), Concerned Businessmen's Assn. Am. (v.p.), Phi Beta Kappa. Republican. Editor-in-chief: (poetry anthology) Golden Horses, 1975.

REINES, FREDERICK, physicist, educator; b. Paterson, N.J., Mar. 16, 1918; s. Israel and Gussie (Cohen) R.; m. Sylvia Samuels, Aug. 30, 1940; children: Robert G., Alisa K. M.E., Stevens Inst. Tech., 1939, M.S., 1941; Ph.D., NYU, 1944; D.Sc. (hon.), U. Witwatersrand, 1966, D. Engring. (hon.), 1984. Mem. staff Los Alamos Sci. Lab., 1944-59; group leader Los Alamos Sci. Lab. (Theoretical div.), 1945-59; dir. (AEC expts. on Eniwetok Atoll), 1951; prof. physics, head dept. Case Inst. Tech., 1959-66; prof. physics U. Calif.-Irvine, 1966—, dean phys. scis., 1966-74. Contbr. numerous articles to profl. jours.; Contbg. author: Effects of Atomic Weapons, 1950. Mem. Cleve. Symphony Chorus, 1959-62. Recipient J. Robert Oppenheimer meml. prize, 1981, Nat. medal of Sci., 1983; Guggenheim fellow, 1958-59; Sloan fellow, 1959-63. Fellow Am. Phys. Soc., AAAS; mem. Am. Assn. Physics Tchrs., Argonne U. Assn. (trustee 1965-66), Am. Acad. Arts and Scis., Nat. Acad. Sci., Phi Beta Kappa, Sigma Xi, Tau Beta Pi. Co-discoverer elementary nuclear particle, free antineutrino, 1956. Office: U Calif at Irvine Irvine CA 92717

REINGOLD, JACK ALLAN, podiatrist; b. Bklyn., Nov. 2, 1954; s. Louis K. and Leah (Green) R. BA in Biology and Psychology, SUNY, Buffalo, 1976; D Podiatric Medicine, Calif. Coll. Podiatric Medicine, 1976. Diplomate Am. Bd. Podiatric Surgery. Resident Coll. Park Hosp., San Diego, 1979-80; practice medicine specializing in podiatry San Diego, 1980—; Commr., expert witness state of Calif. Bd. Med. Quality Assurance, 1986—. Surg. attending Baja Project for Crippled Children, Mexico, 1984—. Fellow Am. Coll. Foot Surgeons; mem. San Diego Podiatric Medicine Soc. (pres.1986-88). Democrat. Jewish. Avocations: running, skiing, cycling. Office: 6244 El Cajon Blvd #25 San Diego CA 92115

REINHARDT, STEPHEN ROY, judge; b. N.Y.C., Mar. 27, 1931; s. Gottfried and Silvia (Hanlon) R.; children: Mark, Justin, Dana. B.A. cum laude, Pomona Coll., 1951; LL.B., Yale, 1954. Bar: Calif. 1958. Law clk. to U.S. Dist. Judge Luther W. Youngdahl, Washington, 1956-57; atty. O'Melveny & Myers, Los Angeles, 1957-59; partner Fogel Julber Reinhardt Rothschild & Feldman (L.C.), Los Angeles, 1959-80; judge U.S. Ct. Appeals for 9th Circuit, Los Angeles, 1980—; Mem. exec. com. Dem. Nat. Com., 1969-72, nat. Dem. committeeman for Calif., 1976-80; pres. Los Angeles Recreation and Parks Commn., 1974-75; mem. Coliseum Commn., 1974-75, Los Angeles Police Commn., 1975-78, pres., 1978-80; sec., mem. exec. com. Los Angeles Olympic Organizing Com., 1980—; bd. dirs. Amateur Athletic Found. of Los Angeles, 1984—. Served to 1st lt. USAF, 1954-56. Mem. Am. Bar Assn. (labor law council 1975-77).

REINHART, ARTHUR SULLIVAN, consultant; b. Sabinal, Tex., Dec. 1, 1919; s. A.F. and Pocahontas E. (Sullivan) R.; B.S., Tex. Tech. U., 1941; postgrad., Air War Coll., 1961, Air Force Inst. Tech., 1962; M. Internat. Affairs, George Washington U., 1966; B.B.A., Boise State U., 1977; m. Hilma H. Ruuttila, Feb. 22, 1947; children—Arthur K., LauriAnne, Robin M., Brian M. Engr., U.S. Bur. Reclamation, Denver, 1946-51; commd. 2 lt. C.E., 1941, transferred to U.S. Air Force, advanced through grades to col., 1969; engaged in personnel, planning, ops.; dir. plans, comptroller Air Res. Personnel Center, Denver, 1969-74; ret., 1974; pvt. practice cons., Boise, Idaho, 1974—. Community adv. Downtown Boise Urban Renewal; chmn. Boise City Transit Com.; vice chmn., treas. Ada County Air Quality Bd. Served with USAAF, 1941-46; Decorated Legion of Merit. Mem. Ret. Officers Assn., Air Force Assn., Acad. Polit. Sci., Boise Com. on Fgn. Relations, Tex. Tech U. Dad's Assn. (trustee). Episcopalian. Clubs: Masons, Kiwanis. Home and office: 4933 Sunderland Dr Boise ID 83704

REINHART-COOK, LAURIE ANNE, social service agency administrator, dietitian; b. Bend, Oreg., July 8, 1953; d. Roger Dale and Eloyce Ann (Roy) Reinhart; m. David Lynn Cook, Dec. 22, 1973; children—Benjamin Lee Reinhart Cook, Susan Elizabeth Reinhart Cook, Brian Allen Reinhart Cook. B.S. in Dietetics and Inst. Mgmt., Oreg. State U., 1975; postgrad. in Mgmt., Willamette U. Registered dietitian, Oreg. Dietetic intern U. Oreg. Health Sci. Ctr., Portland, 1975-76; clin. dietitian Salem Memorial Hosp., Oreg., 1976-80; cons. dietitian Community Dialysis Services, Salem, 1978-81; supr. nutrition and meal planning MPY Council on Aging, Salem, 1980-83; dietitian MWY Sr. Services Agency, Salem, 1983, Nutrition program mgr., 1983—; mem. nat. conf. planning com. Nat. Assn. Meal Programs, Portland, 1981; bd. dirs. Townhouse Meal Program, 1983—. Pres. Rebekah Circle, Presbyterian Ch., Salem, 1982-84; mem. adv. com. Marion County Food Service Program, 1986—. Recipient Distinguished Service award Mid Willamette Valley Sr. Service Agency, 1986. Mem. Am. Assn. Univ. Women (corr. sec. 1980-81, v.p. membership 1981-82), Willamette Dietetic Assn. (pres. elect 1980-81, pres. 1981-82), Oreg. Dietetic Assn. (planning com. 1981-82), Oreg. Renal Council, Oreg. Nutrition Project Dirs. Assn., Nat. Assn. Nutrition and Aging Services Programs (Oreg. Rep. 1986-87). Democrat. Office: Mid Willamette Valley Sr Services Agency 220 High St N E 410 Senator Bldg Salem OR 97301

REINING, BETH LAVERNE (BETTY), public relations consultant, journalist; b. Fargo, N.D.; d. George and Grace (Twiford) Reimche; student N.D. State Coll., U. Minn., Glendale Community Coll., Calif. State Coll., Carson; 1 dau., Carolyn Ray Toohey Hiett; m. Jack Warren Reining, Oct. 3, 1976 (div. 1984). Originated self-worth seminars in Phoenix, 1970-76; owner Janzik Pub. Relations, 1971-76; talk show reporter-hostess What's Happening in Ariz., Sta. KPAZ-TV, 1970-73; writer syndicated column People Want to Know, Today newspaper, Phoenix, 1973; owner JB Communications, Phoenix, 1976-84; owner, pres. Media Communications, 1984—; free-lance writer; tchr. How to Weigh Your Self-Worth courses Phoenix Coll., Rio Solado Community Coll., Phoenix, 1976-84; muralist, works include 25 figures in med. office. Founder Ariz. Call-A-Teen Youth Resources, Inc., pres., 1975-76, v.p., 1976-77, now bd. dirs. Recipient awards including 1st pl. in TV writing Nat. Fedn. Press Women, 1971, numerous state awards in journalism Ariz. Press Women, 1971-76, Good Citizen award Builders of Greater Ariz., 1961. Mem. Ariz. Press Women, No. Ariz. Press Women (pres. 1983), Nat. Fedn. Am. Press Women, Pub. Relations Soc. Am., Phoenix Pub. Relations Soc., Nat. Acad. TV Arts and Scis., Phoenix Valley of Sun Convention Bur., Verde Valley C. of C. (bd. dirs., tourism chmn. 1986-87, Best Chair of Yr. award 1986), Phoenix Metro C. of C. Inventor stocking-tension twist footlet, 1962. Club: Phoenix Press. Office: PO Box 10509 Phoenix AZ 85064 Address: PO Box 10509 Phoenix AZ 85016

REINISCH, NANCY RAE, social worker, consultant; b. Chgo., Mar. 31, 1953; d. Charles Richard and Marianne (Gross) R.; m. Paul A. Salmen, June 14, 1980; children: Chas, Marcus. BA in Sociology cum laude, Colo. Coll., 1975; cert. drug and alcohol counseling, U. Minn., 1980; MSW, U. Denver, 1982. Counselor Rampart Boys' Home, Colorado Springs, Colo., 1975; advocate bilinqual community Migrants in Action, St. Paul, 1976; therapist Chrysalis Ctr. for Women, Mpls., 1979; team leader and prevention specialist Project Charlie, Edina, Minn., 1977-80, also trainer, cons., 1985—; mental health worker Bethesda Mental Health Ctr. and Hosp., Denver, 1980-83; therapist Gateway Alcohol Recovery Ctr., Aurora, Colo., 1983-84; pvt. practice therapy, also dir. Family Practice Counseling Service, Glenwood Springs, Colo., 1984—; bd. dirs. Garfield Youth Services Teen Assistance Program, Glenwood Springs; mem. Valley View Hosp. Ethics com., Glenwood Springs, 1986—. Mem. Nat. Assn. Social Workers, NOW, Nat. Abortion Rights Action League, Common Cause, Colo. Pub. Interest Research Group. Democrat. Jewish. Office: Family Practice Counseling Service 1905 Blake St Glenwood Springs CO 81601

REINSCH, HARRY ORVILLE, power company executive; b. Los Angeles, Feb. 12, 1922; s. Harry Orville and Olive Gladys (Cooper) R.; m. Helen Marsh, Oct. 19, 1942; children: E. James, John H.(dec.), Richard M., Linda Reinsch Marshall. Student engring., U. Calif.-Davis, 1940-42. Asst. supt. Bechtel Power Corp., San Francisco, 1950-55; gen. supt. to mgr. bus. devel. Bechtel Power Corp., San Francisco and Washington, 1955-68; v.p. Bechtel Power Corp., San Francisco, 1968-72, v.p., dir., 1972-73, exec. v.p., dir., 1973-75, pres., 1975-86, dir., 1973-87; dir. Wells Fargo & Co., Wells Fargo Bank; hon. chmn. Korean-Am. Bus. Inst. Dir. No. Calif. Soc. to Prevent Blindness, 1983; dir. That Man May See, 1982; dir., exec. com. Republic of China Econ. Council, U.S.; trustee U. Mont. Found., 1981-85; pres. Korean-Am. Co. of C., 1982-83; dir. Com. Energy Awareness Calif. Council Environ. and Econ. Balance. Mem. ASCE, ASME, Atomic Indsl. Forum (dir., vice chmn., exec. com.). Clubs: World Trade, Bankers, Pacific Union (San Francisco). Home: 1940 Broadway Apt 10 San Francisco CA 94109 Office: Bechtel Power Corp 50 Beale St San Francisco CA 94105

REINSTEDT, ROBERT NELSON, educational administrator; researcher, lecturer; b. Detroit, May 21, 1926; s. Albert Peterson and Mayme May (Bowlin) R.; m. Jean Kirkup; children by previous marriage: Lee N., Bruce R., Jane Barry. A.B., DePauw U., 1950, M.A., 1955; postgrad. Ind. U. 1955, Whittier Coll., 1957, UCLA, 1960. Dean of students Whittier Coll., Calif., 1955-58; with Rand Corp., 1958-86, assoc. dept. head, 1972-77, sr. researcher behavioral scis. dept., 1977-86; pres. computer personnel research group 1970-72; lectr. in field; dir. Rand Employees Fed. Credit Union, trustee Pension Trust Fund; lectr. in field. Contbr. chapters various books. Mem. AAAS, Am. Psychol. Assn., Calif. Psychol. Assn., Western Psychol. Assn., DePauw U. Alumni Assn. (past pres. Los Angeles chpt.) Office: Rand Corp 1700 Main St Santa Monica CA 90406

REINSTEIN, HENRY ALLEN, real estate management and franchising consultant, mail order executive; b. Bklyn., July 8, 1922; s. Harry M. and Jennie (Blam) R.; m. Claire Steckman, Nov. 9, 1947; children: Jon Eric (Rick), Lisa. BA, Bklyn. Coll., 1949; MBA, Wichita U., 1954; postgrad., UCLA; grill master cert. (hon.), McDonald's Hamburger U., Los Angeles, 1975. Gen. mgr. Hurley Distbg., Jamaica, N.Y., 1946-50; ptnr. Geneva Electronics, Elmhurst, N.Y., 1950-55; regional sales mgr. Philco-Bendix Laundercenters, Woodside, N.Y., 1955-68; real estate and franchise dir. Internat. House of Pancakes, Los Angeles, 1969-76; real estate dir. West Winchell's Donuts, La Mirada, Calif., 1976-80; pres. Henry Allen Co., Northridge, Calif., 1980—; cons. Papallini Hair Inst., Los Angeles, 1965-67, Permac Dry Cleaner, Los Angeles, 1968-69, Gibraltar Transmission, San Diego, 1980-84, Auto Oil Changers, Long Beach, Calif., 1985—. Served with U.S. Army Air Corps, 1942-46, ETO. Mem. City of Hope (Northridge, Calif. chpt.), Assn. Corp. Real Estate Execs., Am. Entrepreneurs Assn., Kitco Internat. Inc. Import-Export Assn. Democrat. Jewish. Avocations: reading, writing, photography, woodworking. Home and Office: Henry Allen Co 11641 Viking Ave Northridge CA 91326

REISINGER, GEORGE LAMBERT, management consultant; b. Pitts., Aug. 28, 1930; s. Eugene Merle and Pauline Jane (Lambert) R.; m. Judith Ann Brush, Nov. 24, 1967; children—Douglas Lambert, Christine Elizabeth. B.S. in Bus. Adminstrn., Central Coll., 1953; postgrad., Cleveland-Marshall Law Sch., 1962-67. Asst. personnel mgr. Continental Can Co., Houston, 1958-60; mgr. labor relations The Glidden Co., Cleve., 1960-67; dir. employee relations Mobil Oil Corp., N.Y.C., Caracas, Dallas, Denver, 1967-78; sr. v.p. Minton & Assocs., Denver, 1978-82; v.p., ptnr. Korn-Ferry Internat., Denver, 1982-86; pres., mng. ptnr. The Sigma Group, Inc., Denver, 1986—. Bd. dirs. Ponderosa Hills Civic Assn., 1977-80, Arapahoe County Youth League; Republican campaign dir. for county commr., 1978; pres. Douglas County Youth League. Served with USAF, 1953-58. Mem. Am. Soc. Personnel Adminstrs., N.Y. Personnel Mgmt. Soc., Colo. Soc. Personnel Adminstrn., Am. Soc. Profl. Cons., Rocky Mountain Inst. Fgn. Trade and Fin., Employment Mgmt. Assn. Republican. Methodist. Clubs: Denver Petroleum, Denver Athletic, Pinery Country, Republican 1200. Home: 7924 Deertrail Dr Parker CO 80134 Office: 717 17th St Suite 1440 Denver CO 80202-3314

REISS, W. RANDOLPH (RANDY), entertainment company executive; b. Augusta, Ga., June 13, 1945; m. Carolyn DeFoe, Nov. 14, 1981. BS, U. Md., 1968. Tchr. N.Y. Bd. Edn., N.Y.C., 1968-69; media buyer Grey Advt. Agy., N.Y.C., 1969-70; account exec. Metromedia TV Sales, N.Y.C., 1970-75; nat. sales mgr. Chris Craft Broadcasting, N.Y.C., 1975-77; pres. domestic TV and video programming Paramount Pictures Corp., Los Angeles, 1977-85; pres., chief exec. officer Act III Communications, Inc., Los Angeles, 1986—. Office: Act III Communications Inc 1800 Century Park E Suite 200 Los Angeles CA 90067

REISTER, BARRY WARD, psychologist, university administrator; b. Lexington, Ky., Jan. 15, 1946; s. John Ward and Mildred (Davis) R. BA, U. Ky., 1969; MS, Ind. U., 1973, EdD, 1975. Lic. psychologist, Mass., Calif. Staff psychologist univ. counseling services Boston Coll., 1975-77, asst. dir., 1977-80; adj. faculty Loyola Marymount U., Los Angeles, 1980—, dir., asst. dean for counseling and health services, 1980—; adj. faculty counseling psychology Boston Coll., 1975-77, Northeastern U., 1977-80, U. So. Calif., 1980. Contbr. articles to profl. jours. Served to 1st lt. U.S. Army, 1969-71. Decorated Bronze Star. Mem. Union Concerned Scientist, Jaycees, Am. Psychol. Assn., Am. Coll. Personnel Assn., Am. Assn. Counseling Devel., Assn. Univ. Coll. Counseling Ctr. Dirs., Orgn. Coll. Counseling Ctr. Dirs. in Higher Edn. (steering com. chair 1982-84). Democrat. Mem. Christian Ch. Home: 809 Coeur d'Adlene Ave Venice CA 90291 Office: Loyola Marymount U Loyola Blvd at W 80th St Los Angeles CA 90045

REISWIG, ROBERT DAVID, metallurgist; b. Wichita, July 14, 1929; s. David and Helen Catherine (Glenn) R.; m. Karolyn S. Bloom; children: Martin, George. BS, U. Kans., 1951; MS, U. Wis., 1953, PhD, 1956. Research engr. Battelle Meml. Inst., Columbus, Ohio, 1951-52; staff mem., sect. leader Los Alamos (N.Mex.) Nat. Lab., 1955—. Contbr. articles to profl. jours. Mem. Am. Soc. for Metals (chpt. chmn. 1957-58), AIME, Sigma Xi. Democrat. Methodist. Avocation: photography. Home: 90 Tecolote Los Alamos NM 87544 Office: Los Alamos Nat Lab MS G-770 Los Alamos NM 87545

REITAN, HAROLD THEODORE, social psychologist, management consultant; b. Max, N.D., Nov. 3, 1928; s. Walter Rudolph and Anna Helga (Glesne) R.; m. Margaret Lucille Bonsac, Dec. 29, 1954; children—Eric, Karen, Chris, Jon. B.A., St. Olaf Coll., 1950; M.A. in Social Psychology, U. Fla., 1962, Ph.D., 1967. Commd. officer U.S. Air Force, 1951, advanced through grades to col.; comdr., U.S. Air Force Spl. Treatment Ctr., Lackland, Tex., 1971-74, U.S. Air Force Corrections and Rehab. Group, Lowry, Colo., 1974-76, Tech. Tng. Wing, 1976-78, ret., 1978; mgr. health services Coors Industries, Golden, Colo., 1978-84, mgr. tng. and organizational devel., 1984—. Decorated Legion of Merit with oak leaf cluster, D.F.C. with oak leaf cluster, Bronze Star, Meritorious Service medal, Air medal with four oak leaf clusters. Mem. Am. Psychol. Assn., Phi Kappa Phi. Republican. Lutheran. Contbr. articles to profl. jours. Home: 12098 E Colorado Pl Aurora CO 80012 Office: Coors Industr Golden CO 80401

REITE, MARTIN LAWRENCE, medical educator, research psychiatrist; b. Oakland, Calif., May 22, 1936; s. Martin Luther and Esther (Anderson) R.; m. Julie Deckebach; 1 child, Jennifer; m. Carolyn Jean Osborne, July 3, 1972; children—Erik, Aaron. A.A., U. Calif.-Berkeley, 1955; M.D. cum laude, Yale U., 1960; M.S., UCLA, 1964. Diplomate in Psychiatry, Am. Bd. Psychiatry and Neurology; accredited clin. polysomnographer. Intern med. service UCLA Med. Ctr., Los Angeles, 1960-61, resident in psychiatry Neuropsychiat. Inst., 1961-64; prof. psychiatry U. Colo. Sch. Medicine, Denver, 1979—, mem. NIMH Small Grant Rev. Com., Washington, 1979-82; dir. CPH/Davis Pavilion Regional Sleep Disorders Ctr., Denver, 1983—. Editor: (with T. Field) The Psychobiology of Attachment and Separation, 1985; (with N. Caine), Child Abuse: The Non Human Primate Data, 1983. Contbr. articles to med. and sci. jours. Served to capt. USAF, 1964-67. NIMH research grantee, 1971—; U. Calif.-Berkeley alumni scholar, 1957-58.

Fellow Am. Psychiat. Assn., Am. Electroencephalographic Soc., Clin. Sleep Soc.; mem. Alpha Omega Alpha. Home: 1601 Pontiac St Denver CO 80220 Office: U Colo Sch Medicine 4200 E 9th Ave Denver CO 80262

REITEMEIER, (TIMOTHY) GEORGE, chamber of commerce executive; b. Pueblo, Colo., Jan. 17, 1931; s. Paul John and Ethel Regina (McCarthy) R.; m. JoAnn Lillian Perkins, May 19, 1952 (div. July 1977); children: Michael Douglas, Ann Ellen Loutzenhiser; m. Joy Arline Little, Nov. 16, 1985. A of Arts and Scis., U. So. Colo., 1951. Cert. chamber exec. Mgr. C. of C., Florence, Colo., 1952-53; asst. mgr. C. of C., Cheyenne, Wyo., 1953; mgr. C. of C., Longmont, Colo., 1953-55; dist. mgr. southwest div. C. of C., Washington, 1955-57; mgr. C. of C., Canon City, Colo., 1957-59, Casper, Wyo., 1959-64; v.p. C. of C., Niagara Falls, N.Y., 1965-70; pres., gen. mgr. C. of C., Spokane, Wash., 1970—; bd. dirs. Spokane Unltd. Bd. dirs. Expo '74 Worlds Fair, Spokane, SEACAB. Served with USAF, 1949-50. Mem. Am. C. of C. Execs. (sec.-treas, bd. dirs. 1972-75), Wash. C. of C. Execs. (past v.p., pres.), Colo. C. of C. Execs. (v.p.), Oreg.-Wash. Idaho Chamber Officers/Mgrs. Assn. (pres. 1973-74). Republican. Roman Catholic. Avocations: golf, skiing. Home: 4717 Pittsburg Spokane WA 99223 Office: Spokane Area C of C PO Box 2147 Spokane WA 99210

REITER, GAYLA DENISE, labor union official, government official; b. Beloit, Kans., Sept. 12, 1945; d. Gail Francis and Vivian Maxine (Lagle) R.; m. Stephen C. Chappell, Apr. 10, 1976 (div. 1980); m. Wilfred Joseph Scott, July 4, 1982; 1 child, Layla Diana Scott (dec.), B.S. magna cum laude, Portland State U., 1967; cert. Chemeketa Community Coll., 1973; labor studies credential San Francisco City Coll., 1982; grad. trade union program Harvard U., 1987. Pub. affairs specialist Social Security Adminstrn., San Francisco, 1974-75, mgr., 1975-80, claims specialist, 1980—; pres. local 3172, Am. Fedn. Govt. Employees, San Francisco, 1979-86, exec. v.p. nat. council 220, Chgo., 1982—, pres. regional council 147, San Francisco, 1982—; chief litigator, 1982—; del. San Mateo County Labor Council, Calif., 1982—. Co-editor Union Line from Region Nine, 1980— (outstanding Regional Paper 1983). Co-dir., fundraiser SIRS Hunger Project, San Francisco, 1982; legis. chmn. SIDS Found., 1984—; co-chmn. combined fed. campaign United Good Neighbors, San Francisco, 1984-86; chmn. Nat. Legis. Polit. Action Comm., 1984—, regional chmn. 1980-84. Recipient Gov.'s award State of Oreg., 1971, Superior Achievement award Social Security Adminstrn., Seattle, 1973, Nat. SIDS Found. Congl. Leadership award 1986; named to San Mateo Womens Hall of Fame. Mem. Am. Fedn. Govt. Employees (polit. action coordinator for Calif., Nev., Ariz. 1980-84, legis. rep. Congl. testimony 1982-84; del., com. chmn. nat. conv. Cleve., 1984; del., 1st v.p. officer no. council of locals 1982—; nat. leadership award 1982), ACLU, NOW, Women Execs. San Francisco (v.p., publicist 1975—), Coalition Labor Union Women, Phi Beta Kappa (v.p. Outstanding Speaker award 1967), Alpha Sigma Omega (Outstanding Woman award 1966). Democrat. Clubs: Masters Program Swim, Soroptimist (pres., v.p. 1976-80), Women's Spiritual Network. Office: Social Security Adminstrn 5815 3d St San Francisco CA 94124

REITER, JOSEPH ROMAN, psychotherapist; b. Saukville, Wis., May 8, 1948; s. Clarence Peter and Alice Mary (Loof) R.; children: Marisa, Matthew. BA, U. Wis., 1971; MSW, Wash. U., St. Louis, 1973. Registered clin. social worker, Oreg. Caseworker Family Services Agy., Dekalb, Ill., 1974-75; social worker Chileren's Services, Stockton, Calif., 1975-78; outpatient therapist Sierra View Mental Health, Auburn, Calif., 1978; child sexual abuse therapist Children Service Div., Roseburg, Oreg., 1978-83, supr. sex abuse and family therapy program, 1983—; ptnr., psychotherapist Whitewater Counseling Ctr., Roseburg, 1985—; pres. Reiter's Limestone Acres Inc., Saukville, 1985—. Mem. adv. bd. for guidance and counseling Roseburg Sch. Dist., 1985—, adv bd. youth intervention project Douglas Ednl. Service Dist., Roseburg, 1983-85. Mem. Nat. Assn. Soc. Workers (bd. dirs. 1983-85, mem. nominations and leadership coms. 1985-87, chairperson Douglas County unit 1986—). Avocations: tennis, softball, basketball, home remodeling. Home: 1543 NW Grove Ln Roseburg OR 97479 Office: Children's Services Div 1937 W Harvard Roseburg OR 97470

REITHEL, ROBERT JAMES, physics and mathematics educator; b. Rosiclare, Ill., Oct. 15, 1917; s. Fred Arthur and Ruth Jane R.; B.S., Western Ky. U., 1939; M.S., U. Ky., 1953; m. Ada Louise Emmick, July 15, 1939; children—Mary Elaine, Theresa Louise, Robert Julian, Catherine June, James Fredrick, Brian Joseph. Grad. asst. dept. physics U. Ky., 1939-40; tchr. math. and sci., Henderson County, Ky., 1947-51; instr. dept. physics U. Ky., Lexington, 1951-53; physicist, staff mem. U. Calif., Los Alamos Sci. Lab., 1953-69; tchr. math. Clovis (N.Mex.) Mcpl. Schs., 1969-81; dir. SW Capital Corp., Albuquerque. Democratic chmn., Precinct 31, Curry County, N.Mex.; Scoutmaster Boy Scouts Am., 1958-61, 74-77, 80-82, dist. commr. Los Alamos dist., 1961-65, v.p. Kit Carson council, 1965; chmn. Los Alamos United Fund, 1966-67; chmn. Los Alamos City-wide PTA, 1962. Served with U.S. Army, 1940-47, lt. col. Res. ret. Decorated Bronze Star medal with V, Purple Heart. Mem. AAAS, Am. Assn. Physics Tchrs., Am. Phys. Soc., NEA, Ret. Officers Assn., Air Force Assn., Clovis Edn. Assn., Sigma Xi. Democrat. Methodist. Club: Kiwanis (pres. El Desayuno, lt. gov. Div. 13, SW Dist.). Home: 1004 W Christopher Dr Clovis NM 88101

REITLER, CHARLES WILLIAM (BILL), real estate developer; b. Lakewood, Colo., Aug. 16, 1926; m. Lillian R. Churches; children: Sharon Reitler Rhodes, Carol Ann Reitler Gutke. BBA, U. Denver, 1952. Prin. Reitler Realty, Lakewood, 1952-63, GBM Corp., Lakewood, 1963-1973; pres. Reitler & Co. (formerly GBM Corp.), Lakewood, 1973—; bd. dirs. United Bank Lakewood. Mayor City of Lakewood, 1979-83; mem. gov.'s. round table Water for Met. Denver; past member citizen adv. com. Denver Water Bd.; past chmn. Lakewood Bd. Water and Sewer Commrs.; 1st v.p. Water for Colo. Served with U.S. Army, 1944-47. Mem. Lakewood C. of C. (bd. dirs., past pres., Bus. Man of Yr. 1972, Elected Official of Yr. 1982), Jefferson County Bd. Realtors (Realtor of Yr. 1960), Colo. Assn. Realtors (past bd. dirs.), Nat. Assn. Realtors, Met. Denver Homebuilders Assn. Office: Reitler & Co 1675 Carr St Suite 200 Lakewood CO 80215

REITMAN, LINDA, organizational consultant; b. Rochester, Pa., Sept. 27, 1949; d. Paul and Mary (Jacko) Opsatnik; m. Thomas H. Reitman, Sept. 15, 1979. AS, Robert Morris Coll., Pitts., 1970. Office policies and procedures coordinator MSI Data Corp., Costa Mesa, Calif., 1980-83; adminstrv. asst. Environ. Communications Inc., Costa Mesa, 1983-84; office orgn. cons. Productive Office Cons., Costa Mesa, 1984—; communications services mgr. TMI Corp., Newport Beach, Calif., 1985; seminar leader Orange Coast Community Coll. Mem. Nat. Assn. Profl. Organizers (sec. 1986—), Am. Cons. League, Women in Mgmt.(press release coordinator). Republican. Avocations: reading, collecting miniatures, music. Home and Office: 621 Seaview Ln Costa Mesa CA 92626

REITZ, RICHARD ELMER, physician, laboratory administrator; b. Buffalo, Sept. 18, 1938; s. Elmer Valentine and Edna Anna (Guenther) R.; m. Gail Ida Pounds, Aug. 20, 1960; children—Richard Allen, Mark David. B.S., Heidelberg Coll., 1960; M.D., SUNY-Buffalo, 1964. Intern Hartford (Conn.) Hosp., 1964-65, resident in medicine, 1966-67; asst. resident in medicine Yale U., 1965-66; vis. research assoc. NIH, Bethesda, Md., 1967-68; research fellow in medicine Harvard Med. Sch., Mass. Gen. Hosp., Boston, 1967-69; asst. dir. clin. investigation ctr. Naval Regional Med. Ctr., 1969-71; dir. Endocrine Metabolic Center, Oakland, Calif., 1973—; asst. prof. medicine U. Calif.-San Francisco, 1971-76; assoc. clin. prof. medicine U. Calif.-Davis, 1976-86 ; clin. prof. med. 1986—; chief endocrinology Providence Hosp., Oakland, Calif., 1972—. Contbr. articles to profl. jours., chpt. to book. Mem. scholarship com., Bank of Am., San Francisco, 1983. Served to lt. comdr. USNR, 1969-71. Mem. Endocrine Soc., Am. Soc. Bone and Mineral Research, Am. Fedn. Clin. Research, Am. Fertility Soc., Am. Soc. Internal Medicine, AAAS. Democrat. Lodge: Rotary. Home: 867 Stonehaven Dr Walnut Creek CA 94598 Office: Endocrine Metabolic Ctr 3100 Summit St Oakland CA 94623

REKENTHALER, GREGORY PAUL, graphic systems supervisor; b. Sioux City, Iowa, May 2, 1952; s. Reynold E. and Laura L. (Lill) R.; m. Darlene L. Krueger, May 28, 1977 (div. Apr. 1986). BA, Iowa State U., 1980. Mgr. ITT Fin. Corp., Mpls., 1976-79; graphics supr. Norwest Corp., Mpls., 1979—.

RELYEA, GARY NEAL, food services administrator; b. Honolulu, Mar. 9, 1948; s. Charles Percival and Belle (Reid) R.; m. Christine Crewes Clarke, Apr. 13, 1977; children: Darren Elliot, Adam Stuart. BBA, U. Hawaii, 1971. Regional controller Pan Am Corp., Honolulu, 1968-84; ops. mgr. Ogden Allied Services, Honolulu, 1985-86; gen. mgr. Ogden Allied Services, Las Vegas, Nev., 1986—. Mem. bd. dirs. Aina Haina PTA, Honolulu, 1985-86, Aina Haina Community Assn., Honolulu, 1986. Fleischman scholar Max Fleischman Assn., 1966, Hawaii Hotel Assn. scholar, 1969. Mem. Travel Industry Mgmt. Internat. (pres. Honolulu chpt. 1984-86). Republican. Episcopalian. Avocations: tennis, golf, carpentry. Office: Ogden-Allied Services 4945 Paradise Rd Las Vegas NV 89119

REMER, DONALD SHERWOOD, engineering educator, administrator; b. Detroit, Feb. 16, 1943; s. Nathan and Harriet R.; m. Louise Collen, Dec. 21, 1969; children: Tanya, Candace, Miles. B.S., U. Mich., 1965; M.S., Calif. Inst. Tech., 1966, Ph.D., 1970. Registered profl. engr., Calif., Mich., La. Tech. service engr., chem. raw materials div. coordinator, sr. running plan coordinator, task team leader Exxon, Baton Rouge, 1970-75; assoc. prof. engring. Harvey Mudd Coll., Claremont, Calif., 1975-79; prof. Harvey Mudd Coll., 1980—, dir. Energy Inst., 1981-83; cons. Jet Propulsion Lab., Calif. Inst. Tech., 1976—; co-founder, ptnr. Claremont Cons. Group, 1979—; mem. adv. council Nat. Energy Found., N.Y.C., 1981-85. Contbr. articles to profl. jours.; case study editor: Am. Soc. Engring. Edn., Engring. Economist, 1977—. Shelter mgr. ARC, Baton Rouge, 1965-70. Recipient Outstanding Chem. Engr. award U. Mich., 1965, First Place Pub. Relations award Am. Inst. Chem. Engring., 1975, Outstanding Alumni Fund Achievement award Calif. Inst. Tech., 1976, Outstanding Young Man of Am. award, 1976, NASA award, 1983; named Outstanding Research Seminar Speaker Occidental Research Corp., 1976. Mem. Am. Soc. Engring. Mgmt. (bd. dirs. 1981-83). Club: Toastmasters (pres. Claremont-Pomona chpt.) (1978).

REMER, SUSAN MARIE, accountant; b. New Ulm, Minn., Dec. 24, 1953; d. Walter James and Grace Victoria (Nelson) Rolloff; B.A., Central Wash. State U., 1975; m. Larry Ronal McBride, Dec. 18, 1971 (div. Dec. 1975); adopted children—Michael Allen Stay, Melissa Ann Stay; m. 2d, Francis Leon Remer, Feb. 14, 1984. Staff acct. Dolsen, Synoground, Smith & Martin, Yakima, Wash., 1975-76; office mgr. Simco Mechanical Inc., Yakima, 1976-78; state examiner IV, Office State auditor, Olympia, Wash., 1978—. Mem. Wash. Soc. C.P.A.'s. Democrat. Lutheran. Office: Office State Auditor Legis Bldg Olympia WA 98504

REMERS, WILLIAM ALAN, medicinal chemistry educator; b. Cinn., Oct. 14, 1932; s. Clifford Nelson Remers and Mary Virginia (German) Blakely; m. Ann Bloodworth Jordan, Feb. 25, 1961; children: Julian Jordan, Laurel Ann. BS, MIT, 1954; PhD, U. Ill., 1958. Postdoctoral researcher Oxford (Eng.) U., 1958-59; research chemist Lederle Labs., Pearl River, N.Y., 1959-70; from assoc. prof. to prof. medicinal chemistry Purdue U., Lafayette, Ind., 1970-76; prof. U. Ariz., Tucson, 1976—, dept. head, 1979-85. Author: Chemistry of Antitumor Anitiotics, 1980, Antineoplastic Agents, 1984; contbr. articles to profl. jours.; patentee in field. Mem. AAAS, Am. Chem. Soc., Am. Soc. Microbiology, Am. Assn. Colls. Pharmacy. Episcopalian. Avocations: hiking, swimming. Home: 5022 E Calle Guebabi Tucson AZ 85718 Office: U Ariz Coll Pharmacy Tucson AZ 85721

REMINGTON, JACK SAMUEL, physician; b. Chgo., Jan. 19, 1931; s. Nathan and Sylvia R.; children—David Nathan, Lynne Denise. B.S., U. Ill., Chgo., 1954, M.D., 1956. Diplomate Am. Bd. Internal Medicine. Intern U. Calif. Service, San Francisco County Hosp., 1956; research assoc. NIH, Bethesda, Md., 1957-59; resident in medicine U. Calif. Med. Center, San Francisco, 1959-60; sr. postdoctoral fellow Harvard U. Sch. Medicine, Thorndike Meml. Lab., Boston City Hosp., 1960-62; mem. faculty dept. medicine, div. infectious diseases Stanford (Calif.) U. Sch. Medicine, 1962—, prof., 1974—; chmn. dept. Immunology and Infectious Diseases, Research Inst. Palo Alto (Calif.) Med. Found., 1962—; chief cons. in infectious diseases Palo Alto Med. Clinic, 1962—; cons. VA Hosp., Palo Alto, 1962—; cons. in infectious diseases WHO, 1967—, Pan Am. Health Orgn., 1967—, Dept. Army, 1971—; cons. Letterman Gen. Hosp., 1975—; sci. cons. Merit Rev. Bd. in Infectious Diseases VA, 1972-76; mem. adv. sci. bd. Gorgas Meml. Inst. of Tropical and Preventive Medicine, 1972—; mem. com. on infectious diseases Am. Bd. Internal Medicine, 1973-78; mem. adv. panel Am. Bd. Med. Lab. Immunology, 1978—, Sci. Adv. Com. Am. Found. for AIDS Research, 1985—. Editor: (with J.O. Klein) Infectious Diseases of the Fetus and Newborn Infant, 1976-83, (with M.N. Swartz) Current Clinical Topics in Infectious Diseases, 1980; Mem editorial bd.: Antimicrobial Agts. and Chemotherapy, 1973-76, Jour. Clin. Investigation, 1975—, Am. Rev. Respiratory Disease, 1978—, Jour. Immunopharmacology, 1978—, European Jour. Clin. Microbiology, 1981. Served with USPHS, 1957-59. Recipient Maxwell Finland award. Fellow A.C.P.; mem. Infectious Diseases Soc. Am. (bd. dirs. 1974-77, pres. elect 1987), Western Soc. Clin. Research (pres. 1975, mem. council 1975-77), Western Assn. Physicians (councillor 1980), AAAS, Am. Assn. Immunologists, Am. Fedn. Clin. Research, AMA, Am. Soc. Clin. Investigation, Am. Soc. Microbiology, Am. Soc. Parasitologists, Am. Soc. Tropical Medicine and Hygiene, Assn. Am. Physicians, Internat. Coll. Tropical Medicine, Soc. Protozoologists, Reticuloendothelial Soc., Assn. Am. Physicians, Alpha Omega Alpha. Office: 860 Bryant St Palo Alto CA 94301 also: Stanford U Sch Medicine Stanford CA 94305

REMLEY, MARLIN EUGENE, nuclear company executive; b. Walcott, Ark., Apr. 25, 1921; s. Aubrey James and Kate (Clarida) R.; m. Ruth Neoma Evens, Apr. 4, 1943; children: Carol Sue Bothwell, Nancy Ann Hedges, Barbara Jean Taylor. AB, Southeast Mo. State U., 1941; postgrad., Iowa State U., 1941-42; MS, U. Ill., 1948, PhD, 1952. Registered profl. nuclear engr., Calif. Instr. physics and math. Southeast Mo. State U., Cape Girardeau, 1946-47; research asst. U. Ill., 1947-51; with Atomics Internat. div. Rockwell Internat., Canoga Park, Calif., 1951—, dir. reactor devel., 1958-60, dir. reactor physics, instrumentation, 1960-61, dir. health, safety, radiation services, 1961-84, dir. nuclear safety and licensing, 1984—; lectr. nuclear engring. UCLA extension; exec. dir. Atomic Energy Info. Services. Contbr. articles to profl. jours. Served to capt., Signal Corps U.S. Army, 1942-46. Recipient Southeast Mo. State U. Alumni Merit award, 1973. Fellow Am. Nuclear Soc. (officer reactor ops. div. 1972-76, chmn. 1975-76, mem. nuclear power plant standards com.), Atomic Indsl. Forum (reactor safety com.), Nat. Mgmt. Assn. (pres. Valley chpt. 1969, Silver Knight Mgmt. award 1983), Calif. Mfrs. Assn., Pacific Coast Electric Assn., Chatsworth C. of C. (pres. 1972-78), Sigma Xi, Phi Kappa Phi, Pi Mu Epsilon, Alpha Phi Omega. Republican. Presbyterian. Home: 19112 Halsted St Northridge CA 91324 Office: Rockwell Internat 6633 Canoga Ave Canoga Park CA 91303

REMPEL, ARTHUR GUSTAV, biology educator; b. Marinskaya, USSR, Jan. 5, 1910; came to U.S., 1923; s. Gustav Aron and Elisabeth Electra (Dirks) R.; m. Lucile Elma Sommerfield, June 19, 1934; children: Robert Arthur (dec.), Herbert Frank, Paul Leonard (dec.), Margaret Louise, Roland Richard. Cert., Pasadena Jr. Coll., 1931; AB, Oberlin Coll., 1934; PhD, U. Calif., Berkeley, 1938; DSc (hon), Whitman Coll., 1987. Acting curator Mus. Anthropology and Zoology Oberlin (Ohio) Coll., 1931-34; teaching asst. U. Calif., Berkeley, 1934-38; mem. faculty biology Whitman Coll., Walla Walla, Wash., 1938—, prof., 1949-75, prof. emeritus, 1975—; vis. prof. biology U. Calif., Berkeley, 1949, U. Wash., Seattle, 1957, 58, 66, 67; research assoc. Wash. State U., Pullman, 1956; ranger, historian Nat. Park Service, 1953, 54; ranger, naturalist Nat. Park Service, Yosemite, Calif., 1955. Fellow AAAS; mem. N.W. Sci. Assn., Phi Beta Kappa, Sigma Xi. Avocations: traveling, wildlife photography, gardening. Home: 635 University St Walla Walla WA 99362

REMUS, WILLIAM EDWARD, decision science educator; b. Benton Harbor, Mich., Feb. 5, 1944; s. Franklin G. and Erma O. (Hoffman) R.; m. Pauline Sheldon, Mar. 31, 1986. BSEE, U. Mich., 1967; MSEE, Calif. State U., Santa Barbara, 1968; MBA, Mich. State U., 1972, PhD, 1974. Prof. decision sci. U. Hawaii Manoa, Honolulu, 1975—. Contbr. articles to profl. jours. NSF grantee 1985. Office: U Hawaii Manoa 2404 Maile Way Honolulu HI 96822

REMY, IRMA MARJORIE, educational administrator; b. Maywood, Calif., Oct. 16, 1925; d. Charles Henry and Irma (Page) Bowers; m. Edward Earl Remy, Oct. 3, 1946; children—Christine Ann, Shelly Katherine. Student U. Redlands, 1943, Long Beach City Coll., 1959-60, Pepperdine U., 1974; B.A., Calif. State U.-Long Beach, 1963; M.A., 1966. Cert. secondary tchr., adminstr. Calif. Tchr. home econs. Westminster High Sch., Huntington Beach (Calif.) Union High Sch. Dist., 1963-72, dept. chmn., 1967-72, dist. dept. chmn., 1970-72; coordinator home econs., women's occupations Orange County Dept. Edn., Santa Ana, Calif., 1972-73; regional supr. home econs. vocat. cons. Specialist Regional Occupational Ctrs./Programs, State of Calif. Dept. Edn., Los Angeles, 1973-82, regional coordinator (so. region) vocat. edn., 1982-84; asst. supt. So. Calif. Regional Occupational Ctr., Torrance, 1984—.Mem. Am. Vocat. Assn., Calif. Assn. Vocat. Adminstrs., Calif. Assn. Regional Occupational Programs/Ctrs., So. Calif. Council Vocat. Edn. Adminstrs., Calif. Assn. Vocat. Educators. Democrat. Mem. Ch. Jesus Christ of Latter-day Saints. Office: So Calif Regional Occupational Ctr Occupational Ctr 2300 Crenshaw Blvd Torrance CA 90501

REMY, RAY, chamber of commerce executive; b. San Francisco. B in Polit. Sci., Claremont Men's Coll. (now Claremont McKenna Coll.); M in Pub. Adminstrn., U. Calif., Berkeley. Adminstrv. intern City of Berkeley, 1962-63; with So. Office League of Calif. Cities, 1963, then asst. to exec. dir. and mgr., to 1969; exec. dir. So. Calif. Assn. Govt., 1969-76; appointed dep. mayor City of Los Angeles, 1976-84; pres. Los Angeles Area C. of C., 1984—, also prin. spokesman. Mem. editorial adv. bd. Los Angeles Bus. Jour. Past chmn. bd. councilors Sch. Pub. Adminstrn. U. So. Calif., Los Angeles; vice chmn. bd. dirs. Rose Inst. for state and local govt.; mem. state adv. com. Revision of Master Plan for Higher Edn. Recipient numerous awards including Fletcher Bowron award, Donald Stone award, Mus. of Sci. and Industry Fellowship award, others. Mem. Nat. Acad. Pub. Adminstrn. (past pres.), Jr. Statesmen Found. (trustee, vice chmn. so. Calif. region), Constitutional Rights Found. (bus. adv. council). Office: Los Angeles Area C of C 404 S Bixel St PO Box 3696 Los Angeles CA 90017

RENARD, KENNETH GOERGE, civil engineer; b. Sturgeon Bay, Wis., May 5, 1934; s. Harry Henry and Margaret (Buechner) R.; m. Virginia Rae Heibel, Sept 8, 1956; children: Kenlynn T., Craig G., Andrew T. BCE, U. Wis., 1957, MCE, 1959; PhD in Civil Engring., U. Ariz., 1972. Registered profl. civil engr., Ariz. Hydraulic engr. Agrl. Research Service, USDA, Madison, Wis., 1957-59; resident engr. Agrl. Research Service, USDA, Tombstone, Ariz., 1959-64; resident hydraulic engr. Agrl. Research Service, USDA, Tucson, 1964-72, research leader, 1972—. Contbr. articles to profl. jours. Recipient Superior Service award USDA, 1984. Fellow Soil Conservation Soc. Am. (pres. Ariz. sect. 1975, Conservationist of Yr 1983), ASCE (pres. Ariz. sect. 1981, editor Jour. of Irrigation and Drainage Engrs. 1983-85, John C. Park award 1987); mem. Am. Soc. Agrl. Engrs. (pres. Ariz. sect. 1976), Am. Geophys. Union. Roman Catholic. Lodge: Lions (pres. Tombstone chpt. 1963). Home: 4822 E Paseo Del Bac Tucson AZ 85718 Office: Agrl Research Service USDA 2000 E Allen Rd Tucson AZ 85719

RENCEHAUSEN, LINDA MARY, industrial hygienist; b. Springfield, Mass., Feb. 1, 1950; d. Victor Frank and Lorraine Ruth (Perusse) Antienowicz; m. Walter William Rencehausen, Apr. 16, 1970; 1 child, Will. BS in Microbiology, Ariz. State U., 1977. Microbiology technician Armour-Dial, Phoenix, 1976; histology technician Phoenix Meml. Hosp., 1977-78; soils technician U.S. Forest Service, Flagstaff, Ariz., 1979; secondary sch. tchr. Logan (N.Mex.) Schs., 1980-81, Ft. Sumner (N.Mex.) Schs., 1981-83; industrial hygienist Westinghouse Electric Co., Carlsbad, N.Mex., 1984—. Served with USMC, 1968-70. Mem. Am. Soc. Safety Engrs., Am. Indsl. Hygiene Assn., Am. Chem. Soc. (div. chem. health and safety). Republican. Roman Catholic. Avocations: gardening, crafts, biking. Home: 2835 Western Way Carlsbad NM 88220 Office: Westinghouse Electric PO Box 2078 Carlsbad NM 88221

RENCK, RICHARD TROY, marketing research company executive; b. Rock Island, Ill., Aug. 26, 1925; s. Troy Walker and Doreene Frances (Welch) R. Ph.B., U. Chgo., 1948, M.A., 1953, Ph.D., 1965. Dir. measurement research Indsl. Relations Ctr., U. Chgo., 1950-65; v.p. Social Research Inc., Chgo., 1965-74; v.p. KPR Assocs., Inc. Scottsdale, Ariz., 1974-80, pres., 1980—; sr. cons. Greenleigh Assocs., Inc., N.Y.C., 1960-64. Active Art Inst. of Chgo., Field Mus. Natural History, Heard Mus. (Phoenix), Scottsdale Ctr. for the Arts. Served with USNR, 1943-46. Decorated Presdl. citation. Mem. Am. Sociol. Assn., Am. Mktg. Assn., Mktg. Research Assn. Office: KPR Assoc 7321 Shoeman Ln Scottsdale AZ 85251

RENDINA, ALAN RALPH, research biochemist; b. Lawrence, Kans., Sept. 24, 1951; s. George and Irma (Esner) R.; m. Cathie Smestad, Jan. 20, 1970 (div. Dec. 1979); 1 child, Michael Allen; m. Nancy Susan Coan, Mar. 5, 1982. BS, Ohio State U., 1974; PhD, U. Wis., 1980. Lab. technician Doehler Jarvis div. NL Industries, Toledo, 1970-72; postdoctoral research assoc. U. Wis., Madison, 1980-84; research biochemist Chevron Chem. Co., Richmond, Calif., 1984—. Contbr. articles to profl. jours. Mem. AAAS, Am. Chem. Soc., Am. Soc. Biol. Chemists (assoc.), N.Y. Acad. Scis., Sigma Xi. Avocations: photography, skiing, running. Office: Chevron Chem Co PO Box 4010 Richmond CA 94804

RENFREW, MALCOLM MACKENZIE, chemist, educator; b. Spokane, Wash., Oct. 12, 1910; s. Earl Edgar and Elsie Pauline (MacKenzie) R.; m. Carol Joy Campbell, June 26, 1938. B.S., U. Idaho, 1932, M.S., 1934, D.Sc., 1976; Ph.D., U. Minn., 1938. Asst. chemistry U. Idaho, 1932-35; asst. chemistry U. Minn., 1935-37, duPont fellow, 1937-38; research chemist plastics dept. duPont Co., 1938-44, supr. process devel., 1944-46, supr. product devel., 1946-49; head chem. research dept., research labs. Gen. Mills, Inc., 1949-52, dir. chem. research, 1952-53, dir. chem. research and devel., 1953-54; dir. research and devel. Spencer Kellogg & Sons, Inc., 1954-58; phys. sci. div. head, prof. chemistry U. Idaho, 1959-73, prof., 1973-76, emeritus, 1976—; dir. U. Idaho (Coll. Chem. Cons. Service), 1969-76; on leave as sr. staff asso. Adv. Council Coll. Chemistry, Stanford, 1967-68; mem. materials adv. bd. Nat. Acad. Scis.; exec. v.p. Idaho Research Found., 1977-78, patent dir., 1978—. Editor: Safety in the Chemical Laboratory, Vol. IV, 1981; safety editor: Jour. Chem. Edn, 1977—; Contbr. to tech. and trade publs. on plastics, coatings, safety, chem. edn. Recipient Excellence in Teaching award Chem. Mfrs. Assn., 1977, Outstanding Achievement award U. Minn., 1977; named to U. Idaho Hall of Fame, 1977. Fellow AAAS, Am. Inst. Chemists; mem. Am. Chem. Soc. (councilor 1948, 59, 67—, chmn. paint varnish and plastics div. 1949, chmn. chem. mktg. and econs. div. 1958-59, chmn. chem. health and safety div. 1982, James Flack Norris award 1976, Chem. Health and Safety award 1985, Mosher award 1986), Am. Inst. Chem. Engrs., Soc. Chem. Industry, Soc. Univ. Patent Dirs., Phi Beta Kappa, Sigma Xi, Phi Kappa Phi, Sigma Pi Sigma, Phi Gamma Delta (disting. Fiji 1986). Presbyterian. Home: 1271 Walenta Dr Moscow ID 83843

RENFRO, DONALD WILLIAM, architect; b. Bakersfield, Calif., Nov. 13, 1931; s. Donald Francis and Lennie Lorraine (Despain) R.; student Bakersfield Coll., 1949-51; cert. energy auditor, Calif.; registered, cert. Nat. Council Archtl. Registration Bds.; m. Nancy M. Henry, Aug. 6, 1982; children—Dayna, Trisha, Donna. Staff designer Whitney Biggar, Architect, 1955-61; asso. Eddy & Paynter Assos., Bakersfield, Calif., 1961-70; prin. Eddy Paynter Renfro & Assos., Bakersfield, 1970-78; pres. Donald Renfro & Assocs., Bakersfield, 1978-84; pres. Renfro-Russell & Assocs., Inc., 1984—; pres., dir. Design Research Assos., Inc. Mem. Bakersfield Coll. Archtl. Adv. Com.; mem. Bakersfield Design Rev. Bd. Served with U.S. Army, 1952-54. Mem. AIA (past pres. Golden Empire chpt.) past dir. So. Calif. chpt.). Republican. Lodge: Kiwanis (past dir.). Office: 4800 Stockdale Hwy Suite 304 Bakersfield CA 93309

RENGARAJAN, SEMBIAM RAJAGOPAL, electrical engineering educator, researcher, consultant; b. Mannargudi, Tamil Nadu, India, Dec. 12, 1948; came to U.S., 1980; s. Srinivasan and Rajalakshmi (Renganathan) Rajagopalan; m. Kalyani Srinivasan, June 24, 1982; 1 child, Michelle. BE with honors, U. Madras, India, 1971; MTech, Indian Inst. Tech., Kharagpur, 1974; PhD in Elec. Engring., U. N.B., Fredericton, Can., 1980. Mem. tech. staff Jet Propulsion Lab., Pasadena, Calif., 1983-84; asst. prof. elec. engring. Calif. State U., Northridge, 1980-83, assoc. prof., 1984—; cons. Hughes Aircraft Co., Canoga Park, Calif., 1982—; vis. researcher UCLA, 1984—. Contbr. sci. papers to profl. publs. Recipient Outstanding Faculty award Calif. State U., Northridge, 1985, Meritorious Performance and Profl. Promise award, 1986; Nat. Merit scholar Govt. India, 1965-71. Fellow Inst. Advancement Engrs.; mem. IEEE (sr., Los Angeles chpt. sec., treas.

Antennas and propagation Soc. 1981-82, vice chmn. 1982-83, chmn. 1983-84), Calif. Faculty Assn., Am. Soc. Engring. Edn., Sigma Xi. Avocations: swimming, camping, jogging, tennis. Office: Calif State U 18111 Nordhoff St Northridge CA 91330

RENGEL, RICHARD JAMES, architect; b. Pasadena, Calif., Nov. 7, 1957; s. Richard Julius and Lois Ann (Gardner) R.; m. Karen Christine Petersen, May 11, 1985. BArch, Calif. Poly. State U., San Luis Obispo, 1980, MBA, 1981. Registered architect, Calif. Designer Neil Palmer, Palos Verdes, Calif., 1974-80; project architect Pulaski and Arita, Newport Beach, Calif., 1981-84; prin. Rengel & Co., Newport Beach, 1984—. Mem. AIA, Delta Sigma Phi (pres. San Luis Obispo chpt. 1980-81). Republican. Roman Catholic. Office: Rengel & Co 333 El Camino Real Tustin CA 92680

RENIGER, HENRY AUSTIN, III, sales and marketing executive; b. Lansing, Mich., June 21, 1952; s. Henry Austin and Shirley Ann (Cummings) R.; m. Carol Davis, Aug. 3, 1975; 1 child, Peter Austin. Student U. Salzburg, 1969; B.S. in Mass Communications, U. Utah, 1979; Print/graphic specialist U. Utah, Salt Lake City, 1973-77; advt. mgr. Oscar E. Chytraus Co., Salt Lake City, 1977-79; store mgr. H. J. Davis Co., Van Nuys, Calif., 1979-81; key accounts mgr. Allegretti & Co., Chatsworth, Calif., 1981-82, regional mgr., 1982-84; nat. sales and mktg. mgr. Home Improvement Products div. Forecast Lighting Co., Inglewood, Calif., 1984-86; regional mgr. Chgo. specialty Beatrice Home Specialties, Inc., Sun Valley, Calif., 1987—. Mem. Sigma Nu. Home: 3150 Travis Ave Simi Valley CA 93063 Office: Beatrice Home Specialties 9301 Borden Ave Sun Valley CA 91532

RENLUND, DALE GUNNAR, cardiologist, educator; b. Salt Lake City, Nov. 13, 1952; s. Mats Ake and Ranghild Mariana (Anderson) R.; m. Ruth Lybbert Renlund, June 16, 1977; 1 child, Ashley Ruth. BA in Chemistry, U. Utah, 1976, MD, 1980. Diplomate Am. Bd. Internal Medicine (cardiovascular medicine); ordained bishop Mormon Ch., 1983. Intern Johns Hopkins Hosp., Balt., 1980-81, resident in internal medicine, 1981-83, fellow in cardiology, 1983-85; asst. prof. cardiology U. Utah, Salt Lake City, 1986—; attending cardiologist Utah Heart Transplant Program, Salt Lake City, 1986—. Contbr. articles to profl. jours. Missionary Morman Ch., Sweden, 1972-74. Recipient Leon Waters award U. Utah Dept. Chemistry, 1975, Bonner Meml. award U. Utah Dept. Chemistry, 1976. Mem. AAAS, Am. Heart Assn. (Council on Basic Sci.), Am. Fedn. Clin. Research. Democrat. Home: 1653 Westminster Ave Salt Lake City UT 84105 Office: U Utah Med Ctr div Cardiology 50 N Medical Dr Salt Lake City UT 84132

RENNE, JANICE LYNN, interior designer; b. Los Angeles, July 16, 1952; d. George Joseph and Dolly Minni (Neubaurer) R.; m. William Lee Kile, Dec. 6, 1975 (div. Sept. 1983). BA, Sweet Briar Coll., 1974; AA, Interior Designers Inst., 1985. Student designer Ultimate Designs, Irvine, Calif., 1984, sr. designer, 1985-86; draftsperson JBI Inc., Carson, Calif., 1985; prin. Janice Renne Interior Designs, Costa Mesa, Calif., 1985, Corona Del Mar, Calif., 1986—. Created and published house design for Easter Seals; weekly radio show host on restaurant design. Recipient scholarship Calif. Inst. Applied Design, Newport Beach, 1984. Mem. Internat. Soc. Interior Designers (grad. assoc., designer Butler's Pantry, Orange County chpt. 1986), Nat. Assn. Female Execs., Color Assn. of U.S., Women's Bus. Network Calif., Constrn. Specifier Inst., C. of C., Orange County and Newport Harbor. Republican. Lutheran. Avocations: weight lifting, rollerskating, biking, photography. Office: 2732 E Coast Hwy Suite C Corona Del Mar CA 92625

RENNER, GEORGE R., Mayor city of Glendale, Ariz. Office: Office of the Mayor 7022 N 57th Dr Glendale AZ 85301 *

RENSCH, JOSEPH ROMAINE, public utility holding company executive; b. San Bernardino, Calif., Jan. 1, 1923; s. Joseph R. and Lucille (Ham) R.; m. June Elizabeth Burley, Mar. 25, 1946; children: Steven R., Jeffrey P. BS, Stanford U., 1947; JD, Golden Gate U., 1955. Bar: Calif.; registered profl. engr., Calif. Successively sales engr., regional gas engr., asst. regional gas supt., asst. mgr. gas supply and control Coast Counties Gas & Electric Co., San Francisco, 1947-54; sr. pipeline operations engr. Pacific Gas & Electric Co., 1954-56; prodn. control supt. Western div. Dow Chem. Co., Pittsburg, Calif., 1956; asst. counsel So. Counties Gas Co. of Calif., Los Angeles, 1957-58; asst. v.p., spl. counsel Pacific Lighting Gas Supply Co., Los Angeles, 1958- 61, v.p., bd. dirs., 1962-65; sr. v.p. Pacific Lighting Service Co., 1965-67, exec. v.p., 1967-69, pres., 1969-71, chmn. bd., 1971-73; exec. v.p., dir. Pacific Lighting Corp., Los Angeles, 1968-72, pres., 1972-86, vice chmn., 1986—; bd. dirs. Union Bank, McKesson Corp., Lockheed Corp., Pacific Mut. Life Ins. Co. Served with USNR, 1942-46. Mem. Pacific Coast Gas Assn. (pres. 1966-67), Am. Gas Assn., Tau Beta Pi, Alpha Tau Omega. Office: Pacific Lighting Corp 810 S Flower St Los Angeles CA 90017

RENTERIA, ESTHER G., public relations executive; b. East Los Angeles, Calif., May 1, 1939; d. Oliver Jay and Violet Gatfield; AA, East Los Angeles Coll., 1958; BA, Calif. State U., Los Angeles, 1974; m. Martin Renteria, Feb. 13, 1971; children: Christopher, David. Reporter, Alhambra (Calif.) Post Advocate, 1959-61; reporter, soc. editor East Los Angeles Tribune & Gazette, 1962-68; desk editor, newswriter Sta. KNX, Los Angeles, 1968; asso. producer, hostess-moderator Ahora! TV Series, Public Broadcasting Sta. KCET, 1969-70; public info. dir. East Los Angeles Coll., 1970-83; pres. Esther Renteria Pub. Relations, Inc., 1983—; producer Sta. KNXT TV Series: Bienvenidos and The Siesta is Over, 1970-74, ednl. cons. bilingual edn. series Juntos, 1979-82; sec., dir. Future Broadcasting Corp., 1980—; v.p. Trojan Security Services, Inc. Bd. dirs. Bilingual Found. of Arts; public relations dir. Los Angeles Street Scene Festival, 1978—. Mem. Hispanic Pub. Relations Assn. (v.p., bd. dirs.), Hispanic Acad. Media Arts and Scis (bd. dirs. Hollywood chpt.), Latin Am. Assn. (bd. dirs.), Nat. Hispanic Media Coalition, Bilingual Found. of Arts, Latin Bus. Assn. Democrat. Roman Catholic. Club: Job's Daus. (life). Home: 301 Dochan Circle Montebello CA 90640 Office: 5400 E Olympic Blvd Los Angeles CA 90022

REPIC, EDWARD MICHAEL, aerospace executive, consultant; b. Cleve., June 7, 1935; s. Michael and Ann Mary (Purkeli) R.; m. Patricia Rae Deblass, June 30, 1956; children: Terri Lynn, Raymond Anthony, Toni D'Ann, Edward Michael. BS in Aero. Engring., Ohio State u., 1962; MS in Aerospace Engring., U. So. Calif., 1964; MBA, Pepperdine U., 1975. Cert. profl. mgr. Engr. Rockwell Internat., Anaheim, Calif., 1962-68, mgr., 1968-81, dir. shuttle processing, 1981-82; pres. Effective Mgmt. Resources Corp., Anaheim, 1979—; prof. West Coast U.; bd. dirs. Key to Travel Inc. Author: Managing Engineers, 1981, Project Management for Engineers, 1981, Improving Engineering Productivity, 1982, Business Development, Planning and Capture, 1983. Mem. ASME, AIAA, Am. Inst. Indsl. Engrs., Internat. Soc. Philos. Inquiry, Mensa. Club: Diogenes (Anaheim).

RESH, TERESE ELAINE, clinical social worker; b. Inglewood, Calif., July 19, 1958; d. Toros Kiritjian and Gloria Mae (Siraganian) Kies; m. Richard James Resh, Nov. 5, 1977. AA, Pasadena City Coll., 1977; BSW, Calif. State U., Los Angeles, 1979; MSW, U. So. Calif., 1982. Lic. clin. social worker, Calif. Clin. social worker Huntington Meml. Hosp., Pasadena, Calif., 1981—; pvt. practice specializing in psychotherapy and biofeedback/stress mgmt. counseling Sierra Madre, Calif., 1985—; coordinator biofeedback program, clin. social worker Presbyn. Intercommunity Hosp., Whittier, Calif., 1986—; cons., Sierra Madre, 1983—. Vol. Child Passenger Safety Assn., Altadena, Calif., 1983—. Mem. Nat. Assn. Social Workers, Biofeedback Cert. Inst. Am., Biofeedback Soc. Am. Democrat. Club: Garden. Avocations: cross country skiing, gardening. Office: 122 N Baldwin Ave #B Sierra Madre CA 91024

RESKO, JOHN ALLEN, physiology educator; b. Patton, Pa., Oct. 28, 1932; s. Eli Joseph and Mary Veronica (Haluska) R.; m. Magdalen Ester Redmond, June 23, 1962; children: Rebecca E., John T. PhB, St. Charles Sem., 1956; MS in Zoology, Marquette U., 1960; PhD in Animal Sci., U. Ill., 1963. Postdoctoral fellow U. Utah, Salt Lake City, 1963-64; asst. scientist Oreg. Regional Primary Research Ctr., Beaverton, 1964-67, assoc. scientist, 1967-71, scientist, 1971-81; prof., chmn. dept. physiology Oreg. Health Sci. U., Portland, 1981—; mem. reproductive biology study sect. NIH, Bethesda, Md., 1981-85. Recipient Wyeth award West Coast Fertility Soc., 1972. Mem. AAAS, Soc. Study Reproduction (bd. dirs. 1981-84), Soc. Exptl. Biol. Medicine (mem. council 1981-84), Am. Physiol. Soc., Endocrine Soc., Am. Soc. Zoologists. Democrat. Roman Catholic. Home: 1787 SE Brookwood Ave Hillsboro OR 97123 Office: Oreg Health Sci U Dept Physiology 3181 SW Sam Jackson Park Rd Portland OR 97201

RESTIVO, CHARLES DENNIS, academic administrator, contracting consultant; b. N.Y.C., Dec. 4, 1944; s. Domenico Pontilioni and Frances (Amato) R.; m. Martha Ann Moody, Feb. 14, 1967; children: Kristin E., Lisa M., Charles J. BA, St. Martin's Coll., 1966; MBA, U. Nev., 1972; MA, Calif. State U., Los Angeles, 1979. Lic. building contractor, energy auditor, Calif. Dir. facilities Glendora (Calif.) Unified Schs., 1976-81; dir. facilities Santa Barbara (Calif.) City Coll., 1981-86, also cons., 1984; asst. bus. bgr. Oxnard (Calif.) Union High Sch. Dist., 1986—; energy cons. Pleasant Valley Schs., Oxnard, Calif., 1985. Fund raiser Monticito (Calif.) YMCA, team capt. 1984, 1985. Served to maj. USAF, 1967-72. Recipient Energy Conservation award So. Calif. Gas Co., Glendora, 1979, Energy Conservation award Edison Co., Santa Barbara, 1985, 86. Mem. Calif. Assn. Sch. Bus. Officials (community coll. rep. adminstrs. 1984-86), Pacific Coast Phys. Plant Adminstrs., Calif. Bldg. Contractors Assn. Republican. Roman Catholic. Clubs: Morgan, Lincoln Owners, Van Nuys AFB Officer's (bd. dirs.). Avocation: classic automobiles. Office: Oxnard Union High Sch Dist 309 K St Oxnard CA 93030

RETTERER, RONALD J., management consultant, engineer, author; b. Chgo., July 24, 1940; s. Russell M. and Marietta T. Retterer; B.S., Ill. Inst. Tech., 1963; m. Karen E. Berg, Oct. 5, 1963; children—Kathryn, Anne, Laura, Dan. With Booz-Allen & Hamilton, Chgo., 1965-66; pres. Bus. Growth Services, Sacramento, Entron. Mem. Calif. Inventors Council (state bd.), Am. Assn. Small Research Cos., Soc. Venture Founders, Calif. State Assn. (assembly bus. com.), Clubs: Comstock, Rollingwood. Office: PO Box 1918 Fair Oaks CA 95628

REVAK, SUSAN DIANE, medical researcher; b. Newark, July 21, 1948; d. Philip and Minnie (Silber) Sitzer; m. David John Revak, Jan. 22, 1972; children: Eric Keith, Paul Nathan, Kelly Rachel. BA magna cum laude, UCLA, 1969. Research technician Scripps Clinic and Research Found., La Jolla, Calif., 1969-72, research asst., 1972-78, sr. research asst., 1978-84, sci. assoc., 1984—. Contbr. articles to profl. jours. Treas. Boy Scouts Am., Univ. City, Calif., 1986—. Grantee NSF, 1968. Mem. N.Y. Acad. Scis., AAAS, Phi Beta Kappa. Democrat. Jewish. Avocations: camping, reading, ice skating. Home: 6561 Cascade St San Diego CA 92122 Office: Scripps Clinic and Research Found 10666 N Torrey Pines Rd La Jolla CA 92037

REVEAL, ARLENE HADFIELD, librarian, consultant; b. Riverside, Utah, May 21, 1916; d. Job Oliver and Mabel Olive (Smith) Hadfield; children—James L., Jon A. B.S. with hons., Utah State U., 1938; grad. in librarianship San Diego State U., 1968; M.L.S., Brigham Young U., 1976. librarian, Calif. Social case worker Boxelder County Welfare, Brigham City, Utah, 1938-40; office mgr. Strawberry Inn, Strawberry, Calif., 1950-65, Dodge Ridge Ski Corp., Long Barn, Calif., 1948-65; adminstrv. asst. Mono County Office of Edn., Bridgeport, Calif., 1961-67; catalog librarian La Mesa-Spring Valley Sch. Dist., La Mesa, Calif., 1968-71; librarian Mono County Library, Bridgeport, Calif., 1971—. Author: Mono County Courthouse, 1980. Recipient John Cotton Dana award H.W. Wilson Co., 1974. Mem. Delta Kappa Gamma (pres. Epsilon Alpha chpt. 1984—), Beta Sigma Phi (treas. Xi Omicron Epsilon chpt. 1981, 83-85, pres. 1982, 85), Beta Phi Mu. Lodge: Rebekah (treas. 1973—). Home: PO Box 532 Bridgeport CA 93517 Office: Mono County Free Library PO Box 398 Bridgeport CA 93517

REVELL, JOHN HAROLD, dentist; b. Lead, S.D., Dec. 12, 1906; s. Aris LeRoy and Margaret (O'Donnell) R.; A.B. in Engring., Stanford, 1930; postgrad. McGill Med. Sch., 1930; D.D.S. summa cum laude, U. So. Calif., 1941; postgrad. in Maxillo Facial and Plastic Surgery, Mayo Found., U. Minn., 1944; m. Catherine Cecelia Gerrard, Sept. 14, 1936; children—Mary Margaret (Mrs. Irwin Goodwin), Kathleen Dianne Revell, Timothy John, Maureen Frances Brown, Dennis Cormac. Engaged as instr. U. So. Calif. Dental Coll., Los Angeles, 1941-42; practice oral surgery, maxillo facial-plastic surgery, Shafter, Calif., 1946—; mem. staff Mercy Hosp., Bakersfield, Calif., 1948—, chmn. dental sect., 1955-60, 70-71; mem. surg. staff San Joaquoin Hosp., Bakersfield; lectr. on applied nutrition; internat. pioneer lectr. surg. orthodontics. Served with AUS, 1932-37, 42-46; now maj. ret. Recipient of Special Clinic award Am. Soc. Dentistry for Children, 1964; Rotary Internat. Presdl. citation, 1982. Diplomate Internat. Bd. Applied Nutrition. Fellow Internat. Coll. Applied Nutrition; mem. ADA (life), Calif. Dental Assn. (life), Ventura Dental Soc. (life), So. Calif., Kern County (dir.), Los Angeles County (award 1941), Santa Barbara-Ventura County dental assns., Am. Acad. Dental Medicine, Am. Acad. Applied Nutrition, Am. Soc. Dentistry for Children (life), Pierre Fauchard Acad., Shafter C. of C. (dir. 1948-50), Alpha Tau Epsilon, Omicron Kappa Upsilon, Phi Kappa Phi, Theta Xi. Democrat. Roman Catholic. Rotarian (pres. Shafter 1950-51, dir. 1951-52). Patentee precisioner. Research on maxillary dental papilloma, rotation unerupted impacted teeth, channeling for extensive movement of teeth; also clin. research in cleft palate surgery; inventor rapid fabrication device for infant feeding; pioneer in pre-fab. bldgs. and homes while constrn. officer U.S. Army, 1932; developer prototype WW-2 Jeep machine gun mount. Author publs. in field; all research data presented to and housed at La. State U. Dental Coll., New Orleans. Home: 5173 Aurora Dr Ventura CA 93003

REVELLE, KEITH, librarian; b. Woodland, Calif., Dec. 20, 1942; s. Robert Keith and Cleo Imogene (Adams) R. B.A., U. Calif., Berkeley, 1964; M.S., Simmons Coll., 1967. Jr. librarian Latin Am. Library of the Oakland (Calif.) Public Library, 1967, sr. librarian, 1967-70, dir., 1970-74; asst. municipal librarian Municipality of Anchorage, 1974-76, municipal librarian, 1977—. Mem. Municipal Art Selection Adv. Com., Anchorage, 1978-81; bd. dirs. Basically Bach Festival, 1980-86, Anchorage Concert Assn., 1975—; mem. artistic adv. com. Anchorage Civic Opera, 1979-83, chmn., 1980-83; vice chmn. Alaska Gov.'s Adv. Council Libraries, 1984—. Mem. ALA, Alaska Library Assn. Home: 1811 Commodore Dr Anchorage AK 99507 Office: Municipality of Anchorage 3600 Denali St Anchorage AK 99503

REVENKO, VICTOR JOHN, oil company executive; b. N.Y.C., July 6, 1941; s. Nicholas M. and Martha (Zastra) R.; m. Maude Seaman, Dec. 28, 1966; children: Laura E., Elizabeth L. BA, Columbia Coll., 1963, BS in Engring., 1964, MS in Engring., 1968; cert. in bus., U. Calif., Berkeley, 1971. Registered profl. engr., Calif. Research engr. Chevron Research Co., Richmond, Calif., 1965-71; asst. mgr. benefits Chevron Corp., Richmond, 1981-85, mgr. orgn., 1985—; analyst, advisor Standard Oil Co. Calif., San Francisco, 1971-81. Mem. Am. Chem. Soc., Am. Inst. Chem. Engrs., Assn. Internat. Mgmt. Cons., Commonwealth Club Calif. (chmn. bus. econs. com. 1985—). Republican. Roman Catholic. Avocations: skiing, jogging, tennis, photography. Home: 16 Deer Park Ave San Rafael CA 94901 Office: Chevron Corp 575 Market St San Francisco CA 94104

REY, ARSENIO, language educator; b. Valle de las Casas, Spain, Mar. 12, 1938; came to U.S., 1959; s. Eustaquio Rey and Celerina Tejerina; m. Marianne Tampier; 1 child, Indíbil Rey. BA, El Abrojo, Valladolid, Spain, 1958; MDiv, El Pilar, Madrid, Spain, 1959; PhD, N.Y.U., 1974; diplôme, Sorbonne, Paris, 1976. Adj. asst. prof. CUNY, 1972-77; asst. prof. SUNY, Geneseo, 1977-81; from asst. to assoc. prof. U. Alaska, Anchorage, 1981—, chmn. dept. fgn. langs., 1981—; vis. prof. U. Hawaii, Manoa, 1985. V.p. Hispanic Alaskans, Anchorage, 1983-85; bd. dirs. Alaska Humanities Forum, 1983—, vice-chmn. Mem. MLA (del. 1985—), Alaska Fgn. Lang. Assn. (v.p. 1982-84), Pacific Northwest Council Fgn. Langs. (exec. bd. mem. 1986—), Am. Assn. Teaching of Spanish and Portuguese (mem. com. on hon. fellows 1981—), League of United Latin-Ams. Avocations: traveling, bicycling. Home: 7427 Hennings Way Anchorage AK 99504 Office: U Alaska Dept Fgn Langs 3211 UAA Dr Anchorage AK 99508

REYES, CANDACE MULCAHY, business administrator; b. Chgo., Feb. 16, 1946; d. Robert Emmet and Rita Helen (Schultz) Mulcahy; m. Phillip John Manzella, Aug. 18, 1964 (div. May 1967); 1 child, Janet Manzella; m. James Theodore Shell, Aug. 13, 1971 (div. May 1976); 1 child, Julia; m. Jaime Magbual Reyes, Aug. 12, 1978. Commodity broker Earl K. Riley, Chgo., 1968-72; acct. R.J. O'Brien, Chgo., 1974-75; commodity broker E.F. Hutton, Chgo., 1975-77; make-up artist Elizabeth Arden, Chgo., 1977-78; acct. Crocker Nat. Bank, San Francisco, 1978-80; bus. adminstr. Jaime Reyes, Casa Grande, Ariz., 1980—. Fund raiser Pinal County Med. Soc. Aux., Casa Grande, Ariz., 1983—. Fellow AMA Aux. (del. 1984), Pinal County Med. Soc. Aux. (pres. 1984-85), Assn. Phillippine Practicing Physicians Ariz. Aux. (sec. 1983, treas. 1982). Roman Catholic. Avocations: investing, reading, writing, dancing. Home and Office: 1131 Avenida Fresca Casa Grande AZ 85222

REYES, JOHN BEDFORD, physicist; b. Tucumcari, N.Mex., Nov. 28, 1948; s. Roscoco William and Maria Janet (Watson) R.; m. Angela Constance Dodson, Jan. 1, 1971; children: Raymond, Edward, Sophia. BS, U. So. Calif., 1966; MBA, Harvard U., 1968; PhD in Physics, MIT, 1971. Researcher Strategic Planning Inst., Boston, 1968-71, Rand Corp., Santa Monica, Calif., 1971-72; researcher CIA, Washington, 1972-75, cons., 1976—; prin. Reyes & Edwards, Beverly Hills, Calif., 1975—; Cons. Internat. AEC, Washington, 1979—, Goldman Sachs & Co., N.Y.C., 1984—, IBM, Armonk, N.Y., 1985—. Author: Rational Psychotics, 1982, Drop the Bomb & Save the World, 1977, Water Politics, 1980. Bd. dirs. Dept. Water and Power, City of Los Angeles, 1980-84; chmn. Commn. on Pornography, Washington, 1970-72; benefactor Music Ctr., Los Angeles, 1968—. Recipient Keffsmere Key Ohio Intellects Soc., 1972, Gernalders award Riders Club, 1985. Mem. Phi Beta Kappa. Clubs: Janus Soc. (Marina Del Rey, Calif.); Beaver Builders (Blue Earth, Minn.) (pres. 1979—); Comstock (San Francisco); Calif. (Los Angeles). Avocations: carpentry, computers, photography. Office: Reyes & Edwards 8306 Wilshire Blvd #499 Beverly Hills CA 90211

REYNALDO, JOSÉ, advertising executive recruiter; b. La Habana, Cuba, Dec. 26, 1943; s. O. Reynaldo and M. (Menes) Ramsey; m. Diane Snyder; children: Adrian, Alisha. BA in Econs., Calif. State U., Los Angeles; MBA, UCLA. Dir. econ. devel. Campesinos Unidos Inc., El Centro, Calif., 1975-76; exec. recruiter Dunhill Inc., Tarzana, Calif., 1979-81; prin. Reynaldo & Assocs., Seattle, 1981-85, Comsearch, Lake Oswego, Oreg., 1985—. Served with U.S. Army, 1965-67, Vietnam. Mem. Am. Mktg. Assn. (v.p. membership Seattle chpt. 1983), Portland Advt. Fedn., Am. Advt. Fedn., Internat. Honor Soc. in Econs. Republican. Methodist. Avocations: mountain climbing, hiking, squash, hunting, real estate investments. Office: Comsearch 15800 SW Boones Ferry Rd Lake Oswego OR 97034

REYNOLDS, CHRISTINE DIANE, language arts educator; b. Frankfurt, Fed. Republic of Germany, May 23, 1947; came to U.S., 1947; d. Theodore Alexander and Mary (Omelianuk) Kiersch; m. Carl L. Reynolds, Feb. 1, 1969; children: Catherine Elizabeth, Richard Gregory. BA with honors, U. Ill., 1969; EdM, U. Wyo., 1978. Cert. tchr., Wyo. Tchr. secondary schs. Ill., Wyo., 1969-78; teaching asst. U. Wyo., Laramie, 1977-78; tchr.'s aide Thayer Elem. Sch., Laramie, 1978-79; tchr. Higher Edn. Project, Laramie, 1981-82, Rock River (Wyo.) Sch., 1979—; Bd. dirs. Wyo. High Sch. Student Press Assn., Casper, also past pres. Contbr. news articles to U. Wyo. Alumni News. Dir. and coordinator Rock River Sch. Drama Fest., 1982—; Rep. block worker, Laramie, 1980. Mem. Albany County Edn. Assn. (union sec. 1986—), Nat. Council Tchrs. English, Kappa Delta Pi, Phi Kappa Phi, Phi Delta Kappa (pres. 1983-84), Delta Kappa Gamma, Delta Zeta (sec. 1967, pledge trainer 1968). Episcopalian. Avocations: horses, tending sheep ranches. Home: 4612 Oriole Ln Laramie WY 82070 Office: Rock River Sch Box 128 Rock River WY 82083

REYNOLDS, D. LU, architect; b. Pendleton, Oreg., June 25, 1921; d. Jesse Cyrus and Dorothy Harvey (Wood) Simonsen; m. John Laurin Reynolds, Jan. 25, 1952; 1 child, Heather. BS, U. Oreg., 1946, BArch, 1949. Registered architect, Oreg. Apprentice architect John Laurin Reynolds Architects, Eugene, Oreg., 1946-56; pvt. practice architecture Eugene, Oreg., 1956—. Republican. Lutheran. Avocations: piano, painting, gardening, tennis, swimming. Home: 3300 Hawkins Ln Eugene OR 97405 Office: 364 E Broadway #6 Eugene OR 97401

REYNOLDS, DONALD WORTHINGTON, publisher; b. Ft. Worth, Sept. 23, 1906; s. Gaines Worlie and Anna Louise (Elfers) R. B.J., U. Mo., 1927. Pub. Southwest Times Record, Ft. Smith, Ark., Okmulgee (Okla.) Times, 1940—, Moberly (Mo.) Monitor-Index, Las Vegas (Nev.) Rev. Jour., 1949—, Ely (Nev.) Times and Carson City (Nev.) Appeal, 1950—, Blackwell (Okla.) Jour. Tribune, 1955—, Chickasha (Okla.) Express, 1956—, Guthrie (Okla.) Leader, 1958—, Hawaii Tribune-Herald of Hilo, 1961—, Pawhuska (Okla.) Daily Jour.-Capital, 1964—, Guymon (Okla.) Daily Herald, 1966—, Aberdeen (Wash.) Daily World, 1968, The Daily Report, Ontario, Calif., Northwest Arkansas Morning News, Rogers, Pomona (Calif.) Progress-Bull., Frederick (Okla.) Daily Leader, Borger (Tex.) News Herald, 1977, Pauls Valley (Okla.) Daily Democrat, Wewoka (Okla.) Daily Times, 1967—, Jacksonville (Tex.) Progress, 1978, Cleburne (Tex.) Times Rev., 1976, Red Bluff (Calif.) Daily News, 1968—, Booneville (Ark.) Democrat, 1968—, Holdenville (Okla.) News, 1969—, Weatherford (Tex.) Democrat, 1967, Washington (Ind.) Times Herald, 1972—, Sherman (Tex.) Democrat, 1977, Springdale (Ark.) News, Kailua-Kona (Hawaii) West Hawaii Today, 1968—, Henryetta (Okla.) Freelance, Lompoc (Calif.) Record, Picayune (Miss.) Item, Bartlesville (Okla.) Examiner-Enterprise, Kilgore (Tex.) News Herald, Gainesville (Tex.) Daily Register, Chico (Calif.) Enterprise-Record, Auburn (Wash.) Daily Globe News, Sweetwater (Tex.) Reporter, Glasgow (Ky.) Daily Times, Oskaloosa (Iowa) Herald, Redlands (Calif.) Daily Facts, Vallejo (Calif.) Times-Herald, Poplarville (Miss.) Democrat, Durant (Okla.) Daily Democrat; pres., chief exec. officer Donrey Cablevision, Guymon, Bartlesville, and Blackwell, Okla., Vallejo, Calif.; Pub. Donrey Cablevision, Rogers, Ark.; pres., chief exec. officer Donrey Outdoor, Inc., Las Vegas, Reno, Albuquerque, Spokane, Tulsa, Oklahoma City and Ft. Smith, Donrey Outdoor Advertising, Little Rock, Columbus, Ohio, Amarillo, Tex.; owner, pres. and chief exec. officer radio stas. KEXO, Grand Junction, Colo., radio stas. KBRS, Springdale, Ark., radio stas. KOCM-FM, Newport Beach, Calif., KOLO, Reno, 1955—, KOLO-TV, Reno, 1954—, Wichita (Kans.) Donrey Outdoor Co., 1973—. Hon. disch., maj. M.I. 1945. Awarded Legion of Merit, Bronze Star, Purple Heart, 5 combat stars; Broadcaster of Year award Nev. Broadcasting Assn., 1978. Mem. Nat. Assn. Radio-TV Broadcasters, Am. Soc. Newspaper Editors, So. Newspaper Pubs. Assn., Am. Legion, Sigma Delta Chi, Pi Kappa Alpha. Clubs: Overseas Press (San Francisco); Hillcrest Country (Bartlesville); Tulsa, Dallas Athletic; Hardscrabble Country (Ft. Smith); Prospector's (Reno); Pacific (Honolulu).

REYNOLDS, GARDNER MEAD, civil engineer; b. Ithaca, N.Y., Oct. 29, 1918; s. Minos Mead and Ruth Louise (Gardner) R.; m. Kathleen Kane, July 31, 1945; children: Marcia, Stephen, Timothy, Richard. B.C.E., Cornell U., 1948. With Dames & Moore (civil engrs.), 1948-85, partner, 1954-85; mng. partner cons. div. Dames & Moore (civil engrs.), N.Y.C., 1960-74; sr. partner, chmn. exec. com. Dames & Moore (civil engrs.), Los Angeles, 1974-85; partner Dames & Moore-U.K., 1967-85, Dames & Moore Australia, 1976-85; dir. Chiyoda/Dames & Moore. Mem. Planning Bd. Wyckoff, N.J., 1965-68. Served with USAAF, 1942-46. Decorated Purple Heart. Fellow ASCE (nat. dir. 1966-68, chmn. exec. com. engring. mgmt. div. 1977); mem. Assn. Soil and Found. Engrs. (1st v.p., past treas., pres. 1978-79), The Beavers, World Dredging Assn. Clubs: Palos Verdes Golf, Breakfast (Palos Verdes, Calif.). Home: 2740 Via Campesina Palos Verdes Estates CA 90274

REYNOLDS, JOHN GORDON, research chemist, chemical engineer; b. Oakland, Calif., Nov. 10, 1949; s. Oliver Clyde and Elizabeth Mary (Lorang) R. AA in Chem. Tech., Merritt Coll., 1972; BS in Chemistry, U. Calif., Berkeley, 1976; PhD in Inorganic Chemistry, Stanford U., 1980. Research asst. Lawrence Berkeley (Calif.) Lab., 1974-76, Stanford (Calif.) Magnetic Resonance Lab., 1976-79; postdoctoral assoc. Calif. Inst. Tech., Pasadena, 1980-81; research engr. Chevron Research Co., Richmond, Calif., 1981—; owner, operator Bay Cellars Winery, Everyville, Calif., 1982—. Contbr. articles to profl. jours.; mem. editorial bd. Vortex mag.; patentee in field. Mem. Am. Chem. Soc. (petroleum, fuel, inorganic and small bus. divs.). Home: 330 Summit Pl #1 Point Richmond CA 94801 Office: Chevron Research Co PO Box 1627 Richmond CA 94802

REYNOLDS, JOHN HAMILTON, physicist, educator; b. Cambridge, Mass., Apr. 3, 1923; s. Horace Mason and Catharine (Coffeen) R.; m. Ann Burchard Arnold, July 19, 1975; children from previous marriages: Amy, Horace Marshall, Brian Marshall, Karen Leigh, Petra Catharine. AB,

Harvard U., 1943; MS, U. Chgo., 1948, PhD, 1950; D. honoris causa, U. Coimbra, Portugal, 1987. Research asst. Electroacoustic Lab., Harvard, 1941-43; assoc. physicist Argonne Nat. Lab., 1950; physicist U. Calif. at Berkeley, 1950—, prof. physics, 1961—, chmn. dept. physics, 1984-86, faculty research lectr., 1974. Contbr. articles to profl. jours. Served to lt. USNR, 1943-46. Recipient Wetherill medal Franklin Inst., 1965, Golden Plate award Am. Acad. Achievement, 1968, Exceptional Sci. Achievement award NASA, 1973; Guggenheim fellow U. Bristol, Eng., 1956-57, Los Alamos Nat. Lab., 1987, NSF fellow U. São Paulo, Brazil, 1963-64; Fulbright-Hays research grantee U. Coimbra, Portugal, 1971-72; U.S.-Australia Coop. Sci. Program awardee U. Western Australia, 1978-79. Fellow Am. Acad. Arts and Scis.; mem. Nat. Acad. Scis. (J. Lawrence Smith medal 1967), Am. Phys. Soc., Am. Geophys. Union, Geochem. Soc., Meteoritical Soc. (Leonard medal 1973), AAAS, AAUP, Phi Beta Kappa. Democrat. Club: Faculty (Berkeley). Office: Dept Physics Univ of Calif Berkeley CA 94720

REYNOLDS, JOHN SPENCER, architect, educator; b. Muncie, Ind., Jan. 31, 1938; s. Eugene Spencer and Lura Mae (Schield) R.; divorced; children: Nathan, Vaughan, Hannah. BArch, U. Ill., 1962; MArch, MIT, 1967. Registered architect, Mass., Oreg. Structural designer Scholer & Fuller, Tucson, 1962-63; designer Shepley, Bulfinch, Richardson & Abbott, Boston, 1964-67; prof. architecture U. Oreg., Eugene, 1967—; cons. Equinox Design, Eugene, 1978—. Author: Mechanical and Electrical Equipment for Buildings, rev. 7th edit., 1986. Bd. dirs. Eugene Water and Electric Bd., 1973-76. Fulbright scholar, 1963-64; recipient Ersted Teaching award U. Oreg., 1976. Mem. Am. Solar Energy Soc. (vice-chmn. 1986—). Democrat. Avocation: music. Office: U Oreg Dept Architecture Eugene OR 97403

REYNOLDS, JOHN WESTON, pediatric medicine educator; b. Portland, Oreg., Aug. 5, 1930; s. Lloyd Jay and Virginia (Bliss) R.; m. Phyllis Cantrell, Sept. 19, 1954. BA, Reed Coll., 1951; MD, U. Oreg., 1956. Diplomate Am. Bd. Pediatrics. Asst. prof. pediatrics U. Minn., Mpls., 1961-66, assoc. prof., 1966-70, prof., 1970-77; prof. Oreg. Health Scis. U., Portland, 1977—. Contbr. numerous articles to profl. jours. Bd. dirs. Planned Parenthood of Portland, 1984—. Recipient Research Career Devel. award NIH, 1964-74. Fellow Am. Acad. Pediatrics (nutrition com. 1981—); mem. Am. Pediatric Soc., Soc. Pediatric Research, Endocrine Soc. Avocations: hiking, skiing. Home: 4471 SW Fairview Circus Portland OR 97221 Office: Oreg Health Scis U 3181 SW Sam Jackson Park Rd Portland OR 97201

REYNOLDS, J(OSHUA) PAUL, JR., electronic executive; b. Wilmington, N.C., Aug. 12, 1941; s. Joshua Paul and Martha Rebecca (Ward) R.; m. Janet Ruth Carlton, Nov. 18, 1963; children: J. Paul III, Virginia Ruth. BS with honors, Fla. State U., 1963, MS with honors, 1964. Program mgr. Harris Corp., Melbourne, Fla., 1966-70, mktg. engr., 1970-73, mktg. mgr., 1973-76, sales mgr., 1976-79; program dir. Kaiser Electronics, San Jose, Calif., 1979-83, exec. dir., v.p., 1983—. Mem. City Adv. Council, West Melbourne, 1987-77. Named Mktg. Man of Yr., Harris Govt. Systems, 1972. Mem. Sigma Alpha Epsilon (v.p. 1963). Democrat. Methodist. Avocations: horse breeding and tng., snow skiing, hunting, flying. Office: Kaiser Electronics 2701 Orchard Park Way San Jose CA 95134

REYNOLDS, PETER CARLTON, anthropologist; b. N.Y.C., Nov. 13, 1943; s. Walter Carlton and Maria Bernadette (King) R. AB, U. Calif., Berkeley, 1965; PhD, Yale U., 1972. Postdoctoral fellow Stanford (Calif.) U., 1972-74; research fellow Australian Nat. U., Canberra, 1974-80; dir. Corp. Anthropology Group, Kirkland, Wash., 1982-87; co-founder Intermedia, Inc., Sausalito, Calif., 1987—. Author: On the Evolution of Human Behavior, 1981. Guggenheim fellow, 1980-82. Mem. Sierra Club (exec. com. Chgo. chpt. 1985), Sigma Xi.

REYNOLDS, PETER JAMES, physicist; b. N.Y.C., Nov. 19, 1949; s. Rudolph and Lydia Mary (Schanzer) R.; m. Louise Perini, Aug. 7, 1982. A.B. in Physics, U. Calif.-Berkeley, 1971; Ph.D., MIT, 1979. Research assoc. and lectr. Boston U., 1979, asst. research prof., 1979-83; mem. sci. staff Nat. Resource for Computation in Chemistry, Lawrence Berkeley Lab., U. Calif., 1980-81, mem. sci. staff materials and molecular research div., 1981—; vis. scientist NEC Fundamental Research Lab., Kawasaki, Japan, 1986; lectr. and researcher in field of chem., statis. and computational physics. NSF fellow, 1971-74; IBM fellow, 1975; Lawrence Berkeley Lab. grantee, 1982-83 Mem. AAAS, Am. Phys. Soc., N.Y. Acad. Scis., Phi Beta Kappa, Sigma Xi. Lutheran. Contbr. chpts. to books and articles in field to profl. jours. Office: Lawrence Berkeley Lab Mailstop 50D-106 Berkeley CA 94720

REYNOLDS, R. WALLACE, technical writer, emeritus educator; b. Pitts., Apr. 30, 1914; s. Raymond O. and Anna May (Kime) R.; B.S., State Tchrs. Coll. (California, Pa.) 1940; M.S., Purdue U., 1946; postgrad. U. Pitts., 1946, U. So. Calif., 1948; m. Marjorie Frances Johnson, June 25, 1943; children—Marjorie Wallace, Timothy Lincoln. Engr., Douglas Aircraft Co., 1942, Naval Ordnance Lab., 1942-46; prof., chmn. engring. drawing Washington & Jefferson Coll., 1946-47, U. Santa Clara, 1947-48, West Coast U., 1949-52, Calif. Poly. State U., 1953-79, prof. emeritus, 1979—; mgr. R. Wallace Reynolds Drafting Service, San Luis Obispo, 1968-78; cons. U.S. Bur. Ships, 1955-58; sr. engr. design sect. Jet Propulsion Lab., Pasadena, 1975. Dem committeeman, San Luis Obispo County, 1956-63. Recipient certificate of commendation, U.S. Naval Ordnance Lab., 1945; Excellence award Visual Communications Industry, 1968. Fellow Am. Soc. Cert. Engring. Technicians; mem. Am. Soc. Engring. Edn. (sec. Pacific Southwest sect. 1969-75, chmn. 1976-77, 78-80, nat. dir. 1978-80, life mem.), Am. Inst. Drafting and Design (v.p. edn. Calif. chpt. 1967-69, dir. Central Coast 1972-75), Nat. Assn. Civilian Conservation Corps Alumni, (exec. dir. 1981-82, gen. chmn. 5th biennial nat. conv. 1987), Northwest Area Found. (project dir. 1986—), Phi Sigma Pi, Tau Alpha Pi. Author: Problems for Modern Engineering Drawing, 1956-67. Home: 577 Princeton Pl San Luis Obispo CA 93401

REYNOLDS, RALPH ELVIN, psychology educator; b. Madison, Wis., Nov. 12, 1948; s. Elvin Walter and Elaine Mavis (Brager) R. B.A., U. Wis., 1971; M.A., Ariz. State U., 1975; Ph.D., U. Ill., 1979. Research assoc. U. Ill., Champaign, 1979-80; prof. ednl. studies and ednl. psychology U. Utah, Salt Lake City, 1980—. Served with USAF, 1971-75. Recipient Nat. Ednl. Research award, 1979. Mem. Am. Ednl. Research Assn., Am. Psychol. Assn., Nat. Reading Conf. Presbyterian. Contbr. articles on psychology to profl. jours. Office: University of Utah 130 MBH Salt Lake City UT 84112

REYNOLDS, RICHARD HENRY, art educator; b. N.Y.C., May 16, 1913; s. Raymond R. and Sarah Alice (Weeks) R.; m. Marjorie Merrihew Sharrer, Aug. 10, 1939; 1 dau., Barbara Gwynne Nagata. A.B., U. Calif., 1936; student U. Calif., Los Angeles, 1939, Mills Coll., 1940; M.A., Coll. Pacific, 1942; postgrad. Oreg. State U., 1962; D.F.A., Morningside Coll., Sioux City, Iowa, 1976. Window display artist Emporium, San Francisco, 1936-37. Foreman-Clark, 1937, Hastings Clothing Co., 1937-38; asst. chmn. div. arts and letters Stockton Jr. Coll., 1939-43; prof. art, chmn. dept. U. of the Pacific, 1948-73, sr. prof., 1973-80, prof. emeritus, 1980, faculty research lectr., 1960, chairman academic council (senate), 1967-68, chmn. president's task force on acad. programs, 1980; mem. Stockton Arts Commn., 1980-81; guest lectr. Alaska Meth. U., Liberal Arts Inst., Anchorage, 1962; lectr. in field; judge numerous competitive art exhbns.; judge art sect. Ariz. State Fair, 1971; one-man show (sculpture) John Muir Gallery, Modesto, Calif., 1956, (painting) Lanai Gallery, Sacramento, 1956, (polychromed wood-reliefs) Stockton Fine Arts Gallery, 1972, 74, U. Pacific Alumni House Gallery, 1972; mem. show, Five Artists, invited E. B. Crocker Gallery, Sacramento, 1956; sculpture accepted for national exhbn. 10th Ann. New Eng. Exhbn., New Canaan, Conn., 1958; invited exhibit sculpture Eric Locke Gallery, San Francisco, 3d Ann. West Coast Sculptors, 1960; exhibited painting Purdue U., 1966; 2-man show (with wife) Stockton Savs. Loan Bank Invitational, 1968; exhibited paintings at No. Calif. Arts Exhbn., Sacramento, 1970; exhibited selected paintings Mother Lode Art Assn. Annual Show, Sonora, Calif., 1968; commd. sculptures buildings and campus U. of the Pacific, 1958, 60, 62, 63, bronze relief Swenson Golf Course, Stockton, 1968, metal falcon sculpture Atwater (Calif.) High Sch., 4 foot bronze relief for Stockton Record Bldg., bronze plaque Quemado (N.Mex.) Library, 1973; TV and radio lectr., 1955—; pvt. architectural sculpture commns., 1956—; exhibited Da Vinci Internat. Exhbn., N.Y.C., 1970, U. Pacific, 1973, Modesto Jr. Coll., 1973, Unitarian Arts Festival, Stockton, 1976, Ann. Delta Art Assn. show, Pittsburgh, Calif., 1976, Stockton Art League Show, annually, 1976-80; judge Merced Art Assn., 1976. Bd. dirs. Stockton Art League, 1978-79 hon. bd. dirs. Stockton Symphony Ballet Assn., 1978—, San Joaquin Concert Ballet Assn. Served as lt. (j.g.), U.S. Naval Res., active duty, 1943-46. Awarded prize in oils Spring Art Festival, Stockton Art League, 1951; Bronze medal sculpture, Oakland Art Gallery's Oil Painting-Sculpture Ann. Exhbn., 1952; Kingsley award for sculpture Crocker Art Gallery, Sacramento, 1952, 53, 79; San Joaquin Pioneer Museum, 1953; 2d prize, Nat. Mag. Cover Contest, 1957; sculpture prizes Unitarian Arts Festival, Stockton, 1959, 61; jurors mention Nat. Exhbn. Small Paintings, Tour Gallery Assos., N.Mex., 1962; hon. mention Stockton Art League, 1964, 68; Best of Show award, 2d prize (painting), honorable mentions in Calif. exhibitions, 1966; Transparent Painting award No. Calif. Spring Art Festival Haggin Mus., Stockton, Calif., 1968; Acrylic Painting award Unitarian Arts Festival, Stockton, 1968; purchase prize, painting Lodi Art Ann., Acampo, 1971, 79; 2d prize, painting San Joaquin County Fair and Expn., 1972, drawing and painting awards, 1974, 3d award, mixed media, 1981; 3 painting awards Stockton Art League Ann., 1974, purchase award, 1975; 1st prize sculpture San Joaquin County Fair and Expn. Art Show, 1976, 82; spl. award sculpture Crocker Kingsley Exhbn., 1982. 2d prize and hon. mention Bank of Stockton, 1976; 2d prize, other media San Joaquin County Fair, 1978; 2d award Lodi Spring Wine Show, 1982, 3d award, 1983; hon. mention Lodi Grape Festival and Nat. Wine Show, 1982; 2d award Unitarian Arts Festival, Stockton, 1982; hon. mention No. Calif. Arts, Inc. Exhbn., Sacramento, 1982; 2d award San Joaquin County Fair, also hon. mention, 1983; 1st prize junk sculpture Alan Short Gallery, Stockton, Calif., 1983; 3d award Lodi Spring Wine Show Art Exhbn., 1983, 2 Exhibitor awards No.Calif. Arts Exhbn., Sacramento, 1983, 3d award San Joaquin County Fair Art Exhbn., 1984, Bronze Relief plaque for San Joaquin County Hosp., 1984, Columnist Stockton Art League's newsletter, The Collagraph, 1984-86, 3 2d Place awards, Hon. Mention for sculpture, 1985; 1st prize Stockton Symphony program cover competition, 1984; Order of Pacific award U. of Pacific, 1980; honorable mention Spring Wine Show Art Exhibition, Lodi, Calif., 1986; judge's choice 16th annual Nat. Small Painting Show, Albuquerque, N.Mex., 1987, numerous others. Shell grantee, 1960. Life fellow International Inst. Arts and Letters, 1960. Mem. Coll. Art Assn. of Am., Pacific Arts Assn. (editor Journalette 1951-52; pres. No. Cal. sect. 1951-52), Stockton Art League (pres. 1952-53, 80-82), Nat. Art Edn. Assn. (nat. chmn. membership com. 1952-53), AAUP (v.p. local chpt. 1958-59), Navy League U.S. (dir. Stockton br. 1981-83), Phi Kappa Phi (pres.-elect 1980-81, emeritus), Delta Epsilon, Phi Sigma Kappa, Phi Delta Kappa (emeritus). Episcopalian. Richard H. Reynolds Gallery named in his honor U. Pacif, Stockton, 1986. Contbr. articles to art publs. Exhibitor paintings, sculptures. Home: 1656 W Longview Ave Stockton CA 95207

REYNOLDS, ROBERT HARRISON, export co. exec.; b. Mpls., Sept. 6, 1913; s. Clarence H. and Helen (Doyle) R.; student pub. schs., Vinton, Iowa; m. Gladys Marie Gaster, Apr. 7, 1934; 1 dau., Shirley Anne (Mrs. Frank S. Potestio); m. 2d, Viola E. Shimel, June 26, 1982. Export sales mgr., rolled products sales mgr. Colo. Fuel & Iron Corp., Denver, 1938-46; pres. Rocky Mountain Export Co., Inc., Denver, 1941—; dir. Electromedics, Inc. Club: Denver. Home: 580 S Clinton St Denver CO 80231 Office: Rocky Mountain Export 11111 Mississippi Ave Aurora CO 80012

REYNOLDS, WILLIAM MASON, JR., editor, writer; b. Bremerton, Wash., Sept. 3, 1945; s. William Mason Sr. and Mary Marguerite (Jackse) R.; m. Pamela Christine Hall, Mar. 1972 (div. Jan. 1976). BA, U. Wash., 1972, MS, 1974; PhD, U. Calif., Berkeley. Freelance writer 1967; editor in chief Muscle & Fitness Mag., Woodland Hills, Calif., 1978—. Author numerous books; contbr. numerous articles to profl. jours. Served with USN, 1963-69. Mem. Nat. Strength and Conditioning Assn. Avocation: traveling. Home: PO Box 1475 Santa Monica CA 90406 Office: Weider Health & Fitness 21100 Erwin St Woodland Hills CA 91367

REYNOLDS, W(YNETKA) ANN, university system administrator, educator; b. Coffeyville, Kans., Nov. 3, 1937; d. John Ethelbert and Glennie (Beanland) King; m. Thomas H. Kirschbaum; children—Rachel Rebecca, Rex King. B.S. in Biology-Chemistry, Kans. State Tchrs. Coll., Emporia, 1958; M.S. in Zoology, U. Iowa, Iowa City, 1960, Ph.D., 1962; D.Sc. (hon.), Ind. State U., Evansville, 1980. Asst. prof. biology Ball State U., Muncie, Ind., 1962-65; asst. prof. anatomy U. Ill. Coll. Medicine, Chgo., 1965-68, assoc. prof. anatomy, 1968-73, research prof. ob-gyn, 1973—, prof. anatomy, 1973—, acting assoc. dean acad. affairs Coll. Medicine, 1977, assoc. vice chancellor, dean grad. coll., 1977-79; prof. ob-gyn Ohio State U., Columbus, 1979-82, prof. anatomy, 1979-82, provost, 1979-82; chancellor Calif. State Univ. System, Long Beach, 1982—, prof. biology, 1982—; cons. and lectr. in field. Contbr. chpts. to books, articles to profl. jours. Active numerous civic activities involving edn. Recipient Disting. Alumni award Kans. State Tchrs. Coll., 1972. Fellow Calif. Acad. Scis.; mem. AAAS, Am. Assn. Anatomists, Am. Diabetes Assn., Am. Soc. Zoologists, Endocrine Soc., Perinatal Research Soc., Soc. Exptl Biology and Medicine, Soc. Gynecologic Investigation, Sigma Xi. Office: Calif State U 400 Golden Shore Long Beach CA 90802

REZNIK, DAVID, chemical engineer, food technologist; b. Tel Aviv, Israel, Dec. 18, 1935; came to U.S., 1982; s. Israel Reznik and Zelda (Cohen) R.; m. Miriam Wiener, Oct. 22, 1959; children: Assaf, Omry. BS in Chemistry, Technion, Haifa, Israel, 1960, MS in Food Tech., 1963. Research engr. Technion Research Station, Haifa, 1960-61, chief engr., 1964-67; teaching asst. Technion, Haifa, 1961-63; research engr. Metal Box, London, 1963-64, Lageen Can Mfg., Yagur, Israel, 1968-73; owner, pres. Raz Machinery and Tech., Haifa, Israel, 1973-82; dir. tech. research ctr. Tri Valley Growers, Menlo Park, Calif., 1982—; cons. Tri Valley Growers, Modesto, Calif., 1981-82; food engring. expert UNIDO, Mex., 1979-80; research and devel. cons. Canners and Can Makers, Europe & Israel, 1974-82. Patentee in field. Lord Simon Marks grantee, 1963. Mem. Golden Gate Soc. Coatings, Nat. Assn. Metal Decorators, Nat. Assn. Food Processors, Inst. Food Technologists. Avocations: skiing, hiking. Office: Tri/Valley Growers Tech Research Ctr 179 Jefferson Dr Menlo Park CA 94025

REZNIKOFF, CAROLYN FRANCES, social worker; b. St. Louis, June 3, 1947; d. Simon and Ruth (Shear) R.; m. David Porter, Dec. 21, 1979; 1 child, Sasha. BA, Pitzer Coll., 1968; MSW, San Diego State U., 1971. Lic. clin. social worker, Oreg. Social worker Los Angeles County Dept. Adoptions, 1968-69; med. social worker U. Oreg. Health Sci. U., Portland, 1971-73, Emanuel Hosp., Portland, 1976-79; pvt. practice social work Portland, 1981—; med. social worker Vis. Nurses Assn., Portland, 1983-86; social services supr. Kaiser Permanent Home Health Agy. Hospice, Portland, 1986—; tchr. Re-Evaluation Co. Counseling, Portland, Oreg. Mem. Nat. Assn. Social Workers, Acad. Cert. Social Workers. Democrat. Jewish. Office: Kaiser Permanent Home Health Agy 7201 N Interstate Portland OR 97217

RHEA, ANN CRAWFORD, interior designer; b. Somerville, Tenn., Oct. 30, 1940; d. James Samuel and Annie Marie (Crawford) R. BA in Edn., U. Miss., 1962; BFA, Memphis Coll. Arts, 1967; postgrad., Scottsdale Community Coll., 1975-85. Cert. Nat. Council Interior Design. Designer Holiday Inns Inc., Memphis, 1970-72, Ramada Inns Inc., Phoenix, 1972-78; assoc. Continental Design, Scottsdale, Ariz., 1978-80, Hauser Designs, Scottsdale, 1980-82; prin. Design Criteria, Scottsdale, 1983—; cons. Embassy Suites Hotels Inc., Scottsdale, 1985—. Mem. Nat. Arts and Crafts Assn., Ariz. Hotel Motel Assn., Nat. Mus. Women in the Arts, Smithsonian Orgn., Heard Mus. Democrat. Methodist. Avocations: audio and visual art, travel. Home and Office: 6801 E Camelback S-305 Scottsdale AZ 85251

RHEE, SHIN WOONG, manufacturing company engineer; b. Seoul, Dem. Republic of Korea, June 19, 1943; came to U.S., 1971.; s. Mal Ryong and Sang Kum (Chang) R.; m. Jin Woo Nam, Dec. 22, 1974; children: Grace, Jason. BSEE, Seoul Nat. U., 1967; MSEE, Calif. State U., Northridge, 1979. Research and devel. engr. Am. Tech, Northridge, 1975-78; v.p. Clean Water System, Camarillo, Calif., 1978-79; gen. mgr. Rec Specialties Inc., Camarillo, 1979—; pres. Rhetronics, Northridge, 1980—. Music dir. and conductor Valley Korean Ctr. Presbyn. Ch., Sepulvera, Calif., 1982—. Served to 2d lt. Korean Army, 1967-71. Avocation: fishing. Home: 11626 Killimore Ave Northridge CA 91326 Office: Rec Specialties Inc 530 Constitution Ave Camarillo CA 93010

RHEIN, ROBERT ALDEN, research chemist; b. San Francisco, Aug. 18, 1933; s. Reginald Walter and Gaynelle Kathleen (Brunner) R.; m. Ellen Jane Emerson, June 9, 1956; children: Robert Alden Jr., Mark E., Kathleen E., Dirck N., Jane M. BS in Engring. Physics, U. Calif., Berkeley, 1955; MSME, U. Pitts., 1958; PhD in Chemistry, U. Wash., 1962. Sr. scientist Jet Propulsion Lab., Pasadena, Calif., 1962-79; research chemist Naval Weapons Ctr., China Lake, Calif., 1979—; postdoctoral appointee U. Mass., Amherst, 1983-84. Camping chmn. Boy Scouts Am., La Canada, Calif., 1969-78. Mem. Am. Chem. Soc. Democrat. Roman Catholic. Avocations: swimming, walking, hiking. Office: Naval Weapons Ctr Code 3244 China Lake CA 93555-6001

RHETT, WILLIAM MEANS SMITH, marketing professional; b. Miami Beach, Fla., Jan. 25, 1930; s. Haskell Smith and Eunice Campbell (Emery) R.; m. Ethelyn Eddy, May 29, 1965 (div. July 1971); children: Ian Christopher, Allison Wingate; m. Mary Frances Amill, Jan. 1, 1980. BA, Hamilton Coll., 1952; MBA, Harvard U., 1957. Account group exec. McCann-Erickson Internat., N.Y.C., 1957-60; dir. client services Colón S.A., Madrid, 1960-61; mgr. mktg. devel. and advt. Motorola Overseas Corp., Chgo., 1962-66; account mgr. Marsteller Internat., N.Y.C., 1966-67; area dir. Latin Am. Wells, Rich, Greene Internat., N.Y.C., 1968-69, account supr., 1969-70; v.p. Mktg. Control Inc., N.Y.C., 1971-73; internat. mktg. mgr. consumer products div. Nat. Semiconductor Corp., Sunnyvale, Calif., 1974-75; mng. dir. Intermarkets Ltd., Orinda, Calif., 1975—. Contbr. articles to profl. jours. Served to commdr. USNR, 1954—. Mem. Internat. Advt. Assn. (dir. at large, 1966-68), Midwest Internat. Mktg. Caucus (founder, chmn. projects com.), Hamilton Alumni (pres. 1964-66, pres. North Calif. Assn. 1983—), Marines Meml. Club., San Francisco Advt. Club, U.S. Naval Inst. Republican. Episcopalian. Club: Am. (Madrid); Hamilton (N.Y.C.); Lawn Tennis de la Exposición (Lima, Peru); Stamford (Conn.) Yacht. Avocations: traveling, tennis, classic automobiles. Office: Intermarkets Ltd PO Box 141 Moraga CA 94563

RHINEHART, DERRELL LEE, optometrist; b. Belen, N.Mex., July 29, 1935; s. James Bonar and Dolores (Gilbertson) R.; m. Charlene Lenore Jones; children—Sandra Rhinehart Trevison, Linda Rhinehart Riner, James, Charles. B.A., U. Kans., 1959; B.S., U. Calif., 1962, O.D., 1964. Pvt. practice optometry, Escondido, Calif., 1964—; instr. pub. health Community Coll. Calif., 1976—; cons. optometry Project Concern Hosp., Tijuana, Mex.; sight conservation chmn. Lions Club, 1972. Mem. Am. Optometric Assn., Calif. Optometric Assn., Sports Vision Inc., Coll. Optometry in Vision Devel., San Diego County Optometric Soc. (dir. 1972-77, pres. 1977). Bd. dirs. Valley Center (Calif.) Community Ch. Club: Rotary Internat. Office: 1299 E Pennsylvania St Escondido CA 92027

RHOADES, BARTLETT REUEL, publishing company executive; b. Littleton, N.H., Aug. 22, 1938; s. Gilbert R. and Catherine (Reuell) R.; m. Susan Giannitti; children: Matthew, Andrew, Elizabeth. AB, Harvard U., 1960, MBA, 1967. Exec. v.p. MBA Communications, N.Y.C., 1968-73; group mktg. dir. Doubleday & Co., N.Y.C., 1973-78; exec. v.p., pub. Med. Econs. Co., Cradell, N.J., 1978-84; pres., chief exec. officer PC World Communications, San Francisco, 1984—; bd. dirs. Bus. Publs. Audit of Circulation Inc., N.Y.C., Infoworld Publs., Menlo Park, Calif. Served to lt. USN, 1960-65. Home: 1164 Upper Happy Valley Rd Lafayette CA 94549 Office: PCW Communications Inc 501 Second St San Francisco CA 94107

RHOADS, GERALD AUSTIN, safety executive; b. Thatcher, Ariz., May 9, 1933; s. Gerald Austin and Margaret (Altman) R.; m. Marsha Yandry (div. Jan. 1963); children: Leigh Ann, Robert, Guy; m. Nancy Jean Lucas, Mar. 23, 1963; children: Julie, Mark, Matthew. Student, USAF Ill., Chgo., 1951; pilot officer tng., USN Flight Sch., Pensacola, Fla., 1952; student, Texas A&M U., 1972. Lic. polygraph examiner, N.Mex.; cert. comml. multi-engine pilot, ballon pilot. Commd. ensign USN, Hawaii, 1950; advanced through grades to lt. (j.g.) USN, 1956, resigned, 1957; pilot Flying Service, Plano, Tex., 1957-60; patrolman Tex. Dept. Pub. Safety, Austin, 1960; pilot Frontier Airlines, Omaha, Nebr., 1960-61; recovery pilot Raven Industries, Sioux Falls, S.D., 1961; launch dir., pilot Nat. Ctr. Atmospheric Research, Palestine, Tex., 1973; co-propr. Polygraph Service Inc., Phoenix, 1973-76; v.p. X-PERT-B&M, Hobbs, N.Mex., 1976—. Co-inventor emergency escape device, 1984, traveling block control, 1986. Mem. Assn. Oilwell Service Contractors (chmn. 1983-84, 2d v.p. 1985-86, 1st v.p. 1986—, Watchdog award 1986), Am. Soc. Safety Engrs. (chmn. 1982-83). Republican. Methodist. Avocations: flying, woodworking. Office: X-Pert-B&M PO Box 1918 Hobbs NM 88241

RHODE, EDWARD ALBERT, veterinary medicine educator, university administrator; b. Amsterdam, N.Y., July 25, 1926; s. Edward A. and Katherine (Webb) R.; m. Dolores Bangert, 1955; children: David E., Peter R., Paul W., Robert M., Catherine E. DVM, Cornell U., 1947. Diplomate Am. Coll. Veterinary Internal Medicine. Prof. vet. medicine U. Calif., Davis, 1964—, chmn. dept. vet. medicine, 1968-71, assoc. dean instrn. Sch. Vet. Medicine, 1971-77, 78-81, dean sch. Vet. Medicine, 1982—. Mem. Am. Vet. Medicine Assn., Calif. Vet. Medicine Assn., Am. Acad. Vet. Cardiology, Am. Physiol. Soc., Calif. Biomed. Research Assn. Office: U Calif Sch Vet Medicine Davis CA 95616

RHODES, ANNE LOU, social service administrator; b. Richmond, Ind., Oct. 9, 1935; d. George E. and Margaret (Jones) R. BA, Whittier Coll., 1957; MSW, Fresno State Coll., 1968. Social worker San Bernardino (Calif.) County Welfare Dept., 1959-62, social work supr. I, 1962-63, social work supr. II, 1963-68, social service supr. III, 1968—; instr. social welfare U. Calif., Riverside, 1969; cons. Headstart program Riverside County Econ. Opportunity Bd., 1970, Delman Heights Welfare Rights Orgn., 1968-71.; participant German profl. minority exchange program, 1979, Statehouse Cong. on Children and Youth, 1979; mem. Calif. Com. on Credentials, 1980; bd. dirs. Inland Area Adolescent Clinic, 1970—. Mem. task force YWCA, 1976; bd. dirs. Inland Area Urban League, 1970-71, v.p. leadership devel., 1970-71, Arrowhead United Way, 1980. Mem. NAACP (pres. 1960-61), Acad. Certified Social Workers, LWV (pres. San Bernardino chpt. 1981-82, friends welfare rights), Nat. Urban League (mem. com. 1970-71), Friends Welfare Rights Orgn., Nat. Council Negro Women, Zonta Internat., Alpha Tau Chi (dir. 1979-80). Home: 5710 Belvedere Ave Highland CA 92346 Office: St Bernardine Hosp 2101 N Waterman Ave San Bernardino CA 92404

RHODES, CECIL GLENN, metallurgist; b. Leesville, Ohio, Oct. 17, 1933; s. Lloyd Howard and Sibyl Imogene (Price) R.; B.S. in Math., Calif. State U., Northridge, 1968; m. Lois Irene Spellman, Jan. 1, 1953; children—Pamela Kay, Diane Christine. Metallographer, Battelle Meml. Inst., Columbus, Ohio, 1953-56, Gen. Electric Co., Cin., 1956-59; mem. tech. staff Rockwell Internat. Co., Thousand Oaks, Calif., 1959—. Mem. AIME (publns. com. Metall. Soc.), Electron Microscopy Soc. Am., So. Calif. Electron Microscopy Soc. Author papers in field. Office: PO Box 1085 Rockwell Internat Co Thousand Oaks CA 91360

RHODES, JOHN J., III, congressman, lawyer; b. Mesa, Ariz., Sept. 8, 1943; s. John J. II and Betty (Harvey) R.; m. Peggy Withers (div.); children: John, Taylor, Jeremy; m. Ann Chase, May 27, 1978; 1 child, Arthur. BA in History, Yale U., 1965; JD, U. Ariz., 1968. Bar: Ariz. 1968, U.S. Dist. Ct. Ariz. 1968, U.S. Supreme Ct. 1973. Ptnr. Killian and Legg, Mesa, 1970-77; v.p., gen counsel Health Maintenance Assocs., Phoenix, 1977-80; ptnr. Rhodes and Golston, Mesa, 1980-86; mem. 100th Congress from Ariz. dist. 1, 1987—; mem. gov.'s exec. com. for Plan 6 and CAP financing, Phoenix, 1985-86. V.p. Cen. Ariz. Water Conservation Dist., Phoenix, 1982-87; pres. Mesa Bd. Edn., 1972-76; chmn. Dist. 29, 1973-75; pres. Mesa C. of C., 1973-77. Served to capt. U.S. Army, 1968-70, Vietnam.. Republican. Club: HoHoKams. Lodge: Rotary. Office: 510 Cannon House Office Bldg Washington DC 20515

RHODES, ROY HARLEY, physician, medical researcher; b. Cleve., July 8, 1944; s. Lloyd Harley and Bernice Rae (Simon) R.; m. Jan Mary Edwards, Oct. 1, 1975; children: Jonathan, David. BA, UCLA, 1966; MS, U. So. Calif., Los Angeles, 1968, MD, PhD, 1973. Cert. anatomic and neuropathology. Asst. prof. U. Tenn., Memphis, 1978-82, U. So. Calif., Los Angeles, 1982—; chief of eye pathology U. Tenn., Memphis, 1979-82; cons. neuropathology Baptist Meml. Hosp., Memphis, 1978-82. Contbr. articles to profl. jours.; also chpts. to books. Mem. AAAS, Assn. Clin. Scientists, Am. Assn. Neuropathologists, Assn. Research in Vision and Ophthalmology. Jewish. office: U So Calif Dept Pathology 2011 Zonal Ave Los Angeles CA 90033

RHODY, RONALD EDWARD, banker; b. Frankfort, Ky., Jan. 27, 1932; s. James B. and Mary M. (Clark) R.; m. Patricia Schupp, Apr. 23, 1955; children: Leslie K., Mary M., Virginia K., Ronald C. Student, Georgetown Coll., Ky., 1950-52, U. Ky., 1953-55. Accredited pub. relations Pub. Relations Soc. Am. Pub. relations dir. Kaiser Aluminum & Chem. Corp., Ravenswood, W.Va., N.Y.C., 1959-67, N.Y.C., 1959-67; corporate v.p. Kaiser Aluminum & Chem. Corp., Oakland, Calif., 1967-83; sr. v.p. corp communications Bank of Am. NT&SA, San Francisco, 1983—. Contbr. articles to profl. jours. Mem. exec. steering com. St. Mary's Coll., Moraga, Calif.; mem. adv. bd. U. Calif.-Berkeley Bus. Sch. Program in Bus. and Social Policy, Calif. Named Pub. Relations Profl. of Yr. Pub. Relations News, 1981. Mem. Pub. Relations Soc. Am. (pres.'s adv. council Rex Harlow award), Internat. Assn. Bus. Communicators (Gold Quill award 1980), Pub. Relations Roundtable San Francisco (bd. govs., awards 1980, 85). Clubs: San Francisco Press; International (Washington). Office: Bank of America 555 California St San Francisco CA 94103

RHYNE, THERESA-MARIE, computer graphics consultant, university administrator; b. Denver, Sept. 20, 1954; d. Jimmie Lee and Marie Baker (Britt) R. BSCE, Stanford U., 1976, MS, 1977; MS, Stanford U., 1981. Systems analyst adminstrv. computing dept. Stanford (Calif.) U., 1981-82, long range planner, 1982-83, budget and planning officer, 1983-85; fine artist, cons. Stanford, 1986—; teaching fellow English for Fgn. Students, Stanford, 1977-81 (summers). One woman shows include Old Uncle Gaylord's Expresso and Ice Cream Parlor, Palo Alto (Calif.), 1981, numerous others on the East coast and in the San Francisco Bay Area. Mem. Accessibility Cons. Team for Physically Handicapped, Stanford, 1978-80; coordinator Celebration '85 Palo Alto Celebrates the Arts, 1985. Mem. Council Arts of Palo Alto (membership chmn. bd. dirs. 1985-86, pres. 1986—), Assn. Computing Machinery, Western Art Dirs. Club, Am. Craft Council, Nat. Assn. Female Execs., Nat. Mus. Women in Arts (charter), Pacific Art League, Menlo Art League, San Jose Art League. Avocations: mountain and rock climbing, jazz music, fashion design. Office: PO Box 3446 Stanford CA 94305

RIACH, DOUGLAS ALEXANDER, marketing and sales executive; b. Victoria, B.C., Can., Oct. 8, 1919; s. Alex and Gladys (Provis) R.; came to U.S., 1925, naturalized, 1942; student U. Calif. at Los Angeles, 1937-38, Fenn Coll., 1959, Grad. Sch. Sales Mgmt. and Mktg., 1960, U.S. Army Command and Gen. Staff Coll., 1966, Armed Forces Staff Coll., 1968; m. Eleanor Montague, Mar. 28, 1942; 1 dau., Sandra Jean. Field rep. Gen. Motors Acceptance Corp., 1940-41, 46-47; with Ridings Motors, 1947-48; with Gen. Foods Corp., 1948-80, ter. sales mgr., San Francisco, 1962-80; with Mel-Williams Co., Elgaaen-Booth Co., 1980-86, summit mktg., 1986—; exec. v.p. Visual Market Plans Inc., Novato, Calif., 1984—. Asst. scoutmaster Boy Scouts Am., Los Angeles, 1936-39, asst. dist. commr., 1940-41; co-chmn. Long Beach Tournament Roses, 1947. Served to capt. AUS, 1941-46; comdr. inf. Res. Decorated Bronze Star with V and cluster, Legion of Merit, Purple Heart, Combat Infantryman's badge; Medaille de la France Liberee (France); Commemorative War Cross (Yugoslavia); knight Order of the Compassionate Heart (internat.); knight Sovereign Mil. Order, Temple of Jerusalem; named to U.S. Army Inf. Hall of Fame, 1982; recipient Calif. Medal of Merit. Mem. Long Beach Food Sales Assn. (pres. 1950), Asso. Grocers Mfrs. Reps. (dir. 1955), Am. Security Council (nat. adv. bd. 1975—), Res. Officers Assn. (San Francisco presidio pres. 1974-76, v.p. 1977-82, v.p. dept. Calif. 1979, exec. v.p. 1980, pres. 1981, nat. councilman 1981-82), Assn. U.S. Army (gov. East Bay chpt. 1974-82, San Francisco chpt. 1982—). Republican. Presbyterian. Clubs: Exchange (v.p. Long Beach 1955); Merchandising Execs. (dir. 1970-75, sec. 1976-77, v.p. 1978-79, pres. 1980, bd. dirs. 19816) (San Francisco), Commonwealth of Calif. (nat. def. sect. vice chmn. 1964-66, chmn. 1967-72). Lodge: Elks. Home: 2609 Trousdale Dr Burlingame CA 94010 Office: 1601 Bayshore Hwy Burlingame CA 94010 Office: 1179 Midway Ct Novato CA 94947

RICARDO-CAMPBELL, RITA, economist, educator; b. Boston, Mar. 16, 1920; d. David and Elizabeth (Jones) Ricardo; m. Wesley Glenn Campbell, Sept. 15, 1946; children—Barbara Lee, Diane Rita, Nancy Elizabeth. B.S., Simmons Coll., 1941; M.A., Radcliffe Coll., 1945, Ph.D., 1946. Instr. Harvard U., Cambridge, Mass., 1946-48; asst. prof. Tufts U., Medford, Mass., 1948-51; labor economist U.S. Wage Stabilization Bd., 1951-53; economist ways and means com. U.S. Ho. of Reps., 1953; cons. economist 1957-60; vis. prof. San Jose State Coll., 1960-61; sr. fellow Hoover Instn. on War Revolution and Peace, Stanford, Calif., 1968—; lectr. Health Service Adminstrn., Stanford Med. Sch., 1973-78; dir. Watkins-Johnson Co., Palo Alto, Calif., Gillette Co., Boston. Author: Voluntary Health Insurance in the U.S., 1960, Economics of Health and Public Policy, 1971, Food Safety Regulation: Use and Limitations of Cost-Benefit Analysis, 1974, Drug Lag: Federal Government Decision Making, 1976, Social Security: Promise and Reality, 1977, The Economics and Politics of Health, 1982, 2d edit., 1985; contbr. articles to profl. jours. Commr. Western Interstate Commn. for Higher Edn. Calif., 1967-75, chmn., 1970-71; mem. Pres. Nixon's Adv. Council on Status Women, 1969-76; mem. task force on taxation Pres.'s Council on Environ. Quality, 1970-72; mem. Pres.'s Com. Health Services Industry, 1971-73, FDA Nat. Adv. Drug Com., 1972-75; mem. Pres. Reagan's Econ. Policy Adv. Bd., 1981—, Pres. Reagan's Nat. Council on Humanities, 1982—; bd. dirs. Ind. Colls. No. Calif., 1971-87; mem. com. assessment of safety, benefits, risks Citizens Commn. Sci., Law and Food Supply, Rockefeller U., 1973-75; mem. adv. com. Ctr. Health Policy Research, Am. Enterprise Inst. Pub. Policy Research, Washington, 1974-80; mem. adv. council on social security Social Security Adminstrn., 1974-75; bd. dirs. Simmons Coll. Corp., Boston, 1975-80; mem. adv. council bd. assocs. Stanford Libraries, 1975-78; mem. council SRI Internat., Menlo Park, Calif., 1977—. Mem. Am. Econ. Assn., Mont Pelerin Soc., Phi Beta Kappa. Home: 26915 Alejandro Dr Los Altos Hills CA 94022 Office: Hoover Instn Stanford CA 94305

RICE, BARBARA POLLAK, advertising and marketing executive; b. Ft. Scott, Kans., Nov. 11, 1937; d. Olin N. and Jeanette E. (Essen) Brigman; student N. Central Coll., 1955, Elmhurst Coll., 1956; B.A. in Communications, Calif. State U., Fullerton, 1982; m. Stanley Rice, Apr. 28, 1978; 1 dau., Beverly Johnson. Art dir. Gonterman & Assos., St. Louis, 1968-71; advt. mgr. Passpoint Corp., St. Louis, 1971-73; advt., pub. relations mgr. Permaneer Corp., St. Louis, 1973-74; advt. cons., advt. mgr. Hydro-Air Engring., Inc., St. Louis, 1974-76; mgr. mktg. services Hollytex Carpet Mills subs. U.S. Gypsum Co., City of Industry, Calif., 1976-79; pres. B.P. Rice & Co., Cerittos, Calif., 1979—; press affiliate Inst. Bus. Designers. Recipient Designer Best Exhibit award Nat. Farm Builders Trade Show. Mem. Am. Advt. Fedn. (dist. officer), Los Angeles Advt. Women (pres., dir.), Bus. Profl. Advt. Assn., Calif. State U.-Fullerton Sch. Communications Alumni Assn. (bd. dirs.), Beta Sigma Phi (past pres., outstanding mem.). Author: Truss Construction Manual, 1975. Home: 8178 Havasu Circle Buena Park CA 90621 Office: 13079 Artesia Blvd Suite 228 Cerritos CA 90701

RICE, BART FRANCIS, mathematician, engineer; b. Miami Beach, Fla., Mar. 12, 1943; ; 1 son, Brian Edward; m. Jane P. Shatto, Jan. 16, 1971; 1 dau., Melissa Layne Rice. B.A., Rice U., 1965; Ph.D. in Math., La. State U., 1969; M.S.C.S., Johns Hopkins U., 1976, M.S.E.E., 1982. Math. instr. La. State U., Baton Rouge, 1967-69; mathematician Nat. Security Agy., Ft. Meade, Md., 1972-84; cons. engr. Lockheed Missiles & Space Co., Sunnyvale, Calif., 1984—; adj. prof. Va. Poly. Inst., 1983-84 , U. Md.-Balt. County, 1983, George Washington U., 1976-79. Contbr. articles to math. and engring. jours. Served to lt. USN, 1969-72, to comdr. Res., 1964—. Mem. IEEE (sr. mem., chmn. Santa Clara Valley chpt.), Acoustics, Speech, and Signal Processing Soc., Naval Res. Assn., Armed Forces Communications and Electronics Assn. Republican. Presbyterian. Office: Lockheed Missiles & Space Co 111 Lockheed Way Sunnyvale CA 94089

RICE, DAVID GORDON, archaeologist, consultant; b. Seattle, Nov. 30, 1942; s. Gordon Alfred and Marion Anna (McGonigle) R.; m. Signe Lynn Johnson, Apr. 25, 1970 (div. Feb. 1975). BA in Anthropology, U. Wash., 1965; MA in Anthropology, Wash. State U., 1967, PhD in Anthropology, 1972. Instr. anthropology Wash. State U., Pullman, 1968; asst. prof. U. Idaho, Moscow, 1969-74, assoc. prof., 1974-79; archaeol. cons. Troy (Idaho) and Seattle, 1979-81; archaeologist U.S. Army Corps of Engrs., Seattle, 1981—; archeol. cons. Rockwell Hanford Ops., Richland, Wash., 1981—, Wash. Pub. Power Supply System, Richland, 1975-82, Richland Ops. U.S. Dept. Energy, 1974-77; exec. com. mem. Wash. Archeol. Research Ctr., Pullman, 1984—. Author: Cultural Resources at Hanford, 1982, Windust Phase in Lower Snake River Region Prehistory, 1972; contbr. articles to profl. jours. Del. Idaho State Dem. Conv., Sun Valley, 1972, chmn. Human Rights subcom. of platform com. Named one of Outstanding Young Men Am., Jaycees, 1979. Fellow Am. Anthrop. Assn.; mem. Soc. Am. Archaeology, Soc. Hist. Archaeology, Mid-Columbia Archeol. Soc. (tech. adv. 1967-81), Assn. Humanities in Idaho (chmn. 1980), Sigma Xi, Alpha Kappa Delta. Avocations: photography, hiking, collecting old books and maps, foreign auto history. Home: 1114 17th Ave 201 Seattle WA 98122 Office: US Army Corps Engrs 4735 E Marginal Way South Seattle WA 98134

RICE, DEVEREUX DUNLAP, manufacturer's representative; b. Johnson City, Tenn., Jan. 28, 1952; s. Charles Bailey and Hazel Hunt (Donaldson) R.; m. Marcia Diane Fish, Mar. 20, 1980; 1 child, Melissa Susanne. B.S.E.E., Ga. Inst. Tech., 1974; M.B.A., U. Santa Clara, 1979. Engr. Motorola Semicondr., Phoenix, 1974-75, McDonnell Douglas Co., St. Louis, 1975-76; mktg. mgr. Fairchild Semicondr., Mountain View, Calif., 1976-80; pres. N.W. Mktg., Bellevue, Wash., 1980—. Contbr. articles to mags. Office: Northwest Mktg Assocs Inc 12835 Bel-Red Suite 330N Bellevue WA 98005

RICE, DONALD BLESSING, research institute executive; b. Frederick, Md., June 4, 1939; s. Donald Blessing and Mary Celia (Santangelo) R.; m. Susan Fitzgerald, Aug. 25, 1962; children: Donald Blessing III, Joseph John, Matthew Fitzgerald. B.S. in Chem. Engring., U. Notre Dame, 1961, D.Engring. (hon.), 1975; M.S. in Indsl. Adminstrn., Purdue U., 1962, Ph.D. in Econs., 1965, D. Mgmt. (hon.), 1985. Dir. cost analysis Office Sec. Def., Washington, 1967-69; dep. asst. sec. def. resource analysis Office Sec. Def., 1969-70; asst. dir. Office Mgmt. and Budget, Exec. Office Pres., 1970-72; pres., chief exec. officer Rand Corp., Santa Monica, Calif., 1972—; dir. Vulcan Materials Co., Pacific Lighting Corp., Wells Fargo Bank, Wells Fargo & Co.; mem. Nat. Sci. Bd., 1974-86; chmn. Nat. Commn. Supplies and Shortages, 1975-77; mem. Nat. Commn. on U.S.-China Relations; mem. nat. adv. com. oceans and atmosphere Dept. Commerce, 1972-75; mem. adv. panel Office Tech. Assessment, 1976-79; adv. council Coll. Engring., U. Notre Dame, 1974—; mem. Def. Sci. Bd., 1977-83, sr. cons., 1984—; U.S. mem. Trilateral Commn.; dir. for sec. def. and Pres. Def. Resource Mgmt. Study, 1977-79. Author articles. Served to capt. AUS, 1965-67. Recipient Sec. Def. Meritorious Civilian Service medal, 1970; Ford Found. fellow, 1962-65. Fellow AAAS; mem. Am. Econ. Assn., Council Fgn. Relations, Inst. Mgmt. Scis. (past pres.), Los Angeles Area C. of C. (dir.), Los Angeles World Affairs Council (dir.), Tau Beta Pi. Office: Rand Corp 1700 Main St Santa Monica CA 90406 *

RICE, DOROTHY PECHMAN (MRS. JOHN DONALD), medical economist; b. Bklyn., June 11, 1922; d. Gershon and Lena (Schiff) Pechman; m. John Donald Rice, Apr. 3, 1943; children: Kenneth D., Donald B., Thomas H. Student, Bklyn. Coll., 1938-39; B.A., U. Wis., 1941; D.Sc. (hon.), Coll. Medicine and Dentistry N.J., 1979. With hosp., and med. facilities USPHS, Washington, 1960-61; med. econs. studies Social Security Adminstrn., 1962-63; health econs. br. Community Health Service, USPHS, 1964-65; chief health ins. research br. Social Security Adminstrn., 1966-72, dep. asst. commr. for research and statistics, 1972-75; dir. Nat. Center for Health Stats., Rockville, Md., 1976-82; prof. Inst. Health & Aging, U. Calif.-San Francisco, 1982—. Contbr. articles to profl. jours. Recipient Social Security Adminstrn. citation, 1968, Disting. Service medal HEW, 1974, Jack C. Massey Found. award, 1978. Fellow Am. Public Health Assn. (domestic award for excellence 1978), Am. Statis. Assn.; mem. Inst. Medicine, Am. Econ. Assn., Population Assn. Am., LWV. Developer, mgr. nationwide info. system. Home: 1055 Amito Ave Berkeley CA 94705 Office: Sch Nursing U Calif N631 San Francisco CA 94143

RICE, GERI E(ILEEN), law office management consultant; b. Chgo., Apr. 13, 1947; d. Benjamin Louis and Perle Bertha Friedman. Paralegal cert., Mallinckrodt Coll., 1975; BSBA, U. Phoenix, San Jose, Calif., 1983. Staff asst. Urban Investment Co., Chgo., 1972-79; office mgr. Coffield, Ungaretti & Harris, Chgo., 1979-80; office adminstr. Dinkelspiel & Dinkelspiel, San Francisco, 1980-82; mgmt. cons. San Francisco, 1982—; instr. San Francisco State U., 1981—; instr., program dir. Law Office Adminstrn. cert. program St. Mary's Coll., Moraga, Calif., 1987—. Contbr. articles on law office mgmt. to profl. jours. Vol. Internat. Visitors Ctr., San Francisco, 1985—, San Francisco Suicide Prevention, 1986—. Named one of Outstanding Young Women of Am., Mobile, Ala., 1979. Avocation: acting.

RICE, JERRY DARREL, architectural designer; b. Longview, Wash., Mar. 14, 1939; s. Harry Franklin and Alma Ida (Skalitzky) R.; Frank Lloyd Wright Found. fellow, apprentice archtl. designer Frank Lloyd Wright Sch. Architecture, 1963-68; A.A. in Horticulture, Central Ariz. Coll., 1977. Mem. staff Frank Lloyd Wright Sch. Architecture-Taliesin Asso. Architects, Spring Green, Wis., Scottsdale, Ariz., 1968-70; owner, pres., chief exec. officer, developer, cons. Habitats of Optimum Mobility and Environ. Systems, Inc., (subs.) Criterion Consortium Network, Joint Ventures, Cockeyed Cowgirl Silver and Saddle Shop, Critter's Corner, Western Trader; div. mgr. Joint Ventures; instr. landscape design, archtl. drafting and design. Served with U.S. Army, 1961-63. Mem. Am. Inst. Bldg. Design (designer registration), Nat. Ski Patrol (Nat. Honor award 1957). Prin. archtl. work includes Wintergreen Ski Area; research and devel. in solar energy systems, earth covered and berm structures. Office: 2027 N 39th St Phoenix AZ 85008

RICE, JOHN ANDREW, entrepreneur; b. San Pedro, Calif., May 23, 1955; s. James E. and Jane (St. Pierre) R. AA, Calif. State U., Fullerton, 1975; BA, Calif. State U., Chico, 1978. Ops. asst. U.S. Olympic Com., Olympic Valley, Calif., 1978; dir. Mount. Ops. Squaw Valley USA, Olympic Valley, 1977-82; asst. area mgr. Sierra Summit Ski Area, Lakeshore, Calif., 1982-85; risk mgr. Snow Summit Ski Corp., Big Bear Lake, Calif., 1985—; cons. risk mgmt.; expert witness; presenter seminars. Contbr. articles to ski mag. Recipient Nat. Ski Areas Assn. award of Excellence, 1986; Calif. State scholar, 1973. Mem. Am. Soc. Safety Engrs., Risk Ins. Mgmt. Soc., Sierra Ski Areas Assn. Democrat. Roman Catholic. Avocations: music, modeling, skiing, baseball. Home: PO Box 6075 Big Bear Lake CA 92315 Office: Snow Summit Ski Corp PO Box 77 Big Bear Lake CA 92315

RICE, JULIAN CASAVANT, lawyer; b. Miami, Fla., Jan. 1, 1924; s. Sylvan J. and Maybelle (Casavant) R.; m. Dorothy Mae Haynes, Feb. 14, 1958; children—Scott B., Craig M. (dec.), Julianne C., Linda D., Janette M. Student, U. San Francisco, 1941-43; J.D. cum laude, Gonzaga U., 1950. Bar: Wash. 1950, Alaska 1959. Practice law Spokane, 1950-56; practice law Fairbanks, Alaska, 1959—; mem. firm Rice & Ringstad and predecessor firms, Fairbanks, 1959; dir. Alaska Pacific Bank, Anchorage, Alaska Pacific Trust Co., Anchorage; dir., mem. exec. com. Key Bancshares Alaska, Anchorage; mayor Fairbanks, 1970-72; founder, gen. counsel Mt. McKinley Mut. Savs. Bank, Fairbanks, 1965—, chmn. bd., 1979-80; v.p., dir., gen. counsel Skimmers, Inc., Anchorage, 1966-67; gen. counsel Alaska Carriers Assn., Anchorage, 1960-71, Alaska Transp. Conf., 1960-67. Served to 1st lt. AUS, 1943-46. Decorated Bronze Star. Fellow Am. Bar Found.; mem. ABA, Wash. Bar Assn., Alaska Bar Assn., Am. Judicature Soc., Assn. Transp. Practitioners, Transp. Lawyers Assn. Office: Rice Bldg 330 Wendell St Fairbanks AK 99701

RICE, ROGER EUGENE, systems engineer; b. Maywood, Calif., Jan. 25, 1943; s. Robert William and LaVerne Louise (Elsasser) R.; m. Terri Lynn Shaw, Aug. 22, 1970 (div. May 1976); m. Judy Eileen Tice, May 31, 1980; children: Adam Eugene, Rachael Elizabeth. ASET, Los Angeles Pierce Coll., 1968; BS in Indsl. Tech., Calif. State U., Long Beach, 1971; MSSM, U. So. Calif., 1973. Systems analyst Litton Guidance Control, Woodland Hills, Calif., 1966-68; prodn. coordinator Aerospace Corp., El Segundo, Calif., 1968-70; mem. tech. staff Aerospace Corp., El Segundo, 1971-80, mgr., 1980-83; sr. prodn. coordinator Tech. Media Systems, Los Angeles, 1970-71; mgr. systems engr. Ultrasystems Inc., El Segundo, 1983—. Served with USNR, 1960-63. Mem. IEEE, Assn. for Computing Machinery, Data Processing Mgmt. Assn., Project Mgmt. Inst., AAAS, AIAA, Armed Forces Communications and Electronics Assn., Assn. Old Crows, U.S. Defense Com., Am. Def. Preparedness Assn., U.S. Naval Inst. (assoc.). Democrat. Lutheran. Club: Equestrian Trails Inc. (Simi Valley, Calif. pres. 1985-86). Avocations: skiing, tennis, sailing, equestrian activities, reading. Home: 1013 Nonchalant Dr Simi Valley CA 93065 Office: Ultrasystems DSSI 525 S Douglas St El Segundo CA 90245

RICE, THOMAS HILARY, lawyer; b. Richmond, Va., Apr. 10, 1954; s. Spencer Victor and Kathleen Francis (Reney) R.; m. Judy Clare Clarke, Dec. 31, 1975. BA in Sociology, Furman U., 1976; JD summa cum laude, Calif. Western Sch. Law, 1986. Travel cons. TMT Travel, La Jolla, Calif., 1977; mgr. TLC Travel, San Diego, 1977-80; mgr. passenger, interline sales Pinehurst Airlines, Greenville, S.C., 1980-81; gen. mgr. Western Sun Aviation, El Cajon, Calif., 1981-82; customer service and pub. relations coordinator Balboa Travel, San Diego, 1982-83; assoc. Luce, Foreward, Hamilton & Scripps, San Diego; aviation cons. Calif. Air Express, Marina del Ray, 1982; instr. Nat. U., San Diego, 1982—, San Diego Community Coll. Dist., 1979-80. Mem. Nat. Assn. Criminal Def. Lawyers, Am. Trial Lawyers Assn., ABA, San Diego Trial Lawyers Assn., Nat. Transp. Safety Bd., Calif. Trial Lawyers Assn. Democrat. Roman Catholic. Avocations: flying, photography, cycling. Home: 3575 Alabama St San Diego CA 92104 Office: Luce Foreward Hamilton Scripps 110 W "A" St San Diego CA 92101

RICE, V(IRGIL) THOMAS, lawyer; b. La Harpe, Ill., June 29, 1920; s. Vilas E. and Jane N. (Robertson) R.; m. Phyllis Ann Carpenter, Feb. 14, 1969; children: Lesley Jean Rice Luke, Sharon Leilani Rice Routt. BA, U. Ill., 1941, JD, 1948. Bar: Ill. Supreme Ct. 1948, U.S. Dist. Ct. Hawaii 1948, Hawaii Supreme Ct. 1949, U.S. Ct. Mil. Appeals 1960, U.S. Ct. Appeals (9th cir.), 1962, U.S. Customs Ct. 1963, U.S. Supreme Ct. 1971. Assoc. Blaisdell & Moore and predecessor firm, 1948-61; ptnr. Moore, Torkildson & Rice, 1961-64, Rice, Lee & Wong, and predecessor firms, Honolulu, 1964-86; of counsel to Lee, Henderson, Chipchase & Wong, Molokai, Hawaii, 1986—. Mem. Hawaii Homes Commn., 1960; chmn., sec. Hawaii State Transp. Commn., 1961-63; life mem., bd. dirs. Child and Family Service, 1960-66, 78-79, treas., 1963, pres. 1964-65; bd. dirs. Health and Community Services Council Hawaii, 1967-77, treas. 1968-71, v.p., 1972-74, pres., 1975-77; bd. dirs., chmn. Hawaii Spl. Olympics, 1972-76; mem. State Hawaii Legis. Reapportionment Commn., 1972; hearing officer spl. needs br. Office Instructional Services, State Hawaii Dept. Edn., 1979-81; del. Hawaii Rep. State Conv., 1953-85, chmn. platform com., 1964, 78, party rules com., 1965, mem. Hawaii State Rep. Cen. Com., 1955, 69-73, chmn. Rep. Party Hawaii, 1969-71, chmn. State Rep. Dist. Com., 1955-61, mem. Rep. Nat. Com., 1969-71, del., mem. resolutions com. Nat. Convs., 1972, 76. Served to flying officer RCAF, 1941-43, to capt. USAAF, 1943-45, to maj. JAGC, USAF, 1950-52; lt. col. Res. ret. Decorated D.F.C., Air medal with 3 oak leaf clusters. Fellow Am. Acad. Matrimonial Lawyers; mem. ABA, Hawaii Bar Assn. (chmn. family law com. 1973-85), Ill. Bar Assn., Judge Advs. Assn., Phi Sigma Kappa, Phi Delta Phi. Club: Pacific. Home: PO Box 97 Maunaloa Molokai HI 96770 Office: Lee Henderson Chipchase & Wong 345 Queen St Suite 700 Honolulu HI 96813

RICE, WILLIAM ELDON, business educator, management consultant; b. Colinga, Calif., June 5, 1946; s. Roy Lilbert and Elizabeth Amarilus (Hoff) R.; m. Gena Mae Kincaid, July 11, 1971; children: Roseann K., Joshua David, Christopher William. BS in Acctg., Calif. State U., Northride, 1973, MS in Mktg., 1975; D in Bus. Adminstrn., U. Colo., 1979. Engr. Lockheed Corp., Burbank, Calif., 1967-72; bus. analyst Compass Computer Services, Hungington Beach, Calif., 1972-74; bus. systems analyst Litton Guidance Control Systems, Woodland Hills, Calif., 1974-75; v.p. mktg. Ground Star Energy Corp., Norwalk, Conn., 1976-78; prof. Coll. William and Mary, Williamsburg, Va., 1978-83; dir. reasearch bur. Calif. State U., Fresno, 1984—; cons. Nat. Paper Box and Packing Assn., N.J., 1980-85, Nat. Assn. Ceiling and Wall Contractors, Washington, 1982-83, Bonner Packing Corp., Fresno, 1983—, Pacific Gas and Electric, Fresno, 1985—, Econ. Devel. Corp., Fresno, 1984—. Author: The Business Experience, 1982, The Marketing Experience, 1980, The Marketing Ombudsmen, 1980; mem. editorial bd. Jour. Mktg., 1980—. Mem. ednl. com. Fresno Pvt. Industry Council, 1984—. Served with U.S. Army, 1969-71, Vietnam. Recipient Nat. Forensics Assn. award, 1964, Vietnamese Community Action award Govt. Vietnam, 1971; Coll. William and Mary Alumni fellow, 1982. Mem. Cen. Calif. Am. Mktg. Assn. (pres. 1985-86), Am. Inst. Decision Scis., Assn. Computing Machinery, Assn. Consumer Research, Fresno C. of C. (internat. chmn. 1986—, bus. affairs com. 1984—), Future Soc., Wycliff Bible Translators (bd. dirs. 1982—). Lodge: Rotary. Avocations: public speaking, seminars. Home: 10523 N Rice Rd Fresno CA 93710 Office: Calif State U Sch Bus Fresno CA 93740-0005

RICE-JONES, ANNIE MAY, educator; b. Nashville, July 28, 1945; d. Gilbert Rice and Carlean (Williams) Frierson; m. Charles Sylvester Alford, June 20, 1970 (div. Feb. 1976); m. Willie R. Jones, July 2, 1983; 1 child, Afiya Shani. BS in Health and Phys. Edn., Tenn. State U., 1966; MS in Pub. Health Edn., U. Tenn., 1967; EdD in Health Edn., U. No. Colo., 1983. Instr. Hartford (Conn.) High Sch., 1968-71, Broughton High Sch., Raleigh, N.C., 1971-72, Jefferson County (Colo.) Pub. Schs., Lakewood, 1980—; real estate salesperso; pres. Wellcare Enterprises; instr. health Meharry Med. Coll., Nashville, 1967-68; asst. prof. health edn. Chgo. State U., 1976-78; regional pub. health educator Ill. Dept. Pub. Health, Springfield, 1978-79; survey statisticain U.S. Bur. Census, Lakewood, 1979-80. Mem. Am. Bus. Women's Assn., Lakewood/ South Jefferson C. of C., Mercedes Benz Club Am., Phi Lamda Theta. Lutheran. Avocations: traveling, reading, doll collecting, tropical fish, sports.

RICH, ADRIENNE, writer; b. Balt., May 16, 1929; d. Arnold Rice and Helen Elizabeth (Jones) R.; m. Alfred H. Conrad (dec. 1970); children: David, Paul, Jacob. A.B., Radcliffe Coll., 1951; Litt.D. (hon.), Wheaton Coll., 1967, Smith Coll., 1979. Tchr. workshop YM-WHA Poetry Center, N.Y.C., 1966-67; vis. lectr. Swarthmore Coll., 1967-69; adj. prof. writing div. Columbia U., 1967-69; lectr. CCNY, 1968-70, instr., 1970-71, asst. prof. English, 1971-72, 74-75; Fannie Hurst vis. prof. creative lit. Brandeis U., 1972-73; prof. English Douglass Coll., Rutgers U., 1976-79; Clark lectr. and Disting. vis. prof. Scripps Coll., 1983-84; A.D. White prof.-at-large Cornell U., 1981-87; Disting. vis. prof. San Jose State U., 1984-85; prof. English and feminist studies Stanford U., 1986—. Author: A Change of World, 1951, The Diamond Cutters and Other Poems, 1955, Snapshots of a Daughter-in-Law, 1963, Necessities of Life: Poems, 1962-65, 1966, Leaflets, Poems, 1965-68, Necessities of Life: Poems, 1965-68, 1969, The Will to Change, 1971, Diving into the Wreck, 1973, Poems Selected and New, 1950-74, 1975, Of Woman Born: Motherhood as Experience and Institution, 1976, 10th anniversary ed., 1986, The Dream of a Common Language: Poems, 1974-1977, 1978, On Lies, Secrets and Silence: Selected Prose, 1966-1978, 1979, A Wild Patience Has Taken Me This Far: Poems, 1978-81, 1981, The Fact of a Doorframe: Poems 1978-81, 1979; Your Native Land, Your Life: Poems, 1986, Blood, Bread and Poetry: Selected Prose, 1986; co-editor: Sinister Wisdom, 1980-84; contbr. to numerous anthologies; contbr. numerous articles, revs. to jours. and mags. Mem. nat. adv. bd. New Jewish Agenda, Boston Women's Fund, Sisterhood in Support of Sisters in South Africa. Recipient Yale Series of Younger Poets award, 1951; Ridgely Torrence Meml. award Poetry Soc. Am., 1955; Nat. Inst. Arts and Letters award poetry, 1961; Bess Hokin prize Poetry mag., 1963; Eunice Tietjens Meml. prize, 1968; Shelley Meml. award, 1971; Nat. Book award, 1974; Fund for Human Dignity award Nat. Gay Task Force, 1981, Ruth Lilly Poetry prize, 1986, Brandeis U. Creative Arts medal for Poetry, 1987; Guggenheim fellow, 1952, 61; Amy Lowell traveling fellow, 1962; Bollingen Found. translation grantee, 1962; Nat. Translation Center grantee, 1968; Nat. Endowment for Arts grantee, 1970; Ingram Merrill Found. grantee, 1973-74; Lucy Martin Donnelly fellow Bryn Mawr Coll., 1975; hon. fellow MLA. Address: care of W W Norton Co 500 5th Ave New York NY 10110

RICH, ROBERT O'NEAL, social work educator; b. Salt Lake City, Mar. 25, 1937; s. Charles O'Neal and Catharine Frost (Aldous) R.; m. Frances Lynette Helme, Dec. 14, 1961; children: Allison C., Stephen O. BA, U. Utah, 1962, MSW, 1964; M Pub. Adminstrn., Auburn U., Montgomery, Ala., 1979; PhD, Brigham Young U., 1970. Psychiat. social worker Calif. Dept. Mental Hygiene, Fresno, 1964-65; instr. Brigham Young U., Provo, Utah, 1969-70; prof. social work Eastern Wash. U., Cheney, 1970—; mem. adv. com. Vol. Action Council, Spokane, Wash., 1982. Contbr. articles to profl. jours. Mem. Gov's. Adv. Com. on Vendor Rates, Olympia, Wash., 1983—; mem. allocation and planning com. United Way, Spokane, 1979-80. Served to maj. USAF, 1967-69, 78-79. Ashael Woodruff scholar Brigham Young U., 1965. Mem. Nat. Assn. Social Workers (bd. dirs. Wash. chpt. 1977-79), Acad. Cert. Social Workers, Am. Assn. Marriage and Family Therapy, Phi Kappa Phi, Alpha Kappa Delta, Pi Sigma Alpha. Mormon. Office: Eastern Wash U Sch Social Work Cheney WA 99004

RICH, ROBERT STEPHEN, lawyer; b. N.Y.C., Apr. 30, 1938; s. Maurice H. and Natalie (Priess) R.; m. Myra N. Lakoff, May 31, 1964; children: David, Rebecca, Sarah. A.B., Cornell U., 1959; J.D., Yale U., 1963. Bar: N.Y. 1964, Colo. 1973, U.S. Tax Ct. 1966, U.S. Sup. Ct. 1967, U.S. Ct. Clms. 1968, U.S. Dist. Ct. (so. dist.) N.Y. 1965, U.S. Dist. Ct. (ea. dist.) N.Y. 1965, U.S. Dist. Ct. Colo. 1980, U.S. Ct. Apls. (2d cir.) 1964, U.S. Ct. Apls. (10th cir.) 1978; conseil juridique, Paris, 1968. Assoc., Shearman & Sterling, N.Y.C., Paris, London, 1963-72; ptnr. Davis, Graham & Stubbs, Denver, 1973—; adj. faculty U. Denver Law Sch., 1977—; dir. Clos du Val Wine Co. Ltd., 1972—, several corps.; mem. Colo. Internat. Trade Adv. Council, 1985—. Bd. dirs. Denver Internat. Film Festival, 1978-79, Alliance Française, 1977—; actor, musician N.Y. Shakespeare Festival, 1960; trustee, sec. Denver Art Mus., 1982—. Served to capt., arty. AUS, 1959-60. Mem. ABA, Union Internationale des Avocats, Internat. Fiscal Assn., Internat. Bar Assn., Colo. Bar Assn., N.Y. State Bar Assn., Assn. of Bar City of N.Y. Clubs: Denver, Yale (N.Y.C.). Author treatises on internat. taxation. Contbr. articles in field to profl. jours. Office: Davis Graham & Stubbs PO Box 185 Denver CO 80201

RICHAN, FREDERIC PARTRIDGE, social science educator; b. Provo, Utah, Oct. 7, 1929; s. Raymond Buckley and Ruth Louise (Partridge) R.; m. Joan Arlene Bullock, Nov. 29, 1953; children: Edward, Pamela, Lynette, William, Dean, Ann, Brenda. BS, Brigham Young U., 1952; MS, U. Utah, 1957; ArtsD, U. N. Colo., 1976. Cert. elem. and secondary edn. tchr. Instr. Chaffey Coll., Alta Loma, Calif., 1965-71, Pasadena (Calif.) City Coll., 1968-71; social sci. instr. Western St. Coll., Gunnison, Colo., 1973-74; program coordinator Brigham Young U., Provo, Utah, 1975-80; social sci. instr. Utah Tech. Coll., Provo, 1981—; great decision coordinator Fgn. Policy Assn., Utah, 1977-79. Election Dist. Sec. Rep. Party, Orem, Utah, 1985-86. Served with USNG, 1948-57. Mem. Coop. Edn. Assn. Mormon. Office: Utah Tech Coll 1395 N 150 Provo UT 84603

RICHARD, ANITA LOUISE, entrepreneur, management consultant; b. Willard, N.Y., June 22, 1951; d. Marvin Gerald and Illene (Rosenberg) Isaacson; m. J.E. Richard, May 16, 1981; stepchildren: Christine, Chad. Student, U. Fla., 1969-70, CUNY, Bklyn., 1972-74, Barnard Baruch U., 1974-76; BA magna cum laude, Golden Gate U., 1981. Mktg. mgr. Exxon Office Systems, N.Y.C., 1976-77; program mgr. Exxon Office Systems, Dallas, 1977-78; br. mgr. Exxon Office Systems, Pasadena, Calif., 1978-79; br. sales mgr. Exxon Office Systems, Century City, Calif., 1979; mgr. regional sales program Exxon Office Systems, Marina Del Rey, Calif., 1979-81; mktg. mgr. Exxon Office Systems, San Francisco, 1981-82; product mgr. Well Fargo Bank, San Francisco, 1984; mgmt. cons. J. Richard and Co., Hillsborough, Calif., 1984—. Mem. Am. Mgmt. Assn., Am. Soc. for Personnel Adminstrn., Calif. Assn. for HMO's (chairperson career placement com.), Am. Compensation Assn., Group Health Assn. Am., No. Calif. Human Resource Council, No. Calif. Health Care Mktg. Assn. Republican. Jewish. Clubs: Los Angeles Athletic. Avocations: jogging, photography, piano, hiking. Home and Office: 576 Stetson St PO Box 910 Moss Beach CA 94038

RICHARD, JOSEPH ERNEST, executive compensation consultant; b. Moncton, N.B., Can., Sept. 12, 1944; came to U.S., 1945, naturalized, 1955; s. Joseph Ernest and Aline Marie (Robichaud) R.; m. Coreen Evelyn LeBlanc, Apr. 16, 1966; m. Anita Louise Isaacson, May 16, 1981; children: Christine, Chad. BBA in Mgmt., Western Mich. U., 1968; M in Labor and Indsl. Relations, Mich. State U., 1970. Personnel dir. Hunt Bldg. Corp., El Paso, Tex., 1971-74; sr. cons. Coopers & Lybrand, Boston, 1974-77; dir. personnel Fox & Jacobs, Dallas, 1977-78; mgr. Arthur Young & Co., Los Angeles, 1979-80; sr. v.p. Olanie, Hurst, Hemrich, Towers, Perrin, Forster and Crosby, San Francisco, 1980-82; dir. exec. compensation services Hay Assocs., San Francisco, 1982-84; pres. J. Richard & Co., Moss Beach, Calif., 1984—; lectr. in field. Bd. dirs. Health Benefits Mgmt. Co.; bd. dirs., founder Exec. Compensation Inst. Recipient research publ. prize Indsl. Relations Research Assn., 1969. Mem. Am. Med. Care and Rev. Assn., Group Health Assn., Practising Law Inst., Nat. Assn. Corp. Dirs., Am. Compensation Assn., Am. Mgmt. Assn., Am. Soc. for Personnel Adminstrn., Conf. Bd. Clubs: Los Angeles Athletic. Home and Office: 576 Stetson St PO Box 910 Moss Beach CA 94038

RICHARD, MICHAEL GAYLORD, environmental scientist, educator; b. Vallejo, Calif., Oct. 28, 1949; s. Marion Dean and Helen Lucile (Luck) R.; m. Joan Claire Fadenrecht, Mar. 25, 1972. AB in Biology, U. Calif., Berkeley, 1972, MS in Environ. Health, 1974, PhD, 1980. Research assoc. U. Calif., Berkeley, 1980-84; asst. prof. Colo. State U., Ft. Collins, 1985—; cons. in field, 1980—. Author: Wastewater Treatment, 1985. Mem. Am. Soc. Microbiology, AAAS, Water Pollution Control Fedn., Nat. Environ. Health Assn., Sigma Xi. Avocations: flyfishing, wildlife photography. Home: 1025 B Davidson Dr Fort Collins CO 80526 Office: Colo State U Dept Microbiology and Environ Health Fort Collins CO 80523

RICHARD, PAUL STUART, financial counselor, nonprofit association executive, writer; b. Endicott, N.Y., Oct. 29, 1945; s. Lisle Francis and Bertha Marie (Allard) R. Student Atlanta Bapt. Coll., 1970-71. Vice-pres. mktg. W. Hobbs Ltd., Atlanta, 1974-78; gen. mgr. Imperial Bronzelite Corp., Los Angeles, 1978-79; sr. v.p., gen. mgr. Brawn of Calif., Inc., San Diego, 1979-80; dir. Western Mktg. Assocs., Ltd., San Diego, 1980-81, also pres. Bullion Res. N.Am., Los Angeles, 1980-81; pres., founder Dollarplan Strategy Seminars, San Diego, 1981—, also chmn., founder Christian Fin. Enrichment Seminars, Las Vegas, 1982-84; v.p., dir. edn. Nat. Ctr. for Fin. Edn., San Fransisco, 1984—; exec. dir. Flying Grandma's Odyssey, Las Vegas, 1984—; mem. faculty San Diego State U. Extension, 1982; workshop leader. Chmn. fin. com. 1st So. Baptist Ch.; hon. mem. O.L. Davis Fire Co. of Endwell (N.Y.) Fire Dept., served as capt., 1965-70; vice chmn. Christian Businessmen's Com., San Diego, 1982. Recipient Outstanding award for achievement Dale Carnegie & Assocs., 1972; (named Entrepreneur of Month, Entrepreneur Mag., June 1984. Republican. Author: The Dollarplan Financial Education Course, 1981, revised in 1984; The Student Dollarplan (Financial Education 101), 1984; producer daily radio Show Money Minutes—Your Dollar plan Strategy, Sta. KRRI-FM, 1984; editor: NCFE Motivator; writer Retail Banking Report, San Francisco Bus. Jour.; contbr. articles to profl. jours.and newspapers. Home: 156 Sproule Ln Suite W-7 San Francisco CA 94102

RICHARD, ROBERT CARTER, psychologist; b. Waterloo, Iowa, Apr. 4, 1938; s. Quentin Leroy and Adeline Pauline (Halverson) R.; student Pomona Coll., 1956-57, Westmont Coll., 1957; BA, Wheaton (Ill.) Coll., 1960; BD, Fuller Theol. Sem., 1963, PhD, 1973; STM, Andover Newton Theol. Sch., 1964; m. Shirley Ruth Jones, Aug. 25, 1962; children: David, John. Ordained to ministry Am. Bapt. Conv., 1963; pastor Peninsula Bapt. Ch., Gig Harbor, Wash., 1965-68; marriage and family counselor Glendale (Calif.) Family Service, 1970-71; psychol. asst., Oakland and Pleasant Hill, Calif., 1972-74; clin. psychologist Rafa Counseling Assos., Pleasant Hill, 1974—; mem. faculty John F. Kennedy U., Orinda, Calif., 1975-78; adj. faculty mem. New Coll., Berkeley, Calif., 1986. Co-founder, bd. dirs. New Directions Counseling Center, 1974-81. Recipient Integration of Psychology and Theology award, 1973; lic. psychologist, marriage, family and child counselor, Calif. Mem. Am., Calif., Contra Costa County (past pres.) psychol. assns., Christian Assn. Psychol. Studies. Republican. Presbyterian. Contbr. articles to profl. publs. Researcher assertiveness tng., stress mgmt., lay counselor tng., psychotherapy and religious experience. Office: Rafa Counseling Assocs 101 Gregory Ln Suite 33 Pleasant Hill CA 94523

RICHARDS, FRANCES GRAY (PEGGY), grants specialist, consultant; b. Chgo., May 25, 1920; d. John and Jessie Marion (Brown) Gray; m. Paul Baker Richards, June 20, 1939; children—Nathan B., Peter G., Alison M., Jonathan T., Joel D. Student Colo. Coll., 1938-39. Chief judge Jicarilla Apache Tribe, Dulce, N.Mex., 1960-66; judge Archuleta County, Pagosa Springs, Colo., 1960-66; exec. dir. So. Ute Community Action, Ignacio, Colo., 1966-70, dir. So. Ute Econ. Devel. Dept., 1972-77; self-employed Peggy Richards & Assocs., Durango, Colo., 1977-80; grants mgmt. analyst City of Durango, 1980-81; housing mgmt. officer Indian div. HUD, 1981-82; self-employed cons. various orgns., agys., local govt., Durango, Colo., 1982—. Pres., Four Corners Sheltered Workshop, 1970-72; mem. Durango Housing Rehab. Com., 1983; mem. finance com. San Juan Hospice, 1983. Mem. Nat. Assn. Female Execs., United Indian Planners Assn., Nat. Congress Community Economic Devel., Kappa Kappa Gamma. Episcopalian. Address: 703 5th Ave Durango CO 81301

RICHARDS, GERALD THOMAS, lawyer, consultant; b. Monrovia, Calif., Mar. 17, 1933; s. Louis Jacquelyn Richards and Inez Vivian (Richardson) Hall; children: Patricia M. Richards Grauf, Laura J., Dag Hammarskjold; m. Mary Lou Richards, Dec. 27, 1986. BS magna cum laude, Lafayette Coll., 1957; MS, Purdue U., 1963; JD, Golden Gate U., 1976. Bar: Calif. 1976, U.S. Dist. Ct. (no. dist.) Calif. 1977, U.S. Patent Office 1981, U.S. Ct. Appeals (9th cir.) 1984, U.S. Supreme Ct. 1984. Computational physicist Lawrence Livermore (Calif.) Nat. Lab., 1967-73., planning staff lawyer, 1979, mgr. tech. transfer office, 1980-83, asst. lab. counsel, 1984—; sole practice, Livermore, 1976-78; mem. exec. com., policy advisor Fed. Lab. Consortium for Tech. Transfer, 1980—; panelist, del. White House Conf. on Productivity, Washington, 1983; del. Nat. Conf. on Tech. and Aging, Wingspread, Wis., 1981. Commr. Housing Authority, City of Livermore, 1977, vice chairperson, 1978, chairperson, 1979; pres. Housing Choices, Inc., Livermore, 1980-84; bd. dirs. Valley Vol. Ctr., Pleasanton, Calif., 1983, pres., 1984-86. Recipient Engring. award Gen. Electric Co., 1956. Served to maj. U.S. Army, 1959-67, Korea. Korea. Mem. ABA, Alameda County Bar Assn., Livermore-Amador Valley Bar Assn. (sec. 1978), Phi Beta Kappa, Tau Beta Pi, Sigma Pi Sigma. Club: Commonwealth Calif. Home: PO Box 9001-129 Pleasanton CA 94566 Office: Lawrence Livermore Nat Lab PO Box 808 L-701 Livermore CA 94550

RICHARDS, JOHN SAMUEL, real estate executive; b. Farnam, Nebr., Oct. 27, 1911; s. Herman and Effie C. (Ainlay) R.; student B.A., U. Colo., 1933; M.A., Tufts U., 1935; m. Leontine M. Subatch, Sept. 14, 1935; children—Ellen K., John Samuel, Suzanne, Anthony J. With fgn. funds control div. U.S. Treasury, Washington, 1942-47, mng. dir., 1946-48; fin. mgr., dir. Ford Co., Brazil, 1950-55; exec. v.p. Ford of Germany, Cologne, 1955-56; v.p., staff exec. Chrysler Corp., 1957-58; pres. RCA Brazil, Sao Paulo, 1958-63; staff v.p. Olin Corp., Stamford, Conn., 1964-65; mgmt. cons., Brazil, 1966-70; pres. Triangle Devel., Inc., San Francisco, 1978-84; mng. dir. Adamuz N.V., San Francisco, 1984—; Braker teaching fellow econs. Tufts U., 1933-35; internat. exec. Exec. Service Corp., N.Y.C. and Rio de Janeiro, Brazil, 1966. Mem. Am. C. of C. for Sao Paulo and Rio de Janeiro, U.S. Navy League, Phi Beta Kappa, Pi Gamma Mu. Republican. Home: 2030 Broadway #3 San Francisco CA 94115 Office: Adamuz NV 111 Pine St #1300 San Francisco CA 94111

RICHARDS, LORETTA JANE, state government clerk; b. New Castle, Pa., Apr. 12, 1931; d. John and Regina (Fleischer) Urban; m. Philip Edward Richards, Aug. 30, 1952; children: Rick Edward, Randy John, Rob Lawrence, Rhonda Jane Patterson, Roxanne Hrinko. Aviation secretarial cert., Thiel Coll., 1950; BS in Bus., Grand Canyon coll., 1973. Sec. Ariz. Ho. of Reps., Phoenix, 1961-69, supr. stenopool, 1969-74, asst. chief clk., 1974-79, chief clk., 1979—. Tchr. Sunday sch. Shepherd of the Valley Luth. Ch., Phoenix, 1961—. Mem. Am. Soc. Legis. Clks. and Secs. (pres.-elect, sec. treas. 1983-85, pres. 1986), Legis. Staff Coordinating Com. of the Nat. Conf. State Legislatures, Mason's Manual Rev. Commn. Avocations: travel, fishing. Home: 2019 W San Juan Phoenix AZ 85015 Office: Ariz House Reps 1700 W Washington House Wing Phoenix AZ 85007

RICHARDS, MORRIS DICK, social work administrator; b. Los Angeles, Aug. 20, 1939; s. Morris Dick Richards and Annette (Fox) Briggs; m. Leslie Sondra Lefkowitz, Mar. 22, 1975. BA cum laude, Claremont Men's Coll., 1962; MA, U. Chgo., 1964; M in Pub. Adminstrn., U. So. Calif., 1965; LLB, La Salle Ext. U., 1971; MS in Hygiene, PhD, U. Pitts., 1973; MBA, Chapman Coll., 1987. Asst. dep. dir. children and youth services Orange County (Calif.) Dept. Mental Health, 1973-77; gen. mgr., indsl. therapist Paragon West, Anaheim, Calif., 1977-83; acting dir. alcohol and drug program Horizon Health Corp., Newport Beach, Calif., 1983; editor, pub. relations rep., sr. social worker Orange County Social Services Agy., 1983-85; adminstrv. analyst Environ. Mgmt. Agy., Orange County, 1985—; adj. clin. prof. Chapman Coll., Orange, Calif., 1974-85; program analyst, head child welfare worker Los Angeles County Pub. Social Services, 1967-71; psychiat. clin. specialist Jewish Big Bros., Los Angeles County, 1964-67; med. social work cons. Whittier (Calif.) Presbyn. Hosp., 1973-76; pvt. practice psychotherapy, Tustin, Calif., 1975-77. Editor newsletter Orange County Adv., 1984-85; contbr. articles to profl. jours. Bd. dirs. Orange County chpt. Am. Jewish Com., 1982—, Broadmore Community Assn., Anaheim Hills, Calif., 1981-83; mem. Orange County Mental Health Adv. Bd., 1981—; mem. Juvenile Diversion Task Force of Orange County, 1977. Served with U.S. Army, 1958-64. Fellow U. Chgo., 1962, NIMH, 1962, 72; Haynes scholar U. So. Calif. Sch. Pub. Adminstrn., 1964; grantee Faulk Program in Urban Mental Health, U. Pitts., 1973. Mem. ACLU (Orange County chpt.), Nat. Assn. Social Workers (mental health liaison, v.p. local chpt. 1975-77, Social Worker of Yr. award Orange County chpt. 1987), Acad. Cert. Social Workers (lic. clin. social worker and marriage, family, child counselor), Registry Clin. Social Workers, Orange County Mental Health Assn., Orange County Chpt. Alliance for Mentally Ill. Home: 6506 E Via Estrada Anaheim CA 92807 Office: Environ Mgmt Agy 12 Civic Ctr Plaza Santa Ana CA 92702-4048

RICHARDS, PAUL A., lawyer; b. Oakland, Calif., May 27, 1927; s. Donnell C. and Theresa (Pasquale) R.; m. Ann Morgans, May 20, 1948 (dec. 1984); 1 child, Paul M.; m. Janet Flyge, Aug. 12, 1982. BA, U. Pacific, 1950; JD, U. San Francisco, 1953. Bar: Nev. 1953, U.S. Dist. Ct. Nev. 1953, U.S. Supreme Ct. 1964, U.S. Ct. Claims 1976, U.S. Ct. Appeals (9th cir.) 1982. Sole practice, Reno, 1953—, prin. Paul A. Richards, Ltd.; prof. environ. law Sierra Nevada Coll., 1970-80. Mem. Washoe Dem. Central Com., 1959-74, chmn., 1964-66, vice chmn., 1966-68; trustee Sierra Nevada Coll., 1970-82, Ducks Unltd., 1964-72; trustee emeritus, 1974—; mem. Fed. Land Law Commn., Nev., 1973-80; bd. dirs. Reno Rodeo Assn., 1963, pres., 1979. Served with U.S. Navy, 1945-46. Recipient Pres.'s Buckle and award Reno Rodeo Assn., 1979. Mem. Nev. Bar Assn., Washoe County Bar Assn. Democrat. Roman Catholic. Club: Press. Lodge: Elks. Office: 248 S Sierra St Richards Bldg Suite 1 Reno NV 89501

RICHARDS, VICTOR, surgeon; b. Ft. Worth, June 4, 1918; s. Jules Kelly and Minnie (Cambert) R.; m. Jennette O'Keefe, June 7, 1941; children—Lane R. Kress, Victoria R. Burris, Victor Frederick, Peter Cromwell. A.B., Stanford, 1935, M.D., 1939. Diplomate: Am. Bd. Surgery (mem. bd. 1964-68), Am. Bd. Thoracic Surgery. Intern Stanford Hosp., 1938-39, asst. resident, 1939-42, resident surgery, 1942-43; successively instr., asst. prof., asso. prof. surgery Stanford, 1943-55, prof., chmn. dept., 1955-58; now clin. prof. surgery U. Calif., San Francisco; also at Stanford; chief surgery Children's Hosp. of San Francisco; cons. surgery USPHS, San Francisco, Travis AFB, U.S. Naval Hosp., Oak Knoll, Calif., Letterman Gen. Hosp., San Francisco; pvt. practice medicine San Francisco.; Mem. surgery study sect. B NIH, 1964-68. Author: Surgery for General Practice, 1955, Abdominal Pain, 1958, Cancer The Wayward Cell, 1972, The Wayward Cell, 1972, 78; Mem. editorial bd.: Continuing Edn. for Physicians; editor: Oncology, 1967-76. Commonwealth research fellow, 1950-51. Fellow ACS; mem. AMA (chmn. surg. sect. 1968-70, del. surg. sect. 1971), Am. Surg. Assn., Internat. Surg. Assn., Pacific Coast Surg. Assn., San Francisco Surg. Assn., Soc. U. Surgeons, Soc. Exptl. Medicine and Biology, Am. Thoracic Assn., Pan Pacific Surg. Assn. (v.p. 1972—), Am. Cancer Soc. (pres. San Francisco br. 1972-74), Sigma Xi, Alpha Omega Alpha. Clubs: Commonwealth (San Francisco), St. Francis Yacht (San Francisco), Bohemian (San Francisco). Home: 2714 Broadway San Francisco CA 94115 Office: 3838 California St San Francisco CA 94118

RICHARDS, VINCENT PHILIP HASLEWOOD, librarian; b. Sutton Bonington, Nottinghamshire, Eng., Aug. 1, 1933; emigrated to Can., 1956, naturalized, 1961; s. Philip Haslewood and Alice Hilda (Moore) R.; m. Ann Beardshall, Apr. 3, 1961; children: Mark, Christopher, Erika. A.L.A., Ealing Coll., London, 1954; B.L.S. with distinction, U. Okla., 1966. Cert. profl. librarian, B.C. Joined Third Order Mt. Carmel, Roman Catholic Ch., 1976; with Brentford and Chiswick Pub. Libraries, London, 1949-56; asst. librarian B.C. (Can.) Pub. Library Commn., Dawson Creek, 1956-57; asst. dir. Fraser Valley Regional Library, Abbotsford, B.C., 1957-67; chief librarian Red Deer (Alta., Can.) Coll., 1967-77; dir. libraries Edmonton (Alta.) Pub. Library, 1977—; pres. Faculty Assn. Red Deer Coll., 1971-72, bd. govs., 1972-73. Contbr. articles to profl. jours., 1954—. Vice pres. Jeunesses Musicales, Red Deer, 1969-70; bd. dirs. Red Deer TV Authority, 1975-76, Alta. Found. Lit. Arts, 1984-86. Served with Royal Army Ednl. Corps, 1951-53. Mem. Library Assn. (U.K.) (chartered librarian), Can. Library Assn., Library Assn. Alta. (pres. 1984-85), Pacific N.W. Library Assn., Council Adminstrs. Large Urban Public Libraries. Club: Rotary. Office: 7 Sir Winston Churchill Sq, Edmonton, AB Canada T5J 2V4

RICHARDS, WILLIAM PETTET, JR., real estate executive; b. Ashville, N.C., Nov. 5, 1936; s. William Pettet and Elizabeth Mead (Barber) R.; B.S. in Indsl. Engring., Stanford U., 1958; M.B.A., Harvard U., 1962; m. Deborah Daves, Sept. 5, 1964; 1 child, Dana Ann. Mgr. fin. planning CBS-TV, Los Angeles, 1962-65; asso. Booz, Allen & Hamilton, Los Angeles, 1965-70; ptnr. P.N.E. Co., San Francisco, 1970-74; v.p. Majestic Realty Co., Los Angeles, 1974-78; pres./prtnr. A.K. Utah Properties, Los Angeles, 1978-81; owner William Richards & Assos., Beverly Hills, Calif., 1981—; ptnr. various real estate groups; corp. cons. real estate fin. Bd. dirs. Big Bros. Los Angeles, 1968-72; mem. adv. bd. Direction Sports, 1966-70; bd. dirs., mem. exec. com. Found. Reearch into Origin of Man, 1977—; mem. adv. com. Los Angeles Olympics, 1982—. Served to lt. (j.g.) USNR, 1958-60. Mem. Stanford Alumni Assn., Harvard Alumni Assn. So. Calif., Los Angeles World Affairs Council, L.S.B. Leakey Found., Tau Beta Pi, Delta Upsilon. Republican. Episcopalian. Clubs: La Jolla Beach and Tennis; Harvard of N.Y.C. Home: 3837 Benedict Canyon Dr Sherman Oaks CA 91403

RICHARDSON, A(RTHUR) LESLIE, med. group cons.; b. Ramsgate, Kent, Eng., Feb. 21, 1910; s. John William and Emily Lilian (Wilkins) R.; came to U.S., 1930, naturalized, 1937; student spl. courses U. So. Calif., 1933-35; m. B. Kathleen Sargent, Oct. 15, 1937. Mgr., Tower Theater, Los Angeles, 1931-33; accountant Felix-Krueper Co., Los Angeles, 1933-35; indsl. engr. Pettengill, Inc., Los Angeles, 1935-37; purchasing agt. Gen. Petroleum Corp. Los Angeles, 1937-46; adminstr. Beaver Med. Clinic, Redlands, Calif., 1946-72, exec. cons. 1972-75; sec.-treas. Fern Properties, Inc., Redlands, 1955-75, Redelco, Inc., Redlands, 1960-67; pres. Buinco, Inc., Redlands, 1956-65; vice chmn. Redlands adv. bd. Bank of Am., 1973-80; exec. cons. Med. Adminstrs. Calif., 1975-83. Pres., Redlands Area Community Chest, 1953; volunteer exec. Internat. Exec. Service Corps; mem. San Bernardino County (Calif.) Grand Jury, 1952-53. Bd. dirs. Beaver Med. Clinic Found., Redlands, 1961—, sec.-treas., 1961-74, pres., 1974-75. Served to lt. Med. Adminstrv. Corps., AUS, 1942-45. Recipient Redlands Civic award Elks, 1953. Fellow Am. Coll. Med Group Adminstrs. (life, disting. fellow 1980, pres. 1965-66, dir.); mem. Med. Group Mgmt. Assn. (hon. life; mem. nat. long range planning com. 1963-68, pres. western sect. 1960). Episcopalian. Mason, Kiwanian (pres. 1951). Home: 1 Verlie Dr Redlands CA 92373

RICHARDSON, DENNIS MICHAEL, lawyer, educator; b. Los Angeles, July 30, 1949; s. Ralph Lee and Eva Catherine (McGuire) R.; 1 child, from previous marriage, Scott Randol; m. Catherine Jean Coyl, July 27, 1973; children: Jennifer Eve, Valerie Jean, Rachel Catherine, Nicole Marie, Marie Christina, Laura Michelle. BA, Brigham Young U., 1976, JD, 1979. Bar: Oreg. 1979. Ptnr. Richardson and Andersen, P.C., Central Point, Oreg., 1979—; bd. dirs. Pacific Coll. Art and Design; guest lectr. in field; Contbr. articles to profl. jours. Scoutmaster Boy Scouts Am., Central Point, 1981—; dist. chmn. Citizens for Am., Oreg. 2d Congl. Dist.; bd. dirs. Oreg. Lung Assn., 1980, Oreg. Shakespearean Festival, Ashland, 1981, Jackson County Legal Services, 1982. Served as helicopter pilot U.S. Army, 1969-71, Vietnam. Decorated Vietnamese Cross Gallantry. Republican. Office: 55 S 5th St Central Point OR 97502

RICHARDSON, DOUGLAS FIELDING, lawyer; b. Glendale, Calif., Mar. 17, 1929; s. James D. and Dorothy (Huskins) R.; m. Leni Tempelaar-Lietz, June 26, 1959; children—Arthur Wilhelm, John Douglas. A.B., UCLA, 1950; J.D., Harvard U., 1953. Bar: Calif. 1953. Assoc. O'Melveny & Myers, Los Angeles, 1953-68, ptnr., 1968-86, of counsel, 1986—. Author: (with others) Drafting Agreements for the Sale of Businesses, 1971, Term Loan Handbook, 1983. Bd. govs. Town Hall of Calif., Los Angeles, 1974—, sec., 1977, v.p., 1978-79, pres., 1984, chmn. sect. on legis. and adminstrn. of justice, 1968-70, pres. Town Hall West, 1975, mem. adv. bd. 1973—; bd. dirs. Hist. Soc. So. Calif., 1976-82, pres., 1980-81. Mem. ABA (com. on devels. in bus. financing, com. state regulation of securities, com. corp. law and acctg., com. employee benefits and exec. compensation of sect corp. banking and bus. law.), Calif. Bar Assn., Los Angeles County Bar Assn. (chmn. com. Law Day 1968, exec. com. comml. law sect. 1974-78, exec. com. corp. law sect. 1975-86), Nat. Assn. Bond Lawyers, Phi Beta Kappa. Presbyterian (elder). Home: 1637 Valley View Rd Glendale CA 91202 Office: O'Melveny & Myers 400 S Hope St Los Angeles CA 90071

RICHARDSON, EVERETT VERN, hydraulic engineer, educator, administrator; b. Scottsbluff, Nebr., Jan. 5, 1924; s. Thomas Otis and Jean Marie (Everett) R.; m. Billie Ann Kleckner, June 23, 1948; children—Gail Lee, Thomas Everett, Jerry Ray. B.S., Colo. State U., 1949, M.S., 1960, Ph.D., 1965. Registered profl. engr., Colo. Hydraulic engr. U.S. Geol. Survey, Wyo., 1949-52; hydraulic engr. U.S. Geol. Survey, Iowa, 1953-66; research hydraulic engr. U.S. Geol. Survey, Ft. Collins, Colo., 1956-63, project chief, 1963-68; prof. civil engring., adminstr. Engring. Research Ctr., Colo. State U., Ft. Collins, 1968-82, prof. in charge of hydraulic progress and dir. hydraulic lab., 1982—; project dir. Egypt Water Use Project, 1977-84, project dir. Egypt Irrigation Improvement Project, 1985—; cons. in field. Editor: Highways in the River Environment, U.S. Bur. Pub. Rds., 1975. Contbr. articles to profl. jours., chpts. to books. Mem. Ft. Collins Water Bd., 1969-84. Served with AUS, 1943-45. Decorated Bronze Star, Purple Heart; U.S. Govt. fellow MIT, 1962-63. Fellow ASCE (J.D. Stevens award 1961); mem. Internat. Congress for Irrigation and Drainage, AAAS, Sigma Xi, Chi Epsilon, Sigma Tau. Home: 824 Gregory Rd Fort Collins CO 80524 Office: Engring. Research Ctr Colo State U Fort Collins CO 80523

RICHARDSON, HAROLD LEE, JR., industrial engineer, aerospace company executive; b. Charlotte, N.C., June 15, 1936; s. Harold L. Sr. and Katherine (McAllister) R.; m. Jean Anne Shouse, Aug. 9, 1958; children: Nora Katherine, Harold Wendell III. BS in Indsl. Engring., U. S.D., 1958. Registered profl. indsl. engr., Calif. Engring. mgr. Lockheed Corp., Sunnyvale, Calif., 1959—; adj. faculty Foothill Coll., Los Altos Hills, Calif., 1969—, Mission Coll., Santa Clara, Calif., 1973—; adj. asst. prof. San Jose (Calif.) State U., 1977—. Active Calif. PTA; bd. dirs. YMCA, Palo Alto, Calif. Named hon. life mem. Calif. PTA. Republican. Roman Catholic. Lodge: KC. Home: 1040 Alegre Ave Los Altos CA 94022 Office: Garrett Corp 9851 Sepulveda Blvd Los Angeles CA 90009

RICHARDSON, H.L., state senator; b. Terre Haute, Ind., 1927; m. Barbara Budrow; children—Laurie R. Paredes, Carrie R. Herbertson, Doug. Student Olympic Coll.; advt. degree, Cornish Conservatory, Seattle. Former owner graphic arts and advt. bus.; mem. Calif. State Senate, 1966—, bd. dirs. minority caucus; mem. elections, judiciary coms.; vice chmn. natural resources and wildlife com. chmn. bd. Computer Caging Corp. Mem. Republican State Central Com. Served with U.S. Navy, 1946. Recipient Outstanding Legislator award Calif. Rep. Assembly, annually 1968-76, Calif. Dist. Attys. Assn., Calif. Correctional Officers Assn., Calif. So. Council of Conservation Clubs, George Washington award Freedom Found., Valley Forge. Mem. Nat. Rifle Assn., Gun Owners Am. (founder, chmn.), Gun Owners Calif., Free Market PAC, Law and Order Campaign Com. (founder). Club: Safari. Office: California State Senate Sacramento CA 95814

RICHARDSON, JACK, department store executive. Chmn. Emporium Capwell Co. div. Carter Hawley Hale, San Francisco. Office: Emporium Capwell Co 835 Market St San Francisco CA 94103 *

RICHARDSON, JOHN EDMON, management educator; b. Whittier, Calif., Oct. 22, 1942; s. John Edmon and Mildred Alice (Miller) R.; m.

Dianne Elaine Ewald, July 15, 1967; 1 child, Sara Beth. BS, Calif. State U., Long Beach, 1964; MBA, U. So. Calif., 1966; MDiv, Fuller Theol. Sem., 1969, D Ministry, 1981. Asst. prof. mgmt. Pepperdine U. Sch. Bus. and Mgmt., Malibu, Calif., 1969—. Author: (leader's guides) Caring Enough to Confront, 1984, The Measure of a Man, 1985; editor: Ann. Editions: Marketing 87/88, 1987. Lay counselor La Canada (Calif.) Presbyn. Ch., 1978-84, mem. lay counseling task force, 1982-84. Mem. Am. Mgmt. Assn., Soc. Bus. Ethics, Christian Writers Guild, Fuller Sem. Alumni Cabinet (pres. 1982-85), Am. Mktg. Assn., Beta Gamma Sigma. Avocations: fishing, woodworking, tennis, photography. Home: 4521 El Camino Corto La Canada Flintridge CA 91011 Office: Pepperdine U Sch Bus and Mgmt 3415 Sepulveda Blvd Los Angeles CA 90034

RICHARDSON, LINFORD LAWSON, protective services official; b. Glendale, Calif., Dec. 31, 1941; s. Linford Lawson and Phillis Anette (German) R.; m. Nancy Jane White, Apr. 9, 1961; 1 child, Robin Anette. AA, Riverside Community Coll., 1972; BA, Calif. Bapt. Coll., 1976. Fireman Riverside (Calif.) Fire Dept., 1964-67; police officer Riverside Police Dept., 1967-82, police chief, 1982—; chmn. adv. bd. POST Basic Acad., Riverside County, 1985; chmn. Law Enforcement Adminstrn., Riverside County, 1985. Mem. adv. com. Calif. Bapt. Coll., Riverside, 1985—; advisor Riverside County Coalition for Alternatives to Domestic Violence, 1983—; chmn. Salvation Army, Riverside, 1985; bd. dirs. Riverside Employee Credit Union, 1984—. Served with U.S. Army, 1960-63. Republican. Baptist. Lodge: Rotary (bd. dirs. Riverside club 1985). Office: City of Riverside Police Dept 4102 Orange St Riverside CA 92501

RICHARDSON, RICHARD COLBY, JR., higher education educator, researcher; b. Burlington, Vt., Sept. 10, 1933; s. Richard Colby and Florence May (Barlow) R.; m. Patricia Ann Barnhart, Dec. 21, 1954; children—Richard Colby III, Michael Donald, Christopher Robin. B.S., Castleton State Coll., 1954; M.A., Mich. State U., 1958; Ph.D., U. Tex., 1963; Litt.D. (hon.), Lafayette Coll., 1973. Instr., counselor Vt. Coll., Montpelier, 1958-61; dean instrn. Forest Park Community Coll., St. Louis, 1963-67; pres. Northampton County Area Community Coll., Bethelehem, Pa., 1967-77; chmn. dept. higher edn. and adult edn. Ariz. State U., Tempe, 1977-84, prof. higher edn., 1984—; assoc. dir. Nat. Ctr. Postsecondary Governancy and Fin., 1985—; pres.-elect Council Univs. and Colls., Am. Assn. Community and Jr. Colls., Washington, 1984—; cons. Community Coll. Governance Project, Sacramento, 1984—. Jr. author: The Two Year College: A Social Synthesis, 1965; sr. author: Governance for the Two-Year College, 1972, Functional Literacy in the College Setting, 1981, Literacy in the Open Access College, 1983, College Access and Achievement for Urban Minorities, 1987. Bd. dirs. Easton Hosp., 1973-77, v.p., 1975-77; exec. council Minsi Trails council Boy Scouts Am., Bethelehem, 1973-77. Named Disting. Grad., Coll. Edn., U. Tex., Austin, 1982, recipient Disting. Service award Council of North Central Community Coll., Chgo., 1983; Outstanding Research Publ. award Council Univ. and Colls.-Am. Assn. Community and Jr. Colls., 1983, Disting. Service award, 1984. Mem. Am. Assn. Higher Edn. (charter life, dir. 1970-73), AAUP, Assn. for Study of Higher Edn. (bd. dirs. 1984), Am. Assn. Community and Jr. Colls. (dir. 1980-83). Democrat. Home: 5654 E Wilshire Scottsdale AZ 85257 Office: Ariz State U Tempe AZ 85287

RICHARDSON, ROBERT DALE, JR., educator; b. Milw., June 14, 1934; s. Robert Dale and Lucy Baldwin (Marsh) R.; m. Elizabeth Hall, Nov. 7, 1959; children: Elisabeth, Anne. A.B. magna cum laude in English, Harvard U., 1956, Ph.D. in English Lit., 1961. Instr. English, Harvard U., 1961-63; asst. prof. English, U. Denver, 1963-68, assoc. prof., 1968-72, prof., 1972-87, chmn. dept., 1968-73, pres. Univ. senate, 1972-73, assoc. dean grad. studies, 1975-76, Lawrence C. Phipps prof. humanities, 1979-82; prof. English U. Colo., Boulder, 1987—; vis. prof. Harvard U. Summer Sch., 1976, CUNY, 1978, Sichuan U., 1983; vis. fellow Huntington Library, 1973-74; dir. David R. Godine Pub. Author: Literature and Film, 1969, (with Burton Feldman) The Rise of Modern Mythology 1680-1860, 1972, Myth and Literature in the American Renaissance, 1978, Henry Thoreau: A Life of the Mind, 1986. Trustee Meadville-Lombard Theol. Sch. Mem. MLA, Rocky Mountain MLA, Am. Studies Assn., Soc. Eighteenth Century Studies, Melville Soc., Thoreau Soc., Hawthorne Soc., Poe Soc. Democrat. Unitarian. Office: U Colo Dept English Boulder CO 80309-0226

RICHARDSON, WILLIAM (BILL) BLAINE, congressman; b. Pasadena, Calif., Nov. 15, 1947; m. Barbara Flavin, 1972. BA, Tufts U., Medford, Mass., 1970; MA, Fletcher Sch. Law and Diplomacy, 1971. Mem. staff U.S. Ho. of Reps., 1971-72, Dept. State, 1973-75; mem. staff fgn. relations com. U.S. Senate, 1975-78; exec. dir. N. Mex. State Democratic Com., 1978, Bernalillo County Democratic Com., 1978; businessman Santa Fe, N. Mex., 1978-82; mem. 98th-100th Congresses, 1982—. Active Big. Bros.-Big Sisters, Santa Fe. Mem. Santa Fe Hispanic C. of C., Santa Fe C. of C., Hispanic Council Fgn. Affairs, Am. G.I. Forum. Office: 332 Cannon House Office Bldg Washington DC 20515

RICHART, DONALD LESLIE, interior designer, director; b. Whittier, Calif., June 1, 1964; s. William Donald and Dorothy Lucille (Whittaker) R. AS, Rio Hondo Coll., 1984; student in Interior Design, Calif. State U., Fullerton, 1986—. Draftsman Richard F. Grene Constrn. Co., San Dimas, Calif., 1983-84; steel detailer U.S Detailers, Whittier, 1984; prin. Hanes-Menser, AIA, Downey, Calif., 1984—; also pres., owner Design Interior Co., Whittier, 1983—. Recipient 1st pl. award archtl. drafting, Vocat. Indsl. Clubs Am. state competition, 1983, 1st pl. award archtl. drafting, Vocat. Indsl. Clubs. Am. nat. competition, 1983, 1st pl. award Dance in Action/Elnor Powell contest, 1983, 1st pl. award percussion, Parade of Stars (Cinco De Mayo), 1980. Mem. Am. Soc. Engrs. and Architects, AIA, Kappa Sigma (art dir. 1985-86). Republican. Methodist. Lodge: Rotaract Club. Home: 11548 E Rincon Whittier CA 90606

RICHELSOPH, MARTIN, archivist; b. Bridgeport, Conn., Mar. 14, 1945; s. Morris and Lillian Charlotte (Frankel) R.; m. Lenore Myrna Binen, July 4, 1968 (div. Mar. 1979); children: Russell Brian, Glenn David; m. Barbara Francine Fine, Feb. 17, 1980. BS in Mktg., U. Bridgeport, 1969, postgrad., 1970-72. Cert. records mgr. With mktg. and sales depts. various cos., 1968-75; records mgr. Ariz. Dept. Trans., Phoenix, 1975-79; div. mgr. Ariz. Dept. Library, Archives and Pub. Records, Phoenix, 1979—; instr. Phoenix Coll., 1980—. Mem. Assn. Records Mgrs. and Adminstrs. (chpt. pres. 1981-83, region VI v.p. 1984-86, Chpt. Mem. of Yr. 1982). Jewish. Home: 2824 E Clarendon Phoenix AZ 85016 Office: Records Mgmt Div 1919 W Jefferson Phoenix AZ 85009

RICHER, STEPHEN BRUCE, state official; b. Newark, N.J., Aug. 18, 1946; s. Seymour Albert Richer and Rosalind (Greenberg) Anderson; m. Kathleen Shagner Richer, Jan. 10, 1981; children—Sean Edmund and Jack Albert. A.B. in Politics, Princeton U., 1968. Dep. dir. N.J. Bicentennial Commn., Trenton, N.J., 1975-77; spl. asst. to gov. N.J., Trenton, 1977-80; dir. N.J. Div. of Tourism, Trenton, 1980-82; pres. Travel & Recreation Info. Products, Randolph, N.J., 1982-83; exec. dir. Nev. Commn. on Tourism, Carson City, 1983—; exec. com. Visit the West; mem. fed. agy. Nev. dist. Export Council, Reno, 1984—. Mayor, councilman Randolph Twp., Randolph, N.J., 1974-80; mem. N.J. County and Mcpl. Govt. Study Commn., Trenton, 1979-82; chmn. Pine Nut (Nev.) dist. merit badge com. Eagle Scouts, 1986—. Recipient Tourism award N.J. Hotel and Motel Assn., 1980. Mem. Nat. Govs. Assn. (staff adv. com. on internat. trade and Fgn. relations 1984—), Nat. Council State Travel Dirs. (bd. dirs. 1980-82, 86—), Nev. Hotel-Motel Assn. (ex. officio bd. dirs. 1984—), Am. Bus. Assn., Nat. Tour Assn., Am. Soc. Travel Agts. Travel Industry Assn. Am. (Outstanding Mkgt. award 1980). Democrat. Jewish. Club: Princeton (chmn. schs. com. Northwestern, N.J. 1972-81, Nev. 1985—). Club: Skal of No. Nev. Lodge: Kiwanis (pres. Dover, N.J. 1974). Office: Nev Tourism Commn State Capitol Complex Carson City NV 89710

RICHERSON, DAVID WALTER, ceramic engineer, educator; b. Llano, Tex., Feb. 13, 1944; s. James Walter and Viola Ruth (Nicholson) R.; m. Michael Anne Todd, Sept. 6, 1967; children: Jennifer, Heather. BS in Ceramic Engring., U. Utah, 1967; MS in Ceramic Engring., Pa. State U., 1969. Research engr. Norton Co., Worcester, Mass., 1969-73; supr. adv. materials Garrett Turbine Engine Co., Phoenix, 1973-85; adj. faculty Ariz. State U., Tempe, 1981-85, U. Utah, Salt Lake City, 1985—; dir. research and devel. Ceramatec Inc., Salt Lake City, 1985—. Author: Modern Ceramic Engineering, 1982; (with others) Oxide Ceramics, 1985; patentee in field; contbr. articles to profl. jours. Recipient Admiral Earle award Worcester Engring. Soc., 1972. Fellow Am. Ceramic Soc. (chmn. and organizer Ariz. sect.); mem. Nat. Inst. Ceramic Engrs., AAAS, Ceramic Edn. Council. Avocations: writing, tennis, skiing, mineralogy, art. Home: 2093 E Delmont Dr Salt Lake City UT 84117 Office: Ceramatec Inc 2425 S 900 W Salt Lake City UT 84119

RICHERT, MAXINE HARPER, corporate secretary; b. Juneau, Alaska, June 12, 1947; d. Thomas Oren Sr. and Constance Helen (Harper) P.; m. Dennis Raymond Richert, Dec. 20, 1969; children: Callen Eric, Nicole Denise. BA, Reed Coll., 1969; M in Pub. Adminstrn., U. Alaska, 1985. Personnel mgmt. specialist Bur. Indian Affairs, Juneau, 1969-70; boarding home coordinator Tlingit & Haida Cen. Council, Juneau, 1973-74, edn. coordinator, 1974-76, econ. and social devel. planner, 1976-80; asst. to corp. sec. Sealaska Corp., Juneau, 1981-83, asst. to chief exec. officer, 1983-84, asst. v.p. adminstrn., 1984-86, corp. sec., 1986—; corp. sec. T.O. Paddock, Inc., Juneau, 1984—, dir., 1969—; grant reader Women's Equity Act program, Juneau, 1980, del. Tlingit & Haida Cen. Council, Juneau, 1982-84. active Johnson O'Malley Parent Com., Juneau, 1976-80; dir. Juneau Women's Resource Ctr., 1983-85. Mem. Alaska Native Sisterhood (Juneau chpt.). Democrat. Presbyterian. Avocations: reading, skiing, boating. Home: 4275 N Douglas Hwy Juneau AK 99801 Office: Sealaska Corp 1 Sealaska Plaza Suite 400 Juneau AK 99801

RICHEY, CLARK, designer; b. Bellflower, Calif., Jan. 16, 1939; s. Donald Brown and Laura Virginia (Bailey) R. BA, U. Calif., Long Beach, 1961, postgrad., 1963-65; postgrad., Coll. of William and Mary, 1962-63. Dept. mgr. Sears Roebuck & Co., Los Angeles, 1963-71; merchandising mgr. Montgomery Ward & Co., Las Vegas, Nev., 1971-76; dir. merchandising Doody Co., Columbus, Ohio, 1976-79; pres., chief exec. officer Creative Retailing, Irvine, Calif., 1979—; pres., chmn. bd. dirs. PER Ltd.; guest lectr., instr. Interior Design Inst., Newport Beach, Calif., 1982-84, 86; guest speaker SEMA/Auto Internat., Las Vegas, 1983, 85-86; speaker in field. Contb. editor Custom and Dealership Mag.; contbr. articles to profl. jours. Served with USN, 1961-63. Recipient Best Actor award Pasadena (Calif.) Playhouse, 1957. Mem. Inst. Store Planners (program chmn. 1985-86), Illuminating Engring. Soc., Nat. Assn. Display Industries, Western Assn. Visual Merchandising, Nat. Retail Mchts. Assn., Phi Kappa Tau. Republican. Avocations: skiing, writing, theater, bicycling, traveling. Home: 12143 Sylvan River #141 Fountain Valley CA 92728 Office: Creative Retailing Inc 2222 Martin St Suite 265 Irvine CA 92715

RICHEY, JAMES MILTON, III, oil company executive; b. Decatur, Ill., Sept. 1, 1936; s. James Milton and Emily (McDavid) R.; m. Mary Rafferty, Jan. 25, 1959; children: James M. IV, Nancy Lynn. BS, U. Ill., 1959; MS, Fla. State U., 1961. Environ. engr. Argonne Nat. Lab., Lamont, Ill., 1961-63; jr. exploration geologist Mobil Oil Corp., New Orleans, 1963-65, exploration geologist, 1965-70; sr. exploration geologist Mobil Oil Corp., Anchorage and Denver, 1971-74; assoc. exploration geologist Mobil Oil Corp., Denver, 1974-76; staff geologist Mobil Exploration and Producing Services, Inc., Dallas, 1976-80; prodn. geology specialist Mobil Oil Corp., Denver, 1980-85, sr. geol. advisor Alaska and Calif., 1985—. Mem. AAAS, Gulf Coast Assn. Geol. Socs., Rocky Mountain Assn. Geologists, Nat. Rifle Assn. (life), Nat. Bench Rest Shooters Assn., Sigma Xi. Republican. Presbyterian. Office: Mobil Oil Corp 1225 17th St Denver CO 80202

RICHHEIMER, STEVEN LEE, pharmaceutical executive, chemist; b. Chgo., Jan. 1, 1946; s. H. Richard and Maureen (Biller) R.; m. Jeanne Petrie, June 26, 1980; children: Julie C., Sara E. BS, Lehigh U., 1968; MS, Stanford U., 1971, PhD, 1975. Instr. chemistry Coll. San Mateo, Calif., 1975-76, Gavilan Coll., Gilroy, Calif., 1976-77; asst. prof. Fresno (Calif.) State Coll., 1977-78, Stephens Coll., Columbia, Mo., 1978-79, Metro. State Coll., Denver, 1979-80; lab. dir. Pharm. Basics, Denver, 1980—; Contbr. articles to profl. jours. Mem. Am. Chem. Soc., Assn. Official Analytical Chemists, Phi Beta Kappa, Tau Beta Pi, Colo. Soaring Assn. Club: Englewood Men's Golf. Avocations: golf, soaring, skiing, yoga. Office: Pharm Basics Inc 301 S Cherokee St Denver CO 80223

RICHINS, KENT ALAN, lawyer; b. Evanston, Wyo., Oct. 13, 1959; s. Robert H. and Betty L. (Evert) R.; m. Rosie Ramos, May 27, 1978; children: Mike, Jason, Jennifer. BS in Psychology, Polit. Sci., Utah State U.; JD, Washburn U. Bar: Kansas 1985, U.S. Dist. Ct. Kans. 1985, Wyo. 1986, U.S. Dist. Ct. Wyo. 1986, U.S. Tax Ct. 1987. Sole practice Worland, Wyo.; v.p. Cloud Peak Investment, Inc., Worland, 1983—, also bd. dirs. Mem. Assn. Trial Lawyers Am., Kans. Trial Lawyers Assn., Wyo. Trial Lawyers Assn. Mormon. Avocation: oil painting, golf. Office: 723 Big Horn Ave PO Box 640 Worland WY 82401

RICHMAN, ANTHONY E., textile rental company executive; b. Los Angeles, Dec. 13, 1941; s. Irving M. and Helen V. (Muchnic) R.; m. Judy Harriet Richman, Dec. 19, 1964; children: Lisa Michele, Jennifer Beth. BS, U. So. Calif., 1964. With Reliable Textile Rental Services, Los Angeles, 1964—, service mgr., 1969, sales and service mgr., 1970-73, plant mgr., 1973-75, gen. mgr., bd. dirs., 1975-78, chief exec. officer, 1978-82, v.p., sec.-treas., 1975-82, exec. v.p., chief exec. officer, 1982-84, pres., chief exec. officer, 1984—. Bd. dirs. Guild for Children, 1979—, Valley Guild for Cystic Fibrosis, 1974—; Cystic Fibrosis Found., 1985—; founding mem. Patrons for Cystic Fibrosis, 1983—. Recipient cert. of Achievement Linen Supply Assn. Am., 1979. Mem. Textile Rental Services Assn. Am. (past bd. dirs.). Office: Reliable Textile Rental Services 3200 N Figueroa St Los Angeles CA 90065

RICHMAN, LARRY LEON, publishing executive, actor; b. Brigham City, Utah, July 10, 1955. BA in Spanish, Brigham Young U., 1979, MS in Instl. Sci., 1981; PhD, Clayton (Calif.) Theol. Inst., 1982. Linguistic cons. New World Languages, 1978-80; publs. project coordinator curriculum dept. Mormon Ch., 1981-82, transl. div. supr., 1982—, internat. prodn. mgr. curriculum dept., 1983—; prin. Richman Pub. and Communications Co., 1981—; bd. dirs. Lowry Investors, Inc. Author: Culture for Missionaries: Guatemalan Indian, 1980, Diccionario Espanol-Cakchiquel-Ingles, 1981, Tales of the Cakchquels, 1984; editor: Prominent Men and Women of Provo, 1982; contbr. articles to profl., missionary jours. Missionary Mormon Ch., Guatemala, El-Salvador, 1974-76. Mem. Am. Translators Assn., Deseret Lang. and Linguistic Soc. (sec., treas.), Delta Sigma Pi. Mormon. Office: Richman Communications PO Box 11307 Salt Lake City UT 84147

RICHMAN, MARVIN JORDAN, real estate developer; b. N.Y.C., July 13, 1939; s. Morris and Minnie (Graubart) R.; m. Amy Paula Rubin, July 31, 1966; children—Mark Jason, Keith Hayden, Susanne Elizabeth, Jessica Paige. B.Arch., MIT, 1962; M.Urban Planning, N.Y. U., 1966, postgrad., 1967-69; M.B.A., U. Chgo., 1977; U.S. Dept. State fellow U. Chile, 1960. Architect, planner Skidmore, Owings & Merrill, N.Y.C., 1964, Conklin & Rossant, N.Y.C., 1965-67; ptnr. Vizbaras & Assos., N.Y.C., 1968-69; v.p. Urban Investment & Devel. Co., Chgo., 1969-79, sr. v.p., 1979; pres. First City Devels. Corp., Beverly Hills, Calif., 1979-80, Olympia & York Calif. Equities Corp., Los Angeles, 1981— Olympia & York Calif. Devel. Corp., 1981—, O&Y Hope St. Mgmt. Corp., 1982—, O&Y Homes Corp., 1983—; lectr. N.Y. U., 1967-69, Nat. Humanities Inst., other univs. Adv. Nat. Endowment for Arts. Served with USAF, 1963-64. Registered architect, lic. real estate broker. Mem. AIA, Am Planning Assn., Am. Arbitration Assn., Internat. Council Shopping Centers, Los Angeles World Affairs Council, Urban Land Inst., Air Force Assn., Lambda Alpha. Home: 3238 Fond Dr Encino CA 91436 Office: 11601 Wilshire Blvd Los Angeles CA 90025

RICHMAN, PETER MARK, actor, painter, writer; b. Phila., Apr. 16, 1927; s. Benjamin and Yetta Dora (Peck) R.; m. Theodora Helen Landess, May 10, 1953; children: Howard Bennett, Kelly Allyn, Lucas Dion, Orien, Roger Lloyd. B.S. in Pharmacy, Phila. Coll. Pharmacy and Sci., 1951; student of Lee Strasberg, N.Y.C., 1952-54. Registered pharmacist, Pa., N.Y. Appeared in little theater, Phila., 1946-51, on stage radio and in live TV, Phila., N.Y.C. and Los Angeles, 1948-62; appeared at Grove Theater, Nuangola, Pa., 1952, Westchester Playhouse, 1953; appeared in Broadway plays End As A Man, 1953, Hatful of Rain, 1956-57, Masquerade, 1959; off-Broadway End As A Man, 1953; The Dybbuk, 1954, The Zoo Story, 1960-61; numerous other theater appearances, including Rainmaker, Funny Girl, Hold Me, Equus, Night of the Iguana; Blithe Spirit, Twelve Angry Men at Henry Fonda Theatre, Los Angeles, 1985; others; motion pictures Friendly Persuasion, 1955; The Strange One, 1956, Black Orchid, 1958, The Dark Intruder, 1965, Agent for HARM, 1965, For Singles Only, 1967; appeared on TV series as Nick Cain in Cain's Hundred, 1961-62; as David in David Chapter III for, CBC, 1966; as Duke Page in series Longstreet, 1971-72; as Andrew Laird in series Dynasty, 1981-84; as Channing Capwell in series Santa Barbara, 1984; voice of God series Heroes of the Bible, 1979, voice of the Phantom in animated series Defenders of the Earth, 1986; guest star numerous TV shows, including: Playhouse 90, Marcus Welby, Dallas, Hart to Hart, Fantasy Island, Twilight Zone, Murder She Wrote, T.J. Hooker, Three's Company, Knight Rider, Crazy Like a Fox, others; starred in: TV movies House on Greenapple Road, 1968, McCloud, 1969, Yuma, 1970, Wide World of Entertainment-Nightmare at 43 Hillcrest, 1974, Mallory, 1975, The Islander, 1978, Greatest Heroes of the Bible, 1979, Blind Ambition, 1979, The PSI Factor, 1981, Dynasty, 1981, Dempsey, 1983, City Killer, 1984; one-man shows of paintings, Am. Masters Gallery, 1967, Orlando Gallery, 1966, McKenzie Gallery, 1969, 73, Hopkins Gallery, 1971, Goldfield Gallery, 1979, all Los Angeles, Crocker Mus., others, group shows include Bednarz Gallery, Los Angeles, 1968, Dohan Gallery, Los Angeles, 1966, Celebrity Art Exhibits, 55-city tour, 1964-65; represented in permanent collections, Crocker Museum, Sacramento; SUNY, Albany, also numerous pvt. collections, U.S. and abroad; playwright: Heavy Heavy What Hangs Over?, 1971; mem., Actors Studio, 1954—; dir.: plays Apple of His Eye, 1954, Glass Menagerie, 1954. Trustee Motion Picture and TV Fund. Served with USN, 1945-46. Mem. Screen Actors Guild, Nat. Film Soc., Actors Equity Assn., AFTRA, Assn. Can. TV and Radio Artists, Acad. Motion Picture Arts and Scis. Office: care Agy for Performing Arts 9000 Sunset Blvd Los Angeles CA 90069

RICHMAN, ROGER, celebrity agent; b. Washington, Jan. 18, 1944. BS, Mt. Union Coll., 1965; JD, Vanderbilt U., 1968. Bar: N.Y. Pres. The Roger Richman Agy., Inc., Beverly Hills, Calif., 1978—. Mem. Licensing Industry Assn. Avocations: backpacking, adventure travel. Office: 7768 Torreyson Dr Los Angeles CA 90046

RICHMOND, CHARLES D., lawyer; b. San Diego, Feb. 8, 1951; s. Earl L. And Lois J. Richmond. BA in History, Philosophy, U.S. Internat. U., 1974; JD, Calif. Western Sch. Law, 1979; postgrad., U. San Diego. Bar: Calif. 1980. Enforcement officer Calif. Coastal Commn., San Diego, 1977-78; law clk. Fred Crane, Riverside, Calif., 1978; sales assoc. Ashwill-Burke, San Diego, 1981; sole practice San Diego, 1981-83, 85—; assoc. Sussman & Siegel CPA, San Diego, 1983-85. Mem. ABA, Calif. Bar Assn. (steering com., subcom. real estate law 1985—), San Diego Bd. Realtors (realtor atty. com. 1983—, real property fin. com. 1983—). Democrat. Avocations: tennis, karate, triathlon. Home: 2721 Mission Blvd San Diego CA 92109 Office: 2802 Juan St Suite 25 San Diego CA 92110

RICHMOND, CLAUDE HARRY, provincial government official; b. Blue, River, B.C., Can., Aug. 3, 1935; s. Francis Joseph and Olive Evelyn (Sloan) R.; m. Dorothy Patricia Simpson, Feb. 28, 1958; children: Bradley Craig, Valerie Dianne, Jeffrey Scott. With 'NL Broadcasting, 1970-78, gen. mgr., 1978-82; mem. Legis. Assembly, Province of B.C., 1981—, minister of tourism, 1982-86, minister responsible for Expo 86, minister social services and housing, 1986—. Alderman, City of Kamloops, 1975-78. Served with RCAF, 1952-55. Mem. Social Credit Party. Club: Kamloops Flying. Lodges: Masons, Shriners. Home: 1051 Ollek St, Kamloops, BC Canada V2B 5B1 Office: 113 Parliament Bldgs, Victoria, BC Canada V8V 1X4

RICHMOND, JOHN WALKER, JR., former library administrator; b. Los Angeles, Oct. 3, 1920; s. John Walker and Mary Eugenia (Ransom) R.; m. Lois Marie Roquet, July 25, 1943; children—Susan Marie, John Walker III, David Arthur. B.A., UCLA, 1943; postgrad. Am. U., 1958-59; grad. Army Command and Staff Coll., 1963; M.L.S., U. Calif.-Berkeley, 1973. Commd. ensign U.S. Navy, 1943, advanced through grades to comdr., 1963; comdg. officer USS Interpreter (AGR 14), 1961-62, USS Donner (LSD 20), 1967-69; ops. officer Amphibious Squadron One, 1963-65; dir. evaluation U.S. Naval Amphibious Sch., Coronado, Calif., 1965-67; U.S. naval attache, Malta, 1969-70; exec. officer U.S. Naval Sta., Bklyn., 1970-72; ret., 1972; mgr. North Bay Coop. Library System Service Ctr., Santa Rosa, Calif., 1973-82; tech. services adminstr. Phoenix Pub. Library, 1982-85. Active various community orgns. including Little League, PTA. Decorated 3 Commendation medals with 2 combat Vs. Mem. U.S. Naval Inst. Home: 217 W Frier Dr Phoenix AZ 85021

RICHMOND, ROSALIND, clinical social worker; b. Boston, May 18, 1938; d. Leonard J. and Esther (Greenberg) R. BS, Simmons Coll., MS. Clin. social worker MGH, Boston, 1962-65; clin. social worker VA Hosp., Livermore, Calif., 1966-67, San Francisco, 1967—; lic. examiner Bd. Behavioral Scis., Sacramento, 1982—; chmn. patient edn. com. San Francisco Hosp., 1983—, social work student supr. psychiat. emergency room. Recipient Dir's. Commendation, San Francisco Hosp., 1982, 83, 85. Mem. Nat. Assn. Social Workers (cert.), Simmons Coll. Alumnae Assn. (v.p. 1972-73, pres. 1973-74). Democrat. Jewish. Home: 1551 Southgate Ave 313 Daly City CA 94015 Office: VA Med Ctr 4150 Clement St San Francisco CA 94121

RICHTER, BURTON, physicist, educator; b. N.Y.C., Mar. 22, 1931; s. Abraham and Fanny (Pollack) R.; m. Laurose Becker, July 1, 1960; children: Elizabeth, Matthew. B.S., MIT, 1952, Ph.D., 1956. Research assoc. Stanford U., 1956-60, asst. prof. physics, 1960-63, assoc. prof., 1963-67, prof., 1967—, Paul Pigott prof. phys. sci., 1980—, tech. dir. Linear Accelerator Ctr., 1982-84, dir. Linear Accelerator Ctr., 1984—; cons. NSF, Dept. Energy; dir. Teknowledge Inc., Middlefield Capital Corp.; sci. adv. com. Gen. Motors Corp. Contbr. articles to profl. publs. Recipient E.O. Lawrence medal Dept. Energy, 1975; Nobel prize in physics, 1976. Fellow Am. Phys. Soc., AAAS; mem. Nat. Acad. Sci. Research elementary particle physics. Office: Stanford U SLAC PO Box 4349 Stanford CA 94305

RICHTER, HERBERT PETER, research chemist; b. St. Paul, Jan. 22, 1939; s. Donald Blake and Helen Alberta (Colbeth) R.; m. Patricia Lee Jones, Sept. 8, 1962; children: Deborah Denise, Steven Gregory. BS, San Diego State U., 1965, MS, 1967. Chemist Naval Weapons Ctr., China Lake, Calif., 1967-69, research chemist, 1969-86, coordinator polymer and composite research, 1979-86, head combustion and detonation research br., 1986—; mem. Joint Army-Navy-NASA-Air Force Interagy. Propulsion Com. Contbr. articles on chemiluminescence polymer structure property relationships and solid propellant behavior to profl. jours.; patentee in field. Mem. Am. Chem. Soc., Sigma Xi. Republican. Roman Catholic. Avocations: radio controlled model aircraft, fishing, hunting. Home: 705 Sydnor Ridgecrest CA 93555 Office: Research Dept Naval Weapons Ctr China Lake CA 93555

RICKARD, WILLIAM HOWARD, JR., research ecologist; b. Walsenburg, Colo., May 15, 1926; s. William Howard and Millie (Zalesny) R.; m. Barbara Jane Hudson, June 14, 1953; 1 child, Howard Mott. BA in Botany, U. Colo., 1950, MA in Botany, 1953; PhD in Botany, Zoology and Soils, Wash. State U., 1957. Asst. prof. N.Mex. Highlands U., Las Vegas, 1957-60; research scientist Gen. Electric Co., Richland, Wash., 1960-65; research scientist Battelle Northwest Labs., Richland, 1965-72, sect. mgr., 1972-80, sr. staff scientist, 1980—; instr. Joint Ctr. Grad. Study, Richland, 1960—. Contbr. articles to profl. jours. Active Boy Scouts Am., Richland, 1967-71. Served with U.S. Army, 1944-46, PTO. Mem. AAAS, Ecol. Soc. Am., Range Mgmt. Soc., Northwest Sci. Assn. (trustee 1960—), Pacific Northwest Bird and Mammal Soc., Lower Columbia Basin Audubon Soc. (pres. 1972, 73), Sigma Xi. Avocation: flyfishing. Office: Battelle Northwest Labs PO Box 999 Richland WA 99352

RICKETTS, WALTER PAXTON, state health official, physical education educator; b. Greensburg, Kans., Mar. 29, 1926; s. Joe Glen and Cora Luella (Dent) R.; m. Winifred Elliott Douglas, Aug. 28, 1949; children—Douglas Paxton, Marla Sue, Kerry Dent. B.A., U. Nebr., 1950; M.A., U. Wyo., 1963. Tchr. phys. edn., coach, jr. and sr. high sch., Torrington, Wyo., 1950-64; tchr. phys. edn., elem. sch., Torrington, 1964-68; head dept. phys. edn. Eastern Wyo. Coll., Torrington, 1968-71; cons. Wyo. State Dept. Edn., Cheyenne, 1971-86; dir. Wyo. State Health, Phys. Edn., Recreation and

Dance, Cheyenne, 1971-83. Contbr. articles to state publs. Explorer leader Wyo.-Nebr. council Boy Scouts Am., 1952-60, council mem., 1955-58; mgr.-lifeguard swimming pool, Torrington; dir. Jaycees summer youth recreation programs, 1950-59; golf pro Goshen County Golf Course, 1965-71; cons. Wyo. and Rocky Mountain Area of Nat. Golf Found., 1974-85. Served with USN, 1944-46, 51-52, Korea. Recipient Outstanding Service award (named in his honor Pax Ricketts Outstanding Service award) Am. Alliance Wyo. Health, Phys. Edn., Recreation and Dance, 1983. Mem. NEA (life), AAH-PERD (life), Central Dist. Alliance Health, Phys. Edn., Recreation and Dance (pres. 1980-81, Appreciation of Service cert. 1980), Wyo. Alliance Health, Phys. Edn., Recreation and Dance (pres. 1969-70, Honor award 1974), Nat. Soc. State Dirs Health, Phys. Edn., Recreation and Dance (sec.-treas. 1982-83), Wyo. Assn. Suprs. and Curriculum Dirs., Wyo. State Employees Assn., Nat. Intramural Assn., Phi Delta Kappa. Republican. Congregationalist. Lodges: Masons, Shriners, Order Eastern Star. Home: 3463 Dover Rd Cheyenne WY 82001

RICKMAN, JOSEPH O., teacher; b. Milw., Sept. 19, 1924; s. E.J. and Cassia (Hawks) R.; m. Kris Ness, June 6, 1956; children: Ricardo, Joel, James, Heidi, Jason. BS, U. Iowa, 1950; MS, U. Minn., 1957. Cert. tchr., N.M. Tchr. Pub. Schs., N.M., 1957-67; prof., dir. Vocat. Indsl. Clubs Am. No. N.M. Community Coll., 1967-70; tchr. Mosquero (N.M.) Pub. Schs., 1971-84; collaborator U. Calif., Los Alamos, N.M., 1984-85; judge Mosquero Magistrate Ct., 1984—. Served to 2d lt. Inf. U.S. Army, 1940-45. Mem. NEA, N.Mex. Edn. Assn. (rep.), N.Mex. Classroom Tchrs. Assn. (past pres.), Indsl. Safety Equipment Assn., Secondary Tchrs. Ednl. Assn. (past pres.). Democrat. Avocations: skiing, hiking, painting. Home: PO Box 194 Nosquero NM 87733

RICKS, MARY FRANCES, university administrator, anthropological researcher; b. Portland, Oreg., July 6, 1939; d. Leo and Frances Helen (Corcoran) Samuel; m. Robert Stanley Ricks, Jan. 7, 1961; children: Michael Stanley, Allen Gilbert. BA, Whitman Coll., 1961; MA, Portland State U., 1977, MPA, 1981. Asst. to dir. auxilliary services Portland State U., 1975-79, instnl. researcher, 1979-85, dir. instnl. research and planning, 1985—. Contbr. articles and presentations to profl. socs. Vol. archeologist BLM-USDI, Lakeview, Oreg., 1983—; com. mem. Met. Citizens League, Portland, 1983-85. Fellow Soc. Applied Anthropology; mem. Soc. Am. Archaeology, Soc. Coll. and U. Planning, Pacific NW Assn. Instnl. Research and Planning (exec. bd. mem.), Assn. Instnl. Research (com. chmn.), Sigma Xi. Home: 5466 SW Dover Loop Portland OR 97225 Office: Portland State U Office of Instnl Research PO Box 751 Portland OR 97207

RIDDER, DANIEL HICKEY, newspaper publisher; b. N.Y.C., May 3, 1922; s. Bernard Herman and Nell (Hickey) R.—m. Frani Cooper Ackerman, Oct. 13, 1971; children by previous marriage—Daniel Hickey, Randy Helen, Richard J. A.B., Princeton U., 1943. Reporter N.Y. Jour. Commerce, Grand Forks, (N.D.) Herald; pub. St. Paul Dispatch and Pioneer-Press, 1952-58; co-pub. Long Beach (Calif.) Ind. Press-Telegram, 1958-69, pub., 1969—; v.p. Knight-Ridder Newspapers, Inc.; pres. Twin Coast Newspapers, Inc.; bd. dirs. AP, 1975-84. Vice chmn. bd. St. Mary's Med. Center; bd. dirs. Los Angeles United Way, Los Angeles County Mus. Art, 1974-84, Sta. KCET; past bd. dirs. Newspaper Advt. Bur., Los Angeles County Mus. Art, Calif. Mus. Found. of Calif. Mus. Sci. and Industry;; former chmn. bd. trustees Calif. State U. and Colls.; trustee Long Beach Mus. Art; bd. govs. Calif. Community Found. Served to lt. (j.g.) USN, 1942-46, ETO; Served to lt. (j.g.) USN, PTO. Clubs: Virginia Country (Long Beach, Calif.); El Dorado Country (Palm Springs, Calif.); Los Angeles Country; Cypress Point (Pebble Beach, Calif.). Home: 5531 Bryant Dr Long Beach CA 90815 Office: 604 Pine Ave Long Beach CA 90844

RIDDER, PAUL ANTHONY, newspaper executive; b. Duluth, Minn., Sept. 22, 1940; s. Bernard H. and Jane (Delano) R.; m. Constance Louise Meach, Nov. 6, 1960; children: Katherine Lee, Linda Jane, Susan Delano, Paul Anthony, Jr. B.A. in Econs., U. Mich., 1962. With Aberdeen (S.D.) Am. News, 1962-63, Pasadena (Calif.) Star News, 1963-64; with San Jose (Calif.) Mercury News, 1964-86, bus. mgr., 1968-75, gen. mgr., 1975-77, pub., 1977-86, pres., 1979-86; pres. Knight-Ridder Newspaper Div., 1986—; bd. dirs. Seattle Times. Chmn. Tech. Ctr. of Silicon Valley, 1983—; bd. regents Santa Clara U.; chmn. adv. bd. San Jose State U.; mem. adv. bd. Ctr. for Econ. Policy Devel. Stanford U.; trustee Ctr. for Fine Arts, Miami. Named Calif. Pub. of Yr., 1983. Mem. Calif. Newspaper Pubs. Assn. (exec. com., bd. dirs. met. newspapers), San Jose C. of C. (chmn. bd. dirs. 1975), Young Presidents Orgn. Clubs: Cypress Point (Pebble Beach, Calif.); Indian Creek, Surf (Miami Beach, Fla.). Avocations: golf; skiing, tennis, water skiing, jogging.

RIDDLE, CHRISTOPHER ROBERT, musician, bandleader, trombonist; b. Santa Monica, Calif., May 8, 1950; s. Nelson Smock and Doreen (Moran) R.; m. Elizabeth Nasserine Molloy, Apr. 1, 1986. Student, U. So. Calif.; Trinity Coll. Music, London. Freelance instrumental musician, bandleader Hollywood, Calif., 1971-86; bandleader various cities, 1986—. Mem. Local chpt. 47 Am. Fedn. Musicians, Local chpt. 369 Am. Fedn. Musicians. Democrat. Roman Catholic.

RIDDLES, LIBBY N., sled-dog racer, trainer and breeder; b. Madison, Wis., Apr. 1, 1956; d. Willard Parker and Mary (Reynolds) R. Grad. high sch., St. Cloud, Minn. Finished 18th place in Iditarod Sled-Dog Race, 1980, 20th place, 1981, completed and finished 1st place, 1985; finished 7th place in Kusko 300 Sled-Dog Race, 1982, 5th place, 1984. Recipient Leonard Seppala Humanitarian award Alaska Airlines, 1985, Victor awards for excellence in sports, 1985; honored by Gov. Alaska with proclamation of Libby Riddles Day, Mar. 21, 1985; named Profl. Sportswoman of Yr., Sports Found. N.Y., 1985; first woman to win 1,049 mile Iditarod Race. Home: Box 545 Teller AK 99778 *

RIDER, KENNETH LLOYD, management consultant; b. N.Y.C., July 8, 1943; s. Frederick Cregier and Mildred Elaine (Cohen) R.; A.B., Columbia, 1965; Ph.D., Yale, 1970; research assoc. dept. physics City Coll. N.Y., 1970-72; mgmt. systems analyst N.Y.C.-Rand Inst., 1972-74, project leader fire protection studies, 1974-75; spl. asst. to state spl. dep. comptroller for N.Y.C., dir. spl. services, 1975-78; sr. cons. Deloitte Haskins & Sells, 1978-80, mgr., 1980-83; dir. Interface Design Assocs., Inc., 1983—, Ford Aerospace, 1986—; adj. prof. Columbia Grad. Sch. Bus., 1980-81, Sch. Engring., 1982-83. NSF fellow, 1965-67; Nat. Merit scholar. Mem. Am. Economic Assn., Inst. Mgmt. Scis. (council mem. Coll. on Practice Mgmt. Sci. 1980—, program chmn. seminar 1984, chmn. Edelman prize com. 1985—), Ops. Research Soc. (fin. com. 1979-80, chmn. bus. applications sect. 1982-84), Cognitive Sci. Soc., IEEE, Assn. for Computing Machinery, Am. Assn. Artificial Intelligence, Nat. Fire Protection Assn. (com. on fire reporting 1973-75), Sigma Xi. Club: Yale of N.Y.C. Asso. editor Mgmt. Sci.; contbr. articles on pub. policy and mgmt. sci. to profl. jours. Home: 501 Forest Ave Palo Alto CA 94301 Office: 3939 Fabian Way Palo Alto CA 94303

RIDGE, GARY R., podiatrist; b. Provo, Utah, Nov. 9, 1946; s. Royce Gerald and Carole Deene (Snyder) R.; m. Judy Ann Brimley, Sept. 9, 1970; children: Monica, Brian, Caroline, Alisha. BS, Brigham Young U.; D of Podiatric Medicine, Calif. Coll. Podiatric Medicine. Diplomate Am. Bd. Podiatric Surgery. Resident in surgical podiatry Good Samaritan Hosp., Aneiheim, Calif.; pub. relations chmn. Utah Podiatry Assn., Salt Lake City, 1982-83; chief of podiatry Orem (Utah) Community Hosp., 1983—, Am. Fork (Utah) Hosp., 1984—; team podiatric physician Orem High Sch., 1980—. Dist. committeman Rep. Party, Pleasant Grove, Utah, 1986-87, county delegate, Utah County, 1986-87; dist. commr. Boy Scouts Am., Pleasant Grove, 1982-86; coach Pleasant Grove Boys Baseball, 1983—. Recipient Doctoriate of Commr. Service, Boy Scouts Am., 1984. Mem. Am. Bd. Podiatric Surgery (chmn. Utah state bd. examiners), Am. Podiatric Med. Assn., Utah Podiatric Med. Assn. (pub. relations chmn.), Timpanogos Podiatric Med. Assn. (pres. 1980-82, 85—). Mormon. Club: Alpine Country. Avocations: family activities, golf, reading, working with youths. Home: 226 N 1350 E Pleasant Grove UT 84062 Office: 560 S State Suire J-1 Orem UT 84058

RIDGLEY, ROBERT LOUIS, gas company executive, lawyer; b. Ft. Wayne, Ind., Mar. 4, 1934; s. Charles Herbert and Margaret (Sparling) R.; m. Marilyn A. Hester, Aug. 24, 1957; children: Gregory C., Derek W. A.B., Cornell U., 1956; J.D., Harvard, 1959. Bar: Oreg. bar 1959. Practice in Portland, 1960-84; assoc. Stoel, Rives, Boley, Fraser and Wyse (and predecessors), 1960-66, ptnr., 1966; exec. v.p. N.W. Natural Gas Co., 1984, pres., chief exec. officer, 1985—. Co-editor: Pleading and Practice Handbook, 1964. Mem. Nat. Adv. Council for Edn. Disadvantaged Children, 1969-70; mem. Nat. Commn. on Reform of Secondary Edn.; Mem. Multnomah County Republican Exec. Com., 1962-66; alt. del. Nat. Conv., 1964; Chmn. bd. dirs. Portland Sch. Dist.; bd. dirs. Cornell U. Council, Nat. Pub. Affairs Center for TV; trustee Cornell U., 1970-76; trustee Lewis and Clark Coll., 1975—, chmn. bd. dirs., 1985—; chmn. bd. visitors Northwestern Sch. Law, 1975-76; bd. dirs. Oreg. Symphony Assn., 1981-84; mem. Exposition-Recreation Commn., 1980-85. Served to 1st lt., arty. AUS, 1959-60. Named Jr. First Citizen Portland, 1968. Mem. Nat. Sch. Bds. Assn. (dir.), Oreg. Sch. Bds. Assn. (pres.), Portland C. of C. (dir. 1981—, v.p. 1986-87). Lodge: Portland Rotary (dir. 1983-85, v.p. 1986—). Home: 4927 SW Downsview Ct Portland OR 97221 Office: Northwest Natural Gas Co 220 NW 2d Ave Portland OR 97209

RIDGWAY, DAVID WENZEL, educational film producer-director; b. Los Angeles, Dec. 12, 1904; s. David Nelson and Marie (Wenzel) R.; A.B., UCLA, 1926; M.B.A., Harvard U., 1928; m. Rochelle Devine, June 22, 1955. With RKO Studios, Hollywood, Calif., 1930-42; motion picture specialist WPB, Washington, 1942-43; prodn. mgr., producer Ency. Brit. Films, Wilmette, Ill., 1946-60; dir. film activities, exec. dir. Chem. Edn. Material Study, U. Calif. at Berkeley, 1960—; producer, on-screen interviewer Am. Chem. Soc. TV series Eminent Chemists, 1981; cons. TV project Mech. Universe, Calif. Inst. Tech., 1983 also Am. Inst. Biol. Scis.; introduced CHEM study films to People's Republic of China, 1983. Served to lt. comdr. USNR, 1943-46. Recipient Chris award for prodn. CHEM Study Ednl. Films in Chemistry, Film Council Greater Columbus, 1962-63; Bronze medal, Padua, Italy, 1963; CINE Golden Eagle awards, 1962-64, 73; Gold Camera award for film Wondering About Things, U.S. Indsl. Film Festival, 1971; diploma of honour Internat. Sci. Film Assn. Festival, Cairo, 1st prize Am. Biol. Photog. Assn. for film MARS: Chemistry Looks for Life, 1978. Mem. Soc. Motion Pictures and Television Engrs. (chmn. San Francisco sect. 1970-72), Am. Sci. Film Assn. (trustee 1974-81), Delta Upsilon, Alpha Kappa Psi. Clubs: Faculty (U. Calif.), Bohemian (San Francisco). Author: (with Richard J. Merrill) The CHEM Study Story, 1969; also articles in ednl. jours. Home: 1735 Highland Pl Berkeley CA 94709 Office: Lawrence Hall of Sci U Calif Berkeley CA 94720

RIDLEY, RICHARD ANDERSON, technical writer; b. Orange, Calif., Oct. 4, 1952; s. Bryce Farnum and Margaret Wilson (McBride) R.; m. Stephanie Ann Flosi, Aug. 4, 1974 (dec. 1983); 1 child, Ian Bryce; m. Elizabeth Marie Bates Pappas, May 12, 1984 (div. 1986). B.A. in English cum laude, U. Santa Clara, 1974; M.A. in Folklore and Mythology, UCLA, 1977. Tchr. Montclair Prep Sch., Van Nuys, Calif., 1977-78; tech. writer BBCSI, Santa Clara, Calif., 1980-82, Sierra Electronics, Menlo Park, Calif., 1982; sr. tech. writer ADAC Labs., San Jose, Calif., 1982-84, sr. tech. writer, 1985—; tech. writer DiaSonics, Inc., Milpitas, Calif., 1984-85. Club: Pacific Escrima Acad. (San Jose). Home: 1554 Sierra Creek Way San Jose CA 95132

RIEDELL, KARYN LEA, English professor; b. Biloxi, Miss., Jan. 29, 1954; d. Paul Albert and Charlene (Samson) R.; m. Michael Robert Case, May 21, 1983. BA in English, Ga. So. Coll., 1976, MA in English, 1978; PhD in English, Ariz. State U., 1983. Teaching asst. Ga. So. Coll., Statesboro, 1975-77; instr. English U. Guam, Agana, 1978-79; teaching assoc. Ariz. State U., Tempe, 1979-82; asst. prof. Coll. So. Idaho, Twin Falls, 1982—, head dept. English, 1984—. Editor, staff writer (newspaper) Womyn's Weekly, Tempe, 1979-80, (book) Socioeconomic Impacts of Nuclear Generating Stations, 1982; asst. editor: Mountain West Research, Tempe, 1979-81. Avocations: photography, scuba diving, skiing. Home: 512 E Jefferson Boise ID 83712 Office: Coll So Idaho Falls Ave Twin Falls ID 83712

RIEDEN, DAVID ANTHONY, air traffic control administrator; b. Portland, Oreg., Aug. 1, 1941; s. Leo Aloysius and Mary (Johnson) R.; m. Bernadine Dolly Stienberg, 1960 (div. 1961); m. Mary Lou Conner, 1962 (div. 1974); m. Ellen Louise Peers, Apr. 30, 1975 (div. Apr. 1979); m. Alberta Lela Ramsey, Aug. 13, 1982; children: Robert Anthony, Lisa Lou, David Keith. Grad. high sch., U. Md. Extension Service, Munich, 1959; $$$. Mgr. Ogg Shoe Co., Missoula, Mont., 1961-70; with FAA, 1970—; instr. FAA Aero. Ctr., Oklahoma City, 1977-81; radar controller Gt. Falls Artic, 1970-76, Albuquerque Artic, 1976-77, FAA, Salt Lake City and Auburn, Wash., 1981-84; team supr. FAA, Salt Lake City, 1982, area supr., 1984—; recording sec. Facility Tech. Adv. Com., Controllers' Ops./ Procedures Com., Rocky Mountain Region, FAA. Active Salt Lake City C. of C. Served with U.S. Army, 1958-60. Recipient numerous awards and commendations from FAA. Lodges: Elks, Eagles, Toastmasters. Home: 100 W 5474 S Ogden UT 84405 Office: Salt Lake ARTCC 2150 W 700 N Salt Lake City UT 84116

RIEDLINGER, LES, school district administrator; b. Mott, N.D., Feb. 25, 1937; s. Herbert and Eva (Schaff) R.; m. Gloria Ann Gallagher, June 9, 1962; children: Carrie Allison, Marc Allen. BS, U. Mont., 1965. Facility analyst U. Calif., Berkeley, 1967-77; planning dir. U. Calif., San Francisco, 1977-80; planning dir. dist. 5 Wash. State Community Coll., Everett, 1980-82; dist. planner Fairbanks (Alaska) Sch. Dist., 1982—. Served with USN, 1954-57. Mem. Council Ednl. Facility Planners Internat. (charter), Am. Contract Bridge League (nat. master 1976), MENSA, Nat. Geographic Soc., Am. Bowling Congress. Roman Catholic. Avocations: poker, bowling, bridge. Home: Box 73594 Fairbanks AK 99707 Office: Fairbanks Sch Dist 9th and Cushman Fairbanks AK 99707

RIEGEL, BARBARA J., nursing educator; b. St. Louis, Apr. 3, 1950; d. Lawrence Virgil and Shirley Jean (Weil) R.; m. m. Thomas A. Gillespie, May 23, 1978. Diploma, Jewish Hosp. Sch. Nursing, 1974; B in Nursing, San Diego State U., 1981; M in Nursing, UCLA, 1983. Staff nurse intensive care/critical care unit Mo. Baptist Hosp., St. Louis, 1974-75; staff nurse coronary care unit Barnes Hosp., St. Louis, 1975-76; exec. dir. Community Health Orgn., Frankfurt, Fed. Republic of Germany, 1977-78; cardiovascular nurse specialist collaborative practice, San Diego, 1983-84, Scripps Clinic, La Jolla, Calif., 1984-85; faculty San Diego State U., 1984—; adv. council San Diego State U. Sch. Nursing, 1983-85. Editor: Dreifus' Pacemaker Therapy: an Interprofessional Approach, 1986; editor Jour. Cardiovascular Nursing, 1986—; mem. editorial rev. bd. Heart and Lung, 1985—, Critical Care Quar., 1986—; contbr. articles to profl. jours. Mem. Am. Nurses Assn. (cert.), Am. Assn. Critical Care Nurses (mem. task force Ethics in Critical Care Research 1983-84), Council of Cardiovascular Nurses of Am. Heart Assn., Sigma Theta Tau. Republican. Home: 5127 Bixel Dr San Diego CA 92115 Office: San Diego State U Sch Nursing San Diego CA 92182

RIEGEL, BYRON WILLIAM, ophthalmologist, educator; b. Evanston, Ill., Jan. 19, 1938; s. Byron and Belle Mae (Huot) R.; B.S., Stanford U., 1960; M.D., Cornell U., 1964; m. Marilyn Hills, May 18, 1968; children—Marc William, Ryan Marie, Andrea Elizabeth. Intern, King County Hosp., Seattle, 1964-65; asst. resident in surgery U. Wash., Seattle, 1965; resident in ophthalmology U. Fla., 1968-71; pvt. practice medicine specializing in ophthalmology, Sierra Eye Med. Group, Inc., Visalia, Calif., 1972—; mem. staff Kaweah Delta Dist. Hosp., chief of staff, 1978-79; mem. staff Visalia Community Hosp.; med. staff ophthalmology Valley Med. Center-Univ. Calif. Fresno Med. Edn. Program, 1972—; asst. clin. prof. ophthalmology U. Calif., San Francisco, 1981—. Bd. dirs., asst. sec. Kaweah Delta Dist. Hosp., 1983—. Ka. Served as flight surgeon USN, 1966-68. Co-recipient Fight-for-Sight citation for research in retinal dystrophy, 1970. Diplomate Am. Bd. Ophthalmology, Nat. Bd. Med. Examiners. Fellow A.C.S., Am. Acad. Ophthalmology; mem. AMA, Calif. (del. 1978-79), Tulare County med. assns., Calif., Am. assns. ophthalmology, Am. Soc. Cataract and Refractive Surgery, Internat. Phacoemulsification and Cataract Methodology Soc. Roman Catholic. Club: Rotary (Visalia). Home: 1101 W Whitendale St Visalia CA 93277 Office: 2830 W Main St Visalia CA 93291

RIEK, ROBERT JAMES, laser company executive; b. Johnson City, N.Y., Aug. 15, 1942; s. Carl Arthur and Margaret R.; children—Robert, John, Stephen. B.E.E., Cleve. State U., 1966; M.B.A., Memphis State U., 1971. With mfg. mgmt. program Gen. Electric Co., 1966-69, sr. quality engr., 1969-72, mgr. shop ops., 1972-76, mgr. quality control, 1976-79; exec. v.p. Lincoln Laser Co., Phoenix, 1979—. Mem. Delta Mu Delta, Tau Kappa Epsilon, Beta Gamma Sigma. Republican. Roman Catholic. Office: Lincoln Laser Co 234 E Mohave Phoenix AZ 85004

RIEKE, WILLIAM OLIVER, university president, anatomist; b. Odessa, Wash., Apr. 26, 1931; s. Henry William and Hutoka S. (Smith) R.; m. Joanne Elynor Schief, Aug. 22, 1954; children: Susan Ruth, Stephen Harold, Marcus Henry. B.A. summa cum laude, Pacific Luth. U., 1953; M.D. with honors, U. Wash., 1958. Instr. anatomy U. Wash. Sch. Medicine, Seattle, 1958; asst. prof. U. Wash. Sch. Medicine, 1961-64, adminstrv. officer, 1963-66, assoc. prof., 1964-66; prof., head dept. anatomy Coll. Medicine U. Iowa, Iowa City, 1966-71; dean protem Coll. Medicine U. Iowa (Coll. Medicine), 1969-70, chmn. exec. com., 1969-70; vice chancellor for health affairs, prof. anatomy U. Kans. Med. Center, Kansas City, 1971-73; exec. vice chancellor, prof. anatomy U. Kans. Med. Center, 1973-75; affiliate prof. biol. structure U. Wash. Sch. Medicine, Seattle, 1975—; pres. Pacific Lutheran U., Parkland, Wash., 1975—; Mem. interdisciplinary gen. basic sci. test com. Nat. Bd. Med. Examiners, 1968-72, chmn. anatomy test com., 1972-75, mem. at large, 1975-79; spl. cons. NIH, 1970-72; mem. adv. com. Inst. Medicine, Nat. Acad. Scis., 1974-76; mem. Commn. on Colls., NW Assn. Schs. and Colls., 1979-84. Editor: Procs. 3d Ann. Leucocyte Culture Conf, 1969; editorial bd.: Am. Jour. Anatomy, 1968-71. Bd. dirs. Luth. Ednl. Council N. Am., 1980-83, pres., 1982-83. Named one of Most Effective Coll. or Univ. Pres., Bowling Green State U. Research Study, 1986, Distinguished Alumnus Pacific Luth. U., 1970, Distinguished Alumnus Pi Kappa Delta, 1977. Fellow A.C.P.; mem. Am. Assn. Anatomists, Am. Soc. Cell Biology, AAAS, Nat. Assn. Ind. Colls. and Univs. (bd. dirs. 1985—, trustee 1986—), Sigma Xi, Alpha Kappa Psi, Beta Gamma Sigma. Lutheran (mem. ch. council 1967-70). Home: 13611 Spanaway Loop Rd Tacoma WA 98444-1118 Office: Office of Pres Pacific Lutheran U Tacoma WA 98447

RIEKEN, WILLIAM M., JR., computer systems consultant, educator; b. Vallejo, Calif., Sept. 12, 1947; s. William M. and Billiemarie (Hall) R.; A.B. in Math., U. Calif.-Berkeley, 1971; M.S. in Math., U. Nev.-Reno, 1975; postgrad. in Computer Sci., Stanford U., 1978. Instr. computer sci., faculty asst. U. Wis.-Oshkosh, 1973-76; instr. computer sci. So. Ill. U., Carbondale and software cons. Modern Urban Systems Tech., St. Louis, 1976-77; sr. programmer Bendix Field Engring. Corp., Sunnyvale, Calif., 1977-78; software instr. Amdahl Corp., Sunnyvale, 1978-79; mgr. mktg. software support, software product mgr., program mgr. micrographic systems div. NCR, Mountain View, Calif., 1979-80; pvt. practice cons. in field, San Mateo, Calif., 1980—; UNIX system con. AT&T Bell Labs., N.J., 1983—; internat. ACM lectr., 1985—. Mem. Assn. Computing Edn. (founder), ACM (pres. Golden Gate Chpt. 1981-82, seminar chmn. 1982, disting. Service award 1981), IEEE-Computer Soc., Assn. Systems Mgmt., Ind. Computer Cons. Assn. (com. chmn.). Democrat. Baptist. Home and Office: 3956 O'Neill Dr San Mateo CA 94403

RIEMENSCHNEIDER, PAUL ARTHUR, physician, radiologist; b. Cleve., Apr. 17, 1920; s. Albert and Selma (Marting) R.; m. Mildred McCarthy, May 12, 1945; children: Barbara Anne, Nancy Emelia, David Andrew, Paul Albert, Mary Elizabeth, Sarah Bache. BS, Baldwin-Wallace Coll., 1941; MD, Harvard U., 1944. Diplomate Am. Bd. Radiology (trustee 1973-85), Nat. Bd. Med. Examiners. Prof., chmn. dept. radiology SUNY, Syracuse, 1945-64; chief diagnostic radiology Santa Barbara (Calif.) Cottage Hosp., 1964—; vis. prof. in residence SUNY, Syracuse, 1983—. Co-editor: N.Y. State Jour. Medicine, 1960-64; mem. editorial adv. bd. Yearbook of Cancer, 1960-64; contbr. articles to profl. jours. Mem. appropriations com. Santa Barbara Found., 1984—; vestryman All STs. Episcopla Ch., 1970-76, sr. warden, 1973; bd. dirs. ARC, Santa Barbara, 1968-72, Am. Cancer Soc., Santa Barbara, 1967-70, Casa Dorinda Retirement Residence, 1975-76, Wood Glen Hall Retirement Residence, 1980—, Cancer Found. Santa Barbara, 1966-82, chmn. equipment com., 1973-82. Served to lt. comdr. USNR, 1945-47, 54-56. Fellow Am. Coll. Radiology (cancer com. 1952-54, council 1956-64, bd. chancellors 1967-73, chmn. commn. standards in radiologic practice 1968-71, v.p. 1972, pres. 1974, chmn. com. manpower 1972-86, chmn. com. manpower in armed servies 1975-86, Gold medal 1982); mem. AMA, Calif. Med. Assn., Santa Barbara County Med. Soc. (chmn. med. sch. com. 1967-71), Am. Roentgen Ray Soc. (mem. publs. com. 1965-75, chmn. 1970-75, exec. council 1970-75, 77-82, chmn. program com. 1977-79, pres.-elect 1977-79, pres. 1979, Disting. Service award 1986), South Coast Radiol. Soc. (pres. 1967), Assn. Univ. Radiologists (sec. 1960, pres. 1961, com. resident tng. 1984—), Radiol. Soc. N.Am., Am. Soc. Neuroradiology, Soc. Pediatric Radiology, Eastern Radiol. Soc. (pres.-elect 1987), Calif. Radiol. Soc., So. Calif. Radiol. Soc., Detroit Roentgen Soc. (hon.), Bluegrass Radiol. Soc. (hon.), Pacific N.W. Radiol. Soc. (hon.), Alpha Omega Alpha. Republican. Clubs: Birnamwood Golf (Santa Barbara); Skaneateles Country (N.Y.). Avocations: tennis, swimming. Home: 2740 Sycamore Canyon Rd Santa Barbara CA 93108 Office: Santa Barbara Radiology Med Group Inc PO Box 689 Santa Barbara CA 93102

RIEMKE, RICHARD ALLAN, mechanical engineer; b. Vallejo, Calif., Oct. 11, 1944; s. Allan Frederick and Frances Jewell (O'Brien) R. BA in Physiology, U. Calif., Berkeley, 1967, MA in Physiology, 1971, PhD in Engring. Sci., 1977. Postdoctoral fellow U. So. Calif., Los Angeles, 1977-78; research engr. Del Mar Avionics, Irvine, Calif., 1979; staff fellow NIH, Bethesda, Md., 1980; engring. specialist Idaho Nat. Engring. Lab. EG&G Idaho, Idaho Falls, 1980—. Served with U.S. Army, 1969-75. Mem. AAAS, Am. Soc. Mech. Engrs., Biomed. Engring. Soc., Soc. Computer Simulation, Soc. Math. Biology, Soc. Engring. Sci., Order of Golden Bear, Alpha Sigma Phi. Republican. Roman Catholic. Avocations: swimming, surfing. Home: 1727 Grandview Dr 4 Idaho Falls ID 83402 Office: EG&G Idaho Idaho Nat Engring Lab Idaho Falls ID 83415

RIES, FRANK WILLIAM DAVID, theater and dance professor; b. St. Louis, Apr. 12, 1950; s. Frank William Jr. and Inez (Lewis) R. BFA, Webster U., 1971; BA with honors, Cambridge U., 1974, MA with honors, 1978; PhD, Ind. U., 1980, MS in Ballet, 1978. Dancer, mime St. Louis Ballet, 1968-70, 71; actor, dancer Cambridge (Eng.) Footlights, 1971-74; assoc. instr. ballet Ind. U., Bloomington, 1975-78, assoc. instr. drama, 1977-78; asst. prof. Western Ill. U., Macomb, 1978-79; assoc. prof. Am. musical dance forms U. Calif., Santa Barbara, 1979—; bd. dirs. Intercampus MA program in dance history, Los Angeles, Drama and Dance Affiliates, Santa Barbara, 1984—. Author: Dance Theater of Jean Cocteau, 1986; Dance Chronical monographs, 1984-86; editorial bd. Dance Scope, N.Y., 1976-80; contbr. articles on dance to profl. jours. Research grantee U. Calif., Santa Barbara, 1981-83, 86-87. Mem. Dance History Scholars (bd. dirs.), Congress on Research in Dance (awards com. 1984-86), Soc. Dance Research, Dance Critics Assn. Roman Catholic. Clubs: Faculty, Union. Avocation: reconstruction of B'way dances. Home: 1770 E Valley Rd Santa Barbara CA 93108 Office: U Calif Dept Dance and Drama Santa Barbara CA 93106

RIETZ, KENNETH CHARLES, advertising executive, political consultant; b. Appleton, Wis., May 3, 1941; s. Howard K. and Catherine (Abbey) R.; 1 child, Kenneth Charles. Grad. George Washington U., 1973. Dep. chmn. Republican Nat. Com., 1973; v.p. MGM Records, Los Angeles, 1974, Mike Curb Prodns., 1974-76; pres. Ken Rietz & Co., Los Angeles, 1976—. Mem. Am. Assn. Polit. Cons., Am. Council Young Polit. Leaders, Rep. Eagles. Presbyterian. Office: PO Box 1821 Los Angeles CA 90069

RIGAS, HARRIETT BADAKER, educational administrator, electrical and computer engineering educator; b. Winnipeg, Man., Can., Apr. 30, 1934; came to U.S., 1956, naturalized, 1962; d. Max and Helen (Pasternak) B.; m. Anthony L. Rigas, Feb. 14, 1959; 1 child, Marc. B.Sc. in Elec. Engring., Queen's U., 1956; M.S.E.E., U. Kans., 1959, Ph.D. in Elec. Engring., 1963. Elec. engr. Biophysics, Mayo Clinic, Rochester, Minn., 1956-57; sr. research engr., aerodynamics Lockhee Missiles, Sunnyvale, Calif., 1963-66; asst. prof. Wash. State U.-Pullman, 1966-71, prof., 1976, chmn. dept. elec. and computer engring. 1979-84; chmn. dept. elec. and computer engring. Naval Postgrad. Sch., Monterey, Calif., 1984—. Co-editor Jour. Computers and Elec. Engring., 1982. Contbr. articles to profl. jours. Recipient Disting. Engring. Service award U. Kans., 1983. Fellow IEEE (Engr. of Yr., Spokane sect. 1980, 84); mem. Soc. Women Engrs. (Achievement award 1982), Sigma Xi, Tau Beta Pi (Disting. Engr. award). Home: 4 Victoria Rise Monterey CA 93940 Office: Naval Postgrad Sch Department of Electrical and Computer Engineering Code 62 Monterey CA 93943

RIGG, JOHN BROWNLEE, JR., oil company executive, lawyer; b. Lincoln, Nebr., May 31, 1947; s. John B. and Shirley A. (Tomlinson) R.; children: John III, Eaton James, Michael Torian; m. Melanie S. Toepfer, July 20, 1985. BA, George Washington U., 1969; JD, U. Denver, 1973. Staff, U.S. Senator Gordon Allott of Colo., Washington and Denver, 1967-73; adminstr. City of Idaho Springs (Colo.), 1973-75; regional rep. Motor Vehicle Mfrs. Assn., Denver, 1975-80; govt. affairs rep., Amoco Corp., Denver, 1980—. Mem. Rocky Mountain Oil and Gas Assn. (govt. affairs com.). Office: PO Box 800 Amoco Corporation 1670 Broadway Suite 1984 Denver CO 80201

RIGGALL, EVISON RONALD, physician; b. Fayetteville, Ark., Oct. 10, 1925; s. Frank and Eva Emma (Mead) R.; B.A. with honors (Kellogg scholar), U. Ark., 1946; M.D., Tulane U., 1948; m. Nelda Jean Varney, July 2, 1949; children—Eric Kneave, Ronelda Surle, Meredydd Ian, Evison Varney; m. Joan Elizabeth Budd Hildreth, June 16, 1984. Rotating intern, So. Pacific Gen. Hosp., San Francisco, 1948-49, resident, then chief med. resident, 1949-51; exchange scholar Postgrad. Med. Sch., U. London, 1951-52; practice medicine, specializing in internal medicine, Prairie Grove, Ark., 1951-55, Walnut Creek, Calif., 1957—; chief of medicine Elizabeth Hosp., Prairie Grove, Ark., 1951-55; dir. pulmonary function lab. Samuel Merritt Hosp., 1960-73, chief pulmonary disease sect., 1962-69, mem. shock com., 1969-72, liaison mem. coronary care com., 1970-75, mem. open heart surgery team, 1960-67; dir. pulmonary function lab. Alameda Hosp., 1969-74, program chmn., 1958-59, sec. to med. staff, 1959-60; mem. inhalation therapy adv. com. Peralta Hosp., 1970-73, mem. med. group planning com., 1973-75; mem. staff Providence Hosp., 1960-75, John Muir Meml. Hosp., Mt. Diablo Community Hosp.; cons. VA Hosp., Martinez, Calif., Blue Cross of No. Calif., Medicare Program and Medi-Cal Program of No. Calif.; mem. teaching staff Highland-Alameda County Hosp., 1957-75; instr. pulmonary diseases U. Calif. Med. Center, San Francisco, 1962-69, U. Calif., Berkeley, 1973-75; internist Rossmoor Clinic, Walnut Creek, 1974—; assoc. clin. prof. U. Calif. at Davis Med. Sch., 1977—. Served with USAF, 1955-57. Diplomate Am. Bd. Internal Medicine, Am. Bd. Pulmonary Disease. Fellow Am. Coll. Chest Physicians, Royal Soc. Medicine, A.C.P., Am. Geriatric Soc., Huguenot Soc. London; mem. AMA, Calif., Alameda-Contra Costa med. assns., Royal Soc. Medicine Found., Am., Calif., East Bay (bd. govs. 1962-68, pres. 1966-67) socs. internal medicine, Tulane Med. Alumni Club, Lamplighters, Californians for Am. Conservatory Theatre, Calif. Acad. Sci., Huff and Puff Club San Francisco, Am. (dir. 1973-79), Calif. (dir.), Alameda County (dir., pres. 1967-68), Contra Costa-Solano Counties (dir., mem. med. adv. bd.) lung assns., Laennec Soc. San Francisco (past pres.), Am. Thoracic Soc., Alpha Epsilon Delta, Psi Chi, Alpha Kappa Kappa. Episcopalian. Clubs: Nat. of London; Nat. Travel. Lodge: Masons. Editor Bull. Calif. Thoracic Soc. Contbr. articles to profl. publs. Home: 4069 Happy Valley Rd Lafayette CA 94549 Office: 1220 Rossmoor Pkwy Walnut Creek CA 94595

RIGGS, DONALD EUGENE, university librarian; b. Middlebourne, W.Va., May 11, 1942; m. Jane Vasbinder, Sept. 25, 1964; children: Janna Jennifer, Krista Dyonis. B.A., Glenville State Coll., 1964; M.A., W.Va. U., 1966; M.L.S., U. Pitts., 1968; Ed.D., Va. Poly. Inst. and State U., 1975; postgrad., U. Colo., 1977-78. Head librarian, tchr. sci. Warwood (W.Va.) High Sch., 1964-65; head librarian, audiovisual dir. Wheeling (W.Va.) High Sch., 1965-67; sci. and econs. librarian California State Coll. of Pa., 1968-70; dir. library and learning center Bluefield State Coll., 1970-72; dir. libraries and media services Bluefield State Coll., Concord Coll., Greenbrier Community Coll., and So. campus W.Va. Coll. of Grad. Studies, 1972-76; dir. libraries U. Colo., Denver, Met. State Coll., and Community Col. of Denver—Auraria Campus, 1976-79; univ. librarian Ariz. State U., 1979—; adj. prof. Calif. State Coll., 1968-70, W.Va. U., 1970-72, U. Colo., 1977-79, U. Ariz., 1985; fed. relations coordinator Am. and W.Va. library assns., 1970-75; chmn. bd. dirs. Central Colo. Library System, 1976-79; chmn. Colo. Council Acad. Libraries, 1977-78; exec. bd. Colo. Alliance Research Libraries, 1978-79; cons. to libraries. Contbr. articles to profl. publs.; editor W.Va. Libraries, 1973-75; assoc. editor: Southeastern Librarian, 1973-75; contbg. author: Libraries in the Political Process, 1980; contbg. author, editor: Library Leadership: Visualizing the Future, 1982; contbg. author: Options for the 80s, 1982, Library and Information Technology: At the Crossroads, 1984; author: Strategic Planning for Library Managers, 1984, History of the Arizona State University Libraries, 1986; editorial bd. Jour. Library Adminstrn., 1987—; editorial bd. Am. Libraries, 1987—, editor Library Adminstrn. and Mgmt., 1987—. Trustee Mesa (Ariz.) Pub. Library, 1980-86, chmn., 1985-86; mem. Ariz. State Library Adv. Council, 1981-84; bd. dirs. Documentation Abstracts, Inc., 1986—; trustee AMIGOS Bibliograph. Council, Inc., 1986—. Named Outstanding Young Educator Ohio County Schs., 1966; Council on Library Resources grantee, 1985. Mem. ALA (councilor-at-large 1982-86, chmn. council's resolutions com. 1985-86), Ariz. Library Assn. (pres. coll. and univ. div. 1981-82, pres. 1983-84, Spl. Service award 1986), Colo. Library Assn. (pres. 1978-79), W.Va. Library Assn. (pres. 1975-76), Assn. Coll. and Research Libraries (pres. Tri-State chpt. 1972-74, pres. Ariz. chpt. 1981-82), So. Library Assn. (chmn. coll. and univ. sect. 1982-83), Assn. Research Libraries (mem. 100th meeting planning com. 1982), Beta Phi Mu, Chi Beta Phi, Phi Delta Kappa, Phi Kappa Phi. Home: 2120 E Knoll Circle Mesa AZ 85203 Office: Ariz State U Tempe AZ 85287

RIGGS, JOHN ARTHUR, real estate appraiser, finance executive; b. Los Angeles, Nov. 29, 1946; s. Robert Clarence Carl and and Marguerite Elizabeth (Kondziella) R. BS in Edn., U. Nev., 1972, MEd, 1975; JD, Nev. Sch. Law, 1985. V.p. Fin. Mgmt. Appraisal Analysts, Reno, 1978—; supr. Nev. State Dept. Prisons, Carson City, 1972-82; prin. cons. Riggs Art, Reno, 1978—; bd. dirs. Reno '87 Bet-On-It, Inc. Contbr. articles to profl. jours. Served with U.S. Army, 1966-69. Mem. Nev. Jaycees (pres. 1979-80), Internat. Real Estate Inst., Phi Delta Kappa, Delta Theta Phi. Roman Catholic. Lodge: KC (outside guard). Avocations: photography, travel. Home: 1140 Monitor Dr Reno NV 89512 Office: Fin Mgmt Appraisal Analysts Inc PO Box 9025 Reno NV 89507

RIGGS, JOHN B., architect; b. Tucson, Ariz., June 26, 1942; s. John Stark and Anna Lee (McAleb) R.; m. Barbara Wynn Bettner, Sept. 1, 1966 (div. Dec. 1976); children—Jeff, Bran; m. Jennifer J. Jewett, June 9, 1979; children—Courtney, Jennifer. B.Arch., U. Ariz., 1966. Registered architect, Ariz., Colo., Utah, Wash., Nev. Draftsman Terry Atkinson, Tucson, 1966-68, CNWC Architects, Tucson, 1968-69; designer Freidman & Jobusch, Tucson, 1969-70; prin., pres. Architecture One, Ltd., Tucson, 1970—; mem. Ariz. State Bd. Tech. Registration, Phoenix, 1980—, chmn., 1983-84; mem. exam. com. Nat. Council Architectural Registration Bds., 1981-86, asst. coordinator exam. A com., 1984, coordinator, 1985, mem. examination planning com., 1986-87. Bd. dirs., v.p. Ariz. Theatre Co., Tucson, 1980—; adv. com. U. Ariz. Coll. Architecture, 1983—. Recipient numerous awards in field. Mem. AIA (bd. dirs. So. Ariz. chpt. 1976-77), Western Conf. Archtl. Bds. (chmn. 1986-87, bd. dirs., v.p. Ariz. chpt.). Democrat. Methodist. Office: Architecture One Ltd 6303 E Tanque Verde Suite 200 Tucson AZ 85715

RIGGS, JUNE ROSEMARY, interior design educator; b. Portishead, Eng., June 28, 1927; came to U.S. 1946; d. Arthur William Edward and Joan Ashworth (Keyte) Clarke; m. Francis Porter, Sept. 13, 1945; children: John Prescott, Gillian Anne, Jacqueline June. Assoc. degree, Utah Tech. Coll., 1973; BS magna cum laude, Brigham Young U., 1975. Interior designer Jordan Marsh Co., Peabody, Mass., 1961-69; instr. Brigham Young U., Provo, Utah, 1970—. Author: Material and Components of Interior Design, 1985. Pres. PTA, Gloucester, Mass., 1955; mem. Highland (Utah) Civic Devel. Com., 1981-86; bd. dirs. Girl Scouts U.S., Gloucester, 1957. Mem. Phi Kappa Phi. Republican. Mormon. Avocation: weaving. Home: 11107 N Gambol Oak Circle Highland UT 84003 Office: Brigham Young U 292 BRMB Provo UT 84603

RIGGS, KERSHNER GAIL, restorative medicine educator, administrator; b. Pottsville, Pa., Dec. 24, 1938; d. Russell Jesse and Evelyn Jean (Heebner) Kershner; m. Frank Lew Riggs, June 28, 1960. B.S. cum laude, U. Ariz., 1961, postgrad., 1980—; M.A., Ariz. State U., 1968. Div. merchandising coordinator Kroger Co., Washington, D.C., 1961-62; asst. dist. mgr. Safeway Stores, Inc., Washington, D.C., 1963-64; research assoc. Lybrand, Ross Bros., & Montgomery, Los Angeles, 1966; counselor Ariz. State Employment Service, Phoenix, 1967-68; head acctg. dept. Univ. Ariz. Audiovisual Service, Tucson, 1973-74; dir. edn. Regional Med. Program Arthritis Service, Tucson, 1974-77; assoc. faculty Pima Community Coll., Tucson, 1976-77; dir. Disabled Adult Rehab. Program, Tucson, 1977-78; assoc. dir. SW Arthritis Ctr., U. Ariz., Tucson, 1978-84, assoc. dir. Div. Restorative Medicine, 1984—; cons. NIH, Washington, D.C., 1980—, various med. schs. nationally; chmn. adv. bd. Arthritis Info. Clearinghouse, Washington, D.C., 1982—; keynote speaker various profl. and lay groups nationally. Author/editor: Rheumatic Diseases: Rehabilitation and Management, 1984; Special Learning Series: Arthritis, 1984; Contbr. articles on med. edn. to profl. jours., 1982-84. Vice chmn., trustee Nat. Arthritis Found., 1979-84; bd. dirs. Rehab. Work Adjustment Ctr., Tucson, 1978-80; chmn. bd. Sr. Health Improvement Program, Tucson, 1979-80; v.p. Arthritis Found. (So. Ariz. chpt.), Tucson, 1979-84; trustee Am. Juvenile Arthritis Orgn., 1982—. Named Tucson Woman Yr. Tucson C. of C., 1982; grantee NIH, Rehab. Services Adminstrn., Am. Hosp. Assn. Mem. Nat. Arthritis Health Professions Assn. (pres. 1980-81, Addie Thomas award 1984), Ariz. Arthritis Health Professions Assn. (pres. 1981-82), Am. Pub. Health Assn., Ariz. Pub. Health Assn., (Health Educator of Yr. 1982), Tucson Rheumatism Soc., Kappa Alpha Theta, Pi Lambda Theta, Beta Beta Beta. Home: 5348 E 10th St Tucson AZ 85711 Office: Univ Ariz Div Restorative Medicine 1821 E Elm St Tucson AZ 85719

RIGGS, LEW, medical center official; b. Indpls., Apr. 1, 1937; s. Frank Lloyd and Marie Loretta (Shaner) R.; m. Gail Evelyn Kershner, July 28, 1960. B.S., U. Ariz., 1961, Ed.D., 1976; M.B.A., George Washington U., 1964. Contracts adminstr. TRW Systems, Los Angeles, 1964-67; asst. mgr. Electric League Ariz., Phoenix, 1967-68; asst. pub. affairs Ariz. regional med. program U. Ariz. Coll. Medicine, Tucson, 1968-73; dir. community affairs Tucson Med. Ctr., 1973-82; dir. pub. relations Good Samaritan Med. Ctr., Phoenix, 1982—; chmn. pub. relations com. Nat. Arthritis Found., Atlanta, 1985; speaker mktg., pub. relations, mgmt., 1977—; cons. physicians and hosps., 1979—. Author: (with others) Designing the Future Through Alternative Careers, 1973. Editor: The Health Care Facility's Public Relations Handbook, 1982. Contbr. articles to profl. jours. Bd. dirs. Ariz. Opera Co., Tucson, 1973; co-chmn. pub. relations com. Pima County chpt. Cancer Soc., Tucson, 1973. Lt. col. USAFR. Recipient Mac Eachern citation Acad. Hosp. Pub. Relations, 1975, Golden Mike award Am. Legion Aux., 1964. Mem. Am. Hosp. Assn. (council affiliated soc. 1982, pub. affairs adv. panel 1978), Pub. Relations Soc. Am. (com. chmn. 1981, Silver Anvil award 1964, Pres's Citation 1981), Am. Soc. Hosp. Mktg. and Pub. Relations (pres. 1978-79), Phoenix C. of C. (devel. com. 1984). Republican. Methodist. Home: 1608 E Gardenia Phoenix AZ 85020 Office: Pub Relations Good Samaritan Med Ctr 1111 E McDowell Rd Phoenix AZ 85062

RIGNEY, ROBERT BUFORD, county ofcl.; b. Long Beach, Calif., May 1, 1926; s. Harold Nevins and Nelly Amanda (Buford) R.; A.B., Stanford U., 1950; postgrad. Mexico City Coll., 1951, U. Redlands, Claremont, 1956, U. So. Calif., 1972; m. Lowenda May Morris, Dec. 21, 1952; children—Michael Owen, Jeffrey Owen. Sr. adminstrv. analyst, coordinator spl. dist. County of San Bernardino (Calif.), 1960-66, asst. county adminstrv. officer, 1966-73, 80, county adminstrv. officer, 1980—, adminstr., exec. officer Environ. Improvement Agy., 1973—; chmn. Nat. Acad. Scis. NRC Panel on Earthquake Estimation exec, officer San Bernardino County Redevel. Agy.; mem. Calif. Seismic Safety Com., chmn., 1977-78; mem. Governor's Earthquake Preparedness Task Force Steering Com., 1981-83, chmn. Long-Range Reconstruction and Recovery Com.; del. Governor's Commn. of Californians, 1980—, chmn. environ. com. 1985—; mem. Energy Resources Com., 1983; mem. County Relations with Cities Com., 1984; chmn. Infrastructure Fin. Com., 1984; chmn. Housing Land Use and Transp. Com., 1984; chmn. Peoples Republic of China/U.S. Construction Specialists Exchange Tour, 1978; chmn. Peoples Republic of China Local Govt. Exchange Tour, 1980; cons. U.S. Office of Sci. and Tech. Policy; bd. dirs. City-County Joint Powers Authority for a Greater San Bernardino, 1983—; chmn. program adv. bd. on public adminstr. Calif. State U., San Bernardino, 1983—; bd. dirs. Kimberly-Shirk Found.. Bd. dirs. Calif. Inland Empire council Boy Scouts Am. 1974-79, pres., 1983—; bd. dirs. Inland Empire Cultural Found., 1982—, Kimberly Shirk Found. Recipient 16 Achievement awards Nat. Assn. Counties, Silver Beaver award Boy Scouts Am., 1977, Community award Lighthouse for Blind, 1977. Teachers Hall of Fame, 1983; Community award Public Relations Soc. Am., 1979; govt. medal Shizuoka Prefecture, Japan, 1984; mem. County Supervisors Assn. of Calif., 1980—, League of Calif. Cities, Earthquake Engring, Research Inst., Nat. Assn. of Counties, Nat. Assn. County Adminstrs., Phi Alpha Theta, Phi Delta Kappa. Author publs. in field. Clubs: Native Sons of the Golden West, Rotary, Redlands Dance (pres.), Redlands Roundtable (pres. 1959—). Home: 1101 Cajon St Redlands CA 92373

RIGROD, WILLIAM WALTER, research engineer; b. N.Y.C., Mar. 29, 1913; s. Benjamin and Elizabeth (Block) R.; m. Elisabeth Gill, Oct. 8, 1939. BS cum laude, Cooper Union Inst., 1934; MS in Communication Engineering, Cornell U., 1941; DEE in Electrophysics, Poly. U., 1950. Research scientist Ignatyev Research Inst., Moscow, 1934-35, All-Union Electro-Tech. Inst., Moscow, 1935-39; sec., translator N.Y. Times Bur., Moscow, 1939-40; electronics engr. Westinghouse Elec. Corp., Bloomfield, N.J., 1941-51; mem. tech. staff Electronics Research Dept. Bell Telephone Labs, Murray Hill, N.J., 1951-77; team mem. Project Echo, BTL, Holmdel, N.J., 1960; cons. Los Alamos Nat. Lab., N.Mex. 1979—. Holder of 22 U.S. patents; contbr. articles to profl. jours. Mem. IEEE (life sr.), Am. Optical Soc. (emeritus), Sigma Xi. Club: German (Los Alamos and Santa Fe). Avocations: swimming, hiking, travel, Russian and German lit.

RIGSBY, JOHN NEWTON, cable TV executive; b. Easton, Pa., Aug. 18, 1946; s. John M. and Shirley J. (Johnson) R.; m. Virginia L. Blackwell, July 11, 1976; children: John B., David G. AB, Brown U., 1968; MBA, Harvard U., 1976. Western Regional mgr. Am. TV and Communications Corp., San Diego, 1976-79; div. mgr. Am. TV and Communications Corp., Denver, 1979-82, v.p. video product devel., 1982-85, v.p. consumer satellite services, 1985—. Served to lt. USN, 1968-74. Decorated Navy Achievement medal, Navy Commendation medal. Mem. Calif. Community TV Assn. (bd. dirs.). Republican. Presbyterian. Club: Harvard Bus. Sch. Lodge: Rotary. Home: 2391 Oakridge Rd Sedalia CO 80135 Office: Am TV Communications 160 Inverness Dr W Englewood CO 80112

RILEY, B. GRESHAM, college president; b. Jackson, Miss., June 27, 1938; married; 2 children. B.A., Baylor U., 1960; M.A., Yale U., 1963, Ph.D., 1965. Asst. instr. philosophy Yale U., 1963-64; from asst. prof. to assoc. prof. New Coll., 1965-75, acting provost, 1972-73, provost, 1973-75; prof. philosophy, dean faculty arts and sci. U. Richmond, 1975-81; pres. Colo. Coll., Colorado Springs, 1981—; younger scholar fellow Nat. Found. Arts and Humanities, 1968-69; vis. fellow Ctr. Advanced Studies Behavior Sci Stanford U., 1968-69; cons. Nat. Endowment for Humanities, 1971—; mem. adv. bd. Project Gen. Edn. Models, 1978-81. Contbr. articles to profl. jours. Bd. dirs. Ind. Coll. Fund of Colo., 1981—; chmn. selection com. Colo. Rhodes Scholarship, 1981—. Mem. Am. Philos. Assn., CS Peirce Soc., Soc. Values Higher Edn., Assn. Am. Colls. (oversight com., project on redefining the meaning and purpose of Baccalaureate degrees 1981-85), Commn. on Women in Higher Edn., Am. Council on Edn., North Cen. Assn. Assn. (cons., evaluator 1984—), Associated Colls. of the Midwest (bd. dirs. 1981—). Office: Colorado Coll Office of the Pres Colorado Springs CO 80903

RILEY, BENJAMIN KNEELAND, lawyer; b. Pompton Plains, N.J., June 3, 1957; s. Christopher Sibley and Katharine Louise (Piper) R.; m. Janet Welch McCormick, Sept. 15, 1984. AB, Dartmouth Coll., 1979; JD, U. Calif., Berkeley, 1983. Bar: Calif. 1983, U.S. Dist. Ct. (ea., and no. dists.) Calif. 1983, U.S. Ct. Appeals (9th cir.) 1983, U.S. Dist. Ct. (ea. dist.) Calif. 1985, U.S. Dist. Ct. (cen. dist.) Calif. 1987. Assoc. McCutchen, Doyle, Brown & Enessen, San Francisco, 1983-84, Cooley, Godward, Castro, Huddleson, & Tatum, San Francisco, 1984—; Mem. San Francisco Legal Services Clinic, 1983—. Assoc. editor Calif. Law Rev. Democrat. Club: Barrister of San Francisco. Office: Cooley Godward et al One Maritime Plaza 20th Floor San Francisco CA 94111

RILEY, DENNIS MARTIN, insurance company executive; b. Wyatt, Mo., Oct. 4, 1953; s. James Clifton and Earlene (Nolen) R.; m. Annette Belnap, Feb. 22, 1980; 1 child, Tyler. BS in Safety and Health, Utah State U., 1976. Cert. safety profl. Loss control rep. Hartford Ins., Little Rock, 1976-78, Comml. Union Ins. Co., Salt Lake City, 1978-80; loss control cons. Fireman's Fund Ins. Co., Salt Lake City, 1980-85, loss control mgr., 1985—. Vol. Big Bros., Little Rock, 1977. Mem. Am. Soc. Safety Engrs. Democrat. Mormon. Avocation: softball. Home: 5150 S Heather Hill Circle Salt Lake City UT 84118 Office: Fireman's Fund Ins 420 E South Temple Salt Lake City UT 84147

RILEY, DERRELL WAYNE, coal company executive; b. East St. Louis, Ill., Nov. 5, 1951; s. Elmo Martin and Wilma Irene (Hale) R.; m. Barbara Ann Milton, Apr. 15, 1972 (div. May 1985); children: Jonathan, Lauren; m. Dianne Carol Arp Stricker, June 21, 1985; stepchildren: Jeremy Stricker, Nathan Stricker. BBA, So. Ill. U., Edwardsville, 1979. Constrn. clerk Peabody Coal Co., St. Louis, 1979-80, constrn. auditor, 1980-82, office mgr., 1982-83; acctg. mgr. N. Antelope Coal subs. Peabody Holding Co., Gillette, Wyo., 1983-85; materials mgr. Powder River Coal subs. Peabody Holding Co., Gillette, Wyo., 1985—; instr. materials mgmt. assocs. art program Sheridan Coll., Gillette. Served with U.S. Army, 1970-73. Mem. Purchasing Mgmt. Assn. Wyo. (bd. dirs., dir. at large 1986—). Avocations: skiing, golf. Office: Powder River Coal PO Box 3034 Gillette WY 82716

RILEY, ELIZABETH REGINA, speech pathologist; b. Lynwood, Calif., Nov. 20, 1957; d. Thomas James and Marie Agnes (Remas) Brennan; m. Peter Judson Riley, Mar. 21, 1981. AA, Cypress Coll., 1977; BA in Speech Pathology, Whittier Coll., 1979, MA in Speech Pathology, 1980; postgrad., U.S. Internat. U., 1983—. Lic. speech pathologist, Calif. Speech/lang. specialist Lowell Joint Sch. Dist., Whittier, Calif., 1980-83; pvt. practice speech pathology Anaheim, Calif., 1983—. Vol. children's religious edn. program St. Martin de Porres Ch., Yorba Linda, Calif., 1984-86. Mem. Am. Speech Lang. and Hearing Assn. (cert.), Calif. Speech Lang. and Hearing Assn. Democrat. Roman Catholic. Avocation: needle crafts.

RILEY, MERLE EUGENE, chemical physicist; b. Waterford, Ohio, Mar. 23, 1941; s. Wilbur George and Amy Charlotte (Linscott) R.; m. Cecilia Osorio, July 16, 1966; children—Natalie, Kevin. B.S., Marietta Coll., 1963; Ph.D., Calif. Inst. Tech., 1968. Research fellow Harvard U., Cambridge, Mass., 1968-69; postdoctoral appointee Sandia Nat. Labs., Albuquerque, 1969-71, mem. research staff, 1971—. Contbr. articles to profl. jours. Mem. Am. Phys. Soc., Phi Beta Kappa, Kappa Mu Epsilon. Office: Sandia Nat Lab Box 5800 Albuquerque NM 87185

RILEY, PATRICK JAMES, professional basketball coach; b. Rome, N.Y., Mar. 20, 1945; s. Leon R.; m. Chris Riley. Grad., U. Ky., 1967. Guard San Diego Rockets, NBA, 1967-70; guard Los Angeles Lakers, NBA, 1970-75, asst. coach, 1979-81, coach, 1981—; guard Phoenix Suns, NBA, 1975-76; broadcaster Los Angeles Lakers games Sta. KLAC and Sta. KHJ-TV, Los Angeles, 1977-79; player NBA Championship Team, 1972, coach, 1982, 85, 87. Office: care Los Angeles Lakers PO Box 10 Inglewood CA 90306 *

RIMOIN, DAVID LAWRENCE, physician, pediatrician, geneticist; b. Montreal, Que., Can., Nov. 9, 1936; s. Michael and Fay (Lecker) R.; m. Mary Ann Singleton, Sept. 9, 1962 (div. 1979); 1 dau., Anne; m. Ann Piilani Garber, July 27, 1980; children: Michael, Lauren. BSc, McGill U., Montreal, 1959, MSc, MD, CM, 1961; PhD, Johns Hopkins U., 1967. Asst. prof. medicine, pediatrics Washington U., St. Louis, 1967-70; assoc. prof. medicine, pediatrics UCLA, 1970-73, prof., 1973—, chief med. genetics, Harbor-UCLA Med. Ctr., 1970-86; dir. dept. pediatrics, dir. Med. Genetics and Birth Defects Ctr., Cedars Sinai Med. Ctr., 1986—. Co-author: Principles and Practice in Medical Genetics, 1983; contbr. articles to profl. jours., chpts. to books. Recipient Ross Outstanding Young Investigator award Western Soc. Pediatric Research, 1976, E. Mead Johnson award Am. Acad. Pediatrics, 1976. Fellow ACP; mem. Am. Fedn. Clin. Research (sec./treas. 1972-75), Western Soc. Clin. Research (pres. 1978), Am. Bd. Med. Genetics (pres. 1979-83), Am. Soc. Human Genetics (pres. 1984), Am. Pediatric Soc., Soc. Pediatric Research, Am. Soc. Clin. Investigator, Assn. Am. Physicians. Home: 512 N Palm Dr Beverly Hills CA 90210 Office: UCLA Cedars Sinai Med Ctr 8700 Beverly Blvd Los Angeles CA 90048

RINDE, JOSEPH, marketing professional; b. Paris, Mar. 24, 1947; came to U.S., 1952; s. Maurice and Stella (Klein) R.; m. Sheila Lesley Levin, July 2, 1981; 1 child, David Abraham. BS with high honors, Stevens Inst. Tech., 1968; MS in Computer Sci., Carnegie Mellon U., 1972. Math. programmer Lawrence Livermore (Calif.) Lab., 1972-73; mgr. network architecture Tymshare, Cupertino, Calif., 1974-83; dir. future products Communications div. Amdahl, Marina del Rey, Calif., 1983-85; dir. product planning Equatorial Communications Co., Mountain View, Calif., 1985—. V.p. Congregation Am Echad, San Jose, Calif., 1981. Mem. Assn. Computing Machinery. Republican. Jewish. Avocations: skiing, photography. Home: 3725 Ortega Ct Palo Alto CA 94303 Office: Equatorial Communications Co 300 Ferguson Dr Mountain View CA 94043

RINDERKNECHT, HEINRICH, biochemist; b. Zurich, Switzerland, Jan. 21, 1913; came to U.S., 1949; s. Heinrich and Pauline (Rebmann) R.; m. Peggy Wark, Aug. 26, 1939; children: Margaret Rinderknecht de Beixedon, H. Robin, John. F., Y. Susan. MS, Swiss Fed. Inst. Tech., Zurich, 1936; PhD, U. London, 1939, DSc, 1980. Research chemist Roche Products, Ltd., Welwyn Garden City, Eng., 1939-46; assoc. dir. research Aligena Co., Basel, Switzerland, 1946-49; research fellow Calif. Inst. Tech., Pasadena, Calif., 1949-54, sr. research fellow, 1963-71; dir. organic research The Crookes Labs., London, 1954-55; dir. research and devel. Calbiochem, Inc., Los Angeles, 1955-62; assoc. prof. medicine U. So. Calif., Los Angeles, 1964-70, prof., 1970-85; chief, med. biochemistry VA Med. Ctr., Sepulveda, Calif., 1970-85; cons. Geigy Co., Basel, 1955-57, Stuart Pharm. Co., Pasadena, 1959-61. Co-author: The Exocrine Pancreas, 1985; mem. editorial com. Internat. Jour. Pancreatology; contbr. over 150 articles to profl. jours.; holder 24 patents. Served to 1st lt. cav. Swiss Army, 1939. Fellow Royal Soc. Health; AAAS, Swiss Biochem. Soc., British Biochem. Soc., Internat. Assn. Pancreatology, Am. Pancreatic Soc., Am. Fedn. Clin. Research, N.Y. Acad. Scis., Sigma Xi. Avocations: gardening, writing children's mystery stories, travel. Home: 1971 Cielito Ln Santa Barbara CA 93105

RINEARSON, PETER MARK, journalist, author; b. Seattle, Aug. 4, 1954; s. Peter Morley and Jeannette Irene (Love) R. Student, U. Wash., 1972-78, 87. Editor Sammamish Valley News, Redmond, Wash., 1975-76; reporter Seattle Times, 1976-78, govt. and politics reporter, 1979-81, aerospace reporter, 1982-84, Asian corr., 1985-86. Author: Word Processing Power with Microsoft Word, 2d edit., 1986, Microsoft Word Style Sheets, 1987. Recipient Spl. Paul Myhre award-series Penney-Mo. Newspaper Awards, 1983, Disting. Writing award Am. Soc. Newspaper Editors, 1984, Pulitzer prize for feature writing, 1984, Lowell Thomas travel writing award, 1984, John Hancock award,1985, semi-finalist NASA Journalist-in-Space Project, 1986. Office: Seattle Times PO Box 70 Seattle WA 98111

RINEHART, DONALD RAYMOND, psychotherapist; b. Bellingham, Wash., Dec. 14, 1926; s. Jack Edgar and Cecil Kathleen (Stenger) R.; m. Delores Overdorff, June 21, 1952 (div. Mar. 1976); children: Sarah K., Michelle; m. Paula Panting, July 9, 1982. BA, U. Wash., 1951, MSW, 1956; PhD, Columbia Pacific U., 1983. Reg. clin. social worker. Counselor Wash. State Reformatory, Monroe, 1952-54; dir. intake and counseling King County Juvenile Ct., Seattle, 1956-60; dir. tng., probation and parole Wash. State Probation and Parole Div., Seattle, 1960-62; dir. Lane County Youth Project, Eugene, Oreg., 1962-67; assoc. prof. Portland (Oreg.) State U., 1963—, U. Oreg., Eugene, 1963—; pvt. practice counseling, psychotherapy Salem, Oreg., 1974—; dir. Juvenile Court Summer Sessions U. Oreg., Eugene, 1963-67; advisor Joint Commn. on Correctional Manpower and Tng., Washington, 1970-71. Contbr. articles to profl. jours. Mem. profl. devel. com. Western Correctional Assn., San Jose, Calif., 1969-71; chmn., vice chmn., hospitality and program coms. and planning commn. Nat. Inst. on Crime and Delinquency, 1962-72. Mem. Oreg. Psychol. Assn., Nat. Assn. and Acad. Cert. Social Workers, Jaycees, Sigma Nu (pres. pledge com. council). Office: Security Bldg Suite 142 161 High St SE Salem OR 97301

RINEHART, NERL DAVID, design and engineering company executive; b. Bakersfield, Calif., Jan. 26, 1941; s. Nerl Delbert and Dorothy Lorraine (Bennett) R.; m. Beverly June Smith, Aug. 3, 1979; children—Michael, James, David, Bill, Jeff. A.A., Solano Coll., 1969. Lab. technologist Biol. Research Ctr., San Francisco, 1966-69; electrician St. Joseph's Hosp., Stockton, Calif., 1969-71; chief electrician Kern Valley Packing, Bakersfield,

Calif., 1971-73, Consol. Fiberglass Products, Bakersfield, 1973-74; chief electrician and instrumentation Camay, Sunmarine Drilling, Alaska, 1974-76, Sunland Refining Corp., Bakersfield, 1977-82, owner, pres., chief exec. officer design and engrng. Alpha Gauge and Instrumentation, Bakersfield, 1982—; instr. U.S. Navy and U.S. Navy Res., 1971-79. Patentee in field. Active Boy Scouts Am. Served to chief petty officer USN, 1959-66, Res., 1972—. Mem. Naval Reserve Assn. Am. Democrat. Lodge: Moose. Home: 206 Dogwood Ln Bakersfield CA 93308 Office: Alpha Gauge & Instrumentation 3008 Antonio Ave Bakersfield CA 93308

RINER, REED DOUGLAS, anthropologist, researcher; b. Mentone, Ind., Dec. 22, 1941; s. Kenneth Alden and Yolande Kara (Bunker) R.; m. Beatrice M. von Rotz, Sept. 22, 1967; children: Andrea I., Nicole A., Urs Alden von Rotz. Student, Ind. U., 1959-62; BA in Art History, U. Colo., 1963, MA in Anthropology, 1971, PhD in Anthropology, 1977. Teaching assoc. Undergrad. Pre-Service Tchr. Edn. Program, U. Colo., Boulder, 1971-75; from instr. to assoc. prof. anthropology No. Ariz. U., 1975—; bd. dirs. CONTACT: Cultures of the Imagination, Inc., Capitola, Calif.; cons. Ariz. Town Hall, Ariz. Acad.; cons., lectr. Ariz. Humanities Consortium. Editor: Cultural Futures Research, 1982—; contbr. articles to profl. jours. Served with USNR, 1964-67. Fellow Soc. Applied Anthropology; mem. High Plains Soc. Applied Anthropology (pres. 1983-84), Am. Anthrop. Assn., Nat. Assn. Practicing Anthropologists, World Future Soc., World Future Studies Fedn., Internat. Union Anthrop. and Ethnol. Scis. Lodge: Masons. Home: 506 Charles Rd Flagstaff AZ 86001 Office: No Ariz U Dept Anthropology Box 15200 Flagstaff AZ 86011

RING, BARBARA ANN, management consultant; b. St. Louis, Mar. 7, 1945; d. Oliver C. and Ann (McCarron) Garleb; AA in Nursing, El Camino Coll., 1964; BA, UCLA, 1967; JDUCLA, 1971; BS in Mgmt., Pacific Christian Coll., 1976, MBA Am. Nat. U., 1982. m. Douglas Ralph Ring; 1 son, Michael Francis. With Harbor Gen. Hosp., Torrance, Calif., 1964-66, Gardena Meml. Hosp., 1967-68, UCLA Med. Center, 1969-70, Brotman Meml. Hosp., Culver City, 1971-73; cardiac specialist Calif. Hosp. Med. Center, Los Angeles, 1974-77; asst. dir. nurses Fountain Valley Community Hosp. (Calif.), 1978-79; cons. Upjohn Health Care Services, 1980-84; mgmt. cons. Ind. Contractor . Youth camp dir. YMCA, also caravan dir. Bank Am. scholar, 1962; Westmont Coll. scholar, 1962. Mem. Am. Mgmt. Assn., Nat. Assn. Female Execs., Critical Care Nurses Assn. NOW, ACLU, Christian Bus. Women's Fellowship. Club: Soroptimist.

RINGER, THOMAS LATTA, executive management consultant; b. Lafayette, Ind., June 8, 1931; s. Alfred Victor and Dorothy (Slabaugh) R.; m. Juanita Louise Barwick, June 6, 1954; children: Daniel W., Richard A. BS, Ind. U., 1954, MBA, 1958; postgrad., U. So. Calif., 1961-62. CPA. Mktg. rep. IBM, Los Angeles, 1958-61, 62-65; mgr. mktg. IBM, Santa Monica, Calif., 1965; mgr. market evaluation IBM, Harrison, N.Y., 1966-67; mgr. fin. planning IBM Data Processing, Harrison, N.Y., 1967; v.p. fin. and adminstrn. Gene B. Glick Co., Indpls., 1967-69; v.p. mktg. Xerox Computer Services, Los Angeles, 1969-71; v.p. mktg. and domestic ops. Computer Machinery Corp., Los Angeles, 1971, pres., chief exec. officer, 1972-75; pvt. practice cons. fin. and mgmt. Los Angeles, 1975-81; pres., chief exec. officer TRW-Fujitsu Co., Los Angeles, 1982-83, Fujitsu Systems of Am., Inc., Los Angeles, 1983-84; mgmt. cons. Thomas L. Ringer & Assocs., Los Angeles, 1984—; asst. prof. Calif. State U., Northridge, 1961-62; bd. dirs. Wedbush, Noble, Cooke, Inc., 1981—, Recognition Equipment Inc., The Del Mar Group, Inc., Computer Machinery Corp., Fujitsu Systems Am., Inc., So. Calif. Tech. Exec. Network; chmn. Wedbush Corp., 1981—. Active Malibu Lagoon Mus.; active Malibu Township Council; Served to 1st lt. U.S. Army, 1955-57. Mem. Computer and Communications Industry Assn. (bd. dirs. 1973), Am. Electronics Assn. (bd. dirs. 1973-74), Ind. Soc. CPA's., Univ. Athletic Club, Crest Club of Pepperdine U. Republican. Presbyterian. Avocations: reading, traveling, automobiles. Home: 3520 Cross Creek Ln Malibu CA 90265 Office: Thomas L Ringer & Assocs 22837 Pacific Coast Hwy Suite F PO Box 785 Malibu CA 90265

RINGERT, WILLIAM FREDERICK, lawyer, state senator; b. Castleford, Idaho, June 1, 1932; s. Frederick William and Elizabeth (Knypstra) R.; m. Lynne Bing Kutchback, Mar. 20, 1959; children—John Franklin, Beth Anne. B.S. in Agronomy, U. Idaho, 1953; postgrad. San Angelo (Tex.) Coll., 1955; LL.B., So. Meth. U., Dallas, 1962. Bar: Idaho 1962, U.S. Dist. Ct. Idaho, 1962, U.S. Ct. Appeals (9th cir.) 1978, U.S. Supreme Ct. 1979. Flight engr. Braniff Internat. Airways, Dallas, 1956-62; ptnr. Ringert, Clark, Harrington, Reid, Christenson & Kaufman, Ltd., Boise, 1962—; sec., dir. Farm Devel. Corp., Boise, 1964—, Grindstone Butte Mut. Canal Co., Boise, 1972—; pres., dir. B & B Farms, Inc., Boise, 1973—; mem. Idaho Senate, 1982—; commr. Idaho State Building Authority, 1985—. Served to 1st lt. USAF, 1953-56. Mem. ABA (vice chmn. agrl. law com. gen. practice sect. 1979—), Idaho Bar Assn., Delta Theta Phi. Republican. Methodist. Club: Crane Creek Country (Boise). Lodge: Elks. Office: 599 W Bannock St Boise ID 83702

RINKENBERGER, RICHARD KRUG, geological consultant; b. Gridley, Ill., May 15, 1933; s. Burl E. and Olive J. (Krug) R.; divorced; children; Janice L., Ginger R., Rebekah P.; m. Ida Lee Vaughn, Mar. 22, 1985; children: Douglas W., Angela D. BA in Geology, U. Colo., 1959. Dir. prospecting Grubstake Assn., Sask., Can., 1958-59; engr. Martin-Marietta Aerospace Co., Denver, 1960-75; geologist U.S. Geol. Survey, Denver, 1975; geologist remote sensing U.S. Mine Safety and Health Adminstrn., Denver, 1975-79; pres., exploration geologist Banner Set, Ltd., Denver, 1980-84; pres., cons. geologist R.K. Rinkenberger & Assocs., Aurora, Colo., 1979—; educator prospecting Denver Sch. Prospecting, 1968-71, U. Colo, Denver, Boulder, 1970-75; research geochemist Heritage Chem. Co., Englewood, 1984-85; prospecting researcher R.K. Rinkenberger & Assocs., Aurora, 1979—. Contbr. articles to profl. jours. Mem. parent adv. bd, supt. of schs. Westminster, Colo., 1982-83. Recipient High Quality Performance award U.S. Mine Safety and Health Dept., 1977; grantee U.S. Geol. Survey, 1978. Mem. Am. Soc. Photogrammetry and Remote Sensing, Assn. Exploration Geochemists, Sigma Gamma Epsilon. Republican. Mem. Ch. Nazarene. Avocations: cross country skiing, geol. theory research. Home: 3170 S Pitkin St Aurora CO 80013 Office: PO Box 441473 Aurora CO 80044

RIORDAN, MICHAEL JAMES, banker; b. San Francisco, June 16, 1940; s. James Jerome and Helen (Dolan) R.; m. Judith Elaine Darville, Aug. 24, 1961 (div. 1981); children—Paul, Patrick, Stephen. B.S. in Mgmt., No. Ariz. U., 1966; post-grad. Pacific Coast Banking Sch., U. Wash., 1977-79. Asst. cashier 1st Interstate Bank, Santa Ana, Calif., 1966-71; sr. v.p. Ariz. Bank, Phoenix, 1971—. Bd. dirs. Valley Leadership, Phoenix, 1984—, Valley Forward Assn., Phoenix, 1981—, Goodwill Industries, Flagstaff, Ariz., 1973-76. Served with U.S. Army, 1959-61. Republican. Roman Catholic. Office: Ariz Bank Phoenix AZ 85002

RIPARBELLI, CARLO, aerospace engineer; b. Rome, Nov. 15, 1910; came to U.S., 1946, naturalized, 1953; s. Vittorio and Maria (Bernabei) R.; m. Ellen Johnston Dennis, Dec. 20, 1958. DCE, U. Rome, 1933, Dr. Aero Engring., 1934, Libero Docente Costruzioni Aeronautiche, 1940. Research asst. DSSE, Guidonia, Italy, 1937-41; chief designer Aeroplani Caproni, Milan, Italy, 1941-43; research assoc. Princeton (N.J.) U., 1947-48; design specialist Convair, San Diego, 1955-59; design specialist Gen. Atomics div. Gen. Dynamics Corp., San Diego, 1959, mem. research and devel. staff, 1960-65; engring. staff specialist Gen. Dynamics Corp., Pomona, Calif., 1965-72; engring. cons. Aerospace Corp., El Segundo, Calif., 1973-80, Sci. Applications, Inc., La Jolla, Calif., 1973-86; asst. prof. aero. structures U. Rome, 1937-41, Poly. of Milan, 1941-42, asst. prof. Cornell U. Grad. Sch. Aero. Engring., 1949-51; assoc. prof., 1951-55; lectr. U. Calif. San Diego, 1960, 63; cons. Cornell Aero. Lab., Buffalo, 1951, Aeronautica Macchi, Varese, Italy, 1949-55, Bur. Ships, Dept. Navy, 1953-55; participant Allied Govts. Aero. Research devel. meeting in Copenhagen, 1958. Contbr. articles to profl. jours.; patentee in field. Served to capt. Italian Air Force, 1936-45, permanent officer, 1938-48. Italo-Am. Com. scholar Princeton U., 1946-47. Fellow AIAA (assoc.); mem. Soc. for Exptl. Stress Analysis, Associazione Italiana di Aeronautica e Astronautica, Inst., Aero Scis. (chmn. com. for sci. meetings San Diego chpt. 1960-61, chmn. programs 1961-62), Sigma Xi. Home and Office: 4429 Arista Dr San Diego CA 92103

RIPINSKY-NAXON, MICHAEL, archaeologist, art historian; b. Kutaisi, USSR, Mar. 23, 1944; s. Pinkus and Maria (Kokielov) R.; div.; 1 son, Tariel. A.B. in Anthropology with honors, U. Calif.-Berkeley, 1966, Ph.D. in Archeology and Art History, 1979. Research asst. Am. Mus. Natural History, N.Y.C., 1964, U. Calif.-Berkeley, 1964-66; mem. faculty dept. anthropology and geography of Near East, Calif. State U.-Hayward, 1966-67; asst. prof. Calif. State U.-Northridge, 1974-75; researcher, assoc. UCLA, 1974-75, sr. research anthropologist Hebrew U., Hadassah Med. Sch., Jerusalem, 1970-71; curator Anthropos Gallery of Ancient Art, Beverly Hills, Calif., 1976-78; chief research scientist Archaeometric Data Labs., Beverly Hills, 1976-78; dir. Ancient Artworld Corp., Beverly Hills, 1979-82; conducted excavations Israel, Egypt, Jordan, Mesopotamia, Mexico, Cen. Am; specialist in phenomenon of origins of domestication and camel ancestry; expert on art works from French Impressionists to ancient Egypt and classical world. Contbr. articles to sci. and scholarly jours. Recipient Cert. of Merit for Sci. Endeavour, Dictionary of Internat. Biography, 1974. Mem. Archaeol. Inst. Am. (life), Soc. for Am. Archaeology, Israel Exploration Soc., Am. Anthropol. Assn., Royal Anthropol. Inst., Am. Oriental Soc., Am. Geog. soc., Am. Ethnol. Soc., History of Sci. Soc., Ancient Art Council of Los Angeles County Museum of Art, Am. Chem. Soc., Soc. Archeol. Scis. (life), New England Appraisers Assns. Home: 5315 Zelzah Ave Encino CA 91316

RIPLEY, BRITT JUHLIN, architect; b. Salt Lake City, Sept. 7, 1948; s. Robert Lawrence and Lillian (Juhlin) R.; m. Rosanne Love, June 4, 1971; children—Telacia, Treg, Tys, Tristin. B.Arch., U. Ariz., 1973; M.Arch. Ariz. State U., 1976. Registered architect, Ariz. Draftsman Wadsworth and Jensen, Phoenix, 1973-75; project dir. Alan Turley & Assocs., Mesa, Ariz., 1976-79; owner, prin. Ripley Architects, Mesa, 1979—; instr. solar energy archtl. drawing Mesa Community Coll., 1976—. Evaluation chmn. Mesa Uniform Building Code, 1981; participant leadership and tng. City of Mesa, 1983—; campaign officer Mesa Republican Com., 1983. Recipient best new constrn. award Mesa C. of C., 1980, best remodel award, 1983; best office building award Tempe C. of C., 1978. Mem. AIA, Internat. Solar Energy Assn., Ariz. Solar Energy Soc. Republican. Mem. Ch. of Jesus Christ of Latter-day Saints. Club: Exchange (Mesa) (pres. 1981-82). Office: 606 N Stapley Mesa AZ 85203

RIPLEY, ROBERT KENYON, industrial management consultant; b. Spokane, Wash., May 27, 1927; s. Sherwood Lyman and Hazel Elaine (Rue) R.; m. Martha Van Patten, June 4, 1949; children—Robert Kenyon, Alfred V. P., Martha Lynne. B.S., U.S. Naval Acad., 1949; M.A., Stanford U., 1959. Announcer Stas. KGEZ and KGHL, Mont., 1942-44; commd. ensign U.S. Navy, 1949, advanced through grades to capt., 1969; Commdg. officer USS Chittenden County, 1956-58, USS Weiss, 1962-64, USS Comstock, 1969-70; Pentagon duty officer, 1961-63, 70-74, 76-77; with Joint Chiefs of Staff, 1965-68; with Navy Material Command, 1977-79; ret., 1979; sr. assoc. Maxfield Assocs. Ltd., Falls Church, Va., 1979-81, Missoula, Mont., 1981-86. Contbr. articles to Naval Inst. Procs., 1952—. Democratic candidate for U.S. Senate from Mont., 1984. Decorated Legion of Merit, Navy Commendation medal, Navy Meritorious Service medal. Mem. AIAA, Internat. Hydrofoil Soc. (bd. dirs. N.Am. chpt. 1979-82, 83-85), U.S. Naval Acad. Alumni, Am. Legion, VFW. Lodge: Rotary. Home: 1709 Cyprus Ct Missoula MT 59801

RIPLEY, STUART MCKINNON, real estate cons.; b. St. Louis, July 28, 1930; s. Rob Roy and Nina Pearl (Young) R.; B.A., U. Redlands, 1952; M.B.A., U. Calif., Berkeley, 1959; m. Marilyn Haerr MacDiarmid, Dec. 28, 1964; children—Jill, Bruce, Kent. Vice pres., dir. J.H. Hedrick & Co., Santa Barbara and San Diego, 1958-63; v.p. mktg. Cavanaugh Devel. Co., San Gabriel, Calif., 1963-65; v.p. mktg. dir. Calabasas Park, Bechtel Corp., Calabasas, Calif., 1967-69; v.p. mktg. Avco Community Developers, Inc., La Jolla, Calif., 1969-74; mktg. dir. U.S. Home Corp., Fla. Div., Clearwater, 1974-75; pres., dir. Howard's Camper Country, Inc., National City, Calif., 1975-77; v.p., mktg. dir. Valcas Internat. Corp., San Diego, 1976-77, pres., 1977-79; pres. Stuart M. Ripley, Inc., 1977—, Sunview Realty, Inc., a Watt Industries Co., Santa Monica, Calif., 1979-80; owner Everett Stunz Co., Ltd., La Jolla, 1981—; exec. v.p. Harriman-Ripley Co., Fallbrook, Calif.; avocado rancher, Fallbrook, 1978—; lectr. UCLA, 1961. Served with USN, 1952-55. U. Redlands fellow, 1960—. Mem. Nat. Assn. Homebuilders, Sales and Mktg. Council, Sales and Mktg. Execs., Pi Chi. Republican. Episcopalian. Club: Elks. Home: 13180 Portofino Dr Del Mar CA 92014 Office: 7644 Girard Ave La Jolla CA 92037

RIPLEY, THERESA MARGARET, academic administrator; b. Pontiac, Ill., Sept. 24, 1944; s. William Raymond and Blanche Margaret (Phillips) R. BS, Ill. State U., 1966; MS, Ind. U., 1968; PhD, U. Oreg., 1971. Program coordinator U. Portland, Oreg., 1968-69; mem. faculty U. Oreg., Eugene, 1972—, coordinator career planning, 1972-86; pres. New Directions, Eugene, Oreg., 1980—. Co-author: This Isn't Quite What I Had in Mind, 1974, Career & Life Planning Guide, 1976, Helping Others Help Themselves, 1979. NDEA fellow, 1971; Fulbright grantee, 1979. Mem. Am. Assn. Counseling and Devel., Nat. Career Devel. Assn. Avocation: traveling. Home: PO Box 5441 Eugene OR 97405 Office: U Oreg Dept Counseling Eugene OR 97403

RIPPER, RITA JO (JODY), financial executive; b. Clarion, Iowa, May 8, 1950; d. Carl Phillip and Lucille Mae (Stewart) Ripper; B.A., U. Iowa, 1972; M.B.A., N.Y.U., 1978. Contracts and fin. staff Control Data Corp., Mpls., 1974-78; regional mgr. Raytheon Corp., Irvine, Calif., 1978-83; v.p. Caljo Corp., Des Moines, Iowa, 1983-84; asst. v.p. Bank of America, San Francisco, 1984—. Vol. and alt. del. Republican Party, Edina, Minn., N.Y.C., 1975—; vol. Cancer, Heart, Lung Assns., Edina, N.Y.C., Calif., 1974-78, 84—; Lita, 1986—. Mem. Internat. Mktg. Assn., World Trade Ctr. Assn., Acctg. Soc. (pres. 1975-76), Mensa, Beta Alpha Psi (chmn. 1977-78), Phi Gamma Nu (v.p. 1971-72) Presbyterian. Clubs: Corinthian Yacht, Engrs., Mt. Tam Racquet. Home: 22 Marinero Circle #46 Tiburon CA 94920 Office: Bank of America 2 Embarcadero Ctr San Francisco CA 94111

RIRIE, CRAIG MARTIN, periodontist; b. Lewiston, Utah, Apr. 17, 1943; s. Martin Clarence and VaLera (Dixon) R.; m. Becky Ann Ririe, Sept. 17, 1982; children: Paige, Seth, Theron, Kendall, Nathan, Derek, Brian, Amber, Kristen. AA, San Bernadino Valley Coll., 1966; DDS, Creighton U., 1972; MSD, Loma Linda U., 1978. Staff mem. Flagstaff (Ariz.) Med. Ctr., 1974—; pvt. practice dentistry specializing in periodontics Flagstaff, 1974—; assoc. prof. periodontics No. Ariz. U., Flagstaff, 1979—, chmn. dept. dental hygiene, 1980-81; med. research cons. W.L. Gore, Flagstaff, 1983—. Contbr. articles to profl. jours. Health professions scholarship Creighton U., Omaha, 1969-71; recipient Mosby award Mosby Pub. Co., 1972; research fellowship U. Bergen, Norway, 1978-79. Mem. ADA, Am. Acad. Periodontology (cert.), Western Soc. Periodontology (chmn. com. on research 1982—, bd. dirs. 1983—), No. Ariz. Dental Soc., Am. Acad. Oral Implantologists, Internat. Congress Oral Implantologists, Ariz. Dental Assn. Republican. Mormon. Lodge: Rotary. Avocations: skiing, tennis, golf. Home: 1320 N Aztec Flagstaff AZ 86001 Office: 1421 N Beaver Flagstaff AZ 86001

RISCH, JAMES E., state senator, lawyer; b. Milw., May 3, 1943; s. Elroy A. and Helen B. (Levi) R.; m. Vicki L. Choborda, June 8, 1968; children—James E., Jason S., Jordan D. B.S. in Forestry, U. Idaho, 1965, J.D., 1968. Dep. pros. atty. Ada County, Idaho, 1968-69, chief dep. pros. atty., 1969-70, pros. atty., 1971-75; mem. Idaho Senate, 1974—, majority leader, 1977-82, pres. pro tem, 1983—; ptnr. Risch Goss, Insinger & Salladay, Boise, Idaho, 1975—; prof. law Boise State U., 1972-75. Mem. ABA, Idaho Bar Assn., Boise Bar Assn., Am. Judicature Soc., Nat. Dist. Attys. Assn. (bd. dirs. 1977), Idaho Pros. Attys. Assn. (pres. 1976), Phi Delta Theta, Xi Sigma Pi. Republican. Roman Catholic. Avocations: hunting; fishing; skiing; horseback riding; tennis. Home: 5400 S Cole Rd Boise ID 83709 Office: Risch Goss Insinger & Salladay 407 W Jefferson Boise ID 83702

RISKAS, HARRY JAMES, constrn. co. exec.; b. Shelton, Wis., Mar. 27, 1920; s. James and Anna (Pappeoanou) R.; student St. Mary's Naval Coll., 1941-43; m. Joan Evelyn Clark, Aug. 1, 1964; children—Lawrence, Douglas, Kimberly. Pres., Pacific Western Contractors, Inc., Millbrae, Cal., from 1951; pres., dir. Riskas Baker Riskas Devel. Corp., San Luis Properties, Inc.; pres., chmn. bd. Pacific Western Contractors, Inc., Sanfo-Bay Corp., H.J.R. Developers, Inc., Windrock Corp. Dir., Am. Pro- perties, & Investment Fund, 1970. Served to lt. comdr. USNR, 1942-46. Mem. Young Pres.'s Orgn. Clubs: Bankers, K.C. (San Francisco). Home: 2020 Fairmont Dr San Mateo CA 94402 Office: 1103 Juanita Suite B Burlingame CA 94010

RISLEY, TODD ROBERT, educator, scientist; b. Palmer, Alaska, Sept. 8, 1937; s. Robert and Eva Lou (Todd) R.; 1 child, Todd Michael. A.B. with distinction in Psychology, San Diego State Coll., 1960; M.S., U. Wash., 1963, Ph.D., 1966. Asst. prof. psychology Fla. State U., Tallahassee, 1964-65; research assoc. Bur. Child Research, U. Kans., Lawrence, 1965-77, sr. scientist, 1977—, asst. prof. dept. human devel., 1967-69, assoc. prof., 1969-73, prof., 1973-84; prof. psychology U. Alaska, Anchorage, 1982—; pres. Ctr. for Applied Behavior Analysis, 1970—; dir. Lawrence Day Care Program, 1970—, Johnny Cake Child Study Ctr., Mansfield, Ark., 1973-74; vis. prof. U. Auckland (N.Z.), 1978; acting dir. Western Carolina Ctr., Morgantown, N.C., 1981; cons. in field to numerous orgns. and instns. Editor: Jour. Applied Behavior Analysis, 1971-74, mem. editorial bd., 1967-70, 76-79, Jour. Exptl. Child Psychology, 1969-71, Behaviorism: A Forum for Critical Discussion, 1971—, Jour. Personalized Instruction, 1975—, Jour. Organizational Behavior Mgmt., 1977—, Jour. Applied Research in Mental Retardation, 1979—, Edn. and Treatment of Children, 1979—, Behavior Modification, 1980—, Analysis and Intervention in Developmental Disabilities, 1980—; contbr. revs. and numerous articles to profl. jours.; adv. editor: Advances in Child Clin. Psychology, 1976—; mng. editor: Behavior Therapy, The Behavior Therapist, Behavioral Assessment, 1977-80; co-author: The Infant Center, 1977, Shopping With Children: Advice for Parents, 1978—, The Toddler Center, 1979; contbr. chpts. to books. Co-chmn. Fla. task force on use of behavioral procedures in state programs for retarded, 1974—; mem. resident abuse investigating com. div. retardation Fla. Dept. Health and Rehab. Services, 1972—; mem. adv. com. Social Research Inst., U. Utah, 1977—; mem. Alaska Gov.'s Council on Handicapped and Gifted, 1983—. Grantee NIMH, 1971-72, 72-73; research grantee Nat. Ctr. Health Services, 1976-79; grantee Nat. Inst. Edn., 1973, NIH, 1967—. Fellow Am. Psychol. Assn. (council of reps. 1982-85); mem. AAAS, Am. Assn. Mental Deficiency, Assn. Advancement of Behavior Therapy (dir. 1975-80, pres. 1976-77, chmn. profl. rev. com. 1977—, series editor Readings in Behavior Therapy 1977—), Soc. Behavioral Medicine, Assn. Behavior Analysis, Sigma Xi. Office: U Alaska Dept Psychology Anchorage AK 99508

RISSE, GUENTER BERNHARD, physician, historian, educator; b. Buenos Aires, Argentina, Apr. 28, 1932; s. Francisco B. and Kaete A. R.; m. Alexandra G. Paradzinski, Oct. 14, 1961; children—Heidi, Monica, Alisa. M.D., U. Buenos Aires, 1958; Ph.D., U. Chgo., 1971. Intern Mercy Hosp., Buffalo, 1958-59; resident in medicine Henry Ford Hosp., Detroit, 1960-61, Mt. Carmel Hosp., Columbus, Ohio, 1962-63; asst. dept. medicine U. Chgo., 1963-67; asst. prof. dept. history of medicine U. Minn., 1969-71; asso. prof. dept. history of medicine and dept. history of sci. U. Wis., Madison, 1971-76; prof. U. Wis., 1976-85, chmn. dept. history of medicine, 1971-77; prof., chmn. dept. history health scis. U. Calif., San Francisco, 1985—; Mem. project com. Center for Photog. Images in Medicine and Health Care. Author: Paleopathology of Ancient Egypt, 1964; Hospital Life in Enlightenment Scotland, 1986; editor: Modern China and Traditional Chinese Medicine, 1973, History of Physiology, 1973, Medicine Without Doctors, 1977; mem. editorial bd.: Jour. History of Medicine, 1971-74, Clio Medica, 1973—, Bull. History of Medicine, 1980—. Served with Argentine Armed Forces, 1955. NIH grantee, 1971-73; NIH grantee, 1982-83; WHO grantee, 1979. Mem. Am. Assn. History of Medicine (pres.), History Sci. Soc., Soc. Health and Human Values, Internat. Acad. History Medicine (v.p.), Deutsche Gesellschaft fur Geschichte der Medizin, Internat. Soc. History Medicine, AAAS, Am. Soc. Eighteenth-Century Studies, Mexican Soc. History and Philosophy of Medicine, Peruvian Assn. Med. Ethnology and History, Brit. Soc. for Social History of Medicine, Argentine Ateneo de Historia de la Medicina., Deutsche Gesell. Wissenschaftsgeschichte. Home: 600 Noriega St San Francisco CA 94122 Office: Univ Calif Dept History Health Scis Box 0726 San Francisco CA 94143

RISSER, JAMES CONRAD, philosphy educator; b. Allentown, Pa., Aug. 23, 1946; s. Jay Hershey and Kathryn Mary (Raup) R.; m. Jean T. Austin, May 13, 1972; children: Elizabeth, Jonathon. BA, Calif. State U., Long Beach, 1971; MA, Duquesne U., 1973, PhD, 1978. Instr. philosophy La Roche Coll., Pitts., 1974-77; asst. prof. Villanova (Pa.) U., 1978-79; assoc. prof. Seattle U., 1979—. Contbr. articles to profl. jours. Recipient Faculty Fellowship award Seattle U., 1983, 85. Mem. Internat. Assn. Philosphy and Lit., Am. Philos. Assn., Northwest Soc. Phenomenology Existentialism and Hermeneutics (sec. 1981—). Home: 1840 N 177th St Seattle WA 98133 Office: Seattle U 12th and Columbia Seattle WA 98122

RISSER, JAMES VAULX, JR., journalist, educator; b. Lincoln, Nebr., May 8, 1938; s. James Vaulx and Ella Caroline (Schacht) R.; m. Sandra Elizabeth Laaker, June 10, 1961; children: David James, John Daniel. B.A., U. Nebr., 1959, cert. in journalism, 1964; J.D., U. San Francisco, 1962. Bar: Nebr. bar 1962. With firm Perry, Perry, Witthoff & Guthery, Lincoln, 1962-64; reporter Des Moines Register and Tribune, 1964-85, Washington corr., 1969-85, bur. chief, 1976-85; dir. John S. Knight fellowships for profl. journalists, prof. communication Stanford U., 1985—; lectr. Wells Coll., 1981; mem. com. on agrl. edn. in secondary schs. Nat. Acad. Scis., 1985-86. Profl. Journalism fellow Stanford U., 1973-74; recipient award for disting. reporting public affairs Am. Polit. Sci. Assn., 1969; Thomas L. Stokes award for environ. reporting Washington Journalism Center, 1971, 79; Pulitzer prize for nat. reporting, 1976, 79; Worth Bingham Found. prize for investigative reporting, 1976; Raymond Clapper Meml. Assn. award for Washington reporting, 1976, 78; Edward J. Meeman award for Conservation Reporting, 1985. Mem. Nebr. Bar Assn., Sigma Delta Chi (Disting. Service award 1976). Club: Gridiron. Home: 725 Evergreen St Menlo Park CA 94025 Office: Communication Dept Stanford Univ Stanford CA 94305

RISSO, GIORGIO, marketing professional; b. Lavagna, Italy, Nov. 14, 1939; came to U.S., 1984; s. Bartocomeo and Alma (Bertagnon) R.; m. Kerstin Krantz, Aug. 16, 1980; children: Ulrica, Damele. Student, In Memoria dei Mortici per la Patria, Chiavari, Italy, 1955-59, Geneva U., Switzerland, 1959-63. Mgr. sales Olivetti SpA, Paris, 1965-69; mgr. sales and mktg. Ferrero Suandlinavie, Malmoe, Sweden, 1969-73; mgr. exports, mktg. SNIPS S.P.A., Lugand, Switzerland, 1973-76; mktg. mgr. Rimecuano SA, Lausanne, Switzerland, 1975-86; mgr. mktg. v.p. USA Products, Stockton, Calif., 1984—. Served to 2d lt. Italian Fantery Alpini, 1963-64. Avocations: skiing, tennis, photography. Home: 2153 Piccardo Circle Stockton CA 95207 Office: USA Products 83 W March Ln Stockton CA 95207

RISTOW, BRUNO VON BUETTNER, plastic surgeon; b. Brusque, Brazil, Oct. 18, 1940; came to U.S., 1967, naturalized, 1981; s. Arno and Ally Odette (von Buettner) R.; student Coll. Sinodal, Brazil, 1956-57, Coll. Julio de Castilhos, Brazil, 1957-58; M.D. magna cum laude, U. Brazil, 1966; m. Urania Carrasquilla Gutierrez, Nov. 10, 1979; children by previous marriage: Christian Kilian, Trevor Roland. Intern in surgery Hosp. dos Estrangeiros, Rio de Janeiro, Brazil, 1965, Hospital Estadual Miguel Couto, Brazil, 1965-66, Instituto Aposentadoria Pensão Comerciarios Hosp. for Gen. Surgery, 1966; resident in plastic and reconstructive surgery, Dr. Ivo Pitanguy Hosp. Santa Casa de Misericordia, Rio de Janeiro, 1967; fellow Inst. of Reconstructive Plastic Surgery, N.Y. U. Med. Center, N.Y.C., 1967-68, jr. resident, 1971-72, sr. and chief resident, 1972-73; practice medicine specializing in plastic surgery, Rio de Janeiro, 1967, N.Y.C., 1968-73, San Francisco, 1973—; asst. surgeon N.Y. Hosp., Cornell Med. Center, N.Y.C., 1968-71; clin. instr. surgery N.Y. U. Sch. of Medicine, 1972-73; chmn. plastic and reconstructive surgery div. Presbyn. Hosp., Pacific Med. Center, San Francisco, 1974—. Served with M.C., Brazilian Army Res., 1959-60. Decorated knight Venerable Order of St. Hubertus; Knight Order St. John of Jerusalem; fellow in surgery Cornell Med. Sch., 1968-71; diplomate Am. Bd. Plastic and Reconstructive Surgery. Fellow A.C.S., Internat. Coll. Surgeons; mem. Am. Soc. Aesthetic Plastic Surgery, Am. Soc. Plastic and Reconstructive Surgeons, Internat. Soc. Aesthetic Plastic Surgeons, Calif. Soc. Plastic Surgeons, AMA (Physician's Recognition award 1971-83), Calif. Med. Assn., San Francisco Med. Assn. Republican. Mem. Evang. Lutheran Ch. Club: San Francisco Olympic. Contbg. author: Cancer of the Hand, 1975; contbr. articles on plastic surgery to profl. publs. Office: Pacific Presbyn Profl Bldg 2100 Webster St Suite 502 San Francisco CA 94115

RITALA, KEITH EDWARD, physicist; b. Virginia, Minn., July 29, 1946; s. Robert Edward and Violet (Jalonen) R.; m. Janis Lee Pedlar, Dec. 30, 1972; children: Stacey Lynn, Kraig Edward. BA in Physics, Hamline U., 1968; MD in Physics, U. Oreg., 1970. Research geophysicist UCLA, 1971-73; devel. engr. Cominco Electronic Materials, Inc., Spokane, Wash., 1973-77, mgr. prodn., 1977-83, product mgr., 1983-86, mgr. research and devel., 1986—. Contbr. articles to profl. jours. Geographic feature in Antarctica, Ritala Spur, named in his honor, NSF. Mem. Am. Soc. Metals (treas. 1977-78, sec. 1978-79, vice chmn. 1979-80, chmn. 1980-81, Engr. of Yr. 1981). Unitarian. Avocations: skiing, volleyball, photography, zymology. Office: Cominco Electronic Materials Inc E 15128 Euclid Spokane WA 99216

RITCHEY, MICHAEL LEE, lawyer; b. Salem, Oreg., July 3, 1956; s. Roger Gulik and Leora Marjorie (Goodrich) R.; m. Connie Marie Earnest, Nov. 25, 1978; children: Joshua, Taylor. BA in History and Polit. Sci., U. Oreg., 1978; JD cum laude, Willamette U., 1983. Bar: Oreg. 1983. Legis. aide Oreg. Ho. of Reps., Salem, 1980-81; clk. Oreg. Ct. Appeals, Salem, 1983-85; assoc. Bricker, Zakovics & Querin, Portland, Oreg., 1985—. Pres. Mid-Valley Children's Guild, Salem, 1983-85. Mem. ABA, Am. Trial Lawyers Assn., Am. Judicature Soc. Democrat. Lutheran. Avocations: hiking, fishing, bicycling. Office: Bricker Zakovics & Querin 506 SW 6th Ave 1200 Wilcox Bldg Portland OR 97204

RITCHEY, SAMUEL DONLEY, JR., retail store executive; b. Derry Twp., Pa., July 16, 1933; s. Samuel Donley and Florence Catherine (Litsch) R.; m. Sharon Marie Anderson, Apr. 6, 1956; children: Michael Donley, Tamara Louise, Shawn Christopher. B.S., San Diego State U., 1955, M.S., 1963; postgrad. (Sloan Found. fellow), Stanford, 1964. Store mgr. supermarkets Lucky Stores Inc., San Diego and Phoenix, 1957-61; store supr. Gemco div. Lucky Stores Inc., 1965-66, dist. mgr., 1966-68, nonfood mdse. mgr. parent co., 1968-69, div. mgr., v.p. parent co., 1969-72; sr. v.p. Lucky Stores Inc., Dublin, Calif., 1972-75; exec. v.p. Lucky Stores Inc., 1975-78, pres., chief operating officer, 1978-80, pres., chief exec. officer, 1980-81, chmn., chief exec. officer, 1981-85, chmn. bd., 1981-86, also dir.; dir. Pacific Telesis, McClatchey Newspapers, York Internat. Corp., De La Salle Inst.; grad. mgr. San Diego State U., 1961-63; lectr. in field. Bd. dirs. Sloan Alumni Adv. Bd., Stanford U., Bay Area Council. Mem. Western Assn. Food Chains (dir.), Food Mktg. Inst. (dir., vice chmn. industry relations). Office: Lucky Stores Inc 6300 Clark Ave PO Box BB Dublin CA 94568

RITCHIE, FRAN A., interior designer; b. Seminole, Tex., Nov. 23, 1940; d. Homer C. and Margret A. (Simmons) Kyle; m. Byron D. Ritchie, Dec. 23, 1959. Grad. Seminole High School; interior design student LaSalle Extension U., Chgo., 1967. Designer and sales staff Miller-Waldrop Furniture, Hobbs, N.Mex., 1967—, mgr., buyer, 1976—; buyer, part-owner Eileen's Bed, Bath, and Kitchen, Hobbs, 1976—; co-owner Chapperal Racing Farm, 1985; leader seminars and high school programs on design. Recipient Woman of Yr. award Am. Bus. Women's Assn., 1970. Mem. Am. Soc. Interior Design (assoc.), Am. Bus. Women's Assn., Hobbs C. of C. (bd. dirs. 1983-86—, pres.-elect 1987), Beta Sigma Phi. Home: 620 Luna St Hobbs NM 88240 Office: 100 W Bender St Hobbs NM 88240

RITCHIE, JOHN BENNETT, commercial and industrial realtor; b. West Point, N.Y., Sept. 23, 1924; s. Isaac and Charlotte (Bennett) R.; B.A., Yale, 1946; postgrad. student George Washington U., 1946, U. Wash. Law Sch., 1948-50; m. Suzanne Raisin, Dec. 27, 1952; children—Randolph, Charlotte, Mark, Victoria. Pres. Ritchie & Ritchie Corp., indsl. and comml. realtors, San Francisco, Oakland, San Jose, Calif., Ritchie & Ritchie Ins. Brokers, Inc.; v.p. Cotton-Ritchie Corp., San Diego, Ritchie MacFarland Corp., Portland, Oreg.; owner, trustee Ritchie-Chancery Bldg., Barrett-Ritchie Block, Ritchie & Ritchie Devel. Co., Ritchie Western Mortgage Corp., Ritchie Western Devel. Co.; mem. exec. com. Am. Realty Services Group (nationwide), Colliers Internat. Property Cons. (worldwide). Past mem. San Francisco Planning Commn.; mem. San Francisco Landmarks Bd. Served with AUS. Mem. Soc. Indsl. Realtors, Calif. Real Estate Assn. (v.p. 1967), San Francisco (pres. 1966), Oakland, San Jose real estate bds., San Francisco C. of C., Calif. Hist. Soc. (pres. 1973, trustee), Japan Soc. San Francisco (pres. 1976). Republican. Mem. Ch. of Jesus Christ of Latter-day Saints (elder). Clubs: Concordia Argonaut (San Francisco); Athenian-Nile, Oakland Athletic (Oakland, Calif.); Alta (Salt Lake City); Brook (N.Y.); Caledonian (London); Outrigger Canoe (Honolulu). Home: 2 Presidio Terr San Francisco CA 94118 Home: 209 S Meadow Rd Glenbrook NV 89413 Office: 41 Sutter St San Francisco CA 94104 Also: 363 15th St Oakland CA 94612 Also: 99 N 1st St San Jose CA 95112 Also: 233 A St Suite 1400 San Diego CA 92101 Also: 133 SW 2d Ave Portland OR 97205

RITCHIE, ROBERT WELLS, computer scientist, researcher; b. Alameda, Calif., Sept. 21, 1935; s. W.Z. and Frances E. (Wells) R.; m. Audrey Lee Kelly, July 20, 1957; children: Scott Allen, Lynne Frances. BA, Reed Coll., 1957; MA, Princeton U., 1959, PhD, 1961. J.W. Young Research instr. math. Dartmouth Coll., Hanover, N.H., 1960-62; from asst. prof. to prof. math. and computer sci. U. Wash., Seattle, 1962-83, assoc. dean grad. sch., 1966-69, vice provost, 1969-72; mgr. computer sci. lab. Xerox PARC, Palo Alto, Calif., 1983—. Editor: New Directions in Mathematics, 1963. Mem. IEEE, AAAS, Computer Sci. Bd. (vice chmn. 1985—), Assn. Computing Machinery, Am. Math. Soc., Assn. Symbolic Logic, Sigma Xi, Phi Beta Kappa. Office: Xerox Palo Alto Research Ctr 3333 Coyote Hill Rd Palo Alto CA 94304

RITENOUR, ELSTON RUSSELL, medical physicist; b. Harrisonburg, Va., May 2, 1953; s. Elston Russell and Doris Belle (Spitzer) R.; m. Julia Rebecca Gilkeson, July 30, 1977; 1 child, Jason Alexander. Student, James Madison U., 1971-73; BA in Physics, U. Va., 1975, PhD in Physics, 1981. Research asst. U. Va., Charlottesville, 1977-80; postdoctoral fellow U. Colo. Sch. Medicine, Denver, 1980-82, instr. radiology, 1982-84, asst. prof., 1984—, dir. edn. for radiology, 1985—; cons. physicist Radiation Specialists Inc., Denver, 1981-85. Author: Health Effects of Low Level Radiation, 1983, Seminars in Nuclear Medicine, 1986; co-author: Computer Applications in Diagnostic Radiology, 1983, Magnetic Resonance Imaging; Physical Principles and Clinical Use, 1984, Radiation Protection for Student Radiographers, 1984, Radiation Protection for Dental Radiographers, 1984; contbr. articles to profl. jours. Recipient Research Service award Nat. Cancer Inst., 1980. Mem. Health Physics Soc. (pres. Cen. Rocky Mountain chpt. 1985-86), Am. Assn. Physicists in Medicine, Nat. Health Physics Soc. Avocations: skiing, racketball, microcomputer hardware, software design. Office: U Colo Sch Medicine Radiology C 278 4200 E 9th Ave Denver CO 80262

RITENOUR, JAMES KENNETH, hotel chain executive; b. Ft. Wayne, Ind., Feb. 13, 1931; s. Kenneth W. and Helen L. (Ricks) R.; m. Marilyn Miles, June 18, 1961 (dec. Aug. 1980); children: Michael J., David K. BS in Art and Econs., Purdue U., 1958; MA, Ariz. State U., 1971, PhD, 1983. Cert. purchasing mgr. Customer service mgr. Gen. Colorgraphics, Ft. Wayne, 1962-68; buyer Motorola, Phoenix, 1968-71; dir. purchasing Ramada Inn, Inc., Phoenix, 1971-81; dir. Best Western Internat., Phoenix, 1981—. Pres., bd. dirs. Assn. for Supportive Child Care, Phoenix, 1986; bd. dirs. Friends of Tempe (Ariz.) Library, 1983-86. Served to sgt. USAF, 1952-56. Mem. Nat. Assn. Purchasing Mgrs. Republican. Presbyterian. Lodge: Masons. Avocation: oil painting. Home: 2073 E Pebble Beach Tempe AZ 85282 Office: Best Western Internat 6201 N 24th Pkwy Phoenix AZ 85016

RITTENHOUSE, CARL HARRIS, psychologist; b. Garden City, S.D., Feb. 17, 1922; s. Carl Harris and Helen Alice (Doxrude) R.; m. Marilyn Jeanne Hawkins, Sept. 24, 1947; children—Eric Carl, Christine Amanda. B.A., Stanford U., 1947, M.A., 1949, Ph.D., 1951. Lic. psychologist, Calif. Research psychologist U.S. Air Force, Lowry AFB Colo., 1951-53; research scientist Human Resources, Monterey, Calif., 1953-58; head tng. group Philco Western Devel. Labs., Palo Alto, Calif., 1958-59; research psychologist Stanford Research Inst., 1959-66; asst. dir. edn. dept. SRI Internat. Menlo Park, Calif., 1966-78; cons. Oreg. Shakespeare Festival Assn., 1978-79; Rockwell-Patterson, Palo Alto, 1978-79; mng. prtnr. Roth-Kolker-Rittenhouse Assocs., 1979-82. Contbr. articles to profl. jours. Mem. Am Psychol. Assn., Phi Beta Kappa, Sigma Xi. Democrat. Lutheran.

RITTER, DALE WILLIAM, physician; b. Jersey Shore, Pa., June 17, 1919; s. Lyman W. and Weltha (Packard) R.; m. Winnie Mae Bryant, Nov. 13, 1976; children—Eric, Lyman, Michael, Gwendolyn, Daniel. A.B., UCLA, 1942; M.D., U. So. Calif., 1946. Diplomate Am. Bd. Obstetrics and Gynecology. Intern, Los Angeles County Hosp., Los Angeles, 1945-46, resident, 1949-52, admitting room resident, 1948-52; practice medicine specializing in obstetrics and gynecology, Chico, Calif., 1953—; founder, mem. staff, past chmn. bd. dirs. Chico Community Meml. Hosp.; guest lectr. Chico State Coll., 1956—; mem. staffs Enole Hosp., Chico, 1952—, Glenn Gen. Hosp., Willows, Calif., 1953—, Gridley Meml. Hosp., Calif., 1953-80; spl. cons. obstetrics Calif. Dept. Pub. Health, No. Calif., 1958-70. Contbr. articles to med. and archeol. jours. Bd. dirs. No. dist. Children's Home Soc., Chico, 1954-70. Served with AUS, 1943-45, with M.C., AUS, 1946-48. Fellow ACS, Am. Coll. Obstetrics and Gynecology; mem. AMA, Calif. Med. Assn., Internat. Soc. Hypnosis, Am. Soc. Clin. Hypnosis, Am. Fertility Soc., Pacific Coast Fertility Soc., Soc. for Sci Study of Sex, Assn. Am. Physicians and Surgeons, Pvt. Doctors of Am., Butte-Glenn County Med. Soc. (past pres.), Am. Cancer Soc. (former bd. dirs. Butte County), AAAS, Christian Med. Soc., Am. Assn. Pro-Life Obstetricians and Gynecologists, Butte-Glenn County Tumor Bd., Anthrop. Assn. Am., Archaeol. Inst. Am., Soc. Calif. Archaeology, Oreg. Archaeology Soc., Archeol. Survey Assn., Southwestern Anthrop. Soc., Oreg. Archaeol. Soc., Internat. Assn. for Study of Prehistoric and Ethnologic Religions, Fretted Instrument Guild Am. (dir. Banjo Kats 'n Jammers), North Valley Banjo Band, Am. Philatelic Soc., Am. Horse Council, Am. Horse Shows Assn., Internat. Peruvian Horse Assn., Assn. Owners Breeders Peruvian Paso Horses, Phi Chi, Lambda Sigma, Zeta Beta Sigma. Republican. Lodge: Rotary. Office: 572 Rio Lindo Chico CA 95926

RITTER, MARY L., interior decorator; b. Glencoe, Ill.; children: Caroline Victoria, Mark Henry. BA, Leland Stanford Jr. U., 1948; cert. N.Y. Sch. Interior Design. Interior decorator, N.Y.C., 1951-56; model, N.Y.C., 1951-56; editorial scout numerous shelter mags. and advt. agys., N.Y.C. area, 1951-56, San Francisco area, 1956-63; interior decorator, San Francisco, 1956—; model home decorator Joseph Eichler Corp., San Francisco, 1958; cons. Earl W. Smith Devel. Corp., 1958-60, Draper Shopping Ctrs., Inc., 1959-61; instr. interior design adult edn. div. Redwood City Dept. Recreation (Calif.), 1968, West Valley Community Coll., 1976-78, Can. Coll., 1977—; rep. sculptor Richard Lippold, 1983—. Bd. dirs. Children's Home Soc. Calif., 1966, sec. bd. dirs., 1968; chmn. internat. social services spl. event WAIF, 1976, v.p. spl. events, 1969; chmn. benefit March of Dimes, 1979; bd. dirs. San Francisco Host Com., 1979, mem., 1984, chmn. dinner honoring mayor and consuls gen., 1979. Recipient Cert. Merit World Disting. Service in Field of Interior Design, London, 1968, Gold medal Pro-Am Ski Races, Sun Valley, Idaho, 1971; named as model room designer Children's Home Soc. Decorator Showhouse, 1968, San Mateo County Jr. Mus. Aux. Decorator Showcase, 1972; decor designer San Francisco City Hall, Opus I, Symphony Ball, 1984. Mem. Nat. Home Fashion League, Internat. Platform Assn., Stanford U. Alumni Assn., Calif. Palace Legion of Honor, San Francisco Mus. Art, English Speaking Union, San Francisco Ballet Guild, Am. Soc. Interior Designers (bd. dirs. 1983-84), Profl. Women's Network, Patrons of Art of Vatican Museums, Friends of Les Vieilles Maisons Françaises. Clubs: Far West Ski, Far World Ski, Menlo Park Tennis. Contbr. articles to profl. mags. Home and Office: 349 Selby Ln Atherton CA 94025

RITTER, R(ONALD) DALE, chemistry educator; b. Aberdeen, S.D., Oct. 12, 1942; s. Russell Vernon and Ruth Elizabeth (Anderson) R.; m. Toni Ann Rater, July 19, 1969; children: Deborah Ann, Mark Allan, David Jay. BA, Westmont Coll., 1964; PhD, Oreg. State U., 1969. Asst. prof. chemistry Malone Coll., Canton, Ohio, 1969-74, assoc. prof., 1974-78; chmn. sci. dept. Umpqua Community Coll., Roseburg, Oreg., 1978—. Youth sponsor 1st Conservative Baptist Ch., Roseburg, 1978—. NSF grad. teaching asst. fellow Oreg. State U., Corvallis, 1967, Weyerhauser research fellow Oreg. State U., 1966, DuPont fellow 1966-67; grantee Danforth Found. Malone Coll., 1974, Spectroscopy Soc. Pitts., 1977. Mem. Am. Chem. Soc. (div. chem. edn.), Com. Chemistry in 2-Yr. Colls., Am. Sci. Affiliation, Sigma Xi. Republican. Baptist. Avocations: hunting, fishing, backpacking. Home: 155 W Tanager Roseburg OR 97470 Office: Umpqua Community Coll PO Box 967 Roseburg OR 97470

RITTER, RUSSELL JOSEPH, mayor, college official; b. Helena, Mont., July 22, 1932; s. Walter A. and Sally C. (Mellen) R.; m. Linaire Wells, Aug. 4, 1956; children—Michael, Leslie, Teresa, Gregory, Daniel. Student Carroll Coll., Helena, 1950-53; A.B. in History, U. Mont.-Missoula, 1957, M.A. in History and Polit. Sci., 1962, postgrad. in History, 1963. Salesman, Capital Ford, 1953-54, 56-57; tchr., coach Billings (Mont.) Central High Sch., 1957-58, Loyola High Sch., Missoula, 1958-62, Flathead High Sch., Kalispell, Mont., 1962-69; dir. devel. and community relations Carroll Coll., Helena, 1969-76, v.p. for coll. relations, 1976—; commr. City of Helena, 1977-80, mayor pro-tem, 1980, mayor, 1981—; exec. sec.-treas. Carroll Coll. Found., Inc.; owner Danny's Drive In, Kalispell, 1965-69; ptnr. R-B Enterprises, Inc., Kalispell, 1967-71; bd. dirs. Brubaker & Assos., Inc., Kalispell, 1971-74; v.p. Capital Investment, Inc. (KMTX Radio), Helena, 1973-80; pres. Swinging Door Art Gallery, Inc., Helena, 1973—. Bd. dirs. All Am. Indian Hall of Fame, 1972-78, Jr. Achievement, 1975-79, Mont. Physicians Service, 1984-86, Blue Cross/Blue Shield Mont., 1986—, Mont. C. of C., chmn., Mont. Community Fin. Corp., 1986; bd. govs. Mt. Spl. Olympics, 1984—; mem. Citizen's Adv. Council, 1975-76; chmn. City-County Bldg., Inc., 1978; mem. Mont. Friendship Force. Served with USMC, 1953-56. Mem. Helena C. of C. (dir. 1972-75, v.p. 1973, pres. 1974, Ambassador's Club 1976—, chmn. 1978), Mont. Ofcls. Assn., Mont. Ambassadors (Ambassador of Yr. 1986). Club: Montana. Lodge: K.C. (4th degree). Office: Carroll Coll Room 258 Helena MT 59601

RITTER-DE ROO, ROBIN ANN, biochemist, educator; b. Davenport, Iowa, Aug. 23, 1954; d. Richard Phillip and Sybil Corine R.; m. Robert Allan De Roo, Apr. 26, 1986. B, Calif. State U., Fullerton, 1976, M, 1983. Lectr. Calif. State U., Fullerton, 1980-82, Statewide Nursing, Long Beach, Calif., 1983-86; faculty Calif. State U., Long Beach, 1984-86, instructional design assoc., 1984-86, cons., 1985-86. Publicity dir. Mason Ballet Ctr., Placentia, Calif., 1983; mother advisor Internat. Order Rainbow Girls, Orange, Calif., 1985. Mem. Am. Chem. Soc., Iota Sigma Pi (sec. 1979-80).

RITZ, WILLIAM CARL, educational administrator, science educator; b. Buffalo, Dec. 8, 1929; s. William Frederick and Wilhelmina Maria (Fuchs) R.; m. Joyce Elaine Gocella, June 23, 1956; children: Lynne Elaine Ritz Estabrook, Lisa Ellen. BA, U. Buffalo, 1951, EdM, 1959; EdD, SUNY, Buffalo, 1969; postgrad., Cornell U., Syracuse U., others. Cert. secondary sch. tchr., N.Y. Sci. tchr. Scottsville (N.Y.) High Sch., 1952; sci. tchr., head sci. dept. Amherst Cen. Jr. High Sch., Snyder, N.Y., 1954-67; staff assoc., sci. edn. cons. Eastern Regional Inst. for Edn., Syracuse, N.Y., 1967-71; adminstrv. dir., assoc. prof. Environ. Studies Inst., Syracuse, 1971-77; dir. Sci. and Math. Edn. Inst. Calif. State U., Long Beach, 1977—, prof., coordinator sci. edn., 1977—; cons. U.S. Dept. Def. Dependent Schs., Wiesbaden, Germany, 1985-86; numerous lectures, speaking engagements, presentations to profl. assns.; mem. various coms. Calif. State Dept. Edn., 1982—; co-developer filmstrip program When Science Happens... in conjunction with Los Angeles County Supt. Schs., Downey, Calif., 1979; adj. prof. SUNY, Geneseo, 1975-77; cons. Xerox Corp., 1970-71, Delta Edn. Co., Nashua, N.H., 1982-85, numerous others. Contbr. numerous articles to profl. jours.; co-developer numerous multi-media instructional modules for sci. edn. Mem. Environ. Mgmt. Tech. Adv. Com. Cen. N.Y. Regional Planning and Devel. Bd., 1974-76; bd. dirs. Onondaga Nature Ctrs., Inc., Syracuse, 1973-77; mem. profl. edn. com. Am. Cancer Soc., Long Beach, 1977-79; musician Amherst Symphony, 1947-67, Syracuse U. Symphony, 1968-74; mem. Luth. Ch. Council Buffalo, 1964-67, Liverpool, N.Y., 1971-74; bd. dirs. Syracuse Luth. Student Found., 1968-71. Served to sgt. U.S. Army, 1952-54. Grantee NSF at Syracuse Univ., 1975-77, at Calif. State U., 1977, Calif. Dept. Edn. Environ. Edn. Program at Calif. State Univ., 1983, numerous other grants; recipient 3 spl. inst. awards NSF, Exceptional Merit Service award Calif. State Univ., 1984, 85, 86, numerous other awards. Fellow AAAS, Sci. Tchrs. Assn. N.Y. State; mem. Nat. Sci. Tchrs. Assn. (life) (dir. tchr. edn. 1983-85), NEA (life), Assn. for Supervision and Curriculum Devel., Assn. Edn. Tchrs. in Sci. (pres. 1987—), Am. Cetacean Soc., World Future Soc., Nat. Audubon Soc., Chi Beta Phi, Phi Delta Kappa, others. Avocations: music, gardening, reading, sports, bowling. Office: Calif State Univ 1250 Bellflower Blvd Long Beach CA 90840

RIVIER, JEAN EDOUARD FREDERIC, chemistry educator, laboratory researcher; b. Casablanca, Morocco, July 14, 1941; came to U.S., 1969; s. Etienne Edouard and Edmée Jessie (Henrotin) R.; m. Catherine L. Gafner; children: Lauraine, Cédric. ChemE, U. de Lausanne, Switzerland, 1965; PhD in Organic Chemistry, U. de Lausanne, 1968. Postdoctoral research U. de Lausanne, Switzerland, 1969, Rice U., Houston, 1969-70; research assoc. Salk Inst., La Jolla, Calif., 1970-73, asst. prof., 1973-78, assoc. prof., 1979—, sr. research mem., 1984—. Grantee NIH. Mem. Am. Chem. Soc., Am. Peptide Symposium (organizing com.), Endocrine Soc. Avocation: tennis. Office: The Salk Inst 10010 N Torrey Pines Rd La Jolla CA 92138

RIVIERA, DANIEL JOHN, lawyer; b. N.Y.C., May 28, 1927; s. Charles Adrian and Ruth Blanche (Sinclair) R.; B.A. cum laude, Syracuse U., 1950; LL.B., Georgetown U., 1953; children—Daniel C., Sara J., Jeffrey, Gloria, Spencer. Bar: Wash. 1953, Idaho 1981. Practiced in Seattle, 1953—; mem. firm Foster, Pepper & Riviera, Seattle, 1953—, ptnr., 1968—. Instr. bus. law U. Wash., 1957-59, Journalism law Seattle U., 1965-67, 75-77; mem. Statute Law Com., 1963-72; mem. Bench, Bar, Press Com., 1964-72. Mem. Mercer Island City Council, 1961-68; bd. visitors J. Reuben Clark Law Sch., Brigham Young U., Provo, Utah, 1978-80. Served with AUS, 1946-47. Mem. ABA (vice-chmn. projects com. jr. bar conf. 1959-60), Wash. State Bar Assn. (mem. subcom. of local adminstrv. com. 1967-70), Seattle-King County Bar Assn. (labor law com. 1967—). Clubs: Bellevue (Wash.) Athletic; Harbor (Seattle). Home: 4818 102nd Lane NE Kirkland WA 98033 Office: 1111 Third Ave Bldg Seattle WA 98101

RIVIERE, HOLLISTON LEE, anatomy educator; b. Moline, Ill., Aug. 27, 1944; s. John Mitchel and Mary Lee (Szekely) Brown; m. George Robert Riviere, Aug. 14, 1971; children: Michael Andrew, Kathryn Holliston. AB, Augustana Coll., Rock Island, Ill., 1966; MS, U. Ill., Chgo., 1969, PhD, 1971. Lectr. anatomy UCLA Med. Sch., 1975-76; instr. West Los Angeles Coll., Culver City, Calif., 1978—, Cerritos Coll., Norwalk, Calif., 1980—. Author: Anatomy and Embryology of the Head and Neck, 1982; contbr. articles to profl. jours. Vol. UCLA Hosp., 1977-78, Rancho Palos Verdes (Calif.) Elem. Sch. Dist., 1979—; vol. coach Rancho Palos Verdes Youth Soccer Orgn., 1981; den leader Cub Scout Pack 922, Rancho Palos Verdes, 1982-84. Recipient Hon. Service award Soleado PTA, Rancho Palos Verdes, 1984. Mem. AAAS, Dental Hygiene Edn. Assn., Sigma Xi.

RIX, JAMES HART, public relations consultant; b. Denver, Apr. 19, 1932; s. James Herbert and Blanche (Daniels) R.; m. Marjorie Anne Graham, Aug. 16, 1958; children: James C., Amy Dianne. BS, BA, U. Denver, 1955; grad., Squadron Officer Sch., 1960; cert., Indsl. Coll. Armed Forces, 1977. Enlisted USAF, 1956, advanced through grades to col., 1977, ret., 1985; exec. officer USAF, Turkey and Iran; exec. Office of Sec. Def. Dept., Wash.; dir. adminstrn. Air Force Logistics Command, Dayton, Ohio, NORAD Space Command, Colorado Springs, Colo.; dir. vets. and mil. affairs Shrine of Rest, Colorado Springs, 1985—, also bd. dirs. Decorated Bronze Star, Legion of Merit. Mem. Air Force Assn., U.S. Space Found., Ret. Officers Assn. (editor 1985—, mem. bd. officers 1985), Air Force Acad. Quarterback Club, DAV, Alpha Kappa Psi. Lodges: Masons, Lions, Rotary. Avocations: gardening, recreational motor homes, global traveling. Home: 2730 Alteza Ln Colorado Springs CO 80917 Office: Shrine of Rest 1730 Fountain Blvd Colorado Springs CO 80910

RIZNIK, JOSEPH QUENTIN, editorial consultant; b. Czernowitz, Bukowina, Austria, Apr. 22, 1900; brought to San Francisco, 1907; s. Leizer and Sarah (Brenner) R.; A.B., U. Calif.-Berkeley, 1925, M.A. in Journalism, 1952; postgrad. U. Munich, 1926, Columbia U., 1927; m. Charlotte Barnes, Aug. 22, 1927; 1 son, Barnes. Editor, The Hamiltonian, San Francisco, 1914; correspondent U.P., San Francisco, 1924-25; social service publicity aide Charity Orgn. Soc. N.Y.C., Fellowship House, Fedn. Jewish Charities, N.Y.C., 1926; writer Chgo. Tribune, Paris, France, 1927-31; feature writer Hearst newspapers, San Francisco, 1933-34, N.Y.C., 1934-36, editor Peninsulan Mag., San Fancisco, 1932-34; spl. projects writer Universal Service, N.Y.C, 1935-36; book manuscript cons., 1936—; assoc. editor Crowell-Collier Am mag., N.Y.C., 1936-38; script writer Columbia Pictures, Hollywood, 1938-39; columnist Gayways: Treasure Island Expo., Call-Bulletin, San Francisco, 1939; network news writer, editor CBS, N.Y.C., 1940-42; coordinator media OWI, Washington, 1942-44; exec. editor Nat. Polit. Action Com., N.Y.C., 1944; exec. producer (TV series) Money Ain't Everything; dir. Am. Newsmaker Documentaries, San Francisco, N.Y.C., 1944-50; west coast corr. Overseas Press Bull., 1948-60; founder Grad. Sch. Journalism at U. Calif., Berkeley, 1950; editor mass communications research project U. Calif.-Berkeley, 1950-52. Exec. editor Q Press Found., 1975-76, chmn. bd., 1977-79; founding mem. Hist. Commn., San Anselmo, 1976-79; chmn. Paint-the-Golden Gate Bridge-Gold Commemorative Project, 1977—; exec. dir. Center for Patriotic Revision of Am. Presidency, 1980; founding dir. Office of Peace Info.; dean Sch. for Presidents. Mem. U. Calif. Alumni Assn. (JQR Meml. awards Berkeley Undergrad. Campus Writers), Am. Newspaper Guild (founding). Clubs: Downhold; Hammer and Coffin; XCBS Nat. Alumni Assn. (permanent nat. sec.); Overseas Press Am.; Press (San Francisco, sr. assoc. Unit Am. Newspaper Guild). Author: Propaganda and Counter-propaganda, 1952; The Bad President, 1975; Winter: The JQR Autobituary, 1985; columnist Along the Way. Contbr. to periodicals. Address: Casa Riznik 1 25 Plum Tree Ln San Rafael CA 94901

RIZNYK, RAYMOND ZENON, biology educator; b. N.Y.C., July 20, 1942; s. Walter Albin and Paula (Myhal) R.; m. Natalia Kurkchi, Sept. 30, 1960; children: Nicholas, Larissa, Kira. BS, U. N.Mex., 1965; PhD, Oreg. State U., 1969. Asst. prof. Moss Landing (Calif.) Marine Lab., 1969; prof. Calif. Poly. State U., Pomona, 1969-80; water quality biologist City of Portland, Oreg., 1980-81; prof. Alaska Pacific U., Anchorage, 1983—; cons. So. Calif. Ocean Studies Consortium, 1973-74, Winzler & Kelly Cons. Engrs., Eureka, Calif., 1976-77, City of Long Beach, Calif., 1977. Contbr. articles to profl. jours. NASA fellow, Corvallis, Oreg., 1965-68. Mem. AAUP, Am. Inst. Biol. Scis., AAAS, Sierra Club, Beta Beta Beta, Phi Sigma. Democrat. Home and Office: 4101 University Dr Anchorage AK 99508

RIZZUTO, CARMELA RITA, nursing educator, continuing professional education consultant; b. Waterbury, Conn., Aug. 26, 1942; d. Joseph Anthony and Carmella Rose R.; m. Thomas Lee Chernesky, Aug. 28, 1982. B.S., St. Joseph Coll., 1965; M.S., Boston Coll., 1971; Ed.D., Sch. Edn., UCLA, 1983. R.N., Calif. Nursing instr. Samaritan Hosp. Sch. Nursing, Troy, N.Y., 1969; med. nursing coordinator, clin. specialist Harvard Community Health Plan, Boston, 1971-72; instr. inservice edn. Tufts-New Eng. Med. Center, Boston, 1972-73; instr. inservice edn. St. John's Hosp. and Health Center, Santa Monica, Calif., 1974-76; asst. clin. prof. Sch. Nursing, UCLA, 1976-79; educator, continuing edn. for nurses, Calif. State U., Los Angeles, 1979-80, U. Calif., Santa Barbara, 1981-83; assoc. dir. nursing edn. St. Francis Hosp. of Santa Barbara, 1981-83; asst. dir. nursing edn. and research Stanford U. Hosp., 1983—; USPHS coronary care nurse trainee, 1968; USPHS nurse trainee, 1969-71; recipient Chancellor's Patent Fund, UCLA, 1972-73. Mem. Am. Assn. Critical Care Nurses. Contbr. articles to profl. publs. Office: Dept Nursing Research Stanford U Hosp Stanford CA 94305

ROACH, THOMAS BANKSON, aerospace executive; b. N.Y.C., Sept. 17, 1938; s. Thomas Bankson and Katherine Walter (Hunter) R. BA in History, U. N.C., 1960. Pres. Shrike Software, Cupertino, Calif., 1982-85; dir. microcomputer systems Lockheed Missile and Space Co., Sunnyvale, Calif., 1984—. Club: Merlin (Cupertino) (pres. 1980-82), Piwacket. Avocations: birding, photography. Home: 1330 Copper Peak Ln San Jose CA 95120-4271

ROBB, JAMES ARTHUR, surgical pathologist; b. Pueblo, Colo., Nov. 13, 1938; s. William Arthur and Mary Ann (Hutchinson) R.; m. Carla May Felte, June 16, 1962; 4 children. BA, U. Colo., 1960, postgrad., 1960-61, MD, 1965. Diplomate Am. Bd. Anatomic Pathology, Am. Bd. Dermatopathology. Intern then resident in anatomic pathology Yale U., New Haven, 1965-68; research assoc. NIH, Bethesda, Md., 1969-71; asst. prof. pathology U. Calif., San Diego, 1971-75, assoc. prof., 1975-78; staff pathologist Scripps Clinic, La Jolla, Calif., 1978-81, vice chmn. pathology, 1981—; assoc. adj. prof. U. Calif., San Diego, 1978-84, adj. prof., 1984—. Contbr. articles to profl. jours. Treas. San Diego Jr. Theatre, 1981. Served with USPHS, 1962-80. Grantee NIH, Am. Cancer Soc. Mem. AMA, AAAS, Am. Soc. Cell Biology, Am. Soc. Microbiology, Fedn. Am. Scientists, Am. Assn. Pathologists, Calif. Med. Assn., San Diego Med. Soc., San

Diego County Soc. Pathologists, Internat. Soc. Dermatophatology, Internat. Acad. Cytology, Am. Soc. Dermatopathology, Internat. Acad. Pathology, Am. Soc. Virology, Alpha Omega Alpha, Sigma Tau, Sigma Pi Sigma. Home: 13645 Pine Needles Dr Del Mar CA 92014 Office: Green Hosp Scripps Clinic 10666 N Torrey Pines Dr La Jolla CA 92037

ROBBINS, ALAN, state senator; b. Phila., Feb. 5, 1943; s. Martin and Gladys (Kessler) R.; B.A., UCLA, 1963, J.D., 1966; m. Miriam Elbaum, Sept. 27, 1967 (div. 1980); children—Jacob Harold, Leah Susan. Bar: Calif. 1966. Practice law, San Fernando Valley, Calif., 1966—; mem. Calif. Senate from 20th Dist., 1973—, chmn. com. on ins., claims and corps. Democrat. Office: State Capitol Room 5114 Sacramento CA 95814

ROBBINS, DICK LAMSON, physician, educator; b. Boston, May 13, 1941. BA, Lawrence U., 1963; MD, U. Vt., 1967. Diplomate Am. Bd. Internal Medicine, Nat. Bd. Med. Examiners, Am. Bd. Rheumatology. Intern Good Samaritan Hosp., Phoenix, 1967-68; resident in internal medicine U. Oreg. Med. Sch., Portland, 1968-71; research fellow rheumatology Scripps Clinic and Research Found., La Jolla, Calif., 1973-76; asst. prof. medicine dept. internal medicine sect. rheumatology U. Calif., Davis, 1976-82, assoc. prof., 1982—; program chmn. Soc. Fellows Scripps Clinic and Research Found., 1974-75, pres., 1975-76; adminstrn. coms. held at U. Calif. Med. Ctr. include med. records 1976-78, patient care 1978-79, capital equipment 1979-80, quality assurance outpatient rev. subcom. 1985—; chmn. patient care 1979-81; coms. held with dept. Internal Medicine include internship-residency selection 1979-80, residency rev. 1980-82, internal medicine research 1984—, internal medicine quality assurance rev. 1984—, chmn. 1982-84; coms. held with Sch. Medicine include grad. group immunology 1977—, comparative pathology group 1977—, faculty affaris 1977-78, faculty exec. 1984-85; exec. com. grad. group in immunology 1985—; grade change 1979-81, chmn. 1981-85; coms. held with U. Davis include gen. edn. ad hoc 1981-82; chmn. grad. research awards 1983-84; coms. held Div. Rheumatology/Allergy and Clin. Immunology include dir. postgrad. fellowship program 1977—, dir. rheumatology-orthopedics combined clinics 1978-81, acting chmn. 1985-86; cons. San Joaquin Gen. Hosp., Stockton, Calif., 1976—, Calif. Crippled Children Services, Sacramento, 1976—, Kaiser Hosp., Sacramento, 1979—, VA Hosp., Martinez, Calif., 1979—, Woodland (Calif.) Meml. Hosp., 1979-81, David Grant Meml. Hosp., Travis AFB, Calif., 1980—. Contbr. numerous articles to profl. jours. Recipient Earle C. Anthony award 1976-77, Faculty Research award 1976-81; New Eng. Bd. Higher Edn. scholar 1963-67; NIH fellow 1974-76; research grantee NIH, 1976-83, Calif. Lung Assn., 1977-79, NIH, 1978-81, Am. Heart Assn., 1980-81, NIH, 1983—. Mem. AAAS, Am. Rheumatism Assn., Am. Soc. Zoologists (comparative immunology sect.), Western Soc. Naturalists, Internat. Soc. Devel. and Comparative Immunology.

ROBBINS, HARRY R., auditor, consultant; b. North Braddock, Pa., Apr. 3, 1942; S. Idris R. and Florence E. (Stoll) R.; m. Audrey D. Andrascik, Mar. 21, 1964; children: Douglas, Robert, Julie. BS, Pa. State U., 1964; MBA, Pepperdine U., 1975. CPA. Mgr. Deloitte, Haskins & Sells, Pitts. and Denver, 1963-71; gen. auditor So. Calif. 1st Bank, San Diego, 1971-75, 1st Interstate Data Processing, Los Angeles, 1975-76; dir. mgmt. audit U.S. Leasing Internat., San Francisco, 1976-85; pres. Audit World, Moraga, Calif., 1985—; lectr. John F. Kennedy U., Orinda, Calif., 1985—. Mem. Inst. Internal Auditors (we. region dir., internat. treas., bd. dirs. 1984, Soc. Emeritus award), Am. Inst. CPA's. Republican. Office: Audit World 755 Camino Ricardo Moraga CA 94556

ROBBINS, ROBERT RAYMOND, biology educator, researcher; b. Des Moines, May 28, 1946; s. Harold Raymond and Marjorie Eunice (Brown) R.; m. Susan Ann Lohr, May 11, 1985. BS, Iowa State U., 1968; MS, U. Ill., 1973, PhD, 1977. Instr. human anatomy U.S. Army Med. Field Service Sch., San Antonio, 1969-71, Ctr. for Electron Micrscopy, Urbana, Ill., 1973-74; lectr. botany U. Ill, Urbana, 1976; asst. prof. biology Colo. Coll., Colorado Springs, 1984-85; asst. prof. botany U. Wis., Milw., 1977-84, Idaho State U., Pocatello, 1985—; Contbr. articles to sci. jours. Vol. Nat. Pub. Radio Sta. WUWM, Milw., 1978-84. Served with U.S. Army, 1969-71. Named Disting. Tchr. of Yr., Amoco Found., 1984. Mem. AAAS, Bot. Soc. Am., Am. Inst. Biol. Scis., Am. Bryol. and Lichenol. Soc., Idaho Acad. Sci. Avocations: photography, cross country skiing, hiking. Office: Idaho State U Dept Biol Scis Pocatello ID 83209

ROBENSON, JAMES MELFORD, protective services official; b. Brookhaven, Miss., Oct. 28, 1941; m. Susan Burt. BA in Sociology, Calif. State U., Los Angeles, 1972; M in Pub. Adminstrn., U. So. Calif., 1976; postgrad., Pub. Exec. Inst., Lyndon B. Johnson Sch. Pub. Affairs, 1986. Police officer Pasadena (Calif.) Police Dept., 1964, police agt., 1969, police sgt., 1971, police lt., 1974, police commdr., 1979, police chief, 1985. Contbr. articles to profl. jours. Mem. Pasadena Hispanic Scholarship Com., Rose Bowl Aquatics Bd. Recipient Law Enforcement award Crown City Optimist Club, 1975, Community Service award Pasadena Alliance of Substance Abuse Agys., 1982, Respect for Law commendation Altadena Optimist Club, 1986. Mem. Nat. Orgn. Black Law Enforcement Execs., Los Angeles County Chief's of Police, San Gabriel Valley Police Chiefs, Internat. Assn. Chief's of Police, Calif. Police Chiefs' Assn., San Gabriel Valley Mental Health Edn. Found., Alpha Kappa Delta. Club: University (Pasadena). Office: Pasadena Police Dept 142 N Arroyo Pkwy Pasadena CA 91103

ROBERSON, BEVERLY BUD, physician; b. Lemoore, Calif., Apr. 29, 1922; s. Alexander Grace and Flossie Mae (Gregory) R.; B.A., Pacific Union Coll., 1942; M.D., Loma Linda U., 1945; m. Eleanor June Gourly, June 26, 1949 (div. 1974); children—Donald Edward, Cheryl Diane. Intern Glendale Sanitarium and Hosp., Glendale, Calif., 1945-46; practice medicine specializing in gen. practice, Clearlake Highlands, Calif., 1950-70; resident in anesthesiology White Meml. Med. Center, Los Angeles, 1970-72, instr., 1972-74, dir. anesthesiology, 1980-84; asst. prof. anesthesiology Loma Linda (Calif.) U., 1974-85; practice anesthesiology, Los Angeles, 1972-74, Loma Linda, 1974-80, 84-85, Los Angeles, 1980-84; pres. Lakeshore Investment Corp., 1963-77. Bd. dirs. Lakeshore Fire Protection Dist., 1968-70, Redbud Hosp., 1968-70; comdr. med. emergency team Los Angeles County Sheriff's Dept., 1979-86, sgt., 1986—; ship surgeon Am. Hawaii Cruises, 1985-86. Served with U.S. Army, 1946-48. Diplomate Am. Bd. Anesthesiology. Fellow Am. Coll. Anesthesiologists; mem. Calif., Am. socs. anesthesiologists, Los Angeles County med. assns., AMA. Republican. Home: 3805 Karen Lynn St Glendale CA 91206

ROBERSON, KIM ELIZABETH, nurse; b. Seattle, Sept. 20, 1955; d. Frank Tracey and Zetta Elizabeth (Jacobson) R. BS in Nursing, Seattle U., 1977. Commd. 2d lt., U.S. Army, 1977, advanced through grades to capt., 1980; asst. head nurse, Frankfurt-W.Ger., 1980-81, chief nurse Health Clinic, 1981-83, clin. staff nurse, San Francisco, 1983-85,; house supr. Seattle VA Med. Ctr., 1985—; co-chairperson dept. nursing quality assurance com., 1980-81; mem. affiliate faculty Am. Heart Assn., San Francisco, 1984-85. Capt. USAR, 1985—. Decorated Commendation medal; recipient letter of Commendation. Mem. Nurses Orgn. of VA. Avocations: kayaking, study of wines, music, reading. Home: 8730 Wabash Ave S Seattle WA 98118 Office: Seattle VA Med Ctr 1660 S Columbian Way Seattle WA 98108

ROBERSON, MICHAEL EUGENE, mechanical engineer; b. Wahoo, Nebr., July 15, 1954; s. Marvin E. and Bernice Ann (Pospisil) R.; m. Mary Celeste Welsh, May 25, 1974 (div. May 1978); children: Jessica, Paul. BS in Physics, U. Utah, 1980, MSME, 1985. Prodn. engr. EIMAC div. Varian Assocs., Salt Lake City, 1982-85, tube design engr., 1985—. Supr. EIMAC Credit Union, Salt Lake City, 1985-86. Served to sgt. U.S. Army, 1973-76.

ROBERTS, ALAN H., psychologist, researcher; b. Chgo., Mar. 2, 1929; s. Carl and Kay (Radford) R.; m. Shirley Boe (div. 1963); children: Kenneth Richard, Karen Elizabeth; m. Myrna Morrison, Mar. 18, 1967; children: Joel Philip, Jennifer Elaine. BA, Mich. State U., 1951, MS, 1952; postgrad., U. Colo., 1953-54; PhD, U. Denver, 1958. Diplomate Am. Bd. Profl. Psychology. Sch. psychologist Colo. Rocky Mountain Sch., Carbondale, 1953-54; from research psychologist to supr. psychology Elgin (Ill.) State Hosp., 1956-69; from asst. to assoc. prof. behavioral sci. N. Mex. Highlands U., Las Vegas, 1960-64; asst. prof. clin. psychology U. Colo., Denver, 1964-65; prof. div. health care psychology U. Minn. dept. phys. medicine and rehabilitation, Mpls., 1966-80, dir. autonomic learning lab., 1973-80, dir. pain clinic and pain treatment program, 1973-80; dir. behavioral medicine program Scripps Clinic and Research Found., La Jolla, Calif., 1979—; research assoc. Nat. Tng. Labs., Bethal, Maine, 1955, Group Devel. Labs., U. Colo., Boulder, 1954-55, also teaching assoc.; supr. Walk-In Counseling Ctr., Mpls., 1970-79; mem. rev. bd. St. Peter State Hosp., Minn. Dept. Welfare, 1972-79; mem. community adv. bd. grad. sch. pub. health, San Diego State U., 1983—, also adj. faculty mem.; vis. prof. Stanford U., Palo Alto, Calif., 1972; assoc. clin. prof. U. Calif., San Diego, 1983—. Contbr. chpts. to books, articles to profl. jours. Served with U.S. Army, 1946-47. Named Sr. Stipend fellow Nat. Inst. Mental Health, NIH, 1962-63. Fellow Am. Psychol. Assn.; mem. Acad. Behavioral Medicine Research, Assn. Advancement of Behavior Therapy (behavior medicine spl. interest group), Internat. Assn. Study Pain, Minn. Psychol. Assn. (chmn. legislative com. 1972-73, mem. exec. com. 1974-79, sec. 1976-77, exec. officer 1977-79, life 1980—), Acad. San Diego Psychologists, Soc. Behavioral Medicine, Am. Coll. Sports Medicine, Soc. Behavioral Medicine, Sigma Xi. Avocations: computer sci., running, rare books. Office: Scripps Clinic and Research Found 10666 N Torrey Pines Rd La Jolla CA 92023

ROBERTS, ALAN SILVERMAN, physician; b. N.Y.C., Apr. 20, 1939; s. Joseph William and Fannie (Margolies) S.; B.A., Conn. Wesleyan U., 1960; M.D., Jefferson Med. Coll., 1966; children—Michael Eric, Daniel Ian. Rotating intern, Lankenau Hosp., Phila., 1966-67; resident orthopaedics Tulane U. Med. Coll., 1967-71; pvt. practice medicine, specializing in orthopedics and hand surgery, Los Angeles, 1971—; mem. clin. faculty UCLA Med. Coll., 1971-76; mem. staff Brotman Meml. Hosp., Culver City, Calif. Served with AUS, 1961. Recipient Riordan Hand fellowship, 1969; Boyes Hand fellowship, 1971. Mem. Riordan Hand Soc., Western Orthopaedic Assn., A.C.S., AMA, Calif., Los Angeles County med. assns. Republican. Jewish. Contbr. articles to profl. jours.

ROBERTS, ARCHIBALD EDWARD, retired army officer, author; b. Cheboygan, Mich., Mar. 21, 1915; s. Archibald Lancaster and Madeline Ruth (Smith) R.; grad. Command and Gen. Staff Coll., 1952; student U.S. Armed Forces Inst., 1953, U. Md., 1958; m. Florence Snure, Sept. 25, 1940 (div. Feb. 1950); children—Michael James, John Douglas; m. 2d, Doris Elfriede White, June 23, 1951; children—Guy Archer, Charles Lancaster, Christopher Corwin. Enlisted U.S. Army, 1939, advanced through grades to lt. col., 1960; served in Far East Command, 1942, 1953-55, ETO, 1943-45, 57-60; tech. info. officer Office Surgeon Gen., Dept. Army, Washington, 1950, Ft. Campbell, Ky., 1952-53, info. officer, Camp Chicamauga, Japan, Ft. Bragg, N.C., Ft. Campbell, Ky., 1953-56, Ft. Campbell, 1956-57, Ft. Benning, Ga., Wurzburg, Germany, 1957-58, spl. projects officer Augsburg, Germany, 1959-60, U.S. Army Info. Office, N.Y.C., 1960-61; writer program precipitating Senate Armed Services Hearings, 1962; ret., 1965; mgr., salesman Nu-Enamel Stores, Ashville, N.C., 1937-38; co-owner, dir. Roberts & Roberts Advt. Agy., Denver, 1946-49; pres. Found. for Edn., Scholarship, Patriotism and Americanism, Inc.; founder, nat. bd. dirs. Com. to Restore Constn., Inc., 1965—; Recipient award of merit Am. Acad. Pub. Affairs, 1967; Good Citizenship medal SAR, 1968; Liberty award Congress of Freedom, 1969; Man of Yr. awards Women for Constl. Govt., 1970, Wis. Legislative and Research Com., 1971; medal of merit Am. Legion, 1972; Speaker of Year award We, The People, 1973; Col. Arch Roberts Week named for him City of Danville, Ill., 1974. Mem. Res. Officers Assn., Airborne Assn., SAR, Sons Am. Colonists. Author: Rakkasan, 1955; Screaming Eagles, 1956; The Marne Division, 1957; Victory Denied, 1966; The Anatomy of a Revolution, 1968; Peace: By the Wonderful People Who Brought You Korea and Viet Nam, 1972; The Republic: Decline and Future Promise, 1975; The Crisis of Federal Regionalism: A Solution, 1976; Emerging Struggle for State Sovereignty, 1979; How to Organize for Survival, 1982; The Most Secret Science, 1984; also numerous pamphlets and articles. Home: 2218 W Prospect PO Box 986 Fort Collins CO 80522

ROBERTS, BARBARA, state official; b. Corvallis, Oreg., Dec. 21, 1936; m. Frank Roberts, 1974; children—Mark, Michael. Mem. Multnomah County Bd. Commrs., Oreg., 1978; mem. Oreg. Ho. of Reps., 1981-85; sec. of state State of Oreg., 1985—. Mem. Parkrose Sch. Bd., 1973-83. Office: Office of Sec State 136 State Capitol Salem OR 97310 *

ROBERTS, CAROL MARIE, educational adminstrator, management consultant; b. Los Angeles, Nov. 7, 1939; d. Earl Hugene and Marie Alberta (Royle) Peltier; m. Edward Earl Roberts, July 2, 1964; stepchildren—Linda Pezzopane, Dennis, Mark, Scott. BAEd, Calif. State U.-Long Beach, 1965; MSEd, Calif. State U.-Fullerton, 1977, MS Sch. Adminstrn., 1978; EdD U. So. Calif., 1987. Tchr., Tustin (Calif.) Unified Sch. Dist., 1965-80; tchr. reading and writing U. Calif.-Irvine, 1977; tchr. reading Saddleback Coll., Mission Viejo, Calif., 1977-80; asst. prin. Greenville Fundamental Sch., Santa Ana, Calif., 1980-82; prin. MacArthur Fundamental Intermediate Sch., Santa Ana, 1982-86; cons. adminstrv. tng. ctr. Orange County Dept. Edn., Costa Mesa, Calif., 1986—; tchr.-trainer, staff devel. workshops presenter Orange County Conf. Gifted and Talented, 1980-81. Mem. Assn. Supervision and Curriculum Devel., Internat. Reading Assn., Assn. Calif. Sch. Adminstrs., Calif. Scholarship Fedn. (life), So. Counties Women Mgrs. in Mgmt. Edn. Presbyterian. Home: 1681 Cameo Dr Santa Ana CA 92705 Office: Orange County Dept Edn 200 Kalmus Dr Costa Mesa CA 92628

ROBERTS, DENNIS WILLIAM, association executive; b. Chgo., Jan. 7, 1943; s. William Owen and Florence Harriet (Denman) R.; B.A., U. N.Mex., 1968; M.A., Antioch U., 1982, St. John's Coll., 1984. Cert. assn. exec. Gen. assignment reporter Albuquerque Pub. Co., 1964, sports writer, 1960-64, advt. and display salesman, 1967-68; dir. info. N.Mex. bldg. br. Asso. Gen. Contractors Am., Albuquerque, 1968-79, asst. exec. dir., 1979-82, dir., 1982—. Active United Way, Albuquerque, 1969-78; chmn. Albuquerque Crime Prevention Council, 1982. Recipient Pub. Relations Achievement award Assoc. Gen. Contractors Am., 1975, 78. Mem. N.Mex. Pub. Relations Conf. (chmn. 1975, 82-83), Pub. Relations Soc. Am. (accredited, pres. N.Mex. chpt. 1981, chmn. S.W. dist. 1984), Am. Soc. Assn. Execs. (cert.), Contrn. Specifications Inst. (Outstanding Industry Mem. 1974, Outstanding Com. Chmn. 1978), Sigma Delta Chi (pres. N.Mex. chpt. 1969). Republican. Lutheran. Clubs: Toastmasters (dist. gov. 1977-78, Disting. Dist. award 1978, Toastmaster of Year 1979-80), Masons, Shriners, Elks. Home: 1709 Hiawatha NE Albuquerque NM 87112 Office: Assn Gen Contractors 1615 University Blvd NE Albuquerque NM 87102

ROBERTS, DONALD JOHN, economics and business educator, consultant; b. Winnipeg, Man., Can., Feb. 11, 1945; came to U.S., 1967; s. Donald Victor and Margaret Mabel (Riddell) R.; m. Kathleen Eleanor Taylor, Aug. 26, 1967. B.A. with honours, U. Man., 1967; Ph.D., U. Minn., 1972. Instr. dept. managerial econs. and decision scis. J.L. Kellogg Grad. Sch. Mgmt., Northwestern U., Evanston, Ill., 1971-72, asst. prof., 1972-74; assoc. prof. J. L. Kellogg Grad. Sch. Mgmt., Northwestern U., Evanston, Ill., 1974-77; prof. J.L. Kellogg Grad. Sch. Mgmt., Northwestern U., Evanston, Ill., 1977-80, Grad. Sch. Bus., Stanford U., Calif., 1980; Jonathan B. Lovelace prof. Grad. Sch. Bus., Stanford U., 1980—; vis. research faculty U. Catholique de Louvain, (Belgium), 1974-75; cons. econs. and antitrust, 1976—; spl. econs. cons. U.S. Dept. Transp., Washington, 1978-79. Assoc. editor: Jour. Econ. Theory, 1977—, Econometrica, 1985—; contbr. articles to profl. jours. NSF grantee, 1973—; Ctr. Ops. Research and Econometrics research fellow Heverlee, Belgium, 1974. Fellow Econometric Soc.; mem. Am. Econ. Assn., Beta Gamma Sigma. Home: 835 Santa Fe Ave Stanford CA 94305 Office: Stanford U Grad Sch Bus Stanford CA 94305

ROBERTS, DWIGHT LOREN, historian/novelist, publishing executive; b. San Diego, June 3, 1949; s. James Albert and Cleva Lorraine (Conn) R.; B.A., U. San Diego, 1976, M.A., 1979; m. Phyllis Ann Adair, Mar. 29, 1969; children—Aimee Renee, Michael Loren, Daniel Alexandr. Engring. aide Benton Engring. Inc., San Diego, 1968-73; pres. Robert's Tech. Research Co., also subs. Marine Technique Ltd., San Diego, 1973-76; pres. Research Technique Internat., 1978—; freelance writer, 1979—; owner Agrl. Analysis, 1985—. Served with U.S. Army, 1969-71. Mem. ASTM, AAAS, Nat. Inst. Sci., N.Y. Acad. Scis., Nat. Inst. Cert. in Engring. Techs., Soil and Found. Engr. Assn., Phi Alpha Theta. Baptist. Author: Geological Exploration of Alaska, 1898-1924, Alfred Hulse Brooks, Alaskan Trailblazer; contbr. articles to profl. jours. Office: 3111 Victoria Dr Alpine CA 92001

ROBERTS, GEORGE ADAM, metallurgist; b. Uniontown, Pa., Feb. 18, 1919; s. Jacob Earle and Mary M. (Bower) R.; m. Betty E. Matthewson, May 31, 1941; children: George Thomas, William John, Mary Ellen; m. Jeanne Marie Polk. Student, U.S. Naval Acad., 1935-37; B.Sc., Carnegie Tech., 1939, M.Sc., 1941, D.Sc., 1942. Technician Bell Telephone Labs., N.Y.C., 1938; research dir. Vasco Metals Corp. (formerly Vanadium Alloys Steel Co.), Latrobe, Pa., 1940-45; chief metallurgist Vasco Metals Corp. (formerly Vanadium Alloys Steel Co.), 1945-53, v.p., 1953-61, pres., 1961-66; pres., dir. Teledyne, Inc. (merger with Vasco Metals Corp.), Los Angeles, 1966—, chief exec. officer, 1986—; hon. lectr. Societe Francaise de Metallurgie, 1960. Author: Tool Steels, 1944, 62; Contbr. articles trade jours. Recipient silver medal from Paris, 1955. Fellow Metall. Soc. Am. Inst. Mining, Metall. and Petroleum Engrs., Am. Soc. for Metals (chmn. Pitts. chpt. 1949-50, internat. pres. 1954-55, trustee Found. Edn. and Research 1954-59, 63-64, pres. Found. 1955-56, Gold medal 1977); mem. Nat. Acad. Engring., Metal Powder Industries Fedn. (dir. 1952-55, pres. 1957-61), Am. Soc. Metals, Am. Iron and Steel Inst., Soc. Mfg. Engrs., Tau Beta Pi; hon. life mem. several fgn. socs. Methodist. Office: Teledyne Inc 1901 Ave of the Stars Suite 1800 Los Angeles CA 90067 *

ROBERTS, GEORGE CHRISTOPHER, mfg. exec.; b. Ridley Park, Pa., May 27, 1936; s. George H. and Marion C. (Smullen) R.; m. Adriana Toribio, July 19, 1966; children—Tupac A., Capac Y. Sr. engr. ITT, Paramus, N.J., 1960-65; program mgr. Arde Research, Mawah, N.J., 1965-67; Space-Life Sci. program mgr., research div. GATX, 1967-69; dir. research and devel. Monogram Industries, Los Angeles, 1969-71; chmn. Inca Mfg. Corp, 1970-72; pres. Environ. Protection Center, Inc., Los Angeles, 1970-76. Bd. dirs., trustee Fairborn Obs.; trustee Buckley Sch., 1984—; chmn. solar and stellar physics Mt. Wilson Research Corp., 1984—; mem., dir., v.p. Peruvian Found. Mem. Am. Astron. Soc., Astron. Soc. Pacific. Patentee advanced waste treatment systems, automotive safety systems.

ROBERTS, HARRY FREDERICK, marketing consultant; b. Kingston, N.Y., June 27, 1942; s. Theresa Grace (Salanitro) Roberts; m. Lynda M. Hamilton; children: Christina, Robin, Becky, Melissa, Serra. New products mgr. J.C. Penney Co., N.Y.C., 1965-71; pres. Everfast Inc., N.Y.C., 1971-75; founder, pres. Kitchen Kaboodle, Portland, Oreg., 1975-82, The Roberts Group, Portland, 1982—; cons. Support Techs. Inc., Portland, 1985—; bd. dirs. Inter-Lock Inc., Ramagon Toys, Inc. Inventor workshop tools. Active March of Dimes Gourmet Gala, Portland, 1984, chmn., 1980. Named one of Top Ten Retail Execs. in U.S., entree mag., N.Y.C., 1981. Club: Portland Yacht. Avocations: boating, photography. Home: 4702 NE Alameda Portland OR 97213 Office: The Roberts Group 618 NW Glisan Portland OR 97209

ROBERTS, HOWARD CREIGHTON, acoustics engineer, educator; b. Wayne County, Ill., Nov. 1, 1910; s. Franklin Ebenezer and Sarah Jane (Phelps) R.; m. Elizabeth Clifford, Sept. 25, 1937; children: Anne Clifford, Margaret Ruth. AB, U. Ill., 1933, BEE, 1944. Registered profl. engr., Ill., Colo. Asst. Ill. Geol. Survey, Urbana, 1932-36; seismologist Gen. Geophys. Corp., Houston, 1937-38; mem. research staff Assn. Am. Railroads, Chgo., 1939-46; assoc. prof. civil engring. U. Ill., Champaign-Urbana, 1946-52, prof. engring., 1946-68; lectr. in acoustics U. Colo., Denver, 1977—; cons. Askania Regulator Co., Chgo., 1945-46, Koehring Co., Milw., 1950-69, Nat. Bur. Standards, Washington, 1948. Author: Mechanical Measurements by Electrical Methods, 1951, Instrumental Analysis, 1953, Acousticks--a lecture series, 1984; contbr. articles to profl. jours. Fellow Instrument Soc. Am., AAAS; mem. Inst. of Noise Control Engring., Sigma Xi. Republican. Methodist. Avocations: photography, music, drama. Home: 7199 S Vine Circle Littleton CO 80122

ROBERTS, JAMES GARFIELD, II, cost engineer; b. Tacoma Park, Md., June 13, 1952; s. James Garfield and Mary Louise (Markle) R.; m. Germaine Eleanor Dall-Winther, Sept. 25, 1982. B.S. in Mech. Engring., U. Colo., 1974. Cert. engr.-in-tng., Colo. Design engr. Gt. Western Sugar Co., Ft. Morgan, Colo., 1975-76; field engr. Colo. Interstate Gas Co., Denver, 1976-77, cost engr., Colorado Springs, 1977-79, sr. cost engr., 1979-86; sr. design and evaluation engr., 1986, staff design and evaluation engr., 1987—. Mem. ASME, Am. Assn. Cost Engrs., NSPE (Outstanding Service award 1982). Methodist. Clubs: Phlashers Photo (pres.), CIG Personal Computer Users (v.p.), Sno Jet Ski. Home: 2898 Maverick Dr Colorado Springs CO 80918 Office: PO Box 1087 Colorado Springs CO 80944

ROBERTS, JAMES MCGREGOR, professional association executive; b. Moncton, N.B., Can., Nov. 24, 1923; came to U.S., 1949, naturalized, 1956; s. Roland M. and Edith M. (Shields) R.; m. Thelma E. Williams, May 6, 1944; 1 dau., Jana M. B.Commerce, U. Toronto, Ont., Can., 1949. Auditor Citizens Bank, Los Angeles, 1949-54; auditor Acad. Motion Picture Arts and Scis., Hollywood, Calif., 1954—; controller Acad. Motion Picture Arts and Scis., 1956-71, exec. dir., 1971—, exec. sec. acad. found., 1971—. Served as pilot Royal Can. Air Force, World War II. Mem. Beverly Hills (Calif.) C. of C. Home: 450 S Maple Dr Beverly Hills CA 90212 Office: Acad Motion Pictures Arts Scis 8949 Wilshire Blvd Beverly Hills CA 90211

ROBERTS, JEAN SHAW, public relations executive; b. Pitts., May 22, 1950; d. Joseph L. and Helen B. (Shaw) R. BA, U. Denver, 1973. Caseworker, personal asst. to congressman John Murphy U.S. House Reps., Washington, 1974-76; acct. exec. Ketchum Pub. Relations, Pitts., 1976-78; pres., owner Market Survey Reports, Pitts., 1978-79; pub. relations mgr. Union Nat. Bank, Pitts., 1979-83; asst. v.p., pub. relations mgr. Great Am. 1st Savs. Bank, Tucson, 1984-86, v.p., pub. relations dir., 1986—. Mem. Pub. Relations Soc. Am. (accredited, bd. dirs. Pitts. chpt. 1983-84, Tucson chpt. 1986—), Internat. Assn. Bus. Communicators (chmn. Tucson dist. conf. 1985—). Republican. Office: Great Am Bank 1750 E Benson Hwy PO Box 2871 Tucson AZ 85702

ROBERTS, JOAN DUNKEL, biology educator; b. Norfork, Nebr., Sept. 24, 1924; d. Marion Murray and Hilda Johanna (Hansen) Dunkel; m. Bruce Allen Roberts, May 19, 1967; 1 child, David Allen. BA, Columbia Union Coll., 1948; MA, Walla Walla Coll., 1951; PhD, Oreg. State U., 1963. Assoc. prof. biology George Fox Coll., Newberg, Oreg., 1954-63, Andrews U., Berrien Springs, Mich., 1963-67; tchr. Wenatchee Valley Coll., Omak, Wash., 1984—. Mem. AAAS. Home: PO Box 36 Pateros WA 98846

ROBERTS, JOHN ARTHUR, analytical chemist, translator; b. Oceanside, Calif., June 4, 1954; s. Arthur Renfrew and Mary Nell (Boone) R. B.S., U. Calif-Berkeley, 1976; postgrad. U. So. Calif., 1978-81, Kokusai Kiristokyo U., Tokyo, 1981. Engring. technician Geo Ekta Labs, Fullerton, Calif., 1976-77; tech. English instr., translator Japan Atomic Energy Research Inst., Tokai-mura, 1977-78; analytical chemist Associated Labs., Orange, Calif., 1978—. Mem. Soil Conservation Soc. Am., Am. Agronomy Soc., Calif. Profl. Soil Scientists Assn. Episcopalian. Club: Brotherhood of St. Andrew. Translator tech. and sales lit. Office: Associated Labs 806 N Batavia St Orange CA 92668

ROBERTS, JOHN BARRETT, otolaryngologist; b. Phila., Mar. 3, 1928; s. Bennett Franklin and Helen Josephine (Barrett) R.; B.Sc., U. N.Mex., 1949, M.Sc., 1952; M.D., U. Colo., 1955; m. Joan Turner, May 24, 1958; children—Linda, Susan, Thomas, Amy, Bennett. Intern, Phila. Gen. Hosp., 1955-56; resident Henry Ford Hosp., 1960-61, Mass. Eye and Ear Infirmary, 1961-63, U. Pa. Grad. Sch. Medicine, 1959-60; practice medicine specializing in otolaryngology Ear, Nose and Throat Assocs., Albuquerque, 1963—; mem. staff St. Joseph, Presbyn., VA hosps. (all Albuquerque); clin. asso. U. N.Mex. Med. Sch., 1963—; examiner Am. Bd. Otolaryngology, 1978-79. Served to lt. comdr., M.C., USNR, 1957-59. Fellow A.C.S., Am. Acad. Otolaryngology (gov. 1983—), Oto-Ophthalmology Soc. Pacific Coast; mem. Albuquerque and Bernalillo County Med. Soc. (pres. 1971-72), N.Mex. Otolaryngol. Soc. (pres. 1975-76), Am. Coll. Surgeons N.Mex. (pres. El Paso chpt. 1976-77), N.Mex. Med. Soc. (sec.-treas. 1975—). Clubs: Albuquerque Rotary (pres. 1979-80), Albuquerque Country, Petroleum, Four Hills, Tanoan Country (Albuquerque). Home: 1309 Stagecoach Rd SE Albuquerque NM 87123 Office: W-15 La Mesa Med Ctr 7000 Cutler Ave NE Albuquerque NM 87110

ROBERTS, JOHN D., chemist, educator; b. Los Angeles, June 8, 1918; s. Allen Andrew and Flora (Dombrowski) R.; m. Edith Mary Johnson, July 11, 1942; children: Anne Christine, Donald William, John Paul, Allen Walter. A.B., UCLA, 1941, Ph.D., 1944; Dr. rer. nat. h.c., U. Munich, 1962; D.Sc., Temple U., 1964. Instr. chemistry U. Calif. at Los Angeles, 1944-45; NRC fellow chemistry Harvard, 1945-46, instr. chemistry, 1946; instr. chemistry Mass. Inst. Tech., 1946, asst. prof., 1947-50, asso. prof., 1950-52; vis. prof. Ohio State U., 1952, Stanford U., 1973-74; prof. organic chemistry Calif. Inst. Tech., 1953-72, Inst. prof. chemistry, 1972—, dean of faculty, v.p., provost, 1980-83, chmn. div. chemistry and chem. engring., 1963-68, acting chmn., 1972-73; Foster lectr. U. Buffalo, 1956; Mack Meml. lectr. Ohio State U., 1957; Falk-Plaut lectr. Columbia U., 1957; Reynaud Found. lectr. Mich. State U., 1958; Bachmann Meml. lectr. U. Mich., 1958; vis. prof. Harvard, 1958-59, M. Tishler lectr., 1965; Reilly lectr. Notre Dame U., 1960; Am.-Swiss Found. lectr., 1960; O.M. Smith lectr. Okla. State U., 1962; M.S. Kharasch Meml. lectr. U. Chgo., 1962; K. Folkers lectr. U. Ill., 1962; Phillips lectr. Haverford Coll., 1963; vis. prof. U. Munich, 1962; Sloan lectr. U. Alaska, 1967; Disting. vis. prof. U. Iowa, 1967; Sprague lectr. U. Wis., 1967; Kilpatrick lectr. Ill. Inst. Tech., 1969; Pacific Northwest lectr., 1969; E.F. Smith lectr. U. Pa., 1970; vis. prof. chemistry Stanford U., 1973-74; S.C. Lind lectr. U. Tenn.; Arapahoe lectr. U. Colo., 1976; Mary E. Kapp lectr. Va. Commonwealth U., 1976; R.T. Major lectr. U. Conn., 1977; Nebr. lectr. Am. Chem. Soc., 1977; Leermakers lectr. Wesleyan U., 1980; Iddles Meml. lectr. U. N.H., 1981; Arapahoe lectr. Colo. State U., 1981; Winstein lectr. UCLA, 1981; Gilman lectr. Iowa State U., 1982; Marvel lectr. U. Ill., 1982; vis. lectr. Inst. Photog. Chemistry, Beijing, People's Republic of China, 1983, King lectr. Kans. State U., 1984, Lanzhou U., People's Republic of China, 1985, Davis lectr. U. New Orleans, 1986; dir., cons. editor W.A. Benjamin, Inc., 1961-67; cons. E.I. du Pont Co., 1950—; mem. adv. panel chemistry NSF, 1958-60, chmn., 1959-60, chmn. divisional com. math., phys. engring. scis., 1962-64, mem. math. and phys. sci. div. com., 1964-66; chemistry adv. panel Air Force Office Sci. Research, 1959-61; chmn. chemistry sect. Nat. Acad. Scis., 1968-71; chmn. Nat. Acad. Scis. (Class I), 1976-78, councillor, 1980-83; dir. Organic Syntheses, Inc. Author: Basic Organic Chemistry, Part I, 1955, Nuclear Magnetic Resonance, 1958, Spin-Spin Splitting in High-Resolution Nuclear Magnetic Resonance Spectra, 1961, Molecular Orbital Calculations, 1961, (with M.C. Caserio) Basic Principles of Organic Chemistry, 1964, 2d edit., 1977, Modern Organic Chemistry, 1967, (with R. Stewart and M.C. Caserio) Organic Chemistry-Methane To Macromolecules, 1971; cons. editor: McGraw-Hill Series in Advanced Chemistry, 1957-60; editor-in-chief: Organic Syntheses, vol. 41; editorial bd.: Tetrahedron, Nouveau Chimie, Spectroscopy, Organic Magnetic Resonance. Trustee L.S.B. Leakey Found.; bd. dirs. Huntington Med. Research Insts. Recipient Alumni Profl. Achievement award UCLA, 1967; Guggenheim fellow, 1952-53, 55-56; recipient Am. Chem. Soc. award pure chemistry, 1954; Harrison Howe award, 1957; Roger Adams award in organic chemistry, 1967; Alumni Achievement award UCLA, 1967; Nichols medal, 1972; Tolman medal, 1975; Michelson-Morley award, 1976; Norris award, 1978; Pauling award, 1980; Theodore Wm. Richards medal, 1982; Willard Gibbs Gold medal, 1983; Golden Plate award Am. Acad. Achievement, 1983; Priestley medal, 1987. Mem. Am. Chem. Soc. (chmn. organic chemistry div. 1956-57, exec. com. organic div. 1953-57), Nat. Acad. Scis., Am. Philos. Soc. (council 1983-86), Am. Acad. Arts and Scis., Sigma Xi, Phi Lambda Upsilon, Alpha Chi Sigma. Office: Calif Inst Tech Div of Chem 164-30CR Pasadena CA 91125

ROBERTS, JOHN WARREN, environmental engineer, consultant; b. Albany, Oreg., May 16, 1924; s. Bryan Jefferson Roberts and Selma (Staff) Blodgett; m. Phyllis Mae Latimer, Dec. 21, 1947 (div.), remarried Jan. 9, 1982; children: Wendy Lou Davis, Kelly Roberts Backman; m. Bernice Standish, May 7, 1976 (div. Dec. 1977). BS in Marine Engring., U.S. Merchant Marine Acad., 1944; BS in Physics, Oreg. State U., 1948; MEd, U. Wash., 1956, MS in Engring. Air Pollution, 1973. Registered profl. mech. engr. Marine engr. U.S. Merchant Marine, various locations, 1943-52; advanced through ranks to lt. (j.g.) USNR, resigned, 1950; tchr. Highline Schs., Seattle and Monroe, Oreg., 1949-53; prin. personnel analyst Civil Service Commn., Seattle, 1958-70; source test engr. Puget Sound Air Pollution Control Agy., Seattle, 1970-83; pres., environ. engr. Engring. Plus Inc., Seattle, 1983—; founder, pres. May Valley Coop Community, Seattle, 1955-70; founder, bd. dirs. Youth Enterprises, Seattle, 1965-70; pres., bd. dirs. Theosophical Soc., Seattle, 1974—. Democrat precinct committeeman, Seattle, 1954-55, 83, 85; organizer Citizens for Better Govt., Seattle, 1962; mem. human resources com. LWV, Seattle, 1983; bd. dirs. Orcas Island (Wash.) Found., 1962-68. Mem. Pacific Northwest Internat. Air Pollution Control Assn. (chmn. air toxics com. 1984-86), Air Pollution Control Assn. (interaction with total environ. com. 1985-86). Democrat. Avocations: practicing therapeutic touch healing, metaphysics, meditation. Home and Office: 1425 E Prospect #3 Seattle WA 98112

ROBERTS, KELYN HOWE, social science educator; b. Grand Rapids, Mich., July 12, 1940; s. Richmond M. and Barbara (Howe) R.; m. Ruth Weisberg, July 24, 1966; children: Alicia Weisberg, Alfred Weisberg. BA, U. Mich., 1962, MA, 1969, PhD, 1971. Asst. prof. psychology UCLA, 1969-76; cons. Rand Corp., Santa Monica, Calif., 1977-78; mem. staff Pacific Western U., Los Angeles, 1980—, dir. grad. tchr.'s sch., 1983—; vis. assoc. prof. U. Tex., Odessa, 1978-79; mem. staff U. Redlands, Calif., 1980-83, Chapman (Calif.) Coll., 1983, Clayton U., St. Louis, 1984. Cons. editor Acad. Press, 1974-76;. Chmn. Ocean Park Community Orgn., Santa Monica, 1980-82; pres. John Muir Elem. PTA, Santa Monica, 1981-84, Site Improvement Council, Santa Monica, 1984—; treas. Com. Responsive Sch. Bd., Santa Monica, 1983-87. Mem. AAAS, Western Psychol. Assn. Democrat. Home: 2421 3d St Santa Monica CA 90705

ROBERTS, KENNETH ARTHUR BLAIR, JR., lawyer; b. Springfield, Mass., Nov. 25, 1957; s. Kenneth Arthur Blair and Betty Lou Roberts. BA, U. Colo., 1980; MA, Universite de Bordeaux, France, 1980; JD, U. Pacific, 1984. Bar: Colo. 1984, U.S. Dist. Ct. Colo. 1984, U.S. Ct. Appeals (10th cir.) 1984, U.S. Tax Ct. 1986. Paralegal Manville Corp., Denver, 1980-81; staff paralegal Inst. Adminstrv. Justice, Sacramento, 1982-84; assoc. Weller, Friedrich, Hickisch, Hazlitt & Ward, Denver, 1984-86, Hall and Evans, Denver, 1986—. Contbr. articles to profl. jours. Recipient Recognition of Disting. Youth Leadership and Service to Community award Am. Biog. Inst., 1985; McCarthy Found. Meml. scholar, McGeorge Sch. Law Merit scholar, Gary V. Schaber Meml. scholar U. Pacific, 1981-84. Mem. ABA, Colo. Bar Assn. (Pro Bono award 1985), Denver Bar Assn., Assn. Trial Lawyers Assn., Colo. Trial Lawyers Assn., Colo. Def. Lawyers Assn., Colo. Lawyers for Arts. Club: Sporting (Denver). Home: 636 Washington St Denver CO 80203 Office: Hall & Evans 1200 17th St Suite 1700 Denver CO 80202

ROBERTS, LARRY MICHAEL, lawyer; b. Sacramento, July 23, 1957; s. Ernest Roth and Verna Roberts. Student, Université Paul Valery III, Montpellier, France, 1977-78; BA in Bus., U. Calif., Riverside, 1979; JD, Loyola U., 1982; LLM in Internat. Law, Cambridge U., 1983. Bar: Calif. 1982, U.S. Dist. Ct. (cen. dist.) Calif. 1982. Assoc. Lee Barker & Assocs., Pasadena and Los Angeles, 1984—; dir. Grafin Engerprises, Los Angeles. Mem. ABA (asst. editor Young Lawyers newsletter 1986—), Los Angeles County Bar Assn., Pasadena Bar Assn., Lawyers Com. on Arts, Phi Alpha Delta. Club: Greater Los Angeles Press. Avocations: art dealer, collector, skiing, equitation. Office: Lee Barker & Assocs 35 S Raymond #400 Pasadena CA 91105

ROBERTS, LARRY PAUL, broadcasting executive; b. Marengo, Iowa, June 17, 1950; s. Paul V. and Marcheta Jean (Moore) R.; m. Sheryl Irene Delamarter, Aug. 18, 1972; children: Jason, Stacey, Adam. Student, Northwestern U., 1968-69; BS, U. Minn., 1972. Ops. mgr. Sta. WPEO Radio, Peoria, Ill., 1969-70, Sta. WAYL Radio, Mpls., 1970-76; program dir. Sta. KXL and KXL-FM, Portland, Oreg., 1976-82; pres. Sunbrook Broadcasting, Inc., licensee of stas. KCSJ and KUSN, Pueblo, Colo., 1982—, Sunbrook Communications Corp., licensee of stas. KDXT and KGRZ, Missoula, Mont., also stas. KQUY and KXTL, Butte, Mont. Pres. Salvation Army Bd., Pueblo; v.p. United Way, Pueblo; bd. dirs. Rocky Mountain council Boy Scouts Am., Wayside Cross Rescue Mission, Pueblo; Christian edn. dir. Rocky Mountain Conf., Free Meth. Ch., mem. ofcl. bd., lay minister. Recipient Outstanding Radio Broadcaster award So. Colo. Press Club, 1986; named Radio Copywriter of Yr., Mont. Broadcasters Assn., 1983, Editorial Writer of Yr., Sigma Delta Chi, 1979, one of Outstanding Young Men in Am., Jaycees, 1980, 85. Republican. Lodges: Lions (v.p. Portland club 1982), Rotary (v.p., pres. elect Pueblo club). Home: 1 Sandcastle Pueblo CO 81001 Office: Sta KCSJ-AM 1st and Main Box 236 Pueblo CO 81003

ROBERTS, MALCOLM BLAIR, government and community relations consulting company executive; b. Hollywood, Calif., Nov. 25, 1936; s. Charles Erling and Muriel (Beaufoy) R.; m. Cynthia Ann Graham, Nov. 28, 1970; children—Cheyenne, Bret McKinley, Alexis Michelle. B.A. in History, Princeton U., 1958. Asst. mng. editor Pace Mag., Los Angeles, 1966-69; spl. asst. to U.S. Sec. Interior, 1970; adminstrv. asst. to Gov. Walter J. Hickel, State of Alaska, 1971-74; pres. Malcolm B. Roberts & Assocs., Anchorage, 1974-79, 82—; exec. dir. Commonwealth North, Inc., Anchorage, 1979-82, 1987—; Mem. Alaska State Rep. Cen. Com., 1974—; Rep. candidate for lt. gov. of Alaska, 1982, candidate for state senate, 1986; mem. Alaska State Bd. Edn., 1976-77; mem. Alaska adv. bd. U.S. Civil Rights Commn., 1977. Recipient Francisco Zarco award Mexican Govt., 1968. Clubs: Commonwealth North, World Affairs Council. Editor: Does One Way Of Life Have To Die So Another Can Live?, 1975; Solutions to the National Energy Crisis: Why Not Alaska?, 1979. Office: 2001 Churchill Dr Anchorage AK 99517

ROBERTS, MARTIN, research chemist consultant; b. N.Y.C., May 8, 1920; s. Barnett and Rachel (Schneider) Rabinowitz; m. Ada Jean Goldman, Jan. 30, 1949; children: Jefery, Beth, Darel, Gary. BS, CCNY, 1942; MA, Bklyn. Coll., 1947; PhD, U. So. Calif., 1951. Research chemist Schwarz Labs., Orangeburg, N.Y., 1944-47; research biochemist McGaw Labs., Irvine, Calif., 1951-66; mgmt. dir. Seattle Artificial Kidney Supply Co., 1966-71; dir. med. and regulatory Organon Teknika, Oklahoma City, 1971-86; cons. Robert's Enterprises, Los Angeles, 1986—. Contbr. articles to profl. jours.; patentee in field. Mem. Am. Soc. Artificial Internal Organs, Am. Men Sci., Am. Soc. Nephrology, Internat. Soc. Artificial Organs, Sigma Xi. Avocations: camping, photography, windsurfing. Home and Office: 16022 Parthenia St Sepulveda CA 91343

ROBERTS, NORMAN FRANK, English composition educator; b. Guilford, Maine, Aug. 18, 1931; s. John Francis and Pearl Estelle (Crozier) R.; m. Shoko Kawasaki, Sept. 18, 1959; children: Norman F. Jr., Kenneth K., Kathryn M. BA, U. Hawaii, 1960, MA, 1963, cert. in linguistics, 1972. Instr. ESL, U. Hawaii, Honolulu, 1962-68; instr. of English, Linguistics Leeward Community Coll., Pearl City, Hawaii, 1968—, chmn. language arts, 1975-81; cons. Nat. Council Tchrs. of English, 1972—. Co-author: Community College Library Instruction, 1979. Contbr. articles to profl. jours. V.p. Pacific Palisades Community Assn., Pearl City, pres., 1973-74; Aloha council Boy Scouts of Am., Honolulu, 1972—, dir. wood badge course, 1985. Served with U.S. Army, 1951-55. Recipient Dist. award of Merit Boy Scouts Am., 1986. Mem. Nat. Council Tchrs. of English, Hawaii Council Tchrs. of English (program chmn. 1974), Am. Dialect Soc. (program chmn. Honolulu conf. 1977), Linguistic Soc. Am., Phi Kappa Phi. Avocations: music, outdoor life. Office: Leeward Community Coll Language Arts Div 96 045 ALA IKE Pearl City HI 96782

ROBERTS, RONALD ELDRIDGE, minister, educator; b. Mt. Holly, N.J., Jan. 30, 1942; s. Benjamin Charles and Juanita Odessa (Jacobs) R.; m. Gertrude Inez Timpson Carney, Jan. 30, 1965; children: Ronald E. Jr., Reginald E. BS, Phila. Coll. Bible, 1970; ThM, Dallas Theol. Sem., 1975, D.Min., 1985. Ordained to ministry Bethany Bap. Assn. Assoc. minister Mt. Calvary Bapt. Ch., Camden, N.J., 1965-70, 75-77, Golden Gate Bapt. Ch., Dallas, 1970-71; minister Christian edn. St. John Bapt. Ch., Dallas, 1972-75; dean students, faculty Manna Bible Inst., Phila., 1975-77; sr. pastor Baldwin Hills Bapt. Ch., Los Angeles, 1977—; mem. faculty Talbot Sch. Theology of Biola U., La Mirada, Calif., 1982-86, faculty, 1986—; bd. dirs., co-founder Black Evangelistic Enterprise, Dallas, 1972—. Contbr. articles to profl. jours. Served with USAF, 1960-64. Mem. S.W. Bapt. Conf. Missions (bd. dirs. 1980-82, 84-87), Evang. Tchrs. Tng. Assn., Nat. Black Evang. Assn. (past dir. Christian edn. dept. 1973-75). Democrat. Club: Camera. Office: Baldwin Hills Bapt Ch 4700 W King Blvd Los Angeles CA 90016

ROBERTS, TERRY, country music promoter; b. Vernal, Utah, Mar. 9, 1954; d. Burnett and Reva Alberta (Dean) R. Fast food mgr. Burger Pit, Roosevelt, Utah, 1972-76; forestry technician, Ashley Nat. Forest, Roosevelt, Utah, 1976-79; gen. maintance person Seagull Refinery, Roosevelt, Utah, 1979—; country music promoter. Sec., treas. Oil, Chem., Atomic Workers Internat. Union Local 2-941, 1979-84. Mem. Country Music Assn. Baptist. Home: 168 N State St 82-1 Roosevelt UT 84066

ROBERTS, THOMAS D., research engineer, educator; b. N.Y.C., June 21, 1935; s. Idwall David and Lucille Anne Roberts; m. Jo Baker, June 14, 1957; children: Lynneth, Evan, Eiluned. BS, U. Ala., 1959; PhD, Oregon State U., 1965. Registered profl. elec. engr., Alaska. Engr. Chrysler Corp., Huntsville, Ala., 1959, Bur. Mines, Albany, Oreg., 1960-63.; research physicist Nat. Bur. Standards, Boulder, Colo., 1965-66; prof. engring. and head dept. U. Alaska, Fairbanks, 1966—, dir. Inst. No. Engring., 1983—; cons. Fryer-Pressley Assocs., Meteor Data, Inc., Anchorage, Alaska. Contbr. articles to profl. jours. Treas. Fairbanks Symphony Assn., 1982-85. Served with U.S. Army, 1953-56. Fellow Nat. Defense Edn. Act, 1960-63. Mem. IEEE, Am. Soc. Engring. Edn., Am. Phys. Soc. Avocations: classical piano, amateur radio, cross country skiing. Home: 740 Goldfinch Fairbanks AK 99701 Office: U Alaska Inst Northern Engring Fairbanks AK 99775

ROBERTS, VICKI MICHELE, lawyer; b. Bklyn., July 3, 1959; d. Stanley Benjamin and Adele (Klein) R. Student, Mt. Holyoke Coll., 1976-77; BA in TV and Flim Prodn., Calif. State U., Northridge, 1980; JD, Southwestern U., Los Angeles, 1982. Bar: Calif. 1983, N.J. 1986, U.S. Dist. Ct. (cen. dist.) Calif. 1983, U.S. Dist. Ct. N.J. 1986. Sole practice Los Angeles, 1983-86, Santa Monica, Calif., 1986—; judge pro tem Los Angeles Mcpl. Ct., Van Nuys, Calif., 1984—. Composer music and lyrics, 1972—. Mem. Synagogue for the Performing Arts., Beverly Hills, Calif., 1978—. Named one of Outstanding Young Women of Am., 1982. Mem. Women Lawyers Assn. Los Angeles (legis. com.), Assn. Trial Lawyers Am., Los Angeles County Bar Assn., ABA (entertainment and sports com.), Mensa. Avocations: piano composition, writer. Office: 1250 6th St Suite 401 Santa Monica CA 90401

ROBERTS, WILBUR EUGENE, dental educator, research scientist; b. Lubbock, Tex., Nov. 16, 1942; s. Wilbur Eugene Roberts and Elva Etna (Chance) Turnwall; m. Cheryl Ann Jones, June 6, 1967; children: Jeffery Alan, Carrie Jean. DDS, Creighton U., 1967; PhD in Anatomy, U. Utah, 1969; cert. in orthodontics, U. Conn., 1974. Diplomate Am. Bd. Orthodontics. Research fellow U. Utah, Salt Lake City, 1967-69; postdoctoral fellow U. Conn., Farmington, 1971-74; from asst. prof. to prof. dentistry U. Pacific, San Francisco, 1974—; research assoc. NASA Ames Research Ctr., Moffett Field, Calif., 1980—, NRC sr. research assoc., 1982-83; dir. Bone Research Lab., U. Pacific, 1980-84—, Oral Devel. Clinic, 1980—; research cons. Neodontics Corp., Laguna Niguel, Calif., 1982—, Denar Corp., Anaheim, Calif., 1985—. Contbr. sci. articles to profl. jours. Rep. campaign worker, Contra Costa County, Calif., 1980-82; ch. sch. supt. San Ramon Valley Meth. Ch., Alamo, Calif., 1979-81; adult ministries council San Ramon Valley Meth. Ch., Danville, Calif., 1984-86; sci. cons. St. Isadore Sch. and San Ramon Valley High Sch., Danville, 1978-86. Served to lt. comdr. USN, 1969-71, Vietnam. Recipient Cosmos Achievement award NASA, 1981. Fellow Internat. Coll. Dentists; mem. Med. Dental Guild Calif. (pres. 1982-83, gold key award 1985), Am. Assn. Dental Research, Pacific Dental Research Found (pres. 1978-80), Am. Sportman's Club, Omicrom Kappa Upsilon. Avocations: fishing, hunting, backpacking. Home: 75 Saint Timothy Ct Danville CA 94526 Office: U Pacific Sch Dentistry Bone Research Lab 2155 Webster St San Francisco CA 94115

ROBERTS, WILLIAM BYRON, II, director of engineering consulting firm; b. Bklyn., Feb. 22, 1944; s. William Byron I and Regina Maria (Beardsworth) R.; m. Alison Jane Raymond; children: Elizabeth Frances, Annamarie Regina, Candace Alexandra, William Byron III. BME, U. Santa Clara, 1966; MS, NYU, 1968; diploma, Von Karman Inst., Belgium, 1970; DSc, U. Brussels and Von Karman Inst., 1973. Lic. comml. pilot. Research engr. FAA, Atlantic City, 1969; research asst. Von Karman Inst., Rhode-St-Genese, Belgium, 1969-73; sr. engr. Westinghouse Electric Corp., Sunnyvale, Calif., 1973-76; asst. prof. U. Notre Dame, South Bend, Ind., 1976-78; project engr. Nielsen Engr., Mountain View, Calif., 1978-80; dir. Flow Application Research, Fremont, Calif., 1980—; cons. Ames Research Ctr., NASA, Mountain View, 1976, USAF, Tullahoma, Tenn., 1976-80, Sverdrup Tech., Tullahoma, 1980—, Westinghouse Electric Corp., Sunnyvale, 1980—. Author more than 50 tech. articles; inventor tech. patent Fan Blade Research. Fellow Nat. Edn. Def. Act., NYU, 1968-69, USAF, Von Karman Inst., 1969-70, NASA, Lewis Res. Ctr., Cleve., 1976-77; NASA grantee, Lewis Research Ctr., 1977—. Mem. ASME, AIAA, Sigma Xi. Avocations: flying, hunting, shooting, travel. Office: Flow Application Research 1543 Vernal Ave Fremont CA 94539

ROBERTSON, ANN, librarian; b. Los Angeles, Sept. 28, 1937; d. Charles John Sr. and Eve (Jarmosh) McNeal; m. Michael Paul Robertson, Sept. 9, 1961 (div.); 1 child, Michele Ann. BA, Calif. State U., Fresno, 1981; MLS, San Jose State U., 1982. Med. librarian David Grant USAF Med. Ctr., Travis AFB, Calif., 1965-74; mgr. library services Community Hosps. Cen. Calif., Fresno, 1974-85; dir. library services Virginia Mason Med. Ctr., Seattle, 1985—. Mem. Spl. Libraries Assn., Med. Library Assn. (cert.). Home: 12718 100th Ave NE Kirkland WA 98034 Office: Med Library Virginia Mason Med Ctr 925 Seneca St Seattle WA 98101

ROBERTSON, BILLY B., insurance executive, consultant; b. Red Cloud, Nebr., July 1, 1929; s. Earl and Ruby LaVerne (Christensen) R.; m. Nettie L. Hogan, Sept. 25, 1948; children: Christine L. Pollard, Janet B. Cert. hazard control mgr., master level. Patrol inspector U.S. Border Patrol, Calexico, Calif., 1953-54; officer La Mesa (Calif.) Police Dept., 1954-56; sr. agt. Dept. Justice, San Diego, 1956-66; tech. advisor Fireman's Fund Ins., Santa Ana, Calif., 1966-74; mgr. loss control Mission Ins., Los Angeles, 1974-79; v.p. UniCare Ins. Co., Irvine, Calif., 1979—. Served with U.S. Army, 1946-53. Mem. Am. Soc. Safety Engrs., Systems Safety Soc., Justice Systems Soc., So. Calif. Engring. Soc., So. Calif. Off-Track Racing Assn. (track ofcl. 1972). Republican. Lodge: Masons. Avocation: lawn bowling. Office: UniCare Ins Co 2361 Campus Dr #105 Irvine CA 92715

ROBERTSON, FRANCIS E. (ROBIN), JR., data processing specialist; b. Bryan, Tex., May 9, 1944; s. Francis Elmer and Virginia M. (Dunman) R.; m. Katherine Esmela Mitchell, May 28, 1971. BS in Math., BA in English, U. Md., 1967; MA in Psychology, Internat. Coll., 1981, PhD in Psychology with distinction, 1985. Asst. v.p. Occidental LIfe Ins. Co., Los Angeles, 1969-81; cons. actuary, data processing specialist McGinn Assocs., Anaheim, Calif., 1982-86, Mercer-Meidinger-Hansen, Los Angeles, 1986—; cons. Western Conf. Teamster's Supplemental Pension Plan, Seattle, 1983—. Author: Handle with Care, 1964, Card Modes, 1983, C.G. Jung and the Archtypes of the Collective Unconscious, 1987; book rev. editor Psychol. Perspectives; contbr. articles to hobby jours. Mem. Soc. Actuaries, Western Pension Conf., Internat. Brotherhood of Magicians. Democrat. Avocations: magic, reading, microcomputers. Office: Mercer-Medinger-Hansen 3303 Wilshire Blvd Los Angeles CA 90010

ROBERTSON, GERALD RANKIN, physician, internist; b. Lawton, Okla., July 12, 1944; s. Nathan Ellsworth and Lameda (Newton) R.; m. Martha Elizabeth Marvel, June 23, 1968; children: Eleanor, Rebecca, Douglas, Sharon, Stephen. AA, Cameron Coll., 1964; BS, Okla. U., 1966; MD, Tufts U., 1970. Diplomate Am. Bd. Internal Medicine. House staff officer U. N.Mex. Teaching Hosp., Albuquerque, 1970-71, 73-77; internist, pres. Cibola Med. Found., Gallup, N.Mex., 1977—. Served to capt. U.S. Army, 1971-73. Democrat. Methodist. Lodge: Rotary. Office: Cibola Med Found Vanden Basch Pkwy Po Box 1100 Gallup NM 87301

ROBERTSON, JACQUELINE LEE, entomologist; b. Petaluma, Calif., July 9, 1947; d. John Lyman and Nina Pauline (Klemenok) Schwartz; m. Joseph Alexander, Sept. 12, 1970 (div. Jan. 1978). BA, U. Calif., Berkeley, 1969, PhD, 1973. Registered profl. entomologist. Research entomologist USDA Forest Service, Berkeley, 1969—. Editor Jour. Econ. Entomology, 1982—; contbr. articles to profl. jours.; patentee lab. device, 1982. Mem. Entomol. Soc. Am., Entomol. Soc. Can., AAAS. Democrat. Office: US Forest Service PSW Sta 1960 Addison St Berkeley CA 94704

ROBERTSON, JAMES ALLEN, risk mgmt. consultant, writer, lecturer; b. Burlington, Iowa, Jan. 24, 1948; s. George Allen and Betty Irene (Beck) R.; student Knox Coll., 1965-66; B.A., U. Iowa, 1969; postgrad. San Francisco Theol. Sem./Grad. Theol. Union, 1969-70; M.S.A., Pepperdine U., 1976; m. Stephanie Peacock. Casualty underwriter Hartford Ins. Group, San Francisco, 1970-72, supervising underwriter, 1972-73, Los Angeles, 1973-74; asst. v.p. Tausch Ins. Brokers, Santa Ana, Calif., 1974-75; cons. Warren, McVeigh, Griffin & Huntington, 1975-76; sr. v.p. Reed Risk Mgmt., San Francisco, 1976-78; pres. James A. Robertson & Assoc., Inc., 1978-87; prin. cons., Warren, McVeigh & Griffin, Newport Beach, Calif., 1979-83; pres. Ins. Litigation Cons., 1984-87; sr. cons., nat. dir. profl. ins. publs. Coopers & Lybrand, Newport Beach, 1987—; assoc. in risk mgmt. C.P.C.U. Mem. Soc. Chartered Property Casualty Underwriters (pres. Orange Empire chpt. 1985-86, nat. publs. com. 1984-87), Soc. Risk Mgmt. Cons. (chmn. profl. practices com. 1986-87), Omicron Delta Kappa. Republican. Author: The Umbrella Book, 1976, 2d edit., 1979-83; Key Financial Ratios, 1978; ISO Commercial Liability Forms, 1984, 4th edit., 1986; It's Time to Take the Mystery Out of Umbrellas, 1984; editor Risk Mgmt. Letter, 1981-83. Office: Coopers & Lybrand One Newport Place 1301 Dove St Newport Beach CA 92660

ROBERTSON, JEANNE BENNETT, interior designer, artist; b. San Francisco, May 21, 1916; d. Willard Winslow Bennett and Mary Louise (Weymann) B.; m. Charles Bennett Robertson, July 5, 1941; children: David Bennett, Philip Bennett, Anne Louise Thomas. AB, U. Calif., Berkeley, 1938. Sales mgr. Furniture and Design Co., Mill Valley, Calif., 1966; owner, designer Jeanne Robertson Interiors Co., Belvedere, Calif., 1967-74; pres. Clarke-Robertson, Ltd., 1974—; coordinator artists workshops. Exhibited in ome-woman and group shows; represented in permanent collections City Hall of Honolulu; also pvt. and corp. collections. Formerly active Girl Scouts U.S., Camp Fire Girls; past pres. local PTA. Served with Women Airforce Service Pilots, 1943-44. Mem. AAUW (past pres.), Nat. Home Fashion League, Nat. League Am. Penwomen, Am. Soc. Interior Designers (assoc.), Hawaii Watercolor Soc. (past pres.), Assn. Honolulu Artists. Republican. Presbyterian. Home: 1480 Kamole St Honolulu HI 96821 Office: 812B Kawaiahao Honolulu HI 96821

ROBERTSON, KAREN LEE, county administrator, acoustical consultant; b. Whittier, Calif., Mar. 21, 1955; d. Lethal Greenhaw Robertson and Lloydine Ann (Pierce) Robertson-Reese; 1 child, Kimberlee Ann Kubski. Student Calif. State U. Acoustical technician Hilliard & Bricken, Santa Ana, Calif., 1977-79, John J. Van Houten, Anaheim, Calif., 1979; prin. Robertson & Assocs., Boulder, Colo., 1980; acoustical technician David Adams & Assocs., Denver, 1980; v.p. engring. John Hilliard & Assocs., Tustin, Calif., 1985—; acoustical specialist County of Orange, Santa Ana, 1980-87; airline access, noise officer John Wayne Airport Adminstrn. of Orange County, 1987—. Co-author Land Use/Noise Compatibility Manual, 1984; editor Noise Element of General Plan, 1984. Speaker in field. Mem. acoustical adv. bd. Orange County, 1985—. Recipient Achievement award Nat. Assn. Counties, 1986. Mem. Acoustical Soc. Am. (bd. dirs. 1985-86), Transp. Research Bd. (tech. mem. 1985—), Nat. Assn. Noise Control Ofcls., Community/Indsl. Noise Control Assn., Inst. Noise Control Engring. (affiliate), Calif. Assn. Window Mfrs. (STC Task Group 1985). Republican. Home: 220 N Kodiak #B Anaheim CA 92807 Office: John Wayne Airport Adminstrn County of Orange 3151 Airway Ave Bldg K #101 Costa Mesa CA 92626

ROBERTSON, LAWRENCE MARSHALL, former electric utility executive, consulting engineer; b. Denver, Jan. 20, 1900; s. Hugh Lawrence and Grace (Worden) R.; m. Mildred Eleanor Blackwood, Nov. 15, 1924 (dec. 1971); 1 son, Lawrence Marshall. B.S.E.E. with honors, U. Colo., 1922, E.E., 1927, M.S.E.E., 1938, D.Engring. (hon.), 1955; J.D., U. Denver, 1979. Profl. engr., Colo., Calif., Wash., Wyo., Ill., N.Y. Engr. to chief elec. engr. Pub. Service Co. Colo., Denver, 1922-53, chief elec. engr., mgr. engring., 1953-59, mng. engr., v.p. engring., 1959-68; cons. engr. elec. utilities Colo., Wash., Ill., Argentina, Dominican Republic, 1968—, U.S. Bur. Reclamation, Denver, 1969, Pub. Utilities Dist., Wenatchee, Wash., 1975-79, Power Authority, Buenos Aires, 1969, Dominican Republic, 1981. Contbr. chpts. to books, articles to publs. Chmn. Solid Waste Disposal Denver Region, 1968-73; mem. Fed. Power Commn. Adv. Com., Washington, 1962-67; mem., pres.

Colo. State Bd. Registered Profl. Engrs., 1957-69. Served with U.S. Army, 1918. Named Disting. Engring. Alumnus, U. Colo., 1968; recipient Gold Medal award Colo. Engring. Council, 1954. Life fellow IEEE (v.p. 1945, dir. 1956, Habirshaw award 1963, Centennial award 1984); mem. Profl. Engrs. Colo. (A.J. Ryan award 1969), Conference Internationale (Paris, Attwood award 1982), Denver C. of C. (dir. 1949), Sigma Xi, Alpha Tau Omega. Republican. Methodist. Lodges: Masons, Shriners. Home: 320 Ash St Denver CO 80220

ROBERTSON, LAWRENCE MARSHALL, JR., neurosurgeon; b. Denver, Feb. 4, 1932; s. Lawrence M. and Mildred Eleanor (Blackwood) R.; m. Joan T. White, May 13, 1958 (div. Oct. 1973); children: Colette M., Michele E., Laurienne J., Lawrence M. III; m. Lee Ann Crawford, Sept. 24, 1982; one child, William M. BA, U. Colo., 1954; MD, U. Colo., Denver, 1957; post-grad., U. Denver, 1981-85. Intern Kings County Hosp., Bklyn., 1957-58; resident in gen. surgery St. Joseph Hosp., Denver, 1958-59; resident in neurology U. Colo., Denver, 1959-60; resident in neurosurgery Boston City Hosp., 1960-64; fellow in neurosurgery Lahey Clinic, Boston, 1963; practice medicine specializing in neurosurgery Denver, 1964—; arbitrator Am. Arbitration Assn., 1983—. Contbr. articles on malpractice to legal jours. Served to capt. USNR, 1979-83, 85. Recipient Continuing Edn. Cert., Am. Assn. Neurol. Surgeons and Cong. Neurol. Surgeons, 1976, 1980-83, Physicians Recognition award AMA 1976-79, 80-83, 84-87. Mem. Colo. Neurosurg. Soc., Interurban Neurosurg. Soc., Rocky Mountain Traumatologic Soc., Colo. Bar Assn., Denver Bar Assn., N.Y. Acad. Scis., Assn. Trial Lawyers Am., Nat. Railway Hist. Soc., Assn. Mil. Surgeons of U.S., Naval Re. Assn., Res. Officers Assn., U.S. Naval Inst., AAAS, Phi Alpha Delta. Office: Colo Neurosurgery PC 1635 Gilpin St Denver CO 80218

ROBERTSON, MALCOLM RAY, educator; b. Stockton, Calif., Dec. 12, 1922; s. Malcolm Crawford Robertson and Selma Charlotte (Halvorsen) Pribble; m. Ruth Lois Smith, Oct. 15, 1944; children: Kenneth Ray, Kathleen Joy. BA, Pasadena Coll., 1948; ThB, Pacific Bible Coll., 1950; MA, Calif. State U., Los Angeles, 1961; EdD, U. So. Calif., 1967; HHD (hon.), Azusa Pacific U., 1973. Instr. Pacific Bible Coll., Azusa, Calif., 1948-50; registrar, instr. Pacific Bible Coll., Azusa, 1950-53; dean of instrn. Pacific Bible Coll., 1953-59; v.p., dean of instrn. Azusa Pacific Coll., 1957-63, acad. v.p., 1965-72, exec. v.p. acad., instl. affairs, 1972-75, chmn. presdl. team, acting pres., 1975-76; prof. in religion and psychology Azusa Pacific U., 1977—; U.P. Planning, Research and Evaluation Azusa Pacific Coll., 1977—; assoc. pub. Travelhoat Mag., Orange County, Calif., 1977-80; adminstr. Thaddeus Found, Glendora, Calif., 1979—; chmn. of adminstrn. Calif. Baptist Coll., Riverside, 1981—. Elder Wesleyan Ch., 1952—. Served with U.S. Army, 1944-46. Spl. award Free Meth. Insts. Higher Edn., 1974. Mem. Calif. Tchrs. Assn., Phi Delta Kappa, Kappa Phi Kappa. Republican. Wesleyan. Lodge: Kiwanis (pres. Glendora chpt. 1971-72). Home: 179 Oak Forest Circle Glendora CA 91740 Office: Azusa Pacific U 921 E Alosta Azusa CA 91702

ROBERTSON, MARIAN ELLA (HALL), handwriting company analyst; b. Edmonton, Alta., Can., Mar. 3, 1920; d. Orville Arthur and Lucy Hon (Osborn) Hall; m. Howard Chester Robertson, Feb. 7, 1942; children: Elaine, Richard. Student, Willamette U., 1937-39; BS, Western Oreg. State U., 1955. Cert. elem., jr. high. tchr., supt. (life) Oreg.; cert. graphoanalyst. Tchr. pub. schs. Mill City, Albany, Scio and Hillsboro, Oreg., 1940-72; cons. Zaner-Bloser Inc., Columbus, Ohio, 1972-85, assoc. cons., 1985—; pres. Write-Keys, Scio, 1980—; tchr. Internat. Graphoanalysis Soc., Chgo., 1979. sr. intern 5th Congl. Dist. Oreg., Washington, 1984; precinct committeem. Rep. Cen. Com., Linn County, 1986, alt. vice-chair, 1986; candidate Oreg. State Legis., Salem, 1986. Mem. Altrusa Internat. (internat. chmn. 1985-86), Soc. Integrative Graphology. Republican. Mem. Soc. of Friends. Avocations: piano, organ, violin, gardening, writing. Home: 37929 Kelly Rd Scio OR 97374 Office: Write-Keys PO Box 54 Jefferson OR 97352

ROBERTSON, MATTHEW ROGER, computer scientist; b. Tacoma, Dec. 23, 1957; s. Roger Raymond and Karolina (Högel) R. AA in Computer Sci., U. Puget Sound, 1979, BS in Math., 1979, BS in Chem. Physics, 1979. Programmer, system mgr. Boeing Computer Services, Seattle, 1979-82; software instr. Boeing Aerospace Co., Seattle, 1982-85; systems analyst CADDEX Corp, Woodinville, Wash., 1985-86; computer cons. Redmond, Wash., 1986—. Musician Tacoma Concert Band, 1982—. Mem. Boeing Mgmt. Assn., Digital Equipment Corp. Users Soc., Boeing Employees VAX User Group. Republican. Presbyterian. Avocations: sailing, rock climbing, raquetball, music performance. Home and Office: 15922 NE 42d Ct Redmond WA 98052

ROBERTSON, ORAN B., retail company executive; b. Turner, Ore., 1917; married; student, U. Wash. With Boeing Aircraft Co. until 1946, Fred Meyer, Inc., Portland, Oreg., v.p., dir. engring., now chmn., chief exec. officer, also dir. Office: Fred Meyer Inc 3800 SE 22d St Portland OR 97202 *

ROBERTSON, RAYMOND ELIOT, research chemist; b. St. Louis, Aug. 17, 1940; married;. BS, Cen. Mo. State U., 1962; MS, Colo. State U., 1971; PhD, U. Wyo., 1976. Research chemist Tretolite Co., Webster Groves, Mo., 1963-69; instr. E. Wyo. Coll., Torrington, 1975-76; research chemist Laramie (Wyo.) Energy Tech. Ctr., 1976-83; sr. research chemist Western Research Inst., Laramie, 1983—. Mem. Am. Chem. Soc., Sigma Xi. Office: Western Research Inst PO Box 3395 University Station Laramie WY 82071

ROBERTSON, TED WALTER, artist, educator; b. Dunmor, Ky., Nov. 21, 1942; s. Fred and Gertie Ann (Covington) R.; m. Phyllis Ann Mayfield, Apr. 28, 1967 (div. July 1974); children—Anathea, Tanya Lea; m. Linda Carol Jones, Sept. 17, 1977; children—Jessica Ann, Jason Lewis. Student Colo. State U., Bergman Art Sch., Denver, Austin Peay Coll., Clarksville, Tenn. Designer, Tesco Signs, Inc., Roswell, N.Mex., 1967-72; tchr. art Carizzo Art Sch., Ruidoso, N.Mex., 1972-74, 83, 85; judge, juror Carlsbad Art Mus., 1982, Roswell Fine Arts League, 1982, Pastel Soc., Dallas, 1984. Served with U.S. Army, 1961-64. Recipient 1st place award Colo. Art Symposium, 1967. Mem. Pastel Soc. S.W., Pastel Soc. Am., Am. Portrait Soc., United Internat. Artists Assn., Roswell Fine Arts League (hon.), Roswell Art Mus. Republican. Mem. Ch. of Christ. Office: PO Box 735 Roswell NM 88201

ROBERTSON, WILLIAM RAY, sales and marketing professional; b. Covington, Ky., Jan. 4, 1945; s. William Rolf and Joan Wanda (Ward) R.; m. Charlotte Ann Robertson, Oct. 5, 1968 (div.); children: Merry Sue, Scott, Steve. Grad. high sch., Detroit. Broker Roberston Assocs. Ins., Cleve., 1970-80; owner Network Enterprises, San Diego, 1980-83; v.p. United Resources, Torrance, Calif., 1983-85; pres. Performance Strategies, Inc., San Diego, 1985—. Served with USAF, 1963-68. Mem. Nat. Speakers Assn., Am. Soc. Tng. and Devel. Avocation: photography. Home: 10329 Caminito Rio Branco San Diego CA 92131

ROBIDOUX, PEGGY ANNE, biological sciences, researcher; b. Joliet, Ill., Aug. 30, 1986; d. Robert Frank and Adeline Delores (James) Kweiser; m. Phillip Henri Robidoux, June 12, 1982; 1 child, Scott. AAS, Joliet Jr. Coll., 1977; BS in Biology, Coll. St. Francis, 1979. Phlebotomist St. Joseph Hsop., Joliet, 1978-79; quality control technician Durkee Foods, Joliet, 1979-80; technician Amoco Corp., Naperville, Ill., 1980-82; assoc. chemist Beckman Instruments Co., Palo Alto, Calif., 1982-83; research sci. Travenol-Genentech Diagnostics, Mountain View, Calif., 1983—. Mem. AAAS. Roman Catholic. Home: 38 Devonshire Ave Townhouse 1 Mountain View CA 94043-2162 Office: Travenol Genentech Diagnostics 110 C Pioneer Way Mountain View CA 94041

ROBINDER, RONALD CHARLES, engineer; b. Davenport, Iowa, July 27, 1939; s. Carl Albert and Helen Louise (Clark) R.; m. M. Elaine Scott, Sept. 5, 1959; children: Kevin Wade, David Vaughn, Jennifer Lynn, Jeanette Lee. BA, Linfield Coll., 1961; MA, Duke U., 1968, PhD, 1973. Engr. Tektronix Inc., Beaverton, Oreg., 1962-65, 74-86, Zenith Radio, Niles, Ill., 1968-72, Raytheon Co., Quincy, Mass., 1972-74; real estate salesman Oreg. Realty, Portland, 1983-86; with Sperry Def. Systems div. Honeywell, Inc., Albuquerque, 1986—. Contbr. articles to profl. jours.; patentee in field. Mem. Am. Chem. Soc., Electro Chem. Soc., Sigma Xi. Republican. Baptist. Avocations: stamp collecting, computers, camping. Home: 10312 Trevino Loop NW Albuquerque NM 87114 Office: Sperry Def Systems div Honeywell Inc PO Box 9200 Albuquerque NM 87119

ROBINETTE, MARIANNE SUSAN, federal official; b. San Francisco, July 7, 1949; d. George Robert and Mary Cornelia (Colbert) R. Grad. high sch., San Francisco, 1967. Clk. U.S. Civil Service Commn. (now U.S. Office of Personnel Mgmt.), San Francisco, 1967-73, supr., 1973-76, investigator, 1976-81; lead investigator U.S. Office Personnel Mgmt., Los Angeles, 1981-83, Menlo Park, Calif., 1983-85; supervisory investigator U.S. Office Personnel Mgmt., San Francisco, 1985—. Recipient Sustained Superior Performance award U.S. Office Personnel Mgmt., 1979, 82, 83, 84, Dir.'s award U.S. Office Personnel Mgmt., 1984-85; named San Francisco Region Investigator of Yr., U.S. Office Personnel Mgmt., 1984, 85. Democrat. Roman Catholic. Avocations: bowling, gold panning, boat restoration. Office: U S Office Personnel Mgmt 211 Main St 7th Floor San Francisco CA 94105

ROBINS, JUDY ROSELYN, interior designer; b. Cleve., Sept. 2, 1948; d. Stanley and Esther (Resnick) Waxman; m. Kenneth Michael Robins, Sept. 26, 1971. A.A.S., Fashion Inst. Tech.; B.S., N.Y.U., 1970, M.A., 1972. Fabric coordinator Celanese Corp., N.Y.C., 1970-71; merchandiser Bayly Corp., Denver, 1973-74; instr. Metro State Coll., Denver, 1977-81; self-employed interior designer, Denver, 1975—; mem. bd. Waxman Industries. Mem. steering com. Alliance Contemporary Art; women's bd. Nat. Jewish Hosp., 1978-80, bd. dirs., 1984—; trustee Denver Art Mus., 1986—, collections com., devel. com.; bd. dirs., v.p. leadership Allied Jewish Fedn., assoc. campaign chmn., 1985, gen. chmn. 1987—; bd. govs. Nat. Jewish Ctr. for Immunology and Respiratory Medicine; bd. dirs. congregation Jewish Family and Children's Service Colo., 1975-83; founding mem. Young Women's Leadership Cabinet United Jewish Appeal, 1977-82, nat. women's bd., 1984; mem. steering com. Denver Art Mus., trustee, 1986—. Recipient Young Leadership award Allied Jewish Fedn., 1977. Mem. United Jewish Appeal (nat. women's div. exec. com. 1986—). Address: 755 Lafayette St Denver CO 80218

ROBINS, KIKANZA NURI, educator; b. Boston, Jan. 3, 1950; d. Winston Hersley Robins and Barbara Estelle (Latimer) Brown; B.A., M.A., Occidental Coll., 1972; Ed.D., U. So. Calif., 1982. Head tchr. Kawaida Ednl. and Devel. Ctr., Los Angeles, 1972-75; program coordinator Sch. Pub. Adminstrn. U. So. Calif., 1976-79; adj. prof. edn. U. Redlands, 1977; cons. Desegregation Tng. Inst., Calif. State U., Northridge, 1978-82; lectr. ethnic studies U. So. Calif., 1978-82; owner Nuri Webber Assocs. Cons. Services; cons. in field. Pres. bd. dirs. People Coordinated Services, Los Angeles. Mem. Am. Soc. Tng. and Devel., Sociology of Edn. Assn., Assn. Supervision and Curriculum Devel., Nat. Alliance Black Sch. Educators, Nat. Council Tchrs. English, Phi Delta Kappa. Contbr. articles to profl. jours., confs. Office: 2152 Terminal Annex Los Angeles CA 90051

ROBINS, MIRIAM CLAIR, former insurance company executive, former interior design consultant; b. Denver, Sept. 19, 1935; d. H. Rupard and Mildred L. (Opie) R. BA, Colo. Coll., 1957; MA, U. Denver, 1959. Instr. piano and organ, Denver, 1957-62; v.p. Olinger Life Ins. Co., Denver, 1961-63, exec. v.p., 1963-73, pres., 1973-78, vice chmn. bd., 1978-85; v.p. Robins Agy., Inc., Denver, 1963-85; cons. Cherry Creek Interiors, Denver, 1984. Tchr., music arranger for talent competition Miss America, 1958. V.p. Colo. Life Conv., Denver, 1966-67; mem. Pres.'s Council Colo. Coll. Mem. AAUW, Denver Art Mus., Chancellor's Soc. U. Denver, Kappa Delta Pi, Mu Phi Epsilon, Kappa Alpha Theta. Republican. Clubs: Denver, Denver Athletic, Cherry Hill Country; Garden of the Gods (Colorado Springs, Colo.); Met. Home: Polo Club North 2552 E Alameda Ave # 61 Denver CO 80209

ROBINSON, BERNARD LEO, lawyer; b. Kalamazoo, Feb. 13, 1924; s. Louis Harvey and Sue Mary (Starr) R.; B.S., U. Ill., 1947, M.S., 1958, postgrad. in structural dynamics, 1959; J.D., U. N.Mex., 1973; m. Betsy Nadell, May 30, 1947; children—Robert Bruce, Patricia Anne, Jean Carol. Research engr. Assn. Am. Railroads, 1947-49; instr. architecture Rensselaer Poly. Inst., 1949-51; commd. 2d lt. Corps Engrs., U.S. Army, 1945, advanced through grades to lt. col., 1965, ret., 1968; engr. Nuclear Def. Research Corp., Albuquerque, 1968-71; admitted to N.Mex. bar, 1973, U.S. Supreme Ct. bar, 1976; practiced in Albuquerque, 1973-85, Silver City, N.Mex., 1985—; lectr. bus. adminstrn. Western N.Mex. U., Silver City, 1986—. Dist. commr. Boy Scouts Am., 1960-62. Vice chmn. Republican Dist. Com., 1968-70. Decorated Air medal, Combat Infantryman's Badge, Joint Services Commendation medal. Mem. ASCE, Soc. Am. Mil. Engrs., ABA, N.Mex. Bar Assn., Grant County Bar Assn., Ret. Officers Assn., DAV, Assn. U.S. Army. Home: 3306 Royal Dr Silver City NM 88061 Office: PO Box 4070 Silver City NM 88062

ROBINSON, CALVIN, JR., librarian; b. Saginaw, Mich., June 19, 1950; s. Calvin and Vertis Mae (Frierson) R. BA in Social Services, BA in Speech Psychology, Goshen Coll., 1972; MLS, Rosary Coll., 1974. Cert. community coll. instr., Calif. Library & audio-visual asst. Goshen (Ind.) Coll., 1968-72; reference librarian Chgo. Pub. Library, 1973-77, mem. staff adv. bd., 1975-76; library asst. U. So. Calif., Los Angeles, 1977-78; CADRE-substitute Chgo. Bd. Edn., 1978-79; with young adult Spanish library Los Angeles Pub. Library, 1979-84, mem. young adult adv. bd., 1982-84, acting sr. librarian, 1984—. Active So. Calif. Community Choir, Los Angeles, 1980—. Mem. ALA (Ill. Manpower scholar), Librarian Guild, Rosary Coll. Alumni Assn., Z&Z Prodn. Club (mem. exec. bd.), SW Ark. Genealogy Soc., Los Angeles County Afro-Am. Mus. Genealogy Soc. Avocations: genealogy, dance, theatre, writing book revs. Home: 5749 1/2 Corbett St Los Angeles CA 90016 Office: Los Angeles Pub Library Inner City Bookmobile Unit 1636 W Manchester Ave Los Angeles CA 90047

ROBINSON, CHARLES WESLEY, energy company executive; b. Long Beach, Calif., Sept. 7, 1919; s. Franklin Willard and Anna Hope (Gould) R.; m. Tamara Lindovna, Mar. 8, 1957; children: Heather Lynne, Lisa Anne, Wendy Paige. AB cum laude in Econs., U. Calif., Berkeley, 1941; MBA, Stanford U., 1947. Asst. mgr. mfg. Golden State Dairy Products Co., San Francisco, 1947-49; v.p., then pres. Marcona Corp., San Francisco, 1952-74; undersec. of state for econ. affairs Dept. State, Washington, 1974-75, dep. sec. of state, 1976-77; sr. mng. partner Kuhn Loeb & Co., N.Y.C., 1977-78; vice chmn. Blyth Eastman Dillon & Co., N.Y.C., 1978-79; chmn. Energy Transition Corp., Santa Fe and Washington, 1979—; bd. dirs. Arthur D. Little, The Allen Group, Northrop Corp., NIKE, Inc.; internat. adv. bd. Pan Am. World Airways. Patentee slurry transport. Trustee Trilateral Commn., N.Y.C., 1972-74, 77—, Brookings Instn., Washington, 1977—. Served to lt. USN, 1941-46. Recipient Disting. Honor award Dept. State, 1977. Mem. Council on Fgn. Relations N.Y.C. Republican. Methodist. Club: Pacific Union (San Francisco). Office: PO Box 2224 Santa Fe NM 87501

ROBINSON, DAVID LEON, public relations executive, educator, writer; b. Los Angeles, May 16, 1948; s. Gilmer George and Jewell Rita (Starkweather) R.; m. Jacqueline McCurdy, Jan. 21, 1978. B.A. in English, San Diego State U., 1971, M.S. in Mass Communications, 1980. Promotion cons. Project Concern Internat., 1976; communications coordinator Home Fed. Savs. & Loan, San Diego, 1977-78; asst. pub. relations dir. Phillips-Ramsey Inc., San Diego, 1978-81; pub. relations mgr. Hewlett-Packard, San Diego Div., 1981-82; dir. pub. relations services Young & Rubicam, San Diego, (Young & Rubicam acquired by WFC 1982), v.p. WFC/Westcom, San Diego, 1982—; instr. pub. relations San Diego State U., 1982-86; v.p., gen. mgr. CMF&Z Pub. Relations, San Diego, 1986—. Co-author: The Basic Guide to Fly Fishing, 1979; The Far End of America, A Book About Ocean Beach, California, 1975, 76; contbr. articles to newspapers and mags. Bd. dirs. fundraising campaign Combined Health Agys. Drive, 1983; mem. Mex. and Am. Found. Com. Recipient news media award San Diego County Fire Chiefs, 1974. Mem. Pub. Relations Club San Diego (pres. 1982), Internat. Assn. Bus. Communicators (pres. 1981, communications awards 1977-82, Communicator of Yr. 1983), Pub. Relations Soc. Am., (Counselors Acad.), San Diego Communications Council (co-founder). Presbyterian. Home: 4070 Apore St La Mesa CA 92041 Office: CMF&F Pub Relations 10665 Sorrento Valley Rd San Diego CA 92121

ROBINSON, DAVID ROGER, infosystems specialist; b. Coshocton, Ohio, Aug. 10, 1951; s. Roger Linzey and Hazel Lucille (Snedeker) R.; m. Kathleen Margaret Carpenter, Aug. 12, 1972; children: Kristina Rose, Kimberley Gayle. BS in Math., BS in Physics, Ohio U., 1973; MS Indsl. Engring., U. Wis., Madison, 1975. Cert. systems profl. Systems analyst Burroughs Corp., Detroit, 1975-77, project leader, 1977-83, mgr. data networks, 1980-83, mgr. tech. services, 1983-85; mgr. data communications Joseph & Cogan, Woodland Hills, Calif., 1985-86; project mgr. network integration Burrough and Sperry Corp., Woodland Hills, 1986-87; mgr. tech. services Joseph & Cogan, Woodland Hills, 1987—; adjunct lectr. U. Mich., Ann Arbor, 1985; guest lectr. U. Detroit, 1985. Author: (software) Bitnet, 1979. Mem. founders soc. Detroit Inst. Arts. Mem. GTE Telenet Users Group (pres. 1982-84, 84-86, sec. 1981-82). Republican. Baptist. Club: Econ. of Detroit. Avocations: woodworking, photography.

ROBINSON, DONALD WILFORD, mathematics educator; b. Salt Lake City, Feb. 29, 1928; s. Wilford Allen and Thirza (Cornick) R.; m. Helen Ruth Sorensen, Aug. 27, 1952; children: Diane, Allen Conrad, Karen, Janette, Marilyn, Lynae, David William. BS, U. Utah, 1948, MA, 1952; PhD, Case Inst. Tech., 1956. Asst. prof. math. Brigham Young U., Provo, Utah, 1956-59; assoc. prof. Brigham Young U., Provo, 1959-62, prof., 1962—; sr. research fellow Calif. Inst. Tech., Pasadena, 1962-63; vis. prof. U.S. Naval Postgrad. Sch., Monterey, Calif., 1969-70, Rijksuniversiteit, Ghent, Belgium, 1986. Contbr. articles in field to profl. jours. Dist. chmn. Rep. Party, Provo, 1972-74. NSF Faculty fellow, Pasadena, 1962-63; Fulbright-Hayes lectr. State Dept., Valencia, Venezuela, 1976-77. Mem. Math. Assn. Am. (chmn. Intermountain sect. 1982-84, sect. gov. 1986—), Sigma Xi (pres. Brigham Young U. chpt. 1967-68). Republican. Mormon. Avocations: gardening, singing. Home: 2380 N 930 E Provo UT 84604 Office: Brigham Young Univ 316 TMCB Provo UT 84602

ROBINSON, ELIZABETH ANNE, psychology educator; b. N.Y.C., July 23, 1944; d. John M. and Mary Margaret R.; m. John Richard Garner, Sept. 8, 1979. BS, Cornell U., 1966; PhD, U. S.C., 1977. Lic. psychologist, Wash., 1980. Field adviser Green Valley council Girl Scouts U.S., 1966-67; tchr. Northridge High Sch., Dayton, Ohio, 1967-69; psychology asst. II Willard (N.Y.) State Hosp., 1969-72; psychology trainee VA, Richmond, Va., Cannadaigua, N.Y. and Columbia, S.C., 1973-74; research asst. U. S.C., Columbia, 1974-75, instr. psychology, 1974-76; intern med. psychology U. Oreg. Health Scis. Ctr., Portland, 1976-77; asst. prof. psychology U. Wash., Seattle, 1979-87; prin. investigator Family Interaction Project, 1980-83; practice psychology Everett, Wash.; vis. asst. prof. U. Oreg., Eugene, 1977-79. Contbr. articles to profl. jours. NIMH grantee, 1980-83; Neidich fellow, 1975. Mem. Am. Psychol. Assn., Western Psychol. Assn., Wash. State Psychology Assn. Home: 1609 Baker Ave Everett WA 98201 Office: 1602 Hewitt Ave Suite 514 Everett WA 98201

ROBINSON, FRANK ERNEST, water scientist; b. Oaklyn, N.J., Oct. 29, 1930; s. Wallace Andrew and Ida Mary R.; m. Barbara M. Robinson, May 28, 1983; children: David, Robert, June. BS, Rutgers U., 1952, PhD, 1958. Research assoc. Purdue U., West Lafayette, Ind., 1955-58; with agronomist expt. sta. Hawaiian Sugar Planters, Honolulu, 1958-64; water scientists U. Calif., Davis, 1964—; Mem. adv. bd. Water Quality Control Bd.; mem. Internat. Commn. Irrigation and Drainage. Contbr. articles to profl. jours. Leader boy Scouts Am.; judge sci. fairs. Served to 1st lt. AUS, 1953-55, Korea. Named Man of Yr. Irrigation Assn., 1973; Rep. Geothermal, Inc. grantee. Mem. Am. Soc. Agronomy, Am. Soc. Agrl. Engrs., Am. Geophys. Union, Am. Soc. Hort. Sci., Western Soc. Soil Sci., Soil Sci. Soc. Am. Clubs: Commonwealth Calif., Toastmasters. Home and Office: 1004 E Holton Rd El Centro CA 92243

ROBINSON, FRANK MALCOLM, writer, editor; b. Chgo., Aug. 9, 1926; s. Raymond and Leona (White) R. BS in Physics, Beloit Coll., 1950; MS in Journalism, Northwestern U., 1955. Asst. editor Family Weeklysupplement, Chgo., 1955-56, Sci. Digest mag., Chgo., 1956-59; editor Rogue mag., Evanston, Ill., 1959-65; mng. editor Cavalier, Los Angeles, 1966-67; editor Censorship Today, Los Angeles, 1968-69; staff writer Playboy mag., Chgo., 1969-72; writer San Francisco, 1972—. Author: The Power, 1956; co-author: The Glass Inferno, 1974, The Prometheus Crisis, 1975, The Nightmare Factor, 1978, The Gold Crew, 1980, The Great Divide, 1982, Blow-Out, 1987; co-editor: The Truth About Vietnam, 1966, Sex, American Style, 1971. Served with USN, 1944-46, 50-52. Mem. Phi Beta Kappa, Pi Kappa Alpha (pres. 1949-50). Democrat. Avocation: collecting books, sci. fiction mags. Home and Office: 4100 20th St San Francisco CA 94114

ROBINSON, FRANK ROBERT, radio station executive; b. Hollywood, Calif., Sept. 17, 1938; s. Frank Robert and Helen Macdonnel (James) R.; m. Ann Katherine Carman, Apr. 24, 1965 (div. 1984); children: Geoffrey Scott, Hilary Ann. BS, Westminster Coll., 1967. Account exec. Sta. KLUB, Sta. KISN, Salt Lake City, 1965-69, ops. mgr., 1970-73, gen. mgr., 1974-85; sta. mgr. Sta. KUER U. Utah, 1986—. Bd. dirs. Salt Lake City chpt. ARC, 1975, Salt Lake City YMCA, 1976, Salvation Army, Salt Lake City, 1984, Jr. Achievement, Salt Lake City, 1984; mem. pub. utilities adv. com. Salt Lake City, 1986—. Mem. Utah Broadcasters Assn. (bd. dirs. 1982-83, pres. 1983—), Salt Lake Radio Broadcasters Assn. (sec. 1981-82). Republican. Roman Catholic. Lodge: Kiwanis (Salt Lake City chpt. bd. dirs. 1976-77, pres. 1982-83).

ROBINSON, GWYNN HERNDON, financial executive; b. N.Y.C., Sept. 16, 1920; s. E. Gwynn and Corinne (Herndon) R.; m. Natalie Thompson, Dec. 31, 1959; children—Catherine, Gwynn; 1 stepdau., Kendall Thompson Fewell. Grad., Choate Sch., Wallington, Conn., 1938; student, MIT, 1940. Mgr. exports Rochester Ropes Inc., N.Y.C., 1946-48, Mathieson Chem. Corp., 1948-51; mng. partner Feldt & Robinson (ind. oil producers), Colorado Springs, Colo., 1953-57; with Northrop Corp., 1958-67, v.p., mgr. European ops., 1965-67; pres. Diners Club Internat., 1967-70, Internat. Market Mgmt., Inc., Los Angeles, 1970-73; v.p. Boyden Assos., Inc., Los Angeles, 1973-77; sr. v.p. Eastman & Beaudine, Inc., Los Angeles, 1977-79, THinc Cons. Group Internat., Los Angeles, 1979—. Bd. dirs. Air Acad. Found. Served to maj. USAAF, 1941-45; Served to col. USAF, 1951-53; maj. gen. Res. (ret.). Decorated D.S.M., Legion of Merit, Purple Heart, D.F.C., Air medal with clusters. Mem. Air Force Assn. (past regional v.p., dir.), Am. Fighter Pilots Assn. (life), Res. Officers Assn., Delta Psi. Clubs: MIT of So. Calif; St. Anthony (N.Y.C.). Home: 10701 Wilshire Blvd Los Angeles CA 90024 Office: THinc Cons Group Internat Suite 700 1900 Ave of the Stars Los Angeles CA 90067

ROBINSON, HERBERT FISK, newspaper executive; b. Seattle, Nov. 22, 1924; s. Wallace Craig and Gladys (Lillie) R.; m. Mary Mulligan, Aug. 25, 1949 (div. 1984); children—Michael, Mark, Susan. B.A., U. Wash., 1949; M.S., Columbia U., 1950. Reporter The Times, Seattle, 1941-53, assoc. editor, 1965-77, editorial page editor, 1977—; news dir. Sta. KOMO-TV, Seattle, 1953-65; Served to capt. U.S. Army, 1943-46, CBI. Recipient Spot TV News Reporting award Sigma Delta Chi, 1956, Top Local TV News award Sylvania Corp., 1960, Outstanding Govt. Reporting award Mcpl. League, 1983; Pulitzer scholar, 1950. Mem. Am. Soc. Newspaper Editors, Nat. Conf. Editorial Writers. Clubs: Rainier, Wash. Athletic (Seattle). Office: Seattle Times PO Box 70 Seattle WA 98111 *

ROBINSON, JANET KAY, real estate executive; b. Borger, Tex., Aug., 19, 1943; d. Millard Jerome and Mamie Elizabeth (Miller) Newman; m. Christopher Turner, Nov. 9, 1986; 1 dau. Alisa. B.S. in Bus. Adminstrn. with distinction, U. Redlands, 1982. Regional escrow mgr. Gulf Oil Corp., Los Angeles, 1962-64; asst. mgr. Guild Mortgage Co., San Diego, 1967-69; asst. mgr. real estate dept. Mitsui Mfrs. Bank, Los Angeles, 1969-76; v.p., mgr. loan/equity adminstrn. Wells Fargo Realty Advisors, Marina del Rey, Calif., 1976-81, v.p., mgr. legal adminstrn., 1981—; gen. ptnr. Dynamic Info. Services, 1984—; dir. seminars for loan/equity officers; lectr. colls. and univs. Publicity chmn. Los Angeles Escrow Assn., 1975; bd. govs. Arthritis Found. So. Calif. Mem. Nat. Assn. Corp. Real Estate Execs. Republican. Author: A Short History of WFRA, 1983; The Advisor, 1983; contbr. articles to profl. jours.

ROBINSON, JESSE LEE, personnel mgmt. cons.; b. Hattiesburg, Miss., Jan. 17, 1912; s. Jerry L. and Pearlie L. (Harrison) R.; m. Myrtle Elizabeth Comfort, Dec. 25, 1936; 1 dau., Pearl Elizabeth (Mrs. Dale Roussell). Tng. dir. Los Angeles P.O., 1955-67; prof. East Los Angeles City Coll., 1955-70; pres. Robinson's Research, Los Angeles, 1967—; chmn. bd. Enterprise Savs.

& Loan, 1970-74; treas. Hi-Pro Foods, 1969-71; chmn. bd., comptroller Avalon Med. Mgmt. Inc. Co-chmn. Greater Los Angeles Urban Coalition, 1970—. Trustee Compton Union High Sch., 1963-69; bd. dirs. Los Angeles Heart Soc., Interracial Council Bus. Opportunity, Salvation Army; foreman Los Angeles County Grand Jury, 1974-75, pres., 1986—. Recipient Los Angeles County Suprs. award 1969, Disting. award of Yr., Interracial Council Bus. Opportunity, 1970. Mem. Am. Soc. Tng. and Devel., So. Pacific Assn.-Amateur Athletic Union (pres. 1973—), NAACP (pres. 1954-57). Rotarian. Address: 1702 N Wilmington Ave Compton CA 90222

ROBINSON, JOHN ALEXANDER, football coach; b. Chgo., July 25, 1935; s. Matthew and Ethlyn (Alexander) R.; m. Barbara Lee Amirkhan, July 31, 1960; children: Teresa, Lynn, David, Christopher. B.S., U. Oreg., 1958. Asst. football coach U. Oreg., Eugene, 1960-71, U. So. Calif., Los Angeles, 1971-74, Oakland (Calif.) Raiders, 1975; head fooball coach U. So. Calif., 1976-82, v.p., 1982-83; head coach Los Angeles Rams Football Team, 1983—; coached winning Rose Bowl teams, 1977, 79, 80. Served with U.S. Army, 1958-59. Named NFC Coach of Yr., UPI, 1983-84 season. Roman Catholic. Office: care Los Angeles Rams 2327 W Lincoln Ave Anaheim CA 92801 *

ROBINSON, JOHN DENNIS, data processing and infosystems executive; b. Niigata, Japan, Feb. 2, 1953; came to U.S., 1959; s. Allison and Eiko (Kikuchi) R.; m. Catherine Ellen Hielen, Feb. 13, 1971; children: Joseph, Genie, Nicholas. Constrn. sales rep. Overland Lumber, Boise, Idaho, 1971-75; program analyst County of Ada, Boise, 1975-78; dist. mgr. RGIS, Salt Lake City and Boise, 1978-79; data processing ops. mgr. Waremart Inc., Boise, 1979-85; cen. services mgr. County of Walla Walla, Wash., 1985—; chmn. credit com. Mountain States Wholesale Credit Union, Boise, 1983-85; cons. Meridian (Idaho) Data Service, 1983-84. Mem. editorial bd. Computer World Info. Mgrs., 1986—. Vol. Expanded Food and Nutrition Edn. Program, Boise, 1985. Mem. Assn. County Info. Services, Common Cause. Avocations: photography, outdoors. Home: 1809 Plaza Way Box 10 Walla Walla WA 99362 Office: County of Walla Walla 315 W Main Room 103 Walla Walla WA 99362

ROBINSON, MARK LEIGHTON, oil company executive, petroleum geologist, horse farm owner; b. San Bernardino, Calif., Aug. 4, 1927; s. Ernest Guy and Florence Iola (Lemmon) R.; m. Jean Marie Ries, Feb. 8, 1954; children—Francis Willis, Mark Ries, Paul Leighton. A.B. cum laude in Geology, Princeton U., 1950; postgrad. Stanford U., 1950-51. Geologist Shell Oil Co., Billings, Mont., Rapid City, S.D., Denver, Midland, Tex., 1951-56, dist. geologist, Roswell, N.Mex., 1957-60, div. mgr., Roswell, N.Mex., 1961-63, Jackson, Miss., 1964-65, Bakersfield, Calif., 1967-68, mgr. exploration econs., N.Y.C., 1969; mgmt. advisor BIPM (Royal Dutch Shell Oil Co.), The Hague, The Netherlands, 1966; pres., chmn. bd. dirs. Robinson Resource Devel. Co., Inc., Roswell, 1970—. Campaign chmn. Chaves County Republican Com., Roswell, 1962; mem. alumni schs. com. Princeton U., 1980—. Served with USNR, 1945-46. Mem. Roswell Geol. Soc. (trustee 1972), Am. Assn. Petroleum Geologists, Stanford U. Earth Scientists Assn., Yellowstone Bighorn Research Assn., Am. Horse Shows Assn., Sigma Xi. Episcopalian. Discovered Lake Como oil field, Miss., 1971, McNeal oil field, Miss., 1973, North Deer Creek Gas Field, Mont., 1983, Bloomfield East Oil Field, Mont., 1986. Home: Route 1 Box 31D Roswell NM 88201 Office: Robinson Resource Devel Co Inc PO Box 1227 Roswell NM 88201

ROBINSON, MARY BETH, academic program administrator; b. Hinsdale, Ill., Sept. 2, 1943; d. Lee Fulton and Freda Margaret (Doehle) Higman; m. John Thomas Robinson, June 1, 1974. BA, UCLA, 1965; MA, Stanford U., 1974; PhD, Ohio State U., 1978. Secondary tchr. Berkeley (Calif.) Unified Sch. Dist., 1966-75; teaching evaluator Ohio State U. Sch. Vet. Med., Columbus, 1975-78; lectr., curriculum evaluator Calif. State Poly. U., Pomona, 1978-80; program evaluator Sch. Dist. Phila., 1980-81; coordinator field edn., tchr. edn., sch. edn. Stanford (Calif.) U., 1982-86; reading specialist East Side Union High Sch. Dist., San Jose, Calif., 1986—; instl. program evaluator Commn. on Tchr. Credentialing, Sacramento. Mem. Credential Counselors and Analysts Calif., Calif. Council on Tchr. Edn., Nat. Assn. Female Execs., Friends of Stanford U. Sch. Edn., Assn. Supervision and Cirriculum Devel., Phi Delta Kappa. Democrat. Episcopalian. Avocations: stamp collecting, football, baseball. Home: 444 Saratoga Ave Santa Clara CA 95050-6280 Summer Home: 1249 Via Romero Palos Verdes Estates CA 90274

ROBINSON, NAOMI JEAN, training systems analyst; b. Storm Lake, Iowa, Oct. 10, 1951; d. Wendell and Norma (Wright) R.; B.A., Buena Vista Coll., 1973; M.A.Ed., George Washington U., 1978. Tchr., elem. schs., Storm Lake, Iowa, 1973-75; edn. specialist intern U.S. Army, Fort Monroe, Va., 1976-78, edn. specialist, Fort Eustis, Va., 1978-79, tng. systems analyst, White Sands Missile Range, N.Mex., 1979-82, TRADOC tng. effectiveness analysis study coordinator, 1982—, career program mgr. for edn. and tng., 1984—. Vice pres., Young Republicans, 1972-73. Mem. Nat. Assn. Exec. Females, Federally Employed Women (1st v.p. chpt. 1982-83, 84-85), Human Factors Soc., Iowa Edn. Assn. Republican. Presbyterian. Club: Bus. and Profl. Women. Author: Guidelines for Development of Skill Qualification Tests, 1977. Home: 2850 Fairway Dr Apt 4 Las Cruces NM 88001 Office: US Army TRAC Attention ATOR-THE White Sands Missile Range NM 88002

ROBINSON, RALPH CONRAD, building materials company executive; b. Toronto, Ont., Can., Feb. 18, 1922; s. Ralph Conrad and Helen Herschel (Henderson) R.; m. Mary Elizabeth Swartz, Jan. 3, 1947; children: Judith Carolyn, Kathryn Louise. BS in Geology, U. Wash., 1946. Asst. mgr. Olympian Stone Co., Seattle, 1947-55, v.p. prodn., 1955-65; pres., chief exec. officer Olympian Stone Co., Redmond, Wash., 1965—. Patentee bldg. materials. Served to staff sgt. USAF, 1944-46, CBI. Recipient Craftsman award AIA, Seattle, 1964. Mem. Am. Concrete Inst. (com. chmn.), ASTM (com. chmn.), Constrn. Specifications Inst. (President's award 1976, 79), The Concrete Soc., Redmond C. of C. (pres. 1972), Interclub Boating Assn. Wash. (dir.). Republican. Clubs: Meyden Bauer Bay Yacht (Bellevue, Wash.) (commodore 1983), Bellevue Athletic (Wash.). Lodge: Rotary. Office: Olympian Stone Co Inc PO Box 539 Redmond WA 98073

ROBINSON, RICHARD ALLEN, JR., consultant, human resources development trainer; b. Ellensburg, Wash., Aug. 21, 1936; s. Richard Allen and Rosa Adele (Oswalt) R.; m. R. Elaine Whitham, Sept. 8, 1956; children—Sharon E. Robinson Losey, Richard Allen, René L. B.A., U. Wash., 1958; postgrad. U.S. Army Command and Gen. Staff Coll., 1969-70; M.A., U. Mo., 1971. Commd. 2d lt. U.S. Army, 1958, advanced through grades to lt. col., 1972, various infantry assignments including command, 1958-72, research and devel. assignments including dep. dir. test of behavioral sci., dep. commandant U.S.A. Organizational Effectiveness, 1975-77, ret., 1979; chief mgmt. devel. Wash. Dept. Social and Health Services, Olympia, 1979—; pvt. practice orgn. and mgmt. devel. cons./trainer, 1979—. Decorated Legion of Merit with oak leaf cluster, Bronze Star. Mem. Am. Soc. Tng. and Devel., Organizational Devel. Network, Internat. Platform Assn., Mass. Hort. Soc. Contbg. author: Games Trainers Play, vol. II, 1983. Office: DSHS Mail 8315 W 27th St Tacoma WA 98466

ROBINSON, RICHARD GARY, management consultant; b. Oakland, Calif., Aug. 17, 1931; s. William Albert and Inez Wilhelmina (Zetterblad) R.; B.B.A., U. Minn., 1955; grad. Indsl. Coll. Armed Forces, 1972; M. Internat. Mgmt., Am. Grad. Sch. Internat. Mgmt., 1980; m. Lorraine Mary Deshaies, Nov. 13, 1965 (dec.); children—Elisabeth Claudine (dec.), Christopher Paul. CPA, Colo.; cert. mgmt. cons. Commd. 2d lt. U.S. Air Force, 1956, advanced through grades to maj.; dir. radar ops. tactical air warfare, comdr. strategic missile operation and maintenance functions, project mgr., dir. mgmt. info. systems Dept. Def. activities, S.E. Asia; ret., 1976; mgmt. cons., Colorado Springs, Colo., 1976—; pres. Bus. Devel. Specialists; dir., chief fin. officer Unique Equipment Co. dir. Stage Engring. & Supply; bd. dirs. United Air Freight Ltd.; mem. adj. faculty Embry Riddle Aero. U., Luke AFB, Ariz.; asst. prof. econs. and bus. Colorado Springs br. Regis Coll.; U. So. Colo. Mem. bus. adv. council Colo. Internat. Trade Office. Decorated Meritorious Service medal with oak leaf cluster, AF Commendation medal with 2 oak leaf clusters. Mem. Internat. Trade Assn. Colo. (pres.), Am. Mktg. Assn., Armed Forces Communications and Electronics Assn., Am. Mgmt. Assn., Nat. Assn. Accts., Inst. Mgmt. Cons., Assn. Polit. Risk Analysts, N.Am. Soc. Corp. Planning. Lutheran. Home: 1610 McKay Way Colorado Springs CO 80915 Office: 105 E Kiowa St Suite 406 PO Box 2714 Colorado Springs CO 80901

ROBINSON, ROB (WILLIAM A.), advertising executive; b. Yonkers, N.Y., Nov. 5, 1929; s. Raymond and Marie Elise (Cuddy) R.; m. Yolanda Robinson, Jan. 27, 1957; children: William A. Jr., Mark. BA in History, Franklin & Marshall Coll., 1951. Pres., owner Rob Robinson Advt., Inc., Santa Fe Springs, Calif., 1969—. Pres. local chpt. Chain of Hope, 1986. Served as cpl. U.S. Army, 1951-53. Recipient Belding Advt. award, 1st Pl. award Printing Industries of Am., East-West Network award. Democrat.

ROBINSON, ROBBY WAYNE, research and development engineer; b. Park Ridge, Ill., Sept. 10, 1960; s. Simon and Dolores Juanita (Owens) R. BS in Mech. Engring. Tech., Purdue U., 1982. Mfg. engr. Sundstrand Aviation, Rockford, Ill., 1979-80; sr. engr. McDonnell Douglas Corp., Long Beach, Calif., 1983—. Mem. AIAA (assoc.), Soc. for Advancement Materials and Process Engring., Nat. Computer Graphics Assn., Am. Soc. Metals. Democrat. Presbyterian. Club: Purdue of Los Angeles. Avocations: music, theater, film, softball, spectator car racing.

ROBINSON, ROBERT BLACQUE, association executive; b. Long Beach, Calif., Apr. 24, 1927; s. Joseph LeRoi and Frances Hansel R.; m. Susan Amelia Thomas, Jan. 21, 1960; children: Victoria, Shelly, Blake, Sarah. Student, Oreg. State Coll., 1946; B.A., UCLA, 1950. Partner, Pritchard Assocs. (Mgmt. Cons.), Honolulu, 1956-58; asst. dir. Econ. Planning and Coordination Authority, Hawaii, 1959; dep. dir. Dept. Econ. Devel., State of Hawaii, 1960-62; with Pacific Concrete and Rock Co., Ltd., Honolulu, 1963-77; exec. v.p. Pacific Concrete and Rock Co., Ltd., 1966-68, pres., 1968-75, chmn., 1976-77; pres. C. of C. of Hawaii, Honolulu, 1977—; dir. Bank of Honolulu, N.A., Fed. Home Loan Bank of Seattle. Bd. govs. Hawaii Employers Council, 1969-74, mem. exec. com., 1969-74, vice chmn., 1973-74; bd. dirs. Pacific Aerospace Mus., 1982—; mem. Hawaii Tourism Conf., 1977—, chmn., 1981-82; bd. dirs. Aloha United Fund, 1970-76, sec., 1972, v.p., 1973-76; bd. dirs. Oahu Devel. Conf., 1970-75; treas., bd. dirs. Crime Stoppers Hawaii, 1981—; mem. Hawaii Joint Council on Econ. Edn., 1985—; bd. dirs. Jr. Achievement Hawaii, 1967-73, pres., 1969; bd. dirs. Hawaii Ednl. Council, 1974-75, Health and Community Services Council Hawaii, 1982-84; mem. Hawaii Conv. Ctr. Council, 1984—, Interagency Energy Conservation Council, State of Hawaii, 1978—; trustee Central Union Ch., 1983-86 . Served with USNR, 1945-46; lt. comdr. USNR; ret. Mem. Japan-Am. Conf. of Mayors and C. of C. Pres. (mem. Am. exec. com. 1974—), Am. Soc. Assn. Execs. (past dir. Hawaii chpt.), C. of C. Hawaii (dir. 1972-75, chmn. 1975), Cement and Concrete Products Industry of Hawaii (pres. 1968), Hawaii Mfrs. Assn. (past dir.), Navy League of U.S. (Hawaii council), Engring. Assn. Hawaii, Sigma Chi. Club: Pacific. Lodge: Rotary. Home: 1437 Kalaepohaku St Honolulu HI 96816 Office: C of C of Hawaii 735 Bishop St Honolulu HI 96813

ROBINSON, ROBERT WADE, II, dentist; b. Stillwater, Okla., Jan. 16, 1948; s. Robert Wade and Margery (Le Vern) R.; m. Valerie Ann Tag, Feb. 12, 1971 (div. June 1976); 1 child, Robert Wade III. B.S., Okla. State U., 1971; D.M.D., U. Louisville, 1978. Gen. practice dentistry, Wasilla, Alaska, 1978—; pres. Petro Marine Services Inc., Anchorage, 1980-83; pres., owner RWR Investing Inc., Wasilla, 1980—; ptnr. Alaska Burglar & Fire Alarm Co., Wasilla, 1982-83, Century Park Subdiv., Wasilla, 1984—, Creek Cliff Ltd., Wasilla, 1984—; cons. on floridation Wasilla City Council, 1983—, Alaska Dental Hygiene Sch., Anchorage, 1984—. Charter mem. Iditarod Trail Com., 1978—; founder, bd. dirs. Wasilla Iditarod Days Inc., 1981—; coach, mgr. Wasilla Little League, 1980-83; mem., planner South Central Health Planning Commn., Matanuska-Susitna Borough, Alaska, 1980; fin. chmn. Lacher for Senate, Wasilla, 1984. Served with U.S. Army, 1971-74. Decorated Army Commendation medal; named Small Employer of Yr., Alaska Gov.'s Com. on Employment of Handicapped, 1983. Mem. ADA, Alaska Dental Assn., Acad. Gen. Dentistry, Wasilla C. of C. (pres. 1983), Beta Delta, Phi Delta, Psi Omega. Republican. Presbyterian. Lodges: Rotary, Elks. Home: PO Box 871687 Wasilla AK 99687 Office: Valley Dental Clinic PC PO Box 871687 Wasilla AK 99687

ROBINSON, RONALD HOWARD, aeronautical engineer; b. Boise, Idaho, Oct. 21, 1945; s. Jesse Dwite Robinson and Annie Belle (Baxter) Robinson Bruner; m. Linda Anne Kibble, June 17, 1967; children: James Edward, Kristine Marie. AS, Boise State U., 1966; BSAeroE, U. Wash, 1968; MBA with honors, City U., Seattle, 1980. Registered profl. engr., Wash.; lic. pilot, FAA. Various engring. duties Gen. Electric Corp., Evendale, Ohio, 1969-73; various engring. duties Boeing Co., Seattle, 1966-69, with comml. airplane div., 1973—, aerodynamics tech. engr., 1973-78, flight ops. engr., jet transport ops. cons., 1978-82, spl. projects mgr., 1982-84, tech. requirements mgr., 1984-85, mgr. airline support 7J7 div., 1986-87, mgr. maintenance and reliability 7J7 div., 1987—. Patentee in field. Mem. No. Assn. Retarded Citizens, Seattle, 1978-83, Northwest Gifted Child Assn., 1980, Port of Seattle Joint Com. on Aircraft Overflights, 1983-86; com. mem. Boy Scouts Am., Seattle, 1984—. Mem. AIAA. Republican. Avocations: flying, golf, fishing, skiing. Home: 16813 NE 33d St Bellevue WA 98008 Office: Boeing Comml Aircraft Co PO Box 3707 Seattle WA 98124

ROBINSON, ROSS UTLEY, consulting firm executive; b. Mpls., July 30, 1928; s. Howard Hadley and Doris (Utley) R.; m. Barbara Aitken Brown, Oct. 3, 1953; children: Brian, Emily, Judith, Ross Stuart, Rachel, John. BA, Colgate U., 1949; MA, Wesleyan U., 1951; MS, MIT, 1953. Dir. advanced systems Abbott Labs., North Chicago, Ill., 1953-79; assoc. dir. research and development Boehringer Mannheim, Tustin, Calif., 1979-81; v.p. research and devel. ICL Scientific, Fountain Valley, Calif., 1981-84; pres., chief exec. officer Mesa Diagnostics, Los Alamos, N.Mex., 1984-85; pres. Cardinal Associates, Santa Fe, 1984—; lectr. U. Calif., Irvine, 1984, U. N.Mex., Albuquerque, 1986—; bd. dirs. Los Alamos Diagnostics. Contbr. articles to profl. jours. Bd. dirs. Los Alamos Econ. Devel. Corp. Mem. Am. Chem. Soc., AAAS, Assn. Advancement. Med. Instrumentation (nat. sec. 1973-75), Sigma Xi (club pres. 1964-65), Los Angeles C. of C. (task force mem. 1978). Presbyterian. Home: 2393 Botulph Rd Santa Fe NM 87505 Office: Cardinal Assocs 2801 Rodeo Rd Suite B600 Santa Fe NM 87505

ROBINSON, SHIRLEY JEAN, educational counselor; b. Gibsland, La., Feb. 19, 1941; d. George W. and Clara (Hewitt) Pearson; m. Cecil R. Robinson, July 31, 1939; 1 son, Taiye. B.A., San Francisco State Coll., 1968, M.A., 1972; EdD U. So. Calif., 1986. Counselor, Calif. Blind Sch., Berkeley, 1965-68; counselor Peralta Community Coll. Dist., Coll. of Alameda (Calif.), 1968—. Recipient Outstanding Service award Coll. Alameda, 1982. Mem. Calif. Personnel and Guidance Assn., Am. Personnel and Guidance Assn., Am. Coll. Personnel Assn., Calif. Community Coll. Counselors Assn., East Bay Lit. Guild, Oakland Mus. Assn., Nat. Vocat. Assn., Delta Sigma Theta. Democrat. Office: Coll Alameda 555 Atlantic Ave Alameda CA 94501

ROBINSON, WILLIAM JAMES, mining company executive; b. Butte, Mont., May 15, 1943; s. Harry Ellsworth and Hazel Mary (Crosby) R.; m. Jadeen Marie Flynn, June 15, 1963; children: Bill, Mari, Lance. BS, Mont. Coll. Mineral Sci. & Tech., 1967, Engr. Mines (hon.), 1982. With Anaconda Co., Butte, Mont., 1965-74; proj. mgr. Anaconda Co., Tonopah, Nev., 1974-76; sr. mining engr. Getty Oil Co., Los Angeles, 1977-80; mgr. corp. devel. Western Energy Co., Butte, 1980-84, v.p. adminstrv. and tech. services, 1984-86, v.p. metals, 1986—; western area coord. Emergency Solid Fuels Res. of Nat. Def. Exec. Res., U.S. Dept. Energy, 1982-86. Scoutmaster Boy Scouts Am., Tonopah, 1976; bd. dirs. Mont. Spl. Olympics, Butte, 1983—. Named Outstanding Bd. Mem., Mont. Spl. Olympics, 1984. Mem. AIME (chmn. local sect. 1972-83, Outstanding Service award 1972), Mont. Coal Council, Mont. Tech. Alumni Assn. (pres. 1972-73), Mont. Tech. Found. Bd. Roman Catholic. Club: Mont. Tech. Boosters (Butte) (v.p. 1967-69). Lodge: Elks, Rotary. Avocations: music, skiing. Home: 11 N Lake Butte MT 59701 Office: Western Energy Co 16 E Granite Butte MT 59701

ROBISON, BARBARA ANN, data processing executive; b. Buffalo, Mar. 26, 1953; d. Kenneth William and Gloria Jane (Fischer) V.; m. Gary David Robison, Apr. 17, 1982; children: Carrie Anne, Melissa Lynn. AS in Data Processing, Erie Community Coll., 1981. Programmer, analyst Printronix, Irvine, Calif., 1982-83; sr. programmer, analyst Application Devel. Services, Irvine, 1983-84; mgr. data processing Lifestyle Calif., Irvine, 1984-86; mgmt. info. cons. Barbara A. Robison Assocs., Irvine, 1986—. Mem. Profl. Assn. Computer Technicians (se. 1985), So. Calif. PRISM. Methodist.

ROBISON, LAREN R., agricultural scientist, research and academic administrator; b. Georgetown, Idaho, Mar. 25, 1931; s. Roy Hyrum and Melba Vilate (Weaver) R.; m. Patricia Fredine Bischoff, Aug. 3, 1955; children: Mark, Douglas, James, PattiAnn, Jarred, Leslie. BS, Brigham Young U., 1957, MS, 1958; PhD, U. Minn., 1962. New crops leader U. Nebr., Lincoln, 1962-65, leader extension, 1965-71; chmn. dept. agronomy Brigham Young U., Provo, Utah, 1971-81, assoc. dean Coll. Biol. Agrl. Scis., 1980—, dir. Ezra Taft Benson Inst. Food and Agriculture, 1981—. Contbr. articles to profl. jours. Served with U.S. Army, 1953-55. Mem. Am. Soc. Agronomy, Am. Weed Sci. Soc., Council for Agrl. Sci. and Tech., Am. Registry Cert. Profls. in Agronomy Crops and Soils. Mormon. Avocations: singing, reading, gardening, fishing. Home: 1230 W 860 N Provo UT 84604 Office: Brigham Young U Dept Agronomy Provo UT 84602

ROBISON, MARSHA GAIL, counseling company executive; b. Charleroi, Pa., Nov. 24, 1953; d. Lou H. and Marian Alice (Robinson) Skokut; children—Justin, Maya. Student in Mech. Engring., Mt. San Antonio U., 1977-80. CAD packaging designer Gen. Dynamics, Pomona, Calif., 1972-80, Singer Librascope, Glendale, Calif., 1980-81; ind. cons. Hughes, ITT, Rockwell, Los Angeles, 1981-83; pres. CAD Counsel, North Hollywood, Calif., 1982—. Mem. Nat. Computer Graphics Assn. Avocation: back-packing. Office: CAD Counsel 1590 Lydia Circle Simi Valley CA 93065

ROBLEDO, ARMANDO RAMOS, consulting geographer; b. Palo Alto, Calif., Oct. 25, 1957; s. Edward Garcia and Mary Virginia Robledo. AS in Gen. Sci., Foothill Coll., 1977; BA in Geography, U. Calif., Santa Barbara, 1980. Math. tchr. U.S. Peace Corps, Cen. African Republic, 1980-81; math. tchr. U.S. Peace Corps, Swaziland, 1981-84, meteorologist, 1984-85; pvt. practice geography Mountain View, 1985—; lectr. U. Swaziland, 1984-85. Mem. Assn. Am. Geographers. Democrat. Roman Catholic. Avocation: flying, automobile restoration.

ROBY, KENNETH BRUCE, hydrologist, fishery biologist; b. San Francisco, Jan. 6, 1951; s. William and Wanda Jane (Miller) R.; m. Marsha Adelle Hess, Aug. 7, 1976; children: William Nelson, Erin May. BS, U. Calif., Berkeley, 1973, MS, 1975. Cert. tchr. community colls., Calif. Research asst. U. Calif., Berkeley, 1973-75; fisheries biologist U.S. Forest Service, San Francisco, 1975-76; hydrologist U.S. Forest Service, Greenville, Calif., 1979-83, supervisory hydrologist, 1983—; water mgmt. specialist East Bay Regional Park Dist., Oakland, Calif., 1977-79. Dir. Greenville Community Services Dist., 1983—; pres. Indian Creek Presch., Greenville. Mem. Am. Fisheries Soc. Home: PO Box E261 Greenville CA 95947 Office: US Forest Service PO Box 329 Greenville CA 95947

ROCHA, GUY LOUIS, archivist, historian; b. Long Beach, Calif., Sept. 23, 1951; s. Ernest Louis and Charlotte (Sobus) R.; m. Pamela Marie Parsons, Jan. 4, 1980. B.A. in Social Studies and Edn., Syracuse U., 1973; M.A. in Am. Studies, San Diego State U., 1975; postgrad., U. Nev., 1975—. Tchr., Washoe County Sch. Dist., Reno, Nev., 1975-76; history instr. Western Nev. Community Coll., Carson City, 1976; curator manuscripts Nev. Hist. Soc., Reno, 1976-81, interim asst. dir., 1980, interim dir., 1980-81; state archivist Nev. Div. Archives and Records, Carson City, 1981—; hist. cons. Janus Assocs., Tempe, Ariz., 1980, Rainshadow Assocs., Carson City, 1983—. Co-author The Ignoble Conspiracy: Radicalism on Trial in Nevada, 1986; contbr. to book and govt. study. Mem. Washoe Heritage Council, Reno, 1983-85; editorial bd. Nev. Hist. Soc., Reno, 1983—; mem. Washoe County Democratic Central Com., Reno, 1984—. Mem. Conf. Intermountain Archivists (Council mem 1979-87, v.p. 1984-85, pres. 1985-86), State Hist. Records Adv. Bd. (dep. coordinator 1984-86, coordinator 1986—), Westerners Internat. Nev. Corral (dep. sheriff 1980-81, sheriff 1984-85, mem. state coordinators steering com. 1985-87, vice chmn. 1986-87), Soc. Am. Archivists, Western History Assn., Nat. Assn. Govt. Archives and Records Adminstrs. Democrat. Home: 14485 Huron Trail Reno NV 89511-9012 Office: Nev State Library and Archives Div Archives and Records 101 S Fall St Carson City NV 89710

ROCHA, MARILYN EVA, clinical psychologist; b. San Bernardino, Calif., Oct. 23, 1928; d. Howard Ray Gonding and Laura Anne (Johanson) Walker; m. Hilario Ursala Rocha, Mar. 25, 1948 (dec. Feb. 1971); children: Michael, Sherry, Teri, Denise. AA, Solano Jr. Coll., 1970. BA, Sacramento State U., 1973, MA, 1974; PhD, U.S. Internat. U., 1981. Psychologist, Naval Drug Rehab. Ctr., U.S. Navy, San Diego, 1975-85, chief psychologist, 1983-84; staff clin. psychologist Calif. Youth Authority No. Reception Ctr. Clinic, 1985—; dir. Self-Help Agys., San Diego. Author short story. Vol. counselor Hamonium, San Diego, 1976-77; SMRC Planning Group Scripps/Miramor Ranch, 1982-85; leader Vacaville council Cub Scouts Am., Calif., 1957-62, 4-H, also Brownie's. Mem. Calif. Scholastic Fedn., PTA (hon. life), Am. Psychol. Assn., Am. Assn. Suicidology, Bus. and Profl. Women, Delta Zeta. Democrat. Unitarian. Home: 4919 Gastman Way Fair Oaks CA 95628

ROCHETTE, EDWARD CHARLES, association executive; b. Worcester, Mass., Feb. 17, 1927; s. Edward Charles and Lilia (Viau) R.; m. Mary Ann Ruland, July 29, 1978; children by previous marriage—Edward Charles, Paul, Philip. Student, Washington U., St. Louis U., Clark U. Exec. editor Krause Publs., Iola, Wis., 1960-66; acting exec. dir. Am. Numismatic Assn., Colorado Springs, Colo., 1967-68, exec. v.p., 1972—; editor jour. The Numismatist, Colorado Springs, Colo., 1968-72. Bd. overseers Inst. Philatelic and Numismatic Studies, Adelphi U., Garden City, N.Y., 1979-81; chmn. medals com. Colo. Centennial Bicentennial Commn., 1976; mem. adv. panel Carson City Silver Dollar program Gen. Services Adminstrn., 1979-80; mem. U.S. Assay Commn., 1965. Served with USN, 1944-46. Recipient Gold medal for syndicated column Numistic Lit. Guild, 1980, 86. Mem. Am. Numismatic Assn. (life; medal of merit 1972), Am. Soc. Assn. Execs. Democrat. Roman Catholic. Lodge: Pikes Peak Kiwanis (bd. dirs. 1972). Office: Am Numismatic Assn PO Box 7083 Colorado Springs CO 80933

ROCK, KENNETH WILLETT, history educator; b. Abilene, Kans., Dec. 12, 1938; s. Kenneth Melvin and Marjorie (Taylor) R.; m. Mercedes Alice de Sola, Aug. 22, 1964; children: Kenneth Teodoro, Laurel Elizabeth. BA, U. Kans., 1960; MA, Stanford U., 1962, PhD, 1969. Instr. history Colo. State U., Ft. Collins, 1965-68, asst. prof., 1968-72, advisor Fulbright, Marshall, Rhodes scholarships, 1968-80, assoc. prof., 1972-83, prof., 1983—, acting dir. Office Internat. Edn., 1984-85. Author (booklet) German Footprints in Colorado, 1983; contbr. articles to profl. jours.; chpts. to books. Fulbright scholar Inst. Internat. Edn., Vienna, Austria, 1964-65; fellow NEH, Vienna, 1972-73, NEH, U. Va., 1978; assoc. Danforth Found., 1978-84. Mem. Am. Assn. Advancement Slavic Studies, Conf. Group Cen. European History, Am. Hist. Assn., Am. Hist. Soc. Germans from Russia, Rocky Mountain Slavic Studies Assn., Phi Beta Kappa, Phi Alpha Theta. Democrat. Episcopalian. Avocations: reading, hist. miniatures, travelling, photography, painting. Home: 3212 Shore Rd Fort Collins CO 80524 Office: Colo State U Dept History Fort Collins CO 80523

ROCKLIN, ROY DAVID, chemist; b. San Francisco, Aug. 3, 1953; s. Albert L. and Isobel M. (Saiger) R.; children: Gabriel, Rachel. AB, U. Calif., Santa Cruz, 1975; PhD, U. N.C., 1980. Applications mgr. Dionex Corp., Sunnyvale, Calif., 1980—. Mem. Am. Chem. Soc. Office: Dionex Corp 1228 Titan Way Sunnyvale CA 94088-3603

ROCKSTAD, HOWARD KENT, physicist; b. Ada, Minn., Aug. 5, 1935; s. Gust A. and Petra C. (Ramstad) R. BA in Physics and Math., St. Olaf Coll., 1957; MS in Physics and Math., U. Ill., 1959, PhD in Physics, 1964. Research physicist Corning (N.Y.) Glass Works, 1963-70, Energy Conversion Devices, Troy, Mich., 1970-74; project engr. Micro-Bit Corp., Lexington, Mass., 1974-79; sr. project engr. Control Data Corp.-Micro Bit, Lexington, 1979-81; sr. research scientist ARCO Solar Industries, Calabasas, Calif., 1981-82, Atlantic Richfield Co., Chatsworth, Calif., 1982-86, Jet Propulsion Lab. Calif. Inst. Tech., Pasadena, 1987—; math. lectr. Elmira (N.Y.) Coll. 1967. Contbr. articles to profl. jours.; patentee in field. Mem. World Hunger Appeal com. Luth. Ch. Am., 1985—; treas. CWS/CROP, Thousand Oaks, Calif., 1985-86; bd. dirs. Ventura County Hunger Coalition, Calif., 1984—. Mem. Am. Phys. Soc., Microbeam Analysis Soc., Microbeam

Analysis Soc. So. Calif. (treas. 1984-85), Materials Research Soc., Am. Vacuum Soc., Alfa Romeo Owners Club (nat. pres. 1980-83), Sigma Pi Sigma (pres. St. Olaf Coll. chpt. 1956-57).

ROCKSTROM, ALBERT RAYMOND, former grocer; b. Spokane, Aug. 10, 1917; s. Claes Albert and Ruth Elizabeth (Jonsson) R.; B.S. in Chemistry and Biol. Scis., U. Oreg., 1947; m. Emma Alice Doran, Mar. 14, 1942; children—Thomas Albert, Ronald Charles, David Keith. Self-employed in grocery bus., 1948-75; maj. stockholder Sta. KARY-AM, Prosser, Wash., 1953-59, pres., 1957-58; engaged in real estate investing, 1950-75. Pres. Grandview (Wash.) Jr. C. of C., 1951-52, Grandview C. of C., 1977; mem. Grandview Kiwanis Club, 1971-78, pres., 1975-76; treas. Yakima (Wash.) chpt. S.P.E.B.S.Q.S.A., 1978-79, 83, sec. 1982-83, sec.-treas., 1983-86, adminstrv. v.p. Grandview chpt., 1978-79, pres., 1981-82, Barbershopper of Yr., 1980, area counselor, 1982—; mem. Grandview Sch. Bd., 1956-69, chmn., 1968-69; mem. Citizens Adv. Com. Sch. Dist. Grandview, 1976-77; mem. KYVE-TV Bd., 1962-69. Named Distinguished Club Pres. in Kiwanis Pacific NW Dist., 1976, recipient new club bldg. award, 1977. Mem. Delta Tau Delta. Republican. Methodist. Club: Toastmasters (adminstrv. v.p. Grandview 1978). Lodge: Yakima Kamiakin Kiwanis (lt. gov. Pacific N.W. dist. 1982-83, 2d v.p. 1985-86, 1st v.p. 1986—, honors award 1982-83, disting. club mem. award 1986). Address: 120 Terrace Park Dr Yakima WA 98901

ROCKWELL, DON ARTHUR, psychiatrist; b. Wheatland, Wyo., Apr. 24, 1938; s. Orson Arthur and Kathleen Emily (Richards) R.; m. Frances Pepitone-Arreola, Dec. 23, 1965; children: Grant, Chad. BA, Wash. U., 1959; MD, U. Okla., 1963; MA in Sociology, U. Calif., Berkeley, 1967. Diplomate Am. Bd. Psychiatry and Neurology. Intern in surgery San Francisco Gen. Hosp., 1963-64; resident in psychiatry Langley-Porter Neuropsychiatric Inst. U. Calif. Med. Ctr., San Francisco, 1964-67; instr. dept. psychiatry U. Calif. Sch. Medicine, Davis, 1969-70, asst. prof., 1970-74, assoc. prof., 1974-80, acting. assoc. dir., dean curricular affairs, 1979-80, acting assoc. dean student affairs, 1980, assoc. dean student affairs, 1980-82, prof., 1980-84; career tchr. NIMH, 1970-72; assoc. psychiatrist Sacramento Med. Ctr.; med. dir. U. Calif. Med. Ctr., Davis, 1982-84; prof., vice chmn. dept. psychiatry and biobehavioral scis. UCLA, 1984—; dir. UCLA Neuropsychiat. Hosp., 1984—; exec. assoc. dir. UCAL Neuropsychiat. Inst., 1984—, chief of profl. staff, 1984-85, acting assoc. dir. adminstrn., 1984—; cons. Nat. Commn. on Marijuana, Washington, 1971-73. Co-author: Psychiatric Disorders, 1982; contbr. chpts. to books; articles to profl. jours. Bd. dirs. Bereavement Outreach, Sacramento, 1974-84, Suicide Prevention, Yolo County, 1969-84; bd. visitors U. Okla. Sch. Medicine. Served to capt. USAF, 1967-69. Fellow Am. Psychiat. Assn.; mem. AMA, Am. Coll. Psychiatrists, Soc. Biol. Psychiatry, Soc. Health and Human Values, Am. Sociologic Assn., Cen. Calif. Psychiatric Assn. (sec.-pres. 1977-78), U. Okla. Alumni Assn. (trustee 1981—), Alpha Omega Alpha. Home: 1061 Palisair Pl Pacific Palisades CA 90272

ROCKWELL, MARTIN GUY, eletrical engineer; b. Seattle, Mar. 5, 1954; s. Robert E. and Anne M. (Frogue) R.; m. Laura Jeanne Stockton, Dec. 23, 1978 (div.). B.S.E.E., U. Wash., 1976, M.S.E.E., 1979. project mgr. MTS, Hewlett Packard Co., McMinnville, Oreg., 1979—; cons. in field. Mem. Planetary Soc. Contbr. articles to profl. jours. Office: Hewlett Packard Co 1700 S Baker St McMinnville OR 97128

ROCKWELL, RICHARD THORNTON, military officer, naval engineer; b. Portland, Oreg., Feb. 5, 1946; s. Robert Thorton and Norma Lee (Barron) R.; m. Cheryl Lee Freeman, June 17, 1967; 1 child, Tia Marie. BS Aerospace and Astronautical Engring., U. Wash., 1972; MS in Shipping Mgmt., MIT, 1979. Commd. ensign USN, 1964, advanced through grades to comdr., 1986—; type desk officer SRF Subic, Subic Bay, Philippines, 1979-81; LSD-41 project officer Supship Seattle, 1981-85; asst. repair officer Pearl Harbor Naval Shipyard, Hawaii, 1985—. Mem. Naval Inst., Am. Soc. Naval Engrs. (Brand award 1979), Sigma Xi, Tau Beta Pi.

ROCKWELL, ROBERT GOODE, electrical engineer; b. La Junta, Colo., Aug. 20, 1922; s. Leroy Elwood and Laura Belle (Mc Clain) R.; m. Betty Jean Crawford, Dec. 29, 1945 (div. July 1960); children: Laura Amundsen, Melanie Barham; m. Norma Jean Fosnaugh, Mar. 25, 1961; children: Michael, Robyn Rockwell-Elkins. BSEE, U. Colo., 1944; MSEE, Stanford U., 1948, postgrad., 1949. Mem. tech. staff Hughes Aircraft Corp., Culver City, Calif., 1949-52, Los Angeles, 1969-70; sect. mgr. Varian Assocs., Palo Alto, Calif., 1952-66; mem. tech. staff Fairchild Semiconductor, Palo Alto, 1966-68; mgr. tube tech. Zenith Radio Corp., Glenview, Ill., 1971-82; prin. engr. Rank Electronic Tubes, Scotts Valley, Calif., 1982-86; CRT dispenser cathode cons. Ceradyne Electron Sources, Costa Mesa, Calif., 1986—. Contbr. articles to profl. jours.; patentee in field. Served to lt. (j.g.) USNR, 1942-45. Mem. IEEE (sr., Centennial medal 1984), Soc. Info. Display, Sigma Xi, Tau Beta Pi, Eta Kappa Nu. Democrat. Mem. Christian Ch. Clubs: Bucks and Does Square Dance (Elk Grove Village, Ill.) (pres. 1979-80), Manakin Huguenots (Calif.) (pres. 1986—). Lodge: Masons. Avocations: bicycling, surfing, camping, photography, genealogy. Home: 17242 Chesnut S Irvine CA 92627 Office: Ceradyne Electron Sources 3169A Red Hill Ave Costa Mesa CA 92626

ROCZNIAK, STEVEN OREST, biochemist; b. Vancouver, B.C., Can., Nov. 1, 1955; came to U.S., 1958; s. Stephen and Anastasia (Tinyszin) R.; m. Regina Josephine Mancini, Feb. 4, 1984; 1 child, Daniel Paul. BA, MS, U. Chgo., 1978, PhD, 1984. Postdoctoral scholar U. Calif., San Francisco, 1984-85; research scientist Hybritech, Inc., San Diego, 1986—. Contbr. articles to profl. jours. Mem. AAAS. Avocations: painting, sports.

RODE, EDDIE, real estate broker; b. North Chicago, Ill., Aug. 21, 1920; s. Jacob and Mary (Kosir) R.; m. Marguerite W. Wagner, Nov. 15, 1947; children—Susan, Mark, Joanne, Patricia. Student, U. Md., 1954-58; real estate broker, Calif. Commd. lt. col., U.S. Air Force, 1942, advanced through grades to lt. col., 1959, ret., 1963; mil. adviser, Yugoslavia, 1951-54; owner/broker Rode Realty, Santa Barbara, Calif., 1968—. Decorated Air Medal with 7 oak leaf clusters. Mem. Santa Barbara Bd. Realtors, Lompoc Bd. Realtors, Apt. Owners Assn., Channel City Air Force Assn., Ret. Officers Assn. Republican. Home: 3360 Braemer Dr Santa Barbara CA 93109 Office: 3114 State St Sanat Barbara CA 93105

RODEN, GUNNAR IVO, oceanographer; b. Tallinn, Estonia, Dec. 27, 1928; s. Johannes and Edith (Mueller) R.; m. Ingegerd Willig, Jan. 5, 1958; children: Christopher-Yngve, Lennart, Einar. MS in Oceanography, UCLA, 1956. Postgrad. research fellow U. Calif., La Jolla, 1956-63, asst. specialist in oceanography, 1964-65; research assoc. U. Wash., Seattle, 1966-68, sr. research assoc., 1968-74, 75-81, prin. research assoc., 1982—. Contbr. 50 sci. papers and articles. Mem. Am. Geophys. Union (translations editor 1962—), Am. Meteorol. Soc. (profl.), U.S. Naval Inst., Sigma Xi. Avocations: hiking, photography. Home: 7011-38 Ave NE Seattle WA 98115 Office: U Wash Sch Oceanography WB-10 Seattle WA 98195

RODENGEN, JEFFREY LEE, columnist, motion picture producer and director; b. Mpls., June 5, 1949; s. Marvin Albany and Geraldine Maude (Wooley) R.; m. Susan H. Olsonoski, June 23, 1973 (div. 1985); m. Karine N. Chapus, Nov. 3, 1985; student Moorhead (Minn.) State U., 1967-68, Universidad de las Americas, 1968-69, Riverside City Coll., 1969-70; B.A., U. Calif., Riverside, 1972; M.S., Ph.D. in Systems and Design Engring., U. Beverly Hills, 1982. Pres., Pythagoras Instruments, 1972, D.C. Recording Studios, Riverside, Calif., 1972, AVIII, Inc., 1973-78, AV Am., 1979-80; exec. producer, dir. mktg. Lights & Sounds Images, Tustin, Calif., 1979-81; pres. Grand Illusions Unltd., Las Vegas, 1981-83; Write Stuff Syndicate, 1986—; maj. prodns. include: Libra Colony, 1977, Latin Lasers, 1978, Galactic Laser Experience, 1978, Beyond Magic, 1981; Knowledge, 1978; Achieving Excellence, 1979; Celebrate, 1978; Fiesta Fantastico, 1979. Mem. Riverside Adminstrv. Bd. Appeals, 1973-77. Named Best Actor, Riverside Community Players, 1974; recipient Silver Cindy award, 1977; Honor award Soc. Tech. Communicators, 1984; holder Black Belt in Karate; lic. single and multi-engine pilot, instrument rating. Mem. Internat. Film Producers Am., Assn. Multi-Image, Aircraft Owners and Pilots Assn., Soc. Tech. Writers, Boating Writers Assn. Democrat. Presbyterian. Inventor photo-optical laser and holographic devices, electronic ruler, space-docking game for Am.-Soviet space flight; patentee in field. Home: 1108 Citrus Isle Fort Lauderdale FL 33315

RODEY, PATRICK MICHAEL, state senator; b. San Francisco, Jan. 22, 1943; s. James and Martha Leora (Phillips) R.; B.Ed., U. Alaska, 1966; J.D., U. Ariz., 1973; m. Barbara Jean Coffey, June 25, 1976. With Safeway Corp., 1963-66, U. Alaska, 1968-69, Peter Kiewits Sons, 1973; admitted to Alaska bar, 1973; ptnr. firm Abbott, Lynch & Farney, and predecessor firm, Anchorage, 1975-83, Aglietti, Pennington and Rodney, 1983—; mem. Alaska Senate, 1974—, chmn. statutory revision commn., 1976—, Senate majority leader, 1980-82. Researcher, Inst. Social, Econ. and Govt. Research U. Alaska, 1968-69. Mem. Am., Alaska bar assns., Phi Alpha Delta. Democrat. Episcopalian. Home: 2335 Lord Baranof Anchorage AK 99503

RODGERS, ANTHONY EDWIN, environmental services administrator; b. Los Angeles, May 16, 1949; s. Elihu C. and Bernadine (Armelin) R.; m. Debra Sue Woods, May 10, 1969 (div. 1983); children: Shelean, Myesia, Edwin. Cert. with honors, Long Beach City Coll., 1967; cert., Compton Jr. Coll., 1970, AS, 1974; cert., Los Angeles City Coll., 1981; BSBA, U. Phoenix, Costa Mesa, Calif., 1987. Mechan. inspector N. Am. Rockwell, Downey, Calif., 1967-68; lead custodian Los Angeles County, 1969-74; supr. gen. services Los Angeles County, Long Beach, 1974-78, dir. environ. services, 1978-83; plant mgr. III BellFlower (Calif.) Unified Sch. Dist., 1983; dir. environ. services Ingleside Hosp., Rosemead, Calif., 1983—; instr. bldg. maintenance Baldwin Park (Calif.) Unified Sch. Dist., 1985—. Flickinger scholar County of Los Angeles, 1980. Mem. Nat. Exec. Housekeepers Assn. (program chmn. 1983—, v.p. San Gabriel Valley chpt. 1987—), Environ. Mgmt. Assn., Am. Hosp. Assn., Am. Bowling Congress, U.S. Jaycees. Democrat. Methodist. Avocations: running, swimming, reading, drawing, painting. Office: Ingleside Hosp 7500 E Hellman Ave Rosemead CA 91770

RODGERS, AUDREY PENN, government official; b. Berkeley, Calif., Aug. 8, 1923; d. Lewis and Edith Penn; A.B., U. Calif., Berkeley, 1944; m. David Leigh Rodgers, June 13, 1943 (div. Mar. 1982); children—Timothy Leigh, Janice Leigh Rodgers Bracken. Research asst. U. Rochester (N.Y.) Sch. Medicine, 1943-46, 49-51, NIH, Bethesda, Md., 1948-49; design/cons. landscaping pvt. homes and gardens, 1960-69; pres. Campaign Data Service, Inc., San Francisco, 1970-80; public info. dir. East Bay Infiltration/Inflow Study, Oakland, 1980-85; pub. info. officer East Bay Infiltration/Inflow Correction Program and East Bay Mcpl. Utility Dist. Wet Weather Programs, 1985—. Mem. San Francisco Charter Revision Com., 1968-70; chmn. design group Seward St. Park Task Force, Eureka Valley Promotion Assn., 1970-73; chmn. Dolores Heights Spl. Use Dist. Com., 1978-80; bd. dirs. The Urban Sch., 1968-69, Dolores Heigts Improvement Club, 1962-64, 86—, San Francisco Planning and Urban Research Assn., 1968-78. Mem. Pub. Relations Soc. Am. (chmn. accreditation com. 1984-86, bd. dirs.), Water Pollution Control Fedn., Nature Conservancy, LWV (chpt. bd. dirs. 1966-67), Acad. Polit. Sci., Orgn. Women in Landscape, Sierra Club, People for Open Space, Alpha Xi Delta. Democrat. Club: Met. Office: PO Box 24055 Oakland CA 94623

RODGERS, FREDERIC BARKER, judge, lawyer; b. Albany, N.Y., Sept. 29, 1940; s. Prentice Johnson and Jane (Weed) R.; m. Judy Reed, Feb. 24, 1973. AB, Amherst Coll., 1963; JD, Union U., 1966. Bar: N.Y. 1966, U.S. Ct. Mil. Appeals 1968, Colo. 1972, U.S. Supreme Ct. 1974, U.S. Ct. Appeals (10th cir.) 1981. Chief dep. dist. atty., Denver, 1972-73; commr. Denver Juvenile Ct., 1973-79; mem. Mulligan Reeves Teasley & Joyce, P.C., Denver, 1979-80; pres. Frederic B. Rodgers, P.C., Breckenridge, Colo., 1980—; county judge County of Gilpin, 1987—; presiding mcpl. judge cities of Breckenridge, Blue River, Black Hawk, Central City, Empire, Idaho Springs and Westminster, Colo., 1979—; chmn. com. on mcpl. ct. rules of procedure Colo. Supreme Ct., 1984—. Mem. Colo. Commn. on Children, 1982-85. Served with JAGC, U.S. Army, 1967-72; to maj. USAR, 1972—. Decorated Bronze Star with oak leaf cluster, Air medal. Recipient Spl. Community Service award Colo. Am. Legion, 1979. Mem. ABA, Colo. Bar Assn. (bd. govs. 1986—), Denver Bar Assn. (bd. trustees 1979-82), Continental Divide Bar Assn., First Judicial Dist. Bar Assn., Colo. Mcpl. Judges Assn. (pres. 1986-87), Denver Law Club (pres. 1981-82), Am. Judicature Soc., Marines Meml. Club. Episcopalian. Club: University (Denver). Contbr. articles to profl. jours.. Home: 210 E 4th High St Central City CO 80427-0398 Office: Bank of Breckenridge Bldg 106 N French St Suite 220 Breckenridge CO 80424-0567

RODGERS, JOHN CHARLES, health physicist; b. Wickenburg, Ariz., Aug. 11, 1938; s. George Washington and Dorothy Ann (Eichenwald) R.; m. Sally Ann Suhm, Apr. 1, 1968 (div.); 1 child, Rachael Kate; m. Elizabeth Ann Rohn, Sept. 25, 1978; children: Paul William, Casey John. BS in Physics, Oreg. State U., 1960; MS in Physics, Calif. State U., Los Angeles, 1963; MA in History, Philosophy of Sci., Ind. U., 1965. Cert. Am. Bd. Health Physics. Tutor St. John's Coll., Santa Fe, 1968-71; environ. scientist N. Mex. Environ, Improvement Div., Santa Fe, 1971-75; mem. staff Health div. Los Alamos (N.Mex.) Nat. Lab., 1975-85, Environ. Evaluation Group, Santa Fe, 1985—; mem. Gov.'s rev. com. N.Mex. Radiation Protection Regulations, Santa Fe, 1983-85. Contbr. articles to profl. jours. NSF fellow, Washington U., St. Louis, 1966-67. Mem. AAAS, Health Physics Soc. (pub. info. com. 1982-84), Air Pollutuion Control Assn. Democrat. Home: 2795 Via Caballero del Sur Santa Fe NM 87505 Office: Environ Evaluation Group PO Box 968 Santa Fe NM 87501

RODGERS, LARAINE, financial services executive; b. N.Y.C., Jan. 14, 1947; adopted d. Frank Clark and Connie Mary (Cerrato) Tufaro; m. Bruce Alan Fairman, Nov. 4, 1966; children—Michael Cory, Carolyn Jean; m. Thomas Ramon Daigle, Mar. 2, 1979. BS U. San Francisco, 1986. Programmer/analyst N.Y. Blood Ctr., N.Y.C., 1965-66; cons., instr. data processing, N.Y. and N.J., 1966-74; project mgr. Am. Express, Ft. Lauderdale, Fla. and Phoenix, 1974-79; project mgr. Ryder Truck Rental, Miami, Fla., 1979-80; dir. systems devel. Citicorp Diners Club, Englewood, Colo., 1980-81, regional v.p., 1982-83; v.p. systems devel. MasterCard Internat., St. Louis, 1983; v.p. electronic banking systems Security Pacific Automation Co., Los Angeles, 1983-85, 1st v.p. Capital Markets Services, 1985—. Office: Security Pacific Automation Co 611 N Brand Glendale CA 91203

RODINE, JAMES DWAIN, land developer; b. Smith Center, Kans., Dec. 30, 1940; s. Wallace L. and Dorothy M. Rodine; m. Marcia C. Neilsen, May 10, 1975; children: Charity, Wendy, Heidi, Joshua, Jenica. BS, Calif. State U., Los Angeles, 1969; PhD, Stanford U., 1975. Registered engring. geologist, Calif. Ptnr. Rodine Cos.,, Monrovia, Calif., 1960—; cons. engring. geology, Western U.S., 1970—. Contbr. articles to Debris Flows, 1975. Mem. Assn. Engring. Geologists, Mining Engrs. Soc. of AIME, Geologic Soc. Am. Republican. Home: 2247 N Villa Heights Rd Pasadena CA 91107 Office: Rodine Cos Inc 147 E Olive Monrovia CA 91016

RODMAN, ALPINE CLARENCE, art wholesaler, entrepreneur; b. Roswell, N.Mex., June 23, 1952; s. Robert Elsworth and Verna Mae (Means) R.; m. Sue Arlene Lawson, Dec. 13, 1970; 1 child, Connie Lynn. Student Colo. State U., 1970-71, U. No. Colo., 1983—. Ptnr. Pinel Silver Shop, Loveland, Colo., 1965-68, salesman, 1968-71; real estate salesman, Loveland, 1971-73; mgr. Traveling Traders, Phoenix, 1974-75; owner Deer Track Traders, Loveland, 1975-85, pres. Deer Track Traders, Ltd., 1985—. Author: The Vanishing Indian: Fact or Fiction?, 1985. Cadet comdr. CAP, Ft. Collins, Colo., 1968, 70, Colo. rep. to youth tng. program, 1969, U.S. youth rep. to Japan, 1970. Mem. Bur. Wholesale Sales Reps., Mountain States Men's, Boy's and Western Apparel Club, Eastern States Western Salesman's Assn., Nat. Rifle Assn., Internat. Platform Assn., Indian Arts and Crafts Assn. Republican. Baptist. Clubs: Crazy Horse Grass Roots. Office: Deer Track Traders Ltd PO Box 448 Loveland CO 80539

RODMAN, SUE ARLENE, wholesale Indian crafts company executive, artist; b. Fort Collins, Colo., Oct. 1, 1951; d. Marvin F. and Barbara I. (Miller) Lawson; m. Alpine C. Rodman, Dec. 13, 1970; 1 child, Connie Lynn. Student Colo. State U., 1970-73. Silversmith Pinel Silver Shop, Loveland, Colo., 1970-71; asst. mgr. Traveling Traders, Phoenix, 1974-75; co-owner, co-mgr. Deer Track Traders, Ltd., Loveland, 1975-85, exec. v.p., 1985—. Author: The Book of Contemporary Indian Arts and Crafts, 1985. Mem. Rep. Presdl. Task Force, 1982—; mem. U.S. Senatorial Club, 1982—. Recipient Beta Loveland Women's Club scholarship, 1969; Valley Airpark, Inc. Gordon M. Walker aviation meml. flight scholarship, 1970. Mem. Internat. Platform Assn., Nat. Assn. Female Execs., Indian Arts and Crafts Assn., Internat. Platform Assn. Baptist. Club: Crazy Horse Grass Roots (S.D.). Avocations: museums, recreation research, fashion design, reading, pvt. pilot. Office: Deer Track Traders Ltd PO Box 448 Loveland CO 80539

RODNEY, PETER MARC, theatre educator; b. N.Y.C., Apr. 29, 1948; s. Benjamin Mordecai and Tessie (Federoff) R.; m. Barbara Renee Fields, June 19, 1977. B.A., Queens Coll., 1971; M.A., U. Conn., 1972; Ph.D., Case Western Reserve U., 1980. Lectr. in theatre Baldwin-Wallace Coll., Berea, Ohio, 1973-74; asst. prof. of theatre Elmira Coll., N.Y., 1975-79, Humboldt State U., Arcata, Calif., 1979-82; assoc. prof. of theatre, CSU Dominquez Hills, Carson, Calif., 1982—; chmn. theatre arts program CSU Dominquez Hills. Mem. Am. Theatre Assn., Am. Assn. U. Profs., Calif. Ednl. Theatre Assn., Southern Calif. Ednl. Theatre Assn. Office: Calif State U Dominguez Hills 1000 Victoria Carson CA 90747

RODRIGUE, CHRISTINE M., geography educator, business consultant; b. Los Angeles, Oct. 27, 1952; d. John-Paul and Josephine Genevieve (Gorsky) R. AA in French, German, Los Angeles Pierce Coll., 1972; BA in Geography summa cum laude, Calif. State U., Northridge, 1973, MA in Geography, 1976; PhD in Geography, Clark U., 1986. Computer analyst Jet Propulsion Labs., Pasadena, Calif., 1977; teaching asst. Clark U., Worcester, Mass., 1976-79, research asst., 1977-78; instr. geography Los Angeles Pierce Coll., Woodland Hills, Calif., 1981—; cons. Area Location Systems, Northridge, 1984—; asst. prof. geography Calif. State U., Northridge, 1980—. Mem. NOW, AAAS, Assn. Am. Geographers (chmn. specialty group 1983-84), Los Angeles Geog. Soc. (v.p. 1987—, editor 1981-84), Union Concerned Scientists, The Planetary Soc., Sierra Club, Internat. Arabian Horse Assn., Arabian Horse Registry. Democrat. Avocations: Arabian horses, sci. fiction, hiking, camping, baroque music. Office: Calif State U Dept Geography Northridge CA 91335

RODRIGUES, ALFRED BENJAMIN KAMEEIAMOKU, telephone company executive; b. Honolulu, Jan. 23, 1947; s. Alfred Benjamin Kameeiamoku and Ruth Shiegeko (Kameda) R.BA, U. San Francisco, 1969; postgrad. U. Wis., 1977. Pub. info. mgr. Hawaiian Telephone-GTE, Honolulu, 1979-80, pub. affairs program mgr., 1980-84, dir. pub. affairs, 1984-85, dir. mktg. communications, 1986—. Bd. dirs., pub. relations chmn. Am. Lung Assn., 1981—; trustee, v.p. Hawaii Army Mus. Soc., 1982—; bd. dirs. ARC Hawaii, 1983—; budget com. Aloha United Way. Served to capt. U.S. Army, 1969-79. Decorated Bronze Star with three bronze oak leaf clusters, Meritorious Service medal with oak leaf cluster, Army Commendation medal with oak leaf cluster, Purple Heart with oak leaf cluster, Air medal with oak leaf cluster. Mem. Am. Mktg. Assn., Am. Advt. Fedn., Hawaii Advt. Fedn. (bd. dirs.), Pub. Relations Soc. Am. (pres. Hawaii), Res. Officers Assn., Hawaii C. of C. Republican. Roman Catholic. Lodge: Rotary.

RODRIGUES, GREGORY KENT, structural engineer; b. San Jose, Calif., Sept. 19, 1957; s. Orlando William and Mary Jean (Minhoto) R. BSCE, U. Santa Clara, 1979; MSCE, U. Calif., Berkeley, 1980. Registered profl. civil engr. and structural engr., Calif. Engring. asst. State of Calif., San Jose, 1977; engring. trainee City of San Jose, 1977-79; structural engr. Pregnoff & Matheu, Palo Alto, Calif., 1980—. Mem. ASCE, Structural Engrs. Assn. No. Calif. Democrat. Roman Catholic. Avocations: baseball, basketball, guitar. Home: 460 Shadow Graph Dr San Jose CA 95110 Office: Pregnoff & Matheu 299 Calif Ave Suite 309 Palo Alto CA 94306

RODRIGUES, RAYMOND JOSEPH, academic administrator; b. Somerville, N.J., May 2, 1938; s. Joseph Batiste and Vera (Fedechena) R.; m. Dawn Droskinis; 1 child, Brad. AB, Rutgers U., 1960, MEd, 1965; PhD, U. N.Mex., 1974. Cert. secondary tchr. From asst. prof. to assoc. prof. English and Edn. U. Utah, Salt Lake City, 1974-78, head dept. secondary education, 1978-79; head dept. Curriculum and Instruction N.Mex. State U., Las Cruces, 1982-86; dir., tchr. edn. U. Colo., Colorado Springs, 1979-82; assoc. acad. v.p. Colo. State U., Ft. Collins, 1986—. Author: Teaching Writing with a Word Processor, 1986, A Guide Book for Teaching Literature, 1978. Served to 1st lt. U.S. Army, 1960-62. Mem. Nat. Council Tchrs. English (exec. bd. conf. English edn. 1984—, editorial bd. 1987—). Office: Colo State U Office VP Acad Affairs Fort Collins CO 80523

RODRIGUEZ, ELOY, toxicology educator; b. Edinburg, Tex., Jan. 7, 1947; s. Everardo and Hilaria (Calvillo) R.; m. June 5, 1982; children: Pilar, Eloy Francisco. BA in Zoology, U. Tex., 1969, PhD in Phytochemistry and Plant Biology, 1975. Asst. prof. phytochemical lab., devel. and cell biology U. Calif., Irvine, 1975-76, assoc. prof. phytochem. lab., dpets. ecology, evolutionary biology and devel. and cell biology, 1979-83, prof. phytochemical lab., devel. and cell biology and coll. Medicine, 1983—, dir. internat. Chicano studies program, 1985—; lectr. Indo-Am. and Fulbright Sr. Scholarship, 1983; vis. prof. and research scientist dept. botany Univ. B.C., 1984, dept. pharm. chemistry sch. of pharmacy, 1985; dir. Nat. Chicano Council Higher Edn. Sci. Fellowship Program for Hispanics, 1986—. Author: BIology and Chemistry of Plant Trichomes, 1984; contbr. over 100 articles to profl. jours.; editor (newsletters) Parthenium, 1976-79, Ciencias, 1986—; Internat. Soc. Chem. Ecology Jour., 1984-87; reviewer profl. jours. Recipient Sr. Scholar Lectureship award Fulbright-Hayes, 1978, Letter of Recognition for US-Mex. Symposium on Renewable Phytochem. Resources U. of Calif., 1983, Research Career Devel. award Nat. Inst. of Allergy and Infectious Diseases NIH, 1982-87, First Ann. Hispanic Educator award League of United Latin Am. Citizens, 1984; grantee Am. Cancer Soc., 1977, NIH, 1978-80, 1982-85, 1985-1990, 1987-1990; Ford Found. Mexican-Am. Grad. fellow, 1972-74; Can. Med. fellow, depts. Botany and Dermatology, U.B.C., Vancouver, 1975-76. Mem. Phytochem. Soc. N.Am., Phytochem. Sect. of the Am. Bot. Soc., Calif. Native Plant Soc., Mexican Bot. Soc., Soc. for the Advancement of Chicanos and Native Ams. in Sci., Am. Chem. Soc., AAAS, Internat. Soc. of Chem. Ecology editor newsletter 1984-86), Am. Pharmacognosy Soc., Fulbright Alumni Assn. Office: U Calif Sch Biol Scis Phytochem Lab Depts Developmental and Cell Biology Irvine CA 92717

RODRIGUEZ, FABIAN VICTOR, news photographer; b. Quito, Ecuador, Jan. 20, 1948; came to U.S., 1953; s. Gonzalo and Lola Lea (Torres) R.; m. Patricia Anne Decker, July 9, 1983. BA, Queens Coll., 1974. Photographer Sta. KOB-TV, Albuquerque, 1978-81; engr. ABC-TV, Los Angeles, 1981-83, Sta. KNBC-TV, Los Angeles, 1983—. Recipient APE award Albuquerque Press Club, 1979. Mem. Am. Film Inst., Nat. Assn. Broadcasters Engrs. and Technicians, Nat. Press Photographers Assn., Acad. TV Arts and Scis. (Emmy award 1985). Democrat. Roman Catholic. Avocations: scuba diving, martial arts instruction, chess, equestrian. Office: Sta KNBC-TV 3000 W Alameda Ave Burbank CA 91523

RODRIGUEZ, GERALD, educator; b. Los Angeles, May 21, 1951; s. William and Lupe (Anguiano) R.; m. Mary Ann Zoria, Oct. 29, 1977; children—Roxanne Nicole, Veronica Ann. A.A., E. Los Angeles Coll., 1971; A.B., U. Calif.-Santa Cruz, 1973; M.A., U. San Francisco, 1978-82. Cert. tchr., adminstr., Calif. Tchr., Alum Rock Union Sch. Dist., San Jose, Calif., 1973-74; instr. Met. Adult Edn. Program, San Jose, 1975; tchr. social studies Berryessa Union Sch. Dist., San Jose, 1975—; coordinator San Jose City Coll., 1981-83. Mem. Rep. Nat. Com. Calif. Opportunity grantee, 1969-73; Stanford U. fellow, 1983-84. Mem. Assn. Supervision and Curriculum Devel., Calif. Tchrs. Assn., Nat. Assn. Christian Educators, Christian Educators Assn., Council Basic Edn., NEA, Nat. Soc. for Study of Edn., Nat. Council Social Studies, Nat. Orgn. Legal Problems of Edn., Christian Legal Soc., U. Calif.-Santa Cruz Alumni Assn., U. San Francisco Alumni Assn., Phi Delta Kappa, Pi Lambda Theta. Evang. Christian. Author: Mexican-American Selected Annotated Bibliography, 1970, others. Home: 152 Harriet Ave San Jose CA 95127 Office: Berryessa Union Sch Dist 3155 Kimlee Dr San Jose CA 95132

RODRIGUEZ, LEONARD, public relations executive; b. Phoenix, Jan. 27, 1944; s. Jesus H. and Manuela (Razo) R.; m. Jo Ann Gama, Jan. 16, 1965; 1 child, Lena Teresa. BS in Mktg., Ariz. State U., 1981. Adminstrv. services officer Title XX Adminstrn., Phoenix, 1979-81, Block Grants Adminstrn., Phoenix, 1981-84; property mgmt. mgr. State of Ariz., Phoenix, 1984-86; pres. LTR Mgmt. Services, Phoenix, 1986—; adj. clin. instr., faculty assoc. Ariz. State U., 1979—. Chmn. community relations Ariz. State U. Minority

Recruitment Program, Tempe, 1985-86; bd. dirs. Friendly House Inc., Phoenix, 1985—, vice chmn., 1986, pres., 1987.. Mem. Ariz. Adminstrs. Assn., Counterparts (founder 1986), Hispanic C. of C. Club: Vesta (Phoenix) (chmn. scholarship com. 1983). Lodge: Rotary (sgt. at arms 1985-86, sec. 1986—87, pres. 1987—). Avocations: painting, sculpture, late 19th century art. Home: 7650 S 14th St Phoenix AZ 85040 Office: LTR Mgmt Services 3225 N Central Ave Suite 1618 Phoenix AZ 85012

RODRIGUEZ, LIONEL, SR., transportation company executive; b. Falfurrias, Tex.; s. Vicente and Albertina (Azocar) R.; m. Patricia Ann Wanchick, Dec. 11, 1969; children: Lionel Jr., Leon. BS, Robert Morris Coll., 1976; cert. food service mgmt., Harvard U., 1981. With customer relations United Airlines, Pitts., Pa., 1972-77, catering rep., 1977-80; food service rep. United Airlines, Boston, 1980-83; inflight service rep. United Airlines, Los Angeles, 1983—; organizer Uniter Airlines Flight Attendant Recognition Program, 1985-86. Bd. dirs. Rolling Hills Little League, pres. 1983—, Bay Harbor Hockey Assn. mgr. 1986—; speaker Los Angeles Youth Council, 1986—; chmn. United Way Campaign for United Airlines, 1985; advisor, coach Palos Verdes Basketball Assn., 1983-84; com. mem. Boy Scouts Am., asst. scout master, 1986—. Served as staff sgt. U.S. Army, 1968-71, Vietnam. Decorated Medal of Valor, Bronze Star. Avocations: golf, basketball. Home: 6315 Ridgepath Ct Rancho Palos Verdes CA 90274 Office: United Airlines Los Angeles Internat Airport Los Angeles CA 90045

RODRIGUEZ, LUIS ALCIDES, social worker; b. Colon, Republic of Panama, July 1, 1945; s. Jose E. and Sara Maria (Gutierrez) R. AAS, Niagara County Community Coll., 1966; BA in Anthropology, U. Buffalo, 1970, MA in Latin Am. Studies, 1977; hon. degree, Community Coll. USAF, Randolph AFB, San Antonio, 1971. Psychiat. technician USAF, Wiesbaden, Fed. Republic W. Germany, 1971-75; psychiat. asst. Del Amo Hosp., Torrance, Calif., 1975-78, Edgemont Hosp., Hollywood, Calif., 1978-80; therapist Erikson Ctr., Tarzana, Calif., 1980-82; med. caseworker U. So. Calif. Alternatives Program, Los Angeles, 1982—. Mem. Am. Assn. Retired Persons, Nat. Assn. Social Workers., Am. Film Inst., Air Force Assn. Democrat. Roman Catholic. Home: PO Box 29306 Los Angeles CA 90027 Office: USC Alternatives to Hosp Program 2611 S Portland St Los Angeles CA 90007

RODRIGUEZ, MARJORIE ANN KENWARD, food inspector; b. Fullerton, Calif., Jan. 25, 1951; d. Gordon Herbert and Edna Cleo (Hoffman) Kenward; m. Hector Mayagoitia Rodriguez, Sept. 10, 1977; children—Cristal Nikomi, Jessica Kathleen. B.S. in Animal Sci., Calif. State Poly. U., Pomona, 1973. Food insp. U.S. Dept. Agr., Vernon, Calif., 1974—. Treas., women's program mgr. Am. Fedn. Govt. Employees Local 0926. Home: 9608 Pinehurst Ave South Gate CA 90280 Office: US Dept Agr FSIS MPI 400 Oceangate Blvd Suite 609 Long Beach CA 90802

RODRIGUEZ, RODRI J., entertainment executive; b. Havana, Cuba, Jan. 2, 1955; came to U.S., 1962; d. Leoncio Alejo and Luz Marina (Castaneda) R. Grad., Immaculate Heart High Sch., Hollywood, Calif., 1973. Prin. The Rodri Group, Los Angeles, 1976—. Commr., v.p. Cultural Affairs Commn., City of Los Angeles, 1984—; commr. Legal Services Trust Fund Commn., State Bar Calif., 1986—. Mem. The Vikki Carr Scholarship Found. (bd. dirs. 1983—), The Nat. Network Hispanic Women (bd. dirs. 1986—, named outstanding entrepreneur 1985), The Latin Bus. Assn., State Bar Calif. (legal services trust fund Commn. 1986—). Republican. Avocations: public speaking, the arts, yachting, deep-sea fishing, snow skiing. Office: The Rodri Group 8721 W Sunset Blvd Penthouse Suite Los Angeles CA 90069

RODRIGUEZ, ROMAN, physician, child psychiatrist, educator; b. N.Y.C., Jan. 21, 1951; s. Roman Rodriguez and Margarita (Castillo) Torres. BS in Biology, St. Mary's Coll. of Calif., 1972; MD, U. Calif.-San Francisco, 1976. Diplomate Nat. Bd. Med. Examiners. Resident in gen. psychiatry Menninger Found., Topeka, 1976-79, fellow in child psychiatry, 1978-80; resident physician Topeka VA Med. Ctr., 1976-79; dir. psychiat. services Youth Ctr. Topeka, 1979-80; assoc. med. dir. mission SE Adolescent Day Treatment Ctr., San Francisco, 1980-81; staff psychiatrist, med. advisor Youth Guidance Ctr., San Francisco, 1980-82; clin. dir. Growing Mind Corp., San Rafael, Calif., 1980-85; pvt. practice child psychiatry, San Francisco and San Rafael, Calif., 1980-85; child team leader dept. psychiatry Kaiser Permanente Med. Ctr., South San Francisco, 1985—, med. staff Children's Hosp., San Francisco, 1980-85; St. Luke's Hosp., San Francisco, 1981-85; Marin Gen. Hosp., Greenbrae, Calif., 1983-87; asst. clin. prof. U. Calif., San Francisco, 1981—; mem. admissions com. Sch. Medicine, 1980-85. Bd. dirs. Canal Community Alliance, San Rafael, 1985-86, Community Health Ctr. Marin, Fairfax, Calif., 1985-86, Bahia de Rafael Fourplex, San Rafael. Mem. Am. Psychiat. Assn., Am. Acad. Child Psychiatry, AMA, No. Calif. Psychiat. Soc. Republican. Roman Catholic. Home: 275 Bahia Ln San Rafael CA 94901 Office: Kaiser Permanente Med Ctr Dept Psychiatry 1200 El Camino Real South San Francisco CA 94080

RODVIEN, ROBERT, hematologist, oncologist; b. N.Y.C., Apr. 9, 1942; s. Morris and Esther (Cohn) R.; m. Rayna Rosenzweig, Sept. 7, 1968; children: Brian, Jeffrey. AB, Columbia U., 1963, MD, 1967. Diplomate Am. Bd. Internal Medicine. Intern New England Med. Ctr. Hosps., Boston, 1967-68, resident, 1968-69, fellow in hematology Blood Research Lab., 1969-72, staff physician med. clinic, 1969-72; vis. physician, 1972-73; research assoc. dept. biology MIT, Cambridge, 1972-74; research assoc. dept. surgery Beth Israel Hosp.-Harvard U. Med. Sch., Boston, 1973-74; attending physician dept. medicine Presbyn. Hosp., San Francisco, 1974—, attending physician dept. cardiovascular surgery, 1979—; dir. perfusion Pacific Med. Ctr., San Francisco, 1981—, chief div. hematology, 1982—; instr. medicine Tufts U., Boston, 1969-71; assoc. scientist Insts. Med. Scis., San Francisco, 1974-77, sr. scientist, 1977—; asst. clin. prof. medicine U. Calif., San Francisco, 1974-83, assoc. clin. prof., 1983—; lectr. hematology San Francisco State U., 1974-76; cons. dept. bio-med. engrng. U. Tex., Austin, 1974-76; trustee Hospice of Marin, 1981-84. Contbr. articles to profl. jours. Fellow ACP; mem. Am. Soc. Clin. Oncology, Am. Heart Assn., Am. Soc. Hematology, Am. Soc. Artificial Internal Organs, N.Y. Acad. Scis., AAAS, Internat. Soc. Hemostasis and Thrombosis, Internat. Soc. Artificial Internal Organs, San Francisco Med. Soc. Jewish. Home: 185 Bayview Dr San Rafael CA 94901 Office: Pacific Med Ctr 2100 Webster St Suite 225 San Francisco CA 94120

RODZACH, CHARLOTTE ELIZABETH, educator; b. Lima, Ohio, Apr. 1, 1950; d. Charles Edward and Sara Virginia (Dean) Radabaugh; m. Edward Rodzach, Oct. 19, 1968 (div. Jan. 1984); children: Tiffany Deane, Tonya Caprice. BA with honors, San Diego State U., 1980, MA, 1983; postgrad., U. So. Calif., 1986. Cert. tchr., Calif. Tchr. Lemon Grove (Calif.) Sch. Dist., 1981—. V.p. Lemon Grove PTA, 1985-86. USC fellow, 1987, Godfrey Scholar, 1987. Mem. Lemon Grove Tchrs. Assn., Pi Lambda Theta (scholar 1982). Republican. Avocations: reading, beach activities. Home: 10659 Caminito Derecho San Diego CA 92126 Office: Lemon Grove Sch Dist PO Box 128 Lemon Grove CA 92145

ROE, BENSON BERTHEAU, surgeon, educator; b. Los Angeles, July 7, 1918; s. Hall and Helene Louise (Bertheau) R.; m. Jane Faulkner St. John, Jan. 20, 1945; children: David B., Virginia St. John. A.B., U. Calif.-Berkeley, 1939; M.D. cum laude, Harvard U., 1943. Diplomate Am. Bd. Surgery, Am. Bd. Thoracic Surgery (dir. 1971—, chmn. program com. 1977, chmn. exam. com. 1978, chmn. long-range planning com., chmn. bd. 1981—83). Intern Mass. Gen. Hosp., Boston, 1943-44; resident Mass. Gen. Hosp., 1946-50; nat. research fellow dept. physiology Harvard U. Med. Sch., 1947; Moseley traveling fellow (Harvard U.) U. Edinburg, Scotland, 1951; instr. surgery Harvard Med. Sch., 1950; asst. clin. prof. surgery U. Calif., San Francisco, 1951-58; chief cardiothoracic surgery U. Calif., 1958—, prof. surgery, 1966—; pvt. practice medicine specializing in cardiothoracic surgery San Francisco, 1952—; cons. thoracic surgery VA Hosp., San Francisco Gen. Hosp., Letterman Army Hosp., St. Lukes Hosp.; cons. Baxter Labs., Ethicon, Inc. Mem. editorial bd. Annals of Thoracic Surgery, Pharos, 1969-82; editor 2 med. texts; author 18 textbook chpts.; contbr. numerous articles to profl. jours. Bd. dirs. United Bay Area Crusade, 1958-70, mem. exec. com., 1964-65; bd. dirs. chmn. exec. com. San Francisco chpt. Am. Cancer Soc., 1955-57; bd. dirs. San Francisco Heart Assn., 1964-72, pres., 1964-65, chmn. research com., 1966-71; mem. various coms. Am. Heart Assn., 1967—; pres. Miranda Lux Found.; trustee Avery Fuller Found. Served with USNR, 1944-46. Fellow Am. Coll. Cardiology, ACS (chmn. adv. council thoracic surgery, program chmn. thoracic surgery, mem. cardiovascular com.), Polish Surg. Assn. (hon.); mem. Am. Assn. Thoracic Surgery (chmn. membership com. 1974-75), AMA (residency rev. com. for thoracic surgery), Am., Pacific Coast surg. assns., Calif. Acad. Medicine (pres. 1974), Calif. Med. Assn., Howard C. Naffziger Surg. Soc., Internat. Cardiovascular Soc., Mid Century Surgeons Club, Samson Thoracic Surg. Soc., San Francisco County Med. Soc., Thoracic Surgery Dirs. Assn. (pres. 1979-80), San Francisco Surg. Soc., Soc. Thoracic Surgeons (council 1971—, pres. 1972), Soc. Univ. Surgeons, Soc. Vascular Surgery (past v.p.), Western Soc. Clin. Research, Chilean Soc. Cardiology, Am. Soc. Artificial Internal Organs, Harvard U. Med. Alumni Assn. (councillor at large, pres. No. Calif. chpt. 1974). Clubs: Cruising of Am, Pacific Union, St. Francis Yacht, Calif. Tennis. Office: U Calif Dept Surgery M896 San Francisco CA 94143

ROE, JADEL LYN, police administrator; b. Austin, Minn., Aug. 11, 1950; d. Galen J. and Ardella M. (Laging) H.; m. Russell K. Roe, Jan. 15, 1971 (div. June 1975). BS in Bus. Adminstrn., U. Phoenix, 1981. Cert. law enforcement officer, Ariz. Lt., div. comdr. Maricopa County Sheriff's Office, Phoenix, 1984-87, maj., div. comdr., 1987—. Mem. FBI Nat. Acad. Assocs., Internat. Assn. Women Police. Avocations: river rafting, hiking. Home: 529 W Encanto Blvd Phoenix AZ 85003 Office: Maricopa County Sheriff's Office 102 W Madison Ave Phoenix AZ 85003

ROE, JAMES ALOYSIUS, research chemist; b. N.Y.C., Apr. 9, 1955; s. James Aloysius and Marie Nash (Oliver) R. AB in Chemistry, Classics, Williams Coll., 1977; PhD in Chemistry, U. Calif., Berkeley, 1984. Educator chemistry U. Calif., Berkeley, 1984; research fellow UCLA, 1985—. Mem. Am. Chem. Soc., Phi Beta Kappa, Sigma Chi. Democrat. Roman Catholic. Office: UCLA Dept Chemistry 405 Hilgard Los Angeles CA 90024

ROE, WILLIAM THOMAS, human factors engineer, college official; b. N.Y.C., July 7, 1944; s. William T. and Harriet E. (Higgins) R.; m. Susan C. Kane, Aug. 30, 1972. B.A. in Engining./Indsl. Psychology, Calif. State U.-Northridge, 1971, M.A. in Human Factors and Applied Exptl. Psychology, 1978. Research asst. XYZYX Info. Corp., Canoga Park, Calif., 1973-74; mem. psychol. staff Manned Systems Scis. Inc., Northridge, 1974-75; research psychologist Inst. for Safety and Systems Mgmt., U. So. Calif., Los Angeles, 1975-76; mgr.-acct. exec. systems and data processing Mgmt. Recruiters of So. Calif., Encino, 1976-79; resource evaluation analyst Samaritan Health Service, Phoenix, 1979; sr. methods analyst Valley Nat. Bank, Phoenix, 1979-81; indsl. engr. City of Scottsdale, Ariz., 1981-84; dir. systems and human factors tech. program Phoenix Coll., 1984—. Author: Ergonomic Models of Human Performance: Source Materials for the Analyst, 1975. Contbr. articles to profl. jours. Served with USN, 1961-67, Vietnam. Recipient Certs. of recognition San Fernando Valley chpt. Data Processing Mgmt. Assn., 1978, Phoenix chpt. 1983. Mem. Assn. Systems Mgmt. (pres. Phoenix chpt. 1983-84, dir. western div. 19986—, Outstanding Service award 1982, 84, 86), Am. Inst. Indsl. Engrs., Am. Assn. for Counseling and Devel., Human Factors Soc., Improvement Inst. (trustee), World Future Soc. Office: Phoenix Coll 1202 W Thomas Rd Phoenix AZ 85013

ROEGNER, ROBERT ALAN, mayor; b. Tacoma, Oct. 22, 1948; s. Kathleen Teague Creso; m. Sally Strickler, Nov. 3, 1973; children—Jeffrey Joseph, Janai Noel. M.S. in Sociology, Pacific Luth. U., 1975. Program mgr. Wash. Dept. Employment Security, Auburn, 1970-77, mgr., Tacoma, 1977-78, dep. regional dir., 1978-79, statewide adminstr., Olympia, 1979-81; mayor City of Auburn, 1982—, mem. City Council, 1975-81; pres. King County Suburban Mayors Assn., 1983-84; chmn. Valley Communications Bd., 1983-84, 86-87. Recipient Disting. Service award Wash. Jaycees, 1976; Internat. Merit award Internat. Assn. Personnel in Employment Security, 1976. Mem. Assn. Wash. Cities (bd. dirs. 1983—, pres. 1987-88), Puget Sound Council Govts., Suburban Cities Assn., King County 2000, Jaycees (v.p. 1974-76). Democrat. Lutheran. Lodges: Kiwanis (v.p. 1980-81), Elks, Eagles (Auburn). Office: 25 W Main St Auburn WA 98001

ROEHL, JERRALD J(OSEPH), lawyer; b. Austin, Tex., Dec. 6, 1945; s. Joseph E. and Jeanne Foster (Scott) R.; m. Nancy J. Meyers, Jan. 15, 1977; children: Daniel J., Katherine C., J. Ryan, J. Taylor. BA, U. N.Mex., 1968; JD, Washington and Lee U., 1971. Bar: N.Mex. 1972, U.S. Ct. Appeals (10th cir.) 1972, U.S. Supreme Ct. 1977. Practice of Law, Albuquerque, 1972—; pres. Jerrald J. Roehl & Assocs., 1976-84, Roehl & Henkel, P.C., 1984—. lectr. to profl. groups; real estate developer, Albuquerque. Bd. dirs. Rehab. Ctr. of Albuquerque, 1974-78; mem. assocs. Presbyn. Hosp. Ctr., Albuquerque, 1974-82. Recipient award of recognition State Bar N.Mex., 1975, 76, 77. Mem. ABA (award of achievement Young Lawyers div. 1975, council econs. of law practice sect. 1978-80, exec. council Young Lawyers div. 1979-81, fellow div. 1984—, council tort and ins. practice sect. 1981-83), N.Mex. Bar Assn. (pres. young lawyers sect. 1975-76), Albuquerque Bar Assn. (bd. dirs. 1976-79), N.Mex. Def. Lawyers Assn. (pres. 1983-84), Sigma Alpha Epsilon, Sigma Delta Chi, Phi Delta Phi. Roman Catholic. Clubs: Albuquerque Country, Albuquerque Petroleum. Bd. advs. ABA Jour., 1981-83; bd. editors Washington and Lee Law Rev., 1970-71. Home: 4000 Aspen Ave NE Albuquerque NM 87110 Office: Roehl & Henkel 300 Central Ave SW 3d Central Plaza Suite 2500 E Albuquerque NM 87102

ROEHRS, ROBERT CHRISTIAN, exploration company executive, geologist; b. Graniteville, Mo., May 6, 1931; s. Paul Martin and Margaret Marie (Dinger) R.; m. Shirley Lucille McHenry, Mar. 30, 1956; children: Lizabeth Anne, Robert Christian Jr., Louis Fulton. BA, U. Mo., 1957, MA, 1958. Geologist Shell Oil Co., Casper, Wyo. and Denver, 1958-65; exploration geologist Davis Oil Co., Denver, 1965-68; ptnr. Lotus Petroleum Co., Denver, 1968-69; v.p., dir. Westgate Oil Co., Inc., Denver, 1969-71; pvt. practice in geology Denver, 1971-79; pres. ROMAC Exploration Co., Inc., Denver, 1979—, also bd. dirs. Served with USAF, 1948-52. Recipient Betty McWhorter Meml. award Desk and Derrick Club, 1980. Mem. Am. Assn. Petroleum Geologists, Rocky Mountain Assn. Geologists, Wyo. Geol. Assn., Ind. Petroleum Assn. Am. (bd. dirs. 1982—, v.p. Mountain States chpt. 1978, pres. 1979, bd. dirs. 1979—). Republican. Lutheran. Clubs: Denver Exec., Denver Petroleum. Home: 4 Waring Ln Greenwood Village Littleton CO 80121 Office: ROMAC Exploration Co Inc 621 17th St Denver CO 80293

ROELKE, ADA E(LLEN), social services adminstrator; b. Cumberland, Md., Aug. 24, 1928; d. George William Knock and Mary Emma (Roelke) Eichelberger; children: Karen Bahnsen, Steven Leveen. BA, Syracuse U., 1950; MSW, San Diego State U., 1967; PhD, Profl. Sch. of Psychol. Studies, 1986. Lic. clin. social worker, Calif. Tchr. pub. schs., Syracuse, N.Y., 1960-61; social worker Dept. Pub. Welfare, San Diego, 1964-66; psychiat. social worker State of Calif., Bakersfield, 1967-68; child protection worker Dept. Social Service, San Diego, 1968-77; coordinator, psychotherapist, Chronic Program Grantville Day Treatment Ctr., San Diego, 1977-81; chief social services Edgemoor Geriatric Hosp., Santee, Calif., 1981—; pvt. practice psychotherapy, La Mesa, Calif., 1969—. Fellow Nat. Assn. Social Workers; mem. Marriage Family and Child Counselors Assn., Lic. Clin. Social Workers Assn., Mineral and Gem Soc., Lapidary Soc. Unitarian. Home: 4015 King St La Mesa CA 92041 Office: Edgemoor Geriatric Hosp 9065 Edgemoor Dr Santee CA 92071

ROEMER, ELIZABETH, educator, astronomer; b. Oakland, Calif., Sept. 4, 1929; d. Richard Quirin and Elsie (Barlow) R. B.A. with Honors (Bertha Dolbeer scholar), U. Calif. at Berkeley, 1950, Ph.D. (Lick Obs. fellow), 1955. Tchr. adult class Oakland pub. schs., 1950-52; lab technician U. Calif. at Mt. Hamilton, 1954-55; grad. research astronomer U. Calif. at Berkeley, 1955-56; research asso. Yerkes Obs. U. Chgo., 1956; astronomer U.S. Naval Obs., Flagstaff, Ariz., 1957-66; asso. prof. dept. astronomy, also in lunar and planetary lab. U. Ariz., Tucson, 1966-69; prof. U. Ariz., 1969—; astronomer Steward Obs., 1980—; Chmn. working group on orbits and ephemerides of comets commn. 20 Internat. Astron. Union, 1964-79, 85—, v.p. comm. 20, 1979-82, pres., 1982-85, v.p. commn. 6, 1973-76, 85—, pres., 1976-79; Mem. adv. panels Office Naval Research, Nat. Acad. Scis.-NRC, NASA. Recipient Dorothea Klumpke Roberts prize U. Calif. at Berkeley, 1950, Mademoiselle Merit award, 1959; asteroid (1657) named Roemera, 1965; Benjamin Apthorp Gould prize Nat. Acad. Scis., 1971; NASA Spl. award, 1986. Fellow AAAS (council 1966-69, 72-73), Royal Astron. Soc. (London); mem. Am. Astron. Soc. (program vis. profs. astronomy 1960-75, council 1967-70, chmn. div. dynamical astronomy 1974), Astron. Soc. Pacific (publs. com. 1962-73, Comet medal com. 1968-74, Donohoe lectr. 1962), Internat. Astron. Union, Am. Geophys. Union, Brit. Astron. Assn., Phi Beta Kappa, Sigma Xi. Research and numerous publs. on astrometry and astrophysics of comets and minor planets including 79 recoveries of returning periodic comets; visual and spectroscopic binary stars, computation of orbits of comets and minor planets, photog. astrometry. Office: U Ariz Lunar and Planetary Lab Tucson AZ 85721

ROEN, DUANE HARLEY, English educator; b. River Falls, Wis., Feb. 19, 1949; s. Harley Eldon and Doris June (Bennett) R.; m. Margaret Lee Karbon, May 28, 1972 (div. July 1976); m. Maureen Ann Earley, Apr. 3, 1978; 1 child, Nicholas James. Cert. secondary English tchr., Wis. English tchr. New Richmond (Wis.) High Sch., 1972-77; instr. U. Minn., 1977-81; asst. prof. U. Nebr., Lincoln, 1981-82, U. Ariz., Tucson, 1982—; cons. in field. Contbr. articles to profl. jours. Kelly Research grantee U. Nebr, 1982. Mem. Am. Edn. Research Assn., Ariz. English Tchrs. Assn. (exec. bd., treas. 1983-85). Avocations: genealogy, softball, refinishing furniture. Home: 1503 E Linden St Tucson AZ 85719

ROENKE, KARL GUESS, archaeologist, forester, historian; b. Geneva, N.Y., Dec. 4, 1947; s. Henry Merrill and Marion (Guess) R.; m. Anne Stothoff Chase, Dec. 20, 1970; children: Laura Chase, Keith James. BA in History, Hartwick Coll., 1970; MA in Anthropology, U. Idaho, 1977. Scientist, archaeologist N.Y. State Office of Parks, Recreation and Hist. Preservation, Waterford, 1977-80; forest archaeologist Clearwater Nat. Forest, Orofino, Idaho, 1980—. Pres. parish council Clearwater Luth. Ch., Orofino, Idaho, 1986. Served with U.S. Army, 1970-73. Mem. Soc. Hist. Archaeology, Idaho Archaeol. Soc., Nat. Trust Hist. Preservation, Idaho Adv. Council Profl. Archaeologists, Sigma Xi, Alpha Chi Rho. Democrat. Avocations: photography, carpentry, furniture refinishing. Home: 12453 Hartford Ave Orofino ID 83544 Office: Clearwater Nat Forest 12730 Hwy 12 Orofino ID 83544

ROEPKE, DOLORES MAE, hospital volunteer services administrator; b. Hampton, Iowa, May 25, 1931; dau. Leslie Roy Krafft and Pearlina Ida Osterland; children—Deborah, Janine, Nancy; B.A. cum laude, Westmar Coll., Le Mars, Iowa, 1953; M.A. in Mgmt., U. Phoenix, 1982. Home econs. tchr. Mooseheart (Ill.) High School, 1953-55; music tchr. Bern (Kans.) High School, 1959-60; exec. sec. Willmar (Minn.) United Fund, 1966-70; spl. edn. teacher, Willmar High School, 1969-70; dir. vol. services, Willmar State Hosp., 1973-75; dir. vol. services Scottsdale Meml. Hosp., 1976—; dir. handicapped children's camp, 1966-68. Contbr. articles to profl. jours. Active AAUW, 1962-65, Common Cause, 1962-65. Mem. Dirs. Vol. Services, Ariz. Hosp. Assn. (pres. 1980, dirs. of Vols. in Agys.). Presbyterian. Office: Scottsdale Meml Hosp 7400 East Osborn Rd Scottsdale AZ 85251

ROESCH, WARREN DALE, retail company executive; b. Oakland, Calif., Aug. 8, 1945; s. George Oscar and Dorothy Wenifred (Smith) R.; AA, Coll. of San Mateo, 1966; BA, Calif. State U., 1968; m. Marguerite Mary Whitman, Aug. 1, 1970; 1 son, Warren Whitman. Programmer, operator Western Title Ins. Co., San Francisco, 1973-74, mgr. data processing, 1974; mgr. data processing E. Bay Regional Park Dist., Oakland, 1974-78, Jacuzzi Whirlpool Bath, Walnut Creek, Calif., 1978-82; sr. bus. programmer Bechtel Corp., San Francisco, 1978; cons. systems analyst Packaging div. Crown Zellerbach, San Francisco, 1979, project mgr. MIS installations, 1980; founder, chief exec. officer Total Resource Group, Inc., San Mateo, Calif., 1982—; project mgr. Point-of-Sale and Service Systems, Businessland, Inc., 1984-86, mgr. service MIS, 1986—. Home: 646 Alhambra Rd San Mateo CA 94402 Office: Total Resource Group 1001 Ridder Park Dr San Jose CA 95131

ROFER, CHERYL KATHERINE, chemist; b. Hackensack, N.J., May 7, 1943; d. Christian and Evelyn Fredericke (Grapatin) R. AB, Ripon Coll., 1963; MS, U. Calif., Berkeley, 1964. Mem. staff Los Alamos (N.Mex.) Nat. Lab., 1965—. Contbr. articles to profl. jours.; patentee in field. Fellow Am. Inst. Chemists; mem. AAAS, Am. Chem. Soc., N.Y. Acad. Scis., Assn. Women in Sci. Office: Los Alamos Nat Lab PO Box 1663 MS D462 Los Alamos NM 87545

ROGENSKI, THEODORE JOSEPH, leasing company executive; b. Moline, Ill., Mar. 20, 1941; s. Felix Joseph and Stella Agnes (Borowski) R.; m. Nancy Elizabeth Moore, July 2, 1966; children: Jeffrey, Mark, Kerry. BBA, U. Wis., 1964; MBA, U. Chgo., 1970. Loan officer Am. Nat. Bank, Chgo., 1964-69; dist. mktg. mgr. Greyhound Leasing and Fin, Phoenix, 1969-70; v.p. mktg. Am. Fletcher Leasing Corp., Indpls., 1970-74; sr. v.p., chief mktg. officer Wells Fargo Leasing Corp., San Francisco, 1972-80, pres., chief exec. officer, 1981—, also bd. dirs.; bd. dirs. Wells Fargo Agrl. Credit, Denver, 1983—, Wells Fargo Capital Markets, San Francisco, 1983—. Mem. Assn. Equipment Lessors. Republican. Roman Catholic. Avocations: offshore sailboat racing, tennis, skiing. Office: Wells Fargo Leasing Corp 101 California St San Francisco CA 94111

ROGERS, BARBARA ANN, educator; b. Frackville, Pa., Aug. 25, 1941; d. John R. and Clara M. (Chudzwick) R. BA in Edn., Millersville State Coll., 1963; MA in Chemistry, Bowling Green State U., 1968. Cert. tchr. Scis. tchr. N. Penn High Sch., Lansdale, Pa., 1963-68; sci. tchr. McKinley High Sch., Honolulu, 1968—; mem. adv. com. Hawaii State Sci. and Engring Fair, 1983-85, chmn. sci. tour com., 1979—; coordinator Dreyfus Chemistry Workshop, State of Hawaii, 1985; mem. staff Ann. Student Symposium on Marine Affairs, 1983—; advanced placement chemistry workshop leader Hawaii Bd. Edn., Coll. Bd., 1979, 85. Mem. Ellison Onizuka Scholarship Com., State of Hawaii, 1986-87. Named Sci. Tchr. of Yr., Hawaii Acad. Sci., 1980; recipient Presdl. Excellence in Sci. and Math. Teaching award Pres. of U.S., 1985, Dedication to Teaching Sci.and Encouragement of Research award Sigma Xi, 1983, Teaching Excellence award Nat. Marine Educators Assn., 1984, 85, 86; grantee NSF, Dreyfus Found. Mem. Am. Chem. Soc. (sec. Hawaii sect. 1982-84, chmn. 1984-86, numerous subcoms., grants, awards), Acad. Alliance in Chemistry (dir. Hawaii chpt.), Nat. Sci. Tchrs. Assn., Hawaii State Sci. Tchrs. Assn., NEA, Hawaii State Tchrs. Assn., Smithsonian Honolulu Acad. Arts. Democrat. Home: 425 Ena Rd #607-C Honolulu HI 96815 Office: McKinley High Sch Dept Sci 1039 S King St Honolulu HI 96814

ROGERS, BARBARA ANNE, social worker, psychotherapist; b. Portland, Oreg., Jan. 9, 1934; d. George L. and Dorothy (Melton) Brunner; children: Roby L., Lianne R., Brian D. BS in Social Scis., U. Oreg., 1968; MSW, U. Denver, 1972. Prin. social worker Boulder (Colo.) County Dept. Social Services, 1973-78; pvt. practice calligraphy San Diego, 1980-84; substance abuse counsellor C.O.D.A., Portland, 1984-85; life/work planner and trainer The Employment Connection, Portland, 1984-86; asst. dir. The Exchange Club Ctr. for the Prevention of Child Abuse, Oreg. Children's Med. Ctr., Portland, 1986—; trainer MidLife Debut Seminars, Boulder, 1984—, Change Consortium, Portland, 1986—; mem. mktg. com. The Employment Connection, 1985-86. Calligrapher: Traveling The Road of Success, 1985; artist, calligrapher (greeting cards) Am. Expressions Co., 1982-84. Mem. Nat. Assn. Social Workers (cert.), Nat. Speakers Assn. (assoc. mem. Colo. chpt.), Psi Chi. Avocations: writing, walking. Home and Office: 2790 Vassar Dr Boulder CO 80303

ROGERS, BRYAN LEIGH, artist, art educator; b. Amarillo, Tex., Jan. 7, 1941; s. Bryan Austin and Virginia Leigh (Bull) R.; m. Cynthia Louise Rice, Feb. 3, 1984. BE, Yale U., 1963; MS, U. Calif., Berkeley, 1966, MA, 1969, PhD, 1971. Design engr. Monsanto Co., Texas City, Tex., 1962; research engr. Rocketdyne, Canoga Park, Calif., 1963-64; research scientist Lawrence Livermore (Calif.) Lab., 1966; lectr. U. Calif., Berkeley, 1972-73; fellow Akademie der Bildenden Künste, Munich, 1974-75; prof. art San Francisco State U., 1975—; fellow Ctr. Advanced Visual Studies MIT, Cambridge, Mass, 1981. Editor Leonardo Jour., San Francisco, 1982-85. One-man shows include: Laguna Beach (Calif.) Mus. Art, 1974, DeSaisset Art Gallery U. Santa Clara, Calif., 1974, San Francisco Mus. Modern Art, 1974, Baxter Art Gallery Calif. Inst. Tech., Pasadena, 1979; group exhbns. include: Berkeley (Calif.) Art Ctr., 1969, Hansen-Fuller Gallery, San Francisco, 1970, San Francisco Arts Commn. Gallery, 1984, Clocktower Gallery, N.Y.C., 1984, Otis-Parsons Gallery, Los Angeles, 1985, P.P.O.W. Gallery, N.Y.C., 1985, 18th Internat. Bienal, São Paulo, Brazil, 1985. Fellow NEA, Washington, 1981, 82, Deutscher Akademischer Austauschdienst, Fed. Republic of Germany, 1974, NSF, Washington, 1965-69; recipient SECA award San Francisco Mus. Modern Art, 1974. Office: San Francisco State U Art Dept 1600 Holloway Ave San Francisco CA 94132

ROGERS, CARL STEVEN, entrepreneur, consultant; b. Hermosa Beach, Calif., May 29, 1945; s. George Bernard and Verna Bertha (Fekete) R.; m. Barbara Ann Mealer, Oct. 25, 1969; children: Steven, Rachel. BBA, U. Toledo, 1971. Br. mgr. Savin Corp., San Leandro, Calif., 1966-68; bus. mgr. Labor Union of N.Am., Toledo, 1968-72; ops. mgr. Nat. Semicondr., Santa Clara, Calif., 1972-74; pres., prin. Rainbow Memories, Colorado Springs, Colo., 1984-86; pres. CSR Cons., Lakewood, Colo., 1985—; prin. Real Estate Investments, Colorado Springs, 1986—; pres. Handiman Enterprises, Colorado Springs, 1974-76, Am. Telemktg., Colorado Springs, 1974—; cons. Consortia Inc., Boulder, Colo. Author: Basic Telephone Salesmanship, 1974. Served with USNR, 1965-67. Avocations: physical exercise, golf, reading, fishing. Home and Office: 857 S Van Gordon Ct H101 Lakewood CO 80228

ROGERS, CHARLES THEODORE GRAHAM (TED ROGERS), metapsychologist; b. N.Y.C., Oct. 8, 1907; s. Charles T. and May (Church) G-R.; B.S., Wagner Coll., 1933; M.S., San Diego State U., 1962; certificate in counseling U. So. Calif., 1965; D.Sc., Miss. State Christian Coll., 1969; C.H., Dominion Coll., 1975; Ph.D., Newport U., 1977; Ph.D. in Metapsychology, U. Humanistics Studies, 1978; M.S.D., Inst. Metapsychology, 1980; m. Consuelo Yvonne d'Aguilar, March 11, 1933 (dec. July 1975); 1 dau., Patricia Suzanne. Dir. delinquency prevention N.Y.C. schs., 1934-39; assistant dir. personnel tng. Pub. Works Adminstrn., N.Y.C., 1940-41; mem. N.Y. State Div. Parole, 1941-46; chief probation officer San Diego County, San Diego, 1947-67; cons., researcher parapsychology, psychic phenomena, survival, metaphs. healing, 1967—; dir. Center for Edn. and Research, 1965-78; chmn. metapsychology U. Humanistic Studies, 1977-78, mem. psychology faculty, 1977-83 , dean Inst. Metapsychology, 1981—; guest lectr. San Diego State Coll., 1948; lectr. Calif. Western U., 1958-61; cons. Nat. Probation and Parole Assn., Ariz. Correctional Study, 1958; cons. Deliquency Control Inst., Ariz. State U., 1959-64; cons. Youth Studies Center U. So. Calif., 1963-65, youth problems Bishopric of Fiji, 1966; mem. County Parole Bd., 1961-67; mem. com. Probation Study, Dependent Child Study, State of Calif., 1963-67; mem. profl. advisory com. social work curriculum San Diego State Coll., 1959-61; probation adv. com. Calif. Youth Authority, 1958-67; v.p., chmn. research com. Parapsychology Found., lectr., 1962-67. Served to capt. USAAF, 1942-46; PTO. Recipient Legion of Honor, Order of DeMolay. Fellow Am. Soc. Psychial Research, Royal Soc. Health, Inst. Parapsychol. Research, Coll. Psychic Studies; mem. Soc. Psychical Research, Internat., Am. assns. social psychiatry, Acad. Parapsychology and Medicine, Am. Orthopsychiatric Assn., Assn. for Humanistic Psychology, Soc. for Sci. Study of Religion, Acad. Religion and Psychical Research, Nat. Assn. Social Workers (charter), Acad. Religion and Mental Health, Internat. Assn. Metapsychology (pres. 1980—), So. Calif. Soc. Psychical Research, Cosmosophy Soc. (pres.), Am. Assn. Study Mental Imagery, Assn. Past-Life Research and Therapy, Assn. Transpersonal Psychology, Spiritual Frontiers Fellowship, Calif. Probation, Parole and Correctional Assn. (pres. 1961-62), Acad. Certified Social Workers, Church's Fellowship for Psychic Studies, Pi Sigma Alpha. Contbr. articles to various publs. Address: 962 Greenlake Ct Cardiff-by-the-Sea CA 92007

ROGERS, DENNIS LEE, architect; b. Athens, Tenn., Jan. 26, 1953; s. Franklin O'Dean and Mary Nell (Benson) R.; m. Hada Luz Chavarria, Dec. 17, 1977; children—O'Dina Maria, Angela Emperatriz. B.Arch., U. Tenn., 1980. Archtl. design draftsman U.S. Air Force, Luke AFB, Ariz., 1980-81; engring. design draftsman Marathon Steel Co., Tempe, Ariz., 1981-82; facilities design engr. Hughes Helicopter, Inc., Mesa, Ariz., 1982-83; facilities engr./planner Four-Phase/ISO, Inc., Tempe, 1983-84; architect Motorola, Inc., Mesa, 1984-85; cons. Ariz. Architects and Planners, Inc., Phoenix, 1985-86; project architect Greyhound Lines, Inc., Phoenix, 1986—. Prin. works include passive solar home, Lake Tahoe, Nev., 1982. Recipient Outstanding Performance award Hughes Helicopter, Inc., 1983. Mem. AIA (assoc.), Toastmasters, Mesa Jaycees (treas. 1984-85). Office: Greyhound Lines Inc Phoenix AZ 85077

ROGERS, DOUGLAS BENNETT, physicist; b. Kansas City, Mo., Jan. 16, 1947; s. Elmer Bennett and Betty (Walker) R. AS, Met. Jr. Coll., Kansas City, 1967; BS in Physics, U. Mo., Rolla, 1969; MS in Physics, U. Mo., Kansas City, 1974. Physicist Cook Paint, Kansas City, 1975-78, Naval Weapons Ctr., China Lake, Calif., 1979—. Inventor retroreflectometer. Served with U.S. Army, 1970-72. Mem. China Lake Astron. Soc., Sigma Pi Sigma. Home: 996 Strecker Ridgecrest CA 93555 Office: Naval Weapons Ctr Code 3337 China Lake CA 93555

ROGERS, DOUGLAS GARY, television production executive; b. Salt Lake City, Aug. 13, 1942; s. George Harold and Elizabeth Margaret (Williams) R.; m. Marjorie Jean Sharp, Dec. 10, 1974; children—Lisa Marie, David Mark. Student Brigham Young U., 1960-61. Sales mgr. Los Angeles Times, 1967-69; tng. mgr. Western region 3M Co., Los Angeles, 1969-76; nat. tng. dir. Pertec Computer Corp., Los Angeles, 1976-78; ind. tng. cons. Mattel Toys, Gen. Electric, Sears, Roebuck & Co., other cos., 1974-78; v.p. mktg. Common Carrier Advt., Los Angeles, 1978-81; exec. v.p., co-founder Admedia Internat., Inc., Midvale, Utah, 1981-84, also dir.; founder, pres., owner Internat. TV Prodns., Midvale, 1984—; pres., bd. dirs. Plastic Surgery Video, Inc., 1985—; v.p., bd. dirs. Video Dentistry, Inc., 1986—. Served with USAF, 1964-70. Recipient Utah Film and Video Festival award, 1986. Mem. Sales and Mktg. Execs. Assn., Am. Soc. Tng. and Devel., Internat. TV Assn. Republican. Mormon. Home: 2528 E Montebello Dr Sandy UT 84092 Office: Internat TV Prodns 948 E 7145 S Suite B-101 Midvale UT 84047

ROGERS, DWANE LESLIE, management consultant; b. Maywood, Calif., Oct. 6, 1943; s. Lloyd Donald and Della (McAlister) R.; B.S., Ariz. State U., 1967; M.S., Bucknell U., 1968; m. Doris L. Fantel, Aug. 22, 1970; 1 dau., Valerie Lynn. Successively mktg. research coordinator, customer service analyst, merchandising mgr., product planning mgr., order processing mgr. Samsonite Corp., Denver, 1968-74; dir. adminstrn. WISCO Equipment Co., Inc., Phoenix, 1974-75; dir. discontinued ops. Bowmar Instrument Corp., Phoenix, 1975-77; mgmt. cons., dir. Ariz. ops. Mariscal & Co., Phoenix, 1977-80; mgmt. cons. Ariz. Small Bus. Devel. Center, 1980-81; dir. accounts payable, accounts receivable, crude and finished product acctg. Giant Industries, Phoenix, 1981—; instr. Maricopa County Community Coll., 1979-83. Mem. Am. Mktg. Assn., Mass Retailing Inst. Republican. Episcopalian. Home: 2844 E Acoma Dr Phoenix AZ 85032

ROGERS, HELEN EVELYN WAHRGREN, newspaperwoman; b. Tacoma, Jan. 24, 1924; d. John Sigurd and Emma Elina (Carlson) Wahrgren; B.A., U. Wash., Seattle, 1946; m. Charles Dana Rogers, July 24, 1948. Mem. editorial staff Holiday mag., Phila., 1946; civilian public relations writer, Ft. Lewis, Wash., 1946-47; asst. society editor Tacoma News Tribune-Sunday Ledger, 1947-51, radio-TV editor-columnist, 1951-86. Author: What's Your Line? vol. I: Delila Sprague Sherburne Harrington: Her Ancestors and Descendants. Mem. Newspaper Guild, Wis. Geneal. Soc., Tacoma-Pierce County Geneal. Soc., U. Wash. Alumni Assn. Democrat. Lutheran. Home: 2906 N 24th St Tacoma WA 98406 Office: 2906 N 24th St Tacoma WA 98406

ROGERS, HOWARD H., chemist; b. N.Y.C., Dec. 26, 1926; s. Julian Herbert and Minnie (Jaffa) R.; m. Barbara Kniaz, Mar. 27, 1954 (div. 1978); children: Lynne, Mark David, Susan; m. Maureen Dohn, Dec. 28, 1978. BS in Chemistry, U. Ill., 1949; PhD in Inorganic Chemistry, MIT, 1952. Research group leader Allis-Chalmers Mfg. Co., West Allis, Wis., 1952-61; sr. tech. specialist Rocketdyne div., Rockwell, Canoga Park, Calif., 1961-70; chief research scientist Martek Instruments, Newport Beach, Calif., 1970-73; sr. scientist Hughes Aircraft Co., El Segundo, Calif., 1973—. Developer nickel-hydrogen battery; patentee; contbr. sci. papers to profl. publs. in field. Served with USN, 1944-46. Mem. Electrochem. Soc. (chmn. So. Calif./Nev. sect. 1976-78), Am. Chem. Soc., Forth Interest Group, Sigma Xi. Home: 18361 Van Ness Ave Torrance CA 90504 Office: Hughes Aircraft Co S41/A315 PO Box 92919 Los Angeles CA 90009

ROGERS, JOSEPH WILSON, sociology educator; b. Pensacola, Fla., Oct. 13, 1925; s. Joseph Wilson and Florida Mary (Wallace) R.; m. Doris Gay Ellsworth, Sept. 26, 1953; children: Diana, Suzanne, Jefferson, David. AB, San Diego State Coll., 1949; MA, U. Wash., 1959, PhD, 1965. Asst. probation officer San Diego County Probation Dept., 1949-55; acting inst. sociology U. Wash., Seattle, 1958-61; instr. Wash. State U., Pullman, 1961-62; asst. prof. Kansas State U., Manhattan, 1962-68; chmn. dept. sociology, anthropology N.Mex. State U., Las Cruces, 1968-73, prof. sociology, 1973—, chmn. Pres.' Com. Coll. Teaching; cons. Juvenile Probation Dept., Las Cruces, Gov.'s Council Criminal Justice Planning Region IV, Las Cruces. Author: Why Are You Not a Criminal, 1977; contbr. articles to profl. jours. Pres. adv. bd. Children in Need of Supervision, Las Cruces; vice chmn. screening panel Community Corrections, Las Cruces; bd. dirs. Boys' and Girls' Club, Las Cruces. Served as cpl. U.S. Army, 1943-46, ETO. Recipient Community Leadership award Dona Ana Consortium, 1981. Mem. Am. Sociol. Assn., Soc. Study Social Problems, Am. Soc. Criminology, Acad. Criminal Justice Scis., Circus Hist. Soc. Democrat. Avocations: circus study, tennis. Home: 306 Capri Arc Las Cruces NM 88005 Office: NMex State U Dept Sociology/Anthropology Las Cruces NM 88003

ROGERS, JUDY KAY HAWKINS, educator; b. Madill, Okla., Sept. 22, 1946; d. Cliff Leon and Stella Aline (Teel) Hawkins; m. Robert A. Rogers, Apr. 8, 1965 (div.); children—Robert Chad, Roc Ann. M.E., Okla. State U., 1973; Vocat. cert. Eastern N.Mex. U., 1979; postgrad. U. N.Mex., 1980, Amarillo Coll., 1981, U. Houston 1981. Cert. tchr., Okla., Tex., N.Mex., Kans., Tchr., Dodge City Jr. Coll., Kans., 1968-69, Calera High Sch., Okla., 1969-73; tchr. Grayson Coll., Denison, Tex., 1973-77; tchr. House High Sch., N.Mex., 1977-79, Ft. Sumner High Sch., N.Mex., 1980-81; tchr. 2d grade, Sunray, Tex., 1980-81; tchr. Tucumcari Area Vocat. Sch., N.Mex., 1981—; bus. instr. Amarillo Coll., Tex. Nat. rep. Adv. Council for Bus. Tchrs., 1982—. Mem. NEA, Office Edn. Assn. N.Mex. Office Edn. Assn. (Outstanding Service award 1981), Vocat. Edn. Assn., Nat. Vocat. Edn., Tucumcari Area Vocat. Sch. Office Edn. Assn., Phi Omega Phi. Democrat. Methodist. Clubs: Profl. and Bus. Women, Altrusa. Home: 3402 E Stonehill Ln Salt Lake City UT 84121 Office: Tucumcari Area Vocat Sch PO Box 1143 Tucumcari NM 88401

ROGERS, LAURA ELLEN, electronic engineer; b. Phila., Dec. 7, 1956; d. William B. and Hazel B. Rogers. BSEE, Calif. Poly. State U., San Luis Obispo, 1984. Mem. tech. staff Santa Barbara Research Ctr. subs. Hughes Aircraft Co., Goleta, Calif., 1984—. Mem. IEEE, Eta Kappa Nu. Avocations: surfing, bicycling, skin diving.

ROGERS, MARY NELL, engineer; b. Sao Paulo, Brazil, Jan. 26, 1934; came to U.S., 1950; d. Paul Atherton and Bess Alice (Kerfoot) Applegate; m. Robert G. Rogers, Sept. 26, 1955; children: Robert George Jr., Beverly June, Elizabeth Anne, Mary Paule. BSEE, U. Okla., 1954; MBA, Santa Clara U., 1981. Test engr. Gen. Electric Co., Syracuse, N.Y., 1954-55; system analyst Gen. Electric Co., Ithaca, N.Y., 1955-57, project engr., 1957-58; systems analyst Lockheed Missile & Space Co., Sunnyvale, Calif., 1976-79, program engr., 1979-85, sr. systems test engr., 1985—. Bd. dirs. Santa Clara Council Girl Scouts U.S., San Jose, Calif., 1982—. Mem. NOW, AAUW, Soc. Women Engrs. (bd. dirs. 1984—), Santa Clara Valley sect. Soc. Women Engrs. (pres. 1982-83), Alpha Delta Pi. Democrat. Episcopalian. Club: Commonwealth. Office: Lockheed Missiles and Space Co 1111 Lockheed Way Sunnyvale CA 94089

ROGERS, MICHAEL HOLMES, corporate planner, naval pilot; b. Natick, Mass., Nov. 1, 1949; s. Harrison Holmes and Amelia Mary (Remidies) R.; m. Carole Rose Anderson, Mar. 27, 1976 (div. Dec. 1981); m. Melanie Marie Carl, July 28, 1984. BS in Indsl. Tech., Calif. State Poly. U., 1972; postgrad. San Francisco State U., 1984—. Lic. helicopter pilot. Food service clk. United Airlines, San Francisco, 1972-73; configuration analyst Kaiser Electronics, San Jose, Calif., 1980-81; corp. sr. planner U.S. Sprint, Burlingame, Calif., 1981—. Served to lt. comdr. USN, 1973-79, USNR, 1980—. Mem. Armed Forces Communications and Electronics Assn., Res. Officers Assn. Democrat. Office: US Sprint 985 Masson Ave San Bruno CA 94066

ROGERS, NATHAN, oral and maxillofacial surgeon; b. San Francisco, Aug. 22, 1912; s. Dr. Nathan and Maria (de la Luz Urtuzuastegui) R.; A.B., Stanford U., 1937; B.S., U. Calif., 1943, D.D.S., 1943, postgrad., 1949, 55; postgrad. U.S. Nat. Naval Med. Center, 1944; m. Eleanor Marie Ludes, July 5, 1941; children—Ann Lenore, James William, Craig Edward, Glenn Joseph, Wayne Phillip. Grad. in oral and maxillofacial surgery Columbia-Presbyn. Med. Center, N.Y.C., 1947-48; resident oral and maxillofacial surgery Presbyn. Hosp., N.Y.C., 1948-49; pvt. practice oral and maxillofacial surgery, San Francisco, 1950-60; mem. exec. med. staff French Hosp., 1950-59, vis. oral and maxillofacial surgeon, 1950-60, lectr. in oral and maxillofacial surgery, 1955-60; vis. oral and maxillofacial surgeon St. Francis Meml. Hosp., 1951-61, cons. oral and maxillofacial surgery Cleft Palate Guidance Group Clinic, 1951-60; vis. oral and maxillofacial surgeon St. Mary's Hosp., 1951-60; oral and maxillofacial surgeon to Disaster Council and Corps, City and County of San Francisco, 1950— (all in San Francisco). Contributor U.S. Dept. Interior, Fish and Wildlife Service, 1961—. Instnl. rep. San Francisco council Boy Scouts Am., 1957-63, merit badge counselor, 1972—. Served as surgeon Dental Corps, USN, 1943-47. Mem. ADA, Calif. State, San Francisco dental assns., Internat. Assn. Anesthesiologists (charter mem.), Am. Dental Soc. Anesthesia, Pacific Marine Research Soc., No. Calif. Soc. Oral and Maxillofacial Surgeons (emeritus), Stanford (life), U. Calif. (life), Columbia Dental (life), Presbyn. Hosp. N.Y.C. alumni assns., San Francisco Opera Assn. (contbg.), San Francisco Symphony Assn. (contbg.), VFW (life), Ducks Unltd. (contbg.), Nat. Rifle Assn. Am. (life), Nat. Bench Rest Shooters' Assn., Original Pa. 1000 Yard Bench Rest Club, Alpha Sigma Phi (life, pres. San Francisco grad. chpt. 1953), Delta Sigma Delta (life mem., pres. San Francisco grad. council 1954). Republican. Episcopalian. Clubs: Chabot Gun; Associated Sportsmen of California; Refuge Gun 2 (pres. 1976-82). Home: 22 Lopez Ave San Francisco CA 94116

ROGERS, PATRICIA LOUISE, public health nurse; b. Ellensburg, Wash., June 17, 1926; d. Benjamin Bab and Ethel Mae (Cheney) Colwell; m. Clifford J. Rogers, Jr., Mar. 20, 1949. Diploma in nursing Swedish Hosp., Seattle, 1948; B.Sc. in Nursing, U. Wash., 1962. Staff nurse Swedish Hosp., Seattle, 1948-49, White Pass Hosp., Skagway, Alaska, 1949-51; physician's office nurse, Whitehorse, Y.T., Can., 1954-57; staff nurse, acting head nurse Doctor's Hosp., Seattle, 1960-61, pub. health nurse Seattle-King County Health Dept., 1962-64; staff and head nurse Fairbanks Clinic (Alaska), 1965-67; pub. health nurse Fairbanks Health Center, 1967-69, regional pub. health nursing supr. II, 1970-75, nursing mgr., 1975-81, regional nursing mgr., 1981—. Served with Cadet Nursing Corps, 1945-48. Mem. Am. Pub. Health Assn., Alaska Pub. Health Assn., Am. Nurses Assn., Alaska Nurses Assn., Fairbanks Rehab. Assn., Arctic Alliance for People, Fairbanks Community Health Assn. Episcopalian. Office: State Alaska Dept Health Social Services Div Pub Health Office Regional Nursing 1001 Noble St Suite 450 Fairbanks AK 99701

ROGERS, RICHARD WARREN, independent financial planner; b. Washington, Aug. 19, 1931; s. Ulys Samuel and Helene Burland (L' Hommedieu) R.; B.S. in Bus. Adminstrn., St. Benedicts Coll., Atchison, Kans., 1969; B.S. in Accounting, Humphreys Coll., Stockton, Calif., 1974; M.B.A., Pepperdine U., 1977; m. Mary Catherine Antonelli, May 1, 1954; children—Cynthia Jean, Victoria Lynn, Richard Warren, James Ulys. Commd. 2d lt. C.E., U.S. Army, 1953; advanced through grades to lt. col., 1967; dir. maintenance Sharpe Army Depot, Calif., 1971-72; ret., 1972; dep. dir. for adminstrn. San Joaquin County (Calif.) Dept. Pub. Assistance, Stockton, 1977-82; ret., 1982; independent fin. planner, 1985—; tchr. San Joaquin Delta Coll., Humphreys Coll. Decorated D.F.C. Mem. Nat. Assn. Security Dealers, Nat. Assn. Life Underwriters, VFW, Am. Legion. Republican. Roman Catholic. Clubs: Elks, K.C. Home: 6863 Gettysburg Pl Stockton CA 95207

ROGERS, ROBERT G., Canadian provincial lieutenant governor; b. Montreal, Que., Can., Aug. 19, 1919; m. Elizabeth Jane Hargrave; 3 children. Student, U. Toronto. Ptnr. Norman A. Smith Co., 1945-47; gen. mgr. Philip Carey Ltd., Montreal, 1947-50; various exec. positions Domtar Ltd., 1950-60; with Crown Zellerbach Can. Ltd., 1960-84, pres., 1964-76, chmn., 1976-82; lt. gov. Province of B.C., Victoria, Can., 1983—; former dir. Can. Imperial Bank of Commerce, Genstar Corp., Gulf Can. Ltd., Can. Reins. Co., Can. Reassurance Co., Hilton Can. Ltd., RCA Ltd., Rockwell Internat. (Can.); mem. Can. Bus. and Industry Internat. Adv. Council; Export Trade Devel. Bd. B.C. Mem. adminstrv. adv. bd. U. Western Ont. Sch. Bus.; chmn. Can. Forestry Adv. Council; hon. v.p. Nat. council Boy Scouts Can.; chmn. Pacific region, mem. nat. bd. govs. Can. Council Christians and Jews; bd. dirs. Can. Geriatrics Research Soc.; chmn. Crofton House Sch.; vice chmn. bd. govs. Lester B. Pearson Coll. Pacific; convocation founder Simon Fraser U.; dir. internat. council United World Colls.; dir. nat. bd. World Wildlife Fund Can. Mem. Vancouver Bd. Trade (council). Clubs: Vancouver, Shaughnessy Golf and Country. Avocations: golf; fishing. Office: Government House, 1401 Rockland Ave, Victoria, BC Canada V8S 1V9

ROGERS, ROBERT REED, manufacturing company executive; b. Oak Park, Ill., Feb. 22, 1929; s. Glen Charles and Lucile (Reed) R.; m. Barbara June Fain, Feb. 22, 1951 (div.); children—Robin, Janeen, Kevin. B.S. in Chemistry, Berea Coll., 1951; M.B.A., Ill. Inst. Tech., 1958, postgrad., 1959-62. Asst. mgr. metallurgy research dept. Armour Research Found., Ill. Inst. Tech., 1955-56, mem. faculty, econs. dept., 1956-62; cons. McKinsey & Co., Inc., 1962-64; mgr. devel. planning, profl. group Litton Industries, Inc., 1964-67; pres. N.Am. subs. Muirhead & Co., Ltd., 1967-68; group v.p. Am. Electric Inc. subs. City Investing Co., 1968-70; pres. Cleartight Corp., 1971-73; pres. Newport Internat. Metals Corp., 1973-76; pres. Kensington Assocs., Inc., Newport Beach, Calif., 1976-83; pres., chmn. bd. Proteus Group, Inc., Newport Beach, 1981-85, pres., chmn. bd. Comparator Systems Corp., Costa Mesa, Calif., 1983—. Served as officer USN, 1951-55. Decorated Knight of Honor Sovereign Order St. John; Machinery and Allied Products Inst. fellow, 1956-62; Berea Coll. grantee, 1947-51. Mem. Navy League, Ferrari Owners Club. Libertarian. Mem. Ch. of Religious Sci. Club: Lido Isle Yacht. Home: 2800 Broad St Newport Beach CA 92663 Office: Comparator Systems Corp 930 W 16th St E-2 Costa Mesa CA 92627

ROGERS, WILLIAM CORDELL, financial executive; b. Louisville, Apr. 16, 1943; s. Delbert Clifton and Nelle Frances (Grimsley) R.; m. Elaine Elizabeth Nicolay, Apr. 10, 1966; children: William C. II, Erin D., Nicole M., Shannon D. AA, Lincoln Coll., 1969; BS, Ill. State U., 1971. With Ill. Dept. Revenue, Springfield, 1971-72; controller Old Heritage Life Ins. Co., Lincoln, Ill., 1972-77, DEN, Inc. CPAs, Tempe, Ariz., 1977-83; corp. fin. cons. Dahlberg Industries, Scottsdale, Ariz., 1983—; econ. instr. Lincoln Coll., 1972-77, real estate taxation instr. Real Estate Sch., Mesa, Ariz., 1978-80. Served with U.S. Army, 1964-67, Vietnam. Recipient Dow Jones award Dow Jones-Wall St. Jour., 1969. Mem. Nat. Assn. Pub. Accts., Ariz. Soc. Pub. Accts. Republican. Lodge: Rotary (bd. dirs. Scottsdale club 1986—, Paul Harris fellow 1985—). Avocations: golf, sailing, reading, music. Home: 8549 E Turney Ave Scottsdale AZ 85251 Office: Dahlberg Industires 6535 E Osborn Rd Scottsdale AZ 85251

ROGERS, WINSLOW SMITH, university administrator; b. Boston, Jan. 4, 1944; s. Lockhart Burgess and Eleanor (Greene) R.; m. Kathryn Therese Simpson, May 31, 1969; children: Alice Whitney, David Winslow. BA in English magna cum laude, Amherst Coll., 1966; AM, Harvard U., 1967, PhD, 1972; MA in Mgmt., Webster U., 1983. Teaching fellow in English and gen. edn. Harvard U., Cambridge, Mass., 1968-71; asst. prof. English U. Mo., St. Louis, 1971-77; asst. prof. lit. and lang. Webster U., St. Louis, 1977-78, assoc. prof., 1978-82, chmn. dept. lit. and lang., 1980-81, coordinator instl. devels., 1981-83, coordinator mktg. planning and instl. devels., 1983-85; assoc. dean Claremont (Calif.) Grad. Sch., 1986—. Contbr. articles to profl. publs. Amherst Meml. fellow and Henry P. Field fellow, 1966-68. Mem. Phi Beta Kappa. Office: Claremont Grad Sch Office of Assoc Dean 154 E 10th St Claremont CA 91711

ROGGE, RICHARD DANIEL, former government executive, security consultant, investigator; b. N.Y.C., July 5, 1926; s. Daniel Richard and Bertha (Sarner) R.; m. Josephine Mary Kowalewska, June 6, 1948; children—Veronica Leigh Rogge Erbeznik, Richard Daniel, Christopher Ames, Meredith Ann. B.S. in Bus. Adminstrn., N.Y.U., 1952. Cert. internat. investigator. Clerical worker FBI, N.Y.C., 1947-52, spl. agt., Phila., 1952-54, Washington, 1954-58, supr., 1958-65, asst. spl. agt. in charge, Richmond, Va., 1965-66, Phila., 1966-67, Los Angeles, 1967-69, inspector, 1969, spl. agt. in charge, Honolulu, 1969-72, Richmond, 1972-74, Buffalo, 1974-77, now security cons., investigator, Calif.; police tng. instr.; writer, lectr. in field. Served with USMC, 1944-46; PTO. Recipient Order of Arrow award Boy Scouts Am., 1943; Service to Law Enforcement awards Va. Assn. Chiefs Police, 1975, N.Y. State Assn. Chiefs Police, 1977, others. Mem. Am. Soc. Indsl. Security, Calif. Assn. Lic. Investigators, Calif. Peace Officers Assn., Council Internat. Investigators, Soc. Former Agts. FBI, Inc., Am. Legion. Republican. Roman Catholic. Lodge: K.C. Home and Office: 32010 Watergate Ct Westlake Village CA 91361

ROGNSTAD, JO PAUL, architect; b. Mpls., May 14, 1929; s. Joseph Edwin and Lillian (Evenson) R.; m. Betty Ann Quisenberry, Sept. 9, 1951 (div. 1981); children: Heather, Mark, Eric, Laurel; m. Diane Kim, May 21, 1982; children: Walter, Linda. Student, Pasadena City Coll., 1947-49, Pomona Coll., 1949-51, U. So. Calif., 1951-54. Registered architect, Calif., Hawaii, Nev. Pvt. practice architecture Jo Paul Rognstad, Design, Arcadia, Calif., 1954-56; pres. Rognstad & Sorenson, Arcadia, Calif., 1956-59, Johnson & Rognstad, Pasadena, Calif., 1959-63, Jo Paul Rognstad & Assocs., Inc., Honolulu, 1963-84, Century Computerized Architects, Inc., Honolulu, 1984—, Phoenix Octadome Devel. Co., Honolulu, 1985—. Rep. Boy Scouts Am., Honolulu, 1966-70; chief YMCA Indian Guides, Honolulu, 1967-68; pres. PTA Stevenson Sch., Honolulu, 1972; mem. Common Cause. Recipient Spl. Honor award Bicsayne Nat. Design Competition, 1980, Excellence award Am. P.T. Inst., 1984, Honor award Am. Concrete Inst., 1978, Honor award Am. Engring. Soc., 1982. Mem. AIA (design, housing and urban design and planning comm.), Nat. Council Archtl. Registration Bds., Am. Arbitration Assn., Smithsonian Inst., Amateur Athletic Union (hospitality com. 1972, 76, 80, 84). Democrat. Lutheran. Avocations: photography, athletics, barbershop quartet singing, painting, sculpture. Home and Office: 1750 Kalakaua Ave Suite 4000 Honolulu HI 96826

ROGOFF, ARNOLD M., book dealer, publisher, management consultant; b. Oak Park, Ill., Nov. 8, 1930; s. Julius J. and Lucile E. (Wingerhoff) R.; m. Janet E. Percy, July 16, 1968; children: Hilary, Peter. Student, U. Mo., 1948-49, Harvard Coll., 1951; BS, Boston U., 1951. Pres., Opus Prodns., Los Angeles, 1959-61, CGR Labs., Los Angeles, 1961-63; With McGraw-Hill Book Co., N.Y.C., 1963-77, sales mgr. Gregg div., 1974-75, dir. mktg., 1975-77; prin. ptnr. Arnold M. Rogoff & Assocs., Mill Valley, Calif., 1977—; pres. Ethnographic Arts Pubs., Mill Valley, 1978—. Home: 1040 Erica Rd Mill Valley CA 94941 Office: Ethnographic Arts Publs Indsl Ctr Bldg Suite 108 Gate 5 Rd Sausalito CA 94965

ROHALY, ANDREA TOWERS, travel agency executive; b. Atlanta, Dec. 7, 1948; d. Abner Alexander Towers and Marica (Cok) Miller; m. Michael Edward Rohaly, Oct. 30, 1982. BA, Hollins Coll., 1970. Account exec. Am. Express Co., Atlanta, 1973-76; mgmt. trainee Am. Express Co., New York City, 1976-77; mgr. Am. Express Co., Charlotte, N.C., 1977-80; mgr., dir. Am. Express Co., Dallas, 1980-84; dir. Am. Express Co., Phoenix, 1984—; candidate Inst. Cert. Travel Counselors, Wellesley, Mass., 1981—. Mem. Inst. Cert. Travel Counselors (candidate). Episcopalian. Avocations: swimming, tennis, hiking, reading. Home: 4315 E Shangri-La Rd Phoenix AZ 85028 Office: Am Express Travel Related Services Co Inc 1661 E Camelback Rd Phoenix AZ 85016

ROHDE, JAMES VINCENT, software systems company executive; b. O'Neill, Nebr., Jan. 25, 1939; s. Ambrose Vincent and Loretta Cecilia R.; children: Maria, Sonja, Daniele. BCS, Seattle U., 1962. Sales dir. GCE Telephone Co., Oakland, Calif., 1971-74; chmn. bd. dirs., pres., Applied Telephone Tech., Oakland, 1974; v.p. sales and mktg. Automation Electornics Corp., Oakland, 1975-82; pres., chmn. bd. dirs. Am. Telecorp, Inc., 1982—. Pres. Council Regents Heritage Coll., Toppenish, Wash., 1985—; chmn. exec. com., pres. Council Regents Heritage Coll. Republican. Roman Catholic. Office: Am Telecorp Inc 10 Twin Dolphin Dr Redwood City CA 94065

ROHM, C. E. TAPIE, JR., management educator; b. Long Beach, Calif., June 2, 1947; s. C.E. Tapie and Dorothy Elizabeth (Farrow) R.; m. Karen Diane Bird, May 24, 1972; children: C.E. Tapie III, B.W. Trevor, J.D. Tucker, M.S. Terrell, R.S. Ty Joseph, Kirsti Grace, S.K. Taylor Cody. BS, Brigham Young U., 1973, MA, 1974; PhD, Ohio U., 1977. Treas. Ohio U.

Med. Assocs. Inc., Athens, Ohio, 1977-78; dir. informational planning Ohio U., Athens, 1978-79, asst. to dean, 1977-79; asst. prof. mgmt. Calif. State Coll., San Bernardino, 1979-81, prof., dir. info. programs, 1983—; assoc. prof. Whittier (Calif.) Coll., 1981-83, dir. Small Bus. Inst., 1981-83; cons. in field; series editor Holt, Reinhart & Winston Pub. Co., N.Y.C., 1985-87. Author: EMERGENCY Preparedness, 1986; editor: Crisis Management in Higher Education, 1986; contbr. articles to profl. jours. Dist. commr. Calif. Inland Empire council Boy Scouts Am., 1985; organizer The Gt. Am. Family, San Bernardino, 1986. Recipient Merit award, Arrowhead District of Calif. Inland Empire council Boy Scouts Am., 1985. Mem. Internat. Info. Mgmt. Assn. (pres.-elect 1986-87), Internat. Communication Assn., Assn. Computing Machinery, Acad. Mgmt. Republican. Mormon. Lodge: Native Sons Golden West. Home: 5804 N Acacia St San Bernardino CA 92407 Office: Calif State U 5500 University Pkwy San Bernardino CA 92407

ROHRBERG, RODERICK GEORGE, cons.; b. Minneola, Iowa, Sept. 26, 1925; s. Charles H. and Emma (Minsen) R.; BS in Naval Sci., Marquette U., 1946; BSCE, Iowa State U., 1949; m. Genevieve Mary Sogard, June 19, 1949; children—Karla (Mrs. George H. Witz, Jr.), Roderick K., Cheries, Timothy, Christopher. Bridge design engr. Alaska Rd. Commn., U.S. Dept. Interior, 1949-51; sr. tech. specialist North Am. Rockwell, research, Los Angeles, 1951-69; pres. Creative Pathways, Inc., advanced welding services, Torrance, Calif., 1969—; pvt. practice as cons. advanced welding process, equipment design and devel., Torrance, Calif., 1972—. Served with USNR, 1944-46. Recipient 1st nat. Airco Welding award, 1966, commendation NASA, 1965, Engrng. Profl. Achievement citation Iowa State U., 1973, 3d pl. Von Karman Meml. Grand award, 1974. Registered profl. engr., Calif. Mem. Am. Welding Soc. Lutheran. Patentee in field. Home: 2742 W 234th St Torrance CA 90505 Office: Creative Pathways Inc 3121 Fujita St Torrance CA 90505

ROHRER, BEVERLY JEAN, school district administrator; b. Loma Linda, Calif., Apr. 19, 1937; d. Charles Lesley and Gertrude (Montgomery) Woods; m. Don Charles Rohrer, Apr. 7, 1958; children: Jeffrey Charles, Matthew Charles. BS cum laude, U. So. Calif., 1960, MS, 1966, EdD, 1982. Tchr. Mira Costa High Sch., Manhattan Beach, Calif., 1960-70, counselor, activity dir., 1970-76, dean students, 1976-78; bus. mgr. So. Bay Union High Sch. Dist., Redondo Beach, Calif., 1979-83; dep. supt. Redondo Beach. City Sch. Dist., 1983—; treas., bd. dirs. Centinela South Bay Sch. Ins. Authority, Redondo Beach, 1979—; bd. dirs. Alliance for Sch. Coop. Ins. Purchasing, Downey, Calif., 1985—; sec. bd. dirs. Los Angeles County Schs. Non Profit Corp., Downey, 1984—. Mem. Redondo Beach Coordinating Council, 1983—, PTA Mira Costa High Sch., 1960—. Recipient Life Service award PTA, 1967, Youth Service award City of Manhattan Beach, 1976, Service award March of Dimes, South Bay, Service award ARC, South Bay. Mem. Western Assn. Schs. and Coll. Accreditation (chmn. 1976—), Calif. Assn. Sch. Bus. Officials (pres. South Bay chpt. 1982—, mem. legis. com. South Bay chpt. 1983), Assn. Calif. Sch. Adminstrs., Assn. Supervision and Curriculum Devel., EDUCARE, U. So. Calif. Alumni Assn., U. So. Calif. Edn. Alumni Assn., Phi Delta Kappa (Leadership award 1981), Delta Gamma. Republican. Club: South Bay Trojan League (Palos Verdes, Calif.).

ROHRER, PAUL GEORGE, project management company executive, claims and automation consultant; b. Tacoma, Dec. 3, 1945; s. George and Luella (Loughlin) R.; m. Pamela A. Rohrer, Oct. 10, 1970. BA, Seattle U., BS, MS, 1969. Chief exec. officer Paul Rohrer & Co., Federal Way, Wash., 1970—, R-W Consultants, Federal Way, Wash., 1970—, N.W. Controls, Seattle, 1970—; bd. dirs. Dykes & Assocs., Edmonds, Wash., Automated Project Group, Seattle; dealer and chmn. Group Health, Seattle, 1965—, Rohrer Group, Puyallup, Wash., 1972—. Bd. dirs. My Fathers House, Tacoma, 1981-83; procurator, adminstr. Spl. Olympics, Kent, Wash., 1979—; active Am. Heart Assn., Federal Way, 1978—, Am. Cancer Soc., 1978—. Recipient Spl. Service award Soc. Advancement Mgmt., N.Y.C., 1970, Am. Soc. Cost Engrs., N.Y.C., 1985, Am. Arbitration Assn., N.Y.C., 1986; Advisor of Yr. award Jr. Achievement, Seattle, 1975, 76. Mem. Architect and Engrs. Systems Group, Constrn. Specifications Inst., Soc. Mil. Engrs., Project Mgmt. Inst., Cons. Engrs. Counsel. Avocations: cross-country and alpine skiing, photography, cooking. Office: 28815 Pacific Hwy S Federal Way WA 98003

ROHRING, CLAUDIA MYRTLE (BROWN), magazine production manager; b. Los Angeles, Mar. 13, 1944; d. Claude Morrison Brown and Lois Frances (Canepa) Brown Reymond Pugh; m. John Gary Rohring, Sept. 7, 1962; children: Jeffrey Claude, Brett Frank. Student, UCLA, 1960-61, Ventura Coll., 1965-66. Media clk. Fountain Valley (Calif.) Sch. Dist., 1972-75; gen. mgr. Karl Pub., Newport Beach, Calif., 1976-79; prodn. mgr. HBJ Pubs. (formerly Hester Communications)., Irvine, Calif., 1979—. Program chmn. Fountain Valley Newcomers Assn., 1975-76. Republican. Episcopalian. Avocations: bridge, needlework. Home: 6022 Judwick Circle Huntington Beach CA 92708 Office: HBJ Pubs 1700 E Dyer Rd Suite 250 Santa Ana CA 92705

ROIZ, MYRIAM, export import firm executive; b. Managua, Nicaragua, Jan. 21, 1938; came to U.S., 1949, naturalized, 1968; d. Francisco Octavio and Maria Herminia (Briones) R.; m. Nicholas M. Orphanopoulos, Jan. 21, 1957 (div.); children—Jacqueline Orphanopoulos-Doggwiler, Gene E. Orphanopoulos, George A. Orphanopoulos. B.A. cum laude in Interdisciplinary Social Sci., San Francisco State U., 1980. Lic. ins. agt. Sales rep. Met. Life Ins. Co., San Francisco, 1977-79; mktg. dir. Europe/Latin Am., Allied Canners & Pachers, San Francisco, 1979-83; mktg. dir. Europe/Latin Am., M-C Internat., San Francisco, 1983—. Mem. Common Cause; coordinator Robert F. Kennedy Presdl. campaign, Millbrae, San Mateo County, local mayoral campaign, Millbrae, 1975; dir., organizer fund-raising campaign for earthquake-devastated Nicaragua; active Brown U. World Hunger Program. Named Outstanding Employee of Yr. Hillsborough City Sch. Dist., 1973; recipient Sales award Met. Life Ins. Co., 1977. Mem. Am. Soc. Profl. and Exec. Women, AAUW. Democrat. Roman Catholic. Club: Latino de Foster City. Office: M-C Internat 742 Market St 4th Floor San Francisco CA 94102

ROJA, DENNY S., communications executive, financial consultant; b. Quezon City, Philippines, Mar. 26, 1946; came to U.S., 1967; s. M.A. and Amparo (Santa Catalina) R.; m. Maria C. Zamora, 1969; children: Christine Michelle, Melissa Cheryl. BSChemE summa cum laude, U. Santo Tomas, Manila, 1966; MSChemE, U. Wash., 1969; MBA, Stanford U., 1971; JD, Fordham U., 1986. Registered mgmt. acct. Mktg. controller Gen. Foods Internat., Toronto, Can., 1977-78; mgr. fin. div. Gen. Foods Internat., White Plains, N.Y., 1978-80, mgr. strategic analysis, 1980-82, mgr. corp. devel., 1982-84; dir. mergers and acquistions Pacific Telesis Group, San Francisco, 1984-86; dir. strategic alliances Pacific Bell, San Ramon, Calif., 1986—; adj. prof. finance Sacred Heart U., Bridgeport, Conn., 1980-82. Mem. Assn. Corp. Growth, Soc. Mgmt. Accts. Republican. Roman Catholic. Avocations: golf, tennis, cross-country skiing. Home: 14377 Liddicoat Circle Los Altos Hills CA 94022 Office: Pacific Bell 2600 Camino Ramon 3N401 San Ramon CA 94583

ROKS, MARTY JANETTE, telecommunications executive; b. Dyess, Ark., May 15, 1942; d. Marvin Edward and Delma Mae (Crownover) Turman; m. John Roks, Feb. 3, 1960 (div. Jan. 1970); 1 child, Flora Leigh Bettencourt. AS, Miramar Coll.; BA, Nat. U., BBA, MBA. Entertainer Foxey Lady Agy., Fullerton, Calif., 1974-75; coordinator spl. projects Nat. U. Alumni Assn., San Diego, 1981-82; v.p. Rosjum Mining Corp., San Diego, 1983-84; prin. Unipeg Enterprises, Lemon Grove, Calif., 1983-84; acad. asst. continuing edn., conf. facilities, telecommunications Nat. U., Inglewood, 1984-86; ind. contractor Traditional Industries, El Cajon, Calif., 1985. Vol. San Diego Navy League, 1982. Recipient Letter of Commendation, State Atty. Gens. Office, 1985. Mem. Telecommunication Assn., Assn. MBA Execs., Nat. Assn. Female Execs., Nat. U. Alumni Assn., Antique Aircraft Assn. (v.p. 1980). Democrat. Mem. Ch. of Christ. Home: 15 H St Encinitas CA 92024

ROLAND, HAROLD EUGENE, JR., safety engineering educator; b. Lincoln, Nebr., Aug. 10, 1924; s. Harold E. and Nell (Williamson) R.; m. Elayne M. Merriam, Aug. 5, 1947. B.S. in Aero. Engring., Naval Postgrad. Sch., 1956; M.S. in Aero. Engring., U. Minn., 1958; M.S. in Indsl. Engring., U. So. Calif., 1969; Ph.D., UCLA, 1974. Lic. profl. safety engr., Calif. Commd. USMC, 1943, advanced through grades to lt. col., 1963, ret., 1965; assoc. prof. safety sci. dept. U. So. Calif., Los Angeles, 1965—; pres. Rolson & Co., Los Angeles. Decorated DFC (2), Air medal (5). Mem. AAUP, AIAA, System Safety Soc., Am. Soc. Safety Engr., Sigma Xi. Club: Rancho Verde Racquet. Author: System Safety Engineering and Management, 1983; contbr. numerous articles to profl. jours. Office: U So Calif Safety Sci Dept Los Angeles CA 90089-0021

ROLAND, STEVEN DAVID, lawyer; b. Phila., Mar. 24, 1957; s. Arnold Sanford and Diane Louise (Rubinger) R. BA, Cornell U., 1979; JD, U. San Francisco, 1982. Bar: Calif. 1983. Assoc. Sedgwick, Detert, Moran & Arnold, San Francisco, 1982—. Mem. Calif. Bar Assn., San Francisco Bar Assn. Avocations: tennis, skiing, basketball, softball. Office: Sedgwick Detert et al 1 Embarcadero Ctr 16th Floor San Francisco CA 94111

ROLD, TRACY LOUIS, organic chemist; b. Evansville, Ind., Nov. 16, 1950; s. Kenneth Louis and Dorothy Lee (Hammett) R.; m. Janice Irene Lucas, Sept. 7, 1974; children: Pamela Christine, Nicholas Edward, Kimberly Annette. BA, Pasadena Coll. (now Point Loma Coll.), 1972; PhD, U. Wash., 1977. Staff chemist IBM, Boulder, Colo., 1977-81, adv. chemist, 1981—, tech. area mgr., 1985—. Contbr. articles to tech. jours. Mem. Am. Chem Soc. (polymer and analytical divs., chromatography subdiv.), Rocky Mountain Mass Spectrometry Discussion Group, Front Range Assn. Mass Spectrometrists. Mem. Ch. of the Nazarene. Avocations: computer programming, softball, bowling. Home: 1693 Geneva Circle Longmont CO 80501 Office: IBM Corp PO Box 1900 Boulder CO 80301-9191

ROLDAN, KATHLEEN ANN, speech-language pathologist; b. Pueblo, Colo., Jan. 11, 1958; d. William Albert and Paula Joan (Parker) Sexton; m. Robert Paul Roldan, Aug. 25, 1984. BS, U. So. Colo., 1980; MS, Phillips U., 1982. Pvt. practice speech/lang. pathology Pueblo, 1982-83; speech/lang. pathologist St. Mary Corwin Hosp., Pueblo, 1982, Pueblo Sch. Dist. #60, 1982-85; speech/lang. pathologist, autistic program El Paso County Dist. #11, Colorado Springs, Colo., 1985—. Mem. Am. Speech-lang. Hearing Assn. (cert. clin. competency). Home: 4080 Scotch Pine Dr Colorado Springs CO 80918 Office: El Paso County Dist #11 1620 W Bijou Colorado Springs CO 80904

ROLL, SAMUEL, psychologist; b. Medellin, Antioquia, Colombia, Dec. 21, 1942; s. Haime Hirsch and Bertha (Agudelo) R.; m. Elizabeth Jaffee, Jan. 4, 1970; children: Julia, Eric. BA, La. State U., 1964; MS, Pa. State U., 1967, PhD, 1968. Diplomate Am. Bd. Clin. Psychology, Forensic Psychology. Postdoctoral fellow Yale U., 1968-70; vis. prof. U. Antioquia, Medellin, Colombia, 1975; dir. postgrad. tng. Inst. De Salud Mental, Monterrey, Mexico, 1976-77; vis. prof. law U. N.Mex., 1983, prof. psychology, 1970—; cons. Inst. de Salud Mental, Monterrey, 1978—, Sect. de. Edn. Especial, Mexico City, 1979—; practice forensic psychology, Albuquerque, 1973—. Co-author: Culture and Psychotherapy, 1984, (textbook and test) Mexican WISC-RM, 1984; contbr. articles to profl. jours. Fulbright fellow, Washington, 1975; recipient Contribution to Spl. Edn. award Nuevo Leon, Mex., 1983. Fellow Soc. Personality Assessment, Am. Acad Forensic Psychology (bd. dirs. 1983—); mem. N.Mex. Bd. Psychologist Examiners (sec. 1978-79), Am. Psychol. Assn., Am. Psychology Law Soc. Democrat. Home: 1616 San Patricio SW Albuquerque NM 87104 Office: Psychology Dept Univ Hill Albuquerque NM 87131

ROLLINGS, JOANN, nurse, army officer; b. St. Louis, Feb. 13, 1947; d. Edward Charles and Dorothy Jane (Horak) R. B.S. in Nursing, Baylor U., 1969; M.S. in Nursing, U. Tex.-El Paso, 1982; postgrad. U. Calif.-San Francisco, 1984—. Registered nurse, Tex. Commd. Nurse Corps, U.S. Army, 1969, advanced through grades to lt. col., 1986; clin. staff nurse Irwin Army Hosp., 1969-70, 95th Evacuation Hosp., DaNang, Vietnam, 1970-71; chief nursing inservice edn. and tng. Letterman Gen. Hosp., 1971-72; asst. prof. Walter Reed Army Inst. of Nursing, U. Md. Sch. Nursing, Washington, 1974-78; critical care clin. nurse specialist William Beaumont Army Med. Ctr., 1979-82; chief clin. nursing service U.S. Army Community Hosp., Seoul, Korea, 1982-83; quality assurance cons. Letterman Army Med. Ctr., 1985—; adj. clin. faculty Sch. Nursing, U. Tex.-El Paso, 1980-82, Sch. Nursing, San Francisco State U., 1983-84; cons. to Surgeon Gen. for Critical Care Nursing, 1976—; co-chmn. Maryland Ctr. Vietnamese Relocation Project, 1977-78. Contbr. articles to profl. jours. Health cons. Girl Scouts U.S.A., Rockville, Md., 1975-77. Decorated Bronze Star medal, Army Commendation medal with oak leaf cluster, Meritorious Service medal with 2 oak leaf clusters; Commendation medal (Vietnam); U.S. Army Nurse Corps scholar, 1985. Mem. Am. Nurses Assn., Am. Assn. Critical Care Nurses, Calif. Nurses Assn., Officers Christian Fellowship, Sigma Theta Tau.

ROLLINS, JOAN ELISE, personnel services corporation executive; b. Inglewood, Calif., Mar. 3, 1947; d. Richard H. and Irene C. (Morgan) McClellan; m. James Hood Rollins, Aug. 8, 1970; 1 child, James Richard. B.A. in Psychology, U. So. Calif., 1969; M.A. in Psychology, Calif. State U.-Long Beach, 1978. Registered employment cons., Calif. Employment Assn. Personnel counselor Nancy Nolan Agy., Los Angeles, 1969-70; reservation agt. Trans World Airlines, Los Angeles, 1970; personnel counselor, asst. mgr. A.E.A. Employment Agy., Long Beach, 1970-78; pres. Rollins & Assocs. Personnel Service, Inc., Long Beach, 1979—; guest lectr. classes and seminars in field; lectr. internat. trade job opportunities Calif. State U., Long Beach, 1986—; cons. ct. cases involving employment. Mem. Internat. Mktg. Assn. Orange County, Exec. Women Internat. (dir. 1984), Long Beach Area C. of C. (bd. dirs. 1984—, pres. Women's Council 1982-83, dir. 1982-84), Commerce Assocs. U. So. Calif. Sch. Bus., Export Mgrs. Assn. Calif. Club: Harbor Transp. Office: 337 E San Antonio Dr #200 Long Beach CA 90807

ROLLMAN-BRANCH, HILDA SCHURMAN, physician, psychiatrist, psychoanalyst; b. Essen, Germany; came to U.S., 1941; d. Maximilian and Irma Schurmann; m. Ernst E. Rollman, Dec. 8, 1937 (div. 1951); 1 child, Veronia Kaufman; m. Melville Campbell Branch, Mar. 15, 1951. BS in Chemistry, Columbia U., 1943; MD, U. So. Calif., Los Angeles, 1947. Intern Michael Reese Hosp., Chgo., 1947-48; research assoc. dept. medicine U. So. Calif., Los Angeles, 1948-49, lectr. law sch., 1966-70, assoc. clin. prof. of law in psychiatry, 1970-74, clin. prof. of law in psychiatry, 1974-82; resident in psychiatry Brentwood Neuropsychiat. Hosp., VA Ctr., Los Angeles, 1949-52; practice medicine specializing in psychiatry and psychoanalysis Los Angeles, 1952—; staff psychiatrist Los Angeles Psychiatric Services, 1952-53; attending psychiatrist Los Angeles Psychiat. Service and Reiss-Davis Clinic for Child Guidance, 1956-64; clin. instr. U. Calif., Los Angeles, 1957-60, asst. clin. prof., 1960-66, assoc. clin. prof. psychiatry, 1966-74, clin. prof. psychiatry, 1974—. Contbr. articles to profl. jours. Fellow Am. Psychiat. Assn.; mem. Los Angeles County Med. Assn., Calif. State Med. Assn., AMA, So. Calif. Psychiat. Soc., Los Angeles Psychoanalytic Soc./Inst. Tng. and Supervising Analysts (various positions 1958—), Am. Psychoanalytic Assn. (various positions 1960—), Internat. Psychoanalytic Assn., Mex. Psychoanalytic Assn. (corr.), Israel Psychoanalytic Assn. (corr.). Office: 1800 Fairburn Ave Los Angeles CA 90025

ROLSTON, HOLMES, III, philosopher, educator; b. Staunton, Va., Nov. 19, 1932; s. Holmes and Mary Winifred (Long) R.; m. Jane Irving Wilson, June 1, 1956; children: Shonny Hunter, Giles Campbell. BS, Davidson Coll., 1953; BD, Union Theol. Sem., 1956; MA in Philosophy of Sci., U. Pitts., 1968; PhD in Theology, U. Edinburgh, Scotland, 1958. Ordained to ministry Presbyn. Ch., 1956. Pastor Walnut Grove Presbyn. Ch., Bristol, Va., 1959-67; prof. philosophy Colo. State U., Ft. Collins, 1968—; vis. scholar Ctr. Study of World Religions, Harvard U., 1974-75. Author: The Cosmic Christ, 1966, John Calvin versus the Westminster Confession, 1972, Religious Inquiry--Participation and Detachment, 1985, Philosophy Gone Wild, 1986, Science and Religion: A Critical Survey, 1987, Environmental Ethics, 1987; assoc. editor Environ. Ethics, 1979—; mem. editorial bd. Reidel Series in Applied Philosophy and Pub. Policy; contbr. chpts. to books, articles to profl. jours. Recipient Pennock award Disting. Scholarship Colo. State U., 1984; NSF grantee. Mem. Am. Acad. Religion, AAAS, Am. Philos. Assn. Avocation: bryology. Home: 1712 Concord Dr Fort Collins CO 80526 Office: Colo State U Dept Philosophy Fort Collins CO 80523

ROMANO, ENNIO, physician, cancer researcher; b. Assoro, Italy, Jan. 1, 1925; came to U.S., 1981; s. Marcello and Giuseppina (Fasanaro) R.; m. Giuseppina Digrazia, Oct. 25, 1952; children: Marcello, Anita, Maria. MD, U. Rome, 1951; specialist in gen. surgery, U. Catania, Italy, 1967; specialist in oncology, U. Rome, 1969, specialist in gen. pathology, 1978. Gen. surgeon U. Catania, Italy, 1952-54, head gen. surgeon, 1963-81; gen. surgeon U. Rome, 1954-63; cancer researcher UCLA, 1981-86; head surgery cons. Italian Navy, Rome, 1964-81; dir. clin. pathol. St. Louis Hosp., Catania, 1965-81. Author: Tumors of the Thoracic Skeleton, 1981, Intestinal Obstructions, 1982, Gastrointestinal Tumors, 1984. Mcpl. dep. Partito Repubblicano Italiano, Catania, 1975-81; pres. Italian Nat. Assn. Friends of the U.S.A., Rome, 1978—; mem. Nat. Rep. Congr. Com., U.S., 1984—, Nat. Com. to Preserve Social Security, 1984. Recipient commendatore Ordine Repubblica Italiana, 1981. Mem. Am. Cancer Soc., The N.Y. Acad. Sci., AAAS, Internat. Burckhardt Acad. (Switzerland), Italian Am. Med. Assn., Italian Soc. Surgery. Roman Catholic. Lodge: Lions. Avocations: philately, oil painting. Office: 1886 Rosemont Ave Claremont CA 91711

ROMBERG, GEORGE (BUD) HARVEY, science educator; b. White Plains, N.Y., Oct. 2, 1935; s. George H. and Eleanor (Demuth) R.; m. Jane Weil, Aug. 11, 1956; children: Greg Weil, Gail Romberg Sigman, Janet Susan. BS in Animal Nutrition, Colo. State U., 1957; MA in Chemistry, U. No. Colo., 1967. Prodn. mgr., officer Rockmount Ranch Wear Mfg. Co., Denver, 1960-65; tchr. Sch. Dist. Re-2, Steamboat Springs, Colo., 1966—, also bd. dirs.; dir. Schwayder Camp, Idaho Springs, Colo., 1973-74; mng. ptnr. Rabbit Ears Lodge, Kremmling, Colo., 1975; instr. Colo. Mountain Coll., Steamboat Springs, 1975—. Author: Chemistry Lab. Manual, 1973. Chmn. Citizens Adv. Water Commn., Steamboat Springs, 1982. Served to 1st lt. U.S. Army, 1957-59. Recipient Hon. Mention Colo. Tchr. of Yr., Colo. Dept. Edn., 1970, Hon. Mention, Colo. Dept. Edn., 1972. Mem. Steamboat Springs Health and Recreation Assn. (bd. dirs. 1969—), AAAS, Nat. Sci. Tchrs. Assn. Republican. Jewish. Avocation: stamp collecting.

ROME, HERBERT MARK, manufacturing company executive; b. Boston, Sept. 20, 1926; s. Abraham I. and Lilliam (Rosenberg) R.; m. Eileen Shapiro, Apr. 21, 1950; children: Steven, Ann Mason. BS, U. Calif., Berkeley, 1948. Div. pres. Eldon Office Products, Carson, Calif., 1971-80; exec. v.p. Eldon Industries Inc., Inglewood, Calif., 1980—, also bd. dirs. Avocation: golf. Home: 10129 Bridlevale Dr Los Angeles CA 90064 Office: Eldon Industries Inc 9920 La Cienega Blvd Inglewood CA 90301

ROMEO, PAUL PETER, electronics manufacturing administrator; b. Bklyn., Feb. 3, 1949; s. Dominick and Sophie (Dudek) R.; m. Denise Sempien, May 5, 1975 (div. Sept. 1981); 1 child, Paul P. II; m. Alice Soria, Oct. 1986. BS, U. Ill., 1971; MBA, U. Santa Clara, 1975. Procurement agt. Hewlett-Packard, Palo Alto, Calif., 1971-72, systems adminstr., 1972-73, supr. prodn. control, 1973-74, mgr. prodn., 1974-79, mgr. materials, 1979-86; mgr. mfg. High Yield Tech., Mountain View, Calif., 1986—. Mem. Am. Prodn. and Inventory Control Soc. (treas. 1983-86, pres. 1986-87), No. Calif. Purchasing Mgrs. Assn. Republican. Roman Catholic. Clubs: Palo Alto Tennis, Decathlon. Avocations: tennis, softball, skiing, flying, wine making. Office: High Yield Tech 2400 Bayshore Frontage Rd Mountain View CA 94043

ROMER, ROY R., state governor; b. Garden City, Kans., Oct. 31, 1928; s. Irving Rudolph and Margaret Elizabeth (Snyder) R.; B.S. in Agrl. Econs., Colo. State U., 1950; LL.B., U. Colo., 1952; postgrad. Yale U.; m. Beatrice Miller, June 10, 1952; children—Paul, Mark, Mary, Christopher, Timothy, Thomas, Elizabeth. Engaged in farming in Colo., 1942-52; admitted to Colo. bar, 1952; ind. practice, Denver, 1955-66; mem. Colo. Ho. of Reps., Dist., 1958-62, Colo. Senate, 1962-66; owner, operator Arapahoe Aviation Co., Colo. Flying Acad., Geneva Basin Ski Area; engaged in home site devel.; owner chain farm implement and indsl. equipment stores in Colo.; commr. agr. State of Colo., 1975, state treas., 1977-86; gov. State of Colo., 1987—; chief staff, exec. asst. to gov. Colo., 1975-77, 83-84; chmn. Gov. Colo. Blue Ribbon Panel, Gov. Colo. Small Bus. Council; mem. agrl. adv. com. Colo. Bd. Agr. Past trustee Iliff Sch. Theology, Denver. Served with USAF, 1952-54. Mem. Colo. Bar Assn. (gov.), Order of Coif. Democrat. Presbyterian. Bd. editors Colo. U. Law Rev., 1960-62. Office: Office of the Gov State Capitol Bldg Room 136 Denver CO 80203

ROMERO, ARTURO, psychologist, consultant; b. Santa Paula, Calif., June 8, 1948; s. Alfonso Sermeno and Margarita (Morones) R. AA, Moorpark Coll., 1972; BA, U. Calif., Santa Barbara, 1974; MA, UCLA, 1975, PhD, 1982. Cert. psychologist. Research assoc. UCLA, 1974-78, teaching asst., 1978-79; psychology lectr. U. Calif., Riverside, 1979-82; project mgr. Southwest Regional Lab., Los Alamitos, Calif., 1982-85; behavioral sci. cons. Dept. Mental Health, Los Angeles, 1985-86, children's services coordinator, 1986—. Editor: Hispanic Jour. of Behavioral Sci., 1983-85, mem. editorial bd., 1982-86; editor: El Boletin, 1985-86. Mem. legis. council U. Calif., Santa Barbara, 1973-74. Served with U.S. Army, 1968-70, Vietnam. Migrant Workers' scholar Ventura County Migrant Assn., 1973; culture research grantee UCLA, 1978. Mem. AAAS, Am. Psychol. Assn., Div. Devel. Psychology, Nat. Hispanic Psychol. Assn. (sec. 1984-86), Sigma Xi. Roman Catholic. Avocations: skiing, outdoor activities. Home: 1630 Calle Vaquero 506 Glendale CA 91206 Office: Augustus Hawkins Mental Health Ctr 1720 E 120 St Los Angeles CA 90059

ROMERO, GREGORY GEORGE, fire protection executive; b. Las Cruces, N.Mex., July 29, 1942; s. Max Acacio and Lila Juanita (Forbes) R.; m. Patricia Louise Hawn, Feb. 23, 1963; children: Rob Patrick, Raquel Marie. BA in Bus. Adminstrn., U. Colo., 1964. V.p. sales Red Comet Inc., Littleton, Colo., 1964-82; v.p. Romco Internat., Littleton, 1982-84; v.p. sales Ad-X Fire System, Denver, 1984-85; regional sales mgr. Buckeye Fire Equipment, Cleve., 1985-86; br. mgr. Master Protection, Los Angeles, 1986—; instr. vocat. sch., Littleton, Colo., 1979. Mem. Internat. Trade Assn. (bd. dirs. 1980-82). Republican. Roman Catholic. Lodge: Kiwanis. Avocations: coaching, softball, skiing, bridge. Home: 3329 Kimberly Way San Mateo CA 94403 Office: Master Protection Enterprises 2684 Lacy St Los Angeles CA 90031

ROMERO, JOSIE TORRALBA, mental health executive, social worker; b. Piedras Negras, Mex., Sept. 24, 1944; d. Amado Torralba Mann and Isabel (Flores) Torralba; m. Arturo Romero, May 6, 1967; children: Diana Isabel, Arturo Romero Jr. AA, Gavilan Coll., 1972; BA, San Jose State U., 1976, MSW, 1979. Lic. clin. social worker, Calif. Bilingual tchr. aide Gilroy (Calif.) Unified Sch. Dist., 1968-69; mental health community worker Santa Clara County Mental Health, Gilroy, 1969-78; minority program specialist Santa Clara County Mental Health, San Jose, Calif., 1978-80; so. county ctr. dir. Santa Clara County Mental Health, Gilroy, 1980-82; asst. dir. community mental health Santa Clara County Mental Health, San Jose, 1982-84, regional dir., 1984—; pvt. practice psycho-therapist San Jose, 1984—; cons., trainer in field, San Jose, 1978—; bd. dirs. Hispanic Inst. Family Devel., 1984-86. Contbr. articles to profl. jours. Bd. dirs. Gardener Health Ctr., San Jose, 1984-86; mem Hispanic Women Polit. Assn., Gilroy, 1984. Mem. Bay Area Assn. Spanish Speaking Therapists, Nat. Orgn. Spanish Speaking Health and Mental Health Therapists, Assn. Raza Mental Health Adminstrs. (bd. dirs. advocates 1970-78), Nat. Assn. Social Workers. Democrat. Roman Catholic. Avocations: gardening, baseball, reading, doll collecting. Office: Cen Mental Health Ctr 2221 Enborg Ln San Jose CA 95128

ROMIG, ALTON DALE, JR., metallurgist, educator; b. Bethlehem, Pa., Oct. 6, 1953; s. Alton Dale and Christine (Groh) R.; B.S., Lehigh U., 1975, M.S., 1977, Ph.D., 1979; m. Julie H. Romig. Metallurgist, mem. tech. staff Sandia Nat. Labs., Albuquerque, 1979—; adj. assoc. prof. N.Mex. Inst. Mining and Tech., Socorro, 1981—. Mem. Am. Soc. for Metals (various chpt. offices), AIME, Microbeam Analysis Soc. (nat. officer), Materials Reseach Soc., Sigma Xi, Tau Beta Pi. Republican. Mem. United Ch. of Christ. Mem. bd. rev. Metallurg. Transactions; contbr. articles to sci. jours. Home: 4923 Calle de Luna NE Albuquerque NM 87111 Office: Sandia Nat Labs Div 1832 Albuquerque NM 87185

ROMITO, MAUREEN, personnel director; b. Buffalo, Nov. 20, 1953; d. Richard Brady and Catherine Marie (McDonnell) Halloran; m. Richard Michael Romito, Aug. 2, 1975. BA, SUNY, Geneseo, 1975. Adminstrv. asst. Yale U., New Haven, 1977-79; personnel analyst Valley Bank of Nev., Las Vegas, 1979-81, personnel mgr., 1981-83, AVP, mgr., 1983-85, v.p., 1986—; instr. Clark County Community Coll., Las Vegas, 1983—. Mem.

Am. Soc. Personnel Adminstrn., So. Nev. Personnel Assn., Nat. Assn. Banking Affirmative Action Dirs., Personnel Accreditation Inst. (profl. in human resoruces). Avocations: reading, theatre. Home: 6259 Hummingbird Ln Las Vegas NV 89103 Office: Valley Bank of Nevada 1077 E Sahara PO Box 15427 Las Vegas NV 89114

ROMJUE, STEPHEN WALTER, utility company executive, electrical engineer; b. Alton, Ill., Mar. 21, 1940; s. Russell Clark and Georgia Gloria (Elordi) R.; m. Marilyn Kay Dobyns, June 5, 1960; children: Diane Kay, Lisa Marie, Laura Eva. BSEE, Wash. State U., 1967. Registered profl. elec. engr., Wash. Elec. engr. Wash. Water Power Co., Spokane, 1967-71, dist. supr. engring., 1971-74, transmission and distbn. engring. supr., 1974-80, asst. div. mgr., 1980-82, mgr. Spokane div., 1982—. Chmn. Southside Cath. Schs., Spokane, 1978; bd. dirs. Campfire Girls Eastern Wash. div., 1979-82, Connoisseur Concerts, Spokane, 1985—; mem. Cath. Bishop Fin. Council, Spokane, 1985—. Mem. IEEE (chmn. Spokane chpt.), Power Engring. Soc. (chmn. Spokane chpt.), NW Electric Light and Power Assn. (engring and ops. sect. chmn.). . Republican. Avocations: gardening, skiing, running. Office: Wash Water Power Co E 1141 Mission Ave Spokane WA 99202

RONCO, FRANK, JR., research forester; b. Pueblo, Colo., Sept. 23, 1826; s. Frank Jr. and Lucy Marie (Pace) R.; m. Louise Hall, Mar. 21, 1948; children: Tresa Ann, Michael James. BS, Colo. State U., 1951, MS, 1961; PhD, Duke U., 1968. Asst. dist. ranger U.S. Forest Service, Blairsden, Calif., 1953-56; research scientist U.S. Forest Service, Ft. Collins, Colo., 1957-76; project leader U.S. Forest Service, Flagstaff, Ariz., 1977—. Served with USN, 1944-47. Mem. Soc. Am. Foresters. Democrat. Roman Catholic. Lodge: Masons. Avocation: skiing. Home: 1500 Edgewood Flagstaff AZ 86001 Office: No Ariz U Forestry Scis Lab Rocky Mountain Forest Exptl Sta Flagstaff AZ 86001

RONDEAU, DORIS JEAN, entrepreneur, consultant; b. Winston-Salem, N.C., Nov. 25, 1941; d. John Delbert and Eldora Virginia (Klutz) Robinson; m. Robert Breen Corrente, Sept. 4, 1965 (div. 1970); m. Wilfrid Dolor Rondeau, June 3, 1972. Student Syracuse U., 1959-62, Fullerton Jr. Coll., 1974-75; BA in Philosophy, Calif. State U.-Fullerton, 1976, postgrad., 1976-80. Ordained to ministry The Spirit of Divine Love, 1974. Trust real estate clk. Security First Nat. Bank, Riverside, Calif., 1965-68; entertainer Talent, Inc., Hollywood, Calif., 1969-72; co-founder, dir. Spirit of Divine Love, Capistrano Beach, Calif., 1974—; pub., co-founder Passing Through, Inc., Capistrano Beach, 1983—; instr. Learning Activity, Anaheim, Calif., 1984—; chmn. bd., prin. D.J. Rondeau, Entrepreneur, Inc., Capistrano Beach, 1984—; co-founder, dir. Spiritual Positive Attitude, Inc., Moon In Pisces, Inc., Vibrations By Rondeau, Inc., Divine Consciousness, Expressed, Inc., Capistrano Beach. Author, editor: A Short Introduction To The Spirit of Divine Love, 1984; writer, producer, dir. performer spiritual vignettes for NBS Radio Network, KWVE-FM, 1982-84. Served with USAF, 1963-65. Recipient Pop Vocalist First Place award USAF Talent Show, 1964, Sigma chpt. Epsilon Delta Chi, 1985, others. Mem. Hamel Bus. Grads., Smithsonian Assocs., Am. Mgmt. Assn., Nat. Assn. Female Execs. Avocations: long-distance running, body fitness, arts and crafts, snorkeling, musical composition.

RONDEAU, RENÉ, wine importer; b. Holyoke, Mass., Oct. 26, 1948; s. Alfred Joseph and Irene (Brochu) R.; m. Fran Mitchell, June 13, 1976; 1 child, Christina Nicole. Student, U. Bordeaux, France, 1969; BA in French, U. Kans., 1970. Asst. mgr. Liquor Mart, Boulder, Colo., 1970-76; v.p. Draper & Esquin, San Francisco, 1976-80; pres. Woltner & Co., San Francisco, 1980-86; v.p. Draper and Esquin, San Francisco, 1986—. Contbr. numerous articles to wine pubs. Mem. Vintner's Club (cellarmaster 1978-82), Commanderie de Bontemps de Médoc, Jurade De Saint Emilion. Home: 120 Harbor Dr Corte Madera CA 94925 Office: Draper & Esquin 655 Davis St San Francisco CA 94111

RONDINELLI, ROBERT D., rehabilitative medicine physician, educator; b. Utica, N.Y., Apr. 24, 1949; m. Sandra J. O'Brien, Dec. 10, 1983; 1 child, Jamie Lindsey. BA in Anthropology cum laude, SUNY, Buffalo, 1971; MA in Phys. Anthropology, U. Ill, 1974, PhD in Phys. Anthropology, 1977, MD, 1980; MS in Rehab. Medicine, U. Wash., 1983. Diplomate Am. Bd. Phys. Medicine and Rehab.; lic. physician, Colo., Mass., Wash. Vis. lectr. anthropology U. Ill., Urbana, 1975-76; resident in phys. medicine, rehab. U. Wash. Hosp., Seattle, 1983; dir. admissions Rehab. Inst. attending physiatrists, Adult Inpatient Rehab. Unit, New Eng. Med. Ctr. Hosps., Inc., Boston, 1983-85; med. dir. Rehab. Unit, Phys. Medicine and Rehab. dept. Rose Med. Ctr., Denver, 1986—; chief rehab. medicine service Colo. VA Hosp., Denver, 1986—; asst. prof. rehab. medicine Med. Scis. Ctr., U. Colo., Denver, 1986—. Contbr. articles to profl. jours. Recipient Young Investigator award Phys. Medicine and Rehab. Edn. and Research Found., 1984. Mem. AAAS, Rocky Mountain Rehab. Soc., Am. Acad. Phys. Medicine and Rehab., Assn. Acad. Physiatrists, Am. Assn. Phys. Anthropologists, AAAS. Office: Rose Med Ctr Dept Rehab Medicine 4567 E 9th Ave Denver CO 80220

RONÉR, KENT HARRY, public administrator, CPA; b. Stockholm, Aug. 17, 1948; came to U.S., 1956; s. Harry and May (Johansson) R.; m. Janice Larsen, June 6, 1972; children: Lisa, Rachel, Janette, Michael, Allison, Angela. BA, U. Utah, 1973; M Pub. Adminstrn., Brigham Young U., 1987. Lic. health facility adminstr.; CPA. Internal auditor Zions Utah Bancorp., Salt Lake City, 1973-75; mgr. claims payment Dept. Social Services, Salt Lake City, 1975-79; dir. med. asst. Dept. Health, Salt Lake City, 1979—; pvt. practice acctg. Centerville, Utah, 1983—. Rep. del. Davis County, Utah, 1984-86. Recipient Incentive award Dept. Health, 1981. Mem. Utah Pub. Health Assn., Am. Inst. CPA's, Utah Assn. CPA's, Jaycees (sec., treas. 1985-86). Avocations: gardening, photography, reading early Christian writing, oil painting. Home: 239 W 1125 N Centerville UT 84014 Office: Dept Health UMAP 288 N 1460 W Salt Lake City UT 84116-0700

RONFELD, BERNETT LAURA, interior designer, educator; b. Nampa, Idaho, May 10, 1942; d. Carl Frederick and Hilma Marie (Lenz) R.; m. Cecil William Bondurant, Oct. 19, 1964 (div. 1974); children: Ghaery, Laura. Student, U. Idaho, 1960-61; AA, Bassist Coll., 1978; student, Oreg. Sch. Arts and Crafts, 1983-84, Portland State U., 1984. Asst. mgr. Gold's Ltd., Portland, Oreg., 1980; kitchen design Huggy Bear's Cupboards, Tigard, Oreg., 1981; instr. Bassist Coll., Portland, 1981-85, Pacific N.W. Coll. Art, Portland, 1986; prin. Bernette Ronfeld Design, Portland, 1986—; designer textile print Amanda Briggs Textile Studio, Portland, 1985. Mem. Oreg. Hist. Soc., Hist. Preservation League of Oreg. Lutheran. Avocations: crewel embroidery, study of history of interiors, drawing, painting, mixed media fiber art. Home and Office: Bernette Ronfeld Design 3205 SW Underwood Dr Portland OR 97225

RONHOVDE, VIRGINIA SEDMAN, political and civic worker; b. Missoula, Mont., Dec. 17, 1909; d. Oscar Alfred and Harriet Laura (Rankin) Sedman; student U. Mont., 1925-27; B.A., Wellesley Coll., 1929; M.A., Columbia U., 1930; postgrad., 1930-33; postgrad. (Columbia U. fellow) U. Berlin, 1933-35; m. Andreas G. Ronhovde, Apr. 7, 1936; children—Erik Sedman, Andrea Rankin, Nora Montana Ronhovde Hohenlohe, Kent McGregor. Instr. sociology and labor problems Rutgers U., 1935-36; salesman Boss and Phelps, Inc., Simmons Properties, Washington, 1954-76. Sec., League Rep. Women, Washington, 1969-71, bd. dirs., 1971-73, 75-77, 1st v.p., 1973-75; del. Nat. Fedn. Rep. Women Conv., Dallas, 1975; del., mem. permanent orgn. com. Rep. Nat. Conv., 1976; mem. cen. com. D.C. Rep. Com., 1976-80, 80-84, alt. nat. committeewoman, 1980-84; mem. Missoula Design Rev. Bd. Mem. Missoula Rep. Women's Club, Kappa Kappa Gamma. Episcopalian. Home: 600 Beverly Ave Missoula MT 59801

RONSMAN, WAYNE JOHN, insurance company executive; b. Milw., Jan. 21, 1938; s. Harry Martin and Martha Elizabeth (Popp) R.; student Marquette U., 1955-58, U. San Francisco, 1960-66; m. Joan P. Murphy-Mays, Nov. 30, 1974; children—Allison, Alanna; children by previous marriage—Rosemary, Harry, Martha. Accountant, Otis McAllister & Co., 1960-62; accountant, salesman of data processing Statis. Tabulation Corp., San Francisco, 1962-66; chief accountant, gen. mgr. Dillingham Bros. Ltd., Honolulu, 1966-67; ins. salesman Mut. Benefit Life Ins. Co., 1968-72; v.p. Brenno Assos., Honolulu, 1972-85; prin. Ronsman-Brenno, Anchorage, Alaska, 1980—; bd. dirs. Aloha Nat. Bank, Kihei, Maui. Mem. Gov's Task Force to Program Correctional Facilities Land, 1970-72; mem. State Bd. Paroles and Pardons, 1972-75; treas. Spl. Edn. Center of Oahu, 1969-78; pres. Ballet Alaska, 1986-87. Served with USMCR, 1958-60. Mem. Nat. Assn. Accountants, Am. Soc. C.L.U.s, Internat. Assn. Fin. Planning, Inst. Cert. Fin. Planners, Anchorage Estate Planning Council, Honolulu Assn. Life Underwriters (million dollar round table 1973—), Hawaii (state editor 1970-71, nat. dir. 1972-73), Kailua (pres. 1968-69) Jaycees, Honolulu Bd. Realtors, Anchorage C. of C., Small Bus. Mgmt. Assn., Nat. Assn. Securities Dealers, Kailua C. of C. (pres. 1977-78). Roman Catholic. Home: 3251 Eastwind Ct Anchorage AK 99516 Office: Ronsman-Brenno Alaska Anchorage AK 99516

RONSTADT, PETER, city official; b. Tucson, Feb. 1, 1942; s. Gilbert and Ruthmary (Copeman) R.; m. Jacqueline A. Castle, Nov. 26, 1946; children—Philip Charles, Melinda Marie. B.A., U. Ariz., 1969. Cert. peace officer, Ariz. Police officer including var. positions of patrolman, detective, sgt., lt., capt., maj. Tucson Police Dept., 1963-81, chief of police, 1981—. Bd. dirs. Salvation Army, Tucson. Mem. Ariz Acad., Police Exec. Research Forum, Nat. Exec. Inst., FBI Nat. Acad. Assocs., Police Mgmt. Assn., Ariz. Chiefs of Police Assn., Internat. Assn. Chiefs Police, Sigma Alpha Epsilon. Club: Centurions (Tucson). Lodge: Rotary. Office: Tucson Police Dept 270 S Stone PO Box 1071 Tucson AZ 85702 *

ROOF, RAYMOND BRADLEY, crystallographer, analytical chemist; b. Battle Creek, Mich., Mar. 3, 1929; s. Raymond Bradley and Dorothy Genieve (Crawford) R.; m. Shirley June Knoll, June 12, 1951; children: Steven K., Michael B. BSChemE, BSMetE, U. Mich., 1951, MSMetE, 1952, PhD in Mineralogy, 1955; grad., U.S. Army Command and Gen. Staff Inst., 1976. Sr. engr. Westinghouse, Pitts., 1955-57; mem. tech. staff Los Alamos (N.Mex.) Nat. Lab., 1957—; vis. prof. physics U. West Australia, Perth, 1971; adj. prof. chemistry U. N.Mex., Los Alamos, 1972. Contbr. numerous articles to profl. jours. Served to maj. C.E., USAR, 1951-77. Mem. Am. Crystallography Assn., Internat. Ctr. Diffraction Data, Sigma Xi. Avocations: golfing, bowling, reading. Home: 128 Bandelier Los Alamos NM 87544 Office: Los Alamos Nat Lab PO Box 1663 MS G740 Los Alamos NM 87544

ROOK, ALVIN GORDON, chemist; b. Tacoma, Feb. 15, 1923; s. Alvin Stenso and Borghild Sivertson; m. Dirkje Miedema Rook, Jan. 15, 1956; children: John Gordon, Karen Bee. BSChemE, U. Calif., Berkeley, 1949. Mgr. product devel. Pabco Paint Corp., Emeryville, Calif., 1949-73, Napko Corp., Fremont, Calif., 1973-80; tech. mgr. gen. metals lab. Fuller O'Brien, South San Francisco, 1980-83; mgr. western regional tech. services Nuodex Inc., Pleasanton, Calif., 1983—; chmn. tech. program Western Socs. for Coatings Tech. Symposium and Show, San Francisco, 1966, 75, 79, 83, 87, gen. chmn., 1970. Served as cpl. USAAF, 1942-45, ETO. Recipient Disting. Service award Harrison and Crossfield, 1970. Mem. Fedn. Socs. Paint Tech. (bd. dirs. 1966-83), Fedn. Socs. Coatings Tech. (pres. 1972-73, Cert. Appreciation, 1973), Golden Gate Soc. Coatings Tech. (pres. 1964-65, Disting. Service award 1970), Am. Chem. Soc., Alpha Chi Sigma. Republican. Club: Golden Gate Cinematographers (San Francisco) (pres. 1960-61). Avocations: violin and bow making, music, woodworking, photography, playing violin, viola and piano. Home: 33 Greenview Ct San Francisco CA 94131 Office: Nuodex Inc 5555 Sunol Blvd Pleasanton CA 94566

ROONEY, JOHN LOSSIN, telecommunication educator; b. Oak Park, Ill., Oct. 10, 1940; s. James J. and Dorothy W. (Lossin) R.; divorced; children: James, Jenny, Jeffrey. BS, U. So. Calif., 1965, MBA, 1966, MS, 1974. Mgr. Ralphs, Los Angeles, 1961-78; dir. FedMart, San Diego, 1978-83; asst. prof. tech. Nat. U., San Diego, 1983-85, chmn., prof. telecommunications, 1985. Home: 1844 Chickasaw Los Angeles CA 90041 Office: Nat U 6672 University Ave San Diego CA 92115

ROOP, JOSEPH MCLEOD, economist; b. Montgomery, Ala., Sept. 29, 1941; s. Joseph Ezra and Mae Elizabeth (McLeod) R.; B.S., Central Mo. State U., Warrensburg, 1963; Ph.D., Wash. State U., Pullman, 1973; m. Betty Jane Reed, Sept. 4, 1965; 1 dau., Elizabeth Rachael. Economist, Econ. Research Service, U.S. Dept. Agr., Washington, 1975-79; sr. economist Evans Econs., Inc., Washington, 1979-81; sr. research economist Battelle Pacific N.W. Labs., Richland, Wash., 1981—; instr. dept. econs. Wash. State U., 1969-71. Contbr. tech. articles to profl. jours. Served with U.S. Army, 1966-68. Dept. Agr. Coop. State Research Service research grantee, 1971-73. Mem. Am. Econ. Assn., Am. Agrl. Econs. Assn., Econometric Soc., Nat. Assn. Bus. Economists, Internat. Assn. Energy Economists. Home: 715 S Taft St Kennewick WA 99336 Office: PO Box 999 Richland WA 99352

ROORDA, ERVIN GLEN, minister; b. near Pella, Iowa, Sept. 21, 1938; s. Henry C. and Tena Henrietta (Van Roekel) R.; m. Andrea Marie Boat, June 8, 1960; children: Anne Marie, Mary Elizabeth, Lisa Jane, Jonathan Ervin. BA, Cen. Coll., 1960; BD, Western Theol. Sem., 1963; ThM, Princeton Theol. Sem., 1967; postgrad., San Francisco Theol. Sem. Pastor Cen. Ref. Ch., Muskegon, Mich., 1963-69; assoc. pastor Fremont Presbyn. Ch., Sacramento, 1969-76; sr. pastor Manito Presbyn. Ch., Spokane, Wash., 1976—; commr. to gen. assembly Presbyn. Ch., 1974,86; moderator Presbytery of the Inland Empire, 1985-87. Mem. Nat. Campaign Com. for Maj. Mission Fund. Democratic. Avocations: tennis, cross-country skiing, walking, bicycling, canoeing. Home: South 5418 Lloyd Rd Spokane WA 99223 Office: Manito Presbyn Ch East 402-29th Ave Spokane WA 99203

ROOS, ERIC EUGENE, plant physiologist; b. Charleroi, Pa., May 23, 1941; s. Carl F. and Isabelle (McPherson) R.; m. Lois Bonita Bruno, Aug. 24, 1964; children: Michael, Erin. BS, Waynesburg Coll., 1963; PhD, W.Va. U., 1967. Plant physiologist Nat. Seed Storage Lab, Agrl. Research Service of USDA, Ft. Collins, Colo., 1967—. Mem. Am. Soc. Agronomy, Am. Soc. Hort. Sci., Crop Sci. Soc. Am., Sigma Xi, Gamma Sigma Delta. Office: USDA Agrl Research Service Nat Seed Storage Lab Fort Collins CO 80523

ROOS, LEO, chemist; b. Amsterdam, The Netherlands, Nov. 10, 1937; came to U.S., 1950; s. Andries and Rozet (Agsterribbe) R.; m. Sonya Rosenfeld, Jan. 29, 1961; children: Joel, Lori, Robin. BS in Chemistry, CCNY, 1961; PhD in Chemistry, U. Cin., 1965. Sr. research chemist photoproducts E.I. Dupont de Nemours, Parlin, N.J., 1965-76; dir. research and devel. Xidex Corp., Sunnyvale, Calif., 1976-84; tech. mgr. Dynachem div. Morton-Thiokol, Tustin, Calif., 1984—. Contbr. articles to profl. jours.; patentee in field. Mem. zoning com., bldg. com. City of Tinton Falls, N.J., 1970-76, councilman, 1975-76; chmn. Tinton Falls Dems., 1970-76. Grantee NIH, 1960, USPHS, 1962-65. Mem. ACS (chmn. subcom. 1984—, grad. fellow 1961-62), Inst. Interconnecting Packaging Electronic Circuits (chmn. subcom. application dry film and liquid solder masks 1984—), Soc. Photog. Scientists and Engrs., Sigma Xi, Phi Lambda Upsilon. Jewish. Avocations: gardening, computers, sports. Home: 1404 Morning Side Dr Laguna Beach CA 92651 Office: Dynachem div Morton-Thiokol 2631 Michelle Dr Tustin CA 92680

ROOT, CHARLES JOSEPH, JR., finance executive, consultant; b. Pierre, S.D., July 26, 1940; s. Charles Joseph and Hazel Ann (Messenger) R.; 1 child, Roseann Marie Root. Student, San Francisco Jr. Coll., Coll. of Marin, La Salle Extension U., Am. Coll. Life Underwriters. Chartered fin. cons.; registered investment advisor. Estate planner Bankers Life Co., San Francisco, 1966-78; fin. planner Planned Estates Assocs., Corte Madera, Calif., 1978-81; mng. dir. Double Eagle Fin. Corp., Santa Rosa, Calif., 1981—, investment advisor, 1983—. V.p. Big Bros. of Am., San Rafael, Calif., 1976-80; treas. com. to elect William Filante, San Rafael, 1978, Community Health Ctrs. of Marin, Fairfax, Calif., 1982-83, Wellspring. Found., Philo, Calif., 1981-85; treas., bd. dirs. Ctr. for Attitudinal Healing, Tiburon, Calif. Served with USN, 1959-63. Mem. Internat. Assn. Fin. Planners, Nat. Assn. Life Underwriters, Marin County Assn. Life Underwriters (v.p. 1971-76, editor newsletter 1976-80). Republican. Roman Catholic. Lodge: Rotary (Paul Harris fellow 1980). Avocations: pilot, downhill skiing, scuba diving. Office: Double Eagle Fin Corp 2050 W Steele Ln Suite D1 PO Box 6265 Santa Rosa CA 95406

ROOT, JOHN WALTER, research scientist, microcomputer consultant; b. Kansas City, Mo., Oct. 5, 1935; s. Floyd Walter and Alice Elizabeth (duff) R.; m. Jessie Ann Cramer, Aug. 20, 1960; children: Cheryl Ann, Laura Lynn. BA in CHem., U. Kans., 1957, PhD in Chem., 1964; postgrad., UCLA, 1966. Asst. prof. chemistry U. Calif., Davis, 1966-70, assoc. prof., 1970-75, prof., 1975-85; mem. research staff Los Alamos (N.Mex.) Nat. Lab., 1985-87; pres. Los Alamos Computing Services, 1987—; cons. Los Alamos Computing Services, 1984—. Editor: Fluorine Containing Free Radicals: Kinetics and Dynamics of Reactions, 1978, Laboratory Microcomputers (n. Am.); co-editor Short-lived Radionuclides in Chemistry and Biology, 1981; contbg. editor Computers in Sci.; contbr. numerous articles to profl jours. Guggenheim fellow Brookhaven Nat. Lab., 1972-73, Assoc. Western Univs. fellow Los Alamos Nat. Lab., 1985, NSF fellow, 1960-63. Mem. Am. Chem. Soc., Am. Phys. Soc., Radiation Research Soc., Internat. Union Pure and Applied Chemistry, USENIX Assn., USR Group Assn., Sigma Xi. Home: 4568 Ridgeway Dr Los Alamos NM 87544 Office: Los Alamos Computing Services PO Box 986 Los Alamos NM 87544-0986

ROOTLAND, NANCY LYNN, education educator; b. Orange, N.J., Feb. 26, 1946; d. Joseph Daniel and Bridget Angelina (Marino) Sylvestro; m. Harvey Sheldon Rootland, Feb. 12, 1968; children: Matthew Anthony, Eugenia Marie. BS in Art and Early Child Edn., U. Wis., Superior, 1967; MA in Elem. Edn., Calif. State U., San Bernardino, 1974. Cert. tchr., Calif. Tchr. Rialto (Calif.) Schs., 1967-68, San Bernardino Schs., 1974-81, Colton (Calif.) Sch., 1981-82; instr. San Bernardino Valley Coll., 1983—. Mem. Calif. State U. Alumni Assn. San Bernardino. Avocation: illustrations for childrens books. Office: San Bernardino Valley Coll North Hall 701 S Mount Vernon Ave San Vernardino CA 92410

ROPCHAN, JIM R., research chemist, administrator; b. Leamington, Ont., Can., Apr. 14, 1950; s. William George and Katie (Rudyka) R. Degree in chem. tech., St. Clair Coll. Applied Arts and Tech., Ont., Can., 1971; BS with honors, Detroit Inst. Tech., 1972; PhD, U. Detroit, 1981. Quality control chemist Ford Motor Co., Windsor, Ont., 1973-76; postdoctoral scholar UCLA, 1981-85, assoc. investigator div. nuclear medicine and biophysics, 1983-85; dir. radiopharm. chemistry research VA Med. Ctr.-Wadsworth, Los Angeles, 1986—; part-time tchr. high sch. math. and sci., Windsor, Ont., 1977; part-time instr. organic chemistry Detroit Inst. Tech., 1977. Contbr. articles to profl. jours.; inventor lab. accessories. Recipient Outstanding Scholar award Detroit Inst. Tech., 1972; grantee UCLA, 1983. Fellow Am. Inst. Chemists; mem. AAAS, N.Y. Acad. Scis., Am. Chem. Soc. (divs. Carbohydrate, Organic, Medicinal Chemistry), Am. Heart Assn., The Cousteau Soc., The Planetary Soc. Avocations: hockey, sailing, tennis, biking. Office: VA Med Ctr-Wadsworth Bldg 500 Room 0091 Div Nuclear Medicine UltraSound Sawtelle and Wilshire Blvds Los Angeles CA 90073

ROPER, KATHERINE SUE, history educator; b. Houston, June 6, 1941; d. Edward and Margaret Ardell (Switzer) Gelus; m. Lawrence Wesley Larson, June 29, 1962 (div. June 1968); m. Stephen Howard Roper, Oct. 21, 1977. BA, U. Calif., Berkeley, 1962; MA, Stanford U., 1963, PhD, 1968. Instr. history San Jose (Calif.) State U., 1966-67; asst. prof. San Francisco State U., 1968-69; asst. prof. St. Mary's Coll., Moraga, Calif., 1969-73, assoc. prof., 1973-81, prof., 1981—, chmn. history dept., 1986—. Contbr. articles to profl. jours. Woodrow Wilson Found. fellow 1962, 65; NEH stipendee 1970. Mem. Am. Hist. Assn., German Studies Assn., Western Assn. Women Historians, Phi Beta Kappa. Home: 63 Abbott Dr Oakland CA 94611 Office: St Mary's Coll Dept History Moraga CA 94575

ROPER, RICK B., podiatrist; b. Soda Springs, Idaho, June 10, 1954; s. Frank B. and Karma (Cahoon) R.; m. Ila Smith, Oct. 29, 1976; children: Jamie Lyn, Shan Marie, Joshua Michael, Landon B. BS, Brigham Young U., 1979; D of Podiatric Medicine, Calif. Coll. Podiatric Medicine, 1983. Pvt. practice podiatry Albuquerque, 1984—. Contbr. articles to profl. jours. Mem. Pi Delta. Mormon. Office: Albuquerque Associated Podiatrists 121 Sycamore NE Albuquerque NM 87106

ROPER, WALTER WILLIAM, grain cooperative executive; b. American Falls, Idaho, Mar. 31, 1945; s. Allen Dwight and Evelyn Ruth (Schneider) R.; B.A. in Journalism, U. Idaho, 1968; m. Patrica Jo Morgan, June 20, 1970; children—Valorie Jo, Jason William, Alison Evon. Part time elevator operator, Power County Grain Growers, American Falls, summers 1963-68, bookkeeper, 1970, asst. mgr., 1971-76, mgr., sec., treas., 1976—; city, county news reporter, Moscow (Idaho) Daily Idahonian, 1968, Rexburg (Idaho) Standard and Jour., 1969, part time Power County Press, American Falls, 1970-71. Co-chmn. Concerned Citizens for Clean Growth, 1977. Mem. Grain Elevator and Processors Soc. (v.p. Intermountain chpt. 1982-83, pres. 1983-84), Idaho Feed and Grain Assn. (bd. dirs. Eastern dist. 1982—, bull. editor 1986—), Farmers Grain Coop. Mgrs. Orgn. (sec., treas. 1976-85, pres. 1985—). Democrat. Methodist. Clubs: American Falls Toastmasters (sec., treas. 1976-77), Tuesday Nighters Bowling League (pres. 1975-76, 76-77, sec., treas. 1977-78, 78-79). Home: Route 1 Box 90 Sunbeam Rd American Falls ID 83211 Office: 138 Elevator Ave American Falls ID 83211

ROPPOLO, DOMENICK DAN, computer company executive; b. Leechburg, Pa., Dec. 20, 1937; s. Nathan and Mary Roppolo; m. Geraldine Andolsek, Sept. 20, 1958 (div.); children: Christopher David, Marc Daniel; m. Barbara Willis, Aug. 28, 1976. BA, Ohio U., 1961, postgrad. Territory salesman Varityper div. A.M. Internat. Co., 1964-70; br. sales mgr. Varityper div. A.M. Internat. Co., Columbus, Ohio, 1970-73; dist. sales mgr. Varityper div. A.M. Internat. Co., Chgo., 1973-76; field ops. mgr. Varityper div. A.M. Internat. Co., Nashville, 1976-77, Anaheim, Calif., 1977-79; western regional sales mgr. Varityper div. A.M. Internat. Co., 1979-81, nat. sales mgr., 1981-83; regional sales mgr. Varityper div. A.M. Internat. Co., Newport Beach, Calif., 1983—. Republican. Roman Catholic. Avocation: jogging. Office: AM Internat 459 Promentory Pt W Newport Beach CA 92660

RORIPAUGH, ROBERT ALAN, author, educator; b. Oxnard, Calif., Aug. 26, 1930; s. Charles Clifford and Marion (Abbott) R.; m. Yoshiko Horikoshi, Aug. 6, 1956; 1 child, Lee Ann. Student, U. Tex., 1947-49; BA, U. Wyo., 1952, MA, 1953; postgrad., U. N.Mex., 1956-58. Instr. in English U. Wyo., Laramie, 1958-62, asst. prof., 1962-67, assoc. prof., 1967-72, prof. English, 1972—. Author: A Fever for Living, 1961, Honor Thy Father (Western Heritage award Nat. Cowboy Hall of Fame 1963), Learn to Love the Haze, 1976; asst. editor Writing at Wyo., 1958-65; editorial assoc. Sage, 1966-68; contbr. articles, stories, poems to pubs. Served with U.S. Army, 1953-56. Recipient Don D. Walker prize for best essay in Western Lit. Criticism pub. in 1982. Mem. Western Lit. Assn. (exec. council 1968-71), Authors League Am., Wilderness Soc., Phi Beta Kappa. Office: U Wyo Dept English Hoyt Hall Laramie WY 82071

ROSA, EUGENE A., sociologist, educator; b. Canandaigua, N.Y., Sept. 20, 1941; s. Louis Gustaldo and Flora Louise (Brevette) R.; m. Jody Ross, Sept. 7, 1985. BS, Rochester Inst. Tech., 1967; MA, Syracuse U., 1975, PhD, 1976. Research assoc., instr. Stanford U., 1976-78; from asst. to assoc. prof. Wash. State U., Pullman, 1978—; cons. Brookhaven Nat. Lab., Upton, N.Y., 1978—, Nuclear Regulatory Commn., Washington, 1978—. Editor: Public Reactions to Nuclear Power, 1984; contbr. articles to profl. jours. Served with USNR, 1963-71. Mem. Am. Sociol. Assn., AAAS, Am. Acad. Polit. and Social Scis., N.Y. Acad. Scis., Sigma Xi. Avocations: conceptual art constrns., skiing, collecting Mexican masks. Home: NE 1007 Alfred Ln Pullman WA 99163 Office: Wash State U Dept Sociology Pullman WA 99164

ROSA, RICHARD JOHN, mechanical engineer, educator; b. Detroit, Mar. 19, 1927; s. Richard Kellock and Beatrice (Boleau) R.; m. Jane Norton, Sept. 2, 1950 (div. 1970); children: Katrina, Richard Scott, Cynthia; m. Marion Hogarty, Sept. 16, 1978. BEP, Cornell U., 1953, PhD, 1956. Prin. research scientist AVCO Research Lab., Everett, Mass., 1956-75; prof. mech. engring. Mont. State U., Bozeman, 1975—; cons. in field; vis. scholar U. Sydney, Australia, 1977; vis. prof. Tokyo Inst. Tech., 1981; U.S. coordinator U.S.-Japan Coop. Program in Magnetohydrodynamics, 1982-86. Author: MHD Energy Conversion, 1968; contbr. articles to profl jours.; patentee in field. Served to lt. (j.g.) USN, 1945-49. NSF grantee, 1982—. Mem. IEEE (sr.), AIAA (sr., com. mem.), ASME, AAAS. Avocations: skiing, sailing, hiking.

ROSALAGON, JACQUELINE THERESA, architectural resource consultant; b. N.Y.C., July 28, 1931; d. Hyman and Anna I. (Russo) Gubman; m. Leon I. Rosenbluth, Sept. 10, 1955 (div. 1975); children: John Christopher, Charles Adrian, Eric James. BA, Hunter Coll., 1951; postgrad., Parson's Sch. Design, 1968. Asst. to Louis Harris Elmo Roper Co., N.Y.C., 1951-53; researcher Time mag., N.Y.C., 1953-55; interior designer Shepard Martin Assocs., N.Y.C., 1971-74; asst. to shop mgr. Craft and Folk Art mus., Los Angeles, 1976-79; cons. architectural resources Los Angeles, 1978—. Contbr. articles to mags.; designer patented jewel box. Avocations: ballet, jewelry crafting. Home and Office: 1798 Griffith Park Blvd Los Angeles CA 90026

ROSANDER, ARLYN CUSTER, mathematical statistician, management consultant; b. Mason County, Mich., Oct. 7, 1903; s. John Carl and Nellie May (Palmer) R.; m. Beatrice White, Aug. 26, 1933 (div.); children—Nancy Rosander Peck, Robert Richard Roger (dec.); m. 2d, Margaret Ruth Guest, Aug. 15, 1964. B.S., U. Mich. 1925; M.A., U. Wis., 1928; Ph.D., U. Chgo., 1933; postgrad. Dept. Agr., 1937-39. Research asst. U. Chgo., 1933-34; research fellow Gen. Edn. Bd. Tech. dir. Am. Youth Commn., Balt. and Washington, 1935-37; chief statistician urban study U.S. Bur. Labor Stats., Washington, 1937-39; sect. and br. chief War Prodn. Bd., Washington, 1940-45; chief statistician IRS, Washington, 1945-61; chief math. and stats. sect. ICC, Washington, 1961-69; cons. Pres.'s Commn. on Fed. Stats., Washington, 1970-71; cons., Loveland, Colo.; lectr. stats. George Washington U., 1946-52. Recipient Civilian War Service award War Prodn. Bd., 1945; Spl. Performance award Dept. Treasury, 1961. Fellow AAAS, Am. Soc. Quality Control (25 yr. honor award 1980, Howard Jones Meml. award 1984); mem. Am. Statis. Assn. Author: Elementary Principles of Statistics, 1951; Statistical Quality Control in Tax Operations, IRS, 1958; Case Studies in Sample Design, 1977; Application of Quality Control to Service Industries, 1985, Washington Story 1985. Home and Office: 4330 N Franklin Ave Loveland CO 80538

ROSANOFF, ANDREA, chemistry educator; b. Ft. Worth, Nov. 18, 1944; d. William Ross Rosanoff and Margaret Rita (Miller) Dorr; m. Donald Riddick Croper, Dec. 31, 1966 (div. Aug. 1985); children: Jason, Dorea Meridan. AB, U. Calif., Berkeley, 1966, MS, 1979, PhD, 1982. Med. lab. analyst Solano Labs., Berkeley, 1967-68; tchr. sci. Anna Head Sch., Oakland, Calif., 1968-70; tchr. sci. Head-Royce Sch., Oakland, 1974-76, dir. computer programming, 1984—; research asst. U. Calif., Berkeley, 1977-82; dir. research and devel. Pacific Consolidated Mgmt. Inc., San Jose, Calif., 1983-84; sr. chem. info. specialist Dialog Info. Services, Palo Alto, Calif., 1987—; cons. nutrition Shaklee Corp., San Francisco, 1980, nutrition edn. Dept. Edn. State of Calif., Sacramento, 1980, Calif. Dairy Council, Sacramento, 1981, Pacific Consolidated Mgmt. Inc., San Jose, Calif., 1984—. Contbr. articles to profl. jours. Elder St. John's Presbyn. Ch., Berkeley, 1983-85, deacon, 1983-85, moderator of deacons, 1984-85. Grantee Feedstuff Processing Co., 1977, Chancellor's Patent Fund, Faculty Engrichment Head-Royce Sch., 1985—. Mem. Am. Chem. Soc., Nat. Assn. Corrosion Engrs., West Coast Nutrition Anthropology Network. Democrat. Avocations: piano, singing, writing. Home: 202 Santa Rosa Ave Oakland CA 94610 Office: Dialog Info Services Palo Alto CA 94304

ROSCHER, WILLIAM GLEN, financial planner; b. Kansas City, Mo., Mar. 18, 1929; s. Richard Lee and Clara Belle (Bryant) R.; m. Jo Ann Ethel Middlesteadt, Apr. 3, 1954; children—Glenn, Karen, Mary Jo. B.S., U. Md., 1968; M.S.A., George Washington U., 1973. Cert. fin. planner. Served as enlisted man, U.S. Army, 1949-52, commd. 2d lt., 1952, advanced through grades to col., 1973, ret., 1974; v.p. Corp. Assistance, Inc., Scottsdale, Ariz., 1970-79, pres., 1979—; mem. faculty Scottsdale Community Coll., 1979—. Contbr. articles to Nat. Tax Shelter Digest. Decorated Legion of Merit with oak leaf cluster, Bronze Star, Air medal. Mem. Internat. Assn. Fin. Planning (past officer and bd. dirs.), Inst. Cert. Fin. Planners. Democrat. Methodist. Lodge: Rotary (treas. Paradise Valley, Ariz. 1983—). Home: 9836 N 60th Pl Scottsdale AZ 85253 Office: Corp Assistance Inc 8070 E Morgan Trail Scottsdale AZ 85258

ROSCOE, STANLEY NELSON, psychologist, aeronautical engineer; b. Eureka, Calif., Nov. 4, 1920; s. Stanley Boughton and Martha Emma (Beer) R.; m. Margaret Hazel Brookins, Dec. 21, 1948 (dec.); m. Elizabeth Frances Lage, Mar. 12, 1977 (dec.); children: Lee Marin Roscoe Bragg, Jack, Catherine Marie. AB in Speech and English, Humboldt State U., 1943; postgrad., U. Calif., Berkeley, 1942, 46; MA in Psychology, U. Ill., 1947, PhD in Psychology, 1950. Cert. psychologist, Calif. Research asst. U. Ill., Champaign, 1946-50, research assoc., 1950-51, asst. prof., 1951-52; assoc. dir. Inst. Aviation, head aviation research lab., Champaign, 1969-75, prof. psychology and aero. and astronautical engring., 1969-79, prof. emeritus, 1979—; prof. N.Mex. State U., Las Cruces, 1979-86, prof. emeritus, 1986—; with Hughes Aircraft Co., Culver City, Calif., 1952-69, 75-77, dept. mgr., 1962-69, sr. scientist, 1975-77; tech. adviser, cons. in field; pres. Illiana Aviation Scis. Ltd., Las Cruces, N.Mex., 1976—. Author: Aviation Psychology, 1980; contbr. numerous articles to profl. jours.; editor: Aviation Research Monographs, 1971-72. Served to 1st lt. AC, U.S. Army, 1943-46. Fellow Human Factors Soc. (pres. 1960-61, Jerome H. Ely award 1968, 73, Alexander C. Williams award 1973, Paul M. Fitts award 1974), Soc. Engring. Psychologists, Am. Psychol. Assn. (Franklin V. Taylor award 1976), Royal Aero. Soc. (Gt. Brit.); mem. IEEE, AIAA, Inst. Navigation, Assn. Aviation Psychologists (Ann. Career award 1978), Sigma Xi, Phi Kappa Phi, Phi Sigma, Chi Sigma Epsilon. Patentee, inventor in field. Office: ILLIANA Aviation Scis Ltd Las Cruces NM 88003-5095

ROSE, DAVID, painter-printmaker, artist-reporter, educator; b. Malden, Mass., Mar. 10, 1910; s. Isaac and Dora (Susman) R.; m. Ida Claire Shapiro, July 13, 1945 (dec.); children—Marsha Annette, Lisa Joan. B.S. in Art Edn., Mass. Coll. Art, 1934; student Sch. of Mus. Fine Arts, Boston, 1932, Herman Struck, Haifa, 1933, Chouinard Art Inst., Los Angeles, 1938-40, Art. Ctr. Coll. of Design, 1940-42. Exhibited group shows Pa. Acad. Fine Arts, Bklyn. Mus., Los Angeles County Mus. Art, Calif. State Mus., Los Angeles; represented in permanent collections including Skirball Mus., Los Angeles, Israel Mus., Jerusalem, Mus. Modern Art, Haifa; layout artist Walt Disney Studios, 1936-40; art. dir. Erwin Wasey, advt. agy., Los Angeles, from 1945, then Mogge-Privett, advt. agy., Los Angeles, Cunningham & Walsh, advt. agy., Los Angeles, until 1957; art dir. film and TV, Warner Bros., Burbank, Calif., Universal Pictures, Burbank, KCEF Community TV; graphic designer, illustrator-court room sketch artist NBC, Burbank; ind. artist-reporter, court trials and news events for TV, newspapers and mags. including Cable Network News, ABC World News, NBC Nightly News, Newsweek, Time, Los Angeles Herald Examiner, Los Angeles Daily News, Chgo. Tribune, AP, UPI, San Francisco Examiner, Jerusalem Post; mem. faculty continuing edn. dept. Otis Art Inst., Parsons Sch. Design; lectr. various univs. and art socs. Mem. graphic arts council Los Angeles County Mus. Art. Served with Signal Corps, U.S. Army, 1943-45. Recipient award Army Pictorial Service, 1945; 2 medals Art Dirs. Club, Los Angeles; others. Mem. Artists Equity Assn., Artists for Edn., Soc. Illustrators, Los Angeles Printmaking Soc.

ROSE, DAVID JAY, chemist, consultant; b. Gibbon, Nebr., Mar. 30, 1960; s. Richard Lee and Margene Kay (Myers) R. BS, Kearney State Coll., 1982; MS, U. Utah, 1986. Cons. Caliber Coating, Draper, Utah, 1984-85, dir. research and devel., 1985—. Contbr. articles on polymer research. Office: Caliber Coatings 892 E 12300S Draper UT 84020

ROSE, ERNEST DANIEL, communicatons and film producer, educator, university administrator; b. Pitts., May 23, 1926; s. Goodman A. and Alta Sara (Gilberg) R.; m. Bernice H. Gerson, Sept. 5, 1954; children: Abby S., Adam J., Jason W. Student, Pa. State U., 1944-45; BA, UCLA, 1949, MS, 1951; PhD, Stanford U., 1964. From asst. prof. to assoc. prof. theater arts UCLA, 1954-61; prof., head film program, Radio-TV-Film Dept. Temple U., Phila., 1968-77; dean Coll. Liberal Arts Calif. State Poly. U., Pomona, 1977-82; prof. film studies Pitzer Coll., Claremont, Calif., 1983-86; dean Coll. Fine Arts U. N.Mex., Albuquerque, 1986—; cons., lectr., UNESCO, U.S. Infor. Agy, U.S. State Dept., others, 1951—; head film and TV prodn. Statewide U. Calif. Media Ctr., Berkeley, 1963-68; cons. Dirs. Guild of Am., Hollywood, Calif., 1985, to Australian Prime Minister Australian Film and TV Sch., Sydney, 1973. Author, dir., producer, editor, cinematographer more than 200 documentary films, U.S. and abroad; co-author: Telecommunications: Issues and Choice for Soc., 2d rev. edit., 1986, World Film and TV Study Resources; producer-dir., head film unit U.S. Embassy, Tehran, Iran, 1951-53. Commr. Gov's Council on Arts, Pa., 1974; pres. Claremont Community Sch. Mus., 1982-84, Los Angeles Film Council, 1957-58. Ford fellow, 1959-60; Fulbright scholar Communications Inst. Hebrew U., 1973, sr. exchange prof. Vienna Acad. Mus. and Dramatic Arts, Fulbright Found., 1972-73. Mem. Univ. Film and TV Found. (trustee 1968—, Disting. Life Membership award 1985), Centre Internat. de Liaison des Ecoles de Cinema et de Television (treas., mem. governing bur. 1968-76), Fulbright Assn. (co-founder, v.p. 1976-86), Calif. Council of Fine Arts Deans (pres. 1979-80). Democrat. Jewish. Office: U NMex Office of Dean Coll Fine Arts Albuquerque NM 87131

ROSE, GREGORY MANCEL, neurobiologist; b. Eugene, Oreg., Feb. 3, 1953; s. Mancel Lee and Ilione (Schenk) R.; m. Kathleen Ann Frye, June 30, 1979; 1 child, Julian Mancel. BS cum laude, U. Calif., Irvine, 1975, PhD, 1980. Research fellow M.P.I. for Psychiatry, Munich, 1976; research assoc. Miescher Labor, M.P.I., Tuebingen, Republic of Germany, 1980-81; regular fellow dept. pharmacology U. Colo. Health Sci. Ctr., Denver, 1981-84, asst. prof., 1984—; research biologist VA Med. Ctr., Denver, 1981—. Contbr. articles to sci. jours. Grantee VA Research Service, 1984, 86. Mem. AAAS, AM. Aging Assn., Soc. Neurosci. Democrat. Episcopalian. Avocation: fine woodworking. Office: VA Med Ctr Research Service 1055 Clermont St Box 151 Denver CO 80220

ROSE, I. NELSON, law educator; b. Los Angeles, May 23, 1950; s. Bernard and Helen Mae (Nelson) R.; m. Audree Dee Agbayani, Sept. 25, 1982. B.A., UCLA, 1973; J.D., Harvard U., 1979. Bar: Hawaii 1979, Calif. 1980, U.S. Dist. Ct. Hawaii 1979, U.S. Ct. Appeals (9th cir.) 1980. Pvt. practice, Honolulu, 1979-82; asst. prof. law Whittier Coll., Los Angeles, 1982-85, assoc. prof. 1985—; cons. legal gaming. Author: Gambling and the Law, 1986; also articles in profl. jours. Founder, counsel Hawaii Lions Eye Bank, Honolulu, 1979-82; v.p., counsel Calif. Council on Compulsive Gambling. Mem. ABA, Calif. State Bar Assn., Hawaii Bar Assn., Internat. Assn. Gaming Attys. Democrat. Jewish. Home: 1839 Colby Ave #1 Los Angeles CA 90025 Office: Whittier Coll Sch Law 5353 W 3d St Los Angeles CA 90020

ROSE, JEFFREY STEVEN, cardiologist; b. Albany, N.Y., May 21, 1952; s. Leonard Bertram and Beatrice (Kartus) R.; m. Margaret Ann Young, Jan. 16, 1982. BS in Biology, Portland State U., 1974; MD, U. Oreg., 1978. Diplomate Am. Bd. Internal Medicine, Am. Bd. Cardiovascular Diseases. Resident in medicine U. Mich., Ann Arbor, 1978-81; fellow in cardiology U. So. Calif., Los Angeles, 1982-85, research fellow in electrophysiology, 1982-85; dir. electrophysiology lab. Providence Hosp., Everett, Wash., 1985—; ptnr. Everett Cardiology Assocs., 1985—. Contbr. articles to profl. jours. Recipient Upjohn Achievement award U. Oreg., 1978, Lang Med. Pubs. award U. Oreg., 1976. Mem. AMA, Am. Coll. Cardiology, Am. Heart Assn., Council on Clin. Cardiology. Home: 6701 139th Pl SW Edmonds WA 98020

ROSE, JOHN ELWYN, polymer chemist, consultant; b. Van Nuys, Calif., July 12, 1949; s. Richard Elwyn and Melba Cecilia (Fink) R.; m. Elaine Marie HIllman, May 11, 1968 (div. Dec. 1982); children: Ellen Marie, Michelle Renee; m. Lynette Susan Pierce, Apr. 30, 1983. AA in Electronics, USAF Tech. Sch., 1969; BS in Chemistry, San Jose State U., 1978. Research chemist SRI Internat., Menlo Park, Calif., 1979-83; sr. polymer technologist optics div. CooperVision, Inc., San Jose, Calif., 1983-85; pvt. practice polymer technologist, cons. San Jose, 1985—; cons. Polymer Labs., Inc., Stow, Ohio, 1986—. Contbr. articles to profl. jours. Served with USAF, 1969-76. Mem. Am. Chem. Soc., Soc. Plastics Engrs. (chmn. 1981-83, treas. 1984-85), No. Pharm. Discussion Group, Profl. Assn. Diving Instrs. (open water scuba instr.), Clark AFB Scuba Diving Club (life), N.Am. Thermal Analysis Soc. Democrat. Avocations: orchids, cycling, photography.

ROSE, MARK ALLEN, humanities educator; b. N.Y.C., Aug. 4, 1939; s. Sydney Aaron and Rose (Shapiro) R.; divorced; 1 son, Edward Gordon; m. Rachel Warner Liebes, 1979; 1 stepson, Jonah Liebes. A.B. summa cum laude, Princeton, 1961; B.Litt., Merton Coll., Oxford (Eng.) U., 1963; Ph.D., Harvard, 1967. From instr. to asso. prof. English Yale, 1967-74; prof. English U. Ill., Urbana, 1974-77, U. Calif., Santa Barbara, 1977—. Author: Heroic Love, 1968; fiction Golding's Tale, 1972; Shakespearean Design, 1972, Spenser's Art, 1975, Alien Encounters, 1981; Editor: Twentieth Century Views of Science Fiction, 1976, Twentieth Century Interpretations of Antony and Cleopatra, 1977, (with Slusser and Guffey) Bridges to Science Fiction, 1980. Woodrow Wilson fellow, 1961; Henry fellow, 1961-62; Dexter fellow, 1966; Morse fellow, 1970-71; Nat. Endowment for Humanities fellow, 1979-80. Mem. Modern Lang. Assn., Renaissance Soc. Am., Shakespeare Soc. Am., Phi Beta Kappa. Home: 859 Jimeno Rd Santa Barbara CA 93103

ROSE, NORMAN CARL, chemistry educator; b. Seattle, Mar. 15, 1929; s. Sidney Albert and Rose Marie (Matzner) R.; m. Myra Natalie Rosenthal, Aug. 13, 1954; children: Mark Craig, Bruce Wayne, Paul David, Nancy Cathryn. BS, U. Calif., Berkeley, 1950; PhD, U. Kans., 1956. From asst. to assoc. prof. chemistry Tex. A&M U., College Station, 1956-66; assoc. prof. Portland (Oreg.) State U., 1966-72, prof., 1972—, asst. dean coll. liberal arts and scis., 1979—. Author: Organic Chemistry, 1966. Served to 1st lt. U.S. Army, 1951-53, Korea. Recipient Mosser award Oreg. State System Higher Edn. Mem. Am. Chem. Soc. Office: Portland State Univ Dept of Chemistry Portland OR 97207

ROSE, ROBERT R., JR., lawyer, former state justice; b. Evanston, Ill., Nov. 1, 1915; s. Robert R. and Eleanor B. R.; m. Kathryn Lorraine Warner, June 14, 1948; children: Robert R. III, Cynthia Ann. LL.B., U. Wyo., 1941. Bar: Wyo. bar 1941. Atty. Dept. Justice, 1941; with UNRRA, China; asst. sec. Dept. Interior, 1951-52; sr. partner firm Rose, Spence, Dobos and Duncan, Casper, Wyo., 1968-75; justice Wyo. Supreme Ct., 1975-85, chief justice, 1981-82; assoc. Spence, Moriarity and Schuster, Cheyenne, Wyo., 1985—; organizer, past pres., chmn. bd. Title Guaranty Co. Wyo.; faculty Nat. Coll. Criminal Def., 1977-83, Western Trial Advocacy Inst., 1981—; vis. prof. trial practice U. Wyo. Coll. Law, 1985-86; Milward Simpson chmn. in polit. sci. U. Wyo., 1985-86. Author legal articles. Past chmn. fund drive Casper Community Chest, Am. Cancer Soc.; mem. Wyo. Ho. of Reps., 1949-51; mayor of, Casper, 1950-51; past trustee Casper Coll. Served with USAAF, World War II. Recipient Jud. Achievement award Nat. Assn. Criminal Def. Lawyers, 1983. Mem. Am. Law Inst. Episcopalian. Address: PO Box 1006 Cheyenne WY 82003

ROSE, ROBERT STANLEY, lawyer; b. Chgo., Dec. 23, 1921; s. Olin Stanley and Opal Beatrice (McCall) R.; m. Vivian Marguerite Rickert, Nov. 5, 1945 (div. Jan. 1970); children: Kathleen Sharon, Kevin Patrick. BBA, Loyola U., Los Angeles, 1952; JD, Loyola U., 1955; cert. oil and gas law, So. Meth. U., 1957. Bar: Calif. Dep. atty. gen. State Calif., Los Angeles, 1955-56; dir., gen. counsel McCulloch Oil Corp., Los Angeles, 1957-62; dir., v.p., gen. counsel Occidental Petroleum Co., Los Angeles, 1962-67; sole practice Los Angeles, 1969—; bd. dirs. Jefferson Lake Petrochems. of Can. View Engring., Simi Valley, Calif., 1964-67. Bd. dirs. Santa Monica (Calif.) Hosp. and Med. Ctr. Found., 1983—; bd. regents Loyola Marymount U., 1983—. Served with USN, 1940-46. Recipient Oxford Gold Medal Debate award Loyola U., 1952. Mem. ABA, AAAS, Calif. State Bar Assn., Am. Mgmt. Assn., Los Angeles Bar Assn., Century City Bar Assn., Am. Judicature Soc., Am. Petroleum Inst., Calif. Gas Producers Assn. (v.p. 1961-63), Alpha Delta Gamma, Phi Alpha Delta. Democrat. Roman Catholic. Club: Bel Air Country (Los Angeles). Avocations: boating, hunting, flying, golf. Home: 4050 Via Dolce Suite 143 Marina Del Rey CA 90292 Office: 10100 Santa Monica Blvd Suite 210 Los Angeles CA 90067

ROSE, TED, graphic designer; b. Milw., Aug. 13, 1940; s. Francis John and Ann (Voelkel) R.; m. Polly Towers, July 1, 1967; children: Jesse, Molly. BFA, U. Ill., 1962. Artist, illustrator, book designer Kalmbach Pubs. Co., Milw., 1959-63; cartographer City of Santa Fe, 1967-69, art dir., 1971-76; art dir. Eberline Inst Co., Santa Fe, 1969-71; graphic designer Hod Carriers Ink, Santa Fe, 1971—; art dir. Stereophile Mag., Santa Fe, 1985-86; watercolor artist, 1954-60, 80—; graphic cons. Los Alamos (N.Mex.) Nat. Lab., 1978-80; instr. color graphics Santa Fe Community Coll., 1984-85. Designer, artist (calendar) The Chili Line, 1984; photographer N.Am. Steam Locomotives, 1973; photo exhibits, 1973, 76. Graphic designer Santa Fe Rape Crisis Ctr., 1983, Santa Fe Symphony, 1985—, Santa Fe Dance Found., 1987—. Served with U.S. Army, 1963-65, Vietnam. Mem. No. N.Mex. Advt. Fedn. (pres. 1987, graphic design awards 1982, 83, 84, 86, print advt. awards 1982, 83, 84, 86), Am. Advt. Fedn. (print advt. awards 1982, 85), Santa Fe C. of C. Democrat. Club: Santa Fe Soccer. Avocation: photography. Office: Hod Carriers Ink PO Box 266 Santa Fe NM 87504

ROSEBROCK, DONALD WAYNE, reporter; b. St. Louis, May 3, 1950; s. Ralph Henry and Grace Amanda Ruth (Homier) R.; m. Brenda Joyce Fassel, Oct. 6, 1979. B, U. Mo., 1972. Reporter Sun City (Ariz.) News-Sun, 1972-75; editor then mng. editor Wood River Jour., Sun Valley, Idaho, 1975-79; reporter, editor Ogden (Utah) Standard Examiner, 1979-84; reporter, bur. chief Deseret News, Salt Lake City, 1984—. Mem. Kanganark Mushers (pres. 1984—). Avocations: raising, showing and racing Siberian Huskies. Home: 493 S 1100 W PO Box 441 Farmington UT 84025 Office: Deseret News 30 E 1st S Salt Lake City UT 84110

ROSEHNAL, MARY ANN, educational administrator; b. Bklyn., July 25, 1943; d. Frank Joseph and Mary Anna (Corso) R.; 1 son, Scott Stoddart. BA in Sociology, San Francisco State U., 1968; M in Sch. Bus. Adminstrn., No. Ariz. U., 1985. Lic. substitute tchr., Ariz.; lic. vocat. nurse, Calif.; cert. sch. bus. mgr., Ariz. Deliquency counselor, Calif., 1969-73; office mgr. Nurses Central Registry, Sun City, Ariz., 1973-75; bus. mgr. Nadaburg sch. dist., Wittmann, Ariz., 1975-78, Morristown (Ariz.) sch. dist., 1978—; served on 1st Assessment Handbook editing task force, Fair Employment Practices Handbook task force, 1979-80. Clk. Morristown sch. bd., 1974-76; pres. Morristown PTA, 1977-78; sec. Wickenburg area bd., 1979; bd. dirs. Future Frontiers, 1979-81; rep. HUD block grant adv. com., 1979-85; active Wickenburg Friends of Music, 1984—; sec. of bd. dirs., 1986—. Mem. Ariz. Assn. Sch. Bus. Ofcls. (fin. dir. bd. dirs.), Assn. Sch. Bus. Ofcls. U.S. and Can., Assn. Govt. Accts. Roman Catholic. Club: Morristown Federated Women's. Columnist Wickenburg Sun, 1975—. Office: PO Box 98 Morristown AZ 85342

ROSELL, SHARON LYNN, physics and chemistry educator; b. Wichita, Kans., Jan. 6, 1948; d. John Edward and Mildred Cleona (Binder) R. BA, Loretto Heights Coll., 1970; postgrad., Marshall U., 1973; MS, Ind. U., 1977; postgrad., U. Wash., 1985—. Cert. profl. educator, Wash. Assoc. instr. Ind. U., Bloomington, 1973-74; instr. Ft. Steilacoom (Wash.) Community Coll., 1976-78, 81, Olympic Coll., Bremerton, Wash., 1977-78; instr. physics, math. and chemistry Tacoma (Wash.) Community Coll., 1979—; instr. physics and chemistry Green River Community Coll., Auburn, Wash., 1983-86. Mem. Am. Assn. Physics Tchrs. (rep. com. on physics 2 yr. coll. 1986—), Am. Chem. Soc. Democrat. Roman Catholic. Avocations: leading scripture discussion groups, reading, writing poetry, needlework. Home: 1204 N 7th Apt A Tacoma WA 98403 Office: Tacoma Community Coll 5900 S 12th Tacoma WA 98465

ROSEMAN, CYRIL, health planning and administration educator; b. Phila., Aug. 6, 1936; s. Samuel Isadore and Iryne Edith (Carson) R.; m. Rosalind May Schwartz, Aug. 25, 1957 (div. 1968); children: Laurie, Bonnie. BA, Temple U., 1957; PhD, Princeton U., 1963. Instr. dept. polit. sci. Swarthmore (Pa.) Coll., 1961-62; dir. urban studies San Francisco State U., 1963-68; assoc. prof. sch. pub. health U. Calif., Berkeley, 1970-73; exec. dir. PACT Region VIII Health Planning Ctr., Dnever, 1977-78; assoc. prof. sch. pub. health U. Tex., Houston, 1978-79, U. Hawaii, Honolulu, 1979—; sr. policy advisor Senate Heatlh Commn. of Hawaii Legis., 1980, House Health Commn., 1984; cons. HEW, San Francisco, Phila. and Rockville, Md., 1971-77; advisor Inst. Personal and Career Devel., Cen. Mich. U., Mount Pleasant, 1984—. Author: Introduction to Political Analysis, 1965; contbr. articles to profl. jours. WHO fellow, New Zealand and Australia, 1985. Mem. Am. Pub. Health Assn. Democrat. Jewish. Avocations: photography, videography, poetry. Office: 25480 Hatton Rd Carmel CA 93923

ROSEN, ALBERT LEONARD, professional baseball team executive; b. Spartanburg, S.C., Feb. 29, 1924; s. Louis and Rose (Levine) R.; m. Rita Kallman, July 24, 1971; children: Robert, Andrew, James, Gail, David. B.B.A., U. Miami, 1947. Profl. baseball player Cleve. Indians Baseball Team, 1947-56; with Bache & Co., Cleve., 1955-73, 1st Continental Investment Corp., Cleve., 1973-75; br. office mgr. Caesars Palace, 1975-77; pres. N.Y. Yankees, N.Y.C., 1977-79; with Bally's Park Pl., Atlantic City, N.J., 1979-80; pres., gen. mgr. Houston Astros Baseball, 1980-85, San Francisco Giants Baseball Club, 1985—. Served to lt. (j.g.) USNR, 1943-46, PTO. Named Most Valuable Player Am. League, 1953. Jewish. Club: Westwood Country. Office: care San Francisco Giants Candlestick Park San Francisco CA 94124 *

ROSEN, LOUIS, physicist; b. N.Y.C., June 10, 1918; s. Jacob and Rose (Lipionski) R.; m. Mary Terry, Sept. 4, 1941; 1 son, Terry Leon. B.A., U. Ala., 1939, M.S., 1941; Ph.D., Pa. State U., 1944; D.Sc. (hon.), U. N.Mex., 1979, U. Colo., 1987. Instr. physics U. Ala., 1941-44, Pa. State U., 1943-44; mem. staff Los Alamos Sci. Lab., 1944—, group leader nuclear plate lab., 1949-65, alt. div. leader exptl. physics div., 1962-65, dir. meson physics facility, 1965-85, div. leader medium energy physics div., 1965-86, sr. lab. fellow, 1985—; Sesquicentennial hon. prof. U. Ala., 1981. Author papers in nuclear sci. and applications of particle accelerators.; bd. editors: Applications of Nuclear Physics. Mem. Los Alamos Town Planning Bd., 1962-64; mem. Gov.'s Com. on Tech. Excellence in N.Mex.; mem. Nat. Acad. Panel on Nuclear Sci., chmn. sub-panel on accelerators; mem. N.Mex. Cancer Control Bd., 1976-80 , v.p., 1979-81; mem. panel on future of nuclear sci. Nat. Research Council of Nat. Acad. Scis., 1976; mem. panel on intl. arrangements for orbiting space telescope NRC-Nat. Acad. Scis., 1976; mem. U.S.A.-USSR Joint Coordinating Com. on Fundamental Properties of Matter, 1976—; Co-chmn. Los Alamos Vols. for Stevenson, 1956; Democratic candidate for county commr., 1962; bd. dirs. Los Alamos Med. Center, 1977-83, chmn., 1983; bd. gov's Tel Aviv U., 1986. Recipient E.O. Lawrence award AEC, 1963; Golden Plate award Am. Acad. Achievement, 1964; N.Mex. Disting. Public Service award, 1978; named Citizen of Year, N.Mex. Realtors Assn., 1973; Guggenheim fellow, 1959-60; alumni fellow Pa. State U., 1978. Fellow Am. Phys. Soc. (mem. council 1975-78, chmn. panel on public affairs 1980, chmn. div. nuclear physics 1985), AAAS. Louis Rosen prize established in his honor by bd. dirs. Meson Faculty Users Group, 1984. Home: 1170 41st St Los Alamos NM 87544 Office: PO Box 1663 Los Alamos NM 87545

ROSEN, MARTIN JACK, lawyer; b. Los Angeles, Sept. 9, 1931; s. Irving and Sylvia (Savad) R.; B.A., UCLA, 1953; J.D., U. Calif.-Berkeley, 1956; m. Joan D. Meyersieck, Oct. 22, 1954; children—Dirk Rosen, Marika. Bar: Calif. 1957. Pvt. practice, Merced, Calif., 1960-62, San Francisco, 1962-82; mem. Silver, Rosen, Fischer & Stecher, P.C., San Francisco, 1964—. Pres. Trust for Pub. Land, 1979—. Served with USAF, 1958-60. Fellow internat. legal studies U. Calif. Law Sch./Inst. Social Studies, The Hague, 1956-57.

ROSEN, MICHAEL JAY, foundation executive, public relations officer; b. Wausau, Wis., June 19, 1954; s. Irving and Evie (Cohen) R.; m. Sharon Howard, Aug. 18, 1985. Photographer Sta. WAOW-TV, Wausau, Wis., 1971-73; ptnr. Concept Films, Wausau, 1973-75; project coordinator Wausau Area Performing Arts Found., Wausau, 1975-78; sr. producer spl. programs Sta. KIRO-TV, Seattle, 1978-83; pub. relations dir. Wash. affiliate Am. Heart Assn., Seattle, 1983—; mem. vis. com. sch. pharmacy U. Wash., Seattle, 1985—. Mem. exec. com. Childhaven, Seattle, 1984—, Leadership Tomorrow Class of 87', pub. relations com. Washington Centennial; adv. Gov.'s Council on Fitness. Recipient Iris award 1983, 7 awards Sigma Delta Chi, 1979-83, 4 awards Internat. Film and TV Festival of N.Y., 1980-83; nominated for Emmy award 1982, regional Emmy award 1983, 85. Mem. Nat. Press Photographers Assn., Nat. Acad. TV Arts and Scis. (Emmy nomination, 2 regional Emmy awards), Internat. Assn. Bus. Communicators, Wash. Press Assn. Office: Am Heart Assn Wash Affiliate 4414 Woodland Park Ave N Seattle WA 98103

ROSEN, MOISHE, religious organization administrator; b. Kansas City, Mo., Apr. 12, 1932; s. Ben and Rose (Baker) R.; m. Ceil Starr, Aug. 18, 1950; children: Lyn Rosen Bond, Ruth. Diploma, Northeastern Bible Coll., 1957; DD, Western Conservative Bapt. Sem., 1986. Ordained to ministry Bapt. Ch., 1957. Missionary Am. Bd. Missions to the Jews, N.Y.C., 1956; minister in charge Beth Sar Shalom Am. Bd. Missions to the Jews, Los Angeles, 1957-67; dir. recruiting and tng. Am. Bd. Missions to the Jews,

N.Y.C., 1967-70; founder, chmn. Jews for Jesus Movement, San Francisco, 1970-73, 78—, San Rafael, Calif., 1973-78; speaker in field. Author: Sayings of Chairman Moishe, 1972, Jews for Jesus, 1974, Share the New Life with a Jew, 1976, Christ in the Passover, 1977, Y'shua, The Jewish Way to Say Jesus, 1982. Trustee Western Conservative Internat. Bapt. Sem., Portland, Oreg., 1979-85, Bibl. Internat. Council on Bibl. Inerrancy, Oakland, Calif., 1980—. Office: Jews for Jesus 60 Haight St San Francisco CA 94102

ROSEN, PHILIP TERRY, history educator; b. Syracuse, N.Y., Mar. 22, 1946; s. Theodore and Martha (Mason) R.; m. Jackie McGillivray, May 2, 1970; 1 child, Philip Terry Mason. Student, U. Philippines, 1966-67; BA, Sterling Coll., 1968; postgrad., Universidad Indsl. de Santander, Colombia, 1970; MA, Emporia State U., 1970; PhD, WAyne State U., 1975. Instr. Am. History Wayne State U., Detroit, 1970-73; fellow Smithsonian Inst., Washington, 1974-75; asst. dir. council continuing edn. Marygrove Coll., Detroit, 1977-78, dean div. continuing edn., 1978-80; dean Erie (Pa.) Met. Coll., 1980-84; dir. continuing edn., assoc. prof. history U. Alaska, Anchorage, 1984—. Author: The Treaty Navy, 1919-1937, 1979, Peace and War: U.S. Naval Policies, 1776-1979, 1979, The Modern Stentors: Radio Broadcasters and the Federal Government, 1920-34, 1980. Gannon U. Liberty Fund fellow, 1977. Mem. Am. Hist. Assn., So. Hist. Assn., Orgn. Am. Historians, Council Advancement Exptl. Learning. Address: 3211 Providence Dr Anchorage AK 99508

ROSEN, ROBERT STANLEY, career military officer; b. N.Y.C., Mar. 23, 1936; s. George F. and Mildred S. (Leibowitch) R.; m. Annette Teresa Conley, Dec. 22, 1963; children: Laura Ellen, George William. BA, Columbia Coll., 1958; MS, George Washington U., Washington, 1971, Naval Postgrad. Sch., 1975. Commd. ensign USN, N.Y.C., 1958; advanced through grades to capt. USN, Washington, 1980; budget dir., commdr. submarine forces Atlantic USN, Norfolk, Va., 1975-79; Dept. Navy liason to U.S. Sen. and House Appropriations com. USN, Washington, 1979-81; comptroller USN, Norfolk Naval Base, 1981-84; commdg. officer Naval mag. Lualualie(Hawaii) Naval Weapons Sta. USN, 1984—. Contbr. articles to profl. jours. Mem. Am. Soc. Milit. Comptrollers (pres. Tidewater, Va. chpt. 1983-84, Best Budget Officer Nat. award 1979, Comptroller Nat. award 1984). Lodge: Rotary Internat. Avocation: golf. Home: Qtrs A 66th St Waianae HI 96792-4304 Office: Commdg Officer Naval Mag Lualualei Bldg #1 Lualualei HI 96792-4301

ROSENAU, JAMES NATHAN, political scientist, author; b. Philadelphia, Nov. 25, 1924; s. Walter Nathan and Fanny Fox (Baum) R.; m. Norah McCarthy, Aug. 5, 1955 (dec. July 5, 1974); 1 child, Heidi Margaret. A.B., Bard Coll., 1948; A.M., Johns Hopkins U., 1949; Ph.D., Princeton U., 1957. Instr. Rutgers U., New Brunswick, N.J., 1949-54; asst. prof. Rutgers U., New Brunswick, 1954-60, assoc. prof., 1960-62, prof., 1962-70; prof. Ohio State U., Columbus, 1970-73; prof. polit. sci. U. So. Calif., Los Angeles, 1973—; research asst. Inst. Advanced Study, Princeton, N.J., 1953-54; research assoc. Princeton U., N.J., 1960-70; dir. Sch. Internat. Relations U. So. Calif., Los Angeles, 1976-79; dir. Inst. for Transnat. Studies, U. Southern Calif., Los Angeles, 1973—. Author: Public Opinion and Foreign Policy, 1961, National Leadership and Foreign Policy, 1963, The Dramas of Politics, 1973, Citizenship Between Elections, 1974, The Scientific Study of Foreign Policy, 1980; co-author: American Leaders in World Affairs, 1984. Trustee Bard Coll., Annandale-on-Hudson, 1968-70. Served with U.S. Army, 1942-46. Ford Found. fellow, 1958-59; research grantee NSF, 1970, 73, 78, 79, 83; Guggenheim fellow, 1987—; recipient stipend NEH, 1976. Mem. Internat. Studies Assn. (pres. 1984-85), Am. Polit. Sci. Assn. (mem. exec. council 1975-77). Democrat. Home: 1700 San Remo Dr Pacific Palisades CA 90272 Office: Inst Transnat Studies U So Calif University Park Los Angeles CA 90089

ROSENBERG, BARR MARVIN, economist; b. Berkeley, Calif., Nov. 13, 1942; s. Marvin and Dorothy Fraser R.; m. June Diane Weinstock, Sept. 8, 1966. B.A., U. Calif., Berkeley, 1963; M.S. in Econs, London Sch. Econs., 1965; Ph.D., Harvard U., 1968. Asst. prof. Univ. Calif., Berkeley, 1968-74; asso. prof. Univ. Calif., 1974-77, prof. bus. adminstrn., 1978-83, dir. program in fin., 1979-81; prin. Barr Rosenberg Assos., Berkeley, Calif., 1975-81; mng. partner Barr Rosenberg Assos., 1981-83, cons., 1983-86; mng. ptnr. Rosenberg Instnl. Equity Mgmt., Orinda, Calif., 1985—. Marshall scholar, U.K., 1963-65. Mem. Am. Econ. Soc., Econometric Soc., Am. Statis. Assn., Am. Fin. Assn., Western Fin. Assn. Office: Rosenberg Instnl Equity Mgmt 4 Orinda Way Suite 200E Orinda CA 94563

ROSENBERG, DAN YALE, plant pathologist; b. Stockton, Calif., Jan. 8, 1922; s. Meyer and Bertha (Naliboff) R.; A.A., Stockton Jr. Coll., 1942; A.B., Coll. Pacific, 1949; M.S., U. Calif. at Davis, 1952; m. Marilyn Kohn, Dec. 5, 1954; 1 son, Morton Karl. Jr. plant pathologist Calif. Dept. Agr., Riverside, 1952-55, asst. plant pathologist, 1955-59, asso. plant pathologist, 1959-60, pathologist IV, 1960-63, program supr., 1963-71, chief exclusion and detection, div. plant industry, 1971-76, chief nursery and seed services div. plant industry, 1976-82, spl. asst. div. plant industry, 1982—; pres. Health, Inc., 1972-73; cons. in field; mem. Gov.'s Interagy. Task Force on Biotech., 1986—; bd. dirs. Health Inc., Sacramento, 1967, pres., 1971-72, 79-81, 81-83. Served with AUS, 1942-46; ETO. Mem. Am. Phytopath. Soc. (fgn. and regulatory com. 1975—, grape diseases sect. 1977-79, grape pests sect. 1979-84), Calif. State Employees Assn. (pres. 1967-69). Contbr. articles to profl. jours. Home: 2328 Swarthmore Dr Sacramento CA 95825 Office: 1220 N St Sacramento CA 95814

ROSENBERG, LESTER ALAN, mechanical engineer; b. Bklyn., Sept. 6, 1946; s. Paul and Jeanette (Eisdorfer) R.; m. Lynne Tyler Kelly, June 18, 1977. BME, CCNY, 1968. Registered profl. engr. V.p. Syska & Hennessy, N.Y.C., 1968-84, Daniel, Mann, Johnson & Mendenhall, Los Angeles, 1984—; lectr. engring. Los Angeles Community Coll., 1981-83. Mem. ASHRAE, Am. Soc. Hosp. Engrs., Dean's Council UCLA Sch. Architecture, Los Angeles C. of C., Los Angeles Hdqrs. Assn. Republican. Jewish. Avocations: skiing, cabinetry. Home: 2229 23d St Santa Monica CA 90405 Office: Daniel Mann Johnson & Mendenhall 3250 Wilshire Blvd Los Angeles CA 90010

ROSENBERG, PAUL HERSCHEL, lawyer; b. Des Moines, July 14, 1951; s. Raymond and Gene Louise (Bowman) R. BA, Drake U., 1975, JD, 1978. Bar: Iowa 1978, U.S. Dist. Ct. (so. dist.) Iowa 1978, U.S. Ct. Appeals (8th cir.) 1978. Assoc. Rosenberg, Rosenberg & Reade, Des Moines, 1978-82; ptnr. Rosenberg Law Firm and predecessor firm Rosenberg, Rosenberg & Reade, Des Moines, 1982—. Mem. ABA, Iowa Bar Assn. (criminal law com.), Polk County Bar Assn., Assn. Trial Lawyers Am., Iowa Trial Lawyers Assn. Democrat. Jewish. Office: Rosenberg Law Firm 505 5th Ave Suite 1010 Des Moines IA 50309

ROSENBERG, RICHARD MORRIS, banker; b. Fall River, Mass., Apr. 21, 1930; s. Charles and Betty (Peck) R.; m. Barbara K. Cohen, Oct. 21, 1956; children: Michael, Peter. B.S., Suffolk U., 1952; M.B.A., Golden Gate Coll., 1962, LL.B., 1966. Publicity asst. Crocker-Anglo Bank, San Francisco, 1959-62; banking services officer Wells Fargo Bank, N.A., San Francisco, 1962-65; asst. v.p. Wells Fargo Bank, N.A., 1965-68, v.p. mktg. dept., 1968, v.p., dir. mktg., 1969, sr. v.p. mktg. and advt. div., 1970-75, exec. v.p., 1975—, vice chmn., 1980-83; vice chmn. Crocker Nat. Corp., 1983-85; pres., chief operating officer Seafirst Corp., 1986-87, also dir.; pres., chief operating officer Seattle First Nat. Bank, 1985-87; vice chmn. bd. BankAmerica Corp., San Francisco, 1987—; dir. Saga Corp., Am. Magnetics Corp.; chmn. Mastercard, Internat. Bd. dirs. Marin Ecumenical Housing Assn.; bd. regents Sch. Bank Mktg., U. Colo. Served from ensign to lt. USNR, 1953-59. Mem. Am. Bankers Assn. (exec. com. mktg./savs. div.), Bank Mktg. Assn. (dir.), State Bar Calif. Jewish. Clubs: Ranier, Hillcrest. Office: BankAmerica Corp Bank of Am Ctr San Francisco CA 94104 *

ROSENBERG, SANDERS DAVID, propulsion system chemist; b. N.Y.C., Dec. 21, 1926; s. Philip and Rose (Levine) R.; m. Rita Bernice Strauss, June 30, 1946; children—Nathan Lynn, Robert Bruce. A.B. in Chemistry with honors, Middlebury Coll., 1948; Ph.D. in Chemistry, Iowa State U., 1952. Postdoctoral research fellow Harvard U., Cambridge, Mass., 1953—; research chemist M & T Chems., Rahway, N.J., 1953-57; scientist Aerojet Tech Systems, Sacramento, 1958—. Contbr. numerous articles on chemistry and space propulsion systems to profl. jours. Patentee in field. Served with USN, 1943-46. Recipient NASA Service award, 1977, 86. Fellow AIAA (assoc.). Home: 628 Commons Dr Sacramento CA 95825 Office: Aerojet TechSystems Co PO Box 13222 Sacramento CA 95813

ROSENBLATT, GERD MATTHEW, chemist; b. Leipzig, Fed. Republic Germany, July 6, 1933; came to U.S., 1935, naturalized, 1940; s. Edgar Fritz and Herta (Fisher) R.; m. Nancy Ann Kaltreider, June 29, 1957 (dec. Jan. 1982); children: Rachel, Paul. BA, Swarthmore Coll., 1955; PhD, Princeton U., 1960. Chemist Lawrence Radiation Lab., Univ. Calif., 1960-63, cons., guest scientist, 1968-84; from asst. to assoc. prof. chemistry Pa. State U., University Park, 1963-70, prof., 1970-81; assoc. div. leader Los Alamos (N.Mex.) Nat. Lab., 1981-82, chemistry div. leader, 1982-85; dep. dir. Lawrence Berkeley (Calif.) Lab., 1985—; lectr. U. Calif., Berkeley, 1962-63; vis. prof. Vrije Univ. Brussels, 1973; vis. fellow Southampton U., 1980, King's Coll., Cambridge, 1980; adj. prof. chemistry U. N.Mex., 1981-85; cons. Aerospace Corp., 1979-85, Solar Energy Research Inst., 1980-81, Xerox Corp., 1977-78, Hooker Chem. Co., 1976-78, Los Alamos Nat. Lab, 1978, mem. external adv. com. Ctr. for Materials Sci., 1985—, mem. rev. com. chemistry div., 1985—; mem. rev. com. for chem. engring. div. Argonne Univ. Assn. , 1974-80, chmn. 1977-78; mem. rev. com. for chem. sci. Lawrence Berkeley Lab. , 1984; chmn. rev. com. for chem. and material sci. Lawrence Livermore Nat. Lab. , 1984—; mem. bd. advs. Combustion Research Facility, Sandia Nat. Lab., 1985—; mem. bd. advs. research and devel. div. Lockheed Missiles & Space Co., 1985—; mem. U.S. Nat. Com., Com. on Data for Sci. and Tech., 1986—, Internat. Union of Pure and Applied Chemistry, 1986—. Editor: (jour.) Progress in Solid State Chemistry, 1977—; mem. editorial bd. High Temperature Sci., 1979—; contbr. articles to profl. jours. Du Pont grad. fellow, Princeton U., 1957-58; fellow Solvay Inst., 1973, U.S. Research Council, 1980. Fellow AAAS; mem. Am. Chem. Soc., Am. Physical Soc., Nat. Research Council(chmn. high temperature sci. and tech. com. 1977-79, 84-85, mem. panel on exploration of materials sci. and tech. for nat. welfare, 1986—, mem. commn. on materials sci. and engring., 1986—). Home: 1177 Miller Ave Berkeley CA 94708 Office: Lawrence Berkeley Lab Cyclotron Rd Berkeley CA 94720

ROSENBLATT, MURRAY, mathematics educator; b. N.Y.C., Sept. 7, 1926; s. Hyman and Esther R.; m. Adylin Lipson, 1949; children—Karin, Daniel. B.S., CCNY, 1946; M.S., Cornell U., 1947, Ph.D. in Math., 1949. Asst. prof. statistics U. Chgo., 1950-55; assoc. prof. math. Ind. U., 1956-59; prof. probability and statistics Brown U., 1959-64; prof. math. U. Calif., San Diego, 1964—; vis. fellow U. Stockholm, 1953; vis. asst. prof. Columbia U., 1955; guest scientist Brookhaven Nat. Lab., 1959; vis. fellow U. Coll., London, 1965-66, Imperial Coll. and Univ. Coll., London, 1972-73, Australian Nat. U., 1976, 79; overseas fellow Churchill Coll., Cambridge U., Eng., 1979; Wald lectr., 1970; vis. scholar Stanford U., 1982. Author: (with U. Grenander) Statistical Analysis of Stationary Time Series, 1957, Random Processes, 1962, (2d edit), 1974; editor: Time Series Analyis, 1963, Markov Processes, Structure and Asymptotic Behavior, 1971, Studies in Probability Theory, 1978, The North Holland Series in Probability and Statistics, 1980, Birkhauser Boston Inc Progress in Probability and Statistics Series, 1980; mem. editorial bd.: Jour. Multivariate Analysis, Ind. Jour. Mathematics. Recipient Bronze medal U. Helsinki, 1978; Guggenheim fellow, 1965-66, 71-72. Fellow Inst. Math Statistics, AAAS; mem. Internat. Statis. Inst., Nat. Acad. Scis. Office: Dept Math Univ Calif at San Diego La Jolla CA 92093

ROSENBLUM, DALE MARK, podiatrist; b. Akron, Ohio, Aug. 1, 1947; s. Irvin Robert and Frances (Taras) R.; student U. Akron, 1965-67; D.P.M., Ohio Coll. Podiatric Medicine, 1971; diplomate Am. Bd. Podiatric Surgery; children—Rachel, Reegen, Shifra. Postgrad. tng. assoc. Calif. Coll. Podiatric Medicine, San Francisco, 1971-72; chief podiatry, mem. surg. com. Riverview Hosp., Santa Ana, Calif., 1977-82; mem. credentials com., chmn. podiatric medicine div. med. staff, podiatric residency edn. com. Good Samaritan Hosp., Anaheim, Calif., 1977-83; mem. attending staff So. Calif. Podiatric Med Center, Los Angeles, 1978-83; mem. clin. staff Baja Foot Center, Mexacali, Mexico, 1978—. Mem. Pub. Edn. and Info. Com., 1979; chmn. Foot Health Week, 1978, 79; active March of Dimes Walkathon, Civic Foot Health Screenings. Fellow Am. Coll. Foot Orthopedists; mem. Am. Podiatry Assn., Am. Assn. Hosp. Podiatrists, Acad. Ambulatory Foot Surgery, Am. Coll. Foot Surgeons, Calif. Podiatry Assn., Orange County Podiatry Assn. Democrat. Jewish. Club: Toastmasters Internat. (treas. 1983). Office: Baja Foot Ctr 704 N Harbor Blvd Fullerton CA 92632

ROSENBLUM, RICHARD MARK, utility executive; b. N.Y.C., Apr. 28, 1950; s. Victor Sigmund and Julia (Kessler) R.; B.S., M.S., Rensselaer Poly. Inst., Troy, N.Y., 1972-73; m. Michele E. Cartier, Aug. 30, 1979; children—Gialisa, Jeremy Scott. Startup engr. Combustion Engring. Inc., Windsor, Conn., 1973-76; engr. So. Calif. Edison Co., Rosemead, 1976-82, project mgr. San Onofre Nuclear Generating Sta., 1982-83, tech. mgr., 1983-84, nuclear safety mgr., 1984-86, mgr. quality assurance, 1986—. N.Y. State Regents scholar, 1968-73; registered profl. engr., Calif. Mem. Am. Nuclear Soc. (STD com.), Electric Power Research Inst. (nuclear safety analysis com.). Office: 2244 Walnut Grove Rosemead CA 91770

ROSENBLUM, STEPHEN SAUL, physicist, researcher; b. Bklyn., Sept. 26, 1942; s. Leon Abraham and Gertrude (Kantrowitz) R.; m. Ellen Patricia McLaughlin, Jan. 5, 1972; children: Andrew Edward, Leah Frances. AB in Chemistry, Columbia U., 1963; PhD in Chemistry, U. Calif., Berkeley, 1969. Research fellow in physics Calif. Inst. Tech., Pasadena, 1969-70; guest lectr. physics Freie U., Berlin, Federal Republic of Germany, 1970-72; vis. staff mem. Hahn-Meitner Institut, Berlin, Federal Republic of Germany, 1972-74; postdoctoral Los Alamos (N.Mex.) Nat. Lab., 1974-77; staff scientist Lawrence Berkeley Lab., 1977-85; sr. engr. Varian Assocs., Palo Alto, Calif., 1985—. Contbr. articles on physics to profl. jours.; patentee in field. Mem. Fedn. Am. Scientists, ACLU, Am. Phys. Soc., Am. Chem. Soc., IEEE, Sierra Club, Phi Beta Kappa. Avocations: gardening, sailing. Office: Varian Assocs 611 Hansen Way Mail Stop K307 Palo Alto CA 94303

ROSENBOOM, DAVID, composer, performer; b. Fairfield, Iowa, 1947. Student, U. Ill., NYU. Rockefeller fellow SUNY, Buffalo, 1967-68; artistic coordinator Electric Circus, N.Y.C., 1968-69; assoc. prof. fine arts and interdisciplinary studies York U., Toronto, Can., 1970-79, founder Elec. Media Studios, founder Lab. of Exptl. Aesthetics, coordinator div. interdisciplinary studies; assoc. prof. music, dept. head Mills Coll., Oakland, Calif., 1979—, dir. Ctr. Contemporary Music; tchr. San Francisco Art Inst., 1981-85; lectr. on music writing, producing, composing; co-founder Aesthetic Research Ctr., Can., 1971-79; developer of intermedia systems techs., computer langs. for music and edn., other tech. mus. accomplishments; organizer various performing groups. Home and Office: David Rosenboom Pub 235 Greenbank Piedmont CA 94611 Office: Mills Coll Ctr Contemporary Music Oakland CA 94613

ROSENDIN, RAYMOND JOSEPH, electrical contracting company executive; b. San Jose, Calif., Feb. 14, 1929; s. Moses Louis and Bertha C. (Pinedo) R.; m. Jeanette Marie Bucher, June 30, 1951 (dec. Feb. 1967); children: Mark R., Patricia A., Debra M., Cynthia C., David R.; m. Nancy Ann Burke, July 6, 1984; children: Raymond M., Callie R. Student engring., San Jose State U., 1947-48; B.S.E.E., Heald's Engring. Coll., San Francisco, 1950. Vice pres. Rosendin Electric, Inc., San Jose, Calif., 1953-59, exec. v.p., 1959-75, pres., 1975—; former dir. Community Bank, San Jose. Bd. fellows U. Santa Clara, Calif., 1966—, pres. bd., 1969-72, bd. regents, 1972-82; bd. dirs. United Way, Santa Clara, 1970-74, O'Connor's Hosp., San Jose, 1979—, Community Hosp., Los Gatos, Calif., 1968-74. Recipient Man of Yr. award Santa Clara Valley Youth Village, 1963, Optimist of Yr. award Optimist Club, San Jose, 1970. Mem. C. of C. Greater San Jose (past dir.), Nat. Elec. Contractors Assn. (past pres., gov., dir.). Republican. Roman Catholic. Club: St. Claire (San Jose). Avocation: boating. Office: Rosendin Electric Inc 880 N Mabury Rd San Jose CA 95133

ROSENFELD, MICHAEL D., banker; b. St. Louis, Sept. 5, 1943; s. David C. and Bee (Gale) R. B.S. in Bus. Adminstrn., Washington U., St. Louis, 1965; M.B.A., St. Louis U., 1971. Analyst commodities Clayton Brokerage Co., Mo., 1966-68; investment officer Merc. Trust Co., St. Louis, 1968-75; asst. v.p., investment officer Hawaiian Trust Co., Ltd., Honolulu, 1975-80; v.p. investments Wells Fargo Bank, Newport Beach, Calif., 1980-84; v.p. pvt. banking Bank of Am., Newport Beach, 1984-85; v.p. Winrich Captial Mgmt., Lake Forest, Calif., 1986—; instr. Am. Inst. Banking, Honolulu, 1979-80. Mem. investment com. Harbor Area Youth Found., Newport Beach and Irvine, Calif., 1982—. Fellow Fin. Analysts Fedn.; mem. St. Louis Soc. Fin. Analysts (chmn. membership 1973-74), Investment Soc. Hawaii, Orange County Soc. Investment Mgrs., (bd. dirs., pres. 1985—), Am. Inst. Banking, Alpha Kappa Psi. Jewish. Home: 12 Springacre Irvine CA 92714 Office: Winrich Capital Mgmt 23702 Birtcher Dr Lake Forest CA 92630

ROSENFIELD, STANLEY WILLIAM, communications company executive; b. Oklahoma City, Jan. 1, 1939; s. Stanley W. and Bertha (Angelman) R.; m. Casey Zekley, Sept. 5, 1971; children: Chase Alexandra, Zachary Houston. BBA, U. Okla., 1962. Agt. trainee Creative Mgmt., Los Angeles, 1963-64; exec. v.p. Jay Bernstein Pub. Relations, Los Angeles, 1964-75; prin. Stan Rosenfield Pub. Relations, Los Angeles, 1975—; instr. entertainment and pub. relations U. So. Calif., Los Angeles, 1984—. Mem. Motion Picture Acad. Arts and Scis., TV Acad. Arts and Scis., Italian-Am. Lawyers Assn. So. Calif. (hon.). Jewish. Club: Variety of So. Calif. (bd. dirs. 1975—). Office: Stan Rosenfield Pub Relations 9701 Wilshire Blvd Beverly Hills CA 90212

ROSENGRANT, BARRY LEE, commercial real estate consultant, hospital director; b. Des Moines, Feb. 1, 1933. BS in Bus. and Psychology, Tarkio Coll., 1955; postgrad., U. Minn., 1960=61. Div. mgr. Abbott Labs., Chgo., 1960-62, Knoll Internat., Dallas and St. Louis, 1962-65; exec. v.p. Group Artec, Los Angeles, 1965-70, pres., 1970-77; pres. Metroscape Corp., Los Angeles, 1977—; co-founder At Choice, Los Angeles, 1983; chmn. Century Hosp., Los Angeles, 1985—. Lodge: Rotary. Home: 2705 Krim Dr Los Angeles CA 90064 Office: Metroscape Corp 11726 San Vicente Blvd Los Angeles CA 90049

ROSENHEIMER, LILIA, home health care administrator; b. Rome, Feb. 14, 1938; came to U.S., 1960; d. Emanuele Guido and Ninetta (Fano) Cesana; m. Michael Oscar Rosenheimer, July 15, 1962 (div. May 1977); children: David, Joan, Edward. BS, U. Reading, Eng., 1960; MS, Va. Poly. Inst. and State U., 1962; RN, Merritt Coll., 1973; pub. health nurse, U. Calif., San Francisco, 1977. Staff nurse Herrick Hosp., Berkeley, Calif., 1973-78; case mgr. Home Health and Counseling, Richmond, Calif., 1978-80; asst. supr. Home Health and Counseling, Oakland, Calif., 1980-81, supr., 1981—; pres. So. Alameda (Calif.) County Com. on Aging, 1984—; mem. long term care com. Calif. Assn. Health Services At Home, Sacramento, 1986; dir. Vesper Home Care Leandro, Calif., 1984—. Grantee Korea Found., San Francisco, 1985, Walker and Evelyn Haas, San Francisco, 1985, Mary and Steven Birch, Del., 1984. Democrat. Jewish. Avocations: remodelling, gardening, photography, hiking. Office: Vesper Home Care 311 MacArthur Blvd San Leandro CA 94577

ROSENKILDE, CARL EDWARD, physicist; b. Yakima, Wash., Mar. 16, 1937; s. Elmer Edward and Doris Edith (Fitzgerald) R.; m. Bernadine Doris Blumenstine, June 22, 1963; children: Karen Louise, Paul Eric. B.S. in Physics, Wash. State Coll., 1959; M.S. in Physics, U. Chgo., 1960, Ph.D. in Physics, 1966. Postdoctoral fellow Argonne (Ill.) Nat. Lab., 1966-68; asst. prof. math. NYU, 1968-70; asst. prof. physics Kans. State U., Manhattan, 1970-76, assoc. prof., 1976-79; physicist Lawrence Livermore (Calif.) Nat. Lab., 1979—, cons., 1974-79. Contbr. articles on physics to profl. jours. Woodrow Wilson fellow, 1959, 60. Mem. Am. Phys. Soc., Am. Astron. Soc., Soc. for Indsl. and Applied Math., Am. Geophys. Union, Acoustical Soc. Am., Phi Beta Kappa, Phi Kappa Phi, Phi Eta Sigma, Sigma Xi. Republican. Presbyterian. Club: Tubists Universal Brotherhood Assn. (TUBA). Current Work: Nonlinear wave propagation in complex media. Subspecialties: Theoretical physics; Fluid dynamics.

ROSENMAN, SETH LEWIS, architect; b. N.Y.C., Nov. 10, 1954; s. Richard L. and Rhoda J. (Gottesman) R. B in Environ. Design, U. Colo., 1976, MArch, 1978. Registered architect, Colo. Architect Johnson, Hopson & Ptnrs., Denver, 1978-82; assoc. Anderson, Mason & Dale, Denver, 1982-85, JH/P Architecture, Interior Design & Planning, Denver, 1985—; guest critic U. Colo. Coll. Design & Planning, Denver, 1983—. Coach youth soccer Aurora (Colo.) YMCA, 1979—. Mem. AIA (chmn. urban design com. 1987; Service award 1984). Avocations: photography, downhill skiing, hot air ballooning.

ROSENSTEIN, ADAM MARK, mfg. co. exec.; b. Los Angeles, Mar. 26, 1957; s. Allen B. and Betty R. (Lebell) R. Dir. info. services Pioneer Magnetics, Santa Monica, Calif., 1978—. Mem. Am. Prodn. and Inventory Control Soc. Office: Pioneer Magnetics 1745 Berkeley St Santa Monica CA 90404

ROSENSTEIN, ALLEN BERTRAM, electrical engineering educator; b. Balt., Aug. 25, 1920; s. Morton and Mary (Epstein) R.; m. Betty Lebell; children: Jerry Tyler, Lisa Nan, Adam Mark. B.S. with high distinction, U. Ariz., 1940; M.S., UCLA, 1950, Ph.D., 1958. Elec. engr. Consol. Vultee Aircraft, San Diego, 1940-41; sr. elec. engr. Lockheed Aircraft Corp., Burbank, Calif., 1941-42; chief plant engr. Utility Fan Corp., Los Angeles, 1942-44; prof. engring. UCLA, 1946—; founder, chmn. bd. Inet, Inc., 1947-53, cons. engr., 1954—; founder, chmn. bd. dirs. Pioneer Magnetics, Inc., Pioneer Research Inc., Anadex Instruments Inc.; dir. Internat. Transformer Co., Inc., Fgn. Resource Services; cons. ednl. planning UNESCO, Venezuela, 1974-76. Author: (with others) Engineering Communications, 1965, A Study of a Profession and Professional Education, 1968; contbr. articles to profl. jours.; patentee in field. Bd. dirs. Vista Hill Psychiat. Found. Served with USNR, 1944-46. Fellow IEEE; mem., Am. Soc. Engring. Edn., N.Y. Acad. Scis., AAAS, Sigma Xi, Phi Kappa Phi, Delta Phi Sigma, Tau Beta Pi. Home: 314 S Rockingham St Los Angeles CA 90049

ROSENSTEIN, LEON, philosophy educator; b. Newark, July 4, 1943; s. Lazarus Maximilien and Clara (Elovici) R.; m. Sara Ellen Smith, Oct. 14, 1972. AB, Columbia U., 1965, PhD, 1972. Asst. prof. philosophy San Diego State U., 1969-72, assoc. prof., 1972-77, prof., 1977—, dir. European Studies Research Ctr., 1978—, also dir. Humanities Programs, 1980—; acad. dir., lectr. study tours of world. Contbr. articles to profl. jours. Fellow Adam Leroy Jones, Columbia U., 1966, Pres.'s, 1968, Fulbright, La Sorbonne, Paris, 1968-69, U. Nice, France, 1986; recipient most influential prof. award San Diego State U., 1982, 83. Mem. Classical Alliance of Western States (pres. 1986—), Am. Philos. Assn., Am. Soc. for Aesthetics, Internat. Assn. Philosophy and Lit., Internat. Soc. Comparative Study of Civilizations. Office: San Diego State U Dept Philosophy San Diego CA 92182

ROSENTHAL, JACK, broadcasting executive; b. Chgo., Aug. 7, 1930; s. Samuel J. and Celia (Weinberg) R.; m. Elaine Lois Brill, May 2, 1954; children: Michael Bruce, Robert Joseph, Richard Scott. B.A. in History, U. Wyo., 1952. Sec.-treas. Buffalo Theatre Corp., 1952-57, No. Wyo. Broadcasting Corp., 1957-64; v.p., gen. mgr. KTWO Radio and TV, Casper, Wyo., 1964-69; exec. v.p. Harriscope Broadcasting Corp., 1969-77; pres. broadcast div. Harriscope Broadcasting Corp., Los Angeles, 1977—; also dir. Harriscope Broadcasting Corp.; chmn. Wyo. industry adv. com. FCC; dir. Wyo. Nat. Bank, Affiliated Bank Corp. of Wyo.; dir. TV Info. Office, 1984. Producer: TV film Conrad Schwiering-Mountain Painter (Western Heritage award 1974). Mem. Wyo. Travel Commn., 1969-71, Wyo. Land and Water Commn., 1965-66, Yellowstone Nat. Park Centennial Commn., 1972, Wyo. Council Arts, 1969, City of Casper Art Fund, 1979-80; bd. dirs. Milward Simpson Endowment, U. Wyo. Found., 1970—; adv. Nat. Park Service, Dept. Interior, 1974-76; mem. jud. planning com. Wyo. Supreme Ct., 1976-77; mem. citizens stamp adv. com. U.S. Postal Service, 1985—; trustee The Philatelic Found. Served to 1st. lt. U.S. Army, 1952-54, Korea. Recipient Alfred I. DuPont Found. award broadcast journalism, 1965, U.S. Conf. Mayors award for outstanding community service, 1966, Disting. Alumnus award U. Wyo., 1982, Commendation Casper C. of C., 1984; named hon. mem. Shoshoni and Arapahoe Indian Tribes, 1965. Mem. Nat. Assn. Broadcasters (Grover C. Cobb meml. award 1983, nat. chmn. TV and radio polit. action com. 1977-79), Wyo. Assn. Broadcasters (pres. 1963), Fedn. Rocky Mountain States Ednl. TV Com. Office: Sta KTWO-TV 4200 E 2d St Casper WY 82609

ROSENTHAL, NEIL BRUCE, psychotherapist; b. Chgo., Oct. 7, 1947; s. Stanley and Florence (Podolsky) R. BS, U. Colo., 1973; MA in Behavioral

Sci., U. Houston, 1979. Colo. state pres. Council Internat. Relations and UN affairs, 1968-69; founder, dir., Denver Free U. (Learning Unltd.), 1969-70; project coordinator exptl. schs. program, Craig Sch. Dist., Alaska, 1973-75; adj. asst. prof. Okla. State U., 1979-80; instr. U. Colo., 1981—, U. Denver, 1981—; dir. Assoc. Mgmt. Cons. Internat., 1980; psychotherapist, keynote speaker, seminar leader. Mem. Rocky Mountain Psychol. Assn., Am. Assn. Marriage and Family Therapists, Assn. Humanistic Psychology (pres. Colo. 1981-84). Author: The Psychology of Intimacy. Office: 1385 S Colorado Blvd #714 Denver CO 80222

ROSHOLT, JOHN NICHOLAS, JR., research chemist, science administrator; b. Denver, Nov. 1, 1923; s. John Nicholas and Fay Rita (Schmidt) R.; m. Nora Agnes Guiney, June 12, 1948 (dec. June 1979); children: Jane, Jill, John. BSChemE, U. Colo., 1948; MS in Marine Sci., U. Miami, 1961, PhD in Marine Sci., 1963. Chemist U.S. Geol. Survey, Denver, 1948-53, research chemist, 1953-85, br. chief, 1985—. Served to sgt. U.S. Army, 1942-45. Recipient Meritorious Service award U.S. Dept. Interior, 1985. Mem. Am. Chem. Soc., Geol. Soc. Am., Colo. Sci. Soc. Avocation: golf. Home: 125 Dudley St. Lakewood CO 80226 Office: US Geol Survey Box 25046 MS 963 Fed Ctr Denver CO 80225

ROSICH, RAYNER KARL, physicist; b. Joliet, Ill., Aug. 28, 1940; s. Joseph F. and Gretchen (Cox) R.; BS in Physics cum laude, U. Mich., 1962, MS in Physics, 1963; PhD, U. Colo., 1977; MBA, U. Denver, 1982; m. Judy Louise Jackson, Aug. 20, 1966; children: Heidi Ann, Kimberly Ann, Dawn Ann. Teaching fellow and research asst. U. Mich., Ann Arbor, 1962-67; staff, Argonne (Ill.) Nat. Lab. Applied Math. Div., summers 1961-63; physicist, project leader Inst. for Telecommunication Sci., U.S. Dept. Commerce, Boulder, Colo., 1967-80; sr. scientist and program mgr. Electro Magnetic Applications, Inc., Denver, 1980-82; applications mgr. Energy Systems Tech., Inc., Denver, 1982-83, mgr. R&D, 1983; prin. scientist, program mgr. Contel Info. Systems, Inc., Denver, 1983-84, dir. tech. audits, 1985, dir. basic and applied research and devel., 1986; lab. scientist for systems engring. lab. Hughes Aircraft Co., Denver, 1986—. Vol. judo instr., county recreation dist., 1976-77. Recipient Spl. Achievement award U.S. Dept. Commerce, 1974, Outstanding Performance award, 1978, Sustained Superior Performance award, 1979; Libbey-Owens-Ford Glass Co./U. Mich Phoenix Meml. fellow, 1964-66; NSF Summer fellow, 1965. Mem. Am. Phys. Soc., AAAS, IEEE, Assn. Computing Machinery, Am. Assn. Artificial Intelligence, Sigma Xi, Phi Kappa Phi. Home: 7932 W Nichols Ave Littleton CO 80123 Office: Hughes Aircraft Co Space and Communications Group 8000 E Maplewood Ave Suite 226 Englewood CO 80111

ROSINSKI, EDWIN FRANCIS, health sciences educator; b. Buffalo, June 25, 1928; s. Theodore Joseph and Josephine M. (Wolski) R.; m. Jeanne C. Hueniger, Oct. 27, 1951; children: John T., Mary E., Sarah J. BS, SUNY, Buffalo, 1950; EdM, U. Buffalo, 1957, EdD, 1959. Prof. health scis. Med. Coll. Va., Richmond, 1959-66; dep. asst. sec. HEW, Washington, 1966-68; exec. vice chancellor U. Calif., San Francisco, 1968-72, prof., 1972—; adv. Rockefeller Found., N.Y.C., 1962-67, WHO, Geneva, 1962-78, Imperial Com. Health, Tehran, Iran, 1974-77; cons. Stanford Research Inst., Menlo Park, Calif., 1975-79. Author: The Assistant Medical Officer, 1965; contbr. over 100 articles to profl. jours. Served with USAF, 1950-54. Recipient spl. citation HEW, 1968; named disting. prof. Australian Vice Chancellors Office, 1974, disting. vis. prof. Tulane U., New Orleans, 1983. Fellow AAAS; mem. Assn. Am. Med. Colls., Am. Ednl. Research Assn., Soc. Health and Human Values (founding mem.), Phi Delta Kappa. Roman Catholic. Avocation: long-distance running. Home: 80 Sotelo Ave San Francisco CA 94116

ROSINSKI, PATRICE ANN, speech therapist, educator; b. Columbus, Ohio, Apr. 9, 1945; d. William Alonzo and Yolanda Inez (Auteri) Cosgrove; m. Dennis Alvin Pauletich, May 2, 1968 (div. 1980); m. Gerald Frank Rosinski, May 28, 1984; children: Kelsey Lynn, Courtney Ann. Student, U. Nebr., 1963-68; BA in Speech Pathology, Calif. State U., Chico, 1983, MA in Speech Pathology. Cert. clin. competence in speech pathology, Calif. Speech pathologist Chico (Calif.) Nursing Home, 1982; itinerant speech therapist San Diego City Schs., 1983-84, speech therapist, severe lang. disorders, 1984-87; dir. speech/lang. pathology Havasu Regional Hosp. div. Good Samaritan Health Services, Lake Havasu City, Ariz., 1987—. V.p. Redding (Calif.) Newcomers Club, 1979. Mem. Am. Speech Hearing Assn. (cert.), Sigma Kappa. Democrat. Roman Catholic. Avocations: golf, art, reading, travel. Home and Office: 3432 Indian Peak Dr Lake Havasu City AZ 86403

ROSKY, BURTON SEYMOUR, lawyer; b. Chgo., May 28, 1927; s. David T. and Mary W. (Zelkin) R.; m. Leatrice J. Darrow, June 16, 1951; children: David Scott, Bruce Alan. Student, Ill. Inst. Tech., 1944-45; B.S., UCLA, 1948; J.D., Loyola U., Los Angeles, 1953. Bar: Calif. 1954, U.S. Supreme Ct 1964, U.S. Tax Ct 1964; C.P.A., Calif. Auditor City Los Angeles, 1948- 51; with Beidner, Temkin & Ziskin (C.P.A.s), Los Angeles, 1951-52; supervising auditor Army Audit Agy., 1952-53; practiced law Los Angeles, Beverly Hills, 1954—; partner Duskin & Rosky, 1972-82, Rosky, Landau & Fox, 1982—; lectr. on tax and bus. problems. Judge pro tem Beverly Hills Mcpl. Ct.; mem. Los Angeles Mayor's Community Adv. Council. Contbr. profl. publs. Charter sponsor Los Angeles County Mus. Arts; contbg. mem. Assocs. of Smithsonian Instn.; charter mem. Air and Space Mus; mem. Am. Mus. Natural History, Los Angeles Zoo; sustaining mem. Los Angeles Mus. Natural History; mem. exec. bd. So. Calif. council Nat. Fedn. Temple Brotherhoods, mem. nat. exec. bd. Served with USNR, 1945-46. Walter Henry Cook fellow Loyola Law Sch. Fellow Jewish Chautauqua Soc. (life mem.); mem. Am. Arbitration Assn. (nat. panel arbitrators), Am. Assn. Attys.-C.P.A.s (charter mem. pres. 1968), Calif. Assn. Attys.-C.P.A.s (charter mem., pres. 1963), Calif. Soc. C.P.A.s, Calif., Beverly Hills, Century City, Los Angeles County bar assns., Am. Judicature Soc., Chancellors Assocs. UCLA, Tau Delta Phi, Phi Alpha Delta.; mem. B'nai B'rith. Jewish (mem. exec. bd., pres. temple, pres. brotherhood). Club: Mason. Office: 8383 Wilshire Blvd Beverly Hills CA 90211

ROSS, CAROL D(RING), management consultant; b. Los Angeles, Dec. 1, 1944; d. Buddy and Ruth C. (Lawrence) Burlingame; m. Bruce C. Ross, Apr. 2, 1975; children: Andrew, Tiffany. Student, UCLA, 1963-66; MBA, Pepperdine U., 1979. Internal auditor Planning Research, Westwood, Calif., 1966-68; acct. Calif. Aero Dynamics, Van Nuys, Calif., 1968-69; pvt. practice acctg. 1969-74; office mgr. J.M. Carden Sprinkler, Los Angeles, 1974-77; chief fin. officer Am. Dietary Lab., Burbank, Calif., 1977; v.p. Ziegler Ross, San Francisco, Los Angeles, 1982—; dir. bus. services Internal Edn. Found., Los Angeles, 1977-81; speaker Continuing Legal Edn.; chmn. personnel commn. Glendale (Calif.) Community Coll., 1980—. Author: Part-Time Employment, 1979; author/editor (newsletter) L.O.G.I.C. Mem. ABA, Nat. Assn. Accts. Unitarian. Avocations: youth soccer. Home: 430 Coutin Ln Glendale CA 91206 Office: Ziegler Ross 1201 N Pacific Ave Glendale CA 91202

ROSS, CHARLOTTE PACK, suicidologist; b. Oklahoma City, Oct. 21, 1932; d. Joseph and Rose P. (Traibich) Pack; m. Roland S. Ross, May 6, 1951 (div. July 1964); children: Beverly Jo, Sandra Gail. Ed. U. Okla., 1949-52, New Sch. Social Research, 1952-53. Cert. tchr. Exec. dir. Suicide Prevention and Crisis Ctr. San Mateo County, Burlingame, Calif., 1966—; pres., exec. dir. Youth Suicide Nat. Ctr., Washington, 1985—; pres. Calif. Senate Adv. Com. Youth Suicide Prevention, 1982-84; speaker Menninger Found., 1983, 84; instr. San Francisco State U., 1981-83; conf. coordinator U. Calif., San Francisco, 1971—; cons. univs. and health services throughout world. Contbg. author: Group Counseling for Suicidal Adolescents, 1984; Teaching Children the Facts of Life and Death, 1985. Mem. editorial bd. Suicide and Life Threatening Behavior, 1976—. Mem. regional selection panel Pres.'s Commn. on White House Fellows, 1975-78; mem. CIRCLON Service Club, 1979—, Com. on Child Abuse, 1981—; founding mem. Women for Responsible Govt., co-chmn., 1974-79. Recipient Outstanding Exec. award San Mateo County Coordinating Com., 1971; Koshland award San Francisco Found., 1984. Mem. Internat. Assn. Suicide Prevention (v.p. 1985—), Am. Assn. Suicidology (sec. 1972-74), bd. govs. 1976-78, accreditation com. 1975—, chair region IX, 1975-82), Assn. United Way Agy. Execs. (pres. 1974), Assn. County Contract Agys. (pres. 1982). Club: Peninsula Press Club. Office: 1811 Trousdale Dr Burlingame CA 94010

ROSS, CONNIE SUE, public relations executive; b. Topeka, May 7, 1947; d. Norlan W. and Ruth Eileen (Leech) Foster; m. David E. Ross II, June 9, 1968; 1 child, Sean David. BA summa cum laude, Washburn U., 1969. Dir. communications Salt Lake City (Utah) Area C. of C., 1981; v.p. Gulf Energy Corp., Salt Lake City, 1981-84; sr. v.p. Communications Mgmt. Co., Salt Lake City, 1984; pres. Profl. Communications Ltd., Salt Lake City, 1984—; pres. Commpat Fin. Corp., 1986—. Producer: (TV programs) Infonet and OTC Expo, co-host, 1986. Mem. Commn. Edn. Excellence, Utah Bd. Edn., 1984; bd. dirs. Utah Council Econ. Edn., 1983—. Named Outstanding Young Woman in Salt Lake City, Salt Lake City Jaycees, 1985, Outstanding Young Woman in Utah, Utah Jaycees, 1985. Mem. Pub. Relations Soc. Am. (past newsletter editor), Internat. Assn. Bus. Communicators, Women in Bus. of Salt Lake Area C. of C. (pres. 1986-87), Kappa Alpha Theta, Phi Kappa Psi, Tau Delta Pi. Democrat. Methodist. Avocations: bridge, skiing. Office: Profl Communications Ltd 4636 S Highland DrSuite C Salt Lake City UT 84117

ROSS, CYNTHIA WILLIAMS, international consultant, therapist; b. Kansas City, Mo., Sept. 6, 1937; d. Barnett Ray Williams and Mary Lucinda (Alexander) W.; m. Arthur L. Kelly, Oct. 27, 1956; children—Mary Lucinda, Thomas Lloyd, Alison Williams; m. 2d, David L. Ross, Aug. 22, 1982. Student Smith Coll., 1955-56, Yale U., 1956-57; B.S., Northwestern U., 1975; M.A., Lone Mountain Coll., 1977; Ph.D., Fielding Inst., 1984. Lic. marriage, family and child therapist, Calif. Counselor Extended Family Ctr., San Francisco, 1975-76; counselor Human Sexuality Program, U. Calif.-San Francisco, dept. psychiatry, 1976-77; counselor Family, Youth and Children's Ctr., Berkeley, Calif., 1976, Adult Outpatient Clinic, Berkeley, 1976-79; asst. staff mem. U. Calif.-San Francisco, 1977-79; practice psychotherapy, San Francisco, 1977-81; dir. Counseling Ctr. Motivation Mgmt. Service, San Francisco, 1979-80; crisis counselor Napa County Mental Health Crisis Service, 1980-81; family cons. Travis AFB, Fairfield, Calif., 1980-81, dir. Family Support Ctr., 1981-84; orgn. devel. cons., 1984-87. Mem. Calif. Assn. Marriage and Family Therapists, Orgn. Devel. Network, Am. Assn. Marriage and Family Therapists. Independent. Clubs: Yale of Peninsula, Marine Memorial (San Francisco). Home and Office: 1335 Grandview Napa CA 94558 Office: 609 Cabot Way Suite 706 Napa CA 94559

ROSS, DENNIS ANDREW, real estate development executive, architect; b. Detroit, Jan. 13, 1952; s. Burton A. and Rosalyn (Morgenstern) R.; m. Nathalie Marie LaJarige, June 15, 1977 (div. 1979); 1 child, Shannon Melody. B in Bldg. Scis., Rensselaer Poly. Inst., 1975, BArch, 1975. Registered architect, N.Y., Colo. Project designer Pellegren Corp., Denver, 1978-79; project architect Duff, Reck, Lehman P.C., Denver, 1979-81, R.N.L. Architects, Denver, 1981; project capt. Luckman Ptnrs., Denver, 1981-83; project mgr. H.D.C. Devel. Corp., Englewood, Colo., 1983-84; devel. mgr. Osprey Devel. Corp., Denver, 1984-86; mgr. real estate acquistion and devel. Kambridge Bldg. Co., Colorado Springs, 1986—; cons. in field. Mem. Nat. Council Archtl. Registration Bd, Phi. Kappa Tau. Avocations: moutain climbing, skiing, basketball, horticulture, photography. Home: 4250 S Galapago Englewood CO 80110

ROSS, ERNEST, poultry nutritionist; b. N.Y.C., Dec. 23, 1920; s. George and Mary (Mendelson) R.; m. Mary Elizabeth Krausnick, Jan. 9, 1949; children: Stephanie Ann, Walter Patrick, Jonathan McDonough, Sean Nuuan. BS, U. Ariz., 1946; MS, Ohio State U., 1951, PhD, 1955. Asst. prof. U. Hawaii, Honolulu, 1957-60, assoc. prof., 1960-65, prof. poulty nutrition, 1965—. Contbr. articles to sci. jours. Served to sgt. USAF, 1946-47. Fulbright scholar U. Queensland, Brisbane, Australia, 1962-63. Mem. Poultry Sci. Assn., Worlds's Poultry Sci. Assn. Democrat. Mem. Unitarian Ch. Avocations: tennis. Home: 1909 Kakela Dr Honolulu HI 96822 Office: U Hawaii at Manoa Dept of Animal Sci 1800 East West Rd Honolulu HI 96822

ROSS, GLYNN, opera administrator; b. Omaha, Dec. 15, 1914; s. Herman and Ida (Carlson) R.; m. Angelamaria Solimene, Nov. 15, 1946; children: Stephanie, Claudia, Melanie, Anthony. Student, Leland Powers Sch. Theater, Boston, 1937-39. bd. dirs. O.P.E.R.A. Am., Nat. Opera Inst., Soc. for Germanic Music Culture; founder, dir. Pacific N.W. Festival, 1975—. Opera stage dir., U.S., Can., 1939-63, debut, San Francisco Opera, 1948, gen. dir., Seattle Opera Assn., Inc., 1963-83, dir., Ariz. Opera, 1983—. Served to 1st lt. AUS, 1942-47. Office: Ariz Opera Assn 3501 N Mountain Ave Tucson AZ 85719

ROSS, HUGH COURTNEY, electrical engineer; b. Dec. 31, 1923; s. Clare W. and Jeanne F. Ross; m. Sarah A. Gordon (dec.); m. Patricia A. Malloy; children: John C., James G., Robert W. Student, Calif. Inst. Tech., 1942, San Jose State U., 1946-47; BSEE, Stanford U., 1950, postgrad., 1954. Registered profl. elec. engr., Calif. Instr. San Benito (Calif.) High Sch. and Jr. Coll., 1950-51; chief engr. vacuum power switches Jennings Radio Mfg. Corp., San Jose, Calif., 1951-62; chief engr. ITT Jennings, San Jose, Calif., 1962-64; pres. Ross Engring. HV Cons., Campbell, Calif., 1964—. Contbr. articles to tech. jours.; patentee in field. Mem. IEEE (chmn. Santa Clara Valley subsect. 1960-61), Am. Vacuum Soc., Am. Soc. Metals, Pacific Coast Electronics Assn. Avocations: electronics, electric autos, solar power camping, ranching. Home: 11915 Shadybrook Ct Saratoga CA 95070 Office: 540 Westchester Dr Campbell CA 95008

ROSS, JOHN, physical chemistry educator; b. Vienna, Austria, Oct. 2, 1926; came to U.S., 1940; s. Mark and Anna (Krecmar) R.; m. Virginia Franklin (div.); children: Elizabeth A., Robert K.; m. Eva Miller Madarasz. BS, Queens Coll., 1948; PhD, MIT, 1951; D (hon.), Weizmann Inst. Sci., Rehovot, Israel, 1984, Queens Coll., Rehovot, Israel, 1987. Prof. chemistry Brown U., Providence, 1953-66; prof. chemistry MIT, Cambridge, 1966-80, chmn. dept., 1966-71; prof. Stanford (Calif.) U., 1980—, chmn. dept., 1983—; cons. to industries, 1979—; mem. bd. govs. Weizmann Inst., 1971—. Author: Physical Chemistry, 1980; editor Molecular Beams, 1966; contbr. articles to profl. jours. Served as 2d lt. U.S. Army, 1944-46. Fellow AAAS, Am. Phys. Soc.; mem. Nat. Acad. Scis., Am. Chem. Soc. Home: 738 Mayfield Ave Stanford CA 94305 Office: Stanford U Dept Chemistry Stanford CA 94305

ROSS, JUDITH PARIS, life insurance executive; b. Boston, Dec. 23, 1939; d. Max and Ruth Paris; ed. Boston U., 1961, UCLA, 1978; grad. Life Underwriting Tng. Council, 1978; 1 son, Adam Stuart. Producer, co-host Checkpoint TV show, Washington, 1967-71; hostess Judi Says TV show, Washington, 1969; brokerage supr., specialist impaired risk underwriting Beneficial Nat. Life Ins. Co. (now Nat. Benefit Life), Beverly Hills, Calif., 1973-82, dir. Salary Savs. program for W. Coast, 1982—; mktg. dir. Brougher Ins. Group; featured speaker ins. industry sems. Active local PTA, Boy Scouts Am.; mem. early childhood edn. adv. com. Beverly Hills Unified Sch. Dist., 1977; active Beverly Hills local politics. Mem. Nat. Assn. Life Underwriters, Calif. Assn. Life Underwriters (dir. W. Los Angeles 1980—, v.p. chpt. 1982—, chmn. public relations), W. Los Angeles Life Underwriters Assn. (v.p. fin. 1983-84). Office: 9465 Wilshire Blvd Suite 603 Beverly Hills CA 90212

ROSS, JUNE ROSA PITT, biology educator; b. Taree, May 2, 1931; came to U.S., 1957; d. Bernard and Adeline (Nind) Phillips; m. Charles Alexander, June 27, 1959. BS with honors, U. Sydney, New S. Wales, Australia, 1953, PhD, 1959, DSc, 1974. Research assoc. Yale U., New Haven, 1959-60, U. Ill., Urbana, 1960-65; research assoc. Western Wash. U., Bellingham, 1965-67, assoc. prof., 1967-70, prof. biology, 1970—; pres. Western Wash. U. Faculty Senate, Bellingham, 1984-85; conf. host Internat. Bryozoology Assn., 1986. Author: (with others) A Textbook of Entomology, 1982, Geology of Coal, 1984; editor (assoc.) Palaios, 1985—; contbr. articles to profl. jours. Grantee NSF; recipient Western Wash. U. Outstanding Educator award, 1973, Western Wash. U. Research award, 1986. Mem. Am. Soc. Zoologists, The Paleontol. Soc. (councillor 1984-86), U.K. Marine Biol. Assn. (life), Electron Microscope Soc. Am. Avocations: hiking, classical music. Office: Western Wash U Dept Biology Bellingham WA 98255

ROSS, KATHLEEN ANNE, college president; b. Palo Alto, Calif., July 1, 1941; d. William Andrew and Mary Alberta (Wilburn) R. B.A., Ft. Wright Coll., 1964; M.A., Georgetown U., 1971; Ph.D., Claremont Grad. Sch., 1979. Cert. tchr., Wash. Secondary tchr. Holy Names Acad., Spokane, Wash., 1964-70; dir. research and planning Province Holy Names, Wash. State, 1972-73; v.p. acads. Ft. Wright Coll., Spokane, 1973-81; research asst. to dean Claremont Grad. Sch., Calif., 1977-78; assoc. faculty mem. Harvard U., Cambridge, Mass., 1981; pres. Heritage Coll., Toppenish, Wash., 1981—; cons. Wash. State Holy Names Schs., 1971-73; coll. accrediting assn. evaluator N.W. Assn. Schs. and Colls., Seattle, 1975—; dir. Holy Names Coll., Oakland, Calif., 1979—; cons. Yakima Indian Nation, Toppenish, 1975—; speaker, cons. in field. Author: (with others) Multicultural Pre-School Curriculum, 1977; Cultural Factors in Success of American Indian Students in Higher Education, 1978. Chmn. Internat. 5-Yr. Convocation of Sisters of Holy Names, Montreal, Que., Can., 1981; TV Talk show host Spokane Council of Chs., 1974-76. Recipient E.K. and Lillian F. Bishop Founds. Youth Leader of Yr. award, 1986; Holy Names medal Ft. Wright Coll., 1981 Disting. Citizenship Alumna award Claremont Grad. Sch., 1986; Named Youth Leader of Yr., E.K. and Lillian Bishop, Ranier Bank, 1986; numerous grants for projects in multicultural higher edn., 1974—. Mem. Assn. for Study Higher Edn. (proposal evaluator 1979), Nat. Catholic Edn. Assn. (N.W. regional assoc. 1974-82), Am. Assn. Higher Edn., Soc. Intercultural Edn., Tng. and Research, Sisters of Holy Names of Jesus and Mary. Roman Catholic. Office: Heritage Coll Route 3 Box 3540 Toppenish WA 98948

ROSS, LANSON CLIFFORD, JR., broadcaster, author, consultant; b. Killdeer, N.D., June 23, 1936; s. Lanson Charles and Mabel (Smith) R.; m. Mary Louise Freleigh, Dec. 20, 1957; children—David F., Lanson III. B.A. in Biblical Studies, Seattle Pacific U., 1960; M. Sacred Theology, Internat. Coll., 1984; D of Ministries, 1986. Pres. Evangelistic Enterprises, Inc., Seattle, 1960—; v.p. Christa Ministries, Seattle, 1972-75; pres. Ross Assocs., Inc., Seattle, 1977—; founder Planned Living Seminars, Seattle, 1978—. Mem. Evangelical Free Ch. Club: Seattle Yacht. Author: Total Life Prosperity, 1983; Give Your Children a Target, 1985, Take Charge of Your Life, 1986, The Bubble Burst, 1987; producer 5 vol. video seminar A Planned Life Style, 1986, and film on proper learning environment, leader planned living seminars. Home: 13740 Riviera Pl NE Seattle WA 98125 Office: PO Box 400 Yakima WA 98907

ROSS, LISA JOAN, environmental hazards scientist, statistical consultant; b. N.Y.C., Jan. 24, 1957; d. Alfred Seymour and Rosalind (Weisman) R. BA in Biology, SUNY, Binghamton, 1978; MS in Botany, Ariz. State U., 1982. Asst. curator of herbarium N.Y. State Mus., Albany, 1978-79; research asst. Ariz. State U., Tempe, 1980-82; postgrad. research asst. Statewide Air Pollution Research Ctr., Riverside, Calif., 1982-83; environ. hazards scientist Calif. Dept. Food and Agr., Sacramento, 1983—. Contbr. articles to profl. jours. V. p. Friends of Sycamore Canyon, Riverside, 1982; com. mem. Audubon Soc. Wildlife Sanctuary, Riverside and Sacramento, 1983-84. Mem. Sigma Xi. Avocations: aikido, swimming, bird watching, backpacking, hiking. Home: 1219 Cavanaugh Way Sacramento CA 95822 Office: Calif Dept Food & Agr 1220 N St Sacramento CA 95814

ROSS, LOUISE DORILA, personnel director; b. Gibraltar, U.K., Dec. 31, 1937; d. Lawrence Fermin and Magdalena Antonia (Sacarello) Ferrary; m. Alexander Dean Kalei Ross, Feb. 19, 1961; children: Lawrence Joseph, Alexander Kalani, Jessica Kailani, Patrick Kamaheiwa. Grad., Hampstead U., London, 1956. Cert. hotel adminstr., tax preparer; notary pub. Trilingual sec. Lowenstein O'seas, Tangier, Morocco, 1956-59; personnel clk. U.S. Embassy, Rabat, Morocco, 1959-61; tchrs. aide Calif. Schs., 29 Palms, 1971-74; confidential sec. USN Ship Repair Facility, Subic Bay, Philipines, 1975-77; personnel dir., exec. sec. Napili Kai, Napili, Hawaii, 1977—. Editor: (monthly newsletter) Talk Story Time, 1980—. Mem. Presdl. Task Force for Vietnam Refugees, Subic Bay, 1976; treas. Napilihau Homeowners Assn., Napili, 1986, v.p. 1985. Mem. Ednl. Inst. Am. Hotel & Motel Assn. (pres. Maui chpt. 1982—, cert.), Lahaina Bus. and Profl. Women (pres.-elect 1986—). Republican. Roman Catholic. Avocations: dancing, music. Home: 5161-1 Kohi St Lahaina HI 96761 Office: Napili Kai Beach Club 5900 Honoapiilani Rd Lahaina HI 96761

ROSS, PHILIP DREW, health and environmental scientist, researcher; b. Abington, Pa., Sept. 4, 1952; s. Charles Warren and Charlotte (Drew) R.; m. Martha Bair, Dec. 7, 1979 (div. 1984). BS, Pa. State U., 1973, MS, 1977, PhD, 1979. Research assoc. dept. pharmacology Duke U., Durham, N.C., 1979-80; assoc. researcher Cancer Research Ctr. U. Hawaii, Honolulu, 1980—; assoc. dir. Kuakini Osteoporosis Ctr., Honolulu, 1983—. Contbr. articles to profl. jours. Recipient Research Service award NIH, 1980-82; Am. Cancer Soc. grantee, 1983—. Mem. AAAS, Am. Soc. for Bone Mineral Research. Clubs: Hawaii Aiki Kai (Honolulu) (bd. dirs. 1984-85), Aikido of Honolulu (bd. dirs., v.p. 1986—). Avocations: martial arts, Bonsai, hiking, camping. Home: 3449 Woodlawn Dr Honolulu HI 96822 Office: Kuakini Osteoporosis Ctr 347 N Kuakini St Honolulu HI 96817

ROSS, RICHARD NORMAN, communications executive; b. Huntington Park, Calif., Sept. 20, 1930; s. Robert Norman and Elizabeth (Barrett) R.; m. Connie J. Brown; children—Ronald C., Nancy E., Andrew R. B.S., San Jose State Coll., 1953; Nat. events producer Boy Scouts Am., N.J., 1953-73; dir. entertainment Walt Disney Prodns., Orlando, Fla., 1973-78; creative v.p. Creative Service Group, Salt Lake City, 1978-82; pres. Communication Design Assocs., Salt Lake City, 1982—. Served with USNR, 1947-53. Mem. Meeting Planners Internat., Assn. Multi-Image (chpt. sec.-treas.), Am. Film Inst. Producer TV spls., including: Sing America, 1978; Wonderful World of the Waltz, 1980; Celebration, 1980; Maureen McGovern at Symphony Hall, 1981; Speaking About Economics, 1984; designer AT&T Exhibit, Epcot, Walt Disney World, 1982, Ill. Bell Expocenter, Chgo., 1985-86. Also: Communication Design Assocs Box 520800 North Salt Lake City UT 84106 Also: 1865 Millcreek Way Salt Lake City UT 84106

ROSS, RONALD GRIERSON, JR., aerospace engineer; b. San Diego, Jan. 24, 1942; s. Ronald Grierson and Dorothy (Jenkins) R. AA, Pasadena City Coll., 1962; BS, U. Calif., Berkeley, 1964, MS, 1965, D in Mech. Engring., 1968. Engr. Jet Propulsion Lab., Pasadena, Calif., 1968-76, mgr. reliability and engring. scis., 1976—; lectr. on photovoltaics Ariz. State U. Ctr. Profl. Devel. Contbr. articles to profl. jours.; patentee in field. Recipient Exceptional Service medal NASA, 1981. Mem. Sigma Xi, Tau Beta Pi. Avocations: backpacking, photography. Office: Jet Propulsion Lab Pasadena CA 91109

ROSS, RUSSELL, pathologist, educator; b. St. Augustine, Fla., May 25, 1929; s. Samuel and Minnie (DuBoff) R.; m. Jean Long Teller, Feb. 22, 1956; children: Valerie Regina, Douglas Teller. A.B., Cornell U., 1951; D.D.S., Columbia U., 1955; Ph.D., U. Wash., 1962. Intern Columbia-Presbyn. Med. Center, 1955-56, USPHS Hosp., Seattle, 1956-58; spl. research fellow pathology U. Wash. Sch. Medicine, 1958-62; asst. prof. pathology and oral biology U. Wash. Sch. Medicine and Dentistry, 1962-65, asso. prof. pathology, 1965-69, prof., 1969—, adj. prof. biochemistry, 1978—; asso. dean for sci. affairs Sch. Medicine, 1971-78, chmn. dept. pathology, 1982—; vis. scientist Strangeways Research Lab., Cambridge, Eng.; mem. research com. Am. Heart Assn.; mem. adv. bd. Found. Cardiologique Princess Liliane, Brussels, Belgium; life fellow Clare Hall, Cambridge U.; Guggenheim fellow, 1966-67; mem. adv. council Nat. Heart, Lung and Blood Inst., NIH, 1978-81. Mem. editorial bd. Proceedings Exptl. Biology and Medicine, 1971—, Jour. Cell Biology, 1972-74, Exptl. Cell Research, Jour. Exptl. Medicine; assoc. editor: Arteriosclerosis, Jour. Cellular Physiology, Jour. Cellular Biochemistry; contbr. articles in arteriosclerosis research growth factors, and wound healing to profl. jours. Recipient Birnberg Research award Columbia U., 1975, Gordon Wilson medal Am. Clin. and Climatol. Assn., 1981; Japan Soc. Promotion of Sci. fellow, 1985. Mem. Am. Soc. Cell Biology, Tissue Culture Assn., Gerontol. Soc. Am. Assn. Pathologists, Internat. Soc. Cell Biology, Electron Microscope Soc. Am., Am. Heart Assn. (fellow Council on Arteriosclerosis), Royal Micros. Soc., Harvey Soc. (hon.), AAAS, Am. Soc. Biol. Chemists, Belgian Acad. Medicine (fgn. corr. mem.), Sigma Xi. Home: 4811 NE 42d St Seattle WA 98105 Office: U of Wash Sch Medicine SM-30 Seattle WA 98195

ROSS, SHEILA MAUREEN HOLMES, sales manager; b. San Jose, Calif., Nov. 1, 1951; d. Douglas F. and Mary A. (Zager) Murphy; B.A., San Jose State U., 1973; m. Lawrence Richard Ross, Dec. 20, 1981; 1 child, Vanessa Katherine Ross. Exec. sec. J.M. Mfg., Santa Clara, Calif., 1972-74; mktg. coordinator Chick, Orthopedic/Hosmer-Dorrance, Campbell, Calif., 1974-75; mgr. mktg. adminstrn. Consol. Video Systems, Sunnyvale, Calif., 1975-83; regional mgr., Pacific dist. sales mgr. ADDA Corp., Los Gatos, Calif., 1977-84, N.W. regional mgr., 1983-84; broadcast sales mgr. Aurora Systems, San Francisco, 1984—; dir. U.S. sales Vertigo Systems Internat., Inc., Vancouver,

B.C., Can., 1986—. Mem. Internat. Platform Assn., Soc. Motion Pictures and TV Engrs. Home: 28 Dartmouth Pl Danville CA 94526

ROSS, STANLEY RALPH, writer, publisher, composer; b. N.Y.C., July 22, 1935; s. Morris H. and Blanche (Turer) R.; m. Neila Hyman, Dec. 14, 1957; children: Andrew Steven, Lisa Michelle Turer, Nancy Ellen. Student, Pratt Inst., 1950-51; D.D., Universal Life Ch., 1974, Ph.D., 1978. Self-employed photographer N.Y.C., 1952-56; copywriter Fuller, Smith & Ross, Los Angeles, 1956-60, Universal Pictures, Los Angeles, 1960-61; program exec. ABC-TV, Los Angeles, 1961-63; creative dir. Cole, Fischer & Rogow, Beverly Hills, Calif., 1963-65; self-employed film and TV writer Beverly Hills, 1965—; pres. Neila Corp.; columnist Los Angeles Weekly.; guest lectr. UCLA, U. So. Calif., Calif. Luth. Coll., Los Angeles Coll., Sherwood Oaks U., others; cons. Blanc Advt., N.Y.C. Author: Games For Planes, 1974, Speak When You Hear The Beep, 1975; writer for TV programs All In The Family, The Monkees, Batman, The Man From UNCLE; developer programs Wonder Woman, The Kallikaks, The Electric Co. The Monster Squad, The Challenge of the Sexes; Scriptwriter Banacek, Colombo, others, also 15 TV movies; pub., editor, author: (with Jay Robert Nash) The Motion Picture Guide, feature film ency., 12 vols. Recipient UNICEF award, 1974, West Los Angeles Coll. Presdl. citation, 1974, Carson (Calif.) citation, 1973, also Emmy and Writers' Guild nominations. Mem. Writers Guild, Producers Guild, Dirs. Guild, Screen Actors Guild, AFTRA, ASCAP, Saints and Sinners of Los Angeles (award), Hon. Order Ky. Cols. Republican. Mem. Universal Life Ch. Home: 451 Beverwil Dr Beverly Hills CA 90212 Office: CineBooks Inc 7865 Willoughby Ave West Hollywood CA 90046

ROSS, STEPHEN, film company executive; b. Bklyn., Sept. 12, 1948; s. Irving H. and Muriel M. (Novinsky) R.; m. Rachel Wechselbaum, Dec. 1, 1974; children: Benyamin, Avidan, Oren, Yael. BA, Columbia U., 1970, JD, 1973. Assoc. Barovick, Konecky, Schwartz, Kay and Schiff, N.Y.C., 1974-81; sr. v.p., gen. counsel Telepictures Corp., N.Y.C., Los Angeles, 1981-86, Lorimar-Telepictures Corp., Culver City, Calif., 1986—. Office: Lorimar-Telepictures Corp. 3970 Overland Ave Culver City CA 90232

ROSS, TERENCE WILLIAM, architect; b. Saginaw, Mich., Sept. 27, 1935; s. Oran Lewis and Drucilla (Chadman) R.; B.Arch., U. Mich., 1958; m. Patricia Ann Marshall, Sept. 27, 1974; children by previous marriage—Deborah, David. Designer, Roger W. Peters Constrn. Co., Fond du Lac, Wis., 1958-62; draftsman Kenneth Clark, Architect, Santa Fe, N.Mex., 1962-63, Holien & Buckley, Architects, Santa Fe, 1963-64; office mgr. Philippe Register, Architect, Santa Fe, 1964-68; v.p. Register, Ross, & Brunet architects, engrs., Santa Fe, 1968-71; v.p. Luna-Ross & Asso., 1971-77; staff CNWC Architects, Tucson, to 1981, ADP Architects, 1981—. Vice chmn. N.Mex. R.R. Authority, 1969-74, sec., 1970-72. Bd. dirs. Colo.-N.Mex. Soc. Preservation of Narrow Gauge. Recipient award for hist. preservation N.Mex. Arts Commn., 1971, award for outstanding service to community Santa Fe Press Club, 1972; named col. aide-de-camp State of N.Mex., 1968, hon. mem. staff atty. gen. Mem. AIA (chpt. pres. 1970, dir.), Constrn. Specifications Inst., N.Mex. Soc. Architects (dir. 1972), Ariz. Soc. Architects, N.Mex. R.R. Authorities (chmn. joint exec. com. 1970-74). San Gabriel Hist. Soc. (hon.), Alpha Rho Chi. Clubs: Sashay Rounders Sq. Dance (pres. 1974), Diamond Squares Sq. Dance, Railroad (pres. N.Mex. 1969, 70, dir.). Author: Track of the Cats. Home and Office: 5050 N Avenida de La Colina Tucson AZ 85749

ROSS, THERESA LYNN, speech pathologist; b. Mitchell, S.D., Aug. 25, 1954; d. Thomas Herman and Mary Ann (Schmidt) Hamann; m. Maurice Jay Ross, Aug. 18, 1978. BS, Idaho State U., 1979, MS, 1981. Communication disorders specialist Idaho Sch. Dist. 21, Arimo, 1981-82; staff speech pathologist Pocatello (Idaho) Regional Med. Ctr., 1982-85, mgr. speech pathology, 1985—; mem. adj. faculty Idaho State U., Pocatello, 1985—. Whittenberger Trust fellow, 1980. Mem. Am. Speech Lang. and Hearing Assn. (cert.), Idaho Speech Lang. and Hearing Assn., Nat. Head Injury Found. Democrat. Roman Catholic. Home: 735 Bitterroot Dr Pocatello ID 83201 Office: Pocatello Regional Med Ctr 777 Hospital Way Pocatello ID 83201

ROSS, TIM M., biotechnologist, microbiologist; b. Oakland, Calif.; s. Authur Hjalar Miitbo and Marion Elizabeth (Appelbaum) Petrie. AA, Coll. Redwoods, 1967; BS, San Jose State Coll., 1971; PhD, Neotarian U., 1979. Head researcher Rosstech R & D, Crescent City, Calif., 1979-81; bio-engr. of research and devel. Rosstech Genetics, Crescent City, 1983-84; head research Biotek, Inc., Crescent City, 1984—; owner, operator Blue Skies Travel Agy., Crescent City, 1981—. Contbr. articles to profl. jours. Mem. AAAS, Am. Chem. Soc. (assoc.), Am. Soc. Travel Agts., Del Norte Art Council (charter), Am. Inst. Chemists. Democrat. Methodist. Avocations: botany, oriental art collecting. Home and Office: Biotek Research & Devel Hdqrs Waikiki Grand Suite 718 134 Kapahulu Ave Honolulu HI 96815

ROSS, VICTOR JULIUS, school superintendent; b. Salina, Kans., Mar. 2, 1935; s. Victor J. and Lola Ruth (Sloop) R.; m. Anna Marie Berger, June 15, 1957; children: Victor III, Diane E., Linda M. BA, U. Denver, 1958, MA, 1964; EdD, U. Colo., 1978. Tchr. English Littleton (Colo.) Schs., 1958-65; prin. Littleton Jr. High Sch., 1965-69, Moline (Ill.) High Sch., 1969-72, Lakewood (Colo.) High Sch., 1972-76; asst. supt. Bettendorf (Iowa) Community Sch. Dist., 1976-81; supt. Aurora (Colo.) Pub. Sch., 1981—. Author: The Forbidden Apple, 1985, Bite the Wall, 1986; contbr. articles to profl. jours. City councilman City of Littleton, 1964-68. Named Pub. Servant of Yr., Littleton Ind., 1965. Mem. Nat. Sch. Bds. Assn. (jour. conf. faculty 1982—, named one of 100 Top Exec. Educators, 1984), Collegial Assn. Devel. and Renewal Educators (jour. editor 1982—), Phi Delta Kappa. Episcopalian. Lodge: Rotary. Home: 15890 E 8th Circle Aurora CO 80011 Office: Aurora Pub Schs 1085 Peoria St Aurora CO 80011

ROSS, WILLIAM ARTHUR, florist; b. Artesia, N.Mex., Aug. 20, 1945; s. Carl Ellis and Jean Kathryn (Balzizer) R. BEd, Okla. Christian Coll., 1967; MA, Eastern N.Mex. U., 1974. Tchr. Albuquerque Pub. Schs., 1967-71; purchasing agt. Artesia Gen. Hosp., 1974-75; owner, operator R&B Blossom Shop, Artesia, 1975—; tchr. floral design, Artesia, 1983, 85. Author folk songs, 1969. Liaison bd. mem. Arts Council and Mus., Artesia, 1979-80; bd. dirs. Artesia Arts council, 1976-77; sec. Artesia Hist. Mus., 1982-86; instr. floral desing Artesia Sr. Citizen Ctr., 1982. Mem. Soc. Am. Florists, West. Tex.-N.Mex. Florist Assn. Republican. Mem. Ch. of Christ. Avocations: tennis, swimming, camping, stained glass. Home: 3401 S 13th St Artesia NM 88210 Office: R&B Blossom Shop 106 S 10th St PO Box 155 Artesia NM 88210

ROSS, WILLIAM RICHARD, state agency administrator; b. St. Louis, Dec. 10, 1947; s. William Arthur and Blanche (Mowery) R. BA in Econs., Rice U., 1970; MA in Psychology, Duquesne U., 1975. Assoc. coordinator Dept. Health and Social Services, Juneau, Alaska, 1976-77; assoc. state and fed. coordinator Office of Gov. State of Alaska, Juneau, 1978-80; assoc. coordinator fisheries and environment Office of Gov. State of Alaska, Washington, 1982-85; dep. coordinator Office Coastal Mgmt., Juneau, 1980-82; commr. State of Alaska Dept. Environ. Conservation, Juneau, 1985—; lectr. U. Alaska, Juneau, 1977-78. Producer movies In the Land of the War Canoes, 1973 (NEA grant 1973), Washington, The Capitol, 1983. Chmn. Aiding Women in Assault and Rape Emergencies, Juneau, 1978-82, Women and Juvenile Community Detention Ctr. Bd., Juneau, 1978-82; vice chmn. youth adv. bd. City of Juneau, 1977-82; liaison Cen. Am. Support Group, Juneau, 1979-82. Avocations: hiking, fishing, reading, cooking, golf. Office: Environ Conservation Dept PO Box O 3220 Hospital Dr Juneau AK 99811-1800

ROSSANO, AUGUST THOMAS, emeritus environmental engineering educator; b. N.Y.C., Feb. 1, 1916; s. August Thomas and Rosa (Cosenza) R.; m. Margie Chrisney, Dec. 6, 1944; children: August Thomas III, Marilyn, Pamela, Jeannine, Renee, Christopher, Stephen, Teresa. B.S., M.I.T., 1938; M.S., Harvard U., 1941, S.D., 1954. Diplomate Am. Acad. Environmental Engrs., Am. Bd. Indsl. Hygiene. Commd. lt. (j.g.) USPHS, 1941, advanced through grades to capt., 1955; assigned Hdqrs. USPHS, 1941, 48, Taft Engring. Center, Cin., 1954-59; ret. 1963; prof. air resource engring. U. Wash., Seattle, 1963-81; prof. emeritus U. Wash., 1981—; vis. prof. Calif. Inst. Tech., 1960-63; Mem. expert adv. panel on air pollution WHO, Geneva, 1960—, Pan Am. Health Orgn., 1975—; cons. European office WHO, 1960—, U.S. Dept. HEW, 1962—, U.S. Dept. State, 1962—, U.S. Dept. Commerce, 1962—, State of Wash., 1963—, Puget Sound Air Pollution Control Agy., 1967—; cons. govts. U.S., Can., Greece, Czechoslovakia, Republic of China, Peoples Republic of China, Belgium, Netherlands, Mexico, Syria, Iran, Egypt, Brazil, Peru, Chile, Barbados, P.R., Philippines, Venezuela, Curacao, also; Smithsonian Instn. and World Bank, various other nat. and multi-nat. corps.; mem. subcom. on hydrogen sulfide NRC.; Bd. dirs. Environmental Resources Assos., Bellevue Montessori Sch., Environmental Sci. Service div. E.R.A., N.W. Environmental Scis. Ltd., Inst. Exec. Research, Nat. Air Conservation Commn. Author: (with Hal Cooper) Source Testing for Air Pollution Control, 1971; Editor: Air Pollution Control, 1969; Contbr. 115 articles to tech. jours. Patentee pollution control device. Served with C.E. AUS. Recipient Spl. Service award USPHS, 1958, disting. achievement award Pacific NW-Internat. sect. Air Pollution Control Assn.; HEW tng. grantee, 1964-70; EPA grantee, 1971—. Mem. Harvard Pub. Health Alumni Assn. (pres.), Sigma Xi, Delta Omega, Tau Beta Pi. Clubs: Bellevue Triangle Pool, Bellevue Athletic, Alderbrook (Wash.) Golf and Yacht, Wapato Point Resort, Elliott Bay Yacht, Columbia Towers. Home: 9427 NE 20th St Bellevue WA 98004 Office: More Hall U Wash Seattle WA 98195

ROSSBACHER, LISA ANN, geology educator, science writer; b. Fredericksburg, Va., Oct. 10, 1952; d. Richard Irwin and Jean Mary (Dearing) R.; m. Dallas D. Rhodes, Aug. 4, 1978. BS, Dickinson Coll., 1975; MA, SUNY, Binghamton, 1978, Princeton U., 1979; PhD, Princeton U., 1983. Cons. Republic Geothermal, Santa Fe Springs, Calif., 1979-81; asst. prof. geology Whittier (Calif.) Coll., 1982-84; asst. prof. geology Calif. State Poly. U., Pomona, 1984-86, assoc. prof. geol. scis., 1986—; vis. researcher U. Uppsala, Sweden, 1984. Author: Career Opportunities in Geology and the Earth Sciences, 1983, Recent Revolutions in Geology, 1986; contbr. articles to profl. jours. Recipient scholarship Ministry Edn. of Finland, Helsinki, 1984; grantee NASA, 1983—. Mem. AAAS (geol. nominating com. 1984-87), Assn. Earth Sci. Editors (assoc. editor 1985—), Geol. Soc. Am., Sigma Xi (grantee 1976). Office: Calif State Poly U Geol Scis Dept 3801 W Temple Ave Pomona CA 91768

ROSSEL, EUGENE DAVID, air force officer, electrical engineer; b. Okawville, Ill., July 14, 1937; s. Anthony Paul and Anna Mary (Trost) R.; m. Isabel Martinez Gonzalez, June 19, 1967 (div. Feb. 1983); children: Carlos, Ana Isabel, Eugene Anthony. BSEE, St. Louis U., 1959; MS in Mgmt., Air Force Inst. Tech., 1969; cert., Indsl. Coll. Armed Forces, 1975, Air War Coll., 1976. Registered profl. engr., Pa. Enlisted USAF, 1954, commd. 2d lt., 1959, advanced through grades to lt. col., 1977; officer USAF, worldwide including Vietnam, Laos, Panama and Spain, 1959—; radar engr. USAF, Torrejon AFB, Spain, 1972-77, 1972-77; space shuttle engr. USAF Space and Missile Orgn., Los Angeles Air Force Sta., 1977-80; tech. advisor to Small Bus. Adminstrn. USAF, Los Angeles Air Force Sta., 1980-83, product assurance dir. space div., 1983-84; advanced concepts dir. USAF Ballistic Missile Office, Norton AFB, Calif., 1984—; cons. NASA, SBA, Los Angeles, 1977-80. Author, editor: Counterinsurgency Communications Handbook, 1968; author position papers and policy studies on USAF to U.S. Army and various fgn. mil. orgns. Decorated Bronze Star, Air medal; Gallantry Cross with palm (Republic Vietnam). Mem. Soc. Profl. Engrs. (pub. relations officer 1963-66), AIAA, Air Commando Assn., Air Force Assn., Nat. Rifle Assn., Am. Legion, St. Louis U. Assn. (pres. C.Z. chpt., 1964-66). Roman Catholic. Club: Toastmasters (Madrid)(pres. 1972-74). Avocations: genealogy, amateur radio, writing. Home: 6083 Rosa Ct Chino CA 91710 Office: Ballistic Missile Office BMO/MYS Norton AFB CA 92409-6468

ROSSER, JAMES MILTON, university president; b. East St. Louis, Ill., Apr. 16, 1939; s. William M. and Mary E. (Bass) R.; m. Carmen Rosita Colby, Dec. 27, 1962; 1 son, Terrence. B.A., So. Ill. U., 1962, M.A., 1963, Ph.D., 1969. Diagnostic bacteriologist Holden Hosp., Carbondale, Ill., 1961-63; research bacteriologist Eli Lilly & Co., Indpls., 1963-66; coordinator Black Am. studies, instr. health edn. So. Ill. U., Carbondale, 1968-69; asst. prof. Black Am. studies dir. So. Ill. U., 1969-70, asst. to chancellor, 1970; asso. vice chancellor for acad. affairs U. Kans., Lawrence, 1970-74; asso. prof. edn., toxicology and pharmacology U. Kans., 1971-74; vice chancellor dept. higher edn. State of N.J., Trenton, 1974-79; acting chancellor State of N.J., 1977; pres., prof. health care mgmt. Calif. State U., Los Angeles, 1979—; mem. tech. resource panel Center for Research and Devel. in Higher Edn., U. Calif., Berkeley, 1975-76; mem. health maintenance orgn. com. Health Planning Council, State of N.J., 1975-79; mem. standing com. on research and devel. bd. trustees Ednl. Testing Service, 1976-77; mem. steering com. and task force on retention of minorities in engring. Assembly of Engring. NRC, 1975-78; minority bus. task force; mem. Bd. Med. Examiners, State of N.J., 1978-79; vis. faculty mem. Inst. Mgmt. of Lifelong Edn., Grad. Sch. Edn., Harvard U., 1979; mem. Calif. State U. Trustees Spl. Long Range Fin. Planning Com., 1982—, AFL/CIO Labor Higher Edn. Council, 1983, Nat. Commn. Higher Edn. Issues, 1981-82; mem. Commn. on Confidentiality Am. Council Edn., 1981; mem. So. Calif. Edison, Fedco, Inc., Music Ctr. Performing Arts Council/Edn. Council. Author: An Analysis of Health Care Delivery, 1977. Mem. exec. bd., chmn. varsity scouting program Los Angeles Area council Boy Scouts Am., 1979—; local council rep. Nat. Council Boy Scouts Am., 1980—; bd. dirs. Hispanic Urban Center, Los Angeles, 1979—, Los Angeles Urban League, 1982, Info. and Retrieval Service Los Angeles County, 1982; commr. higher edn. issues Task Force Affirmative Action, Labor/Higher Edn. Council; bd. dirs. Community TV of So. Calif. Sta. KCET, 1980—, United Way, Los Angeles Orthopaedic Hosp., Los Angeles, 1983-86; mem. Citizen's Adv. Council Congl. Caucus Sci. and Tech., 1983—. NSF fellow, 1961; NDEA fellow, 1967-68; recipient award of recognition in Edn. Involvement for Young Achievers, 1981, Pioneer of Black Hist. Achievement award Brotherhood Crusade, 1981, Alumni Achievement award So. Ill. U., 1982, Friend to Youth award Am. Humanics, Inc., 1985. Mem. Am. Assn. State Colls. and Univs. (mem. com. on urban affairs, sci. and tech., health affairs, nominating com.), Am. Ednl. Research Assn., Alhambra C. of C. (bd. dirs. 1979—), Los Angeles C. of C. (bd. dirs. 1984—), Am. Public Health Assn., Los Angeles Philharmonic Assn., Nat. ARC, Kappa Delta Pi, Phi Delta Kappa, Phi Kappa Phi. Roman Catholic. Home: 225 El Cielo Ln Bradbury CA 91010 Office: Calif State U 5151 State University Dr Los Angeles CA 90032

ROSSER, ROBERT WILLIAM, aerospace scientist, chemical researcher; b. Detroit, Mar. 1, 1930; s. William Frank and Ethel Wilma (Rogers) R.; m. Maureen Ann Meister, Mar. 26, 1965; children: Kenneth Wayne, Karin Marie. Music performance, St. Louis Inst. Music, 1949; BS, U. Colo., 1958, PhD, 1961. Organic chemist Shell Devel. Co., Emeryville, Calif., 1961-64; polymer scientist Boeing Sci. Research Labs., Seattle, 1965-68; computational chemist NASA, Moffett Field, Calif., 1969—. Contbr. articles to profl jours.; composer choral works, 1983. Served with U.S. Army, 1953-55. U. Colo. fellow, 1959. Mem. Phi Beta Kappa (assoc.), Sigma Xi (assoc.). Avocations: classical pianist, composing. Office: NASA Ames Research Ctr MS 230-3 Moffett Field CA 94035

ROSSETTI, CARL JOSEPH, government transportation specialist; b. Hillsdale, Mich., Apr. 6, 1926; s. Carl M. and Genevieve Flora (Bonfiglio) R.; student Western Mich. U., 1943-45; B.S. in Mech. Engring., Columbia U., 1946; postgrad. U. Hawaii-Harvard U. Advanced Mgmt. Program, 1962, George Washington U., 1964; m. Margaret N. Mahi, June 5, 1946 (div. 1977); children—Farran F., Carlene A., Jacqueline L., Carl J. III; m. Gloria Aguilar, Dec. 30, 1977. Adminstrv. asst. transp. Pearl Harbor Hawaii Dist. Transp. Office, 1947-51, automotive transp. specialist, 1951-53; v.p. Rossetti Brothers Constrn. Co., Hillsdale, 1953-58; auto transp. specialist Dist. Pub. Works Office, Pearl Harbor, Hawaii, 1958-64; transp. specialist Naval Facilities Engring. Command, Pacific Div., San Francisco, 1964—, mgr. mgmt. br. Transp. Equipment Mgmt. Center, Pearl Harbor, 1965-77, dir., 1975—. Pres., Foster Village Community Assn., Honolulu, 1962, 64-65; pres. West Honolulu Little League, 1963-64. Bd. dirs. Aloha Week Hawaii, Inc., 1958—, pres. 1969. Served as ensign USNR, 1946; lt. (j.g.) Korean Emergency, 1950-52, lt. comdr. Res., ret. Named Fed. Employee of Year, 1964, Fed. Mgr. of Yr., 1985. Mem. Soc. Automotive Engrs. (chmn. Hawaii 1964-65), Am. Legion. Roman Catholic. Elk, Lion. Club: Toastmasters. Home: 1551 Haloa Dr Honolulu HI 96818 Office: Pacific Div Naval Facilities Engring Command FPO San Francisco CA 96610

ROSSI, AMADEO JOSEPH, chemist; b. Seattle, Sept. 23, 1954; s. Amadeo Joseph and Maria Asilia (Chinella) R.; m. Frances Marie Stotts, Sept. 19, 1981. BS in Wood and Fiber Sci., U. Wash., 1979, MS in wood chemistry, 1987. Research aide U. Wash., Seattle, 1978-79; environ. engr. Georgia-Pacific Corp., Eugene, Oreg., 1980; engr., dir. waste research projects Envirosphere Co. subs. EBASCO Services, Inc., Seattle, 1981—. Contbr. articles to profl. jours. Mem. Am. Chem. Soc., Air Pollution Control Assn., Forest Products Research Soc., Xi Sigma Pi. Office: EBASCO Services Inc 10900 NE 8th St Bellevue WA 98004

ROSSO, LOUIS T., scientific instrument manufacturing company executive; b. San Francisco, 1933; married. A.B., San Francisco State Coll., 1955; M.B.A., U. Santa Clara, 1967. Product specialist Spinco div. Beckman Instruments, Inc., Fullerton, Calif., 1959-63; mktg. mgr. Beckman Instruments, Inc., 1963-69, mgr. Spinco div., 1969-70, mgr. clin. instruments div., 1970-74, corp. v.p., mgr. analytical instruments group, 1974-80, corp. sr. v.p., 1980-83, pres., 1983—, also dir. Office: Beckman Instruments Inc 2400-2500 Harbor Blvd Fullerton CA 92634 *

ROST, MICHELE PAULINE, speech-language pathologist; b. Bethesda, Md., July 11, 1956; d. John Paul and Mary Jane (Taubler) R. BS, Northeastern U., Boston, 1979; MS, U. N.Mex., 1981. Library aide Library of Congress, Washington, 1976-77; research aide NIH, Bethesda, 1978-81; speech pathologist Albuquerque Pub. Schs., 1981—. Creator, camera person, dir., producer (TV show) We're Just Kids, 1985. Reader Newman Ctr., Albuquerque, 1979—. Recipient Play it Safe award, Gen. Foods Corp., 1985. Mem. Am. Speech-Lang.-Hearing Assn. (cert., exec. bd. 1976-78, publicity chmn. 1979-80), Beta Sigma Phi. Roman Catholic. Avocations: art work, reading, swimming, stamp collecting, puzzles. Home: 118 Pearl Dr NE Albuquerque NM 87124 Office: Albuquerque Pub Schs MacArthur Elem 1100 Douglas MacArthur Rd NW Albuquerque NM 87107

ROST, PAUL FRANCIS, air force officer; b. N.Y.C., Oct. 27, 1940; s. James Francis and Dorothy Helen (Weiss) R.; m. Janet Louise Bell, June 18, 1962 (div. June 1976); children: John K., Suzanne L.; m. Vickie Lou Westenskow, Apr. 22, 1978; children: Shawn W. Salazar, Sara Ann Salazar. BSME, Stevens Inst. Tech., 1962; MS in Systems Mgmt., U. So. Calif., 1985. Commd. 2d lt. USAF, 1962, advanced through grades to col., 1984; comdr. 34th Tactical Fighter Squadron, Hill AFB, Utah, 1979-81; asst. dir. ops. 388 Tactical Fighter Wing, Hill AFB, Utah, 1981-82; chief fighter trainer br., system safety and engring. div. Air Force Inspection and Safety Ctr., Norton AFB, Calif., 1982-85; chief report and analysis div. Hdqrs. Air Force Inspection and Safety Ctr., Norton AFB, Calif., 1985—. Contbr. articles to profl. jours. Decorated D.F.C. with three bronze oak leaf clusters, 17 Air medals. Mem. Daedalians. Republican. Roman Catholic. Avocations: computers, radio controlled model aircraft, sports. Home: 112 Anita Ct Redlands CA 92373 Office: Hdqrs Air Force Inspection Safety Ctr SER Norton AFB CA 92409

ROST, THOMAS LOWELL, botany educator; b. St. Paul, Dec. 28, 1941; s. Lowell Henry Rost and Agnes Marie (Wojtowicz) Jurek; m. Ann Marie Ruhland, Aug. 31, 1963; children: Christopher, Timothy, Jacquelyn. BS, St. John's U., Collegeville, Minn., 1963; MA, Mankato State U., 1965; PhD, Iowa State U., 1970. Postdoctoral fellow Brookhaven Nat. Lab., Upton, N.Y., 1970-72; prof. botany U. Calif., Davis, 1972—; cons. faculty of agronomy U. Uruguay, 1979; vis. fellow Research Sch. Biol. Sci., Canberra, Australia, 1979-80. Co-author: Botany: A Brief Introduction to Plant Biology, 1979, Botany: An Introduction on Plant Biology, 1982; co-editor: Mechanisms and Control of Cell Division, 1977; also numerous articles to profl. jours. Served to capt. U.S. Army, 1965-67. Fellow Royal Microscopy Soc.; mem. Bot. Soc. Am., Soc. Exptl. Biology, Soc. Devel. Biology, Am. Inst. Biol. Sci. Democrat. Roman Catholic. Avocations: running, reading. Office: U Calif Dept Botany Davis CA 95616

ROSTON, SANDRA MARY, college counseling department director; b. Portland, Oreg., Nov. 9, 1941; d. Booker Taliferro and Frances Marida (Hodges) Kirk; m. John Leslie Roston, Jan. 25, 1962; 1 child, John Michael. BA in Health Edn., U. Wash., 1966, MSW, 1970. Group worker Wash. State Inst. and Martha Washington Sch., Seattle, 1963-66; group life counselor Neighborhood House Inc., Seattle, 1966-70; counselor Shoreline Community Coll., Seattle, 1970-85, acting dir. counseling, 1985—. Chmn. services to youth com. Seattle Links Inc., Seattle, 1984 (mem. 1982—). Recipient Bus. of Yr. award, SBA, Seattle, 1982; named Bus. Woman of Yr., Iota Lambda, Seattle, 1980. Mem. Northwest Coll. Personnel Assn. Democrat. Avocations: travel, antiques, reading, gardening. Home: 20422 2d Ave S Seattle WA 98198 Office: Shoreline Community Coll 16101 Greenwood Ave N Seattle WA 98133

ROSUL, LOUISE C(LARA), real estate broker; b. Rockville Centre, N.Y., Aug. 5, 1942; d. Henry and Rosanna (Musgnug) Dietershagen; m. Ronald C. Rosul, Apr. 8, 1962 (div. 1985); children—Ronald C., Linda, Sean. Student Nassau Hosp. Sch. Radiology, 1962; grad. N.Mex. Real Estate Inst., 1980, Dale Carnegie Courses, 1984, 86. Lic. real estate broker, N.Mex. Real estate sales Kennedy Realty, Los Lunas, N.Mex., 1978-79—, Valencia Valley Real Estate, 1979-82, Camco Realty, 1982-83; founder Real Estate Assocs., 1983; broker Realty World, Inc., Las Lunas, 1983—; mem. Realty World-Land of Enchantment Broker's Council, pres. 1986—; founder Gifts for You, 1983—; mem. Homeowners Mktg. Service. Sec., Los Alamos Republican Central Com., 1973; mem. Planning and Zoning Commn. Valencia County, 1982-85; bd. dirs. Greater Las Lunas Bus. Assn., 1980-82; chmn. Valencia Crimestopper Program, 1980-86. Recipient sales awards Valencia County Bd. Realtors, 1981. Mem. Nat. Assn. Realtors, Realtors Assn. N.Mex. (state bd. dirs. 1985), Albuquerque Bd. Realtors (2d v.p. 1985, pres. 1986) Valencia County Bd. Realtors, Profl. Salespersons Am., U.S. C. of C. Roman Catholic. Address: PO Box 1045 Los Lunas NM 87031

ROTBERG, ALBERT STARR, electronics engineer; b. Chgo., Apr. 30, 1923; s. Morris and Shirley (Hauser) R.; B.Sc.E.E., Pacific Internat. U., 1956; Sc.D.E.E., Universidad Nacional Autonoma de Mexico, 1958; m. Ana P. Kaminesky, May 6, 1952; children—Sheldon Jaime. Chief engr. Canoga Electronics, 1967-69; dir. engring. Data Products, 1970-73; dir. system effectiveness Systems Evaluation, Los Angeles, 1973-74; dir. engring. Besco Industries, Chatsworth, Calif., 1974-78; prin. engr., scientist Hughes Microwave Communications Products, Torrance, Calif., 1978-84; dir. video systems View Engring., Simi Valley, Calif., 1984—; pres. Technilog, Inc., Encino, Calif., 1966—. Recipient Letter of Commendation, USAF, 1975. Mem. IEEE. Patentee in field. Home and Office: 17084 Escalon Dr Encino CA 91436

ROTENBERG, MANUEL, physics educator; b. Toronto, Ont., Can., Mar. 12, 1930; came to U.S., 1946; s. Peter and Rose (Plonzker) R.; m. Paula Weissbrod, June 25, 1952; children: Joel, Victor. BS, MIT, 1952, PhD, 1956. Mem. staff Los Alamos (N.Mex.) Nat. Lab., 1955-58; instr. physics Princeton (N.J.) U., 1958-59; asst. prof. U. Chgo., 1959-61; prof. applied physics U. Calif., San Diego, 1961—, dean grad. studies and research, 1975-84. Author: The 3-j and 6-j Symbols, 1959; founding editor: Methods of Computational Physics, 1963, Jour. of Computational Physics, 1962; editor: Biomathematics and Cell Kinetics, 1981. Fellow Am. Phys. Soc.; mem. AAAS, Sigma Xi. Office: U Calif C-014 La Jolla CA 92093

ROTH, DON R., county official. Formerly mayor of Anaheim, Calif., now mem., bd. of supervisors, Orange County, Calif. Office: Orange Co Bd of Supervisors 10 Civic Ctr Plaza Santa Ana CA 92701 *

ROTH, GARY CLEMENS, lawyer; b. St. Louis, Jan. 31, 1938; s. Clemens and Olga Martha (Zdazinsky) R. BS, Wash. U., St. Louis, 1960; MS, Pa. State U., 1964; JD, Golden Gate U., 1977. Bar: Calif. 1977, U.S. Supreme Ct. 1981. Physicist Monsanto Co., St. Louis, 1956-60; physics instr. Pa. State U., University Park, 1960-64; nuclear weapons designer Lawrence Livermore (Calif.) Lab., 1964-77, patent, 1977—; sole practice Livermore, 1977—. Designer various nuclear devices. Wash. U. scholar, 1956-60. Mem. ABA, Am. Phys. Soc. Republican. Avocations: 5th century Athenian history. Home: 822 Polaris Way Livermore CA 94550 Office: Lawrence Livermore Nat Lab PO Box 808 Livermore CA 94550

ROTH, LEWIS DREXEL, research and development executive, materials engineer; b. Bklyn., June 30, 1955; s. Seymour Matthew and Annette (Drexler) R. B.S., Columbia U., 1976, M.S., 1978, D.Engring. Sci., 1981. Metallurgist Ford Motor Co., Dearborn, Mich., 1976; cons. NASA-Ames, Moffet Field, Calif., 1978-80; sr. engr. Westinghouse Research and Devel., Pitts., 1980-84, mgr. material systems, 1985-86; knowledge engring. cons. Inference Corp., Los Angeles, 1986—. Co-editor: Ultrasonic Fatigue, 1982, Artificial Intelligence Applications in Material Sci., 1987. Contbr. articles to profl. jours. Vol. Dept.Parks-Citiparks Sound Crew, Pitts., 1981-85. Regents scholar N.Y. State, 1972-76; Henry Krumb fellow Krumb Sch. Mines, Columbia U., 1976-77. Mem. Am. Soc. Metals, The Metall. Soc., Sigma Xi. Jewish. Avocations: pilot; video production; camping. Office: Inference Corp 5300 W Century Blvd Los Angeles CA 90045

ROTH, NILES, optometric educator; b. N.Y.C., Sept. 27, 1925; s. Irving Isaac and Sarah Shirley (Weinberger) R.; m. Jean Roth, Aug. 31, 1952; children: Alan, Curtis, Marta. AA, U. Calif., Berkeley, 1953, BS, 1955, MS in Optometry, 1956, PhD, 1961. Research biophysicist UCLA, 1961-69; prof. physiol. optics Pacific U., Forest Grove, Oreg., 1969—. Co-contbr. articles to profl. jours. Served with U.S. Army, 1943-45, PTO. Grantee PHHS, 1961, 64. Fellow Am. Acad. Optometry, Optical Soc. Am.; mem. AAUP, Sigma Xi. Democrat. Mem. Unitarian Ch. Office: Pacific U 2043 College Way Forest Grove OR 97116

ROTH, RANDY NEAL, toxicologist; b. Boulder, Colo., Dec. 6, 1949; s. Albert L. and Dorothy Catherine (Morgan) R.; m. Dorothy Susan Howard, July 2, 1977. BS, SUNY, Albany, 1971; PhD, Union U., Albany, 1977. Diplomate Am. Bd. Toxicology. Toxicologist Diamond Shamrock Corp., Painesville, Ohio, 1977-79, sr. toxicologist, pathologist, 1979-80; sr. toxicologist Atlantic Richfield Co., Los Angeles, 1980-82, cons., 1982-85, toxicology tech. services mgr., 1985—; mem. indsl. adv. bd. N.Mex. State U., 1984—; adj. prof. toxicology U. So. Calif., Los Angeles, 1986. Contbr. articles to profl. jours. Grantee NIH, 1972-77. Mem. Internat. Soc. Regulatory Toxicology and Pharmacology, Soc. Toxicology, Soc. for Risk Analysis, Charles L. Davis Soc., N.Y. Acad. Scis. Home: 3049 E Sierra Dr Westlake Village CA 91362

ROTH, SANFORD HAROLD, rheumatologist, health care administrator, educator; b. Akron, Ohio, June 12, 1934; s. Charles and Rose Marie (Zelman) R.; m. Marcia Ann, June 9, 1957; children—Shana Beth, Sari Luanne. B.Sc., Ohio State U., 1955, M.D., 1959. Intern Mt. Carmel, Columbus, Ohio, 1959-60; fellow Mayo Grad. Sch. Medicine, 1962-65; pvt. practice medicine specializing in rheumatology Phoenix, 1965—; med. dir. Arthritis Ctr., Ltd., Phoenix, 1983—; dir. arthritis rehab. program St. Luke's Hosp., Phoenix, 1978; med. research dir. Harrington Arthritis Research Ctr., Phoenix, 1984—; prof., dir. aging and arthritis program Coll. Pub. Programs, Ariz. State U., Tempe, 1984—; dir. medicine Ariz. Insts., Phoenix, 1985—; past state chmn. Gov.'s Conf. on Arthritis in Ariz., 1967; cons., mem. arthritis adv. com. FDA, 1982—, chmn. anti-rheumatic new drug guidelines, 1984—; cons. Ciba-Geigy, 1983—, Upjohn, 1985-87, Ayerst, 1985—, Pennwalt, 1985—, Arthritis Found. Clinics, 3M-Riker Labs., Inc, 1981—, VA, 1970—, FTC, 1980—, Boots Pharm. Co., 1980-87, Greenwich Pharm., 1986-87, Hoffman-LaRoche, 1986—, FDA Office Compliance, 1987—, G.D. Searle, 1987—, Marion Labs., 1987—; chmn. clin. trials com. Pan. Am. League Against Rheumatism, 1987—; prin. investigator Coop. Systematic Studies of Rheumatic Diseases; vis. scholar in rheumatology Beijing Med. Coll., People's Republic China, 1982; proctor, vis. scholar program U.S.-China Edn. Inst., 1982—; liaison cons. Am. Soc. Clin. Pharmacology and Therapeutics, 1983—; med. research dir., exec. bd., trustee Harrington Arthritis Research Ctr., 1983—. Author: New Direction in Arthritis Therapy, 1980; Handbook of Drug Therapy in Rheumatoloy, 1985; med. contbg. editor RISS, Hosp. Physician, 1960-68, Current Prescribing, 1976-80; hon. internat. cons. editor Drugs, 1977—; editor-in-chief Arthron, 1982-85; editor, contbg. author: Rheumatic Therapeutics, 1985; med. cons. editor Update: Rheumatism, 1985, AMA Drug Evaluations, 6th edit., 1986; mem. editorial bd. VA Practitioner, 1985—, Comprehensive Therapy, 1987; contbr. numerous articles to profl. jours., chpts. to books. Fellow Am. Rheumatism Assn. (founding, liaison com. to regional med. program 1974-76, co-dir. med. info. system ARAMIS, computer com., chmn. antiinflammatory drug study club 1974—, com. on clubs and councils 1977—, western regional co-chmn. 1977—, therapeutic and drug com. 1979—, glossary com. 1981—, ad hoc com. on future meeting sites 1983); mem. AMA, ACP (regional program com., ann. Philip S. Hench lectureship chmn. 1978-79), Arthritis Found. (dir. central Ariz. chpt. 1982-83, past chmn. med. and sci. com. 1967-72), Lupus Found. Am. (bd. 1981—), Internat. Soc. Rheumatic Therapy (bd. dirs. 1987—), Maricopa County Med. Soc. (rehab. com.), Am. Soc. Clin. Rheumatology (past pres. exec. council), Am. Coll. Clin. Pharmacology, Soc. Internal Medicine, Mayo Clinic Alumni Assn., Mayo Clinic Fellows Assn. (sec. 1964-65), Mayo Clinic Fellows Rheumatology Soc. (pres. 1964-65), Mayo Clinic Film Soc. (bd. dirs. 1964-65), Pan Am. League Against Rheumatism (chmn. clin. trials com. 1987—). Office: Arthritis Ctr Ltd 3330 N 2d St #601 Phoenix AZ 85012

ROTHAUPT, RICHARD, industrial engineering educator; b. Chgo., Feb. 27, 1955; s. Ernest and Elin (Miller) R.; m. Jeanne Marie Wittman, May 15, 1981; children: Michael, Kristin. Student, Iowa State U., 1973-74; BS, U. Wis., Menomonie, 1979, postgrad., 1980-81. Lectr. U. Wis., Menomonie, 1980-82; devel. engr. Donaldson Co., Menomonie, 1981-82; instr., dir. machine tool tech. Casper (Wyo.) Coll., 1982—; lectr. Natrona County Sch. Enrichment Program, Casper. Recipient Disting. Service award Donaldson Co., 1982. Mem. Wyo. Vocat. Assn. Democrat. Mem. Soc. Friends. Avocations: wood boat building, auto rebuilding, nordic skiing, fishing. Home: 1144 Oakcrest Casper WY 82601 Office: Casper Coll 125 College Dr Casper WY 82601

ROTHBART, STANLEY GLENN, real estate executive, lawyer; b. Upland, Calif., Aug. 19, 1950; s. Louis and Helen (Friedman) R.; m. Farideh Jahanbin, Dec. 20, 1985. BS, UCLA, 1972, JD, 1975. Bar: Calif. 1975. Dep. pub. defender Office Pub. Defender, Santa Ana, Calif., 1975-79; v.p., gen. counsel Glickman & Assocs., Beverly Hills, Calif., 1979-82; prin. Western Comml., Thousand Oaks, Calif., 1983-86; ptnr. Daniels, Rothbart & Assocs., Sherman Oaks, Calif., 1983-86; pres. Rothbart Devel. Corp., 1986—. Mem. State Bar Assn. Calif., Los Angeles County Bar Assn., Internat. Council Shopping Ctrs., Calif. Commerce Council (bd. dirs. 1986), So. Calif. Comml. Property Owners Assn. (pres., bd. dirs. 1984-86). Home: 1221 Ocean Ave #1405 Santa Monica CA 90401 Office: Daniels Rothbart & Assocs 15315 Magnolia Blvd Suite #130 Sherman Oaks CA 91403

ROTHBLATT, DANIEL MORRIS, fundraiser and community organizer; b. Racine, Wis., Dec. 31, 1958; s. Isaiah and Agnes Rothblatt. BA in Design and Industry, San Francisco State U., 1983; MSW, U. So. Calif., Los Angeles, 1986; M in Jewish Communal Service, Hewbrew Union Coll., 1986. Asst. dir. Shenson's Delicatessen, San Francisco, 1979-83; campaign assoc. San Francisco Jewish Community Fedn., 1983-84; asst. dir. San Fernando Valley Region Jewish Fedn. Council, Los Angeles, 1986—. Mem. Nat. Assn. Social Workers, Second Generation, Assn. Jewish Community Orgn. Personnel, So. Calif. Conf. Jewish Communal Service. Office: Jewish Fedn Council 22634 Vanowen St Canoga Park CA 91307

ROTHE, ANDREW ROBERT, paintings conservator; b. Bozano, Italy, Oct. 12, 1936; came to U.S., 1947; s. Hans Ludwig and Helen Hildegard (Falch) R.; m. Grazia de Santis, May 30, 1965; 1 dau., Elisabeth. Conservation asst. Uffizi labs., U. Pracacci and U. Baldini, Florence, Italy, 1954-57, Bavarian State Gallerie with H. Lohe, Munich, W.Ger., 1957-58, Sch. of Vision with Kokoschka, Salzburg, Austria, 1955-63, Viennese Kunsthistorisches Mus. with Prof. Hajsinek, Austria, 1959; paintings conservator Soprintendeza alle Gallerie, Florence, Italy, 1959-81; head paintings conservation The J. Paul Getty Mus., Malibu, Calif., 1981—; head conservation dept. Palazzo Pitti, Florence, Italy, 1969-81; conservation asst. museums and chs. Urbino, Siena, Arezzo, Naples, Italy, 1966-81. Mem. Internat. Inst. Conservation, Am. Inst. Conservation. Office: J Paul Getty Mus PO Box 2112 Santa Monica CA 90406

ROTHENBERG, ALAN I., lawyer, basketball executive; b. Detroit, Apr. 10, 1939; m. Georgina Rothenberg; 3 children. B.A., U. Mich., 1960, J.D., 1963. Bar: Calif. 1964. Instr. sports law U. So. Calif., 1969, 76, 84; instr. sports law Whittier Coll. Law, 1980, 84; ptnr. Manatt Phelps Rothenberg Tunney & Phillips, Los Angeles; pres. Los Angeles Clippers Basketball Team, 1982—. Mem. soccer commn. 1984 Olympic Games, Equal Edn. Opportunities Commn. State Calif. Bd. Edn., 1972-75. Mem. Nat. Basketball Assn. (bd. govs. 1971-79, 82—, N.Am. Soccer League (bd. govs. 1977-80), Constitutional Rights Found. (dir., pres. 1987—), ABA, local and county bar assns. Office: Los Angeles Clippers 3939 S Figueroa Los Angeles CA 90037 *

ROTHENBERG, HARVEY DAVID, ednl. adminstr.; b. Fort Madison, Iowa, May 31, 1937; s. Max and Cecelia Rothenberg; A.A., Wentworth Mil. Acad., 1957; B.B.A., State U. Iowa, 1960; M.A., U. No. Colo., 1961; postgrad. Harris Tchrs. Coll., 1962-63, St. Louis U., 1962-63; Ph.D., Colo. State U., 1972; m. Audrey Darlynne Roseman, July 5, 1964; children—David Michael, Mark Daniel. Distributive edn. tchr. Roosevelt High Sch., St. Louis, 1961-63, Proviso West High Sch., Hillside, Ill., 1963-64, Longmont (Colo.) Sr. High Sch., 1964-69, 70-71; supr. research and spl. programs St. Vrain Valley Sch. Dist., Longmont, Colo., 1971-72; chmn. bus. div. Arapahoe Community Coll., Littleton, Colo., 1972-75; dir. vocat., career and adult edn. Arapahoe County Sch. Dist. 6, Littleton, 1975—; instr. Met. State Coll., Denver, part-time, 1975—, Arapahoe Community Coll., Littleton, 1975—, Regis Coll., 1979—; vis. prof. U. Ala., Tuscaloosa, summer 1972; dir. Chatfield Bank, Littleton, 1974-83, Yaak River Mines Ltd., Amusement Personified Inc.; pres. Kuytia Inc., Littleton, 1975—; co-owner Albuquerque Lasers, profl. volleyball team. Mem. City of Longmont Long-Range Planning Commn., 1971-72, pres. Homeowners Bd., 1978—. Recipient Outstanding Young Educator award St. Vrain Valley Sch. Dist., 1967. Mem. Am., Colo. (mem. exec. com. 1966-68, treas. 1972-73) vocat. assns., Littleton C. of C., Delta Sigma Pi, Delta Pi Epsilon, Nat. Assn. Local Sch. Adminstrs., Colo. Council Local Sch. Adminstrs. Clubs: Elks, Masons, Shriners. Home: 7461 S Sheridan Ct Littleton CO 80123 Office: Arapahoe County Sch Dist 6 5776 S Crocker St Littleton CO 80120

ROTHENBERG, SIMON JEREMY, aerosol surface chemistry researcher; b. London, Apr. 27, 1940; Came to U.S., 1976; s. Daniel and Hanna Miriam (Weinboum) R.; m. Sheila Yolisa Cingo, July 16, 1970; children: Ronald, Ian, Michelle. BA 1st class, Cambridge U., Eng., 1963, MA, 1965, PhD, 1968. Lectr. Sch. of Sci. U. Botswana, Lesotho & Swaziland, Lesotho, 1968-70, tutor, 1970; assoc. prof. chem. Abadan Inst. Oil Tech., Iran, 1970-72; med. research council fellow U. Essex, Eng., 1973-75; research scientist II Lovelace Biomed., Albuquerque, 1976—. Mem. Am. Chem. Soc., Am. Assn. Aerosol Research, N.Am. Thermal Analysis Soc., Gesellschaft Für Aerosolforschung, Electron Microscopy Soc. Am./Microbeam Analysis Soc. (program chmn. biol. applications, nat. meeting, Albuquerque, 1986), Microbeam Analysis Soc., Am. Vacuum Soc. Office: Lovelace Biomed Inhalation Toxicology Research PO Box 5890 Albuquerque NM 87185

ROTHHAMMER, CRAIG ROBERT, social worker, consultant; b. San Francisco, May 17, 1954; s. Robert Charles and Gloria Lee (Molloy) R. BA, U. Calif., Santa Barbara, 1976; MSW, San Diego State U., 1979. Lic. clin. social worker, Calif. Social work asst. Mercy Hosp., San Diego, 1977; psychiat. social worker Lanterman State Hosp., Pomona, Calif., 1979-83, Sonoma State Hosp., Eldridge, Calif., 1983-84; children's social worker County Adoption Service, San Bernardino, Calif., 1984-86; private practice social work (part-time) Patton, Calif., 1986—; psychiatric social worker Patton State Hosp., 1987—; expert examiner Behavioral Sci. Examiners, Calif. Vol. Social Advs. for Youth, Santa Barbara, Calif., 1974-76, Am. Diabetes Assn., San Diego, 1978-79, San Diego Assn. For Retarded, 1978-80; liason Adoptive Family Assn., San Bernardino, 1986. Mem. Nat. Assn. Social Workers. Democrat. Avocations: scuba diving, bicycling, hiking, writing, ch. related activities. Office: Patton State Hosp 3102 E Highland Ave Patton CA 92369

ROTHMAN, ALBERT JOEL, chemical engineer; b. Bklyn., Jan. 16, 1924; s. Harry and Rose (Chasan) R.; divorced; children: Denise Fagliano, Lynn Iwase, Joel Rothman. BS, Columbia U., 1944; MSChemE, Polytech. U., 1951; PhD, U. Calif., Berkeley, 1954. Research chem. engr. Am. Cyanamid Co., Stamford, Conn., 1944-48; project design engr. Colgate Palmolive, Berkeley, Calif., 1948-50; research assoc. and teaching asst. U. Calif., Berkeley, 1950-53; research chem. engr. Shell Oil Co., Martinez, Calif., 1953-56; mgr. and research assoc. Columbia U., N.Y.C., 1956-57; mgr., project leader, chemist Lawrence Livermore (Calif.) Nat. Lab., 1958-83, sr. research chem. engr., 1983-86, cons., 1987—; cons. McGraw-Hill, 1967-72. Contbr. articles to profl. jours. Vol. Sta. KQED-FM, San Francisco, 1982—. Fellow Cen. Sci. Co., U. Calif.-Berkeley, 1952-53; Pulitzer scholar, Columbia U., 1941-44; recipient Illig award, Columbia U., 1944. Mem. Am. Chem. Soc., Sierra Club, Sigma Xi, Tau Beta Pi. Democrat. Club: Common Cause. Avocations: hiking, music, wine collecting, touring, running. Home and Office: 503 Yorkshire Dr Livermore CA 94550

ROTHMAN, NATHAN FRANK, sailboat manufacturing company executive, trading executive; b. N.Y.C., Mar. 26, 1945; s. Morris and Sylvia (Frank) R.; student Bradley U., 1962-64, Ill. Inst. of Tech., 1964-65, Northwestern U., 1965-67, Roosevelt U., 1967-69; m. Susan Barry Stevens, May 15, 1976. Salesman, Valspar Paint Co., Chgo., 1967; v.p., Count Down, Inc., Chgo., 1968; v.p., treas. The Garment Dist., Inc., Chgo., 1969; pres., Paralines, Chgo., 1969-71; sec.-treas., gen. mgr. Jay R. Benford & Assocs., Inc. and assoc. cos. (Bedford Boat Bldg., Bedford Pub.), Seattle, Wash., 1972-73, chief. exec. and sole proprieter Sea Life, Seattle, 1972-74; pres. Valiant Yacht Corp., Seattle, 1974-80, Trade Interface Corp., 1982—; dir. world sales Valiant Yachts div. Uniflite, Inc., 1981-82; treas., dir. Susan Barry, Inc. Recipient Offshore Cruiser of Decade award Sail mag. Bd. dirs. Wash. State China Relations Council. Club: Wash. State Athletic. Home: 3711 58th Ave SW Seattle WA 98116 Office: 2030 1st Ave Seattle WA 98121

ROTHMAN, STEWART NEIL, photographer; b. Rochester, N.Y., Dec. 27, 1930; s. Morris Zeus and Rose Mary (Cotler) R.; student Wayne State U., 1952-54; m. Shirley Mae Derry, Sept. 12, 1957; children—Leslie Paula, Karen Pat. Free-lance photographer, Detroit, 1952-57; photographer NASA, Gilmore Creek, Alaska, 1965-68; writer, photographer Jessen's Daily, Fairbanks, Alaska, 1968-69; propr. The Lens Unlimited, Fairbanks, 1959—; staff photographer Gen. Mac Arthur's Hdqrs., Tokyo, 1948-50; pres., chmn. bd. Arctic Publs., 1968-72; pres. Public Relations Specialists Co., 1973—; editor Arctic Oil Jour., 1968-72, This Month in Fairbanks, 1974--85; pub. The Fairbanks Mag., 1985—. Publicity adviser to mayor of Fairbanks; pres. Tanana-Yukon Hist. Soc. Served with U.S. Army, 1948-52, Korea, then USAF, 1957-65. Decorated Purple Heart with oak leaf cluster. Fellow Master Photographers Assn. Gt. Britain; mem. European Council Photographers, Fairbanks C. of C. Club: Farthest North Press. Lodges: Lions (pres.), Elks. Author: Nudes of Sixteen Lands, 1971; Hobo and Dangerous Dan McGrew, 1975; The Lens is My Brush, 1977; China, The Opening Door, 1980; Pope John Paul II's First Visit to Alaska, 1981; Window on Life, 1982; The Pope and the President, 1984. Home and Office: 921 Woodway St Fairbanks AK 99709

ROTHSCHILD, RICHARD BARRY, physician, educator; b. N.Y.C., Mar. 30, 1956; s. Walter and Vera (Baar) R. BA in Biochemistry, U. Calif. San Diego, La Jolla, 1977; MD, Harvard U., 1981. Diplomate Am. Bd. Internal Medicine. Intern UCLA, 1981-82, resident in internal medicine, 1982-84, fellow in cardiology, 1984—. Coordinator Tay Sachs Testing Program, La Jolla, 1975. Named Outstanding Citizen of Yr., Los Angeles City Council, 1984; grantee Pres. Undergrad. Fellowship Com., 1975, 76. Mem. ACP, AMA. Los Angeles County Med. Assn., Physicians Social Responsibility (speaker and educator, 1980—), Internat. Physicians for Prevention of Nuclear War (speaker and educator, 1985—), Sierra Club, Amnesty Internat., Nat. Resource Def. Council, Union Concerned Scientists. Democrat. Jewish. Avocations: running, soccer, backpacking, sailing, piano. Home: 938 20th St #7 Santa Monica CA 90403 Office: UCLA Med Ctr 10833 Le Conte Ave Los Angeles CA 90024

ROTHSCHILD, TOBY JAMES, lawyer; b. Los Angeles, Sept. 1, 1944; s. Otto and Sylvia (Singer) R.; m. Elena L. Hyman, Aug. 6, 1967; children: Marnie, Dana. BA, San Francisco State U., 1966; JD, UCLA, 1969. Bar: Calif. 1970, U.S. Dist. Ct. (cen. dist.) Calif. 1970, U.S. Ct. Appeals (9th cir.) 1971, U.S. Supreme Ct. 1973. Staff atty. Los Angeles Neighborhood Legal Service, 1969-71; staff atty. Legal Aid Found., Long Beach, Calif., 1971-73, exec. dir., 1973—; chmn. State Bar Com. on Adminstrn. Justice, 1986—. Author: Automobile Transactions, 1981; contbr. articles to profl. jours. Bd. dirs., vice chmn. Western Ctr. on Law and Poverty, 1973—; v.p. Long Beach Jewish Community Ctr., 1983—. Mem. Am. Arbitration Assn. Office: Legal Aid Found of Long Beach 110 Pine Ave Suite 420 Long Beach CA 90802

ROTHSTEIN, BARBARA JACOBS, federal judge; b. Bklyn., Feb. 3, 1939; d. Solomon and Pauline Jacobs; m. Ted L. Rothstein, Dec. 28, 1968; 1 child, Daniel. B.A., Cornell U., 1960; LL.B., Harvard U., 1966. Bar: Mass. bar 1966, Wash. bar 1969. Individual practice law Boston, 1966-68; asst. atty. gen. State of Wash., 1968-77; judge Superior Ct., Seattle, 1977-80, Fed. Dist. Ct. Western Wash., Seattle, 1980—; faculty Law Sch. U. Wash., 1975-77, Hastings Inst. Trial Advocacy, 1977, N.W. Inst. Trial Advocacy, 1979—. Recipient Matrix Table Woman of Year award, 1980. Mem. Am. Judicature Soc., Am. Bar Assn. (judicial sect.), Phi Beta Kappa, Phi Kappa Phi. Office: US District Court 411 US Courthouse 1010 Fift Ave Seattle WA 98104

ROTHWELL, ROBERT ALAN, investing and consulting company executive, writer; b. Newark, May 13, 1939; s. Albert Robert and Rose Gloria (Cundari) R. B.A., St. Francis Coll., Loretto, Pa., 1961; M.A., Seton Hall U., 1962; M.S., Georgetown U. Sch. Fgn. Service, 1963; Ph.D., Duquesne U., 1967; D.H.L., Georgetown U., 1967; D.Social Scis. (hon.), Fribourgh U., Switzerland, 1969. Prof. psychology U. Steubenville, Ohio, 1966-73; dir. Edn. Dynamics, Las Vegas, 1973-76; pres. Robert's Investing and Cons., Las Vegas, 1976—; U.S. govt. cons. on Russian affairs, Washington, 1976—; spl. UN observer to various countries, 1966-81; mem. Nev. Gov.'s Commn. on Higher Edn., 1978-82; mem. Pres. Commn. on Psychol. Warfare, Washington, 1977-82. Author: (textbook) Existential Psychology, 1972; The Origin of Consciousness, 1974, The Bicameral Mind, 1976, Code Name: Grizzly, 1986. Served to capt. USMC, 1962-66. Decorated Navy D.S.M., Navy and Marine Corps Medal for Heroism, Bronze Star. Recipient Disting. Service award U.S. Def. Dept., 1966, Superior Service Nat. Security award U.S. Def. Dept., 1968; named Mr. Nev. Masters Bodybldg. Champion, 1985, Mr. Silver State Masters Bodybldg. Champion, 1985, Mr. U.S.A. Masters Bodybldg. Champion, 1986. Mem. AAUP, Nat. Assn. Sch. Psychologists, Assn. Advancement Psychology, Nat. Physique Com. (vice chmn. Nev. chpt.), Internat. Assn. Psychologists, Am. Psychologists Assn. Republican. Roman Catholic. Office: Robert's Investing and Cons 7014 La Cienega St Las Vegas NV 89119-4222

ROTTAS, RAY, state official; b. Cleve., Oct. 20, 1927; s. Nicholas and Jessie Mabel (Herpst) T.; m. Barbara Lucas, Sept. 1, 1956; children—Steven, Donna, Paul, Diane. B.B.A., Case Western Res. U., 1951. Owner, operator Auto Warehousing Inc., Phoenix, 1956-83; mem. Ariz. Senate, 1971-74, 77-82; treas. State of Ariz., Phoenix, 1983—. Bd. dirs. YMCA, Phoenix, 1971—; pres. Jr. Achievement, Phoenix, 1979-80, bd. dirs., 1972—; pres. Ariz. Econ. Forum, 1983—. Served to col. USAF, 1951-55, Korea. Republican. Methodist. Lodges: Rotary (pres. Phoenix 1982-83, treas. 1984-85), Masons, Elks. Home: 9424 N 25th St Phoenix AZ 85028 Office: Ariz State Treasurer 1700 W Washington St Phoenix AZ 85007

ROTTER, JEROME ISRAEL, medical geneticist; b. Los Angeles, Feb. 24, 1949; s. Leonard L. and Jeanette (Kronenfold) R.; m. Deborah Tofield, July 14, 1970; children: Jonathan Moshe, Amy Esther, Samuel Alexander. BS, UCLA, 1969, MD, 1973. Intern Harbor-UCLA Med. Ctr., Torrance, Calif., 1973-74; resident in medicine Wadsworth VA Hosp., Los Angeles, 1974-75; fellow in med. genetics Harbor-UCLA Med. Ctr., Torrance, 1975-78, asst. research pediatrician, 1978-79, faculty div. med. genetics, 1978-86; asst. prof. medicine and pediatrics UCLA Sch. Medicine, 1979-83, assoc. prof., 1983—; dir. div. med. genetics and assoc. dir. Med. Genetics Birth Defect Ctr. of Cedars-Sinai Med. Ctr., 1986—; key investigator Ctr. for Ulcer Research and Edn., Los Angeles, 1980—; dir. genetic epidemiology core Ctr. for Study of Inflamatory Bowel Disease, Torrance, 1985—. Recipient Regents scholarship UCLA, 1963-73; recipient Richard Weitzman award for Outstanding Young Investigator, Harbor-UCLA, 1983, Ross award Western Soc. for Pediatric Research, 1985. Mem. Am. Soc. Human Genetics, Am. Gastroent. Assn., Am. Diabetes Assn., Soc. for Pediatric Research, Western Soc. for Clin. Investigation (mem. council 1985—), Am. Fedn. for Clin. Research. Jewish. Avocations: reading, racquetball. Office: Cedars-Sinai Med Ctr Div Med Genetics 8700 Beverly Blvd Los Angeles CA 90048

ROTTO, GARY STEVEN, non-profit corporation executive; b. El Paso, Tex., Apr. 6, 1960; s. Melvin Daniel and Debra (Siegel) R. MSW, U. So. Calif., 1982; MA in Jewish Community Service, Hebrew Union Coll., 1984; BSW, U. Tex., 1984. Lic. clin. social worker, Tex. Asst. dir. community relations Jewish Fedn. Greater Long Beach and West Orange County, Long Beach, Calif., 1984—; ind. pub. relations cons., Long Beach. Author: The Consumers Report. Sports info. officer Los Angeles Olympic Organizing Com., 1984. Scholar Council Jewish Fedns., 1982. Mem. Nat. Assn. Social Workers, Assn. Jewish Communal Orgn. Profls., Jewish Youth Dirs. Assn. (nat. bd. dirs. 1984—), Tex. Ex-Students Assn., Sigma Alpha Mu (Nathan Karcher award 1981). Avocations: volleyball, softball, advising high school groups. Office: Jewish Fedn 3801 E Willow St Long Beach CA 90815

ROUANET, JEAN-PIERRE CHRISTIAN, chemist; b. Paris, Dec. 9, 1957; came to U.S., 1982; s. Jean Louis Yves and Colette (Moret) R.; m. Roxanne Julia Schwartz, May 20, 1983. BS in Chemistry, U. Paris, 1980, Ariz. State U., 1984. Research chemist IRSID, Paris, 1980; research and devel. chemist KTI Chems. Inc., Tempe, 1985; chemist Chemonics Lab., Phoenix, 1985—. Served to chief brigadier Air Force, 1980-81, France. Mem. Am. Chem. Soc. (analytical chemistry div.), Internat. Union Pure and Applied Chemistry (affiliate). Avocations: horseback riding, sailing, classical music. Office: Chemonics Labs 734 A E Southern Pacific Dr Phoenix AZ 85034

ROUANZOIN, CURTIS CLAIR, clinical psychologist, psychology educator; b. Morgan County, Ohio, Mar. 12, 1952; s. Martin Clair and Mary Katherine (McElhiney) R.; m. Denne Jan Pierce, June 1, 1974; children: Erick, Darren, Bryan. B.A., Pacific Christian Coll., Fullerton, Calif., 1974; M.A., Pepperdine U., 1975; Ph.D., Brigham Young U., 1981. Lic. marriage, family and child counselor, clin. psychologist. Marriage, family and child counselor Pacific Counseling Ctr., Fullerton, Calif., 1976-77; marital and family therapist S.E. Christian Ch., Salt Lake City, 1977-80; clin. psychology intern and registered psychol. asst. Child Guidance Ctr., Fullerton, 1980-82; pvt. practice clin. psychology, Fullerton, 1982—; assoc. prof., chmn. depts. social sci. and psychology Pacific Christian Coll., Fullerton; lectr. profl. and religious meetings. Vice pres., bd. dirs. Western Family Inst., 1980-86. Mem. Am. Assn. Marriage and Family Therapy, Am. Psychol. Assn., Orange County Soc. Clin. Hypnosis, Calif. State Psychol. Assn., Christian Assn. for Psychol. Studies, Pi Beta Sigma, Delta Epsilon Chi. Republican.

ROUGH, DAVID S., marketing professional, consultant; b. Lake Placid, N.Y., Dec. 20, 1933; s. Jack and Veva Lillian (Bickford) R.; m. Patricia Anne Healy, June 10, 1962 (div. Sept. 1974); children: Robert Scott, Patricia Anne, Jonathan Lee. BA, U. Conn., 1954; MA, U. Miami, 1963, PhD, 1966. Exec. v.p. Internat. Apparel, Miami, Fla., 1966-69; pres. Outlet Holding Corp., Atlanta, 1969-74; exec. dir. Marco Group, San Bernardino, Calif., 1975-82, Infinity Designs, Anaheim, Calif., 1982—; exec. v.p. Daleco Holographics, Inc., Costa Mesa, Calif., 1984—; cons. Maxines, Encido, Calif., 1982—, Bobbies, San Diego, 1982—. Served with USAF, 1955-58. Democrat. Baptist. Avocations: sports, backgammon, tennis, golf. Office: Daleco Holographics Inc 1603 Monrovia Ave Costa Mesa CA 92627

ROULSTON, LENA MAXINE, language therapist; b. Cisco, Tex., July 25, 1934; d. William Hudson and Maudie Mae (Green) Carlton; B.S., Coll. of Southwest, 1966; M.Ed., Eastern N.Mex. U., 1972, M.Ed. in Reading, 1977; m. Robert Roy Roulston, Jan. 2, 1951; 1 son, Gary. Elem. sch. tchr., Hobbs, N.Mex., 1966—, learning disabilities resource tchr., 1977—; off-campus instr. Eastern N.Mex. U., evenings 1977-79, mem. reading consortium, 1977-79. Mem. Internat. Reading Assn., NEA, N.Mex. Edn. Assn., Hobbs Edn. Assn., Hobbs Assn. Classroom Tchrs., Orton Soc., Delta Kappa Gamma, Phi Kappa Phi. Democrat. Baptist. Home: 608 Luna St Hobbs NM 88240 Office: 1520 Breckon Hobbs NM 88240

ROUMBANIS, THEODORE, microwave engineering physicist, consultant; b. Clinton, Ont., Can., Sept. 10, 1919; came to U.S., 1956; s. Demetrius

Constantine and Lilian Rachel (Kingston) R.; m. Madeleine Sophie Dunphy, Mar. 9, 1943; children: Theodore Kell, Gregory Alexander, Althea Kim. B Engring. in Physics, McGill U., 1953, MS in Microwave Physics, 1956. Profl. engr., Que. Advanced devel. engr. Sylvania Elec. Products, Mountain View, Calif., 1956-63; project mgr. Varian Assocs., Palo Alto, Calif., 1963-70; mgr. microwave engring. Siemens Med. Labs., Walnut Creek, Calif., 1970-84; physicist, microwave engr. Schonberg Radiation Corp., Santa Clara, Calif., 1984—; cons. Teledyne MEC, Palo Alto, 1970, EGG, San Ramon, Calif., 1980, Siemens Med. Labs., Walnut Creek, Calif., 1985-86. Inventor broadbend transition for microwave tube, 1970, centipede circuit for microwave tube, 1970, med. electron accelerator, 1980. Served with RCAF, 1939-45. Mem. IEEE, Am. Welding Soc., Can. Assn. Physicists, Am. Soc. Metals, Sigma XI (br. pres. 1971-72). Greek Orthodox. Avocations: classical singing, mountaineering, tech. rock climbing. Home: 663 Jay St Los Altos CA 94022 Office: Schonberg Radiation Corp 3300 Keller St Santa Clara CA 95054

ROUNTREE, ROBERT BENJAMIN, utility executive; b. Burnsville, N.C., Oct. 20, 1924; s. Benjamin F. and Carrie R.; m. Martha Jane McBee, Feb. 23, 1946; 1 dau., Janet Fay Rountree Wilson. B.S.E.E., U. N.Mex., 1946. With Pub. Service Co. N.Mex., 1948—; beginning as draftsman successively gen. supt. Pub. Service Co. N.Mex., Belen, N.Mex.; mgr. Pub. Service Co. N.Mex., Deming, N.Mex.; asst. div. mgr. Pub. Service Co. N.Mex., Albuquerque, div. v.p., v.p. div. ops., 1948-72; sr. v.p. Pub. Service Co. N.Mex., 1972—, dir.; chmn. bd. Meadows Resources, Inc., 1983—, Sunbelt Minig Co., 1983—. Mem. IEEE, Am. Inst. Mgmt., Nat. Soc. Profl. Engrs.

ROUNTREE, STEPHEN DOUGLAS, arts foundation administrator; b. Pasadena, Calif., Mar. 31, 1949; m. Carol Ann Stassinos, Nov. 5, 1977; children: Kathleen, Emily. BA cum laude, Occidental Coll., 1971; MBA, Claremont Grad. Sch., 1976. Dir. personnel Occidental Coll., Pasadena, 1978-85, asst. exec. v.p., 1978-80; dep. dir. J. Paul Getty Mus., Malibu, Calif., 1980-84; dir. bldg. program Getty Trust, Los Angeles, 1984—. Chmn. U.S. Com. UNICEF, So. Calif. Adv. Council, 1985-86. Mem. Am. Mgmt. Assn., Assn. Phys. Plant Adminstrs. Democrat. Avocations: biking, woodworking, writing. Office: J Paul Getty Trust 1875 Century Park E #2300 Los Angeles CA 90067

ROUSELL, RALPH HENRY, pharmacologist, immunologist; b. Johannesburg, South Africa, Jan. 7, 1933; s. Reginald Henry John and Olive Agnes (Neilson) R.; came to U.S., 1979. M.B., B.Ch., Witwatersrand U., South Africa, 1958; M.Sc., U. London, 1976; diploma in pharm. medicine Royal Colls. Physicians, Edinburgh, Glasgow and London, 1976. Intern in medicine and surgery Johannesburg Gen. Hosp., 1959, resident in surgery and anesthesiology, 1960-63; practice medicine specializing in anesthesiology London Teaching Hosps., 1963; fellow in pharmacology St. Thomas' Hosp., London, 1964-65; med. dir. Pharmacia (Gt. Britain) Ltd., London, 1965-70; head med. services Hoechst U.K., London, 1970-79; dir. clin. research biol. and intravenous nutritionals div. Miles Pharms., Berkeley, Calif., 1979-86, dir. internat. clin. research Cutter div. Miles Pharms., Berkeley, 1986—; mem. sci. council Am. Blood Resources Assn., 1980—. Mem. Brit. Med. Assn., Brit. Soc. Immunology, Royal Inst. Biology, Am. Soc. Clin. Pharmacology, Am. Assn. Clin. Scientists. Methodist. Clubs: Hammersmith Rugby (life), Brockley (London). Editor: Streptokinase in Clinical Practice, 1973; Antilymphocyte Globulin in Clinical Practice, 1976; Intravenous Immune Globulin: Its Use and Potential, 1981. Home: 5585 Cold Water Dr Castro Valley CA 94552 Office: 4th and Parker Sts Berkeley CA 94710

ROUSH, JOHN HUSTON, JR., management consultant; b. Portland, Oreg., Feb. 3, 1923; s. John H. and Josephine (Schuster) R.; m. Virginia Beans, Feb. 24, 1951; children—Paul Huston, Ellard Thomas, Michael Melville. A.A., San Francisco City Coll., 1942; B.A. in Polit. Sci., John F. Kennedy U., 1973, M.P.A., 1973; D.B.A., Western Colo. U., 1975; grad. Command and Gen. Staff Coll., 1967, U.S. Army War Coll., 1970, Fgn. Service Inst., U.S. Dept. State, 1971. Commd. U.S. Army, 1942, advanced through grades to col., 1970; assigned to M.I.; ret., 1970; ins. claims exec. St. Paul Ins. Co., San Francisco, 1970-74; mgmt. cons. to nat. ins. cos., 1975—. Author: Hornets in Our Home: Civil Disturbances and Their Effects upon U.S. National Security, 1971; The Problems of Civil Disturbances as They Relate to Public Administration, 1973; Management Audits of Subordinate Claims Offices of National Insurance Companies, 1974; Successfully Fishing Lake Tahoe, 1976; Enjoying Fishing Lake Tahoe, 1987. Contbr. articles to profl. jours. Decorated Bronze Star, Meritorious Service medal, also others; named Knight Officer Order of Compassionate Heart, 1979, Knight Sovereign Mil. Order of Temple of Jerusalem, K.T., Rome, 1984; named to Inf. Officer Candidate Sch. Hall of Fame, U.S. Army, Ft. Benning, Ga., 1984; recipient George Washington honor medal Freedoms Found. of Valley Forge, Pa., 1968. Mem. Assn. U.S. Army (mem. nat. adv. bd. dirs.), Res. Officers Assn. U.S. (past v.p. for Army, Calif. dept.), Assn. Former Intelligence Officers (past v.p. San Francisco chpt.), Explorers Club, Nat. Writers Club, Outdoor Writers Assn. Am. Republican. Roman Catholic. Clubs: Queens; Commonwealth of Calif. Lodge: Kiwanis. Home: 27 Terrace Ave Kentfield CA 94904

ROUSSIS, JOHN, research electrical engineer; b. N.Y.C., May 23, 1958; s. Harry Thomas and Eleftheria (Papachristodoulos) R. BS, Columbia U., 1978, MA, 1979, PhD, 1982. Registered profl. engr., Calif. Staff scientist semiconductor div. Hughes Aircraft Co., San Diego, 1982—; research semiconductor processing MIT, Cambridge, 1981-82; cons. Dept. Def., Washington, 1983—. Author: Simulating Mos Transistors-The Roussis-Cosworth Model, 1984, Advances in Automated Medical Research Equipment, 1985 (Jaffra C. Paulie Humanitarian award 1986); also articles. Vol. Rep. Organizing Com., San Diego, 1984—; coordinator spl. events Boys Club Am., San Diego, 1985—. Recipient Harvey W. Mudd award Columbia U., 1978, 81. Mem. Optical Soc. Am. Greek Orthodox. Avocations: equestrian events, skiing, classical music. Home: 940 Sealane Dr Apt 3 Encinitas CA 92024 Office: Hughes Aircraft Co 6155 El Camino Real MS 108 Carlsbad CA 92008

ROUTSON, RONALD CHESTER, soil scientist; b. Chewelah, Wash., Dec. 12, 1933; s. Chester A. and Lucille F. R.; Ph.D. in Soil Sci., Wash. State U., 1970; m. Mary Joan Boning, Dec. 26, 1958; 1 dau., Kelly L. Staff soil scientist Battelle Pacific N.W. Lab., 1967-78, Rockwell Hanford Ops., Richland, Wash., 1978—. Served with U.S. Army, 1958-62; mem. Res. NDEA fellow, 1964-68. Mem. Am. Soc. Agronomy, Soil Sci. Soc. Am., Am. Nuclear Soc., N.W. Sci. Assn., Western Soil Sci. Soc. and Geochem. Soc. Sci., Sigma Xi, Alpha Zeta. Republican. Roman Catholic. Home: Route 1 Box 1351 Benton City WA 99320 Office: M0-028 200 W Area PO Box 800 Richland WA 99352

ROUX, WALTER LELAND, electrical engineer; b. Oakland, Calif., Aug. 31, 1929; s. George Francis and Vinnie Alma (Lanfare) R.; B.S., U. Calif., Berkeley, 1957; children—Jeanne Elizabeth, Kevin Alan. Design engr. Westinghouse Electric Co., Emeryville, Calif., 1953-60; with Lockheed Missiles & Space Co., Sunnyvale, Calif., 1960—, research specialist, 1972-81, staff engr., 1981—. Served with USNR, 1948-52. Mem. IEEE. Clubs: Toastmasters (Sunnyvale); Am. Sportsman's. Home: 3163 Loma Verde Dr San Jose CA 95117 Office: Dept 62-24 Box 504 Sunnyvale CA 94088

ROVIRA, LUIS DARIO, state justice; b. San Juan, P.R., Sept. 8, 1923; s. Peter S. and Mae (Morris) R.; m. Lois Ann Thau, June 25, 1966; children—Douglas, Merilyn. B.A., U. Colo., 1948, LL.B., 1950. Bar: Colo. bar 1950. Now justice Colo. Supreme Ct., Denver; Mem. Pres.'s Com. on Mental Retardation, 1970-71; chmn. State Health Facilities Council, 1967-76. Bd. dirs. YMCA, 1969-78; pres. Lowe Found. Served with AUS, 1943-46. Mem. Colo. Assn. Retarded Children (pres. 1968-70), ABA, Colo. Bar Assn., Denver Bar Assn. (pres. 1970-71), Alpha Tau Omega, Phi Alpha Delta. Republican. Clubs: Athletic (Denver), Country (Denver). Home: 4810 E 6th Ave Denver CO 80220 Office: Colo Judicial Bldg Denver CO 80203

ROW, JON DALE, communications executive; b. LaSalle, Ill.; s. Wilbur Dale and Alice Jean Row. Student, Ill. State U. Staff engr. Am. Honda Motor Co., Gardena, Calif., 1977-78; sr. research engr. Am. Honda Motor Co., Gardena, 1978-83, nat. advt. mgr., 1983-86, nat. communications mgr., 1986—. Inventor mfg. antitheft system. Recipient Creative Excellence award U.S. Indsl. Film Festival, 1981. Mem. Am. Motorcycle Assn. Avocations: bicycling, motorcycling, tennis.

ROWAN, BARRY LEE, corporate executive; b. Weiser, Idaho, Oct. 9, 1956; s. Craig and Mary Hortense (Ford) R.; m. Linda Marie Jackson, July 11, 1981. BS in Chem. Biology summa cum laude, Coll. of Idaho, 1979; MBA, Harvard U., 1983. Corp. planner Boise (Idaho) Cascade Corp., 1979; cost and gen. acctg. exec. Hewlett-Packard Co., Boise, 1979-81; with Chelsea Industries, Boston, 1982; v.p. fin. and adminstrn. Comlinear Corp., Ft. Collins, Colo., 1983—. Mem. Nat. Assn. Accts. Roman Catholic. Club: Harvard Bus. Sch. (Colo.). Avocations: snow skiing, water skiing, racquet sports, golf, reading. Office: Comlinear Corp 4800 Wheaton Dr Fort Collins CO 80525

ROWE, ALICE ANN, business educator; b. Washington, Mar. 26, 1949; d. William Edward and Mildred Louise Sue (Heinzman) Virnstein; m. Rodolph R. Rowe, Oct. 21, 1972; children: Sierra, Andy. BA cum laude, Simmons Coll., 1971; MPA, Syracuse U., 1973; cert. Theol. Edn., Pacific Sch. Religion, 1976. Employee devel. specialist IRS, San Francisco, 1973-75; instr. bus. Golden Gate U., San Francisco, 1975-76, Columbia Basin Coll., Pasco, Wash., 1976-82; media coordinator N.W. Regional Found., Pasco, 1977; assoc. Mgmt. Cons., Kennewick, Wash., 1980; instr. Skasit Valley Coll., Mt. Vernon, Wash., 1982—; Cons. U.S. Office Personnel Mgmt., Seattle, 1983—. Officer Meth. Ch., Anacortes, Wash., 1980—. Named one of Outstanding Women Am., 1979, 80. Mem. Am. Assn. Women in Community and Jr. Colls., Anacortes Book Club. Democrat. Avocations: reading, jogging, gardening. Home and Office: 1922 22d St Anacortes WA 98221

ROWE, KENNETH EUGENE, statistics educator; b. Canon City, Colo., Feb. 8, 1934; s. Theodore R. and Helen Mary (Kay) R.; m. Ilene Kay McIntosh, June 6, 1957 (div. June 1970); children: Neeta Beth, Gayle Kay, Tye Neal; m. Linda Agnes Nelson, Aug. 29, 1970; 1 child, Steven Paul. BS, Colo. State U., 1957; MS, N.C. State U., 1960; PhD, Iowa State U., 1966. Animal geneticist USDA Agrl. Research Service, Ames, Iowa, 1961-64; sr. stats. advisor U.S. EPA, Research Triangle Park, N.C., 1978-79; professor statistics Oreg. State U., Corvallis, 1964—; cons. Oreg. Bd. Bar Examiners, Portland, 1965—. Served to capt. U.S. Army, 1957-65. Grantee NSF, 1969. Mem. Am. Statis. Assn., Biometric Soc., Am. Rose Soc. (dist. dir. Pacific N.W.), Sigma Xi (nat. bd. dirs. 1977-82), Phi Kappa Phi, Alpha Zeta. Republican. Roman Catholic. Lodge: Moose. Avocations: rose growing, stamp collecting. Home: 3410 NW Roosevelt Dr Corvallis OR 97330 Office: Oreg State U Dept Statistics Corvallis OR 97331

ROWEN, HENRY S., public management educator; b. Boston, Oct. 11, 1925; s. Henry S. and Margaret Isabelle (Maher) R.; m. Beverly Camille Griffiths, Apr. 18, 1951; children: Hilary, Michael, Christopher, Sheila Jennifer, Diana Louise, Nicholas. BS, MIT, 1949; PhB, Oxford (Eng.) U., 1955. Economist Rand Corp., Santa Monica, Calif., 1950-61, pres., 1967-72; dep. asst. sec. nat security affairs Dept. Def., Washington, 1961-64; asst. dir. Bur. Budget, Washington, 1965-66; prof. pub. policy Stanford (Calif.) U., 1972—, dir. pub. policy program, 1972-75; sr. fellow Hoover Inst., Stanford, Calif., 1983—; Edwin B. Rust prof. pub. policy Stanford (Calif.) U., 1986—; chmn. nat. intelligence council CIA, Washington, 1981-83; mem. organizers group European Am. Workshop, Marina del Rey, Calif., 1974—, Security Council on Asia and the Pacific, Marina del Rey, 1974—; co-founder PanHeuristic div. RDA, Marina del Rey, 1974—. Author: (with R. Imai) Nuclear Energy and Nuclear Proliferation, 1980; editor: Options for U.S. Energy Policy, 1977; contbr. numerous articles to profl. jours. Mem. chief naval ops. exec. panel USN, Washington, 1972-81, def. sci. bd. Dept. Def., Washington, 1983—, World Resources Inst. Served with USN, 1943-46, PTO. Mem. Internat. Inst. Strategic Studies. Republican. Roman Catholic. Office: Stanford U Hoover Inst War Revolution & Peace 10th Floor Stanford CA 94305-6011

ROWEN, MARSHALL, radiologist; b. Chgo.; s. Harry and Dorothy (Kasnow) R.; m. Helen Lee Friedman, Apr. 5, 1952; children: Eric, Scott, Mark. AB in Chemistry with highest honors, U. Ill., Urbana, 1951; MD with honors, U. Ill., Chgo., 1954, MS in Internal Medicine, 1954. Diplomate Am. Bd. Radiology. Intern Long Beach (Calif.) VA Hosp., 1955; resident in radiology Los Angeles VA Hosp., 1955-58; practice medicine specializing in radiology Orange, Calif., 1960—; chmn. bd. dirs. Moran, Rowen and Dorsey, Inc., Radiologists, 1969—; asst. radiologist Los Angeles Children's Hosp., 1958; assoc. radiologist Valley Presbyn. Hosp., Van Nuys, Calif., 1960; dir. dept. radiology St. Joseph Hosp., Orange, 1961—, v.p. staff, 1972; dir. dept. radiology Children's Hosp., Orange County, 1964—, chief of staff 1977-78, v.p. 1978-83; v.p., asst. clin prof. radiology U. Calif., Irvine, 1967-70, assoc. clin. prof., 1970-72, clin. prof. radiology and pediatrics, 1976, pres. clin. faculty assn., 1980-81; trustee Children's Hosp. Found., Choc. Padrinos, Choco Health Services. Mem. editorial bd. Western Jour. Medicine; contbr. articles to med. jours. Founder Orange County Performing Arts Ctr., mem. Laguna Art Mus., Laguna Festival of Arts, World Affairs Council. Served to capt. M.C., U.S. Army, 1958-60. Recipient Rea sr. med. prize U. Ill, 1953; William Cook scholar U. Ill., 1951. Fellow Am. Coll. Radiology; mem. AMA, Soc. Nuclear Medicine (trustee 1961-62), Orange County Radiol. Soc. (pres. 1968-69), Calif. Radiol. Soc. (pres. 1978-79), Radiol. Soc. So. Calif. (pres. 1976), Pacific Coast Pediatric Radiologists Assn. (pres. 1971), Soc. Pediatric Radiology, Calif. Med. Assn. (chmn. sect. on radiology 1978-79), Orange County Med. Assn. (chmn. VCI liason com. 1976-78), Cardioradiology Soc. So. Calif., Radiol. Soc. N.Am., Am. Roentgen Ray Soc., Phi Beta Kappa, Phi Eta Sigma, Omega Beta Phi, Alpha Omega Alpha. Office: 1201 W La Veta Orange CA 92668

ROWLAND, JAMES A., supermarket chain executive. With Safeway Stores, Inc., mgr. ops. Amarillo and So. Calif., 1956-66, mgr. Little Rock div., 1966-70, v.p., 1970-72, v.p., mgr. midwest region, 1972-76, v.p. adminstrn. from 1976, now pres., chief operating officer, dir. Office: Safeway Stores Inc 201 4th St Oakland CA 94660 *

ROWLES, RUSSANA LOUISE, social worker; b. Boonville, Mo., Sept. 25, 1956; d. Russell and Jo Ann (Jackman) Jackman; m. Eddy Dwight Rowles, Nov. 4, 1978; children: Joanna Rochelle, Monique Simone. BSW, Columbia Coll., 1979; MSW, U. Mo., 1981. Work experience counselor Human Devel. Corp., Columbia, Mo., 1979-80; dir. social services Woodhaven Learning Ctr., Columbia, 1981-84; social worker VA Outpatient Clinic, Los Angeles, 1984-85; med. social worker VA Med. Ctr., Los Angeles, 1985—. Co-leader Brownie troop of Girl Scouts U.S., Gardena, Calif., 1985-86; asst. supt. Sunday Sch. dept. Crusaders Christian Community Ch., also tchr. Mem. Nat. Assn. Social Workers (cert.), Delta Sigma Theta. Democrat. Baptist. Avocations: reading, plays, exercising. Home: 3956 Marcasel Ave Los Angeles CA 90066 Office: Wadsworth VA Med Ctr Wilshire & Sawtelle Blvds Los Angeles CA 90073

ROWLEY, DANIEL STEWART, consulting engineer; b. Sherwood, Oreg., Sept. 9, 1935; s. Jesse Alvin and Agnes Teresa (Gangle) R.; m. Jacquelyn LaRae Arbogast, June 15, 1956; children: Jeffrey, Danielle, Kevin. BS, Portland State U., 1961. Registered profl. engr., Oreg., Wash. Project engr. Coe Mfg. Co., Portland, Oreg., 1962-65; head dept. Moore-Oreg., Portland, 1965-68; product mgr. Irvington-Moore, Portland, 1968-73; pres. Dan Rowley and Assocs. Inc., Portland, 1973-82; owner Forest Industries Engring., Portland, 1982—. Author (newsletter) Forest Engineer Datum, 1979—. Served with U.S. Army, 1952-55, Korea. Recipient Design Excellence award Cons. Engring. Council Oreg., 1978. Republican. Presbyterian. Avocation: pvt. pilot. Home and Office: Forest Industries Engring 5220 NE Roselawn St Portland OR 97218-2512

ROWLEY, DEBORAH ANN, nurse; b. Detroit, Feb. 3, 1950; d. Harold Charles and Jennie (Tomasin) Krause; m. Thomas Nathan Rowley, May 10, 1969; children: Thomas, Theresa. Student, Borgess Sch. Nursing, 1968-69; LPN, Portland Community Coll., 1976-77; postgrad., Columbia Basin Coll., 1978-79, Northeastern Ill. U., 1981. Registered nurse, Wash., Oreg. Nurse aide William Beaumont Hosp., Royal Oak, Mich., 1966-70, Bel Air Nursing Home, Mercy Hosp., Burnham City Hosp.; ward clk. Hosp. Clin., Champaign, Ill., 1970-71; poison control nurse State of Oreg., Portland, 1976-78; midnight head RN pediatrics Kennewick (Mich.) Gen. Hosp., 1979-80, head nurse pediatrics, 1979-81; head nurse, patient edn., inservice dir. Richland (Wash.) Clinic, 1983—. Eucharistic minister Holy Spirit Ch., Kennewick, 1985—, instr., 1984-85; mem. Women's Orthopedic Guild, Kennewick, 1982-85, Croatian Fraternal Union, Detroit, 1960—; sec., treas. Kennewick Bowling League, 1979-83. Mem. Wash. State Nurses Assn. Roman Catholic. Avocations: gardening, sewing, water skiing, cooking, bowling. Office: Richland Clinic 1075 Jadwin Ave Richland WA 99352

ROWLEY, RICHARD LEE, chemical engineering educator; b. Salt Lake City, Sept. 1, 1951; s. Marion Hardy and Norma (Anderson) R.; m. Vickie Vay Allred, July 29, 1973; children: Jeremy, Kirsti, Jesse, Johnathan, Justin, Jeffrey, Jordan. BS, Brigham Young U., 1974; PhD, Mich. State U., 1978. Asst. prof. Rice U., Houston, 1978-83, assoc. prof., 1983; assoc. prof. Brigham Young U., Provo, Utah, 1984—. Contbr. articles to profl. jours. Recipient George R. Brown Superior Teaching award Rice U., 1983; named Outstanding Jr. Faculty mem. ARCO CHem., 1981. Mem. AAAS, N.Y. Acad. Scis., Am. CHem. Soc., Am. Inst. Chem. Engrs., Sigma Xi (Research award, 1978). Republican. Mormon. Avocation: recreational water activities. Office: Brigham Young U Dept Chem Engring 350CB Provo UT 84602

ROWLEY, RICHARD THORUP, university center administrator; b. Richfield, Utah, July 10, 1930; s. Andrew William and Nephine (Thorup) R.; m. Maile Jocelyn Perreira, Sept. 25, 1953; children: Richard Andrew, David Thorup. BS, Brigham Young U., 1954; MEd, Utah State U., 1964, EdD, 1970. Cert. gen. adminstr., Utah. Tchr. secondary sch. Sevier Sch. Dist., Richfield, 1954-55; prin. Rowleys, Richfield, 1955-63; tchr. high sch. Salt Lake (City) Sch. Dist., 1964-67; asst. prof. continuing edn. Brigham Young U., Provo, Utah, 1969—; asst. dir. Salt Lake Ctr., Brigham Young U., Salt Lake City, 1985—; instr. ednl. adminstrn. Brigham Young U. Salt Lake Ctr., 1969—, instr. religion, 1980—. Fulbright fellow, 1966, Nat. Ednl. fellow, 1967-69. Mem. Assn. Continuing Higher Edn. (mem. pubs. com., editor annual conf. proceedings 1984-85, Editor award 1984). Mormon. Home: 3050 Bonnie Brae Ave Salt Lake City UT 84124 Office: Brigham Young U Salt Lake Ctr 1521 E 3900 S Salt Lake City UT 84124

ROWLEY, WILLIAM NELSON, consulting engineer; b. Los Angeles, Apr. 16, 1932; s. Robert Ellsworth and Alice Sarah (Nelson) R.; m. Ruth Ann Adrian, Mar. 25, 1961; children: Christopher N., Heidi Ann. B in Mech. Engring., U. So. Calif., 1955, MSME, 1964; PhD in Engring., Kensington U., 1979; postgrad., UCLA, Air Commd. and Staff Coll. Air U., 1971, Nat. Security Mgmt. Indsl. Coll. Armed Forces, 1973, Air War Coll. Air U., 1979. Registered profl. engr., Calif., Fla., Tex., Pa., Ga., N.Mex., Ariz., Hawaii, Nev., Del., Wis., Ky., Ill., Idaho, Colo., Ind., D.C.; lic. gen. engring., solar and plumbing contractor, Calif. Engr. Steam Design and Constrn. Los Angeles Dept. Water and Power, 1955-58; sr. research engr. Marquardt Corp., Van Nuys, Calif., 1958-62; staff engr. Aerospace Corp., El Segundo, Calif., 1962-66; staff engr. to office of v.p., chief scientist United Aircraft Corp., Redondo Beach, Calif., 1966-68; mgr. research Mattel Corp., Hawthorne, Calif., 1968-71; dir. engring. Swimquip subs. Marley Co. and Fluid Filtration Systems, El Monte, Calif., 1971-81; pres. Rowley Internat., Inc., Palos Verdes Estates, Calif., 1981—; lectr. UCLA; gov., chmn. code com. Calif. Spa and Pool Industry Energy Codes and Legis. Council;. Designer 1984 XXIII Olympic Aquatic Complex, Los Angeles; contbr. articles to profl. jours.; patentee in field. Mem. Gov.'s task force on transp., Calif., 1967-68; mem. swimming pool, spa, solar energy code coms. Served to lt. USAF, 1955-58, brig. gen. Res. Decorated Meritorious Service medal with oak leaf cluster. Fellow Internat. Oceanographic Found. (life); mem. ASME, NSPE, Aviation Hall of Fame (charter patron, pres. Los Angeles chpt.), Nat. Spa and Pool Inst. (tech. council), Calif. Spa and Pool Industry Legislative Council, Nat. Swimming Pool Found. (bd. dirs.), Aquatic Products Research Inst. (bd. dirs.), Soc. Plastics Engrs. (sr.), Nat. Assn. Corrosion Engrs. (sustaining), Nat. Sanitary Found. (Spes Hominum award 1985), Internat. Assn. Plumbing and Mech. Ofcls. (solar energy code com.), Nat. Soc. Profl. Engrs., Calif. Soc. Profl. Engrs., Aircraft Owners and Pilots Assn., Am. Def. Preparedness Assn. (life), U. So. Calif. Sch. Engring. Alumni Assn. (past pres., bd. dirs.), Res. Officers Assn. (life), Air Force Assn. (life), U. So. Calif. Gen. Alumni Assn. (life), NRA (life), Air War Coll. Alumni Assn. (life charter), Air Force Aid Soc. (life), Nat. Eagle Scout Assn. (life), Archimedes Circle (charter), Eyre Assocs. (charter), Nat. Engring. Council (cert. single and multi-engine comml. instrument pilot, flight instr., comml. helicopter pilot), Phi Sigma Kappa (life). Republican. Lutheran. Club: Army and Navy (Washington). Home: 225 Rocky Point Rd Palos Verdes Estates CA 90274-2621 Office: Rowley Internat Inc 2325 Palos Verdes Dr W 2d Floor Palos Verdes Estates CA 90274-2755

ROY, CATHERINE ELIZABETH, physical therapist; b. Tucson, Jan. 16, 1948; d. Francis Albert and Dorothy Orme (Thomas) R.; m. Richard M. Johnson, Aug. 31, 1968 (div. 1978); children: Kimberly Anne, Troy Michael. BA in Social Sci. magna cum laude, San Diego State U., 1980; MS in Phys. Therapy, U. So. Calif., 1984. Staff therapist Sharp Meml. Hosp., San Diego, 1984—, chairperson patient and family edn. com., 1986-87, chairperson sex edn. and counselling com., 1987—, chairperson adv. bd. for physical therapy, asst. for edn. program, 1987—; lectr. patient edn., family edn., peer edn.; mem. curriculum rev. com. U. So. Calif. Phys. Therapy Dept., 1982; bd. dirs. Ctr. for Edn. in Health; writer, reviewer licensure examination items for phys. therapy Profl. Examination Services.. Researcher: Consumer Education: Physical Therapy, 1984-85. Tennis coach at clinics Rancho Penasquitos Swim and Tennis Club, San Diego, 1980-81; active Polit. Activities Network, 1985. Mem. Am. Phys. Therapy Assn. (research presenter nat. conf. 1985, del. nat. conf. 1986, 87, rep. state conf. 1987, Mary McMillan student award 1984, mem. exec. bd. San Diego dist. 1985—), AAUW, Nat. Assn. Female Execs., Am. Coll. Sports Medicine, Phi Beta Kappa, Phi Kappa Phi, Chi Omega. Avocations: tennis, reading, piano, travel, puzzles. Home: 13133 Via del Valedor San Diego CA 92129 Office: Sharp Meml Rehab Ctr 7901 Frost St San Diego CA 92123

ROY, CHUNILAL, psychiatrist; b. Digboi, India, Jan. 1, 1935; came to Can., 1967, naturalized, 1975; s. Atikay Bandhu and Nirupama (Devi) R.; m. Elizabeth Ainscow, Apr. 15, 1967; children: Nicholas, Phillip, Charles. MB, BS, Calcutta Med. Coll., India, 1959; diploma in psychol. medicine, Kings Coll., Newcastle-upon-Tyne, Eng., 1963. Intern Middlesborough Gen. Hosp., Eng., 1960-61; jr. hosp. officer St. Luke's Hosp., Middlesborough, Eng., 1961-64, sr. registrar, 1964; sr. hosp. med. officer Parkside Hosp., Macclesfield, Eng., 1964-66; sr. registrar Moorehaven Hosp., Ivybridge, Eng., 1966; reader, head dept. psychiatry Maulana Azad Med. Coll., New Delhi, 1966; sr. med. officer Republic of Ireland, County Louth, 1966; sr. psychiatrist Sask. Dept. Psychiat. Services, Can., 1967-68; regional dir. Swift Current, Can., 1968-71; practice medicine specializing in psychiatry Regina, Sask., Can., 1971-72; founding dir., med. dir. Regional Psychiat. Ctr., Abbotsford, B.C., Can., 1972-82; with Dept. Psychiatry, Vancouver Gen. Hosp., 1987—; cons. to prison adminstrs.; hon. lectr. psychology and clin. asst. prof. psychiatry U. B.C.; ex-officio mem. Nat. Adv. Com. on Health Care of Prisoners in Can.; cons. psychiatrist, Vancouver (B.C.) Hosp.; advisor Asian chpt. Psychosomatic Medicine, World Congress of Law and Medicine, New Dehli, 1985. Author: (with D.J. West and F.L. Nichols) Understanding Sexual Attacks, 1978. Mem. editorial rev. bd. Evaluation, 1977—. Assoc. editor Internat. Jour. Offender Therapy and Comparative Criminology, 1978—. Mem. Bd. Internat. Law Medicine, 1979—; contbr. articles to profl. jours. Recipient Merit award Dept. Health, Republic of Ireland, 1966, Can. Penitentiary Service, 1974, citation by pres. U. B.C., 1982. Fellow Royal Coll. Psychiatry (Can.), Royal Coll. Psychiatry (Eng.), Royal Soc. Medicine (London, assoc.), Pacific Rim Coll. Psychiatrists (a founder); mem. World Psychiat. Assn. (sec. sect. forensic psychiatry 1983), World Fedn. Mental Health, Internat. Council Prison Med. Services (founding sec.-gen. 1977), Can. Med. Assn., Can. Psychiat. Assn., Amnesty Internat., Internat. Acad. Legal Medicine and Social Medicine, Indian Psychiat. Assn. (life), Can. Assn. Profl. Treatment Offenders (founding dir. 1975), Assn. Physicians and Surgeons Who Work in Can. Prisons (founding pres. 1974), Internat. Found. for Tng. in Penitentiary Medicine and Forensic Psychiatry (founding pres. 1980), Australian Acad. Forensic Sci. (corr.). Home: 2030 W 28th Ave, Vancouver Can V6J 2Y9 Office: 750 W Broadway Suite 1417, Vancouver, BC Canada V5Z 1J4

ROY, HAROLD EDWARD, research chemist; b. Stratford, Conn., June 2, 1921; s. Ludger Homer and Meta (Jepsen) R.; B.A., Duke U., 1950; m. Joyce E. Enslin, Oct. 9, 1946 (div. 1975); children—Glenn E., Barbara Anne, Suzanne Elizabeth. Chemist research div. Lockheed Propulsion Co., Redlands, Calif., 1957-61; sec., treas. The Halgene Corp., Riverside, Calif., 1961-

63; self-employed chemist, Glendora, Calif., 1963-64; chief engr. propellant devel. Rocket Power, Inc., Mesa, Ariz., 1964-65; cons., Glendora, 1965-66; engring. specialist Northrop Corp., Anaheim, Calif., 1966-69; pres. Argus Tech., Beverly Hills, 1969-70, dir. Harold E. Roy & Assos., Glendora, 1969—. Served to lt. (j.g.) USNR, 1943-46. Mem. Exptl. Aircraft Assn., Am. Ordnance Assn., Am. Inst. Aeros. and Astronautics, Internat. Platform Assn., Acad. Parapsychology and Medicine, Calif. Profl. Hypnotists Assn., World Future Soc. Republican. Home: 7344 N Barranca Glendora CA 91740

ROY, IRA, microbiology educator; b. Varanasi, India; came to U.S., 1962, naturalized; d. Sourendra Nath and Sobha Roy. BS, Lucknow (India) U., 1952, MS, 1954; PhD, Ohio State U., 1965. Assoc. prof. sci. Banaras U., Varanasi, India, 1955-68; postdoctoral fellow UCLA, 1969-72; microbiologist Martin Luther King. Jr. Hosp., Los Angeles, 1973-78; sr. microbiologist Loma Linda (Calif.) Univ. Med. Ctr., 1978—; co-investigator Animal Health Found., Loma Linda, 1983-84. Contbr. articles to profl. jours. Rockefeller Found. research fellow Ohio State U., 1962-65; NIH spl. postdoctoral fellow, 1969-72. Mem. AAA, AAUW, Am. Soc. Microbiology, Sigma Xi. Home: 3556 Bond St San Bernardino CA 92405 Office: Loma Linda U Med Ctr Anderson St Loma Linda CA 92354

ROY, RAYMOND, bishop; b. Man., Can., May 3, 1919; s. Charles-Borromé e and Zephirina (Milette) R. B.A. in Philosophy and Theology, U. Man., 1942; student, Philos. Sem., Montreal, 1942-43, Major Sem., Montreal, 1943-46, Major Sem. St. Boniface, 1946-47. Ordained priest Roman Catholic Ch. 1947. Asst. pastor, then pastor chs. in Man., 1947-50, 53-66; chaplain St. Boniface (Man.) Hosp., 1950-53; superior Minor Sem., St. Boniface, 1966-69; pastor Cathedral Parish, St. Boniface, 1969-72; ordained bishop 1972; bishop of St. Paul, Alta., Can., 1972—. Club: K.C. Address: 4410 51st Ave, Box 339, Saint Paul, AB Canada T0A 3A0

ROYBAL, EDWARD R., congressman; b. Albuquerque, Feb. 10, 1916; m. Lucille Beserra, Sept. 27, 1940; children: Lucille (Olivarez), Lillian (Rose), Edward R. Student, U. Calif. at Los Angeles, Southwestern U., Kaiser Coll., Los Angeles; LL.D. (hon.), Pacific States U., Claremont Grad. Sch. With Civilian Conservation Corps, 1934-35; social worker, pub. health educator Calif. Tb Assn.; then dir. health edn. Los Angeles County Tb and Health Assn., 1942-49; mem. 88th-100th Congresses from 25th Dist. Calif.; mem. appropriations com., select com. on aging, chmn. Congl. Hispanic Caucus; Mem. L.A. City Council, 1949-62, pres. pro tem, 1961-62. Served with AUS, 1944-45. Recipient Excellence in Pub. Service award Am. Acad. Pediatrics, 1976; Chubb fellow Yale U. Mem. Nat. Assn. Latino Elected Ofcls. (chmn.), Am. Mem. Am. Legion. Democrat. Roman Catholic. Club: K.C. Office: 2211 Rayburn House Office Bldg Washington DC 20515 *

ROYER, CHARLES THEODORE, mayor; b. Medford, Oreg., Aug. 22, 1939; s. Russell Theodore and Mildred Mae (Hampson) R.; m. Rosanne Gostovich, Oct. 19, 1968; children—Jordan, Suzanne. B.S., U. Oreg., 1967; postgrad., Harvard U., Mass. Inst. Tech., 1969-70. Polit. reporter KOIN-TV, Portland, Oreg., 1966-68; news analyst KING-TV, Seattle, 1970-77; mayor City of Seattle, 1978—. Served with U.S. Army, 1961-63. Recipient Am. Polit. Sci. Assn. fellowship, 1969-70; Washington Journalism Center fellow, 1968; Sigma Delta Chi award, 1976; Edward R. Murrow award, 1976. Democrat. Office: Office of the Mayor 1200 Municipal Bldg Seattle WA 98104 *

ROYSTON-JAKES, PENNY JANE, educator; b. Lewistown, Mont., Aug. 4, 1948; d. Keith Richard and Alice Jane (McCandless) Royston; m. David Earl Jakes, Mar. 15, 1970; children: Wendy Rebecca, Aimee Melissa. Student, Eastern Mont. Coll., 1966-67; BS with honors, Montana State U., 1970; MEd, U. Mont., 1981. Cert. vocat. educator, Mont. Sec. Allstate Ins. Co., Missoula, Mont., 1970-73; instr. adult edn. Missoula County High Sch., 1973—; instr. bus., computers Missoula Vocat. Tech. Ctr., 1973—. Active Missoula Humane Soc. Recipient Mont. State Music award Mont. State Music Assn., 1964-66; Mont. State U. scholar, 1967-70. Mem. NEA, Mont. Edn. Assn., Mont. Bus. Edn. Assn. (pres. 1986, v.p. 1985), Mont. Vocat. Assn. (sec. 1986—, Am. Vocat. Assn., Western Bus. Edn. Assn., Nat. Bus. Edn. Assn., Pi Omega Pi, Tau Pi Phi. Avocations: reading, piano, singing, ranching. Home: 3001 Mack Smith Ln Stevensville MT 59870 Office: Missoula Vocat Ctr 909 S Ave W Missoula MT 59801

RUBECK, MARK, managing consultant; b. Rockville Centre, N.Y., Jan. 13, 1951; s. Arnold and Pearl (Kornreich) R.; m. Laurie Heather Larned, Sept. 24, 1983. BS in Applied Math., Brown U., 1973; postgrad., U. Wash., 1974. Systems analyst Boeing Aerospace Co., Seattle, 1973-75; energy systems analyst Boeing Engring. and Constrn., Seattle, 1975-79; cons. Boeing Computer Services, Seattle, 1979-85, mgr. ops. research group, 1985—. Mem. Sigma Xi (assoc.). Avocations: outdoor activities, athletics. Home: 11020 SE 181 St Renton WA 98055 Office: Boeing Computer Services 919 SW Grady Way Renton WA 98055

RUBENSTEIN, EDWARD, physician, educator; b. Cin., Dec. 5, 1924; s. Louis and Nettie R.; m. Nancy Ellen Millman, June 20, 1954; children: John, William, James. M.D., U. Cin., 1947. Intern, jr. asst. resident, sr. asst. resident internal medicine Cin. Gen. Hosp., 1947-50; fellow May Inst., Cin., 1950; sr. asst. resident Ward Med. Service, Barnes Hosp., St. Louis, 1953-54; chief of medicine San Mateo County Hosp., Calif., 1960-70; assoc. dean postgrad. med. edn., clin. prof. medicine Stanford (Calif.) U. Sch. Medicine, 1971—; mem. faculty Stanford Photon Research Lab.; affiliated faculty mem. Stanford Synchrotron Radiation Lab., 1971—; mem. maj. materials facilities com. Nat. Research Council, 1984-85, Nat. Steering Com. 6 GeV Electron Storage Ring., 1986—. Author: textbook Intensive Medical Care; editor-in-chief: textbook Sci. Am. Medicine, 1978—. Served with USAF, 1950-52. Mem. ACP, Inst. Medicine, Calif. Acad. Medicine, Western Assn. Physicians, Soc. Photo-Optical Engrs., Am. Clin. and Climatol. Assn., Alpha Omega Alpha. Research on synchrotron radiation. Office: Med Sch Office Bldg X-365 Stanford Med Center Stanford CA 94305-5423

RUBENSTEIN, LEONARD SAMUEL, creative consultant firm executive, ceramist, painter, sculptor, photographer; b. Rochester, N.Y., Sept. 22, 1918; s. Jacob S. and Zelda H. (Gordon) R.; widowed May 28, 1983; children—Carolinda, Eric, Harley. B.F.A. cum laude, Alfred U., 1939; student Western Reserve, 1938; postgrad. U. Rochester, 1940-41. Creative dir. Henry Hempstead Advt. Agy., Chgo., 1949-55; v.p., exec. art dir. Clinton E. Frank Advt. Agy., Chgo., 1955-63; v.p., nat. creative dir. Foster & Kleiser div. Metromedia, Inc., Los Angeles, 1967-73, v.p. corp. creative cons., Metromedia, Inc., Los Angeles, 1973—; guest lectr. U. Chgo.; instr. Columbia Coll., Chgo.; past. pres. Art Dirs. Club Chgo. (spl. citation); instr. Fashion Inst., Los Angeles; lectr. in field. Mem. Soc. Typog. Arts (past dir.), Am. Ceramic Soc. (design chpt.), Am. Craft Council, Inst. Outdoor Advt. (past plans bd.), Los Angeles County Mus. Art, Palos Verdes (Calif.) Art Ctr., Phi Epsilon Pi. Club: Tennis (Palm Springs, Calif.). Lodge: B'nai B'rith. Author: (with Charles Hardison) Outdoor Advertising; contbr. articles in field to profl. publs. One-man show: Calif. Mus. Sci. and Industry, 1970; numerous juried nat. and regional group shows; creator concept for Smithsonian exhibition Images of China: East and West, 1982. Home: 30616 Ganado Dr Rancho Palos Verdes CA 90274 Office: 5746 Sunset Blvd Metromedia Square Los Angeles CA 90028

RUBENSTEIN, MICHAEL ALAN, architect; b. St. Louis, July 18, 1944; s. Melvin Paul and Miriam (Schwartz) R. BArch, Wash. U., 1966, MArch, 1968. Registered architect, Calif. Architect Skidmore, Owings, Merrill, N.Y.C., 1967-68, Helmuth, Obata, Kassabaum, St. Louis, 1968-69, Peckham/Guyton Assocs., St. Louis, 1969-70, B.A. Berkus, Los Angeles, 1970-71, Gruen Assocs., Los Angeles, 1971-72; design cons. Gruen Assocs., N.Y.C., 1971; architect Studio Works, Los Angeles, 1972; design cons., mem. staff Experiments in Art and Tech., Los Angeles, 1972-73; pvt. practice architecture Los Angeles, 1975-86; ptnr. Anderson & Rubenstein, Santa Rosa, 1986—; prin. Anderson & Rubenstein, Architects, Santa Rosa, 1986—. Exhibited Eugenia Butler Gallery, Los Angeles, 1970, Calif. 101, Monterey Design Conf., 1980, Record Plant Mobile Recording Unit 4, 1984. Mem. Design Rev. Com., Healdsburg, Calif., 1978-80, chmn. 1980-83; mem. Steering Com., Healdsburg, 1981-83; coordinator Regional Urban Design Assistance Team, Healdsburg, 1982; chmn. Cultural Resource Survey Rev. Com., Healdsburg, 1982-83. Recipient Key to City Wine Honorarium, Healdsburg, 1982, Cert. Outstanding Design Lawrence Galleries, 1984, Cert. Distinction Broggini House, 1985, Calif. Solar Cal Council Energy Saving Builder awards (3), 1982, Design and Planning award for pvt. house, 1982, Energy Efficient Housing award for private house P.G.&E., 1978, Excellence in Design award Cultural Arts Council of Sonoma County, 1986. Mem. AIA (bd. dirs. Redwood Empire chpt., v.p., pres. elect Redwood Empire chpt. 1986, pres. 1987—, Plaza St. Cafe award 1984, biennial design awards 1984, 86).

RUBEY, JOHN ALFRED, entertainment company executive; b. Evergreen Park, Ill., Oct. 5, 1951; s. Charles Andrew and Catherine Marie (Whalen) R.; m. Donna M. Holton, Nov. 5, 1977; children: Andrew Joseph, Melissa Erin, Roger Whalen, Timothy John. Staff auditor Price Waterhouse & Co., Denver, 1973-74; with Feyline Presents, Inc., Englewood, Colo., 1974-86, v.p., treas., 1976-86; with Pace Mgmt. Corp., Houston, 1986—, v.p., sec., chief fin. officer, 1986—. Mem. Colo. Soc. CPA's, Am. Inst. CPA's. Democrat. Roman Catholic.

RUBI, LARRY SEBASTIAN, systems engineer; b. Winslow, Ariz., Dec. 20, 1950; s. Frank Robert and Virginia (Smith) R.; m. Silvia Rodriguez, Aug. 27, 1983; 1 child, Frank. AS in Electronics, RCA Inst. Tech. Tng., Flagstaff, Ariz., 1972; AA, Southwestern Coll., Chula Vista, Calif., 1976; BA in Urban Planning, U. Calif., La Jolla, 1978, BA in Math., 1979; MS in Computer Sci. and Engring., San Diego State U., 1980. Systems engr. Lockheed Missles and Space Co., Sunnyvale, Calif., 1981-83; mgr. systems engring. ECR Engring. Cons., Chula Vista, 1981-86; project leader systems engr. Phase Four, Santa Ysabel, Calif., 1983-85, Electronic Data Systems, San Diego, 1985—; program coordinator Assoc. Tech. Coll., San Diego, 1985—; project leader Mgmt. Info. Systems and Strategic Def. Initiative Rocket Propulsion Lab. Strategic Def. Initative, Edward's AFB, Calif., 1986—. Author computer manuals. Fellow NSF, 1978; UN Health Found., 1979. Mem. Am. Cons. Assn., Am. Programing Assn., Am. Assn. Systems Engrs. Avocation: philately, computers. Home: 43526 Kirkland Ave #235 Lancaster CA 93535

RUBIN, ALEJANDRO VICTORIO, electrical engineer; b. Madrid, Sept. 22, 1959; came to U.S., 1961; s. Walter and Pilar (Cortella) R.; m. Maria Victoria Capestany, Jan. 15, 1983. BSEE, U. N.Mex., 1979. Researcher U. Wash., Seattle, 1980-81; engr. Bechtel Power Corp. subs. Bechtel Group Inc., San Francisco, 1981-83; tech. specialist Impell Corp., Walnut Creek, Calif., 1983-86; sr. reliability engr. Lockheed Corp., Palo Alto, Calif., 1986—. Mem. IEEE, Soc. Mfg. Engrs., Nat. Audubon Soc., Nat. Wildlife Fedn. Office: Lockheed Corp 3251 Hanover St Palo Alto CA 94304

RUBIN, DAVID EUGENE, bank executive; b. Plainfield, N.J., May 2, 1947; s. Max and Ruth (Lefkowitz) R.; m. Paula Jan Friewald, May 2, 1982; 1 child, Justin Daniel. BBA, U. Hartford, 1968; MBA, Hofstra U., 1974. Asst. treas. Bankers Trust Co., N.Y.C., 1969-80; asst. v.p Union Bank, Los Angeles, 1980-81; v.p. Am. Internat. Bank, Los Angeles, 1981-86, sr. v.p., 1987—. Bd. dirs. City of Hope, Los Angeles, 1981—. Served with USAR, 1969-72. Mem. Am. Inst. Banking, Am. Mktg. Assn., U. Hartford Alumni Assn., DAV, Am. Legion, Pi Lambda Phi (treas.). Democrat. Jewish. Lodge: B'nai Brith. Avocations: tennis, photography, swimming, traveling. Home: 1675 Chevy Knoll PL Glendale CA 91206 Office: Am Internat Bank 525 S Olive St Los Angeles CA 90013

RUBIN, LAWRENCE IRA, podiatrist; b. Buffalo, Dec. 19, 1945; s. Harold Philip and Rose (Kaiser) R.; m. Janis Bernstein, Sept. 12, 1970 (div. Apr. 1986); children: Alison Meredith, Stacy Heather. Student, Am. U., 1963-65; D of Podiatric Medicine, N.Y. Coll. of Podiatric Medicine, 1969. Diplomate Am. Bd. Podiatric Surgery. Practice medicine specializing in podiatry Clarence, N.Y., 1970-76; chief podiatric surgery and medicine Meml. Hosp. of Gardena, Calif., 1977—; cons. South Bay Free Clinic, Gardena, 1979—. Fellow Am. Coll. Foot Surgeons; mem. Calif. Podiatric Med. Assn. (peer review com. Los Angeles chpt.), Los Angeles County Podiatric Med. Assn. (Pres.'s award 1984). Democrat. Jewish. Lodge: Masons (master mason 1974—). Avocations: jogging, model railroading. Office: Gardena Podiatrist's Group 1141 W Redondo Beach Blvd Gardena CA 90247

RUBIN, LOUIS, materials scientist; b. N.Y.C., Aug. 19, 1922; s. Harry and Mildred (Ziffer) R.; m. Gertrude Berman, June 30, 1946; children: David Mark, Harriet Lynn. BA, NYU, 1943; MA, U. Mo., 1947, PhD, 1950. Head process devel. lab. Winthrop Labs., Rensselaer, N.Y., 1951-59; chief tech. staff space products div. Rohr Corp., Riverside, Calif., 1959-64; project engr. The Aerospace Corp., El Segundo, Calif., 1964—. Contbr. over 30 articles to tech. jours. Served to 1st lt. U.S. Army, 1943-46, PTO. Mem. AIAA, Am. Chem. Soc., Soc. for Advancement of Material and Process Engring. (sect. chmn. 1961-62), Soc. Plastics Engrs. (sect. pres. 1976-77). Avocations: photography, handwriting analysis. Office: The Aerospace Corp 2350 E El Segundo Blvd El Segundo CA 90245

RUBIN, ROBERT TERRY, physician, researcher; b. Los Angeles, Aug. 26, 1936; s. Joseph Salem and Lorraine Grace (Baum) R.; m. Lynne Esther Mathews, Mar. 10, 1962 (div. Dec. 1980); children: Deborah, Sharon, Rachel; m. Ada Joan Mickas, Jan. 18, 1985. AB, UCLA, 1958; MD, U. Calif., San Francisco, 1961; PhD, U. So. Calif., Los Angeles, 1977. Diplomate Am. Bd. Psychiatry, Am. Bd. Neurology. Asst. prof. psychiatry UCLA, 1965-71, prof. psychiatry, 1972—; prof. Pa. State U., Hershey, 1971-72; cons. Naval Health Research Ctr., San Diego, 1969-70; mem. Brain Research Inst. UCLA, 1969—; bd. trustees Kinsey Inst. Sex Research Ind. U., 1986—. Contbr. articles to profl. jours. Served with USNR, 1969. Recipient Research Sci. Devel. awards NIMH, 1972, 77; Research Scientist award NIMH, 1982. Fellow AAAS, Am. Psychiat. Assn., Am. Coll. Psychiatrists; mem. World Psychiat. Assn. (sec. sect. biol. psychiatry, 1983—), Internat. Soc. Psychoneuroendocrinology (pres. 1984—). Avocation: masters' swimming. Office: UCLA Dept Psychiatry Div Biol Psychiatry Harbor Med Ctr Torrance CA 90509

RUBINSTEIN, MOSHE FAJWEL, engineering educator; b. Miechow, Poland, Aug. 13, 1930; came to U.S., 1950, naturalized, 1965; s. Shlomo and Sarah (Rosen) R.; m. Zafrira Gorstein, Feb. 3, 1953; children—Iris, Dorit. B.S., UCLA, 1954, M.S., 1957, Ph.D., 1961. Designer Murray Erick Assos. (engrs. and architects), Los Angeles, 1954-56; structural designer Victor Gruen Assos., Los Angeles, 1956-61; asst. prof. U. Calif. at Los Angeles, 1961-64, asso. prof. dept. engring., 1964-69, prof., 1969—, chmn. engring. systems dept., 1970-75, program dir. modern engring. for execs. program, 1965-70; cons. Pacific Power & Light Co., Portland, Oreg., Northrop Corp., U.S. Army, NASA Research Center, Langley, Tex. Instruments Co., Hughes Space System Div., U.S. Army Sci. Adv. Com., Kaiser Aluminum and Chem. Corp., IBM. Author: (with W.C. Hurty) Dynamics of Structures, 1964 (Yugoslavian trans. 1973), Matrix Computer Analysis of Structures, 1966 (Japanese transl. 1974), Structural Systems, Statics Dynamics and Stability, 1970 (Japanese transl. 1979), Patterns of Problem Solving, 1975, (with K. Pfeiffer) Concepts in Problem Solving, 1980, Tools for Thinking and Problem Solving, 1986. Recipient Disting. Teaching award Acad. Senate, U. Calif. at Los Angeles, 1964; Western Electric Fund award Am. Soc. Engring. Edn., 1965; Distinguished Tchr. trophy Engring. Student Soc., UCLA, 1966; Sussmann Chair for Distinguished Visitor Technion Israel Inst. Tech., 1967-68; Fulbright-Hays fellow Yugoslovia and Eng., 1975-76; Named Outstanding Faculty Mem., UCLA Engring. Alumni award, 1979. Mem. ASCE, Am. Soc. Engring. Edn., Seismol. Soc. Am., Sigma Xi, Tau Beta Phi. Research in use of computers in structural systems, analysis and synthesis; problem solving and decision theory. Home: 10488 Charing Cross Rd West Los Angeles CA 90024 Office: UCLA Sch Engring and Applied Sci Los Angeles CA 90024

RUBLE-TROTTER, ANN, clergywoman; b. Seattle, Oct. 26, 1953; d. Monte Rahe and Stella (Terefinko) Ruble; m. Francis Michael Trotter, Aug. 29, 1984. Cert. sec. Met. Bus. Coll., Seattle, 1972. Ordained to ministry Ch. of Scientology, 1980. Minister, Ch. of Scientology, Seattle, 1980—, dir. pub. affairs, 1983; pres. Ch. of Scientology of Wash. State, 1984—. Bur. chief Jour. Freedom News, 1984—. Mem. Citizen's Commn. Human Rights, Seattle, 1984—, Com. on Religious Liberties, Seattle, 1985—. Office: Ch of Scientology of Wash State 2004 Westlake Ave Seattle WA 98121

RUBY, CHARLES LEROY, educator, lawyer, civic leader; b. Carthage, Ind., Dec. 28, 1900; s. Edgar Valentine and Mary Emma (Butler) R.; certificate Ball State U., 1921-22; AB, Cen. Normal Coll., 1924, LLB, 1926, BS, 1931; MA, Stanford, 1929; JD, Pacific Coll. of Law, 1931; PhD, Olympic U., 1933; m. Rachael Elizabeth Martindale, Aug. 30, 1925; children: Phyllis Arline (Mrs. Norman Braskat), Charles L., Martin Dale. Prin., Pine Village (Ind.) High Sch., 1923-25; Glenwood (Ind.) Pub. Schs., 1925-26; tchr. El Centro (Calif.) Pub. Sch., 1926-27, Central (Calif.) Union High Sch., 1927-29; prof. law Fullerton Coll., 1929-66; prof. edn. Armstrong Coll., summer 1935, Cen. Normal Coll., summers 1929-33; admitted to Ind. bar, 1926, U.S. Supreme Ct. bar, 1970; pres. Ret. Service Vol. Program, North Orange County, Calif., 1973-76, 83-84; dir. North Orange County Vol. Bur., Fullerton Sr. Citizens Task Force. Life trustee, Continuing Learning Experiences program Calif. State U., Fullerton, hon. chmn. fund com. Gerontology Bldg; founder, dir. Fullerton Pub. Forum, 1929-39; founder Elks Nat. Found.; benefactor Gerontology Ctr. Calif. State U., Fullerton; pres. Fullerton Rotary, 1939-40, hon. mem., 1983—; mem. U.S. Assay Commn., 1968—; mem. Orange County Dem. Cen. Com., 1962-78; bd. dirs. Fullerton Sr. Multipurpose Ctr., 1981—; bd. dirs. Orange County Sr. Citizens Adv. Council; mem. pres.'s exec. com. Calif. State U., Fullerton. Recipient Medal of Merit, Am. Numis. Assn., 1954, Spl. Commendation, Calif. State Assembly, 1966, Calif. State Senate, 1978, 86, Commendation, Ind. Sec. of State, 1984, Commendation, Bd. Suprs. Orange County, 1985, Commendation, Fullerton City Council, 1986, Commendation, Orange County Bd. Supervisors, 1986, Commendation, Calif. State Senate, 1986, Commendation, Exec. Com. Pres. Calif. State U., Fullerton, 1986; Charles and Rachel Ruby Gerontology Ctr. named in his and late wife's honor, Calif. State U., Fullerton. Fellow Ind. Bar Found.; mem. Pres. Assocs. Calif. State U. Fullerton, Fullerton Coll. Assocs. (named Spl. Retiree of Yr. 1986, Commendation, 1986), Calif. (life, pres. So. sect. 1962-63, treas. 1964-65, dir. 1956-65), Orange County Tchrs. Assn. (pres. 1953-55), Fullerton Coll. (pres. 1958-60) Tchrs. Assn., NEA (life), Ind. Bar Assn., Stanford U. Law Soc. (pres.'s exec. com.), Calif. State Council Edn., Am. Numismatic Assn. (gov. 1951-53, life adv. bd.), Ind. Bar Assn. (hon. life), Calif. Bus. Educators Assn. (hon. life), Calif. Assn. Univ. Profs., Pacific S.W. Bus. Law Assn. (pres. 1969-70, life), Numismatic Assn. So. Calif. (life, pres. 1961), Calif. Numis. Assn., Indpls. Coin Club (hon. life), Los Angeles Coin Club (hon. life), U.S. Supreme Ct. Hist. Soc., Calif. Town Hall, North Orange County Mus. Assn. (life, benefactor dir.), Stanford U. Alumni Assn., Old Timers Assay Commn. Methodist. Clubs: Elks, Fullerton Jr. Coll. Vets. (hon. life). Contbr. articles in field to profl. jours. Home: 308 N Marwood Ave Fullerton CA 92632

RUCKER, HELEN BORNSTEIN (MRS. B. WALLACE RUCKER), author; b. Seattle; d. Maurice and Julia (Gyle) Bornstein; grad. Nat. Park Coll., 1923; student Cornish Sch. Allied Arts, 1934-35, 46-47, 55-56, U. Wash.; m. B. Wallace Rucker, Jan 30, 1932; children—B. Wallace, Stephen Morley. Librarian, Penwomen's N.W. Collection, Seattle Pub. Library, 1964-65. Unit chmn. ARC, 1940-45; sposoring com. Spirit of Seattle, 1949—; mem. Franklin Guild of Children's Orthopedic Hosp. Trustee, membership chmn., sec., corr. sec., chmn. programs spastic children Seattle Jr. Programs, 1941-56; trustee Cornish Sch. Allied Arts, 1935-38, Friends of Seattle Pub. Library, 1957-60. Recipient Achievement award Past Pres. Assembly, 1960. Mem. Pioneer Assn. State of Wash., Nat. League Am. Pen Women, Seattle Free-Lance Writers, N.W. Internat. Writers Conf., Friends of Crafts, Phi Delta Nu. Clubs: Soroptimist (co-chmn. student loan com. 1968-69), Washington Athletic, Seattle Tennis (Seattle). Author: Cargo of Brides, 1956, 2d edit., 1969; The Wolf Tree, 1960; also short stories. Editor: The Bull., Friends Seattle Pub. Library, 1958-60. Home: 1630 43d Ave E Seattle WA 98112

RUCKER, THOMAS DOUGLAS, purchasing exec.; b. Ottumwa, Iowa, Aug. 30, 1926; s. Everett Henry and Harriett Mary (Evans) R.; A.B., Loyola U., 1951; postgrad. St. Patrick's Coll., 1950-52; m. Rita Mary Rommelfanger, Apr. 18, 1953; children—David, Theresa, Martin, Paul. Asst. purchasing agt. Radio TV Supply, Los Angeles, 1952-53; buyer Consol. Western Steel div. U.S. Steel, Commerce, Calif., 1953-64, S.W. Welding & Mfg. Co., Alhambra, Calif., 1964-70; dir. purchasing Southwestern Engring., Commerce, Calif., 1970—. Served with USAAF, 1945-46. Home: 10642 Abisko Dr Whittier CA 90604 Office: Southwestern Engring 5701 S Eastern Ave Suite 300 Commerce CA 90040

RUDDICK, STEPHEN RICHARD, state representative, lawyer, political consultant; b. Denver, Nov. 6, 1954; s. Paul Richard and Myra Jane (Brooks) R.; m. Ana Maria Peters, June 16, 1984. B.A., Met. State U., Denver, 1977; J.D., U. Denver, 1980. Bar: Colo. 1980, U.S. Dist. Ct. Colo. 1980, U.S. Ct. Appeals (10th cir.) 1980. Steward, I.B. of Teamsters, Denver, 1979; law clk., later assoc. law firm Anderson, Calder & Lembke, P.C., Aurora, Colo., 1979-80; sole practice law, Aurora, Colo., 1980-81; asst. city atty. City Atty.'s Office, Aurora, Colo., 1981—; state rep. Colo. Gen. Assembly, 1987-89. Chmn., 18th Jud. Dist. Dem. Cen. Com., 1983—; vice-chmn. Arapahoe County Dem. Com., 1983—; mem. Colo. ACLU, Colo. Common Cause, Arapahoe-Denver NOW. Mem. Aurora Bar Assn. (sec.-treas. 1983-84, v.p. 1984-85), Colo. Bar Assn. Democrat. Presbyterian. Club: Aurora East Lions. Lodge: Masons (master mason 1983—). Home: 1031 Sable Blvd Aurora CO 80011 Office: Office of City Atty 15001 E Alameda Dr Aurora CO 80014

RUDDY, JOHN MICHAEL, consulting engineer; b. Scranton, Pa., Mar. 24, 1909; s. John A. and Anna R. (Gannon) R.; m. Florence E. Buchan, Mar. 2, 1935 (div. 1965); children: Robert, John, Thomas; m. Gertrude G. Schunk, May 16, 1967; 1 child, Jeffry. BS in Engring., Manhattan Coll., 1931, MCE, 1932. Registered profl. engr., land surveyor. Asst. plant engr. Sperry Gyroscope, Lake Success, L.I., N.Y., 1942-47; chief engr. planning Brookhaven (N.Y.) Atomic Research Lab., 1947-62; resident engr., mgr. Skidmore, Owings & Merril, Puako, Hawaii, 1962-65; chief engr. TAPCO, Honolulu, 1965-77; consulting engr., assoc. Syntech, Ltd., Honolulu, 1977—. Fellow ASCE; mem. ASHRAE. Lodge: Lions. Home: 1058-C Green St Honolulu HI 96822 Office: Syntech Ltd 600 Kapolani Blvd Suite 401 Honolulu HI 96813

RUDE, GARY GORDON, educational administrator; b. Seattle, Apr. 10, 1943; s. Gordon Ross and Marianne (Gleason) R.; m. Kathy Ann Baumunk, Mar. 29, 1980; children—Kristi, Scott, Heather, Charles. B.Ed., Seattle U., 1969, Ed.D., 1985; M.Ed., Western Wash. U., 1973. Cert. elem. and secondary tchr., elem. and secondary prin., Wash. Tchr., North Thurston Sch. Dist., Lacey, Wash., 1969-72, Lake Washington Sch. Dist., Kirkland, Wash., 1972-76, Aberdeen (Wash.) Sch. Dist., 1976-78; prin. Eatonville (Wash.) Sch. Dist., 1978-82, Lake Stevens (Wash.) Sch. Dist., 1982-86, Mt. Pilchuck Elem. Sch., 1982-86; project coordinator Assn. Wash. Sch. Principals, 1986—; condr. conduct effectiveness workshops for sch.-dist. personnel; dir. various ednl. coms.; co-chmn. devel. and implementation of cross-aged micro-computer program for disadvantaged kindergarten students, 1982-83. Active advocacy group for handicapped adults, Aberdeen, sch. levy election campaigns, drama groups; pres. Lake Stevens Food Bank, 1985. Served with U.S. Army, 1963-65. Fed. career edn. grantee, 1982. Mem. Nat. Assn. Supervision and Curriculum Devel., Wash. State Assn. Supervision and Curriculum Devel., Nat. Assn. Elem. Sch. Prins. (participant Nat. Fellows program 1986), Wash. State Assn. Elem. Sch. Prins., Phi Delta Kappa. Home: 2624 118th Dr NE Lake Stevens WA 98258 Office: Wash Assn Sch Prin 12806 20th St NE Lake Stevens WA 98258

RUDEE, MERVYN LEA, university dean, researcher; b. Palo Alto, Calif., Oct. 4, 1935; s. Mervyn C. and Hannah (Mathews) R.; m. Elizabeth Eager, June 20, 1958; children: Elizabeth Diane, David Benjamin. B.S., Stanford U., 1958, M.S., 1962, Ph.D., 1965. Registered profl. engr., Tex. Asst. prof. Rice U., Houston, 1964-68, assoc. prof., 1968-72, prof., 1972-74; provost Warren Coll., U. Calif.-San Diego, La Jolla, 1974-82, dean engring., 1982—; vis. scholar Corpus Christi Coll., Cambridge, Eng., 1971-72; vis. scientist IBM Thomas J. Watson Research Ctr., Yorktown Heights, N.Y., 1987. Served to lt. (j.g.) USN, 1958-61. Guggenheim fellow, 1971-72. Mem. Electron Microscope Soc. Am., Am. Phys. Soc., Tex. Soc. Electron Microscopy (hon., pres. 1966), Sigma Xi, Tau Beta Pi. Home: 1745 Kearsarge Rd La Jolla CA 92037 Office: U Calif San Diego La Jolla CA 92093

RUDESEAL, PATRICIA BRUINGTON, communications executive; b. Owensboro, Ky., Oct. 4, 1948; d. Finis McAdoo and Mary Marzee (Boyd) Bruington; m. George Arthur Rudeseal, Aug. 24, 1985. BA in English, Coll. of William and Mary, 1970; MA in English, U. Tenn., 1972. Instr. Community Coll. Denver N., Westminster, Colo., 1974-81; pvt. practice journalist, photographer Longmont, Colo., 1981-83; anchor, assoc. news dir. Longmont (Colo.) Communications, 1983-84; communications specialist Data and Expert Systems Inc., Westminster, 1984-85; communications dir. Constructors div. CRS Sirrine, Denver, 1985—. Author: Get It in Writing, 1984; contbr. articles to profl. jours. Bd. dirs., fund-raising co-chair Longmont Coalition for Women in Crisis, 1985—. Fulbright Commn. grantee, 1979-80. Mem. Pub. Relations Soc. Am., Soc. of Mktg. Profl. Services, Denver Woman's Press Club, WOmen in Communications, Inc. Congregationalist. Avocations: photography, piano, guitar. Home: 1083 Quince Ave Boulder CO 80302 Office: CRS Sirrine 216 16th St Mall 15th Fl Denver CO 80202

RUDIN, ANNE, mayor; b. N.J.; m. Edward Rudin; 4 children. B.S. in Edn., Temple U.; grad. Sch. Nursing; M.P.A., U. So. Calif. R.N. Mem. Sacramento City Council, 1971-83, vice mayor, 1977, 1st woman mayor, 1983—. Active numerous community orgns.; co-founder Calif. Elected Women's Assn. for Edn. and Research, 1973; bd. dirs. Sacramento Symphony Assn., Crocker Art Mus. Assn., ARC, State Coll. Presidents' Adv. Council. Named Soroptimist of Yr., 1976, Woman of Distinction award, 1985; recipient Hannah G. Solomon award Nat. Council Jewish Women, 1976; Outstanding Service award U.S. Jr. C. of C. Women, 1984. Mem. Sacramento Area Commerce and Trade Orgn. (bd. dirs.), LWV (past local pres.), Golden Key (hon.). Office: Office of Mayor Sacramento City Hall Sacramento CA 95814

RUDLIN, KATHRYN STERN, family therapist; b. Takoma Park, Md., Feb. 20, 1956; d. Leonard and Barbara (Weil) R.; m. donald D. Woolley, Nov. 29, 1986. BA in Psychology, Am. U., Washington, 1978; MSW, U. Denver, 1984; postgrad., Adolescent and Family Inst. Colo., 1985—. Cert. alcoholism counselor, Colo. Counselor Karma Acad., Rockville, Md., 1980-82; intern Northside Empathy Ctr., Aurora, Colo., 1982-83; social worker Warren Village, Denver, 1983; family and group therapist intern Lakewood (Colo.) Human Resources, 1983-84; family therapist Alternative Homes for Youth, Golden, Colo., 1984-86. Mem. Nat. Assn. Social Workers, Council on alcoholism, Sierra Club. Democrat. Jewish. Avocations: scuba diving, photography, cooking, travelling, swimming. Office: 7549 Mission Gorge Rd San Diego CA 92120

RUDNICK, MELANIE RUTH, sales executive; b. Bakersfield, Calif., Sept. 9, 1960; d. Milton and Gloria Diane (Stotts) R. BS, Lewis and Clark Coll., 1982. Dir. mktg. support Western Info. Systems, Bakersfield, Calif., 1983-84; v.p. sales Am. Lifestyle Communications, Bakersfield, 1984—. Mem. Bldg. Industry Assn., Art Council of Kern, Bakersfield C. of C., Bakersfield Trade Club. Office: Am Lifestyle Communications 123 Truxtun Ave Bakersfield CA 93301

RUDOFF, ALVIN, retired sociology educator; b. Bridgeport, Conn., Dec. 10, 1921; s. I. and Rose (Beckman) R.; m. Belle Hellenberg, June 4, 1949. BA, U. So. Calif., 1949, MA, 1960; postgrad., UCLA, 1949-52; PhD, U. Calif., Berkeley, 1964. Lectr. U. Calif., Berkeley, 1960-62; prof. sociology San Jose (Calif.) State U., 1962-80; vis. prof. Chinese U., Hong Kong, 1972-73; lectr. Md. U., Japan, 1981-82; research coordinator Dept. Corrections, Tracy, Calif., 1955-62; cons. Inst. Human Devel., U. Calif., Berkeley, 1959-64, Koba Assocs., Washington, 1980—. Author: Work Furlough, 1975; contbr. articles to profl. jours. Served to sgt. USMC, 1940-46, 48-52. Grantee San Jose State Found., 1963-67, NIMH, 1966-68, HEW, 1967-71. Mem. AAAS, Am. Sociology Assn., Pacific Sociology Assn., Space Studies Inst. Home: 1772 Dalton Pl San Jose CA 95124 Office: San Jose State U Sociology Dept San Jose CA 95129

RUDOLPH, BRUCE ROBERT, computer systems strategist; b. Elgin, N.D., May 1, 1947; s. Ervin and Velma Caroline (Bunse) R.; m. Mary Annette Zipp, Oct. 3, 1971; children: Corey David, Anne Lauren. BA, Westmar Coll., 1969; MBA, U. Denver, 1980. Info. systems applications designer AT&T, Aurora, Colo., 1970, with various depts., 1970-86, chief dept., 1986—. Office: AT&T 111 Havana St Aurora CO 80010

RUDOLPH, FRANCIS RAYMOND, investment sales executive, marketing executive; b. Portsmouth, Ohio, July 13, 1947; s. Clarence Baron Adams and Oma Lee (McGuire) Noble; m. Laura Avery Craig, June 12, 1972 (div. July 1985); m. Joan Louise Rock, Sept. 7, 1985; children: Geoffrey, Hallie, Nathan, Lindsay. BA with honors, U. Cin., 1971; JD, U. Tenn., 1974. Bar: Wash. 1975, U.S. Ct. Appeals (9th cir.) 1975, U.S. Dist. Ct. (we. dist.) Wash. 1975. Assoc. Wendells, Froelich & Powers, Seattle, 1974-77; trust adminstr. Peoples Bank, Seattle, 1977-81; v.p. investment sales U.S. Nat. Bank of Oreg., Portland, 1981-82; with investment sales dept. Columbia Mgmt. Co., Portland, 1982—. Served with USN, 1965-69. Mem. Western Pension Conf., Assn. Investment Sales Execs. Republican. Presbyterian. Club: Tualatin (Oreg.) Country. Avocation: golf. Office: Columbia Mgmt Co PO Box 1350 Portland OR 97207

RUDOLPH, JOHN WILLIAM, marketing professional; b. Little Rock, Sept. 21, 1939; s. Dennis and Thyra (White) R.; children: Dennis, Lauren, Frank. BS, Northwestern U., 1959; MA, U. Calif., Berkeley, 1960, MBA, 1961. Commd. ensign USN, 1958, advanced through grades to lt. comdr., 1962, resigned, 1962; mgmt. cons. Conlon Assocs., San Francisco, 1960-62; v.p. BBB, Berkeley, 1962-63; gen. mgr. Sunset West, San Ramon, Calif., 1963-70; mktg. dir. Town & Country, Palo Alto, Calif., 1970-80, regional mktg. dir., 1980—; faculty Coll. of Marin, Kentfield, Calif., 1970—. Recipient Excellence in Mktg. and Advt. award Nat. Research Bur., 1970-85. Mem. World Trade Com. (pres. 1960-62), No. Calif. Mktg. Dirs. Assn. (past pres.), Beta Beta Beta, Theta Delta Chi, Sigma Phi Epsilon (pres. 1960). Club: Toastmasters (Lafayette, Calif.). Home: 462 Spruce St Berkeley CA 94708

RUDOLPH, RONALD SCOTT, editor; b. Bklyn., Jan. 12, 1959; s. Harry and Shirley (Fox) R. BJ, Utica Coll. Syracuse U., 1981. Copy editor, photographer Idaho Mountain Express, Ketchum, 1981-82; staff writer Sat-Guide & Satellite Orbit Mags., Hailey, Idaho, 1982-83; sr. editor Satellite DEALER mag., Hailey, 1983-85; mg. editor Cablevision mag., Denver, 1985—. Home: 822 S Oneida Denver CO 80224 Office: Cablevision mag 600 Grant St Denver CO 80203

RUDRUD, JUDY LYNN, publishing executive; b. Fargo, N.D., Dec. 30, 1952; d. Ralph Duane and Carol Janis (Anderson) R. BA, U. N.D., 1975. Head copywriter Sta. KTHI TV, Fargo, 1976-77; advt. prodn. mgr. Cardiff Publ. Co., Denver, 1977-78; sales mgr., assoc. pub. Cardiff Pub. Co., Denver, 1978-81, pub., 1981-82, v.p., 1982—, also bd. dirs. Mem. Nat. Women in Cable (treas. 1984, bd. dirs. 1983-84), World Inst. Council (v.p. Rocky Mountain chpt. 1982). Office: Cardiff Publ Co 6530 S Yosemite Denver CO 80111

RUEBE, BAMBI LYNN, environmental designer; b. Huntington Park, Calif., Nov. 13, 1957; d. Leonard John Ruebe and Vaudis Marie Powell. Student, UCLA. Millwright asst. Kaiser Steel Corp., Fontana, Calif., 1976-79; electrician Fleetwood Enterprises, Riverside, Calif., 1977; fashion model internat., 1977-85; freelance draftsman 1982-83; project coordinator Philip J. Sicola Inc., Culver City, Calif., 1982-83; prin. designer Ruebe Inclusive Design, Highland, Calif., 1983—; cons. mfg. design DeRose Industries, Chambersburg, Pa., 1984, Skyline Corp., Redlands, Calif., 1982-84; cons. lighting Lightways Corp., Los Angeles, 1984—. Mem. World Affairs Council, Inland So. Calif., 1986; co-chmn. civil rights com. AFL-CIO, Fontana, 1978-79. Recipient Cert. Merit Scholastic Art award Scholastic Mags. Inc., Southeastern Calif., 1974. Mem. Nat. Trust for Hist. Preservation. Democrat. Avocations: snow skiing, horseback riding, antique sportscar restoration. Office: Ruebe Inclusive Design 27000 Meines St Highland CA 92346

RUECKER, WILLIAM MARTIN, interior architect, urban planner; b. Portland, Oreg., Sept. 30, 1956; s. Robert Lewis and Helen Ruby (Baldwin) R.; m. Mary Louise Cleary, Oct. 31, 1976; children: Jason William, Christopher Michael. BArch, U. Oreg., 1981. Project designer Designers Consortium, Portland, 1981-82; corp. architect, design cons. Papa Aldo's Internat., Portland, 1982—; pvt. practice interior architecture Portland, 1983—. Designed Papa Aldo's pizza shops, 1982 (3d prize, chain unit design award Restaurant Hospitality mag., 1986). Facilitator Portland Cen. City Plan, 1985; active Ladd's Addition Adv. Com., Portland, 1984. Democrat. Lutheran. Club: Tigard (Oreg.) C. of C. Golf League. Avocations: golf, soccer, basketball. Home: 108 SE 39th Ave Portland OR 97214 Office: 1509 SW Sunset Blvd #2B Portland OR 97201

RUETZ, JULIANNE MARGARET, communications educator, consultant; b. Los Angeles, Apr. 6, 1929; d. Paul and Margaret Emma (Zinke) Brueggemann; m. Edward Joseph Ruetz, Sept. 30, 1950 (div.); children—Jeffrey Edward, Lynn Karen Ruetz Hertwig. M.A., U. Denver, 1969; Ph.B., Marquette U., 1950. Tchr. speech, English, Sch. Dist. 6, Littleton, Colo., 1961-71; instr. Arapahoe Community Coll., Littleton, 1971-74, adminstr., 1974-79; media services dir. corp. pub. relations dept. Mountain Bell Co., Denver, 1979-81; asst. prof. pub. relations dept. tech. journalism Colo. State U., Fort Collins, 1982-85; instr. speech Met. State Coll., Denver, 1985—. Mem. Pub. Relations Soc. Am., Internat. Soc. Bus. Communicators, Assn. Edn. in Journalism and Mass Communication. Democrat. Unitarian. Home: 837 E Summer Dr Highlands Ranch CO 80231 Office: Tech Journalism Dept Colo State U Fort Collins CO 80523

RUFF, GEORGE ROBERT, advertising agency executive; b. Salt Lake City, Nov. 5, 1918; s. George Alma and Mary (Jensen) R.; m. Betty Clark, Aug. 28, 1943; children: Alan Robert, Lynn William, Roger Joseph, Robin, Susan. A.B. magna cum laude, Brigham Young U., 1943; postgrad. U. Utah, 1946-50. Account exec. Stevens & Wallis Advt. Agy., Salt Lake City, 1941-42; account exec. David W. Evans & Assocs. Advt. Agy., Salt Lake City, 1943-53, v.p., 1953-65, sr. v.p., 1965-68, vice chmn. bd., 1968-72, exec. v.p., chmn. exec. com., 1972-74; corp. pres. Evans Communications, Inc. (formerly David W. Evans, Inc.), Salt Lake City, 1974-84; v.p., dir. Evans Supply, Inc., 1953-73; pres., sr. cons. Communications Cons., Inc., 1980—; dir. Evans Communications, Inc., Atlanta Evans/Bartholomew, Inc., Denver; chmn. bd. Evans, Pacific, Inc., Seattle and Portland, Oreg.; dir. David W. Evans Calif., San Francisco, Evans/Weinberg, Inc., Los Angeles; dir. Ad Media, Internat. 1981-85; lectr. communications Brigham Young U., 1965-66; lectr. mktg. U. Utah, 1947-54, adj. prof. communications, 1980-82. Vice chmn. Red Butte dist Boy Scouts Am., 1964-65; mem. exec. bd. Great Salt Lake council Boy Scouts Am., 1982—; chmn., exec. com. Friends of Brigham Young U. Library, 1963-67; pres. Brigham Young U. Alumni Assn., 1959-61; mem. nat. adv. council Brigham Young U., 1978—; trustee Ballet West, 1982-86; bd. dirs. Hansen Planetarium; chmn. Com. of 100 for Econ. Devel.; chmn. bus. adv. council Westminster Coll.; bd. dirs., vice chmn. Utah Innovation Found. Served with USAAF, 1942-45. Decorated Air medal with three oak leaf clusters; recipient Presdl. medal for extraordinary service Brigham Young U., 1969, Meritorious Service award in Mass Communications, 1977. Mem. Utah Advt. Fedn. (Recipient Silver Medal award 1984), Am. Mktg. Assn., Pub. Relations Soc. Am. (accredited; pres. chpt. 1970, chmn. N. Pacific dist. 1972-73, dist. bd. 1979, del. nat. assembly 1980-86), Utah Mfrs. Assn. Salt Lake City C. of C. (vice chmn. indsl. and econ. subcom. 1982-85, chmn. com. of 100 1984-85), Air Force Assn. Republican. Mormon. Clubs: University, Timpanogos, Bonneville Knife and Fork. Lodge: Kiwanis (bd. dirs.). Co-chmn. editorial com. Instr. mag., 1960-71, contbr. articles to profl. jours. Home: 658 17th Ave Salt Lake City UT 84103 Office: Evans Communications Inc 110 Social Hall Ave PO Box 115020 Salt Lake City UT 84147-5020

RUFFCORN, JOHN DOUGLAS, health science facility administrator, academic dean; b. Mpls., May 1, 1927; s. John McKinley and Agnes Lorraine (Sproed) R.; m. Carol Jean Johnson, Aug. 24, 1950; children: Susan Marie, Sharon Kay. BBA, Union Coll., 1951; postgrad., U. So. Calif., 1955; cert. internat. acctg. soc. program, 1957. Acct. Ford Motor Co., St. Paul, Minn., 1951-52; acct. Glendale (Calif.) Adventist Hosp., 1952-60, controller, 1960-64, asst. adminstr., 1964-66, assoc. adminstr., 1966-67; adminstr. Washington Adventist Hosp., Takoma Park, Md., 1967-76; assoc. adminstr. Loma Linda (Calif.) Med. Ctr., 1976-77, pres., adminstr., 1977—; exec. v.p. Adventist Health System, Loma Linda, 1982—; assoc. dean Sch. Medicine Loma Linda U., 1983—; trustee Glendale Adventist Med. Ctr., 1960-67, Washington Adventist Hosp., 1967-76, Loma Linda U. Med. Ctr., 1976—; bd. dirs. Adventist Health System U.S., Adventist Health System Loma Linda, Sub Area Council Health Systems Agy; chmn. So. Calif. sect. Calif. Hosps. Polit. Action Com. Past pres. Seventh-day Adventist Hosp. Assn.; past mem. Mental Health Adv. Bd.; mem. Blue Cross Adv. Com.; past bd. dirs. local ARC, Am. Heart Assn. Served with U.S. Army, 1945-46. Mem. Am. Coll. Healthcare Execs., Am. Hosp. Assn., Am. Mgmt. Assn., Am. Protestant Hosp. Assn., Calif. Hosp. Assn., Council Teaching Hosps., Hosp. Council So. Calif., Assn. Adventist Healthcare Execs. Republican. Lodge: Kiwanis. Home: 23187 Glendora Dr Grand Terrace CA 92324 Office: Loma Linda Univ Med Ctr Office of the President 11234 Anderson St Box 2000 Loma Linda CA 92354

RUFFINI, MICHAEL JOHN, chemist; b. Rock Springs, Wyo., Jan. 8, 1958; s. Leno Joseph and Norma Jeanne (Dona) R.; m. Margaret Ann Jakobson, Aug. 14, 1981 (div. July 1982); m. Rhonda Jean Schad, June 16, 1984; 1 child, Krista Jean. AA, Western Wyo. Community Coll.; BS, U. Wyo. Environ. engr. FMC Wyo. Corp., Green River, 1980-83, foreman-phosphate prodn., 1983-85, foreman Sesqui prodn., 1985-86, lead foreman Sesqui prodn., 1986-87, tech. asst. Sesqui prodn., 1987—. Active Sweetwater County (Wyo.) Search & Rescue, 1980—; active Sweetwater County Underwater Recovery Team, 1981—. Mem. Am. Chem. Soc. Democrat. Roman Catholic. Lodge: Elks. Avocations: scuba diving, skiing, hunting. Home: 325 Jade St Rock Springs WY 82901 Office: FMC Wyo Corp PO Box 872 Green River WY 82935

RUFFNER, JEFFREY WILLIAM, project engineer; b. Fontana, Calif., July 12, 1957; s. William Ruffner and Lynette (Gunderson) Fleck; m. Cindy Lee Henrich, July 8, 1978; children: Kelly Lynn, Laura Michelle. BS in Engring. Sci., Mont. Coll. Mineral Sci. and Tech., 1982. Field service engr. Westinghouse Electric Corp., Salt Lake City, 1982-83; reliability engr. Westinghouse Idaho Nuclear Co., Idaho Falls, 1984—, project engr., 1985—; maintenance engr. Exxon Nuclear Idaho Co., Idaho Falls, 1983-84. Mem. ASME (assoc.). Avocations: golf, raquetball, hunting, fishing, cross-country skiing.

RUGGE, HUGO ROBERT, physicist; b. South San Francisco, Calif., Nov. 7, 1935; s. Hugo Heinrich and Marie (Breiholz) R.; m. Coral Loy Irish, Dec. 28, 1969; children—Leslie Anne, Robert David. A.B., U. Calif.-Berkeley, 1957, Ph.D., 1962. Research physicist Lawrence Berkeley Lab., 1961-62; mem. tech. staff Aerospace Corp., Los Angeles, 1962-68, dept. head, 1968-79, prin. dir., 1979-81, lab. dir., 1981—. Contbr. numerous articles on space sci. and astrophysics to profl. jours. Fellow Am. Phys. Soc.; mem. Am. Astron. Soc., Am. Geophys. Union, Internat. Astron. Union, Phi Beta Kappa, Sigma Xi. Office: Aerospace Corp (M2-254) PO Box 92957 Los Angeles CA 90009

RUGGERI, ZAVERIO MARCELLO, medical researcher; b. Bergamo, Italy, Jan. 7, 1945; came to U.S., 1978; s. Giovanni and Anna (Dolci) R.; m. Rosamaria Carrara, June 12, 1971. MD magna cum laude, U. Milan, 1970; degree in Clin. and Exptl. Hematology magna cum laude, U. Pavia, Italy, 1973, degree in Internal Medicine magna cum laude, 1981. Asst. clin. prof. hematology U. Milan, 1972-80; assoc. dir. hemophilia ctr. Policlinico Hosp., Milan, 1980-82; vis. investigator Scripps Clinic and Research Found., La Jolla, Calif., 1978-80, asst. mem., 1982-85, assoc. mem., 1985—; vis. investigator St. Thomas/St. Bartholomews Hosps., London, 1974-76. Editor: Clinics in Haematology, 1985; contbr. articles to profl. jours., chpts. to books. Research scholar Italian Ministry of Edn., 1970, Italian Hemophilia Found., 1970-72. Mem. AAAS, Italian Hemophilia Found., Am. Soc. Clin. Investigation, Italian Soc. Thrombosis and Hemostasis, Internat. Soc. Thrombosis and Hemostasis, Am. Heart Assn. (council on thrombosis), World Fedn. Hemophilia, Am. Fedn. Clin. Research, N.Y. Acad. Scis., Am. Soc. Hematology. Office: Scripps Clinic Research Found 10666 N Torrey Pines Rd La Jolla CA 92037

RUHLING, ROBERT OTTO, academic administrator, educator; b. Takoma Park, Md., Dec. 3, 1942; s. Otto Henry Ruhling and Gertraud Anna Ellie (Lademacher) Daugherty; m. Holly Louise Gilbert, Sept. 5, 1964; children: Alice, Grant, Lara, Erin, Minna, Blair, Jeanne, Roy, Heidi. BS, U. Md., 1964, MA, 1966; PhD, Mich. State U., 1970; postdoctoral cert., U. Calif., Santa Barbara, 1972. Vis. prof. U. Utah, Salt Lake City, 1972-74, asst. prof. exercise physiology, 1974-78, assoc. prof., 1978-80, prof., 1980—, chmn. dept. phys. edn., 1984-86, assoc. dean, 1986—; dir. Human Performance Research Lab., U. Utah, 1972-84. Contbr. numerous papers to profl. publs. and chpts. to books. Del. People's Republic of China, 1985. Gardner fellow, U. Utah, 1982, Park Tchrs. fellow, 1985. Fellow Am. Coll. Sports Medicine (mem. research consortium, Human Biology council, also pres. Southwest regional chpt., appreciation award 1985); mem. N.Y. Acad. Scis. Republican. Mormon. Avocations: reading, walking, writing poems, jigsaw puzzles. Home: 83 H St Salt Lake City UT 84103 Office: U Utah Coll of Health HPR N 221 Salt Lake City UT 84112

RUIS, STEPHEN PAUL, chemistry educator; b. Palo Alto, Calif., Oct. 23, 1946; s. Roy James and Catherine Clara (Long) R.; m. Nancy Myrtle Ray, Aug. 29, 1969 (div. July 1985); 1 child, Andrew Ray; m. Elisabeth Mann, Sept. 7, 1985. BS, San Francisco State Coll., 1969; MS, San Diego State Coll., 1971. Lectr. San Diego State Coll., 1971-72; instr. Skyline Coll., San Bruno, Calif., 1972—. Pres. acad. senate Skyline Coll., San Bruno, 1980-81. Mem. Calif. Assn. Chem. Tchrs., Acad. Senate for Calif. Community Colls. (mem. exec. com. 1982-84, v.p. 1984-85). Avocations: photography, playing piano, woodworking. Home: 4 Lillian Ln Mill Valley CA 94941 Office: Skyline Coll 3300 College Dr San Bruno CA 94066

RUIZ, CARL PHILLIP, nuclear chemist; b. Santa Barbara, Calif., Feb. 1, 1934; s. Charles C. and Augusta (Besson) R.; m. Joyce Donna Guiver; children: Gregory Michael, Susan Marie. BA in Chemistry, U. Calif., Santa Barbara, 1956; PhD in Nuclear Chemistry, U. Calif., Berkeley, 1960. Chemist Gen. Electric Co., Pleasanton, Calif., 1961-69, tech. specialist, 1969-73, mgr., 1973-82, 85—, cons. engr., 1982-84. Contbr. articles and reports to profl. jours.; patentee in field. Served to 1st lt. U.S. Army, 1960. Mem. Am. Chem. Soc., Am. Nuclear Soc., AAAS, Am. Inst. Chemists, Sigma Xi. Republican. Roman Catholic. Home: 1901 Ocaso Camino St Fremont CA 94539 Office: Gen Electric Co PO Box 460 Pleasanton CA 94566

RUIZ, CARLOS BUENO, mechanical engineer; b. Guadalajara, Mex., Nov. 4, 1951; came to U.S., 1955; s. Roque Del Valle Ruiz and Consuelo (Medina) Bueno. AA in Gen. Engr., Los Angeles City Coll.; BSME, Calif. Poly. State U. Product mgr. Sierra Instruments, Cucamonga, Calif., 1978-80; gen. mgr. Sierra Instruments, Puerto Rico, 1980-83; v.p. mfg. Siltron Illumination, Cucamonga, Calif., 1983—. Troop advisor Boy Scouts Am., Los Angeles, 1982. Served to capt. U.S. Army, 1974-78. Mem. ASME, Soc. Am. Mil. Engrs. Roman Catholic. Avocations: skiing, tennis, racketball. Office: Siltron Illumination Inc 7915 Center Ave Cucamonga CA 91730

RUIZ, DELIA, assistant school principal; b. La Barca, Mex., Apr. 4, 1957; came to U.S., 1966; d. Gabriel Ruiz-Gonzalez and Andrea (Hinojoza) R. Student, U. Madrid, 1976-77; BA in Spanish Lit. magna cum laude, UCLA, 1978, teaching credential, 1979; MA, Stanford U., 1982; adminstv. credential, Calif. State U., Hayward, 1983. Bilingual tchr. Alhambra (Calif.) Sch. Dist., 1979-81; bilingual tchr. Redwood City (Calif.) Sch. Dist., 1982-83, coordinator curriculum and tng., 1983-84; curriculum and staff devel. asst. Oakland (Calif.) Unified Sch. Dist., 1984-85, asst. prin., 1985—. Co-author: Project Family Learning: Adult Instructional Manual, 1984; editor: Action Sequence Stories, 1984; editor and contbg. author: Operational Procedures Manual for Bilingual Education, 1985. Scholar Stanford U., 1981, UCLA, 1975-78. Mem. Calif. Assn. Bilingual Edn., Nat. Council Yr.-Round Edn., Phi Delta Kappa, Sigma Delta Pi, Alpha Mu Gamma (v.p. 1974-75). Avocations: baseball, basketball, fgn. flims. Office: Jefferson Elem Sch 2035 40th Ave Oakland CA 94601

RUIZ, JOSE ALEJANDRO, construction company executive; b. Lima, Peru, Feb. 20, 1948; s. Pedro Alejandro and Estela Aida (Correa) R.; B. Mech. and Elec. Engring., Universidad Nacional de Ingenieria, Lima, Peru, 1968; B.S in E.E., Bucknell U., 1970; M.S. in E.E., Stanford U., 1974; m. Teresita Jesus Marquez, June 17, 1971; children—Noe Alfredo, Saul Efrain, Daniel Alejandro. Project engr. Amdhal Corp., Sunnyvale, Calif., 1972-74; owner, mgr. Reliable Packaging, San Jose, Calif., 1974-75; land officer Techo Inc., Watsonville, Calif., 1975-77, project devel. officer, 1977-78, chief exec. officer, 1978—; cons. Appropriate Tech. Internat. Cons., Capitola, Calif. Mem. adv. com. on tech. edn. U. Calif., Santa Cruz, 1978; bd. dirs. El Pajaro Community Devel. Corp., 1980—; bd. dirs. Santa Cruz Community Credit Union, Inc., 1979—, Santa Cruz County United Way, 1984—; bd. dirs., treas. South County Commn. on Alcoholism, 1979—; bd. dirs. Watsonville Area Devel. Corp., 1982—. Stanford U. fellow, 1970-74. Mem. IEEE, Nat. Soc. Profl. Engrs., Alexander Hamilton Inst., Soc. for Internat. Devel., Nat. Assn. Housing and Redevel. Ofcls., Calif. Coalition for Rural Housing, Internat. Assn. for Housing Sci. Home: PO Box 1133 Watsonville CA 95077 Office: PO Box 1138 Watsonville CA 95077

RULEY, STANLEY EUGENE, cost analyst; b. Akron, Ohio, Jan. 24, 1934; s. Royal Lovell and Opal Lenora (McDougall) R.; m. Annie Adam Patterson, Dec. 15, 1962; children: Cheryl Ann, Janice Lynn. Student, Kent State U., 1951-53; BSBA, Ohio State U., 1955. Registered profl. engr., Calif. Indsl. engr. Gaffers & Satler Inc., Hawthorne, Calif., 1961-62; mfg. engr. data systems div. Litton Industries Inc., Van Nuys, Calif., 1962-65; contract price analyst Naval Plant Rep. Office Lockheed, Burbank, Calif., 1966-72; contract negotiator Naval Regional Procurement, Long Beach, Calif., 1972-75; cost/price analyst Def. Contract Adminstrn. Services, Van Nuys, 1975-82; chief of contract pricing, dir. contracting Air Force Flight Test Ctr., Edwards AFB, Calif., 1982—; cons. engr., Northridge, Calif., 1971—. Served as sgt. U.S. Army, 1956-59. Recipient Sustained Superior Performance award Air Force Flight Test Ctr., 1984, Excellent Performance award Air Force Flight Test Ctr., 1982-83, Outstanding Performance award NAVPRO Lockheed, 1970. Mem. Am. Inst. Indsl. Engrs., IBM Computer User Group (Madison, Wis., Conn., San Fernando Valley), Air Force Assn. (life), Nat. Contract Mgmt. Assn. Republican. Presbyterian. Clubs: Lockheed Employee Recreation (treas. Gem and Mineral 1976, pres. 1976), Camper (Burbank) (pres. 1974). Lodge: Masons. Avocations: flying, golf, camping, travel, computers. Home: 18751 Vintage St Northridge CA 91324 Office: Air Force Flight Test Ctr Directorate of Contracting Stop 130 Edwards AFB CA 93523

RUMBLE, EDMUND TAYLOR, III, engineering manager, consultant; b. Phila., Oct. 26, 1942; s. Edmund Taylor and Dorothy (Brookes) R.; m. Katja Maria Kost, Aug. 14, 1976; children—Natalie Michelle, Nadine Vanessa. B.S., U.S. Naval Acad., 1965; M.S., UCLA, 1971, Ph.D., 1974. Registered profl. engr., Calif. Ensign, USN, 1965, advanced through grades to lt., 1970, resigned; corp. v.p. Sci. Applications Internat. Corp., Palo Alto, Calif., 1974—. Author numerous technical publs. Mem. Am. Nuclear Soc. Club: Foothills Tennis and Swimming. Office: Science Applications Internat Corp 5150 El Camino Real Suite C-31 Los Altos CA 94022

RUMPEL, HELEN BARBARA, artist; b. Lancaster, Pa., Mar. 31, 1937; d. Paul Hophni and Olive Deane (Morris) Johnson; m. Clarence Arthur Henry Rumpel, June 14, 1959; children—Warren Dean, Wesley Morris. A.A., Stephens Coll., 1957; B.S. in Art Edn., U. Wis., 1959. Art tchr. Santa Fe Pub. Schs., 1959-61; free-lance in contemporary embroidery, painting and clay, Santa Fe, 1960—; color cons. Register & Assocs. Architects, Inc., Santa Fe, 1977—; U.S. Nat. tchr. Can. Embroidery Seminar, Ontario, 1987, Am. Seminar Nat. Standard's Council, New Orleans, 1987; lectr. mus. and guilds, U.S.A. and abroad, 1978—. Contbr. cover to Delta Kappa Gamma Internat. Bull., 1984. Participant 11th ann. Biennial Needlework Show, Indpls. Art Mus., 1984; one-woman shows include Sheldon Meml. Fine Arts Mus., U. Nebr., 1978, N.Mex. Govs. Gallery, Santa Fe, 1980, Wichita Art Assn., Kans., 1983, Baker Fine Art Gallery, Lubbock, Tex., 1984, 85, Kokopelli II Galleries, Inc., Albuquerque, 1985, Sol del Rio, San Antonio, 1984-85; group show: Pittsburg Art Ctr., 1985; represented in permanent collections Sheldon Meml. Gallery U. Nebr., Fine Arts Mus. of Mus. N.Mex., N.Mex. State Fair (purchase award), St. Luke's United Methodist Ch., Oklahoma City, Wichita Art Assn. Mem. Nat. Artist Equity Assn. (pres. 1972-74), Designer Craftsmen of N.Mex. (pres. 1974-76), Nat. Standards Council Am. Embroiderers (nat. tchr.), Embroidery Guild Am. (nat. tchr., exhibitor, challenge cons. 1987), DAR (officer Heritage chpt.), AAUW (past officer), Pilots Club Internat. (speaker), Dig and Hope Garden Club, Delta Kappa Gamma, Delta Zeta. Republican. Presbyterian. Home: 320 Cadiz Rd Santa Fe NM 87501 Office: Rumpel Art Studio PO Box 1552 Santa Fe NM 87501

RUNDGREN, LINDA SELLERS, public relations executive; b. Peoria, Ill., Mar. 15, 1952; d. William Dale and Margaret Mary (Backes) Sellers; m. James Russell Rundgren, May 17, 1975; children: Soren William, Malachi James. BS with honors, U. Ill., 1973. Reporter The Journal Star, Peoria, 1970-76; pub. info. rep. Caterpillar Tractor Co., Peoria, 1976-80; owner LSR Communications, Seattle, 1981—; pub. relations executive Peoples Bank, Seattle, 1983-85. asst. editor Caterpillar World mag., 1977-78, Caterpillar Folks newspaper, 1976-77. Bd. dirs. N. Seattle Fives Sch., Seattle, 1986—, The Birthplace, Seattle, 1981-82; mem. adv. com. Heart of Ill. Chpt. ARC, Peoria, 1978-80. Mem. Pub. Relations Soc. Am. (sec. Puget Sound chpt. 1986-87, v.p. membership 1987—, newsletter editor 1985, bd. dirs. 1985—), Women in Communications Inc. (pres. Cen. Ill. chpt.). Office: LSR Communications 7352 19th Ave NW Seattle WA 98117

RUNDLE, JOHN BELTING, research geophysicist; b. Somerville, N.J., Aug. 31, 1950; s. David Bradford and Dorothy (Belting) R.; m. Marie Cardoza, July 27, 1974; children: Paul Belting, Daniel Edgar. Student, U. Ill., 1968-69, 74; BS in Engring., Princeton U., 1972; MS, UCLA, 1973, PhD, 1976. Postdoctoral fellow UCLA, 1976-77; research scientist Sandia Nat. Labs., Albuquerque, 1977—; vis. assoc. Calif. Inst. Tech., Pasadena, 1981-84; cons. various govtl. agys, 1980—; mem. Nat. Acad. Scis. NRC com. on Geodesy, 1986—, NASA geophysics sci. working group, 1986—. Contbr. articles to profl. jours. Grantee NASA, U.S. Dept. Energy. Mem. Am. Geophys. Union, Seismol. Soc. Am. Soc. Natural Philosophy, Sigma Xi, Phi Beta Kappa, Tau Beta Pi, Phi Eta Sigma. Republican. Club: Princeton (Albuquerque) (v.p. 1985). Avocations: cabinet-making, athletics, flying. Office: Sandia Nat Labs 1541 Albuquerque NM 87185

RUNICE, ROBERT E., corporate executive; b. Fargo, N.D., Aug. 20, 1929; s. E.M. and Ruth (Soule) R.; m. Geraldine Kharas, June 26, 1954; children—Michael, Christopher, Paul, Karen. B.S., N.D. State U., 1951. Sr. v.p. Northwestern Bell Telephone Co., Omaha, Nebr., 1945-81; v.p. Am. Tel. & Tel. Co.-Info. Systems, Morristown, N.J., 1981-83; v.p., pres. comml. devel. div. U.S. West, Inc., Englewood, Colo., 1983—; bd. dirs. Tandy Brands, Inc., Ft. Worth. Republican. Episcopalian. Club: Metropolitan. Home: 7665 S Yampa St Aurora CO 80016 Home: Mt Crested Butte CO 80114 Office: 7800 E Orchard Rd Suite 200 Englewood CO 80111

RUNKLE, KATHERINE GATES, educator; b. Cleve., Nov. 3, 1944; d. Charles Edward and Helen Mary (Hazel) Gates; m. Clifford Charles Runkle, Feb. 1, 1975. BA, Case Western Res. U., 1966; MS, U. Calif., Davis, 1981. Cert. jr. coll. tchr., Calif.; cert. adult edn. thcr. hazardous materials handling, Calif. Tchr. Byzantine Cath. High Sch., Parma, Ohio, 1967-68; teaching asst. chemistry Kent (Ohio) State U., 1968-69, U. Calif., Davis, 1978-80; chemist I Memorex Corp., Santa Clara, Calif., 1975-76, Mare Island Naval Shipyard, Vallejo, Calif., 1977; technician Castle and Cook, Inc., San Jose, Calif., 1976-77; substitute tchr. Vallejo Unified Sch. Dist., 1978, 82—, Benicia (Calif.) Unified Sch. Dist., 1982—. Mem. Chancellor's com. on handicapped, Davis, 1980. Fellow NSF, 1963, 65, 66, U. Calif., Davis, 1980-81. Mem. AAAS, NEA, Am. Chem. Soc., Calif. Acad. Scis., Smithsonian Instn., Am. Mus. Natural History, Calif. Tchrs. Assn. Republican. Byzantine Catholic. Avocations: philately, target shooting, writing, reading. Home: 1759 Mini Dr Vallejo CA 94589 Office: Vallejo City Unified Sch Dist 211 Valle Vista Vallejo CA 94590

RUNYAN, DONALD RALPH, data processing executive; b. Inglewood, Calif., Oct. 10, 1945; s. Ivan Dady and Genevieve Ruth (Stoner) R.; m. Elizabeth Ann Chenier, Mar. 15, 1974. Student, Iowa State U., 1966-69; BS in Computer and Mgmt. Sci. magna cum laude, Met. State Coll., 1986. Programmer Olivetti Corp., Des Moines, 1972-74; sr. progrmmer 1st Fed. Savs. and Loan Assn., Detroit, 1975; mortgage originator James T. Barnes Co., Detroit, 1976-77; project leader Citicorp Homeowners, Detroit, 1978-80; v.p. software engring. Darama Corp., Howell, Mich., 1981; v.p., dir. data processing Wood Bros. Homes, Inc., Denver, 1982-86; v.p. info. services Colo. Student Obligation Bond Authority, Denver, 1987—. Served with USN, 1963-66. Mem. Data Processing Mgmt. Assn. Republican. Clubs: Trout Unlimited, Ducks Unlimited (Denver). Avocations: fly fishing, duck hunting. Home: 2393 S Holland St Lakewood CO 80227 Office: Colo Student Services 7000 Broadway Denver CO 80221

RUNYON, STEVEN CROWELL, university administrator; b. San Rafael, Calif., June 20, 1946; s. Charles A. and Katherine C. (Pease) R.; m. Lynna Lim, Mar. 9, 1974. BA in Econs., U. San Francisco, 1971, postgrad., 1978—; MA in Radio and TV, San Francisco State U., 1976. Radio producer Sta. KGO, San Francisco, 1965-68; engr., announcer Stas. KSFR, KSAN, San Francisco, 1966-68; publicist Kolmar Assocs./Chuck Barris Prodns., San Francisco, 1970; instructional media technician U. San Francisco, 1968-72; technician, archivist, mgr. Wurster, Bernardi & Emmons, San Francisco, 1972-73; projectionist So. Pacific R.R., San Francisco, 1974; broadcast ops. engr. Stas. KPEN, KIOI, KIQI, San Francisco, 1968-74, public and community affairs program producer, 1971-74, AM transmitter engr., 1974; lectr. communication arts, U. San Francisco, 1974—, gen. mgr. Sta. KUSF-FM, 1974—, dir. mass media studies program, 1975—, acting chmn. communication arts dept., 1976; TV historian; producer, engr., cons. radio and TV programs; communications and audiovisual cons. Author: A Study of the Don Lee Broadcasting Systems' Television Activities, 1930-41, 1976; Educational Broadcast Management Bibliography, 1974. Contbr. articles to profl. jours. Grantee Calif. Council Humanities in Public Policy, Rockefeller Found., Father Spieler Meml. Trust, NSF; recipient cert. of merit for documentary radio series Peninsula Press Club, 1979, Diploma of Honor, Internat. Robert Stolz Soc., 1981, Fr. Dunne award U. San Francisco, 1986; lic. 1st class radiotelephone operator FCC. Mem. Soc. Broadcast Engrs., Broadcast Edn. Assn., Western Edn. Soc. Telecommunications, Assn. for Edn. in Journalism and Mass Communication, AAUP, Assn. Recorded Sound Collections, Pres.'s Ambassadors of U. San Francisco, Internat. Communication Assn., Com. Ethics in Pub. Affairs Broadcasting. Club: Press of San Francisco. Office: U San Francisco 2130 Fulton St San Francisco CA 94117-1080

RUPAAL, AJIT SINGH, physics educator; b. Mangwal, India, June 25, 1933; came to U.S., 1964; s. Puran Singh and Panmaisary Kaur (Panesar) R.; m. Evelyn O. Dzugalo, June 1, 1963; children: Amrit Kaur, Rajin Singh. BS, Panjab U., Hoshiarpur, India, 1954, MS, 1955; PhD, U. B.C., Vancouver, Can., 1963. Postdoctoral fellow Atomic Energy Can., Chalk River, Ont., 1963-64; prof. physics Western Wash. U., Bellingham, 1964—, chmn. physics/astronomy dept., 1980—; sr. research scientist Battelle Meml. Inst., Richland, Wash., 1976, 77. Contbr. articles to sci. jours. Mem. Am. Assn. Physics Tchrs., Can. Assn. Physicists. Democrat. Mem. Sikh Ch. Avocations: tennis, skiing, golf. Office: Western Wash U Dept Physics & Astronomy 516 High St Bellingham WA 98225

RUPEL, PHILIP HUGH, space laboratory engineer; b. Andrews, Ind., Jan. 11, 1933; s. Hildra Richard and Hazel Erdine (Jones) R.; m. Patricia Anne Browne, Sept. 8, 1962 (div. Mar. 1983). BSEE, U. Fla., 1957. Tchr. Peace Corps, Lyallpur, Pakistan, 1961-64; programmer Bunker-Ramo, Ft. Huachuca, Ariz., 1964-65; analyst Lockheed Corp., Sunnyvale, Calif., 1965-72; project engr. Sperry Corp.-Ames Research Ctr., Moffett Field, Calif., 1972-83; space lab. mission planner MATSCO GE-Ames Research Ctr., Moffett Field, 1983—; pvt. pilot San Jose, Calif., 1975-78. Served with U.S. Army, 1958-61. Republican. Roman Catholic. Club: Toastmasters (Santa Clara, Calif.) (pres. 1982-83, area gov. 1983, Best Speaker award 1982). Avocations: scuba diving, wind surfing, flying, dancing. Home: 2886 Taper Ave Santa Clara CA 95051 Office: MATSCO GE PO Box 138 Moffett Field CA 94035

RUPERT, CAROLA G., museum director; b. Washington, Jan. 2, 1954; d. Jack Burns and Shirley Ann (Orcutt) Rupert. B.A. in history cum laude, Bryn Mawr Coll., 1976; M.A., U. Del., 1978, Cert. in Mus. Studies, 1978. Personnel mgmt. trainee Naval Material Command, Arlington, Va., 1972-76; teaching asst. dept. history, U. Del., Newark, 1976-77; asst. curator/exhibit specialist Hist. Soc. Del., Wilmington, 1977-78; dir. Macon County Mus. Complex, Decatur, Ill., 1978-81; dir. Kern County Mus., Bakersfield, Calif., 1981—; tchr. mus. studies course U. Calif.-Santa Barbara Extension, 1982; advisor Kern County Heritage Commn., Historic Records Commn. sec.-treas. Arts Council of Kern, 1984-86, pres. 1986—; county co-chmn. United Way, 1981, 82; chmn. steering com. Calif. State Bakersfield Co-op Program, 1982-83; mem. Community Adv. Bd. Calif. State Bakersfield, Anthro; Soc. 1986—; bd. dirs. Mgmt. Council, 1983-86, v.p. 1987; bd. dirs. Calif. Council for Promotion of History, 1984-86; Community Adv. Bd. mem. Calif. State U.-Bakersfield Sociology Dept., 1986-88. Hagley fellow Eleutherian Mills-Hagley Found., 1977-78; Bryn Mawr alumnae regional scholar, 1972-76. Mem. Nat. Trust for Hist. Preservation, Am. Assn. Mus., Am. Assn. for State and Local History. Unitarian Universalist. Office: Kern County Mus 3801 Chester Ave Bakersfield CA 93301

RUPORT, MARVIN ALBERT, electronics engineer; b. Concord, Calif., Jan. 30, 1960; s. Jacob Charles and Inez Renee (Jefferson) R.; m. Belinda Kenfield, Sept. 22, 1984. Student, Diablo Valley Coll.; BSEE, U. Calif., Berkeley, 1983. Electronics engr. McDonnell Douglas Aircraft Co., Long Beach, Calif., 1982, Varian Inst. Group, Walnut Creek, Calif., 1983—. Republican. Baptist. Office: Varian Inst Corp 2700 Mitchell Corp Walnut Creek CA 94598

RUPP, MATTHEW WILLIAM, laboratory executive; b. St. Louis, Mar. 7, 1947; s. William Stuart and June Evelyn (Dennis) R.; divorced; children—Melissa, Elizabeth. B.S. in Mech. Engring., U. Mo.-Rolla, 1970. Sales engr. The Trane Co., LaCrosse, Wis., 1970-71, Systemaire-Trane, St. Louis, 1971-73; mktg. engr. Olin Brass, East Alton, Ill., 1973-77, sr. market devel. engr., 1977-78; mgr. mktg. DSET Labs., Inc., Phoenix, 1978-83, v.p., 1983—, also dir. Editor: Weathering Technical Handbook, 1985. Contbr. articles to profl. jours. Area coordinator Missouri Valley Jr. Achievement, East Alton, Ill., 1976; mem. regional energy com. Regional Commerce and Growth Assn., St. Louis, 1977. Served with U.S. Army, 1971-72. Decorated Army Commendation medal. Recipient Cert. of Achievement, R. B. Harris Co., 1979. Mem. Solar Energy Industries Assn. (standards com. sec. 1976-77), ASTM (vice chmn. com. 1978-79, award of appreciation 1984), Soc. Mktg. Profl. Services, Inst. Environ. Scis., Ariz. Electric League, Ill. Solar Energy Industries Assn. (dir., sec. 1977-78), Solar Industries Ariz. (dir., pres. 1981-82), Ariz. Solar Energy Industries Assn. (dir. v.p. 1982-83), Am. Mgmt. Assn., Soc. Advancement Materials and Process Engring. Office: DSET Labs Inc Black Canyon Stage 1 Box 1850 Phoenix AZ 85029

RUPP, SIGRID LORENZEN, architect; b. Bremerhaven, Republic of West Germany, Jan. 3, 1943; came to U.S., 1953; d. Harry Wilhelm and Mary Sophie (Gernert) Lorenzen; m. Steven Rupp, June 8, 1963 (div. 1976). BArch, U. Calif., Berkeley, 1966. Registered architect, Calif. Mont., Colo., Wash, Utah, Ariz., Tex. Assoc. Spencer Assocs., Palo Alto, Calif., 1971-76; pres. SLR Architects, Palo Alto, 1976—; chmn. Archtl. Review Bd., Palo Alto, 1975-77. Trustee Am. Inroads, 1983—. Mem. AIA, Constrn. Specification Inst., Orgn. Women Architects. Democrat.

RUPPEL, STEPHEN ALLEN, management infosystems director; b. Madison, Wis., Apr. 10, 1951; s. Richard Walter and Lois Margaret (Griffith) R.; m. Melody Ann Draves, Apr. 20, 1977; 1 child, Lucas Allen. Assoc., U. Wis.-Barron County, Rice Lake, 1971; BS in Edn., U. Wis., Superior, 1973. Systems analyst N. Idaho Coll., Coeur d'Alene, 1982-84, dir. computer services, 1984—. Co-founder Pinecone Alliance, Coeur d'Alene, 1979, CANWE, Coeur d'Alene, 1983. Mem. Data Processing Mgmt. Assn., 1984-86. Avocations: backpacking, whitewater rafting. Office: N Idaho Coll 1000 W Garden Ave Coeur D'Alene ID 83814

RUSAY, RONALD JOSEPH, chemical company executive; b. New Brunswick, N.J., Dec. 21, 1945; s. Stanley G. and Edna (Michalowski) R.; m. Suzanne Lee Hendrickson, Sept. 9, 1967; children—Christopher, Sylvie. B.A., U. N.H., 1967, M.S., 1969; Ph.D., Oreg. State U., 1976. Tchr. Bridgton Acad., North Bridgton, Maine, 1971-73; research fellow Oreg. State U., Corvallis, 1973-76; research chemist Stauffer Chem. Co., Richmond, Calif., 1976-80, bus. analyst, San Francisco, 1980-82, internat. bus. mgr., 1982—. Patentee in field. Served to 1st lt. U.S. Army, 1969-71, Vietnam. Mem. AAAS, Am. Chem. Soc., N.Y. Acad. of Sci., Sigma Xi. Home: 1030 Leland Dr Lafayette CA 94549 Office: Stauffer Chem Co 636 California St San Francisco CA 94108

RUSH, RICHARD WILLIAM, geologist, consultant; b. Austin, Minn., July 14, 1921; s. James Francis and Irene Evelyn (Peterson) R.; m. Florence Allison Rayman, Sept. 6, 1945 (div. 1972); children: Richard William, Lucy E., Frederick J., Cynthia I. B.A., U. Iowa, 1945; M.A., Columbia U., 1948; Ph.D., 1954; tchrs. cert. U. Iowa, 1961; diploma Nat. Tech. Schs., Los Angeles, 1976. Registered geologist, Calif., Ariz., Alaska. Instr. Colby Coll., Waterville, Maine, 1949-51; chief geologist Plateau Exploration & Devel. Corp., Cortez, Colo., 1951-52; asst. prof. U. Tex., Austin, 1952-57; sr. scientist Creole Petroleum Corp., Caracas, Venezuela, 1957-59; vis. prof. U. Iowa, Iowa City, 1960; cons. River Products Co., Iowa City, 1961-64; assoc. prof. No. Ariz. U., Flagstaff, 1963-69; cons. geologist, Phoenix, 1969—; cons. U.S. Steel, Que., Can., 1960; chief geologist Plateau Exploration and Devel. Corp., Cortez, Colo., 1951-52; cons. Exxon Corp., Midland, Tex., 1971, Mobil Oil Corp., Houston, 1972-73, Seneca Upshur Petroleum Co., Buckhannon, W.Va., 1981, 84; pres. JLC Corp., Los Angeles, 1974-75, WESGOE, Denver, 1982. Editor, geologist: Conceptual Design and Engineering, Economic and Environmental Analysis of Surface Pit Slope Caving Mining System, 1977. Supt. Episcopal Ch. Schs., Flagstaff, Ariz., 1965-67. Mem. enforcement adv. com. Ariz. Bd. Tech. Registration Geologists, 1984—. Recipient medal of merit Presdl. Task Force, 1984; Fulbright scholar, Brazil, Boliva, 1967, 68. Fellow AAAS, Geol. Soc. Am.; mem. Am. Inst. Profl. Geologists (charter, mem. exec. com. Ariz. sect.), Am. Assn. Petroleum Geologists (cert. of recognition 1982, 84), Am. Geophys. Union. Republican. Episcopalian. Office: 337 W Pasadena Suite 16 Phoenix AZ 85013

RUSKIN, ARNOLD MILTON, engineering management consultant, educator; b. Bay City, Mich., Jan. 4, 1937; s. Dave Burnard and Florence Shirley (Ruttenberg) R.; m. Dorothy Lee Darrah; 1 child, Sandra. BSChemE, BS in Materials Engring., U. Mich., 1958, MS in Engring., 1959, PhD, 1962; M in Bus. Econs., Claremont Grad. Sch., 1970. Registered profl. engr., Calif., Colo. Lectr. Rugby (Eng.) Coll. Engring. Tech., 1962-63, asst. prof. engring., 1963-66, assoc. prof., 1966-72; prof. engring. Harvey Mudd Coll., Claremont, Calif., 1972-73; engr. mgr. Everett/Charles, Inc., Pomona, Calif., 1973-74; v.p., program mgr. Claremont Engring. Co., 1974-78; system engr. Jet Propulsion Lab., Pasadena, Calif., 1978-80, mgr. strategy devel., 1980-86, dep. mgr. system engring. resource ctr., 1986—; founder, ptnr. Claremont Cons. Group, 1979—; lectr. UCLA, 1974-77, adj. prof. engring., 1977-84, coordinator engring. exec. program, 1978-84; lectr. Indsl. Relations Ctr., Calif. Inst. Tech., Pasadena, 1985—. Author: Materials Considerations in Design, 1967, What Every Engineer Should Know About Project Management, 1982; patent thermally metamorphosing oil shale to inhibit leaching, 1980; book rev. editor Engring. Mgmt. Internat., 1981-84, mem. editorial bd. 1984—; contbr. papers to profl. publs. Mem. Archtl. Commn., Claremont, 1974-76, chmn. 1976; mem. Profl. Adv. Group, Claremont, 1968; bd. dirs. ARC, Claremont, 1970-72. Mem. Am. Soc. Engring. Edn. (founding chmn., engring. mgmt. com. 1972-73, vice chmn. materials div. 1972-73, sec. materials div. 1963-67, editor Pacific Southwest sect. 1965-66, editorial com. Engring. Edn. 1970-71), Project Mgmt. Inst., AIAA (tech. com. on mgmt. 1986—), Am. Inst. Chem. Engrs., Assn. Mgmt. Cons., Am. Soc. Engring. Mgmt.. Office: Claremont Cons Group 545 W 12th St Claremont CA 91711

RUSNAK, JAMES EUGENE, infosystems specialist; b. Seattle, Aug. 1, 1937; s. Frank Loren and Clara Grace (McKee) R.; m. Dawn Rae Arnold, Apr. 15, 1957 (div. Dec. 1964); m. Catherine Ann McGovern, Dec. 30, 1964 (div. Apr. 1987); children: Christian Lance, James Loren, Nicole Marie; m. Claudia Gail Reed, Apr., 1987; children: Emily, Cass. BA, U. Wash., 1961. Systems and program mgr. Blue Shield Co., San Francisco, 1966-69; systems engr. Honeywell Info. Systems, Waltham, Mass., 1969-71; cons. Computer Synergy, Fresno, Calif., 1971-75; dir. data services Washington Hosp., Fremont, Calif., 1975-83; dir. mgmt. infosystems Marian Health Ctr., Sioux City, Iowa, 1983-84; dir. data Calif. Med. Review, San Francisco, 1984-86; health care systems cons. Fremont, Calif., 1986—; mental health systems mgr. Santa Clara County, San Jose, Calif., 1987—. Author: (book chpt.) Information Systems for Patient Care, 1984; contbr. articles to profl. jours. Served to 1st lt. USAF, 1960-66. Mem. Internat. Hosp. Fedn., Hosp. Mgmt. Systems Soc. (advisor Chgo. chpt. 1984-87), Computer Applications Med. (symposium mem.), Data Processing Mgmt. Assn., Am. Assn. Med. Systems and Informatics, Jaycees (state rep. Seattle chpt. 1963), Medinfo. Republican. Roman Catholic. Lodge: Odd Fellows (grand master 1980-81). Home: 37155 Aspenwood Common #102 Fremont CA 94536 Office: County of Santa Clara 645 S Bascom Ave San Jose CA 95128

RUSS, ROBERT MORRIS, JR., microprocessor manufacturing company executive, financial consultant, real estate broker; b. Atlanta, July 18, 1956; s. Robert Morris and Carol Marie (Hodapp) R. B.S. in Mech. Engring., MIT, 1977, B.S. in Mgmt. Scis., 1977, M.M.E., 1978; M.B.A., Stanford U., 1983. Registered profl. engr. Calif.; real estate broker, Calif. Research asst. MIT, Cambridge, Mass., 1978; systems engr. Lawrence Livermore Labs., Livermore, Calif., 1978-80; group leader product devel. Raychem. Corp., Menlo Park, Calif., 1980-81; cons. Stanford U., Palo Alto, Calif., 1981-83, teaching asst., 1983; pres. Unity Systems Inc., Palo Alto, 1983—; bus. tutor Stanford U., Palo Alto, 1981-83; mktg. cons., Palo Alto, 1981-83. Inventor actively controlled energy mgmt. system, variable air flow damper, 1984. Contbr. articles to profl. jours. Arjay Miller scholar Stanford U., 1983. Mem. ASME, Am. Assn. Energy Cons., Tau Beta Pi. Home: 836 Bruce Dr Palo Alto CA 94303

RUSSELL, BILL, coach, former sportscaster, former professional basketball player; b. Monroe, La., Feb. 12, 1934. Grad., San Francisco State Coll., 1956. Player, NBA Boston Celtics Profl. Basketball Club, 1956-69, coach, 1966-69; sportscaster ABC-TV, 1969-80, CBS-TV, 1980-83; coach NBA Seattle Supersonics, 1973-77, Sacramento Kings, 1987—; mem. U.S. Olympic Basketball Team (Gold medal), 1956. Appeared in: TV series Cowboy in Africa; also commls.; co-host: The Superstars, ABC-TV, 1978-79; Author: Second Wind: Memoirs of an Opinionated Man, 1979. Inducted into Basketball Hall of Fame, 1974; mem. 11 NBA championship teams. Office: Sacramento Kings 1515 Sports Drive Sacramento CA 95834

RUSSELL, CHRISTOPHER THOMAS, geophysics educator; b. St. Albans, Eng., May 9, 1943; came to U.S., 1964; s. Thomas Daniel and Teresa Ada Susan (Mary) R.; m. Arlene Ann Thompson, June 25, 1966; children: Jennifer Ann, Danielle Suzanne. BS in Physics, U. Toronto, Ont., Can., 1964; PhD in Space Physics, UCLA, 1968. Research geophysicist Inst. Geophysics UCLA, 1969-81, prof. geophysics dept. earth and space sci., Inst. Geophysics, 1982—; chmn. com. on data mgmt. and computation Nat. Acad. Scis. Space Sci. Bd., 1985—, commn. D. Com. on Space Research, 1982-86. Editor: Solar Wind Three, 1974, Auroral Processes, 1979, The IMS Source Book, 1982. Fellow AAAS, Am. Geophys. Union (pres. solar planetary relations sect. 1988-90, Macelwane award 1977); mem. Planetary Scis. div. Am. Astron. Soc., European Geophys. Soc. Office: UCLA Inst Geophys & Planetary Physics Los Angeles CA 90024

RUSSELL, DIANE HADDOCK, pharmacology educator; b. Boise, Idaho, Sept. 9, 1935; d. Grove Marden and Eileen Flora (Gridley) H.; m. Kenneth S. Russell, May 27, 1953 (div. Apr. 1975); children: Shauna, Keri. AA, Boise Jr. Coll., 1961; BS summa cum laude, Coll. Idaho, 1963; PhD, Wash. State U., 1967; postdoctoral student, Johns Hopkins U., 1969. Research chemist Balt. Cancer Research Ctr., 1969-73; assoc. prof. pharmacology dept. pharmacology U. Ariz., Tucson, 1973-76, research assoc. dept. internal medicine, 1973-76, prof. dept. pharmacology, 1976-84, prof. dept. pharmacology, molecular cell biology, 1984—; mem. Nat. Cancer Inst. Manpower Rev. Com., 1977-81. Mem. editorial bd. Life Scis., N.Y.C.; contbr. numerous articles to profl. jours. Fellow Am. Chem. Soc., Endocrine Soc., Am. Soc. Clin. Pharmacology and Exptl. Therapeutics, Soc. Toxicology; mem. AAAS, Am. Soc. Biol. Chemists, Am. Physiol. Soc., Am. Assn. Cancer Research (bd. dirs. 1979-82), Am. Soc. Cell Biology, Soc. Devel. Biology, Sigma Xi. Avocations: jogging, racquetball. Office: U Ariz Coll Medicine Dept Pharmacology Tucson AZ 85724

RUSSELL, DONALD GAMMELL, public relations executive; b. Ogden, Utah, July 21, 1953; s. Donald Anderson and La Dona (Gammell) R.; m. Esther Blackham, Aug. 7, 1976; children: Rebecca, Brian, Michelle, James. BA, Brigham Young U., 1977. Pub. relations rep. Brigham Young U. Housing Dept., Provo, Utah, 1975-77; asst. pub. relations dir. Gardiner Pub. Relations, Salt Lake City, 1976-77; sr. info. specialist Latter-day Sts. Pub. Communications Dept., Salt Lake City, 1977-80, asst. zone mgr., 1980-85, zone mgr., 1985—. Columnist Deseret News, 1981—. Publicity dir. Salt Lake Sister Cities Com., 1983—; missionary Ch. of Jesus Christ Latter-day Sts., Sao Paulo, Brazil, 1972-74; trustee Kearns Improvement Dist. Named Eagle Scout, Boy Scouts Am., 1969. Mem. Pub. Relations Soc. Am. (v.p. Intermountain chpt. 1985—). Republican. Club: Cougar. Avocations: coins, sports, mass media, music, travel. Home: 5455 Rockford St Salt Lake City UT 84118 Office: Latter-day Sts Pub Communications Dept 50 E N Temple St Salt Lake City UT 84150

RUSSELL, DOUGLAS SPENCE, chemistry educator; b. Oakland, Calif., July 20, 1940; s. Alexander Spence and Lois June (Zurilgen) R.; m. Patricia Kaye Nall, Sept. 5, 1964; children: Todd Spence, Brian Douglas, Erin Helene, Seth Wesley, Sarah Juneane. AA, Santa Rosa Jr. Coll., 1961; BA, Calif. State U., Sonoma, 1967; MS, San Jose State U., 1969. Prof. San Jose City Coll., 1969-70, Shasta Coll., Redding, Calif., 1970—; cons. for attys., Redding, 1970—. Author General Chemistry Experiments, 1972, PSI Quantative Analysis, 1976. Mem. Bishop's counsel, High Priest group leader Ch. Jesus Christ Latter-Day Saints, 1987, Palo Cedro Ward, Redding, Calif., 1982—; scoutmaster Boy Scouts Am., Palo Cedro, Calif., 1979-81, coordinator, 1984—. Served with U.S. Army, 1963-69. Mem. AAAS, Am. Chem. Soc., Calif. Assn. Chemistry Tchrs., Red Barons Flying Club (pres. 1971-84). Republican. Lodge: Masons. Avocations: hunting, fishing, restoring automobiles, camping. Office: Shasta Coll 1065 N Old Oregon Trail Redding CA 96099

RUSSELL, FRANCIA, ballet director, teacher; b. Los Angeles, Jan. 10, 1938; d. W. Frank and Marion (Whitney) R.; m. Kent Stowell, Nov. 19, 1965; children—Christopher, Darren, Ethan. Pupil of, George Balanchine, Vera Volkova, Felia Doubrouska, Antonina Tumkovsky, Benjamin Harkarvy. Mem. faculty Sch. Am. Ballet, 1963-64. Dancer, then soloist, N.Y.C. Ballet, 1956-61, mem., Jerome Robbins Ballets U.S.A., 1961-62, ballet mistress, N.Y.C. Ballet, 1965-70; staged 90 prodns. of Balanchine ballets in, Europe, U.S. and People's Republic China, 1964—; co-dir., Frankfurt Ballet, 1975-77, co-artistic dir., dir., Sch. Pacific NW Ballet, Seattle, 1977—. Home: 2833 Broadway E Seattle WA 98102 Office: 4649 Sunnyside Ave N Seattle WA 98103

RUSSELL, GAY MARTIN, television and film educator; b. Alpine, Tex., June 3, 1933; d. St. John and Ada (Harris) Martin; m. Harley E. Russell (div. 1981); children: Melodie Gay Russell McAheen, Howard Wesley Russell. AS, Arlington (Tex.) State U., 1952; BA, San Diego State U., 1967, MA, 1969. Cert. lifetime community coll. instr., Calif. Grad. asst. San Diego State U., 1967-69; prof. TV and film Grossmont Coll., El Cajon, Calif., 1969—, chmn. dept. TV and film, 1984—. Writer, producer, dir., editor, advisor several videos and film: Who? Me, In College, 1969, Expressions of Love-James Hubbell, 1982, Half of Heaven-The New China, 1983-84, Empowering Children Against Molestation-No, It's My Body, 1985, A Montage of Preschool Days, 1985, Cooking With Preschoolers, 1985, A Directed Movement, 1985. Pres. Murray Hill Homeowners Assn., La Mesa, Calif., 1985-87. Mem. Calif. Tchrs. Assn. (officer, community coll. assn. exec. bd. 1979, communication liaison, caucus chmn. Region IV , state council 1986-88), Broadcast Edn. Assn., Western Edn. Soc. Telecommunications, Am. Film Inst., NEA. Democrat. Home: 7200 Melody Ln #76 La Mesa CA 92041 Office: Grossmont Coll 8800 Grossmont Coll Dr El Cajon CA 92020

RUSSELL, JOHN ALBERT, astronomer; b. Ludington, Mich., Mar. 23, 1913; s. Albert James and Orra Emeline (Woodruff) R.; m. Phyllis Mae Rock, June 13, 1936; children: Carolyn Frances, Stanton James. AB, UCLA, 1935; AM, U. Calif., Berkeley, 1937, PhD, 1943. Instr. astronomy Pasadena (Calif.) City Coll., 1939-41; instr. astronomy extension div. U. Calif., Berkeley, 1941; asst. prof. astronomy U. So. Calif., Los Angeles, 1946-49, head dept., 1946-69, assoc. prof., 1949-56, faculty research lectr., 1956-57, prof., 1956-78, chmn. div. phys., scis. and math., 1959-63, assoc. dean natural scis. and math., 1963-68, prof. emeritus, 1978—; lectr. Griffith Obs. Planetarium, 1953-63; lectr. astronomy course Beyond the Earth Sta. CBS-TV, 1962, Nat. Ednl. TV, 1963—, Project Universe TV series, 1978. Served with USAAF, 1942-46. Recipient Teaching Excellence award U. So. Calif. Assocs., 1960, Disting. Emeritus award U. So. Calif., 1983. Fellow AAAS,

Meteoritical Soc. (sec. 1949-58, pres. 1958-62); mem. Am. Astron. Soc., Astron. Soc. Pacific (bd. dirs. 1961-63), Inst. Nav. (exec. com. 1949-56), Internat. Astron. Union, Sigma Xi, Phi Beta Kappa (hon.), Phi Kappa Phi. Home: 5654 Coliseum St Los Angeles CA 90016

RUSSELL, JOHN KENNETH, psychologist, screenwriter, novelist, producer; b. Belfast, No. Ireland, Oct. 18, 1948; s. William Edward and Nancy R.; m. Denise Louise, June 6, 1981; children—James Allen, Christina Michelle, Darren Christopher. B.A., U. So. Calif., 1970; M.A., Pepperdine U., 1971; Ph.D., U.S. Internat. U., 1974. Lic. psychologist. Pvt. practice Affiliated Psychotherapy Assocs., Lakewood, Long Beach and Cerritos, Calif., 1974—; ptnr. Russell-McCartney Prodns., 1980—. Mem. Am. Psychol. Assn., Calif. State Psychol. Assn., Am. Fitness Assn. (pres.). Author numerous psychol. writings, screenplays, novels. Office: 6700 E Pacific Coast Hwy Suite 295 Long Beach CA 90803

RUSSELL, KATHARINE ANNE, public relations executive; b. Schenectady, N.Y., Mar. 20, 1948; d. Joseph Solomon and Jane (Welsh) R. BA in History, Northwestern U., 1970, MBA in Mktg., 1980; MS in Journalism, Boston U., 1971. Assoc. producer Scientificom, Chgo., 1971-74, v.p., 1974-77; asst. market service mgr. Baxter-Travenol, Deerfield, Ill., 1977-80, mgr. corp. communications, 1980-81, group mgr. corp. communications, 1981-83; dir. pub. relations and investor communications Cetus Corp., Emeryville, Calif., 1983-86, v.p. pub. relations and investor communications, 1986—. Mem. Pub. Relations Soc. Am. Republican. Episcopalian. Club: Press San Francisco. Avocations: tennis, horseback riding, photography. Home: 150 Arbor St San Francisco CA 94131 Office: Cetus Corp 1400 53rd St Emeryville CA 94608

RUSSELL, LOUISE, educator, folklorist; b. Stratford, Okla., Aug. 9, 1931; d. Virgel Wylie and Louise J. (Hayden) R. B.A. magna cum laude, Oklahoma City U., 1953; M.A., Northwestern U., 1955; Ph.D., Ind. U., 1977. Tchr., Sterling, Colo., 1958-59, Washington-Lee High Sch., Arlington, Va., 1959-62, John Handley High Sch., Winchester, Va., 1962-63, Weld Sch. Dist. No. 6, Greeley, Colo., 1963-68, 72-87, Northland Pioneer Coll., St. John's, Ariz., 1987—, Colegio Internacional, Valencia, Venezuela, 1968-69, Holmdel Schs., N.J., 1971-72; ethnographer. Author: Understanding Folklore, 1975; Understanding Folk Music, 1977; also articles. Named Tchr. of Yr. Masons. Mem. Am. Anthrop. Assn., Am. Folklore Soc., NEA, Greeley Tchrs. Assn., Colo. Edn. Assn., Blue Key, Phi Delta Kappa. Office: Northland Pioneer Coll Saint Johns AZ 85936

RUSSELL, NEWTON REQUA, state senator; b. Los Angeles, June 25, 1927; s. John Henry and Amy (Requa) R.; m. Diane Henderson, Feb. 12, 1953; children—Stephen, Sharon, Julia. BS, U. So. Calif., 1951; postgrad. UCLA, Georgetown U., Webb Sch. Spl. agt. Northwestern Mut. Life Ins. Co., Calif., 1954-64; mem. Calif. State Assembly, 1964-74, Calif. Senate, 1974—; mem. com. on energy and pub. utilities, vice-chmn. com. on energy and pub. utilities, mem. subcom. on cable TV, mem. com. on local govt., vice chmn. com. on banking and commerce, mem. com. on budget and fiscal review, joint com. on rules, joint com. on state's economy, task force on legis. efficience. Mem. Republican State Central Com., former precinct chmn.; former chmn. residential campaign Tujunga United Way; past bus. solicitor Community Chest; bd. dirs. Hollywood Presbyn. Med. Ctr., Los Angeles. Served with USN, 1945-46. Recipient Outstanding Legislator award Calif. Rep. Assembly, 1968, 76, 81, Mayor's commendation City of Burbank, 1978, Disting. Service award County Suprs. Assn. Calif., 1980, Nat. Rep. Legislator of Yr., 1981, Legislator of Yr. award Los Angeles County Fedn. Rep. Women, 1982, Legislator of Yr. award Calif. Credit Union League, 1983, numerous honors from community orgns. and instns. Mem. Delta Tau Delta, Alpha Kappa Phi. Mem. Church on the Way. Club: Squires. Office: State Capitol Room 5061 Sacramento CA 95814

RUSSELL, PAUL EDGAR, electrical engineering educator; b. Roswell, N.Mex., Oct. 10, 1924; s. Rueben Matthias and Mary (Parsons) R.; m. Lorna Margaret Clayshulte, Aug. 29, 1943; children: Carol Potter, Janice Russell Gregory, Gregory. BSEE, N.Mex. State U., 1946, BSME, 1947; MSEE, U. Wis., 1950, PhDEE, 1951. Registered elec. engr., Ariz. From instr. to asst. prof. elec. engring. U. Wis., Madison, 1947-52; sr. engr., design specialist Gen. Dynamics Corp., San Diego, 1952-54; from prof. to chmn. elec. engring. dept. U. Ariz., Tucson, 1954-63; dean engring. Kans. State U., Manhattan, 1963-67; prof. Ariz. State U., Tempe, 1967-85; dir. engring. Ariz. State U. West, Phoenix, 1985—; cons. in field, 1954—; programs evaluator, mem. engring. commn. Accreditation Bd. for Engring. and Tech., N.Y.C., 1968—. Contbr. articles to jours. and chpts. to books. Served as sgt. U.S. Army, 1944-46. Recipient Disting. Service award N.Mex. State U., 1965. Mem. IEEE (chmn. Ariz. sect. 1960), Am. Soc. Engring. Educators. Home: 5902 E Caballo Ln Scottsdale AZ 85253 Office: Ariz State U West 2636 W Montebello Phoenix AZ 85017

RUSSELL, RICHARD BRIAN, fisheries biologist; b. Portland, Oreg., May 18, 1947; s. Frank R. and Phyllis A. Russell; m. Marilyn J. D'Alfonso, Dec. 17, 1983; 1 child, Amy J. BS in Fishery Sci., Oreg. State U., 1970. Sport fish biologist Alaska Dept. Fish & Game, King Salmon, 1973-80, comml. fish biologist, 1980—; acting statewide fish and game adv. com. coordinator, Alaska Dept. Fish & Game, Juneau, 1978. V.p., treas. Bristol Bay Hist. Soc. (life mem.), Naknek, Alaska, 1975-76. Mem. Am. Fisheries Soc., East African Wildlife Soc., Nat. Wildlife Fedn., Alpha Zeta, Chi Phi (pres. 1969). Avocations: river rafting, hiking, wildlife observation, scuba diving, travel. Home: PO Box 66 King Salmon AK 99613 Office: Alaska Dept Fish & Game Comml Fish Div PO Box 37 King Salmon AK 99613

RUSSELL, ROBERT BONNELL, petroleum geologist; b. Wylie, Tex., Oct. 5, 1919; s. Vaughn Heywood and Maude Louise (Adams) R.; m. Lettye Louise Smith, Oct. 16, 1948; children: Susan Jo McDaniel, Robert Van, Robin Everett. BA in Geology, Tex. Christian U., 1953. Cert. petroleum geologist. Geologist, Conoco Inc., 1953-55, petroleum geologist, Midland, Tex., 1955-65, staff geologist, Casper, Wyo., 1966-67, sr. geologist, Denver, 1967-81; ind. petroleum geologist, Lakewood, Colo., 1981—; exploration ptnr. cons. petroleum exploration cos. Compiler data: RMAG Guide Book, 1954. Served with U.S. Army, 1940-42; to 1st lt. USAAF, 1942-48, ETO. Mem. Am. Assn. Petroleum Geologists, Fifteenth Air Force Assn. Baptist. Club: Caterpillar. Home: 2696 S Ammons Way Lakewood CO 80227

RUSSELL, THOMAS FLETCHER, mathematician; b. N.Y.C., July 12, 1951; s. James Earl and Jane (Seaver) R.; m. Alene Merle Bycer, Dec. 23, 1979; children: Pamela Harriet, Jeffrey Daniel. AB in Math., Princeton U., 1972; SM in Math., U. Chgo., 1973, PhD, 1980. Lectr. U. Chgo., 1974-80; research mathematician Marathon Oil Co., Littleton, Colo., 1980-85, advanced research mathematician, 1985-86, sr. scientist, 1986-87; assoc. prof. dept. math. U. Colo., Denver, 1987—. Contbr. articles to profl. jours. Mem. Soc. Indsl. and Applied Math., Am. Math. Soc., Soc. Petroleum Engrs., Sigma Xi. Avocations: skiing, mountain climbing. Home: 1648 E Geddes Circle N Littleton CO 80122 Office: U Colo Dept Math Campus Box 170 1100 14th St Denver CO 80202

RUSSELL, THOMAS WYNNE, not-for-profit organization director, consultant; b. N.Y.C., Dec. 9, 1941; s. Ralston William and Margaret (Hall) R.; m. Mary Ann Reynolds, Sept. 4, 1968. BA, Miami U., Oxford, Ohio, 1964; MA, Antioch U., 1969. Coordinator Project Self Help, Austin (Tex.)-Travis County Mental Health Ctr., 1973-74, asst. to dir., 1974-75, partial care services dir., 1975-77, children and adolescent services coordinator, 1977-78; adminstr. Provo (Utah) Canyon Boys Sch., 1978; dir. Utah County Council on Drug Abuse, Orem, 1979—; cons. in field, 1976—. Pres. bd. trustees Utah Bach Choir, Provo, 1985; scoutmaster Boy Scouts Am., Utah and Tex.; coach Utah Youth Soccer League, 1984-85; bd. Parent's Edn. Resource Ctr., Orem, 1984-86. Named Citizen of Yr. Utah County Bd. Realtors, 1982, Exec. of Yr. Profl. Secs. Internat., 1985; recipient 2d Miler award Boy Scouts Am., Provo, 1984. Mem. Nonprofit Mgmt. Assn. (exec. bd. 1985—), Utah Assn. Alcohol and Drug Program Dirs. (pres. 1983). Mormon. Office: Utah County Council on Drug Abuse 347 E 1200 S Orem UT 84058

RUSSO, SALVATORE FRANKLIN, chemistry educator; b. Hartford, Conn., Feb. 6, 1938; s. Sebastiano and Serafina (Corpaci) R.; m. Betty McConaughy, July 3, 1964 (div. Feb. 1967); m. Judy Lee Watke, Aug. 19, 1967; children: Amy Kathryn, Alan Sebastian. BA, Wesleyan U., Middletown, Conn., 1960; PhD, Northwestern U., 1964. Lectr. Northwestern U., Evanston, Ill., 1963-64; research assoc. U. Wash., Seattle, 1964-67; asst. prof. Sacramento State Coll., 1967-68, Western Wash. State Coll., Bellingham, 1968-72; assoc. prof. Western Wash. U., Bellingham, 1972-83; prof. West Wash. U., Bellingham, 1983—; vis. faculty U. Colo., Boulder, 1977-78, 1984-85, Wash. State U., Pullman, summer 1980; vis. scientist COBE Labs., Lakewood, Colo., summer 1981. Contbr. numerous articles to profl. jours. NIH fellow 1965-66, 66-67; grantee Research Corp. 1968, Western Wash. State Coll., 1969, COBE Labs., 1983. Mem. Am. Chem. Soc., AAUP, Sigma Xi (local v.p. 1985-86, local pres. 1986—). Presbyterian. Avocations: hiking, jogging. Home: 2100 Niagara Dr Bellingham WA 98226 Office: Western Wash U Chemistry Dept Bellingham WA 98225

RUSSO HALEY, SALLY FULTON, artist; b. Bridgeport, Conn., June 29, 1908; d. John Poole and Elizabeth (Akers) Haley; m. Michele Russo, June 29, 1935; children—Michele Haley, Gian Donato. B.F.A., Yale U., 1926-31. One-man shows include Marylhurst Coll., 1965, Maryhill Mus. Fine Arts, Washington, 1975, Portland Art Mus., 1960, 75, Woodside Gallery, Seattle, 1971, 76, 79, Gov.'s Office, Oreg. State Capitol, 1976, Wentz Gallery, Pacific N.W. Coll. Art, 1984, Fountain Gallery Art, Portland, 1962, 72, 77, 80, 81, 84, 86; exhibited in group shows 3d Pacific Coast Biennial Exhbn., 1960, Francis J. Newton's Collection, Bush House, 1964, Seattle Ctr. Art Pavilion, 1976, Womans Bldg., Los Angeles, 1977; represented in permanent collections Fred Meyer Trust, Wash. State U., State Capitol Bldg., Salem, Portland Art Mus., The Laura Russo Gallery, Portland, Lynn McAllister Gallery, Seattle. Recipient Oreg. Gov.'s Art award, 1982.

RUSSOM, JERRY RAYMOND, public relations executive; b. Clarendon, Tex., June 7, 1935; s. Raymond R. and Elsie L. (Eoff) R.; B.A. in English Lit., Long Beach (Calif.) State Coll., 1958; m. Margaret M. Jackson, June 18, 1966; children—Anne Leslie, Amy Lind. Vice pres. Lennen & Newell, Inc., San Francisco, 1964-71; exec. v.p. Russom & Leeper, San Francisco, 1971-86; pres. Russom & Co., San Francisco, 1986—. Trustee Dixie Dist. Bd. Edn., San Rafael, 1977-81; bd. dirs. Marin Symphony Assn., 1981—, Marin YMCA, 1982-84, San Rafael Public Edn. Found., 1982—; mem. city council City of San Rafael, 1983—. Served with USCGR, 1958-61. Mem. Public Relations Soc. Am. Home: 97 Upper Oak Dr San Rafael CA 94903 Office: 350 Pacific St San Francisco CA 94111

RUST, FRANK WALTER, electronics company executive; b. Billings, Mont., Sept. 19, 1942; s. Ashley F. and Laura A. (Young) R.; m. Charlotte C. Eppens, June 24, 1964; children: Gerald L., Stacey K. BSEE, Mont. State U., 1972. Registered profl. engr., Mont. Engr.-in-tng. Mont. Power Co., Butte, 1972-73, automations engr., 1973-78, mgr. engring. services, 1978-79, mem. productivity com., 1979-81; v.p., gen. mgr. Tetragenics Co., Butte, 1981—. Pack master Butte council Cub Scouts Am., 1974; mem. high tech. subcom. Build Mont. Orgn., Helena, 1984; mem. elec. engring. adv. com. Mont. State U., Bozeman, 1983—. Served with U.S. Army, 1968-69. Mem. IEEE (chmn. Montana sect. 1979). Republican. Methodist. Avocations: camping, skiing, hunting, fishing. Office: Tetragenics Co PO Box 1338 Butte MT 59701

RUST, KATHLEEN GILLIS, speech-language specialist; b. Sheridan, Wyo., July 4, 1957; d. Neil Joseph and Joan Marie (Dittrich) G.; m. Gregory Joseph Rust, June 25, 1983. BS in Communication Disorders, Colo. State U., 1979, MS in Communication Disorders, 1981. Speech-lang. specialist Jefferson County Pub. Schs., Lakewood, Colo., 1981—. Mem. Am. Speech-Lang.-Hearing Assn. (cert.), Colo. Speech-Lang.-Hearing Assn. Avocations: gardening, sewing, cross stitching. Home: 11186 W Wisconsin Ave Lakewood CO 80226

RUST, THOMAS GRANT, pulp and paper company executive; b. Stratford, Ont., Can., Sept. 23, 1919; s. Stanley Rust; m. Mary Rust, Jan. 26, 1945 (dec.); children: James T., Anne. Student, Avon Sch., Stratford, Ont., Stratford Coll. Inst.; BSc in Chem. Engring., Queen's U. Quality control engr. Dominion Rubber Co., Kitchener, Ont., Can., 1946-47; groundwood control engr. Ont. Paper Co., Thorold, 1947-51; groundwood supt. Que. North Shore Paper Co., Baie Comeau, 1951-59, asst. gen. supt., 1959-61, div. mgr., 1961-64; v.p. Pulp & Paper Co., B.C., 1964-68, exec. v.p., 1968-70; pres., chief exec. officer Weyerhaeuser Can. Ltd. (formerly Kamloops Pulp & Paper Ltd.), 1970-73, chmn., chief exec. officer, from 1973; now chmn. Crown Forest Industries, Ltd., Vancouver; bd. dirs. Inland Natural Gas Co., Ltd., Trans. Mountain Pipeline Co., Ltd., The Bank of Nova Scotia, Can. Pacific, Ltd., Can. Energy Services, Ltd. Commr. B.V. Pavilion Expo '86. Served with Royal Can. Ordnance Corps, 1942-46. Mem. Can. Pulp and Paper Assn., Pulp and Paper Research Inst. Can. Clubs: The Vancouver, Shaughnessy Golf and Country. Avocation: golf. Office: Crown Forest Industries Ltd, 815 W Hastings St, Vancouver, BC Canada V6C 2Y4 *

RUTELIONIS, ALGIMANTAS JONAS, information technology executive; b. Kaunas, Lithuania, May 19, 1939; came to U.S., Sept. 12, 1949; naturalized, 1956; s. Vytautas and Julika (Malinauskas) R.; m. Lolita Anne Borzello, May 6, 1967 (div. 1979); 1 child, Aras Andrius; m. Sue Ellen Vandenberg, Dec. 8, 1982. A.A., Montgomery Jr. Coll., 1962; B.S., U. Md., 1964. Vice pres. internat. devel. Info. Handling Services Inc., Englewood, Colo., 1975-76, research and devel., 1976-77, internat. planning, 1977-78, internat. sales, mktg., 1978-79, v.p. new product devel., Denver, 1979-81, pres. internat., Englewood, 1983—; pres. Internat. Info. Tech. Group, London, 1981-83. Served to lt. U.S. Army, 1958-60. Mem. Info. Industries Assn., Internat. Micrographics Council, Nat. Micrographics Assn., Standards Engring. Soc. Republican. Roman Catholic.

RUTH, MICHAEL D., chemist; b. Santa Monica, Calif., Apr. 6, 1948; s. Edward A. and Macel G. (Mace) R.; children: David M. (dec.), Paul M., John M., Suzanne M. BS in Chemistry, Calif. State U., Northridge, 1975; MS in Chemistry, U. Ill., 1977, PhD in Alalytical Chemistry, 1982. Postdoctoral fellow U. Tex. Med. Sch. dept. pathology and lab. medicine, Houston, 1982-84; research scientist Abbott Labs., Dallas, 1984-85; sr. scientist Beckman Instruments, Brea, Calif., 1985—; cons. in analytical and clin. systems design, Houston, Los Angeles, 1983—. First aid instr. ARC, Urbana, Ill., 1980-82; Explorer post adv. Boy Scouts Am., Urbana, 1980-82, leader Weblos Boy Scouts Am. San Diego, 1986—. Served with USN, 1967-71. Research grantee U. Ill. Mem. Am. Chem. Soc. (editor newsletter 1985-86, publicity chmn. 1985-86, sec. Orange County Sect. 1987, 88), Am. Assn. Clin. Chemistry, Soc. Applied Spectroscopy, AAAS, Sigma Xi, Phi Lambda Upsilon, Chi Gamma Iota, Alpha Phi Omega (chpt. pres. 1980, adv. bd. chmn. 1980-82). Office: Beckman Instruments 200 S Kraemer Blvd Brea CA 71496

RUTHERFORD, THOMAS TRUXTUN, II, state senator, lawyer; b. Columbus, Ohio, Mar. 3, 1947; s. James William and Elizabeth Whiting (Colby) R.; m. Linda Sue Rogers, Aug. 28, 1965; 1 son, Jeremy Todd. BBA (N.Mex. Broadcasting Assn. scholar), U. N.Mex., 1970, J.D., 1982. Page, reading clk. N.M. State Legislature, 1960-65; mem. N.Mex. Atty. Gen. Environ. Adv. Commn., 1972; radio broadcaster Sta. KOB Radio and TV, 1963-72; mem. N.Mex. Senate, Albuquerque, 1972—, majority whip, 1978—, chmn. econ. devel. and new tech. interim com., mem. sci. and new tech. oversight com.; pres. Rutherford & Assos., public relations, Albuquerque, 1978-83; practice law, Albuquerque, 1983—; bd. dirs. Union Savs. Bank, Albuquerque; past chmn. Albuquerque Cable TV adv. bd. Mem. N.Mex. Gov.'s Commn. on Public Broadcasting; bd. dirs., v.p. Rocky Mountain Corp. for Pub. Broadcasting; mem. Am. Council Young Polit. Leaders, del. mission to Hungary, Austria, Greece, 1983; mem. Fgn. Trade Adv. Com. Bd. Econ. Devel. and Tourism; trade del. to People's Republic of China, 1985—. Home: 1133 Montclaire NE Albuquerque NM 87110 Office: PO Box 1610 Albuquerque NM 87103

RUTHERFORD, WILLIAM DRAKE, state treasurer; b. Marshalltown, Iowa, Jan. 14, 1939; s. William Donald and Lois Esther (Drake) R.; m. Janice W. Rutherford, Feb. 4, 1965 (div. Mar. 1982); children—Wayne Donald, Melissa Drake. B.S., U. Oreg., 1961; LL.B., Harvard U., 1964. Bar: Oreg., 1964, U.S. Dist. Ct. Oreg., 1966. Assoc. Maguire, Kester & Cosgrave, Portland, Oreg., 1966-69; house counsel May & Co., Portland, 1969-70, chief exec. officer, 1970-71; pvt. practice law McMinnville, Oreg., 1971-84; mem. Oreg. Ho. of Reps., Salem, 1977-84; state treas. State of Oreg., Salem, 1984—. Served to 1st lt. Q.M.C., U.S. Army, 1964-66. Recipient Contbn. to Individual Freedom award ACLU, 1981. Mem. Nat. Assn. State Treas. (elected exec. v.p. 1985, 86, elected pres. western region 1985, 86), Nat. Assn. State Auditors, Comptrollers and Treas. (exec. com. 1987—). Republican. Home: 1118 Springwood Ln McMinnville OR 97128 Office: State Treasury State Capitol Room 159 Salem OR 97310

RUTLAND, GEORGE ADAMS, electronics executive; b. Demopolis, Ala., July 30, 1944; s. Robert Horton Rutland and Mary Louise (Torbert) Sherrill; m. Patricia Helen Trawick, July 2, 1965; children: Adam, Will, Caroline Elizabeth. BS in Applied Physics, Auburn U., 1966. Mng. dir. Nat. Semiconductor (UK), Ltd., Greenock, Scotland, 1973-75; gen. mgr. Asia/Pacific div. Nat. Semiconductor Corp., Singapore, 1975-77; group dir. Nat. Semiconductor Corp., Santa Clara, Calif., 1977-80; v.p. Synertek, Inc., Santa Clara, 1980-81; pres. Solid State Sci., Inc., Willow Grove, Pa., 1981-84; pres., chief exec. officer Ultratech Stepper, Inc., Santa Clara, 1984—; bd. dirs. Bipolar Integrated Tech., Beaverton, Oreg., 1984—. Mem. Semiconductor Equipment and Materials Inst. (govt. relations com. 1986), Young Presidents Orgn. Club: Toastmasters (Campbell, Calif.) (pres. 1980-81). Office: Ultratech Stepper Inc 3230 Scott Blvd Santa Clara CA 95054

RUTLAND, GEORGE PATRICK, banker; b. Tifton, Ga., Sept. 4, 1932; s. George Patrick Sr. and Peggy (Roberts) R.; m. Dawn Mary O'Neill, Jan. 2, 1954; children: Michael, Kathleen, Dawn Kelly, Mary Linderman. BBA, Pace Coll. N.Y., 1961; postgrad., Stonier Sch. of Banking, Rutgers U., 1962-64. With Citicorp, N.Y.C., 1954-75; sr. v.p. corp. services Citicorp, 1970-73; exec. v.p. Citicorp (Advance Mortgage subs), 1973-75; exec. v.p., cashier Crocker Nat. Bank, San Francisco, 1975-81, sr. exec. v.p. ops, 1981-82; exec. v.p. Calif. Fed. Savs. and Loan Assn., Los Angeles, 1982-83, pres., chief exec. officer, 1983-84, vice chmn., 1984—, also bd. dirs.; pres., chief exec. officer CalFed Inc., Los Angeles, 1985—, also bd. dirs. Served with USN, 1950-53. Mem. Town Hall of Calif., The Newcomen Soc., Los Angeles World Affairs Council, USC Assocs., Pepperdine U. Assocs., The Fla. Council of 100, Los Angeles Area C. of C. (bd. dirs. 1984—). Republican. Roman Catholic. Clubs: The Los Angeles Country, The Wilshire Country (Los Angeles); Desert Horizon Country (Indian Wells, Calif.); Les Ambassadeurs (London). Home: 7220 Avenida Altisima Rancho Palos Verdes CA 90274

RUTLEDGE, SHIRLEY, employee relations executive; b. Detroit, Oct. 25, 1941; d. Arthur P. and Henrietta G. (Lauderdale) Manning; m. Thomas F. Jackson, May 30, 1958 (div. Feb. 1973); children: Gary Jackson, Angela M. Williams; m. James L. Rutledge, July 30, 1977. AA, Saddleback Community Coll., 1984; BAM, U. Redlands, 1985. Cert. profl. human resources generalist. Asst. to dir. personnel Guardian Industries, Novi, Mich., 1964-72; payroll sec. C.M. Hall Lamp Co., Detroit, 1972-74; assoc. dir. Profl. Skills All, Detroit, 1974-77; supr. personnel Traub Mfg. Co., Detroit, 1977-80; adminstr. employee relations Huck Mfg. Co., Detroit, 1980-86; supr. employee relations Huck Mfg. Co., Irvine, Calif., 1986—; chmn. edn. com. Internat. Tng. in Communications, Irvine, 1984-85, pres., 1985. Mem. Personnel-Indsl. Relations Assn. (treas. 1985-86, Achievement award 1985). Avocations: ceramics, reading, poetry. Home: 26591 Otay Circle Mission Viejo CA 92691 Office: Huck Mfg Co 6 Thomas Irvine CA 92718

RUTTENBERG, STANLEY, geophysicist, research director; b. St. Paul, Mar. 12, 1926; s. Edward and Goldene R.; m. Patricia Lee, Feb. 16, 1955; children: Alison L., Rebecca S. BS, MIT, 1946; MA, UCLA, 1951. Research scientist Inst. Geophysics UCLA, 1949-55; mem. Internat. Geophys. Yr. staff Nat. Acad. Scis., Washington, 1955-64; asst. to dir. Nat. Corp. Atmospheric Research, Boulder, Colo., 1964-72, mem. sr. managerial staff, 1972-80; dir. new projects Univ. Corp. Atmospheric Research, Boulder, 1980-84, dir. projects, 1984—; chief scientist film series Planet Earth, 1960-61, Nat. Acad. Sci. tech. cons., 1984-85. Mem. Am. Geophysical Univ., AAAS, Internat. Assn. Meteorology and Atmospheric Physics (sec. gen. 1975-87). Office: Univ Corp Atmospheric Research PO Box 3000 Boulder CO 80307

RUTTER, WILLIAM J., biochemist, educator; b. Malad City, Idaho, Aug. 28, 1928; s. William H. and Cecilia (Dredge) R.; m. Jacqueline Waddoups, Aug. 31, 1951 (div. Nov. 1969); children: William Henry II, Cynthia Susan; m. Virginia Alice Bourke, 1972 (div. 1978). BA, Harvard U., 1949; MA, U. Utah, 1950; PhD, U. Ill., 1952. USPHS postdoctoral fellow U. Wis., Madison, 1952-54, Nobel Inst., Stockholm, 1954-55; from asst. prof. to prof. biochemistry, dept. chemistry U. Ill., 1955-65; prof. biochemistry U. Wash., 1965-69; Hertzstein prof. biochemistry U. Calif., San Francisco, 1969—, chmn. dept. biochemistry and biophysics, 1969-82, dir. Hormone Research Inst., 1983—; chmn. bd. dirs. Chiron Corp.; mem. USPHS Biochemistry and Nutrition Fellowship Panel, 1963-66; cons. physiol. chemistry study sect. NIH, 1967-71; mem. basic sci. adv. exec. com. Nat. Cystic Fibrosis Research Found., 1969-74, chmn., 1972-74, pres.'s adv. council, 1974-75; exec. com. div. biology and agr. NRC, 1969-72; mem. developmental biology panel NSF, 1971-73; mem. biomed. adv. com. Los Alamos Sci. Lab., 1972-75; pres. Pacific Slope Biochem. Conf., 1972-73; mem. bd. sci. counselors Nat. Inst. Environ. Health Scis., 1976—; mem. adv. com. biology div. Oak Ridge Nat. Lab., 1976-80; adv. bd. Oak Ridge Nat. Lab. and Martin-Marietta Energy Systems, 1984-87; basic research adv. com. Nat. Found., 1976—; bd. dirs. Keystone Life Sci. Study Ctr; sci. adv. bd. German Ctr. Molecular Biology, U. Heidelberg, 1983—; panel sci. advisors Internat. Ctr. Genetic Engring. and Biotechnology, 1984—. Asso. editor: Jour. Exptl. Zoology, 1968-72; editor: PAABS Revista, 1971-76, Jour. Cell Biology, 1976-78, Archives Biochemistry and Biophysics, 1978—, Developmental Genetics, 1979—; editorial bd. various jours. Served with USNR, 1945. Guggenheim fellow, 1962-63. Mem. Am. Soc. Biol. Chemists (treas. 1970-76, mem. editorial bd. jour. 1970-75), Am Soc. Cell Biology, Am. Chem. Soc. (Pfizer award enzyme chemistry 1967), Am. Soc. Developmental Biology (pres. 1975-76), Nat. Acad. Scis. Home: 80 Everson St San Francisco CA 94131 Office: U Calif Hormone Research Inst San Francisco CA 94143-0534

RUTZ, RICHARD EMIL, JR., environmental analyst; b. Detroit, May 27, 1952; s. Richard E. Sr. and Dawn Rutz. BS in Zoology, Mich. State U., 1973; MS in Zoology, U. Wis., 1975, PhD in Zoology, 1978. Postdoctoral fellow U. Wash., Seattle, 1978-84; environ. analyst Seattle City Light, 1984—. Contbr. articles to profl. jours. Bd. dirs. N.W. Conservation Act Coalition, Seattle, 1983—; mem. conservation exec. com. The Mountaineers, Seattle, 1982—; mem. Mayor's Environ. Adv. Com., Seattle, 1985—, conservation liasion com. Mount Baker-Snoqualmie Nat. Forest, Seattle, 1982—, citizen's rate adv. com. Seattle City Light, 1983-84. Named Vol. of Yr., Wash. Environ. Council, Seattle, 1984. Mem. AAAS, Am. Soc. Zoologists, Am. Inst. Biol. Scis., Ecol. Soc. Am., Soc. Devel. Biology, Am. Soc. Cell Biology, Sierra Club, Seattle Audubon Soc. (bd. dirs. 1983—, sci. advisor 1983, 86, 2d v.p. 1984, 1st v.p. 1985). Avocations: hiking, backpacking, climbing, music, theatre. Home: 4141 Brooklyn Ave NE #406 Seattle WA 98105 Office: Seattle City Light Environ Affairs Div 1015 Third Ave Seattle WA 98104

RUYBALID, LOUIS ARTHUR, social worker, community development consultant; b. Allison, Colo., Apr. 6, 1925; s. Mike Joseph and Helen Mary (Rodriguez) R.; m. Seraphima Alexander, June 12, 1949; children: Mariana, John. BA, U. Denver, 1946-49, MSW, 1951; PhD, U. Calif., Berkeley, 1970; Professor Ad-Honorem (hon.), Nat. U., Caracas, Venezuela, 1964. Social worker Ariz., Calif., Colo., 1951-62; advisor community devel. Unitarian Service Com., Caracas, 1962-64, U.S. Agy. for Internat. Devel., Rio de Janeiro, Brazil, 1964-66; area coordinator U.S. Office Econ. Opportunity, San Francisco, 1966-68; prof., dept. head U. So. Colo., Pueblo, 1974-80; licensing analyst State of Calif., Campbell, 1984—; cons. UN, Caracas, 1978, Brazilian Govt., Brazilia, 1964-66, Venezuelan Govt., Caracas, 1962-64. Author: (books) Favela, 1970, Glossary for Hominology, 1978, (research instrument) The Conglomerate Hom., 1976. Mem. exec. com. Pueblo (Colo.) Regional Planning Com., 1974-79, Nat. Advisory com. The Program Agy. United Presbyn. Ch., 1978-79. Served with USN, 1944-46. Recipient Pro Mundo Beneficio medal Brazilian Acad. Human Sci., Sao Paulo, 1976; United Def. Fund fellow U. Calif., Berkeley, 1961-62. Mem. Nat. Assn. Social Workers (cert.), Ethnic Minority Commn., IMAGE (nat. edn. chair), Am. Hominol. Assn. (nat. pres. 1975-79), U. Calif. Alumni Assn., Phi Beta Kappa, Phi Sigma Iota. Democrat. Avocations: tennis, boxing history. Home: 1048

Wade Circle NE Albuquerque NM 87112 Office: State of Calif Social Services Dept 1799 S Winchester Blvd Campbell CA 95008

RUZO, LUIS OCTAVIO, research chemist; b. Lima, Peru, Aug. 15, 1949; came to U.S., 1966; s. Daniel and Olga (Mosselli) R.; m. Jacquelyn Evans, Apr. 28, 1984. BA in Chemistry, Boston U., 1970; PhD in Chemistry, Mich. State U., 1974. Postgrad. fellow U. Guelph, Ont., Can., 1974-75; vis. scientist U. Amsterdam, The Netherlands, 1975-76; asst. specialist U. Calif., Berkeley, 1976-78, assoc. specialist, 1979-81, assoc. profl. research chemist, 1981-86, profl. research chemist, 1986—; advisor Nat. Research Council Can., 1982-84; cons. Office for Evaluation of Natural Resources, Lima, 1984—; bd. dirs. Inst. Study Traditional Scis., Berkeley; mem. adv. bd. Jour. Agrl. and Food Chemistry, 1985—. Contbr. numerous articles to profl. jours. Forscheimer fellow, Fed. Republic of Germany and Israel, 1986. Mem. AAAS, Am. Chem. Soc., InterAm. Photochem. Soc., Internat. Soc. Study Xenobiotics. Avocations: archaeology, chess. Office: U Calif Dept Entomol Scis 101 Wellman Hall Berkeley CA 94708

RYAN, ARTHUR NORMAN, movie company executive; b. Gloucester, Mass., Dec. 22, 1938; s. Arthur Stanley and Mary (Ross) R.; children: Maya, Mark. B.S. in Polit. Sci, Suffolk U., Boston, 1962. Sr. acct. Price Waterhouse & Co., N.Y.C., 1962-66; asst. treas. Paramount Pictures, N.Y.C., 1966-67; dir. adminstrn. and bus. affairs Paramount Pictures, Los Angeles, 1967-70; v.p. prodn. adminstrn. Paramount Pictures, 1970-75, sr. v.p. prodn. ops., 1975-76; pres., chief operating officer Technicolor, Inc., Los Angeles, 1976-83, vice chmn., chief exec. officer, 1983-84; chmn., chief exec. officer Technicolor, Inc., 1985—; chmn. bd., chief exec. officer Compact Video Services, Inc., 1984—; chmn. exec. com. Four Star Internat. Inc., 1984—; dir. MacAndrews & Forbes Holdings Inc. Bd. dirs. Hollywood Canteen Found., trustee Calif. Inst. Arts, vice chmn., 1985—. Served with inf. U.S. Army, 1963. Mem. Acad. Motion Picture Arts and Scis., Acad. TV Arts and Scis. Office: Technicolor Inc 4050 Lankershim Blvd North Hollywood CA 91608

RYAN, CATHRINE SMITH, publisher; b. Calif., May 9, 1930; d. Owen W. and Margarette D. (Grimsley) Griffin; A.A., Bellevue Jr. Coll., Denver, 1948; grad. Barnes Sch. Commerce, Denver, 1950; student N.Y. Ballet Acad., 1954; m. Patrick J. Ryan, Apr. 28, 1972. Dir. Ballet Workshop, Enumclaw, Wash., 1958-64; dir. confs. and seminars San Francisco Theol. Sem., 1977-80; pres., dir. Cathi, Ltd., pub. and cons. office orgn. and mgmt., San Francisco, 1980—; freelance travel photographer, 1968-80; guest instr. in field. Active local PTA, March of Dimes, ARC. Recipient various certs. of recognition. Republican. Mormon. Author: Face Lifting Exercises, 1980, Sullivan's Chain, 1986; procedure and policy manuals.

RYAN, HAROLD L., federal judge; b. Weiser, Idaho, June 17, 1923; s. Frank D.R. and Luella Neibling R.; m. Ann Dagres, Feb. 17, 1961; children: Michael C., Timothy F., Thomas P. Student, U. Idaho, 1941-43, U. Wash., 1943-44, U. Notre Dame, 1944; LL.B., U. Idaho, 1950. Bar: Idaho. Atty. 1950—; pros. atty. Washington County, Idaho, 1951-52; mem. Idaho State Senate, 1962-66; judge U.S. Dist Ct. Idaho, 1981—. mem. Idaho State Senate 1962-66. Mem. Am. Bd. Trial Advocates. Office: US Courthouse PO Box 040 Federal Bldg Boise ID 83724

RYAN, JANE FRANCES, business manager; b. Bronxville, N.Y., Nov. 1, 1950; d. Bernard M. and Margaret M. (Griffith) R.; m. Kevin Horan, Dec. 26, 1982; 1 child, Kevin. BS in Journalism, Ohio U., 1972; postgrad., Golden Gate U., 1984—. Asst. promotion mgr. Fawcett Publs., Greenwich, Conn., 1972-75; mktg. coordinator Fawcett Mktg. Services div. CBS, Greenwich, Conn., 1975-78; dist. sales mgr. CBS Publs., San Francisco, 1978; prodn. mgr. Cato Inst., San Francisco, 1979-80; account supr. Bus. Media Resources, Mill Valley, Calif., 1980—. Office: Bus Media Resources 150 Shoreline Hwy B27 Mill Valley CA 94941

RYAN, JOAN SUE, business educator; b. Klamath Falls, Oreg., Mar. 28, 1948; d. John and Susan Elvara (Fenton) Cacka; m. Tom Edward Ryan, Feb. 20, 1976; children—Michael Edward, Christie Susan. B.S., So. Oreg. Coll., 1970; M.S., Oreg. State U., 1976, MBA 1977. Teaching, vocat. cert., Oreg. Legal sec. Luvaas, Cobb & Richards, Eugene, Oreg., 1970-73; escrow closer Lane County Escrow Dept., Eugene, 1974; tchr. jr. high sch. Bethel Sch. Dist., Eugene, 1974-78, high sch., 1978-81; instr. bus. Lane Community Coll., Eugene, 1982—; speaker ednl. confs., Calif., Idaho, Utah, Oreg., Mont., 1983—. Author: Managing Your Personal Finances, 1985, Personal Business Management, 1986; creator bus. math. video tapes for computer interactive telecourse Lane Community Coll., 1984. Mem. Oreg. Bus. Edn. Assn. (sec. 1986-87), Delta Pi Epsilon (v.p. Gamma Omicron chpt. 1985-87, pres. 1987—). Democrat. Baptist. Avocation: oil painting. Home: 1305 Flintridge PO Box 5354 Eugene OR 97405 Office: Lane Community Coll Bus Dept 4000 E 30 Ave Eugene OR 97405

RYAN, KENNETH EDWARD, insurance company executive; b. Bklyn., July 20, 1940; s. Raymond A. Helen R. (Browning) R.; m. Barbara Ann Williamson, Oct. 11, 1963; children: Kenneth E., Karen Ellen. BBA in Indsl. Psychology, Baruch Coll., 1973; MA in Safety Edn., NYU, 1976. Loss control rep. Continental Ins. Co., N.Y.C., 1970-72; sr. loss control rep. Hanover Ins. Co., N.Y.C., 1972-74; loss control mgr. Zurich Am. Ins. Co., N.Y.C., 1974-77; regional risk control mgr. The Atlantic Cos., N.Y.C., 1977; risk control mgr. Comml. Union Ins. Co., Los Angeles, 1977—. Mem. Am. Soc. Safety Engrs. (cert., chmn. sects. and divs. com. 1983-84, treas. chpt. 1984-85), Beta Gamma Sigma. Democrat. Avocations: reading, camping, snorkeling. Office: Comml Union Ins Co 520 S Lafayette Park Pl Los Angeles CA 90057

RYAN, KENNETH JOSEPH, organic chemist; b. Palo Alto, Calif., Sept. 22, 1938; s. Joseph P. and Josephine M. (Pallavicini) R. BS in Chemistry, San Jose State U., 1960. Organic chemist SRI Internat., Menlo Park, Calif., 1961—. Contbr. articles to profl. jours. Mem. Am. Chem. Soc. Office: SRI Internat 333 Ravenswood Ave Menlo Park CA 94025

RYAN, MARY PATRICIA, trade association executive, public relations executive; b. Stanford, Calif., Mar. 16, 1955; d. Lawrence Vincent and Patricia Ann (Tomsicek) R. BA, Stanford U., 1977. Advt. mgr. Taylor Properties, Menlo Park, Calif., 1977-78; account coordinator Foote, Cone & Belding, San Francisco, 1979-81; advt. and pub. relations staff Dreyer's Grand Ice Cream Co., Oakland, Calif., 1981-85; dir. communications Calif. Beef Council, Foster City, 1985—. Mem. Pub. Relations Soc., Am. Women Radio and TV. Clubs: Spinsters (San Francisco). Avocations: dance, tennis, reading. Office: Calif Beef Council 551 Foster City Blvd Suite A Foster City CA 94404

RYAN, RANDEL EDWARD, JR., airline pilot, union officer; b. N.Y.C., Jan. 11, 1940; s. Randel Edward and Ann Augusta (Horwath) R.; m. Pamela Michael Wiley, May 12, 1962; children—Katherine, Gregory. B.S. in Sci., Trinity Coll., 1961. Quality control supr. Ideal Toy Corp., Jamaica, N.Y., 1961-62; airline pilot United Airlines, San Francisco, 1968—, chmn. speakers panel, 1983—. Editor: The Bayliner, 1984-86, The Lowdown, 1980-83. Pres., Highlands Community Assn., San Mateo, Calif., 1975; chmn. Com. to Reelect County Supr., San Mateo, 1976; rep. Highlands Community Assn., San Mateo, 1970-86; coach Little League and Babe Ruth Baseball, San Mateo, 1979-83. Served to capt. USAF, 1962-68. Recipient Vandor award San Mateo PTA, 1976, awards of merit United Airlines, San Francisco, 1975, 79. Mem. Air Line Pilots Assn. (editor newspaper 1984-86, chmn. community relations com. 1983—, mem. contract study com. 1984—, chmn. grievance com. 1982-86, vice chmn. 1986—).Democrat. Club: Highland Tennis (San Mateo). Home: 1768 Lexington Ave San Mateo CA 94402 Office: United Airlines San Francisco Internat Airport San Francisco CA 94128

RYAN, RONALD EUGENE, engineering executive; b. Kansas City, Mo., July 30, 1945; s. Raymond Leslie and Thelma Pearl (Williamson) R.; m. Sharon Lee Stokes, Aug. 18, 1968; children: Gregory James, Kelly Kathryn, Sara Alison. BS, U. Kans., 1968; MS, Pa. State U., 1973. Registered profl. engr., Nev., Ariz., Colo., Wyo. Design engr. Westinghouse Nuclear Energy Systems, Monroeville, Pa., 1968-71, 73-75; teaching asst. Pa. State U., College Park, 1971-73; project mgr. Wyo. Mineral Corp., Denver, 1975-81; program mgr. CER Corp., Las Vegas, Nev., 1981—. Cubmaster Boy Scouts Am., Greenvalley, Nev., 1982-84. Mem. ASME (assoc.), Am. Soc. Quality Control. Republican. Roman Catholic. Home: 2401 Marshall Ct Naperville IL 60565 Office: CER Corp 2225 E Flamingo Rd Las Vegas NV 89119

RYAN, RONALD FRANKLIN, real estate finance executive; b. Kenedy, Tex., Sept. 4, 1946; s. Arthur Franklin and Etta Jane (Bodden) R.; m. Mary Alice Spencer, Aug. 27, 1966; children: Tiffany Marie, Gregory Franklin. BBA, U. Tex., 1968. CPA, Nev., Tex. Asst. mgr. Americana Theatre, Austin, Tex., 1967-68; mgr. Deloitte, Haskins & Sells, Dallas, 1968-74; audit mgr. Summa Corp., Las Vegas, Nev., 1974-76, asst. to treas., 1976-79, dir. corp. cash mgmt., 1979-82; v.p., treas., controller Howard Hughes Properties, Las Vegas, 1982-86; v.p. The Ribeiro Corp., Las Vegas, 1986—. Bd. dirs. Frontier Girl Scouts U.S. Council, 1983-84, Arthritis Found., 1980-81; active Boy Scouts Am., 1978-80; coach Cen. Little League, 1976, 78-79, all in Las Vegas. Mem. Am. Inst. CPA's, Nev. Soc. CPA's. Republican. Methodist. Avocations: photography, backpacking, jogging, racquetball. Home: 2470 W Oakey Las Vegas NV 89102 Office: The Ribeiro Corp 195 E Reno Ave Las Vegas NV 89119

RYAN, SALLY (ANNE), public relations consultant; b. Van Nuys, Calif., Dec. 8, 1935; d. Walter Ralph and Nellie Lou (Ramsey) Smith; m. David Philip Ryan, Aug. 22, 1959 (dec.); 1 dau., Elizabeth Maria. B.A. in Speech and English, UCLA, 1958; postgrad. UCLA, 1959. Cert. gen. secondary sch. tchr. Social worker Los Angeles County Dept. Social Service, 1960-63; asst. regional mgr. corp. relations dept. ITT, Woodland Hills, Calif., 1965-81; owner, pub. relations cons. Ryan and Assocs., Granada Hills, Calif., 1981—. Bd. dirs. United Way Region I, Los Angeles County, 1979-81; bd. dirs. St. Mark's Parish Day Sch., Van Nuys, 1969-72, San Fernando Valley council Girl Scouts U.S.A., 1969-71, San Fernando Valley Pub. Relations Roundtable, 1970-76, 82—, San Fernando Valley Child Guidance Clinic, 1978-82; mem. Republican Central Com. 37th Assembly Dist., Los Angeles County, 1980-82, 39th Assembly Dist., 1982-84. Mem. Women in Communications (v.p., dir.), Valley Interchange Exec. Women (founding dir.), Granada Hills C. of C. (bd. dirs. 1983-85), Valley Press Club (dir.). Mem. Ch. of Religious Science. Columnist Herald Community Newspapers, 1982—. Office: Ryan and Assocs PO Box 33996 Hills CA 91344

RYAN, STEPHEN JOSEPH, JR., ophthalmologist, educator; b. Honolulu, Mar. 20, 1940; s. S.J. and Mildred Elizabeth (Farrer) F.; m. Anne Christine Mullady, Sept. 25, 1965; 1 dau., Patricia Anne. A.B., Providence Coll., 1961; M.D., Johns Hopkins U., 1965. Intern Bellevue Hosp., N.Y.C., 1965-66; resident Wilmer Inst. Ophthalmology, Johns Hopkins Hosp., Balt., 1966-69; chief resident Wilmer Inst. Ophthalmology, Johns Hopkins Hosp., 1969-70; fellow Armed Force Inst. Pathology, Washington, 1970-71; instr. ophthalmology Johns Hopkins U., Balt., 1970-71; asst. prof. Johns Hopkins U., 1971-72, assoc. prof., 1972-74; prof., chmn. dept. ophthalmology LAC-USC Med. Ctr., Los Angeles, 1974—; acting head ophthalmology div., dept. surgery Children's Hosp., Los Angeles, 1975-77; med. dir. Estelle Doheny Eye Found., Los Angeles, 1977—, chief of staff, 1985—; mem. advisory panel Calif. Med. Assn., 1974—. Editor: (with M.D. Andrews) A Survey of Ophthalmology—Manual for Medical Students, 1970, (with R.E. Smith) Selected Topics in the Eye in Systemic Disease, 1974, (with Dawson and Little) Retinal Diseases, 1985; assoc. editor: Ophthalmol. Surgery, 1974—; mem. editorial bd.: Am. Jour. Ophthalmology, 1981—, EYESAT, 1981—, Internat. Ophthalmology, 1982—, Retina, 1983—, Graefes Archives, 1984—; contbr. articles to med. jours. Recipient cert. of merit AMA, 1971; Louis B. Mayer Scholar award Research to Prevent Blindness, 1973; Rear Adm. William Campbell Chambliss USN award, 1982. Mem. Wilmer Ophthal. Inst. Residents Assn., Am. Acad. Ophthalmology and Otolaryngology (award of Merit 1975), Am. Ophthal. Soc., Pan-Am. Assn. Ophthalmology, Assn. Univ. Profs. of Ophthalmology, Los Angeles Soc. Ophthalmology, AMA, Calif. Med. Soc., Los Angeles County Med. Assn., Pacific Coast Oto-Ophthal. Soc., Los Angeles County Acad. Medicine, Pan Am. Assn. Microsurgery, Macula Soc., Retina Soc., Nat. Eye Care Project, Research Study Club, Jules Gonin Club, Soc. of Scholars of Johns Hopkins U. (life). Office: Estelle Doheny Eye Found Bldg Dept Ophthalmology 1355 San Pablo St Los Angeles CA 90033

RYAN, WILLIAM FRANCIS, JR., communications specialist; b. Phila., Feb. 29, 1936; s. William Francis and Anne (Van Horn) R.; m. Doreen Ann Beliveau, Oct. 21, 1971; children: Sally Ann, Brenda Kathleen, Theresa Lee, Mary Beth, Jennifer Lynn, Ann Marie. Cert., Indsl. Coll. Armed Forces, 1971; AA, Cochise Coll., 1972; MA, U. No. Colo., 1977; diploma, U.S. Army War Coll., 1982. Lab. technician Triangle Pubs., Phila., 1953-54; metall. technician E.G. Budd Co., Phila., 1954-56; liaison engr. Burroughs Corp., Radnor, Pa., 1956-62; communications specialist U.S. Army Communications Command, Ft. Huachuca, Ariz., 1962-82; program mgr., system engring. Pacific, Worldwide Mil. Command and Control System, Honolulu, 1982—. Recipient Comdr.'s award for Civilian Service, U.S. Army, 1982. Mem. IEEE (sr.), Assn. of U.S. Army, Armed Forces Communications Elecs. Assn. Republican. Roman Catholic. Avocations: aviation, classical music, photography. Home: 555 Paakiki Pl Kailua HI 96734 Office: WWMCCS System Engring-Pacific PO Box 29 Camp H M Smith HI 96861

RYASON, PORTER RAYMOND, research chemist; b. Bridgeport, Nebr., Jan. 18, 1929; s. Ray and Kathleen Gertrude (Dunn) R.; m. Mary Elizabeth Waterbury, Aug. 26, 1952 (div. Jan. 1987); children: Rhian, Arne Preston, Heather, Sten. BA, Reed Coll., 1950; MA, Harvard U., 1957, PhD, 1954. Research chemist Chevron Research Co., Richmond, Calif., 1953-73, sr. research assoc., 1978—; mem. tech. staff Jet Propulsion Lab., Pasadena, Calif., 1973-78; mem. papers subcom. Internat. Combustion Symposium, Pitts., 1971-78, various com. Am. Petroleum Inst. on Air Pollution, Washington, 1968-73. Mem. editorial adv. bd. Combustion and Flame, University Park, Pa., 1974-77; contbr. articles to profl. jours.; patentee in field. Bd. dirs. Marin Council for Civic Affairs, Marin County, Calif., 1969-70; mem. campaign com. Peter R. Arrigoni for Supr., Marin County, 1968. Dreyfus Found. fellow Harvard U., Cambridge, Mass., 1952-53. Mem. AAAS, Am. Chem. Soc., Am. Phys. Soc., Phi Beta Kappa. Avocation: backpacking.

RYCHETSKY, STEVE, civil engineer, consultant; b. Phoenix, Oct. 9, 1951; s. Edward and Maria (Zabroni) R.; m. Dawna Marie Strunk, June 10, 1972 (div. Oct. 1985); children: Brian, Melissa; m. Michaele Ann Turner, Dec. 28, 1986; stepchildren: Mike, Kristi, Jaye, Karly Reeves. AA in Engring., Oreg. Inst. Tech., 1972, BTech, 1976. Registered profl. civil engr., Oreg., Calif. Mgr. sales engring. Varcopruden, Turlock, Calif., 1976-79, AMCA Internat., Winston-Salem, N.C., 1979-82; civil engr. USDA Soil Conservation Service, Klamath Falls, Oreg., 1983-85, tech. advisor, 1983-85; civil engr., tech. advisor USDA Soil Conservation Service, Tillamook, Oreg., 1985—. Democrat. Roman Catholic. Avocation: outdoor activities. Home: PO Box 338 Tillamook OR 97141 Office: USDA Soil Conservation Service 2204 4th St Suite B Tillamoook OR 97141

RYDEN, JOHN K., electronics executive; b. Mt. Vernon, N.Y., Mar. 9, 1953; s. John V. and Dorothy Ryden. BS in Mgmt. Engring., Rensselaer Poly. Inst., 1975; MBA in Fin., U. Colo., 1979. Engr., supr. Guilford (Conn.) Gravure, 1976-77; dept. mgr. Bic Pen Corp., Milford, Conn., 1977-78; founder, pres., chief exec. officer Unisyn, Boulder, Colo., 1980—; cons. in field, Denver, 1979-80. Republican. Avocation: skiing. Office: Unisyn 3300 Mitchell Ln Boulder CO 80301

RYDER, DEAN MATTHEW, film producer, distributor, consultant; b. Amityville, N.Y., Aug. 10, 1956; s. Donald and Ellen (Wyman) R. B.A. with honors, U. Vt., 1977, M.A., 1979. Dealer ancient, medieval and modern coins, Burlington, Vt. and Madison, Wis., 1975-84, Hollywood, Calif., 1984—; cataloger John H. Kent collection Greek, Roman, and Byzantine coins U. Vt., 1975; mgr. ancient and medieval dept. Internat. Coins and Currency, Montpelier, Vt., 1976, 77; founder Dean M. Ryder Co., 1978, pres. Dean M. Ryder Corp., Madison, 1979-84, Hollywood, 1984—; film prodn. and distbn., cons. Author: Index to the Canadian Numismatic Journal, 1967-76, 1977; The John H. Kent Collection of Greek, Roman, and Byzantine Coins, 1977; The Development of Greek Coinage, 1977; also articles. John H. Kent scholar, 1977. Fellow Royal Numis. Soc.; mem. Am. Numis. Soc., Can. Numis. Assn., Soc. Ancient Numismatics, Am. Film Inst., Internat. Platform Assn. Office: Dean M Ryder Corp 1930 N Vermont Ave Suite 310 Hollywood CA 90027

RYDER, EDWARD JONAS, geneticist, civil servant; b. N.Y.C., Oct. 6, 1929; s. Wilfred Oliver and Tillie (Brown) R.; m. Elouise Jones Viales, Mar. 10, 1962; 1 child, Deborah Lynn; stepchildren: Robert Glenn Viales, Lawrence Dale Viales. BS, Cornell U., 1951; PhD, U. Calif., Davis, 1954. Geneticist Agrl. Research Service, USDA, Salinas, Calif., 1957-72, research leader, 1972-82, location leader, 1982—. Author: Leafy Salad Vegetables, 1979; contbr. articles to profl. jours. Served as pvt. U.S. Army, 1954-56. Recipient award Grower mag. 1982. Mem. AAAS, Internat. Soc. Horticultural Sci., Am. Soc. Horticultural Sci., Am. Genetics Soc. Democrat. Avocations: reading, writing, hiking. Home: 77 Paseo Hermoso Salinas CA 93908 Office: Agrl Research Service USDA 1636 E Alisal St Salinas CA 93905

RYDER, SANDRA SMITH, communications specialist, publicist; b. Great Lakes, Ill., July 6, 1949; d. Dennis Murrey and Olga (Grosheff) Smith. B.S., Northwestern U., 1971; M.A., Annenberg Sch. Communications at U. So. Calif., 1986. Columnist Camarillo Daily News (Calif.), 1971-76; editor Fillmore Herald (Calif.), 1976-78; pub. info. officer Oxnard Union High Sch. Dist. (Calif.), 1980-82; pub. info. officer Ventura County Community Coll. Dist., 1982-83; pub. relations dir. Murphy Orgn., Oxnard, Calif., 1983-84; pub. affairs rep. Gen. Telephone Calif., Santa Monica, 1984—. Sec. Ventura County Commn. for Women, 1981—. Mem. Women in Communications, Soc. Profl. Journalists, Pub. Relations Soc. Am. Home: 177 W Green Vale Dr Camarillo CA 93010 Office: GTE Calif 11333 Sepulveda Blvd Mission Hills CA 91346

RYGIEWICZ, PAUL THADDEUS, plant ecologist; b. Chgo., Feb. 19, 1952; s. Sigismund Thaddeus and Regina (Korpalski) R. BS in Forestry, U. Ill., 1974; MS in Wood Sci., U. Calif., Berkeley, 1976; PhD in Forest Resources, U. Wash., 1983. Research wood technologist ITT Rayonier, Inc., Shelton, Wash., 1977; research assoc. Centre National de Recherches Forestières, Nancy, France, 1983-84; research soil microbiologist U. Calif., Berkeley, 1984-85; research ecologist EPA, Corvallis, Oreg., 1985—; asst. prof. dept. forest sci. Oreg. State U., 1987—. Contbr. articles to profl. jours. Vol. Big Bros. of Am., Urbana, Ill., 1972-74. Fellow Regents U. Calif., Berkeley, 1973-74, Weyerhaeuser U. Calif., Berkeley, 1978-79, Inst. Nat. de la Recherche Agronomique, France, 1983-84, French Ministry of Fgn. Affairs, 1983-84. Mem. AAAS, Ecol. Soc. Am., Am. Soc. Plant Physiologists, Sigma Xi, Gamma Sigma Delta, Xi Sigma Pi (officer 1973-74). Clubs: Cascade Bicycle; Forestry (Urbana and Berkeley). Avocations: bicycling, skiing, mountain climbing, camping, hiking. Office: EPA 200 SW 35th St Corvallis OR 97330

RYKER, NORMAN J., JR., aircraft and missile equipment manufacturing company executive; b. Tacoma, Dec. 25, 1926; s. Norman Jenkins and Adelia Gustine (Macomber) R.; m. Kathleen Marie Crawford, June 20, 1947 (div. 1983); children: Jeanne Ryker Flores, Christina, Vickie Ryker Risley, Norman Jenkins, Kathy; m. Judith Kay Schneider, Dec. 18, 1983. B.S., U. Calif.-Berkeley, 1949, M.S., 1951; postgrad. Advanced Mgmt. Program, Harvard U., 1973. Asst. chief engr. space div. Rockwell Internat., Downey, Calif., 1962-68, v.p. research engring. and testing, 1968-70, v.p. research and engring. graphic systems group, 1970-74, v.p., gen. mgr. Webb div., 1974, v.p., gen mgr. transp. and equipment div., 1974-76; pres. Rocketdyne div. Rockwell Internat., Canoga Park, Calif., 1976-83; sr. v.p. aerospace and indsl. group Pneumo Corp., Boston, 1983-84, exec. v.p., chief operating officer, 1984-85; pres., chief exec. officer Pneumo Corp. subs. IC Industries, 1985-86, Pneumo Abex Corp., 1986—; lectr. in field. Contbr. articles to profl. jours. Served with U.S. Army, 1944-46. Recipient cert. of appreciation NASA, 1969, merit award, 1979, Silver Knight award Nat. Mgmt. Assn., 1979, Tech. Mgmt. award Calif. Soc. Profl. Engrs., 1979. Fellow Inst. Advancement Engring., AIAA; mem. ASCE, Am. Astronautical Soc., Nat. Mgmt. Assn., Instn. Prodn. Engrs. (elected companion). Republican. Office: Pneumo Abex Corp 4800 Prudential Tower Boston MA 02199

RYLAND, MERLE EDWARD, JR., bankruptcy consultant; b. Key West, Fla., Oct. 11, 1944; s. Merle Edward and Maria R. (Rodrigues) R.; m. Michele Gordon Eddy, Mar. 21, 1978; children: Tahereh Marisa, Tatiana Jordan, Tabitha Ryland. BBA, Nat. U., 1982; postgrad. in bus. adminstrn., U. Colo. Pres. Surfer Pub. Group-Products, Capistrano Beach, Calif., 1977-79; gen. mgr. Baha'i Pub. Trust, Wilmette, Ill., 1979-80; prof. bus. dept. Palomar Coll., San Marcos, Calif., 1981-83; pres. Ryland Fin., San Marcos, 1981-83; v.p. fin. Sullins Electronics, San Marcos, 1981-83, also bd. dirs.; gen. counsel Anisa, Inc., 1981-83; bd. dirs. Crutchfield Concessions; adj. lectr. Coll. Aurora (Colo.) Bus. Dept. Pub.: Anisa Process Curriculum, 1981. Served with USN, 1962-64. Mem. Nat. Assn. Accts. (past founding bd. dirs.), Nat. Mgmt. Assn., Am. Arbitration Assn. (panel of arbitrators). Baha'i. Office: 3333 Colorado Ave #1-5A Boulder CO 80303

RYLAND, STEPHEN LANE, consulting geologist; b. Springfield, Mo., Sept. 27, 1949; s. Hollis Ivan and Juanita Elizabeth (Lane) R.; BS, U. Mo., 1970, M.A. (Woodrow Wilson fellow), 1971; MS (NSF fellow), Calif. Inst. Tech., 1973; m. Rose Mary Eissler, June 26, 1971. Research asso., geology Calif. Inst. Tech., Pasadena, 1971-73; geophysicist Geophys. Systems, Pasadena, 1973; seismologist Dames and Moore, Los Angeles, 1973-76, spl. cons., Los Angeles, 1976-80; dir. Seismosearch, Pasadena, 1976—; adj. instr. geology Calif. Poly. U., 1976—; partner Ryland, Cummings & Assos., 1979-83; pres. Ryland Assocs., Inc., 1983—; dir. CalGold Mining. Mem. Phi Beta Kappa. Baptist. Home: 470 N Sunnyside Ave Sierra Madre CA 91024

RYLANDER, ROBERT ALLAN, financial service executive; b. Bremerton, Wash., Apr. 8, 1947; s. Richard Algot and Marian Ethelyn (Peterson) R.; m. Donna Jean Marks, June 28, 1984; children: Kate, Josh, Erik, Meagan. BA in Fin., U. Wash., 1969; postgrad., U. Alaska, 1972-74. Controller Alaska USA Fed. Credit Union, Anchorage, 1974-77, mgr. ops., 1977-80, asst. gen. mgr., 1980-83, exec. v.p., chief operating officer, 1983—; pres., chief exec. officer, treas. Alaska Option Services Corp., Anchorage, 1983—. Served to capt. USAF, 1969-74. Mem. Credit Union Execs. Soc., Shared Networks Exec. Assn. Avocations: audio electronics, music. Home: 6514 Lakeway Dr Anchorage AK 99502 Office: Alaska USA Fed Credit Union PO Box 196613 Anchorage AK 99519-6613

RYLEY-COBEAN, HELEN, educator, administrator, author, lecturer; b. San Antonio, Oct. 20, 1940; d. William A. and Janet G. (Smith) King; m. Frederick G. Ryley, Apr. 21, 1962; children—Tami, Troy and Scott (twins), Christiania, Jay; m. 2d, Kelly J. Cobean, May 6, 1979. B.A. in Elem. Edn., Blackburn Coll., 1962; M.S. in Speech Pathology and Audiology, No. Ill. U., 1965. Tchr. elem. schs., Forest Park, Ill., 1962-63; tchr. deaf, hard hearing and drop-out prone pub. schs., Springfield, Ill., 1965-68; dir. Enrichment Ctr., Taipei, Taiwan, 1968-72; coordinator staff devel., material resources Boulder Valley Schs., Boulder, Colo., 1972-83; v.p. program design and devel. Am. Tng. Ctr., Boulder, 1981—; adj. prof. U. No., Colo. U. Mem. Boulder Youth Symphony Bd. Mem. Assn. Supervision and Curriculum Devel., Colo. Assn. Tchr. Educators, Human Resource Devel., Nat. Staff Devel. Council, Boulder C. of C., Phi Delta Kappa. Author: Discipline With Love and Logic: A Guide for Teachers, 1981; You've Got to Be Kid-ding! A Look at Adolescents, 1984; editor: Who Says You're So Great, 1982; (audio tapes) Discipline with Love and Logic for Parents, 1982, You've Got to Be Kid-ding! The Elementary Years, 1987. Office: Am Tng Cos 2300 Central Ave Boulder CO 80303

RYMER, PAMELA ANN, federal judge; b. Knoxville, Tenn., Jan. 6, 1941. A.B., Vassar Coll., 1961; LL.B., Stanford U., 1964. Bar: Calif. 1966, U.S. Ct. Appeals (9th cir.) 1966, U.S. Ct. Appeals (10th cir.), U.S. Supreme Ct. Assoc. Lillick McHose & Charles, Los Angeles, 1966-72, ptnr., 1973-75; ptnr. Toy and Rymer, Los Angeles, 1975-83; judge U.S. Dist. Ct. (cen. dist.) Calif., Los Angeles, 1983—; faculty The Nat. Jud. Coll., 1986. Mem. Calif. Postsecondary Edn. Commn., 1974—, chmn., 1980-84; mem. Los Angeles Olympic Citizens Adv. Commn.; bd. visitors Stanford Law Sch., 1986—; bd. dirs. Constl. Rights Found., 1985—. Mem. ABA, Los Angeles County Bar Assn. (chmn. antitrust sect. 1981-82), Assn. of Bus. Trial Lawyers. Office: US District Court cen dist Calif 312 N Spring St Los Angeles CA 90012

RYNIKER, BRUCE WALTER DURLAND, industrial designer, manufacturing executive; b. Billings, Mont., Mar. 23, 1940; s. Walter Henry and Alice Margaret (Durland) R.; B. Profl. Arts in Transp. Design (Ford scholar), Art Ctr. Coll. Design, Los Angeles, 1963; grad. specialized tech. engring. program Gen. Motors Inst., 1964; m. Marilee Ann Vincent, July 8, 1961; children—Kevin Walter, Steven Durland. Automotive designer Gen. Motors Corp., Warren, Mich., 1963-66; mgmt. staff automotive designer Chrysler Corp., Highland Park, Mich., 1966-72; pres., dir. design Transform Corp., Birmingham, Mich., 1969-72; indsl. designer, art dir. James R. Powers and Assocs., Los Angeles, 1972-75; sr. design products mgr. Mattel Inc., Hawthorne, Calif., 1975—; dir. design and devel. Microword Industries, Inc., Los Angeles, 1977-80, also dir.; exec. mem. Modern Plastics Adv. Council, 1976-80; elegance judge LeCercle Concours D'Elegance, 1976-77; mem. nat. adv. bd. Am. Security Council, 1980; cons. automotive design, 1972—. Served with USMC, 1957-60. Mem. Soc. Art Ctr. Alumni (life), Mattel Mgmt. Assn., Second Amendment Found., Am. Def. Preparedness Assn., Nat. Rifle Assn. Designer numerous exptl. automobiles, electric powered vehicles, sports and racing cars, also med. equipment, electronic teaching machines, ride-on toys. Home: 21329 Marjorie Ave Torrance CA 90503 Office: 5150 Rosecrans Ave Mail Stop 11-337 Hawthorne CA 90250

RYPKA, EUGENE WESTON, microbiologist; b. Owatonna, Minn., May 6, 1925; s. Charles Frederick and Ethel Marie (Ellerman) R.; m. Rosemary Speeker, June 1, 1967; 1 child, Barbara. Student, Carleton Coll., 1946-47; BA, Stanford U., 1950, PhD, 1958. Prof. microbiology, systems, cybernetics U. N.Mex., Albuquerque, 1957-62; bacteriologist Leonard Wood Meml. Lab. Johns Hopkins U., Balt., 1962-63; sr. scientist Lovelace Med. Ctr., Albuquerque, 1963-71, chief microbiologist, 1971—; adj. prof. U. N.Mex., 1973—; cons. Hoffmann-LaRoche Inc., Nutley, N.J., 1974—, Airline Pilots Assn., Washington, 1976, Pasco Lab., Denver, 1983—; advisor Nat. Com. Clinic Lab. Standards, Pa., 1980-84. Contbr. articles to profl. jours. Served with USN, 1943-46. Fellow AAAS; mem. IEEE, Soc. Gen. Systems Research. Republican. Presbyterian. Avocations: bicycle racing, pets. Home: PO Box 8345 Albuquerque NM 87198

SAAR, FREDERICK ARTHUR, data processing executive; b. Charlotte, N.C., Aug. 30, 1946; s. Frederick Arthur and Mary (Gray) S.; m. Linda Keziah, Feb. 27, 1968; children: Frances Alisa, Jennifer Elizabeth. Sr. programmer Fed. Reserve Bank, Charlotte, 1967-74; EDP auditor 1st Commerce Corp., New Orleans, 1974-76; audit dir. 1st Interstate Bancorp, Phoenix, 1976-84; mgr. info. resource mgmt. 1st Interstate Bank div. 1st Interstate Bancorp, Phoenix, 1984—; pres. Hogan Users Group, Dallas, 1983-84. Served with U.S. Army, 1964-67, Vietnam. Named Auditor of Yr. Inst. Internal Auditors, Phoenix chpt., 1981-82. Mem. EDP Auditors Assn. (pres. Phoenix chpt. 1985, cert. info. systems auditor), Am. Assn. Artificial Intelligence, Inst. Cert. Computer Profls. (cert. systems profl.). Republican. Episcopalian. Club: Ariz. Athletic (Tempe). Office: 1st Interstate Bank 114 W Adams Phoenix AZ 85001

SAARI, LISE MARGARET, organizational psychologist, educator; b. Oakridge, Tenn., Dec. 30, 1953; d. John Matthew and Cecilia (Vogelsang) S.; m. Steven B. Young, Dec. 19, 1980. BS in Psychology cum laude, U. Wash., 1977, MS in Psychology, 1979, PhD in Organizational Psychology, 1982. Lic. organizational psychologist. Research cons. Weyerhauser Co., Seattle, 1977-80; human resources researcher G.P. Latham, Inc., Seattle, 1980-82; research scientist Battelle Research Inst., Seattle, 1982—; affiliate prof. bus. U. Wash., Seattle, 1982—. Contbr. articles to profl. jours. Mem. Am. Psychol. Assn., Acad. of Mgmt. Assn. Democrat. Home: 2015 Condon Way W Seattle WA 98199 Office: Battelle Research Inst 4000 NE 41st St Seattle WA 98105

SAAVEDRA, CHARLES JAMES, banker; b. Denver, Nov. 2, 1941; s. Charles James and Evangeline Cecilia (Aragon) S.; B.S.B.A., Regis Coll., Denver, 1963; postgrad. U. Calif., San Francisco, 1964-66; m. Ann Helen Taylor, 1967; children—Michael, Kevin, Sarah. Vice-pres., Western States Bankcard Assn., San Francisco, 1969-77; dir. info. systems World Airways, Inc., Oakland, Calif., 1977-79; v.p. computer services First Nationwide Savs., San Francisco, 1979-83; sr. v.p. Wells Fargo Bank, San Francisco, 1983—; instr. Programming and Systems Inst., San Francisco, 1968-69; lectr. Am. Mgmt. Assn., 1984—. Served in USNR, 1963-64. Mem. Data Processing Mgrs. Assn. (bd. dirs., chmn. program com. 1981), Am. Nat. Standards Inst., Am. Bankers Assn., San Francisco Jaycees. Clubs: Commonwealth of Calif.; Lake Lakewood Assn. Home: 210 Lakewood Rd Walnut Creek CA 94598 Office: Wells Fargo Bank 394 Pacific Ave San Francisco CA 94163

SABATH, RICHARD HANS NIKOLUS, mechanical engineer; b. Erlangen, Bavaria, Fed. Republic Germany, Mar. 21, 1953; came to U.S., 1957; s. Jakob and Gertrude Eva (Keilbach) S.; m. Karen Jo Jackson, Jan. 8, 1983. BS in Biochemistry, UCLA, 1975, cert. in electric power engring., 1984, M in Engring, 1986; postgrad., U. Nev., 1976. Registered profl. mech. engr. Quality control chemist Miller Brewing Co., Azusa, Calif., 1976-77; supr. start up and prodn. Miller Brewing Co., Azusa and Irwindale (Calif.), 1977-79; start up engr. McGaw Pharm., Irvine, Calif., 1979-80; mech. engr. Bechtel Power Corp., Norwalk, Calif., 1981—. Mem. Nat. Assn. Corrosion Engrs. Republican. Roman Catholic. Avocations: sailing, skiing, scuba diving, golf. Home: 1141 Caladay St Los Angeles CA 91740 Office: Bechtel Power Corp 12400 E Imperial Hwy Norwalk CA 90550

SABATINE, PHILIP JOHN, electronics company executive, consultant; b. Bethlehem, Pa.; s. Philip M. and Linda Ann (Dally) S.; m. Sally Ann McNamara. BS in Physics, MIT, 1976; postgrad., Boston U., 1978-80; postgrad. bus. mgmt., Harvard U., 1985. Systems programmer IPL Systems, Waltham, Mass., 1977-78; software engr. Raytheon Co., Sudbury, Mass., 1979-82; sr. systems analyst Xerox Corp., Wellesley, Mass., 1982-83; prin. devel. engr. GTE Telenet, Burlington, Mass., 1983-85; mem. tech. staff Logicon, San Pedro, Calif., 1985—; cons. QED Computer Service, Inc., Santa Monica, Calif., 1985—. Active YMCA. Nat. Merit scholar, 1970. Mem. AAAS, Assn. Computing Machinery, Delta Psi. Avocations: classical guitar, motor sports, mountain climbing, scuba. Home: Box 4186 San Pedro CA 90731 Office: Logicon 255 W 5th St San Pedro CA 90732

SABBADINI, ALEX, fine arts appraiser; b. Rome, Italy, Oct. 26, 1916; s. Umberto and Silvia (Schunnach) S.; came to U.S., 1939, naturalized, 1942; student U. Rome, 1935-37; children—Roger, Steven; m. Mandy Lee Stermer, June 8, 1984. Owner Alex Sabbadini, Sacramento; fine arts appraiser, 1952—; auctioneer, 1950—; lectr. in field. Active Boy Scouts Am., Am. Cancer Soc.; hon. life mem. PTA; bd. dirs. Am. Soc. Appraisers Edn. Found., 1972-78, Sacramento Symphony Assn., 1971-81; bd. advisors Calif. Auctioneer Commn. Served with AUS, 1942-45. Decorated Purple Heart. Fellow Inc. Soc. Valuers and Auctioneers (life), Am. Soc. Appraisers (internat. sr. v.p. 1976-77, pres. 1977-78); mem. Am. Arbitration Assn., Calif. Appraisers Council, V.F.W. Contbr. articles on tech. personal property valuation to profl. publs. Home: 661-4 Woodside Sierra #3 Sacramento CA 95825 Office: 601 University Ave Suite 150 Sacramento CA 95825

SABEL, ROBERT WALTER, security company executive; b. Chgo., Oct. 22, 1920; s. Walter Reuben and Ella Elizabeth (Andersson) S.; student Coe Coll., 1939-40, U. Md., 1948-49, El Camino Coll., 1980; m. Faith Carol Hammarlund, Dec. 9, 1950; children—Karen L., Ingrid M., James R., John G., Paul F., Kristin E. Mgr. nuclear research and devel. Cook Electric Co., Chgo., 1952-55; mem. tech. staff Ramo-Wooldridge Corp., Los Angeles, 1955-57; western regional mgr. Control Data Corp., Los Angeles, 1957-62; v.p. Electro Vision Industries, Los Angeles, 1962-65; owner Sabel Assos., Los Angeles, 1965-79; pres., dir. Zenith Internat. Protection, Inc., Redondo Beach, Calif., 1979—; lectr. Internat. Police Acad., 1969-72, U. So. Calif. Pres., chmn. Liaison League Rehab. Group, Inc. Served to lt. col. USAF, 1941-50. Decorated D.F.C. with 1 oak leaf cluster, Air medal with 3 oak leaf clusters; Croix de Guerre with Palm (France). Mem. Internat. Assn. Identification, Calif. Peace Officers Assn., Internat. Acad. Criminology, Calif. Assn. Lic. Investigators, Res. Officers Assn. U.S., Am. Law Enforcement Officers & Assn., VFW. Republican. Baptist. Clubs: Army-Navy (Washington); Elks, Masons. Home: 341 Paseo de Gracia Redondo Beach CA 90277

SABHARWAL, RANJIT SINGH, mathematician; b. Dhudial, India, Dec. 11, 1925; came to U.S., 1958, naturalized, 1981; s. Krishan Ch and Devti (An) S.; m. Pritam Kaur Chadha, Mar. 5, 1948; children—Rajinderpal, Amarjit, Jasbir. B.A. with honors, Punjab U., 1944, M.A., 1948; M.A. U. Calif, Berkeley, 1962; Ph.D., Wash. State U., 1966. Lectr. math. Khalsa Coll., Bombay, India, 1951-58; teaching asst. U. Calif., Berkeley, 1958-62; instr. math. Portland (Oreg.) State U., 1962-62, Wash. State U., 1963-66; asst. prof. Kans. State U., 1966-68; mem. faculty Calif. State Hayward, 1968—, prof. math., 1974—. Author papers on non-Desarguesian planes. Mem. Am. Math. Soc., Math. Assn. Am., Sigma Xi. Address: 27892 Adobe Ct Hayward CA 94542

SABIN, GARY BYRON, financial company executive, investment advisor; b. Provo, Utah, Apr. 7, 1954; s. Marvin Elmer and Sylvia (Wall) S.; m. Valerie Purdy, Aug. 18, 1976; children: Kimberly, Justin, Spencer, Jennifer. AA in Lang., Brigham Young U., 1976, BS in Fin., 1977; CFP, Coll. Fin. Planning, 1981; postgrad. (Sloan fellow) Stanford U. Grad. Sch. Bus., 1984-85. Regional gen. mgr. Investors/N. Am. Mgmt., Sioux Falls, S.D., 1975-77; pres., chief exec. officer Excel Interfin. Corp., San Diego, 1977—; chmn. Warner Beck, Inc., San Diego, 1983—; gen. ptnr. various cos., San Diego, 1979—. Recipient Outstanding Young Man of Am. award U.S. Jaycees, 1983. Mem. Inst. Cert. Fin. Planners, Nat. Assn. Securities Dealers (registered prin. 1982—), Young Pres.'s Orgn. Republican. Mormon. Home: 16289 Oak Creek Trail Poway CA 92064 Office: Excel Interfin Corp 15010 Ave of Science Suite 100 San Diego CA 92128

SABIN, JACK CHARLES, engineering and construction firm executive; b. Phoenix, June 29, 1921; s. Jack Byron and Rena (Lewis) S.; B.S., U. Ariz., 1943; B.Chem.Engring., U. Minn., 1947; m. Frances Jane McIntyre, Mar. 27, 1950; children—Karen Lee, Robert William, Dorothy Ann, Tracy Ellen. With Standard Oil Co. of Calif., 1947-66, sr. engr., 1966—; pres., dir. Indsl. Control & Engring., Inc., Redondo Beach, Calif., 1966—; owner/mgr. Jack C. Sabin, Engr.-Contractor, Redondo Beach, 1968—; staff engr. Pacific Molasses Co., San Francisco, 1975-77; project mgr. E & L Assos., Long Beach, Calif., 1977-79; dir. Alaska Pacific Petroleum, Inc., 1968—, Marlex Petroleum, Inc., 1970, 71—. Served with U.S. Army, 1942-46; capt. Chem. Corps, Res., 1949-56. Registered profl. engr., Calif., Alaska; lic. gen. engring. contractor, Ariz., Calif. Mem. Nat. Soc. Profl. Engrs., Ind. Liquid Terminals Assn., Conservative Caucus, Calif. Tax Reduction Com., Tau Beta Pi, Phi Lambda Upsilon, Phi Sigma Kappa. Republican. Clubs: Elks; Town Hall of Calif. Address: 151 Camino de las Colinas Redondo Beach CA 90277

SABLE, ARTHUR JUSTIN, electrical engineer; b. Hartford, Conn., Oct. 2, 1924; s. Israel and Tillie (Oliver) S.; m. Barbara Rowe Kinsey, Nov. 3, 1973. BS, U. Chgo., 1949; MA, Boston U., 1965. Sr. engr. Robertshaw-Fulton, Stratford, Conn., 1954-58; engring. mgr. Polaroid Corp., Cambridge, Mass., 1958-63; tech. dir. IBM, Armonk, N.Y., 1963-70; pres. Sable Photo Works, Inc., Boulder, Colo., 1970-74, Sable Instruments, Inc., Boulder, 1974—. Patentee in field. Served as sgt. U.S. Army, 1942-46. Recipient Naval Ordnance Devel. award, 1954. Mem. IEEE, Soc. Photographic Scientists and Engrs., Optical Soc. Am., Sigma Xi. Democrat. Jewish. Lodge: Rotary. Home: 3430 Ash Ave Boulder CO 80303 Office: Sable Instruments Inc PO Box 3008 Boulder CO 80307

SABLE, EDWARD GEORGE, research geologist; b. Rockford, Ill., Dec. 12, 1924; s. William and Marion (Linsky) S.; m. Vera Mae Hosley, Mar. 20, 1954; children: Alan N., Carol L. BA, U. Minn., 1948; MS, U. Mich., 1959, PhD, 1965. Geologist U.S. Geol. Survey, Washington, 1948-54, Elizabethtown, Ky., 1960-69, Denver, 1969—; instr. U. Ky., Elizabethtown, 1965-66. Chmn. Mt. Vernon Fire Dist., Golden, Colo., 1972-75. Recipient Case Meml. award Sigma Xi, 1959. Mem. Arctic Inst. N.Am., Colo. Sci. Soc. Club: Mt. Vernon Country (Golden) (pres., chmn. bd. dirs. 1972-74). Home: 680 Range View Trail Golden CO 80401 Office: US Geol Survey Denver Fed Ctr Denver CO 80225

SABSAY, DAVID, library administrator; b. Waltham, Mass., Sept. 12, 1931; s. Wiegard Isaac and Ruth (Weinstein) S.; m. Helen Glenna Tolliver, Sept. 24,1 966. AB, Harvard U., 1953; BLS, U. Calif., Berkeley, 1955. Circulation dept. supr. Richmond (Calif.) Pub. Library, 1955-56; librarian Santa Rosa (Calif.) Pub. Library, 1956-65; dir. Sonoma County Library, Santa Rosa, 1965—; coordinator North Bay Coop. Library System, Santa Rosa, 1960-64; cons. in field, Sebastopol, Calif., 1968—. Contbr. articles to profl. jours. Commendation, Calif. Assn. Library Trustees and Commrs., 1984. Mem. Calif. Library Assn. (pres. 1971, cert. appreciation 1971, 80), ALA. Club: Harvard (San Francisco). Home: 667 Montgomery Rd Sebastopol CA 95472 Office: Sonoma County Library Third and E Sts Santa Rosa CA 95404

SACHDEVA, YESH PAUL, research chemist; b. Muzzafargarh, Punjab, India, July 10, 1945; came to U.S., 1978; s. Chander Bhan and Dharma (Verma) S.; m. Meena Malik, Apr. 30, 1974; children: Manish, Amit. BS in Chemistry with honors, Kurukshetra (India) U., 1967, MS in Chemistry, 1969, PhD in Chemistry, 1976; postgrad., SUNY, Stony Brook, 1978-79. Research assoc. Va. Poly. Inst. and State U., Blacksburg, 1980-83; polymer chemist Siemens Corning Corp., Hickory, N.C., 1983-84; project leader Dexter-Hysol, Pittsburg, Calif., 1984—. Contbr. articles to profl. jours. Mem. Am. Chem. Soc., Polymer Div. Am. Chem. Soc. Avocations: photography, outdoor sports. Home: 4421 Pembroke Dr Concord CA 94521 Office: Dexter Hysol 2850 Willow Pass Rd Pittsburg CA 94565

SACKETT, HUGH F., financial services executive; b. Tulsa, Sept. 6, 1930; s. Hubert F. and Frances (Cozier) S.; B.S. in Bus. Adminstrn., Ind. U., 1955; m. Claudette Despres, Aug. 31, 1968; children—Michael Stanton, Deborah Faye, Stephanie Frances. Vice pres., gen. mgr. vender products group Cornelius Co., Anoka, Minn., 1969-72; group v.p. automotive Stellar Industries, Inc., Los Angeles, also pres. lawn care group, 1972-74; exec. v.p. Jefferson Mint, San Diego, 1974-79; pres. Graver Energy Systems, Inc., East Chicago, Ind., 1976-80, HFS, Inc., Costa Mesa, 1976—, New H.S. Industries, Inc., 1980-82, Calif. Design Group, 1980-83, Am. Prins. Holdings, Inc., 1982-84, also dir.; chmn. Pacific Capital Ltd., 1984—, West Coast Securities Ltd., 1979—; dir. Pacific Capital Realty Services Inc., Pacific Captial Fin. Services Inc. Mem. chancellors council Purdue U., Calumet, Ind., 1977. Served with USNR, 1951-52. Mem. Conf. Bd., Am. Mgmt. Assn., Soc. Mayflower Desc., Alden Kindred Am., Ind. U. Alumni Assn. (life), Delta Tau Delta. Republican. Presbyterian. Club: Canyoncrest Recreation. Home: 28761 Hedgerow Mission Viejo CA 92092 Office: 150 Paularino #130 Costa Mesa CA 92626

SACKTON, FRANK JOSEPH, retired army officer, university official, lecturer; b. Chgo., Aug. 11, 1912; m. June Dorothy Raymond, Sept. 21, 1940. Student, Northwestern U., 1936, Yale, 1946, U. Md., 1951-52; B.S., U. Md., 1970; grad., Army Inf. Sch., 1941, Command and Gen. Staff Coll., 1942, Armed Forces Staff Coll., 1949, Nat. War Coll., 1954; M.Pub. Adminstrn., Ariz. State U., 1976. Mem. 131st Inf. Regt., Ill. N.G., 1929-40; commd. 2d lt. U.S. Army, 1934, advanced through grades to lt. gen., 1967; brigade plans and ops. officer (33d Inf. Div.), 1941, PTO, 1943-45; div. signal officer 1942-43, div. intelligence officer, 1944, div. plans and ops. officer, 1945; sec. to gen. staff for Gen. MacArthur Tokyo, 1947-48; bn. comdr. 30th Inf. Regt., 1949-50; mem. spl. staff Dept. Army, 1951; plans and ops. officer Joint Task Force 132, PTO, 1952; comdr. Joint Task Force 7, Marshall Islands, 1953; mem. gen. staff Dept. Army, 1954-55; with Office Sec. Def., 1956; comdr. 18th Inf. Regt., 1957-58; chief staff 1st Inf. Div., 1959; chief army Mil. Mission to Turkey, 1960-62; comdr. XIV Army Corps, 1963; dep. dir. plans Joint Chiefs Staff, 1964-66; army general staff mil. ops. 1966-67, comptroller of the army, 1967-70, ret., 1970; spl. asst. for fed./state relations Gov. Ariz., 1971-75; chmn. Ariz. Programming and Coordinating Com. for Fed. Programs, 1971-75; lectr. Am. Grad. Sch. Internat. Mgmt., 1973-77; vis. asst. prof., lectr. public affairs Ariz. State U., Tempe, 1976-78; dean Ariz. State U. Coll. Public Programs, 1979-80; prof. public affairs Ariz. State U., 1980—, v.p. bus. affairs, 1981-83, dep. dir. intercollegiate athletics, 1984-85. Contbr. articles to public affairs and mil. jours. Mem. Ariz. Steering Com. for Restoration of the State Capitol, 1974-75, Ariz. State Personnel Bd., 1978-83, Ariz. Regulatory Council, 1981—. Decorated D.S.M., Silver Star, also Legion of Merit with 4 oak leaf clusters, Bronze Star with 2 oak leaf clusters, Air medal, Army Commendation medal with 1 oak leaf cluster, Combat Inf. badge. Mem. Ariz. Acad. Public Adminstrn., Pi Alpha Alpha (pres. chpt. 1976-82). Clubs: Army-Navy (Washington); Arizona (Phoenix). Home: 7814 E Northland Dr Scottsdale AZ 85251 Office: College Public Programs Ariz State U Tempe AZ 85287

SADAVA, DAVID ERIC, biology educator; b. Ottawa, Ont., Can., Mar. 14, 1946; came to U.S., 1967; s. Samuel and Ruth (Bloom) S.; m. Angeline Douvas, June 15, 1972; 1 child, Dana Louise. BS, Carleton U., Ottawa, 1967; PhD, U. Calif. San Diego, La Jolla, 1971. Prof. biology Scripps Coll., Claremont, Calif., 1972—, chmn. Joint Sci. Program, 1980—; vis. prof. dept. pediatrics U. Colo., Denver, 1979—, dept. molecular biology, 1981—. Co-author: Plants, Food, People, 1977; contbr. articles to profl. jours. Woodrow Wilson Found. fellow, 1968. Office: Claremont Colls Joint Sci Dept Claremont CA 91711

SADEGHI, ALI, architectural planner; b. Tehran, Iran, May 10, 1955; came to U.S., 1973; s. Mohammad Sadeghi and Homay Sadeghi-Nejad; m. Mitra Afsaneh Farokhpay, Apr. 18, 1980; 1 dau., Sanam Elika. BS in Architecture, Ohio State U., 1978, MArch, M in City and Regional Planning, 1981. Registered profl. architect, Ohio. Phys. planner Karlsberger Cos., Columbus, Ohio, 1981-83; med. planner Rochlin & Baran Assocs., Los Angeles, 1983-84; facility planner Am. Med. Internat., Los Angeles, 1984-86; sr. med. planner URS Corp, Los Angeles, 1986—. Mem. AIA, Calif. Council Architects, Los Angeles Inst. Architects. Avocation: photography. Office: URS Corp 249 E Ocean Blvd Long Beach CA 90802

SADILEK, VLADIMIR, architect; b. Czechoslovakia, June 27, 1933; came to U.S., 1967, naturalized, 1973; s. Oldrich and Antoine (Zlamal) S.; Ph.D. summa cum laude in City Planning and Architecture, Tech. U. Prague, 1957; m. Jana Kadlec, Mar. 25, 1960; 1 son, Vladimir, Jr. Chief architect State Office for City Planning, Prague, 1958-67; architect, designer Bank Bldg. Corp., St. Louis, 1967-70, asso. architect, San Francisco, 1970-74; owner, chief exec. officer Bank Design Cons., San Mateo, Calif., 1974-81, West Coast Development Co., San Mateo, 1975—; pres., chief exec. officer Orbis Devel. Corp., San Mateo, 1981—. Served with Inf. of Czechoslovakia, 1958. Recipient awards of excellence from Bank Building Corp. and AIA for planning and design of fin. instns. in Hawaii, Calif. (1971), Ariz., N.Mex., Tex. (1972), Colo., Wyo. (1973), Idaho, Oreg., Washington (1974); lic. architect, 28 states. Republican. Roman Catholic. Home: 80 Orange Ct Hillsborough CA 94010 Office: 1777 Borel Pl San Mateo CA 94402

SADLER, ERNEST ELMORE, electronics company executive; b. Bklyn., May 15, 1932; s. Ernest Elmore and Faith Myrtle (Jeffers) S.; B.A., U. Mass., 1959, M.S., 1961; m. Maureen Sheila Downey, Feb. 19, 1955; children—Kathleen, Faith, Amy, Sean. Research asst. U. Mass., 1958-61; research engr. N. Am. Rockwell, Anaheim, Calif., 1961-64; mem. tech. staff Rockwell Internat., Anaheim, 1964-70; v.p., gen. mgr. Good Taste Ltd., Reseda, Calif., 1970-74; v.p. ops. Unisen, Inc., Irvine, Calif., 1974-85, pres., 1985—, also dir. Served with USN, 1949-54; ETO. Mem. Human Factors Soc., Am. Psychol. Assn., Soc. Engring. Psychologists, AMVETS, Vets. Fgn. Wars, DAV, Sigma Xi. Lodge: Elks. Contbr. articles to profl. jours. Home: 405 S West St Anaheim CA 92805 Office: Unisen Corp 14352 Chambers Rd Tustin CA 92680

SADLER, THEODORE R., JR., thoracic and cardiovascular surgeon; b. St. Louis, Mar. 26, 1930; s. Theodore R. and Nellie R. (Guffey) S.; m. Roberta Cary Moody, Nov. 26, 1953; children: Michael, Patrick, Susan, Daniel, Shelley. AB, U. Mo., 1951, BS in Medicine, 1954; MD, Washington U., 1956. Diplomate Am. Bd. Thoracic and Cardiovascular Surgery. Commd. U.S. Army, 1956, advanced through grades to col.; chief of surgery Noble Army Hosp., Ft. McClellans, Ala., 1964-66; comdr. 3d Surgery Hosp., Vietnam, 1966-67; chief thoracic surgery Fitzsimmons Army Hosp., Denver, 1968-71; resigned U.S. Army, 1971, with Res., 1971-82; comdr. 181st Thoracic Det., 1971-73, 5502d USAH Aug. Fitzsimmons Army Hosp., Denver, 1974-77; brig. gen. 2d Hosp. Ctr., Hamilton AFB, Calif., 1977-81; ret. Res. U.S. Army, 1982; rotating intern Walter Reed Hosp., Washington, 1956-57; resident in gen. surgery Brooke Gen. Hosp., San Antonio, 1958-61, resident thoracic and cardiovascular surgery, 1964-66; practice medicine specializing in thoracic and cardiovascular surgery St. Joseph's Hosp. and Presbyn. Hosp., Denver, 1971—; cons to surgeon gen. Fitzsimmons Army Hosp., 1983—; past pres. bd. dirs. St. Joseph's Hosp. Contbr. articles to profl. jours. Vice chmn. Bd. of Health and Hosps., 1982—; mem. Commn. Mental Health, Denver, 1985—. Fellow ACS, Am. Coll. Chest Physicians; mem. Soc. Thoracic Surgeons, Western Thoracic Assn., AMA, Colo. Med. Soc. (pres.-elect 1986, bd. dirs., house speaker), Denver Med. Soc. (bd. dirs., past pres.). Republican. Presbyterian. Clubs: Denver Athletic, Pinehurst Country, Metropolitan. Avocations: golf, sports, stamp collecting. Home: 1777 Larimer #2010 Denver CO 80202 Office: 2005 Franklin 700 Denver CO 80205

SADOYAMA, NANCY ARTIS, administrative operations analyst; b. Oakland, Calif., June 12, 1947; d. Robert Lee and Norma Lee (Dyches) Artis; m. Edward T. Sadoyama, June 18, 1978. BA, Calif. State U., Hayward, 1974, M in Pub. Adminstrn. with highest deptl. honors, 1987. Personnel rep. Mack Western, Hayward, 1970-73; ops. coordinator Calif. State U., Hayward, 1974-87, adminstrv. ops. analyst, 1987—; microcomputer cons. Meiklejohn Hall, Calif. State U., Hayward, 1984—. Recipient Vivian Cunniffe Outstanding Staff award Calif. State U., Hayward, 1986. Mem. Calif. Women in Higher Edn., Am. Soc. Pub. Adminstrn., Data Processing Mgmt. Assn., Nat. Assn. Female Execs. Avocations: tennis, swimming, cats. Office: Calif State U Liberal Studies Hayward CA 94542

SADRI, SHARIAR MOSTOFL, manufacturing company executive; b. Tehran, Iran, Feb. 20, 1955; came to U.S., 1978; s. Jafar Mostofi and Pouran (Mosleh) S. BSME, U. So. Calif., 1979, MSME, 1983. Registered profl. engr., Calif. Product engr. Deutsch Corp., El Segundo, Calif., 1979-80; sr. project engr. Monogram Industries, Los Angeles, 1980-86; supr. research and devel. Huck Mfg., Irvine, Calif., 1986—; cons. in field, Los Angeles, 1982—; instr. engring. and math. Los Angeles Community Coll., 1983—. Author: Energy Calculation Software for Non-Residential Buildings, 1986. Mem. NSPE, Soc. Mfg. Engrs. Avocation: photography. Office: Huck Mfg Tech Ctr 6 Thomas Irvine CA 92718

SADRUDDIN, MOE, oil company consultant; b. Hyderabad, India, Mar. 3, 1943; came to U.S., 1964; m. Azmath Oureshi, 1964; 3 children. BSME, Osmania U., Hyderabad, 1964; MS in Indsl. Engring., NYU, 1966; MBA, Columbia U., 1970. Cons. project engr. Ford, Bacon & Davis, N.Y.C., 1966; staff indsl. engr. J.C. Penney, N.Y.C., 1966-68; sr. cons. Drake, Sheahan, Stewart & Dougall, N.Y.C., 1968-70, Beech-Nut Inc. subs. Squibb Corp., N.Y.C., 1970-72; founder, pres. Azmath Constrn. Co., Englewood, N.J., 1972-77; crude oil cons., fgn. govt. rep. 1977—; pres. A-One Petroleum Co., Fullerton, Calif., 1985—; govt. advisor Puerto Rico 1980-82, Kenya 1983-84, Belize 1984-85, Costa Rica 1983-86, Paraguay 1984—. Mem. Los Angeles World Affairs Council. Address: A-One Petroleum Co 2656 Camino Del Sol Coyote Hills Fullerton CA 92633

SADUN, ALFREDO ARRIGO, neuro-ophthalmologist; b. New Orleans, Oct. 23, 1950; s. Elvio H and Lina (Ottoleghi) S.; m. Debra Leigh Rice, Mar. 18, 1978; children: Rebecca Eli, Elvio Aaron. BS, MIT, 1972; PhD, Albert Einstein Med. Sch., Bronx, N.Y., 1976, MD, 1978. Intern Huntington Meml. Hosp. U. So. Calif., Pasadena, 1978-79; resident Harvard U. Med. Sch., Boston, 1979-82, HEED Found. fellow in neuro-ophthalmology Mass. Eye and Ear Inst., 1982-83, instr. ophthalmology, 1983, asst. prof. ophthalmology, 1984; dir. residential tng. U. So. Calif. Dept. Ophthalmology, Los Angeles, 1984-85; asst. prof. ophthalmology and neurosurgery U. So. Calif., Los Angeles, 1984—; prin. investigator Howe Lab. Harvard U., Boston, 1981-84, E. Doheny Eye Found., Los Angeles, 1984—. Contbr. articles to profl. jours. Fellow Am. Acad. Ophthalmology; mem. NIH (Med. Scientist Tng. award, 1972-78), Soc. to Prevent Blindness, Nat. Eye Inst. (New Investigator Research award 1983-86), Soc. Neuroscis., Assn. Research in Vision and Ophthalmology, Am. Assn. Anatomists, N.Am. Neuro-Ophthal. Soc. Avocation: writing. Home: 2070 Robin Rd San Marino CA 91108 Office: U So Calif E Doheny Eye Found 1355 San Pablo Los Angeles CA 90033

SAEGER, LOUIS CARL, anesthesiologist, pain research; b. Richmond, Ind., Aug. 16, 1953; s. Armin Louis and Mary Jane (Hindman) S.; m. Karla Peyton, July 4, 1983. Student, N.E. Okla. State U., 1971-73, Miami U., Oxford, Ohio, 1976; AB in Biology and Psychology, Earlham Coll., 1977; MD, U. Okla., 1981. Diplomate Am. Bd. Anesthesiology. Resident in internal medicine Tulsa Med. Coll., 1981-82; resident in anesthesiology U. Wash., Seattle, 1982-85; sr. research fellow Fred Hutchinson Cancer Research Ctr., Seattle, 1983—; clin. and lab. investigator, palliative care cons. Pain and Toxicity Research Program, U. Wash. Pain Ctr., Fred Hutchinson Cancer Research Ctr., Seattle, 1983—. Contbr. articles to profl. jours. NIH Nat. Research Service fellow U. Wash., Seattle, 1983-84, 85-86. Mem. AAAS, Internat. Assn. Study of Pain, Internat. Anesthesia Research Soc., Am. Soc. Anesthesiologists. Office: Pain and Toxicity Research AB-122 FHCRC 1104 Columbia St Seattle WA 98104

SAELMAN, BENJAMIN, aerospace engineer; b. Los Angeles, Nov. 15, 1917; s. Samuel Henry and Ray (Kashtan) S.; m. Phyllis Markman, July 28, 1964; children: David, Raymond. BA with honors, UCLA, 1939. Registered profl. engr., Calif. With Lockheed Aircraft Corp., Burbank, Calif., 1940-85, group engr., 1969—; cons. aerospace engring., lectr. Contbg. editor Design News, 1953-74; reviewer Prentice-Hall Pubs., 1971; contbr. numerous articles to profl. jours. Mem. AIAA (tech. papers com. 1961-63), Soc. Allied Weight Engrs. (book preparation com. 1970—, lectr.,), Sierra Club, Pi Mu Epsilon. Democrat. Jewish. Home: 7762 Melita St North Hollywood CA 91605

SAENGER, THEODORE JEROME, telephone company executive; b. Pomona, Calif., July 28, 1928; s. Carl Louis and Anna Magdalene (Mangold) S.; m. Catherine MacDonald, 1949 (dec.); children: Lynne Anne, Jeffrey Joseph, Tracey Susan, Brian Louis; m. Gayle Inez Johnson, Oct. 19, 1963. B.S., U. Calif.-Berkeley, 1951. With Pacific Telephone & Telegraph (now Pacific Bell), 1952—, v.p., 1974-77, pres., chief operating officer, 1977-84, pres., chief exec. officer, 1984—, also dir.; vice chmn., dir. parent co. Pacific Telesis Group, San Francisco, 1984—. Trustee San Francisco Theol. Sem., Drew Med. Found.; mem. adv. bd. U. Calif. Bus. Sch.; div. chmn. United Way, Los Angeles, 1980-81. Served with U.S. Army, 1946-47. Mem. Phi Beta Kappa, Theta Chi. Republican. Presbyterian. Club: California, Pacific Union. Office: Pacific Telesis Group 140 New Montgomery St San Francisco CA 94105 *

SAENZ, HULBERTO, chemical company executive, management consultant, educator; b. San Antonio, Aug. 8, 1934; s. Jesus G. and Maria M. (Mendiola) S.; m. Emma Lucy Monrreal, June 3, 1953; children: Elizabeth Ann, David Michael; m. Anita Grace Buckley, Nov. 15, 1969; children: Brett, Maria, Juliana, Angela; m. Marta Rosa Machicado, July 5, 1980; children: Hulberto Javier, Carlos Francisco, Marta Michelle. B.A., U. of Tex., 1963; M.A., Ball State U., 1972; B.S., Weber State Coll., 1978; doctoral candidate U. So. Calif., 1983—. Cert. tchr., adminstr., Utah, Tex. Commd. 2d lt. U.S. Air Force, 1959, advanced through grades to maj., 1969; various assignments air def. fighter squadrons, 1960-70; 115 combat missions Vietnam, 1970-71; liaison to Spanish Air Force, 1973-77; ret., 1978; tchr. Franklin Elem. Sch., Salt Lake City, 1978-79, sch. adminstr. Salt Lake Dist., 1979-81; mgmt. trainer Hercules, Inc., Magna, Utah, 1981-82, sr. mgmt. devel. rep., 1983; tchr. San Antonio Ind. Sch. Dist.; vice prin. Southside Ind. Sch. Dist., 1984-85, prin. 1985—. Mem. Utah Tech. Coll. Adv. Bd., 1981-83. Mem. League United Latin Am. Citizens, 1980—; mem. Gov. Hispanic Adv. Council, 1981-84; pres. Latin Am. Edn. Found., 1982-83; state pres. Spanish Speaking Orgn. Community Integrity and Opportunity, 1982-84. Decorated D.F.C.; recipient cert. Appreciation Gov. Utah, 1982. Mem. Am. Mgmt. Assn., Am. Soc. Tng. and Devel., Tex. Assn. Secondary Sch. Prins., State of Utah Assn. Bilingual Edn. Roman Catholic. Clubs: Officer's (Hill AFB, Utah), Am. Mil. Scottish Rite Bodies. Home: 2713 Perez St San Antonio TX 78207

SAFARJAN, WILLIAM ROBERT, psychologist; b. Visalia, Calif., Feb. 17, 1943; s. Robert and Alice Joy (Sharp) S.; m. Paula Tinder, May 26, 1978; 1 child, Erin Tinder. BA in Internat. Relations, U. Calif., Berkeley, 1966; AB in Psychology, San Diego State U., 1971, MA, 1976; PhD in Research Psychology, Rutgers U., 1980; cert. clin. psychology Calif. Sch. Profl. Psychology, 1985. Lic. psychologist, Calif. Research asst. San Diego State U., 1971, Naval Personnel Research and Devel. Ctr., San Diego, 1972-73, Bell Telephone Lab., Homdel, N.J., 1977; teaching asst., instr. Rutgers U., New Brunswick, N.J., 1974-78, research intern, 1978-80; exptl. psychologist Porterville (Calif.) Devel. Ctr., 1980-84; clin. psychologist/postdoctoral fellow Atascadero State Hosp. (Calif.), 1984-85; model treatment coordinator, 1986—. Served to lt. USN, 1966-69. Mem. Am. Psychol. Assn., Assn. for Advancement of Psychology, San Luis Obispo County Psychol. Assn., Psi Chi, Delta Sigma Phi. Lodge: Rotary Internat. Contbr. articles to profl. jours, chpts. to books. Office: PO Box A Atascadero CA 93423

SAFFIR, ARTHUR JOEL, pharmaceutical company executive; b. Chgo., May 11, 1941; s. Jacob Abraham and Ethel (Smith) S.; m. Donna Zenobia, Aug. 4, 1963; children: Duncan, Jason. Student, Calif. Inst. Tech., 1957-59; DMD, Tufts U., 1964; PhD, MIT, 1970. Dir. research and devel. Materials Analysis Co., Palo Alto, Calif., 1970; cons. Sunnyvale, Calif., 1970-73; dir. oral health research Cooper Labs., Cedar Knolls, N.J., 1973-81; pres. Bio-Systems Research Corp., Lake Oswego, Oreg., 1982—. Mem. Regulatory Affairs Profl. Soc., Internat. Assn. Dental Research. Office: Bio-Systems Research 2057 Summit Dr Lake Oswego OR 97034

SAFFO, MARY BETH, research biologist; b. Inglewood, Calif., Apr. 8, 1948; d. Paul Laurence and Joan (Wilson) S.; m. Erik Alfred Whitehorn, Sept. 2, 1978; one child, Nathan Alexander Whitehorn. BA, U. Calif., Santa Cruz., 1969; PhD, Stanford U., 1977. Miller research fellow U. Calif., Berkeley, 1976-78; asst. prof. Swarthmore (Pa.) Coll., 1978-85; ind. investigator Marine Biol. Lab., Woods Hole, Mass., 1979-84; assoc. research marine biologist U. Calif., Santa Cruz, 1985—; vis. scholar U. Wash., Seattle, 1982. Grantee Research Corp., 1980, 84, Am. Philos. Soc., 1980, 83, NSF, 1981, 84, 85, Whitehall Found., 1984; Steps Toward Independence fellow, 1979; AAUW fellow U. Calif., Berkeley, 1981-82. Mem. Western Soc. Naturalists, Am. Soc. Zoologists (program officer 1985—). Democrat. Office: Inst Marine Scis U Calif Santa Cruz CA 95064

SAFRAN, WILLIAM, political science educator; b. Dresden, Germany, July 8, 1930; s. Abraham Joshua and Golda (Chajes) S.; m. Marian Celia (Folk) S.; Mar. 25, 1961; children: Gabriella Sarah, Joshua Abraham. BA, CUNY, 1953, MA, 1955; PhD, Columbia U., 1964. Lectr., instr. Bklyn. Coll., CUNY, 1960-65, Hunter Coll., 1962; asst. prof. U. Colo., Boulder, 1965-68, assoc. prof., 1968-73, prof. polit. sci., 1973, assoc. chmn. polit. sci. dept., 1974-76, adminstr. internat. relations program, 1971-73, 79, 81, 86; vis. prof., Jerusalem, Paris, Nice. Served with U.S. Army, 1955-57. Social Sci. Found. fellow, 1966; U. Colo. faculty research grantee, 1966, 69-70; NEH grantee, 1980-81; recipient history honors award CUNY, 1953. Mem. Am. Polit. Sci. Assn., Internat. Studies Assn., Am. Acad. Polit. Sci., Western Polit. Sci. Assn., Assn. Française de Sci. Politique, Conf. Group French Politics and Soc., Conf. Group German Politics, Tocqueville Soc. Democrat. Jewish. Author: Veto-Group Politics, 1967, The French Polity, 1977, 79, 2d edit., 1985, Ideology and Politics: The Socialist Party of France, 1979, Comparative Politics, 1982; co-author: The Political Economy of Collectivized Agriculture, 1979, Global Human Rights, 1981, The Fifth Republic at Twenty, 1981, Constitutional Democracy: Essays in Comparative Politics, 1983, Europe and the Super Powers, 1985, Political Economy in Western Democracies, 1985, Antisemitism in the Contemporary World, 1986. Office: Dept Polit Sci U Colo Boulder CO 80309

SAGAR, BOKKAPATNAM TIRUMALA ANANDA, consulting mechanical engineer; b. Guntur, India, Mar. 6, 1929; came to U.S., 1969; s. Bokkapatnam Tirumala M. Raghavachari and Sakuntala Sagar; m. B.T. Yashoda, May 17, 1962; children: B.T. Mohan Raghav, B.T. Sangeetha. BE with honors, Andhra (India) U., 1950; MS, U. Colo., 1959; PhD, Colo. State U., 1973. Dir. Cen. Water Power Commn. Govt. of India, New Delhi, 1950-69; sr. mech. engr. PRC Engring. Cons. Inc., Denver, 1964-73, prin. engr., 1973-77; asst. chief PRC Engring. Cons. Inc., Englewood, Colo., 1977—; cons. cons. DGWRD Directorate and Rivers, Indonesia, 1978—; Hidrandina, Peru, 1984, Chilectra, Chile, 1986; UN expert (token) Govt. of India, 1986; mem. U.S. com. on Large Dams. Contbr. articles to profl. jours. Chmn. Denver-Madras Sister Cities Internat., Denver, 1985-86. Fellow USAID, 1956-57; NSF grantee 1979. Mem. ASCE, Internat. Water Resources Assn., Sigma Xi. Hindu. Home: 5727 S Lowell Littleton CO 80123 Office: PRC Engring Cons Inc 7935 E Prentice Englewood CO 80111

SAGAWA, YONEO, horticulturist; b. Olaa, Hawaii, Oct. 11, 1926; s. Chikatada and Mume (Kuno) S.; m. Masayo Yamamoto, May 24, 1962; children: Penelope Toshiko, Irene Teruko. A.B., Washington U., St. Louis, 1950, M.S., 1952; Ph.D., U. Conn., 1956. Postdoctoral research asso. biology Brookhaven Nat. Lab., Upton, N.Y., 1955-57; guest in biology Brookhaven Nat. Lab., summer 1958; asst. prof., then asso. prof. U. Fla., 1957-64; dir. undergrad. sci. ednl. research participation program NSF, summer 1964; cons. biosatellite project NASA, 1966-67; prof. horticulture U. Hawaii, 1964—; dir. Lyon Arboretum, 1967—; asso. dir. Hawaiian Sci. Fair, 1966-67, dir., 1967-68; research asso. in biology U. Calif., Berkeley, 1970-71; mem. Internat. Orchid Commn. on Classification, Nomenclature and Registration; sci. adv. bd. Pacific Tropical Garden, 1975—; councillor Las Cruces Bot. Garden, Costa Rica, 1975—; cons. UN/FAO, Singapore, 1971; dir. Hawaii Tropical Botanical Garden. Editor: Hawaii Orchid Jour, 1972—, Pacific Orchid Soc. Bull, 1966-71; editorial bd.: Allertonia, 1976; contbr. numerous articles to profl. jours. Hon. trustee Friends of Foster Garden, 1973—. Served with AUS, 1945-47. Recipient Disting. Service award South Fla. Orchid Soc., 1968; grantee Am. Orchid Soc., AEC, NIH, HEW, Stanley Smith Hort. Trust, Honolulu Orchid Soc., 1958—; fellow Agrl. U., ITAL, Wageningin, Netherlands, 1979-80. Hon. life mem. Am. Anthurium Soc., Am. Orchid Soc., Kaimuki Orchid Soc., Honolulu Orchid Soc., Garden Club Honolulu; mem. Bot. Soc. Am., Am. Soc. Hort. Sci., Internat. Assn. Hort. Sci., AAAS, Am. Assn. Bot. Gardens and Arboreta, Hawaiian Bot. Soc., Internat. Assn. Plant Tissue Culture, Palm Soc., Lyon Arboretum Assn. (trustee 1974—), Phi Kappa Phi (past chpt. pres.). Democrat. Club: Aloha Bonsai (Honolulu). Office: Lyon Arboretum 3860 Manoa Rd Honolulu HI 96822

SAGE, E(MILY) HELENE, biochemistry educator; b. Phila., Oct. 6, 1946; d. Robert Charles and Helen (Daumann) S. A.B. cum laude with distinction, Mt. Holyoke Coll., 1969; Ph.D., U. Utah, 1977. Sr. fellow dept. biochemistry U. Wash., Seattle, 1977-80, research asst. prof. dept. biochemistry, 1980-82, asst. prof. dept. biol. structure, 1982-85, assoc. prof. dept. biol. structure, 1985—; invited lectr. numerous confs. and instns., 1979-87. Contbr. numerous articles on connective tissue proteins and vascular cell biology to profl. jours. Recipient citation Twenty-fifth Rheumatism Rev., 1980; established investigator Am. Heart Assn., 1981-86; genetics tng. grantee NIH; fellow R.J. Reynolds Industries, Inc., 1978-80. Mem. Am. Soc. Cell Biology, Am. Chem. Soc., Phi Beta Kappa. Office: Univ Wash Dept Biol Structure SM-20 Seattle WA 98195

SAGE, VINCENT FRANCIS, holding company executive; b. N.Y.C., Mar. 7, 1933; s. Sal Joseph and Nancy (Camuto) Selvaggio; Electronic Engr., Valparaiso Inst. Tech., 1953; children—Catherine, John, Nancy, Mark, Robert; (by previous marriage), Marco, Holly. Field engr. Page Communications Engrs., Inc., Washington, 1956-61; stock broker, N.Y.C., 1961-65; pres. Sageco, Inc., Honolulu, 1965-70; chmn. bd., dir. World Wide Distbrs., Ltd., 1971-76; chmn. bd. The Diamond Co., Inc., 1977—; dir. The Jewel Gallery, Liberty House Fine Jewelry, World Wide Distbrs., Inc. Chmn. state finance com. 1964 Republican Presdl. campaign; del. Nat. Young Republican Conv., 1965, 67, mem. platform com., 1967. Served with AUS, 1954-56. Mem. Young Pres. Orgn., I.E.E.E., Investment Analyst Soc. Hawaii (pres. 1966), World Trade Assn., Navy League. Clubs: Oahu Country, Rotary, Waikiki Yacht, Honolulu. Home: 1686 Laukahi St Honolulu HI 96821

SAGER, JON SIMON, social worker, educator; b. N.Y.C., May 4, 1946; s. Leslie and Edith (Simon) S. BA, UCLA, 1970; MSW, U. Mich., 1973, MS in Psychology, 1975. Dir. Evaluation and Treatment Ctr., Ann Arbor, Mich., 1972-75; instr. U. Mich., Ann Arbor, 1974-75; mgmt. program dir. U. Redlands, Calif., 1979-81, mem. faculty, 1977-86; instr. in mgmt. adminstrn. of community orgns. UCLA, 1986—; mgmt. cons. North Hollywood, Calif., 1978-84; pres. Los Angeles Valley Coll., Van Nuys, 1967-68. Author: Statistics and Evaluation in Public Service Management, 1978, 4th rev. edit., 1984; contbr. articles to profl. jours. Recipient Outstanding Faculty award U. Redlands, 1984; NIMH fellow, 1970-71. Mem. Nat. Assn. Social Workers (clin. lic., membership chmn. region H 1986—), Assn. for Study of Community Orgn., Phi Beta Kappa. Democrat. Jewish. Avocation: piano. Office: UCLA Sch Social Welfare 405 Hilgard Los Angeles CA 90024

SAGHRI, JOHN ABDOLVAHID, engineering specialist; b. Tehran, Iran, Oct. 23, 1948; came to U.S., 1968; s. Kasem and Masroreh (Atai) S. BSEE, Calif. Poly. U., 1973; MSEE, Oreg. State U., 1975; PhD in Elec. Engring., Rensselaer Poly. Inst., 1979. Teaching asst. Oreg. State U., Corvallis, 1973-76; research asst. Rensselaer Poly. Inst., Troy, N.Y., 1976-78, instr., 1978-79; engring. specialist signal processing dept. Aerospace Corp., El Segundo, Calif., 1979—. Contbr. articles to profl. jours. Recipient Outstanding Accomplishment award Aerospace Corp., 1985. Mem. IEEE (sr.), Soc. Photo-Optical Instrumentation Engrs. Club: Tennis (Aerospace Corp.). Avocations: tennis, jogging, hiking, electronics. Home: PO Box 1727 Redondo Beach CA 90278 Office: The Aerospace Corp 2350 E El Segundo Blvd El Segundo CA 90245

SAGINIAN, ARMEN ASHLY, mechanical engineer; b. Tabriz, Iran, Feb. 2, 1933; came to U.S., 1955, naturalized, 1966; s. Hovsep and Varditer (Melik-Djhanian) S.; m. Assik Stella Saginian, Sept. 13, 1959; children: Arthru George, Alan Patrick. BSME, U. Tenn., 1961; cert., UCLA, 1979. Registered profl. engr., Calif. Engr. Boeing Co., Seattle, 1961-63, Gen. Dynamics, San Diego, 1963-64, North Am. Aviation, Van Nuys, Calif., 1964-65; engr., mgr. Garrett Corp., Los Angeles, 1965-85; gen. mgr. TTL Turbo-Supply, Los Angeles, 1985—; bd. dirs. Paysage Devels., Telex Terminals, LTD. Pres. Iran Armenian Soc., Los Angeles, 1970; sec. Iran Nat. Affairs Council, Los Angeles, 1984. Mem. ASME. Republican. Lodges: Mason, Arabic. Home: 9841 Tunney Ave Northridge CA 91324 Office: TTL Ltd 9841 Tunney Ave Northridge CA 91324 address: Turbo-Supply 4523-C San Fernando Rd Glendale CA 91204

SAGSTETTER, ELIZABETH MILLER, writer; b. Fremont, Nebr., May 3, 1947; d. Argie Jay and Helen Maxine (Barnes) Miller; m. William Edward Sagstetter, Apr. 16, 1976. BA magna cum laude, Met. State Coll., 1976. Corr. Denver Post, 1981-82; freelance writer Denver, 1978—. Scriptwriter prime time TV films, incl. Perspectives on Aging, The Mystery of Huajatolla, The Bartered Tribe, Tarahumara: The People Who Run, Caverna del Oro, Cave of Legend. Recipient Colo. Competition award Aspen Arts Festival, 1978. Home: 2217 Grove Denver CO 80211

SAGSTETTER, WILLIAM EDWARD, freelance film producer; b. Denver, Jan. 10, 1945; s. William Edward and Pauline Elizabeth (Strouse) S.; m. Elizabeth Miller, Apr. 16, 1976. Freelance filmmaker, photographer Denver, 1970—; instr. filmmaking U. Colo., Denver, 1977-82; freelance photographer Denver Post, 1981-82; instr. history Denver Auraria Community Coll., 1984; cons. Adrienne Hynes & Assocs., Denver, 1984—; freelance photographer for mags. and newspapers, 1978—. Producer (TV films) Mystery of Huajatolla, 1978, Caverna del Oro, 1970, The Bartered Tribe, 1973, Tarahumara: The People Who Run, 1976, Perspectives on Aging, 1982. Recipient Spl. Film award Aspen Arts Film Festival, 1978. Home and Office: 2217 Grove Denver CO 80211

SAGUM, ROLAND DIAZ, former state official, investment company executive; b. Batangas, Phillippines, Jan. 1, 1912; s. Macario A. and Dionicia (Diaz) S.; came to U.S., 1912, naturalized, 1946; certificate Pub. Adminstrn., U. Hawaii, 1935; certificate Delinquency Control, U. So. Calif., 1958; m. Genevieve Anguay, Aug. 27, 1932; children—Roland Diaz, Ginger Vea, Marvin I., Nelson A., Catherine A. Hudson. With Honolulu Police, 1934-70, capt. of police, 1960-67, community relations coordinator, 1967-68, maj. in charge night ops., 1968-69, police commr., 1969, v.p., dir. pub. relations, 1969-75; chmn. bd. United Hawaiian Investment Corp.; pres. Ambassador Travel Agy., Inc.; dir. United Hawaiian Acceptance, Inc., Paterrin Co., Nuuanu Meml. Park, Financial Security Ins. Co. Chmn. state bd. lay activities Meth. Ch., 1963-65, del. 1st world conf. Human Relations, 1958, del. 1st nat. conf. Christian Social Concerns, Washington, 1960, del. Jurisdictional Conf., World Meth. Conf. and World Meth. Conf. on Family Life, 1964. Mem. Gov.'s Com. on Sex Deviations, 1960-61, Com. on Alcholism, 1960-69, State Com. on Correction, 1968-69; commr. State Criminal Injuries Compensation, 1971-79; mem. Mayor's Com. on Children and Youth to study Drug Abuse, 1962-70, Citizens Com. on Municipal Auditorium, 1964-66; pres. Nat. Polio Found. Hawaii, Police Relief Assn.; pres. United Filipino Council, 1959-61, Hauola Club, 1950, pres. Honolulu Council Chs., Police Activities League; youth dir. Internat. Assn. Y's Men's Clubs; pres. Mental Health Assn. Hawaii, 1972-73, Palama Inter-Church Council, Filipino C. of C., 1979-82; treas. Internat. Christian Leadership, Hawaii Council on Crime and Delinquency, 1980; pres. Palama Settlement, 1970-72, Philippine Meml. Found., 1950; mem. Hawaii CD Adv. Council, 1979-85; bd. dirs. Oahu Tb and Health Council, Nat. Assn. Mental Health, Liliuokalani Adv. Council, Child and Family Service, Pacific and Asian Affairs Council, Hawaiian Govt. Assn., Hawaii Cancer Soc., John Howard Assn., Nat. Soc. for Crippled Children and Adults, Honolulu Community Chest, Honolulu Met. YMCA, Nuuanu br. YMCA, Goodwill Industries; adv. bd. Salvation Army, Hawaii Commn. Criminal Justice. Recipient award U.S. Bur. Prisons, 1962; Nat. Lane Bryant award for civic achievements, 1967; Outstanding Service to Youth award Pacific S.W. Area YMCA. 1964; certificate of appreciation Nat. Bd. YMCA, 1963; named Father of Year, Hawaii chpt. World Brotherhood, 1960; Am. of Week, Honolulu C. of C., 1950, Man of Week, 1952; Outstanding Citizen of Year, Hawaii Govt. Assn., 1964, Outstanding Community Worker, 1973; recipient Hawaii Pioneer award, 1986. Mem. Internat. Assn. Chiefs of Police, Nat. Police Officers Assn., Am. Soc. Tng. Dirs., Am. Soc. Pub. Adminstrn. (dir.). Internat. Juvenile Officers Assn. (award merit 1966), Acad. Sci. Interrogation. Hawaii Assn. Parliamentarians, Am. Inst. Parliamentarians (cert.), Am. Correctional Assn. Methodist (del. numerous world confs.). Clubs: Masons, Knights of Rizal (comdr.). Home: 3008 Makini St Honolulu HI 96815 Office: Suite 407 33 S King St Honolulu HI 96813

SAGUNSKY, BYRON THOMAS, surgeon; b. Butte, Mont., June 30, 1944; s. Walter Gustav and Edith (Schoenek) S.; m. Katherine Leone, May 6, 1972; children—David Lee, Anita Marie. B.A., Ripon Coll., 1966; M.D., U. Utah, 1970. Diplomate Am. Bd. Surgery. Intern Good Samaritan Hosp., Phoenix, 1970-71; resident in surgery U. Calif. Med. Ctr., Sacramento, 1974-78; practice medicine specializing in gen. surgery, Klamath Falls, Oreg., 1978—. Served as capt. USAF, 1971-74. Fellow ACS. Home: 1973 Benson Klamath Falls OR 97601 Office: 2300 Clairmont Dr Klamath Falls OR 97601

SAHARA, ROBERT FUMIO, veterinarian; b. Ogden, Utah, Mar. 13, 1942; s. William Hiroshi and Chiyo (Shimada) S.; m. Joyce Michiko Sanwo, July 23, 1967; 1 child, Jennifer Yuki. A.A. in Zoology, Santa Monica City Coll., 1962; A.B. in Zoology, U. Calif.-Davis, 1965, M.S. in Animal Physiology, 1967, D.V.M., 1972. Staff veterinarian, Romie Lane Vet. Hosp., Salinas, Calif., 1972-73, Bay Pet Hosp., Monterey, Calif., 1972-73, Midtown Animal Hosp., Sacramento, 1973-74; chief of staff Sacramento Emergency Vet. Clinic, 1974-76; co-owner, veterinarian Greenhaven Vet. Hosp., Sacramento, 1976—, reserve warden Calif. Dept. Fish and Game, 1985—. ; Bd. dirs. Jan Ken Po Gakko, Sacramento, 1981-84. Mem. AVMA, Calif. Vet. Med. Assn. (gov. dist V, 1983—), Sacramento Valley Vet. Med. Assn. (exec. bd. 1978-82, pres. 1981). Republican. Buddhist. Home: 4023 El Macero Dr Davis CA 95616 Office: Greenhaven Veterinary Hosp 1 Valine Ct Sacramento CA 95831

SAHIN, TURGUT, chemical engineering professor; b. Hisarardi, Mugla, Turkey, Jan. 16, 1954; came to U.S. in 1979; s. Mustafa and Güllü (Kocaaslan) S.; m. Hatice Aslan, May 4, 1979; 1 child, Koray. BS, Middle East Tech. U., Ankara, Turkey, 1979; MS, Mont. State U., 1982, PhD in Chem. Engring., 1983. Postdoctoral work Mont. State U., Bozeman, 1983-84, asst. prof., 1984—. contbr. articles to profl. jours. U.S. Dept. Energy grantee, 1985. Mem. Am. Chem. Soc., Inst. Am. Chem. Engrs., Am. Vacuum Soc. Avocations: hiking, skiing, racquetball. Office: Mont State U Chem Engring Dept 306 Cableigh Hall Bozeman MT 59717

SAHLEIN, DON, manufacturing executive; b. Jackson, Mich., Mar. 7, 1924; s. David A. and Pauline (Byoir) S.; m. Lee Silver, Mar. 28, 1952; children: Gail Laurie, Stacey Anne. BS, UCLA, 1948. V.p. Leoff & Rose, Hollywood, Calif., 1949-51; pres. Hollywood Camera Co., 1951-71; chief exec. officer Alan Gordon Enterprises, Inc., North Hollywood, Calif., 1971—; bd. dirs. Alpha-Metric Corp., 1984—. Mem. Los Angeles Internat. Visitors Com., 1963—, Los Angeles-Bordeaux Sister City Com., 1974—; chmn. Help the Helpless Assn., 1986-87. Served to 1st lt. USAAF, 1943-45, ETO. Decorated D.F.C., Air medal with three oak leaf clusters. Mem. Am. Soc. Photogrammetry, Soc. Photo-instrumentation Engrs., Soc. Motion Picture and TV Engrs., Internat. Micrographic Congress, Assn. Records Mgrs. and Adminstrs. Inc., Mensa, World Affairs Council, Wine and Food Soc. Hollywood. Republican. Jewish. Lodges: Masons, Vikings. Avocations: photography, waterskiing, flying. Home: PO Box 6038 North Hollywood CA 91603 Office: Alan Gordon Enterprises Inc 5361 Cahuenga North Hollywood CA 91601

SAHLSTROM, E(LMER) B(ERNARD), lawyer; b. Seattle, Feb. 25, 1918; s. August Waldimer and Alma Carolyn (Ostrom) S.; m. Phyllis May Horstman, June 18, 1946; children—Gary Bernard, Sherry Lynn Sahlstrom Monohan, Gregory Lane. B.S., U. Oreg., 1945, J.D., 1947. Bar: Oreg. 1947, U.S. Dist. Ct. Oreg. 1977, U.S. Dist. Ct. Hawaii, 1977, U.S. Ct. Appeals (9th cir.), 1977, U.S. Supreme Ct. 1977; CPA, Oreg. Acct. Haskins & Sells, N.Y.C., 1941-44; mem. Thompson & Sahlstrom, Eugene, Oreg., 1947-57, Sahlstrom, Lombard, Starr & Vinson, and predecessor, Eugene, 1957-76, Sahlstrom & Lombard, Eugene, 1976-78; sole practice Eugene, 1978-80; ptnr. Sahlstrom & Dugdale, Eugene, 1980—. Bd. visitors U. Oreg. Law Sch., 1977-79. Mem. Oreg. State Bar, ABA, Assn. Trial Lawyers Am. (1st v.p. western regional conf. 1954, 4th v.p. conf. 1956, dir. 1955-56, v.p. Oreg. chpt. 1970-71, pres. So. Oreg. chpt. 1972-74), Am. Judicature Soc., Assn. Attys. and CPA's, Oreg. State Bar (com. taxations, unauthorized practice of law, procedure and practice, continuing legal edn., council on ct. procedures), U. Oreg. Sch. Law Alumni Assn. (bd. dirs., pres., bd. vis.), Phi Alpha Delta, Beta Alpha Psi. Clubs: Country, Town (dir. 1970-71, pres. 1978) (Eugene). Lodge: Elks. Home: 715 Fair Oaks Dr Eugene OR 97401 Office: Sahlstrom & Dugdale 915 Oak St Eugene OR 97401

SAHNI, JAGMOHAN SINGH, health product manufacturing company executive; b. New Delhi, Apr. 24, 1949; came to U.S., 1971; s. Tara Singh and Darshan (Kapur) S.; m. Kawaljit K. Kohli, Oct. 9, 1974; children: Deepa, Harleen. BSEE, Thapar Engring. Coll., Patiala, India, 1969; M in Tech. EE, IIT Delhi, New Delhi, 1971; MBA, Pepperdine U., 1980. Engr. Control Data Corp., Schenectady, N.Y., 1972-77; sr. engr. Mohawk Data Scis., Los Gatos, Calif., 1977-81; prin. engr. Omex System, Santa Clara, Calif., 1981-82; reliability engring. mgr. Nat. Semiconductor Corp., Sunnyvale, Calif., 1982; reliability availability maintainability engring. mgr. Rolm Corp., Santa Clara, 1982-84; pres., chief exec. officer Vivix Corp., San Jose, Calif., 1984—. Mem. IEEE, Assn. Advancement Med. Instrumentation. Home: 204 Cheltenham Pl San Jose CA 95139 Office: Vivix Corp 6410 Via Del Oro San Jose CA 95119

SAIFEE, JUZER, printing company executive; b. Hyderabad, Pakistan, Dec. 5, 1950; Came to U.S., 1978; s. Saifuddin and Mehfuza (Merhaba) S.; m. Tasneem Chinwala, Nov. 11, 1979. BS in Chemistry, U. Sind, Hyderabad, 1971, MS Organic Chemistry, 1972. Med. promotional officer Searle Ltd., Hyderabad, 1972-77; field officer Ciba-Giegy, Hyderabad, 1977-78; mgr. Curry Copy Ctr., St. Louis, 1978-82; owner, mgr. Fremont Press, Burbank, Calif., 1982—; pvt. bus. cons., Burbank, 1982—. Office: Fremont Press 624 N Victory Burbank CA 91502

SAIFER, MARK GARY PIERCE, pharmaceutical executive; b. Phila., Sept. 16, 1938; s. Albert and Sylvia (Jolles) S.; m. Phyllis Lynne Trommer, Jan. 28, 1961; children: Scott David, Alandria Gail. AB, U. Pa., 1960; PhD, U. Calif., Berkeley, 1966. Acting asst. prof. zoology U. Calif., Berkeley, 1966, postdoctoral fellow, 1967-68; sr. cancer research scientist Roswell Park Meml. Inst., Buffalo, 1968-70; lab. dir. Diagnostic Data Inc., Palo Alto, Calif., 1970-78; v.p. DDI Pharms., Inc., Mountain View, Calif., 1978—. Patentee in field. Mem. AAAS (life), N.Y. Acad. Scis., Parenteral Drug Assn. Office: DDI Pharms Inc 518 Logue Ave Mountain View CA 94043

SAIFER, PHYLLIS LYNNE, physician, writer; b. Phila., May 19, 1940; d. Philip R. and Evelyn (Milgram) Trommer; m. Mark Gary Pierce, Jan. 28, 1961; children: Scott David, Alandria Gail. Student, Wellesley Coll., 1957-58; BA, U. Pa., 1961; MD, U. Calif., San Francisco, 1966; MPH, U. Calif., Berkeley, 1971. Intern Mt. Zion Hosp. and Med. Ctr., San Francisco, 1966-67, resident in pediatrics, 1967-68, 71-72; practice medicine specializing in allergy and environ. medicine Berkeley, 1972—. Author: Detox, 1984. Fellow Am. Acad. Environ. Medicine (pres. elect 1985-86, pres. 1986-87, editor newsletter 1982—); mem. Am. Acad. Pediatrics, Am. Coll. Allergists,

Brit. Soc. Allergy and Environ. Medicine. Office: 3031 Telegraph Ave Suite 215 Berkeley CA 94705

SAIKI, LOREL KEIKO, art director, photographer; b. Chgo., May 8, 1954; d. Hiroshi and Jessie Keiko (Kawasuna) S. Student U. Colo., Colorado Springs, 1972-73, Art Ctr. Coll. Design, Los Angeles, 1973-76. Art dir. Robertson Co., Los Angeles, 1975-76, Bozell & Jacobs, Inc., Los Angeles, 1976-82; sr. art dir. Evans/Weinberg Advt., Inc., Los Angeles, 1982-84; freelance art dir., advt. cons., 1984—. Recipient award Art Dirs. Club Los Angeles Advt. Show, 1978, cert. of merit Am. Advt. Fedn. Show, 1978, Lulu awards Los Angeles Advt. Women, 1978, Gold medal Indsl. TV Assn., Los Angeles, 1982. Mem. Am. Soc. Mag. Photographers, Los Angeles Advt. Industry Emergency Fund, U.S. Polo Assn.

SAIKI, PATRICIA (MRS. STANLEY MITSUO SAIKI), congresswoman; b. Hilo, Hawaii, May 28, 1930; d. Kazuo and Shizue (Inoue) Fukuda; B.S., U. Hawaii; m. Stanley Mitsuo Saiki, June 19, 1954; children—Stanley Mitsuo, Sandra S., Margaret C., Stuart K., Laura H. Tchr., Dept. Edn. Hawaii, 1959-66; research asst. Hawaii State Senate, 1966-68; mem. Hawaii Ho. of Reps., 1968-74, Hawaii State Senate, 1974-82; mem. 100th Congress from 1st Hawaii Dist., 1987—. Dir. Amfac, Inc., Hawaiian Airlines. Mem. Pres.'s Adv. Council on Status of Women, 1969-76; mem. Nat. Commn. Internat. Women's Year, 1969-70; commr. Western Interstate Commn. on Higher Edn.; fellow Eagleton Inst., Rutgers U., 1970. Mem. Kapiolani Hosp. Aux. Sec. Hawaii Rep. Com., 1964-66, vice chmn., 1966-68, chmn., 1983-85; del. Hawaii Constl. Conv., 1968; alt. del. Rep. Nat. Conv., 1968, del., 1984; Rep. nominee for lt. gov. Hawaii, 1982; mem. Fedn. Rep. Women. Trustee Hawaii Pacific Coll.; bd. dirs. Nat. Fund for Improvement of Post-Secondary Edn., 1982-85. Hawaii Visitors Bur., 1983-85; trustee U. Hawaii Found., 1984—. Episcopalian. Address: 784 Elepaio St Honolulu HI 96816 Office: Room 1407 Longworth House Office Bldg Washington DC 20515

ST.-AMAND, PIERRE, geophysicist; b. Tacoma, Wash., Feb. 4, 1920; s. Cyrias Z. and Mable (Berg) St.-A.; m. Marie Pöss, Dec. 5, 1945; children—Gene, Barbara, Denali, David. B.S. in Physics, U. Alaska, 1948; M.S. in Geophysics, Calif. Inst. Tech., 1951, Ph.D. in Geophysics and Geology, 1953. Mem., asst. dir. Geophys. Lab., U. Alaska, also head ionospheric and seismologic investigations, 1946-49; physicist U.S. Ordnance Test Sta., China Lake, Calif., 1950-55; head optics br. U.S. Ordnance Test Sta., 1955-58, now cons. to tech. dir., head spl. projects office; fgn. service with ICA as prof. geol. and geophys. Sch. Earth Scis., U. Chile, 1958-60; originator theory rotational displacement Pacific Ocean Basin; adj. prof. McKay Sch. Mines, U. Nev., U. N.D.; v.p., dir. Covillac Corp.; cons. World Bank, Calif. Div. Water Resources, Am. Potash & Chem. Co., OAS; mem. U.S. Army airways communications system, Alaska and Can., 1942-46; cons. Mexican, Chilean and Argentine govts.; mem. Calif. Gov.'s Com. Geol. Hazards; mem. com. magnetic instruments Internat. Union Geodesy and Geophys., 1954-59; charter mem. Sr. Exec. Service. Adv. bd. GeoScience News. Presented papers at profl. meetings. Chmn. bd. dirs. Ridgecrest Community Hosp.; chmn. bd. dirs. Indian Wells Valley Airport Dist.; v.p. bd. dirs. Kern County Acad. Decathlon. Recipient certificate of merit OSRD, 1945, certificate of merit USAAF, 1946, letter of commendation USAAF, 1948, Spl. award Philippine Air Force, 1969; Fulbright research fellow France, 1954-55; Diploma de Honor Sociedad Geologica de Chile; disting. civilan service award USN, 1968; L.T.E. Thompson medal, 1973; Thunderbird award Weather Modification Assn., 1974; Distinguished Pub. Service award Fed. Exec. Inst., 1976; decorated knight Mark Twain. Fellow AAAS, Geol. Soc. Am., Earthquake Engr. Research Inst.; mem. Am. Geophys. Union, Weather Modification Assn., Am. Seismol. Soc., Sigma Xi. Club: Rotary (past pres.), Footprinters Internat. (mem. grand bd.). Patentee photometric instrument, weather and ordnance devices. Address: Office of Tech Dir Code 013 Naval Weapon US Naval Ordnance Test Sta China Lake CA 93555

ST. CLAIR, FREDERICK LARRY, retired fisherman's fund administrator; b. Bridgeport, Wash., Sept. 28, 1927; s. Frederick Luther and Ruth Lena (Hopp) St. C.; m. Joyce Elaine Williams, Aug. 9, 1950; children—Frederick III, Lori, Brian, Vicki, Jick. Student Walla Walla Coll., 1949; B.A., Eastern Wash. State U., 1952; degree in med. tech. St. Luke's Hosp., Spokane, Wash., 1953; cert. in exofolic cytology U. Wis., 1961; student U. Alaska. Lab. technologist various locations, 1953-68, Everett Gen. Hosp., 1968, Bartlett Meml. Hosp., 1970-78; bldg. contractor, owner St. Clair Constrn. Co., Juneau, Alaska, 1979-82; adminstr. Fishermen's Fund, Juneau, 1982—. cons. United Med. Labs., 1961-65, Enzomedic Labs., Seattle, 1966-68. Mem. Alcohol and Drug Abuse Adv. Com., Juneau, 1976-84; chmn. Gastineau chpt. Nat. Council on Alcoholism, 1975; Served with AUS, 1946-48. Mem. Am. Soc. Clin. Pathologists, Med. Technologists Soc. Adventist. Home: PO Box 1614 Juneau AK 99802

ST. CROIX, JUDIE ANN, sculptor, dance educator; b. Oakland, Calif., Apr. 4, 1948; d. John William and Marjorie Mary (Saatzer) Hill; m. Jeff A. Miller, June 13, 1970 (div. 1974); m. Robert Bruton St. Croix, Aug. 21, 1981. Student, San Francisco U.; AA, Diablo Valley Coll.; BA, U. Hawaii. Dir. pub. relations Cystic Fibrosis Found., Oakland, 1970-73; exec. dir. Arthritis Found., Oakland, 1973-76; profl. dancer Piilani Rainbow Revue, Honolulu, 1980-85; dance instr. Lokolani Studios, Calif., Hawaii, 1975—; sculptor St. Croix Sculptures and Art Foundry, Sacramento, 1977—. Prin. works include sculpture Tiny Dancer life-size statue, 1985, Justice Enduring, Tom's Dream; contbr. articles on dance to pubs. Democrat. Avocations: English riding and jumping, skiing, photography, piano, guitar. Home: 1933 Church St LaPorte CA 95981 Office: St Croix Sculptures PO Box 986 Newcastle CA 95658

ST. JOHN, ANTHONY DREXEL, videographer; b. San Francisco, May 9, 1951; s. Eric Bischoff and Mary Elizabeth (Story) St. John; m. Ann Humphrey, Oct. 22, 1972. BA in Art and Film, Sonoma State U., 1973. Cameraman NBC News, San Francisco, 1979; system designer Zoetrope Studios, San Francisco, 1980; cameraman Zoetrope Studios, Los Angeles, 1981-84, cons., 1984—; pvt. practice videography Hollywood, Calif., 1985—; speaker Venice Film Festival, 1983, Mill Valley Film Festival, 1984. Camerman (TV spl.) In Celebration of Tut, 1980 (Emmy award), (documentary) Broken Rainbow, 1986 (Oscar award). Sponsor Hollywood Heritage, 1986. Mem. Internat. Alliance of Thatrical Stage Employees and Moving Picture Machine Operators of U.S. and Can. Avocation: sailing. Home: 5127 Willowcrest Ave North Hollywood CA 91601

ST.JOHN, CHARLES EDWARD, management consultant; b. Chgo.; s. Constantine and Mary O. (Johnsos) Zmay. BA, Marquette U., 1965. Restaurateur Stowe, Vt., 1965-67; with TWA Corp., N.Y.C., 1967-72, corp. mgr. tour devel., 1972; dir. mktg. Vail (Colo.) Assocs. Inc., 1972-77; pres. Advantage Vail Advt., 1979-80; founder, chmn. The Results Group, Vail and Denver, 1977—; prin., bd. dirs. Foto-Tek, Denver, 1982-85, Cashback Travel Inc., Denver, N.Y.C., Chgo., 1985—; bd. dirs. Dynavac Inc.; mem. adv. bd. Exec. Ventures Group, Denver, 1986—; mem. adv. bd. 1989 World Ski Championships, Vail, 1986—. Office: The Results Group 1760 Lafayette St Denver CO 80218

ST. JOHN, JUANITA C., university administrator; b. South Bend, Ind., Nov. 5, 1931; d. William and Ethelwyn Ida Isabella (Ryan) Svenson; m. John Joseph St. John, June 8, 1956; children—Michael Bryan, Kathleen Ida Mae. B.A., St. Mary's Coll. for Women, 1952; Ph.C., U. Mich., 1955. Coordinator, Peace Corps Tng. for Africa, UCLA, 1964-68, asst. to dir. African Studies Ctr., 1968-78, asst. to vice chancellor, 1978—, dir. Mayor's Task Force for Africa/Los Angeles Relations, 1979—. Bd. dirs. Los Angeles Ethnic Arts Council, 1975-79, Friends of Cal-Tech Library, 1979-82; Fund African Students, Inc., 1980—; bd. dirs. Internat. Alert, Mus. African-Am. Art, 1980—, v.p., sec., 1980-84; bd. dirs. Precision Planning, 1980—; Town Hall West, 1980—; sec. African Task Force; mem. exec. com. Los Angeles Sister Cities, 1980—; chmn. opening night Treasures of Ancient Nigeria, Mus. Sci. and Industry, 1981, Jewels of the Orient, Pacific Asia Mus., 1984; mem. Com. Fgn. Relations, 1979—; mem. citizens adv. commns. Los Angeles Olympic Organizing Com., 1982-84, envoy African countries, 1984; exec. sec. Internat. Alert, 1985—; chmn. Mayor's Council for Sister Cities and Internat. Visitors, 1985—. Democrat. Author: African Arts Study Kit for Elementary Schools, 1976. Office: UCLA Los Angeles CA 90024

ST JOHN, LAWRENCE WALLIS, educational administrator; b. Coweta, Okla., June 22, 1922; s. Glen Eric and Vera Ann (Bell) St. J.; m. Eva Belle Stout, Nov. 16, 1944; children—Larry, Russell, Sheila. B.S. in Agr., Colo. State U., 1949; M.A. in Ednl. Adminstrn., Western State Coll., 1955. Cert. tchr., Colo. Secondary tchr. Sch. Dist. 16, Parachute, Colo., 1949-51, supt. schs., 1951-52, 1954-60; supt. schs. Sch. Dist. 10, New Castle, Colo., 1960-63, Sch. Dist. 16, Parachute, 1975-85; asst. supt. schs. Sch. Dist. Re-2, Rifle, Colo., 1963-75; retired 1985. Mayor, Town of Grand Valley (now Parachute), Colo., 1958-60. Served to lt. USN, 1942-46, 1952-54; PTO, Korea. Mem. Colo. Assn. Sch. Execs. (Dept. Gen. Adminstrs. award 1985), Rural Edn. Assn. (Colo. rural supt. of yr. 1981), Am. Legion (comdr. 1954-56). Lodges: Lions, Masons. Home: 311 Brennan Ln Box 445 Parachute CO 81635

ST. JOHN, THEODORE VERNE, ecologist, researcher; b. Orange, Calif., Nov. 2, 1944; s. Roscoe Raymond and Marie (Jones) St. J.; m. Kathleen Frances Schultz, May 30, 1976; children: Natalie Christine, Colleen Marie. BS, U. Calif., Irvine, 1971, PhD, 1976. Researcher Instituto Nacional de Pesquisas Da Amazônia, Manaus, Brazil, 1976-78; postdoctoral fellow Nat. Resource Ecology Lab. Colo. State U., Ft. Collins, 1978-82; research assoc. NREL Colo. State U., Ft. Collins, 1982-85; assoc. researcher UCLA Biomed. and Environ. Sci. Lab., 1985—. Contbr. articles to profl. jours. Served with USAF, 1965-68. Chevron Chem. grantee, 1982, NSF grantee, 1983, USAID grantee, 1984, Calif. Air Resources Bd. grantee, 1984, 85, 86. Democrat. Avocation: wood sculpture. Home: 25285 Bundy Canyon Rd Sun City CA 92380 Office: UCLA Biomed & Environ Sci Lab 900 Veteran Ave Los Angeles CA 90024

ST. PIERRE, PAUL, writer; b. Chgo., Oct. 14, 1923; immigrated to Can., 1924; s. Napoleon and Pearl Clayton (Stanford) St. P.; m. Carol Mildred Roycroft, Dec. 12, 1950 (dec. 1972); children—Paul Robert, Michelle Anne, Suzanne Ellen; m. Melanie Anne McCarthy, Nov. 17, 1978. Newspaperman, mostly Vancouver Sun, B.C., 1948-79; M.P. from Coast Chilcotin riding, 1968-72; parliamentary sec. external affairs, Ottawa, Can., 1971-72; del. UN Spl. Com., 1971-72; rapporteur Sci. and Cultural Com. NATO Parliamentary Group, 1972; chmn. B.C. Govt. Caucus, 1970-72; Can. observer Orgn. Am. States, 1972; police commr. Province of B.C., 1979-83. Author: Smith and Other Events, 1983; Breaking Smith's Quarter Horse, 1967; Chilcotin Holiday, 1970; Sister Balonika, 1971; British Columbia Our Land, 1973; Boss of the Namko Drive, 1966; others; playwright over 25 plays including Cariboo (CQ) Country; contbr. articles to mags. Recipient Spur Award (Western Writers of Am.) for best short fiction of 1984 for story Sale of One Small Ranch. Served with RCAF, 1941-42. Club: University (Vancouver).

SAITO, FRANK KIYOJI, import/export firm executive; b. Tokyo, Feb. 28, 1945; s. Kaoru and Chiyoko S.; LL.B., Kokugakuin U., 1967; m. Elaine Tamami Karasawa, Feb. 22, 1975; children—Roderic Kouki, Lorine Erika. With import dept. Trois Co. Ltd., Tokyo, Japan, 1967-68; founder import/export dept. Three Bond Co., Ltd., Tokyo, 1968-71; sales mgr. Kobe Mercantile, Inc., San Diego, 1971-76; pres. K & S Internat. Corp., San Diego, 1976—. Office: K & S Internat Corp 7626 Miramar Rd Suite 3200 San Diego CA 92126

SAITO, KATHLEEN KEIKO, architect, interior design; b. Honolulu, May 4, 1955; d. Raymond Mitsuyoshi and Midlred Tomiko (Kuromoto) Kawano; m. Sanford Sadamu Saito, July 31, 1982. BArch, U. Hawaii. Registered architect, Hawaii. Intern architect Group 70, Honolulu, 1979-81, assoc. architect, interior design, 1982—; interior designer, draftsperson Paul Kamada and Assocs., Honolulu, 1981-82; archtl. draftsperson Zephyr Archtl. Ptnrship, Honolulu, 1981-82. Recipient Lishman award for Interior Design, Bldg. Industry Assn. and Am. Soc. Interior Designers, 1984. Mem. AIA. Avocations: golfing, aerobics.

SAKAKIHARA, PHILIP MITSUO, computer scientist; b. Newell, Calif., June 8, 1943; s. Philip Kazuo and Hisa (Kurosaki) S.; m. Barbara Ruri Shiotsuka, June 24 1967; children: Ryan, Joel. BA in Math., San Jose State U., 1966; MS in Applied Math., U. Santa Clara, Calif., 1972. System test engr. Lockheed Missiles & Space Co. subs. Lockheed Corp., Sunnyvale, Calif., 1966-72; project mgr. Hewlett-Packard Co., Cupertino, Calif., 1972-78, advanced networks mgr., 1979-80; research and devel. lab. mgr. Hewlett-Packard U.K., Pinewood, Eng., 1980-83, Hewlett-Packard Co., Santa Clara, 1983—; vis. prof. U. Calif., Davis, 1978-79; research reviewer MICRO (Microelectronics Innovation and Computer Research Opportunities) program, U. Calif., 1986—; conductor profl. seminars, U.S. and Eng., 1974—. Contbr. articles to profl. jours. Vol. aid Cub Scouts Am., San Jose, 1984-86; asst. coach Community Youth Service, San Jose, 1986—. Recipient Merit and Outstanding Contbn. awards USAF Lockheed Missile and Space Co. Mem. IEEE, Assn. Computing Machinery. Avocations: traveling, snow and water skiing, fishing, jogging. Home: 608 Mindy Way San Jose CA 95123 Office: Hewlett-Packard Co 3410 Central Expy Santa Clara CA 95051

SAKANIWA, YASUO, watch manufacturing company executive; b. Tokyo, Sept. 29, 1925; came to U.S., 1952; s. Yoshio and Misao (Tsurumi) S.; m. Kayoko Ishibashi, Mar. 11, 1961; children—Hiroaki Robert, Hiromi Jane. B.A., Keio U., 1951; B.A., Tusculum Coll., 1953; M.B.A., Temple U., 1955; postgrad. U. Pa., 1959. With pub. relations dept. Hattori Trading Co., Ltd., Tokyo, 1959-61; mgr. Toyo Metall. & Chem. Co. Ltd., Seattle, 1961-70; pres. Seiko Instruments, Inc., Torrance, Calif., 1970-80, 1981-85, also bd. dirs.; bd. dirs. Micro Power Systems, Inc., Gato S.A. Brazil, Daini Seikosha Co., Ltd., Tokyo. Presbyterian. Clubs: Tokyo Lawn Tennis, Asahigaoka Golf; Rolling Hills Country. Home: 4 Silverbit Ln Rolling Hills Estates CA 90274 Office: 2990 W Lomita Blvd Torrance CA 90505

SAKARA, MARILYN JUDITH, social worker; b. Youngstown, Ohio, Nov. 21, 1949; d. Michael Joseph and Mary Jane (Makar) S.; m. Gregory Patrick Hungerford, June 10, 1972 (div.). AB, Youngstown State, 1967-71; MSW, La. State, 1973. Social worker Los Lunas (N.Mex.) Hosp. and Tng. Sch., 1977-78; social worker Dept. Human Services, Albuquerque, 1978-79, Santa Fe, 1979-80; social worker Child Devel. Ctr., Santa Fe, 1980-83; social worker supr. Children's Med. Services, Santa Fe, 1983—; pres. Field Research, Inc., Santa Fe, 1978—. Mem. Nat. Assn. Social Workers (recipient Acad. Cert. Social Workers award 1975). Democrat. Avocation: weight lifting. Home: PO Box 632 Santa Fe NM 87504 Office: HED Children's Med Services PO Box 968 Santa Fe NM 87504

SAKIMURA, KANJYO, entomologist, researcher; b. Koriyama, Japan, Mar. 6, 1903; came to U.S., 1923, naturalized, 1953; m. Bertha Hanaoka, Feb. 12, 1938; children: Pualani Kiku, Ronald Kinji Kaala, Glenn Kilohana. Attended, higher sch., Yamaguchi, Japan, 1923. From asst. entomologist to entomologist and head, entomology dept. Pineapple Research Inst., Honolulu, 1930-68; research assoc., Guggenheim fellow U. Calif., Berkeley, 1956, Bernice P. Bishop Mus., Honolulu, 1964—; entomologist FAO, Jamaica, 1964; retired 1968; vis. investigator Rockefeller Inst. Med. Research, Princeton, N.J., 1948; affiliated mem. grad. faculty, U. Hawaii, Manoa, 1955—. Contbr. articles on plant disease research to profl. jours. NSF grantee, 1965. Mem. Entomol. Soc. Am., Entomol. Soc. Wash., Fla. Entomol. Soc., Hawaiian Entomol. Soc. (pres. 1946), Am. Inst. Biol. Scis., Sigma Xi. Home: 1834 Bertram St Honolulu HI 96816

SAKKAL, MAMOUN, interior designer; b. Damascus, Syria, Dec. 31, 1950; came to U.S., 1978; s. Lutfi Sakkal and Dourieh Khatib; m. Seta K. Sakkal, Mar. 13, 1980; children: Aida, Kindah. BArch with honors, U. Aleppo, Syria, 1974; MArch, U. Wash., 1982, cert. urban design, 1982. Registered architect, Syria; lic. interior designer, U.S. Archtl. designer MCE, Damascus, 1974-75; dir. design MCE, Aleppo, 1975-76; prin. Sakkal & Assocs., Aleppo, 1976-78; archtl. designer Arch. Assocs., Seattle, 1978-82; sr. designer RD&S, Bellevue, Wash., 1982-84; prin. Restaurant/Hotel Design, Seattle, 1984—; lectr. U. Aleppo, 1974-75, Applied Arts Inst., 1977-78. Author: Geometry of Muqarnas in Islamic Architecture, 1981; designer Oct. Mus., Damascus, Syria, 1977 (1st prize award Syrian Ministry Def.); one man shows include: Nat. Mus. Aleppo, Syria, 1969, U. Aleppo, 1974, U. Wash., 1979, 80; contbr. articles to profl. jours. Recipient Best Logo Design award Arab Union Sports, 1976, Best Project Design award Aleppo Ministry of Culture, 1975, Best Moderization Project award Holiday Inns. System, 1986. Mem. Am. Soc. Interior Designers. Avocations: typeface design, illustration. Office: Restaurant/Hotel Design 315 NW 85th Suite B Seattle WA 98117

SAKLAD, HOWARD MARC, analyst/programmer, real estate investor; b. N.Y.C., Apr. 5, 1954; s. Eugene Leonard and Joan Estelle (Feldman); m. Chayyah Susan Baxter, Apr. 12, 1987. B.A. magma cum laude, Boston U., 1977, M.A., 1978. Computer sci. teaching fellow Boston U., Mass., 1977-78; analytical engr. Hamilton Standard, Windsor Locks, Conn., 1978-82; computer sci. educator U. Alaska, Fairbanks, 1982-83, analyst/programmer Inst. Marine Sci., 1982—; owner, property mgr. Residential 4-Plex and 5-Plex, Fairbanks, 1983—. Past composer, arranger, performer piano, trumpet. Designer, builder all-digital polyphonic synthesizer controlled by computer. Lay leader Jewish Congregation Fairbanks, 1983—; marriage commr. State Alaska, 1984, 85, 86; bd. dirs. and chmn. ritual com. Congregation Beth Ahm, Windsor, Conn., 1980. Mem. Computer Music Assn., Great Land Sounds Barber Shop Quartet Singing Soc. (music librarian Fairbanks chpt., 1985—, treas., asst. dir., 1987—, Recognition Merit award 1984, 85, Outstanding Barbershopper 1986). Jewish. Home: 307 Bias Dr E Fairbanks AK 99712 Office: U Alaska Inst Marine Sci O'Neill Bldg Fairbanks AK 99775-1080

SALAMAN, MAUREEN KENNEDY, nutritionist; b. Glendale, Calif., Apr. 4, 1936; d. Ted and Elena (Peters) Kennedy; m. Frank Salaman; children—Sean, Coleen. M.Sc. in Nutrition, Donsbach U., Huntington Beach, Calif., 1981. Hostess show Gift of Health Sta. KFAX AM, 1977—, Totally Yours with Maureen Salaman, Sta. KEST-AM, San Francisco, 1977—, West Coast Report, Sta. WMCA-AM, N.Y.C., 1980—; hostess Maureen Salaman's Accent on Health Sta. KFCB, Concord, Calif.; feature writer Best Ways mag., 1978—; pres. Nat. Health Fedn., Monrovia, Calif., 1982—; cons., lectr., researcher on cancer research and metabolic medicine, nutrition; freedom of choice lobbyist; v.p. Project Freedom; vice presidential candidate Populist Party, 1984. Author: Nutrition: The Cancer Answer, 1983. Editor: Choice Mag., 1972-77, Public Scrutiny, 1978-80, Health Freedom News, 1982-85. Contbr. articles to profl. jours.; hostess TV42 Maureen Salaman's Accent on Health. Developer nutrition programs for radio and TV. Decorated Freedom Fighters medal Korean Govt. Mem. Nat. Health Fedn. (pres. 1981-87, Patrick Henry Liberty award). Office: Nat Health Fedn PO Box 688 Monrovia CA 91016 Office: Sta KFCB-TV Concord CA 94524

SALAMEH, ANTHONY MICHAEL, restaurateur; b. Manila, Sept. 28, 1951; came to U.S., 1972; s. Abraham George and Mary Therese (Nazzal) S.; m. Maria Josephine Linehan, July 15, 1977; children: Anton, Stefan. M in Hotel and Restaurant Mgmt., Hotel Sch. of Lausanne, Switzerland, 1972. Food and beverage mgr. Quail Lodge, Carmel Valley, Calif., 1973-77; club mgr. Carmel Valley Golf and Country Club, 1977-80; pres. MAST Restaurant Group, Carmel, Calif., 1980—; bd. dirs. Calif. Wine Festival. Mem. Monterey Peninsula Hotel and Restaurant Assn. (pres. 1985-86). Republican. Roman Catholic. Avocations: tennis, guitar. Home: 1361 Sylvan Rd Monterey CA 93940 Office: MAST Restaurant Mgmt Group PO Box 4425 Carmel-by-the-Sea CA 93921

SALAMY, JACQUE LEE NOLL, speech pathologist, department chairman; b. Phoenix, Nov. 23, 1944; d. Henry Christopher and Jacqueline (Forney-Overstreet) Noll; m. Joseph George Salamy, Aug. 15, 1969; 1 child, Elissa Brooke. EdB, Okla. State U., 1967; MS in Speech and Lang., U. Okla., 1969. Speech-lang. pathologist Palo Alto (Calif.) Unified Sch. Dist., 1969-71, U. Tex. Med. Br., Galveston, 1971-77; dir. speech-lang., neurosensory ctr. Meth. Hosp., Houston, 1977-79; mem. adj. faculty Baylor Coll. Medicine, Houston, 1977-79; dir. speech-lang. Spalding Rehab. Hosp., Denver, 1979—; cons., lectr. on mastery of communications skills for execs., tchrs., attys., mgrs. Nat. Stroke Assn., Denver, 1985—, Houston Stroke Club, 1977-79, Houston Laryngectomy Assn., 1977-79. Mem. Am. Speech-Lang.-Hearing Assn. (cert. clin. competence), Colo. Speech-Lang.-Hearing Assn. (v.p.-elect 1985, v.p. edn. com. 1986). Methodist. Club: P.E.O. Avocations: skiing, reading. Office: Spalding Rehab Hosp 1919 Ogden St Denver CO 80218

SALANE, DOUGLAS EDWARD, mathematician, researcher; b. Bklyn., July 10, 1952; s. Edward Peter and Helen (Serravalle) S. BA in Math., Queen Coll., Flushing, N.Y., 1976; MS in Applied Math., SUNY, Stonybrook, 1978, PhD in Applied Math., 1981. Research mathematician Exxon Research and Engring. Co., Linden, N.J., 1981-83, Sandia Nat. Labs., Albuquerque, 1984—. Editor: Applied Numerical Mathematics Special Issue on Optimization, 1986. Mem. Soc. Indsl. and Applied Math., Am. Math. Soc., Assn. Computing Machinery. Avocations: personal computers, study of Spanish and French. Office: Sandia Nat Labs Numerical Math 1642 Albuquerque NM 87185

SALANT-MIRFIELD, LYNN NORA, manufacturing company executive; b. N.Y.C., Dec. 16, 1941; d. Samuel and Betty (Katz) Grupp; m. Leon Salant, Jan. 21, 1968 (div. 1976); 1 child, Samuel Evan; m. Andrew George Mirfield, Feb. 9, 1985. BA in Edn. and Broadcasting, Queens Coll., Flushing, 1962; MA in Art History, Calif. State U., Los Angeles, 1966. Tchr. 28th Sch. Dist., East Los Angeles, Calif., 1966-67; founder, pres. Travelite Internat. Inc. formerly Lynn Leigh Inc., Los Angeles, 1968—. Mem. Women in Film, Women in Bus. Jewish. Avocations: tennis, riding, travel, reading. Office: Travelite Internat Inc 12449 Chandler Blvd North Hollywood CA 91604

SALAS, BENNIE, agency realty officer; b. Santa Fe, Feb. 23, 1936; s. Remejio and Emma (Gallegos) S.; m. Pearl Mary Vallo, Apr. 23, 1939; children—Benjamin R., Ira V., Jerry P., Crystal I. B.S. in Bus. Adminstrn., U. Albuquerque, 1977. Edn. Coordinator All Indian Pueblo Council, Albuquerque, 1969-70; edn. technician Bur. Indian Affairs, 1970-74, realty officer, 1976—; aide to war chief Pueblo of Zia, 1961, 62, lt. gov., 1967, gov., 1972, 82-83; pres. T.S.I.A., Inc., Zia Pueblo, N. Mex. 1983—. V.p. Nat. Congress Am. Indians, 1982-86. Served with USN, 1955-59. Ford Found. fellow, 1971. Democrat. Roman Catholic. Address: Zia Pueblo Route Box 1 San Ysidro NM 87053

SALAS, MARILYN SUE, director, headmaster of academic institution; b. Sabetha, Kans., June 4, 1943; d. lee R. and Agnes M. (McPeak) Cashman; m. Henry C. Salas, Aug. 1, 1970. Student, Kans. State U., 1961-62, Kans. U., 1962-64; BA in Bus. Adminstrn., Emporia State U., 1966. Cert. secondary bus. edn. and psychology tchr., Kans., Calif. High sch. tchr. Pacifica High Sch., Garden Grove, Calif., 1966-68; word processor Orange County, Calif., 1968-72; ednl. service rep. IBM, Anaheim, Calif., 1969-70; coll. instr. Cerritos Coll., Norwalk, Calif., 1970-74; adult edn. instr. Lincoln Edn. Tng., Garden Grove, 1972-78; coll. instr. Golden West Coll., Huntington Beach, Calif., 1973-80, Orange Coast Coll., Costa Mesa, Calif., 1976-79, Cypress (Calif.) Coll., 1977-79; freelance word processor Burlington Northern, Newport Beach, Calif., 1978-79; cons. in field, Orange County, 1979; coll. instr. Saddleback Coll., Mission Viejo, Calif., 1979; dir. The Word Processing, Anaheim, 1980—. Mem. Assn. Info. Systems Profls. (mem. ednl. task force), Am. Soc. Tng. and Devel., Calif. Bus. Educators Assn., Anaheim C. of C., Nat. Assn. Trade and Tech. Schs. Accrediting Agy. (accredited). Democrat. Methodist. Avocations: gardening, music, travel, water skiing, animals. Home: 41105 Valle Vista Murrieta CA 92362 Office: The Word Processing and Computer Sch 350 W Cerritos Ave Anaheim CA 92805

SALAZAR, ANITA TERESA, business educator; b. Greeley, Colo., Apr. 2, 1947; d. Fermin and Helen (De La Torre) S. BA, U. No. Colo., 1968, MA, 1969; PhD, Ohio State U., 1981. Instr., coordinator Centennial High Sch., San Luis, Colo., 1969-72; evaluation specialist State Bd. Community Colls. and Occupational Edn., Denver, 1972-74; instr., coordinator Red Rocks Community Coll., Golden, Colo., 1973-77; adminstrv. asst., grad. research asst. Nat. Ctr. Research in Vocat. Edn. Ohio State U., Columbus, 1978-81; assst. prof. U. No. Colo., Greeley, 1982—. Contbr. articles to profl. jours. Named Rookie Tchr. Yr. Colo. State Bd. Community Colls. and Occupational Edn., 1971. Mem. Greeley C. of C. (mem. leadership class 1986). Democrat. Roman Catholic. Avocations: skiing, tennis, jogging, reading, music. Home: Box 305 La Salle CO 80645 Office: U No Colo Coll Edn Greeley CO 80639

SALAZAR, LUIS ADOLFO, architect; b. New Orleans, Sept. 17, 1944; s. Gustavo Adolfo and Luz Maria (Florez) S.; m. Sandra Kay Bucklew, May 30, 1969 (div. Jan. 1984); 1 child, Staci Dahnal. AA, Harbor Coll., 1966; BArch, Ariz. State U., 1971. Registered architect, Ariz., Calif., N.Mex. Area architect Peace Corps, Sierra Leone, 1971-73; project architect Van Sittert Assocs., Phoenix, 1973-77; pres., owner Salazar Assoc. Architects, Ltd., Phoenix, 1977—; Prin. works include bldg. design Kenema Cathedral,

Kenema, Sierra Leone, West Africa, 1980. Bd. dirs. Community Behavioral Services, Phoenix, 1983— Phoenix Meml. Hosp., 1984—, Terraco Properties. mem. Subcom. on Bond Election, Phoenix, 1984; mem. Visual Improvement Awards Com., City of Phoenix, 1985—. Mem. AIA (chmn. program com., honor award Ariz. chpt. 1984), Soc. Am. Value Engrs., Inst. Architects. Roman Catholic. Office: Salazar Assocs Architects Ltd 4518 N 12th St Suite 100 Phoenix AZ 85014

SALAZAR, MICHAEL JOSEPH, engineering company executive; b. Santa Fe, Sept. 27, 1931; s. Michael and Anna (Baca) S.; m. Marilyn Lucille Lobato, Dec. 29, 1956; children: Michael L. (dec.), Sherry, Gregory, Renee. BS, Coll. Santa Fe, 1959; MPH, Tulane U., 1962; postgrad., U. N.Mex., 1969-74. Registered profl. engr., Colo., Wis. Chief environ. health Ill. Health Dept., Springfield, 1962-65; regional environ. supr. N.Mex. EPA, Albuquerque, 1969-71; assoc. prof. N.Mex. Highlands U., Las Vegas, 1971-74; chief engr. EPA, Denver, 1974-83; pres. Salazar Assocs., Westminster, Colo., 1983—. Patentee in field. Served to lt. comdr. USPHS, 1965-69. Mem. NSPE, Colo. Soc. Profl. Engrs., Profl. Engrs. in Pvt. Practice. Democrat. Roman Catholic. Avocations: golfing, swimming, tennis. Home: 4650 W 99th Ave Westminster CO 80030 Office: Salazar Assocs Internat 8791 Wolf Ct Bldg 15 Westminster CO 80030

SALBERG, RICHARD LETFORD, bank executive; b. Longmont, Colo., Nov. 27, 1937; s. Arthur G. and Margaret (Letford) S.; m. Anne Scholberg, June 4, 1960; children: Suzanne, Katherine. BS, U. Colo., 1959; diploma, Colo. Sch. Banking, 1966; student, Am. Inst. Banking, 1967-78. Asst. cashier First Nat. Bank, Johnstown, Colo., 1963-67, v.p., 1967-69, exec. v.p., 1969-84, pres., 1984—, also bd. dirs. Trustee Town of Johnstown, 1970-76, Mayor, 1976-84; bd. dirs. Hospice Inc. Weld County, Greeley, Colo., 1984—; bd. dirs. North Colo. Med. Ctr. Found., 1983—. Served with U.S. Army, 1959-61. Recipient Outstanding Service award Town of Johnstown, 1984, Cert. of Appreciation Larimer Weld Council of Govt's. Loveland, 1984. Republican. Methodist. Lodge: Lions (1st, 2d, 3d v.p. Milliken, Colo. club, pres., treas., 1969—, Outstanding Service award, 1983). Avocations: hiking, golfing, model trains, gardening. Home: 1111 N Park Ave PO Box 457 Johnstown CO 80534-0457

SALE, GEORGE EDGAR, pathologist, cancer researcher; b. Missoula, Mont., Apr. 18, 1941; s. George Goble and Ruth Edna (Polleys) S.; m. Nancy Current, 1978; children: George Gregory, Teo Marie. AB, Harvard U., 1963; MD, Stanford U., 1968. Intern U. Oreg., Portland, 1968-69; sr. asst. surgeon USPHS, Albuquerque, 1969-71; resident in pathology U. Wash., Seattle, 1971-75, instr. pathology, 1975-78, asst. prof., 1978-81, assoc. prof., 1981—; mem. faculty dept. oncology Hutchinson Cancer Ctr., Seattle, 1975—. Author, editor: Pathology of Bone Marrow Transplantation, 1984. Mem. AAAS, Internat. Acad. Pathology, Coll. Am. Pathologists, Am. Assn. Pathologists, Physicians for Social Responsibility. Home: 12146 Sunrise Dr NE Bainbridge WA 98110 Office: Fred Hutchinson Cancer Research Ctr 1124 Columbia Pathology Seattle WA 98104

SALEM, SUSANNE FRANCES, consulting executive; b. San Francisco, Mar. 25, 1945; d. Edward L. and Mary F. (Adams) Ledinski; m. Lee C. Salem, July 14, 1979. B.S., Ariz. State U., 1979. Ins. agt. Atlantic Mut. Ins. Co. and Harris & Assocs., Los Angeles, 1964-73; ptnr. Acero Enterprises, Sierra Vista, Ariz., 1973-77; lease account mgr. Truck Leasing, Phoenix, 1979-80; sales and cons. Internat. Transp., Phoenix, 1980; owner Corp. Directions Cons. & Recruiting, Phoenix, 1980-86; v.p., bd. dirs. The Prism Group, Inc., Cons.; guest speaker. Bd. dirs. Southeastern Ariz. Drug Abuse Council, 1975-77. Am. Trucking Assns. scholar, 1977-79, outstanding transp. grad., 1979. Contbr. articles to profl. jours.

SALES, GROVER, music educator, writer; b. Louisville, Oct. 26, 1919; s. Grover Grauman and Rosalind Esther (Harris) S.; m. Enid Thompson (div. 1955); m. Georgia Ann Schwartz, Dec. 30, 1972; 1 child, Rachel. Student, Reed Coll.; BA, U. Calif., Berkeley, postgrad. Mem. Critics Circle O'Neill Theater Found., Waterford, Conn., 1967-71; instr. Dominican Coll., San Rafael, Calif., 1982-84, U. Calif. extension, Berkeley, 1970—, San Francisco State U., 1980—, San Francisco Conservatory of Music, 1982—, Stanford U., 1987—; publicist San Francisco, 1960-63, Monterey Jazz Festival, Calif., 1958-65; critic (newsroom) Sta. KQED-TV, San Francisco, 1972-75. Author: John Maher of Delancey Street, 1976, Jazz: America's Classical Music, 1984; (with Georgia Sales), Clay-Pot Cookbook, 1974. Served to sgt. USAAF, 1942-46, CBI. Recipient Spl. Mention First Sang prize for drama criticism, 1968, Peabody award for Chevron's Music Makers Series, 1976, nominee Grammy award for Best-Liner Notes Broadway Musical Amadeus, 1985. Phi Beta Kappa. Democrat. Jewish. Avocations: collecting records, folk art, cooking, photography, jazz.

SALGO, JEFFERY DALE, broadcast executive; b. Los Angeles, May 1, 1951; s. Julius and Shirley (Halmos) S. Student, Los Angeles Community Coll., 1969-71. Mgr. ops. Sta. KFXM/KDUO, San Bernardino, Calif., 1976-78; dir. program Sta. KBZT, San Diego, 1980-82; mgr. ops. Sta. KMGG, Los Angeles, 1982-84; pres. Salgo & Assocs., Los Angeles, 1976-84; pres., chief exec. officer New Frontier Broadcasting, Inc., Anaheim, Calif., 1984—; v.p. Anaheim Broadcasting Corp., 1985—; speaker Fullerton (Calif.) City Coll., 1986; cons. Anaheim (Calif.) Broadcasting Corp., 1985—, Alta Broadcasting, San Jose, 1982-85, Duffy Broadcasting, N.Y.C., 1981-84. Author (video tng. course) Broadcast Sales Breakthroughs, 1986, (manual) Research Advances, 1979; editor-in-chief Internat. Radio Report, 1978-80. Advisor Seattle Dept. Parks and Recreation, 1974-75. Mem. World Inst. Scientology Enterprises. Republican. Scientologist. Office: New Frontier Broadcasting Inc 1190 E Ball Rd Anaheim CA 92805

SALIBELLO, COSMO, optometrist, consultant, lecturer; b. N.Y.C., Sept. 21, 1943; s. Joseph and Maria (Patalano) S.; B.Mgmt.Engring., Rensselaer Poly. Inst., 1965; B.A. in Biology summa cum laude, Central Wash. U., 1979; D. D.Optometry, Pacific U., 1983. Diplomate Nat. Bd. Examiners in Optometry; cert. comml. pilot, FAA. Dep. aircrew tng. dir. Grumman Aerospace Corp., Tehran, Iran, 1974-76; practice optometry, Salem, Oreg., 1983—; cons. to industry; lectr. edn. Mem. Ellensburg Community Choir, 1977-79; chmn. Laurel West Homeowners Assn., Forest Grove, Oreg., 1980-83. Served to lt. comdr. USN, 1966-74. Decorated Air medal; recipient Outstanding Student award Naval Schs. Command, 1966. Mem. Am. Optometric Assn., Oreg. Optometric Assn. Patentee design elbow rest, 1982. Home: 12880 SW Scout Dr Beaverton OR 97005 Office: Franz Optical 1580 Lancaster Dr NE Salem OR 97301

SALIBI, BAHIJ SULAYMAN, neurosurgeon; b. Omdurman, Sudan, May 16, 1922; s. Sleiman Khalil and Salva Ibrahim (Salibi) S.; came to U.S., 1946, naturalized, 1961; B.A., Am. U. Beirut (Lebanon), 1941, M.A., 1944; postgrad. U. Mich., 1946; M.D., Harvard, 1950; m. Margaret Elizabeth Beverley, May 16, 1954; children—Lillian Salwa, Charles Khalil, Ernest Kamal. Intern in pathology and clin. pathology Children's Hosp., Boston, 1950-51, research fellow in neurosurgery, 1956; intern in surgery Barnes Hosp., St. Louis, 1951-52, asst. resident in surgery, 1952-53; resident in neurosurgery St. Lukes Hosp., Chgo., 1953-54; resident in neurosurgery U. Ill. Neuropsychiat. Inst., Chgo., 1954-56, chief resident in neurosurgery, 1955-56; asst. in surgery (neurosurgery) Harvard Med. Sch., Boston, 1956; neurosurgeon Marshfield Clinic, Marshfield, Wis., 1958-86; mem. staff St. Joseph's Hosp.; asso. clin. prof. neurol. surgery U. Wis. Med. Sch., Madison. Served as capt. MC, U.S. Army, 1956-58. Diplomate Am. Bd. Neurol. Surgery. Fellow A.C.S.; mem. AMA, Wis. State Med. Soc., Wood County Med. Soc., Congress Neurol. Surgeons, Central Neurosurg. Soc. (pres. 1968-69), Am. Assn. Neurol. Surgeons, Internat. Med. Soc. Paraplegia. Democrat. Episcopalian. Contbr. articles in field to profl. jours. Inventor artery clamp. Home: 1020 Mountain Hwy, North Vancouver Can V7J 2L9

SALIMENO, FRANK LOUIS, optometrist; b. Ogden, Utah, Aug. 31, 1943; s. Frank A. and Jolene (Ruger) S.; children—Nick Anthony, Kristin Lin; m. Linda Knight, May 23, 1986. B.S., Weber State Coll., 1965; O.D., Pacific U. Coll. Optometry, 1969; cert. in gen. and ocular pharmacology U. Calif., 1977; cert. in ocular therapeutics Pa. Coll. Optometry, 1985. Practice optometry, Ogden, 1972—. Vol. probation officer Utah Dept. Social Services, 1981-83; bd. dirs. St. Benedicts Hosp. Found., Ogden, 1982-83. Served to capt. MC., U.S. Army, 1970-72. Decorated Army Commendation medal. Fellow Am. Acad. Optometry; mem. Am. Optometric Assn., Utah Optometric Assn. (pres. 1977-79, contbg. editor and author jour. 1976-79, Spl. award 1977, Optometrist of Yr. 1982), Beta Sigma Kappa. Club: Exchange (club Exchangite of Yr. 1982, pres. club 1982-83) Ogden. Office: 5089 S Adams Ave Ogden UT 84403

SALISBURY, DAVID FRANCIS, newspaper science writer; b. Seattle, Feb. 24, 1947; s. Vernon H. and Lurabelle (Kline) S. BS, U. Wash., 1969. Sci. editor Christian Sci. Monitor, Boston, 1972-76; correspondent Christian Sci. Monitor, Los Angeles, Boulder (Colo.) and San Francisco, 1976-85; sci. and tech. writer U. Calif., Santa Barbara, 1985—; mem. research adv. com. Pub. Service Electric and Gas Co., Newark, N.J., 1979-83. Author: Money Matters, 1982. contbr. many articles to popular mags. and tech. jours. Recipient Sci. Writing awards AAAS, 1976, NSPE, 1978, Aviation Space Writers Assn., 1981. Mem. Nat. Assn. Sci. Writers (Sci.-in-Soc. award 1974), No. Calif. Sci. Writers Assn., Computer Press Assn. Christian Scientist. Avocations: tennis, sailing. Office: U Calif Pub Info Office Santa Barbara CA 93106

SALISBURY, FRANK BOYER, educator, plant physiologist; b. Provo, Utah, Aug. 3, 1926; s. Frank M. and Catherine (Boyer) S.; m. Lois Marilyn Olson, Sept. 1, 1949; children—Frank Clark, Steven Scott, Michael James, Cynthia Kay, Phillip Boyer (dec.), Rebecca Lynn, Blake Charles. B.S., U. Utah, 1951, M.A., 1952; Ph.D., Calif. Inst. Tech., 1955. Asst. prof. botany Pomona Coll., Claremont, Calif., 1954-55; faculty Colo. State U., Ft. Collins, 1955-66; prof. plant physiology Colo. State U., 1961-66; plant physiologist Expt. Sta., 1961-66; prof. plant physiology Utah State U., Logan, 1966—; head dept. plant sci. Utah State U., 1966-70; tech. rep. plant physiology AEC, Germantown, Md., 1973-74; vis. prof. U. Innsbruck, Austria; Lady Davis fellow Hebrew U. Jerusalem, 1983; mem. life scis. adv. com. NASA, 1986—. Author: The Flowering Process, 1963, (with R.V. Parke) Vascular Plants, Form and Function, 2d edit, 1970, Truth by Reason and by Revelation, 1965, (with C. Ross) Plant Physiology, 1969, 3d edit., 1985, The Biology of Flowering, 1971, (with W. Jensen) Botany: An Ecological Approach, 1972, Botany, 2d edit., 1984, The Utah UFO Display, 1974, The Creation, 1976, (with E. Kormondy, T. Sherman, N. Spratt, and G. McCain) Biology, 1977. Trustee Colo. State U. Research Found., 1959-62. Served with USAAF, 1945. NSF sr. postdoctoral fellow Germany and Austria, 1962-63. Fellow AAAS; mem. Am. Soc. for Gravitational and Space Biology, Am. Soc. Plant Physiologists (editorial bd.), Ecol. Soc. Am., Utah Acad. Sci., Arts and Letters, Am. Inst. Biol. Scis. (governing bd. 1976-79), Bot. Soc. Am., Sigma Xi, Phi Kappa Phi. Mem. Ch. of Jesus Christ of Latter-day Saints. Home: 2020 North 1250 E North Logan UT 84321 Office: Utah State U Dept Plant Sci Logan UT 84322-4820

SALK, JONAS EDWARD, physician, scientist; b. N.Y.C., Oct. 28, 1914; s. Daniel B. and Dora (Press) S.; m. Donna Lindsay, June 8, 1939; children: Peter Lindsay, Darrell John, Jonathan Daniel; m. Francoise Gilot, June 29, 1970. B.S., CCNY, 1934, LL.D. (hon.), 1955; M.D., NYU, 1939, Sc.D. (hon.), 1955; LL.D. (hon.), U. Pitts., 1955; Ph.D. (hon.), Hebrew U., 1959; LL.D. (hon.), Roosevelt U., 1955; Sc.D. (hon.), Turin U., 1957, U. Leeds, 1959, Hahnemann Med. Coll., 1959, Franklin and Marshall U., 1960; D.H.L. (hon.), Yeshiva U., 1959; LL.D. (hon.), Tuskegee Inst., 1964. Fellow in chemistry NYU, 1935-37, fellow in exptl. surgery, 1937-38, fellow in bacteriology, 1939-40; Intern Mt. Sinai Hosp., N.Y.C., 1940-42; NRC fellow Sch. Pub. Health, U. Mich., 1942-43, research fellow epidemiology, 1943-44, research asso., 1944-46, asst. prof. epidemiology, 1946-47; asso. research prof. bacteriology Sch. Medicine, U. Pitts., 1947-49, dir. virus research lab., 1947-63, research prof. bacteriology, 1949-55, Commonwealth prof. preventive medicine, 1955-57, Commonwealth prof. exptl. medicine, 1957-63; dir. Salk Inst. Biol. Studies, 1963-75, resident fellow, 1963-84, founding dir., 1976—, 1976—, disting. prof. internat. health scis., 1984—; developed vaccine, preventive of poliomyelitis, 1955, cons. epidemic diseases sec. war, 1944-47, sec. army, 1947-54; mem. commn. on influenza Army Epidemiol. Bd., 1944-54, acting dir. commn. on influenza, 1944; mem. expert adv. panel on virus diseases WHO; adj. prof. health scis., depts. psychiatry, community medicine and medicine U. Calif., San Diego, 1970—. Author: Man Unfolding, 1972, The Survival of the Wisest, 1973, (with Jonathan Salk) World Population and Human Values: A New Reality, 1981, Anatomy of Reality, 1983; Contbr. sci. articles to jours. Decorated chevalier Legion of Honor France, 1955, officer, 1976; recipient Criss award, 1955, Lasker award, 1956, Gold medal of Congress and presdl. citation, 1955, Howard Ricketts award, 1957, Robert Koch medal, 1963, Mellon Inst. award, 1969; Presdl. medal of Freedom, 1977; Jawaharlal Nehru award for internat. understanding, 1976. Fellow AAAS, Am. Pub. Health Assn., Am. Acad. Pediatrics (hon., assoc.); mem. Am. Coll. Preventive Medicine, Am. Acad. Neurology, Assn. Am. Physicians., Soc. Exptl. Biology and Medicine, Inst. Medicine (sr.), Phi Beta Kappa, Alpha Omega Alpha, Delta Omega. Office: Salk Inst Biol Studies PO Box 85800 San Diego CA 92138

SALKIN, BARBARA RUTH, social worker; b. Washington, Sept. 16, 1938; d. David and Bess Marguerite (Adelman) S. BA, UCLA, 1960; MSW, U. Calif., Berkeley, 1962. Lic. clin. social worker, Calif. Clin. social worker Neuropsychiat. Inst. UCLA, 1962-79, Kaiser-Permanente, Woodland Hills, Calif., 1979—. Contbr. articles to profl. jours. Mem. Nat. Assn. Social Work (cert.), Soc. Clin. Social Work, So. Calif. Blues Soc. (treas. 1986—). Democrat. Jewish. Avocations: travelling, music, dancing. Office: Kaiser Permanente Dept Psychiatry 5855 DeSoto Ave Woodland Hills CA 91367

SALKIN, GERALDINE (JERI) FAUBION, dancer, dance therapist, educator; b. Denver, Mar. 18, 1916; d. George Everett and Hanna Viola (Harvey) Faubion; student Lester Horton Dance Theater, Carmelita Maracci, Trudi Schoop, Los Angeles, 1937-47, Doris Humphrey, N.Y.C., 1952-53, Rudolf Von Laban, London, 1956-57, Hanna Fenichel, Ph.D.,Westwood, Calif., 1965-70, UCLA, 1959-60; Ph.D., 1978; m. Leo Salkin, June 29, 1936; 1 dau., Lynn Salkin Sbiroli. Concert dancer Lester Horton Dance Group, Los Angeles, 1937-47, tchr. creative modern dance, 1939-47; tchr. creative modern dance Dance Assos., Hollywood, Calif., 1949-53, Am. Sch. of London (Eng.), 1956-57, Jeri Salkin Studio and Ctr. for Child Study, Hollywood, 1968-73; developer body ego technique Camarillo (Calif.) State Hosp., 1957-64; movement specialist Nat. Endowment Arts grantee, 1973—; dir., body ego technique dept. Cedars-Sinai Thalians Community Mental Health Ctr., Los Angeles, 1965—; dance cons., tchr. Nat. Head Start Program, Calif., 1964; conductor yearly workshops for tchrs., dancers, psychologists, psychiatrists, therapists, Rome, 1979—, mem. aux. faculty Goddard Coll., Antioch Coll., various hosps. and univs. Calif. Dept. Mental Hygiene grantee, 1960-63. Mem. Am. Dance Therapy Assn., AAHPER, Calif. Dance Educators Assn., Calif. Assn. Health, Phys. Edn. Dance and Recreation, Nat. Assn. Edn. Young Children, Assn. Child Devel. Specialists, Com. Research in Dance. Democrat. Author: Body Ego Technique, an Educational and Therapeutic Approach to Body Image and Self-Identity, 1973; author, choreographer film (with Leo Salkin and Trudi Schoop) Body Ego Technique, 1962 (U.S. Golden Eagle Council on Internat. Nontheatrical Events award 1963). Home: 3584 Multiview Dr Hollywood CA 90068 Office: 8730 Alden Dr Los Angeles CA 90048

SALLEE, ALVIN LLOYD, social work educator, consultant; b. Albuquerque, Jan. 19, 1950; s. Lloyd Alvin and Carol (Williams) S.; m. Kathleen Estelle Bickerstaff, Jan. 1, 1971; children: Charles, Shawn, Joan. BA, Phillips U., Enid, Okla., 1972; MSW, Ariz. State U., 1974. Adminstrv. asst. Ariz. Tng. Program at Tucson, 1972-73; research asst. Community Council, Phoenix, 1973-74; instr. S.W. Tex. State U., San Marcos, 1974-76; assoc. prof., head dept. social work N.Mex. State U., Las Cruces, 1976—; cons. Ctr. for Social Work Research, U. Tex., Austin, 1975-79, City of Lubbock, Tex., 1982, Santa Fe Community Found., N.Mex., 1983-84, Social Services div. N.Mex. Human Services Dept., Santa Fe, 1983-84. Author: (with Elaine LeVine) Listen to Our Children: Clinical Theory and Practice, 1986; editor Jour. of Alliance of Info. and Referral Systems, 1978-80. Southwest coordinator Dem. presdl. and congl. campaigns, Las Cruces, 1980; mem. exec. bd. Baccalaureate Program, 1985—, Family Impact Com., 1985—, nomination com. house of dels. Council of Social Work Edn., 1985—; chmn. Gov.'s Family Impact Com., Santa Fe, 1983—, N.Mex. Family Policy Task Force, Santa Fe, 1980-83, United Way of Orange County, Calif., 1985; bd. dirs. Colo. Christian Home, Denver, 1983—. Grantee N.Mex. Human Services Dept., 1977-81, N.Mex. State Agy. on Aging, 1983. Mem. Alliance of Info. and Referral Systems (bd. dirs. 1978—, sec. 1981—), Nat. Assn. Social Workers (bd. dirs. 1972-74), Council of Social Work Edn., N.Mex. Council Social Work Edn., Internat. Schs. of Social Work, Am. Orthopsychiatry Assn. Home: 2700 Crestview Dr Las Cruces NM 88001 Office: New Mexico State U Dept Social Work Box 35 W Las Cruces NM 88003

SALLEE, WESLEY W(ILLIAM), nuclear chemist; b. Perry, Okla., June 5, 1951; s. Jimmie Richard and Nadine A. (Barnes) S.; m. Exine Mamie Clark, Mar. 21, 1979; children: Rachel Nadine, Daniel Mason. BS in Chemistry, Okla. State U., 1974; PhD in Chemistry, U. Ark., 1983. Commd. 1st lt. USAF, 1976, advanced through grades to capt., 1978, resigned, 1979; chemist U.S. Army White Sands Missile Range, 1983—. Author technical reports and symposium papers; contbr. articles to profl. jours. Mem. ASTM, Am. Nuclear Soc., Am. Chem. Soc. Republican. Mem. Ch. of Christ. Avocations: golf, fishing, hunting, reading. Home: 1515 Dorothy Circle Las Cruces NM 88001-1625 Office: Nuclear Effects Lab PO Box 333 Missile Range NM 88002

SALLY, MARK J., chemical engineer. BS in Chemistry, San Diego State U., 1980; MSChemE, U. Calif., San Diego, 1986. Indsl. chemist Shell Oil Co., Martinez, Calif., 1980-83; research engr. U. Calif., San Diego, 1984-86; research and devel. engr. Athens Corp., Oceanside, Calif., 1986—. U. Calif. Research fellow. Mem. Am. Inst. Chem. Engrs. (affiliate), Am. Chem. Soc. Home: 712 Garfield Ave El Cajon CA 92020 Office: Athens Corp 602 Airport Rd Oceanside CA 92054

SALMERON, MIQUEL, physicist; b. Santa Coloma, Catalonia, Spain, Sept. 19, 1944; came to U.S., 1975; s. Francisco Salmeron and Maria Batalle; m. Marta Viver, July 31, 1970; children: Joel, Ausias, Roger. BS, U. Barcelona, Spain, 1967; Diplome D'Etudes Approfondies, U. Paul Sabatier, Toulouse, France, 1968, M in Solid State Physics, 1970; PhD Scis. in Physics, U. Autonoma of Madrid, 1975. Asst. prof. U. Autonoma of Madrid, 1970-73; staff scientist Spanish Nat. Research Council, Madrid, 1973-84, Lawrence Berkeley Lab. Ctr. Advanced Materials, Berkeley, Calif., 1984—. Contbr. articles to profl. jours. Mem. Am. Phys. Soc. Office: Lawrence Berkeley Lab 1 Cyclotron Rd Berkeley CA 96720

SALMON, CHARLES RAY, manufacturing company executive, professional engineer; b. Stockton, Mo., Oct. 18, 1927; s. John Ray and Eunice May (Jones) S.; m. Billie Jean Finnell, Sept. 5, 1950; children: Jon Wheaton, Steven Clay, Christopher Craig. B.A., Pomona Coll., 1950; postgrad. U. Wis., 1950-51, UCLA, 1951-52. Registered profl. engr., Calif. Pres. Evans Industries West, Los Angeles, 1975—, Le Clos de Salmon, Inc., Lafayette, Calif., 1979—; vice chmn. Ball Brass & Aluminum, Auburn, Ind., 1979—; dir. Evans Industries, Inc., Detroit; cons., dir. various corps. Mem. Am. Inst. Indsl. Engrs. (sr.), Phi Beta Kappa. Republican. Calvinist. Author: The Book of Purpose, 1974; Introduction to the Fourth Dimension, 1974, Les Croyances Normandes, 1984.

SALMON, MERLYN LEIGH, lab. exec.; b. Macksville, Kans., June 24, 1924; s. Kenneth Elbert and Inez Melba (Prose) S.; student U. Kans., 1943-44; B.S., U. Denver, 1951, M.S., 1952; m. Flora Charlotte Sievers, Mar. 20, 1948; children—Charla Lee, Merlyn Leigh. Research engr. Denver Research Inst., U. Denver, 1951-56; owner-operator Fluo-X-Spec Lab., Denver, 1956—; cons. in field. Served with AUS, 1943-45, 45-47. Mem. Am. Chem. Soc., Soc. for Applied Spectroscopy (Outstanding Service award 1970), Am. Soc. Metals, Sigma Xi, Tau Beta Pi, Phi Lambda Upsilon. Omicron Delta Kappa. Democrat. Contbr. articles to profl. jours; editor column Applied Spectroscopy. Address: 718 Sherman St Denver CO 80203

SALMON, VINCENT, acoustical consultant; b. Kingston, Jamaica, Jan. 21, 1912; came to U.S., 1914; s. Albert James and Ethlin (Baruch) S.; m. Madeline L. Giuffra, June 11, 1937 (dec. 1977); children—Margaret Elizabeth, Jean Louise. B.A., Temple U., 1934, M.A., 1936; Ph.D., MIT, 1938. Registered profl. engr., Calif., Ill. Physicist research and devel. Jensen Mfg. Co., Chgo., 1939-49; mgr. sonics sect. Stanford Research Inst., Menlo Park, Calif., 1949-65; staff scientist SRI Internat., Menlo Park, Calif., 1965—; acoustical cons., Chgo., 1946-49, Menlo Park, 1949-71, 76—; dir. Acoustical Services, v.p., sec. Indsl. Health, Inc., 1971-76; cons. prof. dept. aeronautics and astronautics Stanford U., Calif., 1977—. Contbr. articles to profl. jours.; inventor new family of horns, 1942, 46. Pres. Palo Alto Sr. Housing Project, Calif., 1966; v.p. Stebbins Found. for Community Facilities, San Francisco, 1966; pres. Planned Parenthood Assn. of Santa Clara County, 1967, Sr. Coordinating Council of Palo Alto, 1971. Recipient Disting. Alumnus award Temple U., Phila., 1964. Fellow Acoustical Soc. Am. (pres. 1970-71, Biennial award 1946, Silver Medal in engring. acoustics 84), Audio Engring. Soc. (life charter, western v.p. 1958-59); mem. Chgo. Audio and Acoustical Group (founder, pres. 1948), Inst. Noise Control Engring. (pres. 1974-75), Nat. Council of Acoustical Cons. (pres. 1969-71). Democrat. Unitarian. Club: Stanford Faculty. Avocations: chamber music; photography; automobile technology. Home: 765 Hobart St Menlo Park CA 94025

SALOMON, LOTHAR LUDWIG, science administrator, biochemist; b. Buedingen, Fed. Republic of Germany, Nov. 8, 1921; came to U.S., 1938; s. Max and Bertha (Mayer) S.; m. Erica Oppenheimer, June 18, 1950; children: Roberta Dee, Carolyn Jean, Barbara Ann. BS, Columbia U., 1949, MA, 1950, PhD, 1952. From instr. to assoc. prof. med. sch. U. Tex., Galveston, 1952-64; chief, biol. div. Dugway (Utah) Proving Ground, 1964-71, dir. test ops. directorate, 1972-75, dir. material testing directorate, 1976-82, sci. dir., 1982—. Contbr. chemistry articles to profl. jours.; devel. sci. methods. Served with U.S. Army, 1943-46. Grantee NSF, 1955-57, NIH, 1956-64. Fellow AAAS; mem. Am. Chem. Soc., Am. Soc. Biol. Chemists, Biol. Soc. Eng., Sigma Xi, Phi Lambda Upsilon. Avocations: silversmithing, photography. Home: 2 Armitage Dr Dugway UT 84022 Office: Dugway Proving Ground Office Commdr Dugway UT 84022

SALOT, STUART EDWIN, testing laboratory executive; b. Los Angeles, Oct. 23, 1937; s. David and Betty S.; children—Douglas, Deborah; m. Martha Corian, 1986. A.B., U. Calif.-Berkeley, 1960; Ph.D., U. So. Calif., 1969. Diplomate Am. Bd. Indsl. Hygiene. Asst. prof. chemistry Calif. State U. System, Los Angeles, 1969-72; dir. tech. services Daylin Corp., Los Angeles, 1972-74; pres. CTL Environ. Services, Los Angeles, 1974—; cons. Author tech. papers. Mem. Am. Chem. Soc., Am. Indsl. Hygiene Assn., Air Pollution Control Assn. Office: CTL Environ Services 2905 E Century Blvd South Gate CA 90280

SALRIN, ROBERT EUGENE, manufacturing company executive; b. Elyria, Ohio, Nov. 16, i927; s. Raymond Augustus and Helen Marie (Brucken) S.; student Fenn Coll., 1950; m. Mary Jean Kohl, Jan. 3, 1947; children—Robert Eugene, michael Thomas, Sheila Marie. Chief mfg. engr. Lear, Inc., Santa Monica, Calif. and Elyria, 1959; mfg. mgr. Litton Industries, Woodland Hills, Calif., 1959-62; dir. ops. Northrop Cdrp., Hawthorne, Calif., 1962-68; group v.p. internat. Rectifier Corp., El Segundo, Calif., 1968-70; v.p. A.C. & C., Inc., Torrance, Calif., 1970; pres. indsl. products group Aeronca, Inc., Montebello, Calif., 1971-73, corp., v.p. environ. controls group, Charlotte, N.C., 1973-76; pres. Western Methods Corp., Gardena, Calif., 1976-77, dir., 1976-78; gen. mgr. So. Calif. Signal Industries, Carlsbad, 1976-77; staff v.p. mfg. Bourns, Inc., Riverside, Calif., 1977-78, pres. Bourns Instruments, Inc. subs. Bourns, Inc., 1978—, sr. v.p. tech. products, 1980—. Registered profl. engr., Calif. Commnr. Riverside Airport. Mem. Am. Prodn. and inventory Control Soc., Instrument Soc. Am., Soc. Mfg. Engrs. Republican. Roman Catholic. Club: Victoria. Lodge: Elks. Home: 6718 Rycroft Dr Riverside CA 92506 Office: Bourns Inc 1200 Columbia Ave Riverside CA 92507

SALSBURY, BARBARA GRACE, consumer specialist, consultant, author, lecturer, enterprises executive; b. Toledo, Dec. 27, 1937; d. Vincent Joseph and Dorothy Minerva (Ramm) Thayer; m. Larry Philip Salsbury, Sept. 24, 1959; children—Erin Scott, Sandi Grace Salsbury Simmons. Student El Camino Coll., 1954-56; student in Resource Mgmt. and Hone Econs., Brigham Young U., 1975—. Spl. faculty mem. Brigham Young U., Provo, Utah, 1972—; consumer specialist Channel 20 TV Salt Lake City; shopping expert Gt. Am. Homemaker Show, U.S.A. Cable TV; guest lectr., condr. workshops and seminars on consumerism, emergency homepreparedness, practical home mgmt., supermarket survival, self improvement, various groups U.S., Can., 1961—. Leader, tchr. Women's Relief Soc. Orgn. Calif.-Wash., 1960—. Author: Just Add Water, 1972; Tasty Imitations, 1973; Just in Case, 1975; If You Must Work, 1976; Cut Your Grocery Bills in Half, 1982; booklets: The Lowly Little Lentil, 1971, Basic Home Drying of Fruits and Vegetables, 1975, Plan or Panic, 1983, The Best Time to Buy, 1985, Supermarket Survival, 1985, Emergency Evacuation!, 1986. Mem. Utah Authors League. Mormon. Office: PO Box 1305 Orem UT 84057

SALTA, STEVEN ANTHONY, infosystems executive; b. Portland, Oreg., Oct. 10, 1955; s. Joseph L. and Juanita M. (Sharp) S. BA, Portland State

U., 1978. Systems specialist Multnomah County Edn. Service Dist., Portland, 1978-79; team leader Tektronix, Inc., Beaverton, Oreg., 1979-81, project mgr., 1981-83, systems devel. mgr., 1983-85, infosystems mgr., 1985—; cons. Custom Software Systems, San Francisco, 1980-85. Contbr. articles to profl. jours. Mem. adv. bd. Boy Scouts Am., 1974; mem. computer sci. adv. bd. Portland Pub. Schs., 1980. Recipient Eagle Scout award Boy Scouts Am., 1969, William T. Hornaday award Boy Scouts Am., 1973. Mem. Data Processing Mgmt. Assn., Assn. Systems Mgmt. (Spl. Achievement award 1984), Assn. Computing Machinery, Computer Soc. of IEEE, Computer Profls. for Social Responsibility. Club: Hampton Court (Portland). Avocation: geology. Office: Tektronix Inc PO Box 500 MS 53/072 Beaverton OR 97077

SALTZBERG, EDWARD WOLFE, consulting mechanical engineer; b. Los Angeles, Oct. 24, 1932; s. Jack and Daisy (Etkin) Wolfe; m. Myrna Rae Kipper, Sept. 4, 1954; children: Diane Louise, Jack David. AA, Los Angeles City Coll., 1953; BS in Plumbing Engring., Calif. State U., Los Angeles, 1956. Registered profl. engr., Calif.; cert. Fire Protections Engr., Calif. Draftsman Febco Inc., 1953; elec. and mech. draftsman Los Angeles Dept. Water and Power, 1953-55; project engr. Gilbert J. Comeau, Cons. Mech. Engr., Los Angeles, 1955-58; asst. dept. head Welton Beckett & Assocs., Los Angeles, 1958-61; assoc. engr. Michael C. Maroko & Assocs., Los Angeles, 1961-67; pres. Edward Saltzberg & Assocs. Inc., Van Nuys, Calif., 1967—; journeyman plumber City of Los Angeles, 1956—, Piping Industry Progress and Edn., Los Angeles, 1985—; adj. extension prof. UCLA, 1968. Mem. editorial rev. bd. Plumbing Engr. mag., 1980—; contbr. articles to profl. jours. Chmn. San Fernando campaign com. United Jewish Welfare Fund; bd. dirs. San Fernando Valley Jewish Fedn. Council, Canoga Park, Calif., 1985—, Brandeis-Bardin Inst., Simi Vally, Calif., 1985—. Familian scholar; recipient Spl. Service awards United Jewish Welfare Fund, several years, Industry Man of Yr. award 1983. Mem. ASHRAE, Am. Soc. Plumbing Engrs. (co-founder, charter mem.), Internat. Assn. Plumbing and Mech. Ofcls., Soc. Fire Protection Engrs. (affiliate), Mech. Engrs. Assn. Calif. (bd. dirs., past pres., past sec.), Assn. Energy Engrs. (cert.), Am. Inst. Plant Engrs., Calif. Soc. Profl. Engrs., Nat. Assn. Forensic Engrs., Nat. Soc. Profl. Engrs. Republican. Avocations: stamp collecting, theater. Office: 14733 Oxnard St Van Nuys CA 91411

SALVATO, ROBERT VINCENT, radio station executive; b. Warren, Ohio, Nov. 24, 1948; s. Vincent Anthony and Frances May (Simone) S.; m. Cynthia Kay Hiner, Aug. 29, 1981. BA in Communications, Ohio State U., 1971; grad. spl. course radio advt., Wharton Sch. U. Pa., 1983. Account exec. Sta. KVOR-KSPZ Radio, Colorado Springs, 1978-79; account exec. Sta. KOSI Radio, Denver, 1979-82, local sales mgr., 1984, gen. sales mgr., 1984-85; gen. sales mgr. Sta. KJQY Radio, San Diego, 1985-87, sta. KKLQ Radio, San Diego, 1987—. Contbg. author: Radio In Search of Excellence. Mem. Denver Advt. Fedn. (bd. dirs. 1982-84), San Diego Advt. Fedn. Club: San Diego Athletic. Avocations: running, skiing, backpacking, squash. Home: 5004 Marlborough Dr San Diego CA 92116 Office: Sta KKLG Radio 8665 Gibbs Dr San Diego CA 92123

SALVERSON, CAROL ANN, theological library administrator, member clergy; b. Buffalo, June 30, 1944; d. Howard F. and Estella G. (Zelie) Heavener; B.A. in Philosophy, SUNY, Buffalo, 1966; M.S. in Library Sci., Syracuse U., 1968; grad. Sacred Coll. Jamilian Theology and Div. Sch., 1976. Library trainee and research asst. SUNY, Med. Center, Syracuse, 1966-67; asst. editor SUNY Union List of Serials, Syracuse, 1967-68; readers services librarian, asst. prof. Jefferson Community Coll., Watertown, N.Y., 1968-75; ordained to ministry Internat. Community of Christ Ch., 1974; adminstr. public services dept. Internat. Community of Christ, Chancellery, Reno, 1975-84, dir. Jamilian Theol. Research Library, 1975—; mem. faculty Sacred Coll. Jamilian U. of the Ordained, Reno, 1979—, Jamilian Parochial Sch., Internat. Community of Christ, 1978—. Chmn. religious edn. com. All Souls Unitarian-Universalist Ch., Watertown, N.Y., 1970-71, treas., 1974-75; trustee North Country Reference and Research Resources Council, Canton, N.Y., 1974-75; dir. Gene Savoy Heritage Museum and Library, 1984—; violist Symphonietta, Reno, 1983—. Mem. ALA, Nev. Library Assn., Friends of Library Washoe County, Friends of Library U. Nev. Club: Coll. Women's. Contbr. articles on library sci. to profl. jours. Home: 2025 La Fond Dr Reno NV 89509 Office: Internat Community of Christ Chancellory 643 Ralston St Reno NV 89503

SALVESON, MELVIN ERWIN, business executive, educator; b. Brea, Calif., Jan. 16, 1919; s. John T. and Elizabeth (Green) S.; m. Joan Y. Stipek, Aug. 22, 1944; children: Eric C., Kent Erwin. B.S., U. Calif. at Berkeley, 1941; M.S., Mass. Inst. Tech., 1947; Ph.D., U. Chgo., 1952. Cons. McKinsey & Co., N.Y.C., 1948-49; asst. prof., dir. mgmt. sci. research U. Calif. at Los Angeles, 1949-54; mgr. advanced data systems Gen. Electric Co., Louisville and N.Y.C., 1954-57; pres. Mgmt. Scis. Corp., Los Angeles, 1957-67; group v.p. Control Data/CEIR, Inc., 1967-68; pres. Electronic Currency Corp., 1968—; chmn. OneCard Internat., Inc., 1983—; dir. Diversified Earth Scis., Inc., Algeran, Inc., Electronic Currency Corp.; founder Master Charge System, Los Angeles, 1966; chmn. Corporate Strategies Internat.; prof. bus. Pepperdine U. 1972-85; adj. prof. U. So. Calif.; adviser data processing City of Los Angeles, 1962-64; futures forecasting IBM, 1957-61; adviser strategic systems planning USAF, 1961-67; info. systems Calif. Dept. Human Resources, 1972-73, City Los Angeles Automated Urban Data Base, 1962-67; tech. transfer NASA, 1965-70, others; mem. bd. trustees, Long Beach City Coll. Contbr. articles to profl. jours. Served to lt. comdr. USNR, 1941-46. Named to Long Beach City Coll. Hall of Fame. Fellow AAAS; mem. Inst. Mgmt. Sci. (founder, past pres.). Republican. Club: Founders (Los Angeles Philharmonic Orch.), Calif. Yacht. Home: 1577 N Bundy Dr Los Angeles CA 90049

SALWAK, DALE FRANCIS, English language educator, writer; b. Greenfield, Mass., Feb. 7, 1947; s. Stanley Francis and Frances Helen (Bachelder) S.; m. Patricia Lynn Dunham, Mar. 19, 1983. BA, Purdue U., 1969; MA, U. So. Calif., 1970, PhD, 1974. Asst. editor dept. agrl. info. Purdue U., West Lafayette, Ind., 1966-69; English instr. U. So. Calif., Los Angeles, 1972-73; prof. English Citrus Coll., Glendora, Calif., 1973—. Author: John Wain, 1981, Literary Voices: Interviews with Britain's "Angry Young Men", 1984, A.J. Cronin: A Reference Guide, 1983, Mystery Voices: Interviews with Britain's Mystery Writers, 1986, The Life and Work of Barbara Pym, 1987; contbr. articles to profl. publs. Fellow NEH, 1985, NDEA Title IV, U. So. Calif., 1969-72. Mem. MLA, Calif. Tchrs. Assn., Soc. Antiquity and Christianity, Acad. Magical Arts (Magician of Yr., 1977, 78). Clubs: Reform, Magic Circle (London). Avocations: piano, golf, magic. Home: 350 E Del Mar Blvd #303 Pasadena CA 91101 Office: Citrus Coll 1000 W Foothill Blvd Glendora CA 91740

SALZMAN, JUDITH B., computer co. exec.; b. Chgo., Sept. 16, 1943; d. Marshall and Helaine (Friedlen) Salzman; B.A., North Park Coll., Chgo., 1976; m. Michael J. Maximov, June 20, 1965 (div. 1983); children—Justin, Marc, Hannah. Cert. fire fighter Ariz., med. first responder. Chairwoman, Ariz. ERA Coalition, 1976-80; owner, operator Judith's Computer Works, Tucson, 1978—; relief postmaster Mt. Lemmon, 1986—. Bd. dirs. Temple Emanu-El, Tucson, 1982-83; bd. dirs., fundraising chairwoman Tucson Center for Women and Children, 1982-84; pres. Tucson sect. Nat. Council Jewish Women, 1982-84, bd. dirs., 1980-82; pres. Women in Tucson, 1982-83; v.p. Mt. Lemmon Homeowners Assn., 1981-82, pres., 1982-83; mem. Mt. Lemmon Vol. Fire Dept., 1983-87; participant Leadership Tucson, 1981, Leadership Tucson Alumni, 1982—. Address: PO Box 675 Mount Lemmon AZ 85619

SALZMAN, MARILYN B. WOLFSON, service company executive; b. Chgo., Dec. 25, 1943; d. Joseph and Sera (Krol) Wolfson; 1 son, Lawrence Todd. Student, U. Ill., Barat Coll., Lake Forest, Ill., 1961-64. Adminstrv. project asst. Sci. Research Assocs., Chgo., 1964-70; reporter Suburban Trib of Chgo. Tribune, 1979-80; pres. MWS Assocs., Los Angeles and Fullerton, Calif., 1980—; exec. adminstrv. dir. Crystal Tips of No. Ill., Inc., 1980-83; dir. adminstrn. Ice Dispensers, Inc., 1981-83, Sani-Serv of Ill., Inc., 1981-83; adminstrv. and organizational cons. 1140 Corp., 1980-83; adminstrv. dir. Iceman's Ico Co., Inc., 1980-83; founder, moderator DWC Workshops, 1984; mgr. data processing Florence Crittenton Services Orange County 1984—; panelist computers in residential treatment Child Welfare League Am. Bienniel Conf. Workshop, 1986. Active Friends of Fullerton Library, Boy Scouts Am.; panelist Child Welfare League Am., Bienniel Conf. Workshop. Mem. Mgmt. Forum, Women's Am. ORT. Contbr. articles to newspapers and indsl. jours. Home: 1112 N Ferndale Dr Fullerton CA 92631

SALZMAN, RICHARD WILLIAM, artist representative; b. Los Angeles, Nov. 22, 1958; s. Paul and Anne (Meyersburg) S.; student public schs., Los Angeles. Stockboy, Marathon Clothing, Los Angeles, 1976-77, salesman, 1977, sales and mgmt. trainee, 1977-78, br. mgr., San Francisco, 1978-80, San Diego, 1980-82; artist rep., 1982—. tchr. freelance bus. practices San Diego City Coll.; mem. adv. bd. Fashion Careers of Calif. Mem. Union of Concerned Scientists, Green Peace, Environ. Def. Fund, Coalition for Non-Nuclear World, Communicating Arts Group San Diego, Internat. Assn. Bus. Communicators, Soc. Photographers and Artists Reps., Am. Inst. Graphic Arts, Graphic Artist Guild, Art Dirs. and Designers of Orange County, San Diego Ad Club, ACLU. Democrat. Home and office: 1352 Hornblend St San Diego CA 92109

SALZMAN, WILLIAM RONALD, chemistry educator; b. Cut Bank, Mont., Feb. 27, 1936; s. Ralph Irwin and Oleta Fern (Owens) S.; m. Virginia Ann Harbin; children: Suzanne R., Sandra R. BS in Chemistry, UCLA, 1959, MS in Physics, 1964, PhD in Chemistry, 1967. Asst. prof. chemistry U. Ariz., Tucson, 1967-72, assoc. prof., 1972-77, prof., 1979—; head dept. chem., U. Ariz., 1977-83. Contbr. numerous articles to profl. jours. Served with U.S. Army, 1959-61. Mem. AAAS, Am. Chem. Soc., Am. Physical Soc., Am. Assn. Univ. Profs., Sigma Xi. Republican. Avocations: computers, music, bicycling. Home: 6736 E Rosewood Circle Tucson AZ 85721 Office: U Ariz Dept Chemistry Tucson AZ 83721

SAM, GORDON KWAI FONG, nuclear engineer; b. Honolulu, July 18, 1937; s. King Chew and Lily Ah See (Zane) S.; m. Betty Navarro, July 3, 1965; 1 child, Stephen. B.S. in Chem. Engring., U. Mich., 1960; M.B.A., U. Hawaii, 1978. Registered profl. engr., Hawaii, Calif. Nuclear test engr. Pearl Harbor Shipyard, Hawaii, 1963-68, chief test engr., 1968-73, nuclear type desk mgr., 1973-80, project mgr., 1983-84, nuclear planning mgr., 1980—. Mem. choir Star of Sea Ch., Honolulu, 1973—; mem. adv. bd. Salvation Army Residential Treatment Facility for Youth and Children. Served to 1st lt. U.S. Army, 1961-63. Recipient Navy Meritorius Civilian Service award, 1984. Mem. Am. Inst. Chem. Engrs., Nat. Soc. Profl. Engrs., Alpha Chi Sigma. Roman Catholic. Club: U. Mich. (Honolulu) (pres. 1978—). Avocation: Karate (black belt). Home: 362 Kikoo Pl Honolulu HI 96825

SAMEK, PAUL HERMAN, apparel manufacturing company exec.; b. New Rochelle, N.Y., May 28, 1923; s. Emil and Sophie (Rich) S.; student U. Wis., 1942; B.A., Dartmouth U., 1945; m. Sibella Oursler, Feb. 16, 1975 (div. 1978); 1 son, Benjamin George; m. Arlene Ellen Du Boff, Dec. 22, 1979; stepchildren—Mark Rosman, Rene Rosman. Actor, Barter Theatre, Abingdon, Va., 1939; radio announcer Sta. WDAE, Tampa, Fla., 1947; newspaper display salesman Tampa Daily Times, 1949; owner, operator women's specialty shop, Winston-Salem, N.C., 1950-57; territorial buyer Sears, Roebuck & Co., Alhambra, Calif., 1957-80; pres. Street Scene of Calif., Inc., Los Angeles, 1980—. Pres., founder Big Bros. Am., Jacksonville, Fla., 1961; v.p. apparel industry div. Save A Life, Los Angeles, 1970-79, pres., 1979-81. Served with USNR, 1942-44; PTO. Mem. Dartmouth Club Fla. (sec. 1960). Lodges: Masons, Shriners. Home: 4461 Van Noord Ave Studio City CA 91604 Office: Street Scene of Calif 530 E 8th St Los Angeles CA 90014

SAMFORD, JUDITH LEE, psychologist, consultant; b. Wayne County, Ill., Nov. 22, 1939; d. Ernest Lawrence and Mary Lutitia (Templeman) L.; m. Donald Francis, Dec. 23, 1967 (div. 1978); 1 child, Lance Adams. BS in Edn., So. Ill. U., 1960, MS, 1963; postgrad., Bradley U., 1965; PhD, Fla. Inst. Tech., 1981. Lic. psychologist, Ill, Hawaii. Psychologist Mo. Dept. Mental Health, St. Louis, 1962-64, Ill. Div. Alcoholism, Chgo., 1964-69; mental health adminstr. Ill. Dept. Mental Health, Chgo., 1969-84; chief of service-geriatrics Chgo. Read Mental Health Ctr., 1985-86; instr. U. Hawaii, Kauai, 1986—; cons. Forkosh Hosp., Chgo., 1981-86; organizer, leader Alateen Group, Carbondale, Ill. Co-author: Illinois State Plan for Alcoholism, 1974. Bd. dirs. So. Ill. Com. on Alcoholic Concerns, Carbondale, 1965-67. Recipient I Dare You award Danforth Found., 1952-57. Mem. Am. Psychol. Assn., Am. Soc. Clin. Hypnosis, Chgo. Soc. Clin. Hypnosis, Internat. Soc. Hypnosis, Nat. Edn. Assn., VFW, Am. Legion, Alpha Lambda Delta, Kappa Omicron Phi. Democrat. Club: 4-H (Wayne County). Avocations: reading, horticulture. Office: Box 845 Waimea Kauai HI 96796

SAMLOFF, I. MICHAEL, gastroenterology educator; b. Rochester, N.Y., Jan. 24, 1932; s. Max and Bluma (Rabinovitz) S.; divorced; children: Ann, David. Student, Cornell U., 1949-52; MD cum laude, SUNY, Syracuse, 1956. From asst. to assoc. prof. gastroenterology U. Rochester (N.Y.) Sch. Med., 1965-68, asst. prof. psychiatry, 1965-68; assoc. prof. U. So. Calif. Sch. Med., Los Angeles, 1968-72; prof. UCLA, 1972—; assoc. chief of staff research VA Med. Ctr., Sepulveda, Calif., 1980—; chief div. gastroenterology Harbor-UCLA Med. Ctr., 1968-80; investigator Ctr. for Ulcer Research and Edn., Los Angeles, 1974—. Editor: The Genetics and Heterogeneity of Common Gastrointestinal Disorders, 1980, Pepsinogens in Man: Clinial and Genetic Advances, 1985. Served to capt. USAF, 1959-61. Fellow ACP; mem. Am. Gastroenterol. Assn., Am. Soc. Clin. Investigation, Western Assn. of Physicians, Western Soc. for Clin. Research. Home: 3611 Sapphire Dr Encino CA 91436 Office: Research 151 VA Med Ctr 16111 Plummer St Sepulveda CA 91343

SAMPLES, KARL CLIFTON, university researcher, educator; b. Seattle, Mar. 20, 1954; s. Loy Clifton and Maryann (Maclellen) S.; m. Carol Elizabeth Campbell, June 17, 1979; 1 child, Kyle C. BS in Fgn. Service, Georgetown U., 1975; MA, U. Wis., 1978, PhD, 1980. Asst. prof. U. Hawaii, Honolulu, 1980-86, assoc. prof., 1986—. Mem. editorial bd. Western Jour. of Agrl. Econs., 1983—; contbr. articles to profl. jours. Mem. Am. Agrl. Econs. Assn., Western Agrl. Econs. Assn., Am. Fisheries Soc., AAUP, Phi Beta Kappa. Office: U Hawaii Dept Agrl Econs 210 Bilger Hall Honolulu HI 96822

SAMPLINER, DONALD WALLACE, psychologist; b. Cleve., May 4, 1928; s. Jerome Mortimer and Charlotte J. Sampliner; B.A., UCLA, 1941, M.A., 1949; postgrad. Calif. State U.-Los Angeles, 1952-53. Tchr., Los Angeles City Schs., 1948-75; lectr. psychology Los Angeles City Coll., 1952-84; host radio program Sta. KPFK, 1971-74, Sta. KMAX-FM, 1973-78; prod., annotator phonograph records, 1982—. Coordinator, CanServ program Good Samaritan Hosp., 1975; pres. Canyon Dr. Hollywood Hills Improvement Assn., 1977-80. Mem. Am. Psychol. Assn., Am. Fedn. Tchrs. Coll. Guild, Theatre Hist. Soc., Am. Theatre Organ Soc. (chmn. Los Angeles chpt. 1961-62). Home: 5823 Green Oak Dr Hollywood CA 90068

SAMPSON, CAROL ANN, interior design firm executive, writer; b. Wabash, Ind., Dec. 5, 1942; d. John Roland Bennett and Virginia Ann (Garthwait) Mulholland; student Bradley U., 1961-62; AA, Riverside City Coll., 1971; BS cum laude, Woodbury U., 1975; children: Tracy Lee, John Russell IV (Arrison). Interior designer Imperial Co., Riverside, Calif., 1971-72; asso. interior designer Booth & Assos., Riverside, 1972-74; owner, prin., project designer Carol Sampson's Interior Designs, Riverside, 1974—; tchr. interior design bus. procedures San Bernardino Valley Coll., 1978—; house and home editor Inland Empire mag., 1978—; interior design staff writer Inland Empire Bus. Quar., 1978-81; home interiors editor for Inland News on cable TV for Falcon, Liberty and Group P-W stas.; interior design cons. radio program Sta. KPRO, Riverside, 1978-81. Recipient Gold Key award (2), Nat. Home Fashions League, 1975, Proclamation award City of Riverside Mayor's Office. Mem. Internat. Soc. Interior Designers (profl.). Episcopalian. Office: Carol Sampson Interior Designs 6876 Indiana Ave Riverside CA 92506

SAMPSON, EARL DELOS, language educator; b. Rifle, Colo., Jan. 26, 1935; s. Charles Earl and Effie (Harvey) S.; m. Eleni Callas, May 21, 1965. Student, Middlebury Coll., 1959; BA, U. Colo., 1960; MA, Harvard U., 1961, PhD, 1968; postgrad., Moscow U., 1973, 83. Instr. Russian Lang. and Lit. U. Colo., Boulder, 1963-64, asst. prof., 1964-74, assoc. prof., 1974—. Author: Nikolay Gumilev, 1979; translator: A History of Pugachev, 1984; contbr. articles to profl. jours. Treas. Greek Orthodox Ch., Boulder 1982-86. Served with U.S. Army, 1954-57. Mem. Am. Assn. Tchrs. Slavic and East European Langs. (pres. Colo. chpt. 1986—), Colo. Congress Fgn. Lang. Tchrs. (scholar 1984), Rocky Mountain Modern Lang. Assn., Pan-Cretan Assn. Am. (conv. com. Cretefs chpt. 1986), Am. Council Tchrs. Russian. Democrat. Avocations: wine appreciation, personal computers. Home: 922 12th St Boulder CO 80302 Office: U of Colo Dept of Slavic Langs & Lit Campus Box 279 Boulder CO 80309

SAMPSON, LOWELL WOOLF, quality control engineer; b. Van Nuys, Calif., June 1, 1958; s. Bon Easton and Sara Dora (Woolf) S.; m. Debra Hurd; children: Anthony Lowell, Tana Charmayne. BS, Utah State U., 1982, postgrad., 1985—. Project mgr. Utah State U. Found., Logan, 1979-80; project developer Utah State U., Logan, 1980-81; quality control mgr. Tri-Miller Packing Co., Logan, 1981—. Ralston Purina scholar, 1981. Mem. Inst. Food Technologists, Am. Soc. Quality Control. Republican. Mormon. Home: 489 E Center Smithfield UT 84335 Office: Tri-Miller Packing Co 510 W 400 N Hyrum UT 84319

SAMPSON, RUTH LOUISE, endocrinologist; b. Providence, Oct. 1, 1947; d. Albert Palmer and Winifred Silk (Lilly) S. AB in Biology, Brown U., 1969; MD, Tufts U., 1973. Diplomate Am. Bd. Internal Medicine, Am. Bd. Endocrinology. Resident NE Deaconess Hosp., Boston, 1973-76; fellow in endocrinology Baystate Med. Ctr., Springfield, Mass., 1976-78; practice medicine specializing in endocrinology Missoula, Mont., 1978—; affiliate Missoula Gen. Hosp., Missoula Community Hosp., St. Patrick Hosp., Missoula, 1978—. Treas. Mont. Libertarians, Missoula, 1980-82, 85-87; vice chairperson Mont. Libertarians, Missoula, 1983. Mem. Am. Diabetes Assn., Am. Thyroid Assn., Phi Beta Kappa, Sigma Xi. Office: 554 W Broadway Missoula MT 59802

SAMPSON, WALLACE IRA, physician, educator; b. Los Angeles, Mar. 29, 1930; s. David J. and Bernice Miriam (Freilich) S.; m. Mary Rita Landry, July 30, 1956; children: Robert T., Paul R., Charles R., Daniel E., David J. AB, U. Calif., Berkeley, 1952; MD, U. Calif., San Francisco, 1955. Diplomate Am. Bd. Internal Medicine. Assoc. clin. prof. medicine Stanford (Calif.) U., 1970—, now clin. prof. medicine; chmn. cancer adv. council Calif. Dept. Health Services, 1985—. Author: chpt. The Health Robbers, 1982. Fellow ACP; mem. Calif. Med. Assn. (chmn. com. health edn. of the pub. 1981—), Santa Clara County Med. Soc. (pres. 1986-87). Office: 515 South Dr Mountain View CA 94040

SAMSON, ANTHONY DONALD, lawyer; b. Huntington Park, Calif., Nov. 27, 1933; s. Nick and Alice Marguerite (Livingston) Hulbert S.; m. Betty White, May 1, 1957 (div. June 1964); 1 child, Nickie Michelle; m. Gloria Perez, Jan. 30, 1965; children—Ixchel Alyssa, Kyra Marina. A.A., Riverside City Coll., 1958; A.B., U. Calif.-Riverside, 1963; J.D., UCLA, 1968. Bar: Calif. 1969, U.S. Dist. Ct. (so. dist.) Calif. 1969. Asst. credit mgr. Sears Roebuck & Co., Riverside, Calif., 1957-65; sole practice, Riverside, 1968-70; chief fraud div. San Diego Dist. Atty.'s Office, 1983—; lectr. Fla. Gov.'s Conf., Orlando, 1975, Nat. Coll. Dist. Attys., Houston, 1978; lectr., cons. Tng. Ctr., Dept. Justice, Sacramento, 1978—. Treas. Democratic Profl. Club, San Diego, 1978—; del. State Dem. Conv., Sacramento, 1983, Conf. Dels. to State Bar, 1985-86; bd. dirs. Utility Consumer Action Network, San Diego, 1983. Served with U.S. Army, 1953-55, Korea, Japan. Recipient Cert. of Appreciation, So. Calif. Fraud Investigators, Ventura, 1982, 83, Disting. Service award Calif. Dist. Atty. Investigators Santa Barbara, 1983. Mem. Consumer Protection Council (sec. 1980-83), State Bar Calif. (exec. com. real property sect. 1986-87, consumer fin. subcom. bus. law sect. 1986-87, del. conf. of dels. 1984-86), Calif. Dist. Attys. Assn., San Diego County Bar Assn., San Diego Lawyer's Club. Democrat. Episcopalian. Office: San Diego Dist Atty 220 W Broadway San Diego CA 92103

SAMUELI, HENRY, electrical engineering educator; b. Buffalo, Sept. 20, 1954; s. Aron and Sala (Traubman) S.; m. Susan Faye Eisenberg, Aug. 22, 1982; children: Leslie Pamela, Jillian Meryl. BS, UCLA, 1975, MS, 1976, PhD, 1980. Staff engr. TRW Inc., Redondo Beach, Calif., 1980-83, section mgr., 1983-85; asst. prof. UCLA, 1985—; cons. TRW, Inc., Redondo Beach, 1985—. Mem. IEEE, Sigma Xi, Tau Beta Pi. Republican. Jewish. Avocations: skiing, basketball, personal computers. Office: UCLA Elec Engring Dept 6731 Boelter Hall Los Angeles CA 90024

SAMUELS, NORRMA, communication company executive; b. N.Y.C., May 18, 1947. BA in Writing, CCNY, 1968. Dir. circulation fulfillment and mailing services Hester Communications Inc., Santa Ana, Calif., 1979-81; gen. mgr. Amrron Data Services div. Mutogo Data Corp., Irvine, Calif., 1981—. Mem. Western Fulfillment Mgmt. Assn. Inc. (v.p. membership 1982-83, 86—, bd. dirs. 1981, 84-85), Mensa, Intertel. Avocations: crafts, reading. Home: 1546 Coriander Dr Costa Mesa CA 92626 Office: Amrron Data Services Div Mutogo Data Corp 1801 Newport Circle Santa Ana CA 92705

SANBORN, DOROTHY CHAPPELL, librarian; b. Nashville, Apr. 26, 1920; d. William S. and Sammie Maude (Drake) Chappell; BA, U. Tex., 1941; MA, George Peabody Coll., 1947; MPA, Golden Gate U., 1982; m. Richard Donald Sanborn, Dec. 1, 1943; children: Richard Donald, William Chappell. Asst. cataloger El Paso (Tex.) Pub. Library, 1947-52, Library of Hawaii, Honolulu, 1953; cataloger Redwood (Calif.) City Pub. Library, 1954-55, 57-59, Stanford Research Inst., Menlo Park, Calif., 1955-57; librarian Auburn (Calif.) Pub. Library, 1959-62; cataloger Sierra Coll., Rocklin, Calif., 1962-64; reference librarian Sacramento City Library, 1964-66; county librarian Placer County (Calif.), Auburn, 1966—; chmn. Mountain Valley Library System, 1970-71, 75-76, 1984-85; cons. county librarian Alpine County Library, Markleeville, Calif., 1973-80. Served with WAVES, 1944-46. Mem. AAUW (pres. chpt. 1982-84), ALA, Calif. Library Assn. Democrat. Mem. United Ch. Christ. Club: Soroptimists. Home: 135 Midway St Auburn CA 95603 Office: Auburn Placer County Library 350 Nevada St Auburn CA 95603

SANBORN, FRANK GEORGE, physiotherapist, acupuncturist; b. Ft. Wayne, Ind., Oct. 23, 1943; s. Frank and Violet (Waring) S.; student No. Coll. Phys. Therapies Life Scis. Inst., 1976; cert. Nat. Acad. Acupuncture, 1978; children—Michael, Tabitha. Physiotherapist, Vienna Clinics, until 1978; owner Stillpoint Clinics, Calgary, Alta., 1977-82; acupuncturist Royal Acupuncture Accupressure Assocs., 1980-81; nutritional cons. Can. Mt. Everest Expdn., 1982, Calgary rowing team, Can. full contact karate team; rep. Can. div. No. Coll. Phys. Therapies, Blackpool, Eng., 1976-79; dir. Northwestern Sch. Massage, Calgary, 1980—; bd. dirs. Calgary Currie Progressive Conservative Assn. Alta., 1979-84, Provincial United Found. Masseurs and Physars, 1980-81. Lic. physiotherapist. Served with USAF, 1962-66. Home: 39 Falsby Way, Calgary, AB Canada T3J 1C2 Office: Stillpoint Clinics Ltd, 10-519 17th Ave SW, Calgary, AB Canada T2S 0A9

SANBURN, ALLYSON ANNE, advertising agency executive; b. Fullerton, Calif., Mar. 21, 1953; d. Donald Duane and LaVerta Anne (Scott) Sanburn; m. Thomas A.E. Shumard, Nov. 11, 1970 (div.); 1 child, Jennifer Anne; m. Safwat Malek, Oct. 4, 1986. AA in Journalism, Fullerton Coll., 1976. Advt. asst. K. Esterley & Assoc., La Habra, Calif., 1977-78; advt. prodn. mgr. Technicolor Audio-Visual Co., Costa Mesa, Calif., 1978-79; graphic cons. Franciscan Graphics Co., Mountain View, Calif., 1979-81; account supr. Collateral Resources Unltd., Mountain View, 1981-82; pres. Sanburn Co., Inc., Palo Alto, Calif., 1982—. Active Calif. Hist. Soc. Recipient Leif Johnson Meml. award Fullerton News Tribune, 1974; Alpha Gamma Eta Woman of Distinction award Associated Students Fullerton Coll., 1975; Mem. Peninsula Women in Advt. (advt. dir.).

SANCHEZ, AMBROSIO, microbiologist, educator; b. Albuquerque, Feb. 26, 1931; s. Francisco Sanchez and Josepha (Montoya) Lucero; m. Melita F. Valencia, Sept. 3, 1960 (dec. Nov. 1970); children: Ricardo A., Carmel T., Phillip A.; m. Kathleen Decker Kadas, Jan. 6, 1973. BS, U. N.Mex., 1960, MS, 1974. Sr. research technologist Lovelace-Inhalation Toxicology Research Inst., Albuquerque, 1962-74, tng. coordinator, 1974-76, investigator, lab. set-up cons., 1976-80, clin. microbiologist, 1976—, support service microbiologist, 1980—. Contbr. articles to profl. jours. Mem. bd. govs. Duke City Marathon, Albuquerque, 1985—. Mem. Am. Soc. Microbiologists, Master Runners Unltd, Sigma Xi. Roman Catholic. Avocations:

running, race walking, reading. Home: 4601 Algiers Dr NE Albuquerque NM 87111

SANCHEZ, GILBERT, university president, microbiologist, researcher; b. Belen, N.Mex., May 7, 1938; s. Macedonio C. and Josephine H. Sanchez; m. Lorena T. Tabet, Aug. 26, 1961; children—Elizabeth, Phillip, Katherine. B.S. in Biology, N.Mex. State U., 1961; Ph.D. in Microbiology, U. Kans., 1967. Research asst. U. Kans., Lawrence, 1963-67; research assoc., postdoctoral fellow Rice U., Houston, 1967-68; prof. N.Mex. Inst. Tech., Socorro, 1968-79; dean grad. studies Eastern N.Mex. U., Portales, 1979-83; v.p. acad. affairs U. So. Colo., Pueblo, 1983-85; pres. N.Mex. Highlands U., Las Vegas, 1985—; cons. NIH, NSF, Solvex Corp., Albuquerque, 1979-83. Contbr. numerous articles to profl. jours. Patentee in field. Pres. Socorro Sch. Bd., 1974-79, Presbyn. Hosp. Bd., Socorro, 1977-79. Research grantee Dept. Army, 1976-79, N.Mex. Dept. Energy, 1979-83, NSF, 1979. Mem. Am. Soc. Microbiology, Am. Soc. Indsl. Microbiology, AAAS, Am. Assn. Univs. and Colls. Roman Catholic. Lodge: Rotary. Avocations: auto mechanics; welding; woodworking; golf. Office: N Mex Highlands U Las Vegas NM 87701

SANCHEZ, RAYMOND G., state legislator; b. Albuquerque, Sept. 22, 1941; s. Gillie and Priscilla S.; m. Elizabeth Stanford, 1964; 1 son, Raymond Michael. B.A., U. N. Mex., 1964, J.D., 1967. Bar: N. Mex. 1967. Mem. N. Mex. Ho. of Reps., 1977—, speaker. Bd. dirs. Community Council, Albuquerque; bd. dirs. NCCJ. Mem. N. Mex. Bar Assn. (mem. con. on jud. selection and reform, law study com.), U. N. Mex. Alumni Assn. (dir.). Democrat. Office: Office of Speaker State Capitol Santa Fe NM 87501 also: PO Box 1966 Albuquerque NM 87103 *

SANCHEZ, ROBERT FORTUNE, archbishop; b. Socorro, N.Mex., Mar. 20, 1934; s. Julius C. and Priscilla (Fortune) S. Student, Immaculate Heart Sem., Santa Fe, 1954, N.Am. Coll., Gregorian U., Rome, 1960. Ordained priest Roman Cath. Ch., 1959; prof. St. Piux X High Sch., Albuquerque, 1960-68; dir. extension lay vols. Archdiocese Santa Fe, 1965-68, chmn. priest personnel bd., 1968-72, vicar gen., 1974, archbishop, 1974—; rep. instl. ministry pastoral care N.Mex. Council Chs., 1968; pres. Archdiocesan Priests Senate, 1973-74; rep. region X Nat. Fedn. Priests Councils, 1972-73; bd. dirs. Mexican Am. Cultural Center; mem. regional com. Nat. Conf. Catholic Bishops, N.Am. Coll., Rome; pres. N.Mex. Conf. Chs. Mem. U.S. Cath. Conf. (chmn. ad hoc com. Spanish speaking). Address: The Cath Ctr Archdiocese of Santa Fe St Joseph Pl NW Albuquerque NM 87120

SANCHEZ, VICTORIA WAGNER, science educator; b. Milw., Apr. 11, 1934; s. Arthur William and Lorraine Marguerite (Kocovsky) Wagner; m. Rozier Edmond Sanchez, June 23, 1956; children: Mary Elizabeth, Carol Anne, Robert Edmond, Catherine Marie, Linda Therese. BS cum laude, Mt. Mary Coll., 1955; MS, Marquette U., 1957; postgrad., U. N.Mex., 1979-86. Cert. secondary tchr., N.Mex. Chemist Nat. Bur. Standards, Washington, 1958-60; tchr., chmn. sci. dept. Albuquerque Pub. Schs., 1979—; chmn. pub. info. area convention Nat. Sci. Tchrs. Assn., 1984, mem. sci. review com. Albuquerque Pub. Schs., 1985-86. Bd. dirs. Encino House, Albuquerque, 1976—, treas., 1977-79; leader Albuquerque troop Girl Scouts U.S., 1966-77. Named Outstanding Sci. Tchr. N.W. Regional Sci. Fair, Albuquerque, 1983; recipient St. George's award N.Mex. Cath. Scouting com., Albuquerque, 1978, Focus on Excellence award Assn. Supervision and Curriculum Devel., Albuquerque, 1985. Mem. AAUW (Albuquerque br. officer 1976-77, N.Mex. div. officer 1977-78), Nat. Sci. Tchrs. Assn., N.Mex. Sci. Tchrs. Assn. (com. mem. 1986), Albuquerque Sci. Tchrs. Assn. (treas. 1984-85, v.p. and pres.-elect, 1986—), Albuquerque Rose Soc. (sec. 1962-63). Democrat. Roman Catholic. Avocations: reading, fishing, hiking, needlecraft, camping. Home: 7612 Palo Duro NE Albuquerque NM 87110 Office: Van Buren Sch 700 Louisiana SE Albuquerque NM 87108

SÁNCHEZ-LANIER, MARY ELIZABETH, virologist, researcher; b. Milw., Sept. 4, 1957; d. Rozier Edmund and Victoria Elizabeth (Wagner) Sánchez; m. Glen Lanier, July 26, 1980; children: Michael Edmund, Suzanne Marie. BS in Biology, U. N.Mex., 1979, PhD in Med. Scis., 1986. Lab. technician medicine dept. U. N.Mex., Albuquerque, 1979-80, research asst. microbiology dept., 1980-86, instr. neurology research, 1986—. Contbr. articles to profl. jours. Active premarital instrn. encounter weekends, Baptism preparation programs for Cath. Ch., Albuquerque, 1981—; judge sci. fairs Albuquerque Pub. Middle Schs., 1981—. Mem. AAAS, Am. Soc. Microbiology (N.Mex. chpt., minority predoctoral fellowship, 1983-85), N.Y. Acad. Sci. Democrat. Roman Catholic. Avocations: hiking, camping, sewing, biking. Office: U NMex Sch Med Microbiology Dept Albuquerque NM 87131

SANCIER, KENNETH MARTIN, research chemist; b. N.Y.C., June 21, 1920; s. Martin M. and Melitta M. (Straus) S. BS in Chemistry, Bklyn. Poly. Inst., 1942; MS in Chemisty, Johns Hopkins U., 1947, PhD in Chemistry, 1949. Gas chemist Linde Air Products Co., Buffalo, 1942-46; tchr. Johns Hopkins U., Balt., 1948; research chemist Brookhaven Nat. Lab., Upton, N.Y., 1949-54, SRI Internat., Menlo Park, Calif., 1954—; vis. scientist NSF Tokyo U., 1966-67. Contbr. numerous articles to profl. jours.; patentee in field. Mem. AAAS, Am. Chem. Soc., Sigma Xi, Phi Beta Kappa, Phi Lambda Upsilon. Avocations: theatre, dancing, pottery, woodworking, travelling. Home: 561 Berkeley Ave Menlo Park CA 94025 Office: SRI Internat 333 Ravenswood Ave Menlo Park CA 94025

SAND, WAYNE RUSSELL, aviation meteorology educator; b. Conrad, Mont., Mar. 2, 1941; s. Harry Palmer and Esther Lucille (Bryant) S.; m. Barbara Jean Walston, May 29, 1970; 1 child, Mark Wayne. BS, Mont. State U., 1963; postgrad., Colo. State U., 1964-66; MS, S.D. Sch. Mines, 1974; PhD, U. Wyo., 1980. Lic. pilot, FAA. Research meteorologist, pilot S.D. Sch. Mines, Rapid City, 1971-76; asst. prof. meteorology, flight facility mgr. U. Wyo., Laramie, 1976-87; deputy mgr. research applications program Nat. Ctr. Atmospheric Research, Boulder, Colo., 1987—; cons. in field, 1983—. Served to capt. USN, 1966-71, USNR 1971—. Grantee FAA, NSF, NOAA. Mem. Am. Meteorol. Soc. (chmn. aviation meteorology com. 1984-87), FAA/Nat. Weather Service Aviation Weather Task Force, AIAA, Naval Res. Assn., Sigma Xi. Republican. Methodist. Avocation: aviation. Home: 3211 Grays Gable Rd Laramie WY 82070 Office: Nat Ctr Atmospheric Research/RAP Box 3000 Boulder CO 80307

SANDBERG, NEIL C., educator, human relations consultant; b. N.Y.C., Apr. 25, 1925; s. Jack Sandberg and Lena Koronczyk; m. Mary Keiser, Dec. 26, 1954; 1 child, Curtis N. BA, Columbia U., 1949; MPL, U. So. Calif., 1971, PhD, 1972. Regional dir. Joint Def. Appeal, N.Y.C. and Los Angeles, 1950-62, Am. Jewish Com., Los Angeles, 1962—; prof. sociology, Loyola Marymount U., Los Angeles, 1964-68, 72—, Hebrew Union Coll., Los Angeles, 1973—; chmn. profl. adv. com. tng. div. Los Angeles Police Dept. Author Ethnic Identitiy and Assimilation: The Polish American Community, 1974; Stairwell 7: Family Life in the Welfare State, 1978, Identity and Assimilation: The Welsh-English Dichotomy, 1981, Jewish Life in Los Angeles: A Window to Tomorrow, 1986; editor New Towns: Why and For Whom?, 1973. Served with USN, 1943-45. Recipient Literary award Kosciuszko Found, 1973, research award, 1982; Research fellow U. Judaism, 1976—. Mem. Assn. for Sociol. Study of Jewry, Assn. of Jewish Community Relations Workers. Office: Am Jewish Com 6505 Wilshire Blvd Los Angeles CA 90048

SANDBORN, VIRGIL ALVIN, civil engineer, educator; b. Conway Springs, Kans., Apr. 30, 1928; s. Kenneth Arthur and Mamie Una (Durham) S.; m. Virginia Ruth Cerny, June 12, 1955; children: Peter Alan, Paticia Marie. B in Aero. Engring., U. Kans., 1950; M in Aero. Engring., U. Mich., 1953. Aero. research scientist NACA-NASA, Cleve., 1951-62; cons. scientist AVCO R&AD, Wilmington, Mass., 1962-63; prof. Colo. State U., Ft. Collins., 1963—; vis. scientist NASA-Ames Research Ctr., Moffett Field, Calif., 1972-73, Navy Underwater Ctr., Newport, R.I., 1984-85. Author: Resistance Temperature Transducers, 1972, Classnotes for Experimental Methods in Fluid Mechanics, 1981. Mem. AIAA, Sigma Xi. Home: 917 Cheyenne Dr Fort Collins CO 80525 Office: Colo State U Fort Collins CO 80523

SANDER, LOUIS WILSON, psychiatry educator, researcher; b. San Francisco, July 31, 1918; s. Louis Francis and Emily (Wilson) S.; m. Betty Estelle Thorpe, Apr. 25, 1953; children—Mark, Rebecca, David. A.B., U. Calif.-Berkeley, 1939; M.D., U. Calif.-San Francisco, 1942. Diplomate Am. Bd. Psychiatry and Neurology. Intern U. Calif. Hosp., San Francisco, 1942-43; resident psychiatry Worcester State Hosp., Mass., 1947, Judge Baker Guidance Ctr., Boston, 1949-50; resident psychiatry Mass. Meml. Hosps., Boston U. Sch. Medicine, 1947-49, resident in neurology, 1950; from instr. to assoc. prof. psychiatry Boston U. Sch. Medicine, 1949-68, prof., 1968-78; prof. psychiatry U. Colo. Sch. Medicine, Denver, 1978-87; prof. emeritus, 1987—; prin. investigator 25 yr. longitudinal study Boston U. Sch. Medicine-U. Colo. Sch. Medicine, 1981—; prin. investigator research Boston U. Sch. Medicine, 1954-78; vis. prof. U. Calif., Davis, 1979; Simpson vis. prof. U. Calif., San Francisco, 1984. Editor: (with others) Infant Psychiatry: A New Synthesis, 1976. Inventor/developer infant bassinet monitor, 1958. Contbr. articles, book chpts., and revs. to profl. publs., 1962-83. Served to maj. USAAF, 1943-46. Recipient Research Career Devel. awards USPHS, 1963-78; research grantee USPHS, March of Dimes, W. Grant Found., MacArthur Found., Spencer Found., Developmental Psychobiology Research Group-Colo. U., Nat. Council on Alcoholism, Univ. Hosp., Boston. Fellow Am. Coll. Psychoanalysts, Denver Psychoanalytic Soc.; mem. Am. Psychiat. Assn., Am. Acad. Child Psychiatry (sec. 1960-61), Boston Psychoanalytic Soc., AAAS, Soc. for Research in Child Devel. (governing council 1975-77), Phi Beta Kappa, Alpha Omega Alpha. Home: 765 15th St Boulder CO 80302 Office: Univ Colo Med Sch 4200 E 9th St Denver CO 80262

SANDER, STEVE DAVID, advertising executive; b. N.Y.C., Nov. 3, 1953; s. Lothar Stephen and Greta (Landwehr) S. BS in Journalism, BA in Geography, U. Colo., 1974, postgrad., 1975-76. Photographer Boulder (Colo.) Daily Camera, 1975-76; account exec. Schentzein & Assocs., Denver, 1976-78; sr. accountant exec. Schenbein & Assocs., Denver, 1978-80; pres. Sander Communications, Denver, 1981-84; v.p. Barnhart & Co., Denver, 1984—; vis. prof. U. Colo., 1985. Mem. Gov.'s Council on Physical Fitness; bd. dirs. Big Bros., Denver, Internat. Film Festival, Williams Street Ctr. Mem. Pub. Relations Soc. Am. (chmn. 1984-85, Gold Pick Awards Com. 1986), Denver Advt. Fedn. (chmn. internship com. 1983-86). Club: Denver (mem. entertainment com.). Avocations: running, squash, tennis, photography, traveling. Home: 669 Washington #705 Denver CO 80203 Office: Barnhart & Co 455 Sherman St #500 Denver CO 80203

SANDER, SUSAN BERRY, environmental planning engineering corporation executive; b. Walla Walla, Wash., Aug. 26, 1953; d. Alan Robert and Elizabeth Ann (Davenport) Berry; m. Dean Edward Sander, June 3, 1978. BS in Biology with honors, Western Wash. U., 1975; MBA with honors, U. Puget Sound, 1984. Biologist, graphic artist Shapiro & Assocs., Inc., Seattle, 1975-77, office mgr., 1977-79, v.p., 1979-84, pres., owner 1984—, also bd. dirs. Merit scholar Overlake Service League, Bellevue, Wash., 1971, Western Wash. U. scholar, Bellingham, 1974-75, U. Puget Sound scholar, 1984. Mem. Soc. Mktg. Profl. Services, Seattle C. of C. Club: Wash. Athletic (Seattle). Avocations: skiing, swimming, hiking, traveling, painting. Office: Shapiro & Assocs Inc 1812 Smith Tower Seattle WA 98104

SANDERS, AUGUSTA SWANN, nurse; b. Alexandria, La., July 22, 1932; d. James and Elizabeth (Thompson) Swann; m. James Robert Sanders, Jan. 12, 1962 (div. 1969). Student, Morgan State U., 1956. Pub. health nurse USPHS, Washington, 1963-64; mental health counselor Los Angeles County Sheriff's Dept., 1972-79; program coordinator Los Angeles County Dept. Mental Health, 1979—. Mem. Assemblyman Mike Roo's Commn. on Women's Issues, 1981—, Senator Diane Watson's Commn. on Health Issues, 1979—; chmn. Commn. Sex. Equity Los Angeles Unified Sch. Dist., 1984—. Mem. Los Angeles County Employees Assn. (v.p. 1971-72), So. Calif. Black Nurses Assn. (founding mem.), Nat. Assn. Female Execs., Internat. Fedn. Bus. and Profl. Women (pres. 1981-82, dist. officer 1982—), Chi Eta Phi. Democrat. Methodist. Avocations: travelling, crocheting, movies, concerts, plays. Office: Augustus F Hawkins Mental Health Ctr 1720 E 120th St Los Angeles CA 90805

SANDERS, CHARLES FRANKLIN, business executive, engineering educator; b. Louisville, Dec. 22, 1931; s. Charles Franklin and Maragret Rhea (Timmons) S.; m. Marie Audrey Galuppo, Dec. 29, 1956; children: Karen Lynn, Craig Joseph, Keith Franklin. B.Chem. Engring., U. Louisville, 1954, M.Chem. Engring., 1958; Ph.D., U. So. Calif., 1970. Research engr. Exxon Research and Engring. Co., Linden, N.J., 1955-62; asst. prof. engring. Calif. State U., Northridge, 1962-68; assoc. prof. Calif. State U., 1968-71, prof., 1971—, chmn. dept., 1969-72; dean Calif. State U. (Sch. Engring. and Computer Sci.), 1972-81; pres., chief exec. officer, dir. Rusco Industries, Los Angeles, 1981-82; exec. v.p. Energy Systems Assocs., Tustin, Calif, 1982-86; bd. dirs. MacBay Energy Corp., Uniforms Unltd. Bd. dirs. San Fernando Valley Child Guidance Clinic, 1979-81. Served to 1st lt. U.S. Army, 1956-57. NSF fellow, 1965-67. Mem. Am. Inst. Chem. Engrs., Nat. Soc. Profl. Engrs., Calif. Soc. Profl. Engrs., Am. Soc. for Engring. Edn., Combustion Inst., Air Pollution Control Assn. Republican. Office: 15591 Red Hill Ave Tustin CA 92680

SANDERS, DANIEL SELVARAJAH, social work educator; b. Sri Lanka, Sept. 18, 1928; came to U.S., 1965, naturalized, 1968; s. David S. and Harriet C. (Handy) S.; m. Christobel C. Niles, Apr. 14, 1959. B.A., U. Ceylon, 1953; diploma social welfare, U. Wales, 1958; M.S.W., U. Minn., 1967, Ph.D., 1971. Assoc. dir., lectr. Ceylon Inst. Social Work, 1955-61; exec. dir., research assoc. Inst. Social Study, Ceylon, 1961-65; spl. projects cons., adminstr. Div. Child Welfare, Minn. Dept. Public Welfare, 1967-69; mem. faculty U. Hawaii, 1971-86, prof. social work, dean, dir. internat. programs, 1974-86; dean, prof. U. Ill., Champaign, 1987—; pres. Lutheran Campus Ministry, 1978-79, 85-86, Interuniv. Consortium for Internat. Social Devel., 1982—. Author: Impact of Reform Movements on Social Policy Changes, 1972, The Developmental Perspective in Social Work, 1982; coauthor: Fundamentals of Social Work Practice, 1981, Education for International Social Welfare; founder, exec. editor Ceylon Jour. Social Work, 1955-60; editorial adv. Internat. Social Work, 1976-86, Social Devel. Issues, 1984—, Jour. Social Devel. in Africa, 1986—; editorial bd. Law and Social Work Quar., 1980-82. Bd. dirs. Hospice Hawaii, 1982-84, Hawaii Council Chs., 1982-84. Brit. Council scholar, 1957-58; Ecumenical scholar World Council Chs., 1965-66; fellow Inst. Internat. Edn. Devel., 1966-67; fellow NIMH, 1969-71. Mem. Nat. Assn. Social Workers, Council Social Work Edn. (bd. dirs. 1983-86), Internat. Assn. Schs. of Social Work (bd. dirs. 1987—), Internat. Soc. Community Devel., Internat. Conf. Social Welfare (U.S. com. bd. dirs. 1986—). Home: 614 W Florida Ave Urbana IL 61801

SANDERS, ERIC PAUL, management educator; b. Bklyn., Apr. 17, 1939; s. Samuel and Sophilyn (Camenick) S.; children: Scott David, Brett Cory. BA, U. Vermont, 1960; MBA, CUNY, 1963; PhD, U. Calif., Berkeley, 1967. Cert. higher edn. tchr., Calif. Asst. prof. San Diego State U., 1967-69; assoc. personnel analyst City of Okland, Calif., 1970-74; assoc. prof. mgmt. Armstrong Coll., Berkeley, 1974-76, North Adams (Mass.) State U., 1976-78; personnel services advisor U. Calif., Berkeley, 1979-81; assoc. prof. mgmt. San Francisco State U., 1980—; cons. psychology Farr Assoc., N.Y.C., 1969-70; mgmt. cons. to ind. airlines and hi-tech. ins. cos., Calif. 1980—. Contbr. articles to profl. jours. Recipient Teaching Excellence award San Francisco State U., 1985. Mem. Indsl. Relations Research Assn., Calif. Bar Assn. (labor and employment law sect.), No. Calif. Human Resources Council (chmn. 1985-86), Am. Inst. Decision Sci. (HRM session chmn. 1984-85), Human Resource Mgmt. and Organizational Behavior (I.R. Session chmn. 1986), Delta Sigma Pi. Club: Commonwealth (San Francisco). Avocations: antique dealer, dancing, weight lifting, playing piano and guitar. Home: 1080 Ygnacio Valley Rd #6 Walnut Creek CA 94598 Office: San Francisco Stat U Sch Bus 1600 Holloway Ave San Francisco CA 94132

SANDERS, GEORGE LORING, architect, photographer; b. Washington, Aug. 24, 1950; s. Spencer Edward and Cornelia Howard (Turrell) S.; m. Paula Ann Duvall, July 30, 1974; children—Lee Duvall, Jessica Duvall. B.F.A., U. N.Mex., 1973, M.Arch., 1975. Registered architect, N.Mex. Draftsman Robert Schwinn Inc., Bethesda, Md., 1973, Mitchell & Wright, Albuquerque, 1974; draftsman, designer G. Patrick Gates & Assocs., Albuquerque, 1975-76; project architect Castillo Preston Ltd., Albuquerque, 1976-79; project architect, assoc. Hutchinson, Brown & Ptnrs., Albuquerque, 1979-83; head architect Craddock Devel., Albuquerque, 1983—. Exhibited photography in numerous shows, 1971-79. Mayor's appointee to the Architects and Engrs. Selection Adv. Com., City of Albuquerque, 1985—. Recipient Weatherhead Found. award Southwest Fine Arts Biennial Mus. N.Mex., 1974, Archtl. and Engring. Excellance award, N.Mex. chpt. Assoc. Gen. Contractors, 1986, Award of Merit AIA Jour., 1981. Mem. AIA, Nat. Trust for Historic Preservation. Democrat. Presbyterian. Club: Albuquerque Coin (v.p. 1983-84). Home: 6000 Rogers NE Albuquerque NM 87110 Office: Craddock Devel 2309 Renard SE Albuquerque NM 87106

SANDERS, KENTON MORRIS, medical educator; b. June 16, 1950; m. Sherryl Lynn Abbott; children: Ryan, Geoffrey, Kendra. BA in Chemistry, U. Calif., Santa Cruz, 1972; PhD in Physiology, UCLA, 1976. NIH postdoctoral fellow UCLA Med. Sch., 1976-78; postdoctoral research fellow Mayo Med. Sch., Rochester, Minn., 1978-79, asst. prof. physiology, 1979-82; assoc. prof. U. Nev., Reno, 1982-85, prof., 1986—. Recipient Research Career Devel. award NIH, 1983—; fellow Am. Heart Assn., 1978-79, U. Coll., London, 1984; NIH grantee, 1980—. Mem. Am. Physiol. Soc., Biophys. Soc., Am. Motility Soc., Am. Gastroenterology Soc. Home: 2324 Desert Flower Ct Sparks NV 89431 Office: U Nev Sch Medicine Dept Physiology Reno NV 89557

SANDERS, RACHEL LYNN, speech-language pathologist; b. Franklin, N.C., July 14, 1961; d. Robert Edward and Darlene (Breedlove) Johnson; m. Vance Alan Sanders, Aug. 6, 1983. BA, U. N.C., 1982, MS, 1984. Speech-lang. pathologist St. Jude Ctr., Inc., Juneau, Alaska, 1984-87, Infant Learning Program, Juneau, 1984-87, City and Borough of Juneau Sch. Dist., 1985, 87—. Grantee USPHS Bur. of Community Health Service, 1983-84; recipient Outstanding Youth award, U.S. Jaycees, 1979. Mem. Am. Speech-Lang.-Hearing Assn. (cert.), Nat. Assn. for Hearing and Speech Action, Alaska Speech-Lang.-Hearing Assn. Democrat. Baptist. Avocations: sports, music, knitting, decorating. Home: 8750 N Douglas Hwy Juneau AK 99801

SANDERS, ROCHELLE SOHL, obstetrician, gynecologist; b. Alpine, Tex., Jan. 29, 1948; d. William James Sohl and Mary Jo (Richardson) Brown; m. Jerry Wayne Johnson, June 17, 1966 (div. Apr. 1970); 1 child, Mary Jo; m. Gregory William Sanders, Oct. 30, 1970; 1 child, Eris Elizabeth. BA, U. Tex., Austin, 1970; MD, U. Tex., San Antonio, 1980. Bookeeper, office mgr. Alpine TV Cable, 1970-72; bookeeper Mobile Home Industries, Austin, 1972-74; resident Bexar County Hosp., Austin, 1980-84; practice medicine specializing in ob-gyn Springerville, Ariz., 1984—. Jr. Fellow Am. Coll. of Obstetrics and Gynecology; mem. AMA, Ariz. Med. Assn., Alpha Omega Alpha. Avocations: alpine and nordic skiing, reading, sewing, classical music, movies. Home: 1570 Sable Way Eagar AZ 85925 Office: Round Valley Clinic PO Box 1578 Springerville AZ 85938

SANDERS, WALTER JEREMIAH, III, electronics company executive; b. Chgo., Sept. 12, 1936; s. Walter J. and Kathleen (Finn) S.; m. Linda Lee Drobman, Nov. 13, 1965 (div. 1982); children: Tracy Ellen, Lara Whitney, Alison Ashley. B.E.E., U. Ill., 1958. Design engr. Douglas Aircraft Co., Santa Monica, Calif., 1958-59; applications engr. Motorola, Inc., Phoenix, 1959-60; sales engr. Motorola, Inc., 1960-61; with Fairchild Camera & Instrument Co., 1961-69; dir. mktg. Fairchild Camera & Instrument Co., Mountain View, Calif., 1961-68, group dir. mktg. worldwide, 1968-69; chmn. bd., chief exec. officer, former pres. Advanced Micro Devices, Inc., Sunnyvale, Calif., 1969—; dir. Donaldson, Lufkin & Jenrette. Mem. Semicondr. Industry Assn. (co-founder, dir.), Santa Clara County Mfg. Group (co-founder, dir.). Office: Advanced Micro Devices Inc 901 Thompson Pl Sunnyvale CA 94086

SANDERSON, CHERYL ANNE, utility company executive; b. Seattle, July 9, 1948; d. Charles F. and Anna Mae (Jones) Bradford; m. Lanny V. DeMoss, Aug. 15, 1968 (div.); 1 child, Sean; m. Von R. Sanderson, Oct. 28, 1977; stepchildren: Gavin, Craig, Todd. Grad. high sch., Seattle, 1966. With Pacific N.W. Bell, Seattle, 1967—, supr. art graphics and typesetting, 1974-75, mgr. word processing ctrs., 1975-77, mgr. staff, advanced office systems, 1977-85, mgr. mechanization, 1985—; tech. advisor N.W. Ctr. Industries, Seattle, 1983-85; advisor Seattle Opportunities Industrialization Ctr., 1982-83; chmn. adv. council South Seattle Community Coll., 1987—. Chmn. Telephone Pioneers, Seattle, 1985—; donor platelets Pheresis program Seattle Blood Ctr. Mem. Soc. Info. Mgmt., Data Processing Mgmt. Assn. Republican. Avocations: skiing, fishing, boating, bowling, camping. Home: 4905 133d St SW Edmonds WA 98020 Office: Pacific NW Bell 1600 Bell Plaza Room 1905 Seattle WA 98191

SANDERSON, SANDY, real estate broker; b. Los Angeles, Nov. 28, 1944; d. Carl Foree and Mildred Anna Bailey; m. Willis Lloyd Pitkin, Jr., June 9, 1965 (div.); children—Joseph Reeves, Sara Love, Mary Faith; m. Howard Sanderson, July 19, 1984. B.A., Whittier Coll., 1966, M.A.T., 1967. Lic. real estate broker, Utah, Idaho, Ariz., Calif.; leadership tng. grad. (LTG). Sales assoc., assoc. broker Aloma Real Estate, Logan, Utah, 1979-82; founder, ptnr. Gold Key Realty, 1982-83; mgr. Wardly Corp.-Better Homes and Gardens, Salt Lake City, 1983—; broker Coldwell Banker Baugh Assocs., Logan, 1984-85; owner, ptnr. Ginny Hays Realty, Inc., Sedona, Ariz., 1985—; founder, pres. Sanderson Data Systems, Sedona, 1986—. Democratic precinct chmn., 1982; sponsor Logan Swim Team. Mem. Cert. Residential Specialists, Nat. Women's Council Realtors (nat. trainer), Logan Women's Council Realtors (pres., founder), Sedona Women's Council Realtors (pres., founder 1985) Internat. Fedn. Realtors, Utah State Farm and Land Inst. (sec.-treas.), Nat. Mktg. Inst., Logan Bd. Realtors (Sales Assoc. of Yr. 1981, Sales Achievement awards, 1980-83), Utah Assn. Realtors, Nat. Assn. Realtors, Ariz. Assn. Realtors, Calif. Assn. Realtors. Contbr. articles to profl. publs. Home: 13 Sycamore Rd Sedona AZ 86336 Office: PO Box HH Sedona AZ 86336

SANDFORD, GORDON THOMAS, music educator; b. Upland, Calif., Oct. 21, 1929; s. Edward Joseph and Margaret (Swan) S.; m. Marguerite Hynes, Aug. 8, 1952 (div. 1985); children: James W., Claire S. Olander, Paul G.; m. Martha Sandstead, Aug. 31, 1985. AB, San Jose State U., 1951; AM, Redlands U., 1952; PhD, U. So. Calif., 1964. Cert. music tchr., Calif. Prof. U. Colo., Boulder, 1966—. Served to cpl. U.S. Army, 1953-55. Mem. Am. Musicol. Soc., Am. Musical Instrument Soc., Viola da Gamba Soc. Am. (v.p. 1984—), Music Educators Nat. Conf., Pi Kappa Lambda (pres.). Avocation: performing early music. Home: 200 Echo Pl Boulder CO 80309 Office: U Colo Coll Music Box 301 Boulder CO 80309

SANDFORD, VIRGINIA ADELE, educator; b. Tacoma, Wash., Nov. 29, 1926; d. Fred John and Lucille Lillian (Skok) Wepfer; student U. Wash., 1946-49; m. Calvert H. Sandford, Sept. 16, 1949 (div. 1970); children—Susan L., Kaye E., James C. Tchr. stringed instruments dept. music Puyallup (Wash.) Sch. Dist., 1944-46; sec. Fife (Wash.) Sch. Dist., 1969-72; exec. sec. Tacoma (Wash.) Sch. Dist., 1972-75; tchr. ednl. sec. program Clover Park Vocat. Tech. Inst., Tacoma, 1975-82; profl. speaker, seminar producer Virginia Sandford & Assocs., 1982—. Violinist, Tacoma Symphony, 1972-75. Mem. Am. Vocat. Assn., Wash. Vocat. Assn., Wash. State Bus. Edn. Assn., Nat. Assn. Ednl. Office Personnel, Internat. Platform Assn., Nat. Speakers Assn., Pacific N.W. Speakers Assn., Alpha Chi Omega.

SANDLER, ALAN PAUL, psychiatrist; b. Phila., Dec. 30, 1944; s. David Joseph and Rae (Hartman) S.; m. Judith Bitman, Dec. 23, 1967 (div. Aug. 1969); m. Elizabeth Bella Goslins, June 11, 1972; children—Danielle Felice, Michael David. B.A., Temple U., 1966, M.D., 1970; M.P.H., UCLA, 1976. Diplomate Am. Bd. Pediatrics, Am. Bd. Psychiatry and Neurology; cert. child psychologist. Pediatric intern and resident Los Angeles County/U. So. Calif. Med. Ctr., 1970-72; fellow in child mental health Children's Orthopedic Hosp., Seattle, 1972-73; fellow in ambulatory pediatrics Los Angeles County/U. So. Calif. Med. Ctr., 1975-76; resident UCLA Neuropsychiat. Inst., 1979-81, fellow in child psychiatry, 1981-83; asst. clin. prof. pediatrics and child psychiatry UCLA Sch. Medicine, 1983—, asst. prof. pediatrics, 1976-79; med. dir. child and adolescent psychiatry Northridge Hosp. Med. Ctr., 1985—. Contbr. articles to med. jours. Bd. dirs. Hollywood Los Feliz Jewish Community Ctr., 1979-86 . Served to maj. USAF, 1973-75; Philippines. Fellow Am. Acad. Pediatrics; mem. Am. Psychiat. Assn., Am. Acad. Child Psychiatry, Ambulatory Pediatrics Assn. (region chair 1978-80), Los Angeles Pediatric Soc., Alpha Omega Alpha, Phi Eta Sigma. Democrat. Jewish. Office: 18531 Roscoe Blvd Northridge CA 91324

SANDOVAL, JAMES PHILIP, concrete company executive; b. Trinidad, Colo., Jan. 14, 1929; s. Philip Joseph and Ermenia Minnie (Vigil) S.; m. Betty C. Loomis, Oct. 24, 1949; children: Patrick, Michael, Christopher, Sue Ann, Eugene, Catherine, Therese. Student, Idaho State U., 1951-52, Tex. Christian U., 1954-56, UCLA, 1960-61. Withacctg. dept. Convair Corp., Ft. Worth, 1954-60; pvt. practice bookkeeping Hacienda Heights, Calif., 1962-71; founder Blue Star Ready Mix, Inc., Moorpark, Calif., 1976—, owner, gen. mgr., 1976—. Served with AUS, 1948-51. Republican. Roman Catholic. Office: Blue Star Ready Mix Inc Box 696 Moorpark CA 93021

SANDS, RUSSELL BERTRAM, insurance broker; b. Santa Cruz, Calif., Feb. 14, 1940; s. Clarence Russell and Betty Ellen (Weeks) S.; m. Jacquelyn Marie Hall, Sept. 9, 1960; children: Douglas Clarence, Gwendolyn Marie. Student, Wheaton Coll., 1957-59, U. Calif., Berkeley, 1960-61; BA, Western Ill. U., 1984. Mgr. CIGNA Corp., San Francisco, 1961-69; v.p. Bayly, Martin & Fay, San Francisco, 1969-76; sr. v.p. Frank B. Hall & Co., San Francisco, 1976-80; mng. gen. ptnr. Wendy Petroleum, San Carlos, Calif., 1980—; bd. dirs. Hammerwell Inc., Los Gatos, Calif.; prin. Sands Properties, San Carlos, Calif., 1972—. Bd. dirs. Fellowship Acad., San Francisco, 1985—, Young Life of San Francisco, 1981—; mem. adv. council Mount Herman Assn., Felton, Calif., 1984—; moderator First. Bapt. Ch., San Carlos, 1979-80. Mem. Ind. Ins. Brokers Assn. Republican. Presbyterian. Clubs: World Trade (San Francisco); Churchill (Palo Alto, Calif.). Avocations: tennis, golf, internat. travelling. Home: 1841 Elizabeth St San Carlos CA 94070 Office: Frank B Hall & Co One Market Pl #2100 San Francisco CA 94105

SANDS, SINDY JEAN, communication disorders specialist; b. Spokane, Jan. 3, 1952; d. Charles Donald and Joann (Clarke) S. BA cum laude, Wash. State U., 1974; MA cum laude, U. Oreg., 1977. Tchr. spl. edn. Bellevue (Wash.) Sch. Dist., 1974-75; communication disorders specialist Evergreen Schs., Vancouver, Wash., 1978—; supr. student interns Wash. State U., 1984-85; seminar leader on Christian growth and alcoholism. Sr. leader Young Life N.W. Vancouver area, 1971—. Mem. Am. Speech and Hearing Assn. (cert. clin. competence), Nat. Educators Hearing Impaired. Mem. Foursquare Ch. Office: Spl Services 7000 NE 117th Ave Vancouver WA 98662

SANDS, WILLIAM ARTHUR, gymnastics coach; b. Madison, Wis., Feb. 8, 1953; s. Arthur Mathew and Joan Marie (Ehredt) S. BS in Phys. Edn. magna cum laude, U. Wis., Oshkosh, 1975; MS in Exercise Physiology, U. Utah, 1985. Asst. coach Am. Acad. Gymnastics, Des Plaines, Ill., 1975-78; dir., founder Mid-America Twisters, Northbrook, Ill., 1978-83; dir. edn. and research U.S. Gymnastics Fedn., Ft. Worth, 1980-81; asst. gymnastics coach U. Utah, Salt Lake City, 1983—; Cons. biomechanics Chgo. Sports Medicine, 1983—, mem. exercise physiology com., biomechanics com. U.S. Gymnastics Fedn., Indpls., 1984—; asst. nat. coach U.S. Gymnastics Fedn. World Championships, 1979, coached U.S. team in various internat. tournaments, 1978-81. Author: Coaching Women's Gymnastics, 1984, Everybody's Gymnastic Book, 1984, Modern Women's Gymnastics, 1982, Beginning Gymnastics, 1981. Recipient Nat. Assn. Intercollegiate Athletics All-Am. Gymnastics award, 1974, 75; nominee U. Wis. Oshkosh Athletic Hall of Fame, 1985. Mem. Am. Coll. Sports Med. (S.W. conf.), AAAS, Phi Kappa Phi. Avocation: writing. Home: 1340 S 2100 East Salt Lake City UT 84108 Office: U Utah Spl Events Ctr Salt Lake City UT 84112

SANDT, SAMUEL HUNTINGTON, anthropology educator; b. Afton, N.Y., June 15, 1939; s. Philip Addison Sandt and Ruth Carroll (Comings) Gibson; m. Merry O'Connell, June 3, 1961 (div. Feb. 1983); children: Caroline Huntington Sandt Bergan, Samuel Addison; m. Patricia Gozawa, Mar. 19, 1983. BA, U. Calif., Santa Barbara, 1966, MA, 1968; postgrad, U. Mich., 1968-70. Instr. Calif. State U., Long Beach, 1970, San Bernardino, 1971; instr. Los Angeles Valley Coll., Van Nuys, Calif., 1971-83; asst. prof. anthropology Los Angeles Pierce Coll., Woodland Hills, Calif., 1983—. Planning commr. City of Redondo Beach, Calif., 1974-75. Served with USN, 1960-64. Nat. def. Fgn. Lang. fellow U. Mich., 1969-70. Mem. AAAS. Democrat. Avocation: sailing. Home: 555 N Harbor Dr #49 Redondo Beach CA 90277 Office: Los Angeles Pierce Coll Winnetka Ave Woodland Hills CA 91371

SANDY, LYMAN GAGE, lawyer; b. Libertyville, Ill., June 20, 1945; s. Robert Edward and Elizabeth Ann (Carroll) S.; m. Alison Kay Schuler, Mar. 30, 1974; 1 child, Theodore Lyman Schuler-Sandy. A.B. magna cum laude, Harvard U., 1967, J.D. cum laude, 1972. Bar: Va. 1973, N.Mex. 1975, U.S. Dist. Ct. N.Mex. 1978, U.S. Ct. Appeals (10th cir.) 1976. Law clk. to presiding justice U.S. Ct. Appeals (5th cir.), New Orleans, 1972-73; assoc. Covington & Burling, Washington, 1973-75; asst. U.S. atty. U.S. Attys. Office, Albuquerque, 1975-78; assoc. Poole, Tinnin & Martin, Albuquerque, 1978-81; dir. Miller, Stratvert, Torgerson & Schlenker, Albuquerque, 1981—. Pres. Harvard-Radcliffe Club of N.Mex., Albuquerque, 1984—, v.p., 1982-84; chmn. N.Mex. Harvard Campaign, Albuquerque, 1982—. Mem. ABA, State Bar N.Mex. Assn., Va. Bar Assn., Albuquerque Bar Assn. Democrat. Lutheran. Home: 632 Cougar Loop NE Albuquerque NM 87122

SANETO, RUSSELL PATRICK, neurobiologist; b. Burbank, Calif., Oct. 10, 1950; s. Arthur and Mitzi (Seddon) S. B.S. with honors, San Diego State U., 1972, M.S., 1975; Ph.D., U. Tex. Med. Br., 1981. Teaching asst. San Diego State U. 1969-75; substitute tchr. Salt Lake City Sch. Dist., 1975; teaching and research asst. U. Tex. Med. Br., 1976-77, NIH predoctoral fellow, 1977-81, postdoctoral fellow, 1981; Jeanne B. Kempner postdoctoral fellow UCLA, 1981-82, NIH postdoctoral fellow, 1982—, lectr. research methods Grad. Sch., 1982; vis. scholar in ethics So. Baptist Theol. Sem., Louisville, 1981. Contbr. articles to profl. jours. Recipient Merit award Nat. March of Dimes, 1978; named one of Outstanding Young Men in Am., 1979, 81, Man of Significance, 1985. Mem. Bread for World, Save the Whales, Sierra Club, Am. Soc. Human Genetics, AAAS, Winter Confs. Brain Research, Neuroscis. Study Program, N.Y. Acad. Scis., Am. Soc. Neurochem., Soc. Neurosci., Am. Soc. Neurochemistry, Soc. Neurosci. Democrat. Mem. Evangelical Free Ch. Club: World Runners. Office: NPIMRRC UCLA 760 Westwood Plaza Los Angeles CA 90024

SANFORD, JOSEPH LEE, architect; b. Tachikawa AFB, Japan, Sept. 19, 1953; (parents Am. citizens); s. George Samuel and Delia Martha Sanford; m. Diane Louise Collison, June 17, 1978; 1 child, Galen Matthew. AA, Am. River Coll., 1974; student, Calif. Poly. State U., San Luis Obispo, 1971-75; BA in Design, Calif. State U., Sacramento, 1980. Registered architect, Calif., Wash. Office mgr., supt. Bansemer Homes Inc., Fair Oaks, Calif., 1976-78; designer Sacramento, 1978-81; design architect HNTB Architects and Engrs., Bellevue, Wash., 1981-82; prin. N.W. Plan Group, Seattle, 1982—; pres., chief exec. officer Specialty Structures Inc., Seattle, 1984—; instr. Am. Acad. Interior Design, Seattle, 1982-83. Mem. Internat. Conf. Bldg. Officials (profl.). Republican. Avocations: sport flying, snow skiing, photography, travel. Office: Speciality Structures Inc 20129 9th Ave S Seattle WA 98198

SANG, JÜRGEN GÜNTER, German educator; b. Coburg, Federal Republic of Germany, Aug. 17, 1937; came to U.S., 1971; s. Rudolf Philipp and Else Johanna (Hittoff) S.; m. Hildegard Hedwig Reindl, Apr. 17, 1964; 1 child Bettina Johanna. Grad., Goethe-Gymnasium, Flensburg, Federal Republic of Germany, 1959; PhD, U. Munich, 1966. Asst. editorial staff mem. Piper Pub., Munich, 1966-67; vis. prof. U. Tokyo, 1967-71; assoc. lectr. Chuno Univ., Tokyo, 1968-71; fgn. lectr. Inst. of Tech., Tokyo, 1968-71; assoc. prof. U. Hawaii, Honolulu, 1971-76, prof. German, 1976—, chmn. German div., 1983—, chmn. German grad. field, 1983—. Contbr. articles to profl. jours. Translator U.S. Dist. Cts., Honolulu; expert witness U.S. Immigration Service, Honolulu. Grantee U. Hawaii Found., 1985. Mem. Am. Assn. Tchrs. German, Hawaii Fgn. Lang. Tchrs., Japanese Soc. for Germanistiks. Avocations: soccer, water-sports. Office: U Hawaii Dept European Langs and Lit Honolulu HI 96822

SANGER, SCOTT HOWARD, lawyer; b. Chgo., Nov. 8, 1948; s. Alvin Beryl and Elaine June (Elman) S.; m. Betty Jane Gordon, June 27, 1971; children—Aaron Lee, Abby Gordon. B.A., Tulane, U., 1970; J.D., Northwestern U., 1973. Bar: Ill. 1973, N.Mex. 1980, U.S. Dist. Ct. (no. dist.) Ill. 1973. Assoc. Altman, Kurlander & Weiss, Chgo., 1973-75; assoc. Newman, Stahl & Shadur, Chgo., 1975-80; sole practice, Taos, N.Mex., 1980—; gen. ptnr. Taos Inn Assocs., Taos, 1981—. Mem. Taos Hist. Commn., 1983—. Mem. Chgo. Bar Assn., Ill. Bar Assn., ABA, N.Mex. Bar Assn.

SANGHA, JANGBIR SINGH, pharmaceutical company executive; b. Lopon, India, July 4, 1945; came to U.S., 1973; s. Pritam S. Pritam and Manjit K. (Dhaliwal) S.; m. Sandra J. Robinson, May 1, 1982. BS, Panjab U., Chandi Garh, India, 1969; MA, Meerut U., India, 1972; BS, Waterloo (Can.) Luth. U., 1976; DSc (hon.), Irvine Inst., 1979. Sr. scientist Nuclear Med. Systems Pharms. Inc., Newport Beach, Calif., 1976-80, v.p. mfg., 1980-86, gen. mgr., 1986—; bd. dirs. Self Care Systems Inc., Newport Beach, sec.; bd. dirs. Synorex Inc., Newport Beach, Animal Biotech Corp., Newport Beach. Mem. AAAS, Am. Assn. Clin. Chemistry. Office: Nuclear Med Systems Pharm Inc 1533 Monrovia Ave Newport Beach CA 92663

SANGUINETTI, EUGENE FRANK, art museum administrator, educator; b. Yuma, Ariz., May 12, 1917; s. Eugene F. and Lilah (Balsz) S.; children: Leslie, Gregory. BA, U. Santa Clara, 1939; postgrad., U. Ariz., 1960-62. Instr. art history U. Ariz., Phoenix, 1960-64; dir. Tucson Mus. and Art Ctr., 1964-67, Utah Mus. Fine Arts, Salt Lake City, 1967—; adj. prof. art history U. Utah, Salt Lake City, 1967—. Contbr. articles to profl. jours. Served with USAAF, 1942-44, to capt. M.I., U.S. Army, 1944-46. Mem. Am. Assn. Museums, Am. Assn. Mus. Dirs., Am. Fedn. of Arts, Coll. Art Assn., Western Assn. Art Museums, Salt Lake City C. of C. Home: 30 S St Salt Lake City UT 84103

SANI, ROBERT LEROY, chemical engineering educator; b. Antioch, Calif., Apr. 20, 1935; m. Martha Jo Marr, May 28, 1966; children: Cynthia Kay, Elizabeth Ann, Jeffrey Paul. B.S., U. Calif.-Berkeley, 1958, M.S., 1960; Ph.D., U. Minn., 1963. Postdoctoral researcher dept. math Rensselaer Poly. Inst., Troy, N.Y., 1963-64; asst. prof. U. Ill., Urbana, 1964-70, assoc. prof., 1970-76; prof. chem. engring. U. Colo., Boulder, 1976—; professeur associe Minister Edn. France, 1982; cons. Lawrence Livermore Nat. Lab., Calif., 1974—. Contbr numerous chpts. to profl. publs.; editorial bd.: Internat. Jour. Numerical Methods in Fluids, 1981—. Guggenheim fellow, 1970. Mem. Am. Inst. Chem. Engrs., Soc. Applied and Indsl. Math. Democrat. Office: U Colo Dept Chem Engring Campus Box 424 Boulder CO 80309

SANKEY, OTTO FRANCIS, research physics educator; b. St. Louis, Jan. 1, 1951; s. Otto Marion and Cecelia Anne (Aug) S.; m. Debra Anne Wibbenmeyer; Aug. 9, 1974; children: Stephanie, Holly, Robyn. BS, U. Mo., 1973; PhD, Wash. U., 1979. Research assoc. U. Ill., Urbana, 1979-80, vis. asst. prof., 1980-82; asst. prof. physics Ariz. State U., Tempe, 1982—, Ctr. Solid State Sci., Tempe, 1982—. Contbr. articles to jours. V.p. Fox Park Neighborhood Assn., St. Louis, 1979. Recipient Research award Office Naval Research, Tempe, 1986. Mem. Am. Phys. Soc. Roman Catholic. Avocations: hiking, fishing. Home: 1646 N Jones Circle Mesa AZ 85203 Office: Ariz State U Dept Physics Tempe AZ 85287

SANNWALD, WILLIAM WALTER, librarian; b. Chgo., Sept. 12, 1940; s. William Frederick and Irene Virginia (Stanish) S.; m. Mary G. Blomberg, May 22, 1965; children—Sara Ann, William Howard. B.A., Beloit Coll., 1963; M.A.L.S., Rosary Coll., River Forest, Ill., 1966; M.B.A., Loyola U., Chgo., 1974. Mktg. mgr. Xerox Univ. Microfilms, 1972-75; assoc. dir. Detroit Public Library, 1975-77; dir. Ventura (Calif.) County Library, 1977-79, San Diego Public Library, 1979—; vis. instr. mktg. San Diego State U.; mem. faculty U. Md. Library Adminstrs. Devel. Program, 1985. Recipient Outstanding Prof. award and Outstanding Mktg. Prof. award, 1985. Mem. ALA, Calif. Library Authority for Systems and Services (pres. congress of mems. 1980), Calif. Library Assn. Roman Catholic. Home: 3538 Paseo Salamoner La Mesa CA 92041 Office: City Adminstrn Bldg 202 C St San Diego CA 92101

SANO, ROY, bishop. Ordained to ministry United Meth. Ch., later consecrated bishop. Bishop Rocky Mountain Conf., United Meth. Ch., Denver. Office: Rocky Mt Conf United Meth Ch 2200 S University Blvd Denver CO 80210 *

SANSONE, FRANCIS JOSEPH, oceanography educator; b. Dayton, Ohio, July 25, 1951; s. C. Joseph and Leah M. (Manninen) S. BS, Rensselaer Poly. Inst., 1973; MS, U. N.C., 1976, PhD, 1980. Asst. prof. oceanography U. Hawaii, Honolulu, 1980—. Contbr. articles to profl. jours. Treas. U. Hawaii Broadcast Communications Authority, Honolulu. Recipient award Best Paper 1982 Organic div. of Geochem. Soc., 1983. Mem. Am. Soc. Limnology and Oceanography, Am. Soc. Microbiology, Am. Geophys. Union, Sigma Xi. Avocations: traveling, water sports. Office: U Hawaii Oceanography Dept 1000 Pope Rd Honolulu HI 96822

SANTIAGO, ESTHER GLORIA, insurance brokerage administrator; b. Los Angeles, Apr. 8, 1944; d. Jesus Barrera and Esther Gutierrez (Alcocer) Campos. Student, U. Calif., Irvine. Exec. sec. Swett & Crawford, Los Angeles, 1968-72; tech. asst. Johnson & Higgins, Los Angeles, 1972-77; tech. adminstr. Frank B. Hall, Los Angeles, 1978-85; ins. adminstr. Emett & Chandler, Los Angeles, 1985-86; acct. rep., loss control specialist Oland Internat. Ins. Brokers, Los Angeles, 1986—. Mem. Am. Soc. Safety Engrs. (pres.-elect and v.p. membership region I 1985-86, spl. recognition for meritorious service, 1978-85), Vets. of Safety. Republican. Club: Toastmasters. Avocations: photography, fine arts, sculpture, reading. Home: 2712 Grand Ave Huntington Park CA 90255 Office: Oland Internat Ins Brokers 655 S Hope St Los Angeles CA 90017

SANTILLAN, ANTONIO, banker, motion picture finance executive; b. Buenos Aires, May 8, 1936; naturalized, 1966; s. Guillermo Spika and Raphaella C. (Abaladejo) S.; children: Andrea, Miguel, Marcos. Grad., Morgan Park Mil. Acad., Chgo., 1954; student, Coll. of William and Mary, 1958. Cert. real estate broker. Asst. in charge of prodn. Wilding Studios, Chgo., 1964; pres. Adams Fin. Services, Los Angeles, 1965-86. Writer, producer, dir. (motion pictures) The Glass Cage, co-writer Dirty Mary/Crazy Harry, Viva Knievel; contbg. writer Once Upon a Time in America; TV panelist Window on Wall Street; contbr. articles to profl. fin. and real estate jours. Served with USNR, 1959. Recipient Am. Rep. award San Francisco Film Festival, Cork Ireland Film Fest, 1961. Mem. Writer's Guild Am., Los Angeles Bd. Realtors, Beverly Hills Bd. Realtors (income/investment div. steering com.), Westside Realty Bd. (bd. dirs.), Los Angeles Ventures Assn. (bd. dirs.). Lodge: Rotary. Avocations: golf, tennis, skiing. Office: Winning Visions Inc 425 N Alfred St Los Angeles CA 90048

SANTLEY, THOMAS SAWYER, public relations executive; b. Los Angeles, Sept. 4, 1935; s. Joseph Mansfield and Ivy Winifred (Sawyer) S.; m. Patricia Caughlan, Aug. 15, 1959; children: Michael, Susan. BA, U. So. Calif., 1957, MBA, 1966. Mgmt. trainee Union Bank, Los Angeles, 1959-60, mgr. advt. and pub. relations, 1960-62; asst. v.p. advt. and pub. relations Western Fed. Savs. and Loan, Los Angeles, 1962-66; account exec. Bowes Co., Los Angeles, 1966-67; asst. v.p. Pacific Mut. Life Ins. Co., Los Angeles, 1967-76; 2nd v.p. Pacific Mut. Life Ins. Co., Newport Beach, Calif., 1976-83; dir. pub. affairs C.J. Segerstrom & Sons, Costa Mesa, Calif., 1983—. Chmn. Orange County Chamber Polit. Action Com., Calif., 1985—. Served to lt. USNR, 1957-59. Mem. Pub. Relations Soc. Am. (accredited; pres. Orange County chpt. 1981, disting. service award 1983), Los Angeles Publicity Club, Orange County C. of C. (bd. dirs.), Santa Ana C. of C. (bd. dirs.). Republican. Episcopalian. Club: Center (Costa Mesa). Home: 715 La Mirada Ave San Marino CA 91108

SANTNER, CHRIS ROBERT, process design engineer; b. Borger, Tex., May 10, 1949; s. Robert Roy and Lois Blanche (Conrad) S.; m. Rhonda Nosker, Mar. 4, 1978; children: Nicholas Robert, Kara Lynelle. BS in Chem. Engring., U. Houston, 1972; MS, Chem. Engring., 1977. Registered profl. engr., Colo. Process engr. M.W. Kellogg Co., Houston, 1977-84; process mgr. Stone & Webster Engring. Corp., Denver, 1984—. Served to lt. USN, 1972-75. Mem. Am. Inst. Chem. Engrs., Am. Chem. Soc. Republican. Avocations: photography, skiing, hiking, tennis. Home: 19798 E Eldorado Dr Aurora CO 80013 Office: Stone & Webster Engring Corp Box 5406 Denver CO 80217

SANTO PIETRO, VINCENT ALBERT, museum education administrator; b. Phila., Apr. 5, 1957; s. Albert Robert and Doris Mae (Sperber) S.P. BA in chemistry, Temple U., 1981; MS in chemistry, U. Pa., 1983. Part-time instr. Franklin Inst. Sci. Museum, Phila., 1972-83, mgr. floor program, 1983-85; supr. visitor edn. Pacific Sci. Ctr., Seattle, 1985—; cons. Ctr. Sci. and Industry, Columbus, 1983-84. Commr. Phila. council Boy Scouts AM., 1975-81. Recipient Service award Temple U. dept. chemistry, Phila., 1981, Outstanding Dramatics award Lincoln Drama Club, Phila., 1976. Mem. Am. Chem. Soc., Am. Assn. Museums. Republican. Methodist. Clubs: Dr. Who, RX-7 (Los Angeles); Sho Bu Kan Karate (Seattle). Lodge: Order of Arrow. Office: Pacific Sci Ctr 200 2d Ave N Seattle WA 98109

SANTOR, KEN, state treasurer. Real estate developer, gen. contracto, treas. state of Nev., 1987—. Served with USMC, Korea. Office: Office of State Treas Capitol Bldg Carson City NV 89710 *

SANTOS, ROLANDO ARQUIZA, social science educator; b. Zamboanga, Philippines, Mar. 21, 1934; came to U.S., 1957; s. Hermenegildo Santos and Josefina (Arquiza) S.; m. Karen Jean Long, Apr. 6, 1963; children: Roland, Fredrick, Leilani, Robert. AB, Ateneo Coll., Zamboanga City, Philippines, 1955, BSEd, 1956; MA, Coll. for Tchrs., 1958; PhD, Vanderbilt-Peabody U., 1961. Dean grad. studies Bur. Pub. Schs., Legazpi City, Philippines, 1962-63; asst. prof. U. Philippines, 1963-65; lectr. UNESCO Tchr. Edn. Ctr. for Asia, Quezon City, Philippines, 1964-65; prof. ednl. foundations Calif. State U., Los Angeles, 1965—; coordinator The Expt. in Internat. Living, São Paulo, Brazil, 1959, Salamanca, Spain, 1960, U.S. Office of Edn. Tchr. Edn., Mex., 1979-80, cross-cultural studies U.S. Peace Corps, 1961, Hilo, Hawaii, 1969, Bellows Falls, Vt., 1970; dir. Indochinese Parent Tng. Inst., San Diego, 1980-83. Contbr. aritcles to profl. jours. Mem. Nat. Com. Multicultural Standards Tchr. Edn., 1976-77. Smith-Mundt/Fulbright scholar, 1957-61; named Outstanding Prof., Calif. State U., 1976; recipient Outstanding Achievement award Ateneo Alumni Assn., 1977. Mem. Nat. Assn. Asian Am. and Pacific Educators (v.p. 1980-82), Nat. Assn. Bilingual Educators, Nat. Adv. Council on Bilingual Edn. of U.S. Dept Edn. (vice chmn. 1975-76), Filipino Am. Educators Assn. (Outstanding Ednl. Achievement award 1978). Republican. Roman Catholic. Clubs: Ala Roma (San Marino, Calif.), Zamboanga Hermosa (Los Angeles, pres.) (bd. dirs. 1978-81). Avocations: travel, antique collecting, swimming, gardening, auctions. Home: 975 Darby Rd San Marino CA 91108 Office: Calif State U Dept Edn Found 5151 State University Dr Los Angeles CA 90032

SANTOSUOSSO, JOSEPH R., defense contracting executive; b. Quincy, Mass, Mar. 14, 1942; s. Frank and Anne D. (Carbotti) S.; m. Diane Drinkwater, Nov. 9, 1963; children: Laurie, Paul, David. BSME, Worcester Poly. Inst., 1963, MSME, 1969; MBA in Fin., Ariz. State U., 1973. Registered profl. engr. Mass., N.Y., N.J., Conn. Colo., Fla., Va., N.C., Wash., La. Engr. Gen. Electric Corp., Schenectady, N.Y., 1965-70, Honeywell Corp., Phoenix, 1970-75; chief engr. EBASCO Services, Inc., N.Y.C., 1975-85; pres. Lockheed Shipbuilding Co., Seattle, 1985—. Mem. ASME, Soc. Naval Architects & Marine Engrs., Am. Soc. Naval Engrs., Sigma Iota Epsilon, Beta Gamma Sigma. Office: Lockheed Shipbldg Co 2929 16th Ave SW Seattle WA 98134

SANVILLE, JEAN BOVARD, social worker, educator; b. Tionesta, Pa., Dec. 6, 1918; d. Forrest Johnson and Ruth (Dimond) Bovard; m. Richard deCordova Sanville (dec. 1971). BA, U. Colo., 1940; MSS in Social Work, Smith Coll., 1942; PhD, Internat. Coll., 1978; doctorate (hon.), Clin. Social Work Inst., Calif., 1984. Caseworker, supr. various Family Service Orgns., Pitts., N.Y.C., Los Angeles, 1942-46; supr. VA Psychiat. Clinic., Los Angeles, 1946-47; chief social worker Hacker Psychiat. Clinic, Beverly Hills, Calif., 1947-58; pvt. practice Los Angeles, 1958—; faculty mem. UCLA Sch. Social Welfare, Los Angeles, 1948-53, 69—; mem. continuing edn. faculty Smith Coll. Sch. for Social Work, 1984—. Editor: Clinical Social Work Journal, 1982—; contbr. articles to profl. jours. Charter mem. Los Angeles County Mus. Art, Mus. Contemporary Art. Fellow Soc. Clin. Social Work, Am. Orthopsychiat. Assn.; mem. Calif. Soc. Clin. Social Work (founder, pres. 1973-75), Inst. Clin. Social Work (founder, dean 1976-79), Los Angeles Inst. Psychoanalytic Studies (founder, pres. 1980-82, supr., tng. analyst), Nat. Assn. Social Workers (charter mem.). Democrat. Avocations: literature, art, travel. Home and Office: 1300 Tigertail Rd Los Angeles CA 90049

SAPERSTEIN, DAVID DORN, spectroscopist, physical chemist; b. N.Y.C., June 30, 1946; s. Charles Levy and Freda (Dornbush) S.; m. Bernelle Hope Welch, Feb. 28, 1976; 1 child, Robert Elliot. BA in Chemistry, Johns Hopkins U., 1967; PhD in Chemistry, NYU, 1973. Sr. research chemist Merck, Sharp, and Dohme Research Labs., Rahway, N.J., 1973-77, research fellow, 1977-81; sr. applications scientist IBM Instruments, Inc., San Jose, Calif., 1981-83; tech. support mgr. IBM Instruments, Inc., San Jose, 1984-85; adv. chemist, gen. products div. IBM, San Jose, 1985—. Contbr. articles to profl. jours.; patentee in field. Mem. Am. Chem. Soc., AAAS, Soc. Applied Spectroscopy,, Coblentz Soc., Western Spectroscopy Assn. (sec. 1983-86, chmn. 1986-87). Democrat. Home: 130 Durazno Way Portola Valley CA 94025 Office: IBM E42/13 5600 Cottle Rd San Jose CA 95193

SAPON, PAULA JO, school psychologist, consultant; b. Wheeling, W.Va., Apr. 30, 1950; d. John and Helen Elvira (Clemente) S. BA in Psychology magna cum laude, UCLA, 1972; MA in Spl. Edn., Calif. State U., Northridge, 1973, MA in Psychology, 1981; MA in Ednl. Psychology, UCLA, 1975, PhD in Ednl. Psychology, 1982. Cert. sch. psychologist; cert. community coll. instr.; registered psychol. asst. Remedial tutor Fernald Sch., Los Angeles, 1971-74; pvt. practice ednl. therapy Encino, Calif., 1973—; lectr., instr. Calif. State U., Northridge, 1979-84; psychol. asst. Clin. and Cons. Assocs., Encino, 1985-86; sch. psychologist Ednl. Resource and Services Ctr., Beverly Hills, Calif., 1981—; teaching asst. UCLA, 1975-77; psychol. cons. Head Start, Compton, Calif., 1978. Mem. Am. Assn. for Counseling and Devel., Down Syndrome Parents Group. Democrat. Avocations: interior decorating, collecting folk art, exercising. Office: Ednl Resource & Services Ctr 9261 W Third St Beverly Hills CA 90210

SAPORITO, PAUL ANTHONY, architect, educator; b. Bklyn., Aug. 1, 1948; s. Frederick Anthony and Dorothy Olive (Reda) S.; m. Kim Dubin, Dec. 6, 1970; children: Alexander, Anna Gabriella. BArch, Cornell U., 1971. Lic. architect, N.Y., Colo. Archtl. intern Marcel Breuer Assocs., N.Y.C., 1974-76; architect James Sudler Assocs., Denver, 1976-77; prin. Paul Anthony Saporito, Architect, Boulder, Colo., 1984—; regional interviewer Cornell U., Ithaca, N.Y., 1983-84; vis. prof. U. Colo., Denver, 1983—, Boulder, 1985—; cons. Downtown Boulder Partnership, 1986; mem. lecture com. U. Colo., Denver, 1985-86. Designer urban plan 13th St. Competition, Boulder, 1985 (3d place award 1985). Mem. AIA. Club: Boulder Road Runners (bd. dirs. 1986-87). Avocation: road racing. Home and Office: 2765 7th Boulder CO 80302

SAPP, DONALD GENE, minister; b. Phoenix, Feb. 27, 1927; s. Guerry Byron and Lydia Elmeda (Snyder) S.; m. Anna Maydean Nevitt, July 10, 1952 (dec.); m. Joann Herrin Mountz, May 1, 1976; children: Gregory, Paula, Jeffrey. AB in Edn., Ariz. State U., 1949; M Sacred Theology, Boston U., 1952, MST, 1960; D in Ministry, Calif. Grad. Sch. Theology, 1975. Ordained deacon, 1950, ordained elder, 1952. Dir. youth activities Hyde Park (Mass.) Meth. Ch., 1950-52; minister 1st Meth. Ch., Peabody, Mass., 1952-54, Balboa Island (Calif.) Community Meth. Ch., 1954-57, Ch. of the Foothills Meth., Duarte, Calif., 1957-63; sr. minister Aldersgate United Meth. Ch., Tustin, Calif., 1963-70, Paradise Valley (Ariz.) United Meth. Ch., 1970-83; dist. supt. Cen. West Dist. of Desert S.W. Conf. United Meth. Ctr., Phoenix, 1983—. Editor Wide Horizons, 1983—; contbr. articles to profl. jours. Chaplain City of Hope Med. Ctr., Duarte, 1957-63; trustee Plaza Community Ctr., Los Angeles, 1967-70; corp. mem. Sch. Theology at Claremont, Calif., 1972-80; pres. Met. Phoenix Commn., 1983-85; del. western jurisdictional conf. United Meth. Ch., 1982 , World Meth. Conf., Nairobi, Kenya, 1986; bd. dirs. So. Calif. Council Chs., Los Angeles, 1963-67, Wesley Community Ctr., Phoenix, 1983—, Orange County (Calif.) Human Relations Council, 1967-70, Interfaith Counseling Service Found., 1982—. Served with USN, 1945-46. Mem. Ariz. Ecumenical Council, Kappa Delta Pi, Tau Kappa Epsilon, Blue Key. Democrat. Lodge: Rotary (pres.). Avocations: camping, backpacking, overseas travel. Home: 5225 E Road Runner Rd Paradise Valley AZ 85253 Office: United Meth Ctr 1807 N Central Ave Suite 100 Phoenix AZ 84004-1508

SAPSOWITZ, SIDNEY H., entertainment company executive; b. N.Y.C., June 29, 1936; s. Max and Annette (Rothstein) Sapsowitz; m. Phyllis Skopp, Nov. 27, 1957; children—Donna Chazen, Gloria Lynn, Marsha Helene. BBA summa cum laude, Paterson State Coll., N.J., 1981. Various fin. and systems positions Metro Goldwyn Mayer, N.Y.C., 1957-68; exec. v.p., chief fin. officer Metro Goldwyn Mayer, Los Angeles, 1980-86, also bd. dirs.; exec. v.p. Penta Computer Assoc. Inc., N.Y.C., 1968-70, Cons. Actuaries Inc., Clifton, N.J., 1970-73, Am. Film Theatre, N.Y.C., 1974-76; exec. v.p., chief fin. officer Cinema Shares Internat. Distributors, N.Y.C., 1976-79; sr. cons. Solomon, Finger & Newman, N.Y.C., 1979-80; various positions leading to exec. v.p.fin. and adminstrn., chief fin. officer MGM/UA Entertainment Co., Beverly Hills, Calif., 1985-86; sr. exec. v.p., bd. dirs. MGM/UA Communications Co., Beverly Hills, Calif., 1986—; sr. exec. v.p. MGM Communications Co., Beverly Hills, Calif., 1986—; dir. Penta Computer Assoc., N.Y.C., 1968-70, Metro Goldwyn Mayer, N.Y.C., 1985-86; MGM/UA Communications Co., Beverly Hills, 1986—. Pres., Wayne Conservative Congregation, N.J., 1970-77. Mem. Am. Mgmt. Assn. (cons., lectr. 1967), Acad. Motion Picture Arts and Scis., Fin. Exec. Inst. Lodge: Knights of Pythias (chancellor 1970).

SARAF, DILIP GOVIND, electronics executive; b. Belgaum, India, Nov. 10, 1942; s. Govind Vithal and Indira Laxman (Divekar) S.; m. Mary Lou Arnold, July 25, 1970; 1 son, Rajesh Dilip. B. Tech with honors, Indian Inst. Tech., Bombay, 1965; M.S.E.E., Stanford U., 1969. Sr. mgmt. trainee Delhi Cloth and Gen. Mills Co. (India), 1965-68; sr. research engr. SRI Internat., Menlo Park, Calif., 1969-78; project dir. Kaiser Electronics, San Jose, Calif., 1978—; cons. teaching U. Santa Clara (Calif.), 1972, 73. Mem. IEEE, Soc. Am. Inventors. Contbr. articles to profl jours. Patentee in field. Home: 28050 Horse Shoe Ct Los Altos Hills CA 94022 Office: 2701 Orchard Pkwy San Jose CA 95134

SARAFIAN, ARMEN, university president emeritus; b. Van Nuys, Calif., Mar. 5, 1920; s. Kevork and Lucy (Gazarian) S.; m. Doris Manoogian, 1941; children: Winston, Norman, Joy. A.B. magna cum laude, La Verne Coll., 1940, LL.D. (hon.), 1967; M.A., Claremont Grad. U., 1947; Ph.D., U. So. Calif., Los Angeles, 1964. Tchr. public elem. and secondary schs. Calif., 1940-47; tchr. English and Am. history and polit. sci. Pasadena (Calif.) Jr. Coll. Dist., 1947-51; mem. part-time faculty various colls. and univs. in Calif., 1947-68; coordinator secondary and jr. coll. edn. Pasadena City Schs., 1951-59; adminstrv. dean for instruction Pasadena City Coll., 1959-65, pres., 1965-76, pres. emeritus, 1976-85; also supt. Pasadena Area Community Coll. Dist., 1966-76; adj. prof. community coll. adminstrn. U. So. Calif., Los Angeles, 1968-78; pres. La Verne (Calif.) Coll. (name changed to La Verne U. 1978), 1976-85, pres. emeritus, 1985—; founder Am. Armenian Internat. Coll., 1976; interim pres. Colo. Mountain Coll., Glenwood Springs, 1986-87; cons. to industry, govt. and bus., 1952—; dir. mgmt. reorgn. of Conn. System of Regional Community Colls., 1974-75; mem. adult and continuing edn. com. for Calif. Community Colls., 1974-75; Delta Epsilon disting. lectr. U. So. Calif., 1973; project dir., cons. joint legis. com. on higher edn. State of Alaska, 1973-77; mem. mgmt. team U. Alaska System, 1977; acad. planning specialist Mary Hardin-Baylor Coll., Belton, Tex., 1974; mem. western regional adv. bd. Coll. Entrance Examination Bd., 1971-75; mgmt. adv. to City of Pasadena Mcpl. Govt., 1972-73; founder Am. Armenian Internat. Coll., 1976; mem. Calif. State Bd. Edn., 1986—; mem. Calif. Ednl. Tech. Com., 1986—; chmn. Joint Vocat. Edn. Com., 1986—. Mem. policy bd. Gt. Plains Nat. Instructional TV Library, 1975-79; founder and mem. exec. com. Pasadena Hall of Sci. Project, 1965-76; founder, adult adv. Pasadena Area Youth Council, 1953-66; mem. St. Luke Hosp. Adv. Bd., 1969-71, Mayor's Com. on Children and Youth, Pasadena, 1960-62; mem. hon. adv. bd. Pasadena Area chpt., ARC, 1956-76; pres. Calif. Conservation Council, 1966-68; mem. nat. adv. council for nurse tng. USPHS, 1967-71; judge Los Angeles Times Scholarship Award Contest, 1974; bd. dirs. Pasadena Urban Coalition, 1973-76; trustee La Verne Coll., 1969-76. Recipient Disting. Community Service award Pasadena Edn. Assn., 1956, Conservation Merit award Calif. Conservation Council, 1960, Meritorious Service award Pasadena City Coll. Faculty Senate, 1960, Ralph Story award Pasadena City Coll. Faculty Assn., 1974, U. So. Calif. Service award, 1974, Recognition award USPHS, 1972, Others award Salvation Army, 1975, Recognition award Pasadena Arts Council, 1976; named Citizen of the Day Sierra Madre City Council, 1972, Arthur Noble disting. citizen City of Pasadena, 1976. Mem. Calif. Scholarship Fedn., Calif. Jr. Coll. Assn. (mem. legis. com. 1973-76), Pasadena Area Sch. Trustees Assn. (founder 1966), Pasadena Arts Council, Pasadena Hist. Soc., La Verne C. of C. (pres. 1978-79), Native Sons of the Golden West, Pasadena Council of Parents and Tchrs. (hon. life), Assoc. Student Body of Pasadena City Coll., Pasadena C. of C. (v.p. 1972), La Verne C. of C. (pres. 1978-79), Calif. State Bd. Edn., Calif. State Ednl. Tech. Com., Phi Delta Kappa (Spl. Recognition award 1970). Home and Office: PO Box 1624 Glendora CA 91740

SARAIYA, ROMIT RAMNIKLAL, mechanical engineer; b. Bombay, Sept. 12, 1945; came to U.S., 1964; s. Ramniklal K. and Nirmala S.; m. Rupa R. Vanlila Sham, Apr. 4, 1969; children: Manish, Tejas. BSME, Christian Bros. U., 1967. Registered profl. engr. Engr. Warwick Electric Co., Niles, Ill., 1967-70; proj. engr. Voice of Music, Benton Harbor, Mich., 1970-71, Magnavox, Ft. Wayne, Ind., 1971-74, Gen. Electric Corp., Decatur, Ill., 1974-75; project mgr. G.T.E. Internat., Burlington, Mass., 1975-79; dir. engring. Megatek Corp., San Diego, 1979—. Mem. Am. Mgmt. Assn., Nat. Computer Graphics Assn. Club: Gujarati Assn. San Diego (sec. 1984-86). Home: 3021 Del Rey Ave Carlsbad CA 92008 Office: Megatek Corp 9645 Scranton Rd San Diego CA 92121

SARCHET, NANCY ANN, social worker; b. Cheyenne, Wyo., Nov. 21, 1953; d. Donald Erwin and Virginia Birdie (Hike) H.; m. Scott David Sarchet, Aug. 12, 1981; children: Virginia Elaine, Justin Marie. AA, Aims Community Coll., Greeley, Colo., 1972; BA, U. No. Colo., 1974; MSW, U. Denver, 1986. Lic. social worker, Colo. Child protection caseworker Weld County Social Services, Greeley, 1977-84; adult caseworker Wash. County Social Services, Akron, Colo., 1975-77; child caseworker Tex. Dept. Pub. Welfare, Houston, 1974-75; social worker Adams County Social Services, Commerce City, Colo., 1985-86; pvt. practice social work Platteville, Colo., 1986—; social worker Weld Boces, LaSalle, Colo., 1986—; cons. Compassionate Friends, Greeley, 1980-81. Mem. Nat. Assn. Social Workers, Am. Assn. Protecting Children, Inc. Republican. Methodist. Avocations: sewing, reading. Home and Office: 14851 WCR 28 Platteville CO 80651

SAREN, DRUCILLA, social science educator; b. N.Y.C., Jan. 8, 1947; d. David and Rita (Doyle) S; divorced; children: Jade, Leila. BA, CCNY, 1967; MA with distinction, U. N.Mex., 1981, PhD, 1986. Cert. tchr. spl. edn. Social worker Welfare Dept., N.Y.C., 1968-69; tchr. Bd. Edn., N.Y.C., 1969-74, New Sch. Santa Fe, 1979-81, Albuquerque Pub. Schs., 1981-83; instr. U. N.Mex., Albuquerque, 1983-86, Diagnostic Sch for Neurologically Handicapped Children, San Francisco, 1986—. Active Citizen Rev. Bd, Albuquerque, 1985, Program Selection Com., Albuquerque; founder Parent Adv. Com., 1978; bd. dirs. Ala Costa Ctr., Berkeley, Calif., 1986; ednl. coordinator Diagnostic Ctr. Neurologically Impaired Children, San Francisco, 1987. Mem. Parents Reaching Out, Assn. Retarded Citizens, Am. Orthopsychiat. Assn., Council for Exceptional Children (convention presenter 1985, 86). Home: 1512 Bonita Ave San Francisco CA 94709 Office: Diagnostic Sch Neurologically Handicapped Children No Calif Lake Merced Blvd and Winston San Francisco CA 94132

SARGENT, ARLENE HONDL, nursing educator; b. Little Falls, Minn., Jan. 11, 1944; d. Anton Clarence and Eleanor (Buerman) Hondl; m. Kenneth William Sargent, June 16, 1972; children: Lisa, Michelle. BS, Coll. St. Catherine, St. Paul; MS, U. Minn., 1972; EdD, No. Ill. U., 1980. Staff nurse U. Wash. Hosp., Seattle, 1969-70; asst. head nurse U. Minn. Hosp., Mpls., 1970-72; instr. nursing Loyola U., Chgo., 1972-75; asst. prof. No. Ill. U., De Kalb, 1975-79; chmn. dept. nursing U. Dubuque, Iowa, 1980-83; assoc. prof. Holy Names Coll., Oakland, Calif., 1983—; cons. Mercy Health Ctr., Dubuque, 1980-83; reviewer textbooks Mosby & W.B. Saunders Pub. Co. Chmn. bioethics com., Lafayette, Calif., 1985—. Mem. Am. Nurses Assn., Calif. Nurses Assn., Am. Assn. Adult Continuing Edn., Sigma Theta Tau, Kappa Delta Pi, Pi Lambda Theta. Presbyterian. Avocations: running, reading. Home: 237 Vagabond Ct Danville CA 94526 Office: Holy Names Coll 3500 Mountain Blvd Oakland CA 94619

SARGENT, DIANA RHEA, bookkeeper; b. Cheyenne, Wyo., Feb. 20, 1939; d. Clarence and Edith (de Castro) Hayes; grad. high sch.; m. Charles Sargent, Apr. 17, 1975; children—Rene A. Coburn, Rochelle A. Riddle, Weldy, Clayton R. Weldy, Christopher J.; stepchildren—Laurie E. Sargent, Leslie E. Sargent. IBM proof operator Bank Am., Stockton, Calif., 1956-58, gen. ledger bookkeeper, Modesto, Calif., 1963-66; office mgr., head bookkeeper Central Drug Store, Modesto, 1966-76; pres. Sargent & Sargent, Modesto, 1976—. Mem. Haven Stanislaus Women's Refuge Center, Stanislaus County Commn. on Women, Stanislaus County Women's Resource Ctr. Mem. NOW, San Francisco Mus. Soc., Nat. Soc. Public Accts., Modesto C. of C., Merced Accts. Soc. Republican. Humanist. Office: 915 14th St Modesto CA 95353

SARGENT, WARREN NICHOLS, JR., consulting company executive; b. New London, Conn., Sept. 17, 1946; s. Warren Nichols and Janice Caroyln (Warner) S.; B.S.M.E., U. Conn., 1968, M.S., 1970, M.B.A., 1971; M.A., U. Tex., Dallas, 1980. Systems analyst, programmer U. Conn., 1965-71, City of Hartford (Conn.), 1968-71; instr. UCCEL, Arlington, Tex., 1973, cons., Nashville, 1973-74, mgr. bus. planning, Dallas, 1974-75, bus. devel., 1975-77; gen. mgr. Bonanza Internat., Houston, 1977, dir. franchising, Dallas, 1978; dir. computer services programs INPUT, Palo Alto, Calif., 1979-81; pres. The Strategist, Visalia, Calif., 1981—. Served to lt. USAF, 1971-73. Decorated D.S.M. Mem. Computer Industry Guide, Share, Adapso, Beta Gamma Sigma. Clubs: Sports, Internat. Mgmt. Address: PO Box 81 Visalia CA 93279

SARIAN, JIRAIR NERSES, radiologist; b. Aintab, Turkey, Aug. 16, 1915; s. Nerses Sarkis and Nourita Hagop (Philipbossian) S.; B.A., Am. U. Beirut, 1937; M.D., U. Lausanne (Switzerland), 1940; B.D., Nazarene Theol. Sem., 1949; m. Jessie Helen Maghakian, Jan. 28, 1950; children—Norita, June, John. Rotating intern U. Lausanne Hosps., 1940-41, resident, 1941-44, chief asst., 1944-46; rotating intern Herrick Meml. Hosp., Berkeley, Calif., 1950-51; research and teaching fellow dept. oncology and radiology U. Kans. Med. Ctr., Kansas City, 1948-49, dept. radiology Huntington Meml. Hosp., Pasadena, Calif., 1951; practice medicine specializing in radiology, Los Angeles, 1951; asst. clin. prof. radiology U. Calif. Coll. Medicine, Irvine, 1965—. Treas. bd. trustees Haigazian Coll. Recipient cert. of appreciation AMA, Am. Roentgen Ray Soc., 1963; Physicians Recognition award AMA, 1969, 72, 76. Diplomate Am. Bd. Radiology. Mem. Armed Forces Inst. Pathology (cert.), AMA, Calif., Los Angeles County med. assns., Am. Roentgen Ray Soc., Am. Coll. Radiology, Physicians Club. Author articles, books and booklets in English, Armenian and French. Home: 5305 Shenandoah Ave Los Angeles CA 90056 Office: 727 W 7th St Los Angeles CA 90017

SARIKAYA, MEHMET, metallurgy educator; b. Ankara, Turkey, Oct. 1, 1953; came to U.S., 1977; s. Mehmet and Hatice (Demirbas) S. BS in Matallurgy, Middle East Tech. U., Ankara, 1977; MS in Materials Sci. and Engring., U. Calif., Berkeley, 1979, PhD in Material Sci. and Engring., 1982. Lectr. U. Calif., Berkeley, Calif., 1982-84; research engr. Lawrence Berkeley Lab., 1982-84; asst. prof. U. Wash., Seattle, 1986—. Mem. Northwestern Soc. of Electron Microscopy (sec. gen. 1986—), Am. Soc. Metals (mem. exec. com. 1985—). Office: U Wash Roberts Hall FB-10 Dept Materials Sci and Engring Seattle WA 98195

SARLAT, GLADYS, public relations company executive; b. Elizabeth, N.J., July 22, 1923; d. Max and Dora (Levin) S. B.S., U. Wash., 1946. Asst., Kay Sullivan Assocs. N.Y.C., 1949-50; fashion dir. Warsaw & Co., N.Y.C., 1950-54; asst. fashion coordinator Emporium Dept. Store, San Francisco, 1955-56; asst. prodn. mgr. Cunningham & Walsh Advt., San Francisco, 1958-59; v.p., pub. relations dir. Harwood Advt. Inc., Tucson and Phoenix, 1959-68; v.p., dir. Waller & Sarlat Advt. Inc., Tucson, 1968-69; pres. Godwin & Sarlat Pub. Relations, Inc., Tucson, 1970—. Active Tucson Tomorrow, 1980—; mem. adv. com. Downtown Devel. Corp., 1979-85. Named Woman of Year for Bus., Ariz. Daily Star, 1963; recipient Lulu award Los Angeles Woman in Advt., 1962. Mem. Pub. Relations Soc. Am. (past bd. mem., counselors acad.), Fashion Group, Tucson Met. C. of C. (v.p., dir. 1976-85, chmn bd. 1986-87), Tucson Trade Bur. (dir. 1977-80). Republican. Jewish. Club: Old Pueblo, La Paloma Country (Tucson). Home: 5530 N Camino Arenosa Tucson AZ 85718 Office: Godwin & Sarlat Pub Relations Inc 110 S Church Ave Suite 411 Tucson AZ 85701

SARNA, LINDA PATTI, nursing educator; b. San Francisco, May 14, 1947; d. Salvatore and Evelyn Alice (Forsmark) Patti; m. Gregory Paul Sarna, Sept. 21, 1969; children: Vanessa, Evan. BS, UCLA, 1969, MN in Nursing, 1976; postgrad, U. Calif., San Francisco, 1986—. Asst. clin. prof. UCLA Sch. Nursing, 1976—. Co-author: Concepts in Oncology, 1981 (named Book of the Year Am. Jour. Nursing). Grad. opportunity fellow, U. Calif. San Francisco, 1983; Recipient nat. research service award NIH, 1985; Am. Cancer Soc. grantee, 1986. Mem. Am. Nurse's Assn., Oncology Nursing Soc., UCLA Jonsson Comprehensive Cancer Ctr., UCLA Sch. Nursing Alumni Assn. (exec. bd. dirs. 1980-82), Sigma Theta Tau, Gamma Tau (exec. bd. dirs. 1979-81). Democrat. Office: UCLA Sch Nursing Cen Health Scis Los Angeles CA 90024

SAROSIEK, ANA MARIA, materials and processes specialist; b. La Guaira, Venezuela, Mar. 2, 1951; d. Kazimierz and Jadwiga (Wojewodzki) Sarosiek; m. David Bruce Laning, Aug. 5, 1978; children: George Peter-David, Kathleen Ann. BSME, U. Simon Bolivar, Caracas, Venezuela, 1974; MS in Materials Sci., MIT, 1977, Phd in Metallurgy, 1982. Instr. Simon Bolivar U., 1974-75, asst. prof., 1977-78; postdoctoral assoc. dept. materials sci. and engring. MIT, Cambridge, 1982-83; sr. scientist G.A. Techs., San Diego, 1983-84; assoc. research scientist Lockheed Missiles and Space Co. Palo Alto (Calif.) Research Lab., 1984-86; materials and processes specialist Lockheed Missiles and Space Co., Sunnyvale, Calif., 1986—. Contbr. articles to profl. jours. Fellow AMAX Found., 1976, 78-82. Mem. Metall. Soc. of AIME, Am. Soc. for Metals (mem. exec. com. 1985—), Sigma Xi. Avocations: running, swimming, hiking. Office: Lockheed Missiles and Space Co PO Box 3504 Sunnyvale CA 94088-3504

SARSFIELD, GEORGE P., lawyer; b. Vancouver, B.C., Can., Jan. 14, 1913 (parents Am. citizens); s. John M. and Margaret (LaValle) S.; B.A., J.D., U. Mont., 1950; m. Margeret Davis, May 23, 1942. Blk., laborer, miner, 1930-41; admitted to Mont. bar, 1950, since practiced in Butte. Past pres. Butte YMCA. Republican nominee Congress, 1st dist. Mont., 1960. Chmn. exec. bd. Mont. Coll. Mineral Sci. and Tech., 1968-71; chmn. bd. trustees U. Mont. Devel. Fund, 1967-70; adv. bd. Salvation Army, 1952—. Served from pvt. to capt. U.S. Army, 1941-46. Recipient Disting. Service award U. Mont., 1971, Pantzer award, 1975. Mem. Am., Mont. (past v.p.) bar assns., Am. Trial Lawyers Assn., U. Mont. Alumni Assn. (pres. 1964, chmn. bd. 1964-66), Mont. State Golf Assn. (past pres.), U.S. Golf Assn. (mem. sectional affairs com. 1968—), Phi Delta Phi, Alpha Kappa Psi, Phi Delta Theta. Clubs: Rotary (past local pres.; dist. gov. 1963-64, chmn. internat. constn. and by-laws com. 1969-70, internat. dir. 1973-75, internat. 1st v.p. 1974-75, chmn. exec. com. internat. bd. dirs. 1974-75). Club: Butte Country (past pres.). Former Mont. open golf champion; Mont. amateur golf champion, 4 years. Home: 2700 Floral Blvd Butte MT 59701 Office: Mayer Bldg Butte MT 59701

SARVAS-PALM, ARLENE FRANCES, educational program administrator; b. Bethlehem, Pa., July 2, 1947; d. James Stephen and Elizabeth (Petanovics) Sarvas; m. Vincent John Palm, July 4, 1985. B.S., Pa. State U., 1970, D.Ed., 1976; M.Ed., Lehigh U., 1973. Cosmetology instr. Bethlehem Area Vocat. Tech. Sch., Pa., 1970-73; asst. dir. Franklin County Area Vocat. Tech. Sch., Chambersburg, Pa., 1975-76; supr. instrn. Bethlehem Area Vocat. Tech. Sch., 1976-81; dir. Carbon County Area Vocat. Tech. Sch., Jim Thorpe, Pa., 1981-85; dir. Baldy View Regional Occupation Program, Claremont, Calif., 1985—; instr. Lehigh U., Bethlehem, 1973-74, Pa. State U., University Park, 1974-75. Co-author: Evaluation of Vocational Technical Schools, 1977. Mem. Am. Assn. Sch. Adminstrs., Nat. Council Local Adminstrs., Calif. Assn. Health Career Educators, Pa. Vocat. Assn. (life, pres.-elect 1985), Calif. Assn. Regional Occupational Ctrs. Programs, Pi Lambda Theta, Iota Lambda Sigma, Phi Delta Kappa. Club: Soroptimist (v.p. 1975). Office: Baldy View ROP 135 S Spring St Claremont CA 91711

SARVER, SHARON MARIE, accountant; b. Wapato, Wash., May 17, 1942; d. Roy Clifton and Mila Ann (Logan) S.; children: Jeffrey Dale Taylor, Rebecca Anne Johnston, Donald Gene Taylor, Jerry Dean Sims. Student Edison Tech. Sch., 1960-63, Data Control Systems, 1964-65, Ventura Coll., 1966-67, Bellevue Community Coll., 1969-71, U. Wash., 1975; Emergency Med. Technician cert., 1974; Acct., Rochester Electronics, Redmond, Wash., 1972, Adby Industries, Seattle, 1973, Koenigsberg, Brown, Sin-Seimer, Stone & Meltzer, Seattle, 1975; bus. mgr. Community Psychiat. Centers, Kirkland, Wash., 1976; acct., owner Gen. Office Services, Woodinville, Wash., 1977—. Bd. dirs. Lower Snoqualmie Valley Sch. Bd., 1974-78, Redmond Miss Pageant, 1977-78. Mem. Nat. Assn. Accountants, Redmond C. of C. (dir.), U.S. C. of C., Nat. Fedn. Ind. Businesses, Assn. Wash. Bus. Office: Gen Office Services 16810 NE 185th Woodinville WA 98072

SASAKI, Y. TITO, business services company executive; b. Tokyo, Feb. 6, 1938; came to U.S., 1967, naturalized, 1983; s. Yoshinaga and Chiyoko (Imada) S.; m. Janet Louise Cline, June 27, 1963; 1 child, Heather N. BS, Chiba U., 1959; postgrad. Royal Coll. Art, London, 1961, U. Oslo, 1962; MS, Athens Tech. Inst., Greece, 1964; postgrad. U. Calif., Berkeley, 1969. Chief designer Aires Camera Industries Co., Tokyo, 1958-59; tech. officer London County Council, 1961-62; researcher Athens Ctr. Ekistics, 1964-66; sr. researcher Battelle Inst., Geneva, 1966-68; project engr. Marin County Transit Dist., San Rafael, Calif., 1968-69; chief planning, research Golden Gate Bridge Dist., San Francisco, 1969-74; pres. Visio Internat. Inc., Somona, Calif., 1973—; chmn. steering com. Kawada Industries Inc., Tokyo, 1974-82; chief exec. officer Quantum Mechanics Corp., Somona, 1981—; bd. dirs., sec. Sonoma Skypark, Inc., 1986—. Mem. Rep. Nat. Com. Mem. ASME, Am. Welding Soc., Experimental Aircraft Assn., Am. Welding Soc., Am. Inst. Cert. Planners, World Soc. Ekistics, Brit. Soc. Long-Range Planning, Am. Vacuum Soc., Aircraft Owners and Pilots Assn. Roman Catholic. Office: Visio Internat Inc PO Box 1888 Sonoma CA 95476

SASAKI, YUKI-HIKO, research associate; b. Tokyo, Aug. 2, 1937; came to U.S., 1970; s. Rin-ichi and Shizuko (Ogawa) S.; m. Fumiko Miyawaki, Mar. 31, 1963; children: Hiroshi, Yumiko, Akira. BA, Internat. Christian U., Tokyo; PhD, McMaster U., Can., 1970. Postdoctoral fellow U. Ariz., Tucson, 1970-71, U. Ala., Tuscaloosa, 1971-73; chem. engr. Chiyoda Chem. Engring. and Constrn. Co., Tokyo, 1961-65; sr. research chemist Avery Internat., Pasadena, Calif., 1973-76, group leader, 1976-81, sr. research assoc., 1981—. Contbr. articles to profl. jours; patentee in field. Recipient Tech. Dir.'s Hon. award Fasson, Europe, Leiden, The Netherlands, 1986, Cleve., 1982. Mem. Am. Chem. Soc., TAPPI. Home: 170 Armstrong Dr Claremont CA 91711 Office: Avery Internat 325 N Altadena Dr Pasadena CA 91107

SASSO, CASSANDRA GAY, lawyer; b. Washington, Feb. 5, 1946; d. Phillip Francis and Lois Aileen (Ayers) S.; m. David John Stephenson, Jr., Feb. 12, 1982; 1 child, Gabriel David. BS magna cum laude, U. Nebr., 1967; MA, U. Calif., Santa Barbara, 1970; JD, Northwestern U., 1974. Bar: Ill., 1974, Colo., 1976. Law clk. Schiff Hardin & Waite, Chgo., 1973; assoc. Sidney & Austin, Chgo., 1974-76; instr. antitrust and securities U. Denver Law Sch., 1978-79, 1985-86; instr. trial practice U. Colo. Law Sch., Boulder, 1983-85; instr. Nat. Inst. Trial Advocacy, 1985-86; ptnr., trial lawyer Sherman & Howard, Denver, 1975—. Bd. dirs. Colo. Judicial Inst., 1982—, v.p. 1984; bd. dirs. Colo. Lawyers Com., Denver, 1980-82, Legal Aid Soc. of Met. Denver, 1981-83; mem. Denver Com. Fgn. Relations, 1981-86; chmn. bd. dirs. Colo. ACLU, Denver, 1982-83; mem. steering com. Colo. Lawyers for Nuclear Arms Edn., Denver, 1982-83. Mem. Colo. Womens Bar Assn., Colo. Bar Assn. (bd. govs. 1980-83), ABA, Chgo. Council Lawyers (sec. 1974-75), Denver Bar Assn. (bd. trustees 1978-81), Colo. Trial Lawyers Assn. (bd. dirs. 1984-85), Alpha Omicron Pi, Mortar Bd. Democrat. Presbyterian. Home: 1781 Holly St Denver CO 80220 Office: Sherman & Howard 633 17th St Suite 2900 Denver CO 80202

SASSOON, MAUREEN HANNAH, industrial hygiene and safety professional, consultant; b. Hollywood, Calif., Jan. 23, 1956; d. Moe George and Margaret Joyce (Eardley) S. BS, Calif. State U., Northridge, 1979, MS, 1980, MPH, 1985; DPub. Adminstrn., U. La Verne, 1987. Registered sanitarian, Calif., cert. community coll. tchr., Calif., ordained elder Presbyn. Ch. Pre-sch. tchr. aid French Nursery Sch., Hollywood, 1971-78; phys. therapy aid Kaiser Hosp., Los Angeles, 1975-80; health and safety officer intern Calif. State U., 1980; indsl. hygiene intern ARLI, Monrovia, Calif., 1980; health and safety coordinator Globe Battery, Fullerton, Calif., 1979-81; indsl. hygiene and safety profl. Cal-Surance, Torrance, Calif., 1981—. CPR and first aid tchr. ARC, Los Angeles, 1980—. Award for Services Above and Beyond, ARC, 1981. Mem. Am. Cancer Soc. (pub. health com. 1984—, chmn. smoking cessation com. 1985—), Am. Indsl. Hygiene Assn. (respiratory com. 1983—), Nat. Environ. Health Assn., Calif. Environ. Health Assn., Am. Soc. Safety Engrs. (v.p., treas. 1983-84, pres. 1984-85), Eta Sigma Gamma. Republican. Avocations: missionary work, photography, swimming, singing, tennis. Office: Cal-Surance 2790 Skypark Dr Torrance CA 90505

SASSOON, VIDAL, hair stylist; b. London, Eng., Jan. 17, 1928; s. Nathan and Betty (Bellin) S.; divorced 1980; children—Catya, Elan, Eden, David. Ed., N.Y. U. Founder, chmn. bd. Vidal Sassoon, Inc. (beauty treatment products, appliances, wearing apparel and boutiques), Europe and Am.; Pres. Vidal Sassoon Found.; lectr. in field. Author: autobiography A Year of Beauty and Health, 1976. Served with Palmach Israeli Army. Recipient award French Ministry of Culture, award for services rendered Harvard Bus. Sch.; Intercoiffure award Cartier, London, 1978; Hair Artists Internat. fellow. Clubs: Anabelle (London, Eng.), Ambassadeurs (London, Eng.), Claremont (London, Eng.); Le Club (N.Y.C.). Office: Vidal Sassoon Inc 2049 Century Park E Los Angeles CA 90067 *

SATHER, GLEN CAMERON, professional hockey team coach and executive; b. High River, Alta., Canada, Sept. 2, 1943. Former professional hockey playe; pres., gen. mgr., coadh Edmonton Oilers, Nat. Hockey League, Alta., Can.; Coach winning team in Stanley Cup competition, 1987. Recipient Jack Adams Award for NHL Coach of the Yr., 1986. Coach NFL Champions, 1984-85. Office: care Edmonton Oilers, Northlands Coliseum, Edmonton, AB Canada T5B 4M9 *

SATHER, RICHARD WALLACE, retail executive; b. Coalville, Utah, Mar. 24, 1947; s. Richard Wayne Sather and LaVon Mable (White) Cornia; m. Cynthia Louise Riley, Mar. 1, 1973; children, Kelly, Rikki, Elisa, Emily, Chelsea. BA, U. Wyo., 1970. With Sathor's Jewelry, Evanston, Wyo., 1972-73, ptnr., 1973-75, corp. pres., 1975—. Mem. Evanston City Council, Evanston Planning and Zoning Bd., Evanston Recreation Bd. Mem. Evanston C. of C. (Bus. Person of Month award 1985). Democrat. Mormon. Home: 1125 Uinta Evanston WY 82930 Office: Sather's Jewelry 932 Main St Evanston WY 82930

SATIR, KEMAL, electrical engineer, consultant; b. Mersin, Turkey, Sept. 3, 1928; s. Hüsnü H. and Emine Seyde (Hasan) S.; m. Gulten Atilla, July 17, 1957; children: Deniz, Filiz, Yasemin, Cengiz, Derya. BSEE, Yildiz Tech. Coll., Istanbul, Turkey, 1949; MSEE, U. Mich., 1955; MSEE in Power, Wash. State U., 1972. Registered profl. engr., Wash., Minn. Jr. elec. engr. Etibank, Ankara, Turkey, 1949-54, system engr., 1956-58; assoc. engr. Boeing Airplane Co., Renton, Wash., 1959-60; chief engr. Inland Power & Light Co., Spokane, Wash., 1961-69; cons. engr. Seattle, 1969—. Served to lt. Signal Corps Turkish Army, 1950-51. Mem. IEEE (sr.), NSPE, Wash. Soc. Profl. Engrs. Club: The Statesman's (Spokane). Avocations: fishing, backgammon, classical music. Home and Office: 11300 1st Ave NE #115 Seattle WA 98125

SATOH, YOSHIHARU, banker; b. Tokyo, Nov. 18, 1928; came to U.S., 1967; s. Sotoji and Miyuki (Odake) S.; m. Ikuko Nakatsuka, May 6, 1955; children: Kaoru, Keiichi. Law degree, Tokyo U., 1952. Sr. v.p., dir. Sumitomo Bank of Calif., San Francisco, 1967-72; sr. v.p. Central Pacific Bank, Honolulu, 1972-73; exec. v.p., dir. Central Pacific Bank, 1973-78, pres., chief exec. officer, 1978—; trustee Kuakini Health Systems, Honolulu, 1983—. Trustee, U. Hawaii Found.; bd. regents Chaminade U. of Honolulu. Mem. Hawaii Bankers Assn. (pres. 1978-79), C. of C. of Hawaii (dir. 1980-83), Honolulu Japanese C. of C. (dir.), Japan-Am. Soc. of Honolulu, United Japanese Soc. of Hawaii, Hawaii Joint Council on Econ. Edn. Clubs: Waialae Country, Honolulu Internat. Country, Pacific. Office: Central Pacific Bank 220 S King St Honolulu HI 96813

SATRE, PHILIP GLEN, business executive, lawyer; b. Palo Alto, Calif., Apr. 30, 1949; s. Selmer Kenneth and Georgia June (Sterling) S.; m. Jennifer Patricia Arnold, June 30, 1973; children—Malena Anne, Allison Neal, Jessica Lilly. B.A., Stanford U., 1971; J.D., U. Calif.-Davis, 1975; postgrad sr. exec. program MIT, 1982. Bar: Nev., Calif. Assoc. Vargas & Bartlett, Reno, 1975-79; v.p., gen. counsel, sec. Harrah's, Reno, 1980-83, sr. v.p., 1983-84, pres. Harrah's East, Atlantic City, 1984; pres., chief exec. officer Harrah's Hotels and Casinos, Reno, 1984—. Mem. ABA, Nev. Bar Assn., Calif. Bar Assn., Order of Coif, Phi Kappa Phi, Stanford Alumni Assn. (pres. Reno chpt. 1976-77). Office: Harrah's 300 E 2d St PO Box 10 Reno NV 89504

SATRE, WENDELL JULIAN, former utilities executive; b. Post Falls, Idaho, July 3, 1918; s. Julian J. and Myrtle A. (Clark) S.; m. Jessie E. Stewart, June 1, 1941; children: Janet Elizabeth, Clark Wendell, Jeanne Ellen Satre Kanikeberg, Glen Walter. B.S. in Elec. Engring, U. Idaho, 1939. With Wash. Water Power Co., Spokane, 1939-85; mgr. constrn., maintenance Wash. Water Power Co., 1958-63, exec. asst. to pres., 1963-64, asst. v.p., 1964-65, v.p., dir., 1965, exec. v.p., 1965-71, pres., 1971-82, chmn. bd., 1975-85; past pres., dir. Devel. Assocs., Inc.; past chmn. Wash. Irrigation & Devel. Co.; past pres., dir. Limestone Co., Water Power Improvement Co., Spokane Indsl. Park, Inc.; past trustee Fidelity Mut. Savs. Bank; past chmn. bd. ITRON, Inc.; chmn. N. Am. Energy Services Co., Empire Health Services; dir. Pacific Telecom. Mem. Gov.'s adv. council Wash. Dept. Commerce and Econ. Devel., 1974-80, chmn., 1976-80; mem. Wash. Energy Policy Council, 1973-75, Council for Wash.'s Future, 1973-85; past dir. Wash. Council Econ. Edn., 1973-80; co-chmn. Com. of 1000, 1974-77; mem. Spokane Little Hoover Commn., 1968-71; past mem. Spokane Area Devel. Council.; Bd. dirs. Inland Empire chpt. A.R.C., 1964-69, United Crusade of Spokane County, 1965-67; mem. exec. bd. Inland Empire council Boy Scouts Am., 1974-82; past pres. Greater Spokane Music and Allied Arts Festival, 1967; trustee Spokane Symphony Soc., 1966-79; past trustee Whitworth Coll.; past mem. adv. bd. Wash. State U. Coll. Engring., 1972-80; adv. bd. U. Idaho Coll. Engring., 1972-82; pres. Wash. Citizens Com. for Pub. Higher Edn., 1976-79; bd. dirs. United for Wash., 1977-80; past mem. Gov.'s Council Econs. Advisers, Greater Spokane Community Found., U. Idaho Found. Served to lt. (j.g.) USNR, 1944-46. Mem. Am. Gas Assn. (dir. 1976-79, exec. com. 1976-77), Pacific Coast Gas Assn. (past pres., past dir.), N.W. Electric Light and Power Assn. (past dir., past pres.), Assn. Wash. Gas Utilities (past trustee, past pres.), Wash. Council Internat. Trade (v.p. 1973-80), Western Environ. Trade Assn. (past 1st v.p., dir. 1973-76), Edison Electric Inst. (dir. 1976-78), NAM (dir. 1974-77, 82-84), Nat. Assn. Electric Cos. (dir. 1974-77), Spokane C. of C. (v.p., dir., vice chmn. 1978-80, chmn. 1982-83), Assn. Wash. Bus. (dir. 1971-83, exec. com. 1975-83, vice chmn. 1978-80, chmn. 1980-82). Presbyterian (elder). Lodge: Rotary. Home: W 39 33d Ave Spokane WA 99203

SATTIZAHN, SAHEDRAN, consulting psychologist, writer, educator; b. Petaluma, Calif., Oct. 17, 1951; d. Alexander Laurence and Eleanor Glades (Orr) Cunninghame. B.A. in Liberal Arts, San Jose State U., 1975; M.A. in Psychology, Sonoma State U., 1978; postgrad. Union Grad. Sch., 1980-86, Columbia Pacific U., 1986—. Research asst. Law Enforcement Tng., Research Assocs., Mountain View, Calif., 1974; paralegal research asst. Varian Assocs., Palo Alto, Calif., 1975; assoc. dir., tchr. Centre of Well-Being, Sebastopol, Calif., 1976; dir., writer Love Letter Press, Sebastopol, 1977—; counselor Pickett House, Santa Rosa, Calif., 1979-80; counseling intern Phobia Recovery Ctr., San Francisco, 1981; pvt. practice astrological cons., Sebastopol, 1983—; acting v.p., sec. Inst. Clin. Philosophy, San Francisco, 1981-82. Mem. Women for Nuclear Disarmament, 1982-85; mem. Orgn. for Women, 1983-85; mem. Nat. Coalition Democracy in Educ., 1982-85; mem. United Neighbors in Action, 1982-85; mem. Sonoma County Farmlands Group, 1981—. Named Outstanding Young Woman of Am., 1981. Author: Love Letters: A Journal of Sharing (Vol. I-II), 1979; Journey within the One, 1975; In Search of God, 1975, The Lotus Is Blooming; The Language of Feeling. Office: PO Box 996 Sebastopol CA 95472

SAUCEDO, ROBERT, engineer; b. El Paso, Tex., Oct. 25, 1932; s. Joseph Delgado and Consuelo (Valencia) S.; m. Maria Christina Grajeda; children: Robert, Teresa, Susan, Carol, Elizabeth, Adela, John, Elena, Connie, Kathy. BSEE, U. Tex., 1955; MSEE, U. Pitts., 1957, PhD, 1961. Lead engr. Westinghouse Electic, Pitts., 1955-62; chief scientist Northrop Corp., Palos Verdes, Calif., 1962-65; lead engr. Aerospace Corp., El Segundo, Calif., 1965-68; mgr. IBM, Westlake, Calif., 1968-70; dir., engr. Litton Industries, Culver City, Calif., 1970-73; pres., founder Casde Corp., Torrance, Calif., 1978—; lectr. U. Pitts., 1959-61, UCLA, 1962-68. Author: Introduction to Digital Controls, 1968; contbr. articles to profl. jours. Bd. dirs. Little League Baseball, Palos Verdes, Calif., 1970-74, Am. Youth Soccer Orgn., Palos Verdes, 1971-74. Named Prime Contractor of Yr., Dept. Def., Washington, 1984, Small Businessman of Yr., SBA, 1984; Westinghouse fellow, 1956. Mem. IEEE, Soc. Naval Architects and Marine Engrs., Acoustical Soc. Am., Am. Soc. Naval Engrs. Office: 2707 Toledo St #604 PO Box 1291 Torrance CA 90505

SAUCKE, GARY B., advertising agency executive; b. Rochester, N.Y., Oct. 31, 1953; s. Oliver Heech and Ida Christine (Schulz) S. AB, Syracuse U., 1975. Cert. real estate broker, Mass. Various account mgmt. positions HBM/Creamer, Boston, BBDO, Inc., N.Y.C., Scali McCabe Sloves, N.Y.C.; now v.p. consumer services Ayer Pacific, San Francisco. Named Eagle Scout, Boy Scouts Am.; recipient Disting. Service award ARC. Mem. Advt. Club San Francisco. Avocations: outdoors, arts. Home: 2919 Pacific Ave No 10 San Francisco CA 94115 Office: Ayer Pacific 909 Montgomery St San Francisco CA 94133

SAUER, HENRY JACK, educator; b. Portland, Oreg., Oct. 23, 1946; s. Henry Jack and Pauline Catherine (Rahn) S.; B.A., Wash. State U., 1970, M.Ed., 1981; m. Nancy Lee Lauber, July 25, 1970. Tchr., coach schs. in Wash., 1970—; learning mgr. experienced based career edn. Kennewick Sch. Dist., 1979-80, project mgr. CETA employer-edn. demonstration project, 1980-81, project dir. CETA employer-edn. project, 1981-82; asst. prin. Desert Hills Middle Sch., 1982—; cons. social studies. Active local United Way, Boy Scouts Am. Mem. Wash. Assn. Sch. Adminstrs., Assn. Supervision and Curriculum Devel., Phi Delta Kappa. Lutheran. Club: Kiwanis. Home: 2306 S Anderson Pl Kennewick WA 99337 Office: Desert Hills Middle Sch 6011 W 10th Pl Kennewick WA 99337

SAUER, JAMES EDWARD, JR., hospital administrator; b. Sanborn, N.D., Feb. 14, 1934; s. James Edward and Rose Marie (Grafton) S.; m. Sharon Ann Groom, Aug. 18, 1962; children—Scott Michael, Jeffrey William, Steven Douglas. B.S. in Bus. Adminstrn., U. N.D., 1956; M.H.A., U. Minn., 1964. Adminstrv. asst. Meth. Hosp., Madison, Wis., 1961-62; adminstrv. resident San Jose Hosp. and Health Ctr., Calif., 1963-64; asst. adminstr. Providence Hosp., Portland, Oreg., 1967-69, assoc. adminstr., 1969-73; pres., exec. dir. Calif. Hosp. Med. Ctr., Los Angeles, 1973-79; adminstr. St. Joseph Med. Ctr., Burbank, Calif., 1979—; mem. hosp. adv. com. Blue Cross So. Calif., 1976-79. Trustee, Sisters of Providence in Calif., 1979—; mem. exec. com. retirement bd. Sisters of Providence, 1983—. Contbr. articles to profl. jours. Served to capt. USAF, 1956-62. Fellow Am. Coll. Hosp. Adminstrs.; mem. Am. Hosp. Assn. (chmn. 1982-84), Oreg. Conf. Cath. Hosps. Assn. (pres. 1973-74), Hosp. Council So. Calif. (bd. dirs. 1975-81, exec. com. 1977-81, chmn. 1979-80), Calif. Hosp. Assn. (trustee 1979-84, chmn. 1983, Walker Fellow 1983), Calif. Assn. Cath. Hosps. (trustee 1981-82), Am. Arbitration Assn. (Los Angeles adv. council), Hollywood Acad. Medicine, Central Area Teaching Hosps. (bd. dirs. 1976-79). Lodge: Rotary. Office: St Joseph Med Ctr Buena Vista and Alameda Sts Burbank CA 91505

SAUER, JON ROBERT, physicist; b. Schenectady, N.Y., Nov. 24, 1940; s. Robert Olvin and Beula Jean (Carson) S.; m. Patricia Ann Fay Valcke, Dec. 15, 1972; children: Alexis, Nadine. BS, Stanford U., 1962; PhD, Tufts U., 1970. Physicist Ind. U., Bloomington, 1975-77, Argonne (Ill.) Nat. Labs., 1977-81; mem. tech. staff Bell Labs., Naperville, Ill., 1981-83, AT&T, Denver, 1984—. Home: 15005 E Grand Ave Aurora CO 80015 Office: AT&T 11900 N Pecos St Denver CO 80234

SAUFLEY, HAROLD FROST, III, consultant, retired chemical company executive; b. New Orleans, Jan. 30, 1928; s. Harold Frost and Henrietta (Miller) S.; m. Barbara Sue Lee, May 3, 1948; children: Suzanne, H. Frost, Heidi, Stefanie, S. Charles, Camilla. BGen. Studies, La. State U., 1955. With Diamond Shamrock Corp., 1956-83; research chemist Diamond Shamrock Corp., Redwood City, Calif., 1956-57, sales mgr. tech. sales, 1957-68, dept. mgr., div. gen. mgr., 1968-78, mgr. internat., 1978-83; cons., mgmt. rep. Saufley & Assocs., Mountain View, Calif., 1983—. Served to capt. US Army Chem. Corps, 1951-54. Mem. Am. Chem. Soc. Republican. Episcopalian. Avocation: sailing. Home and Office: 3490 Bruckner Circle Mountain View CA 94040

SAUGUES, EDMOND PIERRE, chemical company advertising executive, writer; b. N.Y.C., Apr. 11, 1934; s. Edmond Pierre and Andree (Moutier) S.; m. Sally Ann McManus, Apr. 20, 1963; 1 dau., Marcy M. B.A. in English, Northwestern U., 1956; postgrad. UCLA, 1965-68. Advt. mgr. br. store Barker Bros., Los Angeles, 1959-62; sales promotion specialist Gen. Electric, Los Angeles, 1963-64; advtg. mgr. Rexall Drug Co., Los Angeles, 1964-68; advt. mgr. Cooper's Lumber, Los Angeles, 1969-72; sales promotion mgr. Hyland Labs., Costa Mesa, Calif., 1973-78; advt. mgr. Am. Metal Products Co., Los Angeles, 1978-80; advt. mgr. Filon div. Sohio Chem. Co., Los Angeles, 1981—. League commr., coach, referee Am. Youth Soccer Orgn., Palos Verdes Estates, Calif. Served with U.S. Army, 1956-58. Republican. Roman Catholic. Contbr. articles to trade and consumer publs. Home: 28126 Peacock Ridge Dr Palos Verdes Peninsula CA 90274 Office: Sohio Chem Co 12333 S Van Ness Hawthorne CA 90250

SAUL, WILLIAM EDWARD, academic administrator, civil engineering educator; b. N.Y.C., May 15, 1934; s. George James and Fanny Ruth (Murokh) S.; m. J. Muriel Held Eagleburger, May 11, 1976. BSCE, Mich. Tech. U., 1955, MSCE, 1961; PhD in Civil Engring., Northwestern U., 1964. Registered profl. engr., Wis., Idaho, Mich. Mech. engr. Shell Oil Co., New Orleans, 1955-59; instr. engring. mechanics Mich. Tech. U., Houghton, 1960-62; asst. prof. civil engring. U. Wis., Madison, 1964-67, assoc. prof., 1967-72, prof., 1972-84; dean Coll. Engring. U. Idaho, Moscow, 1984—; cons., Madison, 1961-84. Co-editor Conf. of Methods of Structural Analysis, 1976. Fulbright fellow 1970-71; von Humboldt scholar, 1970-71. Mem. ASCE (pres. Wis. sect. 1983-84), Internat. Assn. Bridge and Structures Engrs., Am. Soc. Engring Edn., Sigma Xi, Phi Kappa Phi, Tau Beta Pi, Chi Epsilon. Avocations: hiking, reading, travel, gadgets. Home: 1221 Ponderosa Dr Moscow ID 83843 Office: U Idaho Coll Engring Moscow ID 83843

SAULS, FREDERICK INABINETTE, artist; b. Seattle, Mar. 22, 1934; s. Frederick Inabinette and Borghild Caroline (Zakarison) S.; div.; children—Karoline, Fritz. Student, Stanford U., 1951-57, San Francisco Acad. Art, Calif. Coll. Arts and Crafts, Assoc. in art U. Calif.-Berkeley, 1960-65; vis. artist U. Ky., 1966-68; asst. prof. U. Minn., 1969-70; prof. U. Calif.-Santa Cruz, 1972-73. One-man shows: R.J. Reynolds Gallery, U. Ky., 1966, Tortue Gallery, Santa Monica, Calif., 1972, Gille Mansillon Gallery, Santa Monica, 1984; group shows: travelling exhibit internat. art UNESCO; works represented in permanent collections including: Skopje (Yugoslavia) Mus. of Modern Art, Cornell U., Berkeley Mus., Mus. Modern Art, N.Y., Woodrow Wilson Sculpture Garden, N.Y., Oakland (Calif.) Art Mus., Calif. Served with U.S. Army, 1952-54. Recipient Harry Lord Ford prize U. Calif.-Berkeley, 1962, grand prize for sculpture Paris Biennale, 1965. Mem. Dramatists Guild. Address: 1110 N Hudson Ave Studio C Los Angeles CA 90038

SAUNDERS, ALAN KEITH, professional football coach; b. London, Feb. 1, 1947; m. Karen Saunders: children: Korrin Elizabeth, William Joseph, Robert Charles. Grad., San Jose State U., 1969; M, Stanford U., 1970. Football coach U. Mo., 1972, Utah State U., 1973-75; asst. head coach U. Calif., 1976-81; offensive coordinator, quarterback coach U. Tenn., 1982; coach San Diego Chargers, NFL, 1983—, asst. head coach, 1985-86, head coach, 1986—. Address: San Diego Chargers San Diego Stadium PO Box 20666 San Diego CA 92120 *

SAUNDERS, JOHN RAMSEY, coin and bullion gallery executive; b. Detroit, Aug. 16, 1949; s. Gordon Joseph and Ruth (Ramsey) S.; m. Masako Susukida, Feb. 2, 1979. children—Robert, Sakura, Michelle. B.S., Eckerd Coll., 1971; M.B.A., U. Pa., 1973. Asst. treas. fgn. exchange trading, medium term lending loan officer Euro-Dollar market Am. Express Internat. Banking Corp., London, 1971-73; pres. London Coin Galleries, Mission Viejo, Calif., 1973—. Mem. Am. Numis. Assn. (life), Nat. Assn. Coin and Precious Metal Dealers, Space Studies Inst. Presbyterian. Contbr: Standard Catalogue of World Coins, 1981-83. Office: London Coin Galleries Suite 132 Mission Viejo Mall Mission Viejo CA 92691

SAUNDERS, LAUREL BARNES, librarian; b. Ainsworth, Nebr., Aug. 17, 1926; d. Howard Enos and Flossie Agnes (Marr) Barnes; married; 1 child, Kelvin Edwin Saunders. BA, U. S.D., 1948; MA, U. Mich., 1950. Librarian pub. schs. Howell, Mich., 1950-51; asst. librarian, U.S. Army post Ft. Bliss, Tex., 1951-53; librarian, USAF base Biggs AFB, Tex., 1953-62; supervisory librarian U.S. Air Def. Sch., Ft. Bliss, 1962-64; chief cataloguing and acquistions U.S. Army Tech. Library, White Sands Missile Range, N.Mex., 1964-74, chief librarian, 1975—. Pres. Quaestors Sunday Sch. class, Trinity First Meth. Ch., 1985-86, also adminstrv. bd., 1986—. Mem. Fed. Mgrs. Assn. (2d v.p. 1982-83, pres. 1984-87, bd. dirs., Mgr. of Yr. award 1985), N.Mex. Library Assn. (vice-chmn. Documents Roundtable 1984-85, chmn. 1985-86), Border Regional Library Assn., U.S. Army Library Inst. (active procurement working group 1980-84). Republican. Club: Past Matrons (Anthony, N.Mex.). Lodge: Order of Eastern Star (Worthy Matron 1970, treas. 1982-87).

SAUNDERS, PETER PAUL, financial company executive; b. Budapest, Hungary, July 21, 1928; emigrated to Can., 1941, naturalized, 1946; s. Peter Paul and Elizabeth (Halom) Szende; m. Nancy Louise McDonald, Feb. 11, 1956; children: Christine Elizabeth, Paula Marie. Student, Vancouver Coll., 1941-44; B.Com., U. B.C., 1948. Acct. Canadian Pacific Ry. Co., 1948-50; founder, pres. Laurentide Fin. Corp., Ltd., 1950-66, vice chmn., 1966-67; pres. Coronation Credit Corp. Ltd., Vancouver, B.C., Can., 1968-78; chmn., pres. Cornat Industries Ltd., Vancouver, B.C., Can., 1969-78, Versatile Corp. (formerly Coronation Credit Corp. and Cornat Industries Ltd.), Vancouver, B.C., Can., 1978—; dir. Bralorne Resources Ltd., B.C. Broadcasting Co. Ltd., Wajax Ltd., N.W. Sports Enterprises Ltd., WIC Western Internat. Communications Ltd., Laurentian Pacific Ins. Co., Jannock Ltd.; mem. Vancouver adv. bd. Nat. Trust Co. Ltd. Adv. com. inmate employment Correctional Service Can.; gov. Vancouver Opera Assn.; pres. Vancouver Symphony Soc., 1968-70, Can. Cancer Soc., B.C. and Yukon region, 1975-77, Vancouver Art Gallery Assn., 1981-83; bd. dirs. Conv. Bd. Can., Bus. Council of B.C., Council for Bus. and the Arts in Can., C.D. Howe Inst., Council for Can. Unity. Clubs: Vancouver Lawn Tennis and Badminton, Shaughnessy Golf and Country, Royal Vancouver Yacht; Thunderbird Country (Rancho Mirage, Calif.). vocations: golf, skiing, hunting, boating. Home: 2186 SW Marine Dr, Vancouver, BC Canada V6P 6B5 Office: Versatile Corp, PO Box 49153 Bentall Centre, Vancouver, BC Canada V7X 1K3

SAUNDERS, REYNOLDS J., medical educator, anesthesiology researcher; b. Phila., Nov. 15, 1945; s. Maurice Monroe and Florence (Tokar) S.; m. Marie Weatherred, Feb. 28, 1967; children: J. Eric, Elizabeth Anne. BS, St. Mary's U., San Antonio, 1965; MD, U. Tex., 1973. Intern then resident U. Iowa Hosps., Iowa City, 1973-76; chief anesthesiology St. Mary's Hosp., Rhinelander, Wis., 1976-79; pres. Northwoods Anesthesiologists Ltd., Rhinelander, 1977-79; instr. anesthesiology U. Ariz. Coll. Medicine, Tucson, 1979-83, asst. prof., 1983-87; adj. prof. electronic and computer engring. U. Ariz. Coll. Engring., Tucson, 1979-87; chief anesthesiology services VA Med. Ctr., Tucson, 1982-87; bd. dirs. Orgn. for Multidisciplinary Anesthesia Research, Tucson, 1985-87; staff anesthesiologist Cedars-Sinai Med. Ctr., Los Angeles. Co-editor: Future Anesthesia Delivery Systems, 1984; contbr. articles to profl. jours., chpts. to books. Med. dir. Reachout, Tucson, 1985. VA Research and Devel. Service grantee, 1984. Mem. AMA, Am. Soc. Anesthesiologists, Am. Soc. Regional Anesthesia, Assn. Advancement Med. Instrumentation, Soc. Clin. Data Mgmt. Systems, Assn. Computing Machinery, Assn. VA Anesthesiologists (pres.-elect 1986). Avocations: bread baking, writing, gardening. Office: Ariz Health Sci Ctr Dept Anesthesiology Tucson AZ 85723

SAUNDERS, ROBERT MALLOUGH, engineering educator, college administrator; b. Winnipeg, Man., Can., Sept. 12, 1915; s. Robert and Mabel Grace (Mallough) S.; m. Elizabeth Lenander, June 24, 1943. BEE, U. Minn., 1938, MS, 1942; D.Eng., Tokyo Inst. Tech., 1971. Design engr. Electric Machinery Co., Mpls., part-time 1938-42; teaching asst. elec. engring. U. Minn., 1938-42, instr., 1942-44; faculty U. Calif.-Berkeley, 1946-65, prof. elec. engring., 1957-65, chmn. dept., 1959-63; asst. to chancellor for engring. U. Calif.-Irvine, 1964-65, prof. elec. engring., 1965—, dean Sch. Engring., 1965-73; vis. assoc. prof. MIT, 1954-55; cons. Gen. Motors Research Lab., Apollo Support Dept., Gen. Electric Co., Aerospace Corp., Rohr Corp.; sec. Nat. Commn. for Elec. Engring. films, 1962-71; mem. ECPD Engring. Edn. and Accreditation Com., 1965-71, chmn., 1969-70, bd. dirs., 1971-75; mem. engring. adv. com. NSF, 1968-71; mem. Sec. Navy's Bd. Edn. and Tng., 1972-78. Co-author: Analysis of Feedback Control Systems, 1956; contbr.: Ency. Brit.; tech. jours. Bd. visitors U.S. Army Transp. Sch., 1970-73. Served to lt. (j.g.) USNR, 1944-46. Simon fellow engring. Manchester U., Eng., 1960. Fellow AAAS, IEEE (chmn. ednl. activities bd. 1973-74, mem. exec. com., dir. 1973-79, v.p. regional activities 1975-76, pres. 1977, Centennial medal 1984), mem. Am. Soc. Engring. Edn. (chmn. elec. div. 1965-66), Am. Assn. Engring. Socs. (organizing com. 1977-80, exec. com. 1982-84, chmn. bd. govs. 1983, chmn. awards com. 1984-85, nominating com. 1984-85), Nat. Research Council (mem. com. on edn. and utilization of engr., 1983-84), Sigma Xi, Tau Beta Pi, Eta Kappa Nu. Lodge: Rotary. Office: Univ Calif Sch Engring Irvine CA 92717

SAUNDERS, TIMOTHY, telecommunications company executive; b. Dayton, Ohio, Sept. 2, 1954; s. Peter and Ruth (Holtz) S. B.A., Amherst Coll., 1977; M.S., Northeastern U., 1978; M.B.A., Harvard U., 1983. C.P.A., Ohio. Sr. acct. Arthur Andersen & Co., Cin., 1978-81; asst. to v.p., treas. The Boston Co., 1982; sr. fin. analyst ROLM Corp., Santa Clara, 1983-85, mgr. materials, 1985—. Mem. Am. Inst. C.P.A.s, Ohio Soc. C.P.A.s. Republican. Episcopalian. Clubs: Amherst of No. Calif., Harvard Bus. Sch. of No. Calif. (San Francisco). Home: 6 Garden Ct Belmont CA 94002 Office: ROLM Corp 4900 Old Ironsides Dr Santa Clara CA 95054

SAUSEN, JOHN HIGDON, consulting mechanical engineer; b. Great Falls, Mont., May 1, 1919; s. Alfred Leo and Estelle E. (Higdon) S; m. Jane Mary Mathews, Jan. 3, 1942; children: David, Janet, Mark, Kevin, Karen, Nancy, Gretchen. BS in Petroleum Engring., U. Minn., 1941. Staff engr. Reserve Mining Co., Minn., 1952-65; mgr. Brobeck Engrs., Berkeley, Calif., 1965-71; dir. Ladco Engrs., Hong Kong, 1971-75; pres. JHS Cons. Engrs., Las Vegas, Nev., 1975-82; project mgr. Sverdrup Corp., San Francisco, 1983—. Mem. Soc. Profl. Engrs., Nat. Soc. Energy Engrs., Nat. Soc. Heating Ventilation Air Conditioning Engrs. Republican. Avocations: sailing, golf, tennis. Home: 312 Indian Way Novato CA 94947 Office: Sverdrup Corp 417 Montgomery San Francisco CA 94104

SAVABI, FATEMEH, pharmacologist, pharmacist; b. Yazd, Iran, Dec. 24, 1948; came to U.S., 1977; s. Ali Asghar and Nezhat (Daliri) S.; m. Jamshid Ahmadi, May 11, 1983. PharmD, Tehran (Iran) U., 1976; PhD in Pharmacology and Nutrition, U. So. Calif., 1982. Researcher Tehran U., 1975-77, instr. organic chemistry, 1976-77; postdoctoral fellow U. So. Calif. dept. pharmacology, Los Angeles, 1983-85, research assoc., 1985-86; instr. nutrition and pharmacology U. So. Calif. Sch. Medicine, Los Angeles, 1986—; instr. lab. pharmacology U. So. Calif. Sch. Medicine, 1978-83. Contbr. articles to profl. jours. Avocations: gardening, cooking, reading, sports. Home: 3804 Via La Selva Palos Verdes Estates CA 90274 Office: U So Calif Sch Medicine 2025 Zonal Ave Los Angeles CA 90033

SAVAGE, ELDON PAUL, environmental health educator; b. Bedford, Iowa, Apr. 4, 1926; s. Paul and Nora (Arthur) S.; m. Ella May, June 5, 1948; children: Steven P., Michael D. BS, U. Kans., 1950; MPH, Tulane U., 1958; PhD, Okla. U., 1968. Coordinator environ. sanitation demonstration projects USPHS, Kans., Iowa and Pa., 1950-64; chief state aids sect. pesticide ctr. Ctr. for Disease Control, Atlanta, 1964-70; chief chem. epidemiology sect. Inst. Rural Environ. Health, Colo. State U., Ft. Collins, 1970-84, prof., dir. environ. health div., 1984—, dir., 1984—; dir. environ. health services Colo. State U., 1986—. Contbr. articles to profl. jours. Mem. Am. Acad. Sanitarians (sec., treas., diplomate), Nat. Environ. Health Assn., Sigma Xi, Gamma Sigma Delta. Home: 5220 Apple Dr Fort Collins CO 80523 Office: Inst Rural Environ Health Colo State U Fort Collins CO 80523

SAVAGE, JOHN LAWRENCE, agriculturist, provincial government official; b. Qualicum Beach, B.C., Can., Feb. 23, 1936; s. Harold Roland and Veronica Mary (Wolfe) S.; m. Margaret Johnson; children: Kim, Pamela, Lori. Alderman Dist. of Delta, 1985-87; mem. B.C. Legis. Assembly, Victoria, 1986—, minister of agr. and fisheries, 1986—. Pres., dir. Delta C. of C., 1981-82; pres. B.C. Fedn. Agr., 1983-85, dir. 1976-86; chmn. Delta Parks and Recreation Com., 1985; exec. dir. Can. Fed. Agr., Ottawa, 1981-85. Office: Minister of Agr and Fisheries, Parliament Bldgs, Victoria Can V8V 1X4

SAVAGE, LINETTE, talent agent, health and fitness professional; b. San Fernando, Calif., Aug. 16, 1952; d. Charles Philip and Leticia (Murillo) S. Student, Calif. State U., 1970-72, 79-80, 84—, UCLA, 1982-83. Paralegal Atty. Gen., Los Angeles, 1973-76, Harry L. Usher APC, Beverly Hills, Calif., 1979-80; with contract and loan adminstrn. Union Bank, Century City, Calif., 1977-78; fin. mgr./fitness dir. Los Angeles Olympic Com., 1980-84; pres., co-owner PaVage Fitness, Playa del Rey, Calif., 1984—; cons. Reebok USA Ltd., Boston, 1983—, Dick Clark Productions, Burbank, Calif.; judge City Sports Mag., Los Angeles, 1985, Fit Mag., San Francisco, 1984; Los Angeles judge Nat. Aerobic Championships. Author: MuscleAerobics, 1985; contbr. articles to profl. jours. Counselor Big Sisters Am., Dorothy Kirkeby Ctr. for Girls, 1971-77. Cert. Pres.' Council on Phys. Fitness, 1983. Mem. Am. Coll. Sports Medicine, Assn. Fitness Bus., Nat. Strength and Conditioning Assn., Am. Alliance Health, Phys. Edn. Recreation and Dance, Hispanci Pub. Relations Assn. Roman Catholic. Clubs: Marina City (Marina del Rey, Calif.); Mid Valley Athletic (Reseda, Calif.). Avocations: dancing, writing, reading, weight tng., aerobics. Office: PaVage Fitness Images 200 E Culver Blvd Playa del Rey CA 90291

SAVAGE, MICHAEL JOHN, oil company executive; b. Birmingham, Eng., Oct. 28, 1934; came to U.S., 1962, naturalized, 1981; s. Leonard W. H. and Hilda C. (Fletcher) S.; m. Elisabeth Karl, June 21, 1965 (div.); m. Virginia Hooper, Aug. 31, 1978; 1 child, Matthew Nicholas. MA in Econs. and Law, Cambridge U., 1958; postgrad., Manchester (Eng.) Bus. Sch., 1965; Diploma in Arabic, Middle E. Ctr. for Arab Studies, Shemlan, Lebanon, 1967. Various positions The British Petroleum Co. Ltd., England, Kuwait, Lebanon, Abu Dhabi, Alaska, Can., U.S., 1958-82; pres. BP Alaska Inc., San Francisco, 1977, Sohio Petroleum Co., San Francisco, 1978-82; internat. dir. The Brit. Petroleum Co. Ltd., London, 1982; pres. Merlin Petroleum Co., San Francisco, 1983—. Trustee Alaska Pacific U., 1982-86, San Francisco Conservatory of Music, 1983—. Served to 2d lt. Royal Arty., Brit. Army, 1953-55. Clubs: Bankers (San Francisco); Belvedere (Calif.) Tennis. Avocations: Music, tennis, skiing, mountain walking. Office: Merlin Petroleum Co 101 California St San Francisco CA 94111

SAVAGE, WAYNE, biology educator; b. Sudan, Tex., Oct. 31, 1931; s. Raymond Lee and Mellie (Long) S.; m. Sandra Joanne Stallings, Sept. 14, 1957; children: Scott Matthew, Alison Diana, Stephen Andrew. AB, San Francisco State U., 1958; PhD, U. Calif., Berkeley, 1967. Biology tchr. Capuchino High Sch., San Bruno, Calif., 1959-62; asst. prof. biology San Jose (Calif.) State U., 1966-70, assoc. prof., 1970-76, prof., 1976—, chmn. dept. biol. scis., 1985—; sr. cons. Harvey and Stanley Assocs., Alviso, Calif., 1970—; sr. scientist Wellspring Corp., Cupertino, Calif., 1983-85. Pres. Youth Sci. Inst., San Jose, 1979-81. Grantee NSF, 1972, NASA, 1983—. Mem. AAAS, Am. Inst. Biol. Scis., Assn. Biologists Computing (pres. 1982-85), Bot. Soc. Am., Calif. Bot. Soc. (pres. 1980), Internat. Assn. Plant Taxonomy, Soc. Archimedes (bd. dirs. 1985—). Office: San Jose State U Dept Biology San Jose CA 95192-0100

SAVARA, BHIM SEN, health science educator; b. Sialkote, India, Dec. 4, 1924; came to U.S., 1947; s. Amar Nath and Attur S. (Kaur) S.; m. Mary Lu Baldra, June 1, 1968; children: Lisa, Raj, Shanta. BSD, Demontmorency Coll., 1946; Lic. in Dental Surgery, Royal Coll. Surgery of Eng., London,

1947; postgrad., U. Detroit, 1947-48; MS, U. Ill., 1950; DMD, U. Oreg., 1957. Prof., chmn. child study clinic Oreg. Health Sci. U., Portland, 1957—. Office: Oreg Health Scis U Child Study Clinic SD 611 SW Campus Dr Portland OR 97201

SAVEDRA, MANUEL ANGEL, dentist; b. Los Angeles, Oct. 22, 1943; s. Manuel Diaz and Evangeline (Vasquez) s.; m. Cheryl Dana Silver, Sept. 11, 1982; children: Carli Dana, Richard Evan. A.A., East Los Angeles Coll., 1967; B.A., UCLA, 1969, D.D.S., 1974; cert. Queens Med. Center, Honolulu, 1975. Lic. dentist, Calif., Hawaii. Dentist, Queens Med. Ctr., Honolulu, 1974-75; dentist, lectr. to asst. prof. UCLA, 1975-76; pvt. practice dentistry, Hawthorne, Calif. and Los Angeles, 1976—; mem. med.-dental staff St. Joseph Med. Center, Burbank, Calif., 1976; mem. exam. com. Calif. Bd. Dental Examiners, 1981. Served with Dental Corps, U.S. Army, 1963-66. Named Outstanding Dental Resident, Queen's Med. Ctr., 1974-75. Mem. ADA, Calif. Dental Assn., Acad. Gen. Dentistry, Western Dental Soc. (area rep. 1986), UCLA Dental Alumni Assn. (exec. com. 1978-83, v.p., pres.), Am. Legion, Omicron Kappa Upsilon, Alpha Gamma Sigma. Republican. Jewish. Home: 1727 Port Stirling Pl Newport Beach CA 92660 Office: 13416 Inglewood Avenue Hawthorne CA 90250

SAVITT, TODD DAVID, marketing professional; b. Mpls., Aug. 3, 1958; s. Jory Ralph and Phyllis Sue (Greenberg) S. BS, Occidental Coll., 1980; MS, Calif. State U., Long Beach, 1982. Dir. Organizational Stress Testing, San Diego, 1982-83; mgr. mktg. communications Computer Accessories Corp., San Diego, 1983—; cons. Brainstorms, San Diego, 1985—. Author test instrument specifications, 1982, 84. Mem. Computer and Electronics Mktg. Assn. Avocations: cycling, tennis, stock and bond investments. Home: 8945 Lombard Pl Suite 512 San Diego CA 92122 Office: Computer Accessories Corp 6610 Nancy Ridge Dr San Diego CA 92121

SAVONA, MICHAEL RICHARD, physician; b. N.Y.C., Oct. 21, 1947; s. Salvatore Joseph and Diana Grace (Menditto) S.; B.S. summa cum laude, Siena Coll., 1969; M.D., SUNY, Buffalo, 1973; m. Dorothy O'Neill, Oct. 18, 1975. Intern in internal medicine, Presbyn. Hosp., Columbia U., N.Y.C., 1973-74, resident in internal medicine, 1974-76, vis. fellow internal medicine Delafield Hosp./Columbia U. Coll. Physicians and Surgeons, 1974-76; practice medicine specializing in internal medicine, Maui Med. Group, Wailuku, Hawaii, 1976—; dir. ICU, Maui Meml. Hosp., also dir. respiratory therapy, CCU., chmn. dept. medicine, 1980—; clin. faculty John A. Burns Sch. Medicine, U. Hawaii. Bd. dirs. Maui Heart Assn.; dir. profl. edn. Maui chpt. Am. Cancer Soc.; mem. Maui County Hosp. Adv. Commn.; mem. council Community Cancer Program of Hawaii. Recipient James A. Gibson Wayne J. Atwell award, 1970, physiology award, 1970, Ernest Whitebsky award, 1971, Roche Lab. award, 1972, Pfiser Lab. award, 1973, Phillip Sang award, 1973, Hans Lowenstein M.D. Meml. award, 1973. Diplomate Am. Bd. Internal Medicine. Mem. AMA, Am. Thoracic Soc., Hawaii Thoracic Soc., Maui County Med. Assn. (pres.), Hawaii Med. Assn., Hawaii Oncology Group, A.C.P., SW Oncology Coop. Group, Alpha Omega Alpha, Delta Epsilon Sigma. Office: 1830 Wells St Wailuku Maui HI 96793

SAVORY, ALLAN REDIN, ecologist; b. Bulawayo, Zimbabwe, Sept. 15, 1935; came to U.S., 1979; s. James Harry Redin and Elaine Verna (Muir) S.; m. Shirley Garbutt, 1956 (div. 1974); m. Janet Barnes, 1976 (div. 1980); children: Megan Savory-Davis, Rodger, Claire, Sarah; m. Jody Butterfield, Jan. 4, 1982. BSc, U. Natal, Pietermaritzburg, South Africa, 1955. Provincial game officer N. Rhodesia Game Dept., Zambia, 1956-58; research officer Dept. Tsetse Control, Rhodesia, now called Zimbabwe, 1959, Game Dept., Rhodesia, now called Zimbabwe, 1960-63; cons. Africa, S.Am., and U.S., 1964-84; exec. dir. Ctr. Holistic Resource Mgmt., Albuquerque, 1984—; dir. Wildlife Utilization Services, Rhodesia, 1964-67; prin., dir. Kazuma Res. Station, Rhodesia, 1965-73; lectr. Internat. Stockmens Sch., Tex. and Ariz., 1978-80; cons. UN Food and Agriculture Orgn., Democratic Yemen, 1981, World Bank, Pakistan, 1983. Contbr. articles on wildlife and land deterioration to jours. Mem. Parliament of Rhodesia, 1968-75; pres. Rhodesia Party, 1970-75, Nat. Unifying Force, 1977; pres. Natural Resources Soc., Rhodesia, 1971-72. Served to capt. Rhodesian Army, 1955-79. Mem. Am. Soc. Agrl. Cons., Soc. Range Mgmt., Soil Conservation Soc. Am., AAAS, Explorers Club. Club: Spl. Forces (London). Avocations: falconry, fishing, hunting. Home: PO Box 7128 Albuquerque NM 87194

SAWATZKI, SUSEN CHRISTINE, publisher; b. Salt Lake City, July 23, 1959; d. Frank Julius and Gisela Christel (Horn) S. BS, U. Utah, 1980. Dir. pub. relations High Desert Adventures, Salt Lake City, 1985—; founder, pub. Utad News, Salt Lake City, 1982, owner, 1983. Correspondent Photo Dist. News, 1984—, Photo/Design, 1984—, Adweek, 1983—, Advt. Age mag.; mem. editorial bd. Am. Advt. Fedn. mag. Mem. Utah Advt. Fedn., Art Dirs. of Salt Lake City, Women in Communication (v.p. 1985-86, pres. 1986-87). Avocation: piano. Office: Utad News PO Box 11426 Salt Lake City UT 84147-0426

SAWCHUK, ALEXANDER ANDREW, data processing professional; b. Washington, Feb. 20, 1945; s. Henry A. and Neddie (Vonick) S.; m. Mariette Timmins, Oct. 16, 1971; children: Stephen, Mark. BSEE, MIT, 1966; MSEE, Stanford U., 1968, PhDEE, 1972. Tech. staff mem. Comsat, Washington, 1967; dir. Signal and Image Processing Inst. U. So. Calif., Los Angeles, 1978—, prof. elec. engring., 1982—; cons. Aerospace Corp., Los Angeles, 1981—; dir., founder Optivision, Inc., Davis, Calif., 1983—. Co-author: Digital Image Processing and Analysis Vol. I, II, 1985; contbr. chpt.s to books; patentee in field. Recipient Halliburton award U. So. Calif., 1980. Fellow Optical Soc. Am. (bd. dirs. 1986—, chmn. tech. council 1986—), Soc. Photo-Optical Instrumentation Engrs.; mem. IEEE (sr.), Optical Soc. So. Calif. Office: U So Calif MC 0272 Signal and Image Processing Inst Los Angeles CA 90089

SAWDON, STUART JOSEPH, advertising executive; b. N.Y.C., Oct. 26, 1942; s. Frank Burke Sawdon and Minerva (Feyden) Williams; m. Johanna Marina deRoode, Nov. 11, 1974; 1 child, Stephanie. BA, Worcester Coll., 1964; degree in media mgmt. (hon.), Advt. Inst., N.Y.C., 1969. V.p. Frank B. Sawdon Advt., N.Y.C., 1968-75; advt. mgr. Shakey's Inc., Englewood, Colo., 1975-80; prin. Sawdon Sales Concepts, Poway, Calif., 1980—; sales mgr. Sales and Mktg. Search, San Diego, 1982—; creator concept books and bd. dirs. TKO Enterprises, Q Beef Distbrs., Double Q Ranch, Pup 'n Pop Restaurants. Served with U.S. Army, 1964-67. Mem. Sales and Mktg. Club, Am. Mgmt. Assn. (hon. cert. 1973). Republican. Episcopalian. Avocations: golf, boats, stockmarket.

SAWICKI, EDWARD JAMES, corporate consulting service executive; b. Phila., Aug. 24, 1946; s. Edward Joseph and Catherine (Rita) S.; m. Anita Gale Sottler, July 15, 1972. AS in Sci. and Math., West Valley Coll., 1972; student, San Jose State U., 1973-76, U. San Francisco, 1977-78. Watch comdr. Ampex Corp., Redwood City, Calif., 1973-74; watch comdr., safety engr. Signetics, Sunnyvale, Calif., 1974-76; corp. safety dir. Intel Corp., Santa Clara, Calif., 1976-82; pres. Microsafe, Inc., Santa Clara, 1982—. Served as staff sgt. U.S. Army, 1966-70, Vietnam. Decorated Bronze Star with V device; recipient Plaque City of Santa Clara, 1980, Award of Merit City of Sunnyvale, 1981. Mem. World Safety Orgn. (cert.), Am. Soc. Safety Engrs. (pres. San Jose chpt. 1985-86), Am. Indsl. Hygiene Assn., Health Physics Assn., Nat. Safety Council (research and devel. com.), Nat. Fire Protection Assn., Semiconductor Safety Assn. (bd. dirs. Cen. Counties Nat. Safety Council), Bay Area Electronics Safety Group (founder 1978). Avocations: hunting, fishing. Home: 854 Hilmar St Santa Clara CA 95050 Office: Microsafe Inc 1500 Wyatt Dr Suite #5 Santa Clara CA 95051

SAWICKI, MYRON, lawyer; b. Elizabeth, N.J., Sept. 15, 1954; s. Wasyl and Elizabeth (Zoppa) S. AA, Santa Monica Coll., 1976; BS, Calif. State U.-Long Beach, 1978; JD, Southwestern U., 1980. Bar: Calif. 1980, U.S. Ct. Appeals (9th cir.) 1981, U.S. Dist. Ct. (cen. dist.) Calif. 1981. Spl. investigator William J. Burns, Internat. Detective Agy., Los Angeles, 1977-78; sole practice law, Los Angeles, 1981-83; dep. dist. atty. Mendocino County, Ukiah, Calif., 1983—. Mem. Calif. Dist. Atty. Assn., Nat. Dist. Atty. Assn. Home: PO Box 1095 Ukiah CA 95482 Office: Mendocino County Dist Atty Courthouse Ukiah CA 95482

SAWYER, CHARLES HENRY, anatomist, educator; b. Ludlow, Vt., Jan. 24, 1915; s. John Guy and Edith Mabel (Morgan) S.; m. Ruth Eleanor Schaeffer, Aug. 23, 1941; 1 dau., Joan Eleanor. B.A., Middlebury Coll., 1937, D.Sc. (h.c.), 1975; student, Cambridge U., Eng., 1937-38; Ph.D., Yale, 1941. Instr. anatomy Stanford, 1941-44; assoc., asst. prof., assoc. prof., prof. anatomy Duke U., 1944-51; prof. anatomy UCLA, Los Angeles, 1951-85; prof. emeritus UCLA, 1985—, chmn. dept., 1955-63, acting chmn., 1968-69, faculty research lectr., 1966-67. Editorial bd.: Endocrinology, 1955-59, Proc. Soc. Exptl. Biology and Medicine, 1959-63, Am. Jour. Physiology, 1972-75; Author papers on neuroendocrinology. Mem. Internat. Brain Research Orgn. (council 1964-68), AAAS, Am. Assn. Anatomists (v.p. 1969-70, Henry Gray award 1984), Am. Physiol. Soc., Am. Zool. Soc., Neurosci. Soc., Endocrine Soc. (council 1968-70, Koch award 1973), Am. Acad. Arts and Scis., Nat. Acad. Scis., Soc. Exptl. Biology and Medicine, Soc. Study Reprodn. (dir. 1969-71, Hartman award 1977), Internat. Neuroendocrine Soc. (council 1972-76), Hungarian Soc. Endocrinology and Metabolism (hon.), Nat. Acad. Scis., Japan Endocrin Soc. (hon.), Phi Beta Kappa, Sigma Xi. Home: 466 Tuallitan Rd Los Angeles CA 90049 Office: U Calif Sch Medicine Los Angeles CA 90024

SAWYER, CONSTANCE BRAGDON, astronomer; b. Lewiston, Maine, June 3, 1926; d. William Hayes and Beatrice Goulding (Burr) S.; m. James Walter Warwick, Sept. 6, 1947 (div. 1966); children: Sarah Haskell Warwick Charlock, David Irwin, Rachel Joan, Joel Howard McCulloch. AB, Smith Coll., 1947; AM, Radcliffe Coll., 1948, PhD, 1952. Astronomer Sacramento Peak Obs., Sunspot, N.Mex., 1953-55, High Altitude Obs., Boulder, Colo., 1955-58; physicist, astronomer NOAA, Boulder, Colo.; Miami, Fla.; Seattle, Wash., 1958-82; mem. research staff Radiophysics Inc., Boulder, 1983—; cons. D-PEEK, Boulder, 1983. Co-author: Solar Flare Prediction, 1986; contbr. articles to profl. jours. Mem. Am. Astron. Soc., Solar Physics Div. Am. Astron. Soc. (sec. 1982-85), Am. Geophys. Union, Internat. Astron. Union, Sigma Xi, Phi Beta Kappa. Democrat. Mem. Soc. Friends. Home: 850 20th St #705 Boulder CO 80302 Office: Radiophysics Inc 5475 Western Ave Boulder CO 80301

SAWYER, KATHERINE H. (MRS. CHARLES BALDWIN SAWYER), librarian; b. Cleve., July 11, 1908; d. Willard and Martha (Beaumont) Hirsh; A.B., Smith Coll., 1930; M.S. in Library Sci., Western Res. U., 1956; m. Charles Baldwin Sawyer, Aug. 19, 1933; children—Samuel Prentiss, Charles Brush, William Beaumont. With Cleve. Pub. Library, profl. librarian hosps., instns. dept., 1956-61; med. librarian St. Luke's Hosp., Pittsfield, Mass., 1965-66; library cons. Ministry of Health, Guyana, S. Am., 1966-68; curator Sophia Smith Collection; counselor Friends of Smith Coll. Library, chmn. exec. com., 1959-65; chmn. Friends of Western Res. Hist. Library, 1973-78, trustee, 1980—; trustee Episcopal Ch. Home, 1965— ; bd. govs. Western Res. U., 1957-66, bd. visitors Sch. Library Sci., 1958-68, 69—; trustee Friends of Cleve. Pub. Library, 1962-67, Christian Residences Found., 1976-82, WRHS, 1979—; counselor Friends of Smith Coll. Library, 1962-68. Mem. Ohio Library Assn., Western Res. Hist. Soc., Archeol. Inst., Spl. Libraries Assn., Nat. League Am. Pen Women. Episcopalian (vestryman 1974-77). Clubs: Union, Kirtland Country; Intown. Co-author (talking books for blind) Gardening for Blind Persons, 1962; Beauty, Glamour and Style, 1963. Home: 525 Paseo del Mundo Green Valley AZ 85614

SAWYER, PEGGY DOLAN, public relations executive; b. Chgo., Aug. 17, 1933; s. Earl Jeremiah and Maybelle Delight (Knox) Dolan; m. Robert B. Sawyer, Sept. 4, 1954 (div. Aug. 1982); children: Robert Jr., Patrick, John, Mary, Joseph, Michael. BA, U. Colo., 1955, MA, 1981; postgrad., Nat. Theatre Conservatory. Cert. tchr., Colo., cert. real estate broker, Colo. Realtor Billings & Co., Denver, 1972-76; tchr. Denver Pub. Schs., 1979-81; advt. agt. Sam Lusky Assocs., Denver, 1976-77, Darcy Communications, Denver, 1977-78; news dir. Majority Office Colo. Gen. Assembly, Denver, 1982—; cons. Teleprompter, Denver, 1980-81. Contbr. articles to profl. publs. Vice chmn. Denver GOP Cen. Com., 1976-78; del. alt. GOP Nat. Conv., Detroit, 1980; candidate Colo. Gen. Assembly, Denver, 1976; bd. dirs. Denver U. Theatre, 1969-72, Denver Jr. League, 1962—, Colo. Easter Seals, Denver, 1982—. Mem. Colo. Press Assn., Pub. Relations Soc. Am., Colo. Women's Press Assn., DAR, Colonial Dames. Republican. Roman Catholic. Clubs: Denver Athletic, Denver Country, Denver Press. Avocations: music, theater. Home: 515 Franklin St Denver CO 80218 Office: Colo Gen Assembly State Capitol Room 308 Denver CO 80203

SAWYER, ROBERT FENNELL, mechanical engineering educator, consultant; b. Santa Barbara, Calif., May 19, 1935; s. Clarence Robert Sawyer and Virginia Margaret (Fennell) Waugh; m. Barbara Lee White, June 23, 1957; children: Lisa Marie, Allison Jean Sawyer Shaffer. BS, Stanford U., 1957, MS, 1958; MA, Princeton U., 1963, PhD, 1966. Rocket engr. USAF Rocket Lab., Edwards AFB, Calif., 1958-61; instr. Antelope Valley Coll., Lancaster, Calif., 1959-61; prof. mech. engring. U. Calif., Berkeley, 1966—. Contbr. numerous tech. papers to sci. jours. Mem. Calif. Air Resources Bd.; mem. Health Effects Inst., Cambridge, Mass., 1981—. Served to capt. USAF, 1958-61. Mem. ASME, Am. Chem. Soc., Combustion Inst., Soc. Automotive Engrs., Air Pollution Control Assn. Office: U Calif Dept Mech Engring Berkeley CA 94720

SAWYER, THOMAS ARTHUR, information officer, consultant; b. Pocatello, Idaho, Apr. 26, 1946; s. Fred Ellis and Bertha Elizabeth (Adkins) S.; m. Cora Ada Davis, Sept. 4, 1969; children—Gaylan Thomas, Rebecca Lynn, Bradley Arthur, Mark Twain, Joseph Edward, James Ellis. Student Idaho State U., 1966-69, Boise State U., 1970-77; cert. data processing mgmt., 1971 cert. in prodn. and inventory mgmt., 1979, cert. system devel. profl., 1984. Programmer, FMC Corp., Pocatello, 1967-70; mgr. systems and programming Ore Ida Foods, Inc., Boise, Idaho, 1970-77; mgr. systems devel. Tektronix, Inc., Beaverton, Oreg., 1977-83; dir. mgmt. info. systems and adminstrn. Sidereal Corp., Portland, Oreg., 1983—; cons., instr. mfg. system principles. Served in USAF, 1966-73. Mem. Assn. Systems Mgmt. Data Processing Mgmt. Assn., Am. Prodn. and Inventory Control Soc. Republican. Mormon. Home: 12295 SW Tippitt Pl Tigard OR 97223 Office: Sidereal Corp 9600 SW Barnes Rd Portland OR 97225

SAWYER, THOMAS EDGAR, management consultant; b. Homer, La., July 7, 1932; s. Sidney Edgar and Ruth (Bickham) S.; B.S., UCLA, 1959; M.A., Occidental Coll., 1969; m. Joyce Mezzanatto, Aug. 22, 1954; children—Jeffrey T., Scott A., Robert J., Julie Anne. Project engr. Garrett Corp., Los Angeles, 1954-60; mgr. devel. ops. TRW Systems, Redondo Beach, Calif., 1960-66; spl. asst. to gov. State of Calif., Sacramento, 1967-69; prin., gen. mgr. Planning Research Corp., McLean, Va., 1969-72; dep. dir. OEO, Washington, 1972-74; asso. prof. bus. mgmt. Brigham Young U., 1974-78; pres. Mesa Corp., Provo, 1978-82, chmn. bd., 1978-82; pres. and dir. Sage Inst. Internat., Inc., Provo, Utah, 1982—; dir. Insul Chem. Corp., World Dairy and Food Research, Inc., Nooraid Chem. Corp., Nat. Applied Computer Tech., Inc., Indian Affiliates, Inc. Chmn. Nat. Adv. Council Indian Affairs; chmn. Utah State Bd. Indian Affairs; mem. Utah Dist. Export Council; mem. Utah dist. SBA Council; chmn. So. Paiute Restoration Com.; mem. adv. council Nat. Bus. Assn.; mem. Utah Job Tng. Coordinating Council. Served with USMC, 1950-53. Mem. Am. Mgmt. Assn., Am. Soc. Public Adminstrn., Utah Council Small Bus. (dir.). Republican. Mormon. Club: Masons. Author: Assimilation Versus Self-Indentity: A Modern Native American Perspective, 1976; Computer Assisted Instruction: An Inevitable Breakthrough. Home: 548 W 630 S Orem UT 84058 Office: Sage Inst Internat Inc 226 W 2230 N Provo UT 84604

SAXBY, DOYLE BRYAN, municipal agency administrator; b. College Place, Wash., Jan. 23, 1925; s. Glenn H. and Alice E. (Conklin) S.; m. Lorelei L. Pierce, July 27, 1947; children: Kent Pierce, Monte Arthur, Gayle Lucille. BABA, Walla Walla Coll., 1949; postgrad., U. Oreg., 1949-50, McGeorge Coll. Law, 1957-58, Calif. State U., Sacramento, 1962-63, 65. CPA, Oreg., Calif. Staff acct. Stark's Acctg. Services, The Dalles, Oreg., 1950-54, Richard Artis, CPA, Visalia, Calif., 1954-56; supervising auditor Office of Auditor Gen. State of Calif., Sacramento, 1956-69; state controller State of Mont., Helena, 1969-71; dir. State of Mont. Dept. Adminstrn., Helena, 1971-75, dep. dir., 1975-79; auditor, controller Marin Mcpl. Water Dist., Corte Madera, Calif., 1980-85, asst. gen. mgr., auditor controller, 1986—; pro tem internal auditor State of Alaska, Juneau, 1964; cons. to Nat. Audit Council Thailand, Bangkok, 1967. Served with U.S. Army, 1943-46. Mem. Am. Inst. CPA's, Govt. Fin. Officers' Assn., Am. Soc. Pub. Adminstrn., Council State Govt.'s Acctg. Project (chmn. 1975-79), Nat. Council Govtl. Acctg. (advisor 1977-79, chmn. task force 1979), Am. Mgmt. Assn. Republican. Adventist. Avocations: photography, bird watching, hiking, fishing, snow skiing. Home: 70 Santa Maria Dr Novato CA 94947 Office: Marin Mcpl Water Dist 220 Nellen Ave Corte Madera CA 94925

SAXENA, NARENDRA K., professor, researcher; b. Agra, India, Oct. 15, 1936; came to U.S., 1969; s. Brijbasi Lal and Sarbati Saxena; m. Cecilia H. Hsi, Mar. 21, 1970; Sarah Vasanti, Lorelle Sarita. Diploma Geodetic Engring., Tech. U., Hanover, Fed. Republic Germany, 1966; D in Tech Scis., Tech. U., Graz, Austria, 1972. Research assoc. geodetic sci. Ohio State U., Columbus, 1969-74; asst. prof. U. Ill., Urbana, 1974-78; asst. prof. U. Hawaii, Honolulu, 1978-81, assoc. prof., 1981-86, prof., 1986—; adj. research prof. Naval Postgrad. Sch., Monterey, Calif., 1984—; co-chmn. Pacific Congresses on Marine Tech., Honolulu, 1984, 86. Editor Jour. Marine Geodesy, 1976—. Mem. Neighborhood Bd., Honolulu, 1984. Fellow Marine Tech. Soc. (various offices 1974—); mem. ASCE, Am. Geophys. Union, The Tsunami Soc. (sec. 1985—). Office: U Hawaii Dept Civil Engring Honolulu HI 96822

SAXENA-KUMAR, JAY, utility company executive, consultant; b. Jhansi, India, Oct. 2, 1949; came to U.S., 1971; s. Prem Chandra and Shiela Devi (Sahai) Saxena; m. Judith Ann, Sept. 29, 1979; 1 child, Grant M.S. Kumar. BET, Indian Inst. Tech., Madras, India, 1965; BScME, Sir. Harcourt Butler Inst. Tech., Kanpur, India, 1969; MMS, Jawaharlal Nehru Inst. Internat. Mgmt., New Delhi, 1971; MSME, U. Colo., 1974. Registered profl. engr.; cert. energy mgr., infrared thermographer. Proj. engr. Natkin & Co., Englewood, Colo., 1973-75; mgr. div. energy systems Molitor Industries, Englewood, Colo., 1975-80; dist. mgr. Control Data Corp., Denver, 1980-81; project mgr. Flack & Kurtz Cons. Engrs., Denver, 1981-83; dir. energy mgmt. State of Colo., Denver, 1983—; assoc. dir. public office bldgs. div. city and county of Denver. Contbr. articles to profl. jours. Mem. ASHRAE (chmn. enery commn. 1981-84), Assn. Energy Engrs. (pres. 1985-87), Rocky Mountain Gas Assn. (bd. dirs. 1984-87), Rocky Mt. Assn. Energy Engrs. (dir. internat. chpt. devel.). Home: 6804 W Cornell Ave Denver CO 80227-3506 Office: State of Colo 1460 Cherokee St Room 34 Denver CO 80204

SAXON, RICHARD PETER, business executive; b. Sydney, Australia, Jan. 13, 1946; came to U.S., 1974, naturalized, 1983; s. Wilfred G. and Else L. (Schwanke) S. B Commerce, U. New South Wales, Australia, 1968; BA in Psychology, Sydney U., 1969. Dist. mgr. Internat. Harvester Australia, 1969-71; internat. sales dir. Howard Machinery Corp, Norfolk, Eng., 1971-76; internat. ops. dir. Essick div. Figgie Internat., Richmond, Va., 1976-81; export dir. for Middle East Challenge Cook, City of Industry, Calif., 1981-83; pres., chief exec. officer Bio-Med. Life Systems Inc., Los Angeles, 1983—. Assoc. mem. Australian Inst. Mgmt., Am. Mktg. Assn. Club: Hawaii Yacht. Office: Bio-Med Life Systems Inc PO Box 39636 Los Angeles CA 90039

SAXON, ROBERTA P., chemical physicist; b. Chgo., July 19, 1946; s. Alfred and Blanche (Fine) Pollack. BA, Cornell U., 1967; PhD, U. Chgo., 1971. Research assoc. Argonne (Ill.) Nat. Lab., 1972-73, U. Wash., Seattle, 1973-74; chem. physicist SRI Internat., Menlo Park, Calif., 1974-79, sr. chem. physicist, 1979—. Editor: Electronic and atomic Physics, 1986; contbr. articles to profl. jours. Collaborative Research grantee NATO, 1984. Mem. Am. Phys. Soc. Office: SRI Internat 333 Ravenswood Ave Menlo Park CA 94025

SAYANO, REIZO RAY, electrochemical engineer; b. Los Angeles, Dec. 15, 1937; s. George Keiichiro and Miyo (Nakao) S.; m. Tamiko Shintani, May 28, 1967; children—Kiyomi Coleen, Naomi Jennifer. A.A., Los Angeles Community Coll., 1958; B.S., UCLA, 1960, M.S., 1962, Ph.D., 1967. Research asst. electrochem. and shock tube research dept. engring. UCLA, 1961-66; mem. staff TRW Systems, corrosion and advanced battery research and devel. Redondo Beach, Calif., 1966-78; dir. engring. Intermedics Intraocular Inc., Pasadena, Calif., 1978-80, dir. research and devel., 1980-82, v.p. engring. devel. and research, 1982-84; v.p. research and devel. Interpone Internat. Inc., 1984-85; dir. research and devel., product process devel. IOLAB Corp. subs. Johnson & Johnson Co., Claremont, Calif., 1985-87, dir. new tech., research and devel., 1987—. NASA predoctoral trainee, 1964-65. Mem. Electrochem. Soc., Nat. Assn. Corrosion Engrs., AAAS, Am. Mgmt. Assn., Sigma Xi. Home: 209 Casa Grande Ave Montebello CA 90640 Office: 500 IOLAB Dr Claremont CA 91711

SAYKALLY, RICHARD JAMES, chemistry educator; b. Rhinelander, Wis., Sept. 10, 1947; s. Edwin L. and Helen M. (Janda) S. BS, U. Wis., Eau Claire, 1970; PhD, U. Wis., Madison, 1977. Postdoctoral Nat. Bur. Standards, Boulder, Colo., 1977-79; assoc. prof. U. Calif., Berkeley, 1979—; prin. investigator Lawrence Berkeley Lab., 1981—. Contbr. articles to profl. jours. prin. investigator Lawrence Berkeley Lab., 1981—. Dreyfuss Found. fellow, 1977; presdl. investigator NSF, 1983. Mem. Am. Chem. Soc., Am. Phys. Soc., Optical Soc. Am., AAAS. Office: U Calif Dept Chemistry Berkeley CA 94720

SAYLES, JAMES MCKINLEY, marketing professional; b. Seattle, Sept. 11, 1948; s. William McKinley and Ethel Artis (Lewis) S. BA, Eastern Wash. U., 1971; MS, Gonzaga U., 1979. Musician, Spokane, Wash., 1971-74; with admission control and mktg. World's Fair Expo 74, Spokane, 1974-75; case worker Big Bros., 1975-76; adv. mktg. rep. IBM, 1978—. Co-editor: (quarterly newsletter) Future Tense, 1982—. Bd. dirs. NW Regional Found., 1983—, Future Spokane, 1984—; trustee Mus. Native Am. Cultures, 1987—; mem. community adv. com. Jr. League, Spokane, 1987—. Mem. Data Processing Mgmt. Assn., Alpha Kappa Delta, Pi Gamma Mu. Roman Catholic. Office: IBM W 201 N River Dr Spokane WA 99201

SAYLOR, DENNIS ALAN, civil engineer; b. St. Louis, Apr. 1, 1958; s. Dennis Elwood and Helen Lucille (Howe) S. BSCE, N.Mex. State U., 1980. Registered civil engr., Calif. Project engr. Fluor Corp., Irvine, Calif., 1980-83; office dir. George Gouvis Co., Inc., Newport Beach, Calif., 1983-84; project engr. Johnson & Nielsen Assocs., Irvine, Calif., 1984—. Leadership team Mariners Ch. Singles Group, Newport Beach, 1986. Republican. Home: 1121 W Curie Ave Santa Ana CA 92707 Office: Johnson & Nielsen Assocs 18009 L Skypark Circle Irvine CA 92714

SAYRE, EDWARD CHARLES, librarian; b. Longview, Wash., Aug. 15, 1923; s. Kenneth C. Sayre and Clare (Davis) Clingan; m. Virginia A. Hoy, June 9, 1951; children—Steven Anthony, Sabrina Karen. B.A., Coll. of Gt. Falls, 1955; M.A., U. Idaho, 1961; M.L.S., U. Md., 1968. Coordinator library services Thomas Nelson Community Coll., Hampton, Va., 1968-69; dir. Roswell Pub. Library, N.Mex., 1969-70; cons. N.Mex. State Library, Santa Fe, 1970-72; dir. Central Colo. Library System, Denver, 1972-78, Serra Coop. Library System, San Diego, 1978-79, Los Alamos County (N.Mex.) Library System, 1979—; cons., 1976—. Contbr. articles to profl. jours. Served to maj. USAF, 1951-67. HEA Title II fellow, 1968. Mem. ALA, N.Mex. Library Assn. (pres.-elect 1972), Beta Phi Mu (dir. 1973-74). Democrat. Unitarian. Home: 3 Timber Ridge Los Alamos NM 87544 Office: Mesa Public Library 1742 Central Ave Los Alamos NM 87544

SAYRE, JOHN MARSHALL, lawyer; b. Boulder, Colo., Nov. 9, 1921; s. Henry Marshall and Lulu M. (Cooper) S.; m. Jean Miller, Aug. 22, 1943; children—Henry M., Charles Franklin, John Marshall, Ann Elizabeth Sayre Taggart (dec.). B.A., U. Colo., 1943, J.D., 1948. Bar: Colo. 1948, U.S. Dist. Ct. Colo. 1952, U.S. Ct. Appeals (10th cir.) 1964. Law clk. trust dept. Denver Nat. Bank, 1948-49; asst. cashier, trust officer Nat. State Bank of Boulder, 1949-50; ptnr. Ryan, Sayre, Martin, Brotzman, Boulder, 1950-66, Davis, Graham & Stubbs, Denver, 1966—. Bd. dirs. Boulder Sch. Dist. 3, 1951-57; city atty. City of Boulder, 1952-55; gen. counsel Colo. Mcpl. League, 1956-63; counsel No. Colo. Water Conservancy Dist. and mcpl. subdist., 1964-87, spl. counsel, 1987—, bd. dirs. dist., 1960-64; legal counsel Colo. Assn. Commerce and Industry. Served to lt. (j.g.) USNR, 1943-46. Decorated Purple Heart. Fellow Am. Bar. Found.; mem. ABA, Colo. Bar Assn., Boulder County Bar Assn., Denver Bar Assn., Nat. Water Resources Assn. (Colo. dir. 1980—, pres. 1984-86). Republican. Episcopalian. Clubs: Denver Country, Denver, Petroleum. Office: PO Box 185 Denver CO 80201

SBOROV, DAVID WILLIAM, farming and retail food company executive; b. Washington, Oct. 23, 1950; s. Victor Max and Carol (Reimers) S.; student U. Denver, 1968-71; B.A., U. Calif.-Berkeley, 1972. Gen. mgr. 1st Pacific Realty Corp., Palo Alto, Calif., 1972-73; owner, mgr. Sborov & Assocs., Palo Alto, 1973-74; mng. ptnr. 1st Harvest, Palo Alto, 1974-76; pres. Golden West Farming Co., Inc., Palo Alto, 1976-86; pres., chief exec. officer Snapps Fine Fresh Produce, Inc., 1986—87 chief exec. officer McGregor's Fresh Stop, 1987—; dir. Calif. Fruit Co. NSF grantee, 1969-70; Boetcher Found. fellow, 1970-71. Mem. Fin. Planning Forum, Calif. Pistachio Assn., Internat. Platform Assn. Club: Commonwealth. Author: Migrant Community Studies Guide, 1971; Fine Art of Investing During Inflation, 1975. Office: PO Box 1080 525 University Ave Palo Alto CA 94301

SCADRON, MICHAEL DAVID, physics educator; b. Chgo., Feb. 12, 1938; s. Irwin and Joanna (Dopke) S.; m. Arlene Weininger, June 15, 1960; children: Kari M., Lisa I. BS in Physics magna cum laude, U. Mich., 1959; PhD in Physics, U. Calif., Berkeley, 1964. Postdoctoral fellow U. Calif., Livermore, 1964-66; NSF postdoctoral fellow Imperial Coll., London, 1966-68, sr. physics researcher, 1972, 78; asst. prof. Northwestern U., Evanston, Ill., 1968-70; vis. prof. U. Ariz., Tucson, 1970-71, prof., 1971—. Author: Advanced Quantum Theory, 1979; co-author: Stellar Evolution and Cosmology, 1981. Fellow NSF Coop. Sci., U. Tasmania, U. Melbourne, Australia, 1979, 85-86, Fulbright Quaid iAzam U., Islamabad, Pakistan, 1979, Fulbright IISc, Tata Inst., Bangalore and Bombay, India, 1985; grantee NSF, 1974-80, Dept. Energy, 1985—; research contract Dept. Energy, 1981-85. Mem. AAUP, Am. Phys. Soc. Home: 220 N Stewart Tucson AZ 85716 Office: U Ariz Dept Physics Tucson AZ 85721

SCAFE, LINCOLN ROBERT, JR., sales executive; b. Cleve., July 28, 1922; s. Lincoln Robert and Charlotte (Hawkins) S.; student Cornell U., 1940-41; m. Mary Anne Wilkinson, Nov. 14, 1945; children—Amanda Katharine, Lincoln Robert III. Service mgr. Avery Engring. Co., Cleve., 1946-51; nat. service mgr. Trane Co., LaCrosse, Wis., 1951-57; service and installation mgr. Mech. Equipment Supply Co., Honolulu, 1957-58; chief engr. Sam P. Wallace of Pacific, Honolulu, 1958-62; pres. Air Conditioning Service Co., Inc., Honolulu, 1962-84; sales engr. G.J. Campbell & Assocs., Seattle, 1984—. Served with USNR, 1942-45; PTO. Mem. ASHRAE, Alpha Delta Phi. Clubs: Cornell Hawaii (past pres.); Outrigger Canoe. Republican. Author tech. service lit. and parts manuals; contbr. articles to trade pubs. Home: Route 1 Box 444 Vashon WA 98070 Office: GJ Campbell and Assocs 11613 Rainier Ave S Seattle WA 98178

SCAGLIONE, CECIL FRANK, accredited public relations and marketing communications executive; b. North Bay, Ont., Can., Dec. 2, 1934; came to U.S., 1967, naturalized, 1982; s. Frank and Rose (Aubin) S.; student North Bay Coll., 1947-52, Ryerson Tech. Inst., Toronto, Ont., 1955-56, San Diego State U. Inst. World Affairs, 1979; m. Mary Margaret Stewart, Nov. 11, 1954 (div.); children—Cris Ann, Michael Andrew, Patrick Andrew; m. 2d, Beverly Louise Rahn, Mar. 25, 1983. Fin. writer Toronto Telegram, 1955; reporter Sarnia (Ont.) Observer, 1956-57; reporter, editor Kitchener-Waterloo (Ont.) Record, 1957-61; reporter, editor, analyst Windsor (Ont.) Star, 1961-67; writer, editor, photo editor Detroit News, 1967-71; reporter, asso. bus. editor San Diego Union, 1971-80; mgr. corp. communications Pacific Southwest Airlines, San Diego, 1981-83; sr. v.p. media relations Berkman & Daniels, Inc., San Diego, 1984—; v.p. Spl. Info. Services, Inc. Mem. adv. council SBA, accredited pub. relations Soc. Am. Recipient award B.F. Goodrich Can., Ltd., 1962, 66, Spl. Achievement award Nat. Assn. Recycling Industries, 1978, award SBA, 1980; Herbert J. Davenport fellow, 1977; Canadian Centennial grantee, 1966. Mem. San Diego Press Club (hon. life; past pres.; awards 1978, 80, 84), Airline Editors Forum awards 1982, 83), Pub. Relations Soc. Am., Sigma Delta Chi. Roman Catholic. Founding editor-in-chief Aeromexico Mag., 1973; contbr. articles and photographs to various publs. Home: 3911 Kendall St San Diego CA 92109 Office: Berkman and Daniels Inc 1717 Kettner Blvd Suite 100 San Diego CA 92101

SCALAPINO, ROBERT ANTHONY, political science educator; b. Leavenworth, Kans., Oct. 19, 1919; s. Anthony and Beulah (Stephenson) S.; m. Ida Mae Jessen, Aug. 23, 1941; children: Diane Jablon, Sharon Leslie, Lynne Ann Thompson. AB, Santa Barbara Coll., 1940; MA, Harvard U., 1943, PhD, 1948; LLD (hon.), China Acad., Republic of China, 1976; D in Polit. Sci. (hon.), Hankuk U. Fgn. Studies, Seoul, Republic of Korea, 1983. Instr. Harvard U., Cambridge, Mass., 1948-49; asst. prof. U. Calif., Berkeley, 1949-51, assoc. prof., 1951-56, prof., 1956-77, chmn. dept. polit. sci., 1962-65, Robson research prof. govt., 1977—; dir. Inst. East Asian Studies, 1978—; cons. govtl. and ednl. studies; Bernard Moses lectr. U. Calif., 1983. Co-author: Modern China and Its Revolutionary Process, 1985, Communism in Korea, 1972 (Woodrow Wilson Found. Book award 1974); author: Asia and the Road Ahead, 1975, Major Power Relations in Northeast Asia, 1987; editor: The Foreign Policy of Modern Japan, 1977, (jour.) Asian Survey, 1962—. Founder, chmn., bd. dirs. Nat. Com. U.S.-China Relations, 1966—; bd. dirs. Council on Fgn. Relations, N.Y., 1982—; trustee The Asia Found., San Francisco, 1983—; chmn. Com. Internat. Relations Studies with Peoples Republic of China, 1984—; head N.E. Asia Study Mission, Asia Soc., 1982—. Served to lt. (j.g.) USN, 1943-46. Guggenheim fellow, 1965-66, Social Sci. Research Council fellow, 1952-53. Mem. Am. Acad. Arts Scis., Am. Polit. Sci. Assn., Assn. Asian Studies, Pacific Forum (bd. dirs.). Democrat. Avocations: photography, Asian travel. Office: U Calif Inst East Asian Studies 2223 Fulton St Berkeley CA 94720

SCALARONE, GENE MARTIN, microbiology educator; b. Arma, Kans., Feb. 29, 1940; s. John and Florence (Hiett) S.; m. Reiko Kodama, Aug. 10, 1980; children: Geoffrey, Anne. BS, Kans. State Coll., 1962; MS, U. Okla., 1965; PhD, U. Calif., Berkeley, 1970. Assoc. in pub. health U. Calif., Berkeley, 1967-69, research assoc., 1968-70, research bacteriologist, 1970-80; assoc. prof. microbiology Idaho State U., Pocatello, 1980—. Contbr. numerous articles to profl. jours. Served to capt. M.C., U.S. Army, 1965-67. Mem. AAAS, Am. Soc. Microbiology (councilor 1982—), Internat. Soc. Animal Mycology, Med. Mycol. Soc. Ams., Sigma Xi (local sec.-treas. 1983—). Home: 5117 Mahogany Dr Pocatello ID 83204 Office: Idaho State U Dept Biol Scis Box 8007 Pocatello ID 83209

SCALES, PETER CRAIG, family life educator; b. Glen Ridge, N.J., Nov. 13, 1949; s. Robert and Viola (Boise) S.; m. Cynthia Gay Walker, July 25, 1981; children: Thomas N. Grimm, Matthew B. Grimm. BA cum laude in Psychology, Syracuse U., 1971, MS in Child and Family Studies, 1973, PhD in Child and Family Studies, 1976. Research dir. Inst. for Family Research and Edn., Syracuse, N.Y., 1974-77; dir. pub. affairs Nat. Alliance for Optional Parenthood, Balt., 1978; sr. social scientist Mathtech Social Sci. Group, Bethesda, Md., 1978-81; pvt. practice cons. sociologist Denver, 1981; dir. edn. Planned Parenthood Fedn. of Am., N.Y.C., 1982-83; exec. dir. Family Connection, Inc., Anchorage, 1983—; conf. keynote speaker, 1979—; grant proposal reviewer Ednl. Found. Am., Encino, Calif., 1982—; mem. rev. bd. Child Welfare League of Am., N.Y.C., 1984. Author: The Front Lines of Sexuality Education, 1984, (with others) The Sexual Adolescent, 1979, An Analysis of U.S. Sex Educations Programs and Evaluation Methods, 1979; contbr. articles to profl. jours. Chmn. Scenic Park Community Sch. Bd.; mem. Anchorage Sch. Dist. Health Curriculum Com., 1985—, Mayor's Task Force on Runaway and Homeless Youth, Anchorage, 1986—. Grantee Nat. Fund. for Runaway Children, 1984, NIMH, USPHS; named one of Outstanding Young Men of Am., U.S. Jaycees, 1982; recipient Outstanding Contributions award, Mich. State Legis., 1982. Mem. Am. Assn. Sex Educators, Counselors and Therapists (chmn. pub. policy com. 1983, cons. editor Jour. of Sex Edn. and Therapy 1982—), Nat. Council on Family Relations (cons. editor Family Relations 1986—), Freedom to Read Found (bd. trustees 1982-84), Nat. Family Life Edn. Network (Nat. Adv. Bd. mem 1984—). Democrat. Methodist. Avocations: photography, music composition and performance. Home: 8050 Pioneer Dr #104 Anchorage AK 99504 Office: Family Connection Inc 3745 Community Park Loop Suite 201 Anchorage AK 99508

SCALIA, CINDY SUZANNE, real estate developer; b. Fontana, Calif., Apr. 13, 1951; d. Franklin Benedict and Jimmie Sue (Clayton) Rossi; m. Joseph William Scalia, Mar. 22, 1975; children—Tiffany, Todd. B.A. in Sociology, U. Calif.-Davis, 1973. Stewardess, United Air Lines, Washington, 1973-74; asst. to chief employer-employee relations State of Calif., Sacramento, 1974; job developer U. Calif.-Davis, 1974-80; real estate developer S&K Properties, Sacramento, 1980—; v.p. S&K Computers, Inc., Sacramento, 1983—, dir., 1984—; instr. math. Twin Lakes Elem. Sch., Orangevale, Calif., 1983-84. Active Sch. Site Council, Orangevale, 1983—. Republican. Presbyterian. Home: 5337 Dawn Oak Ln Fair Oaks CA 95628

SCALLORN, LESLIE THOMAS, chemist; b. Tupelo, Miss., Apr. 22, 1943; s. Leslie and Dorthy (Tuckor) S.; m. Judy Ann Williams, June 1, 1969; children: Bruce, Dottie. Assoc. in Chemistry, Northwest Miss. Jr. Coll., 1963; BS in Chemistry, Miss. Coll., 1966. Electrician Glorieta (N.Mex.) Baptist Conf. Ctr., 1971-76; water utilities instr. Dona Ana br. N.Mex. State U., Las Cruces, 1976-78; supervising chemist Pub. Service Co. N.Mex., Santa Fe, 1978-86; water ops. instr. Pub. Service Co. N. Mex., Water Flow, 1986—; mem. adv. bd. Dona Ana br. Community Coll. Water Utilities, Las Cruces, 1986-87. Mem. Am. Chem. Soc., N.Mex. Water and Waste Assn. Republican. Baptist. Avocations: camping, electronics. Office: Pub Service Co New Mexico PO Box 227 Water Flow NM 87421

SCARBOROUGH, TONY, state supreme court judge. Former presiding judge 6th Jud. Dist., N. Mex. Dist. Ct.; judge New Mexico Supreme Court, Santa Fe, NM, 1987—. Office: NMex Supreme Ct PO Box 848 Santa Fe NM 87504 *

SCARFF, EDWARD L., diversified company executive; b. 1930. BS, Mich. Tech. U., 1954. With Ansul Chem. Co., 1953-56, Stanford Research Inst., 1956-60; dir. investment research Investors Diversified Services, Inc., 1960-63; pres., chief exec. officer N. Am. Securities Co., 1963-65; v.p., then pres. Transam. Corp., 1965-71; pres. Edward L. Scarff and Assocs., San Francisco, 1971—; with Arcata Corp., San Francisco, 1971—, now chmn. bd. dirs., also bd. dirs. Office: Arcata Corp 601 California St San Francisco CA 94108 *

SCEPER, DUANE HAROLD, lawyer; b. Norfolk, Va., Nov. 16, 1946; s. Robert George and Marion Eudora (Hynes) S.; m. Sharon Diane Cramer, July 4, 1981; stepchildren: Karin Stevenson, Diane Stevenson. BS in Law, Western State U., 1979, JD, 1980. Bar: Calif. 1982, U.S. Dist. Ct. (so. dist.) Calif. 1982. Field engr. Memorex/Tex. Instruments, San Diego, 1968-70; computer programmer San Diego, 1970-81; atty. Allied Ins. Group, San Diego, 1981-85; sole practice San Diego, 1985—; cons. computers 1980—; lectr. estate planning various orgns. Patentee in field. Active Com. to Elect King Golden to Congress, San Diego, 1978. Served with USAF, 1965-68. Recipient Am. Jurisprudence award, 1979. Mem. ABA, San Diego County Bar Assn., Assn. Trial Lawyers of Am., Calif. Trial Lawyers Assn., San Diego Trial Lawyers Assn., Delta Theta Phi. Democrat. Home: 2641 Massachusetts Ave Lemon Grove CA 92045 Office: 707 Broadway Suite 1100 San Diego CA 92101

SCHAAL, BRADLEY ALAN, chemistry educator; b. Vallejo, Calif., Apr. 28, 1955; s. James Wendel Schaal and Betty Lee (Houglan) Wells; m. Darsanne Elizabeth Carroll, Aug. 12, 1979; children: Erich Ernest, Travis Parker. BS, U. Calif., Davis, 1976. Cert. secondary tchr., Oreg. Tchr. chemistry Carroll High Sch., Dayton, Ohio; tchr. biology Hillsboro (Oreg.) High Sch., 1984-85; tchr. chemistry Jesuit High Sch., Portland, Oreg., 1985—; moderator chess club Jesuit High Sch., Portland, 1985-86. Republican. Avocations: fishing, backpacking, hunting, cross-country skiing. Home: 157 NE 35th Ct Hillsboro OR 97124 Office: Jesuit High Sch 9000 SW Beaverton Hwy Portland OR 97225

SCHAAR, JACQUELINE KAY COUCH (MRS. ROBERT L. SCHAAR), public relations executive; b. San Diego, Apr. 2, 1933; d. Edwin Newton and Nina Mae (Sweetwood) Couch; grad. pub. schs., 1951; m. Robert L. Schaar, May 11, 1962; children—Robert, Denise. Exec. sec. various firms, 1951-57; asst. to community relations dir. Convair-Astronautics, San Diego, 1957-59; advt., pub. relations exec. Frederick C. Whitney & Assos., San Diego, 1959-62, J. Jessop & Sons, 1962-64; regional dir. pub. relations United Way, Los Angeles, Calif., 1964-73; dir. pub. relations Orange County United Way, 1973-77; asso. exec. dir. Orange County chpt. Bldg. Industry Assn. Calif., 1977-80; founder, pres., chief exec. officer Jacqueline Schaar Assos., 1980—. Vice pres. bd. dirs. Orange County council Girl Scouts U.S.A.; mem. adv. council Orange County Performing Arts Center, mem. public relations council U. Calif., Irvine; mem. pub. relation curriculum adv. bd. Calif. State U. at Fullerton; founding pres. Friends of KOCE-TV. Recipient Thanks Badge Girl Scouts U.S. Mem. Pub. Relations Soc. Am. (accredited, past pres. Orange County chpt., nat. dir., Disting. Service award), Orange County Press Club. Home: 23282 Morobe Circle Laguna Niguel CA 92677 Office: 2192 Dupont Drive Suite 208 Irvine CA 92715

SCHABRON, JOHN FRANCIS, research institute administrator, research chemist; b. Carson City, Nev., Nov. 2, 1950; s. Rene L. and Marie Schabron; m. Joan Marie Knobloch, May 27, 1972; children: Susan, Robert, Gregory, Philip, Nicholas, Christopher, Paul. BS in Chemistry, Regis Coll., 1972; MS in Chemistry, Creighton U., 1975; PhD in Analytical Chemistry, U. Wyo., 1978. Research chemist Phillips Petroleum, Bartlesville, Okla., 1979-84; sr. research chemist We. Research Inst., Laramie, Wyo., 1984, mgr. analytical services div., 1985—. Contbr. articles to profl. jours.; reviewer articles to profl. jours. Mem. Am. Chem. Soc., Analytical Chemistry div. Am. Chem. Soc., Soc. Petroleum Engrs. Office: Western Research Inst PO box 3395 Laramie WY 82071

SCHACHT, LINDA JOAN, broadcast journalist; b. Berkeley, Calif., Sept. 11, 1944; d. Henry Mevis and Mary (Turnbull) S.; m. John Burdette Gage, May 1, 1976; children: Peter Turnbull, Katharine Burdette. BA, U. Calif., Berkeley, 1966, MJ, 1978. Reporter Sta. KQED-TV, San Francisco, 1974-76, Sta. KPIX-TV, San Francisco, 1976—. Reporter Dem. conv., 1980 (Emmy award 1981), investigative article on second mortgage brokers, 1977 (Emmy award), on children as witnesses, 1984 (Calif. State Bar award 1985, ABA award 1986. Mem. Nat. Acad. TV Arts and Scis.

SCHACHT, WILLIAM EUGENE, accountant; b. Kokomo, Ind., Nov. 6, 1941; s. Francis Albert and Estella Lillian (Brockman) S.; m. Lucia Fatima Camara, Nov. 21, 1985; children: Julie Ann, Susan Ruth, Randolph Lee. BS in Acctg., Ball State U., 1970. CPA, Calif. Acct. Davidson, Dreyer and Hopkins, CPA's, 1973-74, mgr., 1974-77; pvt. practice acctg. San Francisco, 1977—; chmn., treas. Unique Adventures, Inc.; bd. dirs. Rio-Cal, Inc., Tigs of San Francisco, Inc. Treas. Cystic Fibrosis Found. No. Calif. Served with U.S. Army, 1959-62. Recipient Scholastic award Price-Waterhouse, 1968. Mem. Am. Inst. CPA's, Calif. Soc. CPA's, San Francisco C. of C. Republican. Office: 140 2d St 6th Fl San Francisco CA 94105

SCHACK, CARL JOSEPH, research chemist; b. St. Louis, Dec. 26, 1936; s. Charles and Helen (Sanders) S.; m. Merlyn A. Price, June 6, 1959; children: Carl Jr., William. BS in Chemistry, St. Louis U., 1958; PhD, Poly. Inst. Bklyn., 1964. Po. research engr., research specialist, mem. tech. staff Rocketdyne div. Rockwell Internat., Canoga Park, Calif., 1964—. Author, coauthor over 115 tech. papers; patentee in field. Bd. dirs. Chatsworth (Calif.) Jr. Baseball League, 1975—. Mem. Am. Chem. Soc. (exec. com. fluorine div. 1984—), Royal Chem. Soc. Avocations: woodworking, cabinetry. Office: Rocketdyne BA-26 6633 Canoga Ave Canoga Park CA 91303

SCHAEFER, CHRISTOPHER BRIAN, county planning official, geographic information system company official; b. N.Y.C., June 27, 1949; s. Rudolf Franz and Florence (Rittenwagen) S.; m. Doris Bennett, Nov. 13, 1976; children—Justin, Kimberly, Nathaniel. B.S., U. Utah, 1972; M. Urban Planning, U. Pitts., 1979. Cert. planner. Sr. planner Davis County Planning Commn., Farmington, Utah, 1976—; prin. UNI-Graphic Systems Inc., Salt Lake City, 1984—; cons. planner various local communities, Utah, 1977—; speaker profl. conf., 1983. Planning asst. Squirrel Hill Urban Coalition, Pitts., 1975, People's Freeway Group, Salt Lake City, 1972. Mem. Am. Inst. Cert. Planners, Am. Planning Assn., Urban and Regional Info. Systems Assn. Mormon. Home: 445 S 925 E Kaysville UT 84037 Office: UNI-Graphic Systems Inc PO Box 520610 Salt Lake City UT 84152

SCHAEFER, DAN L., congressman; b. Gutenberg, Iowa, Jan. 25, 1936; s. Alvin L. and Evelyn (Everson) S.; m. Mary Margaret Lenney, 1959; children: Danny, Darren, Joel, Jennifer. B.A., Niagara U., 1961, LLD (hon.), 1986; postgrad., Potsdam State U., 1961-64. Pub. relations cons. 1967-83; mem. Colo. Gen. Assembly, 1977-78; mem. Colo. Senate, 1979-83, pres. pro tem, 1981-82, majority whip, 1983; mem. 98th, 99th, 100th Congresses from 6th dist. Colo., Washington, 1983—; mem. house small bus. com., 1983, govt. ops com., 1983, energy and commerce com. 1984-86 (subcoms. on fossil and synthetic fuels; commerce, transp. and tourism; oversight/investigations), environ. and energy study com., Rep. study com.; mem. house sci. and high tech. task force, mil. reform caucus, congl. grace caucus; mem. adv. com., com. of concern for Soviet jewry. Pres. Foothills Recreation Bd., 1973-76; sec. Jefferson County Republican Party, Colo., 1975-76. Served with USMCR, 1955-57. Recipient Colo. Park and Recreation citation, 1976; named Elected Ofcl. of Yr., Lakewood/South Jeffco C. of C., 1986, Leadership award U.S. Congl. Adv. Bd., Am. Security Council Found.; Taxpayers Best Friend award Nat. Taxpayer's Union, 1985-86; Golden Bulldog award Watchdog of Treasury, 1985-86; Best of Colo. award Aspen Assocs., 1986. Mem. C. of C., Beta Theta Pi. Roman Catholic. Lodge: Rotary. Office: 1317 Longworth House Office Bldg Washington DC 20515

SCHAEFER, HALMUTH HANS, mgmt. cons.; b. Wiesbaden, Germany, May 16, 1928; came to U.S., 1952, naturalized, 1954; s. Ernst and Theresa (Fritz) S.; Ph.D., U. Chgo., 1958; m. Doris Marie Leininger, Sept., 1952; children—Shirley Gail, Christopher Garth. Asst. prof. psychology Loyola U., Chgo., 1958-60; asst. prof., asso. dir. behavior research lab. Pitts. U., 1960-61; project dir. Ency. Brit. Films Inc., Palo Alto, Calif., 1962-63; research specialist State of Calif., Atascadero, 1964—; research asso. Stanford U. Med. Center, 1962-63; asso. prof. psychology Claremont Grad. Sch., 1964-67; prof. clin. . psychiatry Loma Linda U., 1967-71; prof., mem. senate U. Auckland (N.Z.), 1971-77; cons. to govt. agys. Served with U.S. Army, 1952-54. Behavior Research Soc. fellow, 1971—; lic. psychologist, Calif. Mem. Am. Psychol. Assn., N.Y. Acad. Sci., Am. Mgmt. Assn., So. Calif. H-P Users Group, AAAS, N.Z. Assn. Behavior Therapy (hon.), Sigma Xi. Republican. Club: santa Lucia Sportmen's Assn. Author books, the most recent being: Learning and Programmed Instruction, 1965, German transl., 1971; Behavioral Therapy, 1969, rev. edit., 1975; contbr. numerous articles, chpts. to profl. publs. Home: 11950 Viejo Camino Atascadero CA 93422 Office: PO Drawer A Atascadero CA 93423

SCHAEFER, HELEN SCHWARZ, civic worker; b. Evanston, Ill., Apr. 26, 1933; d. Irving J. and Marie L. Schwarz; m. John P. Schaefer, May 18, 1958; children: Ann, Susan. BS, U. Mich., 1955; MS, U. Ill., 1957, PhD, 1978; postgrad., Calif. Inst. Tech., 1958-59, U. Ariz., 1967-71. Teaching asst., research asst. U. Ill., Urbana, 1955-60; teaching asst. U. Ariz., Tucson, 1960-61, 62-63. Pres. Tucson Symphony, 1984-85; v.p. Ariz. for Cultural Devel., Phoenix, 1985—; treas. YWCA of Tucson, 1985-86; bd. dirs. Ariz. Acad., Phoenix, 1985—, Carondelet Mgmt. Corp., Tucson, 1985—. Named Woman of Yr., Tucson Advt. Club, 1977. Mem. AAAS, Am. Chem. Soc., Sigma Xi, Iota Sigma Pi, Sigma Delta Epsilon. Avocations: needlepoint, cooking. Home: 7401 E Kenyon Dr Tucson AZ 85710

SCHAEFER, HENRY FREDERICK, III, chemistry educator; b. Grand Rapids, Mich., June 8, 1944; s. Henry Frederick Jr. and Janice Christine (Trost) S.; m. Karen Regine Rasmussen, Sept. 2, 1966; children: Charlotte, Pierre, Theodore, Rebecca, Caleb. BS in Chem. Physics, MIT, 1966; PhD in Chem. Physics, Stanford U., 1969. Asst. prof. chemistry U. Calif., Berkeley, 1969-74, assoc. prof., 1974-78, prof., 1978—; Wilfred T. Doherty prof., dir. Inst. Theoretical Chemistry, U. Tex., Austin, 1979-80; endowed lectr. Nat. U. Mex., 1979, Johns Hopkins U., 1982, Brown U., 1985, U. Canterbury, Christchurch, New Zealand, 1986, U. Kans., 1986. Author: The Electronic Structure of Atoms and Molecules: A Survey of Rigorous Quantum Mechanical Results, 1972, Modern Theoretical Chemistry, 1977, Quantum Chemistry, 1984. Recipient Pure Chemistry award Am. Chem. Soc., 1979, Leo Hendrik Baekeland award, 1983; Sloan fellow, 1972, Guggenheim fellow, 1976-77; named One of the 100 Outstanding Young Scientists in Am., Sci. Digest, 1984. Fellow Am. Phys. Soc.; mem. Internat. Acad. Quantum Molecular Sci. Mem. Evangelical Ch. Office: U Calif Dept Chemistry Berkeley CA 94720

SCHAEFER, WERNER HELMUT, chemistry company executive; b. Arolsen, Fed. Republic Germany, Jan. 16, 1948; s. Heinrich and Elisabeth (Janson) S.; m. Barbara Klimkeit, Dec. 31, 1975. MS in Chemistry, Philipps U., Marburg, Fed. Republic Germany, 1971, PhD in Chemistry, 1974. Asst. tchr. Philipps U., 1971-75; research chemist Behringwerke AG, Marburg, 1975-78, dir. mktg. and planning, 1982-83, asst. dir. research and devel., 1978-79; v.p. internat. affairs Calbiochem-Behring, La Jolla, Calif., 1980-82; pres. Behring Diagnostics, La Jolla, 1983—; mem. indsl. adv. com. U. Calif., San Diego, 1984—. Contbr. articles to profl. jours. Mem. Am. Assn. Clin. Chemistry, Am. Soc. Microbiology. Avocations: windsurfing, skiing, jogging, reading. Home: 319 Glenmont Dr Solana Beach CA 92075 Office: Behring Diagnostics 10933 N Torrey Pines Rd La Jolla CA 92037

SCHAEFER, WILLIAM PALZER, educator, research scientist; b. Bisbee, Ariz., Jan. 13, 1931; s. Peter Leslie and Amelia Rose (Palzer) S.; m. Margaret Ann Durfy, Dec. 27, 1954; children: Peter Leslie, Michael James. BS, Stanford U., 1952; MS, UCLA, 1954, PhD, 1960. Asst. prof. chemistry Calif. Inst. Tech., Pasadena, 1960-66, from research fellow to sr. research assoc., 1968-81, sr. research assoc., 1981—; asst. prof. chemistry U. Calif., Davis, 1966-68; cons. TransTech., Sherman Oaks, Calif., 1985—. Author: Qualitative Elemental Analysis, 1962. Served to lt. (j.g.) USNR, 1954-57. Fellow AAAS, Am. Chem. Soc., Am. Crystallographic Assn. Republican. Office: Calif Inst Tech Chem Dept 127-72 Pasadena CA 91125

SCHAEFFER, PHILLIP FREDERICK, communications executive; b. N.Y.C., Jan. 28, 1926; s. Joseph and Ellen (Goulden) S.; m. Therese Eugenie, Sept. 7, 1958 (div. 1971); children: Phillip Jr., Francois J., Ellen T., Anton H. BFA, U. Denver, 1950. Art dir. Shell Oil Co., N.Y.C., 1950-57; pres., prin. P.F. Schaeffer Studios, N.Y.C., 1957-70; editor-in-chief Calif. Life mag., Carmel, 1972-75; cons. Acad. Communications, N.Y.C. and London, 1978-80; lectr. UN Internat. Trade, Geneva, 1980-81; dir. communications Physics Internat. Co., San Leandro, Calif., 1981—, also bd. dirs.; lectr. UN, Geneva, 1980-86. Author: Discover Guatemala, 1974, Lake Atitlan, 1975; author, pub. California Craftsmen, 1978, California Craftsmen II, 1979. Mem. Bay Area Pub. Affairs Council, San Francisco, 1981—. Served to staff sgt. U.S. Army, 1944-46. Recipient Bronze and Silver Oscars, Fin. World mag., 1968, Maggie award Maggie Found, 1978, Best Ann. Report U.S. award. Mem. Am. Inst. Graphic Arts. Republican. Home: 2325 Cornell St Palo Alto CA 94306

SCHAFER, DIANE MARIE, social worker; b. Norwalk, Ohio, Mar. 5, 1952; d. Harold Robert and Marjorie Magdelina (Stang) S. BA, Bowling Green State U.; MSW, Calif. State U., Fresno. Lic. clinician, Calif. Probation aide Shasta County (Calif.), Redding, 1975-76; group supr. Bachmann Hill Sch., Boonville, Calif., 1976-77; crisis counselor Youth Counseling Ctr., Redding, 1977-80; case mgr. Comprehensive Youth Services, Fresno, 1981-84; practitioner IV Child Protective Services, Visalia, Calif., 1984—; med. social worker Family Health Ctr., Merced, Calif., 1985—; cons. Young Parents Project, Merced, 1986. Counselor Help Line, Redding, 1977-79; vol. Poverello House, Fresno, 1980-84; bd. dirs. Firehouse Youth Ctr., Fresno, 1982-84, I-Care com., Merced, 1985—, Refugee Services, Merced, 1985—, Child Abuse Coordinating Com., Merced, 1985—. Mem. Nat. Assn. Social Workers. Home: 3075 Park Ave #24 Merced CA 95348 Office: Family Health Ctrs Inc 727 Childs Ave Merced CA 95340

SCHAFER, ELSA MURRAY, marketing professional; b. Chgo., Dec. 5, 1950. BA, Wheaton Coll., Norton, Mass., 1972; MBA, U. Pa., 1975. Brand asst. Proctor & Gamble Co., Cin., 1975-77; account exec. Hicks & Griest, N.Y.C., 1977-78; account supr., v.p. Young & Rubicam, N.Y.C., 1978-84; brand mgr. Campbell-Taggart Inc., Dallas, 1984-85; dir. mktg. Oroweat Foods Co., Montebello, Calif., 1985—. Office: Oroweat Foods Co 480 S Vail Ave Montebello CA 90640

SCHAFFER, JOEL LANCE, dentist; b. Bklyn., Oct. 18, 1945; s. Martin Alter and Irene Natalie (Shore) S.; m. Susan Anne Swearingen, Feb. 14, 1980 (div.); 1 child, Jericho Katherine. B.S., L.I. U., 1967; D.D.S., Howard U., 1971. Dental intern Eastman Dental Ctr., Rochester, N.Y., 1971-72; gen. practice dentistry, Boulder, Colo., 1973—; lectr. in field, 1972—. Contbr. articles to dental jours. Named outstanding clinician Boulder County Dental Forum, 1979. Mem. ADA, Am. Acad. Oral Implantology, Boulder County

Dental Soc., Am. Soc. Dental Aesthetics. Jewish. Home: 3874 Campo Ct Boulder CO 80302 Office: 2880 Folsom St Boulder CO 80203

SCHAFFNER, MELINDA REECE, lawyer; b. Johnson City, Tenn., May 13, 1950; d. Oliver V. and Seulah (Calhoun) R.; m. Wesley Ward, Aug. 28, 1971. Student, U. Tenn.; AA, Santa Ana Coll., 1975; BSL, Western State U., 1981, JD, 1982. Bar: Calif. 1983, U.S. Dist. Ct. (cen. dist.) Calif. Claims adjuster Hartford Ins., Santa Ana, Calif., 1970-78; claims supr. Hartford Ins., Brea, Calif., 1978-81, staff atty., 1983-84; supervising atty. Wendell Faile, Long Beach, Calif., 1984—. Mem. Assn. Trial Lawyers Am., Calif. Trial Lawyers Assn., Los Angeles County Trial Lawyers Assn., Los Angeles County Bar Assn., Christian Legal Soc. Baptist. Avocation: music. Office: Wendell Faile 3629 Atlantic Ave Long Beach CA 90807

SCHAIBLE, GRACE BERG, state attorney general. BA in History and Polit. Sci., U. Alaska; MA in History, George Washingron U.; JD, Yale U., 1959. Mem. Alaska Legis. Council, 1953-56, acting dir., 1956; assoc. McNealy and Merdes, 1959-66; ptnr. Schaible, Staley, DeLisio and Cook (formerly Merdes, Schaible, Staley and DeLisio), from 1966; also past gen. counsel U. Alaska; past city atty. Cities of Fairbanks, Barrow, Kotzebue and North Pole; past gen. corp. counsel Arctic Slope Regional Corp.; now atty. gen. State of Alaska, 1987—. Mem. Fairbanks Estate Planning Council; bd. dirs. United Way of Tanana Valley; past bd. dirs., treas. Fairbanks Devel. Authority; mem. bd. regents U. Alaska, 1985—. Fellow U. Alaska Found. (past bd. dirs.); mem. ABA, Alaska Bar Assn., Tanana Valley Bar Assn., Fairbanks C. of C. (past bd. dirs.), U. Alaska Alumni Assn., (past bd. dirs., officer). Office: Office of Atty Gen PO Box K State Capitol Juneau AK 99811

SCHAJER, GARY STEPHEN, research engineer; b. London, Apr. 20, 1952; came to U.S., 1977; BA hons. first class, Cambridge (Eng.) U., 1974, MA, 1978; MS, U. Calif., Berkeley, 1979, PhD, 1981. Registered profl. mech. engr., Wash.; chartered elec. engr., Eng. Elec. engr. Water Resources and Engring. Constrn. Agy., Kano, Nigeria, 1974-75; research scientist Chloride Silent Power Ltd., Runcorn, Cheshire, Eng., 1976-77; research engr. Weyerhaeuser Co., Tacoma, 1982—; vis. scientist Norsk Treteknisk Institutt, Oslo, 1978, 80; lectr. Zhejiang U., Hangzhou, Peoples Republic of China, 1985; vis. scientist Nagoya U., Japan, 1987. Producer (film) Choosing Circular Saws, 1985; contbr. articles to profl. jours.; inventor sealing glass for ceramic. Found. scholar Pembroke Coll., Cambridge, 1974; Wells fellow U. Calif., Berkeley, 1977; recipient Wood award Forest Products Research Soc., 1981. Mem. ASME (Best Paper award 1981), Inst. Elec. Engr., Am. Acad. Mechanics, Soc. Experimental Mechanics, British Soc. Strain Measurement, Inst. Mech. Engrs., Sigma Xi. Clubs: Toastmasters (Tacoma); Mountaineers (Seattle). Avocations: bicycle touring, hiking, cross country skiing, playing viola. Office: Weyerhaeuser Tech Ctr WTC 1G2 Tacoma WA 98477

SCHALL, LAWRENCE DELANO, economics educator; b. Los Angeles, Nov. 5, 1940; s. Lee and Lillian (Seltzow) S.; m. Betty Jane Kay, Aug. 6, 1982; children: Michael Kay, Adam Kent. BA, UCLA, 1962; MA in Econs., U. Chgo., 1967, PhD in Econs., 1969. CPA, Wash. Sec.-treas. Permco Inc., Los Angeles, 1959-61; acting asst. prof. econs. U. Wash., Seattle, 1968-69, asst. prof., 1969-72, assoc. prof., 1972-76, prof., 1976—. Author: (with C. W. Haley) The Theory of Financial Decisions, 1972, 2d edit., 1979, Introduction to Financial Management, 1977, 4th edit., 1986, (with K. Henderson and R. May) Evaluating Business Ventures, 1982; contbr. articles to profl. jours. Mem. Am. Econ. Assn., Am. Fin. Assn., Fin. Mgmt. Assn., Fin. Execs. Inst. Office: U Wash Sch Bus 261 Mackenzie Hall DJ-10 Seattle WA 98195

SCHAMBER, JON FREDERICK, communications educator; b. Stockton, Calif., June 4, 1952; s. Arnold R. and Inez J. (Normington) S. BA, U. Pacific, 1974, MA, 1975; PhD, U. Oreg., 1982. Asst. instr. U. Calif., Berkeley, 1975-76, assoc. instr., 1976-77, dir. debate, 1975-77; grad. teaching asst. U. Oreg., Eugene, 1977-80, dir. debate, 1977-79; asst. prof. communications U. Pacific, Stockton, 1980-85, assoc. prof., 1986—, asst. dir. forensics, 1974-75, dir., 1980—, chmn. dept. communications, 1985—. Editorial asst. Quar. Jour. of Speech, 1979-80. Debate scholar U. Pacific, 1970-74. Mem. Western Forensics Assn. (sec., treas.), Western Communications Assn., Internat. Communications Assn., Speech Communications Assn., Am. Forensics Assn. (researcher). Republican. Lutheran. Home: 1141 Vernal Way Stockton CA 95203 Office: U of the Pacific Dept of Communication Hand Meml Hall Stockton CA 95211

SCHAMING, JAMES SYLVESTER, electronics company executive; b. Pitts., Dec. 18, 1934; s. Sylvester John and Alma Mae (Schultis) S.; m. Sharan Lee Stevenson, Apr. 8, 1961; children—Jana Lee Schaming Ledbetter, Michael James, Sue Ellen Marie. A.A., Fullerton Coll., 1968; B.S. cum laude in Indsl. Electronic Tech., Calif. State U.-Long Beach, 1972. Registered profl. engr. Calif. Programmer/operator Duquesne Light Co., Pitts., 1953-55, 1959-60; electronic tech. lead Rockwell Internat., Anaheim, Calif., 1960-61, reliability engr., 1962-73, reliability/safety mgr., 1973-78; design assurance engring. mgr. Honeywell Inc., Seattle, Wash., 1978—; chmn. Honeywell Aerospace and Def. Reliability Adv. Bd., Mpls., 1981-82, mem. Honeywell Internat. Reliability Com., 1978-87; mem. Rockwell Internat. Corp. Group on Reliability, Quality Assurance and Statistics, Anaheim, 1976-78; instr. Honeywell Mgmt. Devel. Ctr., Mpls., 1984-86. Author: Y-Westerner Group Leader's Manual, 1973. Founder Parent-child Orgn. Y-Westerners (Grades 4-6), 1971, Y-Adventurers (Grades 7-9), 1974; program dir. YMCA, Orange, Calif., 1971-77; pres. Home Owners Assn., Anaheim Hills, Calif., 1977-78; mem. Seattle Speaker's Bur., 1985-86. Served with USN, 1955-58. Recipient Hon. Service award Calif. Congress Parents and Tchrs. Inc., 1976; YMCA Red Triangle award YMCA, 1974. Mem. Am. Soc. Quality Control, Nat. Mgmt. Assn., Inst. Environ. Scis., Toastmasters Internat. (Honeywell Pacesetters pres. 1982, Competent Toastmaster, 1982, Able Toastmaster, 1984). Republican. Methodist. Club: YMCA Century. Home: 14221 SE 41st St Bellevue WA 98006 Office: Honeywell Marine Systems Div 6500 Harbour Hts Pkwy Everett WA 98204

SCHAMMEL, RICHARD MICHAEL, real estate corporate officer; b. Mpls.; s. Leo Andrew and Alice Jane (Friedricks) S. BA in Econs., U. Calif., 1975; MBA, U. Santa Clara, 1980. Mgr. invoice and order office Liberty House, Dublin, Calif., 1975-78; gen. mgr. acctg. Bullock's, Menlo Park, Calif., 1978-80; v.p., controller Coldwell Banker, Los Angeles, 1980—. Served to capt. USAFR, 1975—. Office: Coldwell Banker 201 Continental Blvd El Segundo CA 90245

SCHANDER, EDWIN, law librarian; b. Harbin, Peoples Republic of China, Mar. 9, 1942; came to U.S., 1957; s. Robert and Olga (Linder) S.; m. Mary Lea, July 3, 1971. BA, Calif. State U., Northridge, 1969; postgrad., UCLA, 1969-72, MLS, 1973. Reference librarian Los Angeles County Law Library, 1973-79, sr. reference librarian, 1979-86, head reference services, 1986—; cons. Rand Corp., Santa Monica, Calif., 1975; bd. dirs. library, City Pasadena. Freelance TV producer Community Access Channel, City of Pasadena. Served with U.S. Army, 1964-66. Mem. Am. Assn. Law Libraries, Humane Soc. U.S., LWV. Club: Los Angeles Athletic. Home: 430 C Orange Grove Circle Pasadena CA 91105 Office: Los Angeles County Law Library 301 W First St Los Angeles CA 90012

SCHANDER, MARY LEA, police official; b. Bakersfield, Calif., June 11, 1947; d. Gerald John Lea and Marian Lea Coffman; B.A. (Augustana fellow) Calif. Luth. Coll., 1969; M.A., U. Calif., Los Angeles, 1970; m. Edwin Schander, July 3, 1971. Staff aide City of Anaheim (Calif.) Police Dept., 1970-72, staff asst., 1972-78, sr. staff asst., 1978-80; with Resource Mgmt. Dept., City of Anaheim, 1980-82; asst. to dir. Pub. Safety Agy., City of Pasadena, 1982-85, spl. asst. to police chief, 1985—; freelance musician, publisher Australian Traditional Songs, 1985; lectr. Calif. Luth. Coll. Active Conejo Symphony; bd. dirs. Community Dispute Resolution Ctr. Pasadena. Contbr. articles in field to profl. jours. Mem. Am. Mgmt. Assn., LWV. Club: Los Angeles Athletic. Home: 430-C Orange Grove Circle Pasadena CA 91105 Office: Pub Safety Agy 142 N Arroyo Pkwy Pasadena CA 91103

SCHANIEL, CARL LOUIS, electrical engineer, research center administrator; b. San Diego, Oct. 21, 1926; s. Carl Louis and Mary Magdalen (Henn) S.; m. Willa May Dowd, June 10, 1950; children: Mary, William, Stephen, Judith, Margaret, Thomas. BA in Math., San Diego State U., 1950, MS in Physics, 1958. Registered profl. elec. engr., Calif. Physicist Navy Elec. Lab., San Diego, 1951-62; ops. research analyst Naval Weapons Ctr., China Lake, Calif., 1962-65, head dept., 1965—, asst. tech. dir. devel., 1965—. Served with U.S. Maritime Service, 1944-47. Recipient L.T.E. Thompson award Naval Weapons Ctr., 1960, Meritorious Civilian Service award USN, 1978. Mem. Ops. Research Soc., Research Soc. Am. Republican. Roman Catholic. Avocations: square dancing, fishing. Home: 612 E Laura Ridgecrest CA 93555 Office: Naval Weapons Ctr Code 33 China Lake CA 93555

SCHANKMAN, ALAN ROBERT, ophthalmologist; b. Bklyn., Jan. 1, 1947; s. Barnet and Sylvia (Barken) S.; m. Vicky Barbara Gellman, Dec. 10, 1973; children—Dana, Lauren, Alison, Michael. B.S., Bklyn. Coll., 1968; M.D., Downstate Med. Sch., SUNY-Bklyn., 1972. Diplomate Am. Bd. Ophthalmology. Intern Beth Israel Med. Ctr., N.Y.C., 1973; resident in ophthalmology E.J. Meyer Meml. Hosp., Buffalo, 1973-76; pvt. practice, N.Y.C., 1976-78, Los Angeles, 1978—; co-founder, v.p. and sec. S & S Med. Office Systems, Inc.; clin. instr. Jules Stein Eye Inst., UCLA Med. Sch., 1980—; co-founder, v.p. S&S Med. Office Systems, Inc.; cons. Braille Inst. Developer refractive eye surgery, myopia, 1980; investigator Yag laser surgery, 1982. Fellow Am. Acad. Ophthalmology; mem. Internat. Assn. Ocular Surgeons, Calif. Assn. Ophthalmology, Los Angeles County Ophthal. Soc., Calif. Med. Soc., Los Angeles County Med. Assn., Internat. Glaucoma Congress, Am. Soc. Contemporary Ophthalmology, Am. Assn. Ophthalmology, Keratorefractive Soc., N.Y. Acad. Scis. Office: 12840 Riverside Dr North Hollywood CA 91607

SCHANNEP, JOHN DWIGHT, stock brokerage firm executive; b. Newport News, Va., May 23, 1934; s. Dwight Bahney and Harriet Louise (Quinn) S.; m. Helen Ann Harris, June 21, 1958; children—John Barton, Dwight David, Timothy Michael, Marie Louise. B.S., U.S. Mil. Acad., 1956. Commd. 1st lt. U.S. Air Force, 1956; resigned, 1960; account exec. Dean Witter Reynolds, Phoenix, 1960-68, v.p., resident mgr., Tucson, 1968-83, sr. v.p., 1983—; pres. Tucson Stock/Bond Club, 1971-72. Author, pub. Schannep Timing Indicator Quar. Letter, 1980—. Pres. Big Bros. Tucson, 1972-74. Mem. Nat. Assn. Security Dealers (Ariz. committeeman and chmn. 1971-73), Tucson C. of C. (v.p. 1971). Republican. Episcopalian. Club: West Point Soc. (pres. 1967) (Phoenix and Tucson). Lodge: Lions (pres. Phoenix lodge 1966). Home: 5191 E Hill Place Dr Tucson AZ 85712 Office: Dean Witter Reynolds 6987 N Oracle Rd Tucson AZ 85704

SCHAPER, DONNA JEAN, educator; b. Estherville, Iowa, Feb. 3, 1937; d. William Thomas and Mae Josephine (Kirchner) S. BA in Art, U. Iowa, 1958; MA in Art, U. Colo., 1969. Cert. elem. and secondary art tchr., Ill., Colo. Art tchr. E. Richland Schs., Olney, Ill., 1958-63, Boulder (Colo.) Valley Schs., 1963—. Contbr. photographs to mags. Grantee Colo. Council Arts, 1972. Mem. United Teaching Profession. Republican. Presbyterian. Avocations: travel, horses, reading, watercolors, drawing. Home: 3186 Westwood Ct Boulder CO 80302 Office: Boulder Valley Sch Dist 6500 Arapahoe Boulder CO 80303

SCHAPIRA, MOREY RAEL, electronics sales executive; b. Chgo., Jan. 4, 1949; s. Julius and Rose (Schwartz) S.; BS with honors in Physics (Ill. State scholar 1966, Case scholar 1966-70), Case Western Res. U., 1970; MBA, Harvard U., 1977; m. Barbara Stein, May 29, 1977; children: Rachel, Deborah, Michael. Research scientist research div. Raytheon Co., Waltham, Mass., 1970-75; cons. scientist M.I.T. Lincoln Labs., Lexington, summer 1976; product mktg. engr. microwave semicondr. div. Hewlett Packard Co., San Jose, Calif., 1977-80, domestic sales mgr. optoelectronics div., Palo Alto, Calif., 1980-81, distbr. mktg. mgr. optoelectronics div., 1981-83; corp. distbn. mgr. Hewlett Packard Components, San Jose, Calif., 1983-85; nat. distbr., sales mgr. Micro Power Systems, Santa Clara, Calif., 1985—. Div. chmn. United Way Campaign., 1978; nat. v.p. Union of Councils for Soviet Jews, 1979-84, nat. pres., 1984-86; pres. Bay Area Council on Soviet Jewry, San Francisco, 1980-84. Mem. Am. Mgmt. Assn., Tech. Mktg. Soc. Am., Am. Enterprise Inst. Assos., Am. Phys. Soc., Assn. Old Crows, World Affairs Council, Bus./Profl. Advt. Assn. Democrat. Editor-in-chief, then pub. A Guide to Jewish Boston, 1974-77; pub., editor-in-chief HarBus News, 1976-77. Home: 1154 Crespi Dr Sunnyvale CA 94086 Office: Micro Power Systems 3100 Alfred St Santa Clara CA 95054-0965

SCHAPP, REBECCA MARIA, museum director; b. Stuttgart, Fed. Republic Germany, Dec. 12, 1956; came to U.S., 1957; d. Randall Todd and Elfriede Carolina (Scheppan) Spradlin; m. Thomas James Schapp, May 29, 1979. AA, DeAnza Coll., 1977; BA in Art, San Jose State U., 1979, MA in Art Adminstrn., 1985. Adminstrv. dir. Union Gallery, San Jose, Calif., 1979-82; mus. coordinator de Saisset Mus. Santa Clara (Calif.) U., 1982-84, asst. dir., 1984—. Mem. San Francisco Mus. Modern Art; bd. dirs. Works of San Jose, v.p. 1983-85. Mem. Non-Profit Gallery Assn. (bd. dirs.). Democrat. Avocations: racquetball, Jazzercise, bicycling, camping. Office: Santa Clara U de Saisset Mus Santa Clara CA 95053

SCHARLACH, ANDREW EDMUND, educator; b. San Francisco, July 4, 1951; s. Adrian Edmund and Marilynn Lorraine (Lustig) S.; m. Ilene Benita Conison, Aug. 20, 1983. BA, U. Calif., Berkeley, 1972; MS, Boston U., 1976; PhD, Stanford U., 1985. Lic. clin. social worker. Dir. adolescent services Jewish Community Ctr., San Francisco, 1976-77; social worker Jewish Home for the Aged, San Francisco, 1977-79; pvt. practice specializing in geriatric counseling San Francisco and Los Angeles, 1979—; teaching fellow Stanford (Calif.) U., 1980-83; asst. prof. U. So. Calif., Los Angeles, 1983—; Bd. dirs. Alzheimer's Disease Assn., 1981-83; faculty mem. Pacific Geriatric Edn. Ctr., Los Angeles, 1983—; research assoc. Andrus Gerontology Ctr., Los Angeles, 1984—; cons. Jewish Fedn., Los Angeles, 1985—; commr. Lic. Clin. Social Workers Examination, Calif., 1984. Contbr. articles to profl. jours. Mem. Gerontol. Soc. of Am., Am. Soc. Aging., Am. Psychol. Assn., Nat. Assn. Social Workers, Am. Orthopsychiat. Assn., Nat. Assn. Social Workers (mem. long term care council 1985-86), Jewish Fedn. Com. on Aging, Respite Planning Com. Democrat. Jewish. Avocations: hiking, tennis, bridge, guitar. Home: 14748 Hesby St Sherman Oaks CA 91403 Office: U So Calif MC-0411 Los Angeles CA 90089-0411

SCHAROLD, PAUL GEOFFREY, chemical engineer; b. Cin., Jan. 27, 1956; s. Frank Joseph and Judith Florence (Berquist) S.; m. Joyce Lorena Buck, Aug. 26, 1978; children: Zoae, Jubal. BA in Chemistry, Spring Arbor Coll., 1975; MS in ChemE, U. N.D., 1978. Registered profl. engr., Wash. Engr. Rockwell Hanford Ops., Richland, Wash., 1978-81; engr., supr. United Nuclear Corp. Nuclear Industries, Richland, 1982—. Mem. Am. Chem. Soc., Am. Inst. Chem. Engrs., Soc. Computer Simulation. Mem. Christian Reformed Ch. Home: 610 W Kennewick Ave Kennewick WA 99336 Office: United Nuclear Corp Nuclear Industries PO Box 490 Richland WA 99352

SCHARPEN, LEROY HENRY, business executive; b. Red Wing, Minn., Oct. 15, 1935; s. Roy Leigh and Edna Esther (Fricke) S.; m. Judith Elaine Arnold, Feb. 16, 1963; children: John Christopher, Gregory Scott. AB, Harvard U., 1961; PhD, Stanford U., 1966. Research scientist McDonnell Douglas, St. Louis, 1966-68; mem. tech. staff Hewlett-Packard, Palo Alto, Calif., 1968-77; exec. v.p. Surface Sci. Labs., Mt. View, Calif., 1977-84, pres., 1984-86; v.p. Kevex, San Carlos, Calif., 1986—. Home: 10145 McLaren Pl Cupertino CA 95014

SCHATZ, MONA CLAIRE STRUHSAKER, social worker, educator; b. Phila., Jan. 4, 1950; d. Milton and Josephine (Kivo) Schatz; m. James Fredrick Struhsaker, Dec. 31, 1979; 1 child, Thain Mackenzie. BA, Metro State Coll., 1976; student, U. Minn., 1976; MSW, U. Denver, 1979; D in Social Work/Social Welfare, U. Pa., 1986. Teaching fellow U. Pa., Phila., 1981—; asst. prof. Southwest Mo. State U., Springfield, 1982-85; asst. prof., field coordinator Colo. State U., Ft. Collins, 1985—; cons. Mgmt. and Behavioral Sci. Ctr., The Wharton Sch. U. Pa., 1981-82; resource specialist So. N.J. Health Systems Agy., 1982; adj. faculty mem. U. Mo., Springfield, 1984; med. social worker Rehab. and Vis. Nurse Assn., 1985—. Contbr. articles to profl. jours. Cons., field rep. Big Bros./Big Sisters of Am., Phila., 1979-83; owner Polit. Cons. in Colo., Denver, 1978-79; active Food Co-op, Ft. Collins, Foster Parent, Denver, Capital Hill United Neighbors, Adams County (Denver) Social Planning Council, Co., Colo. Justice Council, Denver, Regional Girls Shelter, Springfield; bd. dirs. Crisis Helpline and Info. Service. Scholar Lilly Endowment, Inc., 1976, Piton Found., 1978; recipient Spl. Recognition award Big Bros./Big Sisters of Am., 1983. Mem. Counsel Social Work Edn., Nat. Assn. Social Workers (nominating chmn. Springfield chpt.), Student Social Work Assn. of Colo. State U. (adv. 1986—), Permanency Planning Council for Children and Youth, NOW (treas. Springfield chpt. 1984-85), Student Nuclear Awareness Group (advisor), Student Social Work Assn. (advisor), Alpha Delta Mu. Democrat. Jewish. Avocations: cooking, traveling, reading. Office: Colo State U Social Work Dept Eddy Bldg Fort Collins CO 80523

SCHATZ, ROBERT KEITH, former police chief; b. Pocatello, Idaho, May 23, 1927; s. John and Irene B. (Blackborn) S.; children—John, Suzanne, Matthew, Michael. B.A., San Jose State U., 1955; postgrad. FBI Nat. Acad., 1966. Police officer, Mountain View Police Dept., Calif., 1950-53, police sgt., 1953-56, police lt., 1956-61, asst. chief of police, 1961-73, chief of police, 1973-84; instr. San Jose State U., 1974. Mem. Mountain View city Council, 1985—; vice mayor, 1986, mayor, 1987—. Served to lt. U.S. Army, 1951-53. Mem. Internat. Assn. Chiefs Police, Calif. Police Chiefs' Assn., FBI Nat. Acad. Grads., Calif. Peace Officers' Assn. Republican. Lodge: Kiwanis. Home: 505 Cypress Point Dr Apt 234 Mountain View CA 94043

SCHATZ, STEVEN HENRY, metallurgical engineer; b. Mitchell, S.D., June 21, 1958; s. James Marvin and Sarah Ann (Ames) S. BSMetE, Colo. Sch. Mines, 1980; postgrad., Colo. State U., 1980—. Registered profl. engr., Colo. Mem. recruit tng. program Woodward Gov. Co., Ft. Collins, Colo., 1973-80, metall. engr., 1980—. Blood donor Poudre Valley Meml. Hosp., Ft. Collins, 1980—; advisor Jr. Achievement, Ft. Collins, 1983-86; vol. Sky Ranch Luth. Camp, Poudre Canyon, Colo., 1985—; mem. United Campus Ministries Clown Troupe, Ft. Collins, 1986—. Am. Soc. Metals (exec. bd. dirs. Rocky Mountain chpt. 1982-86), Am. Powder Metallurgy Inst., Metall. Soc. of AIME, NSPE. Republican. Mem. United Ch. Christ. Avocations: motorcycling, automobile restoration, photography, bicycling, skiing. Home: 1001 Strachan Dr Unit 2 Fort Collins CO 80525 Office: Woodward Gov Co 1000 E Drake Rd Fort Collins CO 80522

SCHATZ, SUSAN MARY, financial consultant; b. N.Y.C., Nov. 1, 1954; d. Eugene James and Laura (Nevins) Schatz. B.S., Colo. State U., 1977. Fin. cons. Merrill Lynch, Denver, 1980—. Mem. Denver Botanic Gardens, Profl. Women Execs., Phi Kappa Phi. Address: 460 S High St Denver CO 80209

SCHAUBERT, LAUREL VIRGINIA, med. illustrator; b. Portland Oreg., Aug. 3, 1923; d. John and Mildred (Hall) Karg; student Reed Coll., 1940-43, U. Calif., 1947-49, Art League San Francisco, 1950-53, U. Calif. San Francisco Med. Center, 1953-55; m. Arvid D. Schaubert, Nov. 10, 1962; children—Gay Lee Schaubert Giannini, Leslie May (dec.). Med. illustrator Ft. Miley VA Hosp., 1955; sr. illustrator dept. surgery U. Calif., San Francisco, 1955-69; prin. illustrator Lange Med. Publs., Los Altos, Calif., 1961—; now also co-owner, pres. Biomed Arts Assocs., Inc., San Francisco; instr. U. Calif., San Francisco, 1959-61, 74-78. Recipient cert. of commendation Calif. Dist. Attys. Assn., 1977; Merit award Fedn. Biocommunication Socs., 1979. Mem. Assn. Med. Illustrators (Outstanding Service award 1972; chmn. bd. govs. 1971-72, v.p. 1975-76, pres. 1976-77), Graphic Artists Guild. Co-author: Scientific Illustration: Standards for Publication; contbr. med. illustrations and articles to textbooks, profl. jours. Office: 350 Parnassus Ave Suite 905 San Francisco CA 94117

SCHAUER, RALPH FLOYD, microelectronics company executive; b. Waterloo, Iowa, May 31, 1930; s. Herman Carl and Louise Emma (Mixdorf) S.; m. Gwen Elaine Maurer, Mar. 31, 1961; children: Wren, Heidi, Rebecca. BSEE, Iowa State U., 1952, MS, 1957, PhD, 1960. Mgr. design, test and research IBM, Fishkill, N.Y., 1960-80; dir. corp. tech. ctr. Wang Labs. Inc., Lowell, Mass., 1980-82; v.p. computer aided design Ford Microelectronics Inc., Colorado Springs, Colo., 1982—. Patentee in field. Pres. Lakeland Sch. Bd., Shrub Oak, N.Y., 1974, Putnam Valley (N.Y.) Free Library, 1968-78. Served to lt. USN, 1952-55. Mem. IEEE. Democrat. Lutheran. Avocations: collecting Am. antique furniture, metal ware, pewter and art. Office: Ford Microelectronics Inc 10340 State Hwy 83 Colorado Springs CO 80908

SCHAUMBERG, GENE DAVID, chemistry educator; b. Rochester, Minn., Oct. 3, 1939; s. LeRoy Leo and Mary Elenor (Busby) S.: m. Caron D. Anderson, Aug. 26, 1981 (div. June 1986); children: Jason, Nathan. BS, Pacific Luth. U., 1961; PhD, Wash. State U., 1965. Dean. div. nat. sci. Sonoma State U., Rohnert Park, Calif., 1969-72, prof. chemistry, 1972—; vis. prof. U. Hawaii at Manoa, Honolulu, 1985-86, U. Calif., Riverside, 1979-80; advisor Cen. Water Resources Devel. and Mgmt., Keralu, India. Author: Concerning Chemistry, 1975; contbr. articles to profl. jours. Fulbright-Hayes Lectrship., USIA, Nepal, 1971, Philippines, 1980; grantee NSF, Nepal, 1975, Am. Inst. Indian Studies, India, 1982. Mem. AAAS, Am. Chem. Soc., Nepal Chem. Soc. (life), SIgma Xi. Avocations: running, reading. Home: 4949 Snyder Ln #12 Rohnert Park CA 94928 Office: Sonoma State U 1801 E Cotati Ave Rohnert Park CA 94928

SCHAUWECKER, KURT HERBERT, equipment manufacturing executive; b. Parkersburg, W.Va., Oct. 11, 1926; s. Walter Christian and Johanna Freda (Hopf) S.; m. Billie B. Franklin, Dec. 1, 1973; children by previous marriage: Joseph, Dana, Daniel, Thomas, Eric. Student in mech. engring., Ohio State U., 1946-50. Prototype shop supr. N.Am. Aviation Inc., Columbus, Ohio, 1951-60; prodn. mgr. Data Systems div. Litton Industries, Van Nuys, Calif., 1961-72; gen. mgr. Atco Spl. Products Div., Calgary, Alta., Can., 1972-75; ops. mgr. Adams-Rite Products Inc, Glendale, Calif., 1976-78; gen. mgr.tech. products div. Bell Industries, Eugene, Oreg., 1978—; Mem. adv. com. mil. engring. Def. Research Bd. of Can., 1973-74. Served with USNR, 1944-46, PTO. Republican. Lutheran. Lodges: Masons, Shriners. Home: 27172 Huey Ln Eugene OR 97402 Office: Bell Industries Box 2510 Eugene OR 97402

SCHAWLOW, ARTHUR LEONARD, educator, physicist; b. Mt. Vernon, N.Y., May 5, 1921; s. Arthur and Helen (Mason) S.; m. Aurelia Keith Townes, May 19, 1951; children: Arthur Keith, Helen Aurelia, Edith Ellen. B.A., U. Toronto, 1941, M.A., 1942, Ph.D., 1949, LL.D. (hon.), 1970; D.Sc. (hon.), U. Ghent, Belgium, 1968, U. Bradford, Eng., 1970, U. Ala., 1984, Trinity Coll., Dublin, Ireland, 1986. Postdoctoral fellow, research asso. Columbia, 1949-51; vis. assoc. prof. Columbia U., 1960; research physicist Bell Telephone Labs., 1951-61, cons., 1961-62; prof. physics Stanford U., 1961—, now J.G. Jackson-C.J. Wood prof. physics, exec. head dept., 1966-70, acting chmn. dept., 1973-74. Author: (with C.H. Townes) Microwave Spectroscopy, 1955; Co-inventor (with C.H. Townes), optical maser on laser, 1958. Recipient Ballantine medal Franklin Inst., 1962, Thomas Young medal and prize Inst. Physics and Phys. Soc., London, 1963, Schawlow medal Laser Inst. Am., 1982; Nobel prize in physics, 1981; named Calif. Scientist of Year, 1973, Marconi Internat. fellow, 1977. Fellow Am. Acad. Arts and Scis., Am. Phys. Soc. (council 1966-70, chmn. div. electron and atomic physics 1974, pres. 1981), Optical Soc. Am. (hon. mem. 1983, dir.-at-large 1966-68, pres. 1975, Frederick Ives medal 1976); mem. Nat. Acad. Scis., IEEE (Liebmann prize 1964), AAAS (chmn. physics sect. 1979), Am. Philos. Soc. Office: Stanford Univ Dept of Physics Stanford CA 94305-4060

SCHEEL, JEAN W., retired adult educator, freelance writer, poet; b. Emporia, Kans., July 1, 1911; s. William H. and Annie (Smith) S.; m. Ada Wiese, Sept. 29, 1935 (dec. Aug. 1981); m. Beatrice Peters, June 23, 1982. BS in Ind. Journalism, Kansas State U., 1934; AM in Edn. Adminstrn., U. Chgo., 1954. Asst. extension editor Kans. State U., Manhattan, 1934-42; extension info. specialist Oreg. State U., Corvallis, 1946-47, asst. to dir. of extension services, 1947-51, asst. dir., 1951-71; Cons. U. Alaska, Fairbanks, 1972. Co-leader poetry com., Benton County Fair, Corvallis, 1979—; mem. civic beautification commn. City of Corvallis, 1983—; exec. com. Adult Edn. Assn. U.S.A., 1973. Served to capt. Signal Corps, U.S. Army, 1942-46. Recipient George award Corvallis C. of C., 1965, Spl. Recognition award, Corvallis C. of C., 1978, Free Enterprise award, Corvallis C. of C., 1976. Mem. Northwest Adult Edn. Assn. (life, pres. 1967-68, Meritorious Service award 1973). Republican. Presbyterian. Lodges: Rotary (local pres. 1966-67, dist. 511 gov. 1974-75), Elks. Avocations: deer and elk hunting, golf, photography. Home: 2641 NW Foothill Dr Corvallis OR 97330

SCHEER, BRADLEY T(ITUS), retired science educator; b. Los Angeles, Dec. 17, 1914; s. William Bradley and Mabel Eleanora (Titus) S.; m. Marlin Ann Ray, Aug. 14, 1936. BS, Calif. Inst. Tech., 1936; PhD, U. Calif., Berkeley and La Jolla, 1940. Ordained to ministry Episcopal Ch. as deacon, 1967, as priest, 1971. Asst. U. Calif., Berkeley and La Jolla, 1936-40; instr. zoology W.Va. U., Morgantown, 1940-42; instr. biochemistry and medicine Columbia U. Coll. Physicians and Surgeons, N.Y.C., 1942-44; instr. biology Calif. Inst. Tech., Pasadena, 1944-46; instr. biochemistry U. So. Calif. Med. Sch., Los Angeles, 1946-48; asst. prof. biology U. Hawaii, Honolulu, 1948-50; from assoc. prof. to prof. biology U. Oreg., Eugene, 1950-77; adj. prof. biology Westmont Coll., Santa Barbara, Calif., 1978-86. Author various sci. textbooks. Deacon St. Mary's Episc. Ch., Eugene, 1964-71, priest, 1971—; served at Ch. of the Holy Spirit, Nice, France, 1969-70, Holy Trinity Ch., 1972-77; with Trinity Ch., Santa Barbara, 1977-86. Fulbright research fellow, 1957-58, Guggenheim fellow, 1964-65. Fellow AAAS (exec. com. Pacific div. 1959-64); mem. Am. Physiol. Soc., Soc. Gen. Physiol. Republican. Avocation: writing. Home: 93 Quarterdeck Way Pacific Grove CA 93950

SCHEIBE, PAUL OTTO, electronics company executive; b. Marion, N.D., Apr. 4, 1934; s. Carl Henry August and Alma Frieda Selma (Koessel) S.; m. Marlene Clarice Monson, Nov. 26, 1955; children: Lynn Marie, Denise Kay, Jay Bradley. BSEE, U. N.D., 1958, MSEE, 1959; PhD, Stanford U., 1962. Registered profl. engr., Calif. Sr. engr. Sylvania EDL, Mountain View, Calif., 1960-64; dir. tech. ESL Inc., Sunnyvale, Calif., 1964-70; v.p. tech. ADAC Labs., San Jose, Calif., 1970-84, Sterling Networks, Redwood City, Calif., 1984—; lectr. U. Santa Clara, Calif., 1962—; cons. Stanford Tech. Corp., Sunnyvale, 1974-77, ESL Inc., 1974—. Contbr. articles to profl. jours.; chpts. to books. NSF fellow, Stanford U., 1960-61, 61-62. Mem. IEEE, AAAS, Assn. Computing Machinery, Soc. Nuclear Medicine, Am. Coll. Nuclear Physicians. Avocation: amateur radio. Home: 3 Still Creek Rd Woodside CA 94062 Office: Sterling Networks 2000 Broadway Redwood City CA 94063

SCHEIBEL, ARNOLD BERNARD, educator, psychiat. researcher; b. N.Y.C., Jan. 18, 1923; s. William and Ethel (Greenberg) S.; m. Madge Mila Ragland, Mar. 3, 1950 (dec. Jan. 1977); m. Marian Diamond, Sept. 1982. B.A., Columbia U., 1944, M.D., 1946; M.S., U. Ill., 1952. Intern Mt. Sinai Hosp., N.Y.C., 1946-47; resident psychiatry Barnes and McMillan Hosp., St. Louis, 1947-48, Ill. Neuropsychiat. Inst., Chgo., 1950-52; asst. prof. psychiatry and anatomy U. Tenn. Med. Sch., 1952-53, asso. prof., 1953-55; asso. prof. UCLA Med. Center, 1955-67, prof. psychiatry and anatomy, 1967—; mem. Brain Research Inst., 1960—; cons. VA hosps., Los Angeles, 1956—. Contbr. numerous articles to tech. jours, chpts. to books.; editorial bd.: Brain Research, 1967-77, Developmental Psychobiology, 1968—, Internat. Jour. Neurosci., 1969—, Jour. Biol. Psychiatry, 1968—, Jour. Theoretical Biology, 1980—. Mem. Pres.'s Commn. on Aging, Nat. Inst. Aging, 1980—. Served with AUS, 1943-46; from lt. to capt. M.C. AUS, 1948-50. Guggenheim fellow (with wife), 1953-54, 59. Fellow Am. Acad. Arts and Scis., Norwegian Acad. Scis.; mem. AAAS, Am. Psychiat. Assn., Am. Neurol. Assn., Soc. Neurosci., Psychiat. Research Assn., Am. EEG Assn., Am. Assn. Anatomists, Soc. Biol. Psychiatry, Am. Acad. Neurology, So. Calif. Psychiat. Assn. Home: 16231 Morrison St Encino CA 91316 Office: U Calif at Los Angeles CA 90024

SCHEIFLY, JOHN EDWARD, tax lawyer; b. Mexico, Mo., Aug. 25, 1925; s. Luke Clauser and Isabella (Sprankle) S.; m. Patricia Ann Lenhart, Dec. 27, 1947; children: John Edward, Jan Ellen. Sc.B., Brown U., 1945; J.D., Washington and Lee U., 1948. Bar: Calif., W.Va. Practice law Los Angeles, 1953—; mem. firm Baker, Scheifly & Porter, Huntington, W.Va., 1949-53, McClean, Salisbury, Petty & McClean, Los Angeles, 1953-57, Willis, Butler, Scheifly, Leydorf & Grant (and predecessors), Los Angeles, 1958-81, Bryan, Cave, McPheeters & McRoberts, Los Angeles, 1981-84, Morgan, Lewis & Bockius, Los Angeles, 1984—; lectr. tax law U. So. Calif., 1960-74. Author lectr. fed. tax matters profl. publs., insts. Served to lt. USNR, 1943-46, 51-53. Mem. Los Angeles County Bar Assn. (chmn. tax. sect. 1965-66), ABA (mem. council sect. taxation 1974-77), State Bar Calif. Clubs: Jonathan (Los Angeles); Hacienda Golf (LaHabra, Calif.); Monterey Country (Palm Desert, Calif.). Home: 9441 Friendly Woods Ln Whittier CA 90605 Office: Morgan Lewis and Bockius 801 S Grand Ave Los Angeles CA 90017

SCHEINBAUM, DAVID, photography educator; b. Bklyn., Apr. 14, 1951; s. Louis and Rhoda (Feerman) S.; m. Vicki Golden, May 30, 1973 (div. 1975); m. Janet Ann Goldberg-Russek, Mar. 21, 1982; stepchildren: Jonathan Russek, Andra Russek. BA, CUNY, 1973. Instr. photography Pace U., N.Y.C., 1974-75, LaGuardia (N.Y.) Community Coll., 1975-78; instr. Coll. Santa Fe, 1979-81, asst. prof. photography, 1981—; printer, asst. to Beaumont Newhall, Santa Fe, 1980—; printer to Eliot Porter, Santa Fe, 1983—; co-dir. Scheinbaum & Russek, Santa Fe, 1979—. Author/photographer: A Homebirth Experience, 1986, BISTI, 1987; photography exhibitions include Pace U., 1974, Park Slope Civic Council, Bklyn., 1975, F-Stop Gallery, Bklyn., 1976, Midtown Gallery, Bklyn., 1977, Exhibitionists Gallery, Jamaca, N.Y., 1978, Santa Fe Gallery for Photography, 1979, 81, The Armory for the Arts, Santa Fe, 1980, 1981, Sea Breeze Gallery, Block Island, R.I., 1982, Highlands U., Las Vegas, N.Mex., 1982, Gov's. Gallery, Santa Fe, 1982, Santa Fe Festival for the Arts, 1982, Coll. Santa Fe, 1983, Dem. Conv., San Francisco, 1984; permanent collections include Norton Gallery Mus., West Palm Beach, Fla, Amon Carter Mus., Ft. Worth, N.Mex. State U., Las Cruces, Ctr. Creative Photography, Tucson, Ariz., Mus. Fine Arts, Santa Fe, Bklyn. Mus., U. Okla., Norman, Bibliothque Nationale France, Paris, Gernsheim Collection. U. Tex., Austin, Albuquerque Mus. Mem. N.Mex. Council on Photography (v.p.), Santa Fe Ctr. Photography (bd. dirs. 1978-85). Jewish. Home: 615 Don Felix St Santa Fe NM 87501 Office: Coll Santa Fe 2001 Saint Michaels Dr Santa Fe NM 87501

SCHELBY, ERIKA KATE, international business consultant; b. Berlin, Oct. 31, 1935; came to U.S., 1970; d. Kurt H. and Edith (Winkler) Mueller; m. Frederick Schelby, June 6, 1982; children by previous marriage—Ulrike, Susanne. B.A., Kans. State U., 1977; M.S., U. Ill., 1978. Asst. to dir. Georg Jensen Silver, Dusseldorf, W.Ger., 1959-60; v.p. Nordlys Ohg., Dusseldorf, 1960-64, pres., 1964-70; bus. research mgr. Goodyear Tire & Rubber Co., Akron, Ohio, 1978-80; mktg. mgr. Mo. Research Labs., Albuquerque, 1980-82; pres. Interteam Assocs., Albuquerque, 1982—. Mem. Am. Mktg. Assn., Greater Albuquerque C. of C., Phi Beta Kappa, Phi Kappa Phi, Gamma Theta Upsilon. Office: Interteam Assocs 1214 Jackson SE Albuquerque NM 87108

SCHELDORF, JAY JOHN, chemical engineering educator; b. Camden, N.J., Jan. 22, 1932; s. Marvel William and Margaret Belle (Knapp) S.; m. Marilyn Anne Hinshaw, Aug. 22, 1953; Jay John Jr., Debora Lynn. BS, U. Ill., 1953; MS, Kans. State U., 1954; PhD, U. Colo., 1958. Asst. prof. chem. engring. U. Colo., Boulder, 1958-66; from assoc. prof. to prof. chem. engring. and engring. sci. U. Idaho, Moscow, 1966—. Mem. Am. Chem. Soc., Am. Inst. Chem. Engrs., Am. Soc. Engring. Edn., Sigma Xi. Avocations: camping, hiking, reading, auto mechanics, modelling. Home: 618 Moore St Moscow ID 83843 Office: U Idaho Dept Chem Engring Moscow ID 83843

SCHELL, GERALD HERBERT, microbiologist; b. Grosse Point Farms, Mich., June 29, 1945. BS in Biology, Wayne State U., 1967, MS in Microbiology, 1968. Cert. microbiology lab. specialist in pub. health and clin. lab. medicine. Microbiologist, sect. head Gen. Foods Corp., Battle Creek, Mich., 1969-70, Battle Creek Community Hosp., 1970-71, Garden City (Mich.) Hosp., 1972-79; dir. quality analysis Miles Labs., Elkhart, Ind., 1979-85; dir. tech. affairs Chiron Corp., Emeryville, Calif., 1985—; cons. Regional Med. Labs., Battle Creek, 1970-71, Huron Med. Labs., Ypsilanti, Mich., 1973-76, Aries Sci., Wyandotte, Mich., 1978-79. Mem. Am. Chem. Soc., Am. Soc. Quality Control, Regulatory Assocs. Profl. Soc., Am. Soc. Microbiology, Soc. Indsl., Microbiology. Avocation: antique cars. Home: 804 Richard Ln Danville CA 94526 Office: Chiron Corp 4560 Horton St Emeryville CA 94608

SCHELLER, JAMES CHARLES, patent lawyer; b. Balt., Oct. 8, 1956; s. James Charles and Mary Dora (Naglieri) S.; m. Myung-Hee Lee, Sept. 8, 1984. BA in Biophysics, Johns Hopkins U., 1978; MBA, Carnegie-Mellon U., 1980; JD, U. Calif., Los Angeles, 1983. Patent atty. Blakely, Sokoloff, Taylor and Zafman, Beverly Hills, Calif., 1982—. Editor UCLA jour. of Environ. Law and Policy, 1981-83. Mem. ABA, AAAS. Office: Blakely Sokoloff Taylor & Zafman 12400 Wilshire Blvd Suite 700 Los Angeles CA 90025

SCHEMENT, JORGE REINA, information scientist, educator, consultant, writer; b. San Antonio, Jan. 13, 1948; s. Vincent Joseph and Berta (Reina) S.; m. Susan Heck, Apr. 18, 1976; 1 child, Elisa Rebeca Schement-Heck. BBA in Indsl. Mgmt., So. Meth. U., 1970; MS in Mktg., U. Ill., 1972; PhD in Communication, Stanford U., 1976. Asst. prof. to assoc. prof., Radio-TV-Film dept. U. Tex., Austin, 1976-81; assoc. prof. communication U. So. Calif., 1981-84; vis. assoc. prof. library and info. sci. UCLA, 1984—; vis. scholar Stanford U. Inst. Communication Research, Palo Alto, Calif., 1981; bd. dirs. Media Access Project, Washington, 1980—; mem. acad. adv. com. Nat. Citizens Com. Broadcasting, Washington, 1979-82; adv. com. Polit. Implications of Telecommunications in Calif., 1981-83, Joyce Hakansson Assocs., Berkeley, 1982-85. Co-Author: Spanish-Language Radio in the Southwestern United States, 1979; co-editor Telecommunications Policy Handbook, 1982, Media Flows in Latin America, 1984, Competing Visons Complex Realities: Social Aspects of Information-Oriented Society, 1986. Post-doctoral fellowship the Southern Fellowships Fund, 1980, Nat. Chicano Council on Higher Edn., 1980; Fullbright Sr. Research fellow, U. Helsinki, Finland, 1986. AAAS, Internat. Communication Assn., Am. Soc. Info. Sci., Latin Am. Studies Assn. Democrat. Roman Catholic. Avocations: World War II history, camping, cooking. Home: 1770 Loma Vista Pasadena CA 91104 Office: UCLA Powell Library 405 Hilgard Los Angeles CA 90024

SCHEMNITZ, SANFORD DAVID, wildlife biology educator; b. Cleve., Mar. 10, 1930; s. David Arthur Schemnitz; m. Mary Margaret Newby, July 8, 1958; children: Ellen Kay, Steven, Stuart. Student, U. Wis., 1948-50; BS in Wildlife, U. Mich., 1952; MS in Wildlife, U. Fla., 1953; PhD in Wildlife, Olka. State U., 1958. Cert. wildlife biologist. Conservation aide State of Mich. Dept. Conservation, Ann Arbor, 1951-52; game research biologist State of Minn. Dept. Conservation, St. Paul, 1958-59; asst. prof. wildlife Pa. State U., University Park, 1960-61; prof. wildlife resources U. Maine, Orono, 1962-75; dept. head fish and wildlife sci. N.Mex. State U., Las Cruces, 1975-81, prof. wildlife scis., 1981—. Editor: Wildlife Management Techniques Manual, 1980; contbr. articles to profl. jours. Fulbright Prof. Council for Internat. Exchange Scholars, Kathmandu, Nepal, 1983. Mem. Am. Soc. Mammalogists, The Wildlife Soc. (life, S.W. regional rep. 1979-80), Ecol. Soc. Am., Wilson Ornithol. Soc., N.Mex. Wildlife Fedn. (bd. dirs. 1983—), Sigma Xi. Home: 8105 N Dona Ana Rd Las Cruces NM 88005 Office: NMex State U Dept Fish & Wildlife PO Box 4901 Las Cruces NM 88003

SCHENCK, WILLIAM ZIEGLER, librarian; b. Orange, N.J., May 2, 1945; s. Alfred Kenneth and Mary Kathleen (Ziegler) S.; m. Lynn Christopher, 1987. BA, Johns Hopkins U., 1967; MA, MLS, U. N.C., 1972. Asst. acquisitions librarian Yale U. Library, New Haven, 1972-76; head, acquisitions U. N.C. Library, Chapel Hill, 1976-82; collecton devel. librarian U. Oreg. Library, Eugene, 1982—; advt. mgr. Info. Tech. and Libraries, Chgo., 1983—. Contbr. articles on acquisition of library materials to profl. jours. Active allocation com. United Way, Eugene, 1985-87. Mem. ALA. Democrat. Episcopalian. Office: U Oreg Library 15th and Kincaid Eugene OR 97403

SCHENDEL, WINFRIED GEORGE, insurance company executive; b. Harpstedt, Germany, June 19, 1931; s. Willi Rudolf Max and Anna Margarete (Sassen) S.; came to U.S., 1952, naturalized, 1956; B.S. in Elect. and Indsl. Engring., Hannover-Stadthagen U., Hannover, W. Germany, 1952; m. Joanne Wiest, Aug. 24, 1953; children—Victor Winfried, Bruce Lawrence, Rachelle Laureen. Elec. draftsman Houston Lighting & Power Co., 1954-57; elec. draftsman, corrosion technician Transcontinental Gas Pipeline Co., Houston, 1957-59; elec. engr. Ken R. White Cons. Engrs., Denver, 1959-61; sales engr. Weco div. Food Machinery & Chem. Corp., various locations, 1961-64; ins. field underwriter N.Y. Life Ins. Co., Denver, 1964-66, asst. mgr., 1966-70, mgmt. asst., 1970-71, gen. mgr., 1971-77, mgr., 1979-85, field underwriter, 1985—; ind. gen. agt., Denver, 1978-79. Instl. rep., advancement chmn. Denver Area council Boy Scouts Am., Lakewood, Colo., 1968-72; precinct chmn. Republican Party, Jefferson County, Colo., 1976, 78; founder, mem. (life) Sister City Program, Lakewood, Colo. Recipient Centurion award, 1966; Northwestern Region Leader Manpower Devel. award N.Y. Life Ins. Co., 1968, Salesman of Yr. award Jefferson County Salesman with a Purpose Club, 1983. Mem. Nat. Assn. Life Underwriters, Gen. Agents and Mgrs. Assn. (recipient Conf. Nat. Mgmt. award, 1975), Mile High Assn. Life Underwriters (pres. 1986—), Lakewood C. of C. (pres. people-to-people, Trailblazer of Yr. award 1982, 83, Trail Boss of Yr. 1983). Presbyterian (elder). Clubs: Lions, Edelweiss, Internat. Order Rocky Mountain Goats, N.Y. Life Star (leading asst. mgr. Continental region 1980), Masons, Shriners. Home: 13802 W 20th Pl Golden CO 80401 Office: NY Life Ins Co 3100 Arapahoe Suite 310 Boulder CO 80303

SCHENK, RAY M(ERLIN), electronics co. exec.; b. Logan, Utah, Dec. 18, 1946; s. Merlin F. and Thelma E. (Birch) S.; B.S. in Acctg. magna cum laude, Utah State U., 1969. C.P.A., Utah. Staff acct. Haskins and Sells, Phoenix, 1969, Salt Lake City, 1969-71; controller Kimball Electronics, Salt Lake City, 1971—. Recipient Scholastic Achievement cert. Phi Kappa Phi, 1967, 68; 1st Security Found. scholar, 1968; Alpha Kappa Psi scholarship award, 1969; C.P.A. medallion, 1970. Mem. Nat. Assn. Accts., Am. Acctg. Assn., Utah Assn. C.P.A.s, Am. Inst. C.P.A.s. Home: 5044 S Boabab Dr Salt Lake City UT 84117 Office: Kimball Electronics 350 Pierpont Ave Salt Lake City UT 84101

SCHENK, THEODORE ERNEST, financial counsultant, insurance agency executive; b. Gonzales, Calif., Aug. 11, 1922; s. Gottfried and Anna Marie Schenk; m. Joan Bickerton Whitehouse, July 13, 1943; children—Timothy Michael, Deborah Lynn Schenk Chretien. Agy. mgr. Calif. Western States Life Ins. Co., San Jose, 1953-69, New Eng. Mut. Life Ins. Co., San Jose, 1969-83; fin. cons., 1972—; pres. Schenk Ins. Agy., Inc., San Jose, 1978—, Pacific Retirement Cons., Inc., San Jose, 1981—. Mem. Los Gatos Planning Commn., 1972-78; past trustee, mem. adminstrv. bd. Los Gatos 1st United Methodist Ch.; mem. devel. bd. Good Samaritan Hosp. Annuities and Trust Com. Served with USNR, 1939-40, USN, 1940-47. Mem. San Jose Life Underwriters Assn. (dir. 1971-72), San Jose Gen. Agts. and Mgrs. Assn. (pres. 1967-68), Am. Soc. C.L.U.s (pres. San Jose chpt. 1974-75), Santa Clara County Estate Planning Council (pres. 1980-81), Million Dollar Round Table, New Eng. Life Leaders' Assn. Republican. Lodges: Rotary, Masons.

SCHENKEL, BARBARA ANN, minister, counselor; b. Albuquerque, Mar. 17, 1951; d. Richard Henry and Mildred (Voth) S. BSN, U. N.Mex., 1972; MDiv, Iliff Sch. Theology, 1978; postgrad., Ariz. State U., 1986—. RN, N.Mex.; ordained to ministry Meth. Ch., 1979. Minister intern Christ Ch. U. Meth. Ch., Denver, 1975-77; parish minister Herman (Nebr.) Federated and Riverside Bapt. Ch., 1978-82, Cambridge (Nebr.) Bartley U. Meth. Ch., 1982-85; family minister Red Mountain U. Meth. Ch., Mesa, Ariz., 1986—; Christ Ch. Caring Community Coordinator, Denver, 1975-77; advisor alcohol treatment program Immanuel Hosp., Washington County, Nebr., 1980-82; mem. task group to study Ministry Effectiveness in Nebr., 1981; vis. del. to World Meth. Conf., Honolulu, 1981; registrar for candidacy Bd. or Ordained Ministry, 1980-84, strategy com., 1984-85. Chaplain Jackson-Peck Am. Legion Post, Herman, 1980-82. Served to 1st lt. USAF Nurse Corps, 1973-75. Mem. Nebr. Ann. Conf. U. Meth. Chs., Mesa Ministerial Assn., Cambridge Ministerial Assn. (pres. 1984), Tekamah-Herman Ministerial Assn. (pres. 1981), Southwest Dist. Council Ministries (past com. memberships), Common Cause, Sierra Club, Amnesty Internat., Nat. Assn. Social Workers. Avocations: horseback riding, bowling, crochet, needlepoint, crewel. Office: Red Mountain United Meth Ch 2936 N Bush Hwy Mesa AZ 85205

SCHERER, MARY ELLEN, mathematics educator; b. Pomona, Calif., Nov. 10, 1942; d. William Baker and Hulda Anna (Bierman) Worrell; m. Milo Winston Scherer, June 13, 1965; children: Jonathan, Anne. BA, Pomona Coll., 1964; MA, Claremont Grad. Sch., 1967, postgrad., 1984-86. Tchr. math. Rowland (Calif.) High Sch., 1965-68; instr. math (part-time) San Bernardino (Calif.) Valley Coll., 1978-80; instr. math (part-time) Redlands (Calif.) U., 1975-76, 78-80, 84-85, vis. asst. prof. math., 1980-84, asst. prof. math., 1985—. Mem. Gifted and Talented Edn. Parent Adv. Bd., San Bernardino, 1980—. Recipient Faculty Research award U. Redlands, 1986. Mem. Am. Ednl. Research Assn., Math. Assn. Am., Phi Beta Kappa, Phi Mu Epsilon. Democrat. Lutheran. Avocations: music performance, walking, reading, gardening, sewing. Office: U Redlands Dept Math PO Box 3080 Redlands CA 92373-0999

SCHERICH, ERWIN THOMAS, consulting civil and design engineer; b. Inland, Nebr., Dec. 6, 1918; s. Harry Erwin and Ella (Peterson) S.; student Hastings Coll., 1937-39, N.C. State Coll., 1943-44; B.S., U. Nebr., 1946-48; M.S., U. Colo., 1948-51; m. Jessie Mae Funk, Jan. 1, 1947; children—Janna Rae Scherich Thornton, Jerilyn Mae Scherich Dobson, Mark Thomas. Civil and design engr. U.S. Bur. Reclamation, Denver, 1948-84, chief spillways and outlets sect., 1974-75, chief dams br., div. design, 1975-78, chief tech. rev. staff, 1978-79, chief div. tech. rev. Office of Asst. Commr. Engring. and Research Ctr., 1980-84; cons. civil engr., 1984—. Mem. U.S. Com. Internat. Commn. on Large Dams. Served with AUS, 1941-45. Registered profl. engr., Colo. Fellow ASCE; mem. Nat. Soc. Profl. Engrs. (nat. dir. 1981—), Profl. Engrs. Colo. (pres. 1977-78), Wheat Ridge C. of C. Republican. Methodist. Home and office: 3915 Balsam St Wheat Ridge CO 80033

SCHERMER, EUGENE DEWAYNE, college administrator; b. Spokane, Wash., June 21, 1934; s. John W. and Anna E. (Leitz) S.; m. Eileen J. Reider, Aug. 23, 1958; children: Douglas M., Kristin A. BA, Eastern Wash. U., 1958; MS, Oreg. State U., 1962; PhD, La. State U., 1970. Tchr. high schs. Cheney and Stevenson, Wash., 1958-61; instr. chemistry Grays Harbor Coll., Aberdeen, Wash., 1962-84, v.p. for instrn., 1984—. Contbr. articles to profl. jours. Bd. dirs. YMCA, Aberdeen, 1972-85, pres. bd. dirs. 1978; chmn. Grays Harbor County Shoreline Mgmt. Bd., Montesano, Wash., 1982—. Served with U.S. Army, 1953-55, Korea. Fellow NSF. Mem. Am. Chem. Soc. Democrat. Lutheran. Lodge: Lions. Home: 522 W 5th St Aberdeen WA 98520 Office: Grays Harbor Coll Aberdeen WA 98520

SCHERRER, EUGENE FRANK, JR., oil company executive, geophysicist; b. Denver, Jan. 4, 1949; s. Eugene Frank and Martha Louis (Hickson) S.; m. Janet Lynne, June 7, 1969; children: Eric Eugene, Brian Christopher. BS in Math. Engring., Colo. Sch. of Mines, 1971. Geophys. analyst Geophys. Services, Dallas, 1972-76; geophysicist Marathon Oil, Denver, 1976-82, mgr. geophys. services, 1983—. Mem. Denver Geophys. Soc., Soc. Exploration Geophysicists, Sigma Xi. Republican. Avocations: coaching soccer, camping, fishing. Home: 10398 W Weaver Ave Littleton CO 80127 Office: Marathon Oil Co 7400 S Broadway Littleton CO 80164

SCHERY, TERIS KIM, communication disorders educator; b. St. Louis, Apr. 15, 1943; d. Robert W. and Lois J. (Keller) Schery; m. Mark W. Lipsey, Aug. 14, 1980; children: Loren Christopher, Marisa Kim. BA, Stanford U., 1965, MA, 1966; PhD, Claremont Grad. Sch., 1980. Clinician, research asst. Inst. for Childhood Aphasia, Palo Alto, Calif., 1966-70; program specialist for communication disorders Los Angeles County Superintendent of Schs. Office, 1970-80; assoc. prof. communication disorders Calif. State U., Los Angeles, 1981-84, prof. communication disorders, 1984—; cons. in field, 1970—. Contbr. articles to profl. jours. and chpt. to books. Fulbright Teaching grantee, U.S. Ednl. Found., 1985—, grantee Office of Spl. Edn. and Calif. State Univ. System, 1978—. Fellow Am. Speech-Lang.-Hearing Assn.; mem. Calif. Speech Lang.-Hearing-Assn. (cert.), Council for Exceptional Children, Soc. Research in Child Devel., Am. Ednl. Research Assn., Phi Beta Kappa. Avocations: skiing, traveling, winetasting, photography, sailing. Home: 137 W 8th St Claremont CA 91711 Office: Calif State U Dept Communication Disorders 5151 State U Dr Los Angeles CA 90032

SCHERZER, JULIUS, research chemist; b. Czernowitz, Romania, Feb. 17, 1928; came to U.S., 1963; s. Josef and Fanny (Neumann) S.; m. Suzana Latter, 1955 (div. 1963). Phd in Inorganic and Phys. Chemistry, U. Bucharest, Romania, 1963; M Environ. Engring., Johns Hopkins U., 1974. Research asst. Tech. U., Vienna, Austria, 1963; postdoctoral research assoc. Brown U., Providence, 1963-66; research assoc. W.R. Grace & Co., Columbia, Md., 1966-78; research mgr. Filtrol Co., Los Angeles, 1978-83; sr. research assoc. sci. and tech. div. UNOCAL, Brea, Calif., 1983—; Patentee in field; contbr. over 80 articles to profl. jours. Mem. Am. Petroleum Inst. Office: UNOCAL Sci and Tech div 376 S Valencia Ave Brea CA 92621

SCHEUER, ERNEST MARTIN, mathematics educator; b. Bad Nauheim, Germany, July 28, 1930; came to U.S., 1936; s. Sally and Hedwig (Rosenthal) S.; m. Sondra Lee Goldstein, Sept. 20, 1953 (div. June 1972); children: Susan, Michael; m. Mary Jean Aura, June 5, 1972. BA, Reed Coll., 1951; MS, U. Wash., 1954; PhD, UCLA, 1960. Mathematician U.S. Naval Ordnance Test Sta., Pasadena, Calif., 1951-58; statistician Space Tech. Labs., El Segundo, Calif., 1958-62, Rand Corp., Santa Monica, Calif., 1962-69; assoc. dir. CEIR, Inc., Beverly Hills, Calif., 1969-70; assoc. prof. mgmt. Calif. State U., Northridge, 1970-72, prof. mgmt. sci., 1972—, prof. math., 1976—; cons. JPL, Pasadena, 1982—. Co-author books and articles on math. stats. and reliability. Fellow Am. Stats. Assn.; mem. Internat. Stats. Inst., Math. Assn. Am., Inst. Mgmt. Sci. Jewish. Home: PO Box 157 Northridge CA 91328 Office: Calif State U Mgmt Sci Dept Northridge CA 91330

SCHEUER, PAUL JOSEF, emeritus chemistry educator; b. Heilbronn, Germany, May 25, 1915; came to U.S., 1938, naturalized, 1944; s. Albert and Emma (Neu) S.; m. Alice Elizabeth Dash, Sept. 5, 1950; children: Elizabeth E., Deborah A., David A.L., Jonathan L.L. B.S., Northeastern U., 1943; M.A., Harvard U., 1947, Ph.D., 1950. Asst. prof. U. Hawaii, Honolulu, 1950-55; assoc. prof. U. Hawaii, 1955-61, prof. chemistry, 1961-85, prof. emeritus, 1985—, chmn. dept., 1959-62; vis. prof. U. Copenhagen, 1977; Barton lectr. U. Okla., 1967; J.F. Toole lectr. U. N.B., 1977. Author: Chemistry of Marine Natural Products, 1973; Editor: Marine Natural Products: Chemical and Biological Perspectives, Vol. 1, 2, 1978, Vol. 3, 1980, Vol. 4, 1981, Vol. 5, 1983; mem. editorial council: Toxicon; mem. editorial bd.: Toxin Revs. Served with AUS, 1944-46. Recipient Outstanding Alumni award Northeastern U., 1984. Mem. Am., Swiss chem. socs., Royal Soc. Chemistry, AAAS, Sigma Xi, Phi Kappa Phi. Research in molecular structure of natural products from marine organisms, terrestrial plants. Home: 3271 Melemele Pl Honolulu HI 96822

SCHEUERNSTUHL, GEORGE JACOB, III, transportation engineer; b. Cin., Jan. 8, 1940; s. George Jacob Jr. and Erma (Weber) S.; m. Billie Mae Boelter, June 18, 1966; children—Jennifer, William. C.E., U. Cin., 1963, M.S.C.E., M.C.P., 1965. Registered profl. engr., Ohio, Colo. Project engr. Vogt, Ivers & Assocs., Cin., 1965-67; assoc. ptnr. Vogt, Sage & Pflum, Mpls., 1967-71; sr. assoc. Barton Aschman Assocs., Mpls., 1971-77; dir. transp. Denver Regional Council Govts., 1977—; chmn. transp. system com. Transp. Research Bd., Washington, D.C., 1983—. Contbr. articles to profl. jours. Mem. ch. location task force Synod of Rocky Mountains, United Presbyn. Ch. in U.S.A., Denver, 1979; mem. Colo. Front Range Task Force, Denver, 1980. Mem. Inst. Transp. Engrs., ASCE, Am. Planning Assn. (chmn. transp. div. 1984-86), Sigma Phi Epsilon. Office: Denver Regional Council Govts 2480 W 26th Ave Denver CO 80211

SCHEVE, LARRY GERARD, biochemistry educator; b. Palo Alto, Calif., Mar. 1, 1950; s. Gerard M. and Dorothy L. Scheve; m. Gail J. Bergner, July 30, 1983. Bs in Chemistry, Seattle Pacific U., 1972; PhD in Biochemistry, U. Calif., Riverside, 1976. Research assoc. dept. surgery VA Hosp., Martinez, Calif., 1977; asst. prof. chemistry Calif. State U., Hayward, 1977-81, assoc. prof., 1981—. Author: Elements of Biochemistry, 1984; contbr. articles to profl. jours. Mem. AAAS, Am. chem. Soc., N.Y. Acad. Scis., Sigma Xi. Office: Calif State U Dept Chemistry Hayward CA 94542

SCHEWENE, CHARLES BRUCE, pharmacist; b. Covington, Ky., Aug. 14, 1940; s. Louis Elmer and Ruby Anna (Crawford) S. BA, Thomas More Coll., 1961; PhD in Chemistry, U. Wis., 1967; BS in Pharmacy, Phila. Coll Pharmacy and Sci., 1973. Registered pharmacist, Calif. Postdoctoral research fellow Calif. Inst. Tech., Pasadena, 1967-68; research chemist E.I. DuPont de Nemours, Phila. and Wilmington, Del., 1968-70; asst. in chemistry Phila. Coll. Pharmacy and Sci., 1970-73; pharmacist Thrifty Corp., Los Angeles, 1973—. Contbr. articles to Jour. of Am. Chem. Soc. Mem. Am. Pharm. Assn., Calif. Pharmacists Assn., Sigma Xi, Rho Chi. Home:

8162 Manitoba St #102 Playa del Rey CA 90293 Office: Thrifty Corp 3424 Wilshire Blvd Los Angeles CA 90010

SCHICK, SETH HARVEY, land resource economist; b. Kaysville, Utah, June 8, 1936; s. George and Ruth (Harvey) S.; m. Karren Hodgson, Sept. 2, 1960; children: Jeffery, Scott, Daranee, Alison. BS in Econs., Utah State U., 1962, MS in Econs., 1964; postgrad., U. Ariz., 1967-68. Mktg. rep. Proctor and Gamble, Salt Lake City, 1962; economist Fed. Milk Mktg., Denver, 1964; land resource economist Harza Engring. Co., Chgo., 1965-70; land resource economist Schick Internat., Salt Lake City, 1970-74, pres., land resource economist, 1974—; project economist Tipton Kalmback Co., Denver, 1976, Electro Watt Engring. Co., Zurich, Switzerland, 1984-85; spl. assignmenmt rev. economist on Indonesian irrigation project Asian Devel. Bank. Served with USAF, 1954-58. Democrat. Mormon. Office: 317 Continental Bldg Salt Lake City UT 84101

SCHIEFER, GERALD ROBINSON, electronics engineer; b. Zion Nat. Park, Utah, Aug. 1, 1934; s. Arden Guy and Lucy (Crawford) Schiefer; B.S. in Elec. Engring., U. Utah, 1960; m. Loretta McArthur, Dec. 1, 1954; children—Heidi, Gerald Scott, Charles Sidney. Missile design engr. Naval Weapons Center, China Lake, Calif., 1960-70, tech. mgr. high speed antiradiation missile harm, 1970-75, sci. advisor to comdr. operational test and eval. force, Norfolk, Va., 1975-77, head electronic warfare dept., 1977-81, head test and eval. directorate, 1981-82, dep. tech. dir., head lab. directorate, China Lake, 1982-86, tech. dir., 1986—. Chmn., Desert dist. South Sierra council Boy Scouts Am., also scoutmaster. Served with U.S. Army, 1955-56. Recipient Michelson Lab. award for engring. mgmt. Naval Weapons Center, 1974, L.T.E. Thompson award for mgmt., 1978, Superior Civilian Service award, 1985; Silver Beaver award Boy Scouts Am., 1987. Mem. IEEE, AIAA. Mormon (bishop, stake presidency). Author tech. reports. Home: 615 Kevin Ct Ridgecrest CA 93555 Office: Code 01 Naval Weapons Ctr China Lake CA 93555

SCHIEFERSTEIN, ROBERT HAROLD, research agronomist, administrator; b. Klamath Falls, Oreg., May 18, 1931; s. Harold Bernard and Myrtle Charlotte (Ekstrom) S.; m. Joyce Frances Gnos, Dec. 23, 1950; children: Bradley Gordon, Raylene Diane, Terri Carol, Karen Louise, Craig Robert. BS, Oreg. State U., 1954; MS, Iowa State U., 1955, PhD, 1957. Mem. weed control research and devel. staff Chipman Chem. Co., East Palo Alto, Calif., 1957-62; plant physiology research mgr. Shell Devel. Co., Modesto, Calif., 1962-71; research & devel. rep. Shell Devel. Co., Nebr., Colo. and Iowa, 1973-85; herbicide mktg. rep. Shell Chem. Co., Walnut Creek, Calif., 1971-73; field research resources coordinator Shell Agrl. Chem. Co., Modesto, Calif., 1985—; com. mem. Coordinating Research Council, Washington, 1969-71. Inventor herbicidals; chmn., chief exec. officer Weeds Today mag., 1980-84; contbr. articles to profl. jours. Scoutmaster Boy Scouts Am., Modesto, 1962-71. Fellow Weed Sci. Soc. Am. (chmn. various coms.); mem. Am. Inst. Biol. Scis., Am. Soc. Plant Physiologists, Council Agrl. Sci. and Tech., N. Cen. Weed Control Conf. (chmn. various coms.), Western Soc. Weed Sci. (chmn. various coms.), Sigma Xi, Alpha Zeta. Avocations: photography, outdoors activities. Home: 6620 Olive Tree Ln Riverbank CA 95367 Office: Shell Agrl Chem Co PO Box 4248 Modesto CA 95352

SCHIELER, LEROY, chemical technology consultant; b. East St. Louis, Ill., Mar. 31, 1924; s. Frederick Ferdinand and Martha Elizabeth (Kuehn) S.; m. Helen-Joyce Olson, Nov. 4, 1968. AB, Washington U., 1948; MS, U. Puget Sound, 1950; PhD, UCLA, 1953. Chem. engr. Hughes Aircraft Co., Culver City, Calif., 1952; research chemist UCLA Med. Sch., 1953; reserch technologist Shell Oil Co., Martinez, Calif., 1954; research group supr. Jet Propulsion Lab., Pasadena, Calif., 1955-58; dept. head. Aerospace Corp., Los Angeles, 1959-70; chem. tech. cons. Auburn, Calif., 1971—; dollar-a-yr. cons. Dept. Def., Washington, 1965-70, Janaf-NASA Thermochem. Panel, Washington, 1961-70, Janaf-NASA Chem. Kinetics Panel, Washington, 1967-70. Author: Energetics of Propellant Chemistry, 1964, Hazardous and Toxic Materials, 1975, Hazardous and Toxic Materials, 1976; contbr. numerous articles to profl. jours. Served to 2d lt. U.S. Army, 1942-46. Mem. Am. Chem. Soc. Home: PO Box 6328 Auburn CA 95604

SCHIESSWOHL, CYNTHIA RAE SCHLEGEL, lawyer; b. Colorado Springs, July 7, 1955; d. Leslie H. and Maime (Kascak) Schlegel; m. Scott Jay Schiesswohl, Aug. 6, 1977; 1 child, Leslie Michelle. BA cum laude, So. Meth. U., 1976; JD, U. Colo., Boulder, 1978; postgrad. U. Denver, 1984. Bar: Colo. 1979, U.S. Dist. Ct. (Colo.) 1979, U.S. Ct. Appeals (10th cir.) 1984, Wyo. 1986. Research clk. City Atty.'s Office, Colorado Springs, 1976; investigator Pub. Defender's Office, Colorado Springs, 1976; dep. dist. atty., 4th Jud. Dist. Colo., 1979-81; sole practice law, Grand Junction, Colo., 1981-82, Denver, 1983-84; assoc. Law Offices of John G. Salmon P.C., 1984-85; sole practice, Laramie, Wyo., 1985—; guest lectr. Pikes Peak Community Coll., 1980. Staff U. Colo. Law Rev., 1977. Advisor, Explorer Law Post, Boy Scouts Am., 1980-81; ex officio mem. ch. devel. com. Cen. Rocky Mt. region Christian Ch. (Disciples of Christ), 1986—; vol. Project Motivation, Dallas, 1974. Mem. ABA, Wyo. Bar Assn., Colo. Bar Assn. (ethics com. 1984-85, long range planning com. 1985—, chairperson 1986—), Pi Sigma Alpha, Alpha Lambda Delta, Alpha Delta Pi. Republican. United Methodist (mem. evangelism commn. 1987—, mem. fin. com. youth and music depts. 1979-81, lay del. to Rocky Mountain Ann. Conf. 1986-88).

SCHIFF, ANSHEL J., research mechanical engineer; b. Chgo., Sept. 24, 1936. BSME, Purdue U., 1958, MS, 1961, PhD, 1967. Prof. engring. Purdue U., West Lafayette, Ind., 1967-86; cons. prof. Stanford (Calif.) U., 1986—; research dir. Precision Measurement Industries Inc., West Lafayette, 1978—. Author: Pictures of Earthquake Damage to Power Systems and Cost Effective Methods to Reduce Seismic Failures, 1982; also articles to profl. jours. Mem. ASCE (chmn. electric power and communications com. 1983—), ASME (chmn. shock and vibration com. 1978-79). Home: 35 Pearce Mitchell Stanford CA 94305

SCHIFF, E. JEAN, artist, art educator; b. Keokuk, Iowa; d. Eli. J. and Miriam M. (Rossman) Brody; divorced; children: Ellen, Robin. Student, Chgo. Art Inst., 1949-52, Washburn U., 1957-60, U. Kans., 1961-63, Coll. San Mateo, 1963-64; BFA, U. Denver, 1966; MFA, U. Colo., 1970. Instr. drawing U. Colo., Denver, 1970, Temple Buell Coll., Denver, 1970-71, Denver Community Coll., Denver, 1970-71; prof. art. Met. State Coll., Denver, 1971—; video workshops U. Colo., Colorado Springs, 1975, Colo. State U., Ft. Collins, 1977, Red Deer Coll., Alta., Can., 1977; video fellowship Chgo. Art Inst., 1982. Exhibited in group shows at Aspen Arts Festival, 1977, Joslyn Museum, 1973, Omaha, Carson-Sapiro Gallery, Emanuel Gallery, Denver, 1985, 86, Kyle Belding Gallery, Denver, 1986; represented in permanent collections including Bucknell U., 1967, St. Paul Art Ctr., 1968, Norfolk Mus. Arts and Scis., 1969, AT&T, Colo. State Bank, 1982, Memphis State U., 1981. Active art commn. Rocy Mountain Mag., Denver, 1980-81, Frederick Ross & Co., Denver, 1982. Mem. Ctr. for Idea Art, Denver Art Mus. (coll. adv. com. 1984—. Jewish. Home: 1276 Corona Denver CO 80218 Office: Met State Coll 1006 11th St Denver CO 80204

SCHIFF, STEVEN HARVEY, lawyer; b. Chgo., Mar. 18, 1947; s. Alan Jerome and Helen M. (Ripper) S.; m. Marcia Lewis, Nov. 8, 1968; children—Jaimi, Daniel. B.A., U. Ill.-Chgo., 1968; J.D., U. N.Mex., 1972. Bar: N.Mex. 1972, U.S. Dist. Ct. N.Mex. 1972, U.S. Ct. Appeals (10th cir.) 1980. Asst. dist. atty. Dist. Atty.'s Office, Albuquerque, 1972-77; sole practice, Albuquerque, 1977-79; asst. city atty., Albuquerque, 1979-81; dist. atty. State of N.Mex., Albuquerque, 1981—; lectr. U. N.Mex., Albuquerque, 1981—. Chmn. Bernalillo County Republican Party Conv., Albuquerque, 1984, 87. Served to lt. col. and staff judge advocate N.Mex. Air N.G. Recipient Law Enforcement Commendation medal SR, 1984. Mem. Albuquerque Bar Assn., N.Mex. Bar Assn., ABA, N.Mex. Dist. Atty.'s Assn., Nat. Dist. Atty.'s Assn. Republican. Jewish. Club: Civitan. Lodge: B'nai Brith (pres. 1976-78). Home: 804 Summit NE Albuquerque NM 87106 Office: Dist Atty's Office 415 Tijeras NW Albuquerque NM 87102

SCHIFFNER, CHARLES ROBERT, architect; b. Reno, Sept. 2, 1948; s. Robert Charles and Evelyn (Keck) S.; m. Iovanna Lloyd Wright, Nov. 1971 (div. Sept. 1981); m. Adrienne Anita McAndrews, Jan. 20, 1983. Student, Sacramento Jr. Coll., 1967-68, Frank Lloyd Wright Sch. Architecture, 1968-77. Registered architect, Ariz., Wis. Architect Taliesin Associated Architects, Scottsdale, Ariz., 1977-83; pvt. practice architecture Phoenix, 1983—; instr. Ariz. State U., Tempe, 1983—. Prin. works include Ahwatukee House of the Future (cert. distinction Am. Architecture 1985), addition to Richard Black Residence, Encanto Park, Ariz. (1st place J. Brock 1986), The Pottery House, Paradise Valley, Ariz., Seventh Day Adventist Exec. Hdqrs., Scottsdale, Condominium Project, Phoenix; author (poem) Yellowstone Stream (2d prize Winter Wheat contest 1986). Named one of 35 Most Promising Young Americans Under 35, US mag., 1979. Democrat. Roman Catholic. Avocations: art, football. Home: 4540 N 44th St #1 Phoenix AZ 85018 Office: 3920 E Indian Sch Rd #9 Phoenix AZ 85018

SCHILBRACK, KAREN GAIL, system analyst; b. Tomahawk, Wis., Sept. 28; d. Edward Richard and Irene Angeline (Ligman) S. Student U. Calif.-Santa Barbara, 1967-69; B.A. in Anthropology, U. Calif.-Davis, 1971; postgrad. in Edn. and Archeology, Calif. State Poly. U., San Luis Obispo, 1971-72. Cert. computer specialist; cert. data processing; lic. cosmetologist. Computer specialist Facilities Systems Office, Port Hueneme, Calif., 1975-78, sr. computer specialist, 1978-80, project mgr. U.S. Naval Constrn. Bn. Ctr., 1980—, tng. cons. FACSO, 1981, 82; curriculum cons. Ventura Community Coll., Calif., 1981—; instr. U.S. Navy, Port Hueneme, 1983, Civil Service Commn., Port Hueneme, 1978-80. Author: AMALGAMAN Run Procedures, 1976; Cobol Programming Efficiencies, 1978; co-author, editor: Training Manual for Direct Data Entry System, 1983. Vol. Vols. for Camarillo State Hosp., Camarillo, 1978—, coordinator Ventura County, 1981; chmn. scholarship fund drive Ventura, Santa Barbara, Los Angeles, Counties, 1980. Named Young Career Woman of Yr., Calif. Bus. and Profl. Women, 1979. Clubs: Toastmistress, Young Ladies Inst. (pres. Santa Paula, dist. dep. Ventura/Santa Barbara Counties). Home: 6993 Wheeler Canyon Santa Paula CA 93060 Office: FACSO Code 18211 USNCBC Port Hueneme CA 93042

SCHILIT-WOZNICA, REBECCA, social worker, educator; b. N.Y.C., July 6, 1957; d. Barry and Henrietta (Rosen) S. BA, U. Mich., 1979, MSW, 1980, PhD, 1984. Teaching asst. U. Mich., Ann Arbor, 1982-84; asst. resident dir. Martha Cook Bldg., Ann Arbor, 1980-82; asst. prof. Ariz. State U., Tempe, 1984—; cons. Tucson Assn. Child Care, 1985-86; adv. bd. mem. Pima Community Coll., Tucson, 1986-87. Contbr. articles to profl. jours. NIMH fellowship, 1980-82; Graduate Studies Block grantee U. Mich. 1982. Mem. Nat. Assn. Social Workers (chmn. programming and continuing edn. 1985-87, chmn. sterring com. 1986-87), Am. Psychol. Assn., Assn. Women in Social Work, Arizonans for Prevention, Bertha Capen Reynolds Soc. (counsel on social work edn.). Avocation: sports. Office: Ariz State U Sch Social Work 1439 E Helen Tucson AZ 85719

SCHILLER, ANITA ROSENBAUM, librarian; b. N.Y.C., June 16, 1926; d. Aaron and Helen (Camnitz) Rosenbaum; B.A. in Econs., N.Y. U., 1949; M.L.S., Pratt Inst., 1959; m. Herbert I. Schiller, Nov. 5, 1946; children—Daniel T., P. Zachary. Reference librarian Nat. Indsl. Conf. Bd., 1960-61; instr. U. Ill. Grad. Sch. Bus. Adminstrn., 1961-62; reference librarian Pratt Inst., 1962-63; successively research asst., research asso., research asst. prof. U. Ill. Library Research Center, 1964-70; reference librarian, bibliographer U. Calif., San Diego, 1970—; Ralph R. Shaw vis. scholar Rutgers U., 1978. Co-recipient award for mag. writing Los Angeles chpt. PEN, 1982. Fellow Council Library Resources, 1976-77. Mem. ALA (councillor 1972-76, sec.-treas. library research round table 1978-80, mem. council com. on status of women in librarianship 1980, Equality award 1985). Contbr. articles to profl. publs.; editor Aware column Am. Libraries, 1971-72; mem. editorial bds. profl. jours. Home: 7109 Monte Vista St La Jolla CA 92037 Office: U Calif Central U Library San Diego CA 92093

SCHILLER, HERBERT I., author, social scientist; b. N.Y.C., Nov. 5, 1919; s. Benjamin Franklin and Gertrude (Perner) S.; m. Anita Rosenbaum, Nov. 5, 1946; children—Daniel T., P. Zachary. B.S.S., CCNY, 1940; M.A., Columbia U., 1941; Ph.D., NYU, 1960. Teaching fellow CCNY, 1940-41, lectr. econs., 1949-59; economist U.S. Govt., 1941-42, 46-48; mem. faculty Pratt Inst., Bklyn., 1950-63; prof. econs., chmn. dept. social studies Pratt Inst., 1962-63; research asso. prof. Bur. Econ. and Bus. Research, U. Ill. at Urbana, 1963-65, research prof., 1965-70; prof. communication U. Calif. at San Diego, 1970—; lectr. Bklyn. Acad. Music, 1961-66; vis. fellow Inst. Policy Studies, Wash., 1968; vis. prof. U. Amsterdam, Netherlands, 1973-74; Thord-Gray vis. lectr. U. Stockholm, 1978; vis. prof. communications Hunter Coll., City U. N.Y., 1978-79. Author: Mass Communications and American Empire, 1969, Superstate: Readings in the Military-Industrial Complex, 1970, The Mind Managers, 1973, Communication and Cultural Domination, 1976, Who Knows: Information in the Age of the Fortune 500, 1981, Information and the Crisis Economy, 1984; editor: Quar. Rev. Econs. and Bus, 1963-70, National Sovereignty and International Communication, 1979. Served with AUS, 1942-45, MTO. Mem. AAAS, Internat. Assn. Mass Communication Research (v.p.), Internat. Inst. Communications (trustee 1978-84), AAUP (sec. Ill. U.), Phi Beta Kappa. Home: 7109 Monte Vista La Jolla CA 92037 Office: Univ Calif San Diego La Jolla CA 92093

SCHILLER, JUDITH D., clinical social worker, psychotherapist; b. Fayetteville, N.C., Feb. 8, 1943; d. Harry A. and Pearl L. (Tannenbaum) Speert. MSW, DSW, U. Calif., Berkeley, 1978. Lic. clin. social worker, Calif. Pvt. practice clin. social worker San Francisco, 1983—; clin. social worker CASARC, San Francisco, 1985—; mem. faculty Calif. Inst. for Clin. Social Work, Berkeley, 1985—. Author: Child Care Alternatives and Emotional Well-Being, 1980.

SCHILLER, NEAL LEANDER, medical microbiologist, educator; b. Lowell, Mass., Nov. 5, 1949; s. Vincent Roger and Lorraine Margaret (Marion) S.; m. Kathleen Mary Pratt, June 30, 1973; children: Matthew, Kevin, David. BS in Biology, Boston Coll., 1967-71; PhD in Microbiology, U. Mass., 1976. Postdoctoral researcher Cornell U. Med. Ctr., 1976-78; asst. prof. microbiology U. Calif., Riverside, 1979-85, assoc. prof., 1985—; vis. staff scientist NIH, Bethesda, Md., 1985-86. Eucharistic minister St. Andrew's Newman Ctr., Riverside, 1981—, coach, referee Am. Youth Soccer Orgn., Riverside, 1981—. Boston Coll. Scholar, 1967-71; NIH trainee, 1972-76, fellow, 1976-78. Mem. Am. Soc. Microbiology (chmn. elect 1985-86, chmn. Div. D 1986-87, So. Calif. chpt.), AAAS. Roman Catholic. Avocations: tennis, softball, racketball, swimming. Office: U Calif Biomed Scis Div Riverside CA 92521

SCHILLER, THOMAS BENNETT, motion picture writer, director; b. Los Angeles, Apr. 12, 1949; s. Robert Achille and Joyce Gloria (Harris) S. Documentary film maker Los Angeles; writer "Saturday Night Live", N.Y.C., 1975-80; writer, dir. MGM, N.Y.C., 1982; writer Paramount Pictures, Hollywood, Calif., 1984; writer, dir. Home Box Office, Los Angeles, 1986; free-lance writer, dir. Los Angeles, 1986—. Producer: (documentary films) Buckminster Fuller on Spaceship Earth, 1968, A Glimpse of De Kooning, 1969, Anais Nin Observed, 1971, The Henry Miller Odyssey, 1974, Henry Miller Asleep and Awake, 1974; writer, dir. (feature film) Nothing Lasts Forever, 1982; (TV film) From Here to Maternity, 1986. Recipient 2 Emmy awards for Saturday Night Live, 1976, 77. Mem. ASCAP, Am. Fedn. TV and Radio Actors, Writers Guild of Am. (annual award 1976, 79), Dirs. Guild of Am. Lodge: Masons.

SCHILLING, JOHN ALBERT, surgeon; b. Kansas City, Mo., Nov. 5, 1917; s. Carl Fielding and Lottie Lee (Henderson) S.; m. Lucy West, June 8, 1957 (dec.); children: Christine Henderson, Katharine Ann, Jolyon David, John Jay; m. Helen R. Spelbrink, May 28, 1979. A.B. with honors, Dartmouth Coll., 1937; M.D., Harvard U., 1941. Diplomate Am. Bd. Surgery (chmn. 1969). Intern, then resident in surgery Roosevelt Hosp., N.Y.C., 1941-44; mem. faculty U. Rochester (N.Y.) Med. Sch., 1945-53, asst. prof. surgery, 1955-56; prof. surgery, head dept. U. Okla. Med. Sch., 1956-74; prof. surgery U. Wash. Med. Sch., Seattle, 1974—; chmn. dept. U. Wash. Med. Sch., 1975-83; mem. bd. sci. counselors Nat. Cancer Inst., chmn., 1969; also mem. diagnosis subcom. breast cancer task force; chmn. adv. com. to surgeon gen. on metabolism of trauma Army Med. Research and Devel. Command; mem. surgery study sect., div. research grants NIH; chief surgery USAF Sch. Aviation Medicine, 1953-55; cons. Surgeon Gen. USAF, 1959-75. Author articles, chpts. in books, abstracts, reports.; editorial bd. Am. Jour. Surgery, Annals of Surgery. Served to maj. M.C. USAF, 1953-55. Grantee Army Office Surgeon Gen., 1956-80. Mem. ACS (bd. govs., chmn. com. surg. edn. in med. schs., 1st v.p. 1984-85), Am., So., Western, Pan-Pacific, N. Pacific, Pacific Coast surg. assns., Soc. Univ. Surgeons, SW Surg. Soc., Central Surg. Soc., Am. Assn. Surgery Trauma, Surg. Biology Club, Am. Physiol. Soc., Soc. Surg. Chmn., Am. Trauma Soc., Seattle Surg. Soc., Soc. Exptl. Pathology, Soc. Surgery Alimentary Tract, Explorers Club, Alpha Omega Alpha. Clubs: Yacht (Seattle), University (Seattle). Home: 9807 Lake Washington Blvd NE Bellevue WA 98004 Office: Dept Surgery (RF-25) Univ Wash Medical Sch Seattle WA 98195

SCHILLIOS, ROLV HARLOW, editor. Grad., Pacific Luth. U. Editor Portland (Oreg.) Mag.; Bd. dirs. Linfield Coll., Am. Scandinavian Found. Contbr. articles to profl. jours. (winner of numerous newspaper and mag. awards). Aide to a U.S. Congressman, Wash. Served with U.S. Army. Recipient Gold medal Freedoms Found., disting. community service award Columbia Christian Coll.; appointed hon. consul Rep. of Korea, 1978; honored by the Phillipine govt., 1985; named Oreg. Scandinavian of the Yr. Mem. Am. Legion Press Assn., Oreg. Consular Corps (dean two terms). Home: 824 S W Fifth Ave Portland OR 97204

SCHIMMELMAN, ARTHUR ERWIN, marketing professional; b. Los Angeles, June 28, 1941; s. Arthur Henry S.; m. Meredith Ann Johnson, Aug. 2, 1969; children: Leigh, Erik, Erin. AA, Orange Coast Coll., 1964; BS, Calif. State U., San Jose, 1971. Mktg. adminstr. Beckman Inst., Fullerton, Calif., 1965-73, Space Labs., Chatsworth, Calif., 1973-74; v.p. Perma-Curbs, Inc., Orange, Calif., 1974-75; br. mgr. A.P.I. Alarms, Culver City, Calif., 1981-84; gen. mgr. Nat. Guardian, Santa Ana, Calif., 1984-86; br. mgr. Paychex Inc., Santa Monica, Calif., 1986—; pres., bd. dirs. Site Mixed Concrete Corp, 1975—; mktg. cons., co-owner Resume Works, Newport Beach, Calif., 1985—; co-owner Meredith's Hairmates, Placentia, Calif., 1985—. V.p. and bd. dirs. Am. Girls Softball League, La Habra, Calif., 1986—; bd. dirs. Am. Youth Soccer Orgn., La Habra, 1986—. Served with USNR, 1958-64. Republican. Avocations: writing, bicycling, jogging, golf, tennis. Office: Paychex Inc 1217 Imperial Way Placentia CA 92670

SCHIMMERLING, WALTER, research biophysicist; b. Milan, Mar. 10, 1937; came to U.S., 1965; m. Cecilia Eizyk, Dec. 3, 1961; children: Ernest, Carol, Karina. MS, U. Buenos Aires, 1961; PhD, Rutgers U., 1971. Staff scientist Princeton (N.J.) U., 1965-72; asst. to dir. Particle Accelerator, Princeton, 1971-72; staff biophysicist Lawrence Berkeley (Calif.) Lab., 1972-81, sr. research scientist, 1981—. Contbr. numerous articles to sci. jours. Grantee Nat. Cancer Inst., 1978—, NASA, 1981—. Mem. Am. Phys. Soc., Radiation Research Soc., Am. Assn. Physicists in Medicine. Office: Lawrence Berkeley Lab 1 Cyclotron Rd Berkeley CA 94526

SCHINDEL, DAVID CLIFTON, English educator; b. Cleve., Dec. 22, 1948; s. Robert Lee and Ilene (Clifton) S.; m. Deborah Ann Doe, June 23, 1973; 1 child, Charles Alexander. BA, The Defiance Coll., 1972; MA, Bowling Green State U., 1974. Instr. Berkeley Preparatory Sch., Tampa, Fla., 1974-77, Tampa Coll., 1978, Vail (Colo.) Mountain Sch., 1978—. Fellow Nat. Assn. Coll. Admissions Counselors, Colo. Assn. Coll. Admissions Counselors, Nat. Council of Tchrs. of English. Episcopalian. Home: PO BOx 3676 Vail CO 81658 Office: Vail Mountain Sch 3160 Katsos Ranch Rd Vail CO 81657

SCHINNELL, LAURA LOUISE KING, environmental scientist; b. Rochester, N.Y.; d. Gordon David and Kathleen (Smyth) King; m. Gary Lee Schinnell, Apr. 26, 1980; children: Matthew Jacob, Emily Joyce. BA, Hamline U., 1974; MS, U. Minn., 1980. Environ. scientist No. States Power, Mpls., 1974-76; research scientist II State of Minn., Mpls., 1976-77; project environ. supr. Wash. Pub. Power Supply System, Elma, 1977-81, environ. scientist, 1986—; cons. No. States Power, 1976. Contbr. articles to profl. jours. NSF grantee, 1973; named Young Careerwoman Wash. Pub. Power, 1978. Mem. Am. Chem. Soc. Republican. Avocations: reading, sewing, home computers. Home: 808 Lake Hill Rd Montesano WA 98563 Office: Wash Pub Power Supply System PO Box 1223 Elma WA 98541

SCHIPMAN, HENRY CHARLES, artist, cartoonist; b. Las Cruces, N.Mex., Oct. 11, 1924; s. Henry Charles and Rose Love (Johnson) S. Student N.Mex. State Coll., 1949-54. Photo retoucher local photographers, 1945-55; staff artist N.Mex. Farm and Livestock Bur., 1955-65; owner, curator Am. Cowboy Mus., Las Cruces, N.Mex., 1975-82. Past bd. dirs. Retarded Children's Assn. Mem. Nat. Fedn. Ind. Bus., John Birch Soc., Spanish Mustang Registry, Am. Donkey and Mule Soc., Tex. Longhorn Breeders, N.Am. Corriente Assn., Internat. Trick and Fancy Ropers Assn. (hon.). Republican. Methodist. Club: Odd Fellows. Author: Different Types of Cowboys and Their Different Jobs, 1968; The Animal of Christmas and Easter, 1971; My Friends, The Cabdrivers, 1979; contbr., illustrator articles in Western Horseman, True West, Hoofs and Horns, Nat. Parks mags. Home: 644 W Court St Las Cruces NM 88005

SCHIRMER, HOWARD AUGUST, JR., civil engineer; b. Oakland, Calif., Apr. 21, 1942; s. Howard August and Amy (Freuler) S.; m. Leslie May Mecum, Jan. 29, 1965; children: Christine Nani, Amy Kiana, Patricia Leolani. B.S., U. Calif., Berkeley, 1964, M.S., 1965. Registered profl. engr., Hawaii, Guam. Engr. in tng. materials and research dept. Calif. Div. Hwys., Sacramento, 1960-64; engring. analyst Dames & Moore, San Francisco, 1964-67; asst. staff engr. Dames & Moore, 1967-68, chief engr., 1969-72; asso. Dames & Moore, Honolulu, 1972-75; partner, mng. prin. in charge Dames & Moore, 1975-78; regional mgr. Dames & Moore, Pacific Far East and Australia, 1978-81; chief operating officer Dames & Moore, Los Angeles, 1981-83; mng. dir. Dames & Moore Internat., Los Angeles, 1983—; chmn. geotech. engring. com. Am. Cons. Engrs. Council, 1976-78; past chmn. adv. com. for engring. tech. Honolulu Community Coll. Important works include AFDM Berthing Wharf, Pearl Harbor. Chmn. engring. sect., mem. budget com. Aloha United Way, 1974; first aid instr. ARC, 1971-79; founder Mauna Kea Ski Patrol, 1969. Mem. ASCE (vice chmn. engring. mgmt. exec. com. 1985-86, co-chmn. engring. mgmt. group 1985-86, Edmund Friedman Young Engr. award for profl. achievement 1974, pres. Hawaii sect.), Cons. Engrs. Council Hawaii (pres. 1972), Engring. Assn. Hawaii (past dir., 2d v.p.), Internat. Soc. Soil Mechanics and Found. Engring., Am. Public Works Assn. (sec. 1977-78, dir. 1979-80), Soc. Am. Mil. Engrs., Structural Engrs. Assn. Hawaii, Federation Internationale des Ingenieurs-Conseils (co-chmn., U.S. rep. standing com. on profl. liability 1986-87), Chi Epsilon (hon. mem. U. Hawaii), Sigma Phi Epsilon. Republican. Episcopalian. Clubs: Outrigger Canoe, Ski Assn. Hawaii, Jonathan (Los Angeles). Home: 827 Inverness Dr La Canada Flintridge CA 91011 Office: Dames & Moore Internat 445 S Figueroa St Los Angeles CA 90071

SCHIRMER, RALPH BERNHARD, international marketing consultant; b. Fukuoka, Japan, Dec. 5, 1936; came to U.S., 1982; s. Friedrich Emil and Claire (Loeffler) S.; m. Astrid Lucia Pedersen, Dec. 9, 1961; children—Lillian, Alberto, Ernesto. Ed. Shanghai Brit. High Sch. (China), Höhere Handelsschule, Cologne, W.Ger.; degree in fgn. trade Berufsschulen, Bremen, W.Ger. With Martin Stürcken Tecnoimport/Martin Stürcken & Co., G.m.b.H., Bremen, W.Ger. and Caracas, Venezuela, 1956-60, Del Monte Corp., 1964-67; from sales rep. to sales mgr. spl. accounts C.A. Firestone Venezolana, Caracas, 1960-64, 67-71; sales mgr. pvt. markets ITT de Venezuela, Caracas, 1971-73; indsl. sales mgr., nat. sales mgr., mktg. mgr. Corimon Group, Caracas, 1973-75; asst. gen. mgr. Vencobre and Griven (Phelps-Dodge Internat.), Caracas, 1976-77; mktg. and export mgr. Grupo Siderpro, Caracas, 1978-81; dir. internat. sales and mktg. IMI-Info. Mktg. Internat. subs. Ziff Davis Pub. Co., Oak Park, Mich., 1983-84; cons. internat. mktg. and bus. mgmt. Spectrum Internat. Assocs., Tucson, 1986—; planner personal fin. IDS/Am. Express, 1985—. Founding pres. Venezuelan-Brit. Sch., Caracas, 1966. Recipient prizes for rowing, Ger., 1956-58. Mem. Venezuela Assn. Exporters (v.p. 1980; founding mem.), World Trade Assn. Home and office: 8955 E Maple Leaf Dr Tucson AZ 85710

SCHIRMER, TAD WILLIAM, oil company exploration geologist; b. Greenwich, Conn., Sept. 10, 1956; s. Howard William and Beatrice (Cody) S.; m. Virginia Picone, Aug. 6, 1983; 1 child, Jennifer Lynn. BS, Weber State Coll., 1982; MS, Utah State U., 1985. Seismic technician United Geophys. Corp., Douglas, Wyo., 1981; field geologist U.S. Geol. Survey, Menlo Park, Calif., 1982; mining geologist Tinglefoot Mining Co., Idaho City, 1982-83; geologist Utah Bur. Hazardous Waste, Salt Lake City, 1985; exploration geologist Chevron U.S.A., Inc., Denver, 1986—; tchg. asst. Weber State Coll., Ogden, Utah, 1981-82; grad. tchg. asst. Utah State U.,

Logan, 1983-84. Conn. State scholar Coll. Testing Bd., 1974; grad. fellow Utah State U., 1984. Mem. Am. Assn. Petroleum Geologists (research grantee 1984), Sigma Xi Scientific Research Soc.(research grantee 1984). Republican. Presbyterian. Avocations: antique bottle collecting, rock and fossil collecting, hiking, cross-country skiing. Office: Chevron USA Inc PO Box 599 6400 S Fiddlers Green Circle Englewood CO 80111

SCHIRRIPA, ROBERT ROCCO, chemical engineer; b. Bklyn., Apr. 13, 1948; s. Dominico Ralph and Carmela Francis (Curro) S.; divorced; m. Virginia Mae Hildebrandt, July 31, 1977; children: Kenneth, Kevin, Jennifer. BChemE, Pratt Inst., 1970; MChemE, U. Conn., 1973. Engr. Exxon Research and Engring. Co., Florham Park, N.J., 1972-73; process engr. Exxon Chem. Co., Linden, N.J., 1973-78; sr. engr. Exxon Chem. Am., Bayway, N.J., 1978-81, Santa Fe Braun, Alhambra, Calif., 1981-86, IT Corp., Irvine, Calif., 1986—. Cubmaster Cub Scout Pack 124, Madison, N.J., 1977-79; chmn. Parent Faculty Assn. Carnival, Madison, 1977-79; coach Madison Little League, 1978; pres. Spina Bifida Assn., Los Angeles, 1986—. Mem. Am. Inst. Chem. Engrs., Am. Chem. Soc., ASTM. Roman Catholic. Avocations: computers, tennis, bowling, electrical kit building, woodworking. Home: 1914 Wheaton Ave Claremont CA 91711

SCHLACHTER, ALFRED S(IMON), physicist; b. Cedar City, Utah, Feb. 18, 1942; s. Max and Rosel (Rosenfeld) S. AB in Physics, U. Calif., Berkeley, 1963; MA in Physics, U. Wis., 1965, PhD in Physics, 1969. Aerospace engr. Ames Research Ctr. NASA, Sunnyvale, Calif., 1963; research asst. dept. physics U. Wis., Madison, 1963-68; prin. research scientist Honeywell Research Ctr., Mpls., 1968-70; scientist Inst. Fundamental Electronics U. Paris Faculty of Sci. at Orsay, France, 1971-73; scientist atomic physics dept. Ctr. Nuclear Studies at Saclay, Gif-sur-Yvette, France, 1971-75; staff scientist Lawrence Berkeley Lab., 1975—; vis. scientist Ctr. Nuclear Studies at Fontenay-aux-Roses, France, 1977, Justus-Liebig-Universität Giessen, Institut für Kernphysik, Fed. Republic of Germany, 1980-81. Contbr. articles to profl. jours.; patentee in field. Fellow NSF, U. Wis., Madison, 1964, Cen. Nat. de la Recherche Scientifique U. Paris, 1971-72, Joliot-Curie Inst. Nat. des Scis. et Tech. Nucleaires, Saclay, 1972-73, Alexander von Humboldt-Stiftung, 1980-81; NATO Research grantee, 1980-82, 85-86; participant Nat. Acad. Sci. exchange with USSR, 1986. Mem. Am. Phys. Soc. (electron, atomic physics and plasma physics divs.), Optical Soc. Am. Office: Lawarence Berkeley Lab U Calif Berkeley CA 94720

SCHLADWEILER, JON CHARLES, government official; b. Menonomie, Wis., Nov. 21, 1945; s. Walter John and Evangeline Francis (Schutz) S.; m. Lauren Johnson, June 15, 1968; children—Scott David, Todd Charles. B.S., U. Wis., 1968; postgrad. in San. Engring., U. Ariz., 1970-73. Registered profl. engr., land surveyor, Ariz. Design engr. engring. div. AMOCO Chems. Corp., Chgo., 1968-69; design engr. dept. water and sewers, City of Tucson, 1973-77; chief engr. Pima County Wastewater Mgmt. Dept., Tucson, 1977-86, dep. dir. engring., 1986—. Contbr. article to profl. publ. Deacon St. Andrew's Presbyn. Ch., Tucson, 1983-86; asst. coach, umpire Canada del Oro Little League, Tucson, 1984-85, mgr. 1986—; asst. coach Am. Youth Soccer Orgn. Served with USAF, 1969-73. Named Outstanding Citizen of Tucson, 1970. Mem. Water Pollution Control Fedn., Ariz. Water and Pollution Control Assn. (program moderator 1985, chmn. tech. program com. 1986 Conf.; mem. Select Soc. San. Sludge Shovelers (bd. dirs. 1986—), Nat. Soc. Profl. Engrs., Theta Tau, Chi Epsilon. Republican. Office: Pima County Wastewater Mgmt 130 W Congress Tucson AZ 85701

SCHLANK, JOHN JAMES (JACK), III, test engineer; b. Groton, Conn., Jan. 31, 1957; s. John James Jr. and Josephine Johanna (Marmo) S.; m. Laurel Lynne Dunbar, July 24, 1982. BSArch, Clemson U., 1978, BSME, 1981. Assoc. engr. Martin Marietta Aerospace Co., Denver, 1981-82; engr. Martin Marietta Aerospace Co., Vandenberg AFB, Calif., 1982-84; test engr. Gen. Dynamics Convair, San Diego, 1984-85; sr. test engr. Gen. Dynamics Space Systems, San Diego, 1985—. Mem. AIAA, Am. Vacuum Soc. Republican. Roman Catholic. Avocation: motorcycle and car restoration. Home: 1626 Capistrano Ave Spring Valley CA 92077 Office: Gen Dynamics Space Systems Div PO Box 85590 MS 23-8390 San Diego CA 92138

SCHLAX, JAMES ALAN, accountant; b. Chgo., June 10, 1946; s. William Francis and Leone Sophie (Musket) S.; m. Barbara Jean Wasilewski, Aug. 29, 1970; children: Jenny, Tracy, Mindy, Jonathan. BS in Acctg., U. Ill., 1972; MBA in Fin., U. Chgo., 1976; JD, DePaul U., 1982. Bar: Ill. 1982; CPA. Staff auditor Kerber, Eck and Braeckel CPA's, Springfield, Ill., 1972-74; various acctg., fin. and planning positions Amoco Corp., Chgo., 1976-82; mgr. acctg. Casper (Wyo.) Refinery div. Amoco Oil Co., 1982—. Served as 1st lt. U.S. Army, 1966-69, Vietnam. Decorated Bronze Star, Purple Heart. Mem. ABA, Ill. Bar Assn., Am. Inst. CPA's, Ill. Soc. CPA's. Home: 2260 E 16th Casper WY 82609 Office: Amoco Oil Co PO Box 160 Casper WY 82602

SCHLEGEL, GARY LEE, podiatrist; b. Los Angeles, Apr. 8, 1953; s. Forrest M. and Ida C. (Oberg) S.; m. Suzanne M. Herrmann, Dec. 15, 1979. BA, U. Calif., Davis, 1975; D.Podiatric Medicine, Pa. Coll. Podiatric Medicine, Phila., 1979. Diplomate Am. Bd. Podiatric Surgery. Intern, resident New Berlin Meml. Hosp., Milw., 1980; pvt. practice podiatric medicine, Carmichael, Calif., also Folsom, Calif., 1980— ; co-founder Sacramento Valley Sports Medicine Clinic, Folsom, 1980—; gen. ptnr. Sacramento Profl. Investment Group, 1983—; asst. prof. Calif. Coll. Podiatric Medicine, San Francisco, 1980-81; research assoc. Dow-Corning Med. Corp., 1980-81; mem. adv. bd. Placer Bank Commerce, Roseville, Calif. Contbr. articles to profl. jours. Co-creator Lower Extremity Mus., Phila., 1978. Bd. dirs. Sacramento Ballet Theatre, 1984; res. dep. Sacramento Sheriff's Dept., 1973. Fellow Am. Coll. Foot Orthopedists (Orthopedics award 1979), Am. Coll. Foot Surgeons (assoc.), Am. Bd. Podiatric Surgery (cert.), Am. Podiatry Assn., Calif. Podiatry Assn. Republican. Lutheran. Office: 6403 Coyle Ave Suite 390 Carmichael CA 95608 Also: 404 Natoma St Folson CA 95630

SCHLEI, NORBERT ANTHONY, lawyer; b. Dayton, Ohio, June 14, 1929; s. William Frank and Norma (Lindsley) S.; m. Jane Moore, Aug. 26, 1950 (div. 1963); children: Anne C. Buczynski, William K., Andrew M.; m. Barbara Lindemann, Mar. 7, 1965 (div. 1981); children: Bradford L., Graham L., Norbert L., Norma Blake. BA, Ohio State U., 1950; LLB magna cum laude, Yale U., 1956. Bar: Ohio 1956, Calif. 1958, D.C. 1963, U.S. Supreme Ct. 1963. Law clk. to Justice Harlan U.S. Supreme Ct., 1956-57; assoc. atty. O'Melveny & Myers, Los Angeles, 1957-59; ptnr. Greenberg, Shafton & Schlei, Los Angeles, 1959-62; asst. atty. gen. U.S. Dept. Justice, Washington, 1962-66; ptnr. Munger, Tolles, Hills & Rickershauser, 1968-70, Kane, Shulman & Schlei, Washington, 1968-70; ptnr.-in-charge Los Angeles office Hughes Hubbard & Reed, 1972—; bd. dirs. Wedbush Corp., Kahala Capital Corp., Wedbush Securities, Inc., Los Angeles. Author: (with M.S. McDougal and others) Studies in World Public Order, 1961 (Am. Soc. Internat. Law ann. book award); State Regulation of Corporate Financial Practices, 1962; editor-in-chief Yale Law Jour., 1955-56. Democratic nominee for Calif. Assembly, 1962, for sec. of state Calif., 1966. Served to lt. (j.g.) USNR, 1950-53. Mem. ABA, Fed. Bar Assn., Los Angeles County Bar Assn., State Bar Calif., Am. Judicature Soc., Am. Soc. Internat. Law, Ctr. for Pub. Resources, Japan-Am. Found., Inc. (bd. dirs.). Mem. Christian. Ch. Clubs: Yale (So. Calif.); Calif. Yacht (Marina Del Rey), Plaza (Honolulu). Avocations: tennis, golf, skiing, sailing. Office: Hughes Hubbard & Reed 555 S Flower St Suite 3700 Los Angeles CA 90071

SCHLESINGER, DEBORAH LEE, librarian; b. Cambridge, Mass., Sept. 13, 1937; d. Edward M. and Edith D. (Schneider) Hershoff; divorced; children: Suzanne, Richard. BA, U. Mass., 1961; MS, Simmons Coll., 1974; postgrad., U. Pitts., 1983. Reference librarian Bently Coll., Waltham, Mass., 1964-65; dir. Carnegie Library, Swissvale, Pa., 1973-77, South Park Twp. Library, Library, Pa., 1977-81, Monessen (Pa.) Library, 1981-82, Lewis & Clark Library, Helena, Mont., 1983—; vis. scholar Pitts. Regional Library Ctr., 1982-83. Editor Pa. Union List, 1982-83. Mem. exec. bd. Mont. Cultural Advocacy, 1983—. Mem. Mont. Library Assn. (chmn. legis. com. 1984—), Mont. Assn. Female Execs. (fin. com. 1986—), AAUW (exec. com. 1985-86). Democrat. Club: Montana (Helena). Avocations: flying, painting, reading, rafting, travel. Home: 507 5th Ave Helena MT 59601 Office: Lewis and Clark Library 120 S Last Chance Mall Helena MT 59601

SCHLESINGER, JUDITH DIANE, computer science and data processing consultant; b. N.Y.C., Dec. 10, 1945; d. Gustav Elliot and Blanche Ethel (Pack) S. BS in Math., CUNY, 1967; MS in Computer Sci., Ohio State U., 1969; PhD in Computer Sci., Johns Hopkins U., 1976. Programmer Honeywell Info. Systems, Waltham, Mass., 1969-71; systems scientist Mgmt. Adv. Services, Columbia, Md., 1974-75; asst. prof. U. Denver, 1976-81; pvt. practice computer cons. Denver, 1981—; mem. adv. bd. Robotic Computers Inc., Golden, Colo., 1983—. Author (manuals) Structured Methodologies, 1984, Introduction to ADP, 1984. Regents scholar N.Y. State, 1963; NSF fellow, 1972-75. Mem. Computer Soc. of IEEE, Assn. Computing Machinery (chmn. Denver chpt. 1983-84, Service Recognition award 1984, 85), Data Processing Mgmt. Assn., Am. Assn. Artificial Intelligence. Avocation: crafts. Office: JDS Cons Services PO Box 24102 Denver CO 80224

SCHLINTZ, GERALD HARVEY, lawyer; b. Milw., Mar. 29, 1953; s. Harvey Alfred and Iona Frances (Weihert) S.; m. Victoria Lynn Johnson, July 5, 1975. Student, U. Wis., Milw., 1971-73; AB, U. Calif., Berkeley, 1975; JD, U. Calif., San Francisco, 1982. Bar: Calif. 1982, U.S. Dist. Ct. (no. dist.) Calif. 1983. Assoc. Orrick, Herrington & Sutcliffe, San Francisco, 1983-85; assoc. counsel Bank of Am., San Francisco, 1985—. Student advisor, parent-tchr. club participant internat./intercultural programs Am. Field Service, Milw., Berkeley and Oakland, Calif., 1971—. Mem. ABA (corp., banking, bus. law sect.), State Bar Calif., San Francisco Bar Assn. (banking, comml. law sect.), Order of Coif, Phi Beta Kappa. Office: Bank of Am Legal Dept 3017 555 California St PO Box 37000 San Francisco CA 94137

SCHLITT, ANNELIES JEANNE, software engr.; b. New Rochelle, N.Y., May 27, 1943; d. Matthew Marcellus and Aukje Hillegonde (Hoogeveen) Dorenbosch; B.S., Columbia U., 1967; m. Gerd Herbert Schlitt, Feb. 27, 1974; children: Lawrence Matthew, Alexander Paul. Systems programmer Ciba-Geigy Corp., Ardsley, N.Y., 1968-70, Basel, Switzerland, 1970-71, Wehr, W.Ger., 1971-73; self-employed systems cons., Wehr, 1973-78; software engr. Intel Corp., Santa Clara, Calif., 1979-84, systems engr., Munich, 1984-86; pvt. practice cons., Cupertino, Calif., 1986—. Home and Office: 22996 Standing Oak Ct Cupertino CA 95014

SCHLOSSER, ROBERT JULES, theatre administrator; b. Stockton, Calif., Jan. 9, 1935; s. Julius Christian and Wilma Marie (Walker) S.; m. Elizabeth Anne Freeman, Oct. 11, 1959; children—Brita Elizabeth, Christian Mark. B.S., U. San Francisco, 1956. Subscription mgr. San Francisco Actors' Workshop, 1962-65; audience devel. dir. Repertory Theatre, Lincoln Center, N.Y., 1965-73, Mark Taper Forum, Los Angeles, 1973—; founding dir. Theatre Audience Project, Los Angeles, 1979—. Founder, Project D.A.T.E. (Deaf Audience Theatre Experience), Los Angeles, 1978; mem. Greater Los Angeles Visitors and Conv. Bur., 1973—. Served with U.S. Army, 1958-60.

SCHLOTTMANN, DAVID HENRY, accountant; b. Olympia, Wash., Oct. 11, 1944; s. David Frank and Phyllis Emily (Cook) S.; Jr. Accountant, Dietz Bus. Coll., 1968; m. Carol Ann Pink, Nov. 22, 1968; children—Julianna Carol, Amy Marie, David Jesse, Caleb Tyrell Henri. Clk., Wash. State Dept. Labor and Industries, 1968, clk. typist Dept. Motor Vehicles, 1968-69, accounting asst. Dept. Hwys. 1969-70, fed. grants accountant Div. Instns., Dept. Social and Health Services, Olympia, Wash., 1970-72, welfare program accountant Div. Pub. Assistance, 1972-73, budget analyst Vets. Program, 1973-76; chief accountant Dep. Vets.' Affairs, 1976-81, budget analyst Dept. Corrections, 1981—; owner, Ookkee's Bookshop, Olympia, 1974—. Mem. 1976 Jack London Centennial Com., 1973-76; mem. Council of State Agy. Fiscal Officers, 1980-81. Bd. dirs. London NW, 1976—. Served with AUS, 1963-66. Decorated Army Commendation medal. Named Jack London Man of Year, 1973. Mem. Ch. of God (Cleve., Tenn., ch. clk. 1974—). Editor, pub.: What's New About London, Jack?, 1971—, The Chaney Chronical (about London's father), 1972—, The Wolf, a Jack London ann., 1973—, non profit lit. jours. centering around life of Am. author Jack London. Home: 929 S Bay Rd Olympia WA 98506

SCHMALTZ, ROY EDGAR, JR., art educator, artist; b. Belfield, N.D., Feb. 23, 1937; s. Roy and Mercedes (Martin) S.; m. Julia Mabel Swan, Feb. 1, 1958; children—Liese Marlene, Jennifer Lynn, Gregory Jason. Student Otis Art Inst., Los Angeles, 1959-60, U. Wash., 1960-61, Akademie der Bildenden Kunste, Munich, W. Ger., 1965-66; B.F.A., San Francisco Art Inst., 1963, M.F.A., 1965. Lectr. art Coll. of Notre Dame, Belmont, Calif., 1968-70, M. H. De Young Meml. Art Mus., San Francisco, 1968-70; prof. art St. Mary's Coll. of Calif., Moraga, 1969—, chmn. dept. art; exhbns. include: Seattle Art Mus., 1959, M. H. De Young Meml. Art Mus., 1969, Frye Art Mus., Seattle, 1957, San Francisco Mus. Modern Art, 1971, U. Calif.-Santa Cruz, 1977, Fine Arts Mus. of San Francisco, 1978, Oakland Art Mus., 1979, Rutgers U., Camden, N.J., 1979, Springfield (Mo.) Art Mus., 1980, Butler Inst. Am. Art, Youngstown, Ohio, 1981, Huntsville (Ala.) Mus. Art, 1982, Haggin Mus., Stockton, Calif., 1982, U. Hawaii-Hilo, 1983, Alaska State Mus., Juneau, 1981, Tex. State U., San Marcos, 1980, Crocker Art Mus., Sacramento, 1982, Hearst Art Gallery, 1986; represented in permanent collections: Richmond Art Ctr. (Calif.), U. Hawaii-Hilo, Las Vegas Art Mus. (Nev.), Hoyt Mus. and Inst. Fine Arts, New Castle, Pa., Frye Art Mus., San Francisco Art Inst., M. H. De Young Meml. Art Mus., Mills Coll., Oakland, Amerika-Haus, Munich, Contra Costa County Art Collection, Walnut Creek, Calif., Western Wash. U., Bellingham, Clemson U., S.C.; dir. Hearst Art Gallery, St. Mary's Coll.; vis. artist lectr. Academie Art Coll., San Francisco, 1971, grad. program Lone Mountain Coll., San Francisco, 1973-74. Coach Little League Baseball Team, Concord, Calif., 1982. Fulbright fellow, 1965-66; Frye Art Mus. traveling fellow, 1957; recipient Painting award All Calif. Ann., 1965; Nat. Watercolor award Chautauqua Inst., 1980; Seattle Art Assn. Painting award, 1957; San Francisco Art Inst. award, 1961; Otis Art Inst. award, 1959; Walnut Creek Civic Art Ctr. award, 1982, San Francisco Art Commn. award, 1985, Calif. State Fair Art award, 1985. Mem. Coll. Art Assn., Fine Arts Mus. of San Francisco, AAUP, San Francisco Art Inst. Alumni Assn. Home: 1020 Whistler Dr Suison City CA 94585 Office: Saint Marys Coll Dept Art Moraga CA 94575

SCHMAVONIAN, GERALD, association executive; b. Los Angeles, June 26, 1946; s. Sarkis Neshan and Berje-Lucia (der Hareutunyan) S. Student, Stanford U., 1964-67, U. Calif., Berkeley, 1967-70. Leader archaeol. excavation team Turkey, Guatemala, 1970-75; pub. City Mags., Visalia, 1975-80; pres. Am. Cultural Orgns., Los Angeles, 1980-82; dir. Ctr. for Study of Propaganda, Stanford, Calif., 1982—; chmn. Am. Nationalities Council, Stanford, 1983—. Host (PBS series) Ethnic Am. Mem. Calif. Scholarship Fedn. (life, pres. 1963), Nat. Forensic League (pres. 1963, degree of honor). Club: Statesmen's (founder). Home: 6821 Balsam Way Oakland CA 94611 Office: Stanford U Am Nationalities Council PO Box 2338 Stanford CA 94305

SCHMERLER, BARBARA ANN, social worker; b. Daytona Beach, Fla., Dec. 6, 1957; d. Bernie and Martha (Walsh) S. BS in Social Work summa cum laude, East Caroline U., 1978; MSW, U. Ark., Little Rock, 1982. Resident crisis counselor Real Crisis Intervention Inc., Greenville, N.C., 1976-78; youth counselor Peace Corps, Palau, Western Caroline Islands, 1979-81; clin. social worker Youth Home, Little Rock, 1981-82; therapist Yellowstone Boys and Girls Ranch, Billings, Mont., 1982-85, Cen. Wash. Comprehensive Mental Health, Yahima, 1985-86, Midwestern Colo. Mental Health Ctr., Montrose, 1986—. Bd. dirs. council for the prevention of adolescent pregnancy Planned Parenthood, Yahima, 1985-86. Mem. AAUW, Nat. Assn. Social Workers (cert.), Sierra Club (vice chmn. Mont. chpt. 1984-85), Phi Kappa Phi, Alpha Delta Mu. Club: Cascadians (Yahima). Avocations: hiking, back packing, cross-country skiing. Home: 540 N 5th St Montrose CO 81401 Office: Midwestern Colo Mental Health Ctr 447 N 3d St Montrose CO 81401

SCHMID, ANNE MARIE, medical writer, editor; b. Columbus, Ohio, Aug. 10; d. Casimir J. and Petrona M. (Klimas) Mattsewecz; student U. San Francisco, 1932-35; m. Frank H. Schmid, Aug. 19, 1936; children: Frank R., Monica, Gregory, Elena. Editor, UN Charter, San Francisco, 1945; editor dept. pediatrics U. Calif. Sch. Medicine, San Francisco, 1949-77, prin. editor, 1971-78; freelance book editor, 1971—, thesis rewriter, 1973—; mng. editor Jour. Parenteral and Enteral Nutrition, 1977-81. Bd. dirs. San Francisco Chamber Music Soc., 1966-81, pres., 1980-82; bd. dirs. Calif. Christians for Israel; bd. dirs. Henry Harris Library Fund, 1975-81; mem. health clin. adv. com. Telegraph Hill Neighborhood Assn., 1962-66, Dist. V Health and Mental Health Services, 1981-84; mem. maternal child and adolescent health local adv. bd. San Francisco Dept. Pub. Health, 1982-86. Fellow Am. Med. Writers Assn. (past pres. No. Calif. chpt., nat. dir. 1975-76); mem. AAAS, MLA. Republican. Roman Catholic. Club: San Francisco Press. Home and Office: 1820 16th Ave San Francisco CA 94122

SCHMID, HORST A., Canadian provincial administrator; b. Munich, Ger.; came to Can. 1952. Gold miner Yellowknife, 1952-56; Alta. agt. for Canola dealer in Europe; active in civic provincial and fed. polit. campaigns, 1960—; advisor preservation of ethnocultural heritage of Alta. to leader Progressive Conservative Assn. Alta., 1965-71; mem. Alta. Legis. Assembly from Edmonton-Avonmore, 1971-86, minister of culture, youth and recreation, 1971, minister govt. services and minister responsible for culture, 1975, minister of state for econ. devel. and internat. trade, 1979, minister internat. trade, 1982-86; commr. gen. trade and tourism Govt. Alta., 1986—; Alta. commr. for Spokane World's Fair. Recipient numerous awards from provincial, nat. and internat. cultural orgns., including Silver Ribbon award City of Edmonton, Spl. award Nat. Music Council for Encouragement to Music in Alta. and Can., Disting. Service award Alta. Motion Picture Industries Assn.; named Hon. Indian Chief Flying Eagle, Man of Yr., Commonwealth Games Found. Address: Commr Gen Trade and Tourism, 1800 Royal Trust Tower, Edmonton Centre, Edmonton, AB Canada T5J 2Z2

SCHMID, LOREN CLARK, research physicist; b. Ypsilanti, Mich., Feb. 1, 1931; s. Clark Randolph and Luella Marie (Renz) S.; m. Carol Nancy Culham, June 10, 1954; children: Joanne Marie, Eileen Leslie, Donald Clark. BA, U. Mich., 1953, MS, 1954, PhD, 1958. Physicist Argonne (Ill.) Nat. Lab., 1956-58; physicist, mgr. Gen. Electric Co., Richland, Wash., 1958-65; mgr. research and devel. Battelle N.W., Richland, 1965-73, dir. energy programs, 1973-79, mgr. planning, 1979-82, program mgr., 1982—; Far west regional coordinator Fed. Lab. Consortium for Tech. Transfer, 1983— Harold Metcalf award 1986; affiliate prof. U. Wash., Richland, 1973—. Author: Critical Assemblies and Reactor Research, 1971; contbr. articles to profl. jours. Bd. dirs. Retirement Home, Richland, 1968-83, TV Media Ministry, Richland. Fellow Am. Nuclear Soc.; mem. N.Y. Acad. Scis., Sigma Xi. Home: 2132 Hamilton Richland WA 99352 Office: Battelle NW PO Box 999 Richland WA 99352

SCHMIDLEN, MICHAEL EVAN, telecommunications and data specialist; b. Keyser, W.Va., Mar. 13, 1959; s. Virgil Lewis Jr. and Donna Lee (Sheetz) Franklin. Warehouseman Gen. Electric, Idaho Falls, Idaho, 1978-80; with inside sales Gen. Electric Co., Idaho Falls, Idaho, 1980-83; with inside sales Gen. Electric Co., Denver, 1983-84, with indsl. outside sales, 1984-86, telecommunications and data specialist, 1986—. Democrat. Presbyterian. Club: Civitan Singles (Idaho Falls) (bd. dirs. 1982). Avocations: bicycling, softball, basketball. Home: 3655 S Verbena #A102 Denver CO 80237 Office: Gen Electric Supply Co 425 Quivas St Denver CO 80204

SCHMIDT, BALDWIN STEPHEN, manufacturing company executive; b. Cin., Aug. 3, 1942; s. William Christian and Edna Marie (Baldwin) S.; m. Barbara Diana Niasby, Feb. 16, 1979. BS, U.S. Naval Acad., 1964; MA, Calif. State U., San Francisco, 1974. Lic. contractor, Calif. Commd. ensign USN, 1964; advanced through grades to lt. USN, Vietnam; resigned USN, 1969; mental health worker Ross (Calif.) Gen. Hosp., 1974-76; pres. Marin Energy Planning, San Rafael, Calif., 1976-81; sales mgr. Le Fiell Co., San Francisco, 1981-83, pres., 1984—; trustee local AFL-CIO Welfare Plan, Oakland, Calif. Marin County dir. Calif. for Nuclear Safety, San Francisco, 1974-76; mem. Dem. cen. com. Marin County, 1977-81; bd. dirs. Acad. World Studies, San Francisco, 1978-81, Golden Gate Energy Ctr., San Francisco, 1979-81, Marin Community Video, San Rafael, Calif., 1976-78. Mem. Calif. Metal Trades Assn. (bd. dirs. 1983—). Home: 375 Texas St San Francisco CA 94107 Office: Le Fiell Co 1469 Fairfax Ave San Francisco CA 94124

SCHMIDT, CAROL, writer; b. Dearborn, Mich., Sept. 10, 1942; d. Emmett R. and Lorraine G. Schmidt. B.A. Marygrove Coll., 1964; postgrad. U. N.C., 1964-65, UCLA extension, U. Soc. Calif. Reporter, city editor Mich. Chronicle Newspaper, Detroit, 1965-68; communications cons. Chrysler Corp., Detroit, 1968; reporter Macomb Daily Newspaper, Mt. Clemens, Mich., 1969-70; editor Brentwood Pub. Co., Los Angeles, 1971-78; communications dir. Research and Edn. Inst., Inc., Harbor-UCLA Med. Center, Torrance, Calif., 1978-84; owner Words & Numbers, Los Angeles, 1984—; free-lance writer, polit. speech writer, cons. in field; part-time instr. Wayne County Community Coll., Detroit, 1969-70. Pub. relations dir. Sunset Junction (Mich.) Neighborhood Alliance and Street Fairs; state del. Mich. Dem. Conv., 1968-69; mem. Los Angeles Women's Community Chorus; founder White Women Against Racism, Los Angeles, 1980-85. Recipient 1st prize Nat. Newspaper Pubs. Assn., 1969; named Outstanding Lesbian Journalist, Gay and Lesbian Press Assn., 1984. Mem. Am. Soc. Assn. Execs., Am. Hosp. Assn. (communications sect.), Soc. for Hosp. Pub. Relations, Nat. Mgmt. Assn. (v.p. Harbor-UCLA chpt.), Women in Communications, Am. Med. Writers Assn., Feminist Women's Writers Guild, CORE, NOW (pres. Beach Cities 1979-80, state bd. dirs. 1977-81). Office: 3932 W Sunset Blvd Los Angeles CA 90029

SCHMIDT, CHRISTINE RUNYON, social services director; b. Newark, June 2, 1941; d. Ernest Peter and Emma (Runyon) Schmidt. B.A., U. Colo., 1966; M.S.W., U. Mich., 1972. Caseworker, Huerfano County Dept. Social Services, Walsenburg, Colo., 1966-72, social service supr., 1972-73, dir., 1973—. Treas. Walsenburg Civic League, 1978—; treas. Huerfano County Sch. Bd., 1985—, mem., 1983—; pres. Huerfano County Hist. Soc., LaVeta, 1978—; chmn. Project Kids Identified for Devel. Screening, 1986—; past chmn. Huerfano County Human Service Council, sec., 1982—; bd. dirs. South Cen. Coop. Ednl. Services, 1983—. Mem. Colo. Dirs. County Dept. Social Services Assn. (sec. 1974-76), Huerfano C. of C. Avocations: drawing, painting, reading, sports. Office: Huerfano County Dept Social Services 121 W 6th St Walsenburg CO 81089

SCHMIDT, CYRIL JAMES, librarian; b. Flint, Mich., June 27, 1939; s. Cyril August and Elizabeth Josephine S.; m. Martha Joe Meadows, May 22, 1965; children—Susan, Emily. B.A., Catholic U. Am., 1962; M.S. in L.S, Columbia U., 1963; Ph.D., Fla. State U., 1974. Asst. bus. and industry dept. Flint Pub. Library, 1963-65; reference librarian Gen. Motors Inst., Flint, 1965; asso. librarian S.W. Tex. State U., San Marcos, 1965-67; head undergrad. libraries, asst. prof. Ohio State U., 1967-70; dir. libraries SUNY, Albany, 1972-79; also mem. faculty SUNY (Sch. Library and Info. Sci.); univ. librarian Brown U., Providence, 1979-81; exec. v.p. Research Libraries Group, Stanford, Calif., 1981—; cons. in field. Fellow Library Services Act, 1962-63, Higher Edn. Act, 1970-72. Author papers in field. Mem. ALA, ACLU, Pi Sigma Alpha, Beta Phi Mu. Home: 69 Peter Coutts Circle Stanford CA 94305 Office: Research Libraries Group Jordan Quadrangle Stanford CA 94305

SCHMIDT, DIANE GAFFNEY, real estate broker, developer, employee benefits consultant; b. Laramie, Wyo., July 12, 1952; d. Harold Max and Margaret Adella (Vincent) Gaffney; A.A., Pasadena (Calif.) City Coll., 1972; B.S. in Mgmt., San Diego State U., 1977. Fin. asst. Cabrillo Med. Center, San Diego, 1974-76, personnel mgr., 1976-78, personnel services adminstr., 1978-80; asst. adminstr., profl. services, 1980-81; owner, pres. Health Care Profls., 1981-82; employee benefits cons. Johnson & Higgins of Calif., 1983-84, ptnr., 1985—; pres. Sharing Vol. Tutoring Program, Inc., also bd. dirs. Bd. dirs. Pres.'s Council San Diego. Active Nat. Kidney Found.; pres. Jr. League San Francisco. Mem. Am. Hosp. Assn., Calif. Hosp. Assn., Globe Guilders. Office: 2200 Union Bank Bldg 525 B St San Diego CA 92101

SCHMIDT, ECKART WALTER, chemist; b. Essen, Germany, Apr. 16, 1935; s. Wilhelm Heinrich and Margot Anna (Kmitta) S.; came to U.S., 1966, naturalized, 1974; m. Hildegard C. Breuninger, Sept. 22, 1962; children—Wolfram G., Andreas U. B.S., U. Marburg (Germany), 1958; M.S., U. Tuebingen (Germany), 1962, Ph.D., 1964. Research chemist Deutsche Versuchsanstalt fuer Luft-und Raumfahrt, Stuttgart, W. Ger., 1964-66; mgr. chem. research Rocket Research Co., Redmond, Wash., 1966-76, sr. staff scientist, 1976—. Assoc. fellow AIAA. Author: Raketentreibstoffe (Rocket Propellants), 1968; Hydrazine and Its Derivatives, 1984; contbr. articles to profl. jours. Home: 55 151st Pl NE Bellevue WA 98007-5019 Office: Rocket Research Co 11441 Willows Rd NE Redmond WA 98052-1012

SCHMIDT, ERIC EMERSON, computer company executive; b. Washington, Apr. 27, 1955; s. Wilson Emerson and Eleanor Schmidt; m. Wendy Susan Boyle, June 28, 1980; children: Virginia Alison, Sophie Elizabeth. BSEE, Princeton U., 1976; MS in Engring., U. Calif., Berkeley, 1979, PhD in Computer Sci., 1982. Research intern Xerox Parc, Palo Alto, Calif., 1979-80, mem. research staff, 1980-83; software mgr. Sun Microsystems, Mountain View, Calif., 1983-84, software dir., 1984-85, v.p., gen. mgr. software products div., 1985—. Patentee in field. Mem. IEEE, Assn. Computing Machinery, Sigma Xi. Office: Sun Microsystems 2550 Garcia Ave Mountain View CA 94043

SCHMIDT, GAYLE VIRGINIA, health science services administrator, tax consultant; b. Cranston, R.I., Sept. 7, 1936; d. Edwin E. and Virginia Louise (Walker) Whipple; m. Walter Henry Schmidt, May 30, 1962; children—Walter III, Stephen Stanley, Kymberlei Gayle. B.S. with honors in Health Sci. Adminstrn., U. Phoenix, 1981, M.B.A., 1983. Accredited record technician. Owner, tax preparer H&R Block Franchise, Benson, Ariz., 1973—; med. and nursing coordinator, Benson Hosp., Benson, Ariz., 1974-79; dir. med. records, 1979-82; supr. data collection Med. Info. Services Ariz. Health Sci. Ctr., Tucson, 1982-83; asst. dir. med. info. services Ariz. Health Sci. Ctr., Tucson, 1983-84; tchr. tax preparation, Tucson, 1983-84; assoc. dir. med. info. services, 1984—; researcher med. record studies. Recipient Extension award Lioness Internat., 1981. Mem. Am. Med. Record Assn. Republican. Episcopalian. Clubs: Sunset Belles Lioness (Huachuca City, Ariz.), Eyeopeners Toastmasters, Lioness (dist. program chmn.), Ariz. Med. Records Assn. (treas).

SCHMIDT, GRANT JACOB, Canadian government official; b. Balcarres, Sask., Can., July 28, 1948; s. George and Helen (Banerd) S.; m. Sheron L. Schmidt, Aug. 28, 1971; children: Kurt, Luke. LLB, U. Sask., 1971. Bar: Sask. 1973. Ptnr. Schmidt & Graff, Melville, Sask., 1973—; mem. Sask. Legis. Assembly, 1982—; dep. chief of fin. Govt. of Sask., 1983-85, minister of labour, 1985-86, minister of social services, 1986—, chmn. legis. rev. com. Mem. Commonwealth Parliamentary Assn., Can. Bar Assn., Law Soc. Sask. Conservative. Lutheran. Lodge: Lions. Avocations: golf, curling, boating. Home: 16 Vanier Dr, Melville Can S0A 2P0 Office: Legis Bldg, Regina, SK Canada S0A 2PO

SCHMIDT, HARVEY MARTIN, economic forecaster, consultant; b. Chgo., Sept. 15, 1925; s. Joseph David and Dorothy Schmidt; m. Barbara Bebe Bloom, Nov. 25, 1961; children—Ellen Louise, Jay Stephen, Gregg Arthur. Student U. So. Calif., 1943; B.A. magna cum laude, Woodbury U., 1947. Assoc. prof. bus. Woodbury U., 1947-48; pvt. practice acctg., Los Angeles, 1948-80; cons. mgmt., taxes and fins., Los Angeles, 1965-82; cons. fins. and econ. forecaster, Pacific Palisades, 1982—; pres. Harvey Schmidt Mgmt. Inc., 1983— pres. Med-Plan Operators, 1969—; lectr. in field. Served with USCG, 1943-44. Life Master, U.S. Contract Bridge League, 1960—. Mem. Calif. Bd. Accountancy, Internat. Platform Assn. Clubs: Exchange (pres. local chpt. 1953-56); Sportsmen of South of UCLA. Contbr. articles to profl. jours.

SCHMIDT, JEAN MARIE, microbiology educator; b. Waterloo, Iowa, June 5, 1938; d. John Frederick and Opal Marie (Lowe) S. BA, U. Iowa, 1959, MS, 1961; PhD, U. Calif., Berkeley, 1965. NIH postdoctoral fellow U. Edinburgh, Scotland, 1965-66; asst. prof. Ariz. State U., Tempe, 1966-71, assoc. prof., 1971-79, prof. microbiology, 1979—, asst. dir. biology Cancer Research Inst., 1982—. Contbr. chpts. to books, articles to jours. NSF grantee, 1981. Fellow AAAS; mem. Am. Soc. Microbiology (div. chmn. 1979-80), Soc. Gen. Microbiology, Phi Beta Kappa, Sigma Xi. Democrat. Methodist. Avocations: backpacking, photography, piano. Office: Ariz State U Dept Microbiology 350 Life Sci Bldg Tempe AZ 85287

SCHMIDT, JOHN LEONARD, software company executive; b. Oakland, Calif., Oct. 21, 1936; s. Guy Wilbert and Hazel English (Bowles) S.; m. Edna Margaret Wilbur, June 8, 1958 (div. Nov. 1976); children: Hazel Ann Lopes, Elizabeth Lynn; m. Suzanne Jane Williams, Nov. 24, 1984. Messenger Crocker Bank, San Francisco, 1956-59; programmer Morris Plan, San Francisco, 1960-66, First Savs., Oakland, Calif., 1966-67; systems programmer Oakland Bank of Commerce, 1967; sect. mgr., data processing tng. Safeway Stores, Oakland, 1967-85; pres. Just Logical Solutions, Antioch, Calif., 1985—. Democrat. Lodge: Moose. Home and Office: 2704 Iris Ct Antioch CA 94509

SCHMIDT, JUSTIN ORVEL, entomologist, researcher; b. Rhinelander, Wis., Mar. 23, 1947; s. Orvel A. and Jane A. (Groh) S.; m. Deborah K. Wragg, Mar. 14, 1972 (dec. Jan. 1980); m. Patricia J. Figuli, May 8, 1981; 1 child, Krista. BS, Pa. State U., 1969; MSc, U. B.C., Vancouver, Can., 1972; PhD, U. Ga., 1977. Editor and compiler films for biol. scis. Pa. State Audio Visual Service, University Park, 1972-73; research and teaching asst. U. Ga., Athens, 1975-77, postdoctoral, 1979-80; research and teaching asst. U. N.B., Can., 1978-79; research entomologist Carl Hayden Bee Research Ctr., Tucson, 1980—. Mem. Internat. Soc. Toxinology, AAAS, Animal Behavior Soc., Internat. Soc. Chem. Ecology, Internat. Union Study of Social Insects, Am. Entomol. Soc., Sigma Xi. Avocation: natural history. Home: 1961 W Brichta Tucson AZ 85745 Office: Carl Hayden Bee Research Ctr 2000 E Allen Rd Tucson AZ 85719

SCHMIDT, KATHRYN JEAN, audiologist; b. Rawlins, Wyo., Mar. 27, 1961; s. Leonard S. and Margery J. (Polzkill) S. BS, U. Wyo., 1983, MS, 1985. Audiology correspondant U. Wyo., Laramie, 1982-84; audiologist Fitzsimons Army Med. Ctr., Aurora, Colo., 1984-85, Profl. Hearing Service, Gillette, Wyo., 1985—. Mem. Am. Speech Lang. Hearing Assn., Wyo. Speech and Hearing Assn., Women on the Grow, Jaycees, Gillette C. of C. Home: PO Box 9062 Gillette WY 82716 Office: Profl Hearing Services 407 S Medical Arts Ct Suite C Gillette WY 82716

SCHMIDT, KLAUS DIETER, univ. adminstr., marketing and management educator; b. Eisenach, Germany, May 8, 1930; came to U.S., 1949, naturalized, 1952; s. Kurt Heinrich and Luise (Kruger) S.; B.A. in Econs., U. Calif., Berkeley, 1951; M.B.A., Stanford U., 1953; Ph.D. in Bus. Adminstrn., Golden Gate U., 1978; m. Lynda Hollister Wheelwright, June 29, 1950; children: Karen, Claudia. Buyer, jr. mdse. mgr. Broadway Hale, 1952-54; sales mgr. Ames Harris Neville Co., 1954-56, ops. mgr., 1956-57; gen. mgr. Boise Cascade Corp., 1957-60; pres., chmn. bd. Kimball-Schmidt Inc., San Rafael, Calif., 1960-73, chmn. subs. Kalwall Pacific, 1962-67, chmn. subs. AFGOA Corp., 1966-69; asst. prof. mgmt. and mktg. San Francisco State U., 1970-75, assoc. prof. mgmt., 1975-80, prof. mgmt. and mktg., 1980-85, chmn. dept. mgmt. and mktg., 1979—, assoc. dean sch. bus., 1985—; dir. Ctr. for World Bus., 1976—, dir. U.S.-Japan Inst., 1981—, editor-in-chief Sch. Bus. Jours., 1980—; U.S. negotiator on Afghanistan issue, 1980—; mem. Dept. Commerce Dist. Export Council, 1982—; research cons. SRI Internat. Republican. Club: University (San Francisco). Author 20-booklet series Doing Business In ..., 1978-80. Home: PO Box 28 North Brooklin ME 04661 Office: 1600 Holloway San San Francisco CA 94132

SCHMIDT, LOUIS BERNARD, JR., industrial distribution executive; b. Ames, Iowa, Sept. 19, 1922; s. Louis Bernard and Georgia Perle (Wilson) S.; m. Jeanette Hook, June 2, 1956. B.S., Iowa State U., 1944; post grad., 1948. Salesman, Agrl. Indsl., Pub. Works Distributive Co., Tucson, 1952-62, v.p. sales, Phoenix, 1962-72; mgr. engine, energy div. Ariz. Engine and Pump Co., div. I.S. Industries, Inc. Phoenix, 1972-85; stationary gas engine use advisor. Active Phoenix Republican Forum; mem. Ariz.-Mexico Commn. . Mem. Am. Water Works Assn., Ariz. Water and Pollution Control Assn., Soc. Mayflower Descs. Ariz. (state treas., nat. asst. gen.), SAR, Ariz. Acad. Pub. Affairs; Gamma Sigma Delta. Unitarian. Clubs: Sky Harbor, Phoenix Press. Lodges: Kiwanis, Elks. Home: 313 W Lewis Ave Phoenix AZ 85003

SCHMIDT, NAOMI ELLEN, research scientist; b. Phila., Dec. 8, 1952; d. George Louis and Eleanor (Schnell) S.; m. Daniel Patrick Singleton, Sept. 6, 1972 (div. Mar. 1980); m. James Bryan Ross, July 6, 1982. BS, N.Mex. State U., 1975, MS in Biology, 1978, postgrad., 1978—. Grad. reserach asst. N.Mex. State U., Las Cruces, 1973-77, research asst. Soil, Plant and Water Testing Lab., 1977-81, research specialist Crop and Soil Sci. Dept., 1981-83, research specialist N.Mex. Solar Energy Inst., 1983-84; tech. writer Lockheed Corp., Las Cruces, 1984-85, scientist, 1985—. Mem. Am. Statis. Assn., Sigma Xi, Beta Beta Beta. Democrat. Lutheran. Avocations: gardening, computing. Home: 805 Cielo Circle Las Cruces NM 88005 Office: Lockheed Corp Box MM Las Cruces NM 88004

SCHMIDT, RAINER SIEGFRIED, naval officer, dermatologist; b. Zeulenroda, Germany, Mar. 2, 1932; came to U.S., 1955, naturalized, 1960; s. Willy Otto Schmidt and Margarete Aline (Rensky) Schmidt Mueller; m. Patricia Agnes O'Hara, Dec. 29, 1962; children—Rene Steffen, Kevin Michael. A.B., Stanford U., 1956, M.D., 1962. Commd. officer U.S. Navy, 1962, advanced through ranks to capt., 1976 intern Naval Hosp., Oakland, Calif., 1962-63; flight surgeon Naval Air Sta., Oak Harbor, Wash., 1963-66; resident in dermatology Naval Hosp., San Diego, 1966-69; staff Naval Hosp., Oakland, 1969-76, head dermatology, 1976—; assoc. clin. prof. U. Calif.-San Francisco, 1979—. Contbr. articles to profl. jours. Fellow Am. Acad. Dermatology, Assn-Mil. Surgeons U.S., Internat. Soc. Tropical Dermatology, Sierra Club. Republican. Lutheran. Office: Naval Hosp 8750 Mountain Blvd Oakland CA 94627

SCHMIDT, ROBERT MILTON, physician, scientist; b. Milw., May 7, 1944; s. Milton W. and Edith J. (Martinek) S.; children Eric Whitney, Edward Huntington. A.B., Northwestern U., 1966; M.D., Columbia U., 1970; M.P.H., Harvard U., 1975; Ph.D., Emory U., 1982. Diplomate: Am. Bd. Preventive Medicine. Intern Univ. Hosp. U. Calif.-San Diego, 1970-71; medicine residency tng. Ctrs. Disease Control, Atlanta, 1971-74; commd. med. officer USPHS, 1971; advanced through grades to comdr. 1973; dir. hematology div. Nat. Ctr. for Disease Control, Atlanta, 1971-78, spl. asst. to dir., 1978-79, inactive res., 1979—; clin. asst. prof. pediatrics Tufts U. Med. Sch., 1976—; clin. asst. prof. medicine Emory U. Med. Sch., 1976-81, clin. asst. prof. community health, 1976—; clin. assoc. prof. humanities in medicine Morehouse Med. Sch., 1977-79; pres., med. dir. Internat. Health Resource Ctr. of Hawaii, Lihue, Kauai, 1979-82; cons. physician dept. medicine Pacific Presbyn. Med. Ctr., San Francisco, 1983—; dir. Ctr. Preventive Medicine and Health Research, 1983—, dir. Health Watch, 1983—; sr. scientist Inst. Epidemiology and Behavioral Medicine, Inst. Cancer Research, Pacific Presbyterian Med. Ctr., San Francisco, 1983—; prof. hematology and dir. health professions program Gerontology Research Council San Francisco State U., 1983—; cons. WHO, FDA, NIH, Govt. of China, Mayo Clinic; Mem. numerous sci. and profl. adv. bds., panels, coms. Mem. editorial bd.: Am. Jour. Clin. Pathology, 1976-82; author: books and manuals, including Hematology Laboratory Series, 4 vols., 1979-86, CRC Handbook Series in Clinical Laboratory Science, 1976—; contbr.: articles to sci. jours. Alumni regent Columbia U. Coll. Physicians and Surgeons, 1980—. NSF and USPHS fellow, 1964-70; Mayo Found. scholar, 1969; Virginia Kneeland Frantz scholar Columbia U., 1969-70; recipient Microbiology, Pharmacology, Urology awards Columbia U., 1970; Borden Research award in medicine, Upjohn Achievement award Columbia U., 1970; Commendation medal USPHS, 1973; Leadership Recognition award San Francisco State U., 1984, 85, 86, 87. Fellow Am. Coll. Preventive Medicine, ACP, Am. Soc. Clin. Pathology, Internat. Soc. Hematology; mem. AAAS, Am. Pub. Health Assn., Internat. Commn. for Standardization in Hematology, Am. Soc. Hematology, Internat. Soc. on Thrombosis and Hemostasis, Acad. Clin. Lab. Physicians and Scientists, Assn. Tchrs. Preventive Medicine, AMA, Am. Soc. Microbiology, Gerontol. Soc. Am., Am. Assn on Aging, Am. Geriatrics Soc. Club: Army and Navy (Washington). Home: 25 Hinckley Walk San Francisco CA 94111 Office: Pacific Presbyn Med Ctr PO Box 7999 San Francisco CA 94120 also: San Francisco State U 1600 Holloway Ave San Francisco CA 94132

SCHMIDT, ROBERT RUDOLPH, management consultant; b. Binghamton, N.Y., Nov. 14, 1931; s. Wilhelm Rudolph and Harriett Arlene (Stone) S.; m. Joan Elaine Burdsall; children: Kathryn Anne, William Robert, Linda Anne (dec.). BSBA, Ind. U., 1958; postgrad., W. Va. U., 1976-77. Cert. safety, health fire protection engr., radiation safety officer, indsl. hygienist, bus. cost analyst. With Ind. Ins. Services, Indpls., 1958-64, field engr., 1964-68; corp. safety and health dir. Meth. Hosp. of Ind., Indpls., 1968-72; corp. internat. safety health mgr. Senco Products Inc., Newtown, Ohio, 1972-74; safety and loss prevention mgr., safety health engring. mgr. Olin Chem. Co., Brandenburg, Ky., 1974-76; corp. fluor engring. Occidental Petroleum's Chem. Group, Tacoma, 1976-78; safety health and bus. mgmt. cons. Gig Harbor, Wash., 1984—; indsl. hygienist Wash. DSHS, King County, 1985—; nat. hosp. health care NSC sect. chmn., Chgo., 1971-72; mem. at large NSC Indsl. Conf., Chgo., 1972-78; initiator Tideflats Indsl. Mut. Aid Plan, Tacoma, 1979-81, chmn. 1982-84. Contbr. articles to profl. jours. Mem. Mayor's City Disaster Edn. Planning Com., Indpls., 1971, Mayor's Fire Protection Improvement Planning Com., Cin., 1973; producer tv safety health programs, Cin., 1973-74. Recipient $10 thousand accident repeater research and devel. grant Med. Research Dept. Meth. Hosp. of Ind., 1970-71. Mem. Am. Soc. Safety Engrs. (profl., Puget Sound chpt. pres. elect 1986-87), Vets. of Safety, World Safety Orgn. (cert.), Crum Forsters Engrs. Profl. Liability Plan. Republican. Mem. Christian Ch. Club: Welcome Club of Gig Harbor. Avocations: international travel, golf, photography. Home and Office: 3923 101st St Ct NW Gig Harbor WA 98335

SCHMIDT, RODNEY ALBERT, computer science educator; b. Bronxville, N.Y., Dec. 10, 1945; s. Rodney Albert and Janet Garner (Allen) S.; m. Judith Lynn Kayser, Mar. 17, 1977 (div. Oct. 1986); 1 child, Melanie Kayser. BSEE, MIT, 1966; MSEE, Stanford U., 1968, PhDEE, 1971. Mgr. computer sci. Electromagnetic Systems Labs, Sunnyvale, 1971-76; systems engr., asst. prof. U. Denver, 1976-78; mgr. software engring. Denelcor, Inc., Denver, 1978-82; asst. prof. U. Colo., Denver, 1982—, assoc. chmn. computer sci., 1986—; cons. ESL Inc., Sunnyvale, 1976-78, Robot Def. Systems, Thornton, Colo., 1983-84, Syntronics Venture, Toronto, 1985. Contbr. articles to profl. jours. Named Outstanding Researcher in Elec. Engring and Computer Sci., U. Colo., 1986. Mem. Soc. Photo-optical Instrumentation Engrs., Computer Soc. of IEEE, Tau Beta Pi (faculty advisor 1986—). Office: U Colo 1100 14th St Denver CO 80202

SCHMIDT, THEODORE ANDREW, librarian; b. Hammond, Ind., Feb. 6, 1949; s. Harry Theodore and Mildred Martha (Farbak) S.; m. Martha Jane Schuldt, July 14, 1973; 1 child, Rachel Elizabeth. B.A., Purdue U., 1971; M.A., U. Denver, 1974. English instr. Addison Trail High Sch. (Ill.), 1971-73; media ctr. dir. Park R-3 Sch. Dist., Estes Park, Colo., 1974-77; asst. library dir. Loveland Pub. Library (Colo.), 1977-80; library dir. Estes Park Library, 1980-85, Missoula (Mont.) County Library, 1985—; bd. dirs. Tamarack Fedn. Libraries. Photographer, producer: slide-audio tape Yesterday Was Not Today, 1979 (CEMA award 1980), others. Pub. edn. chmn. Am. Cancer Soc., Estes Park, 1980-82. Colo. Humanities Program grantee, 1982, 83. Mem. ALA, Colo. Library Assn. (chmn. pub. library div. 1983-84), Mont. Library Assn., Mountain Plains Library Assn. Office: Missoula County Library 301 E Main St Missoula MT 59802

SCHMIDT, WALLACE ALAN, corporate communications executive; b. Loma Linda, Calif., June 4, 1948; s. Elmer Alonzo and B. Irene (Wallace) S.; m. Donna Lynn Rich, June 28, 1970; children: Allison Marie, Emily Alizabeth. BS, Pacific Union Coll., 1970. TV prodn. mgr. audiovisual service Loma Linda Univ. Med. Ctr., 1974-78, dir. audiovisual service, 1978—. Home: 12910 Sixteenth St Redlands CA 92373 Office: Loma Linda U Med Ctr Loma Linda CA 92354

SCHMIEDER, CARL, jeweler; b. Phoenix, Apr. 27, 1938; s. Otto and Ruby Mable (Harkey) S.; m. Carole Ann Roberts, June 13, 1969; children: Gail, Susan, Nancy, Amy. Student Bradley Horological Sch., Peoria, Ill., 1959-61; B.A., Pomona Coll., 1961; Owner timepiece repair service, Peoria, 1959-61; clock repairman Otto Schmieder & Son, Phoenix, 1961-65, v.p., 1965-70, pres., 1970—, chief exec. officer, 1970—. Mem. subcom. Leap Commn., 1966; area rep. Pomona Coll., 1972-76. Cert. jeweler; cert. gemologist, gemologist appraiser; recipient Design award Diamonds Internat., 1965, Cultured Pearl Design award, 1967, 68, Diamonds for Christmas award, 1970; winner Am. Diamond Jewelry Competition, 1973; bd. dirs. Lincoln Hosp., 1983—, Ariz. Mus., 1984—; delegate White House Conf. Small Bus., 1986; col. Confederate Air Force. Mem. Am. Gem. Soc. (dir. 1973-86, nat. chmn. nomenclature com. 1975-77, chmn. membership com. 1977-81, officer 1981-86), Ariz. Jewelers Assn. (Man of Yr. 1974), Jewelers Security Alliance (dir. 1974-78), Jewelers Vigilance Com. (dir. 1981—), Jewelry Industry Council (dir. 1982—), 24 Karat Club So. Calif., Exptl. Aircraft Assn., Deer Valley (Ariz.) Airport Tenants Assn. (dir. 1980—, pres. 1983—), Ariz. C. of C. (bd. dirs. 1985—), Small Bus. Council (bd. dirs. 1985—, chmn. 1987, del. to White House Conf., 1986). Republican. Methodist. Lodges: Kiwanis (pres. Valley of the Sun chpt. 1975-76), Friends of Iberia. Home: 537 W Kaler St Phoenix AZ 85021 Office: Park Central Phoenix AZ 85013

SCHMIEDER, ROBERT WILLIAM, physicist, marine scientist; b. Phoenix, July 10, 1941; s. Otto S. and Ruby Maybel (Harkey) S.; children: Robyn, Russell Otto, Robert Randall. AB, Occidental Coll., 1963; BS, Calif. Inst. Tech., 1963; MA, Columbia U., 1965, PhD, 1968. Mem. research staff Lawrence Berkeley (Calif.) Nat. Lab., 1969-72; mem. tech. staff Sandia Nat. Labs., Livermore, Calif., 1972—; instr. U. Calif., Berkeley, 1971-72; exp. leader Cordell Bank Exps., Walnut Creek, Calif., 1977—; co-host EBIS Workshop, 1985; mem. ion storage rings com. Nat. Acad. Sci., 1986. Editor Def. Research Rev., 1986—; contbr. numerous articles to profl. jours. Co-chmn. Coastline Initiative, No. Calif., 1974; judge Bay Area Regional Sci. Fair, 1979—; mem. Channel Islands Kelp Forest Project, 1985. Fellow Explorers Club; mem. Am. Phys. Soc., Am. Geophys. Union, Am. Inst. Biol. Scis., Western Soc. Naturalists, Sierra Club (chmn. regional group 1974). Avocations: camping, travel, piano. Home: 4295 Walnut Blvd Walnut Creek CA 94596 Office: Sandia Nat Labs Livermore CA 94550

SCHMITT, CARVETH JOSEPH RODNEY, office supplies manufacturing official; b. Manitowoc, Wis., Sept. 10, 1934; s. Clarence C. and Thelma J. (White) S.; m. Carolyn Sue Jarrett, May 14, 1965. diploma in bus. adminstrn. and acctg. Skadron Coll. Bus., 1959; A.A. in Bus. Mgmt., San Bernardino Valley Coll., 1962; B.S. in Bus. Adminstrn., U. Riverside-Calif., 1970; M.A. in Edn.-Manpower Adminstrn., U. Redlands, 1975; B.S. in Liberal Studies, SUNY-Albany, 1977; B.A. in Social Sci., Edison State Coll., Trenton, 1978; cert. in Human Services, U. Calif. Extension, Riverside, 1977, postgrad., 1977-80. Registered rep. Ernest F. Boruski, Jr., N.Y.C., 1956-61; acct. Barnum & Flagg Co., San Bernardino, Calif., 1959-70; registered rep., ins. agt. (part-time) Inland Am. Securities, Inc., San Bernardino, 1966-70; registered rep. (part-time) Parker-Jackson & Co., San Bernardino, 1970-73, LeBarron Securities, Inc., 1973-74. credit mgr. Stationers Corp., San Bernardino, 1970-77, office mgr., credit mgr., 1977-83; internal auditor Stockwell & Binney Office Products Ctrs., San Bernardino, 1983-85, corp. credit mgr., 1985—. Served with USAF, 1954-58. cert. tchr., community coll. counselor and personnel worker, Calif. Mem. Nat. Geog. Soc., Nat. Rifle Assn. (life), Nevada Mining Assn., Colo. Mining Assn., N.W. Mining Assn., Am. Philatelic Soc., Nat. Travel Club, Edison State Coll. Alumni Assn., U. Redlands Fellows, Friends of Library Assn. U. Redlands, Valley Prospectors (life), SUNY Regents Alumni Assn., U. Redlands Alumni Assn., Am. Legion, Am. Assn. Ret. Persons, Gold Prospectors Assn. Am. (life mem.). Republican. Rosicrucian. Clubs: Fontana Tour, Hiking, Badminton, Bowling, Arrowhead Stamp, M & M Tour, Rosicrucian (San Jose). Lodge: Masons. Home: 538 N Pampas Ave Rialto CA 92376 Office: 420 SE St PO Box 5129 San Bernardino CA 92412

SCHMITT, CHARLES ERNEST, government administrator; b. Salt Lake City, Apr. 20, 1931; S. Edward P. and Helen (Gehrmann) S.; m. Grace Allen, Sept. 20, 1958; children: Sandra Kragthorpe, Karen Daderko. BS, U. Utah, 1955, MS, 1958. Cert. disability examiner. Dir. St. Marks Hosp. Rehab. Ctr., Salt Lake City, 1958-62; disability claims examiner Office Rehab. Service, Salt Lake City, 1964-66, rehab. counselor, 1966-67; facilities specialist Utah div. Rehab. Services, Salt Lake City, 1967-70, coordinator, 1970-79; adminstr. Utah Disability Determination Services, Salt Lake City, 1979—; vocat. and rehab. cons. 1964—; vocat. expert Soc. Security Bur. Hearing and Appeals, 1962-79. Mem. Admissions panel United Way of Great Salt Lake Area, 1986, Utah State Health Facility council, 1970-81; mem. and pres. bd. Work Activity Ctr. for Handicapped, Salt Lake City, 1973-80. Served to sgt. USAF, 1951-52. Recipient Cert. Appreciation Div. Rehab. Services, Utah, 1981. Mem. Nat. Assn. Disability Examiners., Sigma Alpha Epsilon. Lutheran. Avocations: golf, skiing. Home: 1237 E 3545 South Salt Lake City UT 84106 Office: Disability Determination Services 250 E 5th St S Salt Lake City UT 84111

SCHMITT, RICHARD GEORGE, computer company executive, industrial engineer; b. St. Cloud, Minn., June 18, 1948; s. George William and Viola Theresa (Mechenich) S.; m. Ligia Marie Pereira, Aug. 29, 1970; children: Christopher Michael, Scott Andrew. B in Indsl. Engring. with honors, Gen. Motors Inst., 1971. Indsl. engr. Gen. Motors, Fremont, Calif., 1966-78; sr. indsl. engr. Gen. Motors, Oklahoma City, 1978-80; indsl. engring. mgr. Shugart Assocs., Sunnyvale, Calif., 1980-81; mfg. tech. mgr. Magnex Corp., San Jose, Calif., 1981-82, prodn. mgr., 1982-83; facilities mgr. Apple Computer, Fremont, 1983, indsl. engring. mgr., 1984-85, robotics mngr., 1985-86, peripherals pack engring. mgr., 1987—. Transp. chmn. Mt. Diablo council Boy Scouts Am., 1984; chief YMCA Indian Guides, San Jose, 1977-83; asst. scout master Boy Scouts Am., Mt. Hamilton Dist., 1986—. Mem. Am. Assn. Indsl. Engrs. (sr.), Soc. Mfg. Engrs. (sr.). Democrat. Roman Catholic. Lodge: Lions (scholar 1966). Home: 1963 Wave Pl San Jose CA 95133 Office: Apple Computer Mfg Div 48105 Warm Springs Blvd Fremont CA 95439

SCHMITZ, ELLEN MARIE, marketing professional; b. St. Louis, May 5, 1956; d. Richard Louis and Jerry Heloise (Farrar) S. BS, U. N.H., 1978; MBA, NYU, 1983. Sr. research dir. Loews Corp., N.Y.C., 1979, from asst. to assoc. mgr., 1979, product mgr., 1979-83; mktg. mgr. Heublein div. R.J. Reynolds Corp., Farmington, Conn., 1983-84; sr. mktg. mgr. Del Monte div. RJR Nabisco Corp., San Francisco, 1984-86, group mktg. mgr., 1986—. Mem. Am. Mktg. Assn. Home: 90 Alhambra #205 San Francisco CA 94123 Office: RJR Nabisco Del Monte Div 1 Market Plaza Box 3575 San Francisco CA 94119

SCHNACK, HAROLD CLIFFORD, lawyer; b. Honolulu, Sept. 27, 1918; s. Ferdinand J. H. and Mary (Pearson) S.; m. Gayle Hemingway Jepson, Mar. 22, 1947; children: Jerrald Jay, Georgina Schnack Hankinson, Roberta Schnack Poulin, Michael Clifford. BA, Stanford, 1940, LLB, 1947. Bar: Hawaii, 1947. Dep. prosecutor City and County Honolulu, 1947-48; gen. practice with father F. Schnack, 1948-60; pvt. practice, Honolulu, 1960-86; pres. Harcliff Corp., 1961—, Instant Printers, Inc., 1971-81, Koa Corp., 1964—, Nutmeg Corp., 1963—, Global Answer System, Inc., 1972-78. Pres. Goodwill Industries of Honolulu, 1971-72. Mem. ABA, Hawaii Bar Assn., Phi Alpha Delta, Alpha Sigma Phi. Clubs: Outrigger Canoe, Pacific. Lodge: Masons. Home: 4261 Panini Loop Honolulu HI 96816 Office: 220 S King St Suite 1085 Central Pacific Plaza PO Box 3077 Honolulu HI 96802

SCHNAPP, ROGER HERBERT, lawyer; b. N.Y.C., Mar. 17, 1946; s. Michael Jay and Beatrice Joan (Becker) S.; m. Candice Jacqueline Larson, Sept. 15, 1979. BS, Cornell U., 1966; JD, Harvard U., 1969; grad. Pub. Utility Mgmt. Program, U. Mich., 1978. Bar: N.Y. 1970, Calif. 1982, U.S. Dist. Ct. (so. dist.) N.Y. 1975, U.S. Dist. Ct. (no. dist.) Calif. 1980, U.S. Dist. Ct. (cen. dist.) Calif. 1982, U.S. Dist. Ct. (ea. dist.) Calif. 1984), U.S. Ct. Appeals (2d cir.) 1970, U.S. Ct. Appeals (4th and 6th cirs.) 1976, U.S. Ct. Appeals (7th cir.) 1977, U.S. Ct. Appeals (8th cir.) 1980, U.S. Supreme Ct. 1974. Atty. CAB, Washington, 1969-70; labor atty. Western Electric Co., N.Y.C., 1970-71; mgr. employee relations Am. Airlines, N.Y.C., 1971-74; labor counsel Am. Electric Power Service Corp., N.Y.C., 1974-78, sr. labor counsel, 1978-80; indsl. relations counsel Trans World Airlines, N.Y.C., 1980-81; sr. assoc. Parker, Milliken, Clark & O'Hara, Los Angeles, 1981-82; ptnr. Rutan & Tucker, Costa Mesa, Calif., 1983-84; ptnr. Memel, Jacobs, Pierno, Gersh & Ellsworth, Newport Beach, Calif., 1985-86; ptnr. Memel, Jacobs & Ellsworth, Newport Beach, 1986-87; sole practice, Newport Beach, 1987—; cons. collective bargaining Am. Arbitration Assn.; commentator labor relations Fin. News Network; lectr. Calif. Western Law Sch., Calif. State U.-Fullerton, Calif. State Conf. Small Bus., Indsl. League Orange County; lectr. collective bargaining Pace U., N.Y.C. N.E. regional coordinator Pressler for Pres., 1979-80. Mem. ABA (R.R. and airline labor law com., internat. labor law com.), Internat. Bar Assn., N.Y. State Bar Assn., Calif. Bar Assn., Conf. R.R. and Airline Labor Lawyers, Newport Harbor Area C. of C., Orange County C. of C. Republican. Jewish. Clubs: Balboa Bay, Lincoln of Orange County, Center. Lodge: Masons. Author: Arbitration Issues for the 1980s, 1981; A Look at Three Companies, 1982; editor-in-chief Industrial and Labor Relations Forum, 1964-66; contbr. articles to profl. publs. Office: PO Box 9049 Newport Beach CA 92658

SCHNAPP, RUSSELL LAWRENCE, computer scientist; b. N.Y.C., June 3, 1955; s. Sol and Irene Schnapp; m. Brigid Hom-Schnapp, July 9, 1978. BA, Queen's Coll., 1977; MS in Engring., Princeton U., 1978. Research scientist Burroughs Corp., San Diego, 1978-84; sr. systems programmer Penultimate Systems, San Diego, 1984—. Author: Macintosh Graphics in Modula-2, 1986; columnist MACazine. Mem. Computer Soc. of IEEE, Assn. for Computing Machinery, Macintosh User Group, Phi Beta Kappa. Office: Schnapp Software Cons PO Box 261091 San Diego CA 92126

SCHNATHORST, WILLIAM CHARLES, plant pathologist; b. Fort Dodge, Iowa, May 8, 1929; s. William Theodore and Elizabeth (Nelson) S.; m. Rosemarie A. Meyer, Dec. 29, 1951; children—Diana Lynn, William John, Douglas Alan. B.S., U. Wyo., 1952, M.S., 1953; Ph.D., U. Calif.-Davis, 1957. Teaching asst. botany U. Wyo., Laramie, 1952-53; research asst. plant pathology U. Calif.-Davis, 1953-56, lectr., 1965-85, plant pathologist, 1985—; research plant pathologist Agrl. Research Service, U.S. Dept. Agr., Davis, 1956-85. Contbr. articles to profl. jours. Mem. Am. Phytopathol. Soc. (assoc. editor 1978-81), Internat. Soc. Plant Pathology, Mycol. Soc. Am., Bot. Soc. Am., Am. Inst. of Biol. Scis., Colo.-Wyo. Acad. Sci., Sigma Xi, Alpha Zeta, Phi Kappa Phi. Methodist. Club: Fly Fishers of Davis (conservation chmn. 1974—). Home: 647 Cleveland St Davis CA 95616 Office: U Calif-Davis Dept Plant Pathology Davis CA 95616

SCHNEIDER, CALVIN, physician; b. N.Y.C., Oct. 23, 1924; s. Harry and Bertha (Green) S.; A.B., U. So. Calif., 1951, M.D., 1955; J.D., LaVerne (Calif.) Coll., 1973; m. Elizabeth Gayle Thomas, Dec. 27, 1967. Intern Los Angeles County Gen. Hosp., 1955-56, staff physician, 1956-57; practice medicine West Covina, Calif., 1957—; staff Inter Community Hosp., Covina, Calif. Cons. physician Charter Oak Found., Covina, 1960—. Served with USNR, 1943-47. Mem. AMA, Calif., Los Angeles County med. assns. Republican. Lutheran. Home: West Covina CA Home: Laguna Beach CA Office: 224 W College Covina CA 91723

SCHNEIDER, DELWIN BYRON, minister, educator; b. Oshkosh, Wis., May 14, 1926; m. Katherine Louise Gesch; children: Kathi Del, Mark, Michael, Lisa. BA, Concordia Coll., 1948; BS, Concordia Sem., 1951; MA, Pepperdine U., 1950; postgrad., U. Chgo., 1954-56, Japanese Lang. Ctr., Tokyo, 1956-58; PhD, Rikkyo U., Tokyo, 1961; postgrad., Harvard U., 1961-62. Ordained to ministry Luth. Ch., 1951. Pastor St. Paul Luth. Ch., Oak Lawn, Ill., 1951-56; dir. Japan Luth. Hour, Tokyo, 1956-61; chaplain, lectr. Boston U., 1962-65; assoc. prof. Gustavus Adolphus Coll., St. Peter, Minn., 1965-70; asst. dean acad. affairs, coordinator internat. programs Gustavus Adolphus Coll., St. Peter, 1968-70; edn. TV lectr. World Religions KTCA-TV, St. Paul, 1967; dir. The Inst. of E. Asian Studies, 1967-70; prof. U. Minn., Mpls., 1968-69; coordinator U. San Diego Ecumenical Ctr. World Religions, 1972—; lectr. Ctr. Theol. Study, Pacific Luth. Theol. Sem., Berkeley, Calif., 1983. Author: Konkokyo: A Japanese Religion, 1962, Historical Perspectives in Christianity's Relation to Other Religions, 1983; contbr. chpts. to books. Mem. Assn. Asian Studies, Am. Acad. Religion. Clubs: Harvard (San Diego), San Diego Yacht. Office: U San Diego Dept Religious Studies San Diego CA 92110

SCHNEIDER, DOROTHY MARYJOHANNA, psychotherapist; b. New Britain, Conn., Apr. 29, 1934; d. Josef Matthew and Meri Catherine (Stifel) Kratka, m. Warren Andrew Schneider, Apr. 26, 1975. BS in Nursing, Columbia U., 1960; MSW, Fordham U., 1969; EdD, U. San Francisco, 1983. Instr. pub. health nursing U. Conn., Storrs, 1963-64; pub. health nurse Jesuit Med. Mission Bd., Tanzania, East Africa, 1965-67; chief psychiat. social worker Knickerbocker Hosp., N.Y.C., 1969-74; coordinator social services Rockefeller U. Hosp., N.Y.C., 1974-77; asst. prof. Calif. State U., Sacramento, 1977—, assoc. prof., 1985—; bd. dirs. Nat. Assn. Soc. Work Refferal Service, San Francisco, 1984-86. Bd. dirs. Health Systems Adv. Com., San Francisco, 1978; interim pres. Cath. Charities Bd., San Francisco, 1985, bd. dirs., 1983-85. NIMH grantee, 1967-69. Mem. Internat. Assn. Profl. Counselors and Psychotherapists (diplomate psychotherapy), Nat. Assn. Social Workers, Am. Psychol. Assn., Register for Clin. Social Workers of Nat. Assn. Social Workers, Kappa Delta Pi. Democrat. Roman Catholic. Avocations: hiking, watercolors, flying. Office: 1010 B St Suite 325 San Rafael CA 94912

SCHNEIDER, HAROLD, research engineer, mathematician; b. Cin., Apr. 8, 1930; s. Kalman and Ethyl (Oscherwitz) S.; m. Joan Shirley Brown; children: Lynn Dee Groden, Steven Kalman. BS in Physics, U. Cin., 1951, MS, 1954, PhD in Physics, 1956. Aero. research scientist NASA Lewis Research Ctr., Cleve., 1951-61; mem. staff MIT Lincoln Lab., Lexington, Mass., 1962-72; sr. systems analyst Dynamics Research Corp., Wilmington, Mass., 1972-78; prin. engring. mem. RCA, Moorestown, N.J., 1978; staff engr. Lockheed Missiles & Space Co., Sunnyvale, Calif., 1978—. Contbr. articles to profl. jours.; inventor in field. Mem. AIAA, Soc. Indsl. and Applied Math., Sigma Xi. Club: Toastmasters (Wilmington) (treas. 1977-78). Avocations: classical music, astronomy reading, checkers. Home: 855 Clara Dr Palo Alto CA 94303 Office: Lockheed Missiles and Space Co Bldg 154 Dept 85-72 Missile Systems Div Sunnyvale CA 94086

SCHNEIDER, HERBERT ANTON, electrical engineer; b. Vienna, Austria, Aug. 7, 1922; came to U.S., 1940; m. Doris Marie Paterson; children: Thomas Dana, Linda Renee. BSEE, MSEE, MIT, 1949. Mem. tech. staff Bell Telephone Labs., Murray Hill, N.J., 1948-69; disting. mem. tech. staff AT&T Info. Systems Labs., Denver, 1969—. Author: Frequency Synthesis, 1963, 1967; patentee in telecommunications and computers. Leader, treas. Am. Youth Hostels Inc., NYC, 1953-69, also bd. dirs.; patrol leader Boy Scouts Am., Austria, 1935-37, N.J., 1965-69; nat. telecommunications advisor, bd. dirs. Nat. Ski Patrol System, Denver, 1953-85. Served with U.S. Army, 1943-46, PTO, ETO. Recipient various grants. Mem. IEEE, AAAS, Sigma Xi, Tau Beta Pi, Eta Kappa Nu. Avocations: skiing, swimming, gardening. Home: 6980 Hunter Pl Boulder CO 80301 Office: AT&T Info Systems 31F47 11900 N Pecos St Denver CO 80234

SCHNEIDER, JOHN FREDRICK, accountant; b. Berkeley, Calif., Apr. 7, 1945; s. George Mathias and Virginia (Watson) S.; m. Roberta Elizabeth Kennedy, Sept. 21, 1970; children: Janet Marie, Julie Ann, George Fredrick Mathias, James Wilhelm. BBA, Calif. State Poly. U., 1971. CPA, Calif. Staff auditor Arthur Anderson & Co., Los Angeles, 1971-73; staff acct. Keith V. Lapp Acctg. Corp., Santa Maria, Calif., 1973-75; fin. v.p. Boston's Pet Supply Inc., Buellton, Calif., 1975-76; fin. officer City of Grover City, Calif., 1977-79; pres. DePauw & Schneider Inc., Los Osos, Calif., 1979—; mgmt., fin. cons. Mem. Nat. Assn. Accts., Calif. Soc. Accts., Calif. Soc. CPA's, Am. Inst. CPA's. Republican. Office: DePauw & Schneider 2115 10th St Suite B Los Osos CA 93402

SCHNEIDER, LAWRENCE PAUL, mayor; b. Regina, Sask., Can., Mar. 23, 1938; s. Paul Martin and Helen Caroline (Exner) S.; cert. in bus. adminstrn. U. Regina; m. Shirley Anne Wolfe, July 20, 1960; children—Janet, Joanne, Jon. Engring. technician Can. Dept. Agr., 1957-69; mgmt. cons., 1970-79; now mayor City of Regina. Mem. Royal Lifesaving Soc. (award of Merit). Roman Catholic. Clubs: Optimist (pres. 1970), Rotary, Toastmasters (pres. 1972), Regina Flying (Regina). *

SCHNEIDER, WALTER ELI, dental anesthesiologist; b. Chgo., Mar. 14, 1948; s. Sidney Aaron and Helen Eleanor (Neiburger) S.; m. Jacqueline Sandra Dunitz, July 3, 1972; children—Amy, Stephanie. Student Roosevelt U., Chgo., 1966-67, Mich. State U., 1967-68, 71; B.S., U. Ill.-Chgo., 1973, D.D.S., 1975. Staff dentist Wis. Pub. Health Dept., Madison, 1975; clin. instr. U. Colo. Sch. Dentistry, Denver, 1976-78; gen. practice dentistry, Denver, 1976-79; resident in anesthesiology Med. Coll. Pa. Hosp., Phila., 1979-80; pvt. practice dental anesthesiology, Denver, 1980—; mem. staff Porter Meml. Hosp./Swedish Med. Ctr.; dental cons. to 11 nursing homes and long term care facilities, Met. Denver area, 1976-78, lectr., cons. dental anesthesiology, Denver, 1981—. Appointed to Colo. State Dental Bd. Sunset Task Force, 1985. Served with USMC, 1969-70, Vietnam. Fellow Am. Dental Soc. Anesthesiology; mem. Colo. Dental Soc. Anesthesiology, (pres. 1984-85), ADA, Colo. Dental Assn., Am. Soc. Clin. Hypnosis, Met. Denver Dental Soc.

SCHNEIDERMAN, BARRY ALAN, lawyer; b. Seattle, June 28, 1933; s. Harry and Margaret S.; m. Judith Arron, July 1, 1968; children: Paul L., Leah. BA, U. Wash., 1955, JD, 1957. Bar: Wash. 1957. Dep. King County Pros. Atty.'s Office, Seattle, 1959-61; ptnr. Burns, Schneiderman & Finkle, Seattle, 1961-67; pres. Burns, Schneiderman & Davis, Seattle, 1977—; asst. to gen. counsel U.S. Army (IMA), 1979-84; commdr. 6th JAG Mil. Law Ctr., 1974-78. Trustee Temple DeHirsch Sinai, Seattle; pres. bd. dirs. Caroline Kline Galland Home Aged, Seattle. Served as officer AUS, 1957-59; col. JAGC res., ret. Mem. ABA, Fed. Bar Assn., Wash. Bar Assn., Seattle-King County Bar Assn., B'Nai B'Rith (pres. 1967-68). Clubs: Wash. Athletic, College (Seattle), Rainier (Seattle), Seattle Tennis. Lodge: Shriners. Home: 5135 NE Latimer Pl Seattle WA 98105 Office: 2200 4th Ave Seattle WA 98121

SCHNEIR, MICHAEL LEWIS, research biochemistry educator; b. Chgo., Nov. 17, 1937; s. Murry and Sylvia (Greenberg) S.; m. Nanette Diane Brizman, June 27, 1965; children: Adam, Aaron. BS, U. Ill., 1959; MS, U. Ill., Chgo., 1962, PhD, 1965. Postdoctorate fellow Tufts Med. Sch., Boston, 1965-66, U. Pitts. Sch. Medicine, 1966-67; asst. prof. U. So. Calif., Los Angeles, 1967-70, assoc. prof., 1970-86, prof., 1986—, chmn. dept. biochemistry, 1970—. Contbr. articles to profl. jours. Commr. Pacific Palisades (Calif.) Baseball Assn., 1983. Nat. Inst. Dental Research grantee, 1967—. Mem. AAAS, Am. Chem. Soc., Internat. Assn. Dental Research (pres. So. Calif. sect. 1974-77), Am. Soc. Biol. Chemists, Sigma Xi. Avocation: teaching a systematic approach to sci. writing. Office: U So Calif ACB 440 MC 1482 Los Angeles CA 90089

SCHNEITER, GEORGE MALAN, golfer, development company executive; b. Ogden, Utah, Aug. 12, 1931; s. George Henery and Bernice Slade (Malan) S.; B.Banking and Fin., U. Utah, 1955; m. JoAnn Deakin, Jan. 19, 1954; children—George, Gary, Dan, Steve, Elizabeth Ann, Michael. With 5th Army Championship Golf Team U.S. Army, 1955-56; assoc. golf pro Hidden Valley Golf Club, Salt Lake City, 1957; golf pro Lake Hills Golf Club, Billings, Mont., 1957-61, sec., 1957-61, pres., 1964—; owner Schneiter Enterprises, Sandy, Utah, 1964—; developer Schneiter's golf course and subdiv., 1975; player PGA tour 1961-75; player PGA sr. tour 1981—. Served with U.S. Army, 1956. Winner Salt Lake City Parks Tournament, Vernal Brigham Payson Open, Yuma Open, Ariz.; named U.S. Army Ft. Carson Post Golf Champ, 1955-56. Mem. Profl. Golfers Assn. Am. Mormon. Office: 8968 S 1300 E Sandy UT 84070

SCHNELL, ROGER THOMAS, military officer; b. Wabasha, Minn., Dec. 11, 1936; s. Donald William and Eva Louise (Barton) S.; m. Barbara Ann McDonald, Dec. 18, 1959 (div. Mar. 1968); children: Thomas Allen, Scott Douglas. A in Mil. Sci., Command and Gen. Staff Coll., 1975. Commd. 2d lt. Alaska N.G., 1959, advanced through grades to col., 1975; shop supt. Alaska N.G., Anchorage, 1965-71, personnel mgr., 1972-74, chief of staff, 1974-87; electrician Alaska R.R., Anchorage, 1955-61, elec. foreman, 1962-64. Mem. Fed. Profl. Labor Relations Execs. (sec. 1974-75), Alaska N.G. Officers Assn. (pres. 1977-79, bd. dirs. 1974-76, 80-82, chmn. membership com. 1980-81, achievement award 1980), Am. Legion, Amvets. Republican. Methodist. Lodge: Elks. Avocations: bowling, photography. Home: 2751 Pelican Ct Anchorage AK 99515 Office: Hdqrs Alaska NG 3601 C St Anchorage AK 99503

SCHNELL, RUSSELL CLIFFORD, atmospheric scientist, researcher; b. Castor, Alta., Can., Dec. 12, 1944; s. Henry Emmanuel and Anna (Traudt) S.; m. Suan Neo Tan, May 25, 1974; children: Alicia, Ryan. BSc with distinction, U. Alta. (Can.), Edmonton, 1967; BSc, Meml. U., St. John's, Nfld., Can., 1968; MSc, U. Wyo., 1971, PhD, 1974. Research scientist U. Wyo., Laramie, 1971-74, Nat. Ctr. Atmospheric Research and NOAA, Boulder, Colo., 1974-76; dir. Mt. Kenya study World Meteorol. Orgn. div. UN, Nairobi, Kenya, 1976-78; research scientist U. Colo., Boulder, 1979-82, dir. Arctic Gas and Aerosol Sampling Program, 1982—, fellow Coop. Inst. Research in Environ. Scis., 1985—; mem. aerobiology com. Nat. Acad. Sci., 1976-79; cons. UN, Geneva, 1977-80, Shell Devel., Modesto, Calif., 1978-79; mem. adv. bd. Frost Tech., Norwalk, Conn., 1983-85; bd. dirs. TRI-S Inc., Louisville, Colo. Editor Geophys. Research Letters, Arctic Haze Edit., 1983-84; discovered bacteria ice nuclei, 1969; patentee in field; contbr. articles to profl. jours. Bd. dirs. Boulder Valley Christian Ch., 1978—; chmn. Boulder Council Internat. Visitors, 1983-85. Rotary Internat. fellow, 1968-69. Mem. Am. Geophys. Union, AAAS, Am. Meteorol. Soc. (cert. cons. meteorologist), Internat. Assn. Aerobiology, Soc. Cryobiology, Sigma Xi, Sigma Tau. Avocations: travel, real estate investing, public speaking, flying. Home: 4865 Lee Circle Boulder CO 80303 Office: U Colo Coop Inst Research Environ Scis Campus Box 449 Boulder CO 80309

SCHNIEWIND, ARNO PETER, forestry educator; b. Cologne, Germany, June 1, 1929; came to U.S., 1949; s. Friedrich H.M. and Liselotte (Plehn) S.; m. Susan E. Freeman, Aug. 30, 1957 (div. 1974); children: Melissa M., Sandra C., Eric T.; m. Toshiko Miyabe, Dec. 27, 1978. BS, U. Mich., 1953, M Wood Tech., 1955, PhD, 1959. Asst. specialist U. Calif., Berkeley, 1956-59, asst. wood technologist, 1959-64, assoc. prof. forestry, 1964-66, prof., 1966—. Subject editor Ency. Material Sci. and Eng., 1986; contbr. numerous articles to profls. jours. Fellow Internat. Acad. Wood. Sci.; mem. Soc. Wood Sci. and Tech. (pres. 1973-74), Forest Products Research Soc. (sect. chmn. 1967-68), Am. Inst. Conservation of Hist. and Artistic Works. Office: U Calif Forest Products Lab 1301 S 46th St Richmond CA 94804

SCHNITZER, ARLENE DIRECTOR, art dealer; b. Salem, Oreg., Jan. 10, 1929; d. Simon M. and Helen (Holtzman) Director; m. Harold J. Schnitzer, Sept. 11, 1949; 1 son, Jordan. Student U. Wash., 1947-48. Founder, pres. Fountain Gallery of Art, Portland, Oreg., 1961-86; v.p. Harsh Investment Corp., 1951—. Bd. dirs. Oreg. Symphony Assn., Oreg. Coast Aquarium, 1987; v.p. Oreg. Symphony; bd. dirs., exec. com. U.S. Dist. Ct. Hist. Soc.; mem. exec. com., bd. dirs. Artquake; mem. adv. bd. New Beginnings; mem. exec com., trustee Reed Coll., Portland; nat. trustee Nat. Symphony Orch., Washington, 1985—; bd. dirs., exec. com. Oreg. Symphony Assn. Recipient Aubrey Watzek award Lewis and Clark Coll., 1981; Pioneer award U. Oreg., 1985; Met. Arts Commn. award, 1985; White Rose award March of Dimes, 1987; Gov's. award for Arts, 1987; honored by Portland Art Assn., 1979; Woman of Achievment award YWCA, 1987. Clubs: University, Multnomah Athletic (Portland), Portland Golf. Office: Harsh Investment Corp 2112 NW Davis Portland OR 97210

SCHNORR, JANET KAY, psychology educator; b. Clintonville, Wis., Dec. 16, 1944; d. Arthur Albert and Louise Martha (Krueger) S. BS, U. Wis., Oshkosh, 1967; MS, Iowa State U., 1969, PhD, 1972. Assoc. prof. psychology No. Ariz. U., Flagstaff, 1971—; research assoc. U. Ariz., Tucson, 1985-86; cons. Lawrence Livermore Nat. Lab., Berkeley, Calif., 1978, Ariz. Energy Data Systems, Phoenix, 1982—. Author: Biomass Feasibility, 1980; contbr. articles to profl. jours. Delegate Ariz. State Dem. Conv., Phoenix, 1984; mem. Ariz. Solar Energy Commn., 1981—; bd. dirs. Ariz. Community Action Assn., Phoenix, 1977-79, Northland Crises Nursery, Flagstaff, 1982—. Named Outstanding Young Woman of Am., 1976-78, Outstanding Faculty Woman, No. Ariz. U., 1976, Alumni Honoris, Clintonville Sr. High Sch., 1984. Mem. Am. Psychol. Assn., Rocky Mountain Psychol. Assn., Man-Environment Systems, Environ. Design Research Assocs. (reviewer jour. 1982—), Sigma Xi, Kappa Delta Pi (pres. 1966-67). Avocations: fly fishing, camping, art, nature. Home: 1100 N Hemlock Way Flagstaff AZ 86001 Office: No Ariz U Psychology Dept Flagstaff AZ 86011

SCHNYDER, LINDSAY ANNE, broadcasting company executive; b. Bloomington, Ill., July 2, 1952; d. Robert John Schnyder and Constance (Sherbert) Chaplin. Grad. high sch., Huntington Beach, Calif. Gen. mgr. KZZX Radio, Albuquerque, 1978-80; account exec. KRDO TV, Colorado Springs, Colo., 1980-81, KVOR Radio, Colorado Springs, 1981; mktg. dir. Columbus (Ohio) Zoo, 1981-83; pres., gen. mgr. KOTE-KKZZ Radio, Lancaster, Calif., 1983—; v.p., gen. mgr. Programming Consultants, Inc., Albuquerque; bd. dirs. Antelope Valley Health Found., Lancaster. Bd. dirs. C. of C., Lancaster. Named Exec. of Yr., KZZX Radio, 1979, KOTE-KKZZ, 1985. Avocations: skiing, horses. Home: 2300 Artesanos Albuquerque NM 87107 Office: Programming Consultants Inc 2000 Randolph Rd SE Albuquerque NM 87106

SCHOAF, THOMAS LEE, corporate executive, lawyer; b. Lynwood, Calif., May 8, 1951; s. Thomas LeRoy and Betty Jane (Petroli) S.; m. Shirley Ann Simeri, May 22, 1971; children—Thomas, Matthew, Kimberley. B.S. cum laude, Notre Dame, 1972; J.D. summa cum laude, 1976. Bar: Ariz., 1976, Ind., 1978. Market specialist Gen. Electric, Fort Wayne, Ind., 1972-73; lawyer Streich, Lang et al, Phoenix, 1976-78, Thornburgh, McGill et al, South Bend, Ind., 1978-80; pres. Adapto, Inc., Litchfield Park, Ariz., 1980—, also dir., Socor, Inc., 1980—, also dir.; bus., legal cons. Litchfield Park, Ariz., 1980—. Editor: Tax Planning for Agriculture, 1977. Contbr. articles to prof. jours. Pres. Litchfield Park Youth Assn., 1982-84; bd. dirs. Phoenix Little Theatre, 1981-83; mem. governing bd. Litchfield Elementary. Recipient Farabaugh award Notre Dame Law Sch., 1976; NSF research grantee, 1971. Mem. ABA, Nat. Student Register, Tau Beta Pi, Alpha Sigma Mu (pres. 1972). Roman Catholic. Office: Adapto Inc PO Box 280 Litchfield Park AZ 85340

SCHOEN, LINDA ALLEN, marketing director; b. Lynch, Ky., July 9, 1936; d. Wert Harvey and Mary Mabel (Ramsey) Allen; m. Stanly M. Schoen, Apr. 8, 1972. B.A., Northwestern U., 1958. Research technician G.D. Searle & Co., Chgo., 1958-60; research assoc., asst. sec. com. cutaneous health and cosmetics AMA, Chgo., 1960-75; dir. mktg. services Neutrogena Corp., Los Angeles, 1975—. Mem. AAAS, Soc. Cosmetic Chemists, The Fashion Group. Episcopalian. Club: Opera Assn. (Northwestern U. Alumni). Editor The Look You Like column Today's Health mag., 1962-74; The AMA Book of Skin and Hair Care, 1976; contbr. articles to Harper's Bazaar, Vogue, Redbook, Beauty Handbook. Home: 2608 Martha Ave Torrance CA 90501 Office: Neutrogena Corp 5755 W 96th St Los Angeles CA 90045

SCHOENBECK, ERIC LEE, aerospace engineer; b. Gary, Ind., June 21, 1939; s. Edwin Frederick and Florence Wilhelmina (Goehring) S.; m. Mary Lynne Reisenweber, Nov. 28, 1964; children: Stephen, Sara. BA in Psychology, U. Colo., 1962; postgrad., U. Calif., Berkeley, 1973-74; MBA in Mgmt., Golden Gate U., 1980. Intelligence officer USAF and NATO, France and England, 1964-67; intelligence research analyst CIA, Washington, 1967-70; sr. mem. tech. staff ESL, Inc., Sunnyvale, Calif., 1970-74; human factors engr. Boeing Aerospace, Seattle, 1974-76; engring. specialist Ford Aerospace, Palo Alto, Calif., 1976-78; advanced systems staff engr. Lockheed Missiles & Space, Sunnyvale, 1978—; cons. Directory Handicapped Scientists, AAAS. Author: (with others) Boeing's Design Handbook for Imagery Interpretation Equipment; contbr. numerous articles on remote sensing to profl. jours. Vol. parent Lyceum Program for Gifted Children, San Jose, 1982. Served to capt. USAF, 1962-67. Mem. Am. Soc. Photogrammetry, Air Force Assn., Soc. Photo-optical Instrument Engrs. Republican. Lutheran. Avocations: swimming, reading, astronomy. Office: Lockheed Missiles & Space Co 1111 Lockheed Way Sunnyvale CA 94086

SCHOENBORN, ROGER LEE, minister; b. Oregon City, Oreg., June 10, 1948; s. Arthur Frank and Doris Naomi (Brown) S.; m. Ili Bieler, Aug. 16, 1980; children: Helena Christine, Priscila Belle, David Lee. BS, Oreg. STate U., 1970; MDiv., Western Evang. Sem., 1982. Ordained to ministry Evang. Ch., 1982. Missionary tchr. OMS Internat., Londrina, Paraná, Brazil, 1973-77, missionary camp developer, 1978-82; sr. pastor Yakima (Wash.) Evang. Ch., 1982—; mem. com. missions and ch. extension Pacific Conf. Evang. Ch., Milwaukie, Oreg., 1982-86. Chmn. Yakima Christian Sch., 1982-86; mem. com. ministerial relations Pacific Evang. Ch. Conf., 1986—, ways and means, 1985-86, trustee, 1985—. Named one of Outstanding Young Men of Am., 1981, 82. Mem. Yakima Assn. Evangelicals (sec. 1987—). Republican. Clubs: Associação Recreativa Esportiva Londrinese (Londrina Parana, Brazil), San Marino (Guaratuba, Paraná, Brazil). Avocations: stamp collecting, reading, gardening, travelling. Office: Yakima Evang Ch 301 S 7th Ave Yakima WA 98902

SCHOENFELD, ALAN HENRY, education and mathematics educator; b. N.Y.C., July 9, 1947; s. Neil Howard and Natalie (Weinberg) S.; m. Jean Snitzer, June 14, 1970. BS in Math., Queens Coll., 1968; MS in Math., Stanford U., 1969, PhD in Math., 1973. Lectr. U. Calif., Davis, 1973-75; from asst. prof. to assoc. prof. Hamilton Coll., Clinton, N.Y., 1978-81, U. Rochester, N.Y., 1981-84; lectr. U. Calif., Berkeley, 1975-78, assoc. prof. edn., math., 1985-86, prof., 1986—; chmn. Grad. Group in Sci. and Math. Edn., U. Calif., Berkeley, 1985—; chief organizer IV Internat. Conf. Math. Edn., 1984. Author: Mathematical Problem Solving, 1985, Mathematical Association of AmericaNotes #1, Problem Solving, 1983. Grantee NSF, 1979, 85, Sloan Found., 1984, Spencer Found., 1983—. Mem. Math. Assn. Am. (chmn. teaching undergrad. math. com. 1982—, mem. editorial bd. Jour. Research Math. 1982-85, chmn. 1984-85), Am. Ednl. Research Assn. (exec. com. Spec. Int. Group Math Edn. 1984-86), Cognitive Sci. Soc., Nat. Council Tchrs. of Math., Spl. Interest Group for Research in Math. Edn. Avocations: food, wine. Home: 830 Colusa Ave Berkeley CA 94707 Office: U Calif Dept Edn Berkeley CA 94720

SCHOENFELD, BARRY HIRSCH, advertising agency executive; b. Yonkers, N.Y., Feb. 25, 1954; s. David and Madalynne Hermine (Geller) S. BS, Cornell U., 1976. Acct. exec. Keenan & McLaughlin, N.Y.C., 1976-77; sr. acct. exec. N.W. Ayer Inc., N.Y.C., 1977-82; acct. supr. LHS&B Inc., N.Y.C., 1982-84; v.p., group acct. supr. Dancer Fitzgerald Sample Inc., Torrance, Calif., 1984—. Active Cornell U. Secondary Schs. Com., N.Y.C., 1976-84, Los Angeles, 1984—. Mem. Am. Mgmt. Assn., Los Angeles Bus. and Profl. Assn., Los Angeles Advt. and Communications Network (chmn. 1985—), Los Angeles Ad Club. Democrat. Avocations: tennis, photography. Office: Dancer Fitzgerald Sample Inc 3501 Sepulveda Blvd Torrance CA 90505

SCHOENFELD, EUGENE LEONARD, physician, healthcare administrator; b. N.Y.C., Mar. 17, 1935; s. Benjamin and Frieda (Fried) S.; 1 child, Benjamin. AB, U. Calif., Berkeley, 1955; MD, U. Miami, 1961; MPH, Yale U., 1964. Pvt. practice medicine Santa Cruz, Calif., 1982-86; med. dir. Steinbeck Treatment Ctr., Salinas, Calif., 1983—. Author: Dear Dr. Hip Pocrates, 1969, Natural Food and Unnatural Acts, 1974, Jealousy, 1979, Health Guide, 1981; mem. adv. bd. Jour. Psychoactive Drugs, 1984—. Mem. Am. Soc. Treatment Alcoholism and other Drug Dependencies, Calif. Med. Assn. Libertarian. Avocations: sailing, writing. Office: 249 Center Ave Aptos CA 95003

SCHOENFELD, LAWRENCE JON, jewelery manufacturing company executive, consultant; b. Los Angeles, Nov. 30, 1945; s. Donald and Trudy (Libizer) S.; Carol Sue Gard, Aug. 24, 1969. AA, Los Angeles Valley Coll., Van Nuys, Calif., 1963; BBA, Wichita State U., 1969, MSBA, 1970. Cert. tchr. (life), Calif. Asst. treas. Advance Mortgage, Los Angeles, 1970-72; v.p. ops. Unigem Internat., Los Angeles, 1972—; bd. dirs. The Telcom Group, Uniorr Corp., Execucentre-West, Schoenfeld & Co.; co-developer Bay-Osos Mini Storage Co., San Luis Obispo, Calif. Mem. Improvement Commn., Hermosa Beach., Calif. 1976-78. Served to maj. US Army Med. Service Corps, 1970-72, with res. 1972—. Mem. Town Hall, Wichita State U. Alumni Assn. (Nat. dist. rep.). Jewish. Office: Unigem Internat 448 S Hill 12th Floor Los Angeles CA 90266

SCHOENFELD, ROBERT GEORGE, biochemist, laboratory director and owner; b. Topeka, Nov. 29, 1926; m. Roberta Dallas Gray, Mar. 30, 1946; children: David, Cynthia, Kevin, Karen, Robin. BS, U. Okla., 1948; MS in Med. Sci., U. Okla., Oklahoma City, 1956, PhD in Biochemistry, 1958. Diplomate Am. Bd. Clin. Chemistry. Asst. chief chemist Nilson & Co., Oklahoma City, 1948-51; research asst. U. Okla. Sch. Medicine, Oklahoma City, 1955-58; biochemist, chief dept. VA Hosp., Albuquerque, 1958-63; prin. Schoenfeld Clin. Lab., Albuquerque, 1961—. Served to 1st lt. USAD, 1951-55. Fellow Assn. Official Racing Chemists (pres. 1974-77), Am. Assn. Clin. Chemists (cert. toxicol. chemistry 1972, chmn. Rocky Mountain sect. 1986), S.W. Assn. Toxicologists; mem. Acad. Forensic Scis. Avocations: radio controlled airplanes, amateur radio, skiing, sailing. Office: Schoenfeld Clin Lab 8100 Constitution Pl NE Albuquerque NM 87110

SCHOENIG, STEVEN HENRY, manufacturing company executive; b. Valley City, N.D., Jan. 5, 1955; s. Henry Nelson and Ella Elizabeth (Clark) S. Student,

Colo. State U., 1973-76. Head teller and teller supr. Home Fed. Savs., Ft. Collins, Colo., 1976-77, asst. br. mgr., 1978-81; purchasing agt., controller Ultimate Support Systems, Ft. Collins, 1981-82, sec.-treas., 1981-85, controller, office mgr., 1982-84, v.p. info. systems, 1984—; sec.-treas. Inst. Fin. Edn., Ft. Collins, 1980-81, Bridge Internat., Ft. Collins, 1983—, also bd. dirs. Minister music Ft. Collins Bible Chapel, 1975—, also deacon, 1979-85, tchr., 1979—, elder, 1985—. Named Pres. scholar Colo. State U., 1975. Mem. Phi Kappa Phi, Phi Alpha Theta. Avocations: travel, photography, skiing, hiking, reading. Home: 2172 Adobe Dr Fort Collins CO 80525 Office: Ultimate Support Systems Inc 2506 Zurich Dr PO Box 470 Fort Collins CO 80522-4700

SCHOEPFLE, GORDON MARK, anthropological researcher, policy analyst; b. St. Louis, Feb. 25, 1946; s. Gordon Marcus and Esther Gertrude (Schoultheis) S.; m. Elizabeth Marie Metz, July 12, 1946; children: Carla, Marie. BA, U. Calif., Berkeley, 1968; MA, Northwestern U., 1972, PhD, 1977. Planner, researcher Div. of Edn., Navajo Indian Tribe, 1974-77; dir. research and devel. Navajo Community Coll., Shiprock, N.Mex., 1977-81, Dine Bi'Olta Assn., Farmington, N.Mex., 1981-86; dir. planning and legislation Dept. of Health, Navajo Indian Tribe, 1986—; cons. Navajo Tribe, Window Rock, Ariz., 1985-86, Jacobs Engring., Albuquerque, 1985, U.S. Nat. Park Service, Santa Fe, 1985—, WESTAT Inc., Rockville, Md., 1985. Co-author: Systematic Field Work, 1986. Grantee U.S. Office Edn., Washington, 1978, EPA, Washington, 1979, NSF, Washington, 1981. Mem. AAAS, Am. Anthrop. Assn., Nat. Assn. Practice of Anthropology. Lutheran. Avocations: skiing, hiking, flute, target shooting. Home: 220 Girard SE Albuquerque NM 87106

SCHOETTLER, GAIL SINTON, state treasurer; b. Los Angeles, Oct. 21, 1943; d. James and Norma (McLellan) Sinton; m. John H. Schoettler, Sept. 11, 1965; children: Lee, Thomas, James. BA in Econs., Stanford U., 1965; MA in History, U. Calif., Santa Barbara, 1969, PhD in History, 1975. Businesswoman Denver, 1975-83; exec. dir. Colo. Dept. of Personnel, Denver, 1983-86; treas. State of Colo., Denver, 1987—; bd. dirs. Pub. Employees Retirement Assn., Denver; past bd. dirs. Women's Bank, Denver; chmn. bd. dirs. Equitable Bank, Littleton, Colo., Equitable Bankshares of Colo., Denver. Mem. Douglas County Bd. Edn., Colo., 1979—, pres., 1983—; trustee U. No. Colo., Greeley, 1981-87; pres. Denver Children's Mus., 1975-85. Mem. Nat. Women's Forum (bd. dirs., pres. 1983-85), Women Execs. in State Govt. (bd. dirs. 1981—), Leadership Denver Assn. (bd. dirs. 1987—, named Outstanding Alumna 1985), Nat. Assn. State Treas., Stanford Alumni Assn. Democrat. Office: Office of Treas 140 State Capitol Bldg Denver CO 80134

SCHOFIELD, JOHN TREVOR, environmental management company executive; b. Manchester, Eng., Mar. 1, 1938; s. John and Hilda May (Mumford) S.; m. Jennifer Ann Wood, June 4, 1960 (div. Aug. 1980); children: Karen Jane, Alistair John; m. Susan B. West, July 24, 1982; 1 child, Kimberly. BS, U. Manchester, 1959. Dir. European ops. Borg-Warner Chem. Corp., Amsterdam, The Netherlands, 1964-70; mng. dir. Tunnel Holdings PLC, London, 1970-78; chief exec. officer, pres. Stablex Corp., Radnor, Pa., 1978-81; sr. v.p. Internat. Tech. Corp., Torrance, Calif., 1981—. Fellow Inst. Dirs.; mem. Am. Mgmt. Assn., Am. Chem. Soc. Avocation: public speaking. Home: 1245 Lakemont Rd Villanova PA 19085 Office: Internat Tech Corp 23456 Hawthorne Blvd Torrance CA 90505

SCHOICHET, SANDOR ROSS, communications executive; b. Los Angeles, May 27, 1953; s. Nathan L. and Muriel (Rosenberg) S.; m. Linda Christine Thorson, May 5, 1978. BA in Philosophy, BA in Info. Sci., U. Calif., Santa Cruz, 1975; SM in Elec. Engring. and Computer Sci., MIT, 1981. Cert. data processor, systems cons. Engr. logic systems Burroughs Corp., Pasadena, Calif., 1974-76; project engr. Dataproducts Corp., Woodland Hills, Calif., 1976-77; sr. cons., project mgr., dir. telecommunications mktg. Data Architects, Inc., San Francisco, 1981-87, v.p. telecommunications mktg., 1987—. Contbr. articles to profl. jours. Mem. Sigma Xi. Avocations: camping, sailing, photography, travel, skiing.

SCHOLES, ROBERT THORNTON, physician, research adminstr.; b. Bushnell, Ill., June 24, 1919; s. Harlan Lawrence and Lura Zolene (Camp) S.; student Knox Coll., 1937-38; B.S., Mich. State U., 1941; M.D., U. Rochester, 1950; postgrad. U. London, 1951-52, U. Chgo., 1953; m. Kathryn Ada Tew, Sept. 3, 1948; 1 dau., Delia. Intern, Gorgas Hosp., Ancon, C.Z., 1950-51; lab. asst. dept. entomology Mich. State U., 1940-41; research asst. Roselake Wildlife Exptl. Sta., 1941; research assoc. Harvard U., 1953-57; served to med. dir. USPHS, 1954-71, med. officer, dep. chief health and sanitation div. U.S. Ops. Mission, Bolivia, 1954-57, chief health and sanitation div., Paraguay, 1957-60, internat. health rep. Office of Surgeon Gen., 1960-62; br. chief, research grants officer, acting assoc. dir. Nat. Inst. Allergy and Infectious Diseases, NIH, Bethesda, Md., 1962-71; pres. The Bioresearch Ranch, Inc., Rodeo, N.Mex., 1977—; cons. Peace Corps, 1961, Hidalgo County Med. Services, Inc., 1979—, N.Mex. Health Systems Agy., 1980-86, N.Mex. Health Resources, Inc., 1981—. Served to capt. USAAF, 1942-45. Commonwealth Fund fellow, 1953. Mem. AAAS, Am. Soc. Tropical Medicine and Hygiene, N.Y. Acad. Sci., Am. Pub. Health Assn., Am. Ornithologists Union, Sembot Hon. Soc. Contbr. papers to profl. publs. Home and Office: PO Box 117 Rodeo NM 88056

SCHOLNICK, JOSEPH B., public relations executive, journalist; b. Bklyn, Dec. 28, 1921; s. Philip and Esther (Kemper) S.; m. Lynne Okon, Aug. 22, 1948; children—Tina M., Eric Nils, Nadia Franzeska. A.B., U. Miami, 1950; M.S., Northwestern U., 1951; postgrad. in gen. mgmt. Am. Mgmt. Assn., 1958-59. Mem. staff Buffalo Evening News, 1951-56; dir. pub. relations Brown-Forman Distillers Corp., Louisville, 1956-62; contbg. editor Argosy Mag., 1962-65; v.p. pub. relations and communications Calif. World's Fair, Long Beach, 1963-65; gen. mgr. internat. expositions div. Am. Express Co., N.Y.C., 1965-69; pres. Communications Workshop, Long Beach, Internat. Group, Long Beach, 1969—, Creative Travel Services Corp., Long Beach, 1973—; mng. dir. admissions mktg. Pacific 21 Council, Century City, Los Angeles, 1974-75; dir. advance admissions mktg. Expo 74, Spokane, Wash., 1973-74; dir. mktg. Lion Country Safari, Inc., 1975-77; exec. v.p., chief exec. officer LA 200 Corp., 1977-82; pub. relations liaison U.S. and Can., Mex. Nat. Tourist Council, 1978-84; columnist Capitol News Service of Sacramento, 1983—. Served with USAAF, 1942-45. Mem. Internat. Pub. Relations Assn., Pub. Relations Soc. Am., Sigma Delta Chi. Clubs: Nat. Press, Overseas Press, Greater Los Angeles Press. Home: 412 Bellflower Blvd Suite 121 Long Beach CA 90814 Office: PO Box 20239 Long Beach CA 90801

SCHONBERGER, ROSLYN ROSENBERG, publishing company executive; b. Warren, Ohio, Aug. 7, 1937; d. Bernard Wayne and Harriet (Goldberger) Rosenberg; m. Ernest Armin Schonberger, July 14, 1963 (div. May 1972); children: David Wayne, Brian Louis. BA in English, Ohio State U., 1960. Sr. assoc. editor Paisano Pubs., Agoura, Calif., 1978-84; contbg. writer Seattle's Child, 1985; mng. editor Ventura County Mag., Oxnard, Calif., 1985; div. editor-in-chief Windsor Pubs. Inc., Northridge, Calif., 1986—. Democrat. Unitarian. Avocations: competition chili cook, quilt designing and making. Office: Windsor Pubs Inc 8910 Quartz Ave Northridge CA 91328

SCHONFELD, WILLIAM ROST, political science educator, researcher; b. N.Y.C., Aug. 28, 1942; s. William A. and Louise R. (Rost) S.; m. Elena Beortegui, Jan. 23, 1964; children: Natalie Beortegui, Elizabeth Lynn Beortegui. Student, Cornell U., 1960-61; B.A. cum laude with honors, NYU, 1964; M.A., Princeton U., 1968, Ph.D., 1970. Research asst. Princeton U., 1966-69, research assoc., 1969-70, vis. lectr., 1970; asst. prof. polit. sci. U. Calif.-Irvine, 1970-75, assoc. prof., 1975-81, prof., 1981—, dean Sch. Social Scis., 1982—; sr. lectr. Fond. Nat. de Sci. Politique, Paris, 1973-74; researcher Centre de Sociologie des Organisations, Paris, 1976-78. Author: Youth and Authority in France, 1971, Obedience and Revolt, 1976, Ethnographie du PS et du RPR, 1985. Recipient Disting. Teaching award U. Calif.-Irvine, 1984; Fulbright fellow Bordeaux, France, 1964-65; Danforth grad. fellow, 1964-69; Fulbright sr. lectr. Paris, 1973-74; NSF-CNRS Exchange of Scientists fellow Paris, 1976-78; Ford Found. grantee France, Spain, 1978-79. Mem. Am. Polit. Sci. Assn., Phi Beta Kappa. Home: 29 Rocky Knoll Irvine CA 92715 Office: U Calif Sch Social Scis Irvine CA 92717

SCHOOLNIK, MICHAEL L., ceramics manufacturing company executive; b. N.Y.C., Dec. 13, 1957; s. Daniel and Roslyn (Weinberger) S. BFA in Painting, R.I. Sch. Design, 1979. Owner, founder Dish Is It, San Francisco, 1981—. Featured in Better Homes and Gardens: Kitchen and Bath Ideas, Interior Design, House Beautiful, others, 1986. Office: Dish Is It PO Box 162 3309 1/2 Mission St San Francisco CA 94110

SCHOOP, E. JACK, land development administrator; b. Olten, Switzerland, Mar. 15, 1929; s. John Charles and Margaret (Fleischmann) S.; m. Marilyn Rita Powers, June 30, 1957; children: Michael, Kelly, John. AB in Govt., Antioch Coll., 1955; M in City Planning, MIT, 1960. Dir. planning Greater Anchorage Bur., 1963-66; chief planner San Francisco Bay Cons. and Devel. Commn., 1944-71; dir. planning State of Wis., Madison, 1971-73; chief planner Calif. Coastal Commn., San Francisco, 1973-79; dir. planning City of Dallas, 1979-82; dir. devel. Santa Clara County, San Jose, Calif., 1982—. Mem. Metr. Transp. Commn., San Francisco, 1970, Pres.'s Task Force on Quake Hazard Reduction, 1968; chmn. Calif. Legis. Post-Earthquake Adv. Commn., Sacramento, 1967. Mem. Am. Planning Assn., Calif. Chpt. Am. Planning Assn. (Disting. Service award 1979). Democrat. Avocations: backpacking, photography, reading. Home: 1507 Alta Glen Dr San Jose CA 95125 Office: County of Santa Clara 70 W Hedding St E Wing San Jose CA 95110

SCHOPPA, ELROY, accountant, financial planner; b. Vernon, Tex., Aug. 25, 1922; s. Eddie A. and Ida (Foerster) S.; m. Juanita C. Young, Aug. 11, 1956 (div.); children: Karen Marie, Vickie Sue; m. Gail O. Martin, May 12, 1984; stepchildren: Veronica, Vanessa. BBA, Tex. Tech U., 1943; postgrad. Law Sch., U. Tex., 1946-47; MA, Mich. State U., 1950. CPA, Tex., Calif.; cert. real estate broker; cert. ins. agt. Mem. faculty Tex. Tech U., Lubbock, 1943, U. Tex., Austin, 1946-47, Mich. State U., East Lansing, 1947-50; auditor Gen. Motors Corp., 1950-56; dir. systems and procedures Fansteel Metall. Corp., 1956-59; gen. auditor Consol. Electro Dynamics Corp., 1959-60; auditor, sr. tax acct. Beckman Inst. Inc., Fullerton, Calif., 1960-70; pres. Elroy Schoppa Acctg. Corp., La Habra, Calif., 1960—; cons. to bus. Treas. La Habra Devel. Corp.; organizer, pres. 4-H Club, Vernon; adviser Jr. Achievement, Waukegan, Ill.; bd. dirs. Klein Ctr. for Prevention of Domestic Violence; asst. football and basketball coach, Manzanola, Colo.; coach Am. Girls Sport Assn., La Habra. Served with USN, 1942-46. Mem. Calif. Soc. CPA's, Alpha Phi Omega, Theta Xi. Republican. Lutheran. Club: Phoenix (Anaheim, Calif.). Avocations: hunting, fishing, camping. Office: 801 E La Habra Blvd La Habra CA 90631

SCHORK, BARBARA F., marketing research executive; b. N.Y.C., Feb. 23, 1946; d. Harry and Sara (Bender) Feuer; m. James Charles Schork, Dec. 27, 1975. BA in Psychology, Hunter Coll., 1966; postgrad., Baruch Coll., 1967-68. Research analyst Avco Radio-TV Sales, N.Y.C., 1966-69; research analyst, acting research dir. Sta. WNEW-TV, N.Y.C., 1969-70; project coordinator Benton & Bowles Advt., N.Y.C., 1970-71; sr. research analyst McCall's mag., N.Y.C., 1971-74; research dir. Ladies Home Jour., N.Y.C., 1974-78; divisional mktg. mgr. Time, Inc./People mag., N.Y.C., 1978-85; dir. ops. DuVal Research Group, Tucson, 1986; market research mgr. Pima Savs., Tucson, 1987—. Avocations: photography, skiing, music, horseback riding, scuba diving.

SCHORR, MORRIS EDWIN, law office administrator; b. N.Y.C., Aug. 30, 1944; s. Joseph Barnett and Molly Elaine (Honixfelt) S.; m. Sharon Kay Amstutz, Dec. 30, 1978; 1 child, Benjamin Morris. BA, SUNY, Binghamton, 1966; MA, U. Ill., 1970. Word processing specialist O'Melveny & Myers, Los Angeles, 1975-82; mgr. info. systems Leff & Mason, Beverly Hills, Calif., 1982-85; adminstr. office Mudge, Rose, Guthrie, Alexander & Ferdon, Los Angeles, 1985-86; adminstr. Cohen & Steimbrecher, Encino, Calif., 1986—; cons. computer MES Assocs., Burbank, Calif., 1985. Vice chmn. adv. com. Boy Scouts Am., Los Angeles, 1981—. Mem. Assn. Legal Adminstr. Jewish. Avocations: swimming, music. Office: Mudge Rose Guthrie Alexander & Ferdon 333 S Grand Ave Suite 2020 Los Angeles CA 91504

SCHORZMAN, MARK HEWIT, industrial hygienist; b. Spokane, Wash., Sept. 6, 1937; s. Lester Richard and Esther Ann (Cowen) S.; m. Judy Kennett Lavender, Aug. 22, 1959; children—Mark Hewit, Douglas Wheeler. B.S., U. Wash., 1961, M.S. in Pub. Health, 1975; grad. with honors, Army Command and Gen. Staff Coll., 1976; registered sanitarian, Wash.; diplomate Am. Acad. Sanitarians, Am. Acad. Indsl. Hygiene. Sanitarian, Thurston-Mason Health Dist., Wash., 1961-62; commd. 2d lt., U.S. Army, 1962, advanced through grades to maj., 1967, ret., 1982, chief environ. sanitation, N. Baveria Med. Dist., W. Germany, 1968-69, chief preventive medicine Madigan Gen. Hosp., Tacoma, 1970-74, preventive medicine cons. Comdr. U.S. Army Health Services Command, Ft. Sam Houston, Tex., 1975-77, chief environ. sci. Fitzsimons Army Med. Center, Denver, 1977-82; risk mgmt. officer Adams County, Colo., 1982-84; cons. in indsl. hygiene Mark H. Schorzman and Assocs., Denver, 1984—; instr. Nat. Inst. for Food Service Industry, 1980-83. Scouting chmn. Centennial dist. Boy Scouts Am., 1977-79, mem. tng. com., 1977-82. U.S. Army Med. Dept. scholar, 1974. Mem. Am. Indsl. Hygiene Assn., Nat. Environ. Health Assn., Automatic Merchandising Assn., Am. Conf. Govtl. Indsl. Hygienists, Royal Soc. Health U.K., Sigma Chi. Anglican. Contbr. articles to profl. jours. Home: 3419 S Nucla Way Aurora CO 80013

SCHOTT, KIRK ROBERT, optometrist; b. Ft. Dodge, Iowa, Nov. 9, 1954; s. Robert Charles and Velda Kathleen (Jones) S.; m. Melissa Susan Thurow, Feb. 14, 1981; children: Joshua, Matthew. B.S. in Zoology, Iowa State U., 1977; student Morningside Coll., 1977; O.D., Ill. Coll. Optometry, 1981. Sports dir. summer camp Prairie Gold Area Council, Boy Scouts Am., 1976, summer camp program dir., 1977; dir. summer camp scoutcraft Pike's Peak Council, Boy Scouts Am., Lake George, Colo., 1978, summer camp program dir., 1979-80; assoc. Gunnison (Colo.) Eye Clinic, 1982-83; pvt. practice optometry, Craig, Colo., 1984—; mem. Health Services Adv. Com. Gunnison Watershed Sch. Dist. Asst. scoutmaster Boy Scouts Am., 1981-85,mem. Nat. Jamboree West staff, 1973, dist. chmn. Western Colo. Council, 1985—, mem. council exec. bd. Western Colo. Council, 1985—; mem. Craig Old Timers Rodeo Com., 1984—. Recipient Vigil Honor Order of the Arrow, Vigil Honor Guide, Boy Scouts Am. Mem. Am. Optometric Assn., Colo. Optometric Assn. (dist. trustee, chmn. membership com. 1986—), Optometric Extension Program, Gold Key Internat. Optometric Honor Soc. Lutheran. Club: Kiwanis (treas. 1982, v.p. 1982-83, pres. 1983-84, bd. dirs.). Home: 355 Meadow Ln Craig CO 81625 Office: 25 W Victory Way Craig CO 81625

SCHOTZ, BARRY R., employee benefits consultant; b. Lorain, Ohio, May 4, 1951; s. Robert Edward and Ruby Katherine (Urquhart) S.; m. Gretchen Strons, Jan. 17, 1987; BS, U. Kans., 1975, MBA, 1975. Pres., Creative Compensation, Inc., Lawrence, Kans., 1972-75, Lorain, Ohio, 1975-81, La Jolla, Calif., 1981—; mem. adv. bd., savs. and loan banks. Mem. Soc. Profl. Benefit Adminstrs., San Diego County Estate Planning Council, San Diego C. of C. Office: 7777 Fay St Suite 180 PO Box 8529 La Jolla CA 92038

SCHOWALTER, TIMOTHY DUANE, entomologist, ecologist, researcher, educator; b. Newton, Kans., Aug. 14, 1952; s. Duane Eugene and Marjorie Eloise (Fast) S.; m. Catherine Ann Senter, Aug. 4, 1979; children: Shannon Marlene, Corin Michelle. BA, Wichita State U., 1974; MS, N.Mex. State U., 1976; PhD, U. Ga., 1979. Postdoctoral researcher Tex. A&M U., College Station, 1979-81; asst. prof. entomology Oreg. State U., Corvallis, 1981—; Reviewer sci. jours., NSF and USDA proposals. Contbr. chpts. to books, articles to profl. jours. Invited panel mem. to U.S. House Reps. subcom. on Pub. lands, Washington, 1986. Research grantee NSF, 1983, 86. Mem. Entomol. Soc. Am., Entomol. Soc. Can., Ecol. Soc. Am., Sigma Xi. Avocations: fishing, backpacking, bicycling, gardening. Office: Oreg State U Dept Entomology Corvallis OR 97331

SCHOWENGERDT, FRANKLIN D., physics educator; b. Bellflower, Mo., Mar. 8, 1936; s. John Hermann and Muriel Juanita (Taylor) S.; m. Ellen Jeanette Johnson, Feb. 10, 1941; children: Anna Kristine, John Stephen. BS in Physics, U. Mo., Rolla, MS in Physics, PhD in Physics. Vis. asst. prof. U. Neb., Lincoln, 1969-73; asst. prof. Colo. Sch. Mines, Golden, 1973-76, assoc. prof., 1976-79, head dept. physics, 1977—, prof., 1980—; chmn. bd. dirs. Advanced Materials Inst., Golden, 1983—. Contbr. articles to profl. jours; patentee in field. Mem. Am. Phys. Soc., Materials Research Soc., Sigma Xi. Democrat. Presbyterian. Home: 2819 Sunset Dr Golden CO 80401 Office: Colo Sch of Mines Physics Dept Golden CO 80401

SCHRADER, HARRY CHRISTIAN, JR., retired naval officer; b. Sheboygan, Wis., Aug. 4, 1932; s. Harry Christian and Edna Flora (Stubbe) S.; m. Carol Joan Gossman, June 23, 1956; 1 child, Mary Clare. B.S., U.S. Naval Acad., 1955; M.S., U.S. Naval Postgrad. Sch., 1963. Commd. ensign U.S. Navy, 1955, advanced through grades to vice adm., 1982; comdr. U.S.S. Tawasa, 1963-64, U.S.S. A. Hamilton, 1970-72, U.S.S. Jackson, 1972-73, U.S.S. Gilmore, 1973-75, U.S.S. Long Beach, 1975-78; dir. MLSF Amphibious, Mine Warfare and Advanced Vehicles div. Office Naval Ops., Washington, 1978-80; comdr. Cruiser Destroyer Group One, San Diego, 1980-82, Naval Surface Forces, U.S. Pacific Fleet, San Diego, 1982-85; ret. 1985; with Rockwell Internat., Anaheim, Calif., 1985-87; pres. Coronado (Calif.) Tech. Internat., 1987—. Mem. Am. Def. Preparedness Assn., Sigma Xi. Office: Coronado Tech Internat PO Box 181978 Coronado CA 92118

SCHRADER, MARGARET ANNE, speech pathologist; b. St. Alban's, N.Y., Nov. 22, 1954. BS in Speech and Hearing Scis. with honors, U. Ariz., 1975, MS in Speech and Hearing Scis., 1977, postgrad. Speech and lang. specialist Tucson Unified Sch. Dist., 1977-80; pvt. practice speech and lang. pathology Tucson, 1980—; ptnr., author, programmer S&S Software Co., Tucson, 1980—; cons. Communication Skill Builders, Tucson, 1984—, EASME, Tucson, 1978-80. Mem. Am. Speech, Lang. and Hearing Assn. (cert.), Am. Speech, Lang. and Hearing Found., Presch. Lang. Programs of Tucson, Computer Users in Speech and Hearing, Phi Kappa Phi. Avocations: swimming, photography, collecting and creating pottery. Office: PO Box 44148 Tucson AZ 85733

SCHRADY, DAVID ALAN, military school dean and official; b. Akron, Ohio, Nov. 11, 1939; s. Marvin G. and Sheila A. (O'Neill) S.; m. Mary E. Hilt, Sept. 1, 1962; children: Peter, Patrick, Matthew. BS, Case Inst. Tech., 1961, MS, 1963, PhD, 1965. Prof., chmn. Naval Postgrad. Sch., Monterey, Calif., 1974-76, dean acad. planning, 1976-80, provost and acad. dean, 1980—. Contbr. articles to profl. jours. Mem. Ops. Research Soc. Am. (pres. 1983-84), Mil. Ops. Research Soc. (pres. 1978-79, Wanner Meml. award 1984), Inst. Mgmt. Scis., Navy League (bd. dirs. Monterey Peninsula council). Avocation: guitar. Office: Naval Postgrad Sch Office of the Provost Monterey CA 93943-5000

SCHRANT, NANCY LANKENAU, lawyer, university administrator; b. Denver, Oct. 10, 1952; d. John Herman and Edith (Shelby) Schrant; m. John Eric Lankenau. B.A., U. Denver, 1974, J.D., 1978, Ph.D., 1980. Bar: Colo. 1978. Law clk. Thomas Schrant, Denver, 1976-78; cons. Colo. Dept. Edn., Denver, 1980-82, exec. asst., 1982-84; asst. to v.p. adminstrn. U. Colo.-Boulder, 1984—; speaker numerous nat. orgns., insts. Contbr. articles to law jours. Councilwoman, City of Glendale, Colo., 1982-84. Recipient Am. Jurisprudence award U. Denver Coll. Law, 1978. Mem. Colo. Bar Assn., Denver Bar Assn., Phi Beta Kappa. Democrat. Unitarian. Home: 5051 Utica St Denver CO 80212 Office: Box B-27 Vice Pres's Office U Colo University Center Boulder CO 80309

SCHREIBER, ARTHUR ADOLPHUS, journalist; b. Canton, Ohio, Nov. 12, 1927; s. Valentine Adolphus and Nora (Harrison) S.; m. Alice Virginia Vogel, June 19, 1953 (dec. July 1975); children: Amy Jo, Mark Arthur. News dir. Sta. KYW, Cleve., 1960, Sta. WCFL, Chgo., 1965; chief Nat. and Fgn. News Service Group W Washington News Bur., 1965-67; asst. gen. mgr. Sta KYW Radio, Phila., 1967-69; asst. gen. mgr. Sta. KFWB Radio, Los Angeles, 1969, gen. mgr., 1969-77; pres. Commuter Transp. Services, Inc., 1977-80, Computer Van Pool, Inc., 1977-80; gen. mgr. Sta. KSTP-AM, St. Paul/Mpls., 1980—; faculty U. So. Calif. Mem. communication arts and sci. adv. council Pepperdine U., Malibu, Calif., Mayor Bradley's Energy Policy Com., Para-Transit Adv. Commn.; bd. dirs. YMCA. Served with Signal Corps, U.S. Army, 1946-48. Named Young Man of Yr. Zanesville, Ohio, 1959, Parma Heights, Ohio, 1963, Alumnus of Yr., Westminster Coll., 1966; recipient Good Samaritan award Ch. of Jesus Christ of Latter-day Sts., 1975, Outstanding Contbns. recognition Los Angeles Pub. Schs., 1975, 77. Address: 13802 Northwest Passage #302 Marina del Rey CA 90291

SCHREIBER, EDWARD, computer scientist; b. Zagreb, Yugoslavia, Mar. 17, 1943; came to U.S., 1956, naturalized, 1960; s. Hinko and Helen (Iskra) S.; m. Barbara Nelson, 1967 (div. 1969); m. Lea Lusia Hausler, Nov. 7, 1983. BSEE, U. Colo., Denver, 1970. Registered profl. engr. Colo.; cert. data processor. Sr. software scientist Autotrol, Denver, 1972-78; software engr. Sigma Design, Englewood, Colo, 1979-82; founder, v.p. Graphics, Info., Denver, 1982-86; dir. engring. Sigma Dynamics, Denver, 1987—; instr. computer sci. U. Colo., Denver, 1971-72, Colo. Women's Coll., Denver, 1972-73, U. Denver, 1983. Contbr. articles on computer graphics to profl. jours. Trustee 1st Universalist Ch., Denver, 1972-78; Dem. candidate for U.S. Ho. of Reps., 1980. Served with U.S. Army, 1960-66. Mem. IEEE, Assn. for Computing Machinery, Nat. Computer Graphics Assn., Mensa. Home and Office: 7250 Eastmoor Dr #226 Denver CO 80237

SCHREIBER, MICHAEL MARTIN, dermatologist; b. Kansas City, Mo., Nov. 28, 1932; m. Elaine Pailet, Dec. 27, 1958; children: J. Keith, Steven R., Jerrold A. BS, Tulane U., 1954, MD, 1958. Diplomate Am. Bd. Dermatology. Intern Touro Infirmary, New Orleans, 1958-59; resident in dermatology Tulane U. Charity Hosp., New Orleans, 1959-62; pvt. practice medicine specializing in dermatology Tucson, 1962—; clin. assoc. prof. medicine, cancer ctr. U. Ariz. Health Scis. Ctr., Tucson, 1984—; instr. dermatology Tulane U. Med. Sch., 1959-62; assoc. internal medicine and dermatology U. Ariz., Tucson, 1971-84; mem. planning com. Ariz. Tumor Registry, 1971-72. Mem. editorial bd. Ariz. Medicine, 1974-77; contbr. articles to profl. jours. Mem. adv. council Ariz. Sonora Desert Mus., Tucson, 1985-87; bd. dirs. Pima County unit Am. Cancer Soc., Tucson, 1962-64. Fellow Am. Acad. Dermatology, Am. Soc. Dermatol. Surgery, Skin Cancer Found. (charter mem. med. council 1987); mem. Internat. Soc. Dermatology, Pacific Dermatol. Assn., Tucson Derm. Assn., AMA, Ariz. Med. Soc. Office: Associated Dermatologists P C 5402 E Grant Rd Tuscon AZ 85712

SCHREIHART, GAIL K., management consultant; b. Albuquerque, Oct. 21, 1948; d. Gardner L. and Lois H. K.; m. James Howard Efting, Feb. 4, 1983. Student Universidad De Salamanca, Spain, 1970; grad. with honors Am. Bankers Assn. Nat. Compliance Sch., 1980; B.A. in Mgmt., St. Mary's Coll., Moraga, Calif., 1983. Mgr. loan adjustment dept. Valley Nat. Bank, Salinas, Calif., 1978, compliance officer, 1978-80; compliance officer The Hibernia Bank, San Francisco, 1980-82; pres. Compliance Mgmt. Info. Services, Inc., Sunnyvale, Calif., 1982—. Instr., Am. Bankers Assn. Grad. Compliance Sch., 1982, 83, Consumer Bankers Assn., Calif. Bankers Assn.; lectr. Recipient cert. of appreciation Consumer Credit Assn., 1982. Recipient Cert. of Appreciation Credit Grantors Assn., 1984, 85. Mem. Am. Mgmt. Assn., Nat. Assn. Female Execs., Calif. Bankers Assn., Calif. Assn. Thrift and Loans (lectr.), Calif. Savs. and Loan League (lectr.). Republican. Contbr. articles to profl. jours. Office: Compliance Info Services 527 S Frances St Sunnyvale CA 94086

SCHREMP, FREDERIC WILLIAM, JR., oil field corrosion consultant; b. Utica, N.Y., Aug. 14, 1916; s. Frederic William and Elizabeth Alice (Doyle) S.; m. Janet May Edwards, Apr. 14, 1948 (widowed Mar. 1957); children: Barbara Ann, Frederic William III; m. Florence Lucille Barmore, Nov. 1, 1958; children: Paula C., Ellen S. BS in Chemistry, Rensselaer Poly. Inst., 1942; PhD in Phys. Chemistry, U. Wis., 1950. Registered profl. engr., Calif. Research engr. Am. Steel & Wire, Worcester, Mass., 1942-44; sr. research assoc. Chevron Oil Field, LaHabra, Calif., 1950-81; pvt. practice cons. Fullerton, Calif., 1981—. Contbr. several papers on corrosion and corrosion control, 3 papers on rheology of high polymers; 4 patents in field. Served to lt. USN, 1944-46, PTO. Mem. Am. Chem. Soc., Nat. Assn. Corrosion Engrs. (chmn. various tech. coms.), Sigma Xi, Phi Lambda Upsilon. Methodist. Avocations: computer programming, amateur radio, golf, backpacking, fishing. Home and Office: 3225 Arbol Dr Fullerton CA 92635

SCHRIEFFER, JOHN ROBERT, research institute administrator; b. Oak Park, Ill., May 31, 1931; s. John Henry and Louise (Anderson) S.; m. Anne Grete Thomsen, Dec. 30, 1960; children: Anne Bolette, Paul Karsten, Anne Regina. B.S., Mass. Inst. Tech., 1953; M.S., U. Ill., 1954, Ph.D., 1957, Sc.D., 1974; Sc.D. (hon.), Tech. U., Munich, Germany, 1968, U. Geneva, 1968, U. Pa., 1973, U. Cin., 1977, U. Tel Aviv, 1987. NSF postdoctoral fellow U. Birmingham, Eng., also; Niels Bohr Inst., Copenhagen, 1957-58; asst. prof. U. Chgo., 1958-59; asst. prof., then assoc. prof. U. Ill., 1959-62; prof. U. Pa., Phila., 1962-79; Mary Amanda Wood prof. physics U. Pa., 1964-79; Andrew D. White prof. at large Cornell U., 1969-75; prof. U. Calif., Santa Barbara, 1980—, Chancellor's prof., 1984—, dir. Inst. for Theoretical Physics,, 1984—; vis. prof. Niels Bohr Inst., summer 1960, 67, U. Geneva, fall 1963, 67; vis. prof. Stanford U., 1978. Author: Theory of Superconductivity, 1964. Guggenheim fellow Copenhagen, 1967; Recipient Comstock prize Nat. Acad. Sci.; Nobel Prize for Physics, 1972; John Ericsson medal Am. Soc. Swedish Engrs., 1976; Alumni Achievement award U. Ill., 1979; recipient Nat. Medal of Sci., 1984; Exxon faculty fellow, 1979—. Fellow Am. Phys. Soc. (Oliver E. Buckley solid state physics prize 1968), Exxon Faculty; mem. Nat. Acad. Sci., Am. Acad. Arts & Scis., Am. Philos. Soc. (Nat. Medal Sci. 1985), Royal Danish Acad. Scis. and Letters. Office: Inst Theoretical Physics U Calif Santa Barbara CA 93106

SCHRODER, DIETER KARL, electrical engineering educator; b. Lübeck, Germany, June 18, 1935; came to U.S., 1964; s. Wilhelm and Martha (Werner) S.; m. Beverley Claire Parchment, Aug. 4, 1961; children: Mark, Derek. BSc, McGill U., Montreal, Que., Can., 1962, MSc, 1964; PhD, U. Ill., 1968. Sr. engr. research and devel. sect. Westinghouse Electric Corp., Pitts., 1968-73, fellow engr., 1973-77, adv. engr., 1977-79, mgr., 1979-81; prof. elec. engring. Ariz. State U., Tempe, 1981—; researcher Inst. Solid-State Physics, Freiburg, Fed. Republic Germany, 1978-79. Author: Advanced MOS Devices, 1986; patentee in field; contbr. articles to profl. jours. Fellow IEEE; mem. Electrochem. Soc., Sigma Xi. Baha'i. Home: 1927 E Bendix Dr Tempe AZ 85283 Office: Ariz State U Dept Elec Engring Tempe AZ 85287

SCHROEDER, ALBERT HENRY, research chemist; b. Jersey City, Oct. 24, 1952; s. Albert Fredrick and Gladys Ethyl (Huneke) S. BS in Chemistry, Rensselaer Poly. Inst., 1974; PhD in Chemistry, U. Chgo., 1978. Postdoctoral research assoc. IBM, Yorktown Hts., N.Y., 1978-80; asst. prof. U. Calif., Berkeley, 1980; research chemist Chevron Research Co., Richmond, Calif., 1981-84, sr. research chemist, 1984—; invited participant U.S.-France Joint Seminar on Modified Electrodes, Bendor, France, 1980; invited lectr. Gordon Conf. on Electrochem., Santa Barbara, Calif., 1984. Translator (book) Working with Ion-Selective Electrodes, 1979; contbr. articles to profl. jours.; patentee in field. Mem. Am. Chem. Soc., Electrochem. Soc. Home: 6 West Chanslor Ct Richmond CA 94801 Office: Chevron Research Co 576 Standard Ave Richmond CA 94802

SCHROEDER, ARNOLD LEON, educator; b. Honolulu, May 27, 1935; s. Arnold Leon and Wynelle (Russell) S.; BS in Math., Oreg. State U., 1960, MS in Stats., 1962; NSF Insts. at UCLA, 1964, U. So. Calif., 1965; m. Maybelle Ruth Walker, Nov. 9, 1956; children: Steven, Michael, Wendy. Computer engr. Autonetics div. N.Am. Aviation Co., 1960-61; NSF fellow, research asst. State of Oreg., Corvallis, 1961; assoc. prof. math. Long Beach (Calif.) Community Coll., 1962—; computer cons. McDonnell-Douglas Corp., 1966-74, statis. researcher in med. and social sci., 1976-80; cons. statis. software including SPSS, BMDP, Minitab and Fortran, 1980—; asst. prof. math. Calif State U., Long Beach, 1985—. Chmn. bd. elders Grace Bible Ch., South Gate, Calif., 1985—. Served with USAF, 1953-57. Mem. Faculty Assn. Calif. Community Colls., Calif. Teaching Assn., Am. Bowlers Tour (life). Home: 5481 E Hill St Long Beach CA 90815 Office: 4901 E Carson St Long Beach CA 90808

SCHROEDER, EDWYNN EDGAR, orthodontist; b. Los Angeles, Dec. 2, 1930; s. Herbert Joseph and Faye (Dunham) S.; B.A., U. So. Calif., 1952, M.S., 1965, D.D.S., Coll. Physicians and Surgeons, 1959; m. Marla Stacy Berk, Dec. 30, 1975; children—Neil Nelson, Leslie Louise, Samuel George, Tarah Rose. Asso., Douglas F. Snow, North Hollywood, Calif., 1959-60; pvt. practice dentistry specializing in orthodontics, Northridge, Calif., 1960-65, Chatsworth, Calif., 1965—; staff Hollywood Presbyn. Hosp., 1962—, Los Angeles County Hosp., 1965—; clin. instr. Sch. Dentistry, U. So. Calif., 1971-75; treas. Orthodontic Assos., Inc., 1976-81; pres. Western Dental Plan Mgmt., Inc., 1978—; cons. Los Angeles City Sch. Dist., 1960-70; dental cons., dir. Dental Service Bur., 1968—; dental cons. Southwest Adminstrs., 1974—, Meat Cutters Trust, 1974—. Served with U.S. Army, 1952-54. Diplomate Am. Bd. Orthodontics. Mem. ADA, Am. Assn. Orthodontists, Fedn. Dentaire Internat., Coll. Physicians and Surgeons Alumni Assn., San Fernando Valley Dental Soc. (chmn. council on profl. services 1967), Pacific Coast Orthodontic Soc. (chmn. dental care com. 1972), Los Angeles City Schs. Physicians and Dentists Assn. (pres. 1963), Tau Kappa Omega, Psi Omega, Phi Kappa Tau. Contbr. articles to profl. jours. Office: 10234 Canoga Ave Chatsworth CA 91311 Office: 2241 Michael Dr Newbury Park CA 91320

SCHROEDER, JOHN SALMON, chemical consultant; b. Oxford, Miss., June 6, 1957; s. Harry L. and Helen W. (Salmon) S. BS, Butler U., 1979, MS, 1984. Research chemist Frekote, Indpls., 1980-81; lab. chemist RCA Corp., Indpls., 1981-84; application developer Dynamic Solutions, Pasadena, Calif., 1984-85; lab. supr. Graphic Research, Chatsworth, Calif., 1985-86; cons. Los Angeles, 1985—. Recipient Outstanding Scholar in Sci. award Sigma Xi. Mem. Am. Chem. Soc. (analytical chemist of yr. 1978), Phi Kappa Phi. Republican. Presbyterian. Avocations: computer hacking, modeling. Home and Office: 3030 Montrose #210 La Crescenta CA 91214

SCHROEDER, MARY MURPHY, judge; b. Boulder, Colo., Dec. 4, 1940; d. Richard and Theresa (Kahn) Murphy; m. Milton R. Schroeder, Oct. 15, 1965; children: Caroline Theresa, Katherine Emily. B.A., Swarthmore Coll., 1962; J.D., U. Chgo., 1965. Bar: Ill. 1966, D.C. 1966, Ariz. 1970. Trial atty. Dept. Justice, Washington, 1965-69; law clk. Hon. Jesse Udall, Ariz. Supreme Ct., 1970; mem. firm Lewis and Roca, Phoenix, 1971-75; judge Ariz. Ct. Appeals, Phoenix, 1975-79, U.S. Ct. Appeals (9th Cir.), Phoenix, 1979—; vis. instr. Ariz. State U. Coll. Law, 1976, 77, 78. Contbr. articles to profl. jours. Mem. Am. Bar Assn., Ariz. Bar Assn., Fed. Bar Assn., Am. Law Inst., Am. Judicature Soc. Democrat. Club: Soroptimists. Office: US Ct Appeals (9th cir) 6421 US Courthouse& Fed Bldg 230 N 1st Ave Phoenix AZ 85025

SCHROEDER, MIKE FRED, public relations director, magazine editor, association executive; b. Rochester, Minn., Dec. 23, 1957; s. Derald Carl and Elsie Mae (Mohr) S. AA, Rochester Community Coll., 1978; BA, St. Cloud State U., 1981. Editor Viking Report newspaper, Bloomington, Minn., 1981; sports writer St. Cloud (Minn.) Daily Times, 1981-82; sports info. dir. St. Cloud State U., 1982-84; pub. relations dir. Amateur Hockey Assn. of U.S., Colorado Springs, Colo., 1984—. Recipient Sports Series award AP Sports Editors Minn., 1982. Mem. Coll. Sports Info. Dirs. Assn. (mem. ethics com., recipient best sports series in nation award 1984, second in nation 1985). Home: 2575 Woodside Ln #5 Colorado Springs CO 80906 Office: Amateur Hockey Assn of US 2997 Broadmoor Valley Rd Colorado Springs CO 80906

SCHROEDER, PATRICIA SCOTT (MRS. JAMES WHITE SCHROEDER), congresswoman; b. Portland, Oreg., July 30, 1940; d. Lee Combs and Bernice (Scott) Scott; m. James White Schroeder, Aug. 18, 1962; children: Scott William, Jamie Christine. B.A. magna cum laude, U. Minn., 1961; J.D., Harvard U., 1964. Bar: Colo. 1964. Field atty. NLRB, Denver, 1964-66; practiced in Denver, 1966-72; hearing officer Colo. Dept. Personnel, 1971-72; mem. faculty U. Colo., 1969-72, Community Coll., Denver, 1969-70, Regis Coll., Denver, 1970-72; mem. 93d-100th congresses from 1st Colo. dist., 1973—; co-chmn. Congl. Caucus for Women's Issues, 1976—; mem. Ho. of Reps. armed services com., judiciary com., post office and civil service com.; chair civil service subcom.; mem. select com. on children, youth and families. Conglist. Office: 2410 Rayburn House Office Bldg Washington DC 20515 *

SCHROEDER, RALPH MICHAEL (TOPPER), fragrance manufacturing company executive, entertainment advertising and marketing consultant; b. Glendale, Ohio, July 26, 1937; s. Ralph Michael and Calista (Eastep) S. Student, Xavier U., 1955-59. Pres. Musicsearch, West Hollywood, Calif., 1978—; chief exec. officer Gendarme, West Hollywood, 1984—. Pres. 9000 Cynthia Homeowners Assn., West Hollywood, 1985-86. Mem. Ind. Cosmetics Mfrs. and Distbrs., Nat. Acad. Recording Arts and Scis., Fragrance and Cosmetic Guild of So. Calif. Home: PO Box 69954 West Hollywood CA 90069

SCHROEDER, RITA MOLTHEN, chiropractor; b. Savanna, Ill., Oct. 25, 1922; d. Frank J. and Ruth J. (McKenzie) Molthen; m. Richard H. Schroeder, Apr. 23, 1948 (div.); children—Richard, Andrew, Barbara, Thomas, Paul, Madeline. Student, Chem. Engring., Immaculate Heart Coll., 1940-41, UCLA, 1941, Palmer Sch. of Chiropractic, 1947-49; D. Chiropractic, Cleve. Coll. of Chiropractic, 1961. Engring.-tooling design data coordinator Douglas Aircraft Co., El Segundo, Santa Monica and Long Beach, Calif., 1941-47; pres. Schroeder Chiropractic, Inc., 1982—; dir. Pacific States Chiropractic Coll., 1978-80, pres. 1980-81. Recipient Palmer Coll. Ambassador award, 1973. Parker Chiropractic Research Found. Ambassador award, 1976. Mem. Internat. Chiropractic Assn., Calif. Chiropractic Assn., Internat. Chiropractic Assn. Calif., Assn. Am. Chiropractic Coll. Presidents, Council Chiropractic Edn. (Pacific State Coll. rep.). Home: 9870 N Millbrook Ave Fresno CA 93710 Office: Schroeder Chiropractic Inc 2535 N Fresno Ave Fresno CA 93703

SCHROEDER, ROY ALLEN, hydrologist; b. Hutchinson, Kans., July 12, 1942; s. Ernest Irvin and Elma Ann (Duerksen) S. BS in Natural Sci., Bethel Coll., 1964; MS in Phys. Chemistry, U. Calif., Berkeley, 1966; PhD in Oceanography, U. Calif., San Diego, 1974. Elem. tchr. Internat. Voluntary Services, Long Xuyen, So. Vietnam, 1966-67; biophysics technician U. Colo. Med. Sch., Denver, 1967-69; instr., J. Willard Gibbs instr. Yale U., New Haven, 1974-76; prof. U. Utah, Salt Lake City, 1976-78; water-quality specialist U.S. Geol. Survey, Albany, N.Y., 1978-82; research hydrologist U.S. Geol. Survey, San Diego, 1982—. Contbr. articles to profl. jours. Fellow NSF, 1969-73, Scripps Indsl. Assocs., 1973-74; Research Corp. grantee, 1977. Mem. Am. Chem. Soc. (grantee 1975). Republican. Mem. Mennonite Brethren Ch. Avocations: ocean swimming, farming, horse racing. Home: 304 N Sierra Ave Solana Beach CA 92075 Office: US Geol Survey 5201 Ruffin Rd San Diego CA 92123

SCHROEDER, WILLIAM ROBERT, actor, entrepreneur; b. Los Angeles, July 9, 1941; s. Robert Manville and Miriam Ruth (Sloop) S.; m. Marie Paule Fautrel, Sept. 7, 1963. B.A., UCLA, 1964; B.F.A., Art Ctr. Coll. Design, Pasadena, Calif., 1971. Mailman U.S. Post Office, Santa Monica, Calif., 1967-71; art dir., producer N.W. Ayer/West, Los Angeles, 1971-75; pres., gen. mgr. Advt. Ctr., Los Angeles, 1976-77, Alouette Internat., Santa Monica, Calif., 1972—; free-lance woodcarver, Santa Monica, 1981—; free-lance actor, Hollywood, Calif., 1983—; appeared in feature films King of the Streets, 1983, The Forbidden Tome, 1984, The End of Innocense, 1985, Poltergeist II, 1986. Producer TV commercials, 1972-75; author, creator computerized lang. courses Mattel Intellivision, 1980-82. Publicity mgr. Concerned Homeowners of Santa Monica, 1981-82. Recipient 1st Pl. award Belding award for Excellence in Advt., Los Angeles, 1974, Cert. of Merit, Art Dirs. Club Los Angeles, 1972. Mem. Am. Fedn. Radio and TV Artists, Santa Monica C. of C., Mensa (Los Angeles), Combat Pilots Assn., Orange County Squadron, Internat. Plastic Modelers Soc., The Found. Brain Research. Libertarian. Office: Alouette Internat 1626 Montana Ave Santa Monica CA 90403

SCHROEN, FRANCES BRANT, police department administrator; b. Salt Lake City, July 21, 1945; d. Albert Lynn and Julia (Rees) Brant; m. John Richard Schroen, May 19, 1979; 1 child, Joseph Thomas. Student, U. Utah. Research technician Geneol. Soc., Salt Lake City, 1963-65; exec. sec. Lang Wang Equipment Co., Salt Lake City, 1969-70; sec. E-Systems, 1971-72; legal sec., 1981-82; supr., examiner Salt Lake City Police Dept., 1972—; cons. in document examination for local and state police agys. Utah; handwriting specialist, lectr. pvt. bus., local and community orgns.; owner Am. Writs. Contbr. articles to profl. publs. Treas. Salt Lake City Ctr./World Messianity, 1984—. Internat. Graphoanalysis Soc. scholar, 1984. Mem. Ind. Assn. Document Examiners, World Assn. of Document Examiners, Nat. Assn. Female Execs., Utah Bus. Women, Sigma Alpha Gamma. Avocations: racquetball, horseback riding, weight lifting. Office: Salt Lake City Police Dept 450 S 300 E Salt Lake City UT 84111

SCHUBER, STEFAN PAUL, editor; b. Sedalia, Mo., Jan. 30, 1950; s. Paul J. and Regina M. (Pritchard) S.; 1 child, Sebastian. BA with honors, U. Mo., 1971; MA, U. Oreg., 1974, PhD, 1976. Prof. U. Oreg., Eugene, 1972-76, grant cons. ednl. opportunities, 1977-78, prof., 1978-83; prof. U. Constantine, Algeria, 1976-78; editor Aster Pub., Springfield, Oreg., 1983—. Contbr. articles to profl. jours. Campaigner Democrats, Eugene, 1976, 81. Mem. AAAS, MLA, Pacific NW Coll. English Assn. (bd. dirs. 1974-76). Democrat.

SCHUBERT, DEXTER RANDELL, university administrator; b. St. Charles, Va., July 27, 1939; s. Oscar H. and Oma (Terry) S.; m. Sherry Lee Hansen, June 14, 1968; children: Michael Jon, Desiree Lee, Bradley Randell. BS, U. Ariz., 1973, MEd, 1976. Cert. community coll. tchr., Ariz. Asst. registrar U. Ariz., Tucson, 1972-85, assoc. registrar, 1985—, cons., 1980; assoc. mem. faculty Pima Community Coll., Tucson, 1982—. Co-author: Records Management—Systems and Administration, 1983, 2d rev. edit., 1987. Mem. Pima County Bd. Elections, Tucson. Served with U.S. Army, 1961-64. Mem. Assn. Records Mgrs. and Adminstrs. (pres. 1982-83, Service award 1980, 82, Mem. of Yr. 1983), Am. Assn. Collegiate Registrars and Admissions Officers, Pacific Assn. Collegiate Registrars and Admissions Officers, U. Ariz. Alumni Assn. (bd. dirs.), Tucson Youth Football Assn. Democrat. Lutheran. Avocations: reading, fishing, watching TV. Office: U Ariz Office Registrar Tucson AZ 85721

SCHUBERT, DONALD KEITH, clinical psychologist; b. Peoria, Ill., Feb. 24, 1951; s. Elliot N. and Eileen (Kranson) S.; B.A., U. Ill.-Urbana, 1972; M.A., U. Colo.-Boulder, 1977, Ph.D., 1979. Intern San Francisco VA Med. Ctr., 1978-79; staff psychologist St. Louis VA Med. Ctr., 1980-82; Long Beach (Calif.) VA Med. Ctr., 1982-84; Orange County Drug Abuse Services, 1985—; pvt. practice clin. supervision, psychotherapy, psychol. testing. NIMH trainee, 1974-75; Univ. fellow, 1975-76. Mem. Long Beach Psychol. Assn. Home: 215 Euclid Ave Apt 214 Long Beach CA 90803 Office: 1133 N Homer St Anaheim CA 92801

SCHUBERT, GERALD, planetary and geophysics educator; b. N.Y.C., Mar. 2, 1939; s. Morris and Helen (Nelson) S.; m. Joyce Elaine Slotnick, Jan. 16, 1960; children: Todd, Michael, Tamara. BS in Engring. Physics, MS in Aero. Engring., Cornell U., 1961; PhD in Aero. Sci. Engring., U. Calif., Berkeley, 1964. Head heat transfer dept. U.S. Naval Nuclear Power Sch., Mare Island, Calif., 1961-65; mem. tech. staff Bell Telephone Research Labs., Whippany, N.J., 1965; asst. prof. planetary and geophysics UCLA, 1966-70, assoc. prof., 1970-74, prof., 1974—. Co-author: Geodynamics, 1982; contbr. articles to profl. jours. Served to lt. USN, 1961-65. Alexander von Humboldt fellow, 1969, Guggenheim fellow, 1972, Berman fellow Hebrew U. Jerusalem, 1982-83, Nat. Acad. Scis. Nat. Research Council fellow, Cambridge, Eng., 1965-66. Fellow Am. Geophys. Union (James B. Macelwane fellow 1975); mem. AAAS, Div. Planetary Sci. Am. Astron. Assn. Avocations: skiing, handball. Office: UCLA Dept Earth and Space Scis 595 Circle Dr E Los Angeles CA 90024

SCHUBERT, RUTH CAROL HICKOK, artist; b. Janesville, Wis., Dec. 24, 1927; d. Fay Andrew and Mildred Willimette (Street) Hickok; m. Robert Francis Schubert, Oct. 20, 1946; children—Stephen Robert, Michelle Carol Schubert Kump. Student DeAnza Coll., 1972-73; A.A., Monterey Peninsula Coll., 1974; B.A. with honors, Calif. State U.-San Jose, 1979. Owner, mgr. Casa De Artes Gallery, Monterey, Calif., 1977-86; dir. Monterey Peninsula Mus. Art Council, 1975-76; one-woman shows: Aarhof Gallery, Aarau, Switzerland, 1977, Degli Agostiniani Recolletti, Rome, 1977, Wells Fargo Bank, Monterey, 1975, 78, 79, Seaside (Calif.) City Hall Gallery, 1979, Village Gallery, Lahaina, Hawaii, 1983, 86, Portola Valley Gallery, 1984, 85, Rose Rock Gallery, Carmel, 1984-86; group shows include: Sierra Nev. Mus. Art, Reno, 1980, Bard Hall Gallery, San Diego, 1980, Rahr-West Mus., Manitowoc, Wis., 1980, Rosicrucian Mus., San Jose, 1981, 84, Calif. State Agri-Images, Sacramento, 1984; XVII Watercolor West, Brea Civic Cultural Ctr., 1985, Marjorie Evans Gallery, Carmel, Calif., 1986, Monterey Peninsula Mus. Art, Monterey, Calif., 1986; represented in permanent collections: Monterey Calif. Peninsula Mus. Art, Nat. Biscuit Co. subs. Nabisco Brands, Inc., San Jose, Muscular Dystrophy Assn., San Francisco, also numerous pvt. collections. Recipient 1st prize Monterey County Fair, 1979 ; numerous other awards for watercolor paintings. Mem. Artists Equity Assn., Am. Watercolor Soc., Soc. Western Artists, Kona Art Assn., Santa Cruz Valley Art Assn., Ariz., Monterey Peninsula Watercolor Soc., Watercolor West (assoc.), Cen. Coast Art Assn. (pres. 1977-78, 1st, 2d, 3d prizes 1977, 1979, 1980), Nat. League Am. Penwomen (pres. 1983-84, 1st prize Norcal State Art 1985), Art Alumni San Jose State U., Monterey Civic Club. Club: Eastern Star (Milw.). Contbr. to profl. publs. Home: 2462 Senate Way Medford OR 97504

SCHUCHART, GEORGE S., SR., holding company executive. Chmn., dir. Wright Schuchart, Inc., Seattle. Office: Wright Schuchart Inc PO Box 3764 Seattle WA 98124 *

SCHUETZ, CARY EDWARD, thermoscience engineer; b. San Diego, Dec. 6, 1953; s. Celestine Edward and Doris Marjorie (Berquist) S.; m. June Wong, Mar. 11, 1983. B.S. in Mech. Engring., U. Calif.-Santa Barbara, 1978. Engr., U. Calif.-Santa Barbara, 1976-78; engr./scientist McDonnell Douglas Corp., Long Beach, Calif., 1978-81; sr. engr. Northrop Corp., Los Angeles, 1981—. Mem. AIAA, Internat. Platform Assn. Designed and built thermoelectric generator, 1978; developed advanced state of the art in aircraft ice-prevention technology, 1980; developed thermal-structural interfacing, 1985; contbr. articles on automatic computational methods for numerical heat transfer, 1982, 84; formulator Thermal-Structural Interface theory 1985. Home: 10961 Roebling Ave Los Angeles CA 90024 Office: Northrop Corp 1 Northrop Ave 3813/82 Hawthorne CA 90250

SCHUFLE, JOSEPH ALBERT, retired chemistry educator, writer; b. Akron, Ohio, Dec. 21, 1917; s. Albert Bernard and Daisy Susanna (Frick) S.; m. Lois Carolyn Mytholar, May 31, 1942; children: Joseph A. Jr., Jean Ann Fagerstrom. BS, U. Akron, 1938, MS, 1942; PhD, Case Western Res. U., 1948. Prof. chemistry N.Mex. Tech. U., Socorro, 1948-64, N.Mex. Highlands U., Las Vegas, 1964; vis. prof. U. Coll. Dublin, Ireland, 1961-62, Uppsala U., Sweden, 1977. Author: Bergman's Dissertation on Elective Attractions, 1968, D'Elhuyar Discover of Tungsten, 1981, Torbern Bergman, 1985, Vicinal Water, 1986. Served to lt. col. U.S. Army, 1942-46. Recipient Disting. Service award N.Mex. Inst. Chemistry, 1982. Fellow N.Mex. Acad. Sci. (pres. 1960, named outstanding scientist 1972), AAAS (regional pres. 1973); mem. Am. Chem. Soc. (chmn. 1960, 64, recipient John Dustin Clark medal 1981), History of Sci. Soc. Lodge: Rotary (pres. Las Vegas club 1972-73). Home: 1301 8th St Las Vegas NM 87701

SCHULER, CAROL MARGARET, advertising professional; b. Lafayette, Ind., Feb. 21, 1959; d. Ernest Alfred and Roberta Katharine (Mitchell) Deagan; m. Thomas Myrl Schuler, Nov. 13, 1982. Student, DePauw U.; BA, Purdue U., 1981. Advt. mgr. Ind. Design Cons., Lafayette, 1982-84; tech. writer Woodward Gov., Ft. Collins, Colo., 1984; dir. devel. Sta. KCSU-FM, Colo. State U., Ft. Collins, 1985-86; creative supr. Teledyne Water Pik, Ft. Collins, 1986—; advt. cons., Ft. Collins, 1984—. Mem. mktg. com. Open Stage Theatre and Co., Ft. Collins, 1984-85, United Way, Ft. Collins, 1985-86; chmn. publicity Summer Arts Festival, Council on the Arts, Ft. Collins, 1985. Mem. Kappa Kappa Gamma. Democrat. Avocations: tennis, bicycling. Home: 629 S Whitcomb Fort Collins CO 80521 Office: Teledyne Water Pik 1730 E Prospect Fort Collins CO 80525

SCHULER, MICHAEL HAROLD, professional basketball coach; b. Portsmouth, Ohio, Sept. 22, 1940; s. Boyd and Dorothy (Seagraves) S.; m. Gloria Sissea, July 20, 1963; children: Kimberly Suzanne, Kristin Ann. BS in Edn., Ohio U., 1962. Asst. basketball coach U.S. Mil. Acad., West Point, N.Y., 1965-66, Ohio U., Athens, 1966-69, U. Va., Charlottesville, 1972-77, NBA N.J. Nets, East Rutherford, 1981-83, NBA Milw. Bucks, 1983-86; head basketball coach Va. Mil. Inst., Lexington, 1969-72, Rice U., Houston, 1977-81, NBA Portland (Oreg.) Trail Blazers, 1986—. Named NBA Coach of the Year, 1987. Mem. Nat. Basketball Coaches Assn. Office: Portland Trail Blazers 700 NE Multnomah Lloyd Bldg Suite 950 Portland OR 97232

SCHULKIND, MARTIN L., research physician; b. N.Y.C., Feb. 22, 1936; s. Maurice Jacob and Helen (Weinberger) S.; m. Myra Lipkowitz, Aug. 24, 1963 (div. Mar. 1970); children: Marlena Joy, Jonathan David, Adam Benjamin. AB, NYU, 1956; MD, Chgo. Med. Sch., 1960. Diplomate Am. Bd. Pediatrics. Intern in pediatrics L.I. (N.Y.) Jewish Hosp., 1960-61, resident in pediatrics, 1961-63; instr. U. Fla. Coll. of Medicine, Gainesville, 1965-67; asst. prof. dept. pediatrics U. Fla. Coll. of Medicine, 1967-73, assoc. prof., 1973-84; assoc. in pediatrics Kern Med. Ctr., Bakersfield, Calif., 1984—; assoc. clin. prof. pediatrics UCLA Sch. Medicine, 1984—; cons. Calif. Children's Services, Bakersfield, 1984—; hosp. appointments include: staff physician L.I. Jewish Hosp., N.Y., 1961-63, program supr. Children's Med. Services Dist. III, 1976-84, health dir. Dixie County Health Dept., 1980-81, assoc. in pediatrics Kern Med. Ctr., 1983—. Author numerous books and chpts. in books; contbr. articles to profl. jours. Served to major USAF, 1970-73. Spl. trainee NIH, 1965-67. Fellow Am. Acad. Pediatrics (chmn. subcom. on 3d party payments, pediatric practice com.); mem. Am. Acad. Pediatrics, Soc. Pediatric Research, Am. Assn. Immunologists, Los Angeles Pediatric Soc., Nat. Bd. Med. Examiners, Fla. Bd. Med. Examiners, Alachua County Med. Soc., AAAS, AAUW, Am. Fedn. Clin. Research, Am. Rural Health Assn., Fla. Med. Assn., Fla. Pediatric Soc., Fla. Pub. Health Assn., Nat. Rural Primary Care Assn., Soc. Pediatric Research, So. Soc. Pediatric Research (council 1981-83, com. to investigate alternative sources of funding, 1982), Sigma Xi. Democrat. Buddhist. Office: Kern Med Ctr 1830 Flower St Bakersfield CA 93305

SCHULLER, GUNTHER, composer; b. N.Y.C., Nov. 22, 1925; s. Arthur E. and Elsie (Bernartz) S.; m. Marjorie Black, June 8, 1948; children—Edwin Gunther, George Alexander. Student, St. Thomas Choir Sch., N.Y.C., Manhattan Sch. Music; Mus. D.D., Northeastern U., 1967; Mus.D., U. Ill., 1968, Colby Coll., 1969, Williams, 1974. tchr. Manhattan Sch. Music, 1950-63; head composition dept. Tanglewood, 1963-84; pres. New Eng. Conservatory of Music, 1967-77; artistic dir. Berkshire Music Center, Tanglewood, 1969-84, Festival at Sandpoint, 1985—; founder, pres. Margun Music Inc., 1975, GM Recs., 1980. French horn player, Ballet Theatre, then first horn player, Cin. Symphony Orch., solo French horn, Met. Opera Orch., 1945-59, Concerto #1 for Horn, 1945; composer: Quartet for Four Double Bass, 1947, Fantasy for Unaccompanied Cello, 1951, Recitative and Rondo for Violin and Piano, 1953, Music for Violin, Piano and Percussion, 1957, Contours, 1958, Woodwind Quintet, 1958, Seven Studies on Themes of Paul Klee, 1959, Six Renaissance Lyrics, 1962, String Quartet No. 2, 1965, Symphony, 1965, opera The Visitation 1966, opera Fisherman and His Wife, 1970, Capriccio Stravagante, 1972, The Power Within Us, 1972, Tre Invenzioni, 1972, Three Nocturnes, 1973, Four Soundscapes, 1974, Concerto No. 2 for Orch., 1975, Triplum II, 1975, Horn Concerto No. 2, 1976, Violin Concerto, 1976, Diptych for organ, 1976, Sonata Serenata, 1978, Contrabassoon Concerto, 1978, Deaï for 3 orchs., 1978, Trumpet Concerto, 1979, Octet, 1979, Eine Kleine Posaunenmusik, 1980, In Praise of Winds (Symphony for Large Wind Orch.), 1981, Symphony for Organ, 1982, Concerto Quaternio, 1983, Concerto for Bassoon and Orch., 1984, Farbenspiel (Concerto No. 3 for Orch.), 1985, On Light Wings (piano quartet), 1984; author: Early Jazz: Its Roots and Development, 1968, Musings: The Musical Worlds of Gunther Schuller, 1985; premiere of Symphony for Brass and Percussion, Cin., 1950, Salzburg Festival, 1957, Dramatic Overture, N.Y. Philharm., 1956, String Quartet, Number 1 Contemporary Arts Festival, U. Ill., 1957, String Quartet Number 3, 1986, Concertino for Jazz Quartet and Orch, Balt. Symphony Orch., 1959, Seven Studies on Themes of Paul Klee, Ford Found., commn., Minn. Symphony, 1959, Spectra, N.Y. Philharm. 1960, Music for Brass Quintet, Coolidge Found., Library of Congress, 1961, Concerto No. 1 for Orch, Chgo. Symphony Orch., 1966, Triplum, N.Y. Philharm. commd. Lincoln Center, 1967, Aphorisms for Flute and String Trio commd, Carlton Coll. Centennial, 1967, Fanfare for St. Louis, St. Louis Symphony, 1968, Museum Piece commd, Boston Mus. Fine Arts and Boston Symphony, 1970, Duologue for Violin and Piano, Library of Congress, 1984. Recipient creative arts award, 1960; Deems Taylor award ASCAP, 1970, Alice M. Ditson Conducting award, 1970, Rodgers and Hammerstein award,

1971; Guggenheim grantee, 1962, 63. Mem. Nat. Inst. Arts and Letters, Am. Acad. Arts and Scis. Address: care Margun Music 167 Dudley Rd Newton Center MA 02159 also: care Festival at Sandpoint Box 695 Sandpoint ID 83864

SCHULLER, ROBERT HAROLD, clergyman, author; b. Alton, Iowa, Sept. 16, 1926; s. Anthony and Jennie (Beltman) S.; m. Arvella DeHaan, June 15, 1950; children: Sheila, Robert, Jeanne, Carol, Gretchen. B.A., Hope Coll., 1947, D.D., 1973; B.D., Western Theol. Sem., 1950; LL.D., Azusa Pacific Coll., 1970, Pepperdine U., 1976; Litt.D., Barrington Coll., 1977. Ordained to ministry Reformed Ch. in Am., 1950; pastor Ivanhoe Ref. Ch., Chgo., 1950-55; founder, sr. pastor Garden Grove (Calif.) Community Ch., 1955—; founder, pres. Hour of Power TV Ministry, Garden Grove, 1970—; founder, dir. Robert H. Schuller Inst. for Successful Ch. Leadership, Garden Grove, 1970—; chmn. nat. religious sponsor program Religion in Am. Life, N.Y.C., 1975—; bd. dirs. Freedom Found. Author: God's Way to the Good Life, 1963, Your Future Is Your Friend, 1964, Move Ahead with Possibility Thinking, 1967, Self Love, the Dynamic Force of Success, 1969, Power Ideas for a Happy Family, 1972, The Greatest Possibility Thinker That Ever Lived, 1973, Turn Your Scars into Stars, 1973, You Can Become the Person You Want To Be, 1973, Your Church Has Real Possibilities, 1974, Love or Loneliness— You Decide, 1974, Positive Prayers for Power-Filled Living, 1976, Keep on Believing, 1976, Reach Out for New Life, 1977, Peace of Mind Through Possibility Thinking, 1977, Turning Your Stress Into Strength, 1978, Daily Power Thoughts, 1978, The Peak to Peek Principle, 1981, Living Positively One Day at a Time, 1981, Self Esteem: The New Reformation, 1982, Tough Times Never Last, But, Tough People Do!, 1983, Tough Minded Faith for Tender hearted People, 1984, Be Happy You Are Loved, 1986; co-author: The Courage of Carol, 1978. Bd. dirs. Religion in Am. Life; pres. bd. dirs. Christian Counseling Service; founder Robert H. Schuller Corr. Center for Possibility Thinkers, 1976. Recipient Disting. Alumnus award Hope Coll., 1970, Prin. award Freedoms Found., 1974; named Headliner of Year in Religion, Orange County, 1977, Clergyman of Year, Religious Heritage Am., 1977. Mem. Religious Guild Architects (hon.), AIA (bd. dirs. 1986—). Club: Rotary. Office: Religion in Am Life 12141 Lewis St Garden Grove CA 92640

SCHULMAN, SANDRA LONDON, reading specialist, English educator; b. N.Y.C., Apr. 9, 1929; d. Nathaniel and Lillian (Berkowitz) London; m. Benson Richard Schulman, May 28, 1950; children: Randolph David, Mark Gerald. BA, Hunter Coll., 1950; MA, Calif. State U., Northridge, 1967. Lic. secondary and community coll. tchr., Calif. Tchr. English N.Y.C. Pub. Schs., 1950-53; tchr. English, reading Los Angeles City Schs., 1953-69; instr. English Los Angeles Valley Coll., Van Nuys, 1969; prof. reading, English Los Angeles Pierce Coll., Woodland Hills, 1970—, dir. Learning Ctr., 1975—, project dir. vocat. programs, 1972—; cons. tutorial and learning ctrs. various community colls., 1975—; presenter, moderator numerous learning orgns., Los Angeles, 1975—. Author/producer (films) Reading and Tutoring, Reading, Tutor Training, 1979, 80; author: Techniques of Reading and Study Skills, 1986. Chmn. community events Los Angeles Jewish Fedn. Council-Israel Independence Day Fair, Woodland Hills, 1963, San Fernando Valley Interfaith Council, Woodland Hills, 1970; sec. Los Angeles Pierce Coll. Acad. Senate, 1978-79, dist. senator, 1985—; founding chmn. Los Angeles Community Coll. Devel. Edn. Com., 1977-79; charter mem. Los Angeles Learning Ctr. Dir.'s Round Table, co-chmn. 1980-82; active Woodland Hills chpt. Hadassah, pres. 1963-65; trustee Temple Solael, Woodland Hills, 1973-74, v.p. 1974-75. Recipient Pres.'s award Hadassah, 1965, David Ben Gurion award State of Israel Bonds Com., 1975, Tchr. Appreciation and Service award Pierce Honor Soc. and ASB, 1977, 81; Grantee Fed. Vocat. Edn. Act, 1984-86. Mem. Western Coll. Reading and Learning Assn. (v.p. 1979-80, dist. senator 1985—), Calif. Community Coll. Tutorial and Learning Assn. (regional chmn. 1974-75). Democrat. Avocations: poet, lyricist, playwright, dancer, art collector.

SCHULTE, HENRY GUSTAVE, college administrator; b. Seattle, Oct. 14, 1920; s. John Henry and Alma (Winter) S.; m. Joan Noel Burton, Aug. 20, 1949; children—Steven Craig, Scott John, Jane Martha. B.A. in Econs. and Bus., U. Wash., 1948. With D.K. MacDonald & Co., Seattle, 1952-67, asst. treas., 1957-60, treas., 1960-67; bus. mgr. legal firm Bogle, Gates, Dobrin, Wakefield & Long, Seattle, 1967; adminstr. Child Devel. and Mental Retardation Ctr. U. Wash., Seattle, 1968-86; mem. steering com. mental retardation research ctrs. group Nat. Inst. Child Health and Human Devel., 1971-85. Mem. exec. bd., treas. Assn. Univ. Affiliated Facilities, 1974-77. Served with AUS, 1940-45. Mem. Soc. Research Adminstrs. (mem. exec. com. 1971-72), Am. Assn. Mental Deficiency. Office: Univ Wash WJ-10 Seattle WA 98195

SCHULTS, DONALD WILLIAM, chemist, environmental scientist; b. Santa Paula, Calif., Mar. 12, 1938; s. Sylvester William and Mary Hanna (Coleman) S.; m. Connie Ruth Taylor, June 9, 1962; children: Kris, Karen, Mike. BS, Fresno State Coll., 1962. Research chemist USAF, Edwards AFB, Calif., 1962-66, U.S EPA, Corvallis, Oreg., 1966-80; research environ. scientist U.S EPA, Newport, Oreg., 1980—, head U.S. Del. to USSR, 1982. Contbr. articles to profl. jours. Mem. Am. Chem. Soc. Republican. Avocations: traveling, skiing. Office: EPA Hatfield Marine Sci Ctr Newport OR 97365

SCHULTZ, CARROLL DEE, interior designer; b. Downey, Calif., Aug. 31, 1946; d. Wilbur Ray and Vera Mae (Rambo) Weekley; m. Jerry R. Schultz III, June 25, 1967 (div. 1976); m. Michael Douglas LaChance, Nov. 22, 1978; children: Jerry R. IV, Carrie Ann. AA, Saddleback Coll., 1975; BA, Calif. State U., Fullerton, 1978. Designer Viejo Equipment, Santa Ana, Calif., 1978-80; sr. designer Wood Assocs., Costa Mesa, Calif., 1981-83; owner Northwood Design, Irvine, Calif., 1984-86; Mem. Community Assn. Instn., El Toro, Calif., 1986—. 1st v.p. Park Paseo Homeowners Assn., Irvine, 1985-86. Home: 20 Christamon E Irvine CA 92720 Office: Northwood Design 3183 Airway Ave Bldg E Costa Mesa CA 92626

SCHULTZ, DOUGLAS ALAN, architect, energy consultant; b. Upland, Calif., Nov. 15, 1951; s. David B. and H. Maxine (Kinnaman) S.; m. Linda L. Likta, Apr. 28, 1979; children—Rebecca Lynn, Heather Michelle, Jeremy Douglas. A.A., San Bernardino Valley Coll., 1973; B.A., Calif. Poly. Inst., 1976. Architect, Michael J. Murphy & Assocs., San Bernardino, Calif., 1972, 76-85; pres. Archtl. Computer, San Bernardino, 1978—. Prin. works include Arbys, Wendys, Popey Chicken and other fast food restaurants, churches, amusement parks. Avocation: puppeteering.

SCHULTZ, GUSTAV HOBART, religious organization administrator; b. Foley, Ala., Sept. 23, 1935; s. Gustav H. and Anna H. (Coaker) Schultz; m. Flora Redd, June 16, 1958; children: Gustav Hobart III, Timothy Martin, Locke Elizabeth, Bettina Pauley. BD, Concordia Sem., 1961; MST, Luth. Sch. Theology, 1977. Pastor Holy Trinity Luth. Ch., Rome, Ga., 1961-65; asst. pastor Ascension Luth. Ch., Riverside, Ill., 1965-69; pastor U. Luth. Chapel, Berkeley, Calif., 1969—; dean of chapel Pacific Luth. Sem., Berkeley, 1977-78; aux. bishop Southwest Province Assn. Evang. Luth. Chs., 1979—; chmn. Nat. Sanctuary Def. Fund, San Francisco, 1985—, SHARE Found., Washington, 1984—. Commr. City Planning, Berkeley, 1981-83; bd. dirs. Berkeley Emergency Food Project, 1983—, No. Calif. Ecumenical Council, San Francisco, 1984—. Recipient Annual Berkeley Peace Prize, Warwick and Assocs. and Mayor of Berkeley, 1985. Office: U Luth Chapel 2425 College Ave Berkeley CA 94704

SCHULTZ, KENNETH A., mayor of Albuquerque; b. Chgo., Oct. 27, 1937; s. William Edward and Marie (Scmitt) Strang S.; m. Diane Jean Capodice, Nov. 11, 1962; children—Kenneth G., Steve H. Student, Gen. Motors Sales Sch., Gen. Motors Fin. and Budget Sch., Gen. Motors Mgmt. Sch. Pres., owner Ken Schultz Buick Inc., Kenosha, Wis., 1970-74; pres., owner Ken. Schultz Buick GMC Inc., Albuquerque, 1974-84; mem. city council City of Albuquerque, 1981-85; owner, pres. KSI, 1984—; mayor City of Albuquerque, 1985—. legis. chmn. N.Mex. Mcpl. League, 1984-85. Served with USMCR, 1960-66. Named Crimestopper of Yr., Albuquerque, 1983. Mem. Nat. League Cities, U.S. Conf. Mayors, Marine Corps League, Navy League, Am. G.I. Forum, Am. Legion. Democrat. Roman Catholic. Lodge: Lions. Avocations: automotive racing. Home: 1601 LaTuna Pl SE Albuquerque NM 87123 Office: City of Albuquerque Mayor's Office 1 Civiv Plaza NW Albuquerque NM 87103 *

SCHULTZ, LANCE MARTIN, marketing executive; b. Detroit, May 22, 1952; s. Jack Martin and Dorothy (Weaver) S.; m. Alice Ross, June 16, 1973; 1 child, Heather Ellen. BA in Econs., Miami U., Oxford, Ohio, 1975; MBA, Pepperdine U., 1982. Mktg. analyst Pepsi Cola of Miami, Fla., 1975-77; ops. analyst Gen. Cinema Corp., Miami, 1977-78; allied brand mgr. 7Up Bottling Co. of Calif., Los Angeles, 1978-79, 7Up brand mgr., 1979-81, 7Up mktg. dir., 1981-86; v.p. mktg. Stars to Go, Los Angeles, 1986—. Organizer March of Dimes, Los Angeles, 1984—. Mem. Westinghouse Mktg. Com., 7Up Nat. Promotional Adv. Council. Home: 6317 E Mabury Ave Orange CA 92667 Office: Stars to Go 4751 Wilshire Blvd Los Angeles CA 90010

SCHULTZ, SHELDON, physics educator; b. N.Y.C., Jan. 21, 1933; s. Myer and Sarah (Hetson) S.; m. Carolyn Gitterman, Dec. 20, 1953; children: Mark S., Laurie P., David A. M in Engring., Stevens Inst. Tech., 1954; PhD, Columbia U., 1959. Research assoc. Columbia U., N.Y.C., 1959-60; asst. prof. physics U. Calif.-San Diego, La Jolla, 1960-67, assoc. prof., 1967-71, prof., 1971—. Alfred P. Sloan fellow, 1962. Fellow Am. Phys. Soc.; mem. Am. Vacuum Soc., Sigma Xi, Tau Beta Pi. Office: U Calif San Diego Dept Physics B-019 La Jolla CA 92093

SCHULTZ, TARA, chemist; b. Balt., Aug. 29, 1950; d. Samuel Henry and Janice Lee (Ganz) Greenwood; m. Rodney Drew Schultz, Jan. 17, 1975. B.S. in Chemistry, Roanoke Coll., 1972. Cert. water IV, distbn. III, wastewater IV, collection III, Wyo. Dept. Environ. Quality; indsl. wastewater D, Ind. Pollution control technician Bethlehem Steel Corp., Burns Harbor Plant, Chesterton, Ind., 1973-74, sr. technician, 1974-75, environ. chemist, 1975-81; wastewater foreman City of Gillette (Wyo.), 1981—. Mem. Am. Chem. Soc., Am. Water Works Assn., Water Pollution Control Fedn. Home: 7890 Robin Drive Gillette WY 82716 Office: PO Box 3003 Gillette WY 82716

SCHULTZ, TIMOTHY WAYNE, state agricultural commissioner; b. Grand Junction, Colo., Nov. 22, 1948; s. Walter H. and Lavina E. (Truester) S.; m. Sally Lou Johnson, July 9, 1972; children: Ty Cameron, Andrea Kay. AA, Mesa Jr. Coll.; BA, Colo. State U. V.p. Mesa United Bank, Grand Junction, 1972-75; rancher Leu Ranch, Rio Blanco, Colo., 1975-83; county commr. Rio Blanco County, Meeker, Colo., 1978-83; commr. agr. State of Colo., Denver, 1983—; chmn. 1st Nat. Bank, Meeker, 1979—, Colo. Wildlife Commn., Denver, 1983—; mem. Colo. Agrl. Leadership Bd., Denver, 1984—. Mem. Colo. State Fair Bd., Pueblo, 1983—. Served with USAR, 1972-78. Named one of Outstanding Young Men in Am., Jaycees, 1984, County Commr. of Yr., Colo. Counties Inc., 1983; Gates Found. fellow, 1980. Mem. Rio Blanco Stock Growers, Nat. Assn. State Depts. Agr. Republican. Episcopalian. Lodge: Rotary. Avocations: golf, hunting, fishing. Office: Colo Dept Agr 1525 Sherman St 4th Floor Denver CO 80203

SCHULTZ, WILLIAM A., JR., health care executive; b. Racine, Wis., Dec. 16, 1949; s. William A. Sr. and LaVerne L. (Qualler) S.; m. Lynnette M. Rykiel, June 20, 1981. BBA in Acctg., U. Wis., Milw., 1972, MBA, 1974. CPA, Ariz.; cert. data processor. Tchr. U. Wis., Eau Claire, 1974-75; cons. Luth. Social Services, Milw., 1975-76; analyst Cen. Ariz. Health Services Assn., Phoenix, 1976-78; cons. Arthur Andersen & Co., Phoenix, 1978-79; v.p. ops. N.Am. Coin & Currency, Phoenix, 1979-82; v.p. mgmt. infosystems St. Luke's Health System, Phoenix, 1982—; dir. St. Luke's Rehab. Ctr., Phoenix, 1985—. Pres. Metro Civitan, Phoenix, 1981—. Mem. Soc. Info. Mgrs., Data Processing Mgmt. Assn. Republican. Methodist. Avocations: flying, music. Home: 1924 E Buena Vista Tempe AZ 85284

SCHULZ, MARIE BURNS, magazine editor, design coordinator; b. Evanston, Ill., Sept. 15, 1923; d. John A. and Esther A. (Hammar) Burns; children—Richard, Janet Schulz DeBard. Student Mich. State U., 1959-60; Northwestern U., 1965-66. Pub. relations rep. Whirlpool Corp., Benton Harbor, Mich., 1951-56; advt. rep. Heath Co., St. Joseph, Mich., 1956-61; pub. relations rep. Selvage & Lee, Chgo., 1961-63; communications coordinator Joanna Western Mills, Chgo., 1963-69; assoc. editor books Better Homes and Gardens, Des Moines, 1969-77; editor Home Beautiful Phoenix Mag., Phoenix, 1977—; coordinator Phoenix Design Plaza, 1980-86. Mem. interior design adv. com. Scottsdale Community Coll., Phoenix Coll.; design coordinator Home Hunter TV show. Mem. Phoenix Art Mus. Recipient Dorothy Daw award Am. Furniture Mart, Chgo., 1972. Mem. Am. Soc. Interior Designers, Inst. Bus. Designers, Ariz. Design Council (press mem.), Phoenix Press Club. Contbr. articles to profl. jours.

SCHULZ, RAINER WALTER, computer co. exec.; b. Berlin, Jan. 29, 1942; s. Horst and Marta S.; came to U.S., 1959, naturalized, 1964; B.A. summa cum laude in Math., San Jose State U., 1964; children—Heidi, Kenneth, Kirsten. System devel. asso. IBM, San Jose, Calif., 1964-65, SDS, Santa Monica, Calif., 1965-67, U. Calif., Berkeley, 1967-70; system mgmt. asso. Stanford (Calif.) U., 1970-77; v.p. Computer Curriculum Corp., Palo Alto, Calif., 1973-81, dir., sec., 1978-81; mgr. Tandem Computers Inc., Cupertino, Calif., 1981-83; v.p. computing and info. systems Teknowledge, Palo Alto, 1983—; cons. NSF., 1974-77. Mem. Am. Electronics Assn., Conf. Bd. Republican. Lutheran. Home: PO Box 50243 Palo Alto CA 94303 Office: Teknowledge 1850 Embarcadero Rd Palo Alto CA 94303

SCHULZ, WALLACE WENDELL, research chemist; b. Bazile Mills, Nebr., Feb. 24, 1926; s. Lawrence Henry and Hilda Lorraine (Degner) S.; m. Dorothy Jean Snook, Sept. 13, 1947; children: Bruce W., David M. BS in Chemistry, U. Nev., 1949, MS in Chemistry, 1950. Sr. chemist Gen. Electric Co., Richland, Wash., 1950-65; sr. research assoc. Pacific Northwest Lab., Richland, 1965-69; prin. chemist Atlantic Richfield Co., Richland, 1969-77; sr. sci. advisor Rockwell Hanford Ops., Richland, 1977—. Author: The Chemistry of America, 1976, Actinide Separations, 1980, Transplutonium Elements- Production and Recovery, 1981, Geochemical behavior of Disposed Radioactive Waste, 1984, Radiochemistry of Ruthenium, 1984, Americium and Curium Chemistry and Technology, 1985, others; contbr. articles to profl. jours.; patentee in field. Served as staff sgt. AUS, 1944-46, ETO. Recipient IR-100 award Indsl. Research Soc., Chgo., 1984; named Engr. of Yr., Rockwell, Internat., 1986. Mem. AIME, Am. Chem. Soc. (named Chemist of Yr. 1986), Am. Nuclear Soc., Sigma Xi. Republican. Avocations: fishing, collecting stamps, rocks. Office: Rockwell Hanford Ops PO Box 800 Richland WA 99352

SCHUMACHER, JAMES DAVID, physical oceanographer; b. Bronx, N.Y., Dec. 6, 1943; s. Raymond Isadore and Mildred Elizabeth (Barr) S.; m. Jean Marie Brakefield, Mar. 3, 1965 (div. July 1976); children: Lori Jean, Kenneth Michael, Melissa Ann; m. Mary Carolyn Franklin, Sept. 29, 1977; stepchildren: Gary Lynn Miller, Felix Alfonse Cuvreau. BS in Physics, Monmouth Coll., 1967, MS in Physics, 1969; PhD in Marine Scis., U. N.C., 1974. Oceanographer C.E., U.S. Army, 1967-70; research asst. U. N.C., Chapel Hill, 1970-71, 73-74, teaching asst., 1970-72; phys. oceanographer Pacific Marine Environ. Lab., NOAA, Seattle, 1974—; cons. Outer Continental Shelf Environment Assessment Program, Anchorage, 1976-81; adj. asst. prof. U. Wash., 1983—; project leader Fisheries Oceanography Coordinated Investigations, 1985—. Co-author: Variability and Management of Large Marine Ecosystems, 1985; contbr. articles to sci. jours. Mem. AAAS, Am. Geophys. Union, Am. Meteorol. Soc., Marine Tech. Soc., Alaska Acad. Engring. Sci., The Nature Conservatory, Pub. Broadcasting Sta., Nat. Wildlife Fed., Sigma Pi Sigma. Avocations: reading, camping, weight lifting, canoeing. Office: NOAA 7600 Sand Point Way NE Seattle WA 98115-0070

SCHUMACHER, JOSEPH CHARLES, chemical engineer; b. Peru, Ill., Sept. 15, 1911; s. Joseph F. and Josephine (Mattes) S.; m. Theresa Flynn, Jan. 28, 1933; children—John Christian, Kathleen Schumacher Hoffman, Stephen Joseph, Paul; m. Mary Margaret Maher, Jan. 5, 1985. Student, U. Ill., 1928-30; A.B., U. So. Calif., 1946. Research chemist, prodn. supr. Carus Chem. Co., LaSalle, Ill., 1931-40; research and devel. chem. engr. Fine Chems., Inc., Los Angeles, 1940-41; co-founder Western Electro-chem. Co., Los Angeles, 1941, v.p., dir. research, 1941-54, dir.; dir. research Am. Potash & Chem. Corp., 1954-56, v.p. research, 1956-67; v.p. AFN Inc., 1956-67, Kerr-McGee Chem. Corp., 1967-69; founder J.C. Schumacher Co., Oceanside, Calif., 1971, pres., 1971-74, chmn. bd., 1974-86. Regional editor Electrochem. Soc. Jour., 1953-59; co-author, editor Perchlorates; mem. editorial adv. bd. Research Mgmt., 1963-69; contbr. articles to profl. jours.; patentee in chem. products, processes and apparatus. Trustee Whittier Coll., 1968-77. Recipient Honors award U. So. Calif. Chemistry Alumni Soc., 1962. Mem. Los Angles World Affairs Council, N.Y. Mus. Modern Art, Nat. Geog. Soc., Electrochem. Soc. (Vittorio de Nora DiamondShamrock Engring. and Tech. gold medal 1982), Am. Chem. Soc., Sigma Xi, Phi Kappa Theta. Roman Catholic. Clubs: Los Angeles Country, Jonathan. Home: 2220 Ave of Stars West Tower #704 Los Angeles CA 90067 Office: 2220 Ave of Stars 704W Los Angeles CA 90067

SCHUMANN, VERNON KENNETH, industrial investigator; b. Chgo., July 8; s. Edward Charles and Clara (Hansen) S.; B.S., Northwestern U., 1934, postgrad., 1935-36; m. Susan Nerney, Dec. 27, 1969. Copywriter, Lord & Thomas, Chgo., 1935-40; mgr. Sedgewick Advt., Chgo., 1940-42; dir. security U.S. AEC, Richland, Wash., 1946-52; mgr. Fed. Services, Inc., San Francisco, 1952-53; pres. Vernon K. Schumann Investigations, San Jose, Calif., 1953—; cons. AEC, Gen. Dynamics; exec. advisor Aetna Custodial, Oakland Sch. Law. Mem. com. for arts Stanford U. Served to 1st lt. Mil. Intelligence, AUS, 1942-46. Mem. Nat. CIC Assn., Northwestern Alumni Assn., Mensa (ombudsman 1983—), Assocs. Stanford Libraries, Stanford Alumni Assn. Republican. Lutheran. Clubs: Elks. Editor Mensa Research Jour., 1968-72. Home: 1042 Oakland Ave Menlo Park CA 94025 Office: PO Box 2283 Menlo Park CA 94026-2283

SCHUPP, PRISCILLA LISTER, publishing company executive; b. La Jolla, Calif., Oct. 31, 1949; d. Keith F. and Margaret Jean (Boman) L.; m. Robert Olds Schupp, Nov. 18, 1982. B.A. in English, Northwestern U., 1971; student U. Wash., 1973-74, Western Wash. State U., 1974-75. Cert. secondary sch. tchr., Wash. Asst. account exec. Cole & Weber, Inc., Seattle, 1975-77; catalog copy chief Recreational Equipment, Inc., Seattle, 1978-80; editor La Mesa (Calif.) Courier, 1980-84, pub., 1981—; city editor San Diego Daily Transcript, 1984—. co-founder, dir. Seattle Women in Advt.; 1976. Office: San Diego Daily Transcript 2131 3d Ave San Diego CA 92101

SCHUREMAN, HOWARD JAMES, museum exhibits designer; b. Corvallis, Oreg., June 17, 1934; s. Earl and Gertrude (Austad) S.; m. Beverly Sharon Burke, Oct. 27, 1969. BS, U. Oreg., 1960; postgrad., Sacramento State Coll., 1960-62. Curator Calif. Jr. Mus., Sacramento, 1960-62; chief curator Riverside (Calif.) Mus., 1962-79; prin. Howard Schureman & Assocs., Riverside, 1979—; prin. Exhibitaus Riverside, 1982—; dir. interpretive services Miralles Assocs., Inc., Altadena, Calif., 1982—. Designer mus., visitor ctr., and park exhibit projects. Bd. dirs. Pacificulture Found., Pasadena, Calif., 1966-68, Riverside Art Mus., 1969-72; mem. Riverside Cultural Heritage Bd., 1969, Riverside Council of Arts, 1972, 75. Served as cpl. U.S. Army, 1957-58. Recipient Merit award AIA, 1975, Calif. Art on the Road award Calif. Arts Council, 1982. Mem. Am. Assn. Mus. (accreditation vis. com. 1972-79), Western Mus. Conf., Sigma Phi Epsilon. Democrat. Lutheran. Avocations: travel, photography. Home: 4056 Park View Terr Riverside CA 92501 Office: Exhibithaus 1230 Dodson Way Riverside CA 92507

SCHURR, DEBORAH ANN, science educator; b. Bloomington, Ill., May 6, 1955; d. George Roy and Gloria Dianne (Litherland) L.; m. Randall Dean Schurr, Dec. 29, 1976; children: Nathan Randall, Jennifer Lynn. Student, Citrus Jr. Coll., 1975; BS, Calif. Poly. U., Pomona, 1977. Cert. tchr., Calif. Clin. microbiologist, ultrasonographer West End Women's Med. Clinic, Montclair, Calif., 1978-81; clin. microbiologist Dr. Patricia Ebaugh, Rancho Mirage, Calif., 1981-84; sci. tchr. Etiwanda (Calif.) High Sch., 1985—. Contbr. articles to sci. jours. Mem. Am. Soc. Ultrasound in Medicine, Nat. Sci. Tchr. Assn., Am. Assn. Microbiologist, Am. Biology Tchr. Assn. Home: 2387 N Palm Rialto CA 92376 Office: Etiwanda High Sch 13500 Victoria Ave PO Box 447 Etiwanda CA 91739

SCHUSTER, ROBERT PARKS, lawyer; b. St. Louis, Oct. 25, 1945; s. William Thomas Schuster and Carolyn Cornforth (Daugherty) Hathaway; 1 child, Susan Michele. A.B., Yale U., 1967; J.D. with honors, U. of Wyo., 1970; LL.M., Harvard U., 1971. Bar: Wyo. 1971, U.S. Ct. Appeals (10th cir.) 1979, U.S. Supreme Ct. 1984. Dep. county atty. County of Natrona, Casper, Wyo., 1971-73; sole practice, Casper, 1973-76; assoc. Spence & Moriarity, Casper, 1976-78; ptnr. Spence, Moriarity & Schuster, Jackson, Wyo., 1978—. Trustee U. Wyo., 1985—. Ford Found. Urban Law fellow, 1970-71; pres. United Way of Natrona County, 1974; bd. dirs. Dancers Workshop, 1981-83. Mem. ABA, Assn. Trial Lawyers Am., Nat. Assn. of Criminal Defense Lawyers. Wyo. Trial Lawyers Assn. Home: PO Box 548 Jackson WY 83001 Office: Spence Moriarity & Schuster 265 W Pearl Jackson WY 83001

SCHUTZ, ALBERT LEON, publisher; b. Vienna, Austria, Apr. 14, 1910; came to U.S., 1952; s. Eugen and Theresa (Winterberg) S.; m. Hilda Widawer de Schutz, May 12, 1972. Master, U. Vienna, 1931. Art tchr. trade sch. Vienna, 1930-32; art restorer for chs., Jerusalem, Palestine, 1933-36; chicken farmer, Ramataim, Israel, 1945-51; worker paint factory, Bklyn., 1952-54; with Holland Shade Inc., Bklyn., 1954-57; owner All-Shades, N.Y.C., 1958-71; pub. Quantal Pub., Goleta, Calif., 1980—, pres., 1980—; v.p. Quetzal Investments Inc., Goleta, 1974-84. Author: Kosher Yoga, 1971; Call Adonoi, 1979; Exodus-Exodus, 1984, A Palestinian in the RAF, 1986, Gods Call, 1986. Inventor incendiary bombs. served with RAF, 1938-45. Decorated George Cross, Africa Star, Def. medal (RAF). Fellow Assn. Jewish Book Pub. Republican. Jewish. Club: Channel City. Lodge: Masons. Address: 375 Moreton Bay Ln Goleta CA 93117

SCHUTZ, JOHN ADOLPH, university dean, historian; b. Los Angeles, Apr. 10, 1919; s. Adolph J. and Augusta K. (Glueker) S. A.A., Bakersfield Coll., 1940; B.A., UCLA, 1942, M.A., 1943, Ph.D., 1945. Asst. prof. history Calif. Inst. Tech., Pasadena, 1945-53; assoc. prof. history Whittier (Calif.) Coll., 1953-56, prof., 1956-65; prof. Am. history U. So. Calif., Los Angeles, 1965—; chmn. dept. history U. So. Calif., 1974-76, dean social scis. and communication, 1976-82. Author: William Shirley: King's Governor of Massachusetts, 1961, Peter Oliver's Origin and Progress of the American Rebellion, 1967, The Promise of America, 1970, The American Republic, 1978, Dawning of America, 1981, Spur of Fame: Dialogues of John Adams and Benjamin Rush, 1980; joint editor: Golden State Series; contbg. author: Spain's Colonial Outpost, 1985, Generations and Change: Genealogical Perspectives in Social History, 1986, Making of America: Society and Culture of the United States, 1987. Trustee Citizens Research Found., 1985—. Nat. Endowment for Humanities grantee, 1971; Sr. Faculty grantee, 1971-74. Mem. Am. Hist. Assn. (pres. Pacific Coast br. 1972-73), Am. Studies Assn. (pres. 1974-75), Mass. Hist. Soc. (corr.), New. Eng. Hist. Geneal. Soc. (council 1979—), Colonial Soc. Mass. (corr.). Home: 1100 White Knoll Los Angeles CA 90012 Office: U So Calif Los Angeles CA 90089-0034

SCHUTZ, RICHARD EDWARD, educational research executive; b. Long Beach, Calif., May 6, 1929; s. Marvin Edward and Caroline Elizabeth (Jones) S.; m. Iris May Horsefield, June 24, 1951; children: Jerrold, Charles, Stephen, Jody. B.A., UCLA, 1951, M.A., 1953; Ph.D., Columbia U., 1957. Test editor World Book Co., 1955-57; prof. ednl. psychology, dir. testing service Ariz. State U., 1957-66; exec. dir. SWRL Ednl. Research and Devel., Los Alamitos, Calif., 1966—; Mem. research and devel. com. Ednl. Testing Service, 1971-79, Calif. Commn. Ednl. Measurement and Evaluation, 1972-75; trustee Council for Ednl. Devel. and Research, 1977-78, 80-83, chmn., 1978. Contbr. articles in field to profl. jours. Editor: Jour. Ednl. Measurement, 1964-68, Ednl. Researcher, 1972-77, Am. Ednl. Research Jour, 1978-80. Mem. adv. bd. Am. Jour. Edn., Jour. Ednl. Psychology. Mem. ednl. council Music Center Los Angeles County, 1980-86. Served to 1st lt. USAF, 1951-53. Fellow ednl. measurement Am. Ednl. Research Assn., 1955-56. Fellow Am. Psychol. Assn.; mem. Am. Ednl. Research Assn. (v.p. 1976-77), Psychometric Soc., Nat. Council Measurement in Edn. (pres. 1972), Soc. Research Child Devel., Psychonomic Soc., Phi Beta Kappa, Sigma Xi, Phi Kappa Phi, Phi Delta Kappa. Home: 259 Claiborne Pl Long Beach CA 90807 Office: SWRL Ednl Research 4665 Lampson Ave Los Alamitos CA 90720

SCHUURMAN, GUY, library administrator; b. Utrecht, The Netherlands, Aug. 22, 1931; s. Dirk and Gysberta (Van den Berg) S.; m. Jeannette Leni Kros, Oct. 21, 1952; children—Ronald, Rene, Richard, Yvonne. B.A., U. Utah, 1958; M.A.L.S., U. Wash., 1961. Librarian Div. of Blind State Library, Salt Lake City, 1961-66; dir. Weber County Library, Ogden, Utah, 1966-71, Salt Lake County Library System, 1971—. Mem. Utah Library Assn. (exec. sec. 1960-72, pres. 1975-76, Disting Service award 1972, 79), Mountain Plains Library Assn., ALA, Am. Soc. Pub. Adminstrs. Mormon.

Office: Salt Lake County Library System 2197 E 7000 St S Salt Lake City UT 84121

SCHUYLER, DONALD SCOTT, safety engineer; b. Greybull, Wyo., May 4, 1948; s. Francis Hedgeman and Edna Jane (Koeppen) S.; m. Audrey Janette Hunt, May 30, 1971; children: Donald S., Michael F. AS, Northwest Community Coll., 1972; BS, U. Ariz., 1975. Cert. assoc. safety profl. and safety specialist. With Pima County Hosp., Tucson, 1973-74; compliance officer State of Wyo. Dept. Labor Occupational Safety and Health Adminstrn., Cheyenne, 1976-80; safety engr. Kerr-McGee Chem. Corp., Trona, Calif., 1980—. Dir. safety Searles Valley Little League, Trona, 1983-86. Served with U.S. Army, 1968-70, Vietnam. Decorated Bronze Star with oak leaf cluster. Mem. Am. Soc. Safety Engrs., Am. Indsl. Hygiene Assn., World Safety Orgn. (cert. safety specialist), Am. Conf. Govtl. Indsl. Hygienists, VFW. Republican. Presbyterian. Lodge: Elks. Avocations: water skiing, fishing, boating. Home: 13850 Pine St Trona CA 93562 Office: Kerr-McGee Chem Corp PO Box 367 Trona CA 93562

SCHUYLER, MICHAEL ROBERT, librarian; b. Denver, May 21, 1949; s. Robert Julius and Mary Eugenia (Russell) S.; m. Virginia Pauline Gardner, June 5, 1977; 1 child, Linnea Gardner. BA, U. Wash., 1971, ML, 1974. Adult services librarian Kitsap Regional Library, Bremerton, Wash., 1977-81; chief, support services Kitsap Regional Library, Bremerton, 1981—; info. systems analyst Zimmerman & Assoc., Poulsbo, Wash., 1980-81; juror Am. Book awards, 1981; cons. in field, 1981—. Author (software) Readability, 1973, Member Tender, 1985; reviewer Library Jour., 1977-84; columnist The Bit Bucket, 1985—; editor, pub. Systems Librarian and Automation Rev., 1986; contbr. articles to profl. jours. Mem. Wash. Library Assn. (sec. 1979-81), ALA. Home: 27921 Lindvog Rd NE Kingston WA 98346 Office: Kitsap Regional Library 1301 Sylvan Way Bremerton WA 98310

SCHWAB, ERNEST ROE, biologist, educator; b. Denver, July 19, 1950; s. Ernest Roe and Mary Ellen (Murray) S.; m. Patty Ann Millspaugh, May 16, 1974. BA, Union Coll., 1975; MS, Andrews U., 1984; postgrad., Loma Linda U., 1986—. Research asst. U.S. Fish/Wildlife Service, Jamestown, N.D., 1971-72, Andrews U., Berrien Springs, Mich., 1975-78, U. Notre Dame, Ind., 1978-80; sci. tchr. South Bend (Ind.) Jr. Acad., 1980-81; research asst. Loma Linda U., Riverside, Calif., 1981-83, instr. biology, 1983—. Mem. Calif. chpt. Nat. Wilflife Fedn., 1981. Mem. AAAS, Entomol. Soc. Am. (news service liaison 1986—), Internat. Bee Research Assn., N.Y. Acad. Scis., Sigma Xi (Grad. Student Research grantee 1979). Democrat. Adventist. Avocations: butterfly collecting, photography, computer programming, bird watching. Home: 1461 Kevin Ave Redlands CA 92373 Office: Loma Linda U Biology Dept 4700 Pierce St Riverside CA 92515

SCHWABE, PETER ALEXANDER, JR., judge; b. Portland, Oreg., July 23, 1935; s. Peter Alexander and Evelyn (Zingleman) S.; A.B., Stanford, 1958; J.D., Willamette U., 1960; m. Bonnie Jean LeBaron, June 21, 1958; children—Mark, Karen, Diane, Patricia, Kurt. Admitted to Oreg. bar, 1960; pvt. practice, Portland, 1960-76; fed. adminstrv. law judge, 1976—. Del. nat. policy council Office of Hearings and Appeals, Social Security Adminstrn., Dept. Health and Human Services, 1980—. Mem. Oreg. State, Am., Multnomah bar assns., Beta Theta Pi, Phi Delta Phi. Home: 4366 Dorking Ct Sacramento CA 95864 Office: 1029 J St Sacramento CA 95814

SCHWALL, RALPH HAROLD, biomedical researcher; b. Sacramento, Jan. 13, 1956; s. Harold Joseph and Betty Ann (Borg) S. BS with highest honors, U. Calif., Davis, 1977; PhD, U. Calif., San Diego, 1983. Postdoctoral fellow Colo. State U., Ft. Collins, 1983-86; assoc. scientist Genentech, Inc., South San Francisco, 1986—. Contbr. articles to sci. jours. Earl C. Anthony fellow U. Calif., San Diego, 1982. Mem. Soc. for Study Reprodn. Avocations: bicycling, skiing, hiking. Office: Genentech Inc Dept Devel Biology 460 Point San Bruno Blvd South San Francisco CA 94080

SCHWAN, DAVID ARTHUR, design engineer; b. Mpls., May 29, 1957; s. Leroy Bernard and Patricia Ann (Hagemann) S. BS in Chemistry, BA in Philosophy, Quincy Coll., 1979. Analyst, programmer LERCO, Inc., Rochester, Ill., 1979-81; CAD mgr. The I.C. Shop, Inc., Dallas, 1981-85; sr. mask designer Micro-Linear Corp., San Jose, Calif., 1985—. Recipient 1st place Chemistry award Internat. Sci. Fair, Oklahoma City, 1975. Mem. Philosophy Sci. Assn., Assn. Symbolic Logic, U. Calif. San Diego Pascal Users Soc., San Francisco Mus. Modern Art, Fine Arts Mus. San Francisco. Home: 1852 Bexley Landing San Jose CA 95132 Office: Micro Linear 2092 Concourse Dr San Jose CA 95131

SCHWANZ, TERRI LEE, marketing communications specialist; b. Orange, Calif., Aug. 5, 1958; d. Ross M. Bishop and Connie M. Christensen; m. Mark J. Schwanz, Oct. 9, 1982; 1 child, Danielle Marie. BA in Bus. Econs., U. Calif., Santa Barbara, 1980. Mgr. athletic tickets U. Calif., Santa Barbara, 1980-82; specialist mktg. and advt. Provident Fed. Savs., Boise, Idaho, 1982-84; mgr. mktg. communications Hewlett-Packard, Boise, 1984—. active March of Dimes, Boise, 1984. Mem. Boise Advt. Fedn. (com. chmn. 1984-85). Republican. Lutheran. Avocations: skiing, bicycling, reading. Office: Hewlett-Packard 11413 Chinden Blvd Boise ID 83714

SCHWARTZ, ARTHUR NATHANIEL, psychologist, educator; b. Chgo., June 14, 1922; s. Isadore Schwartz; m. Patty Murphy; children: Brian, Cynthia, David, Andrew, Jonathan. BA, Concordia Theol. Sem., St. Louis, 1945; PhD, Washington U., St. Louis, 1962. Lic. psychologist, Calif.; lic. marriage, family counselor, Calif. Staff psychologist VA Med. Ctr., Tacoma, 1962-65; chief psychology sect. VA Med. Ctr., Los Angeles, 1965-72; mem. faculty E.P. Andrus Gerontology Ctr., U. So. Calif., Los Angeles, 1972-80; dir. tng. and research Calif. Luth. Homes, Alhambra, Calif., 1981—; mem. faculty Inter-Am. U., San Juan, Puerto Rico, 1980-81; asst. clin. prof. family medicine U. So. Calif. Med. Sch., 1982—, Irvine, 1985—; adj. clin. prof. U. Calif. Med. Sch., Irvine, 1985; dir. sr. assessment ctr. Caring, Inc., 1984—; cons., faculty Pacific Geriatric Edn. Ctr., U. So. Calif., 1984; pres. Gero/Sci. Assocs. Author: Survival Strategy for Children of Aged Parents, 1978, Aging and Life, 1984; co-editor: Professional Obligations to Aged, 1974; contbr. articles to profl. jours. Recipient Spl. Performance award VA, 1971, Jessie L. Terry Community Service award Los Angeles County Affiliated Com. on Aging, 1972, Better Life award Calif. Assn. Health Facilities, 1977, Meritorious Service award, Calif. Assn. Homes for Aging, 1980, Outstanding Service for Edn. and Tng. award Mayor's Office, 1980, Outstanding Service award Bd. Examiners Nursing Home Adminstrs., Calif., 1981, Research award Am. Coll. Health Care Adminstrs., 1987. Fellow Gerontol. Soc. Am.; mem. Am. Soc. on Aging, Am. Psychol. Assn., Nat. Register, Sigma Xi. Lutheran. Home: 1840-53 S Marengo Alhambra CA 91803 Office: Calif Luth Homes 2312 S Fremont Alhambra CA 91803

SCHWARTZ, BARBARA MARIE, educational consultant; b. Bklyn., Sept. 16, 1936; d. John and Stella (Radetski) Farrett; m. George A. Schwartz, Jr., June 6, 1959; children—John D., Robert G., William G. B.S., Fordham U., 1957; M.A., Nat. Christian U. Mo., 1983. Tchr., N.Y.C. Pub. Schs., 1956-57, Englewood (Colo.) Pub. Schs., 1957-61, Denver Pub. Schs., 1961-78; cons. Assocs. in Awareness, Inc., Denver, 1978—; dir. nat. tng., nat. mktg. Personal Growth Found. Inc., 1982—; co-chmn. Marriage Enrichment of Denver; Inc. Mem. Am. Soc. Trainers and Developers, Am. Assn. Female Execs., Am. Soc. Profl. and Exec. Women. Democrat. Roman Catholic. Address: 2425 S Steele St Denver CO 80210

SCHWARTZ, DOUGLAS WRIGHT, archaeologist, anthropologist, academic administrator; b. Erie, Pa., July 29, 1929; s. Harry and Vernon (Schaaf) S.; m. Rita Juanita Hartley, Oct. 4, 1950; children: Steven, Susan, Kelsey. BA, U. Ky., 1950; PhD, Yale U., 1955; LittD (hon.), U. N.Mex., 1981. Instr. U. Okla., Norman, 1955-56; asst. prof. anthropology, dir. mus. of anthropology U. Ky., Lexington, 1956-67; pres. Sch. Am. Research, Santa Fe, 1967—; academic prof. to pres. U. Ky., 1963-64; pres. Witter Bynner Found. for Poetry, Santa Fe, 1974—; v.p. Jane Goodall African Wildlife Research Inst., San Francisco, 1983—; bd. dirs. United N.Mex. Bank at Santa Fe, 1983—, Santa Fe Inst., 1984—. Author: (with others) The Archaeology of Grand Canyon: The Bright Angel Site, 1979, Unkar Delta, 1980, The Walhalla Plateau, 1981, Conceptions of Kentucky Prehistory (Am. Assn. State and Local History award 1968); editor Sch. Am. Research advanced seminar series. Clubs: Kiva, Quien Sabe(Santa Fe). Avocations: skiing, sailing, running, squash. Office: Sch Am Research PO Box 2188 Santa Fe NM 87504

SCHWARTZ, HARRY JEROME, exposition and special events producer; b. San Diego, Apr. 5, 1960; s. Charles H. and BarbaraSue (Tracht) S.; m. Valentina Valente, Jan. 21, 1984. Student, San Diego State U., 1978-82. Salesman, purchasing agt. Pioneer Van Ctrs., San Diego, 1976-78, 79; asst mgr. McDonald's Corp., San Diego, 1978-79; show coordinator Epic Enterprises, Inc., San Diego, 1979-81, v.p., 1981-82, exec. v.p., 1982-86, pres., 1986—. Fundraiser for youth activities Tifereth Israel Synagogue, San Diego, Calif., 1983-86. Mem. Nat. Assn. Exposition Mgrs., Meeting Planners Internat., Internat. Exhibitions Assn. Democrat. Avocations: guitar and saxaphone playing, bicycling, raquetball. Office: Epic Enterprises Inc 3838 Camino Del Rio N Suite 164 San Diego CA 92108

SCHWARTZ, JOHN CHARLES, chemical engineer; b. Seattle, Apr. 30, 1939; s. Charles and Elizabeth Mercy (Dougherty) S.; m. Sandra Helene Waroff, Aug. 20, 1960 (div. Sept. 1982); children: Barry, Allan, Craig. BS in Chemistry, U. Okla., 1960; MS in Chemistry, Rutgers U., 1968. Research chemist FMC Corp., Carteret and Princeton, N.J., 1962-74; sr. process engr. FMC Corp., Green River, Wyo., 1974—; lab. stockroom operator U. Okla., Norman, 1956-60. Contbr. articles to prof. jours.; patentee in field. Founder, v.p. Cong. Beth Israel of Sweetwater County, Wyo. Served to capt. Chem. Corps., U.S. Army, 1960-66. Mem. VFW, Am. Legion, Am. Chem. Soc. (pres. U. Okla. chpt. 1957), Alpha Epsilon Pi, Alpha Chi Sigma, Phi Lambda Upsilon, Phi Eta Sigma. Democrat. Jewish. Lodge: Eagles. Avocations: skiing, backpacking, hunting, fishing, travel. Home: PO Box 648 Green River WY 82935 Office: FMC Wyo Corp PO Box 872 Green River WY 82935

SCHWARTZ, JOYCE BIELENBERG, library media specialist; b. Welcome, Minn.; d. George William and Milda Marie (Simon) Bielenberg; m. William Lee Schwartz, June 30, 1974. BA, San Francisco State U., 1971; MLS, U. Calif., Berkeley, 1973, postgrad.; cert. adminstrn., Calif. State U., Hayward, 1984. Supr. library Lansing (Kans.) Dist., 1974-75; reference librarian U.S. European Hdqrs., Stuttgart, Fed. Republic Germany, 1975-76; learning resource specialist Stuttgart Am. High Sch., 1976-78; dist. library coordinator Oakland (Calif.) Pub. Schs., 1979—; spl. assignment tchr. Follow Through Fed. program, Oakland, 1983. Judge Nat. Ednl. Film Festival, Oakland, 1986; tutor Chinatown, San Francisco, 1972. Grantee Marcus Foster Found., 1975, State Calif., 1985-86; recipient Cert. Appreciation U.S. Dept. Def., 1975. Mem. NEA, Calif. Library and Media Educators (govtl. relations com. 1984—), Oakland Mus. Assn., Oakland Assn. Sch. Librarians (pres. 1980-82), Computer Using Educators, U. Calif. Alumni Assn., Women's Leadership Council. Avocations: guitar, tennis, book collecting, gardening, drawing/painting.

SCHWARTZ, LAWRENCE, aeronautical engineer; b. N.Y.C., Nov. 30, 1935; s. Harry and Fanny (Steiner) S.; m. Cherie Ann Karo, Aug. 12, 1979; children—Ronda, Daran. S.B. in Aero. Engring., M.I.T., 1958, S.M. in Aero. Engring., 1958; postgrad. Ohio State U., 1960, U. Dayton, 1962-63; Ph.D. in Engring., UCLA, 1966. Electronics design engr. MIT. Instrumentation Lab., Cambridge, 1959; aerospace engr., Wright-Patterson AFB, Ohio, 1962-63; mem. tech. staff Hughes Aircraft Co., Culver City, Calif., 1963-65, staff engr., 1965-67, sr. staff engr., 1967-72, sr. scientist, 1972-79, chief scientist lab., 1979—, tech. mgr. 1985-87; chmn., tech. adv. bd., 1987—; cons., tchr. in field. Served with USAF, 1959-62. Registered profl. engr., Colo., Calif. Mem. IEEE, AAAS, Sigma Xi, Sigma Gamma Tau, Tau Beta Pi. Contbr. articles to profl. jours. Home: 996 S Florence St Denver CO 80231 Office: 8000 E Maplewood Ave Englewood CO 80111

SCHWARTZ, LEON, educator; b. Boston, Aug. 22, 1922; s. Charles and Celia (Emer) S.; m. Jeanne Gurtat, Mar. 31, 1949; children—Eric Alan, Claire Marie. Student, Providence Coll., 1939-41; B.A., U. Calif. at Los Angeles, 1948; certificat de phonetique, U. Paris, 1949; M.A, U. So. Cal., 1950, Ph.D., 1962. Tchr. English, Spanish, Latin Redlands (Calif.) Jr. High Sch., 1951-54; tchr. Spanish, French, high sch. 1954-59; prof. French Calif. State U. at Los Angeles, 1959—, chmn. dept. fgn. langs. and lit., 1970-73. Author: Diderot and the Jews, 1981. Served as 2d lt. USAAF, 1942-45. Decorated Air medal with 5 oak leaf clusters; recipient Outstanding Prof. award Calif. State U. at Los Angeles, 1976. Mem. Am. Assn. Tchrs. French, Modern and Classical Lang. Assn. So. Calif., Western Soc. 18th Century Studies, Am. Soc. 18th Century Studies, Phi Beta Kappa, Phi Kappa Phi, Pi Delta Phi, Sigma Delta Pi, Alpha Mu Gamma. Office: Dept Fgn Langs and Literatures Calif State U Los Angeles CA 90032

SCHWARTZ, MARSHALL ZANE, pediatric surgeon; b. Mpls., Sept. 1, 1945; s. Sidney Shay and Peggy Belle (Lieberman) S.; m. Michele Carroll Walker, Oct. 16, 1971; children: Lisa, Jeffrey. BS, U. Minn., 1968, MD, 1970. Diplomate Am. Bd. Surgery, Am. Bd. Pediatric Surgery,. Instr. Med. Sch. Harvard U., Boston, 1978-79; asst. in surgery Childrens Hosp. Med. Ctr., Boston, 1978-79; asst. prof. Med. Br. U. Tex., Galveston, 1979-81, assoc. prof. Med. Br., 1981-83, chief. pediatric surgery Med. Br., 1980-83; assoc. prof., chief. pediatric surgery U. Calif., Davis, 1983-86, prof., 1986—, chief pediatric surgery, 1983—, chmn. helicopter services, 1983—, programmatic subcom., 1984-86. Editor Pediatric Surgery, 1985; contbr. chpts. to books and articles to profl. jours. Recipient Basic O'Connor Research award March of Dimes Found., 1981, Young Investigator award NIH, 1982, Found. for Children Research award, 1982, James W. McLaughlin award U. Tex., 1983. Fellow ACS; mem. Soc. Univ. Surgeon, Am. Pediatric Surg. Assn. Tract, Soc. Surgery of the Alimentary Tract, Sigma Xi. Jewish. Avocations: skiing, fishing, wood working. Office: U Calif Davis Med Ctr Dept Surgery 4301 X St Room 2310 Sacramento CA 95817

SCHWARTZ, MILTON LEWIS, federal judge; b. Oakland, Calif., Jan. 20, 1920; s. Colman and Selma (Lavenson) S.; m. Barbara Ann Moore, May 15, 1942; children: Dirk L., Tracy Ann, Damon M., Brooke. A.B., U. Calif. at Berkeley, 1941, J.D., 1948. Bar: Calif. bar 1949. Research asst. 3d Dist. Ct. Appeal, Sacramento, 1948; dep. dist. atty. 1949-51; practice in Sacramento, 1951-79; partner McDonough, Holland, Schwartz & Allen, 1953-79; U.S. dist. judge Eastern Dist. Calif., 1979—; prof. law McGeorge Coll. Law, Sacramento, 1952-55; Mem. Com. Bar Examiners Calif., 1971-75. Pres. Bd. Edn. Sacramento City Sch. Dist., 1961; v.p. Calif. Bd. Edn., 1967-68; Trustee Sutterville Heights Sch. Dist. Served to maj. 40th Inf. Div. AUS, 1942-46, PTO. Fellow Am. Coll. Trial Lawyers; mem. State Bar Calif., Am. Bar Assn., Am. Bd. Trial Advocates. Office: US Courthouse 650 Capitol Mall Sacramento CA 95814

SCHWARTZ, MORT, automotive distributor; b. Bklyn., Sept. 16, 1934; s. Harry and Helen (Rehr) S.; B.S. in Indsl. Engring., N.Y.U., 1956, M.S. in Indsl. Engring., 1961; m. Marilyn Carol Spill, Oct. 27, 1956; children—Jay, Richard, Andrew. With Westinghouse Electric Co., Pitts. Columbus, O., Metuchen, N.J., 1956-66, controller WASSCO div., Pitts., 1966-67, v.p. consumer service Westinghouse, Pitts., 1967-68; v.p. Maremont Corp., 1968-75; exec. v.p. Chanslor & Lyon, Chgo., 1968-69, pres., 1969-75, chmn. bd., pres., Brisbane, Calif. 1975-85; chief exec. officer, dir. SKU, 1983-84; pres. Import Parts of Am., Palo Alto, Calif., 1985—; chmn. Thermo King of Norcal, San Leandro, Calif., 1986—; faculty Rutgers U., 1959-61, Bd. dirs. Nat. Inst. Automotive Service Excellence, 1976-82. Pacific Auto Show, 1977; chmn. Calif. Automotive Task Force, 1978-80; trustee Nat. Automotive Technicians Edn. Found., 1982-83 . Served to capt. C.E., AUS, 1956-57. Mem. Automotive Warehouse Distbrs. Assn. (chmn. 1981-82, dir. 1975—), Calif. Automotive Wholesalers Assn. (dir. 1978—), Pacific Coast Wholesalers Assn. (dir., v.p. 1975), Automotive Parts and Accessories Assn. (v.p., dir. 1982-85), Perstare Et Praestare, Zeta Beta Tau. Home: 2505 Rolling Hills Ct Alamo CA 94507 Office: 1500 Newell Ave Suite 702 Walnut Creek CA 94596

SCHWARTZ, MORTON DONALD, computer science and engineering educator; b. Chgo., Oct. 11, 1936; s. Seymour and Lillian (Steinberg) S.; m. Laura Ellen Singer, Aug. 26, 1956; children: Karen, Kenneth. BS, UCLA, 1958, MS, 1960, PhD, 1964. Registered profl. engr., clin. engr., Calif. Prof. elec. engring. Calif. State U., Long Beach, 1970-81, prof. computer sci., 1985—, chmn. dept. elec. engring., 1981-83, assoc. dean engring., 1983-85; cons. TRW Systems, Redondo Beach, Calif., 1985—, St. Mary Med. Ctr., Long Beach, 1970—. Co-author: Hospital Information Systems, 1972; editor: Jour. Clin. Engring., 1975-83, Application of Computers in Medicine, 1981. Centennial scholar Johns Hopkins U., 1975. Mem. IEEE, Biomed. Engring. Soc. (pres. 1980-81, centennial scholar 1984), Am. Soc. Elec. Engrs. Home: 5512 Sierra Roja Irvine CA 92715 Office: Calif State U Sch Engring Long Beach CA 90840

SCHWARTZ, MURRAY LOUIS, lawyer, educator; b. Phila., Oct. 27, 1920; s. Harry and Isabelle (Friedman) S.; m. Audrey James, Feb. 12, 1950; children—Deborah, Jonathan, Daniel. B.S., Pa. State U., 1942; LL.B., U. Pa., 1949; LL.D. (hon.), Lewis and Clark Coll., 1977. Bar: Pa. bar 1950, also U.S. Supreme Ct., D.C. Ct. Appeals 1950. Chemist Standard Oil Ind., Whiting, 1942-44; law clk. Fred M. Vinson, Chief Justice U.S, 1949-51; assoc. firm Shea, Greenman, Gardner & McConnaughey, Washington, 1951-53; spl. asst. to U.S. atty. gen. Office Solicitor Gen., 1953-54; 1st dept. city solicitor City Phila., 1954-56; assoc. firm Dilworth, Paxson, Kalish & Green, Phila., 1956-58; prof. law Law Sch., UCLA, 1958—, dean, 1969-75; dir. Mattel, Inc., 1974-84; chmn. exec. com., bd. dirs. Social Sci. Research Council, 1981-85. Author: (with K.L. Karst and A.J. Schwartz) The Evolution of Law in the Barrios of Caracas, 1973, Law and the American Future, 1976, Lawyers and the Legal Profession, 2d edit. 1985; contbr. articles to profl. jours. Served to lt. (j.g.) USNR, 1944-46. Home: 1339 Marinette Rd Pacific Palisades CA 90272 Office: Sch Law U Calif Los Angeles CA 90024

SCHWARTZ, RICHARD CARL, biochemistry researcher; b. N.Y.C., Nov. 25, 1952; s. Jacob Anton and Sydelle Francis (Stelzer) S. BS, U. Calif., Irvine, 1974; PhD, MIT, 1980. Post-doctorate fellow U. Calif., San Diego, 1980-83; research fellow Calif. Inst. Tech., Pasadena, 1983; post-doctorate fellow UCLA, 1983-86; asst. prof. Mich. State U., 1986—. Contbr. articles to profl. jours. NIH fellow, 1974-80,80-83; Calif. Inst. Cancer Research fellow, UCLA, 1983-84; Cancer Research Coordinating Com. fellow, UCLA, 1985-86. Mem. AAAS, Phi Beta Kappa. Democrat. Avocations: hiking, mountaineering.

SCHWARZ, GERARD RALPH, musician; b. Weehawken, N.J., Aug. 19, 1947; s. John and Gerta (Weiss) S.; B.S., Juilliard Sch., 1972; D.M.A. (hon.) m. Jody Greitzer, June 23, 1984; children—Alysandra, Daniel. Trumpet player Am. Symphony Orch., 1965-72, Am. Brass Quintet, 1965-73, N.Y. Philharm., 1973-77; condr. Erick Hawkins Dance Co., 1966-70, Eliot Field Ballet, 1976-80; trumpet player, guest condr. Aspen Music Festival, 1969-75, bd. dirs., 1973-75; music dir., condr. Mostly Mozart Festival, Lincoln Ctr., Seattle Symphony, Music Today, Waterloo Festival, 1976—, New York Chamber Symphony, 1977—, Los Angeles Chamber Orch., 1978-86, White Mountains (N.H.) Music Festival, 1978-80, mem. faculty Juilliard Sch., 1975-83, Mannes Coll. Music, 1973-79, Montclair State Coll., 1975-80; rec. artist Columbia, Nonesuch, Vox, MMO, Desto, Angel, Delos records; guest condr., performer numerous orchs. Bd. dirs. Naumberg Found., 1975—, Young Concert Artists, Pro Musicis, Youth Symphony of N.Y. Recipient award for concert artists Ford Found., 1973; Record of Year award for cornet favorites Stereo Rev., 1975.Asso. Music Publishers, 1975—. Address: 575 W End Ave New York NY 10023

SCHWARZ, MICHAEL HOWARD, lawyer; b. Brookline, Mass., Oct. 19, 1952; s. Jules Lewis and Estelle (Kosberg) S.; B.A. magna cum laude, U. No. Colo., 1975; postgrad. U. N.Mex., Med. Sch., 1977, U. N.Mex. Law Sch. J.D., 1980; research reader in Negligence Law, Oxford U., summer 1978; diploma in Legal Studies, Cambridge U., 1981. VISTA vol., Albuquerque, 1975-77; research fellow N.Mex. Legal Support Project, Albuquerque, 1978-79; law clk. to field solicitor U.S. Dept. Interior, Santa Fe, summer 1979; admitted to N.Mex. bar, 1980, U.S. Dist. Ct. N.Mex. 1980, U.S. Ct. Appeals (10th cir.) 1982, U.S. Ct. Appeals (D.C. cir.) 1982, U.S. Ct. Internat. Trade, 1982, U.S. Tax Ct. 1982, U.S. Ct. Appeals (fed. cir.) 1982, U.S. Supreme Ct. 1983, N.Y. 1987; supr. in law Cambridge (Eng.) U., 1980-81; law clk. to chief justice Supreme Ct. N.Mex., Santa Fe, 1981-82; sole practice, Santa Fe, 1982—; spl. prosecutor City of Santa Fe, 1985; spl. asst. atty. gen., 1986—. Vice dir. Colo. Pub. Interest Research Group, 1974; scoutmaster Great S.W. Area council Boy Scouts Am., 1977-79; mem. N.Mex. Acupuncture Licensing Bd., 1983. Recipient cert. of appreciation Cambridge U., 1981, Nathan Burkan Meml. award, 1980, 82-83. Mem. ABA (scholar 1983), Fed. Bar Assn. (council on adminstrv. law 1983), N.Y. Trial Lawyers Assn., Assn. Trial Lawyers Am., State Bar N.Mex., First Judicial Dist. Bar Assn. (treas. 1987—) Editorial adv. com. Social Security Reporting Service; coauthor N.Mex. Appellate Manual, 1986; contbr. articles to profl. jours. Home and Office: PO Box 713 Santa Fe NM 87504

SCHWARZ, WERNER JULIUS, analytical chemist; b. Mannheim, Fed. Republic Germany, Nov. 3, 1927; came to U.S., 1948, naturalized, 1954; s. Erwin J. and Edith R. (Mansbach) S.; m. Lea Holzer, July 10, 1952; children: Donna Ruth, Ronald Hillel. BS, Marquette U., 1956, MS, 1958; PhD, Pacific Western U., 1981. Research chemist Whirlpool Corp., Benton Harbor, Mich., 1958-62; tech. mktg. dir. LFE Corp., Richmond, Calif., 1962-76; staff scientist U. Calif. Lawrence Berkeley Lab., 1977-84; v.p. ST&E Inc, Livermore, Calif., 1984—; bd. dirs. Calif. Innovative Network, Redwood City, 1985—. Contbr. numerous sci. articles to profl. jours. S.C. Johnson and Son fellow, 1950. Fellow N.Y. Acad. Scis.; mem. UNESCO (del. 1960), Sigma Xi, Sigma Gamma Chi. Lodge: Rotary (internat. gov. 1988—, pres. Richmond, Calif. club 1980-81). Avocations: sailing, swimming, classical music. Home: 130 Mt Whitney Ct San Rafael CA 94903 Office: ST&E Inc 1214 Concannon Blvd Livermore CA 94550

SCHWARZBERG, HENRY, investment banker, consultant; b. Munich, Oct. 27, 1947; came to U.S., 1949; s. Berek and Agnes (Löwinger) S.; m. Sheila Doyschen, Aug. 30, 1969; 1 child, Jonathan David. BA in Polit. Sci., CCNY, 1969; JD, Bklyn. Law Sch., 1973. Bar: N.Y. 1984. Gen. counsel Feldman Bros., Great Neck, N.J., 1975-77; v.p., counsel Ind. Fin. Planners Corp., Parsippany, N.J., 1978-80; asst. gen. counsel Bankers Nat. Life Ins. Co., Parsippany, 1978-80; pres. Phoenix Fin. Corp., Atlanta, 1980-81; v.p. FSC Securities Corp., Atlanta, 1981-82; pres. MAI Securities Corp., Phoenix, 1982-87, MAI Capital Corp., Phoenix, 1986-87. Co-devel.: (software) "Brass", 1985. Sustaining mem. Phoenix Zoo, 1985—; mem. Wildest Club in Town (zoo aux.). Served with USAR, 1970-75. Mem. Internat. Assn. Fin. Planning, N.Y. State Bar Assn., N.Y. County Lawyers Assn. Republican. Jewish. Avocations: piano, skiing, scuba diving, competitive bridge. Home: 19214 N 31st Ln Phoenix AZ 85027 Office: MAI 19214 N 31st Ln Phoenix AZ 85027

SCHWARZER, WILLIAM W, federal judge; b. Berlin, Apr. 30, 1925; came to U.S., 1938, naturalized, 1944; s. John F. and Edith M. (Daniel) S.; m. Anne Halbersleben, Feb. 2, 1951; children: Jane Elizabeth, Andrew William. A.B. cum laude, U. So. Calif., 1948; LL.B. cum laude, Harvard U., 1951. Bar: Calif. 1953, U.S. Supreme Ct. 1967. Teaching fellow Harvard U. Law Sch., 1951-52; asso. firm McCutchen, Doyle, Brown & Enersen, San Francisco, 1952-60; partner McCutchen, Doyle, Brown & Enersen, 1960-76; U.S. dist. judge for No. Dist. Calif., San Francisco, 1976—; sr. counsel Pres.'s Commn. on CIA Activities Within the U.S., 1975; mem. faculty Nat. Inst. Trial Advocacy, Fed. Jud. Center, ABA. Author: Managing Antitrust and Other Complex Litigation, 1982; Contbr. articles to legal publs., aviation jours. Trustee World Affairs Council No. Calif., 1961—; chmn. bd. trustees Marin Country Day Sch., 1963-66; chmn. Marin County Aviation Commn., 1969-76; mem. vis. com. Harvard Law Sch., 1981-86. Served with Intelligence U.S. Army, 1943-46. Fellow Am. Coll. Trial Lawyers; mem. ABA (jud. rep. council antitrust sect.) Am. Law Inst., Am., San Francisco bar assns., State Bar Calif. Office: 450 Golden Gate Ave San Francisco CA 94102

SCHWARZSTEIN, RICHARD JOSEPH, lawyer; b. Yonkers, N.Y., July 6, 1934; s. Jack H. and Beatrice (Florman) S.; m. Ann Sanford Adsley, Aug. 10, 1938; children: Cynthia L., Alisa J., Amy B. AB, Columbia Coll., N.Y.C., 1956; JD, Harvard U., 1959. Bar: N.Y. 1960, U.S. Dist. Ct. (ea. and so. dists.) N.Y. 1974, U.S. Ct. Appeals (2d cir.) Calif. 1974., U.S. Dist. Ct. (cen. dist.) Calif. Clk. White & Case, N.Y.C., 1957-58; assoc. Kramer & Lans, N.Y.C., 1960-62; assoc., then ptnr. Delson & Gordon, N.Y.C., 1961-74; sole practice, Newport Beach, Calif., 1974—; lectr. George Washington U. Law Sch., U. Calif., Irvine, Calif. State U., Fullerton, Long Beach,

Orange Coast Coll., U. So. Calif. Contbr. articles to profl. jours. Bd. dirs. Orange County Philharmonic Soc., 1975—, Econ. Devel. Corp. Orange County, 1983-85, Hist. and Cultural Found. Orange County, 1985—. Mem. ABA, Internat. Bar Assn., Calif. Bar Assn. (econ. and law sect. exec. com. 1977-80, exec. com., internat. practice com. 1986—), Orange County Bar Assn. (chmn. internat. law sect. 1984—), World Trade Center Assn. Orange County (bd. dirs. 1976—, chmn. 1986—), Orange County C. of C., Am. Arbitration Assn. (nat. panel), Union Internationale des Avocats. Lodge: Rotary. Home: 441 El Bosque Laguna Beach CA 92651 Office: 1201 Dove St 6th Fl Newport Beach CA 92660

SCHWEIGERT, LYNETTE AILEEN, interior designer, consultant; b. Sacramento, July 6, 1949; d. Marvin Gerhardt and Aileen Helen (Velcoff) S.; m. Alan H. Randolph, May 1, 1976; 1 child, Tyler Mason Randolph. BS in Design, U. Calif., Davis, 1971. Display designer Weinstock's, Sacramento, 1971-72, Roos-Atkins, Sacramento, 1972-73; prin., project designer Randolph-Schweigert & Co., Reno, 1975—; prin. Design Ctr. Cons., Reno, 1982—, ptnr., project designer Hospitality Design Group, Reno, 1985—; cons. interior design Dan Carne AIA, Reno, 1980—, Paul Huss AIA, Reno, 1985—, U.S. West Investments, Reno, 1984—; cons. space planning Family Counseling Service of No. Nev., Reno, 1986—. Named one of Top 60 Restaurant Designers, Contract Mag., 1985; recipient Finalist prize Sierra Arts Found., Reno, 1980, Cert. Recognition for Participation in Preprofessional Internship Program U. Nev., 1987. Mem. Inst. Bus. Designers (affiliate). Avocations: photography, skiing, vegetable gardening, water ballet. Office: Randolph-Schweigert & Co 547 S Arlington Ave Reno NV 89509

SCHWEIKHER, PAUL, architect; b. Denver, July 28, 1903; s. Frederick and Elisabeth Ann (Williams) S.; m. Dorothy Miller, Dec. 17, 1923; 1 child, Paul. Student, U. Colo., 1921-22; B.F.A. (fellow), Yale U., 1929, M.A. (hon.), 1953. Registered Nat. Council Archtl. Registration Bds., also in 14 states. Practicing architect 1933—; partner Schweikher & Elting, 1945-53; co-founder Chgo. Workshops, 1933-35; vis. critic architecture Yale, 1947, 50-53, chmn. architecture, 1953-56; head dept. architecture Carnegie-Mellon U., 1956-68; now prof. emeritus architecture; vis. prof. Princeton U., 1960-61; vis. critic architecture U. Kans., 1950; lectr. Syracuse U., 1951; Mem. U. Ill. Conf. Archtl. Edn., 1949; mem. panel Sch. Planning Conf., Nat. Art Edn. Assn., N.Y.C., 1951; mem. Conf. on Edn. in Architecture and the Fine Arts, Carnegie Inst. tech., 1953; mem. jury architecture Fulbright awards Inst. Internat. Edn., 1953-54; fellowships Am. Acad. Rome, 1955; mem. Pitts. Planning Commn., 1961-64; Mem. adv. council Sch. Architecture, Princeton, 1961-69. Contbr. articles to profl. publs.; prin. works include Paul Schweikher House and Studio (hist. site), Mus. Modern Art, N.Y.C., Renaissance Soc., U. Chgo., Carnegie Inst. Tech., Akron (Ohio) Art Inst., galleries U. Minn., U. Ill., U. Kans., Yale, Princeton, Ariz. State U., Carnegie Inst. Mus. Fine Arts; 2 one-man exhbns., Harvard U., 1968, Yale, 1968; represented in permanent collection Art Inst. Chgo. Served to lt. comdr. USNR, 1942-45. Recipient Ford Found. research grant in theater design, 1960-61. Mem. Art Inst. Chgo. (life), Chi Psi. Club: Arts (Chgo.). Address: 5110 N 32d St # 202 Phoenix AZ 85018

SCHWEITZER, BERNARD PAUL, engineer; b. N.Y.C., June 16, 1933; s. Max and Jeanne (Periera) S.; m. Masha Frydman, June 28, 1958; children: Leslie Anne, Jennifer Robin. BS in Physics, Calif. Inst. Tech., 1955; MS in Engring., UCLA, 1962, PhD in Engring., 1971. Engr. Hycon Mfg. Co., Pasadena, Calif., 1955-59; chief scientist Hughes Aircraft Co., Culver City, Calif., 1959—. Contbr. articles to profl. jours.; patentee in field. Mem. AAAS, IEEE, Sigma Xi. Democrat. Jewish. Avocations: photography, hiking, traveling. Home: 9626 Monte Mar Dr Los Angeles CA 90035 Office: Hughes Aircraft Co PO Box 92426 Los Angeles CA 90009-2426

SCHWEITZER, FREDERICK VERNON, auditor, educator; b. Amarillo, Tex., May 19, 1907; s. Fred R. and Olive (Smith) S.; student Kans. Wesleyan U., 1924-26; A.B., U. So. Calif., 1928; postgrad. U. Berlin, 1933; M.A. in Pub. Adminstrn., Columbia U., 1943; m. Cora Henderson, 1928 (div. 1931); m. 2d, Ruth Twenhoefel, 1934 (div. 1940); m. 3d, Margaret Cunha, 1942 (div. 1948); m. 4th, Mary Ann Hiatt, 1948 (div. 1971); children by previous marriage—Gordon Mirrell, Fred Karl (dec.). Public acct. Arthur Anderson & Co., Los Angeles, 1927-30; vice consul Dept. State, Brisbane, Queensland, Australia, 1930-33; field auditor Dept. Agr., Washington, 1933-36; sr. public acct. Peat Marwick Mitchell & Co., San Francisco, 1936; chief div. research and statistics Calif. Dept. Social Welfare, Sacramento, 1936-37; chief acct. Marchant Calculators, Inc., Oakland, Calif., 1938-42; dep. dir. vets. preference div. War Assets Adminstrn., San Francisco, 1946-48; sr. adminstrv. analyst Calif. Joint Legis. Budget Com., Sacramento, 1949-53; S.W. div. dir. Olivett Corp. Am., Dallas, 1954-61; mgr. system sales Friden Inc., Sacramento, 1962-66; data processing systems analyst Calif. Water Resources Dept., Sacramento, 1966-72, internal auditor, 1972-75; instr. history dept. Sacramento City Coll., 1951-52; instr. Calif. State Internal Auditors Assn., 1973-75; instr. Dept. Fish and Game, 1973-75; pvt. practice pub. acctg., Sacramento, 1975—; owner, operator walnut orchard, Yuba City, Calif., 1966-79. Mem. Sacramento County Republican Central Com., 1966-70; chmn. data processing com. Calif. Rep. Central Com., 1968-70; pres. chpt. 165 Calif. State Employees Assn., 1964-66. Served to lt. comdr. USNR, 1942-46. Recipient letter of appreciation for services as instr. at Mgmt. Devel. Inst., Gov. Ronald Reagan, 1969. Mem. Nat. Assn. Accountants, Mgmt. Systems Assn., Western Govtl. Research Assn., S.R., VFW, Phi Mu Alpha. Presbyterian. Clubs: Shriners, Scottish Rite (Sacramento); Masons (Cambridge, Mass.). Author articles. Home: 3908 Heights Ct Cameron Park CA 95682 Office: Travelodge 43 902 Del Paso Blvd Sacramento CA 95815

SCHWERIN, KARL HENRY, anthropology educator, researcher; b. Bertha, Minn., Feb. 21, 1936; s. Henry William and Audrey Merle (Jahn) S.; m. Judith Drewanne Altermatt, Sept. 1, 1958 (div. May 1975); children: Karl Frederic, Marguerite DelValle; m. Partha Louise Hake Buell, Jan. 25, 1979; stepchildren: Tamara, Brent, Taryn. BA, U. Calif., Berkeley, 1958; PhD, UCLA, 1965. Instr. Los Angeles State Coll., 1963; asst. prof. anthropology U. N.Mex., Albuquerque, 1963-68, assoc. prof., 1968-72, prof., 1972—, asst. chmn. dept. anthropology, 1983-85, chmn. dept. anthropology, 1987—; prof. invitado Inst. Venezolano de Investigaciones Cientificas, Caracas, 1979. Author: Oil and Steel Processes of Karinya Culture Change, 1966, Antropologia Social, 1969, Winds Across the Atlantic, 1970; editor: Food Energy in Tropical Ecosystems, 1985; contbr. articles to profl. jours. V.p. Parents without Ptnr., Albuquerque, 1976-77. Grantee Cordell Hull Found., Venezuela, 1961-62, N.Y. Zool. Soc., Honduras, 1981; Fulbright scholar Cañar, Ecuador, 1969-70, Paris, 1986. Fellow Am. Anthropol. Assn.; mem. Am. Ethnol. Soc., Am. Soc. Ethnohistory (pres. 1975), Southwestern Anthropol. Assn. (co-editor Southwestern Jour. Anthropology 1972-75), N.Mex. Cactus and Succulent Society (v.p. 1970-71), Maxwell Mus. Assn. (bd. dirs. 1984-85), Internat. Congress of Americanists (35th-40th, 43d), Sigma Xi (chpt. pres. 1980-81). Avocations: photography, hiking, camping, cycling, studying cacti. Office: U NMex Dept Anthropology Albuquerque NM 87131

SCHWINDEN, TED, governor of Montana; b. Wolf Point, Mont., Aug. 31, 1925; s. Michael James and Mary (Preble) S.; m. B. Jean Christianson, Dec. 21, 1946; children: Mike, Chrys, Dore. Student, Mont. Sch. Mines, 1946-47; B.A., U. Mont., 1949, M.A., 1950; postgrad., U. Minn., 1950-54. Owner-operator grain farm Roosevelt County, Mont., 1954—; land commr. State of Mont., 1969-76; lt. gov. 1977-80, gov., 1981—; mem. U.S. Wheat Trade Mission to Asia, 1968. Chmn. Mont. Bicentennial Adv. Council, 1973-76; mem. Mont. Ho. of Reps., 1959, 61, Legis. Council, 1959-61, Wolf Point Sch. Bd., 1966-69, Pub. Employees Retirement System Bd., 1969-74. Served with inf. AUS, 1943-46. Decorated Combat Inf. badge. Mem. Mont. Grain Growers (pres. 1965-67), Western Wheat Assos. (dir.). Democrat. Lutheran. Clubs: Masons, Elks. Office: Office of Gov State Capitol Helena MT 59620 *

SCHWINDT, JON CAMERON, sire analyst, dairy cattle consultant; b. Kingsville, Ont., Can., Dec. 19, 1937; came to U.S., 1947; s. Carl Cameron and Evelyn Violet (Little) S.; m. Doris Carlyn Wiese, June 11, 1960; 1 child, Jon Alan. BS, Calif. Poly. Inst., 1964. Herdsman Golden Top Dairy, Saticoy, Calif., 1964-67; fieldman Calif. Holstein Assn., Fresno, 1967-68; sanitarian Fresno County Health Dept., 1968-72; evaluator, regional program coordinator Genetics, Carnation Genetics, Landmark Genetics, Hughson, Calif., 1972—. Served with U.S. Army, 1961-63. Republican. Home: 1705 Dennis St Clovis CA 93612 Office: Handmark Genetics PO Box 939 Hughson CA 95326

SCHWINGER, JULIAN, educator, physicist; b. N.Y.C., Feb. 12, 1918; s. Benjamin and Belle (Rosenfeld) S.; m. Clarice Carrol, 1947. A.B., Columbia U., 1936, Ph.D., 1939, D.Sc., 1966; D.Sc. (hon.), Purdue U., 1961, Harvard U., 1962, Brandeis U., 1973, Gustavus Adolphus Coll., 1975; LL.D., CCNY, 1972. NRC fellow 1939-40; research asso. U. Calif.-Berkeley, 1940-41; instr., then asst. prof. Purdue U., 1941-43; staff mem. Radiation Lab., MIT, 1943-46; staff Metall. Lab., U. Chgo., 1943; asso. prof. Harvard U., 1945-47, prof., 1947-72, Higgins prof. physics, 1966-72; prof. physics UCLA, 1972-80, Univ. prof., 1980—; Mem. bd. sponsors Bull. Atomic Sci.; sponsor Fedn. Am. Scientists; J.W. Gibbs hon. lectr. Am. Math. Soc., 1960. Author: Particles and Sources, 1969, (with D. Saxon) Discontinuities in Wave Guides, 1968, Particles, Sources and Fields, 1970, Vol. II, 1973, Quantum Kinematics and Dynamics, 1970, Einstein's Legacy, 1985; editor: Quantum Electrodynamics, 1958. Recipient C. L. Mayer nature of light award, 1949, univ. medal Columbia U., 1951, 1st Einstein prize award, 1951; Nat. Medal of Sci. award for physics, 1964; co-recipient Nobel prize in Physics, 1965; recipient Humboldt award, 1981; Guggenheim fellow, 1970. Mem. Nat. Acad. Scis., Am. Acad. Arts and Scis., Am. Phys. Soc., Royal Instn. Gt. Britain, ACLU, AAAS, N.Y. Acad. Scis. Office: Dept Physics U Calif Los Angeles CA 90024 *

SCHWITALLA, STEPHEN EDWARD, food service executive; b. Tacoma, Nov. 16, 1953; s. Alfred M. and Joan E. (Howard) S.; m. Susan Eileen Schwitalla, Mar. 10, 1973; children: Michael Howard, Diane Kelly. Region mgr. Servomation, Fremont, Calif., 1971-73; distbn. supr. Fleming Foods Co., Fremont, 1973-77; warehouse and transp. mgr. Fleming Foods Co., Oakland, Calif., 1977-79; warehouse and purchasing mgr. Distron/Burger King, San Jose, Calif., 1979-80; div. mgr. Nat. Convenient Stores, Los Angeles, 1980-82; v.p. distbn. Circle K Corp., Phoenix, 1982-85, corp. sr. v.p. foodservice, 1985—, pres. Deli Pride Foods Inc. div. Recipient Clio award for Advt. Excellence, 1985. Mem. Am. Mgmt. Assn., Nat. Assn. Convenience Stores, Ariz. Retail Grocers Assn., Internat. Food Mfg. Assn., Internat. Deli/Bakery Assn. Republican. Avocations: investments, wine and antique collecting, tennis.

SCIBOR-MARCHOCKI, ROMUALD IRENEUS, research scientist; b. Highland Park, Mich., Dec. 29, 1926; s Sigismond August and Sophy L. (Scibor-Marchocka) S-M. B.S., Wayne State U., 1947, M.S., 1948; postgrad. Calif. Inst. Tech., U. So. Calif. Asst. physics Wayne State U., 1943-47, spl. instr., 1947-48; sr. engr. labs. div. Hoffman Radio Corp., 1949-59; design specialist Aerojet Gen. Corp. div. Gen. Tire & Rubber Co., 1959-62; sr. scientist Nortonics div. Northrop Corp., 1962-68; mem. tech. staff Jet Propulsion Lab., Pasadena, 1968-72, staff scientist, 1970-72; owner Mädchental Kennels, Baldwin Park, 1955—; with Wells Fargo Security Guard Services div. Baker Protective Services, 1973-81; tutor Mt. San Antonio Coll., 1978—, staff math. dept., 1979—; cons. in math. and computer sci., 1980—. Mem. Calavo Growers Assn., Acoustical Soc., Math. Assn., Am. Def. Preparedness Assn., Assn. Physics Tchrs., N.Y. Acad. Sci., AAAS, Nat. Rifle Assn., Free for All, Mensa, Naturist Soc., Nat. Free Lance Photographers Assn., Sigma Xi. Contbr. articles to profl. jours. Home: 15250 E Arrow Hwy Baldwin Park CA 91706

SCITOVSKY, ANNE AICKELIN, economist; b. Ludwigshafen, Germany, Apr. 17, 1915; came to U.S., 1931, naturalized, 1938; d. Hans W. and Gertrude Margarete Aickelin; 1 dau., Catherine Margaret. Student, Smith Coll., 1933-35; B.A., Barnard Coll., 1937; postgrad., London Sch. Econs., 1937-39; M.A. in Econs., Columbia U., 1941. Mem. staff legis. reference service Library of Congress, 1941-44; mem. staff Social Security Bd., 1944-46; with Palo Alto (Calif.) Med. Research Found., 1963—, chief health econs. div., 1973—; Lectr. Inst. Health Policy Studies, U. Calif., San Francisco, 1975—; mem. Inst. Medicine, Nat. Acad. Scis., Pres.'s Commn. for Study of Ethical Problems in Medicine and Biomed. and Behavioral Research, U.S. Nat. Com. on Vital and Health Stats., 1975-78; cons. U.S. Dept. Health and Human Services, Inst. Medicine Council on Health Care Tech. Assessment. Mem. Am. Econ. Assn., Am. Public Health Assn. Home: 161 Erica Way Menlo Park CA 94025 Office: Palo Alto Med Research Found 860 Bryant St Palo Alto CA 94301

SCLAFANI, ROBERT ANSELMO, research genetics educator; b. Bklyn., June 20, 1953; s. Anthony William and Maria Carmela (Basta) S; m. Christine Marie Roberts, June 12, 1983. BA, Columbia U., 1975, MA, 1976, PhM, 1978, PhD, 1981. Postdoctoral fellow U. Wash., Seattle, 1981-85; asst. prof. genetics U. Colo., Denver, 1985—. Contbr. articles to profl. jours. Fellow Columbia U., 1975, NIH, 1982. Mem. Genetics Soc. Am., Am. Soc. Microbiology, Sigma Chi. Avocations: home brewing of beer and ale, softball. Office: U Colo Med Sch 4200 E 9th Ave Denver CO 80262

SCOGGIN, CHARLES HENRY, physician, educator, research director; b. Goodland, Kans., June 23; s. Charles R. and Charline (Knudson) S.; m. Karen Louise Kareus, June 13, 1970; children: Charles, Tamar. BS, Colo. State U., 1966; MD, U. Colo, 1970. Diplomate Am. Bd. Med. Examiners, Am. Bd. Internal Medicine (pulmonary sect.); lic. physician, N.C., Colo. Intern and resident Duke U., Durham, N.C., 1970-74; postdoctoral fellow U. Colo., Denver, 1974-76, asst. prof. medicine, 1976-80, assoc. prof., 1980—, head, sect. on human genetics, 1985—; co-head div. clin. applications Eleanor Roosevelt Inst., Denver, also trustee and v.p., 1985—; pres. Somatogenetics Internat. Mem. editorial bd. Chest Jour. Recipient Haskil Shiff award Duke U. Med. Ctr., 1974, New Investigator award Nat. Inst. Child Health and Human Devel., 1980; named Best Clin. Tchr. U. Colo. Sch. Medicine, Denver, 1979; Searle-Mark Baier Meml. Career scholar Am. Lung Assn., 1985. Mem. ACP, Am. Coll. Chest Physicians, Profl. Rodeo Cowboys Assn. Republican. Episcopalian. Office: Eleanor Roosevelt Inst Cancer Research 4200 E 9th Ave B129 Denver CO 80262

SCOPATZ, MARY PORPIGLIA, educational administrator; b. Albany, N.Y., July 1, 1934; d. Paul Vincent and Antoinette Mary (Cambareri) Porpiglia; B.S., SUNY, Albany, 1956; M.S., Syracuse U., 1967; Ed.D., Nova U., 1980; m. John Anthony Scopatz, Apr. 1, 1956 (dec. 1973); children—Stephen David, Robert. Tchr. bus. Liverpool (N.Y.) High Sch., 1965-67; tchr. Los Angeles City Schs., 1967-69; tchr. Santa Barbara (Calif.) High Sch., 1970-78, chairperson bus. edn. dept., 1971-78, dir. project for disadvantaged students Santa Barbara County Schs., 1978-79, dir. career and youth employment programs, 1979—; bd. dirs. Santa Barbara Industry Edn. Council. Mem. Am. Vocat. Assn., Calif. Assn. Vocat. Edn. (pres. 1979-80), Calif. Bus. Edn. Assn. (pres. So. sect. 1976), So. Calif. Consortium of Industry Edn. Councils (pres. 1985-86). Home: 26-3 Barranca Santa Barbara CA 93109 Office: Santa Barbara County Schs 4400 Cathedral Oaks Rd Santa Barbara CA 93160

SCOPINICH, JILL LORIE, editor, writer; b. Seattle, Dec. 7, 1945; d. Oscar John and Marcella Jane (Hearing) Younce; 1 child, Lori. AA in Gen. Edn., Am. River Coll., 1969; BA in Journalism, Sacramento State U., 1973. Reporter Carmichael (Calif.) Courier, 1968-70; mng. editor Quarter Horse of the Pacific Coast, Sacramento, 1970-75, editor, 1975-84; editor NRCHA News, Sacramento, 1983—, Pacific Coast Jour., Sacramento, 1984—; mag. cons., 1975—. Editor: Golden State Program Jour., 1978, Nat. Snaffle Bit Assn. News, 1987. Bd. dirs. CWWPH Assn., Carmichael, 1985. Recipient 1st pl. feature award Jour. Assn. Jr. Colls., 1970, 1st pl. editorial award Jour. Assn. Jr. Colls., 1971, 1st pl. design award WCHB Yuba-Sutter Counties, Marysville, Calif., 1985. Mem. Am. River Jaycees (recipient speaking award 1982), Am. Horse Publs. (recipient 1st pl. editorial award 1983), MENSA (bd. dirs., asst. local sec., activities dir. 1987-88). Republican. Roman Catholic. Club: 5th Wheel Touring Soc. (Sacramento) (v.p. 1970). Avocations: sailing, photography. Home: 4333 Glen Vista St Carmichael CA 95608 Office: Pacific Coast Jour Gate 12 Cal-Expo Sacramento CA 95865

SCORCE, JOLI ANNE, social worker; b. Bklyn., Sept. 26, 1960; d. John Matthew and Denise (Fauci) S. BA, U. Va., 1982; MSW, Cath. U. Am., 1985. Psychiat. technician No. Va. Mental Health Inst., Falls Church, 1982-83; counselor Arlington (Va.) Community Residence, 1983-85; psychiat. social worker Napa (Calif.) State Hosp., 1985-86; psychiat. social worker day treatment program San Mateo County Mental Health Ctr., Redwood City, Calif., 1986—. Mem. Nat. Assn. Social Workers. Roman Catholic. Home: 2203 Vista del Mar San Mateo CA 94404 Office: San Mateo County Mental Health Ctr 411 Middlefield Redwood City CA 94063

SCORSINE, JOHN MAGNUS, lawyer; b. Rochester, N.Y., Dec. 3, 1957; s. Frank and Karin (Frennby) S.; m. Susan Nauss, May 31, 1980. BS, Rochester Inst. Tech., 1980; JD, U. Wyo., 1984. Bar: Wyo., 1984, U.S. Dist. Ct. Wyo., 1984. Police officer Casper (Wyo.) Police Dept., 1980-81; intern U.S. Atty. Office, Cheyenne, Wyo., 1983-84; sole practice Rock Springs, Wyo., 1984-85; ptnr. Scorsine and Flynn, Rock Springs, 1986; sole practice Scorsine Law Office, Rock Springs, 1986—; bd. dirs., treas. Youth Home, Inc., Rock Springs. Leader Medicine Bow Ski Patrol, Laramie, Wyo., 1983; legal advisor Rocky Mountain div. Nat. Ski Patrol, 1984; asst. patrol leader White Pine Ski Area, Pinedale, Wyo., 1986; active Jackson Hole Snow King Ski Patrol, 1987. Mem. Wyo. State Bar, ABA, Wyo. Trial Lawyers Assn., Assn. Am. Trial Lawyers, Rock Springs C. of C. Democrat. Lutheran. Lodge: Rotary. Avocations: rock climbing, backpacking, hunting. Home: 519 Wasatch Circle Rock Springs WY 82901 Office: Scorsine Law Office 1400 Dewar Dr Rock Springs WY 82902-1152

SCOTT, ALLEN JOHN, geography educator; b. Liverpool, England, Dec. 23, 1938; came to U.S., 1980; s. William Rule and Nella Maria (Pieri) S.; m. Nga Thuy Nguyen, Jan. 19, 1979. BA, Oxford (Eng.) U., 1961; PhD, Northwestern U., 1965. Asst. prof. dept. regionsl sci. U. Pa., 1965-67; research assoc. dept. town planning U. Coll. London, 1967-69; prof. geography UCLA, 1980—; Professeur associé U. Paris, 1974. Author: Combinatorial Programming, 1971, Urban Land Nexus, 1980. Fellow Com. on Scholarly Communication with People's Republic China, 1986. Croucher fellow U. Hong Kong, 1984; Guggenheim fellow, 1986-87. Office: UCLA Dept Geography 405 Hilgard Ave Los Angeles CA 90024

SCOTT, BEVERLY ANN, distribution company official; b. Scottsbluff, Nebr., Dec. 27, 1941; d. Henry Clay and Illma Elizabeth (Moody) S.; m. Alan S. Davenport, Aug. 29, 1964 (div., 1980); 1 child, Darby Layne. BA with honors in Sociology, U. Puget Sound, 1963; MA in Sociology, U. Iowa, 1966; postgrad. U. Mich., 1976-79. Instr. Cornell Coll., Mt. Vernon, Iowa, 1965-66, Coe Coll., Cedar Rapids, Iowa, 1966-67; program developer Linn Econ. Action Project, Cedar Rapids, 1967-68; exec. dir. Hawkeye Area Community Action Program, Cedar Rapids, 1968-70; program developer YWCA, Detroit, 1972; social planning and devel. analyst City of Detroit, 1972-75; cons. and edn. specialist Wayne County Community Coll., Detroit, 1975-76; sr. ptnr. Change HRD, Detroit, 1976-79; sr. assoc. Cons. Assocs., Detroit, 1979-81; corp. cons. Bendix Corp., Detroit, 1981; mgr. orgn. and mgmt. devel. McKesson Corp., San Francisco, 1982—; speaker NRD Conf., 1987. Author: (with Ronald Kregoski) Quality Circles: How to Create Them, How To Manage Them, How to Profit from Them, 1982. Mem. adv. bd. North End Concerned Citizens Community Council, 1973, dist. adv. com., 1975-76; chair YWCA, 1972-73, mem., 1971-81; fin. chair Montessorri Sch., 1972-73; chair social awareness group Faculty Women's Group U. Mich., 1972-73; pres. Women's Justice Ctr., 1979-80; co-chair Women's Equality Day Planning Com., 1980; steering com. UCS Met. Cam Council, 1977-81; chair program com. Detroit Women's Forum, 1977-80; mem. tng. team People Acting for Change Together, 1972-75. Named Mgr. of Yr., McKesson Foods Group, 1983. Mem. NOW, Am. Soc. Tng. and Devel., The Women's Found. (major donor com. 1986-87), Am. Sociol. Assn., Nat. Council Family Relations, Midwest Sociol. Assn., Youth Employment Service, Iowa Community Action Dirs., United Community Service Execs., Mich. Episcopal Tng. Network, Univ. Assocs., Women Decision Makers of Detroit, Women in Orgn. Devel., Orgn. Devel. Network (co-chmn. program com. conf. 1985, devel. com. Equal Rights Advocates1987), Am. Camping Assn. (camping unlimited com. 1976-77, editor Vision/Action Jour. 1987). Home: 166 Castro St San Francisco CA 94114 Office: McKesson Corp 1 Post St San Francisco CA 94104

SCOTT, CHARLES KENNARD, state senator, cattle rancher; b. Oreg., Aug. 19, 1945; s. Oliver Kennard and Deborah Ann (Hubbard) S.; m. Elaine Fenton, Dec. 20, 1975; children—Daniel, Abigail. A.B., Harvard Coll., 1967; M.B.A., Harvard U., 1969. Analyst, HEW and EPA, 1969-74; v.p., mgr. Bates Creek Cattle Co., Casper, Wyo., 1974—; mem. Wyo. Ho. of Reps., 1979-82; mem. Wyo. Senate, 1982—; co-owner The Country Computer, 1984—.

SCOTT, CHARLES R., diversified company executive; b. 1928. With Dallas Morning News, 1949-51, Branham Co., 1951-55, Southwestern Investment, Inc., 1955-56, Parker Ford and Co., 1957-62; with Intermark, Inc., 1970—, now pres., also bd. dirs. Office: Intermark Inc PO Box 1149 La Jolla CA 92038 *

SCOTT, CLIFFORD MARC, advertising executive; b. Los Angeles, Sept. 4, 1954; s. Stephen Charles Scott and Patricia Joan (Hymson) Reichman; m. Lisa Ann Saks, Mar. 14, 1982 (div. Nov. 1985); m. Susan Lynn Mallet, May 24, 1986. BA, UCLA, 1976. Asst. prodn. mgr. Gumpertz, Bentley, Fried, & Scott, Los Angeles, 1973-74; broadcast producer So. Calif. Rapid Transit Dist., Los Angeles, 1974-76; dir. print and broadcast Scott Lancaster Mills Atha, Los Angeles, 1976-80, v.p. account supr., 1980-86, v.p. account supr., jr. ptnr., 1986—. Recipient 1st Place award (best in west) Am. Advt. Fedn., N.Y., 1981, ANDY award Advt. Club N.Y., 1981, First Place award Hollywood Radio & TV Soc., 1982, CLIO award, N.Y., 1983. Republican. Jewish. Avocations: golf, tennis, skiing, gardening. Office: Scott Lancaster Mills Atha 2049 Century Park E #860 Los Angeles CA 90067

SCOTT, CLIFFORD RAY, minister, broadcasting station executive; b. Wilmington, N.C., June 15, 1930; s. DeWitt Talmadge and Ruth Elvera (Hufham) S.; student Reedley (Calif.) Coll., 1963-64, Internat. Coll., Honolulu, 1977-80; m. Billie Jean Gibson, Jan. 3, 1956; children—Clifford, Lisa, David, Rebecca. Ordained minister Bapt. Gen. Conf. Announcer, Sta. WGBR, Goldsboro, N.C., 1956, Sta. WMFD, Wilmington, N.C., 1956-58, Sta. KBIS, Bakersfield, Calif., 1958; announcer, account exec. Sta. KRDU, Dinuba, Calif., 1958-67; asst. mgr. Sta. WFGW, Black Mountain, N.C., 1967-71; gen. mgr. Sta. KAIM, Honolulu, 1971—. Served with U.S. Army, 1949-52. Mem. Nat. Religious Broadcasters, Nat. Assn. Broadcasters. Republican. Baptist. Club: Kiwanis (past pres.). Office: KAIM 3555 Harding Ave PO Box 375 Honolulu HI 96816

SCOTT, DAN WILLIAM, computer science educator; b. Galveston, Tex., July 13, 1930; s. Daniel William Jr. and Hilda (Jacobson) S.; m. Martha Margaret Hayes (div.); children: John Mason, David Robert, Charlotte Marie, Steven Kellicut. BS in Physics with high honors, U. Tex., 1951, MA, 1952; PhD, MIT, 1962. V.p. research and devel. Univ. Computing Co., Dallas, 1968-71; prof. computer sci. North Tex. State U., Denton, 1971-82; mgr. cryptographic products Teneron Corp., Beaverton, Oreg., 1984-85; assoc. prof. computer sci. Portland (Oreg.) State U., 1985—. Home: 10960-B Garden Park Pl Tigard OR 97223

SCOTT, EDWARD LAWRENCE, manufacturing company executive; b. Phila., July 11, 1914; s. Louis Charles and Frances (Lawrence) S.; m. Margaret Emerson McGregor (div.); 1 child, Heidi Sharp Scott; m. Barbara Jean Lewis, Sept. 22, 1963; 1 stepchild, Timothy Joseph Bushnell. Pres. Scott-USA, Sun Valley, Idaho, 1959-71, Scott-Mathauser Corp., Sun Valley, 1975—. Served as sgt. U.S. Army, 1942-45. Named to Ski Bus. Hall of Fame, Ski Mag., 1986. Home: Box 323 Ketchum ID 83340 Office: Scott Mathauser Corp Box 1333 Sun Valley ID 83353

SCOTT, EDWARD ROBERT DALTON, planetary scientist, researcher; b. Heswall, Eng., Mar. 22, 1947; came to U.S., 1972; s. Alan Dalton and Barbara Joan (Cook) S.; m. Anneliese Victoria Sullivan, May 10, 1980; 1 child, Victoria. BA, U. Cambridge, Eng., 1968, MA, PhD, 1972. Research geophysicist UCLA, 1972-75; post-doctoral researcher U. Cambridge, 1975-78; sr. fellow Carnegie Inst. Washington, 1978-80; research scientist U. N.Mex., Albuquerque, 1980—; mem. meteorite working group NASA, Houston, 1984-86, lunar and planetary geoscis. rev. panel, 1985-87. Contbr. articles to profl. jours. Fellow Meteoritical Soc. (councillor 1977-80); mem. Am. Geophys. Union (assoc. editor 1985-87), Mineral. Soc. (Eng.), Planetary. Soc. Home: 1711 Ross Pl SE Albuquerque NM 87108 Office: U NMex Dept Geology Albuquerque NM 87131

SCOTT, ELIZABETH HUTCHISON, public relations executive; b. Evanston, Ill., Jan. 14, 1951; d. Stanley Philip and Helen Jane (Rush) H. BS in Speech with highest distinction, Northwestern U., 1981. Dir. pub. relations Nat. Assn. Music Mchts., Carlsbad, Calif., 1982—. Editor: (newsletter) Music Retailer News, 1982—. Mem. Pub. Relations Soc. Am. (chmn. by-laws com. Chgo. chpt. 1984), Friends and Music, USA (nat. vice-chmn., sec. 1982—). Avocations: songwriting, singing, music arranging and producing. Office: Nat Assn Music Mchts 5140 Avenida Encinas Carlsbad CA 92008

SCOTT, FRANKLIN ROBERT, electric power research director; b. Portland, Oreg., Aug. 23, 1922; s. Linden Douglas and Mabel Gay (Smith) S.; m. Christine Louise Golter, Aug. 10, 1950; children: Barbara Louise, Deborah Joanne, Kenneth Robert. BA, Reed Coll., 1947; MS, Ind. U., 1949, PhD, 1952. Research staff mem. Los Alamos (N.Mex.) Sci. Lab., 1951-57; asst. dir. thermonuclear program Gen. Atomic, San Diego, 1957-67; prof. physics and astronomy U. Tenn., Knoxville, 1967-73; chief open systems br. U.S. AEC, Germantown, Md., 1973-75; mgr. fusion power systems program Electric Power Research Inst., Palo Alto, Calif., 1975-86; cons. Oak Ridge (Tenn.) Nat. Lab., 1967-73, Dept. Energy, Washington, 1977—, EPRI, 1987—. Patentee in field; 41 pubs. in nuclear physics, neutron physics, optical spectroscopy, plasma physics, fusion. Served to sgt. U.S. Army, 1943-46. Mem. AAAS, Am. Nuclear Soc., Am. Phys. Soc., Sigma Xi. Club: Toastmasters. Avocations: golf, philately. Home: 2708 Wakefield Dr Belmont CA 94002

SCOTT, GENE, engineer, marketing professional; b. N.Y.C., Apr. 23, 1939; s. Frank and Catherine Anna (McNally) Schlossman; m. Linda DeSoucey, Feb. 1, 1969; children: Denise, Eve. BSEE, CCNY, 1969; MS in Indsl. Adminstrn., Union Coll., 1975. Ops. mgr. Gen. Electric Co., Hudson Falls, N.Y., 1969-75; mktg. mgr. Leybold Heraeus, Monroeville, Pa., 1975-77, Material Research, Orangeberg, N.Y., 1977-79; v.p. mktg. Xinix, Santa Clara, Calif., 1982-84; mem. tech. staff Rockwell Internat., Anaheim, Calif., 1979-82, 84—; pres. bd. dirs. Scott Assocs., El Toro Calif., 1980—; mktg. dir. Window Tinting Assocs., Le Habre, Calif., 1985—; pres., mktg. dir. Macro-Search Info. Services, El Toro, 1985—. Inventor high vacuum thin film. Mktg. supporter City of Santa Ana (Calif.) Community Ctrs., 1985, 86, vol. work with poor, 1985, 86; mem. internat. music outreach com. Lake Hills Community Ch., Laguna Hills, Calif., 1985—, mem. choir, 1984—; big brother Big Bros. Big Sisters Orange County, Tustin, Calif., 1984-85. Served with USNG, 1964-69. Ednl. Fin. grantee State of N.Y., 1964-68. Mem. Am. Vacuum Soc. (exec. com. 1985—), Assn. Indsl. Metallizers Coaters Laminators (film quality com. 1975-76). Republican. Home: 25061 Castlewood St El Toro CA 92630 Office: Rockwell Internat 3370 Miraloma Anaheim CA 92803

SCOTT, GEORGE EDMOND, psychiatrist, mental health administrator; b. LaJunta, Colo., Nov. 9, 1924; s. John Ferdinand and Ida Harriet (Spurlock) S.; m. Leila Ruth Hafer, June 24, 1950; children: George E. Jr., John C., James L., Elizabeth A. BA cum laude, U. Colo., 1946; MD, U. Colo., Denver, 1948. Intern, resident U. Iowa Hosp., Iowa City, 1948-50; practice medicine specializing in psychiatry Colo., 1950—; resident in psychiatry and neurology U. Colo. Med. Ctr., Denver, 1951-52, 56-59; assoc. psychiatrist Emory John Brady Hosp., Colorado Springs, Colo., 1950-56; chief neurology Colo. State Hosp., Pueblo, 1961-63; psychiatrist Denver Gen. Hosp., 1964-80, dir. hosp. psychiat. services, 1965-68; clin. dir. N.W. Denver Counseling Ctr., 1969-75, dir. emergency psychiat. services, 1975-76; med. dir. alcohol rehab. unit VA Med. Ctr., Ft. Lyon, Colo., 1980-83; med. dir. S.E. Colo. Family Guidance and Mental Health Ctr., Inc., La Junta, 1983—; cons. Prowers Meml. Hosp., Lamar, Colo., 1984—, Prowers Adolescent Ctr., Lamar, 1984—, Colo. Dept. Rehab., 1959-61, St. Joseph's Sch. for Boys, Denver, 1969-71. Contbr. articles to profl. jours. Served to lt. col. USAR, 1942-44, 48-62, 76-85. NIH grantee, 1967. Mem. AAAS, Colo. State Med. Soc., El Paso County Mental Health Assn. (bd. dirs. 1955-56), Otero County Med. Soc., S.E. Colo. Med. Soc. Democrat. Lutheran. Avocations: music, history, theology, pipe collecting. Home: 504 East C St Box 3-286 Fort Lyon CO 81038 Office: SE Colo Family Guidance and Mental Health Ctr Inc 711 Barnes Ave La Junta CO 81050

SCOTT, GEORGE LARKHAM, IV, architect, consultant; b. Bloomington, Ill., Aug. 11, 1947; s. George Larkham III and Marilyn Louise (Bouseman) S.; m. Patricia Jean Gregurich, Aug. 1, 1969; 1 child, Matthew Larkham. B in Archtl. Studies, Wash. State U., 1973, BArch, 1974. Dir. facilities planning County of Spokane, Wash., 1978-79; project architect Skidmore, Owings & Merrill, Portland, Oreg., 1981-82; owner George L. Scott, Architect and Planner, Portland, Oreg., 1982—. Prin. works include high tech. clean room facilities for nat. and internat. clients, helistop for U.S. Bancorp Tower, U.S. Bancorp Office Bldg., Portland, Oreg., on-base family housing complex trident Submarine Base, Bangor, Washington, interior layout and design of Bonneville Power Adminstrn. 500,000 S.F. hdqrs. bldg.; lectr., contbr. articles on clean room tech. to profl. jours. Chmn. Task Force on Community Devel., Spokane, 1977; active Committee to Elect Gov. Ray, Wash., 1977-78, City of Spokane Planning Commn., 1977-78. Avocations: sailing, photography, travel.

SCOTT, J(AMES) MICHAEL, research biologist; b. San Diego, Sept. 20, 1941; s. James Melvin Scott and Eileen May (Rose) Scott Busby; m. Sharon Louise Middleton, Dec. 18, 1966; children: Kevin Charles, Heather Ann. BS in Biology, San Diego State U., 1966, MA in Biology, 1970; PhD in Zoology, Oreg. State U., 1973. Project dir. U.S. Fish and Wildlife Service, Mauna Loa Station, Hawaii Nat. Park, 1974-84, Condor Research Ctr., Ventura, Calif., 1984-86; leader Coop. Fish and Wildlife Research Unit, Moscow, Idaho, 1986—. Author: Forest Bird Communities of the Hawaiian Islands, 1986; editor: Estimating Numbers of Terrestrial Birds, 1981, Hawaii's Terrestrial Ecosystems: Protection and Management, 1985; also articles. Vol. Peace Corps, Colombia, 1963-65. Recipient R.E. Dimick award, Oreg. chpt. Wildlife Soc., 1973, Spl. Achievement award U.S. Fish and Wildlife Service, 1978, 81. Mem. Ecol. Soc. Am., Am. Ornithologists Union (elective), Pacific Seabird Group (pres. 1973-75). Avocations: bird watching, body surfing, skin diving, stamp collecting. Home: 1130 Kamiakan St Moscow ID 83843 Office: U Idaho Coop Fish and Wildlife Research Inst Moscow ID 83843

SCOTT, JIMMY PAUL, psychologist; b. Beckley, W.Va., Dec. 15, 1938; s. Frazier Paul and Virginia Lawrence (Martin) S.; m. Bettie Hutchins, Sept. 4, 1960 (div. 1971); children: Jay, Jonathan. BA in Psychology, U. N.C., 1959, MA in Psychology, 1962, PhD in Physiol. Psychology, 1966. Research asst. dept. psychology U. N.C., Chapel Hill, 1959-60, teaching asst., 1960-62, research assoc. Med. Sch. dept. psychiatriy, 1962-65; psychologist Human Engring. Lab., Aberdeen Proving Ground, Md., 1960-61; psychology trainee, Unit on Aging VA Ctr., Kecoughtan, Va., 1962; staff fellow Lab. Clin. Psychobiology NIMH, Bethesda, Md., 1966-70; lectr. dept. behavioral biology U. Calif., Davis, 1970-72; research psychologist Langley Porter Psychiatric Inst. U. Calif., San Francisco, 1972-76; dir. Physiobehavioral Tng. Lab., San Francisco, 1973-79, Acos Found., San Francisco, 1977-78; bd. dirs. A Ctr. for Nutrition and Natural Healing, San Francisco, Marin County, Health Kinesiology Ctr. San Francisco, Marin County, Health Kinesiology Inst.; mem. human subjects com. Physiol. Med. Studies, U. Calif., Davis, 1971-72; chmn. instrumentation com. Biofeedback Research soc., 1972-74; chmn. legis. com. Biofeedback Soc. Calif., 1974-75, mem. cert. com., 1974-77. Author: Energy and Allergy, 1984; mem. adv. com. Internat. Jour. Holistic Health and Medicine, 1985—; contbr. numerous articles to sci. jours. Cubmaster Boy Scouts Am., Davis, 1970-72. NIMH grantee, 1973. Fellow Internat. Coll. Applied Nutrition; mem. Am. Psychol. Assn. (exptl. div. 1967-79, 83—, comparative and physiol. div. 1967-79, 83—, health psychology div. 1985—), Nat. Assn. Research Biochemists, Am. Assn. Nutritional Cons., Sigma Xi. Avocations: amateur radio, scuba diving, flying. Home: 1030 Meadowsweet Dr Corte Madera CA 94925 Office: Health Kinesiology Inst 649 Irving St San Francisco CA 94122

SCOTT, J(OHN) CAMPBELL, science research administrator; b. Edinburgh, Scotland, Oct. 5, 1949; came to U.S. 1971; s. John Halliday and Christiana May (McCulloch) S.; m. Joyce Diane Wilson, May 4, 1975. BSc, St. Andrews U., Scotland, 1971; PhD, U. Pa., 1975. Asst. prof. of physics Cornell U., Ithaca, N.Y., 1975-80; research staff mem. IBM Research Corp., San Jose, Calif., 1980-85, mgr., 1985—. Contbr. articles to profl. jours. Mem. AAAS, Am. Phys. Soc., Materials Research Soc. Avocations: squash, windsurfing, golf. Home: 6188 Flowering Plum Rd San Jose CA 95120 Office: IBM Almaden Research Ctr K46/803 650 Harry Rd San Jose CA 95120-6099

SCOTT, JOHN FRANCIS, III, water resources engineer; b. Winchester, Mass., Nov. 21, 1949; s. John Francis Jr. and Vivian Gene (Miller) S.; divorced; children: Lindsey Melissa, Julia Patricia. BS, U.S. Mil. Acad., 1971; MS, Colo. State U., 1979, PhD, 1983. Research assoc. Colo. State U., Ft. Collins, 1977-83; water resources engr. Western Area Power Adminstrn., Loveland, Colo., 1983—; bd. dirs. Ft. Collins Water Bd., 1984—. Served with U.S. Army, 1971-76. Mem. ASCE, Am. Geophys. Union, Sigma Xi. Home: 1309 Kirkwood Dr #405 Fort Collins CO 80525 Office: Western Area Power Adminstrn PO Box 3700 Loveland CO 80539

SCOTT, JOYCE ELIZABETH, production management analyst; b. Mobile, Ala., Sept. 26, 1950. d. Johnnie and Levia Odell (Watts) Williams; AA, Am. River Coll., 1974; BA, San Francisco State U., 1979; MA, U. Calif., Davis, 1981; m. Russell Alan Scott, July 5, 1980; children: Veronica, Jason. Exec. sec. constrn. br. U.S. Army C.E., San Francisco, 1970-73; adminstrv. asst. Calif. Office Mgmt. and Budget, Sacramento, 1974-75; sales mgr. Jocelynn Starr Accessories, Oakland, Calif., 1977-78; electronics technician, quality assurance specialist Dept. Navy, Naval Air Rework Facility, Naval Air Sta., Alameda, Calif., 1978—, participant electronics apprentice program, 1978-82, 83-84; tchr., vocat. counselor in field, Recipient Superior Performance award State of Calif., 1975. Mem. Federally Employed Women, Adminstrv. Assn., Assn. Mgrs. Democrat. Club: Order Eastern Star. Home: 2698 78th Ave Oakland CA 94605 Office: Naval Air Rework Facility Ops Analysis Div (62130) Naval Air Sta Alameda CA 94501

SCOTT, JUANITA FULLER, rehabilitation counselor; b. Sylacauga, Ala., Mar. 26, 1936; d. Allie B. and Mattie (Moon) Fuller; m. Arthur Bohannon, Mar. 17, 1956 (div.); children—Arthur Bohannon, Anthony Bohannon; m. 2d, Cornelius L. Scott. B.A., U. Colo., 1973; M.A., U. No. Colo., 1974. Instr. adj. faculty Met. State Coll., Denver, 1974-82, Community Coll. Denver, 1974-76, Arapahoe Community Coll., 1978-79; social worker Mile High Child Care Assn., Denver, 1974-76; rehab. counselor State of Colo., Denver, 1977; pvt. cons. marriages, substance abuse, 1974—. Bd. dirs. Lutheran Social Services. U. No. Colo. scholar, 1973-74. Mem. Internat. Assn. Black Women in Criminal Justice System, Colo. Juvenile Counselors, Colo. Coalition Black Social Workers, Kappa Delta Pi, Colo. Black Women for Polit. Action, Black Psychologists of Denver, Alpha Kappa Alpha. Democrat. Baptist. Home: 5303 Tucson Way Denver CO 80239 Office: 3500 S Wadsworth Lakewood CO 80235

SCOTT, KONI KIM, designer, artist; b. Seoul, Korea, Dec. 4, 1942; d. Rinsuk Kim and Songeun (Chu) K.; m. Edward A. Scott, June 21, 1969; children: Myron, Bryan. BA in Design Arts, Seoul U., 1965; MFA, UCLA, 1969. Owner, mgr. M. Koni Art, Inc., Los Angeles, 1976—. Designer of KONI Collection; inventor Koniart. Founder, organizer Korean Girl Scouts in USA, 1978, mem. resources council, 1979. Recipient Civic award Los Angeles Lions Club, 1979. Mem. Am. Soc. Interior Designers, Design Am. (charter). Home: 3240 Lombardy Rd Pasadena CA 91107 Office: 2450 Mariondale Ave Los Angeles CA 90032

SCOTT, MARIE ANTOINETTE (TONI), counselor, consultant; b. Norfolk, Va., Sept. 14, 1935; d. Emil Albert Serlich and Minnie Lee (Sykes) Woodham; m. Haskell Carroll Scott, May 13, 1955 (div. 1971). B.A., Loretto Hts. Coll., 1976; M.A., Vt. Coll., 1981. Sec., U. Colo., Boulder, 1968-75, program specialist, 1975-78, counselor, 1978-82, instr. continuing edn. div., 1976—; counselor Front Range Community Coll., Westminster, Colo., 1982-84; pvt. practice as counselor, Boulder, 1984—; instr., counselor Pre-Retirement Planning Inst., Denver, 1976—; cons. various industries, Denver and Boulder, 1978—. Served with USAF, 1954-55. Mem. Am. Assn. Counseling and Devel., Colo. Assn. Counseling and Devel., Nat. Vocat. Guidance Assn., Colo. Coll. Personnel Assn., Women Educators Consortium, Colo. Cactus Succulent Soc., Am. Mental Health Counselors Assn., Colo. Ferret Fancier's Assn. Club: Sports Car Am. Home: Box 1894 Boulder CO 80306 Office: 1280 28th St Frontage Rd Suite 4 Boulder CO 80303

SCOTT, MARILYN JEAN, insurance company specialist; b. Seattle, June 3, 1939; d. Carlton Frederick and Margaret Katherine (Hiester) Wood; m. Robert Eugene Scott, June 14, 1959 (div. Dec. 1977); children: Bret Owen, Eric Leif; m. Charles Bernard Volkey, Sept. 7, 1985. AA, Clatsop Coll., 1975; BA, Marylhurst, 1983. Cert. assoc. risk mgr., assoc. safety profl. Interpreter U.S. Nat. Park Service, Sequoia and Kings Canyon Nat. Parks, Calif., 1972-74; instr. Clatsop Community Coll., Astoria, Oreg., 1975-76; loss control cons. EBI Companies, Portland, Oreg., 1976-82; ins. mktg. cons. SAIF Corp., Salem, Oreg., 1982-84, loss control trainer, 1984—. Author: (manuals) Accident Investigation for Supervisors, 1980, 1986; editor Page Signal newspaper, 1963. Pres. Miramonte (Calif.) PTA, 1973, Mental Health Assn., Page, Ariz., 1963; leader Boy Scouts Am., Kings Canyon Nat. Park, 1971-74, Girl Scouts Am., Grand Canyon Nat. Park, Ariz., 1966-70. Recipient Recognition for Service on Bicentennial Project award U.S. Nat. Park Service Office of Dir., 1975. Mem. Am. Soc. Safety Engrs., Am. Soc. Tng. and Devel., Oreg. Tng. and Devel. Assn., Nat. Safety Mgmt. Soc. Mem. Unitarian Ch. Avocations: skiing, kayaking, scuba, backpacking, sailing. Office: SAIF Corp 400 High St SE Salem OR 97312

SCOTT, MICHAEL JAMES, lawyer; b. Pendleton, Oreg., Jan. 4, 1956; s. Edward Michael and Kathryn Louise (Hague) S.; m. Laurie Anne Johnson, June 6, 1981. BA, Pacific U., 1978; JD, Lewis & Clark U., 1983. Bar: Oreg. 1983, U.S. Dist. Ct. Oreg. 1984. Exec. gen. mgr. Forest Grove (Oreg.) C. of C., 1979-80; assoc. Patrick J. Furrer, Tigard, Oreg., 1983-84; ptnr. Furrer & Scott, Tigard, 1984—. Trustee Pacific U., Forest Grove, 1977-80; mgr. Com. to Elect Paul Phillips State Rep., Tigard, 1983, mgr. Re-elect Paul Phillips State Rep., 1985—. Named one of Outstanding Young Men of Am., U.S. Jaycees, 1979. Mem. Oreg. State Bar (constrn. sect., bd. dirs. 1985—), Oreg. Law Related Edn. (bd. dirs. 1985—), Comml. Law League, Am. Trial Lawyers Assn., Washington County Bar Assn., Multnomah County Bar Assn., Tigard C. of C. (bd. dirs. 1984—), Lewis & Clark Law Sch. Alumni (bd. dirs., chmn. alumni admissions com. 1985). Club: Multnomah Athletic. Office: Furrer & Scott 9185 SW Burnham PO Box 23414 Tigard OR 97223

SCOTT, MICHAEL RAY, social worker; b. St. Paul, Feb. 15, 1948; s. Eugene Ray and Gloria Mae (Galvin) S. Student, St. John's U., Collegeville, Minn., 1966-68; BA, U. Minn., 1968-71; MSW, U. Wis., 1972-74. Social worker IV Dane County Dept. Social Service, Madison, Wis., 1974-76; juvenile probation officer King County Juvenile Ct., Seattle, 1977, juvenile ct. cons., 1977-78; case mgr. Tacoma (Wash.) Treatment Alternatives to Street Crime, 1978—. employee asst. program counselor Human Affairs Internat., Murray, Utah, 1984—. precinct committeeman Pierce County Rep., Tacoma, 1980-86, county conv. del., 1980, 82, 84, 86. Mem. Nat. Assn. Social Workers (ACSW), Am. Correctional Assn., Washington Correctional Assn., Wash. State Cert. Substance Abuse Profls. Republican. Roman Catholic. Avocations: long distance motorcycle tour and camping, theater, music, photography. Office: Tacoma TASC 710 S Fawcett Tacoma WA 98402

SCOTT, MORRIS DOUGLAS, ecologist; b. Mason City, Iowa, Sept. 8, 1945; s. Morris William and Maxine Imogene (Eppard) S.; m. Suvi Annikki Lehtinen, Aug. 12, 1983. B.S., Iowa State U., 1967; Ph.D., Auburn U., 1971. Instr. zoology Auburn U., Ala., 1971-72; asst. prof. So. Ill. U., Carbondale, 1972-74; sr. ecologist Amax Coal Co., Indpls., 1974-75, environ. mgr., Billings, Mont., 1975-77; research assoc. Mont. State U., Bozeman, 1977-80, dir. Inst. Natural Resources, 1980—; cons. mining industry. Author: Heritage from the Wild, Familiar Land and Sea Mammals of the Northwest. Editor Conf. Proceedings Plains Aquatic Research, 1983. Contbr. articles to profl. jours. Bd. dirs. Bridger Canyon Property Owners Assn., Bozeman, 1984—. Auburn U. fellow, 1970. Mem. Ecol. Soc. Am., Wildlife Soc., Animal Behavior Soc., Gamma Sigma Delta. Current work: Land use planning systems for microcomputers; wildlife mgmt. on reclaimed surface mines; behavioral ecology of feral dogs; ecology of waterfowl and grouse. Subspecialties: Behavioral ecology; Resource management. Home: 16257 Bridger Canyon, Bozeman, MT 59715

SCOTT, PETER BRYAN, lawyer; b. St. Louis, Nov. 11, 1947; s. Gilbert Franklin and Besse Jean (Fudge) S.; m. Suzanne Rosalee Wallace, Oct. 19, 1974; children: Lindsay W., Sarah W., Peter B. Jr. A.B., Drury Coll., 1969; J.D., Washington U., St. Louis, 1972, LL.M., 1980. Bar: Mo. 1972, Colo. 1980; diplomate Ct. Practice Inst. Sole practice, St. Louis, 1972-80; assoc. firm McKie and Assocs., Denver, 1980-81; ptnr. firm Scott and Chesteen, P.C., Denver, 1981-84, Veto & Scott, Denver, 1984—; tchr. Denver Paralegal Inst. Served to capt. USAR, 1971-79. Mem. ABA, Mo. Bar Assn., Colo. Bar Assn., Denver Bar Assn. Republican. Mem. United Church of Christ. Home: 26262 Wolverine Trail Evergreen CO 80439 Office: Veto & Scott 6595 W 14th Ave Suite 200 Lakewood CO 80214

SCOTT, PETER FRANCIS, food products company executive; b. Honolulu, 1927; married. B.S., U. Calif., 1952. Staff acct. Touche Ross Bailey & Smart, 1952-58; with Tay-Holbrook, Inc., 1958-63; asst. treas. Di Giorgio Corp., San Francisco, 1963-64, treas., 1964-69, v.p., treas., 1969-74, v.p., chief fin. officer, mem. exec. com., 1974-80, pres., chief operating officer, dir., 1980-84; chmn., pres., chief exec. officer Di Giorgio Corp., 1984—; dir. Hale Tech. Corp./Scott Corp. Calif. Served to capt. U.S. Army, 1946-49. Office: Di Giorgio Corp 1 Maritime Plaza San Francisco CA 94111 *

SCOTT, RICHARD WALTER, biology educator, botany researcher; b. Modesto, Calif., June 30, 1941; s. Frank Houseman and Dorothy Isabel (Betz) S.; m. Beverly Jean Wilson, Sept. 9, 1961; children: Suzanne Elaine, Kevin Richard. BS, U. Wyo., 1964, MS, 1966; MA, U. Mich., 1969, PhD, 1972. Asst. prof. biology Albion (Mich.) Coll., 1969-75; instr. Cen. Wyo. Coll., Riverton, 1975-85, prof., 1985—. Contbr. articles to profl. jours. NDEA fellow U. Mich., 1966-69. Mem. Am. Polar Soc., Sigma Xi, Phi Delta Kappa. Avocations: skiing, mountaineering, hunting, fishing, orchid growing. Home: 841 Christy Dr Riverton WY 82501 Office: Cen Wyo Coll Dept Biology Riverton WY 82501

SCOTT, ROBERT LANE, educator, chemist; b. Santa Rosa, Calif., Mar. 20, 1922; s. Horace Albert and Maurine (Lane) S.; m. Elizabeth Sewall Hunter, May 27, 1944; children: Joanna Ingersoll, Jonathan Armat, David St. Clair, Janet Hamilton. S.B., Harvard U., 1942; M.A., Princeton U., 1944, Ph.D., 1945. Sci. staff Los Alamos Lab., 1945-46; Frank B. Jewett fellow U. Calif. at Berkeley, 1946-48; faculty U. Calif. at Los Angeles, 1948—, prof. chemistry, 1960—, chmn. dept., 1970-75. Author: (with J.H. Hildebrand) Solubility of Nonelectrolytes, 3d edit, 1950, rev., 1964, Regular Solutions, 1962, Regular and Related Solutions, 1970; Contbr. articles to profl. jours. Guggenheim fellow, 1955; NSF sr. fellow, 1961-62; Fulbright lectr., 1968-69. Fellow Am. Phys. Soc.; Mem. Am. Chem. Soc. (Joel Henry Hildebrand award 1984), AAAS, Royal Soc. Chemistry (London), Sigma Xi. Home: 11128 Montana Ave Los Angeles CA 90049 Office: U Calif Dept Chemistry and Biochemistry 405 Hilgard Ave Los Angeles CA 90024

SCOTT, WILLIAM TAUSSIG, physics educator; b. Yonkers, N.Y., Mar. 16, 1916; s. Carl Forse and Dorothea (Taussig) S.; m. Helen Elizabeth Gabel, June 7, 1942 (div. Sept. 1961); children: Jennifer, Christopher (dec.), Stephanie, Melanie; m. Ann Howe Herbert, Sept. 29, 1961; children: Peter, Katherine. Student, Haverford Coll., 1933-34; BA, Swarthmore Coll., 1937; PhD, U. Mich., 1941. Instr. Amherst (Mass.) Coll., 1941-44; asst. prof. Deep Springs (Calif.) Jr. Coll., 1944-45; mem. faculty Smith Coll., Northampton, Mass., 1945-61, prof. physics, 1959-61; prof. physics U. Nev., Reno, 1961-81; research prof. atmospheric physics Desert Research Inst., 1964—; cons. Brookhaven Nat. Lab., Patchoque, N.Y., 1947-53, Nat. Bur. Standards, Washington, 1954-56, Nat. Ctr. Atmospheric Research, Boulder, Colo., 1964; vis. scholar Philosophy Ctr. Oxford U., Eng., 1969-70; vis. research fellow Yale U., New Haven, 1959-60. Author: The Physics of Electricity and Magnetism, 1959, 2d rev. edit., 1966, Erwin Schrödinger, An Introduction to His Writings, 1967, (monograph) The Theory of Small-Angle Multiple Scattering of Fast Charged Particles, 1963; contbr. articles to profl. jours. Mem. Reno Area Program for Am. Friends Service Com., 1961-84, U. Nev. Peace Studies Com., 1983—; chmn., bd. dirs. John Woolman Sch., Nevada City, Calif., 1966-69. NSF grantee, 1962-63, 69-70, NEH, 1968-74, 78-85; sci. faculty fellow NSF, 1960. Fellow Am. Phys. Soc.; mem. Am. Assn. Physics Tchrs., Am. Meteorol. Soc., Phi Beta Kappa, Sigma Xi. Democrat. Mem. Soc. of Friends. Home: 1425 Alturas Reno NV 89503 Office: U Nev Dept Physics Reno NV 89557

SCOTT, WINFIELD W., JR., air force officer, educator; b. Honolulu, Dec. 10, 1927; s. Winfield W. S.; m. Sally Ann Walker; children: Winfield W., Michael W., David, Mark, John, Kathryn. B.S., U.S. Mil. Acad., 1950; M.A. Internat. Law, Cath. U. Am., 1963; grad., Armed Forces Staff Coll., 1964, Naval War Coll., 1967. Commd., 2d lt. USAF, 1950, advanced through grades, lt. gen., 1978; served as tactical reconnaissance pilot USAF, Kimpo Air Base, S. Korea, 1951-52; various operational and maintenance assignments USAF, 1952-59; instr. Air Force Res. Officers Tng. Corps., 1959-62; prof. aerospace studies Cath. U. Am., Washington, 1962-63; asst. dir. ops. 366th Tactical Fighter Wing USAF, Da Nang Air Base, Vietnam, 1968; various command and staff positions USAF, 1969-77; asst. dep. chief staff plans and ops. Hdqrs. USAF, Washington, 1977-78; comdr. USAF, Alaskan Air Command, Elemdorf AFB, 1978-81; dep. comdr. U.S. Forces Korea, 1981—; dep. comdr. in chief UN Command, Korea; chief staff Combined Forces Command; comdr. Air Component Command; now supt. USAF Acad., Colorado Springs. Decorated D.S.M.; decorated Legion of Merit, D.F.C. with two oak leaf clusters, Bronze Star with V device, Meritorious Service medal, Air Medal with eight oak leaf clusters, Air Force Commendation medal, Republic Korea Order Nat. Security Merit; recipient L. Mendel Rivers medal for excellence Air Force Sgts. Assn., 1980. Office: Office of Superintendent USAF Space Academy CO 80840 *

SCOTT-LOWE, EMILY JOYCE, clinical social worker; b. Phila., Sept. 12, 1954; d. John Atwood and Mary Joyce (Forrester) Scott; m. Dennis W. Lowe, Dec. 20, 1975. BA, Pepperdine U., 1976; MSW, U. Tenn., 1979; PhD in Child Devel., Fla. State U., 1984. Lic. clin. social worker, Calif. Clin. social worker Sunland Hosp. for Retarded, Tallahassee, 1979-82; adj. prof. Calif. State U., Long Beach, 1985; adj. prof. Pepperdine U., Malibu, Calif., 1984—, clin. social worker, 1985—; field instr. Sch. of Social Work, Fla. State U., Tallahassee, 1980-82. Lay minister to young married couples Culver-Palms Ch. of Christ, Los Angeles, 1983—. Mem. Nat. Assn. Social Workers (cert.), Nat. Assn. Edn. of Young Children (North Bay chpt. v.p. 1986-88). Office: Pepperdine U 24255 Pacific Cost Hwy Malibu CA 90265

SCOULAR, ROBERT FRANK, lawyer; b Del Norte, Colo., July 9, 1942; s. Duane William and Marie Josephine (Moloney) S.; m. Donna V. Scoular, June 3, 1967; children—Bryan T., Sean D., Bradley R. B.S. in Aero. Engring., St. Louis U., 1964, J.D., 1968. Bar: Mo. 1968, Colo. 1968, N.D. 1968, U.S. Supreme Ct. 1972, Calif. 1979. Law clk. to presiding justice U.S. Ct. Appeals (8th cir.), 1968-69; ptnr. Bryan, Cave, McPheeters & McRoberts, St. Louis, 1969-75; mng. ptnr. Bryan, Cave, McPheeters & McRoberts, Los Angeles, 1979-84, exec. com., 1984-85, sect. leader tech. and computer law sect., 1985—; dir. Mo. Lawyers Credit Union, 1978-79. Contbr. articles to profl. jours. Bd. dirs. St. Louis Bar Found., 1975-76, 79; Eagle Scout leader Boy Scouts Am.; league commr. Am. Youth Soccer Orgn.; mem. alumni council St. Louis U., 1979-82. Mem. ABA (nat. dir. young lawyers div. 1977-78), Am. Judicature Soc., Bar Assn. Met. St. Louis (v.p. 1978-79, sec. 1979, chmn. young lawyers sect. 1975-76), Los Angeles County Bar Assn., Assn. Bus. Trial Lawyers, Calif. Bar. Assn., Mo. Bar (chmn. young lawyers sect. 1976-77, disting. service award), Computer Law Assn., Environ. Bar Assn., Internat. Bar Assn.. Clubs: Mo. Athletic, University Los Angeles. Home: 4 Horseshoe Ln Rolling Hills Estates CA 90274 Office: 333 S Grand Ave Suite 3100 Los Angeles CA 90071

SCRIMGEOUR, GARY JAMES, writer, educator; b. Auckland, New Zealand, Jan. 15, 1934; came to U.S., 1957; s. Colin Graham and Caroline Lenna (Hardie) S. BA with honors, U. Sydney, Australia, 1954; MA in English, Wash. U., 1959; PhD, Princeton U., 1968. Asst. personnel officer Dexion Ltd., London, 1956-57; mem. faculty dept. English Fla. U., Gainesville, 1959-61, Rutgers U., New Brunswick, N.J., 1963-64, Ind. U., Bloomington, 1964-69; editor, writer Benjamin Blom, Inc., N.Y.C., 1969-70; chief of social systems div. and head editorial office Sch. of Pub. and Environ. Affairs, Ind. U., 1970-74; dir. Profl. Studies Assocs., Bloomington, 1973—; cons. for research in alcoholism, ct. systems, hwy. safety and design of seminars to various govt. agys., schs. and social orgns., 1970—. Author: A

Woman of Her Times, 1982; contbr. numerous manuals on ct. systems and alcohol safety to profl. publs. and articles on lit. criticism to lit. jours. Jane E. Procter fellow Princeton U., 1968. Mem. ABA, Am. Judges Assn., Am. Soc. for Theatre Research, ACLU, Women's Equity Action League. Office: PO Box 2809 Reno NV 89505

SCRITSMIER, JEROME LORENZO, lighting fixture manufacturing company executive; b. Eau Claire, Wis., July 1, 1925; s. Fredrick Lorenzo and Alvera Mary (Schwab) S.; B.S., Northwestern U., 1950; m. Mildred Joan Lloyd, June 27, 1947; children—Dawn, Lloyd, Janet. Salesman, Sylvania Elec. Products, Los Angeles, 1951-69; owner, mgr. Real Properties, 1965—; chief fin. officer Environ. Lighting for Architecture Co., Los Angeles, 1973—. Served with USAAF, 1943-46. Mem. Apt. Assn. (pres., dir. Los Angeles County). Republican. Club: Jonathan (Los Angeles). Home: 2454 N Cameron Ave Covina CA 91724 Office: 17891 Arenth St City of Industry CA 91748

SCRUGGS, LARRY GLEN, college administrator; b. White City, Oreg., Oct. 24, 1943; s. William Freeman and Claudia Rae (Constable) S.; m. Patricia Shafer, Sept. 16, 1967; children—Larry Glen, Laura Rae, William Price, Kerry Wright, Berry Monroe. B.S., So. Oreg. Coll., 1971, M.S., 1972; postgrad. Portland State U.; grad. Wacubo Bus. Mgrs. Inst., Stanford U., 1986. Conf. dir. U. Portland, 1975-83, dir. aux. services, 1983—; founder Larry G. Scruggs & Assocs., 1981—, 53 MPG Scruggs Mktg. Mng. Meeting Planning Group, 1985—; cons. on conf. ops. Portland Rose Festival Assn., also grand floral parade chmn.; Bd. dirs. Greater Portland Conv. and Visitors Assn., Columbia-Williamette council Boy Scouts Am.; chmn. Big Thunder dist. Boy Scouts Am. Served with USAF, 1961-65. Recipient Charles A. Miltner award U. Portland, 1986. Mem. Portland C. of C., Western Assn. Coll. Aux. Services, Nat. Assn. Coll. Aux. Services, Oreg. Soc. Assn. Execs., Meeting Planners Internat., Meeting Planning Alert (adv. bd.), Portland Sales and Mktg. Execs. (bd. dirs., Pres.'s Rose award 1986), Portland Rose Festival Assn. (exec. com., bd. dirs.). Roman Catholic. Author: Conferences on Campus: Marketing and Managing, 1982, rev. 3d edit., 1986; contbr. articles to profl. jours. Home: 6942 N Villard St Portland OR 97217 Office: Columbia 107 Univ of Portland Portland OR 97203

SCUDDER, HARVEY ISRAEL, microbiologist, educator, consultant; b. Elmira, N.Y., Jan. 2, 1919; s. Henry Spaulding and Charlotte Evelyn (Draper) S.; m. Florence Viola Graff, June 16, 1945; children: Paul Harvey, Barbara Carol. BS, Cornell U., 1939, PhD, 1953; postgrad., NYU, 1939-42. Commd. scientist officer USPHS, 1943, advanced through grades to capt., scientist dir., 1963; chief viruses and cancer sects. Nat. Cancer Inst., USPHS, Bethesda, Md., 1959-62; chief health and manpower sects. Bur. State Services USPHS, Washington, 1965-66; ret. USPHS, 1966; prof. microbiology Calif. State U., Hayward, 1967-80, head div. biol. and health scis., 1967-70, prof. emeritus, 1980—; malaria cons. AID, Washington, 1979-83, 84-85; coordinator Stewart Valley (Nev.) Paleontol. Inventory, U.S. Bur. Land Mgmt., Reno, 1982—. Contbr. articles on med. entomology and environ. scis. to profl. jours.; pub. over 22 reports on pub. health, disease control and natural hist. Mem. air conservation com. Alameda County Lung Assn., Oakland, Calif., 1970-80; mem. Alameda County Comprehensive Health Planning Council, 1973-76; mem. Alameda County Mosquito Abatement Dist. Bd., 1982—; bd. dirs. Marine Ecol. Inst., Redwood City, Calif., 1971—, chmn. bd. dirs., 1974-80, 82—; bd. dirs. St. Rose Hosp., Hayward, Calif., 1969-83, chmn. bd. dirs., 1973-74. Mem. Am. Mosquito Control Assn., AAAS, Am. Pub. Health Assn., Am. Soc. Microbiology, Am. Soc. Tropical Medicine and Hygiene, Western Regional Assn. Advisors for the Health Profession of Am. Assn. Med. Colls., Entomol. Soc. Am., Sigma Xi, Phi Kappa Phi. Republican. Mem. Disciples of Christ. Club: Pub. Health Service (Bethesda)(pres. 1962). Avocations: philately, decision processing, natural history. Home: 7409 Hansen Dr Dublin CA 94568-2742 Office: Calif Acad Scis Dept Entomology Golden Gate Park San Francisco CA 94118

SCUDDER, RICHARD ALLEN, business educator, training and information systems consultant; b. Fargo, N.D., Oct. 24, 1942; d. Donald Wilfred and Ruth Louise (Swanke) S.; m. Bonnie Elizabeth Todd, Feb. 3, 1968; children: James, Lisa, Darren. Student, Yale U., 1961; BA in Polit. Sci., U. Colo., 1968, MA in Library Media, 1973, PhD in Ednl. Tech., 1980. Tchr., media specialist Denver Pub. Schs., 1970-78; mgr. mgmt. tng. Manville Corp., Denver, 1978-82; prof. bus. U. Denver, 1982—; pres. AECT Indsl. div., 1981, NSPI-FRC, Denver, 1983; cons. Paradigm Corp., Littleton, Colo., 1982—. Cons. editor; Instructional Innovator, 1981-85; reviewer Ednl. Tech., 1981-84; editor: The Criterion, 1983; assoc. editor Educational Media Yearbook, 1984; contbr. articles to profl. publs. Served with USAF, 1960-64. Mem. Am. Mgmt. Assn., Data Processing Mgmt. Assn., Nat. Soc. Performance and Instrn. (v.p. publs. 1982, newsletter editor 1982, Best newsletter award 1982, pres. elect 1983, Best chpt. award 1983, local chpt. pres. 1984), Assn. Ednl. Tech. (pres. indsl. tng. edn. div. 1982, local bd. dirs. 1982, conv. planning com. 1983), Am. Soc. Tng. Devel., Am. Acad. Mgmt., Colo. Soc. Personnel Adminstrs., Phi Delta Kappa. Avocations: photography, community theatre. Home: 922 Gilia Dr Golden CO 80401 Office: U Denver 2020 S Race BA 441 Denver CO 80208

SCUDDER, THAYER, anthropologist, educator; b. New Haven, Aug. 4, 1930; s. Townsend III and Virginia (Boody) S.; m. Mary Eliza Drinker, Aug. 26, 1950; children: Mary Eliza, Alice Thayer. Grad., Phillips Exeter Acad., 1948; A.B., Harvard U., 1952, Ph.D., 1960; postgrad., Yale U., 1953-54, London Sch. Econs., 1960-61. Research officer Rhodes-Livingstone Inst., No. Rhodesia, 1956-57; sr. research officer Rhodes-Livingstone Inst., 1962-63; asst. prof. Am. U., Cairo, 1961-62; research fellow Center Middle East Studies, Harvard U., 1963-64; asst. prof. Calif. Inst. Tech., Pasadena, 1964-66; assoc. prof. Calif. Inst. Tech., 1966-69, prof. anthropology, 1969—; dir. Inst. for Devel. Anthropology, Binghamton, N.Y., 1976—; cons. UN Devel. Program, FAO, IBRD, WHO, Ford Found., Navajo Tribal Council, AID. Author: The Ecology of the Gwembe Tonga, 1962; co-author: Long-Term Field Research in Social Anthropology, 1979, Secondary Education and the Formation of an Elite: The Impact of Education on Gwembe District, Zambia, 1980, No Place to Go: The Impacts of Forced Relocation on Navajos, 1982. John Simon Guggenheim Meml. fellow, 1975. Mem. Am. Anthrop. Assn. (1st recipient Solon T. Kimball award for pub. and applied anthropology 1984), Soc. Applied Anthropology, Am. Alpine Club. Office: 228-77 Calif Inst Tech Pasadena CA 91125

SCULL, JOHN RAYMOND, mechanical engineer; b. Los Angeles, May 16, 1926; s. John Benjamin and Marjorie Lucielle (Cullen) S.; m. Judith Ann Atkinson, 1952 (div. 1964); children: Adrienne, Hilary, Carolyn; m. Sharon Sue Dumont, Apr. 19, 1965; 1 child, David Michael. BSME, Calif. Inst. Tech., 1947; postgrad., UCLA, 1951-53, Stanford U., 1979-80. Engr., supr. Jet Propulsion Lab., Pasadena, Calif., 1949-59, sect. mgr., 1960-64, div. mgr., 1964-79, chief engr., 1981—; scientist NASA Hdqrs., Washington, 1959-60; cons. prof. Stanford (Calif.) U., 1979-80; cons. Inst. Def. Analysis, Washington, 1961-75; chmn. adv. com. Dept. Def., NASA, Washington, 1961—; lectr. in field UCLA, Calif. Inst. Tech., MIT, Tex. A&M, 1961—. Author: Spacecraft Guidance and Control, 1968; contbr. articles to profl. jours. V.p. Theatre Americana, Altadena, Calif., 1957. Served with USNR, 1944-46. Recipient Apollo Achievement award NASA, Washington, 1969, Viking Achievement award NASA, Washington, 1977, Exceptional Service medal NASA, Washington, 1976. Assoc. fellow AIAA (com. chmn. 1971-72); mem. Sigma Xi. Avocations: computers, photography. Home: 1722 Putney Rd Pasadena CA 91109 Office: Jet Propulsion Lab 4800 Oak Grove Dr Pasadena CA 91109

SCULLEY, JOHN, computer company executive; b. N.Y.C., Apr. 6, 1939; s. John and Margaret (Blackburn) S.; m. Carol Lee Adams, Mar. 7, 1978; children: Margaret Ann, John Balckburn, Laura Lee. Student, R.I. Sch. Design, 1960; B.Arch., Brown U., 1961; M.B.A., U. Pa., 1963. Asst. account exec. Marschalk Co., N.Y.C., 1963-64, account exec., 1964-65, account supr., 1965-67; dir. mktg. Pepsi-Cola, Purchase, N.Y., 1967-69, v.p. mktg., 1970-71, sr. v.p. mktg., 1971-74; pres. PepsiCo Foods, Purchase, N.Y., 1974-77; pres., chief exec. officer Pepsi-Cola Co., Purchase, N.Y., 1977-83; pres., chief exec. officer Apple Computer Inc., Cupertino, Calif, 1983—, also chmn., 1986—; bd. dirs. Comsat Corp. Chmn. Wharton Grad. Exec. Bd., 1980; mem. art adv. com. Brown U., 1980; bd. dirs. Keep Am. Beautiful.; mem. bd. overseers Wharton Sch., U. Pa. Mem. U.S. C. of C. Clubs: Indian Harbor, N.Y. Athletic; Coral Beach (Bermuda); Wharton Bus. Sch. of N.Y. (dir.), Camden (Maine) Yacht. Office: Apple Computer Inc 20525 Mariana Ave Cupertino CA 95014

SCULLY, JAMES HENRY, JR., psychiatrist, educator; b. New Britain, Conn., Jan. 14, 1944; s. James Henry and Marietta (Maguire) S.; m. Mary Elizabeth Hailey, Sept. 6, 1969; children—Jennifer, Sarah. A.B., Georgetown U., 1965; M.D., Tulane U., 1969. Diplomate Am. Bd. Psychiatry and Neurology. Resident in psychiatry U. Colo., Denver, 1975-76, instr. psychiatry, 1976-78, dir. med. student edn. psychiatry, 1978-86, asst. prof. psychiatry, 1978-82, assoc. prof., 1983—, dir. residency tng., 1985—; chief cons. Denver VA, 1978—; dir. profl. edn. Colo. State Hosp., 1979—. Served to lt. comdr. USN, 1969-73. Recipient Kaiser Permanente teaching award Colo. U., 1982; co-recipient VA Award for Valor, 1984. Fellow Am. Psychiat. Assn.; mem. Colo. Psychiat. Soc., Assn. of Dirs. of Med. Student Edn. in Psychiatry, Assn. Dirs. Psychiatry Residency Tng., Assn. Acad. Psychiatry. Democrat. Club: Denver Barbarians Rugby Football. Contbr. chpts. to books. Office: 4200 E 9th Ave Denver CO 80262

SCULLY, MARLAN O., physics educator; b. Casper, Wyo., Aug. 3, 1939; s. Orvil O. and Thelma G. (Thoms) S.; m. Judith Bailey, Aug. 16, 1958; children: James, Robert, Steven. AS, Casper Coll., 1959; BS, U. Wyo., 1961; MS, Yale U., 1963, PhD, 1966. Instr. Yale U., New Haven, 1967-69; asst. prof. MIT, Cambridge, 1969-71, assoc. prof., 1971-72; prof. U. Ariz., Tucson, 1972-80; disting. prof. U. N.Mex., Albuquerque, 1980—; diir., cofounder Radtech, 1984. Mem. Max Planck Soc. Avocations: cattle ranching, inventing. Home: Scully Farms Estancia NM 87016

SEABORG, GLENN THEODORE, chemistry educator; b. Ishpeming, Mich., Apr. 19, 1912; s. H. Theodore and Selma (Erickson) S.; m. Helen Griggs, June 6, 1942; children: Peter, Lynne Seaborg Cobb, David, Stephen, John Eric, Dianne. AB, UCLA, 1934; PhD, U. Calif.-Berkeley, 1937; numerous hon. degrees; LLD, U. Mich., 1958, Rutgers U., 1970; DSc, Northwestern U., 1954, U. Notre Dame, 1961, John Carroll U., Duquesne U., 1968, Ind. State U., 1969, U. Utah, 1970, Rockford Coll., 1975, Kent State U., 1975; LHD, No. Mich. Coll., 1962; DPS, George Washington U., 1962; DPA, U. Puget Sound, 1963; LittD, Lafayette Coll., 1966; DEng, Mich. Technol. U., 1970; ScD, U. Bucharest, 1971, Manhattan Coll., 1976; PhD, U. Pa., 1983. Research chemist U. Calif.-Berkeley, 1937-39, instr. dept. chemistry, 1939-41, asst. prof., 1941-45, prof., 1945-71, univ. prof., 1971, leave of absence, 1942-46, 61-71, dir. nuclear chem. research, 1946-58, 72-75, asso. dir. Lawrence Berkeley Lab., 1954-61, 71—; chancellor Univ. (U. Calif.-Berkeley), 1958-61, dir. Lawrence Hall of Sci., 1982—; sect. chief metall. lab. U. Chgo., 1942-46; chmn. AEC, 1961-71, gen. adv. com., 1946-50; research nuclear chemistry and physics, transuranium elements.; chmn. bd. Kevex Corp., Burlingame, Calif., 1972—; mem. Pres.'s Sci. Adv. Com., 1959-61; mem. nat. sci. bd. NSF, 1960-61; mem. Pres.'s Com. on Equal Employment Opportunity, 1961-65, Fed. Radiation Council, 1961-69, Nat. Aeros. and Space Council, 1961-71, Fed. Council Sci. and Tech., 1961-71, Nat. Com. Am.'s Goals and Resources, 1962-65, Pres.'s Com. Manpower, 1964-69, Nat. Council Marine Resources and Engring. Devel., 1966-71; chmn. Chem. Edn. Material Study, 1959-74, Nat. Programming Council for Pub. TV, 1970-72; dir. Ednl. TV and Radio Center, Ann Arbor, Mich., 1958-64, 67-70; pres. 4th UN Internat. Conf. Peaceful Uses Atomic Energy, Geneva, 1971, also chmn. U.S. del., 1964, 71; U.S. rep. 5th-15th gen. confs. IAEA, chmn., 1961-71; chmn. U.S. del. to USSR for signing Memorandum Cooperation Field Utilization Atomic Energy Peaceful Purposes, 1963; mem. U.S. del. for signing Limited Test Ban Treaty, 1963; mem. commn. on humanities Am. Council Learned Socs., 1962-65; mem. sci. adv. bd. Robert A. Welch Found., 1957—; mem. Internat. Orgn. for Chem. Scis. in Devel., UNESCO, 1980—, chmn., 1981; mem. Nat. Commn. on Excellence in Edn., Dept. Edn., 1981—. Author: (with Joseph J. Katz) Chemical Actinide Elements, 1954, 2d ed. (with Joseph J. Katz and Lester R. Morss) Vols. I & II, 1986, The Chemistry of the Actinide Elements, 1957, The Transuranium Elements, 1958, (with E.G. Valens) Elements of the Universe, 1958 (winner Thomas Alva Edison Found. award), Man-Made Transuranium Elements, 1963, (with D.M. Wilkes) Education and the Atom, 1964, (with E.K. Hyde, I. Perlman) Nuclear Properties of the Heavy Elements, 1964, (with others) Oppenheimer, 1969, (with W.R. Corliss) Man and Atom, 1971, Nuclear Milestones, 1972, (with Ben Loeb) Kennedy, Khruschev and the Test Ban, 1981; editor: Transuranium Elements: Products of Modern Alchemy, 1978; asso. editor: Jour. Chem. Physics, 1948-50; editorial adv. bd.: Jour. Inorganic and Nuclear Chemistry, 1954-82, Indsl. Research, Inc, 1967-75; adv. bd.: Chem. and Engring. News, 1957-59; editorial bd.: Jour. Am. Chem. Soc, 1950-59, Ency. Chem. Tech., 1975—, Revs. in Inorganic Chemistry, 1977—; mem. hon. editorial adv. bd.: Internat. Ency. Phys. Chemistry and Chem. Physics, 1957—; mem. panel: Golden Picture Ency. for Children, 1957-61; mem. cons. and adv. bd.: Funk and Wagnells Universal Standard Ency, 1957-61; mem.: Am. Heritage Dictionary Panel Usage Cons, 1964—; contbr. articles to profl. jours. Trustee Pacific Sci. Center Found., 1962-77; trustee Sci. Service, 1965—, pres., 1966—; trustee Am.-Scandinavian Found., 1968—, Ednl. Broadcasting Corp., 1970-72; bd. dirs. Swedish Council Am., 1976—, chmn. bd. dirs., 1978-82; bd. dirs. World Future Soc., 1969—, Calif. Council for Environ. and Econ. Balance, 1974—; bd. govs. Am. Swedish Hist. Found., 1972—. Recipient John Ericsson Gold medal Am. Soc. Swedish Engrs., 1948; Nobel prize for Chemistry (with E.M. McMillan), 1951; John Scott award and medal City of Phila., 1953; Perkin medal Am. sect. Soc. Chem. Industry, 1957; U.S. AEC Enrico Fermi award, 1959; Joseph Priestley Meml. award Dickinson Coll., 1960; Sci. and Engring. award Fedn. Engring. Socs., Drexel Inst. Tech., Phila., 1962; named Swedish Am. of Year, Vasa Order of Am., 1962; Franklin medal Franklin Inst., 1963; 1st Spirit of St. Louis award, 1964; Leif Erikson Found. award, 1964; Washington award Western Soc. Engrs., 1965; Arches of Sci. award Pacific Sci. Center, 1968; Internat. Platform Assn. award, 1969; Prometheus award Nat. Elec. Mfrs. Assn., 1969; Nuclear Pioneer award Soc. Nuclear Medicine, 1971; Oliver Townsend award Atomic Indsl. Forum, 1971; Disting. Honor award U.S. Dept. State, 1971; Golden Plate award Am. Acad. Achievement, 1972; John R. Kuebler award Alpha Chi Sigma, 1978; Founders medal Hebrew U. Jerusalem, 1981; Henry DeWolf-Smyth award Am. Nuclear Soc., 1982, Great Swedish Heritage award, 1984, Ellis Island Medal of Honor, 1986; decorated officier Legion of Honor France; Daniel Webster medal, 1976. Fellow Am. Phys. Soc., Am. Inst. Chemists (Pioneer award 1968, Gold medal award 1973), Chem. Soc. London (hon.), Royal Soc. Edinburgh (hon.), Am. Nuclear Soc., Calif., N.Y., Washington acads. scis., AAAS (pres. 1972, chmn. bd. 1973), Royal Soc. Arts (Eng.); mem. Am. Chem. Soc. (award in pure chemistry 1947, William H. Nichols medal N.Y. sect. 1948, Charles L. Parsons award 1964, Gibbs medal chgo. sect. 1966, Madison Marshall award No. Ala. sect. 1972, Priestley medal 1979, pres. 1976), Am. Philos. Soc., Royal Swedish Acad. Engring. Scis. (adv. council 1980), Am. Nat., Argentine Nat., Bavarian, Polish, Royal Swedish, USSR acads. scis., Royal Acad. Exact, Phys. and Natural Scis. Spain (acad. fgn. corr.), Soc. Nuclear Medicine (hon.), World Assn. World Federalists (v.p. 1980), Fedn. Am. Scientists (bd. sponsors 1980), Deutsche Akademie der Naturforscher Leopoldina (East Germany), Nat. Acad. Pub. Adminstrn., Internat. Platform Assn. (pres. 1981—), Am. Hiking Soc. (dir. 1979—, v.p. 1980), Phi Beta Kappa, Sigma Xi, Pi Mu Epsilon, Alpha Chi Sigma (John R. Kuebler award 1978), Phi Lambda Upsilon (hon.); fgn. mem. Royal Soc. London, Chem. Soc. Japan, Serbian Acad. Sci. and Arts. Clubs: Bohemian (San Francisco); Chemists (N.Y.C.); Cosmos (Washington), University (Washington); Faculty (Berkeley). Co-discoverer elements 94-102, and 106: plutonium, 1940, americium, 1944-45, curium, 1944, berkelium, 1949, californium, 1950, einsteinium, 1952, fermium, 1953, mendelevium, 1955, nobelium, 1958, element 106, 1974; co-discoverer nuclear energy isotopes Pu-239, U-233, Np-237, other isotopes including I-131, Fe-59, Te-99m, Co-60; originator actinide concept for placing heaviest elements in periodic system. Office: Lawrence Berkeley Lab U Calif Berkeley CA 94720

SEADER, JUNIOR DEVERE, chemical engineering educator; b. San Francisco, Aug. 16, 1927; s. George Joseph and Eva (Burbank) S.; m. Sylvia Bowen, Aug. 11, 1961; children: Steven Frederick, Clayton Mitchell, Gregory Randolph, Donald Jeffrey, Suzanne Marie, Robert Clark, Kathleen Michelle, Jennifer Anne. B.S., U. Calif. at Berkeley, 1949, M.S., 1950; Ph.D., U. Wis., 1952. Instr. chem. engring. U. Wis., 1951-52; group supr. chem. process design Chevron Research Corp., Richmond, Calif., 1952-57; group supr. engring. research Chevron Research Corp., Richmond, 1957-59; instr. chem. engring. U. Calif. at Berkeley, 1954-59; prin. scientist heat transfer and fluid dynamics research Rocketdyne div. N.Am. Aviation, Canoga Park, Calif., 1959-65; sr. tech. specialist Rocketdyne div. N.Am. Aviation, summer 1967; prof. chem. engring. U. Idaho, 1965-66; prof. chem. engring., adj. prof. fuels engring. U. Utah, 1966—, chmn. dept. chem. engring., 1975-78; tech. cons.; trustee CACHE Corp., Austin, Tex.; Inst. lectr. Am. Inst. Chem. Engrs., 1983, also dir., 1983-85. Author 5 books; assoc. editor IEC Research jour.; contbr. articles to profl. jours. Author. Served with USNR, 1945-46. Recipient Distinguished Teaching award U. Utah, 1975. Mem. Am. Inst. Chem. Engrs. (dir. 1983—), ACS, Sigma Xi, Phi Lambda Upsilon. Heat transfer research connected with the development of rocket engines associated with the Apollo and Space Shuttle projects, 1960-65. Home: 3786 View Crest Dr Salt Lake City UT 84124 Office: U Utah Dept Chem Engring MEB 3290 Salt Lake City UT 84112

SEAICH, JOHN LAIRD, physician; b. Salt Lake City, May 26, 1941; s. Eric John and Gladys (Jensen) S.; m. Ina Mae Copper, Feb. 5, 1968; children—Joseph, Jennifer, Jessica. B.S., U. Utah, 1965; M.D., Creighton U., 1969. Diplomate Am. Bd. Internal Medicine, Am. Bd. Endocrinology. Intern Riverside Gen. Hosp., Calif., 1969-70, resident in internal medicine, 1970-73; fellow in endocrinology U. Oreg., Portland, 1973-75; assoc. physician Twin Falls Clinic and Hosp., Idaho, 1975—; mem. cons. staff Magic Valley Regional Med. Ctr., Twin Falls, 1975—. Bd. dirs. Magic Valley Alcohol Recovery Ctr., Twin Falls, 1979-84. Mem. ACP, Am. Diabetes Assn. (bd. dirs. Idaho affiliate 1978-84), AMA, Idaho Med. Assn., Alpha Omega Alpha. Republican. Mem. Ch. of Jesus Christ of Latter-day Saints. Home: 2028 Oakwood Dr Twin Falls ID 83301 Office: Twin Falls Clinic 666 Shoshone St E Twin Falls ID 83301

SEALE, ROBERT MCMILLAN, office services company executive; b. Birmingham, Ala., Feb. 1, 1938; s. Robert McMillan and Margaret Sutherland (Miller) S.; B.A., Emory U., 1959. With N.Y. Life Ins. Co., San Francisco, 1960-67; with Dictaphone Office Services div. Dictaphone Corp., San Francisco, 1967-69; pres. Am. Profl. Service, Inc., Dictation West, Miss Jones' Word Processing, San Francisco, Pleasant Hill, South San Francisco, Calif., Los Angeles, Beverly Hills, Riverside, Portland, Phoenix, Las Vegas., Orange County, Calif. and Denver, 1969—, Environments West, 1980—, Los Arcos Properties, 1980—; bd. dirs. The Rose Resnic Ctr. for Blind and Handicapped; med. word processing cons. to hosps., health care insts., office equipment mfrs.; lectr. in field. Chmn. San Francisco Mayor's Com. for Employment of Handicapped, 1971-73; mem. Calif. Gov.'s Planning and Adv. Com. for Vocat. Rehab. Planning, 1968-69; pres. Calif. League for Handicapped, 1968-70, bd. dirs., 1966-73, 84—, adv. council, 1973-77; v.p. Stebbins Found., 1980—; pres Stebbins Housing Corp., 1980—. Recipient Spoke and Spark award U.S. Jr. C. of C., 1967; KABL Outstanding Citizen's award, 1965, 71. Mem. Am. Med. Records Assn., Adminstrv. Mgmt. Soc., Sales and Mktg. Execs. Assn., Am. Assn. Med. Transcription (Disting. Service award 1985), Emory U. Alumni Assn., Emory Lamplighters Soc., Internat. Word Processing Inst., U. S. C. of C., Delta Tau Delta. Republican. Club: Olympic Athletic. Contbr. articles in field to profl. jours. Office: 1177 Mission Rd S San Francisco CA 94080

SEALEY, B. RAPHAEL, professor; b. Middlesbrough, Yorkshire, Eng., Aug. 14, 1927; came to U.S., 1963; s. Bertram Izod and Florence Gladys (Heath) S.; m. Dagmar Schoelermann, Dec. 19, 1972 (div. Oct. 1977); 1 child, Dorte Freyja. MA, Oxford U., Eng., 1951. Lectr. classics U. Coll. of N Wales, Bangor, 1954-58, U. London, 1958-63; prof. SUNY, Buffalo, 1963-67, U. Calif., Berkeley, 1967—. Author: Essays in Greek Politics, 1967, A History of the Greek City States, 1976, The Athenian Republic., 1987. Home: 1206 Milvia St Berkeley CA 94709 Office: U Calif Dept of History Berkeley CA 94720

SEAMAN, DARYL KENNETH, oil company executive; b. Rouleau, Sask., Can., Apr. 28, 1922; s. Byron Luther and Letha Mae (Patton) S.; children: Diane Maureen Lefroy, Robert Byron, Kenneth Alan, Gary Ross Seaman. B.S. in Mech. Engring., U. Sask., 1948, LL.D., 1982. Cert. mech. engr. Pres., chief exec. officer Bow Valley Industries Ltd., Calgary, Alta., Can., 1962-70, chmn., chief exec. officer, 1970-82, chmn., pres., chief exec. officer, 1985—; bd. dirs. Pan-Alta. Gas Ltd., Calgary, NOVA, Calgary, Vencap Equities Alta. Ltd., Edmonton, BioTechnica Internat. of Can., Calgary. Mem. Royal Commn. Econ. Union; mem. Devel. Prospects for Can., Ottawa, Ont., 1982-85. Served with RCAF, 1941-45, Eng., North Africa, Italy. Progressive Conservative. Clubs: Calgary Petroleum (Calgary), Golf and Country (Calgary), Ranchmen's (Calgary). Home: Rural Rt #8, Calgary, AB Canada T2J 2T9 Office: Bow Valley Industries Ltd, Suite 1800, 321 6th Ave SW, Calgary, AB Canada T2P 2V8

SEARER, LARRY ELLIOTT, architect; b. Harrisburg, Pa., Oct. 18, 1948; s. Arthur T. and Maxine L. (Elliot) S.; m. Diana Lee Paxton, June 12, 1971; 1 child, Kirsten Michelle. Student, Ariz. State U., 1967-70. Registered architect, Ariz. Draftsman, Dolan & Dolan Engrs., Camp Hill, Pa., 1966-67, Lenker Architects, Harrisburg, 1967-68; project mgr. Walser-Krause, Scottsdale, Ariz., 1969-73; assoc., ptnr. Fenlason-Krause, Tempe, Ariz., 1973-74; assoc. VSLA Architects, Phoenix, 1974-85, v.p., 1985—. Mem. AIA, Scottsdale Tips Club, Tempe C. of C. Republican. Methodist. Club: Phoenix Breakfast Civitan (v.p. 1983-84). Home: 1206 E Geneva Dr Tempe AZ 85282 Office: VSLA Architects 2001 E Campbell Phoenix AZ 85016

SEARIGHT, MARY DELL (MRS. PAUL JAMES SEARIGHT), nursing educator; b. Cordell, Okla., Jan. 4, 1918; d. John Quitman and Grace Jewel (Giles) Williams; diploma St. Francis Hosp. Sch. Nursing, 1940; B.S. with honors, U. Calif. at Berkeley, 1960; M.S., U. Calif. at San Francisco, 1961; Ed.D., U. San Francisco, 1980; m. Paul James Searight, June 12, 1953; children—Gregory Newton, Sara Ann. Clin. nursing in various hosps., clinics, industries, drs. offices, 1940-59; instr. nursing Merritt Coll., Oakland, Calif., 1961-66; lectr. U. Calif. at San Francisco Sch. Nursing, 1966-68; nursing cons. regional med. programs, lectr. U. Minn., Mpls., 1968-71; chmn. dept. Sonoma State U., 1971-77, prof. nursing, 1971-87, prof. emeritus, 1987—; mem. acad. senate, 1972-75, cons. nursing edn., 1972-77; project dir. Nat. 2d Step Project, 1978-81; cons. Bur. Health Resources Devel., San Francisco, 1973-75; mem. chancellor's liaison com. nursing edn. Calif. State U. and Colls. Office of Chancellor, Los Angeles, 1973-76; chmn. Sonoma County Health Facilities Planning Com., Santa Rosa, Calif., 1970-72; mem. planning com. Sonoma Health Services/Edn. Activities, Santa Rosa, 1972; mem. exec. com., bd. dirs. Sonoma County Comprehensive Health Planning Com., 1970-72. Mem. Nat. League Nursing, Am. Assn. Colls. Nursing, Am., Calif. (Lulu Hassenplug award 1975) Nurses Assns., Santa Rosa Symphony League, Sigma Theta Tau. Author: Your Career in Nursing, 1970, 2d edit., 1977; editor, contbg. author: The Second Step, Baccalaureate Education for Registered Nurses (Book of Year, Am. Jour. Nursing), 1976; contbr. articles to profl. jours. Address: 6398 Stone Bridge Rd Santa Rosa CA 95405

SEARIGHT, PATRICIA ADELAIDE, retired radio, TV cons.; b. Rochester, N.Y.; d. William Hammond and Irma (Winters) S. B.A., Ohio State U. Program dir. Radio Sta. WTOP, Washington, 1952-63, gen. mgr. info., 1964; radio and TV cons., 1964-84; ret., 1984; producer, dir. many radio and TV programs; spl. fgn. news corr. French Govt., 1956; v.p. Micro Beads, Inc., 1955-59; sec., dir. Dennis-Inches, Corp., 1955-59; exec. dir. Am. Women in Radio and TV, 1969-74. Mem. pres.'s council Toledo Mus. Art. Recipient Kappa Kappa Gamma Alumna achievement award. Mem. Am. Women in Radio and TV (program chmn.; corrs. sec.; dir. Washington chpt.; pres. 1958-60, nat. membership chmn. 1962-63, nat. chmn. Industry Info. Digest 1963-64, Mid-Eastern v.p. 1964-66), Soc. Am. Travel Writers (treas. 1957-58, v.p. 1958-59), Nat. Acad. TV Arts and Scis., Kappa Kappa Gamma. Episcopalian. Clubs: Soroptimist, Women's Advt. (2d v.p. Washington 1958-59, pres. 1959-60), Nat. Press. Home: 10549 E Desert Cove Ave Scottsdale AZ 85259

SEARLE-KUBBY, JAN LILLIAN, sculptor; b. Ellensburg, Wash., Aug. 27, 1938; d. Kenneth Gifford and Lillian (Storey) B.; m. Sheldon Walter Searle, Dec. 5, 1969 (div. Nov. 1982); m. Dan Kubby July 24, 1983; children: Scott William, LoyAnne. Student in art and edn., Cen. Wash. State U., 1957-59, U. Colo., 1962-63. Supr., art dir. Yakima (Wash.) Herald, 1963-69; owner, art dir. Ad Mauk, Denver, 1970-72, Nat. Western Mktg., Ft. Worth, 1972-74, Jan Dihel & Assoc., Denver, 1975-81; sculptor Denver, 1976—. Prin. works include permanent exhibits at State Capitol, Bismark, N.D., 1981, Buffalo Bill Cody Mus., 1978-82, Cowboy Hall of Fame, 1978-80, Profl. Rodeo Cowboys Mus., 1978-84, Tex. Tech. U. Western Heritage Art

Mus., 1983-84 (1st and 2d in sculpture 1979-80, 82), Omni Banks one man show, Denver, 1982 and encore, 1983; contbr. articles to profl. jours. Mem. Internat. Sculptor Soc., Woman Artists Am. West (v.p., Best of Show and 1st in sculpture 1979-83), Nat. Western Artists (1st in sculpture Nat. Western Art Show 1980, 82), Profl. Artists of Colo., Am. Artists Profl. League. Avocations: hiking, travel, photography. Home: 2800 S University #65 Denver CO 80210

SEARNS, ROBERT MICHAEL, urban planner, consultant; b. Toronto, Ont., Can., May 14, 1946; s. James Milton and Bernice (Frankel) S.; m. Sally Preston, June 6, 1982; children: Bryn, Noah. BS, SUNY, Binghamton, 1968; MArch, SUNY, Buffalo, 1971, SUNY, Buffalo. Research assoc. BOSTI, Inc., Buffalo, 1969-71; assoc. planner Erie/Niagara Co. Regional Planning, Buffalo, 1971-74; sect. head Denver Planning Office, 1974-76; cons. to mayor City of Denver, 1976-78; prin. Urban Edges, Inc., Denver, 1978—; appointed mem. Gov.'s Open Space & Agrl. Group, Denver, 1981; devel. cons. South Suburban Found., Denver, 1982—. Author (booklet) The Other Colorado, 1981; contbr. articles to profl. jours. Recipient Friend of The River award Denver Greenway Found., 1982, Boettcher Innovations award Denver Council of Govts., 1986. Mem. Am. Planning Assn. (Nat. Current Topic award 1986), Urban Land Inst. (assoc.), Nat. Recreation and Parks Assn., Colo. Urban Design Forum. Avocations: flying, canoeing, rafting, kayaking, skiing. Office: Urban Edges Inc 1660 Gilpin Denver CO 80218

SEARS, JOHN THOMAS, chemical engineering educator; b. LaCrosse, Wis., Nov. 15, 1938; s. Nicholas J. and Angeline (Mattison) S.; m. Carolyn A. Crane, Aug. 12, 1971; children: Russell, Karen, Cheryl Kincaid, Aaron. BS, U. Wis., 1960; PhD, Princeton U., 1965. Research engr. Brookhaven Nat. Lab., Upton, N.Y., 1964-68, Esso R & E Co., Linden, N.J., 1968-69; prof. chem. engring. W.Va. U., Morgantown, 1969-82; chmn. chem. engring. dept. Mont. State U., Bozeman, 1982—. Author: Air Pollution Abatement and Regional Economic Development, 1974; editor (monograph) Problem Solving, 1983; contbr. articles to profl. jours.; patentee in field. Mem. Am. Inst. Chem. Engrs. (chmn. group 4 1980-82), Am. Soc. Engring. Edn. (chmn. N. Cen. sect. 1977-78, Western Electric Fund award 1974), Am. Chem. Soc. Home: 834 Alpine Way Bozeman MT 59715 Office: Mont State U Chem Engring Dept Bozeman MT 59717

SEARS, ROBERT EUGENE, aerospace company executive; b. Los Angeles, Nov. 22, 1921; s. Albert Eugene and Edythe (Lund) S.; m. Marjorie Welch, Dec. 24, 1946; children: Marjorie Camusi, Elizabeth Edythe, Robert E. Jr. BSME, Princeton U., 1947. Registered profl. engr., Calif. From sect. head to div. mgr. Hughes Aircraft Co., El Segundo, Calif., 1949-84, group v.p., 1984—. Mem. Phi Beta Kappa, Tau Beta Pi. Clubs: Los Angeles Country; Salt Air; Princeton (N.Y.C.). Avocations: golfing, traveling, arts, world affairs. Home: 204 S Plymouth Blvd Los Angeles CA 90004 Office: Hughes Aircraft Co PO Box 902 El Segundo CA 90245

SEARS, ROBERT LOUIS, fire chief, management consultant; b. Lakewood, Ohio, Aug. 5, 1928; s. Clarence Gilbert and Esther (Avery) S.; m. Elaine Hartman, Mar. 28, 1953; children—Cynthia, Susan, Janice. Student fire sci. Ohio State U., 1961; grad. in mgmt. III, Nat. Fire Acad., 1982-83. Firefighter Brecksville Fire Dept., Ohio, 1951-57; fire tng. officer Richfield Fire Dept., Ohio, 1957-60, fire chief, 1960-64; fire chief Kerr Magee Corp., Trona, Calif., 1964-69, Boulder City Fire Dept., Nev., 1969—; mgmt. cons. Internat. Assocs.; instr. fire service U. Nev., 1973-79, chmn. fire tng. bd., 1975-77. Pres. Richfield C. of C., 1961-62; Pres. So. Nev. Heart Assn., Las Vegas, 1980-81; chmn. bd. Nev. chpt. Am. Heart Assn., 1981-82. Recipient Steven Phalen M.D. award Am. Heart Assn., Reno, 1982. Mem. Nat. Fire Protection Assn. (charter mem. fire sect.), Internat. Fire Chiefs Assn., Nev. Fire Chiefs Assn. (bd. dirs. 1972—, pres. 1974-75), Internat. Soc. Fire Service Instrs., Western Fire Chiefs Assn. (State v.p. 1975-76), So. Nev. Arson Task Force, Boulder City C. of C. (bd. dirs.). Lodges: Kiwanis, Lions (pres. Tron 1967), Rotary (bd. dirs. Boulder City 1982-84).

SEARS, ROBERT LOUIS, engineer; b. Oakland, Calif., Jan. 28, 1927; s. Louis Francis and Lucille (Hargreaves) S.; m. Phyllis Ann Barnes, Apr. 30, 1955; children—Stephen A., Jeffrey R., Garth E. B.S., U.S. Mil. Acad., 1952; M.S. in Indsl. Engring., Ariz. State U., 1968. Commd. 2d lt. U.S. Army, 1952, advanced through grades to col., 1972, ret. 1973; supt. emergency med. services State of Ariz., 1973-75; gen. mgr. Behavior Modification Clinic, Inc., Phoenix, 1975-78; dir. Indsl. Systems Assocs., Phoenix, 1978-80; assoc. dir. Ariz. Solar Energy Commn., Phoenix, 1980-87; program dir. Cogeneration Research Ctr. for Energy Systems Research Coll. Engring. and Applied Scis. Ariz. State U., Tempe, 1987—; pres. Robert Sears and Assocs., 1985—. Decorated Legion of Merit (2). Mem. Am. Soc. Profl. Engrs., Am. Inst. Indsl. Engrs. (sr.), Assn. Energy Engrs. (pres. Ariz. chpt. 1986—), Am. Solar Energy Soc., Am. Cogeneration Assn. Republican. Episcopalian. Club: Ariz. Road Racers, Greater Ariz. Bicycle Assn. (Phoenix), U.S. Masters Swimming. Contbr. articles to profl. jours.

SEARS, SANDRA MARCOCCIA, social worker; b. Elmira, N.Y., Apr. 16, 1948; d. John Lewis and Alice Nastasia (Serediak) M.; m. Edward John Sears, July 31, 1978. BA in Psychology, SUNY, Buffalo, 1970; MSW, U. Denver, 1980. Crisis counselor Aurora (Colo.) Mental Health Ctr., 1978-80; psychotherapist White Plains (N.Y.) Med. Ctr., 1980-82, Family Service Soc., Corning, N.Y., 1982-84; treatment coordinator Mount. St. Vincent's, Denver, 1984—; staff cons. Right Assocs., Denver, 1984—. Mem. Outreach, Denver, 1985—. Mem. Nat. Assn. Social Workers (cert.), Colo. Soc. Clin. Social Work. Office: Mount St Vincent's 4159 Lowell Blvd Denver CO 80211

SEASTRAND, RICHARD CHIPMAN, banker; b. American Fork, Utah, Mar. 6, 1927; s. Ernest Joakin and Myrtle (Robinson) S.; m. Gay Moesser, Sept. 25, 1954; children—Rick, Brett. Student Latter-day Saints Bus. Coll., 1948, Brigham Young U., 1956, Stanford U., 1966. Gen. mgr. Seastrand Bros. Contrn., American Fork, 1953-54; asst. mgr. investments First Security Bank of Utah, Salt Lake City, 1957-66, asst. v.p. trust investment, 1966-69, v.p. investment div., 1969-83, sr. v.p. First Security Corp., Salt Lake City, 1984—, trainer, 1960—; lectr. in field. Mem. PTA, Salt Lake City, 1959; team leader United Fund, Salt Lake City, 1974; coach, mgr. Am. Legion and Minor League Baseball, American Fork, 1949-54; mem. Utah Bd. Bonding Commrs. Served with USNR, 1945-46, 51-54. Decorated Navy Commendation medal. Mem. Am. Inst. Banking, Utah Bankers Assn., Am. Bankers Assn., Idaho Bankers Assn., Western Region Depository Com., Utah Appaloosa Racing Assn. Republican. Mem. Ch. of Jesus Christ of Latter-day Saints. Club: Ambassador. Home: 4428 Mark Read Circle West Valley City UT 84119 Office: First Security Corp 61 S Main St Salt Lake City UT 84130

SEATON, W. B., steamship line corporation executive; b. 1925; married. B.S., UCLA, 1949. With J.F. Forbes & Co., 1950-53; treas., controller Douglas Oil Co., 1953-66; asst. treas. Occidental Petroleum Co., 1966-70; v.p., sec., treas. Natomas Co., 1970-72, v.p. fin., treas., 1972-74, sr. v.p., 1974-78, exec. v.p. mktg., 1978-79, exec. v.p., dir., 1979—; with Am. Pres Lines Ltd., Oakland, Calif., 1970—, pres., chief operating officer, dir., 1977—; dir. Eagle Marine Services Ltd. Office: Am Pres Lines Ltd 1950 Franklin St Oakland CA 94612 *

SEAVERSON, LOUIS ALAN, software manager; b. Rawlins, Wyo., Dec. 26, 1936; s. Lester Grant and Estella Arlee (Slade) S; m. Mary Ann Havrilo, Feb. 7, 1960 (div. Feb. 1981); children: Brenda Jean Seaverson Savage, Lynnae Ann, Monique Rae. BSME, U. Wyo., 1960. Registered profl. engr., N.Y., Colo. Sales engr. Gen. Electric Co., Schenectady, N.Y., 1963-65, cognizant engr., 1965-68; design engr. Stearns Roger, Denver, 1968-71; software engr. Rockwell Internat. Corp., Golden, Colo., 1971-82, software mgr., 1982—; cons. engr. ZAK, Inc., Troy, N.Y., 1967-68. Pres. Green Mountainside Civic Assn., Lakewood, Colo., 1973-76. Served to 1st lt. USAF, 1960-63. Mem. Nat. Soc. Profl. Engrs., Instrument Soc. of Am., Nat. Mgmt. Assn. (chpt. pres. 1985-86, sec., treas. Colo. council 1986-87). Republican. Avocations: photography, skiing. Home: 10474 Dale Circle Westminster CO 80234 Office: Rockwell Internat PO Box 464 Golden CO 80401

SEAWELL, DONALD RAY, lawyer, publisher, arts center executive; b. Jonesboro, N.C., Aug. 1, 1912; s. A.A.F. and Bertha (Smith) S.; m. Eugenia Rawls, Apr. 5, 1941; children: Brook Seawell Speidel, Donald Brockman. A.B., U. N.C., 1933, J.D., 1936, D.Litt., 1980; L.H.D., U. No. Colo., 1978. Bar: N.C. 1936, N.Y. 1947. With SEC, 1939-41, 45-47, Dept. Justice, 1942-43; chmn. bd., dir., pub., pres. Denver Post, 1966-81; chmn. bd., dir. Gravure West, Los Angeles, 1966-81; dir. Swan Prodns., London; of counsel firm Bernstein, Seawell, Kove & Maltin, N.Y.C., 1975—; chmn. bd., chief exec. officer Denver Ctr. Performing Arts, 1973—; partner Bonfils-Seawell Enterprises, N.Y.C.; dir. Newspaper Advt. Bur., Metro Nat. Bank. Chmn. bd. ANTA, 1965—; mem. theatre panel Nat. Council Arts, 1970-74; bd. govs. Royal Shakespeare Theatre, Eng.; trustee Am. Acad. Dramatic Arts, 1967—, Hofstra U., 1968-69, Central City Opera Assn., Denver Symphony; bd. dirs., chmn. exec. com. Air Force Acad. Found., Nat. Ints. Outdoor Drama, Walter Hampden Meml. Library, Hammond Mus.; mem. Bus. Com. for Arts; pres. Helen G. Bonfils Found.; vice chmn. Mayor's Commn. on Arts; chmn. bd. Bonfils Theatre; pres. Denver Opera Found.; past chmn., mem. founding bd. Civilian/Mil. Inst. Served with AUS, World War II. Recipient Tony award for producing On Your Toes, 1983, Voice Research and Awareness award Voice Found., 1983. Clubs: Bucks (London); Players (N.Y.C.), Dutch Treat (N.Y.C.); Denver Country (Denver), Denver (Denver), Cherry Hills Country (Denver), Mile High (Denver); Garden of Gods (Colorado Springs, Colo.). Office: Denver Center for the Performing Arts 1050-13th St Denver CO 80204

SEBALD, CHARLES WILLIAM, JR., electrical company executive; b. Danville, Ill., Feb. 3, 1947; s. Charles William and Harriet (Hecker) S.; m. Jane Marie Mitchell, Feb. 25, 1967; children: Charles Dale, Delora Marie. BA in Bus., Ball State U., 1969, MA in Mgmt., 1970. Mgmt. trainee Ind. Nat. Bank, Indpls., 1970-71; sr. materials planner Western Electric div. AT&T, Westminster, Colo., 1971-74; sr. buyer Storage Tech., Louisville, Colo., 1974-78, mgr. procurement, 1978-80; gen. mgr. Ren Electronics Corp., Canon City, Colo., 1980—; chmn. Mfg. Round Table, Fremont County, Colo., 1983—; lectr. bus. colls., Colo., 1976—. Chmn. bd. dirs. Jr. Achievement, Fremont County, Colo., 1984—, United Way, 1986—. Mem. Colorado Springs Exec. Assn. Lodge: Rotary. Home: 1006 Beech Canon City CO 81212 Office: Ren Electronics Corp PO Box 1410 Canon City CO 81212

SEBASTIANI, DONALD, winery executive. Chmn. Sebastiani Vineyards, Sonoma, Calif. Office: Sebastiani Vineyards PO Box AA Sonoma CA 95476 *

SEBBY, KENNETH M., lawyer; b. Elgin, Ill., Apr. 19, 1947; s. Silas M. and Olga H. (Erickson) S.; m. Patricia J. Hansen, Sept. 27, 1969; children: Matthew, Thomas. BA, Carthage Coll., 1969; JD with distinction, U. Nebr., 1973. Bar: Idaho 1973, Nebr. 1973. Assoc. The Law Offices of Michael E. McNichols, Orofino, Idaho, 1973-78; ptnr. Sinor, Blount & Sebby, McCook, Nebr., 1978-79; atty. Quane, Smith, Howard & Hull, Boise, Idaho, 1979-85, Elam, Burke & Boyd, Boise, 1985—. Served to lt. USAR, 1969-75. Mem. Idaho State Bar Assn., Nebr. State Bar Assn. Lutheran. Avocations: sports, coaching sports, outdoor activities. Home: 1515 N 26th St Boise ID 83702 Office: Elam Burke & Boyd 702 W Idaho St Boise ID 83701

SECORD, TERRENCE CLYDE, mech. engr.; b. Hollywood, Calif., July 7, 1927; s. Roy Clyde and Una (Vacelle) S.; B.Engring., U. So. Calif., 1950; m. Mary Rose George, June 30, 1951; 1 dau., Debra Ann. Group engr. airconditioning, thermodynamics Douglas Aircraft, Long Beach, Calif., 1950-59; supr. advance projects and mech. systems, Douglas Missile Space Systems div., Santa Monica, 1960-64; br. chief Life support and power MSSD, Santa Monica, 1964-65, asst. chief engr. advance biotechnology dept. McDonnell Douglas Astronautics Co., Huntington Beach, 1966-72; prin. engr. life sci. payloads, 1973-82, program mgr. life sci. research facility, 1983-86, mgr. space sta. advanced devel., 1986—. Served with AUS, 1945-46. Past mem. Daniel Guggenheim and Elmer A. Sperry Medal Bd. Awards. Registered profl. engr., Calif. Fellow ASME (chmn. and mem. numerous coms.), Inst. Advancement Engring. Clubs: Archimedes Circle, (Los Angeles); Trojan (U. So. Calif.). Contbr. to numerous publs. in field. Office: McDonnell Douglas Astronautics 5301 Bolsa Ave Huntington Beach CA 92647

SECRIST, DOLLY ALVAREZ, translator; b. Bucaramanga, Colombia, June 24; d. Justo Jose and Elvira Maria (Rodriguez) Alvarez; grad. John Robert Powers, 1966; A.A., El Camino Coll., 1971; student UCLA, 1971-73; grad. Dale Carnegie Sch., 1976; B.S., U. Beverly Hills, 1982; postgrad. Golden Gate U., 1983; m. Harold B. Secrist, Aug. 30, 1975, Varitypist Biddle Publ. Co., Los Angeles, 1963-67; exec. sec. Alfred M. Lewis Co., Riverside, Calif., 1967-69; multilingual exec. sec. Gen. Electric TEMPO, Santa Barbara, Calif., 1969-71; multilingual exec. sec. UCLA, Westwood, Calif., 1971-73; adminstrv. asst., translator, expediter Bechtel Power Corp., Los Angeles, 1973-83; exec. staff asst. Denny's Internat., 1984—. Mem. Nat. Assn. Female Execs., Calif. Bus. Women's Network, Success Motivation Inst. Roman Catholic. Club: Toastmasters (officer). Office: Dennys Internat 16700 Valley View La Mirada CA 90657

SEDA, PETER EUGENE, physician, cardiologist; b. North Platte, Nebr., Nov. 5, 1946; s. Edward Robert and Irene Germain (Damstrom) S.; m. Carole Celeste Ogoshi, Oct. 25, 1974; children—Erin Aislinn, Jeremy Peter. B.S., U. Nebr., 1969, M.D., 1973. Diplomate Am. Bd. Internal Medicine, Intern U. Oreg. Med. Sch. Hosp. Clinic, Portland, 1973-74; resident in internal medicine U. Oreg. Health Sci. Ctr., Portland, 1974-76, fellow in cardiovascular medicine 1976-78; dir., cardiologist Mid-Columbia Heart and Lung Inst., Richland, Wash., 1978—, Kadlec Hosp., Richland, 1980—; tchr. for physicians, cons. Kennewick Gen. Hosp., Wash., 1984—; dir. Doppler Echocardiography Lab., Our Lady of Lourdes Hosp., Pasco, Wash. Contbr. articles and reports to profl. jours. Regents scholarship U. Nebr., 1971. Fellow Am. Coll. Cardiology, Am. Coll Chest Physicians, Am. Heart Assn., Council Clinical Cardiology; mem. Wash. State Heart Assn. Republican. Methodist. Home: 1301 S Quay St Kennewick WA 99337 Office: Mid-Columbia Heart and Lung Inst 1110 Gilmore Richland WA 99352

SEDEÑO, EUGENE RAYMOND, electronics engineer, consultant; b. Honolulu, Aug. 31, 1952; s. Josephine Marie Sedeño Rosa; m. Theresa Ann Contreras, Dec. 28, 1980; children: Roxanne, Guadelupe. ASET, Heald Engring. Coll., 1974; BSEE, Coll. Allied Sci., 1980. Field service engr. Bausch & Lomb, San Leandro, Calif., 1974-81; project mgr. Tylan Corp., Carson, Calif., 1981-85; field service supr. Sci. Atlanta, Santa Fe Springs, Calif., 1985—; cons. Refractory Composites, Whittier, Calif., 1985—. Served with U.S. Army, 1970-72. Mem. Am. Mgmt. Assn. Democrat. Roman Catholic. Avocations: karate, photography, collecting antique books. Home: 16137 Minnitonka Rd Victorville CA 92392 Office: Sci Atlanta 10039 Pioneer Blvd Santa Fe Springs CA 90670

SEDLER, MICHAEL DEAN, social worker; b. Kansas City, Mo., May 4, 1955; s. Leon Eugene and Mary (Epstein) S.; m. Joyce Morrison, May 19, 1979; children: Jason, Aaron. BA in Polit. Sci., U. Calif., San Diego, 1977; MSW, Eastern Wash. U., 1981. Social worker, dir. spl. edn. Grand Coulee Dam (Wash.) Sch. Dist., 1980-83; coordinator edn. services Ednl. Service Dist., Spokane, Wash., 1983-84; behavior intervention specialist Spokane Pub. Schs., 1984—; on-call mental health profl. Grant County Mental Health Ctr., Coulee Dam, 1982-84. Author: Multi Disciplinary Teams, 1982. Mem. Nat. Assn. Social Workers (cert.), Wash. Assn. Sch. Social Workers (liaison 1985-86). Democrat. Club: Friend to Friend (Spokane) (v.p. 1985-86). Home: E 2632 14th Spokane WA 99202 Office: Spokane Schs Jefferson Guidance Ctr S 3612 Grand Spokane WA 99203

SEDLOCK, JOY, psychiatric social worker; b. Memphis, Jan. 23, 1958; d. George Rudolph Sedlock and Mary Robson; m. Thomas Robert Jones, Aug. 8, 1983. AA, Ventura (Calif.) Jr. Coll., 1978; BS in Psychology, Calif. Luth. U., 1980; MS in Counseling and Psychology, U. LaVerne, 1983; MSW, Calif. State U., Sacramento, 1986. Research asst. Camarillo (Calif.) State Hosp., 1981, tchr.'s aide, 1982; sub. tchr. asst. Vertura County Sch. Dist., 1981; teaching asst. Ventura Jr. Coll., 1980-82, tchr. adult edn., 1980-84; psychiatric social worker Yolo County Day Treatment Ctr., Broderick, Calif., 1986, Napa (Calif.) State Hosp., 1986—. Mem. Nat. Assn. Social Workers, NOW (campaign 1984 presdl. election). Mem. Humanist Orgn. Ch. Home: 17 Griggs Ln Napa CA 94558 Office: Napa State Hosp Napa/Vallejo Hgwy Napa CA 49558

SEEGALL, MANFRED ISMAR LUDWIG, physical science research consultant, educator; b. Berlin, Germany, Dec. 23, 1929; s. Leonhard and Vera Antonie (Vodackova) S.; came to U.S., 1952, naturalized, 1957; m. Alma R. Sterner Clarke; 2 stepchildren—James, Mark. B.S. magna cum laude, Loyola Coll., 1957; M.S., Brown U., 1960; Ph.D., Stuttgart (Germany) Tech. U., 1965. Research engr. Autonetics Corp. div. N.Am. Aviation, Downey, Calif., 1959-61; physicist Astronautics div. Gen. Dynamics, Inc., San Diego, 1961-62; research scientist Max Planck Inst., Stuttgart, 1962-65; instr. stats. and algebra San Diego City Coll., 1966; sr. research engr. Solar div. Internat. Harvester Co., San Diego, 1967-73; research cons. in energy and pollution, San Diego, 1974-83; part-time evening instr. Mesa Coll., San Diego, 1980-81; instr. Grossmont Coll., El Cajon, Calif., 1981; sr. scientist Evaluation Research Corp., San Diego, 1981-82, RCS analyst Teledyne Micronetics, San Diego, 1983-84, Alcoa Defense Systems, San Diego, 1985—. Mem. IEEE (sr.), Internat. Platform Assn., Calif. Parapsychology Found. (sec. research com.), Cottage of Czechoslovakia of House of Pacific Relations, Rosicrucian Order, Loyola Coll., Brown U. alumni assns. Republican. Club: San Diego Lodge AMORC. Contbr. articles on acoustics, pollution and temp. measurement methods to tech. jours.; patentee in field. Address: 8735 Blue Lake Dr San Diego CA 92119

SEELENFREUND, ALAN, distribution company executive; b. N.Y.C., Oct. 22, 1936; s. Max and Gertrude (Roth) S.; m. Ellyn Bolt; 1 child, Eric. BME, Cornell U., 1959, M. in Indsl. Engring., 1960; PhD in Mgmt. Sci., Stanford U., 1967. Asst. prof. bus. adminstrn. Grad. Sch. Bus. Stanford U., Palo Alto, Calif., 1966-71; mgmt. cons. Strong, Wishart and Assocs., San Francisco, 1971-75; various mgmt. positions McKesson Corp., San Francisco, 1975-84, v.p., chief fin. officer, 1984-86, exec. v.p., chief fin. officer, 1986—; bd. dirs. The Harper Group, San Francisco. Bd. dirs. Ind. Colls. of No. Calif., 1982—. Mem. Fin. Execs. Inst., Fin. Officers of No. Calif., World Affairs Council of No. Calif. Club: Bankers, St. Francis Yacht, San Francisco Yacht. Avocations: sailing, skiing, tennis, running. Office: McKesson Corp 1 Post St San Francisco CA 94104

SEELIN, SRIKANTH NAGABHUSHAN, mechanical engineer, consultant; b. Hassan, India, Nov. 13, 1953; came to U.S., 1977; s. Nagabhushan Alur and Saroja Devi (Rajashekhar) S.; m. Kusuma S. Puttappa, June 29, 1981. BME, U. V. Coll. Engring., Bangalore, India, 1976; MBA, Clarkson U., 1979. Mech. engr. MICO/Robert Bosch, Bangalore, 1976-77; mktg. engr. HMT Ltd./Machine Tools, Bangalore, 1980-81; indsl. engr. Cromemco Inc., Mountainview, Calif., 1982-83; process engr. Dysan/Xidex Corp., Santa Clara, Calif., 1983-85; mfg. engr. Varian NMR Instruments, Palo Alto, Calif., 1985-86; program mgr. System Industries, Milpitas, Calif., 1986—. Mem. Am. Inst. Indsl. Engrs. (Peninsula chpt., exec. v.p. 1984-85, pres. 1985-86, pres. bd. dirs. 1986-87, speaker 1981, 83, 85). Avocations: Western and Indian instrumental music, photography.

SEELY, BEN KETROW, research chemist; b. Springfield, Ohio, Apr. 21, 1914; s. David William and Zola Delite (Ketrow) S.; m. Beverly Bodell, Jan. 5, 1937 (dec. 1969); children: Sandra, Cynthia, Tomacia, David; m. Louisa C. Hillis, Sept. 7, 1977. BS, Wittenberg U., 1936. Chief chemist Crowell-Collier, Springfield, 1938-45; research chemist N.Mex. Inst. Mining and Tech., Socorro, 1946-55, assoc. prof. chemistry, 1976—, sr. research chemist, 1986—; supr. chemistry Sandia Nat. Labs., Albuquerque, 1956-74; investigator atmospheric studies Commonwealth Sci. Indsl. Research Orgn. U. Grounds, Sidney, Australia, 1953, Pineapple and Sugarcane Research Inst. U. Hawaii, Honolulu, 1954, project shower Internat. Research Project, Hawaii, 1955; mem. hurricane com. Nat. Weather Bur., Washington, 1955. Contbr. articles to profl. jours.; developed microchem. procedures for identification of sub-micron particles in the atmosphere. Comdr. CAP, Socorro, 1952-55; pres. PTA, Socorro, 1953-54. Mem. AAAS, Am. Chem. Soc., N.Mex. Acad. Sci. Republican. Presbyterian. Lodge: Lions. Avocations: photography, stamp collecting, travelling, electronics. Home: 4923 Alberta Ln NW Albuquerque NM 87120 Office: NMex Inst Mining & Tech Socorro NM 87801

SEEMANN, JEFFREY RANDALL, plant physiology, biochemistry educator; b. Ithaca, N.Y., Apr. 13, 1955; s. Karl William Seemann and Jacqueline Rose (Cantor) Skolnik; m. Charlotte Eileen Borgeson, July 14, 1985. BA, Oberlin Coll., 1977; PhD, Stanford U., 1982. Postdoctoral fellow Australian Nat. U., Canberra, 1982-83; postdoctoral fellow in plant biology Carnegie Instn., Stanford, Calif., 1983-84; asst. prof. plant physiology Desert Research Inst., Reno, 1984-87; assoc. prof. U. Nev., Reno, 1987—. Author: Biological Control of Photosynthesis, 1986; contbr. articles to profl. jours. McKnight fellow, Stanford U., 1982; grantee USDA, 1985, NSF, 1986, U.S. Geol. Survey, 1985, 86. Mem. AAAS, Am. Soc. Plant Physiologists, Sigma Xi. Avocation: downhill skiing. Office: U Nev Biochemistry Dept Reno NV 89557

SEESE, WILLIAM SHOBER, chemistry educator; b. Meyersdale, Pa., June 13, 1932; s. Carmon Doyle and Florence Evelyn (Shober) S.; m. Ann Reeves, July 25, 1958; children: David Scott, John Steven. BS in Pharmacy, U. N.Mex., 1954, MS in Chemistry, 1959; PhD in Chemistry, Wash. State U., 1965. Registered pharmacist. Instr. Ft. Lewis Coll., Durango, Colo., 1958-61; research chemist Internat. Minerals and Chem. Corp., Wasco, Calif., 1965-66; instr. Casper (Wyo.) Coll., 1966—; instr. U. Petroleum and Minerals, Dhahran, Saudi Arabia, 1973-76, U. N.Mex., Gallup, 1976-77. Author: (with Guido H. Daub) Basic Chemistry, 1972, 4th edit., 1985, In Preparation for College Chemistry, 1974, 3d edit., 1985. Recipient Regional award Chem. Mfrs. Assn. for Outstanding Teaching, 1981. Mem. Am. Chem. Soc. Democrat. Presbyterian. Lodge: Masons. Avocations: fishing, jogging. Home: 2915 Ridgecrest Dr Casper WY 82604 Office: Casper Coll 125 Coll Dr Casper WY 82601

SEETHALER, WILLIAM CHARLES, international business executive, consultant; b. N.Y.C., Dec. 4, 1937; s. William Charles and Catherine Frances (Flaherty) S.; student Quinnipiac Coll., Conn., 1955-56; engring. student Ohio State U., 1956-58; B.S. in Bus. Adminstrn., U. San Francisco, 1977; M.B.A., Pepperdine U., 1980. Asst. to v.p. sales T. Sendzimir, Inc., Waterbury, Conn. and Paris, 1960-66; mgr. internat. ops. Dempsey Indsl. Furnace Co., E. Longmeadow, Mass., 1966-67; mgr. internat. sales Yoder Co., Cleve., 1967-74; mng. dir., owner Seethaler & Assocs.; owner, chief exec. officer Seethaler Internat. Ltd., Palo Alto, Calif., 1974—; ptnr. DFS Computer Assocs., San Jose, Calif., 1976—. Bd. dirs. Palo Alto Fund, 1979—, chmn., 1986—; mem. community adv. panel Stanford U., 1986—. Mem. Menlo Park, Palo Alto (v.p. orgn. affairs 1976-77, pres. 1977-78, dir. 1975-79) chambers commerce, Assn. Iron and Steel Engrs., U. San Francisco Alumni Assn., Stanford U. Alumni Assn., Pepperdine U. Alumni Assn., Assn. M.B.A. Execs., Am. Mgmt. Assn. Clubs: Stanford Buck, Stanford Cardinal Cage, Stanford Diamond.

SEGAL, ALEXANDER, acoustical engineer; b. Novograd, USSR, Oct. 10, 1934; came to U.S., 1977; s. Symon Segal and Riva (Feldman) Ferdman; m. Anna Kadashevich, Aug. 27, 1960; 1 child, Svetland Segal. MS, Poly. Inst., Kiev, USSR, 1958; PhD, Inst. of Textile and Light Industry, Leningrad, USSR, 1973. TV engr., cameraman Kiev TV Studio, USSR, 1959-66; sr. elec. engr. State Inst. Communications, Kiev, 1966-68; sr. sci. assoc. Inst. Labor Hygiene, Kiev, 1968-76; mem. tehc. staff Wyle Labs., El Segundo, Calif., 1978-79; acoustical engr. County of San Diego, 1979—; cons. in acoustics Inst. Kievproject, Kiev, 1970-77; adj. prof. San Diego State U., 1983—. Contbr. articles to profl. jours.; patentee in field. Mem. Acoustical Soc. Am., Sigma Xi. Avocations: photography, fishing, traveling. Home: 5222 Trojan Ave #316 San Diego CA 92115 Office: County of San Diego 5201 Ruffin Rd San Diego CA 92123

SEGAL, D. ROBERT, publishing and broadcast company executive; b. Oshkosh, Wis., Oct. 30, 1920; s. Morris Henry and Ida (Belond) S.; m. Kathryn McKenzie; children: Jonathan McKenzie, Janet Elizabeth. Currently pres., chief operating officer dir. Freedom Newspapers, Inc., Irvine, Calif.; pres. Freedom Communications, Inc., Kinston (N.C.) Free-Press, New Bern (N.C.) Sun Jour., Burlington (N.C.) Times-News, Jacksonville (N.C.) Daily News, WLNE-TV, New Bedford, Mass. and Providence, KFDM-TV, Beaumont, Tex., WTVC-TV, Chattanooga, WRGB-TV, Schenectady, Freedom Newspapers of Fla., Inc., Crawfordsville Jour.-Rev. (Ind.), Huron (S.D.) Daily Plainsman, Greenville (Miss.) Delta Dem. Pub. Co., Dothan (Ala.) Progress.; mng. ptnr. Clovis News-Jour. (N.Mex.), Columbus

Telegram (Ohio), Rio Grande Valley Newspaper Group (Tex.), Gastonia Gazette (N.C.), Lima News (Ohio), Odessa Am. (Tex.), Pampa Daily News (Tex.), others. Trustee Children's Hosp of Orange County, Calif., Boy Scout Council of Orange County. Served with USAAF, 1942-45. Office: 17666 Fitch Irvine CA 92714

SEGAL, JACOB, real estate investment executive; b. Iasi, Romania, Aug. 11, 1946; s. Rubin and Tova S.; came to U.S., 1973, naturalized, 1977; B.A. in Econs. and Statistics, Hebrew U., 1972, postgrad., 1972-73; M.B.A., U. Calif., Los Angeles, 1976; m. Geri Slobin, Sept. 20, 1972. Computer operator Computer Center, Hebrew U. Jerusalem, 1969-72, programmer, 1972-73; research asst. dept. fin. UCLA, 1975, teaching asst., 1975; economist Home Savs. & Loan Assn., Los Angeles, 1976-78, sr. research analyst, from 1978, now v.p., mgr. real estate ops.; real estate economist Investor's Research Group, 1978-86; v.p., dir. acquisitions Real Estate Investment Trust Calif., 1986—; instr. econs. Inst. Fin. Edn., Los Angeles, 1977-78. Mem. Am. Mgmt. Assn., U. Calif. Los Angeles Alumni Assn. Home: 3318 Coolidge Ave Los Angeles CA 90066 Office: Real Estate Investment Trust 12011 San Vicente Blvd Suite 700 Los Angeles CA 90049

SEGALMAN, RALPH, sociology educator; b. N.Y.C., July 15, 1916; s. Samuel and Celia S.; m. Anita Cohen, Aug. 25, 1940; children: Robert, Ruth, Daniel. AB in Zoology, Sociology, U. Mich., 1937, MSW, 1944; PhD in Social Psychology, NYU, 1966. Lic. clin. social worker, Calif.; lic. marriage, family, child counselor, Calif. Social worker, exec. dir. various communities, Sioux City, Iowa, Waterbury, Conn., El Paso, Tex., 1940-65; from asst. to assoc. prof. U. Tex., El Paso, 1965-69; vis. prof. social work U. Wis., Madison, 1969-70; prof. sociology Calif. State U., Northridge, 1970-86, emeritus prof. sociology, 1986—. Author: Dynamics of Social Behavior and Development, 1978, The Swiss Way of Welfare, Lessons for the Western World, 1986, (with Asoke Basu) Poverty in America; The Welfare Dilemma, 1981 (Scholarly Work award Calif. State U. 1982); cons. editor, Jour. of Sociology and Social Welfare, Jour. Am. Behavioral Sci. Recipient State Israel award, 1963. Fellow AAAS, Found. Jewish Culture, Council Jewish Fedns. and Welfare Funds; mem. Am. Sociol. Assn., Soc. Study Symbolic Interaction. Avocations: railroad books, photo collections. Home and Office: 18723 Sunburst St Northridge CA 91324

SEGE, THOMAS DAVIS, electronics company executive; b. Novi Sad, Yugoslavia, May 17, 1926; came to U.S., 1941; m. Dorothea Zimmer; children—Kathy, Ron. B.S. in Elec. Engring., Columbia U., 1946, M.S. in Elec. Engring., 1948. With Sperry Gyroscope Co., N.Y.C., 1948-63, chief engr. Electron Tube div., until 1963; mgr. Power Grid Tube div. EIMAC, San Carlos, Calif., 1963-65, v.p. ops., 1965; v.p., gen. mgr. EIMAC div. Varian Assocs., Palo Alto, Calif., 1965-68, v.p. equipment group, 1968-71, pres. electron device group, 1971-81, pres., chief exec. officer, 1981-84, chmn. bd., chief exec. officer, 1984-86, chmn. bd., chief exec. officer, pres., 1986—; mem. adv. council SRI Internat., Menlo Park, Calif.; dir. Calif. Microwave. Patentee microwave output window, 1957, electron beam forming device, 1959. Campaign chmn. United Way Santa Clara County, 1983, chmn. policy com., 1984. Mem. IEEE (sr.), Santa Clara County Mfg. Group (bd. dirs. 1981-86). Avocation: philosophy. Home: Woodside CA Office: Varian Assocs 611 Hansen Way Palo Alto CA 94303

SEGGER, MARTIN JOSEPH, museum director, art history educator; b. Felixtowe, Eng., Nov. 22, 1946; s. Gerald Joseph and Lillian Joan (Barker-Emery) S.; m. Angele Cordonier, Oct. 4, 1968; children: Cara Michelle, Marie-Claire, Margaret Ellen. B.A., U. Victoria, 1969, Diploma in Edn., 1970; M. in Philosophy, U. London, 1973. Prof. art history U. Victoria, 1970-74, dir. Maltwood Art Mus., prof. art history, 1977—; museologist B.C. Provincial Mus., Victoria, 1974-77; cons. Nat. Mus. Corp., Ottawa, 1977, UNESCO, O.E.A., Cairo, 1983; bd. dirs. Canaap Press, Can., 1980—. Author: exhbn. catalogue House Beautiful, 1975, Arts of the Forgotten Pioneers, 1971, Victoria: An Architectural History, 1979, (commendation Am. Assn. State and Local History 1980), This Old House, 1975, This Old Town, 1979, British Columbia Parliament Buildings, 1979, The Heritage of Canada, 1981, Samuel Maclure: In Search of Appropriate Form, 1986 (Hallmark award 1987). Bd. govs. Heritage Can. Found., 1979-83; chmn. City of Victoria Heritage Adv. Com., 1975-79; bd. dirs. B.C. Heritage Trust, 1977-86; mem. B.C. Heritage Adv. Bd., 1977-83. Recipient Heritage Can. Communications award, 1976. Fellow Royal Soc. Arts; mem. Can. Museums Assn. (counsellor 1975-77), Internat. Council Museums (exec.), Internat. Council Monuments and Sites (bd. dirs. 1980—),Soc. Study Architecture Can. (bd. dirs. 1979-81). Roman Catholic. Avocations: travel, carpentry. Home: 1035 Sutlej St, Victoria, BC Canada V8V 2V9 Office: Univ of Victoria, PO Box 1700, Victoria, BC Canada V8W 2Y2

SEGIL, ANNETTE ROSELLE, industrial psychologist, career management specialist; b. Boksburg, S. Africa; d. Arnold and Miriam (Segal) S.; came to U.S., 1980; M.S.W., U. Witwaterstand, South Africa, 1965, Ph.D. in Indsl. Psychology, 1980. Cert. indsl. psychologist, social worker, South Africa. Mktg. services officer, sociologist Rand Mines, Johannesburg, South Africa, 1968-70; sr. profl. officer South Africa Council Child Welfare, Johannesburg, 1971-72; v.p. manpower planning, devel. Greatermans Stores Inc., Johannesburg, 1973-76; chief officer personnel research Council for Sci. and Indsl. Research, Johannesburg, 1977-79; group v.p. The Kenzer Group of Cos., Los Angeles, 1980-84; pres. Exec. Careers, Los Angeles, 1984—; mem. adv. bd. grad. sch. social work Indsl. Social Work program U. So., Calif., fashion mktg. program Woodbury U. Exec. v.p. South Africa Inst. Personnel Mgmt., 1978-80; founder Black Mgmt. Assn. South Africa, 1979; bd. dirs. U.S.-South Africa Leadership Program, 1977-80; founder Adv. Com. on Profl. Personnel Matters to South African Govt., 1978-80; mem. So. Calif. adv. bd. United Negro Coll. Fund. Recipient South Africa Inst. Personnel Mgmt. Disting. Achievement award, 1979; Jaycees Pres.'s Honor award, 1978. Fellow Royal Soc. Encouragement Arts, Manufactures and Commerce; mem. Am. Soc. Tng. and Devel., Am. Soc. Personnel Adminstrs., Nat. Retail Mchts. Assn., Am. Mgmt. Assn., Internat. Assn. Personnel Women, Inst. Personnel Mgmt. South Africa, Witwaterstand Social Workers, South African Psychol. Assn. Transvaal. Developed and implemented first postgrad. program in social adminstrn. at U. Witwaterstand, 1979. Office: 13930 Northwest Passage Suite 301 Marina Del Rey CA 90292

SEGINSKI, WILLIAM ENOCH, sales company executive; b. Englewood, Colo., July 9, 1933; s. Ignatius Albert and Helen Veronica (Mescier) S.; B.S. in Metall. Engring., U. Ariz., 1960; m. Cora Creswell, July 11, 1957; children—Cynthia, Catherine, Joseph. Mechanic, Am. Airlines, 1956-57; nuclear design engr. Gen. Electric Corp., Richland, Wash., 1960-61; sales engr. Worthington Air Conditioning Corp., Los Angeles, 1962; pres., owner J & B Sales Co., Phoenix, 1963—; vice chmn. Ariz. State Boiler Adv. Bd., 1977-82; lectr. solar energy. Served with USN, 1950-55. Mem. U. Ariz. Alumni Assn. (bd. dirs. 1972-73, pres. Phoenix chpt. 1971-72), Ariz. Elec. League (pres. solar div.), Ariz. Solar Energy Industries Assn. (bd. dirs., founding officer), NSPE (sr.), ASHRAE (bd. dirs. 1985-86), Am. Soc. Plumbing Engrs. (affiliate), Ariz. Plumbing Mfrs. Rep. Assn. (pres. 1982), Internat. Solar Energy Soc., U. Ariz. Alumni Assn. (pres. Dean's Assocs. 1981), Roosevelt Rough Riders (bd. dirs. 1986, pres.-elect 1986, pres. 1987), Sigma Gamma Epsilon (pres., founding mem.), Sigma Alpha Epsilon. Episcopalian. Clubs: Moon Valley Country, Kiva, Masons. Home: 7050 N 11th Ave Phoenix AZ 85021 Office: J & B Sales 3441 N 29th Ave Phoenix AZ 85017

SEGRÈ, EMILIO, physicist, educator; b. Tivoli, Rome, Italy, Feb. 1, 1905; came to U.S., 1938, naturalized, 1944; s. Giuseppe and Amelia (Treves) S.; m. Elfriede Spiro, Feb. 2, 1936 (dec. Oct. 1970); children: Claudio, Amelia, Fausta; m. Rosa Mines, Feb. 12, 1972. Ph.D., U. Rome, 1928; Dr. honoris causa, U. Palermo, Italy, Gustavus Adolphus Coll., St. Peter, Minn., Tel Aviv U., Hebrew Union Coll., Los Angeles. Asst. prof. U. Rome, 1932-36; dir. physics lab. U. Palermo, Italy, 1936-38; research asst. U. Calif.-Berkeley, 1938-43, prof. physics, 1945-72, emeritus, 1972—, group leader Los Alamos Sci. Lab., 1943-46; hon. prof. San Marcos U., Lima; vis. prof. U. Ill., Purdue U.; prof. physics U. Rome, 1974-75. Recipient Hofmann medal German Chem. Soc., Cannizzaro medal Accad. Lincei; Nobel prize in physics, 1959; decorated great cross merit Republic of Italy; Rockefeller Found. fellow, 1930-31; Guggenheim fellow, 1959; Fulbright fellow. Fellow AAAS, Am. Phys. Soc.; mem. Nat. Acad. Scis., Am. Philos. Soc., Am. Acad. Arts and Scis., Heidelberg Akademie Wissenschaften, European Phys. Soc., Accad. Scis. Peru, Soc. Progress of Sci. (Uruguay), Società Italiana di fisica, Accad. Naz. Lincei (Italy), Accad. Naz. XL (Italy), Indian Acad. Scis. Bangalore, others. Co-discoverer slow neutrons, elements technetium, astatine, plutonium and the antiproton. Home: 3802 Quail Ridge Rd Lafayette CA 94549 Office: Dept Physics U of California Berkeley CA 94720

SEGUNDO, LESLIE PAUL, environmental health specialist; b. Honolulu, Apr. 17, 1953; s. Miles Melecio and Florence Palisin (Balasbas) S. AA, Leeward Coll., 1974; BA in Chemistry, U. Hawaii, 1983. Environ. health specialist Hawaii Dept. Health, Honolulu, 1983—. Mem. AAAS, Am. Chem. Soc. Roman Catholic. Avocations: jogging, swimming, fishing, music.

SEHNERT, STEPHEN WILLIAM, oil company executive; b. Iowa City, Oct. 3, 1946; s. Harold Glen and Anne Marie (Deisenroth) S.; m. Carol Jo Wood, Aug. 2, 1969; children: Jeffrey Blake, Laura Ann. BA, Coll. Wooster, 1968; MBA, Wharton Sch. U. Pa., 1972. Tchr. Lima (Ohio) Pub. Schs., 1968-70; fin. analyst Marathon Oil Co., Findlay, Ohio, 1972-74; Washington rep. Marathon Oil Co., 1974-76; mgr. wholesale credit Marathon Oil Co., Findlay, 1976-81, mgr. graphic services, 1983-85; mgr. adminstrv. services Denver Research Ctr. Marathon Oil Co., Littleton, Colo., 1985—; mgr. fin. services Marathon Petroleum Co., Findlay, 1981-83. Republican. Lodge: Rotary. Home: 7075 S Niagara Ct Englewood CO 80112 Office: Marathon Oil Co PO Box 269 Littleton CO 80160

SEIBEL, ERWIN, oceanography educator, researcher; b. Schwientochlowitz, Germany, Apr. 29, 1942; came to U.S., 1952; s. Hugo Josef and Berta Seibel. BS, CCNY, 1965; MS, U. Mich., 1966, PhD, 1972. Asst. research oceanographer U. Mich., Ann Arbor, 1972-75, assoc. research oceanographer, 1975-78, asst. dir. sea grant, 1975-78; environ. lab dir. San Francisco State U., 1978-81, chmn. dept. geoscis., 1981—; sr. scientist cruises U. Mich., 1971-78; mem. sea grant site rev. teams Nat. Sea Grant Program, Washington, 1978—; bd. govs. Moss Landing Marine Labs., Calif., 1981— ; exec. sec. Oceans 83 Marine Tech. Soc. IEEE, San Francisco, 1982-83; coordinator Symposium for Pacific AAAS El Nino Effect, 1983-84; dir. environ. monitoring nuclear power plant, 1972-78. Contbr. articles to profl. jours. Developer photogrammetric technique for continuous shoreline monitoring, 1972-78. Advisor MESA program for Minority Students, San Francisco area, 1981—; vol. San Francisco Bay Area council Girl Scouts U.S.A.; 1982-86. Served to capt. U.S. Army, 1967-71, Vietnam. Grantee Am. Electric Power Co., 1972-78, Gt. Lakes Basin Commn., 1975-76. Recipient Exceptional Merit Service award San Francisco State U., 1984. Fellow AAAS, Calif. Acad. Scis., Geol. Soc. Am.; mem. N.Y. Acad. Scis., Am. Geophys. Union, Marine Tech. Soc. (pres. San Francisco Bay chpt. 1982-83), U. Mich. Alumni Assn., Gold Key (hon.), Sigma XI (pres. San Francisco State U. chpt. 1982-84). Office: San Francisco State U 1600 Holloway Ave San Francisco CA 94132

SEIBEL, RICHARD DORLAND, patent lawyer; b. Gary, Ind., Dec. 5, 1930; s. J. Ralph and Margaret (Dorland) S.; m. Stephonie Nakonechny, Nov. 5, 1955; children: Ann Linda, Susan Marie. BS in Metall. Engring., Stanford U., 1952, MS in Metall. Engring., 1953; JD, U. Denver, 1961. Registered profl. engr., 1966. Research metallurgist Denver Research Inst., 1955-62; asst. patent counsel N.Am. Aviation, Downey, Calif., 1962-69; sr. ptnr. Christie, Parker and Hale, Pasadena, Calif., 1969—. Served as sgt. U.S. Army, 1953-55. Mem. ABA, Am. Soc. Metals, Am. Intellectual Property Assn., Los Angeles Bar Assn., Pasadena Bar Assn., Los Angeles Patent Law Assn., Sigma Xi. Republican. Club: University (Pasadena). Avocations: photography, gardening. Home: 276 W Las Flores Arcadia CA 91006 Office: Christie Parker & Hale 350 W Colorado Blvd Pasadena CA 91105

SEIBERT, MICHAEL, research institute administrator; b. Lima, Peru, Nov. 15, 1944; came to U.S., 1950; s. Russell Jacob and Isabelle Lillian (Pring) S.; m. Patricia Ann Philbin, Dec. 20, 1975; children: Nora E., Jillian L., Lauren J. BS in Physics, Pa. State U., 1966; MS in Physics, U. Pa., 1967, PhD in Molecular Biology, 1971. Mem. tech. staff GTE Labs., Waltham, Mass., 1971-77; sr. scientist Photoconversion Research Br. Solar Energy Research Inst., Golden, Colo., 1977-84, mgr., 1984—; mem. U.S./USSR Joint Working Group in Microbiology, Riga, Leningrad, Moscow and Tbilisi, USSR, 1979, U.S./Japan Program in Photosynthesis, Okazaki, Japan, 1986—. Co-editor: Tree Crops for Energy Co-production on Farms, 1981; assoc. editor Advances in Solar Energy; mem. editorial bd. Applied Biochemistry and Biotechnology; contbr. numerous articles to profl. jours.; patentee in field. Grantee NSF, 1985—, U.S. Dept. Energy, 1980—. Mem. AAAS, Am. Solar Energy Soc. (rep. to biol. sci. div. 1979-82, chmn. biotech. and chem. sci. div. 1980), Am. Soc. Photobiology (charter), Am. Soc. Plant Physiology, Biophys. Soc., Internat. Soc. Plant Tissue Culture. Presbyterian. Avocations: gardening, skiing. Office: Solar Energy Research Inst 1617 Cole Blvd Golden CO 80401

SEIDEL, EUGENE MAURICE, entrepreneur; b. Ft. Wayne, Ind., Mar. 18; s. Emil Richard and Tona Therese (Aden) S.; m. Nancy Ward Biddle, Sept. 2, 1950; children: Amy Aden Seidel Marks, Betsy Roberts Seidel Martin. BS in Chemistry, Bus. Adminstrn., Ind. U., 1944. Tech. service chemist Eberbach & Son Co., Ann Arbor, Mich., 1945-46; with tech. purchasing dept. W.A. Sheaffer Pen Co., Ft. Madison, Iowa, 1946-48; dir. chem. labs. Ind. U., Bloomington, 1948-53; mktg. and comml. developer Comml. Solvents Corp., Terre Haute, Ind., 1953-57; mgr. bus. exploration Crown Zellerbach Co., Camas, Wash., 1957-82; pres. Eugene M. Seidel Assocs., Inc., Vancouver, Wash., 1982—, EMSA, Inc., Vancouver, Wash., %. Ruling elder First Presbyn. Ch., Vancouver; mem. Clark County (Wash.) Comprehensive Health Planning Com., 1984 Ad Hoc com.; bd. dirs., past pres., Columbia Bus. Community for the Arts, Vancouver, 1980-86, v.p., 1987—; bd. dirs. Clark Coll. Found., Vancouver, 1983-87, Clark County Arts Council; trustee Neskowin (Oreg.) Valley Sch.; appointed by gov. to 4 yr. term Health Coordination Council; past pres. Southwest Wash. Health Systems Agy., Shorewood West Condominium Owners Assn. Mem. AAAS, Am. Econ. Assn., Am. Mktg. Assn. (past bd. dirs.), Am. Chem. Soc. (past bd. dirs.), Chrm. Mktg. Research Assn. (life), TAPPI. Lodge: Rotary. Avocations: education, community service, the Arts. Home: Shorewood Apts II-206 5555 E Evergreen Blvd Vancouver WA 98661 Home: 142 Salishan Dr PO Box 709 Gleneden Beach OR 97388 Office: EMSA Inc PO Box 61466 Vancouver WA 98663

SEIDEL, GEORGE ELIAS, JR., animal scientist, educator; b. Reading, Pa., July 13, 1943; s. George E. Sr. and Grace Esther (Heinly) S.; m. Sarah Beth Moore, May 28, 1970; 1 child, Andrew. BS, Pa. State U., 1965; MS, Cornell U., 1968, PhD, 1970; postgrad., Harvard U. Med. Sch., Boston, 1970-71. Asst. prof. physiology Colo. State U., Ft. Collins, 1971-75, assoc. prof., 1975-83, prof., 1983—; vis. scientist Yale U., 1978-79. Co-editor: New Technologies in Animal Breeding, 1981; contbr. articles to profl. jours. Recipient Alexander Von Humboldt award, N.Y.C., 1983, Animal Breeding Research award Nat. Assn. Animal Breeders, Columbia, Mo., 1983, Clark award Colo. State U., 1982. Mem. Am. Dairy Sci. Assn., Am. Soc. Animal Sci. (Young Animal Scientist award 1983), AAAS, Soc. for Study of Reprodn., Internat. Embryo Transfer Soc. (pres. 1979). Home: 3101 Arrowhead Rd Laporte CO 80535 Office: Colo State U Animal Reprodn Lab Fort Collins CO 80523

SEIDEN, ARTHUR JOHN, safety engineer; b. Antigo, Wis., Sept. 8, 1945; s. Frank Raymon and Louise Josephine (Savickous) S. BS in Indsl. Mgmt., Purdue U., 1968; MS in Computer Sci., West Coast U., 1986. Cert. safety profl. Indsl. engr. Lykes-Youngstown, East Chicago, Ind., 1968-74; dir. safety Blaw-Knox, Inc., East Chicago, 1974-78; mgr. plant White Advt., South El Monte, Calif., 1978-80; safety engr. Calif. Inst. Tech., Pasadena, 1980—. Served as sgt. U.S. Army, 1968-70, Vietnam. Home: 252 S Mentor Pasadena CA 91106 Office: Calif Inst Tech 1201 E California Pasadena CA 91125

SEIDL, HENRY WILLIAM, advertising executive; b. Balt., Dec. 23, 1924; s. Henry William and Sarah Rebecca (Evans) S.; m. Amelia Alonzo, Nov. 27, 1954; children: Kimberly Melia, Julie Anne. BS in Mktg., St. Louis U., 1949. Mgr. sales promotions Foster & Kleiser, San Francisco, 1953-60; mgr. eastern sales promotions Foster & Kleiser, San Francisco, Detroit, 1960-62; supr. sales Foster & Kleiser, Los Angeles, 1962-65, dir. sales promotions, 1965-71, v.p. mktg. services, 1971-84, sr. v.p., 1984-87, mktg. advisor, cons., 1987—; mem. exec. com., bd. dirs. The Advt. Council. Bd. dirs. Greater Los Angeles Visitors and Conv. Bur., 1985—. Served with USAAC, 1943-46; served to 1st lt. USAF, 1950-53. Decorated D.F.C., Air Medal with oak leaf cluster. Mem. The Advt. Council (bd. dirs., exec. com. 1985—). Republican. Avocations: photography, jewelry designing, bonsai cultivation, geography. Home: 17345 Haynes St Van Nuys CA 91406 Office: Foster & Kleiser 1550 W Washington Blvd Los Angeles CA 90007

SEIL, FREDRICK JOHN, neuroscientist, neurologist; b. Nova Sova, Yugoslavia, Nov. 9, 1933; s. Joseph and Theresa (Krieger) S.; m. Daryle Faith Wolfers, July 2, 1955; children: Jonathan Fredrick, Joel Philip Timothy. BA, Oberlin Coll., 1956; MD, Stanford U., 1960. Intern Kaiser Found. Hosp., San Francisco, 1960-61; resident in neurology Stanford (Calif.) U., 1961-64, fellow in neurology, 1964-66; staff neurologist VA Med. Ctr., Palo Alto, Calif., 1969; clin. investigator VA Med. Ctr., Portland, Oreg., 1976-79, staff neurologist, 1979-81, dir. VA office regeneration research programs, 1981—; asst. prof. neurology Stanford U., 1969-75, assoc. prof. neurology Oreg. Health Sci. U., Portland, 1976-78, prof. neurology, 1978—. Editor: Nerve, Organ and Tissue Regeneration: Research Perspectives, 1983, Neural Regeneration, 1987; contbr. articles to profl. jours. Served to capt. U.S. Army, 1966-68. Grantee VA, 1970—. Mem. AAAS, Am. Neurol. Assn., Internat. Brain Research Orgn., Am. Assn. Neuropathologists, Soc. Neurosci. Democrat. Home: 10306 SW Radcliffe Rd Portland OR 97219 Office: VA Med. Ctr. Office Regeneration Research Portland OR 97201

SEIM, EDWIN CHARLES, soil scientist, agronomist, educator, consultant; b. St. Louis, Oct. 9, 1932; s. Edwin Carl and Philipina (Reeg) S.; m. Livia Pellegrini, Jan. 3, 1959; children—Carla Philipina Seim Morey, Edwin Carlo. B.S. in Agr., U. Mo., 1954; M.S. in Soil Sci., U. Minn., 1966, Ph.D. in Soil Sci., 1970. Cert. profl. soil scientist and agronomist. Sales agronomist Allied Chem. Corp., N.W. Mo., 1956-58, So. Minn., 1958-60; agr. lab. technician Purity Oats, Gen. Mills, Mpls., 1960-62; research asst. dept. soil sci. U. Minn., St. Paul, 1962-68, teaching asst., 1968-70; postdoctoral fellow dept. agronomy, U. Nebr., Lincoln, 1970-72; sr. horticulturist, research and devel. Hunt Wesson Foods, Davis, Calif., 1972-74, group leader, 1974-77; agronomist, agrl. research Basic Vegetable, Inc., King City, Calif., 1977-78; asst. prof. dept. soil sci. Calif. Poly. State U., San Luis Obispo, 1978-82, assoc. prof. dept. crop sci., 1983—; cons., researcher fertilizers, soil and water and plant relationships. Active Italian Cath. Fedn., Republican Party. Served to 1st lt. U.S. Army, 1954-56. Kroger scholar, 1950; Lange fellow, 1953, 54. Mem. AAAS, Council for Agrl. Sci. and Tech., Am. Soc. Agronomy, Soil Sci. Soc. Am., Soil Conservation Soc. Am., Internat. Soil Sci. Soc., Am. Inst. Biol. Sci., Sigma Xi, Alpha Zeta, Alpha Gamma Rho. Author research pubs., abstracts. Home: 292 Charles Dr San Luis Obispo CA 93401 Office: Dept Crop Sci Calif Poly State U San Luis Obispo CA 93407

SEITER, GARY JOSEPH, electrical engineer, researcher; b. Ferguson, Mo., Sept. 18, 1955; s. Curtis Andrew and Marcella Jane (Menetre) S.; m. Lucee Kathleen Bravo, June 25, 1983, 1 child, Olivia Ann; stepchildren—Fara Anese Newland, Sean Elliot Newland. B.S.E.E. with honors, U. Mo.-Rolla, 1978, M.S. in Elec.Engring., 1980. Research engr. advanced products research and devel. lab. Motorola, Inc., Mesa, Ariz., 1980-84, sr. staff engr. Semicondr. Research and Devel. Lab., Phoenix, 1985—. Mem. IEEE, Eta Kappa Nu. Roman Catholic. Home: 1218 W Palo Verde Dr Chandler AZ 85224 Office: Motorola Inc 5005 E McDowell Phoenix AZ 85008

SEITZ, LAURA RUTH, graphic design company executive; b. Detroit, Nov. 29, 1951; d. John Calvin and Charlotte Mary (Collins) S. Student Western Mich. U., 1969-72, Los Angeles Mcpl. Art Galleries, 1975-78, UCLA, 1978. Clothing designer, dressmaker Moonshadow Designs, Ann Arbor and Los Angeles, 1974-77; sales coordinator Edwards Bros. Inc., Ann Arbor, 1973-74; sec. Maher Elen Advt., Los Angeles, 1976-79; account exec., 1979-80, account supr., 1980-81; sales mgr. Sojourn Design Group, Pico Rivera, Calif., 1981-82; dir. sales and mktg. John Anselmo Design Assocs., Santa Monica, Calif., 1982-83, owner O'Mara-Seitz Design Group, Santa Monica, 1983—; cons., freelance copywriting, lectr. Mem. task force NOW, 1977; mem. Olympics Steering Com., Muscular Dystrophy Assn., 1979; mem. Superwalk Steering Com., March of Dimes, 1981. Mem. Los Angeles Ad Club, Nat. Assn. Female Execs., Internat. Assn. Bus. Communicators, Graphic Artists Guild Mktg. Assn. Calif. Office: 1321 7th St Suite 300 Santa Monica CA 90401

SEITZ, S. STANLEY, electronics executive; b. Bklyn., June 13, 1923; m. Florence Rose Balogh, Feb.19, 1949; children: Craig, Brian. MBA, Pepperdine U. Program mgr. ARMA, Garden City, N.Y., 1956-58; dir. indsl. engring. Am. Electronics, Los Angeles, 1958-60; supr. prodn. quality Sperry Corp., Great Neck, N.Y., 1960-65; chief product quality AIL, Deer Park, N.Y., 1965-69; dir. mgmt. info. systems Rockwell Internat., El Segundo, Calif., 1969-82; dir. big safari programs Lockheed Corp., Ontario, Calif., 1982—. Mem. Assn. Old Crows. Avocations: golf, judo, karate. Home: 612 Mt Vernon Way Placentia CA 92670 Office: Lockheed Internat PO Box 33 Ontario CA 91761

SEITZ, THOMAS BING, communications company executive, aerospace engineer; b. Starkville, Miss., Apr. 5, 1941; s. Henry Morris and Mary Bernice (Kennedy) S.; m. Joyce Ann Gastineau, June 5, 1965; children—Bret, Melissa. B.S. in Aerospace Engring., Miss. State U., 1963; M.S. in Aerospace and Mech. Engring., Air Force Inst. Tech., Wright-Patterson AFB, Ohio, 1965; M. in Aerospace Ops. Mgmt., U. So. Calif., 1969. Project mgr. AT&T Long Lines, San Francisco, 1972-73, product mgr., N.Y.C., 1973-75, dist. engr. staff, San Francisco, 1975-77, dist. mktg. mgr., Los Angeles, 1977-79, div. sales mgr., 1982-84; div. mktg. mgr. Pacific Telephone Co., Los Angeles, 1979-82; sr. mgr. nat. accounts MCI Telecommunications, Los Angeles, 1985—. Chmn. fin. Eastern service area Los Angeles council Boy Scouts Am., 1983-84. Served to capt. USAF, 1963-69. Decorated Air Force Commendation medal. Mem. AIAA, Am. Legion, Assn. Communications Profls., Tau Beta Pi, Sigma Alpha Epsilon. Republican. Home: 131 Terraza Santa Elena La Habra CA 90631 Office: MCI Telecommunications 333 S Grand Ave Suite 440 Los Angeles CA 90071

SEKI, HAJIME, research scientist; b. Nishinomiya, Hyogo, Japan, Feb. 11, 1929; came to U.S., 1950; s. Yasuto and Chizuko (Ozeki) S.; m. Keiko Seki, Dec. 4, 1966; children: George, Kent, Eugene. BS, Brown U., 1954; PhD, U. Pa., 1961. Research staff mem. IBM Corp., Yorktown Heights, N.Y., 1961-66, San Jose, Calif., 1966—. Mem. AAAS, Am. Phys. Soc., Japanese Soc. Physics. Office: IBM Almaden Research Ctr K33 802 650 Harry Rd San Jose CA 95120-6099

SELBY, DOUGLAS ALLEN, environmental engineer; b. Onieda, N.Y., Aug. 16, 1953; s. Samuel Emmons and Elizabeth (Stechyshyn) S.; m. Jelaine Laurette Olliffe, July 31, 1976; one child, Nicole Frances. BS, U. Nev., Las Vegas, 1975, MS, 1977; PhD, Utah State U., 1983. Fish and wildlife technician Calif. Dept. Fish and Game, Sacramento, 1977; aquatic biologist Bio/West Inc., Logan, Utah, 1978-80; sr. engr. Clark County (Nev.) Sanitation Dist., Las Vegas, 1983—. Mem. (VITA) Vols. in Tech. Assistance to developing countries. Mem. ASCE (assoc.), NSPE (Young Engr. of Yr., So. Nev. chpt. 1985-86), Am. Water Works Assn., Water Pollution Control Fedn. Avocations: hiking, snow skiing, photography, botany, entomology. Home: 313 Simon Bolivar Dr Henderson NV 89015 Office: Clark County Sanitation Dist 5857 E Flamingo Rd Las Vegas NV 89122

SELDON, MERVYN W. ADAMS, editor; b. Chgo., May 9, 1930; d. Robert McCormick and Janet (Lawrence) Adams; m. M. Robert Seldon, Mar. 25, 1973 (dec. Mar. 1982). Student, Smith Coll., 1947-50, U. Chgo., 1950-51; MA, Columbia U., 1964. Adminstrv. asst. East Asian Inst. Columbia U., N.Y.C., 1964-68; editor Praeger Publs., N.Y.C., 1968-73; self-employed editor, pub. West Covina, Calif., 1973-81; dir. found. and corp. relations Claremont (Calif.) McKenna Coll., 1981-85; program officer W.M. Keck Found., Los Angeles, 1985-86; dir. devel. Performing Tree, Los Angeles, 1986—. Mem. Assn. Asian Studies, Am. Assn. Advancement Slavic Studies. Democrat. Roman Catholic. Clubs: Claremont. Avocation: tennis.

SELF, L. DOUGLAS, pastor, editor; b. Clovis, N.Mex., June 6, 1945; s. A.R. and Oleta (Bilberry) S.; m. Rebecca Ann Cheatheam, June 12, 1966;

children: Daniel, Bethany, David. BD, Wayland U., 1967; DivM, Southwestern Sem., Ft. Worth, Tex., 1972; D in Ministry, Denver Sem., 1986. Pastor Ch. Redstone, Colo., 1977—; pres. Pastoral Ministry Resources, Carbondale, Colo., 1985—. Author: Consumer's Guide to Religious Beliefs, 1985; editor Pastoral Ministry Newsletter, 1985—. V.p. Redstone Community Assn., 1984, pres. 1985. Republican. Avocations: hiking, skiing. Home: 22995 Hwy 133 Redstone CO 81623 Office: Pastoral Ministry Resources Carbondale CO 81623

SELL, ROBERT EMERSON, elec. engr.; b. Freeport, Ill., Apr. 23, 1929; s. Cecil Leroy and Ona Arletta (Stevens) S.; B.S., U. Nebr., 1962; m. Ora Lucile Colton, Nov. 7, 1970. Chief draftsman Dempster Mill Mfg. Co., Beatrice, Nebr., 1949-53; designer-engr. U. Neb., Lincoln, 1955-65; elec. design engr. Kirkham, Michael & Assos., Omaha, 1965-67; elec. design engr. Leo A. Daly Co., Omaha, St. Louis, 1967-69; mech. design engr. Hellmuth, Obata, Kassabaum, St. Louis, 1969-70; chief elec. engr. Biagi-Hannan & Assos., Inc., Evansville, Ind., 1971-74; elec. project engr. H.L. Yoh Co., under contract to Monsanto Co., Creve Coeur, Mo., 1974-77; elec. project engr. Dhillon Engrs., Inc., Portland, Oreg., 1978-85; project coordinator Brown-Zammit-Enyeart Engring., Inc., San Diego, 1985—; instr. Basic Inst. Tech., St. Louis, 1971. Registered profl. engr., Nebr., Mo., Ill., Ind. Ohio, W.Va., Ky., Ark., Tex., Oreg., Wash. Mem. ASHRAE, IEEE. Home: PO Box 261578 San Diego CA 92126 Office: Brown-Zammit-Enyeart Engring Inc 7950 Dunbrook Rd San Diego CA 92126

SELLECK, FREDERIC THOMPSON, chemical engineer, thermodynamicist; b. Loma Linda, Calif., June 7, 1924; s. Willard Martineau and Florence Elizabeth (Broderick) S.; m. Phyllis Mildred MacDowell, July 12, 1952; children—Pamela L. Selleck-Holderman, Jeffrey MacDowell. B.S. in Chemistry, Calif. Inst. Tech., 1949. Research engr. Standard Perlite Corp., Pasadena, Calif., 1949-50; staff research asst. Chem Engring. Lab., Calif. Inst. Tech., Pasadena, 1950-53; sr. research engr. Fluor Corp., Whittier, Calif., 1953-60; supervising process engr. Fluor E & C, Inc., Los Angeles, 1960-82; dir. process methods and data Fluor Engrs., Inc., Irvine, Calif., 1982-87, cons. 1987—; pres., bd. chmn. Fluid Properties Research, Inc., Okla. State U., Stillwater, 1973-83. Author, editor (with others): API-RP37 Monograph II, 1955; 5 books, numerous papers; contbr. articles to profl. jours.; reviewer Jour. Chem. Engring., Data, Jour. Am. Inst. Chemical Engrs. Patentee process of separating acid gases from hydrocarbons. Served with U.S. Army, 1942-46, ETO. Mem. Am. Chem. Soc., Am. Inst. Chem. Engrs. (chmn. awards and honors com.), Inst. for Advancement in Engring. (outstanding engr. award 1986), Calif. Inst. Tech. Alumni Assn. (pres., bd. chmn.), Sigma Xi. Republican. Unitarian. Home: 14304 Bronte Dr Whittier CA 90602 Office: Fluor Engrs Inc Advanced Tech Div 3333 Michelson Dr Irvine CA 92730

SELLS, HAROLD ROBERT, petroleum engineer; b. Effingham, Kans., June 26, 1917; s. William H. and Bertha E. (McPhilimy) S.; m. Alice Plunkett Starbuck, June 25, 1978; 1 child, Jo Jo Starbuck. B.S. in Petroleum Engring., Kans. U., 1940; M.B.A., Columbia U., 1953. Registered profl. engr., Tex. Petroleum engr. Kerr-McGee Corp., Oklahoma City, 1940-42, Sohio Petroleum Corp., Oklahoma City, 1947-50; instr. Kans. U., Lawrence, 1946-47; cons. engr. Amstutz & Yates, Wichita, Kans., 1950-51; petroleum engr. Rockefeller Bros., N.Y.C., 1953-59; pres. Sells Cons. Services, N.Y.C., 1959-79; geothermal engr. San Diego Gas & Electric, 1979—. Served to lt. comdr. USN, 1942-46. Bronfman fellow, 1952. Mem. NSPE, Soc. Petroleum Engrs. (tech. editor; sr. mem.), Am. Assn. Petroleum Geologists, Geothermal Resources Council, Tau Beta Pi, Sigma Tau, Beta Gamma Sigma, Kappa Sigma. Republican. Presbyterian. Lodges: Masons (32 deg.), Shriners, Elks. Home: 3505-F Monair Dr San Diego CA 92117 Office: San Diego Gas & Electric 101 Ash St San Diego CA 92112

SELMAR, JOHN WILLIAM, speech pathologist; b. Greeley, Colo., Mar. 19, 1928; s. H.B. and Alida (McKay) S.; m. Lois Schneider, Mar. 18, 1951; children: Christine Selmar Smith, Katherine Selmar. BA, U. Dubuque, 1951; MA, U. Iowa, 1954. Speech therapist Seattle Pub. Schs., 1954-66; coordinator speech and hearing dept. Lake Washington Sch. Dist., Kirkland, Wash., 1966-84; pvt. practice speech pathologist Selmar Speech Clinic, Seattle, 1984—, also bd. dirs., cons., lectr.; freelance comml. voice-over and film narrator, 1984—. Contbr. articles and book revs. to profl. jours. Chmn. Puget sound Coop. Fedn., Seattle, 1980-86; chmn. Lake Washington Polit. Action Bd., Kirkland, Wash., 1966-84; pres. Broadview Community Council, Seattle, 1963-66; pres. Dist. Exec. Com. Group Health Coop., Seattle, 1978-82, Republican precinct committeeman. Served with USN, 1946-48. Mem. NEA (del. 1954), Am. Speech-Lang.-Hearing Assn. (cert., supr. chmn. 1954—), Wash. Speech-Hearing Assn. (housing chmn. 1954—), Lake Washington Edn. Assn. (com. chmn. 1966—, Cert. Meritorious Service 1984, Letter of Merit 1984), Nat. Stuttering Project, Seattle Tchr.'s Assn. (v.p. 1954-66). Mem. United Ch. Christ. Avocations: stamp collecting, movies. Home and Office: Selmar Speech Clinic 12232 Fremont Ave N Seattle WA 98133

SELMEIER, RICHARD JAMES, consumer financial services executive; b. Grosse Pointe, Mich., Mar. 19, 1943; s. Henry Leroy and Richalou Mae (Hopson) S.; m. Lauren Kay Schueler, Jan. 2, 1983. B.B.A., U. Mich., 1965, M.B.A., 1966. With Procter & Gamble Brand Mgmt., Cin., 1966-76; with Foote, Cone & Belding Advt. Agy., San Francisco, 1976-79; pvt. practice mgmt. cons., San Francisco, 1979—; v.p. Am. Express, San Francisco, 1981—; cons. mktg., advt. Mem. steering com. Boy Scouts Am.; fundraising chmn. Pros for Kids; dir. "cause-related mktg." ARC, San Francisco. Served to lt. USN, 1967-70. Mem. Commonwealth Club San Francisco, Am. Mgmt. Assn., U. Mich. Alumni Assn. (pres. 1973-75), Lambda Chi Alpha. Republican. Clubs: San Francisco Yacht, Tiburon Yacht. Home: 4670 Paradise Dr Tiburon CA 94920 Office: Am Express Co 601 Montgomery St Suite 725 San Francisco CA 94111

SELTH, JEFFERSON P., librarian; b. Adelaide, Australia, June 20, 1930; came to U.S., 1962; s. Victor Poole and Norah Blanche (Ashton) S.; m. Valerie Walton, June 28, 1957 (div. 1978); children: James, Catherine. BA with honors, U. Adelaide, 1951; MDiv, Starr King Sch. Ministry, 1965. Registration cert. Library Assn. Australia, 1958; ordained to ministry Unitarian Ch., 1965. Tchr. St. Peter's Coll., Adelaide, 1951-52; young adult librarian State Library of South Australia, Adelaide, 1955-59; cataloger U. Calif., Berkeley, 1962-65; minister Unitarian Fellowship of Sonoma (Calif.) County, 1964-67, Bux Mont Unitarian Fellowship, Warrington, Pa., 1968-73; bibliographer U. Calif., Riverside, 1973—; research cons. Survey Calculations Jour., Riverside, 1983-85. Author: Alternative Lifestyles, 1986; editor (jour.) Books at U. Calif. Riverside, 1979—; composer/lyricist (mus. play) Masquerade, 1980. Recipient De Mole prize U. Adelaide, 1949; David Murray scholar U. Adelaide, 1950. Mem. ALA, Assn. Coll. and Research Libraries, Calif. Library Assn. (chpt. pres. 1984-85), ACLU (founder, chmn. Sonoma County chpt. 1966-68), So. Calif. Coalition Intellectual Freedom (founder, chmn. 1979-85). Democrat. Avocations: theatre, music.

SELVAGE, ANTHONY KEITH, arranger, composer, film scorer, musician; b. Los Angeles, June 2, 1939; s. Morris Coffin Selvage and Ennid Gayle (Zamboni) Sternoff; m. Gwendolyn Ann Hoyt, Feb. 27, 1966 (div. Jan. 1970); 1 child, Keirstin Jaime; m. Laura Belle Moire, Dec. 22, 1985; 1 child, Ruby Arielle Antoinette. AA, Santa Monica Coll., 1961; student, Calif. Inst. of Arts, 1969-72; cert. completion, Summit Workshops, Fox Hills, Calif., 1984-85. Packaging engr. Overseas Packing Co., Commerce, Calif., 1960-68; hydraulic engr. Vickers Inc., Los Angeles, 1968-69; salesman DeVoss Ltd., Los Angeles, 1969-70; arranger, composer, film scorer, musician Topanga, Calif., 1970—; cons. dept. Psychology and Behavioral Scis., U. So. Calif., Los Angeles, 1985—. Prin. works include film scores for The Clay Pidgeon, America, Simulations of God, The Fine Line, World of the Unknown, Imagine, Slow Morning Rain, Nightmare on Elm St, III, Dream Warriors; TV scores include The Midnight Special, The Mancini Generation, The Dionne Warwick Special, The American Friend Service Commn. Special, The Dave Mason Show; record scored include Distant Shores by Christine McVie, Rings of Saturn and Zodiac Suite by Steven Halpern, Seapeace by Georgia Kelly, Seeds of Peace by Steven Longfellow Fiske. Active Longest Walk Am. Indian Movement, People for Ethical Treatment of Animals, Actors for Animals, Greenpeace, Alliance for Survival; campaigned for Mayor Tom Bradley, Sen. Diane Watson, Tom Hayden. Served with USN, 1963-65, Vietnam. Recipient Silver Medal Am. Song Festival, 1975, Cash award, 1976. Mem. Screen Actors Guild, AFTRA, Am. Fedn. Musicians, AFL-CIO, Am. Soc. Music Arrangers, Visual Music Alliance. Democrat. Avocations: stained glass, leather, jewelry, carpentry, skiing. Home and Office: PO Box 882 Topanga CA 90290

SELWITZ, CHARLES MYRON, chemist; b. Springfield, Mass., July 20, 1927; s. Joseph and May Evelyn (Groffman) S.; m. Ruth Fineman, Mar. 20, 1955; children: Leslie Jay, Lisa Ann. BS, Worcester Polytech. U., 1949; PhD, U. Cin., 1953. Dir. synthetic chemistry Gulf Oil Corp., Harmarville, Pa., 1953-82; cons. 1982—; conservation scientist Getty Conservation Inst., Los Angeles, 1984—. Contbr. articles to profl. jours.; patentee in field. Mem. Am. Chem. Soc., Petroleum div. of Am. Chem. Soc. (nat. membership chmn. 1976-82), Am. Inst. Conservation, Am. Def. Preparedness Assn. Home: 3631 Surfwood Rd Malibu CA 90265

SELWOOD, ALEXIS FUERBRINGER, psychotherapist; b. N.Y.C., Jan. 9, 1943; d. Otto and Winona (Gunn) Fuerbringer; m. Pierce Taylor Selwood, June 8, 1964; children: Allison Taylor, Jonathan Gunn. BA, Smith Coll., 1964; MSW, U. So. Calif., 1980, postgrad., 1983—. Journalist Calif. Apparel News, Los Angeles, 1964-68; dir. vol. services Family Services of Los Angeles, 1977; caseworker, dir. student programs Catholic Social Service, Long Beach, Calif., 1980-83; pvt. practice psychotherapy Los Angeles, 1982—; lectr. U. So. Calif. and UCLA, 1984-85. Fellow Soc. Clin. Social Work; mem. Nat. Assn. Social Workers (cert.), Nat. Registry Health Care Providers in Clin. Social Work. Avocations: traveling, tennis. Office: 420 1/2 N Larchmont Blvd Los Angeles CA 90004

SELZNICK, STEPHEN ANDREW, computer software executive; b. N.Y.C.; s. Murray and Gertrude S.; m. Cynthia A.; children—Jonathan, Marc, Kimberly. BSEE, U. Miami (Fla.), 1963. Programmer, Boeing Corp., Huntsville, Ala., 1963-64; systems analyst Gen. Dynamics, Pomona, Calif., 1964-66, Walter V. Sterling, Inc., Claremont, Calif., 1966-69; dir. data processing Genge, Inc. (Systems Planning Corp.), Los Angeles, 1970-77; pres. Professional Software Applications, Inc., Los Angeles, 1977-86; v.p. PPS, Inc., 1986—, Los Angeles; instr. Calif. Poly. U., 1974-77. Office: 283 S Lake Ave Suite 214 Pasadena CA 91101

SEMEL, TERRY, motion picture executive; b. N.Y.C., Feb. 24, 1943; s. Ben and Mildred (Wenig) S.; m. Jane Bovingdon, Aug. 24, 1977; 1 child, Eric Scott. BS in Acctg., L.I.U., 1964; postgrad. in market research, CCNY, 1966-67. Domestic sales mgr. C.B.S. Cinema Center Films, Studio City, Calif., 1970-72; v.p., gen. mgr. Walt Disney's Buena Vista, Burbank, Calif., 1972-75; pres. W.B. Distbn. Corp., Burbank, 1975-78; exec. v.p., chief operating officer Warner Bros., Inc., Burbank, from 1979, now pres., chief operating officer. Office: Warner Bros Inc 4000 Warner Blvd Burbank CA 91522 *

SEMSEN, LEE ARTHUR, librarian; b. Portland, Oreg., Jan. 3, 1950; s. James Arthur and Kathleen (Lee) S. BA in Anthropology cum laude, U. Wash., 1972, MLS, 1975. Cert. profl. librarian, Wash. Tech. processes librarian Green River Community Coll., Auburn, Wash., 1980—. Mem. Community Coll. Librarians and Media Specialists of Wash., Phi Beta Kappa, Beta Phi Mu. Avocations: hiking, book collecting, classical music. Home: 1655 22nd Way NE Auburn WA 98002 Office: Green River Community Coll 12401 SE 320th St Auburn WA 98002

SENEAR, ALLEN EUGENE, research chemist, retired; b. Chgo., Nov. 2, 1919; s. Francis E. and Anne E. (Seitz) S.; m. Virginia H. Koch, July 10, 1948; children: Allen W., Elizabeth Anne, Donald F., Virginia R. BA, Williams Coll., 1941; PhD, Calif. Inst. Tech., 1946. Postdoctoral fellow U. Ill., Urbana, 1946-47; from instr. to asst. prof. U. Calif., Santa Barbara, 1947-55; research chemist Boeing Co., Seattle and Renton Wash., 1955-85; ret. 1985—. Contbr. articles to profl. jours. Mem. AAAS, Am. Chem. Soc. (chmn. Puget Sound sect. 1986—), Phi Beta Kappa, Sigma Xi. Republican. Episcopalian. Club: Overlake Golf and Country (Medina, Wash.); Coll. (Seattle); Cen. Park Tennis (Kirkland, Wash.). Avocations: traveling, tennis, gardening. Home: 1446 92d Ave NE Bellevue WA 98004

SENGA, ROBERT MAUNDU, environmental scientist, microbiologist; b. Machakos, Kenya, East Africa, Oct. 16, 1947; s. Gedion M. Senga; m. Dorcas M. Mutungi, July 7, 1979; children—Grace Wanza, Esther Nzilani, William K. Mutuku. B.S., Calif. Poly. U., Pomona, 1975; M.S., U. LaVerne, 1978; M.S., Calif. State U.-Fullerton, 1984. Tech. dir., mgr. Electronic Reclamation Service, Anaheim, Calif., 1979; v.p. Reliable Recovery, Inc., Anaheim, 1980; environ. specialist Donald Bright & Assocs., Inc., Anaheim, 1981; prodn. chemist Armstrong Rubber, Inc., South Gate, Calif., 1982—; waste mgmt. specialist Calif. Dept. Health Services, Los Angeles, 1984—; cons. environ. problems. Mem. AAAS, Am. Soc. for Indsl. Microbiology. Developer chem. method for precious metal refining, also non-chrominated aluminium cleaning compound.

SENGER, JOHN DAVID, behavioral scientist; b. Rochelle, Ill., Feb. 21, 1922; s. Frank Herbert and Estella (Bachman) S.; B.S. in Mgmt., U. Ill., 1945, M.S. in Econs., 1948, Ph.D. in Bus., 1965; m. Doris Graham Schuler, Dec. 31, 1971; children—Sara, Susan, Konrad, Miles. Instr., U. Ill., Urbana, 1946-50; indsl. engr. Englander Co., Chgo., 1950-51; mgmt. cons. Cresap, McCormick, & Paget, Chgo., 1951-55; mgmt. engr. Gardner Board & Carton Co., Middletown, Ohio, 1955-57; prof. behavioral sci. Naval Postgrad Sch., Monterey, Calif., 1957-83, prof. emeritus, 1983—; guest prof. W. Ger. U. of Fed. Armed Forces, Munich, 1983-84; vis. prof. U. Wash., 1969-70, San Francisco State U., 1970-71. Ford Found. grantee, 1964; Office Naval Research grantee, 1966, 77; Naval Personnel Research and Devel. Center grantee, 1974, 76. Fellow Inter Univ. Sem. for the Armed Forces; mem. Am. Psychol. Assn., Acad. Mgmt., Internat. Assn. Applied Psychology, AAUP (chpt. pres. 1981), Phi Delta Theta. Author: Individuals, Groups and the Organization, 1980. Contbr. articles to profl. jours. Home: 25475 Flanders Dr Carmel CA 93923 Office: 513 West Wing Herrman Hall Naval Postgrad Sch Monterey CA 93940

SENGER, LESLIE WALTER, environmental consultant; b. Buffalo, June 8, 1945; s. Walter and Clara Mary (Jakubiak) S. BA, UCLA, 1967, MA, 1969, PhD, 1972. Research geographer U. Calif., Santa Barbara, 1970-73; cons. Dames & Moore, Santa Barbara, 1973—. Co-editor: Remote Sensing: Techniques for Environmental Analysis, 1974; contbr. numerous articles to profl. jours. Mem. AAAS, Assn. Am. Geographers (honoraria cons. 1968-70), Am. Soc. Phogrammetry. Avocation: reading. Home: 831 Cliff Dr #B-1 Santa Barbara CA 93109 Office: Dames & Moore 175 Cremona Dr Santa Barbara CA 93117

SEN GUPTA, RATAN, utility company executive, consultant; b. Calcutta, West Bengal, India, May 22, 1947; s. Ranendra Lal and Anjali (Dutta Choudhury) Sen G.; m. Shikha Choudhury, Feb. 19, 1976; 1 child, Indranil. BTech with honors, Indian Inst. Tech., Kharagpur, West Bengal, 1969; MS, U. Cin., 1971; MBA, Syracuse U., 1973. Sr. project estimator The Ralph M. Parson Co., Pasadena, Calif., 1980-81; supr., project cost engr., estimator Bechtel Petroleum Inc., San Francisco, 1981-83; supr. cost estimating sect. Pacific Gas & Electric Co., San Francisco, 1983—. Mem. Expt. in Internat. Living, Putney, Vt., 1969-76; treas. Bay Area Prabasi, San Francisco, 1985-86. Mem. ASCE, Am. Assn. Cost Engrs. (treas. 1986—). Hindu. Avocations: tennis, photography. Home: 265 Quinault Way Fremont CA 94539 Office: Pacific Gas & Electric Co 345 Mission St Room 4A/12 San Francisco CA 94106

SENKEVICH, JOHN CHARLES, brewery executive; b. Sewickley, Pa., Nov. 2, 1948; s. Joseph and Sylvia (Lamb) S.; children: John, Jeffrey. BSC, U. Louisville, 1970. CPA. Auditor Arthur Andersen & Co., Indlps., 1970-71; analyst Joseph Schlitz Brewing Co., Milw., 1971-76; controller Joseph Schlitz Brewing Co., Van Nuys, Calif., 1976-79; pres. Geyser Perk Winery, Geyserville, Calif., 1979-84, Arroyo Seco Vineyards, Santa Rosa, Calif., 1984-85, Xcelsior Brewery Inc., Santa Rosa, Calif., 1985—. Mem. Am. Inst. CPAs, Ind. Soc. CPAs. Republican. Lutheran. Home: 3328 Parker Hill Rd Santa Rosa CA 95404 Office: Xcelsior Brewery Inc 99 6th St Santa Rosa CA 95401

SENNETTE, LESLIE MARK, interior designer, design consultant; b. Oakland, Calif., Aug. 2, 1949; s. Lionel James Sennette and Dorothy (Hunter) Bradshaw; m. Alfredetta Helena, Oct. 29, 1967 (div. 1976); children: Mark Damon, Nicole Felicia; m. Michel Deyon Bateman, Aug. 22, 1982. AA, Laney Jr. Coll., 1974; student, Coll. of Design Research, 1975-76, San Francisco State U., 1977-78; BFA, Calif. Coll. of Arts and Crafts, 1980. Cert. interior designer, Calif. Space planner Kaiser Ctr. Inc., Oakland, 1970-72; archtl. designer Adv. Design Assn., Berkeley, Calif., 1976-78; sr. interior designer Baldwin Clarke, San Francisco, 1980-81; area mgr. Kaiser Found. Health Plan, Oakland, 1981-87; ptnr. Interior Designer Fairfax Architex, Oakland, 1982—; cons. Minority Bus. Assn., Oakland, 1985. Recipient Scholastic award Cannemex Commodities Corp. Mem. Inst. of Bus. Designers (profl.), Fairfax Businessmen's Assn. Republican. Roman Catholic. Avocations: chess, cycling, swimming. Office: Fairfax Architex 5363 Fairfax Ave Oakland CA 94601

SENST, JAMES ALLAN, broadcasting executive; b. Billings, Mont., Aug. 24, 1953; s. Mervin Otto and Ethel Glenn (Skillin) S. Grad. high sch., Gt. Falls, Mont. Mgr. Import Depot, Gt. Falls, 1974-78; account exec. Sta. KCVL Radio, Colville, Wash., 1978-80; media cons. Beam Pub. Relations Firm, Gt. Falls, 1980-81; sales mgr. Sta. KCAP Broadcasters, Helena, Mont., 1981—. Chmn. March Dimes Pub. Relations, Helena, 1983; fundraiser Helena YMCA, 1986; pub. relations officer Mil. Affairs Com., Helena, 1983—, Last Chance Stampede, Helena, 1982—. Mem. Helena C. of C. (chmn. bus. fair 1984-85). Avocations: bow hunting, fishing, skiing, windsurfing. Home: 1212 Leslie Helena MT 59601 Office: Sta KCAP/KZMT Broadcasters 110 Broadway Helena MT 59601

SENUNGETUK, VIVIAN RUTH, lawyer; b. Syracuse, N.Y., Sept. 27, 1948; d. George Albert and Ethel Margaret (Hearl) Bender; children: Adam George Moore, William Guugzhuk Senungetuk. BA, SUNY, Binghamton, 1968; MAT, U. Alaska, 1972; JD, Boston U., 1984. Bar: Alaska 1985, Mass. 1985, U.S. Dist. Ct. Alaska 1985. Adminstr. Indian Edn., Sitka, Alaska, 1974-76, Cook Inlet Native Assn., Anchorage, 1977-80; assoc. Erwin, Smith & Garnett, Anchorage, 1984-86; sole practice Anchorage, 1986—; adj. prof. constitutional law U. Alaska, Anchorage, 1986—. Author: A Place for Winter, 1987. Mem. ABA, Assn. Trial Lawyers Am., Nat. Assn. Women Lawyers. Democrat. Methodist. Avocations: creative writing, song writing. Office: 400 D St Suite 310 Anchorage AK 99501

SENZER, STEPHEN NEIL, research chemist; b. Bronx, N.Y., July 7, 1956; s. Raymond and Rosalind (Horn) S. BS, Lehigh U., 1978; PhD, Pa. State U., 1984. Research chemist Lockheed Missiles and Space Co., Palo Alto, Calif., 1984—. Author: (software) Statistical Analysis and Plotting, 1985 (Product Improvement Program award 1986); contbr. articles to chemistry jours. Recipient Math. Assn. Am. award, 1974. Mem. Am Chem. Soc. Avocations: basketball, tennis, baseball, volleyball. Home: 1000 Escalon Ave Sunnyvale CA 94086 Office: Lockheed Missiles and Space Co 3251 Hanover St Palo Alto CA 94304

SEPICH, JOHN EVAN, secondary educator; b. Rock Springs, Wyo., Dec. 6, 1946; s. John Evan and Pauline Marie (Slavec) S.; m. Leslie Jean Arnold, Dec. 21, 1968; children: Kathryn Jean, Tanya Lynne. BS in Biol. Scis., Colo. State U., 1969; MA in Secondary Sci. Edn., U. No. Colo., 1980. Cert. tchr. biol. sci. secondary edn., Colo. Tchr. sci. Adams County (Colo.) Dist. 50, Westminster, 1969—; instr., preparation tchr. NSF-Colo. Sch. Mines, Golden, 1974-76, cons. 1978; chmn. dept. sci. M.Scott Carpenter Middle Sch., Denver, 1973—: NSF participant leadership conf., Washington, 1975, Boulder, Colo., 1975. Co-author: Colorado Science Safety Guide, 1978. Bd. dirs. East Jefferson County (Colo.) Sanitation Dept., Lakewood, 1971-86, pres., 1981-86; sec. credit com. Dist. 50 Credit Union. Mem. Nat. Sci. Tchr. Assn. (nat. com. 1975, conv. evaluator 1979, 81), Nat. Sci. Suprs. Assn. (dir. 1975-79), Nat. Assn. Secondary Sch. Prins., Colo. Assn. Sci. Tchrs., Sci. for Handicapped, Colo. Assn. Middle Level Edn. Democrat. Roman Catholic. Avocations: jogging, travel. Home: 7155 W24th Ave Lakewood CO 80215 Office: Scott Carpenter Middle Sch 7001 Lipan Denver CO 80221

SEPPALA, SANDRA KAY, publishing executive; b. Marianna, Fla., Jan. 9, 1944; s. Leslie William and Katherine Annette (Seaman) S.; m. Gary Gene Wilcox, Aug. 26, 1965 (div. Dec. 1979); children: Jeffrey William, David Michael. Student, U. Mich., 1964; BS in Elem. Edn., Wayne State U., 1966. Tng. dir. Bullock's, Stanford, Calif., 1974-77; high sch. tchr. Peace Corps, Mariakani, Kenya, 1977-79; tech. tng. coordinator Cromemco, Inc., Mountain View, Calif., 1980-81; mktg. communications mgr. Portec, Inc., Sunnyvale, Calif., 1981-82; mktg. publs. mgr. TeleVideo, Inc., Sunnyvale, 1982-85; tech. publs. mgr. Counterpoint Computers, San Jose, Calif., 1985—. Founder, sec., Amigos De Las Americas, Silicon Valley, Calif., 1984-85; mem. Nat. Women's Polit. Caucus, Santa Clara County, Calif., 1973-86; founder, bd. dirs. newsletter chair NorCal Council of Returned Peace Corps Vols., San Francisco, 1981-83; sec. Sch. Site Council at Homestead High Sch., Cupertino, Calif., 1985-86; founder Status Women Commn. Organizing Com., Santa Clara County, 1972-73. Mem. AAUW, Soc. Tech. Communication. Democrat. Presbyterian. Avocations: needlepoint, reading, cooking, films, piano. Home: 1624 Hollenbeck Ave #3 Sunnyvale CA 94087 Office: Counterpoint Computers 2127 Ringwood Ave San Jose CA 95131

SERA, KATHRYN K., audiologist; b. Boulder, Colo., Dec. 6, 1953; d. T. Tetsuo and Shizuko G. (Kimura) S. BS, Colo. State U., 1975, MS, 1976. Audiologist Colorado Springs, 1978-80, Pikes Peak Bb. Cooperative Services, Colorado Springs, Colo., 1978-81, Colorado Springs Pub. Schs., 1981-86, Ear Nose and Throat Clinic, 1986—; audiologist Cedar Springs Psychiat. Hosp., Colorado Springs, 1986—. Mem. Am. Speech, Lang. and Hearing Assn. (cert.), Colo. Speech, Lang. and Hearing Assn., Am. Auditory Soc. Avocations: skiing, scuba diving, arts and crafts. Home: 919 N Cedar Colorado Springs CO 80903 Office: Ear Nose and Throat Clinic 715 N Cascade Colorado Springs CO 80903

SERAFINI, VICTOR RENATO, aerospace engineer; b. Chgo., June 9, 1934; s. Renato Victor and Stella (Koch) S. BS in Aero. Engring., U. Ill., 1957, postgrad., 1957-65; postgrad., UCLA, 1957-65. Research and project engr. Rocketdyne Div. N.Am. Aviation, Canoga Park, Calif., 1957-67; program/project mgr. TRW Inc., Redondo Beach, Calif., 1967-78; asst. dir. spacecraft engring. Communications Satellite Corp., El Segundo, Calif., 1978—; bd. dirs. Autobahn West, Westlake Village, Calif.; mgmt. cons. Westoaks Realty, Westlake Village, 1975—; pres. STD Assocs., Rancho Palos Verdes, Calif., 1965—. Recipient award of Recognition, TRW Inc., 1965, Recognition of Outstanding Effort award NASA and TRW, 1963-64. Mem. AIAA (liquid rocket tech. com. 1985-86). Mem. Christian Ch. Avocations: flying, sailing, swimming, mountain climbing, toy collecting. Home: PO Box 2665 Rancho Palos Verdes CA 90274 Office: Communications Satellite Corp 2250 E Imperial Hwy Suite 750 El Segundo CA 90245

SERBEIN, OSCAR NICHOLAS, business educator, consultant; b. Collins, Iowa, Mar. 31, 1919; s. Oscar Nicholas and Clara Matilda (Shearer) S.; m. Alice Marie Bigger, Sept. 16, 1952; children: Mary Llewellyn Serbein Parker, John Gregory. BA, U. Iowa, 1940, MS, 1941; PhD, Columbia U., 1951. Grad. asst. math. U. Iowa, Iowa City, 1940-41; clk. Met. Life Ins. Co., N.Y.C., 1941-42; lectr. U. Calif., Berkeley, summer 1948, 50; lectr., asst. prof., assoc. prof. Columbia U., N.Y.C., 1947-59; prof. ins. Stanford (Calif.) U., 1959—; cons. Ins. Info. Inst., N.Y.C., 1971-78, N.Am. Re-Assurance Life Service Co., Palo Alto, 1973, SRI Internat., Menlo Park, Calif., 1980-81, other bus.; cons., expert witness various law firms. Author: Paying for Medical Care in the U.S., 1953, Educational Activities of Business, 1961; co-author: Property and Liability Insurance, 4 ed., 1967, Risk Management: Text and Cases, 2 ed., 1983; also articles. Bd. dirs. Sr. Citizens Coordinating Council, Palo Alto, 1986. Served to maj. USAF, WWII. Decorated Bronze star 1944. Mem. Am. Risk and Ins. Assn., Western Risk and Ins. Assn., Phi Beta Kappa, Sigma Xi, Beta Gamma Sigma. Democrat. Methodist. Club: Stanford Faculty. Avocation: gardening. Home: 731 San Rafael Pl Stanford CA 94305 Office: Stanford U Grad Sch Bus Stanford CA 94305

SERBIN, MARK DWIGHT, safety administrator; b. Takoma Park, Md., June 20, 1953; s. Alfred James and Edith (Ginsberg) S. BA, Oglethorpe U., 1975. Balance cl. First Ga. Bank, Atlanta, 1976-77; sr. auditor Mut. of Omaha, Rockville, Md., 1977-79; adjuster III Crawford & Co., Las Vegas, 1979-80, 84-85; dir. safety Las Vegas Hilton Hotel, 1985—. Author: Population & Housing Projection for Cobb County, Georgia. For year 1983, 1974. Compensation officer State of Nev. Aid to Certain Victims of Crime Program, Las Vegas, 1984-85. Mem. So. Nev. Claims Assn., Am. Soc. Safety Engrs., Las Vegas Jaycees. Democrat. Jewish. Avocations: cars, cinema, travel. Home: 713 E Sahara Ave #418 Las Vegas NV 89104 Office: Las Vegas Hilton Hotel 3000 Paradise Rd Las Vegas NV 89109

SERIGHT, ORIN DALE, linguistics educator; b. Boulder, Colo., Nov. 23, 1932; s. Orin Dale Seright and Fern Evelyn (Watson) Hilliard. BA magna cum laude, U. Colo., 1955; MA, U. Ark., 1956; PhD, Ind. U., 1960. Teaching fellow U. Ark., Fayetteville, 1955-56; teaching assoc. Ind. U., Bloomington, 1956-60; asst. prof. linguistics U. So. Calif., Los Angeles, 1960-67; prof. San Diego State U., 1967—, founder, first chmn. dept. linguistics, 1972-74. Contbr. articles to scholarly jours. Bd. dirs. Rancho San Diego Archtl. Com., 1979—; mem. San Diego Opera Assn. Mem. MLA, Linguistic Soc. Am., Nat. Council Tchrs. English (panel chmn. 1982), Phi Delta Kappa, Delta Phi Alpha. Democrat. Avocations: playing classical piano, gardening, traveling. Home: 2207 Durasno Ln Rancho San Diego CA 92078 Office: San Diego State U Dept Linguistics San Diego CA 92182-0299

SERVIS, NANCY JANE, mental health counselor; b. Compton, Calif., Oct. 15, 1943; d. Johnnie and Angelina Katherine (Bello) Vigario; children—Sandra, James, Mary, Stephanie. Student Long Beach State Coll., 1961-64; B.S. in Recreation Leadership/Theraputic summa cum laude, No. Ariz. U., 1981; M.S.W., Ariz. State U., 1985. Mental health counselor Coconino Community Guidance Ctr., Flagstaff, Ariz., 1981—; supr. residential mental health program, 1986—; cons. County Atty. Office, Flagstaff; guest speaker in field; mem. Crisis Intervention Backup, 1981—, Sexual Assault Intervention, 1983—; leader recreation and leisure activities for mentally retarded, mentally ill and minority groups, 1980—. Rotary scholar, 1961; Dougherty Found. scholar, 1982-83. Mem. Ariz. Parks and Recreation Assn., Nat. Assn. Social Workers, Phi Kappa Phi. Democrat. Clubs: Recreation, Latin, Girls' State, Service. Home: 430 W Pine Ave Flagstaff AZ 86001

SESAK, JOHN ROBERT, control and aerospace engineer; b. Latrobe, Pa., Jan. 19, 1942; s. John and Margaret (Brillo) S. Student, St. Vincent Coll., 1960-62; BSEE, Pa. State U., 1965; MS, U. Conn., 1967; PhD, U. Wis., 1974. Sr. engr. Gen. Dynamics Co. div. Convair, San Diego, 1976-79, engring. specialist, 1979-82, sr. engring. specialist, 1982-83, program mgr., 1983-85; sr. staff engr. guidance and control dept. Astronautics div. Lockheed Missiles and Space Co., Sunnyvale, Calif., 1985—. Inventor flexible satellite control algorithmns; model error sensitivity suppression; filter accomodated optimal control; passive damping control algorithmns; originator Nat. Short Course on Flexible Spacecraft Control, 1981. Mem. AIAA (guidance and control com. 1981-84, council 1982-83, adminstrv. chmn. 1982, Outstanding Contbn. to Aerospace Engring. award 1979), IEEE, Am. Soc. Engring. Edn., Sigma Xi. Office: Lockheed Missiles and Space Co Astronautics Div 1111 Lockheed Way Bldg 578 Org 59-31 Sunnyvale CA 94089-3504

SESHAN, VENKATACHALAM, business management educator, consultant; b. Kottayam, Kerala, India, Dec. 25, 1938; s. C.S. and Lakshmi Venkatachalam; m. Rosalie J. Tanner, Oct. 19, 1962; 1 child, Sheila. AS, U. Bombay, 1956; B Chem. Engring., U. Bombay, India, 1960; M Chem. Engring., U. Louisville, 1962; PhD, Lehigh U., 1965. Sr. bus. analyst E.I. du Pont de Nemours and Co., Wilmington, Del., 1965-72; prof. mgmt. Am. Grad. Sch. Internat. Mgmt., Glendale, Ariz., 1972-74; bus. mgr. Olin Corp., Stamford, Conn., 1974-80; sr. planning cons. Atlantic Richfield Co., Los Angeles, 1980-85; pres. VS Exec. Cons., Westlake Village, Calif, 1985—; prof. mgmt. Seaver Coll. Pepperdine U., Malibu, Calif., 1986—; adj. prof. U. So. Calif. Sch. Bus., Los Angeles, 1985—, internat. bus. systems mgmt. Calif. Luth. U., Thousand Oaks, 1986—. Creator Spl. Mgmt. Tng., 1975-77 (Excellence award) and other mgmt. projects. Supporter Global Tomorrow Coalition. Research fellow IBM, Inst. Indsl. Research, Louisville, 1961-62; William C. Gotshall Scholar, Lehigh U., 1962-65. Mem. Acad. Mgmt., World Future Soc., Inst. Mgmt Scis., Am. Inst. Chem. Engrs., Ops. Research Soc. Am., Global Futures Network, Action Linkage, Sigma Xi. Lodge: Rotary (internat. dir. 1965-71). Home: 120 Helecho Ct Thousand Oaks CA 91362 Office: Pepperdine U Seaver Coll Dept Bus Adminstrn Malibu CA 90265

SESSA, WILLIAM LAWRENCE, journalist, state official; b. Pitts., Nov. 21, 1947; s. Lawrence Joseph and Mary (Summers) S.; children by previous marriage—Rebecca Lynn, Sara Lynn; m. Sheila Dee Marsee, Dec. 20, 1981. B.S. in Journalism, Calif. State U.-Sacramento, 1969; A.A., American River Coll., 1967; postgrad. NYU, 1976-79. Communications advisor Air Resources Bd., Sacramento, 1979-84; press sec., communication dir. Calif. Office Environ. Affairs, Sacramento, 1983—; contbg. editor Peterson Pub. Co., Los Angeles, 1981—, Lopez Pub. Co., Alexandria, Va., 1979—. Mem. State Info. Officers Council (pres. 1978-79). Democrat. Club: Sacramento Press (bd. dirs. 1981—, chmn. scholarship com. 1982—). Office: Calif Air Resources Bd PO Box 2815 Sacramento CA 95812

SESSLER, ANDREW MARIENHOFF, physicist; b. Bklyn., Dec. 11, 1928; s. David and Mary (Baron) S.; m. Gladys Lerner, Sept. 23, 1951; children: Danial Ira, Jonathan Lawrence, Ruth. BA in Math. cum laude, Harvard U., 1949; MA in Theoretical Physics, Columbia U., 1951, PhD in Theoretical Physics, 1953. NSF fellow Cornell U., N.Y., 1953-54; asst. prof. Ohio State U., Columbus, 1954, assoc. prof., 1960; on leave Midwestern Univs. Research, 1955-56; vis. physicist Lawrence Rediation Lab., 1959-60, Niels Bohr Inst., Copenhagen, summer 1961; researcher theoretical physics U. Calif. Lawrence Berkeley Lab., Berkeley, 1961-73, researcher energy and environment, 1971-73, dir., 1973-80, sr. scientist plasma physics, 1980—; U.S. advisor Panjab U. Physics Inst., Chandigarh, India; mem. U.S.-India Coop. Program for Improvement Sci. Edn. in India, 1966, high energy physics adv. panel to U.S. Atomic Energy Commn., 1969-72, adv. com. Lawrence Hall Sci., 1974-78; chmn. Stanford Synchrotron Radiation Project Sci. Policy Bd., 1974-77, EPRI Advanced Fuels Adv. Com., 1978-81, BNL External Adv. Com. on Isabelle, 1980-82. Mem. editorial bd. Nuclear Instruments and Methods, 1969—; correspondent Comments on Modern Physics, 1969-71; contbr. articles in field to profl. jours. Recipient E.O. Lawrence award U.S. Atomic Energy Commn., 1970; fellow Japan Soc. for Promotion Sci. at KEK, 1985. Fellow Am. Phys. Soc. (chmn. com. internat. freedom scientists 1982, mem. study of directed energy weapons panel 1985-87, vice chmn. panel pub. affairs 1987), AAAS (nominating com. 1984-87); mem. Fedn. Am. Scientists Council (vice chmn. 1987-88), Com. Concerned Scientists Council, Sigma Xi. Home: 225 Clifton St Apt 201 Oakland CA 94618 Office: U Calif Lawrence Berkeley Lab 1 Cyclotron Rd Berkeley CA 94720

SESTINI, VIRGIL ANDREW, educator; b. Las Vegas, Nov. 24, 1936; s. Santi and Merceda Francesca (Borla) S. B.S. in Edn., U. Nev., 1959; postgrad., Oreg. State U., 1963-64; M.N.S., U. Idaho, 1965; postgrad., Ariz. State U., 1967, No. Ariz. U., 1969; cert. tchr., Nev. Tchr. biology Rancho High Sch., 1960-76; sci. chmn., tchr. biology Bonanza High Sch., Las Vegas, 1976—. Served with USAR, 1959-65. Recipient Rotary Internat. Honor Tchr. award, 1965, Region VIII Outstanding Biology Tchr. award, 1970, Nev. Outstanding Biology Tchr. award Nat. Assn. Biology Tchrs., 1970, Nat. Assn. Sci. Tchrs., Am. Gas Assn. Sci. Teaching Achievement Recognition award, 1976, 1980, Gustov Ohaus award, 1980, Presdl. Honor Sci. Tchr. award, 1983; Excellence in Edn. award Nev. Dept. Edn., 1983; Presdl. award excellence in math. and sci. teaching, 1984, Celebration of Excellence award Nev. Com. on Excellence in Edn., 1986, Commemorative Medal of Honor, Am. Biog. Inst., 1986. Mem. NEA, Nat. Sci. Tchrs. Assn., Nat. Assn. Biology Tchrs., Am. Soc. Microbiology, Nat. Audobon Assn., Nat. Sci. Suprs. Assn., Am. Inst. Biol. Scis. Roman Catholic. Office: Bonanza High Sch 6665 W Del Rey Ave Las Vegas NV 89102

SETCHKO, EDWARD STEPHEN, minister theological educator; b. Yonkers, N.Y., Apr. 27, 1926; s. Stephen John and Mary Elizabeth (Dulak) S.; m. Penelope Sayre, Nov. 18, 1950; children—Marc Edward, Kip Sherman, Robin Elizabeth, Jan Sayre, Dirk Stephen. B.S., Union Coll., 1948; M.Div. cum laude, Andover Newton Theol. Sch., 1953, S.T.M., 1954; Th.D., Pacific Sch. Religion, 1962. Ordained to ministry United Ch. of Christ, 1954; cert. profl. hosp. chaplain. Psychometrician, Union Coll. Character Research Project, Schenectady, N.Y., 1947-50; asst. pastor Eliot Ch., Newton, Mass., 1950-54; clin. tng. supr. Boston City Hosp., 1951-54; intern, chaplain Boston State Mental Hosp., 1953-54; univ. campus minister U. Wash., Seattle, 1954-58; Danforth grantee, 1958-59; grad. fellow in psychotherapy Pacific Sch. Religion, Berkeley, Calif., 1959-60, instr. dept. pastoral psychology, 1960-61, grad. fellow, lectr. theology and psychology, 1961-62, asst. prof. psychology and counseling, 1962-63, dir. continuing theol. edn., 1962-63; field research sec. laity div. United Ch. Christ, Berkeley, Calif. and N.Y.C., 1963-68; vis. prof. psychology Starr King Ctr. for Religious Leadership, Berkeley, 1967-69; assoc. prof. religion and soc. Starr King Ctr., Grad. Theol. Union, Berkeley, Calif., 1969-71, prof., 1971—; career counselor The Ctr. for Ministry, Oakland, Calif., 1986—; mem. faculty, chmn. curriculum and faculty com. Layman's Sch. Religion, Berkeley, 1960-67; cons. and lectr. in field. Mem. Peace Del., Mid-East, 1983; lectr. Internat. Conf. on the Holocaust and Genocide, Genocide, Tel Aviv, 1982, Nuclear Disarmament Conf., W.Ger., 1980, 81, 82, Internat. Ctr. for Peace in the Middle East, Resource Ctr. for Non-Violence, Clergy & Laity Concerned, Ecumenical Peace Inst., Internat. Peace Acad.; World Policy Inst., Inst. Peace and World Order, Am. Friends Service Com. (bd. dirs.), Ristad Found.; dir. The Project for Peace and Reconciliation in the Middle East (non-profit Calif. Corp.). Served as lt. (j.g.) USNR, 1944-46, WW II. Mem. Am. Psychol. Assn. (cert.), Calif. State Psychol. Assn., Assn. Clin. Pastoral Edn., World Future Soc., Soc. Sci. Study of Religion, Inst. Noetic Scis., Com. for Protection Human Subjects (U. Calif.-Berkeley). Democrat. Contbr. articles to profl. jours.; condr. seminars: Futurology; Intracacies of Being Human, Images of Women and Men; Changing Values in Roles Between the Sexes in a Technological Society; developer curriculum: Peace and Conflict Studies (U. Calif., Berkeley).

SETH, OLIVER, judge; b. Albuquerque, May 30, 1915; s. Julien Orem and Bernice (Grefe) S.; m. Jean MacGillivray, Sept. 25, 1946; children: Sandra Bernice, Laurel Jean. A.B., Stanford U., 1937; LL.B., Yale U., 1940. Bar: N.Mex. 1940. Practice law Santa Fe, 1940, 46-62; judge U.S. Ct. Appeals 10th Circuit, 1962—, chief judge, from 1976, now senior judge; dir. Santa Fe Nat. Bank, 1949-62; chmn. legal com. N.Mex. Oil and Gas Assn., 1956-59, mem. regulatory practices com., 1960-62; counsel N.Mex. Cattlegrowers Assn., 1950-62, N.Mex. Bankers Assn., 1952-62; govt. appeal agent SSS, 1948-52. Mem. bd. regents Mus. of N.Mex., 1956-60; Bd. dirs. Boys Club, Santa Fe, 1948-49, N.Mex. Land Resources Assn., 1956-60, Ghost Ranch Mus., 1962—; mng. bd. Sch. Am. Research, 1950—. Served from pvt. to maj. AUS, 1940-45, ETO. Decorated Croix de Guerre (France). Mem. Santa Fe C. of C. (dir.), N.Mex., Santa Fe County bar assns., Phi Beta Kappa. Presbyterian. Office: US Ct Appeals PO Drawer 1 Santa Fe NM 87501 *

SETO, JOSEPH TOBEY, microbiologist, educator; b. Tacoma, Aug. 3, 1924; s. Toraichi and Kiyo Morita Seto; m. Grace K. Nakano, Aug. 9, 1959; children: Susan L., Steven F. BS, U. Minn., 1949; MS, U. Wis., 1955, PhD, 1957. Postdoctoral fellow UCLA, 1958-59; asst. prof. San Francisco State U., 1959-60; prof. microbiology Calif. State U., Los Angeles, 1960—; cons. U.S. Naval Biology Lab., Oakland, Calif., 1959-61; vis. prof. Inst. Virology, Giessen, Fed. Republic Germany, 1965-66, 72-73, 79-80, WHO Exchange Worker, 1972. Served to sgt. U.S. Army, 1945-46. United Health Found. fellow, 1965; Humboldt Found. fellow, 1972. Fellow Am. Soc. Microbiology; mem. AAAS, Electron Microscope Soc., Sigma Xi. Office: Calif State U Dept Microbiology Los Angeles CA 90032

SETTLEMYER, GEORGE BERNARD, public administrator; b. San Francisco, Oct. 27, 1936; s. Dewey Lee and Hazel Ella (Bessett) S.; m. Marijane Dorothy Crawford, June 10, 1958; children: Linda Marie, James Bernard. BBA, U. Ariz., 1958; MBA, Golden Gate U., 1985. Jr. adminstrv. asst. City of Los Angeles, 1960-64, adminstrv. asst., 1964-66, sr. adminstrv. asst., 1966-72, prin. adminstrv. asst., 1972—. Sponsor Camp Fire Girls, N. Hollywood, Calif., 1973-74; com. chmn. Great Western Council Boy Scouts Am., N. Hollywood, 1976-81. Served to 1st lt. U.S. Army, 1958-60. Recipient Outstanding Service award YMCA, 1972; Disting. Merit award Boy Scouts Am., 1976. Mem. Telecommunications Assn. (Mem. of Yr. So. Calif. chpt., 1983), U. Ariz. Alumni Assn. (pres. 1970-71). Republican. Episcopalian. Clubs: Men's Garden (pres. 1968), Toastmasters (Able Toastmaster award 1976). Lodges: Plaza de Los Angeles (master 1975), So. Calif. Research (master 1980), Internat. Order of Job's Daughter (hon.). Avocations: reading, camping. Home: 4848 Ledge Ave North Hollywood CA 91601

SETTLES, F. STAN, JR., manufacturing executive; b. Denver, Oct. 3, 1938; s. Frank S. and Dorothy Marie (Johnson) S.; m. Evelyn Brown, June 10, 1961; children: Frank S. III, Richard, Charles, Michael. BS in Prodn. Tech., Indsl. Engring., LeTourneau Coll., Longview, Tex., 1962; MS in Indsl. Engring., Ariz. State U., 1967, PhD in Indsl. Engring., 1969. Sr. systems analyst AiResearch Mfg. Co., Phoenix, 1968-70, project mgr., 1970-74, mgr. operational planning, 1974-80; mgr. indsl. engrs. Garrett Pneumatic Systems, Phoenix, 1980-83; mgr. indsl. mfg. engring. Garrett Turbine Engring. Co., Phoenix, 1983-85; v.p. mfg. ops. AiResearch Mfg. Co., Torrance, Calif., 1985-87; dir. indusl. mfg. engring. The Garrett Corp., Phoenix, 1987—; faculty assoc. Ariz. State U., Tempe, 1974-85. Mem. sch. bd. Tempe Elem. Sch. Dist., 1976-80; mem. YMCA Indian Guides, nat. chief, 1978-79. Fellow Inst. Indsl. Engrs. (pres. 1987-88, Ops. Research award 1980); mem. Soc. Mfg. Engrs. (sr.), Inst. Mgmt. Sci. (sr.). Republican. Presbyterian. Home: 1627 E La Jolla Tempe AZ 85282 Office: The Garrett Corp PO Box 5217 Dept 1-1 Bldg 301-2X Phoenix AZ 85010

SEVERAID, RONALD HAROLD, lawyer; b. Berkeley, Calif., July 13, 1951; s. J. Harold and Irene Ann (Clark) s.; m. Peggy R. Chappus. B.A., U. Calif.-Davis, 1973; J.D., Georgetown U., 1977. Bar: Calif. 1977, D.C. 1979, U.S. Dist. Ct. (ea. and cen. dists.) Calif. 1977. Assoc. Kindel & Anderson, Los Angeles, 1977-79; exec. v.p., gen. counsel Pacific Mktg. Devel., Sacramento, 1979-80, pres., 1980-81; sec. Aaron-Ross Corp., Glendora, Calif., 1983-84; sole practice, Sacramento, 1979-84; sr. atty. Severaid & Seegmiller, Sacramento, 1984—. Co-editor Internat. Cts. of Justice Opinion Briefs, 1978; sr. topics editor Law and Policy in Internat. Bus., 1975-76; contbr. articles to profl. jours. Asst. sec. Internat. Relations Sect.-Town Hall, Los Angeles, 1978-79; pres. Pacifica Villas Homeowners Assn., 1978-79. Mem. ABA, Calif. State Bar Assn., Sacramento County Bar Assn., Community Assns. Inst., Calif. Trustees Assn. Republican. Roman Catholic. Office: Severaid & Seegmiller 601 University Ave Suite 125 Sacramento CA 95825

SEWARD, DORIS KLUGE, service executive, consultant; b. Washington, Dec. 12, 1920; d. Russell O. and Edna Ashford Kluge; m. Robert F. Seward, June 18, 1947. BA, Tex. U., 1943; MS in Edn., U. So. Calif., 1968, M in Pub. Adminstrn., 1972, D in Pub. Adminstrn., 1974. Mgmt. analyst U.S. Dept. Air Force, Columbus AFB, Miss., 1959-62; tng. asst. Los Angeles City Schs., 1963-66; tng. officer Los Angeles County, 1967-79, specialist personnel mgmt., 1979-84; pres. Pub. Adminstrn. Research and Edn., Whittier, Calif., 1981—, Temporary Tng. Skills, Whittier, 1984—; instr. UCLA extension, Los Angeles, 1973—, Calif. State U., Long Beach, 1975—, Northrop Corp., Hawthorne, Calif., 1984—; cons. Exec. Service Corps So. Calif., 1984—. Mem. Los Angeles County Grand Jury, 1986-87; chmn. Editorial, Continuity Com., Govt. Ops. and Audit Com. Recipient Research award Western Govt. Research Assn., 1974, Henry Reining Jr. award U. So. Calif., 1975. Mem. Am. Soc. Pub. Adminstrn. (exec. council mem. Los Angeles Met. chpt., 1974-76, membership chmn. 1974-76), Women's Equity Action League (nat. pres. 1974-75), Am. Soc. Tng. and Devel. (exec. council mem., dir. programming Los Angeles chpt., 1976), Internat. Personnel Mgmt. Assn., So. Calif. Personnel Mgmt. Assn. (life, hon.), Los Angeles County Mgmt. Council (chmn. mgmt. devel. com.,1972, editor jour. 1972-75, chmn. program com. for mgmt. conf., 1976, mem. edn. and tng. com. 1980-84). Democrat. Methodist. Club: Whittier Women's. Avocations: aerobic dancing, raising cocker spaniels.

SEWARD, MARILYN BETTY, educator; b. Red Oak, Iowa, May 16, 1928; d. Morris Bishop and Fern Evelyn (Anderson) Reed; m. Wendell Herbert Seward, June 1, 1947; children—David, Meri Hecker. B.S. with high honors, Portland State U., 1965; M.Sch. Adminstrn. with honors, Calif. State U.-Chico, 1983. Tchr. pub. schs., Burwell, Nebr., 1947-48, Colton, Oreg., 1958-67; prin., tchr. Quartz Valley Sch., Ft. Jones, Calif., 1967—; pvt. practice family and marriage counseling, 1967-83. Started 1st elem. sch. computer program in county, 1st elem. fgn. lang. program in French; provided foster home for 35 teenagers, 1970-83. Developer Kidder Creek Orchard Camp, 1975-82; area rep. Youth for Understanding, 1972-83; active Evangelical Women's Caucus, Scott Valley Berean Ch. Named Scott Valley Citizen of Yr., 1984. Mem. Assn. for Curriculum and Devel., Internat. Reading Assn., Siskiyou County Reading Assn. (pres.), Computer Using Educators, Am. Council Sch. Suprs., Project Leadership, Phi Delta Kappa. Republican. Office: 11033 Quartz Valley Rd Fort Jones CA 96027

SEWELL, CHARLES ROBERTSON, geologist, exploration company executive; b. Malvern, Ark., Feb. 7, 1927; s. Charles Louis and Elizabeth (Robertson) S.; m. Margaret Helen Wilson, Dec. 26, 1953 (dec. July 1985); children—Michael Stuart, Charles Wilson, Marion Elizabeth; m. Louise T. Worthington, Nov. 29, 1985. B.S., U. Ark.-Fayetteville, 1950; M.A., U. Tex.-Austin, 1955, postgrad., 1961-64. Registered geologist, Calif., Ariz. Well logging engr. Baroid, Houston, 1950; asst. metallurgist Magcobar, Malvern, Ark., 1951; geologist Socony-Mobil Petroleum Co., Roswell, N.Mex., 1955; sr. geologist Dow Chem. Co., Freeport, Tex., 1956-61; spl. instr. U. Tex., Austin, 1962-65; pvt. practice cons. geologist, Austin, 1962-65; dist. geologist, mgr. Callahan Mining Corp., Tucson, 1965-68; owner, cons. geologist Sewell Mineral Exploration, worldwide, 1968—. Contbr. articles to profl. jours. Elder, Presbyn. Ch., Tucson, 1973—. Served with USN, 1944-46, 51-53. NSF grantee, 1962-64, 63. Mem. AIME, Ariz. Geol. Soc., Mining Club Southwest (bd. govs. 1982-86, pres. 1984), Colo. Mining Assn., Sigma Xi. Republican. Lodge: Masons. Discoverer/co-discoverer numerouis metallic and non-metallic ore deposits. Home and Office: 9950 E Broadway Tucson AZ 85748

SEWELL, ROBERT GRANVILLE STAHL, physicist; b. Santa Rosa, Calif., July 18, 1922; s. Edward Granville and Pauline (Stahl) S.; m. Barbara Ann Currul, Nov. 4, 1944 (dec. June 1985); children: Margaret Busch, Christine Clapp, Katherine Leckey, Deborah Benson; m. Carrol Diane Evans West, Jan. 25, 1986; children: Lance West, Kevin West, Darin West, Galen West. AA, Taft Jr. Coll., 1942; AB, U. Calif., Berkeley, 1948, MA, 1950. Physicist Naval Weapons Ctr. (formerly NOTS), China Lake, Calif., 1950-86, sr. scientist engring. sci. div., 1983-86; physicist COMARCO, Ridgecrest, Calif., 1986—. Contbr. articles to profl. publs.; patentee in field. Served to 1st lt. USAF, 1942-47. Mem. IEEE, Am. Def. Preparedness Assn. (Crozier Gold medal 1979). Episcopalian. Lodges: Rotary (pres. China Lake club 1965-66), Masons. Avocations: folk singing, golf. Home: 313 E Far Vista Ridgecrest CA 93555 Office: COMARCO 1201 N China Lake Blvd Ridgecrest CA 93555

SEWELL, ROBERT HERBERT, retired advertising executive; b. Seattle, Sept. 4, 1927; s. Robert Herbert and Helen Louise (Servis) S.; m. Patricia Ann Corson, June 19, 1947; children—Sandra Ann, Robert L. Acct. exec. Budget Ln., Seattle, 1952-56; retail sales rep. Stokely Van Camp, Seattle, 1956-58; v.p., acct. exec. Graves Chambers, Seattle, 1958-67; Western Wash. mgr. Fenwick Pickett, 1967-68; food sales exec. Tacoma (Wash.) News Tribune, 1969-84, gen. advt. mgr., 1980-84. Served with USN, 1945-49. Mem. Mfrs. Rep. Club, The Illuminators Inc. Elks, Masons.

SEXTON, JOYCE FORRESTER, audiologist; b. Dillon, Mont., May 20, 1957; d. Roy William and Dorothy Anne (Davis) Forrester; m. Shaun Edward Sexton, Aug. 20, 1983. AA, Cottey Coll., 1977; BS, Purdue U., 1979; MA, U. Mont., 1981. Cert. clin. competence audiologist, speech pathologist. Tchr. infant learning Tanana Chiefs Native Corp., Fairbanks, Alaska, 1981-82, coordinator infant program, 1982-83; audiologist Anchorage Sch. Dist., 1983—; mem. health bd. Chugiak (Alaska) Children's Services, 1985—. Vol. audiologist Chevron Alaska Health Fairs, Anchorage, 1986, 87. Mem. Am. Speech Lang. and Hearing Assn. (cert.), Alaska Speech and Hearing Assn. (treas. 1985—), Ednl. Audiologists Assn., Presbyn. Women's Assn. (pres. Eagle River chpt. 1986-87). Club: Anchorage Women's Rugby, Quota Internat. Avocations: running, reading, fishing, sewing, rugby. Office: Whaley Ctr Audiology Dept 2220 Nichols St Anchorage AK 99508

SEXTON, ROBERT DAYTON, consulting engineer; b. San Francisco, Oct. 15, 1941; s. Lyle Gates and Dorothy Lloyd (Upton) S.; m. Helen Valios, Apr. 20, 1969; 1 child, Dorothy Marie. Student, Fresno City Coll., 1963-65; BSEE, Calif. Poly. State U., San Luis Opispo, 1968. Engr. AV Electronics, Fresno, 1970-71; chief engr., founding employee Dantel, Inc, Fresno, 1971-79; staff engr. GTE-Lenkurt, San Carlos, Calif., 1979-80, Buckner Sprinklers, Fresno, 1980-83; prin. Rosexton-Design Cons., Fresno, 1983—; co-founder, chief engr. J-Tec Corp., Fresno, 1969-70, Picotel, Inc., Fresno, 1983-85. Contbr. numerous articles to profl. jours. Sec. St. George Greek Orthodox Ch., 1982, pres. 1983, mem. parish council 1982-85. Served with USN, 1959-63. Mem. IEEE, Profl. and Tech. Cons. Assn., Scottish Soc. Calif. (steward 1986—). Democrat. Avocations: skiing, photography, sailing, reading sci. and history. Home: 3225 W Minarets Fresno CA 93711 Office: Rosexton Design Cons 320 W Bedford #206 Fresno CA 93711

SEYEDIN, SAEID MIR, biology researcher; b. Mashhad, Iran, Feb. 28, 1948; came to U.S., 1970; s. Abolegasim and Eesmat (Segari) S.; m. Sedigheh Ghodrat, Mar. 20, 1980; children: Melissa, Steven. BS, U. Wis., River Falls; PhD, U. S.C.; postdoctoral, U. Calif., Berkeley. Research scientist Collagen Corp., Palo Alto, Calif., 1981-83, mgr. biology sect., research leader, 1983—. Contbr. articles to profl. jours. Avocations: tennis, racquetball, running. Home: 645 Cheshire Way Sunnyvale CA 94087

SEYFERT, HOWARD BENTLEY, JR., podiatrist; b. Clifton Heights, Pa., July 10, 1918; s. Howard Bentley and Mabel (Ashenbach) S.; m. Anna Mary van Roden, June 26, 1942; 1 child, Joanna Mary Irwin. D of Podiatric Medicine, Temple U., 1940. Cert. Nat. Bd. Podiatry Examiners (past pres.), Ariz. State Bd. Podiatry Examiners (past pres.). Pvt. practice podiatry Phoenix, 1950-82, Sedona, Ariz., 1982—; mem. med. staff Marcus J. Lawrence Meml. Hosp., Cottonwood, Ariz. Served to capt. USAAF, 1942-46, ETO, lt. col. Res. ret. Decorated Bronze Star. Fellow Acad. Ambulatory Foot Surgery, Am. Coll. Foot Surgeons; mem. Ariz. Podiatric Med. Assn. (past pres.), Am. Podiatric Med. Assn. Republican. Presbyterian. Clubs: OakCreek Country (Sedona); Fairfield Flagstaff Country (Flagstaff, Ariz.). Avocations: golf, gardening, landscaping. Home: 370 Oakcreek Dr Sedona AZ 86336 Office: Roadrunner Profl Plaza 105 Roadrunner Dr Sedona AZ 86336

SEYFERTH, HAROLD HOMER, real estate appraising company executive, educator; b. Stockton, Calif., Jan. 22, 1922; s. Lester L. and Bernice (Perkins) S.; m. Betty Jean Stanley, Apr. 12, 1943; children—Mary B., Laurence P. B.A., San Jose State U., 1948; M.B.A., Ph.D., Pacific Western U., 1981. Locomotive engr. Western Pacific R.R., 1939-50; asst. planner City of San Jose, 1950-54; mgr. City of Hollister (Calif.), 1959-63; property mgr. City of Salinas (Calif.), 1963-68; redevel. chief land officer City of Seaside (Calif.), 1968-69; pres. H. Seyferth Assocs., Monterey, Calif., 1969—; lectr. in field. Chmn., bd. dirs. Carmel Riviera Mut. Water Co.; bd. dirs. Boy's City Boy's Club, San Jose, Am. Cancer Soc., San Jose; trustee Enterprise Sch. Dist., Hollister, Calif. Served with USN, 1942-45. Coro fellow, 1950. Mem. Am. Assn. Cert. Appraisers (cert.), Am. Planning Assn., Calif. Assn. Real Estate Tchrs., Internat. Coll. Real Estate Cons. Profls., Internat. Inst. Valuers, Internat. Orgn. Real Estate Appraisers, Internat. Right of Way Assn., Nat. Assn. Cert. Real Property Appraisers, Nat. Assn. Rev. Appraisers, Real Estate Educators Assn., Urban Land Inst. Office: 734 Lighthouse Ave Pacific Grove CA 93950

SEYMORE, WILLIAM ANDREWARTHA, finance company executive; b. Greensburg, Pa., Jan. 16, 1943; s. Francis Gerald and Rosehannah (Andrewartha) S.; student Duffs Bus. Sch., 1960-62, U. Hawaii, 1967-68, U. Calif. at Los Angeles, 1969-71; m. Elizabeth A. Waters, Feb. 20, 1971; children—Mary Elizabeth, David Matthew, Joshua William. Staff accountant Davies & Mulvihill, Pitts., 1962-65; mgr. Haskins & Sells, Honolulu, 1968-69, Los Angeles, 1969-74; exec. v.p. Calif. Life Corp., Los Angeles, 1974-79, also dir.; controller, treas. Allianz Ins. Co., Los Angeles, 1979-84; pres.. chief operating officer, chief fin. officer TMIC Ins. Co., Inc., Los Angeles, 1984—. Served with USNR, 1966-67. C.P.A., Pa. Mem. Am. Inst. C.P.A.'s. Republican. Episcopalian. Club: Jonathan (Los Angeles). Home: 2353 E Burnside St Simi CA 93065 Office: TMIS Ins Co Inc 3255 Wilshire Blvd Los Angeles CA 90010

SEYMOUR, B(ARBARA) J(EAN), social work administrator; b. Chgo., Feb. 7, 1930; d. Louis C. and Amelia (Potasch) Jacobson; m. Douglas Seymour, Sept. 15, 1963 (div. 1984); children: Colin, Leif. PhB, U. Chgo., 1948, MA in Social Service Adminstrn. with honors, 1962; MA in English, Portland State U., 1982; PhD in English, U. Oreg., 1985. Caseworker Oreg. Pub. Welfare Commn., Portland, 1950-51, 54-60; asst. to adminstr. Oreg. Pub. Welfare Commn., Salem, 1963-71; info. dir. Oreg. Dept. Environ. Quality, Portland, 1971-74; lobbyist Tri-Met Transit Dist., Portland, 1974-76, Oreg. Environ. Council, Portland, 1977; dir. social services Pacific U. Optometry Clinics, Portland, 1978-86; pvt. practice psychotherapy Portland, 1976—; asst. prof. social work, English Pacific U., Forest Grove, Oreg., 1986—; lectr. social work Portland State U., 1972, 76; adj. prof. Pacific U., Forest Grove, Oreg., 1986; cons. in field. Bd. dirs. Columbia-Willamette Planned Parenthood, Portland, 1975-81, 1st v.p., 1978. Grantee Met. Arts Commn., 1978. Mem. Nat. Assn. Social Workers (cert., chmn. local chpt. 1978-79), Am. Pub. Welfare Assn. (bd. dirs. 1969-70), Mensa, U. Chgo. Alumni Assn. (local pres. 1983—, v.p. programs 1986—). Clubs: City (Portland). Avocations: community theater, poetry. Home: 1405 SW Park Ave Apt 34 Portland OR 97201

SEYMOUR, JEFFREY ALAN, governmental relations consultant; b. Los Angeles, Aug. 31, 1950; s. Daniel and Evelyn (Schwartz) S.; m. Valerie Joan Parker, Dec. 2, 1973; 1 child, Jessica Lynne. A.A. in Social Sci., Santa Monica Coll., 1971; B.A. in Polit. Sci., UCLA, 1973, M.P.A., 1977. Councilmanic aide Los Angeles City Council, 1972-74; county supervisor's sr. dep. Los Angeles Bd. Suprs., 1974-82; v.p. Bank of Los Angeles, 1982-83; pres. Morey and Seymour Assocs., Los Angeles, 1985—; prin. Jeffrey Seymour & Assocs., Los Angeles, 1983-84; pres. Morey/Seymour & Assocs., Los Angeles, 1985—; mem. comml. panel Am. Arbitration Assn., 1984—; Chmn. West Hollywood Parking Adv. Com., Los Angeles, 1983-84; chmn. social action com. Temple Emanuel of Beverly Hills., 1986; mem. Pan Pacific Park Citizens Adv. Com., Los Angeles, 1982—; bd. dirs. William O'Douglas Outdoor Classroom, Los Angeles, 1981—; exec. sec. Calif. Fedn. Young Democrats, 1971; mem. Calif. Dem. Cen. Com., 1979-82; pres. Beverlywood-Cheviot Hills Dem. Club, Los Angeles, 1978-81; v.p. Community Relations Com. Met. Region Jewish Fedn. Council of Los Angeles, 1985—; co-chmn. Westside Chancellor's Assocs. UCLA; mem. Los Angeles Olympic Citizens Adv. Com.; mem. liaison adv. commn. with city and county govt. for 1984 Olympics, 1984; mem. platform on world peace and internat. relations Calif. Dem. Party, 1983; pres. 43d Assembly Dist. Dem. Council, 1975-79; arbitrator Better Bus. Bur., 1984—. Recipient Plaques for services rendered Beverlywood Cheviot Hills Dem. Club, Los Angeles, 1981, Jewish Fedn. Council Greater Los Angeles, 1983; Certs. of Appreciation, Los Angeles Olympic Organizing Com., 1984, County of Los Angeles, 1984. Mem. Am. Soc. Pub. Adminstrn., Am. Acad. Polit. and Social Scis., Town Hall of Calif., So. Calif. Planning Congress, Bldg. Industry Assn. So. Calif., Greater Los Angeles C. of C., UCLA Alumni Assn. (govtl. affairs steering com. 1983—). Office: Morey/Seymour and Assocs 2007 Sawtelle Blvd Suite 6 Los Angeles CA 90025

SEYMOUR, RICHARD BURT, medical and social service administrator, writer, consultant; b. San Francisco, Aug. 1, 1937; s. Arnold Burt-Oakley and Florence Marguerita (Burt) S.; m. Michele Rhodehamel, Sept. 15, 1963 (div. 1970). children—Brian Geoffrey, Kyra Dalath; m. Sharon Harkless, Jan. 5, 1973. B.A., Calif. State U.-Sonoma, 1969; M.A., 1970. Freelance reporter, novelist, columnist, San Francisco, 1960—; co-founder, adminstr. Coll. of Mendocino, Calif., 1971-73; bus. mgr. Youth Projects, Inc., San Francisco, 1973; exec. adminstr. Youth Projects, Inc. Haight Ashbury Free Med. Clinic, San Francisco, 1973-77; dir. Haight Ashbury Free Clinic Tng. and Edn. Projects, San Francisco, 1977—; asst. prof. Calif. State U.-Sonoma, 1985—; instr. John F. Kennedy U., 1986—; lectr., tchr. to health profls. on drug abuse treatment. Author: The Chemical Muse, 1981; Haight Ashbury Clinic Reflections, 1982; The Client with a Drug Abuse Problem, 1982; Alternatives to Drugs, 1983; The Little Black Pill Book, 1983; Prescribing Psychoactive Drugs, 1983; Physician's Guide to Psychoactive Drugs, 1984, The Coke Book, 1985, MDMA, 1986, Drug Free: Alternatives to Alcohol and Other Drugs, 1987, The Haight Ashbury Free Medical Clinic: Still Free After All These Years, 1987; (novels) Summer Come Loudly, 1970; Compost, 1972. Contbr. numerous articles on drug abuse treatment and adminstrn. to profl. jours. Treas., bd. dirs. Youth Projects, Inc., 1973—; active Calif. Health Profls. for New Health Policy, 1976, 80; mem. Drug Abuse Adv. Bd. Marin County, 1979, chmn., 1981-83. Served with USAF, 1955-59. Recipient Disting. Service award Haight Ashbury Free Med. Clinic, 1982; grantee NIMH, Nat. Inst. Drug Abuse, Mem. Calif. Drug Abuse Services Assn. (chmn.), Calif. Primary Prevention Network, San Francisco Delinquency Prevention Com., Smith Pub. Group, Internat. Platform Assn., Calif. Alcoholism and Drug Counselors Edn. Project. Club: Commonwealth Calif. Democrat. Episcopalian. Home: 2313 5th Ave San Rafael CA 94901 Office: 409 Clayton St San Francisco CA 94117

SFERRAZZA, PETER JOSEPH, lawyer, mayor of Reno; b. N.Y.C., Apr. 30, 1945; s. Peter Joseph and Jane S. (Terry) S.; m. Vivian Ann Carry, 1968 (div.); children—Jessica, Joey. B.A., Mich. State U., J.D. Bar: Wis. Legal intern Wis. Judicare, Madison, 1971-72; staff atty. Wis. Judicare, Wausau, 1972-75, Dane County Legal Services, Wausau, 1972; sole practice Wausau, 1975-76; dir. Nev. Indian Legal Service, Carson City, 1976-79; ptnr. Howard, Cavallera & Sferrazza, Reno, 1979-81; sole practice Reno, 1981—; mayor City of Reno, 1983—; tribal judge Washoe Tribe, Carson City, 1979-80. Alderman city of Wausau, 1976; councilman City of Reno, 1981-83; del. Nat. Democratic conv., 1984; chmn. Nev. Dem. Conv., 1984. Roman Catholic. Home: Reno NV 89505 Office: City of Reno PO Box 1900 Reno NV 89505 •

SHABEN, LAWRENCE, Canadian provincial official; b. Hanna, Alta., Can., Mar. 20, 1935; s. Albert Mohammed and Lila (Kazeil) S.; m. Alma Amina Saddy, July 8, 1960; children—Linda, Carol, Larry, James, Joan. student U. Alta., 1954-55. Real estate agent Lawrence Agys., Alta., 1962-66; dept. mgr. Sears Can. Ltd., Alta., 1966-67; retail merchant, Alta., 1967—; mem. legis. assembly from Lesser Slave Lake dist. Govt. of Alta., Edmonton, 1975—, minister of utilities, 1979-82, minister of housing, 1982—; pres. Lawrence Devels. Ltd., High Prairie, Alta., 1967—, Shaben Stores Ltd., High Prairie, 1967—; minister Econ. Devel. and Trade, Alta., 1986—. Pres. High Prairie Housing Assn., 1967—; mem. High Prairie Town Council, 1969-74, High Prairie Recreation Bd., 1969-74; pres. Lesser Slave Lake Progressive Conservative Assn., 1969-74, High Prairie Minor Hockey Assn., 1973-74; v.p., bd. dirs. Peace Tourist Assn., 1970-72. Moslem. Lodges: Kiwanis (Northgate, Alta.) (bd. dirs. 1965-66), Lions, Elks, Optimists (sec. local club 1967-71). Office: Dept Housing, 403 Legislature Bldg, Edmonton, AB Canada T5K 2B7

SHABOT, MYRON MICHAEL, surgeon, critical care educator; b. Houston, Aug. 5, 1945; s. Sam and Mona Doris (Stalarow) S.; m. Charlotte Shabot, July 6, 1966; 1 child, Samuel Laib. Student, Tulane U., 1963-64; BA, U. Tex., Austin, 1966; MD, U. Tex., Dallas, 1970. Lectr. surgery UCLA, 1977-78, asst. prof. surgery, 1978-82, clin. assoc. prof. surgery and anesthesiology, 1983—; dir. surg. intensive care unit Los Angeles County Harbor Med. Ctr.-UCLA Sch. Medicine, 1980-82; assoc. dir. surgery, dir. surg. intensive care units Cedars-Sinai Med. Ctr., Los Angeles, 1982—. Mem. editorial bd. Internat. Jour.Clin. Monitoring and Computing; contbr. articles to profl. jours. Served to lt. comdr. USPHS, 1971-73. Fellow ACS; mem. Western Surg. Assn., Pacific Coast Surg. Assn., Soc. Critical Care Medicine, Soc. Clin. Data Mgmt. Systems (pres. 1985-86), Phi Eta Sigma. Jewish. Office: Cedars-Sinai Med Ctr 8700 Beverly Blvd Los Angeles CA 90048

SHACK, WILLIAM ALFRED, anthropology educator, researcher, consultant; b. Chgo., Apr. 19, 1923; s. William and Emma (McAvoy) S.; m. Dorothy Nash, Sept. 1, 1960; 1 child, Hailu A. B.A.E., Sch. of the Art Inst., Chgo., 1955; M.A., U. Chgo., 1957; Ph.D., London Sch. Econs., 1961. Asst. prof. sociology and anthropology Northeastern Ill. State Coll., Chgo., 1961-62; asst. prof. sociology Haile Selassie I Univ., Addis Ababa, Ethiopia, 1962-65; assoc. prof. anthropology U. Ill., Chgo., 1966-70; prof. anthropology U. Calif.-Berkeley, 1970—, dean, grad. div., 1979-85. Author: The Gurage, 1966, The Central Ethiopians, 1974; co-author: Gods and Heroes, 1974; co-editor: Strangers in African Societies, 1979. Trustee, bd. dirs. World Affairs Council of No. Calif., San Francisco. Served with USCG, 1943-46; PTO. Fellow AAAS, Am. Anthrop. Assn., Royal Anthrop. Inst. (pres. N.Am. com. 1983-86), Internat. African Inst. (exec. council 1984—, vice chmn. 1985—). Club: The Athenaeum (London). Avocation: vintage motor racing. Home: 2597 Hilgard Berkeley CA 94709 Office: U Calif-Berkeley Dept Anthropology 232 Kroeber Hall Berkeley CA 94720

SHACKELFORD, GORDON LEE, JR., educator; b. South Bend, Ind., Apr. 7, 1948; s. Gordon Lee and Leatha Mae (Andrews) S.; BS in Physics, San Diego State U., 1970, MS in Radiol. Physics, 1974; m. Janis Elizabeth Mead, Apr. 6, 1974. Electronic designer for physics dept. San Diego State U., 1969-70; electronic engr. Naval Electronics Lab., Point Loma, Calif., 1970; electronic engr. product design Info. Machine Corps., Santee, Calif., 1970-71; lectr. physics San Diego State U., 1971—, asst. dir. alumni and devel. Coll. of Scis., 1980-81, assoc. dean scis., external relations, 1981— , project mgr. Biomass Power Plant, 1984—; cons. power supply design, 1970—. Mem. quality life bd. City of San Diego. Mem. Health Physics Soc. Author lab. manuals. Home: 9716 Red Pony Ln El Cajon CA 92021 Office: San Diego State U Physics Dept San Diego CA 92182

SHACKELFORD, LYNE THROCKMORTON (BUD), artist, painter, educator; b. Washington, Nov. 15, 1918; s. Lyne Throckmorton and Frances (Ackerly) S.; m. Dorothy Meacham, Dec. 28, 1946; children—Charles, Leigh, Jean, Todd. Student U. Ala., 1937-38, Chouinard Sch. Art. 1938-39, Art Students' League, N.Y.C., 1940-41. Animator Walt Disney Studios, Burbank, Calif., 1939-40; art dir. Phillips Ramsey Advt. Co., San Diego, 1953-58; pres. Art Assocs., Inc., San Diego, 1958-63; condr. painting workshops throughout U.S., 1963-79; lectr., demonstrator watercolor painting throughout U.S., 1963-79. Author: As I See It, 1942; Fun With Watercolor, 1972; Experimental Watercolor Techniques, 1980. Exhibited in numerous group shows including Am. Watercolor Soc., N.Y.C., Nat. Watercolor Soc., Palm Springs, Calif., Watercolor U.S.A., Springfield, Mo., NAD, N.Y.C., Butler Art Inst., Youngstown, Ohio, Audubon Artists Ann., N.Y.C., West Coast Watercolor Soc. Ann., Royal Watercolor Soc. Invitational, London, Watercolor West Ann., Riverside, Calif., Maxwell Galleries, San Francisco, Cassidy Gallery, Albuquerque, Bonfoey Gallery, Tucson, Schramm Gallery, Ft. Lauderdale, Fla., Ctr. Street Gallery, Orlando, Fla., Challis Galleries, Laguna Beach, Calif., Laguna Beach Mus. Art, Calif., San Diego Mus. Art. Served with Signal Corps, U.S. Army, 1941-45. Recipient over 200 awards in painting. Mem. Am. Watercolor Soc., Nat. Watercolor Soc., Nat. Soc. Art Dirs., Los Angeles Soc. Illustrators, West Coast Watercolor Soc., San Diego Watercolor Soc. (past pres.), San Diego Art Inst. (past. dir.), San Diego Art Guild (past dir.). Republican. Methodist. Lodge: Kiwanis. Home and office: 11532 Rolling Hills Dr El Cajon CA 92020

SHACKLETT, ROBERT LEE, retired physics educator, lecturer, consultant; b. Van Nuys, Calif., Apr. 5, 1926; s. Lee Richard and Rowena (Rowe) S.; m. Jeanne Allison, Apr. 2, 1947 (div. Jan. 1979); children: Richard and David (twins); m. Edie Fischer, May 5, 1979. BA in Physics, Calif. State U., 1949; PhD in Physics, Calif. Inst. Tech., 1956. Prof. Calif. State U., Fresno, 1955-79, asst. acad. v.p., 1967-68, asst. dean grad. studies, 1968-75, acting dean grad. studies, 1975-76, prof. emeritus, 1979—; exec. dir. Found. for Mind-Being Research, Los Altos, Calif., 1982—; curriculum cons. Coll. Ganado, Ariz., 1980. Contbr. sci. papers to profl. publs.; co-inventor digital communication systems. Bd. dirs. U. Religious Ctr., Fresno, 1970-79; pres. Planned Parenthood Cen. Calif., Fresno, 1974, 76-78. Served with USN, 1944-46. Sci. faculty fellow NSF, 1961-62. Fellow Am. Sci. Affiliation; mem. Am. Assn. Physics Tchrs., Am. Phys. Soc., Sigma Xi, Phi Kappa Phi. Democrat.

SHACTER, DAVID MERVYN, lawyer; b. Toronto, Ont., Can., Jan. 17, 1941; s. Nathan and Tillie Anne (Schwartz) S. BA, U. Toronto, 1963; JD, Southwestern U., 1967. Bar: Calif. 1968, U.S. Supreme Ct. 1982. Law clk., staff atty. Legal Aid Found., Long Beach, Calif., 1967-70; asst. city atty. City of Beverly Hills, Calif., 1970; ptnr. Shacter & Berg, Beverly Hills, 1971-83, Capalbo, Lowenthal & Shacter Profl. Law Corp., 1984—; del. State Bar Conf. Dels., 1976-86; lectr. Calif. Continuing Edn. of Bar, 1977, 82, 83, 86; judge pro tem Los Angeles and Beverly Hills mcpl. cts., also Los Angeles Superior Ct.; disciplinary examiner Calif. State Bar, 1986. Bd. dirs. and pres. Los Angeles Soc. Prevention Cruelty to Animals. Mem. Beverly Hills Bar Assn. (bd. govs. 1985—, editor-in-chief jour., bd. govs. award 1986), Los Angeles County Bar Assn., Am. Arbitration Assn. (nat. panel arbitrators), City of Hope Med. Ctr. Aux., Wilshire C. of C. (bd. dirs., gen. counsel). Office: 3580 Wilshire Blvd Suite 1510 Los Angeles CA 90010

SHADIOW, LINDA KAYE, English educator, university administrator; b. Hibbing, Minn., Aug. 7, 1947; d. George LeRoy and Kathryn (Wold) Christofferson; m. Robert Frank Shadiow, Mar. 22, 1969. BS, Bemidji State U., 1969; EdM, Mont. State U., 1976; PhD, Ariz. State U., 1982. Cert. secondary tchr., Mont., Ariz. Tchr. English Walker (Minn.) High Sch., 1969-70, Bozeman (Mont.) Sr. High Sch., 1970-75; state English supr., office pub. instrn. State of Mont., Helena, 1976-78; mem. English faculty Mont. State U., Bozeman, 1978-85; assoc. exec. dir. Ctr. for Excellence in Edn. No. Ariz. U., Flagstaff, 1985—; instr. Southwest Inst. for Research on Women, U. Ariz., Tucson, 1980-82. Contbr. articles to profl. jours. and mags. Mem. Nat. Council Tchrs. English (commn.), Internat. Reading Assn., Assn. Supervision and Curriculum Devel., Faculty Women's Assn. No. Ariz. U. (pres. 1986), Ariz. English Tchrs. Assn. (bd. dirs. 1986—, sec. 1987), AAUW, Phi Delta Kappa (v.p. 1987). Avocations: distance running, reading, hiking. Home: 2041 Timberline Flagstaff AZ 86004 Office: No Ariz U Ctr for Excellence in Edn Box 5774 Flagstaff AZ 86011

SHAFAAT, SYED TARIQ, mechanical engineer; b. Karachi, Pakistan, Oct. 28, 1953; came to U.S., 1975; s. Syed Shafaat Ali and Azra (Sufi) Shafaat; m. Melanie Alison Malchman, July 10, 1976; 1 dau., Hannah Syeda. Student, Middle East Tech. U., Ankara, Turkey, 1973-75; BSME, Mich. Tech. U., 1977; postgrad., U. Ariz., 1979-80, 86—. Jr. engr. CPU products IBM Corp., Endicott, N.Y., 1977-79; assoc. engr. IBM Corp., Tucson, 1979-81, sr. assoc. engr. Servowriter Test Engring., 1981-83, staff engr., scientist Tape Drive Devel. Engring., 1983-86, staff engr., scientist Optics/Actuator Technology, 1987—. Advisor Explorers Tucson council Boy Scouts Am., 1982; coach Pantano Soccer League, Tucson, 1980; mem. Tucson YMCA, 1986—. Recipient Cert. Merit Bd. Edn., Sargodha, Pakistan, 1972, Cert. Recognition IBM Corp., Tucson, 1985; Merit scholar Regional Cooperation for Devel., Ankara, Turkey, 1973, 74, 75, Merit scholar Mich. Tech. U., 1976-77. Mem. Robotics Internat., Soc. Mfg. Engrs. (activity coordinator 1982-83). Republican. Moslem. Club: IBM Ski (Tucson). Avocations: personal computing, skiing, racquetball, soccer, woodworking. Home: 10016 E Leila Dr Tucson AZ 85730 Office: IBM Corp 78G/021-2 9000 S Rita Rd Tucson AZ 85744

SHAFER, JAMES ALBERT, health care administrator; b. Chgo., Aug. 26, 1924; s. James Earl and Kathleen (Sutterland) S.; m. Irene Jeanne Yurcega, June 20, 1948; children: Kathleen Mary Shafer-Petras, Patricia Ann. Technician Zenith Radio Corp., Chgo., 1946-47; owner, operator Eastgate Electronics, Chgo., 1947-61; applications engr. Perfection Mica Co., Bensenville, Ill., 1961-71; pres. Electronics Unltd., Northbrook, Ill., 1972-73, Ariz. Geriatric Enterprises Inc., Safford, 1974—; bd. dirs. Mt. Graham Community Hosp., Safford. Mem. Ariz. Nursing Home Assn. (pres. 1985-86), Am. Coll. Health Care Aminstrs. (cert. 1985). Republican. Roman Catholic. Avocations: computers, photography. Home: Skyline Ranch Pima AZ 85543-0630 Office: Ariz Geriatric Enterprises Inc 1706 20th Ave Safford AZ 85546

SHAFER, RONALD JOE, hospital administrator; b. Dallas, Apr. 21, 1951; s. Jesse Charles and Betty Jo (Etier) S.; m. Sharon Diane, July 9, 1977; children: Shannon Dee, Stephen Lee. AS in Biology, El Central Coll., 1973; BS in Biology, U. Tex., 1975. Lab. technologist Mt. San Rafael Hosp., Trinidad, Colo., 1976-77, lab. dir., 1977-79, asst. adminstr., 1979-86, adminstr., 1986—. Vice pres. Trinidad Legis. Forum, 1984-86. Mem. Am. Soc. Med. Technicians, Am. Soc. Clin. Pathologists, Colo. Soc. Med. Technicians, Colo. Hosp. Assn. (data council mem. 1985—), Trinidad C. of C. (bd. dirs.). Democrat. Baptist. Lodge: Lions (pres. Trinidad chpt. 1986-87). Avocations: hiking, fishing, photography. Home: Rte 1 Box 365 Trinidad CO 81082 Office: Mt San Rafael Hosp 410 Benedicta Ave Trinidad CO 81082

SHAFFER, AUDREY JEANNE, medical records administrator, educator; b. Hutchinson, Minn., Nov. 24, 1929; d. Floyd R. and Edna C. (Seppman) Kleiman; m. Frank L. Shaffer, July 15, 1948; 1 child, Cynthia Louise Shaffer Wilkinson. B.S., Loma Linda U., 1973; M.A., Central Mich. U., 1982. Registered records adminstr. Med. records clk. San Bernardino County Hosp., Calif., 1948-50; radiology receptionist White Meml. Med. Ctr., Los Angeles, 1950-52; med. records clk. Portland Adventist Hosp., Oreg., 1952-53; med. record mgr. Tempe Community Hosp., Ariz., 1953-54; clin. faculty Loma Linda U., Calif., 1975—; dir. med. info. services Corona Community Hosp., Calif., 1973—; med. records cons. Calif., Utah and Philippines Pilot, med. asst. Liga Internat., Mex., 1964-68; chmn. Corona Blood Bank, 1957-68; chmn. vols. Corona Community Hosp. Aux., 1965-68; archaeology supr. Caesarea Expdn., Am. Schs. Oriental Research, Israel, summers 1974—. Recipient Vol. Service award Corona Community Hosp., 1968; Congeniality award Caesarea Archeol. Expdn., 1975. Mem. Loma Linda U. Med. Record Alumni (pres. 1979-81), Am. Med. Record Assn., Calif. Med. Record Assn. (quality assurance com. 1980-81), Nat. Assn. Quality Assurance Profls., Archeol. Inst. Am. Clubs: Women's Improvement (program chmn. 1960-61), Corona Flying (sec. 1960-68) (Corona). Home: 880 Encanto Dr Corona CA 91719 Office: Corona Community Hosp 800 S Main St Corona CA 91720

SHAFFER, CAROLYN (CARI) LEE, temporary staffing service executive; b. Denver, June 3, 1944; d. Richard Michael, Sr. and Joyce Adele (Carnahan) Knoll; m. Charles Larry Shaffer, Dec. 11, 1965; 1 child, Kelly Michael. Student, So. Oreg. Coll., 1962-64, U. Nev., 1964-78. Free lance sec. Colorado Springs, Colo., 1977-80; mgr. Accel Temporaries Colorado Springs, 1980-82, MG Temps div. Marshall Group, Colorado Springs, 1982-84; owner, mgr. Add Staff, Inc., Colorado Springs, 1984—; bd. dirs. Tech. Research Assocs., Colorado Springs, 1971-73. Spl. events chmn. London county unit Am. Cancer Soc., Sterling, Va., 1975-77; speaker for Goodwill, Colorado Springs, 1980—, Wagon Wheel council Girl Scouts U.S., Colorado Springs, 1980—, Jr. Achievement, Colorado Springs, 1980—. Mem. Internat. Assn. Personnel Women (v.p. 1982-83), Colorado Springs Personnel Women (pres. 1983—), Adminstrv. Mgmt. Soc. (salary survey chmn. 1980—), Am. Soc. For Tng. and Devel., Amigos de Ser, Colorado Springs C. of C. (life mem., chmn. ambassador club, chamber vice chmn. exec. com. 1985-86, Ambassador of Yr. award 1984, exec. com. 1986). Republican. Roman Catholic. Club: Little People of Am. (Colorado Springs). Office: Add Staff Inc 6155 Lehman Dr Suite 205 Colorado Springs CO 80907

SHAFFER, JULIET POPPER, statistics educator; b. N.Y.C., May 23, 1932; d. Abraham Louis and Harriet Estelle (Marcus) Popper; m. Harry George Shaffer, Aug. 11, 1960 (div. May 1975); children: Ronald Eric, Leonard Joseph, Tanya Elaine; m. Erich Leo Lehmann, Feb. 24, 1977. BA, Swarthmore Coll., 1953; PhD, Stanford U., 1957. Postdoctoral fellow Ind. U., Bloomington, 1957-58; SSRC research tng. fellow U. Calif., Berkeley, 1973-74, lectr. dept. stats., 1977-81, sr. lectr. dept. stats., 1981—; from. asst. prof. to prof. dept. psychology U. Kans., Lawrence, 1958-77. Stats. editor: Computer Studies in the Humanities and Verbal Behavior, 1970-74, (assoc.) Psychometrika, 1983-85; assoc. editor Jour. Ednl. Stats. 1980-85, editor, 86—; contbr. articles to profl. jours. Mem. Psychometric Soc. (bd. trustees 1982-84), Am. Stats. Assn. (bd. dirs. 1984-86). Office: U Calif Dept Stats Berkeley CA 94720

SHAFFER, LANCE MERITT, geologist; b. Henderson, Nev., Apr. 22, 1947; s. Clinton and Sylvia (Katz) S.; m. Barbara Jean Smith, Dec. 30, 1971; children—Tamara Lynn, Cathleen Kay. B.S. in Geology, Tex. A&M U., 1970. Registered profl. geologist. Logger/command engr. Imco Services, Houston, 1970-74; cons. geologist Tooke Engring., Casper, Wyo., 1974-76; cons. geologist, Boulder, Wyo., 1976—. Past bd. dirs. Fayette Irrigation Ditch Assn., Boulder, 1984. Mem. Am. Inst. Profl. Geologists, Am. Assn. Petroleum Geologists, Wyo. Geol. Assn., Nat. Geog. Soc. Republican. Club: Boulder Community. Address: PO Box 144 Boulder WY 82923

SHAFFER, MARY LOUISE, art educator; b. Blufton, Ind., Nov. 23, 1927; d. Gail H. and Mary J. (Graves) S. AB, Northwest Nazerene Coll., 1950; MA, Ball State Tchrs. Coll., 1955; EdD, MS, Ind. U., 1964. Art and music tchr. Kuna (Ind.) High Sch., 1950-55; asst. prof. art Northwest Nazerene Coll., Nampa, Idaho, 1955-56, head art dept., 1971—; asst. prof. art Pasadena (Calif.) Coll., 1956-61; prof. art Olivet Nazerene Coll., Kankakee, Ill., 1964-71; dir. music Kankakee Congl. Ch., 1964-71, Nampa Christian Ch., 1971-76, Nampa Meth. Ch., 1976-81; speaker various civic clubs and confs., 1965-81. E.I. Lilly grantee, 1961-62; women's singles tennis champion Boise (Idaho) Racquet and Swim Club, 1973; Idaho Sr. Tennis champion Sun Valley, 1984. Mem. Nat. Art Edn. Assn., Idaho Arts Edn. Assn. Avocations: travel, music, renovating buildings, watercolor painting, tennis. Home: 4755 E Victory Rd Meridian ID 83642 Office: Northwest Nazerene Coll Holley at Dewey Nampa ID 83651

SHAFFER, ROBERT CLARENCE, aeros. materials co. exec.; b. Kalamazoo, Mich., Oct. 4, 1918; s. Clarence Daniel and Grace Virginia (Garlick) S.; B.A. in Chemistry, Western State Coll., 1939; postgrad. Wayne U., 1943-44; m. Delores Rita Burns, Nov. 22, 1943; children—Rita Ann (Mrs. Ronald Joseph Bucholtz), Mary Kay (Mrs. Donald Earl Hackett, Jr.). Chemist, Ford Motor Research, Dearborn, Mich., 1940-42; head dept. chem. research Bendix Aviation Central Research, Detroit, 1942-49; supr. high polymer research lab. Ford Motor Sci. Center, Dearborn, 1949-53; research engr. North Am. Aviation, Los Angeles, 1953-56; dir. research Adhesive Engring., San Carlos, Calif., 1956-60; dir. research Westech Plastics, Menlo Park, Calif., 1960-65; mgr. materials research and devel. HITCO Materials Sci. Ctr., Gardena, Calif., 1965-72, staff asst. to v.p. research and engring. Hitco Def. products div., 1972-82, mgr. materials research and new material pilot plant ops. Hitco Fabricated Composites Div., 1982—. Cons. developed, planned and supervised research programs for def. contractors in fields of missile re-entry materials, 1960-65. Mem. Soc. Materials and Process Engrs. (treas. chpt. 1961-62). Patentee in field. Home: 8040 W 83d St Playa Del Rey CA 90291 Office: HITCO 1600 W 135th St Gardena CA 90249

SHAH, GIRISH POPATLAL, data processing services company executive; b. Junagadh, India, Apr. 11, 1942; came to U.S., 1963; s. Popatlal Gulabchand and Lalitaben Popatlas (Kamdar) S.; m. Devmani Manilal Jhaveri, June 18, 1968; children: Nivisha, Munjal, Bhavin. B in Tech., Indian Inst. Tech., Bombay, 1963; MS, U. Calif., Berkeley, 1965. Project analyst IBM Corp., Palo Alto, Calif., 1965-67; v.p. Optimun Systems, Inc., Palo Alto, 1967-72; pres. Banking Systems Internat. Corp., Jakarta, Indonesia and Campbell, Calif., 1972—; dir. software services Tymshare Transactions Services, San Francisco, 1980-83; sr. scientist McDonnell Douglas Corp., Fremont, Calif., 1984-86; dir. corp. devel. Sysorex Internat., Inc., Cupertino, Calif., 1986—. Mem. adv. bd. Goodwill Industries, San Francisco; bd. dirs. Gujarate Cultural Assn., 1982; pres. Jain Ctr. of No. Calif., 1983-84. J.N. Tata Trust nat. scholar, 1963. Mem. IEEE, Ops. Research Soc. Am., Assn. Indians in Am. (v.p. 1980). Democrat. Home: 4048 Twyla Ln Campbell CA 95008 Office: Sysorex Internat Inc 10590 N Tantau Ave Cupertino CA 95014

SHAH, JAMI J., mechanical engineering educator, researcher; b. Karachi, Pakistan, July 11, 1950; came to U.S., 1975; s. Maqsood A. and Nasim K. Shah. BSME, NED Engring. Coll., Karachi, 1973; MSMetE, U. Pitts., 1976; PhDME, Ohio State U., 1984. Engr. Pakistan Steel, Karachi, 1973-75; prodn. engr. Pakistan Oxygen, Karachi, 1976-80; teaching assoc. Ohio State U., Columbus, 1981-84; asst. prof. Ariz. State U., Tempe, 1984—; cons. Gen. Electric, Schnectady, N.Y., 1986. Mem. Computer Soc. of IEEE, ASME, Sigma Xi. Avocations: hiking, climbing, desert plants. Home: 2635 N Hayden Rd #209 Scottsdale AZ 85257 Office: Ariz State U Dept Mech Engring Tempe AZ 85287

SHAH, SHANTILAL NATHUBHAI, biochemist, researcher; b. Nandurbar, India, Aug. 5, 1930; came to U.S., 1956; s. Nathubhai Raojidas and Ratanben Shah; m. Snehlata P. Mahajan, July 13, 1956; children: Deepak, Ajit, Anita. BS, Bombay U., 1951; BS in Tech., Nagpur (India) U., 1954, MS in Tech., 1956; PhD, U. Ill., 1960. Research specialist Sonoma devel. ctr. U. Calif. at San Francisco, Eldridge, 1967-73, asst. research biochemist, 1973-78, assoc. research biochemist, 1978-82, research biochemist, 1982—. Contbr. articles to research jours. Mem. Am. Soc. Neurochemistry, Am. Soc. Biol. Chemistry, Am. Inst. Nutrition, Internat. Soc. Neurochemistry. Hindu. Lodge: Lions (pres. Santa Rosa, Calif. club 1970-71). Home:

1873 Los Olivos Santa Rosa CA 95404 Office: U Calif Sonoma Devel Ctr Eldridge CA 95431

SHAHSHAHANI, AHMAD MADANI, economics educator; b. Tehran, Iran, Sept. 14, 1947; came to U.S., 1971; s. Housein Shahahshani and Zahra (Heshmat) Zommorodian. BS, U. Tehran, 1969; MA, U. Colo., 1973, PhD, 1976. Asst. prof. econs. Tehran U., 1976-80; research fellow Hoover Instn., Stanford, Calif., 1980-82; fin. analyst Unity in Diversity Council, Los Angeles, 1983-84; asst. prof. Calif. State U., Los Angeles, 1984—, Northridge, 1985—; mem. corp. fin. team Baraban Securities, Culver City, Calif., 1983—; fellow Internat. Research Ctr. Energy and Econ. Devel., Boulder, 1976—. Author: Economics for Students, 1972, 2d edit., 1977, An Introduction to the Theory of Employment, 1974, 2d edit., 1977, An Econometric Model of Iran, And Its Application, 1978; also articles to profl. jours. Fellow Tehran U., 1974-76, scholar U. Colo., Boulder, 1973-74. Mem. Omicron Delta Epsilon. Republican. Moslem. Avocations: tennis, jogging, travelling. Home: 1042 6th St #15 Santa Monica CA 90403 Office: Calif State U Dept Econs Northridge CA 91330

SHAIKH, SALEEM, electronics company executive; b. Karachi, Pakistan, Sept. 9, 1950; came to U.S., 1971; s. Rehmat Ali Shaikh and Iqbal Bano. BS, U. Karachi, 1970, U. So. Calif., 1976; MS, U. So. Calif., 1979. Asst. mgr. L.A.A.C., Los Angeles, 1975-76; mgr. Sharp, Irvine, Calif., 1976-84; pres., founder TFD Inc., Anaheim, Calif., 1984—, also chmn. bd. dirs.; analyst G.T.E., 1985; receiver, Stanford Resurces, Palo Alto, Calif., 1985; pres., chmn. bd. dirs. Kay Tex Industries, Los Angeles. Contbr. articles to profl. jours. Fellow Soc. Indsl. Designers; mem. IEEE, Am. Vacumm Soc., Am. Inst. Physics, Electrochem. Soc. Republican. Avocations: skiing, traveling, sailing, tennis, tech. study. Office: Thin Film Device Inc 2021 Via Burton St Unit F Anaheim CA 92806

SHAIN, JOSEPH R., civil engineer; b. Brookline, Mass., June 21, 1945; s. George and Florence Dorothy (Reinholtz) S. BCE, Rensselaer Poly. Inst., 1967. Registered profl. engineer, N.Mex., Alaska, Guam. Engr. Chas. T. Main Inc., Boston, 1969-71; airport engr. Alaska Aviation Div., Anchorage, 1971-74, 76-77; engr. Ter. of Guam, Tumon, 1974-76, N.Mex. Transp. Dept., Santa Fe, 1977-80; engring. v.p. PAJO Tech. Services, Mesilla, N.Mex., 1980—; engring. instr. U. N.Mex., Los Alamos, 1980-83; constrn. claims arbitrator HOW, Dallas, 1980—; tech. advisor Lincoln County, Carrizozo, N.Mex, 1983—, Sierra County, Truth or Consequences, N.Mex., 1985—. Mem. orgn. com. Whole Enchilida Fiesta, Las Cruces, N.Mex., 1984; airport commr. Santa Teresa Airport Commn., Las Cruces, 1985; mem. planning com. Mt. View Water Assn., Las Cruces, 1985; pub. works advisor Town of Mesilla, N.Mex., 1986. Recipient Letter of Commendation, Govt. Guam, 1975, Letter of Commendation N.Mex. Aviation Div., 1983, Letter of Commendation Rural Water Users Assn., 1985. Democrat. Jewish. Avocations: stamp and coin collecting, physical fitness, horseshoe pitching, golf, skiing. Home and Office: PAJO Tech Services Inc PO Box 312 Mesilla NM 88046

SHAKARIAN, STEPHEN DEMOS, association executive; b. Downey, Calif., July 12, 1947; s. Demos Dee and Rose S.; m. Debra G. Shakarian, Mar. 14, 1975; children—Stephanie Lynn, Stephen Demos. BSM, Pepperdine U., 1983; MBA, UCLA, 1985. Vice pres., Omega Advt., Los Angeles, 1973-74, exec. v.p., mgr., 1974-75, pres., 1975-82; dir. ministries Full Gospel Bus. Men's Fellowship Internat., Irvine, Calif., 1978-80, dir. ministries and ops., 1980, chief operating officer, Costa Mesa, Calif., 1980—, also dir. Mem. Nat. Religious Broadcasters. Republican. Office: Full Gospel Bus Mens Fellowship 3150 Bear St Costa Mesa CA 92626

SHAKELY, JOHN (JACK) BOWER, foundation executive; b. Hays, Kans., Jan. 9, 1940; s. John B. and Martha Jean (Gaston) S.; 1 son, Benton. B.A., U. Okla., 1962. Vol. Peace Corps, Costa Rica, 1963-64; editor publs. Dept. Def., 1967-68; dir. devel. U. Okla., 1968-70, Resthaven Mental Health Ctr., Los Angeles, 1970-74; pres. Jack Shakely Assocs., Los Angeles, 1974-75; sr. adv. Grantsmanship Ctr., Los Angeles, 1975-79, Council on Founds., Washington, 1979; pres. Calif. Community Found., Los Angeles, 1980—; lectr. in field. Bd. dirs. Coro Found., Los Angeles, 1982-85; bd. dirs. So. Calif. Assn. Philanthropy, 1980—, Calif. Hist. Soc., 1985—, Watts Towers Trust, 1985—, Treepeople, 1983-85. Served to 1st lt. U.S. Army, 1965-68. Decorated Army Commendation medal. Democrat. Office: Calif Community Found 3580 Wilshire Blvd Suite 1660 Los Angeles CA 90010

SHALETT, JOHN STEVEN, family therapist, educator; b. Washington, Jan. 8, 1946; s. Sidney Melvin and Anita (Effron) S.;m. EllenRae Webber, May 28, 1968; children: Scott, Jeremy. BS, U. Chattanooga, 1967; MSW, La. State U., Baton Rouge, 1969. Instr. La. State U. Sch. Medicine, New Orleans, 1975-77; dir. profl. affairs Am. Assn. Marriage and Family Therapy, Upland, Calif., 1977-78, exec. dir. commn. accreditation for Marriage and family therapy edn., 1978-83; dir. Claremont (Calif.) Family Inst., 1984—; adj. prof. behavioral scis. U. LaVerne, Calif. Mem. changing family task force Union of Am. Hebrew Congregations, Los Angeles, 1983-85; pres. Temple Beth Israel, Pomona, Calif., 1985—, bd. dirs. 1978—. Served to capt. U.S. Army, 1969-75. Fellow Am. Assn. Marriage and Family Therapy (local bd. dirs. 1982-85); mem. Am. Family Therapy Assn. (charter), Nat. Assn. Social Workers. Home: 6829 Ramona Ave Alta Loma CA 91701 Office: Claremont Family Inst 341 W 1st St Claremont CA 91711

SHALKOP, ROBERT LEROY, museum director; b. Milford, Conn., July 30, 1922; s. Bertram Leroy and Dorothy Jane (Boardman) S.; m. Antoinette Joan Benkowsky, Dec. 7, 1963; 1 son, Andrew Goforth. Student, Maryville (Tenn.) Coll., 1940-42; M.A., U. Chgo., 1949; postgrad., Sorbonne, 1951-52. Dir. Rahr Civic Center, Manitowoc, Wis., 1953-56, Everhart Mus., Scranton, Pa., 1956-62, Brooks Meml. Art Gallery, Memphis, 1962-64; assoc. dir. Colorado Springs (Colo.) Fine Arts Center, also curator Taylor Mus., 1964-71; dir. Anchorage Mus. History and Art, 1972—; archaeologist Smithsonian Instn., 1948, 50, Am. Found. Study Man, 1951, U. Wash., 1953, State U. Idaho, 1960. Author: Wooden Saints, the Santos of New Mexico, 1967, A Comparative View of Spanish Colonial Sculpture, 1968, Arroyo Hondo, the Folk Art of a New Mexican Village, 1969, A Comparative View of Spanish Colonial Painting, 1970, A Show of Color: 100 Years of Painting in the Pike's Peak Region, 1971, Russian Orthodox Art in Alaska, 1973, Sydney Laurence, an Alaskan Impressionist, 1975, Eustace Ziegler, 1977, Contemporary Native Art of Alaska, 1979, Henry Wood Elliott, 1982; Editor: An Introduction to the Native Art of Alaska, 1972; assoc. editor: Exploration in Alaska, 1980. Served with USAAF, 1942-45. Mem. Am. Assn. Museums, Assn. Art Mus. Dirs., Art Museum Assn. Am. (regional rep.), Internat. Council Museums. Home: 4248 Charing Cross Circle Anchorage AK 99504 Office: 121 W 7th Ave Anchorage AK 99501

SHAMAS, JIM E., trading and transportation executive. Office: Texaco Trading & Transp Co 1670 Broadway Denver CO 80202 *

SHAMBAUGH, STEPHEN WARD, lawyer; b. South Bend, Ind., Aug. 4, 1920; s. Marion Clyde and Anna Violet (Stephens) S.; m. Marilyn Louise Pyle; children—Susan Wynne Shambaugh Hinkle, Kathleen Louise Shambaugh Thompson. Student San Jose State Tchrs. Coll., 1938-40, U. Ark., 1951; LL.B., U. Tulsa, 1954. Bar: Okla. 1954, Colo. 1964. Mem. staff Reading & Bates, Inc., Tulsa, 1951-54; v.p., gen. mgr., legal counsel Reading & Bates Drilling Co. Ltd., Calgary, Alta., Can., 1954-61; sr. ptnr. Bowman, Shambaugh, Geissinger & Wright, Denver, 1964-81; sole practice, Denver, 1981—; dir., fin. counsel various corps. Served to col. USAF ret. Mem. ABA, Fed. Bar Assn., Colo. Bar Assn., Okla. Bar Assn., Denver Bar Assn., P-51 Mustang Pilots Assn., Phi Alpha Delta. Clubs: Spokane; Petroleum of Bakersfield (Calif.); Masons, Shriners, Elks.

SHAMS, KAMRUDDIN, infosystems executive; b. Chittagong, Bangladesh, July 4, 1953; came to U.S., 1972; s. Shamsuddin and Sherbano Shams; m. Mahin Hashemian, Oct. 29, 1983. BS in Quantitative Methods and Info. Systems, St. Cloud State U., 1978; M Healthcare Adminstrn., Webster U., 1983. Analyst Fed. Res. Bank, Mpls., 1973-77; cons. fin. systems Traveletter Corp., Mpls., 1978-79; cons. Mpls., 1979-81; dir. info. systems Alexian Bros., Schaumburg, Ill., 1981-83; v.p. info. systems Meml. Hosps. Assn., Modesto, Calif., 1984—; pres. The Shams Group, Modesto, 1986—. Chmn. Internat. Friendship com. Modesto City Council, 1986. Mem. Am. Mgmt. Assn., Am. Coll. Healthcare Execs., Am. Assn. Systems Info., Healthcare Fin. Mgmt. Assn., Meditech User's Synergy Exchange (governing). Lodge: Rotary. Avocations: tennis, table tennis, reading, traveling. Home: 3748 Terneuzen Ave Modesto CA 95356 Office: Meml Hosps Assn 1700 Coffee Rd Modesto CA 95355

SHANAHAN, MICHAEL GEORGE, police officer; b. Seattle, Oct. 14, 1940; s. Raymond Roderick and Carletta (Anderson) S.; m. Jo-Anne Genevieve David, Sept. 16, 1961; children: Patrick, Matthew, Raymond. BA in Psychology, Stanford U., 1962. Asst. police chief U. Wash., Seattle, 1970-71, police chief, 1971—; mem. law enforcement task force interim mcpl. com. Wash. State Legis., 1970-71, campus law enforcement task force-higher edn. com., 1970-71; co-chmn. Wash. Law Enforcement Standards Task Force; founding chmn. Washington Law Enforcement Exec. Forum, 1981; others. Author: Private Enterprise and the Public Police: The Professionalizing Effects of a New Partnership, 1985; contbr. articles to profl. jours. Mem. nat. exploring com. Boy Scouts Am., 1977, exec. bd., chief Seattle council; mem. Blanchet High Sch. Bd., Seattle, 1978-79. Decorated Bronze Star; recipient Award for Pub. Service, U.S. Dept. Transp., 1984, Humanitarian award Seattle chpt. NCCJ, 1985, Silver Beaver award Boy Scouts Am., 1986. Mem. Wash. Assn. Sheriffs and Police Chiefs (exec. bd. 1976-79, pres. 1980-81), Internat. Assn. Chief of Police (exec. com. 1986-87), FBI Nat. Acad. Assocs. Roman Catholic. Lodge: Rotary (pres. Univ. club. Seattle 1985-86). Avocations: fishing, gardening. Office: U Wash Police Dept 1117 NE Boat St Seattle WA 98105

SHANAMAN, RICHARD LOWELL, business executive; b. Tacoma, Apr. 30, 1935; s. Fred Charles and Marjorie Blanch (Jefferies) S.; m. Nancy Jean Cottrell, Nov. 8, 1975; children: Christa Ann, Kurt Arik. A.B., Dartmouth Coll., 1958; postgrad., Stanford U., 1967-69. Asst. cashier City Bank, N.Y.C., 1958-62; v.p. Bank of Calif. N.A., San Francisco, 1963-69, F.S. Smithers & Co., Inc., San Francisco, 1969-72; pres. Pacific Intermountain Capital, Sun Valley, Idaho, 1972-74; sr. v.p., treas. Skaggs Cos., Inc., Salt Lake City, 1974-79; exec. v.p., treas. Skaggs Cos., Inc., 1979—; exec. v.p., treas., chief fin. officer, dir. Am. Stores Co., 1979-82, vice-chmn., dir., chief fin. officer, 1982-83; sr. v.p., chief fin. officer Triad Am., 1983-84; sr. exec. v.p., chief operating officer, dir. Prudential Fin. Services, 1985-86; gen. ptnr. Utah Tech. Venture Fund I, 1986—; pres. Impetus, Inc. Served with Army NG, 1959.

SHANE, LAURIE, communications director; b. Los Angeles, Apr. 16, 1955; d. Robert Bernard and Joyce Ruth (Sasner) Sherman. B.A., Stanford U., 1977; postgrad. Canberra Coll., 1981; M.A., Pepperdine U., 1984. Mem. staff, minority specialist Paul N. McCloskey, U.S. Ho. of Reps., Palo Alto, Calif., 1975-77; dir. Australian Environment Ctr., Canberra, 1977-81; exec. dir., pres. The Communication Works, Inc., Los Angeles, 1982-86; dir. communications div. AIDS Project, Los Angeles, 1986—; cons. Laguna Outreach, Laguna Beach, Calif., 1982—. Editor Bogong Mag., 1978-81, (award 1980). Contbr. to poetry mags. Mem. editorial bd. Lesbian News, Los Angeles, 1982—. Sec. Gay Press Assn., Los Angeles, 1982-84. Recipient Golden Advocate award Healthcare Pub. Relations and Mktg. Assn., 1985. Mem. Advt. Club of Am., Pub. Relations Soc. Am. (accredited; Prisms award 1984, award 1985), Nat. Assn. Bus. Councils (del.), Bus. and Profl. Assn. (pres.). Democrat. Jewish. Avocations: creative writing; yoga; hiking; camping; travel. Office: AIDS Project Los Angeles 3670 Wilshire Blvd Suite 300 Los Angeles CA 90010

SHANE, LEONARD, savings and loan executive; b. Chgo., May 28, 1922; s. Jacob and Selma (Shayne) S.; m. Marjorie Cynthia Konecky, Jan. 14, 1941; children: Judith Shane Shenkman, Marsha Kay Shane Palmer, William Alan, Shelley Rose Shane Asidon. Student, U. Chgo., 1939-41, Ill. Inst. Tech., 1941-42. Writer-editor UPI, 1942-44; cons. indsl. areas 1944-46; writer-rancher Tucson, 1946-48; writer-producer ABC, Los Angeles, 1948-49; owner cons. agency Los Angeles, 1949-64; chmn. bd., dir., chief exec. officer Mercury Savs. and Loan Assn., Huntington Beach, Calif., 1964—. Chmn. United Jewish Welfare Fund of Orange County, 1972-73; pres. Western region, mem. internat. bd. govs. Am. Assos. Ben Gurion U., Israel; pres. Los Angeles Recreation and Park Commn., 1960-63, Jewish Fedn. Council of Orange County, 1973-74; trustee Ocean View Sch. Dist., 1970-72, City of Hope, 1968—. Mem. U.S. League Savs. Instns. (vice chmn. 1981-82, chmn. 1982-83, legis. chmn. 1987—), Calif. Savs. and Loan League (dir. 1969-73, v.p. 1979-80, pres. 1980-81), Phi Sigma Delta. Clubs: Big Canyon Country, Masons, Shriners. Office: Mercury Savs and Loan Assn 7812 Edinger Ave Huntington Beach CA 92647

SHANGRAW, ROBERT EDWARD, physician, researcher; b. Troy, N.Y., Mar. 16, 1954; s. Robert Dixon and M. Janice (Bonacker) S.; m. Patricia Mary Ford, May 25, 1985; Kirsten Celanire. BS, Rensselaer Poly. Inst., 1976; PhD, Albany (N.Y.) Med. Coll., 1981, MD, 1985. Resident in surgery U. Wash., Seattle, 1985-86; research assoc. U. Tex. Med. Br., Galveston, 1986—. Contbr. articles on biomedicine to profl. jours. Fellow NIH, 1977-80, 82, 83. Mem. Am. Physiol. Soc. (assoc.), AMA (resident), Biochem. Soc., Sigma Xi, Alpha Omega Alpha. Roman Catholic. Avocations: skiing, sailing, hiking, kayaking, swimming. Home: 7302 Heards Ln Apt 426 Galveston TX 77551 Office: Dept Surgery Harborview Med Ctr U Wash 325 9th Ave Seattle WA 98104

SHANI, JASHOVAM, pharmacology educator, radiopharmacist; b. Tel Aviv, Dec. 30, 1937; s. Moshe Avraham Miszkinsky and Esther Stein; m. Esther Klein, Mar. 23, 1972; 1 child, Mori. MS in Chemistry, Hebrew U. Jerusalem, 1963, MPharm, 1964, PhD in Pharmacology, 1967; MS in Radiopharmacy, U. So. Calif., 1975. Assoc. prof. Hebrew U. Jerusalem, 1980; vis. assoc. prof. U. So. Calif., Los Angeles, 1975-77, 82-87; vis. prof. radiology U. Wis. Sch. Medicine, Madison, 1979; vis. scientist Med. Dept. Brookhaven Nat. Lab., Upton, N.Y., 1975; cons. radiopharmaceuticals Minister of Health, Israel. Contbr. over 120 articles to profl. jours. Mem. Am. Soc. Nuclear Medicine, Internat. Soc. Neuroendocrinology, European Soc. Radiation Biology, Internat. Assn. Radiopharmacology. Office: Hebrew Univ, School of Pharmacy, Ein Kerem, Jerusalem Israel 91120

SHANK, MARY ANN, business analyst company executive; b. Santa Cruz, Calif., June 29, 1943. BA, Calif. State U., San Jose, 1967, MA in Librarianship, 1974. Vol., Peace Corps, Somalia, East Africa, 1967-69; sr. research librarian Santa Cruz, Calif., 1969-76; exec. v.p. Romac Western Corp., San Jose, 1976-81; pres. Trans-M Corp., Los Angeles, 1981—; prin. SBC Ventures, Ventura, Calif., 1986—; speaker Small Bus. Clinic, San Jose, 1976—. Author: Financial Plans for Small Business, 1980, Financial Ratios in Small Business Planning, 1981. Columnist Small Bus. Jour., 1980—. Contbr. articles to profl. jours. Recipient Woman of Distinction award YWCA, 1985. Trustee The Roop Found. Fund, Montecito, Calif., 1981—. Mem. Internat. Assn. Fin. Planners, Amnesty Internat. Sierra Club. Avocations: photography, bicycling. Office: Trans-M Corp 11693 San Vicente Blvd Suite 271 Los Angeles CA 90049

SHANKER, JAMES LEE, education educator, writer; b. Lansing, Mich., Sept. 9, 1946; s. Jack and Ida Shanker; m. Susan E. Edelman, June 22, 1969; children: Michael Eric, Kenneth Louis. BA, U. Mich., 1968; PhD, Mich. State U., 1973. Tchr. Toledo Pub. Schs., 1968-71, Lansing Pub. Schs., 1971-72; instr. Mich. State U., East Lansing, 1971-73; prof. edn. Calif. State U., Hayward, 1973—; cons., Pleasanton, Calif., 1973—. Author: (monograph) Staff Devel., 1982, (books) Diagnosis and Remediation, 1983, Teaching Reading, 1985; contbr. articles to profl. jours. Recipient Meritorious Performance award Calif. State U., Hayward, 1986. Mem. Internat. Reading Assn., Calif. Assn. Tchr. Educators, Calif. Profs. of Reading (pres. 1979-80). Home: 1061 Riesling Dr Pleasanton CA 94566 Office: Calif State U Dept Tchr Edn Hayward CA 94566

SHANKS, LORNA EVELYN, marketing manager; b. Johannesburg, South Africa, May 24, 1938; came to U.S., 1968; d. Andrew Cunningham Shanks and Elizabeth Comfort (Bailie) Challinor. Diploma in graphic design Witwatersrand Tech. Coll., Johannesburg, 1959; postgrad. Ravensbourne Coll. Art and Design, Bromley, Eng., 1965. Graphic designer Henrion Design Assocs., London, 1965, Corning Glass Works, N.Y., 1971-73; cons. graphics White House/Nat. Endowment for Arts, Washington, 1973-74; mktg. mgr. Mergenthaler Linotype Co., Plainview, N.Y., 1975-78; dir. Internat. Typeface Corp., N.Y.C., 1979-82; mktg. mgr. Xerox Corp., El Segundo, Calif., 1983—; guest lectr. Pratt Inst., 1981, Smithsonian Instn., 1981, MIT, 1980, R.I. Sch. Design, 1980, AAUW, 1972. Mem. Am. Inst. Graphic Arts (bd. dirs. 1979-82), Type Dirs. Club. Office: Xerox Corp 701 S Aviation Blvd El Segundo CA 90245

SHANNON, EDFRED L., JR., transportation company executive; b. 1926; (married). B.S., U. Calif., Berkeley, 1951. Petroleum engr. Union Oil Co. of Calif., 1951-53; with Santa Fe Internat. Corp., 1953—, v.p., 1960-63, chmn., chief exec. officer, 1963—, pres., chief exec. officer, 1986—, also dir. Office: Santa Fe Internat Corp 100 S Fremont Ave Box 4000 Alhambra CA 91802

SHANNON, ROBERT RENNIE, optical sciences center administrator, educator; b. Mt. Vernon, N.Y., Oct. 3, 1932; s. Howard A. and Harriebell (Rennie) S.; m. Helen Lang, Feb. 13, 1954; children—Elizabeth, Barbara, Jennifer, Amy, John, Robert. B.S., U. Rochester, 1954, M.A., 1957. Dir. Optics Lab., ITEK Corp., Lexington, Mass., 1959-69; prof. Optical Scis. Ctr., U. Ariz., 1969—, dir., 1983—, prof., 1969—; cons. Lawrence Livermore Lab., 1980—; trustee Aerospace Corp., 1985—; mem. Air Force Sci. Adv. Bd., 1986—. Editor: Applied Optics and Optical Engineering, Vol. 7, 1980, Vol. 8, 1981, Vol. 9, 1983, Vol. 10, 1987. Fellow Optical Soc. Am. (pres. 1985), Soc. Photo-Optical Instrumentation Engrs. (pres. 1979-80, recipient Goodard award 1982), Sigma Xi. Club: Tucson Soaring (past pres.). Home: 7040 E Taos Pl Tucson AZ 85715 Office: Optical Scis Ctr U Ariz Tucson AZ 85721

SHANOR, CLARENCE RICHARD, clergyman; b. Butler, Pa., Dec. 26, 1924; s. Paul L. and Marion (McCandless) S.; B.A., Allegheny Coll., 1948; S.T.B., Boston U., 1951, Ph.D., 1958; m. Anna Lou Watts, June 23, 1948; 1 son, Richard Watts. Ordained to ministry Methodist Ch., 1950; pastor Meth. Ch., South Hamilton, Mass., 1951-54; research asso. Union Coll., Schenectady, 1954-55; prof. Christian edn. Nat. Coll., Kansas City, Mo., 1956-58; asso. minister First United Meth. Ch., St. Petersburg, Fla., 1958-61, First United Meth. Ch., Fullerton, Calif., 1961-66; coordinator Met. dept. San Diego dist. United Meth. Union, San Diego, 1966—; pres. Human Services Corp., 1972-77. Treas. San Diego County Ecumenical Conf., 1970-71, pres., 1975-77; chmn. Coalition Urban Ministries, 1970-71, Cultural and Religious Task Force Rancho San Diego, 1970-74; chmn. western jurisdiction Urban Network United Meth. Ch., 1978. Chmn. San Diego Citizens Com. Against Hunger, 1969-72; bd. dirs. Interfaith Housing Found., chmn., 1979; mem. Gaslamp Quarter Project Area Com., San Diego, 1978, mem. council, 1980-84; chmn. bd. Horton House Corp., 1978; mem. Mayor's Task Force on the Homeless, 1983-84; chmn. Downtown Coordinating Council, 1983-84; mem. regional Task Force on Homeless, 1986—; vice-chmn. Community Congress, 1987. Recipient San Diego Inst. for Creativity award, 1969, Boss of Yr. award Am. Bus. Women's Assn., 1972, Christian Unity award Diocesan Ecumenical Commn., 1984, Congl. Disting. Service award, 1984, Helen Beardsley Human Rights award, 1986. Lodge: Lions. Author: (with Anna Lou Shanor) Kindergartner Meet Your World, 1966. Home: 6919 Maury Dr San Diego CA 92119 Office: 861 6th Ave Suite 810 San Diego CA 92101

SHANSBY, JOHN GARY, investment banker; b. Seattle, Aug. 25, 1937; s. John Jay and Jule E. (Boyer) S.; m. Joyce Ann Dunsmore, June 21, 1959 (div.); children: Sheri Lee, Kimberly Ann, Jay Thomas.; m. Barbara Anderson De Meo, Jan. 1, 1983. B.A., U. Wash., 1959. Dist. sales mgr. Colgate-Palmolive Co., N.Y.C., 1959-67; subs. pres. Am. Home Products Corp., N.Y.C., 1968-71; v.p. Clorox Co., Oakland, Calif., 1972-73, Booz, Allen & Hamilton, San Francisco, 1974-75; chmn. bd., chief exec. officer, dir. Shaklee Corp., San Francisco, 1975-86; gen. ptnr. Montgomery Securities, San Francisco, 1986—. Bd. dirs. Bay Area Council; bd. dirs. U. Calif. at Berkeley Bus. Sch., San Francisco Symphony, U. Calif., San Francisco, Calif. Econ. Devel. Corp.; mem. Pres.'s Adv. Com. for Trade Negotiations, Pres.'s Com. for Internat. Youth Exchange; chmn. Calif. State Commn. for Rev. of Master Plan Higher Edn.; bd. govs. NFL Alumni; founded J. Gary Shansby chair Mktg. Strategy, U. Calif., Berkeley. Mem. Calif. Roundtable, Harold Brunn Soc. Med. Research, San Francisco C. of C. (past pres.), Sigma Nu. Republican. Clubs: Commonwealth (San Francisco), Villa Traverna (San Francisco), Olympic (San Francisco), Silverado (Calif.) Country, Lincoln of No. Calif, Pennask Lake Fishing (B.C.), St. Francis Yacht, Sky Club (N.Y.). Office: Montgomery Securities 600 Montgomery St San Francisco CA 94111

SHAO, SHIU, financial executive; b. Taipei, Taiwan, Rep. of China, Nov. 13, 1951; came to U.S., 1975; s. Chi-Ching and Tintz (Yu) S. B.S. in Physics, Chan Yuan U., 1973; M.B.A. in Fin., U. Pitts., 1977. Programmer analyst Standard Brands, Inc., Burlingame, Calif., 1977-78; acctg. analyst Watkins Johnson Co., Palo Alto, Calif., 1978-81; controller Oromeccanica Inc., Burbank, Calif., 1981-82; v.p. fin., chief fin. officer Oroamerica, Inc., Burbank, 1982—; dir. Am. Internat. Chain Co., Emex Corp. Author: Financial Credit Line Tie to Commodity Index for Precious Metals Industries, 1982. Jr. Achievement advisor, Santa Clara County, Calif., 1979. Served to 2d lt. Chinese Marine Corps, 1973-75. Mem. Nat. Assn. Accts. Home: 250 W Fairview Ave #308 Glendale CA 91202 Office: Oroamerica Inc 443 N Varney St Burbank CA 91502

SHAPERO, HARRIS JOEL, physician, surgeon; b. Winona, Minn., Nov. 22, 1930; s. Charles and Minnie Sara (Ehrlichman) S.; m. Byong Soon Yu, Nov. 6, 1983; children by previous marriage—Laura, Charles, Won Jin. A.A., UCLA, 1953; B.S., Northwestern U., 1954, M.D., 1957. Diplomate and cert. specialist occupational medicine Am. Bd. preventive medicine; cert. aviation medicine FAA. Intern, Los Angeles County Harbor Gen. Hosp., 1957-58, resident in pediatrics, 1958-60, staff physician, 1960-64; attending physician Perceptually Handicapped Children's Clinic, 1960-63; disease control officer for tuberculosis, Los Angeles County Health Dept., 1962-64; practice medicine specializing in pediatrics and occupational medicine, Cypress, Calif., 1965-85; pediatric cons. Los Angeles Health Dept., 1963-85; pediatric cons. Bellflower Clinic, 1952-85; disease control officer sexually transmitted diseases, Los Angeles County Health Dept., 1984-85; emergency room dir. AMI, Anaheim, Calif., 1968-78; staff Anaheim Gen. Hosp., Beach Community Hosp., Norwalk Community Hosp.; courtesy staff Palm Harbor Gen. Hosp., Bellflower City Hosp.; pediatric staff Hosp. de General, Ensenada, Mex., 1978—; founder Calif. Legal Evaluation Med. Group; health care provider, advisor City of Anaheim, City of Buena Park, City of Cypress, City of Garden Grove, Cypress Sch. Dist., Magnolia Sch. Dist., Savanna Sch. Dist., Anaheim Unified Sch. Dist., Orange County Dept. Edn.; pediatric and tuberculosis cons. numerous other orgns. Author: The Silent Epidemic, 1979. Named Headliner in Medicine Orange County Press Club, 1978. Fellow Am. Coll. Preventive Medicine; mem. Los Angeles County Med. Assn., Los Angeles County Indsl. Med. Assn., Am. Coll. Emergency Physicians, Los Angeles County Pediatric Soc., Orange County Pediatric Soc., Am. Pub. Health Assn., Mex.-Am. Border Health Assn. Republican. Jewish. Address: 12235 Woods Rd PO Box 228 Wilton CA 95693-0228

SHAPIRO, ARTHUR MAURICE, zoology educator; b. Balt., Jan. 6, 1946; s. Bernard Robert and Rose (Pogach) S.; m. Adrienne Ruth Austin, Aug. 3, 1969; 1 child, Austin Warren. BA, U. Pa., 1966; PhD, Cornell U., 1970. Asst. prof. CUNY, 1970-71; asst. prof. U. Calif., Davis, 1972-75, assoc. prof., 1975-80, prof., 1980-84, prof. zoology, 1984—, vice chmn. dept., 1984—. Research on Lepidoptera, 1982; contbr. over 200 articles to profl. jours. Grantee NSF, 1977-79, 84-87, Nat. Geog. Soc. 1976-82. Fellow AAAS, Explorers Club, Calif. Acad. Scis.; mem. Soc. Study of Evolution, Lepidopterists' Soc. (v.p. 1974-76, exec. council 1976-79). Avocations: Andean exploration, photography, botany, polit. sci. Office: U Calif Dept Zoology Storer Hall Davis CA 95616

SHAPIRO, BARRY, toy company executive; b. Bklyn., Apr. 18, 1942; s. Sidney and Anne (Sokol) S.; m. Frances Rosenfeld, Apr. 5, 1970; children: David Scott, Sean Jonathan. BA in English, Rutgers U., 1963. Asst. buyer J.C. Penney Co., N.Y.C., 1966-69; dir. product planning and internat. ops. Gabriel Industries, Inc., N.Y.C., 1969-78; exec. v.p. Lakeside Games div. Leisure Dynamics, Inc., Mpls., 1978-79, pres., 1979-80; exec. v.p. Toy Game & Hobby Group div. Leisure Dynamics, Inc., Mpls., 1980-81; exec. v.p., gen. mgr., chief exec. officer Wham-O, San Gabriel, Calif., 1981-83; exec. v.p., gen. mgr. Imagineering, Inc., Phoenix, 1984—; cons. to various toy cos. Coach Little League, Mpls., Arcadia, Calif., 1979—; v.p. Temple Shaarei Tikvah, Arcadia, 1982-84. Served to 1st lt. U.S. Army, 1963-66. Recipient

Army Commendation medal. Mem. Assn. Toy Mfg. Am. Jewish. Avocations: tennis, reading. Home: 5421 E Via Buena Vista Paradise Valley AZ 85253

SHAPIRO, BENNETT MICHAELS, biochemist, educator; b. Phila., July 14, 1939; s. Simon and Sara (Michaels) S.; m. Fredericka Foster, Mar. 13, 1982; children: Lisa, Lise, Jonathan. BS, Dickinson Coll., 1960; MD, Jefferson Med. Coll., 1964. Research assoc. NHLI, NIH, 1965-68, med. officer, 1970-71; vis. scientist Inst. Pasteur, Paris, 1968-70; from assoc. prof. to full prof. biochemistry U. Wash., 1971—, chmn. biochemistry dept., 1985—. Contbr. articles to profl. jour. Served as surgeon USPHS, 1968-70. John S. Guggenheim fellow, 1982; Japan Soc. for Promotion Sci., 1984. Mem. Am. Soc. Biol. Chemists, Am. Soc. Cell Biology, Am. Soc. Devel. Biology, Phi Beta Kappa, Alpha Omega Alpha. Office: Univ of Washington Sch of Medicine Dept of Biochemistry Seattle WA 98195

SHAPIRO, GARY JOHN, lawyer; b. San Francisco, Oct. 4, 1941; s. Herbert H. and Raye (Wall) S.; BS, U. Calif. at Berkeley, 1963; JD, 1966; m. Dana Bloom, July 5, 1964; children— Karen Hillary, Anne Rebecca. Admitted to Calif. bar, 1966, Fed. Dist. Ct., U.S. Ct. Appeals, 1967; law clk., Oliver D. Hamlin, U.S. Ct. Appeals, 9th Cir., 1966-67; assoc. Dinkelspiel & Dinkelspiel, San Francisco, 1967-69; ptnr. firm Buchman, Kass & Shapiro, Profl. Corp., Oakland, Calif., 1970-75; bd. dira. Gary J. Shapiro, P.C., San Francisco; of counsel Steefel, Levitt & Weiss, 1985—; judge pro tem Alameda County Municipal Ct., San Leandro-Hayward Jud. Dist., 1972; ptnr. Shapiro Assocs., Mill Valley; mem. faculty San Francisco Law Sch., 1968-71; mem. faculty John F. Kennedy U. Sch. Law Sch. Bus. Adminstrn., 1977-79, Am. Coll., Bryn Mawr, Pa., 1977-79, Golden Gate U. Grad. Sch. Banking, Fin. and Real Estate, 1979-81; lectr. various tax and real estate seminars. Bd. dirs., pres. Endowment Found. of Jewish Welfare Fedn., 1985-87; bd. dirs., treas. Jewish Family Service Agy., Alameda County; bd. dirs. Am. Friends Shaare Zedak Hosp., Am. Friends Ben Gurim U., Jewish Fedn. Greater East Bay, Jewish Nat. Fund; pres. Estate Planning Council of East Bay, 1980; v.p., trustee Judah L. Magnes Meml. Mus.; trustee, sec. Jacques and Esther Reutlinger Found. Mem. ABA, Am. Israel Pub. Affairs Com. of No. Calif. (bd. dirs., vice chmn., nat. exec com.), Bar Assn. San Francisco, Order of Coif. Republican. Jewish. Club: Concordia-Argonaut. Contbr. articles to legal jours. Office: One Embacadero Center 29th Floor San Francisco CA 94111

SHAPIRO, ISADORE, chemist, cons.; b. Mpls., Apr. 25, 1916; s. Jacob and Bessie (Goldman) S.; B. Chem. Engring. summa cum laude, U. Minn., 1938, Ph.D., 1944; m. Mae Hirsch. Sept. 4, 1938; children—Stanley Harris, Jerald Steven. Asst. instr. chemistry U. Minn., 1938-41, research fellow, 1944-45; research chemist E. I. duPont de Nemours and Co., Phila., 1946; head chem. lab. U.S. Naval Ordnance Test Sta., Pasadena, Calif., 1947-52; dir. research lab. Olin-Mathieson Chem. Corp., 1952-59; head chemistry Hughes Tool Co., Aircraft div., Culver City, Calif., 1959-62; pres. Universal Chem. Systems Inc. 1962—, Aerospace Chem. Systems, Inc., 1964-66; dir. contract research HITCO, Gardena, Calif., 1966-67; prin. scientist Douglas Aircraft Co. of McDonnell Douglas Corp., Santa Monica, Calif., 1967; prin. scientist McDonnell Douglas Astronautics Co., 1967-70; head materials and processes AiResearch Mfg. Co., Torrance, Calif., 1971-82, cons., 1982—. Rater U.S. Civil Service Bd. Exam., 1948-52. Served 1st lt. AUS, 1941-44. Registered profl. engr., Calif. Fellow Am. Inst. Chemists, Am. Inst. Aero and Astronautics (asso.); mem. AAAS, Am. Ordnance Assn., Am. Chem. Soc., Soc. Rheology, Soc. Advancement Materials and Process Engring., Am. Inst. Physics, AIM, Am. Phys. Soc., N.Y. Acad. Sci., Am. Assn. Contamination Control, Am. Ceramic Soc., Nat. Inst. Ceramic Engrs., Internat. Plansee Soc. for Powder Metallurgy, Sigma Xi, Tau Beta Pi, Phi Lambda Upsilon. Author articles in tech. publs. Patentee, discoverer carborane compounds. Home: 5624 W 62d St Los Angeles CA 90056

SHAPIRO, JACK, importer and distributor, former advertising and public relations executive; b. Salinas, Calif., Dec. 6, 1924; s. Morris and Rebecca (Kuperman) S.; m. Loretta Lowell, Oct. 11, 1946 (dec.); m. 2d, Jeannette Pearson, June 4, 1955; children: Karen Lynn Peterson, David Douglas, Victor Morris. Student, Hartnell Coll., 1946-47, Los Angeles City Coll., 1948-49; Dir., Sta. KFI-TV, Los Angeles, 1949-50; v.p. Inter-Mountain Network, Salt Lake City, 1956-59; mgr. Los Angeles office Forjoe Co., 1960-62; founder, pres. Shapiro Advt. and Pub. Relations, Salt Lake City, from 1963, now semi-ret.; importer, distbr. Myford High Precision Metal Turning Lathes to 1986; lectr. Brigham Young U., 1979, U. Utah, 1981; chmn. 1st Ann. Intermountain Pub. Relations Seminar, 1980. Mem. adv. bd. The Salvation Army, Salt Lake City Police Dept. Honorary Cols.; mem. steering com. Taxpayers for Accountable Govt.; mem. Utah Rep. Party Exec. Com., 1971-73, Ctr. Com., 1971-73; chmn. Recreation Vehicle Adv. Council, 1973-83; mem. Days of '47 Parade Com., 1965-67. Served with AUS, 1943-45, 50-51; PTO, Korea. Mem. Public Relations Soc. Am. (pres. local chpt. 1979), Utah Assn. Advt. Agys. (pres. local chpt. 1976-77). Jewish. Clubs: Utah Westerners (sec.), Masons, Shrine (editor Minaret 1977-85). Office: 68 South Main Suite 600 Salt Lake City UT 84101

SHAPIRO, RICHARD STANLEY, physician; b. Moline, Ill., June 11, 1925; s. Herbert and Esther Dian (Grant) S.; B.S., St. Ambrose Coll., 1947; B.S. in Pharmacy, U. Iowa, 1951, M.S. in Preventive Medicine and Environ. Health, 1951, M.D., 1957; m. Arlene Blum, June 12, 1949; children—Michele Pamela, Bruce Grant, Gary Lawrence; m. 2d, Merry Lou Cook, Oct. 11, 1971. Pharmacist, Rock Island, Ill., 1951-53; research asst. U. Iowa Coll. Medicine, Iowa City, 1950-51, 53-57; practice medicine specializing in allergy, Beverly Hills, Calif., 1958-62, Lynwood, Calif., 1962—; attending physician Good Hope Found. Allergy Clinic, Los Angeles, 1958-62, Cedars of Lebanon Hosp., Hollywood, Calif., 1959-68, U. So. Calif.-Los Angeles County Med. Center, 1962—; physician St. Francis Hosp., Lynwood, 1962—; assoc. clin. prof. medicine U. So. Calif., 1978-84, emeritus, 1984—. Bd. dirs. Westside Jewish Community Center, 1961-65, Camp JCA, 1964-65. Served with USNR, 1943-45; PTO. Diplomate Am. Bd. Allergy and Immunology. Fellow Am. Geriatric Soc., Am. Coll. Allergy, Am. Assn. Clin. Immunology and Allergy; mem. Am. Soc. Tropical Medicine and Hygiene, Am. Acad. Allergy, Los Angeles Allergy Soc., AMA, Calif., Los Angeles County med. assns., West Coast Allergy Soc., AAAS, Am., Calif. socs. internal medicine, Calif. Soc. Allergy, Am. Heart Assn., Sierra Club, Sigma Xi. Jewish. Mason; mem. B'nai B'rith. Contbr. articles to profl. jours. Office: 11411 Brookshire Ave Downey CA 90241

SHAPIRO, RODNEY JULIAN, psychologist; b. Bloemfontein, Republic of South Africa, May 26, 1935; came to U.S., 1966; s. Maurice Aaron and Matilda (Green) S.; m. Lucy Kaplan (div. 1971); children: Justine, Meagan; m. Jacqueline Dunn, Apr. 12, 1986. BA, U. Witwatersrand, Johannesburg, Republic of South Africa, 1959, PhD, 1965; BA with honors, U. Pretoria, Republic Of South Africa, 1961; MA, U. South Africa, Republic Of South Africa, 1963. Lic. psychologist, N.Y., Calif. Sr. research officer Nat. Inst. for Personnel Research, Johannesburg, 1961-66; postdoctoral internship Ill. State Psychiat. Inst., Chgo., 1966-67; postdoctoral fellowship Michael Reese Hosp., Chgo., 1967-68; assoc. prof. med. sch. U. Rochester, N.Y., 1968-80; family therapy program dir. VA Med. Ctr., San Francisco, 1981—; dir. Family Therapy Clinic, Pacific Presbyn. Med. Ctr., San Francisco; assoc. clin. prof. U. Calif. Med. Ctr., San Francisco, 1982—. Contbr. articles to profl. jours. Mem. Am. Psychol. Assn., Assn. Family Therapists No. Calif. (pres. 1984-86), Am. Family Therapy Assn. (editorial bd. Contemporary Family Therapy, The Family Therapy Collections, Family Therapy). Jewish. Avocations: fiction writing, photography, long distance running. Home: 111 10th Ave San Francisco CA 94118 Office: VA Med Ctr 116C 4150 Clement St San Francisco CA 94121

SHAPIRO, TERI RASK, advertising executive; b. Abilene, Tex., Jan. 5, 1958; d. Robert Reynold and Laverne Elaine (Kimbrough) R.; m. William David Shapiro, Mar. 13, 1982. AA, Crafton Hills Coll., 1980; BA, Calif. State U., Fullerton, 1982. Mgr. traffic Young & Rubicam(name later changed to DYR), Los Angeles, 1982-83; asst. account exec. Young & Rubicam (name later changed to DYR), Los Angeles, 1983-84, acct. exec., 1984—. Recipient Spl. Achievement award DHHS, Calif., 1981; Soc. Calif. Accountants scholar, 1980. Mem. Los Angeles Advt. Club, Am. Mktg. Assn. (alumni mem. Calif. State U. Fullerton chpt.). Avocations: skiing, running, commuting. Home: 410 S Canyon Ridge Dr Anaheim Hills CA 92807 Office: DYR 4751 Wilshire Blvd Los Angeles CA 90010

SHARMA, BRAHAMA DATTA, chemistry educator; b. Sampla, Punjab, India, June 5, 1931; s. Des Raj and Kesara Devi (Pathak) S.; m. Millicent M. Hewitt, Dec. 22, 1956; children: Nalanda V. Sharma Bowman, Renuka D.; BS with honors, U. Delhi, India, 1949, MS, 1951; PhD, U. So. Calif., 1961. Chemist Govt. Opium Factory, Ghazipur, India, 1951-52; lab. assoc., sci. asst. Nat. Chem. Lab., Poona, India, 1952-55; lab. assoc. U. So. Calif., Los Angeles, 1955-61; research fellow Calif. Inst. Tech., Pasadena, 1961-65; asst. prof. chemistry U. Nev., Reno, 1963-64, Oreg. State U., Corvallis, 1965-70; asst. prof. chemistry Calif. State U., Northridge, 1973-75, assoc. prof., 1975; prof. Los Angeles Pierce Coll., Woodland Hills, Calif., 1976—; part time assoc. prof. chemistry Calif. State U., Los Angeles, 1973-85, part time prof., 1985—; pres. Los Angeles Pierce Coll. Senate, 1981-82; chmn. Acad. Rank Los Angeles Pierce Coll., 1985—. Contbr. articles to profl. jours. Grantee E.I. duPont de Nemours, Los Angeles, 1961, Am. Chem. Soc. Petroleum Research Fund, Washington, 1965-69, NSF, Washington, 1967-69. Mem. Am. Chem. Soc. (chmn. edn. com. So. Calif. chpt. 1981-82). Avocations: playing bridge, reading, history. Office: Los Angeles Pierce Coll Woodland Hills CA 91371

SHARMA, KISHANDUTT JAYDAYAL, management and research consulting company executive; b. Sabarmati, India, July 29, 1937, came to U.S. 1967; s. Jaydayal S. and Satyavati J. Sharma; m. Meera K. Dixit; 1 child, Seema. B.E. in Mech. Engring., Gujarat U., India, 1959, B.E. in Elec. Engr., 1960; M.S. in Elec. Engr., U. Ottawa, 1964; Ph.D. in Systems Sci., Portland State U., 1974. Sr. Scientist Sperry Rand Corp., Montreal, Que., Can., 1963-67; sr. engr. Bechtel Corp., San Francisco, 1974-77; sr. staff mem. SRI Internat. (formerly Stanford Research Inst.), Menlo Park, Calif., 1977-79; project mgr. Calif. Energy Commn., Sacramento, 1979; pres., chief ops. officer Nero & Assocs., Portland, Oreg., Inc., 1981—; cons. Recipient Nat. Research Council of Canada award for grad. edn., 1963. Mem. AAAS, Internat. Club, World Future Soc., Smithsonian, Portland C. of C. Hindu. Author, co-author numerous publs. Office: Nero & Assoc Inc 520 SW 6th Ave Suite 1120 Portland OR 97204

SHARMA, MANORAMA, obstetrician, gynecologist; b. Indore, India, Apr. 22, 1945; came to U.S., 1975; s. Shiu Kumar and Premwati (Trivedi) Vyas; m. Satish Kumar Sharma, Mar. 8, 1975 (div. Feb. 1985); children: Maneesh, Sima; m. Madhu Sudan Gupta, May 29, 1985; children: Jay M., Vinit. BS, Govt. Degree Coll., Bareli, India, 1963; MBBChir, Ghandi Med. Coll., Bhopal, India, 1968, Diploma in Child Health, 1974. Diplomate Am. Bd. Ob-Gyn. Practice medicine specializing in ob-gyn. Mt. Clemens, Mich., 1981-86, Westminster, Calif., 1986—. Mem. research panel Med. World News, 1984-86. Fellow Am. Coll. Ob-Gyns.; mem. AMA, World Med. Assn., Am. Women Med. Assn., Orange County Med. Assn., Orange County Indian Physician Assn. Avocations: music, dance, travel. Office: 7631 Wyoming St #203 Westminster CA 92683

SHARMA, PRAMOD KUMAR, research chemical engineer; b. New Delhi, Oct. 30, 1946; s. Shankar Das and Vidyavati (Joshi) S.; m. Dheera Joshi, Mar. 27, 1978; children: Anvita, Saurabh. B Tech. in Chem. Engring., Indian Inst. Tech., New Delhi, 1968; M. Tech. in Chem. Engring., Indian Inst. Tech., Kanpur, 1972; PhD in Engring., UCLA, 1976. Postdoctoral scholar UCLA, 1976-77; lectr. U. Calif., Santa Barbara, 1977-78; mem. tech. staff MIT, Cambridge, 1978-81; chem. engr. Energy Resources Co., Cambridge, 1981-82; sr. engr. Energy & Environ. Engring, Inc., Cambridge, 1982-83; sr. research assoc. Jet Propulsion Lab., Pasadena, Calif., 1984—. Contbr. articles to profl. jours. Mem. Am. Inst. Chem. Engrs., Am. Chem. Soc., Sigma Xi. Avocations: hiking, camping. Home: 266 N Mar Vista #1 Pasadena CA 91106 Office: Jet Propulsion Lab 4800 Oak Grove Dr Pasadena CA 91109

SHARMA, RAJINDER KUMAR, instrumentation engineer; b. Hoshiarpur, Punjab, India, Sept. 29, 1953; s. Jagdish Mitter and Ramlubhai (Vashishat) S.; m. Sita Devi Salwan, May 20, 1978; children: Ripple, Aroma, Beamy. BSEE, G.N. Engring. Coll., Punjab, 1974; postgrad in computer sci., Chabot Coll., Hayward, Calif., 1983-1984; postgrad in enging. mgmt., San Jose State U., 1986—. Registered profl. engr., Calif. Elec. engr. P.S.E.B., Punjab, 1974-78, Salem Engring., Oak Brook, Ill., 1979-80; elec. engr. Bechtel Corp., San Francisco, 1980-81, control system engr., 1981-84; sr. instrumentation engr. Lockheed Corp., Sunnyvale, Calif., 1984—. Founder, bd. dirs. Vedic Dharam Samaj Temple, Fremont, Calif., 1982-83; exec. mem. Hindu Fedn. Am., 1985—. Mem. India Engrs. Assn. Democrat. Avocations: reading, walking, helping needy persons, traveling. Home: 34877 Starling Dr Union City CA 94587

SHARMAN, WILLIAM, basketball executive; b. Abilene, Tex., May 25, 1926; m. Joyce Sharman; children by previous marriage: Jerry, Nancy, Janice, Tom. Student, U. So. Calif. Basketball player Washington Capitols, 1950-51, Boston Celtics, 1951-61; coach Los Angeles/Utah Stars, 1968-71; coach Los Angeles Lakers, 1971-76, gen. mgr., 1976-82, pres., 1982—. Author: Sharman on Basketball Shooting, 1965. Named to Nat. Basketball Assn. All Star First Team, 1956-59, 2d Team, 1953, 55, 60, All League Team, 7 times; named Coach of Year Nat. Basketball Assn., 1972, Naismith Basketball Hall of Fame, 1976. Office: PO Box 10 Inglewood CA 90306

SHARON, TIMOTHY MICHAEL, physicist; b. Portsmouth, Va., Aug. 21, 1948; s. Lester Clark and Ruth May (Banister) S.; student Santa Ana Coll., 1966-68; B.A., U. Calif.-Irvine 1970, M.A., 1972, Ph.D., 1976; m. Carla Deon Colley, Dec. 17, 1977. Jr. specialist solid state theory U. Calif.-Irvine, 1976, research asst. radiation physics Med. Center and Sch. Medicine, 1976-77, cons. to attending staff Research and Edn. Found., 1976-77; mktg. physicist Varian Assos., Irvine, 1977-78; prin. engr., program mgr. Spectra Research Systems, Newport Beach, Calif., 1977-82; v.p. Brewer-Sharon Corp., Newport Beach, 1981-86, Micor Instruments, Inc., Irvine, Calif., 1983-86; pres., chief exec. officer Medelec Instruments Co., Inc., Newport Beach, 1986—; adj. faculty physics and engring. Columbia Pacific U., San Rafael, Calif., 1981—; dean Sch. Engring., Newport U., Newport Beach, Calif., 1983—; mem. adv. panel on pub. Am. Inst. Physics, 1974-75; mem. research council Scripps Clinic and Research Found. Brython P. Davis univ. fellow, 1973-74. Mem. AAAS, Am. Phys. Soc., Brit. Interplanetary Soc. (asso. fellow), Am. Assn. Physicists in Medicine, IEEE, Internat. Microwave Power Inst., Am. Security Council Found., N.Y. Acad. Scis., Assn. Advancement Med. Instrumentation, Soc. Sci. Exploration, Smithsonian Instn., Am. Film Inst., Nat. Hist. Soc., Nat. Geog. Soc., Internat. Platform Assn., Festival of Arts Laguna Beach, Newport Harbor Area C. of C. Mensa, Intertel, Sigma Pi Sigma, Phi Theta Kappa, Alpha Gamma Sigma. Clubs: Acad. Magical Arts, Magic Island, Club 33. Contbr. articles to profl. jours. Office: 3900 Birch St Suite 201 Newport Beach CA 92660

SHARP, CYNTHIA MAE, real estate broker; b. Detroit, Oct. 25, 1949; d. Theo Frederick and Jean Harriet (Whittemore) S.; m. William Charles Ligety, May 22, 1976; children: Theodore Sharp, Charles. BS, Am. U., 1973. RN; lic. real estate broker, Utah. Broker Gump and Ayers Real Estate, Park City, Utah, 1980—; expert witness for real estate trials, Salt Lake City, 1986. Mem. Nat. Assn. Realtors, Park City Bd. Realtors Million Dollar Club, Salt Lake City Bd. Realtors Million Dollar Club. Avocations: racing sailboats, skiing, windsurfing. Home: PO Box 340 Park City UT 84060 Office: Gump and Ayers Real Estate 1500 Kearns Blvd Park City UT 84060

SHARP, DAVID LEE, advertising executive, consultant; b. Chgo., Apr. 18, 1952; s. Homer Glenn and Jo Ann (Harbour) S.; m. Christine Rowe, Oct. 18, 1975; 1 child, Tara Ann. B.S., Bradley U., 1974; M.S., U. Ill., 1975. Advt. exec. Caterpillar Tractor, Peoria, Ill., 1975-76; sales promotion supr. Armstrong Cork Co., Lancaster, Pa., 1976-78; sr. account exec. Kraft Smith Advt., Seattle, 1978-80; pres. Sharp, Hartwig Advt., Inc., Seattle, 1980—; chmn. Response Mktg., Inc., Seattle, 1982—; instr. Cornish Inst., 1980; cons. Simpson Timber Co., Port of Seattle. Trustee, Eastside Community Mental Health Center, 1983—. Bus. Profl. Advt. Assn. (v.p. 1982-83), Intermarket Assn. Advt. Agy., Am. Assn. Advt. Agy. (gov. 1984—, vice chmn. 1984-85, chmn. 1986-87), Seattle Advt. Fedn. Republican. Methodist. Clubs: Wash. Athletic; Juanita Bay Athletic; Univ. Rotary (program chmn. 1982-83). Home: 11647 73d Pl NE Kirkland WA 98034 Office: 100 West Harrison Plaza South Tower Seattle WA 98119

SHARP, FRANK RAY, neurologist, researcher; b. Sacramento, Nov. 1, 1946; s. Oscar and Jolee (West) S.; m. Mary Lynn Howlett, June 10, 1972; 1 dau., Renee. B.S., U. Calif.-Davis, 1968; M.D., U. Calif.-San Diego, 1972. Diplomate Am. Bd. Psychiatry and Neurology. Med. intern Duke U., Durham, N.C., 1972-73; research assoc. NIH, Bethesda, Md., 1973-76; resident in neurology U. Calif.-San Francisco, 1976-79, assoc. prof. neurology, 1984—; asst. prof. neurology, U. Calif.-San Diego, 1979-83, assoc. prof., 1983-84. Contbr. articles to profl. jours. Served to lt. comdr. USPHS, 1973-76. Recipient Tchr. Investigator Devel. award NIH, 1980-84; Basil O'Connor award March of Dimes, 1980-84. VA grantee, 1984. Mem. Am. Acad. Neurology, Soc. Neuroscis., AAAS. Home: 1806 Scott St San Francisco CA 94115 Office: VA Med Ctr Dept Neurology V127 4150 Clement St San Francisco CA 94121

SHARP, JANICE ANNE, molecular biologist, researcher; b. Sydney, Australia, Nov. 17, 1951; came to U.S., 1978; d. A. Leslie and Betty Joan (Olsson) New; m. Stephen Jefferson Sharp, Jan. 12, 1974 (div. Oct. 1985). BS with honors, U. New South Wales, Sydney, 1975, PhD, 1979. Postdoctoral fellow Yale U., New Haven, Conn., 1978-83, U. Calif., Irvine, 1983-84; dir. research Am. Biogenetics Corp., Irvine, 1985—. Contbr. articles to sci. jours. Deans Postgrad. fellow U. New South Wales, 1975-78, Postdoctoral Research fellow James Hudson Brown-Alexander B. Coxe, 1982-83, Beckman Postdoctoral fellow, 1983-84. Mem. AAAS, Am. Soc. Microbiology. Avocations: sports, squash, tennis, bicycling, drawing. Office: Am Biogenetics Corp 19732 MacArthur Blvd Suite 130 Irvine CA 92715

SHARP, JONATHAN EDWARD, industrial and forensic consultant; b. York, Nebr., Jan. 25, 1921; s. Lorenzo Dow and Ethel May Sharp; m. Alice Louise Paramore, Mar. 16, 1946 (div. Jan. 1969); children: Jon Charles, Jeannette Louise, Christina Marie Sharp Grant; m. Peggy Dare Sachry, Jan. 22, 1978. BA, U. Okla., 1947, postgrad., 1948. Cert. safety profl., Colo. Plant mgr. Rose Mfg. Co., Denver, 1949-64, pres., 1964-75; pres. Rose Mfr. Co., Englewood, Colo., 1977-79, Sharp, Inc., Denver, 1975-77, Sharp Internat. Ltd., Littleton, Colo., 1980—; bd. dirs. RSR Systems, Inc., Denver. Patentee in field. Pres. Rocky Mountain Planned Parenthood, Denver, 1970-72; mem. Gov.'s Phys. Fitness Council, Denver, 1976—, Colo. Seat Belt Coalition, Denver, 1985—. Served to capt. USAF, 1942-46, ETO. Mem. Am. Soc. Safety Engrs. (chpt. pres. 1964-65), Soc. Automotive Engrs., Colo. Soc. Safety Engrs. (pres. 1964-65), Vets. of Safety. Lodge: Lions. Avocations: skiing, scuba diving, sailing, bicycling. Home and Office: 7009 W Stetson Pl Littleton CO 80123

SHARP, PAMELA ANN, engineer, geochemist; b. Pullman, Wash., Dec. 20, 1950; d. Robert Melvin and Vivian Lois (Steele) Olson; m. David William Sharp, June 16, 1973; children: Jaime David, Erik Scott. Student, Big Bend Community Coll., Moses Lake, Wash., 1969-70; BS in Zoology, Wash. State U., 1973; postgrad., Portland State U., 1976. Lab. technician The Carter Mining Co., Gillette, Wyo., 1977-79, lab. supr., 1979-80, quality control supr., 1980-81, enging. analyst, 1982—. Supt. Campbell County Fair, Gillette, 1985—. Mem. ASTM (proximate analysis chmn. 1985—), Am. Water Ski Assn. (regular judge 1974—, eastern regional water ski trick record 1975, 3d nat. trick title 1962, state champion in tricks Wash., Idaho, Mont. 1961-73). Republican. Presbyterian. Club: Takedown (Gillette). Avocations: handball, photography, water skiing. Office: The Carter Mining Co PO Box 3007 Gillette WY 82716

SHARP, TERRY LEE, municipal government official; b. New Castle, Ind., Jan. 13, 1952; s. Karl Morris and Marjorie Ann (Peters) S.; m. Elizabeth Ann Loftus, May 19, 1973; children: Adrienne, Erin. BA in Econs. and Polit. Sci., The Am. U., 1974; MPA, U. Kans., 1976. Mgmt. intern City of Phoenix, 1975-76, mgmt. asst., 1976-83; dir. budget and research City of Glendale, Ariz., 1983-85, dep. city mgr., 1985—; guest lectr. Ariz. State U., Tempe, 1979, Golden Gate U., Luke AFB, Ariz., 1983. Recipient Kinsman-Hurst award The Am. U., Washington, 1974. Mem. Govt. Fin. Officers Assn., Internat. City Mgmt. Assn. (assoc.), Ariz. City Mgmt. Assn. (bd. dirs. 1983), Ariz. Mcpl. Mgmt. Assts. (pres. 1983), Omicron Delta Kappa, Delta Sigma Rho, Tau Kappa Alpha. Roman Catholic. Club: Toastmasters (Phoenix) (pres. 1981, Competent Toastmaster award 1981). Avocations: old movies, swimming, spectator sports, music. Home: 6122 W Corrine Glendale AZ 85304 Office: City of Glendale 5850 W Glendale Glendale AZ 85301

SHARPE, ROLAND LEONARD, engineering company executive, consultant; b. Shakopee, Minn., Dec. 18, 1923; s. Alfred Leonard and Ruth Helen (Carter) S.; m. Jane Esther Steele, Dec. 28, 1946; children—Douglas Rolfe, Deborah Lynn, Sheryl Anne. B.S. in Civil Engring., U. Mich., 1947, M.S.E., 1949. Registered civil engr. and structural engr., Calif. Designer, Cummins & Barnard, Inc., Ann Arbor, Mich., 1947-48; instr. engring. U. Mich., 1948-50; exec. v.p. John A. Blume & Assocs., engrs., San Francisco, 1950-73; chmn., founder Engring. Decision Analysis Co., Inc., Palo Alto, 1974—; mng. dir. EDAC, GmBH, Frankfurt, Germany, 1974-82; dir. EDAC; pres. Calif. Devel. & Engring. Co., Inc., Las Vegas, Nev., 1973-81. Author: (with J. Blume, E.G. Kost) Earthquake Engineering for Nuclear Facilities, 1971. Mem. Planning Commn., Palo Alto, 1955-60; mng. dir. Applied Tech. Council, Palo Alto, 1973-83; dir. Earthquake Engring. Research Inst., 1972-75, now mem.; project dir., editor Tentative Provisions for Devel. of Seismic Regulations for Buildings, 1978. Served with USMCR, 1942-46. Fellow ASCE (chmn. dynamic effects com., 1978-80, exec. com. structural div. 1980-84, chmn. 1983); mem. Structural Engrs. Assn. Calif. (dir. 1971-73, chmn. seismology com. 1972-74), Structural Engrs. No. Calif. (dir. 1969-71), Am. Concrete Inst. Home: 10320 Rolly Rd Los Altos CA 94022 Office: Engring Decision Analysis Co 10051 Pasadena Ave Cupertino CA 95014

SHARPES, DONALD KENNETH, graduate program educator; b. Yakima, Wash., Nov. 16, 1934; m. Linda Bamberg; June 27, 1964; children: Michael, Mary. AB, Gonzaga U., 1959, MA, 1961; MA, Stanford U., 1967; PhD, Ariz. State U., 1968. Research asst. Stanford U., Palo Alto, Calif., 1966-67; faculty assoc. Ariz. State U., Tempe, 1967-68; sr. program officer U.S. Office Edn., Washington, 1968-73; assoc. prof., dir. Ctr. for Internat. Edn. Va. Poly. Inst. and State U., Blacksburg, 1973-78, Weber State U., Ogden, Utah, 1978—, Utah State U., Ogden, 1978—; vis. fellow U. Sussex, Lewes, Eng., 1984-85. Author: (with F. English) Strategies for Differentiated Staffing, 1972; An Asian Enquiry, 1986; contbr. articles to profl. jours. Chmn. bd. dirs. Rocky Mountain Symphony Orch., Ogden, 1980-83. Sr. Fulbright scholar, Cyprus, 1985-86, Malaysia, 1976-77, Washington, 1976, 85. Club: Exchange (Ogden) (bd. dirs. 1982-84). Avocations: tennis, private pilot. Home: 4245 Edgehill Dr Ogden UT 84403 Office: Utah State U Sch Edn Ogden UT 84408

SHARPE-WORKER, ROBIN ANN, social worker; b. Santa Monica, Calif., Feb. 28, 1957; d. John Loftes and Marie Ann (Sartorio) Sharpe; m. John Stephen Worker. AA, Santa Ana Coll., 1980; BS in Social Work, Chapman Coll., 1982. Program asst. New Horizons Santa Ana (Calif.) Coll., 1978-81; social worker, discharge planner Chapman Hosp., Orange, Calif., 1981-82; hospice social worker Town & Country Home Nursing, Garden Grove, Calif., 1982-85; program coordinator ElderMed/United Western Med. Ctrs., Anaheim and Santa Ana, 1985—. Vol. Vols. in Probation, Orange, Calif., 1975-78; mem. Anaheim (Calif.) Chamber Health Services Com., 1986—; vol. English tchr. St. Norbert's Ch. for Vietnam Regugees, Orange, 1975-76; vol. counselor Orange Police Dept. Crisis Intervention, 1981-83. Mem. Nat. Assn. Social Workers, Oncology Social Workers Orange County, Sr. Round Table. Democrat. Avocations: art, music, hiking, skiing, camping. Office: ElderMed Western Med Ctr 1001 N Tustin Ave Santa Ana CA 92705

SHARPTON, THOMAS, physician; b. Augusta, Ga., July 15, 1949; s. Thomas and Elizabeth (Dozier) S. BA, Northwestern U., 1971; MS, Stanford U., 1973, MD, 1977. Intern Martinez (Calif.) VAMC, 1977-78, resident, 1978-80; mem. staff Kaiser Permanente Med. Group, Oakland, Calif., 1980—; cons. Berkeley (Calif.) Free Clinic, 1977—; chmn. peer review Kaiser Permanente Med. Group, Oakland, 1985-86. Mem. Alameda County Profl. Adv. Com., Oakland, 1984—, Alameda County AIDS Task Force, Oakland, 1985—. Mem. ACP, Mensa, Sigma Pi Sigma, Phi Beta Kappa. Democrat. Club: Phi Beta Kappa of No. Calif. Avocations: classical piano. Office: Kaiser PMG 280 W MacArthur Blvd Oakland CA 94611

SHAUDYS, VINCENT KIRKBRIDE, geography educator, academic administrator; b. Newtown, Pa., Oct. 2, 1927; s. Vincent P. and Anna (Kirkbride) S.; m. Jean Hazeltine, Sept. 1956; children: Frederick Ezra, Helen Marie. BA, Duke U., 1950; MA, Ohio State U., 1953, PhD, 1956. From asst. to assoc. prof. geography Mont. State U., Missoula, 1956-62, chmn. dept. geography, 1957-62; asst. to pres. Calif. State U., Hayward, 1963-67, prof. geography, 1963—, chmn. dept. geography, 1983—; Fulbright lectr. U. Dacca, Bangladesh, 1958-59. Served with USN, 1946-47. Named Man of Yr., South Bend (Wash.) C. of C., 1984. Mem. Assn. Am. Geographers, Assn. Pacific Coast Geographers, Calif. Geog. Soc., Soc. Wine Educators. Republican. Mem. Soc. of Friends. Lodge: Kiwanis. Office: Calif State U Dept Geography Environ Studies Hayward CA 94542

SHAUGHNESSY, DONALD JOSEPH, retired personal investor; b. Chgo., Mar. 11, 1932; s. Emmett Michael and Margaret Mary (Shaughnessy) S.; m. Mary Ann Wall, Feb. 11, 1956; children: Mary Rita, Donald Jr., Molly, Joseph, Margaret. BS, Loyola U., Chgo., 1953; MBA, U. Chgo., 1966. With Armour-Dial Inc., Chgo., 1955-66; pres. Armour-Dial Inc., Phoenix, 1966-78, Armour & Co., Phoenix, 1978-80; prin. Sawtooth Beverage Co., Ketchum, Idaho, 1981-85. Served with U.S. Army, 1953-55. Roman Catholic. Club: Tavern (Chgo.). Home: PO Box 142 Sun Valley ID 83353

SHAUGHNESSY, MICHAEL FRANCIS, psychology educator; b. N.Y.C., May 1, 1951; s. Daniel and Agnes (Antol) S.; m. Virginia Anne Shaughnessy, July 3, 1984; children: Lauri, Kaaren, Kurt, Travis. BA, Mercy Coll., Dobbs Ferry, N.Y.C., 1973; MEd, PhD, Bank Street Coll. Edn., 1976; MS, Coll. New Rochelle, 1981; DEd, U. Nebr., 1983. Cert. sch. psychologist. Counselor Children's Village, Dobbs Ferry, 1971-74; tchr. Sch. Sts. Peter and Paul, Bronx, N.Y., 1974-76; social worker Crystal Run Sch., Fallsburg, N.Y., 1976-80; instr. S.E. Community Coll., Lincoln, Nebr., 1980-83; asst. prof. psychology Eastern N.Mex. U., Portales, 1983—. Contbr. articles to profl. jours. Recipient Cooper Found. award Nebr. State Dept. Edn., 1982. Mem. Nat. Assn. Creative Children and Adults (pres. 1985-86), Rocky Mountain Psychol. Assn., Inst. Logotherapy. Lodge: Lions. Home: 23 Paseo Village Clovis NM 88101 Office: Eastern NMex U Dept Psychology Portales NM 88130

SHAVER, CHARLES MACK, park agency administrator; b. Kansas City, Mo., Feb. 25, 1943; s. Charles Howard and Lois Francis (McClain) S.; m. Janet C. Shaver, June 20, 1964; children: Lorine Lynn, Gari Jo. Student, Colo. State Coll., 1961-63; BS, Colo. State U., 1967; postgrad., Coll. of Sequoias, 1971. Park ranger Sequoia/King County Nat. Park, Three Rivers, Calif., 1967-72; sub-dist. ranger Lake Mead Nat. Recreation Assn., Boulder City, Nev., 1972-74; chief ranger Channal Islands Nat. Monument, Ventura, Calif., 1974-76; unit mgr. Glen Canyon Nat. Recreation Assn., Bullfrog, Utah, 1977-80; supt. NW Alaska areas Nat. Park Service, Kotzebue, Alaska, 1980—; comml. pilot Nat. Park Service, Kotzebue, 1981—, emergency med. technician, Nev., Utah, Calif., 1973-80, advanced scuba diver, Nev., Utah, Calif., Alaska, 1973—, prescribed fire mgr., Calif., Utah, Alaska, 1974—. Pilot Civil Air Patrol, Kotzebue, 1980—. Mem. Assn. Nat. Park Rangers, Xi Sigma Pi. Avocations: carpentry, hiking, flying, skiing. Home: PO Box 599 Kotzebue AK 99752

SHAVER, JAMES PORTER, educator; b. Wadena, Minn., Oct. 19, 1933. B.A., U. Wash., Seattle, 1955; M.A. in Teaching, Harvard U., 1957, Ed.D., 1961. Instr. Grad. Sch. Edn., Harvard U., 1961-62; mem. faculty Coll. Edn., Utah State U., Logan, 1962—; prof. edn. Coll. Edn., Utah State U., 1965—; chmn. Coll. Edn., Utah State U. (Bur. Research Services), 1965—, asso. dean research, 1978—; asso. prof. Ohio State U., 1964-65; adv. commn. Com. Youth Edn. for Citizenship, ABA, 1975-81; education task force Am. Hist. Assn.-Am. Polit. Sci. Assn. Project '87, 1981-84. Co-author: Teaching Public Issues in the High School, 1966, Facing Value Decisions: Rationale-building for Teachers, 1976, 2d edit., 1982; also others. Mem. Nat. Council Social Studies (pres. 1976), Am. Ednl. Research Assn., AAAS, AAUP, Am. Soc. Curriculum and Devel., Nat. Council Measurement in Edn., Assn. Supervision and Devel. Home: PO Box 176 Hyrum UT 84319 Office: Edn 412 UMC 28 Utah State U Logan UT 84322

SHAW, ALAN ERIC, state official, actor; b. Bklyn., Sept. 6, 1948; s. Eric Paul and Helen (Pochynok) S. A.A. cum laude, Skyline Coll., 1972; B.A. magna cum laude, San Francisco State U., 1975; M.B.A. magna cum laude, Golden Gate U., 1978. Draftsman, printer Coen Co., Burlingame, Calif., 1970-75; mgmt. intern HHS, San Francisco, 1975-78; sr. budget analyst Office Hearings and Appeals, Arlington, Va., 1978-80; fin. mgr. and adminstr. officer White House, Washington, 1980-84; assoc. dir. for adminstrn. Minerals Mgmt. Service, Los Angeles, 1985—; pvt. practice cons., San Francisco, 1977-78, Washington, 1978-80. Actor ABC film documentary: Saving of the President, 1982 (winner 11 maj. internat. awards); actor various theater and TV performances, 1979—. Mem. Republican Nat. Com., 1983. Served with U.S. Army, 1968-70, Vietnam. Decorated Vietnamese Cross of Gallantry with Palm, Bronze Star and other various decorations. Recipient Achievement award, Exec. Office of Pres., 1981, Presdl. letter of commendation, 1983. Mem. Assn. M.B.A. Execs., Golden Gate U. Alumni Assn., Am. Film Inst., Beta Gamma Sigma. Home: PO Box 17541, Los Angeles, CA 90017 Office: Minerals Mgmt Service, 1340 W 6th St, Suite 100, Los Angeles, CA 90017

SHAW, ARNOLD, author, composer, educator; b. N.Y.C., June 28, 1909; s. David and Sarah (Coller) S.; m. Ghita Milgrom; children—Mindy Sura, Elizabeth Hilda. M.A., Columbia, 1931. Exec. editor Musette Pubs., N.Y.C., 1941; dir. pub. relations, advt. Big Three Music Corp., 1944; editor Swank mag., 1945; dir. pub. relations, advt. Leeds Music Corp., 1946; v.p., gen. profl. mgr. Duchess Music Co., 1949, Hill & Range Songs, 1953, Edward B. Marks Music Corp., 1955-66; Lectr. Juilliard Sch. Music, 1945, New Sch., 1957; Fairleigh Dickinson U., 1964-65, U. Nev., Reno, U. Okla., 1971, U. Nev., Las Vegas, 1977—; Mem. nat. adv. bd. Fisk U. Inst. for Research in Black Music; dir. Popular Music Research Ctr. U. Nev., Las Vegas, 1985—. Pianist on radio, 1926; orch. leader, 1932; TV producer-narrator-writer-composer: series Curtain Time-Gt. Musicals; host: series Window on the Arts, 1972-73; author: Lingo of Tin Pan Alley, 1950, The Money Song, 1953, Belafonte, 1960, Sinatra: 20th Century Romantic, 1968, The Rock Revolution: What's Happening in Today's Music, 1969, The World of Soul, 1970, The Street that Never Slept: N.Y.'s Fabled 52d St, 1971, The Rockin' '50s, 1974, 2d edit. 1987, 52d St.: The Street of Jazz, 1977, Honkers and Shouters: The Golden Years of Rhythm & Blues, (ASCAP-Deems Taylor award), 1978, Music Scene, New Book of Knowledge Annuals, 1970-87, Sinatra: The Entertainer, 1982, Dictionary of American Pop/Rock, 1982 (Ambassador of Honor award English Speaking Union), Black Popular Music in America, 1986, The Jazz Age: Popular Music in the 1920's, 1987; Let's Dance: Popular Music in the 1930's; editor: Mathematical Basis of the Arts by Joseph Schillinger, 1948; co-editor: Schillinger System of Musical Composition, 1946; composer: Sing a Song of Americans, 1941, A Man Called Peter and Other Songs, 1956, Mobiles for Piano, 1966, Stabiles for Piano, 1968, Plabiles for Piano, 1971, One Finger Piano, Kiss Me Another, Night Lights, A Whirl of Waltzes for Piano, 1974, The Mod Moppet: 7 Nursery Rip-Offs for Piano, 1975, They Had a Dream: An American Musical Odyssey, 1975-76, The Bubble-Gum Waltzes, 1977, An American Sonata, 1978, Snapshots of Three Friends, 1980, The Lights of Christmas/Chanukah, 1980, Felicidad!, 1981, The Promise of Easter/Passover, 1981, The IASPM, 1986, Snapshot of Leonard, 1987. Bd. dirs. Popular Music Research Ctr. U. Nev.-Las Vegas, 1985—. Mem. Authors Guild, Am. Musicological Soc., ASCAP (Deems Taylor award 1968, 79), Am. Guild Authors and Composers, Nat. Acad. Rec. Arts and Scis., Nat. Soc. Lit. and The Arts, Nat. Music Tchrs. Assn., Nev. Music Tchrs. Assn. (Nev. Composer of Yr. award 1973), Las Vegas Music Tchrs. Assn. (pres. 1975-77), Sonneck Soc., Univ. Music Soc. of U. Nev. Las Vegas (pres. 1980), Internat. Assn. Study Popular Music (co-chmn. Am. br. 1984—). Address: 2288 Gabriel Dr Las Vegas NV 89119

SHAW, CARL BRADLEY, nondestructive testing engineer; b. Boston, Sept. 30, 1924; s. Nathan and Pauline Marian (Maldowsky) S.; m. Marian Adelia Jensen, Sept. 1952; children—Paul Bradley, Nathaniel Timothy, Twila Ethel Colby. Student U. Tex.-Galveston, 1950-51; B.S. in Radiation Physics, Dow Chem. Co. Coop. Program, Golden, Colo., 1956. Registered profl. engr., Calif. Sr. mfg. engr. Westinghouse Electric Co., Pitts., 1958-62; supr. quality assurance Stearns Roger Co., Denver, 1962-65; nat. mgr. Sperry Labs. Automation Industries, Boulder, Colo., 1965-67; mgr. nondestructive testing Hanford Engring. Lab., Richland, Wash., 1967-73; mgr. quality assurance Sandvik Spl. Metals, Finley, Wash., 1973-76; staff engr. Portland Gen. Electric Co., 1976—; utility indsl. advisor Electric Power Research Inst., Palo Alto, Calif., 1977-85 ; advisor welding com. Portland Community Coll., 1984—; cons. Oreg. Grad. Ctr., Beaverton, 1979—; dir. Internat. Pipeline Technologies, Inc., Portland. Contbr. articles to profl. jours. Patentee neutron camera. Precinct committeman, Washington County, Oreg., 1980—. Fulbright scholar, 1957. Fellow Am. Soc. Nondestructive Testing (chmn. tech. council 1970-71, pres., chmn. bd. 1974-76, Gold medal 1984); mem. ASTM, ASME, Am. Welding Soc. Baptist. Office: Portland Gen Electric Co SB-B 121 SW Salmon St Portland OR 97204

SHAW, CAROLE, editor in chief; b. Bklyn., Jan. 22, 1936; d. Sam and Betty (Neckin) Bergenthal; m. Ray Shaw, Dec. 27, 1957; children: Lori Eve Cohen, Victoria Lynn. BA, Hunter Coll., 1962. Owner The People's Choice, Los Angeles, 1975-79; founder, editor-in-chief BBW Mag., Encino, Calif., 1979—; creator BBW label clothing line. Author: Come Out, Come Out Wherever You Are, 1982; singer: Capitol Records, Hilton Records, Rama Records, Verve Records; TV appearance: Ed Sullivan, Steve Allen, Jack Paar, Colgate Comedy Hour, George Gobel Show. Avocations: piano, painting, swimming, travel. Home: 16756 Morrison St Encino CA 91316 Office: BBW Big Beautiful Woman Fashions for Large Size Woman 5535 Balboa BlvdSuite 214 Encino CA 91316

SHAW, CHARLES BERGMAN, JR., physicist; b. Dallas, June 7, 1927; s. Charles Bergman and Estelle (Goldstein) S.; m. Luchia Evelyn Alcott Powers, June 6, 1966; children: David Elliot, Suzanne Roberta. B.S., Calif. Inst. Tech., 1947; M.S., U. So. Calif., 1950, Ph.D., 1958. Research asst. Los Alamos Sci. Lab., 1949; physicist Nat. Bur. Standards, Corona, Calif., 1951, Lockheed Missile Systems Div., Van Nuys, Calif., 1954-56, Hughes Research Labs., Malibu, Calif., 1956-64, Electro-Optical Systems, Pasadena, Calif., 1964-66; group scientist Autonetics div. N.Am. Rockwell Corp., Anaheim, Calif., 1966-70; scientist Rockwell Internat. Sci. Ctr., Thousand Oaks, Calif., 1970-86, group leader, 1971-86; prin. scientist EG&G Idaho, Inc., Idaho Falls, 1986—; lab. assoc. physics U. So. Calif., 1947-49, lectr. math., 1951-54; vis. prof. physics Loyola U., Los Angeles, 1960; U.S. del. Internat. Inst. Welding. Contbr. articles to profl. jours.; research engring. physics and applied math. Served with USNR, 1945. Mem. Am. Phys. Soc., Soc. Indsl. and Applied Math., IEEE, Am. Welding Soc., Assocs. Calif. Inst. Tech., Sigma Xi. Club: Athenaeum. Office: PO Box 1625-ILF Idaho Falls ID 83415

SHAW, CHENG-MEI, pathology educator; b. Changhua, Republic of China (Taiwan), Oct. 24, 1926; came to U.S., 1954; s. Ching-Keng and Shok Chian S.; m. Shiu-Thi Koo, Nov. 2, 1955; children: Wen-Yee, Andrey, Robert, Katharyn. MD, Nat. Taiwan U., Taipei, Republic of China, 1950. Diplomate Am. Bd. Pathology, Am. Bd. Neurol. Surgery. Research instr. pathology U. Wash., Seattle, 1960-62, research asst. prof., 1962-64, asst. prof. pathology, 1964-68, assoc. prof., 1968-74, prof., 1974—. Contbr. articles to profl. jours. Mem. Internat. Acad. Pathology, Am. Assn. Neuropathologists, Am. Assn. Pathologists, Wash. State Med. Soc., King County Med. Soc. Home: 6541 29th NE Seattle WA 98115

SHAW, EDWARD ALLEN, association executive, consultant; b. Tucson, Ariz., Oct. 18, 1933; s. Allen A. and Zelma (Arootian) S.; m. DeeAnn Olson, Jan. 22, 1966; children: Leslie, Andrea. B.S., U. Calif.-Berkeley, 1955, M.B.A., 1958; Ph.D., UCLA, 1970. Human resources exec. System Devel. Corp., Santa Monica, Calif., 1959-66; human resources exec. Bank of Calif., San Francisco, 1966-67; asst. vice chancellor UCLA, 1967-80; human resources exec. TRW, Redondo Beach, Calif., 1980-81; chief exec. officer Am. Assn. Critical Care Nurses, Newport Beach, Calif., 1981-86; prin. mgmt. cons. Brennan-Thomsen Assocs., Newport Beach, 1986—; mgmt. cons. Edward A. Shaw Assocs., Los Angeles, Newport Beach, Calif., 1967—. Contbr. articles on mgmt. to profl. jours. Bd. dirs. Palisades Village Sch., Pacific Palisades, Calif., 1977-80; mem. adv. bd. Ctr. for Behavior Therapy, Beverly Hills, Calif., 1970-76; bd. dirs. Internat. Student Ctr., Los Angeles, 1974-80. Mem. Acad. Mgmt., Am. Psychol. Assn. Home: 1362 Morningside Dr Laguna Beach CA 92651 Office: Brennan-Thomsen Assocs 901 Dove St Newport Beach CA 92660

SHAW, FREDERIC JOHN, psychotherapist, lawyer; b. Bklyn., July 29, 1920; s. John Harris and Sybil (Galt) S.; divorced; children: John Harris, Elizabeth Shaw Buckley, Susan Marie McGury. BA, Bklyn. Coll., 1941; JD, NYU, 1954; MA, Fairleigh-Dickinson U., 1977; MSW, Ariz. State U., 1980; PhD in Clin. Psychology, Internat. U., 1983. Bar: N.Y., Ariz., U.S. Supreme Ct. Flight capt. Am. Airlines, N.Y.C., 1945-80, dir. flight adminstrn., 1954-61; lawyer N.Y.C. and Ariz., 1954—; pvt. practice psychotherapy Scottsdale, Ariz., 1972—; instr., psychotherapy Franciscan Renewal Ctr., Scottsdale, 1980—, resident Faculty Inst. Reality Therapy, 1981—; vis. lectr. Ariz. State U., Tempe, 1981—; adj. faculty Ottawa U., Phoenix, 1985—; pres., bd. dirs. Profl. Corp., Ariz., 1977—; ops. cons. Nat. Research Corp., Manhasset, N.Y., 1960-63. Author: (monograph) 50 Years After Kitty Hawk, 1954, (research study) Conciliation in Marriage, 1979. Counselor Sr. Citizens Ctr., Scottsdale, 1985—; sponsor Scottsdale Boys Club, 1983—. N.Y.U. scholar, 1952, 53, 54. Mem. Nat. Assn. Social Workers (cert. clin. social worker), Am. Assn. Marital and Family Therapy, Ariz. Soc. Clin. Social Work and Psychotherapy, Assn. Family Conciliation Cts., Allied Pilots Assn., Ariz. Bar Com. Law and Counseling, Am. Arbitration Assn. (div. mediator 1979—, mem. family dispute panel 1979—, cons. family law, domestic relations, 1980—), Airline Pilots Assn. (bd. dirs., rep. 1946-54), Phi Delta Phi. Lutheran. Lodge: Masons (32 degree). Avocations: internat. traveling, sailplane flying. Office: 7505 E Angus Dr Scottsdale AZ 85251

SHAW, GEORGE WILLIAM, II, microsystems analyst consultant, psychotherapist; b. Castro Valley Calif., Oct. 13, 1959; s. George William and Julia Anna (Holmes) S. AA in Data Processing with honors, Chabot Coll., 1981, AA in Bus. Adminstrn. with honors 1982. Asst. mgr., computer technician Computer Systems Unltd., San Lorenzo, Calif., 1976; warehouse mgr. Tech. Rep. Assocs./TRA Sales, Hayward, Calif., 1976-77; mgr. Byte Shop, Hayward, 1977-78, Mountain View, Calif., 1978; owner, mgr. Shaw Labs, Ltd., Hayward, 1977—; ptnr., mgr. Acropolis, Hayward, 1981-82; cons. microsystems analysis, systems and application programming, 1977—; psychotherapists, 1987—; tchr., speaker in field. Contbr. papers to profl. jours and confs.; inventor TaskForth computer lang. Mem. Forth Interest Group, Forth Internat. Standards Team (referee, publs. com. chmn. 1982—), IEEE, Mensa, Assn. Computing Machinery, Aircraft Owners and Pilots Assn., Sierra Club. Office: Shaw Labs 24301 Southland Dr Suite 216 Hayward CA 94545

SHAW, GHITA MILGROM, elementary school principal; b. N.Y.C., Dec. 25, 1929; d. Max and Getrude Etta (Lemberg) Milgrom; m. Arnold Shaw, May 18, 1959; 1 dau., Mindy Sura. B.S., U. Nev.-Las Vegas, 1971, M.Ed., 1974. Cert. spl. edn. tchr., sch. adminstr., Nev. Asst. to dir. N.Y. Herald Tribune Forum, N.Y. Herald Tribune, N.Y.C., 1950-52; asst. to dir. publicity Edward B. Marks Music Corp., N.Y.C., 1954-56; tchr. spl. edn. Clark County Sch. Dist., Las Vegas, Nev., 1972-75, coordinating cons., cons. in spl. edn., 1975-84, site adminstr. elem. summer sch., 1983-85; prin. Tom Williams Elem. Sch., North Las Vegas; guest lectr. U. Nev. Bd. dirs. Temple Beth Sholom Pre-Sch., Las Vegas, 1970-79; bd. dirs. Jewish Family Service Agy., 1982-85. Mem. Assn. Supervision and Curriculum Devel., Council Exceptional Children Assn. Children with Learning Disabilities (mem. Nev. profl. adv. bd.), Internat. Reading Council (corr. sec. Las Vegas council), Phi Delta Kappa, Kappa Delta Pi. Author: Special Education Dictionary for Regular Classroom Teachers and Parents, 1981; (with Cansdale and Reid) Guidelines for Elementary Special Education, 1975, Developing Prerequisite Skills, 1980. Home: 2288 Gabriel Dr Las Vegas NV 89109 Office: Tom Williams Elementary Sch 3000 E Tonopah Ave N Las Vegas NV 89030

SHAW, GLENN EDMOND, atmospheric scientist, educator; b. Butte, Mont., Dec. 5, 1938; s. Joseph E. and Camille C. (DeCelles) S.; m. Gladys Roberta Culver, May 27, 1957; children: Susan, Joseph, Raymond, Glenn Jr., Sarah. BS, Mont. State U., 1963; MS, U. So. Calif., 1965; PhD, U. Ariz., 1971. Research assoc. Argonne Labs., Idaho Falls, Idaho, 1962; Hughes fellow Hughes Aircraft Co., Inglewood, Calif., 1965-67; research asst. U. Ariz., Tucson, 1965-71; asst. prof. geophysics, Geophys. Inst. U. Alaska, Fairbanks, 1971-74, assoc. prof. geophysics, Geophys. Inst., 1974-81, prof. geophysics, Geophys. Inst., 1981—; sabbatical leave at World Radiation Ctr., Davos, Switzerland, 1977. Co-discoverer Arctic Haze; founding mem. Internat. Symposium Arctic Haze, 1985; contbr. numerous articles to profl. jours. Served with USN, 1956-63. Recipient Meritorious teaching award, U. Alaska Alumnus Assn., 1980. Mem. AAAS, Am. Geophys. Union, Am. Meteorol. Soc., Royal Instn., Phi Kappa Phi, Tau Beta Pi, Sigma Xi. Republican. Avocations: biogeochem. cycling, astronomy, exploring sci., history. Home: 3293 Edby Rd Fairbanks AK 99709 Office: Geophys Inst U Alaska Fairbanks AK 99707

SHAW, GRAHAM CAMPBELL, III, chemist; b. Price, Utah, Apr. 18, 1932; s. Graham Campbell Sr. and Sarah Irene (Fitt) S.; m. Doris Fay Marsh, Sept. 29, 1955; children: Pamela J., Gaylene D., Gary G., William C., Michael C., Suzette D. BS, Brigham Young U., 1954, MS, 1955. Research chemist Lawrence Radiation Lab., Livermore, Calif., 1957-61; chemist Thiokol Chem., Brigham City, Utah, 1961—; scientist assoc. Morton Thiokol Inc., Brigham City, 1969—. Contbr. articles to profl. publs.; inventor auto crash bags and propellant devel.; patentee in field. Cub scoutmaster, committeeman Boy Scouts Am., Garland, Utah, 1974-84; mem. sch. bd. com. Box Elder Sch. Dist., Brigham City, 1983-84. Served to capt. USAFR, 1955-73. Brigham Young U. fellow, 1953-55. Avocations: photography, electronics, carpentry, camping, hiking. Home: 936 S Main Garland UT 84312 Office: Morton Thiokol Inc Propellant Research Brigham City UT 84302

SHAW, HARLEY GENE, research biologist; b. Geary, Okla., Mar. 16, 1937; s. Walter David Shaw and Edith Mae (Folks) Saloum; m. Ella Jean Misenheimer, Dec. 23, 1957 (div. 1973); 1 child, Jean Elaine Shaw Debono; m. Patricia Mary Woodruff, Apr. 26, 1985. BS, U. Ariz., 1960; MS, U. Idaho, 1963. Research biologist Ariz. Game and Fish Dept., Phoenix, 1963—. Author: Mountain Lion Field Guide, 1980; contbr. articles to profl. jours. Mem. The Wildlife Soc. (cert.), Sigma Xi. Democrat. Avocations: flying, camping. Home and Office: PO Box 370 Chino Valley AZ 86323

SHAW, HENRY FRANCIS, geochemist; b. Boston, June 5, 1955; s. Henry Francis Jr. and Elizabeth (Cavaliere) S. BA in Geology, Amherst Coll., 1977; MS in Geology, Calif. Inst. Tech., 1978, PhD in Geology/Chemistry, 1984. Vis. assoc. Calif. Inst. Tech., Pasadena, 1983-84; postdoctoral fellow Lawrence Livermore (Calif.) Nat. Lab., 1983-85, geochemist, task leader, 1985—. Contbr. articles to profl. jours. Fellow Anthony Inst., Calif. Inst. Tech., 1977. Mem. Am. Mineral. Soc., Am. Geophys. Union, Am. Geochem. Soc., N.Y. Acad. Scis., Sigma Xi. Avocations: photography, mycology, travel, fine wine and dining. Office: Lawrence Livermore Nat Lab L-204 Livermore CA 94550

SHAW, JAMES RUSSELL, fire technology scientist; b. Jeffersonville, Ind., July 3, 1943; s. James Quinten and Vivian Elizabeth (Hall) S.; m. Gay Lee Hansen, Sept. 10, 1971; children: Nicole Jennifer and Ryan James. BA, Berea (Ky.) Coll., 1966; PhD, U. Utah, 1973; postgrad., U. Wash., 1972-74. Vis. instr. Bowling Green (Ohio) State U., 1971-72; instr. Olympic Coll., Bremerton, Wash., 1974-77; scientist Weyerhaeuser Co., Longview, Wash., 1977—. Mem. Am. Chem. Soc., Forest Products Research Soc., ASTM, Nat. Found. Applied Combustion Toxicology. Republican. Baptist. Home: 2 Northlake Pl Longview WA 98632 Office: Weyerhaeuser Co Fire Tech PO Box 188 Longview WA 98632

SHAW, JOHN FIRTH, orchestra administrator; b. Chesterfield, U.K., June 28, 1948; s. Jack Firth and Mary Stuart (MacPherson) S.; m. Julia Valette Phillips, Dec. 29, 1973; children—Mary Valette, Mark Firth, Andrew Nicholas. Licentiate Royal Acad. Music, 1968; grad. Royal Schs. of Music, 1970. Freelance musician, 1966-70; prin. musician Calgary Phil. Orch., 1970-77, asst. mgr., 1977-78, asst. gen. mgr., 1978-79, gen. mgr., 1979—. Bd. dirs. Calgary Philharm. Soc., 1974-77, Calgary Centre for Performing Arts, 1980-85. Mem. Assn. Can. Orchs. (dir. 1982-84, 86—). Office: Calgary Philharmonic, 205 8th Ave SW, Calgary, AB Canada T2G 0K9

SHAW, KEITH BRIAN, theatrical designer, writer; b. Hartford, Wis., Feb. 24, 1951; s. Harold Wayne and Nancy Ann (Piscetello) S.; m. Kathee Anne Tracy, Dec. 31, 1971; children: Christen Elizabeth, Christopher Brian. BS, U. Wis., LaCrosse, 1972; MFA, U. Okla., 1976. Resident designer Wis. Touring Theatre Co., LaCrosse, 1975-79; lectr. U. Wis., LaCrosse, 1976-79; resident designer Phoenix Little Theatre, 1979-81; asst. prof. dept. music Ariz. State U., Tempe, 1981-86; pres. Shaw Designs, Chandler, Ariz., 1985—; cons. Blue Star Childrens Products, Chandler, 1986—. Author: (playscript) Stormfield, 1974; designer (Opera for TV) Marriage of Figaro, 1983, Cunning Little Vixen, 1985; designer computer software. Avocations: fishing, reading, camping, films. Home and Office: 1605 W Stottler Dr Chandler AZ 85224

SHAW, LEONARD MELVIN, psychotherapist; b. Seattle, Aug. 23, 1935; s. Leonard Hilton Shaw and Fay Elizabeth (Inlow) Sweeney; m. Anne Sylvia Odion, Sept. 19, 1954 (div. Aug. 1979); children: Cynthia Gayle, Mathew Scott; m. Dana Grace Walton, Sept. 1986. BA, U. Wash., 1959, MSW, 1963. Psychotherapist Family Counseling Service, Seattle, 1963-66; pvt. practice psychotherapy Seattle, 1966—; faculty mem. Gestalt Inst., Frankfurt, Fed. Republic Germany, 1981—; cons. Fed. Offenders Rehab. Project, Fla., Ga., Tex., Colo., Wash., 1967-69; asst. dir. Rehab. Research Inst., Seattle, 1966-67; asst. prof. Shoreline Community Coll., Seattle, 1964-66. Mem. Nat. Assn. Social Workers (cert.). Avocation: basketball. Home and Office: 702 11th Ave E Seattle WA 98102

SHAW, LINDA, city executive. Mayor City of Lakewood, Colo. Office: Office of the Mayor 445 Allsion Pkwy Lakewood CO 80226 *

SHAW, MARK HOWARD, religious organization administrator; b. Albuquerque, Aug. 26, 1944; s. Brad Oliver and Barbara Rae (Mencke) S.; m. Ann Marie Brookreson, June 29, 1968 (div. 1976); adopted children: Daniel Paul, Kathleen Ann, Brian Andrew; m. Roslyn Jane Ashton, Oct. 9, 1976; children: Rebecca Rae, Amanda Leith. BA, U. N.Mex., 1967, JD, 1969. Law clk. to presiding justice N.Mex. Supreme Ct., Santa Fe, 1969-70; ptnr. Gallagher & Ruud, Albuquerque, 1970-74, Schmidt & Shaw, Albuquerque, 1974-75; sr. mem. Shaw, Thompson & Sullivan P.A., Albuquerque, 1975-82; chief exec. officer United Ch. Religious Sci. and Sci. Mind Publs., Los Angeles, 1982—. Trustee 1st Ch. Religious Sci., Albuquerque, 1974-77, pres. 1977; trustee Sandia Ch. Religious Sci., Albuquerque, 1980-82, pres. 1981-82; trustee United Ch. Religious Sci., Los Angeles, 1981-82, chmn. 1982; trustee Long Beach (Calif.) Ch. Religious Sci., 1983-86, chmn. 1983-86; chmn. Bernalillo County Bd. Ethics, Albuquerque, 1979-82. Served as sgt. USMCR, 1961-69. Mem. Pres.'s Assn., Am. Mgmt. Assn. Avocation: sailing. Home: 4039 Locust Ave Long Beach CA 90807 Office: United Ch Religious Sci 3251 W Sixth St Los Angeles CA 90020

SHAW, RALPH ROGER, venture capital and investment counselor; b. Bronx, N.Y., Aug. 23, 1938; s. Bernard and Lillian (Forest) S.; m. Elba Rosa Alicea, Mar. 14, 1970; children: Russell Robert, Lorraine Robin, Renee Leora. BBA in Pub. Acctg., Hofstra Coll., 1959; JD, NYU, 1965. Exec. v.p. Terracor, Salt Lake City, 1973-74; v.p. U.S. Nat. Bank, Portland, Oreg., 1974-80; pres. Shaw Mgmt. Co., Portland, Oreg., 1980—; gen. ptnr. Shaw Venture Ptnrs., Portland, Oreg., 1982—; bd. dirs. Costco Wholesale Corp., Seattle, Star Techs., Sterling, Va., Sentrol, Inc., Portland, Riedel Environment Tech., Portland. Mem. Oreg. Grad. Ctr's. Editorial Bd., 1985—. Trustees Portland Youth Philharm., 1979, Oreg. Episcopal Ch. Sch., Portland, 1978-83, Portland Ctr. Visual Arts, 1980-81, Oreg. Mus. Sci. Industry, Portland, 1979-83. Mem. Fin. Analysts' Fedn. (mem. ethics com. 1976—). Home: 3438 SW Brentwood Dr Portland OR 97207 Office: Shaw Mgmt Co 851 SW 6th Ave Suite 800 Portland OR 97204

SHAW, RICHARD JOSHUA, botany educator; b. Ogden, Utah, June 25, 1923; s. David M. and Gwendolyn (Williams) S.; m. Marion Abplanalp, June 27, 1947; children: Richard, Margaret, Sandra. BS, Utah State U., 1947, MS, 1950; PhD, Claremont (Calif.) Grad. Sch., 1961. Instr. botany Utah State U., Logan, 1950-53, asst. prof., 1953-58; instr. Occidental Coll., Los Angeles, 1958; assoc. prof. botany Utah State U., 1959-66, prof. botany, 1966—; dir. Intermountain Herbarium, Logan, 1984—. Author: Plants of

Yellowstone and Grand Teton, 1976, Field Guide to Vascular Plants of Grand Teton National Park, 1976, Manual of Vascular Plants of Cache and Rich Counties, Utah, 1983. Served with USN, 1942-45, PTO. Mem. Am. Soc. Plant Taxonomists, Am. Bot. Soc., Sigma Xi. Democrat. Avocations: photography, mountaineering. Office: Utah State U Dept Biology Logan UT 84322

SHAW, RICHARD LOUIS, remote sensing cons.; b. Champaign, Ill., Apr. 27, 1924; s. Scott Neuton and Helen Elizabeth (Breen) S.; B.S. in Geology, Colo. Sch. Mines, 1949; m. Raquel Ferreira Sanchez, June 13, 1969; children—Kieran, Liam. Sr. resident engr. ITT, Can., Europe, 1961-67; cons. Louis Berger, Inc., 1968-73; pres., owner Am. Infrared & Ground Radar Cons., Inc., Beaverton, Oreg., 1973—. Served with U.S. Army, 1942-45. Roman Catholic. Club: Elks. Contbr. tech. papers to profl. jours.; pub. Remote Sensing News (newsletter). Home: PO Box 1103 Beaverton OR 97005 Office: Am Infrared & Ground Radar Cons 14755 SW Carolwood Dr Beaverton OR 97007

SHAW, RICHARD MELVIN, gemologist, gold company executive; b. Los Angeles, Jan. 14, 1947; s. Melvin and Harriet Louise (Hammond) S.; m. Deanna Lee Revel, Mar. 9, 1968 (div. 1973); 1 child, Katharine Lillian; m. Janet Lynne Gribble, Dec. 31, 1981; 1 child, Jacquelyn Louise. Student Los Angeles Valley Coll.-Van Nuys, 1965-67; grad. Gemological Inst. Am., 1976. Design coordinator Foxy Jon's Smokehouse Cabins, Inc., Los Angeles, 1968-71; Pantera specialist, used car mgr. Bricker Lincoln-Mercury, Los Angeles, 1971-74; designer Melvin Shaw & Assos., Santa Monica, Calif., 1974-76; instr. Gemological Inst. Am., Santa Monica, 1976-79, dir. research and devel., 1979-82; ptnr., dir. sales and mktg. Northwest Gold Mktg., Woodland Hills, Calif., 1982-83; exec. v.p. Nat. Gold Distbr., Ltd., Canoga Park, Calif., 1983-86; pres., chief exec. officer Campbell Shaw, Inc., 1987—; founder, chief exec. officer Campbell-Shaw, Inc., Woodland Hills, 1986—. Developer, designer Diamond Pen instrument. Mem. Los Angeles County Mus. Alliance, Mineral. Soc. So. Calif., Nat. Assn. Underwater Instrs., Instrument Soc. Am.

SHAW, SANDRA CLEAVE, clinical social worker; b. Moscow, Idaho, Nov. 12, 1946; d. Walter R. and Joan Anderson (Ward) S.; m. John Robert Battista, Sept. 8, 1969 (div. Dec. 1984); children: Jennifer Cleave, Jessica Adagia. BA cum laude, Carleton Coll., 1968; MSW, U. Calif., Berkeley, 1973. Lic. clin. social worker. Pub. welfare caseworker Morris County Welfare Dept., Morristown, N.J., 1969; social systems analyst Stanford Research Inst., Menlo Park, Calif., 1970-71; psychiat. social work intern Yolo County Mental Health, Woodland, Calif., 1981-82; clin. social worker Family Physicians of Sacramento, 1983-85, EuResources, Sacramento, 1985—; counselor Interlogue, Palo Alto, Calif., 1971-74, Yolo County Battered Women's Ctr., Davis, Calif., 1979-81, Yolo County Rape Crisis Ctr., 1979-81; community educator, cons. Davis Women's Peer Counseling Ctr., 1980-85. Fellow Soc. Clin. Social Work; mem. Acad. Cert. Social Workers div. Nat. Assn. Social Workers (diplomat), Sacramento Area Career Women's Network, NOW, ACLU, Amnesty Internat. Democrat. Avocations: camping, backpacking, arts and crafts, hiking, reading. Home: 820 Cherry Ln Davis CA 95616 Office: EuResources A Psychol Corp 1451 River Park Dr Suite 285 Sacramento CA 95815

SHAW, SUSAN PFENNINGER, speech pathologist; b. Goliad, Tex., Sept. 23, 1950; d. Roland William and Loretta Marie (Eichman) Pfenninger. BS, Southwest Tex. State U., MEd. Lic. speech pathologist, Tex. Speech pathologist Snook (Tex.) Ind. Sch. Dist., 1976-77; instr., supr. Southwest Tex. State U., San Marcos, 1977-80, 84-85; speech pathologist Mishelle W. Jensen, Gainesville, Fla., 1980-82, Poudre Valley Hosp., Ft. Collins, Colo., 1982-84, 86—. Local Head Injury Support Group, Ft. Collins, 1986. Mem. Am. Speech Lang. Hearing Assn., Colo. Head Injury Found. Avocations: needle point, writing. Office: Poudre Valley Hosp LeMay St Fort Collins CO 80524

SHAWSTAD, RAYMOND VERNON, computer specialist; b. Brainerd, Minn., Mar. 17, 1931; stepson Klaas Ostendorf, s. Ruth Catherine Hammond; student West Coast U., 1960-62, UCLA Extension, 1966-81, Liberal Inst. Natural Sci. and Tech., 1973-83, Free Enterprise Inst., 1973-83. Salesman, Marshalltown, Iowa, 1952-53; asst. retail mgr. Gamble-Skogmo, Inc., Waverly, Iowa, 1953-54, retail mgr., Iowa Falls, 1954-57; sr. programmer County of San Bernardino (Calif.), 1958-64; info. systems cons. Sunkist Growers, Inc., Van Nuys, Calif., 1965-75, sr. systems programmer, 1975—; univ. extension instr. UCLA, 1980-81; propr., artificial intelligence researcher Lang. Products Co., Reseda, Calif., 1980—; cons., tchr. in field, 1961-63. Vol. VA Hosp., 1983—; bedside music therapist Vets, Adminstrn., 1983—; musician Project Caring, 1983—. Fellow Internat. Biographical Assn.; mem. Assn. Computing Machinery, Bus. Data Processing and Software Engring., Assn. Systems Mgmt., Data Processing Mgmt. Assn. (cert.), Los Angeles MVS User Group, Am. Def. Preparedness Assn., Res. Officers Assn., Jewish Vegetarian Soc., Aircraft Owners and Pilots Assn., Math. Assn. Am. Author numerous software programs; editor VM Notebook of GUIDE Internat. Corp., 1982—. Lodge: B'nai B'rith. Home: PO Box 551 Van Nuys CA 91408 Office: PO Box 1667 Reseda CA 91335

SHAY, LYNN KEITH, research oceanographer; b. Newton, N.J., July 22, 1954; s. Donald Jacob and Betty Jane (Hedricks) S.; m. Sally Ann Eiler, Sept. 10, 1977; children: Melissa Ann, Kimberly Marie. BS in Phys. Oceanography, Fla. Inst. Tech., 1976; postgrad., La. State U., 1978-82; MS in Phys. Oceanography, Naval Postgrad. Sch., 1983, postgrad., 1983—. Oceanographer Naval Oceanographic Office, Bay St. Louis, Mo., 1977-82; oceanographer Naval Postgrad. Sch., Monterey, Calif., 1982-84, research oceanographer, 1984—. Named Outstanding Employee U.S. Naval Oceanographic Office, 1979; Navy scholar U.S. Naval Oceanographic Office, 1982. Mem. Am. Geophys. Union, Am. Meteorol. Soc., Sigme Xi (assoc.). Avocations: softball, sailing, skiing. Home: 9640 Oracle Oak Pl Salinas CA 93907 Office: U S Naval Postgrad Sch Monterey CA 93943

SHAY, PETER YUNGCHING, investment company executive; b. Shanghai, China, July 17, 1934; came to U.S., 1974, naturalized, 1980; s. Chung Liu and Chi Chiou (Chen) S.; B.S., Cheng Kung U., 1958; M.S., Va. Poly. U., 1962; m. Jean Wu, Aug. 31, 1963; children—Shirley, Thomas, Dennis. Chief engr. Mayer Steel Pipe Mfg. Co., Tapei, Taiwan, 1963-65; v.p., plant mgr. Kuo Hwa Chem. Corp., Taiwan, 1965-77; pres. Golden Cosmos Investment Corp., Palos Verdes Estates, Calif., 1977—. Served to 2d lt. Engring. Corps., Republic of China, 1958-60.

SHAYNE, ALAN, TV production company executive; b. Boston; s. Ralph and Bertha S. Student public schs., Mass. V.p. creative affairs Warner Bros. Inc., 1974, pres. TV programming, 1976-86, producer, 1986—; v.p. talent CBS, 1975-76. Actor, 1943-60, casting dir., David Merrick Prodns., 1961-62, producer, Talent Assos., 1964-72, producer, creator, Snoop Sisters, TV series, 1973, House Without a Christmas Tree; and various spls., 1972; (Recipient Christopher award for House Without a Christmas Tree 1973). Office: Warner Bros Inc 4000 Warner Blvd Burbank CA 91522

SHEA, TIMOTHY PETER, podiatrist; b. San Diego, July 11, 1947; s. Peter E. and Patricia M. (White) S.; B.S. in Biology, U. San Francisco, 1969; D. Podiatric Medicine, Calif. Coll. Podiatric Medicine, 1973; m. Angela Marie Neville, Sept. 4, 1971; 1 son, Matthew Taylor. Resident in surgery Calif. Coll. Podiatric Medicine, 1973-75; practice podiatric medicine, San Francisco, 1976-78, Concord, Calif., 1979—; assoc. prof. podiatric medicine Calif. Coll. Podiatric Medicine, San Francisco, 1975-79, prof. podiatric surgery, 1975—, prof. podiatric medicine and surgery 1979—, chief of staff, dir. clinics Podiatric Med. Center, 1975-78; chief podiatric surgery Mt. Diable Hosp., Concord, 1984—; mem. med.-surg. staff Calif. Podiatry Hosp., San Francisco., Concord; mem. courtesy staff Port Hueneme Hosp., Ventura, Calif., John Muir Hosp., Walnut Creek, Calif.; mem. cons. staff Vallejo Gen. Hosp., Vallejo, Calif.; clin. instr. home care dept. U. Calif. Med. Center, San Francisco, 1974-78, guest lectr. podiatric medicine in primary care medicine, 1976—; podiatric cons. and guest speaker Over Easy, Sta. KQED-TV, 1977—; guest lectr. podiatric medicine local TV and radio programs, 1975—, Western Podiatry Congress, 1978-81; guest lectr. Am. Diabetes Assn., 1976, 77, 79, 81. Author: Over Easy Foot Care Book. Recipient Man of Yr. award Calif. Podiatry Student Assn., 1972; diplomate Am. Bd. Podiatric Surgery. Fellow Am. Foot Orthopedists, Am. Soc. Laser Medicine and Research; mem. Am. Public Health Assn., Am. Podiatry Assn. (lectr. convs. 1975, 81), Calif. Podiatry Assn., Am. Coll. Foot Surgeons (asso. mem.), Cousteau Soc., Condord C. of C., Alameda-Contra Costa Podiatry Soc., Calif. Coll. Podiatric Medicine Alumni Assn., Pi Omega Delta, Pi Delta, Omicron Theta Chi. Clubs: Kiwanis, Rotary. Home: 647 Augustine Ln Lafayette CA 94549 Office: Bacon-East Med Center 2425 East St Concord CA 94520

SHEAFOR, BRADFORD WARRING, social work educator; b. Topeka, Mar. 31, 1937; s. Leonard A. and Maria (Warring) S.; m. Nadine Louise Harrison, June 13, 1958; children: Christopher Warring, Perry Douglas, Brandon Andrew, Laura Kirsten. BS in Bus., U. Kans., 1959, MSW, 1961; PhD, U. Denver, 1971. Exec. dir. Topeka Welfare Planning Council, 1961-64; assoc. prof. social work, assoc. dean Sch. Social Welfare U. Kans., Lawrence, 1964-74; prof., interim dean Coll. Applied Human Scis. Colo. State U., Ft. Collins, 1974—; lectr. Fulbright Found., New Zealand, 1982; pres. Council on Social Work Edn., Washington, 1984-86. Co-author: Social Work: A Profession of Many Faces, 4th rev. edit., 1986; co-editor: Quality Field Instruction in Social Work, 1982. Pres. Ft. Collins United Way, 1981-82. Recipient Outstanding Service to Baccalaureate Social Work Edn. award Baccalaureate Program Dirs. Assn. ,1986, Outstanding Alumni award U. Kans., Lawrence, 1986. Mem. Nat. Assn. Social Work (classification study 1980—, pub. com. 1976-78), Council on Social Work Edn. (pres. 1984-86, sec. 1977-80, accreditation commn. 1975-78). Democrat. Episcopalian. Home: 2667 Shadow Mountain Dr Fort Collins CO 80525 Office: Colo State U 104 Gibbons Bldg Fort Collins CO 80523

SHEARER, RUTH EVELYN WHISLER (MRS. JACK ERIC SHEARER), molecular geneticist; b. Portland, Oreg., Mar. 23, 1930; d. Hugh Levan and Alice Gertrude (Gilstrap) Whisler; m. Jack Eric Shearer, Dec. 29, 1951; children: Daniel Jack, Alice Joy, Donald Hugh, James Edward. BS, Oreg. State U., 1953; MS, U. Wash., 1966, PhD in Genetics, 1969. Nat. Cancer Inst. postdoctoral fellow in pathology U. Wash., Seattle, 1969-71; head dept. molecular biology Pacific N.W. Research Found., Seattle, 1971-76; asst. mem. Fred Hutchinson Cancer Research Ctr., Seattle, 1973-76; program dir. cancer research Issaquah (Wash.) Health Research Inst., 1976-80, also bd. trustees, 1982-86; mem. sci. council Pacific Sci. Ctr., Seattle, 1972-77, cons. in genetic toxicology for pub. agys. and citizens' groups, 1977—. Contbr. articles to profl. jours. Bd. dirs. Seattle Country Day Sch., 1975-79, Issaquah Valley Community Services, 1986—; elected commr. King County Water and Sewer Dist. 82, Issaquah, 1981—. Nat. Cancer Inst. grantee, 1973-80; Damon Runyon Meml. Fund grantee for cancer research, 1971-74. Mem. AAAS, AAUW, Pacific N.W. Assn. Toxicologists, Phi Kappa Phi. Home and Office: 2017 E Beaver Lake Dr SE Issaquah WA 98027

SHEARER, STEVE LANCE, management company executive; b. Portland, Oreg., Feb. 11, 1947; s. Helmer Rasmus and Wilda Marie (Farmer) Johnson; m. Rose Marie Molling, July 15, 1965 (div. Nov. 1969); 1 child, Tammy Michelle; m. Vickie Lynn Bilton, Nov. 29, 1969; children: Sean Lance, Ryan Eugene, Dana Lynn. Student, San Jose State U., 1962-63, Harper Coll., 1972-73. Customer engr. Xerox Corp., Santa Monica, Calif., 1972-80, mgr. field service, 1980-83, system support engr., 1983-84; br. mgr. Wang Labs., Anaheim, Calif., 1984-85; gen. mgr. field ops. Advanced Image Systems, Glendale, Calif., 1985-86; western dist. mgr. ModComp, La Palma, Calif., 1986—. Instr. CPR ARC, Copley, Ohio, 1977. Served with USN, 1965-69. Mem. Mchts. and Mfrs. Assn. Republican. Baptist. Avocation: woodworking. Home: 1555 O'Mally Ave Upland CA 91786 Office: ModComp 1 Centerpointe Dr Suite 360 La Palma CA 90623-1089

SHEEHY, JOHN C., state supreme court justice; b. Butte, Mont., Jan. 27, 1918. Ed., Mont. Sch. Mines; LL.B., Mont. State U., 1943. Bar: Mont. 1943, U.S. Tax Ct. 1969. Chief dep. ins. commr. State of Mont., 1944-47; sole practice Billings, Mont., 1947-78; assoc. justice Mont. Supreme Ct., 1978—; mem. Mont. Ho. of Reps., 1959, 65, Mont. Senate, 1969. Mem. ABA, Yellowstone County Bar Assn. (pres. 1968-69), Mont. Bar Assn. (sec.-treas. 1953-58). Office: Supreme Court Justice Bldg 215 N Sanders St Helena MT 59620

SHEETS, JOHN WESLEY, JR., research scientist; b. Jacksonville, Fla., Sept. 17, 1953; s. John Wesley and Alice Marie (Hagen) S. BS in Zoology, U. Fla., 1975, MS in Materials Sci., 1978, PhD in Materials Sci., 1983. Grad. research asst. U. Fla., Gainesville, 1976-78, grad. research assoc., 1978-82; biomaterials engr. Intermedics Intraocular, Pasadena, Calif., 1982-84, mgr. biomaterials research, 1984-87; dir. research Pharmacia Intermedics Opthalmics, Pasadena, 1987—; lectr. Calif. State Poly. U., Pomona, 1984. Contbr. articles to profl. jours. Mem. AAAS, Soc. Plastics Engrs., Am. Chem. Soc., Soc. Biomaterials, Jaycees, Sigma Xi, Tau Beta Pi, Alpha Sigma Mu, Mensa. Club: So. Calif. Gator Club (Los Angeles). Avocations: weight tng., scuba diving, cooking. Home: 339 S Catalina #339 Pasadena CA 91106 Office: Pharmacia Intermedics Opthalmics 2650 E Foothills Blvd Pasadena CA 91107

SHEETS, PAYSON DANIEL, anthropology educator, medical researcher; b. Boulder, Colo., Jan. 1, 1944; s. Charles D. and Charlene E. (Spaulding) S.; m. Francine Mandel, Dec. 19, 1971; children: Kailah Mandel, Gabrielle Mandel. BA, U. Colo., 1967, MA, 1969; PhD, U. Pa., 1974. Asst. prof. anthropology Calif. State U., Fresno, 1972-74; assoc. prof. U. Colo., Boulder, 1974-86, prof., 1986—; pres. Fracture Mechanics Ltd., Boulder, 1980—. Author: Archaology and Volcanism in Central America, 1983; editor: Volcanic Activity and Human Ecology, 1979. Grantee NSF, 1973—, Nat. Geographic Soc., 1979, 84. Mem. AAAS, Soc. Am. Archeology, Am. Anthropol. Assn., Colo. Archeol. Soc. Home: 520 Marine Boulder CO 80309 Office: U Colo Dept Anthropology CB 233 Boulder CO 80309

SHEETS, SARA RAE, social worker; b. Manhattan, Kans., July 25, 1949; d. Norman Ray and Phyllis Doris (Van Meter) S.; m. Larry Merl Spier, Dec. 14, 1973; one child, Kari Kimberly. BA, U. Nebr., 1971, MSW, 1975. Registered clin. social worker, Oreg. Social worker U. Nebr., Lincoln, 1974-75, Portland (Oreg.) Pub. Schs., 1976-77, Dammasch State Hosp., Wilsonville, Oreg., 1977-84; social worker, pediatrics renal program Oreg. Health Scis. U., Portland, 1984—; allied health assoc. Cedar Hills Hosp., Portland, 1984—; mem. region 2 pediatrics end stage renal disease task force. Active Oreg. State Pub. Interest Research Group. Mem. Nat. Assn. Social Work. Democrat. Methodist. Avocations: karate, volleyball, vocal and instrumental music, pinochle. Office: Oreg Health Scis U 3181 SW Sam Jackson Park Rd Portland OR 97213

SHEFFIELD, WILLIAM JENNINGS, former governor of Alaska; b. Spokane, Wash., June 26, 1928; s. William J. and Hazel L. (Kraudelt) S. Student pub. schs., Silverdale, Wash. With service dept. Sears, Roebuck & Co., Seattle, 1951-53; with sales and service depts. Sears, Roebuck & Co., Anchorage, 1953-60; owner, mgr. Sheffield Hotels, Anchorage, 1960-82; gov. State of Alaska, Juneau, 1982-86; dir. Alaska Title Guaranty, Nat. Bank Alaska. Regent Alaska Pacific U.; past chmn. Easter Seal Telethon, Anchorage; past pres. March of Dimes, Anchorage; mem. planning commn. City of Anchorage, 1960-63. Served with U.S. Army, 1946-49. Mem. Alaska C. of C. (past pres.), Alaska Visitors Assn. (past pres.). Democrat. Presbyterian. Lodges: Lions, Elks. Office: Governor's Office State Capital PO Box A Juneau AK 99811

SHEFRIN, HAROLD (HERSH) MARVIN, economist, educator, consultant; b. Winnipeg, Man., Can., July 27, 1948; came to U.S., 1974, s. Samuel and Clara Ida (Danzker) S.; m. Arna Patricia Saper, June 28, 1970. B.Sc. with honors, U. Man., Winnipeg, 1970; M.Math., U. Waterloo, Can., 1971; Ph.D., London Sch. Econs., 1974. Asst. prof. econs. U. Rochester, N.Y., 1974-79; asst. prof. U. Santa Clara, Calif., 1979-80, assoc. prof., 1981, chmn. econs., 1983—, full prof., 1986—; cons. Nuclear Regulatory Commn., Livermore, Calif., 1979-82, Syntex Corp., Palo Alto, Calif., 1983—. Contbr. articles to profl. jours. Mem. Am. Econ. Assn., Econometric Soc., Western Econ. Assn. Jewish. Co-developed econ. theory of self control, behavioral finance; contbr. econ. theory of uncertainty, and consumer aggregation. Office: Santa Clara U Dept Econs Santa Clara CA 95053

SHEFVELAND, KENNETH MARTIN, data processing executive; b. Spokane, Wash., Dec. 3, 1947; s. Harvey Norman and Jane Marie (Stirn) S.; m. Janet Elaine Ebaugh, Sept. 16, 1973 (div. July 1975); m. Linda Louise Ernst, June 18, 1977; 1 stepchild, Henry Ludwig Freymueller IV. Student Everett Community Coll., 1966-67, U. Md., London, 1969-70; A.A., Shoreline Community Coll., 1973; B.B.A., U. Wash., 1975. Ops. supr. N.W. Data Systems, 1975-77; systems analyst Seafirst Bank, Seattle, 1977-78, prodn. control mgr., 1978-79, ops. support mgr., 1979-80, computer ops. v.p., mgr., 1980-85; dir. data processing services Pay 'n Save Corp., Seattle, 1985-86;dir. mgmt. info. techs. Seattle Standard Corp., 1986—. Vice chmn. registration com. Seafair Boat Club, Seattle, 1978; fire marshal Snohomish County Fire Protection Dist. 7, 1979 fire investigator Snohomish County Arson Task Force, Everett, Wash., 1984; dep. sheriff Snohomish County, 1984. Served with USAF, 1967-71. Recipient Firefighter of Yr. award Snohomish County Fire Protection Dist. 7, 1981, 85. Mem. Phi Theta Kappa, Alpha Kappa Psi. Congregationalist. Office: Seattle Standard Corp 1511 6th Ave Seattle WA 98101

SHEINBAUM, MARK L., data processing manager, consultant; b. N.Y.C., Sept. 4, 1949; s. Nathan and Florence (Rubenstein) S.; m. Nancy Karen Smith, Mar. 14, 1981; 1 child, Scott. Mem. Assn. for Computing Machinery. Home: 1723 Kansas St Redwood City CA 94061

SHEINBAUM, STANLEY K., economist; b. N.Y.C., June 12, 1920; m. Betty Warner, May 29, 1964; 4 children. AB in Far East History summma cum laude, Stanford U., 1949, postgrad., 1949-56. Mem. faculty dept. econs. Stanford (Calif.) U., 1950-53, Mich. State U., East Lansing, 1955-60, U. Calif., Santa Barbara, 1963. cons. in econs. Ency. Brit., 1961-64, Calif. State Commn. Manpower and Tech., 1063-65; campus dir. project U.S. Fgn. Aid Program, Mich. State U., 1955-59; cons. fiscal policy Govt. South Vietnam, Saigon, 1957-59; cons. on Vietnam Spl. Ops. Research Office, Am. U., Washington, 1958-59; economist fellow Ctr. for Study of Dem. Instns., Santa Barbara, 1960-70; econ. cons. Los Angeles, 1970—; v.p. Warner Ranch, Inc., Los Angeles, 1965-69, Warner Industries, Inc., Los Angeles, 1968-73,. Dem. candidate Congress from Santa Barbara, 1966-68; bd. govs. Calif. Dem. Council, 1968-72; del. Dem. Nat. Conv., 1968-72So. Calif. fin. chmn. McGovern presdl. campaign, 1972; exec. dir. Com. to Improve Tchr. Edn., Calif. Citizens Lobbying Effort, 1961-62; bd. dirs. Scenic Shoreline Preservation Conf., Santa Barbara, 1967—, Council on Econ. Priorities, N.Y.C., 1970-75, Com. for Pub. Justice, 1972—, Bill of Rights Found., N.Y., 1973—, Ctr. for Law in the Pub. Interest, Los Angeles, 1976—, Am. Jewish Com., Los Angeles, 1977—, People for the Am. Way, Washington, 1980—; organizer, coordinator legal def. team Pentagon Papers Trial, Los Angeles, 1971-73; mem. ACLU Nat. Adv. Council, N.Y.C., 1974—; chmn. bd. dirs. ACLU Found. So. Calif., Los Angeles, 1973—; founder, dir. Energy Action Com., Washington, 1975—; mem. ofcl. salaries authority City of Los Angeles, 1976-78; chmn. Clarence Darrow Found., 1977—; mem. Calif. Postsecondary Edn. Commn., 1978—; bd. dirs. Music Ctr. Dance Assn., Los Angeles, 1978-79, chmn. 1979—; trustee Fedn. Am. Scientists Fund, Washington, 1979—; mem. adv. bd. Breast Ctr., Valley Med. Ctr., Van Nuys, Calif., 1979; regent U. Calif., 1977—, now vice-chmn. Fellow Scientists Inst. for Pub. Info.; mem. Phi Beta Kappa, Phi Eta Sigma. Home: 345 N Rockingham Ave Los Angeles CA 90049

SHEINBERG, SIDNEY JAY, recreation and entertainment company executive; b. Corpus Christi, Tex., Jan. 14, 1935; s. Harry and Tillie (Grossman) S.; m. Lorraine Gottfried, Aug. 19, 1956; children: Jonathan J., William David. A.B., Columbia Coll., 1955; LL.B., Columbia U., 1958. Bar: Calif. 1958. Asso. in law UCLA Sch. Law, 1958-59; with MCA, Inc., Universal City, Calif., 1959—, pres. TV div., 1971-74, corp. exec. v.p., 1969-73, corp. pres., chief operating officer, 1973—. Mem. Assn. Motion Picture and Television Producers (chmn. bd.). Office: MCA Inc 100 Universal City Plaza Universal City CA 91608

SHEINFELD, DAVID I(AN), lawyer; b. Atlantic City, June 2, 1954; s. Irving and Lorna (Wesler) S.; married. B.S., Am. U., 1976; J.D., Calif. Western Sch. Law, 1980; postgrad So. Meth. U., 1976-77. Admitted to Calif. bar, 1980; asst. to legal counsel Zale Corp., Dallas, 1977; law clk. firm Augustine & Delafield, San Diego, 1978-79; mem. firm Delafield & Gattis, 1979, Oliver, Sullivan & Cummins, 1980; ptnr. firm Lazarian, Sivas, Martinez, Vanian & Sheinfeld, San Diego, 1981-85; of counsel Aylward, Kintz, Stiska, Wassenaar & Shannahan, 1985-86. Vol. Fedn. Jewish Agys. Mem. ABA, Calif. State Bar, San Diego County Bar Assn., San Diego Barristers. Author: The Insider's Guide to the Capitol, 1977; From Warsaw to Tenerife: Journal of Air Law and Commerce, 1980. Home: 13583 Caminito Carmel Del Mar CA 92014 Office: Aylward Kintz Stisko 550 West B St San Diego CA 92101

SHEINFELD, RICHARD BENNETT, plumbing manufacturing company executive; b. Boston, Jan. 5, 1936; s. Leonard and Sarah (Koffman) S.; B.S., Northeastern U., Boston, 1959; m. Leslie Felicia Fechtor, Nov. 5, 1955; children—William S.M., Terri Lynne. With Treasury Dept., Boston, 1959-60; exec. trainee L. Grossman & Sons, Boston, 1960-62; sales mgr. Glesby Bldg. Materials Co., Van Nuys, Calif., 1963-67; partner Cohart Products Co., mfrs. reps., 1968—, partner Western Am. Mfg. Inc., plumbing supplies, Valencia, Calif., 1974—, Pacific Am. Mfg. Inc., bath accessories, Valencia, 1981—, Hartco Indsl. Real Estate, 1970—; founder Top 10 Products Inc., Top 10 Mktg., Top 10 Properties. Served with Mass. N.G., 1954-62. Recipient various sales awards. Mem. Nat. Hardware Mfg. Assn., Am. Hardware Wholesales Assn., Calif. Retail Hardware Assn. (past v.p.), Nat. Hardware Assn. Republican. Jewish. Clubs: Mid Valley Racquetball and Athletic, Masons. Office: 25395 Rye Canyon Rd Valencia CA 91355

SHEKELL, LESLIE JUDSON, lawyer; b. Birdsville, Ky., Dec. 4, 1955; s. Billy Gene and Ouida Frances (Cress) S. BJ, Murray State U., 1973, BS, 1978; JD, Pepperdine U., 1982. Bar: Calif. 1983, U.S. Dist. Ct. (cen., so. dists.) Calif. 1983, U.S. Ct. Appeals (9th cir.) 1984. Assoc. Law Offices of Donald R. Hall, Santa Ana, Calif., 1983, Law Offices of John H. Wegge, Pasadena, Calif., 1984-85, Pachter, Gold & Schaffer, Los Angeles, 1985—. Mem. ABA, Fed. Bar Assn., Los Angeles County Bar Assn. Republican. Baptist. Avocations: auto racing, sports. Home: 847 Lincoln Blvd #F Santa Monica CA 90403 Office: Pachter Gold & Schaffer 5757 Wilshire Blvd Suite 600 Los Angeles CA 90036

SHELBY, NANCY JANE, research immunologist; b. Powell, Wyo., May 2, 1950; d. Samuel Grantham and Joyce (Churchill) S.; m. Paul E. Lofgreen, Sept. 6, 1969 (div. Mar. 1977); m. James Hosmer Martin, Feb. 21, 1981; children: Kassia Ann, Sara Nicole. Student, U. Utah, 1986—. Research specialist dept. surgery and pathology U. Utah, Salt Lake City, 1969-80, research assoc., 1985—, dir. surg. immunology dept. surgery, 1985—; research asst. U. Iowa, Iowa City, 1981-84. Contbr. numerous articles to profl. jours. Mem. AAAS, Internat. Transplantation Soc. Episcopalian. Avocation: painting. Office: Dept Surgery 50 N Med Dr Salt Lake City UT 84132

SHELDON, GERALD ERNEST, mechanicial engineer, acoustician; b. N.Y.C., July 1, 1942; s. John Gerald and Dorothy Louise (Smith) S.; m. Diane Christine Gould, June 12, 1965; children: Gerald E. Jr., David P. BA, U.S. Naval Acad., 1965; MS in Mech. Engring. and Operating Engr. in Ocean Engring., MIT, 1976. Commd. seaman USN, 1960, advanced through grades to comdr., 1979, ret., 1984; dir. ship silencing, sea systems command USN, Washington, 1981-84; dir. field support Tracor, Inc., San Diego, 1984—. Mem. Soc. Naval Architects and Marine Engrs., Naval Submarine League, Acoustical Soc. Am., Mensa, Triumph Sports Car Club, Sigma Xi. Republican. Avocation: restoring vintage Triumph automobiles. Home: 6712 Cibola Rd San Diego CA 92120 Office: Tracor Applied Scis Inc 9150 Chesapeake Dr San Diego CA 92123

SHELESNYAK, MOSES CHAIM, biodynamicist, physiologist; b. Chgo., June 6, 1909; s. Jonas and Fay (Leavitt) S.; m. Roslyn Benjamin, Jan. 28, 1942; children: Betty Jane (Mrs. Franz Sondheimer), Henry Lawrence. B.A., U. Wis., 1930; Ph.D. (U. fellow), Columbia, 1933; postgrad., Alliance Française, summer 1929, N.Y. Sch. Social Work, 1935-36. Instr. physiology, pharmacology Chgo. Med. Sch., 1935-36; lectr. human growth New Coll., Tchrs. Coll., Columbia, 1936-37; research asso. Mt. Sinai Hosp., N.Y.C., 1936-40; research asso. Friedsam fellow Beth Israel Hosp., N.Y.C., 1940-42; acting head biophysics br. U.S. Office Naval Research, Washington, 1946-47; head human ecology br. U.S. Office Naval Research, 1946-49; lectr. ecology

Johns Hopkins U., 1949-50; dir. Arctic Inst. N.Am., Balt.-Washington, 1949-50; sr. scientist Weizmann Inst. Sci., Rehovoth, Israel, 1950-58; asso. prof. Weizmann Inst. Sci., 1958-59, prof., 1959, head dept. biodynamics, 1960-68; asso. dir. Interdisciplinary Communications Program, Office Asst. Sec. Sci., Smithsonian Instn.-N.Y. Acad. Scis., 1967-68; exec. sec. Council Communication, 1968-72; dir. Interdisciplinary Communications Program, Smithsonian Instn., 1968-77, research asso., 1977—; dir. Internat. Program Population Analysis, 1972-77; pres., chmn. bd. Interdisciplinary Communication Assos., 1969-84; vis. lectr. geography McGill U., 1948; vis. prof. Coll. de France, 1960; mem. bd. human ecology arid zones UNESCO, 1954-72; research com. Internat. Planned Parenthood Fedn., 1959-72; selection and adv. com. Internat. Tng. Program Physiology Reprodn., Worcester, Mass., 1959-70; neuroendocrinology panel Interdisciplinary Brain Research Orgn., 1961—; expert adv. panel biology human reprodn. WHO, 1965-70; cons. Am. Physiol. Soc., 1977-83. Editor: Ovum Implantation, 1969, Growth of Population, 1969; co-editor: Frontiers in Teaching of Physiology: Computer Literacy and Simulation; editorial bd.: Contraception; contbr. articles to profl. jours. bd. dirs. Santa Ynez Valley Hosp., Solvang, Calif. Served to lt. comdr. USNR, 1942-46. Gen. Edn. Bd. fellow, 1936-38; Sir Simon Marks fellow Birmingham (Eng.) U., 1957-58; U. Research fellow Birmingham U., 1957-59. Fellow AAAS, Arctic Inst. N.Am., Eugenics Soc.; mem. Aerospace Med. Assn., AAUP, Israel, Am. chem. socs., Am. Inst. Biol. Sci., Am. Physiol. Soc. (dir. task force commemorative com., exec. editor The Physiology Tchr. 1977-83, exec. editor hist. sect. The Physiologist 1979-83), Am. Polar Soc., Am. Soc. Study Sterility, Animal Behavior Soc., Arctic Circle, Biochem. Soc. Israel, Brit. Glaciological Soc., Ecol. Soc. Am., Endocrine Soc. Am., Endocrine Soc. Israel, European Soc. Drug Toxicity, History Sci. Soc., Inst. Aero. Scis., Soc. Exptl. Biology and Medicine, Israel Fertility Soc., Israel Soc. Exptl. Biology and Medicine, Israel Soc. Undersea Exploration, N.Y. Acad. Scis., Internat. Soc. Research in Reprodn. (founding), Soc. Internat. Devel., Soc. Research Child Devel., Soc. Gen. Systems Research, Am. Acad. Polit. and Social Sci., Acad. Polit. Scis., Population Assn. Am., World Future Soc., Acad. Medicine Washington, Sigma Xi; fgn. mem. La Sociedad Chilena d'Obstetricia y Ginecologia, Societa Italiana per il progresso della zootecnica, Societe Royale Belge de Gynecologie et d'Obstetrique. Clubs: Cosmos (Washington); Explorers (N.Y.C.). Home: 674 Chalk Hill Rd Solvang CA 93463

SHELL, PHIL A., electronic engineer; b. Anaheim, Calif., June 30, 1962; s. John McClain and Kathleen Faye (Ruhs) S.; m. Linda Sue Wakup, Apr. 13, 1985; 1 child, Tiffany. BSEE, DeVry Inst. Tech., 1983. MTS engr. Hughes Aircraft Co., Los Angeles, 1983—. Home: 16809 Crenshaw Blvd Torrance CA 90504-2726 Office: Hughes Aircraft Co PO Box 92919 Space Communication Bldg S1/D347 Los Angeles CA 90009

SHELLHART, CHARLES GUY, real estate broker, rancher; b. Cheyenne, Wyo., Mar. 3, 1933; s. Roye Francis and Marguerite Ailene (Johnson) S.; m. Eloise E. Sandberg, May 3, 1953; children—Rodney Dean, Janet Lea. Grad. high sch., Cheyenne. Gen. agent Ry. Express, Denver, 1955-57; prin. Cross-Arrow Ranches, Albany County, Wyo., 1957—; broker, owner Laramie Peak Realty, Wheatland, Wyo., 1965—; treas. Wyo. Mut. Ins. Co., Wheatland, 1969—; dir. Norwest Bank, Wheatland. Pres., Platte County Meml. Hosp., Wheatland, 1979—; chmn. Platte County Planning Com., Wheatland, 1982—. Mem. Nat. Assn. Realtors, Wyo. Assn. Realtors, Nat. Inst. Farm and Land Brokers, Wyo. Stock Growers Assn., Laramie Peak Stock Growers, Nat. Assn. Real Estate Appraisers, Nat. Assn. Rev. Appraisers. Republican. Baptist. Clubs: Rock Lake Grange, North Albany. Lodges: Masons, Odd Fellows, Moose. Home: 246 Sybille Creek Rd Wheatland WY 82201 Office: Laramie Peak Realty 855 Gilchrist St Wheatland WY 82201

SHELTON, FRANK HARVEY, physicist; b. Flagstaff, Ariz., Oct. 5, 1924; s. Mark Harvey and Jessie Frankie (Foster) S.; m. Lorene Gregory, Dec. 29, 1947; children—Jill Jeannette, Joyce Lynn, Gwen Elaine. B.S., Calif. Inst. Tech., 1949, M.S., 1950, Ph.D., 1953. Mem. staff Sandia Corp., Albuquerque, 1952-55; tech. dir. Armed Forces Spl. Weapons Project, Washington, 1955-59; mem. staff Kaman Nuclear Corp., Colorado Springs, Colo., 1959-65; v.p., chief scientist Kaman Scis. Corp., Colorado Springs, 1965—. Author papers in field. Served to 2d lt. AUS, 1943-46. Fellow Am. Phys. Soc.; mem. Sigma Xi. Methodist. Club: Winter Night (Colorado Springs). Home: 1327 Culebra Ave Colorado Springs CO 80903 Office: Kaman Scis Corp 1500 Garden of Gods Rd Colorado Springs CO 80907

SHELTON, JOEL EDWARD, clinical psychologist, consultant; b. Havre, Mont., Feb. 7, 1928; s. John Granvil and Roselma Fahy (Ervin) S.; m. Maybelle Platzek, Dec. 17, 1949; 1 child, Sophia. AB, Chico (Calif.) State Coll., 1951; MA, Ohio State U., 1958, PhD, 1960. Psychologist Sutter County Schs., Yuba City, Calif., 1952-53; tchr., vice prin. Lassen View Sch., Los Molinos, Calif., 1953-55; tchr. S.W. Licking Schs., Pataskala, Ohio, 1955-56; child psychologist Franklin Village, Grove City, Ohio, 1957; clin. psychologist Marion (Ohio) Health Clinic, 1958; intern Children's Mental Health Ctr., Columbus, Ohio, 1958-59; acting chief research psychologist Children's Psychiat. Hosp., Columbus, 1959-60; cons. to supt. schs. Sacramento County, Calif., 1960-63; mem. faculty Sacramento State Coll., 1961-69; clin. psychologist DeWitt State Hosp., Auburn, Calif., 1965; exec. dir. Children's Ctr. Sacramento, Citrus Heights, Calif., 1965-66, Gold Bar Ranch, Garden Valley, Calif., 1964-72; clin. psychologist El Dorado County Mental Health Ctr., Placerville, Calif., 1968-70; clin. psychologist Butte County Mental Health Ctr., Chico, 1970—, dir. dept. consultation, edn. and community services, 1974-85, outpatient supr., 1985-86; mgmt. cons. 1972—; advisor to pres. Protaca Industries, Chico, 1974—; exec. sec. Protaca Agrl. Research, 1974—; small bus. cons., 1983—. Mem. Am. Pychol. Assn., Western Psychol. Assn. Home: 1845 Veatch St Oroville CA 95965 Office: Butte County Mental Health 18-C County Ctr Dr Oroville CA 95965

SHELTON, ROBERT CHARLES, electronics engineer; b. Los Angeles, July 31, 1934; s. Weir Mitchell and Martalena (Scavarda) S.; B.S. in Elec. Engring., Calif. State Poly. U., 1961; m. A. Corinne, May 28, 1962; 1 son, Kevin Lyle. Mgr. ops. Halcyon, Palo Alto, Calif., 1971-74; mgr. mfg. Programmed Power, Menlo Park, Calif., 1974-78; pres. Shelton Electronics, Menlo Park, 1976—. Bd. dirs. Herbert Hoover Boys Club, Menlo Park. Served with USN, 1952-56. Mem. IEEE, Profl. and Tech. Cons. Assn. Clubs: Elks (chmn. Palo Alto public relations); Rotary (bd. dirs., pres. 1981—) (Menlo Park). Research and publs. in telecommunications, short arc mercury lamps, frequency domain multiplexer, fixed head disc drive, disc. drive controller, digital Ion gauge controller, automatic call sequencer; patentee various crygenics and computer systems. Address: PO Box 2573 Menlo Park CA 94026 Office: 1259-351 El Camino Real Menlo Park CA 94025

SHELTON, ROXANNE BENAY, social worker; b. Des Moines, Dec. 26, 1938; d. Robert Bruce and Maxine Virginia (Seaton) S. BA, U. Mont., 1961; MSW, U. Denver, 1968; postgrad., U. Colo., Denver, 1981. Lic. social worker. Caseworker to lead supr. Adams County (Colo.) Dept. Social Services, Commerce City, 1962-70; team mgr. Adams Community Mental Health Ctr., Commerce City, 1970-80; clin. social worker Aurora (Colo.) Mental Health Ctr., 1981-83; pvt. practice social work Arvada and Denver, Colo., 1983—; field instr. Denver U. Grad. Sch. Social Work, 1972-79. V.p. bd. dirs. Alternatives to Family Violence, Commerce City, 1981-83; pres. bd. dirs. Park East Community Mental Health Ctr., Denver, 1982, 83. Mem. Nat. Assn. Social Workers (cert., mem. com. 1968—), Colo. Soc. Clin. Social Work (mem. com. 1985-86), Interdisciplinary Com. on Child Custody, Colo. Mental Health Assn., Colo. Assn. Community Mental Health Ctrs. and Clinics (exec. com. 1981, 82). Democrat. Club: Toastmasters. Avocations: skiing, mountaineering, music. Office: 7850 Vance Dr Suite 280 Arvada CO 80003

SHELTON, STEPHEN RALPH, association manager; b. Las Vegas, Nev., Nov. 16, 1937; s. Ralph Verl and Virginia (Golden) S.; m. Sally Anne Long, Dec. 4, 1977 (div. Apr. 1983). BS, Brigham Young U., 1961. Prodn. control mgr. Hercules Powder Co., Bacchus, Utah, 1961-63; mktg. rep. Sinclair Refining Co., Salt Lake City, 1963-66, Shell Oil Co., Santa Monica, Calif., 1966-70; exec. dir. So. Calif. Service Station Assn., Irvine, 1970—; cons. and guest lectr. U. So. Calif., Calif. Poly. Inst. and Japanese Gasoline Retailers, 1975—; pres. Pro-Calif. Inc., Irvine, 1980—. Author: Energy Crisis Reports, 1974; writer: (TV series) Family Devel., 1972; contbr. articles to profl. jours. Com. person Transportation Adv., Orange City, Calif., 1980, Fuel Shortage Contingency, Orange City, 1981. Served to sgt. U.S. Army, 1957-63. Mem. Am. Soc. Assn. Execs. Democrat. Avocations: scuba diving, travel. Office: So Calif Service Station Assn 16750 Hale Ave Irvine CA 92714

SHEN, NIEN-TSU, statistical quality control manager; b. Taipei, Taiwan, Nov. 25, 1953; came to U.S. 1975; s. Kung-Peh and Shiang-Ho (Tseng) S.; m. Ching-Chih Hstao, June 8, 1980; children—Elaine C. Hstao, Alexander P. Hstao. B.S., Nat. Taiwan U., Taipei, 1975; M.A., U. Calif.-Santa Barbara, 1976; Ph.D., Purdue U., 1982. Teaching asst. U. Calif.-Santa Barbara, 1975-78, Purdue U., West Lafayette, Ind., 1979-82; vis. lectr. U. Calif.-Davis, 1982-83; asst. prof. dept. decision scis. and computers Rider Coll., Lawrenceville, N.J., 1983-84; mgr. statistical quality control, Nat. Semiconductor Corp., 1984—. Mem. Am. Math. Soc., Math. Assn. Am., Assn. Computing Machinery, Omicron Delta Epsilon. Office: Nat Semiconductor 2900 Semiconductor Dr M/SD 1790 Santa Clara CA 95051

SHENENBERGER, TED WARREN, association executive, educator; b. Bremerton, Wash., Apr. 3, 1946; s. Ralph I. and Ruth (Rust) S.; m. Debra Ann Nelson, Sept. 1, 1984; 1 child, John Eric. AA, Olympic Coll., 1966; BS in Psychology, Wash. State U., 1968; MA in Edn., Ariz. State U., 1974. Cert. edn. dir. Instructional devel. Ariz. State U., Tempe, 1974-76; instructional media specialist Seattle Community Coll., 1976-78; edn. dir. Am. Compensation Assn., Scottsdale, Ariz., 1979—; faculty assoc. Ariz. State U., Tempe, 1974—; instr. Glendale (Ariz.) Community Coll., 1976. Author: Creative Photography, 1976; editor: Am. Compensation Assn. News, 1980-84. Served with USAF, 1968-72. Mem. Am. Soc. Assn. Execs. (gold circle award 1983, award of excellence 1984), Am. Soc. Tng. and Devel. Lutheran. Avocations: musician, composer. Office: Am Compensation Assn 6619 N Scottsdale Rd Scottsdale AZ 85253

SHENKER, MORRIS ABRAHAM, lawyer, hotel exec.; b. Kalius, Russia, Jan. 10, 1907; s. Abraham and Tziporah (Meshurith) S.; m. Lillian Rose Koplar, Dec. 23, 1939; children: Morris Arthur, Patricia Ann. A.B., St. Louis U., 1932; J.D., Washington U., St. Louis, 1932. Bar: Mo. 1932, U.S. Dist. Ct. 1936, U.S. Circuit Ct. Appeals 1939, U.S. Supreme Ct. 1940. Sole practice Las Vegas, 1975-84; chmn. bd. Dunes Hotel, Las Vegas, 1975—; parent corp. M & R Investment Corp., 1975-84, Vegas Village, Inc., 1975-79, Sierra Charter Corp., Los Angeles; chmn. exec. com. M & R Investment Corp., from 1975; bd. dirs. Continental Connector Corp., chmn. bd., 1977; pres., dir. I. J. K. Nev., Inc.; bd. dirs. Royal Bank of Mid-County, Aptos Seascape Inc.; v.p., dir. Nat. States Ins. Co., St. Louis; lectr. Washington U. Sch. Law, St. Louis U., Mo. U., Law Sci. Inst. of U. Tex.; mem. faculty Nat. Coll. Criminal Def. Lawyers and Public Defenders, 1972—, also regent; prof. charter session Nat. Coll., 1972. Contbr. articles to mags. and profl. jours. Pres., bd. dirs. Max and Thelma Manne Found., St. Louis, Morris and Lillian Shenker Found.; sec., bd. dirs. Sam and Janet Koplar Found.; bd. dirs. Israel Investors Corp., N.Y.C., Bd. Jewish Edn., 1954-64, Jewish Hosp. St. Louis, 1964-66, Am. Friends of Hebrew U., 1964—, Am. Friends of Tel Aviv U., 1965—, St. Louis Heart Assn., 1965-70, Council of Jewish Fedns. and Welfare Funds, Inc., 1969-73, Jewish Community Center Assn., 1970-75; hon. chmn. Nat. Meml. Day Observance for John F. Kennedy, Nov. 22, 1964; hon. bd. govs. Hebrew U. Jerusalem, 1973—; cons., adv. to Pres. John F. Kennedy, 1960, 62; Mo. coordinator Johnson-Humphrey campaign, 1964; former mem. Democratic Com. of Mo.; del. Dem. Nat. Conv., 1948, 52, 64, 68, former Democratic committeeman, mem. nat. exec. council Am. Jewish Com., bd. govs., 1970, mem. exec. com., 1963, 64; life mem. bd. dirs. Jewish Fedn. St. Louis, pres., 1966-68; chmn. St. Louis Commn. Crime and Law Enforcement, 1969-72; asso. chmn. bequest and legacy com. Nat. Jewish Hosp., 1964; mem. nat. cabinet United Jewish Appeal, 1970-73; del. 1st constituent assembly Jewish Agy. for Israel, 1971; mem. nat. steering com. Washington U., 1966-68; internat. bd. govs. Hebrew U., 1965-73; bd. govs. Devel. Corp. Israel, 1959-77, Child Center of Our Lady of Grace, 1964-68, Technion, 1970-80; trustee United Israel Appeal, Inc., 1966; mem. adv. bd. Am. Jewish Congress, 1964—; bd. overseers Jewish Theol. Sem. Am., 1964—; mem. cabinet Midwest Leadership Inst., United Jewish Appeal, 1969, mem. nat. cash com., 1971; mem. bd. nat. adv. council of Am. com. Weizmann Inst. Sci., 1967—; bd. regents Congregation of B'nai Amoona; mem. adv. bd. Am. Med. Center, 1953-66; mem. adv. com. United Way Las Vegas, 1976, chmn. corp. gifts, 1975. Recipient citation City of St. Louis March of Dimes Telethon, 1960; Merit award Cardinal Glennon Meml. Children's Hosp.; Louis Marshall award Jewish Theol. Sem. Am., 1963; Human Relations award St. Louis U., 1964; Disting. Service award Am. Jewish Com., 1965; Nat. award Sertoma; Merit award Louisville Bar Assn., 1965; Honor award Lawyers Assn. St. Louis, 1966; Disting. Alumni award Washington U., 1967; cert. of merit Nat. Coll. Criminal Def. Lawyers and Public Defenders, 1974; Guardian of Menorah award B'nai B'rith Found. U.S., 1975; David Ben-Gurion award Israel Bonds, 1975; Humanitarian award Nat. Jewish Hosp. and Research Center, 1977; Keser Torah award St. Louis Rabbinical Coll., 1979; Human Relations award Inst. Human Relations of Am. Jewish Com., 1979; sect. of Little City dedicated in his honor, 1979; award Boys' Clubs Am., 1980. Fellow Nat. Coll. Criminal Def. Lawyers and Public Defenders; mem. Am. Bar Assn., Nat. Assn. Def. Lawyers in Criminal Cases (dir. 1961—, pres. 1968), Lawyers Assn. St. Louis (v.p. 1958, 59), Mo. Bar Assn., Bar. Assn. St. Louis, Order of Coif, Alpha Kappa Psi.

SHENKER, M(ORRIS) ARTHUR, JR., hotel executive; b. St. Louis, June 24, 1947; s. Morris Arthur and Lillian R. (Koplar) S.; m. Deborah J. Hary, Dec. 27, 1970 (div.); 1 dau., Jennifer Ann. Student, Babson Inst.-Wellesley Coll., St. Louis U., U. Salford, Eng. Account exec. I.M. Simon Co., St. Louis, 1970-73; exec. v.p. Murietta (Calif.) Hot Springs, 1973-75; v.p. Dunes Hotels and Casinos Inc., Las Vegas, 1975-80, pres., 1980-83, sr. v.p., 1984—. Chmn. exec. com. Arthritis Found., from 1979; bd. dirs. Big Bros./Big Sisters, 1979, Boulder Dam Area council Boy Scouts Am., from 1979; mem. new leadership div. State of Israel Bonds, 1979; chmn. gifts com. Nev. U. Judaism, 1980; fund raiser Variety Club. Served with USCG, 1969. Named Man of Yr., City of Hope, 1982. Jewish. Club: Las Vegas Country. Office: Dunes Hotels & Casinos Inc 3650 Las Vegas Blvd S Las Vegas NV 89109

SHEN-MILLER, JANE, research plant physiologist, university administrator; b. Shanghai, China, Apr. 29, 1933; came to U.S., 1951; d. Yi and Yeening (In) Shen; m. J. William Schopf, Jan. 16, 1980. Student, Colo. A&M Coll., 1952; BS, Wash. State Coll., 1955; MS, Mich. State U., 1956, PhD, 1959. Postdoctoral fellow-botanist Argonne (Ill.) Nat. Lab., 1959-79; assoc. program dir. NSF, Washington, 1977-79; from assoc. research chemist to research chemist UCLA, 1981-84, research biologist, 1985—, asst. vice chancellor, research programs, 1985-86; vis. prof. U. Ill., Chgo., 1975; vis. research scholar The Agrl. U., Wageningen, The Netherlands, 1980-81; del. Am. Delegation of Botanist to People's Republic of China, 1978, U.S. Delegation to U.S.-Japan Seminar, Kyoto, 1972. Contbr. articles to profl. jours. NASA grantee, 1963-78; recipient travel awards NSF, NAS, NATO, Japan Sci. Council, Canberria (Australia) Nat. Acad. Sci., Swiss Nat. Sci. Found., others. Mem. AAAS, Am. Soc. Plant Physiologists (editorial bd. 1972-77), Assn. for Women in Sci. (exec.com. 1974), Am. Inst. Biol. Scis. (governing bd. 1973-80), Internat. Plant Growth Substance Assn., Common Cause, Nature Conservancy, Sierra Club. Avocations: art, pre-Cambrian bio-geology, sports, stamp collecting. Office: UCLA Dept Biology Hilgard Ave Los Angeles CA 90024

SHEP, ROBERT LEE, editor, publisher, textile book researcher; b. Los Angeles, Feb. 27, 1933; s. Milton and Ruth (Miller) Polen S. B.A., U. Calif.-Berkeley, 1955; student Royal Acad. Dramatic Art, London, 1956; B.Fgn. Trade, Am. Inst. Fgn. Trade, 1960. Asst. area mgr. fgn. dept. Max Factor, Hollywood, Calif., 1960-65; editor, pub. The Textile Booklist, Lopez Island, Wash., 1980-84; free-lance writer, book reviewer, library appraiser, book repairer. Author: Cleaning and Repairing Books, 1980, Cleaning and Care for Books, 1983, Bhutan - Fibre Forum, 1984; co-author: (annotated edit.) The Costume or Annals of Fashion, 1986; editor: The Handbook of Practical Cutting, 2d rev. edit., 1986; pub. Ladies' Guide to Needle Work, 1986. Mem. Costume Soc. (London), Costume Soc. Am. (bd. dirs. 1985-87), Costume Soc. Ont., Australian Costume and Textile Soc., Can. Costume and Archives of B.C. Home: Box C-20 Lopez Island WA 98261

SHEPARD, ALLAN GUY, state chief justice; b. Gardner, Mass., Dec. 18, 1922; s. Guy H. and May (Kendall) S.; m. Donna K. Soderlund, 1972; children: Lynn Kendall, Paul Vernon, Ann Kendall. Student, Boston U., 1942-43; B.S., U. Washington, 1948, J.D., 1951; LL.M., U. Va., 1984. Bar: Idaho 1951. Asst. atty. gen. Idaho, 1951-57; chief counsel Idaho Dept. Hwys., 1952-57; pvt. practice Boise, 1957-63; mem. Idaho Ho. of Reps. from Ada County, 1958-63; atty. gen. Idaho, 1963-69; justice Idaho Supreme Ct., 1969—, chief justice, 1974—; Mem. Western States Hwy. Policy Com., 1959-63. Mem. youth and govt. com. YMCA Idaho, 1953—, chmn., 1969; Adv. bd. Booth Meml. Hosp., Boise. Mem. Am., Idaho, 3d Dist. bar assns., Western Assn. Attys. Gen. (chmn. 1965-66), Nat. Assn. Attys. Gen. (pres. 1968), Delta Theta Phi. Republican. Episcopalian. Home: 4023 Del Monte St Boise ID 83704

SHEPARD, EARL ALDEN, government official; b. Aurora, Ill., Sept. 30, 1932; s. Ralph George and Marcia Louise (Phelps) S.; A.S. magna cum laude in Bus. Adminstrn. (fed. and local govt. employee scholar), Southeastern U., 1967, B.S. magna cum laude in Bus. Adminstrn., 1969; M.B.A. (Ammunition Procurement Supply Agy. fellow), U. Chgo., 1974; m. Carolyn Mae Borman, Sept. 1, 1959; 1 son, Ralph Lyle. Chief program budget div. U.S. Army Munitions Command. Joliet, Ill., 1971-73; comptroller, dir. adminstrn. U.S. Navy Pub. Works Center, Gt. Lakes, Ill., 1973-77; dep. comptroller U.S. Army Electronics Command/U.S. Army Communications Electronics Materiel Readiness Command, Ft. Monmouth, N.J., 1977-79; dir. resource mgmt., comptroller, dir. programs U.S. Army White Sands Missile Range, N.Mex., 1979—; adv. com. Rio Grande Bancshares/First Nat. Bank of Dona Ana County, 1983-84. Bd. govs., Southeastern Univ. Ednl. Found., 1969-71; chmn. fin. com. No. Va. Assn. for Children with Learning Disabilities, 1966-67, treas., 1968-70; pres. West Long Branch (N.J.) Sports Assn., 1979. Mem. Assn. U.S. Army, Am. Soc. Mil. Comptrollers. Assn. Govt. Accts., Fed. Mgrs. Assn. Republican. Home: 2712 Topley Ave Las Cruces NM 88005 Office: Attention: STEWS-RM White Sands Missile Range NM 88002

SHEPARD, JOSEPH WILLIAM, physical chemist, consultant; b. St. Paul, Aug. 16, 1922; s. Joseph N. and Margaret (Hinderschied) S.; m. Elfreda Lemiesz, July3, 1943; children: Mark W., Margaret M., David A., Janet C. Dir. imaging research Cen. Research Labs. 3M Co., St. Paul, 1963-67, tech. dir. Micrographic Products div., 1967-75, tech. dir. copying div., 1975-78, tech. dir. Micrographic Systems div., 1978-80, v.p., gen. mgr. Engring. Systems div., 1980-85; cons., gen. ptnr. JES Assocs., Albuquerque, 1986—. Served with USN, 1943-45, PTO. Mem. AAAS, Am. Chem. Soc., Soc. Photographic Scientists and Engrs., Inf. Mgmt. Congress, 3M Carleton Soc. (tech. council 1977), Sigma Xi, Phi Kappa Phi, Phi Lambda Upsilon.

SHEPHERD, GEORGE WILLIAM, JR., political science educator; b. Shanghai, People's Republic of China, Oct. 26, 1926; came to U.S., 1936; s. George William and Clara Sargent Shepherd; m. Shirley Brower, June 1948; children: Mary-Claire, Holland, Sharon, Harold. BA, U. Mich., 1949; PhD, London Sch. Econs. and Polit. Sci., 1952; DDL, Mercy Coll., 1986. Advisor African Farmers Coop., Uganda, 1953-54; exec. sec. Am. Com. on Africa, N.Y.C., 1954—; lectr. polit. sci. Bklyn. Coll., 1956-58; asst. prof. polit. sci. St. Olaf Coll., Minn., 1958-60; asst. prof. internat. relations U. Denver, 1961-63, prof. internat. relations, 1965—; research assoc., Unitar, N.Y.C., 1972; lectr. USIA, Africa, 1979; pres. Africa Today Assocs., Denver and N.Y.C., 1985—. Author: They Wait in Darkness, 1956, Politics of African Nationalism, 1962, Nonaligned Black Africa, 1970, Anti-Apartheid, 1977, Human Rights in the Third World, 1985, The Trampled Grass, 1987; editor: Africa Today mag., 1966—. Active Colo. Open Space Council, Am. Friends Service Com., Indo-Am. Task Force on the Indian Ocean, Washington, 1984; mem. adv. council Am. Com. Africa, 1958—; chmn. internat. relations com. Council for Social Action United Ch. of Christ., 1970-72. Served with mil. communication, U.S., 1944-45. Fellow Unitar, 1973, Ford Found., 1973; grantee Soc. Sci. Research Council, 1984. Fellow: African Studies Assn., Internat. Studies Assn. Independent democrat. Congregationalist. Club: Tennis and Racquet (Denver). Avocations: tennis, hiking, sailing. Home: 4838 N Lariat Dr Castle Rock CO 80104 Office: U Denver Grad Sch Internat Studies Univ Park Denver CO 80208

SHEPHERD, GILBERT B., computer company executive; b. Quincy, Mass., Nov. 14, 1937; s. James Gilbert and Muriel (Bowen) Freer; children—Darlene, Lynette, Denise. Site engr. Philco Ford Corp., 1963-65; field engr. Gen. Electric Corp., Kannapolis, N.C., 1965-67, Sci. Data Systems subs. Xerox Corp., Beltsville, Md., 1967-68, sr. sales rep., 1968-69; dist. sales mgr. Varian Data Machines, Cheverly, Md., 1969-71, Caelus Memories, 1971-72, OEM Peripheral div. Control Data Corp., Sunnyvale, Calif., 1974-80; regional sales mgr. Decision Inc. subs. Ball Computer Co., Oakland, Calif., 1972-74; regional sales mgr., acting dir. Wangco div. Perkin Elmer, Santa Clara, Calif., 1980-81; v.p. mktg. Cynthia Peripheral Corp. subs. Cii Honeywell Bull Corp., Palo Alto, Calif., 1981-82; chmn., chief exec. officer, chief fin. officer Applied Intelligence Corp., Mountain View, Calif., 1982-86; mgmt. cons. to image processing, storage/retrieval cos., 1986—. Contbr. articles to tech. jours. Served with USAF, 1955-63. Mem. Computer Soc. of IEEE. Home: 1360 Fairway Dr Los Altos CA 94022 Office: Applied Intelligence Inc 1043 Stierlin Rd Mountain View CA 94043

SHEPPARD, ASHER RAPHAEL, neurophysiologist; b. N.Y.C., Apr. 4, 1943; s. Abraham Issac and Ethel Ruth (Kimbrig) S.; m. Ann Schlesinger, June 27, 1965; children: Eva, Julia, Abraham. BS, Union Coll., Schenectady, N.Y., 1963; MS, SUNY, Buffalo, 1964, PhD, 1974. Nat. Inst. Environ. Health Scis. fellow NYU Med. Ctr., 1974-76; postdoctoral fellow UCLA Brain Research Inst., 1976-78; research physicist J.L. Pettis Meml. VA Hosp., Loma Linda, Calif., 1978—; asst. research prof. Loma Linda U., 1979—; sci. advisor Am. Inst. Biol. Scis., Mont. Dept. Natural Resources, WHO. Author: Biological Effects of Electric and Magnetic Fields of Extremely Low Frequency; contbr. articles to profl. jours. Mem. Am. Phys. Soc., Soc. Neurosci., AAAS, Bioelectromagnetics Soc. (mem. editorial bd. 1984—, bd. dirs. 1986—). Office: J L Pettis Meml VA Hosp 11201 Benton St Loma Linda CA 92357

SHEPPERD, WAYNE DELBERT, research forester; b. Sterling, Colo., June 28, 1947; s. Delbert Maine and Berneice Alvyra (Ficken) S.; m. Colleen Sue Billings, Apr. 4, 1970; children: Ryan, Marnie. BS, Colo. State U., 1970, MS, 1974. Research technician U.S. Forest Service, Ft. Collins, Colo., 1970-76; silviculturist U.S. Forest Service, Monte Vista, Colo., 1976-78; research forester U.S. Forest Service, Ft. Collins, 1978—; mem. affiliate faculty Colo. State U., Ft. Collins, 1978—. Authr slide/tape series Silviculture of Species in Rockies (USDA cash award 1985); contbr. articles to profl. jours., chpts. to books. Recipient Courageous Conduct in an Emergency award USDA Forest Service, Ft. Collins, 1975. Mem. Soc. Am. Foresters, Sigma Xi, Xi Sigma Pi. Congregationalist. Office: Rocky Mountain Forest Range Experiment Sta 240 W Prospect Fort Collins CO 80526

SHERER, DAVID MATTHEW, clinical pathologist, laboratory director; b. N.Y.C., Mar. 19, 1943; s. Leslie and Fay (Spiwak) S.; m. Barbara Rose Franco, Feb. 14, 1976; children: Robert H., Charles I., Margaret. BS in Math. and History, NYU, 1963; MD, SUNY, Buffalo, 1969. Diplomate Am. Bd. Pathology. Intern U. Calif., San Diego, 1969-70; resident in viral oncology NIH, Bethesda, Md., 1970-72; resident, chief resident clin. pathology Bellevue Med. Ctr., NYU, N.Y.C., 1972-74; staff physician Schaefer Brewery, Bklyn., 1973-74; dir. clin. labs. Group Health Coop. of Puget Sound, Seattle, 1974—; tchr. math. N.Y.C. Sch. System, 1962-65; mem. clin. adv. bd. Shoreline Community Coll., Seattle, 1976—; chmn. infection and control com. Group Health Coop. of Puget Sound, 1976-78, transfusion com., 1979—, staff pension com., 1975—, mem. deferred compensation com., 1976—, lab. com., 1974—, info. policy com., 1978-82. Mem. Town of Clyde Hill (Wash.) Community Activities Group, 1984—; bd. dirs. Bellevue (Wash.) and Sun Valley (Idaho) Homeowners Assns., Group Health Credit Union, 1987—; choir dir. Herzl Ner Tamid Conservative Congregation, Mercer Island, 1976-82, 84—; tenor Seattle Opera Auxiliary Chorus, 1976-85, Seattle Chorale, 1975-78; patroller Snoqualmie Summit Ski Patrol, Snoqualmie, Wash., 1975-78, 85—. Served to lt. comdr. USPHS, 1970-72. Recipient Winthrop Ranney award NYU, 1972. Fellow Am. Soc. Clin. Pathology, Am. Assn. Blood Banks; mem. A.P.P.L.E. Coop. Jewish. Club: Glendale Country (bd. dirs.) (Bellevue). Avocations: reading, gardening, skiing, singing, computers. Home: 1900 94th Ave NE Clyde Hill WA 98004 Office: Group Health Coop Puget Sound 200 15th Ave Seattle WA 98112

SHERER, KEITH ROGER, civil engineer; b. Klamath Falls, Oreg., Oct. 8, 1935; m. Carolee Davidson, 1956; children: Diane, Keith Jr., Julie. BSCE,

Oreg. State U., 1960; MS in Environ. Scis., U. Okla., 1971. Registered profl. engr.; diplomate Am. Acad. Environ. Engrs. Environ. engr. Oreg. State U., Medford, 1960-63; field engr. USPHS, Oreg. and Idaho, 1964-67; staff engr. USPHS, Okla., 1967-70; dist. engr. USPHS, Ariz., 1970-77; engr. dir. USPHS, Washington, 1978-82; cons. Wash-Aid, 1982-84, U.S. Peace Corps, 1982-84, CRS, Addis Ababa, Ethiopia, 1985-86. Recipient Meritorious Service award USPHS, 1982. Mem. NSPE, Am. Acad. Environ. Engrs., Pub. Health Service Commd. Officers Assn., Pan Am. Health Assn., Jaycees Internat. Republican. Episcopalian. Club: Desert Trails. Lodge: Elks. Avocations: hiking, rafting. Office: Keith Sherer and Assocs Box 346 Madras OR 97741

SHERER, TIM JOHN, financial consultant; b. Saratoga, Calif., Mar. 6, 1948; s. James E. and Reva A. Sherer; B.B.A. cum laude, Ohio U., 1970; M.B.A., U. Santa Clara, 1979; m. Theresa Marie, Apr. 6, 1974. Mgr. Provident Mut. Ins. Co., Campbell, Calif., 1979—; pres. Fin. Clinic, Inc., FCI Investment Adv. Inc. Bd. dirs. U. Santa Clara Grad. Sch., 1979-82. Mem. Nat. Assn. Life Underwriters, San Jose Assn. Life Underwriters (dir. 1984—, v.p. fin. 1986—), San Jose Gen. Agts. and Mgrs. Assn. (dir. 1983—, pres. elect 1986), Nat. Assn. Securities Dealers, Million Dollar Round Table. Served as capt. USMC, 1970-76. Home: 15172 Peach Hill Rd Saratoga CA 95070 Office: Provident Mutual Ins Co 2105 S Bascom Ave Suite 350 Campbell CA 95008

SHERICK, JOHN (JACK) MATTHEW, utilities company executive; b. Butte, Mont., May 9, 1941; s. Mark William and Victoria (Bugni) S.; m. Diane Harriet Meyer, Dec. 28, 1963; children: Michael, Vicki, Heidi. BSChemE, Mont. State U., 1963; MBA, U. Idaho, 1970. ETR reactor engr. Phillips Petroleum Co., Idaho Falls, Idaho, 1963-66; ETR asst. shift supr. Idaho Nuclear Corp., Idaho Falls, 1966-71; ETR shift supr. Aerojet Nuclear Corp., Idaho Falls, 1971-76; ETR experiment br. mgr. EG&G Idaho Inc., Idaho Falls, 1976-79; mgr. projects and engring. div. Mountain States Energy Inc., Butte, 1979-83, pres., gen. mgr., 1983—, also bd. dirs.; bd. dirs. MHD Devel. Corp., Butte. Scoutmaster Boy Scouts Am., Butte, 1972—; bd. dirs. Jr. Achievement, Butte, 1984—, Butte-Silver Bow C. of C., 1986—; loaned exec. Butte-Silver Bow United Way, 1983; pres. Butte High Athletic Council, 1981-82. Recipient Disting. Eagle Scout award Boy Scouts Am., 1986. Mem. Am. Nuclear Soc. Roman Catholic. Club: Butte Exchange. Home: 122 Rampart Dr Butte MT 59701 Office: Mountain State Energy Inc PO Box 4078 Butte MT 59702

SHERIDAN, CHRISTOPHER FREDERICK, labor relations executive; b. Syracuse, N.Y., June 7, 1953; s. Frederick John and Patricia Ann (McCormick) S.; m. Diane Marie Harman, Dec. 31, 1977; children: Ryan, Kelly. BS in Indsl. Relations, LeMoyne Coll., 1975. Employee relations trainee Anaconda Co., Buffalo, 1975-76; employee relations rep. Anaconda Co., Los Angeles, 1976-78; personnel mgr. HITCO, Gardena, Calif., 1978-80; labor relations rep. Miller Brewing Co., Fulton, N.Y., 1980-82; labor relations mgr. Miller Brewing Co., Los Angeles, 1982—. Mem. Indsl. Relations Research Assn., Am. Soc. Personnel Adminstrn., Soc. Profls. Dispute Resolution. Roman Catholic. Avocations: golf, basketball, reading, music, art. Office: Miller Brewing Co 15801 E First St Irwindale CA 91706

SHERIDAN, CLAIRE EILEEN, dance educator, choreographer; b. Oakland, Calif., July 25, 1954; d. Thad Stephens Sheridan Jr. and Sally (Taylor) Sheridan-Bird. AA, Diablo Valley Coll., 1974; BA, St. Mary's Coll., Moraga, Calif., 1978, MA, 1986. Tchr., choreographer Athenian Sch., Danville, Calif., 1977—; lectr., choreographer St. Mary's Coll., Moraga, Calif., 1977—; guest tchr., dir. summer dance programs St. Anne's Sch., Windermere, Eng., 1979—, The Lawrence Sch., Sanawar, India, 1984, Schule Schloss Salem, Fed. Republic Germany, 1981-83, Aiglon Coll., Chesieres-Villars, Switzerland, 1983-84, Sundai Gakuen Sch., Tokyo, 1985-86, Homerton Coll. Cambridge U., England, 1987—. Office: St Mary's Coll Moraga CA 94575

SHERIDAN, DONALD WILLIAM, electrical engineer; b. Devils Lake, N.D., May 16, 1932; s. Richard William and Emily Ida (Utzerath) S.; m. Jane Patricia Shatto, Sept. 25, 1955 (div. Oct. 65); children: Lisa Ellyn, Lynne Patrice, Robert William, Stephen Donald; m. Jeannette Anniece Lowe, Nov. 14, 1965; 1 child, Tiffany Elizabeth. BSEE, U. N.D., 1955; postgrad., U. Ala., 1959-60. Project engr. NASA, Huntsville, Ala., 1961-73; gen. contractor Sheridan Constrn. Co., Lake Arrowhead, Calif., 1978-83; engring. proposal mgr. Northrop, Pico Rivera, Calif., 1983—. V.p. Huntsville (Ala.) Jaycees, 1960; bd. dirs. Woodbridge Archtl. Commn., Irvine, Calif., 1984—. Served to capt. U.S. Army, 1955-58. Recipient Achievement award, NASA, 1968. Fellow Brit. Interplanetary Soc.; mem. The Planetary Soc., Am. Bldg. Contractors Assn., Mensa. Republican. Avocations: astronomy, golfing, singing. Home: 14 Fallbrook Irvine CA 92714 Office: Northrop 8900 E Washington Blvd Pico Rivera CA 90660

SHERIDAN, GEORGE EDWARD, manufacturing company executive; b. Emporia, Kans., July 4, 1915; s. George and Josephine Frances (Benson) S.; m. Edith Joye Card, July 4, 1940; 1 dau., Phyllis Lynne. Liberal arts student Coll. of Emporia, 1934-36; engring. student Nat. Schs., 1936-37, Los Angeles City Jr. Coll., 1937-38. Cert. mfg. engr.; registered profl. engr., Calif. With Douglas Aircraft, Santa Monica, Calif., 1939-40, Northrop Aircraft, Hawthorn, Calif., 1940-45; pres. Sheridan Products, Inc., Inglewood, Calif., 1940—. Active, YMCA, Inglewood, 1960—. Mem. Soc. Mfg. Engrs. (life, award 1979-80, Industrialist of Yr. 1982 past chmn.), U.S. Power Squadron, Am. Ordnance Def. Preparedness Assn., Nat. Rifle Assn., Smithsonian Assos., Cutting Tool Mfg. Assn., Nat. Fedn. Ind. Bus., Mech. Bank Collectors Am., Antique Toy Collectors Am. Republican. Quaker. Patentee double edge scraper. Home: 27692 Via Rodrigo Mission Viejo CA 92692 Office: 1054 E Hyde Park Blvd Inglewood CA 90302

SHERIDAN, JOHN BRIAN, librarian; b. N.Y.C., Aug. 30, 1947; s. John Bernard and Margaret Ann (Hefferon) S.; m. Dindy Reich, Aug. 20, 1972; children: Molly, Jonah. BA in Classics, CCNY, 1970; AM in Classical Studies, Ind. U., 1972; MLS, U. Wis., Milw., 1973. Cataloguer, acquisitions librarian Kearney (Nebr.) State Coll., 1973-75; head tech. services Knox Coll., Galesburg, Ill., 1975-77; head librarian Transylvania U., Lexington, Ky., 1977-84, The Colo. Coll., Colorado Springs, 1984—; chmn. Ky. Gov.'s pre-White House Conf. libraries and info. services, Louisville, 1978-79. Contbr. articles to profl. jours. Commr. Environ. Improvement Commn., Lexington, 1978-81; coach Colorado Springs Youth Soccer Assn., 1984—; bd. dirs. North End Homeowners Assn., Colorado Springs, 1985—. Fellow U. Wis., Milw., 1972; recipient Ward medal in Latin, CCNY, 1970; Regents scholar, CCNY, 1965-69. Mem. Am. Library Assn. (chmn. coll. libraries sect. com. 1980-85, sec. social responsibilities round table 1984-85, chmn. 1985-86), Mind and Body. Democrat. Club: Rogers Lunchers (Colorado Springs). Home: 1731 N Nevada Colorado Springs CO 80907 Office: The Colo Coll Charles Leaming Tutt Library Cascade & San Rafael Sts Colorado Springs CO 80903

SHERIDAN, JOHN ROGER, software developer, educator; b. Helena, Mont., Sept. 24, 1933; s. Maxwell Clark and Blanche Alta (Roberts) S.; m. Carol Marguerite Buckner, June 27, 1959; children: Lenita Lynn, Timothy Patrick. BA in Physics, Reed Coll., 1955; PhD in Physics, U. Wash., 1964. Research engr. Boeing Co., Seattle, 1955-60; research instr. U. Wash., Seattle, 1964; asst. prof. physics U. Alaska, Fairbanks, 1964-67, head, dept. physics, 1966-76, 1978-81, 1985-86, assoc. prof. physics, 1967-71, prof. physics, 1971—, asst. to dean Coll. Math., Phys. Scis., Engring., 1974-75; vis. physicist Stanford Research Inst., Menlo Park, Calif., 1969; hon. prof. physics Queen's U., Belfast, No. Ireland, 1975-76; chmn. U. Alaska budget com., 1981-83, U. Alaska tenure com. 1979-80; mem. president's planning and budget com., 1981-83, U. Alaska planning and budget council, 1981, U. Alaska tenure com., 1979-81, no. region instructional council, 1973-75, faculty council U. Alaska, 1965-68. Contbr. articles to profl. jours. Pres. United Campus Ministry, 1973-75, 78-80, bd. dirs., 1965—, sec., 1981-84, 85—; active Cen. Dist. Democrat Com., 1972-75, 78-82; mem. Dist. 19 Dem. com., 1982-84; treas. Chena-Goldstream Vol. Fire Dept., 1982-84; chmn. Statewide Assembly Budget Com., 1981-83; mem. Adminstrv. Com. of Fairbanks Assembly. Grantee NSF. Fellow Am. Phys. Soc. (div. electron and atomic physics); mem. AAAS, NEA, Am. Assn. Physics Tchrs. (membership com. 1966-68), Terak Pascal Physics Educators Users Group, Nat. Research Council Grad. Fellowship Evaluation Panel (chmn. 1984), Nat. Research Council Minority Grad. Fellowship Evaluation Panel (chmn. 1982), Pacific N.W. Assn. Coll. Physics (bd. dirs. 1966-68), Soc. Physics Students (advisor 1979-85), Fairbanks Faculty Assn. (pres. 1983-84), Microcomputer Users Group, Fairbanks Faculty Assn., Sigma Xi. Presbyterian. Avocations: bridge, swimming, tennis, computers. Home: 2053 Toboggan Ln Fairbanks AK 99709 Office: U Alaska Physics Dept Fairbanks AK 99701

SHERIDAN, KIM ALAN, computer software company executive; b. Lima, Ohio, Jan. 24, 1948; s. Charles Joseph and Jayn Elizabeth (Kassner) S.; m. Mary Margaret Gray, July 17, 1970; children: Nathan, Ben, Siovhan, Otto, Stephani; 1 foster child, Greg. BS in Mktg., U. Ariz., 1970; MBA in Quantitative Analysis, U. Cin., 1971. Salesman Sears, Roebuck and Co., 1969-70; with customer service Sheridan Assocs., Cin., 1970-73, div. v.p., 1973-76; pres. Interactive Info. Systems, Inc., Cin., Tucson, 1984—. Bd. dirs. Cath. Big. Bros., 1971-80, mem. adv. bd., 1981, Tucson, 1984—; mem. adv. bd. Fan Kane Fund for Brain Injured Children, Tucson, 1986—. Mem. Am. Inst. Decision Scis., Assn. Data Processing Orgn. Office: IIS Inc 4541 S Butterfield Suite 405 Tucson AZ 85714

SHERIDAN, MARY STOEBE, social worker; b. Pasadena, Calif., Aug. 5, 1948; d. Jacob G. and Virginia Elizabeth (Gould) S.; m. Harold C. Sheridan, Aug. 23, 1969. BA, Northwestern U., 1969; MSW, U. Ill., Chgo., 1972; PhD, U. Hawaii, 1985. Caseworker Cook County Pub. Aid, Chgo., 1969-70; instr., asst. prof. social work U. Ill. Hosp., Chgo., 1972-77; social worker Hawaii Dept. Edn., Waipahu, 1978-80; social work edn. coordinator Kapiolani Hosp., Honolulu, 1980-82, home monitor coordinator, 1982—; adj. instr. Hawaii Pacific Coll., Honolulu, 1978-79; instr./lectr. U. Hawaii, Honolulu, 1982-85. Author: (novel) To Michael with Love, 1977; contbr. articles to profl. jours. Recipient Cert. Merit Council of Nephrology Social Workers, 1977, Continuing Edn. award March of Dimes, Honolulu, 1985. Mem. Nat. Assn. Social Workers (sec. Honolulu chpt. 1984-85, cert.). Democrat. Roman Catholic. Office: Kapiolani Med Ctr for Women & Children 1319 Punahou Honolulu HI 96826

SHERK, WARREN ARTHUR, counselor, educator; b. Buffalo, July 12, 1916; s. Warren E. and Jennie (Taylor) S.; m. Martha Jean Kritzer, June 11, 1954; children: Elena E., Adra K., Lydian M., Warren M., Wilson E. Student Hiram Coll., 1934-35, U. Rangoon, Burma, 1938-39, Duke U., 1939-40; AB, Allegheny Coll., 1938; BD, Berkeley Bapt. Div. Sch., 1945, ThM, 1952; STD, Burton Sem., 1958. Minister, Meth. chs. in western N.Y., 1941-43; Protestant chaplain Ariz. State Prison, 1971-72; vis. prof. Iliff Sch. Theology, U. Denver, 1945-47; field sec. to Pearl S. Buck, 1948-49; minister edn., Indiana, Pa., 1949-51; minister Waitsburg Meth. Ch., Washington, 1951-52, Community Ch., Watertown, Mass., 1955-58, Savanna, Ill., 1958-59, Nogales (Ariz.) United Ch., 1960-61; exec. Dynamics Found., Tucson, 1962—; personal counselor, 1962—; faculty Phoenix Coll., 1963-66, Mesa Community Coll., Eastern Ariz. Coll., Pima Coll., 1963-78, Western International U., 1984—; cons. spl. seminars Pepsi Cola Mgmt. Inst., 1967-68; dir. bus. and profl. seminars for execs., 1968—; lectr. U. Durham (Eng.), summer 1981, Iliff Sch. Theology, summer 1982, Elder Hostels, N.Y., summer 1983, St. Deinels Library, Wales, summer 1985, S.S. Rotterdam N.Y.C. to South Africa, 1984; founder, exec. sec. Valley of Sun Forum, Phoenix, 1963-67; coordinator Assoc. Bus. Execs. Phoenix, 1963-67. Author: Wider Horizons, 1941, Agnes Moorehead: A Biography, 1976, Pearl Buck, 1987; contbr. numerous articles to mags. Chmn. spl. gifts div. Maricopa County Heart Fund. Corporate mem. Perkins Sch. for the Blind; bd. dirs. Boston World Affairs Council, N.E. Assn. UN; hon. bd. govs., bd. dirs. Pearl S. Buck Found. Fellow Am. Acad. Polit. Sci., Am. Geog. Soc.; mem. Thoreau Soc., Emerson Soc., Watertown Hist. Soc., Pimeria Alta Hist. Soc., Maricopa Mental Health Assn., Internat. Winston Churchill Soc., Theodore Roosevelt Assn., Execs. Internat. (founder, exec. dir. 1967—), Nat. Assn. Approved Morticians (exec. sec. 1967-69), Internat. Platform Assn., Tucson Com. Fgn. Relations, Phoenix Com. Fgn. Relations, NCCJ, AAUP, Theta Chi. Republican. Clubs: Ariz., Univ., Kiva. Address: 10032 N 8th St Phoenix AZ 85020

SHERLOCK, EMMANELL PHILLIPS, educator, painter; b. Monroe, La., Oct. 27, 1914; d. Clarence Leroy and Amy Wallace (Holmes) Phillips; B.A. in Edn., Northwestern La. U., 1939; M.A. in Elem. Edn., Calif. State U., Long Beach, 1966; m. Frank J. Sherlock, Sept. 3, 1948 (div. Feb. 1973); children—Patricia, Michael (twins), Dan. Classroom tchr. St. Tammany and Calcasieu Parishes, La., 1934-41, Orange, Tex., 1941-42; elec. engring. draftsman Consol. Steel, Orange, 1942-43, H. Newton Whitlesey, Chgo., 1943-44, George G. Sharp, New Orleans, 1944-45; music tchr. Orange Public Schs., 1945-47; reading cons. Silver Burdett Publs., 1947-48; tchr., resource tchr. Cypress (Calif.) Elem. Sch. Dist., 1963-83. Cert. tchr., La., Tex., Calif.; cert. adminstr., supr., reading specialist, Calif. Mem. Calif. Tchrs. Assn., NEA, Calif. Reading Assn., Internat. Reading Assn., Orange County (Calif.) Reading Assn. (past exec. bd.), Assn. Supervision and Curriculum Devel. Home: 3701 Green Ave Apt D Los Alamitos CA 90720

SHERMAN, ARTHUR WESLEY, JR., psychology educator; b. Lakewood, Ohio, Feb. 11, 1917; s. Arthur Wesley Sr. and Mabel Hortense (Becker) S.; m. Mary Leneve Crites, May1, 1942; children: Judith D., Beverly R., Sandra A. BA, Ohio U., 1940; MA, Ind. U., 1942; PhD, Ohio State U., 1952. Lic. psychologist, Calif. Instr. Ohio U., Athens, 1946-48, 50-51; asst. prof. psychology Calif. State U., Sacramento, 1954-58, assoc. prof. psychology, 1958-64, prof. psychology, 1964—; pvt. practice psychology, Sacramento, 1955-70. Author: Personnel Practices of American Companies in Europe, 1972, Managing Human Resources, 1984, Practical Study Experiments in Managing Human Resources, 1984, Readings in Managing Human Resources, 1984. Served to lt. col. USAF, 1941-45, 51-54. Mem. Am. Psychol. Assn., Sacramento Valley Psychol. Assn. (pres. 1964-65), Acad. Mgmt. Club: River Park Community (Sacramento) (pres. 1960-61). Office: Calif State U Dept Psychology 6000 J St Sacramento CA 95819

SHERMAN, BARRY MICHAEL, physician; b. Toledo, June 9, 1941; s. Max and Clara (Fingerhut) S.; m. Esther Mallon, Aug. 18, 1963; children: Bruce, Miriam, David, Greg. AB with honors, U. Mich., 1964, MD, 1966. Diplomate Am. Bd. Internal Medicine. Intern Bronx (N.Y.) Mcpl. Hosp., 1966-67; resident in internal medicine Albert Einstein Coll. Medicine, N.Y.C., 1967-68; prof., dir. U. Iowa, Iowa City, 1971-85; dir. clin. research Genentech Inc., South San Francisco, 1985—; prof. internal medicine Stanford (Calif.) U., 1986—; med. researcher. gen. clin. research ctrs. NIH, Bethesda, Md., 1982-86, breast cancer task force NIH, 1977-87. Contbr. numerous articles to profl. jours. Served to lt. cpl., USPHS, 1968-70. NIH grantee, 1973-85. Fellow ACP; mem. Edocrine Soc., Am. Soc. Clin. Investigation, Cen. Soc. Clin. Research. Home: 2830 Churchill Dr Hillsborough CA 94010 Office: Genentech Inc 460 Point SanBruno Blvd South San Francisco CA 94080

SHERMAN, DANIEL ADAM, psychiatrist; b. N.Y.C., Oct. 21, 1948; s. Morris R. and Dorothy (Salomon) S. BA in Human Biology, Johns Hopkins U., 1969, MD, 1972. Diplomate Am. Bd. Psychiatry and Neurology, 1977. Intern then resident in psychiatry Denver Gen. Hosp., 1972-75; staff psychiatrist Am. Lake VA Hosp., Tacoma, 1975-76; program dir. Harborview Med. Ctr., Seattle, 1976-77; acting instr. U. Wash. Sch. Medicine, Seattle, 1976-77; psychiat. med. dir. Providence Med. Ctr., Seattle, 1977-81; practice medicine specializing in psychiatry Seattle, 1977—; research asst. Md. Psychiat. Research Ctr., Catonsville, 1971. Mem. Am. Psychiat. Assn., AMA, Wash. State Psychiat. Assn. (sec. Seattle chpt. 1979-80). Office: 550 16th Ave Suite 300 Seattle WA 98122

SHERMAN, ERIC, filmmaker, writer, educator; b. Santa Monica, Calif., June 29, 1947; s. Vincent and Hedda (Comorau) S.; B.A. cum laude, Yale U., 1968; m. Eugenia Blackiston Dillard, Apr. 1, 1978; children—Cosimo, Rocky. Film producer, dir., writer, photographer and editor; films include: Charles Lloyd—Journey Within, 1968; Paul Weiss—a Philosopher in Process, 1972; Waltz, 1980; Inside Out, 1982; Measure of America, 1983; Michael Reagan's Assault on Great Lakes, 1983; represented in film festivals N.Y.C. Melbourne, Australia, Bilbao, Spain, others; books include: (with others) The Director's Event, 1970; Directing the Film, 1976; Frame by Frame, 1987; pres. Film Transform, Nat. Video Pub. Co.; film tchr. Art Center Coll. Design, Pepperdine U., UCLA; guest lectr. Yale, Calif. Inst. Tech., U. So. Calif.; Andrew Mellon lectr. on arts Calif. Inst. Tech., 1977; contbr. numerous articles to film publs. and distbn. catalogues, book dedication; works include three oral histories for Am. Film Inst. under Louis B. Mayer Found. grant. Trustee Am. Cinematheque. Mem. Soc. Motion Picture and TV Engrs. (asso.), Assn. Ind. Video and Filmmakers, Univ. Film Assn., Assn. Visual Communicators, Nat. Alliance Media Arts Ctrs. Office: 3755 Cahuenga W #B Studio City CA 91604

SHERMAN, FREDERIC JOEL, dentist; b. N.Y.C., Jan. 27, 1937; s. Jules Howard Sherman and Irma (Hirsch) Strumpf; m. Margaret Jane Annand, Sept. 14, 1968; 1 child, Andrew Jules. Student, Cornell U., 1954-57; DDS, N.Y.U., 1961. Cert. State Bd. Dental Examiners, Calif. Dental intern VA Hosp., Long Beach, Calif., 1961-62; pvt. practice Beverly Hills, Calif., 1965-69; dentist Mnich & Sherman, D.D.S., Los Angeles, 1964-86, S. Rowe, D.D.S., Sherman Oaks, Calif., 1976-82, Northridge (Calif.) Dental Assocs., 1987—. Asst. commr. Am. Youth Soccer Orgn., Encino, Calif., 1984, treas. 1981—, coach and referee; mgr. and coach Youth Baseball; pres. Campbell Hall Parent-Tchrs. Council, No. Hollywood, Calif., 1984-85. Served with U.S. Army, 1962-64. Mem. ADA, Calif. Dental Assn. (judicial council 1984—, del. to ho., 1984-86), Los Angeles Dental Soc. (ethics com. chmn. 1983-84, by laws com.-chmn. 1982-83, dental care com. chmn. 1985-87). Democrat. Jewish. Avocations: scuba diving, softball. Home: 7862 Lulu Glen Dr Los Angeles CA 90046 Office: Northridge Dental Assocs 8349 Reseda Blvd Northridge CA 91325

SHERMAN, JOHN LESLIE, physician; b. Mpls., May 23, 1948; s. Bruce and Marion (Kvasnik) S.; m. Noga Pessia Amir, Aug. 15, 1971; children: Lauren, David. BA, UCLA, 1970; MD, U. So. Calif., 1974. Diplomate Am. Bd. Internal Medicine. Practice medicine specializing in internal medicine Northridge, Calif., 1974—. Named UCLA Resident of Yr, 1977. Fellow Am. Coll. Chest Physicians, Am. Coll. Physicians. Office: 8333 Reseda Blvd Northredy CA 91324

SHERMAN, KAREN TAYLOR, elected school board member, civic leader; b. Indpls., Oct. 13, 1946; d. William Howard and Jessie Marcella (Williams) Taylor; m. Edward B. Lasher, June 4, 1967 (div. 1969); m. Byron Jay Sherman, June 3, 1971; children: Carrie Victoria, Taylor Karsten. Student, Ind. U., 1964-67; BA in English and Russian, BS, Dickinson State U., 1968; postgrad., U. N.D., 1969-70. Cert. secondary tchr., N.D. Tchr. Dickinson (N.D.) Pub. Sch., 1968-69, Grand Forks (N.D.) Pub. Sch., 1969-71; bd. dirs. Issaquah (Wash.) Sch. Bd., v.p. 1986, pres. 1984, 87. Candidate State House of Reps. Wash. 41st Legis. Dist., 1984; adv. com. Metro Transit, Seattle, 1983-85; steering com. Ballot Issue HJR22, Wash., 1985; issues and research dir. Gubernatorial campaign, Wash., 1980; chmn. legis. com. Wash. State Sch. Dirs. Assn., 1985-86, 2d. v.p. 1986—; bd. dirs. Elected Wash. Women (treas. 1982-84); chmn. edn. com. Sta. KCTS 1985—; mem. Leadership Tomorrow Seattle C. of C., 1986-87. Mem. Issaquah Women Profls. (pres. 1985). Avocations: reading, politics. Home and Office: 4337 182nd Pl SE Issaquah WA 98027

SHERMAN, KENNETH NEWTON, electrical engineer; b. Balt., Oct. 5, 1958; s. Stanley Newton and Helen Marie (Ridgeway) S. BSEE, George Wahington U., 1980; MSEE, UCLA, 1982. Assoc. engr. Arens Applied Electromagnetics, Gaithersburg, Md., 1978-79; staff engr. Hughes Aircraft Co., Los Angeles, 1980-86; pres. Cybercom Systems, Gaithersburg, Md., 1986—. Mem. IEEE. Republican. Club: Toastmasters (Manhattan Beach, Calif.)(chpt. v.p. 1985-86). Avocations: skiing, scuba diving, piano, guitar. Home: 15804 White Rock Rd Gaithersburg MD 20878 Office: Hughes Aircraft Co PO Box 92919 S&CG S12/W319 Los Angeles CA 90009

SHERMAN, MARY KENNEDY, business executive; b. Chgo., June 17, 1919; d. Robert Thomas and Mary Cecelia (Hammond) Kennedy; A.A., Los Angeles Valley Coll., 1966; B.S., Pepperdine U., 1973; M.B.A., 1974; Accredited Personnel Accreditation Inst. m. Lloyd McBean Sherman, Dec. 1, 1967; children—Tom D. Akins, Mary Patricia Kraakevik. Indsl. relations supr. Douglas Aircraft Co., Inc., Santa Monica, Calif., 1942-61; dir. personnel Helene Curtis Industries, Studio Girl, Glendale, Calif., 1961-65; dir. personnel Semtech Corp., Newbury Park, Calif., 1965-73, v.p., 1973—; lectr., cons. in field. Mem. Am. Mgmt. Assn., Internat. Assn. for Personnel Women (Mem. of Yr. 1982-83), Am. Soc. for Personnel Adminstrn., Personnel and Indsl. Relations Assn., Am. Bus. Women's Assn., Personnel Women of Los Angeles. Republican. Roman Catholic. Club: Zonta Internat. (dist. gov. 1984-86). Office: Semtech Corp 652 Mitchell Rd Newbury Park CA 91320

SHERMAN, MAX HOWARD, research physicist; b. Los Angeles, Apr. 3, 1954; s. Harry and Claire Rose (Walkin) S.; m. Elizabeth Louise Scott, Dec. 26, 1977(div. Nov. 1985). BS in Physics and Chemistry, UCLA, 1975; PhD in Physics, U. Calif., Berkeley, 1980. Teaching asst. U. Calif., Berkeley, 1976-77, research assoc., 1977-80; staff scientist Lawrence Berkeley Lab., 1980—; pres. Harmax Corp., Los Angeles, 1979—; U.S. rep. Annex V of Internat. Energy Agy., London, 1983—. Contbr. articles to sci. jours.; patentee in field. Mem. AAAS, ASTM, ASHRAE (chmn. SPC 119 1983—), Am. Phys. Soc., M.S. De Young Mus. Soc., Calif. Acad. Sci. Exploration, San Francisco Zoo, Am. Contract Bridge League, Sigma Pi Sigma. Home: 461 Hudson St Oakland CA 94618 Office: Lawrence Berkeley Lab 90-3074 Berkeley CA 94720

SHERMAN, RAYMOND BERNARD, electronic engineer; b. N.Y.C., Dec. 28, 1928; s. Samuel and Ethyl Althea (Darby) S.; B. Gen. Studies, U. Nebr., Omaha, 1967; postgrad. Coll. San Mateo, 1972-73; m. Laura Mae Hebert, Aug. 29, 1958; 1 dau., Jennifer Diane (Mrs. Roger Corbello). Electronic engr. Airborne Instruments Lab., 1966-69; div. electronic engr. Continental Can Co., 1969-71; appraisal officer Bank Am., San Jose, Calif., 1972-73, real estate broker, San Mateo, Calif., 1973-75; sr. engr. parts, materials and processes Watkins Johnson Co., Palo Alto, Calif., 1976-79; sr. components engr. TRW Inc., ESL Inc. and Aertech Industries, Sunnyvale, Calif., 1979-81, Quantic Industries, San Carlos, Calif., 1981-82 ; mgr. components engring. Teledyne MEC, 1981-83; electronic components engr. Varian Assocs., Palo Alto, 1983—. Served with USMC, 1946-56, USAF, 1956-66. Mem. Am. Soc. Quality Control, IEEE, Marines Meml. Assn., Am. Legion. Club: Elks. Home: 744 Pinta Ln Foster City CA 94404 Office: Varian Assocs 611 Hansen Way Palo Alto CA 94303

SHERMAN, ROBERT, TV producer; b. N.Y.C., Jan. 9, 1950; s. Allan Sherman and Dolores Miriam (Chackes) Golden. Student, San Fernando Valley State Coll., 1968, UCLA, 1969, Brandeis U., 1970. Co-owner, sec., treas., cons. Sta. KJQN AM-FM, Ogden, Utah. Producer, co-creator Spellbinders, 1978, The Better Sex, 1977-78, Puzzlers, 1980, Blockbusters, 1980-82, 87—, Star Words, 1983; assoc. producer Tattletales, 1974-78, coproducer, 1982; writer, assoc. producer Match Game, 1973-81; producer Password Plus, 1979-82 (Daytime Emmy as Outstanding Game Show award 1981-82); exec. producer Match Game/Hollywood Sqs. Hour, 1983-84, Super Password, 1984—; exec. producer, creator Body Language, 1984-86; producer, creator Oddball, 1986; contbr. articles to profl. jours.; inventor dimmer control system. Mem. Nat. Acad. TV Arts and Scis. (Emmy award 1971-72), Mensa, Acoustic Neuroma Assn., Philatelic Found. Home: 1555 Rising Glen Rd Los Angeles CA 90069 Office: Mark Goodson Prodns 6430 Sunset Blvd Hollywood CA 90028

SHERMAN, ROBERT B(ERNARD), composer, lyricist, screenwriter; b. N.Y.C., Dec. 19, 1925; s. Al and Rosa (Dancis) S.; student UCLA, 1943; BA, Bard Coll., 1949; m. Joyce Ruth Sasner, Sept. 27, 1953; children: Laurie Shane, Jeffrey Craig, Andrea Tracy, Robert Jason. Popular songwriter, 1950-60, including Tall Paul, Pineapple Princess, You're Sixteen (Gold Record); songwriter Walt Disney Prodns., Beverly Hills, Calif., 1960-68, for 29 films including The Parent Trap, 1961, Summer Magic, 1963, Mary Poppins, 1964, That Darn Cat, 1965, Winnie The Pooh, 1965, Jungle Book, 1967, Bedknobs and Broomsticks, 1971; co-composer song It's A Small World, theme of Disneyland and Walt Disney World, Fla.; composer, lyricist United Artists, Beverly Hills, 1969—, songs for film Chitty, Chitty, Bang, Bang, 1969, Snoopy, Come Home!, 1972; song score Charlotte's Web, 1972; composer for Walt Disney's Wonderful World of Color, TV, 1961—; co-producer NBC-TV spl. Goldilocks, 1970; v.p. Musi-Classics, Inc.; co-producer, composer, lyricist stage musical Victory Canteen, 1971; composer-lyricist Broadway show Over Here, 1975; screenplay and song score Tom Sawyer, United Artists, 1972, Huckleberry Finn, 1974, The Slipper and the Rose, 1977, The Magic of Lassie, 1978. Served with inf. AUS, 1943-45; ETO. Decorated

Purple Heart; recipient 2 Acad. awards best score for Mary Poppins, 1964, best song for Chim Chim Cheree, 1965; Grammy award, 1965; Christopher medal, 1965, 74; nine Acad. award nominations; Acad. award nomination for song score Bedknobs and Broomsticks, 1971, for best song The Age of Not Believing, 1971, others; thirteen golden, three platinum and one diamond record album, 1965-83; first prize best composer song score Tom Sawyer, Moscow Film Festival, 1973, B.M.I. Pioneer award, 1977; Golden Cassette awards for Mary Poppins, Jungle Book, Bed Knobs and Broomsticks, 1983, Mouscar award Disney Studios. Mem. Acad. Motion Picture Arts and Scis. (exec. bd. music br. 12 yrs.), AFTRA, Nat. Acad. Rec. Arts and Scis., Composers and Lyricists Guild (exec. bd.), Writers Guild Am., Dramatists Guild, Authors League. Office: care Mike Conner Office 1048 N Carol Dr Los Angeles CA 90069 Address: 9030 Harratt St #2 Los Angeles CA 90069

SHERMAN, ROGER MINOTT, consulting engineer; b. N.Y.C., June 26, 1916; s. Roger and Marjorie (Treat) S.; m. Ruth Laonne Blanchard (div.); m. Lois Bardt, Feb. 6, 1968; children: Roger Sherman II, Susan Tuttle. BSME, U. Calif., Berkeley, 1944. Registered profl. mech. engr., Calif., Hawaii; registered profl. safety engr., Calif., corrosion engr., Calif., agrl. engr., Calif. Patentee in field. Mem. Am. Soc. Safety Engrs., ASTM, Irrigation Assn., Nat. Assn. Corrosian Engrs., Soc. Automotive Engrs., Calif. Soc. Profl. Engrs. Avocations: golf, tennis, swimming, flying. Home and Office: 78-266 Manukai St Kailua-Kona HI 96740

SHERN, DAVID LEN, administrator health research facility; b. Pueblo, Colo., Feb. 23, 1951; s. Lennox Lyle and Louise Marie (Formico) S.; m. Karen Sue Westerman, Nov. 5, 1977. BA in Psychology, U. Colo., 1973, MA in Social Psychology, 1977, PhD in Social Psychology, 1980; cert. in advanced epidemiologic methods, NIMH Staff Coll., 1980. Asst. dir. research and evaluation sect. Denver Dept. Health and Hosps. Mental Health Programs, 1981-82; research assoc. evaluation services sect. Colo. div. Mental Health, Denver, 1982-84, mgr. sponsored research program, 1984—, project dir., investigator estimating residential services for chronically mentally ill, 1983—; investigator validation models for estimating mental health need U. Denver, 1983—; cons. several health facilities, Denver, 1976—. Contbr. articles to profl. jours. Bd. dirs. Traveler's Aid of Denver, 1981-83, Karis Community, 1986—. Mem. Am. Psychol. Assn., Am. Pub. Health Assn., Orgn. for Program Evaluation in Colo. (pres. 1982-83, assoc. editor bull.), Evaluation Research Soc., Am. Evaluation Assn., Sigma Xi. Democrat. Avocations: hiking, camping, cross-country skiing. Office: Colo Div Mental Health 3520 W Oxford Ave Denver CO 80236

SHERRARD, WILLIAM ROBERT, engineering educator; b. Langford, S.D., July 16, 1932; s. Earl George and Isabel Ann (Williams) S.; m. Miriam Elaine Murren, June 11, 1960. BBA, U. Wash., 1957, MBA, 1958, PhD, 1965. Indsl. engr. Boeing Airplane Co., Seattle, 1957-59; prof. Idaho State U., Pocatello, 1959-60, U. N.C., Chapel Hill, 1965-68, San Diego State U., 1968—; cons. various orgns., San Diego, 1968—. Contbr. articles to profl. jours. Mem. Decision Scis. Inst. (program chmn. 1972, pres. 1973-74), Acad. Mgmt., Am. Inst. Mgmt. Scis., Am. Prodn. Inventory Control Soc., Ops. Research Soc. Am., Beta Gamma Sigma, Sigma Iota Epsilon. Avocations: golf, hiking, jogging. Office: San Diego State U Coll Bus 5402 College Ave San Diego CA 92182

SHERRER, CHARLES DAVID, college dean, clergyman; b. Marion, Ohio, Sept. 21, 1935; s. Harold D. and Catherine E. (Fye) S. A.B., U. Notre Dame, 1958, M.A., 1965; S.T.L., Gregorian U., 1962; Ph.D., U. N.C., 1969. Ordained priest Roman Cath. Ch., 1961. Instr. English U. Portland, Oreg., 1963-64, asst. prof., 1969-74, chmn. dept., 1970-74, dean Grad. Sch., 1982-87, mem. Bd. Regents, 1986-87, acad. v.p., 1987—; pres. King's Coll., Wilkes Barre, Pa., 1974-81; dir. studies Holy Cross Fathers, Ind. Province, 1979—. Bd. dirs., v.p. Wyoming Valley United Way; bd. dirs. Greater Wilkes-Barre C. of C. and Indsl. Fund, Osterhout Library; mem. exec. com. Econ. Devel. Council Northeastern Pa. Mem. AAUP, MLA, Shakespeare Soc. Office: Univ Portland Office Acad VP Portland OR 97203

SHERWOOD, ALLEN JOSEPH, lawyer; b. Salt Lake City, Sept. 26, 1909; s. Charles Samuel and Sarah (Abramson) Shapiro; m. Edith Ziff, Jan. 19, 1941; children—Mary (Mrs. John Marshall), Arthur Lawrence. Student, UCLA, 1927-30; A.B., U. So. Calif., 1933, LL.B., 1933. Bar: Calif. 1933, U.S. Supreme Ct. 1944. Practice Los Angeles, 1933-54; practice Beverly Hills, 1954—; legal counsel Internat. Family Planning Research Assn., Inc., 1970-76; bd. dirs. Family Planning Ctrs. Greater Los Angeles, Inc., 1968-84, pres., 1973-76. Mem. editorial bd. So. Calif. Law Rev., 1932-33. Contbr. articles to profl. jours. Mem. Calif. Atty. Gen.'s Vol. Adv. Council and its legis. subcom., 1972-78. Recipient alumni award U. So. Calif. Law Sch., 1933. Fellow Med.-Legal Soc. So. Calif. (bd. dirs. 1966-74); mem. ABA, Los Angeles County Bar Assn., Beverly Hills Bar Assn., State Bar of Calif., Am. Arbitration Assn. (nat. panel arbitrators 1965—), Order of Coif, Tau Delta Phi. Club: Brentwood Country (Los Angeles). Lodge: Masons. Home: 575 Moreno Ave Los Angeles CA 90049 Office: 9033 Wilshire Blvd Penthouse Beverly Hills CA 90211

SHERWOOD, ALLEN RUSSELL, military officer; b. Concord, Calif., Nov. 17, 1942; s. Charles Lloyd and Viola A. (Allen) S.; m. Celeste Marie French, July 25, 1965; 1 child, Alicia Celeste. BA, Calif. State U., 1965; grad., Officer Candidate Sch., USN, 1965; postgrad., U. Okla. Commd. ensign USN, 1966, advanced through grades to comdr., 1980; with Tokyo, 1966-70; lt. comdr., asst. pub. affairs officer U.S. Pacific Fleet, Calif., Hawaii, 1975-80; comdr. Washington, 1980-85; dir. advt. Navy Recruiting Commd., Washington, 1984-86; comdr. Office Pub. Affairs, Naval Postgrad. Sch. Monterey, Calif., 1985—; asst. chief of info. State of Calif., 1971-72, dep. appointments sec. to gov., 1972-75; pub. affairs officer Apollo-Soyuz Manned Spacecraft Recovery, 1985. Bd. dirs. Navy-Marine Corps Mus., San Francisco, 1980-83; Navy chmn. Mayors Fleet Week com., San Francisco, 1982-83; active Reagan for Gov. campaign, 1972. Recipient Freedoms Found. award for essay, 1967. Mem. Navy League of U.S. (v.p. 1974-75), C. of C. (mil. affairs com. 1986—). Republican. Club: Amateur Radio (Chico, Calif.).

SHERWOOD, MORGAN, history educator; b. Anchorage, Oct. 22, 1929; s. Jay Robert and Agnes Elizabeth (Banner) S.; m. Jeanie Woods, June 7, 1963. AB, San Diego State U., 1953; MA, U. Calif., Berkeley, 1958, PhD, 1962; LHD (hon.), U. Alaska, 1983. Research historian U. Calif. at Berkeley, Washington, 1961-64; asst. prof history U. Cin., 1964-65; asst. prof. history U. Calif., Davis, 1965-75, prof., 1975—. Author: Exploration of Alaska, 1965, The Politics of American Science, 1965, Alaska and Its History, 1967, Big Game in Alaska, 1981; editorial advisor Agrl. History, 1965—, Pacific Northwest Quar., 1966-79, Pacific Hist. Rev., Alaska History, 1984—. Served with AUS, 1953-54, Korea. Mem. Am. Soc. Environ. History (pres. 1983-84). Office: U Calif Dept History Davis CA 95616

SHERWOOD, PHILLIP DAVID, training officer; b. Fresno, Calif., Aug. 19, 1949; s. Clifton St. John and Marjorie Louise (Ede) S.; m. Nancy Jean Koealer, June 5, 1971; 1 child: Jeffrey St. John. BA in Polit. Sci., Calif. State U., Fresno, 1973; M in Pub. Adminstrn., Calif. State U., Sacramento, 1975; postgrad., U. Western Australia, 1976-78; PhD in Pub. Adminstrn., U. So. Calif., 1986—. Legis. aide Assemblyman Ken Maddy, Fresno, 1972-73; program analyst Calif. Dept. Fin., Sacramento, 1973-75; lectr. Churchlands Coll., Perth, Australia, 1976-78; assoc. bus. mgmt. analyst Employment Devel. Dept., Sacramento, 1978-80; assoc. govt. program analyst State Dept. Social Services, Sacramento, 1980-84; tng. officer Calif. Dept. Transp., Sacramento, 1984—; instr. Am. River Coll., Sacramento, 1978—, Sacramento City Coll., 1982—; adj. prof. Nat. U., Sacramento, Calif. and Costa Rica, 1984—; cons. San Juan Unified Sch. Dist., Carmichael, Calif., 1986. Chmn. personnell com. Westminster Presbyn. Ch., Sacramento, 1981-83; v.p. Windwood Homeowners Assn., Sacramento, 1984. Grad. fellow Rotary Found., 1976-78. Mem. Calif. Assn. State Trainers (v.p. 1986-87, pres. 1987—), Am. Soc. Tng. and Devel. Republican. Avocations: baseball card collecting, wine. Home: 7325 Flowerwood Way Sacramento CA 95831 Office: State Dept Transp 1120 N St Room 0502 Sacramento CA 95831

SHERWOOD, ROBERT WILLIAM, health department adminstator; b. Anaconda, Mont., Sept. 1, 1921; s. Hazleton Donald and Christine (Murphy) S.; m. Cherril Black, July 27, 1947; children: Robert W. Jr., Leslie D., James M., Teresa C., Peter W. BS, U. Oreg., 1947, MD, 1949; MPH, Harvard U., 1954. Diplomate Am. Bd. Preventive Medicine (fellow 1957—, award 1982, 86). Commd. med. officer U.S. Army, 1949, advanced through grades to col., chief of communicable diseases Office of Surgeon Gen., 1960-63, dir. preventive medicine, 1969-72; asst. dir. Utah Dept. Health, Salt Lake City, 1963-69; health and retirement fund adminstr. United Mine Workers, Evansville, Ind., 1972-76; med. dir. Larimer County Health Dept., Ft. Collins, Colo., 1976—; adj. prof. U. No. Colo., Greeley, 1978—, Colo. State U., Ft. Collins, 1984—. Decorated Legion of Merit. Fellow Am. Assn. Med. Dirs., Am. Pub. Health Assn.; mem. Am. Coll. Physicians Execs. (cert.), Colo. Med. Soc. Avocations: oil painting, photography, fishing, traveling, reading. Home: 717 Dartmouth Trail Fort Collins CO 80525 Office: Larimer County Health Dept 363 Jefferson St Fort Collins CO 80524

SHETH, ROHIT PANALAL, computer engineer; b. Baroda, Gujarat, India, June 22, 1942; came to U.S., 1962; s. Panalal M. and Pushpa (Sheth) S.; m. Nayna R. Sheth, Mar. 7, 1969; children: Nila, Milan, Sanjog. BSc in Chemistry, Bombay U., 1962; BSChemE, U. Mo., Rolla, 1964, MSChemE, 1966; MS in Computer Sci., U. So. Calif., 1979; postgrad., 1979—. Registered profl. engr., Calif. Power control engr. Mobil Oil Co., Nichols, Fla., 1966-69; sr. engr. Revlon, Inc., Bronx, N.Y., 1969-71; engr., programmer ITT Fed. Electric, Vandenberg, Calif., 1971-73; mem. tech. staff TRW Systems, Redondo Beach, Calif., 1973-79; sr. systems engr. Fluer Corp., Irvine, Calif., 1979-83; mgr. systems engring., electronics div. Northrop Corp., Hawthorne, Calif., 1983—; prof. computer sci. Golden State U., Los Angeles, 1984—; mem. part-time faculty U. LaVerne, Calif., 1983—; cons. PRC Assocs., New Port Beach, Calif., 1984—. Mem. Am. Inst. Chem. Engrs. Democrat. Hindu. Avocations: reading, recreational exercises. Home: 3847 W 134th Pl Hawthorne CA 90250 Office: Northrop Corp Electronics div N3673 N4 2301 W 120th St Hawthorne CA 90250

SHIBATA, SHOJI, pharmacology educator, researcher; b. Kyoto, Japan, Nov. 12, 1927; came to U.S., 1963; s. Shuzo and Tetsu Shibata; m. May 1958; children: Toshiyuki, Eri. MD, Nara (Japan) Med. Coll., 1952; PhD, Kyoto U., 1957. Instr. pharmacology Kyoto U. Med. Sch., 1957-60, U. So. Calif., Los Angeles, 1960-62; assoc. prof. Kyoto Coll. Pharmacy, 1962-63; instr. U. Miss., Jackson, 1963-64, assoc. prof., 1964-66; assoc. prof. U. Hawaii, Honolulu, 1967-69, prof., 1970—. Author: Recent Developments in Cardiac Muscle Pharmacology, 1982, Factors Influencing Vascular Reactivity, 1982, Basic Methods of Pharmacology, 1982, Vascular Neuroeffector Mechanisms; 4th Internat. Symposium, 1983; editor Jour. Cardiovascular Pharmacology, Jour. Pharmacol. Methods, Blood Vessels. Fellow Japanese Dept. of Edn., 1954-57, Can. Heart Assn., 1978; sr. fellow Japanese Acad. Scis. Assn. Mem. Am. Physiology Soc., Am. Soc. Pharmaxology and Exptl. Therapy. Home: 3338 Keahi St Honolulu HI 96822 Office: U Hawaii Sch Medicine 1960 East West Rd Honolulu HI 96822

SHIBUTANI, TAMOTSU, research sociologist, educator; b. Stockton, Calif., Oct. 15, 1920; s. Naonosuke and Taka (Aihara) S.; m. Tomika Harano, Apr. 6, 1942 (div. Apr. 1969); m. Sandra Gettman, Nov. 15, 1981 (div. May 1987). AB, U. Calif., Berkeley, 1942; AM, U. Chgo., 1944, PhD, 1948. Instr. sociology U. Chgo., 1948-51; asst. prof. sociology U. Calif., Berkeley, 1951-57; from assoc. prof. to prof. sociology U. Calif., Santa Barbara, 1961—; cons. to chief of naval devel. USN, Washington, 1973-74. Author: Society and Personality, 1961, Improvised News, 1966, The Derelicts of Company K, 1977, Social Processes, 1986; (with K. Kwan) Ethnic Stratification, 1965; editor Human Nature and Collective Behavior, 1970. Served with JAGC, U.S. Army, 1944-46. Fellow AAAS; mem. Am. Sociol. Assn. Office: U Calif Santa Barbara CA 93106

SHICKLE, PAUL EUGENE, educator; b. Bloomington, Ill., Aug. 29, 1927; s. Benjamin Wilson and Eathel Delores (Rowe) S. B.S., Ill. State U., 1949. Cert. secondary tchr., Calif. Tchr. San Marino Unified Sch. Dist., Calif., 1956—, head fgn. lang. dept., 1967—. Mem. performing arts council Music Ctr. Los Angeles County. Mem. Soc. Indian Pioneers, Filson Club, Calif. Classical Assn. (pres. so. sect. 1981-82), Modern and Classical Assn. So. Calif., Am. Council Study Fgn. Lang., Calif. Humanities Assn., Am. Acad. Religion, Nat. Tchrs. Assn., Calif. Tchrs. Assn., Assn. for Supervision and Curriculum Devel., Am. Classical Assn., Am. Acad. Polit. and Soc. Sci., Am. Acad. Polit. Sci., Am. Council for Arts, Ams. United for Separation Ch. and State, Ind. Hist. Soc., Bibl. Archaeology Soc., Calif. Assn. Supervision and Curriculum Devel., Am. Film Inst., Va. Geneal. Soc., Ky. Geneal. Soc., N.Am. Conf. Brit. Studies, History Sci. Soc., Oceanic Soc., Nelson County (Ky.) Hist. Soc., Smithsonian Assocs., Nat. Trust for Historic Preservation, Met. Mus. Art (nat. assoc.), Met. Opera Guild, Asia Soc., Zionist Orgn. Am., ACLU, Amnesty Internat., Ctr. for Study of Presidency, Clan Fraser Soc. North Am., Archeol. Inst. Am., Va. Country Civil War Soc., Nat. Park and Conservation Assn., UN Assn. of U.S., Soc. French Hist. Studies, Am. Com. for Irish Studies, Conf. Group for Cen. European History. Republican. Roman Catholic. Home: 2115 Leafwood Ln Arcadia CA 91006 Office: San Marino Unified Sch Dist 2701 Huntington Dr San Marino CA 91008

SHIEH, JOHN TING-CHUNG, economics educator; b. China. B.S., Chunghsing U., Taiwan, 1956; M.S., Kans. State U., 1960; M.A., U. Calif.-Riverside, 1970; D.Bus. Adminstrn., U. So. Calif., 1981. Asst. prof. Northwestern State Coll., Alva., 1964-67; asst. prof. econs. Calif. State Poly. U., Pomona, 1967-70, assoc. prof., 1970-81, prof., chmn. dept. econs., 1981-84, prof. 1981—; cons. to small bus., So. Calif., Taiwan, 1975—; vis. prof. Tax Inst., U. So. Calif., Los Angeles, 1977-84, U. Calif.-Irvine, 1978-79, U. So. Calif., 1978-81, UCLA, 1982—. Research, publs. in field. NSF fellow, 1965, 66, 67, 73; fellow seminars in econs. and math. U. Wyo., summer 1972. Mem. Am. Econ. Assn., Omicron Delta Epsilon, Omega Rho. Home: 24502 Sandpiper Ln Dana Point CA 92629 Office: Calif State Poly U Dept Econs Pomona CA 91768

SHIEH, PAUL, chemical engineering researcher; b. Taipei, Republic of China, Jan. 15, 1943; came to U.S., 1967; s. Ton-Sun and Pou-Yu (Wu) S.; married; one child, Kate. BS Chem. Engring., Chong-Kung U., Tainan, Taiwan, 1966; MS in Polymer Chemistry, Yale U., 1969; PhD in Biophysics and Polymer Sci., Mich. State U., 1975. Research asst. prof. U. Calif., Berkeley, 1975-79; sr. chemist Ricoh Systems Inc., San Jose, Calif., 1979-83; sr. polymer chemist Primary Diagnostic Co., Santa Clara, Calif., 1983-85; sr. scientist Nellcor Co., Hayward, Calif., 1985—. Author: (with Packer and Sedney) Lipid-impregnated Filter Membranes, 1979; patentee in field. Mem. Am. Chem. Soc., Am. Biophys. Soc., Soc. Plastic Engring. Home: 151 Estrella Rd Fremont CA 94539 Office: Nellcor Inc Hayward CA 94545

SHIELDS, ANTHONY FRANK, research oncologist; b. Highland Park, Ill., Mar. 20, 1952; s. Richard Neil Shields; m. Fayth K. Yoshimura. BS, MIT, 1974, PhD, 1979; MD, Harvard U., 1979. Cert. Am. Bd. Internal Medicine, Am. Bd. Hematology, Am. Bd. Oncology. Intern U. Wash., Seattle, 1970-80, resident in medicine, 1979-81, fellow in oncology, 1981-84; research assoc. Hutchinson Cancer Ctr., Seattle, 1984-85, asst. mem., 1985—. Contbr. articles to profl. jours. Clin. fellow Am. Cancer Soc., 1984-86. Mem. Am. soc. Hematology. Office: Fred Hutchinson Cancer Ctr 1124 Columbia St Seattle WA 98104

SHIELDS, FRED S., JR., office products executive; b. Yakima, Wash., June 11, 1934; s. Frederick S. and Hazel Grace (Meiners) S.; m. María-Inés Terecita Plá, July 9, 1965; children: Keith D., Scott P., Stephanie L. BA in Econs., Whitman Coll., 1956, BA in Polit. Sci., 1961; BA in Fgn. Trade, Am. Grad. Sch. Internat. Trade. Sales rep. Singer Sewing Machines, Latin Am., 1961-62; rep. CARE, Inc., Iran, Iraq and Chile, 1962-66; prin. Shields Office Products, Pasco, Wash., 1966—; Bd. dirs. Benton, Franklin and Walla Walla Pvt. Industry Council. Bd. dirs. Pasco Downtown Devel. Assn., 1983—; active Tri-Cities Indsl. and Econ. Devel. Council, Kennewick, Wash., 1985—; served to lt. (j.g.), USN, 1956-60. Mem. Nat. Office Products Assn. (lt. gov. dist. 8, 1984—), Pasco C. of C., Phi Delta Theta. Republican. Roman Catholic. Club: Meadow Springs Country (Richland). Lodge: Rotary (bd. dirs. 1964-67). Avocations: golf, coaching junior soccer and track programs. Home: 2513 Bluehill Ct Richland WA 99352 Office: PO Box 490 Pasco WA 99301

SHIELDS, LAURA AULL, public relations counselor; b. Taylorville, Ill., Oct. 24; d. Frank and Gladys (Montgomery) Aull; m. Roger V. Shields, Nov. 20, 1940 (div.); children—Deborah, Beth, Roger, Clark, Constance. Student Ill. State U., 1935-37. Freelance writer San Gabriel Valley Tribune, Covina, Calif., 1960; Owner Shields Communications, Santa Monica, Calif., 1974—; speaker in field. Mem. Pub. Relations Soc. Am. and Counselors Acad., Women in Communications, Women in Bus., Santa Monica Bay Area C. of C. Office: 216 A Main St Venice CA 90291

SHIELDS, ROYAL STANLEY, industrial engineer; b. Sandy, Utah, Mar. 20, 1918; s. Archie M. and Mary A. (McLaws) S.; m. Mary Helen Hess, Dec. 24, 1942; children: Michael, John, David, Joe, Rosemary; foster dau., Imogene Antonio. BS in Bus. Adminstrn., Utah State U., 1940; postgrad., U. Utah, 1950. Registered profl. engr., Calif. Buyer ZCMI Dept. Store, Salt Lake City, 1947-49; sr. indsl. engr. Kennecott Copper Corp., Salt Lake City, 1950-60; supr. indsl. engring. Thiokol Chem. Co., Brigham City, Utah, 1960-62; sr. mfg. engr. Lockheed Corp., Sunnyvale, Calif., 1962-63; plant indsl. engr. phosphates and magnesia plants Chem. div. FMC Corp., Newark, Calif., 1963-66; mgmt. cons. Craig Cutten and Assocs., 1967-71; program mgr. electronics Internat. Video Corp., Sunnyvale, 1967-68; sr. indsl. engr., staff writer Marine div. Westinghouse Electric Co., Sunnyvale, 1969-75; sr. mfg. engr., staff writer EIMAC div. Varian Assocs., San Carlos, Calif., 1978—. Contbr. articles on indsl. engring. to profl. publs.; contbr. articles to mags. and newspapers. Served to lt. USN, PTO. Mem. Am. Inst. Indsl. Engrs. (Service to Community award 1974), Calif. Personnel Soc. Mormon. Home: 1456 Owen Sound Dr Sunnyvale CA 94087 Office: Varian Assocs 301 Industrial Way San Carlos CA 94070

SHIELS, JOHN MORSE, leasing company executive; b. San Jose, Calif., Sept. 28, 1937; s. John Burton and Elizabeth Booth (Morse) S.; m. Ai-Ling Cheng, Jan. 27, 1984; Jean. BS, U.S. Naval Acad., 1959; MS with distinction, Naval Postgrad. Sch., 1967. Commd. 2d lt. USN, 1959, advanced through grades to comdr., 1974, ret., 1979; mem. faculty Naval Postgrad. Sch., Monterey, Calif., 1977-79; v.p. mgmt. info. systems Flexi-Van Corp., N.Y.C., 1980-84; v.p. info. systems Equitable Life Leasing Co., San Diego, 1984—; cons. in field, 1977—. Contbr. articles to profl. jours. Pres. local elem. sch. PTA, Alexandria, Va., 1975-76. Decorated Bronze Star, Social Service medal Rep. Vietnam. Mem. Soc. Info. Mgmt., Naval Acad. Alumni Assn., Naval Acad. Athletic Assn. Republican. Mormon. Lodge: Lions. Avocations: reading, gardening, golf, travelling. Home: PO Box 238 Poway CA 92064 Office: Equitable Life Leasing Co PO Box 81224 San Diego CA 92138

SHIFFMAN, MAX, mathematician, educator; b. N.Y.C., Oct. 30, 1914; s. Nathan and Eva (Krasilchick) S.; m. Bella Manel (div. 1957); children: Bernard, David. BS, CCNY, 1935; MS, NYU, 1936, PhD, 1938. Instr. math. St. John's U., N.Y.C., 1938-39, CCNY, 1938-42; researcher Dept. Navy, NYU, 1942-45; assoc. prof. math NYU, 1945-49; prof. math. Stanford U., Palo Alto, Calf., 1949-66; prof. Calif. State U., Hayward, 1967-81; owner, mathematician Mathematico, Hayward and San Francisco, 1970—. Contbr. articles to profl. jours. Blumenthal fellow, 1935-38. Mem. Am. Math. Soc., Math. Assn. Am., Soc. Indsl. and Applied Math. Home and Office: 16913 Meekland Ave 7 Hayward CA 94541

SHIH, CHRISTOPHER CHUNG-YAT, chemical engineer, researcher; b. Shanghai, Peoples Republic of China, Sept. 23, 1942; came to U.S., 1961; s. Pao-Chu and Ying (Yuan) S.; m. Nora Man-Ling Hu, Sept. 7, 1968; 1 child, Stephen. BS, U. Calif., Berkeley, 1964; PhD, Stanford U., 1968. Mem. tech. staff TRW Inc., Redondo Beach, Calif., 1968-74, sect. head, 1974-79, dept. mgr., 1979-83, sr. staff engr., 1983—. Contbr. articles to profl. jours.; inventor cellulosics for the removal of sulfur dioxide. Mem. Am. Inst. Chem. Engrs. Home: 19945 Linda Dr Torrance CA 90503 Office: TRW Inc One Space Park Redondo Beach CA 90278

SHILL, VICTOR LAMAR, architect; b. Phoenix, July 6, 1933; s. Victor David and Olive (Nielsen) S.: m. Patsy Ann Nelson, Nov. 7, 1952; children: Michael, Wayne, Mark, Curt, Tracy. BArch, Ariz. State U., 1955. Registered architect, Ariz. Architect Kistner, Wright & Wright, Los Angeles, 1955-56, Horlbeck, Hickman & Assocs., Mesa, Ariz., 1956-63; pres. Shill, Judd, Richards & Johnson Architects, Mesa, 1963—. Prin. works include Mesa Police Bldg., Mesa Cts. Bldg., Dobson High Sch., Mesa (Lighting award 1981), Rhoder Jr. High Sch., Mesa (AIA award 1978), Ariz. State U. Student Health Bldg., Tempe, Eastern Ariz. Coll. Fine Arts Ctr., Thatcher, Shepherd Jr. High Sch., Mesa, over 100 church projects throughout Ariz. Mem. AIA. Republican. Mormon. Home: 2550 N Gilbert Mesa AZ 85203 Office: Shill Judd Richards & Johnson 1045 E McKellips Rd Mesa AZ 85203

SHILLITO, BARRY JAMES, industrialist; b. Dayton, Ohio, Jan. 1, 1921; s. Lucian W. and Mary Ellen (O'Connor) S.; m. Eileen Elizabeth Cottman, Dec. 2, 1942; children: Barry L., Elaine Tanavage, Daniel G., James K., Colleen Morse. BBA, U. Dayton, 1949; postgrad., UCLA, 1958. Gen. mgr. Harris Lincoln Supply Co., Dayton, 1946-49; sec., chief contracting officer Air Materiel Command, Wright Patterson AFB, Ohio, 1949-54; dir. material sales Hughes Aircraft, 1954-58; exec. v.p., pres. Houston-Fearless Co., Los Angeles, 1958-62; pres. Logistics Mgmt. Inst., Washington, 1962-68; asst. sec. Dept. Navy, Washington, 1968-69, Dept. Def., Washington, 1969-73; pres. Teledyne Ryan., San Diego, 1973-77; v.p. Teledyne, Inc., Los Angeles, 1977-81; chmn. Teledyne Internat., Arlington, Va., 1982-84, La Jolla, Calif., 1984-86; ret. 1986; bd. dirs. Morton Thiokol, Inc., Sci. Applications Internat. Corp., Logistics Mgmt. Inst., Burdeshaw Assocs., Trio Tech. Internat., BR Communications. Campaign chmn. United Way of San Diego County, 1975. Served to 1st lt. USAF, 1942-45. Decorated Purple Heart, Cloud and Banner medal (Taiwan); recipient Disting. Pub. Service award U. Dayton, 1978. Mem. Aerospace Ind. Assn., Armed Forces Mgmt. Assn., Combat Pilots Assn., AIAA, Electronic Industries Assn., Soc. Logistics Engrs. (Founders medal 1976), Indsl. Coll. Armed Forces, Nat. Contract Mgmt. Assn. (Herbert Roback Meml. award 1982), U. Dayton Alumni Assn., UCLA Alumni Assn., Def. Systems Mgmt. Sch., Nat. Alliance Businessmen (met. chmn. 1974-75). Republican. Roman Catholic. Clubs: Burning Tree, Army Navy (Washington); Moraine Country (Dayton); La Jolla Country, Conquistadores del Cielo, San Diego Yacht. Office: 2815 Camino del Rio S Suite C-393 Bldg 2535 San Diego CA 92108

SHIMEK, DEAN TROY, mechanical engineer; b. Austin, Tex., Nov. 4, 1948; s. George Dean and Mary Ellen (White) S. Assoc. in Applied Sci., Austin Community Coll., 1978, Assoc. Sci., 1978; BSME, U. Tex., 1982. Mech. engr. USN Gage and Standards Ctr., Pomona, Calif., 1983—. Chmn. gage and standards ctr. savings bond drive USN, 1986; mgr. Navy Twilight Golf League, Pomona, 1985. Mem. Navy League of U.S. (local chpt. program com., 1984), Precision Measurements Assn., Robotics Internat. (military ststems com.), Air and Space Smithsonian (charter), Ex-Student's Assn. U. Tex. Methodist. Avocations: reading, baseball, collecting space program stamps, yard work, tv. Home: 6846 Plum Way Rancho Cucamonga CA 91739 Office: USN Gage & Standards Ctr 1675 W Mission Blvd Pomona CA 91769-5000

SHIMEK, RONALD LEE, zoologist; b. Great Falls, Mont., Mar. 28, 1948; s. Benin and Sharon Irene (Warner) S.; m. Roxie Lynn Fredrickson. BS in Zoology, Mont. State U., 1970; MS in Zoology, U. Wash., 1973, PhD in Zoology, 1977. Asst. prof. biology U. Alaska, Anchorage, 1977-80, chmn. dept., 1979; ind. investigator Friday Harbor (Wash.) Labs. U. Wash., 1981-82; pvt. practice environ. cons. Friday Harbor, 1982-83; asst. dir. Bamfield (B.C., Can.) Marine Sta., 1983-85; research assoc. U. Ariz., Tucson, 1985-86; affiliate curator malacology Thomas Burke Meml. Wash. State Mus., Seattle, 1987—; environ. cons. Invertebrate Bioanalysis, Anchorage, 1979, WAPORA Inc., St. Louis. Contbr. articles to profl. jours. Fellow ADA, Washington, 1968, NSF, 1970-72. Mem. AAAS, Am. Malacol. Union Inc., Am. Soc. Zoologists, Western Soc. Naturalists (pres. nominating com. 1986), Sigma Xi. Club: Pacific N.W. Shell (Seattle) (v.p. 1974-75). Avocations: scuba diving, photography. Office: PO Box 69793 Seattle WA 98168

SHIMMIN, HAROLD STEVEN, educational administrator; b. Duluth, Minn., Oct. 28, 1948; s. Alfred Earl and Susan May (Lutes) S.; m. Bonnie Louise Walton, Dec. 21, 1969; children: Andrew Callender, Madeleine Haish. BA, UCLA, 1971; MA, Calif. State Coll., Bakersfield, 1978. Cert. standard elem. tchr., adminstrv. service credential. Tchr. Bakersfield Schs., 1971-75, curriculum specialist, 1975-80; research asst. Claremont (Calif.) Grad. Sch., 1981—; tchr. Ontario (Calif.) Schs., 1982-84, program facilitator, 1985; evaluation intern. —, 1985—. Contbr. articles to profl. jours. Mem.

NEA, AAAS, Calif. Sch. Adminstrs., Am. Psychol. Assn., Soc. for Psychol. Study of Social Issues. Democrat. Mem. of Mennonite Brethern. Avocation: collecting musical recordings. Home: 3177 Falcon St Pomona CA 91767 Office: Ontario-Montclair Sch Dist 950 W D St Ontario CA 91762

SHIMMIN, JOHN ALLEN, museologist, archaeologist; b. Detroit, Mar. 29, 1946; s. George Allen and Gertrude (Reeve) S. B.A., Mich. State U., 1975. Artist/cartographer Mich. State U., East Lansing, 1975-76; archaeol. field supr. Mackinac Island State Park Commn., Mich., 1976-79; pres. Archaeographic, Royal Oak, Mich., 1978-82; geophys. data analyst Gold Fields Mining Corp., Denver, 1983—; exec. dir. Archaeographic, Denver, 1982—; archaeol. investigator Western U.S. and Mich.; creator displays for pub. and pvt. mus.; lectr. in field. Illustrator: An Archaeological Inventory and Evaluation of the Sleeping Bear Dunes National Lakeshore, Leelanau and Benzie Counties, Michigan, 1976; The Garfield Orbit, 1978; also numerous other maps and illustrations for profl. jours. Contbr. various articles. Recipient 1st place drawing show Kent State U., 1965-67. Mem. Internat. Platform Assn., Archaeol. Inst. Am., Delta Tau Delta. Presbyterian. Address: 411 Ogden St Denver CO 80218

SHIMODA, WILBERT, chemist, research administrator; b. Denver, May 14, 1931; s. George Gunichi and Ethel Sumiyo (Imai) S.; m. Mary Alice Ague, June 11, 1954; children: Todd Adrian, Matthew George, Gregory John. BS in Chemistry, Colo. State U., 1957, MS in Biochemistry, 1963, postgrad., 1969-72. Sr. research asst. Colo. State U., Ft. Collins, 1957-65; chief chemistry unit Bur. Radiol. Health, Las Vegas, Nev., 1965-68, chief radioiodine studies, 1968-69; research chemist Ctr. Vetr. Medicine, Rockville, Md., 1972-81; dir. research ctr. FDA, Denver, 1981—. Contbr. articles to profl. jours. Advisor Ft. Collins council Boy Scouts Am., 1971, com. mem., Ft. Collins, Las Vegas, Glen Burnie, Md., 1960-75; active PTA, Ft. Collins, Las Vegas, Glen Burnie, 1960-80. Served to capt. USPHS, 1965—. Recipient Dist. Meritorious Service award Boy Scouts Am., 1969, Meritorous Service award USPHS, 1985, Commendation medal USPHS, 1974. Mem. Am. Chem. Soc., Health Physics Soc., Soc. Study Reprodn., Am. Soc. Animal Sci., Assn. Ofcl. Analytical Chemists (com. G 1983-86), Colo. State U. Alumni Assn., Sigma Xi (treas., del. 1980-81). Avocations: auto racing, golf, travel, bowling, fishing. Office: FDA 500 US Customhouse Denver CO 80202

SHIMP, LAWRENCE ALBERT, research chemist; b. Phila., Nov. 17, 1949; s. Hans George and Lydia (Bacon) S. BA, Northwestern U., 1971; PhD, MIT, 1976. Postdoctoral research assoc. U. Tex., Austin, 1976-77, Argonne (Ill.) Nat. Lab., 1977; research chemist FMC Corp., Princeton, N.J., 1977-85; prin. scientist Coors Biomed. Co., Lakewood, Colo., 1985—. Contbr. articles to profl. jours.; inventor tetramethylpentane blood substitutes, others. Fellow Am. Inst. Chemists; mem. Am. Chem. Soc., N.Y. Acad. Scis., Sigma Xi. Home: 7470 Terry Ct Golden CO 80403 Office: Coors Biomed Co 12860 W Cedar Dr Lakewood CO 80228

SHINDE, ANIL SHRAWAN, mechanical engineer; b. Amravati, India, Sept. 30, 1953; came to U.S., 1978; s. Shrawan Tulaji and Babitai S. (Shelkey) S.; m. Snehal Anil Kale, July 5, 1979; 1 child, Aniketa. BS, Govt. Engring. Coll., Amravati, 1975; MS, Indian Inst. Tech. Powai, Bombay, 1977. Registered profl. engr., Wis., Calif. Mech. engr. Environ. Systems Design Inc., Chgo., 1978-81; project engr. Constrn. Control Services Corp., Culver City, Calif., 1981-83; project mgr. Robert M. Young & Assocs., Pasadena, Calif., 1983—. Mem. ASHRAE, Assn. Energy Engrs. (sr.), Inst. Engrs. India. Avocations: games, cricket, soccer, golf. Office: Robert M Young & Assocs 36 N Marengo Ave Pasadena CA 91101

SHINDLER, JACK THOMAS, fin. co. exec., lawyer; b. St. Louis, Jan. 18, 1924; s. Harold Allen and Marie (McCawley) S.; A.B., Georgetown U., 1948; postgrad. Harvard Bus. Sch., 1945, U. Louvain (Belgium), 1949-51; LL.B., Ind. U., 1963, J.D., 1964. With Banque de Bruxelles, N.Y.C., 1951-53, Fidelity Bank and Trust Co., Indpls., 1954-58; admitted to Ind. bar, 1963, U.S. Dist. Ct. bar, 1963; asst. atty. gen. State of Ind., 1963-65; U.S. atty. Dept. Justice, Newburgh and Indpls. 1966-68; practice law, Evansville, Ind., 1968-75; v.p., gen. counsel The Thomas Co., Las Vegas, Nev., 1976—; dir. Nye Enterprises, Las Vegas, Francis Co., Pompano, Fla. Vice chmn. Ind. League Voters, 1954-64. Served as lt. (j.g.), USNR, 1942-52. Recipient Freedom Found. award, 1948. Mem. Theater Arts Soc. of Las Vegas, Georgetown Alumni Assn., YMCA. Democrat. Roman Catholic. Club: Theater Arts, Inc. (Las Vegas). Lectr. Office: The Thomas Co 1111 Las Vegas Blvd S Suite 214 Las Vegas NV 89104

SHINDO, SHOJIRO, aerodynamicist, aeronautical engineer; b. Osaka, Japan, July 18, 1931; s. Mamoru and Ochie S.; m. Kazumi Hisada, Jan. 10, 1960; children—Kaori, Hiroyuki. B.S. in Aero. Engring., U. Wash., 1957. Project engr. Kawasaki Aircraft Co., Gifu, Japan, 1960-62; design engr. U. Wash. Aero. Lab., Seattle, 1958-60, 1963-67, aero. engr., 1967—; cons. in field. Recipient Japanese Govt. Research award Nat. Aerospace Lab., Tokyo, 1974. Mem. AIAA. Author papers and reports on low-speed wind tunnel testing; transl. (with Harold N. Wantiez): Eagles of Mitsubishi, The Story of the Zero Fighter (Jiro Horikoshi), 1981. Home: 20010 Burke Ave N Seattle WA 98133 Office: Dept Aero and Astro U Wash FS 10 Seattle WA 98195

SHINGLETON, GERALD LEE, architect; b. Los Angeles, Jan. 11, 1947; s. Rupert and Marian Augusta (Anderson) S.; m. Karen Jane Keenan; children: William Richard, Johnathan Thomas. AA, El Camino Coll., 1966; BArch, Calif. Poly. State U., San Luis Obispo, 1971. Lic. architect, Calif. Ptnr. Johnson & Shingleton, Lake Arrowhead, Calif., 1974-76; pvt. practice architecture Lake Arrowhead and San Bernardino, Calif., 1976—. Mem. Archtl. Rev. Commn., Lake Arrowhead, 1982-85. Mem. AIA. Home: PO Box 694 Cedar Glen CA 92321

SHIRANE, HARUO, Japanese literature educator; b. Tokyo, Sept. 16, 1951; came to U.S., 1953; s. Gen and Sakae (Uchiyama) S.; m. Tomi Suzuki; 1 child, Seiji. BA, Columbia Coll., 1974; MA, U. Mich., 1977; PhD, Columbia U., 1983. Instr. dept. East Asian Lang. and Cultures U. So. Calif., Los Angeles, 1982-83, asst. prof., 1983—; mem. subcom. Non-Western Civilizations, U. So. Calif., 1984—, senator rep. dept. and div. Humanities, 1985—, Waseda U. Exchange Program com., 1984—; mem. exec. com. So. Calif. Japan Seminar; mem. Nat. Resource Fellowship selection com. 1983-85, Monbusho Fellowship selection com. 1984. Author: The Bridge of Dreams: A Poetics of The Tale of Genji, 1986, The Denial of the Romance, 1982. Fulbright fellow HEW, 1981, Japan Found. fellow, 1980; U. So. Calif. scholar, 1986. Mem. Modern Lang. Assn., Assn. for Asia Studies, Assn. Tchrs. of Japanese, So. Calif. Japan Seminar. Office: U So Calif Dept East Asian Lang Cultures 226 Taper Hall Los Angeles CA 90089-0357

SHIRE, DAVID LEE, composer; b. Buffalo, July 3, 1937; s. Irving Daniel and Esther Miriam (Sheinberg) S.; m. Talia Rose Coppola, Mar. 29, 1970 (div.); 1 son, Matthew Orlando.; m. Didi Conn, Feb. 11, 1984. B.A., Yale U., 1959. Film scores include The Conversation, 1974, The Taking of Pelham 1-2-3, 1974, Farewell, My Lovely, 1975, The Hindenburg, 1975, All the President's Men, 1977, Saturday Night Fever (adaptation and additional music), 1977, Norma Rae, 1979 (Acad. award for best original song It Goes Like It Goes), Only When I Laugh, 1981, The World According to Garp, 1982, Max Dugan Returns, 1983, 2010, 1984, Return to Oz, 1985, Short Circuit, 1986, 'Night, Mother, 1986; TV scores include Raid on Entebbe, 1977 (Emmy nomination), The Defection of Simas Kudirka, 1978 (Emmy nomination, Do You Remember Love?, 1985 (Emmy nomination); theatre scores include: The Sap of Life, 1961, Graham Crackers, 1962, The Unknown Soldier and His Wife, 1967, How Do You Do, I Love You, 1968, Love Match, 1970, Starting Here, Starting Now, 1977, Baby, 1983 (Tony nominee best mus. and best original score); composer: Sonata for Cocktail Piano, 1965; recorded songs include Autumn, 1959, Starting Here, Starting Now, 1965, What About Today?, 1969, Manhattan Skyline, 1977, The Promise, 1978 (Acad. award nomination), It Goes Like It Goes, 1979, With You I'm Born Again, 1979; albums include Saturday Night Fever, 1977 (Grammy award 1978), Starting Here, Starting Now, 1977 (Grammy nomination 1977), Baby, 1984, Return to Oz, 1985. Served with Army N.G., 1960-66. Mem. Composers and Lyricists Guild Am., Am. Fedn. Musicians, Broadcast Music Inc., Acad. Motion Picture Arts and Scis., Nat. Acad. Rec. Arts and Scis., Nat. Acad. TV Arts and Scis. Jewish. Office: care Laventhol & Horwath 2049 Century Park E Suite 3700 Los Angeles CA 90067

SHIRE, HAROLD RAYMOND, legal educator, author; b. Denver, Nov. 23, 1910; s. Samuel Newport and Rose Betty (Herrmann) S.; m. Cecilia Goldhaar; children: Margaret, David, Donna, Darcy, Esti. M.B.A., Pepperdine U., 1972; LL.D. (hon.), 1975; J.D., Southwestern U., Los Angeles, 1974; M.Liberal Arts, U. So. Calif., 1977; Ph.D. in Human Behavior, U.S. Internat. U., San Diego, 1980. Bar: Calif. 1937, U.S. Dist. Ct. (so. dist.) Calif. 1939, U.S. Supreme Ct. 1978. Dep. dist. atty. Los Angeles County, Calif., 1937-38; asst. U.S. atty. So. Dist. Calif., Los Angeles and San Diego, Justice Dept., 1939-42; sole practice, Los Angeles, 1946-56; pres., chmn. bd. Gen. Connectors Corp., U.S. and Eng., 1956-73; prof. mgmt. and law Pepperdine U., Malibu, Calif., 1974-75, U.S. Internat. U., San Diego, 1980-83; dir. Bestobell Aviation, Eng., 1970-74. Bd. dirs. Pepperdine U., 1974-80; nat. bd. govs. Union Orthodox Jewish Congregations Am., 1973—. Served with U.S. Army, 1942-46. Author: Cha No Yu and Symbolic Interactionism: Method of Predicting Japanese Behavior, 1980; The Tea Ceremony, 1984. Patentee aerospace pneumatics; invented flexible connectors. Decorated chevalier du vieux moulin (France); companion Royal Aero. Soc. (U.K.). Mem. Am. Legion (service officer). Republican. Office: PO Box 1352 Beverly Hills CA 90213

SHIREMAN, JOAN FOSTER, social work educator; b. Cleve., Oct. 28, 1933; d. Louis Omar and Genevieve (Duguid) Foster; m. Charles Howard Shireman, Mar. 18, 1967; 1 child, David Louis. BA, Radcliffe Coll., 1956; MA, U. Chgo., 1959, PhD, 1968. Caseworker N.H. Children's Aid Soc., Manchester, 1959-61; dir. research Chgo. Child Care Soc., 1968-72; assoc. prof. U. Ill., Chgo., 1972-85; prof. Portland (Oreg.) State U., 1985—; research cons. child welfare orgns., Ill., 1968-85; mem. adv. bd. Children's Service Div., Salem, Oreg., 1985—; lectr. U. Chgo., 1968-72. Co-author: Care and Commitment: Foster Parent Adoption Decisions, 1985; mem. editorial bd. Jour. Sch. Social Work, 1978-81; contbr. chpts. to books and articles to profl. jours. Bd. mem. Oreg. chpt. Nat. Assn. for Prevention of Child Abuse. Grantee HEW, 1980-82, Chgo. Community Trust, 1982-86. Mem. Nat. Assn. Social Workers, AAUP, Citizens for Children, Acad. Cert. Social Workers, Council on Social Work Edn., Phi Beta Kappa. Home: 2535 SW Sherwood Dr Portland OR 97201 Office: Portland State U Grad Sch Social Work PO Box 751 Portland OR 97202

SHIREY, JOHN FREDERICK, government administrator, lecturer; b. Muncie, Ind., July 10, 1949; s. John Mark and Chloie Marie (Harvey) S.; m. Marilyn Elaine Murden, Apr. 20, 1979; children: Jill Meredith, Gregory Mark. B.S.I.E., Purdue U., 1971; M.P.A., U. So. Calif., 1973. Adminstrv. asst. City of Monterey Park, Calif., 1972-75; legis. analyst City of Long Beach, Calif., 1975-76, dir. intergovtl. relations, 1976-79, asst. city mgr., 1987—; legis. counsel Nat. League Cities, Washington, 1979-82; asst. exec. dir. County of Los Angeles Community Devel. Commn., Calif., 1982-86; asst. chief adminstrv. officer County of Los Angeles, 1985-87; asst. city mgr. City of Long Beach, 1987—; lectr. grad. ctr. for pub. policy and adminstrn., Calif. State U., Long Beach, 1977-79, 83—, sch. pub. adminstrn. U. So. Calif, Los Angeles, 1986—. Contbr. numerous articles to Nation's Cities Weekly, 1979-82. Nat. cert. track and field ofcl. Athletics Congress, So. Calif., 1975—; v.p. Praetors, Sch. Pub. Adminstrn. U. So. Calif., Los Angeles, 1984, pres. 1985-86; bd. councilors Sch. Pub. Adminstrn., U. So. Calif., Los Angeles, 1983—. Named Outstanding Young Man Am., U.S. Jaycees, 1980. Mem. Am. Soc. Pub. Adminstrn. (chpt. council 1978-79, 84—, nat. chmn. sect. on intergovtl. adminstrn. and mgmt. 1979-80), Nat. Assn. County Community Devel. Dirs. (bd. dirs. 1984-85), Govt. Fin. Officers Assn., Internat. City Mgmt. Assn., Mcpl. Mgmt. Assts. So. Calif. (pres. 1974-75). Mem. Christian Ch. (Disciples of Christ). Clubs: Big Ten of So. Calif., Purdue of Los Angeles (Los Angeles). Home: 3721 Cerritos Ave Long Beach CA 90807 Office: City of Long Beach 333 W Ocean Blvd Long Beach CA 90802

SHIRLEY, DAVID ARTHUR, laboratory director; b. North Conway, N.H., Mar. 30, 1934; m. Virginia Schultz, June 23, 1956; children: David N., Diane, Michael, Eric, Gail. B.S., U. Maine, 1955, Sc.D. (hon.), 1978; Ph.D. in Chemistry, U. Calif.-Berkeley, 1959. With Lawrencee Radiation Lab. (now Lawrence Berkeley Lab.), U. Calif., Berkeley, 1958—, assoc. dir., head materials and molecular research div., 1975-80; dir. Lawrence Radiation Lab. (now Lawrence Berkeley Lab.), U. Calif., Berkeley, 1980—, lectr. chemistry, 1959-60, asst. prof., 1960-64, assoc. prof., 1964-67, prof., 1967—, vice chmn. dept. chemistry, 1968-71, chmn. dept. chemistry, 1971-75. Contbr. 300 articles in field to profl. jours. NSF fellow, 1955-58, 66-67, 70; recipient Ernest O. Lawrence award AEC, 1972. Fellow Am. Phys. Soc.; mem. Nat. Acad. Scis., Am. Chem. Soc., AAAS, Am. Acad. Arts and Scis., Sigma Xi, Tau Beta Pi, Sigma Pi Sigma, Phi Kappa Phi. Office: Lawrence Berkeley lab 1 Cyclotron Rd Berkeley CA 94720

SHIRLEY, THOMAS CLIFTON, biology educator; b. Falfurrias, Tex., Sept. 17, 1947; s. Homer Clifton and Julia Justine (Janak) S.; m. Susan McCorkle, Dec. 8, 1979. BS, Tex. A&I U., 1969, MS, 1974; PhD, La. State U., 1982. Instr. La. State U., Baton Rouge, 1978-82; physiologist Nat. Marine Fisheries Service, Juneau, Alaska, 1982; asst. prof. U. Alaska, Juneau, 1982—. Contbr. articles to profl. jours. dir. league Juneau Youth Football League, 1986, coach, 1985; bd. dirs. Baton Rouge Marathon, 1978. Served as sgt. U.S. Army, 1970-71, Vietnam. Decorated Bronze Star; fellow Caesar Kleberg Wildlife Found., 1971-72, Petroleum Refiners Council, 1973-75; named Eagle Scout Boy Scouts Am., 1963. Mem. AAAS (bd. dirs. arctic div.), Am. Inst. Biol. Scis., The Crustacean Soc., Biol. Soc. Wash., Ecol. Soc. Am., Am. Fisheries Soc., Nat. Audubon Soc. (bd. dirs. 1981-82). Avocations: racquetball, basketball, coaching, fishing, hiking. Home: 9345 Northland St Juneau AK 99801 Office: U Alaska Sch Fisheries 11120 Glacier Hwy Juneau AK 99801

SHIROTANI, YU YUU, painter; b. Osaka, Japan, May 20, 1940; came to U.S., 1964; s. Yasuhiko Mohri and Juko Takamatsu; married; 1 child, Akiko. Grad. in Modern Arts with honors, Kohnan U., 1963, grad. in Arts, 1964. Cert. stage costume designer. Pres. Gallery Sawa, Japan, 1964-74; v.p. Zeniya Co. Inc., Torrance, Calif., 1974-85, Howard E. Morseburg Galleries, Los Angeles, 1985—; dir. Takamatsu Interior, Japan, 1971-74. Author: A Part of Bible, 1978. Baptist. Home: 805 N Paulina Ave Redondo Beach CA 90277 Office: Studio Yu 18039 Crenshaw Blvd 204 Torrance CA 90504

SHIRTS, RANDALL BRENT, chemistry professor, researcher; b. Mt. Pleasant, Utah, Apr. 28, 1950; s. Morris Alpine and Dorothy Maxine (Baird) S.; m. Kathryn Adele Hanson, June 12, 1974; children: Michael Brian, Caitlin, Peter, Kristen. BS in Chemistry, Brigham Young U., 1973; AM in Physics, Harvard U., 1978, PhD in Chem. Physics, 1979. Postdoctoral assoc. JILA, Boulder, Colo., 1979-81; asst. prof. chemistry Georgetown U., Washington, 1981-82, U. Utah, Salt Lake City, 1982—. Contbr. articles to profl. jours. Grantee Nat. Sci. Found., 1985-88, Research Corp., 1982-84, Petroleum Research Fund, 1982-84. Mem. Am. Chem. Soc., Am. Phys. Soc., Sigmi Xi. Mormon. Office: U Utah Dept Chemistry Salt Lake City UT 84112

SHIRTS, RUSSELL BAIRD, library director; b. Moroni, Utah, May 26, 1948; s. Morris Alpine and Dorothy Maxine (Baird) S.; m. Marilyn June Stowell, Aug. 6, 1971; children: David Russell, Erin, Casey William, Daniel Bradley, Kimberly Ann. BA, So. Utah State Coll., 1972; MLS, Brigham Young U., 1980. Tchr., coach Duchesne (Utah) Sch. Dist., 1972-74; tchr., coach, librarian Iron County Sch. Dist., Parowan, Utah, 1974-77; librarian Utah State Library, Salt Lake City, 1977-80; dir. Wash. County Library, St. George, Utah, 1980—; cons. Dixie Med. Ctr., St. George, 1984—. Mem. Utah Adv. Council for Library Info. Services, 1983—, Utah Bookmobile Task Force, Utah Network for Cooperating Libraries, 1982-85; pres. Little League Baseball, Parowan, St. George, 1974; coach St. George Recreation, 1980-86. Mem. Am. Library Assn. (Allie Beth Martin award com. 1982), Mountain Plains Library Assn. (nominating com. 1983, Beginning Profl. award 1982), Utah Library Assn. (vice chmn. conv. exhibits 1978-79, rural library com.). Mormon. Avocations: coaching youth sports, jogging, reading. Home: 1407 W 625 N Saint George UT 84770 Office: Wash County Library 50 S Main Saint George UT 84770

SHISHIM, FRANCIS G. (DARK BOB), artist, performer; b. Santa Monica, Calif., May 8, 1953; s. Francis A. and Margaret W. (Addes) S. BFA in Painting, Art Ctr. Coll., 1975. lectr. Art Ctr. Coll. Design, Pasadena, Calif., Otis/Parson Sch. Design, Los Angeles, Calif. Inst. Arts, Valencia, U. Calif.-Berkeley Art Mus., San Francisco Art Inst. and others, 1978—. Exhibitions with Paul Velick (The Light Bob) include Ruth S. Schaffner Gallery, Los Angeles, 1978, Swope Gallery/Art Garden, Venice, Calif., 1979, Los Angeles Inst. Contemporary Art, Los Angeles, 1979, Vanguard Gallery, Los Angeles, 1980, Espace Gallery, Los Angeles, 1981, Upstairs Gallery, Tryon, N.C., 1981, WPA Gallery, Washington, 1981, Marianne Deson Gallery, Chgo., 1982; exhibited in group shows at Los Angeles Inst. Contemporary Art, 1976, 81, Craft and Folk Art Mus., Los Angeles, 1980, Long Beach (Calif.) Mus. Art, San Francisco Internat. Video Festival, 1980, Mus. Contemporary Art, Chgo., 1981, Downtown Gallery, Los Angeles, 1981, Tortue Gallery, Santa Monica, 1981, Am. Gallery, Los Angeles, 1982, UCLA, 1982, WPA Gallery, 1982, Calif. State U., Long Beach, 1983, traveling exhibitions, Los Angeles, Buffalo, 1983, Cochise Fine Arts Gallery, Bisbee, Ariz., Kansas City (Mo.) Art Inst., Spaces ARt Ctr. Cleve. State U., Film in the Cities Jerome Hill Theatre, St. Paul, Randolf St. Gallery, Chgo., Chgo. Art Inst., Inst. Contemporary Art, Boston, Painted Bride Art Ctr., Phila., Swain Sch. Design, New Bedford, Mass., Portland (Oreg.) Ctr. Visual Arts, L.A.C.E. Gallery, Los Angeles, New Langton Gallery, San Francisco, Inst. Contemporary Art, San Jose, Calif., Contemporary Arts Forum, Santa Barbara, Calif., Calif. State U., Long Beach., Sushi Art Gallery, San Diego; appeared in numerous performances, radio interviews, recordings and videos, 1975—. Office: Bob & Bob PO Box 6461 Beverly Hills CA 90212

SHIVELY, JAMES NELSON, animal pathologist, veterinarian; b. Moran, Kans., Feb. 9, 1925; s. Carl Nelson and Clara Wanda (Keith) S.; m. Ruth Ann Webster, June 6, 1953; children: Elizabeth, Susan, Robert. DVM, Kans. State U., 1946; MP H, Johns Hopkins U., 1953; MS, U. Rochester, 1956; PhD, Colo. State U., 1971. Commd. U.S. Army, 1946, advanced through grades to major, resigned, 1960, research veterinarian, 1946-60; animal pathologist and ultrastructurist USPHS, 1961-70; assoc. prof. Cornell U./N.Y. State Vet. Coll., Ithaca, 1971-75; prof. U. Ariz., Tucson, 1975—. Contbr. articles to profl. jours. and chpts. to books. Mem. AVMA, Internat. Acad. Pathology, Electron Microscopy Soc. Am., Sigma Xi. Avocations: photography, cross-country skiing. Office: U Ariz Vet Sci Dept Tucson AZ 85721

SHIVELY, JOHN TERRY, business executive; b. Middletown, N.Y., July 1, 1943; s. Marvin Rathfelder and Esther (Manning) Westervelt; adopted child, Harold Eugene Shively; B.A., U. N.C., 1965. Vol. worker VISTA, Bethel, Yakutat, and Fairbanks, Alaska, 1965-68; health planner Greater Anchorage Area Community Action Agy., 1968-69; health cons. Alaska Fedn. Natives, Anchorage, 1969; dep. dir. Rural Alaska Community Action Program, Anchorage, 1969-70, exec. dir., 1971-72; exec. v.p. Alaska Fedn. Natives, Anchorage, 1972-75; v.p. ops. NANA Regional Corp., Kotzebue, Alaska, 1975-77, NANA Devel. Corp., Anchorage, 1977-82, sr. v.p., 1982-83; chief of staff to gov. of Alaska, 1983-85; cons. bus. and govt., 1985-86; sr. v.p. NANA Regional Corp., Inc., 1986—; chmn. Alaska State Bd. Game, 1983-84. dir. Unicorp. Inc., United Bank of Alaska, NANA Oilfield Services. Mem. Greater Anchorage Area Comprehensive Health Plan Council, 1969-75, chmn., 1969-75; founding mem. bd. dirs. Alaska Pub. Interest Research Group, 1974-75, 86—; mem. Gov.'s Rural Affairs Council, 1971-76, Gov.'s Manpower Commn., 1971, Greater Anchorage Health Bd., 1969-75, Alaska Pipeline Edn. Com., 1973-74; bd. regents U. Alaska, 1979-83. Mem. Alaska Fedn. Natives. Democrat. Episcopalian. Home: PO Box 101758 Anchorage AK 99510 Office: NANA Regional Corp 4706 Harding Dr Anchorage AK 99503

SHIVELY, RUSSELL ALAN, product engineering administrator; b. Long Beach, Calif., Dec. 27, 1940; s. James Latimer and Billie Louise (Cox) S.; m. JoAnn Holland, Dec. 15, 1961; children: Rodney David, Vicki Diane. Student, Long Beach City Coll., 1959-66; AA in Bus. Adminstrn., Yavapai Coll., 1982; BSBA, Ariz. State U., 1986. Product engr. U.S. Elec. Motors Co., Los Angeles, 1961-67; supr. engring. U.S. Elec. Motors Co., Mena, Ark., 1968-70, supr. prodn. control, 1970-72, mgr. materials, 1972-74; sr. project engr. U.S. Elec. Motors Co., Milford, Conn., 1974-76; project mgr. U.S. Elec. Motors Co., Prescott, Ariz., 1976—. Co-author: Electric Power Supply and System Considerations, 1987; contbr. articles to profl. jours. Chmn. bd. deacons Dallas Ave Bapt. Ch., Mena, 1974; chmn. bd. deacons 1st So. Bapt. Ch., Prescott, 1980, trustee, 1981-82; judge Saguaro Internat. Photographic Exhibition, Phoenix, 1981. Mem. Am. Mgmt. Assn., Sigma Iota Epsilon, Beta Gamma Sigma. Republican. Club: Prescott Camera (pres. 1979-81). Lodge: Masons. Avocations: golf, scuba diving, photography, amateur radio. Home: 3032 Chaco Circle Prescott AZ 86301 Office: US Elec Motors Co 200 Ralph Pryne Dr Prescott AZ 86301

SHKURKIN, EKATERINA (KATIA) VLADIMIROVNA, social worker; b. Berkeley, Calif., Nov. 20, 1955; s. Vladimir Vladimirovich and Olga Ivanovna (Lisenko) S. Student, U. San Francisco, 1972-73; BA, U. Calif., Berkeley, 1974-77; MSW, Columbia U., 1977-79; postgrad., Union Grad. Sch., 1986. Cert. police instr. domestic violence, Alaska. Social worker Tolstoy Found., N.Y.C., 1978-79, adminstr., 1979-80; program supr. Rehab. Mental Health Ctr., San Jose, Calif., 1980-81; dir. service counselor Kodiak (Alaska) Crisis Ctr., 1981-82; domestic violence counselor Abused Women's Aid in Crisis, Anchorage, 1982-85; pvt. practice social work specializing in feminist therapy Susitna Therapy Ctr., Anchorage, 1985—; field instr. Abused Women's Aid in Crisis, Anchorage, 1983—; expert witness Anchorage Mcpl. Cts., 1982—; interim faculty U. Alaska, Anchorage, summer 1985, LaVerne U., Anchorage, spring 1986. Coordinator Orthodox Christian Fellowship, San Francisco, 1972-76; pub. speaker Abused Women's Aid in Crisis, Anchorage, 1982—; active nat. and local election campaigns, 1968—. Mem. Nat. Assn. Social Workers (cert.). Democrat. Russian Orthodox. Avocations: organic gardening, reading, crocheting, soccer. Home: 3605 Arctic Blvd #768 Anchorage AK 99503-5704

SHLENKER, SIDNEY L., professional basketball team executive. Attended, Tulane Univ. Former exec. v.p., chief oper. officer Astrodomain Corp., Houston, Tex.; founder PACE Mgmt. Corp.; sr. chmn. Allied Bank West Loop, Houston, Tex.; chmn. Grant Broadcasting System, Inc.; former pres. Houston Astros baseball club; former vice-chmn. Houston Rockets basketball club; majority owner, chmn. Denver Nuggets basketball team, 1985—. Address: care Denver Nuggets McNichols Sports Arena P O Box 4658 Denver CO 80204 Office: Allied Bank West P O Box 4401 Houston TX 77210 *

SHLICHTA, PAUL JOSEPH, research chemist; b. Bklyn., Dec. 4, 1930; s. Joseph and Valerie (Dhervillez) S.; m. Rena Elizabeth Klaiber, Dec. 10, 1966; children: Suzanne, Joseph, Thomas, John, Jennifer. BS in Chemistry, U. Notre Dame, 1952; PhD in Chemistry, Calif. Inst. Tech., 1956. Sr. scientist Jet Propulsion Lab., Calif. Inst. Tech., Pasadena, 1956-65, mem. tech. staff, 1976—; research scientist McDonnell-Douglas Corp., Huntington Beach, Calif., 1966-70; asst. prof., sr. research assoc. U. So. Calif., Los Angeles, 1970-76. Contbr. articles to profl. jours.; patentee in field. Fellow NSF; recipient Pres.'s Fund award Calif. Inst. Tech., 1983, Dirs. Fund award Jet Propulsion Lab., 1985. Mem. Am. Assn. Crystal Growth (mem. regional exec. council 1978-84), Am. Crystallographic Assn., Four Sigma Soc. Republican. Roman Catholic. Home: 1441 Sunnyside Terr San Pedro CA 90732 Office: Calif. Inst. Tech. Jet Propulsion Lab 67-201 Pasadena CA 91109

SHNEOUR, ELIE ALEXIS, neurochemist; b. Neuilly-sur-Seine, France, Dec. 11, 1925; came to U.S., 1941, naturalized, 1945; s. Zalman and Salomea (Landau) S.; m. Joan Haight Brewster, Jan. 22, 1955 (div. 1983); children: Mark Zalman, Alan Brewster. B.A., Columbia U., 1947; M.A., U. Calif. at Berkeley, 1955; Ph.D., U. Calif. at Los Angeles, 1958; D.Sc. (hon.), Bard Coll., 1969. Tchg., research fellowship U. Calif. at Berkeley, 1953-55; Nat. Cancer Inst. research fellow 1956-57; research, tchg. fellowship U. Calif. at Los Angeles, 1958; Am. Heart Assn. research fellow N.Y. U., 1958-59, U. Calif. at Berkeley, 1958-62; research assoc. genetics Stanford, 1962-65; assoc. prof. biology and neurosciences U. Utah, 1965-69; research neurochemist City of Hope Nat. Med. Center, Duarte, Calif., 1969-71; dir. research Calbiochem., 1971-75; pres. Biosystems Assos. Ltd., 1975—; dir. Bio systems Research Inst., 1979—; mem. exec. com. Nat. Acad. Sci. Study Group on

Biology and the Exploration of Mars, 1964; chmn. Western Regional council Research in Basic Bioscis. for Manned Orbiting Missions, Am. Inst. Biol. Scis., NASA, 1966-69. Author: Extraterrestrial Life, 1965, (with S. Moffat) Life Beyond the Earth, 1966, The Malnourished Mind, 1974; Contbr. numerous articles to sci. and lay jours. Chmn. citizens adv. council San Diego Public Schs., 1971-72; mem. adv. council Cousteau Soc., 1977—. Served with U.S. Army, 1944-45. Recipient William Lockwood prize, 1947. Mem. Am. Chem. Soc., N.Y. Acad. Scis., I.E.E.E., A.A.A.S., Am. Inst. Biol. Scis., Am. Soc. Biol. Chemists (chmn. sci. advisers program 1973-75, mem. com. on pub. policy 1974-76), Am. Soc. Neurochemistry (council 1971-73), Soc. Neurosci., Internat. Soc. Neurochemistry, Sigma Xi, Phi Sigma. Office: Biosystems Assocs Ltd Mc Kellar Research Ctr PO Box 1414 La Jolla CA 92038

SHOCKLEY, JAMES THOMAS, physics educator; b. Topaz, Mo., Sept. 16, 1925; s. William Ervin and Minnie Catherine (Turnbull) S.; m. Joan Elsie Griess, June 17, 1950 (div. Aug. 1968); 1 child, John William. BA, Calif. State U., Fresno, 1951, MA, 1953; postgrad., Claremont Grad. Sch., 1955; PhD, U. So. Calif., 1961. Cert. secondary tchr., Calif.; cert. community coll. tchr., Calif. Aerodynamicist N.Am. Aviation, Los Angeles, 1953; instr. Calif. State U., Fresno, 1954-55, asst. prof. physics, 1956-63, instr. workshop in phys. sci. for elem. tchrs., 1961, credential advisor, supr. student teaching, 1956-86, assoc. prof., 1963-68, prof., 1968—; cons. Fresno County Schs., 1971, USAF, Fresno, 1971, 72; validity cons. Commn. Tchr. Preparation and Licensing, San Francisco, 1977; instr. NSF Inst. for high sch. physics tchrs., 1962-63. Author: Physics and Astronomy for Liberal Arts Students, 1970; creator 7 Univ. Courses, 1958-85; textbook reviewer, 1965-77; contbr. articles to profl. jours. Active mem. Civil Def., Fresno, 1952; mem. City-Univ. Edn. Liaison Com., Fresno, 1963-64; judge Bullard High Sch. Sci. Fair, Fresno, 1964-66; sponser Physics Club, Fresno, 1953-55. Recipient I Dare You award Danforth Found., Sanger, Calif., 1944, Tchr. grant Danforth Found., Fresno, 1958; Congress of Parents and Tchrs. scholar, San Diego, 1960. Mem. Am. Inst. Physics, Planetary Soc., Astron. Soc. Pacific, Aero Club, Phi Delta Kappa. Mem. Christian Ch. Avocations: flying, oil painting, internat. travel, reading, photography.

SHOCKLEY, WILLIAM BRADFORD, physicist, emeritus educator; b. London, Feb. 13, 1910; (parent Am. citizens); s. William Hillman and May (Bradford) S.; m. Jean A. Bailey, 1933 (div. 1955); children: Alison, William Alden, Richard Condit; m. Emmy Lanning, 1955. B.S., Calif. Inst. Tech., 1932; Ph.D., M.I.T., 1936; Sc.D. (hon.), Rutgers U., 1956, U. Pa., 1955, Gustavus Adolphus Coll., Minn., 1963. Teaching fellow M.I.T., 1932-36; mem. tech. staff Bell Telephone Labs., 1936-42, 45, became dir. transistor physics research, 1954; dir. Shockley Semicondr. Lab.; pres. Shockley Transistor Corp., 1958-60; cons. Shockley Transistor unit Clevite Transistor, 1960-65; lectr. Stanford U., 1958-63, Alexander M. Poniatoff prof. engring. sci. and applied sci., 1963-75, prof. emeritus, 1975—; exec. cons. Bell Telephone Labs., 1965-75; dep. dir. research, weapons systems evaluation group Dept. Def., 1954-55; expert cons. Office Sec. War, 1944-45; vis. lectr. Princeton U., 1946; vis. prof. Calif. Inst. Tech., 1954-55; sci. adv., policy council Joint Research and Devel. Bd., 1947-49; sr. cons. Army Sci. Adv. Panel.; Dir. research Anti-submarine Welfare Ops. Research Group USN, 1942-44. Author: Electrons and Holes in Semiconductors, 1950, (with A.A. Gong) Mechanics, 1966; editor: Imperfections of Nearly Perfect Crystals, 1952. Recipient medal for Merit; Air Force Assn. citation of honor, 1951; U.S. Army cert. of appreciation, 1953; co-winner (with John Bardeen and Walter H. Brattain) Nobel Prize in Physics, 1956; Wilhelm Exner medal Oesterreichischer Gewerbeverein Austria, 1963; Holley medal ASME, 1963; Calif. Inst. Tech. Alumni Disting. Service award, 1966; NASA cert. of appreciation Apollo 8, 1969; Public Service Group Achievement award NASA, 1969; named to Inventor's Hall of Fame, 1974; named to Calif. Inventor's Hall of Fame, 1983. Fellow AAAS; mem. Am. Phys. Soc. (O.E. Buckley prize 1953), Nat. Acad. Sci. (Comstock prize 1954), IEEE (Morris Liebmann prize 1952, Gold medal, 25th anniversary of transistor 1972, Medal of Honor 1980), Sigma Xi, Tau Beta Pi. Holder over 90 patents. Inventor of junction transistor; research on energy bands of solids, ferromagnetic domains, plastic properties of metals; semicondr. theory applied to devices and device defects such as dislocations; fundamentals of electromagnetic energy and momentum; mental tools for sci. thinking; ops. research on human quality problems. Home: 797 Esplanada Way Stanford CA 94305 Office: Stanford Univ Dept Elec Engring Stanford Electronics Labs Stanford CA 94305

SHOCKLEY-ZALABAK, PAMELA SUE, educator, consultant, author; b. Amarillo, Tex., May 25, 1944; d. James William and Leatha Pearl (Cartwright) Shockley; B.A. (Lew Wentz Tri Delt scholar 1961-65), Okla. State U., 1965, M.A., 1972; Ph.D., U. Colo., 1980; m. Charles Zalabak, Dec. 30, 1975. Account exec., v.p. Ross Cummings & Co., Oklahoma City, 1965-70; cons., pres. CommuniCon, Inc., Colorado Springs, Colo., 1970—; asst. prof., program dir. U. Colo., Colorado Springs, 1980—, chairperson communications dept. Mem. Speech Communication Assn., Internat. Communication Assn., Phi Kappa Phi. Democrat. Home: 5905 Ridge Brook Ln Colorado Springs CO 80907 Office: Univ Colorado Communication Dept Austin Bluffs Pkwy Colorado Springs CO 80907

SHOCTOR, JOSEPH HARVEY, barrister, producer, civic worker; b. Edmonton, Alta., Can., Aug. 18, 1922. B.A., LL.B., U. Alta., 1946, LL.D. (hon.), 1981; diploma (hon.) in theatre adminstrn., McEwan Community Coll., 1986. Barrister, solicitor, sr. ptnr. Shoctor, Mousseau & Starkman, Edmonton; dir. First City Trust, First City Fin. Corp., Harvey Holdings Ltd.; Founder, contbr. Downtown Edmonton newspaper. Producer Broadway plays including Peter Pan, 1965, Henry, Sweet Henry, 1967, Billy, 1969, Hamlet, 1969. Active United Community Fund, 1968—; chmn. Downtown Devel. Corp., 1986; mem. Edmonton Jewish Welfare Bd.; past pres. Edmonton Jewish Community Council; past nat. sec. Federated Zionist Orgn.; past nat. v.p. United Israel Appeal, Inc.; past bd. dirs. Can. Council Jewish Welfare Funds; chmn. div. Brit. Commonwealth Games Found., 1978; founder, pres., exec. producer Citadel Theater, bldg. chmn., campaign chmn.; bd. govs. Nat. Theatre Sch. of Can.; producer Circle 8 Theatre, Civic Opera, Red Cross Entertainment; panelist pub. affairs talk show and sports forum; chmn. Edmonton Downtown Devel. Corp., 1986. Named Man of Hr., Sta. CFRN-TV, 1966, Citizen of Yr., B'nai B'rith, 1966, one of Twelve Top Albertans of the 70's, The Alberta Report; recipient Performing Arts award City of Edmonton, 1972, Theatre Arts Achievement award Province of Alta., 1975, Prime Minister's Medal, State of Israel, 1978; Builder of Community award City of Edmonton, 1979; Queen's Silver Jubilee medal, 1977; The Shoctor Theatre named in his honor, 1976; City of Edmonton Silver Ribbon award, 1985;Edmonton C. of C. Clubs: The Edmonton, The Centre, Eskimo Football (founder, past sec.-mgr.). Office: Shoctor Mousseau & Starkman, 1800 10104 103rd Ave, Edmonton, AB Canada T5J 4A4

SHOEMAKER, CARLYLE EDWARD, chemical engineer; b. Columbus, Ohio, Feb. 19, 1923; m. Violet A. Pacini, Oct. 23, 1948; children: Janet Shoemaker Jerus, John, David. BChemE, Ohio State U., 1943; MS in Chemistry, U. Ill., 1946, PhD in Chemistry and Chem. Engring., 1949. Registered profl. engr. Research chemist Monsanto Mound Lab., 1949-54; research supr. J.T. Baker Chem. Co., Phillipsburg, N.J., 1954-60; mem. tech. staff Bell Telephone Labs., Allentown, Pa., 1960-64; sr. research engr. Bethlehem (Pa.) Steel Co., 1964-77; cons. Gilbert Assocs., Bethlehem and Reading, Pa., 1977-78; project mgr. Electric Power Research Inst., Palo Alto, Calif., 1978—. Contbr. articles to profl. jours.; patentee in field. Mem. Am. Chem. Soc., Am. Soc. for Metals, Nat. Assn. Corrosion Engrs. Club: Toastmasters (Palo Alto) (pres. 1985). Home: 3561 Amber Dr San Jose CA 95117

SHOEMAKER, HAROLD LLOYD, computer system consultant; b. Danville, Ky., Jan. 3, 1923; s. Eugene Clay and Amy (Wilson) S.; A.B., Berea Coll., 1944; postgrad. State U. Ia., 1943-44, George Washington U., 1949-50, N.Y. U., 1950-52; m. Dorothy M. Maddox, May 11, 1947. Research physicist State U., Ia., 1944-45, Frankford Arsenal, Pa., 1945-47; research engr. N.Am. Aviation, Los Angeles, 1947-49, Jacobs Instrument Co., Bethesda, 1949-50; asso. head systems devel. group The Teleregister Corp., N.Y.C., 1950-53; mgr. electronic equipment devel. sect., head planning for indsl. systems div. Hughes Aircraft Co., Los Angeles, 1953-58; dir. command and control systems lab. Bunker-Ramo Corp., Los Angeles, 1958-68, v.p. Data Systems, 1968-69, corp. dir. data processing, 1969-75; tech. staff R & D Assocs., Marina Del Rey, Calif., 1975-85; info. systems cons., 1985—. Served with AUS, 1945-46. Mem. IEEE. Patentee elec. digital computer. Home: PO Box 3385 Granada Hills CA 91344

SHOEMAKER, MICHAEL JOHN, structural engineer; b. Washington, May 20, 1956; s. Robert Frank and Andrea (Lyons) S.; m. Robin Southworth, Oct. 15, 1983. BSCE, U. Va., 1979. Registered profl. engr., Alaska. Engr. Byrd, Tallany, McDonald & Lewis, Falls Church, Va., 1979-82; project engr. Tryck, Nyman & Hayes, Anchorage, 1982—. Contbr. articles to profl. jours. Recipient Cert. Spl. Recognition, Prestressed Concrete Inst., 1985, Award for Excellence, Wash. Precast Concrete Industry, 1985, Excellence in Design award Office of Sec. Def., 1986. Mem. ASCE, Structural Engrs. Assn. Alaska. Office: Tryck Nyman & Hayes 911 W 8th Ave Anchorage AK 99501

SHOEN, SAMUEL W, rental company executive; b. Feb. 26, 1945. B.A., Holy Cross Coll., 1967; M.D., U. Ariz., 1971; M.B.A., Harvard U., 1977. Pres. U-Haul Internat., Phoenix, 1981—. Office: U-Haul Internat 2727 N Central Phoenix AZ 85004

SHOMER, ROBERT BAKER, employee benefit consultant; b. Lakewood, Ohio, Aug. 26, 1943; s. John Edward and Margaret Jeannette (Yeager) S.; BA in Psychology, Cen. Wash. State U., 1966; m. Phyllis B. Newman, Apr. 25, 1985. Brokerage Supr. Aetna Life and Casualty Co., San Francisco, 1971-73; regional dir. Hartford Variable Annuity Co., 1973-75; dir. deferred compensation dept. Galbraith & Green, Inc., Tempe, Ariz., 1976-79, v.p., 1980-82; sr. v.p. Fred S. James, 1983-86; sr. v.p. mktg./nat. accounts Alta Health Strategies, Inc., Salt Lake City, 1986—. Served as capt. USAF, 1967-71. Home: 9733 S Quail Ridge Rd Sandy UT 84092 Office: Alta Health Strategies Inc 2614 S 1935 W Salt Lake City UT 84119

SHONK, ALBERT DAVENPORT, JR., publishers representative; b. Los Angeles, May 23, 1932; s. Albert Davenport and Jean Spence (Stannard) S.; B.S. in Bus. Adminstrn., U. So. Calif., 1954. Field rep. Los Angeles Examiner, 1954-55, asst. mgr. mktg. div. 1955-56, mgr., 1956-57; account exec. Hearst Advt. Service, Los Angeles, 1957-59; account exec., mgr. San Francisco area Keith H. Evans & Assos., 1959-65; owner, pres. Albert D. Shonk Co., Los Angeles, 1965—; pres., Signet Circle Corp., Inc., 1977-81, dir., 1962-81, hon. life dir., 1982-86. Bd. dirs., sec., 1st v.p. Florence Crittenton Services of Los Angeles, exec. v.p., 1979-81, pres., 1981-83, chmn. bd., 1983-85, hon. life dir., 1986—; founding chmn. Crittenton Assos. Recipient Medallion of Merit Phi Sigma Kappa, 1976, Founders award, 1961. Mem. Advt. Club Los Angeles, Bus. and Profl. Advt. Assn., Pubs. Rep. Assn. of So. Calif., Nat. Assn. Pubs. Reps. (past v.p. West Coast 1981-83), Jr. Advt. Club Los Angeles (hon. life; dir., treas., 1st v.p.), Trojan Club, Skull and Dagger, Inter-Greek Soc. (co-founder, hon. life mem. and dir., v.p. 1976-79, pres. 1984-86), Phi Sigma Kappa (dir. grand council 1962-70, 77-79, grand pres. 1979-83, chancellor 1983—, trustee, v.p. meml. found. 1979-84, pres. 1984, trustee pres. Phi Sigma Kappa found. 1984—), Alpha Kappa Psi. Home: 3460 W 7th St Los Angeles CA 90005 Office: 3156 Wilshire Blvd Los Angeles CA 90010

SHONKA, THOMAS EDWARD, podiatrist; b. Chgo., May 12, 1953; s. Francis R. and Louise M. (Cuchna) S.; m. Rene Murphy, Sept. 30, 1983. D Podiatric Medicine, Ill. Coll. Podiatric Medicine, 1978. Diplomate Am. Bd. Podiatric Surgery. Resident in surgery Hine VA Med. Ctr., Maywood, Ill., 1978-79; pvt. practice Boulder (Colo.) Podiatric Sports Medicine Clinic, 1979—. Contbr. articles on sports medicine to mags. Fellow Am. Coll. Foot Surgeons, Am. Acad. Podiatric Sports Medicine; mem. Am. Coll. Sports Medicine, Am. Podiatric Med. Assn., Colo. Podiatric Med. Assn. Office: Boulder Podiatric Sports Medicine Clinic 1120 Alpine Suite E Boulder CO 80302

SHONNARD, LUDLOW, III, agricultural operations executive; b. Pasadena, Calif., Dec. 12, 1950; s. Ludlow Jr. and Christy (Fox) S.; m. Catherine B. Bradley, Aug. 5, 1975; children: Lisa C., Sarah F., Elizabeth L. BA in Psychology, Colo. Coll., 1973. Mgr. Newhall Land & Farming Co., Firebaugh, Calif., 1975-86; pres. Leshon Internat., Inc., Clovis, Calif., 1986—; Bd. dirs. Columbia Canal Co., Firebaugh. Bd. dirs. Lower San Joaquin River Assn., Los Banos, Calif., 1982—; alt. Calif. Wheat Commn., Sacramento, 1983—. Mem. Calif. Wheat Growers Assn. (bd. dirs. 1983—), Calif. Beet Growers Assn. (bd. dirs., sec.-treas. adv. bd.). Home: 1365 E Portals Fresno CA 93710 Office: Leshon Internat Inc 55 Shaw Ave Suite 112 Clovis CA 93612

SHOOK, ROBERT MICHAEL, health care administrator; b. Yuma, Ariz., Mar. 5, 1943; s. William Arthur and Eleanor Eloise (Downey) S.; m. Jacqueline Palma Cetinich, July 5, 1970; children—Justin, Alexandra. B.S., No. Ariz. U., 1966. Program dir. Contra Costa Med. Services, Martinez, Calif., 1968-71; coordinator community mental retardation services, State of Oreg., 1971-74; exec. dir. Oreg. Devel. Disabilities Council, 1974-76; dir. child neurology clinic and comprehensive epilepsy program Good Samaritan Hosp. and Med. Ctr., Portland, Oreg., 1976-80, dir. planning and program devel., 1980-83, coordinator med. staff affairs, 1983—; past project dir. nat. model demonstration grants U.S. Dept. Edn.; lectr. on handicapped infants and children; del. White House Conf. on Handicapped Individuals, 1977. Author: Program Actions for Children with Epilepsy, 1985. Mem. Nat. Assn. Retarded Citizens, Nat. Epilepsy Found. Am., Hosp. Planning Soc., Am. Assn. Mental Deficiency (pres. Region I 1979), Assn. Severely Handicapped. Office: Good Samaritan Hosp and Med Ctr 1015 NW 22d Ave Portland OR 97210

SHORAKA, FEREYDOUN, chemist; b. Tehran, Iran, Jan. 14, 1950; came to U.S., 1975; s. Youssef and Flora (Cohen) S. BS in Materials Engring., Queen Mary Coll., London, 1973; MPhil in Polymer Physics, U. London, 1975; PhD in Chem. Engring, SUNY, Buffalo, 1979. Prin. engr. Carborundum, Niagara Falls, N.Y., 1979-82; devel mgr. Standard Oil of Ohio, Niagara Falls, N.Y., 1982-84; research, devel. mgr., polymer technology mgr. INTEL, Chandler, Ariz., 1984—. Mem. IEEE, Am. Inst. Chem. Engrs., Am. Ceramic Soc. Home: 10592 E Caron Scottsdale AZ 85258 Office: Intel Corp 145 S 79th St Chandler AZ 85224

SHORT, HEDLEY VICARS ROYCRAFT, retired bishop; b. Toronto, Ont., Can., Jan. 24, 1914; s. Hedley Vicars and Martha (Parke) S.; m. Elizabeth Frances Louise Shirley, Apr. 14, 1953; children: Martha, Elizabeth, Janet, Margaret, Desmond. B.A., U. Toronto, 1941; L.Th., Trinity Coll., Toronto, 1943, B.D., 1945, D.D., 1964; D.D. (hon.), U. Emmanuel, St. Chad, 1985. Ordained deacon Anglican Ch. of Can., 1943 ordained priest Anglican Ch. of Can., 1944, consecrated bishop Anglican Ch. of Can., 1970. Asst. curate ch. Toronto, 1943-46; jr. chaplain St. Michael's Cathedral, Coventry, Eng., 1946-47; lectr., sr. tutor, dean of residence Trinity Coll., Toronto, 1947-51; rector Cochraine, Ont., 1951-56, St. Catharines Ch., Ont., 1956-63; canon Diocese of Niagara, 1963-70; dean, rector St. Alban's Cathedral, Prince Albert, Sask., Can., 1963-70; archdeacon of Prince Albert 1966-70, bishop of Sask., 1970-85; pres. council Coll. Emmanuel, St. Chad; chancellor U. Emmanuel Coll., Saskatoon, chmn. doctrine and worship coms., 1971-83; mem. no. devel. adv. council Gov. of Sask., 1985-86. Chmn. high sch. bd., Cochrane, 1953-56, Prince Albert, 1970; chmn. bd. dirs. Prince Albert Community Coll., 1974-77; mem. No. Devel. Adv. Council, Govt. of Sask. Named hon. fellow Coll. Emmanuel and St. Chad, 1980.

SHORT, ROBERT HENRY, utility executive; b. Klamath Falls, Oreg., Oct. 15, 1924; s. Judge Haywood and Henrietta Luella (Lyon) S.; m. Ruby Madalyn Rice, Aug. 1, 1946; children—Robert L., Victoria (Mrs. Gregory Baum), Casey. BS in Journalism, U. Oreg., 1950; PhD in Humane Letters (hon.), Linfield Coll., 1984. City editor Klamath Falls Herald and News, 1950-52; dir. pub. relations Water and Elec. Bd., Eugene, Oreg., 1952-55; mgr. pub. info. Portland Gen. Electric Co., Oreg., 1955-57, asst. to chmn., 1957-62, v.p., 1962-71, sr. v.p., 1971-73, exec. v.p., 1973-77, pres., 1977-80, chmn. bd., chief exec. officer, 1980—, also dir.; dir. First Interstate Bank of Oreg. Bd. dirs. Oreg. Ind. Colls. Found., Oreg. United Way; trustee Oreg. Grad. Center, Willamette U., St. Vincent Hosp. and Med. Center. Served with USNR, 1942-45. Clubs: Astoria Country, Portland Golf, Arlington. Home: 1210 SW 61st Ct Portland OR 97221 Office: Portland Gen Electric Co 121 SW Salmon St Portland OR 97204

SHORTLE, PATRICK JOSEPH, training and management development consultant; b. Detroit, Nov. 16, 1951; s. Emmett Francis and Anne Mary (Mainville) S. BA, U. Santa Clara, 1973. Cert. personnel mgmt. and employee relations U. Calif.-Irvine, 1979. Tng. and devel. officer United Calif. Bank, Los Angeles, 1978-81; tng. and devel. rep. First Interstate Bank, Los Angeles, 1981-82; tng. and devel. cons. Hosp. Council of So. Calif., Los Angeles, 1982-84; adminstr. mgmt. devel. Douglas Aircraft Co., McDonnell Douglas Corp., 1984-85; dir. tng. and devel., Domino's Pizza Distbrn. Corp., Ontario, Calif., 1985—. Procs. editor 2d Ann. Health Care Interaction Mgmt. User's Conf., 1984; presenter 43d Am. Soc. for Tng. and Devel. Nat. Conf. and Expn. Mem. Am. Soc. for Tng. and Devel., Hosp. Personnel Mgmt. Assn., Am. Soc. for Health Care Edn. and Tng. Office: Domino's Pizza Distbrn Corp 301 S Rockefeller Ave Ontario CA 91671

SHORTRIDGE, RUSSELL CHARLES, trade association administrator; b. Hannah, N.D., Aug. 18, 1921; s. Wesley John and Nancy Louise (Bloomquist) S.; m. Isabelle Mae Ryan, Jan. 15, 1944; children: Sharon Faye, James Russell. BS, N.D. State U., 1943. Cert. tchr., N.D. Tchr. Walsh County Tng. Sch., Park River, N.D., 1946-52; farmer Nekoma, N.D., 1952-57; field rep. Holstein Assn., Fresno, Calif., 1957-67; dir. edn. Dairy Council of Calif., Los Angeles, 1967-87; cons. B.C. Dairy Found., Vancouver, 1985—. Author: The Precepteer, 1980, Motivation Generating Model, 1985; contbr. articles to profl. jours. Elder Presby. Ch. of Fresno, Calif., 1962, deacon, 1964. Served to capt. U.S. Army, 1943-47, ETO. Recipient Meritorious Service award Calif. Dietetic Assn., 1986. Mem. Assn. Curriculum and Supervision. Republican. Club: Dairyshrine. Home: 745 E Robin Ln Fresno CA 93710

SHOTWELL, JOHN RALPH, clergyman, administrator; b. Brookneal, Va., Sept. 30, 1926; s. John Henry and Ada Mildred (Puckett) S.; m. Virginia Lambeth, June 22, 1947; children: Donna Lynn, Jo Ann. BA, U. Richmond, 1946; BD, MDiv, Colgate Rochester Divinity Sch., 1949. Ordained cleric. Pastor Union Ave Bapt. Ch., Paterson, N.J., 1949-52; dir. religious activities U. Richmond, Va., 1952-56; sr. pastor Greece Bapt. Ch., Rochester, N.Y., 1956-65, Cen. Bapt. Ch., Hartford, Conn., 1965-75, Flossmoor (Ill.) Community Ch., 1975-81; exec. dir. Internat. Council Community Chs., Homewood, Ill., 1981—, pres., 1980-81; bd. dirs. U.S. Conf. World Council Chs., N.Y.C.; exec. com., bd. dirs. Nat. Council Chs., N.Y.C.; exec. com. mem. Consultation on Ch. Union, Princeton, 1981—. Author: Unity Without Uniformity, 1984, Manual for Ministry, 1986; co-author: Postscript, 1985; contbr. articles to profl. jours. Pres. Family Service Soc., Rochester, 1960-65. Lodge: Rotary (pres. Rochester chpt. 1964-65).

SHOUP, JUNE ELEANOR, speech scientist, research laboratory administrator; b. Sturgis, Mich., Feb. 1, 1929; d. Gail Leo and Sarah Marguerite (Ball) S. BA, U. Mich., 1950, MA, 1956, PhD, 1964. Assoc. dir. Speech Communication Research Lab., Fallbrook, Calif., 1966-67, dir., 1967—; assoc. prof. speech sci. U. So. Calif., Los Angeles, 1979—; dir. U. So. Calif. Speech Sci. and Tech. Program, 1980—, Speech Sci. Research Lab., Los Angeles, 1983—; cons. Interstate Voice Products, Orange, Calif., 1984—, Research and Devel. Assocs., Marina del Rey, Calif., 1985—. Author: (with G.E. Peterson) A Physiological Theory of Phonetics, 1966; contbr. articles to profl. jours. Fellow Acoustical Soc. Am.; mem. Am. Assn. Phonetic Scis. (pres. 1983), Alexander Graham Bell Assn., Am. Speech Lang. and Hearing Assn., Sigma Xi. Office: U So Calif Speech Sci & Tech 3375 S Hoover St Suite A Los Angeles CA 90007

SHOUSE, DAVID SINCLAIR, data processing executive, consultant; b. Joplin, Mo., Mar. 19, 1952; s. Sidney Sinclair and Ethelreda (York) S.; m. Denise Earline Burnham, Nov. 13, 1976 (div. Oct. 1980); m. Mary Charlotte Johnson Voss, Sept. 24, 1983; 1 stepchild, Addie Marie Voss. AS in Data Processing and BS in Bus. Adminstrn., Mo. So. StateColl., 1976. With Fed. Civil Service div., Dept. Defense, White Sands Missile Range, N.Mex., 1977-78; sr. programmer, analyst CE NATCO, Tulsa, Okla., 1978-80, KN Energy, Lakewood, Colo., 1980-81; owner, cons. Shouse Services, Denver, 1981; v.p. Vanguard Techs. Corp., Golden, Colo., 1982—; cons. various govt. agys., banks and oil cos., Denver, 1981. Mem. Soc. Info. Mgmt. (bd. dirs. 1984—), Data Processing Mgmt. Assn. Republican. Mem. Unity Ch. Avocation: comml. photography. Office: Vanguard Techs Corp PO Box 1370 Golden CO 80402

SHOUSE, JACK, artistic director; b. Dec. 8, 1944; s. Clovis and Ruby (Weldon) S.; m. Carolyn Norton, May 30, 1971; children: Amy Kathleen, Sarah Elizabeth. BA, Fresno State U., 1966; MA, San Francisco State U., 1969. Drama instr., artist in residence, designer, dir., assoc. artistic dir. Pacific Conservatory Performing Arts, Hancock Coll., Santa Maria, Calif., 1969-86, artistic dir., 1986—. Mem. Santa Maria C. of C. Home: 325 S Scott Dr Santa Maria CA 93454 Office: Allan Hancock Coll 800 S College Dr Santa Maria CA 93454

SHOWALTER, ROBERT DEAN, lawyer; b. Denver, Mar. 1, 1938; s. Ward Bonnett Showalter and Ruth Elizabeth (Weber) Young; m. Lucy Jeanette Carpenter, Apr. 6, 1968; children: Catherine Lee, Steven Dean, Mark Christopher. BS in Bus., U. Colo., 1961, JD, 1964; postgrad., U. Va., 1964-65. Assoc. Hindry, Erickson & Meyer, Denver, 1965-69; ptnr. Hindry & Meyer, Denver, 1969-79, Wegher & Fulton, Denver, 1979-85, Massey, Graham & Showalter, Denver, 1985—; lectr. U. Denver Tax Inst., 1966-68, Colo. Practice Insts., Denver, 1965-72, N.Mex. Tax Inst., Albuquerque, 1967; mem. edn. appeal bd. U.S. Dept. Edn., Washington, 1985—. Bd. dirs. Cen. City Opera House Assn., Denver, 1970—, gen. counsel and mem. exec. com. Served with U.S. Army, 1956-62. Recipient Service award Com. Non-polit. Selection of Judges, Colo., 1966. Mem. ABA, Colo. Bar Assn., Denver Bar Assn., Computer Law Assn., Computer Law Forum, Am. Arbitration Assn., SAR, Mensa, Delta Sigma Pi, Phi Delta Phi, Beta Alpha Psi (pres. 1961), Sigma Nu (pres. 1963). Republican. Methodist. Clubs: Denver Athletic (pres. 1982), Denver, 26, (pres. 1986) (Denver). Avocations: reading, piano. Home: 5020 S Elmira St Greenwood Village CO 80111 Office: Massey Graham & Showalter 518 17th St Suite 1100 Denver CO 80202

SHREVE, THEODORE NORRIS, construction company executive; b. St. Louis, Feb. 14, 1919; s. Truxtun Benbridge and Beulah (Dyer) S.; B.S., U. Colo., 1942; m. Caroline Prouty, Jan. 7, 1943; children—Sara Ann Caile Shreve, Suzanne Godfrey Shreve, Theo Carol. Sec., treas. Trautman & Shreve, Inc., Denver, 1946-68, pres., 1969—, chmn. bd., 1984—; pres. Race Corp.; pres. T & S Investment Co., Denver, 1965—. Rep. County Assembly, 1962. Served with USNR, 1942-45. Registered profl. engr., Colo. Mem. Mech. Contractors Assn., Colo. Soc. Profl. Engrs., Sigma Phi Epsilon. Republican. Episcopalian. Clubs: Rotary, Gyro, Denver Country. Home: 1510 E 10th Ave #13W Denver CO 80218 Office: T&S Investment Co 4406 Race St Denver CO 80216

SHRONTZ, FRANK ANDERSON, airplane manufacturing executive; b. Boise, Idaho, Dec. 14, 1931; s. Thurlyn Howard and Florence Elizabeth (Anderson) S.; m. Harriet Ann Houghton, June 12, 1954; children: Craig Howard, Richard Whitaker, David Anderson. LL.B., U. Idaho, 1954; postgrad., George Washington U., summer 1953; M.B.A., Harvard U., 1958; postgrad., Stanford U., 1969-70. Bar: Fed. 1954. Asst. contracts coordinator Boeing Co., Seattle, 1958-65, asst. dir. contract administrn., 1965-67, asst. to v.p. comml. airplane group, 1967-69, asst. dir. new airplane program, 1969-70, dir. comml. sales operations, 1970-73; asst. sec. Dept. Air Force, Washington, 1973-76, Dept. Def., 1976-77; v.p. planning and contracts Boeing Co., Seattle, 1977-78; v.p., gen. mgr. 707/727/737 div. Boeing Comml. Airplane Co., Seattle, 1978-82, v.p. sales and mktg., 1982-84, pres., 1986—; pres., chief exec. officer The Boeing Co., Seattle, 1986—; Chmn. bd. Lake Hills Assn., Bellevue, Wash., 1968; mem. bd. Ctr. for Strategic and Internat. Studies, 1986; mem. adv. bd. Stanford Bus. Sch., 1986; mem. The Bus. Council, 1987. Mem. Seattle Met. bd. YMCA, 1981. Served to 1st lt. AUS, 1954-56. Mem. Blue Key, Phi Eta Sigma, Phi Alpha Delta, Beta Theta Pi. Clubs: Rainier, Overlake Golf and Country, Columbia Tower. Home: 8434 W Mercer Way Mercer Island WA 98040 Office: Boeing Co 7755 E Marginal Way S Seattle WA 98108

SHROPSHIRE, DONALD GRAY, hospital executive; b. Winston-Salem, N.C., Aug. 6, 1927; s. John Lee and Bess L. (Shouse) S.; m. Mary Ruth Bodenheimer, Aug. 19, 1950; children: Melanie Shropshire David, John Devin. B.S., U. N.C., 1950; Erickson fellow hosp. adminstrn., U. Chgo.,

1958-59. Personnel asst. Nat. Biscuit Co., Atlanta, 1950-52; asst. personnel mgr. Nat. Biscuit Co., Chgo., 1952-54; adminstr. Eastern State Hosp., Lexington, Ky., 1954-62; asso. dir. U. Md. Hosp., Balt., 1962-67; adminstr. Tucson Med. Center, 1967-82, pres., 1982—; Pres. Tucson Hosps. Med. Edn. Program, 1970-71, sec., 1971—; pres. So. Ariz. Hosp. Council, 1968-69; bd. dirs. Ariz. Blue Cross, 1967-76, chmn. provider standards com., 1972-76; chmn. Healthways Inc., 1985—. Bd. dirs., exec. com. Health Planning Council Tucson, 1969-74; chmn. profl. div. United Way Tucson, 1969-70; chmn. dietary services com. Md. Hosp. Council, 1966-67; bd. dirs. Ky. Hosp. Assn., 1961-62, chmn. council profl. practice, 1960-61; past pres. Blue Grass Hosp. Council; trustee Assn. Western Hosps., 1974-81, pres., 1979-80; mem. accreditation Council for Continuing Med. Edn., 1982-87, chmn., 1986; bd. govs. Pima Community Coll., 1970-76, sec., 1973-74, chmn., 1975-76, bd. dirs. Found., 1978-82; bd. regents U. Ariz., 1982—, sec., 1983-86; pres. Tucson Airport Authority, 1987—; v.p. Tucson Econ. Devel. Corp., 1977-82; bd. dirs. Vol. Hosps. Am., 1977—, treas., 1979-82; mem. Ariz. Adv. Health Council, 1976-78; bd. dirs. Tucson Tomorrow, 1983—. Named Ky. col. Mem. Am. Hosp. Assn. (trustee 1975-78, ho. dels. 1972-78, chmn. council profl. services 1973-74, regional adv. bd. 1969-78, chmn. joint com. with Nat. Assn. Social Workers 1963-64), Ariz. Hosp. Assn. (bd. dirs. 1967-72, pres. 1970-71, nominating com. 1983-86), Assn. Am. Med. Colls. (mem. assembly 1974-77), Tucson C. of C. (bd. dirs. 1968-69), United Comml. Travelers, Nat. League Nursing, Ariz. Acad., Tucson Tomorrow (bd. dirs. 1983—), Tucson Community Council. Baptist (ch. moderator, chmn. finance com., deacon, ch. sch. supt., trustee). Club: Rotarian. Home: 5301 E Grant Rd Tucson AZ 85712 Office: PO Box 42195 Tucson AZ 85733

SHUBERT, GUSTAVE HARRY, research executive; b. Buffalo, Jan. 18, 1929; s. Gustave Henri and Ada Shubert (Smith) S.; m. Rhea Brickman, Mar. 29, 1952; children—Wendy J., David L. B.A., Yale U., 1948; M.A., NYU, 1951. Staff mem. Lincoln Lab., MIT, 1955-57; adminstr. systems engring. Hycon Eastern, Inc., Paris, 1957-59; with RAND Corp., Santa Monica, Calif., 1959—, v.p. domestic programs, 1968-75, sr. v.p. domestic programs, 1975-78, sr. v.p., 1978—; dir. Inst. Civil Justice, 1979—, trustee, 1973—; trustee N.Y.C. Rand Inst., 1972-79, pres., 1972-73; trustee Housing Allowance Offices of Brown County and South Bend, Ind., 1973—; mem. adv. council Sch. Engring., Stanford U., 1976-79; mem. policy adv. com. Clin. Scholars Program, UCLA; mem. program evaluation of methodology div. GAO, 1986—; mem. Commn. on Professionalism sect. litigation ABA, 1985—; mem. Calif. jud. system com. Los Angeles County Bar Assn., 1984-85; mem. adv. bd. Program Evaluation of Methodology div. U.S. Gen. Acctg. Office, 1986—; bd. govs. Josephson Found. Bd. gov.'s Josephson Found., 1986—; mem. Nat. Acad. Scis. Com. on Evaluation of Poverty Research. Served with USAF, 1951-55. Decorated Air medal with 2 oak leaf clusters, Commendation medal. Mem. Am. Judicature Soc., Inst. Strategic Studies (London), Los Angeles World Affairs Council, Council on Foreign Relations. Clubs: Commonwealth (San Francisco); Town Hall of Calif. (Los Angeles), Jonathan (Los Angeles); Yale (N.Y.C.). Home: 13838 Sunset Blvd Pacific Palisades CA 90272 Office: Rand Corp 1700 Main St Santa Monica CA 90406

SHUBSDA, THADDEUS A., bishop; b. Los Angeles, Apr. 2, 1925. Grad., St. John's Sem. Ordained priest Roman Catholic Ch., 1950. Ordained titular bishop of Trau and aux. bishop of Los Angeles 1977-82; apptd. bishop of Monterey Calif., 1982—. Office: 580 Fremont Blvd PO Box 2048 Monterey CA 93940 *

SHUE, GENE, Head coach Los Angeles Clippers (Nat. Basketball Assn.), 1987—. Office: Los Angeles Clippers 3939 S Figueroa Los Angeles CA 90037 *

SHUEY, PHIL JAMES, lawyer; b. Trinidad, Colo., Oct. 12, 1943; s. Phil B. and Alice M. (Smith) S.; m. Jorja L. Winn, June 22, 1967 (div. 1980); children: Dawn, Tyler. BA, Colo. U., 1966; JD, U. Denver, 1969. Bar: Colo. 1969, U.S. Dist. Ct. Colo. 1969, U.S. Ct. Appeals (10th cir.). Ptnr. Decker, Robertson, Shuey & Miller, P.C., Denver, 1969-71; sole practice Denver, 1971-74; ptnr. Shuey & O'Malley, P.C., Denver, 1974-80; pres., chief exec. officer Critique Cons. Corp., Denver, 1978—; prof. U. Denver Coll. Law; mem. bd. advisors MS in Jud. Adminstrn. program; bd. dirs. Denver Paralegal Inst., 1981—. Editor The Colo. Lawyer, 1982—; contbr. articles to profl. jours. Mem. Rep. Precinct com., Denver, 1980. Mem. ABA (chmn. impact tech. com. 1985-86, chmn. div. V facilities and tech. econs. sect. 1986-87), Colo. Bar Assn. (chmn. legal assts. com. 1978-81, chmn. law and tech. com. 1986—), Colo. Region Sports Car Club Am. (regional exec. 1978). Club: Rocky Mountain Vintage Racing, Ltd. (Denver) (bd. dirs. 1983-84). Avocations: tennis, gourmet cooking. Home: 8365 S Bronze Ln Highlands Ranch CO 80126 Office: 6093 S Quebec Suite 203 Englewood CO 80111-4544

SHUGARMAN, PETER MELVIN, biochemistry; b. Duluth, Minn., July 28, 1927; s. Bernard and Lena (Kernes) S. BS, UCLA, 1951, PhD, 1966. Asst. prof. biochemistry U. So. Calif., Los Angeles, 1966-70, assoc. prof., 1970—, asst. dean natural scis. and math., 1972-85, assoc. dean, 1985—. Served with U.S. Army, 1945-46. Office: U So Calif Univ Park MC4012 Los Angeles CA 90089-4012

SHUKMAN, SOLOMON JOSEPH, artist; b. Bobr, Minsk, USSR, July 5, 1927; came to U.S., 1974, naturalized, 1980; s. Joseph Solomon Shukman and Eugenia (Aaron) Shukman Golden; m. Ludmila N. Berman, Nov. 14, 1954; children—Janna, Roman. Student, Coll. of Fine Arts and Theatre, Moscow, 1946-49, Stroganof Inst. of Art, Moscow, 1949-52. Dep. adviser artistic councils Artists Found. of USSR, 1952-74; painter frescoes and murals for internat. exhibits; also artist in graphics, painting, drawing and lithography; mem. of Union of Soviet Artist Internat. Exhibits, 1963-74. One man shows include Denver, 1974, Transam. Pyramid, San Francisco, 1975, Los Altos, Calif., 1976, 80, Nathan Gallery, San Francisco, 1977, Pantheon Gallery, San Francisco, 1978, Magnes Mus., Berkeley, Calif., 1979-80, Internat. Art-Expo, N.Y.C., 1985, Los Angeles, 1985, JBM Gallery, San Francisco, 1985, Koret Gallery, Palo Alto, Calif., 1985, Civic Arts Gallery, Walnut Creek, Calif., 1986; exhibited in group shows N.Y.C., 1956, Paris, 1959, Brussels, 1961, Warsaw, Poland, 1964, Progue, 1967, Ehrfort, German Democratic Republic, 1969, also at Skolnike, Moscow; represented in permanent collections Nathan Gallery, Pantheon Gallery, Magnes Mus., Godfrey Gallery; also numerous pvt. collections. Contbr. articles to profl. jours. Subject of numerous newspaper and mag. articles; works pub. in Print World Directory, 1985. Mem. Graphic Arts Council of Achenbach Found. for Graphic Arts, Internat. Soc. Artists, World Prints Council, Ctr. for Visual Arts. Democrat. Jewish. Home: SoloArt Studio PO Box 1337 Menlo Park CA 94026

SHULER, BRIGHAM SAMUEL, military officer; b. Bainbridge, Ga., Dec 17, 1941; s. Samuel Roy and Ruth M. (Evans) S.; m. Charlotte R. Hutto, Feb. 19, 1962; children: Mark J., Beth C. BA, Brigham Young U., 1972; MA, Cen. Mich. U., 1978; postgrad., U.S. Army War Coll., 1985. Enlisted in U.S. Army, 1959, commd. 2d lt., 1962, advanced through grades to lt. col., 1979; chief pub. affairs U.S. Army Criminal Investigation Command, Washington, 1972-77; student Armed Forces Staff Coll., 1977-78; pub. info. officer Office Sec. Def., Washington, 1978-79; comdr. Ft. Knox dist. U.S. Army Criminal Investigation Command, 1979-83; prof. mil. sci., chmn. dept. Brigham Young U., Provo, Utah, 1983—; instr. Coll. Law Enforcement, Eastern Ky. U., Richmond, 1980-81. Editor: The Detective: Jour. Army Criminal Investigation, 1972-77; contbr. articles to mil. jours. Decorated Silver Star, Bronze Star with oak leaf cluster, Meritorious Service medal with oak leaf cluster, Air medal, Purple Heart, numerous others. Mem. Internat. Assn. Chefs of Police, Nat. Rifle Assn., Nat. Sheriffs Assn., Phi Kappa Phi. Democrat. Mormon. Lodges: Masons, Shriners. Home: 3890 Devonshire Dr Provo UT 84604 Office: Brigham Young U Dept Mil Sci Provo UT 84604

SHULER, CRAIG EDWARD, wood science educator; b. Wichita, Kans., Aug. 27, 1938; s. William Edward and Lois (Marshall) S.; m. Lorraine Luck, Dec. 28, 1960; children: Bren, Dain, Tor, Tiana. BS, Colo. State U., 1960, MS, 1966, PhD, 1969. Lic. forester, Maine. From asst. to assoc. prof. U. Maine, Orono, 1969-79; assoc. prof. wood sci. Colo. State U., Ft. Collins, 1979—; cons. in field. Contbr. articles to profl. jours. Served to 1st lt. USMC, 1960-64. Mem. Soc. Wood Sci. and Tech. (pres. 1983-85), Forest Products Research Soc., ASTM. Republican. Methodist. Avocations: basketball official, civic theater, stamp collecting, sports, camping. Home: 2413 Constitution Fort Collins CO 80526 Office: Colo State U Wood Sci Lab Fort Collins CO 80523

SHULL, HARRISON, chemist, educator; b. Princeton, N.J., Aug. 17, 1923; s. George Harrison and Mary (Nicholl) S.; m. Jeanne Louise Johnson, 1948 (div. 1962); children: James Robert, Kathy, George Harrison, Holly; m. Wil Joyce Bentley Long, 1962; children: Warren Michael Long, Jeffery Mark Long, Stanley Martin, Sarah Ellen. A.B., Princeton U., 1943; Ph.D., U. Calif. at Berkeley, 1948. Assoc. chemist U.S. Naval Research Lab., 1943-45; asst. prof. Iowa State U., 1949-54; mem. faculty Ind. U., 1955-79, research prof., 1961-79, dean Grad. Sch., 1965-72, vice chancellor for research and devel., 1972-76, dir. Research Computing Center, 1959-63, acting chmn. chemistry dept., 1965-66, acting dean arts and scis., 1969-70; acting dean faculties Ind. U. (Research Computing Center), 1974; mem. faculty, provost, v.p. acad. affairs Rensselaer Poly. Inst., 1979-82; chancellor U. Colo., Boulder, 1982-85; prof. dept. chemistry U. Colo., 1982—; asst. dir. research, quantum chemistry group Uppsala (Sweden) U., 1958-59; vis. prof. Washington U., St. Louis, 1960, U. Colo., 1963; founder, supr. Quantum Chemistry Program Exchange, 1962-79; chmn. subcom. molecular structure and spectroscopy NRC, 1958-63; chmn. Fulbright selection com. chemistry, 1963-67; mem. adv. com. Office Sci. Personnel, 1957-60; chmn. First Gordon Research Conf. Theoretical Chemistry, 1962; mem. com. survey chemistry Nat. Acad. Sci., 1964-65; mem. adv. panel chemistry NSF, 1964-67; mem. adv. panel Office Computer Activities, 1967-70, cons. chem. information program, 1965-71, mem. adv. com. for research, 1974-76; mem. vis. com. chemistry Brookhaven Nat. Lab., 1967-70; mem. adv. com. Chem. Abstracts Service, 1971-74; dir. Storage Tech. Corp.; chief of Naval Ops. Exec. Panel, 1984—. Asso. editor: Jour. Chem. Physics, 1952-54; editorial adv. bd.: Spectrochimica Acta, 1957-63, Internat. Jour. Quantum Chemistry, 1967—, Proc. Nat. Acad. Scis, 1976-81; cons. editor, Allyn and Bacon.; Contbr. articles to profl. jours. Trustee Argonne U. Assn., 1970-75, Asso. Univs., Inc., 1973-76. Served as ensign USNR, 1945. NRC postdoctoral fellow phys. scis. U. Chgo., 1948-49; Guggenheim fellow U. Uppsala, 1954-55; NSF sr. postdoctoral fellow, 1968-69; Sloan research fellow, 1956-58. Fellow Am. Acad. Arts and Scis. (v.p. 1976-83, chmn. Midwest Center 1976-79), Am. Phys. Soc.; mem. Nat. Acad. Scis. (com. on sci. and public policy 1969-72, council, exec. com. 1971-74, chmn. U.S.-USSR sci. policy subgroup for fundamental research 1973-81, naval studies bd. 1974-79, chmn. Commn. on Human Resources 1977-81, nominating com. 1978), Univs. Research Assn. (trustee 1984—), Am. Chem. Soc., AAAS, Inst. for Def. Analyses (trustee 1984—), Assn. Computing Machinery, Royal Swedish Acad. Scis. (fgn. mem.), Royal Acad. Arts and Scis. Uppsala (corr. mem.), Phi Beta Kappa, Sigma Xi, Phi Lambda Upsilon. Club: Cosmos (Washington). Office: U Colo Dept Chemistry Boulder CO 80309-0215

SHULTZ, EMMET LAVEL, oil company executive; b. Blackfoot, Idaho, Apr. 23, 1934; s. Emmet Franklin and Alba Elizabeth (Larsen) S.; m. Joan C. Kirby, Nov. 7, 1953; children: Joanne M., Jeanette G.; m. Marilyn Barney, Aug. 4, 1978. Asst. to pres. Flying Diamond Corp., Salt Lake City, 1973-74; pres., also bd. dirs. Shuhart Industries, Inc., Salt Lake City, 1974-75; v.p. Hunstman Chem. and Oil Corp., Salt Lake City, 1975-76; exec. v.p. Huntsman Coal Corp., Salt Lake City, 1975-76; pres., chmn. bd. Gulf Energy Corp., Salt Lake City, 1976—, Channel Energy Corp., 1983—, Kita Corp., 1985—. Served with USN, 1952-56. Republican. Office: Gulf Energy Corp 144 S 500 E Salt Lake City UT 84102

SHULTZ, RUSSELL DON, graphic designer, art director; b. Springfield, Minn., Dec. 8, 1944; s. Russell John and Lorraine Elizabeth (Mielke) S.; m. Jane Elizabeth Schwager, June 14, 1969 (div. Dec. 1980). BS, Mankato State U., 1968. Layout artist Skaggs Drug Ctrs., Phoenix, 1972-74; staff artist Skaggs Drug Ctrs., Salt Lake City, 1974-76; art dir. Am. Vet. Publs. Inc., Santa Barbara, Calif., 1976—. Artist: (caricatures) Corp. Card , 1979 (excellence award 1980); editorial cartoons Ariz. Republic, 1973-74. Mem. Dem. Fundraising Bd., Santa Barbara, 1985. Served to staff sgt. USAF, 1968-72. Club: Ad (Santa Barbara). Avocations: golfing, reading, music. Home: 3731 B Amalfi Way Santa Barbara CA 93105 Office: Am Vet Publs Inc 300 E Canon Perdido St Santa Barbara CA 93105

SHUMAKER, MAURICE CALVIN, banker; b. Spokane, Wash., Jan. 13, 1921; s. John Calvin and Alice Mabel (Henderickson) S.; B.A. in Fin., U. Wash., 1947; postgrad. Pacific Coast Banking Sch., 1961; cert. comml. lender U. Okla., 1974; postgrad. Exec. Mgmt. Acad., U. Mich., 1978; m. Beth Ramsey Harius, Apr. 29, 1944; children—Margaret Ann, John William, Mary Beth, David Calvin. With Rainier Bank, Spokane, 1946—, v.p., 1964-76, sr. v.p., mgr. Eastern region, office, 1976-79, sr. v.p. Spokane main office, 1979-81; sr. v.p., mgr. Comml. Banking Ctr. Eastern Wash., Spokane, 1981-83; mem. adv. bd. Small Bus. Devel. Ctr., Wash. State U. Pres., Twin Harbors council Boy Scouts Am., 1971-74, v.p. Inland Empire council, 1976-82, pres., 1983—, mem. internat. bd., 1980—; treas. U.S. Found. Internat. Scouting, 1982—; trustee St. George's Sch., 1983—. Served with USAAF, 1943-45; ETO. Decorated D.F.C., Air medal with 3 oak leaf clusters. Recipient Silver Beaver award Boy Scouts Am., 1970, Silver Antelope award, 1981, Disting. Eagle Scout award, 1982. Mem. Am. Inst. Banking, Wash. Bankers Assn., Robert Morris Assos. Presbyterian. Clubs: Manito Golf, Spokane City, Wash. Athletic (bd. govs. 1967-69), Elks. Home: E1503 Woodcliff Rd Spokane WA 99203 Office: PO Box 366 Spokane WA 99210

SHUMAKER, ROBERT HARPER, naval officer; b. New Castle, Pa., May 11, 1933; s. Alvah Manora and Eleanor Blanche (Harper) S.; m. Lorraine Malvina Shaw, Dec. 28, 1963; 1 child, Grant Harper. B Marine Engring., U.S. Naval Acad., 1956; M in Aero., Naval Postgrad. Sch., 1964, MEE, 1975, PhD in Elec. Engring., 1977; DSci (hon.), Westminster Coll., 1985. Commd. ensign U.S. Navy, 1956, advanced through grades to rear adm., jet fighter pilot, 1956-64; prisoner of war U.S. Navy, Vietnam, 1964-72; maj. product mgr. for missile acquisitions U.S. Navy, 1977-83; supt. Naval Postgrad. Sch., Monterey, Calif., 1983—. Decorated Purple Heart, D.S.M., Silver Star, Legion of Merit, D.F.C., Bronze Star. Mem. Naval Inst., IEEE, Assn. Naval Aviators, Sigma Xi, Eta Kappa Nu. Republican. Presbyterian. Club: Old Capital. Lodge: Rotary. Avocations: horseback riding; golf; farming. Home: Quarters A Naval Postgrad Sch Monterey CA 93943 Office: Supt Naval Postgrad Sch Monterey CA 93943

SHUMATE, CHARLES ALBERT, physician; b. San Francisco, Aug. 11, 1904; s. Thomas E. and Freda (Ortmann) S.; B.S., U. San Francisco, 1927, H.H.D., 1976; M.D., Creighton U., 1931. Pvt. practice dermatology, San Francisco, 1933-73, ret., 1973; asst. clin. prof. dermatology Stanford U., 1956-62; pres. E Clampus Vitus, Inc., 1963-64; hon. mem. staff St. Mary's Hosp. Mem. San Francisco Art Commn., 1964-67, Calif. Heritage Preservation Commn., 1963-67; regent Notre Dame Coll. at Belmont, 1965-78, trustee, 1977—; pres. Conf. Calif. Hist. Socs., 1967; mem. San Francisco Landmarks Preservation Bd., 1967-78, pres., 1967-69; trustee St. Patrick's Coll. and Sem., 1970-86. Served as maj. USPHS, 1942-46. Decorated knight comdr. Order of Isabella (Spain); knight Order of the Holy Sepulchre, knight of St. Gregory, knight of Malta. Fellow Am. Acad. Dermatology; mem. U. San Francisco Alumni Assn. (pres. 1955), Calif. Book Club (pres. 1969-71), Calif. Hist. Soc. (trustee 1958-67, 68-78, pres. 1962-64), Soc. Calif. Pioneers (dir. 1979—). Clubs: Bohemian, Olympic, Roxburghe (pres. 1958-59) (San Francisco); Zamorano (Los Angeles). Author: Life of George Henry Goddard; The California of George Gordon, 1976, Francisco Pacheco of Pacheco Pass, 1977; Life of Mariano Malarin, 1980; Boyhood Days: Y. Villegas Reminiscences of California 1850s, 1983, The Notorious I.C. Woods of the Adams Express, 1986. Home: 1901 Scott St San Francisco CA 94115 Office: 490 Post St San Francisco CA 94102

SHUMWAY, FORREST NELSON, corporation executive, lawyer; b. Skowhegan, Maine, Mar. 21, 1927; s. Sherman Nelson and Agnes Brooks (Mosher) S.; m. Patricia Ann Kelly, Aug. 12, 1950; children: Sandra Brooks, Garrett Patrick. Student, Deerfield (Mass.) Acad., 1943-45; B.A., Stanford U., 1950, LL.B., 1952; LL.D. (hon.), U. So. Calif., 1974, Pepperdine U., 1978. Bar: Calif. bar 1952. Staff Office County Counsel, Los Angeles, 1953-57; sec. Signal Oil & Gas Co., Los Angeles, 1959-61; gen. counsel Signal Oil & Gas Co., 1961-64, group v.p. operations, 1963-64, pres., 1964-68; pres., chief exec. officer The Signal Cos., 1968-80, chmn. bd., chief exec. officer, 1980-85; vice chmn. Allied-Signal Inc., 1985—, also bd. dirs.; dir. Transamerica Corp., First Interstate Bancorp, Aluminum Co. Am., Clorox Co. Trustee U. So. Calif. Served to 1st lt. USMCR, 1945-46. Mem. State Bar Assn. Calif., Phi Delta Theta. Clubs: Cypress Point (Pebble Beach, Calif.); California (Los Angeles); Newport Harbor Yacht (Newport Beach, Calif.); Tuna (Avalon, Calif.); Bohemian (San Francisco); San Diego Yacht, La Jolla Country. Lodges: Masons, Shriners. Office: 11255 N Torrey Pines Rd La Jolla CA 92037-1059

SHUMWAY, NORMAN D., congressman; b. Phoenix, July 28, 1934; m. Luana June Schow; children: Jennifer, Neal, Perry, Tyler, Stuart, Brenda. A.A., Stockton Coll., 1954; B.S., U. Utah, 1960; J.D., Hastings Coll. Law, U. Calif., 1963. Bar: Calif. 1964. Practice law Downey, Calif.; formerly partner firm Cavalero, Bray, Shumway & Geiger; mem. 96th-100th congresses from 14th Calif. Dist. Mem. San Joaquin County Bd. Suprs., 1974-78, chmn. bd., 1978; past chmn. Goodwill Industries of San Joaquin Valley, Inc.; bd. dirs. Goodwill Industries Am.; former bishop, missionary to Japan Ch. Jesus Christ of Latter-day Saints. Office: Room 1203 Longworth House Office Bldg Washington DC 20515 *

SHUMWAY, NORMAN EDWARD, surgeon, educator; b. Kalamazoo, Mich., 1923. M.D., Vanderbilt U., 1949; Ph.D. in Surgery, U. Minn., 1956. Diplomate: Am. Bd. Surgery, Am. Bd. Thoracic Surgery. Intern U. Minn. Hosps., 1949-50, med. fellow surgery, 1950-51, 53-54, Nat. Heart Inst. research fellow, 1954-56, Nat. Heart Inst. spl. trainee, 1956-57; mem. surg. staff Stanford U. Hosps., 1958—, asst. prof. surgery, 1959-61, assoc. prof., 1961-65, prof., 1965—, head div. cardiovascular surgery Sch. Medicine, 1974—; Frances and Charles D. Field prof. Stanford U., 1976—. Served to capt. USAF, 1951-53. Mem. AMA, Soc. Univ. Surgeons, Am. Assn. Thoracic Surgery, Am. Coll. Cardiology, Transplantation Soc., Samson Thoracic Surg. Soc., Soc. for Vascular Surgery, Alpha Omega Alpha. Office: Stanford U Med Ctr Dept Cardiovascular Surgery Stanford CA 94305 *

SHUNK, DAN LOUIS, academic director; b. LaPorte, Ind., Oct. 18, 1947; s. Frank Michael and Mary (Jonas) S.; m. Gail Diane Steffen, Nov. 24, 1972; children; Michael, Benjamin, Carolyn, Kathryn. BS in Indsl. Engring., Purdue U., 1971, MS in Indsl. Engring., 1972, PhD, 1976. Indsl. engring. mgr. Rockwell Internat., Dallas, 1979-80; group tech. mgr. Internat. Harvester, Chgo., 1980-81; v.p. GCA Corp., Chgo., 1981-84; dir. Research Ctr. Ariz. State U., Tempe, 1984—; chmn. Autofact 1985, Detroit, 1985. Editor Systems Integration, 1985—; contbr. articles to profl. jours. Served to capt. USAF, 1975-79. Mem. Inst. Indsl. Engrs. (sr.), Computer and Automated Systems Assn. of Soc. Mfg. Engrs. (sr., bd. dirs. 1983—, Outstanding Young Engr. award 1983), NRC. Office: Ariz State U Coll Engring Ctr Automated Engring & Robotics Tempe AZ 85287

SHUR, NICOLAI, industrial architect; b. Hamburg, Fed. Republic of Germany, Apr. 4, 1947; came to U.S., 1950, citizen, 1966; s. Iwan and Anna (Leschenko) S. BArch, U. Oreg., 1971; MArch, U. Calif., Berkeley, 1974. Registered architect, Oreg. Mem. office staff Esherick, Homsey, Dodge & Davis, San Francisco, 1973-74; pvt. practice architecture Corvallis, Oreg., 1974-82; sr. indsl. engr. Freighliner/Mercedes Benz Truck Co., Portland, Oreg., 1982—. Prin. works include Benton County (Oreg.) Bank, 1977, Freightliner Truck Plant Expansion, Portland, 1982, Mercedes-Benz/Unimog Assembly Line, Hampton, Va., 1986. Bd. dirs. YMCA, Corvallis, 1979-80, mem., Portland, 1984—; mem. Madison Ave. Task Force, Corvallis, 1975-79, Dem. Cen. Com., Multnomah County, Oreg., 1984—; active Mill Race Fund, Portland, 1981—. John K. Branner Travelling fellow U. Calif. Sch. Environ. Design, Berkeley, 1974. Mem. Nat. Council Archtl. Registration Bds. Lodge: Rotary. Avocations: skiing, photography, travel. Home: 1607 SE Spokane Portland OR 97202 Office: Freightliner/Mercedes Benz Truck Co 4747 N Channel Ave Portland OR 97208-3849

SHUYLER, WAYNE LEIGH, land use planner; b. West Lafayette, Ind., Dec. 5, 1948; s. Harlan R. and Sedley G. (Miller) S.; m. LouAnne C. Theobald, Aug. 26, 1972; children: Kristen Sedley, Leah Carey, Roy Breckenridge. B in Phys. Edn., Purdue U., 1970; MS, U. Mo., 1980. Div. coordinator U.S. Peace Corps, Lipa City, Phillipines, 1970-72; project cons. Dept. Natural Resources, Jefferson City, Mo., 1975-77, natural resource planner, 1977-79; planning officer Ariz. Outdoor Recreation Coordinating Commn., Phoenix, 1979-81, asst. dir., 1981-84; planning mgr. Ariz. State Parks, Phoenix, 1984-86, chief of statewide planning, 1986—; regent Pacific Revenue Sources Mgmt. Sch., San Diego, 1986-88. Lee C. Fine scholar Mo. Parks and Recreation Assn., 1975. mem. Nat. Recreation and Parks Assn., Mem. Ariz. Parks and Recreation Assn. (pres. 1986), Nat. Assn. State Recreation Planner, Nat. Assn. State River Conservation Program Adminstrs., Nat. Assn. State Outdoor Recreation Liaison Officers (alternate state liaison officer). Home: 2001 W Mulberry Phoenix AZ 85015 Office: Ariz State Parks 800 W Washington Phoenix AZ 85007

SIBBESTON, NICK, Canadian government official; b. Ft. Simpson, N.W.T., Can.; m. Karen Benoit; 6 children. BA, U. Alta., JD, 1975. Sec., mgr. Village of Ft. Simpson; mem. legis. assembly 1970-74, 79, 83; sole practice law Yellowknife, N.W.T., two yrs.; govt. leader N.W.T. Legis. Council, Yellowknife, 1985—. Mem. exec. council Priorities and Planning Com., Aboriginal Rights and Constitutional Devel. Com. Roman Catholic. Office: NWT Legis Council, Box 1320, Yellowknife, NT Canada X1A 2L9

SIBBITT, TINA ROBERTA, lawyer; b. Los Alamos, N.Mex., Apr. 15, 1958; d. Wilmer L. and Selma Doris (Otte) S. BA, U. N.Mex., 1980; postgrad., Georgetown U. Law Ctr., 1980-81; JD, U. N.Mex., 1983. Bar: N.Mex. 1984. Law clk. N.Mex. Supreme Ct., Santa Fe, 1984-85; assoc. Budagher & Assocs., Albuquerque, 1985—. Mem. ABA, Am. Trial Lawyer Assn. (young lawyers div.), Phi Beta Kappa, Kappa Mu Epsilon, Phi Kappa Phi, Delta Theta Phi. Office: Budagher & Assocs 1115 Third St NW Albuquerque NM 87102

SIBITZ, MICHAEL WILLIAM, superintendent of schools; b. San Francisco, July 22, 1937; s. Michael Jacob and Erna Anna Elsa (Altendorf) S.; m. Marilyn Joyce Pricco, Nov. 19, 1966; children—Elizabeth, Ryan. B.A., San Francisco State U., 1959, M.A., 1964, Ed.D., U. San Francisco, 1980; postgrad. Notre Dame U. of Calif., Stanford U. Tchr., Pacifica, Calif., 1959-64, Dept. Def., 1964-65; tchr. Belmont, Calif., 1965-70, specialist, 1970-71, adminstr., 1971-80; asst. supt. Sylvan Union Sch. Dist., Modesto, Calif., 1980—, supt., 1984—; supr. recreation City of Daly City (Calif.). Mem. Stanislaus Arts Commn.; past pres. United Way Stanislaus County. Served with U.S. Army, 1960-66. Mem. Assn. Calif. Sch. Adminstrs. (charter), NEA, Assn. Supervision and Curriculum Devel., Phi Delta Kappa. Roman Catholic. Club: Kiwanis. Contbr. articles to profl. jours. Home: 2019 Woodhaven Circle Riverbank CA 95367 Office: Sylvan Union Sch Dist 605 Sylvan Ave Modesto CA 95350

SIDDALL, MARK BERNARD, research physicist; b. Astoria, Oreg., Oct. 18, 1935; s. Mark Montague and Olivine Minerva (Fisch) S.; m. Marian Virginia Giedd, Mar. 19, 1966; 1 child, Lisa Karen. BS in Physics, Oreg. State U., 1957, MS in Material Sci., 1965. Jr. engr. Westinghouse Electric Corp. Research Labs., Pitts., 1957-60; physicist Teledyne Wah Chang, Albany, Oreg., 1961—, sr. research physicist, 1981—. Contbr. articles to profl. jours.; chpt. to book; patentee in field. Gen. chmn. Pacific N.W. Metals and Minerals Conf., Portland, Oreg., 1981; treas. Campaign Com. for State Rep., Albany, 1982, sec.-treas. First Assembly of God Ch., Albany, 1975—. Mem. Metall. Soc. (pres. Oreg. sect. 1975), Sigmi Xi (sec.-treas. Albany chpt. 1986, v.p. 1987). Republican. Club: Toastmasters (Albany) (dir. lt. gov. 1974). Avocations: bicycle touring, cross-country skiing, photography. Home: 1218 13th Ave NE Albany OR 97321 Office: Teledyne Wah Chang 1600 Old Pacific Hwy Albany OR 97321

SIDDIQUI, TOUFIQ ALIUDDIN, science administrator, researcher, educator; b. Hyderabad, India, Sept. 6, 1937; came to U.S., 1967; s. Raziuddin and Khurshid S.; m. Ulrike Wetzel, Dec. 9, 1966. BA with honors, Cambridge U., Eng., 1959; D in Nuclear Physics, Johann Wolfgang Goethe U., Frankfurt, Fed. Republic of Germany, 1966. Research assoc. Ind. U., Bloomington, 1967-69, 70-72, from asst. to assoc. prof., 1972-77; research assoc. East-West Ctr., Honolulu, 1977—, spl. asst. to pres., 1984—; vis. asst. prof. Humboldt State U., Arcata, Calif., 1969-70. Author: World Energy, 1976; co-editor: Coal Transportation in Asia and the Pacific, 1985, Newer

Coal Technologies, 1986; contbr. articles to profl. jours. Mem. Am. Phys. Soc., AAAS, Sigma Xi. Avocations: tennis, photography, reading, computers. Home: 250 Kawaihae St 17F Honolulu HI 96825 Office: East-West Ctr 1777 East-West Rd Honolulu HI 96848

SIDERIUS, LINDA L., lawyer; b. Kalispell, Mont., Nov. 23, 1953; d. Henry Lewis and Josephine Rose (Barry) D. BS in Nursing, U. Pa., 1975; JD, U. Denver, 1982. Bar: Colo. 1983, U.S. Dist. Ct. Colo. 1983. Nurse Grad. Hosp., Phila., 1975-76; researcher, lobbyist Nat. Farmers Union, Denver, 1976-82; assoc. Senn & Hoth, Denver, 1982—; cons. Office Energy Conservation, Denver, 1982, Lt. Gov.'s Office, Denver, 1982; bankruptcy trustee U.S. Dept. Justice, Denver, 1984—. Contbr. articles to profl. jours. Mem. Colo. Women's Bar Assn., Denver Bar Assn., Colo. Bar Assn., Sigma Theta Tau. Democrat. Avocations: skiing, cooking. Office: Senn & Hoth 633 17th St #1960 Denver CO 80202

SIDI, JACK ALBERT, educator, state legislator; b. Marseilles, France, Oct. 29, 1928; came to U.S., 1947, naturalized, 1953; s. Albert and Irene (Smadja) S.; m. Bernadette Mary Weisenberger, Jan. 15, 1955; children: Veronica, Michael. Baccalaureate, U. Grenoble, France, 1947; M.A., Northwestern U., 1951. Tchr. Cherry Lawn Sch., Darien, Conn., 1947-50; tchr. Morgan Jr. High Sch., Casper, Wyo., 1955-86; state legislator Wyo. Ho. of Reps., 1969-86, speaker pro tem, 1983-84, speaker, 1985-86; auditor State of Wyo., Cheyenne, 1987—. Served with USAF, 1951-55. Recipient Friend of Edn. award Wyo. Sch. Bds. Assn., 1978. Republican. Club: Casper Country (pres. 1973). Avocations: golf; bridge. Home: Box 113 Cheyenne WY 82003 Office: State of Wyo Wyo State Capitol Cheyenne WY 82002

SIDWELL, ROBERT WILLIAM, scientist, educator; b. Huntington Park, Calif., Mar. 17, 1937; s. Robert Glen and Eva Amalie (Gordy) S.; m. Rhea Julander, May 31, 1957; children: Richard Dale, Jeanette Kathleen, David Eugene, Cynthia Diane, Michael Jason, Robert Odell. B.S., Brigham Young U., Provo, Utah, 1958; M.S., U. Utah, 1961, Ph.D., 1963. Head serology, ricketts and virus research Epizoology Lab., U. Utah, 1958-63; head virus div. So. Research Inst., Birmingham, Ala., 1963-69; head dept. virology ICN Nucleic Acid Research Inst., Irvine, Calif., 1969-72; head div. chemotherapy ICN Nucleic Acid Research Inst., 1972-75, dir. inst., 1975-77; prof. animal, dairy and vet. scis. Utah State U., Logan, 1977—; mem. faculty U. Ala. Med. Sch., 1968-69; speaker in field. Editorial bd.: Antimicrobial Agts. and Chemotherapy, 1972—, Chemotherapy, 1974—, Jour. Antiviral Research, 1980—; Contbr. articles to profl. jours. Mem. Nibley (Utah) City Planning and Zoning Commn., 1978-80; mem. steering com. Irvine Sch. Bd., 1972, chmn. health edn. awareness forum, 1975. Scholar Order Eagles, 1954; Scholar Dept. Interior, 1954. Mem. AAAS, Am. Assn. Immunologists, Soc. Exptl. Biology and Medicine, Pan Am. Med. Assn., Internat. Soc. Chemotherapy, Inter-Am. Soc. Chemotherapy (exec. sec. 1985—), Am. Soc. Microbiology, Am. Soc. Virology, Sigma Xi. Home: 162 Quarter Circle Dr Nibley UT 84321 Office: Utah State U Dept Animal Dairy and Vet Sci Logan UT 84322-5600

SIEBE, MARY SYLVIA, human resource specialist; b. San Jose, Calif., Nov. 21, 1950; d. Norman Earhardt and Frances Carol (Wilson) S.; m. James Louis Agius, Jr., Dec. 6, 1968 (div. 1974); 1 child, Jamie Francine; m. Patrick Cameron Reed, Aug. 28, 1984. BS in Bus. Adminstrn., Calif. State U., Chico, 1978; postgrad., Colo. State U., 1985-86. Personnel performance mgr. Schaeffer Labs., Walnut Creek, Calif., 1978-80; adminstrn. and personnel specialist City of Ft. Collins Light and Power Utilities, Colo., 1980-87; tng. dir. Home Fed. Savs. and Loan Assn. of the Rockies, Ft. Collins, 1987—. Coordinator United Way fund drive for Ft. Collins Light and Power, 1984; mem. fin. com. Foothills Unitarian Ch., Ft. Collins, 1981; bd. dirs. Poudre R-1 Sch. Dist. Performance Evaluation Council, 1984—. Named one of Outstanding Young Women of Am., 1982. Mem. Am. Soc. Tng. and Devel., Alumni Assn. of Calif. State U.-Chico, Tng. Network of Ft. Collins, Phi Kappa Phi, Beta Gamma Sigma. Democrat. Avocations: travel, backpacking. Home: 1430 Freedom Ln Fort Collins CO 80526 Office: Home Fed Savs Loan Assn Rockies PO Box 2182 Fort Collins CO 80522

SIEBERT, ALAN HAROLD, musician, educator; b. Bklyn., July 8, 1955; s. Harold Joseph and Marilyn (Miller) S.; m. Cathy Hoffmann, July 3, 1977; 1 child, Christopher. MusB, SUNY, Fredonia, 1977; MusM in Trumpet, U. Mich., 1978; postgrad., Ariz. State U., 1983-85. Music tchr. Weston (Conn.) Middle Sch., 1978-80; prin. trumpet player Bridgeport (Conn.) Symphony, 1978-80; prof. trumpet U. Bridgeport, 1979-80; dir. bands, prof. trumpet U. Wis., Superior, 1980-82; prin. trumpet player Duluth (Minn.)-Superior Symphony, 1980-82; asst. prin. trumpet player San Diego Symphony, 1983—; trumpet instr. San Diego State U., 1984—; bd. dirs., treas. Pacific Chamber Ensemble, San Diego, 1985—. Mem. Internat. Trumpet Guild, Phi Mu Alpha (province gov.). Methodist. Avocations: camping, sailing, vintage wines. Office: San Diego State U Dept Music San Diego CA 92182-0217

SIEDLECKI, GEORGE KAZIMIER, public relations company executive; b. Newark, May 25, 1951; s. Kazimier and Zoya (Rukasueva) S.; m. Becky Brown, Nov. 7, 1972 (div. Feb. 1973); 1 child, Amy Leeyanna; m. Shawn Renee Graves, Dec. 1, 1982. Student, U. Colo.-Colorado Springs, 1976-79. Vice pres. Bonni Inc., Colorado Springs, Colo., 1979-83; pres. Bellwether Inc., Colorado Springs, 1983—. Served with U.S. Army, 1968-72, Vietnam. Decorated Purple Heart, Combat Infantryman's badge. Mem. Home Builders Assn., Nat. Fedn. Ind. Bus.

SIEGEL, BARBARA Z(ENZ), research biology educator; b. Detroit, July 22, 1931; d. Joseph and Barbara (Justh) Zenz; m. Sanford Marvin Siegel, June 24, 1950; children: Stephanie Siegel Morgan, Andrea Siegel Brill, Peter Marc, David Nathaniel. AB in Philosophy, U. Chgo., 1950; MA in Zoology, Columbia U., 1963; PhD in Biology, Yale U., 1966. Postdoctoral fellow Yale U., New Haven, 1966-67; dir. biology program U. Hawaii, Honolulu, 1967-72, prof. pub. health, sr. researcher Pacific Biomed. Research Ctr., 1975—, interim dir. research adminstrn., dean grad. sch., 1979-82, dir. pesticide hazard assessment project, 1983—, prof. microbiology and botany grad. dept. pub. health, 1986—; co-chmn. radiation sub-com. Com. Space Research Hdqrs., Paris, 1975-82; vis. prof. Heidelberg (Fed. Republic of Germany), 1973, Weizmann Inst., Rehovot, Israel, 1986; vis. scholar People's Republic of China, 1985; vis. colleague Nat. Research Council of Italy, Pisa. Editor: Hawaii Energy Resource Overviews: Geothermal Development, 1980; contbr. numerous articles to profl. jours. Chmn. Govs. Panel on Pesticides, Honolulu, 1985; nominated by gov. to Commn. on Pesticides, Honolulu, 1986—; chmn. research com. U. Hawaii Peace Inst., Honolulu, 1985, univ. commn. status of women Hawaii Assn. Women in Sci. and Faculty Women's Caucus, 1986. Fulbright Research fellow U.S. Info. Services, Yugoslavia and Fed. Republic of Germany, 1972-73. Mem. Am. Chem. Soc., Internat. Chem. Ecology Assn., Sigma Xi. Avocations: arts, travel, internat. coop. Home: 3119 Beaumont Woods Pl Honolulu HI 96822 Office: U Hawaii Pacific Biomed Research Ctr 1997 East-West Rd Honolulu HI 96822

SIEGEL, DAVID IRA, social work educator; b. N.Y.C., Nov. 28, 1946; s. Hyman H. and Anne (Smith) S. BA, Bklyn. Coll., 1968; MSW, U. Mich., 1971; DSW, Columbia U., 1982. Supr. social work Beth Israel Hosp. Alcoholism Program, N.Y.C., 1973-75; field coordinator Adelphi U., Garden City, N.Y., 1976-77, asst. prof. social work, 1977-83; program dir. York Coll. Social Work Program, Jamaica, N.Y., 1983-85; assoc. dir. U. So. Calif. Indsl. Social Work Program, Los Angeles, 1985-86, dir., 1986—; cons. in field, Los Angeles. Contbr. articles to profl. jours. Grantee VA, 1969, U.S. Office Edn., 1970, Can. Field Placement, 1970, NIMH, 1974-75. Mem. Nat. Assn. Social Workers (chmn. Los Angeles div. occupational social work council 1986—), Council Social Work Edn. Democrat. Jewish. Avocations: photography, jogging, racquetball. Home: 11107 Braddock Dr Culver City CA 90239 Office: U So Calif Indsl Social Work Program Montgomery Ross Fisher Bldg Los Angeles CA 90049

SIEGEL, HERMAN, industrial engineer; b. N.Y.C., May 30, 1926; s. Max and Ann (Brociner) S.; B.S. in Indsl. Mgmt., U. So. Calif., 1961, M.B.A. with honors, 1964; m. Rosalyn Geller, Sept. 6, 1947; children—Karen Anne, Jody Ellen. Indsl. engr. Curtiss-Wright Corp., Woodridge, N.Y., 1955-56; asso. corp. dir. Hughes Aircraft Co., Culver City, Calif., 1956-83; pres. Mgmt. Engring. Affiliates; dir. Fluid Power Corp., Meridian Group Cos., Instrument Finders; cons., lectr. in field. Served with USNR, 1943-46. Registered profl. engr., cert. profl. contracts mgr., Calif. Mem. AIAA, Am. Inst. Indsl. Engrs., Nat. Soc. Profl. Engrs., Am. Preparedness Asso., Los Angeles Peace Officers Assn., Beta Gamma Sigma, Alpha Sigma Lambda. Author papers in field. Office: PO Box 8114 Calabasas CA 91302

SIEGEL, LEE JORDAN, journalist, science writer; b. Portland, Oreg., Feb. 25, 1953; s. Sol and Julie (Benton) S. BS in Journalism, Gen. Sci., U. Oreg., 1975; MS in Journalism, Columbia U., 1976. Reporter The Daily News, Longview, Wash., 1976-79; state reporter Daily News of Longview, Jour. Am. of Bellevue (Wash.) and Daily News of Port Angeles (Wash.), 1979-81; newsman, supr. AP, Seattle, 1981-82; newsman, supr. AP, Los Angeles, 1982-84, sci. writer, 1984—. Mem. Wire Service Guild. Avocations: hiking, books, films. Office: AP 1111 S Hill St Room 263 Los Angeles CA 90015

SIEGEL, MARCI WENDY, clinical social worker, consulting psychotherapist; b. The Bronx, N.Y., July 25, 1954; d. Saul and Claire (Josepher) S. BA cum laude, CUNY, 1975; postgrad., Columbia U., 1975-76; MSW, San Diego State U., 1977. Lic. clin. social worker, Calif. (behavioral sci. oral exam commr. 1982—). Clin. social worker Mercy Hosp., San Diego, 1977—; pvt. practice psychotherapy, cons. San Diego, 1982—; field instr. San Diego State U., 1978—; cons. YMCA Human Devel. Ctr., San Diego, 1981—, Congregation Beth Israel, San Diego, 1985—. Active San Diego Community Child Abuse Coordinating Council, 1980—. Named an Outstanding Young Woman of Am., 1983, 84. Fellow Soc. Clin Social Work; mem. Nat. Assn. Social Workers (cert.), Nat. Found. Ileitis and Colitis (San Diego chpt. exec. bd. 1982—, pres. exec. bd. 1983-84), Am. Orthopsychiat. Assn. Democrat. Jewish. Avocations: photography, hiking, traveling. Office: 3356 2d Ave Suite H San Diego CA 92103

SIEGEL, NEIL GILBERT, computer mathematician, musician; b. Bklyn., Feb. 19, 1954; s. Bernard Siegel and Judith Love Cohen; m. Robyn Christine Friend, July 8, 1979. B.A. cum laude, U. So. Calif., 1974, M.S., 1976, Ph.D., 1977. sr. staff mem. TRW, Inc., Redondo Beach, Calif., 1977-80, prin. scientist Compunet, Inc., Inglewood, Calif., 1980-83; prin. software engr. Titan Systems, La Jolla, Calif., 1983—; lectr. UCLA, 1973, cons., 1984—. Contbr. articles to profl. jours. Performer numerous flute recs., 1970—; orch. dir. AMAN Folk Ensemble, 1969-77. Bd. dirs. Inst. Persian Performing Arts. Mem. Phi Beta Kappa. Jewish. Home: 3306 Gibson Pl Redondo Beach CA 90278 Office: Titan Systems Inc 1515 W 190th St Suite 230 Gardena CA 90248

SIEGEL, STUART ELLIOTT, physician, pediatrics educator, cancer researcher; b. Plainfield, N.J., July 16, 1943; s. Hyman and Charlotte Pearl (Freinberg) S.; m. Linda Wertkin, Jan. 20, 1968; 1 child, Joshua. BA, MD, Boston U., 1967. Diplomate Am. Bd. Pediatrics, Am. Bd. Pediatric Oncology. Intern U. Minn. Hosp., Mpls., 1967-68, resident, 1968-69; clin. assoc. NIH, Bethesda, Md., 1969-72; asst. prof. pediatrics U. So. Calif. Sch. Medicine, Los Angeles, 1972-76, assoc. prof., 1976-81, prof., 1981—; head div. hematology-oncology Children's Meml. Hosp. of Los Angeles, 1976—; mem. clin. cancer program project com. NIH, Nat. Cancer Inst., HEW, Bethesda, Md., 1978-82; pres. So. Calif. Children's Cancer Services, Los Angeles, 1977—. Served to surgeon, USPHS, 1969-72. Fellow Am. Acad. Pediatrics. Office: Childrens Hosp Los Angeles Div Hematology Oncology 4650 Sunset Blvd Los Angeles CA 90027

SIEGELE, KENNETH, minister, university administrator; b. Harvey, N.D., Jan. 5, 1933; s. Henry R. and Jeanette T. (Akland) S.; m. Margaret L. Holbrook, Mar. 16, 1955; children: Paul K., Sharon L., Diane K., Carol A. BA, Pacific Luth. U., 1954; M Divinity, Luther Theol. Seminary, 1960. Ordained to ministry Luth. ch., 1960. Pastor Marion (N.D.) Luth. Ch., 1960-63, Milnor (N.D.) Luth. Ch., 1963-69; regional dir. Am. Luth. Ch., Mpls., 1969-71; assoc. dir. Am. Luth. Ch. Found., Mpls., 1971-74; exec. dir. Calif. Luth. U., Thousand Oaks, Calif., 1975—, dir. Office of Planned Giving,, 1975-79, v.p. devel., 1979-82; cons. Am. Luth. Found., Mpls., 1971-74. Editor CLEF Horizons 1982—. Mem. ch. council King of Glory Luth. Ch., Newbury Park, Calif., 1975-77, 85; bd. dirs. Solheim Luth. Home, Eagle Rock, Calif. Served with U.S. Army, 1955-56, Korea. Mem. Council Advancement and Support Edn., Internat. Assn. Fin. Planning (local bd. dirs. 1983—, sec., treas. 1985—), Nat. Soc. Fund-Raising Execs. (cert.), Assn. Luth. Devel. Execs., Conejo Orchid Soc. (v.p. 1984—). Republican. Avocations: gardening, travel. Office: Calif Luth U Calif Luth Ednl Found 60 W Olsen Rd Thousand Oaks CA 91360-2787

SIEMENS, WERNER HANS, engineering consultant; b. Berlin, Mar. 22, 1933; came to U.S., 1964, naturalized, 1973; s. Werner Detlef and Erna (Friedrich) S.; dipl., Mech. Trade Sch., Berlin, 1952; student Tech. U., Berlin, 1952-53; dipl. Internat. Corr. Sch., Montreal, Que., Can., 1960; m. Rosaline McKenna, Oct. 15, 1965; children—Brian Andrew, Bruce David, Kathleen Barbara, Kenneth Alexander. Sr. signal circuit designer Canadian Nat. Rwy., Edmonton, Alta., 1954-64; sr. signal application engr. Gen. Rwy. Signal Co., Rochester, N.Y., 1964-66; signals engr. Mass. Bay Transit Authority, Boston, 1966-71; mgr. electrification control systems Gen. Electric Co., Erie, Pa., 1971-74; chief engr. r.r. electrification Internat. Engring. Co., San Francisco, 1974-78; mgr. r.r. engring. Kaiser Engrs., Oakland, Calif., 1978-83; cons. Fed. R.R. Adminstrn. on design of EMC test facility at Dept. Transp. Test Center, Pueblo, Colo., 1980-81. Com. mem. Boy Scouts Am., Erie, Pa. and San Rafael, Calif., 1971-78. Registered profl. engr., Calif. Mem. Am. Assn. R.R.s, Am. Ry. Engring. Assn., Transp. Research Bd., U.S. Nat. Com. of Internat. Electrotech. Commn. Contbr. articles to profl. jours. Home: 102 Twelveoakhill Dr San Rafael CA 94903 Office: 102 Twelve Oak Hill Dr San Rafael CA 94903

SIEMERS, REBECCA JANE, software engineer; b. Mason City, Iowa, Aug. 18, 1959; d. Paul Herbert and Betty Jane (Hagstrom) Potter. BS in Math., BS in Computer Engring., Iowa State U., 1981; MSEE, Stanford U., 1985. Software devel. engr. Hewlett-Packard co., Cupertino, Calif., 1981-82, project mgr., 1982-86; mgr. software engring. Microsensor Tech., Fremont, Calif., 1986—. Mem. rev. bd. Jour. Clin. Engring., 1984—. Mem. IEEE, Phi Beta Kappa, Sigma Xi, Tau Beta Pi, Eta Kappa Nu (pres. 1980-81). Avocations: music, needlework, tennis. Home: 1303 Hillview Ct Roseville CA 95661 Office: Microsensor Tech Inc 41762 Christy St Fremont CA 94538

SIEMON-BURGESON, MARILYN M., education administrator; b. Whittier, Calif., Nov. 15, 1934; d. John Roscoe and Louise Christina (Secoy) Mason; m. Carl J. Siemon, Aug. 18, 1956 (div. Oct. 1984); children: Timothy G., Melanie A. Siemon Imes; Troy M.; m. James K. Burgeson, Jan. 24, 1987. BA, U. Redlands, 1956; MA, Pacific Oaks Coll., 1975; postgrad., Point Loma Coll., 1979-80. Cert. elem. and early childhood tchr. Tchr. Sierra Madre (Calif.) Community Nursery Sch., 1970-79; tchr. parent edn. and music Pasadena (Calif.) Unified Schs., 1977-79; project coordinator Pasadena (Calif.) United Schs., 1980-81, tchr. curriculum resource dept., 1982-83; head tchr., Washington Children's Ctr. Pasadena (Calif.) Unified Schs., 1983—. Active Arcadia, Calif. Bicentennial Commn., 1974-76, Pasadena Council Women's Clubs; life mem. Sierra Madre Sch. PTA, also chpt. liaison. Ednl. Professions Devel. fellow Pacific Oaks Coll., Pasadena, 1969. Mem. Nat. Assn. Edn. Young Children, So. Calif. Assn. Edn. Young Children (grantee 1970), Child Care Info. Service (bd. dirs., chmn. parent edn. and family affairs 1986—), Women Ednl. Leadership (asst. program v.p.), AAUW (co-chmn. Math.-Sci. Conf. 1983, grantee 1982, 83), Delta Kappa Gamma (pres. 1986—). Republican. Episcopalian. Avocation: music. Home: 1875 Kinneloa Canyon Rd Pasadena CA 91107 Office: Washington Children's Ctr 130 Penn St Pasadena CA 91103

SIERK, ARNOLD JOHN, physicist, researcher; b. Batavia, N.Y., Nov. 10, 1946; s. Norman Lindsey and Dorothy Ida (Wild) S.; m. Christina Hebenstreit, Aug. 24, 1968; children: Michael, Brian, Kimberly. BS, Cornell U., 1968; PhD, Calif. Inst. Tech., 1973. With Los Alamos (N.Mex.) Sci. Lab., 1972-74; asst. prof. Calif. Inst. Tech., Pasadena, 1974-77; staff mem. Los Alamos Nat. Lab., 1977—. Contbr. sci. articles to profl. jours. Fellow Hertz Found., 1970-72, Sloan Found., 1975-77. Fellow Am. Phys. Soc., Sigma Xi. Office: Los Alamos Nat Lab PO Box 1663 T-9 MS B279 Los Alamos NM 87545

SIGBAND, NORMAN BRUCE, management communication educator; b. Chgo., June 27, 1920; s. Max and Bessie S.; m. Joan C. Lyons, Aug. 3, 1944; children: Robin, Shelley, Betsy. B.A., U. Chgo., 1940, M.A., 1941, Ph.D., 1954; L.H.D. (hon.), De Paul U., 1986. Asst. prof. bus. communication De Paul U., 1946-50, assoc. prof., 1950-54, prof., 1954-65; prof. mgmt. communication U. So. Calif., 1965—, chmn. dept. mktg., 1970-72; asso. dean U. So. Calif. (Sch. Bus.), 1975-80; Disting. Centennial lectr. U. Tex., Austin, 1986; cons. to industry; speaker, condr. workshops, seminars in field; Scholar in Residence, Va. Commonwealth U., 1987. Author: books, including Practical Communication for Everyday Use, 25th printing, 1954, Effective Report Writing for Business, Industry and Government, 1960, Communication for Management, 1970, Communicacion Para Directivos, 1972, Management Communication for Decision Making, 1972, Communication for Management and Business, 1976, 4th edit., 1986, Communicating in Business, 1981, 2d edit., 1985; gen. editor: books, including Harcourt Brace Jovanovich Bus. Series; contbr. numerous articles to profl. jours., mags. Served to capt. AUS, 1942-46, ETO. Decorated Bronze Star; recipient Excellence in Teaching award U. So. Calif., 1975, Dean's award, 1972, Outstanding Educator award, 1973. Fellow Am. Bus. Communication Assn. (pres. 1964-65); mem. Internat. Communication Assn., Acad. Mgmt., Anti-Defamation League, Hadassah Assocs. Democrat. Jewish. Home: 3109 Dona Susana Dr Studio City CA 91604 Office: U So Calif Grad Sch Bus University Park Los Angeles CA 90007

SIGEL, CLAUDE ALLEN, computer scientist, researcher; b. Buffalo, Apr. 13, 1950; s. Charles Lowe and Joanne Frances (Martin) Harrell; m. Marlene Aronin, July 23, 1972; children: Corinne, Keeley. BS, Harvey Mudd Coll., 1971; student, Brandeis U., 1971-72; PhD, U. Pa., 1976. Asst. prof. Northeastern U., Boston, 1976-80; ednl. specialist Digital Equipment Corp., Bedford, Mass., 1980-81; software engr. Digital Equipment Corp., Marlboro, Mass., 1981-83; computer scientist Digital Equipment Corp., Albuquerque, 1983—; instr. U. Albuquerque, 1984-85. Contbr. articles to profl. jours. Internal Research grantee, 1978. Mem. Assn. for Research in Vision and Ophthalmology, Optical Soc. Am., Soc. Info. Display, Assn. Computing Machinery. Avocations: long distance running, jazz music. Home: 726-16 Tramway Vista Dr Albuquerque NM 87122 Office: Digital Equipment Corp PO Box 80 Albuquerque NM 87103

SIGGSON, ALBERT NATHAN, aircraft company executive; b. Phila., Sept. 22, 1928; s. Nathan Harry and Grace Elizabeth (Fenester) S.; AA, Long Beach City Coll., 1957; BS cum laude, U. Phoenix, Irvine, Calif., 1983; m. Marjorie Jane Lindblom, July 17, 1966; children: Larry Jay, Randal Roy. Standards engr. Standards, Northrop, Nortronics, Hawthorne, Calif., 1966-67; sr. electronic engr. standards Hughes, Fullerton, Calif., 1967-68; lead engr. standards ITT/Gilfillan, Van Nuys, Calif., 1968-69; sr. standards engr. Northrop Aircraft, Hawthorne, Calif., 1969-82, Northrop Advanced Systems, Pico Rivera, Calif., 1982-83, design specialist, 1983-86, mgr. data and pubs., 1986—, mem. metrication com., and advanced systems div. mgmt. club; instr. blueprint reading evenings El Camino Coll., Torrance, Calif., 1980-86. Served with USN, 1946-49. Registered profl. engr., Calif.; cert. mfg., standards and metrication engr. Fellow Inst. Advancement Engring.; mem. Soc. Mfg. Engrs. (chmn. Long Beach chpt. 1972-73, mem. Northrop Corp. metric com., internat. award of merit and citation), Standards Engring. Soc., U.S. Metric Assn., Am. Soc. Testing and Materials, U.S. Metric Assn. (charter chmn. South Bay chpt. 1975-76), Sigma Xi. Lutheran. Author books on metrication; contbr. articles to profl. jours. Office: Northrop Advanced Systems 8900 E Washington Blvd Pico Rivera CA 90660

SIGLER, MICHAEL FREDERICK, biologist; b. Binghamton, N.Y., Nov. 7, 1957; s. Frederick Louis and Louise Edith (Lowery) S. BS with honors, Cornell U., 1979, MS, 1982. Fishery biologist No. Southeast Regional Aquaculture Assn., Sitka, Alaska, summer 1982; fishery biologist Nat. Marine Fisheries Service Auke Bay Lab., Juneau, summer 1983, fishery technician, 1984, fishery biologist, 1984-85, fishery research biologist, 1985—. Contbr. articles to profl. jours. Sea Grant fellow N.Y. State Research Found., Albany, 1980-82. Mem. AAAS, N.Y. Acad. Scis., Union Concerned Scientists. Democrat. Avocations: skiing, boating. Home: PO Box 211002 Auke Bay AK 99821 Office: Nat Marine Fisheries Service Auke Bay Lab PO Box 210155 Auke Bay AK 99821

SIGLER, WILLIAM FRANKLIN, environmental consultant; b. LeRoy, Ill., Feb. 17, 1909; s. John A. and Bettie (Homan) S.; m. Margaret Eleanor Brotherton, July 3, 1936; children—Elinor Jo, John William. B.S., Iowa State U., 1940, M.S., 1941, Ph.D., 1947; postdoctoral studies, UCLA, 1963. Conservationist Soil Conservation Service, Ill., 1935-37; cons. Central Engring. Co., Davenport, Iowa, 1940-41; research assoc. Iowa State U., 1941-42; 1945-47; asst. prof. wildlife sci. Utah State U., 1947-50, prof., head dept., 1950-74; pres. W.F. Sigler & Assocs. Inc., 1974—; cons. U.S. Surgeon Gen., 1963-67, FAO, Argentina, 1968. Author: Theory and Method of Fish Life History Investigations, 1952, Wildlife Law Enforcement, 1956, 3d edit., 1980, Fishes of Utah, 1963, Fishes of the Great Basin, 1987; also numerous articles. Mem. Utah Water Pollution Control Bd., 1957-65, chmn., 1963-65. Served as lt. (j.g.) USNR, World War II. Named Wildlife Conservationist of Yr. Nat. Wildlife Fedn., 1970, Outstanding Educator of Year, 1971; recipient Disting. Service cert. recognition Iowa Coop. Wildlife Research Unit, 1982, Outstanding Service award Utah State U., 1986, Alumni Achievement award Coll. Natural Resources Utah State U., 1987. Fellow Internat. Acad. Fishery Scientists, AAAS; mem. Ecol. Soc. Am., Wildlife Soc. (hon.), Am. Fisheries Soc., AAUP, Outdoor Writers Am., Sigma Xi, Phi Kappa Phi. Home: 309 E 2d S Logan UT 84321

SIGMAN, MELVIN MONROE, psychiatrist; b. N.Y.C., Dec. 15, 1935; s. Irving and Lillian (Pearlman) S. BA, Columbia U., 1956; MD, SUNY, N.Y.C., 1960; postgrad., William Alanson White Analytic Inst., N.Y.C., 1969. Staff psychiatrist Hawthorne (N.Y.) Cedar Knolls Sch., 1966-68; pvt. practice psychiatry N.Y.C., 1966-72, Fresno, Calif., 1974—; staff psychiatrist Fresno County Dept. of Health, 1974—; attending staff psychiatry Bellevue Hosp., N.Y.C., 1966-68; cons. N.Y. Foundling Hosp., N.Y.C., 1966-72; assoc. attending staff Roosevelt Hosp., N.Y.C., 1967-72; asst. clin. prof U. Calif. San Francisco, Fresno, 1977; chmn. cen. Calif. com. Columbia Coll. Nat. Alumni Secondary Schs. Served to capt. USAF, 1961-63. Fellow Royal Soc. Health, Am. Orthopsychiat. Assn.; mem. Am. Psychiat. Assn. Fresno Racquet. Avocations: piano, tennis. Office: Fresno County Dept Health PO Box 11867 Fresno CA 93775

SIGOLOFF, SANFORD CHARLES, retail executive; b. St. Louis, Sept. 8, 1930; s. Emmanuel and Gertrude (Breliant) S.; m. Betty Ellen Greene, Sept. 14, 1952; children: Stephen, John David, Laurie. B.A., UCLA, 1950. Cons. AEC, 1950-54, 57-58; gen. mgr. Edgerton, Germeshausen & Grier, Santa Barbara, Calif., 1958-63; v.p. Xerox Corp., 1963-69; pres. CSI Corp., Los Angeles, 1969-70; sr. v.p. Republic Corp., Los Angeles, 1970-71; chief exec. officer Kaufman & Broad, Inc., Los Angeles, 1979-82; chmn., pres., chief exec. officer Wickes Cos. Inc., Santa Monica, 1982—. Contbr. articles on radiation dosimetry to profl. jours. Bd. govs. Cedars-Sinai Hosp. Served in USAF, 1954-57. Recipient Tom May award Nat. Jewish Hosp. and Research Ctr., 1972. Mem. AAAS, Am. Chem. Soc., AIAA, Am. Nuclear Soc., IEEE, Radiation Research Soc. Office: Wickes Cos Inc 3340 Ocean Park Blvd Santa Monica CA 90405 *

SIGURDSON, LARRY LEROY, public relations executive; b. Seaside, Oreg., June 16, 1950; s. Clarence Edwin and Beverly Mable (U'Renn) S.; m. Carolyn Lena Foote, July 5, 1980. AA, Clatsop Community Coll., 1979; BS in Journalism, BS in Polit. Sci., U. Oreg., 1980; postgrad., Syracuse U., 1980. Reporter, photographer Oreg. Daily Emerald, Eugene, 1979-80; dir. pub. relations Crawford Advt., Syracuse, N.Y., 1980-81; aviation info. specialist Port. of Portland, Oreg., 1981; account exec. Sta. KEED Radio, Eugene, 1981-83; account rep. Sr. News Newspapers, Eugene, 1984; dir. community relations, advt. and spl. event promotion Umpqua Community Coll., Roseburg, Oreg., 1984—. Editor, pub. (catalog) Umpqua Community Coll., 1985-86, 86-87; asst. editor: Oreg. N.G., Salem, 1979-84; contbr. articles to profl. jours.; photographer various pubs. Precinct committeemen Douglas County Rep. Cen. Com., Roseburg, 1986—, mem. exec. bd., 1986-88; cons. Bruce Long for Congress, Eugene, 1984; vol. Ross Anthony for Congress, Eugene, 1982; chmn. steering com. bur. Douglas County United Way, 1986-87, v.p. and pres.-elect, 1987—; mem. Douglas County Pub. Relations Roundtable. Served with USN, 1969-74. Named State V.P. of Yr., Oreg. Jaycees,

Salem, 1975-76,. Mem. Nat. Council for Community Relations (Dist. VII communicator/pacesetter of Yr. Chair), Douglas County Pub. Relations Roundtable, Roseburg C. of C. Baptist. Avocations: travelling, hiking, music, reading, theatre. Office: Umpqua Community Coll PO Box 967 Roseburg OR 97470

SIKDAR, SUBHAS KUMAR, chemical engineer; b. Calcutta, India, Apr. 1, 1944; came to U.S., 1969; s. Tarapada and Biva (Bhowmick) S.; m. Ruma Das, Feb. 20, 1977; children: Manjie (dec.), Ronjan, Reena. BS, Calcutta U., 1964, BTech., 1966, MTech, 1967; MS, U. Ariz., 1971, PhD, 1975. Sr. research engr. Occidental Research Co., Irvine, Calif., 1975-79; mgr. process tech. Gen. Electric Co., Schenectady, N.Y., 1979-84; group leader transport processes Nat. Bur. Standards, Boulder, Colo., 1984—; founder, owner Sci. Computing and Instrn., Boulder, 1983—. Contbr. articles to profl. jours.; patentee in field. Merit scholar Govt. India, 1960-67; recipient patent award Gen. Electric Co., 1978, 83, Performance awards Nat. Bur. Standards Dept. of Commerce, 1985, 86. Mem. ASTM (chmn. task force 1986), Am. Inst. Chem. Engrs., Am. Chem. Soc., Am. Planetary Soc. Avocations: tennis, reading, non-fiction writing. Home: 4270 Plum Ct Boulder CO 80301 Office: Nat Bur Standards 325 Broadway Boulder CO 80303

SIKOV, MELVIN RICHARD, toxicologist; b. Detroit, July 8, 1928; s. Paul Merrill and Emma (Perlman) S.; m. Shirley Dressler, June 1, 1952; children: Peter H., Stacy J., Thomas R. BS, Wayne U., 1951; PhD, U. Rochester, 1955. Asst. prof. Wayne State U., Detroit, 1955-60, assoc. prof., 1961-65; sr. research scientist Battelle N.W., Richland, Wash., 1965-68, research assoc., 1968-78, mgr. devel. toxicology, 1978-81, sr. staff scientist, 1981—. Contbr. numerous publs. to sci. jours. Served with U.S. Army, 1946-47, ATO. Fellow Am. Inst. Ultrasound in Medicine; mem. Am. Assn. Pathologists, Health Physics Soc., Radiation Research Soc., Teratology Soc., Soc. Toxicology. Office: Battelle Pacific NW Labs PO Box 999 Richland WA 99352

SILBAUGH, PRESTON NORWOOD, savings and loan consultant, lawyer; b. Stockton, Cal., Jan. 15, 1918; s. Herbert A. and Della Mae (Masten) S.; m. Maria Sarah Arriola; children—Judith Ann Silbaugh Freed, Gloria Silbaugh Stypinski, Ximena Carey Silbaugh Braun, Carol Lee Silbaugh Morgan. A.B. in Philosophy, U. Wash., 1940; J.D., Stanford U., 1953. Bar: Calif. With Lockheed Aircraft Corp., 1941-44, Pan Am. World Airways, 1944, Office Civilian Personnel, War Dept., 1944-45; engaged in ins. and real estate in Calif., 1945-54; mem. faculty Stanford Law Sch., 1954-59, asso. prof. law, 1956-59, asso. dean, 1956-59; chief dep. savs. and loan commnr. for Calif., 1959-61, bus. and commerce adminstr., dir. investment, savs. and loan commr., mem. gov.'s cabinet, 1961-63; dir. Chile-Calif. Aid Program, Sacramento and Santiago, 1963-65; chmn. bd. Beverly Hills Savs. & Loan Assn., Calif., 1965-84; dir. Wickes Cos., Inc.; chmn. bd., pres. Simon Bolivar Fund, Del Mar, Calif.; of counsel firm Miller, Boyko & Bell, San Diego. Author: The Economics of Personal Insurance, 1958; also articles. Mem. pres.'s real estate adv. com. U. Calif., 1966—; mem. Beverly Hills Pub. Bldg. Adv. Com., 1970—. Served with USMCR, 1942-43. Mem. ABA, San Diego County Bar Assn., Soc. Internat. Devel., U.S., Nat., Calif. Savs. and Loan Leagues, Inter-Am. Savs. and Loan Union, Internat. Union Building Socs., U. Wash., Stanford Alumni Assns., Calif. Aggie Alumni Assn., Order of Coif, Phi Alpha Delta. Clubs: Commonwealth (San Francisco), Town Hall (Los Angeles). Home: 13059 Caminito del Rocio Del Mar CA 92014 also: Costenera del Sur, Zapallar Chile

SILBERMAN, DONN MICHAEL, fiber optics engineer; b. Los Angeles, Feb. 3, 1959; s. Irwin Alan Silberman and Lynne Hope (Sussman) Stevens; m. Ana Maria Asbun, Aug. 24, 1984; 1 child, Michael Dean. BS in Engring. Physics with honors, U. Ariz., 1983. Laser engr. Melles Griot Lasers, San Marcos, Calif., 1983; research engr. Spectron Devel. Labs., Costa Mesa, Calif., 1984-86, Am. Edwards Labs, Santa Ana, Calif., 1986—. Mem. Soc. Physics Students U. Ariz. (pres. 1981-83, assoc. councillor zone 2 1983-84). Avocation: astronomy. Home: 302 Marguerite Corona del Mar CA 92625 Office: Am Edwards Labs PO Box 11150 Mail Stop 50 Santa Ana CA 92711

SILBURN, ELAINE GWENDOLYN, banker; b. Denver, June 3, 1937; d. Russell Edwin and Genevieve (Johnson) Seay; m. David L. Silburn, June 16, 1957; children—Carla Anne, James Russell. A.B.A., U. Denver, 1957; student Northwestern U., 1960, U. Okla., 1981. Trust officer United Bank of Denver, 1957-65; personal banker, personal banking officer, asst. v.p., v.p. United Bank of Skyline, Denver, 1978-83, sr. v.p., 1983—, dir., 1984—. Bd. dirs. Holistic Approaches to Independent Living, 1984—; vol. Denver Pub. Schs., alumni fund campaign U. Denver, Channel 6 Pub. TV Auction, 1983, Am. Cancer Soc., mem. major gifts fund com. Denver Symphony Orch., 1984—; mem. steering com. Denver Bus. Challenge, 1984; adv. bd. Mile High United Way, 1985; del. Republican county and state assemblies. Mem. Nat. Assn. Bank Women, Mental Health Assn. Colo. (fin. devel. com.), Leadership Denver Assn., Denver C. of C., Cultural Affairs Task Force, Gamma Phi Beta. Episcopalian. Club: Sweet Adelines, (High Country chpt.) (pres. 1977). Home: 3119 S Akron Ct Denver CO 80231 Office: United Bank of Skyline NA 1055 16th St Denver CO 80202

SILFVAST, ROGER OLIVER, management consultant; b. Spokane, Wash., July 1, 1947; s. Oliver William and Martha Emily (Kauppi) S.; m. Joan Fiore, July 14, 1980; children: Brittany Fiore, Brian Fiore. BA in Psychology, Eastern Wash. State U., 1970; MA in Applied Behavioral Sic., Whitworth Coll., 1976; PhD in Organizational Analysis, U. Wash., 1985. Clin. dir. Therapeutic Health Services, Seattle, 1976-79; city mgr. City of Seattle, 1979-82; mgmt. cons. Touche Ross & Co., Seattle, 1982-85; prin. HRD Assocs., Seattle, 1985—. Pres., bd. dirs. Mt. Baker Youth Service Bur., Seattle, 1986—. Mem. Acad. Mgmt., Assn. Human Resource Mgrs., Organizational Devel. Inst., Internat. Registry Orgn. Devel. Profls. Democrat. Lutheran. Lodge: Rotary. Home: 2218 32d Ave S Seattle WA 98144

SILK, JOSEPH IVOR, astronomy educator; b. London, Dec. 3, 1942; came to U.S., 1964; s. Philip and Sylvia Silk; m. Margaret Wendy Kuhn, Aug. 11, 1968; children: Timothy William, Jonathan Charles. MA, Cambridge (Eng.) U., 1963; PhD, Harvard U., 1968. Research fellow Cambridge U., 1968-69, Princeton (N.J.) U., 1969-70; asst. prof. astronomy U. Calif., Berkeley, 1970-73, assoc. prof., 1973-78, prof., 1978—; chercheur associé Institut d'Astrophysique, Paris, 1982-83. Author: The Big Bang, 1980; co-author: The Left Hand of Creation, 1983. Recipient First prize Gravity Research Found., 1975, Bowdoin prize Harvard U., 1968, Bok prize Harvard U., 1970; fellow Sloan Found., 1972-74, Guggenheim Found., 1975-76, Inst. Advanced Study, 1975-76. Fellow AAAS, Royal Astron. Soc.; mem. Internat. Astron. Union, Am. Astron. Soc. Avocations: skiing, sailing. Office: U Calif Dept Astronomy Berkeley CA 94720

SILKWOOD, VALERIE GAIL, speech/language pathologist; b. Carmel, Calif., Dec. 6, 1958; d. Leonard George Silkwood, Donald Robert and Mary Lou (Sivula) Cooper; m. Stephen Allan Myers, Dec. 17, 1983; 1 child, Scott Treven. BA, U. Calif., Santa Barbara, 1981; MS, U. Wyo., 1983. Speech/lang. pathologist Thompson Sch. Dist., Loveland, Colo., 1983-85, Learning Therapy, Inc., Cupertino, Calif., 1985-86, Crippled Children's Soc., Santa Clara, Calif., 1986, Olga Ramirez Assocs., Sacramento, Calif., 1986—. Mem. Am. Speech/Lang. Hearing Assn. (cert. clin. competence). Home: 8454 Los Serranos Way Citrus Heights CA 95610

SILL, ALEXIS MATTOS, computer company executive; b. Rio de Janeiro, Apr. 15, 1949; came to U.S., 1956, naturalized, 1960; s. Bev Arthur and Gigi Lino (Mattos) S.; m. Sandra Sarah Ann Heaslip, Aug. 24, 1974; children: Courtney Jane, Alexis Ryan, Colin George. Student Golden Gate U., San Francisco. Sales mgr. United Calif. Bank, San Francisco, 1971-77; sales exec. Automatic Data Processing, Inc., San Francisco, 1977-84;nat. sales mgr. Digital Research, Inc., Palo Alto, Calif., 1984—; pres. Mega Distbg., Sausalito, Calif. Served with USMCR, 1969-71. Republican. Home: 40 Hillside Ave San Rafael CA 94901 Office: Digital Research Inc 1860 Embarcadero Rd Suite 215 Palo Alto CA 94303

SILLS, RONALD VERNON, general insurance agent; b. Yakima, Wash., Dec. 31, 1946; s. Vernon Forrest and Margarite Elizabeth S.; m. Leslie Howe, Sept. 2, 1970; children—Jason Durand, Adam Vernon, Catherine Anne. B.A. in Anthropology, U. Mont., 1972, B.S. in Fin., 1972. C.L.U. Dist. mgr. Mut. Benefit Life, Missoula, Mont., 1973-79, asst. gen. agt., Spokane, Wash., 1979-80; asst. supt. agys. Nat. Life of Vt., Montpelier, 1980-82, gen. agt., Denver, 1982—; fin. planner; tchr. in field; seminar recruiter and trainer. Served with USN, 1964-67; Vietnam. Mem. Am. Soc. C.L.Us., Denver Assn. Life Underwriters, Nat. Assn. Life Underwriters, Vt. Estate Planning Council, Gen. Agts. and Mgrs. Assn. (bd. dirs.). Episcopalian. Clubs: Masons (Whitefish, Mont.); Shriners (Spokane). Home: 6124 S Jackson St Littleton CO 80121 Office: Nat Life of Vt 1836 Grant St Suite 200 Denver CO 80203

SILVA, RICHARD JAMES, social service administrator; b. French Camp, Calif., Aug. 18, 1939; s. George Faustine and Catherine (Cook) S.; m. Vona Lee Dunning, May 30, 1976; children: Allegra Kyria, Pia Joelle. BA, San Luis Rey Coll., 1963; M in Social Welfare, U. Calif., Berkeley, 1968; M in Pub. Adminstrn., Golden Gate U., 1976. Social service program specialist Office Program Coordination and Rev., San Francisco, 1977-80; day care program specialist Adminstrn. Children and Families, San Francisco, 1980-82; regional dir. Adminstrn. Devel. Disabilities, San Francisco, 1982-86; dep. regional adminstr. HHS Office Human Devel. Services, San Francisco, 1986—. V.p. Diaconate Community of Oakland, 1984-86; chmn. social justice com. Diocesan Pastoral Council, 1985-86; team leader budget panel United Way, San Francisco, 1975-76; vol. Traverer's Aid Soc., San Francisco, 1972-82; bd. dirs. Jubilee West, Oakland, 1981. Recipient Superior Service award HEW, Washington, 1981. Mem. Am. Assn. Mental Deficiency, Amnesty Internat., Bread for the World. Democrat. Roman Catholic. Avocations: sailing, backpacking, personal computing, church activities. Office: HHS Office Human Devel Services 50 United Nations Plaza San Francisco CA 94102

SILVA, ROBERT OWEN, city official; b. La Junta, Colo., Sept. 5, 1935; s. Owen Delbert and Gertrude H. (Kerr) S.; m. Meredith Ann Ginn, Dec. 18, 1953; children—Edward, Andrew, Colleen. Student Pueblo Jr. Coll., 1953, FBI Nat. Acad., 1975, Police Found. Exec. Program, 1979-80. Cert. peace officer, Colo. Police officer Pueblo Police Dept., Colo., 1958-66, sgt., 1966-72, capt., 1972-77, chief of police, 1977—, dir. Colo. Police Officers Standards and Tng. Bd. dirs. Salvation Army, Pueblo, Easter Seals Soc., Pueblo, Community Corrections Bd., Pueblo, Served with U.S. Army, 1955-57. Mem. Pueblo Community Coll. Criminal Justice Adv. Bd., Leadership Pueblo Steering Com., Pikes Peak Community Coll. Criminal Justice Program (chmn. adv. bd. 1981), Organized Crime Strike Force (bd. dirs. 1977-84, chmn. 1982, 83, 84); Colo. Assn. Chiefs of Police (pres. 1984-85), Rocky Mountain Info. Network (chmn. bd. dirs. 1986—), Presbyterian (elder). Lodges: Kiwanis (bd. dirs. 1982-84), Elks. Office: Pueblo Police Dept 130 Central Main St Pueblo CO 81003

SILVANI, STEPHEN HENRY, podiatrist; b. San Francisco, July 23, 1953; s. Henry L. and Helen (Hagey) S. B.S., U. Calif.-Davis, 1974; D.P.M., Calif. Coll. Podiatric Medicine, 1977. Diplomate Am. Bd. Podiatric Surgery. Staff podiatrist Permanente Med. Group, Hayward, Calif., 1979-86; pvt. practice podiatry, Walnut Creek, Calif., 1986—; asst. clin. prof. surgery, Calif. Coll. Podiatric Medicine, San Francisco, 1980—; clin. prof. podiatry Stanford U., 1986—; examiner Bd. Med. Quality Assurance, State of Calif., 1982—. Lectr. surgery, traumatology, sports medicine, foot care; author articles in field. Fellow Am. Coll. Foot Surgeons; mem. Am. Podiatry Assn., Calif. Podiatry Assn., Alameda-Contra Costa Podiatry Assn., Am. Pub. Health Assn. Office: 1425 S Main St Walnut Creek CA 94596

SILVER, BARNARD STEWART, mech. engr., energy cons.; b. Salt Lake City, Mar. 9, 1933; s. Harold Farnes and Madelyn Cannon (Stewart) S.; B.S. in Mech. Engring., MIT, 1957; M.S. in Engring. Mechanics, Stanford U., 1958; grad. Advanced Mgmt. Program, Harvard U., 1977; m. Cherry Bushman, Aug. 12, 1963; children—Madelyn Stewart, Cannon Farnes. Engr. aircraft nuclear propulsion div. Gen. Electric Co., Evandale, Ohio, 1957; engr. Silver Engring. Works, Denver, 1959-66, mgr. sales, 1966-71; chief engr. Union Sugar div. Consol. Foods Co., Santa Maria, Calif., 1971-74; directeur du complexe SODESUCRE, Abidjan, Ivory Coast, 1974-76; supt. engring. and maintenance U and I, Inc., Moses Lake, Wash., 1976-79; pres. Silver Enterprises, Moses Lake, 1971—, Silver Energy Systems Corp., Moses Lake, 1980—; pres., gen. mgr. Silver Chief Corp., 1983—; pres. Silver Corp., 1984-86, Silver Pubs., Inc., 1986—; v.p. Barnard J. Stewart Cousins Land Co., 1987—; instr. engring. Big Bend Community Coll., 1980-81. Explorer adviser Boy Scouts Am., 1965-66, chmn. cub pack com., 1968-74, chmn. scout troop com., 1968-74, vice chmn. Columbia Basin Dist., 1986—; pres. Silver Found., 1971-84, v.p., 1984—; ednl. counselor MIT, 1971—; pres. Chief Moses Jr. High Sch. Parent Tchr. Student Assn., 1978-79; missionary Ch. of Jesus Christ of Latter-day Saints, Can., 1953-55; 2d counselor Moses Lake Stake Presidency, 1980—; bd. dirs. Columbia Basin Allied Arts, 1986—. Served with Ordnance Corps, U.S. Army, 1958-59. Decorated chevalier Ordre National (Republic of Ivory Coast); registered profl. engr., Colo. Mem. ASME, Assn. Energy Engrs., AAAS, Am. Soc. Sugar Beet Technologists, Internat. Soc. Sugar Cane Technologists, Am. Soc. Sugar Cane Technologists, Sugar Industry Technicians, Nat. Fedn. Ind. Bus.; Utah State Hist. Soc. (life), Mormon Hist. Assn., Western Hist. Assn., Univ. Archeol. Soc. (life), Sigma Xi (life), Pi Tau Sigma, Sigma Chi, Alpha Phi Omega. Republican. Mormon. Lodge: Kiwanis. Home: 1433 Skyline Dr Moses Lake WA 98837 Office: Silver Chief Corp 118 E 3d Ave Moses Lake WA 98837 also: Silver Energy Systems Corp Moses Lake WA 98837

SILVER, ELI ALFRED, earth sciences educator; b. Worcester, Mass.; s. Benjamin and Evelyn (Wellin) S.; m. Mary Elizabeth Wilcox, July 2, 1967 (div. June 1985); children: Monica, Joel. AB, U. Calif., Berkeley, 1964; PhD, Scripps Inst. Oceanography, 1969. Geologist U.S. Geol. Survey, Menlo Park, Calif., 1970-73; prof. earth scis. U. Calif., Santa Cruz, 1974—. Assoc. editor Jour. Geophys. Research, 1985—; mem. editorial bd. Geology, 1978-85. Fellow Geol. Soc. Am.; mem. AAAS, Am. Geophys. Union, Soc. Exploration Geophysicists, Seismol. Soc. Am. Home: 521 Lincoln St Santa Cruz CA 95060 Office: U Calif Dept Earth Scis Santa Cruz CA 95064

SILVER, ERIC AARON, rabbi; b. Bklyn., Apr. 15, 1942; s. Sholom and Marion (Halpern) S.; m. Mary Jennifer Dolcort, Sept. 3, 1978; children: Micah Samuel Dolcort-Silver, Jonathan Baruch Dolcort-Silver. A.B. in Math., U. Mo., 1963; M.A., Hebrew Union Coll., Cinn., 1973; MBA U. Phoenix, 1986. Ordained rabbi, 1974. Rabbi Temple Shalom, Winnipeg, Man., Can., 1977-81, Congregation Kol Ami, Salt Lake City, 1981—. Mem. Utah com. U.S. Civil Rights Commn., 1982—, Gov.'s Blue Ribbon Com. on Med. Rights, Utah, 1984—, Gov.'s Alert Commn. on Edn., Utah Law Enforcement Coordinating Com., 1982—; presdl. appointment to Fed. Judiciary Selection Commn.; trustee United Way of Gt. Salt Lake, Utah, 1982—. Served to lt. comdr., chaplain USN, 1963-77. Decorated Bronze Star medal with combat V, Purple Heart. Mem. Central Conf. Am. Rabbis, Rabbinical Assembly. Club: Kiwanis, Lodges: Masons, Shriners. Home and Office: 4885 Colony Dr Salt Lake City UT 84117

SILVER, H(ENRY) WARD, electrical engineer; b. Port Hueneme, Calif., Mar. 20, 1955; s. Van Allen and Mary Ellen (Hockaday) S.; m. Nancy Lynn Rietzke, Apr. 24, 1982; children: Lowell Evan and Webster Scott (twins). BSEE, U. Mo., 1978. Engr., programmer EMI, St. Louis, 1980-83; design engr. Wesmar, Kenmore, Wash., 1983-84; owner, tech. dir. RBR Engring., Vashon, Wash., 1984—; tech. dir. ISE, Inc., Vashon, Wash., 1985—; chief engr., program dir., announcer KMNR-FM, Rolla, Mo., 1973-80; chief engr. WTAO-FM, Murphyboro, Ill., 1980; operating engr. KETC-TV, St. Louis, 1982-83. Mem. Vashon Island Emergency Radio Group, Vashon Island, Wash., 1983—. Mem. Eta Kappa Nu. Avocations: amateur radio, music, records. Home: Rt 5 Box 290 Vashon WA 98070 Office: RBR Engring PO Box 1608 Vashon WA 98070

SILVER, HOWARD FINDLAY, chemical engineering educator; b. Denver, Sept. 16, 1930; s. Ronald Alexander and Marion (Howard) S.; m. Alice Jane Graham, Feb. 4, 1961; children: Ronald Graham, James Howard, Carol Ann. B.S., Colo. Sch. Mines, 1952; M.S. in Chem. Engring., U. Mich., 1957, Ph.D., 1961. Chem. engr. duPont Co., Buffalo and Chattanooga, 1952-53, 55; research engr. Chevron Research Corp., Richmond, Calif., 1957-58, 61-64; mem. faculty U. Wyo., Laramie, 1964—; prof. chem. engring. U. Wyo., 1968—; program mgr. fossil fuels and advanced systems Electric Power Research Inst., Palo Alto, Calif., 1974-75. Served with AUS, 1953-55. Mem. Am. Inst. Chem. Engrs., Am. Chem. Soc., Sigma Xi, Tau Beta Pi, Sigma Gamma Epsilon, Phi Lambda Upsilon. Home: 607 S 24th St Laramie WY 82070

SILVER, JOEL ART, science associations executive; b. Bklyn., Nov. 1, 1949; m. Mary K. Niedzinski, Apr. 20, 1983. BS in Chemistry, SUNY, Stony Brook, 1971; PhD in Chemistry, MIT, 1976. Prin. research scientist Aerodyne Research Inc., Billerica, Mass., 1979-85; v.p. S.W. Scis., Inc., Santa Fe, 1986—; also bd. dirs. Southwest Scis., Inc., Santa Fe, 1986—. Contbr. articles to profl. jours. Mem. AAAS, Am. Chem. Soc., Am. Phys. Soc., Combustion Inst., Am. Geophys. Union. Avocations: backpacking, photography. Office: Southwest Scis Inc 1570 Pacheco St Suite E-11 Santa Fe NM 87501

SILVER, MEYER, technical engineering administrator; b. N.Y.C., Sept. 12, 1926; s. William and Anna Silver; m. Vivian Yolanda Lamel, May 31, 1947; children: Robin Jeffrey, Barbara June, Bonnie Ellen. BA, Bklyn. Coll., 1949; MS, Rensselaer Poly. Inst., 1957; PhD, U. Notre Dame, 1960. Mem. tech. staff TRW, Redondo Beach, Calif., 1962-66, tech. mgr., 1977—. Served to sgt. U.S. Army, 1945-46. U.S. Naval Ordnance Test Sta. fellow, China Lake, Calif., 1957-59. Mem. AAAS, Am. Phys. Soc., Optical Soc. Am. Avocations: reading, swimming, walking. Home: 1 Oak Tree Ln Rolling Hills Estates CA 90274

SILVER, RAMON RICHARD, city official; b. Los Angeles, Apr. 15, 1949; s. Richard Ramon and Mary Madilyn (D'anna) S.; m. Lynn Ellen Hunter, Jan. 26, 1974; children—Jason Richard, Matthew Raymond. B.A., Calif. State U.-Los Angeles, 1971. Adminstrv. intern City of Pasadena, Calif., 1970-71; adminstrv. analyst city of West Covina, Calif., 1972-73; asst. to city mgr. City of Madera, Calif., 1973-77; dir. adminstrv. services City of Coronado, Calif., 1977-79, city mgr., 1979—. Inventor performance appraisal plan, 1980. Bd. dirs. city mgrs. div. League Calif. Cities, 1982-83, mem. revenue and tax com., 1984; chmn. San Diego County Telecommunications Task Force, 1984. Named hon. student life mem. Calif. State U.-Los Angeles, 1971. Mem. Internat. City Mgmt. Assn., San Diego City/County Mgrs. Assn. (pres. 1981-82), Mcpl. Mgmt. Assts. So. Calif. (hon. mem.). Roman Catholic. Lodge: Rotary (pres. Coronado 1985-86). Home: 714 1st St Coronado CA 92118 Office: City of Coronado 1825 Strand Way Coronado CA 92118

SILVER, SUSAN BACON, management consultant; b. Los Angeles, Dec. 3, 1950; d. Ralph Frankel and Marilyn Marks; m. Donald Philip Silver. B.S. magna cum laude, U. So. Calif., 1972; M.A., Calif. State Poly. U., 1975. Cert., Calif. Tchr., Walnut Valley Unified Sch. Dist., Walnut, Calif., 1972-77; instr. Calif. State Poly. U., Pomona, 1976-77; adult edn. instr. Los Angeles Unified Sch. Dist., 1977-79; writer, editor for Disney, Glencoe Pub., Goodyear Pub., others, Los Angeles, 1977-79; pub. affairs-communications mgr. aircraft div. Northrop Corp., Hawthorne, Calif., 1979-84; editor, writer, photographer trade pubs. Community Report (12 awards) and Small Bus. Report (7 awards), 1981-83; founder, pres. Positively Organized!, Santa Monica, Calif., 1983—; profl. speaker corps. including IBM, Northrop Corp., Mattel Corp., trade assns. including Internat. Assn. Bus. Communicators, Calif. Apt. Assn., colls. and univs. Contbr. to Flowers & Mag., 1985—, Association Management mag., 1986—. Active Richstone Center for Prevention Child Abuse, Hawthorne, Calif., 1980—; vol. Internat. Med. Corps. Mem. Internat. Assn. Bus. Communicators (awards program co-chmn. 1982, hospitality chmn. 1982, Silver 6 Trophy 1982, speaker internat. confs. Montreal and Hawaii 1984), So. Calif. Soc. Assn. Execs., Insiders Network (bd. dirs.), Santa Monica Area C. of C. (bd. dirs., chmn. com.), Calif. Press Women (3 awards 1982-83), Western Publs. Assn. (Maggie trophy 1982), Nat. Speakers Assn., Sierra Club. Office: 3420 Ocean Park Blvd Suite 3060 Santa Monica CA 90405-3305

SILVER, WILLIAM ROBERT, corporate finance executive; b. Oakland, Calif., Mar. 31, 1947; s. Vernon Lowell and Barbara Jean (Zaniboni) S.; m. Joan Ellen Pagani, July 29, 1973. B.S. in Elec. Engring., U. Calif.-Davis, 1970. With sales dept., then area sales mgr. Nuclear Energy div. Gen. Electric Co., San Jose, Calif., 1970-78; western regional mgr. Bankers Leasing & Fin. Corp. sub. So. Pacific Co., San Mateo, Calif., 1978-79, v.p. mktg., 1979-82, sr. v.p. fin., dir., 1982-83, exec. v.p. fin. and mktg., dir., 1983—. Served with Army N.G., 1970-76. Mem. Am. Assn. Equipment Lessors, Pacific Coast Elec. Assn., Mcpl. Fin. Officers Assn., Am. Gas Assn. Republican. Roman Catholic. Club: De Anza Racquet (Cupertino, Calif.). Office: Bankers Leasing & Fin Corp 2655 Campus Dr Suite 200 San Mateo CA 94403

SILVERBERG, STUART OWEN, physician; b. Denver, Oct. 14, 1931; s. Edward M. and Sara (Morris) S.; B.A., U. Colo., 1952, M.D., 1955; m. Joan E. Snyderman, June 19, 1954 (div. Apr. 1970); children—Debra Sue McBride, Eric Owen, Alan Kent; m. 2d, Kay Ellen Conklin, Oct. 18, 1970 (div. Apr. 1982); 1 son, Cris S.; m. 3d, Sandra Kay Miller, Jan., 1983. Intern Women's Hosp. Phila., 1955-56; resident Kings County Hosp., Bklyn., 1958-62; practice medicine specializing in obstetrics and gynecology, Denver, 1962—; mem. staff Luth. Hosp., Rose Med. Ctr., Denver; mem. staff St. Anthony Hosp., chmn. dept. obstetrics and gynecology, 1976-77, 86-87; clin. instr. U. Colo. Sch. Medicine, Denver, 1962-72, asst. clin. prof., 1972—; v.p. Productos Alimenticos, La Ponderosa, S.A.; dir., chmn. bd. Wicker Works Video Prodns., Inc.; cons. Ft. Logan Mental Health Center, Denver, 1964-70; mem. Gov.'s Panel Mental Retardation, 1966; med. adv. bd. Colo. Planned Parenthood, 1966—, Am. Med. Center, Spivak, Colo., 1967—. Mem. Colo. Emergency Resources Bd., Denver, 1965—. Served to maj. AUS, 1956-58; Germany. Diplomate Am. Bd. Obstetrics and Gynecology. Fellow Am. Coll. Obstetricians and Gynecologists, ACS; mem. Am. Internat. fertility socs., Colo. Gynecologists and Obstetricians Soc., Hellman Obstet. and Gynecol. Soc., Colo. Med. Soc., Clear Creek Valley Med. Soc. (trustee 1978, 80, 87), Phi Sigma Delta, AMA, Flying Physicians Assn., Aircraft Owners and Pilots Assn., Nu Sigma Nu, Alpha Epsilon Delta. Jewish. Mem. editorial rev. bd. Colo. Women's Mag.; editor-in-chief Physicians Video Jour., 1984—. Office: 8407 Bryant St Westminster CO 80030

SILVERGLEID, ARTHUR JAY, medical educator, health science facility executive; b. N.Y.C., June 17, 1942; s. David and Dorothy (Hoffman) S.; m. Naomi Gail Schwartzman, June 20, 1964 (div. June 1982); children: Courtenay Sheridan, Jordan Evan; m. Margaret Anderson, Sept. 10, 1983. AB magna cum laude, U. Rochester, 1963; MD, NYU, 1967. Diplomate Am. Bd. Internal Medicine; cert. blood banking, hematology subspecialty. Intern Stanford (Calif.) U. Hosp., 1967-68, asst. resident, 1968-69, sr. asst. resident, 1971-72, fellow in hematology, 1972-74; clin. assoc. hematology NIH, Bethesda, Md., 1969-71; physician specialist in medicine and hematology, clin. asst. prof. Stanford U. Sch. Medicine, 1974-77; assoc. med. dir., sci. dir. ARC-Stanford U. Blood Ctr. and Stanford U. Hosp. Transfusion Service, 1974-77; med., exec. dir. Blood Bank of San Bernardino and Riverside Counties, Calif., 1977—; assoc. clin. prof. medicine Loma Linda (Calif.) U., 1978-80; assoc. clin. prof. UCLA Sch. Medicine, 1980—. Contbr. articles to profl. med. jours. Vice chmn. Aids Adv. Task Force, San Bernardino, 1985-86. Served to lt. comdr. USPHS, 1969-71. Mem. AMA, Am. Assn. Blood Banks (mem. various coms. 1979—), Am. Fedn. Clin. Research, Am. Soc. Hematology (chmn. tranfusion sect. 1978, 81), Calif. Blood Bank System (mem. various com., bd. dirs. 1980—, pres. 1983-84), Calif. Med. Assn. (com. blood banks), Inland Soc. Internal Medicine, San Bernardino County Med. Soc. (publ. com. 1978-79). Democrat. Jewish. Avocations: wine, film, skiing, tennis, lit. Home: 1349 Rhonda Ln Redlands CA 92373 Office: Blood Bank San Bernardino PO Box 5729 San Bernardino CA 92412

SILVERMAN, BARRY LOUIS, psychiatrist, medical group administrator; b. Dallas, Feb. 20, 1949; s. Arthur Sidney and Pearl (Leichter) S. B.A., Duke U., 1971; M.D., U. Tex.-San Antonio, 1974. Diplomate Am. Bd. Psychiatry and Neurology. Resident Washington U.-Barnes Hosp., St. Louis, 1974-77; exec. staff mem. Barnes Hosp., St. Louis, 1976-77; chief psychiatry Dominguez Valley Hosp., Compton, Calif., 1978-81; pres. staff Kaiser Found. Hosp., Harbor City, Calif., 1981-82; asst. clin. prof. UCLA, 1982—; chief consultation psychiatry So. Calif. Permanente Med. Group, Harbor City, 1978—, dir., Los Angeles, 1983—. Mem. Am. Psychiat. Assn., So. Calif. Physicians for Human Rights. Jewish. Home: 506 S Norton Ave Los Angeles CA 90020 Office: So Calif Permanente Med Group 2081 Palos Verdes Dr N Lomita CA 90717

SILVERMAN, CAROL ANN, interior designer; b. Bishop, Calif., Sept. 9, 1936; s. Ivan W. and Laura Harriet (Critchett) Wilson; m. James R. Silverman, Sept. 7, 1957; children: Denise Lynn, Michele Jeanene, Heather Gwenn, Todd Shawn. AA, Sacramento City Coll., 1956; grad., Sacramento State Coll., 1957; BA, San Francisco State U., 1958; postgrad., U. Calif., Davis, U. Calif., Berkeley, Am. River Coll., Sierra Coll. Prin. Environ. Design, Sacramento, 1970—. Elder Fremont Presbyn. Ch., Sacramento; active Jr. Mus. Sponsors, Sacramento. Mem. Am. Soc. Interior Designers (assoc.), Illuminating Engring. Soc. Avocations: tennis, skiing, classical pianist. Office: Environ Design 2222 Sierra Blvd Sacramento CA 95825

SILVERMAN, CHARLES RAYMOND, advertising agency executive; b. Los Angeles, June 25, 1943; s. Raymond and Doris Jean (Pritts) S. AA in Journalism and Advt., Santa Monica Coll., 1963; BA in Journalism and Advt., Calif. State U., Northridge, 1966. Sr. v.p., exec. creative dir. Cunningham and Walsh, Los Angeles; v.p., sr. copywriter Chiat/Day, Los Angeles; v.p. creative dir. Leo Burnett Co., Chgo.; sr. v.p. exec. creative dir. BBDO, Chgo.; mng. ptnr. Scali, McCabe & Sloves, Los Angeles. Recipient Best in the West award Am. Advt. Fedn.

SILVERMAN, PAUL HYMAN, zoologist, former university president; b. Mpls., Oct. 8, 1924; s. Adolph and Libbie (Idlekope) S.; m. Nancy Josephs, May 20, 1945; children: Daniel Joseph, Claire. Student, U. Minn., 1942-43, 46-47; B.S., Roosevelt U., 1949; M.S. in Biology, Northwestern U., 1951; Ph.D. in Parasitology, U. Liverpool, Eng., 1955, D.Sc., 1968. Research fellow Malaria Research Sta., Hebrew U., Israel, 1951-53; research fellow dept. entomology and parasitology Sch. Tropical Medicine, U. Liverpool, 1953-56; sr. sci. officer dept. parasitology Moredun Inst., Edinburgh, Scotland, 1956-59; head dept. immunoparasitology Allen & Hanbury, Ltd., Ware, Eng., 1960-62; prof. zoology and veterinary pathology and hygiene U. Ill., Urbana, 1963-72; chmn. dept. zoology U. Ill., 1964-65, head dept. zoology, 1965-68; sr. staff mem. Center for Zoonoses Research, 1964; prof. biology, head div. natural scis. Temple Buell Coll., Denver, 1970-71; prof. biology, chmn. dept. biology, acting v.p. research, v.p. research and grad. affairs, assoc. provost for research and acad. services U. N.Mex., 1972-77; provost for research and grad. studies SUNY, Central Adminstrn., Albany, 1977-79; pres. Research Found., SUNY, Albany, 1979-80, U. Maine, Orono, 1980-84; fellow Lawrence Berkeley Lab. U. Calif.-Berkeley, 1984—, adj. prof. med. parasitology Sch. Pub. Health, 1986; assoc. dir. head biology and medicine div. Lawrence Berkeley Lab.; dir. Donner Lab.; cons., examiner Middle States Assn. Schs. and Colls., Commn. Colls. and Univs., North Central Assn. Colls. and Secondary Schs., 1964—; chmn. Commn. on Instns. Higher Edn., 1974-76; adj. prof. U. Colo., Boulder, 1970-72; Fulbright prof. zoology Australian Nat. U., Canberra, 1969; adjoint prof. biology U. Colo., Boulder, 1970-72; examiner for Western Assn. Schs. and Colls., Accrediting Commn. for Sr. Colls. and Univs., Calif., 1972—; mem. bd. Nat. Council on Postsecondary Accreditation, Washington, 1975-77; faculty apointee Sandia Corp., Dept. Energy, Albuquerque, 1974-81; project dir. research in malaria immunology and vaccination AID, 1965-76; project dir. research in Helminth immunity USPHS, NIH, 1964-72; sr. cons. to Ministry Edn. and Culture, Brasilia, Brazil, 1975—; cons. to U.S. Senator George Mitchell, Maine; adv. on malaria immunology WHO, Geneva, 1967; bd. dirs. Inhalation Toxicology Research Inst., Lovelace Biomed. and Environ. Research Inst., Albuquerque, 1977—; mem. N.Y. State Gov.'s High Tech. Opportunities Task Force; chmn. research and rev. com. N.Y. State Sci. and Tech. Found.; mem. pres.'s council New Eng. Land Grant Univs.; mem. policies and issues com. Nat. Assn. State Univs. and Land Grant Colls.; bd. advs. Lovelace-Bataan Med. Center, Albuquerque, 1974-77; adv. com. U.S. Army Command and Gen. Staff Coll., Ft. Leavenworth, Kans., 1983-84; corporator Bangor Savs. Bank. Contbr. articles to profl. jours. Bd. dirs. Historic Albany Found.; chmn. Maine Gov.'s Econ. Devel. Conf.; chmn. research rev. com. N.Y. State Sci. and Tech. Found. Fellow Royal Soc. Tropical Medicine, Hygiene, N. Mex. Acad. Sci.; mem. Am. Soc. Parasitologists, Am. Soc. Tropical Medicine and Hygiene, Am. Soc. Immunologists, Brit. Soc. Parasitology (council), Brit. Soc. Immunologists, Soc. Gen. Microbiology, Soc. Protozoologists, Am. Soc. Zoologists, Am. Inst. Biol. Scis., AAAS, N.Y. Acad. Scis., N.Y. Soc. Tropical Medicine, Greater Bangor C. of C. (dir.), Sigma Xi, Phi Kappa Phi. Club: B'nai B'rith. Patentee process for prodn. parasitic helminth vaccine. Office: Lawrence Berkeley Lab U Calif Berkeley CA 94720

SILVERMAN, SIDNEY WILLIAM, electrical engineer; b. N.Y.C., Aug. 27, 1918; s. Max and Eva (Kalfus) S.; m. Charlotte Helen Kant, Sept. 7, 1947; children: Susan Marti, Barbara Ann. BEE, CUNY, 1947; MSEE, U. Mich., 1949. Draftsman Cert. Gauge Co., Long Island City, N.Y., 1934-43; engr. Boeing Co., Seattle, 1949-59; engring. mgr. Boeing Aerospace Co., Seattle, 1959—; mem. adv. com. NASA, Washington, 1983-85. Contbr. articles to profl. jours. Served to 1st lt., 1943-46. Mem. IEEE (chmn. power system com. 1976—), AIAA (chmn. power systems com. 1980-84). Avocations: stamp collecting, photography, leatherwork, skiing, hiking. Home: 19630 Marine View Dr S.W. Seattle WA 98166 Office: Boeing Aerospace Co Elec Power Systems PO Box 3999 Seattle WA 98124

SILVERN, LEONARD CHARLES, engineering executive; b. N.Y.C., May 20, 1919; s. Ralph and Augusta (Thaler) S.; m. Gloria Marantz, June 1948 (div. Jan. 1968); 1 son, Ronald; m. 2d, Elisabeth Beeny, Aug. 1969 (div. Oct. 1972); m. Gwen Taylor, Nov. 1985. B.S. in Physics, L.I. U., 1946; M.A., Columbia U., 1948, Ed.D., 1952. Tng. supr. U.S. Dept. Navy, N.Y.C., 1939-49; tng. dir. exec. dept. N.Y. Div. Safety, Albany, 1949-55; resident engring. psychologist Lincoln Lab., M.I.T. for RAND Corp., Lexington, 1955-56; engr., dir. edn., tng., research labs. Hughes Aircraft Co., Culver City, Calif., 1956-62; dir. human performance engring. lab., cons. engring. psychologist to v.p. tech. Northrop Norair, Hawthorne, Calif., 1962-64; prin. scientist, v.p., pres. Edn. and Tng. Cons. Co., Los Angeles, 1964-80, Sedona, Ariz., 1980, pres. Systems Engring. Labs. div., 1980—; cons. hdqrs. Air Tng. Command USAF, Randolph AFB, Tex., 1964-68, Electronic Industries Assn., Washington, 1963-69, Edn. Research and Devel. Center, U. Hawaii, 1970-74, Center Vocat. and Tech. Edn., Ohio State U., 1972-73, Council for Exceptional Children, 1973-74, Canadore Coll. Applied Arts and Tech., Ont., Can., 1974-76, Centro Nacional de Productividad, Mexico City, 1973-75, N.S. Dept. Edn., Halifax, 1975-79, Aeronutronic Ford-Ford Motor Co., 1975-76, Nat. Tng. Systems Inc., 1976-81, Nfld. Public Service Commn., 1978, Legis. Affairs Office of U.S. Dept. Agr., Rocky Point Techs., 1986; adj. prof. edn., public adminstrn. U. So. Calif. Grad. Sch., 1957-65; vis. prof. computer scis. U. Calif. Extension Div., Los Angeles, 1963-72. Dist. ops. officer, disaster communications service Los Angeles County Sheriff's Dept., 1973-75, dist. communications officer, 1975-76; bd. dirs. SEARCH, 1976—; mem. adv. com. West Sedona Community Plan of Yavapai County, 1986-87. Served with USNR, 1944-46. Registered profl. engr., Calif. Mem. IEEE (sr.), Amateur Radio Satellite Corp, Am. Psychol. Assn., Am. Radio Relay League (life), Friendship Vets. Fire Engine Co. (hon.), Soc. Wireless Pioneers (life), Quarter Century Wireless Assn. (life), Sierra Club, Sedona Westerners., Assn. Bldg. Coms. (chmn. bd. dirs. West Sedona chpt., 1986—), Contbg. editor Ednl. Tech., 1968-73, 81—; reviewer Computing Revs., 1962—. Contbr. numerous articles to profl. jours. Office: PO Box 2085 Sedona AZ 86336

SILVERN, LOUISE ELLEN, psychology educator; b. Long Beach, Calif., Sept. 5, 1946; d. Yale and Ronja (Weisman) Swerdloff; m. Steven Silvern, June 12, 1966; 1 child, Joy Anne. BA magna cum laude, U. Calif., Berkeley, 1967; PhD, UCLA, 1972. Lic. clin. psychologist, Colo. Asst. prof. psychology U. Denver, 1973-74; asst. prof. then assoc. prof. U. Colo., Boulder, 1974—. Cons. editor Sex Roles: A Jour. of Research, 1979—; contbr. articles to profl. jours. Bd. dirs. Colo. chpt. ACLU, 1984-86. NIMH fellow, 1972-73. Democrat. Jewish. Office: U Colo Dept Psychology Campus Box 345 Boulder CO 80309

SILVERS, ARTHUR LEON, planning and policy educator; b. N.Y.C., Dec. 19, 1937; s. David Charles and Fae (Endick) S.; m. Barbara Lois Hyman, Oct. 6, 1968; children: Jessica L., Gabriel D., Michael B. BS, NYU, 1959; MBA, U. Pa., 1962, PhD, 1972. Regional economist Resources for the Future, Washington, 1971-74; chmn. dept. urban studies and planning Va. Commonwealth U., Richmond, 1975-78; prof. mgmt. and policy U. Ariz., Tucson, 1978—, dir. div. of econ. and bus. research, 1981—, chmn. com. on planning, 1983—. Co-author: Urban Planning Analysis, 1974, Rural Development and Urban-Bound Migration in Mexico, 1980; contbr. articles to profl. jours. Mem. Regional Sci. Assn., Western Regional Sci. Assn. Democrat. Jewish. Avocations: tennis, folk music. Office: U Ariz Div Econ & Bus Research Tucson AZ 85721

SILVERSTEIN, JOSEPH HARRY, musician; b. Detroit, Mar. 21, 1932; s. Bernard and Ida (Katz) S.; m. Adrienne Shufro, Apr. 27; children—Bernice, Deborah, Marc. Student Curtis Inst. Music, 1945-50. Violinist, Houston Symphony Orch., Phila. Orch.; concert-master Denver Symphony Orch., Boston Symphony Orch.; formerly chmn. string dept. New Eng. Conservatory Music; also chmn. faculty Berkshire Music Sch.; mem. faculty Boston U. Sch. Music, Yale U. Sch. Music; music dir. Boston Symphony Chamber Players, Boston U. Symphony Orch.; interim music dir. Toledo Symphony Orch.; prin. guest condr. Balt. Symphony Orch., 1981; condr. Utah Symphony; now mus. dir. Worcester Orch., Mass. Recipient Silver medal Queen Elizabeth of Belgium Internat. contest, 1959, Naumberg found. award, 1960; named one of ten outstanding young men, Boston C. of C., 1962. Fellow Am. Acad. Arts and Scis. Address: care Worcester Orch Mechanics Hall Worchester MA 01608 also: care Utah Symphony Orch. 123 W S Temple Salt Lake City UT 84101 *

SILVERSTON, BESS ELLESBERG, educator; b. N.Y.C., Feb. 15, 1947; d. Harold and Rose Leah (Kleban) Ellesberg; m Randall A. Silverston, May 24, 1970; 1 child, Hallie Alana. BA, Calif. State U., Northridge, 1968; MA, U. Mich., 1970; postgrad., So. Ill. U., 1973; PhD, Claremont Grad. Sch., 1984. Cert. handicapped and severely handicapped tchr., cert. English tchr., cert. community coll. instr., Calif. Tchr. pub. schs. Ypsilanti and Romulus, Mich., and Marion, Ill., 1970-74; psychometrician Dean Meml. Learning Ctr., Shelton Sch., Dallas, 1974-76; tchr., counselor Poseidon Sch., Los Angeles, 1976-80; adminstrv. staff assoc. tchr. edn. program Claremont (Calif.) Grad. Sch., 1981-84, placement facilitator, 1985; asst. prof. elem. edn. Calif. State U., Los Angeles, 1984-85; asst. dir., master tchr. Erikson High Sch., Tarzana, Calif., 1985—; resource program specialist Wilson Elem Sch., San Gabriel, Calif., 1984. Mem. Am. Ednl. Research Assn., Council Learning Disabilities, Council for Exceptional Children, Calif. Council Edn. Tchrs., Alliance for Survival, Greenpeace, Kappa Delta Pi, Pi Lambda Theta. Avocations: yardwork, exercising, music, folk dancing. Home: 17147 Gunther St Granada Hills CA 91344

SILVERTHORNE, COLIN PATRIC, dean of university; b. Bristol, Eng., Mar. 17, 1945; s. Leonard Charles and Audrey (Snow) S.; m. Deanna Lyn Morledge, Mar. 28, 1970; children: Wendy, Adam. BS, U. London, 1966; MA in Gen. Psychology, U. Cin., 1966, PhD, 1970. Instr. psychology U. Cin., 1966-69; clin. internship Letterman Gen. Hosp., San Francisco, 1973-74; asst. prof. to full prof. U. San Francisco, 1970-80; sec., treas. Assn. Jesuit Colls. and Univs., 1982-83; pres. Assn. Jesuit Colls. and Univs., 1983-84, 84-85. Author: Common Sense Statistics, 1986; contbr. 50 articles to profl. jours. Mem. San Francisco Suicide Prevention (bd. trustees; pres. 1978-79), Kentfield Sch. Dist. citizens adv. com., 1980-82, Kentfield Planning Area Com., 1982-85. Mem. Am. Psychol. Assn., Western Psychol. Assn., Soc. for the Advancement of Social Psychology, Nat. Univ. Continuing Edn. Assn., Soc. for the Psychol. Study of Social Issues, Council for the Advancement of Exptl. Learning.

SILVIUS, DONALD JOE, educator, administrator; b. Kingman, Kans., July 30, 1932; s. Henry Edgar and Gladys Mae (Beaty) S.; m. Jean Anne Able, Aug. 30, 1931; children—Laurie Dawn Silvius Gustin, Steven Craig, Jonathan Mark, Brian James. Student So. Calif. Coll., 1949-52; A.A., Bakersfield Coll., 1962; B.A., Fresno State Coll., 1963, M.A., 1968. Radio/TV announcer, musician, music arranger and copyist, life ins. underwriter, other positions, 1953-62; jr. high sch. English tchr., elem. jr. high counselor, child welfare, attendance and guidance supr., supr. spl. services Standard Sch. Dist., Oildale, Calif., 1963—; tchr. counseling/guidance and spl. edn. various colls. Recipient Standard PTA-Hon. Service award, Bakersfield "Up With People" Appreciation award, Golden Apple Service award Standard Sch. Dist. Tchrs. Assn., Innovations award Calif. Tchrs. Assn., Hon. Service award Kern chpt. Calif. Assn. Sch. Psychologists, Outstanding Ednl. Leader award West Kern chpt. Assn. Calif. Sch. Adminstrs., 1977-78, 7th Dist. PTA-Silver Service award, Continuing Service award Highland-Wingland PTA, Outstanding Community Service for Developmentally Disabled award. Mem. NEA, Calif. Tchrs. Assn., North of the River Assn., Calif. Assn. Supervision of Child Welfare and Attendance, Assn. Calif. Sch. Adminstrs., Am. Assn. Curriculum Devel., Calif. Assn. Mental Health in Kern County and Calif., Calif. Assn. Counseling and Devel., PTA, CACES, CACAE, CAMECD, Phi Delta Kappa, Kappa Delta Pi. Republican. Home: 611 Linda Vista Dr Oildale CA 93308 Office: Standard School District 1200 N Chester Ave Oildale CA 93308

SIMBURG, EARL JOSEPH, physician, psychiatrist; b. Vonda, Sask., Can., Mar. 21, 1915; came to U.S., 1941; s. Joseph E. and Liza (Yurovsky) S.; m. Virginia Ronan, Feb. 10, 1958; children by previous marriage: Arthur, Melvyn, Sharon. Cert. medicine, U. Sask., Saskatoon, 1935; MDCM, McGill U., Montreal, Que., Can., 1938. Diplomate Am. Bd. Psychiatry and Neurology. Intern Royal Victoria Hosp., Montreal, 1938-39; sr. physician Brandon (Can.) Hosp. Mental Diseases, 1939-41; resident Grace New Haven Hosp., 1941-43; pvt. practice psychiatry Berkeley, Calif., 1947—; mem. faculty San Francisco Psychoanalytic Inst.; instr. psychiatry Yale U., New Haven, 1941-43, U. Calif., San Francisco, 1949-59, Calif. Dept. Health, Berkeley, 1975-76; pres. med. staff Herrick Hosp. and Health Ctr., 1985. Contbr. articles to profl. jours. Served to major M.C. USAF, 1943-47. Fellow Am. Psychiat. Assn. (life); mem. AMA, Am. Psychoanalytic Assn. (life, cert.), Calif. Med. Assn., Alameda Contra Costa County Med. Assn. Avocation: tennis. Home: 86 Tamalpais Rd Berkeley CA 94708 Office: 2006 Dwight Way Berkeley CA 94704

SIMCIK, LUKE JACOB, high energy laser engineer, air force officer; b. Meriden, Conn., Aug. 30, 1962; s. Jacob Alexander and Florence Simcik. BS in Astronautical Engring., USAF Acad., 1984. Enlisted USAF, 1980, advanced through grades to 1st lt., 1986; research assoc. Frank J. Seiler Research Lab., Colorado Springs, Colo., 1984-85; high energy laser engr. Air Force Weapons Lab., Albuquerque, 1985-86, Williams AFB, Ariz., 1986—. Mem. AIAA. Roman Catholic. Avocation: volleyball. Home: 1440 S Val Vista #1012 Mesa AZ 85204

SIME, RUTH LEWIN, chemist, educator; b. N.Y.C., July 2, 1939; d. Norbert and Gerda (Bruno) Lewin; m. Rodney J. Sime, 1968; children: Karen, Jennifer. BA, Barnard Coll., 1960; PhD, Harvard U., 1964. Chemistry educator Calif. State U., Long Beach, 1964-65, Sacramento, 1965-67; chemistry educator Hunter Coll., N.Y.C., 1967-68, Sacramento City Coll., 1968—; cons. Agy. Internat. Devel., Andhra U., 1967. Contbr. articles to profl. jours. NEH grantee, 1981-82, Nat. Sci. Found. grantee, 1984-85. Democrat. Jewish. Home: 609 Shangri Ln Sacramento CA 95825 Office: Sacramento City Coll Sacramento CA 95822

SIMEK, SHERYL LEE, speech pathologist; b. Vincennes, Ind., Dec. 11, 1958; d. Franklin E. and Erna L. (Rozmarynowski) S. BS in Audiology and Speech Sci., Purdue U., 1980, MS in Speech Lang. Pathology, 1982. Cert. in clin. rehab., Calif. Speech pathologist Riverside County Supt. of Schs., Palm Springs, Calif., 1982-83, Palm Springs Unified Sch. Dist., 1983-86, Los Angeles Unified Sch. Dist., 1986—; supr. state licensing Calif. Bd. Med. Quality Assurance, Palm Springs, 1984—. Mem. Am. Speech-Lang.-Hearing Assn. (cert. clin. competence, supr. for cert.), Calif. Speech-Lang.-Hearing Assn., Purdue Alumni Assn., Phi Kappa Phi. Republican. Presbyterian. Avocations: play banjo, play dulcimer, swim, travel. Home: PO Box 7496 Glendale CA 91205 Office: LAUSD Spl Edn Unit Cen Attn Speech-Lang Dept 15530 Hesby St Encino CA 91436

SIMHAN, RAJ GOVINDAN, research glass technologist; b. Visakhapatnam, India; came to U.S., 1973; s. Govindan and Saraswathi (Amma) Pandalai; m. Sushila Balram, Mar. 29, 1972; children: Kalpana, Vijay. BS in Chemistry, Andhra U., Visakhapatnam, 1954; BS in Tech., Banaras (India) U., 1957; MS in Tech., Sheffield (Eng.) U., 1970, PhD, 1973. Glass technologist Indo-Asahi Glass, Bihar, India, 1958-60; design engr. Karrenafuerungsbau, Düsseldorf, Fed. Republic of Germany, 1962-67; glass technologist Consumers Glass, Toronto, Ont., Can., 1967-69; research assoc. Manville Corp., Denver, 1973—; pres. Kairals Assocs., Denver, 1981. Editor Inda Assoc. News, Denver, 1982; author papers on glass durability and surface; inventor glass compositions; patentee in field. Exec. advisor Jr. Achievement, Denver, 1979-81. Mem. Am. Ceramic Soc., Soc. Glass Tech. (U.K.), Materials Soc. Hindu. Office: Manville Corp Research and Devel 10100 UTE Ave Littleton CO 80122

SIMINI, JOSEPH PETER, accountant, financial consultant, author, former educator; b. Buffalo, Feb. 15, 1921; s. Paul and Ida (Moro) S.; B.S., St. Bonaventure U., 1940, B.B.A., 1949; M.B.A., U. Calif.-Berkeley, 1957; D.B.A., Western Colo. U., 1981; m. Marcelline McDermott, Oct. 4, 1968. Insp. naval material Bur. Ordnance, Buffalo and Rochester, N.Y., 1941-44; mgr. Paul Simini Bakery, Buffalo, 1946-48; internal auditor DiGiorgio (Fruit) Corp., San Francisco, 1950-51; tax accountant Price Waterhouse & Co., San Francisco, 1953; sr. accountant Richard L. Hanlin, C.P.A., San Francisco, 1953-54; prof. accounting U. San Francisco, 1954-79, emeritus prof., 1983—; mem. rev. bd. Calif. Bd. Accountancy, 1964-68. Mem. council com. Boy Scouts Am., Buffalo, San Francisco, 1942-65, Scouters Key, San Francisco council; bd. dirs. United Bay Area Fund Drive, U. San Francisco, 1960, Nat. Italian Am. Found., Washington, 1979—. Served to ensign USNR, 1944-46. Recipient Bacon-McLaughlin medal St. Bonaventure U., 1940, Laurel Key, 1940; Outstanding Tchr. award Coll. Bus. Adminstrn., U. San Francisco, 1973; Disting. Tchr. award U. San Francisco, 1975, Joseph Peter Simini award, 1977. Crown Zellerbach Found. fellow, 1968-69; Gold Medal Associzione Piemontese nel Mondo, Turin, Italy, 1984; decorated Knight Order of Merit, Republic of Italy, 1982. C.P.A., Calif. Mem. Am. Inst. C.P.A.s, Calif. Soc. C.P.A.s (past chmn. ednl. standards, student relations com. San Francisco chpt.), Nat. Assn. Accts. (past pres. San Francisco chpt.), Am. Acctg. Assn., Am. Mgmt. Assn. (lectr. 1968-78), Am. Arbitration Assn. (comml. arbitrator), Delta Sigma Pi (past pres. San Francisco alumni club), Beta Gamma Sigma. Roman Catholic. Clubs: K.C., Il Cenacolo (past pres.), Toastmasters (pres. Magic Word). Author: Accounting Made Simple, 1967, 2d rev. edit., 1987; Cost Accounting Concepts for Nonfinancial Executives, 1976; Become Wealthy! Using Tax Savings and Real Estate Investments, 1982. Tech. editor, Accounting Essentials, 1972. Patentee Dial-A-Trig and Verbum Est card game. Home: 977 Duncan St San Francisco CA 94131 Office: PO Box 31420 San Francisco CA 94131

SIMMERMAN, JIM (AMES), English educator; b. Denver, Mar. 5, 1952; s. Wade Darrow and Eleanor Jane (Flowers) S. BS in Edn., U. Mo., 1973, MA in English, 1976; MFA in English, U. Iowa, 1980. Cert. tchr. Teaching asst. U. Mo., Columbia, 1974-76, instr. Project Start, 1976-77; instr. No. Ariz. U., Flagstaff, 1977-78, 81-83, asst. prof. English, 1983—; teaching asst. U. Iowa, Iowa City, 1979-80. Author: Home, 1983 (named Pushcart Writer's Choice Selection, 1984), Bad Weather, 1987; poetry editor Iowa Jour. of Literary Studies, 1980, Shankpainter, 1984-85; mem. editorial bd. Pushcart Press, 1985; advisor Pine Knots (A Literary Mag.), 1981-83. Mem. lit. panel Ariz Commn. on Arts, Phoenix, 1983, 85, 87. Creative writing fellow Fine Arts Work Ctr., 1984-85, Ariz. Commn. On Arts, 1983, Port Townsend Writer's Conf., 1984, Bread Loaf Writer's Conf., 1983; creative writing fellowship grantee Nat. Endowment for Arts, 1984-85. Mem. Poets and Writers Inc., Associated Writing Programs. Avocations: karate, guitar, reading, writing. Home: 3601 Mountain Dr Flagstaff AZ 86001 Office: No Ariz U English Dept Box 6032 Flagstaff AZ 86011

SIMMONDS, A(NDREW) J(EFFREY), curator, columnist; b. Preston, Idaho, Feb. 6, 1943; s. Grant and Cleo (Coburn) S.; m. Jeannie Martha Foersterling, May 20, 1977; children: Andrew Charles, John Jeffrey Ahl. BS in History, Utah State U., 1965, MA in History, 1967. Cert. archives adminstr. Curator spl. collections Utah State U., Logan, 1966—; research cons. Utah Bd. Agr., 1977-78; mem. Univ. Press Council, Logan, 1981—. Author: On the Big Range, 1970, History of Weston, Idaho, 1972, Gentile Comes to Cache Valley, 1976, History of Anderson Lumber Company, 1980, The Bishop's Board: Recipes from the Pantries of the First Three Episcopal Bishops of Utah, 1985, Strength Out of Zion: The History of Anglicanism in Northern Utah and Southern Idaho, 1986; (newspaper column) Looking Back, 1975—; contbr. articles to mags.; exhibitor photogtaphy presentations. Councilman Cornish Town, Utah, 1982-86; bd. dirs. Utah State Hist. Bd., 1979-82.; historiographer Episcopal Diocese of Utah, 1984—. Grantee NEH, 1979-80. mem. Conf. Intermountain Archivists (council mem. 1973-77), Soc. Am. Archivists. Republican. Episcopalian. Lodge: Masons. Home: PO Box 110 Trenton UT 84338 Office: Utah State U Dept Spl Collections and Archives Logan UT 84322

SIMMONS, BRADLEY WILLIAMS, pharmaceutical company executive; b. Paterson, N.J., Apr. 16, 1941; s. John Williams and Grace Law (Van Hassel) S.; m. Diane Louise Simmons, June 6, 1964 (div. May 1986); children: Susan, Elizabeth, Jonathan. AB, Columbia U., 1963, BSChemE, 1964; MBA, NYU, 1974. Chem. engr. Pfizer, Inc., N.Y.C., 1969-73, analyst, 1973-76, dir. planning, 1976-79; dir., bus. analysis Bristol-Myers, N.Y.C., 1979-82, v.p., 1982-85; pres. Oncogen Co., Seattle, 1985—; adj. prof. Farleigh Dickinson U., Teaneck, N.J., 1974-84. Council mem. borough of Allendale, N.J., 1977-82; mem. Bergen County (N.J.) com., 1974-82. Served to lt. USN, 1964-69, Vietnam. Republican. Mem. Unity Ch. Avocations: swimming, reading. Home: 700 Crockett Pl #402 Seattle WA 98109 Office: Oncogen Co 30005 1st Ave Seattle WA 98121

SIMMONS, BRIAN PHILIP, social worker; b. Ridgecrest, Calif., Sept. 28, 1953. AA, Bakersfield Coll., 1973; BA, U. Calif., Berkeley, 1976, M in Social Welfare, 1981, postgrad., 1981-83. Research asst. U. Calif., Berkeley, 1981-83; eligibility worker Kern County Welfare Dept., Bakersfield, Calif., 1973-74, 76-77, social worker, 1977-81, social service practitioner, 1983-86, social service supr., 1986—. Author monthly column, 1986—. Mem. Kern Child Abuse Prevention Council, Bakersfield, 1986—, Kern Foster Parent Support Group, Bakersfield, 1986—; bd. dirs. Kern County Home for Women, Bakersfield, 1978-79. Fellow U. Calif. Bd. Regents, 1982-83; Child Welfare Traineeship U.S. Dept. Health and Human Services, 1980-81. Mem. Nat. Assn. Social Workers, Am. Pub. Welfare Assn., Child Welfare League of Am. (mem. nat. task force 1985—), U. Students Cooperation Assn. (bd. dirs. 1982-83). Democrat. Roman Catholic. Club: Bridge Unit 514 (Bakersfield) (v.p. 1986—). Avocations: bridge, music. Office: Kern County Dept Human Services PO Box 511 Bakersfield CA 93302

SIMMONS, DONALD RALPH, test engineer; b. Longmont, Colo., Mar. 19, 1951; s. Claude Matthew and Theoda Maxine (Packard) S.; m. Elizabeth Louise Cory, May 15, 1970; children: Matthew, Trista, Daniel, Jeremy. AS in Electronics Tech., Grossmont Jr. Coll., 1977; BS in Computer Info. Systems, Regis Coll., 1986. Research electronic technician Naval Ocean Systems Ctr., San Diego, 1976-78; electronic technician Hewlett Packard, Colorado Springs, Colo., 1978-81, test engr., 1981—. Deacon Rustic Hills Bapt. Ch., Colorado Springs, 1980-82, youth leader, 1980—. Served with USN, 1969-75. Mem. IEEE (test tech. com.), Am. Soc. Test Engrs., HP 110 Computer Club. Avocations: backpacking, camping, deer and Waipiti hunting, brook trout fishing. Office: Hewlett Packard 5070 Centennial Blvd Colorado Springs CO 80907

SIMMONS, DWAYNE DEANGELO, biology educator; b. Toledo, Oct. 31, 1959; s. Johnnie Clarance Simmons and Carleen Reid. BS, Pepperdine U., 1980; PhD, Harvard U., 1986. Admissions counselor Pepperdine U., Malibu, Calif., 1979-80; asst. prof. biology Pepperdine U., Malibu, 1985—; Harvard teaching fellow Harvard U., Cambridge, Mass., 1982-85; Harvard resident tutor Harvard U., Cambridge, 1983-85; guest lectr. Los Angeles Elem. Schs., 1986; trustee Mission Jour. Contbr. articles to profl. jours. Mem. Pepperdine U. Alumni Bd. (assoc., sec. 1986), Alpha Chi. Mem. Ch. of Christ. Office: Pepperdine U Natural Sci Div Malibu CA 90265

SIMMONS, HAROLD ERNEST, social worker; b. Clarno, Wis., Jan. 27, 1915; s. Frank Otto and Helen (Louckes) S.; m. Lois-Elaine Hand, June 23, 1937; children: Keith, Catherine, Cynthia. BA, U. Wash., 1938, MSW, 1947. Dir. San Mateo (Calif.) County Social Services Dept., 1954-60; dep. dir. State Dept. Social Welfare, Sacramento, 1960-73; various adminstrv. positions fed. and state agys., 1972-83; pvt. practice social work specializing in stress illness Shingle Springs, Calif., 1983—. Author: Psychogenic Theory of Disease, 1966, Protective Services for Children, 1968, Work Relief to Rehabilitation, 1969, Psychoendocrine Aspects of Epilepsy, 1973, Psychogenic Biochemical Aspects of Cancer, 1979, Side Effects of Estrogen Drug Therapy, 1980, Psychosocial Origins of Mental Retardation, 1980. Mem. Nat. Assn. Social Workers, Soc. for Clin. Social Workers, Am. Acad.

Behavioral Medicine. Democrat. Presbyterian. Club: Cameron Park Country. Avocation: golf. Home and Office: 3571 Sudbury Rd Shingle Springs CA 95682

SIMMONS, JAMES MILLARD, state senator, credit company executive; b. Portland, Oreg., May 20, 1916; m. Margie French, 1938; children—James, Nancy. Student Willamette U., 1933-34; cert. in acctg. Oreg. Inst. Tech., 1938. Operator, mgr. family wholesale grocery bus., 1934-37; acct. Walter D. Whitecomb & Co., 1937-38; loan officer Caldwell Fin. Co., 1938-49; pres., owner Simmons Credit Co., Portland, 1950—; mem. Oreg. Senate, 1980—. Bd. dirs. Portland Rose Festival Assn., 1947—, Consumer Credit Counseling Service, 1968—; precinct committeeman Multnomah County Republican Com., 1955—, Washington County Rep. Com., 1955—. Served with U.S. Army, 1942-46. Mem. Portland C. of C. (mil. affairs com. 1954—, recreational resources com., 1950—). Office: 12160 SW Par 4 Dr Tigard OR 97224

SIMMONS, LEONARD MICAJAH, JR., physicist; b. Hattiesburg, Miss., Nov. 23, 1937; s. Leonard Micajah Sr. and Annie Vivian (Kornegay) S.; m. Margaret Lynn Woodham,June 4, 1959; children: Leonard M. III, Kelly Lynn, David Geoffrey. BA, Rice U., 1959; MS, La. State U., 1961; PhD, Cornell U., 1965. Research assoc. U. Minn., Mpls., 1965-67, U. Wis., Madison, 1967-69; asst. prof. physics U. Tex., Austin, 1969-71; mem. staff Los Alamos (N.Mex.) Nat. Lab., 1973—, asst. div. leader, 1974-76, 83-86, assoc. div. leader, 1977-81, 86—, dep. assoc. dir., 1981-83; vis. asst. prof. U. N.H., Durham, 1971-73; vis. prof. Washington Univ., St. Louis, 1980-81; pres. Aspen (Colo.) Ctr. for Physics, 1985—, trustee, hon. trustee, treas., 1976—; v.p. Santa Fe Inst., 1986—. Co-editor (book series) Los Alamos Series in Basic and Applied Sci., 1976—; contbr. articles to profl. jours. Past. chmn., mem. J.R. Oppenheimer Meml. Com., Los Alamos, 1976—. Mem. AAAS, Am. Phys. Soc., Internat. Assn. Math. Physics. Home: 1047 Camino San Acacio Santa Fe NM 87501 Office: Los Alamos Nat Lab Theoretical div Los Alamos NM 87545

SIMMONS, MEHL LYNDELL, social services administrator; b. Sacramento, Aug. 5, 1934; s. Lydell and Ruth Marie (Mechler) S.; children: Jill and John (twins). BA in Eng., Calif. State U., Sacramento, 1960, MSW, 1970. Lic. clin. social worker, Calif.; cert. secondary tchr., Calif. Asst. dir. Sacramento County Social Services, 1962-84; dir. Tulare County Social Services, Visalia, Calif., 1984—; clinician, dir. Sacramento Gestalt Therapy Inst., 1970-77. Author several bills enacted by Calif. Legislature. Active Sacramento County Children's Commn., legis. and exec. coms., Sacramento Regional Child Care Coalition, Sacramento Emergency Food and Shelter Bd., allocation com., Sacramento Housing and Redevel. Agy., Sr. Gleaners Statewide, Community Services Planning Council; chmn. Sacramento City/County Homeless Task Force; chair teen clinic adv. bd. Am. River Hosp.; chmn. Tulare County Exec. council. Served to sgt. USAF, 1952-56, Korea. Mem. Nat. Assn. Social Workers (state exec. selection com.), Am. Pub. Welfare Assn., Vocat. Counselors Calif., County Welfare Dirs. Assn. (social services, 95/5 ad hoc coms., long term care task force, v.p. 1986—), Vocational Counselors Calif. Democrat. Lodge: Lions. Avocations: golf, fly fishing, travel. Home: 3528 S Oakview Visalia CA 93277 Office: Tulare County Pub Social Services 100 E Center Visalia CA 93279

SIMMONS, MICHAEL ANTHONY, professor of pediatrics; b. Ft. Wayne, Ind., Aug. 9, 1941; s. William David and Mary Gretchen (Roe) S.; m. Margaret Clave Martindale, Aug. 17, 1963; children: Kristen, Jeffrey, Jennifer, Jason. AB, Harvard U., 1963, MD, 1967. Diplomate Am. Bd. Pediatrics, Am. Bd. Neonatal-Perinatal. Asst. prof. pediatrics U. Colo., Denver, 1974-77, assoc. prof. pediatrics, 1977; assoc. prof. pediatrics Johns Hopkins U., Balt., 1977-83, dep. dir. dept. pediatrics, 1981-83; prof., chmn. bd. U. Utah Sch. Medicine, Salt Lake City, 1983—; chmn. sub-bd. Neonatal-Perinatal Medicine, Am. Bd. Pediatrics, Chapel Hill, N.C., 1983—. Mem. bd. trustees Osmond Found., Salt Lake City, 1984—; established investigator Am. Heart Soc., 1976-78. Served to major USAF, 1969-71. Fellow Am. Acad. Pediatrics; mem. Perinatal Research Soc. (pres.-elect 1986, pres. 1987), Soc. Pediatric Research, Am. Pediatric Soc., Western Soc. Pediatric Research Council, Assn. Med. Sch. Pediatric Dept. Chmn. (sec./treas.). Home: 4302 Adonis Dr Salt Lake City UT 84124 Office: Dept Pediatrics U Utah Sch Medicine 50 N Med Dr Salt Lake City UT 84132

SIMMONS, MICHELLE GEORGENE, environmental health professional; b. Los Angeles, Dec. 9, 1959; d. Alonzo Dean and Rae Nell (Lewis) S. BS in Pub. Health Sci., Loma Linda U., 1981; MS in Environ. Studies, Calif. State U., Dominguez Hills, 1984. Registered environ. health officer. Tech. asst. Solid Waste Mgmt. div. City of San Bernardino, Calif., 1981; environ. technician Environ. Health Services div. County of San Bernardino, 1980-81; quality control analyst Van De Kamps Frozen Food, Santa Fe Springs, Calif., 1981-82; environ. health officer Environ. Mgmt. div. County of Los Angeles, 1982-85; asst. mgr. western region Nat. Sanitation Found., Ann Arbor, Mich., 1985-86; loss control and safety cons. Northbrook Property and Casualty, Brea, Calif., 1985—; entrepreneur La Poop Pet Pampering, Century City, Calif., 1984—. Active African Meth. Episc. Ch., Los Angeles, 1984—. Recipient Departmental Commendation Los Angeles County Dept. Environ. Mgmt., 1984, Cert. of Commendation Los Angeles City Council, 1984. Mem. Am. Pub. Health Assn., Calif. Environ. Health Assn. (bd. dirs. 1983-84, v.p. 1984-85, pres. 1985—), Am. Soc. Safety Engrs., Los Angeles County Sanitarians Assn., Nat. Assn. Female Execs., Orlando Flowers Environ. Assn. (Acad. Achievement award 1984), Alpha Kappa Alpha. Democrat. Home: 759 E 91st St Los Angeles CA 90002

SIMMONS, PATRICIA ANNE, university administrative official, accountant; b. Seaside, Oreg., Aug. 20, 1946; d. Richard Edwin and Bonnie Vinona (Enderud) McCosh; m. Larry Eldon Simmons, Aug. 31, 1968 (div. Feb. 1979). BS, U. Colo., 1968, postgrad., 1971-74. From credit analyst to asst. v.p. 1st Nat. Bank Denver, 1968-74; organizer comml. loan credit dept. Bank of Aspen, Colo., 1974-75; acct. Pitkin County, Aspen, Colo., 1975-76, Boulder (Colo.) County, Colo., 1976-78; acct., adminstrv. officer Mont. State U., Bozeman, 1978-82, mgr. within phys. plant div., 1982—. Presenter, equipment room chmn. Expanding Your Horizons, 1985, 86, 87. Recipient Young Career Woman award, Denver Downtown Bus. and Profl. Women, 1972. Mem. Nat. Wildlife Fedn. (Phoenix Western region presenter 1986, alternate del. Mont. to Nat. Conv. 1987), Mont. Wildlife Fedn. (sec., treas., bd. dirs. 1979—), Gallatin Wildlife Assn. (pres., treas., bd. dirs. 1983—), Assn. Coll. and Univ. Telecoms. Adminstrs., Assn. Phys. Plant Adminstrs., Bozeman Bus. and Profl. Women (sec., v.p., pres., com. chairperson 1979—), Mont. Fedn. Bus. and Profl. Women (bd. dirs., treas. 1985-86, Conv. cochairperson 1979—), Nat. Fedn. Bus. and Profl. Women. Democrat. Avocations: fishing, skiing, sewing, reading, photography. Home: 1103 Cherry Dr Bozeman MT 59715 Office: Mont State U Phys Plant Div Bozeman MT 59717

SIMMONS, ROY WILLIAM, banker; b. Portland, Oreg., Jan. 24, 1916; s. Henry Clay and Ida (Mudd) S.; m. Elizabeth Ellison, Oct. 28, 1938; children—Julia Simmons Watkins, Matthew R., Laurence E., Elizabeth Jane Simmons Hoke, Harris H., David E. Asst. cashier First Nat. Bank Layton, Utah, 1944-49; Utah bank commr. 1949-51; exec. v.p. Bank of Utah, Ogden, 1951-53; pres. Lockhart Co., Salt Lake City, 1953-64, Zion's First Nat. Bank, Salt Lake City, 1964-81; chmn., chief exec. officer Zion's First Nat. Bank, 1981—; chmn., chief exec. officer Zion's Utah Bancorp., 1965—; chmn. bd. Zion's Savs. & Loan Assn., 1961-69; pres. Lockhart Co., 1964—; bd. dirs. Salt Lake City br. Fed. Res. Bank San Francisco, 1971-77, Kennecott Copper Corp., 1964-81, Beneficial Life Ins. Co., Hotel Utah, 1964-85, Utah Portland Cement Co., Mountain Fuel Supply Co., 1964-83, Denver & Rio Grande R.R., 1964-83, Rio Grande Industries, 1964-85, Ellison Ranching Co. Chmn. Utah Bus. Devel. Corp., 1969-80; Mem. Utah State Bd. Regents, 1969-81. Mem. Salt Lake City C. of C. (treas. 1964-65), Sigma Pi. Republican. Mem. Ch. of Jesus Christ of Latter Day Saints. Home: Crestwood Rd Kaysville UT 84037 Office: Zion's First Nat Bank 1 Main St Salt Lake City UT 84110

SIMMONS, TED CONRAD, writer; b. Seattle, Sept. 1, 1916; s. Conrad and Clara Evelyn (Beaudry) S.; student U. Wash., 1938-41, UCLA and Los Angeles State U., 1952-54, Oxford (Eng.) U., 1980; m. Dorothy Pauline Maltese, June 1, 1942; children—Lynn, Juliet. Drama critic Seattle Daily Times, 1942; indsl. writer, editor Los Angeles Daily News, 1948-51; contbr. Steel, Western Metals, Western Industry, 1951—; past poetry dir. Watts Writers Workshop; instr. Westside Poetry Center; asst. dir. Pacific Coast Writers Conf., Calif. State Coll. Los Angeles. Served with USAAF, 1942-46. Author: (poetry) Deadended, 1966; (novel) Middlearth, 1975; (drama) Greenhouse, 1977, Durable Chaucer, 1978, Rabelais and other plays, 1980, Dickeybird, 1981, Alice and Eve, 1983, Deja Vu, Deja Vu, 1986; writer short story, radio verse; book reviewer Los Angeles Times; contbr. poetry to The Am. Poet, Prairie Wings, Antioch Rev., Year Two Anthology; editor: Venice Poetry Company Presents, 1972.

SIMMONS, WILLIAM ISAAC, retired dentist; b. Waco, Tex., Feb. 14, 1924; s. Jared Claude and Blanche (Schwarz) S.; D.D.S., Loyola U., New Orleans, 1946; cert. in orthodontics U. Pa., 1950; m. Evelyn Kottle, June 11, 1967; children—Jared Claude, Walter Neil, Gina Denise, Nancy Dayan, Dylan Sara. Tchr., U. Tex. Dental Sch., 1951; individual practice dentistry, specializing in orthodontics, Shreveport, La., 1951-85, ret. Served with USAF, 1946-48. Mem. ADA (v.p. 4th Dist.), Am. Orthodontic Soc., Royal Soc. Health. Jewish. Clubs: Masons, University (Shreveport); Barksdale Air Force Officers. Home: 8120 Via del Lago Scottsdale AZ 85258

SIMON, ALAN HOWARD, lawyer; b. Cleve., Nov. 21, 1938; s. David and Esther (Handler) S.; m. Joan R. Claitman, Aug. 25, 1963; children: Kenneth, Gregory. BA, U. So. Calif., 1960; JD, U. Calif.-Hastings Coll. Law, San Francisco, 1963. Bar: Calif. Chief Juvenile Services div. Los Angeles County Office Pub. Defender, Los Angeles, 1963—. Bd. dirs. Gateways Mental Health Ctr., Los Angeles. Served with USMC, 1957-64. Mem. Calif. Pub. Defenders Assn., Calif. Lawyers for Criminal Justice. Democrat. Jewish. Avocations: old cars, history of Los Angeles and The West. Office: Los Angeles County Office Pub Defender 210 W Temple St Los Angeles CA 90012

SIMON, DAVID HAROLD, public relations executive; b. Washington, Dec. 3, 1930; s. Isaac B. and Marjorie S. (Felstiner) S.; m. Ruth Lurie, Mar. 2, 1962; children: Rachel, Jessie. B.E.E., Cornell U., 1954. Mktg. engr. Sylvania Elec. Products, Inc., Boston, 1957-58; advt. mgr. Sylvania Elec. Products, Inc., Mountain View, Calif., 1958-60; regional sales engr. Sylvania Elec. Products, Inc., Los Angeles, 1960-63; mgr. advt. and public relations Electronic Splty. Co., Los Angeles, 1963-66; corp. dir. advt. and public relations Teledyne, Inc., Los Angeles, 1966-67; pres. Simon/Public Relations, Inc., Los Angeles, 1967—. Contbr. articles on public relations to various publs. Res. dep. sheriff Los Angeles Sheriff's Dept., 1973—; mem. Los Angeles Olympic Citizen's Adv. Commn., 1980-84; trustee Calif. Chamber Symphony, 1981-84. Served with USN, 1954-57. Mem. Public Relations Soc. Am., Nat. Assn. Sci. Writers, Nat. Assn. Corp. Dirs. (founding pres. Los Angeles chpt.), Opera Buffs Inc. (bd. dirs. 1986—), Mensa. Home: 13025 Weddington St Van Nuys CA 91401 Office: Simon McGarry Pub Relations Inc 11661 San Vicente Blvd Suite 903 Los Angeles CA 90049

SIMON, JAMES GEORGE, utility company executive; b. Ohio Camp, Mont., June 29, 1924; s. David Lawrence and Etta Mae (Bruce) S.; m. Alice Jane Olds, Sept. 2, 1950; children: David Edward, Jayme K. Diploma, Chgo. Tech. Coll., 1949; student Jamestown Coll., N.D., 1943; diploma U.S. Army Air Force Navigation Sch., San Marcos, Tex., 1944. Supt., Askevold Constrn. Co., Missoula, Mont., 1949-53; engr., estimator Lease & Leigland, Great Falls, Mont., 1953-54; engr., estimator C.W. Wattnem Constrn., Great Falls, 1954-55, H.S. Leigland & Sons, Great Falls, 1955-63; engr., supt. Lewis Constrn. Co., Great Falls, 1963-81; project mgr. Mont. Power Co., Colstrip and Missoula, Mont., 1981—. Chmn. Colstrip Archtl. Rev. Commn., 1984-85; vice-chmn. Colstrip Property Owners Assn., 1985; chmn. bd. trustees First United Meth. Ch., Great Falls, 1971-72. Served to 2d lt. USAF, 1943-45. Lodges: Elks, Masons, Shriners. Home: 1859 E Broadway Missoula MT 59802 Office: Mont Power Co 725 Juniper Dr Missoula MT 59802

SIMON, NORTON WINFRED, industrialist; b. Portland, Oreg., Feb. 5, 1907; s. Myer and Lillian (Glickman) S.; m. Jennifer Jones, May 30, 1971; children by previous marriage: Donald Ellis, Robert Ellis (dec.). Student, U. Calif., Berkeley, 1923. Founder, former chief exec. officer Norton Simon Inc., N.Y.C.; founder, chief exec. officer 5 corp. founds. and 1 family found. Los Angeles; former dir., chmn. fin. com. Burlington No., Inc. Mem. Courtauld Inst., London; former mem. Carnegie Commn. on Future of Higher Edn., Nat. Programming Council; mem. Nat. Com. on U.S.-China Relations, Founding Friends of Can.; chmn. bd. dirs. The Founders, Los Angeles Music Center; affiliated Calif. Sch. Profl. Psychology; bd. dirs., pres., trustee Norton Simon Mus., Pasadena, Calif.; trustee Inst. Advanced Study, Princeton, N.J.; former bd. dirs. Reed Coll., Inst. Internat. Edn., Los Angeles County Mus. Art; former regent U. Calif.; mem. adv. bd. Columbia U.-McGraw Hill Lectures; fellow Pierpont Morgan Library, N.Y.C.; mem., past chmn. Calif. State Transp. Commn.

SIMON, RICHARD JAMES, reporter; b. N.Y.C., Aug. 9, 1952; s. Jacques Richard and Claire (LeKashman) S. BJ, U. So. Calif., 1974; postgrad., UCLA, 1980—. City hall reporter, asst. city editor The Daily Rev., Burbank, Calif., 1974-76; corr. Copley News Service, Los Angeles, 1976-78; Los Angeles county reporter The Daily News, Van Nuys, Calif., 1978-80; city-county bur. reporter Los Angeles Times, 1980—; instr. journalism U. So. Calif., Los Angeles, 1978, Calif. State U., Northridge, 1985. Recipient Best Human Interest Story award Valley Press Club, 1984. Mem. U. So. Calif. Journalism Alumni Assn. (bd. dirs. 1978—), Investigative Reporters and Editors Inc., Aviation and Space Writers Assn., N.Y. Acad. Scis., Sigma Delta Chi. Avocations: bicycling, marathon running, skiing.

SIMON, SHELDON WEISS, political science educator; b. St. Paul, Jan. 31, 1937; s. Blair S. and Jennie M. (Dim) S.; m. Charlann Lilwin Scheid, Apr. 27, 1962; 1 child, Alex Russell. BA summa cum laude, U. Minn., 1958, PhD, 1964; MPA, Princeton U., 1960; postgrad., U. Geneva, 1962-63. Asst. prof., then prof. U. Ky., 1966-75; prof. polit. sci. Ariz. State U., 1975—, chmn. dept., 1975-79, dir. Ctr. Asian Studies, 1980—; vis. prof. George Washington U., 1965, U. B.C. Can., 1972-73, 79-80, Carleton U., 1976; cons. USIA, Research Analysis Corp., Am. Enterprise Inst. Pub. Policy Research, Hoover Instn., Orkand Corp. Author: The Asean States and Regional Security, 1982; Asian Neutralism and U.S. Policy, 1975. Editor: The Military and Security in the Third World, 1978; other books, research articles; contbr. chpts. to books. Mem. Com. Fgn. Relations, Phoenix, 1976—; bd. dirs. Phoenix Little Theater, 1976-79. Grantee Am. Enterprise Inst., 1974, Earhart Found., 1979, 81, 82, 84; Hoover Instn. fellow, 1980, 85. Mem. Am. Polit. Sci. Assn., Assn. Asian Studies, AAUP, Internat. Studies Assn., Phi Beta Kappa. Democrat. Jewish. Avocations: acting, singer, tennis. Home: 5630 Rocky Point Tempe AZ 85283 Office: Ariz State U Ctr for Asian Studies Tempe AZ 85287

SIMON, WILLIAM LEONARD, film writer; b. Washington, Dec. 3, 1930; s. Isaac B. and Marjorie (Felstiner) S.; m. Arynne Lucy Abeles, Sept. 18, 1966; 1 dau., Victoria Marie; 1 stepson, Sheldon M. Bermont. BEE, Cornell U., 1954; MA in Ednl. Psychology, Golden State U., 1982, PhD in Communications, 1983. Writer features and TV movies, documentary and indsl. films, TV programs 1958—; lectr. George Washington U., Washington, 1968-70. Writer over 500 produced works for motion pictures and TV, including screenplays Fair Woman Without Discretion, Majorca, Swindle. Pres. Foggy Bottom Citizens Assn., 1963-65; mem. exec. bd., 1965-69; v.p. Shakespeare Summer Festival, 1966-67, trustee, 1965-70; mem. interview com. Cornell U., 1987—; mem. jury CINE film festival, 1979—, CINDY film festival, 1985—. Served to lt. USN, 1954-58. Recipient 8 Golden Eagle awards Cine Film Festival, gold medal N.Y. Internat. Festival, gold medal Freedoms Found., IFPA Gold Cindy awards Berlin, Belgrade and Venice film Festivals, numerous others. Mem. Nat. Acad. TV Arts and Scis. (gov. D.C. chpt. 1970-73), Writers Guild Am., Am. Film Inst., Internat. Documentary Assn., Eta Kappa Nu (chpt. pres. 1953-54), Tau Beta Pi. Home: PO Box 2048 Rancho Santa Fe CA 92067

SIMONDS, JOHN EDWARD, editor; b. Boston, July 4, 1935; s. Alvin E. and Ruth Angeline (Rankin) S.; m. Rose B. Muller, Nov. 16, 1968; children—Maximillian P., Malia G.; children by previous marriage—Rachel F., John B. B.A., Bowdoin Coll., 1957. Reporter Daily Tribune, Seymour, Ind., 1957-58, UPI, Columbus, Ohio, 1958-60; reporter, asst. city editor Providence Jour. Bulletin, 1960-65, Washington Evening Star, 1965-66; corr. Gannett News Service, Washington, 1966-75; mng. editor Honolulu Star Bulletin, 1975-80, exec. editor, 1980-87, sr. editor, 1987—. Served with U.S. Army, 1958. Mem. Am. Soc. Newspaper Editors, AP Mng. Editors, Honolulu Press Club. Home: 5316 Nehu Pl Honolulu HI 96821 Office: PO Box 3080 Honolulu HI 96802

SIMONE, ALBERT JOSEPH, academic administrator; b. Boston, Dec. 16, 1935; s. Edward and Mary (DiGiovanni) S.; m. Carolie Roberta Menko, Nov. 7, 1959; children: Edward, Karen, Debra, Laura. BA, Tufts U., 1957; PhD, MIT, 1962. Lectr. Coll. Bus. Adminstrn., Northeastern U., Boston, 1958-59; instr. econs. MIT and Tufts U., Boston, 1959-60; asst. prof. Northeastern U., Boston Coll., 1960-63; prof., dir. quantitative mgmt. program Coll. Bus. Adminstrn., Boston Coll., 1966-68; prof., head dept. quantitative analysis Coll. Bus. Adminstrn. U. Cin., 1968-72, dean Coll. Bus. Adminstrn., 1972-83; v.p. acad. affairs U. Hawaii, Honolulu, 1983-84, acting pres., 1984-85, pres., 1985—; served on, chaired numerous univ. coms.; program chmn. 1970 Nat. Conf. of Am. Prodn. and Inventory Control Soc.; mem. accreditation com. Am. Assembly Collegiate Schs. Bus., 1978-83, visits to U. Ky., Carnegie-Mellon U., 1982; session chmn. various profl. confs.; cons. statis. forecasting, prodn. scheduling and sample design models various cos. including Cin. Gas & Electric Co., Cin. Milacron, Kroger Co.; econ. and mgmt. cons. Atty. Gen.'s Office, State of Mass.; mem. council econ. advisors to Gov., Commonwealth of Mass. Author: Matematica Finita Con Aplicaciones A Las Ciencias Administrativas, 1969, Foundations of Contemporary Mathematics with Applications in the Social and Management Sciences, 1967, Probability: An Introduction with Applications, 1967; (with L. Kattsoff) Finite Mathematics with Applications in the Social and Management Sciences, 1965, (with R. Wessel and E. Willett) Statistics as Applied to Economics and Business, 1965; also articles. Bd. dirs. Cin. Ctr. Econ. Edn., Cin. Minority Contractors Assistance Corp., Goodwill Industries Inc. Rehab. Program in Data Processing; bd. dirs., exec. com. Jr. Achievement Cin., Cin. Better Bus. Bur.; mem. Stadium Authority, Aloha Stadium; bd. govs., exec. com. East-West Ctr.; trustee, exec. com. U. Hawaii Found.; vice chair, bd. dirs. Research Corp. of U. Hawaii. Fellow of grad. sch. U. Cin.; named Prof. of Yr., Delta Sigma Pi, Alpha Theta chpt. U. Cin., 1972. Fellow Am. Inst. Decision Scis. (v.p. publs. 1969-70, v.p. and student liaison 1972, pres. 1974-75; founding editor and editor-in-chief jour. 1970-72; Disting. Service award 1972); mem. Acad. of Mgmt., Am. Econ. Assn., Am. Inst. Indsl. Engrs., Am. Prodn. and Inventory Control Soc., Am. Statis. Assn., Assn. Computing Machinery, Econometric Soc., Fin. Execs. Inst., Inst. Mgmt. Sci., Ops. Research Soc. Am., Phi Beta Kappa, Beta Gamma Sigma. Office: Univ of Hawaii 2444 Dole St Honolulu HI 96822 *

SIMONI, JOSEPH PILIE, banking association official; b. San Francisco, Feb. 26, 1945; s. Joseph Mario and Vittoria (Baldassari) S.; B.A. in Bus., Calif. State U., San Francisco, 1977; M.B.A., Coll. Notre Dame, 1979; m. Patricia Sue Mazza, Mar. 23, 1969. With Wells Fargo Bank, 1970-84, asst. v.p., San Lorenzo, Calif., 1982-84; mgr. program devel. and instrn. Am. Inst. Banking, San Francisco, 1984-86; asst. v.p., mgr. First Comml. Bank, San Francisco, 1986—; mgr. program devel./instrn. Am. Inst. Banking, San Francisco, 1984-86; asst. v.p., mgr. 1st Comml. Bank, San Francisco, 1986—; past gen. partner, prin. cons. ASC Assos.; mem. banking and adv. bd. Foothill Coll.; leader Joe Simoni Orch.; dir. Ohio Valley Gen. Hosp., McKees Rocks, Penn.; instr. music Burlingame Recreation Center. Served with U.S. Army, 1967-70; Vietnam. Decorated Army Commendation medal; recipient various certs. merit. Mem. Am. Inst. Banking (instr. mgmt. skills), Am. Mgmt. Assn., Am. Fedn. Musicians, Native Sons Golden West, Coll. Notre Dame Alumni Assn. (bd. dirs.), Italian-Am. Fedn. San Mateo County, Sons of Italy, Italian-Catholic Fedn. Democrat. Roman Catholic. Home: 55 Club Dr San Carlos CA 94070 Office: 550 Kearny St Suite 310 San Francisco CA 94108

SIMONS, DANNY CHARLES, JR., real estate broker and asset manager; b. Salt Lake City, Feb. 16, 1955; s. Danny Charles and Sally Jane (Andersen) S.; m. Debra Rasmussen, Apr. 6, 1977; children: Danny Chad, Amber Marie, Leslie Ann. Student U. Utah, 1974, 77, Latter-day Saints Bus. Coll., 1978, Lumbleu Real Estate Inst., 1978, 79. Vol. missionary Mormon Ch., Hawaii, 1975-77; sales agt., broker Simons and Co., Salt Lake City, 1977-80; gen. mgr. realty ops. Equitable Life, Salt Lake City, 1980-84; gen. mgr., broker Real Estate Cons., Salt Lake City, 1980-84; ptnr., broker Charles Dunn Co., Realtors, Salt Lake City, 1984; gen. mgr., broker Equitable Real Investment Mgmt., Inc., Salt Lake City, 1985—; Mem. Nat. Assn. Realtors, Utah Assn. Realtors (edn. com. 1979), Salt Lake Bd. Realtors, Bldg. Owners and Mgrs. Assn. Salt Lake City (real property adminstr., sec.-treas. 1982-85, v.p. 1986—, legis. chmn. 1986—), Inst. Real Estate Mgmt. (cert. property mgr., legis. chmn. 1986), Salt Lake City Downtown Retail Mchts. Assn. (bd. dirs. 1982—). Office: Estate Investment Management Inc 466 Lawndale Dr Suite E Salt Lake City UT 84115

SIMONS, KENNETH K., statistician; b. Washta, Iowa, Sept. 18, 1937; s. Kenneth W. and Imogene D. (Koch) S.; m. Shirley Ann Clark, Aug. 28, 1960; children—Deborah, De Ann, Lorie. B.S. in Stats., Iowa State U., 1960, M.S. in Stats., 1962. Reliability engr. Martin Co., Denver, 1962-66; statistician math. modeling IBM, Boulder, Colo., 1966—. Mem. Am. Statis. Assn. Methodist. Clubs: Rocky Mountain Roadrunners, Elks (Denver). Contbr. paper to statis. conf. Office: PO Box 1900 Boulder CO 80302

SIMONS, SANFORD LAWRENCE, design engineer, executive; b. N.Y.C., Apr. 10, 1921; s. Jack And Fay (Provsky) S.; m. Rebecca Jane Blair, Nov. 10, 1947; children: Jane D., Darcie Gale, Douglas Blair. BS, Mo. Sch. Mines, 1944. Cert. profl. engr., Colo. Research engr. Battelle, Columbus, Ohio, 1944; jr. scientist Los Alamos (N.Mex.) Nat. Lab., 1944-46; engr. Alldredge and Simons Lab., Denver, 1947-48; research asst. U. Denver, 1949-50; engr. Gas Mfg., Denver, 1951-60; dir. engring. U. Colo., Denver, 1960—; engr. Simons Engring., Denver, 1954-70; pres. Sienco, Inc., Denver, 1970—. Designer med. instrumentation; patentee in field. Bd. dirs. Inter Canyon Fire Protection Agy., Morrison, Colo., 1958—. Served with U.S. Army, 1944-46. Mem. Am. Soc. Metals, Theta Tau. Home and Office: 9188 S Turkey Creek Rd Morrison CO 80465

SIMONSEN, CHRISTIAN CLINTON, molecular biologist, researcher; b. Gilroy, Calif., Feb. 4, 1953; s. Harry Christian Simonsen and Elizabeth Jean (Rhodes) Poirrier; m. Karen Sue Holth, Dec. 27, 1975; children: Christian Clinton, Daniel Adam. BS, Stanford U., 1975; PhD, U. Utah, 1979. Postdoctoral researcher Stanford U., Calif., 1979-81; scientist Genentech, So. San Francisco, 1981-85; dir. Invitron Corp., Redwood City, Calif., 1985—. Contbr. articles to profl. jours.; inventor hepatitis vaccine. Coach Calif. Youth Soccer Assn., 1984-85, YMCA winter soccer, 1986, Little League Baseball, 1986. Grad. fellow U. Utah, 1977-78; fellow Am. Cancer Soc., 1979, NIH, 1979. Mem. AAAS, Am. Soc. Microbiology. Republican. Episcopalian. Home: 1509 Parkview Ave San Jose CA 95130 Office: INvitron Corp 515 Galveston Redwood City CA 94063

SIMONSON, MICHAEL, lawyer, judge; b. Franklin, N.J., Feb. 5, 1950; s. Robert and Eleanor (Weiss) S. BA, U. Ariz., 1973; JD, Southwestern U., Los Angeles, 1976; LLM in Taxation, Washington U., St. Louis, 1978. Bar: Ariz. 1977, U.S. Dist. Ct. Ariz. 1979, U.S. Tax Ct. 1978. Bailiff, law clk. Superior Ct. Maricopa County Div. 2, Phoenix, 1976-77; sole practice, Scottsdale, Ariz., 1978-79; ptnr. Simonson, Groh, & Lindteigen, Scottsdale, 1979-81, Simonson & Preston, Phoenix, 1984-86, Simonson, Preston & Arbetman, 1986-87, Simonson & Arbetman, 1987—; judge pro tempore Mcpl. Ct., City of Phoenix, 1984—; adj. prof. Ariz. State U Coll. Bus., Tempe, 1984—, Coll. for Fin. Planning, Denver, 1984—, Maricopa County Community Colls., 1984—, Western Internat. U., Phoenix, 1984—; prof. law Univ. Phoenix, 1985—, area chmn. legal studies, 1986—. Mem. Maricopa County Foster Child Care Rev. Bd. No. 17, 1978-81; pres. Camelback Mountainview Estates Homeowners Assn., 1980-81, Congregation Tiphereth Israel, 1979-81. Mem. ABA (taxation sect., various coms.), State Bar Ariz. (cert. specialist in tax law), Maricopa County Bar Assn., Cen. Ariz. Estate Planning Council, Internat. Assn. Fin. Planners, Ariz. Inst. CPA's, Internat. Platform Assn., Phoenix C. of C. (taxation and fin. council 1984—). Democrat. Jewish. Club: Nucleus. Lodge: Masons. Office: Simonson & Arbetman 4645 N 32d St Suite 200 Phoenix AZ 85018

SIMONSON, MILES KEVIN, real estate executive; b. Monmouth, Ill., May 25, 1950; s. John E. and Margaret Katherine (Huston) S. BA, No. Ill. U., 1972. Sgt. DeKalb County Sheriff's Police, Sycamore, Ill., 1972-75;

owner Kishwaukee Realty, DeKalb, 1976-78; v.p and chief ops. officer Realty World, Oak Brook (Ill.), Tampa (Fla.), Phoenix, St. Louis, 1978-84; pres., chief exec. officer Realty 500, Inc., Reno, 1985—, also bd. dirs.; bd. dirs. Realty 500 of No. Nev., Realty 500 Advt. Fund., Reno. Author: Professional Sales, 1985, Professional Listing, 1985. Avocations: golf, swimming, boating. Office: Realty 500 Inc 1539 Vassar 101 Reno NV 89502

SIMONSON, SUSAN KAY, hospital administrator; b. LaPorte, Ind., Dec. 5, 1946; d. George Randolph and Myrtle Lucille (Opfel) Menkes; m. Richard Bruce Simonson, Aug. 25, 1973. BA with honors, Ind. U., 1969; MA, Washington U., St. Louis, 1972. Perinatal social worker Yakima Valley Meml. Hosp., Yakima, Wash., 1979-81, dir. social service, 1982—, dir. patient support and hospice program, 1981—; Spanish instr. Yakima Valley Coll., Yakima, Wash., 1981—; pres. Yakima Child Abuse Council, 1983-85. Mem. Jr. League, Yakima; mem. adv. council Robert Wood Johnson Found. Rural Infant Health Care Project, Yakima, 1980, Pregnancy Loss and Compassionate Friends Support Groups, Yakima, 1982—, Teen Outreach Program, Yakima, 1984—. Recipient NSF award, 1967; research grantee Ind. U., 1968, Fulbright grantee U.S. Dept. State, 1969-70; Nat. Def. Edn. Act fellowship, 1970-73. Mem. AAUW, Soc. Med. Anthropology, Soc. Hosp. Social Work Dirs. of Am. Hosp. Assn., Nat. Assn. Perinatal Social Workers, Nat. Assn. Social Workers, Phi Beta Kappa. Office: Yakima Valley Meml Hosp 2811 Tieton Dr Yakima WA 98902

SIMPLOT, JOHN R., agribusiness executive; b. Dubuque, Iowa, Jan. 4, 1909; m. Esther Becker; children: Richard, Don, Scott, Gay Simplot Otter. Founder, chmn. J.R. Simplot Co., Boise, Idaho, 1941—; bd. dirs. Micron Technology, McDonald's Corp., Ind. Coal and Coke Co., First Security Corp., Continental Life and Accident Co., Morrison-Knudsen, Inc. Former chmn. bd. trustees Coll. Idaho. Avocations: skiing, horseback riding, hunting, fishing. Pioneer in commercial frozen french fries. Office: J R Simplot Co One Capital Ctr PO Box 27 Boise ID 83707 *

SIMPSON, ALAN K., U.S. senator; b. Cody, Wyo., Sept. 2, 1931; s. Milward Lee and Lorna (Kooi) S.; m. Ann Schroll, June 21, 1954; children—William Lloyd, Colin Mackenzie, Susan Lorna. B.S., U. Wyo., 1954, J.D., 1958. Bar: Wyo. bar 1958, U.S. Supreme Ct. bar 1964. Asst. atty. gen. State of Wyo., 1959; city atty. City of Cody, 1959-69; partner firm Simpson, Kepler, Simpson & Cozzens (and predecessor), Cody, Wyo., 1959-78; mem. Wyo. Ho. of Reps., 1964-77, majority whip, 1973-75, majority floor leader, 1975-77, speaker pro tem, 1977; legis. participant Eagleton Inst. Politics, Rutgers U., 1971; mem. U.S. Senate from Wyo., 1978—, asst. majority leader, 1985-87, asst. minority leader, 1987—, ranking majority mem. vets. affairs com., ranking minority mem. vets. affairs com., chmn. subcom. nuclear regulation of comml. environ. and pub. works, ranking minority mem. nuclear regulation subcom., chmn. subcom. immigration and refugee policy of judiciary com., ranking minority mem. subcom. on immigration and refugee policy. Formerly v.p., trustee N.W. Community Coll., Powell, Wyo., 1968-76; trustee Buffalo Bill Hist. Center, Cody; bd. dirs. Western Arts Found.; trustee Grand Teton Music Festival, Gottsche Found. Rehab. Center, Thermopolis, Wyo.; del. Nat. Triennial Episcopal Ch. Conv., 1973, 76. Mem. Wyo. Bar Assn., Park County Bar Assn., Fifth Jud. Dist. Bar Assn., Am. Bar Assn., Assn. Trial Lawyers Am., U. Wyo. Alumni Assn. (pres. 1962, 63, Disting. Alumnus award 1985), VFW (life), Am. Legion, Amvets. (Silver Helmet award). Lodges: Eagles, Elks, Masons (33 deg.), Shriners, Rotary (pres. local club 1972-73). Office: 261 Dirksen Senate Office Bldg Washington DC 20510

SIMPSON, ANDREA LYNN, energy company communications executive; b. Altadena, Calif., Feb. 10, 1948; d. Kenneth James and Barbara Faries Simpson; m. John R. Myrdal, Dec. 13, 1986. B.A., U. So. Calif., 1969, M.S., 1983; postgrad. U. Colo., Boulder, 1977. Asst. cashier United Calif. Bank, Los Angeles, 1969-73; asst. v.p. mktg. 1st Hawaiian Bank, Honolulu, 1973-78; v.p. corp. communications Pacific Resources, Inc., Honolulu, 1978—. Bd. dirs. Hawaii Heart Assn., 1978-83, Child and Family Services, 1984-86 , Council of Pacific, Girl Scouts U.S.A., 1982-85, Arts Council Hawaii, 1977-81; trustee Hawaii Loa Coll., 1984-86; commr Hawaii State Commn. on Status of Women, 1985—. Bd. dirs. Honolulu Symphony Soc., 1986—; active Jr. League of Honolulu. Named Outstanding Young Person of Hawaii, Hawaii Jaycees, 1978; Panhellenic Woman of Yr., Hawaii, 1979; Outstanding Woman in Bus., Hawaii YWCA, 1980; Outstanding Young Woman of Hawaii, Hawaii Legislature, 1980. Mem. Am. Mktg. Assn., Pub. Relations Soc. Am. (bd. dirs. Honolulu chpt. 1984-85, Silver Anvil award 1984), Pub. Utilities Communicators Assn. (Communicator of Yr. 1984), Honolulu Advt. Fedn. (Advt. Woman of Yr. 1984), U. So. Calif. Alumni Assn. (bd. dirs. Hawaii 1981-83), Alpha Phi (dir. Hawaii). Clubs: Outrigger Canoe, Pacific, Jr. League. Office: Pacific Resources Inc PO Box 3379 Honolulu HI 96842

SIMPSON, CHARLES HENDERSON, metallurgical engineer; b. Kershaw, S.C., June 20, 1919; s. William Henderson and Mandy Jane (Williams) S.; m. Thelma Fay Horner, Oct. 9, 1976. Student, Oreg. State Coll.; BBA, Multhnomah Coll., 1952; postgrad., U. Oreg., 1952-54, Carnegie Inst., 1957-59. With geology team UN, South America; pvt. practice metall. engring. Scottsdale, Ariz., 1968—. Patentee metall. extraction processes. Served as cpl. USMC, 1939-45, ETO, PTO, CBI. Decorated Purple Heart with two gold stars; recipient citation Pres. of U.S., 1942, 43. Mem. AIME, AAAS, Am. Inventors Soc. Republican. Presbyterian. Lodge: Elks. Avocations: fishing, bowling, minerology. Home: 7749 E Chapparal Rd Scottsdale AZ 85253 Office: Simpson Research 1035 E Curry Rd Unit G Tempe AZ 85251

SIMPSON, DANIEL CARNEY, clinical social worker; b. McAlester, Okla., Feb. 18, 1944. AA, Eastern Okla. State Coll., 1965; B, E. Cen. U., 1981; M, Okla. U., 1983. Clin. social worker PHS Santa Clara Clinic, Espanola, N.Mex., 1983-85, Albuquerque VA Hosp., 1985—. Served with USN, 1966-69. Mem. Nat. Assn. Social Workers (cert.), N.Mex. Hosp. Dirs. Assn., Okla. Lic. Social Workers. Democrat. Presbyterian. Avocations: photography, astronomy. Home: 11100 Gibson SE-SP#1-196 Albuquerque NM 87123

SIMPSON, GARY ELDRIDGE, electronics company executive; b. Fresno, Calif., Sept. 25, 1937; s. Byron B. Simpson and Bonna M. (Altermatt) S.; m. Sharon Lyn Foletta, July 5, 1969; 1 child, Clay Byron. BA in Journalism, Calif. State U., Fresno, 1959. Copywriter Fresno Bee newspaper, 1959-61; pub. relations staff asst. Pacific Telephone Co., Van Nuys, Calif., 1963-65; dir. info. Calif. Soc. CPA's, Palo Alto, 1965-70; mgr. corp. and div. pub. relations Kaiser Aluminum and Chems., Oakland, Calif., 1970-73, corp. dir. pub. relations and advt., 1974-83, dir. pub. relations and advt., 1975-83; mgr. pub. relations The Clorox Co., Oakland, 1973-74; v.p. corp. communications Varian Assocs. Inc., Palo Alto, 1983—; Chmn. alumni journalism adv. bd. Calif. State U., Fresno, 1981—; mem. pub. relations adv. bd. Golden Gate U., San Francisco, 1985—. Served with U.S. Army, 1961-63. Recipient Nicholson award Nat. Assn. Investors Clubs, 1980, 1981. Mem. Pub. Relations Soc. Am. (Silver Anvil award 1974, 77), San Francisco Pub. Relations Roundtable, San Francisco Publicity Club, Pub. Relations Seminar.

SIMPSON, HOWARD DOUGLAS, research scientist; b. Carrizozo, N.Mex., May 30, 1937; s. Howard Claiborn and Edna Evelyn (Justiss) S.; m. Dianne Kennedy, Sept. 2, 1967; 1 child, Stephen. BS, U. N.Mex., 1959; MS, U. Tex., 1965, PhD, 1969. Research asst. U. Tex., Austin, 1969-71; research engr. Unocal Corp., Brea, Calif., 1971-76, sr. research engr., 1976-81, research assoc., 1981-85, sr. research assoc., 1985—. Contbr. tech. articles to profl. jours.; patentee in field. Served with U.S. Army, 1960-62. Mem. Am. Chem. Soc., Am. Crystallographic Assn., Calif. Catalysis Soc. (sec., treas. 1976-77, program chmn. 1978-79, pres. 1979-80), Sigma Xi. Democrat. Methodist. Avocations: music, hiking, reading. Office: Unocal 376 S Valencia Blvd Brea CA 92621

SIMPSON, HOWARD EDWIN, JR., geologist, consultant; b. Grand Forks, N.D., June 27, 1917; s. Howard Edwin Sr. and Carrie Esther (Bonebrake) S.; m. Elizabeth Jane Taylor, Apr. 10, 1986; children: Anne, Paul, Elizabeth, Laurel. BA in Geology with honors, U. N.D., 1940; MS in Geology, U. Ill., 1942; PhD in Geology with honors, Yale U., 1953. Registered profl. engr., Colo. Geologist U.S. Geol. Survey, Denver, 1947-81; cons. Golden, Colo., 1981—. Author: Geology of the Yankton Area, South Dakota and Nebraska, 1953. Served to lt. USNR, 1942-46, PTO. Fellow Geol. Soc. Am.; mem. Assn. Engring. Geologists, Am. Inst. Profl. Geologists. Methodist. Home and Office: 2020 Washington Ave Golden CO 80401

SIMPSON, JODI ANN, electronics educator; b. Pasadena, Calif., Oct. 7, 1957; d. John Gordon and Cynthia Ann (Fairbairn) S.; m. Lee Randolph Cox, June 21, 1980; 1 child, Perrin Elizabeth. BA in Biology, U. Calif., Santa Barbara, 1979, MS in Sci. Instrumentation Physics, 1982. Software engr. Delco Electronics, Santa Barbara, 1982-83; asst. prof. electronics Santa Barbara City Coll., 1982—, chmn. electronics dept., 1985—; cons. Vetronix Corp., Santa Barbara, 1986—. Co-author: ABE: A Basic Examination of Microcomputer Architecture, 1985. Recipient Outstanding Contbn. to Career and Vocat. Edn. award Santa Barbara Industry Edn. Council, 1985. Democrat. Avocations: bicycle touring, skiing, guitar. Home: 1715 Calle Boca del Canon Santa Barbara CA 93101 Office: Santa Barbara City Coll Dept of Electronics 721 Cliff Dr Santa Barbara CA 93109

SIMPSON, JOHN BARCLAY, psychology educator; b. Oakland, Calif., June 8, 1947; s. Barclay and Joan (Devine) S.; m. Diane C. Pine, Dec. 23, 1967; children: Matthew, Melissa. BA, U. Calif., Santa Barbar, 1969; MA, Northwestern U., 1972, PhD, 1973. Research assoc. U. Pa., Phila., 1973-75; from asst. prof. to prof. psychology U. Wash., Seattle, 1975—, prof., dir. physiology-psychology program, 1984—; vis. researcher U. Calif., San Francisco, 1976-80; vis. prof. Howard Florey Inst. U. Melbourne, Australia, 1983. Contbr. articles to profl. jours. Grantee NIH, 1974—. Mem. Soc. for Neurosci. Club: Mountaineers (Seattle). Avocations: mountaineering, skiing, sailing. Home: 1422 E Roy Seattle WA 98112 Office: U Wash Dept Psychology NI-25 Seattle WA 98195

SIMPSON, ROBERT EMMETT, JR., clinical social worker; b. Bristol, Conn., Mar. 23, 1947; s. Robert Emmett and Helen Virginia (Burckess) S.; m. Genevieve Elizabeth Chandler, Aug. 2, 1975; children: Conor Chandler, Maura Moran, Michael Emmett. BA in Russian, Amherst Coll.; MSW, Simmons Coll.; MPH, Harvard U., Boston; DSW, U. Utah. Asst. dean admissions Amherst (Mass.) Coll., 1969-70; clin. instr. Simmons Coll., Boston, 1975-78; mem. adminstrv. staff Trinity Mental Health Ctr., Framingham, Mass., 1975-78; v.p. med. services, sec., treas. CompHealth, Salt Lake City, 1979-81; exec. dir. Salt Lake (City) Child and Family Therapy Clinic, 1981-86; adj. asst. prof. U. Utah Grad. Sch. Social Work, Salt Lake City, 1982—; with Simpson and Klein Psychotherapy Assocs. of Western Inst. for Neuropsychiatry, Salt Lake City, 1986—. Mem. peer rev. com. Social Work Bd. Examiners, Salt Lake City, 1982-86. Marriner S. Eccles scholar U. Utah, 1982, Shirley Wisenfeld scholar Simmons Coll., 1975, John Simpson scholar Amherst Coll., 1969. Mem. Nat. Assn. Social Workers, Acad. Cert. Social Workers, Nat. Register Clin. Social Workers. Roman Catholic. Avocations: skiing, jogging, piano. Home: 1080 3d Ave Salt Lake City UT 84103 Office: care Western Inst Neuropsychiatry 501 Chipeta Way Salt Lake City UT 84108

SIMPSON, ROBERT GENE, entomology educator, researcher; b. Neodesha, Kans., Aug. 13, 1925; s. Sidney Edward Simpson and Ida Leona (Rufenacht) Todd; m. Annabelle Louise Walek, June 16, 1951; children—Diane Risheill, Kay, Carolyn. B.S. in Zoology, Colo. State U., 1950, M.S. in Entomology, 1952; Ph.D. in Entomology, 1959. Tech. rep. sales Chevron Corp., Grand Junction, Colo., 1952-53; entomologist III, Colo. Dept. Agr., Denver, 1953-56, agr. adv. bd., 1984—; entomologist-extension U.Nebr., Lincoln, 1959-60; prof. entomology Colo. State U., Ft. Collins, 1960—; cons. Analytical Devel. Corp., Ft. Collins, 1976-78. Served with USN, 1943-46. Grantee NSF, 1975, U.S. Dept. Agr.-SEA Adminstrn., 1976-79. Mem. Entomol. Soc. Am. (nat. program chmn. 1979), Lepidopterist Soc., Xerces Soc., Sigma Xi, Gamma Sigma Delta (pres. chpt. 1969-70), Republican. Presbyterian. Lodge: Kiwanis (Ft. Collins). Home: 1317 Lory St Fort Collins CO 80524 Office: Colo State U Dept Entomology Fort Collins CO 80523

SIMPSON, WARREN CANDLER, chemical engineer; b. Gainesville, Tex., Sept. 9, 1919; s. Claude Mitchell and Sarah (Burks) S.; m. Barbara Stocton, June 17, 1946 (div. Sept. 1950); children: Michael, Martha; m. Mary Whitman, Jan. 18, 1952 (div. May 1962); 1 child, Carol; m. Frieda Klein, Nov. 22, 1964; 1 child, Jan. BA, Rice U., 1941, MA, 1943, PhD, 1944. Seismic exploration scientist Texaco Devel. Co., Ruston, La., 1941; core evaluation scientist Humble Oil Co., Houston, 1942; instr. refinery labs. U. Tex., Houston, 1943; teaching fellow Rice U., Houston, 1941-44; supr. research Shell Devel. Co., Everyville, Calif., 1944-73; chem. cons. various oil cos., U.S., Europe, Asia, 1973—; vis. technologist Shell Devel. Co., 1952. Contbr. articles to profl. jours.; patentee in field. Eastman Kodak fellow, Rice U., 1943. Fellow Am. Inst. Chemists; mem. Am. Chem. Soc., Nat. Assn. Corrosion Engrs., Indonesia Engring. Soc. (hon.), Sigma Xi. Methodist. Avocations: woodworking, tennis, sailing, skiing. Home: 1324 Henry St Berkeley CA 94709 Office: Chem Cons PO Box 9134 Berkeley CA 94709

SIMPSON, WILLIAM ARTHUR, insurance company executive; b. Oakland, Calif., Feb. 2, 1939; s. Arthur Earl and Pauline (Mikalasic) S.; m. Nancy Ellen Simpson, Mar. 31, 1962; children—Sharon Elizabeth, Shelley Pauline. B.S., U. Calif.-Berkeley, 1961; postgrad. Exec. Mgmt. Program, Columbia U. C.L.U. Br. mgr. Occidental Life of Calif., Los Angeles, 1965-73, v.p. agys., 1976-79; v.p. mktg. Countrywide Life, Los Angeles, 1973-76; pres., chief exec. officer Vol. State Life, Chattanooga, Tenn., 1979-83; exec. v.p. Transam. Occidental Life Ins. Co., Los Angeles, 1983-86, pres., 1986—, also dir.; dir Am. Nat. Bank., Chattanooga. Pres. Chattanooga council Boy Scouts Am., 1982, bd. dirs., Los Angeles, 1983, v.p., 1983-85; bd. dirs. United Way, Chattanooga, 1982, Chattanooga Symphony, 1982. Served to 1st lt. U.S. Army, 1961-64. Mem. Am. Soc. C.L.U.s, Life Ins. Mktg. Research Assn. (bd. dirs. 1986—). Republican. Presbyterian. Lodge: Rotary. Avocations: golf; skiing. Office: Transam Occidental Life Ins Co 1150 S Olive St Los Angeles CA 90015

SIMPSON, WILLIAM BRAND, economist, educator; b. Portland, Oreg., Nov. 30, 1919; s. John Alexander and Janet Christie (Brand) S.; m. Ruth Laura Decker, June 12, 1957. B.A., Reed Coll., 1942; M.A. in Stats., Columbia U., 1943; Ph.D. in Econs., Claremont Grad. Sch., 1971. Exec. dir. Cowles Commn. Research Econs., Chgo., 1948-53; co-founder, bd. dirs. Inst. Social and Personal Relations, Oakland, Calif., 1955-61; prof. econs. Calif. State U., Los Angeles, 1958—; econs. cons. higher edn. Served with CIC, U.S. Army, 1943-46. Fellow Nat. Social Sci. Research Council; mem. ACLU; Econometric Soc. (internat. sec. 1948-52); AAUP (state pres. 1975-76), nat. council 1978-81, com. govt. relations 1982—), Am. Econs. Assn., Am. Assn. Higher Edn., Western Econ. Assn., Congress Faculty Assns., United Scottish Socs. So. Calif., Sierra Club (Los Angeles chpt.), Phi Beta Kappa. Democrat. Unitarian. Mng. editor, co-editor, Econometrica, 1948-53; contbr. articles to profl. jours. Home: PO Box 1456 South Pasadena CA 91030 Office: Calif State U Los Angeles CA 90032

SIMS, JACK ROBERT, utilities company executive; b. New Orleans; s. Jack Robert and Martha Edith (Davidson) S.; m. Linette Marie Ignots, Feb. 13, 1982; 1 child, Matthew. BS in Biology, Marine Biology, Troy (Ala.) State U., 1975. Environ. control technician Great So. Paper, Cedar Springs, Ga., 1975-80; sr. health physics technician Ala. Power Co., Ashford, 1980-83; emergengy preparedness engr. Ariz. Pub. Light Service, Phoenix, 1983-85; emergency preparedness coordinator Houston Light & Power, Bay City, Tex., 1985—. Named one of Outstanding Young Men Am., 1983. Mem. Am. Soc. Safety Engrs., Am. Nuclear Soc. (chmn. Ariz. sect. 1985), Health Physics Soc. Baptist. Avocation: salt water fishing.

SIMS, JOEL KEVIN, physician, marine toxicologist; b. Shelbyville, Tenn., Aug. 20, 1947; s. John Green III and Mary Georgina (Allen) S.; m. Charlene Mary Maii, Sept. 25, 1976; children—Summer Kaleimakalii Kilika'a, Sarah Clark Lokewaikahuli. B.A., U. So. Fla., 1969; M.D., U. Calif.-San Diego, 1973. Neuroscis. tng. grantee U. Calif.-San Diego, 1970; tng. coordinator, research, devel. and tng. specialist Hawaii Med. Assn. Emergency Med. Services, Honolulu, 1974-79; chief emergency med. services Hawaii Dept. Health, Honolulu, 1980-85; emergency health mobilization physician, 1986—. Author: Advanced Trauma Life Support, 1977. Contbr. articles to profl. jours. Chmn. Hawaii Mil. Assistance to Safety and Traffic Coordinating Com., 1982-83. NSF grantee, 1966; Leahi grantee Am. Lung Assn. Hawaii, 1980. Mem. Am. Physicians Poetry Assn., Am. Coll. Emergency Physicians (pres. Hawaii chpt. 1976), Hawaii Med. Assn. (cons. emergency med. services program 1979-80), AMA. Democrat. Mem. Pentecostal Ch. Home: 2472 Waiomao Rd Honolulu HI 96816 Office: Emergency Med Services Systems Br Hawaii Dept Health P O Box 3378 Honolulu HI 96801

SIMS, MARK LANDON, commercial pilot, aircraft mechanic, police officer; b. Glendale, Calif., June 12, 1952; s. Fred Landon and Naida Jean (Wirth) S.; m. Kathy Lynn Naifeh, June 3, 1979. Student U.S. Army UH-1 Helicopter Mechanic and Door Gunner Sch., 1970, Los Angeles Valley Coll., 1973-74, U.S. Air Force Air Traffic Controller Sch., 1975, Cessna Tng., 1978, Sawyer Sch. Aviation, 1978-79; A.A., Glendale Community Coll., 1976; comml./instrument/multi-engine airplane cert. Airline Ground Sch., 1980. Comml. pilot, aircraft mechanic Monument Valley Air Service, Navaho and Apache Indian Reservation, Ariz., 1979-80; police officer Globe (Ariz.) Police Dept. Res., 1980—; comml. pilot, helicopter and aircraft mechanic NHF Ltd., Houston, 1981—, pilot/mechanic, Malargúe, Argentina, 1981—; geophys. survey pilot Aero Service, comml. aviation co., 1981-83; sky diver, 1972-80; dir. ops. Air Ambulance; search pilot CAP, 1980—. Mem. Republican Nat. Com.; mem. Rep. Presdl. Task Force; mem. U.S. Senatorial Club. Served with U.S. Army, 1969-72, USAF, 1975-77. Decorated Air medal; recipient Don Flower Aviation Safety award World-Wide-Ins., 1979, Presdl. Achievement award; col. Confederate Air Force. Mem. Aircraft Owners and Pilots Assn. (charter mem. Ultralight div.), Nat. Rifle Assn., Cactus Combat League, Air Force Assn. Home: PO Box 856 Litchfield Park AZ 85340

SIMS, MICHAEL ARDEN, information systems specialist; b. Texarkana, Ark., Oct. 12, 1936; s. Arden Ousley Sims and Molly (Merle) Morris; m. Linda Lou Jantz, Aug. 29, 1958; children: Cathryne Lynne Mickels, Janine Renee Mead. BSc, Calif. State U., Los Angeles, 1968; MS, Calif. State U., Fresno, 1974. Sr. ops. analyst Aerojet-Gen. Corp., Azusa, Calif., 1964-68, mgr. adminstrn., 1968-69; adminstrv. analyst Valley Med. Ctr., Fresno, 1970-74; employment adminstr. City of Portland, Oreg., 1974-78; infor. systems mgr. Portland Police bur., 1978—. Home: 505 Roosevelt St Oregon City OR 97045 Office: Portland Police Bur 1111 SW 2d Ave Portland OR 97204

SIMS, WILLIAM ROBERT, broadcast executive; b. Globe, Ariz., Sept. 13, 1940; s. William Harlan and Edna Mae (Whitaker) S.; m. Linda Elizabeth Thomas, July 30, 1960; children: Cheryl Robin, Shannon Lynne. Student, U. N.Mex. Cert. radio mktg. cons. V.p., gen. mgr. Modcom Corp., Casper, Wyo., 1962-69; pres., chief exec. officer Wycom Corp., Laramie, Wyo., 1969-81; chmn., chief exec. officer Classic Media, Inc., Santa Fe, 1981—. Nat. bd. dirs. Jaycees, Tulsa, 1969; pres. Laramie C. of C., 1974. Named one of Outstanding Young Men of Am., 1973, Outstanding Grad. Albuquerque High Sch., 1979, Jaycees Internat. Sen., 1976; recipient Disting. Service award U. Wyo., 1986. Mem. Radio Advt. Bur., Nat. Broadcasters Assn. (bd. dirs. 1976-80, pres. Wyo. chpt. 1972, pres. Rocky Mountain chpt. 1974). Avocation: skiing. Office: Classic Media Inc 121 Sandoval Santa Fe NM 87501

SINBERG, ULO LEMBIT, record company executive; b. Tallinn, Estonia, Feb. 28, 1931; s. Toomas and Maria (Orgo) S.; came to U.S., 1949; B.A. summa cum laude, Yale, 1955; m. Dorothy Garland, Sept. 22, 1978. With Transogram Co., Inc., N.Y.C., 1956-71, dir. distbn. and customer relations, sec. toy and game div., 1969-71; dir. prodn. control MCA Records, Inc., Universal City, Calif., 1971-79, dir. mfg. services, 1979—. Treas., bd. dirs. Estonian Students Fund in U.S.A., Inc., 1968—. Home: 18545 Clark St Tarzana CA 91356 Office: 70 Universal City Plaza Universal City CA 91608

SINCLAIR, JOHN STEPHEN, audiologist, educator; b. Pasadena, Calif., Dec. 1, 1947; s. Gilbert Emerson and Clara Mae (Strubinger) S.; m. Joan Michele Mahon, Dec. 29, 1972; children: Betsy, Laura, Andrew. AB, U. Redlands, 1969, MS, 1974; PhD, Vanderbilt U., 1980. Prof. audiology Calif. State U., Northridge, 1980—; forensic audiologist Associated Specialists in Hearing, Los Angeles, 1983—; assoc. dir. audiology St. Joseph's Med. Ctr., Burbank, Calif., 1985—; co-investigator Use of Hearing Aids in Schs., Siemens Corp., 1978, Auditory Trainers in Schs., U.S. Office of Edn., 1979, multi-channel cochlear implant, Humana Hosp.-West Hills, 1985; prin. investigator Auditory Trainers, U.S. Office of Edn., 1979; mem. instnl. rev. com. Humana Hosp.-West Hills, Canoga Park, Calif., 1985—. Co-editor: Amplification in Education, 1981; contbr. articles to profl. jours. Served to capt. U.S. Army, 1974-76, major Res. Mem. Am. Nat. Standards Inst. (chmn. working group auditory trainers 1981—), Am. Speech and Hearing Assn., Acoustical Soc. Am., Mil. Audiology and Speech Pathology Soc., Calif. Speech and Hearing Assn., Soc. Preservation of Variety Arts. Republican. Mem. Christian Ch. Club: Magic Castle (Hollywood, Calif.). Avocations: magic, racquetball, reading. Office: Calif State U Dept Communicative Disorders Northridge CA 91330

SINCLAIR, THOMAS LOWRY, JR., naval architect; b. Yangchow, China, Feb. 24, 1914; s. Thomas Lowry and Lucy Nelson (Rust) S.; came to U.S., 1919; m. Celina Tio, Nov. 11, 1949; children—Evelyn, Lark, Mary, Lucy, Michael. Student Va. Episcopal Sch., 1932; B.A., Trinity Coll. Conn., 1936; M.A., Harvard U., 1947. Registered naval architect. Commd. ensign U.S. Navy, 1942, advanced through grades to comdr., 1958; ret., 1968; Asst. sect. chief VA, Manila, 1947-49; pres. mgr. Philippine Fleet Industries, Inc., Manila, 1950-52, 55-59; maritime adviser Chinese Navy, Taipei, Taiwan, 1953-54; sr. ptnr. SEABEE Assocs., Manila, 1960-62; ptnr. Ships Unltd., Honolu, 1967-78; sr. ptnr. Sinclair & Assocs., Inc., Honolulu, 1976—. Contbr. articles to profl. jours. Decorated Silver Star, Bronze Star (2). Mem. Soc. Small Craft Designers (area chmn. 1965-84), Soc. Naval Architects and Marine Engrs. (sect. chmn. 1980-82), Am. Boat and Yacht Council, Psi U. Republican. Episcopalian. Home: 1443 Ahuawa Loop Honolulu HI 96816

SINCLAIR, WILLIAM DONALD, ch. ofcl.; b. Los Angeles, Dec. 27, 1924; s. Arthur Livingston and Lillian May (Holt) S.; B.A. cum laude, St. Martin's Coll., Olympia, Wash., 1975; postgrad. Emory U., 1978-79; m. Barbara Jean Hughes, Aug. 9, 1952; children—Paul Scott, Victoria Sharon. Commd. 2d lt. USAAF, 1944, advanced through grades to col., USAF, 1970; service in Italy, Korea, Vietnam and Japan; ret., 1975; bus. adminstr. First United Methodist Ch., Colorado Springs, Colo., 1976-85; bus. adminstr. Village Seven Presbyn. Ch., 1985-87; bus. adminstr. Sunrise United Meth. Ch., 1987—; vice-chmn. council fin. and adminstrn. Rocky Mountain conf. United Meth. Ch., U.S.A., 1979-83. Bd. dirs. Chins-Up Colorado Springs, 1983—, Pikes Peak Performing Arts Ctr., 1985—, Pioneers Mus. Foundn., 1985—. Decorated Legion of Merit with oak leaf cluster, D.F.C. with oak leaf cluster, Air medal with 6 oak leaf cluster, Dept. Def. Meritorious Service medal. Fellow Nat. Assn. Ch. Bus. Adminstrs. (nat. dir., regional v.p., v.p. 1983-85, pres. 1985—; Ch. Bus. Adminstr. of Yr. award 1983), Colo. Assn. Ch. Bus. Adminstrs. (past pres.), United Meth. Assn. Ch. Bus. Adminstrs. (nat. sec. 1978-81), Christian Ministries Mgmt. Assn. (dir. 1983-85), USAF Acad. Athletic Assn. Club: Colorado Springs Country. Lodge: Rotary (pres. Downtown Colorado Springs club 1985—). Home: 3007 Chelton Dr Colorado Springs CO 80909 Office: 420 N Nevada Ave Colorado Springs CO 80903

SINCOFF, STEVEN LAWRENCE, air force officer, laboratory chief; b. N.Y.C., Apr. 17, 1948; s. Murray B. and Lillian (Goldberg) S.; m. Constance Marie Onori, Jan. 17, 1970; children: Kristina Lynne, Carolyn Suzanne. BSChemE, N.J. Inst. Tech., 1969, MSChemE, 1972; PhD in Analytical Chemistry, Ohio State U., 1980. Commd. 2d lt. USAF, 1969, advanced through grades to lt. col., 1987; fuels mgmt. officer USAF, Albuquerque and Galena, Alaska, 1970-74; chem. engr. Aero. Systems Div., Wright-Patterson AFB, Ohio, 1974-77; assoc. prof. chemistry USAF Acad., Colorado Springs, Colo., 1980-84, dir. continuing edn. dept. chemistry, 1982-84; chief gas analysis lab. McClellan (AFB) Cen. Lab., Calif., 1984—; reviewer chemistry textbooks Saunders Pub., Phila., 1983-84. Mem. Am. Chem. Soc., Air Force Assn. Jewish. Avocations: microcomputers, sports, motorcycling. Home: 1863 Hidden View Ln Roseville CA 95661 Office: Tech Ops Div DLG McClellan AFB CA 95652

SINDT, FREDERICK REED, advertising and public relations executive; b. Omaha, Sept. 19, 1936; s. Arthur August and Ruth (Reed); m. Suzanne Haesler, Oct. 21, 1966; 1 child, Petra. Student, Iowa State U., 1957. Account exec. Pikes Peak Broadcasting, Colorado Springs, Colo., 1959-60; asst. pub. relations and advt. dir. The Broadmoor Co., Colorado Springs, Colo., 1960-64, dir. pub. relations and advt., 1964-77; pres., owner Sindt, Inc., Colorado Springs, Colo., 1977—. Pres. Pikes Peak Hillclimb, Colorado Springs, 1974-76, chmn. bd. dirs. Julie Penrose Ctr., Colorado Springs. Mem. Pub. Relations Soc. Am. (founder, pres. Colorado Springs chpt. 1971-73), Am. Assn. Advt. Agys., Am. Advt. Fedn., Internat. Assn. Bus. Communicators, Colo. Assn. Commerce and Industry, Ducks Unltd. (founder), Pikes Peak Advt. Club (founder). Republican. Clubs: Broadmoor, Garden of Gods. Avocations: shooting, hunting, fishing, running. Office: Sindt Inc 306 E Cucharras Colorado Springs CO 80903

SINES, RANDY DWAIN, business executive; b. Spokane, Jan. 16, 1948; s. Myron Jones and Paula Inez (Walls) S.; student Wash. State U., 1966-67, U. Wash., 1968-69; m. Irene Cheng, Mar. 18, 1981. With Boeing Co., 1967; with Winchell's Donut House, Inc. (merged with Denny's Restaurants), Seattle, 1968-71; owner, mgr. bakeries, Wash. and Mont., 1972-78; owner, mgr. Sonsine Inc., Great Falls, Mont., 1976-79; pres. Gardian Port Corp., Oxnard, Calif., 1980-82; pres., chmn. SNS Motor Imports, Inc., Oxnard, 1982—; chmn. Karakal Corp. of Ams., Ventura, Calif., 1984—; gen. mgr. Flasstar Internat., Oxnard. Recipient alumni grant Wash. State U., 1967; lic. water well contractor, Wash., Mont. Patentee sports game apparatus, over 20 patents worldwide. Home: 440 Las Palomas Dr Port Hueneme CA 93041 Office: 500 Esplanade Dr Suite 1000 Oxnard CA 93030 Office: PO Box 6414 Oxnard CA 93031

SING, SANDIE FONG, elementary school educator; b. Oakland, Calif., July 30, 1949; d. Fong Hin Sing and Yuet Sen (Lee) Fong. AA, Modesto Jr. Coll., 1969; BA, Calif. State U.-Stanislaus, Turlock, 1972. Cert. Calif. Elem. Tchr. (life). Jewelry cons. Macy's, Modesto, Calif., 1979-81; tchr. Turlock (Calif.) City Sch. Dist., 1973—. Historian Stanislaus Reading Council, 1985-87; 2d v.p. PTA, 1986-87; sch. improvement program rep., Julien SIP Program, 1985-86; mem. Turlock Sch. Dist.'s Fine Arts Curriculum Com.; art commr. Turlock City Arts Commn., 1984—. Classroom Tchr. Instructional Improvement Program grantee, Turlock Sch. Dist., 1985—. Mem. Calif. Tchrs. Assn., AAUW, Stanislaus Chinese Assn. Avocations: ethnic dancing, making art, aerobics. Office: Turlock Sch Dist Colorado and E Canal Turlock CA 95380

SINGER, DONALD A., geologist; b. Ukiah, Calif., May 11, 1943. BA, San Francisco State U., 1966; MS, Pa. State U., 1968, PhD, 1971. Instr. Pa. State U., 1968-71; system analyst Kennecott Copper Corp., Salt Lake City, 1971-73; geologist U.S. Geol. Survey, Menlo Park, Calif., 1973—. Author: (with others) Mineral Deposits Models, 1986; contbr. articles to profl. jours. Mem. Soc. Econ. Geologists, Am. Statis. Assn., Sigma Xi. Office: U S Geol Survey MS 984 345 Middlefield Rd Menlo Park CA 94025

SINGER, FREDERICK RAPHAEL, medical researcher, educator; b. St. Louis, June 27, 1939; s. Meyer and Lee (Minkle) S.; m. Sandra Joy Barnes, Aug. 16, 1964; children—Stefanie, Jeffrey. Student UCLA, 1956-59; B.S., U. Calif.-Berkeley, 1960; M.D., U. Calif.-San Francisco, 1963. Diplomate Am. Bd. Internal Medicine, Am. Bd. Endocrinology and Metabolism. Intern UCLA Affiliated Hosp., 1963-64; resident VA Hosp., Los Angeles, 1964-65, 68-69; instr. in medicine Harvard U., Boston, 1971-72; asst. prof. medicine UCLA, 1972-73; asst. prof. medicine U. So. Calif., Los Angeles, 1973-74, assoc. prof., 1974-78, prof., 1978—, prof. orthopaedic surgery, 1980—; mem. endocrine and metabolic drug adv. com. FDA, USPHS, Bethesda, Md., 1983-87. Author: Paget's Disease of Bone, 1977. Contbr. numerous articles, revs. to profl. jours. Vice chmn. community adv. com. Univ. High Sch., Los Angeles, 1984. Served as capt. USAF, 1965-67. Calif. State scholar, 1956-60; clin. investigator VA, 1971-73. Mem. Endocrine Soc., Am. Soc. Clin. Investigation, Am. Soc. Bone and Mineral Research (chmn. pub. affairs 1981-86, Council 1987). Office: U So Calif Sch Medicine 2025 Zonal Ave Los Angeles CA 90033

SINGER, GEORGE MILTON, clinical psychologist; b. Phila., Oct. 13, 1924; s. Benjamin and Bessie (Podlisker) S.; m. Carol Ann Horton, June 15, 1977; children: Elizabeth Carol, Susan Theresa, Sonnet Marie-Anne. BA, Temple U., 1950, AM, 1952, PhD, 1958. Chief psychologist Phila. State Hosp., 1953-56; dir. psychol. services Pennhurst State Hosp., Spring City, Pa., 1958-61; clin. psychologist Kern County Mental Health Dept., Bakersfield, Calif., 1961-68; project dir., coordinator Kernview Community Mental Health Ctr., Bakersfield, 1968-70; pvt. practice clin. psychology Bakersfield, 1953—; mem. affiliate Kernview med. staff health ctr. and hosp., Hoag Meml. Hosp., Newport Beach, Calif., 1972-73; cons. psychologist Pioneer Community Hosp., 1976-83. Mem. Kern County Mental Health Adv. Bd., 1976-83, adv. bd. Patton State Hosp., 1979-85; bd. dirs. Orange County Child Guidance Clinic, 1973-74. Served with USAAF, 1943-46, ETO, MTO. Recipient Service award Psi Chi, 1952, Cert. of Achievement Southeast Pa. Mental Health Assn., 1956. Mem. Am. Soc. Clin. Hypnosis, Calif. Soc. Clin. Hypnosis, So. Calif. Soc. Clin. Hypbosis, Kern County Soc. Clin. Psychologists (pres. 1984-85), Kern County Psychol. Assn. (pres. 1968-69), AAAS. Lodge: Rotary (chpt. pres. 1960-61). Home: 1805 Ridgewood Dr Bakersfield CA 93306 Office: 5301 Office Park Dr Suite 125 Bakersfield CA 93309

SINGER, JACK WOLFE, medicine educator; b. N.Y.C., Nov. 9, 1942; s. Leon Eugene and Sarah Betty (White) S.; m. Celestia S. Higano, Dec. 15, 1984; children: Constantine Jeremiah, Emily Savoye. BA, Columbia U., 1964; MD, SUNY, Bklyn., 1968. Diplomate Am. Bd. Internal Medicine, Am. Bd. Hematology, Am. Bd. Oncology. Intern then resident U. Chgo., 1968-70; fellow in hematology and oncology U. Wash., Seattle, 1972-75, asst. prof. medicine, 1975-78, assoc. prof., 1979-85, prof., 1986—; chief med. oncology VA Med. Ctr., Seattle, 1975—; asst. mem. Fred Hutchinson Cancer Ctr., Seattle, 1975—. Author: Cancer Care-A Personal Guide, 1979; contbr. articles to profl. jours. Served to lt. comdr. USPHS, 1970-72. Mem. Am. Soc. Hematology, Am. Soc. Clin. Oncology, Western Soc. Clin. Investigation, Internat. Soc. Exptl. Hematology, Physicians for Social Responsibility. Avocation: classical piano. Office: VA Med Ctr 1660 S Columbian Way Seattle WA 98108

SINGER, LESLEE DELAINE, military officer, educator; b. Houston, Dec. 19, 1952; s. Warren Charles and Irene (Patterson) S. BA in Biology, W. Conn. State Coll., 1976. Enlisted U.S. Army, 1976—; logistics officer U.S. Army, Waegon, Republic of Korea, 1981-82; asst. plans officer U.S. Army, Nellingen, Fed. Republic Germany, 1982-83; ops. officer U.S. Army, Ludwigsburg, Fed. Republic Germany, 1983; co. commdr. U.S. Army, Augsburg, Fed. Republic Germany, 1984; asst. prof. mil. sci. Idaho State U., Pocatello, 1985—; mem. faculty senate com. Idaho State U., 1985—. Mem. Assn. U.S. Army. Episcopalian. Home: 125 S Lincoln Pocatello ID 83204 Office: Idaho State U Dept Mil Sci PO Box 8150 Pocatello ID 83209

SINGER-SAM, JUDITH ANN, molecular biologist; b. N.Y.C., July 14, 1946; d. Herman and Lillian (Simchow) S.; m. Carlton Sam, Mar. 23, 1980; children: Michael, Carolyn. BS cum laude, CUNY, 1967; PhD, U. Calif., Santa Barbara, 1973. Postodoctoral fellow City of Home Nat. Med. Ctr., Duarte, Calif., 1972-75; research assoc. City of Hope Nat. Med. Ctr., Duarte, Calif., 1976-79; asst. research scientist City of Hope Research Inst., Duarte, Calif., 1979-85; assoc. research scientist Beckman Research Inst. City of Hope, Duarte, Calif., 1985—; sabbatical year at Pasteur Inst., Paris, 1981. Contbr. articles to profl. jours. Fellow NIH, 1968, 72, Nat. Cancer Inst., 1973; grantee Muscular Dystrophy Assn. Mem. AAAS, Phi Beta Kappa. Democrat. Office: City of Hope Beckman Research Inst 1450 E Duarte Rd Duarte CA 91010

SINGH, JOYCE HIDEKO, educator; b. Stockton, Calif., July 21, 1942; d. Ichiro and Mitsue (Nakai) Nakahara; BA, San Jose State Coll., 1965, MA, 1968; MA, San Jose State U., 1976; m. Gurnam Singh, Aug. 22, 1970. Substitute tchr. Alumn Rock Sch. Dist., San Jose, Calif., 1965; tchr. Northwood Elem. Sch., Berryessa Union Sch. Dist., San Jose, 1965—; summer sch. tchr. Mem. Soc. Baptist Conv., 1960-67; chmn., coordinator dist. kindergarten com., 1982-86; mem. report card and math. coms., early childhood gesell steering com., presch. caucus, sch. level. Sch. Improvement Program Council and Booster Club, scholarship com. Mem. Santa Clara County Service Ctr. Council, 1984-86; alt. rep. State Council Edn., 1984-87; chmn. fringe benefit com. Berryessa Coalition for Pub. Edn. and County Wide Coalition Pub. Edn.; mem. dist. election and constitution coms.; assembly rep. NEA, Washington, 1985; mem. Mt. Hamilton Council, 1985-86; co-contact coordinator legislature and Calif. Tchrs. Assn.; mem. PTA. Milpitas Metalcraft scholar, 1960; cert. kindergarten-primary tchr., cert. adminstr., Calif. Mem. Calif. Tchrs. Assn. (women's caucus, Asian-Am. caucus, sec. Berryessa chpt. 1983-84, v.p. 1984-85), NEA (Asian Pacific Islanders caucus), Asian Am. Edn. Assn. Assn. Supervision and Curriculum Devel.

SINGH, PARMJIT PAUL, mechanical engineer; b. Romford, Essex, England, July 17, 1959; came to U.S., 1969; s. Mandhir and Kulwant Kaur (Bhangu) S. BS in Aerospace Engring., Calif. State Poly. U., 1983. Scientist and physicist Aerojet Ordnance Co., Tustin, Calif., 1983-85; mech. engr. FMC Corp., San Jose, Calif., 1985—. Mem. AIAA, Am. Def. Preparedness Assn. Republican. Avocations: sports, traveling, reading, flying. Home: 24411 Anna St Hayward CA 94545

SINGH, PRITHIPAL, biotechnology company executive; b. Amritsar, India, Apr. 6, 1939; s. Inder and Sewa (Kaur) S.; m. Rajinder Kaur, Apr. 14, 1963; children: Satinder, Harpinder. BSc, Khalsa Coll., India, 1959; MSc, Benaras U., India, 1961; PhD, Toronto (Can.) U., 1967; postdoctoral, Southampton (Eng.) U., 1969-70. Asst. prof. Benaras Hindu U., India, 1968-69; sr. chemist Syva Research-Syntex, Palo Alto, Calif., 1970-73, group leader, 1973-74, research mgr., 1974-77, asst. dir., 1977-81, v.p., 1981-85; v.p. Idetek, Inc., San Bruno, Calif., 1985—. Contbr. articles to profl. jours.; patentee in field. Trustee Sikh Found.; founding mem. Sikh Temple, Fremont, Calif. Can. Commonwealth scholar, 1963-66. Fellow Chem. Soc. (London); mem. Am. Chem. Soc., Am. Assn. Clin. Chemists, Nat. Com. Clin. Lab. Standards (del.), Am. Soc. Microbiology. Avocation: photography. Office: Idetek Inc 1057 Sneath Ln San Bruno CA 94066

SINGLETON, HENRY EARL, industrialist; b. Haslet, Tex., Nov. 27, 1916; s. John Bartholomew and Victoria (Flores) S.; m. Caroline A. Wood, Nov. 30, 1942; children: Christina, John, William, James, Diana. S.B., S.M., Mass. Inst. Tech., 1940, Sc.D., 1950. Vice pres. Litton Industries, Inc., Beverly Hills, Calif., 1954-60; chief exec. officer Teledyne Inc., Los Angeles, 1960-86; chmn. Teledyne Inc., 1960—. Home: 384 Delfern Dr Los Angeles CA 90024 Office: Teledyne Inc 1901 Ave of the Stars Los Angeles CA 90067 *

SINGLETON, JAMES ROBERT, municipal building official; b. Mineral Wells, Tex., Dec. 21, 1931; s. Robert Floyd and Carrie Lou (Harvey) S.; student Tex. Tech. Coll., 1949-51; B.S.M.E., U. Wyo., 1963; m. Frances Earl Pruitt, June 6, 1953; children—Pamela Jane Singleton Stewart, Victoria Susan. Commd. 2d lt., U.S. Air Force, 1951, advanced through grades to maj., 1966; served as radar observer, pilot, instr. pilot, devel. engr., combat pilot, comdr. Wing Command Center, 1951-71, ret., 1971; civil engr. City of Tucson, 1971-72, plans examiner, 1972-78, bldg. safety adminstr., 1978—. Decorated D.F.C., Air medal with 6 oak leaf clusters, Air Force Commendation medal; cert. bldg. ofcl. Mem. Internat. Conf. Bldg. Ofcls. (past pres. Ariz. chpt., bd. dirs. Internat. Conf. Bldg. Ofcls. 1984—), ASME (past pres. So. Ariz. sect.), Soc. Am. Mil. Engrs. (past pres. Tucson post), Structural Engrs. Assn. Ariz., Air Force Inst. Tech. Assn. Grads., Air Force Assn. Democrat. Baptist. Research on concepts for recovery of radioactive debris using remotely controlled vehicles. Home: 8960 E Rosewood St Tucson AZ 85710 Office: PO Box 27110 Tucson AZ 85726

SINHA, ATIN KUMAR, aerospace engineer; b. Calcutta, India, Sept. 10, 1948; came to U.S., 1979; s. Gobinda Chandra and Sheela (Mitra) S.; m. Shukla Ghosh, May 13, 1975. BME with honors, Jadavpur U., Calcutta, 1970; MAeroE, Indian Inst. Sci., Bangalore, 1973; PhD in Aerospace Engring., U. Tenn., 1984. Engr. Indian Space Research Orgn., Trivandrum, 1973; scientist Nat. Aero. Lab., Bangalore, 1973-79; engr. Gates Learjet Corp., Wichita, Kans., 1984-85; sr. engr. Garrett Turbine Engine Co., Phoenix, 1985—. Contbr. articles to profl. jours. Mem. AIAA, Sigma Xi (assoc.). Avocations: photography, travel. Home: 915 W Diamond Dr Tempe AZ 85283 Office: Garrett Turbine Engine Co 111 S 34th St M/S 93-364 503-4T Phoenix AZ 85010

SINHA, YAGYA NAND, endocrinologist; b. Muzzaffarpur, India, Oct. 21, 1936; came to U.S., 1961; s. Baidyanath Prasad and Rajeshwari (Tiwari) S.; m. Savitri Sinha, May 28, 1958; children: Manjula, Anita, Suman, Arun. Grad., Bihar (India) Vet. Coll., 1957; MS, Mich. State U., 1964, PhD, 1967. Vet. asst. surgeon Bihar Govt., Patna, 1957-59; research asst. Livestock Research Sta., Patna, 1959-61; grad. asst. Mich. State U., East Lansing, 1962-67; research assoc. Cornell U., Ithaca, N.Y., 1967-69; asst. mem. II Scripps Clin. Research Found., La Jolla, Calif., 1969-81; sr. mem. Whittier Inst. for Diabetes and Endocrinology, La Jolla, 1982—, dir. lab. animal care, 1983—, radiation safety officer, 1982—. Contbr. articles to profl. jours. NIH grantee, Balt., 1976—. Mem. AAAS, Soc. Exptl. Biology and Medicine, The Endocrine Soc. Avocations: tennis, badminton, reading. Home: 8385 Aries Rd San Diego CA 92126 Office: Whittier Inst Diabetes Endocrinology 9894 Genesee Ave La Jolla CA 92037

SINNETT, DENNIS FORD, construction company executive; b. Elgin, Ill., June 27, 1942; s. Richard Charles and Helen (Ford) S.; m. Rosalie Austin, June 25, 1977; children: Dan, Jeff, John, Russ. Grad. high sch., Elgin. Carpenter Lamp Constrn. Co., Elgin, 1960-63; gen. supt. Reid Burton Constrn. Co., Ft. Collins, 1969-73; supt. Sinnett Builders, Elgin, 1963-69; prin. Sinnett Builders, Ft. Collins, Colo., 1973—; bd. dirs. 1st Interstate Bank of South Ft. Collins; advisor Indsl. Constrn. Mgmt. dept. Colo. State U., Ft. Collins, 1983—. Vice-chmn. City Builders Bd. Appeals, Ft. Collins, 1981—; mem. Poudre Valley Hosp. Found., Ft. Collins; co-chmn. fund raising com. Ft. Collins Inc., 1986; mem. Ft. Collins Police Res., 1970-77; active United Way (div. coordinator). Mem. Assoc. Builders and Contractors (bd. dirs. 1982-83, pres. 1983, trustee PAC com.), Ft. Collins C. of C. (co-chmn. econ. devel. fund raising com. 1983), Colo. State U. Rams Club. Republican. Methodist. Home: 813 Commodore Pl Fort Collins CO 80525 Office: Sinnett Builders Inc PO Box 1969 Fort Collins CO 80522

SINSHEIMER, ROBERT LOUIS, former educational administrator; b. Washington, Feb. 5, 1920; s. Allen S. and Rose (Davidson) S.; m. Flora Joan Hirsch, Aug. 8, 1943 (div. 1972); children: Lois June (Mrs. Wickstrom), Kathy Jean (Mrs. Vandagriff), Roger Allen; m. Kathleen Mae Reynolds, Sept. 10, 1972 (div. 1980); m. Karen Current, Aug. 1, 1981. S.B., MIT, 1941, M.S., 1942, Ph.D., 1948. Staff mem. radiation lab. MIT, Cambridge, 1942-46; assoc. prof. biophysics, physics dept. Iowa State Coll., Ames, 1949-55; prof. Iowa State Coll., 1955-57; prof. biophysics Calif. Inst. Tech., Pasadena, 1957-77; chmn. div. biology Calif. Inst. Tech., 1968-77; chancellor U. Calif., Santa Cruz, 1977-87. Editor: Jour. Molecular Biology, 1959-67, Ann. Rev. Biochemistry, 1966-72. Named Calif. Scientist of Year, 1968; recipient N.W. Beijerinck-Virologie medal Netherlands Acad. Sci., 1969. Fellow Am. Acad. Arts and Scis.; mem. Am. Soc. Biol. Chemists, Biophys. soc. (pres. 1970), AAAS, Nat. Acad. Scis. (mem. council 1970-73, chmn. bd. editors Proc. 1972-80), Inst. Medicine. Office: University House U Calif at Santa Cruz Santa Cruz CA 95064

SIRCUS, JAN MARTIN, videodisc producer/director, designer; b. Liverpool, Eng., Jan. 6, 1949; came to U.S., 1977; s. Wilfred and Mill-Louisa Katerina Sircus; m. Linda Margaret Cousens, Sept. 6, 1969; children: Jango, Sasha. BArch with honors, Liverpool U., 1972; MArch, UCLA, 1979. Registered architect, Calif. Asst. architect Josef Stöckli, Zug, Switzerland, 1972-73, Piano & Rogers, Paris, 1973-77; instr. design SCI-ARC, Santa Monica, Calif., 1978-83; lectr. design UCLA, 1980-81; v.p. programming and design ISIS/DeJoux, Los Angeles, 1980-83; dir. dialog design Interac, Los Angeles, 1983-86, v.p. interactive applications, 1986; supervising producer The Record Group, Burbank, Calif., 1986—; design cons. H.U.D.D.L.E., Los Angeles, 1980-81; vis. lectr. Sony Interactive Video Ctr., Los Angeles, 1986, UCLA Design Dept., 1985-86. Author: film script Henge, 1986; author/designer videodisc script The Case of the Definitely Dead Director, 1982, Diamond Hunt, 1983; editor teaching text Videoanimation, 1979; codesigner: (bank) Zuger KantonalBank, 1972 (1st prize), (sch.) Leuggern, Switzerland, 1973 (2d prize), (mus.) Center Pompidou, Paris, 1973-75, (acoustic music bldg) IRCAM, Paris, 1975-77, (videodisc program) Monsanto, 1985, (electronic jewelry) Artifax and Glow N Tell, 1985; designer/dir. (videodisc programs) First Nationwide Savs., 1986, Getty Greek Vases, 1986, Gen. Tire, 1986; (CD-I programs) Time Machine Europe, 1986-87, London Tales, 1987—. Robert Abraham scholar Liverpool U., 1970; recipient Charles Reilly medal Liverpool U., 1972, Dean's award Acad. Excellence, UCLA, 1979, Nebby award U. Nebr., 1986, Cindy award Assn. Visual Communicators, 1986; Welton Becket fellow UCLA, 1977-79. Mem. Am. Soc. Engrs. and Architects (bd. dirs. 1986), SIGRAPH, Internat. Interactive Communications Soc., Inst. Future Studies Sci., Sci-ARC. Avocations: photography, song and story writing, reading, sports.

SIRI, WILLIAM EMIL, physicist; b. Phila., Jan. 2, 1919; s. Emil Mark and Caroline (Schaedel) S.; m. Margaret Jean Brandenburg, Dec. 3, 1949; children: Margaret Lynn, Ann Kathryn. B.Sc., U. Chgo., 1942; postgrad. in physics, U. Calif.-Berkeley, 1947-50. Licensed profl. engr., Calif. Research engr. Baldwin-Lima-Hamilton Corp., 1943; physicist Manhattan Project Lawrence-Berkeley Lab., U. Calif. at Berkeley, 1943-45, prin. investigator biophysics and research, 1945-74; mgr. energy analysis program Lawrence Berkeley Lab., 1974-81; sr. scientist emeritus Lawrence-Berkeley Lab., 1981—; exec. v.p. Am. Mt. Everest Expdn., Inc.; Field leader U. Calif. Peruvian Expdns., 1950-52; leader Calif. Himalayan Expdn., 1954; field leader Internat. Physiol. Expdn. to Antarctica, 1957; dep. leader Am. Mt. Everest Expdn., 1963. Author: Nuclear Radiations and Isotopic Tracers, 1949, papers on energy systems analyses, biophys. research, conservation and mountaineering. Pres. Save San Francisco Bay Assn., 1968—; Bd. dirs. Sierra Club Found., 1964-78. Served to lt. (j.g.) USNR, 1950-59. Corecipient Hubbard medal Nat. Geog. Soc., 1963, Elisa Kent Kane medal Phila. Geog. Soc., 1963, Sol Feinstone Environmental award, 1977. Mem. Am. Phys. Soc., Biophys. Soc., Am. Assn. Physicists in Medicine, Sigma Xi. Democrat. Lutheran. Clubs: Sierra (dir. 1955-74, pres. 1964-66, William Colby award 1975), American Alpine (v.p.), Explorers (certificate of merit 1964). Home: 1015 Leneve Pl El Cerrito CA 94530 Office: U Calif Lawrence Berkeley Lab Cyclotron Rd Berkeley CA 94720

SIRIGNANO, WILLIAM ALFONSO, aerospace and mechanical scientist; b. Bronx, N.Y., Apr. 14, 1938; s. Anthony P. and Lucy (Caruso) S.; m. Molly Van Leeuwen, Oct. 29, 1966 (div. 1975); 1 dau., Monica Ann; m. Lynn Haisfield, Nov. 26, 1977; 1 dau., Jacqueline Hope. B.Aero.Engring., Rensselaer Poly. Inst., 1959; Ph.D., Princeton U., 1964. Mem. research staff Guggenheim Labs., aerospace, mech. scis. dept. Princeton U., 1964-67, asst. prof. aerospace and mech. scis., 1967-69, assoc. prof., 1969-73, prof., 1973-79, dept. dir. grad. studies, 1974-78; George Tallman Ladd prof., head dept. mech. engring. Carnegie-Mellon U., 1979-85; dean Sch. Engring., U. Calif.-Irvine, 1985—; cons. industry and govt., 1966—; mem. emissions control panel Nat. Acad. Scis., 1971-73; lectr. and cons. NATO adv. group on aero. research and devel., 1967, 75, 80; chmn. nat. and internat. tech. confs.; chmn. acad. adv. council Indsl. Research Inst., 1985—; mem. space applications adv. com. NASA, 1985—. Assoc. editor: Combustion Sci. and Tech, 1969-70; tech. editor Jour. Heat Transfer, 1985—; contbr. articles to nat. and internat. profl. jours., also research monographs. United Aircraft research fellow, 1973-74. Mem. Combustion Inst. (treas. internat. orgn. and chmn. Eastern sect.), Soc. Indsl. Applied Math., AIAA, ASME. Home: 3 Gibbs Ct Irvine CA 92715 Office: Sch Engring U Calif Irvine CA 92717

SISK, CAROL LYNN, management consultant, educator; b. Los Angeles, July 8, 1949; d. Arthur and Charlotte Babara (Gordon) S.; A.A. in Sociology, Santa Monica Coll., 1969; B.A. in Behavioral Sci., San Jose State U., 1971, M.S. in Therapeutic Recreation, 1975; Ed.D in Leisure Studies and Educational Psychology, Temple U., 1979. Program coordinator San Lorenzo Valley Sch. Dist., Ben Lomond, Calif., 1975-76; research assoc. Am. Inst. Research, Palo Alto, Calif., 1980-81; instr. San Jose (Calif.) State U., U. Phoenix; pvt. practice mgmt. cons., San Jose, 1981-83; tng. devel. officer Bank of the West, San Jose, 1983-86; regional tng. dir. Imperial Corp., San Jose, 1986— . Bd. dirs. San Jose State U. Career Planning and Placement Ctr., 1984—, also adv. bd.; cons. Calif. Planners and Cons., 1986—; instr. San Jose State U. Contbr. articles to profl. jours.; reviewer HRD Rev. Bur. Edn. for Handicapped scholar, 1972-73; Rehab. Services Adminstrn. scholar, 1973-74; Temple U. scholar, 1976-79. Bd. dirs. Silicon Valley Charity Ball Com., 1986. Mem. Peninsula Profl. Women's Network, Women's Community Clinic, Am. Soc. Tng. Devel., Organizational Devel. Network, Edn. Research Assn., Assn. Supervision and Curriculum Devel, Women in Bus. of San Jose C. of C. (bd. dirs. 1981—). Office: Imperial Corp 3190 Stevens Creek Blvd San Jose CA 95117

SISK, CHARLES LANGFORD, lawyer; b. Ann Arbor, Mich., Jan. 27, 1945; s. Fred E. Sisk and Jean L. (Langford) Fussell; children: Michael, Brian, Jennifer; m. Terre L. Rushton, May 24, 1985. BA, U. Colo., 1967, JD, 1970. Ptnr. Hurth, Yeager & Sisk, Boulder, Colo., 1970—; Bd. dirs. Colo. Nat. Bank of East Boulder. Mem. Colo. Bar Assn., Boulder County Bar Assn., U. Colo. Alumni Assn. (pres. 1977-78). Republican. Avocations: football officiating, travel, reading. Home: 671 W Ash St Louisville CO 80027 Office: Hurth Yeager & Sisk 965 Arapahoe Ave PO Box 4585 Boulder CO 90306

SITEMAN, MICHAEL WYNN, realtor; b. Santa Monica, Calif., July 19, 1950; s. Irvin Lee and Edythe (Rouse) S.; m. Barbara Rayliss, Sept. 18, 1983; 1 stepchild, Tessa Christine Ruelas. BA, Calif. State U., Northridge, 1972, postgrad., 1974-75. Studio musician Los Angeles, 1974-78; prin. Broadcast Music Inc., Los Angeles, 1978-86; office leasing specialist Summit Realty, Los Angeles, 1986, Bailes & Assocs., Los Angeles, 1986—; cons. in field, 1984—; freelance photographer, 1985—. Republican. Jewish. Avocations: calligraphy, guitar.

SITES, KENNETH RONALD, electrical engineer, physicist; b. Waynesboro, Pa., July 7, 1939; s. Arthur Kenneth and Nellie Irene (Reid) S.; m. Sharon Ann Reynolds, Oct. 30, 1967 (div. Feb. 1973); children: Mitzi Kay, Dana Lee; m. Mary D. Mulkey, Mar. 19, 1973. BS in Physics and Engring., U. Nev., 1977. Lic. FCC. Electronics tech. EGG, Inc., Las Vegas, Nev., 1962-67, electronics engr., 1968-74; mgr. nuclear instrumentation div. Sci. Applications Internat. Corp., Las Vegas, 1975—. Contbr. tech. articles to profl. jours. Mem. Nat. Rep. Com., Washington, 1984-85, Rep. Presdl. Task Force, Washington, 1983—. Served with USAF, 1957-61. Recipient Midas Myth Quality award Sci. Applications Internat. Corp., 1976. Mem. IEEE, Instrument Soc. Am. (sr.), Soc. Photo-Optical Instrumentation Engrs., ASTM. Presbyterian. Home: 5353 Auburn Av Las Vegas NV 89108 Office: Sci Applications Internat Corp 3351 S Highland Dr Suite 206 Las Vegas NV 89109

SITRICK, MICHAEL STEVEN, communications executive; b. Davenport, Iowa, June 8, 1947; s. J. Herman and Marcia B. (Bofman) S.; m. Nancy Elaine Eiseman, July 1, 1969; children: Julie, Sheri, Alison. BS in Bus. Adminstrn. and Journalism, U. Md., 1969. Coordinator press services Western Electric, Chgo., 1969-70; asst. dir. program services City of Chgo., 1970-72; asst. v.p. Selz, Seabolt & Assocs., Chgo., 1972-74; dir. communications and pub. affairs, pres. Natadco, Ltd. subs. Nat. Can Corp., Chgo., 1974-81; dir. communications Wickes Cos., Inc., San Diego, 1981-82; v.p. communications Wickes Cos., Inc., Santa Monica, Calif., 1982-84, sr. v.p. communications, 1984—. Mem. Pub. Relations Soc. Am., Nat. Investor Relations Inst. Club: Ad of Los Angeles. Office: Wickes Cos Inc 3340 Ocean Park Blvd Santa Monica CA 90405

SITTENFELD, ITAMAR, auditor, consultant; b. Petah Tiqva, Israel, Jan. 13, 1937; came to U.S., 1953; s. Erwin and Yocheved (Gruenberg) S.; m. Anne-Marie A. Hauseux, June 24, 1963; 1 child, Eyal T. AAS, NYC Community Coll., 1961; BBA, Baruch Coll., 1969; MBA, Fordham U., 1979. Bus. analyst Blue Cross Blue Shield, N.Y.C., 1975-80; auditor Salt River Project, Phoenix, 1980—; prof. Western Internat. U., Phoenix, 1986—. Mem. EDP Auditors Assn. (treas. 1984, v.p. 1985). Avocations: flying, chess, classical music. Home: 5336 E Larkspur Dr Scottsdale AZ 85254 Office: SRP PO Box 52025 Phoenix AZ 85072-2025

SITTON, CARL VERNON, music educator, conductor, composer; b. Houston, May 17, 1928; s. Carl Vest and Gussie Iva (Pearce) S.; Mus.B., Tex. Wesleyan Coll., 1949; M.A., Mills Coll., 1951; postgrad. Columbia U., 1954-56, U. So. Calif., 1962-65. Instr. music San Francisco State U., 1960-62, Modesto Jr. Coll., Calif., 1964-68; prof. music, head choral and voice depts. Cañada Coll., Redwood City, Calif., 1968—; choral clinician Calif. Music Educators Assn., also others, 1964—, vocal clinician, 1967—; vocal clinician Greek Orthodox Ch., also others, 1967—, music dir. San Francisco Chamber

Dance Theater, 1978—; dir. Dance Action, Inc., San Francisco, 1969—; guest condr. Am. Choral Dirs. Assn. Nat. Conv., 1968, Calif. Music Edn. Conv., 1966, Calif. Music Educators, 1972/74, San Mateo Council Chs., 1983. Composer 15 choral works and 9 commnd. scores for dance and theatre. Mem. Am. Choral Dirs. Assn. (life mem.), Music Educators Nat. Conf., Nat. Assn. Tchrs. of Singing (pres. San Francisco chpt. 1970-72). Office: Cañada Coll 4200 Farm Hill Blvd Redwood City CA 94061

SITTON, MARYIANN, minister; b. Tex., Jan. 3. BA in Christian Edn., Cen. Bible Coll. Ordained to ministry Christian Ch. Pres., founder Shiloh Christian Ministries Inc., Hamilton, Mont., 1973—; host (TV show) Shiloh Christian Retreat. Office: Shiloh Christian Ministries NW 60 Bowman Rd Hamilton MT 59840

SJOQUIST, STEVEN EDGAR, software engineer; b. Seattle, Sept. 7, 1957; s. Bernard Edgar and Donna Joyce (Stowe) S.; m. Darla Ruth Jacobson, Mar. 29, 1980; children: Christina Marie; Nathan Timothy. BSEE, U. Wash., 1979. Electronic technician A.B. Electronic Systems, Seattle, 1974-79, design engr., 1979-80; software engr. John Fluke Mfg. Co. Inc., Everett, Wash., 1980-83, sr. software engr., 1983-86, chief software engr., 1986—; com. chmn. Shoreline Vocations Electronics Adv. Bd., Seattle, 1978—. Mem. Tau Beta Pi. Lutheran. Avocations: skiing, choral singing, wood working. Home: 4427 154th Pl SW Lynnwood WA 98037 Office: John Fluke Mfg Co Inc 6920 Seaway Blvd Everett WA 98203

SJOSTROM, REX WILLIAM, aerospace executive; b. Norcross, Minn., July 8, 1930; s. William Andrew and Ruth Francis (Cushman) S.; m. Joan Sevier, Mar. 16, 1952; children: Sandra L., Anne M., John W., Sharon M. BSCE, Colo. State U., 1952, MSEE, 1956. Registered profl. engr., Colo. Staff engr. Martin Marietta Corp., Denver, 1956-84, v.p. space systems div., 1984—; dir. engring. Dean's Adv. Bd., Colo. State U., Ft. Collins, 1983-86. Served as col. Colo. N.G., 1948-79. Recipient NASA Pub. Service award, 1976. Mem. IEEE, Sigma Xi. Republican. Lutheran. Avocations: photography, sailing. Home: 2072 W Wolfensberger Rd Castle Rock CO 80104 Office: Martin Marietta Corp MS 8044 Box 179 Denver CO 80201

SKABO, RONALD RICKS, corrosion engineer, consultant; b. Devils Lake, N.D., Dec. 9, 1934; s. Edwin Paul and Grace Minnie (Rice) S.; m. Verona Mae Quale, June 30, 1958; children: Randine Rae, Kari Lynn. BSChemE, Mont. State U., 1957. Registered profl. engr., Mich., Colo., corrosion engr., Calif. Gas engr. Signal Oil & Gas Co., Tioga, N.D., 1957-60; materials engr. Wyandotte (Mich.) Chems., 1960-64; corrosion engr. Hichman Co., Detroit, 1964-67; chief materials engr. BASF Wyandotte, 1967-73; staff corrosion engr. Stearns Catalytic Corp., Denver, 1973-87; lectr. Inst. Applied Tech., Washington, 1976—; cons. in field, Lakewood, Colo., 1982—. Mem. Nat. Assn. Corrosion Engrs. (cert.), Am. Soc. Testing and Materials, Steel Structures Painting Council. Republican. Presbyterian. Avocations: woodworking, camping, fishing, fly tying, singing. Home and Office: 1632 S Garland St Lakewood CO 80226

SKAGGS, DAVID E., congressman; b. Cin., Feb. 22, 1943; m. Laura Driscoll, Jan. 3, 1987; 1 child, Mathew. BA, Wesleyan U., 1964; LLB, Yale U., 1967. Bar: N.Y. 1968, Colo. 1971. Assoc. Newcomer and Douglass, Boulder, Colo., 1971-74, 77-78; staff asst. Congressman Tim Wirth, Washington, 1975-77; assoc. Skaggs, Stone & Sheehy, Boulder, 1978-86; mem. U.S. Ho. of Reps., Washington, 1987—; mem. Colo. Ho. of Reps., Denver, 1980-86, minority leader 1982-85. Served with USMC, 1968-71, to maj. with res. Mem. N.Y. Bar Assn., Colo. Bar Assn. Democrat. Congregationalist. Office: US House of Reps 1723 Longworth Bldg Washington DC 20515

SKAGGS, L. SAM, retail company executive; b. 1922; married. With Am. Stores Co., 1945—, chmn. bd., chief exec. officer, from 1966, formerly pres., now chmn. bd., chief exec. officer, dir.; chmn. Sav-On Drugs Inc., Anaheim, Calif. Served with USAAF, 1942-45. Office: Am Stores Inc PO Box 27447 Salt Lake City UT 84127 *

SKAGGS, SAMUEL ROBERT, materials scientist, energy program manager; b. Philipsburg, Pa., June 23, 1936; s. Samuel Ralph and Martha Amelia (Montes) S.; m. Barbara Jan Hurley, Apr. 7, 1958; children: Russell, Cheryl, Michael, Teresa, Katherine. BSME, N.Mex. A&MA, 1958; MS in Nuclear Engring., U. N.Mex., Los Alamos, 1967; PhDChemE and Materials Sci., U. N.Mex., Albuquerque, 1972. Mech. engr. Argonne (Ill.) Nat. Lab., 1958-60; staff mem. Los Alamos (N.Mex.) Nat. Lab., 1960-61, 62-67, 71—, armor protective systems program mgr., 1986—, program mgr. materials and fossil energy, 1982-86; program mgr. U.S. Dept. Energy, Germantown, Md., 1981-82; cons. USAF, 1970-80. Author 24 tech. pubs. in high temperature ceramics. Field coordinator N.Mex. State Search and Rescue Operation, 1961-87, patrol leader and regional dir. Rocky Mountain div. Nat. Ski Patrol, 1978-84. Served to lt. U.S. Army 1961-62, capt. Res. Mem. Am. Ceramic Soc. (life), AAAS. Roman Catholic. Avocations: skiing, biking, hiking, sailing, ultralight flying. Home: Rt 11 Box 81E Santa Fe NM 87501 Office: Los Alamos Nat Lab PO Box 1663 E549 Los Alamos NM 87545

SKALAGARD, HANS MARTIN, artist; b. Skuo, Faroe Islands, Feb. 7, 1924; s. Ole Johannes and Hanna Elisa (Fredriksen) S.; came to U.S., 1942, naturalized, 1955; pupil Anton Otto Fisher, 1947; m. Mignon Diana Haack Haegland, Mar. 31, 1955; 1 dau., Karen Solveig Sikes. Joined U.S. Mcht. Marine, 1942, advanced through grades to chief mate, 1945, ret., 1965; owner, operator Skalagard Sq., Rigger Art Gallery, Carmel, 1966—; librarian Mayo Hays O'Donnel Library, Monterey, Calif., 1971-73; painter U.S. Naval Heritage series, 1973—; exhibited in numerous one-man shows including Palace Legion of Honor, San Francisco, 1960, J.F. Howland, 1963-65, Fairmont Hotel, San Francisco, 1963, Galerie de Tours, 1969, 72-73, Pebble Beach Gallery, 1968, Laguna Beach (Calif.) Gallery, 1969, Arden Gallery, Atlanta, 1970, Gilbert Gallery, San Francisco; group shows: Am. Artists, Eugene, Oreg., Robert Louis Stevenson Exhibit, Carmel Valley Gallery, Biarritz and Paris, France, David Findley Galleries, N.Y.C. and Faroe Island, Europe, numerous others; represented in permanent collections; Naval Post Grad. Sch. and Library, Allen Knight Maritime Mus., Salvation Army Bldg., Monterey, Calif., Robert Louis Stevenson Sch., Pebble Beach, Anenberg ARt Galleries, Chestlibrook Ltd.,; lectr. Bd. dirs. Allen Knight Maritime Mus., 1973—, mem. adv. and acquisition coms., 1973-77. Recipient Silver medal Tommaso Campanella Internat. Acad. Arts, Letters and Scis., Rome, 1970, Gold medal, 1972; Gold medal and hon. life membership Academia Italia dell Arti e del Honoro, 1980; Gold medal for artistic merit Academia d'Italia. Mem. Navy League (dir. Monterey), Internat. Platform Assn., Sons of Norway (cultural dir. 1974-75, 76-77). Subject of cover and article Palette Talk, 1980, Compass mag., 1980. Home: 25197 Canyon Dr Carmel CA 93923 Office: PO Box 6611 Carmel CA 93921 Also: Dolores at 5th St Carmel CA 93921

SKANNES, GEORGIA CAROL, public relations officer; b. Sitka, Alaska, May 20, 1950; d. George and Rose Mae (Daine) S.; divorced; children—Richard Dapcevich, Steven Dapcevich, Nicole Rhyner. Student U. Alaska, 1975. Traffic mgr. Sitka Broadcasting, 1977; title III/fed. relations staff Sheldon Jackson Coll., Sitka, 1977-78; ptnr. Huckleberry House, Sitka, 1978-79; communications coordinator S.E. Alaska Regional Arts Council, Inc., Sitka, 1979-80; pub. relations dir. Ketchikan (Alaska) Indian Corp., 1980-85; coordinator S.E. Alaska Village Assn. of Presidents, 1981-83; participant Alaska Native Leadership Project, 1982-83. Appointee, Sitka Community Action Group, Sitka Assembly, 1979; mem. Alaska State Pvt. Industry Council, 1984; mem. Ketchikan City Council, 1983-89, vice mayor, 1984-86; mem. legis. com. Alaska Mcpl. League, 1986—; mem. Southeastern Alaska Tourism Conf. Named Woman of Yr., Bus. and Profl. Women, 1979; recipient Broadcasting award Native Programming, 1984. Mem. Pub. Relations Soc. Am., Nat. Congress Am. Indians, Ketchikan Vis. Bur. Democrat. Home: 519 Buren Ketchikan AK 99901

SKARDA, RICHARD JOSEPH, social worker; b. Santa Monica, Calif., Jan. 2, 1952; s. Robert Ralph and Cathryn Marie (Tourek) S. AA, Los Angeles Valley Coll., Van Nuys, Calif., 1976; BA, U. Calif., Berkeley, 1978; MSW, UCLA, 1980. Lic. clin. social worker, Calif. Children's services worker Los Angeles County Dept. Children's Services, Panorama City, Calif., 1980-82; psychiatric social worker Penny Lane, Sepulveda, Calif., 1983; protective services social worker Ventura (Calif.) County Pub. Social Services Agy., 1983-85; head social work dept. Naval Med. Clinic, Port Hueneme, Calif., 1985—; part-time pvt. practice in clin. social work, Ventura, 1986—. Served with USN, 1970-74. Mem. Nat. Assn. Social Workers (cert.), Calif. Soc. Clin. Social Work, U. Calif. Alumni Assn., Fiero Owners Club Am. Democrat. Roman Catholic. Avocations: travelling, reading, films, aerobics, music. Home: 8179 Matilija Ave Panorama City CA 91402 Office: Naval Med Clinic 6630 Webster St Ventura CA 93003

SKEEN, JOSEPH RICHARD, congressman; b. Roswell, N.Mex., June 30, 1927; s. Thomas Dudley and Ilah (Adamson) S.; m. Mary Helen Jones, Nov. 17, 1945; children: Mary Elisa, Mikell Lee. B.S., Tex. A&M U., 1950. Soil and water engr. Ramah Navajo and Zuni Indians, 1951; rancher Lincoln County, N.Mex., 1952—; mem. N.Mex. Senate, 1960-70, 97th-100th Congresses from 2d N.Mex. Dist. Chmn. N.Mex. Republican Party, 1963-66. Served with USN, 1945-46; Served with USAFR, 1949-52. Mem. Nat. Woolgrowers Assn., Nat. Cattle Growers Assn., N.Mex. Woolgrowers Assn., N.Mex. Cattle Growers Assn., N.Mex. Farm and Livestock Bur. Republican. Roman Catholic. Clubs: Elks, Eagles. Office: 1007 Longworth House Office Bldg Washington DC 20515 *

SKEER, NICHOLAS DUGAN, electrical engineer; b. Albany, N.Y., Mar. 21, 1937; s. John Dugan and Helen (Nieman) S.; m. Jean Anne Fisher, Nov. 4, 1984; children: Timothy D., Thomas H. BSEE, Antioch U., 1960. Engr. Sanders Assocs., Nashua, N.H., 1960-72; engr., analyst ARINC Research, Annapolis, Md., 1972-80; mem. tech. staff Kaiser Electronics Corp., San Jose, Calif., 1980-81, mgr. engring., 1983—; mem. tech. staff Teledyne Electronics Corp., Newbury Park, Calif., 1982-83. Avocations: comml. pilot, computer programming. Home: 4653 Powderborn CT San Jose CA 95136 Office: Kaiser Electronics 2701 Orchard Pkwy San Jose CA 95134

SKEETER POSTMUS, JANE ALICE, glass artist, entrepeneur; b. Oakland, Calif., Apr. 7, 1950; d. Lloyd Arnold and Barbara Ellen (Ritz) Thacker; m. Paul Warren Skeeter Jr., Apr. 6, 1968 (div. Apr. 1972); one child, Lisa J. Skeeter; m. Barron Gilbert Postmus, July 8, 1977; stepchildren: Angelle, Lisa, Barron Jr. Student, Pierce Jr. Coll., 1971-73, Calif. State U., Northridge, 1974-75, UCLA, 1982. Dressmaker Jane Skeeter Designs, Northridge, 1968-72; designer Classic Porsche, Canoga Park, Calif., 1972-75; prin. Jane Skeeter Studios, Northridge, 1986—; instr. clothing design, crafts Calif. State U., Northridge, 1970-71, Los Angeles Pub. Schs., 1973-78, Moorpark (Calif.) Jr. Coll., 1975-78. Prin. works include decorative and archtl. glass for homes of Michael Jackson, Earvin "Magic" Johnson, and John Davidson. Democrat. Avocation: flower collecting and propagating. Home: 7251 Bernadine Ave Canoga Park CA 91307 Office: Jane Skeeter Studios 18623 Gresham St Northridge CA 91324

SKELLY, ALICIA KAREN, speech pathologist; b. Bklyn., Apr. 9, 1960; d. Francis Victor and Casimira (Bekarciak) Winski; m. Edward William Skelly, May 20, 1984. BS, Ithaca Coll., 1982; MS, Syracuse U., 1983. Cert. ednl. staff assoc., Wash. Speech pathologist Leeward Oahu Sch. Dist., Waipahu, Hawaii, 1984-85; communication disorders specialist Early Learning Services (formerly Epton Presch.), Pullman, Wash., 1985—; clin. instr. Wash. State U., Pullman, 1985—. Mem. Am. Speech Lang. and Hearing Assn. (cert.), Idaho State Speech and Hearing Assn. Roman Catholic. Home: 529 N Howard St Moscow ID 83843 Office: Early Learning Services 1325 Professional Mall Pullman WA 99163

SKENE, LAURENCE FARTHING, retired chemistry educator; b. Banks, Oreg., July 18, 1911; s. William and Mary (Hilts) S.; m. Rosa Mae Bateman, June 13, 1936; children: David Laurence, Louise Evelyn, Rosemary Skene Allen. Bs, Pacific U., 1933; MS, Oreg. State U., 1936. Prof. chemistry George Fox Coll., Newberg, Oreg., 1935-51, head dept. chemistry and natural sci., 1962-68; bldg. contractor Dundee, Oreg., 1951-82; fin. advisor Friends Cemetery, Newberg, 1980—. Pres. Am. Friends Service Com., Portland, 1940-65; supply officer UN Gaza (Palestine) unit, 1949. Mem. Am. Chem. Soc. Republican. Mem. Soc. Friends. Avocations: woodworking, burls and large clocks, farming. Home: 8595 NE Worden Hill Rd Dundee OR 97115 Office: Newberg Friends Ch 305 N College Newberg OR 97132

SKEWES-COX, BENNET, accountant, educator; b. Valparaiso, Chile, Dec. 12, 1918; came to U.S., 1919, naturalized, 1943; s. Vernon and Edith Page (Smith) S-C.; B.A., U. Calif., Berkeley, 1940; M.A., Georgetown U., 1947; B.B.A., Golden Gate Coll., 1953; m. Mary Osborne Craig, Aug. 31, 1946; children—Anita Page McCann, Pamela Skewes-Cox Anderson, Amy Osborne Skewes-Cox Twiss. Asst. to press officer Am. Embassy, Santiago, Chile, 1941-43; state exec. dir. United World Federalists of Calif., 1948-50; pvt. practice acctg., San Francisco, 1953—; asst. prof. internat. relations San Francisco State U., 1960-62; grad. researcher Stanford (Calif.) U., 1962-63, Georgetown U., Washington, 1963-65; pres. Acad. World Studies, San Francisco, 1969—; sec. Alpha Delta Phi Bldg. Co., San Francisco, 1957—; lectr. in field. Mem. Democratic state central com. Calif., 1958-60, fgn. policy chmn. Calif. Dem. Council, 1959-61, treas. Marin County Dem. Central Com., 1956-62; founder, 1st. chmn. Calif. Council for UN Univ., 1976—; compiler World Knowledge Bank; bd. dirs. Research on Abolition of War; treas. Marin Citizens for Energy Planning. Served as lt. (j.g.), USNR, 1943-46. Mem. Assn. for World Edn. (internat. council 1975—), Am. Soc. Internat. Law, Am. Polit. Sci. Assn., San Francisco Com. Fgn. Relations, Am. Acctg. Assn., Calif. State Univ. Profs., AAUP, Nat. Soc. Public Accts., Fedn. Am. Scientists, UN Assn., Internat. Polit. Sci. Assn. World Federalists Assn. (nat. bd. dirs.). Clubs: University, Commonwealth of Calif., Lagunitas Country. Author: The Manifold Meanings of Peace, 1964; The United Nations from League to Government, 1965; Peace, Truce or War, 1967. Home: Monte Alegre PO Box 1145 Ross CA 94957 Office: Acad World Studies 2820 Van Ess San Francisco CA 94109

SKIDMORE, DONALD EARL, retired manufacturing company executive; b. Tacoma, May 12, 1920; s. Jake and Roxa J. (Young) S.; m. Ingeborg Johnsrud, Feb. 20, 1943; children—Donald E., Marilyn Kay, Sharon Ann. Student Racine Western Inst., 1937-41, Knapp Coll., 1946-48. Bookkeeper, acct. Ace Furnace & Steel Co., Tacoma, 1938-44, acct., 1946-50; ptnr., acct. Central Steel & Tank Co., Yakima, Wash., 1950-58, sec.-treas., dir. 1958-60, v.p., dir., 1966-67, 79-83, pres., dir., 1967-78. Mem. Yakima County Manpower Adv. Com., 1966-73; chmn. Citizens' Adv. Com. Vocat.-Tech. Edn.; bd. dirs. Yakima Sch. Dist. 7, 1965; Mem. council Evangel. Coll., Springfield, Mo., 1960-83, v.p., 1972-75; dir. Yakima Valley Youth for Christ, 1961-64, pres., lay council N.W. Coll. Assemblies of God, Kirkland, Wash., 1965-68, 71-74, bd. dirs., 1972-74, 76-84; internat. dir. Full Gospel Bus. Men's Fellowship Internat., 1974—, chmn. fin. com., 1980-81. Served with U.S. Army, 1944-46. Mem. Sheet Metal and Air Conditioning Contractors Nat. Assn. (local labor advisor 1959-66), Wash. Soc. C.P.A.s. Republican. Lodge: Lions (v.p. 1970-71). Home: 3402 Roosevelt Ave Yakima WA 98902-1559

SKIDMORE, DONALD EARL, JR., government official; b. Tacoma, Apr. 27, 1944; s. Donald E. and Ingeborg (Johnsrud) S.; B.Sc., Evangel Coll., 1968. With Dept. Social and Health Services, State of Wash., Yakima, 1967-74; quality rev. specialist Social Security Adminstrn., Seattle, 1974-76, program analyst, Balt., 1976-79, Seattle, 1979-81, quality assurance officer, mgr. Satellite office, Spokane, Wash., 1981-84, program analyst, Seattle, 1984—. Pres., bd. dirs. Compton County Condo Assn., 1980-81; bd. trustees Norwood Village, 1987—; mem. citizen's adv. com. METRO, 1987—. Mem. Spokane Fed. Execs Assn. Office: 2901 3d Ave M/S 206 Seattle WA 98121

SKIDMORE, JOYCE THORUM, public relations/communications firm executive; b. Murray, Utah, Dec. 30, 1926; d. Rolla Arden and Alice Luetta (Fox) Thorum; m. E. Douglas Jacobsen, Mar. 20, 1956 (dec.); 1 son, Kelly Douglas Jacobsen; m. 2d, Clarence E. Skidmore, Aug. 9, 1969. B.S., U. Utah, 1950, postgrad., 1953-55; postgrad. U. So. Calif., 1964, U. Calif.-Irvine, 1973-74. Sales and promotion devel. JBL Internat., Los Angeles, 1959-69. Adminstrv. asst. world hdqrs. Toastmasters Internat., Santa Ana, Calif., 1973; adj. prof. communications Pepperdine U., 1974, developer human resources, Oran, Algeria, 1975; promotions coordinator Utah Bicentennial Project, Salt Lake City, 1976; editor Saga Weekly Post, and editor Children's Page, Stavanger and Bergen, Norway, 1976-78; press sec. Utah Auditor's Office, Salt Lake City, 1979-81; pres. Joyce Skidmore Cons./Snowflake Prodns., pub. relations, communications and devel. in arts, bus., edn. and govt., Sandy, Utah, 1980—; Utah dir. Nat. Health Screening Council for Vol. Orgns., 1982—; adj. prof. Westminster Coll., 1978-79, Brigham Young U., 1978-83; cons. pub. relations, health costs and tourism C. of C. of Salt Lake Area; adj. prof. mktg. and communications Colo. Mountain Coll., 1985-86; bus. cons. and prof. mktg. and communications Mountainwest Coll. Bus. and Brigham Young U., Salt Lake City; guest dir. Westminster Theatre, 1974; guest dir./writer Cablevision, Newport Beach, Calif., 1975. Author: Happy Holidays, 1968; assoc. editor Utah Symphony newsletter; newsletter editor Nat. Auditor's Assn., 1979-81, State Auditor's Assn., 1979-81, Utah Health Fairs, 1982-83; journalist The Butler Banner; contbr. weekly columns to The Rifle Telegram; contbr. articles to Calif., Norwegian and Utah newspapers; initiated use of old copper from Utah Capitol dome as collector's item, 1980. Organizer Stavanger Theatre Guild and Workshops, 1977, Bookcliffs Arts and Humanities Council, 1984-86; originated and organized Hurlburt Days, Grand Valley and Parachute, Colo.; initiated and directed Reader's Theatre, Community Christmas Fest. and old-time melodrama; mem. steering com. for first nat. competition Utah Playwriting Conf., Sundance, 1979-80; mem. local econ. devel. council.; also polit. dist. delegate, 1986. Dist. pres. LWV, 1976; initiated invitation from Bergen Internat. Festival to Utah Symphony, 1981; campaign mgr. Mayor Lake Valley City (Utah), 1982; cons. Cottonwood Heights (Utah) Council, 1982-83; cons. to Utah pres. Instrumentation Soc. Am.; missionary leader Ch. of Jesus Christ of Latter-day Saints. Recipient 2 Top Editor's awards Calif. Press Women, 1977, 4 writing awards 1977-78; Internat. Yr. of Child award Family Acad., San Francisco and Stavanger, 1979; Colo. Oscar award for Best Dir., 1986; nat. Zeta Phi Eta scholar, 1948; U. Utah fellow, 1953-55; So. Calif. Credit Assn. scholar, 1964. Mem. Pub. Relations soc. Am. (student adv. 1980-82), Utah Press Women (6 writing awards 1979-81; 3d v.p. 1981-82), Instrument Soc. Am., Friendship Force Utah, MMB Reading Arts Soc. (v.p. devel.) Avocations: historian, extensive genealogical research. Home and Office: 2629 Oak Creek Dr Sandy UT 84092

SKIENS, WILLIAM EUGENE, optical systems scientist, polymer engineer; b. Burns, Oreg., Feb. 21, 1928; s. William Poleman and Eugenia Glenn (Hibbard) S.; m. Vesta Lorraine Franz, Nov. 4, 1955; children: Rebecca, Beverly, Michael. Student, N.W. Nazarene Coll., 1946-48; BS in Chemistry, Oreg. State U., 1951; PhD in Phys. Chemistry, U. Wash., 1957. Chemist Dow Chem. Co., Pittsburg, Calif., 1951-53; research chemist Dow Chem. Co., Midland, Mich. and Walnut Creek, Calif., 1957-58, 1958-73, E.I Du-Pont de Nemours, Wilmington, Del., 1955; sr. research chemist Battelle Meml. Inst., Richland, Wash., 1973-84, also cons., 1984—; mgr. media system devel. Optical Data, Inc., Portland, Oreg., 1984—; cons. World Health Orgn., Geneva, 1978-85. Contbr. chpts. to books, articles to profl. jours.; patentee in field. Com. chmn. Concord, Calif. council Boy Scouts Am., 1969-72; sec. Tri-Cities Nuclear Council, Richland, Wash., 1984. Named Alumni of Yr. N.W. Nazarene Coll., 1982. Mem. Am. Chem. Soc. (chmn. Richland sect. 1982), Sigma Xi. Republican. Mem. Ch. Nazarene. Avocations: skiing, photography, backpacking, golf. Home: 7120 Arbor Lake Dr Wilsonville OR 97070 Office: Optical Data Inc 9400 SW Gemini Dr Beaverton OR 97005

SKIFF, RUSSELL ALTON, plastic company executive; b. Waterford, Pa., Feb. 26, 1927; s. Albert Alton and Leah Gladys (Allen) S.; B.S., U. Pitts., 1950; m. Dolores Theresa Molnar, June 25, 1950; children—Russell James, Sandra Lee, Eric Alan, Rebecca Lynn. Metall. chemist Jones & Laughlin Steel Co., Alliquippa, Pa., 1950-51; research and devel. chemist Gen. Electric Co., Erie, Pa., 1951-57; mgr. tech. sales and plant operation Hysol Corp. of Calif., El Monte, 1957-60; sr. research engr. autonetics div. N.Am. Aviation, Downey, Calif., 1960-62; pres. Delta Plastics Co., Inc. (now Delta D.P.C., Inc.), Tulare, Calif., 1962—. Served with USAAF, 1944-46. Mem. Constrn. Specifications Inst. Republican. Presbyterian. Club: Exchange (Calif.-Nevada dist. pres.-elect). Lodge: Lions (dir.). Contbr. articles to profl. jours. Home: 15170 Avenue 260 Visalia CA 93277 Office: Delta Plastics 983 E Levin Tulare CA 93274

SKILES, DONALD KEITH, author, teacher; b. Freeport, Pa., July 23, 1939; s. Raymond Lee and Elizabeth Mary (Canaan) S.; m. Marian Louise Schell, Aug. 23, 1970. BA, San Francisco State U., 1966, MA with honors, 1967. Cert. community coll. tchr., Calif. Instr. of English No. Ill. U., DeKalb, 1967-69; asst. prof. English Williamsport (Pa.) Area Community Coll., 1969-74; instr. lang. arts Chabot Coll., Hayward, Calif., 1975—; sr. systems writer Bank of Am., San Francisco, 1986—; tech. writing cons., San Francisco, 1978—. Author: Miss America, 1982; contbr. numerous articles to profl. and popular mags. and anthologies; reviewer Am. Book Rev., 1978—, San Francisco Chronicle, 1983—. Served with USAF, 1959-62. Avocation: cross-country skiing. Office: Bank of Am Capital Markets 555 California St San Francisco CA 94137

SKILLING, JOHN BOWER, structural and civil engineer; b. Los Angeles, Oct. 8, 1921; s. Harold C. and Helen M. (Bower) S.; m. Mary Jane Stender, May 1, 1943; children: William, Susan, Ann. B.S., U. Wash., 1947. Design engr. W.H. Witt Co., Seattle, 1947-54; partner successor firm Worthington, Skilling, Helle and Jackson, Seattle, 1959-67, Skilling, Helle, Christiansen, Robertson, Seattle, 1967-82; chmn. successor firm Skilling Ward Rogers Barkshire Inc., Seattle, 1983—; mem. Bldg. Research Adv. Bd. Mem. Seattle Found.; mem. Seattle Municipal Art Commn., 1964-67. Fellow ASCE; mem. Nat. Acad. Engring., Am. Concrete Inst., Internat. Assn. Shell Structures, Internat. Assn. Bridge and Structural Engring., Soc. Am. Mil. Engrs., Structural Engrs. Assn. Wash., AIA (hon. mem. Seattle chpt.), Am. Inst. Steel Constrn. (adv. com.). Home: 539 McGilvra Blvd E Seattle WA 98112 Office: Skilling Ward Rogers Barkshire 2200 The Financial Center Seattle WA 98161

SKINNER, EDWARD THOMAS, financial analyst; b. Lansing, Mich., Mar. 7, 1942; s. Baynon Roger and Marjorie Irene (Martha) S.; m. Virginia Burdick, Oct. 07, 1967 (div. Apr. 1979); 1 child, Brian. BS, U. Detroit, 1964. Lic. real estate agt., Ariz. Asst. buyer Jordan Marsh Co., Boston, 1967-68; adminstr. Honeywell Inc., Boston, 1969-70; mgr. incentive compensation adminstrn. Honeywell Inc., Annapolis, Md., 1970-76; mgr. incentive compensation adminstrn. Honeywell Inc., Phoenix, 1977-82, mgr. budgeting and adminstrn., 1983-84, fin. analyst, 1985—. V.p., sec. Birth and Family Ctr. of Phoenix, 1984-85. Served to lt. USNR, 1964-67. Mem. Phoenix Honeywell Credit Union, 1986—. Roman Catholic. Avocations: woodworking, real estate, camping, hiking, reading. Home: 2213 E Paradise Dr Phoenix AZ 85028

SKINNER, HARRY BRYANT, orthopaedic surgery educator; b. Cleve., Oct. 13, 1943; s. Harry Bryant and Marion (Eastlick) S. BS, Alfred U., 1965; MS, PhD, U. Calif., Berkeley, 1970; MD, Med. U. S.C., 1975. Asst. prof. Youngstown (Ohio) State U., 1970-71; postdoctoral research assoc. Clemson (S.C.) U., 1971-72; lectr. Calif. State U., Sacramento, 1977-79; asst./assoc. prof. Tulane U., New Orleans, 1979-82; assoc. prof. orthopaedic surgery U. Calif., San Francisco, 1983-86, prof., 1986—; adj. asst./assoc. prof. Sch. Engring., Tulane U., New Orleans, 1979-82; dir. rehab. research and devel. VA Med. Ctr., San Francisco, 1983—. Mem. editorial bd. Orthopaedics jour., 1984, guest editor, 1985, Jour. Biomed. Materials Research, 1983—; contbr. articles to profl. jours. Grantee NIH, 1978-84, Nat. Inst. Dental Research, 1978-84, VA, 1978—, Schleider Found., 1980-82, Am. Fedn. Aging Research, 1986—. Fellow ACS, Am. Acad. Orthopaedic Surgeons; mem. Orthopaedic Research Soc., Soc. for Biomaterials (charter), Sigma Xi. Office: U Calif Dept Orthopaedic Surgery U-461 San Francisco CA 94143-0728

SKINNER, MARY LOUISE, architect; b. Syracuse, N.Y., June 20, 1949; d. John Borst and Helen Elizabeth (Lucas) S.; m. Richard Owen Kimball, July 28, 1984. BA in Physics, Sweet Briar Coll., 1971; MEd, Antioch Coll., 1974; MArch, U. Pa., 1980. Registered architect, N.Y., N.Mex. Vista vol. U.S. Govt., Frederick, Va., 1971-72; tchr. St. Vrain Valley Elem. Sch., Longmont, Colo., 1974-75, Supervisory Union 22 Elem. Sch., Hanover, N.H., 1975-77; draftsman Architects Atelier, Santa Fe, 1980-81; designer B. Young Architect, Santa Fe, 1981-83; pvt. practice architecture Santa Fe, 1983—. Appointed architect mem. Mayor's Task Force on Affordable Housing, Santa Fe, 1983-84. E. Lewis Dales fellow U. Pa., 1979. Mem. AIA (bd. dirs. Sante Fe chpt.), N.Mex. Soc. Architects, Old Santa Fe Assn. (v.p., bd. dirs.). Democrat. Lutheran. Avocations: skiing, rafting, rock climbing, traveling. Office: 231 Closson St #7 Santa Fe NM 87501

SKINNER, STANLEY THAYER, utility co. exec., lawyer; b. Fort Smith, Ark., Aug. 18, 1937; s. John Willard and Irma Lee (Peters) S.; m. Margaret Olsen, Aug. 16, 1957; children—Steven Kent, Ronald Kevin. B.A. with honors, San Diego State U., 1960; M.A., U. Calif., Berkeley, 1961, J.D., 1964. Bar: Supreme Ct. Calif. bar 1965, U.S. Circuit Ct. Appeals for 9th Circuit bar 1965, 10th Circuit bar 1966. Atty. Pacific Gas and Electric Co., San Francisco, 1964-73; sr. counsel Pacific Gas and Electric Co., 1973, treas., 1974-76, v.p. fin., 1976, sr. v.p., 1977, exec. v.p., 1978-86, exec. v.p., chief fin. officer, 1982-85, vice chmn. bd., 1986—; dir. Pacific Gas and Electric Co., Pacific Gas Transmission Co., Natural Gas Corp. Calif., So. Gas. Ltd. Bd. dirs. Calif. Econ. Devel. Corp.; bd. dirs., trustee United Way of Bay Area; trustee, chmn. bd. dirs. Golden Gate U. Mem. Bankers Club San Francisco, San Francisco C. of C. (bd. dirs.), Calif. State Bar Assn., Fin. Officers No. Calif., Pacific Coast Elec. Assn., Pacific Coast Gas Assn. Republican. Presbyterian. Clubs: Bankers. Office: Pacific Gas & Electric Co 77 Beale St San Francisco CA 94106

SKIPPER, BETTY JEAN, biostatistician; b. Gary, Ind., Apr. 26, 1939; d. William R. and Jean (Adams) Eberle; m. John David Skipper, June 8, 1975; children: David Robert, Elizabeth Jean. AB, Oberlin Coll., 1961; PhD, Case-Western Reserve U., 1968. Asst. prof. biostatistics U. N.Mex., Albuquerque, 1967-74; assoc. prof. biostatistics div. community medicine Sch. Medicine U. N.Mex., Albuquerque, 1974-85; prof. U. N.Mex., Albuquerque, 1985—. Mem. Am. Stats. Soc., Biometric Soc., AAAS, Sigma Xi. Home: 3210 Roma NE Albuquerque NM 87106 Office: U N Mex Sch Medicine Family Practice-Psychiatry Bldg 2400 Tucker NE Albuquerque NM 87131

SKLANSKY, JACK, electrical engineering educator, researcher; b. N.Y.C., Nov. 15, 1928; s. Abraham and Clara S.; m. Gloria Joy Weiss, Dec. 24, 1957; children: David Alan, Mark Steven, Jeffrey Paul. B.E.E., CCNY, 1950; M.S.E.E., Purdue U., 1952; Eng.Sc.D., Columbia U., 1955. Research engr. RCA Labs., Princeton, N.J., 1955-65; mgr. Nat. Cash Register Co., Dayton, Ohio, 1965-66; prof. elec. engring. U. Calif.-Irvine, 1966—; pres. Scanicon Corp., Irvine, Calif., 1980—. Author: (with others) Pattern Classifiers and Trainable Machines, 1981; editor: Pattern Recognition, 1973, (with others) Biomedical Images and Computers, 1982; editor-in-chief: Machine Vision and Applications, 1987. Recipient best paper award Jour. Pattern Recognition, 1977; research grants NIH, 1971-84, Army Research, 1984—. Fellow IEEE; mem. Assn. Computing Machinery. Office: U Calif Dept Elec Engring Irvine CA 92717

SKLAR, RICHARD LAWRENCE, political science educator; b. N.Y.C., Mar. 22, 1930; s. Kalman and Sophie (Laub) S.; m. Eva Molineux, July 14, 1962; children: Judith Anne, Katherine Elizabeth. A.B., U. Utah, 1952; M.A., Princeton U., 1957, Ph.D., 1961. Mem. faculty Princeton U., Brandeis U., U. Ibadan, Nigeria, U. Zambia, SUNY-Stony Brook; now prof. polit. sci. UCLA; mem. fgn. area fellowship program Africa Nat. Com., 1970-73; Simon vis. prof. U. Manchester, Eng., 1975, Fulbright vis. prof. U. Zimbabwe, 1984; Lester Martin fellow Harry S. Truman Research Inst., Hebrew U. Jerusalem, 1979. Author: Nigerian Political Parties: Power in an Emergent African Nation, 1963, Corporate Power in an African State, 1975; contbr. articles to profl. jours. Served with U.S. Army, 1952-54. Rockefeller Found. grantee, 1967. Mem. Am. Polit. Sci. Assn., African Studies Assn. (dir. 1976-78, 80-83, v.p. 1980-81, pres. 1981-82), AAUP (pres. Calif. Conf. 1980-81). Home: 1951 Holmby Ave Los Angeles CA 90025

SKLOVSKY, ROBERT JOEL, physician, educator; b. Bronx, N.Y., Nov. 19, 1952; s. Nathan and Esther (Steinberg) S.; m. Michelle Sklovsky-Welch, Dec. 21, 1985. BS, Bklyn Coll., 1975; MA, Columbia U., 1976; PharmD, U. of Pacific, 1977; D in Naturopathic Medicine, Nat. Coll. Naturopathic Medicine, 1983. Intern Tripler Army Med. Ctr., Honolulu, 1977; prof. pharmacology Nat. Coll. Naturopathic Medicine, Portland, Oreg., 1982-85; pvt. practice specializing in naturopathy Clackamas, Oreg., 1983—; cons. State Bd. Naturopathic Examiners, Oreg., Hawaii, Clackamas County Sheriff's Dept.; cons. Internat. Drug Info. Ctr., N.Y.C., 1983—. Recipient Bristol Labs. award, 1983. Mem. Am. Assn. Naturopathic Physicians. Avocations: classical and jazz music, tap dance, art, botany, acting. Office: 10808 SE Hwy 212 Clackamas OR 97015

SKLOWER, MAX A., broadcasting executive; b. Havre, Mont., Dec. 24, 1927; s. Emanuel M. and Rose S. (Sternglanz) S.; divorced; children: Keith, Nancy Van Eys; m. Linda L. Dennington, July 5, 1974. BA, Mont. U. Asst. mgr. Llewellyn Outdoor Advt., Albuquerque, 1949-51; acct. exec. Sta. KOB Radio-TV, Albuquerque, 1951-58; v.p. gen. mgr. Sta. KOAT-TV, Albuquerque, 1958—. Bd. dirs. N.Mex. Symphony, Albuquerque, 1980—, Albuquerque Jaycees, 1951-54 Albuquerque C. of C., 1964-68, Mayors Future Com., Alubquerque, 1981. Served to lt. (j.g.) USN, 1945-46. Recipient Silver medal Albuquerque Advt. Fedn., 1967; named Crime Stopper of Yr., 1981. Republican. Jewish. Club: Tanoan. Lodge: Rotary. Avocations: tennis, skiing, fishing, piano. Office: Station KOAT-TV 3801 Carlisle NE Albuquerque NM 87107

SKOLD, CARL NELSON, biochemist; b. Knoxville, Tenn., Jan. 24, 1947; s. Laurence Nelson and Mary (Thayer) S.; m. Karen Beck, May 25, 1970; 1 child, Emily. AB, Oberlin Coll., 1968; MS, U. Rochester, 1972; PhD, U. Oreg., 1973. NIH postdoctoral fellow U. Oreg., Eugene, 1974-75; vis. asst. prof. Oreg. State U., Corvallis, 1975-76; sr. scientist Syva Co., Palo Alto, Calif., 1976-81, group leader, 1981—. Contbr. articles to profl. jours.; patentee in field. Mem. Am. Chem. Soc., Am. Assn. Clin. Chemistry. Home: 2487 Dell Ave Mountain View CA 94043 Office: Syva Co 900 Arastradero Rd Palo Alto CA 94304

SKOOG, DOUGLAS ARVID, retired chemistry educator, writer; b. Willmar, Minn., May 4, 1918; s. Arvid C. and Hilma E. (Erickson) S.; m. Judith Bone, Oct. 10, 1942; children: James Arvid, Jon Douglas. BS, Oreg. State U., 1940; PhD, U. Ill., 1943. Research chemist Standard Oil Co. of Calif., Richmond, Calif., 1943-47; asst. prof. chemistry Stanford (Calif.) U., 1947-53, assoc. prof., 1953-62, prof., assoc. exec. head dept. chemistry, 1963-76, prof. emeritus, 1976—; writer Stanford, 1976—. Author: Fundamentals of Analytical Chemistry, 4th rev. edit., 1980, Principles of Instrumental Analysis, 1985, Analytical Chemistry, 4th rev. edit., 1986; contbr. articles to profl. jours. Mem. Am. Chem. Soc. (pres. Santa Clara Valley sect. 1962), Sigma Xi, Phi Kappa Phi, Alpha Chi Sigma. Club: Bohemian (San Francisco). Avocations: flying, skiing. Home: 719 Mayfield Ave Stanford CA 94305

SKOOG, WILLIAM ARTHUR, oncologist; b. Culver City, Calif., Apr. 10, 1925; s. John Lundeen and Allis Rose (Gatz) S.; A.A., UCLA, 1944; B.A. with gt. distinction, Stanford U., 1946, M.D., 1949; m. Ann Douglas, Sept. 17, 1949; children—Karen, William Arthur, James Douglas, Allison. Intern medicine Stanford Hosp., San Francisco, 1948-49, asst. resident medicine, 1949-50; asst. resident medicine N.Y. Hosp., N.Y.C., 1950-51; sr. resident medicine Wadsworth VA Hosp., Los Angeles, 1951, attending specialist internal medicine, 1962-68; practice medicine specializing in internal medicine, Los Altos, Calif., 1959-61; pvt. practice hematology and oncology Calif. Oncologic and Surg. Med. Group, Inc., Santa Monica, Calif., 1971-72; pvt. practice med. oncology, San Bernardino, Calif., 1972—; assoc. staff Palo Alto-Stanford (Calif.) Hosp. Center, 1959-61, U. Calif. Med. Center, San Francisco, 1959-61; asso. attending physician U. Calif. at Los Angeles Hosp. and Clinics, 1961-78; vis. physician internal medicine Harbor Gen. Hosp., Torrance, Calif., 1962-65, attending physician, 1965-71; cons. chemistry Clin. Lab., UCLA Hosp., 1963-68; affiliate cons. staff St. John's Hosp., Santa Monica, Calif., 1967-71, courtesy staff, 1971-72; courtesy attending med. staff Santa Monica Hosp., 1967-72; staff physician St. Bernardine (Calif.) Hosp., 1972—, San Bernardino Community Hosp., 1972—; chief sect. oncology San Bernardino County Hosp., 1972-76; cons. staff Redlands (Calif.) Community Hosp., 1972-83, courtesy staff, 1983—; asst. in medicine Cornell Med. Coll., N.Y.C., 1950-51; jr. research physician UCLA Atomic Energy Project, 1954-55; instr. medicine, asst. research physician dept. medicine UCLA Med. Center, 1955-56, asst. prof. medicine, asst. research physician, 1956-59; clin. asso. hematology VA Center, Los Angeles, 1956-59; co-dir. metabolic research unit UCLA Center for Health Scis., 1955-59, 61-65; co-dir. Health Scis. Clin. Research Center, 1965-68, dir., 1968-72; clin. instr. medicine Stanford, 1959-61; asst. clin. prof. medicine, assoc. research physician U. Calif. Med. Center, San Francisco, 1959-61; lectr. medicine UCLA Sch. Medicine, 1961-62, assoc. prof. medicine, 1962-73, assoc. clin. prof. medicine, 1973—. Served with USNR, 1943-46, to lt. M.C., 1951-53. Fellow ACP; mem. Am. Fedn. Clin. Research, Los Angeles Acad. Western Soc. Clin. Research, Am. Fedn. Clin. Research, Los Angeles Acad. Medicine, San Bernardino County Med. Soc., Am. Soc. Clin. Oncology, Am. Soc. Internal Medicine, Calif. Soc. Internal Medicine, Inland Soc. Internal Medicine, Phi Beta Kappa, Alpha Omega Alpha, Sigma Xi, Alpha Kappa Kappa. Episcopalian (vestryman 1965-70). Club: Redlands Country. Contbr. articles to profl. jours. Home: 30831 Miradero Dr Redlands CA 92373 Office: 399 E Highland Ave Suite 201 San Bernardino CA 92404

SKOPIL, OTTO RICHARD, JR., judge; b. Portland, Oreg., June 3, 1919; s. Otto Richard and Freda Martha (Boetticher) S.; m. Janet Rae Lundy, July 27, 1956; children: Otto Richard III, Casey Robert, Shannon Ida, Molly Jo. BA in Econs., Willamette U., 1941, LLB, JD (hon.), 1946, LLD (hon.), 1983. Bar: Oreg. 1946, IRS, U.S. Treasury Dept., U.S. Dist. Ct. Oreg., U.S. Ct. Appeals (9th cir.), U.S. Supreme Ct. 1946. Assoc. Skopil & Skopil, 1946-51; ptnr. Williams, Skopil, Miller & Beck (and predecessors), Salem, Oreg., 1951-72; judge U.S. Dist. Ct., Portland, 1972-79; chief judge U.S. Dist. Ct., 1976-79; judge U.S. Ct. Appeals (9th cir.), Portland, 1979—; chmn. com. adminstrn. of fed. magistrate system U.S. Jud. Conf.; co-founder Oreg. chpt. Am. Leadership Forum. Hi-Y adviser Salem YMCA, 1951-52; appeal agt. SSS, Marion County (Oreg.) Draft Bd., 1953-66; master of ceremonies 1st Gov.'s Prayer Breakfast for State Oreg., 1959; mem. citizens adv. com., City of Salem, 1970-71; chmn. Gov.'s Com. on Staffing Mental Instns., 1969-70; pres., bd. dirs. Marion County Tb and Health Assn., 1958-61; bd. dirs. Willamette Valley Camp Fire Girls, 1946-56, Internat. Christian Leadership, 1959, Fed. Jud. Ctr., 1979; trustee Willamette U., 1969-71; elder Mt. Park Ch., 1979-81. Served to lt. USNR, 1942-46. Recipient Oreg. Legal Citizen of Yr. award, 1986. Mem. ABA, Oreg. Bar Assn. (bd. govs.), Marion County Bar Assn., Am. Judicature Soc., Oreg. Assn. Def. Counsel (dir.), Def. Research Inst., Assn. Ins. Attys. U.S. and Can. (Oreg. rep. 1970), Internat. Soc. Barristers, Prayer Breakfast Movement (fellowship council). Clubs: Salem, Exchange (pres. 1947), Illahe Hills Country (pres., dir. 1964-67). Office: Pioneer Courthouse Portland OR 97204

SKOTHEIM, ROBERT ALLEN, college president; b. Seattle, Jan. 31, 1933; s. Sivert O. and Marjorie F. (Allen) S.; m. Nadine Vail, June 14, 1953; children—Marjorie, Kris, Julia. B.A., U. Wash., Seattle, 1955, M.A., 1958, Ph.D., 1962; LL.D., Hobart and William Smith Colls., Geneva, N.Y., 1975. Prof. history U. Wash., 1962-63; prof. history Wayne State U., Detroit, 1963-66; prof. UCLA, 1966-67, U. Colo., Boulder, 1967-72; provost, dean faculty Hobart and William Smith Colls., 1972-75; pres. Whitman Coll., Walla Walla, Wash., 1975—. Author: American Intellectual Histories and Historians, 1966, Totalitarianism and American Social Thought, 1971; Editor: The Historian and the Climate of Opinion, 1969; co-editor: American Social Thought: Sources and Interpretations, 2 vols, 1972. Guggenheim fellow, 1967-68. Mem. Phi Beta Kappa (hon.). Office: Whitman Coll Walla Walla WA 99362

SKUJINS, ANDRE J., engineer; b. Oakland, Calif., July 14, 1958; s. John J. and Irena (Vizulis) S. BS in Indsl. Tech., U. State U. Welding engr. Bechtel Power Corp., Palo Verde, Ariz., 1981; quality engr. Morton-Thiokol, Brigham City, Utah, 1982-85, Kaiser-Aerotech, San Leandro, Calif., 1985—. Democrat. Lutheran. Avocations: skiing, tennis, sailing. Home: 2556 Iowa Ogden UT 84401

SKULJAN, ZVONKO DAVID, lawyer; b. Vinkovci, Yugoslavia, Jan. 5, 1955; came to U.S., 1969; s. Stevo and Margita (Mikloucic) S.; m. Julia Maffei, Sept. 10, 1983; 1 child, Grennan William. AB, UCLA, 1981; JD, U. Calif., San Francisco, 1984. Bar: Calif. 1985, U.S. Dist. Ct. (no. dist, cen. dist.) Calif. 1985, U.S. Ct. Appeals (9th cir.) 1985, U.S. Tax Ct.1985. Atty. Edward Otto Cresap Ord, Esq., San Francisco, 1984-85; sole practice Santa Rosa, Calif., 1985—. Bd. dirs. ARC, Santa Rosa, 1986—, 4 Cs, Santa Rosa, 1986—. Served to sgt. USMC, 1973-77. Mem. ABA, Assn. Trial Lawyers Am., San Francisco Bar Assn., Sonoma County Bar Assn. Roman Catholic. Club: UCLA Ski. Avocations: water skiing, wind and body surfing, baseball, scuba diving. Home: 1450 Neotomas Ave Suite 124 Santa Rosa CA 95405 Office: 1499 Hill Rd Glen Ellen CA 95442

SKYLSTAD, WILLIAM S., bishop; b. Omak, Wash., Mar. 2, 1934; s. Stephen Martin and Reneldes Elizzbeth (Danzl) S. Student, Pontifical Coll., Josephinum, Worthington, Ohio; M.Ed., Gonzaga U. Ordained priest Roman Catholic Ch., 1960; asst. pastor Pullman, Wash., 1960-62; tchr. Mater Cleri Sem., 1961-68, rector, 1968-74; pastor Assumption Parish, Spokane, 1974-76; chancellor Diocese of Spokane, 1976-77; ordained bishop 1977; bishop of Yakima, Wash., 1977—. Office: Office of Bishop 222 Washington Mutual Bldg PO Box 505 Yakima WA 98907 *

SLACK, DONALD CARL, agricultural engineering educator; b. Cody, Wyo., June 25, 1942; s. Clarence Ralbon and Clara May (Beightol) S.; m. Marion Arline Kimball, Dec. 19, 1964; children: Jonel Marie, Jennifer Michelle. BS in Agrl. Engring., U. Wyo., 1965; MS in Agrl. Engring., U. Ky., 1968, PhD in Agrl. Engring., 1975. Registered profl. engr., Ky., Ariz. Asst. civil engr. City of Los Angeles, 1965; research specialist U. Ky., Lexington, 1966-70; agrl. engring. advisor U. Ky., Tha Phra, Thailand, 1970-73; research asst. U. Ky., Lexington, 1973-75; from asst. prof. to assoc. prof. agrl. engring. U. Minn., St. Paul, 1975-84; prof. U. Ariz., Tucson, 1984—; tech. advisor Ariz. Dept. Water Resources, Phoenix, 1985—; cons. Winrock Internat., Morrilton, Ark., 1984, Water Mgmt. Synthesis II, Logan, Utah, 1985, Desert Agrl. Tech. Systems, Tucson, 1985—. Contbr. articles to profl. jours. Mem. ASCE, Am. Soc. Agrl. Engrs., Am. Geophys. Union, Am. Soc. Agronomy, Soil Sci. Soc. Am., Sigma Xi, Tau Beta Pi, Alpha Epsilon, Gamma Sigma Delta. Democrat. Lutheran. Avocations: hunting, camping, hiking, model railroading. Home: 9230 E Visco Pl Tucson AZ 85710 Office: U Ariz Agrl Engring Dept Tucson AZ 85721

SLACK, KEITH VOLLMER, aquatic ecologist; b. Louisville, May 20, 1924; s. James Warren and Emily Louise S.; m. Helen Louise Emerson, July 31, 1962; children: Sallie Louise, Keith Thomas, Daniel Emerson, Kathryn Anne. BS in Zoology with honors, with high distinction, U. Ky., 1949, MS, 1950; PhD, Ind. U., 1954. Mil. oceanographer U.S. Navy Oceanographic Office, Suiteland, Md., 1953-60; research project chief U.S. Geol. Survey, Arlington, Va., 1960-64; research project chief U.S. Geol. Survey, Menlo Park, Calif., 1964—, ecology research advisor Water Resources div., 1974-76, 78-84; cons., tchr. Water Resources div. U.S. Geol. Survey, Menlo Park, Denver, Tucson, 1960—. Contbr. articles to profl. jours. Served as sgt. USAF, 1943-46. Recipient Meritorious Service award U.S. Dept. Interior, Washington, 1979. Mem. Ecol. Soc. Am., Am. Soc. Limnology and Oceanography, N.Am. Benthological Soc., Am. Inst. Biol. Scis., Internat. Soc. Theoretical and Applied Limnology, Sigma Xi, Phi Beta Kappa. Avocations: gardening, woodworking, water gardening. Home: 805 Gailen Ave Palo Alto CA 94303 Office: US Geol Survey 345 Middlefield Rd Menlo Park CA 94025

SLADE, SANDRA LYNN, interior designer, educator, consultant; b. Seattle, April 22, 1946; d. Erwin R. Slade, M.D. and Leona Martha (Mears) S.; 1 son, David Slade Privette. B.F.A., U. Wash., 1969, M.F.A. in Interior Design, 1977. owner-designer Image West Inc., Boise, Idaho, 1971-76; asst. prof. interior architecture, U. Idaho, Moscow, 1977-81; asst. prof. interior design Wash. State U., Pullman, 1981-83; pvt. practice interior design Seattle, 1983—; project mgr. MOB; design cons., Seattle; profl. cons. Wilsonart Innova Design Competition, 1983-84. Recipient design award Institution Mag., 1980. Mem. Am. Soc. Interior Designers (cert. 1976), Interior Design Educators Council (NW regional dir.), Alpha Chi Omega. Republican. Episcopalian.

SLAKEY, STEPHEN LOUIS, educator; b. Oakland, Calif., Feb. 7, 1946; s. Louis T. and Vivian (Torrey) S.; m. Sylvia Amanda Loud S., Feb. 5, 1971; children: Stephen Andrew, Stephanie Amanda. BA, Calif. State U., Hayward, 1969; MA, Calif. State U., Fullerton, 1974. Cert. K-12 sch. adminstrn., 7-12 social sci. tchr., Calif. Tchr. geography La Puente (Calif.) High Sch., 1969—, chmn. dept. geography, 1973-80, dir. staff devel., 1985—, mentor tchr., 1984—, staff devel. coordinator, 1985—; co-dir. Geographic Inst. UCLA, 1985; prin. instr. Nat. Geographic Soc. Inst., Washington, 1986-87; cons. bilingual edn. Calif. State Poly. U., Pomona, 1972; curriculum cons. Hacienda-La Puente Unified Sch. Dist., 1972-74. Pres. Glendora Beautiful, 1983-84; researcher Glendora Hist. Resources Survey, 1983. Mem. Calif. Geographical Soc. (bd. dirs. 1977-78, Disting. Teaching award 1975, 79), Calif. Geographic Alliance (founder), Calif. Tchrs. Assn. (chmn. grievance com. 1981-82). Avocations: tennis, volleyball, sailing, traveling, photography. Home: 1149 E Steffen St Glendora CA 91740 Office: Hacienda-La Puente Unified Sch Dist 15615 E Nelson Ave La Puente CA 91744

SLANE, KERRY THOMAS, military officer; b. Pottsville, Pa., Jan. 31, 1960; s. Francis Raymond and Vera Elenor (Paul) S.; m. Pamela Louise Ruscavage, June 30, 1979. Student, Great Lakes Naval Tng. Ctr., 1978-79, Def. Equal Opportunity Mgmt. Inst., Patrick AFB, 1983-84, U. Honolulu, 1986—. Enlisted USN, 1977—; crew mem. USS Indianapolis, 1978-84; effectiveness cons. Orgnl. Effectiveness Ctr., Pearl Harbor, Hawaii, 1984-86; equal opportunity specialist Naval Logistics Commd. U.S. Pacific Fleet, Pearl Harbor, 1986-87; crew mem. USS Cavalla, 1987—. Vol. Boy Scouts Am., Girl Scouts U.S. Mem. Inst. Econometric Research, Am. Assn. Ind. Investors. Republican. Roman Catholic. Avocations: investment analysis, tennis, golf, photography. Home: 1530-A Honeysuckle Pl Honolulu HI 96818

SLATE, JOHN BUTLER, biomedical engineer; b. Schenectady, N.Y., Sept. 27, 1953; s. Herbert Butler and Violet (Perugi) S. BSEE, U. Wis., 1975, MEE, 1977, PhDEE, 1980. Spl. fellow of cardiovascular surgery U. Ala., Birmingham, 1980-81, dept. biomed. research engr., 1981-82; sr. research engr. IMED Corp., San Diego, 1982-83, sr. research scientist, 1983-86; sci. dir. Pacesetter Infusion Ltd. (dba MiniMed Technologies), Sylmar, Calif., 1986-87; v.p. tech. MiniMed Technologies, Sylmar, Calif., 1987—. Fellow Nat. Cancer Inst., 1981-82. Mem. IEEE (Arnyton Premium award), Biomed. Engring. Soc., Sigma Xi. Office: MiniMed Technologies 12774 San Fernando Rd Sylmar CA 91342

SLATER, COLIN, copyright executive, consultant; b. Lincoln, Lincolnshire, Eng., May 5, 1948; s. George William and Muriel Gwendolyn (Barton) S. Student, various colls., univs. worldwide; PhD (hon.), Poly. U., Zurich, 1968. Devel. chemist Croid Adhesives, Newark, Eng., 1965-68; patent cons. 29 European countries, 1968-70; license and copyright cons. James Bond, numerous others, 140 countries, 1970-75; copyright license mgr. Bay City Rollers, 23 countries, 1975-78, USA Clients and John Denver, 1978-86; chief exec. officer The Yankee Energy Group, Garden Grove, Calif., 1986—; owner Sallust Capital, Beverly Hills, Calif., 1986—; lectr. UCLA, 1986, univs. throughout U.S. and western nations, 1968-86; bd. dirs. Marquee Entertainment, Beverly Hills. Author: The Brothers, 1975; patentee in field. Mem. ASCAP (Country Song of Yr. 1984), Broadcast Mus Inc. (Achievment citations 1980-84), Performing Right Soc. Avocations: motor rallys, sailing, photography. Office: Marquee Entertainment 12460 Euclid Garden Grove CA 92640

SLATER, DON AUSTIN, shipyard executive, consultant; b. Bay City, Mich., May 27, 1938; s. William Stuart and Inez Fern (Hagen) S.; m. Sara Belva Sanford, Feb. 3, 1962; children: Shandra Sanford, Nathan Dorman. BS in Naval Architecture and Marine Engring., U. Mich. Naval architect Western Boat Bldg. Corp., Tacoma, 1964; exec. v.p. and gen. mgr. Star Marine Industries, Tacoma; gen. mgr. Shipyard div. Marine Iron Works, Tacoma; pres. and gen. mgr. Marine Industry N.W., Inc., Tacoma, 1976—; cons. to various law firms, Wash. and N.J., 1975—; arbitrator Am. Arbitration Assn., 1985—. 1st v.p. Va. V Found., Seattlem 1986; bd. dirs. Puget Sound Marine Hist. Soc., 1978-80. Avocations: boating, wood carving, collecting antique boats. Home: 30720 43d Ave SW Federal Way WA 98003 Office: Marine Industries NW Inc 313 E F St PO Box 1275 Tacoma WA 98401

SLATER, KENNETH, cinematographer; b. Stillwater, Okla., Dec. 13, 1949; s. Jerry and June Slater; m. Alice Diane Langston, Aug. 6, 1983; 1 child, Diane Kristine. BS in Motion Picture Prodn., Mont. State U., 1973. Owner Western Am. Films, Inc., 1978, Billings, Mont., 1982—; producer, director, writer in various countries throughout Asia, Africa, Europe and U.S.; prin. works include an interview with Mother Teresa, an eight projector multi-image show for Billy Graham World Congress, a film documentary entitled The Potter's House, filming of Olympics in Montreal and a Pat Boone concert tour in Japan.

SLATER, LEONARD, writer, editor; b. N.Y.C., July 15, 1920; s. Max and Jean (Lenobel) S.; m. Betty Moorsteen, 1946; children: Amy, Lucy. BA in Polit. Sci., U. Mich., 1941. Reporter, writer NBC News, Washington, 1941-44; news editor NBC News, N.Y.C., 1941-44; corr. Washington bur. Time mag., 1945-47; assoc. editor Newsweek mag., N.Y.C., 1947-58, corr. Eastern Europe and Middle East; bur. chief Newsweek mag., Los Angeles; sr. editor, columnist Signt and Sound McCalls' mag., N.Y. and Europe, 1959-63; founding editorial cons. San Diego Home-Garden mag., 1979-81; free-lance writer, editor 1963—. Author: Aly, 1965, The Pledge, 1970; contbr. articles to mags. Mem. Authors League of Am. Home: 4370 Arista Dr San Diego CA 92103

SLATER, WILLIAM THOMAS, university administrator, communications researcher; b. Pitts., Oct. 31, 1942; s. William E. and Margaret Ruth (Briggs) S. BA, Tufts U., 1971; AM, Harvard U., 1972; MA, Stanford U., 1973, PhD, 1977. Reporter, editor, Afro-Am. newspaper, 1959-61; reporter Newark News, 1961-62; news dir. Sta. WABQ, Cleve., 1962-64; reporter, anchor Sta. WBZ-TV-AM, Boston, 1964-69; asst. to Gov. of Mass., 1969-71; asst. prof. U. Wash., Seattle, 1973-75; asst. prof. U. So. Calif., Los Angeles, 1975-77; assoc. prof., head div. broadcasting U. Cin., 1977-79; prof., head dept. radio-TV, U. Ariz., Tucson, 1979-83; dean Sch. Fine Arts, Eastern Wash. U., Cheney, 1983-86; v.p. univ. relations Oreg. State U., Corvallis, 1986—; cons. broadcasting and edn. planning. Mem. Phi Beta Kappa. Author: Aspen Handbook on Communication, 1972, 2d edit., 1975; contbr. articles to publs. in field.

SLATON, ALICE MISRAHI, French language educator; b. Alexandria, Egypt, Feb. 11, 1944; came to U.S., 1962; d. Albert and Esther (Cohen) Misrahi; m. Joel Binder, June 10, 1965 (div. 1967); m. Stanley Alvin Slaton, Sept. 1, 1969; children: Ryan Nathan, Daniel Brett. BA, UCLA, 1965, MA, 1966, PhD, 1975. French lang. tchr. Santa Monica (Calif.) Coll., 1966-67, Beverly Hills (Calif.) Unified Sch. Dist., 1967-69; French lang. tchr. Ventura (Calif.) Coll., 1969—, instr. computer literacy, 1985—; research and devel. staff Ventura Coll., 1984—, devel. activities staff, 1985—. Designer laser videodisc; contbr. articles on computer sci. to profl. jours. Mem. Internat. Interactive Communication Soc., Computer Assisted Lang. Instrn. Consortium (editor newsletter 1985—), Ventura Coll. French Club (pres. 1985—). Avocations: swimming, weight training, sailing. Office: Ventura Coll 4667 Telegraph Rd #198 Ventura CA 93003

SLATON, JACK HAMILTON, electrical engineer; b. Riverside, Ill., Mar. 9, 1925; s. Leonard Clyde and Ida Mae (Hamilton) S.; m. Audrey Dorraine Locken, Dec. 9, 1954. BEE, Ill. Inst. Tech., 1945; MEE, Calif. Inst. Tech., 1947; PhD in Engring., UCLA, 1972. Asst. prof. engring. research Pa. State U., U. Park, 1947-50; research scientist U. Tex., Austin, 1950-51; research engr. N. Am. Aviation, Downey, Calif., 1951-53; electronics engr. Naval Ocean Systems Ctr., Pasadena and San Diego, Calif., 1953-83; chief engring. fellow Honeywell, San Diego, 1983—. Patentee in field. Recipient L.T.E. Thompson award Naval Ordnance Test Station, 1962, Superior Civilian Service Award Navy Dept., 1965, David Bushnell award Am. Def. Preparedness Assn., 1984. Home: 1659 Calle Candela La Jolla CA 92037 Office: Honeywell 1663 Rosecrans St San Diego CA 92106

SLATTERY, JAMES ARLEIGH, safety consultant; b. Jackson, Calif., May 10, 1957; s. Paul Harold Slattery and Clifford Antoinette (Smith) Hancock; m. Deirdre Mary Martin, Aug. 19, 1984. AE in Safety Engring. Tech., Cogswell Coll., 1979, BS in Safety Engring., Fire Protection, 1980. Cer. assoc. safety profl. Fire test engr. Warnock-Hersey Internat. Inc., Antioch, Calif., 1982-83; safety coordinator, engring. technologist Tetra-tech Inc., Sausalito, Calif., 1983-84; safety and health profl. Safety Specialists Inc., Santa Clara, Calif., 1984—. Author short story, poem. Mem. Am. Soc. Safety Engrs. Democrat. Roman Catholic. Home: 386 Irving Ave San Jose CA 95128-2222

SLATTERY, THOMAS E., industrial gases company executive; b. Chgo., Aug. 2, 1935; s. James Frederic and Gladys Irene (Pratt) S.; m. Maxine Mary Beebe, Sept. 10, 1955; children: Mary Lynn, David Thomas. B.S. in Mech. Engring., Mich. State U., 1957. Various positions Union Carbide Corp., 1961-79; with strategic planning, mgmt. com. Union Carbide Corp., N.Y.C., 1974-75, v.p., gen. mgr. gases Linde div., 1975-77; v.p. mktg. Union Carbide Corp., 1977-79; pres. indsl. gases div., exec. v.p. Liquid Air Corp., San Francisco, 1979-84; chief operating officer Liquid Air Corp., 1984—, pres., chief exec. officer, 1986—. Served to 1st lt. USAF, 1957-60. Office: Liquid Air Corp 2121 N California Blvd Walnut Creek CA 94596

SLAUGHTER, RONALD JOE, pathologist; b. French Camp, Calif., June 4, 1941; s. Thomas Martin and Martha (Erbele) S.; m. Kathleen Suzanne Florance, Sept. 11, 1965; Thomas, Seth, Ethan. BA, Occidental Coll., 1963; MS, MD, U. Chgo., 1967. Diplomate Am. Bd. Pathology. Resident in pathology Duke U., Durham, N.C., 1971-75; pathologist Humana Hosp. Sunrise, Las Vegas, Nev., 1975—; cons. pathologist William Bee Ririe Hosp., Ely, Nev., 1977—, Grover Dils Med. Ctr., Caliente, Nev., 1979—. Served to lt. comdr. USN, 1967-71. Fellow Coll. Am. Pathologists, Am. Soc. Clin. Pathologists; mem. AMA, Nev. State Med. Assn. (pres. 1986-87), Nev. Med. Lab. Adv. Com. (chmn. 1980-86), Flying Physicians Assn. (bd. dirs. 1983-86), Kappa Sigma. Democrat. Presbyterian. Lodges: Masons, Shriners. Home: 3020 Ashby Ave Las Vegas NV 89102 Office: Lab Medicine Cons Ltd 3186 Maryland Pkwy Las Vegas NV 89109

SLAVIN, ANDREW EDWARD, psychotherapist; b. Phila., Sept. 18, 1954; s. Frederic Albert and Patricia Lynn (Adler) S. BA, Roger Williams Coll., 1977; MSW, U. Ark., 1979. Supr. adolescent group home Luth. Social Service, Seattle, 1979-81; sr. social worker Family Services, Seattle, 1981-83; intake coordinator Seattle Counseling Services, 1983-85; clin. dir. MEN, Inc., Juneau, Alaska, 1985—. Named one of Outstanding Young Men in Am., Jaycees, 1982. Mem. Assn. Cert. Social Workers, Nat. Assn. Social Workers, Internat. Transactional Analysis Assn., Wash. State Shelter Network. Democrat. Jewish. Avocations: swimming, hiking, skiing, singing, reading. Home: PO Box 442 Douglas AK 99824 Office: MEN Inc 222 Seward St 202 Juneau AK 99801

SLAWSON, VIDA, chemist; b. N.Y.C., Oct. 29, 1928; d. Eliot and Lily (Birkmann) Sarasohn; m. Paul Fredric Slawson, June 19, 1951; children: Christina, Paul Fredric. BS, William Smith Coll., 1949. Chemist V.A. Wadsworth Med. Ctr., Los Angeles. Mem. Am. Assn. Clin. Chemistry, Am. Chem. Soc., N.Y. Acad. Sci. Avocations: tennis, book collecting, gardening. Office: Wadsworth Med Ctr Wilshire and Sawtelle Blvd Los Angeles CA 90073

SLAYTON, SASHA ELEANOR, health educator; b. Rahway, N.J., June 27, 1939; d. Clarence Blake and Eleanor Frances (Pippy) Smith. R.N., Orange Meml. Hosp., 1962; B.A., Beloit Coll., 1972; B.S.N., Calif. State U.-Sacramento, 1977; M.S.N., Yale U., 1979. Human sexuality clinician U. Bridgeport, Conn., 1977-79; teaching asst. Yale U., New Haven, 1977-78; family nurse practitioner Siuslaw Rural Ctr., Swisshome, Oreg., 1979-80; joint faculty nursing/medicine Wayne State U., Detroit, 1980-83; dir. staff devel. Kennewick Gen. Hosp., Wash., 1984-85, dir. ednl. services, 1985—. Mem. services com. Community Unitarian Universalist Ch., Kennewick, 1984—, bd. dirs. 1985—; mem. profl. adv. com. Regional March of Dimes, 1985—, Local Head Start, 1986—, Regional Library of Medicine, Wash., Oreg., Idaho, Mont., Alaska, 1985—. Mem. Am. Soc. Tng. and Devel., Eastern Wash. Soc. Healthcare Trainers and Educators, Wash. Orgn. Nurse Execs., Eastern Wash. Soc. Tng. and Devel., Am. Pub. Health Assn., Am. Nurses Assn., Yale Alumni Assn., Sigma Theta Tau. Home: PO Box 5675 Kennewick WA 99337 Office: Kennewick Gen Hosp 900 S Auburn Ave Kennewick WA 99336

SLEICHER, CHARLES ALBERT, chemical engineer; b. Albany, N.Y., Aug. 15, 1924; s. Charles Albert and Beatrice Eugena (Cole) S.; m. Janis Jorgensen, Sept. 5, 1953; children—Jeffrey Mark, Gretchen Gail. B.S., Brown U., 1946; M.S., M.I.T., 1949; Ph.D., U. Mich., 1955. Asst. dir. M.I.T. Sch. Chem. Engring.; Practice Bangor, Maine, 1949-51; research engr. Shell Devel. Co., Emeryville, Calif., 1955-59; asso. prof. chem. engring. U. Wash., Seattle, 1960—; dept. chmn. U. Wash., 1977—; cons. Westinghouse-Hanford Co. Contbr. articles on extraction, heat transfer, fluid mechanics, pesticide transport to profl. jours. Served with USN, 1943-47. NSF postdoctoral fellow, 1959-60; SEED grantee, 1973-74; research grantee NSF; research grantee Chevron Research Corp.; research grantee Am. Chem. Soc. Fellow Am. Inst. Chem. Engrs. (program, awards coms.); mem. Am. Chem. Soc., Council Chem. Research, AAAS, Sigma Xi. Chem. reactor design patentee. Home: 5002 Harold Pl NE Seattle WA 98105 Office: U Wash Dept Chem Engring BF 10 Seattle WA 98195

SLEIGHT, ROBERT BENTON, psychologist; b. Hemlock, N.Y., Sept. 16, 1922; s. Edson F. and Marion (Hoppough) S.; m. Dorothy M. Barden, May 7, 1944; 1 child, Robert Barry. BEd, SUNY, Geneseo, 1946; MS, Purdue U., 1947, PhD, 1949. Lic. psychologist, Va. Research fellow Purdue U., West Lafayette, Ind., 1946-48; asst. prof., research psychologist Johns Hopkins U., Balt., 1948-51; research scientist Naval Research Lab., Washington, 1952; pres., chmn. bd. Century Research Corp., Arlington, Va., 1952—, expert witness, 1976—. Editor Safety Tech. Group Newsletter, 1982-83; contbr. articles to profl. jours. Bd. dirs. ARC, Arlington, 1974-80; mem. exec. bd. Com. of 100, Arlington, 1966-71. Served with USNR, 1943-45. Named Disting. Alumnus SUNY, Geneseo, 1971. Fellow Human Factors Soc. (sec.-treas. 1962-63), Am. Psychol. Assn., AAAS; mem. Walking Assn. (exec. dir. 1976—, newsletter editor 1976—), Sigma Xi. Club: Purdue Club of Washington (v.p. 1962-66). Home: 655 E Rancho Catalina Place Tucson AZ 85704 Office: PO Box 37228 Tucson AZ 85740

SLEMMONS, DAVID BURTON, geology and geophysics educator; b. Alameda, Calif., Dec. 31, 1922; s. Claude Hayes and Gladys Dorothy (Hinton) S.; m. Ruth Marillyn Evans, Sept. 7, 1946; children: David Robert, Mary Anne. BS, U. Calif., Berkeley, 1947, PhD, 1953. Registered geologist, Calif; registered engring. geologist, Nev. From asst. prof. to prof. geology U. Nev., Reno, 1951—; from vis. asst. prof. to assoc. prof. U. Calif., Berkeley, 1952-62, dir. Neotectonics Ctr., 1985—; program dir. Geophysics dept. NSF, Washington; cons. Lawrence Livermore (Calif.) Nat. Lab., U.S. Nuclear Regulatory Commn., Washington. Author: Faults and Earthquake Magnitude, 1977. Served to 1st lt. U.S. Army, 1945-46. Recipient G.K. Gilbert award in Seismic Geology Carnegie Found., 1962. Fellow Geol. Soc. Am. (nat. program chmn. 1984); mem. Seismol. Soc. Am., Am. Geophys. Union, Phi Kappa Phi. Democrat. Methodist. Avocation: fishing. Office: U Nev Mackay Sch Mines Ctr Neotectonic Studies Reno NV 89557

SLIKER, TODD RICHARD, accountant, lawyer; b. Rochester, N.Y., Feb. 9, 1936; s. Harold Garland and Marion Ethel (Caps) S.; B.S. with honors (Ford Found. scholar), U. Wis., 1955; Ph.D., Cornell U., 1962; M.B.A., Harvard, 1970; J.D., U. Denver, 1982; m. Gretchen Paula Zeiter, Dec. 27, 1963; children—Cynthia Garland, Kathryn Clifton. Bar: Colo. 1983. With Clevite Corp., Cleve., 1962-68, head applied physics sect., 1965-68; asst. to pres. Granville-Phillips Co., Boulder, Colo., 1970; v.p., gen. mgr. McDowell Electronics, Inc., Metuchen, N.J., 1970-71; pres. C.A. Compton, Inc., mfrs. audio-visual equipment, Boulder, 1971-77; chief acct. C&S Inc., Englewood, Colo., 1977-80, v.p., 1980-82; sole practice law, Boulder, 1983—. Del., Colo. Rep. Assembly, 1974, 76; Rep. dist. fin. coordinator, 1974-75; precinct committeeman, 1974-86; chmn. Boulder County Rep. 1200 Club, 1975-79; mem. Colo. Rep. State Cen. Com., 1977-81, asst. treas., 1979-87; sect. corr. Harvard U., 1981—. Served to 1st lt. USAF, 1955-57. Recipient paper award vehicular communication group IEEE, 1966. Licensed real estate salesman, securities salesman; CPA, Colo. Mem. Colo. Soc. CPAs (govt. relations task force 1983-86), Colo. Bar Assn. (publs. com. 1982-84), Denver Bar Assn., Am. Phys. Soc., Optical Soc. Am. (referee Jour.), Sigma Xi, Phi Kappa Phi, Theta Chi, Beta Alpha Psi. Club: Rotary. Contbr. articles to profl. jours. Patentee in field. Home: 1658 Bear Mountain Dr Boulder CO 80303

SLILATY, STEVE NASSIF, biochemist, researcher; b. Kab-Elias, Lebanon, Feb. 11, 1952; s. Elias Abraham and Rose Tanons (Filfili) S. AA, Broome Community Coll., 1974; BS, Cornell U., 1976; PhD, U. Ariz., 1983. Postdoctoral fellow U. Ariz., Tucson, 1983—. Recipient Meritorious Performance in Teaching award Ariz. Found., 1981; grantee Ariz. Health Scis. Ctr., 1984. Republican. Roman Catholic. Home: PO Box 40333 Tucson AZ 85717 Office: U Ariz Biochemistry BSW Tucson AZ 85721

SLIND, KATHLEEN CLARA, elementary teacher, consultant on child abuse prevention; b. Seattle, May 27, 1948; d. Donald Gilbert and Juanita Lucille Sinex L.; m. Marvin Gilbert Slind, Feb. 14, 1982; children: Erick Tavis Lee, Kiersten Heather Lee. EdB, Pacific Lutheran U., 1970; EdM, Trinity Coll., Hartford, Conn., 1977. Elem. tchr. White River Sch. Dist., Buckley, Wash., 1970; kgn. tchr. Mercer Day Care Ctr., East Hartford, Conn., 1972-77; elem. tchr. Pullman (Wash.) Sch. Dist., 1979—; cons. Com. for Children and U. Wash., Seattle, 1984—. Editor and pub. Young Writer's Conf., 1984. Nominated as Phoebe Apperson Hearst Outstanding Educator, Jefferson Sch. PTA, Pullman, Wash., 1985. Mem. Nat. Edn. Assn., Wash. Edn. Assn., Phi Delta Kappa. Democrat. Lutheran. Avocations: reading, skiing. Home: SE 1240 Earthtone Ct Pullman WA 99163 Office: Pullman Sch Dist NW 1150 Bryant St Pullman WA 99163

SLOAN, GERALD MARK, plastic surgeon, medical educator; b. New Haven, Jan. 19, 1951. AB, Harvard U., 1972, MD, 1976. Diplomate Am. Bd. Plastic Surgery, Am. Bd. Surgery. Intern Peter Brent Brigham Hosp., Boston, 1976-77, resident in surgery, 1977-78; resident in surgery Tufts-New Eng. Med. Ctr., Boston, 1980-82; resident in plastic surgery U. So. Calif., Los Angeles, 1982-84; clin. assoc. surgery br. Nat. Cancer Inst., Bethesda, Md., 1978-80; asst. prof. surgery U. So. Calif. Med. Sch., Los Angeles, 1984—; cons. City of Hope Nat. Med. Ctr., Duarte, Calif., 1984—. Contbr. articles to profl. jours. Served with USPHS, 1978-80. AMA, Am. Soc. Plastic and Reconstructive Surgeons, Inc., Assn. Acad. Surgery, Los Angeles County Med. Assn., Phi Beta Kappa, Sigma Xi. Office: Childrens Hosp 4650 Sunset Blvd Los Angeles CA 90027

SLOAN, HIRAM COOPER, company executive; b. Amarillo, Tex., Apr. 16, 1929; s. Hiram Cooper and Mary Lou (Thomas) S.; m. Phyllis Mae Hofferbert, Aug. 8, 1959 (div. Dec. 1965); 1 child, Jeffrey Dean. B.S.E.E., Tex. A&M U., 1949; M.B.A. candidate U. Calif.-Berkeley, 1960, Ohio State U., 1954. Registered profl. engr., Ohio, Calif. Test/sales engr. Gen. Electric Co., 1949-53, sales mgr., Waynesboro, Va., 1955-61, mgr. sales, Phila., 1961-62; sales mgr. Internat. Rectifier Corp., El Segundo, Calif., 1962-64; sr. project adminstr. AiResearch/Garrett Corp., Torrance, Calif., 1965-72; pres. UPS Co., Torrance, 1972—, chmn. bd., 1972—; cons. patentee fluorescent light ballast. Served to 1st lt. USAF, 1953-55. Mem. Soc. Automotive Engrs., IEEE, North Orange County Computer Club, Educators Computer Group. Republican. Baptist. Office: UPS 3726 W 172d St Torrance CA 90504

SLOAN, ROBERT FRANCIS, management consultant; b. Los Angeles, June 19, 1935; s. Lafayette F. and Frances (Walsh) S.; B.A. in Zoology, UCLA, 1957; Ph.D. in Oral Radiology, Osaka Dental U., 1977; m. Estela Alarid, June 8, 1961 (dec. May 1982); children—Patrick S., Cristina, Brett. Research asso. U. Calif. Med.-Dental Sch., Los Angeles, 1957-67; founding pres. Rocky Mountain Data Systems, 1967-70; founding exec. dir. Found. Orthodontic Research, 1968-70; exec. dir. InterAm. Orthodontic Seminar, 1964-70; mgmt. cons., Calif., 1978; chmn. bd. Radiol. Mgmt. Communications, Ltd., ITA Ltd., prof. Grad. Sch. of Business, U.S. Internat. U., San Diego, 1977-79; producer documentary and tech. films. Served to capt. M.S.C., U.S. Army, 1957-69. Recipient Bronze N.Y. Film Festival award, 1973, 79, Chris award, 1965, 73, Cine awards, 1964, 65, 74. Mem. ADA, Brit. Inst. Radiology, AMA, Found. Orthodontic Research (hon.), Socieda de Brasileira de Foniatria (hon. mem.). Contbr. articles on radiol. studies to profl. jours. Home: 10342 Wilkins Ave Los Angeles CA 90024

SLOAN, RONALD R., diversified company executive; b. 1934; married. BS, Oreg. State U., 1959. Plant mgr. Albany Frozen Foods, 1960-61; v.p. personnel indsl. relations Lamb-Weston Inc., 1961-72; sr. v.p. mfg. Amfac Foods Inc., Portland, Oreg., 1972-76; with Amfac Inc., parent co., San Francisco, 1976—, dir. indsl. relations, 1976-78, exec. v.p. employee relations, then sr. v.p. adminstrn., then exec. v.p., 1978-84, exec. v.p., chmn. hotels and resorts group, 1984-85, chief operating officer, 1985-86, pres., chief exec. officer, 1986—. Office: Amfac Inc 44 Montgomery St San Francisco CA 94104 •

SLOANE, BEVERLY LEBOV, writer, consultant; b. N.Y.C., May 26, 1936; d. Benjamin S. and Anne (Weinberg) LeBov; AB, Vassar Coll., 1958; MA, Claremont Grad. Sch., 1975, postgrad., 1975-76; grad. exec. program. Sch. Mgmt., UCLA, 1982; grad. pub. course Stanford U., 1982; m. Robert Malcolm Sloane, Sept. 27, 1959; 1 dau., Alison Lori. Circulation librarian Harvard Med. Library, Boston, 1958-59; social worker Conn. State Welfare, New Haven, 1960-61; tchr. English, Hebrew Day Sch., New Haven, 1961-64; instr. creative writing and English lit. Monmouth Coll., West Long Branch, N.J., 1967-69; freelance writer, Arcadia, Calif., 1970—. Mem. public relations bd. Monmouth County Mental Health Assn., 1968-69; adv. council tech. and profl. writing dept. English, Calif. State U., Long Beach, 1980-82; v.p. Council of Grad. Students, Claremont Grad. Sch., 1971-72, mem. campaign com., 1986—; trustee Ctr. for Improvement of Child Caring, 1981-83; mem. League Crippled Children, 1982—; bd. dirs. Los Angeles Commn. on Assaults Against Women, 1983-84; v.p. Temple Beth David, 1983-86; mem. community relations com. Jewish Fedn. Council Greater Los Angeles, 1985—; bd. dirs. Los Angeles Commn. Assaults Against Women, 1983-84. Coro Found. fellow, 1979. Fellow Am. Med. Writers Assn. (dir. 1980—, Pacific S.W. del. to nat. bd. 1980—, chmn. various conv. coms., chmn. nat. book awards trade category 1982-83, chmn. Nat. Conv. Networking Luncheon 1983, 84, chmn. freelance and pub. relations coms. Nat. Midyr. Conf. 1983-84, workshop leader ann. conf. 1984, 85, 86, nat. chmn. freelance sect. 1984-85, gen. chmn. 1985 Asilomar Conf., program co-chmn., 1986-87, nat. exec. bd. dirs. 1985-86, nat. adminstr. sects. 1985-86, pres.-elect Pacific Southwest chpt. 1985—, chairperson general session nat. conf., 1986-87, chairperson Walter C. Alvarez Meml. Found. award 1986-87); mem. Women in Communications (dir. 1980—, v.p. community affairs 1981-82, N.E. area rep. 1980-81, chmn. awards banquet 1982, sem. leader ann. nat. profl. conf., 1985, program adv. com. Los Angeles chpt. 1987, chmn. Los Angeles chpt. 1st ann. Agnes Underwood Freedom of Info. Awards Banquet 1982, recognition award 1983, nominating com. 1982, 83), Am. Assn. for Higher Edn., AAUW (legis. chmn. Arcadia br. 1976-77, books and plays chmn. Arcadia br. 1973-74, creative writing chmn. 1969-70, 1st v.p. 1975-76, networking chmn. 1981-82, Woman of Achievement award 1986), Coll. English Assn., Am. Pub. Health Assn., Calif. Press Women (v.p. programs Los Angeles chpt. 1982-85, pres. 1985—), AAUP, Internat. Communication Assn., N.Y. Acad. Scis., Ind. Writers So. Calif., Hastings Inst., AAAS, Am. Med. Writers Assn. (pres.-elect Pacific S.W. chpt. 1985—, nat. dir. sects. 1985—, exec. bd. dirs. 1985—, chmn. nominating com. 1987—), Calif. Press Women (pres. Los Angeles chpt. 1985—, pres. Calif. state affiliate, bd. dirs. Nat. Fedn. Press Women, Inc. 1987—, chmn. state women of achievement com. 1986—), AAUW (chpt. Woman of Achievement award 1986), Soc. for Tech. Communication (workshop leader, 1985, 86), Kennedy Inst. Ethics, Soc. Health and Human Values, Assoc. Writing Programs. Clubs: Rotary of Duarte; Vassar of So. Calif., Calif. Inst. Tech. Women's, Claremont Colls. Faculty House, Pasadena Athletic, Stock Exchange of Los Angeles, Town Hall of Calif. (vice chmn. community affairs sect. 1982—, speaker, 1986, instr. Exec. Breakfast Inst., 1985-86, mem. study sect. council, 1986—). Author: From Vassar to Kitchen, 1967; A Guide to Health Facilities: Personnel and Management, 2d rev. edit., 1977; mem. adv. bd. Calif. Health Rev., 1982-83. Home and Office: 1301 N Santa Anita Ave Arcadia CA 91006

SLOANE, ROBERT MALCOLM, hospital administrator; b. Boston, Feb. 11, 1933; s. Alvin and Florence (Goldberg) S.; m. Beverly LeBov, Sept. 27, 1959; 1 dau., Alison. A.B., Brown U., 1954; M.S., Columbia U., 1958. Adminstrv. resident Mt. Auburn Hosp., Cambridge, Mass., 1957-58; med. adminstr. AT&T, N.Y.C., 1959-60; asst. dir. Yale New Haven Hosp., 1961-67; assoc. adminstr. Monmouth Med. Center, Long Branch, N.J., 1967-69; adminstr. City of Hope Nat. Med. Center, Duarte, Calif., 1969-80; pres. Los Angeles Orthopedic Hosp., Los Angeles Orthopedic Found., 1980-86, Anaheim (Calif.) Meml. Hosp., 1986—; mem. faculty Columbia U. Sch. Medicine, 1958-59, Yale U. Sch. Medicine, 1963-67, Quinnipiac Coll., 1963-67, Pasadena City Coll., 1972-73, Calif. Inst. Tech., 1973-85, U. So. Calif., 1976-79, UCLA, 1985—; chmn. bd. Health Data Net, 1971-73; pres. Anaheim (Calif.) Meml. Hosp., 1986—. Author: (with B. L. Sloane) A Guide to Health Facilities: Personnel and Management, 1971, 2d edit., 1977; editorial and adv. bd.: Health Devices, 1972—; contbr. articles to hosp. jours. Bd. dirs. Health Systems Agy. Los Angeles County, 1977-78; Bd. dirs. Calif. Hosp. Polit. Action Com., 1979-85, vice chmn., 1980-83, chmn., 1983-85. Served to lt. (j.g.) USNR, 1954-56. Fellow Am. Coll. Hosp. Adminstrs.; mem. Am. Pub. Health Assn., Am. Hosp. Assn., Hosp. Council So. Calif. (dir., treas. 1983, sec. 1982, chmn. elect 1984, chmn. 1985, past chmn. 1986—), Calif. Hosp. Assn. (dir. 1984-86). Home: 1301 N Santa Anita Ave Arcadia CA 91006 Office: 1111 W LaPalma Ave PO Box 3005 Anaheim CA 92803

SLOCUM, RICHARD GENE, nuclear research and development executive; b. Los Angeles, Dec. 12, 1942; s. Donald Gene and Ada May (Condreay) S.; m. Patricia Gail Hayman, Sept. 5, 1963; children: Kenneth James, Kelly Jean. Grad. high sch. Joined Submarine Force, U.S. Navy, 1960, advanced to force master chief petty officer, 1975, ret., 1979; mgr. nuclear research and devel. Westinghouse Hanford Co., Richland, Wash., 1979—. Mem. Am. Nuclear Soc., Nat. Mgmt. Assn., Fleet Res. Assn., Navy Meml. Found. Home: 602 Linda Ct Richland WA 99352 Office: PO Box 1970 Richland WA 99352

SLOVER, ARCHY F., chemist; b. Oshkosh, Wis., July 8, 1920; s. Archie F. and Josephine Petronella (Zindler); B.A., U. Calif., Los Angeles, 1947; m. Mary Beatrice Corkill, May 25, 1946; 1 dau., Mary Kay Slover Eckhardt. Devel. chemist Kelite Products Co., Los Angeles, 1946-49; v.p., gen. mgr. Delco Chems. Inc., Los Angeles, 1949-57; mgr. indsl. spltys. Pennwalt Corp., Los Angeles, 1957-74; chemist Custom Chem. Formulators Inc., Cudahy, Calif., 1974—; mgr. Cherokee Chem. Co., Inc., Compton, Calif., 1976—; cons. in field. Served to capt. U.S. Army, 1942-46. Fellow AAAS, Am. Inst. Chemists; mem. Nat. Assn. Corrosion Engrs., Am. Chem. Soc., Am. Electroplaters Soc., USAF Assn., Soc. Advancement Material Process Engrs., Res. Officers Assn., Sigma Alpha Epsilon. Club: Ky. Cols. Patentee in field. Address: 21 Hacienda Dr Arcadia CA 91006

SLUSSER, ROBERT WYMAN, aerospace company executive; b. Mineola, N.Y., May 10, 1938; s. John Leonard and Margaret McKenzie (Wyman) S.; B.S., MIT, 1960; M.B.A., Wharton Sch., U. Pa., 1962; m. Linda Killeas, Aug. 3, 1968; children—Jonathan, Adam, Robert, Mariah. Assoc. adminstr.'s staff NASA Hdqrs., Washington, 1962-65; with Northrop Corp., Hawthorne, Calif., 1965—, adminstr. mktg. and planning dept., space labs., 1965-68, mgr. bus. and fin. Warnecke Electron Tubes Co. div., Chgo., 1968-71, controller Cobra Program Aircraft div., Hawthorne, 1971-72, mgr. bus. adminstrn. YF-17 Program, 1972-75, mgr. adminstrn. F-18/Cobra programs, also mgr. F-18 design to cost program, 1975-78, mgr. adminstrn. F-18L program, 1978-79, mgr. engring. adminstrn., 1980-82, acting v.p. engring., 1982, mgr. data processing, 1983-84, v.p. info. resources, 1985—. Grumman Aircraft Engring. scholar, 1956-60. Assoc. fellow AIAA. Home: 7270 Berry Hill Drive Rancho Palos Verdes CA 90274 Office: Warnecke Electron Tubes Co One Northrop Ave Hawthorne CA 90250

SMAIL, ANNETTE KLANG, civic leader; b. St. Helena, Calif., July 20, 1920; d. Leon and Victoria Nellie (Hartman) K.; divorced; children: Barry Lee, Karen Smail Poksay. AA, San Francisco Jr. Coll., 1939; AB, U. Calif., Berkeley, 1943; postgrad., U. Chgo., 1945. Cert. adult teaching credential in social studies and English. News reporter Community Newspapers, Chgo., 1945-46; editor textbooks U. Calif., Berkeley, 1948-49; edn. coordinator Econ. Opportunity Council, San Rafael, Calif., 1969-71. Community organizer Novato (Calif.) Human Needs Ctr., 1970-72; founder, leader Older Women's Polit. Caucus, 1977-85, Med. Equality for Dependents, 1977; author of various resolutions passed by Calif. legis. on med. rights, retirement and women's rights; del. White House Conf. on Aging, Washington, 1981; mem. Calif. Task Force on Feminization of Poverty, Sacramento, 1984. Recipient San Francisco Working Woman Achievement award Working Woman mag., 1983, Women Helping Women award Soroptomists, 1979; named Disting. Woman of Yr., Novato Advance Newspaper, 1979. Mem. Nat. Women's Studies Assn., Women's Equity Action League, Am. Jewish Congress. Democrat. Initiator congl. bills: med. rights for former wives, passed 1982; also leading advocate on congl. proposal to create Fed. Council on Women, introduced 1986. Avocations: gardening, reading, walking, visiting friends. Home: 63 Monte Vista Novato CA 94947

SMALL, ELISABETH CHAN, physician, educator; b. Beijing, July 11, 1934; came to U.S., 1937; d. Stanley Hong and Lily Luella (Lum) Chan; m. Donald M. Small, July 8, 1957 (div. 1980); children Geoffrey Brooks, Philip Willard Stanley. Student, Immaculate Heart Coll., Los Angeles, 1951-52; BA in Polit. Sci., UCLA, 1955, MD, 1960. Intern Newton-Wellesley Hosp., Mass., 1960-61; asst. dir. for venereal diseases Mass. Dept. Pub. Health, 1961-63; resident in psychiatry Boston State Hosp., Mattapan, Mass., 1965-66; resident in psychiatry Tufts New Eng. Med. Ctr. Hosps., 1966-69, psychiat. cons. dept. gynecology, 1973-75; asst. clin. prof. psychiatry Sch. Medicine Tufts U., 1973-75, assoc. clin. prof., 1975-82, asst. clin. prof. ob-gyn, 1977-80, assoc. clin. prof. ob-gyn, 1980-82; assoc. prof. psychiatry, ob-gyn U. Nev. Sch. Med., Reno, 1982-85; practice psychiatry specializing in psychological effects of bodily changes on women 1969—; clin. prof. psychiatry U. Nev. Sch. Medicine, Reno, 1985-86, prof. psychiatry, 1986—, clin. assoc. prof. ob-gyn, 1985—; mem. staff Tufts New Eng. Med. Ctr. Hosps., 1973-82, St. Margaret's Hosps., Boston, 1977-82, Washoe Med. Ctr., Reno, Sparks (Nev.) Family Hosp., Truckee Meadows Hosp., Reno, St. Mary's Hosp., Reno; lectr. various univs., 1961—; cons. in psychiatry; mem. psychiatry adv. panel Hosp. Satellite Network; mem. office external peer rev. NIMH, HEW; psychiat. cons. to Boston Redevelopment Authority on Relocation of Chinese Families of South Cove Area, 1968-70; mem. New Eng. Med. Ctr. Hosps. Cancer Ctr. Com., 1979-80, Pain Control Com., 1981-82, Tufts Univ. Sch. Medicine Reproductive System Curriculum Com., 1975-82. Mem. editorial bd. Psychiat. Update Am. (Psychiat. Assn. ann. rev.), 1983-85; reviewer Psychosomatics and Hosp. Community Psychiatry, New Eng. Jour. of Medicine, Am. Jour. of Psychiatry Psychosomatic Medicine; contbr. articles to profl. jours. Immaculate Heart Coll. scholar, 1951-52; Mira Hershey scholar UCLA, 1955; fellow Radcliffe Inst., 1967-70. Mem. AMA, Am. Psychiat. Assn. (rep. to sect. com. AAAS, chmn. ad hoc com. Asian-Am. Psychiatrists 1975, task force 1975-77, task force cost effectiveness in consultation 1984—, caucus chmn. 1981-82, sci. program com. 1982—, courses subcom. chmn. sci. program com., 1986-88), Mass. Med. Soc., Am. Coll. Sports Medicine, Am. Geriatrics Soc., Am. Soc. Psychomatic Ob-Gyn (mem.-at-large 1982-83, curriculum com. 1981-82), New Eng. Soc. Clin. Hypnosis, Assn. Acad. Psychiatry (fellowship com. 1982—), Am. Pain Soc., Nev. Psychiat. Assn., Washoe County Med. Assn., Nev. Med. Soc., Am. Soc. Clin. Hypnosis, Am. Coll. Psychiatrists, Eastern Profl. Ski Instrs. Assn. Avocations: snow skiing, culinary arts. Home: 2105 Chicory Way Reno NV 89509 Office: 1000 Locust St Reno NV 89520

SMALL, LAWRENCE FARNSWORTH, history educator; b. Bangor, Maine, Dec. 30, 1925; s. Irving Wheelock and Geneva May (Turner) S.; m. Elfie Joan Ames, Aug. 9, 1947; children: Kathleen Ann, Linda Jean, Lawrence Farnsworth, Daniel Irving. B.D., Bangor Theol. Sem., 1948; B.A., U. Maine, 1948, M.A., 1951; Ph.D., Harvard, 1955. Ordained to ministry Congregational Ch., 1950; minister Paramus (N.J.) Congl. Ch., 1955-59; asso. prof. history Rocky Mountain Coll., Billings, Mont., 1959-61; prof. Rocky Mountain Coll., 1975—, dean of Coll., 1961-65, acting pres., 1965-66, pres., 1966-75; Chmn. Mont. commn. Higher Edn. Facilities Act, 1965-74; exec. dir. Mont. Assn. Chs. Author: Montana Passage, A Century of Politics on the Yellowstone, Journey with the Law, the Life of Judge William J. Jameson. Pres. Yellowstone County Council Chs., 1968-70; treas. Mont. Conf., United Ch. of Christ, 1970-73; chmn. bd. dirs. Western Independent Colls. Found.; bd. dirs. Community Concert Assn., Yellowstone County Mental Health Assn., Billings Citizens for Community Devel., Billings United Fund; trustee Billings Deaconess Hosp. Mem. Phi Beta Kappa, Phi Kappa Phi. Club: Kiwanis (pres. Billings). Home: 7320 Sumatra Pl Rural Route 4 Billings MT 59106 Office: 1511 Poly St Billings MT 59102

SMALL, LAWRENCE FREDERICK, oceanography educator; b. St. Louis, Feb. 16, 1934; s. Frederick Ruse and Adele Naomi (Edwards) S.; m. Janice Ethel Hammersley; children: Karen Loraine, Stephen Lawrence, Suzanne Marie. AB, U. Mo., 1955; MS, Iowa State U., 1959, PhD, 1961. Asst. prof. oceanography Oreg. State U., Corvallis, 1961-67, assoc. prof., 1967-74, prof., 1974—, assoc. dean oceanography, 1983—; cons. IAEA, Monaco, 1971-72,

78, Pacific Northwest River Basins Commn., Portland, Oreg., 1980-81, Columbia River Data Mgmt. Program, Astoria, Oreg., 1982. Contbr. articles to profl. jours. Served to 1st lt. arty. U.S. Army, 1955-57. Recipient Spl. Service awards IAEA, 1972, 78; grantee NOAA, NSF, Dept. Energy, Office Naval Research, EPA, 1962—. Mem. AAAS, Am. Soc. Limnology and Oceanography, Phycol. Soc. Am., Western Soc. Naturalists, Sigma Xi, Beta Theta Pi. Avocations: birdwatching, hiking, travel with family, phys. exercise, reading. Office: Oreg State U Coll Oceanography Corvallis OR 97331

SMALL, RICHARD DAVID, research scientist; b. Syracuse, N.Y., Jan. 6, 1945; s. Sydney Morton Small and Gertrude (Burman) Goldberg; m. Tsipora Meirson, Dec. 11, 1977; children: Eileen Lara, Carrie Ayala, Sharon Yael. BS, Rutgers U., 1967, MS, 1968, M Phil., 1969, PhD, 1971. Instr. Rutgers U., New Brunswick, N.J., 1970-71; sr. lectr. Technion, Haifa, Israel, 1971-78; sr. engr. Pacific-Sierra Research Corp., Los Angeles, 1979—; vis. asst. prof., U. Calif., Los Angeles, 1977-79, vis. scholar U. Calif., 1979-81; lectr. various univs. and confs. Contbr. over 50 articles to profl. jours. Served with Israeli Army, 1977. Recipient Rothschild Found. prize, 1974; NDEA fellow, 1967-70; N.J. Soc. Profl. Engrs. scholar, 1967. Mem. AIAA, N.Y. Acad. Scis., Nat. Adv. Com. Nuclear Winter Expts., Sigma Xi. Republican. Jewish. Home: 1465 Eastwind Circle Westlake Village CA 91361 Office: Pacific-Sierra Research Corp 12340 Santa Monica Blvd Los Angeles CA 90025

SMALLIE, PAUL (DONALD), author, editor and publisher; b. Madera, Calif., Aug. 22, 1913; s. Robert Samuel and Lillie (Kelly) S.; m. Margret Lloyds, Feb. 8, 1952; children: Marlies Diane Smallie Schaefer, Donald David, Dennis Robert. Doctor of Chiropractic, Ratledge Chiropractic Coll., 1935; HHD (hon.), Columbia U., 1972. Mem. faculty San Francisco Chiropractic Coll., 1946-47; editor/publisher WORLD-WIDE REPORT, Stockton, Calif., 1958—. Author: Chiropractic Encyclopedia, 1972, 2d edit. 1980, Scientific Chiropractic, 1985, Happy Healthy Way to Life, 1985. Served with U.S. Army, 1941-42. Mem. Internat. Chiropractors Assn. (exec. sec. 1972-77), Chiropractic Press Guild (pres. 1968-72), Am. Chiropractic Assn., Calif. Chiropractic Assn. (editor 1964-69). Lodge: Lions (pres. 1960-61). Home: 1056 Friar Stockton CA 95209 Office: World Wide Report 2027 Grand Canal Blvd Stockton CA 95207

SMALLING, RALPH JOHN, regulatory affairs specialist; b. Los Angeles, Sept. 15, 1955; s. Bernard M. and Catherine Louise (Schneider) S.; m. JoEllen Patrice Callaghan, Aug. 16, 1980. BA, Occidental Coll., 1977; MS, Calif. State U., Long Beach, 1981. Research assoc. Amgen, Thousand Oaks, Calif., 1982-85, regulatory affairs specialist, 1985—. Contbr. articles to sci. jours. contbr. to numerous charities; rep. Calif. State U. Career Days; annual vol. sci. fair judge Conejo Valley (Calif.) Unified Sch. Dist. Mem. Regulatory Affairs Profl. Soc., AAAS, Phi Kappa Phi. Lutheran.

SMART, GARY LEE, management company executive; b. Tucumcari, N. Mex., July 10, 1953; s. Alver Lee Smart and Jean (Pack) Rook; m. Joanne Ferguson, Jan. 18, 1975; 1 child, Kara Lee. AA, U. Albuquerque, 1975, BA, 1980. Ops. mgr. Zia Airlines, Albuquerque, 1975-80; exec. officer Mountain Graphics, Albuquerque, 1980-83, Southwest Graphics, Albuquerque, 1983-85; cons. Internat. Mgmt. Assocs., Albuquerque, 1985—; cons. Stallion Software, Houston, Tex., 1984-86, Smart Ideas, Albuquerque, 1985-86. Mem. Albuquerque C. of C. Republican. Methodist. Club: Transp. (Albuquerque). Avocations: racquetball, backpacking, golf, spelunking. Home: 605 High Ave Albuquerque NM 87102 Office: Internat Mgmt 5301 Central NE #200 Albuquerque NM 87102

SMART, WILLIAM BUCKWALTER, newspaper editor; b. Provo, Utah, June 27, 1922; s. Thomas Laurence and Nellie (Buckwalter) S.; m. Donna Toland, July 15, 1945; children: William Toland, Melinda, Kristen, Thomas Toland, Alfred Lawrence. Student, U. Wyo., 1943-44, U. Utah, 1949-51; B.A., Reed Coll., 1948. Reporter Internat. News Service, Portland, Oreg., 1941-43; reporter The Oregonian, Portland, 1946-48, The Deseret News, Salt Lake City, 1948-52; chief editorial writer, editor The Deseret News, 1952-66, exec. editor, 1966-72, editor, gen. mgr., 1972-86, sr. editor, 1986—. Bd. dirs. Western States Arts Found., Deseret Utah Art Found. ; mem. Utah State Commn. on Excellence in Edn., Coll. Commn. N.W. Assn. Schs. and Colls., Provo-Jordan River Pkwy. Found.; mem. nat. adv. bd. Snowbird Inst. for Arts and Humanities; chmn. Utah Innovation Found.; mem. Utah Gov.'s Constn. Bicentennial Commn. Served to 1st lt., inf. AUS, 1943-46, PTO. Mem. Am. Soc. Newspaper Editors (ethics com.), Am. Newspaper Pubs. Assn., Phi Beta Kappa, Sigma Delta Chi, Kappa Tau Alpha. Mem. Ch. of Jesus Christ of Latter-day Saints. Clubs: Bonneville Knife and Fork (Hidden Valley) (past pres.), Timpanogos (Hidden Valley), Fort Douglas (Hidden Valley); Salt Lake Exchange (past pres., nat. v.p. Rocky Mountain region, nat. bd. dirs.), Aztec, Alta. Home: 55 Laurel St Salt Lake City UT 84103 Office: The Deseret News Box 1257 Salt Lake City UT 84110

SMEAD, BURTON ARMSTRONG, JR., lawyer, retired banker; b. Denver, July 29, 1913; s. Burton Armstrong and Lola (Lewis) S.; m. Josephine McKittrick, Mar. 27, 1943; children—Amanda Armstrong-Cassidy, Sydney Hall. B.A., U. Denver, 1934, J.D., 1950; grad. Pacific Sch. Banking Trust Sch., 1955. Bar: Colo., 1950. With United Bank of Denver (formerly Denver Nat. Bank), 1934-78, v.p., trust officer, 1948-78, also sec., dir.; sole practice, Englewood, Colo., 1978—; dir., trust counsel, Resources Trust Co., Englewood, Colo. Pres., trustee Stebbins Orphans Home Assn. Served to maj. U.S. Army, 1941-45; ETO. Decorated Bronze Star; Croix de Guerre (France). Mem. Denver Bar Assn., Colo. Bar Assn. (treas. 1970—), ABA. Republican. Episcopalian. Club: University (Denver). Author: History of the Twelfth Field Artillery Battalion in the European Theater of Operations-1944-45, 1945. Home and office: 3130 Cherryridge Rd Englewood CO 80110

SMEDES, HARRY WYNN, geologist, consultant; b. Spokane, Wash., Sept. 11, 1926; s. Norman and Winifred May (Johnson) S.; m. Marie E. Campbell, Oct. 21, 1945 (div. 1980); children: Richard (dec.), Gerald, Randall, Alan; m. Phyllis J. Robinson, Aug. 22, 1980. BS cum laude, U. Wash., 1948, PhD in Geology, 1959. Instr. Kans. State U., Manhattan, 1951-53; research geologist U.S. Geol. Survey, Spokane, 1953-57, Washington, 1957-66, Denver, 1966-80; sr. tech. advisor U.S. Dept. Energy, Germantown, Md., 1980-82; pres. Harry W. Smedes Assocs., Las Vegas, Nev., 1982—; cons. in field. Recipient Photographic Interpretation award Am. Soc. Photogrammetry, 1975. Fellow Geol. Soc. Am., Mineral. Soc. Am.; mem. Geol. Soc. Washington, Assn. Engring. Geologists, Sigma Xi. Clubs: Explorers (N.Y.) (fellow 1980—), Cosmos (Washington).

SMEGAL, THOMAS FRANK, JR., lawyer; b. Eveleth, Minn., June 15, 1935; s. Thomas Frank and Genevieve (Andreachi) S.; m. Susan Jane Stanton, May 28, 1966; children: Thomas Frank, Elizabeth Jane. BS in Chem. Engring., Mich. Technol. U., 1957; JD, George Washington U., 1961. Bar: Va. 1961, D.C. 1961, Calif. 1964, U.S. Supreme Ct. 1976. Patent examiner U.S. Patent Office, Washington, 1957-61; staff patent atty. Shell Devel. Co., San Francisco, 1962-65; patent atty. Townsend and Townsend, San Francisco, 1965—, now mng. ptnr.; mem. U.S. del. to Paris Conv. for Protection of Indsl. Property. Pres. bd. dirs. Legal Aid Soc. San Francisco, 1982-84, Youth Law Ctr., 1973-84; bd. dirs. Nat. Ctr. for Youth Law, 1978-84, San Francisco Lawyers Com. for Urban Affairs, 1972—, Legal Services for Children, 1980—, Legal Services Corp., 1984—. Served to capt. Chem. Corps, U.S. Army, 1961-62. Recipient St. Thomas More award, 1982. Mem. ABA, Calif. Bar Assn. (v.p. bd. govs. 1986-87), Nat. Council Patent Law Assn. (dir.), Am. Patent Law Assn. (bd. dirs., pres. 1986), Internat. Assn. Intellectual Property Lawyers (dir.), Bar Assn. San Francisco, Patent Law Assn. San Francisco. Republican. Roman Catholic. Clubs: World Trade, Commonwealth, Olympic, Golden Gate Breakfast (San Francisco); Claremont (Berkeley); University (Washington). Contbr. articles to publs. in field. Office: Townsend and Townsend 1 Market Plaza San Francisco CA 94105

SMELICK, ROBERT MALCOLM, investment banker; b. Phoenix, Mar. 27, 1942; s. Valentine and Mary Helen (McDonald) S.; B.A., Stanford U., 1964; M.B.A., Harvard U., 1968; postgrad. U. Melbourne (Australia), 1965-66; m. Gail Paine Sterling, Dec. 10, 1979; children—Christopher Paine Malcolm, Alexandra McBryde, Gillian Sterling. Vice pres. Kidder Peabody & Co., Inc., N.Y.C., 1968-79; mng. dir. First Boston Corp., San Francisco, 1979—; dir. King Broadcasting Corp., The Wine Group, Mayne Nickless Holdings. Home: 615 Sausalito Blvd Sausalito CA 94965 Office: First Boston Corp 101 California St Suite 4300 San Francisco CA 94111

SMELSER, NEIL JOSEPH, sociologist; b. Kahoka, Mo., July 22, 1930; s. Joseph Nelson and Susie Marie (Hess) S.; m. Helen Thelma Margolis, June 10, 1954 (div. 1965); children: Eric Jonathan, Tina Rachel; m. Sharin Fateley, Dec. 20, 1967; children: Joseph Neil, Sarah Joanne. B.A., Harvard U., 1952, Ph.D., 1958; B.A., Magdalen Coll., Oxford U., Eng., 1954; M.A., Magdalen Coll., Oxford U., 1959; grad., San Francisco Psychoanalytic Inst., 1971. Mem. faculty U. Calif.-Berkeley, 1958—, prof. sociology, 1962—, asst. chancellor ednl. devel., 1966-68; assoc. dir. Inst. Internat. Relations, 1969-73, 80-86, Univ. prof. sociology, 1972; dir. edn. abroad program for Inst. Internat. Relations, U.K. and Ireland, 1977-79; bd. dirs. Found. Fund for Research in Psychiatry, 1967-70; bd. dirs. Social Sci. Research Council, 1968-71, chmn., 1971-73; trustee Ctr. for Advanced Study in Behavioral and Social Scis., 1980-86, 87—, chmn., 1984-86; mem. subcom. humanism Am. Bd. Internal Medicine, 1981-85; editor Am. Sociol. Rev., 1962-65; adv. editor Am. Jour. Sociology, 1960-62; mem. com. econ. growth Social Sci. Research Council, 1961-65; chmn. sociology panel Behavioral and Social Scis. survey Nat. Acad. Scis. and Social Sci. Research Council, 1967-69; mem. com. on basic research in behavioral and social scis. NRC, 1980—, chmn., 1982-86, co-chmn., 1984—. Author: (with T. Parsons) Economy and Society, 1956, Social Change in the Industrial Revolution, 1959, Theory of Collective Behavior, 1962, The Sociology of Economic Life, 1963, 2d edit., 1975, Essays in Sociological Explanation, 1968, Sociological Theory: A Contemporary View, 1971, Comparative Methods in the Social Sciences, 1976, (with Robin Content) The Changing Academic Market, 1980, Sociology, 1981, 2d edit., 1984; editor: (with W.T. Smelser) Personality and Social Systems, 1963, 2d edit., 1971, (with S.M. Lipset) Social Structure and Mobility in Economic Development, 1966, Sociology, 1967, 2d edit., 1973, (with James Davis) Sociology, a Survey Report, 1969, Karl Marx on Society and Social Change, 1973, (with Gabriel Almond) Public Higher Education in California, 1974, (with Erik Erikson) Themes of Work and Love in Adulthood, 1980, (with Jeffrey Alexander et al) The Micro-Macro Link, 1987. Rhodes scholar, 1952-54; jr. fellow Soc. Fellows, Harvard U., 1955-58. Mem. Am. Sociol. Assn. (council 1962-65, 67-70, exec. com. 1963-65), Pacific Sociol. Assn. Home: 109 Hillcrest Rd Berkeley CA 94705

SMILEY, DAVID WAYNE, microbiologist; b. Ft. Wayne, Ind., Mar. 24, 1956; s. Dale W. and Virginia L. (Allman) S.; m. Gloria M. Skoniecke, July 29, 1978; 1 dau., Sarah M. AB in Microbiology, Miami U., Oxford, Ohio, 1978; MS in Biol Sci., Ill. State U., 1981. Research assoc. Dept. Biochemistry Colo. State U., Ft. Collins, 1981-84; research scientist Syngene Products and Research, Ft. Collins, 1984-86, Cell Tech., Inc., Boulder, 1986—. Contbr. articles to profl. jours. Mem. Am. Soc. Microbiology, Sigma Xi, Sigma Phi Epsilon (pres. 1977-78, Outstanding Pres. award 1978). Avocations: sports, hiking, camping, skiing, reading. Home: 1500 W Mountain Fort Collins CO 80521 Office: Cell Tech Inc 1668 Valtec Ln Boulder CO 80301

SMILEY, GLEN FRANK, electronics engineer; b. St. Petersburg, Fla., Apr. 15, 1935; s. Russell Glen and Rosila Milldrum (Baker) S.; m. Joyce Anne Dorshow, July 14, 1965; children: Denis Brian, Boyd Alan. BS, U.S. Naval Acad., 1958; BSEE, U. Fla., 1965. Commd. ensign USN, 1958, advanced through grades to lt. (j.g.) Supply Corps, resigned, 1963; ops. and maintenance tng. engr. Bullpup Missile Martin Marietta Corp., Orlando, Fla., 1965-67; field service engr. Martin Marietta Corp., Lemoore, Calif. and Cherry Point, N.C., 1965-67; research and devel., ops. and maintenance tng. engr. Laser Systems, 1967-69; field service engr. Eglin AFB (Fla.), Royal Thai AFB (Ubol, Thailand), 1967-69; maintainability engr. Sprint Missile, Orlando, Fla., 1969-71; field service engr. Army Air Def. Command, Colorado Springs, Colo., 1971-75; prodn./test engr. satellite systems high tech. products Ball Aerospace Systems div. (formerly Ball Bros. Research Corp.), Boulder, Colo., 1976-80, sr. staff engr., troubleshooter, 1980-81, mgr. test ops., 1981-82; sr. prodn. engr. CRRES Spacecraft, 1983-86; prodn. mgr. CRRES Spacecraft, Boulder, Colo., 1986—. Chmn. Coronation Ball, Miss Fla. Pageant, 1971. Mem. IEEE, Nat. Assn. Parliamentarians (v.p. Henry Martyn Robert unit 1973-74), U.S. Naval Acad. Alumni Assn. (life), Smithsonian Instn., U.S. Jaycees (dist. sec. 1970-71). Lodge: Masons (master mason Boulder chpt. 1985). Home: 4738 Ipswich Boulder CO 80301

SMILEY, RICHARD MILLDRUM, leasing company executive, consultant; b. St. Petersburg, Fla., Apr. 22, 1928; s. Russell Glen and Rosila (Milldrum) S.; m. Beryl Jeanne Jensen, Sept. 21, 1956; children: Shannon, Kristin, Brett, Clayton. BA, U. Fla., 1950; BS, Am. Inst. Fgn. Trade, Glendale, Ariz., 1955. CLU. Staff mgr. IBM Corp., Chgo., 1969-73; sr. mktg. exec. IBM Corp., Los Angeles, 1973-84; v.p. Matrix Computer Co., Salt Lake City, 1984—. Rep. dist. chmn., Salt Lake City, 1986; pres. So. Calif. Sch. Adv. Council, Chatsworth, 1977. Served with U.S. Army, 1950-54. Fellow Life Ins. Mgmt. Inst.; mem. Am. Coll. Life Underwriters, Salt Lake City C. of C. (chmn. subcom. 1986), MENSA. Mormon. Lodge: Salt Lake Rotary. Home: 816 16th Ave Salt Lake City UT 84103 Office: Matrix Computer Funding Corp 6925 Union Park Ctr Midvale UT 84047

SMILEY, VERN NEWTON, JR., physicist; b. Goshen, Ind., Sept. 7, 1930; s. Vern Newton Sr. and Dorothy Taylor (Pearce) S.; m. Sylvia Susan Maday, Jan 28, 1956. BS, U. Wis., 1955, MS, 1956; PhD, U. Colo., 1959. Problem mgr. Navy Elec. Lab., San Diego, 1961-71; research prof. Desert Research Inst., Reno, 1971-80, cons., 1980-81; liaison scientist Office Naval Research, London, 1977-79; sci. officer Office Naval Research, Pasadena, Calif., 1986—; sect. head IV EG&G Energy Measurment, Las Vegas, 1980-86; cons. EG&G, Las Vegas, 1987—; cons. Convair, San Diego, 1959-61, USN, San Diego, 1961-64. Author book chpts.; contbr. articles to profl. jours. Served as sgt. U.S. Army, 1951-54. Research assoc. Nat. Acad. Scis. Navy Elec. Lab., 1961; USN fellow, York, Eng., 1966. Mem. Soc. Profl. Indsl. Engrs., Optical Soc. Am., Sigma Xi. Office: Office Naval Research 1030 E Green St Pasadena CA 91106

SMILIE, LARRY ALLEN, banker; b. Tokyo, July 30, 1953; s. Richard Clarence and Atsuko (Nagahashi) S.; Barbara Dean. A.A., Monterey Peninsula Coll., 1973; B.S., U. Calif.-Berkeley, 1976; M.B.A., San Francisco State U., 1978. Asst. v.p. Bank of Am., San Francisco, 1978-82, v.p., mgr., Los Angeles, 1984-87; v.p. lease sydications, asst. v.p. First Interstate Bank of Calif., San Francisco, 1982-84. Mem. Alpha Tau Omega. Clubs: Bachelors (San Francisco); Family. Home: 1441 Jones St #503 San Francisco CA 94109 Office: Bank Amerilease 2 Embarcadero San Francisco CA 94111

SMITH, ALAN HUGGER, dentist; b. Evansville, Ind., Apr. 4, 1942; s. Claude Bryan and Marie (Hugger) S.; m. Bonita Elizabeth Peacock, Oct. 24, 1970; Student Ind. State U., 1960-62, U. Evansville, 1960; D.D.S., Ind. U., 1966; postgrad. U. Nebr., 1966-68, L.D. Pankey Inst. Advanced Dental Edn., 1976, 77, 79, 81, 84, U. Wash., 1982-83. Mem. staff Lincoln (Nebr.) Orthopedic Hosp., Lincoln State Hosp., 1967-68, Berrien County Health Clinic (Mich.), 1968; pvt. practice dentistry, Vancouver, B.C., Can., 1968-71, Portland, Oreg., 1971—; mem. faculty U. Oreg. Health Scis. Ctr., part-time, 1973-78; vol. various local dental programs. Bd. dirs. Mt. Hood Kiwanis Camp for Handicapped Children. Mem. Am. Assn. for Advancement of Tension Control, ADA, Portland Acad. Hypnosis, Oreg. Dental Assn. (del.), L.D. Pankey Alumni Assn., Am. Equilibration Soc., Am. Acad. Gen. Dentistry, Lambda Chi Alpha, Psi Omega. Clubs: East Portland TMJ Study, Kiwanis. Office: 16740 SE Stark St Portland OR 97233 Also: 1110 SW Salmon Portland OR 97205

SMITH, ALBERT CROMWELL, JR., investments consultant; b. Norfolk, Va., Dec. 6, 1925; s. Albert Cromwell and Georgie (Foreman) S.; B.S. in Civil Engring., Va. Mil. Inst., 1949; M.S. in Govtl. Adminstrn., George Washington U., 1965; M.B.A., Pepperdine U., 1975; m. Laura Thaxton, Oct. 25, 1952; children—Albert, Elizabeth, Laura. Enlisted USMC, 1944, commd. 2d lt., 1949, advanced through grades to col., 1970; comdr. inf. platoons, companies, landing force; variously assigned staffs U.K. Joint Forces, U.S. Sec. Navy, Brit. Staff Coll., Marine Staff Coll.; adviser, analyst amphibious systems; ret., 1974; pres. A. Cromwell-Smith, Ltd., Charlottesville, Va., 1973, head broker, cons. A. Cromwell Smith, Investments, La Jolla and Coronado, Calif., 1975—. Bd. dirs. Republicans of La Jolla, 1975-76; vestryman St. Martin's Episcopal Ch., 1971-73. Decorated Legion of Merit with oak leaf cluster, Bronze Star medal with oak leaf cluster, Air medal with 2 oak leaf clusters, Purple Heart. Mem. ASCE, Nat., Calif. assns. Realtors, San Diego, Coronado bds. Realtors, Stockbrokers Soc., So. Calif. Options Soc., SAR, Mil. Order Purple Heart. Club: Kona Kai. Author: The Individual Investor in Tomorrow's Stock Market, 1977; The Little Guy's Stock Market Survival Guide, 1979; Wake Up Detroit! The EVs Are Coming, 1982; The Little Guy's Tax Survival Guide, 1984; The Little Guy's Sailboat Success Guide, 1986; contbr. articles to civilian and mil. publs. Office: 1001 B Ave Suite 319/320 PO Box 192 Coronado CA 92118

SMITH, ALLAN WISTER, retired navy officer, real estate broker; b. Media, Pa., May 14, 1921; s. Allan Meredith and Viola Minerva (Wister) S.; m. Modesta Maria Sousa, June 30, 1974; children—Thomas J., Elizabeth M., Tammy A. Student U. Pa., 1939-40, U. N.C., 1943, U.S. Naval War Coll., Skagit Valley Coll., 1976-77. Registered rep. SEC; cert. real estate broker, Wyo. Enlisted USN, 1941, advanced through grades to comdr., 1959, active duty, 1941-46, 51-67; patrol plane comdr., 1944-45; active NATO ops., Portugal and Greece, 1955-56; comdg. officer USNR Tng. Center, Cadillac, Mich., 1962-67; ret., 1967; pilot TWA, Kansas City, 1947-50; office mgr. Allstate Ins. Co., Sarasota, Fla., 1968-70; mgmt. cons. Snelling and Snelling, Alexandria, Va., 1970-71; real estate broker comml. dept. Mile High Realty, Cheyenne, Wyo., 1978-79, Rosenberg-Storey, Cheyenne, 1979-80; owner, operator real estate co., 1981—; chmn., pres. Great Am. Properties, Ltd., Cheyenne, Wyo., 1981—. Active Republican Party. Decorated Air medal; recipient HOnor award Mil. Police, Goiania, Brazil, 1986. Mem. Wyo. Assn. Realtors, Nat. Assn. Realtors, Cheyenne Bd. Realtors, Cheyenne C. of C. (Mayors bus. adv. com. 1982), Wyo. Ptnrs. of the Americas (pres., chmn. econ. devel. and legis. activity), Wyo. Archaeol. Soc., Wyo. Hist. Soc. Home: 6305 Elk Ave Cheyenne WY 82009 Office: 1611 Morrie Ave Cheyenne WY 82001

SMITH, ALONZO DAVID, marketing executive; b. Detroit, Sept. 25, 1945; s. Robert Hugh and Roxie Minnie (Clowney) S.; m. Brenda Elizabeth Bryson, June 1, 1968; children: Donielle Catrice, Lia Nichole, Robert Hugh II. BA in Mktg., Detroit Coll. Bus., 1971; D (hon.), Napoleon Hill Acad., 1974. Shipping mgr. Chrysler Corp., Detroit, 1964-72; dist. mgr. Equitable Life Ins. Co., Detroit, 1972-74; HQ acct. rep. Chesebrough-Ponds, Inc., Greenwich, Conn., 1974-77; nat. mgr. Exxon Bus. Machines, Los Angeles, 1977-79; sr. systems cons. Gen. Dynamics Corp., St. Louis, 1979-83; PBX acct. exec. U.S. West Info. Systems, Inc., Los Angeles, 1983—; cons. various corps., Calif., 1984—. Pres. Orange County (Calif.) Jr. All-Am. Football League, Cerritos, 1982-84, Distributive Edn. Clubs Am., Detroit, 1972; active Cerritos Civic Leaders, 1981—. Recipient Mayor's award City of Cerritos, 1981-85, Pres.'s award Gen. Dynamics, Los Angeles, 1979-81. Methodist. Club: Meth. Men's (Compton, Calif.). Avocations: football, basketball, racquetball, tennis. Home: 13737 Park St Cerritos CA 90701 Office: US West Info Systems 680 Knox Torrance CA 90502

SMITH, ALVIN JOSEPH, electrical engineering consultant, piano technician; b. Pasadena, Calif., Dec. 3, 1909; s. James and Carrie Louise (Kraus) S.; m. Elizabeth Luella Leist, Dec. 25, 1940; children: Dale Alan, James Conrad. BS, Calif. Inst. Tech., 1933, MS, 1934. Registered profl. elec. engr., Calif. Jr. elec. engr. Los Angeles Dept. Water and Power, 1936-37, 40-41; prin. engring. aide U.S. Engring. Dist., Los Angeles, 1942; chief elec. engr. Pacific Enterprise Prodn., Los Angeles, 1943-47, H.L. Gogerty Orgn., Los Angeles, 1947-64; cons. Montrose, Calif., 1964-79, La Crescenta, 1979—. Patentee in field. Mem. Assn. Cons. Elec. Engrs. (pres. 1970), Illuminating Engring. Soc., IEEE. Republican. Baptist. Avocations: pianist, choir dir. Home and Office: 5004 Ramsdell Ave La Crescenta CA 91214

SMITH, ANDREW VAUGHN, telephone company executive; b. Roseburg, Oreg., July 17, 1924; s. Andrew Britt and Ella Mae (Vaughn) S.; m. Dorothy LaVonne Crabtree, Apr. 25, 1943; children: Janet L., James A. B.S. in Elec. Engring, Oreg. State U., 1950. Registered profl. engr., Oreg. With Pacific N.W. Bell Telephone Co., 1951—; asst. v.p. ops. Pacific N.W. Bell Telephone Co., Seattle, 1965; v.p., gen. mgr. Pacific N.W. Bell Telephone Co., Portland, Oreg., 1965-70; v.p. ops. Pacific N.W. Bell Telephone Co., Seattle, 1970-78, pres., 1978—; bd dirs. U.S. Bank/U.S. Nat. Bank Oreg., Portland, Unigard Mut. and Unigard Ins. Cos., Univar Corp., Seattle, Cascade Natural Gas, Seattle, Airborne Freight Corp., Seattle, Northwest Bell, Seattle, VWR Corp., Seattle, ISC Systems Corp., Spokane; trustee Wash. Mutual Savs. Bank. Trustee Oreg. State U. Found., U. Wash. Grad. Sch. Bus., Seattle U., 1985; chmn. bd. trustees U. Wash. Grad. Sch. Bus., 1984-85; gen. chmn. United Way of King County, 1980-81; trustee Wash. State Internat. Trade Fair; mem. Seattle Urban League. Served with USNR, 1943-46. Mem. Seattle C. of C. (chmn. 1985-86). Episcopalian. Clubs: Harbor, Washington Athletic, Seattle Yacht, Rainier, Overlake Golf and Country, Arlington, Multnomah (Portland), Columbia Tower (Seattle); Anglers (N.Y.). Lodge: Masons. Office: 1600 Bell Plaza Room 3101 Seattle WA 98191

SMITH, ARMISTEAD BURWELL, JR., banker, retired naval officer; b. Gastonia, N.C., Mar. 15, 1921; s. Armistead Burwell and Ruby (Gardner) S.; m. Margaret Pagliotti, Jan. 14, 1944; children—Sandra Smith Wallace, Armistead Burwell, Michael Spencer. Grad., Naval War Coll., Air War Coll.-USAF, Navy Postgrad. Sch., U. N.C., Chapel Hill. Lic. naval aviator. Enlisted U.S. Navy, 1941, served to capt., ret., 1972; trust banker Calif. First Bank, San Diego, 1972-86, advisor to pres., 1986—, also bd. dirs.; chmn. Calif. First Bank Capital Mgmt. Corp., La Jolla, Calif., 1983—; dir. Calif. First Venture Capital Corp., Los Angeles, 1983—. Chmn. bd. dirs. La Jolla Cancer Research Found., 1981—; trustee Powell Scholarship Fund, 1975—; bd. dirs. San Diego Aerospace Mus., 1976—, chmn., 1980—. Decorated Silver Star, Legion of Merit (2), D.F.C. with three clusters, Navy Meritorious Service medal, Air medals (8), Navy Commendation medal. Mem. Am. Fighter Aces Assn. (past pres.), Assn. Naval Aviation, Navy League, San Diego Zool. Soc. Methodist. Clubs: Lomas Santa Fe Country; Naval Order of U.S. Home: 12857 Via Grimaldi Del Mar CA 92014 Office: Calif First Bank 530 B St San Diego CA 92112

SMITH, AUDREY LISETTE, federal commission administrator, consultant; b. El Centro, Calif., Apr. 6, 1936; d. Edward and Charlesetta (Mason) Garmon; children—Deryl, Curve, Thomas. Student pub. schs., San Francisco. With Econ. Opportunity Comm.-Western Addition, 1965-68; founder Audrey L. Smith, Developmental Ctr., San Francisco, 1969-71; coordinator Infant Day Care Project, Mt. Zion Hosp., San Francisco, 1969-71; adminstrv. asst. Infant Day Care Project, Family Service Agy., San Francisco, 1971; asst. dir. Sacramento Neighborhood Health Service Corp., Sacramento, 1971-72; exec. dir. Econ. Opportunity Commn. of Yolo County (Calif.), 1973-82; cons., trainer in field, Sacramento, 1969—. Bd. dirs. Nat. Mental Health Assn., 1978-83, Mental Health Assn. Calif., 1971-79; mem. United Way citizen rev. com., 1980-83; Calif. Gov.'s Adv. Com. on Child Devel. Programs, 1976-85. Recipient Cert. of Honor, San Francisco Bd. Suprs., 1973, others. Mem. Nat. Com. Negro and Bus. and Profl. Workers, Nat. Assn. Female Execs., Cal-Nev. Exec. Dirs. Assn. Democrat. Baptist.

SMITH, BALLARD FLANDERS, JR., baseball club exec.; b. Indpls., June 20, 1946; s. Ballard Flanders and Mildred S.; m. Linda Ardell Smith, Sept. 5, 1970; children—Allison, Amy, Amanda, Holly. B.A. in Sociology, Carleton Coll., 1968; J.D., U. Minn., 1971. Mem. firm Pepicelli & Pepicelli, Meadville, Pa., 1971-76; dist. atty. Crawford County, Pa., 1976; v.p., gen. mgr. San Diego Mariners Hockey Club, 1976-77; exec. v.p. San Diego Nat. League Baseball Club, Inc., San Diego Padres, 1977-79, pres., 1979-87, also dir.; pres., dir. Pares Air Travel, 1970—; bd. dirs. McDonald's Corp. Bd. dirs. Greater San Diego C. of C. Mem. Am. Bar Assn., Pa. Bar Assn., Am. Arbitration Assn., San Diego C. of C. (dir.). Episcopalian. *

SMITH, BARBARA ANN, school administrator; b. Detroit, Jan. 14, 1941; d. Stanley and Bertha (Armstrong) Jackson; m. James Titus Smith, Aug. 19, 1972. BEd, Nat. Coll. Edn., 1963; MS, Pepperdine U., 1973. Tchr. Battle Creek (Mich.) Schs., 1962-64; tchr. Los Angeles Unified Sch. Dist., 1964-71, tchr., cons., 1971-76, asst. prin., 1976-80, prin., 1980-85, adminstr. dist. office, 1985-86, asst. supt. elementary instruction, 1986—. Sec. bd. dirs. Inglewood (Calif.) Philharmonic, 1981—; pres. Pastor Parish Relations Com. MLK United Meth. Ch., 1970, 84, 86; v.p. bd. dirs. Wesley Social Services Ctr., Los Angeles, 1984-86; mem. So. Christian Leadership Conf., Los Angeles, 1986. Named Prin. of Yr., Los Angeles C. of C., 1985; recipient

City Council Scroll, Los Angeles City Council, 1983, Cert. from Mayor City of Los Angeles, 1986; Bishop's Appointee, United Meth. Ch., 1984—; hon. mem. PTA, Los Angeles, 1983. Mem. Council Black Adminstrs. (chmn. scholarship fund raiser 1984), Nat. Assn. Minority Polit. Figures (v.p. 1983—), Assn. Calif. Sch. Adminstrs. (recipient plaque, 1982), Assn. Adminstrs. Los Angeles, United Tchrs. Los Angeles (assoc.). Democrat. Office: Los Angeles Unified Sch Dist Office Elementary Instruction A-309 450 N Grand Ave Los Angeles CA 90012

SMITH, BARBARA GORDON, state official; b. Los Angeles, Oct. 13, 1927; d. Frank and Anna Louisa (Weidauer) Belcher; B.A., Occidental Coll., 1949; M.P.A., U. So. Calif., 1976; m. Kenneth H. Smith, Aug. 29, 1980 (dec.); children—Edward Kermit Parker, Stephen Frank Parker; m. Hugh R. Tassey, Jan. 31, 1987. Tchr., Calif. Public Schs., 1949-72; adminstrv. intern Sacramento (Calif.) Superior Ct., 1975-77; legis. aide, chief of staff Calif. Assembly, Office Speaker Pro Tempore, Sacramento, 1977-80; exec. dir. Calif. Health Facilities Financing Authority, Sacramento, 1980—. Chmn., Contra Costa County Natural Resource Commn., 1965-68; bd. dirs. Pub. Service Skills, Inc., Council Hosp. Fin. Authorities. Named Citizen of Year, Orinda, Calif., 1968. Office: 915 Capitol Mall Room 280 Sacramento CA 94814

SMITH, BARBARA KALO, communications, public relations and advertising executive; b. Lorain, Ohio, Dec. 24, 1950; d. George and Catherine Irene (Repko) K.; m. Robert Mathias Pangburn, May 26, 1973 (dec. July 1974); m. Paul Willis Smith III, Jan. 7, 1977. BA, U. Dayton, 1972. Edit. asst. Hotel and Restaurant Employees Union, Cin., 1973-74; editor Family Motor Coach Assn., Cin., 1974-76; advt. mgr. 3-T's RV Products, Inc., Van Nuys, Calif., 1977-80, 1985—; sec. Lexitron, Thousand Oaks, Calif., 1980-82; editor Micom Systems, Inc., Simi Valley, Calif., 1982-85. Recipient 1st pl. award, Nat. Labor Pubs., 1974. Mem. Internat. Assn. Bus. Communicators (Bronze Quill award 1985). Roman Catholic. Avocations: motor home traveling, flower arranging, reading. Home: 16700 Gledhill St Sepulveda CA 91343 Office: 3-T's RV Products Inc 15216 Stagg St Van Nuys CA 91405

SMITH, BERNALD STEPHEN, pilot, aviation consultant; b. Long Beach, Calif., Dec. 24, 1926; s. Donald Albert and Bernice Merrill (Stephens) S.; m. Marilyn Mae Spence, July 22, 1949; children: Lorraine Ann Smith Foute, Evelyn Donice Smith DeRoos, Mark Stephen, Diane April (dec.). Student, U. Calif., Berkeley, 1944-45, 50-51. Cert. airline transport pilot, flight engr., FAA. Capt. Transocean Air Lines, Oakland (Calif.) and Tokyo, 1951-53, Hartford, Conn., 1954-55; 1st officer United Air Lines, Seattle, 1955, San Francisco, 1956-68; tng. capt. United Air Lines, Denver and San Francisco, 1961-68; capt. United Air Lines, San Francisco, 1968—; founder, v.p. AviaAm., Palo Alto, Calif., 1970-72, AviaInternat., Palo Alto, 1972-74; cons. Caproni Vizzola, Milan, 1972-84; prin., cons. Internat. Aviation Cons. and Investments, Fremont, Calif., 1985—; instr. aviation Ohlone Coll., Fremont, 1976. Author/editor: American Soaring Handbook, 1975, 80; contbr. articles to profl. jours. Trustee Nat. Soaring Mus., 1975—, pres. 1975-78. Served to comdr. USNR, 1944-86. Mem. AIAA (publ. bd. 1977—), Soaring Soc. Am. (pres. 1969-70, chmn. pub. bd. 1971-84, bd.dirs. 1963—, Warren Eaton Meml. Trophy 1977, Exceptional Service award 1970, 75, 82), Soc. Automotive Engring., Nat. Aero. Assn., Exptl. Aircraft Assn., Aircraft Owners and Pilots Assn., Airline Pilots Assn., Seaplane Pilots Assn., Orgn. Scientifique et Technique Internat. du Vol a Voile (bd. dirs., U.S. del. 1981—), Soaring Safety Found. (founder, trustee 1985—), U. Calif. Alumni Assn. (life). Democrat. Methodist. Office: Internat Aviation Cons Investments PO Box 3075 Fremont CA 94539

SMITH, BERNARD JOSEPH, cons. civil engr.; b. Liverpool, Eng., Aug. 29, 1900; s. Thomas J. and Sarah Anne (Crum) S.; came to U.S., 1912, naturalized, 1930; student St. Edward's Coll., Liverpool, 1914-20; ed. Oxford U., Eng., 1918; B.Engring. with honors, U. Liverpool, 1923, M.Engring., 1926; m. Julia Susan Connolly, June 4, 1929; children—Bernard, Sarah Anne Kathleen, Maureen, Una, Aislin, Malachy, Joan, John. Pvt. tutor in math. and physics, Liverpool, 1923-24; field engr. Underpinning & Found. Co., N.Y.C., 1924; underground conduit engr. N.Y. and N.J. Bell Telephone Co., 1924-25, Ohio Bell Telephone Co., Toledo, 1925-26; asst. engr. to Alexander Potter, cons. engr. on water and sewerage systems, N.Y. and N.J., 1926-30; design engr. Humble Oil & Refining Co., Baytown, Tex., 1930-32; city mgr. and engr. City of Baytown, 1932-33, cons. engr., 1930-34; engr. examiner Pub. Works Adminstrn., Ft. Worth, 1935-37; dir. research and personnel City of Ft. Worth, 1938-42; acting state dir. and state planning engr. Tex. Pub. Works Res., 1942; asst. regional dir. and regional economist Nat. Housing Agy., hdqrs. Dallas, 1942-46; cons. engr. on water systems and town planning, Dallas, 1946-65; cons. tides and water resources, San Francisco, 1965—, also Aptos, Calif.; water commr. Santa Cruz County, Calif.; planning engr. and chief San Francisco Bay sect. U.S. Corps of Engrs., 1957-65; lectr. urban devel. Tex. Christian U., Ft. Worth, 1939-43; guest lectr. on town devel. Ala. Poly. Inst., 1940; instr. econs. and engring. So. Meth. U., Dallas, 1943-53; guest panelist Ann. Radio Conf., U. Okla., Norman, 1946; speaker on econs. and town planning to various civic and bus. groups, 1939—; v.p. Southwestern States Water Co., 1949-51. Mem. bd. govs. Dallas Fed. Reference Exchange, 1943-46. Registered profl. engr., Calif., N.J., Tex.; registered pub. surveyor, Tex. Fellow ASCE (com. city planning tng. for civil engrs. 1942); mem. Am. Waterworks Assn., AAAS, Am., Western econ. assns., Assn. Evolutionary Econs., History of Econs. Soc., County Louth (Eire) Archeol. Soc., Irish Lit. and Hist. Soc. of San Francisco (pres. 1959-62), Serra Club. Club: Commonwealth of Calif. Contbr. articles and reports on water systems, flood control, urban devel. and pollution to profl. pubIs. Home: 1446 Day Valley Rd Aptos CA 95003 Office: PO Box 663 Aptos CA 95003

SMITH, BERNARD JOSEPH CONNOLLY, civil engineer; b. Elizabeth, N.J., Mar. 11, 1930; s. Bernard Joseph and Julia Susan (Connolly) S.; B.S., U. Notre Dame, 1951; B.S. in Civil Engring., Tex. A&M U., 1957; M.B.A. in Fin., U. Calif.-Berkeley, 1976; m. Josephine Kerley, Dec. 20, 1971; children—Julia Susan Alice, Teresa Mary Josephine, Anne Marie Kathleen. Asst. Bernard J. Smith, cons. engr. office, Dallas, 1947-57; hydraulic engr. C.E., U.S. Army, San Francisco, 1957-59, St. Paul dist., 1959-60, Kansas City (Mo.) dist., 1960-63, Sacramento dist., 1963-65; engr. Fed. Energy Regulatory Commn., San Francisco Regional Office, 1965—. Served with U.S. Army, 1952-54. Registered profl. engr., Calif., Mo.; lic. real estate broker, Calif. Mem. ASCE (sec. power div. San Francisco sect. 1969), Soc. Am. Mil. Engrs. (treas. Kansas City post 1962), Am. Econ. Assn., Nat. Soc. Profl. Engrs., U.S. Com. on Large Dams, Res. Officers Assn. (chpt. pres. 1973). Clubs: San Francisco Catholic Alumni (pres. 1968), Commonwealth of Calif. Home: 247 28th Ave San Francisco CA 94121 Office: Fed Energy Regulatory Commn 333 Market St San Francisco CA 94105

SMITH, BETTYE L. SEBREE, business college executive; b. Canoga Park, Calif., Feb. 25, 1926; d. Roy Albert and Thelma Hattie (Alexander) Sebree; student Brigham Young U., 1944-45, Links Sch. Bus., Boise, Idaho, 1946, Nampa (Idaho) Bus. Coll. 1956; BSBA, Alaska Meth. U., 1972; cert. adminstrv. mgr.; accredited personnel diplomat; m. George R. Motschman, Feb. 26, 1948 (div. June 1959); children—Jerye Lou, Marie Louise; m. 2d, Leroy I. Smith, Mar. 13, 1961 (div. 1968). Office mgr. Intermountain Surg. Co., Boise, 1945-48; sec. payroll, cost acct. Morrison-Knudsen Co., Fairbanks, Alaska and Boise, 1948-52, Lytle, Green, Birch and Green Construction Co., Fairbanks, 1952-55; owner, operator Fairbanks Secretarial Sch., 1956-59; pres. Alaska Bus. Coll., Inc., Anchorage, 1959—; operator Mars Employment Services and Kelly Girl Services, Anchorage, 1960-62; owner City Employment Ctr., Anchorage, 1962-68, Manpower Bus. Services, Anchorage, 1969-72, Alaska Employment Agy., Anchorage, 1970-72, 86—; pres. Sebree, Ltd. Mem. accrediting commn. Assn. of Ind. Colls. and Schs., accreditation evaluator; bd. dirs. Eastwind Vocat. Services; mem. Gov.'s Council on Vocat. Edn., 1985-87; commr. Alaska Postsecondary Edn. Commn.; pres. Alaska Pvt. Sch. Assn.; past pres. Pacific Northwest Bus. Sch. Assn.; sustaining mem. Community YMCA, past bd. dirs.; mem. Alaskan of Yr. Com., bd. dirs. Mem. Profl. Secs. Assn. (chpt. v.p. 1962, seminar chmn. 1961, 67, 73-77, 80), Profl. Secs. Internat. (Exec. of Yr. award Billikin chpt. 1981-82), Am. Soc. Personnel Adminstrn., Nat. Assn. Student Fin. Aid Officers, Alaska Student Fin. Aid Officers, Commonwealth North, Nat. Bus. Edn. Assn., Western Accredited Career and Schs., Cert. Adminstrv. Mgrs. Assn. Office: 5159 Old Seward Hwy Anchorage AK 99503

SMITH, BOB GENE, biology educator, consultant; b. Floydada, Tex., Nov. 9, 1932; s. C. M. and Carrie A. Smith; m. Thralene Parsons, Dec. 26, 1953; children—Malcolm Shawn, Michael Brian. B.S., Tex. Tech U., 1958, M.S., 1961; credential in adminstrn. Calif. State U.-Los Angeles, 1963-64; M.S. in Biology U. Mont.-Missoula, 1966. Tchr. biology Colton (Calif.) High Sch., 1958-61; athletic dir., vice prin. pub. schs., Bloomington, Calif., 1963-66; asst. prof. biology San Bernardino Community Coll., 1966-70, assoc. prof., 1970—, dean of men, 1968-70; cons. in herpetology, entomology, taxonomy San Bernardino County, Norton AFB. Served with USAF, 1951-53. Mem. Calif. Tchrs. Assn. Calif. Higher Edn. Assn. (state council 1973-74, NEA del. 1973-75), World Wildlife Fund. Democrat. Co-author numerous lab. manuals; designed lab. exercise on metric system; devised method of dating chaparral fires.

SMITH, BODRELL JOER'DAN, architect, city planner; b. Little Rock, Ark., Sept. 21, 1931; s. Robert Stanslaw and Neva (Long) S.; m. Ingrid Elin Kehlet, Oct. 20, 1979; children: Cameron Corbin, Astrid Johannah, Walker Darel. BArch, U. So. Calif., 1956; M in City Planning, U. Paris, France, 1957. Registered architect, Calif. and 17 other states. Designer LeCorbusier, Paris, 1956-57; chief designer W.L. Pereira Assocs., Los Angeles, 1960-61; prin. Bodrell Joer'dan Smith Architects, Los Angeles, 1961-78; pres., chief exec. officer USTEC Architects, Redwood City, Calif., 1978-87; pres. Bodrell Joer'dan Smith Partnership, Mountain View, Calif., 1987—. Trustee Buckley Sch., Encino, Calif., 1965-70. Served to maj. C.E., U.S. Army, 1958-60. Recipient Fulbright Scholarship Dept. of State, Paris, 1956. Mem. AIA, Am. Soc. Military Engrs., Am. Soc. Planning Officials, Am. Corrections Assn. Republican. Methodist. Clubs: Caves des Roys, Outrigger Canoe. Lodge: Eagles. Buildings featured in Time, Fortune, House and Home, Progressive Architecture and other mags. Avocations: skiing, sky diving, backpacking.

SMITH, BRUCE LAWRENCE, broadcast executive; b. Duluth, Minn., Jan. 17, 1952; s. Bruce Robert and Hilda Francis (Schmidt) S. Student, Mich. Tech. U.; BA in Communications magna cum laude, U. Minn., 1973; MS in Radio/TV/Film, Miami U., Oxford, Ohio, 1974; MBA, Murray State U., 1979. Pub. affairs dir. Sta. KUMD-FM, Duluth, 1971-73; program dir. Sta. WGGL-FM, Houghton, Mich., 1975-77; gen. mgr. Sta. WKMS-FM, Murray, Ky., 1977-82, Sta. KSKA-FM, Anchorage, 1982—; sec., treas. Alaska Pub. Radio Network, Anchorage, 1983-85; bd. dirs. Radio Reading Service, Anchorage. Vol. Alaska Congrl. Campaign, Anchorage, 1984, 86; v.p. Murray Civic Music Assn., 1979-82; bd. dirs. radio div. So. Ednl. Communications Assn., 1980-82, Alaska Ctr. for Environment, Anchorage, 1985—, Internship Program for Alaska, 1986—. Mem. Assn. MBA Execs., Anchorage Associated Broadcasters, Alaska Broadcasters Assn., Phi Kappa Phi, Alpha Epsilon Rho. Republican. Home: 140 Eagle St Unit 202 Anchorage AK 99501 Office: Sta KSKA-FM 4101 University Dr Anchorage AK 99508

SMITH, CARTER BLAKEMORE, broadcaster; b. San Francisco, Jan. 1, 1937; s. Donald V. and Charlotte M. (Nichols) S.; children: Carter Blakemore, Clayton M. AA, City Coll. San Francisco, 1958; BA, San Francisco State U., 1960; postgrad. N.Y. Inst. Finance, 1969-70; Assoc. in Fin. PLanning, Coll. for Fin. Planning, 1984. Announcer, Sta. KBLF, Red Bluff, Calif., 1954-56; personality Sta. KRE-KRE FM, Berkeley, Calif., 1958-63, Sta. KSFO, San Francisco, 1963-72, Sta. KNBR, San Francisco, 1972-83, Sta. KSFO, San Francisco, 1983-86, Sta. KFRC, San Francisco, 1986—; mem. faculty radio-TV dept. San Francisco State U., 1960-61. Mem. adv. bd. Little Jim Club Children's Hosp., 1968-71; bd. dirs. Marin County Humane Soc., 1968-73, San Francisco Zool. Soc., 1980—; trustee Family Service Agy. Marin, 1976-85; mem. alumni bd. Lowell High Sch. Recipient award San Francisco Press Club, 1965. Mem. Amateur Radio Relay League (life), Quarter Century Wireless Assn., Alpha Epsilon Rho. Office: Sta KFRC 500 Washington St San Francisco CA 94111

SMITH, CHARLES ANTHONY, businessman; b. Santa Fe, Sept. 16, 1939; s. Frances (Mier) Vigil; student various adminstrv. and law courses; m. Paula Ann Thomas, June 26, 1965; 1 dau., Charlene Danielle. Circulation mgr. Daily Alaska Empire, 1960-63; agt. Mut. of N.Y. Life Ins. Co., Juneau, Alaska, 1964-65; mng. partner Future Investors in Alaska and Cinema Alaska, Juneau, 1961-62; SE Alaska rep. K & L Distbrs., 1966-68; mgr. Alaska Airlines Newspapers, SE Alaska, 1969; dep. Alaska Retirement System, Juneau, 1970-71; apptd. dir. hwy. safety, gov.'s hwy. safety rep., Juneau, 1971-83; pres. Valley Service Ctr., Inc., 1984—. Alaska pres. Muscular Dystrophy Assn. Am.; pres. SE Alaska Emergency Med. Services Council, 1965-72. Served to capt. Army N.G., 1964—. Named Alaska Safety Man of Yr., 1977. Mem. Am. Assn. Motor Vehicle Adminstrs., Alaska Peace Officers Assn., Nat. Assn. Gov.s' Hwy. Safety Reps., N.G. Assn., Internat. Platform Assn. Roman Catholic. Club: Elks (Juneau). Author various hwy. safety manuals and plans, 1971—. Home: PO Box 493 Douglas AK 99824 Office: Pouch N Juneau AK 99811

SMITH, CHERYL LYNN, osteopath; b. Okmulgee, Okla., Sept. 1, 1954; d. Estle Curtis and Wanda Lorene (Fitchett) S. BS in Physiology, Okla. State U., 1976; DO, Okla. Coll. Osteo. Medicine and Surgery, 1979. Diplomate Nat. Bd. Examiners of Osteo. Physicians and Surgeons. Rotating intern Botsford Gen. Osteo. Hosp., Farmington Hills, Mich., 1979-80, resident in gen. surgery, 1980-84, chief surg. resident, 1983-84; practice medicine specializing in general surgery Colorado Springs, Colo., 1984—; lectr. in field. Recipient Cert. Excellence, Alvin Yarrows Meml. award Botsford Gen. Hosp., 1982. Mem. AMA, Am. Acad. Osteopathy, Am. Osteo. Assn., Colo. Med. Soc., Am. Coll. Osteo. Surgeons, Alumni Assn. Okla. Coll. Osteo. medicine and Surgery, Colo. Springs Surg. Soc., El Paso Med. Soc. Republican. Office: 2504 E Pikes Peak Suite 201 Colorado Springs CO 80909

SMITH, CHESTER, broadcasting executive; b. Wade, Okla., Mar. 29, 1930; s. Louis L. and Effie (Brown) S.; m. Naomi L. Crenshaw, July 19, 1959; children—Laurie, Lorna, Roxanne. Country western performer on Capitol records, TV and radio, 1947-61; owner, mgr. Sta. KLOC, Ceres-Modesto, Calif., 1963-81, Sta. KCBA-TV, Salinas-Monterey, Calif., 1981-86; owner, ptnr. Sta. KCSO-TV, Modesto-Stockton-Sacramento, Sta. KREN-TV, Reno, Nev., Sta. KBCP-TV, Paradise-Chico, Calif., Sta. K52AR, Redding, Calif., Sta. KO7TA-TV, Santa Maria, Calif., Sta. KO9UF-TV, Morro Bay, Calif., 1986—. Mem. Calif. Broadcasters Assn. Republican. Mem. Christian Ch. Original rec. Wait A Little Longer Please Jesus, Country Music Hall of Fame, Nashville, 1955.

SMITH, CLIFFORD NEAL, business educator, writer; b. Wakita, Okla., May 30, 1923; s. Jesse Newton and Inez Lane (Jones) S.; m. Anna Piszczan-Czaja, Sept. 3, 1951; children: Helen Inez Smith Barrette. BS, Okla. State U., 1943; AM, U. Chgo., 1948; postgrad. Columbia U., 1960. Selector, U.S. Displaced Persons Commn., Washington and Munich, Germany, 1948-51; auditor Phillips Petroleum Co., Caracas, Venezuela, 1951-58; planning analyst Mobil Internat. Oil Co., N.Y.C., 1960, 65-66, Mobil Oil A.G., Deutschland, Hamburg, Germany, 1961-63; asst. to v.p. for Germany, Mobil Inner Europe, Inc., Geneva, 1963-65; asst. prof. No. Ill. U. Sch. Bus., DeKalb, 1966-69, prof. internat. bus., part-time 1970—; owner Westland Publs.; lectr. in field. Author: Federal Land Series, vol. 1, 1972, vol. 2, 1973, vol. 3, 1980, vol. 4, part 1, 1982, vol. 4, part 2, 1986, Encyclopedia of German-American Genealogical Resources in German Archives, 1977, numerous monographs in German-Am., Brit.-Am., French-Am. geneal. research series, German and Central European Emigration Series; contbg. editor Nat. Geog. Soc. Quar., Geneal. jour. (Utah); contbr. articles to profl. jours. Mem. at large exec. com. Friends Com. on Nat. Legis., 1968-75; mem. regional exec. com. Am. Friends Service Com., 1969-76; v.p. Riverside Dem., N.Y.C., 1959-61; precinct committeeman, 1984—; mem. Ariz. State Central Com. of Dem. Party, 1984—; sec. Dem. Cen. Com. of Cochise County. Recipient Distinguished Service medal Ill. Geneal. Soc., 1973, award for outstanding service to sci. genealogy Am. Soc. Genealogists, 1973. Fellow Geneal. Soc. of Utah; mem. S.R., SAR, Soc. Descs. Colonial Clergy, Soc. Advancement Mgmt., Ill. Genealogic Soc. (dir. 1968-69), Phi Eta Sigma, Beta Alpha Psi, Sigma Iota Epsilon. Mem. Soc. of Friends. Club: American of Hamburg (v.p. 1962-63); contbr. articles to profl. jours. Address: PO Box 117 McNeal AZ 85617

SMITH, COURTLAND LESTER, anthropology educator; b. Hartford, Conn., Nov. 8, 1939; s. Lester Courtland and Nuala (Rommel) S.; m. Linda Varsell, June 21, 1961; children: Kip (dec.), Jonathan, Rebecca. BSME, Rensselaer Poly. Inst., 1961; PhD in Anthropology and Sociology, U. Ariz., 1968. Asst. prof. Carnegie-Mellon U., Pitts., 1968-69; postdoctoral fellow Woods Hole (Mass.) Oceanographic Instn., 1975-76; prof. anthropology Oreg. State U., Corvallis, 1978—; vis. prof. Nat. Sea Grant Coll. program NOAA, Rockville, Md., 1984-85; cons. Seattle Aquarium, Western Rural Devel. Ctr., U.S. Army C.E., Inst. Water Resources, Western Interstate Commn. Higher Edn., New Eng. Fishery Mgmt. Council, Island Resources Found.; bd. dirs. Oreg. State U. Fed. Credit Union, 1986—. Author: Salmon Fishers of Columbia, 1979, The Salt River Project: A Case Study of Cultural Adaptation in an Urbanizing Community, 1972; assoc. editor Human Orgn., 1977-82. Bd. dirs. Ctr. for the Humanities, Oreg. State U. Grantee NSF, NEH, NOAA. Fellow AAAS, Am. Anthropol. Assn., Soc. Applied Antrhopology; mem. Am. Fisheries Soc., Internat. Union Anthropol. Ethnol Scis., Human Dimensions in Wildlife Study Group, Oreg. Acad. Sci. Home: 471 NW Hemlock Ave Corvallis OR 97330 Office: Oreg State U Dept Anthropology Corvallis OR 97331

SMITH, CRAIG PATTERSON, hotel operator; b. Duluth, Minn.; s. Norman Hopkins and Jane (Patterson) S. Grad. in Bus. Adminstrn., U. So. Calif., 1929. Pres., Pacific Western Hotels, San Francisco, 1936-85, Continental Parks Inc., 1962-86. Served to comdr. USN, 1941-46. Mem. Soc. May Flower Descendants, SAR, Calif. Hotel Assn. (past pres.). Home: 825 Sutter St San Francisco CA 94109

SMITH, CYNTHIA JOY, management analyst, computer programmer; b. Glen Ridge, N.J., Dec. 25, 1951; d. Herbert James and Frances Jane (Van Ness) S. BA, Springfield Coll., 1973; MSW, U. Hawaii, 1976; MBA, Pepperdine U., 1982. Coordinator, Pacific Allied Health Project, Honolulu, 1977-78; programmer analyst Computab, Inc., Honolulu, 1980-82; exec. dir. Hale Ho'Ola Hou, Honolulu, 1977-80; med. cons. Microsystems U.S.A. Inc., Honolulu, 1982-84; med. social worker Upjohn's Home Health Agy., Honolulu, 1976-86, Kokua Nurses Home Health Agy., 1986—; analyst, programmer The Queen's Med. Ctr., Honolulu, 1982-83; mgmt. analyst Straub Clinic and Hosp., Inc., Honolulu, 1983—; instr. U. Hawaii Sch. Social Work, 1977-83. Contbr. articles to profl. jours. Mem. Women in Small Bus. Com., SBA, 1983; chmn. pub. affairs, bd. dirs. Hawaii Planned Parenthood Assn., 1981—, pres. 1983-84; bd. dirs. Craigside Condominium, 1987—; mem. friends and alumni U. Hawaii Sch. Social Work. Mem. Hawaii Soc. Hosp. Social Work Dirs. (sec. 1983-85), Hosp. Mgmt. Systems Soc. (sec.-treas. 1985—), Assn. Women Entrepreneurs, Am. Bus. Women's Assn. (pres. 1983-84, Woman of Yr. award 1984-85), Nat. Assn. Social Workers (cert.), Am. Assn. Med. Systems and Info., Computer Profls. for Social Responsibility. Democrat. Home: 2101 Nuuanu Ave #1603 Honolulu HI 96817 Office: Straub Clinic and Hosp Inc 888 S King St Honolulu HI 96813

SMITH, CYRUS DONALD, III, accountant; b. Great Falls, Mont., Sept. 3, 1947; s. Cyrus Donald and Alice Kay (Newman) S.; m. Jane Carol James, Aug. 19, 1977. B.S., Calif. State U.-Hayward, 1971; M.B.A., Wash. State U., 1976. C.P.A., Wash., Calif., Alaska. Sr. auditor Peat, Marwick, Mitchell & Co., C.P.A.s, Oakland, Calif., 1971-73; sr. auditor TransAlaska Pipeline Project, 1974, procurement supr., 1975; asst. prof. acctg., taxation Central Wash. State U., 1976; mgmt. cons. Touche-Ross & Co., Seattle, 1977; pres. Smith-Felez & McLane Co., P.S., C.P.A.s, Tacoma, Wash., 1978—; pres. Constrn. Data Systems, Inc., 1986—, Constrn. DATA Systems, Inc. Chmn., Pierce County Planning Commn., 1982—. Served with AUS, 1966-69. Mem. Associated Gen. Contractors Tacoma, Utility Contractors Assn. Wash., Home Builders Assn. Greater Tacoma, Downtown Tacoma Assn., Tacoma C. of C., Am. Inst. C.P.A.s, Wash. Soc. C.P.A.s. Roman Catholic. Clubs: Propeller, Tacoma. Lodges: Elks. Home: 5310 66th Ave W Tacoma WA 98462 Office: The Fin Bldg 1517 S Fawcett Suite 300 Tacoma WA 98402

SMITH, D. DAVID, chamber of commerce executive; b. Bargesville, Ind., July 10, 1928; s. Donald Edgar and Velva (Whitehead) S.; m. Rachel Irene Maddux, Sept. 4, 1951; children: D. Gregory, Elizabeth A. BS in Bus., Ind. U., 1950. Asst. mgr. San Leandro (Calif.) C. of C., 1956-60; exec. mgr. Woodland (Calif.) C. of C., 1960-65; exec. v.p. Stockton (Calif.) C. of C., 1965—. Pres. Pvt. Industry Council, Stockton, 1981, Jr. Achievement San Joaquin, Stockton, 1986—, Stockton Hall of Fame Assn., 1985-86. Served to sgt. USAF, 1951-55. Named Stocktonian of Yr., Stockton Bd. Realtors, 1974. Mem. Calif. Assn. C. of C. Execs. (pres. 1971). Republican. Avocations: tennis, running, reading, working. Home: 1421 W Alpine Stockton CA 95204 Office: Greater Stockton C of C 445 W Weber Ave Suite 220 Stockton CA 95203

SMITH, DAVID ALDEN, sociologist, educator; b. Lockport, N.Y., Oct. 20, 1956; s. Alden E. and Betty (Carl) S. BA, U. Rochester, 1978; MA, U. N.C, 1981, PhD, 1984. Vis. asst. prof. sociology U. S.C, Columbia, falls 1983, 84; asst. prof. U. Calif., Irvine, 1984—. Contbr. articles to profl. jours. Mem. Orange County Com. on Cen. Am., 1985—, Pledge of Resistance, Irvine, 1985—, Dem. Socialists of Am., N.Y.C., 1981—. Fellow East-West Population Ctr., Honolulu, summer 1984. Mem. Am. Sociol. Assn., Internat. Studies Assn., So. Sociol. Soc. Mem. United Ch. Christ. Club: Crash and Burn Track (Irvine). Home: 47 Cornell Ct Irvine CA 92715 Office: U Calif Sch Social Scis Irvine CA 92715

SMITH, DAVID BERYL DEAN, psychology educator; b. Willows, Calif., Apr. 13, 1933; s. Jack Townsend and Gladys Mae (Clevenger) S.; m. Faith Victoria Smith, June 11, 1960; children: Deborah, Lawrence. BA, UCLA, 1958, PhD, 1964. Instr. psychology UCLA, 1964; research psychologist NASA, Mountain View, Calif., 1965-68; prof. U. So. Calif., Los Angeles, 1969—, chmn. dept. human factors, 1976—, research assoc. gerontology ctr., 1976-86; research assoc. Gerontology Ctr., U. So. Calif., 1976-86. Author: Man and Systems Mgmt., 1974; contbr. articles to profl. jours. Mem. Am. Psychol. Assn., Human Factors Soc., Internat. Human Factors Soc., Internat. Ergonomics Assn., Sigma Xi. Home: 1311 S Brass Lantern La Habra CA 90631 Office: U So Calif Human Factors Dept Los Angeles CA 90089

SMITH, DAVID ELVIN, physician; b. Bakersfield, Calif., Feb. 7, 1939; s. Elvin W. and Dorothy (McGinnis) S.; m. Millicent Buxton; children: Julia, Suzanne, Christopher Buxton, Christopher Buxton-Smith. Intern San Francisco Gen. Hosp., 1965; fellow pharmacology and toxicology U. Calif., San Francisco, 1965-67, assoc. clinical prof. occupational health and clinical toxicology, 1967—, dir. psychopharmacology study group, 1966-70; practice medicine specializing in toxicology and addictionology San Francisco, 1965—; physician Presbyn. Alcoholic Clinic, 1965-67, Contra Cost Alcoholic Clinic, 1965-67; dir. alcohol and drug abuse screening unit San Francisco Gen. Hosp., 2967-68; co-dir. Calif drug abuse info. project U. Calif Med. Ctr., 1967-72; founder, med. dir. Haight-Ashbury Free Med. Clinic, San Francisco, 1967—; research dir. Merritt Peralta Chem. Dependency Hosp., Oakland, Calif., 1984—; chmn. Nat. Drug Abuse Conf., 1977; mem. Calif. Gov.'s Commn. on Narcotics and Drug Abuse, 1977—; nat. health adviser to former U.S. Pres. Jimmy Carter; dir. Benzodiazepine Research and Tng. Project, Substance Abuse and Sexual Concerns Project, PCP Research and Tng. Project; cons. numerous fed. drug abuse agys. Author: Love Needs Care, 1970, The New Social Drug: Cultural, Medical and Legal Perspectives on Marijuana, 1971, The Free Clinic: Community Approaches to Health Care and Drug Abuse, 1971, Treating the Cocaine Abuser, 1985, The Benzodiazepines: Current Standard Medical Practice, 1986, Physicians' Guide to Drug Abuse, 1987; co-author: It's So Good, Don't Even Try it Once: Heroin in Perspective, 1972, Uppers and Downers, 1973, Drugs in the Classroom, 1973, Barbiturate Use and Abuse, 1977, A Multicultural View of Drug Abuse, 1978, Amphetamine Use, Misuse and Abuse, 1979, PCP: Problems and Prevention, 1981, Sexological Aspects of Substance Use and Abuse, Treatment of the Cocaine Abuser, 1985, The Hiaght Ashbury Free Medical Clinic: Still Free After all these Years, 1987; also drug edn. films; founder, editor Jour. Psychedelic Drugs (now Jour. Psychoactive Drugs), 1967—; contbr. over 100 articles to profl. jours. Pres. Youth Projects, Inc.; founder, chmn. bd., pres. Nat. Free Clin. Council, 1968-72. Recipient Research award Borden Found., 1964, AMA Research award, 1966, Community Service award U. Calif. at San Francisco, 1974, Calif. State Drug Abuse Treatment award, 1984, Vernelle Fox Drug Abuse Treatment award, 1985. Mem. Am. Med. Soc. for Treatment of Alcoholism and Other Drug Dependencies, San Francisco Med. Soc., Am. Pub. Health Assn., Calif. Soc.

Treatment of Alcohol and other Drug Dependencies (pres.), Sigma Xi, Phi Beta Kappa. Unitarian. Home: 80 Parnassus Ave San Francisco CA 94131 Office: 409 Clayton St San Francisco CA 94117

SMITH, DAVID RAYMOND, materials scientist; b. London, Dec. 30, 1948; came to U.S., 1957; s. Raymond William and Jean Florence (Craddock) S.; m. Sharon Enid Wong, Oct. 17, 1970; children: Lisa Ann, Kristina Marie. BS in Chemistry, U. Ariz., 1971; MS in Chemistry, U. Oreg., 1972. Analytical chemist Hughes Aircraft Co., Tucson, 1972-77, mgr. materials analysis, 1977-82; staff chemist IBM Corp., Tucson, 1982-84, mgr. materials devel., 1985—. Contbr. articles to profl. jours. Leader Tucson chpt. 4H Club, 1981—; chmn. site com. Univ. High Parents Assn., Tucson, 1985. Mem. Soc. Applied Spectroscopy, Am. Chem. Soc. (younger chem. lectr. 1985), So. Ariz. Soc. Model Engrs. Democrat. Home: 3133 W Alaska Tucson AZ 85746 Office: IBM Corp Bldg 61 Dept 67Y 9000 S Rita Rd Tucson AZ 85744

SMITH, DEAN WARREN, state official; b. Denver, Dec. 15, 1939; s. Clarence Henry and Mabel Ruth (Long) S.; m. Daisy Eugenia Walter, Mar. 5, 1961 (div. 1982); children—Sheri, Kathleen, Scott; m. Joyce Carol Kessinger, Mar. 10, 1984; children—Robert, Roger, Randall, Renee. A.A. in Fire Sci. Tech., Community Coll., Golden, Colo., 1973, A.A. in Criminal Justice, 1975; B.S. in Tech. Mgmt., Regis Coll., 1984. Mgr. Empire Automotive, Arvada, Colo., 1961-68; brewery worker Adolph Coors Co., Golden, 1968-69; fire dist. mgr. Arvada Fire Protection Dist., 1969-85; dir. Colo. Div. Fire Safety, 1985—. Vol. fire fighter Arvada Fire Dept., 1965—; registered lobbyist Colo. Fire Fighters Assn., 1977-84. Served with USNR, 1958-61. Republican. Methodist. Home: 5940 Flower St Arvada CO 80004 Office: Colo Dept Pub Safety Div Fire Safety 700 Kipling St Suite 3000 Denver CO 80215

SMITH, DELMONT KING, textile executive, consultant; b. Pocatello, Idaho, June 9, 1927; s. Leslie H. and Adelia A. (Loveland) S.; m. Velva Lee Stokes, Sept. 18, 1946; children: Linda L., Constance M., Dennis D., Shawna M., David M. BS, Utah State U., 1949, MS, 1955; PhD, Purdue U., 1954. Research mgr. Rayonier, inc., Whippany, N.J., 1956-61; dir. woven products research Chicopee (Mass.) Johnson and Johnson, 1961-70; dir. tech. planning Chicopee (Mass.) Johnson and Johnson, New Brunswick, N.J., 1970-85; cons. Mesa, Ariz., 1985—. Author chpts. in book; contbr. articles to profl. jours.; patentee in field. Served with USNR, 1945-46. Recipient Chmn. award INDA Assn. of Nonwovens Industry, 1977. Mormon. Home and Office: 3112 East Hampton Ave Mesa AZ 85204

SMITH, DENNIS MARKHAM, police officer; b. Oakland, Calif., Mar. 31, 1946; s. Joseph Ward and Elva B. (Kinney) S.; m. Jeanne Marie Griffin, Aug. 26, 1970; children: Sean Markham, Erin Michelle. AA, Santa Rosa (Calif.) Jr. Coll., 1967; BA, Calif. State U., Sacramento, 1969, MS, 1971. Cert. fire fighter, Calif. Govtl. analyst Calif. Dept. Gen. Services, Sacramento, 1970-74; criminal intellegence supr. Calif. Dept. Justice, Sacramento, 1974-82; dep. chief law enforcement div. Gov.'s Office Emergency Services, Sacramento, 1982—. Mem. Placer County (Calif.) Rep. Cen. Com., 1978—, vice chmn., 1982-84. Served with USN, 1965-67. Mem. Calif. Peace Officer Assn. (chmn. 1978-81). Republican. Roman Catholic. Office: Office of Emergency Services Law Enforcement Div 2800 Meadowview Rd Sacramento CA 95832

SMITH, DENNY, congressman; b. Ontario, Oreg., Jan. 19, 1938; children: Maggie, Barrett, Ryan. B.A. in Polit. Sci., Williamette U., Salem, Oreg., 1961. Chmn. bd. Eagle Newspapers Inc.; co-pilot, flight engr. Pan Am. World Airways, 1967-76; mem. 97th-100th Congresses, 1981—; mem. house budget com., mil. reform caucus. Mem. exec. com. Nat. Republican Congl. Com. Served with USAF, 1965-66, Vietnam. Decorated Air medal with six oak leaf clusters. Mem. Vietnam Vets. Caucus, Oreg. Newspaper Pubs. Assn., Nat. Newspaper Assn., Young Pres. Orgn., Associated Oreg. Industries, Aircraft Owners and Pilots Assn., Beta Theta Pi. Office: Room 1213 Longworth House Office Bldg Washington DC 20515 *

SMITH, DONALD E., broadcast engr. and mgr.; b. Salt Lake City, Sept. 10, 1930; s. Thurman A. and Louise (Cardall) S.; B.A. Columbia Coll., Chgo., 1955; B.S.; U. Utah, 1970; postgrad. U. So. Calif., U. Utah; m. Helen B. Lacy, 1978. Engr., Iowa State U., (WOI-TV), 1955-56; asst. chief engr. KLRJ-TV, Las Vegas, 1956-60; studio field engr. ABC, Hollywood, Cal., 1960; chief engr. Teletape, Inc., Salt Lake City, 1961; engring. supr. KUER, U. Utah, Salt Lake City, 1962—, gen. mgr., 1975-85. Free lance cinematography, 1950—; cons. engr. radio and TV prodns., 1965—. Mem. Soc. Motion Pictures and TV Engrs., Lambda Chi Alpha. Home: 963 Hollywood Ave Salt Lake City UT 84105

SMITH, DONALD EVANS, library cons.; b. Shenandoah, Iowa, Dec. 2, 1915; s. William Wesley and Bess Alice (Evans) S.; student Ricks Coll., 1939-40; B.A., Hastings Coll., 1946; M.L.S., U. Wash., 1964. Tchr. English, librarian Tenino (Wash.) High Sch., 1950-51, Rochester (Wash.) High Sch., 1954-59; librarian North Thurston High Sch., Lacey, Wash., 1959-67; head librarian, coordinator instructional materials Lakes High Sch., Lakewood Center, Wash., 1967-80; library cons., 1980—. Mem. awards com. Wash. Library Commn., 1964-66. Served with Signal Corps, AUS, 1942-45; to 1st lt., M.I., U.S. Army, 1951-54; to col. Wash. State Guard, 1971-80, now ret. Mem. Wash. Assn. Sch. Librarians (com. chmn.), Clover Park Edn. Assn. (com. chmn. 1970-71), Am. Legion, Phi Delta Kappa (del. nat. confs.). Home and Office: 4530 26th Loop SE Lacey WA 98503

SMITH, DONALD MACLEAN, broadcasting executive; b. Toronto, Ont., Can., June 25, 1930; s. Donald MacLean and Annie Winnifred S.; m. Lorraine Henderson, Oct. 23, 1955; children: Mary-Catherine, Susan Anne, Donald James. Radio transcription traffic All Can. Radio Facilities Ltd., Toronto, 1951-54; time salesman All-Can. Radio & TV Ltd., Toronto, 1954; group mgr. All-Can. Radio & TV Ltd., 1962-66, Toronto sales mgr., 1966-70; v.p. All-Can. Radio & TV Ltd. (TV), 1970-73; v.p. sales B.C. TV Ltd., Vancouver, B.C., Can., 1973-78; exec. v.p. B.C. TV Ltd., 1978-82, pres., 1982—. Mem. Advt. Guild Toronto (past pres.), TVB Can. (chmn. 1976-78, past dir.), Can. Assn. Broadcasters (chmn. 1979-81), Advt. Standard Council B.C. (chmn.). Anglican. Clubs: Hollyburn Country, Broadcast Execs. Soc, Variety, Celebrity, Capilano Golf. Office: PO Box 4700, Vancouver, BC Canada V6B 4A3

SMITH, DONALD PERRY, lawyer, electrical engineer; b. Bklyn., Feb. 23, 1912; s. Harry N. and Lucy (Perry) S.; m. Frances Carrington, Aug. 1946 (div. 1963); m. Doris Marie Ten Brock, Jan. 12, 1971; 1 child, George A. B.E.E., NYU, 1938; J.D., Am. U., 1951. Bar: D.C. 1951, U.S. Supreme Ct. 1954, N.Mex. 1975. Elec. engr. U.S. Maritime Adminstrn., Washington, 1946; patent examiner U.S. Patent Office, Washington, 1951; div. patent counsel ACF Industries, Riverdale, Mo., 1954; patent counsel Dept. Def., Washington, 1960; ptnr., dir. patent operation Singer, Smith & Powell, P.A., Albuquerque, 1981—. Author: Understanding Patents, 1968. Patentee in field. Recipient Meritorious Civilian Service award U.S. Air Force, Kirtland AFB, 1975, cert. of appreciation St. John's Cathedral, Albuquerque, 1981. Mem. Am. Patent Law Assn., Albuquerque Bar Assn., Sigma Nu Phi. Republican. Episcopalian. Lodges: Masons. Home: 6432 Louise Pl NE Albuquerque NM 87109 Office: Singer Smith & Powell PA 300 Central St SW Box 25565 Albuquerque NM 87125

SMITH, DONNA ELAINE, public relations specialist; b. Franklin, Pa., Nov. 17, 1955; d. Darrell Edwin and Gail (Adams) S. AA, San Diego Mesa Coll., 1976; BA in Journalism, San Diego State U., 1979. Public relations rep. Safeway Stores, Inc., San Diego, Calif., 1973-83; dir. mktg. and promotions Andy Williams Open Shearson Lehman Bros., San Diego, 1983—; advisor mktg. communications U. Calif. San Diego, 1984—. Editor: The Semaphore, 1980-83; mng. editor The Young Republicans, 1984, Republican Record, 1985. Com. chmn. March of Dimes, San Diego, 1983, Holiday Bowl, San Diego, 1985-87; mem. Rep. Cen. Com., San Diego, 1984—; Koala capt. Ctr. for Research Endangered Species, San Diego Zool. Soc., 1985—; advisor jr. world tournament San Diego Jr. Golf Assn. Named Outstanding Young Woman Am., 1984; Tribute to Women and Industry award YWCA, 1983; named to Emerald Club Kyocera Inamori LPGA Classic., 1986—. Mem. Pub. Relations Soc. Am. (San Diego chpt. treas. 1985, dir. 1985—, student sect. advisor 1983-85, sec. 1987, Allen Ctr. Friends of Journalism award 1983), San Diego State U. Young Alumni Assn. Avocations: travel, sailing, flying, skiing. Office: Shearson Lehman Andy Williams Open 9449 Friars Rd Gate P San Diego CA 92108

SMITH, DOUGLAS MCDEVITT, broadcasting executive; b. Akron, Ohio, Mar. 4, 1952; s. James Earl and Nancy Jean (McDevitt) S. BS in Physics, Miami U., Oxford, Ohio, 1974. Media planner Foote, Cone & Belding Communications Inc., Los Angeles, 1976-78; media supr. J. Walter Thompson Co., N.Y.C., 1979-82; field media service mgr. Coca-Cola USA, Atlanta, 1982-84; assoc. media dir. Doyle Dane Bernbach Internat. Inc., Los Angeles, 1984-85; exec. producer Jim Brown Prodns., Santa Monica, Calif., 1986—. Office: James Paul Brown Entertainment 6700 Centinela Ave Culver City CA 90230

SMITH, DWIGHT MORRELL, university chancellor, chemist; b. Hudson, N.Y., Oct. 10, 1931; s. Elliott Monroe and Edith Helen (Hall) S.; m. Alice Beverly Bond, Aug. 27, 1955; children—Karen Elizabeth, Susan Allison, Jonathan Aaron. B.A., Central Coll., Pella, Iowa, 1953; Ph.D., Pa. State U., 1957; ScD (hon.), Cen. Coll., 1986. Postdoctoral fellow, instr. Calif. Inst. Tech., 1957-59; sr. chemist Texaco Research Center, Beacon, N.Y., 1959-61; asst. prof. chemistry Wesleyan U., Middletown, Conn., 1961-66; asso. prof. Hope Coll., Holland, Mich., 1966-69; prof. Hope Coll., 1969-72; prof., chmn. dept. chemistry U. Denver, 1972-83, vice chancellor for acad. affairs, 1983-84, chancellor, 1984—. Editor Revs. on Petroleum Chemistry, 1975-78; contbr. articles to profl. jours. Chmn. Chs. United for Social Action, Holland, Mich., 1968-69; mem. Sch. Bd. Adv. Com., Holland, 1969-70; bd. commrs. Colo. Advanced Tech. Inst., 1984—. DuPont fellow, 1956-57; NSF fellow Scripps Inst., 1971-72; recipient grants Research Corp., grants Petroleum Research Fund, grants NSF, grants Solar Energy Research Inst.; Mem. ch. bds. or consistories Reformed Ch. Am., N.Y., Conn., Mich. Mem. Am. Chem. Soc. (chmn. Colo. 1976, sec. Western Mich. 1970-71, Colo. sect. award 1986), AAAS, Catalysis Soc., Soc. Applied Spectroscopy, Sigma Xi. Clubs: Teknik, Denver; University (N.Y.); Metropolitan. Patentee selective hydrogenation. Home: 7 Sunset Ln Littleton CO 80121 Office: Office of Chancellor Univ Denver 2301 S Gaylord St Denver CO 80208

SMITH, ELAINE JANET, social worker; b. Albert Lea, Minn., Nov. 25, 1939; d. Manville Arthur Frederick and Laura Bertha Louise (Hintz) Pestorious; m. John Vernon Smith, Nov. 27, 1968; stepchildren: E. Michelle, John M., Thomas M., James M. BA, U. Minn., 1960; MSW, U. Denver, 1965. Lic. social worker II, Colo. Social worker Rochester (Minn.) State Hosp., 1961-63, Denver pub. schs., 1965-67, Denver Gen. Hosp., 1967-78; real estate agt. Century 21, Denver, 1978-80; social worker Adams County Social Services, Commerce City, Colo., 1980-85, Sewell Rehab., Denver, 1985—; field instr. Community Coll. Denver, 1980-84. Organist United Ch. Montbello, Denver, 1978—. Recipient Outstanding Achievement Merit Increase award Denver Gen. Hosp., 1974. Mem. Nat. Assn. Social Workers, Alliance for Mentally Ill (asst. sec. local chpt. 1985—). Democrat. Avocations: bowling, sewing, reading, bicycling, travel. Home: 4986 Worchester St Denver CO 80239 Office: Sewell Rehab Ctr 1360 Vine St Denver CO 80206

SMITH, EMERSON EDLYN, III, real estate company administrator; b. Wilmington, Del., Sept. 16, 1949; s. Emerson E. and Patsy (Early) S. BS, Cheyney State Coll., 1973; MEd, Temple U., 1979. Cert. community coll. instr., tchr., counselor, Ariz., N.J., Pa. Counselor No. Homes for Boys, Phila., 1976-78; tchr. Willingboro (N.J.) Sch. Dist., 1973-78, Phoenix Union High Sch. Dist., 1980-82; dir. job career div. No. Ariz. U., Phoenix, 1982; accts. payable supr. Mountain Bell, Phoenix, 1981-82, mgr., 1982—. Vol. counselor Burlington (N.J.) County Probation Dept., 1971; mem. adv. council Burlington County Health Services Administrn., 1972; treas. Valley of the Sun Phoenix United Way, 1982; asst. campaign mgr. Dem. Com. to elect Carolyn Walker, Phoenix 1982-84; coordinator Phoenix March of Dimes, 1984; cons. Black Theatre Troupe, Phoenix, 1984—, bd. dirs., 1985—. Mem. NAACP (bd. dirs. 1985), Black Employees Assn. (bd. dirs. 1983—, pres. 1983-84). Democrat. Baptist. Avocations: photography, travel, jazz, outdoor sports. Home: 608 E Diamond Dr Tempe AZ 85283

SMITH, ERNEST EDWARD, taxi company executive, taximeter repairman; b. Little Rock, Aug. 25, 1944; s. Ernest Edward and Madelyn (Davis) S.; m. Paula Ann Scott, May 1, 1965; children: Michael Paul, Michelle Leann. Student, Riverside (Calif.) City Coll., 1966, Valley Coll., San Bernardino, Calif., 1967. Aircraft mechanic USAF, Calif. and Guam, 1962-66; silverbrazier Bourns Instruments, Riverside, 1966-68; foreman Loma Linda (Calif.) U., 1968-74; owner Paradise Taxi Co., Kailua-Kona, Hawaii, 1974—. Served with USAF, 1962-66. Recipient Best Taxi Service award Bartenders Ocean Breeze, Kailua-Kona, 1985. Republican. Seventh-Day Adventist. Avocations: fishing, rock collecting, coin collecting. Home: 75-221 Aloha Kona Dr Kailua-Kona HI 96745 Office: Paradise Taxi PO Box 1715 Kailua-Kona HI 96740

SMITH, ERNEST KETCHAM, electrical engineer; b. Peking, China, May 31, 1922; (parents Am. citizens); s. Ernest Ketcham and Grace (Goodrich) S.; m. Mary Louise Standish, June 23, 1950; children: Priscilla Varland, Nancy Giovigneri, Cynthia Jackson. BA in Physics, Swarthmore Coll., 1944; MSEE, Cornell U., 1951, Ph.D., 1956. Chief plans and allocations engr. Mut. Broadcasting System, 1946-49; with Nat. Bur. Standards, 1951-65; chief ionosphere research sect. Nat. Bur. Standards, Boulder, Colo., 1957-60; div. chief Nat. Bur. Standards, 1960-65; dir. aeronomy lab. Environ. Sci. Services Adminstrn., Boulder, 1965-67; dir. Inst. Telecommunication Scis., 1968, dir. univ. relations, 1968-70; assoc. dir. Inst. Telecommunications Scis. Office of Telecommunications, Boulder, 1970-72, cons., 1972-76; mem. tech. staff Jet Propulsion Lab. Calif. Inst. Tech., Pasadena, 1976-87; adj. prof. dept. Electrical Engring. U. Colo., Boulder, 1987—; vis. fellow Coop. Inst. Research on Environ. Scis., 1968; assoc. Harvard U. Coll. Obs., 1965-75; adj. prof. U. Colo., 1969-78, 87—; internat. vice-chmn. study group 6, Internat. Radio Consultative Com., 1958-70, chmn. U.S. study group, 1970-76; mem. U.S. commn. Internat. Sci. Radio Union, mem.-at-large U.S. nat. com., 1985—. Author: Worldwide Occurrence of Sporadic E, 1957; (with S. Matsushita) Ionospheric Sporadic E, 1962. Contbr. numerous articles to profl. jours. Editor: Electromagnetic Probing of the Upper Atmosphere, 1969. Served with U.S. Army, 1944-45. Recipient Diploma d'honneur, Internat. Radio Consultative Com., Internat. Telecommunications Union, 1978. Fellow IEEE, AAAS; mem. Am. Geophys. Union. Mem. United Ch. of Christ. Clubs: Harvard Faculty; University (Boulder); Athenaeum, Flint Canyon Tennis (Pasadena). Lodge: Kiwanis. Home: 5159 Idylwild Trail Boulder CO 80301 Office: U Colo Dept Electrical Engring Campus Box 425 Boulder CO 80309

SMITH, FLOYD H., water treatment company executive; b. N.Y.C., Mar. 22, 1932; s. Floyd Harold and Lillian (Pick) S.; m. Johanna Maria Vollebregt, Jan. 28, 1953; children: Donna Maria, Ellen Joanne, Teresa Anne, Shirley June, Susan Kathleen. BS, Oreg. State U., 1959, MS, 1961. Registered profl. engr., Oreg., Wash., Alaska. Engr.-in-tng. Carma Mfg. Co., Torrance, Calif., 1953-55; designer CH2M, Corvallis, Oreg., 1955-62; planner U. Oreg. Bur. Mcpl. Research, Eugene, 1962-66; mgr. spl. projects Neptune MicroFLOC, Corvallis, 1966-77; pres. Nat. Tech. Services, Inc., Corvallis, 1977—. Designer water treatment fabrication method (Design in Steel award 1974). Served as sgt. U.S. Army, 1950-53. Mem. ASCE. Republican. Avocations: hunting, designing mechanical equipment. Home: 1680 Crest Dr Eugene OR 97405 Office: Nat Tech Services Inc 33881 Eastgate Circle Corvallis OR 97333

SMITH, FORREST RANDALL, data processing executive; b. St. Charles, Ill., Mar. 27, 1951; s. Darrell Lemoine and Ruth Lavonne (Jones) S.; m. Judith Ann Hollenbeck, May 29, 1969; 1 child, Denise Renee. Student, Parks Sch. Bus., 1969-70. Mgr. Gigantic Cleaners, Denver, 1969-70; with distbn. maintenance Kan-Nebr. Nat. Gas Co., Holdrege, Nebr., 1970-73; programmer, analyst Kan-Nebr. Nat. Gas Co., Phillipsburg, Kans., 1973-75; supr. property systems Fresno (Calif.) County, 1975-83; asst. v.p. application systems Gesco Corp., Fresno, 1983-86, v.p. application systems, 1986—. Democrat. Office: Gesco Corp 3747 E Shields Ave Fresno CA 93726

SMITH, FRAN KELLOGG, architectural lighting designer; b. Chgo., Oct. 28, 1940; d. James Hull and Jean Mathieson (Defrees) Kellogg; m. Frederick John Bertolone, July 3, 1976; children by previous marriages—Wayne E. McConnell III, Carol Jean McConnell, Scott Kellogg McConnell, Christina L. Smith. B.A., Pomona Coll., 1966; postgrad., Claremont Grad. Sch., 1966-68; B.S. in Interior Design, Woodbury U., 1973. Ptnr., lighting designer Ominia, Los Angeles, 1970-71; staff lighting cons. Black, Swarens & Okada, Los Angeles, 1972-73; founder, owner, operator Luminae Lighting Cons., Los Angeles, 1973-76; chmn. bd. Luminae Inc., Los Angeles and San Francisco, 1976-84; instr. interior design cert. program UCLA, 1980—, U. Calif., Berkeley, 1986; guest lectr. various seminars throughout U.S. Authro: Bringing Interiors to Light, 1986; contbr. articles to Designers West, Miami Herald, Chgo. Tribune, Home Lighting and Accessories, New Shelter. Designer low voltage luminaire (Pacifica cert. of merit 1980). Author: Bringing Interiors to Light, 1986. Founder, charter pres. service sect. Faculty Wives Club, Calif. State U., Los Angeles, 1967, v.p., 1969; bd. dirs. Villa Esperanza Sch. for Retarded, Pasadena, Calif., 1969-72. Recipient 1st place award Los Angeles Art and Antiques Show, 1972, 1st place award for instns. Inst. Bus. Designers, 1974,. Mem. Am. Soc. Interior Designers (2d place Halo award 1980, bd. dirs. No. Calif. 1980-81, liaison to Interior Designer Educators council 1981-83, Presdl. citation 1984, Chpt. citation 1985, del. to Nat. Council Interior Design Qualifications 1984-86), AIA (chpt. affiliate), Designers Lighting Forum (founder, charter pres. Los Angeles chpt. 1972-74), Internat. Assn. Lighting Designers, Illumination Engring. Soc. (CASI award 1976, Sol Cohn award 1984), Interior Design Eudcators Council (hon. life). Republican. Episcopalian. Home: 315 Orange St San Gabriel CA 91776 Office: Luminae 555 De Haro San Francisco CA 94107

SMITH, FRED ALMON, human resources executive; b. Middlebury, Vt., Sept. 20, 1938; s. Maurice Edward and Mabel (Norton) S.; m. Nancy Gail Peterson, June 15, 1967 (dec. Nov. 1977); 1 child, Stephen Peterson; m. Diane Judith DiPinto, July 31, 1981. BA, U. Vt., 1961; MA, NYU, 1983. Dir. food service SAGA Corp., various locations, 1961-67; dir. personnel SAGA Corp., Washington Crossing, Pa., 1968-72; sr. food service dir. SAGA Corp., Burlington, Vt., 1973-75; dir. human resources SAGA Corp., Avon, Conn., 1976-79; div. dir. human resources SAGA Corp., Menlo Park, Calif., 1979-80, v.p. human resources, 1981—; mem. adv. bd. U. New Haven, 1976-69, Rochester (N.Y.) Inst. Tech., 1984—. Mem. Nat. Restaurant Assn., Council Hospitality Restaurant Intstnl. Educators (bd. dirs. 1985—), Human Resources Planning Soc., U. Vt. Alumni Club (chmn. 1982—), Eta Sigma Delta (bd. dirs. 1978—). Republican. Methodist. Avocations: reading, swimming, historical trips. Office: SAGA Corp 4 Main St Los Altos CA 94022

SMITH, GARMOND STANLEY, animal science educator; b. Wayne, W.Va., July 9, 1932; s. Chester Garmond and Pearl (Ferguson) S.; m. Nellie Eileen Hagedorn, May 31, 1953; children: Stephen, Kristina, Amy, David, Susan, Elizabeth. BS, W.Va. U., 1953, MS, 1957, PhD, 1959. Research asst. W.Va. U., Morgantown, 1956-59; research assoc. U. Ill., Urbana, 1959-60, asst. prof., 1960-65; assoc. prof. N.Mex. State U., Las Cruces, 1968-72, prof. animal sci., 1972—; vis. prof. biology Lincoln (Ill.) Christian Coll., 1966-67; vis. prof. vet. medicine, U. Ill., 1967-68; vis. prof. toxicology U. Kans. Med. Ctr., 1982; cons. State Agys., 1968—; cons. Wastetech, Ltd., Johannesburg, S. Africa, 1981, Internat. Atomic Energy Agy., Vienna. Sect. editor Jour. Animal Sci., 1986—; contbr. chpts. to books and articles to profl. publs. Dir. Mimbres Christian Youth Camp, Gila Wilderness Area, N.Mex., 1975—; participant World Conf. on Animal Prodn., Tokyo, 1983. Served to 1st lt. U.S. Army, 1953-55. Recipient Disting. Service award N.Mex. State U., 1974, Disting. Research award N.Mex. State U., 1982, Disting. Service citation U.S. Dept. Energy, 1981. Fellow AAAS; mem. Am. Soc. Animal Sci., Am. Inst. Nutrition, Am. Inst. Biol. Scis., Council Agrl. Sci. Tech., Sigma Xi. Republican. Home: 1840 Myrtle Ave Las Cruces NM 88001 Office: N Mex State U Dept Animal and Range Scis Campus Box 3-I Las Cruces NM 88003

SMITH, GAROLD DAVID, JR., architect-engineer; b. Colorado Springs, Colo., July 4, 1936; s. Garold David and Helen Louise (Sopko) S.; B.S., U. Colo. in Archtl. Engring., 1968; m. Mary Louise Mills, July 4, 1959; children—April Marie-Francine, Heather Anne-Elizabeth, Tiffanie Louise, Garold David III. Lic architect, Colo., N.Mex., Tex.; registered profl. engr., Colo., Tex. Prin., Garold D. Smith Jr., Colorado Springs, 1970-73; project coordinator architect, assoc. Page, Southerland & Page, med. cons., Austin, Tex., 1973-76; prin. Garold D. Smith Jr., AIA, Architect, Structural Engr., Passive Solar Cons., Colorado Springs, 1977-83; pres. Garold D. Smith, Jr. and Assocs., P.C.; 1983—; instr. Bemis Art Sch., 1980—. Bd. dirs. Colorado Springs Regional Bldg. Dept. Plumbing Com., 1979-83, Colorado Springs Fire Bd. Appeals, 1983—. Mem. NSPE, AIA (past pres. S. Colo. chpt., sec. Colo. Soc. Architects 1983), Internat. Solar Energy Soc., Constrn. Specifications Inst., Internat. Platform Assn. Republican. Roman Catholic. Lodge: Sertoma. Home: 1213 High Point Lane E Colorado Springs CO 80904 Office: 104 S Cascade Ave Suite 219 Colorado Springs CO 80903

SMITH, GARY SOREN, music educator, musician; b. Modesto, Calif., July 4, 1938; s. George Alfred Smith and Louise Ann Brand; m. Barbara Faye, Dec. 21, 1968. MusB, U. Calif., Berkeley, 1956, MA in Performance, 1959; PhD in Music Edn., Stanford U., 1975. Cert. adminstrv. supr. Enlisted U.S. Army, 1959; solo clarinetist 6th Army Band, Presidio, Calif., 1959-61, U.S. Army Band, Washington, 1961; resigned U.S. Army, 1961; mus. dir. Oakland (Calif.) Civic Opera, 1972-83; prof. music Ohlone Coll., Fremont, Calif., 1968—, dir. div., 1985—; clarinetist Oakland Symphony Orchestra, 1961-85. Fellow NEH, 1972-73. Fellow Music Educator Nat. Conv.; mem. Music. Assn. Calif. Community Colls. (pres. 1980-81), Am. Fedn. Musicians. Democrat. Episcopalian. Avocations: tennis, bridge, gardening. Home: 43617 Paseo Padre Pkwy Fremont CA 94539 Office: Ohlone Coll 43600 Mission Blvd Fremont CA 94539

SMITH, GENEVIEVE GRANT, educational administrator; b. Meridian, Idaho, Dec. 3, 1922; d. Lawrence Jessie and Melitta Mae (Stiegelmeier) Grant; m. Jasper William Smith, Dec. 13, 1940; children—Lawrence Jasper, Lynda Jean, Eldon Howard, Stanley Dayle. A.A., Boise Jr. Coll., 1957, B.A., Northwest Nazarene Coll., 1964; M.Ed., Coll. Idaho, 1969. Classroom, vocal music tchr./coordinator Boise (Idaho) Ind. Sch. Dist., 1957-73, adminstrv. team leader Lowell Sch., 1973-76; asst. prin. Garfield Sch., 1976-78; prin. Whitney Sch., 1978-85; dir. Capital Educators Fed. Credit Union, 1970-84, v.p., 1978-81, pres., 1981-84; co-founder 3 R's Found., reading workshops for tchrs. and parents; workshop instr., active dist., state edn. coms. Mem. Vista Neighborhood Housing Services; active numerous fund-raising coms. Recipient Idaho Gem award Idaho Assn. Elem. Sch. Prins., Internat. Reading Assn. award, 1985, Spl. Service award Idaho State PTA, 1985, Life Merit award Idaho State PTA, Red Apple award Boise Sch. Dist., Boss of Yr. award Ada County Assn. Ednl. Office Personnel, 1983; named Disting. Citizen, Idaho Statesman Newspaper, 1985; grantee Title IV-C Match Program. Mem. Assn. Supervision and Curriculum Devel., Idaho Soc. Individual Psychology, Idaho Assn. Elem. Sch. Prins., Nat. Assn. Elem. Sch. Prins., Idaho Assn. Sch. Adminstrs., Boise Assn. Sch. Prins., Boise Edn. Assn., Idaho Edn. Assn., NEA, Northwest Women in Ednl. Adminstrn., Alumni Assn. Boise State U., Northwest Nazarene Coll. Assn., Yokefellows Assn., NOW, Phi Delta Kappa, Delta Kappa Gamma, Phi Delta Lambda. Republican. Contbr. articles to local newspapers. Home: 2935 Caradoc Boise ID 83704

SMITH, GEORGE FOSTER, aerospace co. exec.; b. Franklin, Ind., May 9, 1922; s. John Earl and Ruth (Foster) S.; m. Jean Arthur Farnsworth, June 3, 1950; children—David Foster, Craig Farnsworth, Sharon Windsor. B.S. in Physics, Calif. Inst. Tech., 1944, M.S., 1948, Ph.D. magna cum laude (Standard Oil fellow 1949-50), 1952. Founding staff mem. Engring. Research Assos., St. Paul, 1946-48; teaching fellow, resident asso. Calif. Inst. Tech., 1948-52; mem. staff Hughes Research Labs., Malibu, Calif., 1952—; asso. dir. Hughes Research Labs., 1962-69, dir., 1969—; v.p. Hughes Aircraft Co., 1965-81, sr. v.p., 1981—, mem. policy bd., 1966—; adj. asso. prof. elec. engring. U. So. Calif., 1959-62; cons. Army Sci. Adv. Panel, 1975-78. Author. Adv. local Explorer post Boy Scouts Am., 1965-70; bd. mgrs. Westchester YMCA, 1974—, chmn., 1979-81; chmn. trustees Pacific Presbyn. Ch., Los Angeles, 1959-62. Served to lt. (j.g.) USNR, 1944-46. Fellow Am. Phys. Soc., IEEE (pres. Sorenson fellows 1972-73); mem. AAAS, Sierra Club, Sigma Xi, Tau Beta Pi (chpt. pres. 1957-58). Patentee in field. Office: 3011 Malibu Canyon Rd Malibu CA 90265

SMITH, GEORGE LARRY, analytical and environmental chemist; b. Beloit, Kans., Oct. 11, 1951; s. Richard Bailey and Vonda Ellene (Cox) S.; m. Charlene Janell Musgrove, Sept. 4, 1973; 1 child, Brian Lawrence. BA, Augustana Coll., 1973. Lab. technician Sanitary Dist. of Hammond, Ind., 1973; chemist Federated Metals Corp., Whiting, Ind., 1973-77, Air Pollution Technology, Inc., San Diego, 1978-81; staff chemist I Occidental Research Corp., Irvine, Calif., 1981-82; process chemist Chem. Waste Mgmt., Inc., Kettleman City, Calif., 1982-86; lab. analyst for published article in environ. sci. and tech., 1981. bd. dirs. Apostolic Christian Missions, Inc., San Diego, 1978-82. Mem. Am. Chem. Soc., Internat. Union of Pure and Applied Chemistry (affiliate), AAAS, Creation Research Soc. Mem. Pentacostal Ch. Avocations: coin collecting, drawing, reading sci., history and religion. Home: 860 E Grangeville Blvd Space 45 Hanford CA 93230 Office: Chem Waste Mgmt Inc PO Box 471 Kettleman City CA 93239

SMITH, GERALD ARTHUR, museum director; b. Gravette, Ark., June 5, 1915; s. George A. and Mary Grace (Knox) S.; m. Maxine McGowan, June 17, 1938; children: Jerilynn, Geoffrey, Meredith, David. BA, U. Redlands, 1937, MA, 1939; EdD, U. So. Calif., 1953. Tchr. jr. high sch., Bloomington, Calif., 1937-40; coach of freshmen U. Redlands, Calif., 1937-38; tchr. adult edn. Colton (Calif.) High Sch., 1938-40; teaching prin. Warm Springs Elem. Sch., San Bernardino, Calif., 1940-41; dist. supt. Warm Springs Sch. Dist., San Bernardino, 1941-43; adviser Vet.'s Guidance Ctr., San Diego, 1945; coordinator Vet.'s Guidance Ctr., San Bernardino Valley Coll., San Bernardino, 1945-46; dist. supt. Bloomington (Calif.) Sch. Dist., 1946-66; assoc. supt., then dist. supt. Colton Joint Unified Sch. Dist., 1966-71; dir. San Bernardino County Museums, Redlands, 1971-83; vis. prof. edn. U. Redlands, U. Calif., Riverside, 1955; cons. cultural resources and mus., 1984—. Contbr. articles in history and anthropology to profl. jours.; project dir., mem. various archeol. expdns., ethnol. studies. Bd. dirs., sec.-treas. Bloomington Park and Recreation Dist.; bd. dirs. Arrowhead area council Boy Scouts Am., Arrowhead United Fund, ARC, Bloomington, YMCA, San Bernardino; coordinator San Bernardino County Info. Ctr., Calif. Archeol. Inventory. Served with USNR, 1943-45. Decorated Purple Heart; recipient Am. Educators medal Freedoms Found., 1963; spl. award Indian Affairs Conf. of Calif. Hist. Socs., 1971. Mem. Soc. Calif. Archeology, Calif. Conf. Hist. Socs. (pres.), Am. Assn. Museums, Calif. Assn. Museums (v.p.), Am. Assn. State and Local History, Pacific Coast Archaeol. Soc., NEA, Am. Assn. Sch. Adminstrs., Assn. Supervision and Curriculum Devel., Assn. Childhood Edn., Am. Legion (past commdr. Bloomington post), San Bernardino County Hist. Soc. (past pres.), San Bernardino County Mus. Assn. (exec. dir., past pres.), So. Calif. Archeol. Survey Assn. (past pres.), Soc. Profl. Archeology, Calif. Assn. Mus. (v.p.). Office: 1561 Smiley Heights Dr Redlands CA 92373

SMITH, GORDON JAMES, environmental protection administrator; b. Scott AFB, Ill., Apr. 13, 1952; s. George L. and Kikuko T. (Tanabe) S.; m. Gail H. Eshima, Aug. 19, 1977; 1 child, Gregory. BS, U. Hawaii, 1975, MS, 1979. Indsl. hygienist Sandia Nat. Labs., Albuquerque, 1979-84, supr., 1984—; cons. City of Honolulu, 1979. Contbr. articles to profl. jours. Mem. N.Mex. Hazardous Waste Assn. (pres. 1983-84), Am. Indsl. Hygiene Assn., Am. Acad. Indsl. Hygiene. Office: Sandia Nat Labs PO Box 5800 Div 3314 Albuquerque NM 87185

SMITH, GUERDON DIMMICK, investment banker; b. Toledo, Oct. 5, 1916; s. Frederick William and Alice (Winzenreid) S.; m. Jane Shoemaker, July 20, 1946 (dec. 1949); children: Kristin Ann, Guerdon Jr., Frederick II; m. Eleanor Mae McUmber, 1950 (dec. 1977). Student, U. Pa., 1934-36, U. Toledo, 1936-38, N.Y. Inst. Fin., 1945. Exec. trainee Libbey, Owens, Ford & Glass, Toledo, 1938-40; mgr. investments Collin, Norton & Co., Toledo, 1945-51, Dean Witter & J. Barth, Los Angeles, 1951-57; v.p., dir. research Blyth & Co., Inc., N.Y.C., 1965-70, Shelby C. Davis, Wertheim, Kidder & Peabody, N.Y.C., 1970-83; mng. ptnr. Guerdon Smith & Co., Santa Barbara, Calif., 1956—; bd. dirs. Am. Express, N.Y.C.. Author: Barron's, 1969. Mgr. Rep. Party, Toledo, 1945-51; commr. fire and police pensions City of Santa Barbara; dir. Cen. Coast Commn. for Sr. Citizens, Calif. Served to sgt. U.S. Army, 1940-45, ETO, West Pacific, USAF. Decorated 5 combat medals U.S. Army, 1945. Fellow Fin. Analysts Fedn.; mem. N.Y. Soc. Security Analysts. Congregationalist. Clubs: Union League (N.Y.C.), Calif. (Los Angeles), Indian Harbor Yacht (Greenwich, Ct.). Avocations: yachting, golf. Home and Office: PO Box 91739 Santa Barbara CA 93190

SMITH, H. RUSSELL, manufacturing company executive; b. Clark County, Ohio, Aug. 15, 1914; s. Lewis Hoskins and Eula (Elder) S.; m. Jeanne Rogers, June 27, 1942; children: Stewart Russell, Douglas Howard, Jeanne Ellen Smith Akins. A.B., Pomona Coll., 1936. Security analyst Kidder, Peabody & Co., N.Y.C., 1936-37; economist ILO, Geneva, 1937-40; asst. to pres. Blue Diamond Corp., Los Angeles, 1940-46; pres., dir. Avery Internat. Corp., Pasadena, Calif., 1946-75, chmn. bd., 1975-84, chmn. exec. com., 1984-87, retired, 1987; dir. So. Calif. Edison Co., Security Pacific Corp., Security Pacific Nat. Bank, Los Angeles. Bd. dirs., past pres., chmn. Los Angeles Philharm. Assn.; bd. fellows Claremont Univ. Center; chmn. bd. trustees Pomona Coll., Claremont, Calif.; chmn. bd. Children's Hosp. Los Angeles; past chmn. bd. Community TV of So. Calif. (Sta. KCET), Los Angeles. Served with USNR, 1943-46. Home: 1458 Hillcrest Ave Pasadena CA 91106 Office: Avery Internat 150 N Orange Grove Blvd Pasadena CA 91103

SMITH, HAROLD WAYNE, academic principal; b. Granger, Wash., Nov. 16, 1934; s. Harold Max and Gertrude Louisa (Spicer) S.; m. Elsa Chloa Fair, Apr. 30, 1966; children: Heidi Suzanne, Chad Daniel, Brenda Marie. BA, Whitworth Coll., 1958; MEd, Seattle Pacific U., 1965. Elem. sch. tchr. Yakima (Wash.) Pub. Schs., 1958-65, 67-68, Simi Valley (Calif.) Schs., 1965-66; history tchr., vice prin. Schutz Am. Sch., Alexandria, Egypt, 1966-67, 68-70; history tchr. Elma (Wash.) High Sch., 1970-72; counselor Elma Jr.-Sr. High Sch., 1972-76; vice prin. McFarland Jr. High Sch., Othello, Wash., 1976-80, prin., 1980—. Coach Othello Soccer Assn., 1979-81; mem. Theatre Guild, Othello, 1976-81; umpire Othello Little League, 1982—; com. mem. Boy Scouts Am., Othello, 1978—. Mem. Nat. Assn. Secondary Sch. Prins., N. Cen. Wash. Jr. High League (pres. 1978-79), N. Cen. Wash. Jr. High Prins. Assn. (sec. 1977-78), Mid-Columbia Middle Sch. Activities Assn. (pres. 1982-83), Yakima Valley Jr. High Prin.'s Assn. (treas. 1986—), Gideons (pres. 1981-86, treas. 1986-87). Republican. Mem. Christian Ch. Clubs: Y's Men Internat. (Pacific N.W. regional dir. 1972-76, regional award 1979, Internat. Brother award 1984). Lodge: Lions (named Lion of Yr. 1984). Home: 1220 E Hamlet PO Box 148 Othello WA 99344 Office: McFarland Jr High Sch 790 S 10th Othello WA 99344

SMITH, H(AROLD) WENDELL, retired English and journalism educator; b. Topeka, Sept. 26, 1923; s. Harold J. and Marie (Finch) S.; B.A., UCLA, 1948, M.A., 1952; m. Virginia Howson, Apr. 15, 1946; children—Penny Michele, Melanie Kay, Kimberly Ann, Bradley Scott; m. 2d, E. Nadine Andrews, Mar. 29, 1969. Tchr. English, journalism Luther Burbank Jr. High Sch., Burbank, Calif., 1949-50, Santa Monica (Calif.) High Sch., 1950-58; faculty Santa Monica Coll., 1958-84, prof. English 1970-78, chmn. dept. communications, 1979-80, prof. English and broadcast journalism, 1980-84. Served with AUS, 1943-46. Mem. Internat. Soc. Gen. Semantics, MLA. Author: (with A.L. Lazarus) Modern English, 1971, A Glossary of Literature and Composition, 1973, 83; On Paper 1975, 78, 82; (with R. H. Woodward) The Craft of Prose, 1977; Elements of the Essay, 1979, 81, 83, 86; Readable Writing: Revising for Style, 1985, The Belmont Reader: Essays for Writers, 1986. Home and Office: Box 7522 Canyon Lake CA 92380

SMITH, HARRIET FULLEN, author, civic worker; b. Vincennes, Ind., Sept. 12, 1906; d. William Martin and Zola (Stewart) Fullen; m. Lewis Elden Smith, Aug. 12, 1934 (dec. 1964); children—Hannah Kully, Lewis, Deborah, Martin. B.A., U. So. Calif., 1926, M.A., 1927, postgrad., 1927-30, postgrad. in counseling, 1977-78; postgrad. Columbia U. Tchrs. Coll., summer 1929; postgrad. in poetry UCLA, 1960-65. Teaching asst., instr. U. So. Calif., Los Angeles, 1926-30; instr. in psychology, dean of women Compton (Calif.) Jr. Coll., 1930-36; textbook author Ginn and Co., Boston, 1943-76; free-lance writer, 1976—. Bd. dirs. Fullen-Smith Found., 1964—, Child Guidance Clinic, Los Angeles, 1964-71, Los Angeles chpt. ARC, 1965-66, Continuing Edn. Women, Claremont Coll., 1966-76, Internat. Assn. Vol. Edn., 1970—, Blaisdell Inst. Claremont Coll., 1971-83, Otis Art Inst., 1979-80; nat. bd. dirs. Exptl. Internat. Living, 1970-79. Recipient Appreciation award Goodwill Industries So. Calif. Mem. Town Hall Los Angeles, World Affairs Council, Women's Council Community TV of Los Angeles (hon. life), Trojan League, U. So. Calif. Assocs., Claremont Grad. Sch. Assocs., The Amazing Blue Ribbon (music ctr.), Phi Beta Kappa, Phi Kappa Phi, Pi Lambda Theta, Alpha Delta Pi. Democrat. Congregationalist. Author: (with Florence Means) Raphael and Consuelo, 1929; My Shadow Self, 1931; Your Life as a Citizen, 1952, rev. edits., 1961, 65, 67, 70, 76.

SMITH, HARVEY ALVIN, mathematics educator, consultant; b. Easton, Pa., Jan. 30, 1932; s. William Augustus and Ruth Carolyn (Krauth) S.; m. Ruth Wismer Kolb, Aug. 27, 1955; children: Deirdre Lynn, Kirsten Nadine, Brinton Averill. B.S., Lehigh U., 1952; M.S., U. Pa., 1955, A.M., 1958, Ph.D., 1964. Asst. prof. math Drexel U., 1960-65; mem. tech. staff Inst. Def. Analyses, Arlington, Va., 1965-66; assoc. prof. math Oakland U., 1966-68; ops. research scientist Exec. Office of Pres., Washington, 1968-70; prof. math. Oakland U., 1970-77; prof. Ariz. State U., Tempe, 1977—; cons. Inst. Def. Analyses, 1967-69, Exec. Office Pres., 1967-73, U.S. Arms Control and Disarmament Agy, 1973-79, Los Alamos Nat. Lab. Author: Mathematical Foundation of Systems Analysis, 1969. NSF fellow, 1964-65; recipient Meritorious Service award Exec. Office of Pres., 1970. Mem. Soc. Indsl. and Applied Math., Am. Math. Soc., AAAS, Sigma Xi. Home: 18 E Concorda Dr Tempe AZ 85282 Office: Dept Math Arizona State Univ Tempe AZ 85287

SMITH, HELEN REBECCA, clinical social worker; b. Walla Walla, Wash., Jan. 17, 1957; d. Joe Glen and Maxine (Hooper) S. BS in Social Work, Chapman Coll., 1979; MSW, Calif. State U., 1981, M in Pub. Adminstrn., 1982. Lic. clinical soc. worker, Calif. Social worker Sierra Children's Home, Vacaville, CA, 1981-84, San Joaquin Gen. Hosp., Stockton, 1984—; therapist Sexual Abuse Treatment Program, Stockton, 1985-87. Mem. Young Adult Ministry Council, No. Calif. Named one of Outstanding Young Women Am., 1983. Mem. Nat. Assn. Social Workers (bd. dirs. 1980-81), Nat. Assn. Perinatoal Social Workers, Sierra Club. Democrat. Mem. Christian Ch. Avocations: walking, dancing, reading, traveling, music. Office: San Joaquin Gen Hosp 8422 Roxburgh Way Stockton CA 95209

SMITH, HERBERT HARRIS, planning and community development educator, consultant; b. Mayfield, Ky., Aug. 10, 1921; s. George Edward and Emma Jane (Harris) S.; m. Doris Claire Burgess, Oct. 31, 1943 (div.); children—Michael Edward, Merilee Ann Smith Skaar, Tracey Lee Smith Brackett; m. Nancy Ann Dodge, Apr. 30, 1974. Cert. civil engring. S.D. Sch. Mines, 1944; B.Arch., U. Cin., 1947; M.Regional Planning, Cornell U., 1948. Resident planner City of Trenton, 1948-49; chief Planning Bur., State of N.J., Trenton, 1949-54; exec. dir. Community Planning Assocs., Inc., Princeton, N.J., 1954-57; pres. Herbert H. Smith Assocs., West Trenton, N.J., 1957-71; planning dir. Albuquerque/Bernalillo County, 1971-72; city mgr. City of Albuquerque, 1972-75; assoc. prof. planning and community devel. U. Colo.-Denver, 1975-78, prof., 1978-87; cons. Mescalero and Apache reservations, Ruidoso, N.Mex., 1977-78, Denver Urban Obs., 1978-80, Western Colo. Rural Communities Devel. Program, Durango, 1979-80, UFM Services, Inc., Denver, 1981-86. Author: The Ins and Outs of Planning, 1955; (with others) Zoning Primer, 1959; The Citizen's Guide to Planning, 1979; The Citizen's Guide to Zoning, 1983. Precinct judge Denver Election Commn., 1977-82; bd. dirs. Project Colo., Denver, 1981-82; dir. research re-election campaign Gov. Richard Lamm, Denver, 1982; bd. dirs., Colo. Housing Fin. Authority, Denver, 1983—, treas. 1984-86, chmn. pro tem, 1986—. Served to 2d lt. U.S. Army, 1942-46. Recipient Disting. Service award St. Lukes Episcopal Ch., Trenton, 1969, Am. Soc. Cons. Planners, Washington, 1971, N.J. Fedn. Planning Bds., Trenton, 1971, U. Colo. Coll. Design and Planning, Denver, 1982; commendation award Colo. Front Range Project, Denver, 1981. Mem. Am. Soc. Profl. Planners (bd. dirs. 1962-71, pres. 1970-71, Disting. Service award 1971), Am. Planning Assn. (v.p. Colo. chpt. 1980-82), Am. Inst. Cert. Planners, Denver Urban Design Forum. Democrat. Episcopal. Club: City (Denver) (bd. dirs. 1978-86, pres. 1981-82). Home: 100 Marion St Denver CO 80218 Office: U Colo Dept Architecture Denver CO 80202

SMITH, JACK AUBREY, chemist, consultant; b. Wheeler, Tex., Mar. 12, 1922; s. J. Bonner and Annie Laura (Lamberth) S.; m. Laura L. Jacoby, July 3, 1943 (dec. Sept. 1967); children: Jack II, Michael, Aleta; m. Marian Louise Clements, Oct. 23, 1968. BS, Abilene (Tex.) Christian Coll., 1947; MS, N.Mex. Highlands U., 1963. Asst. chief chemist Phillips Chem. Co., Dumas, Tex., 1948-55; chief chemist Sohio Chem. Co., Lima, Ohio, 1955-61; assoc. prof. N.Mex. State U., Carlsbad, 1962-78; devel. dir. Lakeview Christian Home, Carlsbad, 1978-84; cons. City of Carlsbad, 1962—. Contbr. articles to profl. jours. Adult leader Tex. and Ohio councils Boy Scouts Am., 1948-59; mem. N.Mex. Rep. Cen. Com., Carlsbad, 1982—; Served to 1st lt. U.S. Army, 1941-45, with Res. 1949-60. Grantee Summer Inst., NSF, 1962-63, 67, 71. Mem. Am. Chem. Soc., Carlsbad C. of C. (exec. v.p. 1986—, chmn. edn. com. 1983-85). Mem. Ch. Christ. Lodge: Kiwanis (pres. Carlsbad chpt. 1976-77). Home: 1015 N Alameda Carlsbad NM 88220

SMITH, JACK LEE, chemical engineer, business executive; b. Delta, Colo., Oct. 29, 1931; s. Joseph George and Violet Esther (Wilson) S.; m. Barbara H. Jackson, July 7, 1957; children—Beverly Ellen, Leland Andrew. B.S. in Chem. Engring., U. Utah, 1955; B.A. in Bus. Adminstrn. with high honors, Idaho State U., 1969, M.B.A., 1971. Registered profl. engr., Idaho. Dist. corrosion engr. Mountain Fuel Supply Co., Salt Lake City, 1954-56; instrumentation engr. Bechtel Corp., San Francisco, 1956-58; various engring. positions J.R. Simplot Co., Pocatello, Idaho, 1958-65; project engr. Hooker Chem. Co., Tacoma, 1965; various tech. and mgmt. positions Simplot Co., Pocatello, 1965-77, v.p. devel. and planning M & C div., 1977—. Mem. Pocatello Citizens Adv. Council, 1974-76, Pocatello Air Quality Com., 1975-80; mem. adv. bd. Idaho State U. Research and Bus. Park. Served with U.S. Army Res., 1950-60. Recipient project award N.W. Pollution Control Assn., 1981. Mem. Am. Inst. Chem. Engrs. (past chmn. Idaho sect.), Fertilizer Inst. (co. rep., past chmn. mfg. environ. com.), Am. Chem. Soc., Air Pollution Control Assn., AAAS, Am. Mgmt. Assns., Mensa. Contbr. articles on fertilizer prodn. and environ. protection to tech. publs.; patentee in field. Office: Simplot Co 151 N 3d Ave Pocatello ID 83204

SMITH, JAMES ARTHUR, hotel executive; b. Stockton, Calif., July 3, 1942; s. Herbert Leon and Marie Mildred (Mason) S.; m. Saren Wynn Campbell, Jan. 4, 1973 (div. Oct. 1975); m. Michele Raye Robinson, July 15, 1977; 1 child, Michael James Lamont. AA, Sacramento City Coll., 1970; BS, Calif. State U., Sacramento, 1974. Hotel resident mgr. Hollywood (Calif.) Plaza Hotel, 1974-78; hotel gen. mgr. Trusthouse Forte, San Diego, 1978-80; owner J. Glads Restaurant, Sacramento, 1980-83; hotel gen. mgr. Radlow-Gittins, San Diego, 1983-85, Leeds & Strauss, San Diego, 1985—. Author: So You Want to Work on a Cruise Ship--Here's How, 1985; scriptwriter: (film) The Challenge, 1976. Served with USN, 1960-68. Mem. Convention and Vis. Bur., Nat. Assn. Catering Execs. (v.p. 1986—), San Diego Food and Beverage Mgrs. Assn. (1st v.p., 1980), Nat. Assn. Catering Execs., San Diego Hotel Assn. (bd. dirs. 1978-80), Am. Hotel-Motel Assn. (dir. profl. devel. soc. 1977-80), Palm Springs Hotel-Motel Assn. (bd. dirs. 1987—). Republican. Home and Office: Vacation Inn Hotel and Resort 74-715 Hwy 111 Palm Desert CA 92261

SMITH, JAMES EMORY, fin. cons.; b. Fresno, Calif., Sept. 15, 1947; s. Arthur Ralph and Corda Avaleen (Foster) S.; B.A. in Econs., Stanford U., 1969; m. Kathryn E. St. George, Feb. 23, 1974; children—Jessica, Zachary. Acct., Gen. Electric Co., San Jose, Calif., 1969-73; mgr. strategic planning Gen. Electric Japan Ltd., Tokyo, 1974-77; asst. treas. Gen. Electric Tech. Services Co., N.Y.C., 1978-79; pres. Westpro Ltd., San Jose and Monterey, Calif., 1979—; pres. Thompson & Smith, Inc., securities brokers, San Jose and Los Angeles, 1980-83; pres. ZJ Securities Ltd., 1984—. Mem. Soc. Enrolled Agts. Am., San Jose C. of C. Democrat. Unitarian. Office: PO Box 23460 San Jose CA 95153-3460

SMITH, JAMES EMORY, social worker, military officer; b. West Palm Beach, Fla., July 9, 1951; s. William Henry and Josephine (Everett) S. BA in Sociology with high honors, Hampton Inst., 1975; MSW, Va. Commonwealth U., 1977. Lic. master social worker, Kans. Social worker service to mil. families and vets. ARC, Richmond, Va., 1977-78; enlisted U.S. Army, Ft. Riley, Kans., 1978; advanced through grades to maj. U.S. Army; unit social worker U.S. Army Retraining Brigade, Ft. Riley, 1978-80, asst. chief, social work div., 1980-82; chief community mental health U.S. Army, Ft. Greely, Alaska, 1982-83; chief army community service U.S. Army, Ft. Wainwright, Alaska, 1983-85, chief human resources div., 1985-86, dir. personnel and community activities, 1986—; field instr./adj. prof. dept. social work Kans. State U., Manhatten, 1979-82; field placement supr. social work, dept. psychology, sociology and social work U. Alaska, Fairbanks, 1983-84. Bd. dirs. Fairbanks Crisis Line, 1982-85, United Way of Greater Fairbanks, 1986—. Recipient Expert Field Medal badge U.S. Army, 1981, Achievement medal U.S. Army, 1985. Fellow Menninger Found.; mem. Nat. Assn. Social Workers, Acad. Cert. Social Workers (cert.), Nat. Assn. Black Social Workers, Va. Council on Social Welfare, Assn. of U.S. Army (bd. dirs. Polar Bear chpt. 1986—), Nat. Soc. Scabbard and Blade. Avocations: chess, photography, model building, collecting African art and artifacts, hunting. Home: 4351-5 9th St Fort Wainwright AK 99703 Office: US Army 6th Infantry Div Dir Personnel and Community Activities AFVR-FW-PA Fort Wainwright AK 99703

SMITH, JAMES LAWRENCE, research physicist; b. Detroit, Sept. 3, 1943; s. William Leo and Marjorie Marie (Underwood) S.; m. Carol Ann Adam, Mar. 27, 1965; children: David Adam, William Leo. BS, Wayne State U., 1965; PhD, Brown U., 1974. Mem. staff Los Alamos (N.Mex.) Nat. Lab., 1973-82, fellow, 1982-86, dir. ctr. materials sci., 1986—. Contbr. articles to profl. jours. Recipient E.O. Lawrence award, 1986. Fellow Am. Phys. Soc.; mem. AAAS. Office: Los Alamos Nat Lab Ctr for Materials Sci Mail Stop K765 Los Alamos NM 87545

SMITH, JAMES WALKER, horticulturist, consultant, plant breeder; b. Glendale, Calif., Sept. 29, 1946; s. Dale Walker and Eleanor Grace (Hoven) S. Student Los Angeles Pierce Coll., 1964-66, Mira Costa Coll., 1971-72; B.S., Calif. Poly. State U., 1974. Nurseryman, Greenthumb Nursery, Newhall, Calif., 1970-71; instr. Calif. Poly. State U., San Luis Obispo, 1974; grower Pacifica Evergreen Nursery (Calif.), 1975; head estate gardener for pvt. estate, Woodside, Calif., 1975-78; ptnr. landscaping design firm, San Francisco, 1978-79; head estate gardener Whittell Estate Trust, Woodside, 1979-80; horticulturist, plant breeder Plant Smith, Jamestown, Calif., 1980—; hort. cons. Served with USAF, 1966-70. Decorated Bronze Star; commendation medal (Vietnam). Mem. Calif. Hort. Soc., Strybing Arboretum Soc., Calif. Native Plant Soc., Saratoga Hort. Found., Western Hort. Soc. Democrat. Roman Catholic. Home and Office: 11560 La Grange Rd Jamestown CA 95327

SMITH, JEAN, interior design firm executive; b. Oklahoma City; d. A. H. and Goldy K. (Engle) Hearn; m. W. D. Smith, Dec. 2, 1939; children—Kaye Smith Hunt, Sidney P. Student Chgo. Sch. Interior Design, 1970. Vice pres. Billco-Aladdin Wholesale, Albuquerque, 1950—. Pres. Albuquerque Opera, 1979-83, advisor to bd. dirs.; active Civic Chorus, Cen. Meth. Ch.; pres. Inez PTA, 1954-55, life mem.; hon. life mem. Albuquerque Little Theater. Republican. Clubs: Albuquerque County, Four Hills Country, Daus. of the Nile (soloist Yucca Temple). Home: 1009 Santa Ana SE Albuquerque NM 87123 Office: Billco-Aladdin Wholesale 7617 Menaul NE Albuquerque NM 87123

SMITH, JEFF P., grocery and drug stores company executive; b. 1950. Attended, Utah State U. With Smith's Mgmt. Corp., Salt Lake City, 1970—, v.p., then exec. v.p. purchasing ops. mktg., now pres., chief operating officer, dir. Office: Smiths Mgmt Corp 1544 S Redwood Rd Salt Lake City UT 84104 *

SMITH, JEFFRY ALAN, public health administrator, physician; b. Los Angeles, Dec. 8, 1943; s. Stanley W. and Marjorie E. S.; m. Jo Anne Hague. BA in Philosophy, UCLA, 1967, MPH, 1972; BA in Biology, Calif. State U., Northridge, 1971; MD, UACJ, 1977. Diplomate Am. Bd. Family Practice. Resident in family practice NIH, Bethesda, Md., Walter Reed Army Hosp., Washington, Children's Hosp. Nat. Med. Ctr., Washington; dir. occupational medicine and environ. health Pacific Missile Test Ctr., Point Mugu, Calif., 1982-84; dist. health officer State Hawaii Dept. Health, Kauai, 1984-86; asst. dir. health County of Riverside (Calif.) Dept. Health, 1986—. Fellow Am. Acad. Family Practice; mem. AMA, Am. Occupational Medicine Assn., Flying Physicians, Am. Pub. Health Assn. Avocations: pvt. pilot. Home: 30040 Del Rey Rd Rancho California CA 92390 Office: County Riverside Dept Health 3575 11th St Mall Riverside CA 92501

SMITH, JEREMY JOHN, data processing companyexecutive; b. London, June 14, 1954; s. John Bernard and Marion Elaine (Reynolds) S.; divorced; 1 child, Holly Rebecca. Student, London U., 1972-76. Research gardner H.D.R.A., Bocking Braintree, Essex, Eng., 1977; landscape architect C.B. Landscapers, Newport Beach, Calif., 1978-80; computer sales ERA Electronics, San Francisco, 1982; software engr. AMF-SD 1, Irvine, Calif., 1983-85; dir. W & W Software, Costa Mesa, Calif., 1985-86; software system designer Corvallis (Calif.) MicroTech., 1986—. Served as flight sgt. RAF, 1975—. Avocations: running, triathlons, gardening.

SMITH, JEROME ANTHONY, oceanographer, researcher; b. Ann Arbor, Mich., July 6, 1951; s. Frederick Edward and Marguerite (Anderson) S.; m. Pamela Kim Drechsel, July 31, 1985. BA with honors, Reed Coll., 1974; PhD, Dalhousie U., Halifax, N.S., 1980. Postdoctoral researcher MIT, Cambridge, 1980-81; vis. researcher Harvard U., Cambridge, 1981-82; adj. prof. Naval Postgrad. Sch., Monterey, Calif., 1982-84; researcher Scripps Inst. Oceanographer, La Jolla, Calif., 1984—. Contbr. articles to sci. jours. Recipient M.T. Buell award in Physics Ann Arbor Bd. Edn., 1969; Reed Coll. sci. scholar, 1973; Dalhousie U. fellow, 1974-80. Mem. AAAS, Am. Geophys. Union, Am. Meteorol. Soc., Nat. Geographic Soc. Avocations: painting, pottery, bicycling, windsurfing. Office: Scipps Inst Oceanography POSS Bldg A 013 La Jolla CA 92093

SMITH, JOHN ANTHONY, lawyer; b. Poughkeepsie, N.Y., Sept. 10, 1942; s. John Charles and Eunice C. (Hatfield) S.; m. Carol A. Bechtel; children: Jessica R., Michael Anthony. B.S., Cornell U., 1964, J.D., 1971. Bar: U.S. Dist. Ct. Alaska 1971, Alaska 1971, U.S. Supreme Ct. 1978, U.S. Ct. Appeals (9th cir.) 1971. Assoc. firm Kay, Miller, Libbey, Kelly, Christie & Fuld, 1971, ptnr., 1972-73; ptnr. Gruenberg, Willard & Smith, 1973-74; sole practice, Anchorage, Alaska, 1974-77; ptnr. Smith & Taylor, 1978; ptnr. Smith, Taylor & Gruening, Anchorage, 1979, sr. partner, 1979-84; sr. ptnr. Smith, Robinson & Gruening, 1984-85; sr. ptnr. Smith, Robinson, Gruening & Brecht, 1985-86, Smith, Gruening, Brecht, Evans & Spietzfodeu, 1986—; commr. of communication and econ. devel. State of Alaska, 1987—; adj. prof. U. Alaska Sch. Criminal Justice; mem. exec. com. House-Senate Dem. Council; pres. Alaska Inst. Research and Pub. Service; coordinator U. Alaska Paralegal Program; chmn. Bush Justice Com.; chmn. Gov.'s Bodily Injury Reparation Commn., 1979-80. Bd. dirs. Alaska Bus. Monthly; mem. Internat. Relations com. Nat. Olympic Com., 1986—; mem. exec. com. Anchorage Organizing Com. for the Winter Olympics. Columnist Anchorage Times; contbg. editor Alaska Jour. Commerce. Bd. dirs., counsel Anchorage Olympic Devel. Com.; dir. Glacier Creek Acad. Served to lt. (j.g.), USN, 1964-67. Mem. Alaska Bar Assn. (chmn. specialization com.), ABA, Am. Judicature Soc., Am. Trial Lawyers Assn., Anchorage C. of C. Democrat. Quaker. Address: 6861 Covitt Circle Anchorage AK 99576 Address: PO Box D Juneau AK 99811 Office: Smith Robinson & Gruening 801 B St Suite 300 Anchorage AK 99501

SMITH, JOHN ELVANS, chemistry educator; b. Washington, Sept. 6, 1929; s. Carl Bernard and Emily Thornton (Farr) S.; m. Jeanne Mae Cuthbertson, June 11, 1955 (div. 1960); 1 child, David King; m. Eloise Emily Russell, Apr. 11, 1962; children: Katherine Suzanne Beurman, Paul Stanley, Christopher John. AA summa cum laude, Pueblo (Colo.) Jr. Coll., 1950; BA cum laude, U. Colo., 1952, PhD, 1960. Instr. atomic defense USN, San Francisco, 1953-55; head dept. chemistry U. So. Colo., Pueblo, 1964-82, prof. chemistry, 1962—. Author: Conserve Energy and Save Money, 1981; contbr. articles to profl. jours. and mags. Mem. various coms. City of Pueblo. Served to lt. USN, 1953-55. Mem. Am. Chem. Soc., NEA, Colo. Edn. Assn. Episcopalian. Avocations: coin collecting, photography, handguns, hist. sightseeing, music. Home: 809 W Pitkin Ave Pueblo CO 81004 Office: U So Colo Chemistry Dept 2200 Bonforte Blvd Pueblo CO 81001

SMITH, JOHN KEVIN, accountant; b. Monroe, Oreg., Apr. 28, 1949; s. John and Vera Jane (Murray) S. Computer program certificate San Diego Coll. Bus., 1972; B.S., San Diego State U., 1978. Auditor, Atlas Corp., San Diego, 1976, Sheraton Corp., San Diego, 1976-77, Hyatt Corp., San Diego, 1977-78; acct. Hawthorne Machinery Co., San Diego, 1978-79; acct. Presto Foods, Inc., Los Angeles, 1979-81, also chief acct. subs. Jon Donaire Pastries, Inc. until 1981; sr. staff Van de Kamps, Los Angeles, 1981-83; chief acct. La. Pacific Corp., Huntington Beach, Calif., 1983—; owner, mgr. JKS Acctg. Service, Inc., Arcadia, Calif., 1982—. Served with U.S. Army, 1967-71; Vietnam. Mem. Nat. Assn. Accts. Am. Mgmt. Assn. Republican. Lodges: Masons, Rotary. Home and Office: Louisiana-Pac Corp PO Box 1505 Red Bluff CA 96080

SMITH, J(OHN) MALCOLM, political science educator; b. Vancouver, B.C., Can., Jan. 24, 1921; (parents Am. citizens); s. George John and Henrietta E. (Smith) S.; m. Connie Grace Shaw, June 2, 1943; children: Sheila C., Nancy L., Patricia L. BA, U. Wash., 1946; MA, Stanford U., 1948, PhD, 1951. Instr. polit. sci. Stanford (Calif.) U., 1947-50; instr. pub. law and govt. Columbia U., N.Y.C., 1950-52; asst. prof. polit. sci. U. Calif., Riverside, 1952-54; organizer World Affairs Council, Los Angeles, 1954-57; prof. polit. sci. Calif. State U., Hayward, 1965—; cons. Office of Sec. USAF, Washington, 1954-58, Commn. on Civil Rights, Washington, 1958-59; spl. asst. minority whip U.S. Senate, Washington, 1959-61; vis. prof. U. San Diego, 1961-62, Ariz. State U., 1962-63; Merrill prof. Utah State U., 1976; mem. Ctr. for Study fo Presidency. Co-author: Powers of the President During Crisis, 1961, President and National Security, 1972; contbr. articles to profl. jours. Grantee Ford Found., 1955-56, John S. Sheppard, 1951-52. Mem. Acad. Polit. Sci., The Supreme Ct. Hist. Soc. Home: 2289 East Ave Hayward CA 94541 Office: Calif State U Dept Polit Sci Hayward CA 94542

SMITH, JOHNNIE LARRY, civil engineer; b. Ripley, Miss., May 6, 1943; s. Johnnie Willard and Rivie (Clark) S.; m. Deborah Jane Jones, Feb. 10, 1979. B.S.C.E., Miss. State U., 1964; M.B.A. in Fin., U. Colo., 1982. Registered profl. engr., Colo., Tex., Alaska. Sr. engr. Texaco, Inc., Port Arthur, Tex., 1964-69; project engr. Mitchell Engring., Columbus, Miss., 1969-70; sr. engr. Stearns-Roger div. United Engrs., Denver and Vandenberg AFB, 1970-77, 81—; engring. mgr. Stubbs-Overbeck, Houston, 1977-79; project engr. Arco Chem., Houston, 1979-81. Del., Arapahoe County Repubican Assembly, Englewood, Colo., 1984; tutor Calif. Literacy Council. Mem. ASME (bd. dirs. Colo. sect. 1984-85), Nat. Soc. Profl. Engrs., Soc. Piping Engrs. and Designers, Nat. Assn. Corrosion Engrs. Home: 513 E Rice Ranch Rd Santa Maria CA 93455 Office: Stearns Roger div United Engrs PO Box 5276 Vandenberg AFB CA 93437

SMITH, JOSEF RILEY, physician; b. Council Bluffs, Iowa, Oct. 1, 1926; s. George William Smith and Margaret (Wood) Hill; divorced; children: Sarah L. Kratz, David L., Mary E. Loeb, John R., Ruthann P., Mark A.; m. Susan Frances Irwin, Feb. 9, 1973; 1 child, Christopher I. Student, Tulane U., 1944-46; BM, Northwestern U., 1950, MD, 1951; MSEE, Marquette U., 1964. Diplomate Am. Bd. Internal Medicine. Instr. internal medicine U. Miss. Med. Sch., Jackson, 1956-59; asst. prof. Marquette U. Med. Sch., Milw., 1959-63; from assoc. prof. to full prof. U. Mich. Med. Sch., Ann Arbor, 1963-72; physician Youngstown (Ohio) Hosp., 1972-79, Group Health Med. Assn., Tucson, 1979-84, Assn. in Internal Medicine, Tucson, 1985—. Co-author: Clinical Cardiopulmonary Physiology, 1960, Textbook of Pulmonary Disease, 1965, 2d rev. edit., 1974; contbr. articles to profl. jours. Controller Mahoning County TB Clinic, Youngstown, 1973-79. Served to lt. USNR, 1952-54. Fellow ACP, Sigma Xi; mem. AMA, Ariz. Med. Assn., Pima County Med. Assn., Am. Thoracic Soc., Ariz. Thoracic Soc., Bioengring. Med. Soc. (founder). Avocations: photography, computer programming. Office: Assn in Internal Medicine 2122 N Craycroft Rd Suite 110 Tucson AZ 85712

SMITH, JULIA MARGARET, statistician, consultant, educator; b. Radford, Va., May 23, 1943; d. Larry Cooper and Ruby Evelyn (Sale) Smith; m. Lyle E. Delap, Jr., 1969; m. Stephen R. Garinger, June 9, 1984; children—Laura Elaine. B.A. in Math., Chemistry Radford U., 1965; M.S. in Stats., Va. Poly. Inst. and State U., Blacksburg, 1971. Mathematician, Shell Oil Co., Metarie, La., 1966; instr. chemistry Radford U., 1967-69; instr. math. Va. Poly. Inst. and State U., 1970-71; statistician AEC, Washington, 1971-72; statistician Nuclear Fuel dept., Gen. Electric, Wilmington, N.C., 1972-77; statistician Brookhaven Nat. Lab., Upton, N.Y., 1977-81; sr. statistician Rockwell Hanford Ops., Rockwell Internat., Richland, Wash., 1981—; cons. and lectr. in field. Mem. Inst. Nuclear Materials Mgmt., Nat. Mgmt. Assn., Am. Statis. Assn., Phi Kappa Phi., Va. Poly. Inst. and State U. Alumni Assn., Radford U. Alumni Assn., NOW, Rockwell Orgn. for Women. Club: Mensa. Contbr. in field. Office: Rockwell Hanford PO Box 800/200W/2704 S Richland WA 99352

SMITH, KAREN MARGARET, school counselor, counsultant; b. Salt Lake City, Apr. 7, 1944; d. Ray George and Margaret (Howell) S. BS, Utah State U., 1966; MEd, U. Nev., Reno, 1972, ednl. specialist, 1979. Cert. counselor, phys. edn. educator, sch. psychologist, Nev. Tchr. pub. schs., Huntsville, Utah, 1966-68, Ogden, Utah, 1968-69, Reno, 1969-71; counselor Fred W. Traner Middle Sch., Reno, 1971—; guest instr. U. Nev.-Reno, 1980—; cons. region 8, Calif. Dept. Edn., Pyramid House. Bd. dirs. People Inc.; appointed to Gov.'s commn. for profl. standards, State of Nev. Mem. Washoe County Tchrs. Assn., Nev. Tchrs. Assn., NEA, Am. Assn. Counseling and Devel. (nat. awards com.), No. Nev. Counselors Assn., Nev. Sch. Counselors Assn., Am. Sch. Counselors Assn., Am. Personnel and Guidance Assn. (past pres., senator western region).

SMITH, KATHRYN JOYCE, secretarial service executive; b. Maud, Okla., Nov. 29, 1930; d. Elisha Alvin and Doris Louise (Kirk) Dooley; m. Richard A. Smith, Aug. 11, 1950; children—Rick L., John A., Kathy Keele. Student pub. schs., Boise. Steno-clk. Dept. Pub. Assistance, Boise, Idaho, 1948-49; officer Salvation Army, 1949-52; mem. duplicating dept. Suburban Gas Co., Pomona, Calif., 1960-63; sec. to headmistress Girls' Collegiate Sch., Claremont, Calif., 1964-66; steno-clk. FAA, Ontario, Calif., 1968-70; sec. spl. programs office, U. Redlands (Calif.), 1972-73, sec. various offices, 1975-81; owner The Word Co., Redlands. Active Variety Club Telethon; chpt. coordinator Food for All, Redlands. Mem. Nat. Assn. Secretarial Services, Nat. Assn. Female Execs., Soroptimist Internat. Sunrise Club (charter mem. Redlands chpt.). Republican. Mem. Ch. of Christ. Office: 408 E State St Suite B Redlands CA 92373

SMITH, KEITH LARUE, research co. exec.; b. Salida, Colo., Dec. 15, 1917; s. Leroy Holt and Verna Lea (Tunnell) S.; student Marion Coll., 1935-38; A.B. in Math., Ind. U., 1946; postgrad. DePauw U., 1946-47; M.A. in Internat. Affairs, Harvard U., 1955; M.P.A., Calif. State U.-Fullerton, 1979; m. Evelyn May De Bruler, Aug. 29, 1943; 1 son, Eric Douglas. Mil. intelligence research specialist Dept. of Army, Washington, 1951-60; staff engr. Librascope div. Gen. Precision, Inc., Glendale, Cal., 1960-61; sr. operations research analyst Space div. N.Am. Rockwell Corp., Downey, Cal., 1961-71; dir. research Am. Research Corp., Paramount, Calif., 1972—; instr. math. and polit. sci. DePauw U., 1946-47; cons. model bldg. and gaming techniques, 1960—; mgmt. cons., 1970—; instr. math. and sci. Verbum Dei High Sch., 1974—. Adult leader Boy Scouts Am., Long Beach, Calif., 1961-75. Treas., UN Council Harvard, 1947-49, Young Democratic Club, Arlington, Mass., 1949-50. Served to capt. USAAF, 1941-46; ETO. Recipient scholarship award Inst. World Affairs, 1947, Outstanding Efficiency award Dept. Army, 1960, Apollo 11 medallion NASA, 1970. Mem. Am. Mus. Natural History, Nat. Geog. Soc., Harvard Alumni Assn., Pi Sigma Alpha. Methodist. Mason. Research on lunar mission cartography, mil. operations research and war game model bldg. Home: 3451 Curry St Long Beach CA 90805

SMITH, KENNETH C., advertising agency executive; b. Kansas City, Mo., July 18, 1942; s. Clyde M. and Irene Elizabeth (Pitney) S.; m. Ann Hudson Burr, Aug. 24, 1968; 1 son, Aaron Charles. B.A., U. Mo., 1966, B.Journalism, 1967, M.A., 1969. Pres. MSPA Agy., Rockford, 1971-75; pres., owner Kenneth C. Smith & Assocs., La Jolla, Calif., 1975—. Bd. dirs. La Jolla Chamber Orchestra. Mem. San Diego Assn. Advt. Agys., Communicating Arts, Advt. Club San Diego, U. Mo. Sch. Journalism Alumni Assn. (pres. San Diego), Alpha Delta Sigma, Kappa Tau Alpha. Republican. Episcopalian. Clubs: La Jolla Beach and Tennis. Office: 2233 Avenida de la Playa La Jolla CA 92037

SMITH, KENNETH GEORGE, financial analyst, consultant; b. Tokyo, Jan. 8, 1961; came to U.S., 1972; s. Charles Washington and Tokuko (Suzuki) S. BS in Chemistry, U. Hawaii, 1982; MBA in Fin., U. Mich., 1984. Mgmt. analyst Brever Chem. Corp., Honolulu, 1984-86; fin. analyst Am. Hawaii Cruises, Honolulu, 1986-87; sr. cons. Arthur Young & Co., Honolulu, 1987—; Pres., bd. dirs. CWX, Inc., Honolulu, 1979—. Mem. Am. Chem. Soc., U. Mich. Alumni Club. Republican. Avocations: small bus. computers, investments. Home: 4476 Kolohala St Honolulu HI 96816 Office: Arthur Young & Co 700 Bishop St Suite 800 Honolulu HI 96813

SMITH, KENNETH MORRIS, magazine publisher, author; b. Berkeley, Calif., Sept. 1, 1949; s. Malcolm Kellogg Smith and Doris Jean (Fitzsimons) Harrison; m. Patricia Eileen Clyde, Dec. 31, 1983; children: Kimberly, Michael. Grad. high sch., Walnut Creek, 1967. Account exec. M.V Nursery, Inc., Sacramento, 1976-78; v.p. Energy Concepts, Ltd., Sacramento, 1978-80, C.A.F.P.A., Fair Oaks, Calif., 1980-81; publisher, founder, pres. Multi level Mktg. News, Inc., Sacramento, 1982—. Co-author: Financial Freedom Through Multilevel Marketing, 1983; publisher: The Best of M&M News, 1984. Mem. Nat. Assn. for Multilevel Mktg. (founder 1982), Multilevel Mktg. Internat. Assn., Direct Selling Assn., Calif. Alcohol Fuel Producers Assn. (v.p., co-founfer 1980). Libertarian. Unitarian. Avocation: snow skiing. Office: MLM News Inc 9332 Tech Ctr Dr #200 Sacramento CA 95826

SMITH, KENNETH OWLER, communications educator; b. San Jose, Calif., May 13, 1920; s. William Kenneth and Velma Erin (Owler) S.; m. Patricia Ann Nowack, May 23, 1980. A.B., Stanford U., 1941; M.S., UCLA, 1958; Ed.D., 1967. Editor various newspapers and mags., Calif., 1940-42, 46-49; pub. relations dir. Western Airlines Inc., Los Angeles, 1950-60; faculty UCLA, 1960-64, 67-70; adminstr. U. Calif., Berkeley, 1965-67; prof. Sch. Journalism U. So. Calif., Los Angeles, 1970—, dir. Sports Info. Program, 1979—; pub. relations/sports info. mgmt. cons. Served with U.S. Army, 1942-46. Recipient Outstanding Faculty award U. So. Calif. 1974-75; Chasqui award Internat. Pub. Relations Assn. 1977. Mem. Pub. Relations Soc. Am. (accredited, Silver Anvil award, 1969, pres. 1977, Educator of Yr. 1979), AAUP, U.S. Olympic Soc., Sigma Delta Chi, Kappa Tau Alpha, Phi Delta Kappa. Club: Univ. So. Calif. Faculty Ctr. Author: Professional Public Relations, 1968; The Practice of Public Relations, 1976; A Chronology of Sports, 1982; numerous jour. articles. Office: U So Calif Sports Info Program 725 W 27th St Los Angeles CA 90007

SMITH, KENT FARRELL, engineering educator; b. Fish Haven, Idaho, June 26, 1935; s. Elmer Hyrum and Rosella (Calder) S.; m. Colleen Sperry, Aug. 22, 1956; children: Kathryn, Cristine, Jeffrey, Cynthia, Rebekah. BSEE, Utah State U., 1957, MSEE, 1958; PhDEE, U. Utah, 1982. Tech. dir. elec. engring. Gen. Instrument Corp., Salt Lake City, 1966-72; staff engr. U. Utah Research Inst., Salt Lake City, 1972-78; research assoc. prof. U. Utah, Salt Lake City, 1978-82, assoc. prof. computer sci., 1982—, acting chmn. dept., 1985—; v.p., co-owner LSI Testing Inc., Salt Lake City, 1967-72—; tech. reviewer Macmillan Pub., Salt Lake City, 1982—, John Wiley & Sons Pub., Salt Lake City, 1982—; cons. Sperry Univac Corp., Salt Lake City, and various other cos. Author: Advanced Database Machine Architecture, 1983; contbr. articles to profl. jours.; patentee integrated circuits. Grantee NSF, Dept. Def., Gen. Instrument Corp., Dept. Advanced Research Projects Adminstrn. Mormon. Avocations: skiing, motorcycling, hunting, fishing. Home: 1775 Grover Ln Salt Lake City UT 84124 Office: U Utah Computer Sci Dept 3160 Merrill Engring Blvd Salt Lake City UT 84112

SMITH, KEVIN ANTHONY, engineer; b. Los Angeles, Jan. 14, 1958; s. Donald Irving and Norma Shirley (Kooper) S.; m. Antoinette Charlotte George, Feb. 22, 1986. BS in Biology, BS in Psychology, UCLA, 1982; student, Grad. Sch. Bus., Calif. State U., Dominguez Hills. Store mgr. Ralphs Grocery Co., Compton, Calif., 1976-82; project. engr. TRW Inc. Electronics and Def. Sector, Redondo Beach, Calif., 1982—. Pres. Park Avalon Mobile Estates Group, Carson, Calif., 1983-86; scoutmaster Troop 255, Wilmington, Calif., 1987—. Named Eagle Scout, Boy Scouts Am., Torrance, Calif., 1972; Alumni scholar U. So. Calif., Los Angeles, 1976. Mem. AIAA, Inst. Environ. Sci. Mormon. Avocations: music, travelling, exceptional foods, investments. Office: TRW Electronics and Def Sector One Space Park R7/1051 Redondo Beach CA 90278

SMITH, LANGFORD WHEATON, computer company executive; b. San Francisco, Dec. 6, 1928; s. Langford Wheaton and Dorothy Lyman (Leetch) S.; m. Marjorie Francis Roy, June 20, 1950: children: Teresa W., Melissa W., Portia W. BA, St. John's Coll., 1948; MBA, Stanford U., 1951, PhD, 1962. Ops. research analyst Gen. Electric Co., Richland, Wash., 1952-56; mem. tech. staff Ramo Wooldridge Corp., Los Angeles, 1956-57; mem. corp. staff Richfield Oil Corp., Los Angeles, 1957-62; computer scientist, application developer IBM Corp., Los Angeles, 1962-64; computer scientist, application devel. IBM Corp., Palo Alto, Calif., 1964-68; systems assurance mgr. IBM Corp., Palo Alto, 1968-73, systems support adv., 1975-81, mktg. support adv., 1981-84, mktg. support mgr., 1984—; systems support adv. IBM Japan Ltd., Tokyo, 1974-75; asst. research economist UCLA, 1960; dir. Japanese Am. Environ. Conf., Los Altos, Calif., 1979—. Fellow AAAS; mem. Ops. Research Soc., Am. Assn. Computing Machinery, Am. Acctg. Assn., Inst. Mgmt. Sci., Econometrics Soc., Sierra Club. Episcopalian. Office: IBM Corp PO Box 10500 Palo Alto CA 94303-0821

SMITH, LANI KAMIKI, musician, composer; b. Cin., June 9, 1934; s. Leonard Rice and Lillian Grace (Fittz) S.; m. Jama Dianne Dobberstein, Oct. 3, 1980. B.Mus., U. Cin., 1956, M.Mus., 1959. Served as organist and choir dir. for various chs., Ohio and Mich., 1954-81; music editor, composer, arranger Lorenz Pub. Co., Dayton, Ohio, 1967-82; freelance composer arranger 1000 works of sacred mus., numerous other pieces chamber ensemble, ballet, solo voice, orch.; part-time editor Lorenz Pub. Co., Calif., 1982—. Recipient Josef Bearns prize in composition, Columbia U., 1959. Grantee Rockefeller Found., 1967. Mem. Phi Mu Alpha, Pi Kappa Lambda.

SMITH, LARRY DEAN, information systems and data processing executive; b. Idaho Falls, Idaho, Oct. 11, 1946; s. Richard Lorraine and Jean (Hammer) S.; m. LaRae Jensen; children: Kathy, Barbara. AS, Ricks Coll., 1966; BS in Engring., Idaho State U., 1970. Programming mgr. Machine Tabulating Service, Idaho Falls, 1969-74; programmer, analyst ORE-IDA Foods, Boise, Idaho, 1974-76; mgr. info systems Intermountain Milk Products, Salt Lake City, 1976—. Dem. dist chmn., Midvale, Utah, 1983—. Mem. Data Processing Mgmt. Assn. (bd. dirs. awards chmn. Salt Lake City chpt. 1983, treas. Salt Lake City chpt. 1984). Democrat. Mormon. Avocations: woodworking, rock collecting. Home: 639 E 7500 S Midvale UT 84047 Office: Intermountain Milk Producers Assn 175 SW Temple Salt Lake City UT 84110-1228

SMITH, LE ROI MATTHEW-PIERRE, III, municipal administrator; b. Chgo., Jan. 11, 1946; s. Le Roy Matthew and Norma Buckner (McCamey) S.; m. Lois Divine, Jan. 30, 1969; 1 son, Le Roi Matthew Pierre. B.A. in Psychology, Idaho State U., 1969; Ph.D. in Psychology, Wash. State U., 1977. Instr. psychology Idaho State U., Pocatello, 1969-70, Wash. State U., Pullman, 1970-71; mem. faculty dept. psychology Evergreen State Coll., Olympia, 1971-81; equal opportunity officer Port of Seattle, 1981—; cons. in field. Bd. dirs. Thurston-Mason County Community Mental Health Ctr., Olympia; v.p., Idaho State Human Rights Commn., Bannock County, Idaho, 1968-70. Office Edn. fellow, 1969-70; U.S. Dept. Labor grantee, 1968; NSF grantee, 1972; Lilly Found. fellow, 1980. Mem. Am. Psychol. Assn., Am. Personnel and Guidance Assn., Wash. State Black Econs. and Edn. Conf., Assn. Black Psychologists, Am. Assn. of Affirmative Action Officers, Phi Delta Kappa. Democrat. Roman Catholic. Home: 761 S 45th St Tacoma WA 98408 Office: PO Box 1209 Seattle WA 98111

SMITH, LEILA RAE, business educator; b. Bklyn., May 7, 1928; d. Frank and Rose Simon; B.S., NYU; M.A., U. San Francisco; m. Seymour Smith, Sept. 5, 1954; children—Roberta Ellen, Eric Andrew. Instr., Bay Path Jr. Coll., Longmeadow, Mass., 1950-52; instr. secretarial sci. L.A. Pierce Coll., Woodland Hills, Calif., 1956-65; mem. faculty bus. div. L.A. Harbor Coll., Wilmington, Calif., 1965—, prof. office adminstrn., 1970—. Recipient Eugene Pimentel award for excellence in edn., 1982. Mem. Nat. Bus. Edn. Assn., Calif. Bus. Edn. Assn., Am. Bus. Communication Assn., Soc. Accelerative Learning and Teaching, Theta Alpha Delta, Pi Omega Pi, Delta Pi Epsilon. Author: English for Careers, 1977, English for Careers: Business, Professional, Technical, 1981, 3d rev. edit., 1985, Personal Learning Guide for English for Careers, 1981, English for Careers (15 cassettes), 1981, 2d rev. edit., 1985, Basic English for Business and Technical Careers, 1985; Superlearning RSVP, 1982. Contbr. articles to profl. jours. Office: Los Angeles Harbor Coll 1111 Figueroa Pl Wilmington CA 90744

SMITH, LELAND REX, communications specialist; b. Sioux City, Iowa, Sept. 25, 1951; s. Rodney Ream and Beverly (Battey) S. Supr. ops. Computax Corp., El Segundo, Calif., 1975-77; systems analyst Pepperdine U., Malibu, Calif., 1977-79, mgr. tech. support, 197-82, dir. telecommunications, datacommunications dept., 1982-85; owner LRS Assocs., Telecommunications, Data Processing Cons., 1985—. v.p. CTCI Computer Sales Support. Mem. Am. Coll. Univ. Telecommunications Adminstrs., N.Am. Telecommunications Assn.

SMITH, LESLIE ANN, city official; b. Pasco, Wash., Apr. 17, 1945; s. Ralph E. and Melba (Simmonds) S.; div.; A.A., Columbia Basin Coll., 1971; student Wash. State U., 1964-65, Central Wash. State U., 1971-76. Admissions and registration sec. Columbia Basin Coll., 1966-70, scheduling coordinator, 1970-76; mcpl. clk. City of Richland, Wash., 1976—. Mem. LWV, Columbia Basin Chpt. Records Mgrs., Am. Assn. Records Mgrs. and Adminstrs., Wash. State Mcpl. Clks., Internat. Mcpl. Clks., Allied Arts Assn., PEO, Wash. Women in Mcpl. Govt. (bd. dirs.), WMCA (bd. dirs.). Methodist. Lodge: Zonta. Home: 1850 Stevens St Apt 110 Richland WA 99352 Office: PO Box 190 Richland WA 99352

SMITH, LESTER MARTIN, broadcasting executive; b. N.Y.C., Oct. 20, 1919; s. Alexander and Sadie S.; m. Bernice Reitz, Sept. 28, 1962; 1 child, Alexander. B.S. in Bus. Adminstrn, NYU, 1940. Chief exec. officer Alexander Broadcasting Co., radio stas. in, Seattle, Portland, Oreg. and Spokane, 1954—; gen. partner 700 Investment Co.; past dir. Seattle C. of C.; past chmn. dir. Radio Advt. Bur. Served to maj. U.S. Army, 1942-46. Decorated Bronze Star. Mem. Nat. Assn. Broadcasters (past dir.), Oreg. Assn. Broadcasters (past pres.), Broadcast Pioneers. Clubs: Rotary (Seattle), Rainer (Seattle), Wash. Athletic (Seattle). Address: 700 112th NE Bellevue WA 98004

SMITH, LLOYD MUIR, chemist, educator; b. Calgary, Can., Feb. 20, 1917; came to U.S., 1950; s. John Huntly and Lillian Sarah (Muir) S.; m. Edythe Clarissa Dodds, June 26, 1948; children: Michael Bruce, Douglas Lloyd. BS, U. Alberta, Edmonton, Can., 1943, MS, 1949; PhD, U. Calif., Davis, 1953. Instr., lectr. Dairy Industry U. Alberta, Edmonton, 1946-49; grad. asst. Dairy Industry U. Calif., Davis, 1950-52; asst. prof. U. Alta., Edmonton, Canada, 1952-54; asst. prof., then prof. Food Sci. and Tech. dept. U. Calif., Davis, 1954—; cons. edible oils and fats and dairy processing orgns. Served to lt. Can. Army, 1943-46. Fulbright fellow, New Zealand, 1961-62, Brazil, 1986; Nat. Research Council, 1950-52. Mem. Am. Chem. Soc., Am. Oil Chemists' Soc. (award of merit 1983), Am. Dairy Sci. Assn., Inst. Food Technologists. Republican. Presbyterian. Avocations: travel, bridge, biking. Home: 715 Oeste Dr Davis CA 95616 Office: U Calif Dept Food Sci and Tech Davis CA 95616

SMITH, LLOYD PRESTON, management consultant; b. Reno, Nov. 6, 1903; s. Preston Brooks and Ida (Sauer) S.; m. Florence S. Hunkin, Sept. 16, 1928 (dec.); children: Sandra Lee Reynolds, Jacqueline Sue Sullivan; m. F. Irene Anderson, 1971 (dec. 1984). B.E.E., U. Nev., 1925; Ph.D., Cornell U., 1930; D.Sc., U. Nev., 1961. Research engr. Gen. Electric Co., Schenectady, 1925-26; Coffin fellow physics Cornell U., 1926-27, instr. physics, 1927-30, asst. prof., 1932-36, prof., 1936-56, chmn. dept. physics, dir. dept. engring. physics, 1946-56, dir. Research Found., 1948-56, chmn. corp. com. Cornell U. Council, mem. council for Coll. Engring., 1956-64, faculty mem. bd. trustees, 1952-56; NRC fellow Calif. Inst. Tech., 1930-31; Internat. Research fellow U. Munich, U. Utrecht, 1931-32; lectr. Stanford U., 1935; research physicist RCA Labs., Princeton, N.J., 1939; cons. war research RCA Labs., 1941-45, assoc. research dir., 1945-46, cons., 1946-55, mem. research planning commn., 1952-55; mem. council Fund for Peaceful Atomic Devel., 1956-58; cons. atomic bomb research U. Calif., 1942; cons. Union Carbide Nuclear Co. (formerly Carbide & Carbon Chems. Corp.), Oak Ridge, 1947—, Brookhaven Nat. Labs., Upton, L.I., 1947-49, Haloid Co., 1952-53, Detroit-Edison Co., 1953-56; cons. AVCO Mfg. Corp., 1956, 1959, v.p., dir., 1956-59, pres. research and advanced devel. div., 1956-58; research dir. research lab. Aeronutronic div. Ford Motor Co., 1959-63; v.p., dir. applied research labs. Aeronutronic div. Philco Research Labs., 1964-65; v.p. phys. scis. Stanford Research Inst., Menlo Park, Calif., 1965-69; sr. sci. adviser Stanford Research Inst. (Office Research Ops.), 1969-71; cons. on tech. research and devel. of bus. mgmt. 1965—; pres. Lloyd P. Smith and Assocs., 1972—, Desert Research Inst., U. Nev., 1975-80, Wright Energy Nev. Corp., 1980-81; dir. Research Corp. N.Y.; cons. Union Carbide Corp., Douglas Aircraft, Inc., 1959, Crown Zellerbach Corp., 1983-85; mem. exec. com. Def. Sci. Bd., 1961-65; adv. panel for physics NSF, 1956-59; mem. adv. com. anti-submarine warfare Nat. Security Indsl. Assn. Author: Mathematical Methods for Scientists and Engineers, 1953; contbr. articles sci. jours. Bd. dirs. Orange County Philharmonic Soc. Recipient certificate of merit USN, 1947. Mem. Am. Phys. Soc., Am. Assn. Physics Tchrs. (chmn. com. physics engring. edn. 1955-56), Am. Ordnance Assn. (chmn. physics sect. 1959—), Am. Inst. Physics, Am. Soc. Engring. Edn., N.Y. Acad. Scis., Sigma Xi, Theta Chi, Phi Kappa Phi. Club: University (N.Y.C.). Lodge: Masons. Address: 1310 University Dr Menlo Park CA 94025

SMITH, LONNIE LOUIS, vocational educator; b. Electra, Tex., Apr. 24, 1932; s. Robert Lee and Shirley Irene (Walraven) S.; m. O. Winell Towles, Jan. 25, 1957; children—Mark, Mike. A.S., Odessa Coll., 1956; B.S. in Indsl. Arts, North Tex. State U., 1958, M.Ed., 1961; PhD in Adminstrn. and Supervision of Vocat. and Indsl. Arts Edn., Pacific U., 1986. Cert. tchr. Tex., Calif., N.Mex. Tchr. indsl. arts Dallas Ind. Sch. Dist., 1958-62; tchr. indsl. crafts, driver edn., Artesia (N.Mex.) Pub. Schs., 1962-65; tchr. indsl. arts Fremont (Calif.) Unified Schs., 1965-80; instr. mfg. processes Ohlone Coll., Fremont, 1977-80; instr. welding, N.Mex. Jr. Coll., Hobbs, 1980—; sponsor Vocat. Indsl. Clubs Am. Served with USN, 1950-54; Korea. Decorated Am. Spirit of Honor; recipient UN Service medal with two stars, ARC Service award, 1982; named Outstanding Educator of Yr., Hobbs Jaycees, 1983. Mem. Am. Welding Soc., N. Tex. chpt. Am. Welding Soc., Am. Vocat. Assn., N.Mex. Vocat. Assn., Phi Delta Kappa. Democrat. Baptist. Sculpture exhibited in private collections; contbr. articles to profl. jours. Office: NMex Jr College Lovington Hwy Hobbs NM 88240

SMITH, LOUIS DESPAIN, retired microbiologist, consultant; b. Odessa, Wash., Oct. 12, 1910; s. Charles Mortimer and Martha (Wolfe) S.; m. Norma Longeteig, May 5, 1936; children: Celia, Frances, Ellen. BS, U. Idaho, 1932, ScD (hon.), 1971, MS, 1935; PhD, U. Wash., 1948; ScD, Mont. State U., 1976. Diplomate Am. Bd. Microbiology (emeritus). From assoc. prof. microbiology to prof. and dean dept. Mont. State U., Bozeman, 1950-67; prof. Va. Poly. Inst., Blacksburg, 1967-76, prof. emeritus, 1976—; affiliate prof. U. Wash., Seattle, 1976—. Author: Introduction to the Pathogenic Anaerobes, 1955, The Pathogenic Anaerobes, 2d. edit., 1975, Botulism: The Organism, Its Toxins, The Disease, 1977; co-author: Physiologic Effects of Wounds, 1952, The Pathogenic Anaerobes, 1st. edit., 1968, 3d. edit., 1984; contbr. chpts. to books, articles to profl. jours. Served to capt. U.S. Army, 1943-45. Fellow AAAS; mem. Am. Soc. Microbiology (hon). Avocations: winemaking, fishing. Home: 3605 Birchvale Rd Wnatchee WA 98801

SMITH, LOUISE EILEEN, toy manufacturing company executive; b. Hadley, Mass.; d. William J. and Anne (Canavan) S. BA in History, U. Mass. Analyst Lever Bros., N.Y.C., 1965-67; mgr. Chesebrough-Ponds, Greenwich, Conn., 1967-72; assoc. dir. Richardson-Merrill, Wilton, Conn., 1972-78; dir. Gen. Mills Co., N.Y.C., 1978-81; v.p. Mattel Toys, Hawthorne, Calif., 1982—. Mem. Am. Mktg. Assn., Advt. Research Found. Avocations: traveling, reading. Home: 344 31 St Hermosa Beach CA 90254 Office: Mattel Toys 5150 Rosecrans Ave Hawthorne CA 90250

SMITH, LYNWOOD STEPHEN, fisheries educator; b. Snohomish, Wash., Nov. 15, 1928; s. Stephen Johnson and Erna (von Lehe) S.; m. Betty Ann Mars, Sept. 15, 1951; children: Rebecca Jean, Peggy Lynn, Paul Kevin. BS in Biol. Edn., U. Wash., 1952, MS in Zoology, 1955, PhD in Zoology, 1962. Instr. biology Olympic Community Coll., Bremerton, Wash., 1955-60; asst. prof. zoology U. Victoria (B.C.), Can., 1962-65; from asst. prof. to prof. Sch. of Fisheries, U. Wash., Seattle, 1965—, assoc. dir. instrn., 1986—; vis. scientist Biol. Sta., Nemaino, B.C., Can., 1963-65, Cath. U. of Valparaiso, Chile, 1970; resource devel. project P.I., U.S. Agy. for Internat. Devel., Jakarta, Ambon, Indonesia, 1979-84. Author: Introductory Fish Physiology, 1981, Living Shores, 1975, Seashore Animals, 1962; contbr. articles to profl. jours. Mem. Shorelines Hearing Bd., Bothell, Wash., 1975-86. Grantee Fed. Water Pollution Control Adminstrn., 1966-70, U.S. Agy. for Internat. Devel., 1979-83, Wash. Sea Grant, 1981-84. Mem. AAUP, AAAS, Am. Fisheries Soc., Exptl. Aircraft Assn. Avocations: boating, flying, woodworking. Office: U Wash Sch Fisheries Seattle WA 98195

SMITH, LYTTON WILLIAM, physician; b. Montreal, Que., Can., June 11, 1946; came to U.S., 1975; s. William Henry and Daisy Gertrude (Locke) S.; m. Donna Marie Huzel, June 29, 1968. Premed. cert., U. Winnipeg, Man., Can., 1966; MD, U. Man., 1970. Diplomate Am. Bd. Family Practice. Intern U. So. Calif., Los Angeles, 1970-71; gen. practice medicine Emerson Med. Clinic, Terrace, B.C., Can., 1971-72, Vancouver, B.C., 1973-75; gen. practice medicine, also pres. Yorba Linda (Calif.) Med. Group, Inc., 1983—. Served as sub-lt. Can. Navy, 1964-66. Fellow Am. Acad. Family Practice; mem. AMA, Calif. Med. Assn., Orange County Med. Assn., Underseas Med. Soc., Orange County Flyers (pres.). Avocations: pvt. pilot, recreational scuba diver. Home: 5162 Ohio St Yorba Linda CA 92686 Office: Yorba Linda Med Ctr 4900 Prospect Ave Yorba Linda CA 92686

SMITH, MARILYN NOELTNER, science educator, consultant; b. Los Angeles, Feb. 14, 1933; d. Clarence Frederick and Gertrude Bertha (Smith) Noeltner; m. Edward Christopher Smith, Sept. 11, 1971. BA, Marymount Coll., 1957; MA, U. Notre Dame, 1966; MS, Boston Coll., 1969. Cert. tchr.; cert. community coll. tchr., Calif.; cert. adminstr., Calif. Tchr., chmn. sci. dept. Marymount High Sch., Santa Barbara, Calif., 1954-57, Los Angeles, 1957-58, 69-79; tchr., chmn. sci. and math. depts. Marymount High Sch., Palos Verdes, Calif., 1959-69; tchr., chmn. math. dept. Corvallis High Sch., Studio City, Calif., 1958-59; instr. tchr. tng. Marymount-Loyola U., Los Angeles, 1965-71, instr. freshman interdisciplinary program, 1970-71; tchr. math. Santa Monica (Calif.) High Sch., 1971-72; instr. math., chemistry, physics Santa Monica Coll., 1971—; tchr. sci. Beverly Vista Sch., Beverly Hills, Calif., 1972—; cons. Calif. State Sci. Framework Revision Com., Los Angeles, 1975; chmn. NASA Youth Sci. Congress, Pasadena, Calif., 1968-69, Hawaii, 1969-70; participant NASA Educators Conf. Jupiter Mission, Ames, Iowa, Ames Research, San Francisco, 1973, NASA Educators Conf. Viking-Mars Ames Project, San Francisco, 1976-77, NASA Landsat Conf., Edward's AFB, Calif., 1978, NASA Uranus Mission, Pasadena, Calif., 1986. Author articles, books and computer programs on space and physics. Sponsor Social Service Club, Palos Verdes, 1959-69, moderator, sponsor ARC Youth Service Chmn., Beverly Hills, 1974-77, judge Los Angeles County Sci. Fair, 1969, mem. blue ribbon com. Nat. Acad. TV Arts and Scis., 1971—. Recipient Commendation in Teaching cert. Am. Soc. Microbiology, 1962, Salute to Edn. award So. Calif. Industry Edn. Council, 1962, Outstanding Teaching citationCons. Engrs. Assn. Calif., 1967, Cert. Honor, Silver Plaque Westinghouse Sci. Talent Search, 1963-68, Tchr. award Ford-Future Scientists of Am., 1968, Biomed. award Com. Advance Sci. Tng., 1971, Outstanding Tchr. award Los Angeles County Sci. Fair Com., 1975-76, Contbns. to Youth Service citation ARC, 1976-77. Mem. We. Assn. Schs. and Colls. (vis. com. 1968, writing com. 1969—), Assn. Advancement Biomed. Edn. (pres. 1970-71), 1st Internat. Sci. Tchrs. Conf. (presider, evaluator 1977), Nat. Sci. Tchrs. Assn. (presider, evaluator 1976, chmn. contributed papers com. 1977-78), Beverly Hills Edn. Assn. Faculty Council (pres. 1980-81, 85-86), Chemist's Club, Calif. Statewide Math. Adv. Com., So. Calif. Industry Edn. Council, Calif. Assn. Chemistry Tchrs. (program chmn. 1960), Calif. Sci. Tchrs. Assn., Am. Chem. Soc., AAAS, South Bay Math. League (sec. 1967-68, pres. 1968-69, 72, 1969-70), Calif. Math. Council, Nat. Assn. Biology Tchrs. Republican. Roman Catholic. Avocations: stone age architecture, Gaelic. Home: 3934 Sapphire Dr Encino CA 91436 Office: Beverly Vista Sch 200 S Elm Dr Beverly Hills CA 91202

SMITH, MARK ALAN, chemistry educator; b. Oakland, Calif., Jan. 10, 1956; s. Ralph Howard and JoAnn (Fogerty) S.; m. Margaret Helfrich, July 9, 1978. BS, U. Oreg., 1976; SM, MIT, 1978; PhD, U. Colo., 1982. Postdoctoral fellow U. Toronto, Ont., Can., 1982-85; asst. prof. chemistry U. Ariz., Tucson, 1985—. Contbr. articles to profl. jours. Mem. Am. Chem. Soc. Office: U Ariz Dept Chemistry Tucson AZ 85721

SMITH, MARK KUHN, computer software engineer, educator; b. Pitts., Apr. 10, 1951; s. Lewis Oscar and Rachel (Kuhn) S.; m. Marilyn Jo Kern, May 12, 1973 (div. 1982); children: Dana Christian, Travis McKinley; m. Diane Margaret Ritchey, June 1, 1985. BS in Engring., Purdue U., 1972; MS in Computer Sci., U. Colo., 1974; postgrad., St. Martin's Coll., Lacey, Wash., 1983-84. Sr. staff assoc. Nat. Ctr. Higher Edn. Mgmt. Systems, Boulder, Colo., 1974-77; sr. software engr. Boeing Computer Services, Seattle, 1977-83, 87—; asst. prof. St. Martin's Coll., Lacey, 1983-86; sr. software engr. The System Works, Redmond, Wash., 1986-87; adj. prof. Seattle U., 1983-85, Evergreen State Coll., Olympia, Wash., 1984. Coach Midway-Des Moines (Wash.) Soccer Club, 1983—, Cath. Youth Orgn. boys basketball St. Philomena's Ch., 1986—. Mem. IEEE, Assn. Computing Machinery. Roman Catholic. Avocations: mountain climbing, volleyball, tennis, jogging, bird watching. Office: Boeing Computer Services PO Box 24346 Seattle WA 98124

SMITH, MARK MCCONAHA, recording company executive; b. Redwood City, Calif., Oct. 10, 1958; s. Robert Ralph and Margaret (Fish) S. BA in Bus., Portland State U., 1984; MSBA in Internat. Bus., San Francisco State U., 1986. Asst. v.p. Futuretek Communications Inc., San Mateo, Calif., 1984-85; pres. Fashion Records Inc., San Francisco, 1985—, Flame Music Inc., San Rafael, 1987—; cons. for telcommunications and music industry, 1985. Contbr. articles to profl. jours. Mem. ASCAP, Internat. MIDI Assn. Avocation: weight lifting. Address: 3 Cresta Circle #6 San Rafael CA 94903

SMITH, MAUREEN MCBRIDE, chemist, lab. dir.; b. Santa Monica, Calif., Mar. 4, 1952; d. Clayton Laird McBride and Luella (Sullivan) Boudreau; m. Gary Howard Cothran, July 27, 1974 (div. Apr. 1982); m. Guy Gordan Smith, Feb. 12, 1983; stepchildren: Keri Lynn, Scott Allen. BS magna cum laude, Calif. State Coll., San Bernardino, 1978, postgrad., 1983—. Analytical chemist Chalco Engring., Edwards AFB, Calif., 1978-79, 82; microbiol. lab. tech. AVEK Water Agy., Quartz Hill, Calif., 1979-81, chemist, 1982—; instr. Antelope Valley Coll., Lancaster Calif., 1980-82. Mem. AAAS, Am. Chem. Soc. Avocations: skiing, mud drag racing, photography. Office: Antelope Valley E Kern Water Agy 6500 W Ave N PO Box 3176 Quartz Hill CA 93536

SMITH, MICHAEL JAMES, environmental management company executive; b. East St. Louis, Ill., Feb. 18, 1945; s. James Frederick and Dorothy Maxine (Frangen) S.; m. Carolyn Sue Roustio, June 11, 1967; children: Michelle Leann, Sheri Lynn. BA in Chemistry, So. Ill. U., 1967; MA in Analytical Chemistry, U. Mo., 1969, PhD in Environ. Chemistry, 1972. From asst. prof. to assoc. prof. chemistry Wright State U., Dayton, Ohio, 1972-77; dir. Brehm Lab. Wright State U., Dayton, 1974-77; dept. mgr. engineered barriers Rockwell Internat., Richland, Wash., 1977-85, prin. mgr. research, 1985-86; gen. mgr. Internat. Tech., Albuquerque, 1986—; cons. Monsanto Research Corp., Dayton, 1973-74, cons. Miami Conservancy Dist.; rev. panelist NSF, Washington, 1974-77; Atlantic Richfield, Richland, 1976-77; corp. rev. panelist Waste Isolation Pilot Plant, Carlsbad, N.Mex., 1976—. Contbr. numerous articles to profl. jours.; inventor, patentee treatment of acid wastes and waste disposal package. V.p., bd. dirs. Goodwill Industries, Alburquerque, N.Mex., 1979—. Recipient Bicentennial award Am. Bicentennial Commn., 1975. Mem. AAAS, Am. Chem. Soc., Am. Water Works Assn., Nat. Mgmt. Assn., Am. Nuclear Soc., MacIntosh Users Group (pres. 1985-86). Republican. Presbyterian. Avocations: camping, fishing, gardening, computer programming. Home: 1209 Sierra Larga Dr NE Albuquerque NM 87112 Office: Internat Tech Corp 2340 Alamo SE Albuquerque NM 87106

SMITH, NANCY ELIZABETH LAPPLE, mechanical engineer; b. Kansas City, Mo., June 8, 1953; d. Walter Christian and Elizabeth (Stockwell) Lapple; m. Nathan Burnett Smith, June 18, 1977; children: Nikki Elizabeth, Nina Rose. BSME, U. Akron, 1976; MSME, U. Idaho, 1980. Registered profl. engr., Idaho. Engr. EG&G Idaho, Idaho Falls, 1976-78, U. Idaho, Moscow, 1978-79, McKellip Engring., Boise, Idaho, 1979-80, ASC Constructors, Boise, 1980-81, Boise State U., 1984-86, Rockwell-Idaho Nat. Engring. Lab., Idaho Falls, 1986—. Mem. ASME, Soc. Women Engrs. Avocations: skiing, tennis, backpacking. Home: 1302 Tipperary Ct Idaho Falls ID 83401 Office: Rockwell Idaho Nat Engring Lab PO Box 1469 Idaho Falls ID 83403

SMITH, NANCY S(TECKER), speech pathologist; b. Framingham, Mass., Nov. 20, 1942; d. LeRoy Henry and Laura Mary (Harter) Stecker; m. David G. Smith, June 11, 1965; children: Laurie, Julie. BA, U. Ky., 1964; MA, U. Wash., 1966. Speech-lang. pathologist Harborview Med. Ctr., Seattle, 1967-70, Hearing Speech and Deafness Ctr., Seattle, 1970-76, Bellevue (Wash.)-Eastside Assocs., 1976-82, Community Home Health Care, Seattle, 1976-84; pvt. practice speech pathology Seattle, 1976—; cons. to state and pvt. agys., 1972—. Ruling elder Trinity Presbyn. Ch., Seattle, 1986—; circle chmn. Seattle Milk Fund, 1978-80. Mem. Am. Speech-Lang.-Hearing Assn. (cert. clin. competence), Am. Cleft Palate Assn., Wash. Speech and Hearing Assn. Avocations: camping, traveling, bridge, reading, gardening. Address: 135 NW 171st Seattle WA 98177

SMITH, NORMAN LEE, physician, medical educator; b. Logan, Utah, May 7, 1940; s. Norman P. and Alyce (Jorgensen) S.; m. Joan Carrigan, Jan. 31, 1969; children: Ann, Michael, Timothy, Emily, Melanie. BS, U. Utah, 1964, U. Calif., San Francisco, 1965, MD, 1968. Diplomate Am. Bd. Internal Medicine. Intern, then resident U. Utah Med. Ctr., Salt Lake City, 1968-74; chief med. resident U. Utah Affiliated Hosp., Salt Lake City, 1973-74; physician assoc. Meml. Med. Ctr., Salt Lake City, 1974—; clin. faculty U. Utah Sch. Medicine, Salt Lake City, 1975—; chmn. profl. edn. Am. Cancer Soc., Salt Lake City, 1976-77; vice chmn. dept. internal medicine LDS Hosp., Salt Lake City, 1982-84; chmn. Utah State Unproven Health Practices Com., Salt Lake City, 1981-86; v.p. Collegium Aesculapium, Provo, Utah, 1984-86, pres., 1986-87. Contbr. articles to profl. jours. Chmn. Utah State Cost Containment, 1983; instr. Maturation Program, elementary schs., Salt Lake City, 1976-84; coach Little League Basketball, football, Salt Lake City, 1971—. Served to maj. U.S. Army, 1970-72, Korea. Mem. AMA, ACP, Am. Soc. Internal Medicine, Acad. Psychosomatic Medicine, Phi Theta Kappa. Mormon. Lodge: Rotary. Office: Meml Med Ctr 2000 S 900 E Salt Lake City UT 84105

SMITH, ORA EVERETT, corporate executive, lawyer; b. Kennett, Mo., Dec. 24, 1947; s. Everett and Thelma May (Johnson) S.; m. Sue Ellen Caldwell, Sept. 3, 1972; children: Everett Eugene, Nathan Thomas. BME and MME, MIT, 1970; JD, Harvard U., 1976. Bar: Mass. 1977, D.C. 1977, U.S. Dist. Ct. Mass. 1977, Calif. 1983, U.S. Dist. Ct. (cen. dist.) Calif. 1983, U.S. Ct. Appeals (9th cir.) 1983. Mgr. engring. U.S. EPA, Cin., 1970-73; atty. New Eng. Telephone, Boston, 1976-77; mng. dir. Gordian Assocs. Inc., Washington, 1977-79; dir. structural materials integrity Rockwell Internat., Thousand Oaks, Calif., 1979-81, dir. physics and chem., 1981-85, dir. external tech. devel., 1985—; cons. Exec. Office of Pres. of U.S., Washington, 1985—; bd. dirs. N.Mex. TechnetInc., Albuquerque. Patentee impact sensor and coding apparatus; contbr. articles to profl. jours. Trustee Conejo Future Found., Thousand Oaks. Served with USPHS, 1970-72. Mem. ABA, Indsl. Research Inst. (White House fellow 1984-85, program com.), Consortium for Advanced Tech. Edn. (bd. dirs.). Republican. Lodge: Rotary. Home: 447 Arcturus St Thousand Oaks CA 91360 Office: Rockwell Internat PO Box 1085 Thousand Oaks CA 91360

SMITH, OTTO J.M., electrical engineering educator; b. Urbana, Ill., Aug. 6, 1917; s. Otto Mitchell and Mary Catherine (Carr) S.; m. Phyllis P. Sterling, Sept. 3, 1941; children: Candace B., Otto J.A., Sterling M., Stanford D. BS in Chemistry, Okla. State U., 1938; BSEE, U. Okla., 1938; PhDEE, Stanford U., 1941. Registered profl. engr., Calif. Instr. elec. engring. Tufts U., Medford, Mass., 1941-43; assoc. prof. elec. engring. Denver U., 1943-44; research engr. Westinghouse Research Labs., Forest Hills, Pa., 1944-46; sr. research fellow econs. Monash U., Melbourne, Australia, 1966-67; prof. elec. engr. U. Calif., Berkeley, 1947—; chief engr. Smith and Sun, Berkeley, 1976—. Author: Feedback Control Systems, 1958; contbr. articles to profl. jours.; patentee in field. Dist. commr. Boy Scouts Am., Berkeley, 1949-53; trustee South Campus Community Ministry, Berkeley, 1968-70, Wesley Found., Berkeley, 1969-72. Guggenheim fellow, 1960. Fellow AAAS, IEEE; mem. Am. Soc. Engring. Edn., Soc. Social Responsibility Engring., Soc. Social Responsibility in Sci., Am. Solar Energy Soc., Internat. Solar Energy Soc., Am. Wind Energy Assn. Democrat. Methodist. Club: Berkeley City Commons (pres. 1963). Avocations: photography, travel, guitar, violin, chorus. Home: 612 Euclid Ave Berkeley CA 94708 Office: U Calif Elec Engr Computer Scis Dept Berkeley CA 94720

SMITH, PATRICIA ANN, public relations consultant, educator; b. Chgo., June 7, 1933; d. Clarence Richard and Ruth Margaret (Jacobson) Nowack; m. Kurt E. Ferber, Feb. 14, 1954; m. 2d, Robert K. Hunsicker, June 28, 1968; children—Gail, Deborah, Kurt, Lori, Nancy, Janna; m. 3d, Kenneth Owler Smith, May 23, 1980. Student Cornell U., 1951-52; B.A., Centenary Coll., Hackettstown, N.J., 1983. Prodn. asst. Your Hit Parade Batten, Barton, Durstine & Osborne, 1953-54; pvt. practice polit. cons., 1954-66; legal sec., asst. Atty. John C. Cushman, 1966-68; field dep. Los Angeles County Assessor, 1968-69, pub. info. officer Los Angeles County Probation Dept., 1969-73; dir. consumer relations Fireman's Fund, San Francisco, 1973-76; pvt. practice pub. relations cons., 1976-77; spl. projects officer Los Angeles County Transp. Commn., 1977-78; tchr. Calif. State U.-Dominguez Hills, 1979-86; editor, writer Jet Propulsion Lab., 1979-80; pub. info. dir. Los Angeles Dept. Pub. Works, 1980-82; pub. info. cons. City of Pasadena, (Calif.), 1982-84; pub. relations cons., 1983—. Mem. First United Methodist Ch. Commn. on Missions and Social Concerns, 1983—; bd. dirs. Depot, 1983—; mem. devel. com. Pasadena Guidance Clinics, 1984-85. Recipient Pro award Los Angeles Publicity Club, 1978; Outstanding Achievement award Soc. Consumer Affairs Profls. in Bus., 1976. Mem. Pub. Relations Soc. Am. (accredited mem.; award for consumer program 1977, 2 awards 1984, Joseph Roos Community Service award 1985), Nat. Press Women (pub. relations award 1986), Calif. Press Women (awards 1974, 78, 83, 84, 85, community relations 1stplace winner 1986), Nat. Assn. Mental Health Info. Offices (3 regional awards 1986). Republican. Clubs: Pasadena Women's City, Zonta. Contbr. articles to pubs.

SMITH, PAUL GARY, chiropractor; b. Detroit, Sept. 16, 1944; s. Saul Howard and Zelda (Golsky) S.; m. Judy May Klein, Dec. 14, 1968 (div. Aug. 1984); children: Stephen, Lawrence, Jason, Dana; m. Sharon Ann Thompson, Oct. 20, 1984. Student, Highland Park (Mich.) Coll., 1962-64; BS, Pacific Christian Coll., 1977; D Chiropractic, Cleveland Chiropractic Coll., Los Angeles, 1968; cert. in hypnosis, Los Angeles Coll. Chiropractic, 1976, cert. in orthopedics, 1977; MA, U.S. Internat. U., 1979. Diplomate Nat. Bd. Chiropractic Examiners. Practice chiropractic Dr. Dan Parker, Los Angeles, 1968-69, Dr. Dominic LaForte, Redondo Beach, Calif., 1969; pvt. practice chiropractic Los Angeles, 1971-79; practice chiropractic specializing in orthopedics Cambridge Chiropractic Ctr., Las Vegas, Nev., 1979—; appointed Nev. State Bd. Chiropractic Examiners, 1981-85. Co-host (talk show) Back Talk, radio sta. KLAV. Mem. Rep. Nat. Com., Washington, 1985-86, Nev. and local Rep. Coms., 1985-86; res. police officer Clark County (Nev.) Sheriff's Aero Squadron, 1981-87; trustee Rep. Presdl. Task Force, 1985—. Fellow Internat. Coll. Chiropractors; mem. Am. Coll. Chiropractic Orthopedists, Am. Council on Chiropractic Orthopedics, Am. Chiropractic Assn. (Nev. del. 1982—), Nev. State Chiropractic Assn. (pres. 1986—), Am. Pub. Health Assn., Am. Coll. Chiropractic Hypnotists, Clark County Assn. Chiropractic Physicians. Jewish. Club: Rep. Mens (Las Vegas). Lodge: Knights of Malta (Knight of Honor 1983). Avocations: pistol and rifle competition, boxing, flying. Office: Cambridge Chiropractic Ctr 3405 Cambridge Las Vegas NV 89109 Office: Rainbow Chiropractic Ctr 101 S Rainbow Blvd Suite B32 Las Vegas NV 89128

SMITH, PETER BARTLETT, banker; b. West Newbury, Mass., Feb. 21, 1939; s. Norman B. and Alonza E. (Palmer) S.; m. Edna Mae Bourguet, Nov. 30, 1962; children—Kevin Bartlett, Brian Jay, Dwayne Alden. Student N.Mex. State U., 1956-59; diploma Sch. Banking of South, La. State U., 1968. Asst. cashier First Nat. Bank Dona Ana County, Las Cruces, N.Mex., 1958-66; v.p. First Interstate Bank, Roswell, N.Mex., 1967-71; v.p. Bank of Las Vegas, N.Mex., 1971-73; sr. v.p., cashier First Interstate Bank, Albuquerque, 1973—. Bd. dirs. Mountainside YMCA, 1978-81. Mem. N.Mex. Bankers Assn. (chmn. bank ops. com. 1981-82, chmn. EFT com. 1982-85), Greater Albuquerque C. of C. Republican. Clubs: Optimists (pres., 1970-71, lt. gov. dist. 1971), Albuquerque Petroleum (dir. 1983—), Tanoan Country. Office: First Interstate Bank 320 Gold Ave SW Albuquerque NM 87102

SMITH, PETER EDGAR, education educator; b. Potsdam, N.Y., Sept. 19, 1940; s. Edgar Herbert and Delores (Morgan) S.; m. Mardell Sue Hamlin, Aug. 26, 1962; children: Paul, Michael, Anna. BS, Western Oreg. U., 1962, MEd, 1966; PhD, U. Wash., 1974. Tchr. Madison High Sch., Portland, Oreg., 1962-65; research asst. Teaching Research, Monmouth, Oreg., 1965-67; predoctoral teaching assoc. U. Wash., Seattle, 1967-70; prof. edn. Seattle Pacific U., 1970—; cons. Council of Chs., Seattle, 1974-78; mem. adv. bd. media program Bellevue (Wash.) Community Coll., 1978—. Author/editor: Toward a Theory of Instruction, 1985, (instructor's manual) Adolescence, 1970; producer (simulation program) The Fifth Grade, 1985; contbr. articles to profl. jours. Mem. AAUP (pres. Seattle Pacific chpt. 1985-86), Assn. Ednl. Communication and Tech. Presbyterian. Avocations: photography, amateur radio. Home: 2519 8th Ave W Seattle WA 98119 Office: Seattle Pacific U Archer Instructional Media Ctr Seattle WA 98119

SMITH, PHYLLIS STERLING, writer; b. Berkeley, Calif., Aug. 27, 1921; d. Allen and Pearl (Sitzler) S.; m. Otto J.M. Smith, Sept. 3, 1941; children: Candace, Otto J.A., Sterling, Stanford. Student, Stanford U., 1938-41, Tufts U., 1941-43. Interview supr. Am. Psychol. Testing Corp., Boston, 1941-43; art instr. Scranton (Pa.) Studio, 1945-47; freelance author Berkeley, 1947-85; pres. Smith and Sun, Berkeley, 1979-85. Composer lyrics and music, 1972-84; translator TV documentary subtitles, 1985; contbr. articles to profl. publs.; patentee power plant heat rejection. Scout leader Girl Scouts U.S., São Jose Dos Campos, Brazil, 1954-56; switchbd. mgr. South Campus Community Ministry, Berkeley, 1968-70, pres., trustee, 1970-72. Mem. Calif. Writer's Club. Democrat. Methodist. Avocations: guitar, painting, travel.

SMITH, RALPH EARL, virologist; b. Yuma, Colo., May 10, 1940; s. Robert C. and Esther C. (Schwarz) S.; m. Sheila L. Kondy, Aug. 29, 1961 (div. 1986); 1 child, Andrea Denise. BS, Colo. State U., 1961; PhD, U. Colo., 1968. Postdoctoral fellow Duke U. Med. Ctr., Denver, 1968-70; asst. prof. Duke U. Med. Ctr., Durham, N.C., 1970-74, assoc. prof., 1974-80, prof. virology, 1980-82; prof., head dept. microbiology Colo. State U., Ft. Collins, 1983—; cons. Bellco Glass Co., Vineland, N.J., 1976-80, Proctor & Gamble Co., Cin., 1985-86. Contbr. articles to profl. jours.; patentee in field. Asst. scoutmaster Boy Scouts Am., Durham, 1972-82. Eleanor Roosevelt fellow Internat. Union Against Cancer 1978-79. Mem. Am. Soc. Microbiology, N.Y. Acad. Scis., Am. Soc. Virology, Am. Assn. Immunologists, Am. Assn. Avian Pathologists. Democrat. Methodist. Avocations: photography, hiking. Home: 1133 Indian Summer Ct Fort Collins CO 80525 Office: Colo State U Dept Microbiology Fort Collins CO 80523

SMITH, RANDOLPH LELAND, former army, officer, marketing executive; b. Mattoon, Ill., Nov. 3, 1939; s. Leland Prather and Hildred Ruth (Hall) S.; m. Joann Goodwin, Jan. 14, 1967; children—Karron Suzanne, Andrew Michael. B.S. in Aero. Engring., Calif. Poly. State U., 1962; M.B.A., N.Mex. State U., 1975. Commd. 2d lt., Ordnance Corps, U.S. Army, 1962, advanced through grades to lt. col., 1978; air def. officer, Fed. Republic Germany, 1962-64; comdr. 173d Ordnance Detachment, Ansbach, Fed. Republic Germany, 1964-65; chief quality assurance Pueblo Army Depot, 1966; comdr. B Co., 7th Support Bn., 199th Inf. Brigade, Vietnam, 1967-68; material officer 198th Maintenance Bn., Ft. Knox, Ky., 1968-69; spl. asst. to product mgr. Land Combat Support Systems, Redstone Arsenal, Ala., 1970-72; contract ops. officer 277th Supply and Service Bn., Danang, Vietnam, 1972-73; asst. prof. mil. sci. N.Mex. State U., Las Cruces, 1974-77; chief maintenance materiel sect., materiel support br. J-4, UN Command, U.S. Forces Korea, 8th Army, 1978-80; exec. officer U.S. Army Depot System Command, Chambersburg, Pa., 1980-81, dir. engring. and support systems, 1981-83; ret., 1982; v.p. mktg. Pueblo Diversified Industries, Colo., 1983—. Deacon Park Hill Baptist Ch., Pueblo, 1983-86; chmn. troop com. Boy Scouts Am., Pueblo. Decorated Bronze Star, Meritorious Service medal, Army Commendation medal. Mem. Am. Def. Preparedness Assn., Nat. Eagle Scout Assn., Beta Gamma Sigma. Address: 28390 Pongo Dr Pueblo CO 81006

SMITH, RAYMOND EDWARD, health care administrator; b. Freeport, N.Y., June 17, 1932; s. Jerry Edward and Madelyn Holman (Jones) S.; B.S. in Edn., Temple U., 1953; M.H.A., Baylor U., 1966; m. Lena Kathryn Jernigan Hughes, Oct. 28, 1983; children: Douglas, Ronald, Kevin, Doris Jean, Raymond. Commd. 2d lt. U.S. Army, 1953, advanced through grades to lt. col., 1973; helicopter ambulance pilot, 1953-63; comdr. helicopter ambulance units, Korea, 1955, Fed. Republic of Germany, 1961; various hosp. adminstrv. assignments, 1963-73; personnel dir. Valley Forge (Pa.) Gen. Hosp., 1966; adminstr. evacuation hosp., Vietnam, 1967; dep. insp. Walter Reed Gen. Hosp., Washington, 1970; dir. personnel div. Office of Army Surgeon Gen., Washington, 1971-73, ret., 1973; adminstr. Health Care Centers, Phila. Coll. Osteo. Medicine, 1974-76; dir. bur. hosps. Pa. Dept. Health, Harrisburg, 1976-79; contract mgr. Blue Cross of Calif., 1979—. Decorated Bronze Star, Legion of Merit. Mem. Am. Hosp. Assn., Am. Legion, Ret. Officers Assn., Kappa Alpha Psi. Episcopalian. Club: Masons. Home: 7630 Lake Adlon Dr San Diego CA 92119 Office: Blue Cross of Calif 3878 Old Town Ave San Diego CA 92110

SMITH, RAYMOND ROBERT, lawyer, exotic animal breeder; b. Long Beach, Calif., Feb. 15, 1948; s. Glenn R. and Margaret G. (Tweed) S.; m. Christine D. Howard, Aug. 26, 1969; children: Jenavee Marie, Zachary Glenn. BS in Philosophy, Brigham Young U., 1976, BS in Sociology, 1976; J.D., Lewis and Clark Coll., 1979. Bar: Oreg. 1979, U.S. Dist. Ct. Oreg. 1979, U.S. Ct. Appeals (9th cir.) 1979. Law clk. to house counsel Lasko Shipping, Portland, 1978-79; staff atty. Jackson County Legal Services, Medford, Oreg., 1979-80; mng. atty., 1980-82; ptnr. Fishman & Smith, Medford, 1982—; pro-tem mcpl. judge Medford City Ct., 1983; counsel, dir. F.F.R.E.D. Inc., Medford, 1983—; breeder exotic animals, White City, Oreg., 1982—. Mem. Assn. Trial Lawyers Am., ABA, Oreg. Trial Lawyers Assn. Republican. Mormon. Home: 1340 Pine Gate Way White City OR 97503 Office: Fishman & Smith Attys 836 E Main St Suite 3 Medford OR 97504

SMITH, RAYMOND VICTOR, paper products manufacturing company executive; b. Vancouver, B.C., Can., Apr. 28, 1926; s. Stanley Victor and Kathryn Stewart (Hunter) S.; m. Marilyn Joyce Meldrum, Oct. 17, 1947; children—Vicki, Kathi, Stan. Student, U. B.C., Banff Sch. Advanced Mgmt.; student Advanced Mgmt. Program, Harvard U. Trumpeter Dal Richards Band, 1942; ptnr. Warren McCuish Mens' Clothiers, 1947; sales rep. Vancouver Paper Box, 1949-54; with Home Oil Distbrs., 1954-57; with Kraft Paper & Board Sales, 1957-67, asst. mgr., 1961-65; newsprint rep. Powell River-Alberni Sales Corp., Pasadena, Calif., 1965-67; mgr. Powell River-Alberni Sales Corp., Pasadena, 1967-68; mgr. supply control and sales adminstrn. MacMillan Bloedel Ltd., Vancouver, 1968-70; gen. mgr. MacMillan Bloedel Ltd., 1970-71, v.p. mktg. paper and pulp, 1971-73, v.p., gen. mgr. newsprint, 1973-77, group v.p. pulp and paper, 1977-79, sr. v.p. pulp and paper, 1979-80, pres., 1980—, chief operating officer, 1980-83, chief exec. officer, 1983—; bd. dirs. Fibres Internat., Inc., Northwood Mills Ltd., MacMillan Bloedel Forest Products Ltd. U.K.; bd. govs. Bus. Council B.C.; co-chmn. Newsprint Info. Com. Served with Can. Army, 1944. Clubs: Terminal City, Capilano Golf and Country, Vancouver. Avocations: music, golf. Office: Macmillan Bloedel Ltd, 1075 W Georgia St, Vancouver, BC Canada V6E BR9 *

SMITH, RICHARD CLARK, city official; b. New Kinsington, Pa., Mar. 25, 1935; s. Ralph Burdette and Margaret Mary (Maracci) S.; A.S., El Paso Community Coll., 1971; m. Audrey Darlene Montgomery, Dec. 29, 1971; children—Richard Clark, Diane Kay, Gary Allen, David Mark, Carol Lynn.

With Colorado Springs (Colo.) Fire Dept., 1962—, fire capt., 1969-77, bn. chief, 1977-78, div. chief, 1978-79, fire chief, 1979—; program dir. Fire Sci. Asso. Degree, El Paso Community Coll., 1969-72. Mem. Bd. Edn. El Paso County Sch. Dist. 2, 1973-79, treas., 1973-79. Mem. Internat. Assn. Fire Chiefs, Nat. Fire Protection Assn., Colo. Fire Chiefs Assn. Mem. Christian Ch. of Security. Club: Sertoma. Office: Colorado Springs Fire Dept 31 S Weber St Colorado Springs CO 80903 *

SMITH, RICHARD CONWELL, science educator; b. Berkeley, Calif., Jan. 20, 1955; s. Frank Hardin Smith and Elizabeth (Goodfellow) Scott; m. LuAnn Kay Richey, Aug. 13, 1977; children: Jeffrey, Julie. BA, U. Calif., San Diego, 1977; MEd, UCLA, 1983. Research asst. City of Hope, Duarte, Calif., 1977-79; instr. Pacific Christian High Sch., Los Angeles, 1980-83, Downtown Bus. Mag. High Sch., Los Angeles, 1983—. Author: The Historic Atom: from A to Q, 1986. NSF fellow, 1986, Los Angeles Ednl. Partnership fellow, 1985-86, U. So. Calif. Research fellow, 1986. Mem. Greater Los Angeles Tchrs. Sci. Assn. (bd. dirs.), Nat. Sci. Tchrs. Assn., Calif. Sci. Tchrs. Assn., United Tchrs. Los Angeles. Democrat. Avocations: poetry, recorder, wilderness, reading the Bible. Office: Downtown Bus Magnet High Sch 1081 W Temple Los Angeles CA 90012

SMITH, RICHARD HOWARD, banker; b. Tulare, Calif., Aug. 27, 1927; s. Howard Charles and Sue Elizabeth (Cheyne) S.; B.A., Principia Coll, 1958; LL.B., LaSalle U., 1975; postgrad. Sch. Banking U. Wash., 1970-72; m. Patricia Ann Howery, Mar. 12, 1950; children—Jeffrey Howard, Holly Lee, Gregory Scott, Deborah Elaine. Prin., Aurora Elementary Sch., Tulare, 1951-53; prin. Desert Sun Sch., Idyllwild, Calif., 1953-55; trust adminstr. trainee Bank of Am., San Diego, 1955-58, asst. trust officer, Ventura, Redlands, Riverside and Los Angeles, 1958-65; asst. trust officer Security Pacific Bank, Fresno, Calif., 1965-68; trust officer, 1968-72, v.p., mgr., 1972—; instr. San Bernardino Valley Coll., 1962—, Fresno City Coll., 1977—. Served with USN, 1945-46. Mem. Fresno, Bakersfield, Merced estate planning councils. Home: 3222 W Dovewood St Fresno CA 93711 Office: PO Box 5026 Fresno CA 93755

SMITH, RICHARD LEE, information systems executive; b. Marion, Ohio, Sept. 5, 1939; s. Hugh V. and Mildred L. (Bauer) S.; m. Carol L. Danner, Sept. 9, 1961; children: Nancy, Cindy. BS in Bus., Bowling Green State U., 1961. Dir. distbn. O.M. Scott & Sons Co., Marysville, Ohio, 1965-78; v.p. info. service The Toro Co., Mpls., 1978-81; v.p. corp. info. services The Carlson Cos., Mpls., 1981-86; v.p. info. services group The Irvine Co., Newport Beach, Calif., 1986—. Office: The Irvine Co 500 Newport Ctr Dr Newport Beach CA 92668

SMITH, ROBERT ADEN, accountant; b. Gastonia, N.C., July 19, 1937; s. Theodore Roosevelt Sr. and Mandie Elzena (Collette) S.; m. Ruth Evelene Matthews, Apr. 18, 1965; children: Robert Scott, Michael Aden, Howard Kenneth; 1 adopted child, Kellie Denise. BA, Belmont Abbey Coll., 1960. Staff acct. Fred E. Upchurch, Gastonia, 1962-66; comptroller The Gastonia Gazette, 1966-78; pub. Greenhow Newspapers, Hornell, N.Y., 1978-81; acct. mgr. The Register, Santa Ana, Calif., 1981—. Served with U.S. Army, 1960-62. Mem. Nat. Assn. Accts., Inst. Internal Auditors. Republican. Mem. Ch. of God. Home: 1880 Jacalene Ln Anaheim CA 92802 Office: The Register 625 N Grand Santa Ana CA 92711

SMITH, ROBERT EDWARD, JR., electrical engineer; b. Long Beach, Calif., Nov. 15, 1954; s. Robert Edward and Virginia Darlene (Blume) S.; m. Melanie Gilmore, July 21, 1984. AS in Electronics Tech., Don Bosco Tech. Inst., 1973; BS in Electronic and Computer Engring., Calif. State Poly. U., Pomona, 1982. Registered profl. engr., Calif. Test technician Burroughs Corp., Pasadena, Calif., 1973-78, sr. test engring. specialist, 1978-80, assoc. engr., 1980-81, engr., 1981-85, sr. engr., 1985—. Republican. Home: 1650 Royal Oaks Dr Duarte CA 91010 Office: Unisys Corp MS 6085 460 N Sierra Madre Villa Pasadena CA 91109

SMITH, ROBERT FREEMAN, congressman; b. Portland, Oreg., June 16, 1931; m. Kaye Tomlinson, 1966; children: Christopher, Matthew, Tiffany. B.A., Willamette U., 1953. Mem. Oreg. Ho. of Reps., 1960-72, majority leader and speaker pro tem, 1964-66, speaker, 1968-72; mem. Oreg. Senate, 1972-82, Republican leader, 1978-82; mem. 98th-100th Congresses from 2d Oreg. Dist., 1982—; bd. dirs. Key Bank. Trustee Willamette U. Mem. Harney County C. of C. Lodges: Masons; Elks. Office: 118 Cannon House Office Bldg Washington DC 20515

SMITH, ROBERT HAMIL, fund raiser, author; b. Oak Park, Ill., Nov. 8, 1927; s. Henry Garfield and Mary Ellen (Hamil) S.; student U. Denver, 1946-48, LL.B., 1953, J.D., 1960; m. Mary Helen Kingsley, Dec. 29, 1948; children—David H., Mark K., Steven H., Rebecca Anne Smith Quintana. Dep. clk. County Ct., City and County of Denver, 1948-53; with Colo. Ins. Group, 1953-59; mgr. claims dept. R.H. Smith & Assos., 1959-64; pres. Am. Bapt. Home Mission Soc., 1964-68; assoc. dir. devel. Ill. Wesleyan U., 1968-69; asst. to chancellor U. Calif., San Diego, 1969-77; exec. dir. devel. Scripps Clinic and Research Found., La Jolla, Calif., 1977-82, v.p. devel., 1982—; pres. Cartographic Enterprises, 1981—; fund raising cons. deferred giving. Served with USNR, 1945. Mem. Nat. Soc. Fund Raising Execs., Internat. Yachting Fellowship of Rotarians (San Diego fleet comdr. 1979-81). Republican. Baptist. Club: Oceanside Yacht. Author: Guide to Harbors, Anchorages and Marinas So. and No. California edits., 1983.; The Physician as a Fundraiser, 1984. Home: PO Box 2785 Del Mar CA 92014 Office: Scripps Clinic and Research Foundation 10666 N Torrey Pines Rd LaJolla CA 92037

SMITH, ROBYNE MARIA, legal assistant; b. Gary, Ind., Aug. 26, 1959; d. Sylvia Maria Hill. BA, DePaul U., 1981; cert. paralegal U. So. Calif., 1982. Paralegal asst. Fields & Fields, Chgo., 1978-80; legal clk. Walzer & Gabrielson, Los Angeles, 1981-82; legal asst. Northrop Corp., Los Angeles, 1982-85; legal asst. Shea & Gould, Los Angeles, 1985-87, McKenna, Conner & Cuneo, Los Angeles, 1987—. Sec., Provisions, Inc., Los Angeles, 1984—; legal cons. Telview Communications Group, Los Angeles, 1982—. Mem. NAACP, Los Angeles Paralegal Assn., Nat. Fedn. Legal Assts., Am. Film Inst., Nat. Assn. Female Execs. Democrat. Roman Catholic. Avocations: piano, reading. Office: McKenna Conner & Cuneo 3435 Wilshire Blvd Los Angeles CA 90010

SMITH, ROSS QUENTIN, defense electronics systems consultant; b. Nacogdoches, Tex., June 22, 1959; s. Roger Qumil and Mary Hilda (Taylor) S. BS in Computer Engring., U. Tex., 1982. Control systems engr. E.I. duPont de Nemours, Victoria, Tex., 1981-82; research and devel. engr. Geotronics Corp., Austin, Tex., 1982-83; sr. research and devel. engr. Ford Aerospace and Communications Corp., Palo Alto, Calif., 1983-86; def. systems cons., C3I product mktg. mgr. ORI/Intercon Systems Corp., Sunnyvale, Calif., 1986—. Patentee in field. Recipient Ethics in Engring. award Hutchinson Found., 1983; Kmiecik fellow Brookview Inst., 1985. Mem. IEEE, Optical Soc. Am., Assn. Computing Machinery, Soc. Photographic and Imagng Engrs. Lodge: Order of Leon, Hedonism International. Avocations: sport fishing, scuba diving, tennis. Home: 169 Waverly St #C Palo Atlo CA 94301

SMITH, ROULETTE WILLIAM, educational association administrator; b. N.Y.C., Jan. 19, 1942; s. Timothy and Artisse Eulala (Roulette) S.; m. Norma Abe, Dec. 20, 1964; children: Nicole Michelle, Todd Roulette. BS in Math. and Chemistry, Morehouse Coll., 1961; MS in Math., Stanford U., 1964, MS in Computer Sci., 1965, PhD in Math. Models of Edn., 1973; postgrad., U. Calif., San Francisco, 1976-80. Asst. prof. U. Calif., Santa Barbara, 1970-75; sr. staff Far West Labs., San Francisco, 1975-76; pres., chief exec. officer Humanized Technologies, Inc., Palo Alto, Calif., 1973—; dir. Inst. for Postgrad. Interdisciplinary Studies, Palo Alto, 1984—; mgr. math. lab. Cherry Chase Sch., Sunnyvale, Calif., 1986—; cons. San Francisco Head Start, 1978—. exec. editor Instructional Sci., 1970-83; assoc. editor Health Policy and Edn., 1977-82. Mem. AAAS, Am. Psychol. Assn., Am. Ednl. Research Assn., N.Y. Acad. Scis. Democrat. Episcopalian. Mailing Address: PO Box 4061 Stanford CA 94305 Office: Inst Postgrad Interdisciplinary Studies PO Box 60846 Palo Alto CA 94306-0846

SMITH, RUSSELL EVANS, U.S. judge; b. Butte, Mont., Nov. 16, 1908; s. Ernest Clifford and Florence (Evans) S.; m. Mary Ruth Larison, June 21, 1931; children: Sonia Lee (Mrs. Daniel R. Zenk), Russell Evans. LL.B. cum laude, U. Mont., 1931, LL.D. (hon.), 1980. Bar: Mont. 1931. Marshal, law clk. Mont. Supreme Ct., 1931-33; practiced in Cut Bank, Mont., 1933-35, Missoula, Mont., 1935-42, 45-66; counsel for Mont., OPA, 1942-43; judge U.S. Dist. Ct. for Mont., 1966—, chief judge, to 1978, sr. judge, 1978—; lectr. U. Mont. Law Sch.; Mem. Mont. Bd. Bar Examiners. Served to USNR, 1943-45. Mem. Mont. Bar Assn. (past pres. 1956), Alpha Tau Omega, Phi Delta Phi. Office: PO Box 7219 Missoula MT 59807

SMITH, RUSSELL LYNN, JR., engineer, consulting engineer; b. Petaluma, Calif., Dec. 25, 1919; s. Russell Lynn and Marikka (Mikkelson) S.; m. Jean Margaret Austin, July 21, 1942; children: Lynn Suzanne, Dale Austin. Student, Stanford U., 1938-41; B.A., U. Hawaii, 1949. Registered profl. engr., Hawaii, Guam. Pilot, photogrammetric engr., surveyor R.M. Towill Corp., Honolulu, 1947-49; jr. engr. Austin & Towill, Honolulu, 1949-53; assoc. engr. H.A.R. Austin, Honolulu, 1953-56; v.p., sec. H.A.R. Austin & Assocs. Ltd., Honolulu, 1956-64; sec. Austin & Towill Ltd., Honolulu, 1957-59; v.p., treas. Austin, Smith & Assocs., Inc., Honolulu, 1959-75; pres. The Russ Smith Corp., Honolulu, 1975-84; chief engr., dir. pub. works City and County of Honolulu, 1985-86; pres. Smith, Young & Assocs. Inc., 1987—; mem. Honolulu Bd. Water Supply, 1985, 86; cons. on water supplies Pub. Utility Agy, Guam, 1966-74; chmn. Interprofl. Council on Environ. Design, U.S., 1982. Founder Hawaii Air N.G., 1946; mem. Gov.'s Com. on Yr. 2000, Hawaii; mem. budget rev. panel Aloha United Way, 1977-81. Served to 1st lt. A.C. U.S. Army, 1942-46, to lt. col. Air N.G. Decorated Air medal with oak leaf cluster; recipient Hawaii Engr. of Yr. award Hawaii Soc. Profl. Engrs., 1976, cert. of Merit Gov. Samuel W. King, Hawaii, 1956. Fellow ASCE (pres. Hawaii sect. 1961), Am. Cons. Engrs. Council (nat. pres. 1982-83, pres. Hawaii council 1970-71); mem. Water Pollution Control Fedn. (pres. Hawaii assn. 1967), Nat. Soc. Profl. Engrs., Engring. Assn. Hawaii (life), Hawaii Pub. Works Assn. (pres. 1985), Am. Water Works Assn., Am. Legion (vice commdr. Hawaii 1956). Republican. Clubs: Stanford (Hawaii) (pres. 1950-52); Pacific, Plaza. Lodge: Rotary. Home: 1526 Kamole St Honolulu HI 96821 Office: Smith Young & Assocs Inc 677 Ala Moana Suite 1000 Honolulu HI 96813

SMITH, SALLY ANN, telecommunications company executive; b. Mt. Olive, N.C., June 11, 1934; s. Leon Joseph and Ludia Irene (Montague) Simmons; m. Henry Ralph Smith Jr., Mar. 1, 1957 (div. Jan. 1976); children: Molly Montague, Barbara Ellen, Sara Ann, Mary Kathryn. BA in Math., Duke U., 1956; spl. studies, U. Liège, Belgium, 1956-57; postgrad. in bus. econs., Claremont Grad Sch., 1970-72. Mgr. fed. systems Gen. Electric Info. Services Co., Washington, 1976-78; mgr. mktg. support Gen. Electric Info. Services Co., Rockville, Md., 1978-81; dir. bus. devel. info. tech. group div. Electronic Data Systems, Bethesda, Md., 1981-82; v.p. mktg. optimum systems div. Electronic Data Systems, Rockville, 1982-83; v.p. planning and communications Electronic Data Systems, Dallas, 1983-84; dir. comml. devel. U.S. West Inc., Englewood, Colo., 1984—. Recipient Gen. Electric Centennial award, Rockville, 1978. Fellow Rotary Internat. Found.; mem. Phi Beta Kappa, Tau Psi Omega, Pi Mu Epsilon. Democrat. Presbyterian. Home: 1626 S Syracuse St Denver CO 80231 Office: U S West 7800 E Orchard Rd Englewood CO 80111

SMITH, SAM CORRY, foundation executive; b. Enid, Okla., July 3, 1922; s. Chester Hubbert and Nelle Kate (Corry) S.; m. Dorothy Jean Bank, Sept. 21, 1945; children: Linda Jean, Nancy Kay, Susan Diane. Student, Phillips U., 1940-43; BS in Chemistry, U. Okla., 1947, MS in Chemistry, 1948; PhD in Biochemistry, U. Wis., 1951. Asst. and assoc. prof. U. Okla., Oklahoma City, 1951-55; assoc. dir. grants Research Corp., N.Y.C., 1957-65, dir., 1965-68, v.p. grants, 1968-75; exec. dir. M.J. Murdock Charitable Trust, Vancouver, Wash., 1975—. Contbr. sci. articles to profl. jours. Trustee Nutrition Found., Washington, 1977-84, Internat. Life Scis. Inst., Washington, 1984-86; bd. councilors U. So. Calif. Med. Sch., Los Angeles, 1977-82. Served to 1st lt. USAAF, 1943-45, ETO. Named Boss of Yr., Am. Bus. Women's Assn., 1982, Bus. Assoc. of Yr., 1983. Fellow AAAS; mem. Am. Chem. Soc., Am. Inst. Nutrition, Am. Inst. Biol. Scis., N.Y. Acad. Scis. Republican. Presbyterian. Avocations: tennis, photography, gardening. Home: 5204 DuBois Dr Vancouver WA 98661 Office: MJ Murdock Charitable Trust PO Box 1618 Vancouver WA 98668

SMITH, SAMUEL HOWARD, university administrator, plant pathologist; b. Salinas, Calif., Feb. 4, 1940; s. Adrian Reed and Elsa (Jacop) S.; m. Patricia Ann Walter, July 8, 1960; children: Samuel Howard, Linda Marie. B.S. in Plant Pathology, U. Calif.-Berkeley, 1961, Ph.D., 1964. NATO fellow Glasshouse Crops Research Inst., Sussex, Eng., 1964-65; asst. prof. plant pathology U. Calif., Berkeley, 1965-69; assoc. prof. Pa. State U., Arendtsville, 1969-71; assoc. prof. Pa. State U., University Park, 1971-74, prof., 1974-85, head dept. plant pathology, 1976-81, dean Coll. Agr., dir. Pa. Agrl. Expt. Sta. and Coop. Extension Service, 1981-85; pres. Wash. State U., 1985—. Mem. Am. Phytopath. Soc., AAAS. Home: NE 755 Campus Ave Pullman WA 99163 Office: Washington State Univ 422 French Adminstrn Bldg Pullman WA 99164

SMITH, SANFORD LEIGH, architect; b. Long Beach, Calif., July 3, 1957; s. Chester Russell Smith and Marjorie May (Meyer) Buffum; m. Linda Laureen Hall, Aug. 4, 1979; 1 child, Taylor Alexis. BArch, Calif. State Poly. U., Pomona, 1979; cert. mng. archtl. practice, Harvard U., 1985. Registered architect, Calif. Store planning dir. The Harris Co., San Bernardino, Calif., 1979-81; dir. planning John Roberts Assocs., Inc., San Francisco, 1981-83; devel. mgr. The Irvine Co., Newport Beach, Calif., 1983-86; sr. architect U. Calif., Irvine, 1986—; photographer Met. Home mag., 1983. Sponsor Episcopal Youth Council, Irvine, Calif., 1984—. Recipient 3d Place Design award Women's Archtl. League, 1975; Urban Design and Planning scholar The Irvine Co., 1975. Mem. AIA (program com. 1986). Republican. Episcopalian. Avocations: sailing, scuba diving, wind surfing. Office: Univ Calif Irvine 426 Adminstrn Irvine CA 92717

SMITH, SCOTT BENNETT, publishing executive; b. Indpls., June 5, 1940; s. Donald Maxwell and Elsie Ann (Wilson) S.; divorced; children: Don, Laura, Jessie, Huntley. AB in English, Lafayette Coll., 1962. Reporter Allentown (Pa.) Morning Call, 1961-64; polit. journalism asst., nat. editor, metro editor Wash. Star, Washington, 1964-73; prof. journalism U. Ariz., Tucson, 1974-76; mgr. Mgmt. Recruiters, San Francisco and Menlo Park, Calif., 1978-83; pres., pub. San Jose (Calif.) Bus. Jour., 1983—; nat. editor Am. City Bus. Jours. Inc., Kansas City, Mo. Columnist Living Bus.; contbr. articles to profl. publs. Bd. dirs. San Jose Symphony, Jr. Achievement, San Jose, Civic Light Opera, San Jose, Convention and Visitors Bur., San Jose, O'Connor Hosp. Found., San Jose, San Jose Shelter, County Arts Council, San Jose. Stanford U. fellow, 1970-71. Republican. Avocation: golf. Office: The Bus Jour 80 S Market St San Jose CA 95113

SMITH, SCOTT WINFIELD, state administrative official; b. Rochester, N.Y., June 26, 1934; s. Scott Winfield and Thelma (Collins) S.; m. Kay Nadine Long, June 16, 1956; children: Kimberly Karin, Vicky Lee, Michelle Lynn, Scott Winfield IV. BA, Coe Coll., 1956; MS in Aero. Engring., USAF Inst. Tech., 1974; postgrad., Ariz. State U., 1974. Commd. 2d lt. USAF, 1957, advanced through grades to maj., 1968; pilot USAF, various locations, 1957-61, with aircraft missile maintenance, 1961-65; command pilot USAF, Vietnam, 1965-67; test pilot USAF, Warner Robins, Ga., 1967-77; mem. diplomatic corps USAF Joint Mil. Assistance, Phillipines, 1970-72; chief indsl. safety and quality control USAF, Tacoma, 1972-77; retired USAF, 1977; dir. safety and risk mgmt. State of Wash., Olympia, 1977—. Author: (manuals) Employee Benefits, 1979 (Best in State award 1982), Safety Programs, 1980 (Best in State award 1982); (newsletters) Accident Prevention, 1978—, Claims Management, 1978—. Mem. Gov.'s Pub. Employees Safety Panel, Olympia, 1979-86, also pres. Decorated Bronze Star, 4 air medals. Named Career Exec. of Yr., State of Wash., 1985. Mem. Order of Daedalians (local historian 1985-86), Am. Soc. Safety Engrs. (bd. dirs. 1979-86), World Safety Orgn. (cert.), Lacey Daiseys Squaredance Club (pres. 1980-81), Puget Sound Antique Aircraft Club. Republican. Presbyterian. Lodges: Masons, Shriners. Avocations: flying, fishing, music, electronics. Home: 5436 Rehklau Rd SE Olympia WA 98503 Office: Safety and Risk Mgmt Sect Dept Social and Health Services OB-14E Olympia WA 98504

SMITH, SELMA MOIDEL, lawyer, composer; b. Warren, Ohio, Apr. 3, 1919; d. Louis and Mary (Oyer) Moidel; student Los Angeles City Coll., 1936-37, U. Calif., 1937-39, U. So. Calif., 1939-41; J.D., Pacific Coast U., 1942; 1 son, Mark Lee. Bar: Calif. 1943, U.S. Dist. Ct. 1943, U.S. Supreme Ct. 1958. Gen. practice law; mem. firm Moidel, Moidel, Moidel & Smith. Field dir. civilian adv. com. WAC, 1943; mem. nat. bd. Med. Coll. Pa. (formerly Woman's Med. Coll. Pa.), 1953—, exec. bd., 1976-80, pres.-elect, 1980, pres., 1980-82. Decorated La Order del Merito Juan Pablo Duarte (Dominican Republic). Mem. ABA, Calif. Bar Assn. (servicemen's legal com.), Los Angeles Bar Assn. (psychopathic ct. com.), Los Angeles Lawyers Club (public defenders com.), Nat. Assn. Women Lawyers (chmn. com. unauthorized practice of law, social commn. UN, regional dir. western states, Hawaii 1949-57, mem. jud. adminstrn. com. 1960, nat. chmn. world peace through law com. 1966-67), League of Ams. (dir.), Inter-Am. Bar Assn., So. Calif. Women Lawyers Assn. (pres. 1947, 48, chmn. Law Day com. 1966, subject of oral hist. project, 1986), State Bar Conf. Com., Council Bar Assns. Los Angeles County (charter sec. 1950), Calif. Bus. Women's Council (dir. 1951), Los Angeles Bus. Women's Council (pres. 1952), Calif. Pres.'s Council (1st v.p.), Nat. Assn. Composers U.S.A. (dir. 1974-79, ann. luncheon chmn. 1975), Nat. Fedn. Music Clubs (nat. vice chmn. for Western region, 1973-78), Calif. Fedn. Music Clubs (state chmn. Am. Music 1971-75, state conv. chmn. 1972), Docents of Los Angeles Philharmonic (v.p. 1973-83, chmn. Latin Am. community relations 1972-75, press and public relations 1972-75, cons. coordinator 1973-75), Euterpe Opera Club (v.p. 1974-75, chmn. auditions 1972, chmn. awards 1973-75), ASCAP, Iota Tau Tau (dean Los Angeles, supreme treas.), Plato Soc. of UCLA, 1981—, discussion leader UCLA Constitution Bicentennial Project, 1985-87. Composer: Espressivo-Four Piano Pieces (orchestral premiere), 1986. Home: 5272 Lindley Ave Encino CA 91316

SMITH, SHAYN S., career couselor; b. Syracuse, N.Y., Feb. 25, 1952; d. David Bruce and Claudia Rae (Kent) S. BA in Speech Communications, SUNY, Buffalo, 1974; MS in Edn. Counseling, SUNY, Plattsburgh, 1979; PhD in Counseling, U. Colo., 1985. Radio broadcaster Sta. WWOL FM-AM, Buffalo, 1973-77; guidance counselor Agueda Johnston Jr. High, Guam, 1979-80; career counselor Career Services U. Colo., Boulder, 1983—; adj. instr. speech SUNY, Plattsburgh, 1980-81, adj. instr. communications Clinton Community Coll., Plattsburgh, 1979-80; instr. continuing edn. U. Colo., Boulder, 1982, acad. advisor, 1982-84. Singer, producer record album (with others): Suzy Sparkles, 1986. Mem. Colo. Coll. Personnel Assn. (treas., pres. 1982—), Assn. for Past-Life Research and Therapy (therapist), Colo. Assn. for Counseling and Devel. (treas.). Democrat. Methodist. Avocation: composing folk songs. Home: 2952 Glenwood Dr Boulder CO 80301 Office: Career Services U Colo Campus Box 133 Boulder CO 80309

SMITH, SHERMAN UHLER, environmental science professional; b. Burlington, Iowa, July 15, 1947; s. Sherman Allen and Mary Elizebeth (Uhler) S.; m. Diane Rapp, Aug. 6, 1983; 1 child, Summer Lea Nastich-Smith. BA in Gen. Scis., Exptl. Psychology, Monmouth Coll., 1972; MS in Environ. Health/Preventive Medicine, U. Iowa, 1973, postgrad. in environ. mgmt., 1973-74; postgrad. in environ. mgmt., Gov.'s State U., 1975-78. Cert. environ. profl. Mem. staff Congressman E. Mezvinsky, Iowa City, Iowa, 1973; environ. planner H.W. Lockner, Inc., Chgo., 1974-76; supr. environ. services Fluor Power, Inc., Chgo., 1976-78, 80-82; project mgr. Wapora, Inc., Chgo., 1978-80; dir. environ. services Fluor Tech., Inc., Irvine, Calif., 1982-86; mgr. Intellus Corp., Irvine, 1986-87; gen. mgr. ERT, Inc., Irvine, 1987—. Contbr. articles on environ. sci. to profl. jours. Served with U.S. Army, 1966-69, Vietnam. Decorated Bronze Star with Oak Leaf Cluster, Vietnamese Cross of Gallantry. Mem. Nat. Assn. Environ. Profls., Ill. Assn. Environ. Profls. (co-founder, bd. dirs. 1977-82), Air Pollution Control Assn., West Coast Environ. Auditing Bus. Roundtable (co-founder), Inst. Environ. Scis. (nat. com. chmn. 1977-80), Blue Key Soc. (Outstanding Sr. Man. 1971-72). Avocations: skiing, golf, scuba diving, bridge. Home: 3 Springwood Irvine CA 92714 Office: ERT 19782 MacArthur Blvd Irvine CA 92715

SMITH, STANFORD SIDNEY, state treasurer; b. Denver, Oct. 20, 1923; s. Frank Jay and Lelah (Beamer) S.; m. Harriet Holdrege, Feb. 7, 1947; children: Monta Smith Ramirez, Franklin Stanley. Student, Calif. Inst. Tech., 1941-42, Stanford U., 1942-43; BS, U.S. Naval Acad., 1946. Pres. Vebar Livestock Co., Thermoopolis, Wyo., 1961-83; mem. Wyo. Senate, 1974-76; pres. Wyo. Wool Growers, Casper, 1976-78; mem Wyo. ho. of reps., Cheyenne, 1978-82; treas. State Wyo., Cheyenne, 1983—; v.p. Wyo. Wool Growers, 1969-76; dir. Am. Murray Grey, Billings, Mont., 1976-82, Wyo. Prodn. Credit Assn., Casper, 1970-78. County commr. Hot Springs County, Wyo, 1966-72. Served to lt USN, 1943-54. Decorated Bronze Star. Republican. Presbyterian. Lodge: Lions. Office: State Treas State Capitol Cheyenne WY 82002 *

SMITH, STEVEN DENNIS, systems engineer; b. Charleston, W.Va., Nov. 15, 1945; s. Dennis Ray and Katherine Mondaine (Sands) S.; B.A., U. Richmond, 1968; postgrad. Va. Poly. Inst. and State U., 1969, 71-72, UCLA, 1986—. Programmer/analyst Hercules Inc., Radford (Va.) Army Ammunition Plant, also Wilmington, Del., 1968-72; supr. computer systems and ops. Black, Crow and Eidness, Inc., Gainesville, Fla., 1972-74; computer scientist Computer Scis. Corp., Silver Spring, Md., London and Flensburg, W.Ger., 1974-85; mem. tech. staff TRW, Redondo Beach, Calif., 1985—. Hospice vol. St. Agnes Hosps., Balt., 1984-85, Hosp. Home Health Care Agy. Calif., 1985—; active youth work Soccer Assn. Columbia (Md.), 1975-79, Howard County Children's Phys. Devel. Clinic, 1976-79. Mem. AIAA. Home: 606 N Juanita Ave #3 Redondo Beach CA 90277 Office: TRW 1 Space Park Redondo Beach CA 90278

SMITH, STEVEN SIDNEY, molecular biologist; b. Idaho Falls, Idaho, Feb. 11, 1946; s. Sidney Ervin and Hermie Phyllis (Robertson) S.; m. Nancy Louise Turner, Dec. 20, 1974. BS, U. Idaho, 1968; PhD, UCLA, 1974. Asst. research scientist Beckman Research Inst. City of Hope Nat. Med. Ctr., Duarte, Calif., 1982-84, staff Cancer Ctr., 1983—, asst. research scientist depts. Thoracic Surgery and Molecular Biology, 1985—; cons. Molecular Biosystems Inc., San Diego, 1981-84. Contbr. articles to profl. jours. NIH grantee, 1983; Swiss Nat. Sci. Found. fellow Univ. Bern, 1968-73, Scripps Clinic and Research Found., La Jolla, Calif., 1978-82, NIH fellow, Scripps Clinic, 1979-81. Mem. Union Schweizerische Gesellschaften fuer Experimentelle Biologie, AAAS, Pacific Slopes Biochem. Soc., N.Y. Acad. of Scis., Am. Soc. Cell Biology, Phi Beta Kappa. Republican. Club: Pasadena (Calif.) Athletic. Avocations: backpacking, guitar, weightlifting. Office: City of Hope Nat Med Ctr 1500 E Duarte Rd Duarte CA 91010

SMITH, STEWART CRANE, clinical social worker, educator; b. Salt Lake City, May 22, 1936; s. Andrew Delbert and Olive (Crane) S.; m. Mary Louise Snow, June 5, 1964; children: Stewart Randall, David Andrew, Amy Louise, Allen Crane. BS, U. Utah, 1961, MSW, 1963, postgrad., 1965. Salesman Bonneville Life Ins. Co., Salt Lake City, 1958-63; child welfare social worker State of Utah, Salt Lake City, 1963-64, pub. child welfare supr. State Div. Welfare, 1964-66, program dir., 1966-71, dir. spl. demonstration project Utah Div. Family Services, 1971-72, dir. state office comprehensive health planning, 1972-76, dir. state office health planning and resource devel., 1976-77, asst. dir. state planning and research, 1977-78, dir. state office health planning and resource devel., 1978-81; marriage and family counselor Salt Lake City, 1966—, pvt. practice clin. social work, 1978—; chmn. Utah Bd. Social Work Examiners, 1973-78; field instr. U. Utah Grad. Sch. Social Work, 1976-81; field market dir. Personal Dynamics Inst.; mgmt. cons. Performax Systems Internat., 1982—. Mem. Nat. Assn. Wocial Workers (chpt. 1st vice chmn. 1968-71, Utah del. 1976-79, pres. Utah chpt. 1979-80), Phi Delta Phi. Republican. Mormon. Office: 4527 S 2300 E Suite 107 Salt Lake City UT 84117 Home: 4856 Bron Breck Dr Salt Lake City UT 84117

SMITH, SUSAN CAROL, speech and language pathologist, clinical supervisor; b. Milw., Mar. 15, 1959; d. Howard Frank and Mary Susanna (Hawkes) S. BA, Mich. State U., 1981, MA, 1982. Dir., Sacramento area Norma Bork Assocs., Napa, Calif., 1982—; mem. utilization review com. Personalized Home Health, Sacramento, 1984—. Mem. stroke adv. com. Am. Heart Assn., Sacramento, 1984—, Spl. Pioneer Women Arcade Bapt. Ch., Sacramento, 1984—. Mem. Am. Speech, Lang. and Hearing Assn. (cert. clin. competence), Calif. Speech and Hearing Assn. Baptist. Avocations: cycling, needlework, ch. activities. Office: Burger Rehab Agy 101 E Natoma Suite A-1 Folsom CA 95630

SMITH, SUSAN KIMSEY, lawyer; b. Phoenix, Jan. 15, 1947; d. William Lewis and Margaret (Bowes) Kimsey; m. Alfred Jon Olsen, Apr. 15, 1979. Student U. Ariz., 1965-66; B.A., Principia Coll., 1969; M.A., U. Va., 1970; J.D., Ariz. State U., 1975. Bar: Ariz. Atty. trust dept. Valley Nat. Bank Ariz., Phoenix, 1976-77; assoc. Lane & Smith, Ltd., Phoenix, 1977-78; mem. Olsen-Smith, Ltd., Phoenix, 1979—, pres., 1979—; mem. Phoenix Tax Workshop, 1976—, Tax Study Group, 1979—, 401 - II Com., 1982—; chmn. taxation sect. State Bar Ariz., 1985-86; lectr. profl. confs. and univs., 1977, 80—. Author: Estate Planning Practice Manual, 1984; editorial adv. bd. Practical Tax Lawyer, 1985; contbr. writings to profl. publs. Recipient J.P. Walker Am. History award, Principia Coll., 1969, Ethics award, State Bar Ariz., 1974. Mem. ABA (chmn. com. econs. of tax practice 1983-84 , chmn. com. liaison with other ABA sects. and coms., sect. econs. of law practice 1983—, sect. corp., banking and bus law 1976—, com. mem. sect. taxation 1976—, com. mem. sect. real property probate and trust law 1982—, editorial bd. Practical Tax Lawyer), State Bar Ariz. (chmn. taxation sect. 1985—), Maricopa County Bar Assn., Fed. Bar Assn. (vice chmn. estate and gift taxation com., taxation council 1979-80), Valley Estate Planners (pres.), Central Ariz. Estate Planning Council (bd. dirs. 1986—), The Group, Alpha Lambda Delta, Phi Alpha Eta. Republican. Office: Olsen-Smith Ltd 301 E Virginia Ave Suite 3300 Phoenix AZ 85004

SMITH, TERRY GORDON, electronics production manager; b. Cin., Aug. 7, 1937; s. Clifford John and Vivan Aileen (Stone) S.; m. Sylvia Ann Ghel, Jan. 20, 1959 (dec. Dec. 1984); children: Donald Melvin, Terri Ann. Student, Arizona State U.; BA, U. Phoenix, MA in Mgmt., MBA. Mgr., owner Pharmacy, Phoenix, 1959-65; mgr. Super X Pharmacy, Scottsdale, Ariz., 1965-70; supr. Motorola, Inc., Phoenix, 1966-71, prodn. mgr., 1971—; mgmt. lectr. U. Phoenix, 1984—. Author: Metal Finishing Safety Manual, 1975. Mem. World Electroless Nickel Soc., Am. Mgmt. Assn., Am. Electroplaters Soc., Am. Soc. for Metal, Assn. for Mfg. Excellence. Republican.

SMITH, THERESA CATHERINE, ednl. adminstr.; b. San Louis Obispo, Calif., Sept. 9, 1924; d. Michael Mitchell and Lena Evelyn (Onetto) Sullivan; student Immaculate Heart Coll., 1942-44, St. Vincent Hosp. Sch. Nursing, 1944, Hunter Coll., 1944-45, U. Calif., Berkeley, 1947, Ariz. State U., 1947-49; B.S., U. Nev., 1971, M.Ed., 1973; Ph.D., Waldon U., 1982; m. Jack Riley Smith, July 17, 1948 (dec. 1972); children—Linda, David K., Patricia, Nancy. Coordinator spl. services Mohave Valley (Ariz.) Sch. Dist., 1966-72; cons. Diocesan Schs., Las Vegas, Nev., 1972-80; master tchr. U. Nev., Las Vegas, 1973-85; pvt. practice edn. cons., Needles, Calif., 1985—; cons. Title VI-G Child Service Demonstration Centers, Nat. Learning Disabilities Assistance Project, Western States, 1976, Nev. Child Service Demonstration Center, Title VI, Clark County Sch. System, Las Vegas, 1974, Clark County Diagnostic-Prescriptive Center, Las Vegas, 1975; instr. Clark County Community Coll., Las Vegas, part-time, 1974-85; instr., supr. student tchrs. No. Ariz. U., part-time, 1985—; prin. Our Lady of Las Vegas Elem. Sch., 1974-76; dir. spl. services New Horizons Center for Learning, 1975-76 co-founder New Horizons Center for Learning, Las Vegas, 1974, exec. dir., 1976-85; bd. dirs., 1973-80; cons. Structure of Intellect Inst., Las Vegas, 1979—; psychoednl. diagnostician, cons., Las Vegas. Bd. dirs. Mohave Mental Health Center, 1968-71; pres. confs. Nev. Assn. for Children with Learning Disabilities, 1970-80, pres., bd. dirs., 1973-79; mem. Nev. State Title I Adv. Bd., 1975. Served with U.S. Navy Women's Reserve, 1944-46. Roman Catholic. Home: 932 Bailey Ave Needles CA 92363 Office: 13 Broadway Suite 4 Needles CA 92363

SMITH, THOMAS EDGAR, JR., environmental planner, consultant; b. Monrovia, Calif., Nov. 29, 1947; s. Thomas Edgar Sr., and Jean Catherine (Blackburn) S.; m. Lorraine Cordaro, Sept. 23, 1972; children: Julia Renee, Anna Nicole. BA in Social Ecology cum laude (Irvine Co. scholar), U. Calif., Irvine, 1974; MA in Urban Planning (Acad. Senate Research fellow), UCLA, 1976; cert. Am. Inst. Cert. Planners. Research asst. Ultrasystems, Inc., Newport Beach, Calif., 1974-76; environ. planner So. Calif. Assn. Govts., Los Angeles, 1976-79; assoc. Phillips, Brandt, Reddick, Irvine, 1979-82; pres. Michael Brandman & Assocs., Inc., 1982—. Contbr. articles to profl. jours. Mem. dean's council UCLA Sch. Architecture and Urban Planning, 1979—; life mem. UCLA Alumni Assn. Served in USAF, 1967-71. Mem. Am. Planning Assn. (session panelist 1986), Am. Inst. Cert. Planners, Assn. Environ. Profls., Orange County Water Assn., Soc. Am. Mil. Engrs., Soc. Mktg. Profl. Services (bd. dirs.), Water Supply Improvement Assn., Bus. Devel. Assn. of Orange County (v.p.), Phi Beta Kappa. Office: Michael Brandman & Assocs Inc 3140 Redhill Ave Suite 200 Costa Mesa CA 92626

SMITH, THOMAS WINSTON, cotton marketing executive; b. Crosbyton, Tex., Mar. 16, 1935; s. Lance L. and Willie Mae (Little) S.; m. Patricia Mae Zachary, Dec. 13, 1958; children—Janna Olean, Thomas Mark. B.S., Tex. A&M U., 1957; P.M.D., Harvard U., 1964. Various positions Calcot Ltd., Bakersfield, Calif., 1957-77, exec. v.p., pres., 1977—; dir., v.p. Amcot, Inc., Amcot Internat., Inc., Bakersfield, 1977—; v.p. Nat. Cotton Council, Memphis; bd. mgrs. N.Y. Cotton Exchange, N.Y.C. Dir. Greater Bakersfield Meml. Hosp.; mem. president's adv. commn. Calif. State Coll.-Bakersfield; chmn. Continental Data Network, Inc., Bakersfield. Lodge: Rotary.

SMITH, TURK, writer; b. Detroit, June 24, 1917; s. Talbot Truxtun and Constance (Fitch) S.; student U. Ariz., 1935-38; m. Leslie Collie, Apr. 4, 1942 (dec. 1972); children—Talbot Truxtun III, Chopeta Constance. Reporter, feature writer Ariz. Republic, Phoenix, 1952-84, automotive columnist, 1964-84; corr. Newsweek, 1952-64, USIA, 1952-79. Contbr. articles to mags. Home: 4825 E Picadilly St Phoenix AZ 85018 Office: 120 E Van Buren St Phoenix AZ 85002

SMITH, ULRICH WALTER, lawyer; b. Zweibruecken, Fed. Republic Germany, Feb. 6, 1954; came to U.S., 1964; s. John R. and Marlene Lina (Kniprath) S.; m. Karen Lynn Krauss, Oct. 5, 1985. BA, U. Nev., 1980; JD, U. Pacific, 1984. Bar: Nev. 1984, Calif. 1985, U.S. Dist. Ct. Nev. 1985, U.S. Ct. Appeals (9th cir.) 1987. Computer instr. McGeorge Sch. Law U. Pacific, Sacramento, 1982-84; law clk. to presiding justice 8th Jud. Dist. Ct., Las Vegas, Nev., 1984-85; assoc. Jimmerson & Combs, P.C., Las Vegas, 1985-87; dep. dist. atty. Clark County, Nev., 1987—. Served with U.S. Army, 1972-75. Wiche scholar State of Nev., 1981-84. Mem. ABA, State Bar Nev., State Bar Calif., Am. Trial Lawyers Assn., Clark County Bar Assn., Delta Theta Phi. Republican. Baptist. Avocations: parachuting, tennis, golf, culinary arts. Home: 8813 Brescia Dr Las Vegas NV 89117 Office: Dist Atty 200 S 3d St Las Vegas NV 89155

SMITH, VIRGINIA WARE, psychotherapist, consultant; b. Chattanooga; s. Josh H. and Elizabeth (Johnson) Ware; m. Arthur B. Smith, May 30, 1959 (div. Dec. 1969); children: April Liza, Cindy Gaye. BA, Fisk U., 1951; MSW, Howard U., 1955; PhD, St. Louis U., 1980. Lic. clin. social worker, Calif. Social worker, supr. dept. social work Homer Phillips Hosp., St. Louis, 1955-64; instr., asst. prof. St. Louis U., 1965-74; supr. Children's Services, St. Louis, 1974-75; assoc. prof. La. State U., Baton Rouge, 1979-82; psychotherapist, acting social work cons. King Drew Community Health Plan, Los Angeles, 1983—; cons. Golden Key Stroke Program, Los Angeles, 1984—; research study coordinator King Drew Med. Sch., 1985-86; workshop leader Los Angeles County Dept. Health Services, 1986. Staff writer King Drew Hosp. newsletter, 1983—; contbr. articles to profl. jours. Mem. Crenshaw Christian Ctr. Fellow Polio Found., 1954-55, Ford Found., 1975-79. Mem. Nat. Assn. Soc. Workers (sec., treas. 1959-61), Acad. Cert. Soc. Workers, Alpha Kappa Alpha. Democrat. Avocations: travel, music, reading, crocheting. Office: King Drew Community Health Plan 12021 S Wilmington Ave Los Angeles CA 90059

SMITH, W. RAMSAY, wood science educator; b. Asheville, N.C., Apr. 26, 1948. BS in Wood Sci., tech., N.C. State U.; MS in Wood Sci., tech., U. Calif., Berkeley, PhD. Research lab. asst. Calif. Cedar Products Co., Stockton, 1969; assoc. cons. Walton R. Smith Forest Products Cons., Franklin, N.C., 1971-73; instr. Haywood Tech. Inst., Clyde, N.C., 1973; research asst. U. Calif. Forest Products Lab., Richmond, 1973-77; assoc. prof. coll. forest resources U. Wash., Seattle, 1978—; participant Internat. Union of Forestry Research Orgns., Oxford, Eng., 1979, joint Internat. Energy Agy. workshop and study tour, Sweden, 1980; organizer Joint Energy from Forest Biomass Harvesting Session at Internat. Energy Ag. World Congress, 1981; cons. Centre Technique du Bois, Paris, 1981, FAO, Rome; investigator wood products industries and markets, Japan, 1985; organizer Energy from Biomass session Internat. Energy Agy. World Congress, Ljobljana, Yugoslavia, 1986. Contbr. articles to profl. jours. Grantee French govt., 1977-78. mem. Forest Products Research Soc., Soc. of Wood Sci. and Tech., Internat. Union of Forestry Research Orgns., Am. Forestry Assn., W. Coast Dry Kiln Assn. Office: U Wash Coll of Forest Resources AR-10 Seattle WA 98195

SMITH, WALDO GREGORIUS, former government official; b. Bklyn., July 29, 1911; s. John Henry and Margaret (Gregorius) S.; m. Mildred Pearl Prescott, July 30, 1935; 1 dau., Carole Elizabeth Smith Levin. Student CCNY, N.Y., 1928-29; B.S. in Forestry, Cornell U., 1933. Forester, Forest Service, U.S. Dept. Agr., Atlanta, 1933-41, Ala. Div. Forestry, Brewton, 1941-42; engr., civil engring. technician Geol. Survey, U.S. Dept. Interior, 1942-71, cartographic technician, 1972-75; chmn. Public Transp. Council, 1975—. Recipient 40 year Civil Service award pin and scroll; 42 Yr. Govt. Service award plaque. Registered profl. engr., Colo. Fellow Am. Congress Surveying and Mapping (life; sec.-treas. Colo. chpt. 1961, program chmn. 1962, reporter 1969, mem. nat. membership devel. com. 1973-74, rep. to Colo. Engring. Council 1976-77); mem. AAAS, Denver Fed. Center Profl. Engrs. Group (U.S. Geol. Survey rep. 1973-76, Engr. of Yr. award 1975), Nat. Soc. Profl. Engrs. (pre-coll. guidance com. 1986—), Profl. Engrs. Colo. (chpt. scholarship chmn. 1979—, advt. corr., service award 1983), Cornell U. Alumni Assn. (alumni secondary schs. com.), Common Cause, Colo. Engring. Council (chmn. library com., spl. rep. Regional Transp. Dist., 1974-75; mem. sci. fair com. 1970-71; rep. ex officio Denver Pub. Library Found. Bd. Trustees 1975-80), Fedn. Am. Scientists, Am. Soc. Engring. Edn., People for Am. Way. Contbr. proposals to science-for-citizens program and research applied to nat. needs program NSF. Contbr. articles to profl. jours. Home: 3821 W 25th Ave Denver CO 80211

SMITH, WARREN ALBERT, JR., corporate advisor, strategic planner, international business consultant; b. Balt., Nov. 4, 1946; s. Warren Albert Sr. and Mary Virginia (Winter) S.; m. Margery Brook Burt; children—Andara, Elijah. B.A., U. Md., 1970; postgrad. U. Utah, 1977-78; student fin. studies Wharton Sch. Bus., 1980. Educator Prince George's County Schs., Md., 1970-74; exec. dir. Denver Service Ctr., 1974-78; chmn., chief exec. officer Greystone Mgmt. Ltd., The Greystone Corp., Evergreen, Colo., 1978, Greystone Securities Corp., Golden Colo., 1985, Greystone Wealth Mgmt. Ltd., Golden, 1978, Greystone Found, Evergreen, 1985, Greystone Inst., Evergreen, 1985; cons. Forest Oil Corp., Denver, 1980—, Am. TV and Communications, Denver, 1983—, Integrated Resources, Inc., N.Y.C., 1982—. Producer brochure (Swarthmore award 1979), 1979; designer/dir. historic restoration Greystone Estate, Evergreen, Colo., 1981—. Charter mem. U.S. Presdl. Task Force, Washington, D.C., 1982—; mem. U.S. Senatorial Club, Washington, D.C., 1983—, Ctr. for Study of Presidency, 1982—, Acad. Polit. Scis., 1982—, Woodrow Wilson Internat. Ctr. for Scholars, 1982—; mem. U.S. Congl. Adv. Bd., Washington, 1985; assoc. Historic Denver, Inc., 1981—. Mem. Internat. Soc. for Planning and Strategic Mgmt., Strategic Mgmt. Soc., Internat. Platform Assn., Nat. Trust for Hist. Preservation, World Future Soc., Am. Film Inst., The Planetary Soc., The Am. Biographical Inst. Research Assn., Inst. for Study of Consciousness, East West Found., Nat. Geographic Soc., Internat. Assn. Fin. Planning, Nat. Assn. Stragetic Planners, Am. Soc. Tng. and Devel., Pres.'s Assn., Am. Mgmt. Assn., Colo. Assn. Commerce and Industry (bd. dirs. nominee 1984), Denver Mus. Nat. History, Smithsonian Instn., Denver C. of C. Clubs: Brown Palace, Evergreen Athletic. Home: 34513 Upper Bear Creek Rd Evergreen CO 80439 Office: W A Smith and Assocs 222 Greystone Rd Evergreen CO 80439

SMITH, WARREN JAMES, optical engineer, educator; b. Rochester, N.Y., Aug. 17, 1922; s. Warren Abrams and Jessica Madelyn (Forshay) S.; m. Mary Helen Geddes, May 18, 1944; children: David Whitney, Barbara Jamie. BS in Optics, U. Rochester, 1944. Physicist Clinton Engr. Works-Tenn. Eastman Corp., Oak Ridge, 1944-46; chief optical engineer Simpson Optical Mfg. Co., Chgo., 1946-59; mgr. optics sect. Raytheon, Santa Barbara, Calif., 1959-62; v.p. research and devel. Santa Barbara Applied Optics, 1962-87; chief scientist Kaiser Electro-Optics, Inc., Carlsbad, Calif., 1987—. Author: Modern Optical Engineering, 1966; contbr. chpts. to books. Fellow Optical Soc. Am. (pres. 1980), Soc. Photo-Optical Instrumentation Engrs. (pres. 1983, gold medal 1985); mem. Optical Soc. So. Calif. (dir. 1967-68); Sigma Chi (house mgr.). Avocations: sailing, tennis. Home: 2603 Avenida de Anita Carlsbad CA 92008 Office: Kaiser Electro-Optics Inc 6070 Avenida Encinas Carlsbad CA 92009

SMITH, WAYNE EARL, university administrator; b. Franklin, Ind., Jan. 7, 1927; s. John Earl and Ruth (Foster) S.; m. Frances Gary Knause, Aug. 22, 1953; children: Wayne F., Paul A., Donna C. BA, Pomona Coll., 1949; MA, UCLA, 1953, PhD, 1958. Asst. prof. math. Occidental Coll., Los Angeles, 1958-62; asst. prof. applied math. U. Colo., Boulder, 1962-63; vis. asst. prof. biostats. UCLA, 1963-65, lectr. biostats., 1965-68, adminstrv. analyst, 1968—. Mem. Math. Assn. Am., Assn. Instnl. Research, Phi Beta Kappa, Sigma Xi. Home: 554 11th St Santa Monica CA 90402 Office: UCLA Planning Office Los Angeles CA 90024

SMITH, WILLARD GRANT, educational psychologist; b. Sidney, N.Y., June 29, 1934; s. Frank Charles and Myrtle Belle (Empet) S.; m. Ruth Ann Dissly, Sept. 14, 1957; children—Deborah Sue Henri, Cynthia Lynn Koster, Andrea Kay Richards, John Charles. B.S., U. Md., 1976; M.S., U. Utah, 1978, Ph.D., 1981. Cert. sch. psychologist, sch. adminstr., tchr., Utah. Research asst. Med. Ctr., U. Utah, 1977, teaching asst. dept. ednl. psychology, 1976-78, research cons. dept. edn., 1977; program evaluator Salt Lake City Sch. Dist.; program evaluator and auditor Utah State Bd. Edn., 1978; sch. psychologist Jordan Sch. Dist., Sandy, Utah, 1978-82, tchr., 1979-80; exec. dir. Utah Ind. Living Ctr., Salt Lake City, 1982-83; spl. edn. cons. Southeastern Edn. Service Ctr., 1983-85; psychologist Jordan Sch. Dist., Sandy, 1985—. Served to master sgt. USAF, 1953-76. Decorated Air Force Commendation medal with 2 clusters; recipient U. Md. scholastic achievement award, 1975. Mem. Am. Psychol. Assn., Nat. Assn. Sch. Psychologists, Am. Ednl. Research Assn., Assn. Supervision and Curriculum Devel., Air Force Assn., Air Force Sgts. Assn., Ret. Enlisted Assn., Phi Kappa Phi, Alpha Sigma Lambda. Home: 6879 Maverick Circle Salt Lake City UT 84121 Office: Jordan Sch Dist 7500 S 1000 E Midvale UT 84047

SMITH, WILLIAM CLARKE, clergyman; b. Bend, Oreg., Jan. 22, 1926; s. Jay Harvey Smith and Amelia Grace (Starr) Poor; m. Veta Maxine Davidson; children—Carolyn Jean Aldama, Virginia Ann, Barbara Lynn Farstad, Rebecca Ruth Sickler, Donald Allen, Patricia Bea Weinbrenner, Dwight David. A.B. cum laude, Ouachita Baptist U., 1949; postgrad. Golden Gate Baptist Theol. Sem., 1951-53. Ordained to ministry So. Baptist Ch., 1948. Pastor Owensville Baptist Ch., Ark., 1949-50, Grace Bapt. Ch., Corning, Calif., 1951; assoc. pastor 1st So. Bapt. Ch., Richmond, Calif., 1951-53; pastor Montalvin Bapt. Ch., San Pablo, Calif., 1953-60, 1st So. Bapt. Ch., Clovis, Calif., 1961-85, Hillside Bapt. Ch., La Puente, Calif., 1985, Trinity Bapt. Ch. Modesto, Calif., 1986—; mem. exec. bd. So. Bapt. Conv. Calif., 1981-85, cons. stewardship dept., 1976—, parliamentarian, 1964, 69, 74, 78; pres. Calif. So. Bapt. Ministers Conf., 1979, Clovis Ministerial Fellowship, 1963-65, 67-70, 75-77; mem. So. Bapt. Bd. Child Care, 1966-67, chmn., 1966, 67; moderator Mid-Valley So. Bapt. Assn., 1965-66, clk., 1969-78; moderator Fresno Bapt. Assn., 1962-64. Chmn. fin. com. Clovis Civic Improvement Bond Com., Calif., 1976; chmn. religion com. Clovis Bicentennial Com., 1975-76; active Clovis Parks Adv. Com., 1977-78. Served with U.S. Army, 1944-46. Republican. Home: 1817 Scott Ave Modesto CA 95350 Office: Trinity Bapt Ch 1346 Ronald Ave Modesto CA 95350

SMITH, WILLIAM FRENCH, hazardous waste director; b. Bay City, Tex., Nov. 30, 1941; s. William and Willie Mae (Perry) S.; B.S., Tuskegee U., 1964; postgrad. Washington U., 1968-70; m. Sylvia Knight, Feb. 4, 1977; children—William III, Maurice. Equipment engr. Boeing Co., Huntsville, Ala., 1964-67; plant design engr. McDonnell Douglas Corp., St. Louis, 1967-69; project engr. St. Louis County Govt., 1969-72; div. engr. E.I. duPont de Nemours & Co., Inc., Wilmington, Del. and Victoria, Tex., 1972-74; engring. mgr. Westinghouse Corp., Millburn, N.J., 1974-76; bldg. safety engr. Denver Public Schs., 1976—, project adminstr., 1977—, energy conservationist, 1978—; dir. hazardous materials Tuskegee U., Denver, 1985—. Served with USNR, 1979—. Bd. dirs. Denver Opportunities Industrialization Center, 1979-80, Nat. Commn. on Future of Regis Coll.; mem. Mayor's Citizens Adv. Com. on Energy, 1980—. Recipient Pres.'s Nat. award for energy conservation, 1980. Mem. Am. Soc. Safety Engrs., Colo. Assn. Sch. Energy Coordinators, Am. Assn. Blacks in Energy, Denver Pub. Schs. Black Adminstrs. and Suprs. Assn. (treas.), Colo. Environ. Health Assn., Nat. Asbestos Council, Colo. Hazardous Waste Mgmt. Soc., Colo. Hazardous Materials Assn., Nat. Assn. Minority Contractors, Internat. Hazardous Materials Assn., Tuskegee U. Alumni Assn. Republican. Home: 102 S Balsam St Denver CO 80226 Office: Denver Public Schs 900 Grant St Denver CO 80203

SMITH, WILLIAM GORDON, lawyer; b. Los Angeles, Jan. 4, 1933; s. Hughbert Price and Lucile (Gordon) S.; m. Carol Krauthamer, Dec. 22, 1967; children: Diane, Carin, Rhonda. AA, UCLA, 1953, BS, 1955; JD, U. So. Calif., 1963. Bar: Calif., 1964. Dep. pub. defender Los Angeles, 1964-65; ptnr. Margolis, McTernan, Smith, Scope & Sacks, Los Angeles, 1965-74; sole practice Los Angeles, 1974—; chairperson Selective Service Law Panel ACLU and Nat. Lawyers Guild, Los Angeles, 1967—. Served to capt. USAF, 1956-63. Democrat. Home: 5045 Montezuma St Los Angeles CA 90042 Office: 1557 W Beverly Blvd Los Angeles CA 90026

SMITH, WILLIAM RAY, biophysicist, engineer; b. Lyman, Okla., June 26, 1925; s. Harry Wait and Daisy Belle (Hull) S. B.A., Bethany Nazarene Coll., 1948; M.A., Wichita State U., 1950; postgrad. U. Kans., 1950-51; Ph.D., UCLA, 1967. Engr., Beech Aircraft Corp., Wichita, Kans., 1951-53; sr. group engr. McDonnell Aircraft Corp., St. Louis, 1953-60; sr. engr. Lockheed Aircraft Corp., Burbank, Calif., 1961-63; sr. engr. scientist McDonnell Douglas Corp., Long Beach, Calif., 1966-71; mem. tech. staff Rockwell Internat., Los Angeles, 1973-86, CDI Corp.-West, Costa Mesa, Calif., 1986—; tchr. math. Glendale Coll., Calif., 1972; asst. prof. math. and physics Pasadena Coll. (now Point Loma Coll., San Diego), 1960-62, Mt. St. Mary's Coll., Los Angeles, 1972-73. Contbr. articles to sci. jours. Recipent citation McDonnell Douglas Corp., 1968; Tech. Utilization award Rockwell Internat., 1981; cert. of recognition NASA, 1982. Mem. N.Y. Acad. Scis., AAAS, AIAA, UCLA Chancelor's Assocs., Los Angeles Council Internat. Visitors, Town Hall Calif., Yosemite Natural History Assn., Sigma Xi, Pi Mu Epsilon. Republican. Presbyterian. Office: CDI Corp 2405 Roscomare Rd Los Angeles CA 90077

SMITH, WILLIAM RILEY, manufacturing executive; b. Connersville, Ind., Nov. 26, 1936; s. William Edward and Nellie Evelyn (Huber) S.; m. Judith Elaine Penn, Aug. 10, 1954 (dec. 1963); children: Sandra Largen, Deborah Elam, Ronald; m. Patricia Anne Costello, Dec. 29, 1984. BSBA, Ohio State U. Product mgr. Powermatic/ Houdaille, McMinnville, Tenn., 1969-76; gen. sales mgr. Clausing Machine Tools, Elgin, Ill., 1976-80; pres. WRS Cons., Costa Mesa, Calif., 1980-83; mgr. U.S. sales and mktg. Standard Modern, Toronto, Can., 1983-85; pres. Gurutzpe N.Am., Tustin, Calif., 1985—. Served with USAF, 1955-63. Republican. Mem. Bretheren Ch. Lodges: Masons, Rams.

SMITH, WILLIAM WARD, aerospace executive; b. Evanston, Ill., Dec. 20, 1934; s. William Ward and Ina (Riswold) S.; m. Lucy Allene Wakefield, Feb. 14, 1959; children: William Ward III, Ann Wakefield. BSME, Purdue U., 1956; MSME, Calif. Inst. Tech., 1957. Registered profl. engr., Calif. Engring. group supr. Liquid Propulsion Systems, Calif. Tech. JPL, Pasadena, 1957-63; programs dir. Rocket Research Co., Redmond, Wash., 1963-71, v.p., 1971-75, sr. v.p., 1975-76, exec. v.p., 1976-77, pres., 1977-87; pres. Aerospace Div., Olin Defense Systems Group, Redmond, 1987—. Recipient Space Act award NASA, 1964. Mem. AIAA, Sigma Xi, Pi Tau Sigma, Phi Gamma Delta (sec. Purdue chpt. 1954-55). Republican. Episcopalian. Office: Aerospace Div Olin Defense Systems Group PO Box 97009 Redmond WA 98073-9709

SMITH, ZACHARY ALDEN, political science and public administration educator; b. Stanford, Calif., Aug. 8, 1953; s. Alden Wallace and Lelia (Anderson) S.; m. Lisa Friel, May 20, 1983. BA, Calif. State U., Fullerton, 1975; MA, U. Calif., Santa Barbara, 1979, PhD, 1984. Adj. lectr. polit. sci. U. Calif., Santa Barbara, 1981-82; asst. prof. U. Hawaii, Hilo, 1982-87, assoc. prof., 1987—. Author: Groundwater Policy in the Southwest, Interest Group Interaction and Groundwater Policy, Groundwater Policy in the Nineteen Western States, Water and the Future of the Southwest; contbr. numerous articles to profl. jours. Active campaign Jimmy Carter for Pres., 1976, campaign for various state propositions, 1970, 74, 76; elected to Orange County (Calif.) Dem. Cen. Com., 1976—. Research grantee U. Calif., Los Alamos (N.Mex.) Sci. Lab., Water Resources Ctr., Davis., Calif. Mem. Am. water Resources Assn., Am. Polit. Sic. Assn., Western Polit. Sci. Assn., Am. Soc. Pub. Adminstrn. Office: U Hawaii Hilo HI 96720

SMITH-EVERNDEN, ROBERTA KATHERINE, geology educator; b. Los Angeles, Dec. 17, 1931; d. Elmer Harrison and Mary Katherine (Tilley) Smith; m. Mark Newell Christensen, June 12, 1955 (div. 1960); m. Jack Foord Evernden, Dec. 31, 1965. AA, Los Angeles Valley Coll., 1952; BA, U. Alaska, 1957; MA, U. Calif., Berkeley, 1960; PhD, U.B.C., Can., 1966. Registered profl. geologist, Calif. Asst. prof. geology Howard U., Washington, 1967-70; geologist Smithsonian Instn., Washington, 1965-73; lectr., research assoc. dept. earth scis. U. Calif., Santa Cruz, 1974—; prin., cons. Smith-Evernden Assocs., Davenport, Calif., 1976—; geol. reviewer Santa Cruz County, 1977-80; vis. scientist, Beijing, People's Republic China, 1979-80; pres., bd. dirs. Santa Cruz County Resource Conservation Dist.; mem. adv. com. Monterey Bay Area Unified Air Pollution Control Dist.; mem. tech. adv. com. Calif. Bd. Forestry. Contbr. articles to profl. jours. Fellow AAAS; mem. Assn. Engring. Geologists, Paleontol. Research Instn., Cushman Found. for Foraminiferal Research, Soc. Women Geographers, Assn. Women Geoscientists, Sigma Xi. Democrat. Home: 5 San Vicente St Davenport CA 95017 Office: Smith-Evernden Assocs PO Box 174 Davenport CA 95017

SMITH-RITCHIE, JERILYNN SUZANNE, educator; b. Loma Linda, Calif., Aug. 15, 1944; d. Gerald A. and Maxine (McGowan) Smith; m. J. Michael McGinn, July 22, 1966; m. Lynn A. Choate, May 8, 1971; 1 dau., Catherine Anne; m. C. Alen Ritchie, Feb. 17, 1981. B.A., U. Redlands (Calif.), 1966, M.A.T., 1968; M.A.Ed., Calif. State Coll., San Bernardino, 1980. Tchr. elem. sch. Redlands Unified Sch. Dist., 1966-69, tchr. eductionally handicapped, 1969-71, tchr. intermediate grades, 1971-74, tchr. bilingual edn., 1975-79, resource specialist, 1979-84, categorical projects resource tchr., 1984-87; supr. student tchrs. Calif. State Coll., 1975; lectr. in field. Bd. dirs. San Bernardino County Mus. Assn. Recipient Hon. Service award Lugonia PTA, 1982, Tchrs. Hall of Fame award, 1982. Mem. Council for the Exceptional Child, Calif. Assn. Bilingual Edn. (mem. state exec. bd. 1985—), Nat. Assn. Bilingual Edn. Democrat. Office: Redlands Unified Sch Dist 20 W Lugonia Ave Redlands CA 92373

SMITHSON, EDDIE JOE, hotel executive; b. Clovis, N.Mex., Nov. 9, 1933; s. James Clyde and Ruby Laura (Powell) S.; m. Jackie Lou Hunt, Oct. 4, 1951; children—Samie Lou Martinez, Shari Lynn. Student N.Mex. State U. Asst. mgr. Palms Motor Hotel, Las Cruces, N.Mex., 1965-66; gen. mgr. Diamond Jim's Restaurant, Albuquerque, 1966-69; mng. ptnr. Palms Motor Hotel, Las Cruces, N.Mex., 1969-74; regional dir. Don the Beachcomber, Dallas, 1974-75; gen. mgr. Holiday Inn, Las Cruces, 1975-77; mng. ptnr. Best Western of Las Cruces, 1977-83; v.p., mng. dir. La Fonda Hotel, Santa Fe, N.Mex., 1983—. Mem. Gov.'s Econ. Devel. and Tourism Bd., N.Mex., 1981—, chmn. tourism com. 1986; bd. dirs. Pres. Assocs., N.Mex. State U., Las Cruces, 1982-83; mem. Santa Fe Occupancy Tax Bd. Mem. Am. Hotel and Motel Assn. (nat. dir. 1984—), N.Mex. Hotel and Motel Assn. (pres. 1983-84, Innkeeper of Yr. 1986), Santa Fe Lodger's Assn. (bd. dirs.), Las Cruces C. of C. (pres. 1979, Citizen of Yr. 1982, bd. dirs. 1973-80), N.Mex. Restaurant Assn. (pres. 1973-74, state dir. 1969-73, Restaurateur of Yr. 1980). Democrat. Methodist. Club: Skal Internat. (El Paso, Tex.) (pres. 1981-82). Home: PO Box 1209 Santa Fe NM 87504 Office: La Fonda 100 E San Francisco Santa Fe NM 87504

SMITHSON, LUTHER HARRIS, diversified electronics research company executive; b. Birmingham, Ala., July 20, 1932; s. Luther Harris and Mamee

(Champenois) S.; m. Marilyn Anderson, Mar. 24, 1956; children: Kistrina Marie, Paul John. BS in Chemistry, U. Wash., 1957; MS in Phys. Chemistry, UCLA, 1960. Chemist Calif. Research Co., Richmond, 1960-66; lab. mgr. Varian Corp., Palo Alto, Calif., 1966-70; dir. mktg. Smith Kline INst., Palo Alto, 1970-73; dir. biotech. SRI Internat., Menlo Park, Calif., 1973—. Contbr. articles to profl. jours.; patentee in field. Served as cpl. U.S. Army, 1952-55. Avocations: pottery, reading, writing. Home: 2261 Greer Rd Palo Alto CA 94303 Office: SRI Internat 33 Ravenswood Ave Menlo Park CA 94025

SMITH-WILLIAMS, MARGIE MARIAN, consultant and expert witness, designer, automotive engineer; b. June 9, 1942; d. Dann Albert and Anita Pearl Smith; m. Robert E. Williams, Feb. 5, 1977. Student U. Redlands, 1960-62, San Bernardino Valley Coll., 1963-67; B.S.M.E., U. Denver, 1967; postgrad. UCLA Extension, 1970-80; student Healing Light Ctr., Glendale, Calif., 1981—. Registered engr.-in-tng., Calif. Saturday mgr. Dry Clean Agy., Novato, Calif., 1958-60; draftsman Maxwell Surveying, San Bernardino, Calif., 1961; engr. aide II, Calif. Div. Transp., San Bernardino, 1961-66; draftsman Silver Engr. Works, Denver, 1964; designer/draftsman Digmor Equipment & Engring., San Bernardino, 1966; design engr. Mattel Toys, Hawthorne, Calif., 1967-68; project mgr. Spirit of Am. Enterprises, Torrance, Calif., 1968; owner, contract engr. Internat. Racing Designs, Gardena, Calif., 1968-71; pres., chief exec. officer, design engr. IRD Trailers, South El Monte, Calif., 1971-86; owner/designer Illusions, Downey, Calif., 1973—; pub. Trailer Visions, Downey, 1981—; dir. I R D, INC., South El Monte, Structural Dynamics Cons., Pacific Palisades, Calif. Author: Trailers—How to Tow and Maintain, 1982; Trailers—How To Buy and Evaluate, 1983; also tech. mail-order catalogs. Inventor, patentee (16) on trailers and toys. Engr./designer product line of weld-up kit form race car trailers, utility trailers; designer product line stuffed vehicles, decorative cork/fabric bulletin bds., metal planters. Active in effort to change dealer lic. laws and legis. of trailers in Calif., 1969, 73. Mem. Calif. Scholarship Fedn. (life), Healing Light Ctr. Republican. Spiritualist. Avocations: energy healing; metaphysics; sewing; beadwork; creative designs. Office: IRD Inc 7603 E Firestone Suite D-11 Downey CA 90241

SMOLLAN, DAVID LESLIE, tax practitioner; b. Middlesbrough, Eng., June 22, 1928; came to U.S., 1948, naturalized, 1954; s. Philip and Sarah (Freedman) S.; B.B.A., Woodbury Coll., 1950; m. Sheila Joy Glassman, Aug. 5, 1956 (dec.); children—Jeffrey, Debbie; m. June Rolt, Dec. 26, 1985. Chief acct. Lucky Plastic Co., Inc., Los Angeles, 1951-64; self-employed tax practitioner, Encino, Calif, 1965—. Named Kiwanian of Yr., Pacoima Kiwanis Club, 1968; enrolled to practice before the IRS, 1967. Mem. Nat. Assn. Enrolled Agts. (pres. 1973-74), Calif. Soc. Enrolled Agts. Club: Kiwanis (pres. Encino 1985-86). Lodge: B'nai B'rith. Office: 18075 Ventura Blvd Suite 212 Encino CA 91316

SMOOT, LEON DOUGLAS, university dean, chemical engineering educator; b. Provo, Utah, July 26, 1934; s. Douglas Parley and Jennie (Hallam) S.; m. Marian Bird, Sept. 7, 1953; children: Analee, LaCinda, Michelle, Melinda Lee. B.S., Brigham Young U., 1957; M.S., U. Wash., 1958, Ph.D., 1960. Registered profl. engr., Utah. Engr. Boeing Corp., Seattle, 1956; teaching and research asst. Brigham Young U., 1954-57; engr. Phillips Petroleum Corp., Arco, Idaho, 1957; engr., cons. Hercules Powder Co., Bacchus, Utah, 1961-63; asst. prof. Brigham Young U., 1960-63; engr. Lockheed Propulsion, Redlands, Calif., 1963-67; vis. asst. prof. Calif. Inst. Tech., 1966-67; asso. prof. to prof. Brigham Young U., 1967—, chmn. dept. chem. engring., 1970-77, dean Coll. Engring. and Tech., 1977—; dir. Advanced Combustion Engring. Research Ctr. (NSF), 1986—; cons. Hercules, Thiokol, Lockheed, Teledyne, Atlantic Research Corp., Raytheon, Redd and Redd, Billings Energy, Ford, Bacon & Davis, Jaycor, Intel Com Radiation Tech., Phys. Dynamics, Nat. Soc. Propellants and Explosives, France, DFVLR, West Germany, Martin Marietta, Honeywell, Phillips Petroleum Co., Exxon, Nat. Bur. Standards, Eyring Research Inst., Systems, Sci. and Software., Los Alamos Nat. Lab., others. Contbr. over 100 articles to tech. jours.; author 2 books on coal combustion. Mem. Am. Inst. Chem. Engrs., Am. Inst. Aeros. and Astronautics, Am. Soc. Engring. Edn., Combustion Inst., Research Soc. Am., Tau Beta Pi, Phi Lambda Epsilon, Sigma Xi. Republican. Mem. Ch. Jesus Christ of Latter-day Saints. Home: 1811 N 1550 East Provo UT 84604 Office: 270 CB Brigham Young U Provo UT 84602

SMOOT, WENDELL MCMEANS, JR., investment counselor; b. Salt Lake City, Jan. 15, 1921; s. Wendell M. and Rebecca (Clawson) S.; m. Barbara Davis, June 24, 1942; children—Wendell M. III, Margaret, David, John, Mary. B.A., U. Utah, 1942. Gen. ptnr. J.A. Hogle & Co., Salt Lake City, 1945-63, Goodbody & Co., N.Y.C., 1963-70; pres. Smoot, Miller, Cheney & Co., Salt Lake City, 1971—; dir. Grand Central, Inc. Pres. Great Salt Lake council Boy Scouts Am., 1968-70; chmn. Utah State Pioneer Meml. Theatre, 1978-79; pres. Mormon Tabernacle Choir. Served to capt., U.S. Army, 1942-45; ETO. Mem. Fin. Analysts Soc. Republican. Mem. Ch. of Jesus Christ of Latter Day Saints. Club: The Country. Lodge: Rotary.

SMRCKA, ANTONIN KLEMENT JOSEF, college administrator, consultant; b. Humpolec, Czechoslovakia, June 17, 1931; came to Can., 1951; s. Antonin Karel Josef and Bozena (Kristufek) S.; m. Solanges Madeleine Gabrielle Domerson, June 28, 1958; 1 child, Julienne. B.S., Concordia U., Montreal, Que., Can., 1957, B.A., 1967; diploma in edn. McGill U., Montreal, 1971; Ph.D., U. N.Mex., 1978, cert. ednl. spl. adminstrn., 1984. Cert. tchr., Alaska, N.Mex., Tex., Que.; cert. adminstr., Alaska, N.Mex., Tex., Que. Sr. mktg. analyst Allied Chem. Co., Montreal, 1953-68; natural scis. coordinator, tchr. Vaudreuil High Sch., Que., 1968-73; tchr., supv. social scis. Pius X High Sch., Albuquerque, 1973-75; instr. ednl. found. U. N.Mex., Albuquerque, 1975-78; asst. to pres., planning and grants adminstr. and asst. prof. U. Albuquerque, 1978-84; v.p. for bus. affairs Coll. of Santa Fe, 1984-86; pres., dir. P.M.S., Inc., Albuquerque, 1981—; owner Profl. Mgmt. Service, Quebec, 1963—; assoc. G.A. Coombes & Assocs., Toronto, Ont., Can., 1984—. Exec. v.p., sec., treas. bd. trustees Am. U. of Les Cayes (Haiti), 1983—; pres. bd. dirs. S.W. Maternity Ctr., Inc., Albuquerque, 1975; treas. Dorion Garden Community Council, Que., 1961. Named hon. mem. Ecole des Hautes Commerciales et Industrie, Port-Au-Prince, Haiti, 1971. Mem. Chem. Inst. Can., Can. Soc. for Chem. Engrs., AAUP, Assn. for Curriculum and Devel., Am. Accrediting Assn. of Retirement Ctrs. (trustee 1984—, chmn. bd. trustees 1983-84), Greater Albuquerque C. of C., Phi Delta Kappa. Republican. Roman Catholic. Club: Optimist (pres.-elect 1978-79) (Albuquerque). Home: 4224 Roma NE Albuquerque NM 87108

SMULDERS, ANTHONY PETER, biology educator; b. Oss, North Brabant, The Netherlands, July 6, 1942; came to U.S., 1963; s. Arnoldus A.P. and Maria A.A. (Horsten) S. T.C. in Edn. and Psychology, St. Stanislaus T.T.C., Tilburg, The Netherlands, 1962; BS in Biology summa cum laude, Loyola U., Los Angeles, 1966; PhD in Physiology with distinction, UCLA, 1970. Joined Bros. of Our Lady Mother of Mercy, Roman Cath. Ch., 1959. Tchr. Loon op Zand (The Netherlands) elem. schs., 1962-63, Santa Clara High Sch., Oxnard, Calif., 1965-67; research physiologist UCLA, 1970—; prof. biology Loyola Marymount U., Los Angeles, 1970—, assoc. dean sci., 1972—; mem. Los Angeles County Narcotics and Dangerous Drugs Commn., 1973—, Calif. State Adv. Bd. on Drug Programs, 1982—. Contbr. articles to profl. jours. Mem. AAUP, AAAS, The Biophys. Soc., Nat. Assn. Advisors for Health Professions (pres. 1978-84), Western Assn. Advisors for Health Professions, Sigma Xi, Sigma Pi Sigma. Democrat. Lodge: KC. Avocations: stamps, photography, travel, refereeing soccer. Office: Loyola Marymount U 7101 W 80th St Los Angeles CA 90045-2622

SMULLIN, PATRICIA CLARA, broadcasting and cable television executive; b. Eureka, Calif., Dec. 20, 1949; d. William Brothers and Patricia (Duell) S. BS in Communications and Psychology, Oreg. State U.; postgrad. Stanford U., So. Oreg. State U. Office mgr. So. Oreg. Cable TV, Medford, 1973-74, dir. consumer relations, 1974-76, v.p., 1976-82; pres. Calif. Oreg. Inc., Medford, 1982—; pres., bd. dirs. Pacific N.W. Cable Communications; mem. adv. council Rogue Community Coll. Mem. bd. dirs. YMCA, Medford, Rogue Valley Med. Ctr.; apptd. by Gov. to Oreg. Commn. Pub. Broadcasting. Recipient Oreg. Cable TV award. Mem. Oreg. Cable Communications Assn. (past pres., bd. dirs.), Nat. Assn. Broadcasters (bd. dirs., mem. 100 TV market com., congrl. relations com.), Oreg. Assn. Broadcasters (bd. dirs. and past pres.), Medford-Jackson C. of C. (bd. dirs.), Women in Cable TV (charter), Nat. Cable TV Assn., Stanford U. Alumni Assn., Rogue Valley Med. Ctr. (bd. dirs.), Rogue Valley Health Found., Medford-Jackson County C. of C. (bd. dirs.). Office: Calif Oreg Broadcasting Inc 125 S Fir St Medford OR 97501

SMUTNY, ROBERT JAROSLAV, classics educator; b. N.Y.C., Mar. 21, 1919; s. Rudolf V. and Elizabeth (Meskan) S.; m. Ernestine Smith, Aug. 30, 1947. AB, CCNY, 1940; AM, Columbia U., 1949; PhD, U. Calif., Berkeley, 1953. Instr. Latin The Manlius (N.Y.) Sch., 1942, 46-49; teaching asst. U. Calif., Berkeley, 1951-52; asst. prof. classical langs. U. N.Mex., Albuquerque, 1953-55; chmn. dept. classics U. Pacific, Stockton, Calif., 1955—, assoc. prof., 1955-59, prof., 1959—. Contbr. articles to profl. jours. Served with AUS, 1942-46. Mem. Am. Philol. Assn., Archaeol. Inst. Am., Calif. Classical Assn. (pres. No. sect. 1961-62), Philol. Assn. Pacific Coast. Office: U Pacific Dept Classics Stockton CA 95211

SMYSER, (CHARLES ARVIL) SKIP, senator, lawyer; b. Caldwell, Idaho, Nov. 14, 1949; s. Samuel H. and Mildred (Skelton) S.; m. Melinda Sloviaczek, Sept. 22, 1981; 1 child, Lincoln. BA, Eastern Wash. U., 1972; JD, Gonzaga U., 1977. Dep. pros. atty. Ada County, Boise, Idaho, 1977-79; dep. atty. gen. State of Idaho, Boise, 1979-80; ptnr. Connolly & Smyser, Boise and Parma, Idaho, 1980—; senator State of Idaho, 1982—; bd. dirs. Idaho State Sch. and Hosp., Nampa, 1983—. Rep. Idaho Ho. of Reps., Canyon County, 1980-82. Served to capt. Q.M.C., U.S. Amry, 1972-74. Named Legis. of Yr., Idaho Prosecuting Atty.'s Assn., one of Outstanding Young Men of Am., U.S. Jaycees, 1977-86. Mem. Idaho State Bar Assn. Republican. Presbyterian. Lodges: Lions (zone chmn. 1985-86), Masons. Avocations: sports, stamp collecting. Home: Rt 1 Box 1357 Parma ID 83660 Office: Connolly & Smyser 134 S 5th Boise ID 83702

SMYTH, DAVID SHANNON, real estate investor, commercial and retail builder and developer; b. Denver, May 13, 1943; s. William James and Constance Ruth (Sherman) S.; student Regis Coll., 1967-69, USAF Acad., 1961-65, U. No. Colo., 1965-67; m. Sharon Kaye Swiderski, Jan. 3, 1980; children—Julia Caitlin, Alexander Jeremiah, Matthew Davis; 1 son by previous marriage, Shannon David. Accountant, Colo. Nat. Bank, 1966-69; bus. analyst Dun & Bradstreet, 1969-70; pres., dir. Georgetown Valley Water & Sanitation Dist., 1973-74, Realists, Inc., 1973-74, Silver Queen Constrn. Co., 1973-74; v.p., sec., dir. Georgetown Assocs., Inc. (Colo.), 1970-74; pres., chief ops. officer Lincoln Cos., Denver, 1975-76; project mgr., sales mgr., prin. Brooks-Morris Homes, Fox Ridge, Colo., 1976-77; project mgr. U.S. West Homes, Denver, 1977-78; pres., dir. Denver Venture Capital, 1978-81; prin., dir., exec. v.p. Shelter Equities, Inc., 1982—; prin., dir., exec. v.p. Comml. Constrn. Mgmt. Services, Inc., Shelter Equities, Inc., 1984—; owner, dir., exec. v.p. Maple Leaf Realty Corp.; v.p., dir. Gibraltar Devel. Corp., Dominion Properties Ltd., 1978-82. Served with USAF, 1961-65. Lic. real estate broker. Home: 6093 E Briarwood Dr Englewood CO 80112 Office: Shelter Equities 8690 Wolff Ct #120 Westminster CO 80030

SMYTH, DOROTHY LILLIAN, real estate agency executive, musician, florist; b. Albuquerque, July 4, 1934; d. Joseph Franklin and Grace Lillian (Ruppee) Johnson; m. Leo Ralph Smyth, Sept. 2, 1953; children—Robert Lee, Larry Alan, Kathleen Ann Smyth Walsh. Student music edn. U. N.Mex., 1952-54; B.A., U. Tex.-El Paso, 1968. Lic. real estate agt., N.Mex.; cert. floral art designer, Albuquerque. Tchr. pub. schs., Los Lunas, N.Mex., 1952, pvt. tchr. music, Los Lunas, 1953-57, La Cueva, N.Mex., 1957-60, Los Lunas, 1960-64; postmaster, La Cueva, 1958-60; tchr. music, kindergarten pub. schs., El Paso, 1964-69; real estate agent N.Mex. Farm Bur., 1973-75; real estate agt. Century 21, Robertson Realty, Inc., Albuquerque, 1975-83, co-owner, mgr., relocation dir., 1977—, also trainer; owner, mgr. Smyth Flower & Greenhouse, Albuquerque, 1980—. Active extension clubs N.Mex. Extension Service, 1960-64; pres. Mesa Vista PTA, El Paso, 1964-69; sec. Booster Club West Mesa, N.Mex., 1969-75; vol. 4-Seasons Nursing Home, Albuquerque; mem. choir, dir. Sunday Sch. Fruit Avenue Bapt. Ch., Albuquerque. Recipient numerous certs. N.Mex. Extension Service; cert. Albuquerque Bd. Realtors. Mem. Nat. Realtor Assn., Albuquerque C. of C. Republican. Home: 192 Willow Rd NW Albuquerque NM 87107 Office: Norris Realty Inc 2511 Rio Grande NW Albuquerque NM 87102

SMYTH, JACK BORDEN, computer retail company executive; b. Cleve., Jan. 5, 1947; s. Clark Pidgeon and Gladys Marie (Cherna) S.; m. Linn Elizabeth Jensen, Aug. 23, 1969; children—Kristy Newett, Karen Elizabeth, Kim Mc Lean. B.S. in Indsl. Engring., Cornell U., 1969; M.B.A., Stanford U., 1975. Cert. welder, Ohio. Owner, operator Univ. Photo Service, Ithaca, N.Y., 1968-69; tech. rep. Lincoln Electric Co., Cleve. and Chgo., 1969-73; regional dir. Nat. Affiliation Concerned Bus. Students, San Francisco and Chgo., 1973-75; sales mgr. data processing products TAB Products Co., Palo Alto, Calif., 1975-77, nat. mktg. dir., 1977; nat. sales mgr. media products Electronic Memories and Magnetics, San Jose, Calif., 1977-78; product mgr. INMAC, Santa Clara, Calif., 1978-80; co-founder, exec. v.p. Challenge Computer Supplies, Palo Alto, 1980-81, dir., 1980-81; co-founder, pres. Learning Co., Menlo Park, Calif., 1981-82, dir., 1981-82; founder, pres., dir. Add-on Software Inc., Menlo Park, 1983-85; v.p. sales and mktg. Software Access Internat., Inc., Mountain View, Calif., 1984-85; chief exec. officer ChildWare Corp., Menlo Park, 1984-85; product line dir. Businessland, Inc., San Jose, 1985—; dir. Clarence J. Hicks meml. fellow, 1974. Mem. Stanford U. Bus. Sch. Alumni Assn. (dir. 1982-84, Bay Area coordinator 1981-82, pres. Peninsula chpt. 1980-81, v.p. programs 1979-80, v.p. communications 1978-79, founding mem. alumni council 1985—), Peninsula Mktg. Assn. (dir. 1976-79, pres. 1977-78). Republican. Christian Scientist. Clubs: Stanford Golf, Alpine Hills Tennis. Author: (pamphlet) Marketing Research: A Tool for Strategic Planning, 1974. Home: 1899 White Oak Dr Menlo Park CA 94025 Office: Businessland 1001 Ridder Park Dr San Jose CA 95131

SNAPP, BARBARA DENNISTON, biology educator, researcher; b. Oakland, Calif., Oct. 23, 1945; d. Edward Evans and Nancy (Fahnestock) Denniston; m. Craig Pletcher Snapp, Aug. 24, 1968; children: Robyn Christine, Amy Elisabeth. BA, Wells Coll., 1967; postgrad., Duke U., 1967-68; PhD, Cornell U., 1973. Research assoc. Stanford (Calif.) U., 1974-80, lectr. biology, 1984—; safety engr. Hewlett-Packard, San Jose, Calif., 1980; mgmt. analyst Santa Clara County, San Jose, 1981-83. Contbr. articles to profl. jours. Grantee NSF, 1968-71, NIH, 1975-77. Mem. AAAS, Sigma Xi, Phi Beta Kappa. Avocations: natural history, geneal. research. Office: Stanford U Dept Biol Scis Stanford CA 94306

SNARE, CARL LAWRENCE, JR., business executive; b. Chgo., Oct. 25, 1936; s. Carl Lawrence and Lillian Marie (Luoma) S.; B.B.A., Northwestern U., 1968; postgrad. Roosevelt U.; postgrad. in econs. San Francisco State U., 1976-77. Cert. fin. planner. Asst. sec., controller Bache Halsey Stuart & Shields Inc. (now Prudential Bache), Chgo., 1968-73; controller Innisfree Corp. div. Hyatt Corp., Burlingame, Calif., 1973-76; cash mgr. Portland (Oreg.) Gen. Electric Co., 1976-79; chief fin. officer, controller Vistar Fin. Inc., Marina del Rey, Calif., 1979-82; chief fin. officer, v.p., controller Carson Estate Co., Rancho Dominguez, Calif., 1982—; pres. Snare Properties Co., Rialto, Calif., 1984—, Snare Fin. Services Corp., Rialto, 1985—; registered investment advisor. C.P.A., real estate broker, cert. fin. planner, Calif. Mem. Am. Inst. C.P.A.s, Calif. Soc. C.P.A.s (real estate com. Los Angeles Chpt.), Internat. Assn. Fin. Planners, Am. Inst. Fin. Planners. Founder Cash Mgmt. Assn., Portland, Oreg. Home: 1131 Wisteria Ave Rialto CA 92376 Office: 17925 S Santa Fe Ave Rancho Dominguez CA 90220

SNAVELY, ODELL LEROY, businessman, clergyman; b. Lindsay, Okla., June 14, 1918; s. William Patrick and Cenith Dove (Cox) S.; m. Evelyn Marie McDonald, Mar. 27, 1946; children—Gary, Carol. Student Pacific Bible Sem., 1957; M.Th., Reed Coll. Religion, 1959. Salesman, 1950-61; ordained to ministry Christian Ch., 1961; pastor Buena Park, Calif., 1961-67; bus. license supr. City of South Gate (Calif.), 1967-77; owner Del's Gift Shop, South Gate, 1977—; mayor City of South Gate, 1980-81, 82-83. Served with USNR, 1943-46. Mem. South Gate C. of C. Democrat. Clubs: Kiwanis, Eagles. Home: 8992 Annetta Ave South Gate CA 90280 Office: 8650 California Ave South Gate CA 90280

SNEED, JOSEPH DONALD, philosophy educator, author; b. Durant, Okla., Sept. 23, 1938; s. Dabney Whitfield and Sallybelle (Atkinson) S. B.S., Rice U., 1960; M.S., U Ill., 1962; Ph.D., Stanford U., 1964. Prof. Stanford U., Palo Alto, Calif., 1966-73; policy analyst SRI Internat., Menlo Park, Calif., 1973-74; prof. U. Munich, 1974-75, U. Eindhoven, Holland, 1976-77, SUNY, Albany, 1977-79; prof. philosophy Colo. Sch. Mines, Golden, 1980—. Author: The Logical Structure of Mathematical Physics, 1971, (with W. Balzer and C. Moulines) An Architectonic for Science, 1986; editor: (with S. Waldhorn) Restructuring the Federal System, 1974. Mem. Am. Philos. Assn. Office: Colo Sch Mines Golden CO 80401

SNELL, RICHARD, hotel company executive; b. Phoenix, Nov. 26, 1930; s. Frank L. and Elizabeth (Berlin) S.; m. Alice Cosette Wiley, Aug. 1, 1954. B.A., Stanford U., 1952, J.D., 1954. Bar: Ariz. Ptnr. firm Snell & Wilmer, Phoenix, 1956-81; pres., chmn., chief exec. officer Ramada Inns, Inc., Phoenix, 1981—; dir. Ariz. Public Service Co., Western Tech. Inc. Bd. dirs. Am. Grad. Sch. Internat. Mgmt., Phoenix; past pres. YMCA Met. Phoenix and Valley of Sun. Served with U.S. Army, 1954-56. Mem. Am., Ariz., Maricopa County bar assns. Republican. Lutheran. Clubs: Paradise Valley Country, John Gardiner's Tennis Ranch. Office: Ramada Inns Inc 3838 E Van Buren St Phoenix AZ 85008

SNIFFIN, WILLIAM CHARLES, newspaper publisher, editor; b. Wadena, Iowa, Mar. 21, 1946; s. Thomas David and Betty Laverne (Brockmeyer) S.; m. Nancy Rae Musich, May 14, 1966; children—Alicia, Michelle, Amber, Michael. Student Iowa State U., 1964, Midwestern Coll., 1965-66; student U. Wales, 1986. Sports editor Harlan Newspapers, Iowa, 1964-65, news editor, 1966-70; sports editor Denison Newspapers, Iowa, 1965-66; publisher Wyo. State Jour., Lander, 1970—; v.p. Sage Pub. Co., Cody, Wyo., 1971-82; sec. Star Pub. Co., Green River, Wyo., 1975-82; pres. Telemax Corp., Lander, Wyo., 1981—, Mountain Am. Communications, Spearfish, S.D., 1982—; pres. Leader Corp., 1981-83, 84—. Mem. Nat. Newspaper Assn. (nat. com. chmn., recipient 44 awards 1969—), Wyo. Press Assn. (pres. 1980, recipient 163 awards 1970—), Iowa Press Assn. (recipient 29 awards 1964-70), Lander C. of C. Roman Catholic. Lodges: Rotary (dir. 1974), K.C. Home: 28 Boulder Loop Lander WY 82520 Office: Wyo State Jour 188 N 3rd St Lander WY 82520

SNODGRASS, GARY L(ESLIE), consulting firm executive, educator; b. Dec. 12, 1946. BS in Pharmacy, U. Nebr., 1969; PharmD, U. Cin., 1974; MEd in Med. Edn., U. Ill., 1976; MBA, Pepperdine U., 1985. Resident Children's Hosp., Cin., 1974-76; asst. prof. U. Ill., Chgo., 1974-76; dir. clin. pharmacy dept. U. R.I., Kingston, 1976-80; dir. clin. edn. H.P.I. Health Care Services, Los Angeles, 1980-82, asst. v.p., clin. services, 1982-83, v.p. profl. services, 1983-85; pres. Snodgrass, Kean Assoc., Los Angeles, 1985—; cons. Quest Med., Dallas, 1984, Euclid Med., Cleve., 1984; faculty mem. Brown U., Pawtucket, R.I., 1979-80. Co-author Quality Assurance in Hospital Pharmacy, 1983; editor Drug Information Newsletter, 1980-85; exam writer Nat. Assn. of Bds. of Pharmacy; contbr. articles to profl. jours. Fellow Bur. Health Resources and Devel., 1975, Ctr. for Ednl. Devel., 1974; grantee Smith Kline Pharms. Mem. Calif. Soc. Hosp. Pharmacists, Am. Cons. League, Am. Mktg. Assn., Am. Soc. Hosp. Pharmacists. Avocations: billiards, poker, camping. Home and Office: Snodgrass-Kean Assocs 1786 Deerhill Trail Topanga CA 90290

SNOOK, QUINTON, constrn. co. exec.; b. Atlanta, July 15, 1925; s. John Wilson and Charlotte Louise (Clayson) S.; student U. Idaho, 1949-51; m. Lois Mullen, Jan. 19, 1947; children—Lois Ann Snook Matteson, Quinton A., Edward M., Clayson S., Charlotte T. Rancher, Lemhi Valley, Idaho, 1942—; owner, mgr. Snook Constrn., Salmon, Idaho, 1952—; owner Snook Trucking, 1967—, Lemhi Posts and Poles, 1980—. Mem. Lemhi County Commn., Dist. 2, 1980—. Mem. Am. Quarter Horse Assn., Farm Bur., Nat. Rifleman's Assn., Am. Hereford Assn., Idaho Cattlemen's Assn. Republican. Episcopalian. Club: Elks. Home: Route 1 Box 49 Salmon ID 83467

SNOW, DONALD RAY, mathematician, educator; b. Los Angeles, Mar. 19, 1931; s. Eldon Stafford and Mary Lavere (Baker) S.; m. Diane Manwaring, Mar. 21, 1958; children: Donald Ray, Linda, Judy, Kathleen, Jennifer, James Robert. B.S. in Mech. Engring, U. Utah, 1959, B.A. in Math, 1959; M.S. in Mech. Engring, Stanford U., 1960, M.S. in Math, 1962, Ph.D. in Math, 1965. Research asst. Stanford Computation Center, 1961-62; research engr. Lockheed Missiles and Space Co., 1962-64; research asso. U. Minn., Mpls., 1964-66; asst. prof. math. U. Colo., Boulder, 1966-69; assoc. prof. math. Brigham Young U., Provo, Utah, 1969-74; prof. math. Brigham Young U., 1974—; vis. prof., Lima, Peru, 1974; vis. research prof. U. Waterloo, Ont., Can., 1976-77. Contbr. articles to profl. jours. Served with USN, 1953-55. Recipient Hamilton Watch award U. Utah, 1959, Alcuin Gen. Edn. Teaching award, 1986—; fellow AEC, 1959-61, Fulbright-Hayes Found., 1974. Mem. Am. Math. Soc., Math. Assn. Am. (lectr. 1978—), Soc. Indsl. and Applied Math., Utah Council Computers in Edn. (bd. dirs. 1982-85, chmn. ann. programming contest for secondary sch. students 1984-87), Nat. Council Tchrs. Math., Rocky Mountain Math. Consortium (bd. dirs. 1970—), AAAS, Sigma Xi, Phi Kappa Phi, Tau Beta Pi, Pi Tau Sigma. Mormon. Home: 3212 Mojave Ln Provo UT 84604 Office: Dept Math Brigham Young U Provo UT 84602

SNOW, MICHAEL DENNIS, biology educator; b. Sacramento, Nov. 9, 1942; s. George Othur and Margaret C. (Nix) S.; m. Charlene Ann De Cuir, June 11, 1966; children: Julian, Sherman. BA, U. B.C., Vancouver, 1961, Calif. State U., Sacramento, 1965; PhD, Wash. State U., 1974. Prof. biology U. Portland, Oreg., 1970—, chmn. dept. phys. and life scis., 1977-80; research assoc. EPA, Corvallis, Oreg., 1981-82, Oreg. State U., Corvallis, 1982-83. Contbr. articles to profl. jours. Co-founder, chmn. St. Mary's Woods State Park Com., Beaverton, Oreg., 1975-80. Faculty Devel fellow NSF, 1981-82; grantee EPA, 1983, 85. Mem. AAAS, Am. Soc. Plant Physiologists, Sigma Xi. Democrat. Avocation: gardening. Office: U Portland 500 N Willamette Portland OR 97203

SNOW, TOWER CHARLES, JR., lawyer; b. Boston, Oct. 28, 1947; s. Tower Charles and Margaret (Harper) S. AB cum laude, Dartmouth Coll., 1969; JD, U. Calif., Berkeley, 1973. Bar: Calif. 1973, U.S. Dist. Ct. (no. dist.) Calif. 1973, U.S. Dist. Ct. (ea. dist.) Calif. 1979, U.S. Ct. Appeals (fed. cir.) 1980, U.S. Ct. Claims 1980, U.S. Supreme Ct. 1976. Ptnr., chmn. litigation dept. Orrick, Herrington & Sutcliffe, San Francisco, 1973—; arbitrator Nat. Assn. Securities Dealers, N.Y. Stock Exchange, Pacific Coast Stock Exchange, Superior Ct. City and County San Francisco; lectr. Author: numerous law handbooks and articles to prof. jours. Mem. San Francisco Museum Soc., San Francisco Symphony. Mem. ABA (assoc., chmn. subcom. pub. offering litigation), Continuing Edn. Bar (bus. law inst. planning com.), San Francisco Bar Assn., Securities Industry Assn., Nat. Inst. Trial Advocacy. Democrat. Club: Commonwealth (San Francisco). Avocations: internat. travel, skiing, running, scuba diving, photography. Home: 9 Wyngaard Ave Piedmont CA 94611 Office: Orrick Herrington & Sutcliffe 600 Montgomery St San Francisco CA 94111

SNOW, WILLIAM HOWARD, research psychology educator; b. Calumet, Mich., Oct. 15, 1954; s. Wayne Clifford and Rosemary (Rastello) S.; m. Deborah Jean Geesey, Nov. 22, 1954; children: Jared, Tarah, Shelly. AA, N.W. Coll., 1979; BA in Social Welfare, Pacific Luth. U., 1980, MA in Family Therapy, 1981; PhD in Social Work, U. Wash., 1985. Dir. New Hope Counseling, Spanaway, Wash., 1979-81; psychotherapist Lakewood Profl. Counseling Ctr., Tacoma, 1981-86; asst. prof. psychology Bethany Coll., Santa Cruz, Calif., 1986—; researcher U. Wash., Seattle, 1982-86. Contbr. articles to profl. jours. Crisis worker Greater Lakes Mental Health Ctr., Tacoma, 1981-83. Served with U.S. Army, 1973-77. Mem. Nat. Assn. Social Workers, Am. Assn. Marriage and Family Therapy, Soc. Adolescent Research. Mem. Ch. Assemblies of God. Avocations: computer applications, guitar, running, bicycling, camping. Home: 905 Canham Scotts Valley CA 95066 Office: Bethany Coll 800 Bethany Dr Santa Cruz CA 95066

SNOWDEN, DIANA EMILY, utility company executive; b. N.Y.C., Oct. 29, 1947; d. Joseph Philip and Barbara Ellen (O'Mara) Loftus; m. Arthur Holburn Snowden II, June, 1, 1968 (div. Dec. 1982); children: Kirsten M., Arthur Neilan III. BA, Trinity Coll., 1968; MA, U. Alaska, 1983. Asst. v.p., treas. Westwood Mgmt. Corp., Bethesda, Md., 1970-73; dir. employee relations Anchorage Sch. Dist., 1973-79; v.p. indsl. relations Alascom and Tel Utilities, Inc., Anchorage, 1979-81; commr. Alaska Pub Utilities Commn., Anchorage, 1981-85; exec. dir. PNUCC, Portland, Oreg., 1985-86; v.p. human resources Pacific Power and Light, Portland, 1986—; cons. Alaska Gas Pipeline Adv. Bd., Anchorage, 1985—. Commr. Alaska State

Human Rights Commn., Anchorage, 1976-81, chairperson; mem. Alaska Adv. Bd. U.S. Commn. on Civil Rights, 1979-81; bd. dirs. Anchorage Youth Adv. Bd., 1974-76; bd. dirs. Bus Youth Exchange, 1986—; bd. dir. Greater Bus. Group on Health, 1986—. Mem. Nat. Assn. Regulatory Utility Commrs., 1981-84. Republican. Roman Catholic. Home: 4405 SW Council Crest Dr Portland OR 97201 Office: Pacific Power and Light Co 920 SW 6th Ave Portland OR 97204

SNYDER, ALLEGRA FULLER, dance educator; b. Chgo., Aug. 28, 1927; d. R. Buckminster and Anne (Hewlett) Fuller; m. Robert Snyder, June 30, 1951 (div. Apr. 1975, remarried Sept. 1980); children: Alexandra, Jaime. BA in Dance, Bennington Coll., 1951; MA in Dance, UCLA, 1967. Asst. to curator, dance archives Mus. Modern Art, N.Y.C., 1945-47; dancer Ballet Soc. of N.Y.C. Ballet Co., 1945-47; mem. office and prodn. staff Internat. Film Found., N.Y.C., 1950-52; editor, dance films Film News mag., N.Y.C., 1966-72; lectr. dance and film adv., dept. dance UCLA, 1967-73, chmn. dept. dance, 1974-80, acting chair, spring 1985, prof. dance and dance ethnology, 1973—; vis. lectr. Calif. Inst. of Arts, Valencia, 1972; co-dir. dance and TV workshop Am. Dance Fest., Conn. Coll., New London, 1973; dir. NEH summer seminar for coll. tchrs. Asian Performing Arts, 1978, 81; coord. Ethnic Arts Intercoll. Interdisciplinary program, 1974-83, acting chmn., 1986; vis. prof. performance studies NYU, 1982-83; hon. vis. prof. U. Surrey, Guildford, Eng., 1983-84; bd. dirs. Buckminster Fuller Inst.; cons. Thyodia Found., Salt Lake City, 1973-74; mem. dance adv. panel Nat. Endowment Arts, 1968-72, Calif. Arts Commn., 1974; mem. adv. screening com. Council Internat. Exchange of Scholars, 1979-82; mem. dance panelmem. various panels NEH, 1979-85; mem. adv. bd. Los Angeles Dance Alliance, 1978-84; cons. dance film series Am. Film Inst, 1974-75. Dir. film Baroque Dance 1625-1725, in 1977; co-dir. film Gods of Bali, 1952; dir. and wrote film Bayanihan, 1962 (named Best Folkloric Documentary at Bilboa Film Festival, winner Golden Eagle award); asst. dir. and asst. editor film The Bennington Story, 1952; created films Gestures of Sand, 1968, Reflections on Choreography, 1973, When the Fire Dances Between Two Poles, 1982; created film, video loop and text Celebration: A World of Art and Ritual, 1982-83; supr. post-prodn. film Erick Hawkins, 1964, in 1973. Also contbr. articles to profl. jours. and mags. Adv. com. Pacific Asia Mus., 1980-84, Festival of the Mask, Craft and Folk Art Mus., 1979-84; adv. panel Los Angeles Dance Currents II, Mus. Ctr. Dance Assn., 1974-75; bd. dirs. Council Grove Sch. III, Compton, Calif., 1976-81; apptd. mem. Adv. Dance Com., Pasadena (Calif.) Art Mus., 1970-71, Los Angeles Festival of Performing Arts com., Studio Watts, 1970; mem. Technology and Cultural Transformation com., UNESCO, 1977. Fulbright research fellow, 1983-84; grantee Nat. Endowment Arts, 1981, Nat. Endowment Humanities, 1977, 79, 81, UCLA, 1968, 77, 80, 82, 85. Mem. Am. Dance Therapy Assn., Congress on Research in Dance (bd. dirs. 1970-76, chairperson 1975-77, nat. conf. chair 1972), Council Dance Adminstrs., Am. Dance Guild (chairperson com. awards, 1972), Soc. for Ethnomusicology, Am. Anthropol. Assn., Am. Folklore Soc., Soc. Anthropology of Visual Communication, Soc. Anthropol. Study of Play, Soc. Humanistic Anthropology, Calif. Dance Educators Assn. (conf. chair 1972), Los Angeles Area Dance Alliance (adv. bd. 1978-84, selection com. Dance Kaleidoscope project 1979-81), Fulbright Alumni Assn. Home: 15313 Whitfield Ave Pacific Palisades CA 90272 Office: UCLA Dept Dance 124 Dance Bldg Los Angeles CA 90024

SNYDER, CHARLES THEODORE, geologist; b. Powell, Wyo., July 19, 1912; s. Lee G. and Eda Belle (Hansen) S.; m. Marion Ruth Harris, Dec. 22, 1945 (dec. 1973); children: Anita Maria, Kristin Eileen; m. Alberta Irene Dangel, Oct. 15, 1973. BS, U. Ariz., 1948. Registered profl. geologist, Calif. Hydrologist U.S. Geol. Survey, Menlo Park, Calif., 1948-75; dir. Scotts Valley (Calif.) Water Dist., 1980-84; vis. scientist Carter County Mus., Ekalaka, Mont., 1983-84. Author: Effect of Off-Road Vehicles, 1976. Disaster chmn. ARC, 1982-83. Mem. AAAS, Arctic Inst. N.Am., Soc. Vertebrate Paleontologists. Republican. Presbyterian. Home: 552-17 Bean Creek Rd Scotts Valley CA 95066

SNYDER, ERNEST PENNEY, social service director, psychotherapist; b. Somerset, Pa., Dec. 28, 1946. Student, W.Va. U., 1965-68; BA, Northridge State Coll., 1970; postgrad., Met. State Coll., Denver, 1972; MSW, Barry U., 1975; postgrad., Calif. Coast U., 1986—. Coordinator social services St. Patrick's Children's Home, Sacramento, 1977-78; social worker Lane Children's Ctr., Sebastopol, Calif., 1978; coordinator social services Child Opportunity Program, Denver, 1980-81; clin. social worker Family Counseling Services, Monroe, Wash., 1984-86; pvt. practice social work E.P.S. Assocs., Seattle, 1983—; dir. social services Adoption Advocates Internat., Pt. Angeles, Wash., 1983—. Creator Adoption Game, 1984. Chmn. organizing com. United Food and Comml. Workers Union local 7, Denver, 1981; vol. Gay-Lesbian Community Ctr., Denver, 1981. Mem. Nat. Assn. Social Workers (cert.), Register Clin. Social Workers (diplomate). Office: EPS Assocs PO Box 55323 Seattle WA 98155

SNYDER, HOWARD ARTHUR, aerospace engineering sciences educator, industrial consultant; b. Palmerton, Pa., Mar. 7, 1930; s. Howard Franklin and Mary Rachel (Landis) S.; m. Nancy June Simon, Sept. 14, 1961 (div. Feb. 1975); m. Kaye Elizabeth Bache, Mar. 21, 1975. BS in Physics, Rensselaer Poly. Inst., 1952; MS in Physics, U. Chgo., 1957, PhD in Physics, 1961. From asst. prof. to assoc. prof. Brown U., Providence, 1961-68; assoc. prof. aerospace engring. U. Colo., Boulder, 1968—; cons. Storage Tech. Corp., Louisville, Colo., 1980-84, Ball Aerospace Systems, Boulder, 1984—. Contbr. articles to profl. jours. Served to lt. (j.g.) USN, 1948-55. Mem. Am. Phys. Soc. Club: Colo. Mountain (Denver). Home: 251 Gay St Longmont CO 80501 Office: U Colo Dept of Aerospace Engring Sci Campus Box 429 Boulder CO 80309

SNYDER, JAMES JOSEPH, agricultural aviation consultant; b. Chgo., Dec. 14, 1931; s. John Alexander and Estelle Cecelia (Clark) S.; m. Mable Victoria Fagundes, Aug. 31, 1956; children: Audrey, Ravenna, Paul, John. AA, Reedley Coll., 1954. Cert. comml. instrument pilot, airframe and power plant mechanic, journeyman agrl. pilot, Calif. Pilot, mechanic Seaboard World Agrl., Europe, Africa, 1966, Haley Flying Service, Tracy, Calif., 1968-71, Kenny's Crop Dusting, Caruthers, Calif., 1971-77; pilot Western Agrl. Aviation, Tranquility, Calif., 1978-82; agrl. aviation cons. Kingsburg, Calif., 1982—; pilot dir., dist. 3 Calif. Agrl. Aircraft Assn., Sacramento, 1981-85, also safety observer, 1985; cons. Human Resources Research Orgn., Alexandria, Va., 1983—. Co-author: Professional Standards, 1984; co-editor technical appendices for several applications; producer videotape for agrl. aviation; contbr. articles to mags. Served as sgt. USAF, 1949-52. Mem. Nat. Agrl. Aircraft Assn., Calif. Agrl. Aircraft Assn. (outstanding airman award 1983), Nat. Ryan Club, Mensa. Avocation: reading. Home: 2350 19th Ave Kingsburg CA 93631

SNYDER, JANET RUTH, violinist, music educator; b. Berkeley, Calif., Nov. 29, 1932; d. Harry Birge and Marion Virginia (Biggerstaff) O'Brien; m. John Valentine Snyder, Nov. 28, 1952; children—Carol Jeanne, Jeffrey William, Michael William. A.A. in Bus., Armstrong Coll., 1951. Exec. sec. Kaiser Steel Corp., Oakland, Calif., 1951-57; pvt. violin tchr., Idaho Falls, Idaho, 1955—; lectr., violin, viola instr. Idaho State U., Pocatello, Idaho, 1987—; tchr. strings Dist. 91, Idaho Falls, 1980-82; prin. violist Idaho Falls Symphony, 1980—; concert mistress Idaho State Civic Symphony, Pocatello, 1981—; concertmistress Idaho Falls Opera Assn., 1980—; violist Teton Music Festival Seminar, Jackson, Wyo., 1982. Mem. Idaho Music Educators Assn., Pocatello Music Club, Idaho Falls Music Club. Republican. Presbyterian. Home: 1675 Shasta St Idaho Falls ID 83402

SNYDER, JOHN JOSEPH, optometrist; b. Wonewoc, Wis., June 30, 1908; s. Burt Frederick and Alta Lavinia (Hearn) S.; A.B., UCLA, 1931, postgrad., 1931-32; postgrad. U. Colo., 1936, 38, 40, 41, U. So. Calif., 1945-46; B.S. in Optometry, Los Angeles Coll. Optometry, 1948, O.D., 1949. Tchr., La Plata County (Colo.) Pub. Schs., 1927-28; supt. Marvel (Colo.) Pub. Schs., 1932-33; tchr. Durango (Colo.) High Sch., 1933-41; pvt. practice optometry, Los Angeles, 1951-72, Torrance, Calif., 1972-78; now vacation and emergency relief optometrist. Former bd. dirs. Francis Boys' Club, Los Angeles; former pres. Exchange Club South Los Angeles, also sec. Mem. AAAS, Nat. Eye Research Found., Am. Inst. Biol. Scis., Am., Calif., Los Angeles County optometric assns., Internat. Biog. Assn. Republican. Home: 735 Luring Dr Glendale CA 91206

SNYDER, JOYCE COMBS, human services agency administrator; b. Canton, Ohio, Oct. 19, 1927; d. Arthur Oliver and Corinne Louise (Dierker) Combs; m. Ellsworth Snyder, Feb. 18, 1950 (div.); children—Candace Ann, Bradley Andrew. B.A. cum laude, Gettysburg Coll., 1950; M.B.A., Nat. U., 1979. Govt. sales mgr. Gilpin Drug Co., Washington, 1950-52; exec. dir. Community Christian Service Agy. Inc., San Diego, 1973—; cons. North Park and Mid-City Christian Service Agys.; founder Clairemont Friendship Ctr., 1976. Mem. Psi Chi, Alpha Xi Delta. Republican. Lutheran. Home: 4973 Pacifica Dr San Diego CA 92109 Office: Community Christian Service Agy 4167 Rappahannock Ave San Diego CA 92117

SNYDER, LLOYD ROBERT, chemistry consultant; b. Sacramento, July 30, 1931; s. Lloyd and Gladys Emma (Haven) S.; m. Barbara Ann Sheppard, Feb. 3, 1952; children: Julie Ann, Thomas Lloyd, James Paul, David Frederick. BS, U. Calif., Berkeley, 1952, PhD, 1954. Research chemist Shell Oil Co., Houston, 1954-56; sr. research assoc. Union Oil, Brea, Calif., 1956-71; v.p. Technicon Corp., Tarrytown, N.Y., 1971-82; pres. LRS Corp., Yorktown, N.Y., 1982-85; v.p. LC Resources, Orinda, Calif., 1985—; adj. research prof. Pace U., Pleasantville, N.Y., 1979—; cons. E.I. Du Pont de Nemours Co., Wilmington, Del., 1982—. Author: Principles Adsorption Chromatography, 1968, Int. Separation Science, 1973, Int. Modern Liquid Chromatography, 1974, 2d rev. edit., 1979. Recipient Steven Dal Nogare Meml. award Del. Valley Chromatography Forum, 1976, Chromatography Meml. medal Sci. Council Acad. of Scis. of USSR, 1980, Pitts. Soc. award in Analytical Chemistry, 1984, Palmer award Minn. Chromatography Forum, 1985. Mem. Am. Chem. Soc. (chmn. Orange County sect. 1970-71, Petroleum Chemistry award 1970, Chromatography award 1984)., Republican. Presbyterian. Home: 26 Silverwood Ct Orinda CA 94563

SNYDER, THOMA MEES VAN'THOFF, scientist, engineer; b. Balt., May 21, 1916; s. Charles David and Aleida Jacoba (van'tHoff) S.; m. Charlotta Untiedt (dec. Dec. 1981); children—James Arthur, Charles Evans. Ph.D. in Physics, Johns Hopkins U., 1940. Registered profl. engineer, Calif. Instr. Princeton U., N.J., 1940-43; research assoc. Los Alamos Sci. Lab., 1943-45; mgr. physics, later reactor sect. Knolls Atomic Power Lab., Niskayuna, N.Y., 1946-55, mgr. research dept., 1955-57; mgr. physics Vallecitos Lab., Gen. Electric Co., Pleasanton, Calif., 1958-64, cons. scientist, engr. Nuclear Energy Operation, San Jose, Calif., 1964-84; mem. adv. bd. Atoms for Peace Confs. Contbr. articles to profl. jours. Patentee in field. Pres. El Camino Youth Symphony, Santa Clara County, Calif., 1964-67; bd. dirs. Crippled Children's Soc., Santa Clara County, 1969-71. Recipient Steinmetz award, Sec. of War citation, Sec. Navy citation. Fellow Am. Phys. Soc., Am. Nuclear Soc. (charter mem., pres. No. Calif. sect. 1959-62); mem. Astron. Soc. Pacific, Elfun Soc., Phi Beta Kappa, Sigma Xi. Republican.

SO, ALVIN YIU-CHEONG, sociology educator; b. Hong Kong, Sept. 1, 1953; s. Pui-kam and Sam-mui (Au) S.; m. Judy Mei-ling Chan, Jan. 18, 1978. BA, The Chinese U. of Hong Kong, Shatin, 1975; MA, UCLA, 1977, PhD, 1982. Research assoc. Asian Am. Studies Ctr. UCLA, 1980-82; mem. profl. staff Nat. Ctr. Bilingual Research, 1982-83; lectr. U. Hong Kong, 1983-84; asst. prof. sociology U. Hawaii, Manoa, 1984—. Author: The South China Silk District, 1986; contbr. articles to profl. jours. Fellow UCLA, 1979; Hong Kong Spinner scholar The Chinese U. of Hong Kong. Mem. Am. Sociol. Assn., Internat. Sociol. Assn., Assn. Asian Studies, Hawaiian Sociol. Assn., Alumni of East-West Ctr., Phi Beta Kappa. Avocations: chinese and internat. chess, novels, swimming. Office: U Hawaii Dept Sociology Porteus Hall 247 Manoa HI 96822

SO, KENNETH THAY, aerospace engineer; b. Phnom Penh, Peoples Republic of Kampuchea, Dec. 16, 1952; came to U.S., 1973; s. Bun Hor So and Laam Tan; m. Theany Kimchandabot Kim, July 12, 1980; 1 child, Elizabeth Kaliyan. BSChemE, U. Tenn., 1978. Engr. Ampex Corp., Redwood City, Calif., 1978-79, Rockwell Internat., Downey, Calif., 1979—; rep. from Rockwell to NASA Langley Research Ctr., Hampton, Va., 1986-87. Contbr. articles to profl. jours. Recipient Rockwell Internat. award, NASA award. Mem. Phi Kappa Phi, Tau Beta Pi. Republican. Buddhist. Avocations: volleyball, ping pong, bowling, painting. Office: Rockwell Internat 12214 Lakewood Blvd Mail Code FC48 Downey CA 90241

SO, RONALD MING CHO, engineering educator; b. Hong Kong, Nov. 26, 1939; came to U.S., 1966; s. Tsang Yee and Grace W.K. (Chan) S.; m. Mabel Yuen May Wu, Aug. 17, 1968; children: Winnie Wing Ning, Nelson Sing Keen. BS with honors, U. Hong Kong, 1962; M in Engring., McGill U., Montreal, Que., Can., 1966; MA, Princeton U., 1968, PhD, 1971. Engr. Shell Co., Hong Kong, 1962-63; instr. U. Hong Kong, 1963-64; research scientist Union Camp Corp., Princeton, N.J., 1970-72; asst. prof. Rutgers U., New Brunswick, N.J., 1972-76; research engr. Gen. Electric Research and Devel. Ctr., Schenectady, N.Y., 1976-81; prof. engring. Ariz. State U., Tempe, 1981—; cons. Research Cotrell, Piscataway, N.J., 1974-76, Garrett Pneumatic, Phoenix, 1982—; adj. prof. Fairleigh Dickenson U., Teaneck, N.J., 1975-76, Union Coll., Schenectady, 1977-80. Contbr. articles to profl. jours. Commonwealth scholar Can. Govt., Montreal, 1964-66; recipient Publ. award Gen. Electric Co., Schenectady, 1981. Mem. ASME, AIAA, Am. Phys. Soc., N.Y. Acad. Sci., Nev. Acad. Sci., Ariz. Acad. Sci. Home: 10393 E Becker Ln Scottsdale AZ 85260 Office: Ariz State U MAE Dept Tempe AZ 85287

SOALES, MADELYN GEDDES, speech-language pathologist; b. Summit, N.J., Aug. 24, 1953; d. Thomas and Jean Beattie (Sutherland) Geddes; m. Robert Keith Soales, Oct. 10, 1976; 1 child, Brian Keith. BS, Kean Coll. of N.J., 1975; MS, Rutgers U., 1976. Lic. speech pathologist, N.Mex., N.J. Speech/lang. pathologist Albuquerque Pub. Schs., 1976-85, Designs for Learning Differences, Albuquerque, 1985—; adminstrv. asst. Longfellow Community Sch., Albuquerque, 1983-85; supr. grad. students in speech-lang. pathology, Albuquerque, 1985-86. Active Community Edn. Council, Albuquerque, 1983-85; bd. mem. Albuquerque Pub. Schs., 1982-83; mem. steering com. N.Mex. Very Spl. Arts Festival, Albuquerque, 1983-85. Mem. Am. Speech-Lang. and Hearing Assn. (cert.), N.Mex. Speech-Lang. and Hearing Assn. Democrat. Presbyterian. Avocations: snow skiing, needlework. Home: 8132 Irwin NE Albuquerque NM 87109 Office: Designs for Learning Differences 8600 Academy NE Albuquerque NM 87111

SOARES, W. BUDDY, businessman, state senator; b. Honolulu, Sept. 4, 1929; student U. Hawaii; married, 4 children. Pres. Internat. Travel Service; dir. mktg. South Pacific, Aloha Airlines; dir. govt. affairs Hawaiian Electric Co.; sales mgr. hotel and restaurant div. AMFAC, Inc.; dir. mktg. and sales Kaanapali Beach, AMFAC Properties, Inc.; account exec. Pan Am.; gen. sales mgr. Western Dairy Products; mem. Hawaii Ho. of Reps., 1967-75, house leader, 1969, minority floor leader; mem. Hawaii Senate, 1975—, minority floor leader, 1980—. Mem. Hawaii Kai Community Assn., St. Louis Alumni Assn., Pacific Area Travel Assn., Am. Soc. Travel Agts., Hawaii Hotel Assn., Hawaii Visitors Bur., Hawaii C. of C. Office: 674 Pepeekeo St Honolulu HI 96825

SOBEL, KENNETH MARK, research electrical engineer; b. Bklyn., Oct. 3, 1954; s. Seymour Phillip and Marilyn (Nanus) S. BSEE, CCNY, 1976; MEngring, Rensselaer Poly. Inst., 1978, PhD, 1980. Sr. research specialist Lockheed Calif. Co., Burbank, 1980—; adj. asst. prof. U. So. Calif., Los Angeles, 1982—. Contbr. articles to profl. jours. Program vice-chmn. 1986 Am. Control Conf., Seattle. Mem. IEEE (sr., exhibits chmn. 23d conf. on decision and control 1984, tech. assoc. editor Control Systems mag., 1986—), AIAA, Am. Radio Relay League (life), Sigma Xi, Alpha Phi Omega. Office: Lockheed Calif Co D72-33 311 B-6 Burbank CA 91520

SOBIERALSKI, THEODORE JOSEPH, research chemist; b. South Bend, Ind., Dec. 21, 1952; s. Theodore Joseph and Alice Ann Sobieralski; m. Leslie Ann Short, July, 8, 1978; children: Nathan James, Scott Daniel, Brian Thomas. BA, U. Calif., San Diego, 1975; PhD, U. Calif., Davis, 1980. Postdoctoral assoc. MIT, Cambridge, 1980-82; research chemist Dow Chem. Co., Walnut Creek, Calif., 1982—; chemistry instr. Los Medanos Jr. Coll., Pittsburg, 1983—. Contbr. articles to profl. jours.; patentee in field. Eastman Kodak predoctoral fellow, 1976. Mem. Am. Chem. Soc., Internat. Soc. Optical Engring., Materials Research Soc. Republican. Roman Catholic. Avocations: golf, skiing, music. Office: Dow Chem Co 2800 Mitchell Dr Walnut Creek CA 94598

SOBIN, HARRIS JUNIUS, architecture educator, consultant, researcher; b. Boston, Sept. 5, 1931; s. Newton Harrison and Rena (Pearl) S.; m. Francoise Carmen Sanz, June 20, 1964; children—Anne-Christine, Isabelle Rena. A.B., Harvard U., 1953, J.D., 1956, M.Arch., 1961. Bar: Mass. 1957; registered architect, Ariz. Designer, Amaral and Morales, Hato Rey, P.R., 1959-61; researcher, lectr. Archtl. Assn., London, 1962-66; design cons. Urban Renewal and Housing Corp., Rio Piedras, P.R., 1967-68; asst. prof. U. P.R., Rio Piedras, 1967-70; asst. prof. U. Ariz., Tucson, 1970-78, prof., 1978—; vis. assoc. prof. Harvard Grad. Sch. Design, Cambridge, Mass., 1976-77; research cons. Skidmore, Owings & Merrill, Chgo., 1980, Eureka Labs., Inc., Sacramento, 1981, Fla. Solar Energy Ctr., Cape Canaveral, 1982-83; dir. Indsl. Devel. Authority, Florence, Ariz., Hist. Preservation Program, 1973-82. Author: Florence Townsite, A.T., 1977. Contbr. articles to profl. jours. Prin. works include Hotel Delicias, Fajardo, P.R., 1960 (PA Design citation 1961), Parish Ctr., Assumption Cath. Ch., Florence, Ariz., 1987. Bd. dirs. El Tiradito Found., Tucson; mem., acting chmn. Com. to Restore The Chapel of the Gila, Tucson, 1979-83. Fulbright scholar, Archtl. Assn., London, 1961-63, sr. Fulbright research scholar U.S. State Dept., Fondation Le Corbusier, Paris, 1976-77; grantee "City Options" program Nat. Endowment Arts, 1974, Architecture and Environ. Arts grantee 1976-77; recipient Recognition award, creativity in design, Nat. Endowment for Arts, 1980. Mem. AIA. Office: U Ariz Coll Architecture Tucson AZ 85721

SOBIN, SIDNEY S., physiology and biophysics educator, researcher; b. Bayonne, NJ, Jan. 1, 1914; s. Eva (Newman); m. Venus K. Karalis, Nov. 27, 1959; children: Paul B., Dione D. BS, U. Mich., 1935, PhD, 1938, MD, 1941. Diplomate Am. Bd. Internal Medicine. Prof. physiology U. So. Calif., Los Angeles, 1947-56, 1966—; research prof. medicine Loma Linda U., Los Angeles, 1957-66; dir. U. So. Calif. Cardiovascular Research Lab., 1957—. Contbr. numerous articles on microcirculation, aging and hypertension to profl. jours. Fellow ACP (assoc.); mem. Am. Physiol. Soc., Microcirculatory Soc. (pres. 1965-67, Landis award 1980), Alpha Omega Alpha. Office: Cardiovascular Research Lab 1200 N State St 301 Bldg 1 Los Angeles CA 90033

SOBOLEWSKI, JOHN STEPHEN, computer information scientist, director computer services, consultant; b. Krakow, Poland, July 14, 1939; came to U.S., 1966; s. Jan Zygmund and Stefania (Zwolinska) S.; m. Helen Skipper, Dec. 17, 1965 (div. July 1969); m. Carole Straith, Apr. 6, 1974; children: Anne-Marie, Elisa, Martin. BE, U. Adelaide, Adelaide, South Australia, 1962, ME, 1966; PhD in Computer Sci., Wash. State U., 1971. Sci. officer Weapons Research Establishment, Salisbury, South Australia, 1964-66; asst. prof. computer sci. Wash. State U., Pullman, 1966-73; dir. research, assoc. prof. U. Wash., Seattle, 1973-80, dir. computer services, 1980—; cons. govt. and industry, Seattle, 1973—; mem. bd. trustees Fisher Found., Seattle, 1984—. Author: Computers for the Dental Office, 1986; contbr. articles to profl. jours. Served as engr. with Royal Australian Army, 1957-60. Australian govt. scholar, 1954-60, Elec. Res. Bd. scholar CSIRO, Melbourne, Australia, 1961-64. Mem. IEEE, Computer Soc. Roman Catholic. Avocation: mineral collecting. Home: 18722 56th Ave NE Seattle WA 98155 Office: U Wash Mail Stop HG-45 Seattle WA 98195

SOBONYA, RICHARD EMORY, pathologist; b. Lakewood, Ohio, Apr. 15, 1942; s. Emory George and Louise Irene (Bauer) S.; m. Evangeline Ann Eybsen, May 30, 1967; children: Sarah, John, Amy. BS, U. Notre Dame, South Bend, Ind., 1963; MD, Case Western Reserve U., 1967. Resident in pathology Univ. Hosps., Cleve., 1967-72; staff pathologist U.S. Armed Forces Inst. Pathology, Washington, 1972-74; asst. prof. pathology U. Kans. Med. Ctr., Kansas City, 1974-77; assoc. prof. pathology U. Ariz., Tucson, 1977-86, prof. pathology, 1986—. Contbr. 41 articles to med. jours. Served to maj. U.S. Army, 1972-74. Mem. Am. Thoracic Soc., Internat. Acad. Pathology. Avocations: fishing, collecting lepidoptera, natural history. Home: 4825 Via Chapo Tucson AZ 85718 Office: U Ariz Health Scis Ctr Dept Pathology Tucson AZ 85724

SODERLUND, PAUL HENRY, clothing executive, information systems consultant; b. Seattle, July 20, 1937; s. Henry John and Eugenie (Jobe) S.; m. Judith Ann Williams, Nov. 17, 1962; children: Kristin, Jon, Anne Marie. BSBA, U. Wash., 1960; student, U. Oreg., 1964. Cert. systems profl. Sr. systems analyst Evans Products, Portland, Oreg., 1967-69; dir. info. services White Stag Mfg., Portland, 1969-81, v.p. info. services, 1981—; owner, cons. Cascades Mgmt. Systems, Gresham, Oreg., 1985—. Contbr. articles to profl. jours. Served with USNR, 1980-82. Mem. Assn. Systems Mgmt. (div. council chmn. 1986—, Merit award 1981). Republican. Avocations: photography, bicycling, canoeing. Home: 800 New Bella Vista Pl Gresham OR 97030 Office: White Stag Mfg Co 5100 SE Harney Dr Portland OR 97206

SOELBERG, NICHOLAS RAY, chemical research engineer; b. Grand Junction, Colo., Feb. 11, 1956; s. John Adam and Joan Mahalia (Jensen) S.; m. LuAnn Ferkovich, Aug. 14, 1984; children: 1 child, Jeffrey Kent. BS, Brigham Young U., 1980, MS, 1983. Engr. Phillips Petroleum Co., Houston, 1980-81; research asst. Combustion Lab. Brigham Young U., Provo, Utah, 1981-83, cons., 1983; project engr. Babcock & Wilcox Co., Alliance, Ohio, 1983-84; research engr. Energy & Environ. Research Corp., Irvine, Calif., 1984—. Contbr. articles on fuel scis. to profl. jours. Mem. Sigma Xi (assoc.), Tau Beta Pi. Republican. Mormon. Avocations: sports, travel, ham radio. Home: 26204 Via Roble Mission Viejo CA 92691 Office: Energy & Environ Research Corp 8001 Irvine Blvd Santa Ana CA 92705

SOFIA, PAPATHEODOROU, chemistry educator; b. N.Y.C., Feb. 15, 1940; s. Theodore and Stavroula (Koutoupis) P. Student, U. Rochester, 1957-59, Hunter Coll., 1959-60; BS, U. Miami, 1962, MS, 1965, PhD, 1978. Lab. instr. Miami-Dade (Fla.) Community Coll., 1976-78; adj. instr. chemistry Fla. Internat. U., Miami, 1976-78; postdoctoral fellow Papanicolaou Cancer Research Inst., Miami, 1979-81; lectr. chemistry Calif. State U., Fresno, 1981-84; asst. prof. chemistry Calif. State U., Carson, 1985—. Contbr. articles to profl. jours. Active Greek Orthodox Ch. St. Sofia, Los Angeles, 1986, Hellenic Am. Council So. Calif., Los Angeles Community Action Network, Pan-Laconian Fedn. U.S. and Can. Recipient Am. Men and Women of Sci. citation. Mem. AAAS, Am. Chem. Soc., Alumni Assn. U. Rochester, Alumni Assn. U. Miami, Smithsonian Inst., Sigma Xi (sci. research hon.), Phi Kappa Phi (hon. soc.). Democrat. Club: Hellenic U. (So. Calif.). Avocations: photography, stock market, ballet dancing, travel. Home: 2003 W 147th St Gardena CA 90249 Office: Calif State U Dept Chemistry 1000 E Victoria St Carson CA 90747

SOFOS, JOHN NIKOLAOS, food science educator; b. Arachneon, Greece, June 14, 1948; came to U.S., 1972; s. Nicholas John and Marina (Paspaliaris) S.; m. Helen Stamatatos, Oct. 21, 1978; children: Marina, Elvera. BS in Agriculture, Aristotelian U., Thessaloniki, Greece, 1971; MS in Animal Sci., U. Minn., 1975, PhD in Food Sci., 1979. Research asst. U. Minn., St. Paul, 1973-78, research assoc., 1978-80; asst. prof. food sci. Colo. State U., Ft. Collins, 1980-84, assoc. prof., 1984—. Contbr. articles to profl. jours. Mem. Am. Soc. Microbiology, Inst. Food Technologists, Rocky Mountain Inst. Food Tech. (chmn. 1985—), Am. Soc. Animal Sci., Am. Meat Sci. Assn., AAAS., Sigma Xi, Gamma Sigma Delta, Phi Tau Sigma. Home: 1601 Sagewood Dr Fort Collins CO 80525 Office: Colo State U Dept Animal Sci Fort Collins CO 80523

SOKOLOFF, ALEXANDER DIMITROVITCH, biology educator; b. Tokyo, Japan, May 16, 1920; came to U.S., 1938; s. Dimitri Fyodorovitch and Sofia Alexandrovna (Solovieff) S.; m. Barbara B. Bryant, June 24, 1956; children: Alexandra, Elaine A., Michael A. AA, UCLA, 1943, AB, 1948; PhD, U. Chgo., 1954. Instr. Hofstra U., L.I., N.Y., 1955-56, asst. prof., 1956-58; geneticist W.H. Miner Agrl. Research Inst., Chazy, N.Y., 1958-60; assoc. research botanist UCLA, 1960; assoc. research geneticist U. Calif., Berkeley, 1961-66, research geneticist, 1966-68; assoc. prof. Calif. State U., San Bernardino, 1965-66, prof. biology, 1966—. Author: Genetics of Tribolium, 1966, The Biology of Tribolium, vol. 1, 1972, vo. 2, 1975, vol. 3, 1977; mem. editorial bd.: Jour. Stored Product Research, 1965—; assoc. editor: Evolution, 1972-74, Jour. Advanced Zoology, 1980—; editor Tribolium Info. Bull., 1960—. Served to sgt. USAAF, 1942-46. Research grantee USPHS, 1961, NSF, 1957-59, 67-69, 69-71, 71-73, Army Research Office 1973-76, 79. Mem. Soc. Study of Evolution, Genetics Soc. Am., Am. Genetic Assn., Am. Soc. Naturalists, Am. Soc. Zoologists, Genetics Soc.

Can., Japanese Soc. Population Ecology, Entomol. Soc. Am., Sigma Xi. Democrat. Lodge: Elks. Home: 3324 Sepulveda San Bernardino CA 92404 Office: Calif State U 5500 N University Pkwy San Bernardino CA 92407

SOLAK-EASTIN, CRI CRI, public relations executive; b. Glen Cove, N.Y., Feb. 13, 1953; d. Jerzy Jakob and Joan (Thaxter) Solak; m. Richard Verr Eastin, Nov. 17, 1979. BA in Internat. Relations, Pomona Coll., 1975. Mem. staff White House Press Office, Washington, 1975, Domestic Council, U.S. Govt., Washington, 1976, Transnational Investments, Washington, 1977-78; asst. dir. devel. U. So. Calif. Sch. Bus., Los Angeles, 1978-82; acct. supr. N.W. Ayer Pub. Relations Co., Los Angeles, 1982—; West Coast supr. Diamond Info. Ctr., Los Angeles, 1985—. Mem. Pub. Relations Soc. Am. Republican. Avocations: sports, gourmet cooking and wines, classical music. Home: 1036 Armada Dr Pasadena CA 91103 Office: NW Ayer Pub Relations 888 S Figueroa St Los Angeles CA 90017

SOLBERG, RONALD LOUIS, economist, educator; b. Madison, Wis., May 15, 1953; s. Carl Louis and Gladys Irene Evelyn (Oen) S.; m. Anna Maria Teresa Gorgol, May 16, 1983. BA in Econs. with honors, U. Wis., 1975; MA, U. Calif., Berkeley, 1977, PhD, 1984. Country risk analyst Wells Fargo Bank, San Francisco, 1978-79; asst. v.p., economist Wells Fargo Ltd., London, 1979-81; cons. RAND Corp., Santa Monica, Calif., 1982-84; acting instr. econs. U. Calif., Berkeley, 1983; v.p., economist Security Pacific Nat. Bank, Los Angeles, 1984—; adj. asst. prof. U. So. Calif., Los Angeles, 1985—. Author: (monograph with G. Grossman) The Soviet Union's Hard-Currency Balance of Payments and Creditworthiness in 1985, 1983; (book) Sovereign Rescheduling Risk and Portfolio Management, 1987. Research fellow Inst. Internat. Studies, Berkeley, 1982-84. Mem. Am. Econ. Assn., Nat. Assn. for Bus. Economists, Soc. for Internat. Devel. Club: Los Angeles Athletic. Avocations: fly fishing, cross-country skiing. Home: 12621 Rose Ave Los Angeles CA 90066 Office: Security Pacific Nat Bank H8-78 333 S Hope St Los Angeles CA 90071

SOLDNER, PAUL EDMUND, ceramist, educator; b. Summerfield, Ill.; s. Grover and Beulah (Geiger) S.; m. Virginia I. Geiger, June 15, 1947; 1 dau., Stephanie. B.A., Bluffton Coll., 1946; M.A., U. Colo., 1954; M.F.A., Los Angeles County Art Inst., 1956. Tchr. art Medina (Ohio) County Schs., 1946-47; supr. art, asst. county supr. Wayne County Schs., Wooster, Ohio, 1951-54; tchr. adult edn. Wooster Coll., 1952-54; vis. asst. prof. ceramics Scripps Coll., 1957-66, prof., 1970—; prof. Claremont (Calif.) Grad. Sch., 1957-66, prof., 1970—; prof. U. Colo., Boulder, 1966-67, U. Iowa, Iowa City, 1967-68; pres. Soldner Pottery Equipment, Inc., Aspen, Colo., 1956-77; mem. steering com. Internat. Sch. Ceramics, Rome, 1965-77; advisor Vols. for Internat. Assistance, Balt., 1966-75; craftsman, trustee Am. Craft Council, N.Y.C., 1970-74, trustee emeritus, 1976-77; dir. U.S. sect. World Craft Council, 1970-74; dir. Anderson Ranch Center for Hand Art Sch., 1974-76; cons. in field. Author: Kilns and Their Construction, 1965, Raku, 1964; contbr. articles to profl. jours.; subject of 5 films; 155 one-man shows including Cantini Mus. Modern Art, Marseille, France, 1981, Thomas Segal Gallery, Boston, 1982, Elements Gallery, N.Y., 1983, Louis Newman Gallery, Los Angeles, 1985, Esther Saks Gallery, Chgo., 1986, Great Am. Gallery, Atlanta, 1986; group shows include Nelson-Atkins Mus., Kansas City, Mo., 1983, Los Angeles Mcpl. Art Gallery, 1984, 27th Ceramic Nat. Exhibition, Everson Mus. Art, Syracuse, N.Y., 1986, Victoria & Albert Mus., London, 1986, Chicago Internat. New Art Forms Exposition, 1986; works in permanent collections, Nat. Mus. Modern Art, Kyoto, Japan, Victoria and Albert Mus., London, Smithsonian Instn., Washington, Los Angeles County Mus. Art, Oakland Art Mus., Everson Mus. Art, Syracuse Australian Nat. Gallery, Taipei Fine Arts Mus. Served with U.S. Army, 1941-46. Decorated Purple Heart; grantee Louis Comfort Tiffany Found., 1966, 72, Purple Heart. Grantee Nat. Endowment for Arts, 1976, Colo. Gov.'s award for the Arts & Humanities, 1975; voted one of Top Twelve Potters World-Wide, Ceramics Monthly mag., 1981; Scripps Coll. Faculty Recognition award, 1985. Fellow Collequim of Craftsmen of the U.S.; mem. Internat. Acad. Ceramics, Nat. Council on Edn. for Ceramic Arts. Originator Am. Raku philosophy and techniques in ceramics. Originator Am. Raku philosophy and techniques in ceramics. Home: PO Box 90 Aspen CO 81612

SOLEM, JOHNDALE CHRISTIAN, physicist, consultant; b. Chgo., Nov. 8, 1941; s. Henry Richard and Charlotte Ingaborg (Sorenson) S.; m. Ann Montgomery Veirs, July 2, 1966. BS cum laude, Yale U., 1963, MS, 1965, M in Philosophy, 1967, PhD, 1968. Staff mem. theoretical div. Los Alamos (N.Mex.) Nat. Lab., 1969-72, group leader thermonuclear physics, 1973-76, group leader neutron physics, 1977-79, group leader HPD physics, 1978, dep. physics div. leader, 1978-80, assoc. theoretical div. leader, 1980—; mem. USAF Sci. Adv. Bd., 1972-77. Mem. AAAS, Am. Phys. Soc., Am. Nuclear Soc., Soc. Photo Optical Engrs. Republican. Avocations: music, art. Home: 220 Andanada Los Alamos NM 87544 Office: Los Alamos Nat Lab Theoretical Div Los Alamos NM 87545

SOLER, DONA KATHERINE, civic worker; b. Grand Rapids, Mich., Mar. 7, 1921; d. Melbourne and Katherine Anne (Herbst) Welch; 1 child, Suzette Maria. Student pvt. and pub. schs., Grand Rapids, Mich. Artist-instr., metaphys. councilor, researcher, editor, pub. Psychic Exchange, 1979—. Author: What God Hath Put Together, 1979, Our Heritage From the Angels, 1981, Expose the Dirty Devil, 1984, Contemporary Poets of America (anthology), 1984, For Love of Henry, 1985, Greyball, 1986, House of Evil Secrets, 1986. Founder, 1st pres. South Coast Art Assn., San Clement, Calif., 1963-65, Orange Coast Cath. Christian Singles, 1970-73, Psychic Exchange, Orange County, 1979; founder, chief Lake Riverside Estates Communicators, Riverside, 1974-79. Republican. Mem. Animal Assistance League of Orange County, Animal Protection Instn. of Am., Greenpeace, People for the Ethical Treatment of Animals, Internat. Fund for Animal Welfare, World Wildlife Fund-U.S., Humane Soc. of the U.S., Am. Soc. for the Prevention of Cruelty Towards Animals, Ctr. Environ. Edn., Defenders of Wildlife.

SOLES, GAYLE KATHRYN, marketing professional; b. Kansas City, Kans., Sept. 21, 1939; d. Robert Lawrence Garrity and Bertha Katherine (Robbs) Misenhimer; m. R.L. Soles, June 7, 1959; children: Lesa June, Scott R. AA, Moorpark Coll., 1978. Adminstrv. asst. Pertec Computer Corp., Los Angeles, 1978-81; mgr. mktg. communications Callan Data Systems, Westlake Village, Calif., 1982-84; dir. corp. communications Cordata Techs., Inc., Thousand Oaks, Calif., 1984—. Neighborhood chmn. Girl Scouts U.S., Los Angeles, 1967-72; teaching asst. Los Angeles Unified Sch. Dist., 1968-71. Mem. Meeting Planners Internat. Office: Cordata Techs Inc 275 East Hillcrest Thousand Oaks CA 91360

SOLIS, DEBRA LYNNE, marketing professional; b. Toms River, N.J., Mar. 12, 1954; d. Samuel Robert and Sylvia Dorothy (Bushing) Stean; m. Carlos Solis, Aug. 15, 1981. BA, Gettysburg Coll., 1976; MBA, U. So. Calif., 1983. Comml. loan officer Union Bank, Los Angeles, 1976-81; mktg. mgr. Sav-On Drugs Inc., Anaheim, Calif., 1982-85; investment products mktg. mgr. Coast Fed., Los Angeles, 1985-86; dir. product mgmt. Coast Savs., Los Angeles, 1986—. Pres. Los Angeles Open Golf Found., 1985—, Los Angeles Charity Found., 1985—. Mem. Los Angeles C. of C. (bd. dirs. 1986—), Los Angeles Jr. C. of C. (bd. dirs. 1981—, pres. 1985-86, chmn. bd. 1986—, econ. adv. council of Los Angeles 1986—), Am. Mktg. Assn., Am. Mgmt. Assn. Republican. Clubs: Los Angeles Athletic, University. Avocation: internat. travel. Home: 590 Bradford Pasadena CA 91105

SOLIS, MARY ELLEN, oncology social worker; b. Culver City, Calif., Dec. 2, 1956; d. Ascencion and Juanita (Madrigal) S.; m. Klaus Richard Silbermann, Nov. 27, 1982; children: Derek P., Alec K. AA in Human Services, Los Angeles Harbor Jr. Coll., 1976; BA in Psychology, U. Calif., Santa Barbara, 1978; M in Social Welfare, U. Calif., Berkeley, 1981. Lic. clin. social worker. Caseworker Cath. Social Services, Santa Barbara, 1981-84; instr. Zona Seca, Santa Barbara, 1983-84; coordinator patient care Cancer Found., Santa Barbara, 1984—. Author community grant for Housing Relocation Program, 1983 (received $18,000 grant). Fin. review com. mem. United Way of Bay Area, San Francisco, 1980-81; counselor, campaign mgr. YMCA, So. Calif., 1971-84; chmn. Social Welfare Grad. Assembly, U. Calif., Berkeley, 1979-81; bd. dirs. South Coast Coordinating Council, Santa Barbara, Parent and Child Edn. Santa Barbara High Sch., 1983-84. Mem. Nat. Assn. Social Workers, Nat. Assn. Oncology Social Workers, So. Calif. Oncology Social Workers (conf. com. 1984—), Boston Oncology Social Work Group, U. Calif. Berkeley Sch. Social Welfare Alumni Assn. (Outstanding Achievement award 1981), Mid-Atlantic Oncology Social Work Group. Avocations: sports, reading, langs. Home: 3059 Paseo Del Descanso Santa Barbara CA 93105 Office: Cancer Found of Santa Barbara 300 W Pueblo St Santa Barbara CA 93105

SOLIS, RAFAEL, management sciences educator; b. Palizada, Mex., July 31, 1950; came to U.S., 1976; s. Rafael Sr. and Ninfa (Del Rivero) S.; m. Glenda Mary Carberry, Nov. 27, 1981; 1 child, Eric Alexander. BSc, Nat. U., Mex., 1972; MSc, Nat. Sch. Agr., Mex., 1975; PhD, U. Waterloo, Can., 1984. Asst. prof. Fla. Internat. U., Miami, 1982-85; assoc. prof. computer info. systems, ops. research, stats. Calif. State U., Fresno, 1985—; cons. Eastern Airlines, 1984, Can. Fisheries, 1979-80, Dept. Agr., Mex., 1972-76. Rockefeller Found. scholar, 1977-80. Ford Found. scholar, 1972-77. Mem. Inst. Mgmt. Sci., Ops. Research Soc. Am., Assn. Computing Machinery. Avocations: photography, marathon running. Office: Calif State U Dept Info Systems Fresno CA 93740

SOLIVEN, ENRIQUE TUMANG, architect; b. Manila, Jan. 4, 1948; s. Enrique and Paciencia (Tumang) S.; m. Ana Maria Gonzalez, Apr. 8, 1976; children: Alexandra Mariko, Enrico Paolo. BS in Architecture, U. Santo Thomas, Manila, 1968, BSCE, 1971; MS in Indsl. Engring., U. Philippines, 1972. Registered architect, Calif., Philippines. Project superintendent Consuelo Industries, Manila, 1968-69; sr. architect Arcenas Payumo, Manila, 1970-77, practicing architect, 1977-78; sr. draftsperson SMP Architects, San Francisco, 1978-80; job capt. WFEM Architects, San Francisco, 1980-82; regional dir. Hamill McKinney, Walnut Creek, Calif., 1982-86; prin. Facilities Design Group Architecture Engring., Walnut Creek, Calif., 1986—. Mem. AIA, Calif. Resaurant Assn. (bd. dirs. 1983—). Lodge: Rotary, 1983—. Office: Facilities Design Group Architecture Engring 2116 N Main St Suite I Walnut Creek CA 94596

SOLLID, JON ERIK, physicist, consultant; b. Denver, Oct. 1, 1939; s. Erik and Faye (Eising) S.; m. Margaret Louise Bashant, Aug. 18, 1980 (div. Dec. 1985). BS, U. Mich., 1961; MS, N.Mex. State U., 1965, PhD, 1967. Physicist White Sands (N.Mex.) Missile Range, 1961-62, Los Alamos (N.Mex.) Nat. Lab., 1965-66, 1974-85, 86—, Gen. Dynamics Div., Ft. Worth, 1967-72; adj. prof. Tex. Christian U., Ft. Worth, 1971; physicist Ford Motor Co. Sci. Research Lab., Dearborn, Mich., 1972-74; v.p. and gen. mgr. Newport Corp., Los Alamos, 1985-86; also cons. Fountain Valley, Calif. Contbr. articles to profl. jours. Served with USMC, 1958-64. Recipient Top 20 award of Excellence Materials Engring., 1983. Mem. Am. Phys. Soc., Optical Soc. Am., Soc. Photo-Optical Instrumentation Engrs., Sigma Xi, Sigma Pi Sigma. Democrat. Home: 365 Valle del Sol Los Alamos NM 87544 Office: Los Alamos Nat Lab Los Alamos NM 87545

SOLLMAN, GEORGE HENRY, telecommunications company executive; b. Michigan City, Ind., Nov. 2, 1941; s. Henry Charles and Margaret Elisabeth (Gockel) S.; m. Maureen Tosh, July 12, 1968; children: Jennifer, Erich. Spl. student, MIT, 1965-66; BSEE, Northwestern U., 1964; MSEE, Northeastern U., 1967. Engring. dir. Honeywell Info. systems, Waltham, Mass., 1964-73; product line mgr. Control Data, Hawthorne, Calif., 1973-76; v.p., gen. mgr. Shugart/Xerox, Sunnyvale, Calif., 1976-84; spl. ptnr. Sand Hill Venture Group, Menlo Park, Calif., 1984; pres., chief exec. officer Centigram Corp., San Jose, Calif., 1985—. Patentee in field. Home: 32 Anderson Way Menlo Park CA 94025 Office: Centigram Corp 4415 Fortran Ct San Jose CA 95134

SOLOF, BARRY SCOTT, physician; b. Feb. 8, 1948. BA in Psychology summa cum laude, SUNY, Buffalo, 1970; MD, Yale U., 1974. Diplomate Am. Bd. Family Practice (fellow); cert. therapist Biofeedback Certification Inst. Am. Resident in family practice St. Paul-Ramsey County Hosp. and Med. Ctr., 1974-75; employee physician Southeast Med. Ctr., Huntington Park, Calif., 1975-77; med. dir. Victoria Med. Group, Los Angeles, 1977-82, West Jefferson Med. Group, Los Angeles, 1977-82; assoc. Vanowen Med. Group, North Hollywood, 1982-85; med. dir. dept. biofeedback Hollywood Presbyn. Med. Ctr., Los Angeles, 1985—; dir. primary care medicine Western States Psychiatric Inst., Canoga Park, Calif., 1986—; dir. internal medicine A Touch of Care Adult Psychiat. Treatment Program, Los Angeles, 1986—; chief dept. medicine Treatment Ctrs. of Am., Panorama City, Calif., 1986—; med. cons. Edgemont Psychiat. Hosp., Los Angeles, 1980—. Manor West Hosp., Los Angeles, 1985—, Mountainview Lodge Hosp., Glendale, Calif., 1986—; med. dir. Templar Med. Clinic, Los Angeles, 1985—; staff internist Woodview-Calabasas (Calif.) Psychiat. Hosp., 1986—; mem. staff various hosps. Mem. AMA, Calif. Med. Assn., Los Angeles County Med. Assn., Biofeedback Soc. Am., Biofeedback Soc. Calif., Calif. Acad. Physicians. Home: 2463 Solar Dr Los Angeles CA 90046

SOLOLA, ABIODUN SALAUDEEN, obstetrician and gynecologist, medical educator; b. Kano, Nigeria, Oct. 26, 1942; came to U.S. 1974; s. Badru Salaudeen and Alhaja-Rabiat (Layonu) Olorunkemi. M.D., U. Toronto, 1968, D.P.H., 1974. Diplomate Am. Bd. Ob-Gyn. Intern Toronto Gen. Hosp., Ont., Can., 1968-69; resident in ob-gyn Met. Hosp. Ctr.-N.Y. Med. Coll., N.Y.C., 1974-78; asst. prof. ob-gyn, asst. prof. community medicine U. Tenn. Ctr. Health Scis., Memphis, 1978-81; asst. prof. ob-gyn U. Fla., Gainesville, 1982; clin. asst. prof. ob-gyn U. Wash., Seattle, 1983—; chief ob-gyn Pacific Med. Ctr., Seattle, 1982-85; dir. Seattle Gynecology and Fertility Clinic, 1985—. Contbr. articles to profl. jours. Fellow Am. Coll. Ob-Gyn; mem. Am. Pub. Health Assn. Home: 1301 Spring St Seattle WA 98104 Office: Elmer J Nordstrom Med Tower 1229 Madison St Suite 1050 Seattle WA 98104

SOLOMON, ALLEN LOUIS, engineer, researcher; b. Pitts., Oct. 1, 1922; s. Harold Louis and Cecelia (Shrager) S.; m. Elaine Miller, Apr. 15, 1951; children: Ruth Ann, Susan Carol. BS, Yale U., 1942, MS, 1944, PhD, 1948. Solid state device dept. mgr. GTE Labs., Bayside, N.Y., 1956-72; program mgr. Fairchild Camera and Instrument, Palo Alto, Calif., 1973-75; prin. staff engr. McDonnell Douglas Corp., Huntington Beach, Calif., 1977-82; cons. Solocon Co., Fullerton, Calif., 1982-86; sr. engr. Grumman Corp., Irvine, Calif., 1986—. Patentee in field. Served to lt. USNR, 1944-46, PTO. Mem. IEEE (sr.), Elecrochem. Soc., Am. Chem. Soc., Sigma Xi. Home: 1800 Fairford Dr Fullerton CA 92633

SOLOMON, ARTHUR CHARLES, medical corporation executive; b. Gary, Ind., May 30, 1947; s. Laurence A. and Dorothy B. (Klippel) S.; m. Janet Evelyn Irak, Aug. 23, 1969; children: Thomas, Michael, Mark, Jill. BS in Pharmacy, Purdue U., 1970, MS, 1972; PharmD. Registered pharmacist. Clin. prof. pharmacy U. Tex., Austin, 1972-75; v.p. Nuclear Pharmacy, Inc., Atlanta, 1975-83; exec. v.p. Diagnostek, Inc., Albuquerque, 1983—; adj. prof. Mercer U., Atlanta, 1975-82. Contbr. articles to profl. jours. Mem. Am. Pharm. Assn. (author examination 1982-85), Radiology bus. Mgrs. Assn., Soc. Nuclear Medicine, Rho Chi. Republican. Roman Catholic. Lodges: Kiwanis, Elks. Avocations: fishing, gardening, tennis. Home: 1504 Catron SE Albuquerque NM 87123 Office: Diagnostek Inc 3733 Eubank NE Albuquerque NM 87111

SOLOMON, GUY REUBEN, JR., public relations executive; b. Cleve., Jan. 31, 1936; s. Guy Reuben Sr. and Florence Elizabeth (Lomnitz) S.; m. Catherine Pearl Erb, Sept. 9, 1960; children: Christopher Lee, Matthew Brady. BS, Kent State U., 1959. Dir. pub. info. Ohio No. U., Ada, 1965-67; dir. publs. Youngstown (Ohio) State U., 1967-73, dir. news bur., 1973-79; dir. pub. info. Cen. Wash. U., Ellensburg, 1979-85, dir. community relations, 1985—; freelance radio, TV announcer, 1968—; pub. relations dir. Eastern Ohio Podiatry, Youngstown, 1976-79; interview host Sta. KNDO/KNDU-TV, Yakima and Pasco, Wash., 1981—. Served with U.S. Army, 1959-61. Named Kenton, Ohio Young Man of Yr., Jaycees, 1964. Mem. Council for Advancement and Support Edn., Ellensburg C. of C. (bd. dirs. 1982-83), Theta Chi (regional counselor 1966-67). Republican. Lodges: Rotary (Ellensburg chpt. bd. dirs. 1983-84), Elks. Avocations: handball, racquetball, golf, reading, river rafting. Home: Rt 1 Cedar Cove Rd Ellensburg WA 98926 Office: Cen Wash U Community Relations Ellensburg WA 98926

SOLOMON, JULIUS OSCAR LEE, pharmacist; b. N.Y.C., Aug. 14, 1917; s. John and Jeannette (Krieger) S.; student Bklyn. Coll., 1935-36, CCNY, 1936-37; B.S. in Pharmacy, U. So. Calif., 1949; postgrad. Long Beach State U., 1971-72; Southwestern Colls., 1979, 81-82; m. Sylvia Smith, June 26, 1941 (div. Jan. 1975); children—Marc Irwin, Evan Scott, Jeri Lee; m. 2d, Ana Maria C. MacFarland, Apr. 5, 1975; children—George, Anamaria, Gabriella, Arthur. Dye maker Fred Fear & Co., Bklyn., 1935; apprentice interior decorator Dorothy Draper, 1936; various jobs, N.Y. State Police, 1940-45; research asst. Union Oil Co., 1945; lighting cons. Joe Rosenberg & Co., 1946-49; owner Banner Drug, Lomita, 1949-53, Redondo Beach, Calif., 1953-72, El Prado Pharmacy, Redondo Beach, 1961-65; pres. Banner Drug, Inc., Redondo Beach, 1953-72, Thrifty Drugs, 1972-74, also Guild Drug, Longs Drug, Drug King, 1976-83; pres. Socoma Inc., 1983—. Charter commr., founder Redondo Beach Youth Baseball Council; sponsor Little League Baseball, basketball, football, bowling; pres. Redondo Beach Boys Club; v.p. South Bay Children's Health Center, 1974, Redondo Beach Coordinating Council, 1975; founder Redondo Beach Community Theater, 1975; active maj. gift drive YMCA, 1975; mem. SCAG Com. on Criminal Justice, 1974, League of Calif. Environ. Quality Com., 1975; pres. South Bay Democratic Club; mem. Dem. State Central Com., Los Angeles County Dem. Central Com.; del. Dem. Nat. Conv., 1972; chmn. Redondo Beach Recreation and Parks Commn.; mem. San Diego County Parks Adv. Commn., 1982; mem. human resource devel. com., pub. improvement com. Nat. League of Cities; v.p. Redondo Beach Coordinating Council; councilman, Redondo Beach, 1961-69, 73-77; treas. 46th Assembly Dist. Council; candidate 46 Assembly dist. 1966; nat. chmn. Pharmacists for Humphrey, 1968, 72; pres. bd. dirs. So. Bay Exceptional Childrens Soc., Chapel Theatre; bd. dirs. So. div. League Calif. Cities, U.S.-Mexico Sister Cities Assn., Boy's Club Found. of San Diego County, Autumn Hills Condominium Assn. (pres.), Calif. Employee Pharmacists Assn., Our House, Chula Vista, Calif., 1984—; mem. South Bay Inter-City Hwy. Com., Redondo Beach Round Table, 1973-77; mem. State of Calif. Commn. of Californias (U.S.-Mexico), 1975-78; mem. Chula Vista Safety Commn., 1978, chmn., 1980-81; chmn. San Diego County Juvenile Camp Contract Com., 1982—; mem. San Diego County Juvenile Delinquency Prevention Commn., 1983—; spl. participant Calif. Crime and Violence Workshop. Served with USCGR, 1942-45. Recipient Pop Warner Youth award, 1960, 1962, award of merit Calif. Pharm. Assn., 1962, award Am. Assn. Blood Banks, 1982. Diplomate Am. Bd. Diplomates Pharmacy Internat. Fellow Am. Coll. Pharmacists (pres.); mem. South Bay Pharm. Assn. (pres.), South Bay Councilmans Assn. (founder, pres.), Palos Verdes Peninsula Navy League (charter), Am. Legion, U. So. Calif. Alumni Assn. (life), Assn. Former N.Y. State Troopers (life), AFTRA, Am. Pharm. Assn., Nat. Assn. Retail Druggists, Calif. Pharmacists Assn., San Ysidro C. of C. (bd. dirs. 1985—), Fraternal Order of Police, San Diego County Fish and Game Assn., Rho Pi Phi (pres. alumni). Club: Trojan (life). Lodges: Elks (life), Masons (32 deg.; life), Lions (charter mem. North Redondo). Established Lee Solomon award for varsity athlete with highest scholastic average at 10 South Bay High Schs. Home: 1640-57 Maple Dr Chula Vista CA 92011 Office: Socoma Inc 2945 Beyer Blvd San Diego CA 92154

SOLOMON, KENNETH HADLEY, agricultural engineer; b. Los Angeles, June 25, 1945; s. Elmer Whitely and Lois Winifred (Hadley) S. BS in Math., Harvey Mudd Coll., 1967; MA in Math., Claremont Grad. Sch., 1976; MS in Irrigation Sci., Utah State U., 1978, PhD in Agrl. Engring., 1984. Registered profl. agrl. engr., Calif. Agrl. engr. Rain Bird, Glendora, Calif., 1968-80; pres. VON-SOL, Claremont, Calif., 1980-82; dir. ops. Ball Agrl. Systems, Westminster, Colo., 1982-83; agrl. engr., research leader U.S. Salinity Lab., Riverside, Calif., 1983-84, acting dir., 1985; dir. Ctr. Irrigation Tech. Calif. State U., Fresno, 1986—; mem. U.S. Com. on Irrigation and Drainage; vis. scholar U. Nebr., Lincoln, 1983. Contbr. articles to profl. jours.; inventor motor for rotating jet sprinkler. Recipient Research prize U. Council on Water Resources, 1985. Mem. ASCE, Calif. Irrigation Inst. (bd. dirs. 1986—), Am. Soc. Agrl. Engrs., Irrigation Assn., Fla. Irrigation Soc., Nature Conservancy, Audubon Soc., Sierra Club, UN Assn. U.S.A. Office: Calif State U Ctr Irrigation Tech Fresno CA 93740-0018

SOLOMON, MARIAN AUDREY, information systems executive; b. New Orleans, July 31, 1947; d. Ben A. and Jeanette (Arbitter) S.; m. Alan M. Schultz, Oct. 19, 1969 (div. May 1973); m. Howard E. Freeman, Feb. 2, 1979; children: Seth R., Lisa Jill. BS, Fla. State U., 1967, MS, 1969; PhD, UCLA, 1973. Mgmt. analyst HEW, Washington, 1976-79; sr. research mgr. System Devel. Corp., Santa Monica, Calif., 1979-81; project dir. Luth. Hosp. Soc., Los Angeles, 1981-82; dir. mgmt. info. systems Los Angeles County Dept. Mental Health, Los Angeles, 1982—; cons. Inst. Nutrition of Cen. Am. and Panama, Guatemala, 1979-85, Pan Am. Health Orgn., Washington, 1983. Editor: Evaluation Studies Review Annual, vol. 6, 1981, Evaluation Research and Practice: Comparative and Internal Perspectives, 1980. Home: 7911 Hillside Ave Los Angeles CA 90046 Office: Los Angeles County Dept Mental Health 2415 W 6th St Los Angeles CA 90057

SOLOMON, PAUL ALAN, environmental and analytical chemist; b. Boston, Dec. 14, 1956; s. Maurice and Ethel (Goodman) S.; m. Jocelyn Ileen Kritzer, June 9, 1985. BS in Chemistry with honors, U. Md., 1978; PhD in Chemistry, U. Ariz., 1984. Teaching asst. U. Ariz., Tucson, 1978-79, research asst., 1979-83, research assoc., 1983-84; research scientist Calif. Inst. Tech., Pasadena, 1984—; cons. Environ. Monitoring Services, Inc., Newbury Park, Calif., 1986—, Calif. Air Resources Bd., El Monte, Calif., 1986—. Contbr. articles to profl. jours. Biochemistry scholar NSF, 1973; recipient John C. Ingang award U. Md., 1978. Mem. Am. Inst. Chemists, Phi Eta Sigma, AAAS, Am. Chem. Soc. (Coryell award in Basic and Applied Nuclear Chemistry 1978), Alpha Chi Sigma (award 1978). Democrat. Jewish. Avocations: traveling, golfing, racquetball, jogging. Home: 511 W Puente St #2 Covina CA 91722 Office: Calif Inst Tech Mail Code 138-78 Pasadena CA 91125

SOLOMON-RICE, PATTI LYNN, speech pathology director; b. Milw., Sept. 27, 1955; d. Armin Irving and Sylvia (Nashban) S.; m. Gerald William Rice, Apr. 27, 1986. BEd in Speech Pathology with honors, U. Wis., 1977; M in Communication Scis. and Disorders, U. Mont., 1980. Lic. speech pathologist, Calif. Staff speech pathologist San Jose (Calif.) Speech and Lang. Clinic, 1981, sr. speech pathologist, 1981-83, supr. clinic, 1984; dir. dept. speech pathology Kentfield (Calif.) Med. Hosp., 1984-86; dir. pvt. practice, Belmont, Calif., 1986—. Mem. Am. Speech Lang. Hearing Assn. (com. mem. 1984—, Continuing Edn. award 1984, cert.), Calif. Speech Lang. Hearing Assn. (adv. bd. 1984-86, program chmn. 1986), San Mateo County Speech Lang. Hearing Assn., Santa Clara County Speech Lang. Hearing Assn., Bay Area Group for Adult Communicative Disorders (pres. 1985, chmn. program com. 1986), Profl. Group for Adult Communicative Disorders (sec. 1982). Libertarian. Jewish. Club: Bottom Watchers Div (Hayward, Calif.). Avocations: reading, current events, aerobics, skiing, hiking. Home and Office: 3206 Upper Lock Ave Belmont CA 94002

SOMERS, JANET DIANE, psychotherapist, consultant, management consultant; b. Los Angeles, Apr. 24, 1954; d. Robert Worth and Carol Jeanne (Strauss) S. BS in Social Welfare, San Diego State U., 1976; MSW, U. Denver, 1979. Therapist Bethesda Mental Health Ctr., Denver, 1977-79; therapist, cons. Greater Fall River (Mass.) Mental Health Assn., 1979-81; v.p. employee assistance program Security Pacific Nat. Bank, Los Angeles, 1981-84; social worker Mount Airy Psychiat. Ctr., Denver, 1984; pvt. practice psychotherapy cons. Denver, 1984—; cons. Adams County Sch. Dist 14, Commerce City, Colo., 1984—; instr. Colo. State U., Ft. Collins, 1984-85, Contemporary Learn Inc., Denver, 1984—; provider of spl. health services Continental Ins. Commn., N.Y. and Colo., 1985—. Vol. Holiday Project Juvenile Hall, Denver, 1985. Grad. Sch. Social Work scholar U. Denver, 1978, Mile High Counsel on Alcoholism scholar, Denver, 1984. Mem. Nat. Assn. Social Workers (cert.), Colo. Assn. Mental Health, Assn. Labor Mgmt. Adminstrs. and Cons. on Alcoholism (chairperson women's issues com. 1986—). Democrat. Jewish. Avocations: outdoor sports, domestic activities, art, music, lit. Office: 280 Columbine St Suite 306 Denver CO 80206

SOMMERFELD, RICHARD ARTHUR, geologist; b. Chgo., July 4, 1933; s. Arthur Frederick Sommerfeld and Leona Marie (Ciarmoli) Calderwood; m. Susan Esmay Wilmer, Sept. 9, 1980. PhD in Geophysics, U. Chgo., 1965. Geologist U.S. Forest Service, Ft. Collins, Colo., 1967—. Contbr. articles to profl. jours. Mem. AAAS, Internat. Glaciol. Soc. Home: 319 N Pearl St Fort Collins CO 80521 Office: US Forest Service 240 W Prospect Fort Collins CO 80526

SOMMERNESS, MARTIN DAVID, journalism educator, media law consultant; b. Fergus Falls, Minn., Dec. 17, 1954; s. Martin Duane and Gertrude L. (Titus) S. B.A., Mich. State U., 1977, M.A., 1979; J.D., Wayne State U., 1981. Bar: Ariz. 1982, U.S. Dist. Ct. Ariz. 1982. Staff writer Traverse City Record-Eagle, Mich., 1972-77, writer, editor State News, East Lansing, Mich., 1972-76; sr. editor Lansing Chronicle, Mich., 1976-77; teaching asst. Mich. State U., East Lansing, 1977-78; shift supr. Free Legal Aid Clinic, Detroit, 1980-81; atty. intern Wayne County Neighborhood Legal Services, Inkster, Mich., 1980-81; asst. prof. No. Ariz. U., Flagstaff, 1981—, adminstrv. asst. to dean, 1984—; cons. Flagstaff Arts Festival, 1984—, Hopi Tribal Housing Authority, 1983, Phoenix chpt. Pub. Realtions Soc. Am., 1983; legal counsel No. Ariz. Com. against Strip Mining, 1982, Kachina Village Fire Bd., Flagstaff, 1982. Editor: Great American Communications Connection, 1982. Author and editor: Communications America, 1983. Author: Free to Inform: A Beginning Journalist's Survival Guide to Self-Preservation in Media Law, 1987. Pres. Lutheran Campus Ministry Flagstaff, 1982—. Recipient Gen. Mgr.'s award East Lansing State News, 1976; Bur. Nat. Affairs scholar, 1981. Mem. Western Social Sci. Assn. (program coordinator 1983), Assn. Edn. in Journalism and Mass Communications, Am. Judicature Soc., Ariz. Humanities Council (grant co-dir. 1983-84), Sigma Delta Chi (Mark of Excellence award 1976, chpt. v.p. 1982—). Republican. Lodge: Rotary (Flagstaff). Home: 5205 Cortland Blvd 119 Flagstaff AZ 86004 Office: No Ariz U Box 6001 Flagstaff AZ 86011

SOMMERS, WILLIAM PAUL, management consultant; b. Detroit, July 22, 1933; s. William August and Mary Elizabeth (Baietto) S.; m. Josephine A. Sommers; children: William F., Clare M., John C. Hughes. B.S.E. (scholar), U. Mich., 1955, M.S.E., 1956, Ph.D. (Riggs fellow, Texaco fellow, Univ. fellow), 1961. Research asso. U. Mich. Inst. Sci. and Tech., Ann Arbor, 1958-61; chief chem. propulsion space and missile systems Martin Marietta Corp., Balt., 1956-58, 61-63; v.p. Booz, Allen & Hamilton, Inc., Bethesda, Md., 1963-70; pres. Tech. Mgmt. Group Booz, Allen & Hamilton, Inc., 1973-79, exec. v.p., 1979—; dir. Kemper Fin. Services; sci. and tech. adv. bd. Celanese Corp. Contbr. articles to profl. jours., also chpt. in book. Pres. Washington chpt. U. Mich. Alumni Club, 1970-71; v.p. Wildwood Manor Citizens Assn., 1968-70; chief Adventure Guide Program, YMCA, 1971-72; dir. Manor Montessori Sch., 1966-68; bd. visitors Coll. Engring., U. Calif.-Davis. Mem. U. Mich. Coll. Engring. Adv. Bd., Sigma Xi, Tau Beta Pi, Pi Tau Sigma. Republican. Roman Catholic. Clubs: Columbia Country (Bethesda); Board Room (N.Y.C.); San Francisco Tennis, Bankers (San Francisco); Millbrae Tennis. Home: 452 Roblar Ave Hillsborough CA 94010 Office: Booz Allen and Hamilton 555 Montgomery St San Francisco CA 94111

SOMORJAI, GABOR ARPAD, chemist, educator; b. Budapest, Hungary, May 4, 1935; came to U.S., 1957, naturalized, 1962; s. Charles and Livia (Ormos) S.; m. Judith Kaldor, Sept. 2, 1957; children: Nicole, John. B.S. in Chem. Engring, U. Tech. Scis., Budapest, 1956; Ph.D., U. Calif., Berkeley, 1960. Mem. research staff IBM, Yorktown Heights, N.Y., 1960-64; prin. investigator materials and molecular research div. Lawrence Berkeley Lab., Calif., 1964—; mem. faculty dept. chemistry U. Calif.-Berkeley, 1964—, assoc. prof., 1967-72, prof., 1972—, Miller prof., 1978; unilever prof. dept. chemistry U. Bristol, Eng., 1972; vis. fellow Emmanuel Coll., Cambridge, Eng., 1969; Baker lectr. Cornell U., 1977. Author: Principles of Surface Chemistry, 1972, Chemistry in Two Dimension, 1981; mem. editorial bd.: Jour. Solid State Chemistry, 1976—, Progress in Solid State Chemistry, 1973—, Nouveau Jour. de Chimie, 1977-80, Colloid and Interface Sci., 1979—, Catalysis Revs., 1981, Jour. Phys. Chem., 1981—, Langmuir, 1985—; contbr. articles to profl. jours. Recipient Emmett award Am. Catalysis Soc., 1977, Kokes award John Hopkins U., 1976, Albert award Precious Metal Inst., 1986; Guggenheim fellow, 1969. Fellow Am. Phys. Soc., AAAS; mem. Am. Acad. Arts and Scis., Nat. Acad. Scis., Am. Chem. Soc. (chmn. colloid and surface chemistry 1981, Surface and Colloid Chemistry award 1981), Am. Phys. Soc., Catalysis Soc. N.Am. Office: U Calif Dept Chemistry Berkeley CA 94720 Home: 665 San Luis Rd Berkeley CA 94707

SONE, PHILIP GEARY, health psychologist, management consultant; b. Detroit, Jan. 16, 1949; s. Geary Masami and Monica Kazuko (Itoi) S. BA in Psychology and Sociology, Bowling Green U., 1971; MA in Clinical Psychology, W. Ga. Coll., 1974; PhD in Psychology, Ariz. State U., 1981. Cert. psychologist, nat. counselor. Family psychologist Family Service Ctr., Canton, Ohio, 1974-77; counselor and trainer Ariz. State U., Tempe, 1977-79; health psychologist Mesa Luth. Hosp., 1979-86, Health Psychology & Counseling Assocs., Phoenix and Mesa, 1983—, Rehab. Medicine Assocs., Mesa, 1986—; trainer, med. staff, Phoenix Gen. Hosp., 1984; cons., trainer ITT Courier, Inc., Phoenix, 1985, Garrett Pneumatic Industries, Inc., Phoenix, 1985, Coen Engring., Inc., Phoenix, 1985. Mem. Am. psychol. Assn. (health psychology div.), Am. Assn Counseling and Devel., Ariz. Assn. for Health Psychology, Phoenix Group for Study of Chronic Pain.. Presbyterian. Avocations: jazz, classical music, swimming, jogging, hiking. Office: Health Psychology & Counseling Assocs Phoenix AZ 85015 Office: Rehab Medicine Assocs 425 5th Pl Suite A Mesa AZ 85201

SONI, PRAVIN L., chemical company executive; b. Nagpur, India, Jan. 29, 1953; came to U.S., 1973; s. Laxminarayan Ramlal and Vimladevi (Laddha) S. BSChemE, Laxminarayan Inst. Technology, Nagpur, 1973; PhD in Polymer Sci., Case Western Res. U., 1979. Mem. research and devel. Raychem Corp., Menlo Park, Calif., 1979-80, group leader research and devel., 1980-82, dept. mgr. research and devel., 1982-84, sect. dir. research and devel., 1984-86, mgr. materials devel., Interconnect Systems div., 1986—. Contbr. articles to profl. jours. Mem. Soc. Plastics Engrs. (seminar instr. 1982—), Soc. Photo-optical Instrumentation Engrs., Am. Chem. Soc., Am. Phys. Soc. Avocations: tennis, soccer, biking, racquetball. Home: 4811 Kenwood St Union City CA 94587 Office: Raychem Corp 300 Constitution Dr Menlo Park CA 94025

SONNENBURG, STANLEY AL, scouting executive; b. El Paso, Tex., May 11, 1940; s. Stanley A. and Ruth (Reyes) S.; m. Sylvia Ann Chavez, Sept. 19, 1964; children: Dennis, Sonja, Aaron, Matthew, Anissa. BA, Calif. State U., 1968. Campaign worker Syder-Smith Advt., Los Angeles, 1961-66; exec. trainee Earl M. Jorgensen Steel, Los Angeles, 1967; exec. Boy Scouts Am., Los Angeles, 1967-74; field dir. Boy Scouts Am., Sacramento, 1974-84; scout exec. Boy Scouts Am., Maui, Hawaii, 1984—. Recipient Woodbadge award Boy Scouts Am., Los Angeles, 1969. Democrat. Roman Catholic. Lodge: Rotary (program dir. Maui club 1985), KC. Home: 1465 Baldwin Ave Makawao HI 96768 Office: Maui County Council Boy Scouts Am 200 Liholiho St Wailuku HI 96793

SONNENSCHEIN, RALPH ROBERT, physiologist; b. Chgo., Aug. 14, 1923; s. Robert and Flora (Kieferstein) S.; m. Patricia W. Niddrie, June 21, 1952; children—David, Lisa, Ann. Student, Swarthmore Coll., 1940-42, U. Chgo., 1942-43; B.S., Northwestern U., 1943, B.M., 1946, M.S., 1946, M.D., 1947; Ph.D., U. Ill., 1950. Research asst. in physiology Northwestern U. Med. Sch., 1944-46; intern Michael Reese Hosp., Chgo., 1946-47; successively research fellow clin. sci., research asst. psychiatry, research asso. psychiatry U. Ill. Med. Sch., Chgo., 1947-51; mem. faculty U. Calif. Med. Sch., Los Angeles, 1951—; prof. physiology U. Calif. Med. Sch., 1962—; liaison scientist Office Naval Research, London, 1971-72. Author papers on pain, innervation of skin, peripheral circulation. Served with AUS, 1943-46. Spl. research fellow USPHS, 1957-58; fellow Swedish Med. Research Council, 1964-65; grantee USAF; grantee Office Naval Research; grantee NIH; grantee NSF. Mem. Am. Physiol. Soc., Microcirculatory Soc., Soc. Exptl. Biology and Medicine, AAAS. Home: 18212 Kingsport Dr Malibu CA 90265 Office: U Calif Sch Medicine Dept Physiology Los Angeles CA 90024

SONNES, ROBERT ALAN, periodontist; b. Bklyn., Apr. 22, 1938; s. Paul and Lettie (Gordon) S.; m. Maxine Faye Berliner, June 29, 1962 (div. July 1983); children: Howard Andrew, Mark Adrian; m. Laurie Simpson, Jan. 22, 1985. BA, Hunter Coll., 1959; DDS, Temple U., 1963; grad. periodontic cert., N.Y.U., 1969. Lic. dentist, Pa., N.Y., N.J., Oreg. Wash. Intern. Madigan Gen. Hosp., Tacoma, 1964; assoc. Gen. Dentistry Clinic, N.Y.C., 1967-69; assoc. of Dr. George Witkin Rockefeller Ctr., N.Y.C., 1969-70; pvt. practice dentistry specializing in periodontics Portland, Oreg., 1970—; dir. Periodontal Assocs., Portland, Oreg., 1984—; clin. assoc. dept. Periodontics U. Oreg. Dental Sch., Portland, 1971-73; grad. clin. instr. dept. Periodontics N.Y.U., 1968; lectr. in field; bd. dirs. Oreg. Dental Service Corp., 1982-85; mng. ptnr. Healthcare Devel. Leasing, Portland, Seahart Investment Co., Seaside, Oreg., Ju-Bob Properties, Hy-Jean Properties, Boson Co.; ptnr. 43d & King Co.; Am. ptnr. Baja Sun Charters; pres. Weighing Sta. Leasing Co., Cannon Beach, Oreg.; owner R. Alan Realty Co. Bd. govs. Spirit of 76. Served with U.S. Army, 1964-67. Mem. Oreg. Soc. Periodontists (chmn. ins. com. 1973-81, PDR com.), Am. Acad. Periodontology (com. dental care programs, asst. ins. advisor 1976-77, state ins. advisor, 1972-81), Western Soc. Periodontology (bd. dirs. 1982-83), Multnomah County Dental Soc. (chmn. ins. com. 1973-78), Lower Columbia County Dental Soc. (hon.), Am. Soc. Preventive Dentistry, Pa. Acad. Gen. Dentistry, John A. Kolmer Hon. Med. Soc., James R. Cameron Hon. Soc. Oral Surgery. Clubs: Willamette Sailing, Mulnomah Athletic, City (Portland). Avocations: skiing, boating, fishing. Office: 833 SW 11th Ave Suite 1010 Portland OR 97205

SOPP, SAMUEL WILLIAM, chemist; b. Hammond, Ind., Aug. 28, 1934; s. Samuel W. and Mary (Radvak) S.; m. Nancy Whitlock, Aug. 24, 1963; children: Mark, Jeffrey. BS, Ind. State U., 1957; MS, Ariz. State U., 1962; PhD, U. Ill., 1965. Tchr. chemistry Highland (Ind.) High Sch., 1957-60; sr. chemist Merck & Co., South San Francisco, Calif., 1965-71; sr. research and development mgr. Calgon/Merck, South San Francisco, Calif., 1971-84; ptnr., owner Chemicon Assocs., Burlingame, Calif., 1984-86. Patentee in field. Recipient research corp. awards, 1982, 83, 84. Mem. Am. Chem. Soc., Fine Particle Soc. Eastern Orthodox. Lodge: Lions (bd. dirs. Foster City club, treas. 1971-73, 85-87). Avocations: golfing, fishing. Home: 221 Shearwater Isle Foster City CA 94404 Office: Chemicon Assocs 1290 Old Bayshore Suite 256 Burlingame CA 94010

SORBY, DONALD LLOYD, university dean; b. Fremont, Nebr., Aug. 12, 1933; s. Lloyd A. and Orpha M. (Simmons) S.; m. Jacquelyn J. Burchard, Nov. 7, 1959; children—Thomas, Sharon. B.S. in Pharmacy, U. Nebr., 1955; M.S., U. Wash., 1958, Ph.D., 1960. Dir. pharm. services U. Calif., San Francisco, 1970-72; chmn. dept. pharmacy practice Sch. Pharmacy, U. Wash., Seattle, 1972-74; dean Sch. of Pharmacy, U. Mo., Kansas City, 1974-84, Sch. of Pharmacy, U. Pacific, Stockton, Calif., 1984—. Contbr. articles in field to profl. jours. Assoc. fellow Am. Coll. Apothecaries; mem. Am. Pharm. Assn., Am. Assn. Colls. of Pharmacy (pres. 1980-81), Fedn. Internat. Pharmaceutique, Calif. Pharm. Assn., Acad. Pharm. Scis., Calif. Soc. Hosp. Pharmacists, Assn. Pharm. Scis., Sigma Xi, Phi Kappa Phi, Rho Chi. Lodge: Rotary. Home: 4362 Yacht Harbor Dr Stockton CA 95204 Office: Sch of Pharmacy U Pacific Stockton CA 95211

SORBY, JOSEPH RICHARD, artist educator; b. Duluth, Minn., Dec. 21, 1911; s. Joseph Austin and Lydia A. (Esterly) S.; m. P. Elizabeth Ferguson, Dec. 9, 1950. B.A., U. Northern Colo., 1937, M.A., 1952; postgrad., UCLA, 1953, U. of Americas, 1952, U. Colo., 1954. Instr. art Greeley High Sch., Colo., 1937-41, U. Nebr., Lincoln, 1941-43; assoc. prof. art U. Denver, 1946-59; prof. design and painting Calif. State U., San Jose, 1959-72, prof. emeritus, 1972—; guest prof. Southern Utah U., Cedar City, June, July 1964. Exhibited in numerous nat. competitive exhbns. various publ. collections. Served with USN, 1943-46. Recipient Purchase award Joslyn Art Mus., Omaha, Mid-Am. Annual, Kansas City, Nat. Watercolor Competition, Washington, Denver Art Mus. Mem. Fifteen Colo. Artists (pres. 1957-58), Coll. Art Assn. Am., Mil. Order World Wars, East Bay art Assn. (v.p. 1966-68), Group 21 (pres. Los Gatos, Calif. 1970-71). Lodge: Lions (dir. Sun City, Calif. 1983-84). Home: 27028 Howard St Sun City CA 92381 Office: Morningsun Studio 15 N Fork Rd Glen Haven CO 80532

SORENSEN, ALAN GAGE, electronics engineer; b. Bagley, Minn., Nov. 15, 1930; s. Sidney Alden and Olga Elida (Erickson) S.; m. Rose Lena Thompson, Aug. 12, 1956; children: George, Bruce, Judith, Kirk. BSEE, San Jose State U., 1958. Engr. Riley Co., Skokie, Ill., 1973-77; sr. engr. Simpson Electric Co., Elgin, Ill., 1977-79, Sperry-Univac, Santa Clara, Calif., 1979-84, Televideo, Sunnyvale, 1984—. Republican. Avocation: music. Home: 678 Briarcliff Dr San Jose CA 95123 Office: Televideo Systems Inc 1170 Morse Ave Sunnyvale CA 94088

SORENSEN, DEBRA LYNNETTE, computer training executive; b. Austin, Tex., Jan. 16, 1954; d. T.D. and Dolores E. (Walton) Williams; m. Audun I. Sorensen, June 10, 1972; children: Shawn M., Emily L. Student, Kelsey-Baird Bus. Sch., Spokane, Wash., 1972-73, Spokane Community Coll., 1974, Lane Community Coll., Eugene, Oreg., 1976, 79, 86—, U. Oreg., 1986—. Secretarial and word processing positions various, 1972-77; word processing mgr. Lane Council of Govts., Eugene, 1977-80; sales and tng. various word processing/computer vendors, Eugene, 1980-84; owner, mgr. Automation Plus, Eugene, 1984—; served on numerous panels related to word processing/computers for bus. and edn., including establishment of courses at Lane Community Coll., Eugene, 1979. Chmn. Lane County Affirmative Action Com., Eugene, 1980-82, Lane Community Coll. Women's Adv. Com., Eugene, 1980-82; Bethel Sch. Dist. #52 Budget Com., Eugene, 1980-84, bd. dirs., 1984—; vice chmn. Lane Council of Govts. Bd. Dirs., Eugene, 1984—; Young Bd. Members Caucus Nat. Sch. Bd., 1986. Recipient scholarship Spokane Ednl. Secs. Assn., 1972. Mem. Eugene Word Processing Assn. (salary survey com. 1978, area dir. Willamette Valley chpt. 1977), Adminstrv. Mgmt. Soc. Republican. Mem. Ch. of Christ. Avocations: reading, cooking, music, civic activities. Office: Automation Plus 3800 Barger Dr Eugene OR 97402

SORENSEN, JACKI FAYE, aerobic dance company executive, choreographer; b. Oakland, Calif., Dec. 10, 1942; d. Roy C. and Juanita F. (Bullon) Mills; m. Neil A. Sorensen, Jan. 3, 1965. B.A., U. Calif., 1964. Cert. tchr., Calif. Ptnr., Big Spring Sch. Dance, 1965; tchr. Pasadena Ave. Sch., Sacramento, 1968; founder, chmn. bd. dirs., choreographer Aerobic Dancing, Inc., Northridge, Calif., 1969—; cons., lectr. on phys. fitness. Author: Aerobic Dancing, 1979, Jacki Sorensen's Aerobic Lifestyle Book, 1983; choreographer numerous dance exercises for records and videocassettes. Trustee Women's Sports Found. Recipient Diamond Pin award Am. Heart Assn., 1979; Individual Contbn. award Am. Assn. Fitness Dirs. in Bus. and Industry, 1981; Spl. Olympics Contbn. award, 1982; Contbn. to Women's Fitness award Pres.'s Council Phys. Fitness and Sports, 1982; Healthy Am. Fitness Leader award U.S. Jaycees, 1984; Lifetime Achievement award Internat. Dance Exercise Assn., 1985; New Horizons award Caldwell (N.J.) Coll., 1985; Legend of Aerobics award City Sports mag., 1985; Pres. Council award Calif. Womens' Leadership Conf., 1986; Hall of Fame award Club Industry mag., 1986. Mem. Am. Coll. Sports Medicine, AAHPERD, Nat. Intramural and Recreation Assn., AFTRA. Office: Aerobic Dancing Inc 18907 Nordhoff St Northridge CA 91324

SORENSEN, JAMES KURT, computer consultant; b. Tacoma, Nov. 27, 1955; s. William Peter and Rita Marie (Lordeman) S. BSEE, U. Calif., Irvine, 1977. Engr. Computer Automation, Irvine, 1977-78, Basic Four, Tustin, Calif., 1978-80; cons. Cybertel, Santa Ana, Calif., 1980—, Garrett Airesearch, Torrance, Calif., 1984-85. Mem. IEEE. Avocations: aerobics, weight lifting, water and snow skiing, photography.

SORENSON, FAY DOYLE, audiologist; b. Corpus Christi, Tex., Mar. 13, 1937; d. Jack C. and Fay (Clemmer) Doyle, m. Dwight T. Sorenson, Aug. 7, 1965; children: John H., Amy Fay. BA, Our Lady of the Lake Coll., San Antonio, 1958; MS, Baylor U. Coll. Medicine, 1962; PhD, Stanford U., 1969. Lic. Bd. Med. Examiners in Audiology, Calif.; cert. pub. sch. audiologist, Calif. Biochemist Stanford Research Inst., Menlo Park, Calif., 1962-65; asst. prof. Portland (Oreg.) State U., 1973-75, San Jose (Calif.) State U., 1975-77, U. of the Pacific, Stockton, Calif., 1977-80; audiologist Sacramento City Unified Sch. Dist., 1981-85, program supr. spl. edn., 1986—. Fellow Coll. Speech, Lang. and Hearing Assn.; mem. Calif. Speech Lang. Hearing Assn. (cert., mem. ednl. standards bd. 1983—, bd. dirs. 1983-85, Outstanding Achievement award, 1986), Am. Speech Lang. Hearing Assn. (ednl. studies bd. 1983-86), Am. Auditory Soc. Avocations: playing piano, reading, gardening. Home: 134 Mokelumne River Dr Lodi CA 95240 Office: Sacramento Unified Sch Dist Spl Edn Dept 1901 60th Ave Sacramento CA 95822

SORESTAD, GLEN (ALLAN), writer, publisher; b. Vancouver, B.C., Can., May 21, 1937; s. John and Myrtle (Dalshaug) S.; m. Sonia D. Talpash, Sept. 17, 1960; children: Evan, Mark, Donna, Myron. M.Ed., U. Sask., 1976. Elem. tchr., Yorkton, Sask., Can., 1957-67; English tchr., Saskatoon, Sask., 1967-81; writer/pub. Thistledown Press, Saskatoon, 1981—, pres., 1975—; pres. Prairie Pubs. Group, 1984-86; exec. mem. Lit. Press Group, Toronto, 1982-85. Author: (poetry) Prairie Pub Poems, 1976; Pear Seeds in My Mouth, 1977; Ancestral Dances, 1979; Jan Lake Poems, 1984; Hold the Rain in Your Hands, 1985. Hilroy fellow, 1976; Can. Council grantee, 1976. Mem. League Can. Poets (exec. mem. 1977-84), Sask. Writers Guild, Assn. Can. Pubs. (council 1984—), Writers Union of Can., Amnesty Internat., Can. Copyright Inst. Home: 668 East Pl, Saskatoon, SK Canada S7J 2Z5

SORGE, JOSEPH ANTHONY, molecular biologist; b. Newark, Mar. 23, 1954; s. Joseph S. and Margaret (Ticken) S.; m. Maryanne Kinchla, July 2, 1984. BS in Biology, MIT, 1975, BS in Chemistry, 1975; MD cum laude, Harvard U., Boston, 1979. Intern Brown U., Providence, 1979-80; postdoctoral fellow Cold Spring Harbor (N.Y.) Lab., 1980-82; asst. mem. Scripps Clinic and Research Inst., La Jolla, Calif., 1983—, staff physician, 1985—; sci. dir. Stratagene, San Diego, 1984-86, chief exec. officer, 1985—. Contbr. articles on molecular biology to profl. jours. Recipient Research Service award NIH, 1981-83, Research Investigator award NIH, 1983-91, Jr. Faculty award Am. Cancer Soc., 1985-86, Pew Scholars award, Pew Meml. Trust, 1985-89. Mem. AAAS, Am. Soc. Microbiology. Avocations: skiing, surfing. Office: Research Inst Scripps Clinic 10666 N Torrey Pines Rd La Jolla CA 92037

SORRELL, JAMES ROBERT, electronics, aerospace, mining and agriculture consultant; b. San Antonio, Apr. 22, 1944; s. Howard Clifton and Pearl (Secrist) Doolittle; m. Trudy Kay Cressy, Apr. 22, 1979; children: Abby Anne, Alissa Rose, Benjamin Alan. BS, Southwestern U., 1966; MA, UCLA, 1969. News dir. Stas. KFXD and KSPD, Pacific Northwest Broadcasting, Boise, Idaho, 1973-78; dir. Revelation, IR&D, Boise, 1979—; radio reporter covering launch of Apollo 15, Cape Kennedy, 1971, launch of Skylab Space Sta., Cape Kennedy, 1973, launch of Apollo-Soyuz (US-USSR), Cape Kennedy, 1975; NASA pool writer USS New Orleans for landing of 2d Skylab crew, 1973; only reporter on bd. final U.S. comml. whaling voyage, 1971, published in Environ. Quality mag., 1972; speaker N.Y. Graphics, 1985. Tchr. Boise Schs. Night Edn., 1975-82; bd. dirs. Crisis Line, Boise, 1982-83; state chmn. Statue of Liberty Fund, Idaho, 1984-86; administr. Faith Community Ch.; vol. Idaho Space Adv. Council; mem. Idaho Centennial Com., 1986—. Helped develop garlic crop in Idaho. Home and Office: 8306 Crenshaw St Boise ID 83709 Mailing: care Liberty Lake Commn PO Box 189 Liberty Lake WA 99019

SORRELL, ROGER D(ARRELL), psychotherapist; b. Esslingen, Republic of Germany, May 21, 1954; came to U.S., 1956; s. James Clifford and Gertrude Virginia (Mitchell) S. BS summa cum laude, Kans. State U., 1975; Master of Letters, Oxford (Eng.) U., 1978; PhD, Cornell U., 1983; MSW, U. Wash., 1985. Clin. therapist West Seattle Mental Health, 1985—. Author: St. Francis of Assisi and Nature, 1986. Rhodes scholar, 1975. Mem. Nat. Assn. Social Workers, Phi Beta Kappa. Democrat. Mem. Unitarian Ch. Home: 1547 17th Ave E Seattle WA 98112 Office: West Seattle Mental Health 500 Wall St Seattle WA 98112

SORTOMME, JEROME CHARLES, landscape horticulture educator; b. Van Nuys, Calif., Jan. 24, 1946; s. Jerome O. and Claire (La Roy) S.; m. Joyce Adams, Nov. 2, 1977 (div. 1986). AS, Pierce Coll., 1966; BS, Calif. State Poly. U., Pomona, 1969. Instr. Widney High Sch., Los Angeles, 1970-73, Mulholland Jr. High Sch., Van Nuys, 1973-77; instr. landscaping Oxnard (Calif.) Coll., 1978-80; instr. landscape horticulture Santa Barbara (Calif.) City Coll., 1980—; horticulturist Old Creek Ranch and Winery, Oak View, Calif., 1976—. Mem. Santa Barbara County Hort. Soc., Rare Fruit Growers of Calif., Calif. Landscape Contractors Assn. (affiliate), Calif. State Poly. U. Alumni Assn. Democrat. Avocations: Xeriscaping, edible landscaping, meteorology, beer can collecting. Office: Santa Barbara City Coll Landscape Horticulture Program 721 Cliff Dr Santa Barbara CA 93109-2394

SORTOR, KATHRYN ELIZABETH, speech and language pathologist; b. San Francisco, Nov. 13, 1955; d. Alan Thorndike and Wanda Jean (Moore) S.; m. Gordon Bruce McKellar, Jan. 7, 1978. BA with honors, Stanford U., 1977, MA, 1980; MA with honors, Northwestern U., 1982. Speech and lang. pathologist Fresno (Calif.) Community Hosp., 1982-83; program developer Fresno Unified Sch. Dist., 1983-84; program developer, clin. researcher Ctr. for Neurolinguistic Research, Fresno, 1983-84; program asst., program devel. specialist Casa Colina Hosp. Rehab. Medicine, Pomona, Calif., 1984—, researcher, 1985—; lectr. Whittier (Calif.) Coll., 1986. Wis. Alumni Research Found. fellow, 1977-78. Mem. Am. Speech Lang. Hearing Assn. Office: Casa Colina Hosp Team I 255 E Bonita Ave Pomona CA 91767

SOSA, DAN, JR., justice Supreme Court New Mexico; b. Las Cruces, N.Mex., Nov. 12, 1923; s. Dan and Margaret (Soto) S.; m. Rita Ortiz, Aug. 31, 1950; 7 children. BSBA, N.Mex. State U., 1947; JD, U. N.Mex., 1951. Bar: N.Mex. 1951. Tchr., coach, public schs. Mesilla, N.Mex., 1947-48; practiced law Las Cruces, 1952-75; judge Las Cruces City Ct., 1952-55; spl. agt. Office of Price Stblzn., 1951-52; asst. dist. atty., then dist. atty. N.Mex. 3d Jud. Dist., 1956-64; spl. asst. atty. gen. for prosecution capital criminal cases Dept. Justice, 1965-66; justice N.Mex. Supreme Ct., 1975—, former chief justice. Served to 1st lt. AC U.S. Army, 1942-45. Democrat. Roman Catholic. Office: Supreme Ct N Mex 327 Don Gaspar Ave Santa Fe NM 87504 *

SOTAK, CHRISTOPHER HOWARD, chemist, educator, computer engineer; b. San Antonio, Dec. 13, 1951; s. Veonor Michael Sotak and Katherine Marianna (Matthews) Glover; m. Sandra Louise Morrow, June 23, 1979; children: Derek Christopher, Onalie Louise. BA in Chemistry, U. No. Colo., 1975, MA in Chemistry, 1980; PhD in Chemistry, Syracuse U., 1983. Toxicologist Consolidated Biomed. Labs., Inc., Denver, 1978-80; teaching asst. Syracuse U., N.Y., 1980-81, research asst., 1981-83; software engr. Gen. Electric Nuclear Magnetic Resonance Instruments, Inc., Fremont, Calif., 1984-86; applications scientist Gen. Electric Nuclear Magnetic Resonance Instruments, Inc., Fremont, 1986—; adj. lectr. chemistry Santa Clara (Calif.) U., 1985; lectr. numerous presentations on indsl., computer and med. chem. applications. Contbr. articles to profl. jours. Mem. Am. Chem. Soc., Soc. Magnetic Resonance in Medicine. Democrat. Avocations: woodworking, skiing, racquetball. Office: Gen Electric Nuclear Magnetic Resonance Instruments Fremont CA 94539

SOTER, NICHOLAS GREGORY, advertising agency executive; b. Great Falls, Mont., Apr. 26, 1947; s. Sam Nick and Bernice (Bennett) S.; m. Kathleen Lyman, Feb. 20, 1970; children: Nichole, Erin, Samuel Scott, Kara, Stephen Andrew, Riley Kyle. BS, Brigham Young U., 1971. With McLean Assocs., Provo, Utah, 1970-75; chmn. bd., pres., chief exec. officer Soter Assocs. Inc., Salt Lake City, 1975—; instr. advt. Utah Tech. Coll., Provo, 1971-75, Brigham Young U., Provo, 1980-84. Author: Journal of Joseph, 1979, Journal of Brigham, 1980, LaVell Edwards, 1980, Amos Wright, 1981, Moments in Motherhood, 1981, What It Means to Know Christ, 1981, Mormon Fortune Builders, 1982, Utah History, 1982; contbr. articles to profl. jours. Bd. dirs. Utah Valley Pub. Communications Council for Ch. Jesus Christ of Latter-day Saints, 1982—; Rep. dist. chmn. Recipient N.Y. Art Dir.'s The One Show award, Salt Lake Art Dirs. Communications Assn. of Utah Valley award. Mem. Communications Assn. Utah Valley (past pres.), Provo C. of C. (bd. dirs.), Innisbrook Network of Advt. Agys. (pres. 1986-87). Home: 1728 S 290 E Orem UT 84058 Office: Soter Assocs Inc 350 S 400 E Suite 300 Salt Lake City UT 84111

SOTO, GARY, poet, educator; b. Fresno, Calif., Apr. 12, 1952; s. Manuel Soto and Angie (Trevino) Oftedal; m. Carolyn Sadako Oda, May 24, 1975; children: Mariko Heidi. BA in English, Calif. State U., Fresno, 1974; MFA in Creative Writing, U. Calif., Irvine, 1976. Lectr. Chicano Studies U. Calif., Berkeley, 1977-81, asst. prof. English and Chicano Studies, 1981-85, assoc. prof. English and Chicano Studies, 1985—; Bd. dirs. Coordinating Council of Literary Mags., N.Y.C., 1985—. Books: The Elements of San Joaquin, 1977 (U.S. Internat. Poetry Forum award), The Tale of Sunlight, 1978, Where Sparrows Work Hard, 1981, Black Hair, 1985, Living Up the Street, 1985 (Am. Book award 1985), Small Faces, 1986. Fellow Nat. Endowment for Arts, 1981, Guggenheim, 1980; recipient Acad. Am. Poets Prize, 1975, The Discovery-The Nation Prize, 1975, Levinson award from Poetry, 1984.

Avocation: karate. Home: 1020 Santa Fe Albany CA 94706 Office: U Calif Dept English Berkeley CA 94720

SOTO, RONALD STEVEN, management trainer, consultant; b. Los Angeles, Feb. 25, 1948; s. Jesse Douglas and Emma Jean (Nieves) S.; m. Sandra Ester Finocchio, June 17, 1972; children: Raul, Renaldo, Celza, Jesse. BS Social Sci., Calif. Poly. State U., Pomona, 1972; MSW, U. Calif., Berkeley, 1974, MPH, 1977. Co-founder El Centro Mental Health Ctr., Oakland, Calif., 1972-77; exec. dir. La Familia Counseling Service, Hayward, Calif., 1977-81; assoc. dir. Spanish Speaking Unity Council, Oakland, Calif., 1981-82; v.p. The Nat. Hispanic U., Oakland, 1982-85; pres. S.W. Mgmt. Systems, Hayward, 1985—. Mem. Hayward Pub. Works and Indsl. Commn., 1978; bd. dirs. Mex. Am. Pol. Assn., 1978—, Regional Ctr. East Bay, Oakland, 1983—, Alameda County Mental Health Assn., Oakland, 1985—. Recipient commendation Calif. Protection and Advocacy Inc., Sacramento, 1982, cert. appreciation Regional Ctr. East Bay, 1982. Mem. Mex. Am. C. of C. Roman Catholic. Avocations: fishing, sports. Home: 27683 Pensacola Way Hayward CA 94544 Office: Southwest Mgmt Systems 191 Harder Rd Suite 178 Hayward CA 94544

SOUCY, DONALD GILLES, chemist, researcher; b. Van Buren, Maine, Nov. 27, 1952; s. Harry and Gertrude (Thibodeau) S.; m. Petrina Elaine Chiovitti, Aug. 31, 1980; 1 child, Sarah Anne. BA, Cen. Conn. State Coll., 1974; MS, U. Colo., 1979. Lab. technician Pfizer Internat., Groton, Conn., 1974-76; instr. U. Colo., Denver, 1979-80; sr. chemist Aerojet Strategic Propulsion Co., Sacramento, 1980—. Mem. Am. Chem. Soc. (cert.). Democrat. Roman Catholic. Avocations: photography, gardening. Home: 8513 Cherry Crest Ct Elk Grove CA 95624 Office: Aerojet Strategic Propulsion Co Dept 2135 00-006 PO Box 15699C Sacramento CA 95813

SOUDER, C(HARLES) WILLIAM, electronics executive, engineer; b. Los Angeles, Jan. 27, 1945; s. Charles Lee and Lillian Josephine (Bradbee) S.; m. Ernestina Aragón, Aug. 27, 1966; children: Patricia Ann, Michael Steven. BSE, UCLA, 1966; MSEE, U. So. Calif., 1971; MBA, Calif. State U., Long Beach, 1982. Registered profl. mfg. engr., Calif. Specialist in engrng. Northrop Electronics div. Northrop Corp., Hawthorne, Calif., 1966-76, research engr., 1983-84; program mgr. Northrop Research Ctr. div. Northrop Corp., Palos Verdes, Calif., 1976-82, Northrop Aircraft Co. div. Northrop Corp., Hawthorne, 1982-83; v.p. engrng. Photonic Automation, Inc., Santa Ana, Calif., 1984—; pres. Automation Applications, Rancho Palos Verdes, Calif., 1980-82. Contbr. articles to profl. jours.; patentee in field. Mem. ASME (sr., machine vision assn.), Robotics Internat., IEEE. Avocation: building and flying radio-controlled gliders. Home: 28621 Mt Rose Rd Rancho Palos Verdes CA 90732 Office: Photonic Automation Inc 3633 W MacArthur Blvd Santa Ana CA 92704

SOULE, ROGER GILBERT, educator; b. Northport, N.Y., Feb. 21, 1935; s. Freeman Gilbert and Rosemond Merecedes (Shanks) S.; m. Janet Carol, June 13, 1959; children: Steven Walker, Thomas Roger, Elizabeth Janet. B.S., SUNY-Cortland, 1957; M.S., U. Ill., 1958; Ph.D., Wash. State U., 1967. Faculty Dutchess Community Coll., Poughkeepsie, N.Y., 1960-64, Wash. State U., Pullman, 1964-67, Boston U., 1967-75, Liberty Baptist Coll., Lynchburg, Va., 1976-77; chmn. dept. phys. edn. and athletics Biola Coll. (now Biola Univ.), La Mirada, Calif., 1978—; research physiologist Natick Labs., summers 1968-74. Contbr. articles to sci. jours. Served with U.S. Army, 1958-60. Fellow Am. Coll. Sports Medicine; mem. Am. Physiol. Soc., Sigma Xi. Baptist. Home: 14203 Figueroa Rd La Mirada CA 90638 Office: Biola U 13800 Biola Ave La Mirada CA 90639

SOUTH, JOHN ALLAN, mortgage company president; b. Salt Lake City; s. George Q. and Melba (Eastman) S.; m. Linda Webster, May 29, 1969; children: David, Michael, John, Matthew, Rachel, Rebecca, Maren, Mark. BS in Chemistry and Math., Brigham Young U., 1969, MS in Chemistry, 1972. Research engr. Kennecott Corp., Magna, Utah, 1971-82, sr. chemist, 1982-84, 84-85, power plant chemist, 1984; operator Energy Services, Orem, Utah, 1978-84; asst. dir. research Timp Environ. Testing Co., Orem, 1985-86; mortgage loan officer Eagle Nat. Mortgage, Provo, Utah, 1986—. Author: The Sense of Survival, 1985. Coach City Sports Teams, Orem, 1975—. John E. Anderson scholar Brigham Young U. Chemistry Dept., Provo, 1969-70. Mem. Am. Chem. Soc., United Steel Workers Am. Union. Republican. Mormon. Avocations: hiking, fishing, hunting, skiing, writing. Home: 683 S 1040 W Orem UT 84058

SOUTHERN, RONALD DONALD, diversified corporation executive; b. Calgary, Alta., Can., July 25, 1930; s. Samuel Donald and Alexandra (Cuthill) S.; m. Margaret Visser, July 30, 1954; children: Nancy, Linda. B.Sc., U. Alta., Edmonton, 1953; LL.D. (hon.), U. Calgary, 1976. Pres., chief exec. officer Atco Ltd., Calgary, 1954-85, dep. chmn., 1985—; chmn. Canadian Utilities Ltd., Edmonton; hon. assoc. mem. Calgary Exhbn. and Stampede Bd.; gov. Olympic Trust Can.; bd. dirs. ATCO Ltd., B.C. Forest Products Ltd., Can. Airlines Internat., Can. Pacific Ltd., Can. Utilities Ltd., Easton United Securities Ltd., LaFarge Corp., Royal Ins. Ltd., Xerox of Can. Inc. Named to Order of Can., 1986; recipient Holland Trade award Govt. of The Netherlands, 1985; co-recipient (with wife) Sportsmen of Yr. award Calgary Booster Club; named Businessman of Yr. U. Alta. Mem. United Church of Can. Clubs: Calgary Petroleum, Earl Grey Golf, U. Calgary Chancellors. Home: 67 Massey Pl SW, Calgary, AB Canada T2V 2G7 Office Address: Canadian Utilities Limited, Suite 1600, 909 11th Ave SW, Calgary, AB Canada T2R 1N6 Other: Canadian Utilities Ltd, 10035 105 St, Edmonton, AB Canada T5J 2V6

SOUTHWARD, GLEN MORRIS, statistician, educator; b. Boise, Idaho, Oct. 8, 1927; s. Glen P. and Emma M. (Martin) S.; m. M. Lorraine Kissack, Oct. 3, 1974; children from previous marriage: Judith Ann, Richard Todd. BS, U. Wash., 1949, MS, 1956, PhD, 1966. Asst. prof. Stats. Wash. State U., Pullman, 1967-71; biometrician Internat. Pacific Halibut Commn., Seattle, 1971-75; assoc. prof. stats. N.Mex. State U., Las Cruces, 1975-80, prof., 1980—. Contbr. articles to profl. jours. Fellow Am. Inst. Fishery Research Biologists; mem. Am. Statis. Assn., Statis. Soc. Can., Biometric Soc. (sec., treas. Western N.Am. region 1984—), Sigma Xi. Avocations: photography, cooking. Office: NMex State U Dept Exptl Stats Box 3130 Las Cruces NM 88003

SOUTHWICK, CHARLES HENRY, zoologist, educator; b. Wooster, Ohio, Aug. 28, 1928; s. Arthur F. and Faye (Motz) S.; m. Heather Milne Beck, July 12, 1952; children: Steven, Karen. B.A., Coll. Wooster, 1949; M.S., U. Wis., 1951, Ph.D., 1953. NIH fellow 1951-53; asst. prof. biology Hamilton Coll., 1953-54; NSF fellow Oxford (Eng.) U., 1954-55; faculty Ohio U., 1955-61; assoc. prof. pathobiology Johns Hopkins Sch. Hygiene and Pub. Health, Balt., 1961-68; prof. Johns Hopkins Sch. Hygiene and Pub. Health, 1968-79; assoc. dir. Johns Hopkins Internat. Ctr. for Med. Research and Tng., Calcutta, India, 1964-65; chmn. dept. environ., population and organismic biology U. Colo., Boulder, 1979-82, prof. biology, 1979—; mem. primate adv. com. Nat. Acad. Sci.-NRC, 1963-75, com. primate conservation, 1974-75; mem. Gov.'s Sci. Adv. Com. State of Md., 1975-78; mem. com. on research and exploration Nat. Geog. Soc., 1979—. Editor: Primate Social Behavior, 1963, Animal Aggression, 1970, Nonhuman Primates in Biomedical Research, 1975, Ecology and the Quality of Our Environment, 1976, Global Ecology, 1985. Recipient Fulbright Research award India, 1959-60. Fellow AAAS, Acad. Zoology, Animal Behavior Soc.; mem. Am. Soc. Zoologists, Ecol. Soc. Am., Am. Soc. Mammalogists, Am. Soc. Primatology, Internat. Primatology Soc., Internat. Soc. Study Aggression. Research, publs. on animal social behavior and population dynamics, influences animal social behavior on demographic characteristic mammal populations, primate ecology and behavior, estuarine ecology and environmental quality.

SOUTO, MARK AVELINO, aerospace research engineer; b. Newark, Mar. 15, 1948; s. Marcal and Mary Helen (Silva) S.; m. Barbara N. Chikami, Aug. 3, 1974; children: Matthew M., Andrew T. BA in Chemistry, Rutgers U., 1969; PhD in Chemistry, UCLA, 1974. Research asst. Engelhard Industries, Newark, summers 1968, 69; teaching asst. UCLA, 1969-71, research asst., 1971-74; research assoc. U. Utah, Salt Lake City, 1974-76; instr. phys. sci. Golden West Coll., Huntington Beach, Calif., 1976-83; research and devel. engr. Hughes Aircraft Corp., Irvine, Calif., 1983—. Contbr. articles to profl. jours. Mem. Am. Chem. Soc., Phi Beta Kappa, Phi Lambda Upsilon. Roman Catholic. Avocations: sports. Office: Hughes Aircraft Corp 17150 Von Karman Ave Irvine CA 92714

SOVERS, OJARS JURIS, research physicist; b. Riga, USSR, July 11, 1937; came to U.S., 1950; s. Karlis and Olga (Kaneps) S.; m. Zinta Armande Aisters, 1959. BS, Bklyn. Coll., 1958; PhD, Princeton U., 1962. Research assoc. Columbia U., N.Y.C., 1962-64; with tech. staff GTE Labs., Bayside, N.Y., 1964-72, Sony Corp., Tokyo, Japan, 1972-78, Jet Propulsion Lab., Pasadena, Calif., 1979—. Contbr. articles on physics and chemistry to profl. jours. Mem. AAAS, Am. Phys. Soc., Am. Geophys. Union, Sigma Xi. Lutheran. Avocation: backpacking. Home: 1367 La Solana Dr Altadena CA 91001 Office: Jet Propulsion Lab 238-700 4800 Oak Grove Dr Pasadena CA 91109

SOWERS, JOHN PHILLIP, industry administrator, consultant; b. Los Angeles, Apr. 22, 1947; s. Norman Joseph and Cora Marie (Cirino) S.; m. Linda Joyce Boyer, Sept. 5, 1980; 1 stepchild, Alisa Joy Boyer. Student, U. Calif., Santa Cruz, 1965-67, U. Calif., Hong Kong, 1967-68; BA, UCLA, 1969; postgrad., U. B.C., 1969-71. Indsl. security investigator U.S. Dept. of Def., Los Angeles, 1976-78; mgr. security and safety Raytheon Co., Santa Barbara, Calif., 1978-81; sr. safety adminstr. Santa Barbara Research Ctr. Hughes Aircraft Co., 1981—; mem. Hughes Aircraft Environ. Affairs Subcom., Culver City, Calif., 1985—; owner, cons. Enviro-Tech, Santa Barbara, 1985—. Mem. Am. Soc. Safety Engrs., Santa Barbara C. of C. (hazardous waste subcom. 1985—). Avocations: reading, landscaping, home improvement, swimming, tennis.

SOWERWINE, ELBERT ORLA, JR., consultant engineering planning and management; b. Tooele, Utah, Mar. 15, 1915; s. Elbert Orla and Margaret Alice (Evans) S.; B. Chemistry, Cornell U., 1937, Chem. Engr., 1938; m. Norma Borge; children—Sue-Ann Sowerwine Jacobson, Sandra Sowerwine Montgomery, Elbert Orla 3d, John Frederick, Avril Ruth Taylor, Albaro Francisco, Octavio Evans, Zaida Margaret. Analytical chemist Raritan Copper Works, Perth Amboy, N.J., summers 1936, 37; research chem. engr. Socony-Vacuum Oil Co., Paulsboro, N.J., 1938-43; prodn. supr. Merck & Co., Elkton, Va., 1943-45; asst. plant mgr. U.S. Indsl. Chems. Co., Newark, 1945-48; project engr. and research dir. Wigton-Abbott Corp., Newark, 1948-50, Cody, Wyo., 1950-55; cons. engrng., planning, indsl. and community devel., resource evaluation and mgmt. Wapiti, Wyo., also C.Am., 1955—. Commr. N.J., Boy Scouts Am., 1938-43; mem. Wapiti and Park County (Wyo.) Sch. Bds., 1954-58; dir. Mont. State Planning Bd., 1959-61; exec. bd. Mo. Basin Research and Devel. Council, 1959-61. Fellow Am. Inst. Chemists; mem. Am. Inst. Chem. Engrs., Am. Planning Assn., Nicaraguan Assn. Engrs. and Architects. Libertarian. Mem. Christian Ch. Researcher desulfurization of petroleum products, process control, alternate energy projects; patentee in petroleum and chem. processes and equipment. Home: Broken H Ranch Wapiti WY 82450 Office: Sowerwine Cons Wapiti WY 82450

SOX, HAROLD CARLETON, JR., physician, educator; b. Palo Alto, Calif., Aug. 18, 1939; s. Harold Carleton and Mary (Griffiths) S.; m. Carol Helen Hill, Aug. 26, 1962; children: Colin Montgomery, Lara Katherine. B.S., Stanford U., 1961; M.D. cum laude, Harvard U., 1966. Diplomate: Am. Bd. Internal Medicine. Intern and resident Mass. Gen. Hosp., Boston, 1966-68; clin. assoc. Nat. Cancer Inst., Bethesda, Md., 1968-70; instr. Dartmouth Med. Sch., Hanover, N.H., 1970-73; assoc. chief staff for ambulatory care VA Med. Ctr., Palo Alto, Calif., 1976—; asst. prof. medicine Stanford U. Sch. Medicine, Calif., 1973-80, assoc. prof., 1980-85; prof. Stanford U. Sch. Medicine, 1985—, chief div. gen. internal medicine, 1976—; panel mem. Nat. Bd. Med. Examiners, Physicians Assts. Nat. Certifying Examination, 1973-76, Physicians Computer-based Certifying Examination, 1984-86. Author books; contbr. numerous articles to med jours., chpts. to books; mem. editorial bd.: Med. Decision Making, 1980—, Jour. Gen. Internal Medicine, 1985—. Fellow ACP (clin. efficacy assessment subcom. 1985—); mem. Soc. for Research and Edn. in Primary Care Internal Medicine (mem. council 1980-83, chmn. com. on health tech. evaluation 1982—), Soc. for Med. Decision Making (pres. 1983-84, trustee 1980-83), Am. Fedn. Clin. Research, Calif. Acad. Medicine, Inst. Medicine Council Health Care Tech. (panel mem.), Alpha Omega Alpha. Home: 1150 Harker Ave Palo Alto CA 94301 Office: Stanford U Sch Medicine Stanford CA 94305

SPADA, GEORGE JOSEPH, exporter; b. Portland, Oreg., Mar. 27, 1943; s. Fred and Josephine Angela (Sprando) S.; m. Marietta Lucia Capri, July 31, 1965; children: Fredric Raymond, Caprice Marie. Student, Portland U. Prin. Spada Distbg. Co. Inc., Portland, 1963—. Recipient Steamer Portland award Port of Portland. Republican. Roman Catholic. Clubs: Portland Golf, Multnomah Athletic. Avocations: golf, flying, skiing, folk-bluegrass and country music, travel. Home: 4416 SW Bernard Dr Portland OR 97201 Office: Spada Distbg Co Inc 1137 SE Union Ave Portland OR 97214-3474

SPADOTTO, BEVERLY THERESE, editor; b. Syracuse, N.Y., July 11, 1951; d. Ted and Beverly Jean (Loughlin) S.; BA in Journalism, George Washington U., 1973; MA, U. So. Calif., 1975. Dir. pub. relations D'Arcy-MacManus & Masius, advt., Los Angeles, 1976-78; editor Rangefinder mag., Santa Monica, Calif., 1978-81; communications editor CIGNA Healthplans of Calif., Glendale, Calif., 1982-85; dir. communications U.S. Adminstrs., Inc., 1985—; ptnr. Flash & Class, Los Angeles, 1982—. Mem. Western Publs. Assn., Publicity Club Los Angeles, Sigma Delta Chi. Democrat. Roman Catholic. Home: 410 S Hobart Blvd Los Angeles CA 90020

SPAETE, RICHARD ROGER, virologist; b. Rice Lake, Wis., Aug. 18, 1947; s. Paul Robert and Helen Margaret (Betz) S. Student, St. Olaf Coll., 1965-67; BS, U. Wis., Eau Claire, 1974; MS, U. Mont., 1978; PhD, U. Chgo., 1982. Postdoctoral fellow U. Chgo., 1982-83; postdoctoral fellow virology Stanford U., 1983-86; scientist Chiron Corp., Emeryville, Calif., 1986—. Contbr. articles to profl. jours. Served with U.S. Army, 1967-70, Vietnam. NIH fellow, 1978-82, 83, Leukemia Research Soc. fellow, 1984-86. Mem. Am. Soc. Microbiology, AAAS, Soc. for Gen. Microbiology. Lutheran. Avocation: skiing. Office: Chiron Corp Dept Virology 4560 Horton St Emeryville CA 94608

SPAFFORD, MICHAEL CHARLES, artist; b. Palm Springs, Calif., Nov. 6, 1935. B.A., Pomona Coll., 1959; M.A., Harvard U., 1960. One man shows include Seattle Art Mus., 1982, U. Puget Sound, Tacoma, Wash., 1973, Tacoma Art Mus., 1975, Utah Mus. Fine Arts, Salt Lake City, 1975, Francine Seders Gallery, Seattle, 1965—; exhibited in group shows at Wilcox Gallery, Swarthmore Coll., Pa., 1977, Seattle Art Mus., 1977, Am. Acad. and Inst. Arts and Letters, N.Y.C., 1980, 83, Seattle Art Mus., 1980, Kobe, Japan, 1981, Eastern Wash. U., 1982, Henry Art Gallery, 1982. Recipient Prix de Rome, 1967-69, award Am. Acad. and Inst. Arts and Letters, 1983; Louis Comfort Tiffany Found. grantee, 1965-66. Home: 2418 E Interlaken Blvd Seattle WA 98112

SPAHR, BLAKE LEE, German educator; b. Carlisle, Pa., July 11, 1924; s. William Alexander and Mary Agnes (Cuddy) S.; m. Herlinde Amelia Baekelmans, Mar. 22, 1980. BA, Dickinson Coll., 1947; MA, Yale U., 1948, PhD, 1951. Instr. German Yale U., New Haven, 1951-55; asst. prof. U. Calif., Berkeley, 1955-59, assoc. prof., 1959-64, prof. German and Comparative Literature, 1964—. Author: Problems and Perspectives, 1981, Anton Ulrich & Aramena, 1966, The Archives of the Pegnesischer Blumenorden, 1960; editor: Peter Lang Verlag, 1982—. French hornist Oakland (Calif.) Community Orch., 1970—. Served to 1st lt. USAAF, 1943-46. Decorated Air medal with six oak leaf clusters; Grand Cross of Merit 1st class (Germany). Avocations: music, computers. Home: 88 Evergreen Dr Orinda CA 94563 Office: U Calif Dept of German Berkeley CA 94720

SPALSBURY, JEFF RICHARD, training information company executive; b. Mt. Pleasant, Mich., Apr. 7, 1935; s. Jeff R. and Marjorie M. (Bell) S.; m. Diane de la Rosa, Aug. 30, 1964 (div. Mar. 1986); children—Lisa E., Sara M. B.A., San Jose State U., 1967; M.A., U. Denver, 1976. Pres., owner JRS Enterprises, San Jose, Calif., 1959—; instructional designer NISC Co., Denver, 1975-79; dir. sales tng. Raychem, Menlo Park, Calif., 1980-81, nat. tng. mgr. Velo-Bind, Sunnyvale, Calif., 1981-83. Author instruction books, prin. works including: Individualized Instruction: Is It The Answer, 1974, The Instructional Media Center Conflict, 1975; Performance Appraisal, 1984; Train-the-Trainer, 1984; monthly bus. column This Business of Training, 1985; also author popular publs., A Pet Porcupine, 1957, Monument to the Enemy, 1975. Editor, dir., writer 31 motion pictures, also actor. Served with U.S. Army, 1956-58. Mem. Am. Soc. Tng. and Devel., Profl. and Tech. Cons. Assn., Assn. Ednl. Communications and Tech. Office: JRS Enterprises PO Box 53630 San Jose CA 95153

SPANGLER, SUSANNE LOUISE, English educator; b. Lynwood, Calif., Dec. 15, 1950; s. Robert Charles and Susanne Anna (Steuer) S.; m. Eric W. Bell, Dec. 18, 1982. Student, Georg-August U., Göttingen, Fed. Republic of Germany, 1970-71; BA magna cum laude, UCLA, 1972, MA, 1976. Cert. in Teaching ESL. Tchr. Gesch-Scholl Gymnasium, Ludwigshafen, Fed. Republic Germany, 1974-75, Indochinese Project, Los Angeles, 1976-78, Evans Adult Sch., Los Angeles, 1976-86; assoc. prof. English East Los Angeles Coll., Monterey Park, Calif., 1980—; instr. UCLA extension, Los Angeles, 1976, 78, Los Angeles Trade Tech. Coll., 1977-80; curriculum developer Los Angeles Unified Schs., 1978-80; chmn. ESL com. East Los Angeles Coll., 1980—; mem. ESL Dist. com. Los Angeles Community Colls., 1986—. Co-author: Rhetorical Modes for ESL Students, 1982. Chmn. membership com. Mus. Ctr. Opera League, Los Angeles, 1985—. Fulbright grantee, Ludwigshafen, Fed. Republic Germany, 1974-75. Mem. Tchrs. English to Speakers of Other Langs., Calif. Assn. Tchrs. English to Speakers of Other Langs., Fulbright Alumni Assn., Phi Beta Kappa. Democrat. Episcopalian. Avocations: music, singing opera, travel. Office: East Los Angeles Coll 1301 Brooklyn Ave Monterey Park CA 91754

SPANIER, THOMAS ALVIN, manufacturing executive; b. San Francisco, Feb. 24, 1946; s. Joseph Julius and Florence Rosella (Anderson) S.; m. Jacqueline Patricia Harney, Sept. 17, 1966 (div. June 1982); children: Heidi June, Brook Thomas; m. Francesca Marie Siviero, Dec. 29, 1985. BS, U. Calif., Berkeley, 1967; MBA, Harvard U., 1969. Program mgr. Sullivan Co., San Francisco, 1969-71, also bd. dirs.; v.p. Am. Nat. Enterprises, Salt Lake City, 1971-73; pres. Brugger Export Corp., Redwood City, Calif., 1973, Cal-Vine Nurseries, Fallbrook, Calif., 1973-74, Sullivan Industries, Sonoma, Calif., 1975—; chmn. bd. dirs. Quality Hosts, Medford, Phoenix Composites, Inc. Mem. Am. Def. Preparedness Assn., Phi Beta Kappa, Delta Sigma Pi. Avocations: winemaking, snowskiing, tennis.

SPANN, KATHARINE DOYLE, marketing/communications executive; b. Holton, Kans.; d. Edward James and Josephine (Hurla) Doyle; B.S., Emporia State Coll.; m. Hugh J. Spann (div. Feb. 1952); 1 dau., Susan Katharine. V.p. Bozell & Jacobs Advt. (formerly L.C. Cole Co.), San Francisco, 1951-76; pres. Katharine Doyle Spann Assos., 1977—; propr. Kate's Vineyard, Napa Valley, Calif.; exec. producer TV shows Doctors News Conf., The Ben Alexander Show, Land of Jazz, 1956—; communications counsel to health professions, 1970—. Bd. dirs. Heritage Fund, Napa Valley Opera House. Named Advt. Woman of Year, 1962; recipient El Capitan award Peninsula chpt. Pub. Relations Soc. Am., 1962, 66, Am. Silver Anvil award, Pub. Relations Soc. Am., 1962, 66, Excellence award Publicity Club of Bay Area, 1966. Mem. Am. Soc. Enology, Napa Valley Women in Wine, Calif. Vintage Wine Soc. (wine com.), Conferie des Chevaliers du Tastevin (events com.), Delta Sigma Epsilon. Club: Metropolitan (San Francisco). Home: 1447 S Whitehall Ln Saint Helena CA 94574

SPANOS, ALEXANDER GUS, professional football executive; b. Stockton, Calif., Sept. 28, 1923; m. Faye Spanos; children: Dean, Dea Spanos Economow, Alexis Spanos Ruhl, Michael. LLD (hon.), U. Pacific, 1984. Owner A.G. Spanos Catering Service, A.G. Spanos Constrn. Co.; pres., chmn. bd. dirs. San Diego Chargers, 1984—. Trustee Children's Hosp., San Francisco, San Francisco Fine Arts Mus., Eisenhower Med. Ctr., Rancho Mirage, Calif. Greek Orthodox. Office: care San Diego Chargers PO Box 20666 San Diego CA 92120 *

SPARE, ANTHONY EDWARD, investment company executive; b. Chgo., Oct. 1, 1939; s. Alexander T. and Rita H. S.; m. Eleanor Doyle, July 14, 1962; children—Alexander, Samantha, James. B.A., Tufts U., 1961; M.B.A., Stanford U., 1963. With Bank of Calif., San Francisco, 1963—, analyst, 1965-74, dir. research, 1975-86; chief investment officer, 1986—. Pres. Hillsborough Schs. Found; active fund-raising various local and univ. groups. Chartered fin. analyst. Mem. Nat. Assn. Bus. Economists, Security Analysts San Francisco (past pres.), Fin. Analyst Fedn. Home: 119 Baywood Ave Hillsborough CA 94010 Office: Bank of California 400 California St San Francisco CA 94145

SPARKS, IRVING ALAN, biblical scholar, educator; b. Ft. Wayne, Ind., June 15, 1933; s. James Edwin and Isabelle Mildred S.; A.B., Davidson (N.C.) Coll., 1954; B.D., Union Theol. Sem., Richmond, Va., 1959; S.T.M., Lancaster (Pa.) Theol. Sem., 1970; Ph.D., Claremont (Calif.) Grad. Sch., 1970; m. Helen Daniels, Sept. 3, 1954; children—Lydia Isabelle Sparkswworthy, Leslie Bishop, Robin Alan. Lectr. philosophy and religion LaVerne (Calif.) Coll., 1965-69; asst. prof. religion Claremont Grad. Sch., 1970-74, assoc. dir. Inst. Antiquity and Christianity, 1970-74; mem. faculty San Diego State U., 1974—, prof. religious studies, 1980—, chmn. dept. religious studies, 1983—, assoc. dean grad. div. and research, 1974-83; founder/pres. Inst. Bibl. Studies, 1983—; cons. photog. archival conservation of Dead Sea Scrolls in Jerusalem, 1980; mem adv. bd. Inst. Antiquity and Christianity, 1974—. Trustee, Claremont Collegiate Sch., 1970-75, pres., 1972-74; trustee, mem. exec. com. Ancient Bible Manuscript Ctr., 1981—. Fellow Lilly Found., 1964-65, Layne Found., 1965-66; disting. vis. scholar James Madison U., 1982. Mem. Am. Soc. Papyrologists, Soc. Bibl. Lit., Phi Beta Delta. Author: The Pastoral Epistles: Introduction and Commentary, 1981; editor Studies and Documents; contbr. articles on papyrology and bibl. studies to scholarly jours. Office: San Diego State Univ San Diego CA 92182

SPARKS, J. E., language arts consultant, writer; b. New Kensington, Pa., Oct. 22, 1916; s. J. E. and Bertha (Harris) S. B.S., Ind. State U., Pa., 1947; M.Litt., U. Pitts., 1948; Ed.D., UCLA, 1962. Chmn. English dept. Delhaas High Sch., Bristol, Pa., 1947-57; reading cons. Beverly Hills Unified Sch. Dist., Calif., 1957-77; free lance lang. arts cons., Los Angeles, 1977—; host NBC TV series, Burbank, Calif., 1968-69. Author textbooks: Reading for Power and Flexibility, 1968; Write for Power, 1982. Served with U.S. Army, 1943-46, CBI. Creator power designations to sentences and paragraphs, 1968. Mem. Internat. Reading Assn. (chmn. Calif. Orgn. 1962-70, Far West Orgn. 1970-73). Home: 2160 Century Park E 201N Los Angeles CA 90067

SPARKS, JOHN F(RANCIS), composer, lyricist; b. Brockton, Mass., June 24, 1941; s. Clement C. and Elinor M. (Ryan) S. BA, Stonehill Coll., 1964; MFA, UCLA, 1976. Cons. pub. relations Atlantic Richfield Co., Los Angeles, 1976—; dean of instrs. Hollywood (Calif.) Scriptwriting Inst., 1977—; founder, director New Tuners Workshop for Composers, Lyricists and Bookwriters, Chgo., 1986. co-dir. Lehman Engel Mus. Theater Workshop, Los Angeles, 1981—; composer/lyricist mus. comedies Babes in Barns, Chgo., 1984-85, Buddy's Plane is Down, Los Angeles, 1977; composer Two by Aesop, One by Us and How's by You, Los Angeles, 1985. V.p. bd. dirs. Hollywood Heritage, 1985-86. Mem. Broadcast Music, Inc. Democrat. Avocations: puzzles, games. Home: 1237 S Bronson Ave Los Angeles CA 90019 Office: Hollywood Scriptwriting Inst 1605 N Cahuenga Blvd #216 Hollywood CA 90028

SPARKS, JOHN WESLEY, physician; b. Elizabeth, N.J., Sept. 14, 1946; s. William Joseph and Meredith (Pleasant) S.; m. Patricia Bauman, Aug. 19, 1967; children: Rebecca, Michael, Sarah. BS in Life Scis., MIT, 1968; MD, Harvard Med. Sch., 1972. Diplomate Nat. Bd. Med. Examiners, Am. Bd. Pediatrics, Sub-specialty bd. Neonatal-Perinatal Medicine. Research assoc. NIH, Bethesda, Md., 1974-76; resident in pediatrics U. Colo., Denver, 1972-74, 76-77, fellow in perinatal medicine, 1977-79, asst. prof. pediatrics, 1979-84, assoc. prof. pediatrics, 1984—; dir. newborn services U. Colo. Hosp., Denver, 1980—. Contbr. articles and revs. to profl. jours. Served with USPHS, 1974-76. Grantee NIH, 1979—. Mem. Soc. Pediatric Research, Perinatal Research Soc., Western Soc. Pediatric Research. Home: 2408 S Evanston St Aurora CO 80014 Office: Newborn Service B-195 4200 E 9th Ave Denver CO 80262

SPARKS, MILDRED THOMAS, educator; b. Montgomery, Ala., Oct. 2, 1943; d. Leon and Annie Lee (Johnson) Thomas; m. John H. Sparks, Aug. 29, 1964; children—Melanie J., Jennifer L., Regina F. B.S., Ala. State U., 1964; M.S., Pepperdine U., 1978. Cert. reading specialist. Tchr., Dayton (Ohio) Schs., 1964-66; tchr. Oxon Hill (Md.) Schs., 1966-70; technician Reading Lab., Grambling (La.) State U., 1972; reading lab. aide California City (Calif.) Schs., 1975; reading instr. Cerro Coso So. Outreach, Edwards AFB, Calif., 1976-78; substitute tchr. San Bernardino City Schs., 1979, Aquinas High Sch., San Bernardino, 1978-79; reading lab. tchr. San Bernardino High Sch., 1979; instr. reading lab. San Bernardino Valley Coll., 1980-81, assoc. prof. reading, 1981—, head dept. reading. Troop vol. Girls Scouts U.S.A. Mem. Calif. Tchrs. Assn., Nat. Council Tchrs. English, Assn. Supervision and Curriculum Devel., Western Coll. Reading Assn., Bus. and Profl. Women's Club, Link's, Jack and Jill of Am. Inc., Delta Kappa Gamma, Alpha Kappa Alpha. Democrat. Roman Catholic (Norton lay lector). Home: 3357 Mirada Rd Highland CA 92346 Office: 701 S Mount Vernon St San Bernardino CA 92310

SPARKS, RAMONA CLIFTON, social worker; b. Jacksonville, Fla., Aug. 14, 1941; d. Nathan J. and Alma L. (Childers) Clifton; m. Walter A. Sparks, Aug. 12, 1961; children: Veronica, Tara, Craig. BA, Calif. Bapt. Coll., 1967; MSW, San Diego State U., 1985. Social worker Riverside (Calif.) County Dept. Social Services, 1967-74; sec. Calif. Bapt. Coll., Riverside, 1977-83; clin. social worker Hemet (Calif.) Valley Hosp., 1985-86, Family Service Assoc., 1986—; med. social worker Home Health Agys., Riverside and San Bernardino, Calif., 1983-85. Mem. Nat. Assn. Social Workers, Nat. Assn. Christian Social Workers, Am. Diabetes Assn. Baptist. Avocations: reading, needlework, fishing.

SPARKS, TERRY DEAN, management consulting company executive; b. Connersville, Ind., Sept. 18, 1948; s. Ernest Jesse and Maedrew (Evans) S.; m. Sondra Louise Garrison, July 19, 1970; children: Tonya Lynn, Rachel Marie, Stephanie Suzanne. BS, Purdue U., 1971; MBA, Calif. State U., San Bernardino, 1977; M Christian Ministry, Internat. Sch. Theology, 1984. Various mgmt. positions Internat. Ministries of Campus Crusade for Christ, San Bernardino, Calif., 1973-84, field preparation dir., 1980-84; sr. cons. Mgmt. Devel. Assocs., Orange, Calif., 1984—; adj. instr. mgmt. and Christian Ministry, Azusa (Calif.) Pacific U., 1986—; mem. adv. bd. The Network, San Diego, 1986—; cons. in field. Co-author: Organization Stewardship Inventory, 1986, Personal Stewardship Inventory, 1986. Sunday sch. tchr. Community Bible Ch., San Bernardino, Calif., 1975-84, chmn. missions com., 1978-80, 85—, mem. bd. elders, 1978-80, 83—. Mem. Christian Ministries Mgmt. Assn. (cert.), Alpha Pi Mu. Republican. Office: Mgmt Devel Assocs 1744 W Katella Suite 22 Orange CA 92667

SPARKS, WALTER CHAPPEL, horticulturist, educator; b. New Castle, Colo., Aug. 22, 1918; s. Lester Elroy and Jean Ivene (Murray) S.; m. Barbara Ferne Gardner, May 31, 1942; children: Robert, Richard, Eugene. Student, Western State Coll., 1936-37; BS, Colo. State U., 1941, MS, 1943; postgrad., U. Minn., 1945, Wash. State U., 1949, 56-57; DSc (hon.), U. Idaho, 1984. Instr., head dept. agr. Pueblo Jr. Coll., 1941; grad. asst. Colo. State U., 1941-43, instr. horticulture, 1943-44, asst. prof., 1944-47, asso. prof., 1947; asso. horticulturist U. Idaho, Aberdeen, 1947-57; acting supt. Aberdeen br. Agrl. Expt. Sta., 1951, 57, 65, horticulturist, 1957—, research prof. horticulture, 1968—, prin. liaison coordinator for potato program, 1976—; exchange prof. Research Inst., Kolding, Denmark, 1972-73; adviser and lectr. on potato problems to various fgn. govts.; cons., adv., Israel, 1980, Philippines, 1981; dir. Postharvest Inst. Perishables, 1980—. Contbr. articles to profl. jours. Recipient 50th Anniversary medal Fed. Land Banks, 1967; Distinguished Service award for service to Potato Industry of Idaho Gov. of Idaho, 1967; named to Hall of Fame Potato Mus. Brussels, 1977; recipient Alumni Service award, 1980, Disting. Faculty award Phi Kappa Phi, 1980; spl. recognition for numerous contbns. to Idaho agr., 1984; elected to Idaho Agrl. Hall of Fame, 1983; Eldred L. Jenne research fellow, 1957. Mem. AAAS, Am. Inst. Biol. Scis., Am. Soc. Hort. Sci. (life), European Assn. Potato Research, N.W. Assn. Horticulturists, Entomologists and Plant Pathologists, Idaho Acad. Sci., Nat. Potato Research and Edn. Found. (cert. appraciation seed potato storage tech. 1986), N.W. Food Processors Assn. (Disting. Service award, 1987), N.W. Fieldman's Assn. (Disting. Agrl. Service award, 1987), Potato Assn. Am. (life mem., past pres., dir.), Western Regional Potato Improvement Group (past pres.), C. of C., Scabbard and Blade, Sigma Xi (Outstanding Research Paper award 1974), Gamma Sigma Delta (Outstanding Research Worker award 1977, award of merit 1978), Alpha Zeta, Beta Beta Beta, Epsilon Rho Epsilon. Club: Rotary. Home: 234 N 1st St Aberdeen ID 83210 Office: U Idaho Research and Extension Center Aberdeen ID 83210

SPATAFORA, RON JAMES, computer executive; b. Neu-Isenberg, W.Ger., Sept. 24, 1951; came to U.S., 1952; s. James Roger and Elfriede (Krueger) S.; m. Katherine Ann Molnar, Dec. 31, 1978. Student in Elec. Engring., So. Ill. U., 1970; BS in Aircraft Maintenance Engring., Parks Coll., 1974; aircraft maintenance officer course USAF; lic. pilot and mechanic, FAA. Chief engr. L-K Electronics, Cahokia, Ill., 1972-74; service mgr. Mt. Hawley Aviation, Peoria, Ill., 1976-77; chief insp. and avionics supr. Am. Jet Aviation, St. Louis, 1977-78; avionics group engr. Gates Learjet Corp., Tucson, 1979; avionics specialist Electrospace Systems Inc., Richardson, Tex., 1980-84; project systems engr., program requirements mgr. Tex. Instruments, Inc., Dallas, 1984-86; prin. ptnr. Compuprod, Plano, Tex., 1983-85; pres. Spl. Techs., Inc., Garland, Tex., 1986—. Contbg. editor Epson Connection, TI Profl. Computing, Star-Text, Avionics Mag. Served to 1st lt. USAF, 1974-76. Mem. Arnold Air Soc., Air Force Assn., VTI Electronics Assn., Aircraft Owners and Pilots Assn. (Air Safety Found.), Internat. Omega Assn., Airborne Law Enforcement Assn., North Tex. Sysop Assn. (chmn.), Aircraft Maintenance Found. Club: Metroplex Epson Users Group. Office: Spl Techs Inc 1919 S Shiloh Rd Suite 225-25 Garland TX 75042

SPATER, SUSAN CLARKE, museum director; b. Buffalo, Jan. 18, 1948; d. M. John and Jane Lewis (Kennedy) Clarke; m. William W. Spater, May 17, 1980. BA, Smith Coll., 1969; MA, U. Mich., 1973. Arts coordinator Inst. Contemporary Art, Boston, 1970; research asst. Heckscher Mus., Huntington, N.Y., 1972; educator Toledo Mus. Art, 1969-71; curator Addison Galley Am. Art, Andover, Mass., 1973-78; dir. Pimeria Alta Hist. Soc. Mus., Nogales, Ariz., 1979—; reviewer Inst. Mus. Services, Washington, 1983-86, panelist 1987; del. Smithsonian History Agenda Conf., 1987. Bd. dirs. Council Cultural Devel., Nogales, 1982—. Mem. Ariz. Mus. Assn. (southern rep. 1982-84), Nogales C. of C. (named co-citizen of yr. 1983), Am. Assn. State and Local History (edn. com. 1985—). Home: 376 Curtis St Nogales AZ 85621 Office: Pimeria Alta Hist Soc Mus Nogales AZ 85628

SPAULDING, CARLETON WINDHAM, computer software company executive; b. Palo Alto, Calif., Dec. 27, 1954; s. Robert Lytton Spaulding and Nancy Dennett; m. Sharon Kay Howard, Aug. 26, 1978.;. BA, U. Calif., Berkeley, 1980; M Mgmt., Northwestern U., 1984. Media supr. Leo Burnett USA, Chgo., 1980-85; pres. MediaPlan Inc., Berkeley, 1985—. Author: (computer software manual) MANAS version 1.0, 1985. Forum supr. Werner Erhard & Assocs., San Francisco, 1985—. Mem. Am. Assn. Artificial Intelligence. Avocation: downhill skiing. Home and Office: 154 Avenida Dr Berkeley CA 94708

SPAULDING, JOHN PIERSON, public relations executive, marine consultant; b. N.Y.C., June 25, 1917; s. Forrest Brisbine and Genevieve Anderson (Pierson) S.; m. Eleanor Rita Bonner, Aug. 18, 1947; children—Anne Spaulding Balzhiser, John F., Mary T.; m. 2d, Donna Alene Abrescia, May 15, 1966. Student Iowa State Coll., 1935-36, Grinnell Coll., 1936-38, U. Chgo., 1938-39. Reporter, Chgo. City News Bur., U.P.I., 1939-40; editor Cedar Falls (Iowa) Daily Record, 1940-41; picture editor Des Moines Register & Tribune, 1941-42, 47-50; pub. relations dir. Motor Club Iowa, Davenport, 1950-51; commd. 2d. lt. USAF, 1942, advanced through grades to maj., 1947, recalled, 1951, advanced through grades to lt. col.; ret., 1968; v.p. Vacations Hawaii, Honolulu, 1969-70; dir. pub. relations, mgr. pub. relations services Alexander & Balwin, Inc., Honolulu, 1970-76; mgr. community relations Matson Navigation Co., Honolulu, 1976-81. Pres., Econ. Devel. Assn., Skagit County, Wash., 1983-85; mem. Anacortes (Wash.) Sch. Bd., 1982—; mem. Gov.'s Tourism Devel. Council, 1983—; mem. adv. com. State Ferry System, 1982—; chmn. Everett chpt. S.C.O.R.E., 1984-86. Decorated Air medal. Mem. Pub. Relations Soc. Am. (pres. Hawaii chpt. 1974), Hawaii Communicators (pres. 1973), Nat. Def. Transp. Assn. (pres. Aloha chpt. 1980-81, Disting. Service award 1978-79), Air Force Assn., Anacortes C. of C., Sigma Delta Chi (life). Clubs: Propeller (pres. Port of Honolulu 1979-80), Honolulu Press, Fidelgo Yacht, Hawaii Yacht, Royal Hawaiian 400 Yacht (comdr. 1977-81), Rotary. Home: 6002 Sands Way Anacortes WA 98221

SPAZIANO, ROBERT ANTHONY, hospital administrator; b. Providence, R.I., Oct. 4, 1937; s. Domenico and Marie Elena (Baldassarre) S.; m. Eleanor Louise McGinn, Oct. 12, 1959; children—Donna Jean, Lori Ann, Denise Marie. B.S. in Bus. Adminstrn., U. R.I., 1963; postgrad. in edn. UCLA, 1966. Cert. tchr., Calif. Mgr. data processing Culver City (Calif.) Unified Sch. Dist., 1965-67; mgr. ops., Pasadena (Calif.) Unified Sch. Dist., 1967-69; gen. mgr. The Data Corp., Los Angeles, 1969-71; with Huntington Mem. Hosp., Pasadena, 1971—, dir. systems services 1971—; adj. faculty hosp. info. systems Calif. State U., Los Angeles, 1977—. Mem. adv. council Calif. State U., Los Angeles, 1980-82. Mem. Hosp. Info. Systems Sharing Group, Data Processing Mgmt. Assn., Assn. Systems Mgmt., Hosp. Mgmt. and Systems Soc. Contbr. articles to profl. jours. Office: 100 Congress St Pasadena CA 91105

SPEAKMAN, LARY LEE, material, quality engineering executive; b. Rangely, Colo., May 13, 1950; s. Theodore and Carrie Lydia (Mehl) S.; children—Danielle, Michael. B.A., U. Colo.-Boulder, 1972; M.A., U. Ill., 1973; M.B.A., U. Denver, 1984. Research chemist Coors Porcelain Co., Golden, 1975-76, process engring. supr., 1976-80, prodn. supt., 1980-81, mgr. metallized prodn., 1981-82, mgr. material engring. and prodn., 1982-86; mgr. quality engring., 1986—. Bd. dirs. Goodwill Industries, Denver, 1981-84. Mem. IEEE (assoc.), Am. Ceramic Soc. Clubs: Shadows of Iga Soc., Bujinkan Internat. (Noda-City, Japan); Yoshin Ryu Ju Jitsu (Aurora, Colo.). Home: 31991 Black Widow Dr Conifer CO 80433 Office: Coors Porcelain Co 17750 W 32d Ave Golden CO 80401

SPEAR, ARTHUR S., toy and game executive; b. 1920. B. in Archtl. Engring., MIT, 1941. Prodn. engr. Artisan Metal Products, 1943-44; prodn. mgr., gen. mgr. Sperry Mfg. Co., 1945-56; plant mgr., gen. mgr. mfg. and distbn. and corp. ops. coordinator Revlon Inc., 1956-64; dir. distbn. Mattel Inc., Hawthorne, Calif., 1964, v.p. ops., 1965, exec. v.p. ops., 1966, pres., 1973, chief exec. officer, 1974, chmn. bd., chief exec. officer, 1978—, also dir. Served with U.S. Army, 1941-42. Office: Mattel Inc 5150 Rosecrans Ave Hawthorne CA 90250 *

SPEAR, CHARLES JUNIOR, manufacturing company executive; b. Columbia City, Ind., July 23, 1933; s. Charles Albertson and Mina Rebecca (Windle) S.; m. Lora Ann Rice, Nov. 22, 1952; children—Veronica Ann, Charles Gregory, Frederick Joseph. Student Gen. Elec. Apprentice Sch., Ft. Wayne, Ind., 1951-55, Lincoln Elec. Welding for Supervision, Cleve., 1979. Field engr. Lab. Equipment Corp., Mooresville, Ind., 1969-72; plant engr. Gen. Tire & Rubber, Wabash, Ind., 1972-79; plant mgr. Kennedy Tank & Mfg., Indpls., 1979-80, Evans Steel & Mfg., Gilbert, Ariz., 1980-81; facilities supr. Honeywell Process Mgmt. Systems Div., Phoenix, 1981-85; mgr. facilities, fleet and maintenance Food Processing div. Circle K Corp., Phoenix, 1985—; cons. elec. design; instr. computer and fluid power. Served with U.S. Army, 1955-61. Mem. Am. Mgmt. Assn., Fluid Power Soc. Clubs: Moose, Masons. Home: 2166 W Farmdale Mesa AZ 85202

SPEAR, STEPHEN LOUIS, data processing executive; b. Boston, Feb. 6, 1943; s. Arthur S. and Phyllis (Grossman) S.; m. Susan H. Auslander, June 26, 1966; children: Joshua M., Ben G. Student, Lehigh U., 1960-63, Rutgers U., 1963-70. Programmer Chubb & Son Inc., Short Hills, N.J., 1961-64; program counselor Bell Telephone Labs., Whippany, N.J., 1964-66; supr. systems support The Singer Co., Wayne, N.J., 1966-76; sr. teleprocessing analyst Transcon Lines, El Segundo, Calif., 1976-77; mgr. corp. systems Twentieth Century Fox, Beverly Hills, Calif., 1977-85; info. services mgr. Carnation Dairies, Los Angeles, 1985, mgr. info./automation services div., 1987—. Developer computer system, TV Print Syndication. Mem. Am. Motorcyclists Assn., Nat. Street Rod Assn, TRW Motorcycle Club. Avocations: antique auto restoration and modification, motorcycle touring. Office: Carnation Dairies 5045 Wilshire Blvd Los Angeles CA 90036

SPEARE, DANIEL BERNARD, broadcasting company executive, consultant; b. Los Angeles, July 29, 1929; s. Frederick H. Speare and Fannie (Goldstein) Speare Rosenberg; m. Mary Magidow, Sept. 11, 1948; children—Eric, Ellen, Marc. Student Profl. Radio and TV Sch. Calif., 1946-48; B.S. in Pub. Relations, UCLA, 1974. Program dir., news dir. Sta. KREO, Indio, Calif., 1950; dir. pub. relations, speech instr. Frederick H. Speare Radio-TV Sch., Los Angeles, 1950-52, pres., 1952-56; program dir. Sta. KGFJ, Los Angeles, 1956-57; program dir., sales staff Sta. KAFY, Bakersfield, Calif., 1957-58, Sta. KLYD, Bakersfield, 1958-62; v.p., gen. mgr. Sta. KGEE, Bakersfield, 1962-76; pres., chief exec. officer Dan B. Speare Broadcast Enterprises, Inc., KPMC Radio, Bakersfield, 1976—. Bd. dirs. YMCA, Bakersfield. pres. Temple Beth El, Bakersfield, 1972-73. Served with USN, 1948-50. Recipient Radio Mmgt. award Nat. Assn. Broadcasters, 1973, cert. of appreciation Fgn. Govts. Press Assn., 1976, honor citation Americanism Edn. League, 1980, Toastmasters award, Bakersfield, 1981. Mem. Broadcast Pioneers, Kern County Broadcasters, Advt. Club Bakersfield, Bakersfield C. of C. (bd. dirs. 1976-78). Republican. Jewish. Club: Exchange (bd. dirs. 1983-84) (Bakersfield). Lodge: Elks. Home: 4912 Panorama Dr Bakersfield CA 93306 Office: Sta KPMC 230 Truxton Ave Bakersfield CA 93301

SPECK, ROBERT CHARLES, geological engineer; b. Bklyn., June 15, 1944; s. Charles Ernest and Helen Gertrude (York) S.; m. Pia Rey Polanco, July 4, 1971; 1 child, Stephen Ruben. BA, Franklin and Marshal Coll., 1968; BS, U. Missouri, Rolla, 1974, MS, 1975, PhD, 1979. Geologist Peace Corps, Domenican Republic, 1968-70; resident geologist Geokinetics, Inc., Dominican Republic, 1970-72; project geologist Hanson-Rodriguez, S.A., Dominican Republic, 1972-73; staff engr. GAI Cons., Inc., Pitts., 1979-84; assoc. prof., dept. chmn. U. Alaska, Fairbanks, 1984—. Contbr. articles to profl. jours. Mem. Assn. Engring. Geologists (sect. vice chmn. 1985—), Soc. Mining Engrs., Am. Inst Profl. Geologists (lic.), Internat. Soc. for Rock Mechanics, Computer Oriented Geol. Soc., Tau Beta Pi, Sigma Gamma Epsilon. Home: 3030 Forrest Dr Fairbanks AK 99709 Office: U Alaska Dept Mining and Geol Engring Fairbanks AK 99775-1190

SPECTOR, HAROLD, construction company executive; b. Boston, Mar. 8, 1921; s. Mier I. and Ann R. (Kamins) S.; m. Joan L. Smith, May 7, 1967; 1 child, Pamela S. Ankerman. Student, New Eng. Conservatory Music; JD, Northeastern U., Boston, 1941. With chem. dept. Am. Factors, Honolulu, 1949-51; credit mgr. Hawaii Builders Supply, Honolulu, 1951-53; ptnr. Island Lumber Co., Honolulu, 1953-56; owner Aloha Lumber Co., Honolulu, 1956-62; v.p. Loyalty Enterprises, Honolulu, 1962-75; exec. v.p. Hadley-Pruyn, Inc., Honolulu, 1975—; pres. Spector Holdings, Ltd.; mng. gen. ptnr. Liliha Sq. Shopping Ctr. Mem. Gov.'s Task Force for Harbors and Airports, 1976-80, Pres.' Dist. Export Bd., 1979. Served to capt. U.S. Army, 1942-49. Jewish. Clubs: Union League (N.Y.C.); Plaza (Honolulu). Home: 141 Poloke Pl Honolulu HI 96822 Office: Hadley Pruyn Inc 745 Fort St Suite 205 Honolulu HI 96813

SPEDDING, GEOFF ROBERT, zoologist, aerospace researcher; b. Hurley, U.K., Mar. 8, 1957; came to U.S., 1981; s. Colin R.W. and Betsy N. (George) S. BS, U. Bristol, Eng., 1978, PhD, 1981. Research assoc. U. So. Calif. Dept. Aerospace Engring., Los Angeles, 1981—. Contbr. articles to profl. jours. Univ. Bristol scholar, 1978; recipient T.H. Huxley Prize, Zool. Soc. London., 1982. Mem. AAAS, Royal Inst. Biology, Soc. for Exptl. Biology, Sigma Chi. Avocations: surfing, tennis, cycling, roller-skating, computer-hacking, philosophy. Home: 2305 Oakwood Ave Venice CA 90291 Office: U So Calif Dept Aerospace Engring Univ Park Los Angeles CA 90089-0192

SPEED, JOHN WILLIAM, city official; b. Fresno, Calif., July 8, 1935; s. John Moody and Dorothy Ann (Lucas) S.; student Diablo Valley Coll., 1963-64, Contra Costa Coll., 1965-67, Solano Community Coll., 1968; m. Virginia H. Polk, Oct. 8, 1958; children—Dorothy Sue, Valorie Lynn, Lorilee. With Vallejo (Calif.) Fire Dept., 1961-71, 73-76, fire chief, 1973-76; fire chief Tracy (Calif.) Fire Dept., 1971-73; fire chief Aurora (Colo.) Fire Dept., 1976—; instr. fire sci. Solano Coll., 1968-75. Mem. adv. bd. Salvation Army, Aurora, 1976—. Served with USAF, 1952-61. Mem. Nat. Fire Protection Assn., Internat. Fire Chiefs Assn., Colo. State Fire Chiefs Assn., Met. Fire Chiefs Assn. Democrat. Episcopalian. Clubs: Masons, Shriners. Office: City of Aurora Fire Dept 1470 S Havana St Aurora CO 80012 *

SPEER, DONALD PIERCE, orthopedic surgeon; b. Kingsport, Tenn., June 18, 1937; s. Donald Devore and Anna Louise (Pierce) S.; m. Laurel Elmendorf, Jan. 27, 1962; children: Kirsten, Marshall Patton, Stephen Anthony. BS, Stanford, 1959; postgrad., UCLA, 1962; MD, U. So. Calif., 1966. Diplomate Am. Bd. Orthopedic Surgery. Asst. prof. surgery U. Ariz., Tucson, 1975-79, assoc. prof. surgery, 1979-83, assoc. prof. anatomy, 1982-83, prof. surgery, 1983—, prof. anatomy, 1983—; assoc. staff mem. Ariz. Crippled Children's Services, Tucson, 1977—, Myelomenignocele Clinic, 1980—, Cerebral Palsy Clinic, 1986—; affiliate teaching staff Tucson Med. Ctr., 1977—. Contbr. articles to profl. jours. Served to maj. U.S. Army, 1967-71. Named Faculty Mem. of Yr., Alpha Omega Alpha, 1986. Fellow ACS, Am. Acad. Orthopedic Surgeons; mem. Pediatric Orthopedic Soc., Pediatric Orthopedic Study Group, Orthopedic Research Soc. Avocations: running, bicycling, tennis, computers. Office: Orthopedic Surgery Ariz Health Scis Ctr 1501 N Campbell Ave Tucson AZ 85724

SPEER, JOHN CARTER, public relations executive; b. East Cleveland, Ohio, Dec. 25, 1952; s. John Joseph and Janet Smith (Brisbin) S.; m. Elizabeth Diane Speer, Apr. 21, 1977; children: Genesis Eve, John Joseph II, Matthew Carter. BA, Brigham Young U., MA. Pub. relations specialist Bonneville Uniserv, Orem, Utah, 1979-81; staff writer Daily Herald, Provo, Utah, 1979-81; editor The Salina (Utah) Sun, The Gunnison Valley News, 1981-84; dir. pub. info. Shipley Assocs., Bountiful, Utah, 1984—. Contbr. articles to newspapers and mags. Mem. Pub. Relations Soc. Am., Utah Press Assn. (sec., treas. Intermountain chpt. 1987), Am. Soc. Tng. and Devel., Jaycees (v.p. North Sevier 1983, sec. Orem chpt. 1980-81, bd. dirs. Utah state, 1981-82, editor Beeline newsletter, 1981-82), C. of C. (pres. Salina, Utah chpt. 1983, v.p. 1982). Republican. Mormon. Lodge: Lions (music chmn. Salina club 1983-84). Home: 1257 N Main Centerville UT 84014 Office: Shipley Assocs 400 N Main Bountiful UT 84010

SPEIGHT, JAMES GLASSFORD, research company executive; b. Murton, Eng., June 24, 1940; s. George Madison and Elizabeth (Glassford) S.; m. Sheila Elizabeth Stout, Dec. 28, 1963; 1 child, James. BSc in Chemistry with honors, Manchester U., Eng., 1961, PhD in Organic Chemistry, 1965. Research fellow Manchester U., 1965-67; research officer Research Council, Edmonton, Alta., Can., 1967-80; research assoc. Exxon Corp., Linden, N.J., 1980-84; dep. mng. dir. Western Research Inst., Laramie, Wyo., 1984—; adv. com. Grant McEwan Community Coll., Edmonton, 1975-80; chmn. petroleum-natural gas research task force, Alta. Research Council, 1978-79; search com. V.P. for Research and Grad. Studies, U. Wyo., 1985; external mem. promotions com. U. Mosul, Iraq, 1985; thesis examiner, Indian Inst. Techn., Bombay, 1974, U. Mosul, 1976, 77, 78; vis. lect. petroleum sci., U. Mosul, Iraq, 1978; lectr. petroleum sci., U. Alberta, Edmonton, Can., 1976-80, U. Calgary, Alta., 1979-80. Editor Coal Tech., 1978—, Synthetic Fuel Series, 1980—, Fuel Sci. and Tech. Internat., 1983—; refereed numerous jours., manuscripts. Fellow Royal Soc. Chemistry (chartered chemist), Chem. Inst. Can. (treas. Edmonton sect. 1971-78, editor newsletter 1975-77); mem. AAAS, Geochem. Soc., Am. Chem. Soc. (program com. petroleum div. 1981—, bus. mgr. petroleum div. 1982-85), Sigma Xi. Office: Western Research Inst PO Box 3395 University Sta Laramie WY 82071

SPEIGHTS, MICHAEL DAVID, editor; b. Owensboro, Ky., May 12, 1951; s. Marion Thomas and Joy Lee (Griffin) S. BJ with honors, Northeastern U., 1973. Researcher, reporter Congl. Quar., Washington, 1974-77; staff asst. Senator Richard Schweiker, Washington, 1977; anchor, reporter Sta. WILM Radio, Wilmington, Del., 1979-80; reporter, producer Sta. WUHY-FM, Phila., 1980-81, Sta. WABE-FM, Atlanta, 1982-83; editor Padres' Trail, St. Michaels, Ariz., 1984—; freelance reporter, producer for Nat. Pub. Radio, 1980-83. Vol. Navajo Nation Spl. Olympics, St. Michaels, 1986, Franciscan Covenant Program, Ft. Defiance, Ariz., 1984-85. Roman Catholic. Avocations: reading, driving. Home and Office: Padres' Trail Franciscan Mission Ctr PO Box 645 Saint Michaels AZ 86511

SPEISER, THEODORE WESLEY, astrophysics, planetary, atmospheric sciences educator; b. Del Norte, Colo., Nov. 23, 1934; s. Alfred Theodore and Virginia Melva (Pickens) S.; m. Patricia Jane McCrummen, June 10, 1956; children: Tanya Lee, Kelly Ann, Tertia Ava. BS, Colo. State U., 1956; MS, Calif. Inst. Tech., 1959; PhD, Pa. State U., 1964. Asst. prof. U. Colo., Boulder, 1969-74, assoc. prof., 1974-85, prof. astrophysics, planetary and atmospheric scis., 1985—; cons. NOAA, Boulder, 1970—. Contbr. articles to profl. jours. Served to capt. U.S. Army, 1960-61. Recipient U.S. Sr. Scientist award A.V. Humboldt Found., 1977; Fulbright fellow, 1956. Mem. Am. Geophys. Union (local br. v.p. 1986-87, pres. 1987—). Avocations: photography, hiking, cross-country skiing, tennis. Home: 2335 Dartmouth Ave Boulder CO 80303 Office: U Colo Dept of APAS C Box 391 Boulder CO 80309

SPELLMAN, DOUGLAS TOBY, advertising executive; b. Bronx, N.Y., May 12, 1942; s. Sydney M. and Leah B. (Rosenberg) S.; BS, Fairleigh Dickinson U., 1964; m. Ronni I. Epstein, Jan. 16, 1966 (div. Mar. 1985); children—Laurel Nicole, Daren Scott; m. Michelle Ward, Dec. 31, 1986. Media buyer Doyle, Dane, Bernbach, Inc., N.Y.C., 1964-66, Needham, Harper & Steers, Inc., N.Y.C., 1966; media supr. Ogilvy & Mather, Inc., N.Y.C., 1967-69; media dir. Sinay Advt., Los Angeles, 1969-70; chief ops. officer S.H.H. Creative Mktg., Inc., Los Angeles, 1969-70; assoc. media dir. Warren, Mullen, Dolobowsky, Inc., N.Y.C., 1970-71; dir. West Coast ops. Ed Libov Assocs., Inc., Los Angeles, 1971-72; media supr. Carson/Roberts Advt. div. Ogilvy & Mather, Inc., Los Angeles, 1971-72; assoc. media dir. Ogilvy & Mather, Inc., Los Angeles, 1972-73; media dir. Vitt Media Internat., Inc., Los Angeles, 1973-74; v.p., dir. West Coast ops. Ind. Media Services, Inc., Los Angeles, 1974-75; owner Douglas T. Spellman, Inc., Los Angeles, 1975-77, pres., chmn. bd., 1977-82; pres., chief operating officer Douglas T. Spellman Co. div. Ad Mktg., Inc., Los Angeles, 1982-85; pres., chief exec. officer, chmn. bd. Spellbound Prodns. and Spellman Media divs. Spellbound Communications, Inc., Los Angeles, 1984-86; gen. ptnr. Faso & Spellman, Los Angeles, 1984-86; chief operating officer, pres. Yacht Mgmt. Internat., Ltd., Los Angeles, 1984-86; v.p. media Snyder, Longino Advt. div. Snyder Advt., Los Angeles, 1985—; guest lectr. sch. bus UCLA, 1975, U. So. Calif., 1976. Served with U.S. Army Res. N.G., 1964-69. Mem. Aircraft Owners and Pilots Assn., Nat. Rifle Assn., Phi Zeta, Phi Omega Epsilon. Jewish. Clubs: Rolls Royce Owners, Mercedes Benz Am., Aston Martin Owners. Office: PO Box 180 Beverly Hills CA 90213

SPELLMAN, JOHN DAVID, engineer; b. Beaver Dam, Wis., July 27, 1935; s. John Joseph and Elsie Marguerite (Schultz) S.; B.S. in Elec. Engring., U. Wis., 1959; m. Kathleen Burns King, May 26, 1972; stepchildren—Kathleen Biegel, Karen Silva, Kimberly Lyon. Jr. engr., part time, Malleable Iron Range Co., Beaver Dam, 1952-59; mem. tech. staff Rockwell Internat., Anaheim, Calif., 1961-85, lead engr., 1969-78, 81-85; mgr. ground instrumentation ops. unit Rockwell Internat., Vandenberg AFB, 1985—; cons. Data Processing, Santa Maria, Calif., 1965. Served to 1st lt. Signal Corps, AUS, 1959-61. Recipient U.S. Army Accomodation award, 1961, USAF Outstanding Achievement award for Civilian Personnel. Mem. Assn. Computing Machinery, Air Force Assn., Res. Officers Assn. Clubs: Birnam Wood Golf (Montecito, Calif.); Santa Maria Country. Contbr. publs. on minutemen data systems, PCM Telemetry systems. Home: 642 Meadowbrook Santa Maria CA 93455 Office: PO Box 5181 Vandenberg AFB CA 93437

SPENCE, SCOTT THOMAS, electromechanical engineer; b. Astoria, Oreg., Feb. 25, 1953; s. Kenneth J. and Georgia V. (Gray) S.; m. Deborah A. Briggs, Dec. 14, 1971; children—Chelsea S., Bethany G. A.A.S. in Electronics Engring., DeVry Inst., Phoenix, 1978, B.S. in Electronics Engring. Tech., 1980. Field service mgr. Rogers Machinery Co., Seattle, 1973-76; field engr. A-V Compressor, Phoenix, 1976-80, Westinghouse Hanford Co., Richland, Wash., 1980-81; with UNC Nuclear Industries, Richland, 1981—, project mgr., 1983-84, staff asst. to dir. shippingport decommissioning project, 1984-85; program adminstr. Dept. Energy Nat. Tech. Transfer Program, 1985-87. Mem. IEEE, IEEE Communications Soc., Profl. Mgmt.

Soc. Home: 2216 S Rainier Kennewick WA 99337 Office: UNC Nuclear Industries PO Box 490 Richland WA 99352

SPENCE, WILLIAM JOHN, tectonophysicist, seismologist; b. Peoria, Ill., July 11, 1937; s. William Rankine and Martha Sunshine (Utt) S.; m. Pamela Emmeline Jones, Aug. 21, 1976 (dec. Aug. 1979); 1 child, Andrew Edwards; m. Susan Frances Edelstein, Nov. 23, 1984. BS, SUNY, Albany, 1959, MS, 1960; PhD, Pa. State U., 1973. Chmn. sci. dept. Spencer (N.Y.) Cen. Sch., 1960-62; research geophysicist U.S. Coast and Geodetic Survey, Washington, 1962-70, NOAA, Boulder, Colo., 1971-74; research geophysicist, project chief global sesmicity and tectonics/induced seismicity projects U.S. Geol. Survey, Denver, 1975—; adj. prof. Colo. Sch. Mines, Golden, 1985—; research assoc. Denver Mus. Natural History, 1981-84. Mem. Denver Symphony Chorus, 1984—. Mem. Seismol. Soc. Am., Am. Geophys. Union (v.p., pres.-elect Front Range chpt.), AAAS. Democrat. Unitarian. Club: Colo. Mountain. Discovered upper mantle source for silent canyon volcanic ctr., Nev., 1974; discovered that slab pull force is primary cause of great subduction earthquakes, 1985; avocations: jazz piano, backpacking, flyfishing. Home: 2118 Race St Denver CO 80205 Office: Nat Earthquake Info Ctr Box 25046 MS 967 Denver CO 80225

SPENCER, CAROL BROWN, public information official; b. Normal, Ill., Aug. 26, 1936; d. Fred William and Sorado (Gross) B.; m. James Calvin Spencer, Dec. 18, 1965 (div. July 1978); children: James Calvin Jr., Anne Elizabeth. BA in English, Calif. State U., Los Angeles, 1964, MA in Pub. Adminstrn., 1986. Cert. secondary edn. tchr., Calif. Corr. Ashland (Ohio) Times Gazette, 1975-78; tchr. English Seneca Vocat. High Sch., Buffalo, 1966-70; pub. info. official City of Pasadena, Calif., 1979—. Editor: Pasadena In Focus monthly mcpl. publ., 1984-86, N.W. Bulletin quarterly mcpl. publ., 1985-86. Bd. dirs. Pasadena Beautiful Found., 1984-86, Pasadena Cultural Festival Found., 1983-86; mayoral appointee Strategic Planning Adv. Com., Pasadena, 1985-86; chmn. pub. events com., United Way Los Angeles County. Mem. Pub. Relations Soc. Am., Calif. Assn. Pub. Info. Ofcls. (exec. bd., Paul Clark Achievement award 1986), Mcpl. Mgmt. Assts. of So. Calif. Democrat. Anglican. Home: 6026 Encinita Ave Temple City CA 91780 Office: City of Pasadena 100 N Garfield Pasadena CA 91109

SPENCER, DEBRA LEE, English teacher; b. Culver City, Calif., Feb. 15, 1951; d. Bishop Copeland and Rose Elizabeth (Michalis) S.; m. James Robert Rolens, Mar. 5, 1983; children: Clare, Samuel. BA, U. Calif., Santa Cruz, 1972. Cert. elem. tchr., spl. edn. tchr., community coll. tchr., Calif. Tchr. Hanford (Calif.) Elem. Sch. Dist., 1977-79; tchr. English Cabrillo Coll., Aptos, Calif., 1980—. Mem. Nuclear Freeze, Santa Cruz, 1984—; sec. Santa Cruz Chamber Players, 1982—. Mem. Nat. Council Tchrs. Eng., Sierra Club. Democrat. Episcopalian. Avocations: writing, gardening, backpacking. Home: 115 Pennsylvania Ave Santa Cruz CA 95062 Office: Cabrillo Coll 6500 Soquel Dr Aptos CA 95003

SPENCER, DICK, III, magazine publisher; b. Dallas, Jan. 28, 1921; s. Richard and Jessie (Burden) S.; m. Jo Anne Nicholson, July 24, 1943 (div. May, 1983); children: Barbara Jo Spencer Corpolongo, Richard Craig (dec.), Debra Jean.; m. Vivian King, June 4, 1983. B.A., U. Iowa, 1942. With promotion dept. Look mag., 1945-47; editor info. service U. Iowa, also instr. Sch. Journalism, 1948-50; publs. editor U. Colo., Boulder, 1950-51; editor Western Horseman mag., Colorado Springs, 1951-69; pub. Western Horseman mag., 1969—. Author: Editorial Cartooning, 1949, Pulitzer Prize Cartoons, 1951, Beginning Western Horsemanship, 1959, Intermediate Western Horsemanship, 1960, Horse Breaking, 1967. Served with AUS, 1942-45, ETO. Decorated Purple Heart with 2 oak leaf clusters, Bronze Star with oak leaf cluster, Combat Inf. badge, Parachutist badge. Mem. Sigma Delta Chi, Alpha Tau Omega. Methodist. Clubs: Pikes Peak Range Riders, Desert Caballeros. Home: 14050 Roller Coaster Rd Colorado Springs CO 80908 Office: Western Horseman Magazine 3850 N Nevada Ave Colorado Springs CO 80907

SPENCER, DOUGLAS LLOYD, chemist, manufacturers' representative; b. Berkeley, Calif., July 19, 1952; s. Alma Glenn and Anna Lea (Lloyd) S.; A.A., Diablo Valley Coll., 1971; B.S., Brigham Young U., 1974; m. Connie Jeanette Whitesel, Aug. 23, 1974; children—Jeanette Dawn, Jared Douglas, Jilissa Annette, Janine Marie, Janelle Renee. Lab. instr. chemistry dept. Brigham Young U., 1973-74; lab. asst., computer cons. Hartley Internat., Provo, Utah, 1974; research chemist Dow Chem. Western div., Pittsburg, Calif., 1975-80; pres. Sunset Distbg., Inc., Brentwood, Calif., 1980-82; pres. Maier & Assocs., Inc., Brentwood, 1982-83; pres. Doug Spencer & Assocs., Inc., Brentwood, 1983—. Mem. Brentwood Planning Commn., 1980-81; missionary, dist. zone leader Eastern States Mission, 1971-73. Rossmoor residents scholar, 1969-71, Brigham Young U. scholar, 1973-74. Mem. Nat. Eagle Scout Assn., Alpha Gamma Sigma (Calif. state treas. 1970). Republican. Mormon. Club: Liahona. Home: PO Box 427 Brentwood CA 94513

SPENCER, JANET LEE, restauranteur; b. Woodward, Iowa, Aug. 1, 1935; d. L. Marvin and Mabel Miller (Schaal) Sturgeon; m. Gerre L. Spencer, June 9, 1956 (dec.); children—Kristen Petersen, Kimberly Spencer, David Spencer; m. Patrick S. Byrne, Nov. 24, 1984. B.S., Iowa State U., 1956; student Lewis Clark State Coll., U. Idaho; M.A., Whitworth Coll., 1980. Cert. mental health profl., Wash. High sch. tchr., dir. homemaker tng., 1956-69; community orgn. specialist Community Action Agy., Hillsboro, Oreg., 1969-70; children's protective services worker Dept. Social Health Services, Clarkston, Wash., 1970-75; tchr. Walla Walla Community Coll., 1974-80; family therapist Asotin County Mental Health Clinic, 1974-80; mktg. mgr. K. Foster & Assoc., Bellevue, Wash., 1980-83, Spencer & Assocs., Bellevue, 1983-84; owner Theodore Bruin's Restaurant & Lounge, Oroville, Wash., 1984—; agy. cons., trainer in family therapy, Seattle, 1980-84. Chmn. Lewiston Arts Festival, 1967-68; bd. dirs., sec. Orchards Swimming Pool Assn., 1967-69; leader Diamond L Club, 1967-69. Named Jr. Women's Club outstanding mem., 1968. Sigma Kappa. Home: PO Box 599 Oroville WA 98844 Office: Theodore Bruin's Restaurant & Lounge 1412 Main Oroville WA 98844

SPENCER, ROGER KEITH, lawyer; b. N.Y.C., July 2, 1946; s. Martin and Ruth Edith (Weiss) S.; m. Barbara Natalie Kipnis, Jan. 31, 1977; children: William Cary, Elizabeth Ann. BS, U. Mich., 1968; JD, Northwestern U., 1976. Bar: Ariz. 1976, U.S. Dist. Ct. Ariz. 1976, U.S. Ct. Appeals (9th cir.) 1976, U.S. Supreme Ct. 1983; cert. real property law, Ariz. State Bar; lic. real property specialist. Mem. Ryley, Carlock & Ralston, Phoenix, 1976-78, Snell & Wilmer, Phoenix, 1978-83, Mohr Hackett Pederson Blakley, Randolph & Haga, P.C., Phoenix, 1983—. Mem. Phoenix Men's Symphony Guild, 1977-78; bd. dirs. Men's Arts Council Phoenix Art Mus., 1983—. Served to capt. USAF, 1968-73. Mem. State Bar Ariz., Maricopa County Bar Assn., ABA (sect. corp., banking and bus. law, sect. real property, probate and trust law), U. Mich. Alumni Assn., Northwestern U. Alumni Assn. Club: Phoenix Sunrise Rotary. Contbr. articles to legal jours. Office: Mohr Hackett Pederson Blakley Randolph & Haga PC 3807 N 7th St Phoenix AZ 85014

SPENCER, WILLIAM EDGAR, II, fruit company executive, marketing consultant; b. Woodland, Calif., Apr. 30, 1948; s. Clarence Veldon and Helen Joan (Logue) S.;m. Anna Victoria Varner, June 14, 1969 (div. May 1975); children: Jason Curtis Varner, William Edgar III; m. Kathleen Sue Johnson, Feb. 26, 1977; 1 child, Grant Thomas Leslie. BS in Mktg., U. Ariz., 1972. Asst. mgr. Allied Citrus Exchange, Phoenix, 1972-75, Lemon Adminstrv. Com., Los Angeles, 1975-76; mgr. Pacific Gamble Robinson, Kingsburg, Calif., 1976-81; sales mgr. Assoc. Citrus Packers Inc., Yuma, Ariz., 1981-84, v.p., 1984—; bd. dirs. Ariz Dist. Export Council, Phoenix; grower mem. Lemon Adminstrv. Com., 1983—. Pres. Yuma Fine Arts Assn, 1984—. Republican. Roman Catholic. Avocation: photography. Office: Assoc Citrus Packers Inc 635 S Main St Yuma AZ 85364

SPENDLOVE, REX S., research laboratory administrator, microbiologist; b. Hoytsville, Utah, Apr. 29, 1926; s. Janus Albern and Hazel Tressie (Stonebreaker) S.; m. Reta Bright Allen, May 9, 1949; children: Cheri Lynn, Rex Alan, Debbi Susan, Lisa Janette, Lori Jeanne. BS, Brigham Young U., 1951, MS, 1952; PhD, Ohio State U., 1955. Instr. U. Conn., Storrs, 1955-58; research microbiologist Calif. State Dept. Pub. Health, Berkeley, 1958-66; head dept. bacteriology Utah State U., Logan, 1966-73, prof. biology, 1973-81; pres. Sci. Advt. and Mktg., Inc., Logan, 1981—, HyClone Labs. Inc., Logan, 1975—. Mem. editorial bd. excerpta medica Internat. Abstracting Service, Amsterdam, The Netherlands; contbr. chpts. to books; also articles to profl. jours. Named Utah Busman. of Yr., 1982. Mem. AAAS, Nat. Com. Clin. Lab. Standards (serum standardization com. 1985—), Tissue Culture Assn. (serum standardization com. 1981-85), Am. Soc. Microbiology (pres. Intermountain Br. 1970), Am. Acad. Microbiology, Am. Assn. Immunologists, Soc. Exptl. Biology and Medicine, N.Y. Acad. Scis., Internat. Com. Nomenclature Viruses (reovirus study group vertebrate virus subcom. 1978-79), Sigma Xi (pres. Utah State U. chpt. 1973-74). Republican. Mormon. Avocation: skiing. Home: 931 Sumac Dr Logan UT 84321 Office: HyClone Labs Inc 1725 S State Hwy 89-91 Logan UT 84321

SPENSLEY, JAMES, physician, educator; b. Detroit, May 19, 1938; s. Herbert A. and Ruth H. (Hurford) S.; m. Jeannette A. Mattern, Feb. 17, 1962; children: Patrick, Michelle, Andrea, Chris. Student, U. Mich., 1956-63, MD, 1963. Diplomate Am. Bd. Psychiatry and Neruology. Practice medicine specializing in psychiatr; faculty mem. U. Calif. Sch. Medicine, Davis, 1969—, asst. prof. in residence, 1973-76, assoc. prof., 1976-82, assoc. clin. prof., 1982—; adj. prof. Pacific Grad. Sch. of Psychology, 1981—; cons. Westminster Counseling, 1970—, Marriage Tribunal, 1980—, Sacramento Right to Life, 1976—. Contbr. articles to profl. jours. Active Cath. Community Services, Sacramento, 1981—, Physicians for Social Responsibility, 1982—, Bread for the World, 1982—. Served to capt. USAR, 1964-67, lt. USNR, 1967-69. Fellow Am. Psychiat. Assn.; mem. Cen. Calif. Psychiat. Soc., Calif. Med. Assn., Am. Soc. for Clin. Hypnosis, Sigma Xi. Democrat. Avocations: tennis, skiing, woodworking. Home: 4217 Winding Woods Way Fair Oaks CA 95628 Office: U Calif 4401 Hazel Suite 205 Fair Oaks CA 95628

SPERA, FRANK JOHN, geologist, educator; b. Phila., Dec. 6, 1950; s. Frank Augustus and Isabella (DiFabio) S.; m. Cathy Jeanne Busby, Dec. 29, 1977. BA, Franklin-Marshall Coll., Lancaster, Pa., 1972; MA, U. Calif., Berkeley, 1974, PhD, 1977. Asst. prof. geology Princeton (N.J.) U., 1977-82, assoc. prof. geology, 1982-85; assoc. prof. geology U. Calif., Santa Barbara, 1985—. Contbr. articles to profl. jours. Office: U Calif Dept Geology Santa Barbara CA 93106

SPERRY, ROGER WOLCOTT, neurobiologist, educator; b. Hartford, Conn., Aug. 20, 1913; s. Francis B. and Florence (Kraemer) S.; m. Norma G. Deupree, Dec. 28, 1949; children: Glenn Tad, Janeth Hope. B.A., Oberlin Coll., 1935, M.A., 1937, D.Sc. (hon.), 1982; Ph.D., U. Chgo., 1941, D.Sc. (hon.), 1977; D.Sc. (hon.), Cambridge U., 1972, Kenyon Coll., 1979, Rockefeller U., 1980. Research fellow Harvard and Yerkes Labs., 1941-46; asst. prof. anatomy U. Chgo., 1946-52, sect. chief Nat. Inst. Neurol. Diseases of NIH, also asso. prof. psychology, 1952-53; Hixon prof. psychobiology Calif. Inst. Tech., 1954-84, Trustee prof. Emeritus, 1984—; research brain orgn. and neural mechanism. Contbr. articles to profl. jours., chpts. to books.; Editorial bd.: Behavioral Biology. Recipient Oberlin Coll. Alumni citation, 1954; Howard Crosby Warren medal Soc. Exptl. Psychologists, 1969; Calif. Scientist of Year award Calif. Mus. Sci. and Industry, 1972; award Passano Found., 1973; Albert Lasker Basic Med. Research award, 1979; co-recipient William Thomas Wakeman Research award Nat. Paraplegia Found., 1972, Claude Bernard sci. journalism award, 1975, Disting. research award Internat. Visual Literacy Assn., 1979; Wolf Found. prize in medicine, 1979; Nobel prize in physiology or medicine, 1981, Realia award Inst. for Advanced Philos. Research, 1986. Fellow AAAS, Am. Acad. Arts and Scis., Am. Psychol. Assn. (recipient Distinguished Sci. Contbn. award 1971); mem. Royal Acad. (fgn. mem.), Nat. Acad. Scis., Am. Physiol. Soc., Am. Assn. Anatomists, Internat. Brain Research Orgn., Soc. for Study of Devel. and Growth, Psychonomic Soc., Am. Soc. Naturalists, Am. Zool. Soc., Soc. Developmental Biology, Am. Philos. Soc. (Lashley prize 1976), Am. Neurol. Assn. (hon.), Soc. for Neurosci., Internat. Soc. Devel. Biologists, AAUP, Pontifical Acad. Scis., Inst. for Advanced Philos. Research (Realia award 1986), Sigma Xi. Office: Calif Inst of Tech 1201 E California St Pasadena CA 91125

SPEZIALE, A. JOHN, organic chemist, consultant; b. Rocky Hill, Conn., Nov. 3, 1916; s. Antonio and Giovina (DiMarco) S.; m. Dorothy Baumeister, May 2, 1942; children: Dona Speziale Luedde, Karen Speziale Hutcheson, Wendy Speziale Tarson. B.S. in Pharmacy, U. Okla., 1942, M.S., 1943; Ph.D., U. Ill., 1948. With Monsanto Co., St. Louis, 1948-79; sr. scientist agrl. div. Monsanto Co., 1960-63; dir. research Monsanto Agrl. Products Co., 1963-79; chem., agrl. and indsl. cons. 1979-86; dir. Mycogen Corp., 1986—; vis. lectr. Washington U., St. Louis, 1950-53. Author publs. Served with U.S. Army, 1944-46. Recipient Kenneth A. Spencer award, 1981. Mem. Am. Chem. Soc. (exec. com. organic div. 1974-76, mem. editorial bd. Jour. Organic Chemistry 1964-69, lectr. 1970-74, St. Louis sect. award 1973), Weed Sci. Soc. Am. (hon.), AAAS, PGRSA, OAST, Sigma Xi. Patentee synthesis and mechanism action pesticides, phoshporus chemistry, enamines, expoxides, heterocyclics, haloamides. Home: 311 Northumberland Ave Redwood City CA 94061

SPICER, ROBERT JOHN, information systems specialist; b. Santa Monica, Calif., Sept. 30, 1940; s. Stanley and Elizabeth (Gardener) S.; m. Linda Ann Pao, Feb. 20, 1960; children: David, Sheryl, Bryan. AA, Coll. San Mateo, 1962; BS, San Jose State U., 1966; MBA, U. Santa Clara, 1974. EDP mgr. Varian Assocs., Palo Alto, Calif., 1966-74; mgmt. info. systems mgr. Litronix, Cupertino, Calif., 1974-75, Carter Hawley Hale Stores Inc., Santa Clara, Calif., 1975-77, Siliconix, Santa Clara, 1977-81; mgmt. info. systems dir. Nat. Semiconductor Corp., Santa Clara, 1981—; EDP curriculum advisor Evergreen Jr. Coll, San Jose, Calif., 1978-79. Mem. Data Processing Mgrs. Assn. (cert., mem. exam com. 1968-69). Club: Sea Ray Boat (No. Calif.). Avocations: power boating, water skiing, photography.

SPIEGEL, ABRAHAM, savings and loan association executive; b. 1906. Chmn. bd. dirs. Columbia Savs. and Loan Assn., Beverly Hills, Calif., also bd. dirs. Office: Columbia Savs & Loan Assn 8840 Wilshire Blvd Beverly Hills CA 90211 *

SPIEGEL, RONALD STUART, insurance company executive; b. Chgo., Sept. 12, 1942; s. Arthur I. and Elaine M. (Young); m. Carol J. Lieberthal, July 25, 1964; children: Eric, Elissa. BA, Calif. State U., Los Angeles, 1966. Pres. Newhouse Automotive, Los Angeles, 1966-78; agt. N.Y. Life Ins. Co., Santa Fe Springs, Calif., 1978-82, sales mgr., 1982-86, assoc. gen. mgr., 1986—; v.p. Cerritos Valley Br. Life Underwriters Assn. of Los Angeles, 1984—. Pres. Temple Shalom, West Covina, Calif., 1975-77, treas., 1978-83; pres. Jewish Fedn. Council Eastern Region, Los Angeles, 1986, v.p., 1984-85. Mem. Am. Soc. CLU's, Gen. Agts. and Mgrs. Assn., Airline Owners and Pilots Assn. Democrat. Lodge: Kiwanis. Avocation: flying. Home: 1720 Orchard Hill Ln Hacienda Heights CA 91745 Office: NY Life Ins Co 10100 Pioneer Blvd #110 Santa Fe Springs CA 90670

SPIEGEL, THOMAS, savings and loan associaiton executive; b. 1946. Pres., chief exec. officer Columbia Savs. and Loan Assn., Beverly Hills, Calif., also bd. dirs. Office: Columbia Savs & Loan Assn 8840 Wilshire Blvd Beverly Hills CA 90211 *

SPIEGEL, ZANE (ELIHU), hydrologist, educator; b. Middletown, N.Y., Nov. 6, 1926; s. Nathan and Anna Rebecca (Mayer) S.; m. Maryanne Geissler, Dec. 19, 1959; children: Austin Gregory, Evan Nathaniel. BS, U. Chgo., 1949, MS, 1952; PhD, N.Mex. Inst. Tech., 1962. Registered profl. engr., N.Mex., N.Y., Mass., Ct., Ohio. Geologist U.S. Geol. Survey, Albuquerque, 1949-53, N.Mex. State Land Office, Santa Fe, 1954; water resource engr. N.Mex. State Engr. Office, Santa Fe, 1954; project mgr. UN, San Juan, Argentina, 1964-66; cons. Santa Fe, 1971—; vis. prof. Imperial Coll., London, 1963-64; prof. Ohio State U., Columbus, 1980-82; vis. lectr. U. Minn., Mpls., 1967-68, N.Mex. Inst. Tech., Socorro, 1971; course coordinator Coll. Santa Fe, N.Mex., 1974-77, 85. Author: Geology and Groundwater Socorro County, New Mexico, 1955, Hydraulics of Certain Stream-Connected Aquifer Systems, 1962; co-author Water Resources of Santa Fe Area New Mexico, 1965; tech. cons. (film) When the Rivers Run Dry, 1976. Trustee Old Santa Fe Assn., 1974-80. Served as pvt. U.S. Army, 1945-46. Grantee Lafayette Coll., 1944; lectr. grantee Fulbright Commn., 1958; Coop. fellow NSF, 1961, Water Resources fellow Harvard U., 1962. Fellow Geol. Soc. Am., ASCE; mem. Am. Geophys. Union, Nat. Council Engrng. Examiners (cert.), Am. Inst. Hydrology (cert.). Avocations: history, history of sci. Home and Office: PO Box 1541 Santa Fe NM 87504-1541

SPIEGELBERG, EMMA JO, educator; b. Mt. View, Wyo., Nov. 22, 1936; d. Joseph Clyde and Dorcas (Reese) Hatch; B.A. with honors, U. Wyo., 1958, MEd, 1985; m. James Walter Spiegelberg, June 22, 1957; children: William L., Emory Walter, Joseph John. Tchr. bus. edn. Laramie (Wyo.) High Sch., 1960-61, 65—, chmn. Bus. Edn. Dept., mgr. computer system, 1974—; guest lectr. U. Wyo., 1979; chmn. Gov.'s and State Supt.'s Task Force on Vocat. Edn., 1982-83. Bd. dirs. Cathedral Home for Children, Laramie, 1967-70, 72—, pres., 1985-87; precinct committeewoman; bd. dirs. Laramie Plains Mus., 1970-79. Author: Branigan's Accounting Simulation, 1986. Named Wyo. Bus. Tchr. of Yr., 1982. Mem. Am. Vocat. Assn. (policy com. region V 1984—, region V Tchr. of Yr. 1986), Wyo. Vocat. Assn. (exec. bd. 1978-80, pres. 1981-82, Outstanding Contbns. to Vocat. Edn. award 1983, Tchr. of Yr. 1985, exec. sec. 1986—), Nat. Bus. Edn. Assn., Mt. Plains Bus. Edn. Assn. (Wyo. rep. to bd. dirs. 1982-85, rep. to Internat. Soc. Bus. Edn. 1985-86, pres. elect 1986-87, pres. 1987—), Wyo. Bus. Edn. Assn. (pres. 1979-80), NEA, Wyo. Edn. Assn., Albany County Edn. Assn. (sec. 1970-71), Laramie C. of C. (bd. dirs. 1985—), U. Wyo. Alumni Assn. (bd. dirs. 1985—, v.p. 1986—), Kappa Delta Pi, Phi Delta Kappa, Alpha Delta Kappa (state pres. 1978-82), Chi Omega. Mem. United Ch. of Christ. Clubs: Zonta, Laramie Jr. Women's (pres. 1962-63). Home: 3301 Grays Gables Laramie WY 82070 Office: Laramie High Sch 1275 N 11th St Laramie WY 82070

SPIES, ROBERT BERNARD, marine scientist; b. Palo Alto, Calif., May 21, 1943; s. Raymond John and Rita Ethel (Bernard) S.; m. Ann Elizabeth Mohun, Aug. 17, 1963; children: Jessica, Brennan, Rebecca. BS, St. Mary's Coll., Moraga, Calif., 1965; MS, U. Pacific, 1965; PhD, U. So. Calif., 1971. Sr. research officer Victorian Govt., Melbourne, Australia, 1970-73; environ. scientist Lawrence Livermore (Calif.) Nat. Lab., 1973—; mem. cons. bd. So. Calif. Coastal Water Research Project, 1986. Contbr. articles to profl. jours.; regional editor Marine Environ. Research Jour., 1982-87, editor, 1987—. NSF predoctoral fellow, 1969; Arthur Vining Davis fellow, 1969. Mem. AAAS, San Francisco Bay and Estuarine Assn. Avocation: sculpture. Home: PO Box 824 Livermore CA 94550 Office: U Calif Lawrence Livermore Nat Lab Box 5507 Livermore CA 94550

SPIKER, J. WES, advertising executive; b. Dover, Ohio, Aug. 26, 1954; s. John Edward Spiker and Carlyn Ann (Cleveland) Quinton; m. Christine Anne Riley, Mar. 23, 1974; children: Jessica Anne, Jared Wesley. BA in Radio/TV, Eastern Wash. U., 1975; postgrad., Inst. Advanced Advt. Studies, U. So. Calif., 1981. Sales mgr. Sta. KEZE-AM-FM, Spokane, Wash., 1975-78; acctg. exec. Young and Rubicam, Los Angeles, 1978-81; account exec. Nordbye Advt., Missoula, Mont., 1981-82, Brooke & Assocs., Missoula, 1982-83; pres. Spiker Communications, Missoula, 1983—. Creative dir. advt. awards Montana Addy's, 1982-85; chmn. Winter Star Festival, 1985-86; mem. Conv. and Visitors Bur. Mem. Missoula Advt. and Mktg. Fedn. (bd. dirs. 1983-86). Republican. Methodist. Avocations: fly fishing, softball, snow and water skiing, trail biking. Office: Spiker Communications PO Box 8567 Missoula MT 59807

SPILLAR, PAUL VICTOR, international marketing consultant; b. Prague, Czechoslovakia, Jan. 30, 1932; came to U.S., 1941; s. Charles V. and Margaret M. (Mandler) S.; m. Anne C. Stephenson, Jan. 10, 1960 (div. 1974); children: Charles, Catherine. BSE, U. Pa., 1953, MBA, 1954. Dir. mktg. and pub. relations Baldwin-Lime-Hamilton, N.Y.C., 1960-67; group creative dir. Cunningham & Walsh Inc. subs. Newcourt Industries Inc., N.Y.C., 1967-69; asst. to pres. internat. group Ted Bates Worldwide Inc., N.Y.C., 1969-73; exec. v.p. Sharp Communications Inc., San Francisco, 1973-78; mgmt. cons. Burlingame, Calif., 1978—. Served with U.S. Army, 1955-57. Mem. Am. Mktg. Soc. (local bd. dirs. 1972—), World Future Soc., Aviation/Space Writers Assn. Club: Wharton (San Francisco). Avocations: music, art, travel. Home: 1136 Laguna Burlingame CA 94010

SPILLNER, CHARLES JOSEPH, chemist; b. Oakland, Calif., Nov. 17, 1947; s. Charles Joseph and Emma Cecilia (Moreno) S.; m. Jill Ann Sweeney, June 19, 1969 (div. Dec. 1985); children: Michael, Charles, Leanne, Christine. BSc, U. Calif., 1969; PhD, U. Utah, 1973. Research chemist Rohm and Haas, Springhouse, Pa., 1973-76, Stauffer Chem., Mountain View, Calif., 1976—. Contbr. articles to profl. jours. NSF scholar, U. Utah, 1971, Stauffer grad. scholar, U. Utah, 1972. Mem. Am. Chem. Soc., Soc. Environ. Chemistry. Republican. Roman Catholic. Avocation: running. Home: 220 Spreckles Dr Aptos CA 95003 Office: Stauffer Chem PO Box 760 Mountain View CA 94042

SPINRAD, RICHARD WILLIAM, oceanographer, researcher; b. N.Y.C., Apr. 6, 1954; s. Leonard William and Thelma (Zipkin) S.; m. Alanna Wynn Thompson, June 1, 1980; 1 child, Gary Brian. BA, Johns Hopkins U., 1975; MS, Oreg. State U., 1978, PhD, 1982. Research asst. Oreg. State U., Corvallis, 1975-82; research scientist Bigelow Lab. for Ocean Sci., West Boothbay Harbor, Maine, 1982-86, prin. investigator, 1986—; pres. Sea Tech., Inc., Corvallis, 1986—. Contbr. sci. articles to profl. jours. Hon. mem. Benton-Linn Council on Alcohol, Corvallis, 1976-77. Mem. AAAS, Am. Soc. Limnologists and Oceanographers, Am. Geophys. Union, Optical Soc. Am. Democrat. Jewish. Avocations: profl. banjo playing, outdoor activities, woodworking. Office: Sea Tech Inc PO Box 779 Corvallis OR 97339

SPINRAD, ROBERT JOSEPH, electronics co. exec.; b. N.Y.C., Mar. 20, 1932; s. Sidney and Isabel (Reiff) S.; m. Verna Winderman, June 27, 1954; children—Susan Irene, Paul Reiff. B.S., Columbia U., 1953, M.S. (Bridgham fellow), 1954; Ph.D. (Whitney fellow), MIT, 1963. Registered profl. engr., N.Y. Project engr. Bulova Research & Devel. Lab., N.Y.C., 1953-55; sr. scientist Brookhaven Nat. Lab., Upton, N.Y., 1955-68; v.p. Sci. Data Systems, Santa Monica, Calif., 1968-69; v.p. programming Xerox Corp., El Segundo, Calif., 1969-71; dir. info. scis. Xerox Corp., 1971-76, v.p. systems devel., 1976-78; v.p. research Xerox Corp., Palo Alto, 1978-83; dir. systems tech. Xerox Corp., 1983-87, dir. corp. tech., 1987—; cons. Contbr. articles to profl. jours. Mem. IEEE, Assn. Computing Machinery, Sigma Xi, Tau Beta Pi. Patentee in field. Office: Xerox Corp 3333 Coyote Hill Rd Palo Alto CA 94304

SPINWEBER, CHERYL LYNN, research psychologist; b. Jersey City, July 26, 1950; d. Stanley A. And Evelyn M. (Pfleger) S.; m. Michael E. Bruich, June 18, 1977; 1 child, Sean Michael Bruich. AB with distinction, Cornell U., 1972; PhD in Exptl. Psychology, Harvard U., 1977. Lic. psychologist, Calif. Asst. prof. psychiatry Tufts U. Sch. Medicine, Medford, Mass., 1977-79; asst. dir. sleep lab. Boston State Hosp., 1973-79; dep. head dept. behavioral psychopharmacology Naval Health Research Ctr., San Diego, 1978-86, head dept. behavioral psychopharmacology, 1986—; research asst. prof. dept. psychiatry Uniformed Services U. of the Health Scis., Bethesda, Md., 1985—; lectr., workshop instr. U. Calif. San Diego, La Jolla, Calif., 1979-81, vis. lectr. 1979-86; adj. assoc. prof. San Diego State U. Grad. Sch. Pub. Health, 1984—; courtesy clin. staff appointee dept. psychiatry Naval Hosp., San Diego, 1984—. Contbr. articles to profl. jours. Scholar Cornell U., Ithaca, N.Y., 1968-72, West Essex Tuition, 1968-72, Cornell U. Fedn. Women, 1917-72, Harvard U., 1972-73, 74-76, NDEA Title IV, 1973-74; postdoctoral associateship Nat. Research Council, 1978-80. Fellow Clin. Sleep Soc.; mem. AASS, Am. Men and Women of Sci., Sleep Research Soc. (exec. com. 1986—), Am. Psychol. Assn., Western Psychol. Assn. (sec., treas. 1986—), Calif. Sleep Soc., Sigma Xi. Office: Naval Health Research Ctr Naval Hosp 36-4 San Diego CA 92134-5000

SPIRA-SOLOMON, DARLENE JOY, industrial chemist, researcher; b. Walnut Creek, Calif., Feb. 7, 1959; d. Erwin Irving and Beverly Sue (Davis) Spira; m. Edward Ira Solomon, Sept. 15, 1984. BS, Stanford U., 1980; PhD, MIT, 1984. Research asst. Beckman Instruments, Palo Alto, Calif., 1978-79; research assoc. MIT, Cambridge, 1980-84; research assoc. Stanford (Calif.) U., 1982-84, asst. in instruction FT-IR spectroscopy, 1982-83; research scientist Hewlett-Packard Labs., Palo Alto, 1984—. Contbr. numerous articles to profl. jours. Coll. recruiter Hewlett-Packard, 1985—. Fellow chemistry dept. MIT, 1980-82, Stanford U., 1976-80. Mem. Am. Chem. Soc., Sigma Xi, Phi Beta Kappa. Avocations: swimming, tennis, travel, internat. dining and cooking, spectator football. Office: Hewlett Packard Labs PO Box 10490 Palo Alto CA 94303-0971

SPIROCK, CLIFFORD ALLEN, land planner, surveyor, real estate developer, consultant; b. Cleve., Aug. 10, 1943; s. Frank Edward and Jeannette (Shabanek) S.; m. Georgia C. Starr, Nov. 27, 1965; children: Deanna K., Clifford F. Graphic supr. Mid Rio Grande Council Govts., Albuquerque, 1967; surveyor, cons. Miller and Walsh, Inc., Albuquerque, 1965-69; exec. v.p. McIntire & Quiros, Inc., Albuquerque, 1969-74; pres., founder Community Sciences Corp., Albuquerque, 1974—; pres. ECOS Bldg. and Devel. Corp., Albuquerque, 1981-84, Las Chamisas Native Plants, Inc., Albuquerque, 1980-83, Albuquerque Urban Adv. Council, also bd. dirs.; devel. regulations council Urban Land Inst., Washington, 1979—. Prin. planner maps for various urban areas. Commr. Planning and Zoning Commn. Village of Corrales, N.Mex., 1986—; appointed mem. Transp. Coordinating Com., Albuquerque, 1985-86. Mem. Am. Inst. Cert. Planners (cert.), Nat. Assn. Surveyors and Mappers. Republican. Avocations: computer graphics and design, quarter horse breeding, furniture making, graphic art. Home: Star Route Box 1437 Corrales NM 87048 Office: Community Scis Corp PO Box 1328 Corrales NM 87048

SPITZ, LEWIS WILLIAM, historian, educator; b. Bertrand, Nebr., Dec. 14, 1922; s. Lewis William and Pauline Mary (Griebel) S.; m. Edna Marie Huttenmaier, Aug. 14, 1948; children: Stephen Andrew, Philip Mathew. A.B., Concordia Coll., 1944; M.Div., Concordia Sem., 1946; M.A., U. Mo., 1947; Ph.D., Harvard U., 1954. With U. Mo., Columbia, 1953-60; asso. prof. history U. Mo., 1958-60; Fulbright prof. U. Mainz, Ger., 1960-61; prof. history Stanford (Calif.) U., 1960—, William R. Kenan Jr. prof., 1974—, assoc. dean humanities and scis., 1973-77; vis. prof. Harvard U., Cambridge, Mass., 1964-65; dir. research Center for Reformation Research, Clayton, Mo., summer 1964, mem. bd. control, 1973—; sr. fellow Southeastern Medieval and Renaissance Inst., Duke U., summer 1968; vis. prof. Barnard Coll., 1980-81. Author: Conrad Celtis—The German Arch-Humanist, 1957, The Religious Renaissance of the German Humanists, 1963, Life in Two Worlds—A Biography of William Sihler, 1968, The Renaissance and Reformation Movements, 2 vols, 1972, Humanismus und Reformation in der deutschen Geschichte, 1980; The Protestant Reformation, 1517-1559, 1985; mem. editorial bd.: Soundings, 1973-79, Ch. History, 1982-86; mng. editor: Archive for Reformation History, 1968-76. Recipient Harbison award for teaching Danforth Found., 1964; Guggenheim fellow, 1956; Nat. Endowment for Humanities sr. fellow, 1965; Am. Council Learned Socs. fellow, 1971; Huntington Library fellow, 1959; Inst. Advanced Study Princeton fellow, 1979-80; Pew Found. fellow, 1983. Mem. Am. Soc. Reformation Research (pres. 1963-64), Am. Hist. Assn., No. Calif. Renaissance Soc. (pres. 1964-65), Am. Soc. Ch. History (pres. 1976-77). Home: 827 Lathrop Dr Stanford CA 94305 Office: Dept History Stanford U Stanford CA 94305

SPITZER, MATTHEW L., retail store exec.; b. Pitts., June 20, 1929; s. Martin and Ruth G. S.; student U. Buffalo, 1948-50; children—Mark, Edward, Eric, Joseph. Product line mgr. Gen. Dynamics, Rochester, N.Y., 1962-67; dir. contracts Friden div. Singer, San Leandro, Calif., 1968-69; asst. v.p. Talcott Computer Leasing, San Francisco, 1970-71; pres. Spitzer Music Co., Inc., Hayward, Calif., 1972—; pres. Current Techs., Inc.; chmn. bd. Leo's Audio and Music Techs., Oakland, Calif.; pres., chief exec. officer Musical Instruments Inc., Fresno, Calif. Clubs: Masons, Mensa. Office: Spitzer Music Co 943 B St Hayward CA 94541

SPIVAK, JACQUE R., bank executive; b. San Francisco, Nov. 5, 1929; d. Robert Morris and Sadonia Clardine Breitstein; m. Herbert Spivak, Aug. 26, 1960; children—Susan, Donald, Joel, Sheri. B.S., U. So. Calif., 1949, M.S., 1950, M.B.A., 1959. Mgr. Internat. Escrow, Inc., Los Angeles, 1960-65, Greater Los Angeles Investment Co., 1965-75; mgr. escrow Transam. Title Ins. Co., Los Angeles, 1975-78; mgr. escrow, asst. v.p. Wells Fargo Bank, Beverly Hills, Calif., 1979-80; adminstr. escrow, v.p. 1st Pacific Bank, Beverly Hills, 1980-85; escrow adminstr. Century City Savs. & Loan Assn., Los Angeles, 1986-87; pres. Producers Escrow Corp., Beverly Hills., 1987—. Recipient awards PTA, Girl Scouts U.S.A., Jewish Fedn. Los Angeles, Hadassah. Mem. Calif. Escrow Assn., Nat. Assn. Bank Women, Inst. Trustees Sales officers. Republican. Jewish. Office: Producers Escrow Corp 9328 Civic Ctr Dr Beverly Hills CA 90210

SPIVEY, BRUCE E., physician; b. Cedar Rapids, Iowa, Aug. 29, 1934; s. William Loranzy and Grace Loretta (Barber) S.; m. Nancy J. Howe, Mar. 31, 1956 (div. Jan. 1977); children: Lisa, Eric. B.A., Coe Coll., 1956; M.D., U. Iowa, 1959, M.S., 1964; M.Ed., U. Ill., 1969; hon. doctorate Sci., Coe Coll., 1978. Diplomate: Am. Bd. Ophthalmology. Asst. prof. U. Iowa Coll. Medicine, Iowa City, 1966, assoc. prof., 1966-71; dean Sch. Med. Scis. U. Pacific, San Francisco, 1971-76; prof., chmn. dept. ophthalmology Pacific Med. Ctr., San Francisco, 1971-87, pres., chief exec. officer, dir., 1971—; exec. v.p., chief exec. officer Am. Acad. Ophthalmology, San Francisco, 1978—; pres., chief exec. officer Calif. Healthcare System, Bay area, 1986—; dir. Ophthalmic Pub. Co., Chgo., 1977—; v.p. Am. Bd. Med. Specialties, 1978-82, pres., 1980-82; chmn. bd. dirs. Vol. Hosps. of Am.-Northern Calif., 1985-87. Editor: Ophthalmology for Medical Students; contbr. numerous articles to profl. jours.; inventor instruments for eye surgery, 1967, 73. Bd. dirs. Pacific Vision Found., San Francisco, 1977—; bd. dirs. United States-China Ednl. Inst., 1978—; trustee Coe Coll., 1985—. Served to capt. U.S. Army, 1964-66. Decorated Bronze Star; recipient Emile Javal Gold medal Internat. Contact Lens Council, San Francisco, 1982, Gradle medal Pan-Am. Assn. Ophthalmol., others. Fellow Am. Acad. Ophthalmology (Disting. Service award 1972, Sr. Honor award 1986), Am. Bd. Ophthalmology (dir. 1975-83), ACS; mem. AMA, Am. Opthalmol. Soc., Academia Ophthalmol. Internationalis, Internat. Congress Opthalmol. (sec.-gen. 1978-82). Republican. Presbyterian. Clubs: Pacific-Union; University (San Francisco). Home: 1142 Filbert St San Francisco CA 94109 Office: Pacific Med Ctr 2340 Clay St PO Box 7999 San Francisco CA 94120

SPOEHR, ALEXANDER, anthropologist, retired educator; b. Tucson, Aug. 23, 1913; s. Herman Augustus and Florence (Mann) S; m. Anne Dinsdale Harding, Aug. 2, 1941; children—Alexander Harding, Helene Spoehr Clarke. A.B., U. Chgo., 1934, Ph.D., 1940; D.Sc. (hon.), U. Hawaii, 1952. From asst. curator to curator Field Mus., Chgo., 1940-53; dir. Bishop Mus., Honolulu, 1953-62; prof. Yale U., New Haven, 1953-62; chancellor East-West Ctr., Honolulu, 1962-63; prof. anthropology U. Pitts., 1964-78, prof. emeritus, 1978; U.S. mem. South Pacific Commn., 1957-60; mem. Pacific sci. bd. NRC, Washington, 1955-61, chmn. 1958-61. N.Am. and Pacific ethnological and archaeol. researcher. Contbr. numerous articles to profl. jours. Trustee Bishop Mus., 1981-84; Served to lt. USNR, 1942-45. Fellow Am. Anthropol. Assn. (pres. 1965), AAAS; mem. Nat. Acad. Scis., Sigma Xi. Avocation: gardening. Home: 2548 Makiki Heights Dr Honolulu HI 96822

SPOONER, CHARLES EDWARD, university administrator, health educator; b. Boston, July 25, 1932; s. Charles Edward and Elizabeth Terese (Mahoney) S.; m. Beth Ann Tillman, Nov. 17, 1962; children: Allison Marie, Deanna Lynn. BA, UCLA, 1956, MS, 1961, PhD, 1963; cert. in Health Systems Mgmt., Harvard U., 1976. Pharmacologist Riker Labs., Boston and Los Angeles, 1951-59; predoctoral fellowship NIMH, 1960-63, postdoctoral fellowship, 1963-65; research pharmacologist UCLA, 1965-68, asst. prof. med. sch., 1968; from asst. prof. to prof. med. sch. U. Calif., La Jolla, Calif., 1968—, assoc. dean, prof., 1974—; cons. VA Hosp., Sepulveda, Calif., 1964-81, NIMH, Bethesda, Md., 1976-81, Bd. Med. Quality Assurance, Sacramento, Calif., 1983; vis. prof. Harvard Med. Sch., 1976. Fulbright fellow U. Oxford Med Sch., 1986-87. Mem. AAAS, Am. Soc. Pharmacology Exptl. Therapeutics, Assn. Am. Med. Colls., Soc. Neuroscis., Sigma Xi. Clubs: Fedn. Fly Fishermen (West Yellowstone), Steamboaters (N. Umpqua River, Oreg.). Avocation: fly fishing for trout, salmon. Home: 14178 Recuerdo Dr Del Mar CA 92014 Office: U Calif San Diego Sch Med La Jolla CA 92093

SPOOR, JAMES EDWARD, company executive; b. Rockford, Ill., Feb. 19, 1936; s. Frank Kendall and Genevieve Eileen (Johnson) S.; B.S. in Psychology, U. Ill., 1958; m. Nancy E. Carlson, Sept. 8, 1962; children—Sybll K., Kendall P., Andrea K., Marcie K. Personnel mgr. Nat. Sugar Refining Co., N.Y.C., 1960-64, Pepsico, Inc., N.Y.C., Auburn, N.Y., 1964-67; mgr. internat. personnel Control Data Corp., Mpls., 1967-75; v.p. personnel and employee relations Vetco, Inc., Ventura, Calif., 1975-79; v.p. employee relations Hamilton Bros. Oil Co., Denver, 1979-84; pres. Spectrum Human Resource Systems Corp., 1984—; cons., speaker on human resources. Mem. adv. bd. Salvation Army, 1978-79; chmn. Spl. Commn. for Ventura County Bd. Suprs., 1978; mem. task force on human resources Colo. Sch. Mines, 1983. Served with U.S. Army, 1958-60. Mem. Am. Soc. Personnel Adminstrn. (contbg. author handbook), Assn. for Human Resource Systems Profls., Colo. Soc. Personnel Adminstrn. Republican. Episcopalian. Clubs: Denver, Masons, Shriners, Lions. Contbg. author: Am. Soc. Personnel Adminstrn. Personnel and Indsl. Relations Handbook.

SPORCK, CHARLES E., electronic products manufacturing company executive; b. 1928. B.S. in Mech. Engring., Cornell U. With semiconductor div. Fairchild Camera and Instrument Co., 1949-67; pres., chief exec. officer Nat. Semiconductor Corp., Santa Clara, Calif., 1967—, also dir. Office: Nat Semiconductor Corp 2900 Semiconductor Dr Santa Clara CA 95051 *

SPRADLIN, DEWEY DONALD, art dealer; b. Durant, Okla., Mar. 19, 1947; s. Jehu Dewey and Margaret (Butcher) S.; m. Linda Gates, Aug. 5, 1975 (div. Jan. 1980). BA, U. Okla., 1970; MBA, Harvard U., 1972. Corp. fin. assoc. Mitchum, Jones & Templeton, Los Angeles, 1972-74; mgr. Roger's Garden, Newport Beach, Calif., 1974-76; owner, mgr. Victoria Garden, Palo Alto, Calif., 1976-77; dir. acquisitions Winthrop Fin. Corp., Menlo Park, Calif., 1977-83; gen. ptnr. August Fin. Corp., San Francisco, 1983-84; art dealer The Spradlin Gallery, Los Angeles, 1985—. Editor, pub. The Fly Fisher's Guide, 1981-84. Mem. Harvard Bus. Sch. Alumni Assn. (pres. No. Calif. chpt. 1982-84), Guardsmen of San Francisco, Mensa. Republican. Club: Olympic (San Francisco). Avocations: fly fishing, painting.

SPRAGG, ROGER GAYLORD, physician, researcher; b. N.Y.C., Sept. 26, 1943; s. S.D. Shirley and Jane (Trace) S.; m. Carole Fiske, July 13, 1968; children: David, Adam. BA, Wesleyan U., 1965; MD, U. Rochester, 1969. Diplomate Am. Bd. Internal Medicine. Asst. prof. medicine U. Calif., San Diego, 1976-82, assoc. prof. medicine, 1982—; adj. assoc. mem. Research Inst., Scripps Clinic, San Diego, 1984—; vis. scientist Boltzmann Inst., Vienna, Austria, 1984. Editor: Respiratory Emergencies, 1982; contbr. articles on lung injury to jours. Served as surgeon USPHS, 1970-72. Recipient Established Investigator award Am. Lung Assn. Calif., 1986. Fellow ACP, Am. Coll. Chest Physicians; mem. Am. Thoracic Soc., Calif. Thoracic Soc., Western Soc. Clin. Investigation. Office: U Calif Med Ctr 225 Dickinson St San Diego CA 92103

SPRAGUE, GARY EARL, chemistry educator; b. Des Moines, May 8, 1945; s. Francis Elliott and Rose M. (Earl) S.; m. Louise Marie Faulstich, Sept. 3, 1967; children: Mark, David, Michael. BS, Moorhead State U., 1967; MS, U. Ill., 1971. Weather instr. USAF, Chanute, Ill., 1969-72; sci. tchr. Belleville Twp. (Ill.) High Sch., 1972-74, various schs., Medford, Oreg., 1974—; chmn. sci. dept. Sch. Dist. 549C, Medford, Oreg., 1978-79, div. leader, 1985—. Contbr. articles to profl. jours. Bd. mem. Luth. Ch., Medford, 1980-83, Jackson County ESD Adv. Com., Medford, 1986; mem. Rogue Valley Air Quality Adv. Com., Medford, 1983. Served to staff sgt. USAF, 1968-72. Mem. Oreg. Sci. Tchrs. (pres. 1978-79), Nat. Assn. Curriculum Supervision. Democrat. Lutheran. Avocations: archeology, mountain climbing, skiing, bow hunting. Home: 2460 E McAndrews Medford OR 97504 Office: Medford N High Sch 1900 N Keenway Medford OR 97501

SPRAGUE, PETER JULIAN, semiconductor and computer company executive; b. Detroit, Apr. 29, 1939; s. Julian K. and Helene (Coughlin) S.; m. Tjasa Krofta, Dec. 19, 1959; children: Carl, Steven, Kevin, Michael. Student, Yale U., 1961, MIT, 1961, Columbia U., 1962-66. Chmn. bd. dirs. Nat. Semiconductor Corp., Santa Clara, Calif.; bd. dirs. Caesars World, Inc. Trustee Strang Clinic, Lenox Library Assn. Clubs: Yale, Marks. Home: 15 E 88th St New York NY 10128 Office: Nat Semiconductor Corp 2900 Semiconductor Dr Santa Clara CA 95051

SPRAGUE, ROLAND EVERETT, electrical engineer, mathematics educator; b. Penn Yan, N.Y., Apr. 30, 1941; s. Everett Griffith and Charity Bessie (Vandercook) S.; m. Elnora Ruth Hill, June 5, 1976; 1 child, Michelle Renee. B.S. in Physics, U. Rochester, 1970; M.S.E., Pa. State U., 1973. Sr. engr. Gen. Electric Co., Syracuse, N.Y., 1964-66; sr. physicist Xerox Corp., Rochester, N.Y., 1968-71, Sperry Remington, Blueball, Pa., 1971-74; sr. engr. Gen. Electric Co., King of Prussia, Pa., 1974-75; sr. field engr. Litton Industries, Woodland Hills, Calif., 1975—; prof. math. U. Md., Ramstein, Germany, 1979-83, Embry-Riddle Aero. U., Ramstein, 1979-83, Fla. State U., Panama City, Panama, 1983—, Antelope Valley Coll., Lancaster, Calif, 1986—. Patentee (7) in field. Baptist. Avocations: hang gliding; parachuting; flying; running. Home: 39745 Golfers Dr Palmdale CA 93551 Office: Litton Guidance and Control Bldg 25 5500 Canoga Ave Woodland Hills CA 91365

SPRAGUE, TED, dancer, choreographer, director; b. Dewey, Okla., Jan. 6, 1939; s. Austin Samuel and Katie Edith (Dobbs) S. Student Okla. Christian Coll., Tex. Christian U. Appeared in numerous TV shows, including 5 Acad. Awards, Barbara Mandrell and the Mandrell Sisters, and others; featured dancer Funny Girl (Broadway); appeared in nightclub acts with Tony Martin and Cyd Charisse, Ann-Margret, and others; appeared in films: Pennies From Heaven, Mel Brooks History of the World Part I, New York, New York, and others; also roles in summer stock; dir., choreographer Annie, Downey Civic Light Opera, 1984, San Jose Civic Light Opera, 1985, Carousel, 1983, South Pacific, 1981, Scrooge, La Mirada Playhouse, 1983, A Christmas Carol, 1981, Rodgers with Hart, Long each Studio Theatre, 1985, Carousel, Whittier-La Mirada Light Opera Assn., 1985, Barnum, San Jose Civic Light Opera, 1986, Bye, Bye Birdie, Downey Civic Light Opera, 1986, Sound of Music, San Jose Civic Light Opera, 1987; dir. dramas including The Happy Time, 1985; choreographer dramas including: Mame, Whittier-La Mirada Light Opera Assn., 1979, Funny Girl, Fullerton Civic Light Opera (Calif.), Downey Civic Light Opera, 1981, San Jose Civic Light Opera (Calif.), 1980, Bells are Ringing, Lyric Theatre of Okla., 1982; The Music Man, San Jose Civic Light Opera, 1984, Song of Norway, Long Beach Civic Light Opera, 1985, The King and I, 1986, I Do, I Do, 1986, The Most Happy Fella, 1986; others. Recipient award Okla. Arts and Humanities Council, 1980. Mem. Actors Equity Assn., Screen Actors Guild, AFTRA. Democrat.

SPRAINGS, VIOLET EVELYN, psychologist; b. Omaha, Aug. 1, 1930; d. Henry Elbert and Straunella (Hunter) S.; A.B., U. Calif., Berkeley, 1948, M.A., 1951, postgrad., 1960-64; Ph.D., U. San Francisco, 1982. Tchr., Oakland (Calif.) Public Schs., 1951-58; psychologist Med. Edn. Diagnostic Ctr., San Francisco, 1959-62; dir. psychol. edn. and lang. services Calif. Dept. Edn., 1963-71; asst. prof. San Francisco State U., 1964-71; assoc. prof. ednl. psychology Calif. State U., Hayward, 1971-79; dir. Lang. Assocs., Orinda, Lafayette and Redwood City, 1971-79; psychologist in pvt. practice, 1962—; dir. Western Women's Bank, Sprainges Acad.; mem. adv. bd. Bay Area Health Systems Agy.; instr. U. Calif., Berkeley extension, 1964—; mem. oral bd. for Ednl. Psychologists, 1972—; mem. Calif. Dept. Task Force on Psychol. Assessment, 1987—. mem. adv. com. Foothill Jr. Coll. Dist. Recipient Phoebe Apperson Heart award San Francisco Examiner, 1968. Mem. Am. Psychol. Assn., Internat. Neuropsychol. Assn. (charter), Calif. Psychol. Assn., Calif. Assn. Sch. Psychologists and Psychometrists, Western Psychol. Assn., Nat. Council Negro Women, AAUP, Delta Sigma Theta, Psi Chi, Pi Lambda Theta. Contbr. articles to profl. jours. Home: 170 Glorietta Blvd Orinda CA 94563 Office: 3408 Deer Hill Rd Lafayette CA 94549

SPREITER, JOHN ROBERT, mechanical and aerospace engineering educator; b. Oak Park, Minn., Oct. 23, 1921; s. Walter F. and Agda E. (Hokanson) S.; m. Brenda Owens, Aug. 7, 1953; children: Terry A., Janet L., Christine P., Hilary M. B in Aero. Engring., U. Minn., 1943; MS, Stanford U, 1947, PhD, 1954. Research scientist Ames Research Ctr. NASA, Moffett Field, Calif., 1943-62, chief theoretical studies br., 1962-69; prof. applied mechanics of aero. and astronautics Stanford (Calif.) U., 1968—; lectr. Stanford U., 1951-68; cons. Nielsen Engring. and Research Inc., Mountain View, Calif., 1968-85, RMA Aerospace, Mountain View, 1985—. Contbr. numerous articles to profl. jours. Served with USN, 1944-46. Fellow AIAA, Royal Astron. Soc.; mem. Am. Geophys. Union, Am. Phys. Soc., Sigma Xi, Tau Beta Pi, Tau Omega. Democrat. Clubs: Saratoga (Calif.) Tennis (treas. 1955-65); Fremont Hills Country (Los Altos Hills, Calif.). Avocations: tennis, swimming, skiing. Home: 1250 Sandalwood Ln Los Altos CA 94022 Office: Stanford U Div Applied Mechanics Stanford CA 94305

SPRINGER, CHARLES EDWARD, state justice; b. Reno, Feb. 20, 1928; s. Edwin and Rose Mary Cecelia (Kelly) S.; m. Jacqueline Sirkegian, Mar. 17, 1951; 1 dau., Kelli Ann. B.A., U. Nev., Reno, 1950; LL.B., Georgetown U., 1953; LL.M., U. Va. Bar: Nev. 1953, D.C. 1953. Practiced in Reno, 1953-80; atty. gen. State of Nev., 1962, legis. legal adv. to gov., 1958-62; legis. bill drafter Nev. Legislature, 1955-57; mem. faculty Nat. Coll. Juvenile Justice, 1978—, U. Nev., Reno, McGeorge Sch. Law, 1982—; juvenile master 2d Jud. Dist. Nev., 1973-80; justice Supreme Ct. Nev., 1981—; chmn. Jud. Selection Commn., 1981—; trustee Nat. Council Juvenile and Family Ct. Judges, 1983-85. Served with AUS, 1945-47. Recipient Outstanding Contbn. to Juvenile Justice award Nat. Council Juvenile and Family Ct. Judges, 1980. Mem. Am. Judicature Soc., Am. Trial Lawyers Assn., ABA. Office: Supreme Ct Bldg Carson City NV 89710

SPRINGER, GLENN EVERETT, JR., safety consultant; b. Chgo., Jan. 28, 1946; s. Glenn Everett and Dorthy Lynn (Bugg) S.; m. Mary June Rose Brown, Feb. 10, 1976 (div. Mar. 1980); 1 child, James Everett; m. Marta Nancy Goldberg, July 4, 1980; children: Shannon and Crystal (twins). AA in Chemistry, U.S. Army, 1971; student in audiometric tech., UCLA; student in Electronics, Las Vegas Tech.; cert. safety engr., Los Angeles Trade Tech., 1974. Sr. cons. Glenn Springer Assoc., North Hollywood, Calif., 1971-79; safety mgr. Robert Shaw Co., Long Beach, Calif., 1979-80; sr. loss control cons. Beaver Ins. Co., Oxnard, Calif., 1980-81, 85—; loss control mgr. Hughes Market, Los Angeles, 1984; sr. loss control cons. Carnation Co., Los Angeles, 1984-85. Served to sgt. U.S. Army, 1968-71, 76-79. Mem. Am. Soc. Safety Engrs. (cons. div. officer elect. 1971-86), Nat. Safety Council, VFW, Am. Legion, Nat. Fire Protection Assn. Home: 3361 Norfolk Dr Riverside CA 92503

SPRINGER, LEANN MARIE, speech pathologist; b. Santa Barbara, Calif., Oct. 16, 1958; d. Clifton John and Luana Louise (Lopez) Tingstrom; m. John Marion Springer, July 18, 1981; children: Stephen Michael, Kimberly Marie. AA, Ventura Community Coll., 1978; BS, Idaho State U., 1981, MS, 1983. Communication disorders specialist Marsh Valley Joint Sch. Dist 21, Arimo, Idaho, 1983—. Named One of Outstanding Young Women Am., 1980, 81, 82, 83, 85, 86. Mem. Am. Speech Lang. and Hearing Assn. (cert.), Idaho Speech and Hearing Assn. Republican. Roman Catholic. Lodge: Woodmen of World. Avocations: needlepoint, reading. Home: 4819 Freedom Ave Pocatello ID 83202 Office: Marsh Valley Joint Sch Dist 21 PO Box 180 Arimo ID 83214

SPRINGER, ROBERT JOHN, educator; b. Chgo., Oct. 21, 1931; s. John Francis and Helen Monica (Mlodzikowski) S.; student Christian Bros. Coll., Memphis, 1955-57; B.S. cum laude, St. Louis U., 1959; M.A. in Spl. Edn., Calif. State U., Los Angeles, 1964; M.A. in Adminstrn. and Supervision, Calif. State U., Northridge, 1967; m. Mary Patricia Ryan, July 1, 1961; children—Martin Bernard, Robert Thomas. Prof. div. continuing edn. Pasadena City Coll., 1970-75, Ambassador Coll., 1979-82; tchr. deaf Pasadena Unified Sch. Dist., 1962-79, chmn. dept. deaf edn., 1964-79; lectr. Calif. State U., Los Angeles; tchr. sign lang. and lipreading Culver City (Calif.) Adult Sch., 1979-81; instr. sign lang. Dominguez Valley Hosp., Compton, Calif., 1981-83, Calif. State U., Dominguez Hills, 1980-85; founder, pres. co. offering services to handicapped. Served with USN, 1951-55. Cert. Council on Edn. of Deaf, Conv. of Am. Instrs. of Deaf. Mem. Nat. Assn. of Deaf, Pasadena Edn. Assn., Calif. Tchrs. Assn., NEA, Registry Interpreters for Deaf, So. Calif. Registry Interpreters for Deaf, Calif. Assn. Tchrs. Deaf and Hard of Hearing Children, Center for Living Independently in Pasadena, Advocates of Quiet Minority, Internat. Assn. Parents of Deaf, Nat. Leadership Tng. Program Alumni Assn., Greater Los Angeles Area Council on Deafness, Psi Chi. Republican. Roman Catholic. Office: PO Box 1417 San Gabriel CA 91778

SPRINGER, WAYNE RICHARD, biochemist; b. Milw., Nov. 16, 1946; s. Richard Andrew and Irma Edna (Richter) S.; m. Jane Bradley, Aug. 19, 1972; children: Matthew Bradley, Katherine Jane. BA, Northwestern U., 1968; PhD, U. Calif., Berkeley, 1977. Vol. Peace Corps, Washington, 1969-72; postdoctoral fellow U. Calif., San Diego, 1977-79, research biochemist, 1979—; research biochemist VA Med. Ctr., San Diego, 1979—. Coach Little League, Bobby Sox. Mem. Am. Soc. Biol. Chemists, Am. Soc. Cell Biology. Avocations: camping, gardening. Office: VA Med Ctr (151) 3350 La Jolla Village Dr San Diego CA 92161

SPROUL, JOHN ALLAN, public utility executive; b. Oakland, Calif., Mar. 28, 1924; s. Robert Gordon and Ida Amelia (Wittschen) S.; m. Marjorie Ann Hauck, June 20, 1945; children: John Allan, Malcolm J., Richard O., Catherine E. A.B., U. Calif., Berkeley, 1947, LL.B., 1949. Bar: Calif. 1950. Atty. Pacific Gas & Electric Co., San Francisco, 1949-52, 56-62; sr. atty. Pacific Gas & Electric Co., 1962-70, asst. gen. counsel, 1970-71, v.p. gas supply, 1971-76, sr. v.p., 1976-77, exec. v.p., 1977—; gen. counsel Pacific Gas Transmission Co., 1970-73, v.p., 1973-79, chmn. bd., 1979—, also dir.; atty. Johnson & Stanton, San Francisco, 1952-56; chmn. bd., dir. Natural Gas Corp. Calif.; dir. Alta. and So. Gas Co. Ltd., Alta. Natural Gas Co. Ltd, Angus Chem. Co., Angus Petroleum Corp. Bd. dirs. Hastings Coll. of Law. Served to 1st lt. USAAF, 1943-46. Mem. Calif. Bar Assn., Am. Gas Assn., Pacific Coast Gas Assn. Clubs: Engineers, World Trade (San Francisco); Commonwealth, Bohemian, Pacific-Union, Orinda Country. Home: 8413 Buckingham Dr El Cerrito CA 94530 Office: Pacific Gas & Electric Co 77 Beale St San Francisco CA 94106

SPROULL, WAYNE TREBER, consultant; b. Racine, Wis., Aug. 3, 1906; s. John Coppess and Mabel Claire (Warner) S.; m. Ethel Lenore Miller, Aug. 18, 1934; children—Thomas Walter, Sally Ruth Sproull Hohn. B.S. in Physics, U. Akron, 1927; M.S. in Physics, Lehigh U., 1929; Ph.D. in Physics, U. Wis., 1933. Sr. scientist Gen. Motors Research Labs., Detroit, 1933-46, Lockheed Research Lab., Burbank, Calif., 1946; head liquid rocket sect. Jet Propulsion Lab., Calif. Inst. Tech., Pasadena, 1947; dir. research Western Precipitation Corp., Los Angeles, 1947-59; chief physicist W.P. Div. Joy Mfg. Co., Los Angeles, 1959-72; cons. indsl. gas cleaning, Glendale, Calif., 1972—; cons. Electric Power Research Inst., Palo Alto, Calif., Dresser Industries Advanced Tech. Ctr., Irvine, Calif., Carolina Power and Light Co., Raleigh, N.C. Author: X-rays in Practice, 1946; Air Pollution and Its Control, 1972, also tech. articles. Recipient Cert. Appreciation, Office Sci. Research and Devel., 1945. Mem. Am. Phys. Soc., AAAS (life), Air Pollution Control Assn. Republican. Methodist. Club: Verdugo Hills Chess (treas. Tujunga, Calif. 1960-84). Home and Office: 3015 San Gabriel Ave Glendale CA 91208

SPROUSE, JOHN ALWYN, merchant; b. Tacoma, Nov. 23, 1908; s. Robert Allen and Jenne (Glaessel) S.; m. Mary Louise Burpee, Dec. 27, 1932 (div. June 1954); children—Lucy (Mrs. Clyde B. Fletcher), Robert Allen II, John Edward; m. Barbara Barker, May 22, 1955 (dec. July 1983). Student, U. Oreg., 1926-28. With Sprouse-Reitz Co., Inc., Portland, Oreg., 1928—; asst. to pres. Sprouse-Reitz Co., Inc., 1945-61, pres., 1961-74, chmn. bd., 1974—; Expert cons. to Q.M. Gen., 1943-45. Mem. U.S. Power Squadron, USCG Aux., Delta Upsilon. Clubs: Rotarian (Portland), Yacht (Portland), Arlington (Portland), Multnomah (Portland). Home: PO Box 8996 Portland OR 97208-8996 Office: Sprouse Reitz Co 1411 SW Morrison St Portland OR 97205

SPROUSE, ROBERT ALLEN, II, retail chain store executive; b. Portland, Oreg., Dec. 25, 1935; s. John Alwyn and Mary.Louise (Burpee) S.; m. Frances Carolyn Russell, June 22, 1957. Student, Williams Coll., 1953-57. With Sprouse-Reitz Stores Inc., Portland, 1957—; buyer, sec. Sprouse-Reitz Stores Inc., 1963-69, v.p., 1969-73, pres., 1973—, chief exec. officer, 1986—; also bd. dirs. Bd. dirs. Jr. Achievement, Good Samaritan Hosp. Found. Mem. Chief Execs. Orgn. Republican. Episcopalian. Clubs: Multnomah Athletic (Portland); Arlington. Lodge: Rotary. Address: PO Box 8996 Portland OR 97208-8996

SPRUGEL, DOUGLAS GEORGE, ecologist, educator; b. Ames, Iowa, Feb. 18, 1948; s. George and Catharine Bertha (Cornwell) S.; m. Katherine Shea Hilliker, June 23, 1984. BS, Duke U., 1969; MPhil, Yale U., 1971,

PhD, 1974. Asst. prof. ecology U. Pa., Phila., 1973-74, Mich. State U., East Lansing, 1979-82; asst. ecologist Argonne (Ill.) Nat. Lab., 1974-79; sr. research assoc. U. Wash., Seattle, 1983—. Contbr. articles to profl. jours. NSF fellow, 1969-72, grantee, 1985. Mem. AAAS, Am. Inst. Biol. Scis., Internat. Assn. Vegetation Sci. (sec. N.Am. chpt. 1985), Ecol. Soc. Am. (mem. editorial bd. 1978-82). Avocations: music, backpacking, orienteering. Office: U Wash Coll Forest Resources Seattle WA 98195

SPUDIS, PAUL D., geologist; b. Bowling Green, Ky., Aug. 29, 1952; s. Frank Paul and M. Erlene (Wren) S.; m. Anne M. Seaborne, Oct. 21, 1982; children: Janelle Kathryn, Diane Michelle. BS, Ariz. State U., 1976; Sc.M., Brown U., 1977; PhD, Ariz. State U., 1982. Research geologist NASA Ames Research Ctr., Mountain View, Calif., 1976-78, U.S. Geol. Survey, Flagstaff, Ariz., 1980—; com. mem. numerous NASA sci. adv. panels, 1983—. contbr. numerous articles to profl. jours. NASA grantee, 1980—. Mem. Am. Geophys. Union. Avocations: reading, tropical fish, boomeranging. Office: US Geol Survey 2255 N Gemini Dr Flagstaff AZ 86001

SQUAIR, JEAN MARIE, educational administrator; b. Vancouver, B.C., Can., Jan. 19, 1925; came to U.S., 1943; d. Alfred Ernest and Bertha Edith (Bailey) Hall; student Stanford U., 1943-47, Boston U., 1964-65, U. Calif., Berkeley, 1965-68; m. Stuart Davidson Squair, Feb. 14, 1948; children—Roslyn Marie, Elizabeth Ann. Mgr., Oakland (Calif.) Symphony Chorus, 1963-70; dir. vol. services Goodwill Industries, Oakland, 1970-80; adj. prof., Golden Gate U., San Francisco, 1976—, dir. Grad. Sch. Arts Adminstrn., 1976—. Bd. govs. San Francisco Symphony, 1976-81; bd. dirs. San Francisco Opera Western Opera Theater, 1970-78; trustee Calif. Hist. Soc., 1970-76; co-chmn. Piedmont Arts Festival, 1970-78; pres. San Francisco Symphony League, 1973-76. Recipient Disting. Service award Oakland Symphony, 1966; award Nat. Aux. to Goodwill Industries, 1978, Disting. Work and Achievement award City and County of San Francisco Arts Commn., 1986, Cert. Honor, Bd. Suprs. San Francisco, 1986. Mem. Assn. Arts Adminstrn. Educators (dir.), Assn. Calif. Symphony Orchs. (founding pres.), Am. Symphony Orch. League (mem. vol. council bd.). Home: 6001 Acacia Ave Oakland CA 94618 Office: Golden Gate 536 Mission St San Francisco CA 94105

SQUIRE, LARRY RYAN, neuroscientist, psychologist, educator; b. Cherokee, Iowa, May 4, 1941; s. Harold Walter and Jean (Ryan) S.; m. Mary Fox.; 1 child. BA, Oberlin Coll., 1963; postgrad., Stanford U., 1963-64; PhD in Psychology, MIT, 1968. Asst. prof. psychiatry U. Calif., San Diego, 1973-76, assoc. prof., 1976-81, prof., 1981—; psychologist VA Med. Ctr., San Diego, 1976-78, cons. neuropsychology, 1978-80, research career scientist, 1980—; lectr. , Univ. fellow Stanford (Calif.) U., 1963-64. Mem. editorial adv. bd. Jour. Clin. Neuropsychology; mem. editorial bd. numerous profl. jours.; contbr. abstracts and articles to profl. jours., chpts. to books. Fellow Am. Psychol. Assn.; mem. Soc. Neurosci., Internat. Neuropsychol. Soc, Psychonomic Soc., AAAS. Address: 2402 Carmel Valley Rd Del Mar CA 92014 Office: VA Med Ctr 8350 La Jolla Village Dr San Diego CA 92161

SQUIRE, RUSSEL NELSON, musician, emeritus educator; b. Cleve., Sept. 21, 1908. B.Mus. Edn., Oberlin Coll., 1929; A.M., Case Western Res. U., 1939; Ph.D., NYU, 1942; postgrad. U. So. Calif. Dir. Oberlin Summer Music Sch., Ohio, 1929; dir. instrumental music instrn. Chillicothe Pub. Schs., Ohio, 1929-37; faculty Pepperdine U., Malibu, Calif., 1937-56, prof. music, 1937-56, now prof. emeritus, also chmn. fine arts div., 1940-56; faculty Calif. State U.-Long Beach, 1956-72, prof. music, 1964-72, now prof. emeritus; vis. prof. Pacific Christian Coll., 1970-74; prof. philosophy Sch. Edn., Pepperdine U., 1972-78; profl. theater orch. pianist, 1926-28; founder/propr./dir. Ednl. Travel Service, Agoura, Calif., 1958—. Author: Studies in Sight Singing, 1950; Introduction to Music Education, 1952; Church Music, 1962; Class Piano for Adult Beginners, 1964, 3d edit., 1984; also contbr. articles to profl. jours. Founder/pres. Council for Scholarship Aid to Fgn. Students, Inc.; mem. Los Angeles County Music Commn., 1948-60; bd. dirs. Opera Guild So. Calif., 1948-60; pres. Long Beach Symphony Assn., 1961-64. Mem. Music Tchrs. Assn. Calif. (br. pres. 1948-51), AAUP (chpt. founding pres. 1948-49), Phi Mu Alpha Sinfonia (life). Club: Twenty (Los Angeles). Lodge: Rotary (Los Angeles). Home: PO Box 8355 Palm Springs CA 92263

SRINIVASAN, VENKATARAMAN, marketing and management educator; b. Pudukkottai, Tamil Nadu, India, June 5, 1944; came to U.S., 1968; s. Annaswamy and Jambagalakshmi Venkataraman; m. Sitalakshmi Subrahmanyam, June 30, 1972; children: Ramesh, Mahesh. B Tech., Indian Inst. Tech., Madras, India, 1966; MS, Carnegie-Mellon U., 1970, PhD, 1971. Asst. engr. Larsen & Toubro, Bombay, 1966-68; asst. prof. mgmt. and mktg. U. Rochester, N.Y., 1971-73, assoc. prof., 1973-74; assoc. prof. Stanford (Calif.) U., 1974-76, prof., 1976-82, Ernest C. Arbuckle prof. mktg. and mgmt. sci., 1982—; cons. in field. Assoc. editor Mktg. Sci, 1980—, Mgmt. Sci., 1974—; contbr. articles to profl. jours. Mem. Am. Mktg. Assn., Inst. Mgmt. Scis., Ops. Research Soc. Am., Psychometric Soc. Hindu. Avocation: classical music.

SRIVASTAVA, SATISH KUMAR, geologist; b. Sitapur, India, June 28, 1935; came to U.S., 1970; s. Hazari Lal and Sheopiari S.; m. Rosalind Ann Catterall, July 14, 1970. B.Sc., D.A.V. Coll.-India, 1954; M.Sc., U. Alta.-Can., 1965, Ph.D., 1968. Research asst. Forest Research Inst., Dehradun, U.P., India, 1954-57; sr. tech. asst. Oil and Natural Gas Commn., Dehradun, 1957-68; research geologist Chevron Oil Field Research Co., LaHabra, Calif., 1970-80, sr. research geologist, 1980-86; ind. cons., 1986—. Contbr. articles to profl. jours. U. Alta. dissertation fellow, 1967; Killam postdoctoral fellow, 1968-70. Fellow Geol. Assn. Can., Linnean Soc. London; fellow Indian Assn. Palynostratigraphers (pres. 1984-85, 85-86), Palynological Soc. India, Am. Assn. Stratigraphic Palynologists, Bot. Soc. Am., Internat. Orgn. Palaeobotany, Soc. Econ. Paleontologists and Mineralogists, Am. Assn. Petroleum Geologists, AAAS, Palentological Soc. Home: 3054 Blandford Dr Rowland Heights CA 91748 Office: Chevron Oil Field Research Co 3282 Beach Blvd La Habra CA 90631

STAAB, KAREN, artist; b. Milw., Jan. 16, 1950; d. Edwin Phillip and Betty (Thomas) S.; m. James Norman Lembke, Sept. 16, 1979; children: Emerson James, Eric Andrew. BFA, Pratt Inst., 1972. Artist M.D. Publs., N.Y.C., 1973, Bercker Studios, Milw., 1976-77, C.P. Gauger, Milw., 1977-78; artist, art dir. HBJ Publs./Industry Media, Denver, 1979—. Home: 9045 Mandel St Federal Heights CO 80221 Office: HBJ Publs 1129 E 17th Denver CO 80218

STACEY, DOUGLAS SCOTT, podiatrist; b. Redwood City, Calif., Apr. 14, 1952; s. Albert Cyril and Sarah (Scott) S.; m. Shellie Bowman, Aug. 26, 1977; children: Jeniece Sarah, Douglas Scott Jr., Kaisha Ann. AA, Brigham Young U., 1975, BS, 1976; BS in Med. Sci., Calif. Coll. Podiatric Medicine, 1982, D in Podiatric Medicine, 1984. Diplomate Nat. Bd. Podiatry Examiners. Resident in podiatric medicine Doxey Hatch Med. ctr., Salt Lake City, 1984-85; pvt. practice podiatry Salt Lake City, 1985—; cons. Blue Cross Blue Shield, Salt Lake City; chmn. residency selection com. Doxey Hatch Med. Ctr.; dir. Utah State Prison Foot Clinic, Salt Lake City, 1985-86. Mem. Am. Podiatric Med. Assn., Utah Podiatric Med. Assn. Republican. Mormon. Lodge: Kiwanis. Avocations: family, softball, skiing. Office: Taylorsville Med Ctr 1760 W 4805 S Salt Lake City UT 84118

STACH, ERIK ANTHONY, electronics technician, safety engineer; b. Harbor City, Calif., Feb. 20, 1961; s. Arnold Gerhardt and Lois Mary (Karn) S. BS, U. So. Calif., 1986, postgrad. Electronics lab. technician Rockwell Internat., Palmdale, Calif., 1983, space vehicle test technician, 1983—. Joseph T. Desilva scholar United Food and Confectionary Workers Union, 1985. Mem. Am. Soc. Safety Engrs. (vice chmn. local chpt. 1986—). Republican. Roman Catholic. Avocations: flying, surfing, skiing, hunting. Home: 19343 Fairweather St Canyon Country CA 91351

STACY, RICHARD DURANT, chemist; b. N.Y.C., May 20, 1928; s. George Sydney and Margaret (McKay) S.; m. Barbara Jean Smith, June 10, 1952; children: Paula R., Tamra A., David L., Liane M. BS, Colo. Coll., 1952; PhD, U. Colo., 1958. Research chemist Denver Research Inst., 1957-60, Lasdon Found., Colorado Springs, 1960-64; sr. research chemist NARMCO, San Diego, 1964-65, Arapahoe Chem., Boulder, Colo., 1965-71; process devel. mgr. Syntex Corp., Freeport, The Bahamas, 1971-78; adv. scientist IBM-GPD, Tucson, 1978—. Served as pvt. USMC, 1946-48. Mem. Am. Chem. Soc., Sigma Xi (pres. local chpt. 1962-63), Phi Lambda Upsilon. Avocations: woodworking, photography. Home: 9421 E Deer Trail Pl Tucson AZ 85710 Office: IBM-GPD 02F-041-2 Tucson AZ 85744

STADLEY, PAT ANNA MAY GOUGH (MRS. JAMES M. STADLEY), author; b. El Paso, Tex., Aug. 31, 1918; d. Thomas and Leona (Plitt) Gough; A.A., Chaffey Jr. Coll., 1936; m. James M. Stadley, Aug. 15, 1936; children—William T., Jerry M. Author books, anthologies, short stories published in over 15 fgn. langs., works include: The Black Leather Barbarians, 1960; Autumn of a Hunter (Edgar Allen Poe spl. award 1970, produced as The Deadly Hunt TV Friday Night Movie Week 1971), 1970; The Deadly Hunt; 1977; The Murder Hunt, 1977; also numerous short stories including The Doe and The Gantlet, 1957, The Waiting Game, 1961, Kurdistan Payload, 1962, Something for the Club, 1963, The Big Measure, 1976, The Tender Trap, 1977, The Stranger, 1980. Democrat. Mem. Christian Ch. Clubs: Calif. Writers (v.p. 1967) (Citrus Heights), Calif. Writers (v.p. 1967—), Mystery Writers Am. Home: 6439 Donegal Dr Apt 2 Citrus Heights CA 95610

STAEHELIN, LUCAS ANDREW, cell biology educator; b. Sydney, Australia, Feb. 10, 1939; came to U.S., 1969; s. Lucas Eduard and Isobel (Malloch) S.; m. Margrit Weibel, Sept. 17, 1965; children: Daniel Thomas, Philip Roland, Marcel Felix. Dipl. Natw., Swiss Fed. Inst. Tech., Zurich, 1963, Ph.D. in Biology, 1966. Research scientist N.Z. Dept. Sci. and Indsl. Research, 1966-69; research fellow in cell biology Harvard U., Cambridge, Mass., 1969-70; asst. prof. cell biology U. Colo., Boulder, 1970-73, assoc. prof., 1973-79, prof., 1979—; vis. prof. U. Freiburg, 1978, Swiss Fed. Inst. Tech., 1984; mem. cellular biology and physiology study sect. NIH, Bethesda, Md., 1980-84. Editor Jour. Cell Biology, 1977-81, European Jour. Cell Biology, 1981—, Plant Physiology, 1986—; contbr. numerous articles to sci. jours. Recipient Humboldt award Humboldt Found., 1978; Sci. Tchr. award U. Colo., 1984. Mem. AAAS, Am. Soc. Cell Biology, Am. Soc. Plant Physiology. Office: U Colo Dept Molecular Cell/Devel Biology Boulder CO 80309-0347 Home: 2855 Dover Dr Boulder CO 80303

STAEHLE, ALAN WALLACE, county police and public safety official; b. Rochester, N.Y., Mar. 13, 1941; s. Henry C. and Isabel M. Staehle. Student, U. Colo., 1959-60, U. Colo., 1973-74. Cert. Peace Officer, Colo., Peace Officer Tng. Instr., Colo. Patrolman Boulder Police Dept., 1968-70, supr., 1971; capt. patrol Boulder County Sheriff's Dept., 1972, 74-76, capt. communications, 1973, capt. detectives, 1977-82, undersheriff, 1983—; chmn. automation task force, Boulder County, 1983. Named Officer of Month Boulder Jaycees, 1968; recipient Disting. Service award Boulder Optimists, 1981. Mem. AMA, Internat. Assn. Chiefs of Police, World Space Found. (founding), Planetary Soc., Smithsonian Instn., Am. Mus. Natural History, Nat. Rifle Assn., Cousteau Soc. Avocations: photography, motorcycling, hiking, hunting, fishing. Office: Boulder County Sheriff's Dept 1777 6th St Boulder CO 80302

STAEHS, JAMES PAUL, mechanical engineer and designer, researcher, company executive; b. Beatrice, Nebr., Jan. 19, 1933; s. Paul Otto and Elsie Margaret (Koenig) S.; m. Dorthy Maxine Sand, Aug. 23, 1953; children—Jerri Lynn Staehs Mills, Sandra, J. Matthew. B.S.C.E., Tex. A&M U., 1955. Hydraulic engr. Waterways Expt. Sta., Vicksburg, Miss., 1955; State of Calif., Sacramento, 1958-61; assoc. mgr., test engr. Aerojet Gen. Corp., Sacramento, 1961-65; v.p. SDS Enterprises, Inc., Dallas, 1965-68; supr. Lockheed Missiles & Space, Sunnyvale, Calif., 1968-73; pres. JASTA, San Jose, Calif., 1974—; bus. cons. Scoutmaster Santa Clara County council Boy Scouts Am., 1972-76, bd. dirs., 1975-81, v.p. council, 1976-80; pres. Almaden Boys Baseball, San Jose, 1975-76; pres. County Eagle Scout Assn., Santa Clara County, 1980-81. Served to capt. USAF, 1955-58. Recipient Dist. Award of Merit, Boy Scouts Am., 1975, Silver Beaver award, 1976. Mem. U.S. C. of C. Republican. Club: Bible Study Fellowship. Patentee swimming pool equipment. Office: JASTA 7013 E Realm Dr San Jose CA 95119

STAFF, ROBERT JAMES, JR., management consultant; b. Memphis, Oct. 18, 1946; s. Robert J. and Harriet G. (Karber) S.; m. Teresa Smith Patka, Aug. 23, 1967 (div.); 1 child, Kirsten Katherine; m. Martha Lee Coleman, Oct. 31, 1976; children: Adrian Devereaux, Marika Stokset. Student Wilhelms Universität, Münster, W.Ger., 1966-67; B.A., Kalamazoo Coll., 1968; postgrad. Ateneo de Manila Univ., Philippines, 1969; M.B.A., Am. Mgmt. Assn., 1970. Exec. dir. Model Cities Program, Juneau, Alaska, 1971-72; sr. cons. George Odiorne Assocs., Ann Arbor, Mich., 1972-74; assoc. cons. Hutchings Orgn., Palo Alto, Calif., 1974-75; sr. mgmt. cons. E.H. White & Co., Inc., San Francisco, 1975-78; pres. The Wavelink Orgn., Honolulu, 1978—; consulting analyst State of Hawaii, Honolulu, 1979—; research mgr. Inst. Philippine Culture, Manila, 1969; sector analysis adviser U.S. Dept. State, Washington, 1978; fiscal project mgr. U. Hawaii, Honolulu, 1980; vis. lectr. Pacific Asian Mgmt. Inst., 1981; coordinator Pacific Devel. Program East-West Ctr., Honolulu, 1981; mem. staff Prime Minister's Disaster Relief Com., Fiji, 1981; mem. adv. staff Kahauale'a Geothermal Energy Project, 1982-83; mem. Gov.'s Adv. Com. on Criminal Justice Info. Systems, 1984. Author: Political Aspects of Modernization: Buddhist Experiences in Southeast Asia, 1968, Assessment of Health Manpower Planning, 1978; Consolidated Fiscal Procedures in Education, 1981. Co-author: MBO Systems Users Manual, 1974; National Manpower Utilization Study HEW, 1976. Dep. dir. Anchorage Community Action Agy., Alaska, 1971-72; diplomatic liaison Coll. Fgn. Study Program, Munster, W.Ger., 1966-67. Served with USAFR, 1970-72. Leo C. Hughes Meml. scholar Kalamazoo Coll., 1965-68. Mem. Am. Soc. Pub. Adminstrn. (nat. conf. speaker 1982). Tai Chi Ch'uan. Home: PO Box 1873 Honolulu HI 96805 Office: State Capitol PO Box 150 Honolulu HI 96810

STAFFORD, J. FRANCIS, archbishop; b. Balt., July 26, 1932; s. F. Emmett and Mary Dorothy S. Student, Loyola Coll., Balt., 1950-52; B.A., St. Mary's Sem., Balt., 1954; S.T.B., S.T.L., Gregorian U., Rome, 1958; M.S.W., Catholic U., 1964; postgrad., Rutgers U., 1963, U. Wis.-Madison, 1969, St. Mary's Sem. and Univ., Balt., 1973-75. Spiritual moderator Ladies of Charity Ch., Balt., 1966-76; spiritual moderator Soc. St. Vincent de Paul, Balt., 1965-76; urban vicar Archdiocese of Balt., 1966-76, vicar gen., 1976-83; bishop Diocese of Memphis, 1983-86; archbishop Diocese of Denver, 1986—; dir. Assn. Catholic Charities, Balt., 1966-76; archdiocesan liaison to Md. Cath. Conf., Balt., 1975-78. Contbr. articles to profl. jours. Bd. trustees Good Samaritan Hosp., Balt., 1973-76, Blue Cross of Md., Inc., 1973-76, Balt. Urban Coalition, 1970-75; mem. bd. Sch. Social Work and Planning U. Md., 1973-76. Recipient Father Kelly Alumni award Loyola High Sch., 1978; Alumni Laureate, Loyola Coll., 1979. Mem. World Methodist Conf. Roman Catholic Dialogue (chmn. 1977—), Oriental Orthodox Roman Catholic Consultation, (chmn. 1979—), Nat. Conf. Cath. Bishops, Lutheran Roman Catholic Dialogue. Address: Archdiocese of Denver 200 Josephine St Denver CO 80206 *

STAFFORD, KENNETH RAY, psychologist, educator; b. Ryan, Okla., Mar. 14, 1922; s. William Henry and DIcie Ray (Morrison) S.; m. Lila Merle Kearns, June, 1952 (div. 1975); m. Rachel Elliot, Feb. 11, 1976. BA, U. Okla., 1948, MEd, 1950, PhD, 1953; postgrad., Oxford U., Eng., 1973, 74. Registered psychologist, Ariz. Asst. prof. U. Ark., Little Rock, 1953-55, E. Tex. State U., Commerce, Tex., 1955-57; asst. prof. Ariz. State U., Tempe, 1957-60, assoc. prof., 1960-65, prof., 1966-79, prof. emeritus, 1979—; pvt. practice psychologist various cities, Ariz., 1979—. Author: Learning Theory, 1973; co-author: Great Psychologists, 1962; contbr. articles to profl. jours. Bd. dirs. Big Bros., Lake Hausu City, Ariz., 1985—, Crisis Line, Lake Hausu City, 1985—. Mem. Am. Psychol. Assn., N.Y. Acad. Sci., Sigma Xi. Office: 2176 McCulloch Blvd Suite 2 Lake Havasu City AZ 86403

STAGLIN, GAREN KENT, finance and computer service company executive; b. Lincoln, Nebr., Dec. 22, 1944; s. Ramon and Darlene (Guilliams) S.; m. Sharalyn King, June 8, 1968; children: Brandon Kent, Shannon King. BS in Engring. with honors, UCLA, 1966; MBA, Stanford U., 1968. Treas. Stanco, Inc., 1968—; assoc. Carr Mgmt. Co., N.Y.C., 1971-75; v.p. Crocker Nat. Bank, San Francisco, 1975-76; dir. fin. Itel Corp., San Francisco, 1976-77, pres. ins. services div., 1977-79; pres. ADP-CES, ADP Autotrack, Hayward, Calif., 1978—; corp v.p. Automatic Data Processing, Roseland, N.J., 1984—. Bd. dirs. Peralta Hosp. Cancer Inst., 1977-78, Berkeley Repertory Theatre, 1979-85. Served to lt. USN, 1968-71. Mem. Stanford Assocs. (bd. govs. 1985—, chmn. spl. gifts program No. Calif. region 1978-79), Stanford Bus. Sch. Assn., Young Pres. Orgn., Internat. Ins. Soc. (bd. govs. 1985—), Blue Key. Democrat. Lutheran. Home: 40 Green Tree Ct Lafayette CA 94549 Office: Automatic Data Processing 2380 W Winton Hayward CA 94545

STAHELI, LANA RIBBLE, psychology counselor, management consultant; b. Battle Creek, Mich., June 21, 1947; d. Vercil LeRoy and Mildred Irene (Sponseller) Ribble; m. Lynn Taylor Staheli, June 11, 1977; children—Linda, Diane, Todd. B.A. cum laude, U. Wash., 1974, M.Ed., 1976; Ph.D., Union Grad. Sch.-San Francisco, 1978. Co-founder, bd. dirs. Human Alternatives, N.W., Seattle, 1973-74; adminstr. orthopedic med. office, Seattle, 1975-76; pres. Profl. Practice Cons., Seattle, 1974-79; pvt. practice psychol. counseling, Seattle, 1978—; pres. Staheli, Inc., 1979—; cons. orthopedic dept. Children's Orthopedic Hosp., 1974-76; exec. cons. Sundance Cruises, 1984-85, v.p. adminstrn., 1985-86; adj. faculty Antioch Coll., 1974. Bd. dirs. Univ. Tutoring Service, 1979-80, J. Silver, Glad Rags and Gt. Things. Founder, pres. Rainier Found. Mem. Am. Psychol. Assn., Wash. Psychol. Assn., Orthopsychiat. Assn. (pres. Psychology Forum 1981-82). Democrat. Club: U. Wash. President's. Home: 2301 Fairview E #404 Seattle WA 98102 Office: 2301 Fairview E #307 Seattle WA 98102

STAHL, JACK LELAND, real estate company executive, state official; b. Lincoln, Ill., June 28, 1934; s. Edwin R. and Edna M. (Burns) S.; B.S. in Edn., U. N.Mex., 1957; m. Carol Anne Townsend, June 23, 1956; children—Cheryl, Nancy, Kellea. Tchr., Albuquerque Public Schs., 1956-59; pres. House Finders, Inc., Albuquerque, 1959-65; v.p. N.Mex. Savs. & Loan Assn., Albuquerque, 1965-67; chmn. bd. Hooten-Stahl, Inc., Albuquerque, 1967-77; pres. The Jack Stahl Co., Albuquerque, 1977—; mem. N.Mex. Ho. of Reps., 1969-70, mem. N.Mex. Senate, 1981-86; lt. gov. N.Mex., 1987—. Bd. dirs. Better Bus. of N.Mex., 1966-82, pres., 1975-76; trustee Univ. Heights Hosp., 1980-85. Named Realtor of Yr., Albuquerque Bd. Realtors, 1972. Mem. Nat. Assn. Realtors, Nat. Homebuilders Assn., N.Mex. Amigos. Republican. Methodist. Clubs: 20-30 (pres. 1963-64), Elks, Rotary. Office: 1911 Wyoming Blvd NE Albuquerque NM 87112

STAHL, JOHN ROLAND, book publisher; b. Concord, N.H., Apr. 1, 1947; s. Roland Chase and Elizabeth Josephine (Boyajian) S.; 1 child, Jade Bamboo. Student, Brown U., 1965-68. Owner Evanescent Press, Laytonville, Calif., 1983—, Montreal, Can., 1971-72; owner Evanescent Press Co., San Francisco, 1972-83; instr. 1972—. Author: Theophany, 1979 (3d prize Sausalito Art Fest., 1979), Patterns of Illusion and Change, 1984. Avocation: chess. Home and Office: 61300 Bell Springs Rd PO Box 968 Laytonville CA 95454

STAHL, RICHARD G.C., journalist, editor; b. Chgo., Feb. 22, 1934; m. Gladys C. Weisbecker; 1 child, Laura Ann. Student, Northwestern U., U. Ill., Chgo. Contbg. editor Railway Age Mag., Chgo., 1960-63; editor pub. relations dept. Sears Roebuck & Co., Chgo., 1963-68; dir pub. relations dept. St. Joseph's Hosp. Med. Ctr., Phoenix, 1968-72; v.p. pub. relations dept. Consultation Service, Inc., Phoenix, 1972-73; creative dir. Don Jackson and Assoc., Phoenix, 1973; editor, pub. relations mgr. Maricopa County Med. Soc., Phoenix, 1974-76; mng. editor Ariz. Highways mag., Phoenix, 1977—. Regional editor: (travel guides) Budget Travel, 1985, USA, 1986, Arizona, 1986; free-lance writer and editor. Mem. Soc. Profl. Journalists. Avocation: woodworking. Office: Ariz Hwys Mag 2039 W Lewis Ave Phoenix AZ 85009

STAHL, ROBERT EDWARD, professional association director; b. Jersey City, Feb. 24, 1931; s. Edward Stahl and Edith (Johnson) Gustafson; m. Lillian Mildred Boland, Nov. 20, 1954; children: Robert, Peter, Mark. BA, Montclair State Coll., 1956, MA, 1962. Cert. secondary tchr. Tchr. pub. schs. N.J., 1956-65; field rep. NEA, Phila., 1964-65; exec. dir. San Bernardino (Calif.) Tchrs. Assn., 1966-67; mgr., cons., organizer Calif. Tchrs. Assn., Burlingame and Campbell, Calif., 1967—; exec. v.p. Inst. Teaching, Burlingame, 1972-78, fiscal officer, 1973-75. Dem. chmn., Westwood, N.J., 1958-62. Served with U.S. Army, 1948-51, Korea. Recipient Econs. award NSF, 1962. Mem. NEA, Calif. Tchrs. Assn. Avocations: reading, travel, gardening. Home: 801 Beaverton Ct Sunnyvale CA 94087 Office: Calif Tchrs Assn 1925 S Winchester Blvd Suite 105 Campbell CA 95008

STALEY, JAMES TROTTER, microbiology educator; b. Brookings, S.D., Mar. 14, 1938; s. Newton Clarence and Isabelle (Trotter) S.; m. Sonja Jean Erickson, Dec. 28, 1963; children: Greg, Wendy. BA, U. Minn., 1960; MS, Ohio State U., 1963; PhD, U. Calif., Davis, 1967. From instr. to asst. prof. Mich. State U., East Lansing, 1967-69; asst. prof. U. N.C., Chapel Hill, 1969-71; asst. prof. U. Wash., Seattle, 1971-74, assoc. prof., 1974-82, prof. microbiology, 1982—; cons. Weyerhauser, Federal Way, Wash., Biotechniques Labs., Redmond, Wash., 1983-84, Biocontrol Systems, Kent, Wash., 1985—. Mem. editorial bd. Microbial Ecology, 1977, Applied Environ. Microbiology, 1975; editor: Bergey's Manual, 1981; contbr. articles to jours. Mem. AAAS, Am. Soc. Microbiology (vice chmn., chmn. gen. microbiology sect. 1975-76, div. lectr. 1983), Internat. Assn. Microbiology Soc. (judicial commn. 1983—), Internat. Symposium on Environ. Biogeochemistry. Office: U Wash Dept Microbiology Seattle WA 98195

STALL, PATRICIA HOPKINS, English educator; b. Perryton, Tex., Mar. 17, 1956; d. Joslin Houston and Vera Josephine (Troutman) Hopkins; m. Robert Jearl Stall, Nov. 25, 1980; 1 child, Joslin Thomas. BA, Northwest Okla. State U. Cert. secondary tchr., N.Mex. Speech and drama tchr. Grants (N.Mex.) High Sch., 1977-78; reading tchr. Wingate High Sch., Ft. Wingate, N.Mex., 1978-82; English tchr. Thoreau (N.Mex.) High Sch., 1982—. Mem. Ways and Means Com., DOES, Gallup, N.Mex., 1985-86. Recipient Silver Screen award Nat. Sci. Tchrs. Assn., 1986. Home: Box 311 Fort Wingate NM 87316 Office: Thoreau High Sch PO Box 96 Thoreau NM 87323

STALLINGS, JEFFREY WARD, energy consultant; b. Teaneck, N.J., Sept. 19, 1945; s. Ward K. and Margaret (Stocker) S.; m. Marilyn Grace Hikida, Aug. 17, 1985. BSChemE, Princeton U., 1967; MA in Internat. Studies, Johns Hopkins U., Washington, 1972; MBA, U. Calif., Berkeley, 1983. Registered profl chem. engr., Calif. Tchr. Am. Community Sch., Beirut, 1967-70; research analyst Nat. Ctr. Resource Recovery, Washington, 1974-75; sr. chem. engr. Energy Inc., Idaho Falls, Idaho, 1976-79; sr. engr., economist SRI Internat., Menlo Park, Calif., 1979-85; program mgr. Sci. Applications Internat. Corp., Los Altos, Calif., 1985—. Contbr. tech. articles to jours. Active Idaho Falls United Way, 1976. Mem. Am. Inst. Chem. Engrs., Am. Chem. Soc. Avocations: tennis, golf, skiing, swimming. Home: 3558 Jefferson Ave Redwood City CA 94062 Office: SAIC 5150 El Camino Real Suite C-31 Los Altos CA 94022

STALLINGS, RICHARD H., congressman; b. Ogden, Utah, Oct. 7, 1940; s. Howard J. and Elizaveth (Austin) S.; m. Ranae Garner, Sept. 5, 1963; children—Richard H., Sallianne, Daniel. B.S., Weber State Coll., 1965; M.S., Utah State U., 1968; student, Colo. Coll., 1968. Tchr. Bonneville High Sch., Ogden, Utah, 1964-69; prof. Ricks Coll., Rexburg, Idaho, 1969-79, chmn. dept. history, 1979-84; mem. 99th, 100th Congresses from 2d Idaho dist., Washington, 1985—. Office: House of Reps Office House Members Washington DC 20515

STAMBAUGH, ROBERT HOWARD, JR., management consultant; b. Leetonia, Ohio, Apr. 9, 1946; s. Robert Howard and Rosemary (Stevens) S. AB, Stanford U., 1969. Analyst SRI Internat., Menlo Park, Calif., 1970-79; mgr. Crocker Bank, San Francisco, 1979-80, Intel Corp., Santa Clara, Calif., 1980-82; cons. VRC Cons. Group Inc., Los Altos, Calif., 1982-83, v.p., 1983—; lectr. Golden Gate U., San Francisco, 1982—; nat. dir. Human Resource Systems Profls. Inc., Walnut Creek, Calif., 1980-84, chpt. dir., San Francisco, 1980—. Editor (jour.) HRSP Rev., 1982-84. Mem. Am. Mgmt. Assn. Lutheran. Office: VRC Cons Group 289 S San Antonio Rd Los Altos CA 94022

STAMES, WILLIAM ALEXANDER, realtor, cost mgmt. exec.; b. Douglas, Ariz., Mar. 26, 1917; s. Alex Basil and Teresa (Ruis) S.; A.A., Long Beach Coll., 1941; postgrad. U. Calif., Berkeley, 1962-64; cert. mgmt.

practices Naval Officers CIC Sch., Glenview, Ill., 1955; grad. Real Estate Inst., Calif.; m. Marguerite Winifred Nelson, June 11, 1943; 1 dau., Wynn Lorain. Owner, Stames Beverage Co., Brawley, Calif., 1945-50; liaison engr. Lockheed Missiles & Space Co., Sunnyvale, Calif., 1958-60, liaison engr. sr., 1960, adminstr., 1960-62, staff adminstr., 1962-63, liaison engr., sr., design engr. sr., 1965-76; owner, mgr. Cost Reduction Equipment Sales & Tech., Sunnyvale, Calif., 1967-76. Served to comdr. USNR, 1941-69, ret.; World War II, Korea, Vietnam. Decorated D.F.C., Air medal with two gold stars, Presdl. citation. Mem. Am. Mgmt. Assn., Mountain View Real Estate Bd. (pres.), Calif. Assn. Realtors (bd. dirs.), Tailhook Assn. Clubs: Commonwealth San Francisco, Ret. Officers (past pres. Peninsula chpt.), Lions. Author: Polaris Electrical Subsystems Design History, 1964; Poseidon Subsystem Invention, 1971. Home: 10640 Ainsworth Dr Los Altos CA 94022 Office: 341 Castro St Mountain View CA 94041

STAMISON, PETER GEORGE, aviation industry executive; b. Chgo., Oct. 25, 1942; s. George Peter and Lucille (Stein) S.; m. Karin Sue Lawrence, Nov. 28, 1964; children: Lisa, Vikky, Krista, Peter Jr. BBA in Mktg., Northwestern U., 1964. Sales mktg. exec. Dow Chem., Midland, Mich., 1964-83; v.p., founder TMC of So. Calif., Pasadena, 1983-85; pres., chief exec. officer Bus. Info. Transmission Systems, Universal City, Calif., 1985-86; v.p. mktg. Lockheed Air Terminal, Inc., Burbank, Calif., 1986—. Republican. Greek Orthodox. Avocations: golf, tennis, running, flying, skiing. Office: Lockheed Air Terminal Inc PO Box 7229 Burbank CA 91510

STAMM, RICHARD WILLIAM, podiatrist; b. Meadville, Pa., July 9, 1944; s. William Henry and Norma Marie (Bertocci) S.; m. Maria Johnine Avdellas, June 16, 1968; children: Aileen Johnine, William Tarkington. AA, Hershey Jr. Coll., 1965; BA, Washington and Jefferson Coll., 1967; D Podiatric Medicine, Ohio Coll. Podiatric Medicine, 1978. Resident in podiatric surgery Cleve. Foot Clinic, 1978-79; practice medicine specializing in podiatry Family Foot Care, Albuquerque, 1979—. Contbr. articles to profl. jours. Bd. dirs. Albuquerque Wild Turkey Fedn., 1984—, SVC, 1984-86, Bernalillo Chpt. Am. Diabetes Assn., 1985-87, Albuquerque Vis. Nurse Found., 1983—, pres. bd. dirs., 1985-86; mem. citizens adv. council Albuquerque Pub. Schs., 1985-86. Served with U.S. Army 1967-71, Vietnam. Fellow Am. Coll. Foot Orthopedists; mem. Am Coll. Podopediatrics, Am. Podiatric Med. Assn., N.Mex. Podiatric Med. Assn. (pres. 1984—, Appreciation awards 1981, 85, 86), Am. Diabetes Assn. (bd. dirs. Albuquerque chpt. 1986—). Republican. Greek Orthodox. Avocations: hunting, photography, landscaping, automobile restoration. Home: 1700 Father Sky NE Albuquerque NM 87112 Office: Family Foot Care 1201 Eubank Ave NE Albuquerque NM 87112

STAMM, ROBERT JENNE, building contractor, construction company executive; b. Albuquerque, Nov. 17, 1921; s. Roy Allen and Elizabeth C. (Baldridge) S.; m. Florence I. Bradbury, May 14, 1943; children—R. Brad, Susan Stamm Evans. BSCE, U. N.Mex., 1942; postgrad. in Naval Architecture, U.S. Naval Acad., 1943. Registered profl. engr. and surveyor, N.Mex. With Bradbury & Stamm Constrn. Co., Albuquerque, 1946—; chmn., chief exec. officer Bradbury & Stamm Constrn. Co., 1975—, former pres.; bd. dirs., CREGO Block Co., Albuquerque, also sec. Mem. U. N.Mex. Found., 1982—; trustee Albuquerque Community Found., 1983—; chmn. U. N.Mex. Devel. Fund Dr., 1985, Greater Albuquerque Community Ednl. Alliance, 1985; mem. N.Mex. Commn. on Higher Edn., 1986—; bd. dirs. Albuquerque Mus. Found., 1986—. Served to comdr. USNR, 1943-69. Recipient Regents Recognition medal N. Mex., 1986. Mem. Nat. Soc. Profl. Engrs., Associated Gen. Contractors of N.Mex. (pres. bldg. br. 1962), Econ. Forum Albuquerque. Episcopalian. Clubs: Albuquerque Country (bd. dirs. 1972-76, 87—), Albuquerque Tennis (bd. dirs. 1978-80). Lodge: Elks. Avocations: tennis; skiing; golf. Home: 1524 Las Lomas St NE Albuquerque NM 87106 Office: Bradbury & Stamm Constrn Co PO Box 25027 Albuquerque NM 87125

STAMP, LINDA LEE, lawyer; b. Council Bluffs, Iowa, Aug. 13, 1957; d. James Edward and LeNeita Jean (Reigle) S. BS in Acctg., U. Denver, 1978; JD, U. Colo., 1981. CPA, Colo. Bar: Colo. 1981. Tax acct. Bow Valley Explanation, Denver, 1981-83; lawyer John Mason, Jr., Denver, 1983—. Del. County and State Rep. Conventions, Boulder, 1986; vol. Denver Art Mus., Denver, 1982—. Mem. ABA, Colo. Bar Assn., Denver Bar Assn., U. Denver Alumni Assn., Denver C. of C. (leadership Denver program 1986-87), Alpha Lambda Delta, Alpha Chi Omega. Republican. Avocations: reading, exercising. meeting peo. Home: 1025 Jasmine #2 Denver CO 80220

STAMPER, MALCOLM THEODORE, aerospace company executive; b. Detroit, Apr. 4, 1925; s. Fred Theodore and Lucille (Cayce) S.; m. Marion Philbin Guinan, Feb. 25, 1946; children: Geoffrey, Kevin, Jamie, David, Mary, Anne. Student, U. Richmond, Va., 1943-44; B.E.E., Ga. Inst. Tech., 1946; postgrad., U. Mich., 1946-49. With Gen. Motors Corp., 1949-62; with Boeing Co., Seattle, 1962—; mgr. electronics ops., v.p., gen. mgr. turbine div. Boeing Co., 1964-66; v.p., gen. mgr. Boeing Co. (747 Airplane program), 1966-69, v.p., gen. mgr. comml. airplane group, 1969-71, corp. sr. v.p. ops., 1971-72; pres. Boeing Co., 1972-85, vice chmn., 1985—; dir. Travelers Ins. Cos., Nordstrom Co., Chrysler Corp. Chmn. Wash. State U.S. Treasury Savs. Bond Campaign, Boy Scouts Am. Devel. Fund State of Wash., Variety Club Handicapped Children Telethon.; Candidate U.S. Ho. of Reps., Detroit, 1952; Trustee Seattle Art Mus.; nat. bd. dirs. Smithsonian Assocs. Served to ensign USNR, 1943-46. Named Industrialist of Year, 1967; recipient Educator's Golden Key award, 1970, Elmer A. Sperry award, 1982, AIEE award, Ga. Inst. Tech. award, Sec. Dept. Health and Human Services award. Mem. Nat. Alliance Businessmen, Phi Gamma Delta. Office: Boeing Co 7755 E Marginal Way S Seattle WA 98108 *

STANARD, JAMES EARL, music educator, performer; b. Great Falls, Mont., Aug. 12, 1944; s. Earl Watt and Cora Aeriol (Klingler) S.; m. Jeana Dee Stowell, Sept. 1, 1968; children: Sherrilyn Jean, Christina Ann, Jonathon Earl. BA, Brigham Young U., 1966; MS, Mont. State U., Bozeman, 1968; DMA, U. Oreg., 1976. Prof. music Humboldt State U., 1972—; gen. dir. Humboldt Light Opera Co., Eureka, Calif., 1983—; tenor soloist various opera cos. and symphony orchs., 1968—. Served with USAR, 1963-69. Mormon. Office: Humboldt State U Music Dept Arcata CA 95521

STANBACK, ELIEHUE, accountant; b. Byhalia, Miss., May 25, 1918; s. Clint and Eva Stanback; m. Sophronia M. Thompson, Dec. 7, 1936 (div. 1939); m. Ellen Richmond, July 18, 1941 (div. Feb. 1962); children: Eliehue Jr., William Earl, DeLores Ann, Alice Marie; m. Celia Anne Davis, Mar. 9, 1962; children: Gwendolyn Ann, Sandra Renee, Anthony, Mildred Cynthia, Eric. Student, Cen. YMCA Coll., Chgo., 1936-37; degree in higher accountancy, Henderson Bus. Coll., 1949-50; student, LeMoyne Coll., 1951-52; cert. pub. accountancy, LaSalle Extension U., 1961, LLB, 1979; postgrad., Mt. San Antonio Coll., Walnut, Calif., 1979-80, Calif. State Poly. U., Pomona, 1969-83. Registered pub. acct. Founder, editor, pub. Indsl. Leader, Chgo. and Memphis, 1939—; U.S. railway mail clk. U.S. Mail, Memphis, 1943-49; pvt. practice acctg. Memphis, 1950—; carrier U.S. Mail, Pomona and Ontario, Calif., 1965-77. Candidate for Tax Assessor, Memphis, 1959; pres. Memphis, Shelby County and Tenn. Voters Assn., 1959-63, civil rights activist 1949-63; chmn. bd. Binghampton Civic League, Memphis, 1958-63. Served as pvt. U.S. Army, 1942-43. Mem. Soc. of Calif. Accts. (bd. dirs. Tri County Chpt. 1982-84), Nat. Soc. Pub. Accts., Nat. Assn. Letter Carriers, Disabled Am. Vets., Pomona Valley Amatuer Astronomers, Postal Sportsmen Rod and Gun Club. Republican. Methodist. Home: PO Box 318 Pomona CA 91766 Office: Stanback's Bus Mgmt and Tax Service 1230 Cromwell St Pomona CA 91768

STANBERY, VENDA T., employment manager; b. Manolo Fortich, Philippines, Jan. 4, 1950; came to U.S., 1969; d. Eustaquio Omo and Rosario (Sanchez) Tuyor; m. James B. Stanbery, June 29, 1968 (div. Apr. 1983); 1 child, Lani S. Stanbery. BS in Edn., Misamis U., Ozamis City, Philippines. Personnel interviewer Sears, Carson, Calif., 1973-79; personnel recruiter Fidelity Fed. Savs. and Loan, Glendale, 1979-82; employment coordinator Lincoln Savs. & Loan, Irvine, Calif., 1982-84; employment mgr. Metmor Fin., Inc., Los Angeles, 1985—. Home: 29641 S Western Ave 414 Rancho Palos Verdes CA 90732

STANBRIDGE, ERIC JOHN, biology educator; b. London, May 28, 1942; came to U.S., 1965; BS, Brunel U., 1964; PhD, Stanford U., 1971. Mem. sci. staff Nat. Inst. Med. Research, London, 1968-69; research assoc. Stanford (Calif.) U., 1972-73, instr., 1973-75; asst. prof. U. Calif., Irvine, 1975-78, assoc. prof., 1978-82, prof., 1982; chmn. Gordon Conf. Cancer Biology, 1985; advisor Office of Tech. Assessment, 1986; co-organizer UCLA-Triton Bioscis. Symposium, 1986. Editorial bd. mem. Microbiol. Revs., 1985—, (assoc.) Cancer Research, 1985; contbr. articles to profl. jours. and chpts. to books. Fellow Internat. Union Against Cancer, 1979, Eleanor Roosevelt Internat., 1983-84; recipient Research Career Devel. award, NIH, 1978-83; named one of Outstanding Young Men of Am., Jaycees, 1979. Mem. AAAS, N.Y. Acad. Scis., Internat. Orgn. Mycoplasmologists, Am. Soc. Microbiology, Sigma Xi. Home: 501 Seaward Cornona del Mar CA 92625 Office: U Calif Microbiology and Molecular Genetics Irvine CA 92717

STANCHFIELD, JOHN BARTLEY, endocrinologist; b. Plymouth, Wis., Oct. 16, 1941; s. Charles Bartley Stanchfield and Irene L. (Sipple) Way; m. Margaret Ann Schmitt, Aug. 25, 1965; children: Joseph, James, Paul, Joshua, Jennifer. BA, Marquette U., 1963, MD, 1967. Diplomate Am. Bd. Internal Medicine, Am. Bd. Endocrinology. Assoc. clin. prof. medicine U. Utah, Salt Lake City, 1973—; ward attendant Salt Lake City VA Hosp., 1973-83; practice medicine specializing in endocrinology Internal Medicine Ltd., Salt Lake City, 1973—. Served to lt. comdr. USN, 1969-70. Named Outstanding Internest of Yr., Utah Soc. Internal Medicine, 1985. Mem. AMA, ACP, Am. Soc. Internal Medicine, Utah Med. Ins. Assn. (med. dir. 1985-86), Utah State Med. Assn. (chmn. computers in medicine com. 1985-86), Salt Lake City C. of C. Roman Catholic. Avocations: marathon running, fly fishing, fly tying, skiing. Office: Internal Medicine Ltd 1377 E 3900 S Salt Lake City UT 84124

STANFIELD, PEGGY SUE, nutrition educator; b. Ala., June 15, 1928. BS, Montevallo U., 1949; MS, Mont. State U., Bozeman, 1973. Registered dietitian. Dietitian Baroness Erlanger Hosp., Chattanooga, 1951-57, Orange Meml. Hosp., Orlando, Fla., 1957-58, U. Tex., Galveston, 1958-59, Magic Valley Hosp., Twin Falls, Idaho, 1959-71; prof. nutrition Coll. So. Idaho, Twin Falls, 1971—. Author: Nutrition and Diet Therapy, 1986, Basic Nutrition: Self Instructional Modules, 1987. Mem. Am. Dietetic Assn., Soc. Nutrition Edn., Nutritionists in Nursing Edn., Idaho Dietetic Assn. (pres. 1964). Episcopalian. Office: Coll Southern Idaho 315 Falls Ave Twin Falls ID 83301

STANFILL, BERNICE HARRIETT, stock broker, investor relations administrator; b. Coalgate, Okla., Feb. 3, 1944; d. Harris Connor and Bernice Cleo (Willis) Shearer; m. Jack L. Stanfill, Nov. 24, 1962 (divorced); children—William L., Theressa J., Michelle C., Jack A. Paralegal cert. Mesa Coll., 1972; student Palomar Coll., 1974-75; Registered securities prin., Fla., Ga., Washington, Calif., Mo., Ohio, N.Y., Kans. Dir. stockholder relations Sci. Applications, Inc., 1972—; v.p., dir., Bull, Inc. subs. Sci. Applications Internat. Corp., La Jolla, Calif., since 1972—. Team rep., mem. North County Women's Soccer Assn., 1981-87; team mem. North County Women's Softball Assn., 1982-83. Mem. Nat. Assn. Female Execs., Am. Assn. Individual Investors, Nat. Assn. Securities Dealers. Republican. Office: 476 Prospect St Suite 237 La Jolla CA 92037

STANFORD, JACK ARTHUR, biological station administrator; b. Delta, Colo., Feb. 18, 1947; s. LeRoy and Wilma (Tucker) S.; children: Jake, Chriss. BS in Fisheries Sci., Colo. State U., 1969, MS in Limnology, 1971; PhD in Limnology, U. Utah, 1975. Fisheries biologist Alaska-Fish and Game, Dillingham, 1968-69; research biologist and limnologist instr. U. Mont., Bigfork, 1973-74, dir. Flathead Lake Biol. Sta., 1980—; research prof. zoology U. Mont., Missoula, 1983-86; research scientist III N. Tex. State U., Denton, 1974-81; mem. ecology panel NSF, Washington, 1985-87. Editor: Ecology of Regulated Streams, 1979; co-editor Internat. Newsletter on Regulated Stream Limnology, 1981—; mem. bd. editors Freshwater Invertebrate Biology, Milw., 1982-85; contbr. chpts. to books. Advisor Nature Conservancy, Boulder, Colo., 1982—. Named Am. Man of Sci., Bierman Prof. Ecology U. Mont., 1986—; grantee N. Tex. State U., EPA, U.S. Army, U.S. Bur. Reclamation, NSF. Mem. Mont. Acad. Sci., Am. Soc. Limnology and Oceanography, Ecological Soc. Am., N.Am. Benthological Soc. (exec. com. 1979), AAAS. Avocations: mountaineering. Home and Office: Flathead Lake Biol Sta East Shore Polson MT 59860

STANFORD, ROBERT AUGUST, editor; b. Akron, Ohio, Mar. 16, 1927; s. George Frederick and Margaret Hannah (Ruthenberg) S. BA with honor, U. Akron, 1956; Lic. et Arts et Lettreswith mention bien, U. Paris, 1958. Asst. to pres. Dover Pubs., N.Y.C., 1962-64; copy editor McKinsey & Co., N.Y.C., 1965-66; gen. mgr. Burt Franklin Pubs., N.Y.C., 1967-68; dep. dir., adv. bd. N.Y.C. Dept. Social Services, 1968-78; mng. editor N.Y. Native Newspaper, 1981-82; editor-in-chief In Touch Pubs., North Hollywood, Calif., 1984—; field ops. asst. U.S. Census Bur., Manhattan, N.Y.C.; partowner That New Mag., Inc., NYC. Vol. Congresswoman Bella S. Abzug, N.Y.C., 1970-76. Mem. Phi Sigma Alpha. Democrat. Mem. United Ch. Christ. Avocations: piano, photography, film history. Home: 6842 Fulton St #7 North Hollywood CA 91605 Office: In Touch Pubs Internat Inc 7216 Varna St North Hollywood CA 91605

STANFORD, VERL ARNOLD, mechanical engineer; b. Fullerton, Calif., July 16, 1943; s. Charles Arnold and Mildred Victoria (Robinson) S.; m. Louise BettyAnn Vargas, Apr. 23, 1983. AA in Engring., Fullerton Jr. Coll., 1966; BSCE with honors, Calif. State Poly. U., Pomona, 1966; MS in Engring., Calif. State U., Long Beach, 1969. Registered profl. mech. engr., Calif. Mem. tech. staff N.Am. Rockwell Space Div., Downey, Calif., 1966-69; sr. staff engr. Bertea Corp., Irvine, Calif., 1969-78; supr. analytical support Control Systems div. Parker-Bertea, Irvine, 1978—. Mem. Parker Mgmt. Club. Lodges: Masons, Elks. Avocation: restoring antique homes. Office: Parker Hamnifin Corp Bertea Control Systems Div 14300 Alton Pkwy Irvine CA 92713

STANGE, DENNIS EARLE, quality assurance engineer; b. Jersey City, Feb. 5, 1952; s. Harry William and Mildred (Earle) S.; m. Barbara Ann Werenko, Dec. 28, 1975; children: Dennis Earle, Martha Ann. BS in Math., U. Albuquerque, 1973; MBA, U. N.Mex., 1984. Quality engr. Stromberg-Carlson, Lake Mary, Fla., 1973-76, Northrop Corp., Rolling Meadows, Ill., 1976-78, Martin Marietta, Orlando, Fla., 1978-79; group leader E Systems div. ECI, St. Petersburg, Fla., 1979-80; sr. engr. EMI div. EG&G, Los Alamos, N.Mex., 1982-83; office mgr. II Quality Assurance EMI div. EG&G, Albuquerque, 1983-86; flight assurance mgr. Goddard Space Flight Ctr. NASA, Greenbelt, Md., 1986—. Coach Lobo Little League, Albuquerque, 1985-86; mem. exec. com. U. N.Mex., Albuquerque, 1985. Mem. Am. Soc. Quality Control (sec. 1977-78, vice-chmn. 1983-84, chmn. 1984-85, nominating com. 1985-86, editor newsletter 1986), Engring. Soc. for Pres. Council, EG&G Employee Recreation Assn. (treas. 1985). Republican. Roman Catholic. Avocations: swimming, traveling, bowling, little league. Office: NASA Goddard Space Flight Ctr Greenbelt MD 20770

STANGELAND, ROGER EARL, retail chain store executive; b. Chgo., Oct. 4, 1929; s. Earl and Mae E. (Shaw) S.; m. Lilah Fisher, Dec. 27, 1951; children: Brett, Cyndi Stangeland Meili, Brad. Student, St. Johns Mil. Acad., 1943-44, Carleton Coll., 1947-48, U. Ill., 1944-47. With Coast to Coast Stores, Mpls., 1960-78, pres., 1972-77; sr. v.p., exec. v.p. Household Merchandising, Chgo., 1978-84; chief exec. officer, chmn. bd. Vons Grocery Co., Los Angeles, 1984-85; chmn., chief exec. officer The Vons Cos., Inc., 1986—; bd. dirs. Coast to Coast Stores Inc., Denver, Frank Purcell Co., Kansas City, Mo. Chmn. Wauconda (Ill.) Bd. Edn., 1957-60, Hopkins (Minn.) Bd. Edn., 1968-74; bd. dirs. Claremont (Calif.) U. Ctr. & Grad. Sch., 1986. Mem. Food Mktg. Inst. (bd. dirs.), Food Employer Council (bd. dirs.), Mchts. & Mfrs. Assn. (bd. dirs.). Clubs: Jonathan (Los Angeles). Home: 842 Oxford Rd San Marino CA 91108 Office: Vons Grocery Co 10150 Lower Azusa Rd El Monte CA 91731

STANGL, KURT OTHMAR, geotechnical engineering company executive; b. Mödling, Austria, July 9, 1949; came to U.S., 1982; s. Othmar J. and Hermine J. (Kraus) S.; m. Carolyn Anne Maitland, Dec. 6, 1975; 1 child, John Ehren. BS with honors, Queen's U., Kingston, Ont., Can., 1972. Registered profl. engr., Alta., N.W.T. Geologist Consumer's Gas Co., Toronto, Ont., Can., 1972-74; geol. engr. EBA Engring Cons. Ltd., Edmonton, Alta., Can., 1974-80; arctic group mgr. EBA Engring Cons. Ltd., Edmonton, Alta., Canada, 1980-82; v.p. EBA Engring., Anchorage, 1986—, also bd. dirs., 1986—; asst. office mgr. McClelland-EBA Inc., Anchorage, 1982-86. Mem. Assn. Profl. Engrs. Geologists and Geophysicists Alta. and N.W. Terrs. Avocations: hunting, fishing, boating. Office: EBA Engring Inc 907 E Dowling Rd #27 Anchorage AK 99518

STANILOFF, HOWARD MEDA, cardiologist, epidemiologist; b. Saskatoon, Sask., Can., Sept. 18, 1948; s. Sidney and Ethel (Epstein) S.; m. Robin Debra Du Shey, June 27, 1981; 1 child, Alexander Drew. B.Sc., U. B.C., 1970, M.D., 1973; M.P.H., UCLA, 1980. Intern, Toronto (Ont.) Gen. Hosp., 1973-74, resident, 1974-75, cardiology fellow, 1975-78; cardiology fellow Cedars-Sinai Med. Ctr., Los Angeles, 1978-80, mem. staff, 1980—, dir. outpatient cardiac rehab., 1981-83, dir. cardiac rehab., 1983-86 ; adj. asst. prof. medicine UCLA, 1980-86 , adj. asst. prof. pub. health, 1981—; vol. Greater Los Angeles affiliate Am. Heart Assn. NIH Research Career Devel. awardee, 1982. Fellow Am. Coll. Cardiology, Royal Coll. Physicians and Surgeons Can. Jewish. Home: 15825 Vose St Van Nuys CA 91406 Office: 301 N Prairie Ave Inglewood CA 90301

STANISLAW, RALPH MICHAEL, architect; b. Toronto, Can., Oct. 10, 1954; came to U.S., 1968; s. Kurt Gustav Adolf and Waltraud Luise (Wenkemann) S.; m. Caren Leslie Krasnoff, Dec. 31, 1982 (dec. 1984); 1 child, Kasey; m. Nancy Ann Sherman, Sept. 1, 1985; 1 child, Rebecca. BA magna cum laude, Yale U., 1976; MArch, UCLA, 1979. Registered architect, Calif. Jr. designer W.L. Pereira Assocs., Los Angeles, 1978-80; sr. designer W.L. Pereira Assn., Los Angeles, 1980-85, design dept. mgr., assoc., 1986—. Prin. works include Citicorp Ctr., San Francisco, 1984, Fox Plaza, Los Angeles, 1986. Mem. Los Angeles Conservancy. Office: Pereira Assocs 6100 Wilshire Blvd Los Angeles CA 90048

STANLEY, FORREST EDWIN, fund raiser, educational administrator; b. Bakersfield, Calif., Sept. 6, 1942; s. James Edwin and Lucile Haworth (Sloan) S.; student U. Calif., Los Angeles, 1960-63, M.S., 1970; B.S., Calif. State U., Northridge, 1969; m. Suzanne Roberts, June 15, 1968 (div. 1984); children—John Forrest, Cheryl Suzanne. Sr. clk. So. Calif. Gas Co., 1963-65, programmer analyst, 1965-70; fin. analyst Continental Bldgs. Co., Burbank, Calif., 1970-72; fin. analyst McKinsey & Co., Inc., Los Angeles, 1972-74; analyst Unionamerica Advisors, Beverly Hills, Calif., asst. v.p., asst. treas., 1974-75; dir. alumni and devel. Grad. Sch. Mgmt., UCLA, 1976-80; dir. spl. campaigns U. Calif., Berkeley, 1980-84; dir. devel. U. Colo., Colorado Springs, 1984-86; dir. devel. pub. affairs, Calif. State Coll., Bakersfield, 1987—; v.p. U. Colo. Found., Inc., 1984-86. Mem. Am. Inst. Cert. Computer Profls., Assn. for Computing Machinery, Council for Advancement and Support of Edn., UCLA Mgmt. Alumni Assn. (v.p. 1974, pres. 1975-77), Sons Am. Colonists, Mensa, Lambda Chi Alpha (UCLA alumni chpt. pres. 1974-77, treas. 1977-80). Clubs: North Kern. Office: 9001 Stockdale Hwy Bakersfield CA 93311-1099 also: Univ Colo Devel Office PO Box 7150 Colorado Springs CO 80933

STANLEY, NORMAN WYLIE, management executive; b. Velma, Okla., Nov. 8, 1934; s. William Arnold and Abbie Louis (Dodson) S.; m. Robbie Maye Cherry, Sept. 1, 1958; children: Raymond A., Katherine C., Scott A. BA, San Jose State Coll., 1961; MBA, U. Mo., 1967. Ordained Bapt. Ch., 1981; lic. to ministry, 1984. Commd. 2d lt. USAF, 1961, advanced through grades to lt. col., 1977; dir. of contracts Pacific Air Command Air Force procurement ctr. USAF, Okinawa, Japan, 1971-73; comdr. Peace Hawk Program USAF, Saudi Arabia, 1976-77; retired USAF, 1979; program mgr. 1st lunar landing NASA, 1967-69; mgr. contracts M/A-Com Linkabit, San Diego, 1980-85; dir. contracts United Techs., San Diego, 1985—. Assoc. minister Bethel Bapt. Ch., Escondido, Calif., 1984—. Mem. Nat. Contract Mgmt. Assn., Ret. Officers Assn. Republican. Avocations: golf, tennis. Home: 265 Vista Grande Glen Escondido CA 92025 Office: Advanced Systems United Techs 10251 Vista Sorrento Pkwy San Diego CA 92121

STANLEY, SANDRA RYAN, civil engineer; b. Florence, Ala., Feb. 24, 1940; d. John H. and Mary Emma (Ryan) Traudt; m. Allen Daniel Stanley, Oct. 28, 1966. BCE, U. Ala., 1964. Registered profl. engr., Wash. Engr. designer Alabama Hwy. Dept., Montgomery and Tuscaloosa, Ala., 1959-64; engr. Rader & Assocs., Miami, Fla. and Helena, Mont., 1964-66; city engr. City of Pasco, Wash., 1966-74; engr. A.D. Stanley & Assocs., Pasco, 1974-82; group mgr. Kaiser Engrs., Richland, Wash., 1982—. Mem. ASCE, Wash. Soc. Profl. Engrs. (sec., v.p.). Republican. Club: 99's. Lodge: P.E.O. Noted as 1st Female City Engr. in State of Wash.; avocations: snow skiing, pvt. piloting, golfing, fishing, reading. Home: 4509 W Sylvester Pasco WA 99301 Office: Kaiser Engrs Hanford PO Box 888 Richland WA 99352

STANNARD, GEORGE PARKER, psychotherapist; b. Youngstown, Ohio, Dec. 9, 1925; s. George M. and Martha L. (Parker) S.; m. Dixie Lee, Oct. 15, 1961; 1 child: Kirby J.; m. Valene Davies, Apr. 11, 1967. B.A., U. Nev., 1960; M.S., Nova U., 1979; D.Sc. (hon.), U. Sri Lanka Coll. Acupuncture. Tchr., Boulder City, Nev., 1963-67, Knudson High Sch., Las Vegas, Nev., 1967-83; addiction psychotherapist, substance abuse counselor; psychotherapist for drug and alcohol abuse, Las Vegas, 1981—; dir. Profl. Sch. Bioenergetic Research Profl. Sch. Bioenergetics Research, 1983—. Served with USN, 1942-46, USCG, 1961-63. Recipient award for excellence in edn. Clark County Sch. Bd., 1983-84. Mem. Assn. Hypnotists of Am., Biofeedback Soc. Am., Assn. Counseling and Devel., N.Am. Acupuncture Assn., Am. Mental Health Counselors Assn. Democrat. Club: Subvets of Am.

STANNARD, JAMES NEWELL, radiation biologist and toxicologist educator; b. Owego, N.Y., Jan. 2, 1910; s. Jay Ellis and Miriam (Newell) S.; m. Grace L. Kingsley, Aug. 7, 1935; 1 child, Susan L. Stannard Stumpf. AB, Oberlin Coll., 1931; MA, Harvard U., 1934, PhD, 1935. Instr. physiology U. Rochester, N.Y., 1935-39, asst. prof. radiation biology and biophysics, 1947-49, assoc. prof. radiation biology and biophysics, 1949-59, prof., 1959-75, prof. pharmacology and toxicology, 1952-75, emeritus prof., 1975—; assoc. dir. Atomic Energy Project U. Rochester, 1959-69; assoc. dean for grad. studies U. Rochester, N.Y., 1959-75; adj. prof. community medicine and radiology U. Calif.-San Diego, La Jolla, 1977—; asst. prof. pharmacology Emory U., Atlanta, 1939-41; sr. pharmacologist to prin. physiologist NIH, Bethesda, Md., 1941-47; vis. prof. U. Calif. Med. Ctr., San Francisco, 1954; cons. Battelle Pacific NW Lab., others; mem. task group Internat. Commn. on Radiol. Protection; chmn., mem. sci. coms., life mem. Nat. Council on Radiation Protection and Measurements; mem. adv. bd. Hanford Environ. Health Found. Author: Radioactivity and Health-A History, 1987; author, editor: Handbook of Experimental Pharmacology, vol. 36, 1973; editor: Radioisotopes in the Aquatic Environment, 1976; contbr. sci. articles to profl. jours. Sec. bd. dirs. Oaks North Mgmt. Corp. Number 1, San Diego. Served to lt. USN, 1944-46. Recipient cert. of appreciation HEW, 1970, cert. appreciation AEC, 1975, cert. appreciation EPA, 1977. Mem. Am. Indsl. Hygiene Assn., AAAS, Am. Soc. Pharmacology and Exptl. Therapeutics, Am. Physiol. Soc., Radiation Research Soc., Health Physics Soc. (dir. 1965-71, pres. 1969-70, editor, mem. editorial bd. 1975-81, Disting. Achievement award 1977), Biophys. Soc., Soc. Gen. Physiologists, Phi Beta Kappa, Sigma Xi. Home: 17441 Plaza Animado Apt 132 San Diego CA 92128 Office: U Calif San Diego M-022 La Jolla CA 92093

STANTON, MICHAEL JOSEPH, film and communications educator; b. South Amboy, N.J., July 15, 1947; s. Michael Joseph Sr. and Mary Ann (Tabasko) S.; m. Julia Adams, Apr. 7, 1979. B, William Paterson Coll., 1969; M, Bowling Green State U., 1970, D, 1977. Lic. radiotelephone operator, FCC; cert. tchr., Calif., N.J. Bus. mgr. Continental Cable, Findlay, Ohio, 1974; asst. prof. Kent (Ohio) State U., 1974-78, Calif. State U., Fullerton, 1978-81; producer news Fin. News Network, Santa Monica, Calif., 1981-82; dir. instrn. TV U. Tex., Arlington, 1982-83; asst. prof. Calif. State U., Northridge, 1984-86, assoc. prof., 1986—; with videotape ops. Nat. Broadcasting Co., Burbank, Calif., 1980; ind. TV producer GFI Enterprises, Huntington Beach, Calif., 1983—; lectr. Fullerton Coll., 1985—. Contbr. articles to profl. jours. Pub. affairs producer Kent, 1974-78, Alliance, Ohio, 1976-78, Anaheim, Calif., 1980-81, Arlington, Tex., 1982-83. Grantee Calif. State U., Northridge, 1986. Mem. Acad. TV Arts and Scis., Broadcast Edn. Assn., Soc. Motion Picture and TV Engrs., Calif. Faculty Assn. Avocations: reading, outdoor sports, computing. Office: Calif State U 18111 Nordhoff St Northridge CA 91330

STANTON, PETER HARRISON, electronics company executive; b. N.Y.C., June 21, 1922; s. Stanley and Margaret (Berndt) S.; B.E.E. cum laude, NYU, 1943; M.B.A. with high distinction, Harvard U., 1948; children—Carol, Peter. Vice pres. fin. and adminstrn. Topp Industries, Inc., Los Angeles, 1955-59; pres. Astro-Sci. Corp., Los Angeles, 1959-64, Infonics, Inc., Santa Monica, Calif., 1966-73, Electroscale Corp., Santa Rosa, Calif., 1974-82, Fluidyne/Electrodata, Inc., Santa Rosa, 1982-84, Electrocorp, Santa Rosa, 1984—. Past pres., bd. dirs. United Way North Bay, 1981—. Served with USNR, 1945-46. Mem. Santa Rosa C. of C. (bd. dirs. 1987—), Young Pres.' Orgn., Psi Chi, Eta Kappa Nu. Republican. Episcopalian. Clubs: Harvard. Lodge: Rotary. Office: Electrocorp 1435 N Dutton Santa Rosa CA 95406

STANTON, TIMOTHY KEELER, university administrator, consultant; b. Ross, Calif., Aug. 9, 1947; s. James Harrison and Lucy Jane (Keeler) S.; m Catherine Pratt Howard, June 18, 1977; children: Caitlin, Erin. AB in English, Stanford U., 1969; MA in Edn., San Francisco State U., 1976; postgrad. in human and orgn. devel., Fielding Inst., 1983—. Cert. secondary, community coll. tchr., Calif. Dir. The Switching Yard, San Rafael, Calif., 1971-76; dir. human ecology field study Cornell U., Ithaca, N.Y., 1977-85; coordinator action research pub. service Stanford (Calif.) U., 1985—; cons. Learning Ctr., San Francisco, 1984-85; evaluator Formative Evaluation Research, Ann Arbor, Mich., 1985-86; orgn. devel. cons. Pacific Gas & Electric Co., San Francisco, 1984-85, Nat. Soc. for Internships and Experiential Edn., 1986-87. Author: The Experienced Hand, 1982; editor: Jour. Experiential Edn., 1984; contbr. articles to profl. jours. Mem. allocations com. United Way Santa Clara County, San Jose, Calif., 1986; mem. mental health adv. com. County of Marin, San Rafael, 1973-76; mem. adv. council Ctr. for Instl. Change San Francisco State U.; bd. dirs. Albany Semester Adv. Bd., 1979-81. Mem. Nat. Soc. for Internships and Experiential Edn. (bd. dirs. 1978-83, chmn. nat. conf. 1980-81, pres. 1981-82, cons. 1986—). Democrat. Avocations: cooking, hiking, photography. Office: Stanford U Pub Service Ctr PO Box Q Stanford CA 94305

STANTON, WILLIAM JOHN, JR., marketing educator; b. Chgo., Dec. 15, 1919; s. William John and Winifred (McGann) S.; m. Imma Mair, Sept. 14, 1978; 1978; children by previous marriage: Kathleen Louise, William John III. B.S., Ill. Inst. Tech., 1940; M.B.A., Northwestern U., 1941, Ph.D., 1948. Mgmt. trainee Sears Roebuck & Co., 1940-41; instr. U. Ala., 1941-44; auditor Olan Mills Portrait Studios, Chattanooga, 1944-46; asst. prof., asso. prof. U. Wash., 1948-55; prof. U. Colo., Boulder, 1955—; head mktg. dept. U. Colo., 1955-71, acting dean, 1963-64; assoc. dean U. Colo. (Sch. Bus.), 1964-67; vis. prof. summers U. Utah, 1946, 1949, U. Calif., Berkeley, 1950, Los Angeles, 1957; mktg. cons. to various bus. firms and govt. agys., 1950—. Author: Economic Aspects of Recreation in Alaska, 1953, (with Richard H. Buskirk) Management of the Sales Force, 7th edit, 1987 (also Spanish transl.), (with others) Challenge of Business, 1975, (with C. Futrell) Fundamentals of Marketing, 8th edit, 1987 (also Spanish, Portuguese and Indonesian transls.); (with M.S. Sommers and J.G. Barnes) Can. edit. Fundamentals of Marketing, 4th edit., 1985 Australian edit. (with K. Miller and R. Layton), 1986, Italian edit. (with R. Varaldo); mem. editorial bd. Jour. Mktg. 1963-69. Mem. Am., So., Southwestern, Western mktg. assns., Beta Gamma Sigma. Roman Catholic. Home: 1445 Sierra Dr Boulder CO 80302 Office: U Colo Campus Box 419 Boulder CO 80309

STANWYCK, STEVEN JAY, lawyer; b. N.Y.C., Sept. 21, 1944; m. Joan Mary Ciapciak, Jan. 18, 1969; children: Kirsten Jane, Michael Peter, Devin Marie, Mark Peter, Joseph Robert. BA, U. Denver, 1967; MBA, U. Calif.-Berkeley, 1971, JD, 1970. Bar: N.Y. 1972, Calif., 1971, U.S. Dist. Ct. (cen. dist.) Calif. 1981, U.S. Ct. Appeals (9th cir.) 1971, U.S. Tax Ct. 1982, U.S. Supreme Ct. 1980. Assoc. Dewey, Ballantine, Bushby, Palmer & Wood, N.Y.C., 1971-73; assoc. Kadison, Pfaelzer, Woodard, Quinn & Rossi, Los Angeles, 1973-74; ptnr. Steven J. Stanwyck, P.C., Los Angeles, 1974—. Corp. adv. bd. Nat. Ctr. for Hyperactive Children. Served with AUS, 1962-64. Recipient Calif. Real Estate Scholarship Found. award 1971; Phi Alpha Delta Nat. scholar, 1970. Mem. Assn. Bar City N.Y., Los Angeles County Bar Assn., N.Y. State Bar Assn., Am. Mgmt. Assn., Calif. Bar Assn., Am. Judicature Soc., ABA, Am. Mgmt. Assn., Phi Alpha Delta. Episcopalian. Club: Regency (Los Angeles). Office: 880 W 1st St Suite 300 Los Angeles CA 90012

STAPLETON, JEAN, journalism educator; b. Albuquerque, June 24, 1942; d. James L. and Mary (Behrman) S.; m. John Clegg, Apr. 15, 1965 (dec. Sept. 1972); m. Richard Bright, Jan. 13, 1973 (div. 1985); children: Paul. BA, U. N.Mex., 1964; MS in Journalism, Northwestern U., 1968. Reporter Glenview (Ill.) Announcements, 1967-68, Angeles Mesa News Advertiser, Los Angeles, 1968-69, City News Service, Radio News West, Los Angeles, 1969-71; press sec. polit. campaign 1972; instr. journalism East Los Angeles Coll., 1973-75, assoc. prof., head dept., 1975—. Co-editor Star, Am. Yankee Assn. Mem. NOW (pres. Los Angeles chpt. 1973-74), Women in Communications, Soc. Profl. Journalists, Nat. Women's Polit. Caucus, Los Angeles Community Coll. Journalism Profs. Assn. Democrat. Methodist. Address: 3232 Philo St Los Angeles CA 90064

STARCHER, RONALD ROSCOE, superintendent of schools; b. Leroy, W.Va., May 15, 1933; s. Orville and Edra (Smith) S.; m. Kathryn Irene Briggs, Aug. 7, 1960. BS in Chemistry and Physics, Marietta Coll., 1955; MEd in Edn. and Chemistry, U. Ariz., 1964, PhD in Edn. Adminstrn., 1971. Cert. Ariz. supr. Sci. tchr. Amphitheater Pub. Sch., Tucson, 1964-66, chemistry tchr., 1966-67; bldg. prin. Suffolk Hills High Sch., Tucson, 1967-71; supt. schs. Antelope Union High Sch., Wellton, Ariz., 1971-75, Santa Cruz Valley Unified High Sch., Eloy, Ariz., 1975-84, Safford (Ariz.) Unified Sch. Dist., 1984—; devel. chemist Am. Cyanamid, Willow Island, W.Va., 1957-62; control chemist Union Carbide Co., Marietta, Ohio, 1954-55. Pres. Safford Airport Authority, 1987; bd. dirs. Southeastern Ariz. Assn. Govt's., 1986, Pvt. Industry Council, 1986. Served with U.S. Army, 1955-57. Recipient Ariz. State Farmers award Future Farmer's Am., 1983. Mem. Am. Assn. Sch. Adminstrs., Am. Chem. Soc., Ariz. Sch. Adminstrs., Aircraft Owners and Pilots Assn., Am. Bonanza Soc., Phi Delta Kappa. Republican. Congregationalist. Lodges: Masons, Rotary (bd. dirs. Safford club). Avocations: flying, traveling, fishing, reading, observing people. Home: 999 W Relation St Safford AZ 85546 Office: Safford Unified Sch Dist #1 734 11th St Safford AZ 85546

STARING, GRAYDON SHAW, lawyer; b. Deansboro, N.Y., Apr. 9, 1923; s. William Luther and Eleanor Mary (Shaw) S.; m. Joyce Lydia Allum-Poon, Sept. 1, 1949; children: Diana Hilary Agnes, Christopher Paul Norman. Student, Colgate U., 1943-44; A.B., Hamilton Coll., 1947; J.D., U. Calif.-Berkeley, 1951. Bar: Calif. 1952, U.S. Supreme Ct. 1958. Atty. Office Gen. Counsel, Navy Dept., San Francisco, 1952-53; atty. admiralty and shipping sect. U.S. Dept. Justice, San Francisco, 1953-60; assoc. Lillick McHose & Charles, San Francisco, 1960-64, ptnr., 1965—; titulary mem. Internat. Maritime Com.; bd. dirs. Marine Exchange at San Francisco, 1984—, pres. 1986—; instr. pub. speaking Hamilton Coll., 1947-48. Assoc. editor: Am. Maritime Cases, 1966—; contbr. articles to legal jours. Mem. San Francisco Lawyers Com. for Urban Affairs, 1972—; bd. dirs. Legal Aid Soc., San Francisco, 1974—, v.p., 1975-80, pres., 1980-82. Served with USN, 1943-46, comdr. Res. ret. Fellow Am. Bar Found., Am. Coll. Trial Lawyers; mem. ABA (chmn. maritime ins. com. 1975-76, mem. standing com. on admiralty law 1976-82, 86—), Fed. Bar Assn. (pres. San Francisco chpt. 1968), Bar Assn. San Francisco (sec. 1972, treas. 1973), Calif. Acad. Appellate Lawyers, Maritime Law Assn. U.S. (exec. com. 1977—, v.p. 1980-84, pres. 1984-86), World Trade Club San Francisco, Mayor's San Francisco Shanghai Friendship Com. Club: Propeller of U.S. Republican. Episcopalian. Home: 195 San Anselmo Ave San Francisco CA 94127 Office: Two Embarcadero Ctr Suite 2600 San Francisco CA 94111

STARK, DAVID CHARLES, military chemical officer; b. Bethesda, Md., June 13, 1953; s. Robert Edward and Grace Burlingame (Cadwell) S.; m. Maureen Ann McDonald, Oct. 1, 1983; 1 child, Christopher Joseph. BS, Rensselaer Poly. Inst., 1975; postgrad., U. Wis., Milw., 1975-77; grad., Army Combined Arms and Services Staff Sch., 1985—; postgrad., Golden Gate U., 1986—. Commd. 2d. lt. U.S. Army, 1975, advanced through grades to capt., 1980; detachment commdr. 242nd Chem. Detachment U.S. Army, Fuerth, Fed. Republic Germany, 1978-79; platoon leader 69th Chem. Co., Fuerth, 1979; brigade security/intelligence officer 1st Armed div. Support Command, Fuerth, 1979-80; brigade chem. officer 3rd Brigade, 1st Armored div. U.S. Army, Bamberg, Fed. Republic Germany, 1980-81; research project officer Chem. Research and Devel. Ctr. U.S. Army, Aberdeen Proving Ground, Md., 1982-85; brigade chem. officer 11th Signal Brigade U.S. Army, Ft. Huachuca, Ariz., 1985—. Inventor improved inturned mask periphery, 1985. referee class 2, U.S. Soccer Fedn. Decorated Armed Forces Res. medal U.S. Army, 1985. Mem. Am. Chem. Soc., Assn. of U.S. Army, Mil. Order of World Wars. Republican. Presbyterian. Club: BMW Car of Am. (Tucson). Avocations: track and soccer, volksmarching, mil. miniatures, photgraphy, coin collecting. Home: 5154 Paseo Las Palmas Sierra Vista AZ 85635 Office: c/o ASG-CE-NBC 11th Signal Brigade Fort Huachuca AZ 85613-5600

STARK, FORTNEY HILLMAN (PETE), JR., congressman; b. Milw., Nov. 11, 1931; s. Fortney Hillman and Dorothy M. (Mueller) S.; children: Jeffrey Peter, Beatrice Ann, Thekla Brumder, Sarah Gallun. B.S., MIT; M.B.A., U. Calif. Teaching asst. MIT, 1953-54; prin. Skaife & Co., Berkeley, Calif., 1957-61; founder Beacon Savs. & Loan Assn., Antioch, Calif., 1961; pres., founder Security Nat. Bank, Walnut Creek, Calif., 1963-72; mem. 93d-100th Congresses from 9th Dist. Calif., Ways and Means Com., D.C. Com., Select Com. on Narcotics. Dir. A.C.L.U., 1971; dir. Housing Devel. Corp.; adv. com. Contra Costa County Coalition; dir. Common Cause, 1971; Del. Democratic State Central Com; trustee Calif. Dem. Council; bd. dirs. Starr King Sch. Served to capt. USAF, 1955-57. Mem. Delta Kappa Epsilon. Office: House of Representatives Washington DC 20515 *

STARK, FRANKLIN CULVER, lawyer; b. Unityville, S.D., Apr. 16, 1915; s. Fred H. and Catherine (Culver) S.; m. Alice C. Churchill, Sept. 16, 1941 (dec. May 1975); children: Margaret C., Wallace C., Judith C., Franklin Culver; m. Carlyn Kaiser Stark, July 18, 1976. J.D., Northwestern U., 1940; A.B., Dakota Wesleyan U., 1937, LL.D., 1959. Bar: Ill. 1940, U.S. Supreme Ct. 1945, U.S. Tax Ct. 1945, U.S. Ct. Appeals (10th cir.) 1945, Calif. 1946; cert. taxation law specialist, Calif. Assoc. firm Sidley, McPherson, Austin & Burgess, Chgo., 1940-41, Fitzgerald, Abbott & Beardsley, Oakland, Calif., 1946-47; sr. mem. firm Stark, Wells, Rahl, Field & Schwartz, Oakland, 1947—; lectr. comml. law U. Calif. Sch. Bus., 1946-66. Editor: Ill. Law Rev, 1939-40; Contbr. articles to legal publs. Staff Office Gen. Counsel, OPA, Washington, 1941-42; Bd. dirs. Merritt Peralta Found., Claremont Sch. Theology, Dakota Wesleyan U., Fred Finch Youth Center, 1970-82, Calif.-Nev. United Meth. Found., 1974-80, Oakland Meth. Found., 1952-82; chmn. bd. trustees Calif.-Nev. Meth. Homes, 1966-73; pres. Oakland Council of Chs., 1954-56; charter mem. World Peace Through Law Center; nat. pres. Campaign for UN Reform. Served with USNR, 1942-45. Named Alumnus of Year for notable achievement Dakota Wesleyan U., 1966. Mem. Am., Calif., Alameda County bar assns., Oakland C. of C., Am. Trial Lawyers Assn., Phi Kappa Phi, Pi Kappa Delta, Phi Alpha Delta, Order Coif. Methodist. Clubs: Lakeview (Oakland); Commonwealth (San Francisco). Lodges: Masons; Shriners. Home: 333 Wayne Ave Apt E Oakland CA 94606 Office: Stark Wells Rahl Field & Schwartz 1999 Harrison St Suite 1300 Oakland CA 94612 also: Peri Exec Centre Suite 900 2033 N Main St Walnut Creek CA 94596

STARK, JACK EVERETT, national park official; b. Arkansas City, Kans., Aug. 27, 1931; s. Daniel Crenshaw and Audra Maxine (Woolridge) S.; m. Gail Karlene White, Dec. 16, 1956; children: Jennifer, Cynthia, John. B.S., Colo. State U., 1954. Park ranger Nat. Park Service, 1957-67; supt. Platt Nat. Park, Sulphur, Okla., 1967-71, Everglades Nat. Park, Homestead, Fla., 1971-76; regional dir. North Atlanta Region, Nat. Park Service, Boston, 1975-79; supt. Grand Teton Nat. Park, Moose, Wyo., 1979—. Served to lt. USNR, 1954-57. Named Conservationist of Yr. Tropical Audubon Soc., Miami, Fla., 1970; recipient Meritorious Service Dept. Interior, 1982. Mem. Sigma Chi. Lodge: Rotary. Office: Nat Park Service Grand Teton Nat Park Office of the Supt Moose WY 83012

STARK, JACK LEE, college president; b. Urbana, Ind., Sept. 26, 1934; s. Lynn C. and Helen (Haley) S.; m. Jil Carolyn Harris, June 14, 1958; children—Janet, Jeffrey, Jennifer, Jonathan. B.A., Claremont McKenna Coll., 1957; hon. degree, Redlands U., LDH, 1973. Asst. to pres. Claremont McKenna Coll., Calif., 1961-70, pres., 1970—; dir. Angeles Corp., Los Angeles. Chmn. Pomona Valley Community Hosp., Region II United Way, El Monte, Calif.; bd. dirs. Foothill Country Day Sch., Claremont. Served to capt. USMCR, 1957-60. Mem. Assn. Ind. Calif. Colls. and Univs. (chmn.), Ind. Colls. So. Calif. (bd. dirs.), Western Coll. Assn. (bd. dirs.). Club: California (Los Angeles). Office: Claremont McKenna College Office of the President Claremont CA 91711 *

STARK, MILTON DALE, sports organization executive; b. Fellows, Calif., Apr. 28, 1932; s. Ernest Esco and Ruth Hazel (Keeney) S.; m. Katherine Margaret Boyd, Dec. 17, 1955 (div. June 1978); children: Mark Boyd, Kimberly Kay, Matthew Scott, Martin Dean; m. Diana Lynn Mead, July 26, 1980; 1 child, Ryan. AA, Taft Coll., 1956; BA, Whittier Coll., 1958, MEd, 1963. Cert. edn1. adminstr., Calif. Sec. Western Softball Congress, Hollywood, Calif., 1962-70; commr. Internat. Softball Congress, Anaheim Hills, Calif., 1966-75, sec., 1975-83, exec. dir., 1983—; sports cons. Whittier (Calif.) News, 1959-70. Editor in chief Softball Illus. mag., 1966-69; contbr. articles to softball mags. Served with USAF, 1951-55. Named to Internat. Softball Congress Hall of Fame, 1981. Republican. Avocations: theater, wine and book collecting, traveling. Home and Office: Internat Softball Congress 6007 E Hillcrest Circle Anaheim Hills CA 92807

STARK, RAY, motion picture producer. m. Fran Stark. Ed., Rutgers U. Publicity agt, lit. agt.; talent agt. Famous Artist Agy., to 1957; founder Seven Arts Prodn. Co., 1957; Ind. film producer 1966—. Producer: films The World of Suzie Wong, 1960, The Night of the Iguana, 1964, Reflections in a Golden Eye, 1967, Funny Girl, 1968, The Owl and the Pussycat, 1970, Fat City, 1972, The Way We Were, 1973, Funny Lady, 1975, The Sunshine Boys, 1975, Murder By Death, 1976, Smokey and the Bandit, 1977, The Goodbye Girl, 1978, The Cheap Detective, 1978, California Suite, 1978, Chapter Two, 1979, The Electric Horseman, 1979, The Hunter, 1980, Seems Like Old Times, 1980, Annie, 1981, The Slugger's Wife, 1985, others. Recipient Thalberg award Acad. Motion Picture Arts and Scis., 1980. Office: care Rastar Prodns 100 Universal City Plaza Universal City CA 91608

STARKEBAUM, GORDON ALAN, rheumatologist, researcher; b. Borger, Tex., Aug. 17, 1944; s. Norman Victor and Florence (Wilshire) S.; m. Mary Kathryn Hiltner, June 10, 1967; children: Elaine Margaret, Paul Michael, David Alan. BS, U. Wash., 1966; MD, Columbia U., 1970. Intern, then resident U. Wash., Seattle, 1970-71, 73-75; fellow in rheumatology U. Wash., 1977-79, assoc. prof. medicine, 1985—; chief arthritis sect. VA Med. Ctr., Seattle, 1981—. Office: VA Med Ctr 1660 S Columbian Way Seattle WA 98108

STARKEY, HARRY CHARLES, geologist; b. Wheeling, W.Va., Dec. 10, 1925; s. Burtice Johannes and Mary Irene (Hilton) S.; B.S., W.Va. U., 1950; m. Ruth Woods, May 16, 1964. With U.S. Geol. Survey, 1955-84, geologist specializing in clay mineralogy, Denver, 1958-84. Served with inf. U.S. Army, 1944-46. Mem. Clay Minerals Soc., Mensa. Methodist. Research in clay mineralogy, ion-exchange in clay and zeolites, chem. reactions involving clays; contbr. articles to profl. jours. Home: 1636 S Yarrow Ct Lakewood CO 80226

STARKWEATHER, FREDERICK THOMAS, data processing executive; b. Sioux City, Iowa, Feb. 24, 1933; s. Fred Ervin and Gertrude Faye (Madden) S.; m. Margot Glassen, Nov. 19, 1959; children: Thomas Frederick, Jerry Russell, Michael Glassen. BA in Math. and Physics, U. Nebr., Omaha, 1955. Mathematician Flight Determination Lab., White Sands Missile Range, N.Mex., 1955-56; supervisory mathematician Analysis & Computation, White Sands Missile Range, N.Mex., 1956-81; chief Data Scis. Div. Nat. Range Ops., White Sands Missile Range, N.Mex., 1981—; Nat. council rep. Am. Def. Preparedness Assn., Washington, 1980—; pres. White Sands Pioneer Group, White Sands Missile Range, 1983-86; bd. dirs. Assn. U.S. Army, Washington. Author hist. and genealog. books; contbr. book reviews and articles to newspapers and mags. Chmn. El Paso (Tex.) City Planning Commn., 1980-84; bd. dirs. El Paso County Hist. Soc., 1983-87; mem. El Paso County Hist. Commn., 1983—. Served with USAR, 1955-63. Named Disting. Alumnus U. Nebr., Omaha, 1985, Mgr. of Yr. Fed. Mgrs. Assn., White Sands Missile Range, 1984; recipient Conquistador City of El Paso award, 1980; cited for Services to Mankind Sertoma, El Paso chpt., 1985. Mem. Fed. Mgrs. Assn. (bd. dirs.), Freedom Found. at Valley Forge (pres. El Paso chpt., George Washington Hon. medal 1982), El Paso C. of C. (assoc. dir. 1984—, bd. dirs.). Club: Toastmasters (dist. gov. 1970-71). Lodge: Masons. Avocations: numismatics, genealogy, books, weaponry. Home: 8010 Tonto Pl El Paso TX 79904 Office: Nat Range Ops Chief Data Scis Div White Sands Missile Range NM 88002

STARR, GRIER FORSYTHE, pathologist, consultant; b. Jamestown, N.D., Oct. 6, 1926; s. Earl Grier and Grace (Forsythe) S.; m. Virginia Lucille Heidinger, June 25, 1948; children: William Grier, Joan Elizabeth Starr Ferguson. BS cum laude, Jamestown (N.D.) Coll., 1947; MD, Northwestern U., 1951; MS in Pathology, U. Minn., 1956. Diplomate Nat. Bd. Med. Examiners, 1952, Minn., Mich. and Oreg. state bds., Am. Bd. Pathology in Clin. Pathology, 1956, and in Pathol. Anatomy, 1957;. Intern Evanston (Ill.) Hosp., 1951-52; sr. resident in pathology Henry Ford Hosp., Detroit, 1955-56; fellow in pathology Mayo Clinic, Rochester, Minn., 1952-55, cons. surgical pathology, 1956-59; cons., pathologist Lab. Pathology and Pathology Cons., Eugene, Oreg., 1959—, pres., 1973-85; mem. staff McKenzie-Willamette Hosp., Springfield, Oreg., 1959—; mem. staff Sacred Heart Gen. Hosp., Eugene, Oreg., 1959—, chief of staff, 1969-71, dir. labs., 1973-81; chmn. bd., chief ops. officer Oreg. Consol. Labs., Eugene, Oreg., 1986—; bd. dirs. Oreg. Blue Cross-Blue Shield, Portland, 1985—; affiliate in pathology Oreg. Health Scis. Ctr., Portland, 1972—; assoc. prof. U. Oreg., Eugene, 1986—. Contbr. articles to profl. jours. Served with USN, 1944-46. Fellow Am. Coll. Pathologists, Am. Soc. Clin. Pathologists; mem. AMA, Lane County Med. Soc. (pres. 1984-85), Am. Soc. Cytology, Internat. Acad. Pathologists, Pacific NW Soc. Pathologists (pres. 1979-80), Oreg. State Soc. Pathologists, Am. Soc. Dermatopathology (chmn. 1984, peer review com. 1976—). Republican. Presbyterian. Avocation: raising, training and showing Am. Quarter Horse Assn.-registered cutting horses. Home: 2455 S Louis Ln Eugene OR 97405 Office: Pathology Cons PO Box 369 Eugene OR 97440

STARR, JILL RENÉ, software development company analyst; b. Tulsa, June 15, 1951; d. George J. Howard and Norma Jeanneane (Butler) Collins; m. H. Michael Smith, June 30, 1974 (div. Oct. 1975); m. James L. Starr II, June 7, 1986. AA in Data Processing, Tulsa Vocat. Tech., 1968. With Cities Service Co., Tulsa, 1970-83; data base specialist Trilogy, Cupertino, Calif., 1983-84; data base analyst FMC Corp., San Jose, Calif., 1984-85; co-owner SCI, Tulsa, 1985; support analyst Boole & Babbage, Sunnyvale, Calif., 1986—. Republican. Avocations: artwork, needlework.

STARR, MELVIN LEE, counselor; b. N.Y.C., Mar. 17, 1922; s. Herman and Martha (Aberman) S.; m. Eileen Ferne Kagan, Sept. 7, 1947; children: Marianne, Lisa Caren. BBA, U. Miami, 1947; postgrad. Columbia U., 1949-53, U. Denver, 1955-56, Ariz. State U., 1956-57; MA, U. Ariz., 1950; EdD, Western Colo. U., 1974. Faculty, adminstrn. Tucson Pub. Schs., 1950—; tchr. Doolen Jr. High Sch., 1951-53, counselor high sch., 1953-62, asst. prin. Alice Vail Jr. High Sch., 1962-64, Catalina High Sch., 1964-68; prin. Rincon High Sch., 1968-71, Tucson High Sch., 1971-74; asst. supt. Tucson Pub. Schs., 1974-78, assoc. supt., 1978-82; pvt. practice family counseling. Mem. Tucson Mayor's Com. on Human Relations, 1969—; mem. Ariz. state com. Anti Defamation League, 1971; Ariz. state adv. bd. Good Shepherd Sch. for Girls, 1971; mem. Dem. Cen. Com., Pima City, Ariz., 1968—; bd. dirs., Mobile Meals of Tucson, Pima County Bd. Health, So. Ariz. Girl Scouts U.S. Council; chmn. Tucson Community Ctr. Commn.; bd. dirs. Amigos dos los Americanos, AnyTown, Ariz., Lighthouse YMCA, Beacon Found., Big Bros., NCCJ, Jr. Achievement, Tucson Community Center, Pacific Western region Anti-Defamation League, Handmaker Nursing Home Pima County, United Way, CODAC, Planned Parenthood, Girl Scouts Am., Ariz. Mobile Meals, Epilepsy Soc. So. Ariz., Drug Abuse and Alcohol Consortium; adv. bd. Tucson Free Med. Clinic; bd. dirs. Los Ninos Crisis Center. Mem. Ariz. Assn. Student Teaching (state treas.), NEA, Ariz. Interscholastic Assn. (pres. conf. 1971, legis. council), Ariz. Personnel and Guidance Assn., Nat. Assn. Secondary Sch. Prins., Am. Assn. Sch. Adminstrs., Assn. Supervision and Curriculum Devel., Ariz. Sch. Adminstrs., Phi Epislon Pi, Phi Delta Kappa. Home: 7101 E River Canyon Rd Tucson AZ 85715 Office: 2096 N Kolb Rd Suite 107 Tucson AZ 85715

STARR, ROBERT IRVING, plant physiologist, chemist; b. Laramie, Wyo., Dec. 11, 1932; s. George Herman and Meriel Louise (Spooner) S.; m. Lavon Fabricius, June 10, 1956; children: Deborah Ann, Kenneth Irving. BS in Chemistry, U. Wyo., 1956, MS in Soil and Biochemistry, 1959, PhD in Plant Physiology and Chemistry, 1972. Ordained deacon, Presbyn. Ch. Chemist Shell Chem. Corp., Dominguez, Calif., 1956-57; biochemist Bur. Sport Fisheries and Wildlife, Denver, 1960-63; plant physiologist U.S. Bur. Sport Fisheries and Wildlife, Denver, 1968-74; plant physiologist Colo. State U., Ft. Collins, 1963-64, chemist, 1965-68, mem. environ. faculty dept. botany and plant pathology, 1973—; analytical chemist FDA, Denver, 1964-65; environ. scientist coal mining U.S. Geol. Survey, Denver, 1974-77, chief environ. tech. unit, 1977-78; chief biol. and ecol. scis. br. Office of Surface Mining U.S. Dept. Interior, Denver, 1979-81, cons. environ. chemistry, 1984—; cons. in environ. chemistry and fin. planning/real estate, 1982-84. Reviewer Jour. Agrl. Food Chemistry, 1970; editor, Reclamation Rev., 1981; contbr. articles to profl. jours. Served to 1st lt., AUS, 1957-64. Fellow Am. Inst. Chemists; mem. AAAS, Am. Chem. Soc., Sigma Xi. Club: Ft. Collins Swimming. Office: Fort Collins CO 80524

STARR, THOMAS C., land surveyor; b. Pasadena, Calif., July 21, 1939; s. Noble White and June Louise (Borkenhagen) S.; m. Pamela Jean Price, Nov. 9, 1974; children: Craig, Amy, Nigel, Jamie. Student, Fullerton Jr. Coll., 1957-59; BS in Indsl. Engring., Calif. Poly. Inst., 1962. Indsl. engr. Autonetics, Anaheim, Calif., 1962-65; sales engr. Collins Radio Co., Newport Beach, Calif., 1965-70, Nat. Semiconductor, Santa Clara, Calif., 1970-71; co-owner Krabbe and Starr, Inc., Friday Harbor, Wash., 1971—. Rep. chmn. San Juan County, Wash., 1985; campaign mgr. Senator Slade Gorton, Wash., 1986; pres. San Juan Econ. Devel. Council, 1985, San Juan County Land Assn., 1983-84. Fellow Am. Congress Surveying and Mapping; mem. Land Surveyors Assn. Wash. (pres. Northwest chpt., 1986—), Nat. Soc. Profl. Surveyors. Presbyterian. Lodge: Lions. Avocations: motorcycle touring, trumpet. Office: Krabbe & Starr Inc PO Box 897 Friday Harbor WA 98250

STATE, DAVID, surgeon, educator; b. London, Ont., Can., Nov. 12, 1914; s. Louis and Sara (Rosenberg) S.; m. Avis Gae Lorberbaum, Nov. 25, 1945; children—Norman, Claudia, Leslie, Rosanne, Mathew. B.A., U. Western Ont., 1936, M.D., 1939; M.S., U. Minn., 1943, Ph.D., 1945. Diplomate Am. Bd. Surgery. Instr. surgery U. Minn. Med. Sch., Mpls., 1946-47, asst. prof., 1947-50, assoc. prof., 1950-52; dir. surgery Cedars of Lebanon Hosp., Los Angeles, 1952-58; prof., chmn. dept. surgery Albert Einstein Coll. Medicine, N.Y.C., 1958-71; prof. surgery Harbor/UCLA Med. Ctr., Los Angeles, 1971—, chmn. dept., 1971-81. Contbr. numerous articles to med. jours. Am. Diabetic Assn. grantee, 1978-83; Nat. Surg. Adjuvant Project grantee, 1979—. Mem. Allen O. Whipple Surg. Soc., AAAS, Am. Assn. History of Medicine, Am. Assn. Thoracic and Cardiovascular Diseases, ACS, Am. Gastroent. Assn., Am. Heart Assn. (sci. council cardiovascular surgery), Am. Soc. Artificial Internal Organs, Am. Surg. Assn., Am. Trudeau Soc., Halsted Soc., Inernat. Soc. Surgery, Los Angeles Surg. Soc., Med. Research Assn. Calif., Pacific Coast Surg. Assn., Transplantation Soc., Soc. Exptl. Biology and Medicine, Soc. Surgery of Alimentary Tract, Soc. Univ. Surgeons, Sigma Xi. Democrat. Jewish. Home: 1 Reata Ln Rolling Hills CA 90274 Office: Harbor/UCLA Med Ctr Dept Surgery Box 25 1000 W Carson St Torrance CA 90509

STATES, JACK STERLING, biology educator, environmental microbiology consultant; b. Laramie, Wyo., Nov. 6, 1941; s. Herbert James and Guenivere A. (Gilfry) S.; m. Diantha Louise Green, June 8, 1965; children: Jeffrey Sterling, Janel Ann. BA, U. Wyo., 1964, MS, 1966; PhD, U. Alta., Edmonton, Can., 1969. Research assoc. U. Wyo., Laramie, 1969-70; tchr. biology Laramie, 1969-70; asst. prof. No. Ariz. U., Flagstaff, 1970-77, assoc. prof., 1977-84, prof. biology, 1984—; environ. cons. Salt River Project Ariz. Pub. Service Co., Phoenix, 1971-75, So. Calif. Edison, 1974-75. Contbr. articles to profl. jours. Recipient Leadership award SAR, 1964. Mem. Mycol. Soc. Am. (chmn. com. on teaching 1978-81), Ariz. Beekeepers Assn. (bd. dirs. 1984,86), Sigma Xi (No. Ariz. chpt. pres. 1985, S.W. regional dir., nat. bd. dirs. 1986-88, mem. nat. com. on membership 1986-88), Kappa Delta Pi, Phi Kappa Phi. Republican. Presbyterian. Avocations: beekeeping, fly-fishing, skiing. Office: No Ariz U Box 5640 Flagstaff AZ 86011

STATES, MITCHELL HUGH, management development consultant, educator; b. San Francisco, Mar. 20, 1945; s. Hugh Wilson and Frances (Peters) S. BS in Bus., Calif. Poly. State U., San Luis Obispo, 1967; MBA in Mgmt. Sci., U. Nev., 1974; postgrad. in bus., U. Ariz., 1975-80. Coordinator Coll. Relations Atlantic Richfield Co., Los Angeles, 1969-76; prof. mgmt. Calif. State U., Chico, 1980-84; mgmt. devel. cons. Pacific Gas & Electric Co., Diablo Canyon Nuclear Power Plant, San Luis Obispo, 1984—; mem. faculty Calif. Poly. State U., San Luis Obispo, 1984—; mem. faculty, advisor U. Ariz., Tucson, 1975-80; registered orgn. devel. cons.; cons. in field, 1967—. Named Disting. Alumnus, Calif. Poly. State U., 1972, Outstanding Bus. Tchr. U. Ariz., Tucson, 1977, Outstanding Mgmt. Tchr. Calif. State U., Chico, 1982, 84. Mem. Acad. Mgmt. (doctoral consortium 1979), Sigma Iota Epsilon, Beta Gamma Sigma, Pi Alpha Alpha. Avocations: fishing, art, philosophy, nature studies.

STATES, STANLEY WILMETH, infosystems specialist; b. Hartman, Colo., Aug. 9, 1930; s. Henry Wilmeth and Lelia Belle (Hopkins) S.; m. Irene Joyce Kestner, May 11, 1956; children: Pamela, Jeffrey. Student, U. Colo., 1949-52; EdB, U. Nebr., 1961. Enlisted USAF, 1952, advanced through grades to lt. col., 1969; sr. systems analyst Inter Am. Devel. Bank, Washington, 1973-74; dep. dir. data automation Fed. Communications Commn., Washington, 1974-79; dir. info. systems Mine Safety and Health Adminstrn., Denver, 1979—. Decorated DFC, 1968. Republican. Avocations: tennis, wood working, automobile restoration. Home: 3 Doral Ln Littleton CO 80123 Office: Mine Safety Health Adminstrn Info Systems Ctr PO Box 25367 Denver CO 80225

STATHAM, DAWN STRAM, social service administrator; b. Arlington, S.D., May 15, 1944; d. Walter Ernest and Thelma (LaDuke) S.; m. William Patrick Statham, Aug. 3, 1974; children: Sean Adrien, Philip Shane, Alonzo Frederick, Emily Elizabeth. BA, Portland State U., 1972; MA, Idaho State U., 1981. Rule making coordinator Dept. Health and Welfare, Boise, Idaho, 1977-82; exec. dir. Council on Domestic Violence, Boise, 1982—; adj. instr. Boise State U., 1982-84; panelist Nat. Victim Rights Forum, Washington, 1986; expert witness U.S. Atty. Gen.'s Task Force on Family Violence, Seattle, 1984. Author: Camas and the Northern Shoshoni, 1982; (poems) roots & wings, 1967. Del. Idaho Dem. Conv., Boise, 1984; founder VANGUARD, Boise, 1985—, pres., 1985. Scholar Idaho State Coll., 1961-63, Portland State U., 1971-72. Mem. Nat. Orgn. for Victim Assistance, Sigma Xi. Avocations: astrology, gardening. Home: 1421 N 21st Boise ID 83702 Office: Council on Domestic Violence 3311 W State PO Box 55 Boise ID 83707

STATHAM, WILLIAM PATRICK, airport planner; b. Boise, Idaho, June 20, 1949; s. Harold Russell and Wilma (Lewis) S.; m. Dawn Stram, Aug. 3, 1974; children: Sean A., Philip S., Alonzo F., Emily E. BA, Boise State Coll., 1972; MA, Idaho State U., 1978. Mus. curator Idaho State Hist. Soc., Boise, 1975-84; spl. lectr. Boise State U., 1984; sr. airport planner Hosac Engineering., Inc., Meridian, Idaho, 1984—; mktg. cons. D&B Assocs., Boise, 1983—. Mem. Idaho State Dept. Health and Welfare task force on pesticide disposal, 1986—; pres. grad. student assn., Idaho State U., Pocatello, 1973-74. Scholar Am. Fedn. Mineral. Socs., 1974-76. Mem. Idaho Archeol. Soc. (pres. local chpt. 1985—, bd. dirs. 1976—, Profl. Service award 1983), Service Employees Union (bd. dirs., pres. 1982-84), Idaho Airport Mgrs. Assn., Sigma Xi (assoc.). Democrat. Club: Anthropology of Boise State Coll. (pres. 1971-72). Avocations: flintworking, making exptl. stone tools. Home: 1421 N 21st St Boise ID 83702 Office: Hosac Engring Inc 2250 N Meridian Rd Meridian ID 83642

STAUBER, SHOSHANA, speech and language pathologist; b. Harrisburg, Pa., Jan. 20, 1961. BA in Speech Pathology, Audiology, San Diego State U., 1982; MS in Communicative Disorders, U. Redlands, 1984. Lic. speech pathologist, Calif. Speech pathologist Irwin Lehrhoff & Assocs., Beverly Hills, Calif., 1984-86, Parker Hearing & Speech Inst., Torrance, Calif., 1986—. Mem. Am. Speech-Language-Hearing Assn. (cert.). Office: Parker Hearing & Speech Inst 4201 Torrance Blvd #140 Torrance CA 90503

STAUDENMIER, KAREN LOUISE, respiratory therapist, educator; b. Wagner, S.D., Apr. 9, 1959; d. Edward Clare and Delores Mae (Minnaert) S. Student in biology and nursing, U. S.D., 1977-80; BA in allied health and edn., Ottawa U., 1986. Cert. respiratory therapy technician; registered respiratory therapist. Respiratory therapist for intensive care unit Phoenix Baptist Hosp., 1981-82; clin. instr. Good Samaritan, Phoenix, 1982-83; clin. instr. Biosystems Inst., Tempe, 1982-83, didactic instr., 1983-86; respiratory therapist Valley Luth. Hosp., Mesa, Ariz., 1986—. Mem. Am. Assn. Respiratory Care, Ariz. Soc. Respiratory Care (numerous coms., cert. recognition 1986, 87, membership ambassador), Kappa Alpha Theta (Alpha Rho chpt., historian 1980). Republican. Roman Catholic.

STAUDERMAN, BRUCE FORD, advertising agency executive; b. Jersey City, Mar. 17, 1919; b. Herbert Henry and Helen Ann (Jacobus) S.; m. Claude Outhier, Mar. 23; 1946. Student, Syracuse U., 1936-38, TV Workshop, N.Y.C., 1949-50, Sch. TV Technique, 1950. V.p. TV, radio, films Meldrum & Fewsmith, Inc. (advt. agy.), Cleve., 1954-62; exec. v.p., chmn. plans bd., exec. creative dir. Meldrum & Fewsmith, Inc. (advt. agy.), 1973—; v.p., creative dir. Ogilvy & Mather (advt. agy.), N.Y.C., 1962-69, Kenyon & Eckhardt, Inc. (advt. agy.), N.Y.C., 1979-83, Barnhart & Co. (advt. agy.), Denver, 1983-84; pres. Stauderman Advt., 1984—; v.p., creative dir. Mktg. Resources Group (advt. agy.), 1985—; dir. TV, advt. cons. Intermarco-Elvinger (advt. co.), Paris, 1969-73; TV cons. gov., Ohio, 1958; council mem., judge C.L.I.O. Festival, 1960—; chmn. Paris jury, 1969-73; jury mem. Internat. Advt. Film Festival, Cannes, Venice, 1976—. Radio, TV program writer: House of Mystery, 1946-51; writer, producer, dir., WXEL-TV, Cleve., 1951-54. Mem. men's com. Cleve. Playhouse, 1958-62; chmn. TV com. Cleve. United Fund, 1958-59. Served from pvt. to 2d lt. AUS, 1941-46; to 1st lt. N.G. Essex Troop AUS, 1948-50. Mem. Am. Assn. Advt. Agys. (TV and radio adminstrs. com. 1958-62), Am. Fedn. of TV and Radio Artists, Denver Advt. Fedn. Home: 6750 E Costilla Circle Englewood CO 80112 Office: 110 16th St Denver CO 80202

STAUFFER, TERRY WELDEN, academic administrator; b. Astoria, Oreg., Jan. 11, 1948; s. Welden Maynard and Grace Bernadine (Cleveland) S.; m. Janice Maxine MacLardy, Oct. 5, 1974; 1 child, Courtney Marie. Student, So. Oreg. State U., Lane Community Coll. Interviewer Oreg. Employment Div., Vancouver, 1974-75; tng. officer Clark County, Vancouver, 1975-80, asst. dir., 1980-81; coll. dir. Trend Colls., Vancouver, 1981-86; dir. Unique Employment Agy., Escondido, Calif., 1986—. Chmn. Jackson County Housing Authority, Medford, 1983-86, Pvt. Industry Council of Medford, 1983-86, Youthworks Inc., Medford, 1981-83, Community Accountability Bd., Vancouver, 1978-79; mem. Area Edn. Dist. Formation Com., Medford, 1981, So. Oreg. Leaders Inc., Medford, 1982-83; sec.-treas. Clark County Jobs for Vets Commn., Vancouver, 1977-81. Named one of Outstanding Young Men of Am., Nat. Jaycees, 1976. Mem. Nat. Bus. Edn. Assn., Western Bus. Edn. Assn., Oreg. Bus. Edn. Assn. (v.p. 1981-86), Oreg. Vocat. Assn., Nat. Assn. Pvt. Industry Councils, Medford C. of C., Calif. Assn. Personnel Cons. Republican. Lodge: Elks. Avocations: community service, music, hunting, fishing, reading. Home: 1651 S Juniper #207 Escondido CA 92025

STAURSKY, GEOFFREY NICHOLAS, geologist; b. Cleve., Aug. 12, 1957; s. Nicholas and Helen (Balasz) S.; m. Karen Leigh Hillen, June 6, 1981. B.A., Miami U., Oxford, Ohio, 1979, M.S., 1981. Grad. asst. Miami U., Oxford, 1980-81; devel. geologist Getty Oil Co., Denver, 1981-86; indsl. mktg. rep. Texaco, Inc., Denver, 1986—. Mem. Am. Assn. Petroleum Geologists, Soc. Econ. Paleontologists and Mineralogists, Rocky Mountain Assn. Geologists, Okla. City Geol. Soc., Sigma Xi. Home: 7384 S Dexter Way Littleton CO 80122 Office: Texaco Inc PO Box 2100 Denver CO 80201

STAVIG, MARK LUTHER, English educator; b. Northfield, Minn., Jan. 20, 1935; s. Lawrence Melvin and Cora (Hjertaas) S.; m. Donna Mae Ring, July 3, 1957; children—Anne Ragnhild, Thomas Edward, Rolf Lawrence. B.A., Augustana Coll., 1956, Oxford U., 1958; M.A., Oxford U., 1962; Ph.D., Princeton U., 1961. Instr. to asst. prof. English U. Wis., Madison, 1961-68; from assoc. prof. to prof. English Colo. Coll., Colorado Springs, 1968—. Editor: Ford, 'Tis Pity She's a Whore, 1966; author: John Ford and the Traditional Moral Order, 1968. Fellow Danforth Found., 1956-61, Woodrow Wilson Found., 1956-57; Fulbright scholar Oxford U., 1956-58. Mem. MLA, Soc. for Values in Higher Edn. Democrat. Home: 1409 Wood Ave Colorado Springs CO 80907 Office: Colo Coll Dept English Colorado Springs CO 80903

STAVROUDIS, ORESTES N., mathematics educator; b. N.Y.C., Feb. 22, 1923; s. Nicholas Andreas Stavroudis and Marguerite (Mizner) Fox; m. Dorothea Franziska Allina, Sept. 2, 1949; children: Christopher Kim, Gregory Andreas. AB, Columbia U., 1948, MA, 1949; DIC, Imperial Coll. Sci. and Tech., London, 1959; PhD, U. London, 1959. Tchr. The Tutoring Sch., N.Y.C., 1949; teaching asst. Rutgers U., New Brunswick, N.J., 1950-51; mathematician Patuxtent River (Md.) N.A.S., 1951, Nat. Bur. Standards, Washington, 1951-67; prof. U. Ariz., Tucson, 1967—; visiting prof. Nat. Chiao Tung U., Hsinchu, Rep. China, 1982-83. Author: The Optics of Rays, Wave Fronts and Caustics, 1972, Modular Optical Design, 1982; co-author: Spot Diagrams, 1965. Treas. Philharmonia Orch. Tucson, 1976—. Served to cpl. USAF, 1943-46, ATO. Fellow AAAS, Optical Soc. Am. (assoc. editor jour. 1970-74, topical editor 1986—); mem. Soc. Photo-Instrumental Engrs., Am. Math. Soc., Math. Assn. Am., Soc. Indsl. & Applied Math. Democrat. Office: U Ariz Optical Scis Annex 1002 N Warren Tucson AZ 85719

STEA, DAVID, urban planner, educator; b. Bklyn., Dec. 12, 1936; s. Armand and Henriette (Lipsky) S. B.S., Carnegie Inst. Tech., 1957; M.S., U. N.Mex., 1960; Ph.D. (NSF fellow), Stanford U., 1964. Human factors engr. Sandia Corp., Albuquerque, 1957-60; engring. psychologist Lockheed Missiles & Space Corp., Sunnyvale, Calif., 1961; asst. prof. geography and psychology Clark U., Worcester, Mass., 1967-69, assoc. prof., 1969-71; asso. prof. architecture, urban design and planning UCLA, 1971-74, prof., 1974-82; disting. prof. architecture U. Wis.-Milw., 1982-86, adj. disting. prof., 1986—, sr. scientist Urban Research Ctr., 1982-86; vis. prof. planning U. N.Mex., 1986—; dir. Internat. Ctr. for Built Environment, Santa Fe, 1985—; co-founder Miniversity, 1970; cons. Navajo Nation and Pima/Maricopa Salt River Community, 1974—, Fed. U. Tech., Yola, Nigeria, 1982-84, Inst. Am. Indian Arts, 1983—; vis. prof. architecture Middle East Tech. U., Turkey, 1981, U. Melbourne, 1982, U. Autónoma de Baja California, Mex., 1983, Gadjah Mada U., Yogyakarta, Indonesia, 1986. Author: Environmental Mapping; co-editor: Maps in Minds, Ethnoscapes; mem. editorial bd. Environment and Behavior, 1969-80, Human Ecology, 1971-76, Jour. Environ. Psychology and Non-Verbal Behavior, 1976-80, Jour. Environ. Psychology, 1980—, Geog. Research Forum, 1982—. Community planning cons. Sawtelle Community, Los Angeles, 1972-75, Confederated Tribes of the Umatilla, 1980, San Ysidro del Norte, N.Mex., 1985—, AIA R/UDAT program, 1976—. NSF grantee, 1961-64; Social Sci. Research Council grantee, 1966-67; Shell Found. grantee, 1969; U.S. Dept. Edn. grantee, 1968-71, 85-88. Mem. AIA (assoc.), Sociedad Interamericana de Psicología, Sociedad Interamericana de Planificación, Internat. Assn. Impact Assessment, Soc. for Intercultural Edn. Tng. and Research. Office: Internat Ctr for Built Environment 54 1/2 E San Francisco St Santa Fe NM 87501

STEAD, JOHN HENRY, industrial technology educator; b. Inglewood, Calif., June 13, 1931; s. Henry E. and Hazel R. Stead; m. Marion Constance Terry, July 30, 1958; children: Stacy, Kevin. AA, Pasadena (Calif.) City Coll., 1951; BA, U. Calif., Santa Barbara, 1956; MA, Calif. State U., Los Angeles, 1959; EdD, U. So. Calif., 1969. Gen. adminstrn. credential, gen. pupil personnel services credential, gen. secondary teaching credential, vocat. teaching credential, gen. elem. teaching credential, Calif. Tchr. Ventura (Calif.) High Sch., 1953-54, 56-63, chmn. indsl. arts edn. dept., 1958-63, counselor, 1964-65; vocat. edn. coordinator Ventura Unified Sch. Dist., 1965-78; co-owner Aazunna Pub., Ventura, 1978-83; asst. prof. indsl. tech. Calif. Poly. State U., San Luis Obispo, 1984; instr. UCLA, 1972-83, coordinator packaging program, 1987—; instr. LaVerne Coll. Residence Ctr., Point Mugu, Calif., 1975; mem. verification team Calif. Dept. Edn., Sacramento, 1973-74; affirmative action complaint resolution hearing officer, Ventura County Pub. Soc. Services Agy., 1976. Pres. Ventura Youth Employment Service, 1969-72, Ventura Girls Club, 1977-78; bd. dirs. Consumer Credit Counselors of Ventura County, 1973-79. Served with U.S. Army, 1954-56. Recipient commendation Ventura County Bd. Suprs., 1973, Pres.'s award Calif. Indsl. Edn. Assn., 1975, Outstanding Service award Ventura County United Way, 1980, Cert. Appreciation Spl. Olympics Program, Santa Barbara, 1981. Mem. Calif. Council Indsl. and Tech. Tchr. Educators, Packaging Edn. Found. (mem. ednl. com.), Soc. Packing and Handling Engrs. (assoc.), Nat. Assn. Indsl. Tech., Epsilon Pi Tau (chpt. v.p. 1985—), Assn. Calif. Sch. Adminstrs. (regional chmn. vocat. com. 1974-77). Republican. Home: PO Box 6306 Los Osos CA 93412 Office: Calif State Poly U Indsl Tech Dept San Luis Obispo CA 93407

STEAD, WILLIAM GEORGE, city official; b. Arlington, Mass., Aug. 7, 1946; s. William Holdsworth and Lillian (Wellhofer) S.; m. Cynthia Ann Gluck, Dec. 19, 1971. BSCE, U. Pa., 1969, MSE, 1970, MS in Anthropology, 1981. Registered profl. engr. Prin. engr. L.T. Klauder & Assocs., Phila. and Sao Paulo, Brazil, 1971-79; chief of staff, asst. v.p. surface ops. N.Y.C. Transit Authority, 1980-83; dir. ops. Mass. Bay Transp. Authority, Boston, 1983-85; gen. mgr. San Francisco Mcpl. Ry., 1985—; assoc. prof. Calif. State U.; instr. Golden Gate U.; bd. dirs. Caltrain Commuter Railway. Contbr. articles to profl. jours. Mem. civilian adv. council U.S. 6th Army. Served to capt. U.S. Army, 1970-71. Ford Found. fellow, 1969-70. Mem. ASCE, NSPE, Soc. Am. Archaeology, Archaeol. Soc. of Am. Republican. Mem. United Ch. Christ. Home: 355 Buena Vista Ave E San Francisco CA 94117 Office: San Francisco Mcpl Ry 949 Presidio Ave San Francisco CA 94117

STEARNS, JOHN WARREN, physicist; b. Santa Barbara, Calif., June 3, 1933; s. Charles Page and Margaret Ellen (Plasterer) S.; m. Grace Ann McCoy, Jan. 10, 1967. AB in Math., U. Calif., Berkeley, 1959, MS in Nuclear Engring., 1967. Sr. engring. aide, design engr. Calif. Div. Hwys., San Francisco, 1953-59; research apparatus operator Lawrence Berkeley Lab., Berkeley, Calif., 1959-62, physicist, 1962—; judge Santa Clara County (Calif.) Sci. Fair, 1983—, San Francisco Sci. and Engring. Fair, 1984—. Contbr. articles to profl. jours.; patentee in field. Served with USNR, 1956-57. Mem. AAAS. Democrat. Avocations: flying, skiing, tennis, softball, cycling. Office: U Calif Lawrence Berkeley Lab MS 5-119 Berkeley CA 94720

STEARNS, STEWART WARREN, charitable association executive; b. Denver, Apr. 8, 1947; s. Vinton H. and Marjorie L. (Tedro) S.; B.S., Eastern N.Mex. U., 1970; M.A., No. Ill. U., 1973; postgrad. SUNY, Albany, 1974—; m. Marjorie L. Fuller, Jan. 25, 1969; children—Theresa Lyn, Gregory Robert. Mng. editor Studies in Linguistics, DeKalb, Ill., 1972-73; instr. No. Ill. U., DeKalb, 1972-73; cons. AID, Guatemala, 1973-74; instr. Skidmore Coll., Saratoga Springs, N.Y., 1975; OAS fellow, Guatemala, 1976-77; asst. dir. Chaves County Community Action Program, Roswell, N.Mex., 1977-78; exec. dir. United Way Chaves County, Roswell, 1978-83,, Levi Strauss Found., 1983-85; exec. dir. Community Trust of Met. Tarrant County, 1985—; bd. dirs. Eastern N. Mex. U.-Roswell, 1982; bd. mem. Chaves County Community Action Program, 1979; treas. Chaves County Interagy. Council, 1980. Mem. All-America City Task Force, Roswell, 1978-79. NDEA fellow, Dallas, 1970-71. Mem. Am. Anthrop. Assn., Latin Am. Anthropology Group, Am. Soc. Applied Anthropology, Sigma Xi. Methodist. Clubs: Rotary (com. chmn. 1979-80), Noonday Toastmasters (adminstrv. v.p. 1979-80) (Roswell).

STEBBINS, GEORGE MCKINLEY, construction company executive; b. Merced, Calif., Nov. 15, 1957; s. George Norton and Mildred Ann (Wigdaul) S.; m. Kathleen Mary Callanan, June 16, 1984; 1 child, Michael Paul. Assoc. in Tech., Ft. Stella Community Coll., 1978; student, U. Puget Sound, 1978-81; BSBA, Evergreen State Coll., 1985. Cert. fire systems evaluation systems surveyor, 1982. Restaurant mgr. 3 brs. 1975-78; engring. draftsman VA Med. Ctr., Tacoma, 1978-81; engring. technician VA Med. Ctr., Portland, Oreg., 1981—; cons. Norton McKinley, Vancouver, Wash., 1985—. Youth leader St. James Cath. Ch., Vancouver, 1981—. Mem. Am. Fedn. Govt. Employees. Lodge: KC. Avocations: sailboat and yacht racing, snow skiing, hiking, cooking, sports cars. Home: 10273 NE Notchlog Dr #108 Vancouver WA 98685 Office: VA Med Ctr Portland PO Box 1034 Portland OR 97207

STEBLAY, CRAIG DOUGLAS, real estate executive, entrepreneur; b. San Bernardino, Calif., Mar. 1, 1948; s. Ralph Edward and Grace J. (Rhody) S.; m. Amina Marie Nickell, Sept. 28, 1968; children: Lavee, Kari Ann, Jennifer. V.p. Phototron Corp., San Bernardino, Calif., 1982—, also dir.; sec., treas. Sunmass Corp., Phoenix, Ariz., 1986—; pres. Sunmass Corp., Phoenix, 1987—. Served with USMC, 1969-71. Lodge: Knights of Malta (named Knight of Honor 1984), Cedam Internat. Avocation: philanthropy.

STECHER, BRIAN MARK, education researcher, consultant; b. Los Angeles, Nov. 18, 1946; s. Arthur Irving and Evelyn Esther (Schon) S.; m. Cheryl Ann Chadurgian, Dec. 30, 1983. BA cum laude, Pomona Coll., 1968; MS, U. Oreg., 1970; PhD, UCLA, 1982. Math. specialst Compton (Calif.) Sch. Dist., 1970-71; dir. Project SEED, Columbus, Ohio, 1972-75; dir. curriculum, instr. Project Spl. Elem. Edn. for Disadvantaged, Berkeley, Calif., 1975-79, also bd. dirs.; teaching assoc. UCLA, 1979-82; profl. assoc. Ednl. Testing Service, Los Angeles, 1982—; cons. Edn. Evaluation Assocs., Los Angeles, 1981-84. Author: The Electronic Schoolhouse, 1985; contbr. articles to profl. jours. Crown-Zellerbach Corp. scholar, 1967-68; fellow UCLA, 1980-82. Mem. Am. Ednl. Research Assn., Nat. Council Measurement in Edn., Phi Delta Kappa. Avocations: woodworking, bicycling. Office: Ednl Testing Service 2 N Lake Ave Suite 510 Pasadena CA 91101

STECKEL, JULIE RASKIN, psychpthereapist, lecturer, consultant; b. Los Angeles, Jan. 3, 1940; d. Edward M. and Selma (Romm-Rosby) Raskin; m. Richard Jay Steckel, June 16, 1960; children: Jan Marie, David Matthew. BA, UCLA, 1960, MSW, 1975; MA in Teaching., Harvard U., 1961. Lic. clin. social worker. Music tchr. Los Angeles, Beverly Hills and Santa Monica, Calif., 1968-70; psychol. cons. BMA Dialysis Units, Torrance, Calif., 1976-83; pvt. practice psychotherapy Los Angeles, 1975—; affiliate staff Del Amo Hosp., Torrance, 1983—; lectr., cons. UCLA Dental Sch., 1984—; lectr. social welfare UCLA Grad. Sch., 1985—. Mem. editorial bd. Contemporary Dialysis and Nephrology Jour.; contbr. articles to jours. Bd. dirs. Palisades Dem. Hdqrs., Pacific Palisades, Calif., 1972; credentials currier Dem. Conv., Miami, Fla., 1972. Fellow Soc. Clin. Social Workers; mem. Nat. Assn. Social Workers, Acad. Psychosomatic Medicine, Am. Orthopsychiat. Assn. Home: 248 24th St Santa Monica CA 90402 Office: 12301 Wilshire Blvd Suite 413 Los Angeles CA 90025 Office: 3250 W Lomita Blvd Suite 304 Torrance CA 90505

STEDJEE, BRIAN JAMES, chemical professional; b. Modesto, Calif., Nov. 12, 1949; s. Allan James and Dorothy Marie (Watkins) S. AS, Modesto Jr. Coll., 1969; BS in Chemistry, Fresno State Coll., 1971. Lab. technician Modesto Jr. Coll., 1973—. Co-author: Experiments in Basic Chemistry, 1985; contbr. articles to profl. jours. Mem. Am. Chem. Soc., Amnesty Internat., ACLU. Home: 1626 Woodland Modesto CA 95351 Office: Modesto Jr Coll Modesto CA 95350

STEED, GERRY (GERALDINE ANN), ceramic tile company executive; b. Seattle, July 9, 1934; d. Edward Thomas and Helen Theresa (Flynn) Murphy; A.A., Los Angeles Valley Coll., 1954; C.T.C., Cermaic Tile Inst., 1976; m. Feb. 11, 1956; children—Edward Lee, Colleen Ann, William Lee, Heather Ann, Amanda Ann. Vice pres., fin. officer William L. Steed Tile, Inc., Ventura, Calif., 1970—; pres., fin. officer Buena Tile Supply, Inc., Ventura, 1978—; assoc. ceramic tile cons. program Ceramic Tile Inst., Los Angeles, 1976—. Treas., Y.L.I., Ventura, 1964-66, v.p., 1967-68, pres., 196-69, trustee, 1969-70; treas., fin. sec. Parent-Tchr. Guild, Our Lady of Assumption Sch., Ventura, 1972-74; mem. ways and means com. St. Bonaventure High Sch., Ventura, 1974-75. Mem. Ceramic Tile Inst. (Woman of Yr. award 1975), Ventura County Contractors Assn., Nat. Ceramic Tile Mktg. Fedn. (treas. 1986-87), Ceramic Tile Distbrs. Assn., Western States Ceramic Tile Contractors Assn., Tile Contractors Assn. Am., Tile Contractors Assn. So. Calif. Republican. Roman Catholic. Office: 11019 Nardo St PO Box 3259 Ventura CA 93006

STEED, ROBERT WILLIAM, geophysicist, geologist; b. Rawlins, Wyo., Feb. 20, 1957; s. Robert Hansen and Flora Mae (Maughan) S.; m. Susan Hopkins, Nov. 20, 1979; children: Robert Hopkins, Ashley Suzanne, Alex Matthew. BS, Brigham Young U., 1981; MS, Duke U., 1983. Geophysicist Exxon Co., U.S.A., Denver, 1983—; seismic processing analyst Casper (Wyo.) Processors, Inc., summers, 1979-81. Mem. AAAS (assoc.), Soc. Exploration Geophysicists (assoc.), Am. Assn. Petroleum Geologists (jr.). Republican. Mormon. Office: Exxon Co USA PO Box 120 Denver CO 80201

STEED, WILLIAM LEE, ceramic tile company executive; b. Los Angeles, July 18, 1934; s. Lee R. and Mary Caroline (Banks) S.; m. Geraldine Ann Murphy, Feb. 11, 1956; children: Edward L., Colleen, William Jr., Heather, Amanda. Grad. high sch., Idaho Falls, Idaho. Installation foreman Selec-Tile Inc., Los Angeles, 1959-69; tile contactor, cons. William L. Steed Tile Inc., Ventura, 1969—. Active Joint Apprenticeship Com., Los Angeles, Orange and Ventura Counties, 1977—. Served with U.S. Army, 1956-58. Mem. Associated Tile Contractors (bd. dirs. 1977-84, pres. 1979), Western States Ceramic Tile Contractors Assn. (pres. 1981—, tile contractor of yr. 1981), Ceramic Tile Inst. (Golden Tile award 1982). Republican. Roman Catholic. Avocations: water skiing, fishing, rebuilding old cars. Office: PO Box 3259 Ventura CA 93006

STEELE, ANITA (MARGARET ANNE MARTIN), law librarian, legal educator; b. Haines City, Fla., Dec. 30, 1927; d. Emmett Edward and Esther Majulia (Phifer) Martin; m. Thomas Dinsmore Steele, June 10, 1947 (div. 1969); children—Linda Frances, Roger Dinsmore, Thomas Garrick, Carolyn Anne; m. James E. Beaver, Mar. 1980. B.A., Radcliffe Coll., 1948; J.D., U. Va., 1971; M.Law Librarianship, U. Wash., 1972. Asst. prof. law U. Puget Sound, Tacoma, 1972-74, assoc. prof. law, 1974-79, prof. law, 1979—, dir. law library, 1972—. Contbr. articles to profl. jours.; mem. editorial adv. bds. various law book pubs., 1980—. Treas., Congl. Campaign Orgn., Tacoma, 1978, 80; mem. adv. bd. Clover Park Vocat.-Tech. Sch., Tacoma, 1980-82. Mem. Am. Assn. Law Libraries, Internat. Assn. Law Libraries, Am. Soc. Info. Sci. Republican. Home: 1502 Fernside Dr S Tacoma WA 98465 Office: U Puget Sound Sch of Law 950 Broadway Tacoma WA 98402

STEELE, DONALD DICKINSON, public relations agency executive; b. Bozeman, Mont., Apr. 17, 1909; s. Fred M. and Cecille Roberta (Heywood) S.; student pub. and pvt. schs.; m. Evelyn Jane de Clairmont, May 8, 1932; 1 son, Donald de Clairmont. Founder, 1941, now chmn., pres. Steele Group, San Francisco; San Francisco ptnr. IPR Group of Cos. Mem. Pub. Relations Soc. Am. (accredited), Pub. Relations Round Table. Republican. Clubs: Rotary, San Francisco Press, Olympic, Metropolitan, Shriners. Address: 703 Market St San Francisco CA 94103

STEELE, JAMES FRANKLIN, human resource management; b. Coeur D'Alene, Idaho, Jan. 14, 1955; s. Hubert N. and Jane O. (Holman) S.; m. Debra K. Anderson, May 29, 1976; children: Bethany K., Matthew J. Student, N. Idaho Coll., 1972-73, Pacific Luth. U., 1975-76; AA, Luth. Bible Inst., 1975, BA in Edn., 1977. Registered profl. in human resources. Edn. dir. Am. Luth. Ch., Seattle, 1977-79, Lake Oswego, Oreg., 1979-81; br. mgr. Western Temp. Services, Portland, Oreg., 1981-84; personnel, adminstrn. mgr. Synektron Corp., Portland, 1984-86; mgr. personnel Am. Kotobuki Electronics Industries, Vancouver, Wash., 1986—. Lay minister Living Savior Luth. Ch., Tualatin, Oreg., 1983—. Nat. Merit scholar, 1972; recipient Nat. Sales award Western Temp. Services, 1983. Mem. Am. Soc. Personnel Adminstrn., Pacific Northwest Personnel Mgmt. Assn. Avocations: music, volunteer work, skiing. Home: 21081 SW Jameco Ct Tualatin OR 97062 Office: Am Kotobuki Electronics Industries PO Box 61427 Vancouver WA 98666-1427

STEELE, JOHN ROY, real estate broker; b. Detroit, Feb. 16, 1945; s. Wallace Lee Roy and Kay F. (Fitzpatrick) S.; B.A., Alma Coll., 1967; M.B.A., Central Mich. U., 1968; m. Beverly Louise Rauh, June 3, 1972; children—Josh Oliver, Matt Edward, Anne Elizabeth. Owner/broker Century 21 Steele, Realtors, Jackson, Calif., 1981—; partner/broker Century 21, Lewis-Steele, Realtors, Inc., Jackson and Truckee, Calif., 1976-81; dir. Amador Title Co., 1978-83, pres., 1978-79; ptnr. Computer World, Jackson, 1983-85. Bd. dirs. Trinity Episcopal Ch., Sutter Creek, Calif., 1978-79, 80-83, jr. warden, 1979; trustee Citizens for Progress, 1981-82; chmn. Amador County chpt. Easter Seals Telethon, 1985, 86, 87. pres. Amador Swim Team, 1986-87; coach Mother Lode Youth Soccer League, 1984, 86, Olympics of The Mind, coach all star tournament, 1986. Mem. Amador County Bd. Realtors (bd. dirs. 1974-82, pres. 1978), Calif. Assn. Realtors (dir. 1978). Club: Friends of the Library. Office: PO Box 210 Jackson CA 95642

STEELE, JON M., lawyer; b. Cedar Rapids, Iowa, Feb. 17, 1950; s. Jack T. and Winifred (Johnson) S.; m. Kathy Susan Kemp, Apr. 14, 1973; children: Jacob Jon, Andrew Benjamin, Nicholas Patrick. BA, U. Iowa, 1972; JD, Drake U., 1975. Bar: Idaho. Staff atty. J.R. Simplot Co., Boise, Idaho, 1976-78; ptnr. Ellis, Brown, Shiels and Steele, Boise, 1979—. Bd. dirs. Big Brothers, Boise, 1983-85, Friends of 4, Boise, 1982-83; chmn. Ada County Zoning Commn., 1984. Mem. ABA, Idaho State Bar Assn., Idaho Trial Lawyers Assn. (bd. dirs. 1982—). Office: Idaho 1st Plaza Suite 1500 Boise ID 83702

STEELE, RODERICK M., lumber and paper company executive; b. 1925. B.A. in Bus., U. Wash., 1947. Sr. acct. Arthur Andersen & Co., 1947-51; contractor Twin Feather Mills Inc., 1951-53; treas. River Lumber Co., 1953-54, Pack River Co., 1943-63; div. contractor Potlatch Corp., San Francisco, 1963, gen. mgr. western ops. wood products group, 1967, v.p. western wood products group, 1968, corp. v.p., 1970, group v.p. wood products, 1972, exec. v.p. ops., 1974, pres., chief operating officer, 1977—; chmn. bd. govs. Nat. Council Paper Industry for Air and Steam Improvements Inc. Mem. Nat. Forest Products Assn. (bd. dirs.), Western Wood Product Assn., Am. Wood Council. Served with USN, 1943-46. Office: Potlach Corp One Maritime Plaza PO Box 3591 San Francisco CA 94119 *

STEELE, TIMOTHY DOAK, water resources company executive, hydrologist; b. Muncie, Ind., Apr. 12, 1941; s. A. Logan and Joan P. (Doak) S.; m. Katherine Kohler, June 19, 1965; children: Tolan Doak, Karina Kohler. AB magna cum laude, Wabash Coll., 1963; MS, Stanford U., 1965, PhD in Hydrology, 1968; cert. in acctg., USDA Grad. Sch., 1968. Research hydrologist U.S. Geol. Survey, Menlo Park, Calif., 1966-68; staff research hydrologist U.S. Geol. Survey, Reston, Va. and Washington, 1968-75; project chief, hydrologist U.S. Geol. Survey, Lakewood, Colo., 1975-80; chief water quality group Woodward-Clyde Cons., Denver, 1980-83; water resources mgr. In-Situ, Inc., Lakewood, 1983—; tech. advisor water quality U.S. AID, Lahore, Pakistan, 1972; affiliate faculty mem. Colo. State U. Dept. Civil Engrs., 1981—. Contbr. articles to profl. publs., chpts. to books. Treas., bd. dirs. Colts Neck Cluster Assn., Reston, Va., 1973-75; singer Evergreen (Colo.) Chorale, 1975—; leader Boy Scouts Am., Evergreen, 1978—. Wabash Coll. honor scholar, 1959-63, scholar Fulbright-Hays, 1963-64, USPHS, 1965-66; research fellow Alexander von Humboldt Stiftung, 1979. Mem. Am. Geophys. Union (life, sec. 1978-80, water quality com. 1972-80), Internat. Assn. Hydrol. Scis. (nat. corr.), Internat. Water Resources Assn., Am. Chem. Soc., Colo. Ground Water Assn. Republican. Avocations: travel, stamp and coin collecting, tennis, racquetball, hiking. Home: 28888 Cedar Circle Evergreen CO 80439 Office: In-Situ Inc 7401 W Mansfield Ave #114 Lakewood CO 80235

STEELE, WILLIAM KENNETH, geology educator; b. Ft. Wayne, Ind., Nov. 2, 1942; s. William Kenneth and Jacquetta Capitola (Clukey) S.; m. Lindell Marie Bergman, Aug. 21, 1965 (div. 1978); 1 child, Steven W.; m. Carol Ilene Lewis, Feb. 15, 1985. BS in Physics, Case Inst. Tech., 1965; PhD in Geology, Case Western Res. U., 1970. Asst. prof. Eastern Wash. U., Cheney, 1970-77, assoc. prof., 1977-82, prof. geology, 1982—. Contbr. articles to sci. jours. NSF grantee, 1974, 80. Mem. AAAS, Am. Geophys. Union, N.W. Sci. Assn., Sierra Club (chmn. Spokane chpt. 1974), Wilderness Soc., Sigma Xi, Tau Beta Pi. Avocations: hiking, horticulture, violin. Home: Rt 1 Box 146 Spangle WA 99031 Office: Eastern Wash U Dept Geology Cheney WA 99004

STEELMAN-BRAGATO, SUSAN JEAN, public relations executive; b. Los Angeles, Aug. 25, 1957; d. Claude and Leota (Chapman) S. B.A. in Journalism and Polit. Sci., Pepperdine U., 1980. Intern, Congl. Environ. Study Conf., Washington, 1978, White House Press Office, summer 1980; regional press coordinator Carter/Mondale Re-election Campaign, Washington, 1980; account exec. DJMC Advt., San Francisco, 1981; communications dir. Calif. Beef Council, Foster, City, 1981—. Leader 4-H Club; YMCA Youth and Govt. program advisor. Recipient Editorial Leadership award Pepperdine U., 1980, 2d place pub. relations program Nat. Agrl. Mktg. Assn.; named best all-around journalist, 1979. Mem. Soc. Profl. Journalists (Outstanding Journalism grad. 1980), Pub. Relations Soc. Am., Calif. Women for Agriculture (v.p.), Am. Women in Radio and TV. Club: Commonwealth of Calif. Editor-in-chief coll. newspaper: Pepperdine Univ. of the Graphic, 1980, coll. mags.: Oasis, 1979, Impressions, 1978. Home: 920 Walnut St San Carlos CA 94070 Office: Calif Beef Council 551 Foster City Blvd Foster City CA 94404

STEEN, JOHN GERALD, convention bureau administrator; b. North Adams, Mass., Aug. 10, 1936; s. James Ralph and Doris Ellen (Booth) S.; divorced; children: Kelly, Shawn. V.p. Hertz Corp., Burlingame, Calif., 1962-72; pres. Pacific Car Rental, Burlingame, Calif., 1972-74; exec. dir. San Mateo County Conv. and Vis. Bur., San Francisco, 1974—. Bd. dirs. Greater San Francisco Bay Area Vacation Council, Western Symphony, Mariners Island Assn. #1, Phoenix in the Hill, Hibernia Club of San Mateo County, Cow Palace; pres. adv. council Easter Seal Soc. of San Mateo County; mem. exec. com. San Mateo Performing Arts Ctr.; mem. exec. bd. Bay Area Super Bowl Task Force; mem. organizing com. Am. Sports, 1996. Mem. Calif. Assn. Meeting. Planners (pres.), No. Calif. Soc. Assn. Execs. (past pres.), Western Assn. Conv. and Vis. Burs. (past pres.), San Mateo County Conv. and Vis. Burs. (exec. dir.), Conquistadors de El Camino Real (exec. dir.), Confrerie De La Chaine Des Rotisseurs (vice conseiller gastronomique), Western Tourism Industry Assn., Sacramento Soc. Assn. Execs., Am. Soc. Assn. Execs., Hotel Sales Mgrs. Assn., U.S. Robotics Soc., Assn. Travel Mktg. Execs., Soc. for Advancement of Travel for the Handicapped, Calif. Travel Industry Assn., Calif. Assn. C. of C. Execs., Nat. Tour Assn., So. Calif. Soc. Assn. Execs., Golden Gate U. Adv. Com., Nat. Assn. Exhibit Mgrs., Wash. Legal Found., Can. Coll. Adv. Com., Internat. Assn. Conv. Vis. Burs. Republican. Roman Catholic. Lodge: Rotary. Office: San Mateo County Conv & Visitors Bur 601 Gateway Blvd South San Mateo CA 94080

STEENSMA, ROBERT CHARLES, English language educator; b. Sioux Falls, S.D., Nov. 24, 1930; s. Anton Charles and Martha (Johnson) S.; m. Sharon Hogge, Sept. 5, 1964 (div. 1985); children: Craig, Michael, Laura, Kathryn, Rebecca. B.A., Augustana Coll., Sioux Falls, 1952; M.A., U. S.D., 1955; Ph.D., U. Ky., 1961. Instr. English Augustana Coll., 1955-57; asst. prof. U. S.D., 1959-62; asst. prof., then asso. prof. Utah State U., Logan, 1962-66; mem. faculty U. Utah, 1966—, prof. English, 1971—; Fulbright lectr., Finland, 1972-73. Author: Sir William Temple, 1970, Dr. John Arbuthnot, 1979; Editor: On The Original and Nature of Government (Sir William Temple), 1965; Contbr. articles to profl. jours. Served to capt. USNR, 1948-83. Mem. Rocky Mountain MLA, U.S. Naval Inst., Am. Soc. 18th Century Studies., MLA. Republican. Lutheran. Office: Dept English Univ Utah Salt Lake City UT 84112

STEEVES, SHERRI LEE, speech pathologist; b. Chgo., Mar. 22, 1960; d. Jack David and Donna Eve (Berquist) S.; m. Jon Conrad Zdechlik, June 25, 1983. BA, U. Colo., 1982; MS, U. Vt., 1983. Cert. clin. competence speech pathology. Speech and lang. pathologist Montpelier (Vt.) Pub. Schs., 1984, Mountain Bd. Coop. Services, Leadville, Colo., 1984—. Vol. advs. for victims of assault, Frisco, Colo., 1986. Mem. Am. Speech, Lang. and Hearing Assn., Colo. Speech and Hearing Assn. Office: Mountain Bd Coop Services 115 W 10th St Leadville CO 80461

STEFAN, ROSS, artist; b. Milw., June 13, 1934; s. Edward and Ivah (Johnson) S.; m. Anne Silverson, July 22, 1955; children—Jon, Gary. Student U. Ariz.-Tucson, 1953-55. One man shows: Rosequist Galleries, Tucson, 1959—, Panhandle Plains Hist. Mus., Canyon, Tex., 1967, Bryan-Scott Galleries, Colorado Springs, Colo., 1969—, Grand Central Galleries, N.Y.C., 1972; group shows include Mountain Oyster Club, Tucson, 1973—, Beijing Exhbn. Ctr., Peoples Republic of China, 1981; represented in permanent collections: Ariz. Bank, Garden of Gods Club, Colorado Srings. Author: John K. Goodman: An Impressionistic Painter of the Contemporary Southwest, 1977, 2d edit., 1984. Recipient Artist of Yr. award Tucson Festival Soc., 1978; Wrangler award Best Western Art Book-Nat. Cowboy Hall of Fame, 1978; Readers Digest Front Cover, 1978. Mem. John F. and Anna Lee Stacey Found (mem. awards com. 1982). Club: Mountain Oyster (Tucson). Office: Rosequist Galleries 39th Ann Tucson Exhibition 1987 1615 E Fort Lowell Rd Tucson AZ 85719 Home: Tucson AZ and Del Mar CA 85718

STEFFAN, WALLACE A., entomologist, educator, museum director; b. St. Paul, Aug. 10, 1934; m. Sylvia Behler, July 16, 1966; 1 child, Sharon. B.S., U. Calif.-Berkeley, 1961, Ph.D., 1965. Entomologist dept. entomology Bishop Mus., Honolulu, 1964-85, head diptera sect., 1966-85, asst. chmn., 1979-85; dir. Idaho Mus. Natural History, Idaho State U., Pocatello, 1985—; mem. grad. affiliate faculty dept. entomology U. Hawaii, 1969-85; liaison officer Bishop Mus., Mus. Computer Network, 1980-85; reviewer NSF, 1976—; mem. internat. editorial adv. com. World Diptera Catalog, Systematic Entomology Lab., U.S. Dept. Agr., 1983—; bd. dirs. Idaho State U. Fed. Credit Union, 1986—; mem. Ft. Hall Replica Commn., 1986—. Acting editor Jour. Med. Entomology, 1966; assoc. editor Pacific Insects, 1980-85. Judge Hawaii State Sci. and Engring. Fair, 1966-85, chief judge sr. display div., 1982, 83, 84; bd. dirs. Ahuimanu Homeowners' Assn., 1972; v.p. Ahuimanu P.T.A., 1977; mem. vestry St. Christophers Episcopal Ch., 1974-76; bd. dirs. Kamehameha Fed. Credit Union, 1975-77, chmn., mem. supervisory com., 1980-84. Served with USAF, 1954-57. Grantee NIH, 1962, 63, 67-74, 76-81, 83-85. U.S. Army Med. Research and Devel. Command, 1964-67, 73-74, NSF, 1968-76, 83-89, City and County of Honolulu, 1977, U.S. Dept. Interior, 1980, 81. Mem. Entomol. Soc. Am. (mem. standing com. on systematics resources 1983-87, mem. awards canvassing com. Pacific br. 1982), Am. Mosquito Control Assn., Pacific Coast Entomol. Soc., Soc. Systematic Zoology, Hawaiian Entomol. Soc. (pres. 1974, chmn. coms. 1966-85, editor procs. 1966), Hawaiian Acad. Scis. (councillor 1976-78), Entomol. Soc. Wash., Sigma Xi. Office: Idaho Mus Nat History Idaho St U Campus Box 8096 Pocatello ID 83209

STEFFEN, THOMAS LEE, state supreme court justice; b. Tremonton, Utah, July 9, 1930; s. Conrad Richard and Jewel (McGuire) S.; m. Lavona Ericksen, Mar. 20, 1953; children—Elizabeth, Catherine, Conrad, John, Jennifer. Student, U. So. Calif., 1955-56; B.S., U. Utah, 1957; J.D. with honors, George Washington U., 1964. Bar: Nev., U.S. Dist. Ct. Nev. 1965, U.S. Tax Ct. 1966, U.S. Ct. Appeals 1967, U.S. Supreme Ct. 1977. Contracts negotiator U.S. Bur. Naval Weapons, Washington, 1961-64; private practice Las Vegas, 1965-82; justice Supreme Ct. Nev., Carson City, 1982—; chmn. Nev. State-Fed. Jud. Council, 1986—. Mem. editorial staff George Washington U. Law Rev., 1963-64; contbr. articles to legal jours. Bd. dirs. So. Nev. chpt. NCCJ, 1974-75; mem. exec. bd. Boulder Dam Area council Boy Scouts Am., 1979-83; chmn. Nev. State-Fed. Jud. Council, 1986—; bd. visitors Brigham Young U., 1985—. Recipient merit citation Utah State U., 1983. Mem. Nev. Bar Assn. (former chmn. So. Nev. med.-legal screening panel), Nev. Trial Lawyers Assn. (former dir.). Republican. Mem. Ch. of Jesus Christ of Latter-day Saints. Avocations: reading, spectator sports. Office: Supreme Ct of Nev Capitol Complex Carson City NV 89710

STEFFEY, CYNTHIA ANN, social worker; b. Columbus, Nebr., July 13, 1954; d. Andrew William and Annabelle Lee (Schmidt) Erickson; m. Micheal Claude Steffey, Nov. 1, 1977; 1 child, Jason Micheal. BA in Social Welfare, U. Nebr., Lincoln, 1976; MSW, U. Nebr., Omaha, 1982. Cert. social worker. Sgt. U.S. Army, 1976-80; commd. 1st lt. USAF, 1982, advanced through grades to capt., 1984; clin. social worker USAF, Moody AFB, Ga., 1982-84, Lowry AFB, Colo., 1984—. Asst. coach YMCA soccer team, Aurora, Colo., 1985; vol. Spl. Olympics, Lowry AFB, 1986, 87. Mem. Nat. Assn. Social Workers, Air Force Assn. Republican. Lutheran. Club: Officer's (Lowry AFB). Avocations: aerobics, jogging, reading. Home: 1762 S Laredo St Aurora CO 80017 Office: USAF 3320th CRS Lowry AFB CO 80230-5000

STEFFEY, EUGENE PAUL, veterinary medicine educator; b. Reading, Pa., Oct. 27, 1942; s. Paul E. and Mary M. (Balthaser) S.; m. Marcia Ann Matzelle, June 10, 1967; children: Michele A., Bret E., Michael R., Brian T. Student, Muhlenberge Coll., 1960-63; D in Vet. Medicine, U. Pa., 1967; PhD, U. Calif., Davis, 1973. Diplomate Am. Coll. Vet. Anesthesiologists (pres. 1980). Research fellow U. Calif., San Francisco, 1973; asst. prof. U. Calif., Davis, 1974-77, assoc. prof., 1977-80, prof. vet. medicine, 1980—, also chmn. dept. vet. surgery; mem. scientific reviewers Am. Jour. Vet. Research, Schaumburg, Ill., 1984—. Contbr. numerous articles to profl. jours. NIH fellow, 1972-73, anesthesiology research fellow U. Calif. Med. Ctr., 1973. Mem. AAAS, AVMA, Am. Coll. Vet. Anesthesiologists, Am. Physiol. Soc., Am. Soc. Pharmacology Exptl. Therapeutics, Am. Soc. Anesthesiologists, Assn. Vet. Anaesthitists, Calif. Soc. Anesthesiologists, Comparative Respiratory Soc., Internat. Anesthesia Research Soc., Pa. Vet. Med. Assn., Sacramento Valley Vet. Med. Assn., Soc. Edn. Anesthesia, Sigma Xi, Phi Zeta. Office: U Calif Sch Vet Medicine Davis CA 95616

STEGALL, BENJAMIN IRVING, JR., financial consultant; b. Griffin, Ga., Oct. 1, 1933; s. Benjamin Irving and Hilda (Span) S.; m. Doris Ilene Schoenberg, Mar. 4, 1962; children—Wendy Lauren, Sheri Dawn. B.Indsl. Engring., Ga. Inst. Tech., 1954; postgrad. UCLA, 1958-61. Registered rep. N.Y. Stock Exchange, 1961. Engr., Douglas Aircraft, Santa Monica, Calif., 1956-60; asst. v.p., sr. account exec. Merrill Lynch Pierce Fenner & Smith, Inc., Los Angeles, Hollywood and Santa Monica, Calif., 1960—. Nation chief Indian Princess program Santa Monica YMCA, 1981-82; trustee Beth Sholom Temple, 1979-81. Served to 1st lt. U.S. Army, 1954-56. Jewish. Clubs: Wilshire Western Optimist (sec. treas. 1963-66, pres. 1966-67), Crescent Bay Toastmasters (pres. 1965-66), Red Ribbon Squares (pres. 1980-81), (Santa Monica), Masons, Shriners. Home: 424 Euclid St Santa Monica CA 90402 Office: Merril Lynch Pierce et al 1299 Ocean Ave Santa Monica CA 90401

STEHSEL, MELVIN LOUIS, biology educator; b. Long Beach, Oct. 3, 1924; s. Louis Joseph Stehsel and Ida Batchelder; m. Beatrice Henrietta Solli, Nov. 30, 1957; children: Dené, Craig. BS in Chemistry, U. Calif., Berkeley, 1945, MS in Plant Physiology, 1947, PhD in Plant Physiology, 1950. Research fellow Calif. Inst. Tech., Pasadena, Calif., 1948-51; chemist Mobil Oil, Los Angeles, 1951-56; sr. engr. Aerojet, Azusa, Calif., 1956-65; prof. biology Pasadena City Coll., 1965—; cons. plant tissue culture LA County Arboretum, Arcadia, Calif., 1975—. Editor: (newsletter) Foothill's Rare Fruit Growers. Rockefellow scholar U. Chgo., 1942; French Govt. fellow, 1951. Mem. AAAS, Am. Chem. Soc., Am. Botanical Soc., Am. Orchid Soc. Republican. Presbyterian. Avocations: orchid growing, hang gliding, piano studies. Home: 1049 Rancho Rd Arcadia CA 91006 Office: Pasadena City Coll 1570 E Colo Blvd Pasadena CA 91106

STEIGER, FRANCES PASCAL, author; b. Columbus, Ohio, Jan. 20, 1938; d. Joseph James Paschal and Velma Louise (Wiggins) Walker; m. Brad E. Steiger, July 7, 1977; children: Christopher, Tia, Michael-Anthony, Regina. Cert. in bus., Sacred Heart Sch. Bus., 1954; student, Ohio State U., 1953-57, Union Coll., 1973. Legal sec. Law Offices Allen & Maxson, Columbus, 1954-55; mgr. personnel Dept. Pub. Welfare, Columbus, 1957-62; gen. mgr., legal sec. Office Dist. Atty., Schnectady, N.Y., 1971-77; free lance writer Scottsdale, Ariz., 1977—; counselor, instr. Columbus, Schnectady, 1963-77. Author: The Star People, 1981, Reflections from Angel's Eye, 1982, The Love Force, 1985, The Transformation: Humankind's Next Evolutionary Step, 1986. Pres. Columbus Sch. Dist. PTA, 1965-66. Mem. NOW, The Star People Found. (founder, pres. 1984—), People for Ethical Treatment Animals, Peace Links, ACLU. Democrat. Avocations: research, science, mysticism. Office: Starbirth 12629 N Tatum Blvd #445 Phoenix AZ 85032

STEIGER, IRWIN HARVEY, obstetrician gynecologist; b. N.Y.C., Aug. 15, 1940; s. Sam and Augusta (Zuckerman) S.; m. Jan Steiger, June 4, 1979; children: Jason, Joshua. BS, L.I. U., 1960; MD, N.Y. Med. Coll., 1965. Cert. Am. Bd. Ob-Gyn. Resident Cedars-Sinai Med. Ctr., Los Angeles, 1969-71, chief resident, 1971-72; practice medicine specializing in ob-gyn Santa Monica, Calif., 1972-75, Los Angeles, 1975—. Columnist Woman's Corner, 1981-84. Served to lt. comdr. USN, 1967-69, Vietnam. Recipient Physician Recognition award AMA, 1986. Mem. Am. Coll. Ob-Gyn. Avocations: photography, mountain climbing. Office: 11980 San Vicente Blvd #618 Los Angeles CA 90049

STEIGHNER, RICHARD LEE, audiologist; b. Butler, Pa., Jan. 30, 1957; s. Harold John and Beatric (Leona) S.; m. Karen Ann Huber, Jan. 12, 1980; children: Richard Lawrence, Megan Elizabeth. BS, Ind. (Pa.) U., 1979; MA, U. Colo., 1981. Cert. clin. competence; lic. hearing aid dispenser. Audiologist Denver EAR Assn., 1981-83, Porter Meml. Hosp., Denver, 1983-85; terr. mgr. Phonic EAR Inc., Denver, 1985—; cons. Bill English & Assocs., Denver. Recipient Judge Schumaker award Butler Rotary, 1976. Mem. Colo. Speech and Hearing Assn. (com. mem. 1981—), Am. Speech-Lang.-Hearing Assn., Colo. Speech-Lang.-Hearing Assn., Wyo. Speech-Language-Hearing Assn., Mont. Speech-Lang.-Hearing Assn., Utah Speech-Lang.-Hearing Assn. Roman Catholic. Lodge: Sertoma. Avocations: golf, fly fishing, tennis, gardening. Home: 3240 S Newland Denver CO 80227 Office: Phonic EAR Inc PO Box 36356 Denver CO 80236

STEIN, ARTHUR OSCAR, physician; b. Bklyn., Apr. 3, 1932; s. Irving I. and Sadie (Brander) S.; A.B., Harvard U., 1953; M.D., Tufts U., 1957; postgrad. U. Chgo., 1963-66; m. Judith Lenore Hurwitz, Aug. 27, 1955; children—Susan, Jeffrey, Benjamin. Intern U. Chgo. Hosps., 1957-58, resident, 1958-59; resident N.Y. Hosp.-Cornell U. Med. Center, 1959-61; practice medicine specializing in pediatrics, 1963—; instr. pediatrics U. Chgo., 1963-66, asst. prof. pediatrics, 1966-70; mem. Healthguard Med. Group, San Jose, Calif., 1970-72; mem. Permanente Med. Group, San Jose, 1972—; asst. chief pediatrics Santa Teresa Med. Center, 1979-87; clin. instr. Santa Clara Valley Med. Center, Stanford U., 1970-72. Served to capt., M.C., AUS, 1961-63. USPHS Postdoctoral fellow, 1963-66. Fellow Am. Acad. Pediatrics. Jewish (v.p. congregation 1969-70, pres. 1972-73). Clubs: Light and Shadow Camera (pres. 1978-80) (San Jose); Central Coast Counties Camera (v.p. 1980-81, pres. 1981-82), Santa Clara Camera. Co-discoverer (with Glyn Dawson) genetic disease Lactosylceramidosis, 1969. Home: 956 Redmond Ave San Jose CA 95120 Office: Kaiser/Permanente Med Group 260 Internat Circle Jose CA 95119

STEIN, FREDRICK MICHAEL, academic dean, chemistry educator; b. Boston, Mar. 15, 1942; s. Sigmund Magnus and Blanche (Tarlin) S.; m. Claudia Schalm, Jan. 30, 1965; children: Mishele, Lisa. BA in Chemistry, U. Colo., 1964; PhD in Chem. Physics, Ind. U., 1971. With Peace Corps, 1965-67; prof. chemistry Western State Coll., Gunnison, Colo., 1971-81, 83-85, dean, 1985—; prof. Amherst (Mass.) Coll., 1981-83. Author jour. Chem. Physics, 1983, Am. Jour. Physics, 1985. Mem. Am. Chem. Soc., Am. Phys. Soc., Philosophy of Sci. Assn., Sigma Xi. Avocations: history and philosophy of science, skiing, sailing. Office: Western State Coll Gunnison CO 81230

STEIN, IRV, mechanical engineer; b. The Bronx, N.Y., Dec. 20, 1926; s. Harry and Esther (Hornstein) S.; m. Bernice Ramer, Mar. 5, 1947 (div. 1977); children: Stephen Robert, Barbara Ann. BME, CCNY, 1957. Designer AMF Inc., Stamford, Conn., 1955-56; design engr. Aerojet Gen. Corp. subs. General Tire & Rubber Co., Azusa, Calif., 1956-58; program mgr. RCA, Princeton, N.J., 1958-76; tech. mgr. Jet Propulsion Lab., Pasadena, Calif., 1976—. Served with U.S. Army, 1945-46. Assoc. fellow AIAA. Republican. Jewish. Lodge: Masons. Avocations: motorcycling, photography, hiking. Home: 1236 N Columbus Ave #42 Glendale CA 91202 Office: Jet Propulsion Lab 4800 Oak Grove Rd Pasadena CA 91109

STEIN, MARJORIE GAIL, sales and marketing professional; b. Oakland, Calif., Mar. 18, 1960; d. Robert Edward and Constance Leigh (Rogers) S. BA in Communications, Calif. State U., 1984. Asst. ops. mgr. The Hdqrs. Co., Walnut Creek, Calif., 1983-84, sales rep., 1984, sr. sales rep., 1985, dir. sales and mktg., 1985—. Mem. Walnut Creek C. of C., Nat. Assn. Female Execs., Am. Mgmt. Assn. Democrat. Avocations: tennis, skiing, travel, classical music, photography. Office: The Hdqrs Co 1990 N California Blvd Suite 830 Walnut Creek CA 94596

STEIN, STEPHEN, lawyer; b. Bklyn., Oct. 22, 1943; s. Alex and Rachel (Osbrach) S.; m. Susan Helane Cooper, Dec. 23, 1965; children: Sharyn Beth, David Marc. BA, NYU, 1964; JD, Bklyn. Law Sch., 1967. Bar: N.Y. 1967, U.S. Ct. Appeals (3d cir.) 1973, Nev. 1974, U.S. Dist. Ct. Nev. 1974, U.S. Ct. Appeals (9th cir.) 1974, U.S. Supreme Ct. 1974, U.S. Ct. Appeals (5th cir.) 1975, U.S. Ct. Appeals (4th cir.) 1976, U.S. Ct. Appeals (10th cir.) 1979, U.S. Ct. Appeals (8th and 11th cirs.) 1982. Spl. atty. U.S. Dept. Justice, Washington, 1971-74; ptnr. Goodman, Stein & Quintana, Las Vegas, Nev., 1974—. Pres. Temple Beth Am, Las Vegas, 1985—. Served to lt. commdr. USN, 1967-71. Mem. Nev. Trial Lawyers Assn. (bd. dirs. 1985—). Republican. Jewish. Office: Goodman Stein & Quintana 520 S 4th St Las Vegas NV 89101

STEINBACH, CHARLES ALBERT, management specialist; b. Elmhurst, Ill., Mar. 27, 1951; s. Albert F. and Barbara Jean (Stretch) S.; m. Debra Seeger, Apr. 19, 1981; children: Andrew Jonathan, Rachel Marie. BSE, Concordia Coll., 1973; M in Human Resource Devel., Univ. Assocs., San Diego, 1985. Cert. tchr. grade and high sch. Tchr. jr. high St. Matthew Sch., St. Louis, 1973-75; tchr. English Luth. Lang. Inst., Tokyo, 1975-78; program dir. Arrowhead Luth. Camp, Lake Arrowhead, Calif., 1978-79; fedn. adminstr. Aid Assn. for Luths., Appleton, Wis., 1979-82, program devel. specialist, 1982-84, mgmt. devel. specialist, 1985-86, mgr. mgmt. devel., 1986—. Bd. dirs. Am.-Indo-Chinese Friendship Soc., Appleton, 1984-85, YMCA Strategic Planning Com., 1985-86, YMCA, Appleton, 1987; bd. dirs. local chpt. Bread for the World; sec. bd. dirs. Ptnrs. in Mission, 1974-75. Avocations: cross country skiing, hiking. Home: 2605 N Appleton Appleton WI 54911 Office: Aid Assn for Luths 4321 N Ballard Appleton WI 54919

STEINBECK, JOHN WITHERUP, II, educational administrator; b. St. Louis, Feb. 14, 1931; s. John William and Fayne Harriet (Witherup) S.; B.A. magna cum laude, Westminster (Mo.) Coll., 1952; postgrad. law U. Mich., Ann Arbor, 1952-53; M.A., Ind. U., 1955, postgrad., 1960-61; Ph.D., La Jolla U., 1983; m. Jeanette Palmer Hubbard, June 16, 1962; children—Jeffrey Alan, John Witherup, Sarah Jane Bunker. Tchr., Judson Sch., Scottsdale, Ariz., 1954-55; research tchr., counselor Imperial Valley Coll., El Centro, Calif., 1955-56; tchr., chmn. dept. social studies Citrus Coll.; tchr. Azusa (Calif.) High Sch., 1957-60; master tchr. Morton Jr. Coll., Cicero, Ill., 1961-63; instr. Ind. U., Bloomington, 1960-61; founder, owner, dir., headmaster The Villa Sch., Casa Grande, Ariz., 1964—. Pres., The Villa Sch. Found. Edn., Inc., 1973—. Mem. S.A.R., Ariz., So. Ariz. assns. ind. acad. schs., English Speaking Union, Phi Gamma Delta, Phi Alpha Theta. Episcopalian. Mason. Home: 3640 N Toltec Rd Toltec AZ 85231 Office: The Villa-Oasis Sch PO Box 1218 Casa Grande AZ 85222

STEINBERG, CLAIRE JAMES, photographer; b. Newport News, Va., Aug. 15, 1942; d. Michael Ronald and Bella Ruth (Herbert) Frisch; m. John Edward Steinberg, Mar. 26, 1967; 1 child Jeremy Adam. BA, UCLA, 1965. cert. high sch.; cert. jr. coll. tchr., Calif. With art and photography dept. Palisades High Sch., Los Angeles, Calif., 1965-69; asst. to Milton Greene N.Y.C., 1969-70; picture editor Popular Photography mag., N.Y.C., 1970-72; profl. photographer People mag., Time mag., Rolling Stone mag., 1972—; mus. curator 1st Exhibition Craft and Folk Art Mus., Los Angeles, 1975; interior designer, photography tchr. Los Angeles, 1975—; photographer Los Angeles Bar Assn., 1978. One woman shows include Craft Folk Art Mus., 1975; exhibited photographs at Egg and Eye Gallery, San Francisco Art Inst., 1973, Paris Mus. Pasadena (Calif.) City Coll., Sunset Ctr., 1973. Organizer Children's Exhbn. at Natural History Mus. Los Angeles County, 1986-87. Mem. Art Mus. Council, Arts Council Barndall Museum. Democrat. Jewish. Avocations: tennis, travel, reading, cooking, design activities. Home and Office: 11731 Crescenda St Los Angeles CA 90049

STEINBERG, DAVE SOLOMON, mechanical engineer; b. Chgo., Oct. 6, 1923; s. Harry P. and Tillie (Solomon) S.; m. Annette H. Shapiro, June 29, 1958; children: Corie Beth, Stacie Susan. BSME, Ill. Inst. Tech., 1948. Registered profl. engr., N.Y., N.J., Mich. Pres. Steinberg & Assocs., N.Y.,

N.J., 1950—, Westlake Village, Calif., 1979—; mgr. mech. engring. Singer Kearfott, Wayne, N.J., 1969-79, Litton, Woodland Hills, Calif., 1979—; lectr. in field, 1970—; vis. prof. U. Wis., Milw., 1975-84. Author: Vibration Analysis for Electronic Equipment, 1973, Cooling Techniques for Electronic Equipment, 1980; also articles to profl. jours.; inventor lift truck. Served to capt. USAAF, 1942-45. Fellow Inst. Environ. Sci. (ednl. chmn. 1980, Dr. Vigness award 1985). Jewish. Lodge: B'nai B'rith. Avocations: model airplanes, jogging, weight lifting. Home: 3410 Ridgeford Dr Westlake Village CA 91361 Office: Litton GCS 5500 Conoga Ave Woodland Hills CA 91367

STEINBERG, GUNTHER, manufacturing executive; b. Cologne, Fed. Republic Germany, Apr. 14, 1924; s. Herbert H. and Hetty (Kohsen) S.; m. Beatrice Rose Steinberg, Aug. 20, 1949; children: Paul G., Julia C. BS, UCLA, 1948, MS, 1950, PhD, 1956. Chemist Shell Oil Research Co., Martinez, Calif., 1956-60, Shell Devel. Co., Everyville, Calif., 1960-64; sr. chemist Stanford U. Research Inst., Menlo Park, Calif., 1964-67; sr. mgr. chem. research Memorex Corp., Santa Clara, Calif., 1967-77; pres., cons. Steinberg Assocs., Portola Valley, Calif., 1977—. Contbr. articles to profl. jours. Served with U.S. Army, 1943-45, ETO. Mem. Magnetics Soc. IEEE, Am. Chem. Soc., N.Am. Thermal Analysis Soc. Home and Office: Steinberg Assocs 95 Lerida Ct Portola Valley CA 94025

STEINBERG, HOWARD, chemical company executive; b. Chgo., Aug. 23, 1926; s. Leo and Hattie (Seskind) S.; m. Eve Taubman, Feb. 10, 1946; children—Gary, Erik, Lisa. B.S., U. Ill., 1948; PhD, UCLA, 1951. AEC postdoctoral fellow MIT, 1951-52; research chemist Aerojet Gen. Corp., Azusa, Calif., 1952; research asso. UCLA, 1952-53; collaborator U.S. Dept. Agr., Pasadena, Calif., 1953-54; with U.S. Borax Research Corp., Anaheim, Calif., 1954—; dir. chem. research U.S. Borax Research Corp., 1961-63, v.p., 1963-69, pres., 1969—; v.p. U.S. Borax & Chem. Corp., Los Angeles, 1969—; dir. U.S. Borax & Chem. Corp., 1973—; mem. sci. and engring. adv. council Calif. State U., Fullerton, 1964—. Author: Organoboron Chemistry, Vol. 1, 1964, Vol. 2, 1966; also articles.; Co-editor: Progress in Boron Chemistry, Vol. 1, 1964, Vol. 2, 1970, Vol. 3, 1970. Served with USAAF, 1945. Mem. Am. Chem. Soc., Soc. Chem. Industry, Indsl. Research Inst., AIME, Brit. Chem. Soc., Sigma Xi, Pi Mu Epsilon, Phi Lambda Upsilon. Patentee in field. Home: 1401 Miramar Dr Fullerton CA 92631 Office: US Borax and Chem Corp 3075 Wilshire Blvd Los Angeles CA 90010

STEINBERG, JEFFREY MARK, physician, researcher; b. Phila., Oct. 7, 1953. BS, UCLA, 1973; MD, U. Guadalajara, Mex., 1977; MS, U. Saskatchewan, Can., 1978. Diplomate Am. Bd. Ob-Gyn, Am. Bd. Med. Reproductive Endocrinology. Dir. InVitro Fertilization program Northridge (Calif.) Hosp. Med. Ctr., 1981-83; fellow reproductive endocrinology U. Calif.-San Diego, La Jolla, 1984-86; dir. fertility InVitro Fertilization program Glendale (Calif.) Adventist Med. Ctr., 1986—; med. dir. Beverly Hills (Calif.) Fertiltiy Inst., 1986—. Contbr. articles to profl. jours. NIH grantee, 1986. Fellow Am. Coll. Obstetricians and Gynelcologists; mem. Am. Fertility Soc., Am. Assn. Gynecologic Lapnrascopists, Pacific Coast Fertility Soc. Avocations: music, recording and sound engring. Office: Glendale Adventist Med Ctr 16260 Ventura Blvd Suite 820 Encino CA 91436

STEINBERG, JOAN EMILY, educator; b. San Francisco, Dec. 9, 1932; d. John Emil and Kathleen Helen (Montgomery) S.; B.A., U. Calif.-Berkeley, 1954; Ed.D., U. San Francisco, 1981. Tchr., Vallejo (Calif.) Unified Sch. Dist., 1959-61, San Francisco Unified Sch. Dist., 1961—, tchr. life and phys. sci. jr. high sch., 1978-85, sci. cons., 1985—. Fulbright scholar U. Sydney (Australia), 1955-56. Mem. Audubon Soc., Nat. Wildlife Fedn., Oceanic Soc., Nature Conservancy, Astron. Soc. Pacific, Am. Fedn. Tchrs., AAAS, Calif. Acad. Scis., Calif. Malacozool. Soc., Nat. Sci. Tchrs. Assn., Elem. Sch. Sci. Assn. (sec. 1984-85, pres. 1986-87), Calif. Sci. Tchrs. Assn., Internat. Reading Assn., Sigma Xi. Democrat. Contbr. articles to profl. jours. Home: 424 43d Ave San Francisco CA 94121 Office: San Francisco Unified Sch Dist San Francisco CA 94102

STEINBERG, RICHARD DAVID, psychologist, educator; b. Chgo., Apr. 22, 1947; s. Martin and Betty (Soglin) S. B.A. with honors in Psychology, U. Calif.-Berkeley, 1968; M.A. in Clin. Psychology, York U., Toronto, Ont., Can., 1970, Ph.D. in Clin. Psychology, 1975. Lic. psychologist, Calif., B.C. Instr., U. Toronto, 1974; clin. psychologist dept. psychiatry Nanaimo (Can.) Regional Hosp., 1975-79; vis. faculty mem. U. B.C., Vancouver, Can., 1977; lectr. U. Victoria (B.C.), 1977; pvt. practice, Santa Barbara, Calif., 1979—; staff psychologist Camarillo (Calif.) State Hosp., 1979-85; psychol. cons. Sansum Med. Clinic, Santa Barbara, 1981—; instr. U. Calif. Extension, Santa Barbara, 1981—. Can. Council doctoral fellow, 1971-73. Mem. Santa Barbara Assn. Clin. Psychologists (pres. 1982), Am. Psychol. Assn., Calif. State Psychol. Assn., Can. Psychol. Assn. B.C. Psychol. Assn., Western Psychol. Assn., Am. Personnel and Guidance Assn., Calif. Neuropsychology Soc., Assn. for Advancement Psychology. Democrat. Jewish. Home: 5058 Ella Ln Santa Barbara CA 93111 Office: Sansum Med Clinic Pueblo at Castillo Sts Santa Barbara CA 93102

STEINBERG, WARREN LINNINGTON, school principal; b. N.Y.C., Jan. 20, 1924; s. John M. and Gertrude (Vogel) S.; student U. So. Calif., 1943-44, U. Calif. at Los Angeles, 1942-43, 46-47, B.A., 1949, M.Ed., 1951, Ed.D., 1962; m. Beatrice Ruth Blass, June 29, 1947; children—Leigh William, James Robert, Donald Kenneth. Tchr., counselor, coach Jordan High Sch., Watts, Los Angeles, 1951-57; tchr. athletic coordinator Hamilton High Sch., Los Angeles, 1957-62; boys' vice prin. Univ. High Sch., Los Angeles, 1962-67, Crenshaw Hig Sch., Los Angeles, 1967-68; cons. Center for Planned Change, Los Angeles City Sch., 1968-69; instr. edn. UCLA, 1965-71; boys' vice prin. LeConte Jr. High Sch., Los Angeles, 1969-71, sch. prin., 1971-77; adminstrv. cons. integration, 1977-81; prin. Gage Jr. High Sch., 1982-83, Fairfax High Sch., 1983—. Pres. Athletic Coordinators Assn., Los Angeles City Schs., 1959-60; v.p. P-3 Enterprises, Inc., Port Washington, N.Y., 1967-77, Century City (Calif.) Enterprises, 1966—. Vice pres. B'nai B'rith Anti-Defamation League, 1968-70; mem. adv. com. Los Angeles City Commn. on Human Relations, 1966-71, 72—, commr., 1976—, also chmn. edn. com.; pres. Los Angeles City Human Relations Commn., 1978—; mem. del. assembly Community Relations Conf. of So. Assembly, 1975—; mem. citizens' adv. com. for student integration Los Angeles Unified Sch. Dist., 1976-79; chmn. So. Calif. Drug Abuse Edn. Month com., 1970. Bd. dirs. DAWN, an anti-narcotics youth group. Served with USMCR, 1943-46. Recipient Beverly Hills B'nai B'rith Presdl. award, 1965; commended Los Angeles City Council, 1968. Mem. West Los Angeles Coordinating Council (chmn. case conf., human relations), Beverly-Fairfax C. of C. (bd. dirs. 1986—). Lodges: Lions (dir. 1960-62), Kiwanis. Contbr. articles on race relations, youth behavior to profl. jours. and newspapers. Home: 2737 Dunleer Pl Los Angeles CA 90064 Office: Fairfax High Sch 450 N Grand Ave Los Angeles CA 90054

STEINBOCK, JOHN T., bishop; b. Los Angeles, July 16, 1937. Student, Los Angeles Diocesan sems. Ordained priest Roman Cath. Ch., 1963. Aux. bishop Diocese of Orange, Calif., 1984-87; bishop Diocese of Santa Rosa, Calif., 1987—; titular bishop of Midila. Office: Diocese of Santa Rosa 547 B St PO Box 1297 Santa Rosa CA 95402 *

STEINBRECHER, JEAN ANN, intern architect; b. Two Rivers, Wis., June 7, 1948; d. William P. and Adele B. (Habeck) S. BS, U. Wis., Oshkosh, 1970; postgrad., U. Wis., Madison, 1970-72; MArch, U. Tex., 1985. Mgr. costume shop N.C. Sch. of Arts, Winston-Salem, 1972-74, Milw. Repertory Theatre, 1974-75; costume technician Brooks-Van Horn Costume Co., N.Y.C., 1975-76; costume designer Musical Theatre Assn., Santa Fe, 1978-79; owner, operator Fashion Fabrics/White Horse Gallery, Ruidoso, N.Mex., 1980-81; intern architect Barker-Bol and Assocs. Architects, Albuquerque, 1986, FMSBM Architects, Inc., Albuquerque, 1986—. Mem. AIA (assoc. dir. Albuquerque chpt. 1987—), Nat. Trust Hist. Preservation, Assn. Preservation Tech., The Albuquerque Conservation Assn., Tex. Ex-Student Assn., Phi Kappa Phi. Avocations: swimming, skiing, sewing, hiking, biking. Home: PO Box 647 Corrales NM 87048

STEINBRENNER, EUGENE CLARENCE, research forester; b. St. Paul, Sept. 3, 1921; s. Clarence Christopher and Sophia Francis (Lesch) S.; m. Erlyse E. Champine, Feb. 12, 1944; children—Peter, David, Joseph, Judy. B.S. with distinction, U. Minn. 1949; M.S., U. Wis., 1951; Ph.D., U. Wash., 1954. Project leader Forest Soils, Weyerhaeuser Co., Centralia, Wash., 1951-82, unit mgr. soil research, 1951-77, dir. soil survey program, 1977-82; cons. in forest soil and forest mgmt., Centralia, 1982—; affiliate prof. U. Wash., 1973-86. Mem. Centralia Planning Adv. Bd., 1982-83. Served with USAAF, 1942-45. Weyerhauser fellow, 1951-52; Bullard fellow, 1968-69, others. Fellow Am. Soc. Agronomy; Soil Sci. Soc. Am.; mem. Soc. Am. Foresters, Forest Sci. Council. Republican. Episcopalian. Club: Grange (master). Contbr. articles to profl. jours. Address: 3315 Tiger Ln Centralia WA 98531

STEINBRICHER, JERRY S., pathologist, physician; b. Glencoe, Minn., Aug. 5, 1947; s. Sam and Bernice Born S.; m. Mary Neumeier, June 18, 1971; children: Kristin, Scott. BS, U. Minn., 1968, MD, 1972. Diplomate Am. Bd. Pathology. Intern, then resident U. Colo. Health Sci. Ctr., Denver, 1972-76; pathologist St. Mary's Hosp., Grand Junction, Colo., 1976-79, Valley View Hosp., Glenwood Springs, Colo., 1979—, Aspen (Colo.) Valley Hosp., 1979—; cons. pathologist St. Vincent's Hosp., Leadville, Colo., 1979—, Cloggett Hosp., Rifle, Colo., 1979—. Served to capt. USAR, 1972-78. Fellow Coll. Am. Pathologists; mem. AMA, Am. Soc. Clin. Pathologists, Colo. Med. Soc. (polit. contact person 1985—), Phi Beta Kappa. Avocations: skiing, running, biking, hiking. Office: Lab Valley View Hosp PO Box 1970 Glenwood Springs CO 81601

STEINBROCK, KAREN J., marketing professional; b. Salina, Kans., Nov. 14, 1962; d. Richard Henry and Mary Alice (Fowler) S. Student, Ft. Hays (Kans.) State U., 1981-83; BS in Journalism, Pub. Relations, U. Nebr., 1986. Mem. staff advt. dept. Shopko, Omaha, 1984-86; mgr. advt. The Gateway newspaper U. Nebr., Omaha, 1985-86; mktg. asst. Network Solutions, Inc., Phoenix, 1986—; cons. Creatif Strategies, Phoenix, 1987—. Mem. Pub. Relations Soc. Am., Phoenix Communicating Arts Soc., Assn. Am. Advt. Fedn. (pub. relations high tech. sect.). Republican. Roman Catholic. Club: Ariz. Road Racers (Phoenix). Avocations: running, biking, bowling, softball. Home: 17435 N 7th St #2122 Phoenix AZ 85022

STEINER, BRUCE ALAN, human factors specialist; b. Santa Monica, Calif., Nov. 23, 1955; s. Carl Joseph and Yetta (Wexler) S.; m. Nancy Ann Olson, Oct. 14, 1984. BA, U. Calif., Santa Cruz, 1977; MA, Miami U., Oxford, Ohio, 1980. Human factors specialist Lockheed Corp., Burbank, Calif., 1980—. Mem. Am. Voice Input/Output Soc., Soc. Infor. Display, Human Factors Soc. Home: 26158 Via Raza Valencia CA 91355 Office: Lockheed Corp D/7465 B/229 P/Z PO Box 551 Burbank CA 91520

STEINER, GEORGE ALBERT, retired educator; b. Norristown, Pa., May 1, 1912; s. Elwood Heacock and Mary (Steele) S.; m. Jean Wood, Sept. 19, 1937; 1 child, John Frederick. BS in Bus., Temple U., 1933, Litt. D. (hon.), 1963; MA in Econs., U. Pa., 1934; PhD in Econs., U. Ill., 1937. Asst. prof. fin. Ind. U., Bloomington, 1937-42; staff specialist War Prodn. Bd., Washington, 1942-43; div. dir. Civilian Prodn. Adminstrn., Washington, 1946-47; prof. econs. U. Ill., Urbana-Champaign, Ill., 1947-50; dir. policy Def. Prodn. Adminstrn., Washington, 1950-53; chief economist Lockheed Aircraft Corp., Los Angeles, 1954-56; Kunin chair in Bus. and Society, prof. of mgmt. emeritus UCLA, 1956—; served as cons. to over 100 corps. throughout the world, 1956—; lectr. numerous univs. and colls. Author: over 30 titles, including Top Management Planning, 1969 (Best Book Yr. award Acad. Mgmt. 1969), Stategic Planning: What Every Manager Must Know, 1979, The New CEO, 1983; (with John B. Miner) Management Policy and Stategy, 1977, 3d rev. edit., 1986 (Best Book Yr. award Am. Hosp. Assn. 1977); (with John F. Steiner) Business, Government, and Society, 4th rev. edit., 1986; also contbr. articles to profl. jours. Served to lt. USNR, 1943-46. Recipient Disting. Service award Exec. Office Pres. of U.S., 1968, numerous grants for research in mgmt. Fellow Acad. Mgmt. (pres. 1972, Dean of the Fellows 1975-78), Internat. Acad. Mgmt., Exec. Planning Inst.; mem. The Planning Forum, Internat. Soc. Strategic Mgmt. (bd. dirs.), Delta Tau Delta, Beta Gamma Sigma, Alpha Kappa Psi. Presbyterian. Avocation: oil painting. Home: 13943 Cumpston St Van Nuys CA 91401 Office: UCLA Grad Sch Mgmt 405 Hilgard Ave Los Angeles CA 90024

STEINER, KENNETH DONALD, bishop; b. David City, Nebr., Nov. 25, 1936; s. Lawrence Nicholas and Florine Marie (Pieters) S. B.A., Mt. Angel Sem., 1958; M.Div., St. Thomas Sem., 1962. Ordained priest Roman Catholic Ch., 1962, bishop, 1978; asso. pastor various parishes Portland and Coos Bay, Oreg., 1962-72; pastor Coquille Ch., Myrtle Point, Powers, Oreg., 1972-76, St. Francis Ch., Roy, Oreg., 1976-77; aux. bishop Diocese of Portland, Oreg., 1977—; vicar of worship and ministries and personnel dir. clergy personnel Portland Archdiocese. Democrat. Office: 2838 E Burnside St Portland OR 97214

STEINER, RICHARD RUSSELL, conglomerate executive; b. Chgo., Feb. 26, 1923; s. Frank Gardner and Ruth (Cowie) S.; m. Colleen M. Kearns, Dec. 6, 1949; children—Robert C., Kevin K., Sheila M. B.A., Dartmouth Coll., 1948. With Steiner Corp., Salt Lake City, 1948—; divisonal dir., v.p. Steiner Corp., 1951-59, pres., 1959—; dir. Am. Uniform Co. Served with USAAF, 1942-46. Decorated D.F.C. Mem. Textile Rental Service Assn., Phi Beta Kappa. Clubs: Alta, Salt Lake Country. Office: Steiner Corp 505 E South Temple St Salt Lake City UT 84102

STEINER, ROBERT, professor, writer; b. Lasalle, Ill., July 16, 1948; s. Robert Alfred and Gertrude (Osborne) S. BA with honors, U. Iowa, 1970; MFA, Bowling Green U., 1971; PhD, U. Mass., 1977. Asst. prof. Bowling Green U., Mass., 1971, Mt. Holyoke Coll., South Hadley, Mass., 1976-77; assoc. prof. U. Colo., Boulder, Colo., 1979—; dir. creative writing program U. Colo., Boulder. Author: Quill, 1973, Bathers, 1980, Passion, 1980, Dread, 1987, Matinee, 1987. Fulbright fellow, 1977-78, NEAfellow, 1978, 82. Mem. Fiction Collective (bd. dirs. 1985—). Office: U Colo English Dept Boulder CO 80309

STEINER, ROBERTA PEARL, not-for-profit foundation administrator; b. N.Y.C., July 11, 1948; d. Charles and Ethel (Fier) S. BA, U. Calif., Berkeley, 1969, MLS, 1973. Specialist community resources, Sch. Resource Vols. Berkeley Pub. Schs., 1975-77; chief librarian Am. Insts. for Research, Palo Alto, Calif., 1973-77; assoc. in bibliography and instr. library sch. U. Calif., Berkeley, 1975-77; dir. Cen. Pacific Region B'nai B'rith Women, Daly City, Calif., 1977-84; dir. Found. Ctr. San Francisco office. Rep. to San Francisco Jewish Community Relations Council; bd. dirs. San Francisco Jewish Vocat. and Career Counseling Service, San Francisco, San Francisco Jewish Community Ctr. Mem. Phi Beta Kappa. Jewish. Home: 57 Wilshire Ave Daly City CA 94015

STEINHAGE, CHRISTINE ANN, marketing professional; b. Milw., Mar. 16, 1955; d. George Anothoy and Eva May (Brown) S. BA in Film Criticism, History and Theory, U. Wis., 1977, MA in Mass Communications, 1979. Media mgr. 20th Century Fox-Film Corp., Los Angeles, 1984-85; west coast ad. dir. Am. Film Inst., Los Angeles, 1984; sr. media planner Doyle Dane Bernback, Los Angeles, 1983-84; media planner J. Walter Thompson, N.Y.C., 1981-83; ad mgr. RCA/Columbia Pictures Home Video, Burbank, Calif., 1985—; cons. Urban Eclipse Film, Santa Monica, Calif., 1984—. Democrat. Roman Catholic. Avocations: film history, art history. Home: 2405 34th #27 Santa Monica CA 90405

STEINHAUER, GENE DOUGLAS, psychology educator; b. Fresno, Calif., Jan. 1, 1944; s. Wilbert Peter and Rosie Nielsen (Askov) S.; m. Linda Bol, July 7, 1985; children: Christopher William, Karlie Elizabeth. BA, Calif. State U., Fresno, 1972, MA, 1974; PhD, U. Mont., 1977. Asst. prof. SUNY, Oswego, 1977-78; assoc. prof. Calif. State U., Fresno, 1978—; pres. Artificial Behavior Inc., Fresno, 1985—; cons. Fresno County Schs., 1980—, NIH Council on Children, Media, Mass., 1980-81; grant reviewer NSF, Washington, 1978—. Author: Artificial Behavior, 1986; contbr. articles to profl. jours., chpts. to books. Served with USAF, 1961-65. NIMH fellow, 1975-77. Mem. Soc. Computer Simulation, Sigma Xi. Office: care Artificial Behavior Inc 2124 Kittredge #215 Berkeley CA 94704

STEINMAN, JOHN FRANCIS, psychiatrist; b. N.Y.C., May 5, 1916; s. David Barnard and Irene Stella (Hoffman) S.; m. Helen G. Meyer (div. 1963); children: James, Judith, Jill; m. Roxane Bear (div. 1972); m. Ellen M. Sears, Nov. 16, 1985. AB with hons., Columbia U., 1936, MD, 1940. Diplomate Am. Bd. Psychiatry and Neurology. Intern Strong Meml. Hosp., Rochester, N.Y. and Cin. Gen. Hosp., 1940-43; resident psychiatry Nebr. Psychiat. Inst., 1948, 58, R.I. Med. Ctr., 1961; psychiatrist, dir. Lincoln (Nebr.) and Lancaster County Child Guidance Ctr., 1948-61; instr. pediatrics, psychiatry and neurology U. Nebr., Lincoln, 1951-52; postdoctoral fellow in psychiatry Yale U., New Haven, Conn., 1962-64; psychiatrist U. Conn., Storrs, 1964-69, Community Mental Health Services, San Francisco, 1971-79; pvt. practice psychiatry San Francisco, 1979—. Delgate, chmn. Nebr. health com. White House Conf. Children and Youth, Washington, 1960. Served to capt. M.C., AUS, 1943-46, PTO. Mem. Am. Psychiat. Assn. (life), Am. Orthopsychiat. Assn., N.Y. Acad. Scis., Phi Beta Kappa. Home and Office: 164 Otsego Ave San Francisco CA 94112

STEINMAN, LISA MALINOWSKI, English literature educator; b. Willimantic, Conn., Apr. 8, 1950; d. Zenon Stanislaus and Shirley Belle (Nathanson) Malinowski; m. James A. Steinman, Apr. 1968 (div. 1980); m. James L. Shugrue, July 23, 1984. BA, Cornell U., 1971, MFA, 1973, PhD, 1976. Asst. prof. English Reed Coll., Portland, Oreg., 1976-82, assoc. prof., 1982—; cons. NEH, Washington, 1984-85; bd. dirs. Portland Poetry Festival. Author: Lost Poems, 1976, Made in America, 1987; editor Hubbub Mag., 1983—; contbr. articles to profl. jours. Fellow Nat. Endowment for Arts, 1984, Oreg. Arts Commn., 1983-84, NEH, 1983, Danforth Found., 1971-75. Mem. MLA, Poets and Writers. Home: 5344 SE 38th Ave Portland OR 97202 Office: Reed Coll Dept English 3203 SE Woodstock Ave Portland OR 97202

STEINMANN, JOHN COLBURN, architect; b. Monroe, Wis., Oct. 24, 1941; s. John Wilbur and Irene Marie (Steil) S.; m. Susan Koslosky, Aug. 12, 1978. BArch., U. Ill., 1964; postgrad. Ill. Inst. Tech., 1970-71; Project designer C.F. Murphy Assocs., Chgo., 1968-71, Steinmann Architects, Monticello, Wis., 1971-73; design chief, chief project architect State of Alaska, Juneau, 1973-78; project designer Mithun Assos., architects, Bellevue, Wash., 1978-80; owner, prin. John C. Steinmann Assos., Architect, Kirkland, Wash., 1980—; bd. dirs. Storytell Internat.; lectr. Ill. Inst. Tech., 1971-72; prin. works include: Grant Park Music Bowl, Chgo., 1971, Menomonee Falls (Wis.) Med. Clinic, 1972, Hidden Valley Office Bldg., Bellevue, 1978, Kezner Office Bldg., Bellevue, 1979, The Pines at Sunriver, Oreg., 1980, also Phase II, 1984, Phase III, 1986, The Pines at Sunriver Lodge Bldg., 1986, 2d and Lenora highrise, Seattle, 1981, Bob Hope Cardiovascular Research Inst. lab. animal facility, Seattle, 1982, Wash. Ct., Bellevue, 1982, Anchorage Bus. Park, 1982, Garden Townhouses, Anchorage, 1983, Vacation Internationale, Ltd. corp. hdqrs., Bellevue, 1983, Torre Vallarta III, Puerto Vallarta, Mex., 1987, also pvt. residences. Served to 1st lt. C.E., USAR, 1964-66; Vietnam. Decorated Bronze Star. Registered architect, Wash., Oreg., Calif., N.Mex., Ariz., Utah, Alaska, Wis., Ill. Mem. AIA, Am. Mgmt. Assn., Nat. Council Archtl. Registration Bds., Alpha Rho Chi. Republican. Roman Catholic. Club: U. Wash. Yacht. Address: 4316 106th Pl NE Kirkland WA 98033

STEINMETZ, WAYNE EDWARD, chemistry educator; b. Huron, Ohio, Feb. 16, 1945; s. Ralph Freeman and Helen Louise (Rossman) S. AB, Oberlin Coll., 1967; AM, Harvard U., 1968, PhD, 1973. Asst. prof. chemistry Pomona Coll., Claremont, Calif., 1973-79, assoc. prof., 1979—; akademischer Gast (vis. prof.) Eidgenössische Technische Hochschule, Zurich, Switzerland, 1979-80, 86-87. Contbr. articles on spectroscopy and molecular structure to profl. jours. Scoutmaster, adult leader trainer Old Baldy council Boy Scouts Am., 1973—. Fellow NSF, Woodrow Wilson Found.; recipient Dist. Merit award Boy Scouts Am., 1978. Mem. AAUP, Am. Chem. Soc., Phi Beta Kappa (local sec.-treas. 1980—). Democrat. Roman Catholic. Avocations: hiking, cross country skiing, choral singing. Home: 1081 Cascade Pl Claremont CA 91711 Office: Pomona Coll Dept Chemistry Claremont CA 91711

STELLRECHT, FRITZ, newspaper publishing executive; b. Ulm, Fed. Republic Germany, Jan. 6, 1941; came to U.S., 1957; s. Karl Wilhelm and Else Kaethe (Schaupp) S.; m. Priscilla Holtz, Feb. 22, 1974. BA, San Jose State U., 1968, cert. secondary teaching, 1969. Tchr. San Jose Pub. Schs., Calif., 1969-75; various mgmt. positions San Jose Mercury, 1978-82; mgr. regional circulation USA Today, Los Angeles, 1982-83; gen. mgr. USA Today, Kansas City, Mo., 1983-84, Chandler, Ariz., 1984—. Served with U.S. Army, 1963-65. Mem. Internat. Circulation Mgrs. Assn., Calif. Western Circulation Mgrs. Assn., Ariz. Newspaper Assn. (assoc.). Republican. Avocations, golf, chess, collecting stamps and WWII memorabilia. Office: USA Today 411 N Roosevelt Ave Chandler AZ 85226

STEMMER, JAY JOHN, safety engineer; b. Wilkes-Barre, Pa., Apr. 29, 1939. Engr. Factory Mut., N.J., 1973-77; cons. McKay & Assoc., Calif., 1977-81, Index Research, Calif., 1981-83, Fireman's Fund, Calif., 1983-85, AIG Cons., Calif., 1985—; assoc. prof. Sierra Coll., Los Angeles, 1979-80. Author: Medical Manual of Industrial Toxicology, 1965, Latin America, A Study of Air Transport, Development and Potential in the Decade Ahead, 1970. Served to lt. USAF, 1962-65. Mem. NSPE, Am. Soc. Safety Engrs., Am. Risk and Ins. Assn., Bd. Motion Pictures and TVEngrs. Avocations: graphology, duplicate bridge, photography, white water rafting. Home: 1517 E Garfield Ave #84 Glendale CA 91205

STENBAKKEN, RICHARD OLIVER, army officer, chaplain; b. Denver, July 27, 1940; s. Oliver T. and Celia E. (Reed) S.; m. Ardis Aleen Dick, Aug. 20, 1962; children: Erik Brent, Rikki Michele. BA, Union Coll., Lincoln, Nebr., 1962; MA, Andrews U., 1964, BD, 1965; MA, Chapman Coll., 1974; MEd, Columbia U., 1980. Commd. U.S. Army, 1969, advanced through grades to lt. col., 1985; battalion chaplain U.S. Army, Vietnam, 1970-71; div. support command chaplain U.S. Army, Ft. Lewis, Wash., 1971-73; family life ctr. dir. U.S. Army, Ft. Leonard Wood, Mo., 1974-78; mem. chaplain bd. Office of the Chief of Chaplains, Ft. Monmouth, N.J., 1978-82; dir. Aliamanu Family Life Ctr. (U.S. Army), Honolulu, 1982-86; div. chaplain, dep. post chaplain 4th Inf. Div., Colorado Springs, Colo., 1986—. Co-editor Mil. Chaplains Rev., 1980; contbr. articles to profl. jours. Pres. Worland (Wyo.) Ministerial Assn., 1966-67; mem. Tri-Services Family Advocacy, Honolulu, 1982-86; advisor Adventist chaplaincy ministries Gen. Conf. Seventh-Day Adventists, Washington, 1983—. Decorated Bronze Star with bronze oak leaf cluster. Mem. Am. Assn. Sex Educators and Counselors (life), Sex Info. and Edn. Council of U.S., Am. Assn. Marriage and Family Therapists (clin.). Avocations: stained glass, wood carving, backpacking, fishing, stamp collecting. Home: 3410 Oak Cree Dr E Colorado Springs CO 80906 Office: Office of Div Chaplain 4th Infantry div (MECH) Fort Carson CO 80913-5030

STENCHEVER, DIANE HANNAH, social worker; b. Buffalo, Aug. 10, 1933; d. Hanford Willard and Rose (Backer) Bilsky; m. Morton Albert Stenchever, June 19, 1955; children: Michael Alan, Marc Russell, Douglas Andrew. Student, Syracuse U.; BS, U. Buffalo, 1955; MSW, U. Utah, 1975. Caseworker Erie County Welfare, Buffalo, 1955-56; group leader Divorce Lifeline, Seattle, 1977-84; pvt. practice counselor Seattle and Renton, Wash., 1977-86; with U. Wash. Dept. of Psychiatry, Seattle, 1977—, researcher. Contbr. to Am. Jour. Psychiatry. Bd. dirs. Woodlake Park Zoo, docents 1982-84, pres., 1984—. Mem. Nat. Assn. Social Workers. Club: Mercer Island Country. Home: 8301 SE 83d St Mercer Island WA 98040

STENHOUSE, DOUGLAS SIMMS, energy research, housing and land planning cons.; b. Washington, June 16, 1932; s. John Warn and Elizabeth (Brent) Simms; m. Susan May Taylor, Jan. 29, 1967; children: Laura Waller, Paula Simms, Richard Douglas, Brent Taylor, David Carroll. BA, Princeton U., 1954; BArch, U. Pa., 1957; MArch in Urban Design, Cath. U. Am., 1970, M City and Regional Planning, 1971. Registered architect D.C., Md., Va., N.J., N.Mex., Calif.; registered planner N.J.; cert. energy auditor, Calif. Designer Faulkner, Kingsbury & Stenhouse, Washington, 1958-63; practice architecture Washington, 1964-69; asst. project mgr. housing systems Operation Breakthrough, HUD, Washington, 1970-72; chief architect and planner Community Tech. Corp. subs. TRW Inc., Redondo Beach, Calif., 1972-74; cons. Torrance Beach, 1972-74; pres. Energy Mgmt. Cons. Inc., Los Angeles, San Diego, 1976—; vis. design critic Howard U., Washington, 1965; asst. to dir. tech. services div. Housing Assistance Adminstrn., 1969; lectr. U. So. Calif., UCLA, So. Calif. Inst. Architecture, Santa Monica, Calif. State Poly. Inst., Pomona. Editor: Archtl. Graphic Standards, 6th edit.; contbr. articles on energy conservation to profl. jours. Mem. Torrance (Calif.) Planning Commn., 1975-78; Los Angeles Solar City Com., 1977-80; past sr. warden Christ Episc. Ch., Redondo Beach, St. Luke's Episc. Ch., Long Beach, Calif.;

bd. dirs. Family and Child Services, 1967-69, Casa de los Amigos, Redondo Beach, 1975-79; adv. bd. Washington Tech. Inst., 1969-72, Citizens Energy Conservation and Solar Devel., 1974-80, So. Calif. Solar Energy Assn., 1975-78. Served with C.E., AUS, 1956-58. Recipient Spl. Achievement award HUD, 1972. Mem. AIA (pres. local chpt. 1977, Disting. Service award 1974, 82, Presdl. commendation 1975, nat. energy com. 1976-80), Am. Inst. Cert. Planners., ASHRAE (assoc.) Internat. Solar Energy Soc., Zeta Psi. Home: 20329 Roslin Ave Torrance CA 90503 Office: Energy Mgmt Cons Inc 2807 Oregon Ct Suite E-1 Torrance CA 90503-2608

STENZEL, DAVID BENTHEIM, historian, educator, small business owner; b. Bellerose, N.Y., Jan. 5, 1927; s. Roland and Mildred (Rich) S.; m. Muriel Rosalie Powers, Sept. 12, 1958; children: Christina Stenzel Randall, Eric Bentheim, Carl Bentheim. BA in Fgn. Service, Georgetown U., 1951; MA in History, U. Calif., Berkeley, 1954, PhD in History, 1957. Acting asst. prof. Stanford (Calif.) U., 1957-61; prof. history Calif. State U., Turlock, 1961—; lectr. Royal Viking Line, Europe, 1983—; ownner Stenzel Travel, Inc. doing bus. as Tempo Travel. Contbr. articles to profl. jours. Chmn. dist. Boy Scouts Am., 1975-77; chmn. Stanislaus County (Calif.) Planning Commn., 1972-81; pres. Calif. County Planning Commn. Assn., 1977. Served to capt. USAF, 1951-53. Mem. Turlock C. of C. (bd. dirs. 1983-86), Phi Beta Kappa. Republican. Lutheran. Lodge: Rotary (pres. Turlock chpt. 1977-78, Paul Harris fellow 1985). Avocation: traveling. Home: 761 E Tuolumne Rd Turlock CA 95380 Office: Calif State U 801 W Monte Vista Turlock CA 95380

STEPANEK, JOSEPH EDWARD, industrial development consultant; b. Ellinwood, Kans., Oct. 29, 1917; s. Joseph August and Leona Mae (Wilson) S.; m. Antoinette Farnham, June 10, 1942; children: Joseph F., James B., Antoinette L., Debra L. BSChemE, U. Colo., 1939; DEng in Chem. Engring., Yale U., 1942. Registered profl. engr., Colo. Engr. Stearns-Roger Mfg., Denver, 1939-45; from asst. to assoc. prof. U. Colo., Boulder, 1945-47; from cons. to dir. UN, various countries, 1947-73; cons. internat. indsl devel., U.S.-China bus. relations Boulder, 1973—; bd. dirs. 12 corps., 1973—. Author 3 books on indsl. devel.; contbr. 50 articles to profl. jours. Exec. dir. Boulder Tomorrow, 1965-67. Recipient Yale Engring. award Yale Engring. Assn., 1957, Norlin award U. Colo. 1978, Annual award India League of Am., 1982. Mem. AAAS. Democrat. Unitarian. Club: Yale (N.Y.C.). Avocation: ranching. Home: 1622 High St Boulder CO 80302

STEPANEK, STEPHEN JOSEPH, podiatric physician; b. Chgo., Mar. 29, 1947; s. Stephen Joseph and Irene Theresa (Pogorzelski) S.; m. Rita Helen Luczynski, Aug. 6, 1977; 1 child, Sarah. AA, Coll. DuPage, 1972; BS, U. Ill., 1974; D Podiatric Medicine, Ill. Coll. Podiatric Medicine, 1979. Resident Community Hosp., Ottawa, Ill., 1979-80; pvt. practice specializing in podiatric medicine Everett, Wash., 1980—; treas. Waldo Hosp. Staff, Seattle, 1985—. Named one of Outstanding Young Men of Am., 1981. Mem. Wash. State Podiatric Med. Assn., Am. Podiatric Med. Assn. Avocations: golf, skiing, fishing. Office: 221 SE Everett Mall Way Everett WA 98204

STEPHENS, CHARLES WILLIAM, aerospace consultant, electronic engineer; b. Liberal, Kans., July 26, 1930; s. Ernest Virgil and Thelma Dorleska (Keating) S.; m. Mary B. Hoofnagle, Aug. 31, 1952; children—Craig A., Cathy J., Kirk M. B.S.E.E., U. Kans., Lawrence, 1952; postgrad. engring. studies, Bell Telephone Labs., N.Y.C., 1953-54. Mem. tech. staff Bell Telephone Labs. Inc., Whippany, N.J., 1953-54; v.p., dep. gen. mgr. Electronics & Def. Sector, TRW Inc., Redondo Beach, Calif., 1957-86, aerospace consultant, 1986—; mem. adv. bd. dept. elec. and computer engring. U. Kans., 1980—, mem. adv. bd. Sch. Engring., 1981—; mem. bd. counselors sch. engring., U. So. Calif. Bd. mgrs. Torrance-South Bay Area YMCA, Calif., 1982; mem. Rolling Hills Covenant Ch., Calif., 1984—. Served with U.S. Army, 1954-56; Army Ballistic Missile Agy. Mem. Nat. Acad. Engring., Am. Men and Women of Science, AIAA, IEEE, Electronic Industries Assn. (bd. govs. 1983-86, bd. dirs. gov. div. 1983-86), Sigma Xi, Sigma Pi Sigma, Eta Kappa Nu, Tau Beta Pi, Sigma Tau. Avocations: tennis; fishing; golf. Home: 2707 W 233 St Torrance CA 90505

STEPHENS, DAVID WILLIAM, biologist; b. Salt Lake City, June 23, 1955; s. Dean Richins and Bonnie (Hansen) S.; m. Anne Elder Sorensen, Aug. 7, 1982. BS in Biology, BS in Math., U. Utah, 1978; PhD, Oxford (Eng.) U., 1982. Vis. scientist Smithsonian Inst., Washington, 1982-83; NATO fellow U. B.C., Vancouver, Can., 1983-84; NSF fellow U. Utah, Salt Lake City, 1984—. Author: Foraging Theory, 1986; contbr. articles to profl. jours. Mem. Am. Behavior Soc. Avocations: fly fishing. Home: 659 E 1200 E #1A Salt Lake City UT 84102 Office: U Utah Dept Biology Salt Lake City UT 84112

STEPHENS, DON RICHARDS, banker; b. San Francisco, June 28, 1938; s. Donald Lewis and Anona Marie (O'Leary) S.; m. Christina Brinkman, Sept. 11, 1971; children—Lane B., Justin H., Nicholas W., Adam H. B.S., U. So. Calif., 1961; J.D., Hastings Coll., 1969. Pres. Campodonico & Stephens, San Francisco, 1963-65; pres., owner Union Investment Co., San Francisco, 1966-69; assoc. Law Offices of Louis O. Kelso, 1969-72; individual practice law, San Francisco, 1972-77; pres. D.R. Stephens & Co., San Francisco, 1976—; chmn., chief exec. officer Bank of San Francisco, 1979—, also bd. dirs.; bd. dirs. A.I.F.S., Inc., Real Estate Research Corp., Skouras Pictures. Bd. dirs. Joffrey Ballet, Bay Area Council; trustee St. Francis Meml. Hosp., San Francisco, 1976-82; mem. San Francisco Stadium Com. Mem. Urban Land Inst., Western Assn. Venture Capitalists, Young Pres.'s Orgn., San Francisco C. of C. Republican. Presbyterian. Clubs: Bohemian (San Francisco), Calif. Avocation: tennis.

STEPHENS, GEORGE EDWARD, JR., lawyer; b. Lawrence, Kans., Mar. 26, 1936; s. George Edward and Mary Helen (Houghton) S.; m. Gretel Geiser, Dec. 31, 1965; children: Thaddeus Geiser, Edward Houghton, Mary Schoentgen. Student, U. Colo., Boulder, 1954-57, U. Colo. Sch. Medicine, Denver, 1957-59; LLB, Stanford U., 1962. Bar: Calif. 1963, U.S. Dist. Ct. (cen. dist.) Calif. 1963, U.S. Ct. Appeals (9th cir.) 1971. Law clk. to judge U.S. Dist. Ct., Los Angeles, 1962-64; ptnr. Pollock & Palmer, Los Angeles, 1964-69, Gates, Morris, Merrill & Stephens, Los Angeles, 1969-72, Paul, Hastings, Janofsky & Walker, Los Angeles, 1972—; Mem. coordinating council on Lawyer Competence, Conf. Chief Justices, 1983—; chmn. porbate sect. Los Angeles County Bar Assn., 1979-80. Nat. chmn. Stanford (Calif.) U. Law Fund Quad Program, 1980-87; mem. bd. visitors Stanford Law Sch., 1982-85; founder Mus. Contempory Art, Los Angeles, 1982. Recipient Stanford Assocs. award, 1982. Fellow Am. Bar Found., Am. Coll. Probate Counsel, Internat. Acad. Probate and Trust; mem. ABA (chmn. standing com. specialization 1979-82, rep. to coordinating council on lawyer competence, 1982-87); mem. Stanford Law Soc. (pres. 1972-73). Episcopalian. Clubs: Chancery (Los Angeles), Amandale Golf (Pasadena, Calif.), Balley Hunt (Pasadena). Office: Paul Hastings Janofsky & Walker 555 S Flower Floor 22 Los Angeles CA 90071

STEPHENS, KAREN MIGNON, banker; b. Beaumont, Tex., May 9, 1946; d. Otis Lester and Thelma Florence (Carter) Quarles; m. Lowell Dene Stephens, July 27, 1963; children—Jeffrey Dene, Gregory Don. Student pub. schs. Caddo Mills., Tex.; student Nat. Compliance Sch., 1984, N.Mex. Sch. Banking, 1985. Ins. claim clk. Employers Group Ins. Co., Artesia, N.Mex., 1964-65; dep. county clk. Otero County, Alamogordo, N.Mex., 1965-69; loan sec., asst. v.p., then v.p., compliance officer First Nat. Bank, Alamogordo, 1969—. Mem. Bus. and Profl. Womens Club (Young Career Woman award 1973). Democrat. Methodist. Club: Jr. Women's (sec.-treas. 1971) (Alamogordo). Home: 3028 Del Cerro Alamogordo NM 88310 Office: First Nat Bank 414 10th St Drawer 9 Alamogordo NM 88310

STEPHENS, MICHAEL GARY, microelectronics packaging engr.; b. Los Angeles, Dec. 12, 1947; s. Stanley Cameron and Aline Mary (Tremblay) S.; A.A. in Engring., Math. and Sci., Cerritos Coll., 1973; m. Bobbie Jo Robertson, Nov. 30, 1974; 1 son, Samuel Cole. Designer, Pacific Sci. Co., Anaheim, Calif., 1966-71; microelectronics engr. Western Digital Corp., Newport Beach, Calif., 1973-75; mgr. microelectronics packaging engring. Xerox Corp., El Segundo, Calif., 1975-81; prin. engr. hermetic packaging Silicon Systems, Inc., 1981-85; mgr. mfg. engr. RF Device div. TRW, El Segundo, 1985—. Mem. Semicondr. Equipment and Materials Inst. Republican. Roman Catholic. Patentee in field. Home: 1013 S Nicklett St Fullerton CA 92631

STEPHENS, MICHAEL JON, automobile industry executive; b. Alpena, Mich., Aug. 30, 1948; s. Byron L. and Jeanne E. (Hackett) S.; B.S. in Indsl. Engring., Gen. Motors Inst., 1972; M.B.A., Wayne State U., Detroit, 1976; m. Marise E. Mundwiler, Apr. 17, 1982. With Gen. Motors Corp., 1967-77, 79-81, sr. quality control engr., Detroit, 1973-77, sr. staff adminstr. corp. mktg. staff, 1979-81; mkt. planning analyst, Toyota Motor Sales USA, Torrance, Calif., 1977-78; nat. mktg. and product mgr., Brit. Leyland Inc., Leonia, N.J., 1978-79; mgr. sales and mktg., Pasha Group, San Francisco, 1981-82; exec. field cons. The Hdqrs. Co., 1982-84; mgr. advance product planning, Chrysler Corp., Detroit, 1984—. adj. prof. bus. Bergen (N.J.) Community Coll., 1978-79. Home: 31625 Auburn Birmingham MI 48009 Office: Chrysler Corp CIMS #415-03-10 PO Box 857 Detroit MI 48009

STEPHENS, RONALD DAVID, academic administrator; b. Sacramento, Oct. 21, 1946; s. Jesse W. and Nancy F. (Rice) S.; m. Kathleen Warford, Jan. 21, 1948; children: David, James, TJ. BS in Bus., Pepperdine U., 1967, MBA, 1969; EdD, U. So. Calif., 1981. Bus. mgr. Columbia Christian Coll., Portland, Oreg., 1971-74; dir. bus. services Pepperdine U., Malibu, Calif., 1974-77, v.p., 1979-82, prof. grad. sch. bus. and edn., 1982-85; ptnr. Regal Constrn., Portland, 1977-79; exec. dir. Nat. Sch. Safety Ctr., Encino, Calif., 1985—. Exec. editor Sch. Safety, 1985—; contbr. articles to profl. jours. Pres. sch. bd. Columbia Christian Schs., 1978-79; bd. dirs. Calif. Christian Schs., San Fernando, 1976-77; elder Ch. Christ, Thousand Oaks, Calif., 1986—. Served with U.S. Army, 1969-71, Vietnam. Avocations: water and snow skiing. Office: Nat Sch Safety Ctr 16830 Ventura Blvd Encino CA 91436

STEPHENS, RONALD W., academic administrator; b. Bellingham, Wash., May 5, 1945; s. Robert Leonard and Iva Della (Willet) S. BA, Wash. State U., 1967; MA, Pacific Luth. U., 1974; PhD, U. Nebr., 1977; JD, U. Puget Sound, 1980. Bar: Wash. 1980, U.S. Dist. Ct. (we. dist.) Wash. 1980, U.S. Ct. Appeals (9th cir.) 1981. Dir. legal services Wash. State Sch. Dir. Assn., Olympia, 1980-84; exec. dir. Vt. Sch. Bds. Assn., Montpelier, 1984-85; faculty mem. Union for Experimenting Colls. and Univs., Los Angeles, 1985—; cons. Assn. Wash. Sch. Prins., Olympia, 1982-85, Nebr. Council Sch. Adminstrs., Lincoln, 1976-77; mem. Wash. Profl. Edn. Adv. Com., Wash. Spl. Edn. Adv. Com., Olympia, 1981-84. Editor Wash. Sch. Law Digest, 1980-82. Mem. task force United Council Chs. on World Hunger, Lincoln, 1977, Wash. task force on Juvenile Facilities, Olympia, 1984; chmn. Tacoma Arts Festival, 1975; bd. dirs. Kent (Wash.) Area Youth Services, 1982-84. Recipient Service award Assn. Wash. Sch. Prins., 1984, Wash. Edn. Assn., 1975. Mem. Wash. Bar Assn., ABA, Wash. Council Sch. Attys., Nat. Council Sch. Attys., Vt. Council Sch. Attys., Phi Delta Kappa, Sigma Phi Epsilon (v.p. Pullman, Wash., chpt. 1967), Pi Kappa Delta. Methodist. Avocations: swimming, travel, reading, writing, designing simulation games. Home: 1840 Garfield Pl #214 Hollywood CA 90028

STEPHENS, WILLIAM JAMES, army officer, communications specialist; b. Detroit, May 30, 1937; s. James Willard and Edythe Viola (Harris) S.; m. Jacqueline Younger, Apr. 2, 1963; children—Leslie Diane, Patricia Elaine. B.S., Eastern Mich. U., 1960; M.S., So. Ill. U., 1968; cert. U.S. Army Command and Gen. Staff Coll., 1973, U.S. Army Signal Sch., 1960, 64, Indsl. Coll. Armed Forces, 1981. Commd. 2d lt. U.S. Army, 1960, advanced through grades to col., 1981; project officer Orgn. Joint Chiefs of Staff, 1978-80, dep. asst. chief of staff, 1981-82; dir. communications Armed Forces Inauguration Com., 1984-85; comdr. dep. chief staff Communications-Electronics, U.S. Army Communications Command, Mil. Dist. of Washington, 1984-85; comdr. Pentagon Telecommunications Ctr., 1982-85, brigade comdr. U.S. Army Info. Systems Command Ops. Command, The Pentagon, 1982-85, mil. asst. for info. Office Asst. Sec. of Army, The Pentagon, 1985; comdr. USAIS Engring. Support Activity, Ft. Huachuca, Ariz., 1985—. Advisor Transatlantic council Explorer Scouts, 1960-64; mem. service team Nat. Capitol Area council Explorer Scouts, 1968-71; asst. dist. commr. Belgium and Netherlands, Boy Scouts Am., 1974-76. Decorated Legion of Merit, Bronze Star with oak leaf cluster, Joint Service Commendation medal with 2 oak leaf clusters, Meritorious Service medal with oak leaf cluster, Air medal. Mem. Armed Forces Communications-Electronics Assn., Assn. U.S. Army, U.S. Army Signal Officers Assn., 101st Airborne Div., Eastern Mich. U. Alumni Assn. (Disting. Alumni award 1985), Indsl. Coll. Armed Forces Alumni Assn., SHAPE Officers Assn. Episcopalian. Club: Lettermen's (Eastern Mich. U.). Lodges: Masons, Shriners. Avocations: basketball; tennis; jogging; horseback riding. Home: 11004 Clara Barton Dr Fairfax Station VA 22039

STEPHENS, WILLIAM LEONARD, univ. dean; b. Covington, Ky., Apr. 19, 1929; s. Leonard Edwin and Mary Blanche S.; m. Claire Neall, Apr. 12, 1957. B.A. with honors, Calif. State U., Sacramento; Ph.D. in Microbiology, U. Calif., Davis, 1963. Research asst. U. Calif., Davis, 1957-63; mem. faculty Calif. State U., Chico, 1963—; prof. biol. scis. Calif. State U., 1970—, chmn. dept., 1968-74; dean Calif. State U. (Sch. Natural Scis.), 1977—. Served with USN, 1950-54. Mem. Am. Soc. Microbiology, Sigma Xi. Research in bacterial pigments, microbial metabolism. Home: 1661 Oak Vista Chico CA 95926 Office: Calif State U Coll Natural Scis Chico CA 95929

STEPHENSON, HERMAN HOWARD, banker; b. Wichita, Kans., July 15, 1929; s. Herman Horace and Edith May (Wayland) S.; m. Virginia Anne Ross, Dec. 24, 1950; children: Ross Wayland, Neal Bevan, Jann Edith. B.A., U. Mich., 1950; J.D., U. Mo. at Kansas City, 1958. Bar: Kans. 1958. Mem. fgn. dept. City Nat. Bank, Kansas City, Mo., 1952-54; asst. sec. City Bond & Mortgage Co., Kansas City, Mo., 1954-59; with Bank of Hawaii, Honolulu, 1959—, asst. cashier, 1960-62, v.p., 1962-68, sr. v.p., 1968-72, exec. v.p., 1972-80, pres., dir., 1980—; v.p., treas. Bancorp. Hawaii, Inc., Honolulu, 1978-80, pres., dir., 1980—; chmn., dir. Bancorp Fin. of Hawaii, Inc.; chmn., dir. Bancorp Life Ins. Co., Bancorp Bus. Systems of Hawaii, Inc.; v.p., dir. Bancorp Fin. of Hawaii, Inc., Bancorp Hawaii Small Bus. Investment Co., Inc., Bancorp Ins. Agy. of Hawaii, Inc.; vice chmn., dir. Hawaii Fin. Corp. (Hong Kong) Ltd., Hawaiian Trust Co., Ltd.; v.p. Bancorp Leasing of Hawaii, Inc. former trustee; chmn., trustee Realty & Mortgage Investors of Pacific (RAMPAC); dir. Banque de Tahiti, Bank of New Caledonia Bank Adv. Corp., Bancorp Fin. of Hawaii-Guam, Inc., Bancorp Hawaii Service Corp., Investors Pacific Ltd., S.I.L., Inc., Bank of Hawaii Internat., N.Y.; pres., treas., bd. dirs. Hawaiian Hong Kong Holdings, Ltd.; pres., bd. dirs. Bank of Hawaii Internat. Corp., Bankoh Adv. Corp., Bancorp Investment Adv. Services, Inc.; vice-chmn., dir. BOH Investment Mgmt. Co., Ltd., Hong Kong. Chmn. urban renewal com. Oahu Devel. Conf., 1966-68, mem. comprehensive planning com., 1970-71; trustee, past pres. Tax Found. Hawaii; former trustee Hawaii Conf. Found., United Ch. of Christ; bd. dirs. Honolulu Symphony, Maunalani Hosp.; chmn., bd. dirs. Aloha United Way; co-chmn. Ellison Onizuka Meml. Scholarship Fund Com.; v.p., treas. Bancorp Hawaii Charitable Found.; mem. adv. group internat. arbitration. Served with U.S. Army, 1950-52. Mem. Am. Bankers Assn. (past chmn. exec. com. housing and real estate fin. div., dir. 1976-77, mem. governing council 1976-77, mem. govt. relations council Banking Leadership Conf.), Am., Kans. bar assns., Mortgage Bankers Assn. Hawaii (past pres.), Hawaii Bankers Assn. (pres. 1984-85), U.S.-Japan Bus. Council, Pacific Asia Travel Assn., Navy League of U.S., Kappa Sigma, Pi Eta Sigma. Clubs: Rotary, Oahu Country, Pacific, Waialae, President's of U. Hawaii Found. Office: PO Box 2900 Honolulu HI 96846

STEPHENSON, IRENE HAMLEN, biorhythm analyst, consultant, editor, teacher; b. Chgo., Oct. 7, 1923; d. Charles Martin and Carolyn Hilda (Hilgers) Hamlin; m. Edgar B. Stephenson, Sr., Aug. 16, 1941 (div. 1946); 1 child, Edgar B. Author biorhythm compatibilities column Nat. Singles Register, Norwalk, Calif., 1979-81; instr. biorhythm Learning Tree Open U., Canoga Park, Calif., 1982-83; instr. biorhythm character analysis 1980—; instr. biorhythm compatibility, 1982—; owner, pres. matchmaking service Pen Pals Using Biorhythm, Chatsworth, Calif., 1979—; editor newsletter Mini Examiner- The Truth-Biorhythm, Chatsworth, 1979—; researcher biorhythm character and compatibility, 1974—, selecting a mate, 1985—. Author: Learn Biorhythm Character Analysis, 1980; Do-It-Yourself Biorhythm Compatibilities, 1982; contbr. numerous articles to mags. Office: Irene Hamlen Stephenson PO Box 3893 Chatsworth CA 91313

STEPHENSON, LARRY KIRK, strategic planner, management and geography educator; b. Seattle, Sept. 22, 1944; s. Norman Eugene and Virginia Dare (Frost) S.; m. Tamara Leah Ladin, June 24, 1967; children—Mathew Alan, Leah Anela. B.S., Ariz. State U., 1966, M.A., 1971; Ph.D., U. Cin., 1973; Manpower research analyst Employment Security Commn. of Ariz., 1969-70; asst. prof. dept. geography U. Hawaii, Hilo, 1973-76, assoc. prof., 1976-78, chmn. dept., 1975-77; vis. lectr. dept. geography Ariz. State U., 1978, adj. assoc. prof., 1979—; planner Ariz. Dept. Health Services, Phoenix, 1978-84; vis. assoc. prof. dept. geography, area devel. and urban planning U. Ariz., 1978; strategic plannner City of Glendale, Ariz., 1984—. Mem. faculty U. Phoenix, 1979—; adj. prof. Golden Gate U., 1981—; ptnr. Urban Research Assocs., Phoenix, 1981—; adj. prof. Coll. St. Francis, 1982—. Mem. Hawaii Island Health Planning Council, 1974-78; mem. Glendale Community Colls. Pres.'s Council, 1986—. Served with U.S. Army, 1966-68. NDEA fellow, 1971-72. Mem. Am. Inst. Cert. Planners, Am. Planning Assn., Assn. Am. Geographers, Ariz. Planning Assn. (pres. 1987—), Southwest Profl. Geog. Assn. Unitarian. Author books in field; contbr. chpts. to textbooks, articles to profl. jours. Home: 306 W Encanto Blvd Phoenix AZ 85003 Office: 94 Commercial St Portland ME 04101

STEPHENSON, TONI EDWARDS, investment management exec.; b. Bastrop, La., July 23, 1945; d. Sidney Crawford and Grace Erleene (Shipman) Little; B.S., La. State U., 1967; m. Arthur Emmet Stephenson, Jr., June 17, 1967; 1 dau., Tessa Lyn. Computer programmer Employers Group Ins., Boston, 1967-68; systems analyst Computer Tech., Inc., Cambridge, Mass., 1968-69; founding ptnr. Stephenson & Co., Denver, 1971—, Stephenson Mcht. Banking, 1980—; gen. ptnr. Viking Fund; ptnr. Stephenson Properties, Stephenson Ventures, Stephenson Mgmt. Co.; sr. v.p., dir. Gen. Communications, Inc., Globescope Corp.; underwriting mem. Lloyd's of London; founder, dir. Charter Bank & Trust. Co-pub. Denver Bus. Mag., 1978—, Denver Mag., 1982—, Vail Mag., 1980—, Development Sales Catalog, 1980—, Colorado Book, 1986—. Founder, bd. dirs. Rocky Mountain Child Health Mgmt. Services, Inc.; mem. Jr. League Denver; past pres. Children's Hosp. Assn. Vols.; mem. Jr. League Denver. Mem. DAR, Delta Gamma. Clubs: Annabel's of London, Thunderbird Country, Petroleum. Home: 11102 E Harvard Dr Aurora CO 80014 Office: Stephenson & Co 100 Garfield St Denver CO 80206

STEPIEN, CAROL ANN, marine ecologist, researcher; b. Cleve., Apr. 21, 1956; d. Theodore John and Anna M. (Bowerman) Stepien; m. Steven Alan Naffziger, Aug. 31, 1984. BS, Bowling Green U., 1977; MS, U. So. Calif., 1979, PhD, 1985. Asst. prof. U. San Diego, 1984-86; research assoc. Hubbs Marine Research Inst., San Diego, 1985-86, NSF and Scripps Instn. Oceanography, La Jolla, Calif., 1986—. Contbr. articles to profl. jours. NSF fellow, 1986; Lerner Marine grantee Am. Mus. Natural History, 1982-84. Mem. Am. Soc. Ichthyologists and Herpetologists (Best Paper 1983), Am. Soc. Zoologists, Western Soc. Naturalists, Ecol. Soc. Am., So. Calif. Acad. Scis. (Best Paper 1983). Avocations: scuba diving, underwater photography. Office: Scripps Instn Oceanography Marine Biology Div A-002 La Jolla CA 92093

STEPOVICH, MICHAEL LEO, orthodontist; b. Fairbanks, Alaska, Nov. 17, 1929; s. Mike and Vuka (Radovich) S.; A.B., San Jose State U., 1956; D.D.S., Marquette U., 1961; M.S., St. Louis U., 1964; m. Arline Audry Gentry, June 10, 1956; children—Michael John, Matthew James, Dean Alexander, Lynn Diane. Intern, USPHS Hosp., Fort Worth, 1961-62; pvt. practice orthodontics, San Jose, Calif., 1964—; mem. staff Good Samaritan Hosp., San Jose. Pres., Orthodontic Edn. and Research Found., St. Louis, 1969; bd. dirs. Tweed Found. for Orthodontic Research, 1978-84, pres. Western sect., 1985-87. Served with AUS, 1953-54; PTO. Diplomate Am. Bd. Orthodontists. Mem. Am., Calif., Santa Clara County dental assns., Am. Assn. Orthodontists, Pacific Coast Soc. Orthodontists (pres. Central sect. 1975), Angle Soc., DeMolay, Interfrat. Council San Jose State U. Alumni (chmn. 1966), Omicron Kappa Upsilon, Delta Upsilon. Contbr. articles to profl. jours. Home: 19557 Arden Ct Saratoga CA 95070 Office: 4110 Moorpark Ave San Jose CA 95117

STEPP, GEORGE ALLAN, JR., state official; b. Inglewood, Calif., Apr. 26, 1922; s. George Allan and Ida Johanna (Wehselau) S.; m. Margit Lindblad, Oct. 15, 1966; 1 dau., Elizabeth. B.A., U. Hawaii, 1948, M.A. in Govt., 1950. Personnel technician and adminstr. Hawaii Dept. Civil Service, Honolulu, 1950-59; asst. dir. research Hawaii Employers Council, Honolulu, 1959-61; mgmt. services adminstr. Hawaii State Dept. Budget and Fin., Honolulu, 1961—. Served with USCG, 1942-45, to comdr. Res. (ret.), 1952-82. Mem. Western Govtl. Research Assn. (pres. 1971-72), Am. Soc. Pub. Adminstrn., Am. Mgmt. Assn., Am. Cons. League. Res. Officers Assn. of U.S. Democrat. Home: 2999 Kalakaua Ave Honolulu HI 96815 Office: Hawaii State Dept Budget & Fin PO Box 150 Honolulu HI 96810

STERGIOU, PANOS, dentist; b. Patras, Greece, June 11, 1944; came to U.S., 1973; s. Ioannis and Altani (Papasaika) S.; m. Yioula Lycou, July 17, 1982; 1 child, Ioannis. Degree, Aristotelian U., Salonica, Greece, 1973; DDS, UCLA, 1974. Practice dentistry specializing in cosmetic dentistry Hawaiian Gardens, Calif., 1974—. Served as sublt. Greek Army, 1967-68. Mem. Acad. Internat. Med. Studies, Am. Acad. Cosmetic Dentistry, Am. Acad. Gnathologic Orthopedics, Am. Acad. Implant Prosthodontics, Am. Assn. Functional Orthodontics. Greek Orthodox. Avocations: golf, sailing, horseback riding, playing the flute, sculpture. Office: 12531 E Carson St Hawaiian Gardens CA 90716

STERKEL, MARY J.K., speech, language, hearing pathologist; b. Ft. Collins, Colo., Oct. 6, 1931; d. Forrest Earl and Bernice Norma (Brooks) Kennedy; m. Manuel William Sterkel, Oct. 8, 1949; children: Susan Annette Sterkel McKinney-Motto, Forrest George, William Louis. AA, Goldenwest Community Coll., 1972; BA, Calif. State U., Fullerton, 1975, MA, 1979; postgrad., U. Calif., Irvine, 1985-86. Coordinator sch. improvement plan Huntington Beach (Calif.) City Sch. Dist., 1985-86, speech/lang. specialist, 1976—. Works include audio slide The Normal Development of Speech and Language from Birth to Six Years Old. Vol. speech/lang. pathologist Wycliffe Bible Translators, Huntington Beach, 1977—. Mem. Calif. Speech Lang. Hearing Assn., Am. Speech. Lang. Hearing Assn., Huntington Beach Tchrs. Assn. (sec. 1983-84), Calif. Tchrs. Assn., Nat. Tchrs. Assn., Calif. PTA (life). Avocations: bowling, knitting, biking, reading.

STERLING, DONALD T., professional basketball team executive. Owner Los Angeles (formerly San Diego) Clippers, Nat. Basketball Assn., Los Angeles. Office: care Los Angeles Clippers Los Angeles Memorial Sports Arena 3939 S Figueroa St Los Angeles CA 90037 *

STERLING, ROBERT RAYMOND, educator; b. Bugtussle, Okla., May 16, 1931; s. Roland Pomeroy and Lillian (Neuman) S.; B.S., U. Denver, 1956, M.B.A., 1958; Ph.D., U. Fla., 1964; children—Robert, Kimberly. Asst. prof. social sci. Harpur Coll., Binghamton, N.Y., 1963-66; Sci. Faculty fellow Yale U., 1966-67; asso. prof., then prof. bus. adminstrn. U. Kans., Lawrence, 1967-70, Arthur Young disting. prof., 1970-74; dir. research Am. Acctg. Assn., 1972-74; Jesse Jones Disting. prof. Rice U., Houston, 1974-80, dean Grad. Sch. Adminstrn., 1976-80; Winspear disting. prof. U. Alta. (Can.), 1980-81; sr. fellow Fin. Acctg. Standards Bd., 1981-83; Garff disting. prof. bus. U. Utah, Salt Lake City, 1983—. Bd. dirs. Nat. Bur. Econ. Research, United Way, Trust Corp. Internat. Recipient Gold medal Am. Inst. C.P.A.s, 1968, 74; Bicentennial Disting. Internat. lectr., Europe, 1976; Hoover Disting. Internat. lectr., Australia, 1979. Fellow Acctg. Researchers Internat. Assn. (pres. 1974-80), Am. (v.p. 1975-76), S.W. (pres.) acctg. assns., Accts. for Public Interest (dir.); mem. Nat. Assn. Accts. (dir.), Houston Philos. Soc. (dir.). Author: Theory of the Measurement of Enterprise Income, 1970; (with William F. Bentz) Accounting in Perspective, 1971; Asset Valuation and Income Determination 1971; Research Methodology In Accounting, 1972; Institutional Issues in Public Accounting, 1974; (with A.L. Thomas) Accounting for a Simplified Firm, 1979; Toward a Science of Accounting, 1980; An Essay on Recognition, 1985; editor: Accounting Classics Series; editorial bd., dept. editor Accounting Rev.; editorial bd. Abacus; pub., editor Scholars Book Co. Home: 4409 Viewcrest Dr Salt Lake City UT 84124 Office: U Utah Coll Bus Salt Lake City UT 84117

STERMER, DUGALD ROBERT, designer-illustrator, writer, consultant; b. Los Angeles, Dec. 17, 1936; s. Robert Newton and Mary (Blue) S.; m. Jeanie Kortum; children: Dugald, Megan, Chris, Colin. B.A., UCLA, 1960. Art dir., v.p. Ramparts mag., 1965-70; freelance designer, illustrator, writer, cons. San Francisco, 1970—; founder Pub. Interest Communications, San Francisco, 1974; pres. Frisco Pub Group Ltd. Cons. editor Communication Arts mag., Palo Alto, Calif., 1974—; designer Oceans mag., 1976-82; editor: The Environment, 1972, Vanishing Creatures, 1980; author: The Art of Revolution, 1970, Vanishing Creatures, 1980; designer 1984 Olympic medals; illustration exhbn. Calif. Acad. Scis., 1986. Bd. dirs. Delancey St. Found., 1976—. Recipient various medals, awards for design and illustration nat. and internat. design competitions. Mem. Soc. Publ. Designers, Am. Inst. Graphics Arts, San Francisco Soc. Communicating Arts. Office: 1844 Union St San Francisco CA 94123 Address: 1635 Grove StY San Francisco CA 94117-1322

STERN, ARTHUR CHARLES, magazine editor; b. Salem, Mass., Oct. 20, 1957; s. Henderson Arthur and Marjorie Farnsworth (Green) S. BFA in Drama, U. So. Calif., 1979. Mng. editor Rona Barrett's Hollywood Laufer Publs., 1980-81; features editor Gambling Times, Inc., Hollywood, 1981-82; mng. editor Real Life mag. D.S. Publs., Cresskill, N.J., 1982-83; freelance writer 1983-84; editor The Rangefinder Pub. Co., Santa Monica, Calif., 1984—; Author: Over 40 and Fabulous, 1984. Democrat. Avocations: video, film, theater, golf. Office: The Rangefinder Pub Co 1312 Lincoln Blvd Santa Monica CA 90401

STERN, ARTHUR PAUL, electrical engineer, electronics manufacturing company executive; b. Budapest, Hungary, July 20, 1925; came to U.S., 1951, naturalized, 1956; s. Leon and Bertha (Frankfurter) S.; m. Edith M. Samuel; children—Daniel, Claude, Jacqueline. Dipl. Ing. in Elec. Engring., Swiss Fed. Inst. Tech., Zurich, 1948; M.S. in Elec. Engring., Syracuse U., 1955. Mgr. electronic devices and applications lab. Gen. Electric Co., Syracuse, N.Y., 1957-61; dir. engring. Martin Marietta Corp., Balt., 1961-64; dir. ops. Bunker Ramo Corp., Canoga Park, Calif., 1964-66; v.p., gen. mgr. advanced products div. Magnavox, Torrance, Calif., 1966-79, pres. Magnavox Advanced Products and Systems Co., 1980—; dir. Magnavox Govt. and Indsl. Electronics Co., Torrance; non-resident staff mem. MIT, 1956-59. Co-author: Transistor Circuit Engineering, 1957; Handbook of Automation, Computation and Control, 1961; also articles. U.S., fgn. patentee in field. Fellow AAAS, IEEE guest editor spl. issue IEEE Trans. on Circuit Theory 1956, invited (guest editor spl. issue Procs. IEEE on Integrated Electronics 1964, Centennial medal 1984). Jewish. Home: 606 N Oakhurst Dr Beverly Hills CA 90210 Office: Magnavox Govt & Indsl Electronics 2829 Maricopa St Torrance CA 90503

STERN, BRONCHA MACHLA, child development educator; b. Los Angeles, July 16, 1935; d. Sidney and Rose (Friedel) Schwartzwald; m. Leon Aron Stern, Dec. 21, 1958; children: Bonnie, Gary, Howard. AA, Los Angeles City Coll., 1955; BS, UCLA, 1957, MEd, 1964, postgrad., 1964—. Tchr. Van Nuys (Calif.) Jr. High Sch., 1958-63; substitute tchr. Los Angeles City Schs., 1964-67; prof. child devel. Los Angeles Valley Coll., Van Nuys, 1967—, chmn. dept. family and consumer relations, 1974-77. Mem. Nat. Assn. Edn. Young Children, Calif. Assn. Edn. Young Children, So. Calif. Assn. Edn. Young Children, San Fernando Valley Childcare Consortium, Calif. Community Coll. Early Childhood Educators, Omicron Nu. Democrat. Jewish. Avocations: travelling, cooking, gardening, reading. Office: Los Angeles Valley Coll 5800 Fulton Ave Van Nuys CA 91401

STERN, DANIEL DAVID, conductor; b. Locarno, Switzerland, July 28, 1943; came to U.S., 1949, naturalized, 1955; s. Frans Martin and Dorette (Tchenio) S.; children: Rebecca, Frances. Mus.B., Eastman Sch. Music, Rochester, N.Y., 1965; Mus.M. (NDEA fellow), U. Oreg., 1969, Mus.D. (NDEA fellow), 1973. String specialist Salem (Oreg.) public schs., 1965-67; asst. prof. music N.Mex. Highlands U., 1971-74. Asst. condr., U. Oreg. Symphony Orch., 1968-71, music dir., Boise (Idaho) Philharm., also, Boise Civic Opera, 1974—, condr.-in-residence, Boise State U., 1974-79, founder, 1975, since dir., Sun Valley, also Idaho music festivals; (Recipient Performers cert. conducting U. Oreg. 1971). Bd. dirs. Idaho Civic Ballet, 1977-79; Religious leader Beth Israel Congregation, Boise, 1981-83. Mem. Am. Symphony Orch. League, Condrs. Guild. Club: Boise Rotary. Office: Boise Philharmonic Assn 205 N 10th Suite 617 Boise ID 83702

STERN, JAMES MAX, computer programmer; b. Chgo., June 30, 1955; s. Leo Adolph and Ethel June (Isaacs) S.; m. Barbara Ellen Geller, Mar. 28, 1982. Bachelors, U. Ill., 1976, Masters, 1979. Computer programmer McDonnell Douglas Corp., Long Beach, Calif., 1979-82, Northrop Corp., Hawthorne, Calif., 1982—. Mem. Sigma Xi, Phi Beta Kappa, Phi Kappa Phi. Home: 4915 Tyrone Ave Apt 209 Los Angeles CA 91423 Office: Northrop Corp 1 Northrop Ave 4540/82 Hawthorne CA 90250

STERN, MARK STEVEN, cardiologist; b. N.Y.C., June 18, 1946; s. David H. and Lillian (Zadan) S.; m. Rochelle, Aug. 2, 1969; children: Jennifer, Allison, Jaime, Karen. MD, N.Y. Med. Coll., 1971. Intern. UCLA, 1971, resident, fellowship; cardiologist TriCity Cardiology, Mesa, Ariz. Served to lt. commdr. USPH, 1971-73. Am. Coll. Cardiology fellowship, 1979, AHA, 1981. Republican. Club: Mesa Country. Avocations: golf, boating. Home: 2143 E Calle Maderas Mesa AZ 85203 Office: TriCity Cardiology 1500 Dobson Rd Mesa AZ 85203

STERN, NORMAN STANLEY, optometrist, research consultant; b. Los Angeles, Feb. 1, 1947; s. Maurice and Marsha (Braff) S.; m. Barbara Gail Cuesta, June 14, 1969. BS, 1969, OD, 1971; MA, Pacific Luth. U., 1973; PhD, U.S. Internat. U., 1976; MEd, Pacific U., 1984. Asst. prof. Pacific U., Forest Grove, Oreg., 1977-84, research cons., 1984—. Served to capt. U.S. Army, 1971-77. Mem. Sigma Xi (pres. 1984). Avocation: painting. Home: PO Box 705 Forest Grove OR 97116

STERN, RICHARD DAVID, investment counseling company executive; b. New Rochelle, N.Y., Nov. 5, 1936; s. Leo and Grace Marjorie (Phillips) S.; m. Phyllis Marlene Edelstein, Nov. 20, 1966; children—Marjorie Anne, Andrew Howard. A.B. Princeton U., 1958; M.B.A., Harvard U., 1962. First v.p. Newburger, Loeb & Co., N.Y.C., 1962-74, also dir.; sr. investment officer Central Trust Co., Cin., 1974-76; owner bus. valuation cons. co., Cin., 1976-78; v.p. Gt. Western Bank & Trust Co. (name now Citibank Ariz.), Phoenix, 1978-84; pres. Stern, Ludke & Co., Phoenix, 1984—. Co-author: Air Cushion Vehicles, 1962. Trustee endowment trust Phoenix Chamber Music Soc., 1982—, v.p., 1986—; pres. Cen. Ariz. chpt. Arthritis Found., 1982-84, chmn. planned giving com., 1986—; chmn. endowments and trusts com. Temple Beth Israel, Phoenix, 1980-83; mem. demographic survey com. Jewish Fedn. Greater Phoenix, 1982-84, mem. planning and budget com., 1983-84, chmn. investment com. Endowment Fund, 1984—; pres. Phoenix chpt. Am. Jewish Com., 1983-84; bd. dirs. Asian Arts Council, Phoenix Art Mus., 1987—. Served to lt. comdr. USCGR, 1959. Mem. Phoenix Soc. Fin. Analysts (chmn. profl. conduct com. 1980-83, bd. dirs.), Anti-Defamation League of B'nai B'rith (dir. cen. Ariz. chpt. 1986—). Republican. Home: 6013 E Donna Circle Paradise Valley AZ 85253 Office: Stern Ludke & Co 2035 N Central Ave Phoenix AZ 85004

STERN, STEVEN ALAN, investment banker; b. Chgo., Dec. 5, 1943; s. Sidney J. and Leona (Bernstein) S.; m. Helena Kerner, July 12, 1975; children: Jeremy, Jessica. AB, Brandeis U., 1965; postgrad. Columbia U. Grad. Sch. Bus., 1965-66. CPCU, Ill. Trust officer, First Nat. Bank Chgo., 1966-69; ptnr., Equicon, Inc., Chgo., 1970-74; coordinator Singer for Mayor, Chgo., 1974-75; mgr. underwriting policy CNA Ins., Chgo., 1976-79; project dir. Gov.'s Blue Ribbon Panel, Denver, 1979-81; dir. capital budget State of Colo., Denver, 1981-82; exec. dir. Ctr. Bus. and Econ. Forecasting, U. Denver, 1982-85; v.p. pub. finance, Kirchner, Moore & Co., Denver, 1986—; mem. adv. task force to capital devel. com. Colo. Gen. Assembly, 1985—, chmn. adv. task force subcom. on privatization, 1986—; mem. adv. council Colo. Advanced Tech. Inst., 1986—; guest lectr., 1982—; adv. task forces on capital budgeting, transp. Denver C. of C., 1980—. Author: Colorado Capital Investment Budget, 1982; (with others) Colorado; Investing in the Future, 1981; editor: Techniques of Economic Research, 1981. Speaker, Adopt-A-Sch., Denver Pub. Schs., 1983, 86; participant Leadership Denver, 1983-84; sec.-treas. Colo. Student Obligation Bond Authority, 1984-86, also bd. dirs.; bd. dirs. Circus Arts Found., 1985-86; chmn. devel. com. Stanley Brit. Primary Sch., Denver, 1984; chmn. corp. gifts Epilepsy Found. Chgo., 1977-79, also bd. dirs.; mem. Colo. Open Space Council. Mem. Denver Zool. Soc., Denver Childrens Mus., Denver Mus. Natural Hist., Wilderness Soc., Brandeis U. Alumni Assn., NAACP (life), Colo. Mcpl. Bond Dealers Assn. (chmn. legis. affairs com.), Denver C. of C. Democrat. Jewish. Office: Kirchner Moore & Co 717 Seventeenth St Suite 2700 Denver CO 80202

STERN, STEVEN LESLIE, lawyer; b. N.Y.C., Aug. 17, 1943; s. Fred D. and Erika (Sonder) S.; children: Jeffrey Michael, Jonathan Gary, Jennifer Rose. AB with great distinction, Stanford U., 1965; JD magna cum laude, Harvard U., 1968. Bar: Calif. 1969, D.C. 1985. Assoc. Irell & Manella, Los Angeles, 1968-70; ptnr. McCormac, Davis, Punelli & Stern, Newport Beach, Calif., 1971-76; sole practice Newport Beach, Calif., 1976-82; ptnr. McDermott & Trayner, Newport Beach, Calif., 1982—; lectr. Orange County Bar Assn., Calif. Judge pro tem. Harbor Mcpl. Court, Newport Beach, 1978—. Served as 1st lt. U.S. Army, 1969. Mem. Orange County Bar Assn. (chmn. Health Care Law sect. 1984-85), Los Angeles County Bar Assn., Calif. Soc. Health Care Attys. Democrat. Jewish. Clubs: Dana West Yacht (Dana Point, Calif.) (judge adv., 1980-82), Balboa Ski (Newport Beach) (bd. dirs. 1975-76, 87—). Avocations: skiing, sailing, photography. Office: McDermott & Trayner 1201 Dove St Suite 600 Newport Beach CA 92660

STESSEL, LARRY ROBERT, record company executive; b. N.Y.C., Dec. 27, 1953; s. Saul and Grace Stessel; B.S. in Mktg., U. Fla., 1975. Nat. mgr. coll. promotion CBS Records, 1975-77, prodn. mgr. E/C, 1977-78, dir. prodn. mgmt. East Coast, 1978-79, dir. mdsg. West Coast, 1979—. Address: CBS Records 1801 Century Park W West Los Angeles CA 90067

STETLER, DAVID HAMLIN, JR, electronics technician; b. Seattle, Mar. 25, 1948; s. David Hamlin Sr. and Doreen May (Hagen) S.; m. Jamie Rebecca Holderbein, Sept. 10, 1977; 1 child, Melissa Claire. Diploma, CTC Edn. Systems Inc., Lynnwood, Wash., 1973. Test technician Tally Corp., Kent, Wash., 1973-78; documentation control mgr. Sercel Inc., Redmond, Wash., 1978-86; test technician Intermec Corp., Lynnwood, Washington, 1987—. Served with USMC, 1967-71. Avocations: reading sci. fiction, inventing, golf, bicycling, camping. Office: Intermec Corp 4405 Russell Rd PO Box 360602 Lynnwood WA 98046-9702

STEUCKE, PAUL THEODORE, professional association administrator, artist; b. Oneida, N.Y., Mar. 3, 1939; s. Erwin Wallace and Alice (Voodre) S.; m. Annette Jo Hagaman, Nov. 4, 1960; children: Catherine, Stacia, Susan, Paul Jr. BFA, Commonwealth U., 1962. Dir. art Va. Extension Service, Blacksburg, 1962-63; visual info. specialist USDA Agrl. Research Service, Washington, 1963-65; pub. info. officer USDA Forest Service, Milw., 1965-68; asst. br. chief audio-visuals USDA Forest Service, Washington, 1968-71; exec. sec. U.S. Water Resources Council, Washington, 1971-74; pub. affairs officer Alaska Land Use Commn., Anchorage, 1974-79; pub. affairs specialist Alaska Natural Gas Pipeline Inspector, Anchorage, 1979-83; pub. affairs officer Alaska region FAA, Anchorage, 1983—. One-man shows include Anchorage, Fairbanks, Alaska, Washington, Honolulu, Richmond, 1980—. Fellow Va. Art Mus., 1960, 62; named Fed. Employee of Yr., 1986. Mem. Pub. Relations Soc. Am. (past pres. Alaska chpt., Merit award 1983), Soc. Fed. Artists and Designers (pres. 1970). Office: FAA DOT AAL-5 701 C St Box 14 Anchorage AK 99513

STEVENS, CAROL DAVIDSON, public relations executive; b. St. Paul, May 30, 1945; d. William John and Muriel (Friedland) Davidson; m. Henry A. Pattiz (div. 1970); 1 child, Davidson Matthew; m. Eugene Aristedes Accas, May 22, 1982. BA, Bard Coll., 1964. Dir. publicity Universal Studios Tour, Universal City, Calif., 1970-73; spl. projects exec. ABC-TV, Los Angeles, 1974-76; v.p. TV Rogers & Cowan, Los Angeles, 1976-77, sr. v.p., 1985—; sr. v.p. ICPR Pub. Relations, Los Angeles, 1977-85. Mem. Acad. TV Arts and Scis., Nat. Assn. TV Program Execs., Nat. Cable TV Assn. Office: Rogers & Cowan 10000 Santa Monica Blvd Suite 400 Los Angeles CA 90067-7007

STEVENS, DAVID, economics educator; b. Burbank, Calif., Jan. 26, 1926; s. Frederick and Alpheus (Perkins) S.; 1 child, David Fancher. B.A., Whitman Coll., 1947; M.B.A., Stanford U., 1949. Asst. prof. Okla. State U., 1949-51; asst. prof. econs. Whitman Coll., Walla Walla, Wash., 1951-54; asso. prof. Whitman Coll., 1954-56, prof., 1956-67, Roger and David Clapp prof. of econ. thought, 1958—, dean adminstrn., 1954-64, chmn. faculty, 1982-85; vis. prof. Glasgow U., Scotland, 1964-66, sr. research fellow, 1980—; instr. Am. Inst. Banking. Author: Adam Smith and the Colonial Disturbances, 1976; Editor: The Wedderburn Manuscript In Adam Smith: Correspondence, 1977. Commr. Regional Planning Commn., Walla Walla County, 1960-64; chmn. Walla Walla County chpt. ARC, 1961-63, 75-77. Served to lt. J.G. U.S. Navy, 1943-46. Mem. Am. Econ. Assn., Western Econ. Assn., History of Econ. Soc. Episcopalian. Clubs: Columbia Tower, Rainier (Seattle). Home: 602 Boyer Ave Walla Walla WA 99362 Office: Whitman College Walla Walla WA 99362

STEVENS, ELEANOR SANDRA, professional services executive; b. Oklahoma City, Nov. 1, 1932; d. Benjamin Franklin and Mary Lou (Smith) Williams; children: Fred W., Nathandra, Benjiman, Ola Enaid. AS in medicine, Fresno State U., 1954; student Fresno Adult Edn., Los Angeles Trade Tech., 1972-73. Radio disc jockey, Fresno, Calif., 1954-55; bookkeeper Los Angeles County Assessor, 1961-69; supervisor Holzman-Begue Real Estate Co., Los Angeles, 1969-73; dist. mgr. United Systems, Inc., Los Angeles, 1973-77; pub. relations cons. Harold G. Simon & Assoc., Vernon, Calif., 1977-81; pres. Stevens Personalized Services, Los Angeles, 1982—. Recipient cert. profl. devel. State of Calif., 1983. Mem. Van Nuys Women's Referral Service, Torrance Bus. Mgmt. Assn., Los Angeles Good Neighbor Council, Nat. Assn. Female Execs. Mem. Ch. of God Holiness. Lodge: Order of Eastern Star. Office: 4614 S Western Ave Los Angeles CA 90062

STEVENS, HELEN GROOM, victim prevention specialist; b. Whittier, Calif., Mar. 23, 1930; d. Homer Pearl and Stella Earl (Hibbs) Groom; m. James Henry Stevens, May 26, 1951; children—Mara, Jamie, Lisa, Kevin, Michael, Michele. Black belt Judo, Aikido. Instr. martial arts, 1947-81; devised self-def. course for women, 1969; founder, dir. instrn. Women's Self-Def. Council, 1977; founder, pres. Victim Prevention, Inc., 1983—; performer with Rockettes, Bob Hope Mil. shows, Earl Carroll Theatre; also in movies, on stage and TV, 1944-51. Mem. Stamp Out Crime Council, Internat. Police Assn., Soc. League Against Molesters. Author: The Privilege of Self-Defense: A Capsule View of the Law, 1975; various self def. tng. and teaching manuals. Home: 552-155 Bean Creek Rd Scotts Valley CA 95066 Office: PO Box 5057 Wheat Ridge CO 80034

STEVENS, JONATHAN LEE, academic administrator; b. Roswell, N.Mex., July 24, 1948; s. Jack Duane Stevens; m. Gale A. Rhine, June 10, 1971; children: Arianne, Mark. BS in Computer Sci., USAF Acad., 1971; MS in Computer Sci., U. Tex., 1979. Cert. data processor. Systems programmer SAGE Command and Control Systems, Phoenix, 1971-73; database adminstr. Mil. Personnel Ctr., Randolph AFB, Tex., 1973-78; chief user services Computer Ctr., USAF Acad., Colorado Springs, Colo., 1979-81, comdr. 30th cadet squadron, 1981-82, dir. edn. and research computer ctr., 1982—; commd. major USAF, 1983—. Contbr. articles on data mgmt. to profl. jours. Named Outstanding Mil. Educator USAF Acad. Faculty Dean, 1980. Mem. Assn. Computing Machinery, Air Force Assn., Data Processing Mgrs. Assn., U.S. Jaycees (sec./treas. San Antonio chpt. 1976-78, Outstanding Jaycee 1977). Republican. Roman Catholic. Avocations: tennis, golf. Home: 6435 Snowbird Dr Colorado Springs CO 80918 Office: USAF Acad Hdqrs USAFA/DFSEC Colorado Springs CO 80840

STEVENS, KENT ALLEN, computer scientist, vision researcher; b. Burbank, Calif., Mar. 1, 1948; s. Arthur C. and Ruth (Penwarden) S.; m. Maike Kueppers, Mar. 1, 1984; children: Scott, Nicholas. BS, UCLA, Westwood, 1969, MS, 1971; PhD, MIT, 1979. Research scientist MIT, Cambridge, 1979-82; asst. prof. computer sci. U. Oreg., Eugene, 1982-84, assoc. prof., 1984—. Contbr. chpts. to books; articles to profl. jours. Served with USN, 1971-72. Vision research grantee Air Force Office Sci. Research, Office Naval Research. Mem. The Behavioral And Brain Scis. Assn., Tau Beta Pi. Office: U Oreg Dept Computer and Info Sci Eugene OR 97403

STEVENS, MARY JAYNE, guidance couselor, teacher; b. Joliet, Ill., Dec. 1, 1950; d. Jay Kendall and Shirley May (Van Duyne) Hubbell; m. Robert Lloyd Stevens, Jan. 3, 1976; 1 child, Julie Christine. BA in English, No. Ill. U., 1972; MeD, Westminster Coll., 1982; MA in Educational Psychology, U. Utah, 1985. Tchr. Lewiston (Idaho) Schs., 1973-74; dir. edn. N. Idaho Children's Home, Lewiston, 1974-76; educational coordinator Girls Village, Salt Lake City, 1976-77; cons. Granite Sch. Dist., Salt Lake City, 1977-82, counselor, 1982—; cons. Boise (Idaho) State U., 1974; adj. tchr. Utah State U., Logan, 1976-81; adj. instr. U. Utah, Salt Lake City, 1978-81. Author: Darwin Dandylion, 1985, Joshua Giraffee, 1986. Mem. Am. Sch. Counselors Assn. (del. to nat. conv. 1986), Utah Sch. Counselors Assn. (v.p. 1984-86), Granite Sch. Counselors Assn. (v.p. 1985). Avocations: skiing, reading, writing. Home: 1505 Colony Dr Salt Lake City UT 84117 Office: Granite Sch Dist 3d E 33d S Salt Lake City UT 84111

STEVENS, MICHAEL BRADLEY, industrial engineer; b. Portland, Oreg., Feb. 27, 1957; s. H. Arthur and Susan (Cattin) S.; m. Linda Susanne Edwards, Oct. 12, 1985. BS, Oreg. State U., 1979. Loss control rep. Chubb Ins. Co., Portland, 1980-86; indsl. engr. Bagaard Automation Systems Inc., Portland, 1986—. Vol. ARC, Portland, 1978—. Mem. Am. Soc. Safety Engrs., Sigma Alpha Epsicon (Spl. award for mgmt. duties, 1978). Republican. Avocations: woodworking, skiing, motorcycling, rafting, bicycling. Office: BaGaard Automation Systems Inc 725 SE Lincoln Portland OR 97214

STEVENS, MICHAEL GEIST, zoologist, international fishery administrator; b. Portland, Oreg., May 20, 1950; s. Howard W. and Delores Alvina (Geist) S. BS in Zoology, U. Wis., 1972. Internat. fisheries observer Alaska Dept. Fish and Game, Juneau, 1975-76; mgr. USSR office U.S.-USSR Marine Resources Co., Inc., Nakhodka, 1977-79, mgr. fishing ops., 1980-83; v.p. ops. Profish Internat., Inc., Seattle, 1984—, also bd. dirs.; chmn. U.S. Industry Join Venture Policy com., 1985—. Fellow Coalition for Open Ocean Fisheries (founder 1981). Avocations: golf, fitness, boating, travel. Home: 2524 Boyer E Apt 108 Seattle WA 98102

STEVENS, MICHAEL H., otolaryngologist; b. Salt Lake City, Jan. 6, 1939; s. Henry C. and Grayce (Needham) S.; m. Ruth C. Stevens, Dec. 29, 1965; children: Lisa, Alyce, Daniel, Elizabeth, Caroline, Jonathan. BS, U. Utah, 1963, MD, 1966. Chief ears, nose and throat div. Salt Lake VA Hosp., Salt Lake City, 1974-84; instr. U. Utah Sch. Medicine, Salt Lake City, 1974-76, asst. prof., 1976-81, assoc. prof., 1981-86, asst. dean, 1981-84, prof. otolaryngology, 1986—. Contbr. articles to profl. jours. Mem. Mormon Tabernacle Choir, Salt Lake City, 1985. Served to maj. U.S. Army, 1967-70. Mem. Am. Acad. Otolaryngology (cert. 1984), Am. Soc. Head and Neck Surgery, Triol. Soc., ACS. Home: 3496 Mill Hollow Circle Salt Lake City UT 84106 Office: Univ Ears Nose Throat Assocs 50 N Medical Dr Salt Lake City UT 84132

STEVENS, ROBERT BOCKING, college adminstrator, lawyer; b. U.K., June 8, 1933; naturalized, 1971; s. John Skevington and Enid Dororthy (Bocking) S.; m. Katherine Booth, Dec. 23, 1985; children by previous marriage: Carey, Richard. BA, Oxford U., 1955, BCL, 1956, MA, 1959, DCL, 1984; LLM, Yale U., 1958; LLD (hon.), N.Y. Law Sch., 1984; LL.D. (hon.), Villanova U., 1985, U. Pa., 1987. Barrister-at-law London, 1956; tutor in law Keble Coll. Oxford U., 1958-59; asst. prof. law Yale U., 1959-61, assoc. prof., 1961-65, prof., 1965-76; provost, prof. law and history Tulane U., 1976-78; pres. Haverford Coll., 1978-87; chancellor U. Calif., Santa Cruz, 1987—; vis. prof. U. Tex., 1961, U. East Africa, 1962, Stanford U., 1966; cons. UN, HEW, U.S. Dept. State. Author: The Restrictive Practices Court, 1965, Lawyers and the Courts, 1967, In Search of Justice, 1968, Income Security, 1970, Welfare Medicine in America, 1974, Law and Politics, 1978, The Law School, 1983. Rockefeller Found. grantee, 1962-64, Ford Found. grantee, 1962-64, 73-74, Nat. Endowment for the Humanities grantee, Nuffield Found. grantee, Russell Sage Found. grantee, 1967-68; Hon. fellow Keble Coll. Oxford U., 1985. Mem. Nat. Council on Humanities. Clubs: Oxford and Cambridge (London); Yale (N.Y.C.). Home: University House Meyer Drive Santa Cruz CA 95064 Office: Office of Chancellor Univ Calif Santa Cruz CA 95064 *

STEVENS, SALLY JEAN, social worker; b. Pontiac, Mich., July 28, 1951; d. John Mitchell and Marjorie (Jones) S.; m. Victor Wyzanski Chapman, July 27, 1979; 1 child, Seth David Chapman. BA, Earlham Coll., 1973; MSSA, Case Western Res. U., 1976. Cert. clin. social worker. Alcohol specialist Project STOP, Portland, Oreg., 1976-79, coordinator women's program, clin. supr., 1979; alcohol specialist, psychiat. social worker Family Counseling Ctr., St. Helens, Oreg., 1979-82; youth and family counselor Westside Youth Service Ctr., Portland, 1982-86; pvt. practice social work specializing in youth , adult and family counseling and substance abuse Portland, 1986—; field instr., supr. Portland State U. Sch. Social Work, 1982-86, field liaison, 1986-87. Avocations: photography, skiing. piano, films, literature. Home: 12417 SW Terwilliger Portland OR 97219 Office: 1525 NE Weidler Portland OR 97232

STEVENS, STEPHEN EDWARD, psychiatrist; b. Phila.; s. Edward and Antonia S.; B.A. cum laude, LaSalle Coll., 1950; M.D., Temple U., Phila., 1954; LL.B., Blackstone Sch. Law, 1973; m. Isabelle Helen Gallacher, Dec. 27, 1953. Intern, Frankford Hosp., Phila., 1954-55; resident in psychiatry Phila. State Hosp., 1955-58; practice medicine specializing in psychiatry Woodland Hills, Calif., 1958-63, Santa Barbara, Calif., 1970-77; asst. supt. Camarillo (Calif.) State Hosp., 1963-70; cons. ct. psychiatrist Santa Barbara County, 1974-77; clin. dir. Kailua Mental Health Center, Oahu, Hawaii, 1977—. Served with M.C., USAAF. Diplomate Am. Bd. Psychiatry and Neurology. Fellow Am. Geriatrics Soc. (founding); mem. Am. Acad. Psychiatry and Law, AMA, Am. Psychiat. Assn., Am. Legion, DAV (Oahu chpt. 1), Caledonia Soc., Am. Hypnosis Soc., Am. Soc. Adolescent Psychiatry. Clubs: Hawaiian Canoe, Honolulu, Elks, Aloha String Band (founder and pres.). Home: PO Box 726 Kaneohe HI 96744 Office: 45-691 Keaahala Rd Kaneohe HI 96744

STEVENS, THEODORE FULTON, U.S. senator; b. Indpls., Nov. 18, 1923; s. George A. and Gertrude (Chancellor) S.; m. Ann Mary Cherrington, Mar. 29, 1952 (dec. 1978); children—Susan B., Elizabeth H., Walter C., Theodore Fulton, Ben A.; m. Catherine Chandler, 1980; 1 dau.; Lily Irene. B.A., U. Calif. at Los Angeles, 1947; LL.B., Harvard U., 1950. Bar: Calif., Alaska, D.C., U.S. Supreme Ct. bars. Pvt. practice Washington, 1950-52, Fairbanks, Alaska, 1953; U.S. atty. Dist. Alaska, 1953-56; legis. counsel, asst. to sec., solicitor Dept. Interior, 1956-60; pvt. practice law Anchorage, 1961-68; mem. Alaska Ho. of Reps., 1965-68, majority leader, speaker pro tem, 1967-68; U.S. senator for Alaska 1968—, asst. Rep. leader, 1977-85. Served as 1st lt. USAAF, World War II. Mem. ABA, Alaska Bar Assn., Calif. Bar Assn., D.C. Bar Assn., Am. Legion, VFW. Lodge: Rotary. Home: PO Box 879 Anchorage AK Office: 522 Hart Senate Bldg Washington DC 20510

STEVENSON, CHARLES EDWARD, chemist, researcher; b. Mt. Vernon, N.Y., Feb. 26, 1913; s. Walter Samuel and Lulu Mae (Helreigel) S.; m. Eleanor Clara Conrad, Apr. 24, 1943; children: Elizabeth Jean, Alan Charles, David Robert. BS, Pa. State Coll., 1934, MS, 1937, PhD, 1941. Research chemist Standard Oil Devel. Co., Elizabeth, N.J., 1942-45; process chemist Diamond Glass Co., Royersford, Pa., 1945-47; assoc. div. dir. Argonne Nat. Lab., Idaho Falls, Idaho, 1947-54, supr. fuel cycle facility, 1960-69, sr. scientist, 1969-78; tech. dir. Phillips Petroleum Co., Idaho Falls, 1954-60; cons. Argonne Nat. Lab., 1978-85. Author: The EBR-II Fuel Cycle Story, 1987. Dem. committeeman, Bonneville County, Idaho, 1985-86; mem. planning and zoning commn. City of Ammon, Idaho, 1982-86. Mem. Am. Nuclear Soc., Am. Inst. Chem. Engrs., Nat. Audubon Soc. Avocation: ornithology. Home: 1538 Falcon Dr Idaho Falls ID 83401 Office: Argonne Nat Lab Idaho Falls ID 83401

STEVENSON, JAMES RICHARD, radiologist; b. Ft. Dodge, Iowa, May 30, 1937; s. Lester Lawrence and Esther Irene (Johnson) S.; B.S., U. N.Mex., 1959; M.D., U. Colo., 1963; JD U. N.Mex. 1987; m. Sara Jean Hayman, Sept. 4, 1958; children—Bradford Allen, Tiffany Ann, Jill Renee, Trevor Ashley. Intern U.S. Gen. Hosp., Tripler, Honolulu, 1963-64; resident in radiology U.S. Gen. Hosp., Brook, San Antonio, Tex., 1964-67; radiologist, ptnr. Van Atta Labs., Albuquerque, 1970—; adj. asst. prof. radiology U. N.Mex., 1970-71; pres. med. staff AT & SF Meml. Hosp., 1979-80, trustee, 1982-83. Served with U.S. Army, 1963-70; Vietnam. Decorated Bronze Star Medal. Diplomate Am. Bd. Radiology, Am. Bd. Nuclear Medicine. Allergy fellow, 1960. Fellow Am. Coll. Radiology (councilor 1981—); mem. AMA (physicians recognition award 1969—), Am. Coll. Nuclear Medicine (charter), Am. Coll. Nuclear Physicians (charter), Soc. Nuclear Medicine (v.p. Rocky Mountain chpt. 1975-76), Am. Inst. Ultrasound in Medicine, N.Mex. (pres. 1978-79), N.Am. radiol. socs., N.Mex. (chmn. grievance com.), Albuquerque-Bernalillo County (scholar 1959) med. socs., Nat. Assn. Health Lawyers, ABA (antitrust sect. 1986—), Sigma Chi. Republican. Methodist. Clubs: Elks, Albuquerque Country, Masons, Shriners. Home: 3333 Santa Clara Dr SE Albuquerque NM 87106 Office: Van Atta Labs 8307 Constitution Dr NE Albuquerque NM 87110

STEVENSON, ROBERT MURRELL, educator; b. Melrose, N.Mex., July 3, 1916; s. Robert Emory and Ada (Ross) S. A.B., U. Tex. at El Paso, 1936; grad., Juilliard Grad. Sch. Music, 1938; M.Mus., Yale, 1939; Ph.D., U. Rochester, 1942; S.T.B., Harvard, 1943; B.Litt., Oxford (Eng.) U.; Th.M., Princeton. Instr. music U. Tex., 1941-43, 46; faculty Westminster Choir Coll., Princeton, N.Y., 1946-49; mem. faculty to prof. music UCLA, 1949—, Faculty Research lectr., 1981; Vis. asst. prof. Columbia, 1955-56; vis. prof. Ind. U., Bloomington, 1959-60, U. Chile, 1965-66; cons. UNESCO, 1977. Author: Music in Mexico, 1952, Patterns of Protestant Church Music, 1953, La musica en la catedral de Sevilla, 1954, 85, Music before the Classic Era, 1955, Shakespeare's Religious Frontier, 1958, The Music of Peru, 1959, Juan Bermudo, 1960, Spanish Music in the Age of Columbus, 1960, Spanish Cathedral Music in the Golden Age, 1961, La musica colonial en Colombia, 1964, Protestant Church Music in America, 1966, Music in Aztec and Inca Territory, 1968, Renaissance and Baroque Musical Sources in the Americas, 1970, Music in El Paso, 1970, Philosophies of American Music History, 1970, Written Sources For Indian Music Until 1882, 1973, Christmas Music from Baroque Mexico, 1974, Foundations of New World Opera, 1973, Seventeenth Century Villancicos, 1974, Latin American Colonial Music Anthology, 1975, Vilancicos Portugueses, 1976, Josquin in the Music of Spain and Portugal, 1977, American Musical Scholarship, Parker to Thayer, 1978, Liszt at Madrid and Lisbon, 1980, Wagner's Latin American Outreach, 1983, Spanish Musical Impact Beyond the Pyrenees, 1250-1500, 1985; contbg. editor: Handbook Latin Am. Studies, 1976—; editor: Inter-Am. Music Rev, 1978—; contbr. to: New Grove Dictionary of Music and Musicians, 9 other internat. encys. Served with AUS, 1943-46. Decorated Army Commendation ribbon.; Recipient Fulbright research awards, 1958-59, 64, 70-71, Carnegie Found. teaching award, 1955-56; Ford Found. fellow, 1953-54; Gulbenkian Found. fellow, 1966, 81; Guggenheim fellow, 1962; NEH fellow, 1974; recipient Gabriela Mistral award OAS, 1985; Gold medal Sociedad Espanola de Musicologia, 1985; Orgn. Am. States medal, 1986. Office: 405 Hilgard Ave Los Angeles CA 90024

STEWARD, PATRICIA ANN RUPERT, real estate consultant; b. Panama City, Panama, Apr. 20, 1945 (parents Am. citizens); d. Paul S. and Ernestina M. (Ward) Rupert; grad. Sch. of Mortgage Banking, Grad. Sch. of Mgmt., Northwestern U., 1979; m. Robert M. Levine, Oct. 28, 1978; children by previous marriage—Donald F. Steward, Christine Marie Steward. Vice pres. Asso. Mortgage & Investment Co., Phoenix, 1969-71; v.p., br. mgr. Sun Country Funding Corp., Phoenix, 1971-72, Freese Mortgage Co., Phoenix, 1972-74, Utah Mortgage Loan Corp., Phoenix, 1974-81; pres. Elles Corp., 1982—; condr. numerous seminars on mortgage fin. State chmn. Ariz. Leukemia Dr., 1977-78, mem. exec. com., 1979-80; troop leader Cactus Pine council Girl Scouts U.S.A., 1979-80; bd. dirs. Nat. Mental Health Assn., 1986—, Ariz. Mental Health Assn., pres., 1986-87, bd. dirs., treas. Maricopa Mental Health Assn., 1984-85, v.p., 1985-86, pres., 1986-87; apptd. by state supreme ct. to Ariz. Foster Care Rev. Bd., 1984—, chairperson Bd. 8, 1986—. Recipient cert. of appreciation Multiple Listing Service, Phoenix Bd. Realtors, 1975, Multiple Listing Service, Glendale Bd. Realtors, 1977. Lic. mortgage broker, Ariz. Mem. Ariz. Mortgage Bankers Assn. (dir. 1981-82, chmn. edn. com. 1981-82, founder continuing edn. seminar series 1981), Young Mortgage Bankers Assn. (chmn. exec. com. 1980-81), Cen. Ariz. Homebuilders Assn. Republican. Author: A Realtors Guide to Mortgage Lending, 1972. Office: Elles Corp 320 E McDowell Rd Suite 100 Phoenix AZ 85004

STEWART, B. CHARLENE, retired data processing manager; b. Bath, N.Y., July 27, 1934; d. Fay Henry and Norma Elizabeth (Gage) Stewart; m. W. B. Stewart, June 18, 1955; children—Jim, Debbie, Shirley. B.A. in Chemistry, Houghton (N.Y.) Coll., 1955. Cert. real estate salesman, Alaska. Tchr. high sch., Bradford, N.Y., 1955-56, Kenai, Alaska, 1956-57; acctg. clk. U.S. Army, Kenai, FHA, Anchorage, 1957-59; EDP prgrammer State of Alaska, Juneau, 1966-71, systems analyst, Anchorage, 1972-80; customer service mgr. Anchorage Data Ctr., 1980-83, ret., 1983—; lectr. on data processing. Mem. Anchorage Republican Women, 1982—, LWV. Mem. Data Processing Mgmt. Assn., Am. Assn. Motor Vehicle Adminstrs. Republican. Methodist. Clubs: Juneau Sweet Adelines, Internat. Women's Barbershop. Designer, programmer state on-line system to issue motor vehicle registrations and titles. Home: PO Box 1007 Willow AK 99688

STEWART, CHERYL MAURINE, social worker; b. Phoenix, Jan. 20, 1944; d. William Frank Wayne and Stella Maurine (Boyd) Edel; m. Richard Alan Stewart, June 7, 1966 (div. July 1982); children: Scott Edel, Michael Boyd. AA, Phoenix Jr. Coll., 1964; BA, Ariz. State U., 1966, MSW, 1972. Social worker Maricopa County Gen. Hosp., Phoenix, 1970-73, Ariz. State Dept. Child Protective Services, Phoenix, 1974, West Yavapai Guidance Clinic, Prescott, Ariz., 1974-81; pvt. practice social work Yavapai Big Bros./ Sisters, Prescott, 1981-83; pvt. practice psychotherapy Prescott, 1981—; expert witness child sexual abuse Yavapai County Superior Ct., Prescott, 1981—; coordinator sexual assault vols. Prescott Police Dept., 1982—; mediator, conciliator Yavapai County Superior Ct., 1985—; therapist Prescott Child Devel. Ctrs., 1981—; contracted therapist Huddleston House Ariz. State Dept. Econ. Security, 1984-86; mem. faculty Prescott Coll., 1986—. Mem. Prescott Town Hall, 1981-86; den mother Boy Scouts Am., Prescott, 1981—; vol. educator Prescott Pub. Schs. Faith House, 1981—. Recipient Women Helping Women award Soroptomists, Prescott, 1986. Mem. Nat. Register Clin. Social Workers (diplomate), Nat. Assn. Social Workers (cert.), Alpha Kappa Delta, Kappa Kappa Gamma (scholarship chmn. 1965-66). Democrat. Presbyterian. Avocations: collecting antiques, piano, swimming, working with children. Home: 1205 Country Club Dr Prescott AZ 86301

STEWART, DONALD CHARLES, chemical research administrator, retired; b. Salt Lake City, Dec. 15, 1912; s. John Caldwell and Nelle Marsh (Flandro) S.; m. Dorothy Wilhelmina Bockhop, Apr. 16, 1948; children: Katharine Ann, Deborah Jean. AB, UCLA, 1935; MS, U. So. Calif., 1940; BS, Va. Poly. Inst., 1944; PhD, U. Calif., Berkeley, 1950. Chemist Knudsen Creamery, Los Angeles, 1935-42; asst. sect. chief Manhattan Project, Chgo., 1944-46; assoc. chemist Argonne Nat. Lab., Chgo., 1950-59, assoc. div. dir., 1959-77, cons., 1978—; observer AEC, Bikini Islands, 1946; cons. Japanese AEC, 1960, Republic of Korea AEC, 1965, Taiwan, Republic of China, 1965; participant staff exchange program U.K. Atomic Research Establishment, Harwell, Eng., 1957-58. Author: Handling Radioactivity, 1981, Data for Radioactive Wast Management, 1985; editor: Progress in Nuclear Energy, Vols. 2-12, 1966-73. Served as sgt. U.S. Army, 1942-46. Fellow AAAS; mem. Am. Chem. Soc., Research Soc. Am. Democrat. Avocations: gardening, writing, reading. Home: 17220 Tamara Ln Watsonville CA 95076

STEWART, DONALD MARTIN, plant pathologist; b. Rembrandt, Iowa, Jan. 20, 1908; s. Alexander Porter and Nellie Louise (Martin) S.; B.S., U. Minn., 1931; postgrad. U. Calif., Berkeley, 1938; Ph.D., U. Minn., 1953; m. Marion G. Christiansen, May 14, 1938; children: Margo Jeanne, Bonnie Ann. Dist. leader White Pine Blister Rust Control, USDA, Duluth, Minn., 1935-51, research plant pathologist U. Minn., St. Paul, 1951-70, liaison officer, project mgr. improvement field crops in Egypt, 1970-74, agronomist, nat. sorghum millet project Yemen Arab Republic, 1977-78; adj. prof., cons. for new crops, dept. plant scis. U. Ariz., Tucson, 1978-86, ret.; pres. Minn. Archeol. Soc., 1965. Fulbright-Hays grantee, Romania, 1965; recipient cert. of appreciation U.S. Dept. Agr., 1974, Mpls. Public Schs., 1968-69; cert. of Merit award U.S. Dept. Agr., 1958. Mem. Am. Phytopath. Soc., Sigma Xi. Club: Mason. Contbr. articles to profl. jours. Home: 9476 E Shiloh St Tucson AZ 85710

STEWART, ISAAC DANIEL, JR., associate chief justice Utah Supreme Court; b. Salt Lake City, Nov. 21, 1932; s. Isaac Daniel and Orabelle (Iverson) S.; m. Elizabeth Bryan, Sept. 10, 1959; children: Elizabeth Ann, Shannon. B.A., U. Utah, 1959, J.D., 1962. Bar: Utah 1962. Atty. Dept. Justice, 1962-65; asst. prof., then asso. prof. U. Utah Coll. Law, 1965-70; partner firm Jones, Waldo, Holbrook & McDonough, Salt Lake City, 1970-79; justice Utah Supreme Ct., 1979-86, now assoc. chief justice, 1986—; lectr. in field; dir. Med. Devel. Corp.; Mem. Utah Bd. Oil, Gas and Mining, 1976-78, chmn., 1977-78; Utah rep. Interstate Oil Compact Commn., 1977-78, exec. com. 1978-79; mem. adv. com. rules of procedure Utah Supreme Ct., 1983—. Contbr. articles to legal jours. Chmn. subcom. on legal rights and responsibilities of youth Utah Gov's Com. on Youth, 1972; pres. Salt Lake Chpt. Council Fgn. Relations, 1982; bd. dirs. U. Utah Alumni. Named Apellate Judge of Year, 1986. Mem. ABA, Am. Judicature Soc., Utah Bar Assn. (Appellate Judge of Yr. 1986), Salt Lake County Bar Assn., U. Utah Alumni Assn. (bd. dirs. 1985—), Phi Beta Kappa, Order of Coif, Phi Kappa Phi, Sigma Chi (Significant Sig award 1987). Mormon. Address: 332 State Capitol Bldg Salt Lake City UT 84114

STEWART, JAMES H., public relations executive; b. Boston, July 15, 1941; s. James Henry and Mary E. (Cummins) St.; m. Linda A. LaFond, Oct. 24, 1964; children: Laurie, Cathi, Brian, Daniel. BS in Pharmacy, Mass. Coll. Pharmacy, 1964. Registered Pharmacist. Pharmacist various pharmacies, Boston, 1964-74; dir. profl. relations Pilgrim Health Applications, Bedford, Mass., 1974-78; exec. dir. Mass. State Pharm. Assn., Boston, 1978-84; mgr. indsl. affairs Syntex Labs., Inc., Palo Alto, Calif., 1984—. Mem. fin. com. Town of Kingston, Mass., 1974-77; mem. capital budget com. Town of Marshfield, Mass., 1980-83. Fellow Am. Coll. Apothecaries; mem. Am. Pharm. Assn., Am. Soc. Hosp. Pharmacists, Soc. Consumer Affairs Profls. Roman Catholic. Lodge: Knights of Columbus (dist. dep.). Avocations: golf, tennis. Office: Syntex Labs Inc 3401 Hillview Ave Palo Alto CA 94304

STEWART, JANICE MAE, lawyer; b. Medford, Oreg., Feb. 13, 1951; d. Glenn Logan and Eathel Mae (Jones) S.; m. F. Gordon Allen III, Aug. 10, 1975; children—Benjamin Stewart, Rebecca Mae. AB in Econs., Stanford U., 1972; JD, U. Chgo., 1975. Bar: Ill. 1976, Oreg. 1977, U.S. Dist. Ct. Oreg. 1977, U.S. Ct. Appeals (9th cir.) 1978. Assoc. Winston & Strawn, Chgo., 1975-76; ptnr. McEwen, Gisvold Rankin & Stewart, Portland, Oreg., 1976—. Mem. Multnomah County Profl. Responsibility Com., Portland, 1979-82, Oreg. Profl. Responsibility Bd., 1982-85, Oreg. State Bar Practice and Prodecure Com., 1985—, Profl. Liability Fund Def. Panel, Portland, 1985—, Multnomah County Judicial Selection com., 1985—. Mem. ABA, Oreg. Bar Assn., Multnomah County Bar Assn., Network of Bus. and Profl. Women, Phi Beta Kappa. Democrat. Club: City (Portland). Office: McEwen Gisvold Rankin & Stewart 1100 SW 6th Ave Standard Plaza Suite 1408 Portland OR 97204

STEWART, JEAN LOUISE, chemist; b. Redlands, Calif., Nov. 22, 1957; d. Elbert Wilton and Lillian Florence (Wolfe) S.; m. Paul Norman Hirtz, June 14, 1986. BA, Sonoma State U., 1982. Analytical chemist Anatec Labs., Inc., Santa Rosa, Calif., 1981-83; lab. teaching asst. Sonoma State U., Rohnert Park, Calif., 1982, 84, tchr. chemistry Upward Bound program, 1984, 85; ptnr. Thermochem Labs., Santa Rosa, 1984—; v.p. Thermochem Labs, Santa Rosa, 1986—. Mem. Am. Chem. Soc., Assn. Women in Sci., LWV, Geothermal Resources Council. Democrat. Avocations: swimming, gardening, botanical study, sailing. Home: 9825 Keith Ct Windsor CA 95492 Office: Thermochem 6119 Old Redwood Hwy Suite A-2 Santa Rosa CA 95401

STEWART, JOHN HARRIS, geologist; b. Berkeley, Calif., Aug. 7, 1928; s. George Rippey and Theodosia (Burton) S.; m. Sarah Elizabeth Dwight, Nov. 3, 1962; children: Edward Dwight, William Rippey. BS, U. N.Mex., 1950; PhD, Stanford U., 1961. Geologist U.S. Geol. Survey, Menlo Park, Calif., 1951—. Contbr. articles to profl. jours. Recipient Meritorious Service award, U.S. Dept. Interior, 1981. Fellow Geol. Soc. Am. Home: 30 Los Cherros Ln Portola Valley CA 94025 Office: US Geol Survey 345 Middlefield Rd Menlo Park CA 94025

STEWART, JOHN ULYSSES, JR., municipal official; b. Oakland, Calif., Apr. 14, 1950; s. John Ulysses Stewart and Emma Lee (Smith) Ford. Housing inspection cert., bldg. inspection cert., Chabot Coll., 1973. Lic. real estate agt., Calif. Housing rep. City of Oakland, 1974—; real estate agt. Better Homes Realty Agy., Oakland, 1977—; housing code cons., Oakland, 1979—. Club: All Seasons (Oakland). Avocations: weightlifting, football, basketball. Home: 6864 Sherwick Dr Berkeley CA 94705 Office: City of Oakland Housing Conservation Div 1417 Clay St Room 305 Oakland CA 94705

STEWART, KATHLEEN JO, social worker; b. Monterey Park, Calif., Jan. 12, 1943; d. Lawrence A. Rogers and Bernice L. (Sprague) Hagar; m. Donald L. Stewart, June 4, 1960 (div. Mar. 1984); children: K. Renee Alexander, Donald Kent. BS, Ariz. State U., 1983, MSW, 1985. V.p. Don Stewart Assn., Phoenix, 1960-84, cons., 1985—; pres., founder Feed My People, Phoenix, 1979-85, cons., 1986—. Guest vocalist White House, Washington, 1980, 82. Mem. Nat. Assn. Social Workers, Am. Psychol. Assn., Masterworks Chorale, Choral Union, Psi Chi (sec. 1981-82). Democrat. Avocations: music, golf, skiing, hiking. Home: 5110 N 32d St 3224 Phoenix AZ 85018 Office: Don Stewart Assn 17602 N Black Canyon Hwy Phoenix AZ 85023

STEWART, LAWRENCE COLM, electrical engineer; b. Mineola, N.Y., July 12, 1955; s. Samuel Woodard and Irene (Colm) S. BSEE, MIT, 1976; MSEE, Stanford U., 1977, PhDEE, 1981. Mem. research staff Xerox Palo Alto (Calif.) Research Ctr., 1977-83, Digital Equipment Corp., Palo Alto, 1984—. Mem. IEEE, Assn. Computing Machinery, Sigma Xi, Eta Kappa Nu. Avocations: ham radio, skiing. Home: 2420 Greer Rd Palo Alto CA 94303 Office: DEC Research Ctr 130 Lytton Ave Palo Alto CA 94301

STEWART, LINDA HOLMES, marketing professional; b. Glendale, Calif., Mar. 17, 1945; d. Leonard Oscar and Ruth Emilie (Young) H.; m. Michael Alexander Stewart, Jan. 2, 1971 (div. Dec. 1978). BS in Bus., Oreg. State U., 1966; MA in Math., U. Wash., 1971. Sr. programmer Burroughs, Pasadena, Calif., 1972-74; mgr. communications TRW Communications Group, Mountain View, Calif., 1974-81; product mgr. Atari Co., San Jose, 1981-83; cons. San Jose, 1983-84; pres. Stewart Enterprises, Mountain View, Calif., 1984—; mgr. mktg. Excelan, San Jose, 1984—. Pres. Palmdale Homeowner's Assn., Mountain View, 1981-84. Office: Excelan 2180 Fortune Dr San Jose CA 95131

STEWART, LUCILLE MARIE, special education program specialist; b. Pittsburgh, Feb. 24; d. William H. and Edna (Hoffman) S. B.Ed. Duquesne U.; M.Ed., U. Pittsburgh; postgrad. courses Columbia U., U. Calif., Calif. State U. Cert. elem. and secondary tchr., spl. edn. tchr., supr., adminstr. Tchr. Lincoln (Ill). State Sch., 1953; group leader Retarded Education Alliance, N.Y.C., 1954-58; program dir. Pomona (N.Y.) Camp for Retarded, summers 1960-63; tchr. Stockton Sch., San Diego, 1964-65; tchr. Cathdral City (Calif.) Sch., 1967-78; prin. elem. summer schs. Palm Springs (Calif.) Unified Sch. Dist., 1971-72; prin.-tchr. Summer Extended Sch. for Spl. Students, 1979—. Mem. NEA, Calif. Tchrs. Assn., Palm Springs Tchrs. Assn., Palm Springs Ednl. Leadership Assn., Calif. Assn. Program Specialists, AAUW, Assn. for Supervision and Curriculum Devel., Am. Assn. Childhood Edn. Alpha Kappa Alpha, Phi Delta Kappa. Clubs: Toastmistress, Cath. Daus. Office: Extended Summer Sch 333 S Farrell Palm Springs CA 92262

STEWART, RALPH LEWIS, electrical engineer; b. Helena, Ark., June 27, 1924; s. John Russell and Martha Virginia (Gearhart) S.; m. Patricia Ann Paris, Sept. 3, 1949 (div. May 1967); children: Ralph Steven, Jacqueline Suzanne Stewart Rader; m. Ruth Mutscher, July 5, 1980. BSEE, U. Ark., 1949. Registered profl. engr., Colo., Okla., Tex., land surveyor, Colo., Okla., Tex. Dist. engr. Ark. Power and Light Co., Helena, 1949-51; chief meters and relays Grand River Dam Authority, Pryor, Okla., 1951-55; field engr. Schlumberger Well Surveying Corp., Borger, Tex., 1955-57; engr. Miner and Miner, Littleton, Colo., 1957-59; mgr. facilities engring. Martin Marietta Corp., Denver, 1959-87. Chmn. planning and zoning commn., Pryor, 1954-55. Served to 2d lt. USAAF, 1942-45. Mem. IEEE, Am. Assn. Contamination Control (pres. 1969-70), Internat. Facilities Mgmt. Assn., Blue Key Soc., Theta Tau. Democrat. Methodist. Lodges: Masons, Shriners. Avocations: photography, model railroading, carpentry. Home: 6533 S Grant St Littleton CO 80121

STEWART, SIGRID JOAN, research scientist; b. Rochester, N.Y., May 21, 1941; d. Edwin Russell and Inez Winifred (Tayler) Westcott; m. Carleton Colburn Stewart, June 22, 1963; children: Cynthia, Gregory. BA, Hartwick Coll., 1963. Chemistry technician Strong Meml. Hosp., Rochester, N.Y., 1963-64; cell biology technician Washington U., St. Louis, 1978-80; life sci. technician Los Alamos (N.Mex) Nat. Lab., 1981—. Instr., camp dir., scoutleader Girl Scouts U.S., St. Louis, 1971-79. Avocations: skiing, hiking, gardening, house renovation. Home: 1137 San Ildefonso Los Alamos NM 87544 Office: Los Alamos Nat Lab Los Alamos NM 87545

STEWART, WARD DOUGLAS, landscape architect; b. Lake City, Iowa, Aug. 23, 1939; s. Edward and Zona Gail (Newcomb) S.; m. Sheryl Elizabeth Snoke, Nov. 26, 1970; children: Sara Lynn, Andrew Douglas. Student, Iowa State U., 1958-59, Drake U., 1959-60; BS, U. Ariz., 1965. Registered landscape architect, Ariz., Tex., Fla., Calif., La. Landscape architect City of Tucson, 1966-75; mgr. AG Middle East, Doha, Qatar, 1975-77; project mgr. Hartwig & Assocs., Jacksonville, Fla., 1977-78; dept. mgr. VTN Consol., Irvine, Calif., 1978-79; project mgr. Oson Assocs., Newport Beach, Calif., 1980-83; owner STEWART 4, Newport Beach, 1983—. Contbr. articles to profl. jours. Mem. Am. Soc. Landscape Architects, Alpha Sigma Phi (v.p, treas.). Democrat. Presbyn. Avocations: camping, stamps, coins, motorcycles, music. Home and Office: 1737 Centella Pl Newport Beach CA 92660

STEWART, WILLIAM HIRAM, minister; b. Washington, Dec. 27, 1935; s. George Moody Stewart and Jane (Halliwell) Biederman; m. Janila Lee Oertel, June 15, 1962; children: Lucinda Kay, Mark William. BA in Bible Studies cum laude, Northwestern Coll., Mpls., 1958; 1st class FCC lic. and diploma, Don Martin Sch. Radio and TV Arts and Sci., 1959; MA, Mennonite Brethren Bibl. Sem., 1978. Ordained to ministry Bapt. ch., 1970. Minister Youth for Christ, Mpls., 1954-58; youth minister Grace Community Ch., North Hollywood, Calif., 1958-59, administr., youth minister, 1965-68; minister Youth for Christ, Los Angeles, 1960-63, Oakland, Calif., 1963-65; minister youth edn. First Bapt. Ch., Modesto, Calif., 1968—; mem. com. Youth for Christ Nat. Club, 1960's. Author: Wittenburg Door, 1970. Mem. Pub. Sch. Com., Modesto, 1970's; vice chmn. 15th Dist. Congl. Awards Com., 1985. Mem. Nat. Network Youth Ministries Bd., Am. Sci. Affiliation. Republican. Avocations: radio, TV, hunting. Home: 909 Meadowood Dr Modesto CA 95355 Office: 1st Bapt Ch 808 Needham PO Box 4309 Modesto CA 95352

STEWART-SMITH, DAVID ALLEN, radiation scientist, state agency official; b. Duluth, Minn., Sept. 11, 1952; s. George Stephen and Vivian Lorraine (Erickson) Smith; m. Carol Ann Stewart, July 9, 1977; 1 child, Kathryn Emma. BS, Lewis and Clark Coll., 1974; M Pub. Adminstrn. with honors, Portland State U., 1985. Radiochemist Oreg. Div. Health, Portland, 1974-78, radiation specialist, 1978-82, legis. coordinator, 1983, health physicist, 1983-84; radioactive materials mgr. Oreg. Dept. Energy, Salem, 1985—; adj. instr. Portland State U., 1983. Mem. Health Physics Soc. (sec. Cascade chpt. 1984-86, editor chpt. newsletter 1984-86). Presbyterian. Avocations: history of physics, camera collecting, family activities. Home: 9095 SW Hill St Tigard OR 97223 Office: Oreg Dept Energy 625 Marion St NE Salem OR 97310

STICCA, PERRY, electronics executive; b. Mt. Vernon, N.Y., June 5, 1957; s. Pat M. and Pauline (Cruciani) S. BA, SUNY, Binghamton, 1979, MBA, 1980. Programmer Texaco, Inc., White Plains, N.Y., 1981; systems analyst Texaco, Inc., Los Angeles, 1981—. Unitarian. Office: Texaco Inc 10 Universal City Plaza Universal City CA 91608

STICHT, DOUGLAS JOHN, electrical engineer; b. N.Y.C., Dec. 21, 1945; s. John Peter and Anna (Gaidis) S.; m. Cathine Woolery, June 3, 1967; children: Jessica, Steven. BSEE, U. Ariz., 1967, MSEE, 1969, PhD, 1975. Elec. engr. Naval Weapons Ctr., China Lake, Calif., 1969-75, supervisory electronics engr., 1975-82, program mgr., 1982—; grad. instr. Calif. State U., Northridge, 1978—. Contbr. articles to profl. jours. Pres., treas. Indian Wells Valley Concert Assn., Ridgecrest, Calif., 1983—; pres. Grace Luth. Ch., Ridgecrest, 1982, Ridgecrest Montessori Sch., 1971-72; team coach China Lake Youth Recreational Soccer League, Ridgecrest, 1981-84. Fellow Naval Weapons Ctr., 1973; recipient Michelson Lab. award, Naval Weapons Ctr., 1986. Mem. IEEE, Old Crows, Valley Vultures, Sigma Xi. Club: China Lake Tennis. Avocations: tennis, radio controlled model aircraft. Home: 820 W Vicki Ridgecrest CA 93555 Office: Naval Weapons Ctr Code 35403 China Lake CA 93555-6001

STICKLER, JOHN COBB, publisher, journalist; b. Washington, July 18, 1937; s. Joseph Harding and Virginia Murray (Cobb) S.; m. Lucy Han, 1964; children: Stephen Han, Alexander Han. BA with honors, Yale U., 1959; cert. Peace Corps, Pa. State U., 1961. Stringer CBS Radio News, Seoul, Republic of Korea, 1967-76; owner, mgr. S/K Internat. Advt., Seoul, 1966-76; pub., owner Jour. Applied Mgmt., Walnut Creek, Calif., 1978-81; account exec. Cunningham & Walsh, San Francisco, 1981; dir. mktg. Neighborhood Housing Services, Tucson, 1982; dir. pub. relations Sheraton Tucson El Conquistador Resort, 1983—. Editor/pub.: Advertising in Korea, 1973, 2d revised edit., 1975; (poetry) Growing Up Afraid, 1985; contbr. articles to mags. Served with U.S. Army, 1962-64. Recipient advt. prize Hotel Sales and Mgmt. Assn., 1974, CLIO award, 1975, poetry award Nat. Writers Club, 1977, poetry award World Order Narrative Poets, 1978. Mem. Pub. Relations Soc. Am., Internat. Assn. Bus. Communicators (pres. Tucson chpt. 1985-86), Soc. Southwestern Authors (v.p. 1986—), Am. Soc. Journalists and Authors, UNESCO Assn. USA (bd. dirs. 1981—), Internat. Advt. Assn. (founder Korea chpt. 1967), Royal Asiatic Soc. (Korea br.). Democrat. Clubs: Tucson Press, Yale of Tucson. Home: 8300 N McCarty Rd Tucson AZ 85704 Office: Sheraton El Conquistador Resort 10000 N Oracle Rd Tucson AZ 85704

STICKNEY, ROBERT ROY, fisheries educator; b. Mpls., July 2, 1941; s. Roy E. and Helen Doris (Nelson) S.; m. LuVerne C. Whiteley, Dec. 29, 1961; children: Robert Roy, Marolan Margaret. BS, U. Nebr., 1967; MA, U. Mo., 1968; PhD, Fla. State U., 1971. Cert. fisheries scientist. Research assoc. Skidaway Inst. Oceanography, Savannah, Ga., 1971-73, asst. prof., 1973-75; asst. prof. Texas A&M U., College Station, 1975-78, assoc. prof., 1978-83, prof., 1983-84; prof. zoology, dir. Fisheries Research Lab., So. Ill. U., Carbondale, 1984-85; dir. Sch. of Fisheries U. Wash., Seattle, 1985—; chmn. S-168 com. So. Regional Coop. Research Project, 1981-84; chmn., bd. dirs. We. Region Agrl. Consortium, 1987. Author: Principles of Warmwater Aquaculture, 1979, Estuarine Ecology of the Southeastern United States and Gulf of Mexico, 1984; also articles; editor Culture of Non-Salmonid Freshwater Fisheries, 1986. Served with USAF, 1959-63. Mem. Am. Fisheries Soc. (pres. fish culture sect. 1983-84, Tex. Aquaculturist of Yr. 1979), Am. Inst. Fish Research Biologists (past Tex. div. dir.), Am. Inst. Nutrition, World Agr. Soc. (bd. dirs.), Am. Soc. Limnology and Oceanography. Home: 17507 NE 133 Redmond WA 98052 Office: U Wash Sch Fisheries WH-10 Seattle WA 98195

STIDD, CHARLES KETCHUM, meteorologist; b. Independence, Oreg., Aug. 12, 1918; s. Charles Leland and Ruth Elizabeth (Ketchum) S.; m. Barbara Jean Mills, May 30, 1942; children: John Mills, Charles Winfield. BS, Oreg. State U., 1941; postgrad., UCLA, 1942-43. Research forcaster U.S. Weather Bur., Honolulu and Washington, 1946-55; pvt. practice meteorology Pendleton, Oreg., 1955-62, 1979—; research assoc. U. Nev., Reno, 1962-71; specialist in meteorology U. Calif. Scripps Oceanography Lab., San Diego, 1971-79. Contbr. articles to profl. jours. Served to capt. USAF, 1942-46, CBI. Mem. Am. Meteorol. Soc. (cert.), Am. Geophysics Union, Assn. Computer Machinery, Sigma Xi. Home and Office: 4005 Carmel View Rd #61 San Diego CA 92130

STIEGHORST, JUNANN JORDAN, seed co. exec.; b. Hydro, Okla., June 8, 1923; d. John Wallace and Myrtle Mae (Harrison) Jordan; student Southwestern Coll., Weatherford, Okla., 1940-41; B.A. in L.S., U. Okla., 1944, B.A. in English, 1947, postgrad., 1959-60; postgrad. So. Meth. U., 1945; m. Guenther Paul Stieghorst, Aug. 13, 1955; 1 son, Theodore Mark.

Stewardess, Braniff Airways, 1944-45; advt. copywriter, model Neiman-Marcus, Dallas, Tex., 1945-46, dir. clientele and charge account promotion, 1947-55; advt. copywriter Wilhelm-Laughlin-Wilson, Dallas, 1946; dir. public relations and clientele Lichensteins, Corpus Christi, Tex., 1955-56; clientele dir. Joskes of Tex., San Antonio, 1957-58; children's librarian Jefferson County Public Library, Golden, Colo., 1967-69; co-owner Stieghorst Seed Co., Golden, 1973—. Recipient award for outstanding book U. Okla., 1966. Mem. AAUW, Colo. Archaeol. Soc., DAR (nat. chairman's award 1975, nat. chmn. western div., state chmn., chpt. regent), Alpha Chi Omega. Republican. Lutheran. Clubs: Soroptimist, Braniff Clipped B's. Author: Bay City and Matagorda County: A History, 1965; Colorado Historical Markers, 1978; History of Mount Lookout Chapter 1923-1960, 1983; contbr. articles on retail bus. to various mags.

STIFEL, FREDERICK BENTON, pastor, biochemist, nutritionist; b. St. Louis, Jan. 30, 1940; s. Carl Gottfried and Alma J. (Clark) S.; m. Gail Joane Stewart, Aug. 10, 1963; children: Tim, Faith, Seth, Elizabeth. BS, Iowa State U., 1962, PhD, 1967; MDiv., Melodyland Sch. Theol., Anaheim, Calif., 1979. Ordained to ministry Evang. Presbyn. Ch., 1981. Lab. supr., research chemist U.S. Army Med. Research and Nutrition Lab., Denver, 1968-74, Letterman Army Inst. Research, San Francisco, 1974-76; intern pastor Melodyland Christian Ctr., Anaheim, 1979-80; assoc. pastor Faith Presbyn. Ch., Aurora, Colo., 1980—; chmn. Care of Candidates Com., Presbytery of West, Denver, 1985—; bd. dirs. Christian Family Services, Aurora, Love, Inc. of Metro Denver. Contbr. clin. med. and nutritional articles to profl. jours. Del. Iowa State Rep. Conv., Des Moines, 1964, Colo. State Rep. Conv., Denver, 1984; mem. parent adv. council, IMPACT drug intervention team Rangeview High Sch., Aurora, 1985—. Served to capt. U.S. Army Med. Service Corps, 1967-70. Recipient Sci. Achievement award U.S. Army Sci. Conf., West Point, N.Y., 1968, 70. Mem. Am. Inst. Nutrition, Am. Soc. Clin. Nutrition, N.Y. Acad. Scis., Am. Sci. Affiliation, Evang. Theol. Soc., Phi Eta Sigma, Phi Kappa Phi, Alpha Zeta, Gamma Sigma Delta, Kappa Sigma. Avocations: reading, hiking, swimming, writing poetry, gardening. Home: 3492 S Blackhawk Way Aurora CO 80014 Office: Faith Presbyn Ch 11373 E Alameda Ave Aurora CO 80012

STIGLICH, JACOB JOHN, JR., engineering consultant; b. Milw., Dec. 21, 1938; s. Jacob John Sr. and Augusta (Prezel) S. BSME, Marquette U., 1961; PhD, Northwestern U., 1970. Chief engr. Boride Products, Traverse City, Mich., 1971-74; mgr. ceramic materials Valeron Corp., Madison Heights, Mich., 1974-76; group leader, asst. dir. tech. Eagle Picher, Miami, Okla., 1976-78; program mgr. San Fernando Lab., Pacoima, Calif., 1978-84; tech. specialist Aerojet Ordnance Co., Tustin, Calif., 1984-85; cons. Newport Beach, Calif., 1985—. Contbr. articles to profl. jours.; patentee in field. Served to col. Ordnance Corps, USAR, 1961—. Mem. AIME, Am. Soc. Metals, Am. Ceramic Soc., Sigma Xi. Avocations: snow skiing, tennis. Office: Ultramet 12173 Montague St Pacoima CA 91331

STILES, ROBERT VERNON, journalism educator; b. Grand Rapids, Mich., Nov. 11, 1948; s. Merton Thomas and Ferne Maxine (Sturges) S.; m. Lise Kristine Carver, Aug. 25, 1984; 1 child, Nicklas John. BA, Stanford U., 1973, MA, 1974. Tchr., coach Woodside Priory Sch., Portola Valley, Calif., 1974-78; instr., coach Menlo Coll., Atherton, Calif., 1979—; field dir. soccer tournament Los Angeles Olympic Organizing Com., Stanford, Calif., 1984; clinician U.S. Army Soccer Clinic, San Jose, Calif., 1985; head clinician Dial Soccer Camp, San Mateo, Calif., 1986. Contbr. revs. on soccer to profl jours. Mem. Nat. Council Editorial Writers, Soc. Newspaper Design, Nat. Soccer Coaches Assn. Am. (state rep. 1984—). Avocations: soccer, writing children's stories, computers. Home and Office: Menlo Coll Dept Mass Communication 1000 El Camino Real Apt 9616 Atherton CA 94025

STILL, ROBERT MILTON, interior designer; b. Madison, Kans., Oct. 13, 1932; s. Orval Alexander and Esther Marie (Helmer) S.; m. Sally Rae Robbins, Apr. 7, 1962; children—Todd, Ross, Erik. A.A., Kansas City (Mo.) Jr. Coll., 1953; B.F.A., U. Wash., 1956. Employed in interior design studio Frederick & Nelson, Seattle, 1958-59, head home furnishings display dept., 1959-60; interior designer B.K. Alsin Imports, Seattle, 1960-70; owner RMS Interior Design, Mercer Island, Wash., 1970—; vis. team mem. Accreditation Com. Found. for Interior Design Edn. Research. Served with USNG, 1951-56, U.S. Army, 1956-58. Mem. Am. Soc. Interior Designers (past pres. Wash. chpt.), Bellevue C. of C. Tau Kappa Epsilon. Home and Office: 4518 W Mercer Way Mercer Island WA 98040

STILLMAN, ALFRED WILLIAM, JR., design/support engineer; b. Biloxi, Miss., Sept. 11, 1942; s. Alfred William and Marie Ann (Hengen) S.; A.A., Am. River Coll., 1966; B.S. in Elec. Engring., Calif. Poly. State U., 1970, B.S. in Applied Math., 1970, M.S. in Applied Math., 1973; M.E. in Indsl. Engring., Tex. A. and M. U., 1976; postgrad. elec. engring. N.J. Inst. Tech., 1977; Ph.D. in Mgmt., Calif. Coast U., 1984; children—Shannon Lynn, Laura Marie. Cert. profl. logistician, instr. Calif. Community Colls. Engring. intern U.S. Army Material Command, Texarkana, Tex., 1973-75, electronic systems staff maintenance engr., Ft. Monmouth, N.J., 1975-77, mil. tactical data system integrated logistics support mgr. Office of Project Mgr., ARTADS, Ft. Monmouth, 1977-78, tactical ADP ILS mgr., ILS dir. CORADOM, Ft. Monmouth, 1978-79, engring. mgr. regional dist. office Office of Project Mgr., Firefinder, Hughes Aircraft Co., Fullerton, Calif., 1979-80; prof. systems acquisition mgmt. Dept. Def. Systems Mgmt. Coll., Ft. Belvoir, Va., 1980-82; integrated logistics support engring. specialist, advanced systems div. Northrop Corp., Pico Rivera, Calif., 1982-83; program mgmt. rep. space systems group Rockwell Internat., Downey, Calif., 1983-84; product assurance project engr. Space Sta. Systems div. Rockwell Internat., Downey, Calif., 1984-85; mgr. product support, 1985-86; sr. mgr. ILS, Amex Systems, Inc., Compton, Calif., 1986—; pres. AWS Assocs. Calif., Inc., Huntington Beach, 1983—; corp. v.p., div. pres. HOPE Assocs., Inc., Huntington Beach, 1983—; Served with USAF, 1962-66. Mem. IEEE, Am. Mgmt. Assn., Am. Inst. Indsl. Engrs. (sr.) Soc. Logistics Engrs. (sr.), Am. Def. Preparedness Assn., Am. Security Council, Tau Beta Pi. Presbyterian. Club: Acacia. Home: 705 W 40th #1 San Pedro CA 90731 Office: 780 Bay Blvd Chula Vista CA 92010

STILSON, WALTER LESLIE, radiologist, educator; b. Sioux Falls, S.D., Dec. 13, 1908; s. George Warren and Elizabeth Margaret (Zager) S.; m. Grace Beall Bramble, Aug. 15, 1933 (dec. June 1984); children: Carolyn G. Palmieri, Walter E., Judith A. Stirling; m. Lula Ann Birchel, June 30, 1985. BA, Columbia Union Coll., 1929; MD, Loma Linda U., 1934. Diplomate Am. Bd. Radiology, Med. Examiners. Intern White Meml. Hosp., Los Angeles, 1933-34; resident radiology Los Angeles County Gen. Hosp., 1934-36; instr. radiology Loma Linda (Calif.) U. Sch. Medicine, 1935-41, asst. prof., 1941-49, exec. sec. radiology, 1945-50, assoc. prof., 1949-55, head dept. radiology, 1950-55, prof. radiology, 1955-83, chmn. dept. radiology, 1955-69, emeritus prof., 1983—; chief radiology service White Meml. Hosp., Los Angeles, 1941-65, Loma Linda U. Med. Ctr., 1966-69; chmn. dept. radiologic tech. Sch. Allied Health Professions, 1966-75, med. dir. dept. radiologic tech., 1975-83. Contbr. articles to health jours. Fellow Am. Coll. Radiology; mem. AAAS, Los Angeles Radiol. Soc. (sec. 1960-61, treas. 1961-62, pres. 1963-64), Radiol. Soc. N.Am., Am. Roentgen Ray Soc., N.Y. Acad. Sci., Inland Radiol. Soc. (pres. 1971), Alpha Omega Alpha. Republican. Adventist. Avocations: photography, classical music, travel. Home: 25045 Crestview Loma Linda CA 92354 Office: Loma Linda Radiology Group Inc 11234 Anderson St Loma Linda CA 92354

STILSON, WARREN RANDOLPH, library administrator; b. Long Beach, Calif., Dec. 4, 1951; s. Malcolm Harvey and Suzanne (Houts) S.; m. Catherine Ann Holmes, Dec. 16, 1982; 1 child, Christopher Peregrin. B.A., Evergreen State Coll., 1977; M.L., U. Wash., 1979. Archivist intern Nat. Archives and Records Ctr., Seattle, 1978-79; records mgmt. technician City of Portland, Oreg., 1980-81; library dir. City of Shelton, Wash., 1981-87. Chmn. trustee Mason Youth Services, Shelton, 1983-84; chmn. Com. for New Community Ctr., Shelton, 1982. Served with USCG, 1970-74. Mem. Soc. Am. Archivists, Wash. Library Assn., West Library Service Area (v. chmn. 1985-86, chmn. 1986-87). Office: Shelton Pub Library 427 W Railroad Ave Shelton WA 98584

STILWELL, JOSEPH GREGORY, podiatrist; b. Durango, Colo., May 10, 1955; s. Charles Allen and Charlotte (Carmon) S.; m. Susan Rochelle Loeff, May 20, 1978; 1 child, Daniel Elliott. BA, Colo. U., 1978; DPM, W.M. Scholl Coll., 1983. Diplomate Nat. Bd. Podiatry Examiners. Podiatrist No. N.Mex. Podiatry Assn., Santa Fe, 1983-84, High Country Foot Clinic, Colorado Springs, Colo., 1984—; podiatrist, Sunnyrest Watt Sanitorium, Colorado Springs, 1984—, Eisenhower Med. Ctr., Colorado Springs, 1984—, Rocky Mountain Osteopathic Hosp., Denver, 1986—, Peak Health Systems, Colorado Springs, 1984—. Contbr. article to profl. jours. Bd. dirs. Spl. Olympics, Colorado Springs, 1985—. Named Outstanding Preceptor No. N.Mex. Podiatry Assn., 1984. Mem. Am. Podiatric Med. Assn., Colo. Podiatric Med. Assn., Colorado Springs C. of C. Republican. Jewish. Club: Ben Lomond Gun (Palmer Lake, Colo.). Lodges: Rotary, Elks. Avocations: golfing, hunting, trap shooting. Home: 5050 Farmingdale Dr Colorado Springs CO 80917-1041 Office: High Country Foot Clinic 6165 Lehman Dr #101 Colorado Springs CO 80907-1456

STINECIPHER, MARY MARGARET, research chemist; b. Chattanooga, Feb. 26, 1940; d. Jesse Franklin and Florence Gladys (Marshall) S.; m. John David Fowler, (div. Mar. 1979); children: John Christopher, Jesse David. AB, Earlham Coll., 1962; PhD, U. N.C., 1967. Postdoctoral researcher Research Triangle Inst., Research Triangle Park, N.C., 1966-68, 74-76; mem. staff Los Alamos (N.Mex.) Nat. Lab., 1976—; vis. scientist AFOSR (AFATL), Eglin AFB, Fla., 1980-81. Contbr. articles to profl. jours.; inventor ammonium nitrate explosive systems. Mem. AAAS, Am. Chem. Soc., N.Mex. Network Women in Sci. and Engring. (v.p. 1985-86, pres. 1986-87). Democrat. Unitarian. Avocations: skiing, whitewater rafting, hiking. Office: Los Alamos Nat Lab MS C920 PO Box 1663 Los Alamos NM 87545

STINI, WILLIAM ARTHUR, anthropologist, educator; b. Oshkosh, Wis., Oct. 9, 1930; s. Louis Alois and Clara (Larsen) S.; m. Mary Ruth Kalous, Feb. 11, 1950; children—Patricia Laraine, Paulette Ann, Suzanne Kay. B.B.A., U. Wis., 1960, M.S., 1967, Ph.D., 1969. Planner cost acct. Kimberly-Clark Corp., Niagara Falls, N.Y., 1960-62; asst. prof. Cornell U., Ithaca, N.Y., 1968-71; assoc. prof. Cornell U., 1971-73, U. Kans., Lawrence, 1973-76; prof. anthropology U. Ariz., Tucson, 1976—; head dept. anthropology U. Ariz., 1980—; panelist anthropology program NSF, 1976-78; cons. NIH, 1974—. Author: Ecology and Human Adaptation, 1975; Nature, Culture and Human History - A Biocultural Introduction to Anthropology, (with Davydd J. Greenwood), 1977; Physiological and Morphological Adaptation and Evolution, 1979; editor-in-chief Am. Jour. Phys. Anthropology, 1983—; assoc. editor Nutrition and Cancer, 1981—; cons. editor Collegium Antropologicum, 1985—; contbr. articles to profl. jours. Mem. Gov.'s Adv. Council on Aging, State of Ariz., 1980-83. Nat. Inst. Dental Research tng. grantee, 1964-68; Clark Found. grantee, Cornell U., 1973; fellow Linacre Coll., Oxford, 1985. Fellow AAAS, Am. Anthrop. Assn., N.Y. Acad. Sci.; mem. Am. Assn. Phys. Anthropologists (exec. com. 1978-81), Soc. Study Human Biology, Human Biology Council (exec. com. 1978-81), Soc. Study Social Biology, Am. Inst. Nutrition, Western Gerontol. Soc., Sigma Xi. Home: 6240 N Camino Miraval Tucson AZ 85718 Office: U of Ariz Dept Anthropology Tucson AZ 85721

STINSON, DAVID JAY, small business owner; b. Los Angeles, Feb. 6, 1942; s. Robert Ward and Florence (Jessen) S.; m. Judith A. Panter, Apr. 2, 1966 (dir. Sept. 1982); children: Todd Robert, Trevor David. BS, U. So. Calif., 1966. Sales rep. Armstrong, Lancaster, Pa., 1966-68, Mobil Chem., Woodland, Ca., 1968-71; nat. sales mgr. Bemis Co., Mpls., 1971-81; dir. mktg. Interpolymer, Los Angeles, 1981-84; owner Creative Concepts, Cerritos, Calif., 1984—. Served with U.S. Army, 1960-62. Republican. Lutheran. Avocation: business, marketing. Home: 21321-149 Norwalk Blvd Hawaiian Gardens CA 90716 Office: Creative Concepts PO Box 758 Cerritos CA 90701

STINSON, DONALD CLINE, electrical engineer; b. Malta, Idaho, Dec. 7, 1925; s. Elton Salem and Neoma (Cline) S.; m. Betty Barbara Green, Apr. 15, 1954; children: Donald George, Laura Neoma, Barbara, Elizabeth, Paul Elton. BEE, Iowa State U., 1947; MEE, Calif. Inst. Tech., 1949; PhDEE, U. Calif., Berkeley, 1956. Research scientist, group leader Missile Systems div. Lockheed Corp., Palo Alto, Calif., 1956-58; prof. elec. engring. U. Ariz., Tucson, 1958-68, U. Tex., Arlington, 1968-69; mem. tech. staff Hughes Aircraft Co., Tucson, 1969-84, Fullerton, Calif., 1984-86; ad tech. specialist Lockheed Aircraft Service Co., Ontario, Calif., 1986—; cons. McGraw Hill, 1958-60, Tex. Instruments, Dallas, 1968-69. Contbr. articles to profl. jours. Served with USNR, 1944-46. NSF grantee, 1960-63. Mem. IEEE, Sigma Xi, Pi Mu Epsilon, Eta Kappa Nu. Home: 4571 Loganlinda Dr Yorba Linda CA 92686 Office: Lockheed Aircraft Service Co PO Box 33 Ontario CA 91762-8033

STINSON, KARL BARRY, environmental engineer; b. Lindsay, Calif., July 14, 1949; s. E. Howard and R. Minalee (Woolsey) S. B.S. magna cum laude in Engring., UCLA, 1971; M.S. magna cum laude, U. So. Calif., 1975. Registered profl. engr., Calif. Asst. san. engr. City of Los Angeles, 1972-76, assoc. san. engr., 1976; assoc. environ. engr. East Bay Mcpl. Utility Dist., Oakland, Calif., 1976-81, sr. engr., 1981-86, mgr. treatment and distbn., 1983, mgr. water distribution planning, 1986—. Bd. dirs. Utility Dist. Credit Union. Mem. ASCE, Am. Water Works Assn., Bay Area Water Works Assn. (dir.), Tau Beta Pi. Contbr. numerous articles to profl. jours. including ASCE Jour. Environ. Engring., Jour. Am. Water Works Assn. Office: East Bay Municipal Dist 2127 Adeline St Oakland CA 94623

STIRLING, ISABEL ANN, science librarian; b. San Jose, Calif., Dec. 4, 1948; d. James H. and Betty Stirling. BA, U. Calif., Riverside, 1970; MLS, Western Mich. U., 1977. Head bio-agrl. library U. Calif., Riverside, 1977-82; head sci. library, assoc. prof. U. Oreg., Eugene, 1982—. Author: Self-Paced Library Instruction Workbook for the Sciences, 1981; contbr. revs. to jours. Mem. ALA, Assn. Coll. and Research Libraries of ALA (various coms.), Spl. Library Assn., Oreg. Library Assn., Oreg. Online Users Group. Avocations: handloom, fiber arts. Office: U Oreg Sci Library Eugene OR 97403

STIRN, REBECCA ATKINSON, health care marketing executive; b. Kansas City, Mo., Feb. 23, 1953; d. Russell Jay and Virginia (Cox) Atkinson; B.A., Smith Coll., 1975; M.B.A., Stanford U., 1978; m. Bradley Albert Stirn, Aug. 30, 1975. Asst. mgr. market devel. So. Pacific Transp. Co. San Francisco, 1978-79, fin. analyst, fin., adminstrn., 1979-80, asst. mgr. fin. adminstrn., 1980-81; mgr. market research Cooper Vision Optics div., Menlo Park, Calif., 1981-82, mgr. new products and planning, 1982-83, dir. profl. mktg., 1983, v.p. mktg., 1983-85; v.p. mktg. CEMAX, Inc., 1986-87; v.p. sales and mktg. CEMAX, Inc., 1987—; market researcher Saga Corp., Menlo Park, Calif., summer 1977; research asst. Fed. Res. Bank of San Francisco, 1975-76. Mem. devel. com. Nairobi Day Sch., 1978; bd. dirs. Wilmer Eye Inst. at Johns Hopkins Hosp.; bd. dirs. Peninsula Smith Coll. Club, 1977-80, pres., 1984-85; mem. gift com. Smith Coll. Leadership, 1986—. Home: 590 Albion Ave Woodside CA 94062 Office: CEMAX 2801 Orchard Pkwy San Jose CA 95134

STITH, JOHN EDWARD, writer, engineering executive; b. Boulder, Colo., July 30, 1947; s. George Allen and Virginia Franklin (Kenway) S.; m. Nancy Ann West, June 8, 1969 (div. 1979); m. Annette Colleen Chamness, May 24, 1981. BA in Physics, U. Minn., 1969. Mission ops. controller Cordura Corp., Seabrook, Md., 1972-73; project leader System Devel. Corp., Colorado Springs, Colo., 1973-75; software engr. Ford Aerospace, Colorado Springs, 1975-76; head software sect. Wyle Labs., Colorado Springs, 1976-79; engring. mgr. Kaman Scis. Corp., Colorado Springs, Colo., 1979—. Author: Scapescope, 1984, Memory Blank, 1986. Served to 1st lt. USAF, 1969-72. Mem. Mystery Writers Am. (regional v.p. 1984-86), Sci. Fiction Writers Am., Sci. Fiction Research Assn., Mensa. Avocation: tennis. Home: 1242 Amsterdam Dr Colorado Springs CO 80907-4004 Office: Kaman Scis Corp 1500 Garden of the Gods Rd Colorado Springs CO 80907

STOBER, QUENTIN JEROME, fisheries researcher, educator; b. Billings, Mont., Mar. 25, 1938; s. Quentin W. and Eva (Lesell) S.; m. Angie Hollingsworth, Dec. 26, 1965; children: Jonathan M., Alyson C. BS in Fish and Wildlife, Mont. State U., 1960, MS in Fish and Wildlife Mgmt., 1962, PhD in Aquatic Zoology, 1968. Aquatic biologist Fed. Water Pollution Control Adminstrn. Southeastern Water Lab., div. EPA, Athens, Ga., 1962-65; research asst. prof. fishery sci. Fisheries Research Inst. U. Wash., Seattle, 1969-72, research assoc. prof., 1972-77, research prof., 1977—; adminstrv. judge environ. sect. Atomic Safety Licensing Bd. panel of U.S. Nuclear Regulatory Commn., 1974—; mem. joint sci. com. Wash. Water Research Ctr. and Wash. State U., Pullman, 1975—; cons. EPA, 1979-82, UNC Nuclear Industries, Inc., Richland, Wash., 1985-86. Contbr. articles to profl. jours. Mem. AAAS, Am. Fisheries Soc. (cert.), Am. Soc. Limnology an Oceanography, Am. Inst. Fisheries Research Biologists (W.F. Thompson award 1969), Sigma Xi, Phi Sigma. Methodist. Avocations: woodworking, fishing, hiking, skiing, hunting. Office: U Wash Fisheries Research Inst WH-10 Seattle WA 98195

STOBIE, LARRY JOSEPH, art educator; b. Spokane, Wash., Jan. 26, 1937; s. James Stobie. BFA, Wash. State U., 1962, MFA, 1966. Cert. tchr., Wash. Instr. art Pub. Sch. Dist. 59, Cusick, Wash., 1962-66, Wash. State U., Pullman, 1966-67; prof. art Nebr. Wesleyan U., Linocoln, 1967-69; prof. art Western Oreg. State U., Monmouth, 1969—, head dept., 1986—. Exhibited work in numerous one man shows. Home: 17055 Oakdale Rd Dallas OR 97338 Office: Western Oreg State Coll Art Dept Monmouth OR 97361

STOCKDALE, RONALD ALLEN, grocery company executive; b. Aplington, Iowa, Apr. 28, 1934; s. Carl Robert and Mildred Louise (Gerhardt) S.; m. Carol Ann Hermeier, Dec. 23, 1956; children—Bryan Ross, Russell Allen, Paul Roderick. B.S. in Commerce, State U. Iowa, 1958. C.P.A. Auditor Arthur Andersen & Co., Chgo., 1958-63; controller Super Food Services, Bellefontaine, Ohio, 1963-66, Mountain States Wholesale Co., Boise, Idaho, 1966-69; exec. v.p., sec. West Coast Grocery Co., Tacoma, 1969-82; pres., chief operating officer West Coast Grocery Co., 1982—; bd. dirs. Profit Sharing Council Am., Chgo., 1977-83. Bd. dirs. Univ. Place Sch. Bd., Tacoma, 1973-75; trustee Humana Hosp.-Tacoma; mem. adv. bd. Sch. Bus. Adminstrn., Pacific Luth. U., 1986—. Served with U.S. Army, 1954-56. Mem. Am. Inst. C.P.A.s, Fin. Execs. Inst., Tacoma-Pierce County C. of C. (bd. dirs. 1986—). Republican. Presbyterian. Home: 2720 Soundview Dr W Tacoma WA 98466 Office: West Coast Grocery Co PO Box 1834 Tacoma WA 98401

STOCKDALE, WILLIAM KENNETH, civil engineer; b. Rock Island, Ill., Oct. 11, 1928; s. Robert Ferguson and Irene Mildred (Kail) S.; B.S., U.S. Mil. Acad., 1951; M.S., U. Ill., 1958, Ph.D., 1959; m. Alice Marie Carr, June 9, 1951; children—Mary, William, Jacqueline, Barbara, Theresa; adopted children—Sharon, David. Commd. 2d lt. C.E., U.S. Army, 1951, advanced through grades to col., 1972; from asst. prof. to prof. civil engring. U.S. Mil. Acad., West Point, 1967-78; ret., 1978; mgr. engring. services Wash. Pub. Power Supply System, Richland, Wash., 1978-81, lead civil/structural engr., tech. services coordinator, 1981—. Served with AUS, 1946-47. Registered profl. engr., Pa., Ill., Wash. Mem. Soc. Am. Mil. Engrs. (pres. West Point-Stewart Post chpt. 1973-74), ASCE, Nat. Soc. Profl. Engrs., Am. Concrete Inst., N.Y. Acad. Scis., Sigma Xi. Roman Catholic. Home: 1873 Marshall Ave Richland WA 99352 Office: Washington Pub Power Supply 3000 George Washington Way Richland WA 99352

STOCKING, BEAU CAROL DIANE, optometrist; b. Arlington, Va., Feb. 28, 1949; d. John Howard and June Lillian (Mathurin) Stapf. m. Reginald Angus Stocking, Mar. 6, 1976. B.S., Whittier Coll., 1970; postgrad. U. So. Calif., 1970-72; O.D., So. Calif. Coll. Optometry, 1976. Lic. optometrist, Calif. Optometrist USAF, 1976-79; gen. practice optometry, Burbank, Calif., 1980—. Served to capt., USAF, 1976-79. Mem. Calif. Optometric Assn., Am. Optometric Assn. Republican. Episcopalian. Office: 2915 W Magnolia Blvd Burbank CA 91505

STOCKMAN, ANN WENTWORTH, social worker; b. Evanston, Ill., Sept. 30, 1953; d. Lynn H. and Barbara W. (Sheafe) S.; m. Eugene Augustine, June 9, 1984; 1 child, Ralph Amouak. BA, U. Alaska, Anchorage, 1979; MSW, U. Wash., 1982. Dir. crisis services STAR, Anchorage, 1982-85, vol. cons., 1986; clin. therapist Charter North Hosp., Anchorage, 1986—; pvt. practice therapy Anchorage, 1987—. Mem. Nat. Assn. Social Workers (social action com. 1982-86, Gold Card award 1985). Democrat. Sufi.

STOCKS, CHESTER LEE, JR., hospital administrator; b. Montgomery, Ala., Oct. 8, 1928; s. Chester Lee and Evelyn (Cooley) S.; m. Mary Gwendoline Hase, June 5, 1954; children: Susan, Bradley Hase, Charles Lee, Sally. B.S., Auburn U., 1949; M.H.A., Washington U., St. Louis, 1955. Resident Baylor U. Med. Center, Dallas, 1954-55; adminstrv. asst. Baylor U. Med. Center, 1955-57, asst. adminstr., 1957-63; exec. v.p. Good Samaritan Hosp. and Med. Center, 1963, Portland, Oreg., 1963—; Preceptor grad. programs in hosp. adminstrn. U. Calif., U. Iowa, Washington U.; lectr., participant programs on health care; mem. exec. com. Oreg. Regional Med. Programs, 1966-74, v.p., 1969-76; mem. Oreg. Commn. on Nursing, 1969-75, Oreg. Health Manpower Commn., 1966-73, Comprehensive Health Planning Assn. Met. Portland, 1969-76, Oreg. Health Commn. Siting Com., 1974-77; dir. Oreg. Med. Polit. Action Com., 1974-77; Oreg. chmn. Wash. U. devel. program, 1967-70. Trustee Fred Hutchison Cancer Center, Seattle, 1972-79, Oreg. Comprehensive Cancer Center, 1973-75, Blue Cross Oreg., 1965—; pres. Oreg. Hosp. Found., 1979; mem. vestry Trinity Episc. Ch., 1983-86. Served to 1st lt. USAF, 1950-53. Fellow Am. Coll. Health Care Execs. (regent 1969-75, gov. 1975-78, chmn. 1979); mem. Assn. Western Hosps. (trustee, pres. 1973-74), Am. Hosp. Assn. (trustee 1984-87, various coms. 1965—), Oreg. Assn. Hosps. (pres. 1967-68, trustee 1973-76), Portland Council of Hosps. (pres. 1966-67), Greater Portland Area Hosp. Council (pres. 1983), NW Oreg. Council Hosps. (exec. com. 1980-83), Tex. Hosp. Assn. ((hon.)), Portland C. of C. (bd. dirs. 1967-69), Nat. Assn. for Practical Nurse Edn. and Service (trustee 1960-86), Voluntary Hosps. Am. (bd. dirs. 1984-87), Voluntary Hosps. Am. Enterprises (bd. dirs. 1986—), Protestant Hosp. Assn., Nat. League for Nursing, Pi Kappa Alpha. Episcopalian (dir. William Temple House 1965-70). Clubs: Rotarian. (Portland), Multnomah Athletic (Portland), Arlington (Portland). Home: 282 NW Macleay Blvd Portland OR 97210 Office: Good Samaritan Hosp 1015 NW 22 Ave Portland OR 97210

STODDARD, MARGERY MIESSNER, editor; b. St. Louis, May 26, 1929; d. George Emil and Myrtle Antoinette (Wolf) Miessner; A.A., Santa Monica Coll., 1948; student U. So. Calif., 1948-50; m. Scott Powell Stoddard, Nov. 5, 1955; children—Scott Wilcox, Janet Faye Stoddard Bouweraerts. Photo and fashion model (part-time) Caroline Leonetti Studios, Hollywood, Calif., 1948-51; tech. artist and scene coordinator Metro-Goldwyn-Mayer. Motion Picture Studios, Culver City, Calif. 1951-54; story editor Playhouse 90, CBS-Television City, Los Angeles, 1954-56, free-lance non-fiction and features writer various publs., 1956-78; mng. editor Plastics mag. (Western Plastics News, Inc.) Santa Monica. Calif., 1978—, public relations and press rep. Western Plastics Expns., Santa Monica, also creative advt. and graphics artist. Patron Santa Monica Coll.; mem. Nat. Rep. Congl. Com. Mem. Soc. Plastics Engrs., Soc. Advancement of Material and Process Engring., Los Angeles Soc. Coatings Tech., Nat. Assn. Female Execs., AAUW (mem.-at-large), Am. Film Inst., Smithsonian Assocs. Republican. Presbyterian. Home: 502-26th St Santa Monica CA 90402 Office: Plastics Mag 1704 Colorado Ave Santa Monica CA 90404

STODDARD, STEPHEN DAVIDSON, state senator, ceramic engineer; b. Everett, Wash., Feb. 8, 1925; s. Albert and Mary Louise (Billings) S.; m. Joann Elizabeth Burt, June 18, 1949; children: Dorcas Ann, Stephanie Kay. Student, Tacoma Coll., 1944, Conn. Coll., 1946; B.S., U. Ill., 1950. Asst. prodn. supr., asst. ceramic engr. Coors Porcelain Co., Golden, Colo., 1950-52; ceramics-powder metallurgy sect. leader Los Alamos (N.Mex.) Sci. Lab., U. Calif., 1952-80; pres., treas. Materials Tech. Assocs., Inc.; Cons. Ceramic Age Mag., 1958-60, Nuclear Applications for Ceramic Materials,

1958-60; Jury commr. Los Alamos County, 1969; justice of peace 1956-62; mem. Los Alamos Sch. Adv. Council, 1966; mcpl. judge 1976-77; chmn. Los Alamos Ordinance Rev. Com., 1958; Mem. Republican County and State Central Com., 1955—; county commr. Los Alamos, N.Mex., 1966-68; mem. Los Alamos County Planning Commn., 1962-63, N.Mex. State Senate, 1981—; adv. dir. Bank of Los Alamos, 1982—. Bd. dirs. Sangre de Cristo council Girl Scouts Am., 1965-71. Served with AUS, 1943-46. Decorated Bronze Star medal, Purple Heart, Combat Inf. badge; recipient Disting. Alumni award U. Ill. Coll. Engring., 1986. Fellow Am. Ceramic Soc. (treas. 1972-74, pres. 1976-77, disting. life mem. 1984), Am. Inst. Chemists; mem. Nat. Inst. Ceramic Engrs. (PACE award 1965, Greaves Walker award 1984), Am. Soc. Metals, U. Ill. Alumni Assn. (Honor award 1986), Sigma Xi, Alpha Tau Omega. Episcopalian. Clubs: Masons, Shriners, Elks, Kiwanis (pres. 1963-64, dist. dep. grand exalted ruler 1968-69, lt. gov. 1968-69), Los Alamos Golf Assn. (dir. 1964-66). Patentee in field. Home: 326 Kimberly Ln Los Alamos NM 87544 Office: PO Box 11 Los Alamos NM 87544

STOEBE, THOMAS GAINES, university dean, materials science educator; b. Upland, Calif., Apr. 26, 1939; s. Wallace Theodore and Martha Thomas (Gaines) S.; m. Jessica Rae Trout, June 20, 1959 (div. Jan. 1981); children: Brian, Paul, Diane; m. Janet Eleanor Dumm, Aug. 7, 1982. BS, Stanford U., 1961, MS, 1963, PhD, 1965. Instr. Imperial Coll., London, Eng., 1965-66; from asst. to assoc. prof. U. Wash., Seattle, 1966-75, prof., 1975—, assoc. dean, 1982-87, chmn. dept. materials sci. and engring., 1987—; vis. prof. U. Sao Paulo, Brazil, 1972-73; fellow USAF Materials Lab, Wright Patterson AFB, 1975. Patentee direct response dosimeter system; contbr. 85 tech. articles to profl. jours. Bd. dirs. Wash. Math., Engring., Sci. Achievement Program, Seattle, 1984—. Spl. fellow Atomic Energy Commn. Mem. Am. Soc. Engring. Edn. (young faculty award, 1972, Western Electric award, 1977), Am. Phys. Soc., Materials Research Soc., Am. Inst. Mining, Metall. and Petroleum Engrs. (chmn. metall. sect. 1973), Am. Ceramic Soc. Club: PRO Sports (Redmond, Wash.). Home: 11106 NE 38 Pl Bellevue WA 98004 Office: U Wash Roberts Hall FB-10 Seattle WA 98195

STOEN, J. THOMAS, energy company executive, land developer, investor; b. Milw., June 20, 1939; s. Joel A. and Lucile V. (Oliver) S.; m. Sara Peterson (div. 1980); children: Eric Thomas, Erin Kristen. BA, Wheaton (Ill.) Coll., 1961. V.p. Columbia Savs., Denver, 1964-72; pres. Crown Properties, Denver, 1972-74, Columbia Corp., Denver, 1972-74, Cimmaron Corp., Colorado Springs, Colo., 1974-79; chmn. Pacific Energy and Minerals Ltd., Colorado Springs, 1979-87; pres. Remington Oil and Gas Co., 1986—; bd. dirs. Bristol Trading Co., Vancouver, B.C., Can. Served to lt. U.S. Army, 1961-64. Clubs: Garden of the Gods, Broadmoor Golf (Colorado Springs). Avocations: golf, tennis, skiing. Home: 8 Pourtales Rd Colorado Springs CO 80906

STOIK, MARY ELIZABETH, corporate administrator, risk mgr.; b. Clinton, Iowa, Oct. 31, 1952; d. Lloyd P. and Mary (Johnson) Stoik; m. Steven H. Dymond. B.A., U. S.D., Vermillion, 1975. Paralegal firm Ross Hardies, Chgo., 1975-77, firm Calkins & Kramer, Denver, 1977-79, firm Holland and Hart, Denver, 1979-81; corp. affairs adminstr., risk mgr. asst. sec. Axem Resources, Denver, 1981—; asst. sec. Laser Oil Co., Axroyalty Inc.; corp. sec. Axem Found., 1981-87; risk mgr. Apache Corp., Denver, 1987—. Active Denver Sym. Orch., 1982-85, choreographer for local dance co., 1982-85. Mem. Risk Ins. Mgrs. Soc., Delta Phi Alpha, Phi Alpha Theta, Pi Beta Phi (v.p., 1974-75). Home: 1616 S Grant St Denver CO 80210 Office: Apache Corp One United Bank Bldg Denver CO 80237

STOKER, HOWARD STEPHEN, chemistry educator; b. Salt Lake City, Apr. 16, 1939; s. Howard Seymour and Alice Maud (Child) S.; m. Sharon Rosella Stevenson, June 16, 1964; children: Rebecca, Deborah, Scott, Stephen, Howard, Alice, Hyrum. BA, U. Utah, 1963; PhD, U. Wis., 1968. Asst. prof. chemistry Weber State Coll., Ogden, Utah, 1968-72, assoc. prof., 1972-76, prof., 1976—. Author: Preparatory Chemistry, 1985, Introduction to Chemical Principles, 2d rev. edit., 1986. Mem. Am. Chem. Soc. Mormon. Home: 765 Ben Lomond Ave Ogden UT 84403 Office: Weber State Coll Dept Chemistry Ogden UT 84408

STOKER, MARK FREDERICK, lawyer; b. Chgo., Apr. 22, 1958; s. Frederick James and Frances Margaret (Jamison) S.; m. Cynthia Kay Hildebrand, June 20, 1981; children: Allyson Marie and Rachel Louise (twins). BBA, U. Wash., 1981; JD cum laude, Lewis & Clark Law Sch., 1984. Bar: Oreg. 1984, Wash. 1984. Assoc. McClaskey, Greig & Troutwine, Portland, Oreg., 1984-85; ptnr. McClaskey, Greig, Troutwine & Stoker, Portland, 1985-86, Williams Kastner & Gibbs (merger McClaskey, Greig, Troutwine & Stoker), Vancouver, Wash., 1986—; gen. counsel Red Lion Inns, Vancouver, Wash., 1984—. Mem. Oreg. State Bar Assn., Wash. State Bar Assn., Oreg. Trial Lawyers Assn., Young Lawyers Assn. Republican. Lutheran. Avocations: sports, raquetball, woodworking. Home: 8318 NW 14th Ct Vancouver WA 98665 Office: Williams Kostner & Gibbs 610 Esther St Vancouver WA 98660

STOKES, BILLIE WESLEY, management analyst; b. Rome, Ga., July 5, 1943; s. Earl Wesley Stokes and Aileen Dawn (Boswell) Carter; m. Edeltraut Gerthild (Schmette), Nov. 22, 1963; children: Patricia Ann, Duane Billy. BS, Regis Coll., 1983, postgrad., 1985—; postgrad., Colo. Tech. Coll., 1984-85. Enlisted U.S. Army, 1960-83, ret., 1983; mgmt. analyst USA Med. Activity, Ft. Carson, Colo., 1985—. Editor monthly newsletter Western Ranger, 1976-79, Home Owners News, 1976-77. Sec. University Park Home Owners Assn., Macomb, Ill, 1976-77; mem. Pres. Sports Awards, Macomb, 1978. Decorated Bronze Star, Purple Heart; recipient Commandant's Trophy U.S. Army Drill Sgts. Sch., 1969, Meritorius Service award U.S. Army, 1976. Mem. Mil. Comptroller's Assn., Sgts. Maj. Assn., Future Farmers Am. Democrat. Lodges: Masons, Elks. Avocations: bowling, fishing, golf, camping, interior design and decorating. Home: 7209 Millbrook Ct Fountain CO 80817 Office: USA Meddac Comptroller div Fort Carson CO 80913-5207

STOKES, JAMES DIGBY, wildlife biologist, consultant; b. Mill Valley, Calif., Apr. 2, 1914; s. Charles J. and Annette J. (Jeffreys) S.; m. Blanche Hattie Evan, Mar. 13, 1946; children—James, Charles, John. Student Santa Rosa Jr. Coll., 1931-32, Merritt Coll., Oakland, Calif., 1933-35. With Calif. Dept. Fish and Game, 1936-70, regional mgr. No. Calif., 1952-64, chief planning, Sacramento, 1964-70; co-founder, v.p., treas. Jones & Stokes Assocs. Inc., wildlife and environ. investigations, Sacramento, 1970-76; cons. wildlife biology, environ. problems, 1976—; condr. wildlife planning seminars U.S. Fish and Wildlife Service, nationwide, 1965-70; wildlife biologist member Earthwatch, Chilean expdn. Search for the Huemul, 1981-82. Mem. adv. council Ukian Dist. (Calif.), U.S. Bur. Land Mgmt.; speaker, mem. adv. com. Vina Plains Preserve, Nature Conservancy, Chico, Calif. Served to 1st lt. inf. U.S. Army, 1942-45. Decorated Bronze Star, Purple Heart (U.S.); Order of Leopold (Belgium); Recipient Commr.'s award U.S. Fish and Wildlife Service, 1970; resolution of commendation Assembly Rules Com., Calif. Legislature, 1970. Mem. Wildlife Soc. (cert. wildlife biologist), Audubon Soc., Sierra Club. Republican. Episcopalian. Prin. author: Calif. Wildlife Resources Plan, 1965; Fish and Wildlife Planning Guide, 1969; Hawaii Fish and Wildlife Resources Plan, 1973. Home: 8758 Churn Creek Rd Redding CA 96002

STOKES, JOHN DENNIS, physician; b. Tacoma, June 26, 1946; s. John Franklin and Mildred (Trump) S.; m. Gayle Eileen Weeden, Dec. 20, 1969; children: Jonathan Patrick, Michael Stephen. BA, Ind. U., 1968; MS, Loyola U., 1973; MD, U. Ill., Chgo., 1976. Diplomate Nat. Bd. Med. Examiners, Am. Bd. Internal Medicine, Am. Bd. Endocrinology and Metabolism. Resident, fellow U. Calif., Irvine, 1976-81; practice medicine specializing in endocrinology and internal medicine San Clemente, Mission Viejo, Calif., 1981—; instr. OC paramedic program, 1977—; lectr. CME program and diabetes edn. South Coast Med. Ctr., Mission Community Hosp., San Clemente Hosp, 1981—. E. James scholar U. Ill. Med. Ctr., Chgo., 1973-76. Mem. ACP, AAAS, AMA, Am. Chem. Soc., Am. Heart Assn., Am. Diabetes Assn., Internat. Diabetes Fedn., Am. Assn. Diabetes Educators, Am. Fedn. Clin. Research, Calif. Med. Assn., Orange County Med. Assn., Am. Soc. Internal Medicine. Methodist. Avocations: photography, scuba diving, bicycling, racquetball. Office: 647 Camino de Los Mares #234 San Clemente CA 92672 Office: 27800 Medical Ctr Rd #232 Mission Viejo CA 92691

STOKES, ROBB LYLE, psychologist; b. Albany, Ore., Aug. 13, 1949; s. Lyle Eldon and Ellenor Isabelle S.; m. Cleo Klemzak, Nov. 19, 1977. BS, Portland (Oreg.) State U., 1972, MS, 1976; PhD, Walden U., Naples, Fla., 1983. Lic. clin. psychol. assoc., Alaska. Counselor, Sheldon Jackson Coll., Sitka, Alaska, 1976-77; program dir. Mt. Edgecumbe Comprehensive Alcohol Program (Alaska), 1977-79; psychologist Norton Sound Health Corp., Nome, Alaska, 1980-83; pvt. practice clin. psychology, Petersburh and Sitka, Alaska, 1983—. Mem. Western Psychol. Assn. (Alaska area coordinator), Christian Assn. Psychol. Studies, Am. Psychol. Assn. (assoc.). Home and Office: PO Box 9 Petersburg AK 99833

STOKKE, ROBERT J. (BOB), training adminstrator; b. Salt Lake City, Aug. 20, 1943; s. Otto John and Barbara (Parkison) S.; m. Margaret Louise Whitford, Apr. 23, 1976; children—John, Brian, Michele, Justin, Aaron, Philip. B.A. in Social Scis., Eastern Wash. U., 1965; M.S. in Human Resources Mgmt., Gonzaga U., 1976; M.A. in Human Relations, Pacific Luth. U., 1977. With Skipper's Inc., Bellevue, Wash., 1976—, successivley mgmt. trainee, unit mgr., corp. tng. mgr., dist. mgr., corp. adminstr. tng., 1982—. Served to capt. U.S. Army, 1965-74, lt. col. Res. USAR. Decorated Bronze Star, Meritorious Service medal. Mem. Am. Soc. Tng. and Devel., Res. Officers Assn. U.S. Home: 1848 226th Pl NE Redmond WA 98053 Office: 14450 NE 29th Pl Suite 200 Bellevue WA 98007

STOLLER, JEFFREY MARK, publishing executive; b. Brookline, Mass., Oct. 5, 1953; s. Eugene and Ruth (Sklar) S. BS in Bus., U. So. Calif., 1975, MBA, M in Bus. Taxation, JD, 1978. Bar: Calif. 1978; cert. mgmt. acctg., real estate and securities broker. Tax acct. Peat Marwick Mitchell & Co, Los Angeles, 1978; pres. Entertainment Funding Corp., Los Angeles, 1979-81, Stoller Publs., Los Angeles, 1984—; adj. prof. bus. law and real estate U. So. Calif., Los Angeles, 1979-82. Recipient Arthur Young Tax award, 1977. Mem. Inst. Mgmt. Acctg. (cert. disting. performance), Beta Gamma Sigma, Order of Coif. Office: 8306 Wilshire Blvd 196 Beverly Hills CA 90211

STOLPER, EDWARD MANIN, geology educator; b. Boston, Dec. 16, 1952; s. Saul James and Frances A. (Liberman) S.; m. Lauren Beth Adoff, June 3, 1973; children: Jennifer Ann, Daniel Aaron. AB, Harvard U., 1974; M Philosophy, U. Edinburgh, Scotland, 1976; PhD, Harvard U., 1979. Asst. prof. geology Calif. Inst. Tech., Pasadena, 1979-82, assoc. prof. geology, 1982-83, prof. geology, 1983—. Recipient F.W. Clarke medal Geochem. Soc., 1985; Marshall scholar Marshall Aid Commemoration Commn., 1974-76. Fellow Meteoritical Soc. (Nininger Meteorite award 1976); mem. AAAS (Newcomb Cleveland prize 1984), Geol. Soc. Am., Mineral. Soc. Am., Am. Geophys. Union (James B. Macelwane award 1986), Sigma Xi. Office: Calif Inst Tech Div Geol Planetary Sci Pasadena CA 91125

STOLPMAN, THOMAS GERARD, lawyer; b. Cleve., June 2, 1949; s. Joseph Eugene and Katherine Ann (Berry) S.; m. Marilyn Heise, Aug. 17, 1974; children: Jennifer, Peter. BA, UCLA, 1972; JD, Los Angeles, 1976. Bar: Calif. 1976, U.S. Dist. Ct. (cen. dist.) Calif. 1976, U.S. Dist. Ct. (ea. dist.) Calif. 1985. Ptnr. Silver, McWilliams, Stolpman, Mandel and Katzman, Wilmington and Los Angeles, Calif., 1976—. Editor-in-chief The Advocate legal jour., 1984—; contbr. articles to profl. jours. Bd. dirs. Miraleste Recreation and Park Dist., Rancho Palos Verdes, Calif., 1982—, Citizens Against Forced Annexation, Rancho Palos Verdes, 1978-83; del. Rancho Palos Verdes Council of Homeowners Assns., 1979-86, v.p. 1986; v.p., gov. Miraleste Assn., Rancho Palos Verdes, 1976-82. Named Trial Lawyer of Yr. So. Calif., Verdictum Juris, 1984. Mem. Los Angeles Trial Lawyers Assn. (treas. 1984, sec. 1985, v.p. 1986-87, bd. govs., 1979-83), Calif. Trial Lawyers Assn. (bd. govs. 1987—), Assn. Trial Lawyers of Am., Am. Bd. Trial Advocates, Nat. Bd. Trial Advocacy (cert.), Los Angeles County Bar Assn., South Bay Bar Assn., Long Beach Bar Assn. Democrat. Roman Catholic. Office: Silver McWilliams Stolpman Mandel & Katzman 1121 N Avalon Blvd Wilmington CA 90744-3598

STOLTENBERG, CARL HENRY, university dean; b. Monterey, Calif., May 17, 1924; s. George L. and Eloise (Hyatt) S.; m. Rosemary Johnson, Apr. 20, 1973; children by previous marriage—Bruce C., Gail L., Susan I., Paul L., Shirley J.; stepchildren—Michael Johnson, Jillean Johnson. B.S., U. Calif.-Berkeley, 1948, M.F., 1949; Ph.D., U. Minn., 1952. Instr. U. Minn., 1949-51; asst. prof. Duke U., 1951-56; forest economist U.S. Forest Service, Washington, 1956; chief div. forest econs. research N.E. Forest Expt. Sta., Forest Service, USDA, Upper Darby, Pa., 1956-60; head dept. forestry Iowa State U., 1960-67; dean, prof. Oreg. State U. Coll. Forestry, Corvallis, 1967—; mem. adv. bd. Coop. Forestry Research, USDA, 1963-67, 86—, mem. adv. com. for state and pvt. forestry, 1970-74; mem. Oreg. Bd. Forestry, 1967—, chmn., 1974-83; bd. dirs. Resources for Future, 1980—. Author: Research Planning for Resource Decisions, 1970. Served with AUS, 1943-45, ETO. Mem. AAAS, Soc. Am. Foresters (pres.-elect, 1987, past mem. council, com. chmn.), Forest Products Research Soc., Am. Econ. Assn., Sigma Xi, Xi Sigma Pi. Methodist. Home: 7890 NW Ridgewood Dr Corvallis OR 97330

STONE, CAROL BEALL, science writer; b. Coloma, Mich., Aug. 8, 1937; d. Henry Reginald and Isabelle Maud (Anderson) Beall; m. Thomas Dean Leth, July 5, 1959 (div. 1967); m. Harold Joseph Stone, July 3, 1971. BA, Kalamazoo Coll., 1958; MA, Govs. State U., 1975; PhD, Stanford U., 1984. Med. editor AMA, Chgo., 1961-64; sci. editor Rand McNally & Co., Skokie, Ill., 1964-69, 74-78, Random House/Singer, N.Y.C., 1969-71; prin. The Stone Cottage, Alameda, Calif., 1983—. Co-author: Biology TRB, 1984; BSCS Green Version, 6th edition, 1987. Democrat. Unitarian. Home and Office: The Stone Cottage 1719 Fifth St Alameda CA 94501

STONE, DAVID ULRIC, management executive; author; b. Santa Cruz, Calif., Feb. 4, 1927; s. Ernest Marshall and Grace (Stone) S.; student Theol. Ministry Sch., San Jose, Calif., 1945-48; grad. Real Estate Inst., Nat. Inst. Real Estate, 1964; m. Iva Dell Frazier, July 20, 1947; children—Katherine LaVerne, Russell Keith, Susan Marie. With E.M. Stone Realty, San Jose, 1945-48; mgr. Broadway-Hale Co., San Jose, 1948-52; sales mgr. William Perry Co., San Francisco, 1952-56; gen. mgr., ptnr. Stone & Schulte, Inc., San Jose, 1956-66; pres., chmn. bd. dirs. Stone Inst., Los Gatos, Calif., 1966; chmn. bd. Sunchoke Internat., Inc. 1983—, Custon One Internat. Inc., 1986—; pres. The Mktg. Forum, Inc., Mpls., 1986—; dir. Realty Programming Corp. St. Louis; chmn. bd. dirs. Custom One Internat., Inc., Mpls.; pres. Sunchoke Internat. San Juan Bautista, Calif, 1984. Named Realtor of Yr. Homes for Living Network, 1982. Mem. Nat. Inst. Real Estate Brokers (faculty mem. 1965—), Nat. Assn. Real Estate Bds. (chmn. joint task force 1966-68), Builder's Mktg. Soc. (founder, chmn. 1985), Calif. Real Estate Assn. (dir.), Nat. Assn. Home Builders (award 1960, Sales Mgr. of Year 1960, chmn. joint task force 1966-68, faculty mem. Inst. Residential Mktg. 1982—), The Builder Marketing Soc. (founder, chmn. bd.). Author: How to Operate a Real Estate Trade-In Program, 1962; Training Manual for Real Estate Salesmen, 1966; Guaranteed Sales Plan for Realtors and Builders, 1968 New Home Sales Training Course; The Professional Approach To Selling Real Estate; How To Communicate with Persuasive Power; How to Sell New Homes and Environmental Communities; How to Market and Sell Condominiums; How to Hire, Train and Motivate Real Estate Salespeople, How to Profitably Manage a Real Estate Office, 1977; The Road to Success in Real Estate, 1978; New Horizons in Real Estate, 1980; New Home Sales, 1982, Sales Power: American Sales Masters, 1986, New Home Marketing, 1987. Home: 236 Camino Del Cerro Los Gatos CA 95030

STONE, DEVON MERLIN, construction and engineering executive; b. Preston, Idaho, Mar. 27, 1942; s. Merlin Porter and Leota (Corbridge) S.; B.S. in Engring., Brigham Young U., Provo, Utah, 1966; M.S. in Civil Engring., U. Santa Clara (Calif.), 1972; m. Linda Marie Brown, July 26, 1963; children—Robert, Sandra, Richard, Rodney, Annette, Aaron, Jessica, Jennifer. Project engr. Philco-Ford Corp., Palo Alto, Calif., 1966-72; chief structural engr. Food Industries Research & Engring., Inc., Yakima, Wash., 1972-76; supr., mgr. engring. Pullman Torkelson Co., Salt Lake City, 1976-79; pres. Devon M. Stone & Assocs., Midvale, Utah, 1979—, Sanders, Stone & Allred Inc., Salt Lake City, 1980-81, Stone & Assocs. Inc., Salt Lake City, 1981-82; spl. insp. Salt Lake County. Registered profl. engr., Calif., Utah, Idaho, Wash, Wyo. Mem. ASCE, Am. Concrete Inst. Republican. Mormon. Home: 7847 Willowcrest Circle Salt Lake City UT 84121 Office: 6909 S State Midvale UT 84047

STONE, DONALD D., investment and sales executive; b. Chgo., June 25, 1924; s. Frank J. and Mary N. (Miller) Diamondstone; student U. Ill., 1942-43; B.S., DePaul U., 1949; m. Catherine Mauro, Dec. 20, 1970; 1 child, Jeffrey. Pres., Poster Bros., Inc., Chgo., 1950-71, Revere Leather Goods, Inc., Chgo., 1953-71; owner Don Stone Enterprises, Chgo., 1954—; v.p. Horton & Hubbard Mfg. Co., Inc. div. Brown Group, Nashua, N.H., 1969-71, Neevel Mfg. Co., Kansas City, Mo., 1969-71. Mem. adv. bd. San Diego Opera; founder Don Diego Meml. Scholarship Fund; mem. bd. overseers U. Calif., San Diego, chancellor's assoc.; mem. exec. bd. Chgo. Area council Boy Scouts of Am. Served with U.S. Army, 1943-46. Clubs: Bryn Mawr Country (Lincolnwood, Ill.) (dir.), Carlton, La Jolla Beach and Tennis, La Jolla Country, Del Mar Thoroughbred. Home: 8240 Caminito Maritimo La Jolla CA 92037

STONE, ELIZABETH (BETSY) CAMPBELL, marketing executive; b. Kingston, Ont., Can., June 15, 1957; d. Henry Snively and Eileen (Driscoll) C.; m. Jeffrey Todd Stone, Aug. 7, 1982. Student, U. Wash., 1978; BA, U. Puget Sound, 1979; postgrad., U. Calif., Davis, 1981. Resident, traveling field rep. Pi Beta Phi, St. Louis, 1979-81; asst. acct. exec. Dancer Fitzgerald Sample, Los Angeles, 1981-82; account exec. Girvin Conrad Girvin, Sacramento, 1982-83; dir. communications Sacramento Bd. Realtors, 1983-84; community relations rep. Sutter Health System, Sacramento, 1984-85; mktg. mgr. Sutter Meml. Hosp., Sacramento, 1985-86; mktg. dir., Saramento div. Sutter Health Systems, Sacramento, 1987—. Bd. dirs. United Cerebral Palsy Bd., Sacramento, 1984—. Recipient Gold Circle award Am. Soc. Assn. Execs., 1985; named Best Publ. Nat. Assn. Realtors, 1984; Women on the Move award C. of C.; Showcase award of Excellence IABC. Mem. Internat. Assn. Bus. Communicators (pres. 1987, Silver award, 1986), Soc. Hosp. Pub. Relations and Mktg., Women's Network Sacramento. Republican. Episcopalian. Lodge: Soroptimists (del. 1986, recording sec. 1985). Avocations: hiking, aerobics, winetasting, reading. Office: Sutter Health System IIII Howe Suite 600 Sacramento CA 95825

STONE, HARRY RONALD (RON), insurance company executive, retired professional baseball player; b. Corning, Calif., Sept. 9, 1942; s. Harry Marshall and Dorothy (Morris) S.; m. Arlene Ann Marcello (div. 1982); 1 child, Jonathan McKenzie; m. Marian Agnes Aniot, July 8, 1984; 1 child, Jennifer Paige. AA, Stockton Coll., 1962; BS, Calif. State U., Sacramento, 1965. cert. life and health gen. lines ins. agt. Player Balt. Orioles, 1963-65, 67-68, Kansas City (Mo.) Athletics, 1966-67, Phila. Phillies, 1969-73; div. mgr. Payment Insured Plan, Eugene, Oreg., 1976-84; owner Cascade F&I Agy., Portland, Oreg., 1984—; cons. Conductor clinics amateur baseball teams, Oreg. Served with U.S. Army, 1964-69. Named 1st Team All-Star Internat. League, 1967. Mem. Airplane Owners and Pilots Assn., Active and Oldtimers Baseball Assn. Republican. Club: Oreg. Duck Hunters (Portland). Avocations: flying, boating, golf, shooting, white water rafting. Home: 7560 Downs Post Rd Wilsonville OR 97070

STONE, HERBERT ALLEN, management consultant; b. Washington, Sept. 14, 1934; s. Joseph and Marion (Solomon) S.; m. Marjorie Nelke Sterling, June 14, 1964; children: Joanna, Lisa. BSc, U. Mass., 1955, MSc, 1958; PhD, U. Calif., Davis, 1962. Specialist Exptl. Sta. U. Calif., Davis, 1961-62; food scientist SRI, Menlo Park, Calif., 1962-67, dir. food and plant sci., 1967-74; pres. Tragon Corp., Redwood City, Calif., 1974—. Author: Sensory Evaluation Practices, 1985; assoc. editor Jour. Food Sci., 1977-80; contbr. sci. and tech. articles to profl. jours.; patentee in field. Fellow Inst. Food Technology (pres. S.E. div. 1977-78), mem. AAAS, Am. Soc. Enology, European Chemoreception Orgn. Club: Ladera Oaks (Menlo Park). Home: 990 San Mateo Dr Menlo Park CA 94025 Office: Tragon Corp 365 Convention Way Redwood City CA 94063

STONE, JAMES MATTHEW, food service industry executive; b. Flushing, N.Y., June 5, 1951; s. Michael and René (Rudich) S.; m. Maria Kathleen Ruiz, June 16, 1974; children: Stella Ochian, Jessica Amber. BFA, Fairleigh Dickinson U.; postgrad., U. Nev. Stage technician I.A.T.S.E., Las Vegas, 1975—; owner, operator La Paloma Restaurant, Sant Fe, N.Mex., 1980-87; gen. mgr. McBurnie Coachcraft, Sante, Calif., 1987—. producer, dir. Dryfus Community Theatre, 1974, Tenth St. Players, 1975; dir. UNLU Little Theatre, 1975. Active Youth exchange; advisor United Synagogue Youth Program, Louisville, 1971-72. Mem. Casa de Analco Mchts. Assn. (sec. 1985). Democrat. Jewish. Avocations: stained glass, woodwork. Home: 17119 W Bernardo Dr San Diego CA 92127

STONE, JOAN ELIZABETH, English educator, writer; b. Port Angeles, Wash., Oct. 22, 1930; d. William David and Florence Iva (Burdick) Duncan; m. Donald Harwood Stone, Sept. 7, 1949 (div. 1980); children: Bruce, Duncan, Duane, Todd, Anne. BA magna cum laude, U. Wash., 1970, MA, 1974, postgrad., 1976—. Vis. prof. poetry U. Mont., Missoula, 1974; assoc. prof. English U. Wash., Seattle, 1975; poetry cons. Yakima (Wash.) schs., 1975-77; asst. prof. English The Colo. Coll., Colorado Springs, 1977—. Author: The Swimmer, 1975, Alba, 1976, A Letter to Myself to Water, 1982, Our Lady of the Harbor, 1986. Bd. advisors Press at The Colo. Coll., 1978—. Recipient Acad. Am. Poets award, U. Wash., 1969, 70, 72, 74, Borestone Mountain award, 1973, 74. Avocations: restoring houses, cooking, drawing. Home: 312 E Yampa Colorado Springs CO 80903 Office: The Colo Coll Armstrong Hall Colorado Springs CO 80903

STONE, LINDA, sales executive, TV broadcaster, writer; b. Atlanta, Nov. 11; student Forrell Sch. Entertainment Arts, 1960-61, Phoenix Coll., 1960-61, Ga. State U., 1962-63; m. Howard Corbett Bloomer, July 1, 1978. Owner, Acad. Playhouse of Entertainment Arts, Charleston, S.C., 1969-70; promotion mgr. WUSN-TV, Charleston, 1967-69; promotion mgr., broadcaster KPHO-TV, Phoenix, 1970-78; creative dir. KJJJ and KXTC Radio Stas., 1978-79; promotion dir., pub. service dir. Sta. KTAR-KBBC-FM, Phoenix, 1980-81; v.p. sales and promotion Aerolight Flight Devel., Inc., Mesa, Ariz., 1982-83; pilot, dir. Services Superstition Mountain Airpark, 1982-83; program and advt. dir. Short Excursions in Ariz.; author children's books; contbr. articles to various jours. and publs. including: Phoenix mag., Ariz. Sports News Weekly, Ariz. Host; instr. communication Ariz. State U., 1977. Mem. Broadcast Promotion Assn., Acad. TV Arts and Scis., Am. Women in Radio and TV (past dir.), Phoenix Press Club, LWV, Mu Rho Sigma (life). Editor: Ad-Libber, Phoenix Ad Club, 1975-76. Address: PO Box 2313 Phoenix AZ 85002

STONE, NORMAN CLEMENT, psychologist, foundation administrator; b. Evanston, Ill., Apr. 28, 1939; s. W. Clement and Jessie Verna (Tarson) S.; m. Norah Grace Sharpe, June 1, 1986; children: Bryan C., Norman Clifford, Mark C., Amy M. ABA, Nichols Jr. Coll., 1959; BA, Stanford U., 1962; PhD, Wright Inst., 1985. Pvt. investor, 1964—; gen. ptnr., founder San Francisco Venture Capital, 1970-76; trustee, co-founder Nueva Day Sch. and Learning Center, Hillsborough, Calif., 1967-76; psychotherapist Bay View Hunter's Point Found. for Community Improvement Mental Health Ctr., San Francisco, 1981—; pres. W. Clement and Jessie V. Stone Found., 1985—; chmn. bd. Golden West Sales.

STONE, RICHARD ARNOLD, podiatrist; b. Buffalo, Apr. 22, 1954; s. Sol and Geraldine (Swerdloff) S.; m. Margaret J. MacPherson, Nov. 24, 1985. BA, SUNY, Buffalo, 1976; DPM, Calif. Coll. Podiatric Medicine, 1979. Practice medicine specializing in podiatry Burlingame, Calif., 1982—; asst. clin. prof. Calif. Coll. Podiatric Medicine, San Francisco, 1982—; chmn. dept. podiatric surgery Peninsula Hosp., Burlingame, 1982—. Mem. Am. Podiatric Med. Assn., San Francisco/San Mateo County Podiatry Assn. (v.p. 1983—), Pi Delta. Avocations: running, windsurfing, tennis. Office: Calif Coll Pediatric Medicine 1515 Trousdale Burlingame CA 94010

STONE, ROBERT MAURICE, lawyer; b. Great Lakes, Ill., Apr. 6, 1956; s. Herman and Leah Sara (Horberg) S.; m. Kathleen Ferguson, Jan. 23, 1981; children: Alexander, Brian. BA, UCLA, 1978; JD, U. Calif., San Francisco, 1982. Bar: Calif. 1982, U.S. Dist. Ct. (no. dist.) Calif. 1982, U.S. Dist. Ct. (cen. dist.) Calif. 1983, U.S. Dist. Ct. (ea. dist.) Calif. 1985. Assoc. atty. Simon, McKinsey & Miller, Long Beach, Calif., 1983—; cons. Long Beach City Coll., 1985. Mem. ABA, Long Beach Bar Assn., Los Angeles County Bar Assn., Phi Alpha Delta. Democrat. Jewish. Avocations: gardening, baseball. Office: Simon McKinsey & Miller 2750 Bellflower Blvd Suite 100 Long Beach CA 90815

STONE, ROBYN LYNN, advertising executive; b. Denver, Mar. 2, 1950; d. Marvin Leon and Marian Rhea (Leiser) S. Student, U. Calif., Berkeley, 1969-71; BA, U. Denver, 1972. Account coordinator Sam Lusky Assocs., Denver, 1972-74; pub. relations asst. Shaw Elliott, Inc., N.Y.C., 1975-76; ptnr. Kathryn Stone & Co., N.Y.C., 1976-78; pub. relations dir. PA Internat., N.Y.C., 1978-82, Mile Hi Cablevision, Denver, 1982-83; owner Stone Advt., Denver, 1984—. Bd. dirs. Hospice of Metro Denver, 1984—. Mem. Denver Advt. Fedn. (Alfie award 1984, 85), Pub. Relations Soc. Am. (Gold Pick award Denver chpt. 1985, 1986), Bus. Profl. Advt. Assn. (Gold Key award Denver chpt. 1984), Denver Sales and Mktg. Council (Mame award 1986). Democrat. Jewish. Avocations: jogging, travel, tennis. Office: Stone Advt 1565 Gilpin Denver CO 80218

STONE, TERRY ANN, advertising executive, media and market researcher; b. Pueblo, Colo., Dec. 27, 1938; d. Kenneth Calvin and Maxine Grace (McKendry) Mead; m. Donald R. Stone, June 12, 1959; children: Robert K., Katherine M. BA, U. Denver, 1960; MBA, U. Santa Clara, 1981. Cert. bus. communicator, U.S., Can. Var. tching. positions Colo. and Calif., 1960-70; vol. in schs., personal growth orgn. City Palo Alto and San Mateo and Santa Clara Counties, Calif., 1970-77; mktg., adminstrn. exec. Surface Sci. Labs., Mt. View, Calif., 1977-80; mktg., com. exec. TAB Products, Palo Alto, Calif., 1980-82; media, mkt. researcher Imahara & Keep, Sunnyvale, Calif., 1982-85, Ebey, Utley & Co., Mt. View, Calif., 1985—. Creator Peace Ribbon panel Families, 1985 (part of perm. collection Oakland, Calif. Mus). Active Com. Against U.S. Intervention in Cen. Am., Palo Alto, 1984—. Mem. Bus. Profl. Advt. Assn. (bd. dirs. 1985-86, v.p. membership 1986—). Democrat. Club: AAUW (Palo Alto chpt.). Avocations: fiber arts, folk music, dance.

STONE, WILLIAM, JR., ophthalmologist; b. N.Y.C., Mar. 1, 1916; s. William and Gabriella S.; m. Margaret Saunders Fyles, Jan. 22, 1963; children: Heather Fyles, Hollice Fyles. BA, Columbia U., 1937, MD, 1941. Diplomate Am. Bd. Ophthalmology. Asst. resident in neurology Colombia U., N.Y.C., 1941-42; intern Lenox Hill Hosp., N.Y.C., 1942-43; resident Mass. Eye & Ear Inst., Boston, 1947-49, dir. eye research lab., 1949-64, asst. surgeon, 1950-64; pres. Nat. Inst. Sci. Research, Los Angeles, 1968—; assoc. clin. prof. Loma Linda U., Los Angeles, 1965-71, U. So. Calif., Los Angeles, 1967-71; cons. C.R. Bard, Murray Hill, N.J., 1975-80, Gambro Inc., 1980—; pres. Am. Membrane Corp., 1970—. Inventor plastic artificial cornea. Pres. Bishops Sch. Fathers Club, La Jolla, 1984-85, La Jolla Homeowners Summit, 1986. Served to maj. Air Surgeons Office, 1943-47. Recipient Bronze medal for original research AMA, 1950. Mem. U. Calif San Diego Chancellors Club. Clubs: Rancho Santa Fe Tennis (Calif.); La Jolla Beach and Tennis.

STONE, WILLIAM EDWARD, association executive; b. Peoria, Ill., Aug. 13, 1945; s. Dean Proctor and Katherine (Jamison) S.; m. Deborah Ann Duncan; children: Jennifer Duncan, Allison Duncan. A.B., Stanford U., 1967, M.B.A., 1969. Asst. dean Stanford U., 1969-71, asst. to pres., 1971-77; exec. dir. Stanford Alumni Assn., 1977—. Bd. dirs. North County YMCA, 1975-76; bd. dirs. and chmn. nominating com. faculty club Stanford U., 1979-81; trustee Watkins Discretionary Fund., 1979-82; mem. community adv. bd. Resource Ctr. for Women. Mem. Council for Advancement and Support of Edn., Stanford Hist. Soc., Stanford Assocs., Bay Area Profl. Women's Club. Democrat. Club: Stanford Faculty. Home: 543 Junipero Serra Blvd Stanford CA 94305 Office: Bowman Alumni House Stanford CA 94305

STONE, WILLIAM ROSS, research and development company executive, physicist; b. San Diego, Aug. 26, 1947; s. William Jack and Winifred (Beckcom) S.; m. Susan Letita Lane, Aug. 8, 1970; 1 child, Ann Michele. A.B. in Earth Sci., U. Calif.-San Diego, 1967, M.S. in Applied Physics, 1973, Ph.D. in Applied Physics, 1978. Research asst. U. Calif.-San Diego, 1967-69; sr. physicist Gen. Atomic, La Jolla, 1969-72; sr. engr. engring. div. Gulf Gen. Atomic, La Jolla, Calif., 1972-73; sr. scientist Megatek Corp., San Diego, 1973-80; prin. physicist, inverse scattering group leader IRT Corp., San Diego, 1980-86, research advisor, 1986—; pres. Stoneware, Ltd., La Jolla, Calif., 1976-13 ; dir., chmn. Samaritan Inst., San Diego, 1984—. Editor: Vol. New Methods for Optical, Quasioptical, Acoustic and Electromagnetic Synthesis, 1981. Contbr. articles to various publs. Recipient medal San Diego Soc. Tech. Writers and Pubs., 1962. Mem. NRC, Nat. Acad. Sci., Internat. Radio Sci. Union, Optical Soc. Am., Acoustical Soc. Am., Soc. Exploration Geophysics, AAUP, Nat. Acad. Scis., IEEE Antennas and Propagation Soc. (coordinator profl. activities 1980-83, editor procs. 1984—), Assn. Computing Machinery Soc. Indsl. and Applied Maths., Soc. Photooptical Instrumentation Engrs., Phi Eta Sigma. Home: 1446 Vista Claridad La Jolla CA 92037 Office: IRT Corp 3030 Callan Rd San Diego CA 92121

STONE, WILLIAM RUSSELL, newspaper publisher; b. Wheeling, W.Va., Aug. 27, 1951; s. James Marvin and Juanita (Tracewell) S. BA, W.Va. Wesleyan Coll., 1974; MBA, U. Va., 1979. Auditor U.S. GAO, Falls Ch., Va., 1974-77; fin. mgr. Miss. Pubs. Corp., Jackson, 1979-82, dir. fin., 1982-84; dir. ops. Statesman-Jour., Salem, Oreg., 1984-86, pub., 1986—. Mem. Am. Newspaper Pubs. Assn., Oreg. Newspaper Pubs. Assn., Allied Northwest Newspapers. Methodist. Club: Illahe Country (Salem). Office: Statesman Jour Co 280 Church St NE Salem OR 97306

STONEBRAKER, WILLIAM ERNEST, toxicologist, pharmacist; b. Evanston, Wyo., Sept. 15, 1934; s. John William and Beulah Lillian (Stacy) S.; m. Jacquelyn Marie Igo, June 30, 1962; 1 child, Cynthia Anne. BS in Chemistry, U. Wyo., 1957; BS in Pharmacy, U. Utah, 1968. Registered pharmacist, Utah, Wyo.; registered clin. chemist, Am. Soc. Clin. Pathologists. Chemist Morton Thiokol Corp., Brigham City, Utah, 1959-63; sales rep. Beckman Instruments, Inc., Denver, 1963-65; chemistry supr. Wasatch Pathology Labs., Salt Lake City, 1968-76; toxicologist Utah State Labs., Salt Lake City, 1976-81, chief pub. safety toxicology, 1981—; expert witness Utah Courts, 1977-86—; part-time pharmacist Zions. Coop. Merchantile Instn., Salt Lake City, 1976-86, Smith's Food and Drug, 1986—. Served with U.S. Army, 1957-59. Mem. Am. Chem. Soc., Calif. Assn. Toxicologists, Am. Acad. Forensic Sci. (provisional mem.). Republican. Mormon. Club: Cowboy Joe (Laramie, Wyo.). Lodge: Elks. Avocations: golf, swimming, fishing, hunting. Home: 4931 Laura Dr Murray UT 84107 Office: Utah State Health Labs Toxicology Dept 44 Medical Dr Salt Lake City UT 84113

STONEBRIDGE, JERRY BERT, construction company executive, consultant; b. Issaquah, Wash., June 2, 1941; s. Harold William and Phoebe Kay (Hoye) S.; m. M. Suzanne Carlson, July 28, 1976; children—Jerry Edward, Jeffrey Scott. B.S. in Zoology and Chemistry, Wash. State U., 1963; cert. in operating engring. Northwest Heavy Equipment Sch., 1964; postgrad. U. Wash., 1970-75. Research asst. rehab. medicine dept. U. Wash., Seattle, 1964-72, research assoc., 1972-78; ophthalmic med. asst. Am. Assn. Ophthalmology, 1971-72; pres. Stonebridge Constrn. Co., Inc., Whidbey Island, Wash., 1978—; cons. on-site sewage disposal systems and their mgmt., 1978—. Pres. Freeland Community Assn., 1980-82; trustee Saratoga Beach Community Assn., 1982—; mem. tech. rev. bd. Island County Health Dept., 1980-82. Bausch & Lomb grantee, 1959-60; Nellie Martin grantee, 1960; recipient 1st place prize for research exhibit Am. Phys. Therapy Assn., 1973; Silver medal Am. Congress Rehab. Medicine, 1974. Mem. Internat. Platform Assn., Am. Bibliography Inst., Pi Ti Iota. Republican. Contbr. articles to profl. jours. Home and Office: 3329-S E Harbor Rd Langley WA 98260

STONEHAM, EDWARD BRYANT, technical company executive; b. Coronado, Calif., Oct. 13, 1946; s. Samuel Camp and Jennie Lynn (Reagor) S.; m. Haesook Nam, July 4, 1972; children: Anita Lynn, Trina Ann. AB, U. Calif., Berkeley, 1968; PhD, Stanford U., 1975. Devel. engr. Hewlett-Packard Corp., Palo Alto, Calif., 1971-75; project mgr. Hewlett-Packard Corp., Santa Rosa, Calif., 1975-84; mgr. research and devel. Microwave Tech., Inc., Fremont, Calif., 1984—; ptnr. Tamler-Stoneham Instruments, San Francisco, 1977-83; owner Stoneham Innovations, Santa Rosa, 1980-84. Patentee in field; contbr. articles to profl. jours. Served with U.S. Army, 1969-71. Mem. Sigma Xi, Phi Beta Kappa. Republican. Avocations: sailplane piloting, mus. compositions. Office: Microwave Tech Inc 4268 Solar Way Fremont CA 94538

STONEHOUSE, JAMES ADAM, lawyer; b. Alameda, Calif., Nov. 10, 1937; s. Maurice Adam and Edna Sigrid (Thuesen) S.; A.B., U. Calif., Berkeley, 1961; J.D., Hastings Coll. Law, U. Calif., San Francisco, 1965; m. Marilyn Jean Kotkas, Aug. 6, 1966; children—Julie Aileen, Stephen Adam. Bar: Calif. 1966. Assoc. Hall, Henry, Oliver & McReavy, San Francisco, 1966-71; partner firm Whitney, Hanson & Stonehouse, Alameda, 1971-77; individual practice law, Alameda, 1977-79; partner firm Stonehouse & Silva, Alameda, 1979—; judge adv. Alameda council Navy League, 1978—. Founding dir. Alameda Clara Barton Found., 1977-80; mem. Oakland (Calif.) Marathon-Exec. Com., 1979; mem. exec. bd. Alameda council Boy Scouts Am., 1979—, pres., 1986—; mem. Nat. council Boy Scouts Am., 1986—; trustee Golden Gate Scouting, 1986—; bd. dirs. Lincoln Child Ctr. Found., 1981—, pres., 1983-85. Named Boss of Yr. Alameda Jaycees, 1977; Coro Found. fellow in pub. affairs, 1961-62. Mem. ABA, State Bar Calif., Alameda County Bar (vice chmn. com. office econs., 1977-78). Republican. Roman Catholic. Club: Commonwealth. Lodges: Rotary (dir. club 1976-78), Elks (past exalted ruler, all state officer 1975-76, all dist. officer 1975-77, 78-79) (Alameda). Home: 2990 Northwood Dr Alameda CA 94501 Office: 512 Westline Dr Suite 204 Alameda CA 94501

STONEMAN, DOUGLAS GRAYSON, oil company executive; b. Ottawa, Ont., Can., May 21, 1931; s. John A. and Muriel L. (Grayson) S.; m. Barbara Joan Damery, Oct. 12, 1957; children—Sharon, Michael, William. B.S.C.E., U. Man., Can., 1954. Registered profl. engr., Alta., Can. Gen. mgr. prodn. Shell Can. Ltd., Calgary, Alta., 1973-75, gen. mgr. pub. affairs, Toronto, Ont., 1975-77, gen. mgr. environ. and govt. affairs, 1977-78, v.p. devel., Calgary, 1978-82, sr. v.p. oil and gas, 1982-84, sr. v.p. bus. devel., 1984—; chmn. Sultran Ltd., Calgary, 1978—, Pacific Coast Terminals, Vancouver, B.C., 1982—. Recipient Gold medal U. Man., 1954. Mem. Assn. Profl. Engrs., Geologists and Geophysicists Alta. (membership chmn. 1975, young mem. task force 1979, admission requirements task force 1981), Can. Petroleum Assn. (past chmn. bd. govs. 1986), Sulphur Inst. (dir. 1981—), Can. Energy Research Inst. (dir. 1981), Calgary Petroleum Club. Club: Canyon Meadows Golf (Calgary). Office: Shell Can Ltd, 400 4th Ave SW, Calgary, AB Canada T2P 0S4

STONER, BARTINE ALBERT, JR., advertising executive; b. Trenton, N.J., Apr. 18, 1926; s. Bartine Albert and Estella (Hart) S.; m. Elizabeth Ann Bond, Mar. 18, 1949 (div. 1973); children: Bartine Albert III, Jonathan West; m. Madeleine Ruskin, 1973. B.S., Princeton U., 1948. With Westinghouse Electric Corp., Boston, Newark and Phila., 1948-56; account exec. N.W. Ayer & Son, Inc., Phila., 1956-65; v.p., dir. account service N.W. Ayer & Son, Inc., 1965-67; dir., exec. v.p., gen. mgr. N.W. Ayer & Son, Inc., Phila. region, 1967-73; dir. internat. ops. N.W. Ayer & Son, Inc., N.Y.C., 1974-76; also bd. dirs. N.W. Ayer & Son, Inc.; pres. Ayer Baker Advt., Seattle, 1974-75; mng. dir. Ayer Barker Hegemann Internat. B.V., London, 1976-79; pres., chief exec. officer Ayer, Jorgensen, Macdonald, Los Angeles, 1979-80; exec. v.p., dir. N.W. Ayer Inc.; pres. N.W. Ayer Inc. (Western div.), 1981-83, chmn., chief exec. officer, 1983—; dir., pres. Settembrini and Tecchio ABH Internat., Milan, Italy, 1976-79; Charles Barker, Gmbit, Frankfurt, Fed. Republic of Germany, 1978-79; dir Moussault ABH Internat., Amsterdam, Holland and Antwerp, 1976-79, O'Hara, Hannigan and Reid, ABH Internat., Toronto, 1975-76. Bd. dirs. Greater Phila. Movement, 1973-74, Elwyn Inst.-Hosp., 1967-76; bd. pensions U.P. Ch. U.S.A., 1971-76; trustee Internat. Assn. Shipboard Edn. Served to lt. (j.g.) USNR, 1944-46. Mem. Pa. Soc. Presbyterian (elder). Clubs: Phila. Racquet; Hurlingham (London); Princeton (N.Y.C.); Jonathan (Los Angeles), Rotary (Los Angeles), Riviera Tennis (Los Angeles). Home: 10475 Wyton Dr Los Angeles CA 90024 Office: NW Ayer & Co 888 S Figueroa St 12th Floor Los Angeles CA 90017 also: 1345 Ave of Americas New York NY 10019

STONEY, JAMES MARSHALL, microbiology and biology educator, consultant; b. San Francisco, Feb. 27, 1930; s. Reed J. and Leola (McCoy) S.; m. Joan E. Harrison, Jan. 20, 1970 (div.); children: Scot, Renee, Paul, David; m. Maureen Ann Gallagher, Jan. 21, 1984; children: Nicole, Sean. BA, MA, San Francisco State U., 1953; postgrad., Claremont Coll., 1975, Oreg. State U., 1959. Instr. microbiology and biology City Coll. San Francisco, 1954, Stockton (Calif.) Coll., 1954-59, Coll. of San Mateo, Calif., 1959-68, Canada Coll., Redwood City, Calif., 1969—; researcher San Francisco Coll. Parasitology Found., 1952-55; cons. bacteriology, chem. and food processing cos., 1964—. Trustee San Mateo County Mosquito Abatement Dist., Millbrae, Calif., 1975-77; coach Am. Youth Soccer Assn., Woodside and Redwood City, 1973—. Mem. Am. Assn. Microbiology, Nat. Ednl. Assn., Calif. Tchrs. Assn. Office: Canada Coll 4200 Farm Hill Blvd Redwood City CA 94061

STONG, JOHN ELLIOTT, retail electronics company executive; b. Elkater, Iowa, Sept. 20, 1921; s. Elliott Sheldon and Nora Elizabeth (Daly) S.; ed. U. Colo., 1943; m. Olive Miriam Foley, Dec. 11, 1943; children—Mary Mandelson, Jon, Miriam, Salesman, Purucker Music, Medford, Oreg., 1946-48, dept. mgr., 1949-56, store mgr., 1957, partner, 1958-61, owner, 1962-64; pres. Purucker Music Houses, Medford, 1965-67, Music West, Inc., Eugene, Oreg., 1968-70, Magnavox Centers, Medford, 1971—, Exec. Assist., Consultants Internat., 1972—. Served with USAF, 1943-45. Decorated Air medal. Mem. Nat. Assn. Music Mchts. (dir. 1969-72), Scull Mchts. Research Group (dir., chmn.). Republican. Roman Catholic. Home: 2120 Woodlawn St Medford OR 97501 Office: Cons Internat 117 N Central St Medford OR 97501

STONICK, VICTOR H., instructional technologist; b. Clairton, Pa., Feb. 25, 1930; s. Joseph John and Mary Agnes (Sprites) S.; B.A., UCLA, 1956, postgrad., 1964; postgrad. Calif. State U., Fullerton, 1972; m. Patricia Ann Sims, Mar. 25, 1967; children—Mark A., Cynthia L., Lyndell M., Timothy M., Christopher P., Amelia D., Jennelle D. Comml. TV dir., prodn. supr., Los Angeles, 1953-59; supr., coordinator Ednl. TV Broadcasting, Los Angeles, 1959-62; dir. communications Loyola U., Los Angeles, 1962-65; dir. motion pictures, supr., writer, producer Gen. Dynamics, Pomona, Calif., 1967-69; motion picture producer, writer N.Am. Rockwell Autonetics, Anaheim, Calif., 1965-67; sr. multi media producer So. Calif. Regional Occupational Center, Torrance, 1969-74; dir. ops. and spl. projects Hoffman Occupational Learning Systems, El Monte, Calif., 1974-76; pres. Multi Communications div. Nat. Tech. Assn. div. Nat. Tech. Schs., Anaheim, 1976-81, group dir. WICAT Systems, Orem, Utah, 1981-82; with Trainex-Saudi Arabia Ltd., 1982; dir. spl. projects Medcom., 1984-85; pres. HighTech., Inc., Orem, 1985—; cons. Stonick & Assos.; v.p. Varcon Industries Internat. Mktg. Group, 1977. Served with USAF, 1948-52. Mem. Calif. Assn. Media and Ednl. Tech., Am. Soc. Tng. and Devel. Home: 616 E 445 S Orem UT 84058

STOPHER, PETER ROBERT, transportation executive, consultant; b. Crowborough, Eng., Aug. 8, 1943; came to U.S., 1968; s. Harold Edward and Joan Constance (Salmon) S; m. Valerie Anne Alway, Apr. 11, 1964; children: Helen Margaret Anne, Claire Elizabeth. BSCE, U. Coll., London, 1964, PhD, 1967. Research officer Greater London Council, London, 1967-68; asst. prof. transp. planning, applied statistics, math. modeling Northwestern U., Evanston, Ill., 1968-70, from assoc. prof. to prof., 1973-79, vis. prof., 1980-81; asst. prof. McMaster U., Hamilton, Ontario, 1970-71; assoc. prof. Cornell U., Ithaca, N.Y., 1971-73; tech. v.p. Schimpeler Corradino Assoc., Miami, Fla., and Los Angeles, 1980-84, v.p., 1984—; spl. advisor Nat. Inst. Transp. and Rd. Research, Pretoria, S. Africa, 1976-77; vis. prof. U. Syracuse, N.Y., 1971-73, U. Lovain, Belgium, 1980. Co-author Urban Transportation Planning and Modeling, 1974, Transportation Systems Evaluation, 1976, Survey Sampling and Multivariate Analysis, 1978; contbr. articles to profl. jours. Recipient Fred Burgraaf prize Hwy. Research Bd., 1968. Fellow Inst. Hwy. Engrs., Royal Stats. Soc.; mem. ASCE, Am. Stats. Assn., Transp. Research Bd. (com. chmn. 1970-77). Democrat. Methodist. Avocations: jogging, gardening, photography, reading, classical music. Home: 3913 Via Cardelina Palos Verdes Estates CA 90274-1110 Office: Schimpeler Corradino Assocs 425 S Main St Los Angeles CA 90013

STOREY, SHERRIELL EDWARD, transportation safety trainer, consultant; b. Leaksville, N.C., Jan. 6, 1947; s. Sherriell Edward and Ellen Ray (Hall) S.; m. Roma Jane Warfel, Dec. 22, 1967; children: Gregory Edward, Brian Lee. Student, Milligan (Tenn.) Coll., 1965-66, Johnson Bible Coll., 1966-69; BA in Ministry and Edn., Dakota Bible Coll., 1971. Safety tng. and personnel supr. Tundra Towers, Inc., Palmer, Alaska, 1981-85; safety tng. cons. Alaska State Dept. Edn., Juneau, 1985—; prin., cons. J&E Transp., Palmer, 1985—; safety tng. cons. Mat-Su Borough Sch. Dist., Palmer, 1983-85, Railbelt Sch. Dist., Hedly, Alaska, 1985; lectr. seminars on safety. Author safety procedure manuals. Pack leader Boy Scouts of Am.; vol. instr. ch. camp, Sherrod Elementary Sch.; coach Matanuska Youth Activities Com., Palmer, 1985. Mem. Am. Soc. Safety Engrs. Alaska chpt. Mem. Ch. of Christ. Avocations: reading, landscaping, sports, hunting, fishing. Home: Outer Springer Loop Rd Palmer AK 99645 Office: J and E Transp Outer Springer Loop Rd Palmer AK 99645

STORM, DAVID LYNN, chemist, toxicologist; b. Hawarden, Iowa, Aug. 10, 1939; s. Charles Rauworth and Lola Ethel (Olson) S.; m. Jane Mary Kostrovnova, Apr. 8, 1967; children: Paul, Matthew. BS in Chemistry, U. Wash., 1962; PhD in Organic Chemistry, Iowa State U., 1967. Postdoctoral research fellow Dartmouth Coll., Hanover, N.H., 1966-67; research chemist Celanese Chem. Co., Corpus Christi, Tex., 1967-70; postdoctoral biochemist U. Calif., Berkeley, 1970-73; research chemist Calif. Dept. Health, Berkeley, 1973-84; staff toxicologist Calif. Dept. Health, Sacramento, 1984—; instr. chemistry San Francisco State U., 1976-77; mem. Colo. Intergovtl. Sci., Engring. and Tech. Adv. panel, 1978-79; cons. EPA to City of Colorado Springs, Colo., 1979-80; mem. Western Fed. Regional task force for hazardous waste, San Francisco, 1973-77. Contbr. articles to profl. jours. Mem. Am. Chem. Soc., Zeta Mu Tau. Avocations: running, gardening, computers. Home: 8697 River Rd Sacramento CA 95832 Office: Calif State Dept Health Services 714 P St Sacramento CA 95832

STORM, DAVID RUSSELL, civil engineer, consultant; b. Ross, Calif., May 7, 1931; s. Walter Ernst and Nanetta V. (Adams) S.; m. Leona Kathryn Hickey, Aug. 8, 1954; children: Timaurie Anne, Tyghe Adams, Todd Anthony. BSCE, U. Nev., Reno, 1954; MS, U. Calif., Davis, 1969, PhD, 1973. Registered civil engr., Calif., Oreg., Nev., Wyo., Utah. Hydraulic engr. Tudor Engring. Co., San Francisco, 1958-61; project engr. Leeds-Hill, Inc., San Francisco, 1961-63; br. office mgr. Metcalf-Eddy, Inc., San Francisco, 1963-68; cons. engr. Storm Engring., Winters, Calif., 1968—; chmn. SWI, Inc., Davis, 1973—, Winters Winery, Inc., 1979—. Tech. editor Practical Winery Jour., 1983—. Served with USN, 1954-58, commdr. Res. Republican. Roman Catholic. Avocations: skiing, tennis. Office: Storm Engring 15 Main St Winters CA 95694

STORM, MICHAEL CRAIG, research nutritionist; b. Santa Ana, Calif., Mar. 19, 1947; s. Clyde Ernest and Hazel Alfreda (Boyd) S. BA, Calif. State U., Fullerton, 1974, MA, 1976; PhD, U. Calif., Riverside, 1980. Clin. coordinator Am. McGaw, Irvine, Calif., 1980-84; mgr. nutrition sect. Kendall McGaw, Irvine, 1984—. Contbr. articles to profl. jours. Mem. Am. Chem. Soc., Nat. Assn. Underwater Instrs., Profl. Assn. Diving Instrs. Democrat. Lutheran. Avocations: scuba diving, photography. Home: 25212 Nueva Vista Laguna Niguel CA 92677 Office: Kendall McGaw 2525 McGaw Ave Irvine CA 92714

STORMER, KENT ALLEN, corporate lawyer; b. Los Altos, Calif., Sept. 20, 1945; s. John Frederick and Margery (Pickett) S. BA, Stanford U., 1966, JD, 1970. Legal advisor U.S. Office of Edn., Washington, 1970-73; asst. regional atty. U.S. Dept. HEW, San Francisco, 1973-79; atty. Syntex (U.S.A.) Inc., Palo Alto, Calif., 1979-84, dir. environ. and adminstrv. law, 1984—. Office: Syntex (USA) Inc 3401 Hillview A2-112 Palo Alto CA 94304

STORMS, KATE, industrial safety consultant; b. Easton, Pa., Nov. 13, 1954; d. Carl Richard and Phyllis Elizabeth (Taylor) S. BA, U. Del., 1976; postgrad., Tulane U., 1980—. Cert. safety profl. Safety/security adminstr. Stewart Enterprises Inc., New Orleans, 1978-79; safety coordinator Ragnar Benson Inc., Pitts., 1979-80; safety rep. Middle South Services Inc., New Orleans, 1980-85; loss control rep. AIG Cons. Inc., Los Angeles, 1985-86; sr. loss control rep. CIGNA Loss Control Services, Inc., Orange, Calif., 1986—; sales leader, part-time trainer Shaklee Corp., New Orleans, 1981-83; instr. Cameron Coll., New Orleans, 1983-84; mgmt. cons. Wellbeing, New Orleans, 1984. Mem. health services com. ARC, New Orleans, chmn. promotion subcom., 1984-85. Mem. Am. Soc. Safety Engrs. (treas. New Orleans chpt. 1984-85, Cert. Recognition 1984), Nat. Safety Mgmt. Soc., Am. Council Career Women (bd. dirs. 1981-83), Bus. and Profl. Women's Club, Inst. Self-Actualization (coordinator 1980). Democrat. Avocations: running, sailing, metaphysics. Home: 38 Horizon Ave Apt D Venice CA 90291 Office: CIGNA Loss Control Services Inc 1120 W La Veta Ave Orange CA 92668

STORY, HARRY JOE, economics educator; b. Long Beach, Calif., July 16, 1937; s. Harry Ervin and Margaret Marietta (Herrick) S.; m. Barbara Elizabeth Sedgwick, Jan. 28, 1966; children—Elizabeth Ann, Bruce Robert. B.A., U. Calif.-Santa Barbara, 1959; M.A., Calif. State U., 1968; Ph.D., U. Oreg., 1975. Lic. real estate broker, Oreg. Faculty, Pacific U., Forest Grove, Oreg., 1968—, prof. econs. and chmn. dept. bus. and econs., 1978—; cons. in field. Trustee, Pacific U., 1976-79; mem. Forest Grove Planning Commn., 1975-77. Served to lt. USN, 1959-62. U. Oreg. grad. fellow, 1970-72; Pacific U. research grantee, 1970-71; Danforth assoc., 1976-82; Dept. Energy grantee, summer 1978; Joseph P. Malone fellow, 1985. Mem. Am. Econs. Assn., Western Econs. Assn., Danforth Assocs. Democrat. Contbr. articles to profl. jours.

STOTHART, ROBERTA BATES, bookstore manager; b. Long Beach, Calif., Mar. 29, 1934; d. Morley DaCosta and Dorothy Clarice (Graham) Bates; student U. Ariz., 1952-53; children—Lisa, Camille, Anna, Elizabeth. Library asst. Am. Sch. Switzerland, Lugano, 1967-70; mus. bookstore mgr. J. Paul Getty Mus., Malibu, Calif., 1974-85, mgr. publs. dept., 1985— . Mem. Mus. Stores Assn. (dir.). Home: 1472 Palisades Dr Pacific Palisades CA 90272 Office: J Paul Getty Mus 17985 Pacific Coast Hwy Malibu CA 90265

STOTLAR, SUZANNE CORA, solid state physicist; b. Niagara Falls, N.Y., Aug. 27, 1947; d. Harvey Lewis and June Catherine (Mark) Wince; M. James Christopher Stotlar, June 10, 1972; children—Leslie Diane, James Harvey. B.S. with honors, Ohio U., 1969; postgrad. U. Calif.-Irvine, 1969-70. Mem. tech. staff Rockwell Internat., Anaheim, Calif., 1969-70; supr. infrared detectors group Harshaw Chem. Co., Solon, Ohio, 1970-76; staff psysicist, sect. leader Los Alamos Nat. Lab., 1976-85; engring. mgr. Advanced Detector Corp. div. Applied Solar Energy Corp., City of Industry, Calif., 1985—; chmn. Los Alamos Conf. on Optics, 1979, 81; co-chmn. 81 Expanding Your Horizons Conf.; chmn. S.W. Conf. on Optics, 1985. Mem. Optical Soc. Am., IEEE, Quantum Electronics and Applications Soc., IEEE (sr.), Soc. Photo-Optical Instrumentation Engrs., Los Alamos Optical Soc. (pres. 1978-82). Roman Catholic. Editor QEAS/IEEE Newsletter; contbr. articles profl. jours. Patentee in field. Home: 6048 Avenida Barcelona Yorba Linda CA 15251 Office: 15251 E Don Julian Rd City of Industry CA 91749

STOTT, CHARLES BUCKLEY, personal computer management consultant; b. Quincy, Mass., June 27, 1924; s. Charles Buckley and Gladys Selina (Warhurst) S.; m. Barbara Ann Wood, Apr. 10, 1948; children: Richard F., Janet L., Warren C., Robert A. Student, Clark U., 1943-44, Brown U., 1947; BSEE, Tufts U., 1949; MS, Cornell U., 1963. Registered profl. engr., Colo. Customer engr. IBM Corp., Boston, 1949-50; reliability mgr. IBM Corp., Endicott, N.Y., 1950-66; engring. design systems mgr. IBM Corp., Boulder, Colo., 1966-78; power systems mgr. IBM Corp., Tucson, Ariz., 1978-81, tech. coordinator IBM PC, 1981-84; pres. Charles B. Stott Assocs., Tucson, 1984—. Patentee in field. V.p. Longs Peak Council Boy Scouts Am., 1976-78; chmn. Ariz. Council Engring. and Sci. Orgns., Tucson, 1982-83. Served with U.S. Army, 1943-46, ETO. Recipient Dist. award of Merit Boy Scouts Am., 1974, Silver Beaver award, 1976. Mem. IEEE (sr., chmn. Tucson sect. 1980, adminstrv. com. Engring. Mgmt. Soc. 1972-84, pres. 1980-81, dir. div. VI 1985-86, bd. dirs. U.S. activities 1985-86, chmn. employment assistance com. 1987—), Sigma Xi, Tau Beta Pi. Republican. Methodist. Lodges: Masons, Elks. Avocation: camping. Home and Office: 8434 E Brookside Ln Tucson AZ 85710

STOTT, PETER WALTER, trucking company executive; b. Spokane, Wash., May 26, 1944; s. Walter Joseph and Rellalee (Gray) S.; m. Carole Ann Sizer, Aug. 20, 1972. Student Portland State U., 1962-63, 65-68, U. Americas, Mexico City, 1964-65. Founder, chmn. bd. dirs., pres. Market Transport Ltd., Portland, Oreg., 1969—; bd. dirs., officer United Express Ltd.; bd. dirs., officer, prin. share holder Columbia Tree Farms, Inc. Bd. dirs. Sunshine div. Portland Police Bur. Served with USAR, 1966-72. Mem. Nat. Football Found. and Hall of Fame, Oregon Sports Hall of Fame (bd.

dirs.), Oreg. Trucking Assn., Western Hwy. Inst., Internat. Platform Assn. Republican. Roman Catholic. Clubs: Mazamas, Multnomah Athletic, Univ. Office: Market Transport Ltd 110 N Marine Dr Portland OR 97217

STOUDT, GEORGE STEPHAN, organic chemist; b. Evanston, Ill., Sept. 8, 1955; s. Edward Oberst and Rosemary Margaret (Rhein) S. BS cum laude, N.Mex. Highlands U., 1976; PhD, U. Colo., 1984. Research asst. NASA Ames Research Ctr., Moffett Field, Calif., 1974-75; research assoc. U. Colo. Sch. Pharmacy, Boulder, 1983-85; postdoctoral scholar U. Calif. Dept. Chemistry and Biochemistry, Los Angeles, 1986—; cons. Celestial Seasonings Inc., Boulder, 1986—, Mile-High Labs. Inc., Denver, 1985; program adminstr. computer lit. searches in chemistry U. Colo. Sch. Pharmacy, 1985-86. NASA fellow, 1974-76. Mem. Am. Chem. Soc., Am. Soc. Pharmacognosy, Am. Inst. Chemists, Internat. Union Pure and Applied Chemistry (U.S. affiliate), Phi Kappa Phi. Home: 1228 N Sycamore Ave Los Angeles CA 90038 Office: U Calif Dept Chemistry and Biochemistry 405 Hilgard Los Angeles CA 90024

STOUT, ARDATH ARLAINE, social worker; b. Portland, Oreg., Jan. 22, 1939; d. Elmo Leslie and Anna Ellen (Braden) T.; m. Donald Gary Stout, Feb. 9, 1957; children: Maria, Julia, Laura, Marla, Joe. BSW with high honors, Portland State U., 1981, MSW, 1983. Cert. clin. social worker, Oreg. Sch. cons. Tillamook (Oreg.) Counseling, Inc., 1983-86; pvt. practice clin. social work Tillamook, 1986—; cons. Co-author: Washington County Wanderings, 1970. Active Interagency group for Prevention and Treatment of Sexual Abuse, 1984—. Mem. Nat. Assn. Social Workers. Republican. Mem. Christian Ch. Club: Jr. Women's (Hillsboro) (pres. 1969). Avocations: skiing, hiking, reading. Office: Counseling Assocs 503 Pacific Tillamook OR 97141

STOUT, LEONARD MARVIN, management consultant; b. Sterling, Kans., Apr. 23, 1948; s. Clifford Marvin Stout and Eithel I. (Thode) Gibson; m. Kathryn Randall Groves, Dec. 30, 1970 (div. June 1982); 1 child, Scott Franklin; m. Marion Nichols Hamill, Nov. 25, 1982. BS in Engring. Mgmt., U. Mo., Rolla, 1970. Engr. Bechtel Corp., San Francisco, 1970-71; supr. Bechtel Corp., N.Y.C., 1971-74, San Francisco, 1974-77; cons. Tera Corp., Berkeley, Calif., 1977-85; prin. Stout and Assocs., Orinda, Calif., 1985—. Office: Stout and Assocs 18 Greenwood Ct Orinda CA 94563

STOUT, RAY BERNARD, physicist; b. Georgetown, Ohio, June 16, 1939; s. Beryl Bernard and Mary Florence (Edenfield) S.; m. Tanya Kay Kuenzli, Aug. 28, 1965; 1 child, Natasha Kay. BSME, Ohio State U., 1964, MSME, 1969; PhD, Ill. Inst. Tech., 1970; MBA, U. Pitts., 1972. Engring. fellow Bettis Atomic Power Lab. div. Westinghouse Electric Corp., West Mifflin, Pa., 1969-79; physicist Lawrence Livermore Nat. Lab., Livermore, Calif., 1979—. Mem. Am. Phys. Soc., ASME, N.Y. Acad. Scis. Avocations: racquetball, woodworking, hiking. Home: 954 Venus Way Livermore CA 94550 Office: Lawrence Livermore Nat Lab PO Box 808 L-200 Livermore CA 94550

STOVER, WILLIAM JAMES, political science educator; b. Blakely, Pa., July 1, 1945; s. Russell James and Gwendolyn (Williams) S.; m. Sinikka Christina Vennola, June 12, 1963 (div. Jan. 1981); children: Jussi Vennola-Stover, Ellen Vennola-Stover; m. Diane Elizabeth Dreher, May, 6, 1982. AB, Nyack Coll., 1966; MA, Am. U., 1968, SUNY, Buffalo, 1972; PhD, SUNY, Buffalo, 1974. Diplomat U.S. Dept. State, Washington, 1968-70; research assoc. Ctr. for Crisis Studies, Buffalo, 1968-70; instr. Coll. Wooster, Ohio, 1973-75; prof. U. Santa Clara, Calif., 1975—, chmn. polit. sci. dept., 1978-82; cons. Am. Council on Nationalities, San Jose, Calif., 1980—, Exec. Leadership Ctr., Santa Clara, 1976-82; assoc. dir. Danforth Found., St. Louis, 1982-85, Forum for Refugee Affairs, San Jose, 1979-83. Author: Military Politics, 1981, International Crisis Simulation, 1983, Information Technology in the Third World, 1984. Commnr. Santa Clara County Commn. on Women, 1981-84. Fellow NSF, 1971, Am. Scandinavia Found., 1975, Mass Media Inst., 1979. Mem. No. Calif. Polit. Sci. Assn. (councillor), Welsh Am. Soc., Internat. Polit. Sci. Assn. Club: Flying Aces (San Jose). Avocations: aviation, music. Home: 1143 S Daniel Way San Jose CA 95128 Office: U Santa Clara Dept Polit Sci Santa Clara CA 95053

STOWE, MICHAEL WILLIAM, information systems executive; b. Denver, July 18, 1953. BA, U. No. Colo., 1974. Data processing operator Signode, Glenview, Ill., 1974-75, programmer, 1976-78, systems programmer, 1979-80; capacity planner Baldwin-United, Denver, 1981-83; info. systems mgr. US West, Englewood, Colo., 1984-87, processor architect, 1987—. Mem. Internat. Computer Measurement Group. Avocations: reading, camping. Home: 1636 S Field Ct Lakewood CO 80226 Office: US West 6200 S Quebec Englewood CO 80111

STOWELL, JAY LEROY, communications specialist; b. Spokane, Wash., Nov. 29, 1940; s. David Jay and Roberta Grace (Edson) S.; m. Martha Jo Spurlin, June 30, 1973. BA, Eastern Wash. State U., 1963; student, U.S. Army Security Agy., Fort Devens, Mass., 1964, Western Coll. of Electronics, 1968, Miami Bible Coll., 1969, John O'Connell Sch., San Francisco, 1972-73, Computer Learning Ctr., 1984-85. Resident engr. Blue Ridge Broadcasting, Black Mountain, N.C., 1970-72; mgr. WLTR FM S.C. Ednl. TV, Columbia, 1973-77; asst. chief engr., announcer Sta. KRDU, Sta. KLTA-FM, Dinuba, Calif., 1977-82; mgr. trainee Radio Shack, Alameda, Calif., 1983-84; communications specialist NASA, Moffett Field, Calif., 1984—. Served with U.S. Army, 1964-67. Recipient cash prize Army Security Agy. Incentive Award Com., Taiwan. Baptist. Club: Ames Amateur Radio, Moffett Field. Avocations: amateur radio. Home: PO Box 5195 Redwood City CA 94063 Office: Nat Aero and Space Adminstrn Ames Research CtrMail Stop 200-24 Moffett Field CA 94035

STOWERS, HARRY E., JR., state supreme court justice; b. 1926. B.A., U. N.Mex.; J.D., Georgetown U. Former judge N.Mex. 2d Jud. Dist., Albuquerque; assoc. justice N.Mex. Supreme Ct., Santa Fe, 1983—. Office: Supreme Court New Mexico Supreme Ct Bldg 327 Don Gasper Ave Santa Fe NM 87501 *

STRAIGHT, JAMES WILLIAM, research mechanical engineer; b. Wichita, Aug. 5, 1940; s. Russell James and Marian (Ringer) S.; m. Roberta Marie Cunningham, Aug. 12, 1961; children: William Herbert, Suzanne. BSME, MSME, U. Kans., 1963; PhDME, U. Ariz., 1967. Registered profl. engr., Tenn., N.Mex. Prof. mech. engring. Vanderbilt U., Nashville, 1969-71; prof. Christian Bros. Coll., Memphis, 1971-77; from staff mem. to group leader Los Alamos (N.Mex.) Nat. Lab., 1977—; prin. cons. Brown & Straight, Memphis, 1971-77. Contbr. articles to profl. jours. Mem. dist. council Boy Scouts AM., Los Alamos, 1983-84. Served to capt. U.S. Army, 1967-69. Mem. ASME (pres., v.p., sec., treas., bd. dirs., nat. agenda conf. del. 1971-83), Am. Soc. Engring. Edn. (instrumentation div. chmn. 1982). Club: Los Alamos Mountaineers (v.p., treas., bd. dirs. 1982-85). Avocations: rock climbing, backpacking, fishing, hunting. Home: 1 Comanche Los Alamos NM 87544 Office: Los Alamos Nat Lab MS J960 Los Alamos NM 87545

STRAIN, JOHN WILLARD, aerospace engineering executive, consultant; b. Ottumwa, Iowa, Dec. 31, 1929; s. John Wells and Agnes Gertrude (Kearns) S.; m. Elizabeth LaVonne Moment, Dec. 27, 1952 (dec.); children—James Anthony, Mary Therese, Michael Douglas, Meagan Kathleen. Student Upper Iowa U., 1947-48; B.A., U. No. Iowa, 1952. Supr., aero. rocket power plant engr. White Sands Proving Ground, N.Mex., 1954-55; mgr. Santa Cruz test and Hunters Point, Missile Systems div. Lockheed Missiles & Space Co., Sunnyvale, Calif., 1960-63, mgr. Ea. Test Range support, 1966-73, chief test engr. Aquila RPV/STD Program, 1975-78, factory test mgr. Army RPV Program, 1979-82, qualification and test engring. div. mgr., chief test engr., 1982-84, mgmt. proposal assignment, 1984—; owner Indsl. Systems Co. Bd. dirs. San Jose Civic Light Opera, 1971-73; treas. Assn. Unmanned Vehicle Systems, 1982-84. Served with AUS, 1952-54. Recipient Alumni Service award U. No. Iowa, 1981. Assoc. fellow AIAA; mem. Nat. Mgmt. Assn., AAAS, Inst. Environ. Scis. (sr.). Republican. Roman Catholic. Assoc. editor Missile Away mag. Am. Rocket Soc., 1954-55. Office: 1111 Lockheed Way Box 504 Sunnyvale CA 94086

STRAIN, ROBERT JOSEPH, semiconductor manufacturing company executive; b. Bloomington, Ind., July 21, 1936; s. William Joseph and Ethel Louise (Moore) S.; m. Janet Lucille Majors, June 10, 1961; children: Douglas, Margaret, Ellen. BS, U. Ill., 1958, MS, 1959, PhD, 1963. Research engr. Standard Tel. Lab., Harlow, Essex, Eng., 1963-65; supr. mem. tech. staff Bell Labs., Murray Hill, N.J., 1965-73; mgr. devel. liaison Harris Semiconductor, Melbourne, Fla., 1973-80; mgr. engring. Fairchild Semiconductor, San Jose, Calif., 1980-82; mgr. tech. Nagasaki project Fairchild Semiconductor, Palo Alto, Calif., 1982-85; mgr. bus. devel. Fairchild Semiconductor, Cupertino, Calif., 1986—. Contbr. articles to profl. jours.; patentee in field. Mem. IEEE (sr.), Am. Mgmt. Assn. Republican. Avocation: art. Office: Fairchild Semiconductor Corp 10400 Ridgeview Ct Cupertino CA 95014

STRAKA, GEORGE JOHN, police chief; b. Hazleton, Pa., Mar. 14, 1937; s. George and Mary (Orach) S.; m. Gloria Helen Newton, Feb. 18, 1956; children—Leslie Anne, Stephen John. A.A., Fullerton Jr. Coll., 1964; B.A. in Police Sci., John F. Kennedy U., 1972, M.A. in Pub. Adminstrn., 1975; grad. FBI Nat. Acad., 1980. Advanced cert. peace officer's standards and tng., Calif. Police officer, Fullerton, Calif., 1958-65; police officer, Concord, Calif., 1966-68, police sgt., 1968-71, police lt., 1971-81, police chief, 1981—; instr. No. Calif. Peace Officer's Acad., 1965-72. Mem. exec. bd. Mt. Diablo Council Boy Scouts Am., 1981—. Served with USMC, 1954-57. Mem. Internat. Assn. Chiefs Police, FBI N.Am. Assn., Calif. Police Chiefs Assn., Calif. Peace Officers Assn. Republican. Lutheran. Club: Century (Concord). Office: Concord Police Dept Willow Pass and Parkside Concord CA 94519 *

STRAKA, JOSEPH JOHN, oil company executive; b. Chgo., Mar. 19, 1942; s. Joseph John and Elaine Marie (Sindelar) S.; m. Margaret Ann Mailliard, Sept. 5, 1964; children—Joseph John, Robert, Ann, Rita. B.A., Cornell Coll., Mt. Vernon, Iowa, 1964; M.S., U. Iowa, 1966, Ph.D., 1969. Geologist, sr. geologist Shell Oil USA, Denver and Midland, Tex., 1968-74; exploration mgr. Shell Can., Calgary, 1974-81, Can. Hunter Exploration Co., Calgary, 1981—, Am. Hunter Exploration, Denver, 1983—. Contbr. articles to profl. jours. Mem. Am. Assn. Petroleum Geologists. Roman Catholic. Office: Am Hunter Exploration Ltd 1700 Lincoln St Suite 2300 Denver CO 80203

STRALING, PHILLIP FRANCIS, bishop; b. San Bernardino, Calif., Apr. 25, 1933; s. Sylvester J. and Florence E. (Robinson) S. B.A., U. San Diego, 1963; M.S. in Child and Family Counseling, San Diego State U., 1971. Ordained priest Roman Catholic Ch., 1959, consecrated bishop, 1978. Mem. faculty St. John Acad., El Cajon, Calif., 1959-60; mem. faculty St. Therese Acad., San Diego, 1960-63; chaplain Newman Club, San Diego State U., 1963-72; mem. faculty St. Francis Sem., San Diego, 1972-76; pastor Holy Rosary Parish, San Bernardino, 1976-78; bishop Diocese of San Bernardino, 1978—; pub. Inland Catholic newspaper, 1979—; bd. dirs. Calif. Assn. Cath. Campus Ministers, 1960s; exec. sec. Diocesan Synod II, 197-76; 1972-76; Episcopal vicar San Bernardino Deanery, 1976-78. Office: Diocesan Pastoral Ctr 1450 N D St San Bernardino CA 92405

STRAND, JENS ALVIN, colon and rectal surgeon; b. Portland, N.D., Jan. 9, 1946; s. Robert Bernard and Opal Marie (Anderson) S.; m. Rosalinda Mastricola, Feb. 22, 1969; 1 child Jens Christian. PhB, U. N.D., 1971, BS in Medicine, 1973; MD, Wash. U., St. Louis, 1975. Diplomate Am. Bd. Colon and Rectal Surgeons, Am. Bd. Surgery. Intern Med. Coll Wis. Affiliate Hosp., Milw., 1975-76; resident in gen. surgery U. Minn. Hosp., Mpls., 1976-77, Hennepin County Gen. Hosp., Mpls., 1977-78; commd. U.S. Army, 1979, advanced through grades to maj.; resident in gen. surgery Tripler Army Med. Ctr., Honolulu, 1979-81; staff surgeon Nuermberg (Fed. Republic Germany) Army Med. Ctr., 1981-83; fellow in colon-rectal surgery Carle Clinic and Hosp., Urbana, Ill., 1983-84; chief colon-rectal surgery Madigan Army Med. Ctr., Tacoma, 1984-86. Mem. AMA, Am. Soc. Colon and Rectal Surgeons, Soc. Am. Gastraintestinal Endoscopic Surgeons, Am. Soc. for Gastrointestinal Endoscopy, Assn. Mil Surgeons of US. Republican. Lutheran. Avocations: skiing, golf. Home: 10902 Glenwood Dr SW Tacoma WA 98498 Office: Madigan Army Med Ctr 902 S L St Tacoma WA 98405

STRANDE, M. SAM, corporate officer; b. Granite City, Ill., Feb. 19, 1949; d. Joseph Stephen and Esther Merel (Wright) Apponey; m. Carl Angelo Strande, Jan. 31, 1982. Diploma in bus., Ft. Collins Community Coll., 1973; cert. real estate, Cagy Real Estate Sch., 1978; student, Boise State U., 1979-82, U. Alaska, 1983. Sec. TX AgrCul Ext Services, Amarillo, Tex., 1968-70; exec. sec. Maytag Aircraft Co., Colorado Springs, Colo., 1971-75; adminstrv. asst. Miniutti & Co., Denver, 1976-78, Morrison Knudsen Co., Denver and Boise, 1978-81; corp. officer Bordax Alaska, Ltd., Fairbanks, Anchorage, Alaska, 1982—, also bd. dirs.; prin. Almanor Cons., Fairbanks, Anchorage, 1981—; bus. mgr. Harrison-Western Corp., Anchorage, 1984-86. Home and Office: 143 S Devinney St Golden CO 80401

STRANGE, WILLIAM JOSEPH, former library director; b. Winchester, Kans., Sept. 13, 1924; s. William Carl and Effie Francis (Hull) S.; m. Wilda Louise Jones, June 19, 1952 (div.); children—Carol, Joy, Shannon, Eric; m. Barbara Strange. B.S. in Edn., Emporia State U., 1950, M.L.S., 1962. Tchr., librarian Bern Rural High Sch. (Kans.), 1950-52, Lincoln High Sch. (Kans.), 1952-54, Ilwaco High Sch. (Wash.), 1954-55; librarian Delano High Sch. (Calif.), 1955-57, La Puente High Sch. (Calif.), 1957-61, Palos Verdes High Sch. Palos Verdes Estates, Calif., 1961-64, Los Angeles Harbor Coll., Wilmington, Calif., 1962-64; library dir. Glendale Coll., (Calif.), 1964-84. Served with USN, 1943-46. Mem. ALA, Calif. Library Assn., Alpha Kappa Lambda.

STRANGWAY, DAVID WILLIAM, geologist, university president; b. Can., June 7, 1934. B.A. in Physics and Geology, U. Toronto, 1956, M.A. in Physics, 1958, Ph.D., 1960. Sr. geophysicist Dominion Gulf Co. Ltd., Toronto, 1956; chief geophysicist Ventures Ltd., 1956-57, sr. geophysicist, summer 1958; research geophysicist Kennecott Copper Corp., Denver, 1960-61; asst. prof. U. Colo., Boulder, 1961-64, M.I.T., 1965-68; mem. faculty U. Toronto, 1968-85, prof. physics, 1971—, chmn. dept. geology, 1972-78, v.p., provost, 1980-83, pres., 1983-84; pres. U.B.C., 1985—; chief geophysics br. Johnson Space Center, NASA, Houston, 1970-72, chief physics br., 1972-73, acting chief planetary and earth sci. div., 1973; vis. prof. geology U. Houston, 1971-73; interim dir. Lunar Sci. Inst., Houston, 1973; vis. com. geol. scis. Brown U., 1974-76, Meml. U., St. John's, Nfld., 1974-79, Princeton U., 1980. v.p. Can. Geosci. Council, 1977; chmn. proposal evaluating team Univs. Space Research Assos., 1977-78, Ont. Geosci. Research Fund, 1978—; Pahlavi lectr. Govt. of Iran, 1978; cons. to govt. and industry, mem. numerous govt. and sci. adv. and investigative panels. Author numerous papers, reports in field. Recipient NASA Exceptional Sci. Achievement medal, 1972; hon. mem. Can. Soc. Explotation Geophysicists. Fellow Royal Astron. Soc., Royal Soc. Can.; mem. Soc. Exploration Geophysicists (Virgil Kauffman Gold medal 1974), Geol. Assn. Can. (pres. 1978-79), Can. Geophys. Union (chmn. 1977-79), Am. Geophys. Union (sect. planetology sect. 1978—), European Assn. Exploration Geophysicists, Soc. Geomagnetism and Geoelectricity Japan, Can. Geosci. Council (pres. 1980), AAAS, Can. Exploration Geophysicists. Address: U BC Office of Pres, 6328 Memorial Rd, Vancouver, BC Canada V6T 2B3

STRATHEARN, RICHARD ALAN, military officer; b. Warsaw, N.Y., Oct. 31, 1955; s. LaVerne and Alicia (Wawrzycki) S. BS in Indsl. Tech., Ohio U., 1977; M Mgmt. Info. Systems, West Coast U., 1985. Commd. USAF, 1977, advanced through grades to capt.; satellite system controller, dir. SAC, Offutt AFB, Nebr., 1979-81, asst. chief ops. tng., 1980-81; pilot Air Tng. Command, Williams AFB, Ariz., 1981-82; chief systems mgmt. br. Space Command, Vandenberg AFB, Calif., 1982-85; chief navigation/weather br. Space Command, Peterson AFB, Colo., 1985—. Asst. master Boy Scouts Am., Omaha, 1979-81. Mem. AIAA, Inst. of Navigation, Air Force Assn., L5 Soc. Republican. Home: 3727 Adirondack Dr Colorado Springs CO 80918 Office: Hdqrs AF Space Command/XPSS Peterson AFB CO 80914

STRATTON, HAL, state attorney general; b. Muskogee, Okla., Dec. 6, 1950; s. Mr. and Mrs. H. Duane S. BS in Geology, U. Okla., 1973, JD, 1976. Bar: N.Mex., Okla., U.S. Dist. Ct. N.Mex., U.S. Dist. Ct. (we. dist.) Okla., U.S. Ct. Appeals (10th cir.), U.S. Supreme Ct. Spl. asst. dist. atty. Bernalillo County Dist. Atty.'s Office, Albuquerque, 1978; mem. N.Mex. Ho. Reps., 1979-86, mem. house jud. com., 1979-86, chmn. house jud. com., 1985-86, mem. house energy and natural resources com., 1979-82, 85-86, vice-chmn. house energy and natural resources com, 1981-82, mem. house transp. com., 1983-84, mem. house rules and order of bus. com., 1981-82, mem. radioactive wast consultation com., 1979-81, mem. N.Mex. mortgage fin. authority oversight com., 1983-84; mem. N.Mex. workmens compensation com. Coors, Singer and Broullire, 1986; assoc. Coors, Singer and Broullire, Albuquerque, 1977-81; ptnr. Stratton and Barnett, Albuquerque, 1981-86; atty. gen. State of N.Mex., 1987—; mem. N.Mex. Supreme Ct. com. on rules governing magistrate cts., mcpl. cts. and met. cts., 1984-86; mem. N.Mex. Jud. Council, 1981-82. Sec./treas., bd. dirs. N.Mex. Rep. legis. campaign com., 1981-85; state counsel Rep. Nat. Com., 1984—; mem. juvenile justice project adv. bd. Rose Inst., Claremont-McKenna Coll., 1984—, Bur. of Land Mgmt. Citizens Adv. Com., Albuquerque, 1983-86; state dir. The Consrevative Caucus; state chmn. Nat. Tax Limitation Com., Citizens for Am.; founding chmn. N.Mexicans for Tax Limitation. Phillips petroleum scholar, 1969, Union Oil of Calif. scholar, 1969-73, George Wyatt Brown scholar, 1972-73; recipient George Wyatt Brown award, 1971-72. Mem. Council of State Govts. (western conf. 1981-84), Nat. Conf. of Commrs. on Uniform State Laws. Office: Office of Atty Gen PO Drawer 1508 Santa Fe NM 87504-1508

STRATTON, HAROLD SEAY, marketing executive; b. Nashville, Apr. 18, 1932; s. John Lee and Rena Mae (Lockwood) S.; m. Patricia Ann Cheatham. BSME, Wayne U., 1954. Dir. bus. mgmt. Rocketdyne div. Rockwell Internat., Canoga Park, Calif., 1963-76, project engr., advanced propulsion, 1976-79, dir. advanced propulsion system, 1979-83, dir. internat. bus. devel., 1983-85, dir. mktg. bus. devel., 1985—; cons. GCE, Rome, 1981—. Inventor propulsion system. Served to 1st lt. USAF, 1954-56. Mem. AIAA. Republican. Avocation: fishing. Home: 5046 Escobedo Dr Woodland Hills CA 91364 Office: Rocketdyne 6633 Canoga Ave Canoga Park CA 91303

STRATTON, LOIS JEAN, state legislator; b. Springdale, Wash., Jan. 5, 1927; d. Charles B. and Ann B. (Hill) Brunton; m. Allen F. Stratton, 1946; children—Alan Edward, Kathleen Prater, Mark Charles, Scott D., Karen Jeanne. Student Kinman Bus. U., 1944-45. Democratic precinct committeewoman, Spokane County, Wash., from 1958; mem. Spokane County Dem. Exec. Bd.; alt. del. Dem. Nat. Conv., 1976; co-chmn. Gov. Dixy Lee Ray Com., 1976; committeewoman Wash. State Dem. Com., from 1977; now mem. Wash. Senate, Dist. 3; exec. sec. pub. affairs Kaiser Aluminum & Chem. Corp., Spokane, from 1963; adminstrv. asst., exec. sec. to pres. Expo 74 World's Fair, Spokane. Recipient World's Fair Expo 74 Vol. Service citations Gov. of Wash. and Wash. State Commn., 1974. Mem. Spokane County Dem. Club (sec.), Jane Jefferson Dem. Club (1st v.p.). Roman Catholic. Office: State Capitol Olympia WA 98504 Address: 1724 W Mansfield Spokane WA 99205

STRATTON, RICHARD MUNRO, medical doctor; b. Syracuse, July 11, 1945; s. Hubert Charles Stratton and Margaret Cotter (Munro) McLennan; m. Janet Lee Rike, Feb. 10, 1968; children: Richard Charles, Reid Munro. BS cum laude, Hillsdale Coll., 1967; MD, SUNY, Syracuse, 1971. From intern to resident family practice St. Joseph Hosp.-Health Ctr., Syracuse, N.Y., 1971-74; commd. USAF, 1974—, advanced through grades to lt. col., 1980; staff mem. family practice dept. USAF Hosp. Patrick AFB, Cocoa Beach, Fla., 1974-83, chief. family practice dept., 1976-83; chief. dept. family practice and primary care Elmendorf AFB Regional Hosp., Anchorage, 1983—. Mem. Am. Acad. Family Practice. Republican. Avocations: volley ball, cross country and downhill skiing. Home: 2420 Banbury Dr Anchorage AK 99504 Office: USAF Regional Hosp Elmendorf AFB Anchorage AK 99506

STRAUB, HOWARD NICHOLAS, eye surgeon. s. J. Harold and Helen (Loftus) S.; m. Joan Theresa Modica, Dec. 26, 1971; children: Jessica, Howard, Marissa, Lauren. BA, William Paterson Coll., 1970; DO, Kansas City (Mo.) Coll. Osteo. Medicine, 1975. Med. dir. Colo. Eye Inst., Aurora, 1979—; dir. ophthalmology Rocky Mountain Hosp., Denver, 1979—; asst. clin. prof. ophthalmology Mich. State U., 1985—. Mead Johnson Research fellow, 1976-79. Mem. Am. Acad. Ophthalmology, Osteo. Coll. Ophthalmology and Otolaryngology, Colo. Med. Soc., Colo. Soc. Osteo. Medicine, Denver Med. Soc. Presbyterian. Avocations: skiing. Office: Colo Eye Inst 1421 S Potomac St Aurora CO 80012

STRAUS, LEONARD H., retail company executive; b. 1914; married. LL.B., Harvard U., 1938. With Thrifty Corp., Los Angeles, 1945—, officer legal dept., from 1948, chmn., 1979—, now chief exec. officer, also dir. Served with USCG, 1943-45. Office: Thrifty Corp 3424 Wilshire Blvd Los Angeles CA 90010 *

STRAUSER, JEAN MARIE, accountant; b. Sheridan, Wyo., Jan. 25, 1949; d. Alfred Fredrick and Justine Aileen (Long) Germann; m. Robert Dee Strauser, Aug. 22, 1970; children—Kelly Dee, Dawn Marie. B.S., U. Wyo., 1971, M.S., 1972. C.P.A., Wyo. Bookkeeper, Skiles & Wickersham, Pub. Accts., Laramie, Wyo., 1971; staff acct. Jeffreys & Jeffreys, C.P.A.s, Laramie, 1972-74, Harris Huffsmith & Assocs. P.C., C.P.A.s, Casper, Wyo., 1975-78, Curtis W. Christensen, C.P.A., Sheridan, 1978-81, Mulholland & Strauser, C.P.A.s, Sheridan, 1981; ptnr. Strauser & Strauser, C.P.A.s, Sheridan, 1981—. Community leader 4-H, 1986—. Mem. Am. Inst. C.P.A.s, Wyo. Soc. C.P.A.s (v.p. Sheridan chpt. 1982-83, pres. 1983-84), Beta Alpha Psi, Beta Gamma Sigma, Phi Gamma Nu, Beta Sigma Phi (rec. sec. 1983-84, pres. 1985-86). Home: PO Box 287 Ranchester WY 82839 Office: PO Box 4068 Sheridan WY 82801

STRAUSS, JANICE DILDAY, social worker; b. Monticello, Ark., Mar. 14, 1933; d. James C. and Annie Quinn (Coulter) Dilday; m. Melvin G. Strauss, Aug. 11, 1962; children: Michael, Nancy, Douglas. BSE, U. Ark., 1954; MSW, U. Denver, 1976. Lic. social worker I, Colo. Airline flight attendant Continental Air Lines, Denver, 1955-62; sch. social worker Adams County Sch. Dist. 12, Northglenn, Colo., 1976—. Chmn. Sisterhood Recording for the Blind, Denver, 1972-81; mem. Temple Emmanuel Caring Com., Denver, 1984—; del. Dem. County Conv., Denver, 1984; mem. Colo. Coalition of Missing and Exploited Children Legis. Com., 1985—, v.p. 1986—. Mem. Nat. Assn. Social Workers, NEA, LWV (Denver unit leader 1968). Club: Golden Penguins (Denver, pres. 1970-71). Avocations: racquetball, tennis, skiing, sewing, reading. Home: 3545 S Oneida Way Denver CO 80237 Office: Adams County Sch Dist 12 10280 N Huron Northglenn CO 80221

STRAUSS, VICKI LYNN, graphic designer, public relations, marketing consultant; b. Salt Lake City, Mar. 30, 1942; d. William Joseph Selman and Verna Mayne (Arnold) Allem; m. Dennis J. Strauss, Oct. 15, 1961 (div. Dec. 1975); children: Richard Scott, Sean Eric. AA, Cypress (Calif.) Coll., 1973; BA with honors, Calif. State U., Fullerton, 1984. Instructional aide, coordinator Centralia Sch. Dist., Buena Park, Calif., 1973-76, sec., fed. project dir., 1976-80, pub. info. officer, 1980-85; ptnr., owner The Graphics Haus, Tustin, Calif., 1985—; cons. Calif. Assn. Program Specialists, Anaheim, 1985—. Mem. Buena Park chpt. Am. Cancer Soc., 1983-85, region 17 legis., political action com. Assn. Calif. Adminstrs., Orange County, 1982-85; vol. trainer of witnesses Huntington Beach, Irvine, Costa Mesa, Westminster (Calif.) Police Victim Assistance and Crisis Program, 1985—; presenter state conf. Calif. Sch. Bd. Assn., Anaheim, 1985. Recipient Outstanding Service award, Centralia Adminstrs. Assn., 1985; Hon. Silver Service award, Buena Park PTA Council, 1985; Outstanding Employee award, Buena Park Classified Sch. Employees Assn., 1979. Mem. So. Counties Women in Ednl. Mgmt. (exec. com., pub. info. officer 1984—), Am. Bus. Women's Assn., Nat. Sch. Pub. Relations Assn. Democrat. Avocation: photography. Home: 7871 Comstock Circle La Palma CA 90623 Office: The Graphics Haus 12932 Newport Ave #11 Tustin CA 92680

STRAUSS, WILLIAM ISADORE, JR., industrial market researcher, electrical engineer; b. Augusta, Ga., Dec. 11, 1939; s. William Isadore and Marion Mosley (Hamilton) S.; m. Barbara Ann Couch, Apr. 12, 1969; children—Eric Hamilton, Kathryn Elizabeth, Mark Lawrence. B.E.E., Ga. Inst. Tech., 1961; M.S. in Engring Adminstrn., So. Methodist U., 1969. System design engr. Collins Radio Co., Richardson, Tex., 1961-69; sr. sales rep. Digital Equipment Corp., Maynard, Mass., 1970-78; dir. mkgt. Gen. Instrument Corp., Chandler, Ariz., 1978-79; v.p. Integrated Circuit Engring. Corp., Scottsdale, Ariz., 1979-84; v.p. In-Stat, Inc., Scottsdale, 1984; pres. Forward Concepts, Inc., Tempe, Ariz., 1984—; sr. staff cons. Integrated

Circuit Engring. Corp., Scottsdale, 1984-85. Editor: (ann. series) Status of the Integrated Circuit Industry, 1980-84; Electronic Packaging Strategies for the '80s, 1982. Editor ICECAP Report, 1982-83, In-Stat Research Letter, 1984. Asst. cubmaster, Boy Scouts Am., Mesa, Ariz, 1980-82, asst. scoutmaster, 1983—. Mem. IEEE. Office: Forward Concepts Inc 1228 N Stadem Dr Tempe AZ 85281

STRAWBRIDGE, KATHLEEN VOLPE, education coordinator, consultant; b. Knoxville, Tenn., Sept. 15, 1939; d. James and Kathleen Mary (O'Brien) Volpe; m. Lawrence William Strawbridge, Mar. 21, 1964; children: Sean Christopher, Mark Brien, Gregory James. BA, U. Ariz., 1962; postgrad., Calif. State U., San Jose, 1963-65. Cert. tchr., Ariz., Calif. Classroom tchr. Washington Sch. Dist., Phoenix, 1961-63, Alum Rock Sch. Dist., San Jose, 1963-68; research coordinator U. Ariz., Tucson, 1977-79; edn. coordinator Internal Medicine, Spokane, Wash., 1979—, also cons., 1981—. Active Southeast Asian Refugee Consortium, Spokane, 1980-83; coordinator services Spokane Urban Indian Health Ctr., 1982-84. Mem. Am. Pub. Health Assn., Wash. State Pub. Health Assn., Spokane Edn. Council, U. Wash. Residency Selection Com. (coordinator 1980—). Republican. Roman Catholic. Avocations: theater, music, reading. Home: N 28403 Cottonwood Rd Chattaroy WA 99003 Office: Internal Medicine W 101-8th TAF C-9 Spokane WA 99220

STRAWHUN, DEBRA ANN, speech, language patholgist; b. Lancaster, Calif., Mar. 14, 1955; d. Amos Lincoln and Annabelle (Tabor) S.; m. William James Reedy, July 22, 1982; 1 child, William Lincoln. AA, Allan Hancock Jr. Coll., 1975; BA, Sonoma State U., 1977; MS, Arizona State U., 1981. Speech, lang. pathologist Creighton Sch. Dist., Phoenix, 1982—. Severely Lang. Impaired grantee U.S. Govt., 1986. Mem. Am. Speech Lang. Hearing Assn., Ariz. Speech Lang. Hearing Assn., Ariz. State Reading Council. Democrat. Home: 7257 E Wilshire Dr Scottsdale AZ 85257 Office: Creighton Sch Dist Squaw Peak Sch 4601 N 34th St Phoenix AZ 85018

STRAWN, ROGER CLAYTON, aerospace engineer; b. Syracuse, N.Y., Sept. 27, 1956; s. Ralph Kenneth and Barbara Jean (Greenly) S. ScB, Brown U., 1978; MS, Stanford U., 1981, PhD, 1983. Staff engr. Acurex Corp., Mountain View, Calif., 1983-85; research scientist U.S. Army Aeroflightdynamics Directorate, Ames Research Ctr., Moffett Field, Calif., 1985—. Mem. AIAA. Democrat. Lutheran. Home: 227 Ada Ave Unit M Mountain View CA 94043 Office: US Army Aeroflightdynamics Directorate Ames Research Ctr Mail Stop 215-1 Moffett Field CA 94035

STRAYER, RICHARD LEE, accounting educator, electronic manufacturing executive; b. Ocheyedan, Iowa, Sept. 14, 1934; s. Glayde Watters and Mary Ann (Graves) S.; m. Eileen Curtis, July 28, 1956; children—Susan Rae, Wendy Anne, Richard Curtis. Student S.D. Sch. Mines and Tech., 1952-53, S.D. State U., 1953, Bakersfield Jr. Coll., 1958-59; B.S. in Acctg. with highest honors, UCLA, 1960, M.B.A., 1961; D.B.A., U. So. Calif., 1970. C.P.A., Calif. Instr. acctg. UCLA, 1961; sr. acct. Peat, Marwick & Co., C.P.A.s, Los Angeles, 1962-65; lectr. U. So. Calif., 1965-68; prof. acctg. Calif. State U.-Northridge, 1968—, chmn. dept. 1983-85; co-founder, dir. Kronos, Inc., Torrance, Calif., 1969-73; fin. v.p., treas., 1969-71, pres., 1971-73; pres., co-founder, dir. Maxtek, Inc., Torrance, Calif., 1975—; cons. in field, 1965—. Chmn., treas. East Valley Youth Assn.; mem., treas. N. Hollywood Adv. Council; trustee, treas. Congregational Ch. of Chimes; mem. San Fernando Valley Youth Athletic Assn. Served with USAF, 1954-58. Mem. Am. Inst. C.P.A.s, Calif. Soc. C.P.A.s, Fin. Execs. Inst., Am. Acctg. Assn., Alpha Gamma Sigma, Beta Gamma Sigma, Beta Alpha Psi. Republican. Home: 7901 Mary Ellen Ave North Hollywood CA 91605 Office: Calif State U 2908 Oregon Ct Northridge CA 91324 Office: Maxtek Inc 2908 Oregon Ct I-1 Torrance CA 90503

STREET, CHRIS ROBERT, leasing company executive; b. Cuckfield, Sussex, Eng., Apr. 3, 1943; came to U.S., 1977; s. Harry James and Rose Maud Hilton; m. Dian Helfer, Aug. 29, 1981; children: Samantha, Tamara. Student, U. London, U. Southampton, Eng. Buyer Freeman's, London, 1965-67; chmn. North Midland (Eng.) Fin. Centre, 1968-77; pres. WWUSA, Inc., Encino, Calif., 1978-86, A.C. Leasing & Assocs., Inc., Van Nuys, Calif., 1985—; cons. Creative Force, Malibu, Calif., 1979-83. Patentee automatic confectionary dispenser, 1981. Republican. Episcopalian. Clubs: Lake Lindero Yacht (vice commodore, 1985), Lake Lindero Country (mem. world tennis bd. 1986—). Avocations: scuba diving, sailing, skiing, tennis, golf. Office: A C Leasing & Assocs Inc 6100 Sepulveda Blvd Suite 303 Van Nuys CA 91411

STREET, JOHN MALCOLM, forester, arborist, educator; b. McIntosh, S.D., May 28, 1924; s. Thomas Malcolm and Alta Maud (Jones) S.; m. Fuyu Nakamura, Sept. 14, 1960; children: Susan Yoko, Sarah Sakuko. BA summa cum laude, U. Calif., Berkeley, 1948, PhD, 1959. Prof. U. Calif., Davis, 1960, U. Hawaii, Honolulu, 1960—. Author: Historical Geography of Haiti, 1960, co-author Geography in Asian Universities, 1972, Oahu Environments, 1980; co-editor Proceedings of Land Use Symposium Taiwan, 1978. Served to sgt. U.S. Army, 1943-46. Mem. Pacific Sci. Assn., Lyon Arboretum Assn., Phi Beta Kappa. Avocation: commodity futures speculation. Home: 3591 Woodlawn Dr Honolulu HI 96822 Office: U Hawaii Geography Dept Honolulu HI 96822

STREET, ROBERT LYNNWOOD, civil and mechanical engineer; b. Honolulu, Dec. 18, 1934; s. Evelyn Mansel and Dorothy Heather (Brook) S.; m. Norma Jeanette Ensminger, Feb. 6, 1959; children: Brian Clarke (dec.), Deborah Lynne, Kimberley Anne. M.S., Stanford U., 1957, Ph.D. (NSF grad. fellow 1960-62), 1963. Mem. faculty Stanford U. Sch. Engring., 1962—, prof. civil engring., asso. chmn. dept., 1970-72, chmn. dept., 1972-80, prof. fluid mechanics and applied math., 1972—; assoc. dean research Sch. Engring., 1971-83, vice provost for acad. computing and info. systems, 1983-85, vice provost and dean of research and acad. info. systems, 1985—, acting provost, 1987; vis. prof. U. Liverpool, Eng., 1970-71; trustee Univ. Corp. Atmospheric Research, 1983—, chmn. sci. programs evaluation com., 1981, treas. corp., 1985, vice chmn. bd., 1986, chmn. bd., 1987; cons. in field. Author: The Analysis and Solution of Partial Differential Equations, 1973; co-author: Elementary Fluid Mechanics, 6th edit, 1982; asso. editor: Jour. Fluids Engring, 1978-81; author articles in field; mem. editorial bds. profl. jours. Served with C.E., USN, 1957-60. Sr. postdoctoral fellow Nat. Center Atmospheric Research, 1978-79; sr. Queen's fellow in marine sci., Australia, 1985; fellow N.E. Asia-U.S. Forum on Internat. Policy Stanford U. Mem. Am. Soc. Engring. Edn., ASCE (chmn. publs. com. hydraulics div. 1978-80, Walter Huber prize 1972), ASME (R.T. Knapp award 1986), Am. Geophys. Union, Phi Beta Kappa, Sigma Xi, Tau Beta Pi. Office: Stanford U Office of Provost Bldg 10 Stanford CA 94305

STREETER, EUGENE CLARENCE, museum director, college administrator, educator; b. Fond du Lac, Wis., Apr. 14, 1924; s. Clarence L. and Lillian R.S. 1 adopted son, Vincent J. DeMarco-Streeter. B.A., Brooks Inst. Photography, 1965. Civilian adv. U.S. Army, Fond du Lac, 1951-63; faculty Brooks Inst. Photography, Santa Barbara, Calif., 1965—, chmn. colortech. dept., 1967-80, v.p., 1970-72, 78—, prof. history of photography, 1982-84; pres. Brooks Photographic Research and Devel. Found., 1977—; dir., curator Western States Mus. Photography, Santa Barbara, 1977—; nat. exec. committeeman State of Wis. AMVETS, 1952-55; mem. registrars com. Western Region Mus. Dirs. Served with U.S. Army, 1942-51, to maj. Res. ret., 1951-67. Decorated Bronze Star. Mem. Western Photog. Collectors Assn., Soc. Tchrs. Profl. Photography, Assn. Ind. Colls. and Schs. (accreditation liaison officer 1984—), Am. Soc. Camera Collectors, Camera Collectors Assn. Cen. Calif., Smithsonian Inst. (assoc.). Home: 1323 Rialto Ln Bel Air Knolls Santa Barbara CA 93105 Mailing Address: Brooks Inst Photography 801 Alston Rd Santa Barbara CA 93108

STREETER, STEPHEN ALAN, county planner; b. Mt. Holly, N.J., May 15, 1951; s. Noble Mason and Betty Jane (Breuer) S.; m. Nancy Ellen Jones, Apr. 3, 1977. AA in Social Sci., Shasta Coll., 1971; BA in Environ. Studies, San Jose State U., 1974; MA in Environ. Planning, Calif. State U., Chico, 1982. Planning aide City of Anderson, Calif., 1975-76; environ. rev. specialist Butte County Environ. Rev., Oroville, Calif., 1977-81; assoc. planner Butte County Planning, Oroville, Calif., 1981, sr. planner, 1981—; tchr. Parson Jr. High, Redding, Calif., 1974. Councilman City of Oroville, 1983—; active local govt. adv. commn. Calif. Commn. on Econ. Devel., Sacramento, 1984—. Mem. Am. Planning Assn., Assn. Environ. Profls. Democrat. Presbyterian. Lodge: Rotary. Avocations: tennis, reading, bicycling, singing, theater. Office: Butte County Planning 7 County Center Dr Oroville CA 95965

STREIGHT, ROBIN JOY, chemist; b. Pasadena, Calif., July 7, 1957; d. Glen Duane and Charlotte Ann (Culver) S. BS in Biology and Chemistry, Azusa Pacific U., Calif., 1979. Research chemist Lee Pharm., El Monte, Calif., 1980-82; analytical chemist Envirogenics, Rosemead, Calif., 1982-85; quality assurance supr. Fasson div. Avery Internat., Rancho Cucamonga, Calif., 1985—. Mem. Am. Chem Soc., Internat. Union of Pure and Applied Chemistry. Republican. Office: Fasson div Avery Internat 9292 9th St Rancho Cucamonga CA 91730

STREITWIESER, ANDREW, JR., chemistry educator; b. Buffalo, June 23, 1927; s. Andrew and Sophie (Morlock) S.; m. Mary Ann Good, Aug. 19, 1950 (dec. May 1965); children—David Roy, Susan Ann; m. Suzanne Cope Beier, July 29, 1967. A.B., Columbia U., 1949, M.A., 1950, Ph.D., 1952; postgrad. (AEC fellow), MIT, 1951-52. Faculty U. Calif.-Berkeley, 1952—, prof. chemistry, 1963—; cons. to industry, 1957—. Author: Molecular Orbital Theory for Organic Chemists, 1961, Solvolytic Displacement Reactions, 1962, (with J.I. Brauman) Supplemental Tables of Molecular Orbital Calculations, 1965, (with C.A. Coulson) Dictionary of Pi Electron Calculations, 1965, (with P.H. Owens) Orbital and Electron Density Diagrams, 1973, (with C.H. Heathcock) Introduction to Organic Chemistry, 3d edit, 1985; also numerous articles.; co-editor: Progress in Physical Organic Chemistry, 11 vols, 1963-74. Recipient Humboldt Found. Sr. scientist award, 1976, Humboldt medal, 1979. Fellow AAAS; mem. Am. Chem. Soc. (Calif. sect. award 1964, award in Petroleum Chemistry 1967, Norris award in phys. organic chemistry 1982), Royal Soc. Chemistry, AAAS, Nat. Acad. Scis., Am. Acad. Arts and Scis., Phi Beta Kappa, Sigma Xi. Research on organic reaction mechanisms, application molecular orbital theory to organic chemistry, effect chem. structure on carbon acidities, rare earths organometallic chemistry. Office: Dept Chemistry U Calif Berkeley CA 94720

STREMBITSKY, MICHAEL ALEXANDER, school administrator; b. Smoky Lake, Alta., Can., Mar. 5, 1935; s. Alec and Rose (Fedoretz) S.; m. Victoria Semeniuk, Aug. 12, 1954; children—Michael, William-John. B.A., U. Alta., 1955, B.Ed., 1958; M.A., Columbia U., 1968, M.Ed., 1972. With Edmonton (Alta.) pub. schs., now supt. of schs. Bd. dirs. Glenrose Hosp. Mem. Can. Coll. Tchrs., Can. Edn. Assn., Am. Mgmt. Assn., Council Ednl. Facility Planners Internat., Edmonton-Harbin Frindship Soc., U. Alta. Faculty Club, Ukrainian Profl. Bus. Club, Conf. Alta. Sch. Supts., Am. Assn. Sch. Adminstrs., Assn. Sch. Bus. Ofcls., Edmonton Edn. Soc., Assn. for Supervision and Curriculum, Can. Assn. Sch. Adminstrs., Nat. Assn. Ednl. Negotiators, World Council for Curriculum and Instrn., Edmonton C. of C., Phi Delta Kappa. Lodge: Rotary. Office: Edmonton Public Schools, Ctr for Edn, 1 Kingsway, Edmonton, AL Canada T5H 4G9

STREVEY, TRACY ELMER, JR., army officer, surgeon; b. Shorewood, Wis., Apr. 24, 1933; s. Tracy Elmer and Margaret (Rees) S.; m. Victoria Crowley; children: Virginia Ann, Tracy Elmer III, Andrew Victor. Student, Pomona Coll., 1951-54; MD, U. So. Calif., 1958; student, Armed Forces Staff Coll., 1970-71, U.S. Army War Coll., 1977-78. Diplomate Am. Bd. Surgery, Am. Bd. Thoracic Surgery. Intern Los Angeles County Gen. Hosp., 1958-59; commd. officer U.S. Army, 1959, advanced through grades to maj. gen., 1983; resident in gen. surgery Letterman Gen. Hosp., San Francisco, 1962-66; resident in thoracic and cardiovascular surgery Walter Reed Gen. Hosp., Washington, 1968-70; comdg. officer 757 Med Detachment OA Walter Reed Gen. Hosp., Ludwigsburg, Fed. Republic Germany, 1959-61; ward officer orthopaedic service 75th Sta. Hosp. Walter Reed Gen. Hosp., Stuttgart, Fed. Republic Germany, 1961-62; chief profl. service, chief surgery 85th Evacuation Hosp. Walter Reed Gen. Hosp., Qui Nhon, Vietnam, 1967; comdg. officer 3d Surg. Hosp. Walter Reed Gen. Hosp., Dong Tam, Vietnam, 1967-68; asst. chief thoracic and cardiovascular surgery service Fitzsimons Army Med Ctr., Denver, 1971-73, chief thoracic and cardiovascular surgery service, 1973-75; asst. dir. med. activities and dir. Profl. Edn. Gorgas Hosp., Panama Canal Zone, 1975-77; chief dept. surgery Walter Reed Army Med. Ctr., Washington, 1978-81; comdr. Brooke Army Med. Ctr., Ft. Sam Houston, Tex., 1981-83, Tripler Army Med. Ctr., Tripler AMC, Hawaii, 1983—; asst. clin. prof. surgery U. Colo. Med. Ctr., Denver, 1973-75; prof. surgery Uniformed Services U. Health Scis., Bethesda, 1978—, vice chmn. dept. surgery, 1978-81. Contbr. articles to profl. jours. Decorated Legion of Merit, Meritorious Service medal with 2 oak leaf clusters, Purple Heart, Army Commendation Medal for Valor, Vietnam Cross of Gallantry with Palm; recipient Outstanding Service award U. So. Calif. Med. Alumni Assn., 1983. Fellow ACS, Am. Coll. Chest Physicians, Am. Coll. Cardiology; mem. Assn. Mil. Surgeons of U.S., Soc. Thoracic Surgeons, Western Thoracic Surg. Assn., Am. Assn. Thoracic Surgery, Am. Acad. Med. Dirs., Am. Coll. Physician Execs., Am. Cancer Soc., Bexar County Med. Soc., ARC (bd. dirs. 1984—), Honolulu-Pacific Fed. Exec. Bd. Lodges: Masons, Rotary. Avocations: ham radio; scuba diving; golf; computer science. Office: Comdg Gen Tripler Army Med Ctr Tripler AMC HI 96859

STRINGER, WILLIAM JEREMY, university official; b. Oakland, Calif., Nov. 8, 1944; s. William Duane and Mildred May (Andrus) S.; BA in English, So. Meth. U., 1966; MA in English, U. Wis., 1968, PhD in Ednl. Adminstrn., 1973; m. Susan Lee Hildebrand; children: Shannon Lee, Kelly Erin, Courtney Elizabeth. Dir. men's housing Southwestern U., Georgetown, Tex., 1968-69; asst. dir. housing U. Wis., Madison, 1969-73; dir. residential life, asso. dean student life, adj. prof. Pacific Luth., Tacoma, 1973-78; dir. residential life U. So. Calif., 1978-79, asst. v.p., 1979-84, asst. prof. higher and post-secondary edn., 1980-84; v.p. student life Seattle U., 1984—. Bd. dirs. N.W. area Luth. Social Services of Wash. Danforth Found. grantee, 1976-77. Mem. N.W. Assn. Coll. and Univ. Housing Officers, Am. Assn. Higher Edn., Nat. Assn. Student Personnel Adminstrs., Am. Personnel and Guidance Assn., Phi Eta Sigma, Sigma Tau Delta, Phi Alpha Theta. Democrat. Lutheran. Author: How to Survive as a Single Student, 1972; The Role of the Assistant in Higher Education, 1973. Home: 4553 169th Ave SE Issaquah WA 98027 Office: Seattle U Seattle WA 98122

STRNAD, LYDIA JOAN, social worker; b. Rogers, Tex., Mar. 4, 1918; d. Leonard David and Filomena (Sasin) S. BA, Marylhurst Coll., 1947; MSW, St. Louis U., 1953. Caseworker Clackamas County Welfare, Oregon City, Oreg., 1947-51, Family and Children's Service of Greater St. Louis, 1951-57; social worker then aging services dir. Family Counseling Service (name changed to Met. Family Service), Portland, Oreg., 1957-81; pvt. practice social worker with aging people Portland, 1981—. Mem. Nat. Assn. Social Workers (cert.). Avocations: camping, beachcombing, gardening, fishing. Home: 6125 NE Clackamas Portland OR 97213

STROBEL, SHAWNA ELLISON, interior design educator; b. Salt Lake City, Dec. 23, 1929; d. Edward James and Oneita (Rees) Ellison; m. Joseph Edwin Strobel, Dec. 16, 1950; children: James, Heidi, Joseph, David, Dirk, Oneita, John, Richard, Angela, Tiffany, Joshua. Student, Woolf Sch. Design, summers 1948, 49; BS in Clothing and Textiles, U. Utah, 1950; M in Child Devel., Brigham Young U., 1968; D, U. Minn., 1984. Asst. dress designer Lily Claire of Calif., Los Angeles, 1950; with ZCMI, Salt Lake City, 1951-52; instr. adult edn. program Brigham Young U.-Ricks Coll., Idaho Falls, Idaho, 1965-69; mem. faculty home econs. dept. Ricks Coll., Rexburg, Idaho, 1969—, chmn. dept., 1983—; pvt. practice interior design, Rexburg, 1968—. Mem. Am. Soc. Interior Designers (v.p. Utah chpt. 1984-85), Interior Design Educators Council (regional chair 1984-85), Inst. Bus. Designers (continuing edn. units com. 1986—), Illuminating Engrs. Soc. Mormon. Avocations: reading, sewing. Home: 444 Morgan Rexburg ID 83440 Office: Ricks Coll 244 Clarke Bldg Rexburg ID 83440

STROBER, MICHAEL ARTHUR, psychiatry educator, clinical psychologist; b. N.Y.C., Feb. 22, 1949; s. Emanuel and Joan (Kristal) S.; m. Sheila Shapiro, Aug. 7, 1971; children: Nicole, Meredith. BA magna cum laude, Queens Coll., 1971; MS, U. Pitts., 1973, PhD, 1975. Asst. prof. psychiatry UCLA, 1975-83, assoc. prof., 1983—. Editor Internat. Jour. Eating Disorders, 1983—; contbr. articles to jours. and chpts. to books. Mem. AAAS, N.Y. Acad. Sci., Am. Psychol. Assn., Phi Beta Kappa. Office: UCLA Neuropsychiat Inst 760 Westwood Pl Los Angeles CA 90024

STROCK, ARTHUR VAN ZANDT, architect; b. Los Angeles, Sept. 14, 1945; s. Arthur and Eileen (Cortelyou) S.; m. Hallie vonAmmon, Mar. 22, 1969. BArch, U. Calif., Berkeley, 1971. Registered profl. architect. Asst. dean Sch. Architecture and Fine Arts U. So. Calif., Los Angeles, 1970-71; designer Allied Architects, Long Beach, Calif., 1971-73; architect Langdon and Wilson, Newport Beach, Calif., 1973-77, Lee & Strock Architects, Newport Beach, 1978-82, Strock Architects, Inc., Newport Beach, 1982—; guest lectr. U. Calif., Irvine; guest speaker AIA of Orange County, 1986, Pacific Coast Design Conf., Monterey, Calif.; archtl. examiner State of Calif. Prin. works include I.R.W.D. Bldg., 1979 (Merit award 1982), Newport/Irvine Ctr., 1980 (Merit award 1982), Bay Corp. Ctr., 1982 (Merit award 1984), Scripps Ctr., 1985, Long Beach Airport Bus. Park, 1986, Orange County Register Hdqrs., 1986. Pres. Beacon Bay Community Assn., Newport Beach, 1985-86; bd. dirs. Nat. History Found. of Orange County, 1982. Mem. AIA (Merit award 1981), Urban Land Inst., Nat. Assn. Indsl. and Office Parks, Sigma Chi. Republican. Clubs: Newport Harbor Yacht, Newport Beach Tennis. Avocations: yachting, fishing, tennis. Home: 23 Beacon Bay Newport Beach CA 92660 Office: Strock Architects 3300 Irvine Ave Newport Beach CA 92660

STROCK, HERBERT LEONARD, motion picture producer, director, editor, writer; b. Boston, Jan. 13, 1918; s. Maurice and Charlotte (Nesselroth) S.; m. Geraldine Polinger, Dec. 25, 1941; children—Leslie Carol, Gail Ellen, Candice Dell. B.A., U. So. Calif., 1941, M.A., 1942. Editorial dept. Metro-Goldwyn-Mayer, 1942-46; producer 13 TV films for CBS, Cases of Eddie Drake 1948-50; assoc. producer, film editor Storm over Tibet, 1951; dir., editor Dragnet, 1952; assoc. producer, dir., film editor Magnetic Monster, 1952, Donovan's Brain, Riders to the Stars; dir. and editor Gog, 1953; producer, dir. I Led Three Lives, Mr. District Attorney, Favorite Story, Corliss Archer, Sci. Fiction Theatre, Hwy. Patrol, Dr. Christian, Man Called X, Harbor Command, 1954; dir. Battle Taxi; exec. producer, dir. Tom Swift Series; TV shows: Mann of Action, Red Light and Siren; Sky King; (for Warner Bros.): Maverick, Alaskans, Colt 45, Bronco, Cheyenne, 77 Sunset Strip; (for Paramount Studios) Bonanza, for NBC Hans Brinker spl., Decisions-Decisions; feature pictures; Perfect World of Rodney Brewster, I Was a Teenage Frankenstein, Blood of Dracula, How to Make a Monster, Rider on a Dead Horse, Strike Me Deadly, Search the Wild Wind; editor, dir. The Crawling Hand, One Hour of Hell; editorial supr. Shark; writer, dir. Brother on the Run; editor So. Evil My Sister, Chamber-Mades; co-producer Small Miracle on Hallmark Playhouse; editor, dir. They Search for Survival documentary, supervising film editor Hunger Telethon (both for World Vision, Internat.); editor the Making of America, 2 hour spl. for BBC and NBC; cowriter, film editor Hurray for Betty Boop; dir., chief prodn. coordinator for U.S., Miss World, 1976, NBC; editor documentaries; UFO Journals, UFO Syndrome, Legends, all 1979; pres. Herbert L. Strock Prodns.; co-dir., film editor: Witches' Brew, 1979; pres., chmn. bd. Hollywood-World Films, Inc.; writer, film editor Flipper TV series, 1981; lectr. U. So. Calif. Editor post prodn. services China-Mao to Now, Eucatastrophe, Tibet, El Papa, Night Screams, King Kung Fu; dir., editor Deadly Presence; co-dir., editor Deadly Presence. Mem. Acad. Motion Picture Arts and Scis., Dirs. Guild Am., Am. Cinema Editors (dir.), Motion Picture Editors Guild, Delta Kappa Alpha (pres.). Office: 6500 Barton Ave Hollywood CA 90038

STROEVE, PIETER, chemical engineering educator, consultant; b. Velp, Gelderland, The Netherlands, Sept. 15, 1945; came to U.S., 1959; s. Antonie and Frederika Wilhelmina (Smolders) S.; m. Barbara Leonard Nichols, Sept. 5, 1967; children: Dale, Maryke, Yuly. Student, Contra Costa Coll., 1962-65; BSChemE, U. Calif., Berkeley, 1967; MSChemE, MIT, 1969, ScD, 1973. Sr. scientist Weizmann Inst. Sci., Rehovot, Israel, 1973-74; asst. prof. U. Nijmegen, The Netherlands, 1974-77; from asst. to assoc. prof. SUNY, Buffalo, 1977-81; assoc. prof. U. Calif., Davis, 1981-83, prof., 1983—; cons. Los Alamos (N.Mex.) Nat. Lab., 1983—. Author, editor: Integrated Circuits, 1985, Biomedical Engineering, 1983; editor: Transport with Chemical Reaction, 1981; contbr. 70 articles to profl. jours. Recipient teaching award U. Calif., Davis, 1984; grantee NSF, 1985, NATO, 1982. Mem. Am. Inst. Chem. Engrs., Am. Chem. Soc., Soc. Plastics Engrs., Soc. of Rheology. Office: U Calif Dept Chem Engring Davis CA 95616

STROHM, BEVERLEY FRANCELLA, advertising executive; b. Sharon, Pa., July 9, 1937; d. Charles Patric and MaryLouise (Feeney) S.; m. John W. Swenson, Sept. 7, 1961 (div. June, 1965); children: Joyce, Claudia, Collene. BS in Graphic Arts Mgmt., Rochester Inst. Tech., 1960; MBA in Advertising, UCLA, 1973, MB in Purchasing. Maj. WAC, 1955-65; direct mail mgr. May Co., Los Angeles, 1965-75; dir. of purchasing Mass Mktg. Systems Internat., Agoura, Calif., 1975-83; mktg. v.p. Times Lithograph, Forest Grove, Oreg., 1983-84; dir. prodn. Wunderman West, Los Angeles, 1984-86, Ogilvy & Mather Direct, Los Angeles, 1987—. Treas. South Bay Arts Alliance, Torrance, Calif., 1969-80; mem. adv. bd. Los Angeles City Schs., 1960-73. Mem. Direst Mail Assn., Women in Advt. Avocation: supporting the arts. Office: Ogilvy & Mather 5757 Wilshire Blvd Los Angeles CA 90036

STRONG, DOUGLAS M., biotechnology company executive; b. Newport, Wash., Sept. 4, 1941; s. George Leslie Strong and Dorothea Gwenyth (Rednour) Foulkes; m. Geraldine Anne O'Melveny, Jan. 30, 1965; children: Michael Phillip, David Richard, Patricia Anne. BS, Gonzaga U., 1963; cert. med. technician, Sacred Heart Sch. Med. Tech., Spokane, Wash., 1964; PhD, Med. Coll. Wis., 1973. Commd. ensign USN, 1965, advanced through grades to comdr., ret., 1985; v.p. diagnostic research and devel. Genetic Systems, Seattle, 1985—; cons. Alta. (Can.) Govt., Edmonton, 1978-82, Pa. Regional Tissue and Transplant Bank, Scranton, 1978—, Controlled Chems., Inc., Ann Arbor, Mich., 1985—, Armed Forces Radiobiology Research Inst., Bethesda, Md., 1982-85. Contbr. articles to profl. jours.; mem. numerous jour. editorial bds. Coach soccer Wheaton Boy's Club, Montgomery United Soccer Club, Montgomer County, Md., 1976-84, Rockville United Soccer Club. Recipient commendations Nat. Jud. Coll., Nat. Inst. Justice, Nat. Conf. Spl. Ct. Judges, Nat. Orgn. for Victims Assistance, Montgomery County Police Tng. Acad., Walter Reed Army Med. Ctr. Mem. AAAS, Am. Assn. Tissue Banks, Am. Assn. Immunology, Internat. Inst. Refrigeration (sec. council U.S. 1976—), Soc. Cryobiology (sec. 1975-76), Am. Soc. Hist. Immunology (standards com. 1986). Roman Catholic. Home: 18624 94th Ave W Edmonds WA 98102 Office: Geneti Systems Corp 3005 1st Ave Seattle WA 98020

STRONG, GARY EUGENE, librarian; b. Moscow, Idaho, June 26, 1944; s. Arthur Dwight and Cleora Anna (Nirk) S.; m. Carolyn Jean Roetker, Mar. 14, 1970; children: Christopher Eric, Jennifer Rebecca. BS in Edn., U. Idaho, 1966; AMLS, U. Mich., 1967. Adminstrv. and reference asst. U. Idaho, 1963-66; extension librarian Latah County Free Library, Moscow, 1966; head librarian Markeley Residence Library, U. Mich., 1966-67; library dir. Lake Oswego (Oreg.) Public Library, 1967-73, Everett (Wash.) Public Library, 1973-76; asso. dir. services Wash. State Library, Olympia, 1976-79; dep. state librarian Wash. State Library, 1979-80; state librarian Calif. State Library, Sacramento, 1980—; chief exec. Calif. Library Services Bd., 1980—; founder, bd. dirs. Calif. State Library Found., 1982—; bd. dirs. No. Regional Library Bd., 1983—; mem. adv. bd. Ctr. for Book, 1983-86; vis. lectr. Marylhurst Coll., Oreg., 1968, Oreg. Div. Continuing Edn., 1972. Host, producer: cable TV Signatures program, 1974-76, nationwide videoconfs. on illiteracy, censorship, 1985; editor Calif. State Library Found. Bull., 1982—, Western Americana in the Calif. State Library, 1986; contbr. articles to profl. jours.; editor, designer and pub. of various books. Bd. dirs., v.p. Pacific N.W. Bibliog. Center, 1977-80; bd. dirs. Thurston Mason County Mental Health Center, 1977-80, pres., 1979-80; bd. dirs. Coop. Library Agy. for Systems and Services, 1980—, vice chmn., 1981-84; bd. dirs. Sr. Services Snohomish County, 1973-76, HISPANEX (Calif. Spanish lang. data base), 1983-86; bd. govs. Snohomish County Hist. Assn., 1974-76; mem. Oreg. Council Public Broadcasting, 1969-73; mem. psychiat. task force St. Peters Hosp., Olympia, 1979-80; mem. adv. bd. Calif. State PTA, 1981—. Recipient Disting. Alumnus award U. Mich., 1984; Disting. Service award Calif. Literacy Inc., 1985. Oreg. Library scholar, 1966. Mem. ALA (legis. com. 1980-82, Commn. on Freedom and Equality of Access to Info. 1983-86), Library Adminstrn. and Mgmt. Assn. (dir. 1980-86, pres. 1984-85), Oreg. Library Assn. (hon. life mem., pres. 1970-71), Pacific N.W. Library Assn. (hon. life mem., pres. 1978-79), Calif. Library Assn. (govt. relations com. 1980—), Chief Officers of State Library Agys. (pres. 1984-86), Everett Area C. of C. (bd. dirs. 1974-76). Clubs: Book of Calif., Press of San

Francisco, Sacramento Book Collectors. Office: PO Box 2037 Sacramento CA 95809

STRONG, GAY, industrial relations and human resources executive; b. Santa Monica, Calif., Jan. 13, 1930; d. Claude Roderick and Katherine Anna (Brown) Riley; student UCLA, 1947-49; A.A., Pierce Coll., Los Angeles, 1969; B.A. in English, Calif. State U.-Northridge, 1973; m. Duane Gordon Strong, Aug. 20, 1949; children—Philip, Katherine, Patricia, Barbara. With credit office, store ops., then asst. personnel mgr. Builders Emporium, Van Nuys, Calif., 1969-74, personnel mgr., 1974-78; dir. indsl. relations GC Internat., Hawthorne, Calif., 1978-81; personnel mgr. Lok Products Co., Fullerton, Calif., 1981-82; chief exec. officer Asset Recovery, Santa Monica, Calif., 1982-83; dir. Human Resource Targeted Coverage, Inc., Pomona, Calif., 1983—; editor house organ, 1983—. Mem. Am. Mgmt. Assn., Personnel and Indsl. Relations Assn., Electronic Assn. Calif. Republican. Editor Builders Emporium house organ, 1972-78. Office: 3200 "A" Pomona Blvd Pomona CA 91768

STRONG, MAYDA NEL, psychologist, educator; b. Albuquerque, May 6, 1942; d. Floyd Samuel and Wanda Christmas (Martin) Strong; 1 child, Robert Allen Willingham. BA in Speech-Theatre cum laude, Tex. Western Coll., 1963; EdM, U. Tex., Austin, 1972, PhD in Counseling Psychology, 1978; lic. clin. psychologist, Colo., 1984; cert. alcohol counselor III, Colo., 1987. Asst. instr. in ednl. psychology U. Tex., Austin, 1974-78; instr. psychology Austin Community Coll., 1974-78, Otero Jr. Coll., La Junta, Colo., 1979—; dir. outpatient and emergency services S.E. Colo. Family Guidance and Mental Health Ctr., Inc., La Junta, 1978-81; pvt. practice psychol. therapy, La Junta, 1981—; exec. dir. Pathfinders Alcohol Dependency program, 1985—. Co-star The Good Doctor, Picketwire Theatre, La Junta, 1980, On Golden Pond, 1981. AAUW fellow. Mem. Bus. and Profl. People (legis. chairperson 1982-83), Colo. Psychol. Assn. (legis. chair for dist.). Contbr. articles in field to profl. publs. Author poems in Chinook: Paths through the Puzzle, Decisions, Passion. Home: 1 Opera House Apts La Junta CO 81050 Office: #21 Town Square Mall La Junta CO 81050

STRONG, WILLIAM JAMES, physicist; b. Idaho Falls, Idaho, Jan. 1, 1934; s. William A. and June (Engberson) S.; m. Charlene Fuhriman, June 8, 1959; children—William, Stephen, Kathleen, John, David, Richard. B.S., Brigham Young U., Provo, 1958, M.S., 1959; Ph.D., M.I.T., 1964. Mem. staff Lincoln Labs., M.I.T., 1960-61, Air Force Cambridge Research Labs., Bedford, Mass., 1963-66; lectr. physics Holy Cross Coll., Worcester, Mass., 1963-64, Northeastern U., Boston, 1964-66; mem. faculty Brigham Young U., 1967—, prof. physics, 1976—; vis. scientist Gallaudet Coll., Washington, 1974; Fulbright sr. scholar U. New Eng., Armidale, N.S.W., Australia, 1980. Author: Music, Speech and High Fidelity, 1977, 2d edit., 1983. Served with USAF, 1964-67. Fellow Acoustical Soc. Am.; mem. IEEE, Sigma Xi. Mormon. Patentee in field. Address: Dept Physics Brigham Young Univ Provo UT 84602

STRONG, WILLIAM LEE, former manufacturing company executive; b. Jacksonville, Fla., Sept. 17, 1919; s. William M. and Hedwig C. (Ulm) S.; m. Betty Jean Stream, Dec. 13, 1941; children—William Lee, Thomas B., Robin E. Strong Vandever. A.B. in Econs., Occidental Coll., 1942; M.B.A., Harvard U., 1947. Budget dir. Byron-Jackson div. Borg Warner Corp., Los Angeles, 1954-56, controller, 1956-57; budget dir. Consol. Freightways, Inc., Menlo Park, Calif., 1957-60, treas., chief fin. officer, 1960-62; v.p. fin., treas., dir. Packard-Bell Electronics Corp., Los Angeles, 1962-65; treas. Allis-Chalmers Mfg. Co., Milw., 1965-68; v.p., treas. Continental Can Co., Inc., (now Continental Group, Inc.), 1968-75; sr. v.p., chief fin. officer Firestone Tire & Rubber Co., Akron, Ohio, 1976-77, exec. v.p., dir., 1978-81; dir. Transatlantic Fund, U.S. Life Corp.; guest lectr. various grad. bus. schs., other groups. chmn. bd. advisors Sch. Acctg. U. So. Calif. Served to lt. comdr. USN, 1942-54; PTO. Mem. Treas. Club N.Y., Phi Gamma Delta. Club: Harvard Bus. Sch. (N.Y.C.). Home: 4020 Calle Marlena San Clemente CA 92672

STRONGE, WILLIAM JAMES, JR., mechanical engineer; b. Chgo., Mar. 6, 1937; s. William James and Lillian Mae S.; B.S., Oreg. State U., 1960; M.S., UCLA, 1964; Ph.D. in Applied Mechanics, Stanford U., 1969; children—Brent R., Leslie Ann; m. Katerina Homenidou, 1983. Mech. engr. Naval Weapons Center, China Lake, Calif., 1960-81, head structural dynamics br., 1979-81; prof. dept. engring. Cambridge (Eng.) U., 1981—, invited lectr. Beijing (People's Republic of China) Inst. Tech., 1984, 87. Fellow Jesus Coll. Pres., China Lake Mountain Rescue, 1979-80. Mem. AIAA, Am. Acad. Mechanics, Sigma Xi. Contbr. articles to profl. jours. Research on wave propagation, dynamic plasticity, impact mechanics. Office: Dept Engring, U Cambridge, Cambridge England

STROOCK, THOMAS FRANK, state senator; b. N.Y.C., Oct. 10, 1925; s. Samuel and Dorothy (Frank) S.; B.A. in Econs., Yale U., 1948; m. Marta Freyre de Andrade, June 19, 1949; children—Margaret, Sandra, Elizabeth, Anne. Landman Stanolind Oil & Gas Co., Tulsa, 1948-52; pres. Stroock Leasing Corp., Casper, Wyo., 1952—, Alpha Exploration, Inc., 1980—; partner Stroock, Rogers & Dymond, Casper, 1960-82; dir. Wyo. Bancorp., Cheyenne, First Wyo. Bank, Casper, Century Oil & Gas Corp., Denver; mem. Wyo. Senate, 1967-69, 71-75, 79—, chmn. appropriations com. 1983, co-chmn. joint appropriations com., 1983—, mem. mgmt. and audit com. P; mem. steering com. Edn. Commn. of States. Pres. Natrona County Sch. Bd., 1960-69; pres. Wyo. State Sch. Bds. Assn., 1965-66; chmn. Casper Community Recreation, 1955-60; chmn. Natrona County United Fund, 1963-64; chmn. Wyo. State Republican Com., 1975-78; chmn. Western States Rep. Chmn. Assn., 1977-78; chmn. Wyo. Higher Edn. Commn., 1969-71; mem. Nat. Petroleum Council, 1972-77; chmn. trustees Sierra Madre Found. for Geol. Research, New Haven; bd. dirs. Ucross Found., Denver; mem. Nat. Pub. Lands Adv. Council, 1981-85. Served with USMC, 1943-46. Mem. Rocky Mountain Oil and Gas Assn., Petroleum Assn. Wyo. Republican. Unitarian. Clubs: Kiwanis; Casper Country; Casper Petroleum; Denver. Office: PO Box 2875 Casper WY 82602

STROOP, WILLIAM GEORGE, neurology and pathology educator; b. Klamath Falls, Oreg., June 17, 1952; s. John William and Constance Salome (Truchan) S.; m. Janice Louise Brandenburg, June 22, 1974. BS, Oreg. State U., 1975; PhD, U. Calif., San Francisco, 1981. Staff research assoc. dept. neurology U. Calif. Sch. Medicine, San Francisco, 1975-78, predoctoral fellow dept. pathology, 1978-81, research asst. dept. medicine, 1980-81; postdoctoral fellow The Slow Virus Group The Wistar Inst., Phila., 1981-83, sec., 1982-83; postdoctoral fellow U. Penn., Phila., 1981-83; instr. dept. neurol. U. Utah, Salt Lake City, 1983-84, instr. dept. pathology, 1983-85, asst. prof. dept. pathology, 1985—, asst. prof. dept. neurology, 1984—, faculty mem. program in neurosci., 1984—; participant workshop on DNA, Nat. Cancer Inst., Rockville, Md., 1984; coordinator Neurol. Diseases Tissue Ctr., U. Utah Med. Sch., 1983—; mem. research safety subcom. Research Adminstrn. Service, VA Med. Ctr., Salt Lake City, 1984—, animal research subcom., 1984—, research and devel. com., 1986—; grant reviewer NSF, 1984-85; cons. VA Merit rev. bd. for neurobiology, prin. investigator, 1985—; ad hoc mem. NIH site visit team, 1985. Reviewer Sci., Jour. Neuropathology and Exptl. Neurology, Infection and Immunity, Annals of Neurology, Jour. Infectious Diseases; contbr. articles to profl. jours., chpts. to books. Founder, sec. Fairway Park Neighborhood Assn., Pacifica, Calif., 1979-81. Walter H. Beane Meml. scholar, 1970-74; Earl C. Anthony fellow U. Calif., 1980-81; recipient Nat. Research Service award U. Penn. Sch. Medicine, 1981-83, prin. investigator grant U. Utah, 1983-84, 1984-85. Mem. AAAS, Am. Assn. Neuropathologists, Am. Soc. Microbiology (co-convenor ann. meeting 1982), Am. Soc. Neurologic Investigation, Am. Soc. Virology, N.Y. Acad. Scis., Soc. Exptl. Biology and Medicine, Sigma Xi. Republican. Roman Catholic. Avocations: zoology, gardening, stamp collecting, salt water aquariums. Home: 8126 S Scandia Circle Sandy UT 84092 Office: VA Med Ctr Neurovirol Research 500 Foothill Dr Salt Lake City UT 84148

STROTTMAN, DANIEL, physicist; b. Waverly, Iowa, Apr. 15; s. Arnold and Alice (Schwake) S.; m. Theresa Anne Short, Dec. 22, 1966; 1 child, Nissa. BA, U. Iowa, 1964; MA, SUNY, Stony Brook, 1966, PhD, 1969. Fellow Niels Bohr Inst., Copenhagen, 1969-70; research officer Oxford (Eng.) U., 1970-73; asst. prof. physics SUNY, Stony Brook, 1974-78; mem. staff Los Alamos (N.Mex.) Nat. Lab., 1978—; vis. prof. U. Oslo, 1973-74; adv. com. Los Alamos Meson Physics Facility (now Clinton P. Anderson Meson Physics Facility at Los Alamos) program, 1986—. Mem. editorial bd. Internat. Rev. Nuclear Phusics, 1982—, Modern Physics A., 1986—; contbr. articles to profl. jours. Pres. Los Alamos Youth Soccer League, 1985—. Fellow Am. Phys. Soc.; mem. AAAS, No. N.Mex. Soccer Referees Assn. (pres. 1981-84). Home: 613 47th St Los Alamos NM 87544 Office: Los Alamos Nat Lab Theoretical Div MS B279 Los Alamos NM 87545

STROUD, ROBERT MICHAEL, biophysicist, educator, biotechnologist; b. Stockport, Eng., May 24, 1942; came to U.S., 1968; BA in Natural Sci., Cambridge U., Eng., 1964, MA in Natural Sci., 1968; MS in Crystallography, London U., 1965, PhD, 1968. Asst. prof. chemistry Calif. Inst. Tech., Pasadena, 1971-77, assoc. prof., 1975-77; assoc. prof. U. Calif., San Francisco, 1977, prof., 1980—; cons. NIH, 1976—. Contbr. articles to profl. jours. Research grantee NIH, 1971—, NSF, 1971—. Fellow Royal Soc. of Medicine (U.K.), Mem. U.K. Biophys. Soc., U.S. Biophys. Soc. (council, pres.), Fedn. Exptl. Biologists. Avocation: surf-sailing.

STROUSE, WILLIAM A., contract computer consultant, writer; b. Los Angeles, Apr. 22, 1945; s. Wilbert W. and Ruth Strouse. Diploma, Control Data Inst., San Jose, Calif., 1971. Systems designer, Klystrom dept. Stanford Linear Accelerator, Menlo Park, Calif., 1984—; cons. Tech. Services Corp., Sunnyvale, Calif., 1984—; founder Wild Bill's Pub. Remote Access System, 1984. Mem. Micro Bull. Bd. Systems (on-line support provider 1984—), Pub. Domain Software and Info. Exchange, Trail Info. and Vol. Ctr. (on-line support provider), Bay Area Morrow Designs Users Assn. (asst. systems operator 1985), Pub. Remote Access Computer Standards Assn. (trustee San Josechpt.). Office: PO Box 28684 San Jose CA 95159

STROZIER, WENDELL, nuclear medical technologist; b. St. Louis, Sept. 21, 1952; s. Harvey and Hattie Beatrice (Bell) S.; m. Juanita L. Watts, Sept. 1983. A.A., Los Angeles City Coll., 1977; B.S., Calif. State U., 1980; postgrad. U. Redlands, 1980-81; diploma Excel Security Acad., 1982. Distbr. Amway Products, Los Angeles, 1979—; radiol. technologist USAFR, North AFB, Calif., 1974-78; nuclear medicine staff technologist NuclearMedico Services, Van Nuys, Calif., 1977-81, nuclear medicine mgr., Los Angeles, 1981; staff technologist Kaiser Permanente of West Los Angeles, 1982—; call technologist Meml. Hosp., Gardena, Calif., 1982—; dist. mgr. A.L. Williams, 1985—; rep. Mass. Indemnity and Life Ins. Co. and First Am. Nat. Securities, Inc., 1986—; pres. The Akili Network; lectr. in field. Vol., UCLA Med. Ctr., 1979-80; counselor Watts Labor Community Action Com., 1982; union steward Local 399 Hosp. and Service Employees Union AFL-CIO, 1986—. Served with USAF, 1972-73. Mem. Soc. Nuclear Medicine, Am. Mgmt. Assn., Am. Legion. Club: Kaiser Employee (treas. 1986—). Home: PO Box 88184 Los Angeles CA 90009 Office: 2310 La Cienaga Blvd Los Angeles CA 90019

STRUBLE, GEORGE WARING, computer science educator; b. Phila., July 6, 1932; s. George Goodell and Lillie O. (Strand) S.; m. Elsa Laura Bennett, June 18, 1955; children: Andrew, Jennifer, Laura. BA with honors, Swarthmore Coll., 1954; MS, U. Wis., 1957, PhD, 1961. From asst. to assoc. prof. U. oreg., Eugene, 1961-82, research assoc., dir. computer ctr., 1961-74; prof. computer sci. Willamette U., Salem, Oreg., 1982—. Author: Assembler Language Programming, 3d rev. edit. 1984, Business Information Processing with Basic, 1979; contbr. articles to profl. jours. Served with U.S. Army, 1954-56. Mem. Assn. Computing Machinery, Greater Eugene Stamp Soc., Sigma Xi. Democrat. Mem. Unitarian Ch. Club: Chemeketans (Salem). Avocation: chamber music. Home: 210 18th St NE Salem OR 97301 Office: Willamette U Computer Sci Dept Salem OR 97301

STRUCINSKI, MITCH, public relations executive; b. Chgo., Feb. 23, 1922; s. Joseph and Salomea (Madura) S.; m. Joanne De Eds, 1960 (div. 1961); 1 child, Gregory Joseph; m. Rosanne Baskir, July 1, 1967. BA, Coll. Notre Dame, Belmont, Calif., 1970; MSW, Fresno State U., 1972; MPH, U. Calif., Berkeley, 1976; MBA, Stanford U., 1980. Lic. clin. social worker, Calif. Dir. social services Mill Meml. Hosp., San Mateo, Calfi., 1977-79; bus. mgr. Computer Faire, Woodside, Calif., 1979-80; pres. White Eagle Communications Inc., Menlo Park, Calif., 1980—; researcher, cons. Santa Clara County Health Systems Agy., San Jose, Calif., 1976-79. Author: The Corridor, 1960, Santa Clara County Health Profile, 1979, Super Computers, 1986; also short stories. Served to comdr. USNR, 1950-57. Stegner Creative Writing fellow Stanford U., 1960. Mem. Pub. Relations Soc. Am., Nat. Assn. Social Workers, Charles Babbage Inst. Avocations: sailing, collecting Am. Ephemera.

STRUDTHOFF, JEAN MARIE, speech pathologist; b. Alta, Iowa, Sept. 30, 1950; d. Stanley Leo and Loraine Kathryn (Reinicke) S.; m. David Earl Vorland, Sept. 25, 1971 (div. July 1981). BA in English Teaching, U. Northern Iowa, 1974, MA in Speech Pathology, 1982. Speech pathologist S.W. Mont. Ednl. Coop., Dillon, 1982—; instr. Western Mont. Coll., Dillon, 1984; cons. Parkview Convalescent Ctr., Dillon, 1984—, Social Service, Dillon, 1985—; supr. Dillon Sch. Dist. 10, 1984-85, S.W. Mont. Ednl. Coop., Deer Lodge, 1983—. Mem. Am. Speech Lang. and Hearing Assn. (cert.), Mont. Speech Lang. and Hearing Assn. Democrat. Lutheran. Avocations: downhill skiing, back packing, crocheting, quilting. Home: 833 S Atlantic Dillon MT 59725 Office: SW Mont Ednl Coop Box 48 WMC Dillon MT 59725

STRUGACH, MICHAEL GRIGORY, engineer, scientist; b. Leningrad, USSR, Nov. 23, 1939; came to U.S., 1978; s. Grigory I. and Berta S. (Soloveychik) S.; m. Ellen V. Ionova, Nov. 30, 1969; children: Gregory, Victor, Natalie. BEE, Mil. Mech. Inst. of Leningrad, 1960, MME, 1963; PhD in Control and Instrumentation, Acad. Krilov Cen. Sci. Research Inst., Leningrad, 1972. Registered profl. engr., USSR. Engr. Kulakov Ship's Instrumentation Plant and Inst., Leningrad, 1962-65; sr. engr. Acad. Krilov Cen. Sci. Research Inst., Leningrad, 1965-73; cons. Leningrad, 1973-78; mem. tech. staff Litton Guidance and Control Systems, Woodland Hills, Calif., 1979—. Contbr. articles to profl. jours.; patentee gyroscopes, accelerometers, inertial instrumentation. Mem. Inst. of Navigation. Republican. Jewish. Avocations: hiking, pantomime.

STRUHL, STANLEY FREDERICK, real estate developer; b. Bklyn., Oct. 10, 1939; s. Isidore and Yvette (Miller) S.; B.S. with honors in Engring., UCLA, 1961, M.B.A. in Data Processing, 1963; m. Patricia Joyce Wald, Feb. 26, 1966; children—Marc Howard, Lisa Lynn. Mem. tech. staff Hughes Aircraft Co., Fullerton, Calif., 1963-65; sr. asso. Planning Research Corp., Los Angeles, 1965-70; mgr. corporate info. systems Logicon, Inc., Torrance, Calif., 1970-73; mgr. operations analysis System Devel. Corp., Santa Monica, Calif., 1973-77; gen. partner TST Developers, Canyon Country, Calif., 1977-81; pres. Struhl Enterprises, Inc., Northridge, Calif., 1977-85; owner Struhl Properties, Northridge, 1979—. Lic. real estate broker, Calif. Mem. Assn. For Computing Machinery, San Fernando Valley Bd. Realtors, Tau Beta Pi, Beta Gamma Sigma, Alpha Phi Omega. Home: 17074 Knapp St Northridge CA 91325

STRYER, LUBERT, biochemist, educator; b. Tientsin, China, Mar. 2, 1938. B.S. with honors, U. Chgo., 1957; M.D. magna cum laude, Harvard U., 1961. Helen Hay Whitney fellow Harvard U., also Med. Research Council Lab., 1961-63; from asst. prof. to assoc. prof. biochemistry Stanford U., 1963-69; prof. molecular biophysics and biochemistry Yale U., 1969-76; Winzer prof. cell biology Stanford U. Sch. Medicine, 1976—, chmn. dept. structural biology, 1976-79; cons. NIH, NRC.; mem. sci. adv. bd. Jane Coffin Childs Fund, Research to Prevent Blindness, 1984—. Mem. editorial bd.: Jour. Molecular Biology, 1968-72, Jour. Cell Biology, 1981—; assoc. editor: Annual Revs. Biophysics and Bioengineering, 1970-76. Recipient Am. Chem. Soc. award in biol. chemistry Eli Lilly & Co., 1970. Fellow Am. Acad. Arts and Scis.; mem. Nat. Acad. Sci., Am. Chem. Soc., Am. Soc. Biol. Chemists, Biophys. Soc., Phi Beta Kappa. Office: Fairchild Center D133 Stanford Sch Medicine Stanford CA 94305

STUART, CHARLES ROSSITER, sales executive; b. San Rafael, Calif., Nov. 9, 1957; s. Charles Rossiter and Marilyn Brauer (Morse) S.; m. Mimi McIntosh, Oct. 9, 1982. BA in Econs., U. Calif., Berkeley, 1979. Research analyst Sta. KTTV, Los Angeles, 1980, account exec., 1980-85, nat. sales mgr., 1985—. Mem. Town Hall, Cousteau Soc. Republican. Episcopalian. Club: Los Angeles Athletic. Avocations: travelling, scuba diving, skiing, rowing. Office: Fox TV Stations Inc 5746 Sunset Blvd Los Angeles CA 90028

STUART, DAVID EDWARD, anthropologist, columnist; b. Calhoun County, Ala., Jan. 9, 1945; s. Edward George and Avis Elsie (Densmore) S.; B.A. (Wesleyan Merit scholar 1965-66), W.VA. Wesleyan Coll., 1967; M.A. in Anthropology, U. N.Mex., 1970, Ph.D., 1972, postdoctoral student, 1975-76; m. Cynthia K. Morgan, June 14, 1971. Research assoc. Andean Center, Quito, Ecuador, 1970; continuing edn. instr. anthropology U. N.Mex., 1971, research archeologist Office Contract Archeology, 1974, research coordinator, 1974-77, asst. prof. anthropology, 1975-77, assoc. prof. anthropology, 1984—; asst. prof. Eckerd Coll., St. Petersburg, Fla., 1972-74; cons. archeologist right-of-way div. Pub. Service Co. N.Mex., Albuquerque, 1977-78; cons. anthropologist Bur. Indian Affairs, Albuquerque, 1978, Historic Preservation Bur. N.Mex., Santa Fe, 1978-81, Nat. Park Service, 1980, Albuquerque Mus., 1981; sr. research assoc. Human Systems Research, Inc., 1981-83, Quivira Research Center, Albuquerque, 1984-86; bd. dirs. Table Ind. Scholars, 1979-83, pres., bd. dirs. Rio Grande Heritage Found., Albuquerque and Las Cruces, 1985-87; advisor Human Systems Research, Inc., Tularosa, N.Mex., 1978-80, Albuquerque Commn. on Hist. Preservation, 1984-86. Grantee Eckerd Coll., 1973, Historic Preservation Bur., 1978-80. Essayist award N.Mex. Humanities Council, 1986. Mem. Am. Anthrop. Assn., Royal Anthrop. Inst. Gt. Britain, N.Mex. Archeol. Council, N.Mex. Press Assn., Albuquerque Archeol. Soc. (pres. 1986—), Descs. Signers Declaration Independence, Sigma Xi, Phi Kappa Phi. Presbyterian. Co-author: Archeological Survey: 4 Corners to Ambrosia, N.Mex., 1976; A Proposed Project Design for the Timber Management Archeological Surveys, 1978; Prehistoric New Mexico, 1981, 2d edit., 1984; Ethnoarcheological Investigations of Shepherding in the Pueblo of Laguna, 1983; Author: Ancient New Mexico, 1986, The Ona and Yahgan of Tierra del Fuego, 1987, others; columnist New Mexico's Heritage, 1983-87, Glimpses of the Ancient Southwest, 1985, others. Editor: Archeological Reports, No. 1, 1975, No. 2, 1981. Address: U NMex Dept Anthropology Albuquerque NM 87131

STUART, GERARD WILLIAM, JR., bus. exec.; b. Yuba City, Calif., July 28, 1939; s. Gerard William and Geneva Bernice (Stuke) S.; student Yuba Jr. Coll., 1957-59, Chico State Coll., 1959-60; A.B., U. Calif., Davis, 1962; M.L.S., U. Calif., Berkeley, 1963; m. Lenore Frances Loroña, 1981. Rare book librarian Cornell U., 1964-68; bibliographer of scholarly collections Huntington Library, San Marino, Calif., 1968-73, head acquisitions librarian, 1973-75; sec.-treas., dir. Ravenstree Corp., 1969-80, pres., chmn. bd., 1980—; pres., chmn. bd. William Penn Ltd., 1981—. Lilly fellow Ind. U., 1963-64. Mem. Bibliog. Soc. Am., Phi Beta Kappa, Alpha Gamma Sigma, Phi Kappa Phi. Clubs: Rolls-Royce Owners; Grolier (N.Y.C.); Zamorano (Los Angeles). Home: 1472 Gateway Dr Yuma AZ 85364 Office: 2424 W 5th St Yuma AZ 85364

STUART, GILBERT EDWARD, banker; b. Gooding, Idaho, Apr. 3, 1929; s. Floyd Jack and Olivia Alice (Hurt) S.; m. Neva Marie Weathers, Apr. 2, 1955; children—Susan Alice, Mark Edward. B.A. in Econs., Coll. of Idaho, 1951; postgrad. in comml. banking Am. Inst. Banking, 1962, Pacific Coast Banking, U. Wash., 1965. Cert. comml. lender. Br. mgr. U.S. Nat. Bank, Portland, Oreg., 1956-69; v.p., head office mgr. Gt. Western Nat. Bank, Portland, 1970-74; v.p., corp. banking officer First State Bank, Portland, 1974-78; chief exec. officer Bus. Banking Corp., Beaverton, Oreg., 1979-85; chief. fin. officer Valley Nat. Bank, 1985— . chmn. bd. dirs. Pacific N.W. Trust Co. Served to 1st lt. U.S. Army, 1951-60. P.G. Batt scholar Coll. of Idaho, 1950. Mem. Am. Inst. Banking (pres. 1962-63), Oreg. Bankers Assn. Club: Kiwanis (pres. 1979—). Lodge: Elks. Home: 13550 SW 29th Ct Beaverton OR 97005 Office: Bus Banking Corp 4875 SW Griffith Beaverton OR 97005

STUART, JOHN GOODSPEED, school administrator; b. Utica, N.Y., Sept. 28, 1926; s. Donald Cameron and Gertrude (Goodspeed) S.; m. Ann Mulroy, June 23, 1951; children: John, Mary, Rosemary, Elizabeth, William. BA, Denver U., 1949; MA, Columbia U., 1952, EdD, 1954. Prin., Jefferson (Colo.) Sr. High Sch., 1960-62; supt. schs. Gunnison (Colo.) Sch. Dist. Re-1J, 1962-65, Adams County Sch. Dist. 14, Commerce City, Colo., 1965-70; assoc. sec. Am. Assn. Sch. Adminstrs., Arlington, Va., 1970-74; supt. schs. Aurora (Colo.) Pub. Schs., 1974-86. Mem. Nat. Assn. Sch. Security Dirs., NEA, Am. Assn. Sch. Adminstrs., Nat. Acad. Sch. Execs., Colo. Assn. Sch. Execs., Colo. Schoolmasters, Denver Sch. Supts. Council, Phi Delta Kappa. Episcopalian.

STUART, JOHN MICHAEL, mechanical engineer; b. Mexico, Mo., Feb. 1, 1954; s. John Leslie and Margaret Loree (Spencer) S. BS in Mech. and Aerospace Engring., U. Mo., 1977; postgrad., MIT, 1984. Cert. engr. in tng. Assoc. engr. Gen. Foods, Kankakee, Ill., 1977-78; engr. Am. Hosp. Supply Co., Irvine, Calif., 1978-82; mfg. engr. Emhart Corp., Anaheim, Calif., 1982-85; prin. engr. Smith Tool Co., Irvine, 1985-86; supr. prodn. Allergan Pharms. Co., Irvine, 1986—. Patentee in field. Pres. Laguna Owner's Assn., Laguna Hills, Calif., 1985-86. Scholar Mexico Key Club, 1972. Mem. Robotics Internat. Republican. Avocations: photography, amateur radio, outdoor activities, off road vehicles. Home: 22275 Caminito Danubo Laguna Hills CA 92653 Office: Allergan Pharms 18600 Von Karman Irvine CA 92713

STUART, MICHAEL GEORGE, lawyer; b. N.Y.C., May 24, 1951; s. George Bernard and Diana (Porikos) S.; 1 child, Jennifer. BBA, Pace U., 1973, JD, 1980. Bar: Oreg. 1981, U.S. Dist. Ct. Oreg. 1981, U.S. Tax Ct. 1981, U.S. Ct. Appeals (9th cir.) 1982; CPA, Oreg. Acct. Cambridge Instrument Inc., Ossining, N.Y., 1973-76; fin. cons. Bronxville, N.Y., 1976-78; legal asst. Frank B. Hall & Co., Briarcliff Manor, N.Y., 1978-79; supr. tax specialist Coopers & Lybrand, Portland, Oreg., 1979-81; sole practice Beaverton, Oreg., 1981—; com. mem. Atty. Realtors, Beaverton, 1986. Pres. Young Adult League, Portland, 1983-85; sec. Portland Parish Council, 1983, treas. 1984; mem. Greek Civic Club Oreg., Portland, 1982—. Mem. Washington County Bar Assn., Oreg. State Bar Assn. (tax bus. sect.), ABA (econs. of law practice sect.), Beaverton C. of C., Am. Hellenic Ednl. Progressive Assn. Democrat. Greek Orthodox. Lodge: Masons. Avocations: guitar, backpacking, woodworking, racquetball. Home: 3950 SW 102d St #72 Beaverton OR 97005 Office: 4540 SW 110th Ave Beaverton OR 97005

STUART, TRACY CLEVELAND, educator; b. Albuquerque, Oct. 2, 1941; s. Tracy Cleveland and Anita Jane (Baker) S.; m. Loretta Marie Regusa; children: Tracy Christophere, Scott Anthony. BA, Adams State Coll., 1970; M in Sci. Tchg., N.Mex. Inst. Mining and Tech., 1976. Cert. tchr., N.Mex. Tchr. Raton (N.Mex.) Pub. Schs., 1971—, chmn. sci. dept., 1976—; instr. N.Mex. State U., Raton, 1983—. Contbr. articles to sci. jours. Served with USAF, 1960-65. Mem. Am. Chem. Soc., NEA, N.Mex. Acad. Sci., N.Mex. Sci. Tchrs. Assn. (sec. 1976-78), Raton Classroom Tchrs. Assn. (2nd v.p. 1975-76). Democrat. Roman Catholic. Avocation: golfing. Office: Raton Pub Schs S 4th St Raton NM 87740

STUBBERUD, ALLEN ROGER, educator; b. Glendive, Mont., Aug. 14, 1934; s. Oscar Adolph and Alice Marie (LeBlanc) S.; m. May B. Tragus, Nov. 19, 1961; children: Peter A., Stephen C. B.S. in Elec. Engring, U. Idaho, 1956; M.S. in Engring, UCLA, 1958, Ph.D., 1962. From asst. prof. to assoc. prof. engring. UCLA, 1962-69; prof. elec. engring. U. Calif., Irvine, 1969—; assoc. dean engring. U. Calif., 1972-78, dean engring., 1978-83; chief scientist U.S. Air Force, 1983-85; bd. dirs. ECSE div. NSF. Author: Analysis and Synthesis of Linear Time Variable Systems, 1964, (with others) Feedback and Control Systems, 1967; assoc. editor: IEEE Transaction on Automatic Control. Contbr. articles to profl. jours. Recipient USAF Exceptional Civilian Service medal, 1985. Fellow IEEE (centennial medal 1984), AIAA (assoc.), AAAS; mem. Ops. Research Soc. Am., Sigma Xi, Sigma Tau, Tau Beta Pi, Eta Kappa Nu. Home: 19532 Sierra Soto Rd Irvine CA 92715 Office: U Calif Dept Elec Engring Irvine CA 92717

STUBBLEFIELD, THOMAS MASON, educator, agricultural economist; b. Taxhoma, Okla., Apr. 16, 1922; s. Temple Roscoe and Martha Lacy (Acree) S.; B.S., N.Mex., State U., 1948; M.S., A. and M. Coll. Tex., 1951, Ph.D., 1956; postgrad. U. Ariz., 1954; m. Martha Lee Miller, Mar. 7, 1943; children—Ellen (Mrs. Richard Damron), Paula (Mrs. James T. Culbertson),

Thommye (Mrs. Gary D. Zingsheim). Specialist cotton mktg. N.Mex. State U., 1948; extension economist, then asst. agrl. economist U. Ariz., Tucson, 1951-58, from assoc. prof. to prof., 1958-64, prof. and agrl. economist, 1964-83, emeritus prof., 1983—, acting asst. dir. agrl. expt. sta., 1966-68, asst. to dir. sta., 1973-74, chief party Brazil contract, 1968-70. Mem. Pima Council Aging, 1974-77, 83-87; chmn. adv. com. Ret. Sr. Vol. Program, Pima County, 1974-77, 80-87. Chmn. bd. Saguaro Home Found. Served with AUS, 1942-45. Mem. Soc. Range Mgmt. Author bulls. Home: 810 Calle Milu Tucson AZ 85706

STUBBS, CAP, marketing executive; b. Los Angeles, Jan. 30, 1936; s. Milton A. and Lillian M. (Sutton) S.; B.S. in B.A., U. So. Calif., 1957; postgrad. U. Calif., 1960-62; postgrad. Pepperdine U.; m. Nancy Shirey, Jan. 31, 1958; children: Lea Anne, David Michael. Lic. pvt. pilot. With Air Supply Co. div. Garrett Corp., Beverly Hills, Calif., 1959-60; ptnr. Arielco, Beverly Hills, Calif., 1960-62; sales mgr. Eldema Corp., El Monte, Calif., 1962-63; distbn. sales mgr./advt. mgr. Master Spltys. Co., Los Angeles, 1963-64; Western regional engring. mgr., dist. sales mgr. wire & cable div. ITT, Los Angeles, 1964-67; corp. dir. mktg. Raychem Corp., Menlo Park, Calif., 1967—; co-founder govt./industry forum on warranties Ariz. State U.; guest lectr. UCLA Grad. Sch. Bus. and Exec. Mgmt., Ariz. State U. Author: In Search of Mediocrity, 1986. Served to lt. (j.g.) USN, 1957-59. Recipient Apollo Achievement award NASA, 1969. Mem. Am. Mktg. Assn. (exec. council indsl. mktg. div.), Delta Tau Delta, Commerce Assn. U. So. Calif. Office: Raychem Corp 96 Laburnam Rd Atherton CA 94025

STUBBS, DANIEL GAIE, management consultant; b. Charleston, S.C., Nov. 13, 1940; s. Daniel Hamer and Esther Virginia (Garlow) S.; m. Sherrill Ann Sloan, July 8, 1984; children: Kimberly, Allison, Don; student U. Fla., 1959-60; B.A., W.Va. U., 1965; postgrad. Temple U., 1965-67. Tchr., Sch. Dist. of Phila., 1965-67; rep. Am. Fedn. Tchrs., Washington, 1967; exec. sec. Calif. State Coll. Council, Am. Fedn. Tchrs., AFL-CIO, Los Angeles, 1967-68; rep. Am. Fedn. Tchrs., AFL-CIO, Los Angeles, 1968-69, dir. orgn. Balt. Tchrs. Union, 1969-70; employee relations specialist Calif. Nurses Assn., Los Angeles, 1971-72; exec. dir. United Nurses Assn. Calif., Los Angeles, 1972-74; labor relations cons. Social Services Union, Service Employees Internat. Union, Local 535, AFL-CIO, Los Angeles, 1974-76; exec. dir. Met. Riverside UniServ Unit, Calif. Tchrs. Assn., 1976-79, exec. dir. San Bernardino/Colton Uniserv Unit, 1979-80; gen. services adminstr. Housing Authority, City of Los Angeles, 1980-82; cons. Blanning & Baker Assocs., Tujunga, Calif., 1983-84; asst. exec. dir. adminstrv. services Los Angeles Housing Authority, 1984-86; mgmt. con., Los Angeles, 1986—, pres. Esquire Mgmt. Services Inc., 1986—; lectr. in field. Served with U.S. Army, 1961-62. Recipient W.Va. U. Waitman Barbe Prize for creative writing, 1965. Mem. So. Calif. Indsl. Relations Research Assn., Orange County Indsl. Relations Research Assn., Indsl. Relations Research Assn., UCLA Inst. Indsl Relations Assn., Soc. of Profls. in Dispute Resolution. Presbyterian. Club: Town Hall of Calif. Home: 3200 Fairesta St #11 La Crescenta CA 91214

STUDARUS, PHILIP GLENN, internat. fin. cons.; b. San Francisco, June 3, 1944; s. Glenn W. and Ruth E. (Robinson) S.; B.A., Am. U. Beirut, 1966; M.B.A., U. Oreg., 1970; m. Tahere Abharroudi, Feb. 8, 1969; children—John Philip, James Joseph. Sr. auditor Price Waterhouse & Co., San Jose, Calif., 1971-74; asst. controller Triad Holding Corp., Beirut, 1974-75; chief fin. officer Triad Internat. Mktg. Group, London and Paris, 1976-81; internat. fin. cons., San Francisco, 1981—; underwriting mem. Lloyds of London, 1981—. C.P.A., Calif. Mem. Am. Inst. C.P.A.s, Calif. Soc. C.P.A.s. Home: 25 Van Tassel Lane Orinda CA 94563

STUDLEY, HELEN ORMSON, artist, poet, writer, designer; b. Elroy, Wis., Sept. 8, 1937; d. Clarence Ormson and Hilda (Johnson) O.; m. William Frank Studley, Aug. 1965 (div.); 1 son, William Harrison. Owner RJK Original Art, Sherman Oaks, Calif., 1979—; designer Aspen Series custom greeting cards and stationery notes, lithographs Love is All Colors, 1982; represented in numerous pub. and pvt. collections throughout U.S., Can., Norway, Sweden, Austria, Germany, Eng., France. Active Luth. Brotherhood, Emmlanuel Luth. Ch. Honors include display of lithograph Snow Dreams, Snow Queens at 1980 Winter Olympics, Lake Placid, N.Y., lithograph Summer Dreams, Summer Queens at 1984 Summer Olympics, Los Angeles; named finalist in competition for John Simon Guggenheim fellowship. Mem. Soc. Illustrators, Am. Watercolor Soc., Internat. Soc. Artists, Internat. Platform Assn., Calif. Woman's Art Guild. Club: Sons of Norway. Office: RJK Original Art 5020 Hazeltine Ave Sherman Oaks CA 91423

STUECKLE, DONALD NORMAN, interior designer; b. Whitman County, Wash., Oct. 6, 1929; s. Arthur and Mary (Walters) S.; m. Wilma Merle Divine, Apr. 24, 1954; children—Shannon, Tamera, Megan. B.A., Wash. State U., 1952. Interior designer Barclay Brown Co., Spokane, Wash., 1952-55; ptnr. Larson & Assocs., Spokane, 1955-59; interior designer Paul Schatz Co., Portland, Oreg., 1959-63, Velte Home Furnishings Co., Vancouver, Wash., 1963-66; co-owner, mgr. Designed Interiors, Inc., Portland, 1966-86; ptnr. New Market South Partnership, 1982-83; instr. Mt. Hood Community Coll., 1972-73. Arbitrator Am. Arbitration Assn., 1978, pres. Skidmore Fountain Village Assn., 1975; chmn. bd. Community Design Ctr., 1977; mem. Portland Hist. Landmark Commn., 1976-83; bd. dirs. Portland Beautification Assn., 1970-86. Named Disting. Alumnus, Wash. State U., 1978; recipient Urban Devel. Action Grant Excellence award, 1981. Mem. Am. Soc. Interior Designers (dir. Oreg. chpt. 1960—, pres. chpt. 1962-63, 1978-79, v.p. No. Pacific region 1982-83, nat. bd. dirs. 1981-84, nat. chmn. and innovator, chief exec. officer program 1983), outstanding contbr. in community service award 1974, presdl. citation 1974), Council Continuing Edn. Republican. Office: 79 SW First St Portland OR 97204

STULBERG, NEAL HOWARD, conductor, pianist; b. Detroit, Apr. 12, 1954; s. Samuel and Judith (Victor) S. B.A. magna cum laude, Harvard Coll., 1976; M.Mus., U. Mich., 1978; postgrad., Juilliard Sch. Music, 1979-80. Condr. MIT Symphony Orch., Cambridge, 1980-82, Young Musicians Found. Debut Orch., Los Angeles, 1981-84; Exxon Arts Endowment asst. condr. Los Angeles Philharm. Orch., 1983-85; music dir., condr. N.Mex. Symphony Orch., 1985—. Recipient 2d prize Balt. Symphony Orch. Young Condrs. Competition, 1980; Henry Russell Shaw fellow, 1976-77. Office: New Mexico Symphony Orchestra PO Box 769 Albuquerque NM 87103

STUMBLES, JAMES RUBIDGE WASHINGTON, multinational company executive; b. Salisbury, Zimbabwe, Aug. 13, 1939; came to U.S., 1980; s. Albert R.W. and Mary Dallas (Atherstone) S.; m. Vyvienne Clare Shaw, Dec. 19, 1964; children: Christopher, Timothy, Jonathan. BA, U. Cape Town, Republic of South Africa, 1960, LLB, 1962. Adv. Supreme Ct. of S. Africa. Mng. dir. Pritchard Services Group of South Africa, Johannesburg, 1972-80; dir. security, pres. subs. security cos. Pritchard Services Group Am., Columbus, Ohio, 1980-83; sr. v.p., pres. subs. Mayne Nickless/ Loomis Corp., Seattle, 1984—. Sec. Boy Scouts, Johannesburg, 1978-80. Episcopalian. Clubs: Rand (Johannesburg), Mercer Island (Wash.) Country. Lodges: Rotary, Kiwanis, Round Table (officer 1969-80). Avocations: tennis, boating, fishing. Office: Mayne Nickless Inc 720 Olive Way #625 Seattle WA 98101

STUMP, BOB, Congressman; b. Phoenix, Apr. 4, 1927; s. Jesse Patrick and Floy Bethany (Fields) S.; children: Karen, Bob, Bruce. B.S. in Agronomy, Ariz. State U., 1951. Mem. Ariz. Ho. of Reps., 1957-67; mem. Ariz. Senate, 1967-76, pres., 1975-76; mem. 95th-100th Congresses from 3d Ariz. Dist., 1976—. Active Com. for Survival of Free Congress, Citizens Com. for Right to Keep and Bear Arms. Served with USN, 1943-46. Mem. Am. Legion, Ariz. Farm Bur., Gun Owners Am. Democrat. Seventh-day Adventist. Office: 211 Cannon House Office Bldg Washington DC 20515 *

STUMP, CARY JOHANSON, construction manager, educator; b. Glendale, Calif., July 22, 1948; s. John Philip and Christine (Laubach) S.; m. Viola Johanson, Apr. 5, 1975; children: Jason, Alexander. BA, Pomona Coll., 1970; MArch, U. Minn., 1979. Constrn. mgr. Place Makers, St. Paul, 1976-80, M.H. Golden Co., San Diego, 1980—; instr. San Diego State U., 1983—. Constrn. Commonweatlh Bank Bldg., 1982, Rio Vista Bldg., 1984 (orchid award 1984), West Tower of Plaza at La Jolla (Calif.) Village, 1986 (Gold Nugget award 1986), Magnetic Resonance Imaging Ctr. at Sharp Meml. Hosp., 1986, East Tower of Plaza at La Jolla Village, 1987. Mem. Project Mgmt. Inst., Mensa. Avocation: photography. Home: 1103 Alberta Pl San Diego CA 92103 Office: M H Golden Co 123 Camino de la Reina San Diego CA 92108

STUMP, D. MICHAEL, librarian; b. Santa Monica, Calif., Dec. 22, 1947; s. H. Walter and Margaret June (Stetler) S. B.A. in History, Pasadena Coll., 1971; M.L.S., U. So. Calif., 1977. Library asst. Calif. Inst. Tech., Pasadena, Calif., 1970-74; librarian First Baptist Ch. of Van Nuys, Calif., 1974-81, 1982—, Laurence/2000, Van Nuys, 1981-82; Van Nuys Christian Coll., 1975-76. Asst. scoutmaster San Fernando council Boy Scouts Am., 1970-73. Named to Outstanding Young Men Am. U.S. Jaycees, 1976. Mem. Spl. Libraries Assn., Evang. Ch. Library Assn. (So. Calif. chpt.). Republican. Baptist. Office: First Baptist Ch Van Nuys 14800 Sherman Way Van Nuys CA 91405

STURDEVANT, BRUCE LAYTON, mech. engr.; b. What Cheer, Ia., Dec. 5, 1922; s. Louis A. and Ethel (Phillips) S.; B.S., U. Ia., 1948; m. Helen L. Clevenger, Apr. 17, 1943; children—Celeste, Christine, Constell. With Stanley Engring. Co., Muscatine, 1948-69, successively engr.-in-tng., design engr., asst. chief coordinating engr., chief coordinating engr., asst. chief mech. engr., head mech. dept., head power dept., head design group, head indsl. dept., 1948-65, head power and indsl. group, v.p., 1965-66, head power group, 1966-69; dir. Stanley Consultants, Inc., 1966-69; asst. mgr. Central Design Office, R.W. Beck & Assos., Denver, 1969-70, asso., asst. mgr., 1970-71, partner, asst. mgr., 1971-76, partner, mgr., 1976—, mem. exec. com., 1978-85. Chmn. budget and admissions com. United Fund, 1963, 64, pres., 1966, 67, bd. dirs.; mem. adv. com. tech. curriculum devel. Muscatine Community Coll., 1962; v.p., dir. Ia. Children's and Family Services. Bd. dirs. Douglas County Sch. Dist., 1975, 78. Trustee Hillcrest Services to Children and Youth. Served from cadet to 2d lt. USAAC, 1943-46. Registered profl. engr., Colo. Mem. Nat. Rifle Assn. (life), Am. Mgmt. Assn., ASME, Nat. Soc. Profl. Engrs., ASTM, Iowa Engring. Soc. (chmn. constrn.-industry relations com. 1963, 64). Methodist (lay del. to ann. conf. 1956-69, chmn. adminstrv. bd. 1971, 73, chmn. pastor parish relations 1974, 75, chmn. fin. com. 1979, 80). Mason. Author articles in field. Home: 505 Wrangler Rd NEDC Castle Rock CO 80104 Office: RW Beck & Assos 660 Bannock Denver CO 80204

STURGES, STANLEY G., administrative psychiatrist; b. Ngoma, Zaire, Oct. 14, 1929; (parents Am. citizens); s. John Hubert and Violet Katherine (Floding) S.; m. Raylene Ethel Duncan, July 26, 1953; children—Cheri, Stanley, James, Charlene, Mark. B.A. in Biology, Pacific Union Coll., 1951; M.D., Loma Linda U., 1955. Diplomate Am. Bd. Psychiatry and Neurology. Resident in psychiatry Menninger Sch. Psychiatry, Topeka, 1964-66; med. dir. Scheer Meml. Hosp., Banepa, Nepal, 1957-62; med. dir. psychiatry Kettering Med. Ctr., Dayton, Ohio, 1970-82; dir. psychiatry St. Vincent Hosp., Portland, 1983—; assoc. clin. prof. Wright State U. Sch. Medicine, Dayton, 1977-82. Author: In the Valley of Seven Cities, 1965. Recipient Ten Oustanding Young Men award Jr. C. of C., 1961. Mem. Am. Psychiat. Assn., AMA. Republican. Seventh Day Adventist. Home: 2411 Saddle Ct West Linn OR 97068 Office: St Vincent Hosp and Med Ctr 9205 SW Barnes Rd Portland OR 97225

STURGULEWSKI, ARLISS, state senator; b. Blaine, Wash., Sept. 27, 1927; B.A., U. Wash. Mem. Assembly Municipality of Anchorage; vice chmn. New Capital Site Planning Commn., mem. Capital Site Selection Com.; chmn. Greater Anchorage Area Planning and Zoning Commn.; mem. Alaska State Senate, 1978—; dir. Denali Drilling, Inc. Address: 1024 W Sixth Ste 304 Anchorage AK 99501

STURMAN, EUGENE GOCH, painter, sculptor, educator; b. N.Y.C., Jan. 28, 1945; s. Eugene John and Frances Marie (Goch) S. BFA, Alfred (N.Y.) U., 1967; MFA, U. N.Mex., 1969; postgrad., Tamarind Lithograph Workshop, 1970. Instr. printmaking Long Beach (Calif.) State U., 1972-74; lectr. printmaking, painting, drawing U Calif., Los Angeles, 1974—, Otis-Parson Sch. of Design, Los Angeles, 1984—; represented by Koplin Gallery, Santa Monica, Calif. Exhibited in group shows at LA Six, 1974, Los Angeles County Mus., 1974, 82, (New Talent award 1974), 24 from Los Angeles, Barnsdall Munic Gallery, Los Angeles, 1974, Basle (Switzerland) Art Fair, 1974, 75, Whitney Mus. Art Biennial, 1975, Chgo. Art Fair, 1982. Recipient Michael Levins award Alfred U., 1966, Sculpture award NEA, 1986; Nat. Endowment Arts grantee, 1975. Home and Office: 190 Loma Metisse Malibu CA 90265

STUSSY, NORRIS A., library director. Multi-state library network dir. Western Library Network, Olympia. Office: Western Library Network AJ-11W Olympia WA 98504-0111

STUTZMAN, THOMAS CHASE, lawyer; b. Portland, Oreg., Aug. 1, 1950; s. Leon H. and Mary L. (Chase) S.; B.S. with high honors, U. Calif., Santa Barbara, 1972; J.D. cum laude, Santa Clara U., 1975; m. Wendy Jeanne Craig, June 6, 1976; children: Sarah Ann, Thomas Chase. Bar: Calif. 1976; individual practice law, San Jose, Calif., 1976-79; pres., sec., chief fin. officer Thomas Chase Stutzman, P.C., San Jose, 1979—; legal counsel, asst. sec. Robt. A. Greenley, O.D. and Charles P. Wolf, O.D., Inc., 1978—, Leon H. Stutzman & Assocs. Phys. Therapy, Inc., 1978—; legal counsel, asst. sec. Marina Assocs. Inc., Meadows Graphic Arts Inc., Pacific Internat. Trade Corp., Midnight Fraction Mine Inc., C. Harrington Enterprises Inc., Santa Teresa Fin. Services, Forbord Enterprises, S&SK Packaging Inc., Trans Pacific Profl. Investment Services Inc., GHA Imports Inc., numerous others; instr. San Jose State U., 1977-78. Bd. dirs. Santa Cruz Campfire, 1978-80, Happy Hollow Park, 1978-80, 83—. Mem. Calif. Bar Assn., Santa Clara County Bar Assn. (chmn. environ. law com. 1976-78), San Jose Jaycees (Dir. of the Year 1976-77), Phi Beta Kappa. Congregationalist. Lodges: Lions (dir. 1979-81, 2d v.p. 1982-83, 1st v.p. 1983-84, pres. 1984-85), Masons, Scottish Rite. Office: 1625 The Alameda Suite 309 San Jose CA 95126

STYNE, DENNIS MICHAEL, physician; b. Chgo., July 31, 1947; s. Irving and Bernice (Coopersmith) S.; m. Donna Petre, Sept. 5, 1971; children: Rachel, Jonathan. BS, Northwestern U., 1969, MD, 1971. Intern in pediatrics U. Calif., San Diego, 1971-72, resident in pediatrics, 1972-73; resident in pediatrics Yale U., New Haven, 1973-74; fellow in pediatric endocrinology U. Calif., San Francisco, 1974-77, asst. prof. pediatrics, 1977-83; assoc. prof. U. Calif., Davis, 1983—. Author numerous book chpts., contbr. articles to profl. jours. Mem. Endocrine Soc., Soc. Pediatric Research, Lawson Wilkins Soc. for Pediatric Endocrinology. Avocations: sailing, music. Office: U Calif Dept Pediatrics Davis CA 95616

STYSKAL-O'KEEFE, LUKI, financial consulting firm executive; b. Los Angeles, June 7, 1937; d. Ladislav Jakup and Lucia Marie (Matulich) Styskal; children by previous marriage—Thomas Lad, Jerome David, Tricia Marie. B.S. in Mktg., Loyola-Marymount U., Los Angeles, 1959. Registered securities prin. Nat. Assn. Securities Dealers. Vice pres. mktg. Burlingame Mortgage Investors, Tustin, Calif., 1980-83; pres. Investors Equity Council, Inc., Tustin, 1983-84; regional v.p. Diversified Properties Inc., 1984-85; owner Luki S. O'Keefe & Assocs.; dir. San Clemente (Calif.) Sav. & Loan, 1978-84. Pres. Children's Home Soc., San Clemente, 1972-74; chmn. Council Mem. Election Com., San Clemente, 1966-78; chmn. pro-tem Orange County Grand Jury, 1978-79. Mem. Western Pension Conf., Internat. Assn. Fin. Planners.

SUAREZ, ORLANDO GOMEZ, management executive; b. Havana, Cuba, Oct. 20, 1930; s. Francisco and Virginia Suarez G.; m. Cristiana Maria Vazquez, Aug. 23, 1964 (div. Aug. 1978); children: Glenn, Orlando Jr., Regina. BS in Bus. Adminstrn., Ind. U., 1952; postgrad., Harvard U., 1970. Auditor Peat, Marwick & Mitchell, N.Y.C., 1960-63; chief fin. officer Philip Morris, Buenos Aires, 1966-75; group chief fin. officer Warner-Lambert, Barcelona, Spain, 1975-79; port dir. City of Port Everglades, Fla., 1980; v.p. Revlon Corp., Sao Paulo, Brazil, 1980-82, CooperVision, Menlo Park, Calif., 1983—. Mem. Fin. Execs. Inst., Harvard U. Alumni Assn. Roman Catholic. Office: CooperVision Inc 75 Willow Rd Menlo Park CA 94025

SUBLETTE, SALLIE ELLEN, social worker; b. Washington, June 5, 1947; d. William Ezra and Bernice (Felton) Bowers. BS in Edn., Concord Coll., 1969; MSW, W.Va. U., 1975. Cert. social worker. Tchr. W.Va. State Sch. System, various, 1969-73; mental health specialist Community Mental Health Ctr., Huntington, W.Va., 1976-78; statewide health and welfare trainer Idaho State U., Pocatello, Idaho, 1978-81; asst. prof. social work Idaho State U., Pocatello, 1981-85; creative arts therapist Aspen Crest Hosp., Pocatello, 1984-85, pvt. practice as clin. social worker, 1985—; pvt. cons. and trainer, 1979—; dir., social work program Idaho State U., 1982-83. Facilitator Parents United, Pocatello, 1983-84; crisis intervention vol. Women's Advocates, Pocatello, 1980-85. Mem. Nat. Assn. Social Workers (state exec. bd. 1980-81, 84-86, southeast Idaho pres. 1984-86), Acad. Cert. Social Workers, Am. Art Therapy Assn. Democrat. Avocations: music, hiking, camping, cross-country skiing. Home: 4865 Kim Dr Pocatello ID 83204 Office: Aspen Crest Hosp 155 S 2d Ave Pocatello ID 83201

SUBRAMANIAN, CHITTOOR VISWANATHAN, research civil engineer; b. Kozhikode, India, May 21, 1939; came to U.S., 1968; s. Chittoor Subramanian and Rajam Viswanathan; m. Jayalakshmi, May 19, 1964; 1 child, Lakshmi Subramanian. BS, Benares (India) Hindu U., 1961; MS, U. Calif., Davis, 1969, PhD, 1972. Registered civil engr., Calif. Asst. project engr. IIS Co., Kulti, India, 1961-68; cons. Nuclear Services Corp., Campbell, Calif., 1972-76; mgr. Gen. Elec. Co., San Jose, Calif., 1976-83; project leader Sandia Nat. Labs., Albuquerque, 1983—. Contbr. articles to profl. jours. Mem. ASCE (dynamic analysis com., nuclear standards working group), Structural Engrs. Assn. No. Calif. Hindu. Avocations: tennis, bridge, gardening, reading. Office: Sandia Nab Labs 6311 PO Box 5800 Albuquerque NM 87111

SUBRAMANIAN, RAMASWAMY, research chemist; b. Nagapattinam, Tamilnadu, India, Apr. 20, 1953; came to U.S., 1981; s. Ramaswamy Iyer and Sampoornam Subramanian; m. Linda Fay Van Arsdale; children: Gail Ann, Marla Fay, Kelly Sue. BS, St. Joseph's Coll., Trichy, India, 1973, MS, 1975; PhD, U. Madras, India, 1980. Asst. prof. phys. chemistry Am. Coll., Madurai, Tamilnadu, India, 1980-81; research assoc. U. Notre Dame, Ind., 1981-85; postdoctoral scholar U. Calif., Davis, 1985—. Contbr. articles to profl. jours. Mem. Am. Chem. Soc., Am. Soc. Photobiology, N.Y. Acad. Scis., AAAS, Interam. Photochem. Soc., Am. Inst. Biol. Scis. Avocation: travel. Home: 520 Alvarado Ave Apt #103 Davis CA 95616 Office: U Calif-Davis Davis CA 95616

SUBRAMANIAN, SUNDARAM, electronics engineer; b. Emaneswaram, Madras, India, July 9, 1934; came to U.S., 1968; s. Sundaram and Velammal (Subbiah) S.; m. Hemavathy Vadivelu, Feb. 18, 1968; children: Anand Kumar, Malathy. BE, Madras (India) U., 1959; PhD, Glasgow (Scotland) U., 1967; MBA, Roosevelt U., Chgo., 1977. Research engr. Zenith, Inc., Chgo., 1968-75; project engr. Motorola, Inc., Chgo., 1975-77; prof. Chapman Coll., Orange, Calif., 1977-78; cons. MCS, Orange, 1978-80; project engr. Endevco, San Juan Capistrano, Calif., 1980-84; project mgr. Unisys Corp., Rancho Santa Margarita, Calif., 1984—; bd. dirs. P.S.B. Inc., Torrance, Calif., 1984—. Patentee in field. Bd. dirs. Tamil Nadu Found. Inc., Balt. and Washington, 1976-79; pres. S. India Cultural Assn., Villa Park, Calif., 1977-78. Mem. IEEE, Inst. Environ. Sci. (sr.). Avocations: internat. travelling, Vedantic research. Office: Unisys Corp 30200 Bandaras Ranco Santa Margarita CA 92688

SUBRAMANYA, SHIVA, aerospace systems engineer; b. Hole-Narasipur, India, Apr. 8, 1933; s. S.T. Srikantaiah and S. Gundamma; m. Lee. S. Silva, Mar. 3, 1967; children: Paul Kailas, Kevin Shankar. BSc, Mysore U., Bangalore, India, 1956; MSc, Karnatak U., Dharwar, India, 1962; postgrad., Clark U., 1963; MBA, Calif. State U., Dominguez Hills, 1973; D in Bus. Adminstrn., PhD in Bus. Adminstrn., Nova U., 1986. Sr. scientific officer AEC, Bombay, India, 1961-63; chief engr. TEI, Newport, R.I., 1964-67; prin. engr. Gen. Dynamics Corp., San Diego, 1967-73; asst. project mgr. TRW Def. Systems Group, Colorado Springs, Colo., 1973—. Contbr. over 100 articles to profl. jours. V.p. VHP of Am., Berlin, Conn., 1984-87; pres. IPF of Am., Redondo Beach, 1981-86; appointed to Atomic Energy Commn., India. Mem. Armed Forces Communications and Electronics Assn. (v.p.-elect Rocky Mountain chpt. 1986—, Meritorious service award 1985). Hindu. Avocation: social service. Home: 65 Polo Pony Dr Colorado Springs CO 80906 Office: TRW Def Systems Group 1555 N Newport Rd Colorado Springs CO 80916

SUCCAR, JORGE K., food products research engineer; b. Lima, Peru, June 1, 1949; came to U.S., 1978; s. Jorge and Georgina (Knudsen) S.; m. Michele V. Maier, Dec. 8, 1985. BS, Agrarian U., Lima, 1974, degree in engring., 1976; MS, Rutgers U., 1980, PhD, 1984. Prin. researcher Dept. Food Tech. and Agrl. Products, Lima, 1974-76; food products engr. Ministry of Industry, Lima, 1976-78; project analyst Ministry of Agriculture, Lima, 1977-78; researcher Rutgers U., New Brunswick, N.J., 1979-84; engr. Beatrice Hunt-Wesson Inc., Fullerton, Calif., 1984—; cons. internat. agrl. food program, 1984. Contbr. articles to profl. jours. Mem. AAAS, ASHRAE (reviewer Jour. Food Sci. Publs., com. mem.), Inst. Food Technologists (AMFAC Nat. fellow 1981, Nestle Nat. fellow 1982), Sigma Xi, Phi Tau Sigma. Avocations: track and field, discus throwing, guitar. Office: Beatrice Hunt Wesson Foods 1645 W Valencia Dr Fullerton CA 92634

SUDER, JOHN MICHAEL, TV director; b. Phila., Nov. 14, 1948; s. Michale Paul and Rose Marie (Jaworski) S.; m. Maureen Danca, May 19, 1973 (div. 1981); 1 child, Laura Rose; m. Carol Ann Lainio, Feb. 19, 1983. BS, Syracuse U., 1970. Account exec. Petry TV, N.Y.C., 1971-72, Peters, Griffin & Woodward, N.Y.C., 1972-73; nat. sales mgr. Sta. WTOG-TV, N.Y.C., 1973-77; gen. sales mgr. Sta. WTOG-TV, Tampa and St. Petersburg, Fla., 1977-81; dir. mktg. Tribune Broadcasting Co., Chgo., 1981-83; v.p., gen. mgr. Sta. KWGN-TV, Denver, 1983—; bd. dirs. Denver Ptnrship., Denver Civic Ventures. Mem. adv. bd. YMCA, Denver, 1985—; mem. Chem. People Blue Ribbon Com., Denver, 1984. Recipient Media award Chic Chicana Youth Group, 1983, Youth award Joint Effort, 1985, Bobby Wilkerson Community award Success Services Inc., Denver, 1984. Mem. U.S. Congrl. Adv. Bd., Nat. Assn. Broadcasters, Colo. Broadcasters Assn., TV Bur., Ind. TV Stas., Denver C. of C., Denver Advt. Fedn. Republican. Roman Catholic. Clubs: Metropolitan, Columbine Court, Brown Palace (Denver). Home: 7765 S Madison Circle Littleton CO 80122 Office: Sta KWGN TV 6160 S Wabash Englewood CO 80111

SUDLER, BARBARA WELCH, historical society administrator; b. Honolulu, Apr. 20, 1925; d. Leo F. and Barbara Lloyd (Petrikin) Welch; m. James Stewart Sudler, Dec. 30, 1950 (dec. 1982); children—Eleanor, James S.; m. William H. Hornby, Oct. 22, 1983. B.A., U. Colo., 1944. Exec. adminstr. Historic Denver, 1974-79; exec. dir. Colo. Hist. Soc., Denver, 1979-81, pres., 1981—; historic preservation officer State of Colo., Denver, 1983—; dir. Women's Bank, Denver. Editor: Nothing Is Long Ago, 1975. Bd. dirs. Denver Symphony Assn., 1983—, Met. State Coll. Found. Recipient Soroptomist award, 1980, Contbn. to Arts award Big Sisters, 1981, Contbns. to Community award AIA, 1982, Community Service award U. Colo., 1986. Mem. Am. Antiquarian Soc., Nat. Conf. State Historic Preservation Officers, Colo. Hist. Records Commn. (coordinator), Colo. Commn. on Bicentennial of Constitution, Martin Luther King Jr. Holiday Commn. Republican. Episcopalian. Clubs: Denver Country, University. Home: 180 High St Denver CO 80218 Office: Colo Hist Soc 1300 Broadway St Denver CO 80203

SUE, LAWRENCE GENE, statistician; b. Portland, Oreg., Sept. 22, 1939; s. Henry Lock Sue and Dorothy Helen (Wong) Chung. BS in Math., Brigham Young U., 1967, MS in Statistics, 1973. Assoc. engr. Boeing Co., Seattle, 1967-69; math. statistician Ultrasystems Inc., Hill AFB, Utah, 1974-77; mem. tech. staff TRW Systems, Hill AFB, 1977-81; sr. staff engr. Motorola Inc., Phoenix, 1981-84, mgr. engring., 1984-85, statis. engr., 1985—; statis. cons. Motorola Semiconductor Research and Devel. Lab., Phoenix, 1985—; instr. Rio Salado Community Coll., Phoenix, 1984—, Brigham Young U. Extension, Salt Lake City, 1975-81, Highline Coll., Midway, Wash., 1967-69. Single adult adminstr. Ch. Jesus Christ Latter-day Saints, Salt Lake City, 1973-81; voting del. Salt Lake County Rep. Conv., 1973. Mem. Am. Statis. Assn. (2d v.p. Utah chpt.), Am. Soc. Quality Control (cert. quality engr.), Sigma Xi. Avocations: ham radio, tour bus driver, sound reproduction. Home: 2308 W Sagebrush Dr Chandler AZ 85224

SUENRAM, BRUCE WILLIAM, protectice services official; b. Lakeport, Calif., Nov. 25, 1950; s. Beverly Bernice Suenram; m. Karen Marie Stout, Jan. 21, 1984; children: Sara Elizabeth, Kathleen Marie. BA in Biol. Scis.,

Calif. State Coll., 1973. Fire chief Kelseyville (Calif.) Fire Sta., 1974-80, Missoula (Mont.) Rural, 1980—; Instr. Mont. Fire Services Tng. Sch., Coll. of Great Falls, Missoula Vocat. Tech. Ctr., No. Regional Tng. Ctr. Contbr. articles to profl. jours. Adv. bd. mem. 911; mem. Disaster Planning Steering Com., Missoula Symphony Assn.; deputy dir. Disaster and Emergency Services. Mem. Missoula County Fire Protection Assn., Mont. State Fire Services Tng. Sch. (mem. Master Planning Task Force, mem. adv. bd.), Mont. Fire Chiefs Assn., Western Fire Chiefs Assn., Internat. Fire Chiefs Assn., Internat. Soc. Fire Service Instrs., Nat. Fire Protection Assn. (mem. Fire Service sect.). Avocations: camping, hunting, fishing. Office: Missoula Rural Fire Dist 2521 S Ave W Missoula MT 59801

SUGARMAN, MYRON GEORGE, lawyer; b. San Francisco, Nov. 7, 1942; s. Irving Garden and Jane Hortense (Weingarten) S.; m. Cheryl Ann Struble, June 8, 1968; children: Andrew, Amy, Adam. BS, U. Calif., Berkeley, 1964, JD, 1967. Judge advocate gen. U.S. Army, Washington, 1968-71; assoc. Cooley, Godward, Castro, Huddleson & Tatum, San Francisco, 1972-77, ptnr., 1977—. Served to capt. U.S. Army, 1968-71. Fellow Am. Coll. Probate Counsel; mem. U. Calif. Alumni Council (councilor), San Francisco Grid Club. Avocations: skiing, tennis. Home: 3807 Palo Alto Dr Lafayette CA 94549 Office: Cooley Godward Castro et al 1 Maritime Plaza San Francisco CA 94111

SUGIHARA, THOMAS TAMOTSU, scientist, administrator; b. Las Animas, Colo., June 14, 1924; s. William Bansaku and Takeyo (Kubota) S.; m. Fumi Anraku, Mar. 15, 1952; children—Sara Toshi, Edna Michi. A.B., Kalamazoo Coll., 1945; S.M., U. Chgo., 1951, Ph.D., 1952. Research asso. chemistry Mass. Inst. Tech., 1952-53; mem. faculty Clark U., 1953-67, prof. chemistry, 1962-67, chmn. dept., 1963-67; prof. chemistry Tex. A&M U., 1967-81; dir. Cyclotron Inst., 1971-78, dean of sci., 1978-81; prof. chemistry Oreg. State U., Corvallis, 1981-86; dean sci. Oreg. State U., 1981-86; dep. assoc. dir. for research, chemistry and materials sci. Lawrence Livermore Nat. Lab., 1986—; assoc. geochemistry Woods Hole Oceanographic Instn., 1954-70; vis. scientist Lawrence Radiation Lab., Berkeley, Calif., summer 1964, Brookhaven Nat. Lab., Upton, N.Y., summer 1965, Oak Ridge Nat. Lab., 1977. Contbr. articles on nuclear chemistry, nuclear physics, geochemistry, analytical chemistry to tech. jours. Served with AUS, 1945-46. Guggenheim fellow, 1961-62. Fellow AAAS, Am. Phys. Soc.; mem. Am. Chem. Soc., Sigma Xi, Delta Kappa Epsilon, Phi Beta Kappa. Office: Chemistry and Materials Sci Lawrence Livermore Lab Livermore CA 94550

SUH, BO YOUNG, physician, researcher; b. Pusan, Republic of Korea, Jan. 28, 1948; came to U.S., 1976; s. Jong D. and Doo S. (Lee) S.; children: Angela, Daniel. BS, Pusan Nat. Premedical Sch., 1969; MD, Pusan Nat. Medical Sch., 1973. Physician Army, Republic of Korea, 1973-76; resident in ob-gyn Bklyn. Hosp., 1978-79, Mt. Sinai Hosp., Hartford, Conn., 1979-82; practice medicine specializing in ob-gyn Portsmouth, R.I., 1982-83; research fellow U. Calif., San Diego, 1983-85; asst. prof. ob-gyn U. Colo., Denver, 1986—. Contbr. articles to profl. jours. Served to capt. 8th div. Korean Army, 1973-76. Mem. Am. Coll. Ob-gyn (assoc.). Office: U Colo Dept Ob-Gyn 4200 E 9th Ave Denver CO 80262

SUINN, RICHARD MICHAEL, psychologist; b. Honolulu, May 8, 1933; s. Maurice and Edith (Wong) S.; m. Grace D. Toy, July 26, 1958; children: Susan, Randall, Staci, Bradley. Student, U. Hawaii, 1951-53; B.A. summa cum laude, Ohio State U., 1955; MA in Clin. Psychology, Stanford U., 1957, PhD in Clin. Psychology, 1959. Lic. psychologist, Colo. Counselor Stanford U., 1958-59; research assoc. Stanford U. Med. Sch., 1964-66; asst. prof. psychology Whitman Coll., 1959-64; assoc. prof. U. Hawaii, 1966-68; prof. Colo. State U., 1968—, head dept. psychology, 1973—; cons. in field; psychologist U.S. Ski Teams, 1976 Olympic Games, U.S. Women's Track and Field, 1980 Olympic games; mem. sports psychology adv. com. U.S. Olympic Com., 1983—; mem. Colo. Bd. Psychologist Examiners, 1984-86; reviewer NIMH, 1977-80. Author: The Predictive Validity of Projective Measures, 1969, Fundamentals of Behavior Pathology, 1970, The Innovative Psychological Therapies, 1975, The Innovative Medical-Psychiatric Therapies, 1976, Psychology in Sport: Methods and Applications, 1980, Fundamentals of Abnormal Psychology, 1984, Seven Steps to Peak Performance, 1986; editorial bd.: Jour. Cons. and Clin. Psychology, 1973-86, Jour. Counseling Psychology, 1974—, Behavior Therapy, 1977-80, Behavior Modification, 1977-78, Jour. Behavioral Medicine, 1978—, Behavior Counseling Quar, 1979-83, Jour. Sports Psychology, 1980—; author: tests Math. Anxiety Rating Scale. Mem. City Council, Ft. Collins, 1975-79, mayor, 1978-79; mem. Gov.'s Mental Health Adv. Council, 1983, Colo. Bd. Psychologist Examiners, 1983-86. Recipient cert. merit U.S. Ski Team, 1976; NIMH grantee, 1963-64; Office Edn. grantee, 1970-71. Fellow Am. Psychol. Assn. (bd. ethnic minority affairs 1981-83, chmn. 1982-83, mem. edn. and tng. bd. 1985—, chmn. 1986, 87), Behavior Therapy and Research Soc. (charter); mem. Assn. Advancement Psychology (trustee 1983-86), Assn. Advancement Behavior Therapy, (sec.-treas. 1986—), Asian Am. Psychol. Assn. (bd. dirs. 1983—), sec. treas. 1986-88), Phi Beta Kappa, Sigma Xi. Home: 808 Cheyenne Dr Fort Collins CO 80525 Office: Dept Psychology Colo State U Fort Collins CO 80523

SUKONECK, HARRIET, psychologist, computer scientist; b. Newark, Jan. 30, 1945; d. Edward and Mae S.; B.A., Rutgers U., 1966; M.A., U. So. Calif., 1968, Ph.D. (NIMH fellow), 1971. NIMH clin. postdoctoral fellow, div. psychiatry Children's Hosp. of Los Angeles, 1971-73; lectr. Calif. State U., Los Angeles, 1971-76; core faculty research series Calif. Sch. Profl. Psychology, Los Angeles, 1973-78, clin. psychologist in pvt. practice, Santa Monica, Calif., 1973-78; vis. asst. prof. Loyola Marymount U., Los Angeles, 1976-78; research assoc. Neuropsychiat. Inst., UCLA, 1978-79, adminstrv. analyst office of vice chancellor UCLA, 1979; sr. mem. tech. staff, project leader Computer Scis. Corp., El Segundo, Calif., 1979-81; systems cons./ project adminstr. First Interstate Services Co., El Segundo, Calif., 1981-83; dir. research and product planning Data Line Service Co., 1983-84; project mgr. Xerox Corp., El Segundo, 1984—; founder Brainstorms, Los Angeles, 1985—; also bd. dirs. Brainstorms, Los Angeles, 1985—; Lic. psychologist, Calif. Mem. Assn. Computing Machinery, Am. Psychol. Assn., AAAS. Contbr. articles to profl. jours. Editor et. al, social sci. jour., 1971-76.

SUKUT, DARWIN LEE, city official, bridgetender; b. Fredonia, N.D., Oct. 25, 1941; s. Gustav and Pearl Emma (Templein) S.; children—Gordon Lee, Sybil Anne, Margie Eileen. Student Shoreline Community Coll., 1966-69, U. Wash., 1969-76. Asst. dock agt. Matson Navigation Co., Seattle, 1963-64; sta. agt. W. Coast Airlines Co., Seattle, 1965; design, liaison engr. Boeing Co., Seattle, 1966-71; bridgetender city of Seattle, 1971—. Mayor City of Snoqualmie 1982-85, councilman, 1978-81, 86—; mem. Puget Sound Council Govts., 1978—; chmn. SnoValley Juvenile Ct. Conf. Com., 1979—. Served with USMC, 1959-63. Mem. Bridgetenders Assn. (treas.). Clubs: Rotary, Snoqualmie. Home: 718 Spruce Snoqualmie WA 98065 Office: PO Box 987 Snoqualmie WA 98065

SULLIVAN, CORNELIUS WAYNE, research marine biology educator; b. Pitts., June 11, 1943; s. John Wayne and Hilda Sullivan; m. Jill Hajjar, Oct. 28, 1966; children: Shane, Preston, Chelsea. BS in Biochemistry, Pa. State U., 1965, MS in Microbiology, 1967; PhD in Marine Biology, Scripps Inst. Oceanography, 1971. Postdoctoral fellow Scripps Inst. Oceanography, La Jolla, Calif., 1971-74; asst. prof. marine biology U. So. Calif., Los Angeles, 1974-80, assoc. prof., 1980-85, dir. marine biology sect., 1982—, prof., 1985—; vis. prof. U. Colo., Boulder, 1981-82, MIT, Cambridge, 1981-82; field team leader Sea Ice Microbial Communities Studies, McMurdo Sound, Antarctica, 1980-86; chief scientist/cruise coordinator Antarctic Marine Ecosystem Research at the Ice Edge Zone Project, Weddell Sea, 1983, 86; mem. BIOMASS Working Party on Pack-Ice Zone Studies, 1983-86, ecol. research rev. bd. Dept. Navy, 1982-85; so. ocean ecology group specialist Sci. Com. on Antarctic Research. Editorial bd. Jour. Microbiol. Methods, 1982-85; contbr. articles to profl. jours. USPHS fellow; recipient Antarctic Service Medal of U.S., NSF, 1981. Mem. Nat. Acad. Sci. (polar research bd., 1983—, chmn. com. to evaluate polar research platforms, 1985-86). Office: U So Calif Dept Biol Scis University Park Los Angeles CA 90089-0371

SULLIVAN, DANIEL J., stage director; b. Wray, Colo., June 11, 1940; s. John Martin and Mary Catherine (Hutton) S.; m. Cecilia Ward, Nov. 1, 1974; children—John, Rachel M. 1 dau. by previous marriage, Megan Anne. B.A., San Francisco State U. Actor, Actor's Workshop, San Francisco, 1963-65; actor, dir. Lincoln Center Repertory, N.Y.C., 1965-73; dir. numerous regional theatres, 1973-79; resident dir. Seattle Repertory Theater, 1979-81, artistic dir., 1981—; instr. acting Calif. Inst. Arts, Valencia, 1973-74. Translator play, The Mandrake, 1984. Recipient Drama Desk award N.Y. Theatre Critics, 1972. Mem. Nat. Endowment for Arts, Theatre Communications Group (bd. dirs. 1982—), Commonwealth Award Panel, Democrat. Office: Seattle Repertory Theatre 155 Mercer St Seattle WA 98109 *

SULLIVAN, DANIEL JOHN, information system executive; b. Butte, Mont., May 3, 1955; s. Daniel William and Mary Catherine (Evankovich) S.; m. Lauri Lee Johns, Aug. 13, 1976; children: Shannon Marie, Maureen Elizabeth. BS in Computer Sci., U. Mont. Programmer Mont. Power Co., Butte, 1977-79, sr. programmer, 1979-81, system analyst, 1981-83, mgr. application program, 1983-85, cons., 1983—, mem. design and rev. bd., 1983—, mgr. system plan and devel., 1985—. Canvasser United Way of Butte, 1984-85, Heart Found, Butte, 1984-86, Boy Scouts Am., Butte, 1984. Recipient Bronze award, United Way, Butte, 1984. Mem. Mont. Data Processing Assn., Summit Valley Investment Club (presiding ptnr. 1985), Phi Kappa Psi. Roman Catholic. Club: Grizzly Athletic Assn. Lodge: KC. Avocations: running, basketball, volleyball, camping, hiking. Home: 2022 Wall St Butte MT 59701

SULLIVAN, DENNIS MICHAEL, lawyer, fin. cons.; b. San Francisco, Jan. 6, 1945; s. Albert Gifford and Eileen Winona (Ganshirt) S.; m. Evie Ellen Rankin, Oct. 26, 1971; children—Dennis, Ethan, Jennifer, Meghan, Patrick. B.S.C., U. Santa Clara, 1966; postgrad. Internat. Sch. Law, The Hague, Netherlands, 1967; J.D. (Dean Snodgrass scholar), U. Calif., 1969. Bar: Calif. 1970, U.S. Supreme Ct. 1978. Sr. acct. Boitano & Sargent, Santa Clara, Calif., 1963-66; dep. dist. atty. Alameda County, Calif., 1971-74; ptnr. Sullivan, Nakahara, DuBois & Hove, Oakland, Calif., 1974-80; sole practice, Oakland and San Francisco, 1980—; spl. cons. to consulate gens. of W.Ger. and Switzerland, San Francisco; judge pro tem Oakland-Piedmont Mcpl. Ct. 1978—; ct. commr. for local and dist. cts. of W.Ger.; referee Calif. bar ct. 1982—; ct. arbitrator Alameda County Superior and San Francisco County Superior Cts., 1982—; dir., chief fin. officer various closely-held corps. Served to capt. M.I., U.S. Army 1970-71. Mem. ABA, Alameda County Bar Assn., Oakland C. of C., Swiss-Am. C. of C., Grand Avenue Mchts. Assn. (dir.), Am. Arbitration Assn. (comml. arbitrator 1982—), Order of Coif. Democrat. Roman Catholic. Club: Piedmont (Calif.) Swimming; Lakeview (Oakland). Mem. editorial bd. Hastings Law Jour. 1968-69; contbr. articles to legal publs. Home: 9 Sea View Ave Piedmont CA 94611 Office: One Kaiser Plaza Suite 1115 Oakland CA 94612 Office: Mills Bldg 220 Montgomery St Suite 1094 San Francisco CA 94104

SULLIVAN, DONAL D., federal judge; b. 1931. Attended, Loyola U., Chgo.; LLB, De Paul U. Bar: U.S. Dist. Ct. Oreg., 1957. Bankruptcy judge U.S. Dist. Ct. Oreg. Office: 900 Orbanco Bldg 1001 S W 5th Ave Portland OR 97204 *

SULLIVAN, FRANK PATRICK, lawyer; b. Las Vegas, Nev., Feb. 2, 1953; s. Thomas Michael and Joan Patsy (Corrigan) S.; m. Annette Vivian DeJulio, Oct. 20, 1979; children: James, Joseph, Corrin, Frank. BA with honors, Northeastern Ill. U., 1975, tchr. cert., 1978; JD, DePaul U., 1984. Bar: Ill. 1985, Nev. 1985, U.S. Dist. Ct. Nev. 1985, U.S. Ct. Appeals (9th cir. 1986). Tchr. Chgo. Bd. Edn., 1978-85; assocs. Hilbrecht and Assocs., Las Vegas, 1985-86; dep. atty. gen. Atty. Gens. Office, Las Vegas, 1986—. Vol. various agencies abused, neglected, abandoned children. Mem. ABA, Ill. State Bar Assn., Nev. State Bar Assn., Assn. Trial Lawyers Am., Nev. Trial Lawyers Assn. Democrat. Roman Catholic. Avocations: horseback and bull riding. Home: 95 E Windmill Las Vegas NV 89123 Office: Atty Gens Office 300 S Fourth St #1100 Las Vegas NV 89101

SULLIVAN, GERALD JAMES, ins. co. exec.; b. Olympia, Wash., Sept. 30, 1937; s. John F. and Elizabeth J. (Yater) S.; B.B.A., U. Wash., 1959; M.B.A., Wharton Sch. U. Pa., 1966; children—Gerald James, Thomas, Katheleen, Shannon. Security analyst Hartford Ins. Group (Conn.), 1966-67; chief dep. ins. commr. State of Wash., Olympia, 1967-68; sec. John F. Sullivan Co., Seattle, 1968-71; pres. Walker Sullivan Co., Los Angeles, 1971-80, chmn., 1979; chmn. bd., pres. Gerald J. Sullivan & Assocs., Inc., ins. brokers, 1980—; mem. exec. com., chmn. security com. Calif. Surplus Lines Assns., San Francisco, 1974; mem. NAIC Industry Adv. Com. on Surplus Lines Laws and Reins. Served to capt. USAF, 1959-64. C.P.C.U., C.L.U. Roman Catholic. Clubs: Wilshire Country, Pauma Valley Country, Jonathan, Calif., Stock Exchange, K.C. Author: Trends in International Reinsurance Affecting American Reinsurers, 1966. Office: 800 W 6th St Los Angeles CA 90017

SULLIVAN, JAMES KIRK, forest products company executive; b. Greenwood, S.C., Aug. 25, 1935; s. Daniel Jones and Addie (Brown) S.; m. Elizabeth Miller, June 18, 1960; children: Hal N., Kim J. B.S. in Chemistry, Clemson U., 1957, M.S., 1964, Ph.D., 1966. Prodn. supr. FMC Corp., South Charleston, W.Va., 1957-62; tech. supt. FMC Corp., Pocatello, Idaho, 1966-69; mktg. mgr. FMC Corp., N.Y.C., 1969-70; v.p. Boise Cascade Corp., Idaho, 1971—; dir. Idaho Bank & Trust Co. Contbr. articles to profl. jours.; patentee in field. Mem. bus. roundtable, environ. com. staff services subcom., mem. Coll. of Forest and Recreation Resources Com. Clemson U.; mem. Idaho Found. for Pvt. Enterprise and Econ. Edn., Idaho Research Found., Inc.; mem. adv. com. Idaho Task Force on Higher Edn.; chmn. adv. bd. U. Idaho Coll. Engring., Idaho Research Found.; chmn. bd. trustees Bishop Kelly High Sch. Served to 1st lt. U.S. Army, 1958-59. Mem. Am. Chem. Soc., Am. Inst. Chem. Engrs., Am. Paper Inst. (govtl. affairs com.), Idaho Assn. Commerce and Industry (bd. dirs.), C. of C. of U.S. (pub. affairs com.). Republican. Home: 5206 Sorrento Circle Boise ID 83704 Office: Boise Cascade Corp One Jefferson Sq Boise ID 83728

SULLIVAN, JEREMIAH THOMAS, clergyman, educator; b. Butte, Mont., July 16, 1937; s. Jeremiah Joseph and Sadie Katherine Meagan Ogrin. A.B. in Philosophy, Carroll Coll., 1959; S.T.B. in Theology, Gregorian U., 1961, S.T.L., 1963; M.A. in History, St. Louis U., 1970. Ordained priest Roman Catholic Ch., 1962. Instr., asst. prof. Carroll Coll., Helena, Mont., 1963-78, assoc. prof., 1978—, head dept. history, 1978—. Recipient Fulbright-Hayes award, 1970-71. Mem. Delta Epsilon Sigma, Phi Alpha Theta. Office: Dept History Carroll Coll Helena MT 59601

SULLIVAN, JOANN MARIE, safety engineer; b. Oakland, Calif., June 10, 1951; d. Bennett William and Barbara Jean (Johnson) Brown; m. Thomas Leo Sullivan, Aug. 19, 1972; children: Benjiman, Natalie. BA in Indsl. Edn., Ariz. State U., 1974, MTech., 1980. Cert. safety profl. Tchr. indsl. arts Lafayette Elem. Sch., Phoenix, 1974-75, Chualar Sch. (Calif.), 1975-76; chef, mgr. Steinbeck House, Salinas, Calif., 1977-78; grad. asst. safety office Ariz. State U., Tempe, 1979-80, now faculty assoc. dept. tech., also chmn. curriculum adv. bd.; sr. loss control rep. Transamerica Ins. Services, Phoenix, 1980—. Sec., del.-at-large Ariz. Young Republican League, 1980, 81-82; sec. Dist. 30 Rep. Com., 1982-84, precinct capt., 1981-85. Recipient Outstanding Sr. award Ariz. State U. Coll. Edn., 1974; cert. of merit Ariz. Indsl. Arts Assn., 1975; Service award Ariz. Young Rep. League, 1982. Mem. Am. Indsl. Arts Assn., Ariz. Indsl. Arts Assn., AAUW, Am. Soc. Safety Engrs. (profl. devel. com. 1986-87, chmn. edn. com. Ariz. chpt. 1982-83, treas. 1983-84, 2d v.p. 1984-85), Ariz. State U. Alumni Assn., Queen of Peace Sch. Bus. Assn. (sec. 1985-86). Roman Catholic.

SULLIVAN, JOANN MARIE, medical technologist; b. Butte, Mont., May 31, 1938; d. Joseph D. and Ann E. (Melvin) Bracco; m. Thomas Roy Sullivan, Jan. 25, 1964; children—Michelle Ann, Renee Marie. B.S., Carroll Coll., 1960; grad., internship for medical tech. Sacred Heart Hosp., Spokane, Wash., 1960. Lic. med. technologist, Calif. Med. technologist, hematology U. Wash. Hosp., Seattle, 1960-63, Stanford U. Hosp., Palo Alto Calif., 1963-64; med. technologist, hematology supr. Guam Meml. Hosp., Tamuning, 1964-65; med. technologist Seventh-Day Adventist Clinic, Agana Heights, Guam, 1965-67; co-owner, med. technologist, dir. Physicians Diagnostic Lab., Tamuning, 1972—; mem. adv. council for med. technologist program U. Guam, 1975. Bd. dirs. Am. Cancer Soc., 1971-78, P.E.A.C.E. Found., 1975—; mem. Comprehensive Health Planning Bd., 1973-75; pres. Blood Exchange Bd., 1977-79. Mem. Am. Soc. Clin. Pathologists (affiliate; med. technologist), Am. Soc. Med. Technologists, Beta Sigma Phi. Roman Catholic. Home: PO Box 7 Agana GU 96910 Office: 388 Ypao Rd Suite A Tamuning GU 96911

SULLIVAN, JOHN ALLAN, engineer, physicist; b. White Water, Colo., Dec. 31, 1937; s. Leo Lester and Carrie Elizabeth (Blackman) S.; m. Phyllis Lorraine Rogers, June 6, 1958; children: Elizabeth, Lorraine, John A. AS, Mesa Jr. Coll., 1956; BS in Aero. Engring., U. Colo., 1958, MS in Aero. Engring., 1960; PhD in Mech. Engring., U. Mich., 1966. Design engr. Research Service Lab. U. Colo., Boulder, 1958-59, research asst., 1959-60, instr. aero. engring., 1959-60; instr. mech. engring. U. Mich., Ann Arbor, 1960-63; asst. prof. Colo. State U., Ft. Collins, 1966; mem. staff Los Alamos (N.Mex.) Sci. Lab., 1966-74, group leader, 1974-77, mem. staff, project leader applied photochemistry div., 1978-81, program mgr. Molecular Laser Isotope Separation Office of Energy Programs, 1981-82, asst. to dep. assoc. dir. for Nuclear Programs, 1982-83, mgr. KrF PAM, project P-DO, 1983-86; alt. dir. Reactor Behavior div. EG&G, Idaho Falls, Idaho, 1977-78; adj. prof. mech. engring. U. N.Mex., 1971; presenter seminars on laser isotope separation and applied photochemistry numerous corps., including Union Carbide Corp., N.Am. Rockwell, Dow Chem. Co., others. Contbr. articles to profl. jours.; patentee in field. Various offices Los Alamos Ski Patrol, 1969—, instr. first aid and ski mountaineering; counselor first aid and skiing Boy Scouts Am., Los Alamos; instr. hunting safety State N.Mes. Game and Fish Dept., 1970-81. Mem. Internat. Arabian Horse Assn., Nat. Arabian Horse Assn., Sigma Xi, Sigma Tau. Clubs: Los Alamos Mountaineers, Los Alamos Sportsmen's (pres. 1969, 80, bd. dirs. 1968, 75, 76, 79). Home: Rt 1 PO Box 373 Espanola NM 87532 Office: Los Alamos Nat Lab PO Box 1663 Los Alamos NM 87545

SULLIVAN, JOHN LOUIS, JR., executive search company executive; b. Macon, Ga., Aug. 27, 1928; s. John Louis and Elizabeth (Macken) S.; m. Barbara Boyle, Aug. 17, 1974; children: John, Katherine, Betsy, Ted. A.B. in Econs., Duke U., 1950; M.B.A., U. Pa., 1957; postgrad. Advance Mgmt. Program, Harvard U., 1975. Br. mgr. IBM, Phila., 1962-63; mgr. edn. IBM, Endicott, N.Y., 1963-64; asst. to pres. Data Procesing Div. IBM, White Plains, N.Y., 1965-67; dist. mgr. Data Processing Div. IBM, Washington, 1967-69; mgr. eastern and fed. regions Memorex Corp., 1969-71; v.p. mktg. Infonet div. Computer Sci. Corp., El Segundo, Calif., 1971-75; exec. v.p. Fin. Service Group-ADP Inc., Clifton, N.J., 1975-77; sr. v.p. Heidrick & Struggle's Inc., San Francisco and Los Angeles, 1977-82, dir., 1977-82, office mgr., 1979-82; pres. Korn-Ferry Internat., Los Angeles, 1982—, v.p., mng. dir., mem. exec. com., 1982—. Bd. dirs., mem. exec. com. March of Dimes, Los Angeles County; bd. regents Mount St. Mary's Coll., Los Angeles. Served to lt. (j.g.) USN, 1950-53. Mem. Harvard U. Bus. Sch. Alumni Assn. (dir.). Democrat. Clubs: Regency (Los Angeles); Bankers (San Francisco); Flint Canyon Tennis, Atheneum; Mission Hills (Rancho Mirage); Calif. Yacht (Los Angeles). Home: 244 Inverness Dr Flintridge CA 91011 Office: Korn Ferry Internat 911 Wilshire Los Angeles CA 90017

SULLIVAN, MARK DAVID, producer, writer, consultant; b. Chgo., Dec. 2, 1934; s. John Martin and Amelia Marie (Stauder) S.; B.A., Northwestern U., 1958. Various exec. positions Jack Morton Prodns., Inc., producers, Dallas and Chgo., 1959-64; v.p., gen. mgr., producer Michael John Assocs., Inc., N.Y.C., 1965-66; ind. producer, cons., Dallas and N.Y.C., 1962-71; exec. producer Wilding div. Bell and Howell Co., Detroit, 1971-75, Sandy Corp., Detroit, 1975-78, Jack Morton Prodns., Inc., N.Y.C., 1978-80; pres., producer Mark D. Sullivan, Inc., N.Y.C., 1980-83; ind. producer, writer, cons., San Francisco and Monterey, 1983—. Author: Location: Monterey County, 1986; contbg. author Monterey Life (magazine), 1986—. Served with AUS, 1954-57. Named Alumnus of Year, Phi Kappa Psi N.Y. Alumni Assn., 1971. Mem. Producers Guild (nat. pres. 1981-83), Advt. Club Monterey Peninsula (honorary 1987—), Nat. Writers Union, Phi Kappa Psi (nat. pres. 1972-74, Quarter Century Commn. 1975-78; North Tex. pres. 1960-61, 63-65; N.Y. chmn. bd. 1970-71, pres. 1968-70 alumni assns.), Monterey Peninsula C. of C. 1985—. Office: Box A-3793 177 Webster St Monterey CA 93940

SULLIVAN, MICHAEL EVAN, investment and management company executive; b. Phila., Dec. 30, 1940; s. Albert and Ruth (Liebert) S.; BS, N.Mex. State U., 1966, MA (Ednl. Research Tng. Program fellow), 1967; BS, U. Tex., 1969; MBA, U. Houston, 1974; MS, U. So. Calif., 1976, MPA, 1977, PhD in Adminstrn., 1983; BS in Acctg., U. La Verne, 1981. Sr. adminstrv. and tech. analyst Houston Lighting & Power Co., 1969-74; electronics engr. U.S. Govt., Point Mugu, Calif., 1974-77; mem. tech. staff Hughes Aircraft Co., El Segundo, Calif., 1977-78; staff program adminstr. Ventura div. Northrop Corp., Newbury Park, Calif., 1978-79; div. head engring. div. Navastrogru, Point Mugu, 1979-82; br. head, div. head spl. programs Pacific Missile Test Ctr. (Calif.), 1983—; pres., chmn. bd. Diversified Mgmt. Systems, Inc., Camarillo, Calif., 1978—. Author: The Management of Research, Development, Test and Evaluation Organizations; Organizational Behavior Characteristics of Supervisors-Public versus Private Sectors, Organizational Behavior Characteristics of Supervisors, Public versus Private Sectors; Self-Actualization in RDT & E Organizations; Self-Actualization in a Health Care Agency; others. V.p., bd. dirs. Ventura County Master Chorale and Opera Assn; bd. dirs. Southern Calif. Assn. of Pub. Adminstrn. (also mem. fin. com., programs com., student aid com.). Served with U.S. Army, 1958-62. Ednl. Research Info. Clearing House fellow, 1965-67. Mem. Am. Math. Soc., Math. Assn. Am., Am. Statis. Assn., IEEE, IEEE Engring. Mgmt. Soc., Am. Soc. Pub. Adminstrn., So. Calif. Assn. Pub. Adminstrn. (bd. dirs., various coms.), Am. Personnel and Guidance Assn., Fed. Mgrs. Assn., Am. Assn. Individual Investors, Mcpl. Mgmt. Assts. So. Calif., Acad. Polit. Sci., Assn. M.B.A. Execs., Phi Kappa Phi, Pi Gamma Mu. Home: PO Box 273 Port Hueneme CA 93041 Office: PO Box 447 Camarillo CA 93010

SULLIVAN, MIKE, governor, lawyer; b. Omaha, Sept. 23, 1939; s. Joseph Byrne and Margaret (Hamilton) S.; m. Jane Metzler, Feb. 28, 1939; children: Michelle, Patrick, Theresa. BS in Petroleum Engring., U. Wyo., 1961, JD, 1964. Assoc. Brown, Drew, Apostolos, Barton & Massey, Casper, Wyo., 1964-67; ptnr. Brown, Drew, Apostolos, Massey & Sullivan, Casper, 1967—; gov. State of Wyo., Casper, 1987—. Trustee St. Joseph's Children's Home, Torrington, Wyo., 1986-87; bd. dirs. Natrona County Meml. Hosp., Casper, 1976-86. Mem. ABA, Wyo. Bar Assn., Assn. Trial Lawyers Am., Wyo. Trial Lawyers Assn. Democrat. Roman Catholic. Lodge: Rotary (pres. Casper club). Avocations: fly fishing, golf, tennis, jogging. Home: 5001 Central Ave Cheyenne WY 82002 Office: Office Gov State Capitol Cheyenne WY 82002-0010

SULLIVAN, RICHARD MICHAEL, JR., systems engineer; b. Worcester, Mass., Jan. 9, 1933; s. Richard Michael and Mary Frances (Fleming) S.; student U. Mass., 1951-52; B.S. in Naval Sci., U.S. Naval Postgrad. Sch., 1964; M.S. in Systems Mgmt., U. So. Calif., 1979; m. Claire Louise Nadean, Sept. 4, 1955 (dec. 1982); children—Richard, Mark, Paul, Mary, Thomas; m. Hope. McCall, Nov. 3, 1984. Commd. ensign U.S. Navy, 1955, advanced through grades to lt. comdr., 1964; aircraft squadrons, 1955-61; USS Forrestal, 1964-66; in Vietnam, 1970; ret., 1974; project mgr. Systems Assocs., Inc., San Diego, 1974-78; systems engr. Rohr Marine, Inc., Chula Vista, Calif., 1978-80; asst. adminstr. ops. Cabrillo Med. Ctr. San Diego, 1980-82; program mgr. J. Allan Flora & Assocs. Inc., San Diego, 1982—; mgr. ILS Engring. Sundstrand Turbomach, 1984—. Mem. Am. Inst. Indsl. Engrs., Republican. Roman Catholic. Home: 3261 Casa Bonita Dr Bonita CA 92002 Office: 4400 Ruffin Rd San Diego CA 92138

SULLIVAN, ROBERT EDWARD, lawyer; b. San Francisco, May 18, 1936; s. Edward C. S. and Mary Jane (Sullivan); m. Maureen Lois Miles, June 14, 1958 (dec. 1972); children: Teresa Ann, Andrew Edward; m. Theda Braddock, 1987. B.S., U. San Francisco, 1958; LL.B., U. Calif-Berkeley, 1961. Bar: Calif. 1962. Assoc. Pillsbury, Madison & Sutro, San Francisco, 1963-70, ptnr., 1971—; lectr. bus. law Calif. Continuing Edn. Bar and Practicing Law Inst.; mem. com. corps. State Bar Calif., 1979-82, chmn., 1981-82; mem. exec. com. bus. law sect., 1982-85, vice chmn., 1983-84, chmn., 1984-85, advisor, 1985-86; v.p., treas., dir. MPC Ins., Cayman, Ltd. Contbr. articles to profl. jours. Served to 1st lt. U.S. Army, 1961-63. Mem. ABA, San Francisco Bar Assn. Democrat. Roman Catholic. Club: Bankers (San Francisco). Office: Pillsbury Madison and Sutro 225 Bush St San Francisco CA 94104

SULLIVAN, STUART FRANCIS, physician, anesthesiology educator; b. Buffalo, July 15, 1928; s. Charles S. and Kathryn (Duggan) S.; m. Dorothy Elizabeth Faytol, Apr. 18, 1959; children: John, Irene, Paul, Kathryn. BS, Canisius Coll., 1950; MD, SUNY, Syracuse, 1955. Diplomate Am. Bd. Anesthesiology. Instr. anesthesiology Coll. Physicians and Surgeons, N.Y.C., 1961-62; assoc. Columbia U., N.Y.C., 1962-64, asst. prof., 1964-67, assoc. prof., 1967-73; prof., vice chmn. dept. anesthesiology UCLA Sch. Medicine, 1973—. Served to capt. M.C., USAR, 1956-58. Fellow NIH, 1960-61; recipient research career devel. award NIH, 1966-69. Mem. Assn. Univ. Anesthetists, Am. Physiol. Soc., Am. Soc. Anesthesiologists. Home: 101 Foxtail Dr Santa Monica CA 90402 Office: UCLA Sch Medicine Dept Anesthesiology Los Angeles CA 90024

SULLIVAN, TIMOTHY REESE, broadcasting executive; b. Los Angeles, June 15, 1938; s. Charles Gardner and Ann Beatrice (May) S.; B.S., U. Ariz., 1961; M.B.A., Pepperdine U., 1978; m. Nancy Lee Robbins, July 6, 1967; children—Kelly Ann, John Casey. Vice-pres., West Coast mgr. Metro Radio Sales, Los Angeles, 1968-71; gen. sales mgr. Sta. KIAC, Los Angeles, 1971-72; v.p., dir. sales Metromedia Radio West Coast, 1972-73; v.p., gen. mgr. Sta. KHJ, Los Angeles, 1973-79; gen. mgr. Sta. KHTZ, 1978-80; v.p., gen. mgr. Sta. KMGG, Los Angeles, 1980-84; pres. Anaheim Broadcasting, Calif., 1984—. Mem. radio adv. com. U. So. Calif.; mem. exec. bd. Los Angeles March of Dimes, treas., 1977-79; mem. exec. bd. Pacific Palisades YMCA, 1978. Served with USMC, 1961-65. Mem. Nat. Assn. Broadcasters, Nat. Radio Broadcasters Assn., So. Calif. Broadcasters Assn. (chmn. 1980-81), Sigma Alpha Epsilon. Republican. Presbyterian. Club: Los Angeles Country, Beach. Office: Anaheim Broadcasting 1190 E Ball Rd Anaheim CA 92805

SULLIVAN, WILLIAM COLLIER, II, physician, psychiatrist, real estate developer; b. Manhattan, N.Y., Dec. 21, 1937; s. William C. I and Rosemary C. (Murray) S. BS, Fordham U., 1960; MD, Med. Coll. Wis., 1964. Lic. physician, Calif.; Diplomate Nat. Bd. Med. Examiners; cert. psychiatrist, Am. Bd. Neurology and Psychiatry, Bd. Med. Quality Assurance, Calif. Intern USPHS Hosp., New Orleans, 1964-65; resident in psychiatry U. Mich. Hosp., Ann Arbor, 1967-68; resident in psychiatry Langley Porter Neuropsychiat. Inst., San Francisco, 1968-70, sr. resident I, community mental health tng. program, 1970-71, sr. resident II, 1971-72; sr. resident II U. Calif. Med. Ctr., San Francisco, 1971-72. Served with USPHS, 1965-67. Grantee NIH, 1970-72. Mem. Am. Psychiat. Assn., No. Calif. Psychiat. Soc. Club: Commonwealth (San Francisco). Avocations: photography, marine botany, physics. Home: 2615 Divisadero St San Francisco CA 94123 Office: 2615 Divisadero St San Francisco CA 94123

SULLIVAN, WILLIAM FRANCIS, broadcasting company executive; b. Denver, Mar. 14, 1941; s. William Francis and Hortense M. (Maroney) S.; m. Kathleen Marie Bowlds, Feb. 10, 1962; children—Daniel, Kevin, Terence, Molly, Brian, Kathleen. Student Colo. U., 1960-61. Salesman The Singer Co., Denver, 1962-64, mgr., Grand Junction, Colo., 1964-65; salesman Sta. KREZ-TV, XYZ-TV, Inc., Durango, Colo., 1965-66, Sta. KREX-TV, Grand Junction, Colo., 1966-70, sales mgr., 1970-77, sta. mgr., 1977-85, Sta. KPAX-TV, Missoula, Mont., 1966-78, gen. mgr. 1986—. Bd. dirs. March of Dimes, Grand Junction, 1971-76, pres., 1973; mem. steering com. for curriculum devel. Sch. Dist. 51, 1981-83; service area chmn. Hilltop Rehab., 1980; com. mem. Project Critical Care, St. Mary's Hosp., 1982; co-chmn. spl. gifts div. Western Colo. Ctr. for Arts, 1982; mem. parish council St. Joseph's Catholic Ch., 1974-76; mem. Holy Family Sch. Bd., 1972-78; bd. dirs. Grand Junction Osteo. Hosp., 1975-79; mem. adv. bd. Phi Beta Lambda, Mesa Coll., 1982-85. Served with USMC, 1959-65. Mem. Grand Junction C. of C. (dir. 1979-82, 1st v.p. 1981-82). Lodges: Masons (32 degree), Lions (pres. local club 1978, dep. dist. gov. 1980), Shriners (pres. local club 1981). Office: Sta KPAX-TV PO Box 4827 Missoula MT 59806

SULLIVAN, WILLIAM RICHARD, pharmaceutical company executive, retired; b. Warren, Ohio, Oct. 22, 1916; s. Daniel Joseph and Ruth (Scholton) S.; m. Dorothy H. Earleywine, Dec. 25, 1941. BA, Western Reserve U., 1937, MA, 1939; PhD, U. Wis., 1942. Sr. chemist Hoffmann-LaRoche Inc., Nutley, N.J., 1942-45, from asst. to dir. research, 1945-57, research coordinator, 1957-62, dir. research services, 1962-79; adj. asst. prof. Oreg. Health Scis. U., Portland, Oreg., 1982—. Contbr. articles to profl. jours. Recipient Meritorious Achievement award, Oreg. Health Scis. U. Med. Sch. Alumni Assn., 1984. Fellow Am. Inst. Chemists, AAAS; mem. Am. Chem. Soc., Sigma Xi. Republican. Avocations: gardening, philately. Home: 13505 SE River Rd Portland OR 97222 Office: Oreg Health Scis U Med Sch Dept Pharmacology 3181 SW Sam Jackson Park Rd Portland OR 97201

SULLIVAN, WOODRUFF TURNER, III, astronomy educator, science historian, researcher; b. Colorado Springs, Colo., June 17, 1944; s. Woodruff Turner Jr. and Virginia Lucille (Ward) S.; m. Barbara Jean Phillips, June 8, 1968; children: Rachel, Sarah. SB in Physics, MIT, 1966; PhD in Astronomy, U. Md., 1971. Astronomer Naval Research Lab., Washington, 1969-71; postdoctoral fellow U. Groningen, The Netherlands, 1971-73; mem. faculty U. Wash., Seattle, 1973—, prof. astronomy, 1986—; advisor NASA Search for Extraterrestrial Intelligence group, Ames Research Ctr., Calif., 1980—. Editor: Classics in Radio Astronomy, 1982, The Early Years of Radio Astronomy, 1984; contbr. articles to profl. jours. Vice chmn. Discovery Park Adv. Com., Seattle, 1976—. Grantee NSF, NASA. Mem. Internat. Astron. Union, Am. Astron. Soc., History of Sci. Soc. Club: Astron. Unit (Seattle). Avocations: hiking, softball, pardating.

SULZBACH, DANIEL SCOTT, computer company executive; b. Iowa City, Feb. 6, 1949; s. John Francis and Elizabeth (Sims) S. BA summa cum laude, St. John's U., Collegeville, Minn., 1971; MS, Queen's U., Kingston, Ont., Can., 1975; PhD, Ind. U., 1979. Research fellow Wesleyan U., Middletown, Conn., 1979-80, U. Calif., San Diego, 1980-82; acad. computing coordinator San Diego State U., 1982-85; cons. mgr. San Diego Supercomputer Ctr., 1985—. Editor Internat. Jur. Supercomputer Applications. Postdoctoral fellow NIH, 1980. Mem. Soc. for Study of Evolution, AAAS. Office: San Diego Supercomputer Ctr Box 85608 San Diego CA 92138

SUMAN, WALTER VICTOR, sales executive; b. Houston, Oct. 15, 1956; s. Robert P. and Jean (Hull) S.; m. Margaret G. Krauss, Nov. 14, 1981; 1 child, Elizabeth Hull. Student, U. Colo., 1974-75, Portland State U., 1975-77; BS in Bus. and Bldg. Constrn., U. Oreg., 1980. Sales mgr. Wiley Bayley Agy., Seattle, 1980—; v.p. N.W. Cos., Seattle, 1986—. Republican. Home: 2520 27th Ave W Seattle WA 98199 Office: PO Box 3822 Seattle WA 98124 Mailing Address: PO Box 84212 Seattle WA 98124

SUMIDA, GERALD AQUINAS, lawyer; b. Hilo, Hawaii, June 19, 1944; s. Sadamu and Kimiyo (Miyahara) S.; m. Sylvia Whitehead, June 23, 1970. AB summa cum laude, Princeton U., 1966, cert. in pub. and internat. affairs, 1966; JD, Yale U., 1969. Bar: Hawaii 1970, U.S. Dist. Ct. Hawaii 1970, U.S. Ct. Appeals (9th cir.) 1970, U.S. Supreme Ct. 1981. Research assoc. Ctr. Internat. Studies, Princeton U., 1969; assoc. Carlsmith, Wichman, Case, Mukai & Ichiki, Honolulu, 1970-76, ptnr., 1976—; mem. cameras in courtroom evaluation com. Hawaii Supreme Ct., 1984—. Mem. sci. and statis. com. Western Pacific Fishery Mgmt. Council, 1979—; mem. study group on law of armed conflict and the law of the sea Comdr. in Chief Pacific, U.S. Navy, 1979—; pres. Pacific and Asian Affairs Council Hawaii, 1982—, bd. govs., 1976—, Paul S. Bachman award, 1978; chmn. internat. com. Hawaii chpt. ARC, 1983—; vice chmn. Honolulu Com. on Fgn. Relations, 1983—; pres., dir., founding mem. Hawaii Ocean Law Assn., 1978—; mem. Hawaii Adv. Group for Law of Sea Inst., 1977—; pres. Hawaii Inst. Continuing Legal Edn., 1979-83, dir., 1976—; pres., founding mem. Hawaii Council Legal Edn. for Youth, 1980-83, dir., 1983—; chmn. Hawaii Commn. on Yr. 2000, 1976-79; exec. com. Honolulu Community Media Council, 1976—, legal counsel, 1979-83; bd. dirs. Hawaii Imin Centennial Corp., 1983—, Hawaii Pub. Radio, 1983—. Legal Aid Soc. Hawaii, 1984; mem. Pacific Alliance Trade and Devel., 1984—. Recipient cert. of appreciation Gov. of Hawaii, 1979, resolutions of appreciation Hawaii Senate and Ho. of Reps., 1979; grantee Japan Found., 1979. Mem. ABA, Hawaii Bar Assn. (pres. young lawyers sect. 1974, v.p. 1984—), Japan-Hawaii Lawyers Assn., Am. Soc. Internat. Law, Japan-Hawaii Lawyers Assn., Hawaii C. of C. (energy com. 1981—, chmn. 1985—), Am. Judicature Soc., AAAS, Asia Pacific Lawyers Assn., Real Estate Securities and Syndication Inst., Phi Beta Kappa. Democrat. Clubs: Yale (N.Y.C.); Plaza (Honolulu); Colonial (Princeton). Author: (with others) Legal, Institutional and Financial Aspects of An Inter-Island Electrical Transmission Cable, 1984, Alternative Approaches to the Legal, Institutional and Financial Aspects of Developing an Inter-Island Electrical Transmission Cable System, 1986, Alternative Approaches to he Legal, Institutional and Financial Aspects of Developing an Inter-Island Electrical Transmission Cable System, 1986; editor Hawaii Bar News, 1972-73; contbr. chpts. to books. Home: 1130 Wilder Ave #1401 Honolulu HI 96822 Office: Pacific Trade Center 190 S King St Suite 2200 Honolulu HI 96813 also: Carlsmith Wichman Case Mukai Ichiki 1001 Bishop St Pacific Tower Suite 2200 Honolulu HI 96813

SUMTER, THOMAS LEE, consultant, educator; b. Topeka, Kans., Sept. 1, 1942; s. Thomas Harden and Viola Mae (Harding) S.; children—Thomas Allen, Michael Patrick; m. Beth Anne Balder, Feb. 14, 1981; 1 stepchild, Keri Lynn Anilionis. Student, Olympic Coll., 1963-64, U. Wash., 1964-66. Supr. Tally Corp., Seattle, 1964-68; project engr. Honeywell, Seattle, 1968-72; mfg. mgr. Contact Telecomm, Seattle, 1972-74; cons. Olympic Assocs., Seattle, 1974-80; prin. T.L. Sumter & Assocs., Kingston, Wash., 1980—; instr. project mgmt. Edmonds Community Coll., Wash., 1979-80. Adv. council on State Govt. Quality Assurance & Productivity, 1975; mem. Consumer Product Safety Commn., Sea Systems Quality Control, 1976. Recipient Letter of Commendation, USS Conquest, 1984. Mem. Am. Soc. Quality Control (sect. chmn. 1974—), Soc. Am. Mil. Engrs., Project Mgmt. Inst. Democrat. Congregationalist. Club: Kingston Yacht. Lodge: Kiwanis. Home: 12101 NE Olive Dr Kingston WA 98346 Office: T L Sumter & Assocs PO Box 7302 Kingston WA 98346

SUN, ANTHONY, venture capitalist; b. Bangkok, July 8, 1952; came to U.S., 1970, naturalized, 1977; s. Chung Ta and Ching Sin (Ho) S.; BSEE, MIT, 1974, MSEE, 1974; MBA, Harvard U., 1979; m. Leslie Shao-Ming Suen, June 21, 1974; children: Christopher Chia-Chun, Timothy Chia-Chieh. Design engr. Hewlett Packard Co., Palo Alto, Calif., 1972-74; product line mgr. TRW, Sunnyvale, Calif., 1975-76; engring. mgr. Caere Corp., Los Gatos, Calif., 1976-77; asst. to pres. Advent Corp., Cambridge, Mass., 1977-79; gen. partner Venrock Assocs., Palo Alto, 1979—; dir. 8 high tech. cos. Contbr. articles on engring. tech. to profl. jours; patentee in field. Home: 415 El Arroyo Rd Hillsborough CA 94010 Office: Venrock Assocs 2 Palo Alto Sq Suite 528 Palo Alto CA 94306

SUN, SAMUEL SAI-MING, plant biochemist, molecular biologist; b. Canton, China, Sept. 15, 1942; s. Kuen and Siu-Ying (Wong) S.; B.Sc. cum laude (Govt. Hong Kong scholar, New Asia Distinction scholar), Chinese U. Hong Kong, 1966; B.Sc. with special honors, U. Hong Kong, 1968, M.Sc., 1971; Ph.D., U. Wis.-Madison, 1974; m. Piera S. Sun, May 25, 1974; 1 son, Bryan K. Demonstrator, U. Hong Kong, 1968-71; research assoc. U. Wis.-Madison, 1971-74, postdoctoral research assoc., 1975-79, asst. scientist, 1979-80; sr. scientist Plant Cell Research Inst., Dublin, Calif., 1980-85, prin. scientist, 1985-86, dir. molecular biology, 1986—. Mem. N.Y. Acad. Sci., Am. Soc. Plant Physiologists, Am. Inst. Biol. Scis., Sigma Xi. Contbr. articles to profl. jours., chpts. to books. Office: Plant Cell Research Inst 6560 Trinity Ct Dublin CA 94568

SUND, JOHN LEONARD, lawyer, state legislator, business executive; b. Ketchikan, Alaska, Feb. 14, 1949; s. Otto Arthur and Karen (Berre) S.; m. Kathleen A. MacKinnon, Aug. 7, 1971; children: Kevin, Theresa. BA in History, Polit. Sci. and Edn., Western Wash. U., 1971; JD, Lewis and Clark Coll., 1974. Bar: Alaska 1974, U.S. Dist. Ct. Alaska 1975, U.S. Ct. Appeals (9th cir.) 1976. Ptnr., Ellis, Sund & Whittaker, Ketchikan, 1974-79; chief counsel to speaker Alaska Ho. of Reps., Juneau, 1979-81; pres. Waterfall Group Ltd., Ketchikan, 1981-84; mem. Alaska Ho. of Reps., 1984—, chmn. house judiciary com., 1987—; apptd. Gov.'s Com. for Study of Bodily Injury Reparations, 1978-79, Fisheries Ctr. Study Com., 1980-81. Chmn. Ketchikan Overall Econ. Study Com., 1977-79. Mem. ABA, Alaska Bar Assn., Am. Judicature Assn. Democrat. Club: Sons of Norway (Ketchikan).

SUNDBERG, JOHN EDWIN, research chemist, computer educator; b. Changsha, Hunan, Peoples Republic of China, Nov. 21, 1947; came to U.S., 1956; s. Rodney August and Vohnie Marie (Spangler) S.; m. Carol Anne Falkenberg, Sept. 4, 1971; children: Heather, Amy. BA, Coll. of Wooster, 1970; PhD, U. Calif., Santa Cruz, 1975. Researcher biol. chemistry U. Calif., Davis, 1972-73; research chemist United Technologies Corp., Sunnyvale, Calif., 1975-77; sr. research chemist Chevron Research Co., Richmond, Calif., 1977—. Mem. Am. Chem. Soc. Avocation: personal computers. Office: Chevron Research Co 576 Standard Ave Richmond CA 94802

SUNDBERG, PATRICIA ANN, union official; b. Santa Barbara, Calif., Feb. 20, 1956; d. George and Kathleen (Campbell) Hotchkiss. A.A., Santa Barbara City Coll., 1983. Cashier, clk. Coronet Stores, Goleta, Calif., 1977; tchr.'s aide Goleta Schs., 1977-78; sec., bookkeeper Hotchkiss Excavations, Carpinteria, Calif., 1978-79; with Sundberg Stamp & Coin, Santa Barbara, 1976-80; office mgr., bus. agt. Culinary Allinace and Bartenders Union, Local 498, Santa Barbara, 1980-81, exec. sec.-treas., bus. mgr., 1981—, chmn. exec. bd., 1981—; co-chmn. Tri-Counties Central Labor Council, 1984—. Trustee Restaurant-Employee-Employer-Union Welfare Fund, Santa Barbara, 1980—, chmn., 1983—; alt. Indsl. Welfare Commn., 1987; adv. Santa Barbara City Coll., 1981—, Santa Barbara High Sch., 1982—; co-chmn. 19th Congl. Dist. Mondale Campaign, 1984. Democrat. Office: Culinary Alliance Union Local 498 1019 Chapala St Santa Barbara CA 93101

SUNDE, ROGER ALLAN, nutritional biochemist, educator; b. Madison, Wis., Jan. 31, 1950; s. Milton Lester and Genevieve Claire (Larson) S. BS in Biochemistry, U. Wis., 1972, PhD. in Biochemistry, 1980. NIH fellowship Rowett Research Inst., Aberdeen, Scotland, 1981-83; asst. prof. U. Ariz., Tucson, 1983—. Contbg. editor Nutrition Reviews, 1984—. Recipient Archer-Daniels-Midland award Am. Oil Chemist's Soc., 1985, Future Leader award Internat. Life Scis. Inst.-Nutrition Found., 1986—. Mem. AAAS, Am. Chem. Soc. Home: 2421 E 7th St Tucson AZ 85719 Office: U Ariz Dept Nutrition and Food Sci 309 Shantz Bldg Tucson AZ 85721

SUNDEL, HARVEY H., marketing research analyst and consultant; b. Bronx, NY, July 24, 1944; s. Louis and Pauline (Brotman) S. BBA, St. Mary's U., San Antonio, 1969, MBA, 1970; PhD, St. Louis U., 1974. Asst. dir. research Lone Star Brewery, San Antonio, 1970-71; cons. Tri-Mark, Inc., San Antonio, 1972-73; asst. prof. mktg. Lewis and Clark Coll., Godfrey, Ill., 1973-74; asst. prof. mktg. Met. State Coll., Denver, 1974-77, chmn., prof. mktg., 1977-86; pres. Sundel Research, Inc., Denver, 1976—; cons. Frederick Ross Co., Denver, 1979-84, U.S. West, Denver, 1986—, Monsanto Chems. Co., St. Louis, 1985—, Mountain Bell, Denver, 1979—; chmn., prof. mktg., 1977-86. Contbr. papers and proceedings to profl. jours. Com. mem. Mile High United Way, Denver, 1975-80. Mem. So. Mktg. Assn., Southwestern Mktg. Assn., Midwestern Mktg. Assn. Jewish. Avocation: handball. Home: 1616 Glen Bar Dr Lakewood CO 80215 Office: Sundel Research Inc 1150 Delaware Denver CO 80204

SUNDEM, GARY LEWIS, accounting educator; b. Montevideo, Minn., Nov. 8, 1944; s. Clifford Leroy and Sylvia Edna (Larson) S.; m. Jennifer McGilvray, Aug. 20, 1969; children: Garth Clifford, Jens Lewis. BA, Carleton Coll., 1967; MBA, Stanford U., 1969, PhD, 1971. Asst. prof. U. Wash., Seattle, 1971-74, assoc. prof., 1974-80, prof., 1980—; vis. prof. Norwegian Sch. Econs., Bergen, 1974-75; vis. assoc. prof. Cornell U., Ithaca, N.Y., 1977-78; vis. prof. INSEAD, Fontainebleau, France, 1987; cons. in field; editor The Acctg. Review, 1982-86. Bd. trustees The Little Sch., 1978-82, also v.p. fin. Named Seattle Newsmaker of Tomorrow, Time Mag. and Seattle C. of C., 1979; recipient Outstanding Acctg. Educator award Wash. Soc. CPA's, 1987. Mem. Am. Acctg. Assn. (exec. com. 1982-85), Am. Fin. Assn., Fin. Execs. Inst., Nat. Assn. Accts. (nat. bd. dirs. 1986—), Fin. Mgmt. Assn., Inst. Mgmt. Sci. Author: Introduction ti Financial Accounting, 1987, Introduction to Management Accounting, 1987; contbr. articles to profl. jours. Home: 12420 Miller Rd NE Bainbridge Island WA 98110 Office: Sch Bus Adminstrn Univ Wash Seattle WA 98195

SUNDQUIST, PAUL MARTIN, safety engineer; b. Boston, Mar. 30, 1957; s. Robert Gustav and Edith Caroline (Setterstrom) S.; m. Cynthia Eleanor Falk, June 29, 1985. BSBA, U. Maine, 1980. Football coach Eastern Mich. U., Ypsilanti, 1980-81; loss prevention rep. Liberty Mutual Ins. Co., Lexington, Mass., 1981-83; sr. loss prevention rep. Liberty Mutual Ins. Co., San Francisco, 1983; loss control rep. Md. Casualty Co., San Bruno, Calif., 1983-85, loss control mgr., 1985-87, regional loss control mgr., 1987—. Coach PopWarner Football League, Chelmsford, Mass., 1982, Chelmsford Youth Basketball, 1981-83. Mem. Am. Soc. Safety Engrs. Republican. Lutheran. Avocations: fishing, sports. Home: 756 Marlin Ave 4 Foster City CA 94404 Office: Maryland Casualty Co 1100 Grundy Ln 125 San Bruno CA 94066

SUNIA, FOFO I. F., congressional delegate; b. Fagasa, Am. Samoa, Mar. 13, 1937; s. Fiti and Savali (Alesana) S.; m. Aioletuna Ta'amu, Feb. 5, 1960; children: Fiti, Merina, Iosefa, Vaaomala, Alexander, Cindy, Lupe, Dwayne. B.A., U. Hawaii. Liaison officer to gov. Am. Samoa govt., elec. commr., 1962-70, dir. tourism office; senator Am. Samoa legislature; del. 97th-100th Congresses. Office: 1206 Longworth House Office Bldg Washington DC 20515 *

SUNLIGHT, CAROLE, psychologist; b. DuBois, Pa., Aug. 19; d. Andy and Mary Ann Gaborick; Med. Tech., Carnegie Coll., 1959; BA in Psychology, Cleve. State U., 1971; MA in Psychology (Univ. scholar), Pepperdine U., 1973; PhD in Psychology, U.S. Internat. U., 1980. Med. technologist Doctors Piercy, Fertig, Schneider and Doran, Cleve., 1959-67; chief technologist med. dept. U.S. Steel Corp., Lorain, Ohio, 1967-69; office mgr. dept. philosophy and religious studies Cleve. State U., 1969-70; counselor Gardena Valley Counseling Service, Gardena, Calif., 1971-72; clin. intern Pepperdine U. psychology clinic, 1972-73; testing technician Norco-Corona (Calif.) Sch. Dist., 1973; dir. treatment services Unfinished Symphony Ranch, Inc., Agoura, Calif., 1973-77; pvt. practice, Westlake Village, Calif., 1977-78; staff Kaiser Permanente Mental Health Center, 1977—; pvt. practice, Torrance, Calif., 1980—, Cypress, Calif., 1986—; speaker in field. Bd. dirs. COMOSI Mental Health, Thousand Oaks, Calif., 1977-78. Registered med. technologist. Mem. Am. (sects on psychology of women, clin. neuropsychology, Calif. Psychol. Assn., Los Angeles County (newsletter editor 1982-84) Psychol. Assn., Am. Med. Technologists (Ohio State Soc. Publ. award 1972), Calif. Neuropsychol. Soc., Psychologists for Social Responsibility, NOW, Psi Chi. Office: 765 W College St Los Angeles CA 90012 Office: 19000 Hawthorne Blvd Suite 300 Torrance CA 90503

SUNN, RAY ELDON, real estate and computer executive; b. Henderson, Ky., Mar. 15, 1927; s. Francis Connie S.; m. Jeanne N. Swords, May 7, 1957; children: Steven L., Susan L., Heidi Rae. Cert. in real estate, UCLA, 1964; grad., Realtors Inst., Chgo., 1981. Prin. Sunn Real Estate Co., Palm Desert, Calif., 1952—, Sunn Computer Systems, Palm Desert, Calif., 1967—; cons. investment real estate computer systems, 1967-72; mem. adv. bd. Bank of Am., Anaheim, Calif., 1967-74. Served with USMC, 1944-46, 50-52. Named to Hon. Order Ky. Cols., 1960. Nat. Assn. Realtors, Calif. Assn. Realtors, Palm Desert Calif. Bd. Realtors, Realtors Inst., Am. Farm and Land Inst., Anaheim C. of C. Republican. Lodges: Shriners, Elks, Masons, Rotary. Office: PO Box 1791 Palm Desert CA 92261

SUNSHINE, IRVING, toxicologist; b. N.Y.C., Mar. 17, 1916; s. Samuel Sunshine and Sara Kanter; m. Helen Rogoff, Dec. 24, 1939, (dec.); children: Jonathan Howard, Carl Alan; m. June Singer, Oct. 20, 1985. BS, NYU, 1937, MA, 1941, PhD in Toxicology, 1950. Diplomate Am. Bd. Forensic Toxicology (dir. 1979—), Am. Bd. Clin. Chemistry. Prof. toxicology emeritus Case Western Res. U., Cleve., 1951—; chief toxicologist emeritus Coroner's Office, Cleve., 1951—; toxicologist Univ. Hosps., Cleve., 1951-85; cons. toxicologist VA Hosp., Cleve., 1979-85; vis. prof. U. Ghent, Belguim, 1976; Fulbright prof. Vrije U., Brussels; cons. toxicologist Syva Corp., Palo Alto, Calif., 1985—. Author: Handbook of Analytical Toxicology, 1969, Handbook of Spectrophotometric Data of Drugs, 1981, Handbook of Toxicology Chromotography, 1981, Methods for Analytical Toxicology Vol. 1, 1975, Vol. 2, 1982, Vol. 3, 1985. Fellow Am. Acad. Forensic Scis. (chmn. 1969-71, Gettler award 1980), Am. Assn. Clin. Chemistry (bd. dirs. 1981-84, Internat. fellowship 1984, Ames award 1973); mem. Am. Chem. Soc. (chmn. Cleve. sect. 1968), Calif. Assn. Toxicologists (bd. dirs. 1986—), Internat. Assn. Forensic Toxicologists. Home: 4173 Hubbartt Dr Palo Alto CA 94306

SUPKO, PETER RICHARD, geologist; b. Passaic, N.J., Dec. 8, 1939. BA Geology, Rutgers U., 1961; MS in Geol. Oceanography, U. Miami, 1963, PhD in Geol. Oceanography, 1970. Research scientist Rosenstiel Sch. Marine and Atmospheric Scis., Miami, Fla., 1965-70; chief sci. editor Deep Sea Drilling Project, Scripps Instn. Oceanography, La Jolla, Calif., 1970-75; sci. coordinator Nat. Research Inst. Oceanology, South Africa, 1975-78; mgr. phys. scis. Normandeau Assocs., Bedford, N.H., 1978-79; bus. devel. mgr. McClelland Engrs., Inc., Ventura, Calif., 1979-83, mgr. exploration geology services, 1983—; spl. cons. USN Deep Submergence Systems Rev. Group, 1963; cons. USAF, 1973; vis. prof. oceanography U. Hawaii, 1974; chmn. Internat. Geol. Correlation Program, 1976-79. Contbr. articles to profl. jours. Served to lt. USAF, 1963-65. Mem. Am. Assn. Petroleum Geologists, Am. Geol. Inst., Am. Geophys. Union, Assn. Petroleum Geochem. Explorationists, Soc. Econ. Paleontologists and Mineralogists, Sigma Xi. Home: 618 Colina Vista Ventura CA 93003

SUPPES, PATRICK, educator; b. Tulsa, Mar. 17, 1922; s. George Biddle and Ann (Costello) S.; m. Joan Farmer, Apr. 16, 1946 (div. 1970); children: Patricia, Deborah, John Biddle; m. Joan Sieber, Mar. 29, 1970 (div. 1973); m. Christine Johnson, May 26, 1979; 1 dau., Alexandra Christine. B.S., U. Chgo., 1943; Ph.D. (Wendell T. Bush fellow), Columbia U., 1950; LL.D., U. Nijmegen, Netherlands, 1979; Dr.h.c., Académie de Paris, U. Paris V, 1982. Instr., Stanford U., 1950-52; asst. prof. Stanford, 1952-55, assoc. prof., 1955-59, prof. philosophy, statistics, edn. and psychology, 1959—. Author: Introduction to Logic, 1957, Axiomatic Set Theory, 1960, Sets and Numbers, books 1-6, 1966, Studies in the Methodology and Foundations of Science, 1969, A Probabilistic Theory of Causality, 1970, Logique du Probable, 1981, Probabilistic Metaphysics, 1984, (with Davidson and Siegel) Decision Making, 1957, (with Richard C. Atkinson) Markov Learning Models for Multiperson Interactions, 1960, (with Shirley Hill) First Course in Mathematical Logic, 1964, (with Edward J. Crothers) Experiments on Second-Language Learning, 1967, (with Max Jerman and Dow Brian) Computer-assisted Instruction, 1965-66, Stanford Arithmetic Program, 1968, (with D. Krantz, R.D. Luce and A. Tversky) Foundations of Measurement, Vol. 1, 1971, (with M. Morningstar) Computer-Assisted Instruction at Stanford, 1966-68, 1972, (with B. Searle and J. Friend) The Radio Mathematics Project: Nicaragua, 1974-75, 1976. Served to capt. USAAF, 1942-46. Recipient Nicholas Murray Butler Silver medal Columbia, 1965, Disting. Sci. Contbr. award Am. Psychol. Assn., 1972, Tchrs. Coll. medal for disting. service, 1978; Center for Advanced Study Behavioral Scis. fellow, 1955-56; NSF fellow, 1957-58. Fellow Am. Psychol. Assn., AAAS, Am. Acad. Arts and Scis.; mem. Math Assn. Am., Psychometric Soc., Am. Philos. Assn., Assn. Symbolic Logic, Am. Math Soc., Académie Internationale de Philosophie des Scis. (titular), Nat. Acad. Edn. (pres. 1973-77), Nat. Acad. Scis., Am. Psychol. Assn., Internat. Inst. Philosophy, Finnish Acad. Sci. and Letters, Internat. Union History and Philosophy of Sci. (div. logic, methodology and philosophy of sci., pres. 1975-79), Am. Ednl. Research Assn. (pres. 1973-74), Sigma Xi.

SURACI, JOSEPH MICHAEL, engineer; b. Washington, May 25, 1939; s. Joseph Carmelo and Betty (Driscoll) S.; m. Andrea Catherine Suraci, Dec. 1, 1966; children: Deborah Ann, Teresa Louise, Tammy Jo, Michael Joseph, Steven Francis. BSEE, Cath. U. Am., 1962. Registered profl. engr., Mass., Tex. Elec. engr. Nat. Bur. Standards, Washington, 1960-66; sr. scientist ITT Fed. Elec. Corp., Kennedy Space Ctr., Fla., 1966-69; supr. Lowell (Mass.) Tech. Inst., 1969-70; prin. engr. Lockheed Electronics Co., Houston, 1970-77; lab. mgr. Lockheed Missiles & Space Co., Bremerton, Wash., 1977—. Editor Nat. Conf. Standards Lab. newsletter, 1973-76. Recipient Outstanding Service award Nat. Conf. of Standards Labs., 1972-73, Safety Suggestion award NASA/Lockheed Electronics Co., 1973. Mem. Alpha Delta Gamma (Pres.' award 1962). Club: Meadowmeer Golf and Country. Home: 8522 NE Meadowmeer Rd Bainbridge Island WA 98110 Office: Lockheed Missiles & Space Co Inc PO Box 6429 NSB Bangor Bremerton WA 98315

SURFACE, STEPHEN WALTER, water treatment chemist; b. Dayton, Ohio, Feb. 25, 1943; s. Lorin Wilfred and Virginia (Marsh) S.; m. Suzanne MacDonald, Aug. 29, 1964 (div.); 1 child, Jennifer Nalani; m. Sinfrosa

Garay, Sept. 16, 1978; children: Maria Lourdes, Stephanie Alcantara. BS, Otterbein Coll., 1965; MA, U. So. Calif., 1970; postgrad., U. Hawaii, 1971. Tchr. Hawaii State Dept. Edn., Honolulu, 1970-71; staff chemist Del Monte Corp., Honolulu, 1971; head chemist USNPearl Harbor, Honolulu, 1971-76, staff chemist, 1976—. Contbr. articles to profl. jours. Recipient DuPont Teaching award, U. So. Calif., 1966. Fellow Am. Inst. Chemists; mem. Am. Chem. Soc., Am. Water Works Assn., Sigma Zeta, Phi Lambda Upsilon. Democrat. Methodist. Avocations: traveling, artifact collecting, landscaping. Home: 94-1139 Noheaiki St Waipahu HI 96797 Office: Naval Facilities Engring Command Pacific div Pearl Harbor HI 96860-7300

SURYOUTOMO, HERMAN, engineering executive, food company executive; b. Pati, Indonesia, July 7, 1946; came to U.S., 1970; s. Kiem Hoo Oei and Lies Nio Ong; m. Lusia Amalia Karnoatmodjo, Mar. 1, 1976; children: David Christopher, Nina Amelia, Jason Andrew, Tanya Christina. BS equivalent, Bandung Inst. Tech., Indonesia, 1970; MS, Washington U., St. Louis, 1972, DSc, 1975; MBA, Pepperdine U., 1984. Registered profl. engr., N.C., Ala.; registered civil engr., Calif. Sr. engring. specialist Jack Gillum & Assocs., St. Louis, 1974-75; div. and project mgr. Cygna Corp., San Francisco, 1975-82; chmn., chief exec. officer Innova Corp., Fremont, Calif., 1982—; pres. Innova Corp. of N.C., Raleigh, 1983—; owner, broker Prima Realty, Fremont, 1986—; pres., chief exec. officer Prima Foods Corp., Fremont, 1985—. Author: Organizational Effectiveness, 1984; contbr. articles to profl. jours. Treas., bd. dirs. Companion of Alameda County, Hayward, Calif., 1985—. Named Fulbright Hays scholar, Washington, 1970; recipient Highest Achievement scholarship Dale Carnegie Schs., Oakland, Calif., 1976. Mem. ASCE. Roman Catholic. Lodges: Rotary, Toastmasters (officer 1985—). Avocations: tae kwon do, swimming, skiing, tennis, hiking. Home: 44433 Park Meadow Dr Fremont CA 94539 Office: Innova Corp 5411 Randall Pl Fremont CA 94538

SUSEL, JOEL IRA, marketing executive; b. Denver, May 3, 1957; s. Samuel and Ann (Salomonowicz) S.; m. Leslie Swid, June 17, 1984; 1 child, Jeremy. BA, Claremont McKenna Coll., 1979; MBA, Harvard U., 1983. Research assoc. Booz Allen & Hamilton, Houston, 1979-81; cons. William M. Mercer, Inc., Houston, 1981; asst. mktg. mgr. Pepsi USA, Purchase, N.Y., 1983-84, assoc. mktg. mgr., 1984-85; dir. field mktg. United Cable TV, Denver, 1985—. Jewish. Club: Harvard. Avocations: cooking, travel, personal computer. Office: United Cable TV Corp 4700 S Syracuse Pkwy Suite 1100 Denver CO 80237

SUSSKIND, TERESA GABRIEL, publisher; b. Watford, Eng., came to U.S., 1945, naturalized, 1948; d. Aaron and Betty (Fox) Gabriel; m. Charles Susskind, May 1, 1945; children—Pamela Pettler, Peter Gabriel, Amanda. Student U. London, 1938-40. Profl. librarian Calif. Inst. Tech., Pasadena, 1946-48, Yale U., New Haven, Conn., 1948-51, Stanford U., Calif., 1951-52, SRI Internat., Menlo Park, Calif., 1953; founder, pres. San Francisco Press, Inc., 1959—. Served with Women's Royal Naval Service, 1943-45. Author: A Room of One's Own Revisited, 1977. Active in cultural affairs; pres. East Bay League, San Francisco Symphony, 1984-86, bd. govs. 1986—. Club: Town and Gown (pres. 1984-85) (Berkeley, Calif.). Office: Box 6800 San Francisco CA 94101

SUSSMAN, JUDITH ANNE, interior designer; b. N.Y.C., Jan. 9, 1935; d. Samuel and Paula Rose (Kroll) G.; m. Donald E. Axinn, Mar. 29, 1953 (div. Apr. 1967); children: Meredith, Allison, Michael, Jennifer; m. Sanford Sussman, Nov. 3, 1967. BA, Columbia U., 1955; cert. design, N.Y. Sch. Interior Design, 1974. Interior designer J.C. Penney, Garden City, N.Y., 1974-76, R.H. Macy, Garden City, 1977; pvt. practice interior design Florence, S.C., 1977-78, Phoenix, 1979—; instr. Scottsdale (Ariz.) Community Coll., 1986—. Chmn. Hist. League, Phoenix, 1981-83; mem. Contemporary Forum Phoenix Art Mus., 1982—. Mem. Am. Soc. Interior Design (assoc., bd. dirs., head assoc. com. of yr. 1983, 1st pl. Residential Design award 1982, 1st pl. Model Home Designer award 1985), Nat. Home Fashions League, Jewish Bus. and Profl. Women (bd. dirs.), Phoenix C. of C. Democrat. Jewish. Avocations: tennis, aerobics. Home: 2039 E Pasadena Phoenix AZ 85016 Office: Judy Sussman's Designworks Ltd 2150 E Highland Suite 205 Phoenix AZ 85016

SUTHERLAND, ARTHUR ABBOTT, research company executive; b. Bklyn., Feb. 17, 1937; s. Arthur Abbott and Margaret Louise (Schweitzer) S.; m. Marion Lorraine Oliver, July 6, 1963; children: Amy Lynn, Laurie Ann. B in Aero. Engring., Rensselaer Poly. Inst., 1958; SM, MIT, 1962, PhD, 1966. Registered profl. engr., Calif. Mem. tech. staff Analytic Scis. Corp., Reading, Mass., 1966-69, group leader control systems, 1969-75, dir. energy and environment dept., 1975-79; mgr. nuclear environ. programs Ford, Bacon & Davis, Salt Lake City, 1979-80; mgr. engring. Rogers & Assoc. Engrs., Salt Lake City, 1980-82, v.p., 1982—; mem. faculty Kalman Filtering Inst. U. Wis., Madison, 1970; cons. U.S. Army Electronics Command, 1973-74, Midwest Low-level Radioactive Waste Mgmt.Commn., Tex. Low-level Radioactive Waste Disposal Authority; reviewer, contbr. Dept. of Energy Office Civilian Radiation Wast Mgmt. mission plan and environ. assessments. Author: Applied Optimal Estimation, 1974; contbr. articles to profl. jours.; patentee in field. Served with USMC, 1958-61. Mem. AIAA (reviewer tech. papers 1972-75), Am. Nuclear Soc., Air Pollution Control Assn., Common Cause (charter), Sigma Xi, Tau Beta Pi, Sigma Gamma Tau. Lutheran. Home: 3081 Rainier Ave Salt Lake City UT 84109 Office: Rogers & Assocs 515 E 4500 S Salt Lake City UT 84107

SUTHERLAND, BRUCE, composer, pianist; pupil Halsey Stevens, Ellis Kohs, Ethel Leginska, Amparo Iturbi; b. Daytona Beach, Fla.; s. Kenneth Francis and Norma (Williams) S.; Mus.B., U. So. Calif., 1957, Mus.M., 1959. Harpsichord soloist with Telemann Trio in concert tour, 1969-70; tchr. master class for pianists U. Tex., Austin, 1971; dir. Bach festivals Music Tchrs. Assn. Calif., 1972-73, dir. Artists fo Tomorrow, 1984—; compositions performed in numerous contemporary music festivals in U.S., 1957—; piano faculty Calif. State U. at Northridge, 1977—; adjudicator music competitions and auditions Nat. Guild Piano Tchrs., others; dir. Brentwood-Westwood Symphony ann. competition for young artists, 1981; composer: Allegro Fanfara for Orch., world premiere conducted by José Iturbi with Bridgeport Symphony Orch., 1970; Saxophone Quartet, 1971; Quintet for Flute, Strings, Piano, 1972; Notturno for Flute and Guitar, 1973; also string trio, piano and vocal works. Recipient grand prize Internat. Competition Louis Moreau Gottschalk, 1970; Stairway of Stars award Music Arts Soc., Santa Monica, 1973; named one of Los Angeles' Finest Piano Tchrs., New West Mag., 1977. Mem. Nat. Assn. Am. Composers and Condrs., Music Tchrs. Nat. Assn., Music Tchrs. Assn. Calif., Calif. Assn. Profl. Music Tchrs., Pi Kappa Lambda.

SUTHERLAND, DOUGLASS B., tent and awning company executive, city official; b. Helena, Mont., May 2, 1937; s. Chris and Marie Sutherland; m. Patrica Sutherland, Dec. 15, 1957; children—Karen, Scott. B.A., Central Wash. U., 1959. Program specialist Boeing Co., Tacoma, Wash., 1960-71; owner, pres. Tacoma Tent & Awning, Inc., 1971—. Bd. dirs., chmn. Puget Soung Air Pollution Control Agy.; bd. dirs. Tacoma-Pierce County Bd. Health, Tacoma-Pierce County Employment and Tng. Consortium; mayor City of Tacoma, 1982—. Mem. Assn. Wash. Cities, Tacoma-Pierce County C. of C. Republican. Lodge: Rotary. Avocation: sailing. Address: Office of the Mayor 747 Market St Suite 1220 Tacoma WA 98402 Office: Tacoma Tent and Awning Inc 121 N G St Tacoma WA 98403 *

SUTHERLAND, LOWELL FRANCIS, lawyer; b. Lincoln, Nebr., Dec. 17, 1939; s. Lowell Williams and Doris Genevieve (Peterson) S.; A.B., San Diego State Coll., 1962; LL.B., Hastings Coll. Law, 1965; m. Sandra Gaylynne Stengel, June 12, 1965; children—Scott Thorpe, Mark James, Sandra Doris. With Cooper, White & Cooper, attys., San Francisco, 1963-66; admitted to Calif. bar, 1966; with Wien & Thorpe, attys., El Centro, 1966-67; ptnr. Wien, Thorpe & Sutherland, El Centro, 1967-74, Wien, Thorpe, Sutherland & Stamper, 1973-74, Sutherland, Stamper & Feingold, 1974-77, Sutherland & Gerber, 1977—; ptnr. Sutherland & Sutherland, Ivy Shoppe; instr. bus. law Imperial Valley Coll., 1967. Pres. El Centro Active 20-30 Club, 1968-69; finance chmn. Salvation Army, 1972. Pres. bd. dirs. Boys Club of El Centro, 1969-71; bd. dirs. Imperial Gen. Hosp., 1971. Mem. Am., Calif., Imperial County bar assns., Am., Calif. (Recognition of Experience awards), San Diego (named outstanding trial lawyer April 1981, Oct. 1983 trial lawyer of yr. 1982), trial lawyers assns., Thurston Soc., Am. Bd. Trial Advocates (diplomate), Theta Chi. Mem. editorial staff Hastings Law Jour., 1964-65. Home: 1853 Sunset Dr El Centro CA 92243 Office: 300 S Imperial Ave 7 El Centro CA 92243

SUTHERLAND, ROBERT LOUIS, engineering company executive, educator; b. Fellsmere, Fla., May 15, 1916; s. John Alexander and Georgia Myrtle (Legg) S.; m. Mary-Alice Reed, May 18, 1945; children—Robert Hynes, Wayne Muzzy, Connie Anne, Nancy Lee, John Gary. B.S., U. Ill., 1939, M.S., 1948. Registered profl. engr., Ill., Iowa, Wyo. Devel. engr. Firestone Tire & Rubber Co., Akron, Ohio, 1939-41; research engr. Borg & Beck div. Borg-Warner Corp., Chgo, 1941; test engr. Buick Motor Div. Gen. Motors Corp., Melrose Park, Ill., 1942-43; sr. engr. research dept. Aeronca Aircraft Corp., Middletown, Ohio, 1943-45; research asso. Coll. Engring., U. Ill., 1945-48; asst., then asso. prof. mech. engring. State U. Iowa, Iowa City, 1948-58; city engr. Coralville, Iowa, 1950-53; prof. mech. engring. U. Wyo., Laramie, 1958-80; prof. emeritus U. Wyo., 1980—, head dept., 1960-70; pres. Skyline Engring. Co. Inc., Laramie, 1972—; research engr. Collins Radio Co., Cedar Rapids, Iowa, summer 1954, cons. engr., 1950-56; staff engr. Environ. Test Lab., Martin Co., Denver, summer 1960; dir. Hunter Mfg. Co., Iowa City, 1955-58, sec. bd., 1956-58. Author: Engineering Systems Analysis, 1958; Contbr. articles to profl. jours. Bus. adviser mfg. group Jr. Achievement, Middletown, 1943-44; mem. Iowa City Sch. Study Council, 1956-58; Mem. Civil Air Patrol, Chgo., 1941-43; legis. fellow to Nat. Conf. State Legislatures, 1982-84. Co-recipient Richard L. Templin award ASTM, 1952. Fellow ASME (life, regional v.p. 1965-67); mem. Soc. Automotive Engrs., Sigma Xi, Sigma Tau, Pi Tau Sigma, Tau Beta Pi. Methodist (steward, chmn. ofcl. bd. 1964-65, trustee 1966-69, pres. bd. 1967-69, lay leader 1969-72, chmn. council ministries 1973-75, chmn. finance com. 1975-79). Club: Kiwanian (dir. Laramie chpt. 1963-65, 79-82, pres. 1966, div. lt. gov. 1970-71, life mem. 1978). Home: 1420 Sanders St Laramie WY 82070

SUTRO, ROBERT, mortgage banker, certified public accountant; b. St. Joseph, Mo., Feb. 21, 1909; s. Ralph C. and Ellabelle (Greensfelder) S.; A.B., Stanford, 1931; M.A. in Econs./Accountancy, 1932; LL.D. (hon.), Linfield Coll., 1980; m. Dora Edith McMullen, Apr. 25, 1946; children—James Bernard, Thomas Lionel, Victoria Belle, William Gower, Margaret Zoe. Teaching asst. Stanford, 1931-32, 34-35; pub. accountant Haskins & Sells, Oscar Moss & Co., R.W.E. Cole & Co., C.P.A.'s, Los Angeles, 1933-36; partner Ralph C. Sutro Co., mortgage bankers, Los Angeles, 1937-41, pres., 1946-68, chmn. bd., 1959-81, chief exec. officer, 1968-79, ret., 1981; chmn. bd. trustees Sutro Mortgage Investment Trust, 1963-79; dir. Investors Mortgage Ins. Co. Pres., Sutro Sch. Music, Dance, Drama. Chmn. So. Calif. Research Council, 1974-76; trustee Pomona Coll.; trustee Linfield Coll., Oreg., chmn., 1974-77; trustee Calif. State U., Northridge Found., past bd. dirs. Trinity Coll. Parents Assn., Hartford, Conn., 1974-76; mem. exec. bd. Art Ctr. Coll. Design. Served to col. AUS, 1941-46; PTO, ETO. Recipient Humanitarian award real estate and constrn. industries div. NCCJ, 1976; C.P.A., Calif. Mem. Am. (past chmn. mortgage market, membership, investor liaison coms.; instr. Sch. Mortgage Banking, regional v.p., gov.-at-large, trustee research and ednl. trust fund, Disting. Service and Aubrey Costa awards 1967), So. Calif. (past dir.), Calif. mortgage bankers assns., Nat. Assn. Real Estate Investment Trusts (past gov.), Hancock Park Home Owners Assn. (dir., treas.), Apt. Assn. Los Angeles (past dir.), Am. Inst. C.P.A.'s, Calif. Soc. C.P.A.'s, Los Angeles, Wilshire (past dir., named Man of Yr. 1973) chambers commerce, Ret. Officers Assn., Nat. Assn. Realty Bds., Mil. Order World Wars, Res. Officers Assn., Lambda Alpha (chpt. pres. 1979-81, internat. v.p. 1981—). Clubs: Los Angeles (dir.), Univ. of Los Angeles, Miracle Mile Lions (Man of Yr. 1978). Office: Robert Realty Investments Inc 1337 S Gaffey St San Pedro CA 90731 Home: 1355 Paseo del Mar San Pedro CA 90731

SUTTER, HARVEY MACK, cons. engr.; b. Jennings, La., Oct. 5, 1906; s. Josiah Harvey and Effie Relief (Murray) S.; A.B., U. Wichita, 1932; m. Julia Genevieve Wright, Sept. 19, 1936; children—James Houston, Robert Mack, Julia Ann (Mrs. Richard D. Boyd), John Norman. Design and prodn. engr. Boeing Aircraft, Wichita, Kans., 1936-38; supr. arts, crafts and coop. activities Bur. Indian Affairs, U.S. Dept. of Interior, 1938-42, chief procurement br. Bur. of Reclamation, Washington, 1946-54, chief div. procurement and property mgmt., 1954-58; asst. to adminstr. Bonneville Power Adminstrn., 1958-61, asst. to chief engr., 1962-66; cons. engr., 1967—; analyst, chief prodn. service WPB, Denver, 1942-44; chief div. supply C.E., Denver, 1944-46. Mem. exec. bd. Portland area Boy Scouts Am. Recipient Silver Beaver award. Presbyterian. Mem. Nat., Western woodcarvers assns., Internat. Wood Collectors Soc. Club: Electric of Oreg. Author or co-author books and articles on woodcarving. Home: 3803 SE Carlton Portland OR 97202

SUTTON, BARBARA POWDERLY, marketing executive; b. Scranton, Pa., Oct. 29, 1940; s. Eugene Thomas and Kathryn Dorothy (Loftus) Powderly; m. Ronald Lewis Sutton, Jan. 7, 1984 (div. Feb. 1985). Student, Miami-Dade Jr. Coll., 1960. Asst. controller Oak Ridge, Inc., Hialeah, Fla., 1959-63; v.p., media dir. Harold Gardner Assoc., Inc., Miami Beach, 1963-67; media dir., adminstr. asst. Stern, Hays & Lang Advt., Inc., Miami, 1967-69; exec. asst. Los Angeles Times, 1969-71; media dir. Greenman Advt., Inc., Hollywood, Fla., 1971-73; various adminstrv. positions Fla. and Nev., 1973-82; owner Dolphin Secretarial Service, Reno, 1982—, Powderly Assocs., Reno, 1982—; pres. Bus.-Promotional Services, Inc., Reno, 1986—. Bd. dirs. March of Dimes, Reno, 1981-82; mem. Presdl. Task Force, Washington, 1982—. Named one of 2,000 Women of Achievement, London, 1971. Mem. Internat. Turquoise Assn. (exec. dir. 1975-76), Nat. Assn. Female Execs., Am. Soc. Profl. and Exec. Women, Nat. Assn. Secretarial Services, Reno Women in Advt., Reno-Sparks C. Of C. Republican. Roman Catholic. Avocations: sculpting, reading, travel, bridge, camping, auto racing. Office: Business-Promotional Services Inc 100 W Grove St #360 Reno NV 89509

SUTTON, DONALD HOWARD, baseball player; b. Clio, Ala., Apr. 2, 1945; m. Patricia Luther, Oct. 1, 1968; children: Daron, Staci. Ed., Miss. Coll., Clinton, Whittier (Calif.) Coll. With Los Angeles Dodgers, 1966-80, Houston Astros, 1980-82, Milw. Brewers, 1982-84, Oakland A's, 1984-85, Calif. Angels, 1985—; Nat. League pitcher in All-Star Game, 1972, 73, 75, 77, in World Series, 1974, 77, 78, 82. Author: How to Throw a Curve, 1977. Office: c/o California Angels Anaheim Stadium 2000 State College Blvd Anaheim CA 92806 *

SUTTON, GEOFFREY WILLIAM, psychologist; b. London, July 20, 1950; came to U.S., 1956; s. Arthur William and Gladys (New) S.; m. Sandra Marie Schmidt, Feb. 3, 1973; 1 child, Nathaniel William. BA in Psychology, Evangel Coll., 1972; MEd in Counseling, U. Mo., 1975, PhD in Psychology, 1981. Diplomate Am. Bd. Psychology; cert. psychologist, N.Mex. sch. psychologist, Mo., sch. psychol. counselor, N.Mex. Counselor, tchr. Teen Challenge, Sunbury, Pa., 1975-77; research asst. U. Mo., Columbia, 1977-79; psychology intern Woodhaven Sch., Columbia, 1979-80, dir. psychology, 1980-81, exec. dir., 1981-84; pvt. practice psychology Albuquerque, 1984—; cons. rural pub. schs. N.Mex., 1984—; staff affiliate Heights Psychiat., Albuquerque, 1985—; affiliate Helen Keller Ctr., N.Y., 1981-83. Author: Psychology: Foundations, 1980 (Author award 1981), Introduction to Personal and Social Psychology, 1980, Youth in Conflict, 1984; contbr. articles to profl. jours. Mem. C. of C., Columbia, 1983-84. Deaf-Blind Project grantee So. Cen. REG Ctr., Dallas, 1981-83. Mem. Am. Psychol. Assn., N.Mex. Psychol. Assn., Nat. Assn. Sch. Psychologists. Republican. Mem. Evang. Free Ch. Office: 5712 Osuna Rd NE Albuquerque NM 87109

SUTTON, GEORGE WALTER, research laboratory executive, professional engineer; b. Bklyn., Aug. 3, 1927; s. Jack and Pauline (Aaron) S.; m. Evelyn D. Kunnes, Dec. 25, 1952; children—James E., Charles S., Richard E., Stewart A. B. Mech. Engring. with honors, Cornell U., 1952; M.S., Calif. Inst. Tech., 1953, Ph.D. magna cum laude, 1955. Research scientist Lockheed Missle Co., 1955; research engr. Space Sci. Lab., Gen. Elec. Co., 1955-61, mgr. magnetohydrodynamic power generation, 1962-63; vis. Ford prof. Mass. Inst. Tech., 1961-62; sci. adviser Hdqrs. USAF, 1963-65; with Avco Research Lab., 1965—, dir. laser devel., 1971—; v.p. Avco Everett Research Lab., Everett, Mass., 1972-82; v.p., tech. dir. Helionetics Laser div. Avco Everett Research Lab., San Diego, 1983-86, v.p., tech. dir., 1985-86; v.p. JAYCOR, San Diego, 1986—; spl. cons. Energy Agy., 1977-79, Arms Control Agy., 1986; lectr. magnetohydrodynamics U. Pa., 1960-63, Stanford, 1964. Author: Proceedings 4th Symposium Engineering Aspects of Magnetohydrodynamics, 1964, (with A. Sherman) Engineering Magnetohydrodynamics, 1965, Direct Energy Conversion, 1966; Editor-in-chief: Jour. Am. Inst. Aeros. and Astronautics, 1967—; Contbr. 72 articles to profl. jours. Served with USAAF, 1945-47. Recipient Arthur Flemming award for outstanding govt. service, 1965. Fellow AIAA (chmn. plasmadynamics tech. com., Thermophysics award 1980), ASME, AAAS; mem. Symposium Engring. Aspects Magnetohydrodynamics (pres.). Spl. research on ablation of heat protection for ICBM re-entry and high energy lasers. Home: 8870-309 Villa La Jolla Dr La Jolla CA 92037 Office: PO Box 85154 San Diego CA 92138

SUTTON, JOHN PAUL, lawyer; b. Youngstown, Ohio, July 24, 1934; m. Jane Williamson, Aug. 20, 1958; children—Julia, Susan, Elizabeth. B.A., U. Va., 1956; J.D., George Washington U., 1963. Bar: Calif. bar 1965. Patent examiner U.S. Patent Office, Washington, 1956, 59-62; law clk. U.S. Ct. Customs and Patent Appeals, Washington, 1962-64; asso. firm Flehr, Holbach, Test, Albritton & Herbert, San Francisco, 1964-68; partner firm Limbach, Limbach & Sutton, San Francisco, 1969—; adj. instr. Practicing Law Inst., 1968-69; continuing edn. program Calif. State Bar, 1972, 75, U. Calif. Law Sch., Berkeley, 1975, 84. Contbr. articles to legal jours. Served with USNR, 1956-59. Mem. Calif. Patent Law Assn. (pres. 1975), San Francisco Patent Law Assn. (pres. 1976), State Bar Calif. (exec. com. patent sect. 1975-77), Am. Chem. Soc. Democrat. Episcopalian. Club: World Trade (San Francisco). Home: 2421 Pierce St San Francisco CA 94115 Office: Limbach Limbach & Sutton 2001 Ferry Bldg San Francisco CA 94111

SUTTON, MARCELLA FRENCH, interior designer; b. Prague, Czechoslovakia, Sept. 4, 1946; came to U.S., 1952, naturalized, 1956; d. Eugen E. and Frances V. (Pruchovia) French; B.S. in Profl. Arts, Woodbury U., 1971; m. Michael D. Sutton, Feb. 11, 1978; 1 son, Kevin Christopher. Mgr. design dept. W. & J. Sloane, Beverly Hills, Calif., 1972-76; project dir. Milton I. Swimmer, Beverly Hills, 1977-78; owner, interior designer Marcella French Designs, Woodland Hills and La Crescenta, Calif., 1969—; property mgmt. coordinator, interior designer Home Savs. and Loan., State of Calif., Los Angeles, 1979-82; regional premises officer, asst. v.p. regional hdqrs. Bank of Am., Los Angeles, 1981-86; v.p. M.D. Sutton Ins. Agy.; prin. designer Marcella French Designs, Woodland Hills; cons. pvt. residences. Active Young Republicans. Recipient various scholarships. Mem. Moravian Brothers Ch.

SUTTON, MICHELE MARIE, printing company executive; b. Hermosa Beach, Calif., Sept. 30, 1945; d. Richard Prentice and Melva Marie (Jensen) Jenkins; m. Darel Lee Sutton, May 25, 1968; 1 child, Joshua James. Paralegal City's Atty.'s Office, Santa Monica, Calif., 1970-77; owner, pres. Kwik-Kopy Printing, Grand Junction, Colo., 1981—; pres. MDJ, Investments Inc. Trustee Western Colo. Ctr. for Arts, Grand Junction, 1985—; bd. dirs. March of Dimes, 1986—. Mem. Nat. Assn. Quick Printers, Nat. Assn. Female Execs., Grand Junction C. of C. (v.p. and mem. bd. dirs. women's div. 1984). Democrat. Avocation: photography. Home: 2695 Wilshire Ct Grand Junction CO 81506 Office: Kwik-Kopy Printing 904 N 7th St Grand Junction CO 81501

SUTTON, MILO WILTON, newspaper executive; b. Hartford, Kans., Dec. 24, 1928; s. Joseph Bernard and Genevieve Loraine (Campbell) S.; m. Erna Doreen Clemmer, Dec. 18, 1946; children—Cynthia, Janet, Rita, Debbie, Wendy, Michael. Student Kans. State Tchrs. Coll., 1948-50, UCLA, 1969. Mem. Kans. Ho. of Reps., 1950-54; adv. mgr. Emporia (Kans.) Times, 1949-52; reporter Emporia Gazette, 1953-54; owner, pub. Salina (Kans.) Advertiser-Sun, 1954-59; with advt. and editorial depts. Los Angeles Mirror-News, 1959-60; promotion mgr. South Bay Daily Breeze, Torrance, Calif., 1960-74; dir. promotion and research Dallas Times Herald, 1974-77; dir. mktg. services, mem. operating com. Los Angeles Herald Examiner, 1977-84; regional mktg. adminstr. Los Angeles Times, 1984—. Bd. dirs., regional pres. Kans. Press Assn., 1956-57. Served with USN, 1946-48. Mem. Internat. Newspaper Mktg. Assn. (internat. bd. dirs. 1975-79, 85-88, pres. So. region 1976-77, pres. Western region 1984-85, internat. v.p. 1986—), Am. Mktg. Assn., Advt. Club Los Angeles. Lutheran. Author numerous trade mag. articles; lectr. USA, Europe. Home: 415 2nd St Hermosa Beach CA 90254 Office: Times Mirror Sq Los Angeles CA 90053

SUTTON, PHILIP D(IETRICH), psychologist; b. Ridgewood, N.J., June 20, 1952; s. Clifton C. and Ida-Lois (Dietrich) S.; m. Kathleen E. Duffy, June 17, 1973; children—Heather, Shivonne. B.A., So. Ill. U., 1974; M.A., U. Chgo., 1975; Ph.D., U. Utah, 1979. Lic. psychologist, Colo. Psychologist VA Hosp., Salt Lake City, 1975-76; psychology intern Salt Lake Community Mental Health Ctr., Salt Lake City, 1976-78; counselor, instr. Counseling Ctr., U. Utah, Salt Lake City, 1976-78; counselor, acting dir. spl. services program Met. State Coll., Denver, 1978-80; staff psychologist Kaiser-Permanente Health Plan, Denver, 1980-83; adj. prof. U. Colo., 1979-83; pvt. practice psychology, Boulder (Colo.) Med. Ctr., 1981—; cons. spl. programs for disadvantaged students in higher edn. Dept. HEW, 1980. Mem. Am. Psychol. Assn., Biofeedback Soc. Am., Soc. Behavioral Medicine. Home: Box 810 Nederland CO 80466 Office: Boulder Med Ctr 2750 Broadway Boulder CO 80302

SUTTON, TONY WAYNE, interior designer; b. Peoria, Ill., Oct. 3, 1955; s. Jerry Dean Sutton and Mary (Guylene) Rhodes; m. Tracey Lynn Matlick, Apr. 11, 1981; children: Alex Rhodes, Blake Rhodes. B in Interior Design, U. Ill., 1978. Interior designer Cen. Design Studio, Springfield, Ill., 1978-79, Est Est, Inc., Scottsdale, Ariz., 1980-84; pres., owner Est Est, Inc., Scottsdale, 1984—. Co-chmn. Scottsdale Culinary Festival, 1981, chmn., 1982. Recipient Mame award Cen. Ariz. Sales and Mktg. Council, 1981. Mem. Men's League Scottsdale Ctr. for Arts (v.p. 1983, pres. 1984), Scottsdale Arts Ctr. Assn., Am. Cancer Soc. Avocations: community projects, traveling, reading. Home: 5210 E Marconi Scottsdale AZ 85254 Office: Est Est Inc 7050 Main St Scottsdale AZ 85251

SUVER, JAMES DONALD, health administration educator, accountant; b. Swords Creek, Va., Oct. 21, 1931; s. Van Dola and Marcia Ellen (Davis) S.; m. Margaret Louise Schindler, Mar. 21, 1958 (div. 1977); children: James A., Amanda M.; m. Jean Claire Cooper, Dec. 31, 1980. BBA, Calif. State Coll., Sacramento, 1962; MBA, Harvard U., 1965, DBA, 1971. Cert. mgmt. acct. Enlisted U.S. Air Force, 1949, advanced through grades to col., 1975; dir. mil. pay Air Force Acctg. and Fin. Ctr., Denver, 1973-75; ret., 1975; prof. acctg. U. Colo.-Colorado Springs, 1975-81, prof. health adminstrn. Health Scis. Ctr., 1978-81; prof. health policy and adminstrn. U. N.C. Sch. Pub. Health, Chapel Hill, 1981-84, dir. masters program, 1982-84; dir. program health adminstrn. U. Colo., Denver, 1984-86, assoc. dean, 1985—; cons. in field. Bd. dirs. Peak Health, Ltd., Colorado Springs, Colo., 1981—; treas. Triangle Hospice, Chapel Hill, 1982-84, dir., chmn. fin. com. Rocky Mountain Multiple Sclerosis Ctr., 1985—; Decorated D.F.C., Legion of Merit, Air medal (8), Bronze Star; recipient Outstanding Teaching award U. Colo., 1977, 78, 81. Mem. Nat. Assn. Acctg. (Cert. of Merit 1977-79), Am. Pub. Health Assn., Health Care Fin. Mgmt. Assn., Assn. Govt. Acctg. (Disting. Research award 1978). Republican. Roman Catholic. Author: Management Accounting for Health Care Organizations, 1981, 84, Financial Management Concepts and Applications for Health Care Provider, 1984; contbr. articles in field to profl. publs. Home: 7878 W 110th Dr Westminster CO 80020 Office: U Colo Coll Bus 1475 Lawrence St Denver CO 80202

SUYENAGA, ELSIE SAKAE, educator; b. Honolulu, Dec. 19; d. Shigeji Jinbo-Shimizu and Misao Jinbo; B.A., Honolulu Christian Coll., 1962; A.B. (Fed. grantee, 1963), Pasadena Coll., 1963; postgrad. U. Hawaii, 1963-81; m. James Saburo Suyenaga; 1 son, Matthew Masao. Sec., Nuuanu Bapt. Ch., 1954-62; tchr. Ewa Beach Elem. Sch., Ewa Beach, Hawaii, 1964—; exchange tchr. Laurel Elem. Sch., Los Angeles Sch. Dist., 1968-69; advisor student council. Sec., Palisades Community Assn., 1977, news editor; active polit. campaigns, 1962, 78, 80, 82, 84, 86; treas. Neighborhood Bd. Pearl City, 1982, legis. chmn. Pearl City Community Assn., also treas., 1984-85; treas. local chpt. PTA. Recipient student council award for advisors, 1978, Dist. award PTA, 1976, cert. of merit Pearl City Community Assn., 1977. Mem. Hawaii State Tchrs. Assn. (cert. of merit 1969, dir. 1981-83, sec. fin. com. 1981, vice-chmn. 1982), Leeward Tchrs. Assn. (treas., polit. action chmn. 1986—), Hawaii Edn. Assn. (bd. trustees 1986—), Am. Mus. Natural History, DAV, Alpha Delta Kappa (treas. Lambda 1980-81). Democrat. Baptist. Home: 2381 Anihinihi St Pearl City HI 96782

SUYETSUGU, GRACE TAMIKO, nurse; b. San Mateo, Calif., Feb. 16, 1957; d. Frank Takiji and Mitsuka (Shimizu) S. BS magna cum laude in Nursing, San Francisco State U., 1979. RN, Calif. Charge nurse med./surg. unit Peninsula Hosp. and Med. Ctr., Burlingame, Calif., 1979-84; staff nurse ICU, 1984—. Mem. Nat. Nurses Assn., Calif. Nurses Assn., Am. Assn. Critical Care Nurses. Democrat. Buddhist. Avocations: traveling, photography, cooking, needlework, sports. Home: 1274 40th Ave San Francisco CA 94122 Office: Peninsula Hosp and Med Ctr 1783 El Camino Real Burlingame CA 94010

SUZUKI, SUSAN JAN, mechanical engineer; b. Santa Barbara, Calif., July 31, 1959; d. John Yoshio and Fumi Suzuki. BS in Environ. Engring., Calif. Poly. State U., San Luis Obispo, 1982. Cert. engr.-in-tng. Mech. and environ. engr. Naval Air Rework Facility, Alameda, Calif., 1982-84; mech. engr.Coal/Air dept. Naval Energy and Environ. Support Acitvity, Port Hueneme, Calif., 1984—. Mem. Air Pollution Control Assn., Soc. Women Engrs., ASME, Am. Electroplaters and Surface Finishers Soc., Nat. Assn. Female Execs. Office: Naval Energy & Environ Support CBC Bldg 1163 Port Hueneme CA 93043-5014

SVEINSSON, JOHANNES, retired electronics engineer, former city and county government official, building material sales engineer; b. Winnipeg, Man., Can., Nov. 30, 1912; m. M. Eleanor Lundstedt, 1938; children—Joleen Sveinsson Kinney, Kenneth J., Johannes. Electronic engr., Fresno State Coll., 1935; student U. Calif.-Berkeley, 1940. With Pacific Rock & Gravel & Paving Co., Los Angeles, 1935-41; counselor Calif. Dept. Corrections, 1941-76. Bd. dirs. Anti Poverty, Monterey County, 1965-75, Monterey County Med. Assn., 1977, Sr. Citizens, Montery County, 1982—; v.p. Monterey Bay Govts., Monterey, Santa Cruz and San Benito Counties, 1960-83; mem. Gonzales City Council Calif., 1960-83; pres. Calif. League of Cities, Monterey Bay Div., 1976-77; mayor Gonzales, 1981-83; mem. Monterey County Grand Jury, Salinas, Calif., 1983—. Served with USAAF, 1942-45. Mem. Calif. League Cities (bd. dirs. pub. safety com. 1962-74), Icelandic Assn. No. Calif. (pres. 1966), Am. Scandanavians of Calif. (pres. 1975). Democrat. Home: PO Box 934 Gonzales CA 93926

SVIKHART, EDWIN GLADDIN, construction equipment manufacturing executive; b. Chgo., July 12, 1930; s. Edwin Gabriel and Mildred Charlotte (Slapnicka) S.; m. Joann Barbara Frisk, Aug. 22, 1954; children: David E., Robert E. BA, Beloit (Wis.) Coll., 1952; postgrad., Bradley U., 1957-59. Western fin. mgr. Caterpillar Tractor Co., Peoria, Ill., 1956-66; chief fin. officer Berglund Inc., Napa, Calif., 1966-71; chief fin. officer, treas. Galion (Ohio) Mfg. Co., Galion, 1971-77; chief operating officer constrn. equip. internat. div. Dresser Industries, Columbus, Ohio, 1977-81; chief operating officer Rocky Mountain Machinery Co., Salt Lake City, 1981—. Speaker at various trade confs. Elder, fin. dir. Westminster Presbyn. Ch., Peoria, 1960-63; v.p., bd. dirs. Galion Community Ctr., 1973-75; elder, personnel chmn. 1st Presbyn. Ch., Salt Lake City, 1981-83. Served to lt. (j.g.) USN, 1952-56. Named an Outstanding Young Man of Am., U.S. C. of C., 1966. Mem. Nat. Assn. Accts., Mountain W. Venture Capital Club (founder). Republican. Avocations: period furniture building, gardening.

SWAGEL, DENNIS JAY, lawyer; b. N.Y.C., May 25, 1946; s. Harry R. and Sah Belle (Fisher) S.; student Harvard U., 1966; certificat de langue pratique U. Paris, 1967; AB (Dana scholar), Hamilton Coll., 1968; JD, Fordham U., 1971; postgrad. U. So. Calif. Sch. Law, Los Angeles, 1976, 79. Bar: N.Y. 1972, Calif. 1974. Law clk. firm Lord, Day & Lord, N.Y.C., 1969; legal asst. Legal Aid Soc., N.Y.C., 1969-70; law clk. Greenbaum, Wolff & Ernst, N.Y.C., 1970-71; ptnr. Casa de Cynjaden Co., Cypress, Calif., 1972-73; assoc. firm William J. Bluestein, Beverly Hills, Calif., 1974; ptnr. firm Bluestein, Heimbach & Swagel, Beverly Hills, 1975; sole practice, Los Angeles, 1975-84, Beverly Hills, Calif., 1984—. Mem. Environ. Def. Fund. Mem. Am., Los Angeles County, Beverly Hills bar assns., Assn. Trial Lawyers Am., Calif. Trial Lawyers Assn., Los Angeles Trial Lawyers Assn., Lawyers Club Los Angeles, Fordham Law Alumni Assn., Am. Film Inst., U.S. Olympic Soc., ACLU, Los Angeles County Mus. Art, Los Angeles Contemporary Exhbns., Greater Los Angeles Zoo Assn., Mus. Contemporary Art Los Angeles, Town Hall, Internat. Platform Assn., Nat. Trust Hist. Preservation, Am. Guild Authors and Composers, Sierra Club. Democrat. Jewish. Club: B'nai B'rith. Home: 4329 Latona Ave Los Angeles CA 90031

SWAIM, JEFFREY LYNN, minister; b. Eugene, Oreg., Aug. 14, 1956; s. Laurence Erven and Winifred Marie (Hansen) S.; m. Kathy Lyn Crow, Aug. 13, 1977; children: Stephanie Ann, Lyndsey Elain Marie. BA in Bible, Cen. Bible Coll., 1978. Ordained minister Assemblies of God Ch., 1981. Youth minister First Assembly, Medford, Oreg., 1978-81, Albany, Oreg., 1981—; lectr. South Albany High Sch., 1982-85; mem. state youth senate Assemblies of God, Salem, Oreg., 1981-85, youth rep., Medford, 1978-81, Albany, 1984-85; named Youth Rep. of Yr., 1980, 81. Author (booklet) Questions for New Teen Christians, 1985; editor (booklets) Youth Leaders Training Manual, 1983, Camp Counselor Manual, 1984. Bd. dirs. Juvenile Services Commn., Linn County, Oreg., 1981-82. Republican. Avocations: big game hunting, jogging.

SWALLEY, CLINTON LAVON, electronic engineer; b. Ponca City, Okla., Nov. 12, 1937; s. Fred Wesley and Mary Lena (Barber) S.; m. Dorothy Elizabeth Flynt, May 31, 1958 (div. Sept. 1973); children: Charles, Lyle, Sherylyn; m. Pansy Loretta Folkerts, Feb. 1, 1976 (div. Sept. 1977); 1 child, Christina; m. Debralee Ann Waite, Mar. 1978 (div. 1983); m. Donna Louise Wood, July 5, 1983; children: Pamela, Jim, Karen, Patricia. AA, USAF Inst., 1963; AS, Allen Hancock Coll., 1972. Enlisted USAF, 1956, advanced through grades to staff sgt., resigned, 1969; test data analyst Lint-Tempco-Vaught, Grand Prairie, Tex., 1969-71; organ installation service rep. Baldwin Piano & Organ Co., Los Angeles, 1972-73; design engr. Schrager Cues, North Hollywood, Calif., 1974-76; electronic technician AMD, Sunnyvale, Calif., 1976-79; electronic engr. Monolithic Memories, Inc., Santa Clara, Calif., 1979—. Instr. CPR and First Aid, ARC, Palo Alto, Calif., 1982-86. Mem. AAAS, Nat. Rifle Assn. Republican. Mem. Ch. Disciples of Christ. Avocations: backpacking, camping, golf. Home: 955 Primrose Ave Sunnyvale CA 94086 Office: Monolithic Memories Inc 2175 Mission Coll Blvd Santa Clara CA 95050

SWAN, DEAN GEORGE, weed scientist; b. Wheatland, Wyo., Sept. 16, 1923; s. Oscar Elvirus and Augusta Marie (Drube) S.; m. Rowena Mae White, Dec. 19, 1948; children: Cynthia, John, Daniel. BS, U. Wyo., 1952, MS, 1954; PhD, U. Ill., 1964. Vocat. agrl. instr. Chadron (Nebr.) High Sch., 1952-53; asst. prof. farm crops Oreg. State U., Pendleton, 1955-65; extension weed specialist U. Ariz., Tucson, 1965-66; sabbatical research Weed Research Orgn., Oxford, Eng., 1972-73, 78-79; extension weed scientist Wash. State U., Pullman, 1966—. Co-author: Weeds of Eastern Washington and Adjacent Areas, 1972; contbr. numerous articles to profl. jours. Served to sgt. USAAF, 1942-45. Mem. Weed Sci. Soc. Am., Western Soc. Weed Scis. (chmn. extension and regulatorysect. 1971, local arrangements com., 1981-84, site selection com. 1981-84), Wash. State Weed Assn. (hon.). Avocations: photography, gardening, sports. Home: SW 822 Crestview Pullman WA 99163 Office: Wash State U 173 Johnson Hall Pullman WA 99164-6420

SWAN, KENNETH CARL, physician and surgeon; b. Kansas City, Mo., Jan. 1, 1912; s. Carl E. and Blanche (Peters) S.; m. Virginia Grone, Feb. 5, 1938; children: Steven Carl, Kenneth, Susan. A.B., U. Oreg., 1933, M.D., 1936. Diplomate: Am. Bd. Ophthalmology (chmn. 1960-61). Intern U. Wis., 1936-37; resident in ophthalmology State U. Iowa, 1937-40; practice medicine specializing in ophthalmology Portland, Oreg., 1945—; staff Good Samaritan Hosp.; asst. prof. ophthalmology State U. Iowa, Iowa City, 1941-44; asso. prof. U. Oreg. Med. Sch., Eugene, 1944-45; prof. and head dept. ophthalmology U. Oreg. Med. Sch., 1945—; Chmn. sensory diseases study sect. NIH; mem. adv. council Nat. Eye Inst.; also adv. council Nat. Inst. Neurol. Diseases and Blindness. Contbr. articles on ophthalmic subjects to med. publs. Recipient Proctor Research medal, 1953; Disting. Service award U. Oreg., 1963; Meritorious Achievement award U. Oreg. Med. Sch., 1968; Howe Ophthalmology medal, 1977; Aubrey Watzek Pioneer award Lewis and Clark Coll., 1979; named Oreg. Scientist of Yr. Oreg. Mus. Sci. and Industry. Mem. Assn. Research in Ophthalmology (trustee), Am. Acad. Ophthalmology (v.p. 1978), Soc. Exptl. Biology and Medicine, AAAS, AMA, Am. Ophthal. Soc. (Howe medal for distinguished service 1977), Oreg. Med. Soc., Sigma Xi, Sigma Chi (Significant Sig award 1977). Home: 4645 SW Fairview Blvd Portland OR 97221 Office: Univ Oregon Med Sch Portland OR 97201

SWAN, RICHARD ALAN, health care administrator; b. Hollywood, Calif., May 5, 1944; s. Morris George and Mary Theresa (Fenusz) S.; m. Carol Ann Jacobs, Apr. 15, 1967; children: David Michael, Jennifer Marie, Matthew Richard. BS in Indsl. Mgmt., U. So. Calif., 1966; MS in Health Care Adminstrn., Trinity U., 1970. Adminstrv. resident Tucson (Ariz.) Med. Ctr., 1971; assoc. cons. A.T. Kearney and Co. Inc., Chgo., 1971-72; v.p. Tribrook Group Inc., Oakbrook, Ill., 1972-82; dir. program and spl. studies div. James A. Hamilton Assocs. Inc., Dallas, 1982-83; v.p. corp. devel. Vincentian Health Services, Los Angeles, 1983—. Contbr. articles to profl. jours. Served to capt. Med. Service Corps, U.S. Army, 1967-69. Fellow Am. Assn. Hosp. Cons.; mem. Am. Coll. Healthcare Execs., Soc. Hosp. Planning and Mktg., So. Calif. Soc. Hosp. Planners (charter), Health Care Execs. of So. Calif., Am. Hosp. Assn. Republican. Roman Catholic. Avocations: golfing, fishing. Office: St Vincent Med Ctr 2131 W Third St Los Angeles CA 90057

SWANN, EUGENE MERWYN, lawyer, economist; b. Phila., Aug. 21, 1934; s. Earl and Doris Burnette (Michell) S.; married (div. 1978); children: Liana, E. Michael, Elliott. BS, Temple U., 1957; MA, U. Mass., 1959; LLB, U. Calif., Berkeley, 1962. Bar: Calif. 1963, U.S. Supreme Ct. 1967. Dep. dist. atty. Contra Costa County, Calif., 1963-67; exec. dir. Contra Costa Legal Found., 1967-77; dir. office of citizens' complaints City of San Francisco, 1982-84; sole practice Contra Costa, 1984—; mem. exec. com. Contra Costa Bar, 1965-69. Democrat. Home: 43 Donald Dr Orinda CA 94563

SWANSON, BARRY GRANT, food science educator; b. Green Lake, Wis., Apr. 16, 1944; s. Orville Edward and Vera Louella (Dressel) S.; m. Marilyn Ann Ribbe, Apr. 4, 1970; children: Alyssa Michelle, Krista Jo, Sara Beth. BS in Secondary Edn., U. Wis., 1966, MS in Food Sci., 1970, PhD in Food Sci., 1972. Asst. prof. food sci. U. Idaho, Moscow, 1972-73; from asst. prof. to prof. Wash. State U., Pullman, 1973—; cons. FAO/UN, India, 1986; chmn. tech. com. Bean/Cowpea Collaborative Research Support Program-U.S. Agy. Internat. Devel., 1985-86. Pres. Emmanuel Luth. Ch., Moscow, 1975-78; legis. rep. Wash. State U. Faculty Senate, 1984-86. Grantee Nalley's Fine Foods, Inc., Tacoma, 1985-86. Mem. AAAS, Am. Chem. Soc., Inst. Food Technologists (councilor 1986—, Travelaward 1974), Am. Council Sci. and Health, Am. Soc. Horticultural Sci. Home: 1141 Highland Dr Moscow ID 83843 Office: Wash State U Dept Food Sci and Human Nutrition Pullman WA 99164-6330

SWANSON, DALE WALTER, chemist, educator; b. Duluth, Minn., Dec. 11, 1954; s. Walter Leon and Alice Henrietta (Helgeton) S.; m. Phyllis Sumiko Fujinami, May 7, 1983. BS in Chemistry, U. Minn., Duluth, 1977; MS in Chemistry, U. Calif., Irvine, 1982. Cert. community coll. tchr., Calif. Semiconductor process and software engr. Rockwell Internat., Anaheim, Calif., 1978-82, polymer chemist, 1983—; chemistry lectr. Calif. State Poly. U., Pomona, 1985—. Mem. Am. Chem. Soc. Democrat. Avocation: tennis. Home: 4545 Avenida Rio Del Oro Yorba Linda CA 92686 Office: Rockwell Internat 3370 Miraloma Ave Anaheim CA 92803

SWANSON, DONALD ALAN, geologist; b. Tacoma, July 25, 1938; s. Leonard Walter and Edith Christine (Bowers) S.; m. Barbara Joan White, May 25, 1974. BS in Geology, Wash. State U., 1960; PhD in Geology, Johns Hopkins U., 1964. Geologist U.S. Geol. Survey, Menlo Park, Calif., 1965-68, 71-80, Hawaii National Park, 1968-71; sr. geologist Cascades Volcano Obs. U.S. Geol. Survey, Vancouver, Wash., 1980—, scientist in charge, 1986—; cons. U.S. Dept. Energy, Richland, Wash., 1979-83; volcanologist New Zealand Geol. Survey, Taupo, 1984; advisor Colombian Volcano Obs., Manizales, 1986. Assoc. editor Jour. Volcanolgy and Geothermal Research, 1976—; editor Bull. of Volcanology, 1985—; contbr. numerous articles to profl. jours. Recipient Superior Service award U.S. Geol. Survey, 1980, Meritorious Service award U.S. Dept. Interior, 1985; postdoctoral fellow NATO, 1964-65. Fellow Geol. Soc. Am.; mem. AAAS, Am. Geophys. Union, Sigma Xi. Avocation: hiking. Home: 15710 NE 31st Ave Vancouver WA 98686 Office: US Geol Survey 5400 MacArthur Blvd Vancouver WA 98661

SWANSON, EDWIN ARCHIE, business educator; b. Boone County, Nebr., July 5, 1908; s. Andrew E. and Alma (Nordgren) S.; student George Washington U., 1933-34; B.S., Nebr. State Tchrs. Coll., Kearney, 1932; M.S., U. So. Calif., 1936, Ed.D., 1949; m. Fern E. Anderson, Aug. 25, 1933; children—Edwin Burton, John LeRoy. Elementary, high sch. tchr., Nebr., 1925-35; instr. Fullerton Jr. Coll., 1936-37, 38-39; teaching and research fellow in edn. U. So. Calif., 1935-36, instr. edn. and commerce, 1937-38; asso. prof., dept. head Ariz. State Coll., 1939-46; prof. bus. San Jose (Calif.) State U., 1946-79, emeritus prof. bus., 1979—, chmn. dept., 1957-68. Vis. faculty mem., summer sessions U. Tenn., Woman's Coll. U. N.C., Armstrong Coll., Colo. State Coll., U. So. Calif., U. Fla. Editor: New Media in Teaching the Business Subjects, 1965; editorial bd. Nat. Bus. Edn. Quar., 1939-48, editor, 1939-41. Mem. AAUP, AAAS, Am. Mgmt. Assn., Nat. (pres. 1950-51, mem. and chmn. publs. com. and editorial bd. 1959-62, editor Yearbook 1965), Western (pres. 1954-55, gen. program chmn. conv. 1965), Cal. bus. edn. assns., NEA, Calif. Tchrs. Assn., Phi Delta Kappa (chpt. pres. 1945-46, 54-55, area coordinator 1955-66), Kappa Delta Pi, Pi Omega Pi, Delta Pi Epsilon (mem. nat. commn. bus. and econ. edn. 1964-65, mem. bd. govs. for research and devel. in bus. edn. 1968-74), Gamma Rho Tau, Xi Phi, Phi Kappa Phi (chpt. pres. 1956-57). Presbyn. Club: Commonwealth (San Francisco). Contbr. publs. in field. Home: 2390 Mazzaglia Ave San Jose CA 95125

SWANSON, GERALD (GERRY) CHANDLER, social worker, health planner; b. Los Angeles, May 28, 1940; s. Conrad De Forrest and Margot Lamb (Spratt Lamb) S.; m. Mary Joan Atichson, Sept. 1, 1967; children: Scott, Kent. BA in Psychology, Vanderbilt U., 1963; MSSW, U. Tenn., 1965; postgrad., San Antonio Group Psychotherapy Inst., 1967-68. Counselor, adminstrv. asst. Kirk Army Hosp., Aberdeen, Md., 1965-66; social worker officer and acting dir., social work service Brooke Gen. Hosp. div. Brooke Army Med. Ctr., Houston, 1966-68; outpatient team leader Bernalillo County Mental Health and Mental Retardation Ctr., Albuquerque, 1968-70, Quebrar, Inc., Albuquerque, 1970-72; dir. client support services Gen. Addictions Treatment Effort program, Albuquerque, 1972-75; dir. Albuquerque Treatment Alternatives to Street Crime project Gen. Addictions Treatment Effort program and Bernalillo County Mental Health and Mental Retardation Ctr., 1975-78; owner and operator Albuquerque Screening and Treatment Referral Assocs., 1978—; dir. planning N.Mex. Health Systems Agy., Albuquerque, 1979-85; co-chmn. N. Mex. Human Services Coalition, 1984-85; adminstrv. coordinator open adult program Vista Sandia Hosp., Aubuquerque, 1985-87. State Dem. vice-ward chair and precinct chair, 1985-86; co-chair N.Mex. Human Services Coalition; acting chair N.Mex. Coalition for Pub. Responsibility; co-chmn. Alliance for the Mentally Ill., Albuquerque. Served to capt. U.S. Army, 1965-68. Mem. N.Mex. Mental Health Assn. (bd. dirs. 1980—), Nat. Assn. Social Workers (cert.), Employee Health Providers Assn., N.Mex. Pub. Health Assn., N.Mex. Substance Abuse Counselors Assn., Am. Hosp. Assn. (social work dirs.), Albuquerque X-C Ski Touring Club, Norski Ski Racing Club, Phi Alpha. Methodist. Club: Albuquerque X-C Ski Touring. Avocations: cross-country ski racing, bicycling, backpacking, canoeing. Home: 910 Adams NE Albuquerque NM 87110 Office: Vista Sandia Hosp 501 Alameda Blvd NE Albuquerque NM 87113

SWANSON, LLOYD VERNON, dairy science educator; b. Isanti, Minn., Oct. 16, 1938; s. Verner S. and Berniece M. (Wick) S.; m. Grace A. Larson, June 18, 1966; children: Andrea, Alan. BS, U. Minn., 1960, MS, 1967; PhD, Mich. State U., 1970. Asst. prof. Oreg. State U., Corvallis, 1971-76, assoc. prof., 1976—. Contbr. articles to profl. jours. Served with USNR, 1960-62. Mem. AAAS, Am. Dairy Sci. Assn., Am. Soc. Animal Sci., Endocrine Soc., Soc. for Study Reprodn., Sigma Xi. Democrat. Lodge: Kiwanis. Avocations: photography, woodworking, travel, reading. Home: 3125 NW Taft Corvallis OR 97330 Office: Oreg State U Dept Animal Sci Corvallis OR 97331

SWANSON, LYNN ALLEN, research chemist; b. Mpls., July 28, 1942; s. Arnold Clinton and Helen Margaret (Horgan) S.; m. Carol Ruth Hurtley, Aug. 12, 1967; children: Erick Olof, Taylor Alexander. B in Chemistry, U. Minn., 1964; MS, U. Iowa, 1968, PhD, 1970. Research chemist Research and Devel. div. IMC Corp., Terre Haute, Ind., 1969-77, asst. mgr., 1977-80; research scientist Researhc and Devel. div. IMC Corp., Terre Haute, Ind., 1980-86, tech. supr., 1984-86, mgr., 1986—. Mem. Am. Chem. Soc. (counselor Wabash Valley Sect. 1985—), Ind. Acad. Sci., Terre Haute Jaycees (treas. 1972-73, adminstrv. v.p. 1973-74, exec. v.p. 1974-75), Sigma Xi, Alpha Chi Sigma (gen. advisor 1986—, pres. edn. found. 1984-86, trustee 1978—). Republican. Lutheran. Avocations: genealogy, philately, gardening. Office: IMC Corp PO Box 207 Terre Haute IN 47808

SWANSON, PHILLIP DEAN, neurologist; b. Seattle, Oct. 1, 1932; s. William Dean and Kathryn C. (Peterson) S.; m. Sheila N. Joardar, Apr. 17, 1957; children—Stephen, Jennifer, Kathryn, Rebecca, Sara. B.S., Yale U., 1954; student, U. Heidelberg, 1952-53; M.D., Johns Hopkins U., 1958; Ph.D. in Biochemistry, U. London, 1964. Intern Boston City Hosp., 1958-59; resident in neurology Johns Hopkins Hosp., Balt. City Hosp., 1959-62; asst. prof. U. Wash. Sch. Medicine, Seattle, 1964-68; assoc. prof. U. Wash. Sch. Medicine, 1968-73, prof., 1973—, head div. neurology, 1967—; mem. med. adv. bd. Puget Sound chpt. Nat. Multiple Sclerosis Soc., 1967—, chmn., 1970-74; mem. com. to combat Huntington's Disease Nat. Sci. Council, 1975-84. Author: (with others) Introduction to Clinical Neurology, 1976; editor: Signs and Symptoms in Neurology, 1984; contbr. articles to profl. jours. NIH spl. fellow, 1962-64; NIH grantee. Fellow Am. Acad. Neurology; mem. Am. Neurol. Assn., Assn. Univ. Profs. Neurology (pres. 1975-76), Am. Heart Assn., Am. Soc. Neurochemistry, Internat. Soc. Neurochemistry, Biochem. Soc. (London), Am. Soc. Clin. Investigation (emeritus). Home: 6537 29th Ave NE Seattle WA 98115 Office: Div Neurology Univ Wash Sch Medicine Seattle WA 98195

SWANSON, RICHARD WILLIAM, operations research analyst; b. Rockford, Ill., July 26, 1934; s. Richard and Erma Marie (Herman) S.; B.S., Iowa State U., 1958, M.S., 1964; m. Laura Yoko Arai, Dec. 30, 1970. Ops. analyst Stanford Research Inst., Monterey, Calif., 1958-62; statistician ARINC Research Corp., Washington, 1964-65; sr. scientist Booz-Allen Applied Research, Vietnam, 1965-67, Los Angeles, 1967-68; sr. ops. analyst Control Data Corp., Honolulu, 1968-70; mgmt. cons., Honolulu, 1970-73; exec. v.p. SEQUEL Corp., Honolulu, 1973-75; bus. cons. Hawaii Dept. Planning and Econ. Devel., Honolulu, 1975-77, tax research and planning officer Dept. Taxation, 1977-82; ops. research analyst U.S. Govt., 1982—. Served with AUS, 1954-56. Mem. Hawaiian Acad. Sci., Sigma Xi. Home: 583 Kamoku St Apt 3505 Honolulu HI 96826 Office: HQ PACAF/OA Hickam AFB HI 96853

SWANSON, ROBERT BOUDINOT, II, film production company executive; b. Crawfordsville. Ind., Sept. 26, 1936; s. Raymond E. and Lucille R. Swanson; B.S. in Elec. Engring., Mich. State U., 1960; M.B.A., U. So. Calif., 1972, M.F.A. in Motion Picture Prodn., 1986; children—Lisa G., Robert B. III. Mktg. rep. Gen. Electric Computer Dept., Los Angeles, 1960-63; mktg. mgr. IBM Corp., Los Angeles, 1964-81; regional sales mgr. Data Gen. Corp., Santa Ana, Calif., 1982-83; pres. Delta Max, Inc, 1983-85; pres. Digital Prodns., 1986—; pres. Digital Prodns., 1986—; instr. U. So. Calif. Grad. Sch. Bus.; cons. personal fin. planning. Bd. dirs. U. So. Calif. Assocs., 1977—, U. So. Calif. Pres.' Circle, 1980-84. Served to capt. USAF, 1960-62. Mem. Eta Kappa Nu, Phi Kappa Phi, Tau Beta Pi, Beta Gamma Sigma, Sigma Alpha Epsilon. Club: Elks. Contbr. articles on computer tech. and fin. planning to profl. jours.; producer various films. Office: PO Box 7188 Newport Beach CA 92660

SWANSON, ROBERT KILLEN, real estate corporation executive; b. Deadwood, S.D., Aug. 11, 1932; s. Robert Claude and Marie Elizabeth (Kersten) S.; m. Nancy Anne Oyaas, July 19, 1958; children: Cathryn Lynn, Robert Stuart, Bart Killen. B.A., U. S.D., 1954; postgrad., U. Melbourne, Australia, 1955. With Gen. Mills, Inc., Mpls., 1955-58, 71-79; v.p. Gen. Mills, Inc., 1971-73, group v.p., 1973-77, exec. v.p., 1977-79; with Marathon Oil Co., Findlay, Ohio, 1958-60; sr. v.p., dir. Needham, Harper & Steers, Inc., Chgo., 1961-69; joint mng. dir. S. H. Benson (Holdings) Ltd., Eng., 1969-71; pres., chief operating officer Greyhound Corp., Phoenix, 1980; chmn. chief exec. officer Del E. Webb Corp., Phoenix, 1981—; dir. United Bancorp.; trustee Scripps Clinic and Research Found., Ariz. State U. Found. Bd. dirs. Phoenix Art Mus., Ariz. Div. Am. Cancer Soc., Univ. S.D. Found. Served to 2d lt. U.S. Army, 1955. Fulbright scholar, 1954-55; Woodrow Wilson scholar. Mem. U.S. Council Fgn. Relations, U.K. Dirs. Inst., U.S. Internat. Scholars Assn. Episcopalian. Clubs: Phoenix Country, Plaza, Mansion, Ariz. State U. Econ.; Econ. Chgo. Lodge: Masons. Office: Del E Webb Corp 3800 N Central Ave Phoenix AZ 85012

SWANSON, ROBERT NELS, meteorologist; b. Ashland, Wis., Feb. 4, 1932; s. Sigurd and Rose (Verville) S.; m. Phyllis Grage, Sept. 22, 1956; children: Robert N. Jr., Richard N., Russell N., Rosanne N. BS in Chemistry, Wis. State U., River Falls, 1953; student, U. Wash., 1953-54; MS in Meteorology, U. Mich., 1958. Meteorologist White Sands (N.Mex.) Missile Range, 1958-61; staff scientist GCA Corp., Salt Lake City, 1961-72; sr. meteorologist Pacific Gas & Electric Co., San Francisco, 1972-84, dir. meteorol. services, 1984—. Contbr. articles to profl. jours. Served to lt. USAF, 1953-57. Fellow Royal Meteorol. Soc.; mem. Air Pollution Control Assn., Am. Meteorol. Soc. (chmn. com. Atmospheric Measurements 1983-85). Avocations: auto repairing, metal working, sports. Home: 1216 Babel Ln Concord CA 94518 Office: Pacific Gas and Electric Co 215 Market St Room 451 San Francisco CA 94106

SWANSON, ROCHELLE ANITA, public relations program coordinator, lecturer; b. Kenmare, N.D., Apr. 16, 1949; d. Arthur Reuben and Verna Waneta (Nederbo) S. Student Phoenix Coll., 1968-69, Ariz. State U., 1966; B.S. in Pub. Adminstrn., U. Ariz., 1971; postgrad. U. So. Calif., 1973-75. Cert. recreation therapist. Recreation supr., Cypress, Calif., 1971; recreation specialist aide County of Los Angeles Dept. Parks and Recreation, 1972-74, recreation specialist, 1974-82; program coordinator Jesse Owens Games, Atlantic Richfield Co., Los Angeles, 1982-84; pres. Promotional Cons. Services, 1984—; cons. Fountain Val, 1980-82; lectr. U. Redlands, U. So. Calif., Calif. State U.-Northridge; cons. U. So. Calif., various confs. Calif. Spl. Olympics gymnastics chmn., 1972-83, mem. adv. com. gymnastics rules, 1985; So. region volleyball tournament dir., 1984; dir. Orange County Spl. Olympics Track and Field Meet, 1983; Dist. IX bowling chmn. Mentally Retarded Citizens, 1974-84; chmn. bd. First Lutheran Day Sch., 1983-84; mem. council First Luth. Ch., sec., v.p. ch. council, 1985; state bowling commn. handicapper Assn. Retarded Citizens. Recipient awards Los Angeles Basin Parks and Recreation Commn. and Bd., 1982; spl. award Koroibos Found., 1984; Am. Legion award, 1963. Mem. Calif. Park and Recreation Soc. (sec. dist. XIII, 1981, program awards 1984), Sons of Norway, VASA, Chi Kappa Rho. Republican. Contbr. article to profl. jour. Home: 1756 N Verdugo Rd #22 Glendale CA 91208 Office: 515 S Flower St AP 3274 Los Angeles CA 90071

SWANSTROM, SIGVARD ANTÖN HOLMSTEDT (SIG), business executive; b. Seattle, Mar. 2, 1951; s. Roy D. and Marie Ann (Sellman) S.; m. Peggy Jo Griffin, Dec. 21, 1975. BA, Seattle Pacific U., 1972; Postgrad., U. So. Calif., 1975. Pres. Advanced Computer Images, Seattle, 1984—; chief exec. officer Alaska Travel Bur., Seattle, 1985—; pres. Webster & Stevens SLIDECRAFT, Seattle, 1985—; bd. dirs. Fellowship Found., Seattle, 1983—, Advanced Bus. Techs. Inc., Seattle, 1984—; chmn. bd. dirs. Firstrav Internat., Boston, 1985—, Internat. Travel Bur., Seattle. Seattle Pacific U. fellow, 1983—. Office: Alaska Travel Bur 411 1st Ave S Suite 650 Seattle WA 98104

SWARD, ROGER WILLIAM, data processing executive, computer software consultant; b. San Jose, Calif., Feb. 15, 1951; s. William Clare and Rhoda Frances (Soares) S.; m. Jean Halpern, Nov. 22, 1972 (div. Jan. 1983). Student, Stanford U., 1969-71. Dir. data processing Behaviordyne, Inc., Palo Alto, Calif., 1971-79, pres., 1983—, also bd. dirs.; pres. Structured Computer Concepts, Inc., Sunnyvale, Calif., 1979—; mem. adv. bd. Omega Assocs., Inc., Santa Clara, Calif., 1986. Mem. Assn. Computing Machinery, Data Processing Mgmt. Assn., Inst. Cert. Computer Profls. (cert.), IEEE (assoc., computer soc.). Avocation: astrology. Home: 1135 Blackfield Way Mountain View CA 94040 Office: Behaviordyne Inc 944 San Antonio Blvd Palo Alto CA 94303

SWARTHOUT, JOHN VANLEWEN, brokerage house professional; b. Tampa, Fla., July 18, 1945; s. John Max and Mary A. (Cianfoni) S.; m. Kathleen A. Deal, Aug. 19, 1984; 1 child; Jaime Michaela. Student, U. Washington, 1963-65, U. Utah, 1965; BA, Portland State U., 1967; MA, Ind. U., 1968. Cert. fin. planner; lic. securities broker, commodities broker. Instr. polit. sci. Tacoma Community Coll., 1968-73; mgmt. coordinator, personnel dir. Multnomah County, Portland, Oreg., 1973-75; indsl. engring. cons. Ritchie & Assoc., Los Angeles, 1976-77; personnel mgr. AAR Western Skyways, Troutdale, Oreg., 1977-80; stockbroker Kidder Peabody & Co., Portland, 1980-85, cons., 1985—; equity mgr. ManEquity Inc., Portland, 1985—; instr., Portland State U., 1973-75. Bd. dirs. Am. Heritage Assn., Lake Oswego Oreg., 1984—. Nat. Def. Fgn. Lang. fellow U. Utah, 1965, NSF fellow Ind. U., 1967-68. Mem. Western Polit. Sci. Assn., Northwest Polit. Sci. Assn., Theta Delta Phi, Sigma Nu. Clubs: City, Willamette Athletic (Portland), Western Fitness and Racquet. Home: 6970 SW Gable Pkwy Portland OR 97225 Office: Man Equity Inc Lincoln Ctr N Tower Suite 345 10220 SW Greenburg Rd PO Box 3425 Portland OR 97208-3425

SWARTZ, ALAN JAY, electrical engineer; b. Boston, Sept. 29, 1957; s. Herbert Jack and Anita (Wertheim) S.; m. Denise Laurie Terrill, Sept. 20, 1981; 1 child, Joseph. BSEE, U. Rochester, 1980. Elec. engr. Prime Computer, Framingham, Mass., 1978-79, Burroughs Corp., Westlake Village, Calif., 1980-82, Raytheon Corp., Sudbury, Mass., 1982-84, Computer Identics Corp., Canton, Mass., 1984-85, Perkin Elmer, Pomona, Calif., 1985—. Inventor in field. Recipient Bausch and Lomb Sci. prize, 1976. Mem. Zeta Beta Tau (treas. 1978-80). Club: Toastmasters (Pomona) (pres. 1985).

SWARTZ, ALLAN JOEL, pharmacist, hospital administrator, educator; b. Phila., July 2, 1935; s. Milton and Rosalie S.; A.B., Central High Sch., 1955; Pharm.D., U. So. Calif., 1958; postgrad. Loyola U. Sch. Law, Los Angeles, 1964-66; M.A. in Edn., Pepperdine U., 1976; m. Roslyn Thelma Holt, Jun 2, 1963. Asst. dir. pharmacy City of Hope Nat. Med. Center, Duarte, Calif. 1966-69; dir. pharm. services, 1969-78; dir. pharmacy services Encino (Calif.) Hosp., 1978—; quality assurance coordinator, 1986—; hazardous materials officer, 1986—; risk and safety mgr., 1987—; asst. clin. prof. pharmacy U. So. Calif., 1971-82, 87—; asst. clin. prof. U. of Pacific, 1978-86 , regional coordinator externship program, 1982-86; chmn. pharm. group purchasing com. Hosp. Council So. Calif., 1978-82; mem. profl. edn. com. Am. Cancer Soc., 1970-78. Bd. dirs. H.O.P.E. Unit Found., 1980-83; bd. dirs. Vis. Nurse Assn. Los Angeles, 1983—; chmn. bd. dirs. Visiting Nurse Home Services, Inc., Los Angeles, 1986—. Served with M.C., U.S. Army, 1958-59. Recipient Order of Golden Sword award Calif. div. Am. Cancer Soc., 1974, cert. merit, 1978, award of recognition U. So. Calif. Comprehensive Cancer Ctr., 1983. Mem. AAAS, Am. Med. Writers Assn., Am. Soc. Hosp. Pharmacists (commendation 1976), Calif. Soc. Hosp. Pharmacists (pres. 1976), QSAD Centurions, Rho Pi Phi. Feature editor for pharmaceutics Cancer Nursing, 1977-81, editorial bd., 1983—; cons. editor Am. Jour. Hosp. Pharmacy, 1978-83. Home: 1353 Comstock Ave Los Angeles CA 90024 Office: 16237 Ventura Blvd Encino CA 91436

SWARTZ, BARBARA ANN, interior designer; b. Edmonton, Alta., Can., Aug. 20, 1930; d. Ian and Beatrice Kathleen (Lutz) Murray; m. Billie Waldo Nichols, July 10, 1949 (div.); m. John Cleland Swartz, Aug. 19, 1951; children—John Cleland, Keith Murray, Janet Elizabeth. Ed. pub. schs., various coll. courses. Cert. Nat. Council Interior Design Qualification. Interior designer, Pasadena, Calif., 1965-68, Westlake Village, Calif., 1968-72; owner, head designer Barbara Swartz Interiors, Westlake Village, 1972—; photographs of design pub. Designers West, 1980, 81, Conejo Mag., 1982, The Designer, 1983. Bd. dirs. Orange County Philharm. Soc., 1958; pres. Pasadena Guild of Rosemary Cottage, 1961; officer San Marino League, 1963; pres., founder Westlake Village Art Guild, 1972; pres. Westlake Village C. of C., 1979. Mem. Am. Soc. Interior Designers, Conejo Assn. Profl. Interior Designers (pres. 1982), Conejo Women in Bus. Republican. Presbyterian. Office: 960 2 Westlake Blvd Westlake Village CA 91361

SWATEK, FRANK EDWARD, microbiology educator; b. Oklahoma City, June 4, 1929; s. Clarence Michael and Bessie (Doubek) S.; m. Mary Frances Over, Jan. 28, 1951; children: Frank Edward, Lorraine Beth, Martha Lynn, Susan Ann, Cheryl Lee. B.S. in Zoology, San Diego State Coll., 1951; M.A. in Microbiology, UCLA, 1955, Ph.D., 1956. Mem. faculty Calif. State U. at Long Beach, 1956—, prof. microbiology, 1963—, chmn. dept., 1960-83; cons. to industry, 1953—; cons. dept. dermatology Long Beach VA Hosp., 1956—; lectr. postgrad. medicine U. So. Calif., 1958—; adj. prof. clin. med. U. Calif., Irvine, 1980—; mem. fuel sect. Coordinating Research Council, 1961—. Author: Textbook of Microbiology, 1967, Laboratory Manual and Workbook for General Microbiology, 1969; also articles. Fellow Royal Soc. Health, Am. Acad. Microbiology; mem. Am. Soc. Microbiology (chmn. bd. edn. and tng., Carski Found. Disting. Teaching award 1974), Internat. Platform Assn., Sigma Xi, Lambda Xi Alpha, Phi Kappa Phi. Club: Long Beach Aquatic (pres. 1963-65). Research on med. mycology. Home: 812 Stevely Ave Long Beach CA 90815

SWEENEY, CHRISTEE A., public relations executive; b. Eugene, Oreg., June 10, 1950; d. Milton Greer and Rosemarie Walsh Johnson; m. Patrick E. Sweeney, Sept. 22, 1973. BS in Journalism, U. Oreg., 1973. Cons. mktg. communications Pacific N.W. Bell Co., Portland, Oreg., 1972, acting mgr. mktg., 1972-73; editor newsletter Hyster Co., Portland, Oreg., 1973-81, coordinator corp. pub. relations, 1981-83; dir. pub. relations Gerber Advt., Portland, 1983—; Bd. dirs. Portland Rose Fest. Assn., Columbia Willamette chpt. Pub. Relations Soc. Am. Active Friends of Timberline, Portland, 1984—. Mem. Pres. Club Portland C. Of C., Pub. Relations Soc. Am., Columbia Wilamette Chpt. Pub. Relations Soc. Am., Pub. Relations Roundtable, Inst. Managerial and Profl. Women. Democrat. Roman Catholic. Avocations: skiing, tennis, reading. Office: Gerber Advt 209 SW Oak Portland OR 97204

SWEENEY, CHRISTOPHER LEE, applied mathematics engineer; b. Denver, Oct. 14, 1959; s. Roger Lee Sweeney and Beverly Ann (Wagoner) Good; m. Susan Ann Merrell, May 24, 1986. Student, Community Coll. Denver, U. Colo., 1986—. Technican Ball Computer Products, Boulder, Colo., 1978-82, devel. engr., 1982-83; devel. engr. Ball Electronic Systems, Westminster, Colo., 1983—. Inventor in field. Mem. Eta Kappa Nu. Home: 9836 Jellison St Westminster CO 80020 Office: Ball Electronic Systems Div 9300 W 108th Circle Westminster CO 80020

SWEENEY, EILEEN HUNTER, child placement agency executive; b. Los Angeles, July 4, 1958; d. Lewis Ray Hunter and Jaye (Newbury) Watson; m. Martin J. Sweeney, Sept. 4, 1982. BA in Social Work, Chapman Coll., 1980; MSW, U. Denver, 1982. Asst. dir. YWCA, Orange, Calif., 1979-81; counselor Loft House, Denver, 1981-82, Excelsior Youth Ctr., Aurora, Colo., 1981-82; therapist Youth Benefits Unltd., Westminster, Colo., 1982-84, dir., 1984—; supr. of therapy Youth Benefits Unltd., Westminster, 1984—. Child Welfare grantee HEW, 1980. Mem. Nat. Assn. Social Workers, Colo. Juvenile Council, Greenpeace, Residential Council Chapman Coll. (judge 1979-80), Alpha Chi Omega (pres. 1979-80). Democrat. Methodist. Avocations: dance, camping, fund-raising. Home: 6302 Harlan Arvada CO 80003 Office: Youth Benefits Unltd PO Box 970 Westminster CO 80030

SWEENEY, GEORGE HARRY, physician; b. Peoria, Ill., Jan. 29, 1930; s. Elmer D. and Mary Jane (Brown) S.; m. Mary Louise Vincent, Dec. 12, 1953; children: Kathryn, Phillip, J. Shannon, Sarah. AB, Wabash Coll., Crawfordsville, Ind., 1951; MD, U. Ill., Chgo., 1955. Diplomate Am. Bd. Psychiatry and Neurology. Intern Albany (N.Y.) Med. Ctr., 1955-56; sr. psychiatrist DeWitt State Hosp., Auburn, Calif., 1961-64; resident Albany (N.Y.) Hosp., 1956-57, 59-61; practice medicine specializing in psychiatry Roseville, Calif., 1963—. Served to capt. M.C., U.S. Army, 1957-59. Fellow Am. Psychiat. Assn.; mem. Calif. Med. Assn., Cen. Calif. Psychiat. Soc. (exec. council), Placer-Nev. County Med. Soc. (pres. 1968). Republican. Avocations: hiking, history. Office: 402 Sunrise Ave Roseville CA 95661

SWEENEY, RICHARD JAMES, economics educator; b. San Diego, Jan. 13, 1944; s. John Joseph and Catherine Scott (Spahr) S.; m. Joan Zita Long, June 19, 1965; children: Robin Scott, Erin Michaela. BA, UCLA, 1965; PhD, Princeton U., 1972. Acting asst. prof. econs. UCLA, 1968-71; asst. prof. Tex. A&M U., College Station, 1971-73; dep. dir. office of internat. monetary research U.S. Dept. Treasury, Washington, 1973-77; Charles M. Stone prof. econs. and fin. Claremont (Calif.) McKenna Coll., 1977—, chmn. dept. econs., 1987—; vis. assoc. prof. econs. U. Va., Charlottesville, 1975; vis. prof. bus. adminstrn. Dartmouth Coll., Hanover, N.H., 1979. Author: Principles of Microeconomics, Macroeconomics, 1980, Wealth Effects and Monetary Theory, 1987; author/editor Exchange Rates, Trade and the U.S. Economy, 1985, A Macro Theory with Micro Foundations, 1974; contbr. articles to profl. jours. Fellow NSF 1966-68, Woodrow Wilson Found. 1965; Gen. Electric Found. grantee, 1980. Mem. Western Econ. Assn. (editor Econs. Inquiry jour. 1984—), Am. Econ. Assn., Am. Fin. Assn., Western Fin. Assn., Phi Beta Kappa. Democrat. Avocations: writing, weightlifting, walking, aerobics. Home: 174 E Radcliffe Dr Claremont CA 91711 Office: Claremont McKenna Coll Dept Econs 890 Columbia Ave Claremont CA 91711

SWEENEY, URBAN JOSEPH, librarian; b. St. John, N.B., Can., Jan. 18, 1922; came to U.S., 1927, naturalized, 1945; s. Urban James and Dorothy E. (Murray) S.; B.S., N.Y. U., 1956; M.S., Pratt Inst., 1957; m. Margaret Stretz, Jan. 12, 1952; children—Dennis, Steven, Edward, Mark, Barbara. Chief librarian Republic Aviation, Farmingdale, N.Y., 1958-66; chief librarian electronics div., Gen. Dynamics, Rochester, N.Y., 1966-71, Convair div., San Diego, 1971-85; project mgr. Integrated Library Systems, US Naval Ocean Systems Ctr., San Diego, 1985—; vis. instr. Sch. Library Sci., SUNY, Geneseo, 1967-70. Served with USAAF, 1941-45; ETO. Mem. Assn. Computing Machinery, Am. Soc. Info. Sci., Spl. Libraries Assn. (chmn. aerospace div. 1978-80, chpt. pres. 1973-74). Contbr. articles to profl. jours. Home: 7311 Borla Pl La Costa CA 92008 Office: PO Box 85386 San Diego CA 92138

SWEERE, TED HARRY, computer company executive; b. Perham, Minn., Oct. 13, 1933; s. Cornelius and Gertrude (Hofland) S.; m. Joan Carol Stollenwerk, Aug. 1, 1957; children: Paul, Thomas, Laura, Linda, Leann, Leslie, Matt, Eric, Nicole. Grad. high sch., New York Mills, Minn. Cert. tchr., Minn. Dir. systems engring. Vanian Data Machines, Irvine, Calif., 1970-75, dir. systems mktg., 1976, dir. customer service, 1976-77; dir. tech. ops. Sperry Corp., Irvine, 1977, dir. systems quality, program mgmt., 1977-82; dir. West devel. ctr. program mgmt. CCI, Irvine, 1982-86; dir. product mktg. Computer Consoles Inc., Irvine, 1986—; mgr. systems engring. VDM-Vanian Assocs., Irvine, 1968-69; design engr. NCR, Hawthorne, Calif., 1963-68. Served with U.S. Army, 1953-55. Republican. Roman Catholic. Home: 23681 Cavanaugh Rd El Toro CA 92630 Office: Computer Consoles Inc 9801 Muirlands Irvine CA 92718

SWEET, CAROL LYNN, compensation analyst; b. N.Y.C., Dec. 11, 1952; d. William John and Vera Edna (Gretschel) Sloan; m. Stanley Karl Sweet, June 16, 1974; children: Kenneth Justin, Kevin David. A.A., Suffolk County Community Coll., 1973; B.S. in Bus. Adminstrn., SUNY-Buffalo, 1980. Internship affirmative action planning Carborundum Bonded Abrasives Co., Niagara Falls, N.Y., 1980; compensation analyst St. Luke's Med. Ctr., Phoenix, 1981—. Mem. Am. Soc. Personnel Adminstrs., Ariz. Hosp. Personnel Assn., Am. Compensation Assn., Am. Mgmt. Assn. Home: 1229 E Claire Dr Phoenix AZ 85022 Office: St Lukes Health System 1800 E Van Buren Phoenix AZ 85006

SWEET, GEORGE ELLIOTT, geophysicist, author; b. Denver, Sept. 26, 1904; s. Leroy F. and Bertie Belle (Cooper) S.; m. Mildred Robison, Oct. 13, 1932 (dec. Aug. 1976); 1 child, J. Eric. B.S., U. Okla., 1927, M.S., 1928; postgrad. Harvard Law Sch., 1940-41. Cert. geophysicist, Calif. Party chief Geophys. Research Corp., Houston, 1928-32; chmn. bd. Am. Seismograph Co., Oklahoma City, 1932-40; pres. Sweet Geophys. Co., Malibu, Calif., 1945—. Author: Shakespeare, The Mystery, 1956; Gentleman in Oil, 1966; The History of Geophysical Prospecting, Vol. I, 1966, Vol. II, 1969; The Petroleum Saga, 1971; Seven Dramas from Seven Centuries, 1978; Beginning of the End, 1982; Murder by Guess, 1984. Pres. Santa Monica Pony League, Calif., 1958-59. Served to lt. USNR, 1942-45. Named Valedictorian U. Okla., 1927. Mem. Soc. Exploration Geophysicists, Am. Assn. Petroleum Geologists, Acacia, Phi Beta Kappa, Alpha Chi Sigma, Sigma Delta Psi. Club: Harvard-Radcliffe of So. Calif. Home: 502 Georgina Ave Santa Monica CA 90402

SWEET, LARRY ROSS, research engineer, state agency administrator; b. Fairbanks, Alaska, June 2, 1940; s Harold Laverne and Florence Edna (Zwiers) S.; m. Frances Claire Tannian, Jan. 11, 1965 (div. May 1979); children: Steven R., Michael S.; m. Barbara Hultin, Nov. 9, 1979. BEE, Wash. State U., 1963; MS in Engring. Mgmt., U. Alaska, 1972. Asst. design engr. Geophys. Inst., U. Alaska, Fairbanks, 1966-69, head tech. services, 1969-70, assoc. supervisory engr., 1970-75, systems engr., 1987—; exec. officer to v.p. for research U. Alaska, Fairbanks, 1975-76, exec. officer to vice chancellor for research and advanced study, 1976-80, research assoc. Inst. No. Engring., 1986—; statewide research mgr. Alaska Dept. Transp. and Pub. Facilities, Fairbanks, 1980-85, chief spl. research projects, 1985-86; mem. adv. bd. Fairbanks North Star Borough Community Research Ctr., Fairbanks, 1983-86, vice-chmn., 1984-86; mem. adv. bd. U. Alaska Transp. Ctr., 1983-86, Alaska Climatol. Ctr., 1983—, Northwest Tech. Transfer Ctr., 1984-86, Gov.'s Sci. Bd., Alaska, 1985-86. Contbr. articles to profl. jours. Active Fairbanks Crisis Line, 1979-80, Gov.'s Commn. on Child Support, 1984-85. Mem. IEEE, ASCE (research com. 1983—), NSPE, AAAS, Alaska Acad. Engring. and Sci. (charter), Soc. Research Adminstrs. (chpt. v.p. 1984), Am. Soc. Engring. Mgmt., Transp. Research Bd. of NRC (conduct of research com. 1985—), Nat. Petroleum Council (Arctic oil and gas resources com. 1980-81), Arctic Inst. N.Am., N.Y. Explorers Club, Pioneers of Alaska, Phi Kappa Phi, Tau Beta Pi. Lodge: Rotary. Avocations: house building, camping. Home: 1923 Swallow Dr Fairbanks AK 99709-8360 Office: U Alaska Geophys Inst Fairbanks AK 99775

SWENERTON, HELENE ELIZABETH, nutrition educator; b. Norfolk, Va.; d. Harry Roupen and Mary Khedrian; m. Arthur Kells Swenerton, Oct. 30, 1943; children: Ross Arthur, Earl Edward, Steven Kells. BS, U. Calif., Davis, 1963, MS, 1965, PhD, 1970. Research nutritionist U. Calif., Davis, 1970-72, extension nutritionist, 1972—. Recipient Health Sci. Advancement award USPHS, 1968-70. Mem. Am. Inst. Nutrition, Soc. Nutrition Edn., Am. Dietetics Assn., Inst. Food Technologists, Sigma Xi. Home: 343 Arizona St Fairfield CA 94533 Office: U Calif Dept Nutrition Davis CA 95616

SWENEY, FREDRIC, artist, writer; b. Holidaysburg, Pa., June 5, 1912; s. Charles Frederick and Ida (Haworth) S.; m. Ruth-B.-Hogan, June 13, 1937; 1 son, William Lee. Student Cleve. Inst. Art, 1931-33. Artist Cleve. Press, 1933-41; supr. tech. pub. Leece-Neville Co., Cleve., 1941-47; wildlife calendar artist Brown & Bigelow, St. Paul, 1949-79; instr. in graphics, head of graphics Ringling Sch. Art and Design, Sarasota, Fla., 1950-76. Author, illustrator: Techniques of Drawing and Painting Wildlife, 1959; Drawing and Painting Birds, 1961; Painting the American Scene, 1964; The Art of Painting Animals, 1983; The Art of Painting Cityscapes and the Urban Environment, 1985. Contbr. illustrations to popular mags., 1943-76. Group shows include Wild Wings Ann.; represented in permanent collections various corps. Recipient Nat. Offset Lithograph 1960-61; Lithographic Competition and Exhibit award, 1961; Design for Printing on Plastics award 2d Ann. Printing Exhbn., Mpls., 1962. Democrat. Presbyterian. Lodge: Masons. Home and Studio: 22244 SE 42d Ln Issaquah WA 98027

SWENNES, THOMAS RICHARD, trucking co. exec.; b. Portland, Oreg., May 27, 1930; s. Alf and Ellen Taylor (Bennison) S.; B.B.A., U. Oreg., 1954; postgrad. transp. mgmt. program Stanford U., 1965; m. Joan Hodges Swennes, Oct. 8, 1955; children—Kimberly Ellen, Clerin Michelle, Thomas Richard II. With Convoy Co., various locations, 1955-84, v.p. ops., Portland, 1974-78, exec. v.p., gen. mgr., Portland, Oreg., 1978, pres., gen. mgr., 1979-84; v.p. Portservice Co., Portland, 1984—; past pres. Western Hwy. Inst.; chmn. motor carrier adv. com. U.S. Dept. Transp., 1982-87 ; trustee Episc. Diocese of Oreg., 1979-82. Served with Army NG, 1951-62. Mem. Am. Trucking Assn. (vice chmn. 1984), Oreg. Trucking Assn. (past chmn.), Nat. Def. Transp. Assn. (life), Pi Kappa Alpha, Delta Nu Alpha. Republican. Office: Portservice Co 6347 N Marine Dr Portland OR 97213

SWENSON, DAVID WAYNE, clinical audiologist; b. Salt Lake City, Sept. 16, 1955; s. Wayen Hyrum and Margo (Fortney) S.; m. Tamara Ray Fairbanks, Aug. 26, 1980; children: Carleen Elizabeth, Robert David. BS in Audiology, U. Utah, 1980, MS in Audiology, 1982. Audiologist, coordinator hearing impaired program Sch. Dist. 93, Idaho Falls, Idaho, 1982-84; clin. audiologist Audiology Assocs., Garden Grove, Calif., 1984-86; chief audiology, clin. audiologist Idaho Elks Rehab. Hosp., Boise, Idaho, 1986—. Mem. Am. Speech-Lang.-Hearing Assn. (cert.). Republican. Mormon. Avocations: golf, basketball, guitar, fishing, boating. Home: 3271 Betsy Ross Way Boise ID 83706-5303

SWENSON, DENNIS MALCOLM, accountant; b. Denver, Apr. 7, 1935; s. Louis Edmond and Clarice Juanita (Stephens) S.; m. Constance Colleen Conroy, July 22, 1961; children—Kristin, Carla, Kathleen, Carolyn. B.S., Brigham Young U., 1958; M.B.A., U. Denver, 1960. C.P.A., Colo. Acct., Ernst & Whinney, Denver, 1960-73, ptnr., 1973—, ptnr.-in-charge privately owned bus. practice, 1982—, nat. com., 1984—, chmn. nat. agr. com., 1977-83. Mem. exec. com. Central YMCA, Denver, 1977-84; v.p. Bow Mar South Homeowners Assn., Littleton, Colo., 1983, pres., 1984; bd. dirs. Early Horizons Child Care, Inc., Denver, 1984—. Named Layman of Yr., Central YMCA, 1975. Mem. Am. Inst. C.P.A.s (spl. agribus. com. 1977-83), Colo. Soc. C.P.A.s, Nat. Soc. Accts. for Coops. (pres. M.W. chpt. 1983-84, mem. nat. acctg. and auditing com.), MIT Forum Denver, Denver C. of C. (high tech. com. 1984-86). Republican. Mormon. Clubs: Denver, Pinehurst Country (Denver), Met. Home: 5360 S Lakeshore Dr Bow Mar CO 80123 Office: 4300 Republic Plaza Denver CO 80202

SWENSON, DONNA EMILIE, speech pathologist; b. Hazen, N.D., Jan. 25, 1958; d. Robert O. and Alma (Galster) S. BS in Speech and Lang. Pathology, Walla Walla Coll., 1980; MS in Speech and Lang. Pathology, Loma Linda U., 1982. Cert. speech pathologist, Calif., clin. rehab. Speech pathologist Oliver-Mercer Spl. Edn., Hazen, 1980-81, Hemet (Calif.) Unified Sch. Dist., 1982—; part-time speech pathologist Sturlaugsen & Assocs., Redlands, Calif., 1984—. Mem. Am. Speech Lang. Hearing Assn. (cert.). Avocations: skiing, biking, reading. Home: 25218 Lawton Loma Linda CA 92354 Office: Hemet Unified Sch Dist 2350 W Latham Hemet CA 92343

SWENSON, ERICK NOAK, data processing executive, retired naval officer; b. Rochester, N.Y., June 12, 1926; s. Noak and Hulda Josephina (Sjellberg) S.; m. Annette Miller, Nov. 22, 1959; 1 child, Erika Margaret. BEE, U. Rochester, 1950; postgrad. U. Pitts., 1950-51, USN Postgrad. Sch., 1960-62. Registered profl. electrical engr., Calif. Enlisted USN, 1944, commd. ensign, 1951, advanced through grades to capt., 1975; electronics div. officer USS Missouri, 1951-52; ships supt. U.S. Navy Yard, San Francisco, 1952-53; quality control engr. Naval Ordnance div. Eastman Kodak Co., Rochester, N.Y., 1953-57; asst. Naval Tactical Data System project officer Dept. Navy, Washington , 1957-60, buships tech. rep. St. Paul, 1962-65, naval tactical data system project officer, Washington, 1965-75, ret., 1975; sr. scientist Hughes Aircraft Co., Fullerton, Calif., 1975-76, project mgr., 1976—; served as mil. adv. to NATO Indsl. Adv. Group on Naval Command and Control; coordinated naval command and control matters for U.S. and Allied Navies and involved in fgn. mil. sales; co-designer Naval Tactical Data System used world-wide for combat warships; instigated update of combat weapons system USN destroyers; pres. Physical Evaluation Bd., U.S. Navy, Washington, 1969-75; Pres. 1st Luth. Ch., Fullerton, Calif., 1981-83; mem. Mil. Service Academy Rev. Bd., 39th Congl. Dist., Fullerton, 1982—. Decorated Meritorious Service Medal; recipient Value Engr. award Hughes Aircraft Co., 1980, Naval Bd. Crest, Australian Dept. Def., 1975; N.Y. State Regents scholar 1946-50. Mem. IEEE, Am. Soc. Naval Engrs., USN League, Am. Def. Preparedness Assn., Nat. Railway Hist. Soc., USS Missouri Assn., Am. Battleship Assn., Fleet Res. Assn., U.S. Naval Inst., Australian Naval Inst. Home: 2073 Smokewood Ave Fullerton CA 92631 Office: Hughes Aircraft Co 1901 W Malvern Fullerton CA 92634

SWENSON, FRANK JOSEPH, microbiologist; b. Oct. 16, 1949. BA in Microbiology with honors, U. Conn., 1973; MS in Microbiology and Immunology, U. Nev., 1977; PhD in Microbiology, U. N.Mex., 1980. Supr. microbiology Day Kimball Hosp., Putnam, Conn., 1973-74; sect. head microbiology Washoe Med. Ctr., Reno, 1974-77; post doctoral fellow in clin. microbiology and infectious diseases Am. Bd. Med. Microbiology, U. Conn. Health Ctr., Farmington, 1980-81; microbiology dir. St. Joseph's Hosp., Albuquerque, 1981-83; sr. clin. research scientist Warner-Lambert Co., Morris Plains, N.J., 1983-85; mgr. microbiology research and devel. Mesa Diagnostics, Inc., Albuquerque, N.Mex., 1985; dir. microbiology research and devel. Mesa Diagnostics, Inc., Los Alamos, N.Mex., 1986—. Contbr. articles to profl. jours. Fellow U. N.Mex, 1978, 79; grantee dept. microbiology U. N.Mex, 1977-80. Mem. Inst. Med. Lab. Scis., Am. Soc. Clin. Pathologists (cert.), Am. Soc. Microbiology, AAAS, Sigma Xi. Home: 2942 Camino Piedra Lumbre Santa Fe NM 87505

SWERDA, PATRICIA FINE, artist, author, educator; b. Ft. Worth, Aug. 10, 1916; d. William Emerson and Margaret Ellen (Cull) Fine; B.S. cum laude, Tex. Woman's U., 1941; student Ikenobo U., Tokyo, 1965-66, Ikenobo Dojo, Kyoto, Japan, 1976, 77, 83; m. John Swerda, July 7, 1941; children—John Patrick James, Susan Ann Mary Swerda Foss, Margaret Rose Swerda Yovino. Pres. N.W. Sakura chpt. Ikenobo Ikebana Soc., Seattle, 1960—; exhibited ikebana in one-person shows including: Bon Marche, Tacoma, 1966, Seattle, 1967, 85, Gallery Kokoro, Seattle, 1972-78; exhibited in group shows including: Takashimaya Dept. Store, 1965, 77, 83, 85, Matsuzakaya Dept. Store, Tokyo, 1966, Ikenobo Center, Kyoto, 1966, 77, Seattle Art Mus., 1974-80, Sangyo Kaikan, Kyoto, 1976, Burke Mus., U. Wash., ann. Cherry Blossom Festival, Seattle; demonstrations in field for various groups. Master of Ikebana of Ikenobo Ikebana Soc., Kyoto. Trustee, pres. Bellevue Sister Cities Assn. 1985—. Mem. Ikenobo Ikebana Soc., Ikebana Internat., Bonsai Clubs Internat., Puget Sound Bonsai Assn., Japan-Am. Soc., Seattle Rose Soc., AAUW. Democrat. Russian Orthodox. Author: Japanese Flower Arranging: Practical and Aesthetic Bases of Ikebana, 1969; Creating Japanese Shoka, 1979; contbr. articles to mags. in field; numerous radio and TV appearances. Home and Office: 23025 NE 8th St Redmond WA 98053

SWERDLOW, SKIP, food service executive; b. Columbus, Ohio, Aug. 12, 1947; s. George and Dorothe (Holzberg) S.; B.S. summa cum laude, Ariz. State U., 1969, M.B.A. summa cum laude, 1970, Ph.D. summa cum laude, 1974. Western region supr. Western Big Wheel, Inc., San Diego, 1974-75; dir. mgmt. systems Bricklin Vehicle Corp., Scottsdale, Ariz., 1975; mgmt. cons., Tempe, Ariz., 1975-76; prof. Mesa (Calif.) Community Coll., 1976, Clark County Community Coll., Las Vegas, Nev., 1976-81; asst prof. fin. U. Nev., Las Vegas, 1981—; v.p. Triple S. of Las Vegas, Inc., Burger King franchisee for 6 restaurants, 1975-86; spl. cons. Coll. Bus. Adminstrn., Ariz. State U., Tempe, 1970-71, mem. exec. council, 1967-68; owner Pecos Center, shopping center, 1981-86; owner Dakotas Restaurant and Saloon, 1986—. Named Businessman of Year, Distributive Edn. Clubs Am., 1977. Mem. Nev. Restaurant Assn. (2d v.p.), Mensa, Phi Kappa Phi, Sigma Iota Epsilon, Beta Gamma Sigma. Republican. Jewish. Office: U Nev Dept Fin 4505 S Maryland Pkwy Las Vegas NV 89154

SWIFT, AL, congressman; b. Tacoma, Sept. 12, 1935; m. Paula Jean Jackson, 1956; children—Amy, Lauri. Student, Whitman Coll., 1953-55, Central Wash. U., 1956; 57. Broadcaster; public affairs dir. Sta. KVOS-TV; adminstrv. asst. to U.S. rep. Lloyd Meeds, 1965-69; mem. 96th-100th Congresses from 2d Wash. dist.; Mem. Bellingham (Wash.) City Charter Revision Com.; chmn., mem. Bellingham Citizens Adv. Com.; mem. Bellingham Housing Authority. Democrat. Office: 1502 Longworth House Office Bldg Washington DC 20515

SWIFT, MYLES JAMES, software company executive; b. Scranton, Pa., Oct. 9, 1948; s. John Joseph and Marie (Geroulo) S.; m. Patricia Condon, May 30, 1970. Student, Georgetown U., 1966-68, Lane Coll., 1974-75. With live news dept. Am. Broadcasting, Washington, 1968-73; prin. M&B Swift Shop, Creswell, Oreg., 1976—; pres. Computer Assistance, Creswell, 1977—. Coordinator Hart for Pres., Eugene, Oreg., 1984. Mem. Equipment and Tool Inst. (com. chmn. 1985), Automotive Service Council, Simulation Soc. Democrat. Avocations: fishing, sailing, aviation theory and history. Office: Computer Assistance 8277 Weiss Rd Creswell OR 97426

SWIHART, H. GREGG, real estate co. exec.; b. San Francisco, Sept. 25, 1938; s. Lawson Benjamin and Violet Mary (Watters) S.; B.A., U. Ariz., 1958; postgrad. U. Heidelberg (W.Ger.), 1958-59, Harvard U., 1959-60;

M.A., Boston U., 1961; postgrad. U. Freiburg (West Germany), 1961-65; m. Ilse Paula Rambacher, Dec. 24, 1958; children—Tatjana Etta, Brett Marc, Natascha Theda. Stock broker Walston & Co., Tucson, 1966-71; with Solot Co., Tucson, 1971-74; pres. Cienega Properties, Inc., property mgmt. and investment, Tucson, 1975-77; pres. GT Realty Assocs., Ltd., Tucson, 1977—. Mem. Tucson Com. Fgn. Relations, 1973—; pres. Forum for Greater Outdoors, 1977-79; bd. dirs. Tucson Mus. Art, 1968-74, pres. 1969-70; pres. and trustee Canelo Hills Sch., 1977-79. Cert. property mgr. Mem. Tucson Bd. Realtors, Inst. Real Estate Mgmt. (pres. Tucson-So. Ariz. chpt. 1982, mem. nat. governing council 1985-87), Inst. Real Estate Mgmt. (governing council 1985-87), Realtors Nat. Mktg. Inst. Clubs: Harvard (pres. 1973-74), Active 20-30 (pres. 1969), Downtown Tucson. Home: PO Box 555 Tunnel Springs Ranch Sonoita AZ 85637 Office: 660 N Swan Tucson AZ 85711

SWIHART, JOHN MARION, aircraft manufacturing company executive; b. New Winchester, Ohio, Dec. 27, 1923; s. Harry Miron and Fay I. (Cress) S.; m. Gail G. Carter, Nov. 8, 1986; children from previous marriages: Vicki Ann, John Richard, Thomas Marion, Mark Andrew, Karen, Laurie, Stacey. B.S. in Physics, Bowling Green State U., 1947; B.S. in Aero. Engring., Ga. Inst. Tech., 1949, postgrad., 1951-53. Asst. group leader propulsion group NASA, 1956-58, group leader spl. projects, 1958-59, head advanced configurations group aircraft, 1959-62, chief large supersonic tunnels br., 1962; with Boeing Co., 1962—; dir. internat. sales for Far East Boeing Comml. Airplane Co. Boeing Co., Renton, Wash., 1971-74, dep. dir. internat. sales, 1974-75; v.p. Japan Boeing Internat. Corp. Boeing Co., Tokyo, 1973-74; program mgr. 7X7 Boeing Co., Kent, Wash., 1975-76; dir. new airplane product devel., sales, mktg. Boeing Co., Seattle, 1976-78; dir. product devel., sales mktg. Boeing Co., 1978-79, v.p. U.S., Can. sales, 1979-83, v.p. govt. tech. liaison, 1983-85, v.p. airplane market analysis, 1985; v.p. internat. affairs Boeing Co., Seattle, 1985—. Contbr. articles to profl. jours. Served to 1st lt. USAAF, 1943-45. Decorated D.F.C., Air medal with 3 oak leaf clusters. Fellow AIAA (chmn. aircraft design com. 1970-72, chmn. Pacific N.W. sect. 1969-70, gen. chmn. aircraft systems and design meeting 1977), Royal Aeronautical Soc.; mem. Am. Ordnance Assn., Japan-Am. Soc. (pres. 1978-79). Office: Boeing Comml Airplane Co PO Box 3707 Seattle WA 98124

SWINDELLS, WILLIAM, JR., lumber and paper company executive; b. 1930; married. B.S., Stanford U., 1953. With Willamette Industries, Inc., Portland, Oreg., 1953—; sr. v.p. prodn., mktg. bldg. materials Willamette Industries, Inc., until 1978, exec. v.p., 1978-80, pres. forest products div., 1980-82, pres., chief exec. officer, 1982—, also dir., chmn., 1984—; dir. Oreg. Bank, Portland. Office: Willamette Industries Inc 1300 SW 5th Ave Portland OR 97201 *

SWINDLER, DARIS RAY, physical anthropologist, forensic anthropologist; b. Morgantown, W.Va., Aug. 13, 1925; s. George Raymond and Minnie Mildred (McElroy) S.; m. Kathryn Pardo, Nov. 10, 1977; children: Gary, Darece, Linda, Dana, Bruce, Geoffry, Jason. AB, W.Va. U., 1950; MA, U. Pa., 1952, PhD, 1959. Instr. Cornell Med. Sch., N.Y.C., 1956-57, W.Va. Med. Sch., Morgantown, 1957-59; asst. prof. Med. Coll. S.C., Charleston, 1959-64; assoc. prof. Mich. State U., East Lansing, 1964-68; prof. phys. anthropology, comparative primate anatomy, dental anthropology U. Wash., Seattle, 1968—; cons. King County Med. Examiner, Seattle, 1968—. Author: A Racial Study of the West Nakani of New Britain, 1962, Dentition of Living Primates, 1976, Systematics, Evolution and Anatomy, Comparative Primate Biology; (with C.D. Wood) Atlas of Primate Gross Anatomy, 1973 (Gov's. award 1973), (with J. Sirianni) Growth and Development of Pigtailed Macaque, 1985. Served with USN, 1943-46. Recipient Alexander von Homboldt Sr. U.S. Scientist award, Frankfurt, Fed. Republic Germany, 1982-83. Mem. Am. Assn. Phys. Anthropologists (v.p. 1976-78), AAAS, N.Y. Acad. Sci., Italian Primatological Assn., Sigma Xi. Office: U Wash Dept Anthropology Seattle WA 98195

SWING, WILLIAM EDWIN, bishop; b. Huntington, W.Va., Aug. 26, 1936; s. William Lee and Elsie Bell (Holliday) S.; M. Mary Willis Taylor, Oct. 7, 1961; children—Alice Marshall, William Edwin. B.A., Kenyon Coll., Ohio, 1954-58; D.Div. (hon.), Kenyon Coll., 1980; M.A., Va. Theol. Sem., 1958-61, D.Div., 1980. Ordained priest Episcopal Ch. Asst. St. Matthews Ch., Wheeling, W.Va., 1961-63; vicar St. Matthews Ch., Chester, W.Va., 1963-69, St. Thomas Ch., Weirton, W.Va., 1963-69; rector St. Columbias Episcopal Ch., Washington, 1969-79; bishop Episcopal Ch. Calif., San Francisco, 1980—; chmn. bd. Ch. Div. Sch. of the Pacific, 1983-84; founder, chmn. Episcopal Found. for Drama, 1976—. Republican. Home: 2006 Lyon St San Francisco CA 94115 Office: Episcopal Ch Diocesan Office 1055 Taylor St San Francisco CA 94108 *

SWINGLE, ARTICE MAY, educational administrator, special education educator; b. Schenectady, Jan. 28, 1939; d. Arto Webster and Ida Elzada (Gosnell) S.; m. Richard Henry Burke, July 29, 1961 (div. 1973); children: Richard Robert, Daniel Douglas; m. John Joseph Wordin, Dec. 31, 1974. BS cum laude, Syracuse U., 1961, MS, 1963; cert. adminstr. spl. edn. Calif. State U., Los Angeles, 1976. Lic. marriage, family and child guidance counselor, Calif.; cert. tchr., adminstr., coll.-level instr., Calif.; cert. elem. tchr., spl. edn. tchr., N.Y. Tchr. educable mentally retarded children, chmn. dept. Tully Central Sch., N.Y., 1961-65; therapist, dir. ednl. services Los Angeles Child Achievement Ctr., 1967-70; diagnostic clinic tchr. Diagnostic Sch. for Neurologically Impaired Children So. Calif., Los Angeles, 1970-78; mem. faculty Calif. State U., Los Angeles, 1974, 77; coordinator spl. services Idaho Falls Sch. Dist. 91, Idaho, 1977—; regional coordinator spl. needs low-incidence programs, Idaho Falls Sch. Dists. 91, 59, 60, 93, 1982-86; lectr. to various profl. and community groups. Co-author: Development of Ordinal Scales of Non-Culturally Biased Development Diagnostic Instrument, 1976. Chmn. bd. trustees 1st Congl. Ch., Idaho Falls, 1983-84, moderator, 1984-85; cons. Human Relations Ctr., Woodland Hills Congl. Ch., also former trustee; den leader Great Western council Boy Scouts Am., 1961. N.Y. Regents scholar, 1957-61; research grantee U.S. Dept. Edn. and ESEA. Mem. Idaho Falls Weavers and Spinners Guild (chmn. spinning study group 1983-87), Pi Lambda Theta. Republican. Avocations: spinning, flying. Home: 735 N 900 E Shelley ID 83274 Office: Idaho Falls Sch Dist 91 690 John Adams Pkwy Idaho Falls ID 83401

SWINK, MICHAEL GEORGE, electronics executive; b. Stillwater, Okla., July 2, 1941; s. Hugh Harold and Carrie Belle (Reynolds) S.; m. Elisabeth Ann Cowtun, May 31, 1969; children: Simone, Nicole. BSEE, U. Kans., 1963, BA in Math., 1967; MBA, Harvard U., 1969. Cons. Banco Central de Nicaragua, 1969-73; lectr. bus. U. Sask., Can., 1973-75; asst. prof. bus. Portland (Oreg.) State U., 1975-76; with product and market devel. dept. Tektronix, Beaverton, Oreg., 1976—, now gen. mgr. color shutter strategic program unit. Served to lt. USN, 1963-67. Mem. Am. Mktg. Assn., Am. Electronics Assn. Club: Harvard Bus. (Portland). Home: 4530 SW Humphrey Ct Portland OR 97221 Office: Tektronix Inc MS 48-300 PO Box 500 Beaverton OR 97077

SWINNEY, MARTHA BROWN, speech and language pathologist; b. Evansville, Ind., Oct. 23, 1959; d. George Walter and Judith Margaret (Nowers) Brown; m. Jay Charles Swinney, July 30, 1983. BA, N.Mex. State U., 1982; MA, Memphis State U., 1984. cert. speech and lang. pathologist, Tenn. Grad. asst. Memphis State U., 1982-84; speech and lang. diagnostician U. Tenn. Child Devel. Ctr., Memphis, 1984; speech and lang. pathologist Esperanza Presch., Albuquerque, 1984—. Mem. Am. Speech Lang. Hearing Assn., Albuquerque Speech and Audiology Profls., N.Mex. Speech Lang. Hearing Assn. Republican. Roman Catholic. Avocations: gardening, fishing, water skiing. Home: Route 5 Box 66 Los Lunas NM 87031 Office: Esperanza Para Nuestros Ninos Presch PO Box 12212 Albuquerque NM 87195

SWINTON, PATRICIA ANN WATERFORD, clinical psychologist; b. Washington, Feb. 19, 1953; d. James Raleigh and Nathalie (Wardy) S. B.S., U. D.C., 1967-70; M.A., Howard U., 1973, Ph.D., 1981; postdoctoral in health services UCLA, 1984—. Counselor, educator D.C. Pub. Sch. System, Washington, 1970-80, sch. psychologist, 1980-82; research and evaluation specialist Howard U., Washington, 1977-80, acad. counselor, 1979-80, residency program asst. dept. psychiatry, 1979-82, research and evaluation specialist, 1981-82; psychology therapist D.C. Gen. Hosp., Washington, 1979-81; clin. staff psychologist Augustus F. Hawkins Mental Health Ctr., Los Angeles, 1983—, asst. ward chief, 1985—, psychiatric inpatient edn. coordinator, 1986—, acting assoc. dir. residency tng. and inpatient psychiat. edn., 1987—; cons. Charles R. Drew Postgrad. Med. Sch., Los Angeles, 1982-84, Child, Youth and Family Services, Los Angeles, 1983-84, psychology liaison cons. Med. Sch. Project Head Start, 1986—; curriculum research specialist Computer Assisted Instructional Resources, Carson, Calif., 1983—. Mem. Compton Community Services, Compton Community Coll., Calif., 1983—, Los Angeles Union PTA, 1983—, Long Beach Mental Health Assn., Calif., 1984—. Recipient Recognition award Los Angeles Sentinel, 1983. Mem. Am. Ednl. Research Assn., Am. Personnel and Guidance Assn., Nat. Assn. for Mental Health Specialists, Long Beach Psychol. Assn., Careers in Health, Kappa Delta Pi, Alpha Kappa Alpha (corr. sec. 1968-70). Democrat. Congregationalist. Club: Carson's Women's (Calif.). Avocations: skiing; painting; classical dance; boating; flying. Office: 1720 E 120th St Augustus F Hawkins Mental Health Ctr Martin Luther King Gen Hosp Los Angeles CA 90059

SWINYARD, SHARON JOAN, language professional, educator; b. Salt Lake City, July 20, 1943; d. Chester Allan and Vivian (Redford) S.; m. David B. Sutton, July 14, 1968. BA in Spanish with honors, NYU, 1965, MA, 1966; PhD, Stanford U., 1972. Program asst. NYU and U. Madrid, 1965; teaching, research asst. Stanford (Calif.) U., 1966-68, 72; assoc. in Spanish U. Calif., Santa Barbara, 1970-72; prof., chmn. Hispanic studies dept. St. Joseph's Coll., Mountain View, Calif., 1974-84, asst. to pres., 1981-84; assoc. prof., chmn. Hispanic studies dept. St. Patrick's Sem., Menlo Park, Calif., 1979-84; dir. ann. giving, assoc. dir., exec. dir. Children's Hosp. San Francisco Found., 1984-86; assoc. dir., campaign dir. for new children's hosp. Office Med. Devel. Stanford U. Med. Ctr., 1986—; dir. humanities program Antaeus Group, 1975—. Translator: El Niño con espina bifida, 2d edit., 1974, 4th edit., 1984. Recipient certificado del rector U. Madrid y del Presidente de NYU, 1964, 66; diploma Iberoamericana de Miembro de Honor del com. Directivo de la Revista Iberoamericana de Rehab. Médica, 1966; N.Y. State Regents scholar NYU, 1965, NYU scholar, 1965-66; Stanford U. grantee 1969-70. Mem. MLA, Am., Am. Assn. Tchrs. Spanish and Portuguese, Nat. Soc. Fund Raising Execs., Nat. Assn. Hosp. Devel., Devel. Execs. Roundtable. Home: PO Box 4050 Stanford CA 94305 Office: Stanford Univ Med Ctr Office Med DevelSch Med Office Bldg Stanford CA 94305

SWISTOK, JOHN EDWARD, electrical engineer; b. Lordstown, Ohio, June 18, 1933; s. John and Matilda Margaret (Mathe) S.; A.A., Long Beach City Coll., 1959; B.S. in Elec. Engring., U. Calif., Berkeley, 1961; m. Nancy Ann Miloch, Mar. 29, 1955; children—John Robert, Paula Marie Swistok Elston, Roberta Paula, Diana Nannette, Nancy Ann, Robert John, Vetura Roberta. Research engr. Autonetics, Anaheim, Calif., 1961-62; engr. Nortronics, Anaheim, 1962-63; elec. engr. Gen. Dynamics, Pomona, Calif., 1963-64; sr. engr. Northrop Corp., Newbury Park, Calif., 1968-69, Hawthorne, Calif., 1969-74; sr. engr. Litton Industries, Woodland Hills, Calif., 1964-68; engring. specialist Litton Industries, 1974-76; reliability engring. specialist Northrop Corp., Hawthorne, Calif., 1977—. Tchr., Religious Sci. Jr. Ch., 1971—. Served with USN, 1952-56; Korea. Mem. IEEE, Northrop Mgmt. Club. Home: 2037 N Chouteau St Orange CA 92665 Office: One Northrop Ave Hawthorne CA 90250

SWITLIK, CLEMENT THOMAS, JR., safety engineer; b. Parsons, Kans., Oct. 19, 1941; s. Clement Thomas Sr. and Margaret Agnes (Currigan) S.; m. Gail Elizabeth Quirk, May 20, 1970 (div. July 1976); 1 child, Jennifer; m. Dorothy Karen Dorn, Jan. 29, 1982; children: Michelle, Dawn, Laurie, Sarah, Crys. BA in Zoology, U. Kans., 1971; postgrad., Golden Gate U., 1974-76; MA in Health Services Mgmt., Webster U., 1980; postgrad., U. Beverly Hills, 1981-82. Registered profl. engr.; cert. hazardous materials mgr., hazard control mgr. Regional mgr. safety and health U.S. Dept. Labor, San Francisco, 1977-78; cons. Switlik & Assocs., Walnut Creek, Calif., 1978-79; mgr. safety Naval Regional Med. Ctr., Long Beach, Calif., 1979-80; regional mgr. safety and health USDA Agrl. Research Service, Peoria, Ill., 1980-84; systems safety engr. Air Force Space Div., Los Angeles, 1984-86. Active CORE, Lawrence, Kans., 1965-66. Served with USN, 1959-63. Mem. NSPE, Am. Soc. Safety Engrs., Am. Conf. Govt. Ind. Hygienists, Nat. Safety Mgmt. Soc. (sec. 1977-78, Recognition award 1975-81), Assn. Fed. Safety and Health Profls. (charter), Fed. Safety Council (vice chmn. 1975), U. Kans. Alumni Assn., Mensa, Am. Legion. Republican. Roman Catholic. Club: Toastmasters. Lodge: Kiwanis (sec. Peoria club 1981-82). Avocations: alpine skiing, traveling. Home: 18535 Mayall St Unit E Northridge CA 91324 Office: Stearns Roger Div United Engrs & Constructors Boy 5888 Denver CO 80217

SWITZER, ALFRED IVAN, civil engineering consultant; b. El Paso, Tex., Apr. 19, 1911; s. Charles Wesley and Anna Adelaide (Sherwood) S.; m. Catharine Johnson, Aug. 9, 1940 (dec. July 1979); m. Eleanor Gregg, Aug. 14, 1983. BSME, Calif. Inst. Tech., 1934. Registered profl. engr., Calif. Pvt. practice civil engring. cons. Los Angeles, 1954-71; pres. Switzer-Jennings, Los Angeles, 1969-71; pvt. practice civil engring. cons. Los Osos, Calif., 1971—. Chmn. County Servic Area Adv. to Bd. Suprs., San Luis Obispo, Calif., 1972—, Water Resources Adv. to Bd. Suprs., San Luis Obispo, 1984—. Served to lt. col. C.E., U.S. Army, 1941-46, 48-50. Mem. ASCE. Republican. Lodge: Lions (pres. Los Osos club 1974, 80). Avocations: golfing, fishgin, hunting. Home: 633 Ramona Ave Sp 68 Los Osos CA 93402

SWITZER, JAY A(LAN), research chemist; b. Cin., May 14, 1950; s. William K. and Virginia H. (Gray) S.; m. Barbara A. Smith, Aug. 18, 1972; 1 child, Eric R. BS in Chemistry, U. Cin., 1973; MA in Inorganic Chemistry, Wayne State U., 1975, PhD in Inorganic Chemistry, 1979. Research chemist Unocal Corp., Brea, Calif., 1979-84, sr. research chemist, 1984—. Mem. Electrochem. Soc. (vice chmn. So. Calif. sect. 1985-86), Am. Chem. Soc., Materials Research Soc., Am. Ceramic Soc. Home: 1668 Sherwood Village Circle Placentia CA 92670 Office: Unocal Corp Sci and Tech Div 376 S Valencia Ave Brea CA 92621

SWOAP, DAVID BRUCE, government relations firm executive; b. Kalamazoo, Aug. 12, 1937; s. Orlo Frederick and Aileen Esther (Hempy) S. B.A. in Govt. with honors, Denison U., 1959; M.A. in Govt, Claremont Grad. Sch., 1961; D.Sci. (hon.), U. Osteo. Medicine and Health Scis., Des Moines, 1981. Asst. sec. Calif. State Personnel Bd., Sacramento, 1972-73; chief dep. dir., acting dir. Calif. State Dept. Social Welfare, Sacramento, 1973; dir. Calif. State Dept. Social Welfare, 1973-74, Calif. State Dept. Benefit Payments, 1974-75; sr. research asso. Republican Study Com., U.S. Ho. of Reps., Washington, 1975-76; profl. staff mem. U.S. Senate Com. on Fin., Washington, 1976-79; legis. dir. U.S. Senator William L. Armstrong, Washington, 1979-81; undersec. Dept. Health and Human Services, Washington, 1981-83; sec. health and welfare State of Calif., Sacramento, 1983-85. Elder Presbyn. Ch.; bd. dirs. Friends of SOS Children's Villages, Inc., 1975—. Rotary Club Found. fellow, 1961-62. Mem. Am. Public Welfare Assn., United Council on Welfare Fraud, Wycliffe Assos., Phi Beta Kappa, Delta Upsilon. Republican. Office: Franchetti & Swoap One Market Plaza Steuart St Tower Suite 1210 San Francisco CA 94105

SYDNOR, ROBERT HADLEY, state government geologist; b. Whittier, Calif., July 1, 1947; s. Thurston Edward and Mary Edith (Thompson) S.; m. Nancie Jeanne Neubert, Mar. 29, 1986. B.A., Whittier Coll., 1969; M.S., U. Calif.-Riverside, 1975. Registered geologist, Calif., Oreg., Alaska, Ariz.; cert. engring. geologist, Calif., Oreg. Asst. petroleum geologist Mobil Oil Corp., Anchorage, 1970-71; staff engring. geologist Leighton & Assocs., Irvine, Calif., 1973-77; assoc. engring. geologist Orange County, Laguna Niguel, Calif., 1977-79; sr. engring. geologist VTN Corp., Irvine, 1979; chief engring. geologist R&M Cons., Inc., Irvine, 1979-82; supervising geologist Calif. Div. Mines and Geology, San Francisco, 1982—; mem. exam. com. Calif. State Bd. of Registration for Geologists and Geophysicists, Sacramento, 1977—, chmn., 1978. Contbr. many cons. reports on landslides and seismicity. Mem. alumni scholarship com. U. Calif.-Riverside, 1978—; mem. City of Los Angeles Grading Appeals Bd., 1979-84; alt. mem. County of Orange Grading Appeals Bd., 1980-84. Donnel Foster Hewett fellow U. Calif., 1972. Mem. Calif. Acad. Sci. (life), Assn. Engring. Geologists (assoc. editor Bull. 1979-86, chmn. So. Calif. sect. 1979-80), Geol. Soc. Am., Seismol. Soc. Am. (life), Am. Assn. Petroleum Geologists, Am. Inst. Profl. Geologists, Nat. Assn. Geology Tchrs., Arctic Inst. N.Am. (life), ASTM, Am. Geophys. Union (life), Sigma Gamma Epsilon (life). Republican. Home: 1859 Stratton Circle Walnut Creek CA 94598 Office: Calif Div Mines and Geology 380 Civic Dr Suite 100 Pleasant Hill CA 94523

SYERS, WILLIAM EDWARD, mfg. co. exec.; b. DeKoven, Ky., Feb. 26, 1926; s. John Benedict and Mary Helen (Watson) S.; student Lockyear's Bus. Coll., Evansville, Ind., 1950-52; m. Veda Marie Swisher, Dec. 23, 1950; children—David Bruce, Drew Edward. With Internat. Harvester Co., Evansville, Ind., 1946-52, IBM, 1952-68, subs. Service Bur. Corp., 1968-70; with Teledyne Econ. Devel. Co., Phoenix, 1970—, dir. adminstrv. services, 1979—, asst. ctr. dir., 1980—. Served with Q.M.C., AUS, 1946-48. Mem. Adminstrv. Mgmt. Soc. (pres. Phoenix chpt. 1977-78, dir. 1978-79), Phoenix C. of C. Republican. Mem. Ch. of Christ. Office: Teledyne Econ Devel Co 518 S 3d St Phoenix AZ 85004

SYLLA, JAMES R., petroleum company executive. Vice pres. Chevron Corp., San Francisco; pres., dir. Chevron U.S.A., Inc., San Francisco. Address: Chevron USA Inc 575 Market St San Francisco CA 94105 *

SYMMS, STEVEN DOUGLAS, U.S. Senator; b. Nampa, Idaho, Apr. 23, 1938; s. Darwin and Irene (Knowlton) S.; m. Frances E. Stockdale, 1959; children: Dan, Susan, Amy, Katy. B.S., U. Idaho, 1960. With Symms Fruit Ranch, Inc., Caldwell, Idaho, 1963-72; mem. 93d-96th Congresses from 1st Idaho Dist., U.S. Senate, 1980—; mem. Com. on Budget, Com. on Fin., Com. on Environment and Public Works, Joint Econ. Com., Nat. Republican Senatorial Com. Served with USMC, 1959-63. Office: 509 Hart Senate Bldg Washington DC 20510 *

SYMONS, ROBERT SPENCER, electronic engineer; b. San Francisco, July 3, 1925; s. Spencer W. and Avesia (Atkins) S.; B.S., Stanford U., 1946, M.S., 1948; m. Alice Faye Smith, Dec. 21, 1960; children—Julia Ann, Robert Spencer. Engr., Eitel-McCullough, Inc., San Bruno, Calif., 47, Heinz & Kaufman, South San Francisco, 1948, Pacific Electronics Co., Los Gatos, Calif., 1949; sr. engring. mgr. Varian Assocs., Palo Alto, Calif., 1950-83; product line mgr. Litton Industries, San Carlos, Calif., 1983—. Served to 1st lt. AUS, 1950-53. Fellow IEEE; mem. Phi Beta Kappa, Tau Beta Pi. Club: Commonwealth of Calif. Assoc. editor IEEE Transactions on Electron Devices, 1980-83. Patentee in field. Home: 290 Surrey Pl Los Altos CA 94022 Office: Litton Industries 960 Industrial Rd San Carlos CA 94070

SYPUTA, ROBERT WAYNE, electronics company executive; b. Chgo., Nov. 30, 1950; s. Phillip Joseph and Leola Murial (Palmer) S. BSEE, So. Tech. Inst. (name changed to So. Coll. Engring. div. Georgia Tech), 1979; MBA, Seattle U., 1985. Owner Blown-In-Insulation, Marietta, Ga., 1977-79; sales engr. Honeywell Comml. div., Seattle, 1979-82; sales engr., mgr. Centralab, Inc., Seattle, 1982-85; sales engr. Fairchild, Inc., Bellevue, Wash., 1985; pres. Microsafe, Inc., Kirkland, Wash., 1985—. Inventor/patentee fiber optic theft alarm, 1985; author bus. plan, Microsafe Products Co., 1986. Vol. United Way, Seattle, 1985-86; mem. Jr. Civitans, Kirkland, 1986. Mem. Northwest Surface Mt. Users Group (panelist 1984-85). Republican. Lutheran. Club: Toastmasters (acting v.p.). Avocations: sailing, microcomputers, traveling.

SZABO, ROBERT MORRIS, orthopedic surgeon, educator; b. N.Y.C., May 8, 1952; s. Gustav and Jette (Schulsinger) S.; m. Mary Lynne Talamo, May 7, 1977. BA in Psychobiology, NYU, 1973; MD, SUNY, Buffalo, 1977. Diplomate Nat. Bd. Med. Examiners, Am. Bd. Orthopedics, Am. Bd. Orthopedic Surgery. Resident in gen. and orthopedic surgery Mt. Sinai Med. Ctr., N.Y.C., 1977-82; fellow in hand/microvascular surgery Univ. Calif. Hosp., San Diego, 1982-83; asst. prof. dept. orthopedics, chief of Hand and Microvascular Service Med. Ctr. U. Calif.-Davis Sch. Medicine, Sacramento, 1982—; Cons. rheumatology service Med. Ctr. U. Calif.-Davis. Contbr. articles to profl. jours. Bd. dirs. Californians for Safe Motorcycling, Sacramento, 1985. Grantee Am. Soc. Surgery of the Hand, U. Calif.-Davis Sch. Medicine, 1985, 86. Mem. Calif. Med. Assn. (adv. panel 1985—), AMA. Avocations: photography, classical music, skiing. Home: 1040 44th St Sacramento CA 95819 Office: U Calif Davis Med Ctr 2230 Stockton Blvd Sacramento CA 95817

SZABO, SHARON LYNN, registered nurse; b. Cleve., Nov. 17, 1946; s. Joseph Steven and Margaret Minerva (Marigaard) S.; m. Ross Earl McFarland Jr., June 15, 1968 (div. June 1972). RN, Mt. Sinai Hosp. Sch. Nursing, 1967. Cert. operating room nurse. Asst. head nurse Mt. Sinai Hosp., Cleve., 1967-68; staff nurse operating room Cedars-Sinai Med. Ctr., Los Angeles, 1969-71; ob-gyn office nurse for med. office of Everett Wood, MD, Burbank, Calif., 1968-69; internal medicine office nurse for Martin Covel, MD, Beverly Hills, Calif., 1971-74; from. staff nurse to asst. head nurse U. Calif., San Francisco, 1974-85, cardiac surgery head, 1985—; cons. Westervelt, Johnson, Nicholl, & Keller, Attys. at Law, Peoria, Ill., 1985—. Contbg. author: Alexander's Care of the Patient in Surgery. Mem. Assn. of Operating Room Nurses (chpt. treas. 1983-84, test specifications com. mem. of nat. cert. bd., 1979-81). Office: U Calif San Francisco Med Ctr 3d & Parnassus Aves San Francisco CA 94143

SZABO, ZOLTAN, medical research organization administrator, continuing education educator; b. Szeged, Hungary, Oct. 5, 1943; came to U.S., 1967; s. Imre and Maria (Szikora) S.; m. Wanda Toy, Dec. 5, 1976; children: Eva, Maria. Student, U. Med. Sch., Szeged, 1962-65; PhD, Columbia Pacific U., 1983. Tech. dir. microsurgery lab. R.K. Davies Med. Ctr., San Francisco, 1972-80; dir. Microsurg. Research Inst., San Francisco, 1980—; research assoc. oral and maxillofacial surgery U. of the Pacific, San Francisco, 1980-83, adj. asst. prof., 1983—. Author: Microsurgery Techniques, vol. 1 1974, vol. 2 1984 (1st Place award for excellence in med. writing, 1982); contbr. chpt. books, articles to profl. jours. Served with U.S. Army, 1969-71, Vietnam. Recipient 1st prize scientific exhibit Am. Soc. Plastic and Reconstructive Surgeons, 1977; Cert. of Merit, AMA, 1978. Fellow Internat. Coll. Surgeons; mem. Hungarian Gynecol. Soc. (hon.), Medico-Dental Study Guild of Calif., Internat. Microsurg. Soc., Am. Fertility Soc., Am. Soc. Reconstructive Microsurgery (assoc.), Soc. for Study of Impotence. Avocations: gardening, landscaping, oil painting, wood sculpture, travel. Office: Microsurg Research Inst 153 States St San Francisco CA 94114

SZALECKI, WOJCIECH JOSEF, research chemist; b. Kutno, Poland, Mar. 18, 1935; came to U.S., 1969; s. Mieczyslaw and Julia (Wojciechowska) S.; m. Zofia Fortuna, Nov. 10, 1959 (div. Mar. 1974); 1 child, Dorota; m. Danuta Grad, Dec. 10, 1977; 1 child, Adam. MS, U. Lodz, Poland, 1959, PhD, 1968. Research asst. U. Lodz, 1959-68, adj. instr., 1970-79; postdoctoral fellow Wayne State U., Detroit, 1969-70; research assoc. U. Colo., Boulder, 1979-83; research chemist Molecular Probes, Inc., Eugene, Oreg., 1983—; abstractor Chem. Abstracts Service, Columbus, Ohio, 1970-82. Contbr. articles to profl. jours. Fellow Am. Inst. Chemists; mem. Am. Chem. Soc. Avocations: chess, bridge, tennis. Home: 4109 Jessen Dr Eugene OR 97402 Office: Molecular Probes Inc 4849 Pitchford Ave Eugene OR 97402

SZARNICKI, ROBERT JOSEPH, pediatric/adult cardiovascular surgeon; b. Natrona Heights, Pa., Oct. 29, 1943; s. Frank John and Xaviera (Zolnowski) S.; AB, Columbia Coll., 1965; MD, Boston U., 1969; m. Mary Donovan, Nov. 21, 1982; children: Timothy Robert, Anna Victoria. Gen. surg. intern Boston City Hosp., 1969-70; resident in surgery, Boston Univ. Hosp., 1971-74; exchange registrar U. Wales, 1972-73; surgery resident St. Luke's Hosp., N.Y.C., 1970-71; cardiac surgery resident Columbia U. and Harlem Hosp., N.Y.C., 1974-76; sr. registrar in pediatric cardiac surgery Hosp. for Sick Children, London, 1976-77; pediatric cardiovascular surgeon Children's Hosp. of San Francisco, 1980; assoc. pediatric and adult cardiovascular surgeon Pacific Med. Ctr., San Francisco, 1977—, mem. critical care com. 1980—, joint clin. practice com., 1979-80; bd. dirs. Pacif. Presbyn. Med. Group. Diplomate Am. Bd. Surgery, Am. Bd. Thoracic Surgery. Fellow ACS, Am. Coll. Cardiology; mem. AMA, Calif. Med. Assn., San Francisco Med. Soc., Soc. Thoracic Surgeons, Soc. Thoracic and Cardiovascular Surgeons Gt. Britain and Ireland, Pan Pacific Surg. Assn., San Francisco Surg. Soc., Pediatric Cardiac Surg. Group. Clubs: San Francisco Bay, Guardsmen, Garfield Gentlemen's. Contbr. articles to profl. jours.; invented exptl. extra cardiac bypass of obstructed mitral valve, 1979. Home: 125 30th

Ave St San Francisco CA 94121 Office: Pacific Presbyn Med Ctr 2100 Webster St Suite 411 San Francisco CA 94115

SZEGO, PETER A., government consultant, mechanical engineer; b. Berlin, July 18, 1925; came to U.S., 1934; s. Gabor and Anne E. Szegö. Sr. cons. Calif. State Senate, Sacramento. Contbr. articles to profl. jours. Served as sgt. U.S. Army, 1944-46, ETO. Mem. ASME, IEEE, SIAM, Am. Math. Soc. ACM. Democrat. Avocation: camping. Home: 75 Glen Eyrie Ave #19 San Jose CA 95125 Office: Office Senator Dan McCorquodale State Capitol Room 4032 Sacramento CA 95814

SZETO, ANDREW YEUN-JONG, biomedical engineer; b. Canton, China, Jan. 8, 1949; s. Daniel Ming and Lien Chu S.; came to U.S., 1957, naturalized, 1967; m. Vivian Lim Ong, Sept. 1, 1979; 1 child, Jonathan Mark. BS, UCLA, 1971, PhD, 1977; MS, U. Calif., Berkeley, 1973, M. in Engring., 1974. Elec. engr. Hughes Aircraft Co., Canoga Park, Calif., summers 1969-72: grad. research asst. biotech. lab. UCLA, 1975-77, postdoctoral scholar, summer 1977, vis. scholar, summer 1978; asst. prof. La. Tech. U., Ruston, 1977-80, assoc. prof. biomed. engring., 1980-82; dir. research and devel. La Jolla Tech., Inc., San Diego, 1982-83; assoc. prof. dept. elec. and computer engring. San Diego State U., 1983-86; prof. dept. elec. and computer engring , 1987; tech. cons. Transcutaneous Nerve Stimulators, La Jolla Tech., Inc., 1983-86; workshop organizer, 1978—. Recipient Ralph Crump award UCLA, 1977, Meritorius Profl. Performance and Promise award San Diego State U., 1986; Vocat. Rehab. grantee, 1978-82, 84-87; NSF grantee, 1979-81. Mem. IEEE, Engrs. in Medicine and Biology Soc., Human Factors Soc., Biomed. Engring. Soc., Internat. Soc. Prosthetics and Orthotics, Am. Soc. Engring. Edn., Am. Med. Instrumentation Inst., Internat. Assn. Study of Pain, N.Y. Acad. Sci., Sigma Xi (Researcher of Yr. 1981), Tau Beta Pi. Baptist. Contbr. articles to profl. jours. Home: 10445 Summerwood Ct San Diego CA 92131 Office: San Diego State U San Diego CA 92182

SZILAGYI, MIKE (MIKLOS) NICHOLAS, electrical and computer engineering educator; b. Budapest, Hungary, Feb. 4, 1936; came to U.S., 1981; s. Karoly and Ilona (Abraham) S.; m. Larissa Dorner, Feb. 23, 1957 (div. July 1970); 1 child, Gabor; m. Julia Levai, May 31, 1975; 1 child, Zoltan Charles. MS in Engring., Physics with honors, Tech. U. Leningrad, USSR, 1960; PhD, Electrotech. U. Leningrad, 1965; D Tech., Tech. U. Budapest, 1965; DSc with exceptional distinction, Hungarian Acad. Scis., 1979. Research asst. phys. electronics Tech. U. Leningrad, 1958-60; research assoc., Inst. Tech. Physics Hungarian Acad. Scis., 1960-66; head electron optics lab. Tech. U. Budapest, 1966-71; prof., head dept. phys. scis. K. Kando Coll. of Elec. Engring., Budapest, 1971-79, pres., 1971-74; cons. Deutsches Elektronen-Synchrotron DESY, Hamburg, Federal Republic of Germany, 1980-81; vis. sr. research assoc., applied and engring. physics Cornell U., 1981-82; prof. elec. and computer engring. U. Ariz., 1982—; sci. adv. Nat. Inst. Neurosurgery, Budapest, 1966-70; vis. prof. Enrico Fermi Inst., U. Chgo., Lawrence Berkeley Lab., U. Calif., Stanford Linear Accelerator Ctr., Stanford U., 1976-77, Inst. Physics, U. Aarhus, Denmark, 1979-81, U. Heidelberg, Fed. Republic of Germany, Max Planck Inst. Nuclear Physics, Heidelberg, 1984. Author nine books, including Introduction to the Theory of Space-Charge Optics, 1974, Fachlexikon Physik, 1979; contbr. 70 articles to profl. jours., also contbr. to internat. confs. UN Indsl. Devel. Orgn. fellow, 1976. Mem. IEEE (sr.), Am. Phys. Soc., Internat. Soc. Hybrid Microelectronics, European Soc. Stereotactic and Functional Neurosurgery, L. Eotvos Phys. Soc. (Brody prize 1964), J. Neumann Soc. for Computer Sci., Danish Phys. Soc., Danish Engring. Soc. Contbr. to devel. of various particle beam devices, provided solution to problem of electron optical synthesis. Avocations: swimming, music, literature and fine arts, hiking, photography. Office: U Ariz Dept Elec and Computer Engring Tucson AZ 85721

SZILAS, PETER, mathematics educator; b. Debrecen, Hungary, Jan. 16, 1948. BS Physics, Munich U., 1968, MS in Physics, 1973, postgrad., 1973-76, PhD, 1983. Grad. teaching asst. U. Tenn., Knoxville, 1976-77; instr. physics and math. Gymnasium, Munich, 1978-81; research assoc. Inst. Theoretical Physics U. Munich, 1977-83; research assoc. Inst. Geophysics and Planetary Sci. UCLA, 1983-84, research assoc. Philosophy dept., 1985; research assoc. Stanford Synchrotron Radiation Lab. Stanford U., Palo Alto, 1984; tchr. math. Le Lycee Francais, Los Angeles, 1985-86; instr. math. Pacific States U., Los Angeles, 1985-86. Contbr. articles to profl. jours. Grantee Ctr. for Advanced Nondestructive Evaluation, Rockwell Internat., 1977, Deutsche Forschungsgemeinschaft, 1978-83; Sci. Contbrs. award, Siemens' Labs. Research div., 1974. Home: 1245 N Kings Rd Apt 16 Los Angeles CA 90069

SZUTU, PETER CHENG, non-profit adminstrator; b. Beijing, Peoples Republic of China, Sept. 18, 1945; came to U.S., 1952; s. Gene Chan and Florence (Chiang) S.; m. Martha Ann McClaren, Apr. 2, 1978 (div. Dec. 1984); m. Janice Rose Eldred, May 26, 1985. BA in Chemistry and Biology, U.S. Internat. U., 1972; MPH, U. Calif., Berkeley, 1981. Adminstr. Beach Area Community Clinic, San Diego, 1973-79; peer counseling U. Calif., Berkeley, 1979-81; spl. asst. State Dept. Health Services, Sacramento, Calif., 1980-82; exec. dir. Oakland (Calif.) Chinese Community Council, 1982-86; mgmt., planning cons. Calif., 1986—. Legis. cons. Bay Area Asian Health Alliance, Oakland, 1980-83; bd. dirs. Chinatown & Cen. Dist. Community Devel., Oakland, 1983-84; mem. State Adv. Council Refugee Affairs, Oakland, Sacramento, 1983-85; mem. steering com. City of 21st Century, Oakland, 1985-86. Served to sgt. USAF, 1966-70. Recipient Cert. of Appreciation, Pub. Adminstrn. U. So. Calif., 1981, Spl. Recognition award Vietnamese Fisherman's Assn., 1985. Mem. East Bay Forum on Refugee Affairs (chmn., pres. 1984—), Fund Devel. Com. (bd. dirs. La Clinica de La Raza, Inc. chpt. 1982—), Community Adult Day Health Services (bd. dirs. 1983—), Nat. Council on Alternate Health (bd. dirs. 1974—). Democrat. Avocations: skiing, woodworking, auto mechanics.

SZWARC, MICHAEL M., chemistry educator; b. Poland, June 9, 1909; came to U.S., 1952; s. Maier and Regina (Prager) Szwarc; m. Marja Frankel, Aug. 6, 1933; children: Raphael, Myra, Rina. Ch.E., Warsaw Poly. Inst., Poland, 1932; Ph.D. in Organic Chemistry, Hebrew U., Jerusalem, 1945; Ph.D. in Phys. Chemistry, Manchester U., Eng., 1947; D.Sc. (hon), Manchester U., 1949, U. Leuven, Belgium, 1974, Uppsala U., Sweden, 1975, Louis Pasteur U., Strasbourg, France, 1978. Researcher Hebrew U., Jerusalem, 1935-45; researcher Manchester U., Eng., 1946-52, univ. fellow, lectr. phys. chemistry, 1949-52; mem. faculty SUNY-Syracuse Coll. Forestry, 1952-79, disting. prof. chemistry, 1964-82, dir. polymer ctr., 1966-82, prof. emeritus, adj. prof., 1982; prof. emeritus, adj. prof. U. Calif.-San Diego, La Jolla, 1982—. Author: Carbanious Ions and Living Polymers, 1968; editor: Ion Pairs in Organic Chemistry, 1972. Recipient award in polymer chemistry Am. Chem. Soc., 1970; recipient Gold medal Internat. Soc. Plastics Engrs., 1972, Benjamin Franklin Soc., 1978. Fellow Royal Soc. (London). Office: Dept Chemistry U Calif-San Diego La Jolla CA 92093

SZYLIOWICZ, JOSEPH SIMON, international studies educator; b. Charleroi, Belgium, Dec. 7, 1931; came to U.S., 1948.; s. Jules and Minka S.; m. Irene R. Lust, Mar. 20, 1960; children: Michael G., Dara M. BA, Denver U., 1953; MA, Johns Hopkins U., 1955; PhD, Columbia U., 1961. Instr. Middle East Studies Bklyn. Coll., 1961-64; asst. prof. Denver U. Grad. Sch. Internat. Studies, 1965-69, assoc. prof., 1969-74, prof., 1974—, acting dean, 1968, dir. placements, 1970-73, 79-81, 85—; tchr. U. Md. extension div., 1960, Hunter Coll., 1961-62, L.I. U., 1966, U. Utah, 1980, Portland State U., 1980, U. Mich., 1982, Oxford U., 1984; sr. assoc. Oxford U. St. Antony's Coll., 1984-85; cons. Office Tech. Assessment, Washington, 1982-83, various other agys. Author: Planning, Managing and Implementing Technological Development Projects:The Case of Eregli Iron and Steel Works, 1982; co-author, editor: The Contemporary Middle East, Tradition and Innovation, 1965, Political Change in Rural Turkey, Erdemli: A Case Study, 1966, Education and Modernization in the Middle East, 1973, The Energy Crisis and U.S. Foreign Policy, 1975, Decision-Making in a Technological Environment: The Case of the Aswan High Dam, 1980, Technology and International Affairs, 1981; referee Am. Polit. Sci. Rev., Comparative Politics, Sage Profl. Papers, Jour. Developing Areas, Econ. Devel. and Cultural Change, others; contbr. articles to profl. jours. Fellow Ford Found., 1955-58, Inst. Advanced Studies, 1979; Fulbright sr. research fellow 1983; named Martin Prof. Harry S. Truman Inst., Hebrew U. Jerusalem, 1977; grantee Ford Found., 1968-69, Social Sci. Research Council, 1968-69, Rand Inst., Sloan Found., HEW Office Edn. Mem. AAAS, Am. Polit. Sci. Assn., Turkish Studies Assn. (pres. 1974-76, exec. council 1983—, sec. 1973-74, exec. com. 1977-79), Internat. Studies Assn. (mem. gov.'s council 1985-87, chmn./pres. comparative interdisciplinary studies sect. 1985-87, sec. 1982-84), Am. Pol. Sci. Assn., Middle East Studies Assn. (chmn. program com. 1972-73, dissertation awards com. 1982-84)., Am. Research Inst. in Turkey (exec. bd. dirs. 1976-78, sr. fellow 1964-65), Am. Profs. for Peace in Middle East (nat. exec. com. 1978—), Phi Beta Kappa, Pi Gamma Mu, Tau Kappa Alpha. Avocations: photography, tennis, travel. Office: U Denver Grad Sch Internat Studies Denver CO 80208

SZYNAKA, EDWARD M., library director, consultant; b. N.Y.C., Sept. 26, 1948; s. Edward J. and Catherine A. (Regan) S.; m. Diane Pickering; children—Edward, Andrew, Emily. B.A. in Polit. Sci., SUNY-Fredonia, 1972; M.L.A., Syracuse U., 1973. Dir. libraries, Massena, N.Y., 1972-75, Midland, Mich., 1975-80; dir. Pasadena (Calif.) Pub. Library, 1980—; mgmt. cons. Bd. dirs. ARC; active Big Bros. Served to lt. U.S. Army, 1966-68. Mem. ALA, Calif. Library Assn., Mich. Library Assn. Democrat. Roman Catholic. Club: Kiwanis. *

TABACCHI, OTAVIO ROBERT, food service company executive; b. Chester, Pa., Oct. 29, 1946; s. Leonard and Amelia Rose (Ziegler) T.; m. Mary Frances Hanlon, Aug. 5, 1972; children—Patricia, Lisa, Robert, Edward. B.S.E.E., U. Dayton, 1968; M.B.A., Wharton U. Pa., Phila., 1970. Analyst, City of Boston, 1971-73; cons. Touche Ross & Co., 1973-76; sr. v.p. Hallsmith-Sysco, Norton, Mass., 1976-85; exec. v.p. Nobel-Sysco, Denver, 1985—. Served to capt. USAR, 1971-76. Club: Wharton. Avocations: tennis; sailing. Home: 3478 E Jamison Ave Littleton CO 80122 Office: Nobel-Sysco PO Box 5566 Denver CO 80217

TABER, ROBERT RUSSELL, advertising executive; b. Richland, Wash., Aug. 4, 1949; s. Robert Russell and Catherine Cordelia (Foote) T.; m. Karen Jean Chrisman, Jan. 23, 1970; 1 son, Benjamin Guy. B.A. in Journalism, U. Idaho, 1971; M.A. in Journalism, U. Oreg., 1973. Acct. exec. Dailey & Assocs. Advt. Agy., San Francisco, 1973-75; acct. supr. Ayer/Baker Advt. Agy., Seattle, 1975-78; v.p., acct. supr. N.W. Ayer Advt. Agy., N.Y.C., 1978-80; asst. prof. advt. U. Oreg., 1980-85; v.p. profl. devel. Assn. Nat. Advertisers, 1985-86; acct. supr. Scali, McCabe and Sloves, Inc., 1986—; cons. in field. Mem. Am. Advt. Fedn. (Northwest Advt. Educator of Yr. 1985), Am. Acad. Advt., Kappa Tau Alpha, Phi Kappa Phi. Contbr. articles to profl. publs.

TABORSKY, GEORGE, biochemist, educator; b. Budapest, Hungary, Feb. 12, 1928; s. Otto and Theresa (Halzl) T.; m. Eva Nemeth, Sept. 12, 1953; children: Peter, Andrea. BS, Brown U., 1951; PhD, Yale U., 1956. Postdoctoral fellow Carlsberg Lab., Copenhagen, 1956-57; faculty Yale U., New Haven, Conn., 1957-70, U. Calif., Santa Barbara, 1970—; mem. editorial bd. Jour. Biological Chemistry, 1975-80; ad hoc reviewer manuscripts and grant proposals for various govt. agys. and jours. Contbr. numerous articles and reviews to profl. jours. and mags. Research grantee NIH, 1962-71, 84—, NSF, 1973-83. Fellow; Am. Inst. Chemists; mem. Am. Soc. Biol. Chemists, Am. Chem. Soc., Biophys. Soc. Office: Univ Calif Dept Biol Sci Santa Barbara CA 93106

TABRISKY, JOSEPH, radiologist; b. Boston, June 23, 1931; s. Henry and Gertrude Tabrisky; B.A. cum laude, Harvard U., 1952; M.D. cum laude, Tufts U., 1956; m. Phyllis Eleanor Page, Apr. 23, 1955; children—Joseph Page, Elizabeth Ann, William Page. Flexible intern U. Ill. Hosp., 1956-57; resident in radiology Fitzsimons Army Hosp., 1958-60; instr. radiology Tufts U. Med. Sch., 1964-65; cons. radiologist Swedish Med. Center, Denver, 1966-68; chief radiologist Kaiser Found. Hosp., Harbor City, Calif., 1968-72; mem. faculty UCLA Med. Sch., 1972—, prof. radiol. scis., 1975—, vice chmn. dept., 1976—, exec. policy com. radiol. scis.; chmn. radiology dept. Harbor-UCLA Med. Center, 1975—, pres. faculty soc., 1979-80, exec. dir. MR/CT Imaging Ctr., bd. dirs. Research Ednl. Inst., Harbor Collegium/UCLA Found.; dir. Vascular Biometrics Inc.; steering com. Harvard U., 1952; cons. Los Angeles County Dept. Pub. Health; chmn. Los Angeles County Radiol. Standards Com., 1979. Mem. Harvard-Radcliffe Schs. Com.; bd. dirs., treas., Harbor-UCLA Med. Found.; chmn. UCLA Council for Ednl. Devel. Served to maj. M.C., U.S. Army, 1957-63. Diplomate Am. Bd. Radiology. Fellow Am. Coll. Radiology (chief exec. officer, univ. radcom assn., 1986); mem. Radiol. Soc. N. Am., Assn. U. Radiologists, Am. Heart Assn. (cardiovascular radiology council), Calif. Med. Assn., Calif. Radiol. Soc., So. Calif. Radiol. Soc., Los Angeles Med. Assn., Los Angeles Radiol. Soc., Alpha Omega Alpha. Contbr. articles to med. jours. Office: 1000 W Carson St Torrance CA 90509

TACHE, YVETTE FRANCE, medical research educator; b. Lyon, Rhone, France, Feb. 1, 1945; came to U.S., 1982; d. Lucien Joseph and Jeanne Marthe (Fouillat) Laurent; m. Jean Arthur Tache, June 1970 (dec. 1979); children: Stephanie, Veronique. Baccalaureat, Lycc, Tarare, France, 1965; Maitrise, Faculty of Scis. U. C. Bernard, Lyon, 1968, DEA, 1969; PhD, U. Montreal, Que., Can., 1974. Asst. researcher U. Montreal, 1977-78, asst. research prof., 1980-81, assoc. research prof., 1981-82; assoc. prof. in residence UCLA, 1982-85, prof. medicine in residence, 1985—; vis. scientist Salk Inst., La Jolla, Calif., 1978-80; mem. selection com. Med. REsearch Council, Montreal, 1982. External referee Specialized Sci. Jours., 1977—, Med. Research Council, Quebec, 1981—; contbr. articles to profl. jours. Fellow MRC, Med. Research Council Que., Montreal and Ottawa, Can., 1974-78; centenial fellow MRC, Ottawa, 1978-80, scholar MRC, Ottawa, 1982; grantee FMRCQ, MRC, NIH, 1977—. Mem. Internat. Soc. Psychoneuroendocrinology, Endocrine Soc., Soc. Neurosci., Am. Physiol. Soc., Am. Gastroenterol. Soc., Hans Selye Found. (v.p. 1984), N.Y. Acad. Scis. Office: CURE VA Wadsworth Bldg 115 Room 203 Los Angeles CA 90073

TACKES, JEROME MATHAU, mechanical engineer; b. Great Falls, Mont., Apr. 1, 1923; s. Joe and Katherine (Keller) T.; m. Lillian A. Nyman, Oct. 22, 1955; children—Gregory J., Todd A. B.S. in Mech. Engring., 1950. Registered profl. engr., Alaska. Mech. design engr. U.S. Army Corps of Engrs., Anchorage, 1952-62, chief mech. design, 1962-80; prin. mech. engr., cons. Morrison-Knudsen Engrs., Inc., Anchorage, 1980—. Chmn. Engr. Week Activities Anchorage Area, 1969, 78. Served to sgt. USAF, 1943-45. Recipient Superior Performance award U.S. Army Corps of Engrs., 1972, 80. Mem. Nat. Soc. Profl. Engrs. (pres. Anchorage chpt. 1969), Soc. Am. Mil. Engrs. (pres. Anchorage chpt. 1979), Alaska Soc. Profl. Engrs. (sec., pres. 1965-84), ASHRAE, ASME, Toastmasters (officer 1969-84). Lodge: K.C. Home: 1437 Sunrise Dr Anchorage AK 99508 Office: Morrison-Knudsen Engring Inc 813 D St Anchorage AK 99501

TAFOYA, ARTHUR N., bishop; b. Alameda, N.Mex., Mar. 2, 1933. Ed., St. Thomas Sem., Denver, Conception (Mo.) Sem. Ordained priest Roman Cath. Ch., 1962; ordained bishop of Pueblo Colo., 1980—. Office: 1426 Grand Ave Pueblo CO 81003 *

TAFT, DAVID ALLAN, surgeon; b. Madison, Wis., Dec. 26, 1933; s. Cyrus Alonso and Margaret Eleanor (Brubaker) T.; m. Sheila Blackwood, Apr. 20, 1968; children: Robert Matthew, Michael Cyrus. BS, Iowa State U., 1955; MD, U. Iowa, 1959; M in Med. Sci., Ohio State U., 1965. Diplomate Am. Bd. Surgery. Intern Ohio State U., Columbus, 1959-60, resident in surgery, 1960-64, chief resident, 1964-65; research fellow and jr. cons. Royal Infirmary U. Edinburgh, Scotland, 1965-66; surgeon The Mason Clinic, Seattle, 1969—; assoc. prof. surgery U. Wash., Seattle, 1979—. Contbr. articles to profl. jours. Served to comdr. USN, 1966-69, Vietnam. Decorated Navy Cross. Fellow ACS, Am. Bd. Surgery, Western Surgical Assn., North Pacific Surgical Assn.; mem. Pacific Coast Surgical Assn., Seattle Surgical Soc., Soc. Surgery Olinentary Tract, Sigma Xi. Republican. Presbyterian. Avocations: camping, hiking, running, outdoor activities. Home: 5757 64th Ave NE Seattle WA 98105 Office: The Mason Clinic 1100 9th Ave Seattle WA 98101

TAFT, PERRY HAZARD, lawyer; b. Los Angeles, Jan. 23, 1915; s. Milton and Sarah T.; m. Callie S. Taft, Aug. 15, 1968; children by previous marriage—Stephen D., Sally L., Sheila R. Student U. Calif.-Berkeley, 1932-35; A.B., UCLA, 1936; LL.B., George Washington U., 1940. Bar: Calif. 1940. Spl. atty. Antitrust div. U.S. Dept. Justice, Los Angeles, 1941-42; dep. atty. gen. State of Calif., San Francisco, 1943-44; regional rep. Council State Govts., San Francisco, 1944-45; regional dir. govt. affairs Trans World Airlines, Los Angeles, 1945-47; Pacific coast mgr. Am. Ins. Assn., San Francisco, 1948-66; gen. counsel Assn. Calif. Ins. Cos., Sacramento, 1967-73; asst. city atty. City of Stockton, Calif., 1973-79; pres. Perry H. Taft, P.C., Stockton, 1979-85; dir. Compair, Inc., Burlingame, Calif. ; arbitrator Surplus Line Assn. Calif., 1965—. Contbr. articles to profl. jours. Bd. dirs. Stockton East Water Dist., 1979-83, pres., 1981-83; mem. San Joaquin County Water Adv. Com., 1982-85. Mem. State Bar of Calif., Psi Upsilon. Democrat. Clubs: Elkhorn Country, Yosemite. Home: 8615 Stonewood Dr Stockton CA 95209 Office: PO Box 7453 Stockton CA 95207

TAFT, PETER R., lawyer; b. Cin., Mar. 3, 1936; s. Charles P. and Eleanor (Chase) T.; m. Diana F. Todd, Nov. 17, 1979. B.A., Yale U., 1958, LL.B., 1961. Bar: D.C. 1963, Calif. 1969. Law clk. U.S. Ct. Appeals (5th cir.), 1961-62; law clk. to Chief Justice Earl Warren, U.S. Supreme Ct., 1962-63; assoc. Williams & Connolly, Washington, 1963-67, ptnr., 1967-69; asst. atty. gen. Land and Natural Resources div. Dept. Justice, Washington, 1975-77; ptnr. Munger Tolles & Olson, Los Angeles, 1969-75, 77—. Mem. D.C. Bar Assn., Calif. Bar Assn., Los Angeles Bar Assn., ABA. Republican. Episcopalian. Home: 17058 Ave de Santa Ynez Pacific Palisades CA 90272 Office: 355 S Grand St 35th Fl Los Angeles CA 90071

TAGGART, SONDRA, financial planner, investment advisor; b. N.Y.C., July 22, 1934; d. Louis and Rose (Birnbaum) Hamov; B.A., Hunter Coll., 1955; children—Eric, Karen. Cert. fin. planner, registered investment advisor; registered prin. Nat. Assn. Securities Dealers. Founder, dir. Copyright Service Bur., Ltd., N.Y.C., 1957-69; dir., officer Maclen Music, Inc., N.Y.C., 1964-69; pres. Westshore, Inc., pub. internat. bus. materials, Mill Valley, Calif., 1965-80; pres. The Taggart Co. Ltd.; securities broker-dealer. Mem. Internat. Assn. Fin. Planners, Registry Fin. Planning Practitioners. Republican. Clubs: Bankers, Beverly Hills Country. Editor: The Red Tapes: Commentaries on Doing Business With The Russians and East Europeans, 1978; exec. producer (film) Second Wind. Office: 2049 Century Park E #1950 Los Angeles CA 90067

TAGLIAFERRI, EDWARD, physicist; b. Providence, Apr. 8, 1938; s. Edward and Madeline (Marianni) T.; m. Veronica Sue Sterrett, Aug. 11, 1962. BA in Physics, UCLA, 1960, MS in Physics, 1963, PhD in Physics, 1966. Mem. research staff Space Tech. Labs. (name changed to TRW), Redondo Beach, Calif., 1965-71; space program researcher Gemini, Apollo, Space Shuttle NASA and U.S. Dept. Def., 1968-83; dir. spl. projects Space and Control Systems div. System Devel. Group of UNISYS Corp., Camarillo, Calif., 1983—. Contbr. articles to profl. jours. Mem. AAAS, AIAA (space systems tech. com.), Nat. Space Indsl. Assn. (various panels), Nat. Acad. Engring.'s Naval Studies Bd. (IR panel), Am. Phys. Soc., Sigma Xi. Avocation: pvt. pilot. Office: System Devel Corp 5151 Camino Ruiz Camarillo CA 93010

TAHARA, STANLEY MAKOTO, biochemistry educator; b. Gardena, Calif., Sept. 17, 1952; s. Masayoshi and Sumiko (Kamimoto) T. BS in Biochemistry, U. Calif., Riverside, 1973, PhD in Biochemistry, 1979. Research asst. U. Calif., Riverside, 1974-79; postdoctoral fellow Roche Inst., Nutley, N.J., 1979-83; asst. prof. Sch. Medicine U. So. Calif., Los Angeles, 1983—. Grantee Wright Found., Los Angeles, 1984-85, Am. Cancer Soc., N.Y.C., 1985—, Life and Health Ins. Med. Research Fund, Washington, 1985—. Mem. AAAS, Am. Chem. Soc., Am. Soc. Biol. Chemists, Am. Soc. Microbiology, Sigma Xi. Office: U So Calif Sch Medicine Dept Microbiology 2011 Zonal Ave Los Angeles CA 90033-1054

TAI, SELWYN C., podiatric surgeon; b. Hong Kong, Oct. 31, 1950; s. En Shui and Jean T.; m. Helen Lim, June 2, 1979; 1 son, Gabriel. B.S.E., U. Pa., 1974; D.P.M., Ohio Coll., Podiatric Medicine, 1980. Dir., Community Foot and Ankle Clinic, Renton, Wash., 1981-85, Federal Way, Wash., 1984—; chief exec. officer Comfac, Bellevue, Wash., 1981—. Mem. Internat. Coll. Podiatric Laser Surgery, Am. Podiatric Med. Assn., Acad. Ambulatory Foot Surgery, Wash. State Podiatric Med. Assn., Internat. Coll. Podiatric Laser Surgery, IEEE, Federal Way C. of C. Home: PO Box 7178 Federal Way WA 98003 Office: Comfac 720 S 320th St Federal Way WA 98003

TAIMUTY, SAMUEL ISAAC, physicist; b. West Newton, Pa., Dec. 20, 1917; s. Elias and Samia (Hawatt) T.; B.S., Carnegie Mellon U., 1940; Ph.D., U. So. Calif., 1951; m. Betty Jo Travis, Sept. 12, 1953 (dec.); children—Matthew, Martha; m. 2d, Rosalie Richards, Apr. 3, 1976. Physicist, U.S. Naval Shipyard, Phila. and Long Beach, Calif., 1942-46; research asst. U. So. Calif., 1947-51; sr. physicist U.S. Naval Radiol. Def. Lab., 1950-52, SRI Internat., Menlo Park, Calif., 1952-72; sr. staff engr. Lockheed Missiles & Space Co., Sunnyvale, Calif., 1972—; cons. physicist, 1971—. Mem. Am. Phys. Soc., Sigma Xi. Episcopalian. Mason. Contbr. articles to sci. publs. Patentee in field. Home: 3346 Kenneth Dr Palo Alto CA 94303 Office: Lockheed Missiles and Space Co PO Box 3504 Sunnyvale CA 94088

TAKAHASHI, TENEY KUNIO, real estate executive; b. Honolulu, May 18, 1938; s. Torao and Takeno (Shimamoto) T.; m. Mae Toyo Yamamoto, Dec. 30, 1968; 1 child, Teney. BS, USAF Acad., 1961; MBA, U. Hawaii, 1971. Commd. 2d lt. USAF, 1961, advanced through grades to capt., resigned, 1969; sr. v.p. devel. Amfac Fin. Corp., Honolulu, 1973-77; pres. Amfac Property Investment Corp., Honolulu, 1977-85; sr. v.p. properties Amfac Hawaii, Inc., Honolulu, 1985—. Bd. dirs. Hawaii Visitors Bur., Honolulu, 1983-85. Mem. Hawaii Resort Developers Conf. (bd. dirs. 1977—). Republican. Episcopalian. Office: Amfac Hawaii Inc 700 Bishop St Honolulu HI 96813

TAKAHASHI, WATARU, environnmental consultant; b. Ewa, Hawaii, Aug. 20, 1925; s. Zenjiro and Matsuno (Kodama) T.; m. Nobuko Toyama, Sept. 17, 1955; 1 child, Ann Eiko. BA in Chemistry, U. Hawaii, 1957; MA in Chemistry, Ind. U., 1959. Organic chemist U.S. Argl. Research Service, Peoria, Ill., 1961-62; indsl. hygiene chemist Dept. Health, Honolulu, 1962-65; marine chemist U. Hawaii, Honolulu, 1965-70, field epidemiologist, 1971-82; cons. Aiea, Hawaii, 1982—. Contbr. articles to profl. jours. Served with U.S. Army, 1950-52, PTO. Mem. AAAS, Am. Chem. Soc., Phi Beta Kappa. Home and Office: 98-1996 Hoala St Aiea HI 96701

TAKAHASHI, YASUNDO, retired educator; b. Nagoya, Japan, June 12, 1912; came to U.S., 1958; s. Sakunosuke Seisen and Teruko Sogyoku (Umemura) T.; m. Kuwako Kusunoki, Apr. 9, 1939; 1 child, Yuri Canfield. BS, U.Tokyo, 1935, PhD, 1945; hon. degree, U. Grenoble, France, 1978. Registered profl. engr., Calif. Engr. Japanese Nat. Ry., Japan, 1935-37; asst. prof. Yokohama (Japan) Tech. Coll., 1937-40, Nagoya U., 1940-44; prof. U. Tokyo, 1944-58, U. Calif., Berkeley, 1958-79, Toyohashi U., Japan, 1979-82; sr. tech. cons. Mikuni Research and Devel., Richmond, 1982—. Author: Control, 1970, Systems and Control, 1970, Digital Control, 1984. Recipient Edn. award Am. Council of Auto Control, 1981. Fellow ASME (life, chmn. control div. 1976, Oldenburger medal 1978), Japan Soc. Instrument and Control (hon.), Japan Soc. Mech. Engrs. (hon.). Avocations: world travel, personal computers. Home: 135 York Ave Berkeley CA 94708 Office: Mikuni Berkeley Research Devel 4000 Lakeside Dr Richmond CA 94806

TAKAKI, RONALD T., ethnic studies educator; b. Honolulu, Apr. 12, 1939; s. Harry Toshio and Catherine Shizuko (Okawa) T.; m. Carol Marie Rankin, June 12, 1961; children: Dana, Troy, Todd. BA, Coll. Wooster, 1961; MA, U. Calif., Berkeley, 1962, PhD, 1967. Asst. prof. ethnic studies, Am. history UCLA, 1967-72; assoc. prof. U. Calif., Berkeley, 1972-80, prof., 1980—. Author: A Pro-Slavery Crusade, 1971, Iron Cages: Race and Culture in 19th Century America, 1979, Pau Hana: Plantation Life and Labor in Hawaii, 1983. NEH fellow, 1970, Rockefeller Found. fellow, 1980. Office: U Calif Dept Ethnic Studies Berkeley CA 94707

TAKAMUNE, ROBERT KATSUTOSHI, life insurance agent; b. Paauilo, Hawaii, Nov. 20, 1929; s. Koichi and Edith Nobue (Nakashima) T.; student Hilo Comml. Coll., 1947-49; m. Janet Tsurue Kawahara; children—Audrey, Claire, Daniel, Joyce. Bookkeeper, Frank Huff Agy., Hilo, Hawaii, 1949-52, Yamada Ins. Agy., Ltd., Honolulu, 1952-63; div. mgr. Investors Equity Life Ins. Co. Hawaii, Ltd., Honolulu, 1963-70; spl. agt. Northwestern Mutual

Life Ins. Co., Honolulu, 1970—. Treas., Life Underwriters Polit. Action Com., 1978-80; treas. Parents Scouters Guild, 1976-81, pres., 1981-82, committeeman, 1981—; past chmn. bd. trustees Harris United Meth. Ch., Honolulu. Recipient Diamond award Northwestern Mutual Life Ins. Co., 1977. Mem. Am. Soc. C.L.U.'s (C.L.U. Jour. discussion moderator Hawaii chpt. 1980-81, dir. Hawaii chpt. 1981-84, treas. 1984-86, sec. 1986-87), Life Underwriting Tng. Council (advanced sales course moderator 1980-81), Nat. Assn. Life Underwriters, East Honolulu Assn. Life Underwriters (treas. 1982-84, sec. 1984-85, v.p. 1985-86, pres.-elect 1986-87), Hawaii Estate Planning Council, Million Dollar Roundtable (life), Honolulu Assn. Life Underwriters (fin. chmn. 1980-81). Home: 4747 Analii St Honolulu HI 96821 Office: 1000 Bishop St Honolulu HI 96813

TAKASHIMA, HIDEO, lawyer, accountant; b. Kobe, Hyogo-Ken, Japan, Mar. 2, 1919; came to U.S., 1956; s. Yoshimitsu and Yoshie (Akagi) T.; m. Adrianna Elizabeth Selch Coe, Oct. 31, 1961 (div. Apr. 1984); children—James, George K., Oliver Sachio; m. Chizu Kojima, Mar. 14, 1986. Chartered Acct., Kanagawa U., Yokohama, Japan, 1941; LL.M., Taihoku Imperial U., Japan, 1943; LL.M. in Bus. Law Yale U., 1957; S.J.D. in Antitrust Laws, N.Y. Law Sch., 1959; postgrad. Yale Sch. Law, 1961-62. Bar: D.C. 1973, U.S. Tax Ct. 1973, U.S. Ct. Appeals (D.C. cir.) 1973, N.J. 1974, U.S. Dist. Ct. N.J. 1974, U.S. Ct. Claims 1974, U.S. Ct. Appeals (3d cir.) 1977, U.S. Supreme Ct. 1977. Lectr. criminology Yen Ping Coll., Taipei, Taiwan, 1946-47; mgr. Taiwan br. Warner Bros. F.N. Pix, Inc., Taipei, 1947-52; with labor union activities dept. FOA MSM/C, Am. embassy, Taipei, 1953-54; tax editor Prentice-Hall, Inc., Englewood Cliffs, N.J., 1961-66; editor-in-chief Washington Publs., Inc., N.Y.C., 1966-69; tax atty., editor Am. Inst. C.P.A.s, N.Y.C., 1971-72; pres., Charles Hideo Coe, P.A., Jersey City, 1973—; dir. Coe & Coe, Inc., Park Ridge, N.J., 1973—; pvt. practice acctg., N.J. 1980—. Author: My Unsuspecting Formosa, 1944. Editor-in-chief The Tax Barometer, 1966-69. Capt. Chinese Kuo-Min-Tang, Taipei, 1945; Judo-Kendo instr. New Milford Recreation Commn., N.J., 1963-69, Park Ridge Recreation Com., 1969-72, Pascack Valley Kendo Club, Park Ridge, 1969-71. Yale Law Sch. fellow, 1956-57; N.Y. Law Sch. scholar, 1958, Prentice-Hall, Inc. scholar grad. div. NYU Sch. Law, 1961-63. Mem. Am. Immigration Lawyers Assn. (sec. N.J. chpt. 1978-83), Assn. Trial Lawyers Am., N.J. Assn. Pub. Accts., Yale Law Sch. Alumni Assn., NYU Law Alumni Assn. Republican, Am. Assn. N.Y. Clubs: Yale (N.Y.C.); Japanese Community Pioneer Ctr. (Los Angeles), Japanese Am. Assn. of N.Y. Home: 15377 Shefford St Hacienda Heights Los Angeles CA 91745 Address: Charles Hideo Coe Journal Sq Station PO Box 16702 Jersey City NJ 07306 Office: 303 Fifth Ave New York NY 10016

TAKASUGI, NAO, mayor, business developer; b. Oxnard, Calif., Apr. 5, 1922; s. Shingoro and Yasuye (Hayashi) T.; m. Judith Shigeko Mayeda, Mar. 23, 1952; children—Scott, Russell, Ronald, Tricia, Lea. B.S., Temple U., 1945; M.B.A., U. Pa. Wharton Sch., 1946. Mem. city council City of Oxnard, Calif., 1976-82, mayor, 1982—; bus. developer, cons. Mem., Oxnard Planning Commn., 1974-76; pres. World Trade Ctr. Assn., Oxnard. Mem. Ventura County Japanese Am. Citizens League, World Trade Ctr. Assn. (pres. Oxnard chpt.). Republican. Methodist. Club: Optimists (Oxnard). Home: 1221 El Portal Way Oxnard CA 93035 Office: City of Oxnard 305 N Third St Oxnard CA 93030

TAKASUGI, ROBERT MITSUHIRO, federal judge; b. Tacoma, Sept. 12, 1930; s. Hidesaburo and Kayo (Otsuki) T.; m. Dorothy O. Takasugi; children: Jon Robert, Lesli Mari. BS, UCLA, Los Angeles, 1953; LLB, JD, U. So. Calif., 1959. Bar: Calif. bar 1960. Practiced law Los Angeles, 1960-73; judge East Los Angeles Municipal Ct., 1973-75, adminstrv. judge, 1974, presiding judge, 1975; judge Superior Ct., County of Los Angeles, 1975-76; U.S. dist. judge U.S. Dist. Ct. for Central Dist. Calif., 1976—; nat. legal counsel Japanese Am. Citizens League; guest lectr. law seminars Harvard U. Law Sch. Careers Symposium; commencement speaker; mem. Atty. Liaison/Lawyers Rep. Circuit Conf. Com.; chmn. affirmative action com., calendar relief com., new judges' calendar com.; mem. pub. defender and indigent def. panel com.; mem. Legion Lex U. So. Calif. Law Center. Mem. editorial bd. U. So. Calif. Law Rev., 1959; contbr. articles to profl. jours. Mem. Calif. adv. com. Western Regional Office, U.S. Commn. on Civil Rights. Served with U.S. Army, 1953-55. Recipient U.S. Mil. Man of Yr. award for Far East Theater U.S. Army, 1954; certificate of merit Japanese-Am. Bar Assn.; other awards; Harry J. Bauer scholar, 1959. Mem. U. So. Calif. Law Alumni (dir.). Club: Optimists (Los Angeles) (hon. dir. local club). Office: US Dist Ct US Courthouse 312 N Spring St Los Angeles CA 90012

TAKATA, SAYOKO, educator; b. Los Angeles, July 12, 1937; d. Henry Takuji and Fujie (Udo) Nishi; m. Isao Jon Takata, Nov. 24, 1961; 1 child, Stephen Isamu. BA in Bus., U. No. Colo., 1959; M.Ed. in Vocat. Edn., Colo. State U., 1980. Life teaching cert., Colo. Tchr. home econs. Erie (Colo.) Jr. and Sr. High Sch., 1959-60; tchr. bus. and office edn. Manual High Sch., Denver, 1960-63, 68-78, chmn. dept., 1977-78; asst. bookkeeper Century Fixtures, Inc., Los Angeles, 1963-64; tchr. bus. and office edn. East High Sch., Denver, 1978-79; tchr. bus. and office edn. Met. Youth Edn. Ctr., Zuni Ctr., 1978-79; tchr. bus. and office edn. East extension, Denver, 1979—, chmn. dept., 1980—; mem. Colo. Spl. Needs Ad Hoc Com., 1980. Mem. Am. Vocat. Assn., Nat. Bus. Edn. Assn., NEA, Colo. Educators For/About Bus. (treas. 1981-83), Internat. Soc. bus. Educators, Colo. Vocat. Assn., Mountain Plains Bus. Edn. Assn. (Colo. rep. 1986—), Denver Classroom Tchrs. Assn., Colo. Edn. Assn., Delta Pi Epsilon, Delta Kappa Gamma (asst. treas. 1986—). Buddhist. Home: 561 W 87th Pl Denver CO 80221 Office: 3800 York St Bldg 1 Unit A Denver CO 80205

TAKEDA, KENNETH KINGO, orthodontist; b. Riverside, Calif., Dec. 24, 1929; s. Orisaburo and Umeko (Ando) T.; m. Mary Yamaguchi, Jan. 28, 1951; children—Matthew Curtis, Kristin Haruko. AA, Riverside Coll. (Calif.), 1949; BSCE, U. Calif.-Berkeley, 1951; DDS, U.Calif., San Francisco, 1965. Engring. draftsman U.S. Bur. Reclamation, Boulder City, Nev., 1949, jr. engr., Marble Canyon, Ariz., 1950; stress analyst Boeing Airplane Co., Seattle, 1951-53; structures engr. Douglas Aircraft Co., Long Beach, Calif., 1953-60; research engr. The Boeing Co., Seattle, 1961, 62, 63; practice dentistry specializing in orthodontics, Stockton, Calif., 1965—. Pres. chpt. Japanese Am. Citizens League, Lodi, Calif., 1984. Recipient Gabbs prize in dentistry U. Calif., 1965. Mem. U. Calif. Dental Alumni Assn., U. Calif. Orthodontic Alumni Assn., Calif. State Soc. Orthodontists, Pacific Coast Soc. Orthodontists, Am. Assn. Orthodontists, Am. Dental Assn., Calif. Dental Assn. (rep. ho. dels. 1972-73), San Joaquin Dental Soc. (pres. 1972-73), Omicron Kappa Upsilon, Delta Sigma Delta. Lutheran. Club: Kiwanis (Disting. Pres. 1977-78). Home: 626 Birchwood Dr Lodi CA 95240 Office: 532 W Harding Way Suite B Stockton CA 95204

TAKEMOTO, CLIFFORD HIROSHI, development engineer; b. San Jose, Calif., Jan. 20, 1953; s. Tsugio and Mitsuye (Onishi) T. BS, San Jose State U., 1976. Chemist Radiation Detection, Sunnyvale, Calif., 1976-78, SRI Internat., Menlo Park, Calif., 1978-80; engr. Nat. Semiconductor, Santa Clara, Calif., 1980—. Mem. Am. Chem. Soc. Avocations: photography, movies, listening to music. Office: Nat Semiconductor M/S C2326 2900 Semiconductor Dr Santa Clara CA 95051

TALBERT, MELVIN GEORGE, bishop; b. Clinton, La., June 14, 1934; s. Nettles and Florence (George) T.; m. Ethlelou Douglas, June 3, 1961; 1 child, Evangeline. B.A., So. U., 1959; M.Div., Interdenominational Theol. Ctr., Gammon Theol. Sem., Atlanta, 1962; D.D. hon., Huston Tillotson Coll., Austin, 1972; LLD (hon.), U. Puget Sound, 1987. Ordained deacon, Methodist Ch., 1960 ordained elder, Methodist Ch., 1962 elected to episcopacy, United Meth. Ch., 1980. Pastor Boyd Chapel, Jefferson City, Tenn., 1960-61, Rising Sun, Sunrise, Tenn., 1960-61, St. John's Ch., Los Angeles, 1961-62, Wesley Ch., Los Angeles, 1962-64, Hamilton Ch., Los Angeles, 1964-67; mem. staff So. Calif.-Ariz. Conf. United Meth. Ch., Los Angeles, 1967-68; dist. supr. Long Beach dist. So. Calif.-Ariz. Conf. United Meth. Ch., 1968-73; gen. sec. Gen. Bd. Discipleship, Nashville, 1973-80; resident bishop Seattle area Pacific N.W. conf. United Meth. Ch., 1980—; mem. exec. com. World Meth. Council, 1976-81, 84—, mem. evangelism com., 1980—; mem. governing bd. Nat. Council Chs., 1980—; v.p., chmn. funding com. Gen. Commn. on Religion and Race, 1980-84, pres., 1984—; chmn. Missional Priority Coordinating com. Gen. Council Ministries, 1980-84; mem. Gen. Commn. on Christian Unity and Interreligious Concerns, 1984—, African Ch. Growth and Devel. Com., 1981-84. Mem. steering com. Student Non-Violent Coordinating com. Atlanta U. Ctr., 1960-61; trustee Gammon Theol. Sem., Atlanta, 1976—, U. Puget Sound, Tacoma, 1980—, Sch. Theology at Claremont, Calif., 1981—. Recipient award of merit for outstanding service in Christian edn. Gen. Bd. Edn., 1971; recipient Spl. achievement award Nat. Assn. Black Bus. Women, 1971; Nat. Meth. scholar, 1960; Crusade scholar, 1961. Mem. Theta Phi. Democrat. Club: Harbor (Seattle). Home: 18135 SE 42d Pl Issaquah WA 98027

TALBERT, WILLARD LINDLEY, JR., research physicist; b. Casper, Wyo., Mar. 8, 1932; s. Willard L. and Ellen L. (Goodlander) T.; m. Mary A. Williams, Aug. 24, 1952; children: Marc A., Kenneth E., Linda S., Cynthia L. BA cum laude, U. Colo., 1954; PhD, Iowa State U., 1960. Research physicist Ohio Oil Co., Littleton, Colo., 1959-62; prof. physics Iowa State U., Ames, 1962-76; mem. staff Los Alamos (N.Mex.) Nat. Lab., 1976—. Contbr. articles to profl. jours. NSF fellow, 1955-59. Fellow: Am. Phys. Soc.; mem. AAAS, Sigma Xi, Phi Beta Kappa, Phi Kappa Phi. Republican. Methodist. Avocations: backpacking, hiking, bicycling. Home: 2 La Flora Ct Los Alamos NM 87544 Office: Los Alamos Nat Lab MS-J514 PO Box 1663 Los Alamos NM 87545

TALBOT, FRANK HAMILTON, museum director, marine researcher; b. Pietermaritzburg, Natal, S. Africa, Jan. 3, 1930; came to U.S., 1982; s. Ralph West and Willemina (Atlmann) T.; m. Mabel Suzette Logeman, July 20, 1953; children: Helen Campbell, Richard Bill, Jonathan Charles, Neil Hamilton. B.Sc., U. Witwatersrand, South Africa, 1949; M.Sc., U. Cape Town, South Africa, 1951; Ph.D., U. Cape, South Africa, 1959. Fisheries research scientist Brit. Colonial Service, Zanzibar, 1954-57; marine biologist South African Museum, Cape Town, 1958-59, asst. dir., 1960-63; curator fishes Australian Mus., Sydney, 1964-65, dir., 1965-74; prof. environ. studies MacQuarie U., Sydney, Australia, 1975-81; exec. dir. Calif. Acad. Scis., San Francisco, 1982—. Contbr. articles to sci. jours. Fellow Linnean Soc. (London), Royal Soc. Arts (London), Royal Zool Soc. (Australia); mem. Mus. Assn. Australia (pres. 1973-74), Australian Marine Scis. Assn. (pres. 1971-72), Explorers Club. Clubs: Bohemian, St. Francis Yacht (San Francisco); Sydney Amateur Sailing (Australia). Office: Calif Acad Scis Golden Gate Park San Francisco CA 94118

TALBOT, MATTHEW J., oil company executive; b. Sept. 4, 1937; s. Matthew J. and Margaret A. (Green) T.; m. Maureen Donlan, June 3, 1958; children: Maureen A., Matthew J., Kathleen M. BBA in Acctg., Iona Coll., 1963. Acct. S.D. Leidesdorf (now Ernst & Whinney), N.Y.C., 1961-67; sr. analyst Gen. Foods Corp., White Plains, N.Y., 1967-68; asst. to comptroller Tosco Corp., Los Angeles, 1968-70, comptroller, 1970-83, v.p., 1972-76, sr. v.p., 1976-78, exec. v.p., 1978-83; pres. Tosco Corp., Santa Monica, Calif., 1983-86, Santa Monica, 1986—. Treas., bd. dirs. Ctr. Theatre Group, Los Angeles; trustee Craft and Folk Art Mus., Los Angeles. Mem. Am. Inst. CPA's, Fin. Execs. Inst. Roman Catholic. Office: Tosco Corp 2401 Colorado Santa Monica CA 90406

TALBOTT, GEORGE ROBERT, physicist, biophysicist, mathematician, educator; b. San Diego, Oct. 1, 1925; s. George Fletcher and Mary (Lanz) T.; B.A. with honors, UCLA, 1960; D.Sc., Ind. No. U., 1973. Physicist, mem. tech. staff Rockwell Internat. Co., Anaheim, Calif., 1960-85; mem. faculty thermodynamics Pacific States U., 1971-77, prof., 1972-80, chmn. dept. math. studies, 1973-80; lectr. computer sci. Calif. State U., Fullerton, 1979—; cons. physics, computer sci.; disting. guest lectr. Brunel U., London, 1974, 76; spl. guest Forschungsbibliothek, Hannover, W. Ger., 1979; assoc. editor KRONOS jour., Glassboro (N.J.) U., 1978—; chief computer scientist and ednl. videotape dir. Specialized Software, Wilmot, Wis., 1982—. Served with M.C., U.S. Army, 1956. Recipient Vis. Scholar's award Western Mich. U., 1979. Mem. Am. Soc. Med. Technologists, Am. Math. Soc., Math. Assn. Am., Am. Soc. Clin. Pathologists (lic. med. lab. technologist). Buddhist. Author: Electronic Thermodynamics, 1973; Philosophy and Unified Science, 1977; co-inventor burner. Home: 4031 Charter Oak Dr Orange CA 92669

TALBOTT, LAURENCE FLETCHER, engineering educator, consultant; b. San Diego, Nov. 17, 1920; s. George Fletcher and Mary (Lanz) T.; m. Ruth Mabel Hanson, July 22, 1942 (dec. May 1944); 1 child, Michael Laurence; m. Patsy Anne Davis, Feb. 14, 1963; children: Mary Anne, Susan Alice. AB in Gen. Engring., San Diego State U., 1951; MBA, U. So. Calif., 1965; EdD in Indsl. Tech. Edn., Utah State U., 1972; MSCE, Calif. Poly. State U., 1979; postgrad. Exeter Coll. Oxford (Eng.) U., 1985; BA in History, U. State N.Y., 1986. Elec. engr. Convair, San Diego, 1950-51, C. F. Braun & Co., Alhambra, Calif., 1951-52; engring. mgr. N.Am. Aviation, Downey, Calif., 1952-66; prof. Calif. Poly. State U., San Luis Obispo, 1966-76, assoc. dean engring., 1976-79, head indsl. tech. dept., 1979—; cons. Fred Schott & Assocs., San Luis Obispo, 1968-75, Calif. Maritime Acad., Vallejo, 1975, Calif. State U.-Chico, 1979, Environ. Design Cons., San Diego, 1981, 84, No. Mich. U., 1986. Contbr. articles to profl. jours. Served with USNR, 1942-45, PTO. Vera Christie fellow Western Coll. Placement, 1968; scholar Utah State U., 1970. Mem. Am. Inst. Plant Engrs. (v.p. 1978-80, service citation 1976), Calif. Assn. Indsl. Tech. (pres. 1975-76), Nat. Assn. Indsl. Tech. (v.p. 1983-84, pres. 1984-85), U. So. Calif. Alumni Assn., Am. Legion, Gamma Delta (trustee chpt. Epsilon Pi Tau 1982-85). Republican. Mormon. Home: 66 Benton Way San Luis Obispo CA 93401 Office: Calif Poly State U Indsl Tech Dept San Luis Obispo CA 93407

TALLEY, GREGORY BRENT, police officer, criminal justice educator; b. Indpls., Apr. 15, 1948; s. Richard Eugene and Vivian Jeanne (Goodman) T.; m. Susan Schofield, Aug. 13, 1970; children: Benjamin, Scott, Nanon, Justin, Megan. Student, Ricks Coll., 1970; BA, Coll. Santa Fe, 1981; cert., U. Va., 1984. Probation officer Johnson Superior Ct., Franklin, Ind., 1970-73; spl. dep. sheriff Marion County Sheriff's Office, Indpls., 1974-75; police officer Los Alamos (N.Mex.) Police Dept., 1975—, detective sgt., 1982—, capt., 1985—. Cubmaster Boy Scouts Am., 1986—; Rep. ward chmn., Los Alamos, 1980; bd. dirs. Family Recovery Ctr., Los Alamos, 1983-86, Family Council, Los Alamos, 1985—. Named one of Outstanding Young Men of Am., U.S. Jaycees, 1983. Mem. FBI Nat. Acad. Assocs., Delta Phi Kappa. Mormon. Office: Los Alamos Police Dept 2500 Trinity Dr Los Alamos NM 87544

TALLEY, WILSON KINTER, foundation executive; b. St. Louis, Jan. 27, 1935; s. Samuel K. and Isabella (McCurtain) T.; m. Sharon Tettemer, July 8, 1961 (div. 1974); children: Steven K., Elaine H., Edward L.; m. Helen A. Mazetis, July 1, 1981. BS, U. Calif., Berkeley, 1956, PhD, 1963; MS, U. Chgo., 1958. Prof. dept. applied sci. U. Calif., Davis, 1963—, asst. v.p. U. Calif.-Statewide, 1971-74; asst. adminstr. EPA, Washington, 1974-77; pres. Fannie & John Hertz Found., Livermore, Calif., 1972—; chmn. Army Sci. Bd., Washington, 1983-86; chmn. Helionetics, Inc., Irvine, Calif., 1984-86; mem. tech. adv. bd. Pa. Cen. Fed. Systems Co., 1985—. Co-author: Constructive Uses of Nuclear Explosives, 1968; contbr. numerous articles to profl. jours. Mem., Presdl. Transition Team, Washington, 1980-81; mem. Pres.-Elect's Com. on Sci. and Tech., Washington, 1980. White House fellow, 1969. Mem. Am. Phys. Soc., Am. Nuclear Soc., Sierra Club, Sigma Xi. Republican. Clubs: Capitol Hill. Home: 3167 Paseo Granada Pleasanton CA 94566 Office: Fannie and John Hertz Found PO Box 2230 Livermore CA 94550

TALLMAN, GARY DEAN, financial analyst educator; b. Omaha, Oct. 14, 1943; s. Howard Jay and Lillian (Yellineck) T.; m. Elizabeth Anne Mangan, June 1972; children: Marsha, Darren. BSBA, U. Nebr., 1965; MBA, Creighton U., 1969; DBA, U. Colo., 1974. Fin. specialist No. Nat. Gas Co., Omaha, 1965-70; teaching asst. U. Colo., Boulder, 1970-71; asst. prof. Kent (Ohio) State U., 1971-75; prof. No. Ariz. U., Flagstaff, 1975—. Author: Financial Analysis and Planning Package, 1985; contbr. articles to profl. jours. Mem. Fin. Mgmt. Assn., Midwest Fin. Assn. Home: 3474 N Andes Flagstaff AZ 86001 Office: No Ariz U Box 15066 Flagstaff AZ 86011

TALLMAN, IRVING, research sociology educator; b. N.Y.C., May 11, 1925; s. Albert and Sue Rae (Sternlicht) T.; m. Beverley Shirley Johnstone, Jan. 27, 1950 (div. 1970); children: Laura, Susan; m. Marilyn Ihinger, Apr. 7, 1977. AB in Psychology, U. Calif., Berkeley, 1948; MSW, Wayne State U., 1950; postgrad., U. Chgo., 1954; PhD in Sociology, Stanford U., 1963. Asst. prof. sociology San Jose (Calif.) State U., 1962-64; asst. prof. to prof. U. Minn., Mpls., 1964-76, dir. family studies, 1975-76; prof. Wash. State U., Pullman, 1976—, chmn. dept., 1976-80; vis. scholar Uppsala (Sweden) U., 1983; cons. Minn. Sch. Pub. Affairs, Mpls., 1982-84; mem. peer rev. NIMH, Washington, 1984—; invited lectr. U. Geneve, Helsinki, Switzerland, Louvain, Belgium, U. Calif., Berkeley, others. Author: Passion, Action and Politics, 1976, Adolescent Socialization, 1983; co-editor: Family Problem Solving, 1970; contbr. articles to profl. jours. Mem. Am. Sociol. Assn. (elected mem. Sociol. Reseach Assn.), Nat. Council Family Relations, Midwest Sociol. Assn., Pacific Sociol. Assn., ACLU. Democrat. Avocations: travelling, tennis, reading. Home: SE 845 Green Hill Rd Pullman WA 99163 Office: Wash State U Dept Sociology Pullman WA 99164

TALMADGE, PHILIP ALBERT, state senator, lawyer; b. Seattle, Apr. 23, 1952; s. Judson H., Jr., and Jeanne C. T.; m. Darlene L. Nelson, Sept. 6, 1970; children—Adam, Matthew, Jessica, Jonathan. B.A. magna cum laude with honors in Polit. Sci., Yale U., 1973; J.D., U. Wash., 1976. Bar: Wash. 1976. Shareholder, Karr, Tuttle, Koch, Campbell, Mawer, Morrow and Sax, P.S., Seattle, 1976—; mem. Wash. Senate, 1978—, chmn. judiciary com., mem. senate ways and means com., mem. govtl. ops. com. Trustee, South Seattle Community Coll. Found.; bd. dirs. Seattle Consumer Credit Counseling Service; mem. Nature Conservancy Bd. Mem. ABA, Wash. State Bar Assn., Seattle-King County Bar Assn. Author: The Nixon Doctrine and the Reaction of Three Asian Nations, 1973; editor Law Rev., U. Wash., 1975-76; contbr. articles to legal publs.

TAMASHIRO, THOMAS KOYEI, electrical engineer; b. Paia, Maui, Hawaii, Aug. 4, 1926; s. Kokichi and Mashi (Shinyashiki) T.; B.E.E., Tri-State U., Angola, Ind., 1951, E.E., 1964; m. Mary E. Oden; children—Cheryl M., Venita. Project engr. Jackson & Church Co., Saginaw, Mich., 1953-55; project mgr. Aerojet-Gen. Corp., Azusa, Calif., 1955-72; sr. staff engr. Aerojet Nuclear Corp., Idaho Falls, Idaho, 1972-75; project mgr. Allied Chem. Corp., Idaho Falls, 1976-79, Exxon Nuclear-Idaho, Idaho Falls, 1979-84, Westinghouse Idaho Nuclear Co., 1984—; lectr. in field. Mem. Am. Nuclear Soc. Club: Eagle Rock Amateur Radio. Lodges: Shriners, Masons. Home: 2544 Barberry Ln Route 9 Idaho Falls ID 83402 Office: Westinghouse Idaho Nuclear Co PO Box 4000 Idaho Falls ID 83403

TAMKIN, CURTIS SLOANE, real estate development company executive; b. Boston, Sept. 21, 1936; s. Hayward and Etta (Goldfarb) T.; B.A. in Econs., Stanford U., 1958; m. Priscilla Martin, Oct. 18, 1975; 1 son, Curtis Sloane. Vice pres., treas., dir. Hayward Tamkin & Co., Inc., mortgage bankers, Los Angeles, 1963-70; mng. ptnr. Property Devel. Co., Los Angeles, 1970-82; pres. The Tamkin Co., 1982—. Bd. govs. Music Center Los Angeles, 1974—; pres. Los Angeles Master Chorale Assn., 1974-78; mem. vis. com. Stanford U. Libraries, 1982-86; bd. dirs. Los Angeles Philharm. Assn., 1985—. Served to lt. (j.g.) USNR, 1960-63. Mem. Founders League of Los Angeles (pres.), Los Angeles Jr. C. of C. (dir. 1968-69). Republican. Clubs: Burlingame Country, Los Angeles, University. Office: 3600 Wilshire Blvd Los Angeles CA 90010

TAMMANY, ALBERT SQUIRE, III, savings and loan executive; b. Paget, Bermuda, Aug. 21, 1946; s. Albert Squire Jr. and Marion Genevieve (Galloway) T.; BA, Stanford U., 1968; MBA (Woodrow Wilson fellow), U. Pa., 1973; m. Teresa Reznor, Sept. 8, 1973. Budget and planning officer Tuskegee Inst., Ala., 1973-74; budget analyst controllers dept. Chase Manhattan Bank, N.Y.C., 1974-75; v.p., div. controller Wells Fargo Bank, San Francisco, 1975-78, v.p., retail group controller, 1978-79; v.p., controller Imperial Bank, Los Angeles, 1979-81, sr. v.p. fin., 1981-83; exec. v.p., Deauville Savs. & Loan Assn., Los Angeles, 1983—, also bd. dirs.; cons. Inst. for Services to Edn., Inc., 1973-74. Served with USMC, 1968-71. Wharton Pub. Policy fellow, 1972. Mem. Am. Bankers Assn. (trust ops. com.). Episcopalian. Clubs: Wharton, Stanford. Office: Deauville Savs & Loan Assn 10100 Santa Monica Blvd Suite 500 Los Angeles CA 90067

TAN, JACK SIN-GIE, architect; b. Sukabumi, W. Java, Indonesia, Dec. 5, 1942; came to U.S., 1971; s. Thomas Peng-Tjiang and Rosanna Tjeng-Nio (Liauw) T.; m. Tineke Giok-Tien Sie, Nov. 7, 1969; children—Roger Kuan-Lee, Elaine May-Ing. Cand.Ing. (B.Arch.), Tech. U. Darmstadt, W. Ger., 1967; Diplom Ing. (M.Arch.), Tech. U. Aachen, W. Ger., 1969. Registered architect, Calif. Dipl.Ing. architect Heinz Mosch, Ent., Bonn, W.Ger., 1969-70; Ir. architect Van der Erve Architects, The Hague, Netherlands, 1970-71; archtl. asst. Wm. Pereira & Assocs., Los Angeles, 1972-73; project mgr. Richard E. Huston Architects, Anaheim, Calif., 1975-79; project architect Carl Karcher, Ent., Anaheim, 1979-81; project architect HMC Architects, Inc., Ontario, Calif., 1981—. Mem. Permai, Los Angeles. Mem. AIA, Bond van Nederlandse Architekten (cert.), Bund Deutscher Architekten. Nichiren Shoshu Soka Gakkai, Nat. Rifle Assn. Home: 16931 Royal View Dr Hacienda Heights CA 91745 Office: HMC Architects Inc 500 East E St Ontario CA 91764

TAN, KONG-MENG, radiologist; b. Malacca, Malaysia, Nov. 9, 1943; s. Hin Jin and May (Woon) T.; came to U.S., 1965; BS, U. Ill., Chgo., 1967, MD, 1971; m. May Chen; 1 child, Jennifer Mei-Sim. Intern, Ill. Masonic Med. Ctr., Chgo., 1971-72; resident radiology, 1972-75; instr. radiology U. Ill. Coll. Medicine, Chgo., 1974-75; chief dept. radiology Kaiser Permanente Med. Ctr., Richmond, Calif., 1976—, dir. med. edn., 1976-83, dir. quality assurance, 1983—; dir. Permanente Med. Group, Inc., 1982—; governing bd. Alameda Contra Costa Health Systems Agy., 1979-83, vice chmn., 1982. Mem. adv. council Bay Area Air Quality Mgmt. Dist., 1978-86, chmn., 1982; bd. dirs. Oakland Chinese Community Council, 1981—, pres., 1983; chmn. Bay Area Asian Health Alliance, 1980. Fgn. scholar U. Ill., 1966-67, Fgn. travel scholar, 1970. Mem. AMA (chmn. com. house staff affairs 1974-75, mem. adv. com. continuing med. edn. 1978-83, com. fgn. med. grads. 1984-86), Ill. State Med. Soc. (com. housestaff affairs 1973-75), Calif. Med. Assn. (cons. com. continuing med. edn. 1979-83, com. accreditation and cert. of continuing med. edn. 1985—, chmn. 1986—, mem. commn. quality care 1986—), Alameda Contra Costa Med. Assn., Phi Delta Epsilon, Omega Beta Pi. Contbr. articles to sci. jours. Home: 952 Sunnyhills Oakland CA 94610 Office: Kaiser Med Center 901 Nevin Ave Richmond CA 94801 *

TAN, WILLIAM LEW, lawyer; b. West Hollywood, Calif., July 25, 1949; s. James Tan Lew and Choon Guey Louie. BA, U. Pa., 1971; JD, U. Calif. Hastings Coll. Law, San Francisco, 1974. Bar: Calif. 1975, U.S. Dist. Ct. (cen. dist.) Calif. 1975, U.S. Ct. Appeals (9th cir.) 1975, U.S. Supreme Ct. 1979. Assoc. Hiram W. Kwan, Los Angeles, 1974-79; ptnr. Mock & Tan, Los Angeles, 1979-80; sole practice Los Angeles, 1980-81; ptnr. Tan & Sakiyama, P.C., Los Angeles, 1981—; bd. dirs. Pacific Career Opportunities, Los Angeles, Am. Bus. Network, Los Angeles; pres., bd. dirs. Asian Research Cons., Los Angeles. Founder Asian Pacific Am. Roundtable, Los Angeles, 1981; chmn. bd. dirs. Leaderhip Edn. for Asian-Pacifics, Los Angeles, 1984; alt. del. Dem. Nat. Conv., San Francisco, 1984; mem. Calif. State Bd. Pharmacy, Sacramento, 1984, Los Angeles City and County Crime Crisis Task Force, Los Angeles, 1981, Los Angeles Asian Pacific Heritage Week Com., 1980—, Asian Pacific Women's Network, Los Angeles, 1981, Los Angeles City Atty.'s Blue Ribbon Con. of Advisors, 1981, community adv. bd. to Mayor of Los Angeles, 1984, allocations vol. liaison team health and therapy div. United Way, Los Angeles, 1986; bd. dirs. Chinatown Service Ctr., Los Angeles, 1983; conf. advisor U.S.-Asia, Los Angeles, 1981-83; atty. Los Angeles City Housing Adv. Com. Named one of Outstanding Young Men of Am., 1979. Mem. ABA (mem. numerous coms.), Calif. State Bar Assn. (vice chmn. com. ethnic minority relations 1983-85, chmn. pub. affairs com. 1981-82, mem. others), Los Angeles County Bar Assn. (vice chmn. 1980-82, mem. numerous coms.), So. Calif. Chinese Lawyers Assn. (pres. 1980-81, mem. various coms.), Minority Bar Assn. (chmn. 1981-82, sec. 1980-81, chmn. adv. bd. 1982-83), Asian Pacific Bar of Calif., Nat. Asian Pacific Am. Bar, Japanese Am. Bar Assn., Assn. Trial Lawyers Am., Bench and Bar Council, Calif. Trial Lawyers Assn., Soc. Intercultural Edn. (conf. coordinator, advisor panelist tng. and research com. 1983),. Club: Marina City (Marina del Rey, Calif.). Avocations: gourmet cooking, bicycling, swimming, tennis, water color painting. Office: Tan & Sakiyama 711 W College St Suite 610 Los Angeles CA 90012

TANADA, YOSHINORI, professor of entomology; b. Honolulu; m. Edna Noriko Saito; children: Karen Miyo, Ruth Kuniyo. BS, U. Hawaii, 1940, MS, 1945; PhD, U. Calif., Berkeley, 1953. Asst. in zoology U. Hawaii, Honolulu, 1943-45; asst. prof. U. Hawaii Exptl. St., Honolulu, 1954-56, assoc. prof., 1956; lectr. U. Calif., Berkeley, 1961-65, assoc. to full prof., 1965—; ju. entomologist U. Hawaii Exptl. Sta., Honolulu, 1945-53, asst.

entomologist, 1953-56, assoc. entomologist, 1956; asst. insect pathologist, U. Calif. Exptl. Sta., Berkeley, 1956-59, assoc. insect pathologist, 1959-64, insect pathologist, 1964—. Co-editor: The Cytoplasmic Polyhedrosis Virus of the Silkworm, 1971, Epizootic Insect Diseases, 1987. Fellow NIH, 1961-71, NSF, 1956-61, 71-87. Fellow AAAS, Soc. Invertebrate Pathology (treas. 1972-74; trustee 1976-80). Office: U Calif Dept Entomological Sci 342 Hilgard Hall Berkeley CA 94720

TANAKA, GENZO, physical chemist; b. Koto-cho, Japan, Feb. 5, 1942; came to U.S., 1977; s. Otozo and Tomi (Katayama) T.; m. Mikiko Hirota, Nov. 2, 1969; children: Ai, Satoshi. BE, Kyoto (Japan) U., 1965, ME, 1967, DE, 1978. Research assoc. Dartmouth Coll., Hanover, N.H., 1977-79, Mich. Molecular Inst., Midland, 1979-80, 81-85; research fellow Kyoto U., 1970-77, 80; vis. scientist Salk Inst., La Jolla, Calif., 1985—. Contbr. articles to profl. jours. Mem. Am. Chem. Soc., Polymer Soc. Japan. Office: The Agouron Inst 505 Coast Blvd S La Jolla CA 92037

TANAKA, JEANNIE E., lawyer; b. Los Angeles, Jan. 21, 1942; d. Togo William and Jean M. Tanaka. BA, Internat. Christian U., Tokyo, 1966; MSW, UCLA, 1968; JD, Washington Coll. Law, 1984. Bar: Calif., 1984, D.C. 1987. Instr. Aoyama Gakuin, Meiji Gakuin, Sophia U., Tokyo, 1968-75; with program devel. Encyclopedia Britannica Inst., Tokyo, 1976-78; instr. Honda, Mitsubishi, Ricoh Corps., Tokyo, 1975-80; assoc. Seki and Jarvis, Los Angeles, 1984-86, Jones, Day, Reavis & Pogue, Los Angeles, 1986—. Active Japan-Am. Soc., Los Angeles, 1984, World Affairs Council, Los Angeles, 1984, Japanese-Am. Citizens League, Los Angeles, 1981; vol. Asian Pacific Am. Legal Ctr. of So. Calif., 1985—. Mem. ABA, L.A. County Bar Assn., Women Lawyer's Assn. of Los Angeles, Asian Bus. Laegue, Japanese-Am. Bar Assn., Mensa, Phi Delta Phi. Home: 100 S Doheny Los Angeles CA 90048 Office: Jones Day Reavis & Pogue 355 S Grand Ave Los Angeles CA 90071

TANAKA, KOUICHI ROBERT, physician, educator; b. Fresno, Calif., Dec. 15, 1926; s. Kenjiro and Teru (Arai) T.; m. Grace Mutsuko Sakaguchi, Oct. 23, 1965; children—Anne M., Nancy K., David K. B.S., Wayne State U., 1949, M.D., 1952. Intern Los Angeles County Gen. Hosp., 1952-53; resident, fellow Detroit Receiving Hosp., 1953-57; instr. Sch. Medicine, UCLA, 1957-59, asst. prof. medicine, 1959-61, assoc. prof. medicine, 1961-68, prof., 1968—; assoc. chmn., chief hematology, dept. medicine Harbor-UCLA Med. Center, Torrance, Calif., 1961—. Served with AUS, 1946-48. Fellow A.C.P.; mem. Am. Fedn. Clin. Research, Western Soc. Clin. Investigation, Los Angeles Soc. Internal Medicine (pres. 1971), Am. Soc. Hematology, Western Assn. Physicians, Am. Soc. Clin. Investigation, Assn. Am. Physicians, Sigma Xi, Alpha Omega Alpha. Research red cell metabolism. Home: 4 Cayuse Ln Palos Verdes CA 90274 Office: Harbor UCLA Med Ctr 1000 W Carson St Torrance CA 90509

TANAKA, MARSHA MIKI, speech pathologist; b. Wailuku, Hawaii, July 6, 1952; d. Hitoshi and Patsy (Murata) Urada; m. Byron Patric Tanaka, July 26, 1974; children: Brooke, Marisa. BS in Edn., Oreg. Coll. Edn., 1974, MS in Edn., 1975. Speech pathologist Easter Seal Soc., Wailuku, 1975-79, Hawaii Dept. Edn., Wailuku, 1979—. Mem. Am. Speech-Lang. and Hearing Assn., Hawaii Speech and Hearing Assn. Democrat. Avocations: reading, sewing. Office: Hawaii Dept Edn PO Box 1070 Wailuku HI 96790

TANAKA, NOBUYUKI, staff physicist; b. Tokyo, May 12, 1937; came to U.S., 1954; s. Yoshio and Yoshiko Tanaka. BA, Harvard U., 1962; PhD, Tufts U., 1969. Staff mem. Los Alamos (N.Mex.) Nat. Lab., 1969—. Democrat. Club: Harvard (N.Mex. chpt.). Avocations: backpacking, travel, photography. Home: 940 Old Bridge Ct Santa Fe NM 87505

TANAKA, STANLEY KATSUKI, optometrist, consultant; b. Honolulu, Sept. 19, 1932; s. Tomikichi and Hatsue T.; m. Esther K. Kokubun, Oct. 31, 1959; children—Glen A., Fay M. Student U. Hawaii, 1950-52; B.S., U. Okla., 1952; O.D. magna cum laude (Jackson award), Ill. Coll. Optometry, 1956. Enlisted U.S. Army, 1957, advanced through grades to col. Res., 1981; optometrist Hawaii Permanente Med. Group, Honolulu, 1968—; cons. opthalmic firms. Named Hawaii Optometrist of Yr., 1984. Mem. Am. Optometric Assn., Hawaii Optometric Assn., Armed Forces Optometric Soc., Contact Lens Soc., Am. Optometric Found., Optometric Extension Program, Beta Sigma Kappa. Democrat. Club: Toastmasters. Home: 2645 Oahu Ave Honolulu HI 96822 Office: 1010 Pensacola St Honolulu HI 96814

TANAKA, TOGO W(ILLIAM), financial executive; b. Portland, Oreg., Jan. 7, 1916; s. Masaharu and Katsu (Iwatate) T.; m. Jean Miho Wada, Nov. 14, 1940; children: Jeannine, Christine, Wesley. AB cum laude, UCLA, 1936. Editor Los Angeles Japanese Daily News, 1936-41; documentary historian War Relocation Authority, 1942; staff mem. Am. Friends Service Com., Chgo., 1943-45; editor to headl. publs. div. Am. Tech. Soc., 1945-52; pub. Chgo. Pub. Corp., 1952-56; pub. School-Indsl. Press, Inc., Los Angeles, 1956-60; chmn. Gramercy Enterprises, Los Angeles; pres. Rossmore Mgmt. Co.; treas. T.W. Tanaka Co., Inc.; city commr. Community Redevel. Agy., Los Angeles, 1973-75; dir. Los Angeles Wholesale Produce Market Devel. Corp., Fed. Res. Bank, San Francisco, 1979; mem. adv. bd. Calif. First Bank, Los Angeles, 1976-78. Author: (with Frank K. Levin) English Composition and Rhetoric, 1948; (with Dr. Jean Bordeaux) How to Talk More Effectively, 1948; (with Alma Meland) Easy Pathways in English, 1949. Mem. citizens mgmt. rev. com. Los Angeles Unified Sch. Dist., 1976-77; adv. council to assessor Los Angeles County, 1981-84; bd. dirs. Goodwill Industries of So. Calif.; trustee Wilshire United Meth. Ch., 1976-78, Calif. Acad. Decathlon, 1978-81; bd. dirs. Meth. Hosp. So. Calif., ARC, Nat. Safety Council, Los Angeles, Visitors and Conv. Bur., Am. Heart Assn., New Careers Opportunities, Inc., YMCA Met. Los Angeles, Boy Scouts Am. Council, 1980-86; mem. adv. council Calif. World Trade Commn. Recipient merit award Soc. Advancement Mgmt., 1950, mag. award Inst. Graphic Arts, 1953, 1st award Internat. Council Indsl. Editors, 1955, UNESCO Literacy award, 1974, Los Angeles Archbishop's Ecumenical award, 1986. Mem. Los Angeles Area C. of C. (dir. 1974-76), Japan-Am. Soc. So. Calif. (council 1960-78), Phi Beta Kappa, Pi Sigma Alpha, Pi Gamma Mu. Clubs: Stock Exchange, Lincoln. Lodges: Masons, Shriners, Rotary (dir., pres. Los Angeles club 1983-84). Home: 949 Malcolm Ave Los Angeles CA 90024 Office: 4500 Wilshire Blvd Los Angeles CA 90010

TANASE, THEODORE TAMEZO, retail lumber company executive; b. Oakland, Calif., Dec. 12, 1941; s. Thomas T. and Claire Y. (Nikaido) Tanase-Whiteman; m. (div. 1975) children—Pamela, Mark; m. Priscilla Bumpus, Apr. 9, 1976. B.S. Engring., U. Mich., 1963; M.B.A., Wayne State U., 1969. Various engring. and mktg. positions Sperry Corp., Troy, Mich., 1964-71, mgr. internat. ops., Phoenix, 1971-78; nat. sales mgr. Rockwell Internat., Cedar Rapids, Iowa, 1978, gen. mgr. adv. programs, 1978-81; dir. Lanoga Corp., Seattle, 1978—, pres., chief exec. officer, 1981—; dir. Laird-Norton Co., Seattle. Bd. visitors U. Puget Sound, Tacoma, Wash., 1983—; bd. dirs. Rainier Found., Seattle. Mem. Young Pres.' Orgn. (chmn. membership com. 1985). Republican. Office: Lanoga Corp 1418 Norton Bldg Seattle WA 98104

TANBARA, DIANE KIMI, health science facility administrator; b. Tacoma, Mar. 22, 1955; d. Ayao George and Kimiko (Fujimoto) T. BA in Human Biology, Stanford U., 1977; M in Health Sci. Adminstrn., U. Mich., 1981. Administr. Pediatrics N.W., Tacoma, 1981—; mem. adv. bd. Knapp Coll. Mem. Am. Pub. Health Assn., Wash. State Med. Group Mgrs. Assn. Home: 710 N Yakima Tacoma WA 98403 Office: Pediatrics NW PS 1811 S K St Tacoma WA 98405

TANDON, SIRJANG LAL, computer corporation executive; b. 1941; married. BS, Punjab U., India, 1959; BSME, Howard U., 1962; MBA, U. Santa Clara, 1970. Project engr. Beckman Co., 1965-66; staff & project engr. IBM Corp., 1966-68, Memorex Co., 1968-73; mgr. recording tech. Pertec Computer Corp., 1973-75; now chmn., chief exec. officer, dir. Tandon Corp., Chatsworth, Calif., also bd. dirs. Office: Tandon Corp 20320 Prairie St Chatsworth CA 91311 *

TANG, CHUNG-SHIH, educator, researcher; b. Anwhei, Peoples Republic of China, Jan. 8, 1938; came to U.S., 1963; d. Chuan-Chi and I-Chuan (Ho) T.; m. Wen-Jing Yang, Jan. 31, 1965. BS, Nat. Taiwan U., Taipei, Republic of China, 1960, MS, 1962; PhD in Agrl. Chemistry, U. Calif., Davis, 1967. Research asst. U. Calif., Davis, 1963-66, postdoctoral, 1966-68; aast. prof. U. Hawaii, Honolulu, 1968-73, assoc. prof., 1973-79, prof., 1979—. Editor: The Science of Allelopathy, 1986. Mem. Am. Chem. Soc., Am. Soc. of Plant Physiology, Internat. Soc. Chem. Ecology, Phytochemistry Soc. N.Am. Office: U Hawaii Dept Agrl Biochemistry 1800 East West Rd Honolulu HI 96822

TANG, JAMES KONG-LEK, medical educator; b. Ayer Tawar, Malaysia, Oct. 5, 1955; came to U.S., 1967; s. Siu T. and Sik (Ling) T. BA, Asbury Coll., Wilmore, Ky., 1971; BS, NYU, Albany, 1972; MS, Murray (Ky.) State U., 1974; MPH, U. Tenn., 1976, EdD, 1978; PhD, Purdue U., W. Lafayette, Ind., 1980; MD, Am. U., Montserrat, Brit. West Indies, 1985. Indsl. hygienist Ind. State Bd. Health, Indpls., 1978-80; adminstrv. profl. asst. Purdue U., 1980; asst. prof. Calif. State U., Northridge, 1980-81; prof. U. So. Calif., Los Angeles, 1981—; cons. UCLA, Torrance, 1985—. Regional dir. VA Med. Ctr., Long Beach, Calif., 1987—. Mem. Am. Pub. Health Assn., Am. Indsl. Hygienist Assn., AAAS, Am. Soc. Safety Engrs. Avocation: traveling. Home: PO Box 15980 Long Beach CA 90815-0980

TANG, THOMAS, judge; b. Phoenix, Jan. 11, 1922. B.S., U. Santa Clara, 1947, law student, 1948-50; LL.B. with distinction, U. Ariz., 1950. Bar: Ariz. 1950, Calif. 1951. Dep. county atty. Maricopa County, Ariz., 1953-57; asst. atty. gen. State of Ariz., 1957-58; judge Ariz. Superior Ct., 1963-70; mem. firm Sullivan, Mahoney & Tang, Phoenix, 1971-77; councilman City of Phoenix, 1960-62, vice mayor, 1962; judge U.S. Ct. of Appeals 9th Circuit, Phoenix, 1977—. Mem. State Bar Ariz. (bd. govs. 1971-77, pres. 1977), State Bar Calif. Office: US Ct of Appeals Federal Bldg 230 N 1st Ave Phoenix AZ 85025

TANGRI, NAVEEN, computer engineer; b. Kharagpur, India, Jan. 20, 1959; came to U.S., 1980; s. Jang Bahadur and Urmil (Dhir) T. B of Tech., Indian Inst. Tech., 1980; MSEE, U. Fla., 1981. Research assoc. U. Fla., Gainesville, 1980-81; design engr. Gould-AMI, Santa Clara, Calif., 1981-83; engring. project mgr. Daisy Systems, Mountain View, Calif., 1983—. Contbr. articles to profl. jours. Avocations: skiing, white-water rafting.

TANIGUCHI, RICHARD RYUZO, wholesale building supplies executive; b. Eleele, Hawaii, Oct. 21, 1913; s. Tokuichi and Sana (Omaye) T.; B.A., U. Hawaii, 1936; m. Sumako Matsui, July 22, 1939; children—Grace Fujiyoshi, Susan Penisten. Acctg. clk. Bank of Hawaii, 1935-36; treas., gen. mgr. Hawaii Planing Mill, 1944-54; pres., gen. mgr. Hawaii Hardware Co., Ltd., Hilo, 1954—; pres., dir. Enterprises Hilo; v.p., dir. Hawaii Funeral Home. Chmn. Hawaii County CSC, 1950-56; vice chmn. Hawaii County Tidal Wave Adv. Com., 1961-68; vice chmn. Hawaii Council Tb and Health Assn., 1965; pres. Am. Cancer Soc., 1969-72, state bd. dirs., 1970-78; pres. Hilo Hongwanji Mission 1968-70, sr. adviser, 1972—; v.p. Hawaii State Hongwanji Mission, 1969—; mem. Hawaii Comprehensive Health Planning Com., 1970-72; gen. chmn. Kanyaku Imin Centennial Com., 1985. Named Hawaii Vol. of Year, Am. Cancer Soc., 1973, recipient Nat. award Am. Cancer Soc., 1978, Fifth Class Order of Sacred Treasure, Emperor of Japan, 1985. Mem. Am. Supply Assn., Nat. Plumbing Wholesalers Assn., Japanese C. of C. and Industry of Hawaii (pres. 1957), Hawaii (dir. 1958-59), Japanese (hon. dir.) chambers commerce, Hawaii Funeral Home (chmn. bd.), Hawaii Island Japanese Community Assn. (pres. 1983-85), Phi Kappa Phi, Pi Gamme Mu. Club: Waiakea. Lodge: Lions (treas., bd. dirs. 1956-60) Home: 572 Iwalani St Hilo HI 96720 Office: Honguanji Mission 550 Kilauea Ave Hilo HI 96720

TANIGUCHI, TOKUSO, surgeon; b. Eleele, Kauai, Hawaii, June 26, 1915; s. Tokuichi and Sana (Omaye) T.; B.A., U. Hawaii, 1941; M.D., Tulane U., 1946; 1 son, Jan Tokuichi. Intern Knoxville (Tenn.) Gen. Hosp., 1946-47; resident in surgery St. Joseph Hosp., also Marquette Med. Sch., Milw., 1947-52; practice medicine, specializing in surgery, Hilo, Hawaii, 1955—; chief surgery Hilo Hosp.; teaching fellow Marquette Med. Sch., 1947-49; v.p., dir. Hawaii Hardware Co., Ltd. Served to capt. M.C., AUS, 1952-55. Diplomate Am. Bd. Surgery. Fellow Internat., Am. colls. surgeons; mem. Am., Hawaii med. assns., Hawaii County Med. Soc., Pan-Pacific Surg. Assn., Phi Kappa Phi. Contbr. articles in field to profl. jours. Patentee automated catheter. Home: 277 Kaiulani St Hilo HI 96720

TANK, GERHARD WILLI, obstetrician, gynecologist; b. Arnswalde, Germany, Jan. 26, 1926; s. Frederick Karl and Martha Marie (Lade) T.; B.S. in Med. Sci., U. Wis., 1951, M.D., 1953. Intern, Swedish Hosp., Seattle, 1953-54; resident in ob-gyn, 1954-56; resident in ob-gyn Calif. Hosp./Orange County Hosp., 1956-57; research asst., dept. physiology U. Wis. Med. Sch., Madison, 1949-51; practice medicine specializing in obstetrics and gynecology, Grants Pass, Oreg., 1957—; partner Grants Pass Clinic, 1957—; pres. Rogue Valley Physicians Service, Medford, Oreg., 1972; mem. staff Josephine Gen. Hosp., 1957—, chief of staff, 1968, bd. dirs., 1984—; clin. asst. prof. U. Oreg. Health Sci. Center. Vol. worker Project Hope, 1967, 72; mem. So. Oreg. State Coll. Found. Diplomate Am. Bd. Obstetrics and Gynecology, Fellow Am. Coll. Obstetricians and Gynecologists; mem. Pacific N.W. Soc. Ob-Gyn, Oreg. Med. Assn. (trustee, mem. exec. com.). Contbr. articles to med. jours. Office: 125 NE Manzanita St Grants Pass OR 97526

TANNEHILL, RICHARD LEE, telecommunications engineer, consulting firm executive; b. Ft. Wayne, Ind., Feb. 1, 1947; s. Donald Lee and Cleo M. (Moudy) T.; m. Carolyn R. Smith, June 14, 1969 (div. 1981); children—Bryan R., Eric J.; m. Susan L. Beckenbach, July 14, 1981 (div. 1984); 1 adopted son, Paul E.; m. Rachel Nagle, Oct. 25, 1986. BSEE, U. Ariz., 1969; M in Advanced Bus. Adminstrn., Ariz. State U., 1981. Registered profl. engr., Ariz., Calif. Jr. design engr. Goodyear Aerospace Corp., Litchfield Park, Ariz., 1969-73; v.p. ATC, Phoenix, 1977-79; sr. communications engr., engring. mgr. Ariz. Dept. Pub. Safety, Phoenix, 1973-84; prin. Richard L. Tannehill, Communications Cons. Engr., Phoenix, 1981—; cons. City of Mesa, Ariz., 1977, Samaritan Health Services, Phoenix, 1978, Navopache Electric, Lakeside, Ariz., 1981, City of Tucson, 1981-83, Rural-Metro Fire, Inc., Scottsdale, Ariz., 1981-84, Mesa Sch. Dist., 1984, City of Glendale, Ariz., 1984-85. Contbr. articles on solar energy, communications to mags. Legis. chmn. Assn. of Fathers and Children, Phoenix, 1982, v.p., 1983, pres., 1986. Mem. IEEE (sr.; chmn. membership Phoenix chpt. 1981). Republican. Mormon. Home: 4821 W Avalon Dr Phoenix AZ 85031 Office: Ariz Dept Pub Safety 2310 N 20th Ave Phoenix AZ 85009

TANNEN, PETER DAVID, physicist, science administrator; b. Bronx, N.Y., Feb. 17, 1936; s. Sydney S. and Lil (Ringel) T.; m. Mary Ninfa Villegas, July 9, 1960; children: David, Elizabeth, Ann-Marie, Roger, Stephen, Rebecca. B in Aero. Engring., Rensselaer Poly. Inst., 1957; MS in Astronautics, USAF Inst. Tech., 1962, PhD in Aerospace Engring., 1973. Commd. 2d lt. USAF, 1957, advanced through grades to col., 1979, retired; aircraft maint. officer USAF, Harlingen, Tex., 1957-60; astronautical engr. AFSWC USAF, Albuquerque, 1962-67; physicist ARL USAF, Dayton, Ohio, 1969-73; chief electric lasers AFWL USAF, Albuquerque, 1973-79; chief guided weapons AFATL USAF, Ft. Walton Beach, Fla., 1979-81; gen. mgr. W.J. Schafer Assocs., Albuquerque, 1981—. Fellow AIAA; mem. Am. Phys. Soc., AAAS, Tau Beta Pi, Sigma Gamma Tau. Avocations: fishing, swimming, reading, travel. Home: 8920 Matthew Ave NE Albuquerque NM 87112 Office: W J Schafer Assocs Inc 2000 Randolph Rd SE Albuquerque NM 87106

TANNER, CLARA LEE FRAPS, anthropology educator; b. Biscoe, N.C., May 28, 1905; d. Joseph Conrad and Clara Dargon (Lee) F.; m. John Frederic Tanner, Jan. 22, 1936; 1 dau., Sandra Lee. BA, U. Ariz., 1927, MA, 1928, LLD (hon.), 1983; postgrad., Nat. U. Mex., Mexico City, 1929, Oriental Inst., Chgo., 1934. Instr. anthropology U. Ariz., Tucson, 1928-35, asst. prof., 1935-57, assoc. prof., 1957-68, prof., 1968-78, prof. emerita, 1978—; vis. asst. prof. Denver U., 1949; vis. prof. Colo. Coll., Colorado Springs, 1980; frequent pub. lectr. on Indians of Southwest, Ariz., Colo., Calif., Tex., Kans., Fla., 1928—; judge Indian craft shows; mem. grant rev. bd. NEH, NSF, Wenner-Gren Found. for Anthropol. Research; numerous com. memberships U. Ariz. Author: Southwest Indian Craft Arts, 1968 (1st Place award Nat. Fedn. Press Women 1969), Southwest Indian Painting, 1973 (1st Pl. award 1974), Prehistoric Southwest Craft Arts, 1975 (1st Pl. award Soc. Southwestern Authors 1976, 2d Pl. award Nat. Fedn. Press Women 1976), Apache Indian Basket, 1983 (3d Pl. award Nat. Fedn. Press Women 1984, Border Regional Library award 1984); editor Ariz. Highways Indian Arts and Crafts (1st Pl. award Soc. Southwestern Authors 1976); contbr. numerous articles to profl. jours. Com. mem. Tucson Fine Arts Assn., Southwest Indian Arts and Crafts Com. Recipient Faculty Recognition award Tucson Trade Bur., 1972-73, Tucson Panhellenic Athena award Profl. Achievement, 1983; named One of Outstanding Tucson Women, 1957. Mem. Am. Anthropol. Assn., Ariz. Archeol. and Hist. Soc. (life, editor The Kiva 1938-48), Southwest Assn. Indian Affairs (life), Am. Ethnol. Soc., Soc. Am. Archaeology, Nat. Fedn. Press Women, Ariz. Acad. Sci. (sec. div. anthropology 1960-61), Ariz. Hist. Soc., Soc. Southwest Authors, Archeol. Soc. N.Mex., Ariz. Press Women (Woman of Yr. 1971-72), Sigma Xi, Phi Beta Kappa, Delta Kappa Gamma. Office: U Ariz Dept Anthropology Tucson AZ 85721

TANNER, JAMES JOSEPH, geologist; b. N.Y.C., Nov. 4, 1947; s. Charles James and Rose Marie (Greico) T.; m. Marie Jennie Mazzarella, June 3, 1972 (div. 1977); m. Ellen Ruth Fickett, July 4, 1981; 1 child, Hope Rose. AA in Liberal Arts, Bronx Community Coll., 1967; BA in Geology, Lehman Coll., 1970; MA in Geology, Hunter Coll., 1975. Phys. scientist U.S. Assay Office, N.Y.C., 1972-76; geologist U.S. Dept. Energy, Washington, 1976-78, U.S. Geol. Survey, Metairie, La., 1978-79; area geologist U.S. Bur. Land Mgmt., Kingman, Ariz., 1980-81; assoc. mineral resources engr. Calif. State Lands Commn., Long Beach, 1981—. Mem. Am. Assn. Petroleum Geologists, AAAS. Republican. Roman Catholic. Office: Calif State Lands Commn 245 W Broadway Suite 425 Long Beach CA 90802

TANNER, LANE RUTH, enologist; b. Lakeport, Calif., Nov. 12, 1955; d. Robert LaVern Tanner and Alice Anett (Beeman) Knauss; m. Frank Robert Ostini, May 28, 1986. BS in Chemistry with gt. distinction, San Jose State U., 1976. Research scientist Environ. Systems and Service, Kelseyville, Calif., 1976-79, MRI, Altadena, Calif., 1979-80; enologist Firestone Winery, Los Olivos, Calif., 1981-83, Zaca Mesa Winery, Los Olivos, 1983-84, L.R. Cons., Santa Maria, Calif., 1984—. Editor: (with others) Geothermal Symposium, 1976. Mem. Am. Chem. Soc., Am. Soc. Enology and Vitaculture, Black Masques, Phi Kappa Phi, Cen. Coast Wine Soc. Democrat. Avocations: collecting glass, flute, wine tasting, family.

TANNER, MARTIN STANLEY, lawyer; b. Salt Lake City, Mar. 27, 1955; s. George Stanley and Nona (Watson) T.; m. Patti Madsen, June 16, 1979; 1 child, David. BA, U. Utah, 1981; JD, Brigham Young U., 1984. Bar: Utah 1984, U.S. Ct. Appeals (9th and D.C. cir.) 1986, U.S. Tax Ct. 1986, U.S. Ct. Appeals (10th cir.) 1987. Assoc. R. Dale Potter P.C., Salt Lake City, 1984-86, Snell & Wilmer, Phoenix, 1986—; vol. atty. Utah Legal Services, Salt Lake City, 1984-86. Articles editor Utah Bar Jour., 1982-84; contbr. articles to profl. jours. Missionary Ch. Jesus Christ Latter-day Sts., Japan, 1974-76; explorer post leader Boy Scouts Am. Mem. ABA, Utah Bar Assn., Phi Delta Phi. Republican. Mormon. Avocations: ski jumping, water skiing, distance running, swimming. Home: 1920 N Arrowhead Circle Chandler AZ 85073-3100 Office: Snell & Wilmer 3100 Valley Bank Ctr Phoenix AZ 85224

TANNER, OWEN RALPH, ophthalmologist; b. Layton, Utah, July 6, 1915; s. Alfonzo Z. and Vera Elizabeth (Noall) T.; m. Dorothy June Phillips, Aug. 10, 1940 (dec. July 1955); children: Dorothy, George, David, Richard; m. Marylou Mc Garry, Oct. 25, 1959; children: Garry, Patrick. AB with honors, U. Utah, 1936; postgrad., U. Mich., 1936; MD, Stanford U., 1940. Diplomate Am. Bd. Ophthalmology. Intern San Francisco City and County Hosp., 1939-40; resident Stanford Lane Hosp., San Francisco, 1940-42; assoc. and teaching asst. Stanford U., San Francisco, 1942-46; chief dept. ophthalmology Palo Alto (Calif.) Med. Clinic, 1946-80; sr. ophthalmologist Palo Alto Med. Found., 1980—; clin. prof. surg. ophthalmology Stanford (Calif.) U. Sch. Medicine, 1980—; guest lectr. Ogden (Utah) Surg. Soc., 1959, Intermountain Ophthal. Soc., 1959. Contbr. articles to profl. jours. Bd. dirs. West Bay Opera Assn.; bd. dirs. Stanford Mus. Guild, trustee. Mem. Am. Acad. Ophthalmology, San Francisco Ophthal. Round Table, Pacific Coast Oto-Ophthal. Soc. (v.p. 1968-69, pres. pro tem 1968, dir. ophthalmic edn. 1955-63), Phi Kappa Phi, Alpha Omega Alpha. Republican. Lodge: Kiwanis (past bd. dirs.). Avocations: golf, climbing, hiking, traveling. Home: 435 Coleridge Ave Palo Alto CA 94301 Office: Palo Alto Med Found 300 Homer AVe Palo Alto CA 94301

TANNER, THOMAS WILLIAM, marketing executive; b. St. Louis, Aug. 7, 1952; s. William Eugene and Betty (Helmering) T. BS in Computer Sci., U. Mo., Rolla, 1974; MBA, So. Ill. U., Edwardsville, 1982. Systems analyst City of St. Louis, 1972-76; adv. mktg. rep. Motorola Corp., San Bruno, Calif., 1976—. Vol. ARC, St. Louis and Calif., 1974-79; vice-chmn. Cambrian Community Council, San Jose, Calif., 1983-86, chmn., 1987; mem. citizen adv. council Housing and Urban Devel., Santa Clara County, Calif. Roman Catholic. Avocations: cycling, running, backpacking. Home: 2301 Saidel Dr Apt 2 San Jose CA 95124

TANNO, JOHN W., librarian; b. Bklyn., Sept. 28, 1939; s. John C. and Hildegarde (Whitaker) T.; m. Dolores Valencia, Aug. 7, 1968; children: Maria Elena, Luisa. AA, Phoenix Jr. Coll., 1959; MusB, Ariz. State U., 1963; MusM, U. So. Calif., 1965, MLS, 1970. Music librarian SUNY, Binghamton, 1965-68; order librarian Claremont (Calif.) Colls., 1970; music librarian U. Calif., Riverside, 1970-72, head monographs sect., 1972-78, asst. univ. librarian, 1978-83, assoc. univ. librarian, 1983—; lectr. in field; mem. ops. com. So. Regional Library Facility, 1984—, task group Intercampus Transp., 1984, negotiating team CLSI, 1981-84, bldg. com. So. Regional Compact Shelving Facility, 1979-82, steering com. Univ. Bibliographic Access System, 1978-82. Editor Soundboard, 1976-80; contbr. articles to profl. jours. Mem. ALA, The Music Library Assn., Coll. Music Soc., Assn. Recorded Sound Collections, Guitar Found. Am. (exec. com. 1976-80), Beta Phi Mu. Home: 20320 Stanford Ave Riverside CA 92507 Office: U Calif Library PO Box 5900 Riverside CA 92517

TANOUYE, ELYSE TOSHIE, magazine editor; b. Honolulu, Sept. 6, 1955; d. Roy S. and Frances T. (Akita) T. BA, Reed Coll., 1979. Editor Hawaii Bus. mag. subs. Hawaii Bus. Pub. Corp., Honolulu, 1981-86; Bagehot felow Columbia U., N.Y.C., 1986-87. Bd. dirs. YWCA of Oahu, Honolulu, 1985, mem. com., 1986. Recipient Overall Excellence award Hawaii Pubs. Assn., Honolulu, 1986, Maggie awards (2) Western Publs. Assn., Los Angeles, 1986, Writing award Am. Inst. Architects Hawaii Soc., Honolulu, 1984. Mem. Hawaii Soc. Corp. Planners (bd. dirs. 1985-86), Investigative Reporters and Editors.

TANSEY, JOHN RAYMOND, architect, consultant; b. Chamblee, Ga., Nov. 8, 1944; s. Charles Milton and Marjorie Evelyn (Shafer) T.; m. Patti Ann Montoya, Jan. 8, 1973: children: Jenny, Hallie. Student, Washington U., St. Louis, 1962-64; BFA, U. N.Mex., 1969. Registered architect, N.Mex., Nev. Project architect Jack Sample & Assocs., Albuquerque, 1974-77; v.p., architect Tansey, Saxton & Assocs., Albuquerque, 1978-81; pvt. practice architecture Albuquerque, 1981—; cons. N.Mex. Property Control Div., Santa Fe, 1985; cons. various Indian housing authorities, Nev., 1978-81. Planner, illustrator: Tajique, Torreon, Manzano, Punta de Agua—A Planning Framework for Revitalization, 1969. Active anti-Vietnam War groups and draft resistance groups, N.Mex., Ariz., and Calif., 1968-72. Mem. AIA, Nat. Council Archtl. Registration Bds. (cert.). Libertarian. Avocations: sculpture, woodworking, winemaking.

TAPP, RONALD GENE, insurance company executive; b. Bloomington, Ind., July 15, 1941; s. Wayne E. and Golda G. Tapp; student Ind. U., 1959-63; m. Helen L. Black, Sept. 24, 1977; children—Rhonda Jean, Randy G., Rita Jean. Printer, Phoenix Newspapers, Inc., 1972-76; ins. agt. Am. Republic Ins. Co., Phoenix, 1976-77; ins. agt. Minn. Protective Life Ins. Co., Phoenix, 1977-78, gen. agt., 1978-82, Southwestern regional mgr., 1978-82; sec.-treas. Internat. Benefit Cons., Ltd., 1981—; mktg. dir. Lincoln Benefit Life, 1982—; regional mgr. Pan Am. Life Ins. Co., 1983-85; pres. Empire-Am. Ins. Cons., Ltd., 1982—, Empire-Am. Bonding, Inc., 1985—. Republican precinct committeeman, also state committeeman for dist. 19. Served with U.S. Army, 1964-65. Recipient various profl. awards, 1977-81. Mem. Ariz. Public Employees Assn. (assoc.). Home: 144 E Bluefield Phoenix AZ 85022 Office: 4215 N 16th St Suite 2 Phoenix AZ 85016

TAPPAN, DAVID S., JR., engineering, construction, natural resources management company executive; b. Hainan, China, May 27, 1922; m. Jeanne Boone. B.A., Swarthmore Coll., 1943; M.B.A., Stanford U., 1948. With sales and engring. dept. U.S. Steel Corp., 1948-52; adminstrv. asst. to v.p. of sales Fluor Corp., Los Angeles, 1952-59, v.p. domestic sales, 1959-62, v.p. domestic and internat. sales, 1962-68, also. bd. dirs., sr. v.p., 1968-71; pres. Fluor Engrs. & Constructors Inc., 1971-76, vice chmn. bd., 1976-82, pres., chief operating officer, 1982-84, chmn., chief exec. officer, 1984—; bd. dirs. Genentech Inc., Allianz Ins. Co., The Nat. Council for U.S.-China Trade Inc., Los Angeles-Guangzhou Sister City Assn., Nat. Energy Found.; bd. overseas exec. council on fgn. diplomats and adv. com. Export-Import Bank of U.S. Bd. dirs. Nat. Bus. Com. for Arts; chmn. Orange County Orgn.; councillor U. So. Calif. Sch. Bus. and Adminstrn., Stanford U. Grad. Sch. Bus. Served to lt. (j.g.) USNR, 1943-46. Mem. Am. Petroleum Inst., Los Angeles C. of C. (vice chmn., bd. dirs.). Office: Fluor Corp 3333 Michelson Dr Irvine CA 92730

TAPSCOTT, ROBERT EDWIN, science research administrator; b. Terre Haute, Ind., June 10, 1938; s. Glenn Daniel and Mary Emiline (Imle) T.; m. Mary Frances Summers, Dec. 31, 1966; 1 child, Michael. BSChemE, U. Colo., 1964; PhD in Chemistry, U. Ill., 1968; postgrad., U. Ill., Chgo., 1967-68. Prof. chemistry U.N.Mex., Albuquerque, 1968-84; sr. research scientist N.Mex. Engring. Research Inst. div. U. N.Mex., Albuquerque, 1984—. Author: Experiments in General Chemistry, 1972, 4th rev. edit., 1982; contbr. reports in chemistry to USAF, articles to profl. jours. Grantee USPHS, 1966, U.S. Rubber, 1967, numerous others. Mem. Am. Chem. Soc. (treas., chmn. bd. dirs. local sect.), Chem. Soc. London, AAAS, Combustion Inst., Am. Soc. Aerosol Research, N.Mex. Hazardous Waste Soc. Democrat. Roman Catholic. Home: 3812 Palomas Dr NE Albuquerque NM 87110 Office: NMex Engring Research Inst U NMex Campus Box 25 Albuquerque NM 87131

TARANIK, JAMES VLADIMIR, geologist, educator; b. Los Angeles, Apr. 23, 1940; s. Vladimir James and Jeanette Downing (Smith) T.; m. Colleen Sue Glessner, Dec. 4, 1971; children: Debra Lynn, Danny Lee. B.Sc. in Geology, Stanford U., 1964; Ph.D., Colo. Sch. Mines, 1974. Chief remote sensing Iowa Geol. Survey, Iowa City, 1971-74; prin. remote sensing scientist Earth Resources Observation Systems Data Center, U.S. Geol. Survey, Sioux Falls, S.D., 1975-79; chief non-renewable resources br., resource observation div. Office of Space and Terrestrial Applications, NASA Hdqrs., Washington, 1979-82; dean mines Mackay Sch. Mines, prof. geology U. Nev.-Reno, 1982—; adj. prof. geology U. Iowa, 1971-79; vis. prof. civil engring. Iowa State U., 1972-74; adj. prof. earth sci. U. S.D., 1976-79; program scientist for space shuttle large format camera expt., for heat capacity mapping mission liaison Geol. Scis. Bd., Nat. Acad. Scis., 1981-82; team mem. Shuttle Imaging Radar-B Sci. Team NASA, 1983—, mem. space applications adv. com. 1986—; chmn. remote sensing subcom. SAAC, 1986—; chmn. working group on civil space commercialization U.S. Dept. Commerce, 1982-84, mem. civil operational remote sensing satellite com., 1983-84; bd. dirs. Newmont Gold Co.; mem. NASA Space Applications adv. com., 1986, chmn. remote sensing subcom., 1986—. Contbr. to profl. jours. Served with C.E. U.S. Army, 1965-67. Decorated Bronze Star medal.; recipient Spl. achievement award U.S. Geol. Survey, 1978, exceptional sci. achievement medal NASA, 1982; NASA prin. investigator, 1973; NDEA fellow, 1968-71. Fellow AAAS (sr. mem.), Explorers Club, Geol. Soc. Am.; mem. Am. Assn. Petroleum Geologists, Soc. Mining Engrs., Am. Inst. Profl. Geologists (certified, pres. Nev. sect. 1985—), AIAA (sr. mem.), Internat. Acad. Astronautics (academician), Am. Astronautical Soc. (sr. mem.), Soc. Exploration Geophysicists, Geosci. and Remote Sensing Soc. of IEEE (bd. dirs., geosat com.), Am. Soc. Photogrammetry (certified), Internat. Soc. Photogrammetry and Remote Sensing (pres. working group II/4 1976-80, working group VIII-5 non-renewable resources 1980—), Sigma Xi. Developer remote sensing program and remote sensing lab. for State of Iowa, ednl. program in remote sensing for Iowa univs.; Office Space and Terrestrial Applications program scientist for 2d space shuttle flight; terrestial geologic applications program for NASA. Home: 3075 Susileen Dr Reno NV 89509 Office: Office of Dean Mackay Sch Mines U Nev Reno NV 89557

TARGOVNIK, SELMA E. KAPLAN, physician; b. N.Y.C., Apr. 22, 1936; d. Harry A. and Helen (Goodstein) Kaplan; m. Jerome H. Targovnik, Dec. 2, 1961; children—Nina Rebecca, Labe Eric, Diane Michelle. B.A., NYU, 1957; M.D., Albert Einstein Coll. Medicine, 1961. Diplomate Am. Bd. Dermatology. Intern Kaiser Found. Hosp., San Francisco, 1961-62; resident in internal medicine Bellevue Hosp., NYU Med. Ctr., 1962-63, U. Colo. Med. Ctr., Denver, 1963-64; research fellow, resident in dermatology Boston U. Med. Ctr., 1968-69; practice medicine specializing in dermatology, Phoenix, 1969—; mem. staff St. Joseph's Hosp., Phoenix, St. Luke's Hosp., Phoenix, Humana Hosp., Phoenix; mem. staff Good Samaritan Hosp., Phoenix, chief div. dermatology, 1985—. Bd. dirs. ACLU, Ariz., 1973-78, 1983—, Congregation Beth El, Phoenix, 1971-75, Flagstaff Festival of the Arts, 1984-86; active Jewish Nat. Fund. Fellow Am. Acad. Dermatology; mem. Dermatology Found., Sonoran Dermatologic Soc. Southwestern Dermatologic Soc., Pacific Dermatologic Soc., Noah Worcester Dermatologic Soc., Galen Soc. (sec. 1982-83), Phi Beta Kappa, Mu Chi Sigma, Pi Delta Phi, Beta Lambda Sigma. Democrat. Jewish. Home: 3706 E Rancho Dr Paradise Valley AZ 85253 Office: 1300 N 12th St Suite 503 Phoenix AZ 85006

TARIO, TERRY C(HARLES), broadcast executive; b. Los Angeles, Aug. 28, 1950; s. Clifford Alexander and Marion Charlene (Olive) T.; divorced; 1 child, Brian Paul. Grad. high sch., Hermosa Beach, Calif., 1968. Gen. mgr. South Bay Power Tools, Hermosa Beach, 1973-76; broadcaster Sta. KEEP/KEZJ, Twin Falls, Idaho, 1976—; dir. mktg. Pet Complex, Boise and Salt Lake City, 1985—. Creator commls. John Lennon Meml. (Best of Yr. award 1982), Pets Unltd., 1983 (Best of Yr. award 1983), Depot Grill, 1984 (Best of Yr. award 1984), Eyecenter (Best of Yr. award 1986). Served with USN, 1968-72. Mem. Idaho State Broadcasters Assn., Advt. and Mktg. Cons. (pres.). Avocations: skiing, running, writing. Office: Sta KEEP/KEZJ 415 Park Ave Twin Falls ID 83301

TARK, SUNG YONG, polymer chemist; b. Andung, Republic of China, May 11, 1939; came to U.S., 1962; s. Yung S. and Kum S. (Kim) T.; m. Sue Jung Kim, Jan. 8, 1972; children: Eunice K., Irene K. BS, Ft. Hays Kans. State U., 1967, MS, 1969; MS, U. Akron, 1972. Research chemist Energy Conversion Devices, Inc., Troy, Mich., 1972-76; project leader Dynachem Corp. div. Morton Thiokol, Inc., Tustin, Calif., 1976-87; sr. research assoc. Swedlow, Inc. div. Pilkington Co., Ltd., Garden Grove, Calif., 1987—. Patentee in field. Pres. Korean Philharmonic Soc., Irvine, Calif., 1980—; chmn. Logos Meth. Youth Choir Supporting Com., Los Angeles, 1986; bd. dirs. Korean Am. Scholarship Found. Mem. Am. Chem. Soc., Korean Scientists Engrs. Assn. Republican. Lodge: Lions (Service award 1983). Home: 16 Field Irvine CA 92720 Office: Swedlow Inc div Pilkington Co Ltd 12122 Western Ave Garden Grove CA 92641

TARLOV, ALVIN RICHARD, physician, educator; b. Norwalk, Conn., July 11, 1929; s. Charles and Mae (Shelinsky) T.; m. Joan Hylton, June 12, 1956 (div. 1976); children: Richard, Elizabeth, Jane, Suzanne, David. BA, Dartmouth Coll., 1951; MD, U. Chgo., 1956. Intern Phila. Gen. Hosp., 1956-57; resident in medicine U. Chgo. Hosps., 1957-58; asst. prof. medicine U. Chgo., 1963-67, assoc. prof., 1967-60, prof., 1970-83, chmn. dept. medicine, 1968-81; chmn. nat. adv. com. on grad. med. edn. HHS, Washington, 1980; pres. Henry J. Kaiser Family Found., Menlo Park, Calif., 1984—. Served to capt. U.S. Army, 1958-61. Recipient Research Career Devel. award NIH, 1962-67; John and Mary Markle Found. scholar, 1966-71. Mem. ACP (master), Inst. Medicine of Nat. Acad. Scis. Office: The Henry J Kaiser Family Found 525 Middlefield Rd Suite 200 Menlo Park CA 94025

TARON, TIMOTHY DALE, lawyer; b. Richmond, Calif., Jan. 20, 1951; s. Willard Warden and Christine B. (Wilberts) T.; m. Lisa Brann, July 15, 1978; children: Joanna, Daniel. BA, Stanford U., 1973; JD, UCLA, 1976. Assoc. Hefner, Stark & Marois, Sacramento, 1976-82, ptnr., 1982—. V.p., bd. dirs. Mather Heritage Found., 1985—. Mem. Sacramento Met. C. of C. (gen. counsel 1983, bd. dirs. 1981—, v.p. govt. affairs 1984, pres. 1986), CAP-PAC (bd. dirs. 1984-85). Republican. Club: Sutter (Sacramento). Lodge: Rotary. Avocations: snow skiing, fishing, hunting, golf. Home: 3102 Barberry Ln Sacramento CA 95864 Office: Hefner Stark & Marois 555 Capitol Mall #1425 Sacramento CA 95814

TARR, DELBERT HOWARD, JR., seminary president, clergyman; b. Aitkin, Minn., June 14, 1934; s. Delbert Howard and Catherine Elizabeth (Boomer) T.; m. Dorothy D. Hill, June 12, 1954; children—Cindy Sharon, Terry Mark, Randel Ray. B.A. in Bible, North Central Bible Coll., 1956; postgrad. Ecole Lemania, Switzerland, 1959-60; M.A. in Communications, U. Minn., 1969; Ph.D. in Communications, 1979. Ordained to ministry Assemblies of God Ch., 1957; pastor Assemblies of God Ch., Hopkins, Minn., 1956-58; apptd. fgn. missionary Burkina Faso (formerly Upper Volta), West Africa, 1960-63; dir. Mossiland Bible Sch., 1964-67; co-founder, dean West African Advanced Sch. Theology, Lome, Togo, 1970-73; prof., coordinator cross-cultural communication studies Assemblies of God Theol. Sem. (formerly Assemblies of God Grad. Sch.), Springfield, Mo., 1973-77, dean missions div., 1977-80, chmn. missions dept., 1980-82; pres. Calif. Theol. Sem., Fresno, 1983—; guest lectr. Far East Advanced Sch. Theology, Manila, Philippines, 1983. Research grantee African speech mannerisms, 1976-77. Mem. Am. Soc. Missiology, Acad. Evangelism, Soc. Pentecostal Studies. Office: Calif Theol Sem 2515 W Shaw St Fresno CA 93711

TARR, MITCHELL A., chemical engineer; b. Waterville, Maine, May 30, 1957; s. Alfred E. and Norene F. (White) T. BS in Chem. Engring., U. Maine, 1979. Sr. process engr. Nat. Semiconductor, Hawthorne, Calif., 1980-83; prodn. mgr. EE Tech., El Segundo, Calif., 1983-85, cons., 1985; mts TRW, Redondo Beach, Calif., 1985—; mgmt. cons. Leemax Corp., Santa Clara, Calif., 1986—. Bd. dirs. Brookfield (Conn.) Baseball Assn., 1980. Mem. Am. Vacuum Soc., Am. Inst. Chem. Engrs. Club: Brookfield Judo (pres. 1980-81), Gardena (Calif.) Judo. Avocations: scuba diving, judo, softball, white water rafting. Home: 34927 Belvedere Terrace Fremont CA 94536 Office: TRW 3375 Scott Blvd Suite 440 Santa Clara CA 95054

TARR, WILLIAM WINSHIP, JR., photographer; b. Los Angeles, 1953; s. William Winship and Shirley (Wright) T.; BA in Biology, Calif. State U., Northridge, 1983; postgrad. Mt. St. Mary's Coll., 1983-84. Cert. sci. and math. secondary tchr., Calif.; m. Catherine Ann Byrer, Oct. 28, 1978. Sales specialist J.C. Penney Corp., Canoga Park, Calif., 1973; customer service technician, tech. demonstrator Berkey Mktg. Corp., West Coast, 1974; show mgr. photo expn. Los Angeles Conv. Center, 1974, publicity and advt. mgr. Olympic Camera, 1975; owner, mgr. Winship Photo Studio, Canyon Country, Calif., 1973—; tchr. sci. Los Angeles Unified Sch. Dist., 1986—; chmn. arts dept. Alemany High Sch., Mission Hills, Calif., 1979-85; flotilla comdr. USCG Aux. Flotilla 14-7, 1986-87. Mem. Los Angeles Mus. Natural History Alliance, Sierra Club, CSUN Sailing Club (commodore 1976-77), Oceanic Soc., USCG Aux. (instr., vessel examiner). Republican.

TARRANT, ROBERT FRANK, soil science educator, researcher; b. Portland, Oreg., Mar. 11, 1918; s. Frank A. and Vera Leona (Tibbils) T.; m. Jean Inez Horton, Sept. 20, 1941; children: Christopher R., Susan J., Brian H., Stephanie A. Tarrant Martin. BS, Oreg. State U., 1941. Soil scientist USDA Pacific N.W. Forest Research Sta., Portland, 1946-71, asst. dir., 1971-74, dep. dir., 1975, dir., 1975-79; prof. forest scis. Oreg. State U., Corvallis, 1979-86. Co-editor: The Biology of Alder, 1968; contbr. articles, reports to profl. jours. Bd. dirs. Oreg. Easter Seal Soc., Portland, 1969-75, pres., 1971-73. Served to lt. comdr. USN, 1942-45, ETO, PTO, also 1950-52. Recipient Superior Service award USDA, Washington, 1971. Fellow Soc. Am. Foresters; mem. Northwest Scientific Assn. (hon. life), Sigma Xi. Episcopalian. Home: 2660 SW Fairmont Dr Corvallis OR 97333

TARSON, HERBERT HARVEY, university administrator; b. N.Y.C., Aug. 28, 1910; s. Harry and Elizabeth (Miller) T.; m. Lynne Barnett, June 27, 1941; 1 son, Stephen. Grad., Army Command Gen. Staff Coll., 1942, Armed Forces Staff Coll., 1951, Adavnced Mgmt. Sch. Sr. Air Force Comdrs., George Washington U., 1954; B.A., U. Calif., Los Angeles, 1949; Ph.D., U.S. Internat. U., 1972. Entered U.S. Army as pvt., 1933, advanced through grades to maj., 1942; transfered to U.S. Air Force, 1947, advanced through grades to lt. col., 1949; adj. exec. officer Ft. Snelling, Minn., 1940-42; asst. adj. gen. 91st Inf. Div., 1942-43; chief of personnel, advance sec. Comd. Zone, ETO, 1944-45; dir. personnel services 8th Air Force, 1946-47; dep. dir. dept. info. and edn. Armed Forces Info. Sch., 1949-51; dir. personnel services Japan Air Def. Force, 1951-53, Continental Air Command, 1953-62; dir. adminstrv. services, spl. asst. to Comdr. 6th Air Force Res. Region, 1962-64; ret. 1964; asst. to chancellor L.I. U., Brookville, 1964-69; dean admissions Tex. State Tech. Inst., San Diego Indsl. Center, 1970-72; v.p. acad. affairs Nat. U., San Diego, 1972-75; sr. v.p. Nat. U., 1975—. Decorated Bronze Star medal with oak leaf cluster, Air Force Commendation medal with 2 oak leaf clusters. Fellow Bio-Med Research Inst.; mem. Doctoral Soc. U.S. Internat. U., Am. Soc. Tng., Devel., World Affairs Council, Air Force Assn., Navy League U.S., Pres.'s Assos. of Nat. U. (presidential life). Home: 4611 Denwood Rd La Mesa CA 92041 Office: Nat U 4141 Camino del Rio S San Diego CA 92108

TARTAR, VANCE, research educator; b. Corvallis, Oreg., Sept. 15, 1911; s. Herman Vance and Stella (Parsons) T.; m. Emogean Eva Saunders, June 19, 1950; children: Helen Sarah, Karl Nicholas, Wanda Gale. BS, U. Wash., 1933, MS, 1934; PhD, Yale U., 1939. Instr. U. Vt., Burlington, 1939041; researcher Dept. Fisheries, Seattle, 1941-48; research prof. U. Wash., Seattle, 1949—. Author: Biology of Stentor, 1961. Recipient Research award Am. Cancer Soc., 1941, Nat. Cancer Inst., 1942. Mem. Soc. Protozoologists, Peninsula Arts Assn. Home: Rural Rt 1 Box 250 Ocean Park WA 98640

TASAKA, MASAICHI, hospital executive; b. Hilo, Hawaii, Feb. 3, 1925; s. Sunao and Shizue (Katayama) T.; m. Toshiko Kohatsu, Aug. 30, 1952; children—Sharon Lei, Russell Ken. M.S. in Hosp. Adminstrn., Northwestern U., 1955. Bookkeeper, Francis Hiu & Co., 1948-50; bus. mgr. South Shore Hosp., 1950-53; asst. adminstr. Highland Park Hosp., 1955-64; asst. adminstr. Kuakini Med. Ctr., Honolulu, 1964-69, pres., 1969—; asst. prof. Sch. Pub. Health. Mem. Am. Hosp. Assn. (life), Am. Coll. Hosp. Adminstrs., C. of C. of Hawaii, Honolulu Japanese C. of C. Club: Lions. Office: Kuakini Med Ctr 347 N Kuakini St Honolulu HI 96817

TASHEY, THOMAS ERNEST, JR., gemologist; b. Highland Park, Mich., Sept. 11, 1947; s. Thomas Ernest and Doris Margaret (Hodgson) T.; m. Myriam Clara Both, July 28, 1980; 1 child, Thomas Ernest III. Student, Kalamazoo Coll., 1965-67, 71-73. Supr. Gemological Inst. Am. Gem Trade Lab., Los Angeles, 1975-78; dir. European Gem Lab., Los Angeles, 1978-79; salesman, wholesaler Luxor Gems, Beverly Hills, Calif., 1979-80; owner IGL, Los Angeles, 1980-86, EGL, Los Angeles, 1985—. Served with USN, 1967-71. Fellow Gemological Assn. Great Brit.; mem. Accredited Gemologists Assn. (1st v.p. 1984-85, sec. 1982-84, master gemolgist appraiser 1983-86), Gemological Inst. Am. (cert. gemologist, alumni assn.). Democrat. Bhuddist. Avocation: tennis. Home: 641 Ocean Park Blvd #2 Santa Monica CA 90405 Office: Ind Gem Lab 608 S Hill St #1013 Los Angeles CA 90014

TATA, GIOVANNI, museum curator; b. Taranto, Italy, Apr. 26, 1954; came to U.S., 1974, naturalized, 1982; s. Vito and Angela (Colucci) T.; m. Brenda Susan Smith, Feb. 14, 1978; children: Elizabeth Ariana, Katherine Allyson. B.S. cum laude (scholar), Brigham Young U., 1977, M.A., 1980; grad. cert. area studies U. Utah, 1980; PhD, 1986; postgrad. U. Turin (Italy), 1980-81. Archaeologist, Utah State Hist. Soc., Salt Lake City, 1979; instr. dept. langs. U. Utah, Salt Lake City, 1983-85; Mediterranean specialist Soc. Early Hist. Archaeology, Provo, Utah, 1978—; mus. curator Pioneer Trail State Park, Salt Lake City, 1982-83; instr. dept. art Brigham Young U., Provo, 1982-84; research fellow Direzione Generale per la Cooperazione Scientifica Culturale e Technica, Rome, 1980-81; research curator Utah Mus. Fine Arts, Salt Lake City, 1985—; chmn. 35th Ann. Symposium on the Archaeology of the Scriptures, 1986. Republican. Mem. Ch. Jesus Christ of Latter-day Saints. Mem. Am. Assn. Mus.'s, Coll. Art Assn. Am., Utah Art History Assn., Utah State Hist. Soc. Home: PO Box 8414 Salt Lake City UT 84108 Office: Utah Mus Fine Arts Salt Lake City UT 84116

TATALOVICH, NICHOLAS STEPHAN, airline administrator; b. McKeesport, Pa., May 26, 1939; s. Milan and Mary (Yambor) T.; m. Marylee Carol Brinson (div. Aug. 1977); children: Nicki, Scott, Michael. BA, U. Calif., Long Beach, 1971. Mgr. avionics and accessory repair Western Airlines, Inc., Los Angeles, 1984—. Served with USN, 1957-61. Republican. Orthodox. Avocations: golf, camping, fishing. Home: 4415 Larwin Ave Cypress CA 90630 Office: Western Airlines 6060 Avion Dr Los Angeles CA 90045

TATE, KAREN ANNE, librarian; b. Jamaica, N.Y., Dec. 22, 1948; d. Thomas and Katherine (Henrickson) Egan; m. Donald Joseph Tate, Aug. 7, 1971; children—Jeanne Renee, Keith Chamberlain. B.A., Coll. New Rochelle, 1971. Tchr., Jackson Sch. Dist., Wyo., 1979, Teton County Sch. Dist., Idaho, 1980, Soda Springs Sch. Dist., Idaho, 1981; library dir. Soda Springs Public Library, 1982—; Columnist, Library News, 1983-84. Mem. Democratic Precinct Com., Denver, 1972-73; sec. Caribou County Hist. Soc., Soda Springs, 1984; chmn. PTO, 1981-84; leader Girl Scouts U.S.; mem. bd. dirs. YMCA Women's Advocates for Battered Women. Mem. ALA, Idaho Library Assn., Pacific Northwest Library Assn., Library Adminstrn. and Mgmt. Assn., Beta Sigma Phi. Republican. Roman Catholic. Club: Art Guild (Jackson, Wyo.). Office: Soda Springs Public Library 149 S Main St Soda Springs ID 83276

TATE, WILLIAM JAMES, business counselor, tax adviser; b. Sarnia, Ont., Can., May 4, 1922; came to U.S., 1924, naturalized, 1940; s. Alfred Carlisle and Myrtle May (Hamilton) T.; m. Nancy Lou Arnold, Mar. 30, 1946; children—William James, Gary S., Cheryl A. Tate Pendergast, Franklin H. B.A., U. Mich., 1947. C.P.A., Mich.; enrolled agt. IRS. Auditor, Touche, Ross, C.P.A.s, Detroit, 1947-52; controller Grinnell Bros., Detroit, 1953-54; div. controller Chrysler Corp., Detroit, 1955-66, dir. and v.p. fin. and adminstrn. Chrysler U.K., London, 1967-70; v.p. fin. and adminstrn. Xerox Data Systems, also controller west region Xerox Corp., Los Angeles, 1970-75; sr. ptnr. Gen. Bus. Services, Oceanside, Calif., 1976—. Served to 1st lt. USAF, 1943-46; ETO. Mem. Nat. Assn. Enrolled Agts., Mich. Assn. C.P.A.s, Calif. Assn. Enrolled Agts., Oceanside C. of C. (ambassador). Club: Oceanside Rotary. Office: Gen Bus Services 1310 Union Plaza Ct Suite 206 Oceanside CA 92054

TATUM, ELSIE LOUISE, psychotherapist; b. LaFayette, Ala., July 14, 1952; s. Glenn Anthony and Margaret (Harrell) T.; m. Charles G. Bellville, Oct. 14, 1978; one child, Ian Burns Tatum Bellville. BA cum laude, Randolph-Macon Women's Coll., 1974; postgrad., U. Reading, Eng., 1972-75; MSW magna cum laude, U. Ga., 1976. Health planner N. Cen. Ga. Health Systems Agy., Atlanta, 1977-79; research instr. psychiatry Oreg. Health Scis. U., Portland, 1979-86, mem. clin. faculty, 1986—; practice psychotherapy, cons. Portland, 1986—; field instr. Portland State U., 1980-84. Contbr. articles to profl. jours. Active Mental Health Assn., Atlanta and Portland, 1974—. Mem. Nat. Assn. Social Workers, Acad. Cert. Soc. Workers. (cert.), LWV, Phi Kappa Phi. Avocations: skiing, backpacking, weightlifting, painting, hiking. Home: 4717 NW Barnes Rd Portland OR 97210 Office: 720 SW Morrison Suite 708 Portland OR 97205

TAUB, LEWIS H., management consultant, engineer; b. Chgo., Nov. 23, 1947; s. Sol and Shirlee Lorraine (Cohn) T.; m. Sharon Rockoff, Mar. 22, 1970 (div. Oct. 1980); children—Elliot, Vanessa. B.S., Calif. State U.-Long Beach, 1970. Cert. mgmt. cons.; cert. in data processing. Engr. IBM, San Jose, Calif., 1970-72; systems engr., Chgo., 1972-76; cons. Booz Allen Hamilton, Chgo., 1976-80; cons., v.p. Gottfried Cons. Inc., Los Angeles, 1980-84; mgr. in charge fin. services practice Deloitte Haskins and Sells, 1984-86, sr. mgr., 1986—. Author: Item Processing Capacity Planning, 1983. Mem. Am. Assn. for Artificial Intelligence, Am. Arbitration Assn. Home: 1717 Stoner St Apt 103 Los Angeles CA 90025 Office: Deloitte Haskins & Sells 333 S Grand Los Angeles CA 90070

TAUBE, HENRY, chemistry educator; b. Sask., Can., Nov. 30, 1915; came to U.S., 1937, naturalized, 1942; s. Samuel and Albertina (Tiledetski) T.; m. Mary Alice Wesche, Nov. 27, 1952; children: Linda, Marianna, Heinrich, Karl. B.S., U. Sask., 1935, M.S., 1937, LL.D., 1973; Ph.D., U. Calif., 1940; Ph.D. (hon.), Hebrew U. of Jerusalem, 1979; D.Sc. (hon.), U. Chgo., 1983, Poly. Inst., N.Y., 1984, SUNY, 1985, U. Guelph, 1987. Instr. U. Calif., 1940-41; instr., asst. prof. Cornell U., 1941-46; faculty U. Chgo., 1946-62, prof., 1952-62, chmn. dept. chemistry, 1955-59; prof. chemistry Stanford U., 1962—, Marguerite Blake Wilbur prof., 1976, chmn. dept., 1971-74; Baker lectr. Cornell U., 1965. Recipient Harrison Howe award, 1961; Chandler medal Columbia U., 1964; F.P. Dwyer medal U. N.S.W., Australia, 1973; Nat. medal of Sci., 1976, 77; Allied Chem. award for Excellence in Grad. Teaching and Innovative Sci., 1979; Nobel Prize in Chemistry, 1983; Bailar medal U. Ill., 1983; Robert A. Welch Found. Award in chemistry, 1983; Guggenheim fellow, 1949, 55. Mem. Am. Acad. Arts and Scis., Nat. Acad. Scis. (award in chem. scis. 1983), Am. Chem. Soc. (Kirkwood award New Haven sect. 1965, award for nuclear application in chemistry 1955, Nichols medal N.Y. sect. 1971, Willard Gibbs medal Chgo. sect. 1971, Disting. Service in Advancement Inorganic Chemistry award 1967, T.W. Richards medal NE sect. 1980, Monsanto Co. award in inorganic chemistry 1981, Linus Pauling award Puget Sound sect. 1981, Priestley medal 1985), Royal Physiographical Soc. of Lund, Nat. Acad. Scis., Am. Philos. Soc., Finnish Acad. Sci. and Letters, Royal Danish Acad. Scis. and Letters, Phi. Beta Kappa, Sigma Xi, Phi Lambda Upsilon (hon.). Office: Stanford Univ Dept of Chemistry Stanford CA 94305

TAUCHER, FRED HORACE, data processing company executive; b. Berlin, Germany, Jan. 29, 1933; s. Julius and Therese (Gerstel) T.; came to U.S., 1946, naturalized, 1954; grad. high sch.; m. Hisako Kawano, Apr. 25, 1955; children—Walter A., Audrey T. Asst. supr. data processing dept. Pacific Hwy. Transport, 1955-60; mgr. data processing dept. Graystone Corp., Seattle, 1960-68, dir. Canal Computer Center, 1962-68; pres. Corporate Mgmt., Inc., Seattle, 1968-86; pres. Corp. Computer, Inc., 1986—. Mem. CAP. Served with AUS, 1951-54. Recipient Individual Performance award Data Processing Mgmt. Assn., 1968. Mem. Data Processing Mgmt. Assn. (dir. Puget Sound chpt. 1962-66, 68-70, treas. 1967-68, sec. 1973-74, internat. dir. Puget Sound chpt. 1968-71, 74-76, div. chmn. Northwestern div. 1971-72, gen. chm. Region 2 conf. 1974), Aircraft Owners and Pilots Assn., DAV (life). Home: 1211 8th Ave S Edmonds WA 98020 Office: 1530 Eastlake Ave E Suite 101 Seattle WA 98102

TAUSCHER, WILLIAM YOUNG, pharmaceutical and cosmetic products executive; b. Hyattsville, Md., 1950; s. Gilbert Young and Dorcas (Jones) T.; m. Janet Mariani, Oct. 25, 1975; children: Lauren M., Joseph William. B.S., Yale U., 1972. With mktg. dept. IBM Co., Chgo., 1972-75; computer exec. MST Co., Chgo., 1975-78; pres. Western Textile Co., Chgo., 1978-79; pres. Foxmeyer Corp., Denver, 1979-85, chmn., 1979—; dir. Far Western, San Jose, Calif., Nat. Wholesale Druggists Assn., Washington. Office: Foxmeyer Corp 1220 Senlac Carrollton TX 75006

TAUSSKY, OLGA (MRS. JOHN TODD), mathematics educator; b. Olomouc, Czechoslovakia, Aug. 30, 1906; came to U.S., 1934, naturalized, 1953; d. Julius David and Ida (Pollach) T.; m. John Todd, Sept. 29, 1938. PhD in Math., U. Vienna, 1930, Golden D diploma (hon.), 1980; MA (hon.), U. Cambridge, Eng., 1937. Fellow Girton Coll., Cambridge, Eng., 1934-40; asst. lectr. U. London, Eng., 1937-43; sci. officer Ministry Aircraft Prodn., London, 1943-46; mathematician Nat. Bur. Standards, Washington, 1947-57; research assoc. Calif. Inst. Tech., Pasadena, 1957-71, prof. math., 1971—. Contbr. articles to profl. jours.; editor numerous books in field. Recipient Ford prize Math. Assn. Am., 1971; Fulbright prof. U. Vienna, 1965; decorated Gold Cross of Honor 1st Class (Austria). Fellow AAAS; mem. Am. Math. Soc. (council 1972-74, 83-85, v.p. 1986—), Austrian Acad. Scis. (corr.), Bavarian Acad. Scis. (corr.). Office: Calif Inst Tech 253-37 Pasadena CA 91125

TAVEGGIA, THOMAS CHARLES, management consultant; b. Oak Lawn, Ill., June 15, 1943; s. Thomas Angelo and Eunice Louise (Harriss) T.; m. Brigitte I. Adams, Jan. 23, 1965; children—Michaela, Francesca. B.S., Ill. Inst. Tech., 1965; M.S., U. Oreg., 1968, Ph.D., 1971. Prof., U. Oreg., Eugene, 1970, U. B.C. (Can.), Vancouver, 1970-73, U. Calif.-Irvine, 1973-74, Ill. Inst. Tech., Chgo., 1974-77; mgmt. cons. Towers, Perrin, Forster & Crosby, Chgo., 1977-80; ptng. Manplan Cons., Chgo., 1980-81; ptnr. Coopers & Lybrand, San Francisco, 1981-86; ptnr. Touche Ross, San Francisco, 1986—. NDEA Title IV fellow, 1967-71; U. B.C. faculty research grantee, 1970, 71, 72. Mem. Am. Compensation Assn., Inst. Mgmt. Cons.

Presbyterian. Author: (with R. Dubin and R. Arends) From Family and School To Work, 1967; (with Dubin) The Teaching-Learning Paradox: A Comparative Analysis of College Teaching Methods, 1968; (with Dubin and R.A. Hedley) The Medium May Be Related to the Message: College Instruction by TV, 1969; contbr. numerous articles to profl. jours. Home: 2188 Lariat Ln Walnut Creek CA 94596 Office: Touche Ross 1 Maritime Plaza San Francisco CA 94111-3578

TAVELLA, MICHAEL JOHN, electrical engineer, patent agent; b. Queens, N.Y., Sept. 13, 1952; s. Anthony T. and Berenice (Perrine) T.; m. Ki Sun Yi, Mar. 9, 1978; children: Min Jung, Anne Marie. BEE, Pratt Inst., 1975. Registered agt. U.S. Patent Office, 1979. Trainee engr. Am. Electric Power Co., N.Y.C., 1971-74; engr. Alaska Village Electric Co., Anchorage, 1976-82; utility engr. Alaska Pub. Utility Commn., Anchorage, 1982—; patent agt., Anchorage, 1980—. Patentee. Chmn. bd. Campbell Community Sch. Assn., 1982; sec. Council Assns. Anchorage Community Schs., 1986-87. Roman Catholic. Home: 6900 Rovena St Anchorage AK 99502 Office: 420 L St Suite 100 Anchorage AK 99501

TAVROW, RICHARD LAWRENCE, lawyer, transportation executive; b. Syracuse, N.Y., Feb. 3, 1935; s. Harry and Ida Mary (Hodess) T.; m. Barbara J. Silver, Mar. 22, 1972; children—Joshua Michael, Sara Hallie. A.B. magna cum laude, Harvard U., 1957, LL.B., 1960, LL.M., 1961; postgrad., U. Copenhagen, 1961-62, U. Luxembourg, 1962. Bar: N.Y. bar 1961, U.S. Supreme Ct. bar 1969, Calif. bar 1978. Atty. W.R. Grace & Co., N.Y.C., 1962-66; asst. chief counsel Gen. Dynamics Corp., N.Y.C., 1966-68; chief counsel office of fgn. direct investments U.S. Dept. Commerce, Washington, 1969-71; ptnr. Schaeffer, Dale, Vogel & Tavrow, N.Y.C., 1971-75; v.p., sec., gen. counsel Prudential Lines, Inc., N.Y.C., 1975-78; v.p., sec., gen. counsel Am. Pres. Lines Ltd., Oakland, Calif., 1978-80, sr. v.p., sec., gen. counsel, 1980-82, sr. v.p. legal and govt. affairs, 1982—, also bd. dirs.; sr. v.p., sec., gen. counsel, bd. dirs. Am. Pres. Cos., Ltd., Oakland, 1983—; instr. Harvard Coll., 1959-61; lectr. Am. Mgmt. Assn., Practising Law Inst. Contbg. author: Private Investors Abroad - Problems and Solutions in International Business, 1970. Recipient Silver Medal award Dept. Commerce, 1970; Fulbright scholar, 1961-62. Mem. ABA, State Bar Calif., Internat. Bar Assn., Am. Soc. Internat. Law, Maritime Law Assn., San Francisco Bar Assn., Asia-Pacific Lawyers Assn., Transp. Lawyers Assn., Am. Steamship Owners Mut. Protection and Indemnity Assn. (dir.), Pacific Mcht. Shipping Assn. (dir., chmn. bd. dirs.), Am. Corp. Counsel Assn., Am. Soc. Corp. Secs. Inc., Calif. C. of C. (state transp. com.), Harvard Law Sch. Assn., Navy League. Democrat. Jewish. Clubs: World Trade, Alpine Hills Swimming and Tennis, Lakeview (Oakland), Harvard (N.Y.C. and San Francisco). Office: Am President Cos Ltd 1800 Harrison St Oakland CA 94612

TAY, DAVID YEE-CHAW, biochemist; b. Rangoon, Burma, June 28, 1953; came to U.S., 1982; s. Tze-Hwa and Tao-Tzu (Fang) T.; m. Julia Shing-Hung, July 27, 1982. BS in Pharmacy, Nat. Taiwan U., Taipei, 1978; MS in Chemistry, Eastern N.Mex. U., 1984. Registered pharmacist, Taiwan. Asst. leader Panlabs Taiwan, Ltd., Taipei, 1979-80; pharmacist Cen. Trust of China, Hwalien, Taiwan, 1980-81; research assoc. City of Hope Med. Ctr., Duarte, Calif., 1984—. Contbr. articles to profl. jours. Mem. Am. Chem. Soc. Home: 3818 Durfee Ave #2 El Monte CA 91732 Office: City of Hope Nat Med Ctr Dept Endocrinology Metabolism Diabetes 1550, E Duarte Rd Duarte CA 91010

TAYLOR, ANDREW CLAYTON, publishing company executive; b. Auburn, Wash., July 16, 1957; s. Walter Clayton and Betty Finch T. m. Junko Yajima, Nov. 18, 1981; 1 child, Samuel Yajima. BS in Journalism and Japanese, U. Oreg., 1976-80. Customs broker George S. Bush Co., Seattle, 1980-81; editor Far East Reporters, Tokyo, 1981-83; pres. Japan Pacific Publs., Gig Harbor, Wash., 1983—; bd. dirs. Knapp Coll. Travel-Tourism Bd.; mem. Wash. State Internat. Tourism Com., 1983—; publisher Pacific Companion visitor guide, 1983. Editor: Far East Traveler mag., 1980. Democrat. Episcopalian. Avocations: skiing, golf, sailing. Office: Japan Pacific Publs PO Box 3092 Seattle WA 98114

TAYLOR, ANN, artist; b. Rochester, N.Y., 1941. Student, Vassar Coll.; BA, The New Sch. Social Research. One-woman shows include Carol Solway Gallery, Cin., 1964, York Gallery, N.Y.C., 1967, Hunter Gallery, Aspen, Colo., 1970, Christopher Gallery, N.Y.C., 1975, 77, Miller Gallery, Cin., 1978, 83, Munson Gallery, Santa Fe., 1980, Oxford Gallery, Rochester, 1980, 84, 87, C.G. Rein Galleries, Mpls., 1981, Scottsdale, Ariz., 1982, 85, Houston, 1983, Yuma (Ariz.) Art Ctr., 1984, Gallery Henoch, N.Y.C., 1984, Scottsdale Ctr. for Arts, 1985, Kauffman Galleries, Houston, 1986, Marilyn Butler Fine Art, Scottsdale, 1987, others; solo exhibition or solo traveling exhibition: Rochester Mus. and Scis. Ctr., 1984-85, Palm Springs Desert Mus., 1984-85, Yuma Art Ctr., 1984-85, Reed Whipple Cultural Ctr., 1984-85, Scottsdale Ctr. for the Arts, 1984-85, Beaumont Art Mus., 1984-85; exhibited in group shows at Indpls. Ctr. for Contemporary Art, Gallery of Modern Art, N.Y.C., Fine Art Ctr., Tempe, Ariz., Everson Mus., Syracuse, N.Y., Walton-Gilbert Galleries, San Francisco, Adelle M. Fine Art, Dallas, Janet Fleischer Gallery, Phila., Peter M. David Gallery, Mpls., Mickelson Gallery, Washington, Julia Black Gallery, Taos, N.Mex., Palm Springs Desert Mus., Scottsdale Ctr. for the Arts, Ariz. State U.; represented in permanent collections Bank of Am., Houston, Am. Express, Phoenix, Bausch & Lomb, Inc., Rochester, A.C. Nielsen Corp., Chgo., 1st Interstate Bank, Phoenix, Honeywell, Inc., Mpls., Xerox, Rochester, Lincoln Chase Trust Co., Rochester, Third Nat. Bank, Dayton, Ohio, Cen. Trust Co., Cin., Valley Nat. Bank, Phoenix, Butterfield Savs. & Loan, Santa Ana, Calif., Sohio Petroleum Co., Houston, A.C. Neilsen Corp., Chgo., others.

TAYLOR, BARBARA KLINE, consultant; b. Phila., Aug. 10, 1945; d. Bernard and Mary Helen (Warren) K.; m. Robert Ellsworth Taylor, Dec. 21, 1985. BS, Temple U., 1969; MA, Mich. State U., 1977; EdD, Va. Tech. U., 1981. Adminstrv. intern Pima Community Coll., Tucson, 1979, Tex. Instruments, Dallas, 1979-80; coordinator, research specialist Nat. Ctr. for Research in Vol. Edn., Columbus, Ohio, 1981-83, asst. dir. nat. acad., 1983-84, dir. nat. acad., 1984-86; cons. Taylor and Taylor, Silver City, N.Mex., 1986—; tech. advisor U.S. Dept. Edn., Washington, 1985-86. Author: Vocational Education and Economic Development in the united States, 1985. Mott Found. scholar, 1970; Univ. Denver Dept. Edn. fellow, 1978-81, Carl Duisberg Soc. exchange fellow, 1985. Mem. Am. Vocat. Edn. Personnel Devel. Assn. (sec., treas. 1985-86, pres.-elect 1986-87), Am. Soc. Tng. and Devel. (sec., 1985-86, v.p. for profl. devel. 1984-85), Am. Vocat. Assn., Am. Vocat. Edn. Research Assn., Phi Delta Kappa. Club: Bus. and Profl. Women (Silver City, N.Mex.). Avocations: cooking, flower arranging, antiques. Home and Office: HCR 88061 35 McMillen Rd Silver City NM 88061

TAYLOR, DELORIS "LOIS", oil company executive; b. Osceola, Ark., Dec. 25, 1931; d. Milo and Roetta (Grogan) Overstreet; m. Virgil N. Taylor, July 3, 1948. Student pub. schs., Conroe, Tex. With McClellan Oil Corp., Roswell, N.Mex., 1959—, head land dept., fin. dept., 1962-80, sec.-treas., head fin., 1972—, also dir.; dir. Sulimar Corp., Cortez Drilling Co., both Roswell; instr. Eastern N.Mex. U., Roswell campus, mem. adv. com. on support personnel program, 1982—; mem. adv. com. Office Edn. for Roswell and Goddard High Schs., 1986-87. Ch. clk. Tabernacle Baptist Ch., Roswell, 1954—, in charge women's prayer group and mem. choir; co-chair. oil and gas div. United Way. Mem. Altrusa. Democrat. Club: Roswell Desk & Derrick (sponsor 198-87). Home: 1012 N Lea Ave Roswell NM 88201

TAYLOR, DOUGLAS GRAHAM, Canadian provincial minister and member legislative assembly; b. Wolseley, Sask., Can., July 4, 1936; s. Robert Douglas and Isabella Roy (Graham) T.; m. Katherine Isabel Garden, Oct. 3, 1959; children—Robert Douglas, Katherine Isabel Marie, Susan Joan, Peter Samuel. B.Ed., U. Regina (Sask.), 1966, Diploma in Ednl. Adminstrn., 1972. Tchr. Kipling (Sask.) High Sch., 1962-64; prin. Wolseley High Sch., 1967-79; mem. Sask. Legis. Assembly for Indian Head-Wolseley, 1979—, minister of health, opposition house leader, 1979, opposition critic for edn. and continuing edn., minister of tourism and small bus., minister-in-charge Sask. Property Mgmt. Corp. (formerly dept. Supply and Services), Sask. Econ. Devel. Corp., No. Affairs Secretariat, Higher Control Bd., Liquor Commn.; mem Cabinet planning and priority coms.; Founder Qu'Appelle Valley Sci. Fair, Sask. Mem. Indian Head Superintendency Tchrs.' Assn., pres., Qu'Appelle Valley Prins.' Assn. Progressive Conservative. Mem. United Ch. of Canada. Club: Lions (Wolseley). Office: Legis Bldg, Room 38, Regina, SK Canada S4S 0B3

TAYLOR, DOUGLAS MICHAEL, podiatrist; b. Oakland, Calif., Aug. 16, 1951; s. David Harwell and Dorothy Mae (Grafe) T.; m. Celeste Rosanne Moe, Aug. 13, 1977; children: Michael Raymond, Rebecca Sarah. BS, U. San Francisco, 1974; D in Podiatric Medicine, Ohio Coll. Podiatric Medicine, 1983. Diplomate Nat. Bd. Podiatry Examiners; cert. tchr. community colls., Calif. Nursing asst. Hayward (Calif.) Hosp., 1970-79; tchr. Hayward Unified Sch. Dist., 1974-79; resident in podiatry VA Med. Ctr., Battle Creek, Mich., 1983-84; pvt. practice podiatry Walnut Creek, Calif., 1986—; podiatrist Mt. Diablo Med. Ctr., Concord, Calif., 1986—, Walnut Creek Hosp., 1986—, Oak Park Convalescent Hosp., Pleasant Hill, Calif., 1986—. Author: Podiatric Dermatology, 1986. Mem. Am. Podiatric Med. Assn., Alameda/Contra Costa Podiatry Soc., Calif. Podiatric Med. Assn., Walnut Creek C. of C. (ambassador 1985—). Republican. Roman Catholic. Lodge: Lions. Avocations: tennis, jogging, swimming. Office: Assoc Podiatry Group Walnut Creek 1844 San Miguel Dr #310 Walnut Creek CA 94596

TAYLOR, EDWARD STEWART, physician, educator; b. Hecla, S.D., Aug. 20, 1911; s. Robert Stewart and Sylvia Frances (Dewey) T.; m. Ruth Fatherson, June 15, 1940; children: Edward Stewart, Elizabeth Dewey Taylor Bryant, Catherine Wells Taylor Lynn. B.A., U. Iowa, 1933, M.D., 1936. Diplomate Am. Bd. Ob-Gyn (dir. 1962-69). Intern, Hurley Hosp., Flint, Mich., 1936-37; splty. tng. ob-gyn L.I. Coll. Hosp., 1937-41; prof. ob-gyn, chmn. dept. Sch. Medicine, U. Colo., 1947-76, clin. prof., 1976-81, prof., chmn. emeritus, 1981—; cons. ob-gyn Fitzsimons Gen. Hosp.; attending obstetrician and gynecologist St. Joseph's Hosp., Rose Hosp. Med. Center, both Denver; nat. cons. ob-gyn to surg. gen. USAF, 1958-62. Author: Manual of Gynecology, 1952, Essentials of Gynecology, 4th edit.; editor: Beck's Obstetrical Practice, 10th edit.; editor-in-chief for obstetrics: Obstetrical and Gynecol. Survey. Trustee Denver Symphony Orch., 1979-85. Served to lt. col. AUS, 1943-45; surgeon 107th Evacuation Hosp., ETO. Fellow ACS, Am. Coll. Obstetricians and Gynecologists (Disting. Service award 1984); mem. AMA, Am. Gynecol. Soc. (v.p. 1974-75), Am. Assn. Obstetricians and Gynecologists (pres. 1970-71), Central Assn. Obstetricians and Gynecologists, S.W. Obstetrical and Gynecol. Soc., Am. Gynecol. and Obstetrical Soc., Assn. Profs. Ob-Gyn (pres. 1974-75), Western Surg. Soc., Finnish Gynecol. Soc. (hon.), Alpha Omega Alpha. Congregationalist. Club: Univ. (Denver). Home: 80 S Dexter St Denver CO 80222 Office: 4545 E 9th Ave Denver CO 80220

TAYLOR, GAYLAND WAYNE, civil engineer, public relations executive; b. Midland, Tex., Aug. 12, 1958; s. Samuel Lee and Ardis Faye (Padgitt) T. BSCE, Prairie View A&M U.; postgrad., U. Phoenix. Civil engr. Ariz. Pub. Service, Phoenix, 1982—; pres. Spartan Studios, Phoenix; com. chmn. minority adv. bd. Sta. KPNX-TV, Phoenix, 1983—. Editor Fundamentals of Electricity, 1986; editor, pub. Unitech News, 1986—. Dem. dep. registrar, Phoenix, 1986; asst. scout master Boy Scouts Am., Phoenix, 1983—; City of Phoenix Equal Opportunity Fair Housing Program, 1987; mem. Phoenix Urban League, 1983; advisor Jr. Achievement, Phoenix, 1982-84, 86. Recipient Leadership award Valley Christian Ctrs., Phoenix, 1982-83, Tng. & Leadership award Boy Scouts Am., Phoenix, 1984. Mem. NSPE, ASCE, ASME, Ariz. Sect. Civil Engrs., Am. Nuclear Soc., Ariz. Small Bus. Assn., Nat. Black Media Coalition, Am. Assn. Blacks in Energy, Inst. Indsl. Engrs., Ariz. Black C. of C. (chmn. pub. relations), U.S. C. of C., Ariz. Council of Black Engrs. and Scientists (chmn. pub. relations 1985-87, Nat. bd. dirs. 1986—, editor newsletter 1982—), Les Beaux Cultural Fraternity (treas. 1977—). Club: Phoenix City, Toastmasters (Phoenix). Lodges: Masons, Optimists. Avocations: photography, scouting, collecting stamps and records. Home: 3834 W Mitchell Dr Phoenix AZ 85019 Office: Ariz Pub Service Co PO Box 21666 Sta 5414 2216 W Peoria Ave Phoenix AZ 85036 address: PO Box 23832 Phoenix AZ 85063

TAYLOR, GORDON THOMAS, biological oceanography educator; b. Buffalo, Apr. 28, 1952; s. Gordon Howard and Marilyn (Naudascher) T.; m. Janice Goodson, May 18, 1986. BA, SUNY, Binghamton, 1974; PhD, U. So. Calif., 1983. Asst. project engr. Betz Environ. Engrs., Plymouth Meeting, Pa., 1974-76; asst. scientist U. Hawaii, Honolulu, 1983—; cons. Harbor Environ. Projects, Los Angeles, 1978-81. Contbr. articles to profl. jours. Mem. AAAS, Am. Soc. Microbiology, Am. Soc. Limnology and Oceanography, Hawaiian Acad. Sci., Sigma Xi (grantee 1978). Democrat. Avocations: underwater photography, scuba, running. Office: U Hawaii Dept Oceanography 1000 Pope Rd Honolulu HI 96822

TAYLOR, HELEN L. (SALLY), education educator; b. Seattle, Apr. 16, 1932; d. Floyd E. and Mabel (Smith) Rowe; m. James Gavin Taylor, Feb. 11, 1955; children: Julianne, Gavin. BA, U. Wash., 1954; MS, Cen. Wash. U., 1978; postgrad., La Catolica U., Lima, Peru, 1983. Cert. vocat. tchr., Wash., hort. therapist. Instr. early childhood edn. Seattle Cen. Community Coll., 1963-70, Edmonds Community Coll., Lynnwood, Wash., 1970—; cons. Seattle Pub. Schs., 1966-69; trainer Wash. State Tech. Assistance Tng. Office, Seattle, 1975-82. Contbr. articles to profl. jours. Vice chmn. Snohomish County Children's Commn., Everett, Wash., 1986; steering com. Human Services Coalition, 1986. Fulbright scholar, 1983. Mem. Nat. Edn. Assn. Young Children, World Orgn. for Early Childhood Edn., Nat. Council Therapy and Rehab. Through Horticulture. Avocations: horses, gardening, reading, swimming. Office: Edmonds Community Coll. 20000 68th W Lynnwood WA 98036

TAYLOR, IRVING, mechanical engineer, consultant; b. Schenectady, N.Y., Oct. 25, 1912; s. John Bellamy and Marcia Estabrook (Jones) T.; m. Shirley Ann Milker, Dec. 22, 1943; children: Bronwen D., Marcia L., John I., Jerome E. BME, Cornell U., 1934. Registered profl. engr., N.Y., Mass., Calif. Test engr. Gen. Electric Co., Lynn, Mass., 1934-37; asst. mech. engr. M.W. Kellogg Co., N.Y.C., 1937-39; sect. head engring. dept. The Lummus Co., N.Y.C., 1939-57; research engr. Gilbert and Barker, West Springfield, Mass., 1957-58, Marquardt Corp., Ogden, Utah, 1958-60, Bechtel, Inc., San Francisco, 1960-77; cons. engr. Berkeley, Calif., 1977—. Contbr. articles to profl. jours. Mem. ASME (life), Pacific Energy Assn., Soaring Soc. Am. (life), Sigma Xi (assoc.). Unitarian. Avocation: sailplane soaring, skiing. Home: 1150 Keeler Ave Berkeley CA 94708

TAYLOR, JACK STANLEY, social worker; b. Atlanta, Mar. 14, 1937; s. Morris David and Ida Fanny (Kovsky) T.; m. Jerri Ann McKee, Apr. 7, 1962; children: Terrell, Sydney, Stuart. BA, Ga. State U., 1962; MSW, Our Lady of the Lake Coll., 1975; postgrad., Command and Gen. Staff. Coll., 1978. Advanced through grades to lt. col. U.S. Army Med. Service Corps., 1962-82; counselor med. dept. The Boeing Co., Seattle, 1983—; cons. Nat. Council Juvenile and Family Ct. Judges, U. Nev., Reno, 1978—; lectr., Seattle U., 1983-85; tchr., Ft. Steilacoom Coll., 1980-81, Columbia Coll., Mo., 1978-79. Tchr. Temple Beth-El, Tacoma, 1977-79. Decorated Bronze Star, 1974, Legion of Merit, 1982. Mem. Nat. Assn. Social Workers (bd. dirs.), Wash. State Substance Abuse Profl. Assn., Phi Gamma Mu, Tau Epsilon Phi (pres. 1960-62). Jewish. Club: Oakbrook Golf and Country. Avocations: water skiing, family outings, stereo and recording equipment. Home: 7115 Zircon Ct SW Tacoma WA 98498 Office: The Boeing Co PO Box 3707 MS 11-40 Seattle WA 98124

TAYLOR, JACQULYN JOYCE, technical services specialist; b. Roswell, N.Mex., Sept. 8, 1955; d. Wilson Dewane and Bernice Irene (Sanderson) T. BS in History, Ea. N.Mex. U., 1978. Library asst. I Golden Library Ea. N.Mex. U., Portales, 1978-80; tech. services asst. Roswell Pub. Library, 1980-81; tech. services specialist N.Mex. Mil. Inst., Roswell, 1981—. Mem. AAUW (pres. Roswell br. 1983—, rep. to capts. adv. com. Roswell Neighborhood Watch, 1985, sec., rep. 1986). Avocations: crafts, painting, collecting. Office: N Mex Mil Inst Toles Learning Ctr College and N Main Roswell NM 88201

TAYLOR, JAMES WALTER, marketing professor; b. St. Cloud, Minn., Feb. 15, 1933; s. James T. and Nina C. Taylor; m. Joanne Syktte, Feb. 3, 1956; children: Theodore James, Samuel Bennett, Christopher John. BBA, U. Minn., 1957; MBA, NYU, 1960; D in Bus. Adminstrn., U. So. Calif., 1975. Mgr. research div. Atlantic Refining, Phila., 1960-65; dir. new product devel. Hunt-Wesson Foods, Fullerton, Calif., 1965-72; prof. Calif. State U., Fullerton, 1972—; cons. Knudsen, Inc., Los Angeles, 1975-82, Chiat Day Advt., Los Angeles, 1982-85, Moray Industries, Devonport, New Zealand, 1985—. Author: Profitable New Product Strategies, 1984, How To Create A Winning Business Plan, 1980, Competitive Marketing Strategies, 1986, The 101 Best Performing Companies In America, 1986. Served with USN, 1952-53. Fulbright scholar Ministry of Industry, Lisbon, Portugal, 1986-87. Mem. North Am. Soc. Corp. Planners, Am. Mktg. Assn., Strategic Mgmt. Assn., Assn. for Consumer Research, Acad. Mktg. Sci. Home: 3190 Mountain View Dr Laguna Beach CA 92651 Office: Calif State U Dept of Marketing Fullerton CA 92634

TAYLOR, JANE CARVEY, real estate consultant; b. Nashville, Apr. 15, 1927; d. Thomas B. and Florence E. (Haney) Carvey; m. Waller Taylor, II, Oct. 31, 1947 (div. 1972); children: Stephen, Grant, Waller. BA, U. Puget Sound, 1977; postgrad. U. Alaska, 1977. Investor, real estate cons. Sun Valley, Idaho, 1970-80; exec. v.p. JDF Fin. Corp., Palm Springs, Calif., 1981-82; account exec. Heinold Commodities, Bellevue, Wash., 1982-83; exclusive agt. Thousand Trails, Bellevue, 1984-85; v.p. Landnet, Inc., Bellevue, 1985-86; co-owner Capstone Corp., Bellevue, 1986—. Active Las Madrinas Children's Hosp., 1959-86; pres. Jr. League Pasadena, 1959-60; docent Council Los Angeles Mus. Art, 1963-66; bd. dirs. Otis Art Inst., 1967-70. Mem. Acad. Real Estate. Republican. Episcopalian. Office: Capstone Corp 405 114th Ave SE Bellevue WA 98004

TAYLOR, JOHN JOSEPH, nuclear engineer; b. Hackensack, N.J., Feb. 27, 1922; s. John J.D. and Johanna F. (Thibideau) T.; m. Lorraine Crowley, Feb. 5, 1943; children: John B., Nancy M., Susan M. BA, St. John's U., Jamaica, N.Y., 1942, PhD, 1975; MS, U. Notre Dame, 1947. Mathematician Bendix Aviation Corp., Teterburo, N.J., 1946-47; engr. Kellex Corp., N.Y.C., 1947-50; v.p. water realtor div. Westinghouse Electric Corp., Pitts., 1950-81; v.p. nuclear power Electric Power Research Inst., Palo Alto, Calif., 1981—; mem. adv. com. Oak Ridge (Tenn.) Nat. Lab., 1973-83, Brookhaven Nat. Lab., Upton, N.Y., 1986—, Argonne (Chgo.) Nat. Lab., 1980-86, bd. dirs.; cons. office of Sci. and Tech., Washington, 1975-78. Co-author Reactor Shielding Manual, 1953, Naval Reactor Physics Manual; contbr. articles to profl. jours. Served to lt. (j.g.) USN, 1942-45. Recipient Order of Merit, Westinghouse Electric Corp., 1957. Fellow AAAS (bd. dirs.), Am. Nuclear Soc. (bd. dirs.); mem. Am. Phys. Soc., Nat. Acad. Engring. Republican. Roman Catholic. Home: 15 Oliver Ct Menlo Park CA 94025 Office: Electric Power Research Inst Palo Alto CA 94303

TAYLOR, JUANITA EDNA, educator; b. Pueblo, Colo., Apr. 22, 1922; d. Mike and Myrtle (Chavalia) Joseph; children—Michael Frank, Peter Adrian. B.A., Adams State Coll., 1952, M.A., 1961; postgrad. U. Calif.-Riverside, 1955-59, U. Okla.-Norman, 1966. Psychiatric nurse Pueblo State Hosp., Colo., 1940-42; chauffeur USAF, Buckley Field, Colo., 1942-44; pharmacist mate U.S. Navy, 1944-46; tchr. pub. schs., Colo., Calif., 1949-59; supt. schs. Costilla County, Colo., 1959-62; supr. resident relations Denver Housing Authority, 1962-66; owner Queen Bee Antiques, 1976—; adminstr. Migrant Ednl. Program, 1957-58 edn. advisor State Dept., Montevideo, Uruguay, 1967-69; program rev. and resources officer Office of Child Devel. HEW, 1969-73; children's services specialist Community Services Adminstrn. HEW, Denver, 1973-76; cons. Office Econ. Ops., State Colo., 1966; asst. dir. Planning for Voc. Rehab., Colo., 1966-67; treas. Fulbright Commn., Montevideo, 1968-69. Vice chmn. Rep. Party, Costilla County, 1956, committee-woman, 1957; sec. Costilla County C. of C., 1955-59. Recipient Cash award, HEW, 1974; Doll Artist award Rocky Mt. region, 1984. Mem. NEA, Colo. Edn. Assn., Colo. Assn. County Supts. (sec. 1958-59), Calif. Edn. Assembly (5th grade rep., del.), DHA Employees Assn. (sec., exec. bd., treas. 1962-65), Am. Legion. Roman Catholic. Club: Catharis Theatre. Office: 2727 W 27th Ave Denver CO 80211

TAYLOR, KENDRICK JAY, microbiologist; b. Manhattan, Mont., Mar. 17, 1914; s. William Henry and Rose (Carney) T.; B.S., Mont. State U., 1938; postgrad. (fellow) U. Wash., 1938-41, U. Calif. at Berkeley, 1952, Drama Studio of London, 1985; m. Hazel Marguerite Griffith, July 28, 1945; children: Stanley, Paul, Richard. Research microbiologist Cutter Labs., Berkeley, Calif., 1945-74; microbiologist Berkeley Biologicals, 1975—. Committeeman Mount Diablo council Boy Scouts Am., 1955, dist. vice-chmn., 1960-61, dist. chmn., 1962-65, cubmaster, 1957, scoutmaster, 1966; active Contact Ministries, 1977-80; bd. dirs. Santa Clara Community Players, 1980-84; vol. instr. English as a Second Lang., 1979-80; vol. ARC Blood Ctr., VA Hosp., Berkeley. Served with AUS, 1941-46, lt. col. Res., ret. Recipient Scout's Wood badge Boy Scouts Am., 1962. Mem. Am. Soc. Microbiology (chmn. local com. 1953, v.p. No. Calif. br. 1963-65, pres. 1965-67), Sons and Daus. Mont. Pioneers. Presbyterian (trustee 1951-53, elder 1954—). Home: 550 S 13th St San Jose CA 95112 Office: Berkeley Biologicals 2d and Hearst Sts Berkeley CA 94710

TAYLOR, LEIGHTON ROBERT, JR., marine biologist; b. Glendale, Calif., Nov. 17, 1940; s. Leighton Robert and Mary A. (Highberger) T.; BA, Occidental Coll., 1962; MS, U. Hawaii, 1965; PhD, Scripps Instn. Oceanography, 1972; MBA, Chaminade U., 1985. m. Linda Louise Pudet, Feb. 2, 1963; children—Leighton, Maria Louise. Mus. curator Scripps Instn. Oceanography, 1971-72; mem. grad. faculty dept. zoology U. Hawaii, Honolulu, 1972—, dir. Waikiki Aquarium, 1975-86; fishery biologist U.S. Fish and Wildlife Service, Honolulu, 1972-75; dep. exec. dir. Calif. Acad. Scis., San Francisco, 1986—; research assoc. Calif. Acad. Scis. Bd. dirs. Lahaina Restoration Found., 1976—; pres. Hawaiian Islands Aquarium Corp., 1984-86. Fellow Am. Assn. Zool. Parks and Aquariums; mem. Bishop Mus. Assn., Hawaii Small Bus. Assn., Explorers Club, Western Soc. Naturalists, Am. Miscellaneous Soc. Clubs: Bohemian, Outrigger Canoe. Contbr. articles to profl. jours. Office: Calif Acad Scis Golden Gate Park San Francisco CA 94118

TAYLOR, LELAND THOMAS, agricultural products executive; b. Topeka. Student in Physics, U. N.Mex., 1967-71. Assoc. engr. Manzano Labs. div. Sandia Corp., Albuquerque, 1967-72; pres. Agronics, Inc. (formerly Farm Guard Products), Albuquerque, 1967—, Nat. Resources Gasification, Albuquerque, 1985; pres., chief exec. officer Kleen Tek, Albuquerque, 1985—. Patentee chemistry devices. Recipient subscription scholarship IEEE, 1963-67. Mem. AAAS. Republican. Home: 701 Madison St NE Albuquerque NM 87110 Office: Agronics Inc 3620 Wyoming NE Suite 205 Albuquerque NM 87111

TAYLOR, LENNY LEE, consultant, corporation executive, writer; b. Weston, W.Va., June 30, 1941; s. Clifford Albert and Monna Madeline (Bonnett) T.; m. Leticia Liwanag Suarez, Apr. 18, 1965; children: Jonathan Len, Timothy Lee, Matthew Paul. Student U. S.C., 1960-61, U. Md., 1965-66; AB, U. Philippines, 1969; postgrad. U. Colo.-Denver, 1975-76. Ordained to ministry Evang. Ch. Alliance; mem. Bible Fellowship Ch.; lic. realtor, ins. broker. Speakers bur. rep., prodn. analyst, merchandising analyst Western Electric Co., Denver, 1970-75; dist./adminstrv. aide, rep. U.S. Congressman James P. Johnson, 4th Dist. Colo., 1975-81; pres., owner, prin. mgr. Taylor Internat. Services, Denver, also Len Taylor and Assocs. and Taylor Communications Group, 1981—; pub. affairs adminstr. United Bank of Denver, 1983-84; mktg. acct. exec. Kaiser Found. Health Plan, Denver, 1985-86; cons. to govs., non-profit orgns., bus. and industry; tchr. seminars, lectures. Bd. dirs. Filipino-Am. Community of Colo., Inc., 1974-82; mem. Leadership Denver Assn; bd. dirs. Denver Christian Servicemen's Cen., Inc.; bd. dirs., co-founder Assocs. in Ministry Chs., Inc., Ramona, Calif.; mem. Metro North Denver C. of C.; bd. dirs. Metro YMCA, 1981; bd. mgrs. Adams County YMCA, chmn., 1981, Vol. of Yr. award, 1981; chmn. State Senate Dist. 17 br. Rep. Cen. Com., 1979-80; mem. U.S. Jaycees, 1973-75. Served with USAF, 1962-67; Vietnam. Mem. Assn. Profl. Cons. Internat., Am. Soc. Pub. Adminstrn., Am. Entrepreneurs Assn., Am. Soc. Tng. and Devel., Am. Soc. Profl. Cons., Pro Denver, Colo. Group Ins. Assn., Nat. Speakers Assn., Internat. Platform Assn. Club: Rotary. Editor News-Notes, 1974-75; contbr. articles to newspapers. Office: 13073 Dyanna Dr Suite 101 Denver CO 80241

TAYLOR, LESTER DEAN, economics educator, consultant; b. Toledo, Iowa, Mar. 8, 1938; s. Samuel George and Willa Emma (Brown) T.; m. Carol Austin, Aug. 13, 1966 (div. May 1980); children—James, Rebecca. B.A., U. Iowa, 1960; Ph.D., Harvard U., 1963. Instr., Harvard U., Cambridge, Mas., 1963, asst. prof. econs., 1964-68; staff economist Council Econ. Advisers, Washington, 1964-65; adviser Harvard Inst. Internat. Devel., Bogotá, Colombia, 1967-68; assoc. prof. econs. U. Mich., Ann Arbor, 1969-74; prof.

U. Ariz., Tucson, 1974—. Author: (with H.S. Houthakker) Consumer Demand in the U.S., 1966, 2d, rev. edit., 1970; Telecommunications Demand, 1980. Woodrow Wilson fellow Harvard U., 1960-62. Mem. Phi Beta Kappa. Home: PO Box 689 Wilson WY 83014

TAYLOR, LINDA BODE, psychotherapist; b. Ann Arbor, Mich., July 20, 1948; d. Frank Carter and Lenore Elizabeth (Bode) T. AB in Psychology, U. Mich., 1970, MSW, 1973. Lic. clin. social worker. Social service practitioner San Joaquin County Children's Services, Stockton, Calif., 1974-76; psychiat. social worker Napa (Calif.) State Hosp., 1976-78; personnel asst. Crocker Bank, San Francisco, 1979-80; psychosocial cons. Work Return, San Francisco, 1981-82; pvt. practice psychotherapy Berkeley, 1980—; mem. creative arts therapy conf. Sonoma State U., Rohnert Park, Calif., 1985-87. Exhibitor Bus. Women's Expo, Oakland, 1985, Oakland Symphony Soc., Oakland C. of C., 1985; planning com. Youth in Bus. Day, San Francisco Jaycees, 1982. Mem. Nat. Assn. Social Workers, Calif. Assn. Marriage and Family Therapists, Assn. Transpersonal Psychology, Bay Area Orgnl. Devel. Network, Wall St. Women (fin. change seminars 1984-86). Democrat. Club: Last Monday. Avocations: music, travel, sailing. Office: 2607 Alcatraz Suite 5 Berkeley CA 94705

TAYLOR, LINDA JEAN THORTON, information systems executive; b. Cambridge, Mass., Apr. 16, 1942; d. Ferdinand and Hazel Irene (Towne) Karamanoukian; m. John Robert Thornton, Jan. 21, 1961; 1 son, John Robert; m. F. Jason Gaskell, Nov. 30, 1978. A.A. in Bus. Adminstrn., West Los Angeles Coll., 1976; B.S., West Coast U., 1978, M.S. in Bus. and Info. Scis., 1980. Asst. to chief indsl. engr. Pitts. Plate Glass Co., Boston, 1960-64; corp. sec., gen. mgr. Seaboard Planning Corp., Boston, 1967-67, Los Angeles, 1969-72; prin. Tay-Kara Mgmt., Los Angeles, 1972-73; chief systems adminstrn. Comp-La, Los Angeles, 1973-74; mgr. systems analysis Trans Tech Inc., Los Angeles, 1974-77; mgr. software engring. and tech. audit depts. System Devel. Corp., Los Angeles, 1977-81; v.p. Gaskell & Taylor Engring., Inc., Los Angeles, 1981-86 ; pres. Taylor & Zeno Systems, Inc., 1986—; sr. lectr. West Coast U., Los Angeles, 1980—; vis. lectr. sr. seminar Calif. Poly. U., Pomona, 1978, 87; appeared in 8 episodes of The New Literacy: An Introduction to Computers, Pub. Broadcasting System. Chmn. bus. and profl. women's com. Calif. Republican Central Com., 1974; mem. White House Com. on Workers Compensation, 1976; mem. fiscal adv. com. Santa Monica Unified Sch. Bd. Edn., 1979-81. Recipient Pub. Service award West Los Angeles C. of C., 1974. Mem. Assn. Women in Computing (pres. 1980-84, v.p. Los Angeles chpt. 1979-80), Nat. Computer Conf. (vice chmn., program com. 1980, mem. adv. com. 1983), Data Processing Mgmt. Assn. (v.p. South Bay chpt. 1979-80, dir. Los Angeles chpt. 1984, chmn. program com., media relations com. 1984 internat. conf., Performance award 1984), IEEE (software engring. terminology task force 1980), Assn. Systems Mgmt. (sec. local chpt. 1974-75), EDP Auditors Assn., Assn. for Computing Machinery, Women in Mgmt., Nat. Assn. Women Bus. Owners, Ind. Computer Cons. Assn. Office: Taylor & Zeno Systems Inc 3572 Greenfield Ave Los Angeles CA 90034

TAYLOR, MARCUS JAMES, geophysicist; b. Fontana, Calif., Oct. 30, 1957; s. Robert William and Audrey Helene (Meek) T. BSME, U. Calif., Davis, 1980, MS in Geophysics, 1983, postgrad., 1983—. Lab. asst. U. Calif., Davis, 1975-79, researcher, 1979-82; contract researcher Calif. State Lands Commn., Sacramento, 1982-86, Gonzo Labs., Davis, 1986—; head scientist western regional div. U.S. Geol. Survey, Sacramento, 1987—. Contbr. articles to profl. jours. Mem. Am. Geophys. Union. Democrat. Buddhist. Home: 3000 Cowell Blvd #251 Davis CA 95616 Office: Western Regional div US Geol Survey 2800 Cottage Way Sacramento CA 95825

TAYLOR, MARIA BROWNETT, medical equipment company executive; b. El Paso, Tex., Sept. 11, 1945; d. Francis Harold and Harriet (Whitehurst) Brownett; m. Maxwell Ford Taylor, Nov. 25, 1967 (div. June 1978); children: Brian Harold, Bradley Ford. BS in Med. Tech., U. N.C., 1967. Cert. med. technologist; cert. vol. personnel administr. Mgr. staff programs City of Colorado Springs, Colo., 1978-85; dir. administrn. Xanar Inc., Colorado Springs, 1985—. Author: (jour.) FBI Law Enforcement Bulletin, 1982; Police Volunteer Program (awarded and recognized by Internat. Assn. of City Mgrs., and Am. Assn. of Retired Persons), Senior Victim Assistance Team, 1980 (named creative program of yr. by Nat. Assn. of Vols. in Criminal Justice, 1983). Chmn. bd. dirs. Colo. Office of Voluntarism, Denver, 1980-85, pres. 1982-85; trustee Colorado Springs Dance Theatre, 1981-85, pres. 1985-87; trustee Meml. Hosp., Colorado Springs, 1983—; bd. dirs. Health Assn., 1981-83; bd. advisors Community Vol. Ctr., 1979-83, pres., 1981-83; mem. community services council Colorado Springs C. of C., 1986—. Named one of Outstanding Young Women of Am., 1980, 81; appointed to state bd. Gov. R. Lamm, Denver, 1980; recipient Outstanding Citizenship award, Mutual of Omaha Ins. Corp., 1985. Mem. Am. Soc. for Personnel Adminstrs., Jr. League (bd. dirs. Colorado Springs 1972—), Exec. Women Internat. Republican. Episcopalian. Avocations: skiing, tennis, whitewater rafting, theatre, art. Home: 120 W Del Norte Colorado Springs CO 80907 Office: Xanar Inc 2868 Janitell Rd Colorado Springs CO 80906

TAYLOR, MICHAEL JAMES, engineering and construction company executive; b. Des Moines, June 20, 1941; s. Robert Phillip and Evelyn (Brown) T.; m. Judith Brissette, Dec. 27, 1966; children: Jason Edmond, Bryan Michael, Jennifer Marie. BSCE, Carnegie Mellon, 1963; MSCE, Carnegie Mellon U., 1965. Registered profl. engr., Colo., Ill., Md., Mich., Minn., Mont., Nev., N.Mex., N.D., Ohio, Pa., Va., W.Va., Wyo. Engr. E. D'Appolonia, Pitts., 1964-65, from asst. project engr. to asst. project mgr., 1967-76; project mgr., v.p. tech. E. D'Appolonia, Denver, 1976-83; from v.p. to sr. v.p. Canonie Environ. Service Corp., Denver, 1983—. Contbr. articles to profl. jours.; chpts. to books; patentee in field. Served to lt. C.E., U.S. Army, 1965-67. Mem. ASCE, Am. Inst. Mining Engrs. Home: 9807 E Bayou Ridge Trail Parker CO 80134 Office: Canonie Environ Service Corp 6551 S Revere Pkwy #155 Englewood CO 80111

TAYLOR, MYRON CLINTON, bank executive; b. Kirtland, N.Mex., Sept. 29, 1940; s. Clinton McKay and Dixie (Dustin) T.; m. Revis Laverne Washburn, Sept. 10, 1963; children: Dean Myron, Alan McKay. BA, Brigham Young U., 1965; grad., U. Ill. Sch. Bank Investment, 1979. Loan officer 1st Nat. Bank, Farmington, N.Mex., 1965, auditor, comml. loans officer, investments officer, 1966—. Chmn. March of Dimes, Farmington, 1960-63, Muscular Dystrophy Assn., 1980—; adv. dir. Farmington Mus. Assn., 1981-86; bd. dirs. San Juan Regional Med. Ctr., 1983—; commr. recreation and cultural affairs City of Farmington Parks, N.Mex., 1987—. Mem. Am. Inst. Banking (cert.), N.Mex. Bankers Assn. (chmn. bank investment seminar 1983-84). Republican. Mormon. Office: 1st Nat Bank 100 E Broadway Farmington NM 87401

TAYLOR, PETER VAN VOORHEES, advertising and public relations consultant; b. Montclair, N.J., Aug. 25, 1934; s. John Coard and Mildred (McLaughlin) T.; BA in English, Duke U., 1956; m. Janet Kristine Kirkebo, Nov. 4, 1978; 1 son, John Coard III. Announcer, Sta. WQAM, Miami, 1956; announcer, program dir. Sta. KHVH, Honolulu, 1959-61; promotion mgr. Sta. KPEN, San Francisco, 1962; with Kaiser Broadcasting, 1962-74, Gen. Electric Broadcasting Co., 1974-78; program/ops. mgr. Sta. KFOG, San Francisco, 1962-66; mgr. Sta. WXHR AM/FM, Cambridge, Mass., 1966-67; gen. mgr. Sta. WJIB, Boston, 1967-70; mgr. FM div. Kaiser Broadcasting, 1969-72; v.p., gen. mgr. Sta. KFOG, San Francisco, 1970-78; pres. Taylor Communications, 1978—, No. Calif. Broadcasters Assn., 1975-77, Broadcast Skills Bank, 1975-76. Trustee, WDBS, Inc., Duke U., 1974-80; bd. dirs. San Francisco Better Bus. Bur., 1976-78. Served to lt. USCGR, 1957-63. Mem. Nat., Internat. radio clubs, Calif. Hist. Soc., Mus. Assn., Calif. Broadcasters Assn., San Francisco Symphony, Bay Area Publicity Club, San Francisco Advt. Club, Pub. Relations Soc. Am., Worldwide TV/FM Dx Assn. Clubs: Advt. Tennis Assn. (pres. 1976-77), San Francisco Tennis, Marina Tennis, Circle de L'Union, Olympic. Lodge: Rotary. Home: 2614 Jackson St San Francisco CA 94115 Office: 490 Post St Penthouse San Francisco CA 94102

TAYLOR, PHILIP CRAIG, physics educator; b. Paterson, N.J., Mar. 17, 1942; s. Philip D. and Elizabeth (Erdman) T.; m. Muriel Allison Taylor, Dec. 20, 1969; children: Allison L., Heather M. AB, Carleton Coll., 1964; PhD, Brown U., 1969. Research physicist Naval Research Lab., Washington, 1971-80, supervisory research physicist, 1980-82; prof. physics U. Utah, Salt Lake City, 1982—, dir. materials sci. research div. Laser Inst., 1986—. Fellow Am. Phys. Soc.; mem. AAAS, Materials Research Soc. Office: U Utah Dept Physics Salt Lake City UT 84112

TAYLOR, R. ERVIN JR., archaeologist; b. Los Angeles, Jan. 15, 1938; s. Royal Ervin and Francys Ellen (McMurtry) T.; m. Marilynn Julia Lampley, Aug. 22, 1959; children: Gregory Michael, Karen Louane. BA, Pacific Union Coll., 1960; MA, UCLA, 1965, PhD, 1969. Asst. prof. Calif. State U., Northridge, 1967-70; from assoc. prof. to prof. archaeology U. Calif., Riverside, 1970—. Author: Radiocarbon Dating, 1987; editor: Chronologies in New World Archaeology, 1978, Advances in Obsidian Glass Studies, 1980. Grantee NSF, 1978—. Fellow AAAS, Am. Anthropol. Assn.; mem. Southwestern Anthropol. Assn. (pres. 1965-76), Soc. Archaeol. Scis. (pres. 1982, gen. sec. 1982—). Home: 25155 Crestview Dr Loma Linda CA 92521 Office: U Calif Radiocarbon Lab Riverside CA 92354

TAYLOR, RICHARD EDWARD, physicist, educator; b. Medicine Hat, Alta., Can., Nov. 2, 1929; came to U.S., 1952; s. Clarence Richard and Delia Alena (Brunsdale) T.; m. Rita Jean Bonneau, Aug. 25, 1951; 1 child, Norman Edward. B.S., U. Alta., 1950, M.S., 1952; Ph.D., Stanford U., 1962; Docteur honoris causa, U. Paris-Sud, 1980. Boursier Lab. de l'Accelerateur Lineaire, Orsay, France, 1958-61; physicist Lawrence Berkeley Lab., Berkeley, Calif., 1961-62; staff mem. Stanford Linear Accelerator Ctr., Calif., 1962-68, assoc. dir., 1982-86, prof., 1968—. Fellow Guggenheim Found., 1971-72, von Humboldt Found., 1982. Fellow Am. Phys. Soc. (council, div. particles and fields 1983-84), Royal Soc. Can.; mem. AAAS. Office: Stanford Linear Accelerator Ctr PO Box 4349 Bin 96 Stanford CA 94305

TAYLOR, ROBERT LEE, mechanical engineer; b. Enid, Okla., Aug. 15, 1931; s. William Osmer and Dorothy Almira (Riggs) T.; m. Barabara Noble, June 11, 1954 (div. Jan. 1968); children: Larry, Michael; m. Josephine Frey, Aug. 28, 1970; children: Joseph, Jefferey, Cynthia. BS, Okla. State U., 1958. Engr. Marquardt Corp., Van Nuys, Calif., 1958-61; from engr. to program mgr. United Technologies, Sunnyvale, Calif., 1961-81; program mgr. Aerojet Tactical Systems, Sacramento, Calif., 1981—. Served to sgt. USAF, 1950-53. Republican. Avocations: skiing, golfing, writing, mktg. computer software. Home: 3011 Driftwood Circle El Dorado Hills CA 95630 Office: Aerojet Tactical Systems PO Box 13400 Sacramento CA 95813

TAYLOR, RONALD J., biology educator; b. Victor, Idaho, Oct. 16, 1932; s. George G. and Elva A. (Drake) T.; m. Gloria M. Wood, May 26, 1955; children: Ryan J., Rhonda L. Ripplinger. BA, Idaho State U., 1954; MS, U. Wyo., 1960; PhD, Wash. State U., 1964. Asst. prof. biology Western Wash. U., Bellingham, 1964-72, prof. biology, 1972—, chmn. dept., 1985—. Author: Sagebrush Country, 1975, Mountain Wildflowers of the Pacific Northwest, 1976, Rocky Mountain Wildflowers, 1979; editor: Mosses of North America, 1978. Served to 1st lt. USAF, 1954-59. Mem. AAAS (bd. dirs. Pacific div. 1983—), Torrey Bot. Club, Bot. Soc. Am., Am. Soc. Plant Taxonomy (past pres.), N.W. Sci. Assn. (past pres.), Wash. Native Plant Soc. (pres. 1985-87), Sigma Xi (past chpt. pres.). Avocation: outdoor photography. Home: 4241 Northwest Rd Bellingham WA 98226 Office: Western Wash U Dept of Biology Bellingham WA 98225

TAYLOR, RUSSELL RICE, lawyer; b. Santa Monica, Calif., Feb. 6, 1949; s. Kenyon Ross and Victoria (Mansfield) T.; m. Marcia Anne Kubley, Feb. 26, 1954. BA in Speech Communications, Calif. State U., Fullerton, 1971; JD, U. So. Calif., 1974. Bar: Calif. 1974, U.S. Supreme Ct. 1976. Lawyer United Pacific Ins., Los Angeles, San Bernadino, Calif., 1972-76; with litigation Orange County Claims Chubb, Irvine, 1980-84; mgr. So. Calif. Oregon Mutual Ins., San Diego, 1984-85; home and office claims examiner Design Profls. Ins. Co., Monterey, Calif., 1985—. Mem. Blue Goose Internat., Pi Kappa Delta. Republican. Episcopalian. Avocations: swimming, tennis, bowling, baseball. Home: 2362 Altisma Way La Costa CA 92008 Office: Design Profls Ins Co 2959 Monterey Salinas Hwy Monterey CA 93942

TAYLOR, SHARON LEE EDABURN, museum director; b. Lennox, Calif., Aug. 31, 1946; d. Hugh and Laura Bernice (Caldwell) E.; m. Gregory Alan Taylor, Dec. 31, 1982. A.A., Am. River Coll., 1966; B.A., Sacramento State Coll., 1970; M.A., Calif. State U.-Sacramento, 1982. Dispatcher, Citrus Heights (Calif.) Fire Dept., 1966-70; dispatcher Reno Police Dept., 1972-75; firefighter U.S. Forest Service, Bridgeport, Calif., 1976; interpretive specialist Calif. State R.R. Mus., Sacramento, 1977-78; mus. dir., curator Churchill County Mus. and Archive, Fallon, Nev., 1978—; guest lectr. U. Nev., Reno and Las Vegas, 1978—; dir. Churchill County Oral History Project, 1979—. Chmn., Carson City Dist. Bur. Land Mgmt. Citizens Adv. Council, 1980-82; founding dir. Fallon Community TV, PBS Channel 25, 1984-86. Mem. Soc. Indsl. Archeology, Am. Assn. State and Local History, Conf. Intermountain Archivists, Nev. Archaeol. Assn., Nev. Council Profl. Archaeologists. Democrat. Office: 1050 S Maine St Fallon NV 89406

TAYLOR, STEVE HENRY, zoologist; b. Inglewood, Calif., Mar. 18, 1947; s. Raymond Marten and Ardath (Metz) T.; 1 child, Michael Travis. B.A. in Biology, U. Calif.-Irvine, 1969. Animal keeper Los Angeles Zoo, 1972-75, assoc. curator, 1975-76; children's zoo mgr. San Francisco Zoo, 1976-81; zoo dir. Sacramento Zoo, 1981—. Bd. dirs. Sacramento Soc. Prevention Cruelty to Animals, 1983-87. Fellow Am. Assn. Zool. Parks and Aquariums (infant care diet advisor 1979, 85, Outstanding Service); mem. Sierra Club, Audubon Soc., Animal Use and Care Adminstrn. Democrat. Lodge: Rotary. Home: 443 De Mar Dr Sacramento CA 95831 Office: Sacramento Zoo 3930 W Land Park Sacramento CA 95822

TAYLOR, SUSAN SEROTA, biochemistry researcher; b. Racine, Wis., June 20, 1942; d. Rudolph M. and Helen L. (Vohs) S.; m. Palmer William Taylor, July 3, 1965; children: Tasha Katherine, Ashton David, Palmer Andrew. AB, U. Wis., 1964; PhD, Johns Hopkins U., 1968. Postdoctoral fellow MRC Lab. Molecular Biology, Cambridge, Eng., 1968-70; postdoctoral fellow U. Calif. San Diego, La Jolla, 1971-72, asst. prof. chemistry, 1972-79, assoc. prof., 1979-85, prof. chemistry, 1985—; mem. biochemistry study sect. NIH, Bethesda, Md., 1978-82; mem. nucleic acids and protein synthesis rev. bd. Am. Cancer Soc., N.Y.C., 1983—; vice chmn. Second Messengers and Protein Phosphorycation, Gordon Conf., 1985, chmn. 1986. Mem. editorial bd. Jour. Biol. Chemistry, 1985—. Recipient Career Devel. award NIH; postdoctoral fellow NIH 1969-72, Fogarty Internat. fellow NIH, 1981-82. Mem. Am. Chem. Soc., Am. Soc. Biol. Chemists (nominating com. 1985-86). Office: U Calif San Diego Dept Chemistry D-006 La Jolla CA 92093

TAYLOR, TIMOTHY DAVIES, counselor; b. Tacoma, Jan. 25, 1945; s. Thomas Gibson and Eleanor Jane (Davies) T.; B.A., Central Wash. U., 1968; M.A., U. Puget Sound, Tacoma, 1975; Ph.D., U.S. Internat. U., 1980. Tchr. schs. in Wash., 1968-72; v.p. Tom Taylor Ins. Brokers, Tacoma, 1972-81; pvt. practice psychology, Tacoma, 1981—. Vice chmn. Pierce County March of Dimes, 1977-78, chmn.-elect, 1979-80, chmn., 1980; active Tacoma-Pierce County YMCA; assoc. chmn. United Way Pierce County, 1981-82. Mem. Ind. Ins. Agts. and Brokers Am., Family Service Assn. Am., Profl. Ins. Agts. Wash., Am. Psychol. Assn., Am. Assn. Marriage and Family Therapy. Democrat. Clubs: W. Tacoma Optimist (pres. 1977, Optimist of Yr. award 1977), Elks. Home: 4412 N 27th St Tacoma WA 98407 Office: Trust Office Bldg 808 N 2d St Tacoma WA 98403

TAYLOR, WALTER WALLACE, lawyer; b. Newton, Iowa, Sept. 18, 1925; s. Carrol W. and Eva (Greenly) T.; A.A., Yuba Coll., 1948, A.B., 1950; M.A., U. Calif., 1955, J.D., McGeorge Coll. Law, 1962; m. Mavis A. Harvey, Oct. 9, 1948; children—Joshua Michael (dec. 1980), Kevin Eileen, Kristin Lisa, Jeremy Walter, Margaret Jane, Melissa E., Amy M. Adminstrv. analyst USAF, Sacramento, 1951-53; personnel, research analyst Calif. Personnel Bd., Sacramento, 1954-56; civil service, personnel analyst, chief counsel, gen. mgr. Calif. Employees Assn., Sacramento, 1956-75; staff counsel, chief profl. standards Calif. Commn. Tchr. Credentialing; tchr. discipline civil service, personnel cons. Served USCGR, 1943-46. Mem. Calif. State Bar, Am., Sacramento County bar assns. Democrat. Author: Know Your Rights, 1963-64. Home: 4572 Fair Oaks Blvd Sacramento CA 95862 Office: 1812 9th St Sacramento CA 94244-2700

TAYLOR, WILLIAM JESSE, III, aircraft co. exec.; b. Wilson, N.C., Nov. 4, 1942; s. William Jesse and Eleanor Matilda (Townsend) T.; m. Linda Kay Baker, May 7, 1977. Student Garden City (Kans.) Jr. Coll., 1960-62; BS in Aero. Engring., Embry Riddle Aero. Inst., 1964. With Gov. Products div. Pratt & Whitney Aircraft, West Palm Beach, Fla., 1964—, Los Angeles rep., 1977—. Mem. AIAA, Exptl. Aircraft Assn., Am. Aviation Hist. Soc., Planetary Soc., Brit. Interplanetary Soc., Air Force Assn., U.S. Naval Inst., Am. Helicopter Soc., L-5 Soc. Home: 21216 New Hampshire Ave Torrance CA 90502 Office: Pratt and Whitney 5200 W Century Blvd Suite 880 Los Angeles CA 90045

TAYLOR, WILLIAM MALCOLM, personnel recruitment executive; b. South Hiram, Maine, June 18, 1933; s. William Myers and Gladys Marie (Weldy) T.; m. Carrie Mae Fiedler, Aug. 31, 1957 (div. Sept. 1980); children: William Stephan, Alyson Marie, Eric Fiedler; m. Elizabeth Van Horn, June 18, 1983. BA in Liberal Arts, Pa. State U., 1956; MEd in Sci., U. N.C., 1961. Cert. secondary sch. tchr. Sci. tchr. Coral Shores High Sch., Tavernier, Fla., 1961-62; park naturalist Nat. Park Service, Everglades Nat. Park, Fla., 1962-65; tech. editor Nat. Park Service, Washington, 1965-67; chief naturalist Nat. Park Service, Canyonlands, Utah, 1967-71; environ. edn. specialist western regional office Nat. Park Service, Calif., 1971-77; programs devel. dir. Living History Ctr., Novato, Calif., 1981-83; ptnr. Van Horn, Taylor & Assocs., Berkeley, Calif., 1983—. Developer: (ednl. program) Environ. Living Program, 1973 (Calif. Bicentennial Commn. award 1974, Don Perryman award Calif. Social Studies Council, 1975, Calif. Conservation Council award 1975). Dir. Novato Environ. Quality Commn., 1973-76, Calif. Conservation Council, 1973-76; sponsor Am. Bicentennial Commn., NEA, 1976. Mem. AAAS, Assn. Biotech. Cos., Assn. Ind. Recruiters, MENSA. Club: Santa Cruz Bird. Avocations: flying, birding, remodeling and woodworking, natural history. Home: 4200 Smith Grade Rd Santa Cruz CA 95060 Office: Van Horn Taylor & Assocs 105 Cooper St Santa Cruz CA 95060

TAYLOR-WALKER, OPHELIA, speech pathologist; b. Gainesville, Fla., Oct. 20, 1952; s. John Oliver and Edna Taylor; m. Wallace Walker, Nov. 15, 1981 (div. May 1983); 1 child, Ebony Maliaka. BA, Fla. A&M U., 1973; MA, U. Iowa, 1978. Drug therapist Western State Hosp., Tacoma, 1975-76; office cl. Rockwell Internat., Cedar Rapids, Iowa, 1976-77; speech pathologist State of Wash., Buckley, 1978-79; speech therapist Tacoma Pub. Schs., 1979—; lectr. Tacoma, 1980—; workshop-coordinator Tacoma Pub. Schs., 1984—; adj. prof. U. Puget Sound, Tacoma, 1985—. contbr. articles on econ. choices to newspaper, 1983. Active Tacoma Urban League, 1983—. Mem. Am. Speech-Lang.-Hearing Assn. (cert. clin. competence). Club: Jack and Jill of Am. (Tacoma). Avocations: aerobics, weight lifting. Home: 4722 41st NE Tacoma WA 98422

TEAGUE, BRUCE WILLIAMS, chiropractor; b. Dayton, Ohio, Sept. 6, 1947; s. Bige Barnett and Lena (Williams) T.; m. Germaine Lee Mullican, Oct. 15, 1977; children—Deanna, Katrina, Bret., Travis, Krystal. B.B.A., Eastern Ky. U., 1970; D.Chiropractic, Palmer Coll. Chiropractic, 1977. Chiropractor, pres., dir. Teague Chiropractic Ctr., Anchorage, 1980—. Mem. Am. Chiropractic Assn. (mem. council nutrition, council on sports injuries and phys. fitness), Internat. Chiropractic Assn., Alaska Chiropractic Soc., Palmer Coll. Alumni Assn. Lodges: Moose, Rotary. Office: Teague Chiropractic Ctr 1515 E Tudor Rd Anchorage AK 99507

TEAGUE, LAVETTE COX, JR., educator, architectural consultant; b. Birmingham, Ala., Oct. 8, 1934; s. Lavette Cox and Caroline Green (Stokes) T.; student Auburn U., 1951-54; B.Arch., MIT, 1957, M.S.C.E., 1965, Ph.D., 1968; M.Div. with distinction, Ch. Div. Sch. Pacific, 1979. Archtl. designer Carroll C. Harmon, Birmingham, 1957, Fred Renneker, Jr., Birmingham, 1958-59; architect Rust Engring. Co., Birmingham, 1959-62, Synergetics, Inc., Raleigh, N.C., 1962-64, Rust Engring. Co., Birmingham, 1964-68; research asst., inst., research assoc. MIT, Cambridge, 1964-68; dir. computer services Skidmore, Owings & Merrill, San Francisco, Chgo., 1968-74; postdoctoral fellow UCLA, 1972; adj. assoc. prof. architecture and civil engring. Carnegie-Mellon U., Pitts., 1973-74; archtl. systems cons., Chgo., 1974-75, Berkeley, Calif., 1975-80, Pasadena, Calif., 1980-82, Altadena, Calif., 1982—; lectr. info. systems Calif. State Poly. U., Pomona, 1980-81, prof., 1981—; Fulbright lectr., Uruguay, 1985. Co-author: Structured Analysis Methods for Computer Information Systems, 1985. Recipient Tucker-Voss award M.I.T., 1967; Fulbright scholar, 1985. Mem. AIA (Arnold W. Brunner scholar 1966), Assn. Computing Machinery, Sigma Xi, Phi Eta Sigma, Scarab, Scabbard and Blade, Tau Beta Pi, Chi Epsilon. Episcopalian. Home: 1696 N Altadena Dr Altadena CA 91001 Office: 3801 W Temple Ave Pomona CA 91768

TEAGUE, WELDON WINSTON, structural design engineer; b. Temple, Tex., Nov. 13, 1933; s. Weldon B. and Lucile E. Teague; m. Norma Jean Jenkins, Aug. 27, 1955; children: Cheryll Teague Jacobs, Lynda Teague Poblete, Michelle Teague Crawford, Janet Teague Carter. BS in Aerospace Engring., U. Tex., 1960. Engr. McDonnell Douglas, Santa Monica, Calif., 1960-84; engr., mgr. structures design spl. space program McDonnell Douglas, Huntington Beach, Calif., 1984—. Republican. Congregationalist. Avocations: camping, woodworking, traveling. Home: 528 Torito Ln Diamond Bar CA 91765

TEASDALE, WARREN EDWARD, geologist; b. Oceanside, N.Y., June 15, 1935; s. Otto Edward and Florence Henrietta (Golden) T.; m. Dagmar Florence Cornell, Apr. 27, 1961; children: Deborah Suzanne, Scott Eugene. Student, Bklyn. Poly. Inst., 1952-53; BA in GeologyB, Hofstra Coll., 1958. Hydrologic technician U.S. Geol. Survey, Mineola (N.Y.), Denver and Sacramento; radiation waste hydrologist water resources div. U.S. Geol. Survey, Idaho Falls, Idaho, 1961-69; geologist geologic div. U.S. Geol. Survey, Lakewood, Colo., 1978-83, hydrologist, research project chief water resources div., 1983—; cons. U.S. Geol. Survey Dhaka, Bangladesh, 1983-87. Recipient Service awards U.S. Dept. Interior, 1967, 77, 86. Mem. ASTM, Idaho Assn. Profl. Geologists. Democrat. Lutheran. Avocations: hunting, fishing, camping, singing, woodworking. Office: US Geol Survey Water Resources Div PO Box 25046 MS 403 Denver Fed Ctr Denver CO 80225

TEDDER, WILLIAM RANDALL, III, chromatography consultant; b. Salinas, Calif., June 10, 1957; s. William Randall Jr. and Edna Claire (Johnson) T. AB in Genetics, U. Calif., Berkeley, 1980. Cert. CPR tchr., Calif. Tutor Hartnell Community Coll., Salinas, 1982; tchr. Salinas Union High Sch. Dist., 1982-84; sales engr. Filtrex Inc., Hayward, Calif., 1984-85; tchr. San Mateo (Calif.) Union High Sch. Dist., 1985-86; tech. specialist indsl. filtration and heating products Montgomery Bros. Inc., Burlingame, Calif., 1986-87; cons. San Francisco, 1987—; cons. Western Analytical Products, San Francisco, 1987—, in fields of filtration and chromatography. Bd. dirs. Salinas Lyceum, 1983. Recipient U. Calif. Berkeley Grant in Aid, 1975-76, fee grant U. Calif., Berkeley, 1975-76; Calif. State scholar, Berkeley, 1976-78. mem. AAAS, N.Y. Acad. Scis., Calif. Alumni Assn., Mensa (chmn. local bylaw com. 1983, editor newsletter 1982). Republican. Presbyterian. Office: PO Box 1757 Temecula CA 92390

TEDFORD, CHARLES FRANKLIN, biophysicist; b. Lawton, Okla., June 26, 1928; s. Charles E. and Loula B. (Waters) T.; B.S. with distinction in Chemistry, S.W. Tex. State U., 1950, M.S., 1954; postgrad. in radiobiology Reed Coll., 1957, in biophysics U. Calif., Berkeley, 1961-63; m. Julie Reme Sauret, Sept. 15, 1951; children—Gary Franklin, Mark Charles, Philip John. Served as enlisted man U.S. Navy, 1945-47, Commd. ensign, 1950, advanced through grades to capt., 1968; biochemist U.S. Naval Hosp., San Diego, 1953-54, U.S. Naval Biol. Lab., Oakland, Calif., 1954-56; sr. instr., radiation safety officer Nuclear, Biol. and Chem. Warfare Def. Sch., Treasure Island, Calif., 1956-61; asst. chief nuclear medicine div. Navy Med. Sch., Bethesda, Md., 1963-66; adminstrv. program mgr. radiation safety br. Bur. Medicine and Surgery, Washington, 1966-72; dir. radiation safety and health physics program Navy Regional Med. Center, San Diego, 1972-74; mgr. Navy Regional Med. Clinic, Seattle, 1974-78, ret., 1978; dir. radiation health unit Ga. Dept. Human Resources, Atlanta, 1978-79; dir. Ariz. Radiation Regulatory Agy., Tempe, 1979—. Decorated Legion of Merit; recipient Meritorious Service award U.S. Navy, 1970. Mem. Health Physics Soc., Am. Nuclear Soc. Contbr. articles on radiation safety to profl. publs. Office: 8414 S 40th St Phoenix AZ 85040

TEEL, DALE, utility company executive; b. Sesser, Ill., Oct. 11, 1925; s. Lester N. and Ruth (Martin) T. B.S. in Chem. Engring., U. Ill., 1946. With chem. div. U.S. Rubber Co., Naugatuck, Conn., 1946-47, plantations div., Penang, Malaya, 1948-52; asst. gen. sales mgr., mgr. Hawaii br. Honolulu Gas Co., Honolulu and Hilo, 1952-60; pres. Anchorage Natural Gas Corp., Anchorage, 1960—, Alaska Pipeline Co., Anchorage subs. Seagull Energy Corp., 1974—. Served with USNR, 1943-45. Office: Alaska Pipeline Co 3000 Spenard Rd Anchorage AK 99502

TEEL, RAYMOND FRANK, landscape engineer and designer, artist; b. Sudan, Tex., July 19, 1929; s. John Hugh and Grace Arizone (Branscum) T.; m. Ruth Ann Gilbert, Mar. 1972 (div. Jan. 1967). Grad. high sch. Real estate developer Los Angeles, 1962-66; prin. Teel Landscape Co., San Pedro, Calif., 1972—; artist, proprietor, distbr. ltd. edition art Teel Gallery, Los Angeles, 1969—. Republican. Avocation: art shows. Office: Teel Landscape Co 28709 Mt Shasta Dr San Pedro CA 90732

TEEPLE, ELIZABETH PERRY, medical information systems director; b. Atlanta, Jan. 9, 1950; d. Robert Perry and Elizabeth Ann (Vanstory) T. BS, U. State N.Y., Albany, 1980; M in Health Service Adminstrn., George Washington U., 1983. Enlisted USAF, 1978, advanced through grades to capt.; research asst. NIH, Bethesda, Md., 1980-81; dep. comdr., ops. officer 60th Air Evac Flight, Andrews AFB, Washington, 1981-82; resident med. adminstr. Malcolm Grow Med. Ctr., Andrews AFB, 1982-83; dir. patient affairs USAF Regional Hosp., March AFB, Calif., 1984-85; dir. med. systems USAFR Hosp., March AFB, 1983—; project mgr. VA/Def. Dept. Software Test, March AFB, 1984—; regional cons. med. systems SAC, March AFB, 1985—. Pub. speaker March AFB, Los Angeles, Riverside, Calif., 1986; leader death & dying seminars, March AFB Community, 1984-85. Mem. Am. Soc. Mil. Surgeons, Am. Coll. Healthcare Execs. Democrat. Avocations: glider flying, cross-country skiing. Office: USAFRH/SGAI March AFB CA 92518-5300

TEER, HAROLD BENTON, JR., marketing educator; b. Eunice, La., June 12, 1945; s. Harold Benton and Kathryn (Weems) R.; m. Faye Peltier, Feb. 9, 1973. BSBA, Northwestern State U., 1969; MBA, Miss. Coll., Clinton, 1977; D in Bus. Adminstrn., La. Tech. U., 1985. Salesman Johnson & Johnson, Jackson, Miss., 1973-76; instr. Hinds Jr. Coll., Raymond, Miss., 1977-78, La. Tech. U., Ruston, 1978-81; prof. Fort Lewis Coll., Durango, Colo., 1981-86, James Madison U., Harrisonburg, Va., 1986—; vice chmn., bd. dirs. Durango Better Bus. Bur., 1984-86. Served as sgt. U.S. Army, 1967-71, Vietnam. Named one of Outstanding Young Men Am. Mem. Am. Mktg. Assn., So. Mktg. Assn., Southwestern Mktg. Assn., Southwestern Small Bus. Assn., Mid-South Acad. Econs. and Fin. Republican. Methodist. Home: 1710-D Park Rd Harrisonburg VA 22801 Office: James Madison Univ Dept Mktg Harrisonburg VA 22807

TEERLINK, J(OSEPH) LELAND, real estate developer; b. Salt Lake City, July 16, 1935; s. Nicholas John and Mary Luella (Love) T.; student U. Utah, 1953-55; m. Leslie Dowdle, Nov. 5, 1975; children—Steven, David, Andrew, Suzanne, Benjamin. Sales rep. Eastman Kodak Co., Salt Lake City, 1960-69; founder Graphic Systems, Inc., Salt Lake City, 1969-82, pres., 1969-79, chmn. bd., 1979-82; founder Graphic Ink Co., Salt Lake City, 1973, pres., 1975-79, chmn. bd., 1979-82; founder G.S.I. Leasing Co., Salt Lake City, 1975, pres., 1975-82; chmn. bd. Graphic Systems Holding Co., Inc., Salt Lake City, 1978-82; dir. leasing and acquisitions Terra Industries, Inc., real estate developers, 1982-86, ptnr., 1986—. Bd. dirs. ARC, Salt Lake City, 1979-82; vice consulate of the Netherlands for Utah, 1977—; mem. active corps of execs., SBA, 1979-83. Named Small Businessman of the Yr. for Utah, SBA, 1978. Mem. Graphic Arts Equipment and Supply Dealers of Am. (dir. 1978-82), Printing Industry of Am., Nat. Assn. Indsl. and Office Parks (pres. Utah chpt., 1986—), Nat. Fedn. Ind. Businessmen, Salt Lake City C. of C., Salt Lake Bd. Realtors, Million Dollar Club. Republican. Mormon. Clubs: Univ., Rotary. Home: 2984 Thackeray Pl Salt Lake City UT 84108 Office: 6925 Union Park Ctr Midvale UT 84047

TEETERS, CLARENCE, salt co. mgr.; b. Mt. Pleasant, Pa., Dec. 22, 1933; s. Clarence and Edna Marie (Grimm) T.; student U. Toledo, 1952-55, U. So. Calif., 1978; m. Sandra Jean Ulery, Aug. 2, 1958; children—Deanna Marie, Douglas James. Buyer, mgr. Tiedtkes, Toledo, 1955-60; sales rep. Morton Salt Co., 1960-69, dist. sales mgr., No. Calif., Nev., Hawaii, 1969-78; mgr. consumer products Leslie Salt Co., Newark, Calif., 1978—. Mem. The Illuminators. Republican. Presbyterian. Clubs: San Francisco Sales Mgrs., Masons. Address: 7200 Central Ave Newark CA 94560

TEETS, GREGG DUNCAN, mining engineer; b. Syracuse, N.Y., May 4, 1961; s. Robert Marvin Sr. and Janet McMillen (Duncan) T.; m. Barbara Jean Brodie, Oct. 6, 1984. BS, Mont. Coll. Mineral Sci. and Tech., 1983. Cert. engr. in tng. Mine laborer Allied Chem. Co., Green River, Wyo., 1980; engring. aid Stauffer Chem. Co., Green River, 1981; pvt. practice engring. Salt Lake City, 1983-84; estimator Gilbert Western Corp., Salt Lake City, 1984; prodn. engr. Black Butte Coal Co., Point of Rocks, Wyo., 1984—. Mem. Soc. Mining Engrs. (vice chmn. 1985-86, Southwestern Wyo. chmn. 1986—), Wyo. Mining Assn. Democratic. Congregationalist. Avocations: basketball, coin collecting, woodworking. Home: 907 Wilderness Green River WY 82935 Office: Black Butte Coal Co PO Box 98 Point of Rocks WY 82942

TEETS, JOHN WILLIAM, diversifed company executive; b. Elgin, Ill., Sept. 15, 1933; s. John William and Maudie T.; m. Nancy Kerchenfaut, June 25, 1965; children: Jerri, Valerie Sue, Heide Jane, Suzanne. Student, U. Ill. Pres., partner Winter Garden Restaurant, Inc., Carpenterville, Ill., 1957-63; v.p. Greyhound Food Mgmt. Co.; also pres. Post Houses, Inc., and Horne's Enterprises, Chgo., 1964-68; pres., chief operating officer John R. Thompson Co., Chgo., 1968-71; pres., chief operating officer Restaurant div., also corp. v.p Canteen Corp., Chgo., 1971-74; exec. v.p., chief operating officer Bonanza Internat. Co., Dallas, 1974-76; chmn., chief exec. officer Greyhound Food Mgmt., Inc., Phoenix, 1976—; group v.p. food service Greyhound Corp., Phoenix, 1976-81, group v.p. services group, 1980-81, vice chmn., 1980-82, chmn., chief exec. officer, 1981—, dir.; chmn., pres. Armour & Co., from 1981; vice chmn. President's Conf. on Foodservice Industry; mem. adv. bd. Phoenix and Valley of Sun Conv. and Visitors Bur., 1979-82. Recipient Silver Plate award, Golden Plate award Internat. Foodservice Mfrs. Assn., 1980. Mem. Nat. Automatic Mdsg. Assn., Nat. Restaurant Assn., Nat. Inst. Foodservice Industry (trustee), Am. Mgmt. Assn., Christian Businessmen's Assn. (chmn. steering com. 1977), Nat. Speakers Assn. Club: Arizona. Office: Greyhound Corp Greyhound Tower Sta 3103 Phoenix AZ 85077 *

TEICHMAN, SOL, store display mfg. co. exec.; b. Mukacevo, Czechoslovakia, May 9, 1929; s. Sam and Lujza (Friedman) T.; came to U.S., 1946, naturalized, 1954; m. Ruth Noe, Nov. 22, 1959; children—Bernard, Lisa, Alan. Salesman Pacific Fixture Co., Los Angeles, 1949-56; owner, sec.-treas. Teichman Enterprises (T & H Store Display), Los Angeles, 1956—. Chmn. bd. Emek Hebrew Acad., Valley Torah Center; bd. dirs. Los Angeles Bur. Jewish Edn. and B'Nei Akiva (youth orgn.), Congregations Mishkan Israel and Shaarey Zedek, UOJCA. Served with AUS, 1951-53. Recipient award for efforts for Jewish community Los Angeles City Council, 1971; Nat. Disting. Service award Union Orthodox Jewish Congregations Am., 1984; Man of Yr. award Emek Hebrew Acad., 1971; David Ben Gurion award Mizrachi Orgn. and State of Israel, 1975, others. Patentee in field. Home: 5323 Genesta Ave Encino CA 91316 Office: 2035 E 46th St Los Angeles CA 90058

TEIGER, DOUGLAS HAUPT, architect; b. Newark, May 23, 1960; s. David Allen and Florence (Haupt) T. BArch, Cornell U., 1982. Pvt. practicer furniture design and prodn. 1981—; archtl. designer Swanke, Hayden & Connell, N.Y.C., 1982-84, Arthur Erickson Archts., Los Angeles, 1984-85, Waldo's Designs, Los Angeles, 1985—. Prin. works include Trump Tower N.Y.C, Hempstead Village N.Y.C., One Seaport Plaza N.Y.C., Am. Express Bldg. N.Y.C., Statue of Liberty renovation, design team San Diego Conv. Ctr., design devel. of Calif. Plaza, design devel. Bunker Hill, design schematics Stockton St. Hotel, competition drawings Ariz. State U. Fine Arts Complex, project design Brentwood Library, Los Angeles, Koala Blue Prototype for franchised boutiques, Trumps Restaurant addition, Moss Residence, Fernandez/Borman Residence, Stivers Residence. Home: 1211 Horn Ave Apt 403 Los Angeles CA 90069

TEITZ, RICHARD STUART, museum director; b. Fall River, Mass., July 18, 1942; s. Alexander George and Lucille T.; m. Elaine Tallmadge Osborn, 1962; children: Rebecca Eve, Jessica Ann, Alexander Osborn. A.B., Yale U., 1963; M.A., Harvard U., 1965. Asst. curator Fogg Art Mus., Harvard U., 1964-65; curatorial asst. Worcester (Mass.) Art Mus., 1965-67, asst. dir., 1969-70, dir., 1970-81; dir. Hood Mus. of Art, Dartmouth Coll., Hanover, N.H., 1981-84, Denver Art Mus., 1984—; dir. Wichita Art Mus., 1967-69; lectr. Boston Archtl. Center, 1964-65; instr. Clark U., 1966-67; asso. dir. Etruscan Found., Siena, 1965, 66—; prof. art Dartmouth Coll., 1981-84; bd. dirs. Ava Gallery, N.H. Visual Artists Coalition. Author: Masterpieces of Etruscan Art, 1967, Art of the Victorian Era, 1969; also articles. Mem. Assn. Art Mus. Dirs., Archaeol. Inst. Am., Internat. Council Mus., Coll. Art Assn. Clubs: Yale (N.Y.C. and Colo.), Denver Athletic. Home: 1968 Ivy St Denver CO 80220

TELESE, ROCCO JOSEPH, systems simulation engineer, researcher; b. Glen Cove, N.Y., Aug. 8, 1954; s. Frank and Antoinette (Congero) T.; m. Reneé Norine Williams, July 3, 1982. B.S. in Elec. Engring. Tech., N.Y. Inst. Tech., 1977. Digital tooling specialist Photocircuits, Glen Cove, N.Y., 1972-77; lab mgr. engr. Grumman Aerospace, Bethpage, N.Y., 1977-81; sr. aviation systems engr. Northrop Aircraft, Hawthorne, Calif., 1981-83; sr. systems engr. Telos Cons. Fullerton Branch, Calif., 1983-84; sr. systems test engr. Systems Software, Inc., Fullerton, 1984; sr. research specialist Kelly Johnson Research Facility, Valenica, Calif., 1984—. Mem. Republican Nat. Com., 1981—. Mem. IEEE, Assn. Computing Machinery, Soc. Computer Simulation, AIAA, Spl. Interest Group in Graphics, Smithsonian Inst., Nat. Geog. Soc. Nat. Rifle Assn., Acad. Sci. Fiction, Fantasy and Horror Films (membership chmn. 1982—), Am. Film Inst., Acad. Family Films and Family TV, Lockheed and Nat. Mgmt. Assn., Assn. Old Crows. Clubs: Group Z Sports Car of So. Calif. Office: Kelly Johnson Research Facility Rye Canyon Valencia CA 91355

TELFORD, JAMES WARDROP, atmospheric physicist; b. Merbein, Australia, Aug. 16, 1927; came to U.S., 1967; s. Alexander Wardrop and Hilda (Georgina) T.; m. Mary Billing, Jan. 7, 1954; children: David, Susan, Catriona. BSc in Physics, Melbourne U., Australia, 1950, DSc in Atmospheric Scis., 1970; Diploma in Numerical Analysis and Automatic Computing, U. Sydney, Australia, 1961. Research officer CSIRO Radiophysics Div., Sydney, 1950-67; vis. scientist Imperial Coll. London U., 1965-66; research prof. Desert Research Inst., Reno, 1967—, dep. dir. Lab. Atmospheric Physics, 1969-78, dir. Air Motions Lab., 1978—; cons. NASA, World Meteorol. Orgn. Lima, Peru; rep. U. Corp. Atmospheric Research, Boulder, Colo.; mem. panel aviation Nat. Ctr. Atmospheric Research, Boulder. Contbr. articles to profl. jours.; patentee in field. Fellow AAAS, Royal Meteorol. Soc., Am. Meteorol. Soc. (com. chmn. atmospheric electricity); mem. Sigma Xi. Club: Cosmos. Home: 1975 Fallen Leaf Ct Reno NV 89509 Office: Desert Research Inst ASC PO Box 60220 Reno NV 89506

TELLEM, SUSAN MARY, public relations executive; b. N.Y.C, May 23, 1945; d. John F. and Rita C. (Lietz) Cain; m. Mark S. Grody, Mar. 25, 1978; children: Tori, Laura, John, Daniel. BS, Mt. St. Mary's Coll., Los Angeles, 1967. Cert. pub. health nurse; RN. Pres. Tellem Pub. Relations Agy., Marina del Rey, Calif., 1977-80, Grody/Tellem Communications, Inc., Los Angeles, 1980—; instr. UCLA Extension, 1983—; speaker numerous seminars and confs. on pub. relations. Editor: Sports Medicine for the '80's, Sports Medicine Digest, 1982-84. Bd. dirs. Marymount High Sch., 1984—, pres. 1984-86; bd. dirs. Los Angeles Police Dept. Booster Assn., 1984—. Mem. Internat. Assn. Bus. Communicators, Acad. Hosp. Pub. Relations, Am. Mktg. Assn., Am. Soc. Hosp. Mktg. and Pub. Relations, Healthcare Mktg. and Pub. Relations Assn., Assn. for Advancement of Med. Instrumentation, Pub. Relations Soc. Am. Roman Catholic. Club: Marina City (Marina del Rey); Publicity (Los Angeles), Mountaingate County. Avocations: reading, tennis, aerobic dance. Office: Grody Tellem Communications 11150 W Olympic Blvd Suite 840 Los Angeles CA 90064-1815

TELLEP, DANIEL MICHAEL, mechanical engineer; b. Forest City, Pa., Nov. 20, 1931. B.S. in Mech. Engring. with highest honors, U. Calif., Berkeley, 1954, M.S., 1955; grad. Advanced Mgmt. Program, Harvard U., 1971. With Lockheed Missiles & Space Co., 1955—, chief engr. missile systems div., 1969-75, v.p., asst. gen. mgr. advanced systems div., 1975-83, exec. v.p., 1983-84, pres., 1984—; pres. Lockheed Missiles & Space Group, 1986—; cons. in field. Author papers, reports in field. Fellow AIAA (Lawrence Sperry award 1964); mem. Nat. Acad. Engring., Sigma Xi, Pi Tau Sigma, Tau Beta Pi. Office: Lockheed Corp Dept 10-12 Sunnyvale CA 94086 Other Office Address: Lockheed Corp 4500 Park Granada Blvd Calabasas CA 91399

TELLER, DAVIDA YOUNG, psychology, physiology and biophysics educator; b. Yonkers, N.Y., July 25, 1938; d. David Aidan and Jean Marvin (Sturges) Young; m. David Chambers Teller, June 18, 1960 (div. May 1986); children: Stephen, Sara. BA, Swarthmore Coll., 1960; PhD, U. Calif., Berkeley, 1965. Lectr., research prof. U. Wash., Seattle, 1965-69, asst. prof. psychology, physiology and biophysics, 1969-71, assoc. prof., 1971-74, prof., 1983—; research affiliate Regional Primate Research Ctr., Child Devel. and Mental Retardation Ctr.; mem. com. on vision Nat. Acad. Scis.-Nat. Research Council, 1971—, vision research program com. Nat. Eye Inst. and NIH, 1973-76, Assn. Research in Vision and Ophthalmology, program com. Visual Psychophysics and Physiol. Optics, 1973-75, visual scis. B study sect. Nat Eye Inst. and NIH, 1981-85, chmn. 1983-85; U. Wash. appointments include chmn. Univ. Com. on Vision, 1971; mem. Univ. Council on Women, 1971-76, Faculty Senate Spl. Com. on Faculty Women, 1972-75, ad hoc com. Evaluation of Dir. of Black Studies Program, 1976, faculty adv. bd. Women Studies, 1980-82, ad hoc com. to search for Chmn. Psychology, 1981, standing com. Women Studies, 1982-83, faculty senate council on Grants and Contract Research, 1985—, Univ. Acad. Council, 1986—; dept. psychology appoints include Exec. Com., 1973-75, 77-79; chmn. Budget and Facilities Com., 1979-81; mem. ad hoc com. Staff Employment, 1982-83; honors advisor and dir. Honors Program, 1982—; mem. planning com. 1984—; reviewer for the following granting agys. NSF, Exptl. Psychology and Visual Sci. B Study Sects. of NIH, Nat Research Council of Can., U.S.-Israel Binational Sci. Found., The Thrasher Research Fund; visited sites for Nat. Inst. Neurol. Diseases and Stroke, Nat. Eye Inst., Vision B. Study Sect. Mem. editorial bd. Infant Behavior and Development, 1981-85, Behavioral Brain Research, 1984—, Vision Research, 1985—, Clinical Vision Sciences, 1986—; contbr. numerous articles to profl. jours.; patentee in field. Recipient Sabbatical award James McKeen Cattell Fund, 1981-82. Fellow AAAS, Optical Soc. Am.; mem. Assn. Research in Vision and Ophthalmology, Assn. Women in Sci., Am. Acad. Ophthalmology (Glenn Fry award 1982). Avocations: hiking, traveling, dancing. Office: U Wash Dept Psychology NI-25 Seattle WA 98195

TEMIANKA, HENRI, violinist, conductor; b. Greenock, Scotland, Nov. 19, 1906; came to U.S., 1940; s. Israel and Fanny (Hildebr) T.; m. Emmy Cowden, Jan. 28, 1943; children: Daniel, David. Ed., Rotterdam, Berlin, Paris; grad., Curtis Inst., 1930; PhD (hon.), DFA (hon.), Pepperdine U., 1986. head violin dept., summer master classes Santa Barbara Music Acad. of West, 1952; artistic adviser Nat. Fedn. Music Clubs; vis. prof. U. Calif. at Santa Barbara, 1960-65; lectr. univs.; prof., music dir. Calif. State U. at Long Beach, 1964-74, prof. emeritus, 1974—; lectr. UCLA; cons. Ford Found. Debut, N.Y.C., 1928, Europe, 1930, soloist with, John Barbirolli, George Szell, Vaughan Williams, Sir Adrian Boult, Fritz Reiner, Otto Klemperer, also with, Amsterdam Concertgebouw Orch., philharm. orchs. of, Warsaw, The Hague, Rotterdam, London, Brussels, Monte-Carlo, Geneva, Stockholm, Copenhagen, Helsinki; toured, Russia at govt. invitation, 1935, 36, founded, Temianka Chamber Orch., London, 1936, toured, U.S., 1942—, leader, Paganini String Quartet, 1946-66; produced, wrote, narrated series ednl. motion pictures commd. by, Ednl. TV Center, 1956; guest condr., Los Angeles Philharmonic Orch., 1958-59, 59-60, U.S. tour of 40 concerts with, Temianka Little Symphony, 1960, 61, 64, concert tours, Europe, Orient, S.Am., Can., 1960—; founder, condr., Calif. Chamber Symphony; concert tours with Temianka Virtuosi, U.S. and Hong Kong, 1980, 82, 85; Author: Facing the Music, 1973; contbr. to magazines. Adviser Young Musicians Found. Served with overseas br. OWI, 1942-44. Decorated officier des Arts et Lettres France). Office: 2219 S Bentley Los Angeles CA 90064

TEMKO, ALLAN BERNARD, writer; b. N.Y.C., Feb. 4, 1924; s. Emanuel and Betty (Alderman) T.; m. Elizabeth Ostroff, July 1, 1950; children: Susannah, Alexander. A.B., Columbia U., 1947; postgrad, U. Calif., Berkeley, 1949-51, Sorbonne, 1948-49, 51-52. Lectr. Sorbonne, 1953-54, Ecole des Arts et Metiers, Paris, 1954-55; asst. prof. journalism U. Calif., Berkeley, 1956-62; lectr. in city planning and social scis. U. Calif., 1966-70; prof. art Calif. State U., Hayward, 1971-80; lectr. art Stanford U., 1981, 82; architecture critic San Francisco Chronicle, 1961—, art editor, 1979-82; archtl. planning cons. Author: Notre Dame of Paris, 1955, Eero Saarinen, 1962; contbr. articles to U.S. and fgn. mags. and newspapers; West Coast editor, Archtt. Forum, 1959-62. Served with USNR, 1943-46. Recipient Gold medal Commonwealth Club Calif., 1956; journalism award AIA, 1961, Silver Spur award, 1985, 1st prize in archtl. criticism Mfrs. Hanover Art/World, 1986; Rockefeller Found. grantee, 1962-63; Twentieth Century Fund grantee, 1963-66; Guggenheim fellow, 1956-57. Office: San Francisco Chronicle San Francisco CA 94119

TEMPELIS, CONSTANTINE HARRY, immunologist, educator; b. Superior, Wis., Aug. 27, 1927; s. Harry and Thelma Marie (Hoff) T.; m. Nancy Louise Foster, Aug. 27, 1955; children: William H., Daniel S. B.S., U. Wis.-Superior, 1950; M.S., U. Wis.-Madison, 1953, Ph.D., 1955. Project asso. immunology U. Wis., Madison, 1955-57; instr. immunology U. W.Va., Morgantown, 1957-58; asst. research immunologist U. Calif., Berkeley, 1958-66; asso. prof. immunology U. Calif., 1966-72, prof., 1972—; vis. scientist Wellcome Research Labs., Beckenham, Kent, Eng., 1977-78, U. Innsbruck, Austria, 1985; cons. in field. Contbr. articles to profl. jours. Served with USNR, 1945-46. Recipient Research Career Devel. award, 1965-70; Fogarty sr. internat. fellow, 1977-78. Mem. AAAS, N.Y. Acad. Scis., Am. Assn. Immunologists, Fedn. Am. Soc. Exptl. Biology, Sigma Xi. Home: 215 Trinity Ave Berkeley CA 94708 Office: U Calif Sch Pub Health Berkeley CA 94720

TEMPEST, BRUCE DEAN, physician; b. Catasauqua, Pa., Nov. 3, 1935; s. Comley Quinton and Eleanor Dorthy (Wenner) T.; A.B., Lafayette Coll., 1957; M.D., U. Pa., 1961; m. Phyllis Rems, June 20, 1959; children—Peter, Rebekah, Andrew. Intern, Phila. Gen. Hosp., 1961-62, resident in internal medicine, 1962-65; fellow in immunology and allergy Hosp. U. Pa., 1965-67; med. dir. USPHS, HEW, 1967; chief medicine USPHS Hosp., Tuba City, Ariz., 1967-70; chief, dep. chief medicine Gallup (N.Mex.) Indian Med. Center, 1970—. Fellow A.C.P. Republican. Mem. Christian Reformed Ch. Contbr. articles to profl. jours.; research epidemiology of pneumonia. Home: 1603 Monterey Dr Gallup NM 87301 Office: Gallup Indian Med Center Gallup NM 87301

TENG, EDWARD FON SAN, computer company executive; b. Taipei, Taiwan, Feb. 6, 1950; came to U.S., 1974; naturalized, 1984; s. Sheng-Siong and Whee-lang (Lee) T.; m. Tsing-ping, Chang, July 1, 1978; children—Tammy, Karen. B.S., Nat. Taiwan U., 1972; M.S., Wash. State U., 1976, Ph.D., 1979. Sr. assoc. engr. IBM, Rochester, Minn., 1979-81; tech. mgr. MPI Div. CDC, Santa Clare, Calif., 1981-83; co-founder, tech. mgr. Lin Data Corp., Santa Clara, 1983—. Contbr. articles to profl. jours. Pres. Chinese Student Assn., Pullman, Wash., 1976. Recipient Outstanding Achievement award Sperry Univac, Santa Clara, 1982. Mem. Am. Chem. Soc., IEEE, Am. Inst. Chem. Engring. Office: Lin Data Corp 2005 Dela Cruz Blvd Santa Clara CA 95050

TENGERDY, ROBERT PAUL, microbiology educator; b. Budapest, Hungary, Dec. 17, 1930; came to U.S., 1957; s. Ferenc and Aranka (Garay) T.; m. Catherine Elizabeth Kokeny, Nov. 14, 1953; children: Thomas, Peter. Diploma in Chem. Engring., U. Tech. Sch., Budapest, 1953; PhD, St. John's U., N.Y.C., 1961. Asst. prof. chem. engring. U. Tech. Sch., Budapest, 1953-56; research biochemist Charles Pfizer & Co., Bklyn., 1957-61; asst. prof. microbiology Colo. State U., Ft. Collins, 1961-64, assoc. prof., 1964-70, prof., 1970—. Contbr. numerous articles on biotechnology and immunology to profl. jours. A. von Humboldt fellow, 1968, Fulbright fellow, 1985. Mem. Am. Soc. Microbiology, Soc. Indsl. Microbiology. Home: 1236 Country Club Rd Fort Collins CO 80524 Office: Colo State U Dept Microbiology Fort Collins CO 80523

TENNANT, FOREST SEARLS, JR., physician; b. Dodge City, Kans., Jan. 23, 1941; s. Forest Searls and Vivian (White) T.; A.A., Hutchinson (Kans.) Jr. Coll., 1960; B.A., U. Mo., 1962; M.D., U. Kans., 1966; M.P.H., U. Calif., Los Angeles, 1973, D.P.H., 1974; m. Miriam Isaac, Sept. 17, 1966. Intern, U. Louisville, 1966-67; resident in internal medicine U. Tex. Med. Br., 1967-68; postdoctoral fellow USPHS, also resident in preventive medicine UCLA, 1972-74; exec. dir. Community Health Projects, Inc., West Covina, Calif., 1974—; assoc. prof. dept. public health UCLA; cons. Calif. Dept. Justice, Los Angeles Dodgers Baseball Club; advisor on drugs NFL. Bd. dirs. Am. Cancer Soc., 1976, Am. Lupus Soc., 1978, ARC, 1979; pres. West Covina Republican Club, 1976; mem. West Covina City Council, 1980-85; mayor West Covina, 1985-86. Served to maj. M.C., AUS, 1968-72. Decorated Army Commendation medal, Meritorious Service medal. Diplomate Am. Bd. Family Practice, Am. Bd. Preventive Medicine, Nat. Bd. Med. Examiners. Fellow Am. Coll. Preventive Medicine; mem. Calif., Los Angeles County med. assns., So. Calif. Assn. Physicians in Drug Dependence (pres.), AMA, Calif. Soc. Treatment of Dependency Disorders, Am., Calif. pub. health assns., Assn. Tchrs. Preventive Medicine, Am. Geriatrics Soc., Am. Assn. Automotive Medicine, AAAS, Calif. Soc. Treatment of Alcoholism and Other Durg Dependencies (dir.). Methodist. Club: Rotary (dir. 1978). Contbr. articles to profl. jours. Home: 1744 Aspen Village Way West Covina CA 91791 Office: Community Health Products 336 1/2 S Glendora Ave Covina CA 91790

TENNEN, LESLIE IRWIN, lawyer; b. Toronto, Ont., Can., Aug. 26, 1952; came to U.S., 1961; s. Edward and Elsie (Liberbaum) T. B.A. with distinction, U. Ariz., 1973, J.D., 1976; Mount Scopus, Hebrew U., Jerusalem, 1975. Bar: Ariz. 1977, U.S. Dist. Ct. Ariz. 1979. Sole practice, Tucson, 1977-79; ptnr. Sterns and Tennen, Phoenix and Tucson, Ariz., 1979—; cons. internat. law and aerospace activities; lectr. Princeton U., U. Ariz., Am. Grad. Sch. Internat. Mgmt., also profl. aviation and aerospace congresses and seminars in N.Am., Europe, Asia; judge Jessup Internat. Moot Court Competition, 1982, 83, 85. Contbr. articles to profl. jours. Precinct committeeman State Democratic Com., 1972-73. Received highest score Ariz. Bar Examination, 1977. Mem. Internat. Inst. Space Law, Am. Soc. Internat. Law, AIAA, Aviation Space Writers Assn., Planetary Soc., Fedn. Aerospace Socs. in Tucson (exec. bd.). Office: Sterns and Tennen 932 N Swan Rd Tucson AZ 85711

TENNEY, ROBERT NELSON, finance company executive; b. Detroit, Jan. 14, 1942; s. Elmer L. and Marguerite E. (Proper) T. BS, Ferris State Coll., 1965. Asst. v.p. Congress Fin. Corp., N.Y.C., 1970-76; sr. v.p. Congress Fin. Corp., Los Angeles, 1984—; v.p. A.J. Armstrong Corp., Los Angeles, 1976-81, Chase Comml. Corp., Los Angeles, 1981-84. Pres. Park Kenwood Homeowners Assn., Glendale, Calif., 1983-84. Mem. Comml. Fin. Conf. of Calif. (bd. dirs. 1981—, pres. 1983-85, chmn. bd. 1985—), Nat. Comml. Fin. Assn. (Far Western edn. com. 1983—, program com. 1985), Tau Kappa Epsilon (chmn. bd. trustees Calif. Poly. State U. Pomona chpt., 1984—). Clubs: Los Angeles, Los Angeles Athletic. Office: Congress Fin Corp 3333 Wilshire Blvd Los Angeles CA 90010

TENNEY, WILLIAM FRANK, physician; b. Shreveport, La., June 5, 1946; s. William Bonds and Pat (Patton) T.; m. Elizabeth Carter Steadman, Oct. 4, 1973; children: Amy Karen, William Allen. BA, Vanderbilt U., 1968; MD, La. State U., New Orleans, 1972. Diplomate Am. Bd. Pediatrics, sub-Bd. Pediatric Nephrology. Intern Grady Meml. Hosp., Atlanta, 1972-73; resident in pediatrics Emory U. Affiliated Hosps., Atlanta, 1973-74, fellow in pediatric nephrology and inorganic metabolism, 1974-76; practice medicine specializing in pediatric nephrology St. Helens, Oreg., 1976-79, Shreveport, 1979-85, Seattle, 1985—; mem. staff Children's Orthopedic Hosp. and Med. Ctr., Seattle; chief dept. pediatrics Swedish Hosp. Med. Ctr., Seattle, 1987—; clin. asst. prof. pediatrics La. State U. Sch. Medicine, 1979-85, U. Wash. Sch. Medicine, Seattle, 1985—; chmn. Renal com. Schumpert Med. Ctr., Shreveport, 1982, co-chmn. 1979-81, mem. 1983-84, co-dir. Renal Dialysis Unit, 1979-84, mem. renal transplantation com., 1984; cons. pediatric nephrology Shriner's Hosp. Crippled Children, Shreveport, 1979-84, Shreveport Regional Dialysis Ctr., 1979-84, Bossier Dialysis Ctr., Bossier City, La., 1983-84,

Natchitoches (La.) Dialysis Facility, 1984. Author: (with others) Pediatric Case Studies, 1985; contbr. articles to profl. jours. Mem. Union Concerned Scientists, Cambridge, Mass., 1986—, Internat. Physicians for Prevention of Nuclear War, Boston, 1986—. Fellow Am. Acad. Pediatrics; mem. Am. Soc. Pediatric Nephrology, North Pacific Pediatric Soc., AMA, Wash. State Med. Assn., Internat. Soc. Peritoneal Dialysis, Empirical Soc. Emory U., King County Med. Soc., AAAS, Northwest Renal Soc., Southwest Pediatric Nephrology (mem. study group 1981-84). Avocations: oil painting, rockhounding, camping, jogging. Home: 1133 16th Ave E Seattle WA 98112 Office: 1221 Madison St Seattle WA 98104

TENORIO, PEDRO PANGELINAN, governor No. Mariana Islands; b. Saipan, Mariana Islands, Apr. 18, 1934; m. Sophia Tenorio; 8 children. Student, Territorial Coll. of Guam (now U. Guam). Formerly sch. tchr., bus exec.; former mem. Congress of Micronesia, also Marianas Dist. Legis.; v.p. Senate, chmn. program com. 1978-80 , pres. Senate, 1980-82; gov. No. Mariana Islands, 1982-. Repulbican. Roman Catholic. Office: Office of Gov No Mariana Islands Saipan CM 96950*

TENOVER, FRED CARRON, microbiologist; b. Kalamazoo, Mich., Oct. 28, 1954; s. Fred and Mary Georganna (Carron) T. BS, U. Dayton, 1976; MS/PhD, U. Rochester, 1981. Lab. asst. U. Dayton, Ohio, 1974-75; technician Borgess Hosp., Kalamazoo, 1975-76; nat. research service U. Rochester, N.Y., 1976-80; sr. fellow U. Wash., Seattle, 1980-82; asst. prof. U. Washington, Seattle, 1982—; assoc. chief microbiolgist VA Med. Ctr., Seattle, 1982—; mem. editorial bd. Jour. Clinical Microbiology, Washington, 1986—, Antimicrobial Agts. and Chemotherapy, Washington, 1986—; cons. USAID-Suez Canal U., Ismailia, Eqypt, 1983-85; visiting scientist Armed Forces Research Inst. for Med. Scis., Bangkok, 1986. Contbr. over 50 scientific articles to profl. jours. Mem. Bread for the World, Washington, 1973—; IMPACT, Washington, 1975—, Smithsonian Inst., Washington, 1985—. Mem. Am. Eagle Scout Assn., Am. Soc. Microbiology (pres.' fellow 1979), Acad. Clinical Physicians and Scientists, Am. Venereal Disease Assn., AAAS. Roman Catholic. Avocations: hiking, tennis, traveling. Home: 123 Blaine St Seattle WA 98109 Office: Lab Service VA Med Ctr 1660 S Columbian Way Seattle WA 98108

TENZER, MICHAEL L., housing development executive; b. N.Y.C., May 7, 1930; s. Sigmund and Rose (Weiss) T.; m. Jacqueline Newmark, Aug. 7, 1952; children—Gary, Marc. Grad. Art Ctr. Coll. Design, 1949. Photojournalist Look mag., 1949-50; free-lance photographer, pub. relations UN, 1950-51; mgr. brand mktg. Modern Globe, Inc., 1953-57; gen. sales mgr. Berkshire Hosiery Mills, Reading, Pa., 1957-60; mktg. mgr. intimate apparal div. Kayser-Roth Corp., N.Y.C., 1960-63; sr. v.p., dir. Larwin Group, Inc., Beverly Hills, Calif., 1963-74; pres. single family div. Tenzer & Co., Inc., Beverly Hills, 1975-76; chmn. bd., pres., chief exec. officer, dir. Leisure Tech., Los Angeles, 1976—; bd. dirs. policy adv. bd. Ctr. for Real Estate and Urban Econs., U. Calif., Berkeley; mem. Nat. Housing Conf. Past regional chmn. Crescent Bay council Boy Scouts Am., 1966-68, chmn. exec. com., exec. bd. Ocean Ctr. council; mem. Ocean County (N.J.) council Boy Scouts Am., Los Angeles council Boy Scouts Am.; mem. Pres. Carter's Housing Task Force; trustee, chmn. bd. emeritus Young Musicians Found.; trustee Friends of Music, U. So. Calif., 1971-79, Washington Inst. for Near East Policy; bd. dirs. Am. Youth Symphony, 1974-80; founder Met. Opera; Gold Circle founder Los Angeles Music Ctr.; chmn. bd. dirs. Am.-Israel Cultural Found.; bd. dirs. John Douglas French Found. for Alzheimer's Disease; mem. Am.-Israel Polit. Action Com. Served with Signal Corps, AUS, 1951-52. Recipient Top Performer award Housing mag., 1968, Disting. Eagle Scout award Nat. council Boy Scouts Am., 1982, Inst. Human Relations civic achievement award Am. Jewish Com., 1984, Nat. Humanitarian award Nat. Jewish Hosp., Denver, 1985. Mem. Urban Land Inst. (fed. policy com.), Nat. Assn. Home Builders (conv. housing, mortgage banking coms. 1965-73). Office: Leisure & Technology Inc 12233 W Olympic Blvd Los Angeles CA 90064

TEPPER, R(OBERT) BRUCE, JR., lawyer; b. Long Branch, N.J., Apr. 1, 1949; s. Robert Bruce and Elaine (Ogus) T.; m. Belinda Wilkins, Nov. 26, 1971; children—Laura Katherine, Jacob Wilkins. A.B. in History, Dartmouth Coll., 1971; J.D. cum laude, St. Louis U., 1976, M.A. in Urban Affairs, 1976. Bar: Mo. 1976, Calif. 1977, Ill. 1978, U.S. Ct. Appeals (7th cir.) 1978, (8th cir.) 1976, (9th cir.) 1978, U.S. Dist. Ct. (cen., no. and so. dists.) Calif. 1978. Asst. gen. counsel St. Louis Redevel. Authority; 1976-77; assoc. Goldstein & Price, St. Louis, 1977-78, Loo, Merideth & McMillan, Los Angeles, 1978-82; sole practice, Los Angeles, 1982-84; ptnr., litigation supr. Weiser, Kane, Ballmer & Berkman, Los Angeles, 1984—; spl. counsel to Solano County, San Diego, Santa Barbara, Hermosa Beach, Anaheim, Oceanside, Moreno Valley, West Covina, Glendale and Hawthorne, Calif.; judge pro tempore Los Angeles County Mcpl. Ct., 1983—; grader State Bar Calif., 1980-84. Assoc. editor St. Louis U. Law Jour., 1974-76. Contbr. articles to legal jours. Grad fellow St. Louis U., 1973-76. Mem. Los Angeles County Bar Assn., Assn. Bus. Trial Lawyers, ABA. Republican. Jewish. Clubs: So. Calif. Dartmouth (bd. dirs. 1980-83), Los Angeles Athletic (Los Angeles). Home: 10966 Wrightwood Ln Studio City CA 91604 Office: Weiser Kane Ballmer & Berkman 354 S Spring St Suite 420 Los Angeles CA 90013

TEPPERMAN, MARGOT EVONNE BAKER, psychotherapist; b. Chgo., Feb. 4, 1936; d. Frank Eastman and Irene Ann (Grosse) Baker; m. David Jay Tepperman, Mar. 26, 1967; children: Elliott Michael, Jonathan Daniel. BA, U. Colo., 1957, MA, 1962; MSW with distinction, Fresno State U., 1976. Lic. clin. social worker, Calif. Therapist Calif., 1976, Visalia (Calif.) Mental Health Ctr., 1977-78; dir. Fresno Vol. Bur., 1979-81; pres. Transitions, Fresno, 1981—; coordinator employee assistance program Human Affairs Inc., San Francisco, 1984—. Developer Nat. award program Cancer Soc., Fresno, 1977-78; mem. speakers bur. Mental Health Assn., 1983—; vol. pub. TV fund drive. Named Woman of Yr., Midstate Bus. and Profl. Women, 1983; finalist to be named Profl. and Bus. Women of Yr. City of Fresno, 1986. Mem. Profl. Sales Women's Assn., Nat. Acad. Social Workers (cert.), Fresno Career Women Assn., Am. Assn. Counseling and Devel., Am. Group Therapy Assn., Folklore Soc., Traditional Jazz Assn., Soc. Creative Anachronism, C. of C., Execs. Assn. Fresno. Democrat. Jewish. Avocations: sailing, cultural arts, travelling. Office: Transitions 171 N Van Ness Fresno CA 93701

TERJUNG, WERNER HEINRICH, climatology educator; b. Mülheim-Ruhr, Fed. Republic Germany, Feb. 27, 1931; came to U.S., 1954; s. Ernst and Mathilde (Bergstein) T.; m. Bettye Jane Kilgore, Sept. 25, 1954; children: Jane, Nancy. BA, Long Beach State U., 1962, MA, 1963; PhD, UCLA, 1966. Tchr. Mayflower High Sch., Bellflower, Calif., 1963-64; prof. climatology UCLA, 1966—. Contbr. numerous articles to profl. jours. Served to sgt. U.S. Army, 1954-57. Research grantee NSF, 1966, 75-78, Dept. of Interior, UCLA, 1969-72. Mem. AAAS, NSF (referee 1966—), Assn. Am. Geographers, Internat. Soc. Biometeorology, Sigma Xi (sec. Los Angeles chpt. 1981-83), Gamma Theta Upsilon. Avocation: hiking. Office: UCLA Dept Geography Los Angeles CA 90024

TERREL, RONALD LEE, civil engineer, executive, former educator; b. Klamath Falls, Oreg., Sept. 2, 1936; s. Theodore Thomas and Ruth Margaret (Fausset) T.; m. Susan Laura Harrower, Feb. 28, 1959 (div. July 1981); children: Douglas Scott, Nancy Dawn, Janet Lynn; m. 2d Alice Marie Blanchard, July 23, 1981. B.S.C.E., Purdue U., 1960, M.S., 1961; Ph.D., U. Calif.-Berkeley, 1967. Estimator J.H. Pomeroy & Co., San Francisco, 1955; lab. asst. Purdue U., 1956-60; asst. field geologist Bear Creek Mining Co., Mpls., 1957-58; materials engr. U.S. Bur. Reclamation, Denver, 1960-64; project engr. J.H. Pomeroy & Co., Antigua, B.W.I., 1964-65; research asst. U. Calif.-Berkeley, 1965-67; asst. prof. civil engr. U. Wash., Seattle, 1967-70, assoc. prof., 1970-75, prof., 1975-85, prof. emeritus, 1985—, head Transp. Constrn. and Geometrics div., 1976-79; pres. Pavement Systems Inc., 1970-82; exec. v.p. Seattle Engring. Internat., Inc., 1979-81; pres. Terrel Assocs., Inc., 1981-85, owner, 1986—; v.p. Pavement Technologies Inc., 1985-86; cons. in field. Co-founder, bd. dirs. Wash. State Transp. Ctr., 1981-84. Nominated Constrn. Man of Yr. Engring. News-Record, 1972; Purdue Alumni scholar, 1959-60; Ford fellow, 1965-67. Mem. ASCE, Transp. Research Bd., Assn. Asphalt Paving Technologists (bd. dirs. 1979-83, W.J. Emmons 1983), ASTM, Triaxial Inst. (chmn. 1971-73), Can. Tech. Asphalt Assn., Sigma Xi, Tau Beta Pi, Chi Epsilon, Sigma Gamma Epsilon. Office: 9703 241st Pl SW Edmonds WA 98020

TERRELL, A. JOHN, university telecommunications director; b. Pasadena, Calif., Dec. 27, 1927; s. Harry Evans and Elizabeth (Eaton) T.; m. Elizabeth Schalk, June 6, 1949; children—Patricia Elyse, Marilee Diane, John Scott. Student, Chaffey Coll., 1947-48; B.B.A., U. N. Mex., 1952. Communications cons. Mountain States Tel. & Tel., Albuquerque, 1951-56; mgr. office and communications services A.C.F. Industries, Inc., Albuquerque, 1956-62; mgr. communications and services Norton Simon Industries, Inc., Fullerton, Ca., 1962-68; v.p. gen. mgr. Wells Fargo Security Guard Service Div. Baker Industries, Fullerton, Ca., 1968-71; adminstrv. mgr., budget adminstr. Hyland div. Baxter-Trevenol Labs. Inc., Costa Mesa, CA, 1971-77; exec. v.p. Am. Tel. Mgmt. Inst Inc., Newport Beach, Calif., 1977-78; telecommunications dir. UCLA, 1978—. Contbr. articles to profl. jours. Republican. candidate for state rep., Albuquerque, 1960; precinct chmn. and mem. Bernalillo County Rep. Central Com., 1961-62; Rep. candidate for N. Mex. State Bd. Edn., 2nd Jud. Dist., 1962; colonial aide-de-camp Gov. N. Mex., Santa Fe, 1968. Served with U.S. Mcht. Marine, 1944-45, U.S. Army, 1946-47, USAR, 1947-50. Mem. Nat. Assn. Accts. (dir. 1967-77) (Most Valuable mem. 1974-75), Telecommunications Assn., Am. Legion, Am. Legion Yacht Club , VFW. Episcopalian. Lodges: Greater Irvine Lions (charter pres. 1975-76), Albuquerque Jaycees (v.p., treas. 1956-62). Home: 1725 Port Charles Pl Newport Beach CA 92660-5319 Office: UCLA 405 Hilgard Ave CSBI Los Angeles CA 90024-1363

TERRELL, CHARLES SHAUL, JR., educational administrator; b. Chgo., Oct. 1, 1930; s. Charles Shaul Sr. and Maxine (Kagley) T.; m. Roberta Lucille Fisher, Aug. 31, 1951; children—Gregory Allen, Kathleen Rae Smith. B.A., LaVerne Coll., 1952; M.A., San Diego State U., 1956; Ed.D., U. So. Calif., 1966. Tchr. Hudson Elem. Sch. Dist., La Puente, Calif., 1952-53, San Diego City Sch. Dist., 1955-56; tchr. social studies Azusa High Sch., Calif., 1956-58, counselor, 1957-60, dir. student activities, 1960-61, unit adminstr., 1961-63, prin., 1963-66; supt. Needles Unified Sch. Dist., Calif., 1966-69, Corona-Norco Unified Sch. Dist., Calif., 1969-77; supt. San Bernardino City Unified Sch. Dist., Calif., 1977-82; supt. San Bernardino County Sch. Dist., 1982—; pres. EDUCARE, sch. Edn., U. So. Calif., Los Angeles, 1964—, also dir.; summer session instr. U. Calif.-Irvine, 1973-75; instr. Calif. State Coll., San Bernardino, 1977—; mem. Coll. Bd. Western Regional Acad. Adv. Panel. Past pres. Nat. Soc. to Prevent Blindness, So. Calif. affiliate; bd. dirs. San Bernardino Community Hosp. Served as cpl. USMC, 1953-55. Recipient Award Merit, Corona C. of C., 1976. Mem. Am. Assn. Sch. Adminstrs. (chmn. Calif. del. 1979-87, mem. Nat. Ctr. for Improvement Learning, 1980-84), Assn. Calif. Sch. Adminstrs. (supt. com. 1978—), Small Sch. Dists. Assn. (exec. com.), San Bernardino Area C. of C. (bd. dirs., v.p.). Republican. Presbyterian. Lodges: Rotary (past pres.), Elks, Masons. Home: 3730 Osbun Rd San Bernardino CA 92404 Office: County Supt Schs 601 N E St San Bernardino CA 92410-3093

TERRELL, (NELSON) JAMES, JR., physicist; b. Houston, Aug. 15, 1923; s. Nelson James and Gladys Delphine (Stevens) T.; m. Elizabeth Anne Pearson, June 9, 1945; children—Anne (dec.), Barbara, Jean. B.A., Rice U., 1944, M.A., 1947, Ph.D., 1950. Research asst. Rice U., Houston, 1950; asst. prof. physics Western Res. U., Cleve., 1950-51; mem. staff Los Alamos Nat. Lab., U. Calif., 1951—. Producer (computer generated movie) The X-Ray Sky, 1969-76; contbr. articles to profl. jours. and encys. Served to 1st lt. AUS, 1944-46. Graham Baker scholar, 1943-44; fellow Rice U., 1946-48, AEC, 1948-50. Fellow Am. Phys. Soc., AAAS; mem. Am. Astron. Soc., Internat. Astron. Union, Phi Beta Kappa, Sigma Xi. Clubs: Los Alamos Ski, Los Alamos Choral Soc. Fields of work include relativity, quasars, x-ray and gamma ray astronomy, nuclear physics, lasers. Home: 85 Obsidian Loop Los Alamos NM 87544 Office: Los Alamos Nat Lab Mail Stop D436 Los Alamos NM 87545

TERRELL, W. GLENN, university president; b. Tallahassee, May 24, 1920; s. William Glenn and Esther (Collins) T.; divorced; children: Francine Elizabeth, William Glenn III. BA, Davidson Coll., 1942, LLD (hon.), 1969; MS, Fla. State U., 1948; PhD, State U. Iowa, 1952; LLD (hon.), Gonzaga U., 1984, Seattle U., 1985. Instr., then asst. prof. Fla. State U., Tallahassee, 1948-55; asst. prof., then assoc. prof., chmn. dept. psychology U. Colo., Boulder, 1955-59, assoc., acting dean Coll Arts and Scis., 1959-63; prof. psychology, dean Coll. Liberal Arts and Scis., U. Ill. at Chgo. Circle, 1963-65, dean faculties, 1965-67; pres. Wash. State U., Pullman, 1967-85, pres. emeritus, 1985—; Pres. Nat. Assn. State Univs. and Land-Grant Colls., 1977-78. Contbr. articles to profl. jours. Served to capt. inf. U.S. Army, 1942-46, ETO. Recipient Disting. Alumnus award U. Iowa, 1985. Fellow APA; mem. Am. Psychol. Assn., AAAS, Sigma Xi, Phi Kappa Phi. Avocations: golf, reading, traveling. Home: SW 410 Crestview #1 Pullman WA 99163 Office: Wash State U Pullman WA 99163

TERRY, KEITH EMERSON, automation systems manager, industrial engineer; b. Portsmouth, N.H., Jan. 20, 1957; s. Paul Vaughn and Barbara Rita (Hitchcock) T.; m. Kimberley Kay Wimsatt, Feb. 16, 1980; 1 child, Michael. BS in Indsl. Engring., Oreg. State U., 1979. Cert. engr.-in-tng. Indsl. engr. Reynolds Metals, Longview, Wash., 1979-84; plant engr. Coaxco Inc., Tualatin, Oreg., 1982-83; automation mgr. Reynolds Metals, Longview, 1984—. Task force mem. Cowlitz County Computer Study, Longview, 1986. Mem. Portland PC Club, Portland Soc. Computer Users, Inst. Indsl. Engrs. Avocations: board sailing, snow skiing, jogging. Office: Reynolds Aluminum Prim Metals PO Box 999 Longview WA 98632

TERRY, LEE MARION, employment company executive; b. Tuatapere, N.Z., May 4, 1937; d. Andrew and Edna (Jordan) Mathieson; came to U.S., 1967; m. Richard Lee Terry, Oct. 26, 1967 (div.). A.A., Southland Coll., Invercargill, N.Z., 1953. Owner, pres. Bruce Personnel Service Inc., San Mateo, Calif., 1978—; lectr. Mem. Calif. Assn. Personnel Cons. (pres.), Nat. Assn. Personnel Cons. (dir. 1981-83), Calif. Employment Assn. (J.R. Pierce award 1976, Jean Widdicombe award 1979, 84), Nat. Assn. Female Execs., Nat. Assn. Personnel Cons. (sec. 1985-86), Am. Soc. Profl. and Exec. Women, Adv. Council Status of Women. Club: Pena Taurina Sol y Sombra (San Francisco). Office: Suite 300 2000 S El Camino San Mateo CA 94403

TERRY, ROBERT DAVIS, educator, neuropathologist; b. Hartford, Conn., Jan. 13, 1924; m. Patricia Ann Blech, June 27, 1952; 1 son, Nicolas Saul. A.B., Williams Coll., 1946; M.D., Albany (N.Y.) Med. Coll., 1950. Diplomate: Am. Bd. Pathology, Am. Bd. Neuropathology. Postdoctoral tng. St. Francis Hosp., Hartford, 1950, Bellevue Hosp., N.Y.C., 1951, Montefiore Hosp., N.Y.C., 1952-53, 54-55, Inst. Recherches sur le Cancer, Paris, France, 1953-54; sr. postdoctoral fellow Inst. Recherches sur le Cancer, 1965-66; asst. pathologist Montefiore Hosp., 1955-59; assoc. prof. dept. pathology Einstein Coll. Medicine, Bronx, N.Y., 1959-64; prof. Einstein Coll. Medicine, 1964-84, acting chmn. dept. pathology, 1969-70, chmn., 1970-84; prof. depts. neuroscis. and pathology U. Calif.-San Diego, 1984—; mem. study sect. pathology NIH, 1964-68; study sects. Nat. Multiple Sclerosis Soc., 1964-72, 74-78; mem. bd. sci. counselors Nat. Inst. Neurol. and Communicative Disorders and Stroke, NIH, 1976-80, chmn., 1977-80; mem. nat. sci. council Huntington's Disease Assn., 1978-81; mem. med. and sci. adv. bd. Alzheimer's Disease Soc., Inc., 1978—. Editorial adv. bd.: Jour. Neuropathology and Exptl. Neurology, 1963-83, 86—, Lab. Investigation, 1967-77, Revue Neurologique, 1977—, Annals of Neurology, 1978-82, Ultrastructural Pathology, 1978—, Am. Jour. Pathology, 1985—. Served with AUS, 1943-46. Mem. Am. Assn. Neuropathologists (pres. 1969-70), N.Y. Path. Soc. (v.p. 1969-71, pres. 1971-73), Am. Soc. Exptl. Pathology, Am. Neurol. Assn., Am. Acad. Neurologists. Research, publs. on Alzheimer's disease and Tay Sachs disease. Office: Dept Neuroscis U Calif San Diego La Jolla CA 92093

TERRY, ROGER, pathologist, consultant; b. Waterville, N.Y., May 8, 1917; s. Orrin and Mary Isabelle (Kennedy) T.; m. Eleanor Virginia, Dec. 13, 1942; children: Robin, Orrin. AB magna cum laude, Colgate U., 1939; MD, U. Rochester, 1944. Cert. anatomic pathologist. Intern then resident Strong Meml. Hosp., Rochester, N.Y., 1944-51; asst. prof. U. Rochester Sch. Medicine, 1951-56, assoc. prof., 1956-61, prof. pathology, 1961-69; prof. pathology U. So. Calif. Sch. Medicine, Los Angeles, 1969-82; pathologist San Gabriel (Calif.) Valley Med. Ctr., 1982—; exec. dir. Calif. Tumor Tissue Registry, Los Angeles, 1969-84. Contbr. articles to profl. jours. Served to capt. USAF, 1954-56. Fellow Am. Soc. Clin. Pathologists, Coll. Am. Pathologists; mem. Internat. Acad. Pathology (councilor 1973-76), Am. Assn. Pathologists, Los Angeles Soc. Pathologists, Am. Soc. Exptl. Pathologists, Phi Beta Kappa, Sigma Xi, Alpha Omega Alpha. Republican. Episcopalian. Avocations: ballroom dancing, scuba diving, underwater photography. Home: 2841 Shakespeare Dr San Marino CA 91108 Office: San Gabriel Valley Med Ctr 218 S Santa Anita St San Gabriel CA 91776

TERRY, STEVEN SPENCER, mathematics educator, consultant; b. Hoodriver, Oreg., July 9, 1942; s. Steven Bliss and Kathryn (Spencer) T.; m. Vivian Hickman, Aug. 20, 1964; children: Yvette, Kathryn, S. Matthew, Spencer, Stuart, Heather. BS, Utah State U., 1964, MS, 1967. Tchr. math Clayton Jr. High, Salt Lake City, 1964-67, 29 Palms (Calif.) High Sch., 1967-68; tchr. math, coach Yucca Valley (Calif.) High Sch., 1968-76; prof. math. Ricks Coll., Rexburg, Idaho, 1976—. Author: (textbook) Elementary Teachers' Math, 1978. Pres. City Council Yucca Valley, Calif., 1972-76, water bd., fire streets bd., lighting bd., recreation bd.; judge Jr. Miss Contests, Idaho; officer Baseball Assn., Madison County, Idaho. Named one of Outstanding Young Men of Am. Jaycees, 1976; recipient Outstanding Tchr. award San Bernardino and Riverside Counties, Calif., 1976, Outstanding Secondary Educator, 1974, 75. Mem. Am. Math. Assn. Two Yr. Colls. (v.p. 1980—, Outstanding Contribution award 1982, 84, 86), Nat. Council Tchrs. of Math., NEA (life), Phi Delta Kappa (life, sec. 1974-76, Outstanding Contribution award 1984). Republican. Mormon. Avocations: raquetball, basketball, computer programming, outdoor activities, skiing. Home: 221 S 2d E Rexburg ID 83440 Office: Ricks Coll Rexburg ID 83440

TERRY, WILLIAM MACK, investment banker; b. Oklahoma City, Sept. 2, 1943; s. O.A. and Helen (McConkey) T.; children: Paul Bryan, Rachel Lynn. BS, MIT, 1968, MS, 1968. Dir. mgmt. scis. Bank of Am., San Francisco, 1973-77, sr. v.p., dep. cashier, 1977-82, sr. v.p. product devel., 1982-84, dir. asset sales, 1984-86; chmn. Tavistock Capital Corp., San Francisco, 1986—. Mem. Fin. Execs. Inst. (program dir. 1981). Republican. Clubs: San Francisco Tennis, Bankers (San Francisco). Avocations: skiing, flying. Office: Tavistock Capital Corp 300 Montgomery Suite 1111 San Francisco CA 94104

TERWILLIGER, NORA BARCLAY, marine biologist; b. Hartford, Conn., Oct. 9, 1941; d. Edward Elwin and Marjorie (Scribner) B.; m. Robert Chapman Terwilliger, May 9, 1967; children: Kelly Jean, Robert Barclay. BS, U. Vt., 1963; MS, U. Wis., 1965; PhD, U. Oreg., 1981. Cert. med. technologist Am. Soc. Clin. Pathologists. Research asst. Boston U., 1967-69; research asst. U. Oreg., Charleston, 1971-78, research assoc., 1981—; instr. State of Oreg., Coos Bay, 1974-75, S.W. Oreg. Community Coll., Coos Bay, 1980-81; vis. scientist Marine Biol. Assn., Plymouth, Eng., 1983-84; cons. Coos Bay Sch. Dist., 1975-76. Contbr. articles to profl. jours. Mem. AAAS, Am. soc. Zoologists, We. Soc. Naturalists, Phi Beta Kappa. Home and Office: Oreg Inst Marine Biology Charleston OR 97420

TERWISCHE, DAVID KENNETH, broadcasting educator, television writer and producer; b. Quincy, Ill., Nov. 30, 1943; s. Kenneth Theodore and Virginia Mary (Dickwish) T. BA, Culver-Stockton Coll., 1965; MA, U. Mo., 1967, PhD, 1970. Asst. prof. So. Ill. U., Carbondale, 1970-78; network publicist Columbia Broadcasting System, Hollywood, Calif., 1978-80; free-lance TV writer Hollywood, Calif., 1980-82; asst. prof. U. Ariz., Tucson, 1982-84; assoc. prof. Eastern Wash. U., Cheney, 1984—; founder and dir. Summer TV drama workshops So. Ill. U., 1970-78, U. Ariz., 1982-84, Eastern Wash. U., 1984—. Author (film script) Great White Virgin, 1980, also radio dramas, including Merry Christmas, Daisy Mae, 1977, Final Visit from Mr. Z, 1976, Ritchie's Angel, 1975. Mem. Broadcast Edn. Assn., Alpha Epsilon Rho. Avocations: restoring player pianos, water skiing. Home: 1817 Fourth Cheney WA 99004 Office: Eastern Wash U Radio-TV Dept Cheney WA 99004

TESAR, GAYE LEE, computer services executive; b. Crete, Nebr., Feb. 14, 1953; d. LaVern J. and Marjory Jean (Beck) T. BS, Colo. State U., 1977. Systems analyst Tech. Info. Systems, Seattle, 1978-80; lead analyst Weights Computing dept. Boeing Computer Services div. Boeing Co., Seattle, 1980-83, mgr., 1983—. Supr. King County Police-Green River Task Force, Seattle, 1985—. Mem. Boeing Mgmt. Assn., Assn. Computer Machinery, N.W. Wash. Steelheaders Assn. Republican. Office: Weights Computing/Boeing Co PO Box 3707 MS 9W/07 Seattle WA 98124

TESKE, JOHN ARTHUR, business executive; b. Merrill, Wis., Jan. 10, 1925; s. Theodore Henry and Nina Mary (Smith) T.; m. Lois Marian Seiske, Apr. 7, 1945 (dec. Nov. 1984); children—John Robert, Meri Katherine Teske Backus, Kristin Marie Teske Dillon, Michael Paul, Margaret Ann Teske O'Reilly, Liesl Bridget. B.S.E.E., U. Notre Dame, 1948, M.S. in Physics, 1949. Mem. sr. staff Johns Hopkins Applied Physics Lab., Silver Spring, Md., 1949-55; project engr. AiResearch Mfg. Co., Torrance, Calif., 1955-63, asst. div. mgr., 1963-69, v.p., mgr., 1970-75; v.p., mgr. AiResearch Mfg. Co., Phoenix, 1975-76; sr. exec. v.p. The Garrett Corp., Los Angeles, 1976-79, pres., 1979-85, chmn., pres., chief exec. officer, now also chief ops. officer, 1985—; Mem. engring. adv. bd. U. Notre Dame, 1976—, trustee Loyola Marymount U., Los Angeles, 1983—, 1985—. Chmn. Region IV United Way, Los Angeles, 1984-85, bd. dirs. Los Angeles County. Served with USN, 1944-46. Recipient Engring. award U. Notre Dame, 1975. Mem. IEEE, Aerospace Industries Assn. Am. (bd. govs.). Roman Catholic. Clubs: Los Angeles Country, California. Avocations: golf; fishing; hunting. Office: The Garrett Corp 9851 Sepulveda Blvd PO Box 92248 Los Angeles CA 90009 *

TESSIER, CLAUDIA JEANNE, medical association administrator; b. Athol, Mass., Mar. 17, 1943; d. Frederic G. Tessier and Alfreda Cora (Ross) Noel; m. David M. Byron, June 12, 1976. Student, Rivier Coll., 1961-62; AS, Fisher Jr. Coll., 1964; BA, San Francisco State U., 1972; MEd, U. Houston, 1981. Med. sec. Children's Hosp., Boston, 1964-66; adminstrv. coordinator Mt. Zion Hosp., San Francisco, 1966-70; adminstrv. asst. San Francisco State U., 1970-72, adminstrv. research technician, 1973-74; adminstrv. asst. New Eng. Edn. Tng. Service, Wiesbaden, Federal Republic of Germany, 1973; med. transcriptionist Dictation West, San Francisco and Riverside, Calif., 1974-78; asst. chief med. records USPHS Hosp., Nassau Bay, Tex., 1979-80; asst. prof. med. records U. Ill., Chgo., 1980-82, U. Wis., MIlw., 1982; dir. edn. Am. Assn. Med. Transcription, Modesto, Calif., 1983-84, exec. dir., 1984—. Author: The Surgical Word Book, 1981; co-author: Style Guide for Medical Transcription, 1985; editor and writer Jour. Am. Assn. Med. Transcription, 1983—. Served to lt. (j.g.) USPHS, 1978-80. Mem. Am. Assn. Med. Transcription, Am. Soc. Assn. Execs., Am. Med. Record Assn., Am. Med. Writers Assn., Am. Soc. Allied Health Profls. Avocations: opera, reading, travel. Office: Am Assn Med Transcription 3460 Oakdale Rd Suite D Modesto CA 95355

TESTA, RICHARD ALAN, computer systems executive; b. Revere, Mass., Sept. 10, 1955; s. Albert and Marilyn (MacNeil) T.; m. Martha Louise Sullivan, Oct. 9, 1976; 1 child, Branden Douglas. BA, Boston U., 1978, M in Urban Affairs, 1981, MS, 1983. Asst. v.p. ops. Towle Silver Co., Boston, 1976-81; sr. system analyst S.F. Techs., San Fernando, Calif., 1981-82; systems mgr. Reisner Metal Co., South Gate, Calif., 1982-85, Korn Ferry Internat., Los Angeles, 1985—. Mem. Digital Equipment User Group. Club: Simi Hills Men's (Simi Valley, Calif.). Avocation: golf. Home: 1340 S Beverly Glen #115 Los Angeles CA 90024 Office: Korn Ferry Internat 1800 Century Park E #900 Los Angeles CA 90067

TESTUT, RICHARD STANTON, corporate executive, consultant; b. N.Y.C., Mar. 2, 1910; s. Lester and Edith (Arnold) T.; m. Ruth Elizabeth Tompkins, Nov. 3, 1934 (div.); children—Richard Stanton, Robert Bruce, Barbara Ruth; m. Ilene Hazel Bennett, June 30, 1950; 1 dau., Beverly Sue. Student Cornell U., 1928-29, NYU, 1929-30. Nat. account exec. Scott Paper Co., Phila., 1933-45; v.p. Muzak Corp., N.Y.C., 1946-50; regional dir. Booz, Allen & Hamilton, N.Y.C., 1950-55; v.p. Servel, Inc., Evansville, Ind., 1955-56; pres. Testut Fin. Corp., San Diego, 1957—, also dir.; chmn. bd. dirs., chief exec. officer CSI Technologies, Inc., San Marcos, Calif., 1973—; bd. dirs. Cam-Stat, Inc., Los Angeles, Am. Electronics, Inc., Fullerton, Calif. Mem. Am. Mgmt. Assn., Alpha Tau Omega. Republican. Presbyterian. Clubs: Lake San Marcos Country; Los Angeles; Thunderbird Country (treas. 1970-76) (Rancho Mirage). Home: 3421 Lomas Serenas Dr Escondido CA

92025 Office: CSI Technologies Inc 810 Rancheros Dr San Marcos CA 92069

TETLOW, WILLIAM LLOYD, computer executive; b. Phila., July 2, 1938; s. William Lloyd and Mary Eleanor (Ferris) T.; m. Amber Jane Riederer, June 13, 1964; children: Jennifer Kay, Rebecca Dawn, Derek William. Student, Cornell U., 1956-60; B in Gen. Edn., U. Omaha, 1961; MA, Cornell U., 1965, PhD, 1973. Dir. instl. research Cornell U., Ithaca, N.Y., 1965-70; dir. planning U. B.C., Vancouver, Can., 1970-82; div. dir. NCHEMS Mgmt. Products, Boulder, Colo., 1982-85; pres., dir., propr. Vantage Info. Products, Inc., Boulder, 1985—; cons. various univs. U.S., Can. and Australia, 1970—. Editor/author: Using Microcomputers for Planning and Decision Support, 1984; contbr. numerous articles to profl. jours. Council mem. Mt. Calvary Luth. Ch., Boulder, 1984-85. Served to 1st lt. AUS, 1961-63. Mem. Assn. Inst. Research (sec. 1973-75, v.p. 1980-81, pres. 1981-82). Republican. Lodges: Concordia, Tsawwassen. Avocations: outdoor sports, camping. Home: 3650 Smuggler Way Boulder CO 80303 Office: Vantage Computer Services 1525 Spruce St Suite 100 Boulder CO 80302

TEVROW, GERALD ALAN, motion picture distribution company executive; b. Milw., Feb. 16, 1953; s. George and Esther (Salloway) T.; m. Judith Beth Traighten, Dec. 26, 1977. BS in Bus. Mgmt., Boston Coll., 1975. Various sales positions Columbia Pictures, Burbank, Calif., 1975-80; mgr. western div. Orion Pictures Corp., Los Angeles, 1980-84; prin. Sutton Mgmt., Sherman Oaks, Calif., 1984—; v.p. distribution New Line Cinema, Los Angeles, 1986—; cons. Monet, Phelps, Rothenberg & Tunny, Los Angeles, 1984-85, Torch Prodns., Los Angeles, 1985. Avocations: film, music, sports. Home: 14955 Sutton St Sherman Oaks CA 91403

TEWARI, ASHOK, materials engineer; b. Lucknow, India, Jan. 9, 1957; came to U.S., 1963; s. Param Hans and Shanti (Dube) T.; m. Deepa Singh, Jan. 5, 1984; 1 child, Anjali Shanti. BS in Chemistry, U. Manitoba, Can., 1978; MS in Chemistry, U. San Francisco, 1983; MS in Material Engring., San Jose State U., 1984. Engr. ESSO Research, Sarnia, Can., 1980, Petro-Can., Calgary, Can., 1981; teaching asst. U. San Francisco, 1981-82; engr. IBM, San Jose, Calif., 1983, Hewlett-Packard, Palo Alto, Calif., 1983-84; materials engr. Hewlett-Packard, Santa Clara, Calif., 1984—. Contbr. articles to profl. jours. Mem. Metall. Soc. of AIME, Am. Soc. Metals, Am. Chem. Soc., Tau Beta Pi. Club: Tennis Assn. (Manitoba). Avocation: tennis. Office: Hewlett-Packard 5301 Stevens Creek Blvd Santa Clara CA 95050

TEWARI, PARAM HANS, research scientist; b. Gorakhpur, India, Jan. 31, 1929; came to U.S., 1962; s. Moham and Rama Tewari; m. Shanti, June 25, 1953; children: Ashok, Anand. MS, 1952, PhD, 1959. Sr. scientist Atomic Energy of Canada, Pinawa, Manitoba, 1969-81; prin. scientist Exxon Enterprises, San Jose, Calif., 1981-84; staff scientist Lawrence Berkeley (Calif.) Lab., 1984—. Contbr. articles to profl. jours. Mem. Am. Chem. Soc., Am. Ceramic Soc., Materials Research Soc. Home: 40 Country Club Blvd Apt #1 Worcester MA 01605 Office: Lawrence Berkeley Lab Applied Sci Div 90-2024 Berkeley CA 94536 Home: 3330 Keslid Pl Fremont CA 94536

THACKER, HERBERT DICKEY, real estate exec.; b. Honolulu, Oct 5, 1929; s. Earl Maxwell and Dorothy Dimond (Dickey) T.; B.A., Stanford U., 1951; M.B.A., Harvard U., 1953; m. Elizabeth Pond (dec. Jan. 1953); children: William Dickey, Peter Earl, Mark Allen (dec.). With Earl Thacker Ltd., Honolulu, 1956—, pres., 1958—. Chmn. Waikiki Beach Improvement Com., 1970-71. Served to lt. USNR, 1953-56; Korea. Named Hawaii Realtor of Yr., 1969; recipient Bus. Achievement award Hawaii C. of C., 1981. Mem. Nat. Assn. Realtors (dir. 1967-82), Nat. Inst. Farm and Land Brokers, Soc. Real Estate Appraisers (v.p. 1967), Hawaii Assn. Real Estate (pres. 1968-69), Honolulu Bd. Realtors (pres. 1968-69), Honolulu C. of C., Stanford U. Alumni Assn. Clubs: Harvard Bus. Sch., Outrigger Canoe, Pacific (Honolulu). Office: 2222 Kalakaua Ave Suite 1415 Honolulu HI 96815

THACKERAY, MILTON HOWARD, accountant; b. Provo, Utah, June 13, 1944; s. Milton Grover and Farol (Hassell) T.; m. Sandra Anne West, Dec. 29, 1966; children: Steven, Anne, William, James, Thomas, Milton, Mark. BS in Acctg., U. Utah, 1968, MBA, 1969. CPA, Utah, Wyo., N.Mex. Missionary, Latter-day Saints Ch., West Germany, 1963-66; staff acct. Main Hurdman, Salt Lake City, 1969-71, sr. acct., 1971-74, mgr., 1974-77; European liason ptnr. KMG Main Hurdman, Brussels, Belgium, 1977-80, ptnr. in charge govt. services, Salt Lake City, 1980-87; ptnr. Peat Marwick Main & Co., Salt Lake City, 1987—; pres. faculty adv. bd. U. Utah, Salt Lake City, chmn. com. on faculty resources devel. chmn. com. on Grad. Sch. Acctg., 1983-84; adj. faculty mem. Westminster Coll., Salt Lake City, U. Utah, 1987. High counselor U. Utah 2d Stake, Ch. of Jesus Christ of Latter-day Saints, Salt Lake City, 1982-85. Mem. Am. Acctg. Assn., Am. Inst. CPA's, Assn. Govt. Accts., Utah Assn. CPAs (v.p., chmn. forums and speakers subcom. state legis. com. 1984—, dir.), Beta Gamma Sigma, Beta Alpha Psi. Republican. Office: KMG Main Hurdman 4th Floor Kennecott Bldg Salt Lake City UT 84133

THAETE, LARRY GENE, research pathobiologist; b. Twin Falls, Idaho, Nov. 3, 1947; s. Ernest Theodore and Hilda Dorothea (Tripple) T. BS in Zoology, Coll. Idaho, 1970; MS in Biology, No. Ariz. U., 1972; PhD in Molecular and Cellular Biology and Pathobiology, Med. U. S.C., 1984. Research assoc. Loma Linda (Calif.) U., 1973-79, U. Colo., Boulder, 1984—. Contbr. numerous articles to profl. jours. Mem. Electron Microscopy Soc. Am., The Histochem. Soc. Republican. Presbyterian. Avocations: classical guitar, scuba diving, underwater photography, cross-country skiing. Office: U Colo Sch Pharmacy Campus Box 297 Boulder CO 80309-0297

THAGARD, SHIRLEY STAFFORD, sales and marketing executive; b. Detroit, Nov. 29, 1940; d. Walter Jay Stafford and Marjorie Gertrude (LaRa) Stafford Goode; m. Charles Wendell Thagard, Sept. 21, 1963; children—Grayson Jay, Devon Charles. Assoc. Bus., Webber Coll., 1961; cert. Pierce Coll., 1973. Dir. pub. relations Miami Herald, Fla., 1963-67; pres. Thagard Enterprises, Woodland Hills, Calif., 1980—; v.p. mktg. R.T. Durable Med. Products, Inc., Miami, also Woodland Hills, 1983-85; investment cons., lectr. investments Palisades Fin. Services, Sherman Oaks, Calif., 1985-86; v.p. real estate investments, M.W. Palmer and Assocs., 1986—; ind. lectr. women's issues and children's health care, 1980—. Editor, pub. Pediatric Network, 1980-85. Contbr. articles to various jours. Creator Med. Moppets healthcare teaching tools, 1983. Chairperson Los Angeles County Mental Health (Expressing Feelings), 1985-87; ind. lobbyist for child abuse legislation Calif. Legislature, 1985—. Recipient commendation Los Angeles City Council, 1983, Calif. Congresswoman Bobbi Fiedler, 1984. Mem. Nat. Assn. Female Execs., San Fernando Valley Bd. Realtors, Assn. Care of Children's Health, Am. Bus. Women's Assn., Pilot Internat. (pub. relations com. 1985-86, San Fernando Valley club commendation 1985), Nat. Assn. Edn. Young Children, Direct Mktg. Council Los Angeles. Avocations: travel, writing. Office: PO Box 8396 Calabasas CA 91302

THALER, MANNING MICHAEL, pediatrics educator; b. Poland, Sept. 29, 1934; came to U.S., 1965; s. Morris and Fanny Thaler; m. Libby L. Fuss, Jan. 24, 1966; children: Eva, Joshua. MD, U. Toronto, Can., 1958. Prof. pediatrics U. Calif., San Francisco, 1967—, also dir. pediatric gastroenterology and nutrition; bd. dirs. U. Calif., San Francisco, 1967—. Contbr. articles to profl. jours. and chpts. to books. Pres. Holocaust Ctr. of No. Calif., San Francisco, 1982. Josiah Macy Jr. Found. scholar, 1974. Mem. Am. Soc. Biol. Chemists, Am. Pediatric Soc., Am. Soc. Clin. Investigation, Assn. for Study Liver Disease, Soc. Pediatric Research, Am. Gastroenterol. Assn. Office: U Calif M680 San Francisco CA 94143

THALL, RICHARD VINCENT, school administrator; b. San Francisco, Sept. 12, 1940; s. Albert Vincent and Alice Stella (O'Brien) T.; m. Ellyn Marie Wisherop, June 15, 1963; children: Kristen Ellyn, Richard Vincent Jr. AA, City Coll. San Francisco, 1961; BA, San Francisco State Coll., 1964; MA, San Francisco State U., 1971. Cert. elem. tchr., Calif.; cert. secondary tchr., Calif.; cert. community coll. tchr., Calif. Tchr. biology San Francisco Unified Sch. Dist., 1965-66; tchr. biology Mt. Diablo Unified Sch. Dist., Concord, Calif., 1966-79, program coordinator, 1979—; ranger/naturalist State of Calif., Brannan Island, 1973-78; naturalist Adventure Internat., Oakland, Calif., 1979-81; lectr. Princess Cruise Lines, Los Angeles, 1982-84. Author: Water Environment Studies Program, 1986; co-author: Project MER Laboratory Manual, 1982. Mem. Contra Costa County (Calif.) Natural Resources Commn., 1975-78, vice-chmn., 1977-78; active Save Mt. Diablo, Concord, 1969-76, v.p., 1974-75; mem. citizens com. Assn. Bay Area Govt. Water Quality, 1979-82, vice-chmn., 1980-82; active John Marsh Home Restoration Com., Martinez, Calif., 1977-78; troop com. chmn. Boy Scouts Am., Concord, 1984—, asst. scoutmaster, 1985—. Recipient Recognition and Excellence cert. Assn. Calif. Sch. Adminstrs., 1984; grantee State Calif., 1982, 84. Mem. AAAS, Nat. Assn. Biology Tchrs., Nat. Audubon Soc., Am. Mus. Natural Hist., Nat. Geog. Soc., Smithsonian Instn. (assoc.). Republican. Roman Catholic. Avocations: skiing, jogging, reading, hiking, photography. Home: 1712 Lindenwood Dr Concord CA 94521 Office: Mt Diablo Unified Sch Dist 1936 Carlotta Dr Concord CA 94519

THALMAN, JAMES STUART, police officer; b. Wilmette, Ill., Sept. 16, 1935; s. Mathew James Thalman and Irma Amy (Christiansen) Townsend; m. Alvena Diane Shirley, July 20, 1958 (div. Mar. 1978); children: Debra Alvena, David Matthew, Peter James, Lawrence Stephen; m. Kristine Elliott, June 10, 1978; children: Lawrence Vincent Gonzales, Jennifer Ann Gonzalez. AA, Fullerton Coll., 1967; BA, Calif. State U., Fullerton, 1973; cert., FBI Nat. Acad., 1983; M in Pub. Adminstrn., Calif. State U., Fullerton, 1986. Police officer Anaheim (Calif.) Police Dept., 1960-70, police sgt., 1970-74, police lt. traffic bur. commdr., 1974—; instr. Fullerton Coll., 1976—, San Bernardino County (Calif.) Sheriff's Dept., 1977-82, J.K. Enterprise, Chino, Calif., 1981—, Chaffey Coll., Alta Loma, Calif., 1981-85, Golden West Coll., Huntington Beach, Calif., 1982-83. Commr. County Service Area #19, San Bernardino County, 1985—; coach Little League Baseball, Chino Hills, Calif., 1981-82; chmn. Am. Host. Found., Anaheim, 1985; bd. dirs. STAR Internat. Police Officer Exchange, Anaheim, 1986—; mem. safety com. Orange County Solid Waste Assn., Anaheim, 1985—. Served with U.S. Army, Korea. Mem. NSC, Internat. Police Assn., Internat. Assn. Auto Theft Investigators, Calif. Peace Officers Assn., Calif. Pub. Parking Assn., Calif. State Sheriff's Assn., Nat. Acad. Assocs., Nat. Rifle Assn. Republican. Roman Catholic. Avocations: wood working, sports. Office: Anaheim Police Dept Traffic 425 S Harbor Blvd Anaheim CA 92805

THATCHER, DICKINSON, lawyer; b. Huntington Beach, Calif., May 26, 1919; s. Charles Harold and Gladys Belle (Dickinson) T.; m. Dale Nadine Mortensen, Feb. 2, 1952; children: Kirk R., Jeffrey L. BS, UCLA, 1941; postgrad. NYU, 1943-44, U. Paris, 1945-46; JD, Stanford U., 1948; LLM in Taxation, U. So. Calif., 1962. Bar: Calif. 1948, U.S. Ct. Claims 1956, U.S. Tax Ct. 1954, U.S. Supreme Ct. 1954. Dep. city atty. City of Los Angeles, 1948-51; credit atty. Union Oil Co., Calif., Los Angeles, 1951-54; trial atty. tax div. Dept. Justice, Washington, 1954-56; asst. U.S. atty. Los Angeles, 1956-57; sole practice Van Nuys, Calif., 1957-59, 72—, North Hollywood, Calif., 1959-72. Contbr. articles to legal jours. Served with AUS, 1942-46. Mem. ABA, State Bar Calif. (disciplinary bd. 1970-72, client security fund 1973-75), Los Angeles County Bar Assn. (chmn. council, affiliated bar pres. 1968-70, exec. com. probate and trust law sect. 1985—), San Fernando Valley Bar Assn. (pres. 1966). Home: 15040 Hamlin St Van Nuys CA 91411 Office: 14540 Haynes St Suite 109 Van Nuys CA 91411

THATCHER, MARILYN, clinical psychologist, lecturer; b. San Francisco, Jan. 23, 1933; d. John Pemberton Thatcher and Mary Frances Hill; m. John P. O'Shea, Oct. 2, 1954 (div. Oct. 1963); children—John, Patrick, Lynne, Kathleen; m. Arthur Back, Apr. 26, 1986. A.B., San Jose State U., 1953; M.A., Stanford U., 1964; Ph.D., Calif. Inst. Integral Studies, 1977. Lic. clin. psychologist, Calif.; lic. ednl. psychologist, Calif. Chief psychologist Golden Gate Regional Ctr., San Francisco, 1971-80; lectr. San Francisco State U., 1974—; pvt. practice, Greenbrae, Calif., 1980—, researcher autism, forensic psychology, Greenbrae, 1980—. Author: Application of Piaget Theory to Autism, 1977; others. Mem. Am. Psychol. Assn., Acad. Neuropsychology, Nat. Assn. Autism. Democrat. Home: 68 Oak Knoll Dr San Anselmo CA 94960

THAXTON, VERA, home economics educator; b. Wenatchee, Wash., Aug. 15, 1933; d. Charles Clay and Ruth Ellen (Parsons) T. A.A., Mt. San Antonio Coll., 1954; B.A., San Diego State U., 1956; M.S., U. Ill.-Urbana, 1958. Cert. secondary tchr., Calif. Child welfare worker I, Lucas County (Ohio) Child Welfare, Toledo, 1958-60; home econs. instr. Bridgewater (Va.) Coll., 1960-62; licensing caseworker I, Los Angeles County Dept. Charities, Bur. Licensing, 1962-63; home econs. tchr. Pomona (Calif.) Unified Sch. Dist., 1963-69, Sonora (Calif.) High Sch., 1969-71, Banning (Calif.) High Sch., 1971-73, Coachella High Sch., Thermal, Calif., 1974—. Sec., La Quinta Property Owners Assn., 1979-82, 83-84. Mem. AAUW, Am. Home Econs. Assn., Calif. Home Econs. Assn. (dist. past pres., treas.), Nat. Assn. Edn. Young Children, Calif. Assn. Edn. Young Children, Future Homemakers Am. (sponsor), Fgn. Affairs Council. Republican. Presbyterian. Club: U. Ill. Alumni (past treas.). Home: PO Box 85 La Quinta CA 92253 Office: 83-800 Airport Blvd Thermal CA 92274

THAYER, HANFORD, consulting engineer; b. Maple Island, Minn., Sept. 12, 1909; s. Nap Bon and Ida May (Purchase) T.; m. Lois Mae Foster, June 12, 1934; children: Roger Hanford, Diane Mae (Mrs. Robert Anthony Hill), Alden Bon, Shirley Anne. BSCE, Iowa State U., 1935. Registered profl. engr., Wash. Field engr. constrn. Stone & Webster Engring. Corp., Rock Island Dam, Wash., 1935-36; field engr. Bur. Fisheries, Seattle, 1936; ju. engr., asst. engr. in design and constrn. of migratory fish program Grand Coulee Dam project, Bur. Reclamation Fish and Wildlife Service, Seattle, 1939-41; regional engr. Fish and Wildlife Service, Portland, Oreg., 1941-42; asst. engr. Office of Div. Engring., CE U.S. Army, Portland, 1942; asst. engr. then assoc. engr. and supervising civil engr. Office of Div. Engring., CE U.S. Army, Seattle, 1942-62, food plain planning engr., 1962, sr. Army project coordinator, chief architecture engring. sect., 1963-67; dir. research and devel. Quinton-Budlong Engring. Corp., Seattle, 1967-69, asst. v.p., 1969-70; cons. engr., planner, mgr. Tudor Engring. Co., 1970-76; mgr. Thayer Studio, Seattle, 1972-76; mem. Puget Sound Engring. Council, chmn., 1959; v.p. Nat. Advanced Tech. Mgmt. Conf., 1962-70; primary organizer Radiation Biol. Lab. U. Wash., 1943-46; project liaison Manhattan Atomic Project, 1943-46; researcher Herbert Hoover Oral History Program, 1967-70. Bd. dirs. Useless Bay Colony, 1985-87; pres. Useless Bay Condo Assn., 1975-87; mem. Island County fire bd., 1985-87. Served to lt. CE U.S. Army, Res. 1934-40. Fellow ASCE (life mem., pres. Seattle chpt. 1956, named Engr. of Yr. 1960), Soc. Am. Mil. Engrs. (life, pres. Seattle chpt. 1950, nat. dir. 1952-67, regional v.p. 1967-76, Engr. of Yr. 1959-60, highest nat. gold medal award 1974); mem. Seattle Mcpl. League, Newcomen Soc. N.Am., NRA, NSPE, Wash. Soc. Profl. Engrs. (dir. 1970-71), Allied Arts of Seattle, Metric Assn., Seattle Area Indsl. Council. Mem. Ch. of Christ. Republican. Clubs: Seattle Engrs.; Wenatchee (Wash.) Fencing (pres. 1937-39); Cascade Sportsmens Rifle (pres. 1951). Home: 5647 S McDonald Dr #202 Langley WA 98260

THAYNE, RICHARD GRANT, photographer, writer; b. Murray, Utah, May 29, 1930; s. Clifton Earl and Mirla (Greenwood) T.; m. Ann C. Nielsen, Apr. 2, 1959; children—Catherene, Kay, Laurie; B.S. in Photography, Brigham Young U., Provo, Utah, postgrad. in photography, still and motion picture, newswriting; cert. Nord Photo Engring., 1972, Photog. Tech., Brigham Young U., 1968. Pub. 1st picture in mag. at age 12; printed 8x10 brown tone prints for Brown Studio, 1947-48; began Creative Art Photography lab at age 18, 1948—; instr. photography Brigham Young U., 1970-75; instr./producer motion pictures and video; past pres. Thayne Family Orgn. Mem. Sons of Utah Pioneers (past pres.). Served in Army N.G., 1950-52. Recipient Kodak Nat. Newspaper award in photography, 1969, 71. Mem. Profl. Photographers Am., Wedding Photographers Internat., Photog. Soc. Am., Fine Arts Club (Salt Lake City), Intermountain Profl. Photographers Assn. Mormon. Patentee in creative art photography. Author: Goodbye for Now 1981, Somethings Are Real, 1986, (video) When He Comes Again; contbr. articles to profl. jours. Home and Office: 992 E 3d N Provo UT 84601

THEE, FRANCIS CHARLES RUDOLPH, educator religion; b. Lexington, Mo., Mar. 8, 1936; s. Paul Rudolph and Yetta Mary (Willer) T.; m. Mary Ellen Bartlett, Jan. 24, 1959; 1 child, Paul Leslie. BA, Cen. Bible Coll., 1957, MA in Religion, 1959; MA, Wheaton Coll., 1963; PhD, U. Chgo., 1980; postgrad., Inst. of Holy Land Studies, Jerusalem, 1983. Ordained to ministry, Ch. Assemblies of God, 1967. Pastor's asst. Woodmere Gardens Tabernacle, Grand Rapids, Mich., 1959-61; assoc. prof. religion N.W. Coll. of the Assemblies of God, Kirkland, Wash., 1963-86, prof., 1986—. Author: Julius Africanus and the Early Christian View of Magic, 1984; contbr. articles to scholarly bibl. jours. Recipient Bible Lands Study Grant N.W. Coll., 1983, Pope Meml. Grant N.W. Coll., 1985. Mem. Am. Acad. Religion, Soc. Pentecostal Studies. Avocations: reading, traveling, hiking, computer programs. Home: 5829 112th Pl NE Kirkland WA 98033 Office: NW Coll PO Box 579 Kirkland WA 98083-0579

THELEN, MAX, JR., foundation executive, lawyer; b. Berkeley, Calif., Aug. 18, 1919; s. Max and Ora Emily (Muir) T.; m. Phyllis J. Barnhill, Mar. 8, 1952; children—Nancy B. Thelen Rehkopf, Jane M. Thelen Greene, Max, III, William B. A.B. with highest honors, U. Calif., Berkeley, 1940; J.D. cum laude, Harvard U., 1946. Bar: Calif. 1946. Since practiced in San Francisco; ptnr. Thelen, Marrin, Johnson & Bridges, 1946-87; pres., trustee S.H. Cowell Found., 1970—; pres., dir. Oramax Fund. Trustee World Affairs Council. Served to lt. USNR, 1942-46. Mem. State Bar Calif., Com. Fgn. Relations. Republican. Presbyterian. Clubs: Commonwealth (past gov.), World Trade, Marines Meml. Home: 199 Mountain View Ave San Rafael CA 94901 Office: 2 Embarcadero Ctr Suite 2200 San Francisco CA 94111

THERIOT, CHRIS BRANDON, plant engineer; b. Port Arthur, Tex., June 1, 1953; s. Carl G. and Jo Ann (Dutton) T.; m. Margaret E. Collins, Sept. 24, 1977 (div. Oct. 1982); children: Sabrina Jo Ann, Tiffany Danae. BSME, Lamar U., 1975. Plant engr. Mobile Chem. Co., Santa Ana, Calif., 1976—; cons. Fredaman's Shipbuilding, Vinton, La., 1979. Campaign coordinator Carl Parker for Senator, Beaumont, 1975. Mem. Pi Tau Sigma (v.p. 1975), Zeta Beta Tau. Republican. Avocations: weightlifting, golf, skiing, soft ball. Home: 14402 Cherrywood Tustin CA 92680 Office: Mobil Chem Co 2530 S Birch Santa Ana CA 92707

THEROUX, DAVID JON, economist, educator, research exec.; b. Lansing, Mich., May 25, 1949; s. Paul Richard and Marjorie Erma (Withrow) T.; m. Elaine Laconia Shipp, Mar. 20, 1976; children—Paul Jacques, Drake Emeri. A.B. in Applied Math., U. Calif.-Berkeley, 1973, B.S.M.E., 1973, M.S.M.E., 1974; M.B.A., U. Chgo., 1977. Research asst. Richmond Field Sta., U. Calif.-Berkeley, 1974; project engr. Exxon Co. U.S.A., 1975-76; research asst. U. Chgo., 1976, dir. vis. lecture program in econ. sci., 1977; v.p., dir. acad. affairs, dir. pub. policy studies Cato Inst., San Francisco, 1977-79; pres., dir. Pacific Inst. Pub. Policy Research, San Francisco, 1979-86; pres. The Ind. Inst., San Francisco, 1986—; pres., gen. ptnr. LibertyTree Network, 1986—; bd. dirs. San Francisco Grocery Express, 1986—; mem. Council for Monetary Reform, adv. bd. No. Calif. Econ. Seminars, 1981—, Jour. Austrian Econs. Trustee, William Koch Found., 1978-79. Served with USAF, 1967-72. Recipient George Washington Honor medal for excellence, 1983. Mem. Am. Econ. Assn., Royal Econ. Soc., Western Econ. Assn., So. Econ. Assn., Nat. Assn. Bus. Economists, Pub. Choice Soc., Direct Mtkg. Assn., Pi Tau Sigma, Omicron Delta Epsilon. Sr. editor: Policy Report, 1978-79; editor: Cato Papers, 1978-79; The Energy Crisis: Government Policy and the Economy, 1978; (with P. Truluck) Private Rights and Public Lands, 1983; Politics and Tyranny: Lessons in Pursuit of Freedom, 1985. Home: 6311 Girvin Dr Oakland CA 94611 Office: 847 Sansome St San Francisco CA 94111

THERRIAN, MICKAELA, lawyer, educator; b. Rapid City, S.D., Oct. 30, 1952; d. Fergus Manfred and Pahla Yuvette (Marvin) T.; m. John Harkey, Nov. 1986. B.S. in Speech and Theatre, Lewis Clark State Coll., 1974. J.D., U. Idaho, 1977. Bar: Idaho 1978, Ariz. 1980, U.S. Dist. Ct. Idaho 1978, U.S. Dist. Ct. Ariz. 1980, U.S. Ct. Appeals (9th cir.) 1983; cert. community coll. tchr., Ariz. Intern, State of Alaska Pub. Defender, Fairbanks, 1977; lawyer, chief staff Bur. Support Enforcement, Boise, Idaho, 1978-79; dep. county atty. Coconino County (Ariz.), Flagstaff, 1980-85; Navajo County (Ariz.), 1986—; prof. law Yavapai Community Coll. Bd. dirs. Theatrikos, Flagstaff, Flagstaff Women's Shelter; mem. Friends Coconino County/Flagstaff City Library, Flagstaff Vol. League, Friends of the River. Caroline Silverthorn scholar, 1972. Mem. Idaho Bar Assn., Ariz. Bar Assn., ABA, Ariz. Women for Agr., Ariz. Women Lawyers Assn., Am. Trial Lawyers Assn., N.Am. Basque Orgn. (pres. local chpt.), Navajo County Bar Assn. (v.p.) Christian Scientist. Office: Navajo County Govtl Complex Holbrook AZ 86025

THERRIAULT, RONALD GREGORY, cultural organization administrator; b. Stockton, Calif., Nov. 2, 1931; s. Paul Elmer Therriault and Gertrude Lousia (Neeham) Allec; m. Dona Rae Pedersen, Jan. 1956 (div. Jan. 1978); children: Kimberley, Heather, Ronald; m. Ginny Ann Wright, Oct. 6, 1978; children: Benjamin John, Renee Carmel. AA, Hartnell Coll., 1976; BA, Antioch U., 1979. Commd. U.S. Army, 1950, advanced through grades to sgt. maj., 1971, ret., 1974; dir. Native Am. studies Salish/Kootenai Coll., Pablo, Mont., 1980—; chmn. tribal council Confederated Salish & Koutenai Tribes, Pablo, 1986; chief cons. Winter Count Inc., St. Ignatius, Mont., 1980—. Author: Drawing a Conclusion, 1977. Home: Box 416 Saint Ignatius MT 59865 Office: Box 278 Pablo MT 59855

THIEL, WARREN HARRY, tech. consultant; b. Grand Rapids, Mich., Jan. 12, 1919; s. Harry and Josephine Johanna (Timmers) T.; Asso. Sci., Grand Rapids Jr. Coll., 1938; B.S. in Chemistry, U. Mich., 1940, M.S. in Chemistry, 1942; grad. AEC Oak Ridge Sch. Reactor Tech., 1953; certificate in Contract Adminstrn., U. Cal., Los Angeles Ext., 1966; m. Vitalina Coello Laborde, June 8, 1957. Research engr. E.H. Sargent & Co., Chgo., 1943-45; project engr. Bell & Howell Co., Chgo., 1945-47; asso. chemist, engr. AEC Argonne Nat. Lab., Chgo., 1947-51; design specialist Convair div. Gen. Dynamics Corp., San Diego, 1951-61; sr. project engr. Aerojet-Gen. Corp., Downey, Cal., 1961-62; prin. engr., scientist Douglas Aircraft Co., Santa Monica, 1962-65; sr. project engr. Hughes Aircraft Co., Culver City and Canoga Park, Cal., 1965-70; ind. cons. in tech., 1968—. Tech. cons. to small bus. on new product ventures, 1968—. E.H. Sargent grantee, 1943. Registered profl. engr., Ill. Mem. Am. Rocket Soc. (pres. San Diego sect. 1960-61), Am. Security Council, Am. Def. Preparedness Assn., Nat. Rifle Assn., Am. Chem. Soc., IEEE, AIAA, Armed Forces Communications and Electronics Assn. Office: PO Box 92232 Long Beach CA 90809

THIERS, EUGENE ANDRES, mineral economist, educator; b. Santiago, Chile, Aug. 25, 1941; came to U.S., 1962, naturalized, 1976; s. Eugenio A. and Elena (Lillo) T.; m. Marie H. Stuart, Dec. 23, 1965 (div. 1979); children: Ximena, Eugene, Alexander; m. Patricia Van Metre, Jan. 29, 1983. B.S., U. Chile, 1962; M.S., Columbia U., 1965, D.Eng.Sc., 1970. Mgr.-tech. Minbanco Corp., N.Y.C., 1966-70; dir. iron info. Battelle Inst., Columbus, Ohio, 1970-75; minerals economist SRI Internat., Menlo Park, Calif., 1975-79, dir.-minerals and metals, 1979-83, sr. cons., 1983-86; bus. mgr. inorganics, 1986—; vis. prof. mineral econs. Stanford U., Calif., 1983—. Contbr. articles, chpts. to profl. publs. Campbell and Krumb fellow Columbia U., 1965-67. Fellow AAAS; mem. AIME (chmn. Columbus sect. of Ohio chpt. 1973-75, chmn. Bay Area chpt. of metall. sect. 1979-80), AIME (San Francisco sect.). Home: 426 27th Ave San Mateo CA 94403 Office: SRI Internat 333 Ravenswood Ave Menlo Park CA 94025

THIES, DAVID BYRON, chemist, researcher; b. Cottage Grove, Oreg., May 8, 1945; s. Byron O. and Muriel Leora (Dickinson) T.; m. Robin Marie Robinette, Jan. 23, 1971 (div. Sept. 1975); 1 child, Laurie. AS, Lane Community Coll., Eugene, Oreg., 1969; BS in Biology, U. Oreg., 1971; postgrad., Oreg. State U., 1973-74. Med. researcher VA Hosp., Albany, N.Y., 1972-73; cons. Water Analysis and Cons., Eugene, 1974-77; chemist, applied research dept. J.H. Baxter Co., Eugene, 1978—. Served with U.S. Army, 1963-66. Mem. ASTM, Am. Chem. Soc., Western Dry Kiln Assn. (com. chmn. 1984-85), Am. Water Works Assn., Am. Wood Preservers' Assn. Democrat. Avocations: woodworking, stained glass art. Office: J H Baxter Co 85 Baxter St PO Box 10797 Eugene OR 97440

THIESEN, RONALD JOEL, science teacher; b. Kingsburg, Calif., Nov. 5, 1959; s. John and Martha Elizabeth (Balzer) T. BA in Natural Sci., Fresno Pacific Coll., 1981. Cert. tchr., Calif. Tchr. sci. Fresno (Calif.) Christian Edn. System, 1982-83; tchr. sci. Immanuel High Sch., Reedley, Calif., 1983—, chmn. dept. sci., 1984—, coach track, 1982—; coach jr. varsity basketball Immanuel High Sch., Reedley, 1984—. Mem. Nat. Sci. Tchrs. Assn. Republican. Mem. Mennonite Brethren Ch. Avocations: basketball, track, skiing, crafts. Home: 479 W Olson Ave Reedley CA 93654 Office: Immanuel High Sch 1128 S Reed Reedley CA 93654

THIESSEN, BRIAN DAVID, lawyer; b. Grass Valley, Calif.; s. John J. and Ellen E.A. (Larsen) T.; A.B., Duke U., 1960; postgrad. SUNY, Plattsburg, 1961-62; J.D., Hastings Coll. Law, 1967; m. Carolyn Owen, June 16, 1962; children—Robert, Erica, William. With Kaiser Industries, 1964-67; admitted to Calif. bar, 1967, U.S. Supreme Ct., 1982; partner, v.p. Merrill, Thiessen, & Gagen, Danville, Calif., from 1967; now ptnr., pres. Thiessen, Gagen & McCoy, P.C.; instr. John F. Kennedy Law Sch., 1977—; sec., dir. 1st Western Savs. and Loan Assn.; judge pro tem Walnut Creek-Danville Mcpl. Ct., Mt. Diablo Mcpl. Ct. Mem. governing bd. Alameda-Contra Costa Counties Community Found., 1973-79; chmn. San Ramon Valley Planning Com., 1973; pres. Mt. Diablo council Boy Scouts Am., 1986-87; mem. Diablo Valley Found. for Aging; mem. Alamo Park and Recreation Commn., 1984—, chmn., 1986-87. Served to capt. USAF, 1960-63. Cert. family law specialist. Mem. Am. Bar Assn., Contra Costa County Bar Assn. (past pres.), Calif. Trial Lawyers, Hastings Coll. of Law Alumni Assn. (mem. bd. govs.). Republican. Congregationalist. Lodges: Lions (past pres.), Rotary. Home: 100 Los Balcones Alamo CA 94507 Office: 279 Front St PO Box 218 Danville CA 94526

THIESSEN, JON ISAAC, utilities executive; b. Mountain Lake, Minn., Jan. 29, 1936; s. John K. and Neina K. (Eitzen) T.; m. Glenna B. Mahan, Feb. 27, 1960; children: Forrest, Daniel, James, Jon Jr., Christy. Student, Pierce Jr. Coll., 1960-61. Dist. mgr. tng. BSCTE, Lisle, Ill., 1971-75; dist. mgr. switched services Mountain Bell, Denver, 1975-78, dist. planning engr., 1978-79, dir. cen. office staff, 1979-82, dir. Colo. switched services, 1982-85, dir. network engring. no. region, 1985-87; dir. network engring. no. region Mountain Bell, Phoenix, 1987—. Home: 7058 W Elmhurst Ave Littleton CO 80123 Office: Mountain Bell Dir Network Engring Room 717 3033 N 3d St Phoenix AZ 85012

THIGPEN, JOE DENNARD, industrial psychologist, management consultant; b. Gainesville, Fla., June 22, 1942; s. Joe Dennard and Doris (Young) T. BA, U. Fla., 1966, Ed.S., 1972, PhD, 1974; MS, George Washington U., 1970. Vol. Peace Corps, Santa Catarina, Brazil, 1963-65; counseling psychologist U. Fla., Gainesville, 1972-73; exec. dir. Suicide and Crisis Intervention Ctr., Gainesville, 1973-75; dir. Alachua County Crisis Ctr., Gainesville, 1975-79, v.p. western region, 1986—; mgmt. cons. Gehlhausen Ruda and Assocs., Chgo., 1979—; adj. prof. U. Fla., Gainesville, 1974-79. Author: (contbr.) Psychological Assessment of Suicidal Risk, 1974; cons. editor Suicide and Life-Threatening Behavior jour., 1982—; contbr. articles to profl. jours. Pres. Alachua County Council on Child Abuse, Gainesville, 1978-79. Served with U.S. Army, 1966-69. Mem. Am. Assn. Suicidology (cert. examiner, treas. 1981-83, bd. dirs. 1981-85, pres. 1983-84, Edward Shneidman Young Contributor award, 1980), Am. Assn. Counseling and Devel. Democrat. Methodist. Home: 222 S Figuersoa St Apt 711 Los Angeles CA 90012 Office: Gehlhausen/Ruda and Assocs 727 W Seventh St Suite 900 Los Angeles CA 90017

THILL, JOHN VAL, communications professional, consultant; b. Milw., Dec. 27, 1953; s. Lewis Dominic and Carol Jean (Werner) T. BS, San Diego State U., 1977; MBA, U. San Diego, 1982. Mgr. Pacific Bell, San Diego, 1979-82; pres. Communication Specialists of Am., San Diego, 1982—; bd. dirs. Communication Research Inst., Los Angeles. Author: Business Communication Today, 1986. Named Outstanding Bus. Communicator Am. Soc. Journalists, 1982. Mem. Assn. Bus. Communication, 1985. Avocations: swimming, racquetball. Office: Communication Specialists Am 7159 Navajo Rd San Diego CA 92119

THIMANN, KENNETH VIVIAN, biology educator; b. Ashford, Eng., Aug. 5, 1904; came to U.S., 1930, naturalized Am. citizen; s. Israel Phoebus and Muriel Kate (Harding) T.; m. Ann Mary Bateman, Mar. 20, 1929; children—Vivianne Thimann Nachmias, Karen Thimann Romer, Linda Thimann Dewing. Student, Caterham Sch., Eng., 1915-21; B.Sc., Imperial Coll. Sci and Tech. London Royal Coll. Sci., 1924, A.R.C.S., 1924, Ph.D., 1928; A.M. (hon.), Harvard U., 1938; Ph.D. (hon.), U. Basel, Switzerland, 1960, U. Clermont-Ferrand, France, 1961. Demonstrator bacteriology Kings Coll., London, 1927-29; instr. biochemistry and bacteriology Calif. Inst. Tech., Pasadena, 1930-35; lectr. botany Harvard U., 1935-36, asst. prof. plant physiology, 1936-39, assoc. prof., 1939-46, prof., 1946-62, Higgins prof. biology, 1962-65, prof. emeritus, 1965—; prof. biology U. Calif.-Santa Cruz, 1965—; provost Crown Coll., 1965-72; dir. Biol. Labs., Harvard U., 1946-50, tutor in biology Eliot House, 1936-52, assoc., 1952-65; master East House, Radcliffe Coll., 1962-65; exchange prof. U. Paris, 1954-55; vis. prof. U. Mass., 1974, U. Tex., 1976; pres. XI Internat. Bot. Congress, 1969; pres. 2d Nat. Biol. Congress, Miami, 1970; pres. Internat. Plant Growth Substance Assn. Triennial Meeting, Tokyo, 1973. Author: (with F. W. Went) Phytohormones, 1937, The Life of Bacteria, 2d edit., 1963, The Natural Plant Hormones, 1972, Hormones in the Whole Life of Plants, 1977, (with J.H. Langenheim) Botany: Plants and Human Affairs, 1982; author, editor (with others) Senescence in Plants, 1981; editor (with R.S. Harris) Vitamins and Hormones (ann.) Vol. 1, 1943, to Vol. 20, 1962, (with G. Pincus) The Hormones, 5 vols., 1948, 55, 63; mem. editorial bd. Archives of Biochemistry and Biophysics, 1949-70, Canadian Jour. Botany, 1966-73, Plant Physiology, 1974—; contbr. numerous articles to tech. jours. Bd. dirs. Found. Microbiology, Biol. Scis. Info. Services. Served as civilian scientist, USN, 1942-45. Recipient Stephen Hales prize research Am. Soc. Plant Physiologists, 1936; Guggenheim fellow, Eng., 1950-51, Italy, 1958; medallist Internat. Plant Growth Substance Assn., 1976, Balzan prize, 1982. Fgn. mem. Royal Soc. (London), Soc. Nazionale dei Lincei (Rome), Akad. Leopoldina (Halle), Acad. Nat. de Roumaine (Bucharest), Acad. des Sci. (Paris), Acad. d' Agr. de France, Bot. Soc. Netherlands, Bot. Soc. Japan, Indian Soc. Plant Physiology; mem. Am. Soc. Biol. Chemists, Am. Philos. Soc. (council 1973-76), Am. Acad. Arts and Scis., Nat. Acad. Scis. (chmn. botany sect. 1962-65, mem. council 1967-71, exec. com. assembly life scis. 1972-76), Bot. Soc. Am. (pres. 1960), AAAS (dir. 1968-72), Am. Soc. Plant Physiologists (pres. 1950-51), Soc. Gen. Physiologists (pres. 1949-50), Biochem. Soc., Am. Soc. Naturalists (pres. 1954-55), Am. Inst. Biol. Scis. (pres. 1965), Soc. Study Devel. and Growth (pres. 1955-56). Office: Thimann Labs U of Calif Santa Cruz CA 95064

THIRLWALL, CAROL SUZANNE, retail communications sales; b. New York, July 1, 1959; d. Daniels Francis and Harriet Suzanne (Nitzburg) T. BS in Bus. Adminstrn., U. So. Calif., 1981; postgrad., Harvard U. Sch. Bus., 1986—. Classified sales advisor Los Angeles Daily News, Van Nuys, 1981-82, contract sales exec., 1982-83, account exec., 1983-85, advt. tng. mgr., 1985, retail sales mgr., 1985-86. Recipient Pioneer of Yr., Area Salesperson of Yr., Los Angeles Daily News, 1984, 85, Young Careerist of Yr., Bus. and Profl. Women, 1985. Mem. CNAEA, Los Angeles Advt. Club, Beta Gamma Sigma. Club: Cosmos (pres. 1985-86), Trojan Jr. Aux. (Los Angeles) (pres. 1984-85). Avocations: reading, skiing, dancing, calligraphy, arts and crafts.

THISTLETHWAITE, DAVID RICHARD, architect; b. Burlington, Iowa, Aug. 24, 1947; s. Robert and Nona (Binder) T.; m. Carol Anne Armstrong, Aug. 22, 1970. BArch, Iowa State U., 1971. Registered architect, Calif., Minn. Designer Morrison Architects, St. Paul, 1971-73, Times Architects, Mpls., 1973-74; project architect Bentz/Thompson Assocs., Mpls., 1974-77; project mgr. Setter Leach Lindstrom, Mpls., 1977-78; project architect Wurster Bernardi Emmons, San Francisco, 1978-79, Strotz & Assocs., Tiburon, Calif., 1979-81, Hood Miller Assoc., San Francisco, 1981-84; prin., ptnr. R S T Architects, San Francisco, 1984—. Mem. AIA (nat. profl. devel. com., 1983—, treas. San Francisco chpt. 1985—). Office: R S T Architects 729 Sansome St San Francisco CA 94111

THODEY, ALAN ROBERT, software development executive; b. East Melbourne, Australia, June 5, 1941. B of Econs. with honors, U. Tasmania, Australia, 1962; PhD, U. Ill., 1969. Economist Stanford Research Inst., Menlo Park, Calif., 1967-71, Ford Found., Chieng Mai, Thailand, 1971-75; economist/cons. U.S. Agy. Internat. Devel., 1977-81; assoc. prof. Calif. State U., Fresno, 1976-79; pres. Argos, Inc., Fresno, 1979—. Office: Argos Inc 1485 W Shaw Ave Fresno CA 93711

THOMA-LAURIE, DEBRA LEE, marketing executive, toxicologist; b. Newport Beach, Calif., Jan. 3, 1956; d. Paul Andrew and Beverly ruby (Bixler) Thoma; m. Louis Daniel Laurie Jr., May 30, 1981. BA magna cum laude, W.Va. U., 1978, PhD, 1982; student, Golden Gate U., 1983—. NIH postdoctoral fellow in toxicology U. W.Va., 1978-82; study dir., toxicologist Syntex Research, Palo Alto, Calif., 1982-85; bus. planning analyst Syntex Labs., Palo Alto, Calif., 1985-86, product devel. mgr., 1986—. Author: Toxicology of The newborn, 1984; contbr. articles to profl. jour. Mem. AAAS, Assn. Women in Sci., Med. Mktg. Assn., Am. Coll. Toxicology, Soc. Toxicology, DAR, Kappa Kappa Gamma (personnel advisor). Avocations: skiing, horseback riding, aerobics, tennis, biking. Home: 7529 DeFoe Dr Cupertino CA 95014 Office: Syntex Labs L1310 3401 Hillview Dr Palo Alto CA 94304

THOMAS, ANDREW ROBERT, urologist; b. Sharon, Pa., Dec. 31, 1940; s. Andrew Theodore and Marie Eva (Varraux) T.; m. Colleen Murray, June 4, 1962; children: David, Matthew, Cynthia, Benjamin. BS, Allegheny Coll., 1963; MD, U. Cin., 1966. Diplomate Am. Bd. Urology. Intern Hennepin County Gen. Hosp., Mpls., 1966-67; resident in urology U. Cin., 1967-71; practice medicine specializing in urology Mesa (Ariz.) Urologists P.C., 1971—; chief of staff Mesa Luth. Hosp., 1985. Fellow ACS; mem. Am. Urol. Assn., AMA, Assn. Clin. Urologists. Republican. Methodist. Club: Mesa Country. Avocations: golf, backpacking. fishing. Office: Mesa Urologists PC 560 W Brown Rd Suite 1004 Mesa AZ 85201

THOMAS, ANTONY ROSS, marketing professional; b. Cleve., Jan. 31, 1956; s. William Granville and Christine (Toles) T.; m. Bonita Catherine Nicholas, Feb. 7, 1981. Cert., Ohio Sch. Broadcasting, 1976, Cleve. Advt. Sch., 1978; student, Compton Coll., 1979-80. Account exec. Wave Newspapers, Los Angeles, 1980, Sta. KBRT, Los Angeles, 1980-81; announcer, engr. Sta. KTYM, Inglewood, Calif., 1981—; mng. dir., chief exec. officer Target Communications Internat., Inglewood, 1983—. Contbr. articles to mags. Active candidates com. Citizens League Greater Cleve., 1978-79; bd. dirs. Mt. Pleasant Community Council, Cleve., 1978-79. Recipient cert. Inglewood C. of C., 1984. Mem. CXSM Users Group. Home and Office: 1123 Rosewood Ave Inglewood CA 90301

THOMAS, BYRON EUGENE, optometrist; b. Colville, Wash., May 18, 1941; s. William Clarke and Mae Deen (Gafford) T.; children—Katherine Marie, Kenneth Clark. B.S., Pacific U., 1963, O.D., 1964. Pvt. practice optometry Ellensburg (Wash.) Vision Clinic, P.S., Inc., 1968—; lectr. Wash. Bd. Optometry, 1977; mem. Western Vision Service Bd., 1978-82; lectr. Pacific U. Student Assn., 1982. Chmn. Ellensburg Sch. Bd., 1979-81, mem. bd., 1977—; campaign chmn. pres. United Way.; active Ft. Simco council Boy Scouts Am. Served to 1st lt. USAF, 1965-68. Recipient Silver Beaver award Boy Scouts Am., 1978. Mem. Am. Optometric Assn., Wash. Optometric Assn., Yakima Valley Optometric Soc., C. of C. Clubs: Lions, Elks, Moose. Office: Ellensburg Sch Bd 301 E 2d St Ellensburg WA 98926

THOMAS, CHARLES WILLIAM, II, urban studies educator; b. Md., Apr. 26, 1926; s. Charles W. and Estella Thomas; m. Shirley Wade, Aug. 30, 1958; children: Charles William III, Shawn. BS, Morgan State Coll., 1951; MA, John Carroll U., 1955; PhD, Western Res. U., 1961. With Highland View Cuyahoga County Hosp., Cleve., 1955-63, acting dir. sheltered workshop research project, 1956-58, co-prin. investigator, dir. aging research project, until 1963; asst. prof., dir. counseling services and personnel devel. Job Corps Ctr., U. Oreg., 1963-66; evaluation design analyst, dir. edn. and tng. South Central Multipurpose Health Service Ctr., U. So. Calif., 1966-69; assoc. prof. community medicine U. So. Calif., Los Angeles, 1966-69; prin., dir. Ctr. for Study Racial and Social Issues, Los Angeles, 1969-71; prof. urban studies and planning U. Calif.-San Diego Third Coll., La Jolla, 1977—, coordinator urban studies and planning, 1977-82; lectr. John Carroll U., 1961-63, Calif. State Coll., Los Angeles, 1967-68, Calif. State Coll., Dominguez Hills, 1970, Claremont Coll. Black Studies Ctr., 1970-71; vis. prof. counseling psychology Ariz. State U., 1970-71; vis. scientist Am. Psychol. Assn., 1979-80, Assn. Black Psychologists, 1969-70; mem. Calif. Psychology Examining Commn.; active Calif. Bd. Edn., 1975-79; facilitator, chmn. pro tem Nat. Ad Hoc Com. on Homicidal Violence Among Blacks; facilitator for devel. Nat. Black Mental Health Workers Assn.; founder, coordinator Ann. Conf. on Issues in Ethnicity and Mental Health; speaker, cons. in field. Contbr. articles, chpts. to profl. publs., popular mags. Served with AUS, 1944-46. Recipient Father of Black Psychology award Black Students' Psychol. Assn., 1970; cert. recognition Nat. Assn. Sch. Psychologists, 1971; commendation Mayor San Diego, 1976; legis. commendation State of Ohio, 1979; Legal Aid Soc. San Diego award, 1979; Outstanding Contbn. award So. Regional Edn. Bd. Community Clin. Psychology Project, 1980; commendation Christ Ch. of San Diego, 1980; San Diego Black Achievement award in sci., 1981, in journalism, 1983; Charles W. Thomas psychology scholarship established in his honor at Morgan State U., 1976; named to Scroll of Honor for Ednl. Leadership, Omega Psi Phi, 1979; Jesse Smith Noyes fellow John Carroll U.; Cleve. Found. fellow Western Res. U.; Danforth assoc., 1979; vis. scholar Howard U. Inst. Urban Affairs, 1979-80; Spl. Achievement award Morgan State U., 1986, Disting. Alumni award Nat. Equal Opportunity Assn. for Higher Edn. Fellow Am. Psychol. Assn. (chmn. edn. and tng. bd. 1971-72, chmn. task force on master's level edn. 1973); mem. Calif. State Psychol. Assn., Nat. Acad. TV Arts and Scis., AAAS (adv. body), Council for Advancement Psychol. Profession and Scis. (gov. 1969), Assn. Black Psychologists (founding chmn. 1968, hon. nat. chmn.), Black Action Council San Diego (hon.), NAACP (pres. San Diego chpt. 1977, San Diego chpt. Outstanding Service award 1976), Nat. Acad. Black Scientists (chmn.). Republican. Home: 610 Bradford Rd El Cajon CA 92021 Office: U Calif-San Diego Third Coll Urban Studies and Planning D-009 La Jolla CA 92093

THOMAS, CLAUDEWELL SIDNEY, psychiatric educator; b. N.Y.C., Oct. 5, 1932; s. Humphrey Sidney and Frances Elizabeth (Collins) T.; m. Carolyn Pauline Rozawsky, Sept. 6, 1958; children: Jeffrey Evan, Julie-Anne Elizabeth, Jessica Edith. BA, Columbia U., 1952; MD, SUNY, Downstate Med. Ctr., 1956; MPH, Yale U., 1964. Diplomate Nat. Bd. Med. Examiners, Am. Bd. Psychiatry. From instr. to assoc. prof. Yale U., New Haven, 1963-68, dir. Yale tng. program in social community psychiatry, 1967-70; dir. div. mental health service programs NIMH, Washington, 1970-73; chmn. dept. psychiatry U.M.D.N.J., Newark, 1973-83; prof., chmn. dept. psychiatry Drew Med. Sch., 1983—; prof., chmn dept. psychiatry UCLA, 1983—; cons. A.K. Rice Inst., Washington, 1978-80. Author: (with B. Bergen) Issues and Problems in Contemporary Soc., 1966; editor: (with R. Bryce LaPorte) Alienation in Contemporary Society, 1976; mem. editorial bd. Internat. Jour. Mental Health, Adminstrn. In Mental Health, Social Psychiatry Internat., World Jour. Psychosynthesis. Served to capt. USAF, 1959-61. Fellow: Am. Psychoanalytic Assn. (hon.), Am. Psychiat. Assn., Am. Pub. Health Assn., Royal Soc. Health, N.Y. Acad. Sci., N.Y. Acad. Medicine; mem. Am. Sociol. Assn. Avocations: tennis, racquetball, violin, piano. Home: 30676 Palos Verdes Dr E Rancho Palos Verdes CA 90274 Office: Charles R Drew Med Sch Dept Psychiatry 1720 E 120 St AFH Bldg Los Angeles CA 90059

THOMAS, DARWIN LAMAR, sociology educator; b. Genola, Utah, Dec. 3, 1933; s. David Bynon and Grace (Hartvigsen) T.; m. Beverly Morrison, Sept. 14, 1959; children: Kim, Suanne, Rebecca, Kristi, Sara, David. BS with honors, Brigham Young U., 1962, MA, 1964; PhD, U. Minn., 1968. Instr. Clara Elizabeth Fund, Flint, Mich., 1962-63; instr. Child Devel. and Family Relations dept. Brigham Young U., Provo, Utah, 1964-65, assoc. prof. sociology, 1972-77, prof., 1977—, dir. Family Research Inst., 1973-77, editor Family Perspective mag., 1983—; asst. prof. sociology Wash. State U., Pullman, 1968-72. Author: Family Socialization and the Adolescent, 1974, Social Psychology, 1980; editor Population Resources and Future, 1972; contbr articles to profl. jours. Served with U.S. Army, 1956-58. NIMH fellow, 1965-68; named Outstanding Social Scientist, Western Behavioral Sci. Inst., La Jolla, Calif, 1973. Mem. Am. Sociol. Assn., Nat. Council Family Relations (pres. family theory com. 1972-73). Republican. Mormon. Avocations: horsemanship, ranching. Office: Brigham Young U Dept Sociology 844 SWKT Provo UT 84602

THOMAS, DAVID WALTER, JR., manufacturing executive; b. Asheville, N.C., May 19, 1938; s. David Walter and Frances (Warren) T.; children—David, Anne. B.S.M.E., N.C. State U., 1962; M.S. in Indsl. Mgmt., U. Tenn., 1974. With Huyck Corp., 1962-80, beginning as field service engr., successively sales engr., product mgr., mfg. services, project mgr., constrn. mgr., start-up engr., plant mgr., mfg. mgr., v.p., div. gen. mgr., 1974-79, corp. dir. planning, Wake Forest, N.C., 1979-80; sr. v.p. corp. devel. Ameron, Inc., Monterey Park, Calif., 1981-83, group v.p., 1984—. Dist. chmn. Boy Scouts Am., 1977-78, exec. com. East Tenn. council, 1976-78; budget com. Tenn. United Way, 1977-78; sect. leader Los Angeles United Way, 82-83. Served with AUS, 1960-61. Mem. Golden Chain, Blue Key, Thirty and Three, Beta Gamma Sigma. Clubs: Lions, Exchange. Contbr. articles to profl. jours. Home: 2141 E Pioneer Ave Fullerton CA 92631 Office: Ameron Inc PO Box 3000 Monterey Park CA 91754

THOMAS, DELBERT DALE, engineering executive, consultant; b. Portland, Oreg., June 14, 1930; s. Theodore C. and Esther E. (Kemnitz) T.; m. Phyllis B. Bartlett, Jan. 8, 1949; children—James, Leonard, Stephen, Timothy, Susan. Student San Jose City Coll., Santa Rosa Community Coll., 1950-51. Lic. contractor, Calif., Ariz., Nev. Pres., Shale Devel. Corp. Redlands, Calif., 1976—; pres. Energy '80 Scientific, Inc., Redlands, 1981—; chmn. bd. Impex, Inc., Redlands, 1982—; exec. v.p., bd. dirs. United Stradtum Corp., San Bernardino, Calif.; developer indsl. projects Govt. of Pakistan. Awarded 3rd place Inventor of Yr., Inventors Workshop Internat., 1976. Mem. ASHRAE. Republican. Baptist. Mech. contractor on space shuttle assembly facility, Palmdale, Calif., 1973. Author: Practical Ductwork Estimating, Synfuel; patentee in field of synthetic fuels. Home: 1522 Cameo Dr Redlands CA 92373 Office: Impex Inc 313 High St Redlands CA 92373

THOMAS, ETHEL COLVIN NICHOLS (MRS. LEWIS VICTOR THOMAS), educator; b. Cranston, R.I., Mar. 31, 1913; d. Charles Russell and Mabel Maria (Colvin) Nichols; Ph.B., Pembroke Coll. in Brown U., 1934; M.A., Brown U., 1938; Ed.D., Rutgers U., 1979; m. Lewis Victor Thomas, July 26, 1945 (dec. Oct. 1965); 1 child, Glenn Nichols. Tchr. English, Cranston High Sch., 1934-39; social dir. and adviser to freshmen, Fox Hall, Boston U., 1939-40; instr. to asst. prof. English Am. Coll. for Girls, Istanbul, Turkey, 1940-44; dean freshman, dir. admission Women's Coll. of Middlebury, Vt., 1944-45; tchr. English, Robert Coll., Istanbul, 1945-46; instr. English, Rider Coll., Trenton, N.J., 1950-51; tchr. English, Princeton (N.J.) High Sch., 1951-61, counselor, 1960-62, 72-83, coll. counselor, 1962-72, sr. peer counselor, 1986—. Mem. NEA, AAUW, Nat. Assn. Women Deans Adminstrs. and Counselors, Am. Assn. Counseling and Devel., Bus. and Profl. Women's Club (named Woman of Yr., Princeton chpt. 1977), Met. Mus. Art, Phi Delta Kappa, Kappa Delta Pi. Presbyn. Clubs: Brown University (N.Y.C.); Nassau.

THOMAS, GEORGE IRVING, editor periodical; b. Balt., July 10, 1949; s. George I. Thomas and Genavie (Difford) Nichols. BA in European History, U. Wash., 1975, BA in Editorial Journalism, 1980. Copywriter REI Co-op, Seattle, 1979-80; editor Sports Northwest mag., Seattle, 1980-85, Canoe mag., Kirkland, Wash., 1985—. Contbr. articles and photos to profl. jours. and mags. Coach U. Wash. ski team, Seattle, 1982—. Served to capt. USMC, 1975-80. Avocations: competitive skiing, cycling, kayaking, climbing, running. Home: 10108 NE 68th #4 Kirkland WA 98033

THOMAS, GERALD WAYLETT, former university president; b. Small, Idaho, July 3, 1919; s. Daniel Waylett and Mary (Evans) T.; m. Jean Ellis, June 2, 1945; children—David Gerald, Peggy Jeane, Marianne. Student, Pasadena Jr. Coll., 1936-38; B.S., U. Idaho, 1941; M.S., Tex. A. and M. Coll., 1951, Ph.D., 1954. With U.S. Forest Service in, Idaho, 1938-40; range conservationist, work unit conservationist Soil Conservation Service, St. Anthony and Rexburg, Idaho, 1946-50; asst. and asso. prof. dept. range and forestry Tex. A. and M. Coll., College Station, 1951-56; research coordinator Tex. Agrl. Expt. Sta., 1956-58; dean agr. Tex. Technol. U., 1958, exec. v.p., 1968; pres., now pres. emeritus N.Mex. State U., Las Cruces; former mem. Nat. Forest Systems Adv. Com.; former mem. Bd. for Internat. Food and Agrl. Devel.; former mem. exec. bd. Assn. State Univs. and Land-Grant Colls., Asso. Western Univs. Author: also numerous publs. on ecology and agrl. subjects. Food and Fiber for a Changing World. Served to lt. comdr. USNR, 1942-45. Decorated D.F.C. (3), Air medal (2). Fellow Am. Soc. Range Mgmt. (bd. dirs.), AAAS; mem. Soil Conservation Soc., Sigma Xi, Phi Kappa Phi. Club: Rotarian. Home: University Park Las Cruces NM 88003

THOMAS, GRACE FERN, physician, psychiatrist; b. Gothenburg, Nebr., Sept. 23, 1897; d. George William and Martha C. (Johnson) Thomas; B.S., U. Nebr., 1924; M.A., Creighton U., 1926; M.D., U. So. Calif., 1935; postgrad. U. Colo., 1942-43, Inst. of Living, 1943, U. So. Calif., 1946, UCLA, Angeles, 1947-50, Columbia U., 1953; M.A. in Religion, U. So. Calif., 1968. Instr. chemistry, biology Duchesne Coll., 1924-27; lab. technician various hosps., 1927-32; intern Los Angeles County Hosp., 1934-35; resident physician Riverside County Hosp., 1935-36; resident psychiatrist Los Angeles County Psychopathic Hosp., 1936-37; staff psychiatrist Calif. State Hosp. System, 1937-42, Glenside San., 1943-44; pvt. practice neuropsychiatry, Long Beach, Calif., 1946-51; chief mental hygiene clinic VA, Albuquerque, 1951-54; dir. psychiat. edn. Miss. State Hosp., Jackson, 1955; dir. Stark County Guidance Center, Canton, Ohio, 1956-58; dir. Huron County Guidance Center, Norwalk, Ohio, 1958-61, Arrowhead Mental Health Center, San Bernardino, Calif., 1962-64; dir. Mendocino County Mental Health Services, Ukiah, Calif., 1964-65; chief psychiat. edn. Porterville (Calif.) State Hosp., 1965-66; dir. Tuolumne County Mental Health Services, Sonora, Calif., 1966-70; psychiatrist-cons. Emanuel Hosp. Mental Health Center, Turlock, Calif., 1970-71; pvt. practice psychiatry, Turlock, 1970-73, Modesto, Calif., 1973—; cons. psychiatrist Stanislaus County Mental Health Dept., Modesto, 1972-73; alienist to Stanislaus County Superior Ct., Modesto, 1972—; psychiatrist-cons. Cath. Social Service Agency, 1974-78. Ordained to ministry United Meth. Ch., 1968. Served as capt. M.C., AUS, 1944-46. Diplomate Am. Bd. Psychiatry and Neurology. Fellow Am. Psychiat. Assn.; mem. AMA, Stanislaus Med. Soc., Central Calif. Psychiat. Assn., Inst. Religion and Health, Am. Med. Women's Assn. Am. Legion, AAUW, Soroptimists, Phi Delta Gamma, Phi Beta Kappa, Sigma Xi, Phi Kappa Phi, Nu Sigma Phi. Methodist. Home: 2001 LaJolla Ct Modesto CA 95350 Office: 1130 Coffee Rd Suite 8B Modesto CA 95355

THOMAS, HAYWARD, manufacturing company executive; b. Los Angeles, Aug. 9, 1921; s. Charles Sparks and Julia (Hayward) T.; m. Phyllis Mary Wilson, July 1, 1943; children: H. David, Steven T. BS, U. Calif., Berkeley, 1943. Registered profl. engr. Staff engr. Joshua Hendy Corp., Los Angeles, 1946-50; prodn. mgr. Byron Jackson Co., Los Angeles, 1950-55; mgr. mfg. Frigidaire div. Gen. Motors Corp., Dayton, Ohio, 1955-70; group v.p. White Motor Corp., Cleve., 1971-73; sr. v.p. Broan Mfg. Co., Hartford, Wis., 1973-85; pres. Jensen Industries, Los Angeles, 1985-87; retired 1987. Served to lt. USNR, 1943-46. Mem. Soc. Mfg. Engrs. (chmn. mfg. mgmt. council 1984-86). Republican. Episcopalian. Avocations: tennis, fishing. Home: 1320 Granvia Altamira Palos Verdes Estates CA 90274 Office: Jensen Industries 1946 E 46th St Los Angeles CA 90058

THOMAS, HERIBERTO VICTOR, scientist, consultant; b. Republic of Panama, Mar. 17, 1917; came to U.S., 1946; s. Alberto Eduardo and Nena Beatricio (Jaén) T.; m. Orvella Amanda Hall, Aug. 1950 (div. May 1971); children: Lesbia Marcia Francis, Fermin A.; m. Margaret Liao Lee, Nov. 13, 1976. BA, U. So. Calif., 1950, MS, 1960; MPH, UCLA, 1964; PhD, U. Calif., Berkeley, 1968. Research fellow U. So. Calif., Los Angeles, 1953-61; research assoc. St. Joseph Hosp., Burbank, Calif., 1961-64; research specialist, unit chief Calif. Dept. Health, Berkeley, 1964-80; sr. lectr. U. Calif., Berkeley, 1973-81; mem. med. quality rev. com. Bd. Med. Quality Assurance, Sacramento, 1979—; chmn. Calif. Med. Bd., San Mateo, 1983-85. Contbr. articles to sci. jours. Recipient A.E. MacGee award Am. Oil Chemists' Soc., 1962. Mem. AAAS, Am. Soc. Human Genetics, Sigma Xi. Republican. Avocations: piano playing and listening. Home: PO Box 9062 Berkeley CA 94709

THOMAS, HOWARD PAUL, civil engineer, consultant; b. Cambridge, Mass., Aug. 20, 1942; s. Charles Calvin and Helen Elizabeth (Hook) T.; m. Ingrid Nybo, Jan. 4, 1969; children: Kent Michael, Lisa Karen. BS in Engring., U. Mich., 1965, MS in Engring., 1966. Registered profl. engr., Alaska, Calif. Engr. Ove Arup & Ptnrs., London, 1966-67; project engr. Woodward-Clyde Cons., San Francisco, 1967-73; assoc. Woodward-Clyde Cons., Anchorage, 1975—; spl. cons. Cowiconsult Cons., Copenhagen, 1973-

75; bd. dirs. Nat. Tech. Council Cold Regions Engring., 1985—, Alaska Profl. Design Council, 1986—; chmn. 4th Internat. Conf. Cold Regions Engring., Anchorage, 1986. Contbr. articles to profl. jours. Mem. Resource Devel. Council, Anchorage, 1985—, Alaska Support Alliance, Anchorage 1985—, World Affairs Council, Anchorage, 1981—. Named Alaskan Engr. Yr., 1986. Mem. NSPE, ASCE (pres. Anchorage chpt. 1985-86), Internat. Soc. Soil Mechs. and Found. Engring., Soc. Am.'s Mil. Engrs., Cons. Engrs. Council of Alaska (v.p. 1986—), Anchorage C. of C. Lutheran. Club: Toastmasters (Anchorage) (pres. 1984). Lodge: Sons of Norway. Avocations: music, travel, skiing, sailing. Home: 2611 Brittany Dr Anchorage AK 99504 Office: Woodward-Clyde Cons. 701 Sesame St Anchorage AK 99503

THOMAS, HUBERT JON, electrical engineer; b. Phila., June 14, 1940; s. Hubert Jon and Olive Beatrice (Nicholas) T.; m. Lynn Partezana, July 4, 1981. BS, Pa. State U., 1962, MS, 1964, PhD, 1969. Asst. prof. Rochester (N.Y.) Inst. Tech., 1969-71, Calif. State U., Los Angeles, 1971-73; logic designer Zenith Radio and Electric Co., Chgo., 1973-77; elec. engr. Litton Systems, Woodland Hills, Calif., 1977—; asst. prof. Midwest Coll. Engring., Lombard, Ill., 1975-77; software cons. ProSen Assocs., Canoga Park, Calif., 1984—. Mem. IEEE, Am. Soc. Engring. Edn. Avocations: chess, photography, miscellaneous computer recreations. Office: Litton Systems 5500 Canoga Ave Woodland Hills CA 91365

THOMAS, JACK EVAN, advertising executive; b. Seattle, May 15, 1919; s. David and Jessie (Jameison) T.; m. Dorothy Edna Powers, May 20, 1944; children: Dianne, Judith, Susan. BA, U. Wash. Prin. Jack E. Thomas & Assocs., Seattle, 1947-70; pres. B&T Importers Inc., Seattle, 1952-70, Monarch Import Co., Seattle, 1952-70, Desert Distbrs., Las Vegas, Nev., 1970-72; advt. exec. Winston Network, Los Angeles, 1973—. Mem. Rep. State Com., Seattle, 1952-56; chmn. United Fund, Seattle, 1960; del. Nat. Rep. Conv., Chgo., 1952; bd. dirs. March of Dimes, Orange, Calif., 1984—; active YMCA youth programs. Served with USN, 1942-46, PTO. Presbyterian. Club: Ad (Los Angeles). Avocation: fishing. Home: 2214 W Palm Orange CA 92668 Office: Winston Network Inc 3255 Wilshire Blvd 1513 Los Angeles CA 90010

THOMAS, JACK WARD, wildlife biologist, civil servant; b. Fort Worth, Sept. 7, 1934; s. Scranton Boulware and Lillian Louise (List) T.; m. Farrar Margaret Schindler, June 29, 1957; children: Britt Ward, Scranton Gregory. BS, Tex. A&M U., 1957; MS, W.Va. U., 1969; PhD, U. Mass., 1972. Wildlife biologist Tex. Game & Fish Commn., Sonora, 1957-60, Tex. Parks & Wildlife Dept., Llano, 1961-66; research biologist U.S. Forest Service, Morgantown, W.Va., 1966-69, Amherst, Mass., 1970-73, LaGrande, Oreg., 1974—. Author, editor: Wildlife Habitats in Managed Forests, 1979 (award The Wildlife Soc. 1980), Elk of North America, 1984 (award The Wildlife Soc. 1985); contbr. numerous articles to profl. jours. Served to lt. USAF, 1957. Recipient Conservation award Gulf Oil Corp., 1983, Earle A. Childs award Childs Found., 1984. Fellow Soc. Am. Foresters; mem. The Wildlife Soc. (cert., pres. 1977-78, Oreg. chpt. award 1980, Arthur Einarsen award 1981, Spl. Services award 1984), Am. Ornithol. Union, Am. Soc. Mammalogists. Lodge: Lions. Avocations: hunting, fishing, white-water rafting. Office: US Forest Service Rt 2 Box 2315 La Grande OR 97850

THOMAS, JANET KENNEDY, educator, account executive; b. Mpls., July 23, 1939; d. Gordon Douglas and Florence Otelia (Nelson) Kennedy; B.S., U. Minn., 1960, M.A., 1964; postgrad. U. Calif. (Santa Cruz and Riverside), Stanislaus State Coll., Calif. State Coll. (Fresno and San Bernadino); postgrad. Calif. Coast U., 1982—; m. Irven Earl Michael Thomas, Feb. 12, 1960. Tchr., Edina, Minn., 1960-61, Hermantown Sch., Duluth, Minn., 1961-65, Pleasant Valley Sch. Dist., Camarillo, Calif., 1966-68, Dept. of Def. Schs., Philippines, 1968-69, Atwater (Calif.) Sch. Dist., 1969-73, Moreno Valley Sch. Dist., Riverside, Calif., 1973-76; sch. site adminstr., prin. Pleasant Valley Sch. Dist., Camarillo, 1976-81; account exec. TMI Equities, Inc., 1981—; pvt. tutor, reading specialist, 1981—; owner Academics Plus, Camarillo. Asst. to state field dir. Calif., Pet Pride, 1969-81, dir. Philippines, 1968-69. Mem. Assn. Calif. Sch. Adminstrs. (conf. leader), Assn. Supervision and Curriculum Devel., Calif. Reading Assn., Internat. Reading Assn., Nat. Assn. Securities Dealers, Ventura County Profl. Women's Network (charter). Author series of books on teaching and adminstering classes for the mentally retarded, 1969; author pamphlets and handbooks. Home: 2545 N Temple Ave Camarillo CA 93010 Office: 600 Temple Ave Camarillo CA 93010 Also: 601 Daily Dr Suite 132 Camarillo CA 93010

THOMAS, JAY CLARK, industrial psychologist; b. Portland, Oreg., July 2, 1951; s. Robert Francis and Ethel Carolyn (Johnson) T.; m. Jerilee Marie Weber, Mar. 16, 1974; children: Caralee Marie, Katie Lynn, Julie Elizabeth. BS, Portland State U., 1974; MA, U. Akron, 1976, PhD, 1981. Research asst. U. Akron (Ohio), 1975-79; asst. prof. Ball State U., Muncie, Ind., 1979-81; vis. asst. prof. Rice U., Houston, 1981-82; staff indsl. psychologist NUS Corp., Houston, 1982-85; cons. NUS Corp., Portland, 1985-86; indsl. psychologist J.C. Thomas & Assocs., Portland, 1985—; cons. in field. Co-author profl. articles to jours. Mem. Am. Psychol. Assn., Soc. Indsl. and Organizational Psychologists, Soc. Engring. Psychologists, Acad. of Mgmt., Oreg. Psychol. Assn. Republican. Avocations: hunting, fishing, outdoors, computers, writing. Home: 4303 NE 34th Ave Portland OR 97211

THOMAS, JOHN RICHARD, chemist; b. Anchorage, Ky., Aug. 26, 1921; s. John R. and Mildred (Woods) T.; m. Beatrice Ann Davidson, Dec. 7, 1944; children: Jonnie Sue Jacobs, Richard G. B.S., U. Calif., Berkeley, 1943, Ph.D., 1947. With U.S. AEC, 1949-51; research chemist Chevron Research Co., Richmond, Calif., 1948-49; sr. research assoc. Chevron Research Co., 1951-60, sr. research scientist, 1961-67; mgr. research and devel. Ortho div. Chevron Chem. Co., Richmond, 1967-68; asst. sec. Standard Oil Co., Calif., 1968-70; pres. Chevron Research Co., 1970—, also dir.; v.p. petroleum research Standard Oil of Calif. Contbr. articles to profl. jours. Mem. Am. Chem. Soc., AAAS, Indsl. Research Inst., Soc. Automotive Engrs. Republican. Patentee in field. Home: 847 McEllen Way Lafayette CA 94549 Office: Chevron Research Co 576 Standard Ave Richmond CA 94802

THOMAS, JOSEPH, marketing executive; b. Chgo., July 25, 1949; s. Raymond and Yolanda Nadolski; m. Shelley Sachs, Sept. 21, 1985; 1 child, Sarah. BS in Journalism, Bradley U., 1971. Dir. Fed. Exec. Bd., Seattle, 1980-82, Seattle Veterans' Action Ctr., 1982-83; prin. The Thomas Mktg. Co., Seattle, 1983-85; sr. v.p. Rebound Dynamics, Lynnwood, Wash., 1985—. Author: Marketing For Profit, 1984. Served to 1st lt. U.S. Army, 1971-75. Recipient ToTem award for Pub. Relations Excellence, 1980, 84. Mem. Pub. Relations Soc. Am. (accredited). Lodge: Rotary (bd. dirs. Seattle chpt. 1983—). Avocations: skiing, sailing, herding cattle, cooking. Home: 4314 Winslow Pl N Seattle WA 98103

THOMAS, JULIA DESSERY, planner; b. Riverside, Calif., Dec. 4, 1938; d. Floyd Gordon and Myrtle (Thomas) Dessery; m. David B. Thomas, Nov. 30, 1963 (div.); 1 child, Leslie; m. Michael Lawrence Bobrow, Mar. 24, 1980; stepchildren—Elizabeth, Erica, David. B.A., Calif. State U.-San Francisco, 1963; M.A., Sch. Architecture and Urban Planning, UCLA, 1974. Dir. communications William L. Pereira Assocs., Los Angeles, 1972-73; sr. assoc. Bobrow/Thomas and Assocs., Los Angeles, 1973-78, pres., 1978-84, chmn. bd., chief exec. officer, 1984—; guest lectr. U. So. Calif., Los Angeles, UCLA, Scripps Coll., Claremont, Calif., Calif. Poly. U., Pomona; mem. exec. com., dean's council UCLA Sch. Architecture and Urban Planning, 1982—; mem. design award jury Progressive Architecture, Stamford, Conn., 1983. Prin. works include: Shriners Hosps. for Crippled Children, Los Angeles, Shreveport, Santa Monica Hosp. Med. Ctr., UCLA Arroyo Bridge, Mus. Cultural History; restoration of adminstrn. bldg. Calif. Inst. Tech., Pasadena; Motion Picture and TV Hosp. and Country Home, Woodland Hills, Calif.; Kings Road Housing for Elderly, Hollywood, Calif. (Los Angeles chpt. AIA award 1981). Contbr. articles to profl. publs. Recipient Los Angeles Conservancy award, 1984. Trustee UCLA Found., 1985—; mem. exec. com. UCLA Grad. Shc. Mgmt. Bd. Vis., 1985—; vice chmn. Calif. Council for Humanities, San Francisco, 1980-83; co-conferrer Bobrow-Thomas Fellowship, UCLA; pres. Com. of 200, 1984-85; bd. regents Mt. St. Mary's Coll. Leadership award Calif. Chpt. Am. Planning Assn., 1986, Design Excellence award U.S. Dept. Def. for Naval Med. Clinic. Mem. Am. Inst. Cert. Planners, Am. Inst. Planners , Nat Assn. Sr. Living Industries. Club: Regency (Los Angeles). Office: Bobrow/Thomas and Assocs 1001 Westwood Blvd Los Angeles CA 90024

THOMAS, KEITH RICHARD, marketing company executive; b. San Francisco, Feb. 11, 1953; s. Richard Cody and Janet Marie (Cope) T.; m. Marcia Hatch, Apr. 15, 1978; children: Cody Shipley, Adam Hatch. B.A. in Mktg., San Francisco State U., 1977. Pres. Joint Commn., San Francisco, 1971-73; ptnr. Pereira, Thomas & Assocs., San Francisco, 1973-78; pres. Keith R. Thomas and Co., Inc., San Francisco and N.Y.C., 1978—; officer Windsor Techs., Inc., San Mateo, Calif., 1983-86, Point 'N Shoot Video, Inc., San Francisco, Honolulu, 1985—. Bd. dirs. Jr. Achievement of Bay Area, Inc. Mem. Am. Advt. Fedn. (nat. chmn. 1977-78) Sales and Mktg. Execs. Assn., Am. Mktg. Assn., San Francisco Advt. Club. Republican. Presbyterian. Club: San Francisco Press. Office: 153 Maiden Ln San Francisco CA 94108 Office: 15 Maiden Ln Suite 1500 New York NY 10038

THOMAS, KEITH VERN, bank executive; b. Provo, Utah, Oct. 21, 1946; s. Vern R. and Lois Doran T.; m. Sherrie Hunter, Oct. 7, 1969; children: Genevieve, Joshua, Rachel, William, Rebecca. AA, Dixie Coll., 1969; BS, Brigham Young U., 1971; MBA, St. Mary's Coll., 1980. Cert. rev. appraiser. Examiner Fed. Home Loan Bank Bd., San Francisco, 1971-79, field mgr., 1979-84, asst. dir., 1984-85; sr. v.p., dir. examinations Fed. Home Loan Bank, Seattle, 1985—; bd. dir., v.p. Thomas Mgmt. Corp., Cedar City, Utah, 1979—; bd. dirs. Inst. Fin. Edn., San Francisco, Calif., 1982-85. Editor: Real Estate Textbook, 1983-84. Recipient Outstanding Service award, Fed. Home Loan Bank Bd., 1976, 77, 85, Disting. Service award, Fed. Home Loan Bank Bd., 1981, 85; named Outstanding Instr. Inst. Fin. Edn. 1984. Mem. Nat. Assn. Rev. Appraisers and Mortgage Underwriters, Brigham Young U. Mgmt. Soc. Republican. Mormon. Avocations: sports, reading, music, family. Home: 13624 171st Ave NE Redmond WA 98052 Office: Fed Home Loan Bank Seattle 1501 4th St Seattle WA 98101

THOMAS, KENNETH GAYLE, computer software engineer; b. Grace, Idaho, June 22, 1943; s. Kenneth Turner Thomas and Nelda (Spackman) Herron; m. Janis Lynn Robb; children—Tracy Mark, Tara Michelle. B.S. in Engring. Math., U. Ariz., 1971. Owner, pres. GTS Software and Desert Valley Office Supply, Tucson, 1972-76; analyst Lockheed Electronics, Sierra Vista, Ariz., 1976-78; tech. dir. Bell Tech. Ops., Tucson, 1978-86, Singer Systems and Software Engring., Tucson, 1986—. Contbr. reports and tech. papers on software to profl. jours. Served with USAF, 1962-66. Mem. Ch. of Jesus Christ of Latter-day Saints. Home: 5161 Camino Del Norte Sierra Vista AZ 85635 Office: Singer Systems and Software Engring 6369 E Tanque Verde Tucson AZ 85715

THOMAS, LAWRENCE EUGENE, academic library director; b. York, Pa., Dec. 8, 1931. BS in Composition, Julliard Sch., 1954; MFA in Composition, Brandeis U., 1957; MLS, Ind. U., 1961. Asst. head circulation Columbia U., N.Y.C., 1961-63; chief circulation services Dartmouth Coll., Hanover, N.H., 1964-67; asst. librarian U. Tex. Med., San Antonio, 1967-69; AUL Coll. Devel. and Pub. Service Simon Fraser U., Burnaby, B.C., Can., 1970-80; university librarian Seattle U., 1980—; adj. faculty music Seattle U., 1983; cons. Bowdoin Coll., Brunswick, Maine, 1966, McDowell Colony, Peterborough, N.H., 1964. Mem. ALA. Office: Seattle U Lemieux Library Seattle WA 98122

THOMAS, LINDA IRENE, former state legislator; b. Seattle, Mar. 14, 1944; d. Donald and Lavada Irene (Doran) Craig; m. Robert Keith Reed Jr., Jan. 9, 1968; m. 2d, Alfred Richard Thomas, Feb. 16, 1972; children—Yvonne Michelle, Sherri Ellen. Student U. Wash., 1962, Tacoma Community Coll., 1968-78. Acctg. clk. Steven Motor Co., Tacoma, 1967-68; office mgr., rate clk. Tacoma Moving and Storage, 1969-72; dist. acct. Fife (Wash.) Sch. Dist., 1973-76; staff acct. Nelson, Johnson & Barlow, Federal Way, Wash., 1976-78; pres. Thomas Acctg., Gig Harbor, Wash., 1978-83; mem. Wash. Ho. of Reps., 1984-86; tchr. SBA classes area community colls. Mem. adv. bd. Steilacoom High Sch.; former bd. dirs. Tacoma Area Coalition Individuals with Disabilities; adv. Women-In-Bus. Wash. State U. Mem. Home Builders Assn. Tacoma (chmn. edn. com., mem. legis. and membership service coms.), Tacoma C. of C. (energy task force), Puget Sound Mgrs. Council (past pres.), Nat. Accts. Assn., Nat. Assn. Female Execs., Greater Gig Harbor Bus. Assn., Nat. Fedn. Ind. Bus., Assn. Wash. Bus., LWV, University Place C. of C. Republican. Author: Payroll Taxes without Tears, 1981. Office: PO Box 708 Gig Harbor WA 98335

THOMAS, MITCHELL, JR., aerospace company executive; b. Terre Haute, Ind., Nov. 25, 1936; s. Mitchell and Carolyn Amalia (Wolff) T.; m. Helen Steimle, June 28, 1970; children: Sheri Helen, Deborah Michal, Mitchell III. AB cum laude, Harvard U., 1958; MS, U. Ill., 1959; PhD, Calif. Inst. Tech., 1964. With McDonnell Douglas, Santa Monica, Calif., 1959-64, group leader launch vehicles, 1964-65, sect. chief ablation and applied research sect., 1965-67; br. chief thermophysics lab. McDonnell Douglas, Huntington Beach, Calif., 1969-75; dir. research and devel. L'Garde Inc., Newport Beach, Calif., 1975-76, pres., 1976—; mem. adv. com. on Gossamer structures NASA, 1981. Contbr. articles to profl. jours. Mem. AAAS, AIAA (assoc. fellow thermophysics com., tech. program chmn. for 8th thermophysics conf.). Home: 9691 Villa Woods Dr Villa Park CA 92667 Office: L'Garde Inc 15181 Woodlawn Ave Tustin CA 92680

THOMAS, PAUL ROGER, English educator; b. Takoma Park, Md., Nov. 30, 1940; s. Edwin Moroni and Dessie Verene (Worthington) T.; m. Sandra Johnson, June 21, 1963; children: John, Geoffrey, Jason, Justin. BA, Brigham Young U., 1964; MA, U. Va., 1967; postgrad., U. Hawaii, 1971-72; D. Phil., U. York, Eng., 1982. Publs. clk. CSC, Washington, 1964-65; instr. English Ch. Coll. Hawaii, Laie, 1967-72; asst. prof. English Brigham Young U., Hawaii campus, Laie, 1972-76, Brigham Young U., Provo, Utah, 1980—, Va. Mil. Inst., Lexington, 1977-78; cons. Motivational Concepts, Inc., Charlottesville, Va., 1977-78. Contbr. articles to profl. jours. Active Pleasant View 3d Ward Bishopric (Mormon Ch.), Provo, 1981-84, 85—, Bishop, 1986—; publicity dir. Ralph Woodward Chorale, Provo, 1985-86. Mem. MLA (chmn. Rocky Mountain sect. 1985-86), Medieval Acad. Am., New Chaucer Soc., Rocky Mountain Medieval and Renaissance Assn., Utah Acad. Arts Scis. and Letters. Democrat. Avocations: singing, camping, European travel. Home: 280 E 2200 N Provo UT 84604 Office: Brigham Young U Dept English 3166 JKHB Provo UT 84602

THOMAS, RICHARD GRANT, electrical engineer; b. San Rafael, Calif., Mar. 14, 1946; s. Robert Richard Thomas and Anna Lee (Adams) Thomas Ector; m. Carol Jean Schroder, Mar. 21, 1971; children: Mathew Robert, Adam McBain, Brian Fredrick. AS in Engring., Coll. Marin, 1966; BS in Aero. Engring., Calif. State Poly. U., San Luis Obispo, 1968. Registered profl. engr., Calif., Oreg., Minn., N.Mex., Colo. Data reprodn. analyst Rockwell Internat., Downey, Calif., 1968-70; elec. engr. Buonaccorsi & Assocs., San Francisco, 1970-72; assoc. Skidmore, Owings & Merrill, Portland, Oreg., 1972-76, Chgo., 1976-77; ptnr., sr. elec. engr. Glumac & Assocs. Inc., San Francisco, 1977—. Active Novato (Calif.) Protestant Ch., 1980—. Mem. Illuminating Engrs. Soc. (sec., treas. 1985—, past chmn.), Bldg. Industry Conf. Bd., Soc. Am. Mil. Engrs. Republican. Avocations: reading, golf, photography. Home: 118 La Merida Ct Novato CA 94947 Office: Glumac & Assocs Inc Cons Engrs 4 Embarcadero Ctr Suite 1570 San Francisco CA 94111

THOMAS, RICHARD STEPHEN, architect; b. Duluth, Minn., July 7, 1956; s. Wallace Norman and Kathleen Anne (Sullivan) T.; m. Joanne Marie Bryndal, Sept. 26, 1981. BArch, U. Cin. Registered architect, Colo. Project designer Pouw, Outland & Murata, Denver, 1980-81; project designer Murata Outland Assocs., Denver, 1981-82, assoc., 1982-84, sr. assoc., 1984-86, prin., 1986—; sr. advisor Coll. Design U. Colo., Denver, 1985, guest critic, 1986—. Recipient Grand Alfie award Denver Advt. Fedn., 1984. Mem. AIA, Nat. Assn. Sr. Living Industries, Soc. Mktg. Profl. Services, Denver C. of C. Roman Catholic. Avocations: photography, volleyball. Office: Murata Outland Assocs Inc 1660 17th St Suite 200 Denver CO 80202

THOMAS, RICHARD VAN, state justice; b. Superior, Wyo., Oct. 11, 1932; s. John W. and Gertrude (McCloskey) T.; m. Lesley Arlene Ekman, June 23, 1956; children: Tara Lynn, Richard Ross, Laura Lee, Sidney Marie. B.S. in Bus. Adminstrn. with honors, U. Wyo., 1954, LL.B. with honors, 1956; LL.M., NYU, 1961. Bar: Wyo. 1956, U.S. Ct. Appeals (10th cir.) 1960, U.S. Supreme Ct. 1960. Law clk. to judge U.S. Ct. Appeals 10th Circuit, Cheyenne, 1960-63; asso. firm Hirst & Applegate, Cheyenne, 1963-64; partner firm Hirst, Applegate & Thomas, Cheyenne, 1964-69; U.S. atty. Dist. Wyo., Cheyenne, 1969-74; justice Wyo. Supreme Ct., Cheyenne, 1974-85, chief justice, 1985-86. Pres. Laramie County United Way, 1972, trustee, 1973-74, chmn. admissions and allocations com., 1968-69, chmn. exec. com., 1973, chmn. combined fed. campaign, 1974; bd. dirs. Goodwill Industries Wyo., Inc., 1974-77; exec. com. Cheyenne Crusade for Christ, 1974; v.p., exec. com. Wyo. Billy Graham Crusade, 1987; bd. dirs. Cheyenne Youth for Christ, 1978-81; chancellor Episcopal Diocese of Wyo., 1972—, lay dep. gen. conv., 1973—, chmn. search evaluation nomination com., 1976-77, lay reader, 1969—; bd. dirs. Community Action of Laramie County, 1977-82; chmn. Cheyenne dist. Boy Scouts Am., 1977-78, mem. nat. council, 1982—, mem. Longs Peak council, 1977—, v.p. membership relationships, 1979-81, pres., 1981-83; mem. North Cen. Region Exec. Bd., 1986—; chmn. Laramie County Health Planning Com., 1980-84. Served with JAGC USAF, 1957-60. Named Boss of Year, Indian Paintbrush chpt. Nat. Secs. Assn., 1974; Civil Servant of Year, Cheyenne Assn. Govt. Employees, 1973; Vol. of Yr., Cheyenne Office, Youth Alternatives, 1979; recipient St. George Episcopal award, 1982, Silver Beaver award Boy Scouts Am., 1985. Mem. Am., Laramie County bar assns., Wyo. State Bar, Phi Kappa Phi, Omicron Delta Kappa, Sigma Nu. Clubs: Kiwanis (Cheyenne) (program com. 1969-70, dir. 1970-72, chmn. key club com. 1973-76, disting. pres. 1980-81), Masons (Cheyenne) (33 deg., past master); Shriners; Nat. Sojourners (Cheyenne). Office: Supreme Ct Bldg Cheyenne WY 82001 *

THOMAS, ROBERT CHESTER, sculptor, art educator; b. Wichita, Kans., Apr. 19, 1924; s. Chester and Alma (Mead) T.; m. Eleanor Louise Brand, July 15, 1944; children—Robin Louise, Elizabeth Catherine. Studies with Ossip Zadkine, Paris, 1948-49; B.A., U. Calif.-Santa Barbara, 1951; M.F.A., Calif. Coll. Arts and Crafts, 1952. Prof. sculpture U. Calif., Santa Barbara, 1954—; executed life size bronze figure U. Calif., Santa Barbara, 1967, sculpture J. Magnin store, Century City, 1966, fountain, Montecito, 1968; represented in permanent collection Hirshhorn Mus., Washington, Whatcom Mus., Bellingham, Wash., Santa Barbara Mus., U. Calif., Santa Barbara. Served with USAAF, 1943-46; ETO. Recipient Bronze medal City of Los Angeles, 1949, Silver medal Calif. State Fair, 1954. Home: 38 San Mateo Ave Goleta CA 93117 Office: Dept Art U Calif Santa Barbara CA 93106

THOMAS, ROBERT DICKINSON, sports association communications director; b. Sacramento, Oct. 2, 1945; s. Jack Irvin and Evelyn Lee (Barnett) T.; m. Jennifer Jean Abels, Sept. 7, 1966 (div. 1974); children: Derek Michael (dec.), Kimberly Jean; m. Nicole Jean Pinard, Aug. 5, 1976; 1 child, William O. Stark. Student, U. So. Calif., 1963-64, 66-68; BA in Journalism, Calif. State U., Los Angeles, 1977. Asst. mgr. pub. relations Transamerica Fin. Corp., Los Angeles, 1977-79; mgr. publs. and media services Beneficial Standard Corp., Los Angeles, 1979-83; dir. communications So. Calif. Golf Assn., North Hollywood, 1983—; pub. relations cons. Los Angeles Opera Theatre, 1982-83. Classical music critic Pasadena (Calif.) Star-News, 1983—; editor and pub. FORE Mag., 1983— (Harry Eckhoff award of Excellance, 1983, 85, 86, 87). campaign chmn. United Way Los Angeles, 1982-83. Recipient 36 awards various civic and bus. agys. Mem. Internat. Assn. Bus. Communicators (pres. Los Angeles 1984, v.p. dist. 6 fin. and adminstrn. 1986-87). Democrat. Presbyterian. Avocations: music, golf, reading. Home: 333 Stowe Terr Los Angeles CA 90042 Office: So Calif Golf Assn 3740 Cahuenga Blvd North Hollywood CA 91609

THOMAS, ROBERT EDWIN, business executive; b. Long Beach, Calif., Apr. 24, 1943; s. Benjamin Edwin and Ruby Marie (Penn) T.; m. Paula Ann Camacho, Mar. 19, 1977; children: Ryan S., Nicole M. B of Profl. Arts, Art Ctr. Coll., Los Angeles, 1966. Mktg. mgr. Craig Corp., Compton, Calif., 1969-75; ops. mgr. Audiovox Corp., Hauppauge, N.Y., 1975-79; gen. mgr. L&M Dist., Corvallis, Oreg., 1979-81, Automotive Mgmt., Portland, Oreg., 1981-84; pres. Direct Profit Systems Inc., Beaverton, Oreg., 1984—; cons. Oreg. Dept. Ins., Salem, 1985—, Oreg. Auto Dealers Assn., Portland, 1985—. Photographer, author: Oregon Coast, 1985. Mem. Beaverton Area C. of C., United Kingdom Atari Club. Republican. Avocations: model railroading, photography, sports. Office: Direct Profit System Inc 14335 SW Allen Blvd Suite 201 Beaverton OR 97005

THOMAS, ROBERT EUGENE, biology educator; b. Salineville, Ohio, Feb. 17, 1936; s. Audrey and Margaret (Auld) T.; m. Judith R. Visintainer, July 9, 1962; children: Elizabeth Ann, Susan Rebecca. BS, Kent State U., 1961, MA, 1963, PhD, 1966. Instr. Kent (Ohio) State U., 1964-65; prof. biology Calif. State U., Chico, 1966—; research physiologist Nat. Marine Fisheries Service, Auke Bay, Alaska, 1973—. Contbr. articles on the physiological effects of pollutants to profl. jours. Served with U.S. Army, 1955-57. Named Outstanding Prof. Calif. State U., Chico, 1983, 84; recipient Cy Conkle Pub. award NOAA/ U.S. Dept. Commerce, 1984, Profl. Achievement award Calif. State U., Chico, 1981, 86, Merit Service award Chico State U., 1984, 86. Mem. AAAS. Home: 1651 Park Vista Dr Chico CA 95928 Office: Calif State U Dept Biol Scis Chico CA 95929

THOMAS, ROBERT LANCEFIELD, psychiatrist; b. Forest Grove, Oreg., Feb. 23, 1909; s. Horace Estes and Georgia (Lancefield) T.; student Reed Coll., 1926-27; A.B. with distinction, Stanford U., 1930; M.D. cum laude, Harvard, 1933; children—Randolph Woodson, Suzanne Chilton, Robert W., Barbara Jelen, Gwen Thomas Intern, Mass. Gen. Hosp., Boston, 1933-36; fellow Lahey Clinic, Boston, 1936-37; practice medicine, specializing in surgery, Portland, Oreg., 1937-42, Oakland, Calif., 1946-64, Whitefield, N.H., 1964, Nev. Test Site, AEC, 1964-66; med. dir. Yolo Gen. Hosp., Woodland, Calif., 1966-67, Yerington, Nev., 1967-68; asst. med. dir. Multnomah Med. Service Bur., Portland, 1938-42; med. dir. Hosp. Service of Calif., Oakland, 1948-58; resident psychiatry Napa-Sonoma State Hosps., 1969-72; staff psychiatrist Napa State Hosp., 1972-80, 84—; practice medicine, specializing in psychiatry, 1969-80; with Rehab. Mental Health Services, San Jose, 1980-84. Served from lt. to capt. M.C., USNR, 1938-69; Res., 1938-42, 46-69; PTO. Decorated Asiatic Pacific medal with 4 bronze stars; diplomate Am. Bd. Surgery. Fellow A.C.S.; mem. Am. Psychiat. Assn., Huguenot Soc., Order First Families of Va., Soc. Mayflower Descs. (mem.-at-large exec. com. gen. soc. 1972-75, surgeon gen. 1969-72, gov. Calif. soc. 1970-73, gov. gen. 1975-78), Soc. of Cincinnati in State of R.I., Hereditary Order Descs. Colonial Govs., Jamestowne Soc., Soc. Calif. Pioneers, SAR, Sons and Daus. Oreg. Pioneers, Naval Order U.S., Sovereign Colonial Soc., Ams. of Royal Descent, Barons of Magna Charta, Soc. Descs. Colonial Clergy, Alden Kindred Am., Order of Crown in Am., Sons of Colonial New England, Phi Beta Kappa, Alpha Omega Alpha, Phi Gamma Delta, Nu Sigma Nu. Club: U. Calif. Faculty. Home: 41359 Whitecrest Ct Fremont CA 94539-4529 Office: Napa State Hosp Imola CA 94558

THOMAS, ROGER PARRY, interior designer, art consultant; b. Salt Lake City, Nov. 4, 1951; s. E. Parry and Peggy Chatterton T.; m. Marilyn Harris Hite, Nov. 21, 1976 (div. Apr. 1979); m. H. Andrea Wahn, Nov. 20, 1982. Student Interlochen Arts Acad., 1969; B.F.A., Tufts U., 1973. Pres. Miller-Thomas, Inc., Las Vegas, 1973-76; v.p. Yates-Silverman, Inc., Las Vegas, 1976-81; v.p. design Atlandia Design a Golden Nugget Co., Las Vegas, 1981—; curator Valley Bank Nev. Fine Art Collection. Treas. bd. trustees Nev. Mus. Fine Art; bd. dirs. Nev. Dance Theatre; mem. McCarren Arts Adv. Bd., dir. Nev. Inst. Contemporary Art. Republican. Mem. Ch. of Jesus Christ of Latter-day Saints. Clubs: Sports Club, Country (Las Vegas). Office: Atlandia Design 3380 Arville St Las Vegas NV 89102

THOMAS, SAMUEL FINLEY, physician; b. Paris, France, Oct. 2, 1913 (parents Am. citizens); s. Edward Russell and Elisabeth (Finley) T.; A.B., Princeton, 1935; M.D., Columbia, 1940; m. Ruth Larson, May 21, 1976; 1 dau. by previous marriage, Susan Faith. Intern St. Lukes Hosp., N.Y.C., 1940-41, resident 1941-42, Neurol. Inst. N.Y., 1942-43; practice medicine specializing in neurology and psychiatry, N.Y.C., 1946—; mem. staff Neurol. Inst., N.Y.C., 1946—, attending neurologist, 1975-80, cons. emeritus, 1980—, clin. prof. neurology, 1975-80; mem. staff St. Luke's Hosp., N.Y.C., 1946-80, attending physician neurology, 1955-80, attending psychiatrist, 1975; cons. physician and psychiatrist emeritus, 1980—. Served to maj., M.C., USAAF, 1943-46. Mem. A.M.A., N.Y. County Med. Soc., Am. Psychiat. Assn., N.Y. Neurol. Soc., N.Y. Acad. Medicine. Republican.

Episcopalian. Clubs: Ambassador Athletic (Salt Lake City); Am. Alpine (N.Y.C.); Wasatch Mountain (Salt Lake City). Contbr. articles to med. jours., poetry to popular mags. and newspapers. Address: 123 2d Ave Salt Lake City UT 84103

THOMAS, SHARLA MARIE, utility company technician; b. Missoula, Mont., June 12, 1950; d. Kenneth Charles and Mary Grace (Caras) T. Student, U. Mont., 1986—. Meter reader Mont. Power Co., Missoula, 1976-77, groundman, 1977-78, apprentice lineman, 1978-81, div. technician, 1981—. Republican. Mormon. Avocations: sci., reading, baseball, basketball, stamp collecting.

THOMAS, STEVE D., info-system specialist; b. Butte, Mont., Aug. 8, 1951; s. William James and Catherine (Murphy) T.; m. Kathy Ann McCarthy, Aug. 22, 1971; children: Shawn, Heather. Programmer analyst Anaconda Co., Butte, 1973-81, systems analyst, 1981-82; systems programmer ARCO Metals, Columbia Falls, Mont., 1982-83, supr. ops. and tech. support, 1983-85; supr. of mgmt. info. systems Columbia Falls Aluminum Co., Columbia Falls, 1985—. Home: 1872 Riverwood Rd PO Box 741 Columbia Falls MT 59912 Office: CFAC 2000 Aluminum Dr Columbia Falls MT 59912

THOMAS, TERENCE MICHAEL, chemist, researcher; b. Ft. Dix, N.J., Apr. 13, 1952; s. William Marion and Elizabeth (King) T.; m. Anita Marie Betzen, June 7, 1975; children: Edmund, Elizabeth, Karen. BA, Benedictine Coll., Atchison, Kans., 1970-74; MS, Colo. State U., 1976; PhD, U. Tenn., 1980. Research asst. Oak Ridge (Tenn.) Nat. Lab., 1978; staff chemist Solar Energy Research Inst., Golden, Colo., 1980—. Contbr. articles to profl. jours.; patentee in field. Vocalist Arvada (Colo.) Ctr. Chorale, 1982—. Mem. Am. Chem. Soc., Am. Vacuum Soc. Democrat. Roman Catholic. Avocations: hiking, climbing, computers, motorcycling, reading. Home: 6346 Fenton St Arvada CO 80003 Office: Solar Energy Research Inst 1617 Cole Blvd Golden CO 80401

THOMAS, TERESA ANN, microbiologist, educator, consultant; b. Wilkes-Barre, Pa., Oct. 17, 1939; d. Sam Charles and Edna Grace Thomas. B.S. cum laude, Coll. Misericordia, 1961; M.S. in Biology, Am. U. Beirut, 1965; M.S. in Microbiology, U. So. Calif., 1973. Tchr., sci. supr., curriculum coordinator Meyers High Sch., Wilkes-Barre, 1962-64, Wilkes-Barre Area Public Schs., 1961-66; research assoc. Proctor Found. for Research in Ophthalmology U. Calif. Med. Center, San Francisco, 1966-68; instr. Robert Coll. of Istanbul (Turkey), 1968-71, Am. Edn. in Luxembourg, 1971-72, Bosco Tech. Inst., Rosemead, Calif., 1973-74, San Diego Community Coll. Dist., 1974-80; instr. math.-sci. div. Southwestern Coll., Chula Vista, Calif., 1980—,pres. acad. senate, 1984-85, del., 1986—; mem. steering com. project CREATE Southwestern Coll.-Shanghai Inst. Fgn. Trade; coordinator Southwestern Coll. Great Teaching Seminar, 1987; mem. exec. com. Acad. Senate for Calif. Community Colls., 1985-86, Chancellor of Calif. Community Colls. Adv. and Rev. Council Fund for Instrnl. Improvement, 1984-86; adj. asst. prof. Chapman Coll., San Diego, 1974-83; asst. prof. San Diego State U., 1977-79; chmn. Am. Colls. Istanbul Sci. Week, 1969-71; mem. adv. bd. Chapman Coll. Community Center, 1979-80; cons. sci. curriculum Calif. Dept. Edn., 1986—. Pres. Internat. Relations Club 1959-61; mem. San Francisco World Affairs Council, 1966-68; chmn. land use, energy and wildlife com. Congressman Duncan Hunter's Environ. Adv. Council, 1982-84; v.p. Palomar Palace Estates Home Owners Assn., 1983-85. NSF fellow, 1965; USPHS fellow, 1972-73; Pa. Heart Assn. research grantee, 1962. Mem. Am. Soc. Microbiology (life), Nat. Sci. Tchrs. Assn. (internat. com., coordinator internat. honors exchange lectr. competition sponsored with Assn. Sci Educators Great Britain, 1986), Nat. Assn. Biology Tchrs., Soc. Coll. Sci. Tchrs. (Calif. membership coordinator 1984—), San Diego Natural History Mus., S.D. Zool. Soc., Calif. Tchrs. Assn., NEA, Am. Assn. Community and Jr. Colls., MENSA, Arab Am. Med. Assn., Am.-Lebanese Assn. San Diego (chmn. scholarship com.), Am. U. of Beirut Alumni and Friends of San Diego (1st v.p. 1984-87) Kappa Gamma Pi (pres. Wilkes-Barre chpt. 1963-64, San Francisco chpt. 1967-68), Sigma Phi Sigma. Club: Am. Lebanese Syrian Ladies (pres. 1982-83). Office: Southwestern College 900 Otay Lakes Rd Chula Vista CA 92010

THOMAS, THOMAS DARRAH, chemistry educator; b. Glen Ridge, N.J., Apr. 8, 1932; s. Woodlief and Jean (Darrah) T.; m. Barbara Joan Rassweiler, Sept. 8, 1956; children: David, Steven, Kathleen, Susan. BS, Haverford Coll., 1954; PhD, U. Calif., Berkeley, 1957. Instr. chemistry U. Calif., Berkeley, 1957-58, asst. prof., 1958-59; research assoc. Brookhaven Nat. Lab., Upton, N.Y., 1959-61; asst. prof. Princeton (N.J.) U., 1961-66, assoc. prof., 1966-71; prof. Oreg. State U., Corvallis, 1971—, chmn. dept. chemistry, 1981-84, dir. Ctr. Advanced Materials Research, 1986—; cons. Los Alamos (N.Mex.) Sci. Lab., 1965. Contbr. articles to profl. jours. Fellow Alfred P. Sloan Found., 1966-68, Guggenheim Found., 1969, U. Liverpool, Eng., 1984-85. Fellow AAAS, Am. Phys. Soc.; mem. Am. Chem. Soc., Sigma Xi, Phi Beta Kappa. Home: 1470 NW Greenwood Pl Corvallis OR 97330 Office: Oreg State U Dept Chemistry Corvallis OR 97331

THOMAS, WALTER DILL, JR., forest pathologist, consultant; b. St. Louis, July 3, 1918; s. Walter D. and Helen (Gardner) T.; m. Dolores B. Thomas, Dec. 31, 1939 (div. May 1984); children: Sandra Thomas Bosworth, Arthur D; m. Nancy McCarthy, Feb. 15, 1985. BS, Colo. State U., 1939; MS, U. Minn., 1943, PhD, 1947. Prof. plant pathology Colo. State U., Ft. Collins, 1947-55; supr. biol. research Chevron Chem. Co., Richmond, Calif., 1955-70; v.p. research Nat. Research Mgmt., Eureka, Calif., 1970-72; pres. Forest Ag Corp., Lafayette, Calif., 1972-86; cons. in field, 1986—. Author: Field manual of forest and shade tree diseases, 1947, Not Long Apart, 1965. Commr. Park and Recreation Com., Ft. Collins, 1949, Concord, Calif., 1959; city forester, Ft. Collins, 1950. Served to commdr. USNR, 1944-80. Fellow AAAS; mem. Am. Phytopathological Soc., Soc. Am. Foresters, Assn. Cons. Foresters, Am. Soc. Cons. Arborists, VFW. Republican. Lodges: Elks, Lions. Avocations: swimming, writing. Home and Office: 2435 Heather Leaf Ln Martinez CA 94553

THOMAS, WILLIAM F., newspaper editor; b. Bay City, Mich., June 11, 1924; s. William F. and Irene Marie (Billette) T.; m. Patricia Ann Wendland, Dec. 28, 1948; children: Michael William, Peter Matthew, Scott Anthony. BS, Northwestern U., 1950, MS cum laude, 1951; LHD (hon.), Pepperdine U., Los Angeles. Asst. chief copy editor Buffalo Evening News, 1950-55; editor Sierra Madre (Calif.) News, 1955-56; reporter, asst. city editor, then city editor Los Angeles Mirror, 1957-62; asst. city editor, then met. editor Los Angeles Times, 1968-71, editor, 1971-72, editor, exec. v.p., 1972—. Served with U.S. Army, 1943-46. Office: Los Angeles Times Times Mirror Sq Los Angeles CA 90053

THOMAS, WILLIAM JENNINGS, physician, pub. health adminstr.; b. Washington County, Va., Dec. 1, 1930; s. William W. and Novella (Eden) T.; B.S., Emory and Henry Coll., 1952; M.D., U. Va., 1956; m. Shirley Mae Conway, Sept. 14, 1954; children—Cheryl Wynne, William Jennings, Sharon Lynn, Douglas Eugene. Intern Watts Hosp., Durham, N.C., 1956-57; pub. health trainee Va. Dept. Health, 1959, dist. health dir., 1959-62; practice medicine specializing in preventive medicine and pub. health, Virgilina, Va., 1962-63, Flagstaff, Ariz., 1963—; mem. clin. staff Flagstaff Community Hosp., 1963-68, cons. staff pub. health and preventive medicine, 1968—; dir. Coconino County (Ariz.) Dept. Pub. Health, Flagstaff, 1967—; asst. coordinator Ariz. Regional Med. Program, 1969-73; mem. Ariz. State Cervical Cancer Screening Adv. Council, 1974-75. Mem. social health adv. council Flagstaff Pub. Schs., 1970-73; Gov.'s Emergency Med. Service Com., Ariz., 1968-73, Ariz. Alcoholism Adv. Com., 1972-75, Ariz. Family Planning Adv. Council, 1970-72; mem. child services mgmt. No. Ariz. U., 1976—; bd. dirs. Coconino Council on Alcoholism, 1971-72, No. Ariz. Comprehensive Guidance Centers, Inc., 1969-70, No. Ariz. Med. Evaluation Systems, 1980; bd. govs. No. Ariz. Health Systems Agy., 1979-83. Served to lt. M.C., USN, 1957-59, to comdr. M.C., Res., 1959-80; col. Army N.G., 1980—. Fellow Am. Acad. Family Physicians, Royal Soc. Health; mem. Am., Ariz. med. assns., Coconino County Med. Soc., Am., Ariz. pub. health assns., Am., Ariz. acads. family physicians, Ariz. Health Officers Assn., N.G. Assn. Ariz., N.G. Assn. U.S., No. Ariz. Mil. Assn., Flagstaff C. of C. (mem. sci. and environ. adv. com. 1971). Methodist. Elk. Home: 2045 N Crescent Dr Flagstaff AZ 86001 Office: 2500 N Fort Valley Rd Flagstaff AZ 86001

THOMAS, WILLIAM MARSHALL, congressman; b. Wallace, Idaho, Dec. 6, 1941; s. Virgil and Gertrude T.; m. Sharon Lynn Hamilton, Jan., 1967; children: Christopher, Amelia. B.A., San Francisco State U., 1963, M.A., 1965. Mem. faculty dept. Am. govt. Bakersfield (Calif.) Coll., 1965-74, prof., 1965-74; mem. Calif. State Assembly, 1974-78, 96th-100th Congresses from 18th Calif. Dist.; Mem. del. to Soviet Union, by Am. Council Young Polit. Leaders, 1977; chmn. Kern County Republican Central Com., 1972-74; mem. Calif. Rep. Com., 1972-80. Office: 2402 Rayburn House Office Bldg Washington DC 20515 *

THOMAS, WILLIAM (WILL) ELWOOD, newspaper editor; b. Willows, Calif., Feb. 5, 1932; s. Ralph E. and Bertha A. (Adam) T.; B.S. in Agrl. Journalism, Calif. State Poly. U., 1956; m. Nancy Rae Eisenbeiss, Aug. 27, 1955; children—William Scott, Brian Edward, Bradley Westlund, Karen Jessica. Reporter, Merced (Calif.) Sun-Star, 1956-57; patrolman-clk. Willows (Calif.) Police Dept., 1957-58; staff announcer, news dir. KHSL-TV and Radio Sta., Chico, Calif., 1958-60; editor Lakeport (Calif.) Record-Bee, 1960-66, North County Publs., San Mateo Times Newspaper Group, South San Francisco, 1966—. Active San Mateo council Boy Scouts Am., 1970-71; pres. Benjamin Franklin Jr. High Sch. PTA, 1971-72, del. state conv., 1971, 76; pres. Broadmoor Property Owners Assn., 1976-77. Served with U.S. Army, 1953-55. Recipient Hon. Service award Jefferson Council of PTA, 1976. Mem. Peninsula Press Club, South San Francisco C. of C. (bd. dirs.). Republican. Home: 723 87th St Colma CA 94015 Office: 1331 San Mateo Ave South San Francisco CA 94080

THOMASCH, ROGER PAUL, lawyer; b. N.Y.C., Nov. 7, 1942; s. Gordon J. and Margaret (Molloy) T. BA, Coll. William and Mary, 1964; LLB, Duke U., 1967. Bar: Conn. 1967, Colo. 1974. Assoc. atty. Cummings & Lockwood, Stamford, Conn., 1967-70; trial atty. U.S. Dept. Justice, Washington, 1970-73; ptnr. Roath & Brega, Denver, 1975-87, Ballard, Spahr, Andrews & Ingersoll, Denver, 1987—; vis. assoc. prof. of law Drake U. Sch. Law, Des Moines, 1973-74; frequent lectr. in field, U.S. and Can.; co-dean comml. litigation program of Atla Nat. Advanced Coll. of Advocacy, 1982-86; adj. faculty mem. U. Denver Coll. Law, 1976-80. Recipient Leland Forrest Outstanding Prof. award, Drake U. Sch. Law, 1973. Mem. ABA, Colo. Bar Assn., Assn. Trial Lawyers Am. (nat. chmn. comml. litigation sect. 1981-82), Colo. Trial Lawyers Assn. (bd. dirs. 1981-86, chmn. comml. litigation sect. 1978-79). Clubs: University, Denver Athletic, Tournament Players (Denver). Office: Ballard Spahr Andrews & Ingersoll 17th St Plaza Bldg 1225 17th St Suite 2300 Denver CO 80202

THOMASON, C. JO, school system administrator; b. Chgo., Mar. 7, 1937; d. Clarence Walker-Failor and Mary (Springer) Dotts; m. Duncan MacDonald, June 4, 1956 (div. 1959); m. Tom William Thomason, June 6, 1960. Student, U. Colo., 1954-56; BA, U. Minn., 1958; MA, U. N.Mex., 1968, Ed.D., 1977. Cert. elem. and spl. edn. adminstr. Tchr. spl. edn. Taos (N.Mex.) Pub. Schs., 1958-59; tchr. elem edn. Albuquerque Pub. Schs., 1959-66, tchr. spl. edn., 1966-69, coordinator spl. edn., 1969-76, area coordinator spl. edn., 1976-78, asst. dir. spl. edn., 1978-86; endl. cons. 1986—; lectr., presentor numerous State Depts. Edn., local dists., pvt. bus. in Ind., Fla., N.Mex., La., Alaska, Tex., 1967—; cons. Malagasy Republic, 1967, White House Conf. on Handicapped, 1978; adj. prof. U. N.Mex., Albuquerque, 1969-80. Author: (chpt.) Managerial Models of Mainstreaming, 1986; contbr. articles to profl. jours. Bd. dirs. Foster Grandparents Program, Albuquerque; pres. YWCA, Albuquerque, 1986-87. Mem. Internat. Council for Exceptional Children (pres. 1981-82, chmn. N.Mex. Polit. Action Network 1982—, Leadership awards, Service award), N.Mex. Council Adminstrn. Spl. Edn. (pres. 1985-86), Found. for Exceptional Children (state coordinator), Assn. for Severely Handicapped, N.Mex. Sch. Adminstrs. (bd. dirs.). Democrat. Mem. Unitarian Ch. Avocations: gardening, reading, traveling, cooking. Home: 615 16th St NW Albuquerque NM 87104 Office: Albuquerque Pub Schs 725 University Blvd SE Albuquerque NM 87106

THOMASON, GAIL ANN, writer and communications consultant; b. Denver, June 22, 1947; d. Galen Arthur and Eva Mary (Lenzen) T.; 1 child, John Folsom Hallett II; m. James H. Harmon, Sept. 30, 1972. Student, U. S.C., 1965-67, U. Colo., 1967-68; BA magna cum laude, Colo. State U., 1980, MA in Teaching, 1982. Various positions 1970-80; owner, ptnr. BCA Resources Tng. (formerly Better Communication), Ft. Collins, Colo., 1983-86; arts cons. Raeburn House Gallery, Palm Springs, Calif., 1986—; instr. Colo. State U., U. Colo., Boulder, 1983-86; tng. cons. McGraw-Hill, N.Y.C., 1985-86. Author/editor Colo. State U. research bull., 1984. Hist. restoration photographer Jr. League, Ft. Collins, 1985-86; head Zonta sponsored battered women's safehouse project, 1985-86. Mem. Ft. Collins C. of C. (future studies commn. 1983-86, leadership program 1985-86), Delta Zeta Alumnae Assn., Ft. Collins Panhellenic Alumnae Assn. Episcopal. Lodge: Zonta (sec., author newsletter 1984-86). Avocations: skiing, needlepoint, hist. research and photography. Home: 2663 Victoria Park Dr Riverside CA 92506

THOMPSEN, DOLORES IRENE, educator; b. Murray, Utah, Mar. 6, 1935; d. Walter Delbert and Afton Irene (Ronneburg) Jensen; B.S., U. Utah, 1970; m. Fergus C. Thompsen, Nov. 6, 1953; children—Pamela, Byron, Candace, Elizabeth. Jewelry examiner O.C. Tanner Co., 1953-54; tchr. schs. in Utah, 1970-73; tchr. home econs. West High Sch., Salt Lake City, 1973—. Pres., Young Women's Mut. Assn., Kearns, Utah, 1963-66, 72-73; chmn. fin. com. Mormon Ch., Kearns, 1980-81. Grantee U. Utah. Mem. Am. Home Econs. Assn., Am. Vocat. Assn., Utah Tchrs. Assn., Utah Home Econs. Assn., Utah Vocat. Assn., Salt Lake Tchrs. Assn. Republican. Author curriculum guides. Office: West High Sch 241 North 3d W Salt Lake City UT 84103

THOMPSON, ANNE MARIE, newspaper publisher; b. Des Moines, Feb. 7, 1920; d. George Horace and Esther Mayer Sheely; m. J. Ross Thompson, July 31, 1949; children—Annette McCracken, James Ross. B.A., U. Iowa, 1940; postgrad. U. Colo., 1971. Co-pub. Baca County Banner, Springfield, Colo., 1951-54; pub. Rocky Ford (Colo.) Daily Gazette, 1954—. Mem. Colo. Ho. of Reps., 1957-61; Colo. presdl. elector, 1972; chmn. Colo. adv. com. SBA, 1979-81. Recipient Community Service award Rocky Ford C. of C., 1975; named Colo. Woman of Achievement in Journalism, 1959; Colo. Bus. Person of Yr., Future Bus. Leaders of Am., 1981; elected to Colo. Community Journalism Hall of Fame, 1981; bd. dirs. Fla. Symphony Orch. Mem. Nat. Fedn. Press Women (dir. 1971-81), Nat. Newspaper Assn. (Emma C. McKinney award 1984), Inland Daily award 1984), Inland Daily Press Assn., Colo. Press Assn. (dir. 1981-83), Colo. Press Women, PEO, Bus. and Profl. Women's Club, AAUW. Republican. Methodist.

THOMPSON, ANSON ELLIS, research plant geneticist; b. Eugene, Oreg., Apr. 9, 1924; s. Anson Victor and Ellis Elizabeth (Rust) T.; m. Ruth Warris, June 6, 1945; children: Rebecca, Diane, Reid, Ann. BS with honors, Oreg. State U., 1948; PhD, Cornell U., 1952. Grad. teaching asst. Cornell U., Ithaca, N.Y., 1948-51; from asst. prof. to prof. U. Ill., Urbana, 1951-71; prof., head dept. U. Ariz., Tucson, 1971-76; field staff plant sci. Rockefeller Found., Yogyakarta, Indonesia, 1976-79; nat. research program leader USDA-Agr. Research Service, Beltsville, Md., 1979-83; research geneticist USDA-Agr. Research Service, Phoenix, 1983—; chief of party and advisor on U. adminstrn, Pantnagar, U.P. India, 1967-69; vis. prof. U. Ky. Internat. Coop. Adminstrn. Contract Team, Bogor, Indonesia, 1958-60. Contbr. articles to profl. jours. and chpts. to books. Served with USNR, 1943-44. Recipient USDA Superior Service award, 1982. Fellow AAAS, Am. Soc. Hort. Sci. (v.p. internat. affairs 1983-84, Asgrow award in Vegetable Crops 1966, Charles G. Woodbury award in Raw Products Research 1965); mem. Soc. Econ. Botany, Internat. Soc. Hort. Sci., Sigma Xi, Alpha Zeta. Republican. Presbyterian. Avocations: gardening, photography. Home: 7741 Via Del Mundo Scottsdale AZ 85258 Office: US Water Conservation Lab 4331 E Broadway Phoenix AZ 85040

THOMPSON, ARLENE RITA, nursing educator; b. Yakima, Wash., May 17, 1933; d. Paul James and Esther Margaret (Danroth) T. BS in Nursing, U. Wash., 1966, Masters in Nursing, 1970, postgrad., 1982—. Staff nurse Univ. Teaching Hosp., Seattle, 1966-69; mem. nursing faculty U. Wash. Sch. Nurses, Seattle, 1971-73; critical care nurse Virginia Mason Hosp., Seattle, 1973—; educator Seattle Pacific U. Sch. Nursing, 1981—. Contbr. articles to profl. jours. USPHS grantee, 1969; nursing scholar Virginia Mason Hosp., 1965. Mem. Am. Assn. Critical Care Nurses (cert.), Am. Nurses Assn., Am. Heart Assn., Nat. League Nursing, Sigma Theta Tau, Alpha Tau Omega. Republican. Presbyterian. Avocations: sewing, swimming, jogging, bicycle riding, hiking. Home: 2320 W Newton Seattle WA 98199 Office: Seattle Pacific U 3307 3d Ave West Seattle WA 98199

THOMPSON, BARRY LEE, computer services director; b. San Francisco, June 8, 1948; s. George Robert and Emolyn Wynworth (Berryhill) T.; m. Etna Noreen Locklar, May 19, 1974; children: Evan Michael, Lyle Christopher. BS in Math., Grand Canyon Coll., 1974; postgrad., Ariz. State U., 1986—. Asst. dir. admissions Grand Canyon Coll., Phoenix, 1975-76, asst. registrar, 1976-80, registrar, dir. computer services, 1980-83, dir. computer services, instl. research, 1983—; systems programmer Ramada Inns, Inc., Phoenix, 1970-72. Mem. com. to elect Brenda Burns, Phoenix, 1986; minister of music/youth West Phoenix Bapt. Ch., 1972-75. Named one of Outstanding Young Men of Am., 1978, 80. Mem. Digital Equipment Corp. Users Soc., Math. Assn. Am. Republican. Avocations: astronomy, music. Office: Grand Canyon Coll PO Box 11097 3300 W Camelback Rd Phoenix AZ 85061

THOMPSON, BRUCE ALLAN, oil company executive, consultant; b. Alliance, Ohio, Apr. 24, 1938; s. George Otho and Gwendoline E. (Copeland) T.; m. Geraldine Ann Manley, June 15, 1963; children—Heather, Bruce, Jayson, Winston. B.S., Kent State U., 1960; M.S., Miami U., Oxford, Ohio, 1963. Cert. profl. geologist. Asst. dist. geologist Texaco Inc., Casper, Wyo., Billings, Mont., 1963-68; regional geologist Inexco Oil Co., Denver, Houston, 1968-79; exploration mgr. United Natural Resource, Denver, 1979-82; owner, mgr. Skull Creek Oil Co., Denver, 1982—; dir. Knee Hill Energy Co., Denver; cons. Synder Oil Co., Denver, 1982-84, Tom Brown, Inc., Denver, 1983—. Author: Stratigraphy of the Dunkard Basin, 1963; exploration guide Hydrocarbon Potential in Wyoming, 1974. Alt. del. Republican Party, Sedalia, Colo., 1984; active Ducks Unlimited, Castle Rock, Colo., 1983-84. Mem. Am. Assn. Petroleum Geologists, Am. Radio Relay League, Wyo. Geol. Assn. Houston Geol. Soc., Rocky Mountain Assn. Petroleum Geologists, Casper Petroleum Club, Denver Petroleum Club, Sigma Gamma Epsilon (Geol. Merit award 1962). Episcopalian. Clubs: Diehl Lake Country (Ohio) (fin. com. 1984—); Brown Palace (Colo.). Office: Skull Creek Oil 1615 California St Suite 615 Denver CO 80202

THOMPSON, BRUCE ALLEN, electrical design engineer; b. Seattle, Mar. 24, 1961; s. Dwaine Leroy and Bette Susan (Engerman) T. BS in Physics, U. Wash., 1983. Design engr. RATELCO Inc., Seattle, 1984—. Avocations: music, electronics design. Home: 18322 9th NE Seattle WA 98155 Office: RATELCO Inc 1260 Mercer St Seattle WA 98109

THOMPSON, BRUCE ASHTON, senior analyst; b. Reading, Pa., May 14, 1958; s. W. Paul Thompson and Sally (Lessig) Leyson. AA, UCLA, 1978. Ops. officer trainee Bank of Am., Sepulveda, Calif., 1979-80; acct., bookkeeper, fin. analyst Angeles Corp., Century City, Calif., 1980-82; part-owner Castle Movers, Encino, Calif., 1982; asst. dir., sr. analyst summer sessions UCLA, 1983—; cons. in field, Los Angeles, 1984—; tchr. summer sch. program workshops, U.S. and Can., 1985—. Chief of security Mercado Fundraiser, Los Angeles, 1986. Mem. Adminstrs. and Suprs. Assn. (bd. dirs.). Republican. Episcopalian. Avocations: skiing, surfing, racquetball, soaring, hang gliding. Home: 1048 Grant Ave Santa Monica CA 90405

THOMPSON, BRUCE RUTHERFORD, judge; b. Reno, July 31, 1911; s. Reuben Cyril and Mabel (McLeran) T.; m. Frances Ellen Creek, Sept. 11, 1938; children: Jeffrey, Judith, Harold. A.B., U. Nev., 1932; LL.B., Stanford U., 1936. Bar: Nev. 1936. Practiced in Ren; asst. U.S. atty. Dist. Nev., 1942-52; spl. master U.S. Dist. Ct., Reno, 1952-53; judge U.S. Dist. Ct. Nev., Reno, 1963—. Mem. Nev. State Planning Bd., 1959—, chmn., 1960-61; bd. regents U. Nev. Mem. Am. Judicature Soc. (dir.), ABA, State Bar Nev., Am. Coll. Trial Lawyers, Am. Law Inst., Alpha Tau Omega. Democrat. Baptist. Club: Elks. Home: 1550 Plumb Ln Reno NV 89509 Office: Fed Bldg 300 Booth St Reno NV 89509

THOMPSON, CAROL ANN, speech pathologist, audiologist; b. Worcester, Mass., Apr. 4, 1953; d. Leroy E. and Wanda J. (Writer) Miller. BS, Worcester State Coll., 1975; MS in Speech Pathology and Audiology, Idaho State U., 1977. Speech pathologist head injury unit Crotched Mountain Rehab. Ctr., Greenfield, N.H., 1984-85; speech pathologist, audiologist Adult, Child Devel. Ctr., Twin Falls, Idaho, 1977-84, Magic Valley Speech and Hearing Clinic, Jerome, Idaho, 1985—. Mem. Am. Speech Lang. Hearing Assn. (cert. clin. competence), Idaho Speech Hearing Assn., Nat. Head Injury Found. Avocations: dog training, cooking, horseback riding, walking. Home: 741 Grant Ave Twin Falls ID 83301 Office: Magic Valley Speech and Hearing Clinic 414 N Lincoln Jerome ID 83328

THOMPSON, CHARLES EDWARD, aviation industry consultant; b. Memphis, Jan. 3, 1933; s. Robert Henry and Nellie Agnes (Johns) T.; m. Beverly Ann Aughey, Sept. 1, 1951; children—Valerie Lynn Hall, Stephanie Lee Hanners. B.S., Tulane U., 1954; grad. Naval Flight and Tng. Coll., 1960; B.S. in Aero. Engring., Naval Postgrad. Sch., 1966; grad. Air War Coll., 1973; M.B.A., Auburn U., 1973. Commd. 2d lt. U.S. Marine Corps, 1954; advanced through grades to col., 1976; spl. asst. to asst. sec. of Navy for research and devel., 1973-76; comdg. officer Naval Air Rework Facility, Cherry Point, N.C., 1976-79; comdg. officer Marine Aircraft Group 36, Okinawa, Japan, 1979-80; battle staff comdr. Atlantic Command, 1980-81; ret., 1981; prodn. mgr. comml. div. Sperry Flight Systems, Phoenix, 1981-84; pres. Nehemiah Corp., Phoenix, 1985—; dir. engring. and devel. Hydroil, Inc., Phoenix, 1986—; cons. aviation industry. Mem. adv. bd. Ariz. Vietnam Vets. Leadership Program Inc.; speaker Full Gospel Businessmen's Fellowship Internat. Decorated Legion of Merit, Air medal with gold star, Purple Heart, others. Mem. AIAA (assoc. fellow; founder, chmn. tech. com. aerospace maintenance), Am. Helicopter Soc., Marine Corps Assn. Republican. Mem. Assembly of God Ch. Contbr. articles to tech. jours. Home: 205 E Acapulco Ln Phoenix AZ 85022

THOMPSON, C(LIFFORD) A(NTHONY) (ANDY), social services administrator; b. Minot, N.D., Jan. 7, 1945; s. Raymond Lee and Madonna (Gamber) T.; m. Debra Kay Bush, Apr. 19, 1980; children: Barbara, David, Andrea. BA in Psychology, San Diego State U., 1973; MA in Social Psychology, Goddard Coll., 1978; PhD in Mgmt., Golden State U., 1984. Dir. Santee (Calif.) Counseling Ctr., 1978-84, Personal and Family Counseling Ctr., San Diego, 1985—; dir. Santee Substance Abuse Project, 1983-84, Santana High Sch. Peer Counseling Ctr., Santee, 1983-84, Santee Dispute Resolution Project, 1982-84, Santee Youth Recreation Ctr., 1980-81, El Cajon (Calif.) Counseling Ctr., 1979-84; cons. adminstr. Child Abuse Prevention Project, Santee, 1982—, Social Advocates for Youth, San Diego, 1985—. Author: Counseling for Paraprofessionals, 1978; (manual) Training Trainers, 1979. Chmn. San Diego County Human Relations Commn., 1985—; co-chmn. Media Community Relations Com., San Diego, 1986—. Served as sgt. USAF, 1965069, Vietnam. Named one of Outstanding Young Men Am., 1979; recipient Service to City and Children award Pure Heart Bapt. Ch., Santee, 1983; Vol. of Yr. award San Diego County, 1986. Republican. Avocations: golfing, camping, landscaping.

THOMPSON, DAVID ALFRED, industrial engineer; b. Chgo., Sept. 9, 1929; s. Clifford James and Christobel Eliza (Sawin) T.; children: Nancy, Brooke, Lynda, Diane, Kristy. B.M.E., U. Va., 1951; B.S. in Indsl. Engring, U. Fla., 1955, M.S. in Engring, 1956; Ph.D., Stanford U., 1961. Registered profl. engr., Calif. Research asst. U. Fla. Engring. and Industries Exptl. Sta., Gainesville, 1955-56; instr. indsl. engring. Stanford U., 1956-58, acting asst. prof., 1958-61, asst. prof., 1961-64, asso. prof., 1964-72, prof., 1972—, prof., asso. chmn. dept. indsl. engring., 1972—; prin. investigator NASA Ames Research Center, Moffatt Field, Calif., 1974—; cons. Dept. of State, Fed. EEO Commn.; maj. U.S. and fgn. cos.; cons. emergency communications center design Santa Clara County Criminal Justice Bd., 1975, Bay Area Rapid Transit Control Center, 1977. Dir., editor: documentary film Rapid Answers for Rapid Transit, Dept. Transp., 1974; contbr. articles profl. jours; editorial adv. bd.: Computers and Graphics, 1970—; reviewer: Indsl. Engring. and IEEE Transactions, 1972—. Served to lt. USNR, 1951-54. HEW grantee, 1967-70. Mem. Am. Inst. Indsl. Engrs., Human Factors Soc., IEEE, Am. Soc. Engring. Edn., Am. Soc. Info. Sci., MTM Assn. Standards and Research, Am. Robotics Soc., Soc. Info. Display. Home: 101 Peter

Coutts Circle Stanford CA 94305 Office: Stanford U Dept Indsl Engring Stanford CA 94305

THOMPSON, DENNIS PETERS, plastic surgeon; b. Chgo., Mar. 18, 1937; s. David John and Ruth Dorothy (Peters) T.; B.S., U. Ill., 1957, B.S., Coll. Medicine, 1959, M.S., 1961, M.D., 1961; m. Virginia Louise Williams, June 17, 1961; children—Laura Faye, Victoria Ruth, Elizabeth Jan. Intern, Presbyn.-St. Lukes Hosp., Chgo., 1961-62; resident in gen. surgery Mayo Clinic, Rochester, Minn., 1964-66, fellow in gen. surgery, 1964-66; resident in gen. surgery Harbor Gen. Hosp., Los Angeles, 1968-70; resident in plastic surgery UCLA, 1971-73, clin. instr. plastic surgery, 1975-82, asst. clin. prof. surgery, 1982—; practice medicine specializing in plastic and reconstructive surgery, Los Angeles, 1974-78, Santa Monica, Calif., 1978—; chief plastic surgery sect. St. John's Hosp., 1986-87; mem. staff Santa Monica Hosp., UCLA Ctr. Health Scis., Brotman Med. Ctr.; chmn. dept. surgery Beverly Glen Hosp., 1978-79. Moderator, Congl. Ch. of Northridge (Calif.), 1975-76, chmn. bd. trustees, 1973-74, 80-82; pres. Coop. of Am. Physicians Credit Union, 1978-80, bd. dirs., 1980—, promotion com. chmn. 1984—, treas. 1985—. Am. Tobacco Inst. research grantee, 1959-60. Diplomate Am. Bd. Surgery, Am. Bd. Plastic Surgery. Fellow ACS; mem. AMA (Physicians Recognition award 1971, 74, 77, 81, 84), Calif., Los Angeles County (sec.-tres. dist. 5, 1982-83, pres.-elect 1984-85, pres. 1985-86, chmn. ethics com. 1980-81, chmn. bylaws com. 1979-80, program chmn. 1983-84), Pan-Pacific med. assns., Am., Calif., Los Angeles socs. plastic and reconstructive surgeons (chmn. Calif. soc. med. liability com., 1983-85, chmn. Calif. soc. bylaws com., 1982-83), Los Angeles Soc. Plastic Surgeons (sec. 1980-81, pres. 1982-87), Lipolysis Soc. N.Am., UCLA Plastic Surgery Soc. (treas. 1983-84), Am. Soc. Aesthetic Plastic Surgery, Western Los Angeles Regional C. of C. (dir. 1981-84, 86-87, chmn. legis. action com. 1978-80), Santa Monica C. of C., Phi Beta Kappa, Alpha Omega Alpha, Nu Sigma Nu, Phi Kappa Phi. Republican. Contbr. articles to med. jours. Office: 2001 Santa Monica Blvd Santa Monica CA 90404

THOMPSON, DENNIS ROY, information management executive; b. Chgo., Apr. 11, 1939; s. Roy Gustav and Charlotte Rose (Schultz) T. BSEE with honors, U. Ill., 1964; MS in Bus. Adminstrn., UCLA, 1967. Ops. research cons. Dart Industries, Los Angeles, 1969-70; pres. Seahill, Inc., Los Angeles, 1971-72; dir. credit analysis Comml. Credit Co., Balt., 1973-77; pres. Epicom, Inc., San Diego, 1978—; pub. RFP Publs., 1983—; lectr. data processing and computer sci. San Diego Community Coll. Patentee matchbook. Founder and past chmn. UNZX/C SIG, San Diego; sec., Annapolis (Md.) Libertarians, 1975; 1986 Libertarian Candidate for Calif. 44th Congl. Dist. Served with U.S. Army, 1959-61. Mem., Assn. Computing Machinery, IEEE, Data Processing Mgmt. Assn., Mensa. Club: Toastmasters. Office: 3647 Fairmount Ave San Diego CA 92105

THOMPSON, DOUGLAS STUART, engineer; b. Richmond, Calif., Dec. 5, 1939; s. Stuart M and Alice Thompson; m. Ann Elizabeth Sloan, Nov. 27, 1970; children: Betty, Louise. BS, U. Calif., Berkeley, 1961; PhD, MIT, 1965; M in Chem. Engring., N.C. State U., 1983. Sr. research phys. chemist Dupont Co., Wilmington, Del., 1968-76; assoc. prof. chemistry Hampden-Sydney (Va.) Coll., 1976-81; sr. process engring. group leader INTEL Corp., Santa Clara, Calif., 1983—. Contbr. articles to profl. jours.; patentee in field. Mem. Am. Inst. Chem. Engrs., Soc. of Photolithographic Engrs., Am. Phys. Soc., Am. Chem. Soc.

THOMPSON, DWIGHT ALAN, vocational rehabilitation specialist; b. Monterey Park, Calif., Mar. 2, 1955; s. Irvin Edward and Lydia (Busch) T.; m. Irene Anita Arden, June 18, 1977; children: Dwight Christopher, Meredith Irene. BA in Social Welfare, U. Wash., 1978, MSW, 1980. Registered vocat. rehab. counselor, Wash. and Oreg.; cert. Emergency Med. Technician. Houseparent Parkview Home for Exceptional Children, Seattle, 1976-77; research analyst Wash. State Ho. Reps., Olympia, 1979-81; v.p. The James L. Groves Co., Everett, Wash., 1982-86; exec. dir. Evaluation & Tng. Assocs., Seattle, 1984-86; pres., owner Rehab. & Evaluation Services, Seattle, 1986—; social work officer 50th Gen. Army Reserve Hosp., Seattle, 1982-87—, San Francisco, 1987—; aide-de-camp 2d Hosp. Ctr., San Francisco; practicum instr. U. Wash., 1985—. Co-author Correction Study Report, 1981. Registered lobbyist Wash. State, 1983—; conf. pres. St. Vincent de Paul Soc., 1975-78; lt. Thurston County Fire Dist #6, East Olympia, Wash., 1980-83; alumni rep. COS Track Com. U. Wash., 1984—; primary candidate Dem. Primary for State Rep., Renton, Wash., 1984. Mem. Acad. Cert. Social Workers, Nat. Assn. Social Workers (cert.), Profl. Rehab. Orgn. Wash., Wash. Self-Insurers Assn. (legislative steering com.), Theta Xi (pres. 1975-77). Roman Catholic. Home: 5119-81st Pl SW #5 Mukilteo WA 98275 Office: Rehab and Evaluation Services 507 Jones Bldg Seattle WA 98101

THOMPSON, GORDON, JR., judge; b. San Diego, Dec. 28, 1929; s. Gordon and Garnet (Meese) T.; m. Jean Peters, Mar. 17, 1951; children—John M., Peter Renwick, Gordon III. Grad., U. So. Calif., 1951, Southwestern U. Sch. Law, Los Angeles, 1956. Bar: Calif. bar 1956. With Dist. Atty.'s Office, County of San Diego, 1957-60; partner firm Thompson & Thompson, San Diego, 1960-70; U.S. dist. judge So. Dist. Calif., San Diego, 1970-84, chief judge, 1984—. Bd. visitors U. San Diego. Mem. Am. Bd. Trial Advocates (treas.), ABA, San Diego County Bar Assn. (v.p. 1970), Delta Chi. Club: San Diego Yacht. Office: 940 Front St San Diego CA 92189 *

THOMPSON, HERBERT ERNEST, tool and die co. exec.; b. Jamaica, N.Y., Sept. 8, 1923; s. Walter and Louise (Joly) T.; student Stevens Inst. Tech., 1949-51; m. Patricia Elaine Osborn, Aug. 2, 1968; children—Robert Steven, Debra Lynn. Foreman, Conner Tool Co., 1961-62, Eason & Waller Grinding Corp., 1962-63; owner Endco Machined Products, 1966-67, Thompson Enterprises, 1974—; pres. Method Machined Products, Phoenix, 1967; pres., owner Quality Tool, Inc., 1967—. Served to capt. USAAF, 1942-46. Decorated D.F.C., Air medal with cluster. Home: 14009 N 42d Ave Phoenix AZ 85023 Office: 4223 W Clarendon Ave Phoenix AZ 85019

THOMPSON, JAMES HOMER, insurance agent, educator; b. Henrietta, Tex., Sept. 11, 1926; s. James Hite and Virginia (Marberry) T.; student U. Okla., 1944-45; Ph.B., U. Chgo., 1947, M.B.A., 1950; M.S. in Fin. Services, Am. Coll., Bryn Mawr, Pa., 1980; m. Ilene Kriss, Mar. 17, 1979; children by previous marriage—Julie A., Laurie J. Dist. sales mgr. Studebaker Corp., South Bend, Ind., 1951-55; assoc. gen. agt. State Mut. Life Assurance Co. Am., Denver, 1955—; instr. U. Colo. 1964—; mem. bd. Nat. C.L.U. Inst. Recipient J. Stanley Edwards award Colo. Ins. Industry, 1985, Alumni Service Citation, U. Chgo., 1987; Inst. Mem. cabinet U. Chgo.; mem. Colo. Ins. Adv. Bd., 1980—. C.L.U., C.P.C.U. Bd. dirs. Adult Edn. Council of Met. Denver, 1977. Mem. Am. Soc. C.L.U.s (v.p. Rocky Mountain chpt. 1967, pres. 1968-69, regional v.p. 1972-73), Denver Assn. Life Underwriters (dir. 1963-66). Home: 180 Ivanhoe St Denver CO 80220 Office: 44 Cook St Denver CO 80206-5898

THOMPSON, JAMES MARTIN, aerospace company executive; b. Glendale, Calif., Sept. 27, 1941; s. Roy James and Ruth Jeannette (Rook) T.; m. Karen Jo Allen, Sept. 7, 1968. BA in Physics, UCLA, 1963, MS in Physics, 1965, postgrad., 1969, PhD in Math., 1970, M Engring., 1976. Computer scientist Lockheed, Burbank, Calif., 1965-75; line mgr. Hughes Aircraft, Culver City, Calif., 1975—; software cons., 1976—. Contbr. articles to profl. jours. Home: 729 N Maria Ave Redondo Beach CA 90277 Office: Hughes Aircraft Co 2141 E Rosecrans Ave El Segundo CA 90245

THOMPSON, JAMES WILLIAM, lawyer; b. Dallas, Oct. 22, 1936; s. John Charles and Frances (Van Slyke) T.; B.S., U. Mont., 1958, J.D., 1962; m. Marie Hertz, June 26, 1965; children—Elizabeth, Margaret, John. Accountant, Arthur Young & Co., N.Y.C., summer 1959; instr. bus. adminstrn. Eastern Mont. Coll., Billings, 1959-60, U. Mont., Missoula, 1960-61; admitted to Mont. bar, 1962; asso. firm. Cooke, Moulton, Bellingham & Longo, Billings, 1962-64, James R. Felt, Billings, 1964-65; asst. atty. City of Billings, 1963-64, atty., 1964-66; partner firm Felt, Speare & Thompson, Billings, 1966-72; partner firm McNamer, Thompson & Cashmore, 1973-86; ptnr. McNamer & Thompson PC, 1986—. Mem. Billings Zoning Commn., 1966-69; v.p. Billings Community Action Program (now Dist. 7 Human Resources Devel. Council), 1968-70, pres., 1970-75, trustee, 1975—; mem. Yellowstone County Legal Services Bd., 1969-70; City-County Air Pollution Control Bd., 1969-70; pres. Billings Symphony Soc., 1970-71; bd. dirs. Billings Studio Theatre, 1967-73; mem. Diocesan exec. council, 1972-75; mem. Billings Transit Commn., 1971-73; mem. City Devel. Agy., 1972-73; bd. dirs. United Way, Billings, 1973-81. C.P.A., Mont. Mem. ABA, State Bar Mont., Yellowstone County Bar Assn. (bd. dirs. 1983—, pres. 1985-86), Mont. Soc. C.P.A.s, C. of C., Sigma Chi (pres. Billings alumni assn. 1963-65). Clubs: Elks, Kiwanis. Episcopalian. Home: 123 Lewis Ave Billings MT 59101 Office: Transwestern 1 Bldg Billings MT 59101

THOMPSON, JENENNE MARIE, dietitian; b. Trinidad, Colo., July 7, 1947; d. Edward Eli and Cecilia Josephine (Castor) Jenkins; m. G. Neal Thompson, July 31, 1964; (div. 1972); 1 child, Shawn Eric. B.S., U. N.Mex., 1975. Dietary dir. San Juan Regional Med. Ctr., Farmington, N.Mex., 1976-78, Meml. Gen. Hosp., Las Cruces, 1978-80; asst. dietary dir. Presbyn. Hosp., Denver, 1980-82; dietary dir. Parkview Hosp., Pueblo, Colo., 1983-85; pres. Cons. in Health and Healing, Denver, 1982—; cons. food service mgmt. St. Joseph's Hosp., Del Norte, Colo., 1984—, Alamosa Hosp., Colo., 1985—, Sangre de Cristo Nursing Facility, Monte Vista, Colo., 1984—, Sanhaven Nursing Facility, Lamar, Colo., 1984—. Mem. Am. Dietetic Assn., Colo. Dietetic Assn., Am. Hosp. Assn., Hosp. Food Service Adminstrn., Am. Diabetes Assn. Democrat. Roman Catholic. Avocations: Skiing; gourmet cooking. Home: 4113 Grove St Denver CO 80211

THOMPSON, JOHN JONES, physician, medical administrator; b. Washington, Feb. 21, 1947; s. Robert Luther and Marjorie (Jones) T.; m. Catherine Ruth Wisswaesser, May 15, 1982; 1 child, Scott Beckett. BS, Yale U., 1969, MD, 1974. Diplomat Am. Bd. Pathology. Intern Yale New Haven Hosp., 1974-75; resident in pathology U. Pa., Phila., 1975-79, fellow in surg. pathology, 1979-80; asst. prof. U. Pa. Hosp., Phila., 1980-82; dir. labs., asst. area med. dir. Kaiser Permanente Med. Ctr., Portland, Oreg., 1983—. Author: Pathology of the Esophagus, 1984. Chmn., blood services com. bd. dirs., ARC, Portland, 1983—. Mem. Am. Soc. Clin. Pathologists (cons. HT/HTC com.), AAAS, Internat. Acad. Pathology, Soc. Med. Decision Making, Soc. Clin. Trials. Democrat. Unitarian. Avocations: hiking, cross country skiing, gardening, music. Home: 2524 SW 17th Ave Portland OR 97201 Office: Kaiser Permanente Regional Lab 10200 SE Sunnyside Rd Clackamas OR 97015

THOMPSON, JOHN LESTER, bishop; b. Youngstown, Ohio, May 11, 1926; s. John Lester and Irene (Brown) T.; m. Shirley Amanda Scott, Aug. 1, 1951; children: Amanda, Ian. B.A., Youngstown Coll., 1948; S.T.B., Episcopal Theol. Sch., Cambridge, Mass., 1951. Ordained priest Episcopal Ch., 1951; curate, then rector chs. Ohio, Oreg. and Calif., 1951-78; bishop Episcopal Diocese No. Calif., Sacramento, 1978—; trustee Ch. Divinity Sch. Pacific, Berkeley, Calif. Pres., Oreg. Shakespeare Festival, 1955-56, chmn. bldg. com. for outdoor theatre, 1957-58. Served with USNR, 1943-46. Office: PO Box 161268 Sacramento CA 95816

THOMPSON, JOHN PHILLIP, city manager; b. Sacramento, June 29, 1949; s. Jack Walter and Kathryn Bernice (Graves) T.; m. Diane Lilly Schmitz, Feb. 14, 1976; children: Kristen Kay, Scott Phillip. BA in Polit. Sci., U. Calif., Santa Barbara, 1971; MA in Urban Studies, Occidental Coll., 1975. Lic. real estate salesman, Calif. Sr. adminstrv. asst. City of Salinas, Calif., 1971-73; adminstrv. analyst State Legis., Sacramento, 1974-76; sr. mgmt. analyst City of Sacramento, 1976-79; asst. mgr. City of Vacaville, Calif., 1979-84, mgr., 1984—; instr. Golden Gate U., San Francisco, 1980-83; mem. policy coms. League of Calif. Cities, Sacramento, 1982-84. Pres. United Way, Vallejo, Calif., 1985. CORO Found. fellow, 1973-74. Mem. Internat. City Mgmt. Assn., Calif. Econ. Devel. Assn., Calif. Redevel. Assn., Urban Land Inst., Vacaville C. of C. (1986—). Republican. Presbyterian. Lodge: Rotary (bd. dirs. 1983-84, pres. 1986—). Avocations: golfing, computers, financial planning, landscaping.

THOMPSON, JOSEPH FRANCIS, insurance loss control consultant; b. Newburgh, N.Y., Feb. 23, 1957; s. Gordon R. and Florence (Kavanaugh) T. Student, Dutchess Community Coll., 1975-76; AAS, Rockland Community Coll., 1978. Cons. loss control Kemper Ins. Co., Melville, N.Y., 1979-80, Continental Ins. Co., Glens Falls, N.Y., 1981-84, Genesis Custom Homes, Inc., Los Angeles; sr. cons. loss control Fireman's Fund Ins. Co., Van Nuys, 1985—; pres., bd. dirs., chief fin. officer, chief exec. officer Genesis Custom Homes, Inc., Los Angeles, 1986—; profl. instr. open water scuba diving. Vol. firefighter Vails Gate (N.Y.) Fire Co., 1973-80. Mem. Am. Soc. Safety Engrs. Republican. Avocations: scuba diving, tennis, white water rafting. Home: 6627 Burnet Ave Van Nuys CA 91405 Office: Firemans Fund Ins Co 3223 W 6th St Los Angeles CA 92233

THOMPSON, JULIA ELIZABETH, correctional counselor; b. Phila., June 14, 1949; d. Jacob Peter and Helena Leota (Caruthers) Hemmert; m. George C. Thompson, July 5, 1969 (div.); 1 son, George C. A.A., Solano Community Coll., 1971; postgrad. Calif. State U.-Sacramento, U. Calif.-Berkeley Extension. Group counselor I, Solano County Probation Dept., Solano County Welfare Dept., Fairfield, Calif., 1971-72, group counselor II, Solano County Welfare Dept., 1973-76; correctional officer Calif. Med. Facility, Vacaville, Calif., 1976-78, corectional sgt., 1981-82; correctional program supr. I, Calif. Correctional Ctr., Susanville, 1978-80; correctional sgt. Calif. State Prison, San Quentin, 1980-81; correctional counselor I, Correctional Tng. Facility, Soledad, Calif., 1982-83, No. Reception Ctr., Vacaville, 1983—. Mem. Calif. Correctional Counselors Assn., Calif. Correctional Peace Officers Assn., Chicano Correctional Workers Assn., Nat. Assn. Exec. Females, Calif. Human Services Orgn. (past pres. Solano County chpt., past state bd. rep.). Republican. Office: PO Box 2000 Vacaville CA 95696

THOMPSON, LOHREN MATTHEW, oil company executive; b. Sutherland, Nebr., Jan. 21, 1926; s. John M. and Anna (Ecklund) T.; m. Ruth A. Stammer, Jan. 2, 1959; children—Terence M., Sheila M., Clark M. Ed., U. Denver. Spl. rep. Standard Oil Co., Omaha, 1948-56; v.p. mktg. Frontier REF. co., 1967-68; mgr. mktg. U.S. region Husky Oil Co., Denver, 1968-72; v.p. Westar Stas., Inc., Denver, 1967-70; pres., chmn. bd. Colo. Petroleum, Denver, 1971—. Served with USAAF, 1944-46. Mem. Colo. Petroleum Council, Am. Petroleum Inst., Am. Legion. Democrat. Lutheran. Clubs: Denver Petroleum, Denver Oilman's Lodge: Lions. Home: 10161 Melody Dr North Glenn CO 80221 Office: Colo Petroleum 4080 Globeville Rd Denver CO 80216

THOMPSON, MALCOLM FRANCIS, elec. engr.; b. Charleston, S.C., Sept. 2, 1921; s. Allen R. and Lydia (Brunson) T.; B.S., Ga. Inst. Tech., 1943, M.S., 1947; postgrad. Mass. Inst. Tech., 1947-49; m. Ada Rose O'Quinn, Jan. 20, 1943; children—Rose Mary, Nancy Belle, Susan Elizabeth, Frances Josephine. Instr. dept. elec. engring. Mass. Inst. Tech., 1947-49; research engr. Autonetics Co., Anaheim, Calif., 1949-70; tech. dir. SRC div. Moxon, Inc., Irvine, Calif., 1970-73; engring. mgr., mgr. computers and armament controls. Northrop Aircraft Div., Hawthorne, Calif., 1973-87; ind. cons., 1987—. Served to capt. AUS, 1943-46. Mem. IEEE, Nat. Geog. Soc., Nat. Rifle Assn., Am. Ordnance Assn., Eta Kappa Nu. Patentee in field. Home and Office: 1602 Indus St Santa Ana CA 92707

THOMPSON, MARGARET THERESE, manufacturing executive; b. Fontana, Calif., Jan. 26, 1950; d. Joseph Robert and Margaret Mary (McKinney) Benchwick; m. Jeffrey Lee Thompson, Sept. 8, 1973; children—Kristen Ashley, Cara Lauren. A.A., Moorpark Jr. Coll., 1970; B.S. in Nursing, B.A. in Psychology, Calif. State U.-Los Angeles, 1974; M.S. in Health Adminstrn., Calif. State U.-Northridge, 1981. Research asst. Los Angeles County Probation Dept., 1972-74; head nurse, group counselor Glendale (Calif.) Adventist Med. Ctr., 1974-76, quality assurance coordinator, 1976-80, nursing unit coordinator, definitive observation unit, 1980-84; assoc. prof. Calif. State U.-Northridge, 1983—; dir. Los Angeles br. Nat. In-Home Health Services, 1984-85, v.p. internal ops., 1985-86; prin. B&T Innovations, Inc., 1986—; cons. West Coast Med. Mgmt. Assocs., Westlake Village, Calif., 1979—. NIMH scholar, 1972-74. Home: 9510 Haines Canyon Ave Tujunga CA 91042 Office: PO Box 211 Tujunga CA 91042

THOMPSON, MARY JEAN, interior designer, lecturer; b. Salem, Oreg., Aug. 6, 1935; d. Lester Wayne and Bernis Laverne (Nelson) Schrunk; m. Newton L. Thompson, July 5, 1962 (div.); children—Craig L., Brooks D., K. Inga, Heidi A. B.A. cum laude in Music, Lewis and Clark Coll., 1957; B.A. cum laude in Interior Design, U. Utah, 1969. Designer, Clark Leaming Co., Salt Lake City, 1967-69; pres. Thompson Design Assocs., Inc., Reno, 1970—. Bd. dirs. Community Concerts, 1975-76, Washoe Landmark Preservation, 1976-82, Sierra Nev. Mus. of Art, 1980—. Recipient McGraw Edison Lighting Excellence award, 1978; AIA honor award, 1981. Mem. Am. Soc. Interior Designers (cert. 1970, Merit award ASID/Wilson design competition 1983), AIA (affiliate mem., dir. No. Nev. chpt. 1981-82). Interiors include: Western Nev. Community Coll., 1976, Reno Internat. Airport, 1981, Sparks Family Hosp., 1982, Westlake Community Hosp., 1984, Panorama Community Hosp., 1984, Harrah's Tahoe, 1983-84, Wellington (Fla.) Regional Med. Ctr., 1986, Inland Valley (Calif.) Med. Ctr., 1986, Roseville (Calif.) COmmunity Hosp., 1986. Interiors featured in Designers West Mag., Dec. 1983, Interior Design Mag., Dec. 1983, Contract Mag., 1984.

THOMPSON, MILTON EARL, protective services official; b. Vincentown, N.J., Apr. 15, 1931; s. Milton and Margaret (Van Bibber) T.; divorced; children: Randa Lee, Carolyn Gayle, Gregory Douglas, Eric Van; m. Carol Lynne Kincaid, Mar. 10, 1973; children: Cynthia Ann Sevier, Kristin Noel Sevier. AA in Fire Sci., San Jose City Coll., 1976; BA in Pub. Service, U. San Francisco, 1977; M in Pub. Adminstrn., Golden Gate U., 1983. Fire fighter Palo Alto (Calif.) Fire Dept., 1953-58; fire fighter San Jose (Calif.) Fire Dept., 1959-85, asst. fire chief, 1975-85; mgr. emergency services Santa Clara County, San Jose, 1985—; instr. fire sci. San Jose City Coll., 1968-71, Mission Coll., Santa Clara County, 1985—. Fund raiser YMCA, San Jose, 1977—; mem. adv. council Salvation Army ARC, San Jose, 1976—. Served with USN, 1949-53. Recipient Spl. Recognition award City of San Jose, 1985. Mem. County Emergency Services Assn. Republican. Lodges: Kiwanis, Rotary. Home: 131 College Ave Los Gatos CA 95030 Office: Santa Clara County 70 W Hedding St San Jose CA 95110

THOMPSON, NATHAN CHRISTOPHER, electronics company executive; b. Newton, Kans., Aug. 21, 1960; s. Ralph James and Virginia Lee (Creighton) T. BSEE, U. Colo., 1983. Pres., founder Western Automation, Inc., Boulder, Colo., 1980—, chmn. bd. dirs. Vol. Sta. KGNU-FM Pub. Radio, Boulder, 1986, Ken Kramer for Senate, Boulder, 1986. Republican. Club: Colo. Mountain (Boulder). Avocations: soaring, flying, bicycling, writing. Home: 3495 Eastman Boulder CO 80303 Office: Western Automation Inc 1700 N 55th Boulder CO 80301

THOMPSON, ORVAL NATHAN, lawyer; b. Shedd, Oreg., Nov. 29, 1914; s. Otto M. and Laura L. (Halverson) T.; m. Jessie Mila Jackson, Nov. 24, 1958 (dec. 1983); children—Kathleen Persons, Richard, Marion Wells. B.S., U. Oreg., 1935, J.D., 1937; LL.M., Northwestern U., 1939. Bar: Oreg., 1937, U.S. Ct. Appeals, 1949, U.S. Supreme Ct., 1945. Practiced, Albany, Oreg., 1938—, pres. firm Westherford, Thompson, Brickey & Quick, P.C., 1972—; dir. Citizens Valley Bank, 1956-86, Key Bank Oreg., 1986—; sec. Oreg. Metall. Corp., 1955—. Mem. Oreg. Ho. of Reps., 1941-42; mem. Oreg. Senate, 1947-50; legal advisor to gov. Oreg., 1957-58. Served to lt. USN, 1942-46. Mem. ABA, Oreg. Bar Assn., Linn County Bar Assn., Albany Area C. of C., Phi Beta Kappa. Democrat. Presbyterian. Clubs: Masons, Springhill Country, Elks. Home: 605 Erin Crest NW Albany OR 97321 Office: Weatherford Thompson Brickey & Quick PC 130 W 1st Ave PO Box 667 Albany OR 97321

THOMPSON, PAULA ANN, restaurant executive; b. Floral Park, N.Y., Sept. 10, 1940; d. Chester H. and Emma P. (Sternberg) Jordan; 1 child, Julie Ann. B.A. in Math., Hofstra U., Hempstead, N.Y., 1962. Research analyst Carter Wallace, N.Y.C., 1964-68; mgr., market research Grey Advt., Los Angeles, 1970-77; v.p., research dir. Larson, Bateman Inc., Santa Barbara, Calif., 1977-80; dir. market research and strategic planning Vicorp Specialty Restaurants, San Diego, 1980—. Recipient Twin award San Diego YWCA, 1985. Mem. Am. Mktg. Assn. Home: 334 S Granados Ave Solana Beach CA 92075 Office: Vicorp Specialty Restaurants 6610 Convoy Ct PO Box 121513 San Diego CA 92112

THOMPSON, PHIL BARR, sub sea consultant; b. Lachute, Quebec, Can., Aug. 14, 1947; s. Stuart E. and Floria Thompson; m. Cynthia Pearson, Apr. 21, 1979; children: Branden, Scott. Grad., Upland (Calif.) High Sch. Deep sea diver Santa Fe Internat., Houma, La., 1969-73; saturation diver Sub Sea Internat., Aber Deen, Scotland, 1973-75; supt. saturation diving Stolt-Nielsen Seaway, Haugesound, Norway, 1975-80; project mgr. Stolt-Nielsen Seaway, Mexico City, 1980-82, Houston, 1982-84; sr. cons. Wet Solutions, Inc., New Orleans, 1984—; experimental diver Inner Space, New Orleans, 1973. Home: PO Box 1130 Idyllwild CA 92349 Office: Wet Solutions Inc 2000 Comet St New Orleans LA 70114

THOMPSON, PHILIP MASON, museum director; b. N.Y.C., June 9, 1942; s. William R. and Marie J. (Buckovecky) T.; m. Vilja Marie Horner, Sept. 4, 1966; children: Philip Jr., Tyra. BA, Ariz. State U., 1969, MA, 1986. Asst. dir. Phoenix Art Mus., 1971-73, Phila. Mus. Art, 1973-78; dir. devels. and community affairs Phoenix Meml. Hosp., 1978-81; dir. devels. St. Joseph's Hosp., Phoenix, 1981-83; dir. Mus. No. Ariz., Flagstaff, 1983—; nat. adv. bd. practitioners No. Ariz. U., Flagstaff, 1986; bd. dirs. Western Mus. Conf., Ariz. Mus. Assn. Mem., vice chmn. Ariz. Hist. Gov.'s Adv. Commn., Phoenix, 1984—; mem. steering com. BLOC Grant Program, 1980-83. Served with U.S. Army, 1963-66. Mem. Am. Assn. Mus., Am. Anthropol. Assn., Sigma Xi. Republican. Presbyterian. Club: Continental Country (Flagstaff). Avocations: fly fishing, skiing, golf. Home: Rt 4 Box 718 Flagstaff AZ 86001 Office: Mus of No Ariz Rt 4 Box 720 Flagstaff AZ 86001

THOMPSON, RAYMOND HARRIS, educator, anthropologist; b. Portland, Me., May 10, 1924; s. Raymond and Eloise (MacIntyre) T.; m. Molly Kendall, Sept. 9, 1948; children: Margaret Kelsey, Thompson Luchetta, Mary Frances. B.S., Tufts U., 1947; A.M., Harvard U., 1950, Ph.D., 1955. Fellow div. hist. research Carnegie Instn., Washington, 1950-52; asst. prof. anthropology, curator Mus. Anthropology, U. Ky., 1952-56; faculty U. Ariz., 1956—, prof. anthropology, 1964—, Riecker Disting. prof., 1980—, head dept., 1964-80; dir. Ariz. State Mus., 1964—; mem. adv. panel program in anthropology NSF, 1963-64, mem. mus. collections program; mem. NSF grad. fellowship panel Nat. Acad. Scis.-NRC, 1964-66; mem. research in nursing in patient care rev. com. USPHS, 1967-69; com. on social sci. commn. edn. in agr. and natural resources Nat. Acad. Scis., 1968-69; mem. anthropology com. examiners Grad. Record Exam., 1967-70, chmn., 1969-70; mem. com. recovery archaeol. remains, 1972-77, chmn., 1973-77; collaborator Nat. Park Service, 1972-76; mem. Ariz. Hist. Adv. Commn., 1966—, chmn., 1971-74, chmn. hist. sites rev. com., 1971-83; chmn. Ariz. Humanities Council, 1973-77, mem., 1979—; mem. research review panel for archaeology NEH, 1976-77, mem. rev. panel for museums, 1978; cons. task force on archaeology Adv. Council on Historic Preservation, 1978. Author: Modern Yucatecan Maya Pottery Making, 1958; editor: Migrations in New World Culture History, 1958; editorial bd.: Science, 1972-77. Trustee Mus. No. Ariz., 1969—; bd. dirs. Tucson Mus. Art, 1974-77. Served with USNR, 1944-45, PTO. Fellow AAAS (chmn. sect. H 1977-78), Tree-Ring Soc., Am. Anthrop. Assn. (Disting. Service award 1980); mem. Soc. Am. Archaeology (editor 1958-62, mem. exec. com. 1963-64, pres. 1976-77); Mem. Am. Soc. Conservation Archaeology (Conservation award 1980); mem. Seminario de Cultura Maya, Am. Assn. Museums, Internat. Council Museums (asso.), Council Museum Anthropology (dir. 1978-79, pres. 1980-83), Assn. Sci. Mus. Dirs. (sec.-treas. 1978—), Ariz. Acad. Sci., Ariz. Archaeol. and Hist. Soc., Ariz. Mus. Assn. (pres. 1983, 84), Phi Beta Kappa, Sigma Xi. Office: Dept Anthropology U Ariz Tucson AZ 85721

THOMPSON, RAYMOND KERMIT, architect, engineer; b. Seaside, Oreg., Aug. 27, 1905; s. Herschel V. and Anna Mathilde (Schirmer) T.; m. Lillian Myrtle Polly Povey, Jan. 5, 1929; children: Kermit Duncan, Priscilla Ann Elizabeth. BArch, U. Oreg., 1929; MS, MIT, 1932. Registered architect Oreg., Wash., Idaho, Ohio, N.Y., Conn.; registered profl. engr., Conn. With design bur. mech. engring. dept. Bklyn. Edison Co., 1930-31; pvt. practice architecture Pittsfield, Mass., 1938-42, Portland, Oreg., 1948-53; ptnr. Thompson & Thompson AIA, Portland, 1953—; assoc. prof. sch. engring. U. Portland, 1965-83; assoc. prof. architecture Ohio State U., Columbus, 1946-48; mem. architecture faculty Wentworth Inst., Boston, 1932-42. Served to lt. comdr. USN, 1942-46. Mem. AIA (sec. Oreg. chpt. 1950), Am. Soc. Engring. Edn. (vice chmn. N.W. region 1967), SAR (pres.

Oreg. chpt. 1987—, v.p. 1985-86, pres. Portland chpt. 1984). Republican. Methodist. Home: 806 SW Vista Ave Portland OR 97205 Office: Thompson & Thompson AIA 320 SW Stark St Portland OR 97204

THOMPSON, RICHARD ARLYN, insurance company executive; b. Vancouver, Wash., Dec. 5, 1946; s. Harold and Joy (Winters) T.; m. Barbara Lynn Sommer, Nov. 21, 1970. Cert. consumer fin. mgr., Portland State U., BA in Bus. Mgmt., 1978. Registered health underwriter. Mgr. field sales Mass. Mut. Life Ins. Co., Boise, Idaho, 1972-79; dir. sales Mountain Lakes Ins. Co., Boise, 1979-80; gen. agt. Security Mut. Life Ins. Co., Boise, 1980-84; sales mgr. State Mut. Life Ins. Co., Boise, 1984-86, Prin. Fin. Group, Boise, 1986—. Author: New Agents Training Manual, 1976. Pres. Briar Hill Inc. Assn., Boise, 1979-83. Served with USN, 1965-71, Vietnam. Recipient Boise's Best Boss award Boise Bus. Assn., 1985; named Agt. of Yr., Mass. Mut. Life Ins. Co., 1977, Dist. Mgr. on Move, Mass. Mut. Life Ins. Co., 1978; rank of col. (hon.) bestowed by DAR, 1978; Outstanding Young Man of Am. Mem. Nat. Assn. Life Underwriters, Boise Assn. Life Underwriters (instr. life underwriters tng. council 1975-79), Nat. Health Underwriters, Idaho Health Underwriters, Boise Jaycees (clubhouse mgr. 1975-77, named Jaycee of Month, 1976), DeLorean Owners Assn. Republican. Lodge: Elks. Avocations: flying, golf, camping, hiking, boating. Home: 4803 Wildrye Dr Boise ID 83703

THOMPSON, RICHARD EARL, artist; b. Oak Park, Ill., Sept. 26, 1914; s. Abijah Snyder and Vera (Koster) T.; m. Mary Munn, June 25, 1937; children—Richard Earl, Bruce, Daniel. Student Chgo. Acad. Fine Arts, 1930-31, Am. Acad. Art, Chgo., 1932-33, Chgo. Art Inst., 1944. Instr., Am. Acad. Art, Chgo., 1935-37; comml. artist Coca Cola, Anheuser-Bush, Standard Oil and Miller Brewing Co., 1937-59; artist in residence U. Wis.-Rhinelander, 1980; numerous one-man exhibits include: Veldman Galleries, Milw., 1970-71, 73, 75, 77, Wild Life Art Gallery, Minocqua, Wis., 1971, John P. Klep Galley, Houston, 1971-74, Richard Thompson Gallery, San Francisco, 1977, 79, 81; group exhbns. include: Vincent Price Collection Fine Art, 1965, Peter Darro Galleries, Chgo., 1969; mus. shows include: Berstorm Art Ctr., Neenah, Wis., 1965, Leigh Yawkey Woodson Art Mus., Wausau, Wis., 1979, R.W. Norton Art Gallery, Shreveport, La., 1982; represented in mus. and corp. collections: Continental Ill. Bank, Chgo., de Sasset Art Gallery and Mus. of U. Santa Clara, Calif., Leigh Yawkey Woodson Art Mus., Lewer Agy., Kansas City, Mo., Marquette U. Collection, Mills Coll., Milw. Jour., Naval Art Collection of Pentagon, Washington, New Britain Mus. Am. Art, R.W. Norton Art Gallery, Robert Louis Stevenson Acad. Collection, Carmel, Calif., Southland Fin. Corp., Irving, Tex., Southland Corp., Dallas, Wis. Meml. Park, Milw., Wood County Nat. Bank, Wisconsin Rapids, Wis. Recipient 1st hon. mention award Salmagundi Club, N.Y.C., 1981. Club: Salmagundi. Subject of book: Richard Earl Thompson—American Impressionist, a Prophetic Odyssey in Paint (Patricia Jobe Pierce), 1982. Office: Richard Thompson Gallery 80 Maiden Ln San Francisco CA 94108

THOMPSON, RONALD EDWARD, lawyer; b. Bremerton, Wash., May 24, 1931; s. Melville Herbert and Clara Mildred (Griggs) T.; m. Marilyn Christine Woods, Dec. 15, 1956; children—Donald Jeffery, Karen, Susan, Nancy, Sally, Claire. B.A., U. Wash., 1953, J.D., 1958. Bar: Wash. 1959. Asst. city atty. City of Tacoma, 1960-61; pres. firm Thompson, Krilich & LaPorte, P.S., Tacoma, 1961—; judge pro tem Mcpl. Ct., City of Tacoma, Pierce County Justice Ct., 1972—; dir. Air Gemini, Inc. Chmn. housing and social welfare com. City of Tacoma, 1965-69; mem. Tacoma Bd. Adjustment, 1967-71, chmn., 1968; mem. Tacoma Com. Future Devel., 1961-64, Tacoma Planning Commn., 1971-72; bd. dirs., pres. Mcpl. League Tacoma; bd. dirs. Tacoma Pierce County Cancer Soc., Tacoma-Pierce County Heart Assn., Tacoma-Pierce County Council for Arts, Econ. Devel. Council Puget Sound, Tacoma Youth Symphony, Kleiner Group Home, Tacoma Community Coll. Found., Pierce County Econ. Devel. Corp.; precinct committeeman Republican party, 1969-73. Served with AUS, 1953-55; col. Res. Recipient Internat. Community Service award Optimist Club, 1970, Patriotism award Am. Fedn. Police, 1974, citation for community service HUD, 1974, Disting. Citizen award Mcpl. League Tacoma-Pierce County. Mem. Am. Arbitration Assn. (panel of arbitrators), ABA, Wash. State Bar Assn. (mem. unauthorized practice com. 1970-73), Tacoma-Pierce County Bar Assn. (sec. 1964, pres. 1979, mem. cts. and judiciary com. 1981-82), Assn. Trial Lawyers Am., Wash. State Trial Lawyers Assn., Tacoma-Pierce County C. of C. (dir., exec. com., v.p., chmn.), Phi Delta Phi, Sigma Nu. Roman Catholic. Clubs: Variety (Seattle); Lawn Tennis, Tacoma, Optimist (Tacoma). Home: 817 N Yakima Ave Tacoma WA 98403 Office: 524 Tacoma Ave S Tacoma WA 98402

THOMPSON, ROSEMARY ANN, environmental consultant, biologist; b. San Diego; m. John Joseph Thompson, June 17, 1967; 1 child, Shawn Nicole. BA, U. Mo., 1967; PhD, U. Calif., San Diego, 1972. Research assoc. U. So. Calif., Los Angeles, 1972-73; sr. biologist Henningson, Durham & Richardson, Santa Barbara, Calif., 1974-84, URS Co., Santa Barbara, Calif., 1984—; cons. EG&G, Santa Barbara, 1974; pres. Swift's Environmental Analysis, Santa Barbara, 1985—. Mem. Am. Fisheries Soc., Desert Fishes Council, The Wildlife Soc. Avocations: camping, hiking, crafts, sewing, carpentry. Home and Office: Swift's Environ Analysis 4634 Mint Ln Santa Barbara CA 93110

THOMPSON, STANLEY OWEN, social worker; b. Sheridan, Wyo., July 24, 1952; s. Merritt James and Mary S. (Smith) T. AS, Casper Coll., 1976; B in Social Work, Ariz. State U., 1978, M in Pub. Adminstrn., 1981. Pub. asst. worker Wyo. Dept. Pub. Assistance and Social Services, Casper, 1981-82, social worker, 1982—. Served with U.S. Army, 1972-74. Mem. Nat. Assn. Social Workers, Am. Soc. Pub. Adminstrn. Democrat. Home: 152 S Washington #11 Casper WY 82601 Office: Dept Pub Assistance and Social Services 475 S Spruce Casper WY 82601

THOMPSON, THOMAS ARTHUR, electrical engineer; b. Niles, Mich., Feb. 8, 1959; s. Mark McKim and Elaine Marie (Smith) T. BSEE, Tri-State U., 1981. Mem. tech. staff Hughes Aircraft Co., El Segundo, Calif., 1983—. Avocations: hiking, reading, softball. Office: Hughes Aircraft Co 2000 E El Segundo El Segundo CA 90245

THOMPSON, THOMAS MILLER, mathematics educator; b. Walla Walla, Wash., Jan. 12, 1946; s. Thomas Russell and Genevra Edelle (Miller) T.; m. Anna Clare Rasmussen, June 4, 1968; children—Trina Marie, Tyler Mark, Heidi Christine. B.A., Walla Walla Coll., 1968; M.A., U. Wash., 1971; Ph.D., U. Calif., 1979. Prof. math. Walla Walla Coll., College Place, Wash., 1971—. Author monograph. Mem. Am. Math. Soc., Math. Assn. Am., Can. Soc. History and Philosophy of Math., Phi Kappa Phi.

THOMPSON, THOMAS WILLIAM, radar astronomer; b. Canton, Ohio, May 25, 1936; s. Clifford Earl and Doris Marie (Flickinger) T.; m. Alicia Kathleen O'Connor, July 16, 1966; children: Kimberly Robin, Marisa Lynn. BS, Case Western Res. U., 1958; M in Engring., Yale U., 1959; PhD, Cornell U., 1965. Research assoc. Arecibo (P.R.) Obs., 1966-69; mem. tech. staff Jet Propulsion Lab., Pasadena, Calif., 1970—. Avocations: skiing, golfing, sailing. Home: 3043 Cloudcrest Rd La Crescenta CA 91214

THOMPSON, VICKI CLAUDETTE, educator, calligrapher; b. Fargo, N.D., Mar. 17, 1952; d. Arthur Melvin and May Druscille (Barney) T.; m. Richard Jerome Benshoof, Apr. 13, 1979 (div.). Vocat. degree, Interstate Bus. Coll., Fargo, N.D., 1970; B.S., Moorhead State U., 1974. Cert. elem. and spl. edn. tchr., Ariz., Minn. Hearing impaired resource tchr. Parkers Prairie Sch. Dist., Minn., 1974-75; kindergarten and 1st grade tchr. Detroit Lakes pub. sch., Minn., 1975-80; spl. edn. resource tchr. Washington Sch. Dist., Phoenix, 1980-81; 1st and 3d grade tchr. Mesa Pub. Schs., Ariz., 1981—; freelance calligrapher, instr., Tempe, Phoenix and Mesa, 1981—; art liaison tchr. Edison Sch., Mesa, 1981—; instr. Salt River Indian Reservation, Scottsdale, Edison Sch., Mesa, 1983—. Editor children's books: How to Scare a Lion, 1983; Just SoSo Stories, 1984. Developer ednl. filmstrips Learning Ctr., Tuskegee Inst., Ala., 1975. Sunday sch. tchr. Bethany Community Ch., Tempe, 1983—. Mem. NEA, Mesa Edn. Assn., Ariz. Calligraphy Soc., Valley Calligraphy Guild, Friends of Calligraphy, Ariz. State Reading Council, Ariz. State Math. Council Smithsonian Instn., Pi Lambda Theta. Republican. Home: 1028 E Bendix St Tempe AZ 85283

THOMPSON, VIRGINIA LOU, agricultural products supplier and importer; b. Malcolm, Iowa, July 15, 1928; d. Isaac Cleveland and Viola (Montgomery) Griffin; m. Alfred Thompson, Mar. 1, 1946; children—Michael Duane, Cathryn Lynn, Steven Curtis, Laura Lue. Student Phoenix Coll., 1962, Phoenix-Scottsdale Jr. Coll., 1973-74. With sales dept. Trend House, Phoenix, 1962-67; importer World Wide Imports, Ft. Collins, Colo., 1974-79; owner, mgr. Windsor Elevator Inc. (Colo.), 1979—; participant in trade shows, seminars. Pres. Am. Luth. Ch. Women, 1973-74. Mem. Nat. Grain and Feed Assn., Colo. Grain and Feed Assn., Rocky Mountain Bean Dealers, Colo. Cattle Feeders Assn., Western U.S. Agrl. Assn., Rice Millers Assn. Democrat. Lutheran. Clubs: Christian Women (Greeley, Colo.); Order of Eastern Star (Iowa). Home: 1627 Adriel Dr Fort Collins CO 80524 Office: PO Box 147 Windsor CO 80550

THOMPSON, WALTER WILLIAM, financial executive; b. S.I., N.Y., June 29, 1927; s. Walter Harold and Rose Veronica (Dugan) T.; B.S. magna cum laude, Wagner Coll., 1950; m. Margaret Ellen Coulson, Mar. 5, 1956; 1 dau., Kathleen. Commd. officer USAF, 1951, advanced through grades to lt. col., 1967, ret., 1970; govt. bond salesman Merrill Lynch Pierce Fenner & Smith, Salt Lake City, 1970-73; staff Blythe, Eastman & Dillon, Salt Lake City, 1973-74, v.p., office mgr., 1974; v.p., mgr. Dean Witter & Co., Spokane, Wash., 1974; sr. govt. bond specialist Merrill Lynch Pierce Fenner & Smith, Seattle, 1975-76; v.p. sales Bache & Co., Seattle, 1976, sr. govt. bond specialist Loeb Rhodes Hornblower, Phoenix, 1976—; pres., chmn. Thompson Fin. Cons., 1978—; apptd. to Com. to Amend the Investment Laws, Utah, 1973, Ariz., 1979. Mem. Ret. Officers Assn., Air Force Assn. Republican. Roman Catholic. Home: 8607 Via Del Sereno Scottsdale AZ 85258

THOMPSON, WILLIAM BELL, educator, physicist; b. Belfast, No. Ireland, Feb. 27, 1922; s. Herbert Ginnif and Mary (Bell) T.; m. Gertrude Helene Goldschmidt, Mar. 24, 1954 (div. 1971); children—Kathleen Susan, Graham Jonathan; m. Johanna Elzelina Ladestein Korevaar, Jan. 29, 1972. B.A., U. B.C., 1945, M.A., 1947; Ph.D., U. Toronto, 1950; M.A. (hon.), Oxford (Eng.) U., 1962. With U.K. AEC, Harwell, Eng., 1950-60; sr. prin. sci. officer, head plasma theory group U.K. AEC, 1959-60; head plasma theory div. Culham Lab. Plasma Physics and Controlled Fusion Research, Culham, Eng., 1960-62; prof. plasma physics U. Oxford, 1962-65; prof. physics U. Calif. at San Diego, 1965—, chmn. dept., 1969-72; cons. in field. Contbr. papers in field.; Joint editor: Advances in Plasma Physics, 1967—; asso. editor: Jour. Plasma Physics, 1966—. Recipient Hulton award achievement Brit. sci., 1958; fellow St. Peters Coll., U. Oxford, 1962-65. Fellow Am. Phys. Soc., Royal Astron. Soc.; mem. Canadian Assn. Physics. Address: U Calif San Diego B-019 La Jolla CA 92093

THOMPSON, WILLIAM RANDALL, international relations educator; b. Great Falls, Mont., July 30, 1946; s. William Wesley and Jacquelyn May (Risley) T.; m. Karen Anne Rasler, Aug. 15, 1981. BA, U. Wash., 1968, MA, 1969, PhD, 1972. From asst. prof.to prof. Fla. State U., Tallahassee, 1973-83; prof. Claremont (Calif.) Grad. Sch., 1983—, prof., chmn., 1986—; vis. prof. U. Minn., Mpls., 1972-73, U. Ariz., Tucson, 1982; asst. program dir. NSF, Washington, 1979. Author: (monograph) The Grievances of Military Coup-Makers, 1973, On Global War: System Time, Change and Continuity, 1987; (with others) The Comparative Analysis of Politics, 1978; Sea Power in Global Politics, 1494-1993, 1987; co-editor: Rhythms in Politics and Economics, 1985; editor Contending Approaches to World System Analysis, 1983; mem. editorial bd. Am. Jour. Polit. Sci., 1982-85, Jour. Politics, 1982—, Western Polit. Quarterly, 1984—, Internat. Interactions, 1984—, Internat. Polit. Economy Yearbook, 1987—; contbr. articles to profl. jours. Fellow NIMH, 1972-73; grantee Nat. Acad. Scis., 1971-72, NSF, 1982-85, 85-87. Mem. Am. Polit. Sci. Assn., Internat. Studies Assn., Peace Sci. Soc., Inter-Univ. Seminar on Armed Forces and Soc. Avocation: martial arts. Home: 4045 La Junta Dr Claremont CA 91711 Office: Claremont Grad Sch Internat Relations Dept Claremont CA 91711

THOMPSON LYONS, KELTON RAE, advertising executive; b. Oklahoma City, Oct. 23, 1959; d. Kenneth Wayne and Barbara Ann (Mitchell) Thompson; m. Brad Edward Lyons, Nov. 29, 1985. BS, Iowa State U., 1982. Corp. trainee Meredith Corp., Des Moines, 1982-83; acct. exec. Meredith Corp., San Francisco, 1983—. Mem. Women in Communications, San Francisco Mag. Reps., Young Profl. Women, Am. Cancer Soc., Sigma Delta Chi, Kappa Alpha Theta Alumnae Assn. (v.p. 1984—). Office: Meredith Corp 300 Montgomery Suite 833 San Francisco CA 94133

THOMSEN, CHRISTOPHER JAY, water treatment consultant; b. Port Angeles, Wash., Dec. 5, 1957; s. James Roger and Barbara Sharon (Wippel) T.; m. Lisa Diane Hille. BA in Chemistry, BS in Biology, St. Martin's Coll., 1980. Lab. dir. CH2O Inc., Olympia, Wash., 1980-81, field engr., 1981-83, exec. dir., 1983—; instr. Clover Park Vocat., Tacoma, 1983—; mgmt. advisor Chem. Week mag., Riverton, N.J., 1985—. Author: Water Treatment Engineering Manual, 1984. Mem. Assn. Wash. Bus. (water quality task force 1986), Instrument Soc. Am. (sr.), Wash. State Soc. Hosp. Engrs., Pacific N.W. Assn. Masters Swimming (editor Wet Set newsletter 1982-83). Republican. Roman Catholic. Avocations: flying, triathlons, painting, photography, cross-country skiing. Home: 1705 5th Ave SW Olympia WA 98502 Office: CH2O Inc PO Box 1190 Olympia WA 98507

THOMSEN, ERICH GOTTFRIED, mechanical engineering educator; b. Geesthacht, Hamburg, Germany, Sept. 9, 1906; s. Richard and Caroline (Meyer) T.; m. Harriette La Rue Harte, May 7, 1932. BS, U. Calif., Berkeley, 1936, MS, 1941, PhD, 1943; honorus causa, U. Louvain, Belgium, 1965, Cath. U. Chile, Santiago, 1984. Lic. mech. engr., Calif. From instr. to assoc. prof. mech. engring. U. Calif., Berkeley, 1941-73, prof., 1956-73, prof. emeritus, 1973—; visiting prof. Tech. U., Aachen, Fed. Republic Germany, 1962; program coordinator Cath. U. Chile, Santiago, 1965-66; dir. U. Calif. Edn. Abroad Program Göttingen, Fed. Republic Germany, 1971-73. Co-author: Mechanics of Plastic Deformation in Metal Processing; contbr. numerous papers on metal processing to profl. jours. Fellow ASME (Blackall award 1960, Taylor award 1980), Soc. Mfg. Engrs.; mem Japan Soc. Applied Plasticity (hon.), Internat. Inst. Prodn. Engrs. (emeritus). Avocations: archaeological metal working. Office: U Calif Berkeley CA 94720

THOMSEN, HALVARD JESSEN, minister; b. Tulsa, Jan. 7, 1917; s. Hans Jessen and Ninni (Hansen) T.; m. Hester Ida Bryan, Sept. 15, 1940; children: Joyce Elaine, Halvard Bryan. BTh, Walla Walla Coll., 1938. Ordained to mininstry Seventh-day Adventist Ch., 1944. Lit. evangelist Mont. Conf., Culbertson, 1938, minister, 1939-47; pastor Humboldt Park Seventh-day Adventist Ch., Chgo., 1947-53, Wash. Conf. Seventh-day Adventists, 1953-64, Bklyn. Seventh-day Adventist Ch., 1967-76, Babylon (N.Y.) Seventh-day Adventist Ch., 1976-86; exec. dir. Soc. Issachar's Offspring, Milton-Freewater, Oreg., 1986—; exec. producer films Bibl. archaeology, 1960-66, including The Marks of Man series, 1962; pub. info. officer Dogubayazit Expdn. to Turkey (search for Noah's ark), 1962, writer, producer, performer radio programs, 1944-62; pres. Griffon Graphics. Co-author: Ahmed, Boy of Jerusalem, 1965; contbr. articles to religious jours. Mem. exec. com. Greater N.Y. Conf. Seventh-day Adventists, Greater N.Y. Acad.; mem. bd. Council Concerned Citizens, Manhattan; founder, pres. Ch. Aid Found.; chmn. bd Bklyn. Seventh-day Adventist Sch. Address: Rt 3 Box 147F-1 Milton-Freewater OR 97862

THOMSEN, HESTER IDA, science and mathematics educator, archaeologist; b. Arlington, Oreg., Nov. 17, 1914; d. Robert and Winnie Ethel (Salisbury) Bryan; m. Halvard Jessen Thomsen, Sept. 15, 1940; children—Joyce Elaine, Halvard Bryan. Student Walla Walla Coll., 1934-36, B.A., 1940; postgrad. U. Wash., 1967, Andrews U., 1966, summers 1968-76, Columbia U., summers 1968, 74, Pratt Inst., summer 1972. Cert. tchr. Elem. tchr. Upper Columbia Conf., Granger, Wash., 1936-38; sci. and math. tchr. Kirkland Jr. Acad., Wash., 1959-67, Greater N.Y. Acad., Woodside, 1967-78; pottery registrar Andrews U. Archaeol. Expdn., Berrien Springs, Mich. (expdn. to Heshbon, Jordan), 1968-76; math. and sci. tchr. Country Garden Sch., Walla Walla, Wash., 1982—; archaeology instr. Walla Walla Coll., College Place, Wash., 1983-84; pottery registrar Andrews U. Archaeol. Expdn. to Madeba Plains, 1984. Author: Study Guide for Health, 1978, also articles to mags. and profl. jours. Student advisor New Rochelle/Ciba-Geigy Biology, Sci. Fair, 1975 (outstanding performance); tchr. Westinghouse Sci. Talent Search, 1971; seminar leader Waldemar Med. Research Found., Woodbury, 1972. Mem. Inst. Archaeology Horn Mus., Nat. Sci. Tchrs. Assn. Seventh-day Adventist. Club: Writers (College Place). Home: Rt 3 Box 147 F-1 Milton-Freewater OR 97862 Office: Country Garden Rt 5 Box 184 Walla Walla WA 99362

THOMSON, BARBARA JEANNE, purchasing executive; b. Cardiff, Calif., Feb. 10, 1929; d. Zack Rowden and Zula Mae (Tuckness) Taylor; m. Robert Allyn San Clemente, Feb. 8, 1946 (div. Aug. 1954); children—Robert Allyn Jr., Frances Irene, Michael George; m. Seeth Lyle Thomson, Aug. 7, 1954; 1 child, David Seeth. Grad. high sch., Encinitas, Calif. Various positions Gen. Dynamics Convair, San Diego, 1957-73; purchasing agt. Systems, Sci. & Software, San Diego, 1973-78; sr. buyer Gen. Dynamics Electronics, San Diego, 1978-80; sr. buyer LSI Products div. TRW, San Diego, 1980-84, purchasing mgr., 1984—. Named Employee of Yr., Gen. Dynamics Electronics, San Diego, 1978. Mem. Ry. Hist. Soc. (sec. San Diego 1957-60), Pacific Beach Model R.R. Club (sec. 1955-65), Nat. Assn. Female Execs., Nat. Mgmt. Assn., San Diego Hospice Assn. Democrat. Avocations: model railroading; photography; baseball; football. Home: 3204 McGraw St San Diego CA 92117 Office: TRW LSI Products Div 4243 Campus POint Ct San Diego CA 92121

THOMSON, HUGH TALBERT, lawyer; b. San Francisco, Nov. 21, 1944; s. Douglas Hugh and Margaret Rose (Coffen) T.; m. Sandy L. Herman; children—Brian, Kimberly. B.A., U. Calif.-Berkeley, 1967; J.D., U. Calif.-Davis, 1970. Bar: Calif. 1971. Sole practice San Jose, Calif., 1971—; lectr. Continuing Edn. of Bar, Judge's Conf. Fellow Am. Acad. Matrimonial Lawyers; mem. State Bar Calif. (writer family law specialization exam. 1981, 82, 84, author Family Law News, mem. exec. com. family law sect. 1979-83), Calif. Bd. Legal Specialization for Family Law. Office: Law Office of Hugh T Thomson 2060 The Alameda San Jose CA 95126

THOMSON, THYRA GODFREY, former state official; b. Florence, Colo., July 30, 1916; d. John and Rosalie (Altman) Godfrey; m. Keith Thomson, Aug. 6, 1939 (dec. Dec. 1960); children—William John, Bruce Godfrey, Keith Coffey. B.A. cum laude, U. Wyo., 1939. With dept. agronomy and agrl. econs. U. Wyo., 1938-39; writer weekly column Watching Washington pub. in 14 papers, Wyo., 1955-60; planning chmn. Nat. Fedn. Republican Women, Washington, 1961; sec. state Wyo. Cheyenne, 1962-86; mem. Marshall Scholarships Com. for Pacific region, 1964-68; del. 72d Wilton Park Conf., Eng., 1965; mem. youth commn. UNESCO, 1970-71, Allied Health Professions Council HEW, 1971-72; del. U.S.-Republic of China Trade Conf., Taipei, Taiwan, 1983; mem. lt. gov.'s trade and fact-finding mission to Saudi Arabia, Jordan, and Egypt, 1985. Recipient Disting. Alumni award U. Wyo., 1969, Disting. U. Wyo. Arts and Scis. Alumna award, 1987; named Internat. Woman of Distinction, Alpha Delta Kappa; recipient citation Omicron Delta Epsilon, 1965, citation Beta Gamma Sigma, 1968, citation Delta Kappa Gamma, 1973, citation Wyo. Commn. Women, 1986. Mem. N.Am. Securities Adminstrs. (pres. 1973-74), Nat. Assn. Secs. of State, Council State Govts. (chmn. natural resources com. Western states 1966-68), Nat. Conf. Lt. Govs. (exec. com. 1976-79). Home: 3102 Sunrise Rd Cheyenne WY 82001

THOMSON, VIRGINIA WINBOURN, history educator, author; b. Oakland, Calif., Aug. 6, 1930; d. Harry Linn and Jennie Cook (Vineyard) T. A.A., San Mateo Coll., 1948; B.A., San Jose State Coll., 1951; M.A., U. Calif.-Berkeley, 1952. Cert. secondary tchr., Calif. Social sci. tchr. Capuchino High Sch., San Bruno, Calif., 1952-54, Watsonville High Sch., Calif., 1954-87; saleswoman and storyteller Home Interiors, San Mateo, 1963-64. Author: The Lion Desk, 1965; Short Talks Around The Lord's Table, 1985. Recipient Silver Pitcher award Home Interiors, 1964. Mem. Nat. Geog. Soc. (life), AAUW (life), Nat. Writers Club Christian Writers Guild, Calif. Alumni Assn. (life), Phi Alpha Theta. Republican.

THOMURE, RANDALL OLIVER, engineering executive; b. St. Louis, Mar. 27, 1949; s. Glennon Oliver and Anita (Schmidt) T.; m. Lynne Palisch, May 26, 1972 (div. June 1983); children: Matthew Oliver, John Glennon; m. Michele Dana, June 16, 1984. BS, U. Mo., 1972. Diesel supr. Mo. Pacific R.R., Chester, Ill., 1974-76; gen. foreman locomotive div. Mo. Pacific R.R., Avondale, La., 1976-78; gen. foreman car div. Mo. Pacific R.R., Sedalia, Mo., 1978-80; mgr. maintenance Rail div. Itel Corp., San Francisco, 1980-84; dir. engring. Itel Rail Corp., San Francisco, 1984—. Mem. ASME, ASTM. Club: Toastmasters, (San Mateo, Calif.). Avocations: running, tennis, golf.

THONG, TRAN, scientist, engineer, researcher; b. Saigon, Vietnam, Dec. 8, 1951; came to U.S., 1969, naturalized, 1980; s. Vy and Vinh-Thi (Nguyen) T.; m. Thuy Thi-Bich Nguyen, Jan. 12, 1978. BSEE, Ill. Inst. Tech., 1972; MS in Engring., Princeton U., 1974, MA, 1974, PhD, 1975. Research scientist Western Geophys. Houston, 1975-76; computer devel. engr. Gen. Electric Co., Syracuse, N.Y., 1976-79; dir. electronic system lab. Tektronix, Inc., Beaverton, Oreg., 1980—; adj. asst. prof. Syracuse U., 1979-81, Oreg. State U., Corvallis, 1980-83, U. Portland, Oreg., 1981-83; adj. assoc. prof. Oreg. Grad. Ctr., Beaverton, 1984. Author numerous sci. papers. Princeton U. fellow, 1974. Sr. mem. IEEE (com. chmn. 1982—, assoc. editor transaction 1979-81, gen. chmn. internat. symposium on circiuts and systems); mem. Soc. Motion Picture and TV Engrs., Eta Kappa Nu, Tau Beta Pi, Sigma Xi. Republican. Office: Tektronix Inc PO Box 500 M S 50-370 Beaverton OR 97077

THOR, RICHARD MARQUETTE, automotive executive; b. Seattle, Mar. 3, 1931; s. Russell Johnston and Hazel (Stowe) T.; m. Ann Lee Shingleton, July, 13, 1959; children: Daniel M., Michael R. B in Econs., U. Wash., 1954; MSW, U. So. Calif., 1958. Cert. social worker; lic. clin. social worker, Calif. Stock trader Blythe & Co., Seattle, 1954-56; clin. social worker Calif. Youth Authority, Los Angeles, 1958-60; asst. dir. relocation Community Redevel., Los Angeles, 1960-64, dir. relocation, 1966-68; asst. to dean Sch. Social Work U. So. Calif., Los Angeles, 1964-66; pres. Russ Thor, Inc., Torrance, Calif., 1968—; clin. social worker Los Angeles Psychiat. Services, Rush Clinic, 1960-65; social work cons. Juvenile Div. Project, Redondo Beach, Calif., 1984—; instr. U. So. Calif. Delinquency Control Inst., 1965, UCLA Crisis Intervention, 1966. Elder Presbyn. Ch., Palos Verdes, Calif., 1986; chmn. adv. bd. Salvation Army, 1986. Served with USAF, 1951-52. Mem. Nat. Assn. Social Workers, Am. Internat. Automotive Dealers Assn. (state chmn. 1986), South Bay Student Attendance Rev. Bd., South Bay Free Clinic (bd. dirs. exec. com. 1986—), Little County Mary Hosp. Centurian Bd. (pres. 1984—). Republican. Presbyterian. Lodge: Rotary.

THORDARSON, WILLIAM, hydrogeologist; b. N.Y.C., Mar. 14, 1929; s. William and Lillian (Hirsch) T. BA, Columbia U., 1950; postgrad., U. Kans., Lawrence, 1953-55, U. Colo., 1975—. Hydrogeologist U.S. Geol. Survey, Denver, 1955—. Author: Perched Groundwater, Nevada, 1965, Hydrogeology Great Basin, Nevada, 1974, Hydrogeology of Test Wells, 1983, Hydrogeologic Monitoring, Nevada, 1985. Served with U.S. Army, 1950-52. Mem. Geol. Soc. Am., Am. Assn. Petroleum Geologists, Am. Geophys. Union, Assn. Groundwater Scientists and Engrs., Am. Water Resources Assn., Am. Inst. Profl. Geologists (cert.), Am. Inst. Hydrology (cert.).

THORESEN, WENDY ANN, architect; b. Boston, July 6, 1953; d. Philip Benjamin and Eleanor F. (Jackson) T.; m. Horace Harrison Beaven, Jr., Nov. 21, 1979. B.F.A., U. Colo., 1977, B.A., 1978; M.Arch., U. Colo., Denver, 1980. Designer Robert C. McHugh Inc., Steamboat Springs, Colo., 1979; Midyette/Seieroe, Boulder, Colo., 1981-84; pvt. practice designing, Louisville, Colo., 1984, NBI, Inc., Boulder, 1984—. Mem. Nat. Trust for Historic Preservation, AIA (assoc., assoc. bd. dirs. Colo. North chpt. 1984-85, bd. dirs. 1986-87). Democrat.

THORINGTON, GLYNE UNDINE, research scientist; b. West Indies, Barbados, Jan. 20, 1941; came to U.S., 1964; d. Charles and Enid Undine (Husbands) T. BS, Andrews U., 1969; MS, U. Conn., 1971; PhD, Boston U., 1980. Tchr. Modern High Sch., St. Michael, Barbados, 1960-61; biology tchr. Alexandra Sch., St. Peter, Barbados, 1961-64; sci. tchr. Westledge Sch., Simsbury, Conn., 1971-73; postdoctoral fellow Oxford U., Eng., 1980-81; postdoctoral fellow Loma Linda (Calif.) U., 1981-85, research scientist, 1985—; presenter papers Internat. Collegium on Endosymbiosis and Cell

Research, Tubingen U., Fed. Republic of Germany, 1980, Am. Soc. Cell Biology, Kansas City, Mo., 1984; invited speaker Internat. Symposia, U. Calif., Irvine, 1984. Contbr. articles to profl. jours. Macy's scholar Marine Biol. Sta., 1977-78; grad. scholar Boston U., 1979-80. Fellow N.Y. Acad. Sci., Sigma Xi. Adventist. Avocation: reading. Office: Loma Linda U Dept Physiology & Pharmocology Loma Linda CA 92350

THORN, ROBERT NICOL, physicist; b. Coeur d'Alene, Idaho, Aug. 31, 1924; s. Harry Grover and Grace (Nicol) T.; m. Betty Vogel, June 15, 1948; children: Karen, Kyle, Gretchen, Robert Nicol; m. Lorraine Patten, Oct. 10, 1962; 1 child, Andrea Kay; m. Nancy MacDonald, Dec. 24, 1983. A.B., Harvard U., 1948, A.M., 1949, Ph.D. in Theoretical Physics, 1953. Mem. staff Los Alamos Sci. Lab., 1953—, div. leader theoretical design div., 1971-76, assoc. dir. for weapons, lasers, computers and reactor safety, 1976-79, acting dir., 1979, dep. dir., 1979-85, acting dir., 1985-86, sr. advisor, 1986—; cons. to bus. and govt., 1959—; mem. USAF Sci. Adv. Bd., 1962; mem. sci. adv. group Def. Atomic Support Agy., 1966-72; mem. sci. adv. com. Def. Intelligency Agy., 1971—. Chmn. Los Alamos County Commn., 1958-60. Served with AUS, 1943-46, ETO. Recipient Ernest Orlando Lawrence award AEC, 1967. Mem. Am. Phys. Soc., AAAS, Los Alamos Ski Club (pres. 1957-58), Los Alamos Ski Racing Club (pres. 1974-76), U.S. Ski Assn. (chmn. Alpine competition com.), Phi Beta Kappa, Sigma Xi. Home: 155 Kimberly Los Alamos NM 87544 Office: Los Alamos Nat Lab Los Alamos NM 87545

THORNBURY, WILLIAM MITCHELL, lawyer, law educator; b. Kansas City, Mo., Feb. 11, 1944; s. Paul Cobb and Marguerite Madellaine (Schulz) T.; m. Joy Frances Barrett, Feb. 2, 1973; children: Barrett Mitchell, Adele Frances. B.A., UCLA, 1964; J.D., U. So. Calif., 1967, postgrad. 1967-69. Bar: Calif. 1968, U.S. Dist. Ct. (cen. dist.) Calif. 1968, U.S. Dist. Ct. (no. dist.) Calif. 1973, U.S. Dist. Ct. (so. dist.) Calif. 1980, U.S. Dist. Ct. (ea. dist.) Calif. 1980, U.S. Ct. Appeals (9th cir.) 1973, U.S. Ct. Claims 1980, U.S. Ct. Internat. Trade, 1981, U.S. Ct. Customs and Patent Appeals 1980, U.S. Ct. Mil. Appeals 1980, U.S. Supreme Ct. 1973, U.S. Ct. Appeals (Fed. cir.) 1984. Dep. pub. defender Los Angeles County Pub. Defender, 1969—, dep.-in-charge traffic ct., 1982-84, supervising atty. Juvenile Services div., 1984, dep. in charge, Inglewood, Calif., 1984-85; legal asst. prof. Calif. State U.-Los Angeles, 1983—; mem. adv. com. on alcohol determination State Dept. Health, 1984—; appointed to apprenticeship council by Gov. Deukmejian State of Calif., 1986—; chmn., vice chmn. Santa Monica Fair Election Practices Commn., Calif., 1981-85; advisor on drunk driving Calif. Pub. Defenders Assn., 1984—; alt. mem. Los Angeles County Commn. on Drunk Driving, 1983-84; mem. steering com. Santa Monica Coalition, nominations com., 1984—; bd. dirs. Westside Legal Services, 1984-86, v.p., 1986—. Columnist Calif. Defender; editor Drunk Driving Manual, 1984; contbr. article to Forum. Exec. bd. dirs. Santa Monica Young Rep., 1967-72, pres. 1972-73, treas. 1973-75, bd. dirs. 1968-72; delegate, precinct chmn., registration chmn. Los Angeles County Young Rep., 1968-70; chmn. legal com. Los Angeles County Rep. Cen. Com., 1977-81, 83-85; chmn. jud. evaluation com., 1978-80; pres. Santa Monica Rep. Club 1986—, bd. dirs., 1966—; bd. dirs. West Los Angeles Republican Club, 1986—; mem. Beverly Hills Rep. Club, Rep. State Cen. com., 1983-85, assoc. mem., 1980-83, 86—, Non-Partisan Candidate Evaluating Council, Inc. (bd. dirs. 1980-86, v.p. 1986—); bd. dirs. Santa Monicans Against Crime, 1979—; chmn. 44th Assembly Dist. Rep. Central Com. 1974-87; chmn. Western part of Los Angeles County for George Murphy for U.S. Senate, 1970, John T. LaFollette for Congress, 1970; campaign chmn. Donna A. Little for City Council, 1984; adv. Pat Geffner for City Council, 1979, 81; campaign mgr. Experienced Coll. Team, 1983. Recipient Outstanding Chmn. award Los Angeles County Rep. Party, 1974, sec.-treas. 1968-75, chmn. legal com. 1977-82, 83-85; named Outstanding Service to Rep. Party Legal Counsel, 1978; recipient award Am. Assn. UN, 1961. Mem. Los Angeles County Bar Assn. (vice chmn. indigent and criminal def. com., jud. qualification com. 1986, criminal justice com. 1986, criminal law and law enforcement com., 1986—), Santa Monica Bar Assn. (trustee 1976-77, 79—, chmn. legis. and publicity com., chmn. jud. evaluation com. 1982-84, pres.-elect 1984, pres. 1985-86, del. to state bar conv. 1974-86, liaison to Los Angeles County Bar Assn. 1986—), Los Angeles County Pub. Defenders Assn. (advisor, bd. dirs. 1980—), ABA, Calif. Pub. Defenders Assn. (advisor), Santa Monica Hist. Soc., San Fernando Valley Criminal Bar Assn. (membership chmn. 1986—, bd. trustees 1986—), Assn. Trial Lawyers Am., Supreme Ct. Hist. Soc., Nat. Legal Aid and Defenders Assn., Nat. Assn. Criminal Def. Attys., Acad. Criminal Justice Scis., U. So. Calif. Law Alumni Assn., UCLA Alumni Assn., N.Y. Acad. Scis., Am. Assn. Polit. Sci., Criminal Law sect. of State Bar of Calif., Am. Soc. Criminology (life), Western Region Criminal Law Educators, Santa Monica C. of C. (inebriate task force 1980), Calif. Hist. Soc., Santa Monica Coll. Patron's Assn., Nat. Assn. Criminal Def. Counsel, Navy League (life, bd. dirs. 1979—, legis. chmn. 1982, judge advocate 1983—), Nat. Rifle Assn. (life), Calif. Rifle and Pistol Assn. (life).

THORNE, LARRIE MARTIN, inforsystems specialist; b. Salt Lake City, June 6, 1952; s. Larrie Ian and Shirley Mae (Anderson) T.; m. Jean Ann Bell, July 14, 1973; 1 child, Gabriel David. AA in Data Processing, Idaho State U. Systems programmer Farm Bur. Mutual, Pocatello, Idaho, 1974-80; programmer, analyst Mont. Deaconess, Great Falls, 1980-83, mgr. tech. services, 1983—. Home: 927 Ave D Northwest Great Falls MT 59404 Office: Mont Deaconess 1101 26th St S Great Falls MT 59405

THORNE, LAWRENCE RAY, research chemist; b. Logan, Utah, Oct. 19, 1949; s. James Perry and Norma (Meyers) T.; m. Nola Mortensen, June 14, 1973. BS, Utah State U., 1973; PhD, U. Calif., Berkeley, 1979. Postdoctoral research Calif. Inst. Tech., Pasadena, 1979-81; mem. tech. staff Sandia Nat. Labs., Livermore, Calif., 1981—. Contbr. articles to profl. jours. Mem. Am. Chem. Soc., Colbentz Soc., Phi Kappa Phi. Home: 419 Murdell Ln Livermore CA 94550 Office: Sandia Nat Labs Div 8353 PO Box 969 Livermore CA 94550

THORNTON, ALICE ADELE, social worker; b. Carson City, Nev., Apr. 11, 1960; s. LaVerne Lewis and Lola Adele (Campbell) Hardy; m. David Wayne Thornton, May 4, 1985. AA, Western Nev. Community Coll., 1980; student, U. Nev., Reno, 1982; BS, Grand Canyon Coll., 1983; postgrad., Ariz. State U., 1985—. Intern Ariz. Ctr. for Women, Phoenix, 1982; counselor Ariz. Bapt. Children's Services, Phoenix, 1984-86, social worker, 1986—. Elected rep. Staff Adv. Council-ABC's, Phoenix, 1985-86, Strategic Planning Com.-ABC's, Phoenix, 1985-86; tchr. Love Bapt. Ch., Phoenix, 1985-86; bd. dirs. alumni rep. Grand Canyon Coll., 1985-86. Recipient Cert. Outstanding Achievement, Shiloh Crisis Counseling, 1983. Mem. Nat. Assn. Social Workers, N.Am. Assn. Christians in Social Work, Ariz. Soc. Clin. Social Work and Psychotherapy, Grad. Student Assn. Social Workers, Ariz. Profl. Child Care Assn. Home: 4401 W Cathy Circle Glendale AZ 85308 Office: Ariz Bapt Children's Services 400 W Camelback Rd Suite 101 Phoenix AZ 85061

THORNTON, CATHERINE LEE, electrical engineer; b. Baton Rouge, Mar. 19, 1938; d. Jess Brooks and Charlene (Roemer) Thomas; m. Thomas Holman Thornton, Apr. 21, 1963; children: Thomas Holman III, Patricia Ann. BA in Math., Vanderbilt U., 1960; MS in Math., Northwestern U., 1961; PhD in Engring., UCLA, 1976. Research engr. Jet Propulsion Lab., Pasadena, 1961-76, mem. tech. staff, 1977-79, mgr. deep space network advanced systems program, 1980-82, dep. mgr. tracking systems and applications sect., 1982—. Contbr. articles to profl. jours. Bd. trustees Arcadia Presbyn. Ch., 1986—, elder, lay counselor. Mem. IEEE, AIAA, Am. Geophys. Union, Sigma Xi, Phi Beta Kappa. Avocations: jogger, gardening, skiing, tennis.

THORNTON, DAVID BEDWELL, information systems specialist; b. Ellsworth, Kans., Mar. 2, 1927; s. David B. and Elizabeth D. (Halford) T.; m. Mary Jane Rathbun, Aug. 14, 1947; children: Randall, David, Kevin, Melany. AA, Riverside Coll., 1948. Cert. data processor and systems profl. Supr. shift Riverside (Calif.) County, 1947-51; supr. Calif. Elec. Power co., San Bernardino, Calif., 1951-60; mgr. mgmt. info. systems Nev. Power Co., Las Vegas, 1960—. Served with U.S. Army, 1945-47. Mem. Pacific Coast Elec. Assn., Data Processing Mgmt. Assn., Edison Elec. Inst./Am. Gas Assn. Lodges: Masons, Shriners. Avocations: reading, fishing, camping, travel. Office: Nev Power Co 6226 W Sahara Las Vegas NV 89102

THORNTON, DEAN DICKSON, airplane company executive; b. Yakima, Wash., Jan. 5, 1929; s. Dean Stoker and Elva Maud (Dickson) T.; m. Joan Madison, Aug. 25, 1956 (div. Apr. 1978); children—Steven, Jane Thornton; m. Mary Shultz, Nov. 25, 1981; children—Volney, Scott, Peter, Todd Richmond. B.S. in Bus., U. Idaho, 1952. C.P.A., Wash. Acct. Touche, Ross & Co., Seattle, 1954-63; treas., controller Boeing Co., Seattle, 1963-70; various exec. positions Boeing Co., 1974-85; pres. Boeing Comml. Airplane Co., 1985—; sr. v.p. Wyly Co., Dallas, 1970-74; dir. Genetic Systems Corp., Seattle; cons. Energy Internat., 1986. Bd. dirs. YMCA, Seattle, 1966-68, Jr. Achievement, Seattle, 1966-68; chmn. Wash. Council on Internat. Trade, Seattle, 1984—. Served to 1st lt. USAF, 1952-54. Mem. Phi Gamma Delta. Republican. Presbyterian. Clubs: Rainier, Seattle Tennis, Seattle Yacht, Conquistadores de Cielo. Avocations: skiing; sailing; fishing. Home: 1602-34 Ct W Seattle WA 98199 Office: Boeing Co PO Box 3707 Seattle WA 98124

THORNTON, JAMES WILLIAM, III, priest; b. Palo Alto, Calif., Jan. 18, 1937; s. James William Jr. and Cyrilla Mary (Dolan) T. BA, BS, U. Notre Dame, 1959; STB, Pontiff Gregorian U., Rome, 1961, Sacrae Theologiae Licentiatus, 1963; PhD, U. Oreg., 1981. Ordained priest Roman Cath. Ch., 1964. Tchr. Notre Dame high Sch., Niles, Ill., 1963-66; spiritual dir. Moreau Sem., South Bend, Ind., 1971-72; assoc. dean students U. Portland, Oreg., 1972-79, asst. acad. v.p., 1981-82; counselor on alcoholism Portland Med. Ctr. Hosp., 1982-83; counselor on alcoholism De Paul Ctr. Inc., Portland, 1983-86, dir. adult treatment services, pres., chief exec. officer, 1986—. Bd. dirs. Oreg. Inst. Alcoholism Studies, Waldport, 1983—, Alcohol and Drug Counselor Cert. Bd. Oreg., 1986—; chmn. Shared Housing, Portland, 1984—. Mem. Assn. Alcohol and Drug Counselors of Oreg. (bd. dirs. 1986—). Democrat. Avocations: computers, reading. Office: De Paul Ctr Inc 8200 NE Sandy Blvd Portland OR 97220

THORNTON, LINDA HERSHBERGER, communications executive, educator, filmmaker; b. Inglewood, Calif., July 28, 1959; d. Richard Ben and Jane Olive (Taylor) Hershberger. B.A. in Communication Studies magna cum laude, UCLA, 1981, M.A. in Motion Pictures/TV Studies (fellow), 1983, postgrad. Motion Pictures/TV Studies, 1983-84. Newswriter, KABC-TV, Los Angeles, 1978-79; account exec. Communication Develop. Assocs., Inc., Los Angeles, 1979, media cons. and pub. relations dir., 1980-84; with Dramatic Devel. Assocs. Embassy Communications, 1985-86; then with Dramatic Devel. Assocs. Columbia Pictures, Entertainment Bus. Sector, Coca-Cola TV, 1987—; assoc. TV devel. Embassy Television, Los Angeles, 1985—; TV writer Alan Thicke Prodns., Los Angeles, 1980-81; grad. teaching assoc. dept. communication studies UCLA, 1981-84; exec. tng. pub. speaking and media relations, career counseling high school and college levels. Mem. Internat. Assn. Bus. Communicators, Soc. Cinema Studies Alumni, Pi Beta Phi (del. Nat. Leadership Conv. 1979). Author: The Training Applications of Interactive Video; contbr. articles to profl. jours. Home: 14044 Panay Way #230 Marina del Rey CA 90292 Office: Columbia Pictures Entertainment Business Sector Coca-Cola Television 956 Seward St Los Angeles CA 90038

THORNTON, ROBERT Y., state judge; b. Portland, Oreg., Jan. 28, 1910; s. Oliver Cromwell and Nellie (Hennessy) T.; m. Dorothy Marie Haberbach, March 13, 1937; 1 child, Thomas. AB, Stanford U., 1932; postgrad., U. Oreg., 1933-35; JD, George Washington U., 1937. Research asst. Legis. Reference Services, Washington, 1935-37; law clk. D.C. Ct. Appeals, Washington, 1937; asst. solicitor Dept. Of Interior, Washington, 1938; sole practice Tillamook, Oreg., 1939-53; atty. gen. State of Oreg., Salem, 1953-69; assoc. judge Oreg. Ct. Appeals, Salem, 1971-83, sr. judge; cons. Ministry of Justice, Tokyo, 1959; bd. dirs. Northwest China Council, Portland, 1983—, Oreg. Judicial Council, Salem, 1983—. Contbr. articles to law reviews. Com. mem. Salem Kawagoe Japan Com. 1986—. Served to lt. col. U.S. Army M.I., 1941-46. Decorated Order of the Sacred Treasure (Japan), 1976; recipient Spl. award Portland State U., 1962, JACL, 1975. Mem. ABA, World Affairs Council, Oreg. Internat. Council (bd. dirs.), Illahe Hills C. of C., Am. Social Health Assn., Nat. Assn. Atty. Gens. Democrat. Episcopalian. Lodge: Kiwanis. Home: 2895 Alvarado Terr S Salem OR 97302 Office: Oreg Ct Appeals Justice Bldg Salem OR 97310

THORNTON, WAYNE ALLEN, naval officer, engineer; b. Manchester, Conn., Dec. 17, 1952; s. Warren George and Dorothy Marie (Brooks) T. BS in Ocean Engring. with honors, U.S. Naval Acad., 1974; MS in Mech. Engring., Stanford U., 1980. Commd. ensign USN, 1974, advanced through grades to lt. comdr., 1982; naval liaison officer to U.S. Senate Office of Legis. Affairs, Washington, 1974; elec. and reactor controls officer USN, San Diego, 1975-77, main propulsion asst., 1977-78, combat systems officer, 1978-79, engring. officer, 1981-84, engring. officer submarine group five staff, 1984-86, engring. officer submarine group 11 staff, 1986, exec. officer, 1987—. Mem. ASME, AIAA, Stanford Alumni Assn., Porsche Club of Am., Sigma Xi. Avocations: fgn. lang., fgn. travel, scuba diving, underwater photography, skiing. Home: 343 Avenida de las Rosas Encinitas CA 92024 Office: USS Pollack (SSN603) Submarine Base San Diego CA 96675

THORNTON, WILLIAM C., loss control specialist; b. Tucson, Oct. 16, 1943; s. Charles Alexander and Margaret (Colborn) T.; m. Susan Ruth Schickedanz, Dec. 27, 1969. BA, U. Ariz., 1966. Elem. tchr. Muroc Sch. Dist., Edwards AFB, Calif., 1966-67; sales rep. Hughes Calihan Corp., Tucson, 1968-70, Am. Greetings Co., Tucson, 1970-72; mktg. rep. State Compensation Fund, Tucson, 1972-84, loss prevention rep., 1984—; pres. Rama Mexican Ins., Tucson, 1977-78. Bd. dirs. ARC, Tucson, mem. exec. com., 1983—. Recipient Retention Team awards State Compensation Fund, 1980-83; named Top Producer State Compensation Fund, 1982. Mem. Am. Soc. Safety Engrs. Democrat. Episcopalian. Avocations: hiking, camping, gardening, reading. Home: 2955 E Chula Vista Dr Tucson AZ 85716 Office: State Comptroller Fund 55 E Helen PO Box 5686 Tucson AZ 85703

THORP, EDWARD OAKLEY, investment management company executive; b. Chgo., Aug. 14, 1932; s. Oakley Glenn and Josephine (Gebert) T.; B.A. in Physics, UCLA, 1953, M.A. (NSF fellow 1954-55), 1955, Ph.D. in Math., 1958; m. Vivian Sinetar, Jan. 28, 1956; children—Raun, Karen, Jeffrey. Instr., UCLA, 1958-59, C.L.E. Moore instr. MIT, 1959-61; asst. prof., then assoc. prof. math. N.Mex. State U., 1961-65; mem. faculty U. Calif., Irvine, 1965—, prof. math., 1967-78, prof. mgmt., 1978-82; pres. Oakley Sutton Mgmt. Corp., investments, 1972—; v.p. Oakley Sutton Securities Corp., 1972—; gen. ptnr. Dorchester Govt. Securities Co. Grantee NSF, 1962-64, Air Force Office Sci. Research, 1964-74. Fellow Inst. Math. Stats.; mem. Am. Math. Soc., Am. Statis. Assn., Math. Assn. Am., Phi Beta Kappa, Sigma Xi. Author: Beat The Dealer: A Winning Strategy for the Game of Twenty-One, rev. edit., 1966; Elementary Probability, 1966; The Mathematics of Gambling 1984; co-author: Beat The Market, 1967; The Gambling Times Guide to Blackjack, 1984; columnist Gambling Times, 1979—. Office: 3 Civic Plaza Suite 100 Newport Beach CA 92660

THORPE, GARY STEPHEN, chemistry educator; b. Los Angeles, Mar. 9, 1951; s. David Winston and Jeanette M. (Harris) T.; m. Patricia Marion Eison, Apr. 13, 1949; children: Kristin Anne, Erin Michelle. BS, U. Redlands, 1973; MS, Calif. State U., Northridge, 1975. Educator Los Angeles Schs., 1975-80, Los Angeles Community Colls., 1976-81, Beverly Hills (Calif.) High Sch., 1980—; pres. 21st Century Software, Los Angeles, 1984—. Recipient Commendation, Los Angeles county Bd. Supers., 1983, 84, Commendation Beverly Hills City Council, 1983, 84, Resolution of Commendation, State of Calif. Senate and Assembly, 1983, 84, Cert. Appreciation, Los Angeles County Bd. Edn., 1984-85, Cert. Appreciation, Gov. George Deukmejian, Sacramento, 1984-85. Mem. Am. Chem. Soc., NEA, Calif. Tchrs. Assn., Phi Delta Kappa. Republican. Lutheran. Lodge: Masons. Avocations: ham radio, computer application. Home: 6127 Balcom Ave Reseda CA 91335 Office: 21st Century Software Inc 1888 Century Park E Los Angeles CA 90067

THORPE, JAMES, humanities; b. Aiken, S.C., Aug. 17, 1915; s. J. Ernest and Ruby (Holloway) T.; m. Elizabeth McLean Daniells, July 19, 1941; children: James III, John D., Sally Jans-Thorpe. A.B., The Citadel, 1936, LL.D., 1971; M.A., U. N.C., 1937; Ph.D., Harvard U., 1941; Litt.D., Occidental Coll., 1968; L.H.D., Claremont Grad. Sch., 1968; H.H.D., U. Toledo, 1977. Instr. to prof. English Princeton, 1946-66; dir. Huntington Library, Art Gallery and Bot. Gardens, San Marino, Calif., 1966-83; sr. research assoc. Huntington Library, San Marino, Calif., 1966—. Author: Bibliography of the Writings of George Lyman Kittredge, 1948, Milton Criticism, 1950, Rochester's Poems on Several Occasions, 1950, Poems of Sir George Etherege, 1963, Aims and Methods of Scholarship, 1963, 70, Literary Scholarship, 1964, Relations of Literary Study, 1967, Bunyan's Grace Abounding and Pilgrim's Progress, 1969, Principles of Textual Criticism, 1972, 2d edit., 1979, Use of Manuscripts in Literary Research, 1974, 2d edit., 1979, Gifts of Genius, 1980, A Word to the Wise, 1982, John Milton: The Inner Life, 1983, The Sense of Style: Reading English Prose, 1987. Served to col. USAAF, 1941-46. Decorated Bronze Star medal.; Guggenheim fellow, 1949-50, 65-66. Fellow Am. Acad. Arts and Scis., Am. Philos. Soc.; mem. MLA, Am. Antiquarian Soc. Democrat. Episcopalian. Clubs: Zamorano, Twilight. Home: 1199 Arden Rd Pasadena CA 91106 Office: Huntington Library San Marino CA 91108

THORPE, JOHN NATHAN, electrical contractor; b. Oakland, Calif., May 18, 1934; s. Carl V. and Margaret B. Thorpe; m. Betty J. Stout, Mar. 9, 1967; children: Nathan Wade, Matthew John. BA, Calif. State U., Chico, 1958. Lic. contractor Calif. Pres., Kutz-Hall-Thorpe Contractors, Chico, Calif., 1966-83; pres. Agri Electric, Chico, 1983—. Bd. dirs., chmn. Durham Parks & Recreation; dir. Durham Irrigation Dist. Mem. Phi Kappa Tau, Iota Sigma. Lodge: Elks (past exalted ruler Chico). Office: Agri Electric 11011 Midway Chico CA 95926

THORSEN, ARTHUR CARL, materials scientist; b. Portland, Oreg., July 27, 1934; s. Arthur C. and Hertha (Arndt) T.; m. Patricia J. Cook, July 6, 1968 (div. 1982); children: Jennifer, Melissa. B.A., Reed Coll., 1956; M.S., Rice U., 1958, Ph.D., 1960; M.B.A., Calif. Lutheran Coll., 1981. Sr. physicist Atomics Internat.-Rockwell, Canoga Park, Calif., 1960-63; mem. tech. staff Rockwell Internat., Thousand Oaks, Calif., 1963-68, Anaheim, Calif., 1968-74; mgr. indsl. research and devel. Rockwell Internat., Thousand Oaks, Calif., 1974-79, mgr. publs., 1977-79, dir. corp. research, 1979-84, dir. materials sci., 1984—. Contbr. numerous articles to profl. jours.; patentee silicon on sapphire oriented for maximum mobility. Home: 3263 W Sierra Dr Westlake Village CA 91362 Office: Rockwell Internat Sci Ctr 1049 Camino Dos Rios Thousand Oaks CA 91360

THORSEN, JAMES HUGH, aviation director, airport manager; b. Evanston, Ill., Feb. 5, 1943; s. Chester A. and Mary Jane (Currie) T.; B.A., Ripon Coll., 1965; m. Nancy Dain, May 30, 1980. Asst. dean of admissions Ripon (Wis.) Coll., 1965-69; adminstrv. asst. Greater Rockford (Ill.) Airport Authority, 1969-70; airport mgr. Bowman Field, Louisville, 1970-71; asst. dir. St. Louis Met. Airport Authority, 1971-80; dir. aviation, airport mgr. City of Idaho Falls (Idaho), 1980—. Named hon. citizen State of Ill. Legislature, 1976, Ky. Col.; FAA cert. comml. pilot, flight instr. airplanes and instruments. Mem. Am. Assn. Airport Execs. (accredited airport exec.), Internat. NW Aviation Council, Greater Idaho Falls C. of C. (bd. dir. 1986—), Mensa, Sigma Alpha Epsilon. Home: 1270 First St Idaho Falls ID 83401 Office: Mcpl Airport Idaho Falls ID 83401

THORSON, GEORGE ALLEN, utility company executive; b. Graceville, Minn., July 11, 1934; s. George Washington and Clara Amelia (Rasmusson) T.; m. Krista June Bly, Nov. 11, 1967; children: Kerry Patrick, Allen David, Kris Vernon. BSAE, U. Idaho; postgrad., U. Mich., 1983. Div. mgr. Mont. Power Co., Great Falls. Bd. dirs. ARC, Great Falls, 1985, United Way, Great Falls, 1983-86; treas. Housing Services Inc., Great Falls, 1985. Mem. Northwest Electric Light Power, Neighborhood Housing Services. Lutheran. Lodge: Elks. Home: 1313 Park Garden Rd Great Falls MT 59404 Office: Mont Power Co 101 Central Great Falls MT 59403

THORSTAD, BRUCE HARDY, magazine editor; b. Mpls., Apr. 16, 1946; m. Ruth Pederson, Oct. 1, 1967; 1 child, Holly Dana. BA, U. Wis., 1973; postgrad., U. Iowa, 1974-75. Editor Holiday Inn Companion, Friedrichsdorf, Fed. Republic Germany, 1975-78, Overseas Life Mag., Friedrichsdorf, Fed. Republic Germany, 1975-78; editor Off Duty, Frankfurt, Fed. Republic Germany, 1978-80, Costa Mesa, Calif., 1980—; copywriter, cons. SCM Walton Printing, Buena Park, Calif., 1984—. Contbr. articles to profl. jours. Home: 17349 Los Amigos Circle Fountain Valley CA 92708 Office: Off Duty Mag 3303 Harbor Blvd Suite C-2 Costa Mesa CA 92626

THORSTENSON, ROBERT M., seafood company executive; b. Vancouver, B.C., Can., Dec. 23, 1931. B.A., U. Wash., 1956. Vice pres. prodn. Pacific Am. Fisheries; with Icicle Seafoods, Inc., Seattle, Wash., 1965—, chmn., 1980—. Office: Icicle Seafoods Inc PO Box C 99309 Seattle WA 98199

THORWALD, STEPHEN JOHN, advertising executive; b. North Bend, Oreg., July 8, 1941; s. Clifford H. and Lila (Endicott) T.; m. Kristen L. Cook, Aug. 10, 1969 (div. 1974). A.A., S.W. Oreg. Community Coll., 1967; B.S. in Journalism, U. Oreg., 1969. Mgmt. trainee Standard Oil Calif., Eugene, Oreg., 1969-72; account exec. Ben H. Smith Advt., Eugene, 1972; owner/pres. Thorwald & Assocs., Advt., Eugene, 1972-84; advt.-sales promotion dir. Emporium Dept. Stores, Eugene, 1984—. Bd. dirs. Lane Humane Soc., Eugene, 1971. Served with U.S. Army, 1963-66. Mem. Mid-Oreg. Ad Club (bd. dirs. 1979-82; Ad Man of Yr. 1980), Sales and Mktg. Execs. Eugene (assoc.), Emerald Execs. Assn., Mid-Oreg. Execs. Assn. Republican. Clubs: Springfield Country (bd. dirs. 1970-71) (Springfield, Oreg.); Willow Creek Racquet (membership dir. 1984) (Eugene). Home: 2285 Ironwood Eugene OR 97401 Office: PO Box 5467 Eugene OR 97405

THRANOW, MARY CHRISTINE, academic administrator; b. Milw., Sept. 20, 1917; d. Frederick William and Mary Margaret Thranow. BA, Immaculate Heart Coll., Los Angeles, 1943, MA in English, 1963; MA in Counseling Psychology, Loyola Marymount U., 1968. Cert. tchr. (life); cert. prin.; cert. pupil personnel. Tchr. pvt. schs., Calif.; prin. St. Luke's Elem. Sch., Temple City, Calif., 1947-54; tchr. Mary Star of Sea High Sch., San Pedro, Calif., 1954-56; dean of girls, chmn. English dept. Pius X High Sch., Downey, Calif., 1956-60; dean of students Immaculate Heart Coll., 1960-70; dean student services Loyola Marymount U, 1970-75; prin. Our Lady of Corvallis High Sch., Studio City, Calif., 1975—. Career counselor, Santa Monica, Calif.; counselor Benjamin Rush Counseling Ctr., Los Angeles, 1968-70. Mem. Nat. Cath. Educational Assn., Nat. Assn. Secondary Sch. Prins., Assn. of Supervision and Curriculum Devel., Sister Cities, Internat. (Studio City chpt.). Roman Catholic. Office: Our Lady of Corvallis 3921 Laurel Canyon Blvd Studio City CA 91604

THRASHER, LINDA JACQUELINE, copier supplies company executive; b. Detroit, May 9, 1946; d. Nolan and Jeannette Leach; m. Paul Cameron Thrasher, Sept. 11, 1965; children—Laura Linda, Matthew Michael. Grad. Pontiac Bus. Inst., 1965. Sales rep. Bliss Supplies, Inc., Troy, Mich., 1975-78; pres. Cactus Copier Supplies, Inc., 1978—. Mem. NOW, Nat. Assn. Women Bus. Owners, Scottsdale C. of C. Democrat. Mem. Soc. Friends. Office: Cactus Copier Supplies Inc 14435 N Scottsdale Rd Suite 600 Scottsdale AZ 85254

THRONSON, RODERICK MORRIS, education educator; b. Helena, Mont., July 22, 1949; s. Rolan Morris and Marjorie Dolores (Gregor) T.; m. Carolyn Claudia Miller, May 26, 1972; children—Kirsten Ann, Paul Roderick. B.S. in Botany, Montana State U., 1971, M.Ed. in Secondary Curriculum and Instrn., 1979, Ed.D in Curriculum and Instrn., 1984; degree in Elem. Edn. Conversion, Carroll Coll., 1977. Class I teaching cert., class III adminstrn. cert., Mont. Commd. 2d lt. U.S. Air Force, 1971, advanced through grades to capt., 1981; wing intelligence officer, Cannon AFB, N.Mex., 1972-74; tchr. middle sch. interdisciplinary team C.R. Anderson Sch., Dist. 1, Helena, 1974-79; tchr. 5th grade, 1979-81; supt. schs. Turner (Mont.) Sch. Dist. #43, 1981-83; asst. prof. adminstrn. and secondary edn. U. Cen. Ark., Conway, 1984-86; asst. prof. edn. Carroll Coll., Helena, Mont., 1987—. Mem. Nat. Sci. Tchrs. Assn., Mont. Sci. Tchrs. Assn., Am. Edn1. Research Assn., Learning Styles Network, Assn. Supervision and Curriculum Devel, Phi Delta Kappa, Kappa Delta Phi. Democrat. Lutheran. Contbg. author: Energy-Environment Simulator Montana Schools, 1980. Home: 620 1st St Helena MT 59601 Office: Carroll Coll. Edn Dept Helena MT 59625

THUILLIER, RICHARD HOWARD, meteorologist; b. N.Y.C., Apr. 3, 1936; s. Howard Joseph and Louise (Schilling) T.; m. Barbara Unger; children: Stephen, David, Lawrence, Daniel. BS in Physics, Fordham U., 1959; MS in Meteorology, NYU, 1963, postgrad., 1963-66. Cert. cons. meteorologist. Instr. SUNY, 1963-66; dir. of research Weather Engrs. of Panama Inc., Panama City, Rep. Panama, 1966-68; cons. Oakland, Calif., 1968—; meteorologist and chief of research and planning Bay Area Air Quality Mgmt. Dist., San Francisco, 1968-76; sr. research meteorologist SRI Internat., Menlo Park, Calif., 1976-80, Pacific Gas & Electric, San Francisco, 1980—; lectr. Hunter Coll., N.Y.C., 1965-66, U. Calif. , Berkeley, 1973-74, San Jose State U., 1984—. Served to capt. USAF, 1959-62. Mem. Am. Meteorological Soc., (pres. Panama Canal Zone chpt. 1967-68, San Francisco Bay chpt. 1971-72), Sigma Xi (hon.). Republican. Roman Catholic. Avocations: skiing, bowling, golf, music, art.

THUMS, CHARLES WILLIAM, designer, consultant; b. Manitowoc, Wis., Sept. 5, 1945; s. Earl Oscar and Helen Margaret (Rusch) T. B. in Arch., Ariz. State U., 1972. Ptnr., Grafic, Tempe, Ariz., 1967-70; founder, prin. I-Squared Environ. Cons., Tempe, Ariz., 1970-78; designer and cons. design morphology, procedural programming and algorithms, 1978—. Author: (with Jonathan Craig Thums) Tempe's Grand Hotel, 1973, The Rossen House, 1975; (with Daniel Peter Aiello) Shelter and Culture, 1976; contbg. author: Tombstone Planning Guide, 5 vols., 1974. Office: PO Box 3126 Tempe AZ 85281

THURBER, MARY B. O'DELL, multiple association executive, political consultant, writer; b. Columbus, Nebr., Aug. 28, 1930; d. Harry C. and Helen A. (Cherny) Brown; m. Robert A. O'Dell, July 26, 1953 (div.); children—Christopher, Mark, Paul; m. Marvin D. Thurber, Aug. 30, 1986. B.A. in Elem. Edn., U. Colo., 1952, Tchr. elem. pub. schs., Kirkwood, Mo., 1952-55; news editor Aurora (Colo.) Sun, 1972-76; cons. various Congl. coms., 1976—; exec. dir. Colo. Assn. Tobacco and Candy Distbrs., 1977—, Colo. Assn. Indsl. Bankers, 1982—, Colo. Fin. Services Assn., Denver, 1982—; exec. dir. Okla. Assn. Tobacco and Candy Distbrs., 1985—; cons. pub. relations; dir. Consumer Credit Counseling Service; dir. Sec. State's Bus. Adv. Council. Pres. Aurora JayCee-ettes, 1960; citywide chmn. March of Dimes, 1961; chmn. bd. dirs. Metro Denver Sewage Disposal Dist. No. 1, 1974-76, dir., 1967-86; mem. Colo. Com. on Women, 1974, Aurora Citizens Adv. Budget Com., 1980-81; bd. dirs. Home Neighborly Service; mem. Arapahoe County Republican Exec. Com., 1974-81, 85-86; pres. Aurora Rep. Women's Club, 1974-76; vice chmn. 62d state rep. dist., 1982-83. Named Colo. TAN activist of Yr., Tobacco Inst., 1980, 82; recipient J. Ernest O'Brien Meml. award Nat. Assn. Tobacco Distbrs., 1981; Leo Marks award Colo. Assn. Tobacco and Candy Distbrs., 1986; key to City of Aurora City Council, 1976. Mem. Colo., Soc. Assn. Execs., Am. Soc. Assn. Execs., P.E.O., AAUW, LWV, Pi Lambda Theta, Tau Beta Sigma. Presbyterian. Avocations: music, swimming, reading mysteries. Home: 2848 S Kenton Ct Aurora CO 80014 Office: 1390 Logan St Suite 304 Denver CO 80203

THURMAN, HAROLD VANBERG, oceanography educator; b. Salem, Ill., May 21, 1934; s. Howard Galloway and Ethel (Berg) T.; Iantha Lou Britton, July 2, 1955; 1 child, Deborah Ann. BS in Geology, Okla. State U., 1957; MA in Edn., Calif. State U., Los Angeles, 1966. Petroleum geologist KErr-McGee Oil Ind., Oklahoma City, 1957-63; tchr. Charter Oak Unified Sch., Covina, Calif., 1964-68, Mt. San Antonio Coll., Walnut, Calif., 1968—. Author: Introductory Oceanography, 1985, Essentials of Oceangraphy, 1986; coauthor: Physical Geology, 1982, Marine Biology, 1984. Mem. AAAS, Geol. Soc. Am., Nat. Assn. Geology Tchrs., Internat. Oceanographic Found. Republican. Avocations: gardening, collecting various rarities. Home: 1909 Scenic Ridge Dr Chino Hills CA 91709 Office: Mt San Antonio Coll 1100 N Grand Ave Walnut CA 91709

TIBBITTS, PAT A., financial corporation executive; b. Tacoma, Dec. 28, 1933; s. Earl P. and Margaret E. (Wolfe) T.; divorced; 1 child, Susan M. BA, U. Wash., 1952. Pres. Internat. Devel. Fin. Corp., Lynnwood, Wash., 1984—. Served to sgt. U.S. Army, 1954-56. Democrat. Avocations: stamps, camping. Home: 5605 34th Ave SW Seattle WA 98126 Office: Internat Devel Fin Corp PO Box 896 Lynnwood WA 98036

TIDBALL, JAMES GORRIE, biomedical science educator; b. Washington, May 14, 1953; s. James Gorman and Helen (Gorrie) T. BS, Duke U., 1975; PhD in Anatomy, Dalhousie U., Halifax, N.S., Can., 1981. Electron microscopist Duke U., Durham, N.C., 1975-77, research assoc., 1981-83; grad. fellow Dalhousie U., 1977-81; asst. prof. biomed. sci. U. Calif., Riverside, 1983—. Contbr. articles to profl. jours. Mem. AAAS, Am. Assn. Cell Biologists, Sigma Xi. Office: U Calif Div Biomed Sci Riverside CA 92521

TIDWELL, JOSEPH PAUL, JR., aviation and product safety administrator; b. Tuscaloosa, Ala., Oct. 29, 1943; s. Joseph Paul and Jeanette (Steinwinder) T.; m. Susan Kay White, Oct. 3, 1970; children: Joseph Paul III, James Boland, Heather Loran, Shawn Damon. A.S., NYU, 1978, BS, 1984; postgrad. Murray (Ky.) State U., 1984-85, Embry Riddle Aero. U., 1986—. Lic. pilot rotorcraft, cert. safety mgr. Commd. aviation ops. officer U.S. Army, 1976, advanced through grades to maj., 1985; aviation safety officer Ft. Campbell, Ky., 1982-85, Chun Chon, Korea, 1981-82; chief aviation and product safety McDonnell Douglas Helicopter, Co., Mesa, Ariz., 1985—. Developer safety engring., safety cons., safety instr. Webelos den leader Clarksville council Cub Scouts Am., Tenn., 1983-85; asst. scout master Clarksville council Boy Scouts Am., 1983-85, scoutmaster Mesa council, 1985—; bd. dirs., exposition mgr. S.W. Health and Safety Congress, 1985-86. Decorated Purple Heart, Meritorious Service medal, recipient Den Leaders Tng. Key Middle Tenn. council Boy Scouts Am., 1985, Woodbadge Beads Middle Tenn. Council Boy Scouts Am., 1985. Named Scoutmaster of Yr., Mesa Dist., Theodore Roosevelt Council Boy Scouts Am., 1986. Mem. Am. Soc. Safety Engrs. (profl.; Safety Officer of Month award 1985, chmn. awards and elections Ariz. chpt. 1985-87), Army Aviation Assn. Am. (air assault chpt. exec. treas. 1983-85, Aviation Safety Officer of Yr. award 1984), U.S. Army Warrant Officer's Assn. (Ky.-Tenn. chpt. pres. 1984-85, Disting. Service plaque 1984, World Safety Orgn. (affiliate), Internat. Soc. Air Safety Investigators). Republican. Roman Catholic. Lodge: WIPALA WIKI, Order of Arrow. Avocations: golfing, camping, cycling. Home: 2338 E Javelina St Mesa AZ 85204 Office: McDonnell Douglas Helicopter Co 5000 E McDowell Rd Mesa AZ 85205

TIEDT, THAO ANN, lawyer; b. Mpls., Apr. 10, 1944; d. John Frederick and Theo Ann (Totushek) Telke; m. Niels F.S. Tiedt, Dec. 7, 1963; children: Jennifer Ann, Kimberly Camille. BS suma cum laude, Southwest Mo. State, 1980; JD with honors, U. Wash., 1983. Bar: Wash., 1983. Freelance writer 1970-80; legal intern Schwabe, Williams, Wyatt, Moore & Roberts, Portland, Oreg., 1981; legal intern Ryan, Swanson, & CLeveland, Seattle, 1982-83, atty., 1983—. Co-chairwoman Com. to Support Bond Inssues, Springfield, Mo., 1980; co-chairwoman Wayzata (Minn.) Sch. Dist. Communication Com., 1975-77; active SKBA Youth and Law Com., 1985—, Pub. Info Com., 1985-86; chairperson Prisoner Counseling Project, Seattle, Wash., 1982-83. Recognized for contbn. to Criminal Justice System Wash. State, 1983. Mem. ABA, Wash. State Bar Assn., Seattle-King County Bar Assn., Am. Soc. Safety Engrs., Order of Coif, Order of Barristers. Avocations: sewing, sailing, wallpapering, walking. Office: Ryan Swanson & Cleveland 3201 Bank of Calif Ctr Seattle WA 98164

TIEN, CHANG LIN, mechanical engineering educator; b. Wuhan, China, July 24, 1935; came to U.S., 1956, naturalized, 1969; s. Yun Chien and Yun Di (Lee) T.; m. Di Hwa Liu, July 25, 1959; children: Norman Chihnan, Phyllis Chihping, Christine Chihyih. B.S., Nat. Taiwan U., 1955; M.M.E., U. Louisville, 1957; M.A., Ph.D., Princeton U., 1959. Acting asst. prof. dept. mech. engring. U. Calif.—Berkeley, Berkeley, 1959-60; asst. prof. U. Calif.—Berkeley, 1960-64, assoc. prof., 1964-68, prof., 1968—, dept. chmn., 1974-81, also vice chancellor for research, 1983-85; tech. cons. Lockheed Missiles & Space Co., Gen. Electric Co. Contbr. articles to profl jours. Guggenheim fellow, 1965. Fellow ASME (Max Jakob Heml. award AS-ME—Am. Inst. Chem. Engrs. 1981, Heat Transfer Meml. award 1974, Larson Meml. award 1975), AIAA (Thermophysics award 1977); mem. Nat. Acad. Engring. Home: 1451 Olympus Ave Berkeley CA 94708 Office: Dept Mech Engring U Calif Berkeley CA 94720

TIETZ, WILLIAM JOHN, JR., university president; b. Chgo., Mar. 6, 1927; s. William John and Irma (Neuman) T.; children: Karen Elizabeth, William John, Julia Wells. BA, Swarthmore Coll., 1950; MS, U. Wis., 1952; DVM, Colo. State U., 1957; PhD, Purdue U., 1961, DSc, 1982. Research assoc. Baxter Labs., Morton Grove, Ill., 1952-53; instr., then assoc. prof. Purdue U., 1957-64; faculty Colo. State U., 1964-77, prof., chmn. physiology and biophysics, 1967-70, v.p. student and univ. relations, 1970-71; dean Colo. State U. (Coll. Vet. Medicine and Biomed. Scis.), 1971-77; assoc. dir. Colo. State U. (Agr. Expt. Sta.), 1975-77; pres. Mont. State U., Bozeman, 1977—; dir. First Bank of Bozeman; mem. Gov.'s Com. on Econ. Devel., 1984—; mem. Mont. Sci. and Tech. Alliance, 1985—. Bd. dirs. Children's House, Montessori Sch., 1966-70, chmn., 1968-70; bd. dirs. Colo. State U. Found., 1970-71, Colo. chpt. Am. Cancer Soc., 1976-79; mem. research bd. Denver Zool. Soc., 1975-77; treas. Mont. Energy Research and Devel. Inst., 1977—, v.p., 1978-80, pres., 1981-83; bd. dirs. Greater Mont. Found., 1979—; mem. Mont. Com. for Humanities, 1980-83; mem. div. research resources adv. council NIH, 1979-82; trustee Yellowstone Park Found., 1981—. Served with USNR, 1945-46. Recipient Service award Colo. Vet. Med. Assn., 1976. Mem. Larimer County Vet. Med. Assn. (pres. 1968-69), Am. Assn. Vet. Physiologists and Pharmacologists (pres. 1971-72), Am. Physiol. Soc., Sigma Xi, Phi Zeta (sec.-treas. 1970-71), Assn. Am. Colls. Vet. Medicine (chmn. council of deans 1975-76), Phi Kappa Phi, Phi Sigma Kappa, Omicron Delta Kappa, Beta Beta Beta. Address: Mont State U Office of Pres Bozeman MT 59717 *

TIFT, MARY LOUISE, artist; b. Seattle, Jan. 2, 1913; d. John Howard and Wilhelmina (Pressler) Dreher; m. William Raymond Tift, Dec. 4, 1948. B.F.A. cum laude, U. Wash., 1933; postgrad., Art Center Coll., Los Angeles, 1945-48, U. Calif., San Francisco, 1962-63. Art dir. Vaughn Shedd Advt., Los Angeles, 1948; asst. prof. design Calif. Coll. Arts and Crafts, Oakland, Calif., 1949-59; coordinator design dept. San Francisco Art Inst., 1959-62. Subject of cover story, Am. Artist mag., 1980; one woman shows, Gumps Gallery, San Francisco, 1977, 1986, Diane Gilson Gallery, Seattle, 1978, Oreg. State U., 1981, group shows include, Brit. Biennale, Yorkshire, Eng., 1970, Grenchen Triennale, Switzerland, 1970, Polish Biennale, Crakow, 1972, Nat. Gallery, Washington, 1973; represented in permanent collections, Phila. Mus. Art, Bklyn. Mus., Seattle Art Mus., Library Congress, Achenbach Print Collection, San Francisco Palace Legion of Honor. Served to lt. USNR, 1943-45. Mem. Print Club Phila., World Print Council, Calif. Soc. Printmakers, Phi Beta Kappa, Lambda Rho. Christian Scientist. Home: 16 West Harbor Dr Sausalito CA 94965 Office: 112 Industrial Center Bldg Sausalito CA 94965

TIGHE, DANIEL JOSEPH, lawyer; b. Oakland, Calif., Apr. 3, 1950; s. Peter Joseph and Rose Ellen (Keegan) T.; m. Antoinette Rafli Diab, Feb. 18, 1977; children: Justin K., Daniel Joseph. BS in History, Portland State U., 1972; JD, Gonzaga U., 1975. Bar: Wash. 1975. Atty. Poyhonen & Tighe, Inc., Montesano, Wash., 1975-81; sole practice Montesano, Wash., 1981—; v.p. DaPaul, Inc., Olympia, Wash., 1972—. Atty. City of Montesano Civil Service Commn., 1981—. Mem. ABA, Fed. Bar. Assn., Grays Harbor County Bar Assn., Wash. State Bar Assn., Wash. State Trial Lawyers., Am. Trial Lawyers Assn. Democrat. Roman Catholic. Lodge: Elks. Avocations: hunting, fishing, cars. Home: PO Box 567 Montesano WA 98563 Office: 120 Main Street S Montesano WA 98563

TILBURY, ROGER GRAYDON, lawyer; b. Guthrie, Okla., July 30, 1925; s. Graydon and Minnie (Lee) T.; m. Margaret Dear, June 24, 1952; 1 dau., Elizabeth Ann. B.S., U. So. Calif., 1945; J.D., U. Kans., 1949; LL.M., Columbia, 1950; postgrad., Oxford (Eng.) U., 1949. Bar: Mo. bar 1950, Oreg. bar 1953. Practiced in Kansas City, Mo., 1950-53, Portland, Oreg., 1953—; asso. firm Rogers, Field, Gentry, Kansas City, Mo., 1950-53, Stern, Reiter & Day, Portland, 1953-56; partner firm Roth & Tilbury, 1956-58, Tilbury & Kane, 1970-72, Haessler, Tilbury & Platten, 1978-81; individual practice law Portland, 1981—; circuit judge pro tem., Oreg., 1972—, arbitrator and fact finder, 1973—; tree farmer; sec. Barrington Properties; mem. nat. panel arbitrators U.S. Mediation and Conciliation Service; atty. Animal Defender League, 1969-73; dir. Consol. Cargos, Inc. Dep. election commr. Kansas City, Mo., 1952-53; bd. dirs. Multnomah Bar Found. Served to lt. (j.g.) USNR, 1943-45. Battenfeld scholar, 1943. Mem. Oreg. State Bar, Soc. Barristers, Am. Arbitration Assn., Save the Redwoods League, East African Wildlife League, Nat. Wildlife Found., Am. Trial Lawyers Assn., Delta Tau Delta, Phi Delta Phi. Home: 9310 NW Cornell Rd Portland OR 97229 Office: 1123 SW Yamhill Portland OR 97205

TILLEMANS, PATRICIA LOUISE, psychiatric social worker; b. Milbank, S.D., June 12, 1937; d. Patrick Henry and Gwendolyn Faye (Schultz) T. BA, Mt. St. Mary's Coll., Los Angeles, 1966; MSW, U. So. Calif., 1978; postgrad., Cambridge Grad. Sch. Psychology, Los Angeles, 1986—. Cert. teacher, Calif.; lic. clin. social worker, Calif. Social worker Good Shepherd Residence, San Francisco, Los Angeles, Chgo., 1967-75; coordinator Status Offender Detention Alternative Program, Los Angeles, 1976; clin. social worker Long Beach (Calif.) Neuropsychiat. Inst., 1978-81; supr. Gateways Conditional Release Program, Los Angeles, 1981-85; dir. Gateways Mentally Disordered Offenders Program, Los Angeles, 1985—; pvt. practice Los Angeles, 1981—; mem. legis. com. Mental Health Council, Los Angeles, 1982-84. Mem. Fellowship of Reconciliation, Los Angeles, 1981—. Mem. Nat. Assn. Social Workers (steering com. 1982-84, Register of Clin. Social Workers 1982—), Acad. Cert. Social Workers, Forensic Mental Health Assn. Democrat. Roman Catholic. Avocations: snorkeling, travel. Office: Gateways Satellite 437 N Hoover Los Angeles CA 90004

TILLER, MICHAEL HEINRICH, environmental engineering consultant executive; b. Huntsville, Ala., Feb. 1, 1953; s. Werner Gerhard and Ruth Lina (Urbanski) T.; m. Margaret Wilkinson, May 21, 1983. BS, Vanderbilt U., 1975; MBA, Pepperdine U., 1982; MS in Environ. Engring., U. So. Calif., 1984. Sr. staff engr. Woodward-Clyde Cons., Santa Ana, Calif., 1980-82; sr. environ. engr. Earth Tech. Corp., Long Beach, Calif., 1983-85; pres. environ. risk div. Tiller Cons. Group, Inc., Corona Del Mar, Calif., 1985—. Contbr. articles to profl. jours. Served to lt. USN, 1975-81. Mem. ASCE, Am. Indsl. Hygiene Assn. (full mem.), Soc. Risk Analysis, World Future Soc. (profl.), ASTM, Nat. Inst. Bldg. Scis. (asbestos task force 1985), Nat. Assn. Ins. Commnrs. (adv. com. environ. impairment liability ins. 1985), Newport Harbor C. of C. Avocations: chess, astromomy, swimming. Office: Tiller Cons Group Inc 509 B Goldenrod Ave Corona Del Mar CA 92625

TILLERY, BILL W., physics educator; b. Muskogee, Okla., Sept. 15, 1938; s. William Earnest and Bessie C. (Smith) Freeman; m Patricia Weeks Northrop, Aug. 1, 1981; children by previous marriage—Tonya Lynn, Lisa Gail. B.S., Northeastern U., 1960; M.A., U. No. Colo., 1965, Ed.D., 1967. Tchr. Guthrie Pub. Schs., Okla., 1960-62; tchr. Jefferson County schs., Colo., 1962-64; teaching asst. U. No. Colo., 1965-67; asst. prof. Fla. State U., 1967-69; assoc. prof. U. Wyo., 1969-73, dir. sci. and math. teaching ctr., 1969-73; assoc. prof. dept. physics Ariz. State U., Tempe, 1973-75, prof., 1976—; cons. in field. Author: (with Ploutz) Basic Physical Science, 1964; (with Sund and Trowbridge) Elementary Science Activities, 1967, Elementary Biological Science, 1970, Elementary Physical Science, 1970, Elementary Earth Science, 1970, Investigate and Discover, 1975; Space, Time, Energy and Matter: Activity Books, 1976; (with Bartholomew) Heath Earth Science, 1984; (with Bartholomew and Gary) Heath Earth Science Activities, 1984, 2d edit. 1987, Heath Earth Science Teacher Resource Book, 1987, Heath Earth Science Laboratory Activity, 1987; editor Ariz. Sci. Tchrs. Jour., 1975—, Ariz. Energy Edn., 1978—. Fellow AAAS; mem. Nat. Sci. Tchrs. Assn., Ariz. Sci. Tchrs. Assn., Assn. Edn. of Tchrs. in Sci., Nat. Assn. Research in Sci. Teaching. Republican. Episcopalian. Home: 8986 S Forest Ave Tempe AZ 85284 Office: Dept Physics Ariz State U Tempe AZ 85287

TILLOTSON, DELBERT EUGENE, college dean; b. Maupin, Oreg., Sept. 22, 1926; s. George A. and Elsie R. T.; m. Doris Kimble, Nov. 25, 1953; children—Stephen, Craig. A.B., Willamette U., 1950; M.A., Miami U., Oxford, Ohio, 1951. Credit reporter Dun & Bradstreet, 1951-52; instr. bus. adminstrn. Skagit Valley Coll., 1954-66, dean adminstrv. services, Skagit Valley Coll., Mt. Vernon, Wash., 1966—, instr. acctg., 1954—. Served to lt. USN, 1952-53. Mem. Nat. Assn. Coll. and Univ. Bus. Officers, Assn. Sch. Bus. Ofcls., Western Assn. Coll. and Univ. Bus. Officers. Republican. Episcopalian. Lodge: Elks. Contbr. articles to profl. jours. Home: 720 N 21st St Mt Vernon WA 98273 Office: 2405 College Way Mt Vernon WA 98273

TILLSON, STEPHEN ALFRED, endocrinologist; b. Flint, Mich., Dec. 29, 1940; s. Harry Alfred and Mary Eva (Hartwig) T.; m. Judith Ann Osterloh, Dec. 30, 1961 (div. June 1978); children: David Alfred, Michael Thomas; m. Elizabeth Tiebout, Nov. 28, 1985. BS, Calif. State Poly Coll., Pomona, 1962; MS, U. Mo., 1965; PhD, Purdue U., 1969. Postdoctoral fellow Worcester Found., Shrewsbury, Mass., 1970; dir. toxicology Alza Corp., Palo Alto, Calif., 1970-78; dir. lab. Cen. Ariz. Vet. Lab., Casa Grande, 1978-81; mgr. clins. Syntex Med. Diagnostics, Palo Alto, 1981—; cons. Los Olivos Med. Lab., Los Gatos, Calif., 1982-84. Author: Immunologic Methods in Steroid Determination, 1970, Research on Steroids IV, 1970, Advances in Steroid Biochemistry and Pharmacology, 1974, Clinical Experience with the Progesterone Uterine Therapeutic System, 1978. Mem. AAAS, Soc. Study Reproduction, N.Y. Acad. Sci., Endocrine Soc., Pacific Coast Fertility Soc. Republican. Baptist. Home: 409 F Cork Harbour Circle Redwood City CA 94065 Office: Syntex Diagnostics 900 Arastradero Rd Palo Alto CA 94304

TILTON, DAVID LLOYD, savings and loan association executive; b. Santa Barbara, Calif., Sept. 21, 1926; s. Lloyd Irving and Grace (Hart) T.; m. Mary Caroline Knudtson, June 6, 1953; children: Peter, Jennifer, Michael, Catharine. A.B., Stanford U., 1949, M.B.A., 1951. With Santa Barbara Savs. & Loan Assn., 1951—, vice-chmn., 1973—, pres., 1965-84, also dir.; chmn., dir. Fin. Corp. Santa Barbara; dir. Collins Ford Internat.; trustee Calif. Real Estate Investment Trust. Mem. pres.'s cabinet Calif. Poly. U. Served with USNR, World War II. Mem. Calif. Savs. and Loan League (dir. 1980), Delta Chi. Home: 630 Oak Grove Dr Santa Barbara CA 93108 Office: Santa Barbara Savs & Loan 3908 State St Santa Barbara CA 93105

TIMBERLAKE, CYNTHIA JANE, librarian; b. Denver, Sept. 1, 1926; d. James Julius and Lillian Mae (Johnson) Alford; m. Lewis George Timberlake, Dec. 22, 1947; children—Stephen Lewis, Phyllis Lynn. B.A. in English, U. Calif.-Berkeley, 1947; M.L.S., UCLA, 1962. Gifts and exchange librarian Am. U., Washington, 1963; rare book cataloger Fairfax County Pub. Library, Fairfax, Va., 1963-68; vol. librarian Micronesian Area Research Ctr., Guam, 1969-70; assoc. librarian Bernice P. Bishop Mus., Honolulu, 1970-75, head librarian, 1975-86; trustee, chmn. publs. com. Hawaiian Hist. Soc., Honolulu, 1981-85; mem. adv. council Pacific Regional Conservation Ctr., Honolulu, 1981-83. Contbr. articles to profl. jours. Librarian, sec. Fairfax County Civil Rights Assn., 1963-68, Laubach Literacy Action, 1963-68. Mem. Hawaii Library Assn. (pres. 1983-84), Hawaii Mus. Assn., ALA, Soc. Am. Archivists, Spl. Library Assn., Beta Phi Mu. Democrat. Roman Catholic.

TIMM, JAMES DONALD, aerospace engineer; b. Plainfield, Wis., Nov. 5, 1934; S. Alvin H. and Martha A. (Helmrick) T.; m. Grace Eileen Rathjen, June 15, 1956; children: Susan, Timothy. BS in Aerospace Engring., Northrop U., 1961. Lic. comml. pilot. Test engr. Gen. Dynamics Corp., Pomona, Calif., 1956-57; project engr. B.H. Hadley, Pomona, 1957-66; engring. specialist Garrett Turbine Engine Co., Phoenix, 1966—; advanced instrument ground instr. Patentee in field. Mem. AIAA, Soc. Automotive Engrs., Exptl. Aircraft Assn., Ariz. Pilots Assn. (pres. 1981—), Aircraft Owners and Pilots Assn. Republican. Lutheran. Avocation: aviation. Home: 220 E Ellis Dr Tempe AZ 85282

TIMMERHAUS, KLAUS DIETER, college dean, chemical engineering educator; b. Mpls., Sept. 10, 1924; s. Paul P. and Elsa L. (Bever) T.; m. Jean L. Mevis, Aug. 3, 1952; 1 dau., Carol Jane. B.S. in Chem. Engring, U. Ill., 1948, M.S., 1949, Ph.D., 1951. Registered profl. engr., Colo. Process design engr. Calif. Research Corp., Richmond, 1952-53; extension lectr. U. Calif., Berkeley, 1952; mem. faculty U. Colo., 1953—, prof. chem. engring., 1961—, asso. dean engring., 1963—, dir. engring. research ctr. Coll. Engring., 1963—, chmn. aerospace dept., 1979-80; chem. engr. cryogenics lab. Nat. Bur. Standards, Boulder, summers 1955,57,59,61; lectr. U. Calif. at Los Angeles, 1961-62; sect. head Engring. div. NSF, 1972-73; cons. in field. Bd. dirs. Colo. Engring. Expt. Sta., Inc., Engring. Measurements Co, both Boulder. Editor: Advances in Cryogenic Engineering, vols. 1-25, 1954-80; co-editor: Internat. Cryogenic Monograph Series, 1965—. Served with USNR, 1944-46. Recipient Disting. Service award Dept. Commerce, 1957; Samuel C. Collins award outstanding contbns. to cryogenic tech., 1967; George Westinghouse award, 1968; Alpha Chi Sigma award for chem. engring. research, 1968; Meritorious Service award Cryogenic Engring. Conf., 1967; R.L. Stearns Profl. Achievement award U. Colo., 1981; Disting. Pub. Service award NSF, 1984. Fellow AAAS; mem. Nat. Acad. Engring., Am. Astron. Soc., Am. Inst. Chem. Engrs. (v.p. 1975, pres. 1976, Founders award 1978, Eminent Chem. Engr. award 1983), Am. Soc. for Engring. Edn. (bd. dirs. 1986—, 3M Chem Engring. div. award 1980), Internat. Inst. Refrigeration (v.p. 1979-87, U.S. nat. commn. 1983-86, pres. 1983-86), Cryogenic Engring. Conf. (chmn. 1956-67, bd. dirs. 1956—), Sigma Xi (v.p. 1986—, dir. 1981-86), Sigma Tau, Tau Beta Pi, Phi Lambda Upsilon. Home: 905 Brooklawn Dr Boulder CO 80303

TIMMINS, JAMES DONALD, investment banker; b. Hamilton, Ont., Can., Oct. 3, 1955; came to U.S., 1979; s. Donald G. and Myrna L. (Seymour) T. B.A., U. Toronto, 1977; J.D., Queen's U., 1979; M.B.A., Stanford U., 1981. Investment banker Wood Gundy, Toronto, 1980, Salomon Bros., San Francisco, 1981-84; mng. dir. and chief exec. officer McKewon & Timmins, San Diego, 1984—; bd. dirs. Instl. Realty Advisors, Inc., McKewon & Timmons, San Diego Stock and Bond Club. Home: 341 Playa Del Sur La Jolla CA 92037 Office: McKewon & Timmins 701 B St San Diego CA 92101

TIMMINS, WILLIAM MONTANA, II, management educator; b. Salt Lake City, Mar. 13, 1936; s. William Montana and Mary Brighton T.; m. Theda Laws, Oct. 14, 1960; children: William Montana III, Clark Brighton, Laurel, Sally, Rebekah. BS, U. Utah, 1960, PhD, 1972; MA, Harvard U., 1962; postdoctoral student, UCLA, 1973. Asst. to gov. State of Utah, Salt Lake City, 1966-69; asst. v.p. U. Utah, Salt Lake City, 1969-71; dir. interstate projects Utah Bd. Edn., Salt Lake City, 1971-74; prof. mgmt. Brigham Young U., Provo, Utah, 1974—; chmn. of bd. TCI, Inc., Paris; vice chmn. Pioneer Valley Hosp., West Valley, Utah, 1985—; chmn. Mountain View Hosp., Payson, Utah; bd. dirs. Nat. Congress Hosp. Governing Bds., Washington, 1984—. Author: Career Education (vols. I and II), 1971, Guide to Improved Employee Relations, 1984, International Economic Policy Coordination, 1985; editor: Comprehensive Educational Planning, 1972; contbr. articles to profl. jours. Chmn. Salt Lake County Youth Services Ctr., 1979-80. Recipient Silver Beaver award Boy Scouts Am., 1974, Carnation Silver Bowl Community Services Council, 1978; Redd fellow Redd Ctr. Brigham Young U., 1982. Mem. Utah Hosp. Assn. Salt Lake City (trustee 1985—), Am. Soc. Pub. Adminstrn. (bd. dirs. 1983-85, com. mem. 1981-86), Soc. Profls. in Dispute Resolution, Am. Arbitration Assn., Nat. Assn. Civil Service Commrs. (hon., life, pres. 1982-83), Rocky Mountain Pub. Employer Labor Relations Assn. (v.p. 1980-83), Utah Assn. Civil Service Commrs. (pres. 1979-80), Internat. Personnel Mgmt. Assn. (publs. com. 1985—), Phi Kappa Phi. Republican. Mormon. Avocations: philately, writing, drawing cartoons, traveling, camping. Office: Brigham Young U 772 Tanner Bldg Provo UT 84602

TIMMRECK, THOMAS C., health sciences educator; b. Montpelier, Idaho, June 15, 1946; s. Archie Carl and Janone (Jensen) T.; m. Ellen Prusse, Jan. 27, 1971; children: Chad Thomas, Benjamin Brian, Julie Anne. AA, Ricks Coll., 1968; BS, Brigham Young U., 1971; MEd, Oreg. State U., 1972; MA, No. Ariz. U., 1981; PhD, U. Utah, 1976. Program dir. Cache County Aging Program, Logan, Utah, 1972-73; asst. prof. div. health edn. Tex. Tech U., Lubbock, 1976-77; asst. prof. dept. health care adminstrn. Idaho State U., Pocatello, 1977-78; program dir., asst. prof. health services program No. Ariz. U., Flagstaff, 1978-84; cons., dir. grants Beth Israel Hosp., Denver, 1985; assoc. prof. dept. health scis. and human ecology Calif. State U., San Bernardino, 1985—. Author: Dictionary of Health Services Management, rev. 2d edit., 1987, editorial bd. Jour. Health Values, 1986—; contbr. articles to profl. jours. Served with U.S. Army, 1966-72, Vietnam. Mem. Assn. Advancement of Health Edn., Am. Acad. Mgmt., Assn. Univ. Programs in Health Care Adminstrn., Assn. Western Hosps. Republican. Mormon. Office: Calif State U Dept Health Scis and Human Ecology San Bernardino CA 92407

TINDALL, ROBERT JAMES, organizational development consultant; b. Salt Lake City, Jan. 10, 1948; s. Thomas Ducharme and Betty Nadine (Frazier) T. BS in Human Relation Organizational Behavior, U. San Francisco, 1981, M. Human Resource and Organizational Devel., 1983.

Customer service rep. Pacific Gas & Electric Co., San Francisco, 1972-79; tng. devel. cons., San Francisco, 1979-82, human resource mgmt., organizational devel. cons., 1982—; intern Drake, Beam, Morin, Inc. Cons. Mgmt. Human Resources, San Francisco, 1982—; cons. human resources and orgnl. devel.; instr. human resource development New Coll Calif., 1986—. Mem. Am. Soc. Tng. and Devel. (steering com. organizational devel. local chpt., chmn. internat. profl. practice exec. com., pres. Golden Gate chpt. 1986), Organizational Devel. Network. Republican. Home and Office: 25 Corwin St #1 San Francisco CA 94114

TINDLE, CHARLES DWIGHT WOOD, broadcasting company executive; b. Bryn Mawr, Pa., Jan. 13, 1950; s. Charles Wood and Nancy (Sapp) T. Student, Kenyon Coll., 1968-71. Pres. Dwight Karma Broadcasting, Mesa, Ariz., 1971-76, Natural Broadcasting System, Mesa, 1976-79; producer, fellow Am. Film Inst. Ctr. for Advanced Film Studies, 1979-80; pres. Network 30, Scottsdale, Ariz., 1985—; owner Sta. KDKB-AM-FM, Mesa, Sta. KSML-FM, Lake Tahoe, Calif., Sta. KNOT-AM-FM, Prescott, Ariz., Sta. KBWA, Williams, Ariz. Recipient Peabody award U. Ga., 1976. Republican. Episcopalian. Home: 4959 E Red Rock Dr Phoenix AZ 85018 Office: Network 30 Inc 4416 N Scottsdale Rd #605 Scottsdale AZ 85251

TINEBRA, CARL PETER, manufacturing executive, electrical engineer; b. Oak Park, Ill., Jan. 23, 1934; s. Peter and Mildred (Difrancesca) T.; m. Irene Beale, Sept. 1, 1956; children—Peter, Jean, Ann, Patricia, Christine. B.S.E.E., Ill. Inst. Tech., 1955; postgrad. Northwestern U., 1959-60, San Jose State U., 1963-64; M.B.A., U. Santa Clara, 1972. Devel. engr. Motorola, Inc., Chgo., 1958-61; project engr. GTE Lenkurt, San Carlos, Calif., 1961-65; chief engr. Bell & Howell, Chgo., 1965-67; engring. mgr. Philco Ford Corp., Palo Alto, Calif., 1967-73; planning mgr. Plantronics Inc., Santa Cruz, Calif., 1973-75; product planning mgr. Ford Aerospace & Communications Corp., Palo Alto, 1975-79; engring. mgr. Anderson Jacobson, Inc., San Jose, Calif., 1979-81; v.p. engring. Lear Siegler, Inc., Menlo Park, Calif., 1981-85; v.p. ops. telecommunications div., 1985—. Patentee in field. Contbr. articles to profl. jours. Basketball coach St. Simon's Roman Catholic Ch., 1976-80, pres., bd. dirs. men's club, 1978-79. Served to capt. USAF, 1956-58. Mem. IEEE (engring. mgmt. group), U. Santa Clara Alumni Assn. (bd. dirs.), Arnold Air Soc., Rho Epsilon. Republican. Office: Lear Siegler Inc 3885 Bohannon Dr Menlo Park CA 94025

TINER, RICHARD HAROLD, broadcasting executive; b. Corpus Christi, Tex., Aug. 29, 1951; s. Kenneth W. and Doris M. (Brown) T.; m. Brenda J. Adams, Jan. 1, 1971; children: Richard Jr., Shawna, Christopher. BS, Gulf-Coast Bible Coll., 1976. Owner, mgr. All Day Sound Co., Houston, 1977-78; program dir. Sta. KFMK-FM, Houston, 1973-78; ops. mgr. Sta. KYND-FM, Houston, 1979-81; cons. Sta. KGOL-FM, Houston, 1981-82; owner, mgr. Tiner Broadcasting Sta. KTNR, Kenedy, Tex., 1982—, Tiner Broadcasting Sta. KRSS, Spokane, Wash., 1985—; lectr. Gulf Coast Bible Coll., Houston, 1979; adj. prof. Ea. Wash. U., 1986; featured panelist Nat. Assn. Broadcasters Nat. Radio Broadcasters Assn. Conv., Los Angeles, 1984, mem. mgmt. roundtable, 1984. Pres. United Way, Kenedy, 1982-85, Little League, Kenedy, 1984. Republican. Mem. Ch. of God. Avocations: Christian work, singing. Office: Tiner Broadcasting Co N 1406 Ash Spokane WA 99201

TINGLEY, HOWARD E., mining company executive; b. Omaha, Apr. 27, 1933; s. Howard Allison and Marjorie Elizabeth (Palmquist) T.; m. Anna Vee Hartman, Sept. 2, 1955 (dec. Nov. 1972); children: Michael Eugene, Mitchell Edward; m. Elizabeth McEwen, July 30, 1976. BS in Internat. Bus., U. Colo., 1970; MS in Human Resource Mgmt., U. Utah., 1978. Engr. Tipton & Kalmbach, Inc., Denver, 1958-71; office mgr., adminstrv. engr. Eldorado Engring., Glenwood Springs, Colo., 1972-76; constrn. cons. Carbondale, Colo., 1976-82; gen. ptnr. R.A. Mining Co., Glenwood Springs, 1982—; pres. R.A.M.O. Corp., Glenwood Springs, 1985—; gen. ptnr., cons. Eagle Gypsum (Colo.) Ltd., 1986—. Served with USNR, 1952-54. Avocations: flying, diving, travel. Home: 12433 Hwy 82 Carbondale CO 81623 Office: Eagle Gypsum Ltd 401 N River Glenwood Springs CO 81602

TINKER, GRANT A., broadcasting executive; b. Stamford, Conn., Jan. 11, 1926. Student, Dartmouth Coll. With radio program dept. NBC, 1949-54; TV dept. McCann-Erickson Advt. Agy., 1954-58, Benton & Bowles Advt. Agy., 1958-61; v.p.-programs West Coast, NBC, 1961-66; v.p. in charge programming West Coast, NBC, N.Y.C., 1966-67; v.p. Universal TV, 1968-69, 20th-Fox, 1969-70; pres. Mary Tyler Moore (MTM) Enterprises, Inc., Studio City, Calif., 1970-81; chmn. bd., chief exec. officer NBC, Burbank, Calif., 1981-86; independent producer Burbank, Calif., 1986—. Office: c/o NBC-TV 3000 W Alameda Blvd Burbank CA 91523

TINKER, ROBERT EUGENE, clergyman, educational consultant; b. Lincoln, Kans., June 10, 1915; s. Eugene F. and Mildred Adelaide (Brown) T.; A.B., Am. U., 1937; M.Div., Garrett Theol. Sem., 1942; postgrad. Northwestern U., 1942-46; m. Anne Elizabeth Hall, June 13, 1942; children—Anne Terrill, Robert Bruce, MaryBeth. Ordained to ministry Methodist Ch., 1942, Congregational Ch., 1947-77, United Ch. Christ; minister Oxen Hill, Md., Tuxedo, Md., 1933-37, Evergreen Park, Ill., 1940-41; assoc. minister 1st Presbyterian Ch., Evanston, Ill., 1942-44; minister Glenview Meth. Ch. (Ill.), 1944-46, Broadway Meth. Ch., Chgo., 1946-47; with Chgo. Theol. Sem., 1947-58, asst. sec., asst. treas., bd. dirs., 1947-58, asst. bus. mgr., 1947-50, bus. mgr., 1951-55, dir. devel., 1953-55, v.p. charge devel., 1955-58; assoc. Gonser and Gerber, 1958-64; ptnr. Gonser Gerber Tinker Stuhr, ednl. cons. in devel. and public relations, Chgo., 1964-82, cons., 1982—; pres. Tabco Corp., Chgo., 1983-85; lectr. Creighton U., Omaha, summers 1978-80. N.J. State scholar, 1933; Larry Foster scholar, 1933; John Wanamaker scholar Lingenon U., Canton, Republic of China, 1935-36; Howes Meml. scholar, 1939-42. Bd. dirs. Hyde Park YMCA, Chgo., Hyde Park Union Ch., Porter Found., U. Chgo., Bryn Mawr Community Ch., Chgo. Mem. (bd. dirs. 1947-58), Phi Sigma Kappa, Phi Beta Zeta, Pi Gamma Mu. Republican. Contbr. articles to profl. books and jours. Home: 8250 Circle Dr Neah Kah Nie Nehalem OR 97131 Home: 63 W Oro Pl Oro Valley AZ 85737

TINSETH, ALAN MELVIN, mechanical engineer; b. Oceanside, Calif., Nov. 23, 1959; s. Eugene Orville and Audrey Margaret (Loraas) T.; m. Gracie Garza, Nov. 10, 1984; children: Shaun Walton, Shannon Michelle. BS in Nuclear Engring., U. Ariz., 1982. Mech./test engr. U.S. Army-Yuma (Ariz.) Proving Ground, 1983—. Mem. Am. Nuclear Soc. (sr. liaison 1981-82), Modern Mus. Masters (treas. 1976-77). Republican. Lutheran. Avocations: music, fgn. coins and currency, tennis, bike riding. Home: 4429 W 16th Ln Yuma AZ 85364 Office: US Army Yuma Proving Ground STEYP-MT-EW Yuma AZ 85365-9103

TIPTON, GARY LEE, personal services company executive; b. Salem, Oreg., July 3, 1941; s. James Rains and Dorothy Velma (Dierks) T.; B.S., Oreg. Coll. Edn., 1964. Credit rep. Standard Oil Co. Calif., Portland, Oreg., 1964-67; credit mgr. Uniroyal Inc., Dallas, 1967-68; partner, mgr. bus. Tipton Barbers, Portland, 1968—. Mem. Rep. Nat. Com., 1980—, Sen. Howard Baker's Presdl. Steering Com., 1980; mem. U.S. Congl. adv. bd. Am. Security Council, 1984—. Recipient Key to Internat. Biog. Cen., Cambridge, U.K., 1983, World Culture prize Accademia Italia, 1984, Presdl. Achievement award, 1982, cert. disting. contbn. Sunset High Sch. Dad's Club, 1972, 73. Fellow Internat. Biog. Assn. (life, Key award 1983) (U.K.); mem. Sunset Mall Mchts. Assn. (co-founder, treas. 1974-79, pres. 1982-83), Internat. Platform Assn., Smithsonian Assocs., Council on Fgn. Relations (vice chmn. steering com. Portland 1983-84, chmn. Portland com. on fgn. relations 1984-86), UN Assn. (steering com. UN day 1985). Office: Tipton Barbers 1085 NW Murray Rd Portland OR 97229

TISDALE, DOUGLAS MICHAEL, lawyer; b. Detroit, May 3, 1949; s. Charles Walker and Violet Lucille (Battani) T.; m. Patricia Claire Brennan, Dec. 29, 1972; children—Douglas Michael, Jr., Sara Elizabeth, Margaret Patricia, Victoria Claire. B.A. in Psychology with honors, U. Mich., 1971, J.D., 1975. Bar: Colo. 1975, U.S. Dist. Ct. Colo. 1975, U.S. Ct. Appeals (10th cir.) 1976, U.S. Supreme Ct. 1979. Law clk. to chief judge U.S. Dist. Ct. Colo., Denver, 1975-76; assoc. Brownstein, Hyatt, Farber & Madden, Denver, 1976-81, ptnr., 1981—; bd. dirs. Employer Services Program, Inc., Denver, Warner Devels., Inc., Vail, Colo.; lectr. Law Seminars, Inc., 1984—, Continuing Legal Edn. in Colo., Inc., 1984—, Nat. Bus. Insts., 1985—; Colo. Law-Related Edn. Coordinator, 1982—. Mem. ABA (mem. litigation sect. trial evidence com. 1981—, vice chmn. real property sect. com on creditors rights in real estate fin. 1984—, vice chmn. real property sect. com. on real property law and needs of public 1984-85, chmn. real property sect. sub-com. on foreclosures in bankruptcy 1982—), Colo. Bar Assn. (conv. com. 1979—), Denver Bar Assn. (jud. adminstrn. com. 1978—), Am. Judicature Soc., Assn. Trial Lawyers Am., Colo. Trial Lawyers Assn., Law Club of Denver (sec. 1984-85), Phi Alpha Delta, Phi Beta Kappa. Democrat. Roman Catholic. Home: 10986 West 77th Ave Arvada CO 80005 Office: Brownstein Hyatt Farber & Madden 410 17th St Denver CO 80202

TISS, GEORGE JOHN, pediatrician, educator; b. Weiser, Idaho, Aug. 24, 1925; s. George Joseph and Mildred Gwendolyn (Barham) T.; m. Catherine Cassady, June 6, 1968; children: Randy, Carolyn, Danny, Mary, Andy. BS, U. Oreg., 1950, MD, 1954. Diplomate Am. Bd. Pediatrics. Intern U. Oreg. Hosps. and Clinics, Portland, 1954-55; resident in pediatrics 1955-57; practice medicine specializing in pediatrics Visalia (Calif.) Med. Clinic, 1957—, chmn. bd., 1959-70; specialist Care Medico, Malaysia, 1969, Indonesia, 1976; specialist Managua, Nicaragua, 1979; cons. Keweah Delta Dist. Hosp., Visalia, Tulare (Calif.) Dist. Hosp., Tulare County Hosp.; chmn. 1st Rubella mass immunization program in U.S., Tulare, 1969; chmn. Visalia Comprehensive Health Planning Bd., 1973-74; mem. bd. consortium San Joaquin Valley, 1975—; co-chmn. Calif. Immunization adv. com., 1973-76, chmn., 1976-77, chmn. Toddler Immunization adv. com., Calif., 1983—; asst. clin. prof. pediatrics U. Calif., San Francisco. Mem. sch. bd. Liberty Sch., 1980—. Served with USAAF, 1945-46. Recipient Lyda M. Smiley award Calif. Assn. Sch. Nurses, 1981. Mem. AMA, Calif. Med. Assn., Tulare CountyMed. Soc. (pres. 1969-70), Am. Acad. Pediatrics, West Coast Allergy Soc., Los Angeles Pediatric Soc., Calif. Thoracic Soc., Am. Legion. Office: 5400 W Hillsdale Rd Visalia CA 93277

TITUS, (STEPHEN) JASON, interior designer, consultant; b. Canton, Ill., Apr. 11, 1938; s. Harry B. Titus and Marjorie A. (Lucas) Larson; m. Kay E. McWhirter, July 21, 1962 (div. June 1971). BS in Interior Architecture, U. Oreg., 1966. Entry and staff designer Design Ctr. Interiors, San Diego, 1966-68; staff designer Cricket Interiors, San Clemente, Calif., 1968-71, Cannell and Chaffin, Newport Beach, Calif., 1971-77, Erickson Assocs., Alhambra, Calif., 1977; owner, designer Jason Titus Interiors, Costa Mesa, Calif., 1977-86, Fullerton, Calif., 1986—; cons. North Orange County Interior Design Com., 1977—. Served with USAF, 1956-61. Mem. Am. Soc. Interior Designers (sec., v.p., edn. chmn. Orange County chpt. 1979-84, career day chmn. 1979-84). Democrat. Mem. Religious Sci. Ch. Avocations: weaving, pottery, adobe bldgs., landscape design and history. Office: Jason Titus Interiors 607 E Chapman Ave Fullerton CA 92631

TOAL, PIETER, civil engineer, city official; b. den Helder, Netherlands, Aug. 25, 1921; came to U.S., 1956; s. Petrus and Maartje (Aker) Tool; m. Matilde Maria Holstege, May 20, 1951; children—Paul, Marya, Rick, Inge. M.C.E., Tech. U., Delft, Netherlands, 1950. Registered profl. engr., Calif., N.D. Project engr. Morrison Knudsen, San Francisco, 1956-67; constrn. mgr. Bay Area Rapid Transit, San Francisco, 1967-77, Clean Water Program, San Francisco, 1977—. Bd. dirs. San Anselmo Elem. Sch. Dist., Calif., 1965-69; councilman Town of San Anselmo, 1974-86. Home: 48 Hawthorne Ave San Anselmo CA 94960

TOBA, H. HAROLD, entomologist; b. Puunene, Hawaii, Aug. 24, 1932; s. Jinsaburo and Haru (Uemae) T.; m. Matsuko Matsuura, Sept. 6, 1958; children: Wynne, Rhonda, Luanne. BS, U. Hawaii, 1957, MS, 1961; PhD, Purdue U., 1966. Entomologist Agr. Research Service, USDA, Riverside, Calif., 1965-74, Yakima, Wash., 1974—. Served with U.S. Army, 1952-54. Mem. AAAS, Entomol. Soc. Am., S.C. Entomol. Soc., Sigma Xi. Home: 771 Ames Rd Selah WA 98942 Office: USDA Agr Research Service 3706 W Nob Hill Blvd Yakima WA 98902

TOBER, GARY PAUL, lawyer; b. Lakewood, Ohio., Dec. 11, 1950; s. Norman Frederick and Eleanor Patricia (Koch) T.; m. Maria Tulele Seumalo, Apr. 28, 1980; children: Ilalia Anne, Brian Paul, Kevin Tulele. BA, Denison U., 1973; JD, U. Toledo, 1976; LLM, Washington U., St. Louis, 1982. Bar: Ohio 1976, Wash. 1983. Judge advocate USAF, 1977-81; tax cons. Touche, Ross & Co., Seattle, 1982-85; assoc. Carney, Stephenson, Bradley, Smith, Mueller & Spellman, P.S., Seattle, 1985—; mem. Wash. Council on Internat. Trade, Seattle, 1983—. Served to capt. USAF, 1977-81. Mem. ABA, Ohio State Bar Assn., Wash. State Bar Assn., Seattle-King County Bar Assn. Clubs: World Trade, Am.-Korea Trade (Seattle). Office: Carney Stephenson Bradley et al 2300 Columbia Center 701 5th Ave Seattle WA 98104

TOBIN, ALLAN JOSHUA, biologist; b. Manchester, N.H., Aug. 22, 1942; s. Maurice and Eve (Alter) T.; m. Elaine Munsey, Apr. 7, 1968 (div.); children: David, Adam; m. Janet Ruth Hadda, Mar. 22, 1981. BS, MIT, 1963; PhD, Harvard U., 1969. Asst. prof. biology Harvard U., Cambridge, Mass., 1971-75; asst. prof. biology UCLA, 1975-81, assoc. prof. biology, 1981-86, prof. biology, 1986—; sci. dir. Hereditary Disease Found., Santa Monica, Calif., 1979—. Recipient Faculty Teaching award UCLA Dept. Biology, 1979. Mem. AAAS, Soc. for Neurosci. Office: UCLA Dept Biology 405 Hilgard Ave Los Angeles CA 90024

TOBIN, HAROLD WILLIAM, lawyer; b. San Francisco, Apr. 7, 1922; s. Robert Douglass and Rita Mary (Lannon) T.; m. Julie DeLaveaga, Aug. 3, 1946; m. Shirley Ellen Traynor, Jan. 5, 1965; children: Douglas Michael, Kathleen, Harold William, Jr., Suzanne, Neil McKinley. Student U. San Francisco, 1940-42, U.S. Air Corp Aviation Cadet Sch., 1942-43; JD, U. San Francisco, 1946. Bar: Calif. 1949, U.S. Dist. Ct. (no. dist.) Calif. 1949, U.S. Ct. Apls. 1949. U.S. atty. War Crimes Trials, Manila, Phillipines, 1946-48; assoc. Hone & Lobree; assoc. Benjamin L. McKinely, 1951-53; ptnr. Jacobsen & Tobin, 1953-57, Tobin and Ransom, 1957-67; sole practice San Francisco, 1970-71, Antioch, Calif., 1971—. Mem. San Francisco Rep. County Central Com., 1949-51, 70-71; pres., VIP San Francisco Archdiocesan Council Cath. Men, 1958-59. chmn. Antioch Police Commn., 1977-81; sec. Bay Area Rapid Transit Citizens. Served with USAAF, 1942-43. Mem. ABA, Contra Costa County Bar Assn., State Bar Calif. (pres. conf. barristers 1957-58), Bar Assn. San Francisco (past dir.), Assn. Trial Lawyers Am. Club: Barristers of San Francisco (past pres.). Catholic. Home: 2100 Reseda Way Antioch CA 94509 Office: 2830 Lone Tree Way Antioch CA 94509

TOBIN, WILLIAM JOSEPH, newspaper editor; b. Joplin, Mo., July 28, 1927; s. John J. and Lucy T. (Shoppach) T.; m. Marjorie Stuhldreher, Apr. 26, 1952; children—Michael Gerard, David Joseph, James Patrick. B.J., Butler U., 1948. Staff writer AP, Indpls., 1947-52, news feature writer, N.Y.C., 1952-54, regional membership exec., Louisville, 1954-56, corr., Juneau, Alaska, 1956-60, asst. chief of bur., Balt., 1960-61, chief of bur., Helena, Mont., 1961-63; mng. editor Anchorage Times, 1963-73, assoc. editor, 1973-85, gen. mgr., 1974-85, v.p., editor-in-chief, 1985—; dir. Alaska Mut. Bank, Anchorage. Mem. devel. com. Anchorage Winter Olympics, 1984—, bd. dirs. Anchorage organizing com., 1985—; bd. dirs. Alaska Council on Econ. Edn., 1978-84, Boys Clubs Alaska, 1979-83, Anchorage Symphony Orch., 1986-87; mem. adv. bd. Providence Hosp., Anchorage, 1974—, chmn., 1980-85. Served to sgt. AUS, 1950-52. Mem. Am. Soc. Newspaper Editors, AP Mng. Editors Assn., Alaska AP Mems. Assn. (pres. 1964), Anchorage C. of C. (bd. dirs. 1969-74, pres. 1972-73), Alaska World Affairs Council (pres. 1967-68), Sigma Delta Chi (chpt. pres. 1947, state chmn. 1960), Phi Delta Theta. Clubs: Alaska Press (pres. 1968-69), Petroleum, Commonwealth North (Anchorage). Home: 2130 Lord Baranof Dr Anchorage AK 99517 Office: Anchorage Times PO Box 40 Anchorage AK 99510

TOBKIN, VINCENT HENRY, venture capitalist; b. Pelican Rapids, Minn., July 4, 1951; s. Henry Edward and Kathryn Mary (Johnson) T.; m. Christine Marie Anderson, Aug. 28, 1976; children: Gregory, Carolyn. BS, MS, MIT, 1973; MBA with high distinction, JD Harvard U., 1977. Elec. engr., cons. various cos., Calif., 1969-76; founder Kodon, Inc., Cambridge, Mass., 1971-73; mgmt. cons. MC Kinsey & Co. N.Y.C., 1976-79; mgmt. cons. MC Kinsey & Co. San Francisco, 1979-84, ptnr., 1983-84; v. p. Woodriver Capitol, Calif. and N.Y., 1984-; gen. ptnr. Sierra Ventures, Calif. and N.Y., 1984-; bd. dirs. Prospect Group, N.Y.C., 1984-85, Stratacom, Cupertino, Calif., 1985-; Lab Support Inc., Woodland Hills, Calif., 1985-. Editor:(mag.) Tech. Engring. News, 1969-73. Hughes PhD fellow, 1973. Mem. IEEE, Assn. Computing Machinery, Assn. Old Crows, Oceanic Soc., Tau Beta Pi, Eta Kappa Nu. Republican. Roman Catholic. Clubs: Lincoln's Inn (Cambridge), Hasty Pudding (Cambridge); Commonwealth (San Francisco). Avocations: scuba diving, skiing ,flying, running. Home: 2644 Webster St. San Francisco CA 94123 Office: Sierra Ventures 3000 Sand Hill Rd Bldg 1 Suite 280 Menlo Park CA 94025

TOBUREN, LARRY HOWARD, research physicist; b. Clay Center, Kans., July 9, 1940; s. Howard H. and Beulah (Boyd) T.; m. Lana L. Henry, June 16, 1962; children: Debra L., Tina L. BA, Emporia State U., 1962; PhD, Vanderbilt U., 1968. Research scientist Battelle Northwest Lab., Richland, Wash., 1967-80, mgr. radiology research, 1980—. Contbr. articles to profl. jours. Fellow Am. Phys. Soc.; mem. AAAS, Radiation Research Soc. Home: 226 Wallace Richland WA 99352 Office: Battelle Northwest Lab PO Box 999 Richland WA 99352

TODD, DAVID KEITH, hydrologist, educator; b. Lafayette, Ind., Dec. 30, 1923; s. Marion W. and Evangeline (Klinkel) T.; m. Caroline Lark, June 15, 1948; children: Stuart K., Brian W. B.S. in Civil Engring., Purdue U., 1948; M.S. in Meteorology, NYU, 1949; Ph.D. in Civil Engring., U. Calif.-Berkeley, 1953. Hydraulic engr. U.S. Bur. Reclamation, Denver, 1948-50; mem. faculty dept. civil engring. U. Calif.-Berkeley, 1950—, prof. civil engring., 1953—, chmn. div. hydraulic and san. engring., 1970-74; pres. David Keith Todd, Cons. Engrs. Inc. (planning, devel., mgmt. and protection groundwater resources), 1978—; cons. to UN, govt. and state agys. and industries. Author: Ground Water Hydrology, 1980, Polluted Groundwater, 1976; also numerous articles.; editor: The Water Ency., 1970, Water Publications of State Agencies, 1972, 76, Ground-Water Resources of the United States, 1983. NSF fellow, 1957- 58, 64-65. Mem. Am. Geophys. Union (pres. sect. hydrology 1964-68), Univs. Council on Hydrology (chmn. 1962-64), ASCE (Research prize 1960), Am. Meteorol. Soc., AAAS, Am. Water Works Assn. Research on frequency rainfall and floods, ground water flow theory, ground water pollution, sea water intrusion of ground water zones, recharge of ground water artificially, mgmt. of ground water resources, application of nuclear energy to water resources, underground storage of energy. Home: 2938 Avalon Ave Berkeley CA 94705

TODD, DOROTHY ANN, psychologist; b. Lexington, Ky., Mar. 30, 1940; d. Joseph Joplin and Jean (Johnson) T.; 1 child, Scott Halliday. BA, Wake Forest U., 1961; MSW, U. Denver, 1963, D in Psychology, 1983. Lic. social worker, clin. psychologist. Social worker U. Colo. Health Scis. Ctr., Denver, 1963-70, Contra Costa County Mental Health Clinic, Martinez, Calif., 1970-71; asst. dir. Denver Children's Home, 1971-78; psychologist Denver Pub. Schs., 1980—; pvt. practice psychology Denver, 1981—. Fellow Am. Orthopsychiat. Assn.; mem. Am. Psychol. Assn., Colo. Psychol. Assn., Nat. Assn. Social Workers, Colo. Clin. Social Work Soc. Avocations: travel, camping, horseback riding. Home: 2555 Dahlia St Denver CO 80207

TODD, ELEANOR FRANCIS, special education consultant; b. Astoria, Oreg., Apr. 4, 1913; d. Eric H. and Beatrice (Masten) Broman; m. William H. Todd, Aug. 20, 1938 (dec. Apr. 1980); children: William Eric, Michael. BA, U. Redlands, 1935; MA, U. Pacific, 1973. Social worker County Welfare Dept., San Bernardino, Calif., 1935-40, 47—; cons. deaf and hearing impaired, screening of new borns for hearing St. Joseph Hosp. and Dameron Hosp., Stockton, Calif. V.p. bd. trustees Lodi (Calif.) Unified Sch. Dist., 1981—; commr. Juvenile Justice and Delinquency Bd., San Joaquin, Calif., 1984—; mem. San Joaquin County Maternal and Adolescence Health Bd., 1980—. Recipient Susan B. Anthony award Edn. Status of Women Commn., 1982. Mem. Am. Speech Lang. and Hearing Assn. (life), Council of Exceptional Children (life, Teacher of Yr. 1970), Bus. and Profl. Women Club (pres. 1978-79, Woman of Yr. 1979), Delta Kappa Gamma (pres. 1979-80, Disting. Career/Profl. Service award 1985). Lodge: Soroptimist (pres. Lodi club, 1984-85). Avocations: travel, bridge. Home: 2208 Cabrillo Circle Lodi CA 95241

TODD, FRANK STURTEVANT, biologist; b. Colon, Panama, Aug. 25, 1942; s. Sturtevant and Pauline (Lucas) T.; m. Sherlyn Timmons, Mar. 12, 1966; children—Suzy, Joseph. B.A. in Biology, U. Mont., 1965. Curator of birds Los Angeles Zoo, Calif., 1966-72; corp. curator of birds Sea World, Inc., San Diego, 1972-85, corp. v.p. aviculture, 1985—; v.p., sr. research fellow Hubbs-Sea World, San Diego, 1983-84. Author: Waterfowl: Ducks, Geese and Swans of the World, 1979; Penguins, 1981. Recipient Headliner of Yr. in Sci. Div. award San Diego Press Club, 1983; U.S. Polar medal Antarctic Sci. Found., Washington, 1976. Profl. fellow Am. Assn. Zool. Parks and Aquariums; mem. Am. Ornithol. Union, Wilson Ornithol. Soc., Cooper Ornithol. Soc., Nat. Audubon Soc., Avicultural Soc. Am., Brit. Aviculture Soc., Internat. Wild Waterfowl Assn. (bd. dirs.), Am. Game Bird Breeders Coop. Fedn., Internat. Found. for Conservation of Birds (bd. dirs.), numerous others. Republican. Home: 8958 Kobe Way San Diego CA 92123

TODD, HARRY WILLIAMS, aircraft power plant assembly company executive; b. Oak Park, Ill., 1922. BSME, U. So. Calif., 1947, BS, 1948, MBA, 1950. With Rockwell Internat., Pitts., 1946-76, former v.p. ops.; pres., chmn., chief exec. officer, bd. dirs. The L.E. Myers Co., Pitts., 1976-80; with Rohr Industries, Inc., Chula Vista, Calif., 1980—, pres., chief operating officer, 1980-82, pres., chief exec. officer, chmn., 1982—, also bd. dirs. Served with U.S. Army, 1944-46. Office: Rohr Industries Inc PO Box 878 Chula Vista CA 92012

TODD, WILLIAM JAMES, aerospace researcher; b. Milw., Aug. 11, 1948; s. Sanford William and Marion Eleanor (Hass) T.; m. Linda Lucille Edgren, June 12, 1971; children: Anna, Kenneth. Student, U. Wis., Milw., 1966-67; BA, Valparaiso U., 1970; MA, Ind. State U., 1972; diploma in photointerpretation, Internat. Inst. Aerial Survey and Earth Scis., Enschede, The Netherlands, 1974. Research geographer Lab. Applications of Remote Sensing Purdue U., West Lafayette, Ind., 1972-73; application scientist Technicolor Graphic Services Inc., EROS Data Ctr., U.S. Geol. Survey, Sioux Falls, S.D., 1974-78; project mgr. Technicolor Graphic Research Ctr., Ames Research Ctr. NASA, Moffett Field, Calif., 1978-80; research analyst Lockheed Missiles & Space Co., Sunnyvale, Calif., 1980—. Contbr. articles to profl. jours. Active First Bapt. Ch. Los Altos, Calif. Mem. Am. Soc. Photogrammetry and Remote Sensing, Planetary Soc., Assn. Old Crows, Sierra Club, Gamma Theta Upsilon, Sigma Gamma Epsilon. Republican. Avocations: astronomy, hiking, urban history, canoeing, reading hist. novels. Home: 837 Gail Ave Sunnyvale CA 94086 Office: Lockheed Missiles and Space Co 1111 Lockheed Way Sunnyvale CA 94088

TODD COPLEY, JUDITH ANN, materials scientist and mechanical engineering educator; b. Wakefield, West Yorkshire, Eng., Dec. 13, 1950; came to U.S., 1978; d. Marley and Joan Mary (Birkinshaw) Booth; m. David Michael Todd, June 17, 1972 (div. June 1981); m. Stephen Michael Copley, Aug. 3, 1984. BA, Cambridge (Eng.) U., 1972, MA, PhD, 1977. Research asst. Imperial Coll. Sci. and Tech., London, 1976-78; research assoc. SUNY, Stonybrook, 1978; research engr. U. Calif., Berkeley, 1979-82; asst. prof. materials sci. and mech. engring. U. So. Calif., Los Angeles, 1982—; mem. task force Metals Property Council, N.Y.C., 1979—. Contbr. articles to profl. jours. Recipient Faculty Research award Oak Ridge (Tenn.) Nat. Lab., 1986,Brit. Univs. Student Travel award 1972, Brit. Fedn. Univ. Women award 1972; Kathryn Kingswell Meml. scholar 1972. Mem. AIME (research award, 1983), ASTM, Soc. Women Engrs. (sr.), Am. Soc. Metals Internat. (chmn. 1986—, council mem. materials sci. div. 1984—), Electron Microscopy Soc. Am., Assn. Women in Sci., Hist. Metallurgy Soc., Nat. Soc. Corrosion Engrs. (Seed Grant award 1983), Microbeam Soc., Microbeam Analysis Soc. Avocations: archaeometry, hiking. Home: 4029 Via Nivel Palos Verdes Estates CA 90274 Office: U So Calif Dept Materials Sci Los Angeles CA 90089-0241

TOENJES, DON ALAN, agricultural scientist, education, researcher, consultant; b. Los Angeles, June 22, 1931; s. Frederick William and Hilda Marian (Williamson) T.; BS, U. Calif., Davis, 1955; m. Virginia Marie Gayaldo, July 17, 1960; children: Carol Ann, Helen Marie, Kurt Alan. Farm advisor U. Calif. Coop. Extension, 1957—; cons. S.M.A.D.E.A. Project, Bou Salem, Tunisia, dairy industry in Taiwan, Republic of China; guest lectr. Chung Hsin U., Taichung, Taiwan, Chico State U. Mem. Rep. Presdl. Task

Force. Served with M.C., USN, 1956-57. Mem. Council Agrl. Sci. and Tech., Am. Inst. Biol. Scis., Am. Dairy Sci. Assn., Calif. Aggie Alumni Assn., N.Y. Acad. Sci., Alpha Gamma Rho. Club: Elks. Research on Calif. agr.; contbr. articles to profl. jours. Home: Route 1 Box 1551A Orland CA 95963 Office: PO Box 697 Orland CA 95963

TOEPKE, BARRY KARLYLE, public relations executive; b. Chgo., Sept. 19, 1960; s. Lyle Edwin Toepke and Karla Vee (Reynolds) Cave; m. Cinny Newman, Sept. 24, 1983. Student, Orange Coast Coll.; BA, Calif. State U., Long Beach, 1982. Communications coordinator Hyatt Hotels, Sarasota, Fla., 1982-84; v.p. Nann Miller Enterprises, Los Angeles, 1984—; guest lectr. mktg. to univs.; pub. dir. Theatre III, Hollywood, Calif., 1986; mktg. advisor vol. talent pool, Sarasota, Fla., 1984; pub. relations cons. Pub. Corp. for the Arts, Long Beach, 1981-82; asst. bus. mgr. Calif. State U. Theatre of Arts, Long Beach, 1981-82. Vol. Starlight Found. Republican. Avocations: sports, theater. Office: Nann Miller Enterprises Inc 1230 W 2d St Los Angeles CA 90026

TOFFEL, PAUL HASKELL, otolaryngologist, maxillofacial surgeon, educator; b. Los Angeles, Mar. 3, 1943; s. Harry and Estelle Charlotte (Kandel) T.; m. Beverly Diane Peterson, June 12, 1965; children—Nicole, Hope, Erica. Student Stanford U., 1961-62; M.D., U. So. Calif., 1968. Intern, Los Angeles County-U. So. Calif. Med. Center, 1968-69, resident in otolaryngology, 1969-73; practice medicine specializing in otolaryngology and maxillofacial surgery, Los Angeles, 1975—; mem. staff Daniel Freeman Med. Center, Centinela Valley Med. Center, Orthopedic, Verdugo Hills hosps.; clin. assoc. prof. U. So. Calif. Med. Sch., 1974—; mem. med. emergency team Los Angeles County Sheriff's Dept., 1973—; head facial plastics div., med. adv. com. Calif. Athletic Commn.; chief med. officer equestrian events 1984 Los Angeles Olympiad. Served to lt. comdr. M.C., USNR, 1973-75. Fellow Am. Acad. Otolaryngology, Soc. Mil. Otolaryngologists, A.C.S., Am. Acad. Facial, Plastic and Reconstructive Surgery; mem. AMA, Calif., Los Angeles County med. assns., Salerni Collegium. Office: 2080 Century Park East Suite 610 Los Angeles CA 90067 Office: 1808 Verdugo Blvd Suite 420 Glendale CA 91208

TOFTNESS, CECIL GILLMAN, lawyer, consultant; b. Glasgow, Mont., Sept. 13, 1920; s. Anton Bernt and Nettie (Pedersen) T.; m. Chloe Catherine Vincent, Sept. 8, 1951. A.A., San Diego Jr. Coll., 1943; student Purdue U., Northwestern U.; B.S., UCLA, 1947; J.D., Southwestern U., 1953. Bar: Calif. 1954, U.S. Dist. Ct. (so. dist.) Calif. 1954, U.S. Supreme Ct. 1979. Sole practice, Palos Verdes Estates, Calif., 1954—; dir., pres., chmn. bd. Fisherman & Mchts. Bank, San Pedro, Calif., 1963-67; dir., v.p. Palos Verdes Estates Bd. Realtors, 1964-65. Chmn. Capital Campaign Fund, Richstone Charity, Hawthorne, Calif., 1983. Served to lt. (jg.) USN, 1938-46, ETO, PTO. Named Man of Yr., Glasgow, 1984. Mem. South Bay Bar Assn., Southwestern Law Sch. Alumni Assn. (class rep. 1980—), Internat. Physicians for the Prevention of Nuclear War (del. 7th World Congress, 1987), Themis Soc.-Southwestern Law Sch., Schumacher Founder's Circle-Southwestern Law Sch. (charter). Democrat. Lutheran. Lodges: Kiwanis (sec.-treas. 1955-83, v.p., pres., bd. dirs.), Masons, K.T. Home: 2229 Via Acalones Palos Verdes Estates CA 90274 Office: 2516 Via Tejon Palos Verdes Estates CA 90274

TOGNERI, ENRICO NATALE, laboratory director, consultant; b. Lucca, Italy, Dec. 23, 1946; came to U.S., 1958; s. Alberto and Annies (Peranzi) T.; m. Cindy Jack, Aug. 14, 1969; 1 child, Marcello. AA, Santa Rosa Jr. Coll., 1971; BA, Sonoma State U., Rohnert Park, 1973; postgrad., U. Calif., Berkeley, 1973-74, FBI Nat. Acad., 1982. Criminalist Contra Costa County, Martinez, Calif., 1974-78; lab dir. Washoe County Sheriff's Dept., Reno, 1978—; instr. Truckee Meadows Community Coll., Reno, 1980—; cons. various firms, Sparks, Nev., 1982—; lectr. various locations, Sparks, 1980—; mem. Com. for Testing of Intoxication, Carson City, Nev., 1983—. Author: Nevada Drunk Driving Laws and Chemical Testing, 1984. Served with USN, 1967-68. Fellow Am. Acad. Forensic Scis. (sec. 1985, chmn. criminalistics 1986); mem. Am. Soc. Crime Lab. Dirs. (pres. 1984), Calif. Assn. Crime Lab Dirs. (pres. 1983), Calif. Assn. Criminalists. Democrat. Roman Catholic. Avocations: skiing, golf, fishing. Office: Washoe County Sheriff's Office PO Box 2915 Reno NV 89505

TOHILL, BRUCE OWEN, geologist; b. Chgo., Oct. 21, 1941; s. Kenneth Fay and Jane Fayette (Dickinson) T.; m. Merrily Jo McCann, Jan. 31, 1965; children—Damon, Kevin, Brian. B.S., U. Nebr., 1964, M.S., 1965. Geologist, Humble Oil & Refining Co., Kingsville, Tex., 1965-67, Amoco Prodn. Co., Denver, 1967-72, Pubco Petroleum Corp., Denver, 1972-73; ptnr. Peppard & Assocs., Denver, 1973-83, Basin Analysis Cons., Denver, 1983—. Contbr. articles to profl. jours. Adv. bd. dept. geology U. Nebr., 1981-85. Mem. Calif. Explorationists Group (founder), Rocky Mountain Assn. Geologists, Am. Assn. Petroleum Geologists (chmn. ho. of dels. 1983-84), Soc. Econ. Paleontologists and Mineralogists (pres. sect. 1975), Am. Inst. Profl. Geologists (bd. dirs. 1977, v.p. 1979), U. Nebr. Alumni Club (pres. 1976). Republican. Methodist. Lodges: Masons, Shriners. Home: 7519 Windwood Way Parker CO 80134 Office: Basin Analysis Cons Suite 201 609 W Littleton Blvd Littleton CO 80120

TOINTON, ROBERT G., construction company executive; b. 1933. BSCE, Kans. State U., 1955. With Martin Eby Constrn. Co., 1959-63, Hensel Phelps Constrn. Co., 1963-82; now pres. Phelps, Inc., Greeley, Colo. Served with USAF, 1956-59. Office: Phelps Inc 420 Sixth Ave Greeley CO 80632 *

TOKAY, RONALD NAYLAND, contract research and devel. company executive, consultant; b. South Bend, Ind., May 5, 1933; s. Emery A. and Sophie C. (Barna) T.; Marlene Marie Serritella, Jan. 29, 1954; children—Brenda Marie, Mark Nayland, Lori Lizabeth. B.S. in Bus., Miami U., 1955; M.B.A., George Washington U., 1970. Cert. profl. contracts mgr. Enlisted U.S. Navy, 1955, advanced through grades to comdr., 1969, ret., 1978; contract specialist Battelle Meml. Inst., Richland, Wash., 1978-85; cons., 1985—. Mem. Nat. Contract Mgmt. Assn., Delta Sigma Pi. Roman Catholic. Clubs: Tri City Country, Clover Island Yacht (bd. dirs. 1981-83). Home and Office: 2615 S Fillmore Ct Kennewick WA 99337

TOKIOKA, FRANKLIN MAKOTO, investment company executive; b. Honolulu, Nov. 17, 1936; s. Masayuki and Harue (Fujiyoshi) T.; m. Suzanne M. Sears, Dec. 11, 1965; children: Franklin M. II, Dana M. BA, Williams Coll., 1958; MBA, Stanford U., 1960. Exec. v.p., sec. Nat. Mortgage and Fin. Co., Ltd., Honolulu, 1960—; sr. v.p., sec. Island Ins. Co., Ltd., Honolulu, 1969—; pres. Mut. Fin. Co., Ltd., Honolulu, 1971—, Nat. Securities and Investment, Inc., Honolulu, 1975—; bd. dirs. 1st Interstate Bank, Oceanic Cablevision, Inc., Honolulu, Intelect, Inc., Honolulu. Bd. dirs. Young People's Support Ctr., Honolulu, Boy Scouts Am., Honolulu, Sex Abuse Treatment Ctr. Recipient Silver Beaver award Boy Scouts Am., 1984. Clubs: Honolulu, Waialae Country. Home: 925 Waiholo St Honolulu HI 96821 Office: Nat Mortgage Fin Co Ltd 1022 Bethel St Honolulu HI 96813

TOKIOKA, LIONEL YUKIO, savings and loan executive; b. Honolulu, Sept. 7, 1934; s. Masayuki and Harue (Fujiyoshi) T.; m. Carole Hisako Saikyo, Aug. 11, 1962; children: Tyler, Darcie. BA, Kenyon Coll., 1956; MS, Columbia U., 1959. Sec. Internat. Savs. & Loan, Honolulu, 1963-68, v.p., sec., 1969-70, exec. v.p., sec., 1970-71, pres., 1971-78, chmn. bd. dirs., 1979—; chmn. bd. dirs. Internat. Holding Capital Corp., Honolulu, 1984—; mem. Hawaii Savs. League, Honolulu, U.S. League of Savs. Insts., Chgo.; bd. dirs. Am. Trust Co., Honolulu. Trustee Hawaii Maritime Ctr., Honolulu, 1985-86, Honolulu Theatre for Youth, Pub. Schs. of Hawaii Found.; mem. U. Hawaii Council Disting. Friends, Honolulu, 1982-83; campaign exec. com. St. Francis Hospice, Honolulu, 1986; chmn. Kuakini Med. Ctr., Honolulu, 1980-81, Hawaii League Savs. Insts., Honolulu, 1983-84; pres. U. Hawaii Found., 1980, Honolulu Japanese C. of C., 1982-83; bd. dirs. Fed. Home Loan Bank Seattle, 1978-80, Aloha Week Hawaii, Inc., Honolulu, 1983, Oahu Devel. Conf., Honolulu, Downtown Improvement Assn., Honolulu, Easter Seal Soc., Honolulu, Arts Council Hawaii, Honolulu, 1981-82, Am. Cancer Soc., Honolulu, Hanahauoli Sch., Honolulu, 1979-83, Aloha Sports Assn., Honolulu, Aloha United Way, Honolulu. Office: Internat Holding Capital Corp 1111 Bishop St Suite 515 Honolulu HI 96813

TOKUYASU, KIYOTERU, biologist; b. Nagasaki, Japan, Oct. 16, 1925; came to U.S., 1964; s. Suginobu and Gino (Honda) T.; m. Suzuko Kumagai, Nov. 3, 1957; children: Setsu, Taku. BS in Physics, Kyushu U., Fukuoka, Japan, 1949, PhD in Med. Sci., 1957. Assoc. prof. Kurume (Japan) U., 1956-58; chief designer Hitachi Naka Works, Katsuta, Japan, 1958-63; assoc. research pathologist UCLA, 1964-69; assoc. research biologist U. Calif. San Diego, La Jolla, 1969-73, research biologist, 1973-77, prof. in residence, 1977—. Contbr. articles to profl. jours. Mem. AAAS, N.Y. Acad. Scis., Histochem. Soc. Am., Electron Microscopy Soc. Am., Am. Soc. Cell Biology. Avocations: music, hiking. Office: U Calif San Diego Dept Biology B-022 La Jolla CA 92093

TOLAN, JOHN CLAIR, utility executive; b. Rockford, Ohio, June 9, 1950; s. Reid Manning and Agnes Ruth (Fleming) T. AA, Pensacola Jr. Coll., 1975; BSBA, City U., Seattle, 1980, MBA, 1984. Engring. technician Lee County (Fla.) Elec. Coop., Ft. Myers, 1976-78; engring. technician Clallam County (Wash.) Pub. Utility Dist., Port Angeles, 1978, adminstrv. aide, 1978-79, mgr. conservation, 1979-82, mgr. adminstrn., 1982—; instr. fin. City U., Seattle, 1984. Served with U.S. Army, 1968-71. Mem. Am. Pub. Power Assn. (personnel com. 1983-86, task force on productivity 1986), Northwest Pub. Power Assn. (conservation contracts com. 1981-82), Western Pub. Agys. Group. Club: Toastmasters (Port Angeles) (pres. 1984-85). Lodge: Rotary. Avocations: computers, reading. Home: 226 Orcas PO Box 3 Port Angeles WA 98362 Office: Clallam County Pub Utility Dist 2419 Hwy 101 E Port Angeles WA 98362

TOLENTINO, CASIMIRO URBANO, lawyer; b. Manila, May 18, 1949; came to U.S., 1959; s. Lucio Rubio and Florence (Jose) T.; m. Jennifer Masculino, June 5, 1982; 1 child, Casimiro Masculino. BA in Zoology, UCLA, 1972, JD, 1975. Bar: Calif. 1976. Gen. counsel civil rights div. HEW, Washington, 1975-76; regional atty. Agrl. Labor Relations Bd., Fresno, Calif., 1976-78; regional dir. Sacramento and San Diego, 1978-81; regional atty. Pub. Employment Relations Bd., Los Angeles, 1981; counsel, west div. Writers Guild Am., Los Angeles, 1982-84; dir. legal affairs Embassy TV, Los Angeles, 1984-86; sole practice Los Angeles, 1986—; mediator Ctr. Dispute Resolution, Santa Monica, Calif., 1986—. Editor: Letters in Exile, 1976; contbr. articles and revs. to Amerasia Jour. Chmn. adv. bd. UCLA Asian Am. Studies Ctr., 1983—; v.p. bd. dirs. Asian Pacific Legal Ctr., Los Angeles, 1983—; v.p. bd. civil service commrs., City of Los Angeles, 1984—. Mem. State Bar Calif. (exec. com. labor law sect. 1985—), Los Angeles County Bar Assn., Minority Bar Assn. (sec. 1984-85), Philippine Lawyers of So. Calif. (pres. 1984—, Award of Merit 1982). Democrat. Roman Catholic. Avocations: history, photography, travel. Office: 10351 Santa Monica Blvd Suite 406 Los Angeles CA 90025

TOLLEFSON, MICHAEL JOSEPH, national park superintendent; b. Seattle, Feb. 9, 1947; s. Harold I. and Emma T.; m. Judy A. Mosset. BA in Mktg. and Fin., U. Wash., 1970. Park ranger Katmai Nat. Monument, King Salmon, Alaska, 1973-77; dist. ranger Denali Nat. Park, McKinley Park, Alaska, 1977-79; chief naturalist V.I. Nat. Park, St. John, 1979-81; chief ops. Lake Clark Nat. Park, Port Alsworth, Alaska, 1981-83; supt. Glacier Bay Nat. Park and Preserve, Gustavus, Alaska, 1983—. Served to capt. USAR, 1971-78. Home: Barlett Cove Gustavus AK 99826 Office: Glacier Bay Nat Park and Preserve Bartlett Cove Gustavus AK 99826

TOLLEY, JOHN STEWART, state transportation administrator, urban planner; b. Greenville, Miss., Feb. 3, 1953; s. Frank Edward and Rachel Lee (Roberts) T. BA, U. Alaska, 1977; M in Urban Planning, Princeton U., 1979. Research asst. Princeton (N.J.) U., 1978-79; planner transp. Alaska Dept. Transp., Anchorage, 1979-81, mgr. statewide planning, 1982-84, chief of planning, 1985—. Mem. AIA, Am. Planning Assn., Transp. Research Bd. of Nat. Acad. Scis. (mem. various coms.). Avocations: travel, reading, hiking. Home: 1200 I St #416 Anchorage AK 99501

TOLMAN, KEITH GRANT, medical sciences educator, physician; b. Vancouver, B.C., Can., Oct. 23, 1941; s. Albert Samuel and Nora (Lawson) T.; m. Susan Dale Markland, Nov. 20, 1971; children: Rebecca Sue, Sarah Dale, David Keith. MD, U. B.C., Vancouver, 1966. Intern, then resident Baylor U. Coll. Medicine, Houston, 1966-68; resident U. Utah, Salt Lake City, 1968-70, asst. prof. medicine, 1972-76; resident U. Utah Affiliated Hosp., Salt Lake City, 1968-70; assoc. prof. U. Utah, Salt Lake City, 1976-85, prof., 1985—, chmn. gastroenterology dept., 1982—; vis. prof. medicine U. Queensland Brisbane, Australia, 1977; dir. drug research ctr. U. Utah, 1981—. Contbr. articles to profl. jours. NIH grantee, 1982—. Fellow ACP, Am. Bd. Internal Medicine, Am. Coll. Clin. Phamacology. Avocations: carving, painting, antique furniture, sports. Office: U Utah Sch Medicine Salt Lake City UT 84132

TOLZIN, KEITH W., superintendent schools; b. Sutherland, Iowa, Oct. 30, 1941; s. Ralph W. and Mable A. (Neisses) Heick T.; m. Leah M. Schultz, June 11, 1966; 1 child, Tara Lea. BA, Augustana Coll., 1964; MS, Utah State U., 1970; PhD, Walden U., 1983; edn. specialist U. Idaho, Moscow, 1985. Student living counselor S.D. Sch. for the Deaf, Sioux Falls, 1960-63; tchr. Nebr. Sch. for the Deaf, Omaha, 1964-65; tchr. Utah State Sch. for the Deaf, Ogden, 1968-69; asst. dir., audiologist Alaska Treatment Ctr. for Crippled Children and Adults, Inc., Anchorage, 1970-73; cons. Div. for Exceptional Children, State Dept. Edn., Juneau, Alaska, 1973-74; exec. dir. Alaska Treatment Ctr. for Crippled Children and Adults, Inc., Anchorage, 1974-76; spl. edn. dir. Matanuska-Susitna Borough Sch. Dist., Palmer, Alaska, 1976-77; supt. Idaho State Sch. for the Deaf and Blind, Gooding, 1977-86; asst. supt. Twin Falls (Idaho) Sch. Dist. 411, 1986—; prof. U. Alaska and Mat-Su Community Coll., 1970-77; cons. Alaska State Program for Deaf Long Range Planning, 1982; mem. adv. com. Office Demographic Studies, 1981-83; mem. adv. bd. Mountain Plains Regional Ctr. for Deaf-Blind, 1981-83, Idaho State Library, 1979-86. Bd. dirs. Walker Alcohol and Drug Treatment Ctr., Gooding, 1978-82; mem. Twin Falls Crime Prevention Council, 1986—; mem. adv. bd. State of Idaho 5th Dist. Dept. Health and Welfare; mem. long range planning com. Magic Valley Regional Hosp., 1987—. Named Boss of Yr., Anchorage Profl. Businesswomen's Assn., 1975. Mem Internat. Assn. Parents of the Deaf, Nat. Assn. Deaf, Con. Am. Instrs. Deaf, Conf. Edn. Adminstrs. Serving the Deaf (bd. dirs. 1982-86), Am. Printing House for the Blind, Idaho Assn. Deaf, Nat. Fedn. Blind of Idaho, Idaho Assn. Sch. Adminstrs. (2d v.p., pres. 1986-87), Idaho Assn. Spl. Edn. Adminstrs. (pres. 1984-86), Idaho Assn. Sch. Supts. (sec.-treas. region IV 1980—, pres. 1986-87), Idaho Tchr. Consortium (bd. dirs. 1977-82), Idaho Fourth Dist. Activities Assn., Gooding C. of C., Twin Falls C. of C. (chmn. membership drive com. 1987), Idaho Horse Show Assn., Phi Delta Kappa. Republican. Lutheran. Lodges: Rotary (Gooding) (newsletter editor 1978-79, dir. 1979-81), Kiwanis. Office: Sch Dist 411 201 Main Ave W Twin Falls ID 83301

TOM, CREIGHTON HARVEY, aerospace engineer, consultant; b. Oakland, Calif., Mar. 29, 1944; s. Harvey and Katherine (Lew) T. BS in Forestry, U. Calif., Berkeley, 1966; MS in Stats., Colo. State U., 1972, PhD in Computer Sci., 1978. Sr. environ. analyst HRB-Singer, Inc., Ft. Collins, Colo., 1977-78; staff scientist Sci. Applications, Golden, Colo., 1979-80; cons. Golden, 1981; scientist, specialist ConTel Info. Systems, Littleton, Colo., 1981-84; sr. staff engr. Hughes Aircraft Co., Englewood, Colo., 1984—; shuttle astronaut cand. NASA, Houston, 1980; cons. to companies and schs. Contbr. articles to profl. jours. Adviser CAP, Golden, 1981—. Served to maj. U.S. Army, 1966-67, with Res. 1967—. Decorated Bronze Star and Air medals, U.S. Army, 1967. Mem. Am. Soc. Photogrammetry, Mensa, Intertel, Sigma Xi, Xi Sigma Pi, Phi Kappa Phi. Republican. Methodist. Avocations: astronomy, fiction writing, photography, sci. fiction, survivalism. Home: 7951 S Cedar St Littleton CO 80120 Office: Hughes Aircraft Co 6251 S Ulster St Englewood CO 80111

TOM, LAWRENCE, computer graphics engineering executive; b. Los Angeles, Jan. 21, 1950; s. Tommy Toy and May (Fong) T. B.S., Harvey Mudd Coll., 1972; J.D. Western State U., San Diego, 1978. Design engr. Rockwell Internat., Los Angeles, 1972-73; design engr. Rohr Industries, Inc., Chula Vista, Calif., 1973-76, sr. design engr., 1980, computer graphics engring. specialist, 1980-83; pvt. practice design engring. cons., Los Angeles, 1975-77; sr. engr. Rohr Marine, Inc., Chula Vista, 1977-79; chief exec. officer Computer Aided Tech. Services, San Diego, 1983—; software cons. Small Systems Software, San Diego, 1984-85; computer graphics engring. specialist TOM & ROMAN, San Diego, 1986—; facilitator Computervision West Coast Users Group, 1986—; cons. in field. George H. Mayr Found. scholar, 1971; Bate Found. Aero. Edn. scholar, 1970-72. Mem. Aircraft Owners and Pilots Assn. Office: 7770 Regents Rd Suite 113-190 San Diego CA 92122

TOM, LYNNELL KA'OPUA A., social worker; b. Hilo, Hawaii, Dec. 11, 1952; d. William Kua and Eva Pearl (Medeiros) Akamu; m. Grifford Lynn Tom, July 2, 1983. BA in Sociology, U. Hawaii, Hilo, 1974; MSW, U. Hawaii, Honolulu, 1977. Adult service worker Hawaii Dept. Social Services and Housing, Honolulu, 1977, Kealakekua, 1977-79; social worker, licensing worker Hawaii Dept. Social Services and Housing, Honolulu, 1979-85; project dir. Ho'opaepae, Kanehoe, Hawaii, 1985—. Sec. Hawaiian Civic Club of Honolulu, 1983-84, bd. dirs. 1985—. Mem. Nat. Assn. Social Workers. Hawaiian Congregationalist. Home: 2434 Waiomao Rd Honolulu HI 96816 Office: Ho'opaepae Project 45-710 Keaahala Rd Kaneohe HI 96744

TOMASH, ERWIN, computer equipment company executive; b. St. Paul, Nov. 17, 1921; s. Noah and Milka (Ehrlich) T.; m. Adelle Ruben, July 31, 1943; children—Judith Freya Tomash Diffenbaugh, Barbara Ann. B.S., U. Minn., 1943; M.S., U. Md., 1950. Instr. elec. engring. U. Minn., 1946; assoc. dir. computer devel. Univac div. Remington Rand Corp., St. Paul, 1947-51; dir. West Coast ops. Univac div. Sperry Rand Corp., Los Angeles, 1953-55; pres. Telemeter Magnetics, Inc., Los Angeles, 1956-60; v.p. Ampex Corp., Los Angeles, 1961; founder, pres. Dataproducts Corp., Los Angeles, 1962-71; chmn. bd. Dataproducts Corp., 1971-80, chmn. exec. com., 1980—; chmn. Tomash Cons., Inc., cons. to high tech. industry; chmn. bd. Tomash Pubs., pubs. computer and physics works, Newport Corp., Fountain Valley, Calif.; dir. Supershuttle Internat., Inc., Los Angeles. Founder, chmn. bd. trustees Charles Babbage Found., U. Minn.; bd. govs. Coro Found., Los Angeles.; trustee Computer Mus., Boston. Served to capt. Signal Corps AUS, 1943-46. Decorated Bronze Star. Mem. IEEE (sr.), Assn. Computing Machinery, Am. Soc. for Technion (exec. v.p., dir.). Home: 110 S Rockingham Ave Los Angeles CA 90049 Office: Dataproducts Corp 6200 Canoga Ave Woodland Hills CA 91365

TOMASSON, HELGI, dancer, choreographer, dance company executive; b. Reykjavik, Iceland, 1942; m. Marlene Rizzo, 1965; children: Kristin, Erik. Student, Sigridur Arman, Erik Bidsted, Vera Volkova, Sch. Am. Ballet, Tivoli Pantomime Theatre, Copenhagen. Debut with, Tivoli Pantomime Theatre, 1958; with Joffrey Ballet, 1961-64; soloist Harkness Ballet, 1964-70; prin. dancer, N.Y.C. Ballet, 1970-85; artistic dir. San Francisco Ballet, 1985—; choreographer Ballet d'Isoline, 1983, others. Decorated Order of Falcon (Iceland), 1974; recipient Silver medal Internat. Moscow Ballet Competition, 1969. Office: care San Francisco Ballet 455 Franklin St San Francisco CA 94102 *

TOMBARI, HENRY ANTHONY, management consultant, business educator; b. Cohoes, N.Y., Oct. 1, 1928; s. Enrico Antonio Tombari and Lena Helen (Ghetti) Serfilippi; m. Josephine M. Martenis, Dec. 6, 1952; children: Henry A., Joseph H., John P. B in Engring. Sci., U.S. Naval Acad., 1952; BCE, Rensselaer Poly. Inst., 1956; MS, U.S. Naval Postgrad. Sch., 1967; D in Bus. Adminstrn., U. Md., 1975. Registered profl. engr., N.Y. Commd. ensign USN, 1952, advanced through grades to comdr., 1967; civil engr. Civil Engr. Corps USN, worldwide assignments, 1955-72; ret. USN, 1972; prof. bus. adminstrn. George Washington U., Washington, 1975-76, Calif. State U., Hayward, 1976—; pres. Tombari Assocs., Berkeley, Calif., 1973—; chmn. bd. dirs. Cafe Americain, San Francisco; bd. dirs. Cocolat, Inc, Berkeley, Original Candy Factory, Hayward. Author: Business and Society, 1984; contbr. articles to profl. jours. Vol. cons. Ctr. for Ind. Living, Berkeley, 1977-78; dir. project Hayward Ahead, 1980-86; research adv. Peace Officer Standards and Tng., Sacramento, 1985-86. Decorated Bronze Star with Combat V device. Mem. Acad. Mgmt., Nat. Assn. Security Dealers, Hon. Bus. Soc., Small Bus. Inst. Dirs. Assn., Issues Network Calif. (steering com. 1984-86). Roman Catholic. Avocations: hiking, golf. Office: Calif State U Dept Mgmt Scis Hayward CA 94542

TOMBERG, ROBERT BRUCE, dentist, real estate developer; b. Tacoma, Mar. 31, 1948; s. Robert Miles and Helen Abigail (Mauseth) T.; m. Jo Ann Brown (div.); m. Marlene Marie King, Aug. 11, 1981; children—Adam, Robert. B.S. in Pharmacy, U. Wash., 1971, D.D.S., 1976. Registered pharmacist, Wash. From stock boy to pharmacist Lakeside Drug, Bellevue, Wash., 1964-77; resident in gen. practice dentistry U. Wash., Seattle, 1976-77; gen. practice dentistry, Bellevue, 1977—. Mem. ADA, King County Dental Soc., Am. Assn. Function Orthodontists (charter), Am. Dental Soc. Anesthesiology, Am. Straight Wire Orthodontics Assn. Republican. Lutheran. Club. Bellevue Athletic. Home: 6005 Hazelwood Ln SE Bellevue WA 98006 Office: 5611 119th St SE Suite 2 Bellevue WA 98006

TOMBLESON, GARY EARL, educational administrator; b. San Diego, Sept. 2, 1937; s. Kenneth John and Bessie Lee (Coburn) T. B.A., San Diego State U., 1964; Ph.D., U. Calif.-San Diego, 1974. Assoc. adj. prof. Chapman Coll., Orange, Calif., 1968—, dean afloat edn., 1974-76; prof. humanities Armstrong U., Berkeley, Calif., 1986—, dean instrn., 1981-82, v.p. acad. affairs, 1982-86; instr. U. Calif. extension, Berkeley, 1981—. Recipient Disting. Service to Coll. award, 1975. Home: 1997 Oak St #6 San Francisco CA 94117 Office: Armstrong U 2222 Harold Way Berkeley CA 94704

TOMLINSON, JOHN LASHIER, materials engingeering educator; b. Salem, Oreg., Sept. 15, 1935; s. Arthur Lewis and Genevieve (Lashier) T.; m. Janice Marlene Cottrell, Aug. 17, 1958; children: Gina-Marie, Contessa. BA, Loma Linda U., 1958; MA, U. Oreg., 1961; PhD, U. Wash., 1967. Physicist Naval Ordnance Lab., Corona, Calif., 1960-63; research engr. Boeing Co., Seattle, 1963-64; research assoc. metall. engring. U. Wash., Seattle, 1964-67; research physicist Naval Weapons Ctr., Corona, 1967-69; prof. materials engring. Calif. State Poly U., Pomona, 1969—; instr. Chaffey Coll., Ontario, Calif., 1961-63; adj. prof. Loma Linda U. (Calif.) Dental Sch., 1970—; cons. Naval Ocean Systems Ctr., San Diego, 1971-78; sr. assoc. RSI Assocs. Inc., Claremont, Calif., 1979—. Contbr. articles to profl. jours.; patentee in field. Recipient Charles Babbage award Inst. Electronic Radio Engrs., London, 1976. Mem. Metall. Soc., Am. Soc. Metals, Am. Phys. Soc., Am. Assn. for Crystal Growth, Sigma Xi. Office: Calif State Poly U Dept Chem and Materials Engring Pomona CA 91768

TOMLINSON-KEASEY, CAROL ANN, psychology educator; b. Washington, Oct. 15, 1942; d. Robert Bruce and Geraldine (Howe) Tomlinson; m. Charles Blake Keasey, June 13, 1964; children: Kai Linson, Amber Lynn. BS, Pa. State U., 1964; MS, Iowa State U., 1966; PhD, U. Calif., Berkeley, 1970. Lic. psychologist, Calif. Asst. prof. psychology Trenton (N.J.) State Coll., 1969-70, Rutgers U., New Brunswick, N.J., 1970-72; assoc. prof. U. Nebr., Lincoln, 1972-77; prof. U. Calif., Riverside, 1977—, assoc. dean coll. humanities and social scis., 1986—. Author: Child's Eye View, 1980, Child Development, 1985; also numerous chpts. to books; articles to profl. jours. Recipient Disting. Tchr. award U. Calif., 1986. Mem. Am. Psychol. Assn., Soc. Research in Child Devel., Riverside Aquatics Assn. (pres. 1985). Office: U Calif Dept Psychology Riverside CA 92521

TOMORI, WILLIAM YUSUKE, neurosurgeon; b. Portland, Oreg., May 28, 1933; s. Frank M. and Martha M. (Takasugi) T.; m. Betty Tazuko Kimura, June 18, 1959. B.A., Reed Coll., 1954; M.D., U. Oreg., 1958. Diplomate Am. Bd. Neurol. Surgery. Intern, Los Angeles County Gen. Hosp., 1958-59; resident in neurosurgery Mayo Clinic, Rochester, Minn., 1961-66; practice medicine specializing in neurol. surgery, La Habra, Calif., 1966—. Served to lt. USN, 1959-61. Mem. Congress of Neurol. Surgeons, Am. Assn. Neurol. Surgeons. Republican. Home: 1711 Rocky Rd Fullerton CA 92631 Office: 1211 W Lambert Rd La Habra CA 90631

TOMPANE, MARY BETH, management consultant; b. Hollywood, Calif., Sept. 27, 1928; d. Richard Earl and Mary Elizabeth (McGregor) Goss; A.A., Phoenix Coll., 1948; postgrad. No. Ariz. U., Ariz. State U., 1946-55; M.Banking Mgmt., U. Calif., Riverside, 1973; m. Eugene F. Tompane, Nov. 4, 1950; children—Michael, Richard, Donald, John. Mgmt. analyst, 1955-69; dept. head Boswell Hosp., Sun City, Ariz., 1969-72; non profit orgn. cons., Phoenix, 1972—; travel agt., Phoenix and Tempe, Ariz., 1972-81; interim exec. dir. Girl Scouts U.S.A., from 1981; mem. nat. women's bd. Northwood Inst., 1980—. Pres. Maricopa County YWCA, 1962-65, Phoenix Day Nursery, 1965-67, Friends of Thunderbird, 1975-77; pres. Family Service Phoenix, 1980; Horizona chmn. Bicentennial City of Phoenix, 1974-76. Named Woman of Year, Phoenix, 1965. Mem. Internat. Assn. Vol. Edn., Dirs. of Vols., Am. Assn. Assn. Execs. Republican. Episcopalian.

TOMPKINS, DOUGLAS, apparel company executive. Pres. Esprit de Corps, San Francisco. Office: Esprit de Corps 900 Minnesota St San Francisco CA 94107 *

TOMPKINS, ROBERT EUGENE, psychologist; b. Fruita, Colo., July 27, 1942; s. Earl W. and Eleanor P. (Reed) T.; BS, Colo. State U., 1964; MA, U. No. Colo., 1966; EdD, U. S.D., 1973; m. Gayle Walters, June 17, 1967; children: Kirstin, Joshua. Psychologist, Winona State Coll., Minn., 1967-70, Yonngdahl Human Relations Ctr., Owatonna, Minn., 1970-72, Scottsdale (Ariz.) Pub. Schs., 1973-75, Mental Health Ctr., Billings, Mont., 1975-79, Billings Clinic, 1979—; dir. Neighborhood Counseling Center, Mental Health Ctr. Lic. psychologist, Mont. Mem. Mont. Psychol. Assn. (dir.), Yellowstone County Psychol. Assn. (sec.-treas., past pres.), Am. Psychol. Assn., Billings Blues and Jazz Soc. (past pres.). Democrat. Home: 3915 Laredo Pl Billings MT 59101 Office: Box 2555 Billings MT 59103

TOMPKINS, SUSIE, apparel company executive. Artistic dir. Esprit de Corps, San Francisco. Office: Esprit de Corps 900 Minnesota St San Francisco CA 94107 *

TOMPKINS-MCGILL, PATRICIA ANN LONGAN, social worker, administrator; b. Oklahoma City, Okla., Oct. 5, 1939; d. John P. and Dorothy Dee (Reynolds) Longan.; m. James Richard Tompkins, Nov. 24, 1962 (div. 1972); children: Timothy John, Mark Patrick; m. John Alexander McGill, Oct. 4, 1980. BA in Sociology, Tex. Tech U, 1960; MSW, Cath. U., 1965; PhD, U. Tex., 1980. Field instr. grad. social work program Our Lady of the Lake Coll., San Antonio, 1972-75; sr. social worker, asst. chief early childhood, social work supr. child welfare San Antonio Children's Ctr., Austin, 1975-76; field instr. faculty unit U. Tex., Austin, 1976-79; from instr. to asst. prof. and coordinator child welfare program Coll. of Santa Fe, 1979-82; exec. dir. Las Cumbres Learning Services, Los Alamos, N.Mex., 1982—; adminstr. various govtl. tng. grants Coll. Santa Fe and Las Cumbres. Mem. Council for Exceptional Children, Am. Group Psychotherapy Assn., Nat. Assn. Social Workers (cert., diplomate in clin. social work), Assn. Retarded Citizens. Democrat. Home: Unit 1 Box 4 Terrace Farm Rd Espanola NM 87532 Office: Las Cumbres Learning Services PO Box 740 Los Alamos NM 87544

TOMPKISON, SARA ANN, social worker; b. Geneva, Ill., Apr. 26, 1955; d. William Gee Kong and Gloria Iona (Paul) Wong; m. John Patrick Tompkison, June 21, 1980; 1 child, Andrew. BS, U. Hawaii, 1977, MSW, 1979. Med. social worker Home Health Care St. Francis Hosp., Honolulu, 1980—, St. Francis Hosp., Honolulu, 1985-86. Adv. mem. Cath. Social Services, Honolulu, 1980-84. Mem. Nat. Assn. Social Workers, Hawaii Pacific Gerontological Soc. Home: 3174 A Kaohinani Dr Honolulu HI 96817 Office: St Francis Hosp Home Care 2230 Liliha St Honolulu HI 96817

TOMSICK, GREGORY DEAN, buyer; b. Denver, Sept. 8, 1954; s. Michael Joseph and Gloria Jean (Henjes) T.; m. Lori Kay Fickes, Aug. 5, 1977; children: Justin, Jeremiah, Brittany. AS in Bus., Community Coll. Denver, 1974, AS in Acctg., 1975. Cert. Food Mktg. Mgmt., U. So. Calif., 1980. Merchandiser King Soopers, Denver, 1971-84; sr. buyer Pace Membership Warehouse, Denver, 1984—. Elder, Our Saviour Luth. Ch., Commerce City, Colo., 1975, pres., 1985-86, chmn. bd. stewardship, 1987. Mem. Am. Mgmt. Assn. Democrat. Home: 7924 Clarkson Ct Thornton CO 80229

TOMSKY, JUDY RACHEL, developer/fundraiser; b. Oklahoma City, Nov. 28, 1959; d. Mervin and Helen (Broude) T. BA in Liberal Studies, Sonoma State U., 1981; postgrad., Hebrew U. of Jerusalem, 1979-80. Internat. tour group dir. Kibbutz Yahel, Israel, 1981-83; telemktg. advisor, mktg. and advt. coordinator The Sharper Image, San Francisco, 1983-85; fundraiser Jewish Nat. Fund, San Francisco, 1985-86; br. mgr., acct. exec. Marin Express Ltd., Corte Madera, Calif., 1986; freelance property mgr. Sausalito, Calif., 1986—; freelance event coordinator, fundraiser 1987—. Democrat. Avocations: folkdancing, hiking, archaeology, world peace projects, earth stewards. Home and Office: 80 Rancho Dr Mill Valley CA 94941

TON, STEVEN EDWARD, manufacturing engineer; b. Inglewood, Calif., Dec. 31, 1951; s. Stanley Edward and Dorothy Grace (Paulicheck) T. BSE, U. Idaho, 1975; BS in Indsl. Tech., U. Calif., Long Beach. Supr. TRW Engring. and Devel.-Mfg. div., Redondo Beach, Calif., 1982-87, mgr., 1985—. Mem. ASME. Republican. Club: TRW Ski (Redondo Beach) (dir. competition 1985-87). Avocations: woodworking, waterskiing, snowskiing, basketball. Office: TRW Electronic and Def Mfg Div MS/1568 One Space Park Redondo Beach CA 90278

TONDREAU, BEVERLY FRANCIS, computerized teleprompting service executive; b. Los Angeles, Dec. 2, 1945; d. Thomas Francis and Beverly Green (Goodrich) Hanley; m. William P. Tondreau, Oct. 26, 1968 (div. Feb. 1971). B.A. in Art, Immaculate Heart Coll., 1967. Dir. rental promotions Compu-Prompt, Hollywood, Calif., 1984, v.p. ops., 1984—; reporter Nat. Pub. Radio, Washington; ind. producer various prodns., Hollywood, 1985—. Mem. Internat. Documentary Assn., Nat. Assn. Female Execs., Women in Film, Assn. Entertainment Industry Computer Profls. Democrat. Avocations: hiking; writing. Home: 152 N Irving Blvd Los Angeles CA 90004

TONELLA, CLAUDIA, former state official; b. Buenos Aires, June 30, 1933; came to U.S., 1957, naturalized, 1963; d. Carlos Cesar and Gabriela Matilde (Raggio) Pineiro; children: Andrea Roxana, Jessica Robin. BBA, Universidad Nacional de la Plata, Buenos Aires, 1955; MALS, Rosary Coll., River Forest, Ill., 1973, MBA, 1979. Tchr. Berlitz Sch., Winnetka, Ill., 1969-70; librarian Northwestern U., Evanston, Ill., 1970-73; purchasing mgr., asst. materials mgr. Materials Mgmt. div., mgr. cen. info. systems Ill. Tollway Authority, Oak Brook, Ill., 1974-84; dir. purchasing Lynwood (Calif.) Unified Sch. Dist., 1985-86, Palos Verdes Peninsula Unified Sch. Dist., Rolling Hills, Calif., 1987—. Bd. dirs., treas. Deerfield Crossing Condominium Assn., 1982-84; mem. South Bay Purchasing Com. Mem. Calif. Assn. Bus. Officials, U.S. Fencing Assn. Clubs: Western Riding. Home: 27900 Ridgebrook Ct Rancho Palos Verdes CA 90274 Office: Palos Verdes Unified Sch Dist 38 Crest Rd W Rolling Hills CA 90274

TONELLI, EDITH ANN, art gallery director, art historian; b. Westfield, Mass., May 20, 1949; d. Albert Robert and Pearl (Grubert) T. B.A., Vassar Coll., 1971; M.A., Hunter Coll., 1974; Ph.D., Boston U., 1981; grad., Mus. Mgmt. Inst. U. Calif.-Berkeley, 1981. Arts curriculum coordinator Project SEARCH, Millbrook, N.Y., 1972-74; curator DeCordova Mus., Lincoln, Mass., 1976-78; dir. art gallery, asst. prof. art U. Md., College Park, 1979-82, dir. mus. studies program, 1979-82; project dir. Summer Inst. Artists U. Md., 1981-82; dir. Frederick S. Wight Art Gallery, 1982—; adj. asst. prof. art UCLA, 1982—; reviewer pub. programs NEH, 1977—. Author exhbn. catalogs. Fellow Nat. Endowment Arts, 1981; predoctoral fellow Smithsonian Instn., 1979; doctoral and teaching fellow Boston U., 1974-76; mem. Helen Squire Townsend fellow Vassar College, 1971-72; recipient dissertation award Boston U. Vis. Com., 1979. Mem. Am. Assn. Museums, Coll. Art Assn., Women's Caucus for Art, Art Mus. Assn. Am. (advisor profl. tng.), Assn. Art Mus. Dirs. (trustee 1987—), Am. Studies Assn., Art Table Inc. Office: Frederick S Wight Art Gallery UCLA 405 Hilgard Ave Los Angeles CA 90024

TONELLO-STUART, ENRICA M., political economist; b. Monza, Italy, Dec. 20, 1926; d. Alessandro P. and Maddalena M. (Marangoni) Tonello; m. Albert E. Smith, May 14, 1947 (div. 1964); m. Charles L. Stuart, Feb. 14, 1975. BA in Internat. Affairs, Econs., U. Colo., 1961; MA, Claremont Grad. Sch., 1966, PhD, 1971. Med. asst. 1971-74, med. adminstr., 1974; sales mgr. Met. Life Ins. Co., 1974-79; pres. E.T.S. Research and Devel., Inc., 1977—; dir. internat. studies program Union U., Los Angeles-Tokyo, 1975-83; lectr. UCLA Extention, Union U. Pub., editor Tomorrow Online Journal, 1963—. Bd. dirs. Caesarea World Monument, Inland Empire, Los Angeles World Affairs Council; active Red Cross Gray Ladies' Service, 1955-58; organized first family assistance program Langley AFB Tactical Air Command, 1958-63; founder U.S.-China Journalists Fellowship Assn., 1986. Recipient vol. service award VA, 1950-55, ARC service award. Mem. Corp. Planners Assn. (treas. 1974-79), Investigative Reporters and Editors, World Future Soc. (pres. 1974—), Nat. Assn. Bus. Economists, World Future Soc., US-China Journalists Fellowship Assn. (founder, pres. 1984—), Los Angeles C. of C., Palos Verdes C. of C., Italian Heritage Found. (pub. relations agt.), Pi Sigma Alpha. Clubs: Los Angeles Press, San Francisco Press. Lodge: Zonta (chmn. internat. com. South Bay). Avocations: travel, research, writing.

TONEY, MICHAEL FOLSOM, materials physicist; b. Los Angeles, Calif., Nov. 26, 1957; s. James Andrew and Carol Marie (Folsom) T.; m. Carol Elaine Rudnick, June 17, 1978. BS, Calif. Inst. Tech., 1979; MS, PhD, U. Wash., Seattle, 1983. Data analyst Cosmic Ray Group, teaching asst. physics dept. Calif. Inst. Tech., Pasadena, 1978-79; research asst. physics dept. U. Wash., Seattle, 1979-83; NATO postdoctoral fellow Riso Nat. Lab., Roskilde, Denmark, 1983-84; mem research staff IBM Corp., San Jose, Calif., 1984—. Contbr. articles to profl. jours. Mem. Am. Physical Soc., European Physical Soc., Am. Vacuum Soc., Sigma Xi, Tau Beta Pi. Avocations: backpacking, skiing, running. Home: 950 Meadowood Dr San Jose CA 95120 Office: IBM Corp 650 Harry Rd San Jose CA 95120

TONG, RICHARD DARE, anesthesiologist; b. Chgo., Oct. 20, 1930; s. George Dare and June (Jung) T.; student U. Calif., Berkeley, 1949-52; M.D., U. Calif., Irvine, 1956; postgrad. U. Calif., Los Angeles, 1965-67; m. Diane Helene Davies, Apr. 12, 1970; children—Erin, Jason. Intern, Phoenix Gen. Hosp., 1956-57; resident in anesthesiology U. Calif., Los Angeles, 1965-67; practice medicine specializing in anesthesiology, Lakewood, Calif., 1967—; clin. instr. U. Calif. Sch. Medicine, Los Angeles, 1968—. Dep. sheriff reserve med. emergency team, Los Angeles County. Served with USNR, 1947-53. Diplomate Am. Bd. Anesthesiology. Fellow Am. Coll. Anesthesiology; mem. Am. Soc. Anesthesiologists, AMA, Calif., Los Angeles County med. assns. Democrat. Office: 3700 South St Lakewood CA 90712

TONG, SIU WING, computer programmer, analyst; b. Hong Kong, Hong Kong, May 20, 1950; came to U.S., 1968; BA, U. Calif., Berkeley, 1972; PhD, Harvard U., 1979; MS, U. Lowell, 1984. Research assoc. Brookhaven Nat. Lab., Upton, N.Y., 1979-83; software engr. Honeywell Info. Systems, Billerica, Mass., 1984-85; sr. programmer, analyst Hui Computer Cons., Berkeley, 1985—. Vol. tchr. Boston Chinatown Saturday Adult Edn. Program of Tufts Med. Sch., 1977-79. Muscular Dystrophy Assn. fellow, 1980-82. Mem. AAAS, IEEE, Assn. Computing Machinery. Home: 131 Chilpancingo Pkwy Apt 265 Pleasant Hill CA 94523 Office: Hui Computer Cons and Services Inc 1483 Campus Dr Berkeley CA 94708

TONG, TIMOTHY WAI-CHEONG, mechanical engineering educator, consultant; b. Hong Kong, Aug. 18, 1953; came to U.S., 1972; s. Chak-Yuen and Wai-Ching (Lee) T.; m. Esther Siu-Kuen, May 21, 1979; children: Ernest K., Patricia K. BS, Oreg. State U., 1976; MS, U. Calif., Berkeley, 1978, PhD, 1980. Teaching, research asst. U. Calif., Berkeley, 1976-80, jr. research specialist, 1980; asst. prof. U. Ky., Lexington, 1980-85, assoc. prof., 1985; assoc. prof. mech. engring. Ariz. State U., Tempe, 1986—; cons. Oak Ridge (Tenn.) Nat. Lab., 1983-85, Lockheed Palo Alto (Calif.) Research Lab., 1984—. Contbr. articles to profl. jours. Mem. ASME (assoc.), AIAA, ASTM, Soc. Automotive Engring. (Ralph R. Teetor Ednl. award 1985), Am. Soc. Engring. Edn. Office: Ariz State U Dept Mech Aerospace Engring Tempe AZ 85287

TONINI, LEON RICHARD, sales professional; b. Pittsfield, Mass., May 16, 1931; s. John Richard and Mabel Grayce (Rushbrook) T.; B.A. in Mgmt., U. Md., 1951; m. Helen Jo, Aug. 15, 1966; 1 son, John Richard, II. Enlisted in U.S. Army, 1947, advanced through grades to master sgt., 1968; service in W.Ger., Vietnam; ret., 1974; dir. vets. employment and assistance Non-Commd. Officers Assn., San Antonio, 1974-75; supr. security Pinkerton's Inc., Dallas, 1975-78; gen. mgr. civic center Travelodge Motor Hotel and Restaurant, San Francisco, 1978-85; sales representative Vernon Co, 1985—. Chmn. San Francisco Vets. Employment Com., 1981. Served as sgt. maj. Calif. N.G., res. Decorated Bronze Star; Republic Vietnam Honor medal 2d class. Mem. San Francisco Hotel Assn. (dir.), Non-Commd. Officers Assn. (dir. Calif. chpt.), Am. Legion, Regular Vets. Assn., Amvets, Patrons of Husbandry. Republican. Baptist. Club: Masons. Home: 205 Collins St Apt 9 San Francisco CA 94118 Office: Vernon Co 655 Ellis St San Francisco CA 94118

TONJES, MARIAN JEANNETTE, reading educator; b. Rockville Center, N.Y., Feb. 16, 1929; d. Millard Warren and Felicia E. (Tyler) Benton; m. Charles F. Tonjes (div. 1965); children: Jeffrey Charles, Kenneth Warren. BA, U. N.Mex., 1951, cert., 1966, MA, 1969; EdD, U. Miami, 1975. Dir. recreation Stuyvesant Town Housing Project, N.Y.C., 1951-53; tchr. music., phys. edn. Sunset Mesa Day Sch., Albuquerque, 1953-54; tchr. remedial reading Zia Elem. Sch., Albuquerque, 1965-67; tchr. secondary devel. reading Rio Grande High Sch., Albuquerque, 1967-69; research asst. reading Southwestern Coop. Ednl. Lab., Albuquerque, 1969-71; assoc. dir., vis. instr. Fla. Ctr. Tchr. Tng. Materials U. Miami, 1971-72; asst. prof. U.S. Internat. U., San Diego, 1972-75; prof. edn. Western Wash. U., Bellingham, 1975—; vis. prof. adult edn. Palamar (Calif.) Jr. Coll., 1974; reading supr. Manzanita Ctr. U. N.Mex., Albuquerque, 1968; mem. numerous coms. at Western Wash. U.; dir. summer study in Eng. at Oxford U., 1975—; speaker, cons. in field. Author: (with Miles V. Zintz) Teaching Reading/Thinking Study Skills in Content Classrooms, 2d rev. edit. 1987; contbr. articles to profl. jours. Mem. Am. Reading Forum (chmn. bd. dirs. 1983-85), Internat. Reading Assn. (travel interchange and study tours com. 1984-86, non-print media and reading com. 1980-83, com. mem. 1982-83, workshop dir. S.W. regional conf. 1982, 85), Nat. Assn. Primary Edn. (Eng.), Nat. Council Tchrs. English, United Kingdom Reading Assn. (speaker), PEO (past pres.), Phi Delta Kappa (nominating com. 1984, alt. del. 1982), Delta Delta Delta. Republican. Avocations: travelling, tennis, bridge, theatre, reading. Office: Western Wash U Dept Edn Bellingham WA 98225

TOOKEY, ROBERT CLARENCE, consulting actuary; b. Santa Monica, Calif., Mar. 21, 1925; s. Clarence Hall and Minerva Maconachie (Anderson) T.; BS, Calif. Inst. Tech., 1945; MS, U. Mich., 1947; m. Marcia Louise Hickman, Sept. 15, 1956; children: John Hall, Jennifer Louise, Thomas Anderson. Actuarial clk. Occidental Life Ins. Co., Los Angeles, 1945-46; with Prudential Ins. Co. Am., Newark, 1947-49; assoc. actuary in group Pacific Mut. Life Ins. Co., Los Angeles, 1949-55; asst. v.p. in charge reins. sales and service for 17 western states Lincoln Nat. Life Ins. Co., Ft. Wayne, Ind., 1955-61; dir. actuarial services Peat, Marwick, Mitchell & Co., Chgo., 1961-63; mng. partner So. Calif. office Milliman & Robertson, cons. actuaries, Pasadena, 1963-76; pres. Robert Tookey Assos., Inc., 1977—. Committeeman troop 501 Boy Scouts Am., 1969-72. Served to lt. (j.g.) USNR, 1943-45, 51-52. Fellow Soc. Actuaries, Conf. Actuaries in Pub. Practice; mem. Am. Acad. Actuaries, Pacific States Actuarial Club, Pacific Ins. Conf. Clubs: San Gabriel Country; Rotary (Pasadena); Union League (Chgo.). Home: 1249 Descanso Dr La Canada CA 91011 Office: 1249 Descanso Dr La Canada CA 91011

TOOLEY, CHARLES FREDERICK, communications executive, consultant; b. Seattle, Sept. 29, 1947; s. Creath Athol and Catherine Ella (Wainman) T.; m. Valerie Adele Gose, Mar. 7, 1981; children: Paige Arlene Higdon, Marni Higdon Tooley. BA, Lynchburg Coll., 1968. Producer, stage mgr., tech. dir. various theatre cos. and performing arts orgns., Ala., Fla., Va., N.Y., Ariz., 1965-74; field underwriter N.Y. Life Ins. Co., Billings, Mont., 1974-77; market adminstr. Mountain Bell Telephone Co., Butte and Billings, Mont., 1978-83; pres. BCC Inc., Billings, Mont., 1983—. Chmn. Mont. Arts Council, chmn. Dance/Drama Grants panel;mem. prodn. com. Billings/Yellowstone County Centennial; deacon Cen. Christian Ch., Billings, chmn. bd. trustees, 1983-85; mem. steering com. Mont. Inst. of the Arts Found.; del. regional assembly Christian Chs. in Mont.; dir. Mont. Dem. Exec. Bd., 1982—; sec., treas. adv. bd. Salvation Army, Billings. Dem. candidate Mont. Ho. Reps., 1986; mem. Billings Com. on Fgn. Relations. Served to sgt. U.S. Army, 1969-72, Vietnam. Recipient Gov's. Cup, Toastmasters Internat., Butte, Mont., 1978. Mem. Disciples of Christ. Lodges: Kiwanis (bd. dirs. 1981-85), Masons, Shriners, Elks. Avocations: theatre productions, political campaigns. Home: 502 Alderson Billings MT 59101 Office: BCC Inc PO Box 555 Billings MT 59103

TOOMBS, MICHAEL GENE, data processing manager; b. Nashville, Dec. 7, 1953; s. Paul Edward and Betty Jean (Wall) T.; m. Juanita Hunt, Aug. 5, 1978; children: Jason, Perry. BS in Bus., U. Tenn., Nashville, 1975; AS in Data Processing, Nashville State Tech. Inst., 1977. Programmer Advanced Data Systems, Nashville, 1977-78; programmer, analyst Creary Systems, Nashville, 1978-80, Tridon Inc., Smyrna, Tenn., 1980-83; systems mgr. Leprino Foods, Denver, 1983-84; data processing mgr. Assocs. Cash Express, Denver, 1984-87, Dallas, 1987—; prin. Creative Innovations, Aurora, Colo., 1983—. Active Denver Young Reps., 1984. Served with U.S. Army, 1972-74. Mem. Common User Group, Data Processing Mgrs. Assn. Baptist. Club: Meadowhills Men's (Aurora) (v.p. 1984-85). Avocations: golf, bowling, skiing.

TOOR, JASWANT SINGH, aerospace scientist; b. Sowaddi, Punjab, India, Sept. 12, 1938; s. Naginder Singh and Ind (Kaur) T.; came to U.S., 1965, naturalized, 1972; B.S. in Math., Punjab U., 1957, B.S. in Mech. Engring., 1961; M.S., Purdue U., 1967, Ph.D., 1971; m. Marlene Spiess; 1 dau., Jasbir Andrea Kaur. Lectr. mech. engring. Punjab Poly., Nilokheri, India, 1961-62; design engr. BBDO Power Plant Design Orgn., Punjab, 1962-65; research asst. mech. engring. Purdue U., Lafayette, Ind., 1966-67, 68-71, David Ross fellow, 1971-72; project engr. Lau Blower Co., Dayton, Ohio, 1967-68; project mgr. Stewart Warner Corp., Indpls., 1968; program mgr. Systems, Sci. and Software, San Diego, 1972-75; ind. cons., 1975-76; sr. scientist Sci. Applications Inc., La Jolla, Calif., 1976-81; program mgr. advanced research and tech. devel. (low observables/survivability) Convair div. Gen. Dynamics Co., San Diego, 1981—; cons. in field. Mem. AIAA, ASME, Soc. Advancement of Materials and Processing Engring., Combustion Inst. Registered profl. engr. Calif. Contbr. articles to sci. jours. on energy, energy conservation, infrared signature, devel. of new and renewable resources of energy, heat transfer and thermodynamics. Office: Gen Dynamics Convair Div 5001 Kearny Villa Rd San Diego CA 92123

TOPILOW, CARL S., symphony conductor; b. Jersey City, N.J., Mar. 14, 1947; s. Jacob Topilow and Pearl (Roth) Topilow Josephs; m. Carol Ruggiero, Dec. 14, 1970; 1 child, Jenny Michelle. B.Mus., Manhattan Sch. of Mus., 1968, M.Mus., 1969. Exxon/Arts Endowment Condr. Denver Symphony Orch., 1976-79, asst. condr., 1979-80; mus. dir. Denver Chamber Orch., 1976-81, Denver Youth Orch., 1977-80, Grand Junction Symphony, Colo., 1977-80, Colo. Philharm., Evergreen, Colo., 1978—; dir. orchs. Cleve. Inst. Mus., 1981—, conducting tchr., 1981—. Recipient Conducting fellowship Nat. Orch. Assn., N.Y.C., 1972-75, Aspen Mus. Festival, Colo., 1976; winner 1st place Balt. Symphony Conducting Competition, Md., 1976. Mem. Am. Symphony Orch. League.

TOPLIKAR, MICHAEL EDWARD, architectural firm executive; b. Los Angeles, May 29, 1950; s. William Anthony Jr. and Mary Louise (Arnold) T. Student, Cypress Coll., Woodbury U. Co-owner, founder Shirt Tale Stores, Los Angeles, 1971-73; owner, designer MTA Design, Newport Beach, Calif., 1973—; co-owner, v.p., chief exec. officer Medarch Inc., Los Angeles, 1985—; design dir., ptnr. Medcon Constrn., Los Angeles, 1985—; ptnr. MDE Resources, Los Angeles, 1986—. Mem. Los Angeles Arts Council, 1985—, Los Angeles County Mus. Art, 1982—. Mem. Inst. Bus. Designers. Office: Medarch Inc 2046 Cotner Ave 2d Floor Los Angeles CA 90025

TOPOL, LEO ELI, environmental scientist; b. Boston, Apr. 15, 1926; s. Samuel E. and Mary (Davis) T.; m. Pauline T. Horvitz, June 27, 1948; children: Marilyn B., Barry C. BS, Northeastern U., 1946; PhD, U. Minn., 1952. Mem. tech staff Oak Ridge (Tenn.) Nat. Lab., 1952-57, Atomics Internat., Canoga Park, Calif., 1957-61, Rockwell Sci. Ctr., Thousand Oaks, Calif., 1961-75; sr. mgr. program Environ. Monitoring and Services, Inc., Newbury Park, Calif., 1975—; reviewer Nat. Acid Precipitation Assessment Program-EPA, Raleigh, N.C., 1986—; vice chmn. quality assurance com. Nat. Atmos. Deposition Program, Raleigh, 1980-81, chmn., 1981-82. Author EPA lab. manuals; patentee in field; contbr. articles to profl. jours. Mem. Am. Chem. Soc., Air Pollution Control Assn. Home: 23435 Strathern St Canoga Park CA 91304 Office: Environ Monitoring and Services Inc 4765 Calle Quetzal Camarillo CA 93010

TOPP, ALPHONSO AXEL, JR., environmental scientist, consultant; b. Indpls., Oct. 15, 1920; s. Alphonso Axel and Emilia (Karlsen) T.; m. Mary Catherine Virtue, July 7, 1942; children—Karen, Susan, Linda, Sylvia, Peter, Astrid, Heidi, Eric, Megan, Katrina. B.S. in Chem. Engring., Purdue U., 1942; M.S., UCLA, 1948. Registered health physicist, N.Mex. Commd. 2d lt. U.S. Army, 1942, advanced through grades to col., 1966, ret., 1970; environ. scientist Radiation Protection Sect., State of N.Mex., Santa Fe, 1970, program mgr., licensing and registration sect., 1978, chief radiation protection bur., 1981-83; cons., 1984—. Decorated Legion of Merit, Bronze Star with 2 oak leaf clusters. Mem. Health Physics Soc., Conf. Radiation Control Program Dirs. (emeritus), Sigma Xi. Republican. Presbyterian. Club: Rotary. Home and Office: 872 Highland Drive Los Osos CA 93402

TOPPEN, DAVID LIVINGSTONE, engineering educator; b. Chgo., Jan. 11, 1944; s. William J. and Gladys M. (Cottam) T.; m. Nina Alexis Klein, Apr. 4, 1981; children: Jason, Monica, Erica. BS, Cornell Coll., 1965; PhD, U. Mo., 1970. From asst. prof. to assoc. prof. Calif. State U., Northridge, 1973-79, prof., 1979-86, univ. planner, 1984-86; v.p. acad. affairs Mont. Inst. Tech., Butte, 1986—. Author: Forth: An Applications Approach, 1985; contbr. articles to profl. jours. Chmn. adv. council Los Angeles Unified Sch. Dist., 1975-79. Recipient Devel. award Carnegie Corp. and InterUniv. Consortium Ednl. Computing, 1986; grantee Research Corp., 1974, NIH, 1980, Digital Equipment Corp., 1983, AT&T, 1985. Mem. IEEE, Am. Chem. Soc., Assn. Computing Machinery, Sigma Xi. Office: Mont Tech VP for Acad Affairs W Park Butte MT 59701

TORBERT, JAMES CARVER, architect; b. Montclair, N.J., May 25, 1950; s. John Keith and Kathelen (Flesch) T.; m. Diana Ross, Sept. 19, 1972; children: Alexander Ross, Jeffrey Eston. BArch, Auburn U., 1972. Registered architect, N.Y., Colo., Calif.; cert. Nat. Council Archtl. Registration Bd. Draftsman Haines, Lundberg & Waehler, N.Y.C., 1969-72; project mgr. Schuman, Lichtenstein, Claman & Efron, N.Y.C., 1972-80, MCB Architects, Denver, 1980-82; prin., v.p., health care facility planning Kentros Group, Inc., Englewood, Colo., 1982—. Chmn. Boulder County Task Force on Elderly Housing Options, 1984-85; mem. Denver Symphony Orch. chorus, 1984—, Colo. Opera Co., 1986. Mem. AIA (com. health architecture 1985—), Nat. Fire Protection Agy. Buddhist. Avocations: hiking, skiing, gardening. Home: 526 Aztec Dr Boulder CO 80303 Office: Kentros Group Inc 5200 DTC Pkwy Englewood CO 80111

TOREN, ROBERT, photojournalist; b. Grand Rapids, Mich., Oct. 9, 1915; s. Clarence J. and Helen (Holcomb) T.; student Winona Sch. Profl. Photography, 1957, West Coast Sch. Photography, 1959-62; m. Miriam Jeanette Smith, July 17, 1940. Photographer, Harris and Ewing, Washington, 1938-39, Versluis Studios, Grand Rapids, Mich., 1939-43, prodn. mgr., 1940-43; owner, photographer Toren Galleries, San Francisco, 1946-70; photographer Combat Tribes of World, Rich Lee Orgn., 1978-84, Darien jungle expdn. Am. Motors, 1979; feature writer Auburn (Calif.) Jour., El Dorado Gazette, 1983—. One man shows various univs.; prints in permanent collections: Photog. Hall of Fame, Coyote Point Mus., San Mateo County Hist. Mus.; photog. column San Mateo Times; lectr. Am. Pres. Lines, Coll. San Mateo, Peninsula Art Assn., Mendicino Art Center. Historian City of Foster City; vice chmn. Art Commn. Foster City. Trustee, West Coast Sch.; bd. dirs. Foster City Art League, Hillbarn Theatre, San Mateo County Arts Council; mem. art com. San Mateo County Fair, 1979—; coordinator, dir. Georgetown (Calif.) Mountain Mus., 1982—. Served from pvt. to staff sgt. AUS, 1943-46. Mem. Calif. Writers (br. pres.), Profl. Photographers Am. Presbyn. Author: Peninsula Wilderness. Illustrator: The Tainted Tree, 1963. Editor: The Evolution of Portraiture, 1965; The Western Way of Portraiture, 1965, Conquest of the Darien, 1984. Home: 3140 Cascade Trail Cool CA 95614

TORGENSEN, A(LLEN) BRENT, chemist; b. Richfield, Utah, Jan. 2, 1947; s. Morris Leaun and Donna Vee (Anderson) T.; m. Debra Peterson, Apr. 21, 1972; children: John Allen, Tiffani K., James Morris, Douglas E. BS, So. Utah State Coll., 1972; recert. secondary edn., U. Utah, 1978. Tchr. Sevier Sch. Dist., Richfield, Utah, 1972-73; analytical chemist Ford

Chem. Lab., Salt Lake City, 1974-75, supr., 1975-79; analytical chemist Utah Biomed. Test Lab., U. Utah Research Inst., Salt Lake City, 1979-81, group leader, 1981-84, project mgr., 1982—, sect. mgr., 1984—; prin. investigator Data Chem (formerly Utah Biomedical Test Lab.), Salt Lake City, 1985—. Cubmaster Boy Scouts Am, Murray, Utah, 1982—, scoutmaster, 1982. Mem. Am. Indsl. Hygiene Assn. Mormon. Office: Data Chem 520 Wakara Way Salt Lake City UT 84108

TORGERSEN, TOROLF ROBERT, research entomologist; b. Bklyn., Jan. 11, 1937; s. Bjarne and Kathinka Emilia (Christiansen) T.; m. Anna Gotschall Sperry, Jan. 20, 1962; children: Elizabeth Karen, Marianne Sperry, Christian Erik. BA, Syracuse U., 1960; BS, N.Y. State Coll. of Forestry, 1960; MS, U. Wis., 1962, PhD, 1964. Research entomologist Inst. No. Forestry, Juneau, Alaska, 1964-75, Forestry Scis. Lab., Corvallis, Oreg., 1975-83, Forestry and Range Scis. Lab., La Grande, Oreg., 1983—. Co-editor, writer Soggy Sneakers Guide to Oregon Rivers, 1980, 2d rev. edit., 1986; contbr. numerous articles to profl. jours. Active City Parks and Recreation Com., Juneau, 1969-71; coordinator Mountain Rescue Council, Juneau, 1972-75. Mem. AAAS, The Wildlife Soc., Entomol. Soc. Can., Entomol. Soc. Am., Sigma Xi. Avocation: whitewater kayaking. Home: 29471 NE Timberline Dr Corvallis OR 97333 Office: Forestry and Range Scis Lab Rt 2 Box 2315 La Grande OR 97850

TORGERSON, LEANN MARIE, elementary school principal; b. Everett, Wash., Oct. 19, 1942; d. Oscar Bernard and Geraldine Gertrude (Holcomb) Benson; m. Larry Ole Torgerson, Dec. 21, 1968; children: Rebecca Jill, Matthew Erik. AA, Everett Jr. Coll., 1962; BEd, Cen. Wash. State Coll., 1964; MEd, U. Wash., 1974; EdD, U. Seattle, 1987. Cert. elem. tchr., Wash. Tchr. pub. schs. Everett, 1964-79; prin. elem. sch., coordinator of elem. edn. Everett Sch. Dist., 1979—. Dist. com. mem. Pilchuck council Camp Fire, Everett, 1985-86, mem. exec. bd. Providence Hosp. Children's Assn., Everett, 1978-82. Grantee Rachel Royston Found. U. Wash., 1985, 86. Mem. Elem. Sch. Prins. Assn. of Wash. (mem. curriculum and instr. com.), Nat. Assn. Elem. Sch. Prins., Internat. Reading Assn. (1st v.p. local chpt. 1984-85), Phi Delta Kappa, Delta Kappa Gamma (pres. local chpt. 1972-73). Episcopalian. Lodge: Soroptimist. Avocations: reading, antiques. Office: Everett Sch Dist Adminstrv Ctr 4730 Colby Everett WA 98203

TORGERSON, LOIS GLOCK, hospital administrative dietitian; b. Appleton, Minn., July 3, 1928; d. Conrad F. and Hilda A. (Brodhagen) Glock; m. Glen O. Torgerson, Nov. 29, 1952. B.S., U. Wis., 1950. Intern Harborview Hosp., Seattle, 1951; diabetic dietitian Firland Sanitorium, Seattle, 1951-52; dir. women's residence halls dining room U. Idaho, Moscow, 1952-54; dietitian mgr. Wash. State U., Pullman, 1954-56; clinic dietitian Rockwood Clinic, Spokane, Wash., 1960-65; therapeutic dietitian Sacred Heart Med. Center, Spokane, 1959-61, chief clin. dietitian, asst. dir., 1961-72, dir. dietetic services, 1972—. Wis. Dietetic Assn. fellow, 1950. Mem. Am. Dietetic Assn. (registered dietitian), Wash. State Dietetic Assn. (past pres.), Greater Spokane Dietetic Assn. (past pres.), Am. Soc. Hosp. Food Service Adminstrs., Wis. Alumni Assn., Wis. Home Econs. Alumni Assn. Home: N 250 Raymond Rd C 12 Spokane WA 99206 Office: Sacred Heart Med Ctr W 101 Eighth Ave Spokane WA 99220

TORIO, MARY CAROL, dietitian; b. Bellevue, Iowa, Sept. 3, 1938; d. Robert A. and Marcella Frances (Even) Hayes; m. Louis F. Torio, Oct. 21, 1972. B.S., Iowa State U., 1960; M.S., Cornell U., 1964; M.P.A., U. So. Calif., 1978. Registered dietitian. Adminstrv. dietitian Stanford U. Hosp. (Calif.), 1964-66, edn. dir., 1966-67, dir. dietetics, 1967-75; asst. prof. Calif. State U.-Los Angeles, 1975-78; dir. food services Mary's Help Hosp., Daly City, Calif. 1978-84; asst. prof. San Jose State U., 1984-86. Mem. San Mateo County (Calif.) Nutrition Council, 1984-86. Mem. Am. Dietetic Assn., Calif. Dietetic Assn. (Disting. Service award 1981, treas. 1969-71, pres. 1975-77). Roman Catholic. Home: 711 Bowhill Rd Hillsborough CA 94010

TORME, MARGARET ANNE, public relations executive, communications consultant; b. Indpls., Apr. 5, 1943; d. Ira G. and Margaret Joy (Wright) Barker; children—Karen Anne, Leah Vanessa. Student Coll. San Mateo, 1961-65. Pub. relations mgr. Hoefer, Dieterich & Brown, San Francisco, 1964-73; v.p., co-founder, creative dir. Lowry & Ptnrs., San Francisco, 1975-83; pres., founder Torme & Co., San Francisco, 1983—; cons. in communications. Mem. Pub. Relations Soc. Am., San Francisco Advt. Club, North Bay Advt. Club (dir.), San Francisco C. of C. Office: 414 Jackson St San Francisco CA 94111

TOROK, LESLIE WILLIAM, circulation manager; b. Toronto, Ont., Can., Oct. 18, 1952; came to U.S., 1964; s. William and Helen Ramona (Konesky) T. BA in English, San Francisco State U., 1981. Tchr. Reading Guidance Ctr., San Francisco, 1980-82; circulation mgr. Antic Pub., San Francisco, 1982—; distbn. cons. Add-on Systems, San Francisco, 1984—. Avocations: music, film, ice hockey. Office: Antic Pub 524 2d St San Francisco CA 94107

TORRANO, STEPHEN JAMES, insurance company executive; b. Oakland, Calif., Dec. 31, 1948; s. Herman Joseph and Barbara (Uhl) T.; m. Paula Christine Lichtenberger, Feb. 14, 1975; 1 child, Alexander. BS in Engring., Cornell U., 1971. Cert. safety profl.; cert. ins. counselor. Loss control rep. Continental Ins., San Francisco, 1972-77; sr. loss control rep. Indsl. Indemnity, Walnut Creek, Calif., 1977-78; loss control mgr. Indsl. Indemnity, Boise, Idaho, 1978-83; account exec. Alexander & Alexander, Boise, 1983-86, producer, account exec., 1986—. Served with USN, 1971-77. Mem. Am. Soc. Safety Engrs., Bd. Cert. Safety Profls., Soc. Cert. Ins. Counselors. Republican. Avocations: tennis, racquetball, scuba diving. Home: 5334 Bainbridge Dr Boise ID 83703 Office: Alexander & Alexander of Idaho Inc 908 Jefferson Boise ID 83701

TORRES, ESTEBAN EDWARD, congressman, business executive; b. Miami, Ariz., Jan. 27, 1930; s. Esteban Torres and Rena Baron (Gomez) T.; m. Arcy Sanchez, Jan. 22, 1955; children: Carmen D'Arcy, Rena Denise, Camille Bianca, Selina Andre, Esteban Adrian. A.A., E. Los Angeles Coll., 1960; grad., Calif. State U., Los Angeles, 1963; postgrad., U. Md., 1965, Am. U., 1966; PhD (hon.), Nat. U., 1987. Chief steward United Auto Workers, local 230, 1954-63, dir. polit. com., editor, 1963; organizer, internat. rep. United Auto Workers (local 230), Washingtdn, 1964; asst. dir. Internat. Affairs Dept., 1975-77; dir. Inter-Am. Bureau for Latin Am., Caribbean, 1965-67; exec. dir. E. Los Angeles Community Union (TELACU), 1967-74; U.S. ambassador to UNESCO, Paris, 1977-79; chmn. Geneva Grp., 1977-78; chmn. U.S. del. Gen. Conf., 1978; spl. asst. to pres. U.S., dir. White House Office Hispanic Affairs, 1979; mem. 98th-100th Congresses from 34th Dist. Calif.; pres., chmn. bd. Internat. Enterprise and Devel. Corp., Washington; campaign coordinator Jerry Brown for Gov., 1974; Hispanic coordinator Los Angeles County campaign Jimmy Carter for Pres., 1976; mem. Sec. of State Adv. Group, 1979-81; v.p. Nat. Congress Community Econ. Devel., 1973-74; pres. Congress Mex.-Am. Unity, 1970-71, Los Angeles Plaza de la Raza Cultural Center, 1974; dir. Nat. Com. on Citizens Broadcasting, 1977; cons. U.S. Congress office of tech. assessment, 1976-77; del to U.S. Congress European Parliament meetings, 1984—; ofcl. congl. observer Geneva Arms Control Talks; chmn. Congl. Hospanic Caucus, 1987—; pres. Congl. Hispanic Caucus Inc. Found., 1987—; speaker Wrights Del. to USSR, 1987. Contbr. numerous articles to profl. jours. Bd. visitors Sch. Architecture U. Calif. at Los Angeles, 1971-73; bd. dirs. Los Angeles County Econ. Devel. Com., 1972-75, Internat. Devel. Conf., 1976-78. Served in AUS, 1949-53; ETO, Korea. Recipient various awards for public service. Mem. Americans for Dem. Action (exec. bd. 1975-77). Office: Room 1740 Longthworth Office Bldg Washington DC 20515

TORRES, JOSE LUIS, hospitality industry executive; b. Tlalpujagua, Michoacan, Mex., Apr. 30, 1936; came to U.S., 1959, naturalized, 1962; s. Rafael Magana and Rosa (Ynsense) T.; m. Nola Ellen Schultz, Dec. 3, 1957; children—Andrea Violet, Ted Jose. Student advanced mgmt. program, U. San Diego, 1977; student mgmt. program for execs., U. Pitts., 1979; student advanced mgmt. program, Harvard U., 1979. Various positions Holiday Inns, Inc., Memphis, 1962-74, sr. v.p. ops., 1974-80; sr. v.p. adminstrn. Harrah's, Reno, 1980-81; exec. v.p. internat., exec. v.p. ops. Ramada Inns, Inc., Phoenix, 1981—; also chmn. assoc. exec. com. Ramada Inns, Inc. Chmn. bd. trustees Phoenix Meml. Hosp., 1984—. Mem. Harvard Alumni Assn., Pitts. Alumni Assn., Nat. Restaurant Assn., Am. Hotel Motel Assn. (adv. council). Roman Catholic. Club: Ariz. Harvard Bus. (Phoenix). Avocations: golf; tennis; swimming. Office: Ramada Inns Inc 3838 E Van Buren Phoenix AZ 85008

TORTOLANO, J(AMES) VINCENT, lawyer; b. San Jose, Calif., Aug. 21, 1949; s. James and Celia Delores Tortolano; m. Joan Marie Sorci, Aug. 2, 1969 (div. June 1971); 1 child, James John. BSEE, U. Santa Clara, 1971; JD, U. Calif., Davis, 1983. Bar: Calif. 1983, U.S. Dist. Ct. (no. dist.) Calif. 1983, U.S. Patent Office 1984. Corp. atty. Advanced Micro Devices, Sunnyvale, Calif., 1983—. Mem. State Bar Calif. (intellectual property sect.), Peninsula Patent Law Assn., San Francisco Patent Law Assn., Santa Clara County Bar Assn. Democrat. Avocations: weightlifing, racquetball, music, film, reading. Office: Advanced Micro Devices Inc 901 Thompson Pl PO Box 3453 Sunnyvale CA 94088

TOSTI, DONALD THOMAS, training company executive, management consultant; b. Kansas City, Mo., Dec. 6, 1935; s. Joseph T. Tosti and Elizabeth M. (Parsons) Tosti Addison; m. Carol J. Curless, Jan. 31, 1957 (dec. 1980); children—Rene, Alicia, Roxanna, Brett, Tabitha, Todd Marcus. B.S. in Elec. Engring., U. N. Mex., 1957, M.S. in Psychology, 1962, Ph.D. in Psychology, 1967. Chief editor Teaching Machines Inc., Albuquerque, 1960-64; div. mgr. Westinghouse Learning Corp., Albuquerque, 1964-70; founder, sr. v.p. Ind. Learning Systems, San Raphael, Calif., 1970-74, pres., 1974-76; chmn. bd. Omega Performance, San Francisco, 1976-77; pres. Operants Inc., San Rafael, 1978-81; v.p. Forum corp., San Rafael, 1981-83; mng. ptnr. Vanguard Cons. Group, San Francisco, 1983—. Author: Programmer Arithmetic Series, 1960-63; Behavior Technology, 1970; A Guide to Child Development; Tactics of Communication; co-author: Learning Is Getting Easier, 1973; Introductory Psychology, 1981, Performance Based Management. Mem. Am. Psychol. Assn., Soc. Performance and Instrn. (v.p. research 1983-85; outstanding mem. award 1984, life membership award 1984, outstanding product award 1974). Home: 41 Marinita Ave San Rafael CA 94901

TOTH, ANTHONY WAYNE, chemist; b. Pueblo, Colo., Nov. 2, 1949; s. Anthony Joseph and Mildred Margaret (Mravich) T.; m. Diane Lynette Baumgartner, Aug. 16, 1975; children: Damian Alex, Chandra DeAnn. BS, So. Colo. State Coll., 1971; postgrad., Tex. A&M U., 1971-72, U. No. Colo., 1972-75. Teaching asst. U. No. Colo., Greeley, 1973-74; research assoc. Colo. State U., Ft. Collins, 1975; sr. level chemist U.S. Dept. Labor, Salt Lake City, 1975-81; analytical chemist Rockwell Internat., Golden, Colo., 1981-86; sr. scientist Rocky Mountain Analytical Labs., Arvada, Colo., 1986—; contract coordinator U.S. Dept. Labor, 1980-81; bd. dirs. Rocky Mountain Thermal Analysis Forum, Boulder, Colo., 1985-86. Contbr. articles to profl. jours. Mem. Am. Chem. Soc. Avocations: composing and performing contemporary and folk music, percussion instruments, hiking, exercise.

TOTH, MIKLOS GEORGE, psychologist; b. Szatmarnemeti, Hungary, Apr. 19, 1946; came to U.S., 1956; s. Miklos and Anna Maria (Klapka) T.; m. Josephine Ann (Jo-Ann) Wirth, Dec. 28, 1977; children: Miklos George III, Krisztina Annamaria. B.A., U. Calif.-Santa Barbara, 1969, M.Ed., 1971; Ph.D., Fla. State U., Tallahassee, 1974. Cert. sch. psychologist, Calif., Nev., Alaska, marriage and family counselor, Nev., substance abuse counselor, program adminstr. Counselor, Panhandle Alcoholism Treatment Ctr., Panama City, Fla., 1975-76; psychologist Bear River Mental Health Ctr., Logan, 1977-79; drug abuse coordinator Umatilla County Mental Health Clinic, Pendleton, Oreg., 1979-81; supervising psychologist State of Nev. Rural Clinics, Ely, 1981—. Bd. dirs. Umatilla County Sch. Guidance Assn., Pendleton, Oreg., 1979-81. Mem. Am. Psychol. Assn., Western Psychol. Assn., Nev. Psychol. Assn., Kappa Delta Pi. Roman Catholic. Lodge: KC. Home: PO Box 684 East Ely NV 89315 Office: PO Box 187 Ely NV 89301

TOTTEN, GEORGE OAKLEY, III, political science educator; b. Washington, July 21, 1922; s. George Oakley and Vicken (von Post) Barrois; m. Astrid Maria Anderson, June 26, 1948 (dec. Apr. 1975); children: Vicken Yuriko, Linnea Catherine; m. Lilia Huiying Li, July 1, 1976; 1 child, Blanche Lemes. Cert., U. Mich., 1943; A.B., Columbia U., 1947, A.M., 1949; M.A., Yale U., 1950, Ph.D., 1954; docent i Japanologi, U. Stockholm, 1977. Lectr. Columbia U., N.Y.C., 1954-55; asst. prof. MIT, Cambridge, 1958-59, Boston U., 1959-61; assoc. prof. U. R.I., Kingston, 1961-64; prof. polit. sci. U. So. Calif., Los Angeles, 1965—, chmn. dept., 1980-86; dir. East Asian Studies Ctr. U. So. Calif., 1974-77; dir., founder U. So. Calif.-UCLA Joint East Asia Ctr., 1976-77; vis. prof. U. Stockholm, 1977-79, dir. Ctr. Pacific Asia Studies, 1985—. Author: Social Democratic Movement in Prewar Japan, 1966; co-author: Socialist Parties in Postwar Japan, 1966, Japan and The New Ocean Regime, 1984; co-editor, author: Developing Nations: Quest for a Model, 1970, 75; co-translator: Traditional Government in Imperial China, 1982. Mem. U.S.-China People's Friendship Assn., Washington, 1974—; mem. Com. on U.S.-China Relations, N.Y.C., 1975—; chmn. Los Angeles-Pusan Sister City Assn., Los Angeles, 1976-77; bd. dirs. Los Angeles-Guangzhou Sister City Assn., 1982—; mem. council of dirs. Japan-Am. Soc. Los Angeles, 1981—. Served to 1st lt. AUS, 1942-46, PTO. Social Sci. Research Council fellow, 1952-53; Ford Found. grantee, 1955-58; NSF grantee, 1979-81; recipient Plaque for program on Korean studies Consulate Gen. of Republic of Korea, 1975. Mem. Assn. for Asian Studies, Am. Polit. Sci. Assn., Internat. Polit. Sci. Assn., Internat. Studies Assn., Japanese Polit. Sci. Assn. Presbyterian. Club: U. So. Calif. Faculty (Los Angeles). Home: 5118 Village Green Los Angeles CA 90016 Office: Dept Polit Sci U So Calif University Park Los Angeles CA 90089 also: Ctr Pacific Asia Studies, U Stockholm, Stockholm Sweden S-10691

TOTTEN, VICKEN YURIKO, physician; b. New Haven, Sept. 20, 1953; d. George Oakley and Astrid Maria (Anderson) T.; m. Paul Sheldon Preitauer, June 22, 1973 (div. Jan 1984); children: Collin Oakley Preitauer, Sanden Oakley Sheldon, Brendan Oakley Jordis. BA in Psychology, U. So. Calif., 1975; MD, Loyola U., Chgo., 1978. Diplomate Am. Bd. Family Practice; cert. neurolinguistic programmer. Intern East Tenn. State U., Johnson City, 1978-79; resident Merced (Calif.) Community Med. Ctr., 1982-84; staff physician Manteca (Calif.) Hosp., 1986—, Los Baños (Calif.) Community Hosp., 1986—; dir. dept. emergency medicine John C. Fremont Hosp., Mariposa, Calif., 1984-85. Served with USPHS, 1980-82. Fellow Am. Acad. Family Practice.

TOTTON, CARL ALLEN, II, rehabilitation counselor; b. Los Angeles, May 10, 1948; s. Carl Allen and Elva (Ezell) T. Student Calif. State U., 1976, BS in Rehab. Counseling, 1978, MS in Counseling, 1980; postgrad. Nova U., Ft. Lauderdale, Fla. Cert. rehab. counselor, Calif.; cert. sch. psychologist, counselor, Calif. Faculty mem. counseling psychology Sierra U., Los Angeles, 1982—; dir. Taoist Inst., North Hollywood, Calif., 1981—; dir., counselor Rehab. Counseling Assocs., North Hollywood, 1981-83; stress mgmt. cons., hypnotherapist. Recipient cert. of appreciation Los Angeles Pub. Library, 1975, Mcpl. Sports Program Los Angeles, 1976. Mem. Calif. Rehab Counseling Assn. (pres. 1983-84), Am. Rehab. Counseling Assn., Nat. Assn. Sch. Psychologists, Calif. Assn. Sch. Psychologists, Am. Sch. Counseling Assn., Am. Assn. Counseling and Devel. Democrat. Taoist. Club: Chinese Physical Health (Los Angeles). Editor: Tui Na: Chinese Healing and Acupressure Massage, 1984. Contbr. articles to mags. Office: Taoist Inst 10630 Burbank Blvd North Hollywood CA 91601

TOUR, ROBERT LOUIS, physician; b. Sheffield, Ala., Dec. 30, 1918; s. R.S. and Marguerite (Meyer) T.; Chem.E., U. Cin., 1942, M.D., 1950. Intern, U. Chgo. Clinics, 1950-51; resident U. Calif. Med. Center-San Francisco, 1951-54; practice medicine, specializing in ophthalmology, San Francisco, 1954-76, Fairbanks, Alaska, 1976-79, Phoenix, 1979—; mem. staff John C. Lincoln Hosp., Humana Hosp., Boswell Meml. Hosp.; clin. prof. ophthalmology U. Calif.-San Francisco, 1974-76. Served to maj. AUS, 1942-45. Diplomate Am. Bd. Ophthalmology. Fellow ACS, Am. Acad. Ophthalmology; mem. Ariz. Ophthal. Soc., Phoenix Ophthal. Soc., Calif. Assn. Ophthalmology, Contact Lens Assn. Ophthalmologists, Pacific Coast Oto-Ophthal. Soc., Pan-Am. Assn. Ophthalmology, AMA, Ariz. Med. Assn., Maricopa County Med. Soc., Assn. Research in Vision and Ophthalmology, F.C. Cordes Eye Soc., Sigma Xi, Nu Sigma Nu, Alpha Tau Omega, Tau Beta Pi, Alpha Omega Alpha, Phi Lambda Upsilon, Omicron Delta Kappa, Kappa Kappa Psi. Clubs: Masons, K.T., Lions. Shriners. Home: 1016 E Lois Ln Phoenix AZ 85020 Office: 755 E McDowell Rd Phoenix AZ 85006

TOW, MARC RAYMOND, real estate executive, lawyer; b. N.Y.C., Jan. 15, 1951; s. Benjamin and Stephanie (Cohen) T.; m. Joanna Pupos, Mar. 26, 1977; children: David Andrew, Stephen Michael. BA, SUNY, Cortland, 1973; JD, Western State U., Fullerton, Calif., 1975. Ptnr. Marc R. Tow & Assocs., Newport Beach, Calif., 1979-84; exec. v.p. CPE Engrs., Inc., Irvine, Calif., 1984-85; real estate advisor Brookstone Realty Advisors, Newport Beach, 1985—; bd. dirs. VTN Corp., Irvine. Mem. Orange County Dem. Found., 1985. Mem. Urban Land Inst., Internat. Council Shopping Ctrs., Bldg. Owners Mgmt., Mortgage Bankers Assn., Irvine C. of C. Democrat. Jewish. Clubs: Balboa Bay, Univ. Athletic (Newport Beach). Home: 300 Canal St Newport Beach CA 92663 Office: Brookstone Realty Advisors 3345 Newport Blvd Newport Beach CA 92663

TOWE, THOMAS EDWARD, lawyer; b. Cherokee, Iowa, June 25, 1937; s. Edward and Florence (Tow) T.; m. Ruth James, Aug. 21, 1960; children: James Thomas, Kristofer Edward. Student, U. Paris, 1956; BA, Earlham Coll., 1959; LLB, U. Mont., 1962; LLM, Georgetown U., 1965. Ptnr. Towe, Ball, Enright & Mackey, Billings, Mont., 1967-71; legislator Mont. House of Rep., Billings, 1971-75, Mont. State Senate, Billings, 1975-87; served on various coms. Mont. Senate, 1973-87. Contbr. articles to law revs. Pres. Alternatives, Inc. Halfway House, Billings, 1985-86; mem. adv. com. Mont. Crime Control Bd. 1971-78, Youth Justice council, 1981-83; mem. State Dem. Exec. com., 1969-71, Yellowstone County Dem. Exec. Com., 1969-73; bd. dirs. Mont. Consumer Affairs Council, Regional Community Services for the Devel. Disabled, 1975-77, Rimrock Guidance Found., 1975-80, Vols. of Am., Billings, 1984—. Served to capt. U.S. Army, 1962-65. Mem. Mont. Bar Assn., Yellowstone County Bar Assn., Am. Hereford Assn., Billings C. of C. Mem. Soc. of Friends. Club: Billings Friends Meeting (clk. 1982-85). Lodge: Optimists. Avocation: outdoor recreation. Home: 2739 Gregory Dr S Billings MT 59102 Office: Mont State Senate 2525 Sixth Ave N Billings MT 59101

TOWERS, BERNARD LEONARD, medical educator; b. Preston, Eng., Aug. 20, 1922; s. Thomas Francis and Isabella Ellen (Dobson) T.; m. Carole Ilene Lieberman; 1 child, Tiffany Sabrina; children by previous marriage: Helena Marianne, Celia Marguerite, Julie Carole. M.B., Ch.B., U. Liverpool, 1947; M.A., U. Cambridge, 1954. House surgeon Royal Infirmary, Liverpool, 1947; lectr. U. Bristol, 1949-50, U. Wales, 1950-54, Cambridge U., 1954-70; fellow Jesus Coll., 1957-70, steward, 1961-64, tutor, 1964-69; dir. med. studies 1964-70; prof. pediatrics UCLA, 1971-84, prof. anatomy, 1971—, prof. psychiatry, 1983—, convenor, moderator medicine and soc. forum, 1974—; co-dir. Program in Medicine, Law and Human Values, 1977-84; cons. Inst. Human Values in Medicine, 1971-84; adv. bd. Am. Teilhard Assn. for Future of Man, 1971—; v.p. Teilhard Centre for Future Man, London, 1974—. Author: Teilhard de Chardin, 1966, Naked Ape or Homo Sapiens?, 1969, Concerning Teilhard, 1969; also articles, chpts. on sci. and philosophy.; Editor anat. sect.: Brit. Abstracts Med. Scis, 1954-56, Teilhard Study Library, 1966-70; adv. bd.: Jour. Medicine and Philosophy, 1974-84. Served to capt. RAMC, 1947-49. NIH grantee, 1974-78; NEH grantee, 1977-83. Fellow Cambridge Philos. Soc., Royal Soc. Medicine; mem. Brit. Soc. History of Medicine, Soc. Health and Human Values (pres. 1977-78), Anat. Soc. Gt. Britain, Worshipful Soc. Apothecaries London, Am. Assn. for Study Mental Imagery, Western Assn. Physicians, Socièté Européenne de Culture Venise. Office: U Calif Ctr Health Scis Los Angeles CA 90024

TOWLE, STEWART WILLIAM, chemical company executive, metallurgical engineer; b. Tucson, Oct. 28, 1932; s. Louis Wallace and Mildred (Maeys) T.; m. Doris Reiner, June 5, 1955; children—Karl Stewart, Heidi Sue, Sharon Kay, Thomas William. Met.E., Colo. Sch. Mines, 1954; M.S. in Metall. Engring., U. Ariz., 1960. Engring. trainee Worthington Corp., Harrison, N.J., 1954-55; metallurgist, gen. plant foreman, asst. supt. Phelps Dodge Corp., Douglas, Ariz., 1957-71, rep. to Smelter Control Research Assn., N.Y.C., 1970-71; smelter supt., Morenci, Ariz., 1971-79; v.p. Apache Powder Co., Benson, Ariz., 1979-80, pres., chief exec. officer, 1980—; bd. dirs. Inst. Makers of Explosives, Washington, AMIGOS, Mining Suppliers Trade Assn., Phoenix. Bd. dirs. Catalina council Boy Scouts Am., Tucson, 1967-70, 80-83, dist. chmn. Cochise South dist., 1970-71, 1st v.p., 1986; pres. Town of Benson Indsl. Devel. Authority, 1983—; bd. dirs. Cochise Coll. Found., 1983—, pres. 1986-87; bd. dirs. Cochise County Indsl. Devel. Authority, 1984—; 48th Ariz. Town Hall, Ariz. Acad., 1986—. Served to 1st lt. U.S. Army, 1955-57, Germany. Ariz. State scholar Colo. Sch. Mines, 1950. Mem. Benson C. of C. (bd. dirs. 1980-86, pres. 1982-83), AIME (subsect. chmn. 1972-73, chmn. extractive metallurgy com. 1978). Republican. Clubs: Mining of Southwest (Tucson), Plaza. Lodges: Rotary (pres. 1986-87), Elks. Home: PO Box 1117 Benson AZ 85602 Office: Apache Powder Co PO Box 700 Benson AZ 85602

TOWNE, DOROTHEA ALICE, III, chiropractor; b. Easton, Ill., Feb. 1, 1910; d. Elnathan and Fairy Alice (Downey) T. D.C., Cleveland Chiropractic Coll., Los Angeles, 1954, Ph.C., 1955, B.S., 1977; student U. Wash., 1928-30; B.A. magna cum laude, U. So. Calif., 1946. Indsl. relations dir. Standard Paper Box Corp., Los Angeles, 1943-54; asso. dean acad. affairs Cleveland Chiropractic Coll., 1956-75, dean, tchr., 1976-82, dir. clin. scis., 1972-78, emerita, 1981—; naturopath, 1986—; lectr. in field; numerous radio and TV appearances. Composer: (with L. Mayberry) The Presidents Parade. Contbr. to poetry anthologies. Recipient numerous awards including appreciation award San Francisco Bay Research Assn., C.S. Cleveland, Sr., award for outstanding service, 1984. Fellow Internat. Chiropractors Assn., Idaho Assn. Naturopathic Physicians (bd. dirs. 1986), Gamma Phi Beta, Psi Chi, Sigma Chi Psi. Address: E 508 Eaton Ave Spokane WA 99218

TOWNER, HOWARD FROST, biologist, educator; b. Los Angeles, Aug. 10, 1943; s. Leonard Wimberley and Caroline Warren (Frost) T.; m. Linda Lorraine Pardee, Aug. 25, 1977; children: Mary, Elizabeth. AB, U. Calif., Riverside, 1965; PhD, Stanford U., 1970. Prof. biology Loyola Marymount U., Los Angeles, 1972—; cons. PCR, Santa Monica, Calif., 1971—. Bd. dirs. Friends of Ballona Wetlands, Los Angeles, 1977—. Mem. Ecol. Soc. Am., Am. Soc. Mammalogists, Calif. Bot. Soc., Phi Beta Kappa, Sigma Xi. Home: 8114 Westlawn Ave Los Angeles CA 90045 Office: Loyola Marymount U Dept Biology 7101 W 80th St Los Angeles CA 90045

TOWNER, LARRY EDWIN, transportation company executive; b. Gallup, N.Mex., Sept. 27, 1937; s. Edwin Robert and Esther Kathryn (Kern) T.; m. D. Yvonne Turner, Mar. 12, 1966; children: Kristina Kay, Jennifer Kate. BS in Tech. Mgmt., Am. U., Washington, 1976. Project mgr. Wolf Research, Houston, 1965-66, Gultom SRG, Arlington, Va., 1966-67; dep. for database devel. USN, Washington, 1967-79; mgr., BTP teleprocessing RCA, Cherry Hill, N.J., 1979-80; mgr., data base adminstrn., solid state div. RCA, Somerville, N.J., 1980-82; mgr., systems devel. Hughes Aircraft, El Segundo, Calif., 1982—. Author: Ads/Online Cookbook, 1986; contbr. articles to profl. jours. Treas. Va. Hills Recreation Assn., Alexandria, 1970-72, pres. 1975-77; active Civil Air Patrol, Alexandria, 1968-79; bd. dirs. Northwest Citizens Radio Emergency Service, Spokane, Wash., 1960-63. Recipient Meritorious Service award Civil Air Patrol, 1976. Mem. IDMS User Assn. (bd. dirs.) (Outstanding Service award, 1984), Hughes Mgmt. Club, Amateur Radio Relay League. Methodist. Avocations: flying, computers, amateur radio. Home: 8702 Delray Circle Westminster CA 92683 Office: Hughes Aircraft Co Bldg E12/C170 PO Box 902 El Segundo CA 90245

TOWNES, CHARLES HARD, physics educator; b. Greenville, S.C., July 28, 1915; s. Henry Keith and Ellen Sumter (Hard) T.; m. Frances H. Brown, May 4, 1941; children: Linda Lewis, Ellen Screven, Carla Keith, Holly Robinson. B.A., B.S., Furman U., 1935; M.A., Duke U., 1937; Ph.D., Calif. Inst. Tech., 1939. Mem. tech. staff Bell Telephone Lab., 1939-47; asso. prof. physics Columbia U., 1948-50, prof. physics, 1950-61; exec. dir. Columbia Radiation Lab., 1950-52, chmn. physics dept., 1952-55; provost and prof. physics Mass. Inst. Tech., 1961-66, Inst. prof., 1966-67; v.p., dir. research Inst. Def. Analyses, Washington, 1959-61; Univ. prof. U. Calif. at Berkeley, 1967—; Guggenheim fellow, 1955-56; Fulbright lectr. U. Paris, 1955-56, U. Tokyo, 1956; lectr., 1955, 60; dir. Enrico Fermi Internat. Sch. Physics, 1963; Richtmeyer lectr. Am. Phys. Soc., 1959; Scott lectr. U. Cambridge, 1963; Centennial lectr. U. Toronto, 1967; Lincoln lectr., 1972-73, Halley lectr.,

1976; dir. Gen. Motors Corp.; mem. Pres.'s Sci. Adv. Com., 1966-69, vice chmn., 1967-69; chmn. sci. and tech. adv. com. for manned space flight NASA, 1964-69; mem. Pres.'s Com. on Sci. and Tech., 1976. Author: (with A.L. Schawlow) Microwave Spectroscopy, 1955; author, co-editor: Quantum Electronics, 1960, Quantum Electronics and Coherent Light, 1964; editorial bd.: (with A.L. Schawlow) Rev. Sci. Instrument, 1950-52, Phys. Rev, 1951-53; bd.: (with A.L. Schawlow) Phys., Rev, 1951-53, Jour. Molecular Spectroscopy, 1957-60, Procs. Nat. Acad. Scis, 1978—; contbr. articles to sci. publs. Trustee Calif. Inst. Tech., Carnegie Instn. of Washington, Pacific Sch. Religion; mem. corp. Woods Hole Oceanographic Instn. Recipient numerous hon. degrees and awards, including; Nobel prize for physics, 1964; Stuart Ballantine medal Franklin Inst., 1959, 62; Thomas Young medal and prize Inst. Physics and Phys. Soc., Eng., 1963; Disting. Public Service medal NASA, 1969; Wilhelm Exner award Austria, 1970; Niels Bohr Internat. Gold medal, 1979; Nat. Sci. medal, 1983; named to Nat. Inventors Hall of Fame, 1976, Engring. and Sci. Hall of Fame, 1983. Fellow Am. Phys. Soc. (council 1959-62, 65-71, pres. 1967, Plyler prize 1977), Optical Soc. Am. (hon., Mees medal 1968), IEEE (medal of honor 1967), Calif. Acad. Scis.; mem. Am. Philos. Soc., Am. Astron. Soc., Am. Acad. Arts and Scis., Nat. Acad. Scis. (council 1969-72, 78-81, chmn. space sci. bd. 1970-73, Comstock award 1959), Société Française de Physique (council 1956-58), Royal Soc. (fgn.), Pontifical Acad. Scis. Patentee masers and lasers; research nuclear and molecular structure, quantum electronics, interstellar molecules, radio and infrared astrophysics. Office: Dept Physics U Calif at Berkeley Berkeley CA 94720

TOWNSEND, JEFFREY FRED, winery executive, infosystems specialist; b. Bklyn., Aug. 20, 1953; s. Richard F. Townsend and Blanche Horgan; m. Jan M. Pathroff, Nov. 25, 1984. BS in Acctg., Rider Coll., 1975; MBA in Fin., Fairleigh Dickinson U., Madison, N.J., 1978. Project mgr. IMS Internat., N.Y.C., 1976-79; dir. research Dun and Bradstreet, N.Y.C., 1979-80, dir. mgmt. info. systems, 1980-83; mgmt. cons. N.Y.C., 1983-84; dir. info. resources Gallo Winery, Modesto, Calif., 1984—. Mem. Data Processing Mgmt. Assn., Am. Info. Assn., Assn. for Computing Machinery, Assn. Systems Mgmt. (speaker), Food Mktg. Inst. Avocation: golf. Home: 2624 Nassau Circle Modesto CA 95355 Office: Gallo Winery PO Box 1130 Modesto CA 95351

TOWNSEND, JOHN HOLT, electronics engineer; b. Chgo., July 15, 1947; s. J. Russell and Virginia Kathern (Holt) T.; m. Susan Elaine Rogers, May 1, 1976. BSEE with honors, Purdue U., 1969. Registered profl. engr., Ind.; ordained to ministry Bible Therapy Ch., 1987. Electronics engr. Naval Ocean Systems Ctr., San Diego, 1971—. Author: Project Manager's Guide, 1977, Suggestions for Designers of Navy Electronic Equipment, 1985; contbr. articles to profl. jours.; inventor protective communications helmet. Sec. Peninsula Community Planning Bd., San Diego, 1983—; religious vol. Met. Correctional Ctr., San Diego, 1983—; mem. San Diego County Jail Ministries, 1978—; deacon Christ Ctr. of Bible Therapy, San Diego, 1977-86. Served to lt. (j.g.) USN, 1969-73. Mem. IEEE, AAAS, U.S. Naval Inst. (life), Purdue Alumni Assn. (life), San Diego Engring. Mgmt. Soc. (chmn. 1974-76), Key Collectors Internat. (bd. dirs. 1979—), Eta Kappa Nu, Phi Eta Sigma. Club: Help Defeat Gloom. Lodge: Order of DeMolay. Avocations: locksmithing, strategic games, golf. Office: Naval Ocean Systems Ctr 271 Catalina Blvd San Diego CA 92152-5000

TOWNSEND, JOSEPH J., safety professional; b. Loma Linda, Calif., July 21, 1941; s. Willard B. and Sara Bell (Denton) T.; m. Doris Marie Schack, Nov. 25, 1967; children: Cheryl Marie, Linda Elaine. AA, Riverside City Coll., 1962; BA in Econs., San Jose State U., 1966; Assoc. in Mgmt., Ins. Inst. Am., 1977. Cert. safety profl., Assoc. Risk Mgmt. Inst. Inst. Am. Loss control engr. Safeco Ins. Co., Seattle, 1970-73, loss control mgr., 1973-76, loss control tng. supr., 1976-78, asst. mgr. loss control, 1978—. Served as lt. USN, 1967-70. Mem. Am. Soc. Safety Engrs. (Safety Profl. of Yr. award Puget Sound chpt. 1987). Republican. Office: Safeco Ins Co Safeco Plaza T-20 Seattle WA 98185

TOWNSEND, PETER LEE, lawyer; b. Glendale, Calif., July 21, 1926; s. Craig and Georgia (Barhyte) T.; m. Irma Mathilde Greisberger, Aug. 12, 1947; children—Ingrid P., Russell T., Dorothy Poole. J.D. summa cum laude, McGeorge Coll. Law, 1958. Bar: Calif. 1959, U.S. Supreme Ct. 1982. Dep. dist. atty., Stockton, Calif., 1959-60; litigation counsel Western Title Ins. Co. of San Francisco, 1960-68; ptnr. Townsend and Bardellini, San Francisco, 1969—. Served to capt., inf., U.S. Army, 1944-54. Republican. Clubs: San Francisco Lawyers, San Rafael Yacht.

TOWNSEND, SUSAN ELAINE, social service institute administrator, hostage survival consultant; b. Phila., Sept. 5, 1946; d. William Harrison and Eleanor Irene (Fox) R.; m. John Holt Townsend, May 1, 1976. BS in Secondary Edn., West Chester State U., 1968; MBA, Nat. U., 1978; PhD in Human Behavior, La Jolla U., 1984. Biology tchr. Methacton Sch. Dist., Fairview Village, Pa., 1968-70; bus. mgr., analyst profl. La Jolla Research Corp., San Diego, 1977-79; pastoral asst. Christ Ctr. Bible Therapy, San Diego, 1980-82, also bd. dirs.; v.p., pub. relations World Outreach Ctr. of Faith, San Diego, 1981-82, also bd. dirs.; owner, pres., cons. Townsend Research Inst., San Diego, 1983—; teaching assoc. La Jolla U. Continuing Edn., 1985—. Author: Hostage Survival-Resisting the Dynamics of Captivity, 1983; contbr. articles to profl. jours. Religious vol. Met. Correctional Ctr., San Diego, 1983—, San Diego County Jail Ministries, 1978—. Served to comdr. USN, 1970-76, USNR, 1976—. Mem. Naval Res. Assn. (life, Outstanding Jr. Officer of Yr. 1982), West Chester Alumni Assn., Nat. U. Alumni Assn. (life), La Jolla U. Alumni Assn., Past Pres.' Assn., Calif. Fedn. Women's Clubs (v.p.-at-large San Diego dist. 25, 1982-84), Gen. Fedn. Women's Clubs (pres. Peninsula Woman's Club 1983-85, pres. Parliamentary Law Club 1984-86, mem. Past Pres.'s Assn.).

TOWNSEND, VICTORIA ELIZABETH, assoc.; b. Cleve., Oct. 9, 1957; d. Colin George and Joyce (Jonap) T. BA in Sociology, Antioch Coll., 1980; JD, UCLA, 983. Assoc. Law Office of Al Schallau, Los Angeles, 1984, Schlothauer & Ellison, Los Angeles, 1984-86, Berger, Kahn, Shafton & Moss, Los Angeles and Marina Del Ray, 1986—. Mem. ABA, Assn. Trial Lawyers Am., Calif. Trial Lawyers Assn., Los Angeles County Bar Assn., Westwood Bar Assn. Office: Berger Kahn Shafton & Moss 4215 Glencoe Ave 2nd Floor Marina Del Ray CA 90292

TOWNSHEND, JACK, geomagnetism and seismology scientist; b. Brandywine, Md., Apr. 24, 1927; m. Frieda Wybenga, Nov. 22, 1952; children—Donna Lynn, Donald Gilbert, Brenda Jean. Student George Washington U., 1950, U. Wis.-Madison, 1960-62. Mail carrier U.S. Post Office, Brandywine, Md., 1943-45; sci. aid Cheltenham Obs., Md., 1946-49; geophysicist Coast and Geodetic Survey, Washington, 1949-55, tng. officer, Fredericksburg, Va., 1955-63; chief Coll. Obs., Fairbanks, Alaska, 1963—; lectr. in field. Contbr. articles to profl. jours. Vice pres. Alaska State Bd. Edn., Juneau, 1979-83; lay leader Methodist Alaska Missionary Conf., Anchorage, 1972-76. Served with U.S. Army, 1945-46. Recipient Silver medal Coast and Geodetic Survey, 1962, Disting. Service award, 1964; Superior Service to Pub. award Dept. Commerce, 1967. Fellow Explorers Club; mem. Am. Assn. Advancement Service, Am. Geophys. Union, Nat. Assn. State Bds. Edn. (bd. dirs. 1981-82). Club: Farthest North Press (Fairbanks) (pres. 1970). Lodge: Kiwanis (lt. gov. Pacific Northwest dist. 1971-72, Layman's award 1969). Office: College Obs 800 Yukon Dr Fairbanks AK 99775-5160

TOY, MADELINE SHEN, chemist; b. Shanghai, Peoples Republic of China, Nov. 6, 1926; came to U.S., 1947; d. Zee and She-Ven (Hwang) Shen; m. Stephen Moy Toy, Dec. 26, 1951; 1 child, Stephanie Moy. BS, Coll. St. Theresa, Winona, Minn., 1949; MS, U. Wis., 1951, Ohio State U., Columbus, 1957; PhD, U. Pa., 1959. Mgr. organic lab. Freelander Research Devel. Lab. div. Dayco Corp., Hawthorne, Calif., 1959-60; staff mem. ITT Fed. Lab., San Fernando, Calif., 1961-62; sec. chief, research scientist McDonnell Douglas Corp., Newport Beach and Huntington Beach, Calif., 1964-70; sr. chemist Stanford Research Inst., Menlo Park, Calif., 1971-75; head chem. lab. Sci. Applications Internat. Corp., Sunnyvale, Calif., 1975—; cons. NASA, Houston, 1972. Author books in field; contbr. numerous articles profl. jours.; patentee in field. Recipient Certs. of Recognition NASA, Houston, 1978,80, Pasadena, Calif., 1977, New Tech. award NASA, Pasadena, 1970. Fellow Royal Chem. Soc. London; mem. Am. Chem. Soc. (exec. com. div. fluorine chems. 1975-77), Am. Inst. Chemists (sec. treas. Golden Gate chpt. 1975). Club: Lydia Health.

TOYODA, HIROO, molecular biologist; b. Tokyo, Sept. 8, 1947; s. Motoo and Toyoko (Yamashita) T.; m. Mieko Onohara, Apr. 7, 1985. MS, Tokyo Coll. Pharmacy, 1974; PhD, Kanazawa U., Japan, 1978. Research fellow Mayo Grad. Sch. Medicine U. Minn., Rochester, 1979-81; research fellow City of Hope Med. Ctr., Duarte, Calif., 1981-82, asst. research scientist, 1982-85; asst. prof. medicine UCLA Sch. of Medicine, 1986—. Grantee Am. Diabetics Assn., 1981-83, Juvenile Diabetics Found., 1983-85, Nat. Found. Ilitis and Colitis, 1983-85. Mem. Am. Soc. Cell Biology, Am. Soc. Bacteriology, Am. Diabetes Assn. Avocations: music, skiing, playing the violin. Home: 810 Fairview Ave Arcadia CA 91006 Office: Harbor-UCLA Med Ctr Dir Med Genetics 1000 W Carson Carson CA 90509

TOYOMURA, DENNIS TAKESHI, architect; b. Honolulu, July 6, 1926; s. Sansuke Fujimoto and Take (Sata) T.; m. Akiko Charlotte Nakamura, May 27, 1949; children—Wayne J., Gerald F., Amy J., Lyle D. B.Sc. in Archtl. Engring., Chgo. Tech. Coll., 1949; cert., U. Ill., Chgo., 1950, 53, 54; student, Ill. Inst. Tech., Chgo., 1953-54; cert., U. Hawaii-Dept. Def., Honolulu, 1966-67, 73. Lic. architect, Ill., Hawaii; lic. real estate broker, Ill. Designer, draftsman James M. Turner, Architect, Hammond, Ind., 1950-51, Wimberly and Cook, Honolulu, 1952, Gregg, Briggs & Foley, Architects, Chgo., 1952-54; architect Holabird, Root & Burgee, Architects, Chgo., 1954-55, Loebl, Schlossman & Bennett, Architects, Chgo., 1955-62; prin. Dennis T. Toyomura, AIA, Architect, Honolulu, 1963-83, Dennis T. Toyomura, FAIA, Architect, Honolulu, 1983—; fallout shelter analyst Dept. Def., 1967—; cert. analyst multi-distaster design, Dept. Def., 1973; cons. Honolulu Redevel. Agy., City and County of Honolulu, 1967-71; sec., dir. Maiko of Hawaii, Honolulu, 1972; mem. steering com. IX world conf. World Futures Studies Fedn., U. Hawaii, 1986; conf. organizer pub. forum 10th Hawaii Conf. in High Energy Physics, U. Hawaii, 1985; bd. dirs. Research Corp. U. Hawaii, 1986-89; archtl. mem. Bd. Registration for Profl. Engrs., Architects, Land Surveyors and Landscape Architects, State of Hawaii, 1974-82, sec. 1980, vice chmn. 1981, chmn., 1982; appointed by commr. Hawaii State Found. on Culture and Arts, 1982-86; mem. gov.'s com. Hawaii Economic Future, 1984. Del. commr. state assembly, Synod of Ill., United Presbyn. Ch. U.S.A., 1958, alt. del. commr. nat. gen. assembly, 1958, del. commr. Los Angeles presbytery, 1965; bd. session 2d Presbyn. Ch., Chgo., 1956-62, trustee, 1958-62; trustee 1st Presbyn. Ch., Honolulu, 1964-66, 69-72, sec., 1965, bd. sessions, 1964-72, 74-79; founding assoc. Hawaii Loa Coll., Kaneohe, 1964; mem. adv. commn. drafting tech. Leeward Community Coll., U. Hawaii, 1965—; bd. dirs. Lyon Arboretum Assn., U. Hawaii, 1976-77, treas., 1976; Served with U.S. Army, 1945-46. Recipient Human Resources of U.S.A. award Am. Bicentennial Research Inst., 1973; Outstanding Citizen Recognition award Cons. Engrs. Council Hawaii, 1975; Cert. Appreciation, Gov. of Hawaii, 1982, 86, commendation, 1983; resolution and cert. commendation Hawaii Ho. of Reps. and Senate, 1983. Fellow AIA (bd. dirs. Hawaii Soc. 1973-74, treas. 1975, Pres.'s Mahalo award 1981); life mem. AAAS, Acad. Polit. Sci., Am. Acad. Polit. and Social Scis., N.Y. Acad. Scis., Chgo. Art Inst., Chgo. Natural History Mus., Honolulu Acad. Arts, Nat. Geog. Soc.; mem. Nat. Coucil Archtl. Registration Bds. (western region del. 1975-82, nat. del. 1976-82), Council Ednl. Facility Planners Internat. (bd. govs. NW region 1980—), Bldg. Research Inst. (adv. bd. of Nat. Acad. Sci.), Ill. Assn. Professions, ASTM, Constrn. Specifications Inst., Constrn. Industry Legis. Orgn. (bd. dirs. 1973-81, 83—, treas. 1976-77), Japan-Am. Soc., Hawaii State C. of C. (bd. dirs. 1984-87), U. Hawaii Kokua O'Hui, O'Nahe Popo (bd. dirs. 1984—), Nat. Council Engring. Examiners, N.Y. Acad. Scis., Alpha Lambda Rho, Kappa Sigma Kappa. Clubs: Presidents (U. Hawaii), Malolo Mariners (purser 1964, skipper 1965) (Honolulu). Home: 2602 Manoa Rd Honolulu HI 96822 Office: 1370 Kapiolani Blvd Honolulu HI 96822

TRACY, C. RICHARD, zoology educator; b. Glendale, Calif., May 24, 1943; s. Clarence Robert and Doris Edith (Borel) T.; m. Barbara Jean Tracy, Oct. 14, 1967 (div. Mar. 1986); 1 child, Christopher Richard. BA, Calif. State U., Northridge, 1966, MS, 1968; PhD, U. Wis., 1972. Asst. scientist U. Wis., Madison, 1972-74; assoc. prof. zoology U. Mich., Douglas Lake, 1974-79; assoc. prof. Colo. State U., Ft. Collins, 1979-82, prof., 1982—; research assoc. prof. U. Wash., Seattle, 1980-81. Contbr. numerous articles to profl. jours. Fellow Guggenheim Found., 1980-81, U. Wis., Madison, 1971-72. Mem. AAAS, Ecol. Soc. Am. (chmn. physiol. ecology sect. 1986—), Am. Soc. Zoologists (pres.-elect div. ecology), Am. Soc. Icthyologists and Herpetologists, Herpetologists League. Democrat. Avocations: hiking, bicycling, racquetball. Home: 640 1/2 S Meldrum Fort Collins CO 80521 Office: Colo State U Dept Zoology Fort Collins CO 80523

TRACY, JOHN MICHAEL, III, speech pathology educator; b. Whittier, Calif., Apr. 29, 1949; s. John Michael and Roberta Josephine (Clay) T.; m. Diane Elaine Kafka, June 21, 1971. BA, Whittier Coll., 1971; MS, Oreg. Coll. Edn., 1974; PhD, U. Oreg., 1983. Cert. clin. competence in speech-lang. pathology. Speech clinician Medford (Oreg.) Pub. Sch., 1974-76; speech pathologist Providence Hosp., Medford, 1977-80, Home Health Agy., Eugene, Oreg., 1981-84; asst. prof. Western Oreg. State Coll., Monmouth, 1984—. Mem. Am. Speech-Lang. Hearing Assn., Oreg. Speech and Hearing Assn. (editor newsletter, 1982-84, pres. 1986—). Avocations: gardening, parenting. Office: Western Oreg State Coll Monmouth OR 97361

TRAEGER, MADELEINE SHEILA, social worker; b. N.Y.C., June 2, 1937; d. Frank E. Fishof; m. Jerome Salzman, Sept. 8, 1979; children: David, Terri, Andrea. BA in Psychology, Boston U., 1957; MSW, U. Calif., Berkeley, 1959. Lic. clin. social worker, lic. marriage counselor. Med. social worker Michael Reese Hosp., Chgo., 1959-60, VA Hosp., Palo Alto, Calif., 1960-62; instr. Stanford U. Med. Sch., Palo Alto, 1962-66, Kaiser Hosp., Santa Clara, Calif., 1966-67; psychotherapist Marital and Sexual Problems Med. Clinic, Los Altos, Calif., 1969-73; dir. Marital Counseling Services, Los Altos, 1973—. Mem. Unitarian Fellowship, Los Gatos, Calif., Hunger Project, San Jose, Calif. Fellow Soc. for Clin. Social Work (bd. dirs. 1984-86, editor state newsletter, cert. appreciation); mem. Acad. Cert. Sex Educators and Therapists, Nat. Assn. Social Workers, Acad. Cert. Social Workers. Democrat. Jewish. Home: 15550 Winchester Blvd Monte Sereno CA 95030 Office: Marital Counseling Services 851 Fremont #208 Los Altos CA 94022

TRAGER, RUSSELL HARLAN, publishing company executive; b. Cambridge, Mass., Sept. 26, 1945; s. Nathan Allan and Shirley (Gibbs) T.; m. V. Jan Adams, Aug. 19, 1968 (div. July 1975); 1 child, Eric Todd; m. Edna Marie Sanchez, Feb. 16, 1980; 1 child, Felice Rosanne. AA, Newton Jr. Coll., 1965; BS, U. Miami, 1968; postgrad., Harvard U., 1968-69. Account rep. Hervic Corp., Sherman Oaks, Calif., 1972-75, Canon USA, Lake Success, N.Y., 1975-78; key account sales rep. Yashica Inc., Glendale, Calif., 1978-79; sales rep. Region I United Pubs. Corp., Beverly Hills, Calif., 1979-81, sales mgr., 1981-83; regional pres. United Pubs. Corp., Carson, Calif., 1983—. Avocations: salt-water fishing, photography, collecting art. Home: 1201 11th St Manhattan Beach CA 90266 Office: United Pubs Corp Region II 550 Carson Plaza Dr Carson CA 90746

TRAN, DIEN THANH, editor; b. Vietnam, Nov. 18, 1938; came to U.S., 1975; s. Seng and Loanh Thi (Lam) T.; m. Thuan Thu, Sept. 16, 1961; children—Trang, Thanh, Giang, Long. Equivalent B.S. degree in Mil. Sci., Nha Trang Naval Acad., 1962; equivalent M.S. degree of Mil. Sci., Armed Forces Coll., Vietnam, 1974. Commd. officer Vietnamese Navy, 1967, advanced through grades to capt., 1975; chief of security Republic of Vietnam Presidency, 1970-75; systems operator Rinconada (Calif.) Water Plant, Los Gatos-Santa Clara County, 1980—; editor, pub. Martial Arts and Sports mag., San Jose, Calif., 1982—. Col. Calif. Res. Pres. Vietnamese Martial Arts Fedn., 1973—. Decorated 5d Nat. Order (Vietnam). Roman Catholic. Home: 705 Orkney Ave Santa Clara CA 95050 Office: Martial Arts and Sports Mag 198 W Julian St San Jose CA 95113

TRANMER, BRUCE IAN, neurosurgeon; b. Cobourg, Ont., Can., Mar. 15, 1954; s. William Edwin and Grace Lois (Nellist) T.; m. Sandra Margaret McCormick, Sept. 7, 1984. MD, Queen's U., Can., 1979. Resident neurosurgery Toronto (Can.) Gen. Hosp., 1981-85; neurosurgeon U. Colo., Denver, 1986; asst. prof. neurosurgery U. Colo., 1986—. Contbr. articles on neurosurgery to profl. jours. Office: U Colo HSC Div Neurosurgery 4200 E 9th Box C307 Denver CO 80262

TRANSPOTA, ROBERT PAUL, artist, teacher; b. Spokane, Wash., Nov. 15, 1923; s. Gerald Garrique and Eleanor Fredrika (Schultz) T.; m. Mary Anne Taylor, June 10, 1946; children—Mary Antia, Allen Paul, Christopher. Student Los Angeles City Coll, 1942-43, Monmouth Coll., 1943-44, Chgo. Acad. Fine Arts, 1949-50. Tech. and fine arts artist, Los Angeles, 1950-60; tchr., cons. in field; one-man shows Freeman Galleries, Beverly Hills, Calif., 1965, Palace Art Gallery, Prescott, Ariz., 1971, House of Bronze, Prescott, 1973; exhibited in group shows Am. Savs. & Loan Assn., Beverly Hills, 1967, Files Gallery of Fine Arts, Big Bear City, Calif., 1980; San Bernardino County (Calif.) Mus., 1982; represented in permanent collection George Phippen Meml. Invitation Western Art Show, Prescott, Nat. Cowboy Hall of Fame, Oklahoma City; paintings include oil portrait of John Mullens, Cowboy, 1976; instr. TV art series The Seven Principles of Drawing, 1975. Bd. dirs. George Phippen Meml. Art Found., 1976. Served with USN, 1944-46; PTO. Recipient gold medals George Phippen Meml. Invitational Western Art Show, 1976, 77, Files Gallery of Fine Arts, 1980; merit cert. award for oils Am. Painters in Paris Exhbn., 1975. Mem. Portrait Club N.Y., Fine Arts Guild, Big Bear Art Assn.

TRAPP, GERALD BERNARD, journalist; b. St. Paul, May 7, 1932; s. Bernard Edward and Lauretta (Mueller) T.; m. Bente Joan Moe, Jan. 29, 1954; children—Eric Gerald, Lise Joan, Alex Harold. B.A., Macalester Coll., St. Paul, 1954. Editor Mankato (Minn.) Free Press, 1954-57; with AP, 1957-80; nat. broadcast exec. charge sales AP, East of Miss., 1966-68; gen. broadcast news editor AP, N.Y.C., 1968-79; dep. dir. broadcast services AP, 1979-80, liaison broadcast networks, 1968-80; v.p., gen. mgr. Intermountain Network, Salt Lake City, 1980-87; v.p., dir. mktg. Travel Motivation, Inc., Salt Lake City, 1987—. Mem. Radio TV News Dirs. Assn., Oratorio Soc. Utah (bd. dirs.), Sigma Delta Chi. Mem. United Ch. Christ. Home: 1615 Millcreek Way Salt Lake City UT 84106 Office: 3487 West 2100 South Suite 105 Salt Lake City UT 84119

TRAUB, JANE TREVARTHEN, scientist, entrepreneur; b. Auckland, N.Z., Aug. 12, 1932; d. William Gordon and Olive Marion (Simpson) Trevarthen; m. Volker Gottfried Traub; children—Niklas, Marcus, Melina, Daniella. B.S., Auckland U., 1953, postgrad., 1953-55. Reference librarian Auckland Pub. Library, 1952-53; vis. research scientist Otago, N.Z. U., 1953; sci. cons. Internat. Sci. Supply Co., N.Z., 1955-57; research asst. to Linus Pauling, Calif. Inst. Tech., 1957-59, research asst. genetics, 1979-82, research asst. in molecular genetics City of Hope, 1982-83; cons., lectr. in field. Founder, pres., bd. dirs. The Book Bridge Inc. Internat. Ednl. Library, Altadena, Calif., 1972—. Contbr. articles to profl. jours. Vice pres. U.S. Ctr. Internat. Performing Arts, 1981—. Calif. Community Found. grantee, 1982. Mem. Auckland Inst. and Mus. (life), Los Angeles World Affairs Council, AAAS. Address: 272 Jaxine Dr Altadena CA 91001

TRAUTENBERG, GERALD ANTHONY, chemical company executive; b. Newark, N.J., Dec. 10, 1935; s. Anthony and Catherine (Galik) T.; m. Joan Marie Freiermuth, 1972 (div. 1982); children: Laurie Jean, Carol Ann, Christopher Neal. AB, Rutgers U., 1959, MS in Biochemistry, 1964. Biochemist Bristol Myers, Hillside, N.J., 1958-62; product mgr. Drew Chem. Corp., Parsippany, N.J., 1962-72; tech. service mgr. Betz Labs., various locations, 1973-78; ptnr. Process Products N.W., Bellevue, Wash., 1979-85; nat. mgr. Chemtex Ltd., Bellevue, 1986—; bd. dirs. Fitness Network Am., Bellevue, 1985—. Contbr. tech. papers to sci. publs. V.P. Bellevue Ski Council, 1983—. Mem. TAPPI. Avocations: skiing, sailing, biking. Home: PO Box 5052 Bellevue WA 98009 Office: Chemtex Ltd, 219-255 W 1st St, North Vancouver Can V7M 3G8

TRAVIS, DENNIS M., botany educator; b. Erie, Pa., Aug. 14, 1944; s. Nelson R. and Mildred E. (Carver) T.; m. Kathryn Brickner, Aug. 21, 1965; children: Grant C., Tyler G., Seth B. BS, Edinboro U., 1966, MEd, 1967; PhD, Miami U., 1974. Asst. prof. botany Miami U., Oxford, Ohio, 1970-78, asst. dean coll. arts and scis., 1974-78; dean arts and scis. Millikin U., Decatur, Ill., 1978-79; v.p. acad. affairs Mansfield (Pa.) State Coll., 1979-81, U. Maine, Presque Isle, 1981-83; dean natural scis. Weber State Coll., Ogden, Utah, 1983—. Contbr. articles to profl. jours. Mem. Utah State Adv. Council on Sci. and Tech., Salt Lake City, 1983—. Mem. AAAS, Council Colls. Arts and Scis. Deans, Sigma Xi, Phi Delta Kappa, Phi Sigma. Lutheran. Lodge: Rotary (chmn. com. 1983—). Avocations: fishing, hunting, boating, golfing. Office: Weber State Coll Sch Natural Scis Ogden UT 84408-2501

TRAVIS, ROBIN, computer conversion specialist, author; b. Bklyn., Dec. 20, 1949; d. Elias and Fay T.; m. Jeffrey Sanchez Hinkle, Dec. 9, 1972; 1 child, Jesse Robin. BA, Hunter Coll., 1971; MA, CUNY, 1974. Chief exec. officer Travis, Campbell, Fisher & Assocs. (formerly TLC Computer Services), 1976-84, sr. tech. ptnr. , 1984—. Author: (novels) China Train, 1979, Entering the Middle Kingdom, 1981; (play) Red Flannel Murders, 1980; contbr. articles to bus. sect. local newspaper, to Calif. Banker Mag.; appeared on local TV show, co-host computer show radio sta. KIEV. Mem. Nat. Assn. for Exec. Females, Ind. Assn. Computer Cons., Nat. Assn. Women Bus. Owners, Smithsonian Inst., Los Angeles Mus. Contemporary Art. Office: Travis Campbell Fisher & Assocs PO Box 3392 Los Angeles CA 90028

TRAYLOR, CHERYL LEE, psychiatric social worker; b. Oswego, N.Y., June 20, 1944; d. Donald Elton and Harriette (Lee) Gais; BA, SUNY, Buffalo, 1966, MSW, 1972; m. Jean LaRue Traylor, Jr., Nov. 11, 1965 (div. Dec. 1970). With Psychiat. Clinic, Buffalo, 1967-70; psychiat. social worker Hillcrest Childrens Ctr., Washington, 1972-74; asst. dir. outpatient services Comprehensive Community Mental Health Ctr. #2, Seat Pleasant, Md., 1974-77; psychiat. social worker Arlington (Va.) Mental Health Ctr., 1977-78, So. Calif. Permanente Med. Group, San Diego, 1978—; pvt. practice psychotherapy La Jolla, Calif., 1983—; NIMH fellow, 1970-72. Mem. Nat. Assn. Social Workers (cert.), Nat. Assn. Black Social Workers. Democrat. Club: Foxtrappe (Washington).

TREANOR, WALTER JOHN, physician; b. County Tyrone, No. Ireland, May 14, 1922; came to U.S., 1949, naturalized, 1954; s. Hugh and Marion (deVine) T.; M.D., Nat. U. Ireland, 1947; m. Mary Stewart, Dec. 29, 1971; children—James P., Wanden, Dona, June. Intern, St. Mary's Hosp., San Francisco, 1949-52; resident Mayo Found., Rochester, Minn.; practice medicine specializing in rehab. medicine, Santa Rosa, Calif.; emeritus prof. medicine U. Nev., Reno, 1979—. Served to capt., M.C., U.S. Army, 1953-55. Fellow ACP, Royal Soc. Medicine; mem. Am. Acad. Neurology, Internat. Med. Soc. Paraplegia, Am. Acad. Phys. and Rehab. Medicine. Republican. Anglican. Contbr. articles to profl. jours. Home: 1370 Spring St Santa Rosa CA 95404 Office: 990 Sonoma Ave Santa Rosa CA 95404

TREDENNICK, HARRY LESLIE (NICK), III, researcher, aeronautical engineer; b. Schenectady, N.Y., June 6, 1946; s. Harry Leslie and Alvera Ida (Wood) T. BEE, Texas Tech U., 1968, MEE, 1970; PhDEE, U. Tex., 1976. Registered profl. engr., Tex. Asst. prof. research and teaching asst. U. Tex., Austin, 1972-77; sr. design engr. Motorola Corp., Austin, 1977-79; vis. faculty mem. U. Calif. Berkeley, 1983-84; indsl. adv. com. Tex. Tech Elect. Engring. Dept., 1984—; mem. Accreditation Bd. Engrs., 1982—. Author: Microprocessor Logic Design; contbr. articles to profl. jours.; patentee in field. Served to capt. USAF, 1970-72, maj. USNG, 1979-84; with res. 1972-79. Mem. IEEE (sr.), Tex. Tech Elec. Engrs. Assn. (life), Assn. Computing Machinery, Sigma Xi, Eta Kappa Nu, Tau Beta Pi, Phi Kappa Phi. Avocations: automobile mechanics and restoration. Office: IBM Micro/370 W A52/029 5600 Cottle Rd San Jose CA 95193

TREECE, JAMES LYLE, lawyer; b. Colorado Springs, Colo., Feb. 6, 1925; s. Lee Oren and Ruth Ida (Smith) T.; m. Ruth Julie Treece, Aug. 7, 1949 (div. 1984); children—James (dec.), Karen, Teryl Wait, Jamilyn Snyser, Carol Crowder. Student Colo. State U., 1943, Colo. U., 1943, U.S. Naval Acad., 1944-46; B.S., Mesa Coll., 1946; J.D., U. Colo., 1950; postgrad. U. N.C., 1976-77. Bar: Colo. 1952, U.S. Dist. Ct. Colo. 1952, U.S. Ct. Appeals (10th cir.) 1952, U.S. Supreme Ct. 1967. Assoc., Yegge, Hall, Treece & Evans and predecessors, 1951-59, ptnr., 1959-69; U.S. atty., Colo., 1969-77;

pres. Treece, Bahr & Arckey, P.C. and predecessor firms, Littleton, Colo., 1977—; mcpl. judge, 1967-68; mem. faculty Nat. Trial Advocacy Inst., 1973-76, Law-Sci. Acad., 1964; lectr. Chmn. Colo. Dept. Pub. Welfare, 1963-68; chmn. Colo. Dept. Social Services, 1968-69; mem. Littleton Bd. Edn., 1977-81. Served with USNR, 1944-46. Recipient awards Colo. Assn. Sch. Bds., 1981, IRS, 1977, FBI, 1977, DEA, 1977, Fed. Exec. Bd., 1977. Mem. Fed. Bar Assn. (pres. Colo. 1975), Colo. Bar Assn. (bd. govs.), Denver Bar Assn. (v.p., trustee). Republican. Lutheran. Home: 7210 E Euclid Dr Englewood CO 80111 Office: 2596 W Alamo Ave Littleton CO 80120

TREESE, DARLENE ANN, counselor, hypnotherapist, writer, speaker; b. Warren, Ohio, Nov. 27, 1946; d. Steven Andrew and Ruth Suomi (Uitto) Dubasik; m. Robert Edward Treese, Sept. 26, 1965 (div.); children—Eric Michael, Craig Allen. BEd, summa cum laude, Ariz. State U., 1975, MEd, 1979, M in Counseling, 1981, PhD in Counseling Psychology, William Lyon U., 1986. Cert. community coll. tchr., Ariz. Tchr. Painesville (Ohio) Twp. Schs., 1968-72; staff instructional leader Washington Elem. Sch. Dist., Phoenix, 1976-81, resource tchr. for gifted children, 1982-84; cons., condr. workshops; coach Ariz. State Championship Olympics of the Mind Teams, 1983, 84, exec. governing bd. 1984-86. Active local polit. campaigns. Recipient various grants. Mem. NEA, Ariz. Edn. Assn., Washington Dist. Edn. Assn., Ariz. Assn. Gifted and Talented, Ariz. Soc. Profl. Hypnotherapists, Kappa Delta Pi, Pi Lambda Theta. Republican. Home: 1452 E Todd Dr Tempe AZ 85283 Office: 1050 E Southern Ave Tempe AZ 85282

TREFETHEN, DANIEL BERTRAND, III, librarian; b. Seattle, Apr. 7, 1954; s. Daniel Bertrand Jr. and Mary Esther (Ross) T.; m. Joanna Marie Golden, July 14, 1977. BA in English, U. Wash., 1977, MA in Librarianship, 1978. Librarian U. Wash., Seattle, 1978-79, Earl R. Combs, Inc., Mercer Island, Wash., 1979-81, TRA Architects, Seattle, 1982—. Contbr. articles to profl. jours. Mem. Spl. Libraries Assn. (sec.-treas. Pacific N.W. chpt. 1984-85, pres. 1985-86). Home: 3441 13th Ave W Seattle WA 98119 Office: TRA Architects-Engrs 215 Columbia Seattle WA 98104

TREFFTZS, KENNETH LEWIS, business and finance educator; b. Sparta, Ill., Dec. 28, 1911; s. John Sydney and Dorothy Nora (Wright) T.; m. Ellen Lois Ryniker, Aug. 7, 1937; children: Jeffrey Lewis, Ellen Sterling. B.S., U. Ill., 1936, M.S., 1937, Ph.D., 1939. Asst. economist, com. on bank research Ill. Bankers Assn., 1937-39; instr. Carnegie Inst. Tech., 1939-41; asst. prof. fin. U. So. Calif., Los Angeles, 1941-45; assoc. prof. U. So. Calif., 1945-50, prof., 1951-82, prof. emeritus, 1982—, head dept. fin., 1945-57, head dept. fin. and real estate, 1959-66, chmn. dept. fin. and bus. econs., 1966-71; vis. assoc. prof. UCLA, 1948; vis. assoc. prof. sch. bus. adminstrn. U. Wash., 1949-50; instr. Pacific Coast Banking Sch., Seattle, summer, 1949; conf. dir. Ann. Inst. Fin., So. Calif., 1962, 63, 64; chmn., dir. Fund of Am., Inc., Provident Fund for Income, Inc., Am. Capital Comstock Fund, Inc., Am. Capital Corp. Bond Fund, Inc., Am. Capital Enterprise Fund, Inc., Am. Capital Govt. Securities, Inc., Am. Gen. Money Market Accumulation Fund, Inc., Am. Gen. High Yield Accumulation Fund, Inc., Am. Capital Mcpl. Bond Fund, Inc., Am. Capital Pace Fund, Inc., Am. Capital Res. Fund, Inc., Am. Capital Venture Fund, Inc., Am. Capital Over-the-Counter Securities, Inc., Am. Capital Harbor Fund, Am. Capital High Yield Investments, Inc.; dir. Source Capital, Inc., MGM/UA Communications Co., Inc., FPA Perennial Fund, Inc., FPA New Income Inc., Fremont Gen. Corp., FPA Capital Fund, Inc., Pacific Horizon Fund, Inc. (govt. money market portfolio, money market portfolio, high yield bond portfolio, aggressive growth portfolio), Pacific Horizon Calif. Tax Exempt Bond Portfolio, The Horizon Funds (Horizon Prime Fund, Treasuary Fund, Tax-Exempt Money Fund, Intermediate Govt. Fund, Intermediate Tax-Exempt Fund); trustee. chmn. Am. Calif. Tax-Exempt Trust, Am. Capital Fed. Mortgage Trust, Am. Capital Govt. Money Mkt. Trust, Am. Capital Life Investment Trust, Am. Capital Tax-Exempt Trust; cons. (under AID) U. Karachi, Pakistan, 1962. Author: Mathematics of Banking and Finance, 1944, (with E.J. Hills) Mathematics of Business and Accounting, 1947, Mathematics of Business, Accounting and Finance, 1956, What Put the Stock Market Where It Is; Contbr. articles to profl. jours. Recipient Dean's award Grad. Sch. Bus., U. So. Calif., 1963; Teaching Excellence award U. So. Calif., 1974-75; Assos. award for excellence in teaching, 1977. Mem. Am. Econ. Assn., Western Econ. Assn. (pres. 1955-56), Western Fin. Assn. (pres. 1965-66), Am. Fin. Assn. (v.p. 1946-48), Beta Gamma Sigma, Phi Kappa Phi, Rho Epsilon, Omicron Delta Epsilon, Lambda Alpha, Beta Alpha Psi, Alpha Kappa Psi. Address: 11131 Briarcliff Dr San Diego CA 92131

TREGARTHEN, TIMOTHY DORAN, journalist, educator; b. Riverside, Calif., Nov. 25, 1945; s. Doran Woodrow and Ethel Mae (Geabhart) T.; m. Karen Sue Angel, June, 1967 (div. 1971); m. Nancy L. Sidener, Aug. 23, 1971 (div. 1985); step-children—Liese Ripley, Susan Rohwer; m. Suzanne Jo Schroeder, Aug. 3, 1985; 1 child, Doran Richard. B.A. in Econs., Calif. State U., 1967; M.A. in Econs., U. of Calif.-Davis, 1970, Ph.D. in Econs., 1972. Lectr., U. of Calif.-Davis, 1970-71; asst. prof. U. Colo., Colorado Springs, 1971-76, assoc. prof., chmn. dept., 1976-78, prof., chmn. dept. 1981—; editor The Margin Mag.; prof. econs. U. Colo.; vis. prof. The Colo. Coll., 1981—; chmn. bd. dirs. The Wright-Ingraham Inst., Colo. Springs, 1982—. Author: Food, Fuel and Shelter, 1978; editor The Margin mag., 1985—; syndicated columnist, 1984—. Chmn., El Paso Country Planning Commn., Colorado Springs, 1981-83, Nat. Multiple Sclerosis Soc., Colo. Springs, 1984. Woodrow Wison Found. fellow, 1967; recipient Disting. Teaching award, U. of Colo., 1976, 81, 86. Mem. Am. Econ. Assn., Atlantic Econ. Assn., Western Econ. Assn. Democrat. Home: 810 Crystal Park Rd Manitou Springs CO 80829 Office: U Colo Dept Econs Colorado Springs CO 80933

TREIMAN, JOYCE WAHL, artist; b. Evanston, Ill., May 29, 1922; d. Rene and Rose (Doppelt) Wahl; m. Kenneth Treiman, Apr. 25, 1945; 1 child, Donald. A.A., Stephens Coll., 1941; B.F.A. (grad. fellow 1943), State U. Iowa, 1943. vis. prof. San Fernando Valley State Coll., 1968; lectr. UCLA, 1969-70; vis. prof. State U. Calif., Long Beach, 1977. One man shows include Paul Theobald Gallery, Chgo., 1942, John Snowden Gallery, Chgo., 1945, Art Inst. Chgo., 1947, North Shore Country Day Sch., Winnetka, Ill., 1947, Fairweather-Garnett Gallery, Evanston, 1950, Edwin Hewitt Gallery, N.Y.C., 1950, Palmer House Galleries, Chgo., 1952, Glencoe (Ill.) Library, 1953, Elizabeth Nelson Gallery, Chgo., 1953, Charles Feingarten Gallery, Chgo., 1955, Cliff Dwellers Club, Chgo., 1955, Fairweather-Hardin Gallery, Chgo., 1955, 58, 73, 81, Marian Willard Gallery, N.Y.C., 1960, Felix Landau Gallery, Los Angeles, 1961, 64, Adele Bednarz Gallery, Los Angeles, 1969-71, 74, La Jolla (Calif.) Mus., 1962-72, Palos Verdes (Calif.) Art Mus., 1976, Forum Gallery, N.Y., 1963, 66, 75, 81, Tortue Gallery, Santa Monica, Calif., 1980, 83, 86, Schmidt-Bingham Galery, N.Y.C., 1986, Fairweather-Hardin Gallery, Chgo., 1986; numerous exhbns. including Carnegie Internat., 1955, 57, Met. Mus., 1950, Whitney Mus., 1951, 52, 53, 58, Art Inst. Chgo., 1945-59, John Herron Art Inst., 1953, Library of Congress, 1954, Cocoran Gallery, 1957, Pa. Acad. Fine Arts, 1958, Mus. Modern Art, 1962, Am. Acad. Arts and Letters, N.Y.C., 1974, 75, 76, Retrospective Exhbn., Mcpl. Art Gallery, Los Angeles, 1978; represented in permanent collections Kemper Ins. Co., Chgo., Met Mus. Art, N.Y.C., Denver Mus. Art, State U. Iowa, Ill. State Mus., Long Beach (Calif.) Mus., Whitney Mus. Am. Art, N.Y.C., Tupperware Art Mus., Orlando, Fla., Art Inst. Chgo., Utah State U., Abbott Labs., Oberlin Allen Art Mus., Internat. Mineral Corp., Pasadena Art Mus., U. Calif. at Santa Cruz, Grunwald Found., UCLA, Santa Barbara Mus. Art, Calif., Oakland Mus., Calif., Security Pacific Nat. Bank, Los Angeles, Rochester (N.Y.) Art Mus.; pub. collections include Art Inst. Chgo., Whitney Mus., Met. Mus., Santa Barbara (Calif.) Mus., Portland (Oreg.) Mus. Recipient numerous awards including Logan purchase prize Art Inst. Chgo., 1951, Martin B. Cahn prize, 1959, 60, Pauline Palmer prize, 1953, Saratosa Am. Painting Exhbn. award, 1959, Ford Found. purchase prize, 1960, Purchase prize Ball State Coll., 1961, prize La Jolla Art Mus., 1961, Purchase prize Pasadena Art Mus., 1961; Tiffany fellow, 1947; Tupperware Art Fund fellow, 1955; Tamerind Lithography fellow, 1961. Address: 712 Amalfi Dr Pacific Palisades CA 90272

TREINEN, SYLVESTER WILLIAM, bishop; b. Donnelly, Minn., Nov. 19, 1917; s. William John and Kathryn (Krausert) T. Student, Crosier Sem., Onamia, Minn., 1935-41; B.A., St. Paul's Sem., 1943. Ordained priest Roman Catholic Ch., 1946; asst. pastor Dickinson, N.D., 1946-50; sec. to bishops Ryan and Hoch, 1950-53; asst. pastor Cathedral Holy Spirit, Bismarck, N.D., 1950-57; chancellor Diocese Bismarck, 1953-59; asst. pastor St. Anne's Ch., Bismarck, 1957-59; pastor St. Joseph's Ch., Mandan, N.D., 1959-62; bishop Boise, Idaho, 1962—. Address: 420 Idaho St PO Box 769 Boise ID 83701 *

TRELEASE, FRANK JOHNSON, III, water engineer; b. Boulder, Colo., May 24, 1937; s. Frank Johnson Jr. and Mary (Thayer) T.; m. Patricia Ann Powers, June 6, 1959; children: Gail F., Anne L., Amy L. BCE, U. Wyo., 1959; MCE, Colo. State U., 1961. Registered profl. civil engr., Colo., Wyo., Mont. From surveyor to civil engr. U.S. Bur. Reclamation, 1956-59; research assoc. Colo. State U., Ft. Collins, 1959-61; with Wright Water Engrs., 1963-64, v.p. and mgr. Wyo. office, 1979-84; with water bd. City of Denver, 1964; with water conservation bd. State of Colo., 1965-66; with nat. resources bd. State of Wyo., 1966-68, dir. water planning program, 1968-78, asst. state engr., engrs. office, 1985—; v.p. BRW/Noblitt, 1978; mem. adv. bd. Wyo. Bur. of Land Mgmt., 1975-77; Wyo. rep. Yellowstone River Basin Fed./State Plan, 1975-78. Contbr. chpts. to engring. and hydrology pubs., articles to profl. jours. Active Cole Community Ctr., Cheyenne, Wyo., 1967-85, treas., 1971-74; mem. Cheyenne Urban Drainage task force, 1985—. Served to 1st lt. U.S. Army, 1961-63. Mem. ASCE (pres. Denver Hydraulics br. 1966, pres. Wyo. sect. 1970, treas. 1969, editor newsletter 1971-74), Wyo. Engring. Soc. (sec.-treas. 1982-83, v.p. 1984, pres. 1985, mem. scholarship com. 1985—), U.S. Com. on Irrigation and Drainage (publs. chmn. 1978-84, tech. activities 1985—), Wyo. Water Devel. Assn. (adv. to bd. dirs. 1968-78), Am. Water Works Assn. (water rights com.), Sigma Xi, Phi Epsilon Phi, Omicron Delta Kappa, Sigma Tau, Phi Kappa Phi. Republican. Congregationalist. Lodge: Rotary (pres.-elect Cheyenne club, 1986—, bd. dirs. 1983-86). Avocations: skiing, camping, fishing, hunting, scuba diving. Home: 3228 Locust Dr Cheyenne WY 82001 Office: Wyo State Engrs Office Hershler Bldg Cheyenne WY 82002

TREMBLAY, FRANCIS WILFRED, education consultant, educator; b. Lebanon, N.H., Mar. 10, 1925; s. Albert Napoleon and Mary Ann (Gagnon) T.; m. Eugenia Howson, July 21, 1952 (div. Feb. 1973); 1 child, Mary Irene; m. Micheline Francoise Poirier, Nov. 25, 1974; children—Sophie, Annie, Catherine, Paul Gauthier. B.A., U. N.H., 1949; B.E., Wash. State U., 1950, M.Ed., 1953; Ed.D., Brigham Young U., 1980. Cert. pub. sch. adminstr., Calif. Tchr. Mullan Pub. Schs., Idaho, 1950-51, Palouse Pub. Schs., Wash., 1951-53; prin. Warm Springs Elem. Sch., Calif., 1954-58; supt. Smith River Union Sch., Calif., 1958-62, Placer Hills Union Sch., Meadow Vista, Calif., 1962-68; cons. Calif. Dept. Edn., Sacramento, 1968—; adj. prof. Chapman Coll., Orange, Calif., 1981—; mem. Nat. Com. on Migrant Student Record Transfer System, 1980. Pres. Del Norte County Tchrs. Assn., Calif., 1963, N. Coast Adminstrs. Assn., Calif., 1963; mem. Common Cause, Sacramento, 1984. Served with USN, 1943-46, PTO. Nat. Def. Inst. Scholar, 1965, 66, 67. Mem. Calif. Assn. Sch. Adminstrs., Calif. Assn. Compensatory Edn., Phi Delta Kappa. Democrat. Unitarian. Home: 6937 Ellsworth Circle Fair Oaks CA 95628 Office: Calif State Dept Edn Sacramento CA 95814

TRENBERTH, KEVIN EDWARD, meteorologist; b. Christchurch, New Zealand, Nov. 8, 1944; came to U.S., 1977; s. Edward Maurice and Ngaira Ivy (Eyre) T.; m. Gail Neville Thompson, Mar. 21, 1970; children: Annika Gail, Angela Dawn. BSc with honors, U. Canterbury, Christchurch, 1966; ScD, MIT, 1972. Meteorologist New Zealand Meteorol. Service, Wellington, 1966-76, supt. dynamic meteorology, 1976-77; assoc. prof. meteorology U. Ill., Urbana, 1977-82, prof., 1982-84; scientist Nat. Ctr. Atmospheric Research, Boulder, Colo., 1984-86, sr. scientist, 1986—; adj. prof. U. Ill., 1984—; cons. NOAA, 1980—, NASA, 1981—. Contbr. articles to profl. jours. Grantee NSF. Fellow Am. Meteorol. Soc. (editor sci. jour. 1981-86, com. chmn. 1983—); AAAS, Royal Soc. of New Zealand, Meteorol. Soc. of New Zealand. Home: 1445 Landis Ct Boulder CO 80303 Office: Nat Ctr Atmospheric Research PO Box 3000 Boulder CO 80307

TRENHOLME, BARBARA ANN, school system administrator; b. Galveston, Tex., Aug. 1, 1948; d. Lawrence Barrett and Mary Thompson (Macon) T.; m. Vipin M. Worah, Aug. 20, 1978; children: Moneka Worah, Sarah Worah. BA with hons., U. Tex., 1969, MEd, 1973, PhD, 1983. Cert. secondary tchr., Colo.; cert. spl. edn. tchr., Colo. Tchr. Dallas Pub. Schs., 1970-72, St. Vrain Pub. Schs., Longmont, Colo., 1972-75, Austin (Tex.) Pub. Schs., 1975-76; tchr. Jefferson County Schs., Lakewood, Colo., 1977-79, spl. edn. supr., 1979-82, staff devel. trainer, 1984—; ednl. cons. Douglas County Schs., Castle Rock, Colo., 1986—. Mem. Assn. Supervision Devel. Democrat. Avocation: cross country skiing. Home: 17260 E Dorado Circle Aurora CO 80015 Office: Jefferson County Schs Staff Acad 1209 Quail Lakewood CO 80226

TRENT, MICHAEL EDWARD, office supply company executive; b. Boulder, Colo., Sept. 17, 1949; s. Michael Collins and Geraldine Elise (Blaser) T.; B.A. in Bus., Hastings Coll., 1975; m. Victoria Bogenschutz, Jan. 16, 1971; children—Elizabeth Louise, Kristin Elise, Donna Michelle, Michael Collins II. Bookkeeper, Standard Office Supply Co., Boulder, 1972, furniture salesman, 1972-77, owner, pres., 1977-84; co-owner, v.p. Western Standard Office Supply, Boulder, 1984-85; acct. mgr. NBI's The Office Place, Aurora, Colo., 1985—. Chmn., Colo. & Northwestern Preservation Com. Mem. Nat. Office Products Assn., Boulder Jaycees, Boulder C. of C., Downtown Assn., Burlington Route Hist. Soc., Nat. Model R.R. Assn., Boulder Model R.R. Club (pres.), Rocky Mountain R.R. Club, Presbyterian. Home: 330 Bates St Boulder CO 80303 Office: NBI's The Office Place 13800 E 39th Ave Aurora CO 80011-1608

TRENT, THOMAS MICHAEL, semiconductor company executive; b. Des Moines, Iowa, Oct. 6, 1945; s. Voight Beason and Millicent Inas (Fenton) T.; m. Marsha Kay Dean, Aug. 2, 1969 (div. 1976); children—Cherelynne, Amy Camille. B.S.E.E., Kans. State U., 1973; M.S.E.E., Ariz. State U., 1976, M.B.A., 1980. Maintenance technician AT&T, Dodge City, Kans., 1963-69; design engr. Motorola, Inc., Mesa, Ariz., 1973-80; design engr. Micron Tech., Boise, 1980-83, engring. mgr., 1983-86; v.p. research and devel., chief tech. officer, 1986—. Served with U.S. Army, 1967-68. Republican. Episcopalian. Office: Micron Technology Inc 2805 E Columbia Rd Boise ID 83706

TRENTANELLI, PATSY LAVERNE, industrial engineer; b. Athens, Tex., Oct. 9, 1934; d. Felton Henry and Anna Laverne (Taylor) Griffin; m. Allan Guinn Sanders, Nov. 17, 1951 (div. 1966); children: Karen Virginia Sanders Oglesby, Mary Jean Baker, Laura Sue; m. Mario Joseph Trentanelli. BS, U.S. Army Engring. Tng. Agy., 1973, MA, 1974. Cancer analyst for Western U.S. David Grant Hosp., Travis AFB, Calif., 1962-67; indsl. engr. 60th Aerial Port, Travis AFB, Calif., 1967-76; cons. Mil. Airlift Command, Scott AFB, Ill., 1976—; cancer analyst con. Am. Coll. Surgeons, 1965-67. Contbr. articles to tech. publs. Active Charleston (S.C.) Operatic Soc., 1959-62. Named Fed. Female Employee of Yr. USAF, 1975, Mil. Airlift Command Transp. Specialist of Yr., 1975. Mem. Morning Music Club, Epsilom Sigma Alpha (sec. 1962-66). Republican. Baptist. CLubs: ARC (Grey Lady, 1959-62). Avocations: music, writing, all types handcrafts, tax cons. Home: 646 Kuliouou Pl Honolulu HI 96821

TRETHEWEY, JAMES ALGER, civil engineer; b. Miami, Ariz., Jan. 5, 1937; s. Alger Perry and Lorna Mary T.; B.S.C.E., U. Ariz., 1960; student law McGeorge Coll. Law, 1964-66, U. Santa Clara, 1973, U. Calif.-Davis, 1978. Sr. engr. Aerojet Solid Propulsion Co., 1961-67; sr. project engr., chief mfg. engr. Lockheed Propulsion Co., 1967-74; dir. engring. Aerojet Solid Propulsion Co., Sacramento, 1974-79; v.p. ops. Aerojet Strategic Propulsion Co., Sacramento, 1979-84; gen. mgr. Aerojet Solid Rocket Ops., 1984—. Bd. dirs. Civic Assn./Sch. Bd., 1963-65. Mem. Lockheed Propulsion Co. Mgmt. Assn. (pres. 1972-73), Nat. Rifle Assn. (life), Am. Mgmt. Assn., Air Force Assn., AIAA, Soc. Advancement Material and Process Engring., Calif. Rifle and Pistol Assn. (life), Sigma Xi. Republican. Office: PO Box 15699C Sacramento CA 95813

TREVITHICK, RONALD JAMES, financial planner; b. Portland, Oreg., Sept. 13, 1944; s. Clifford Vincent and Amy Lois (Turner) T.; m. Delberta Russell, Sept. 11, 1965; children: Pamela, Carmen, Marla, Sheryl. BBA U. Wash., 1966. CPA, Alaska, N.C., Va., La. Mem. audit staff Ernst & Ernst, Anchorage, 1966, 68-70; pvt. practice acctg., Fairbanks, Alaska, 1970-73; with Touche Ross & Co., Anchorage, 1973-78, audit ptnr., 1976-78; exec. v.p., treas., bd. dirs. Veco Internat., Inc., 1978-82; pres., bd. dirs. Petroleum Contractors Ltd., 1980-82; bd. dirs. P.S. Contractors A/S, Norcon, Inc., OFC of Alaska, Inc., V.E. Systems Services, Inc., Veco Turbo Services, Inc., Veco Drilling, Inc., Vemar, Inc., 1978-82; with Coopers & Lybrand, Anchorage, 1982-85; field underwriter, registered rep. New York Life Ins., 1985—; instr. acctg. U. Alaska, 1971-72; lectr. acctg. and taxation Am. Coll. Life Underwriters, 1972; bd. dirs. Ahtna Devel. Corp., 1985-86. Div. chmn. United Way, 1975-76, YMCA, 1979; bd. dirs., fin. chmn. Anchorage Arts Council, 1975-78, Am. Diabetes Assn., Alaska affiliate, 1985—, Am. Heart Assn., Alaska affiliate, 1986—. Served with U.S. Army, 1967-68. Mem. Alaska Soc. CPAs, Am. Inst. CPAs, Petroleum Accts. Soc. (bd. dirs. Alaska 1976; nat. tax com. 1978-80), Fin. Execs. Inst. (pres. Alaska chpt. 1981-83), Internat. Assn. Fin. Planners, Am. Soc. CLUs, Internat. Assn. Registered Fin. Planners, Nat. Assn. Life Underwriters, So. Alaska Assn. Life Underwriters, Alaska Assn. Life Underwriters, Beta Alpha Psi. Clubs: Petroleum; Rainier. Lodge: Rotary. Home: 13200 Floral Ln Anchorage AK 99516 Office: 1400 W Benson Blvd Anchorage AK 99503

TREYBIG, JAMES G., computer company executive; b. 1940. Mkgt. mgr. Hewlett-Packard Co., 1968-72; with Kleiner and Perkins, 1972-74; with Tandem Computer Inc., Cupertino, Calif., 1974—, now pres., chief exec. officer, dir. Office: Tandem Computers Inc 19333 Vallco Pkwy Cupertino CA 95014 *

TRIBBY, JOHN WALLACE, investment service company executive; b. Sewickley, Pa., Aug. 27, 1946; s. John Frederick and Berta Marie (Holfelder) T.; m. Katherine Leslie Morris, July 25, 1980; 1 child, Jesse. BA, Pa. State U., 1968; MLS, U. Pitts., 1972. Reference librarian Carnegie-Mellon U., Pitts., 1975-77; mgr. Intell Research Cons., Coraopolis, Pa., 1977-78; info. mgr. projects div. Westinghouse Power System, Pitts., 1978-79; designer database New Zealand Forest Products, Ltd., Auckland, 1981; supr. Info. Research Ctr., Morrison-Knudsen Co., Inc., Boise, 1981—; gen. mgr., founder Fundamentals Co., Boise, 1986—. Author (software) Finalist: Intell. Inv. Mdls., 1985. Mem. Idaho Library Assn. (chmn. acad. and spl. libraries div. 1983-84), Treasure Valley Library Assn., W.Va. Library Assn., Pitts. On-Line User's Group (sec./treas. 1978-79). Avocations: reading the Bible, running, expert systems. Home: 119 Main St Boise ID 83702 Office: Fundamentals Co 119 Main St Boise ID 83702

TRIBBY, RICHARD LOUIS CALVIN, JR., insurance company executive; b. Arlington, Va., July 3, 1948; s. Richard Louis Calvin Tribby and Doris Faye (Fischer) Zenger; m. Elizabeth Anne Witte, Mar. 20, 1976; children: Louis, Calvin, Mariel. AA, N.Mex. Mil. Inst., 1968; BBA, U. N.Mex., 1973, MBA, 1975. Enlisted U.S. Army, 1970, resigned, 1972; bank examiner FDIC, Chgo., 1975-79; asst. auditor Sunwest Bank, Albuquerque, 1979-84; ins. agt. Farmers Ins. Group, Albuquerque, 1984-86, dist. office mgr., 1986—. Bd. dirs. La Montanita food Coop., Albuquerque, 1981-82; mem. Nob Hill Neighborhood Assn. Named one of Outstanding Young Men of Am., 1983, Outstanding Community Development V.p. of Quarter, U.S. Jaycees, 1984; recipient Jaycee Internat. Sen. award, 1986. Mem. N. Mex. Inst. Internal Auditors (treas. 1984-85), Downtown Jaycees (pres. 1982-83, v.p. adminstrn. 1985—, Jaycee of Yr., 1984, V.P. of Yr. 1986), N.Mex. Jaycees (v.p. community devel. 1983-84, v.p. adminstrn. 1984-85, Outstanding Local Pres. 1983), Maxwell Mus. Assn., Sierra Club (bd. dirs. 1973, 81-82, treas. 1981-82). Republican. Episcopalian. Club: Lobo (Albuquerque). Avocation: philately.

TRIER, WILLIAM CRONIN, medical educator, plastic surgeon; b. N.Y.C., Feb. 11, 1922; s. John and Anne (Cronin) T.; m. Kathleen Emily Renz, June 14, 1947; children: William Cronin, Peter L. AB, Dartmouth Coll., 1943; MD, N.Y. Med. Coll., 1947. Diplomate Am. Bd. Surgery, Am. Bd. Plastic Surgery (dir. 1976-82, vice-chmn. 1981-82). Intern St. Agnes Hosp., White Plains, N.Y., 1947-48; intern Grasslands Hosp., Valhalla, N.Y., 1948-49, resident in surgery, 1949-50; commd. lt. (j.g.) USN, 1948, advanced through grades to capt., 1964; asst. med. officer USS Midway and USS Wasp, 1950-52; residen in surgery St. Albans Hosp., L.I., N.Y., 1952-55; fellow plastic surgery Washington U. Barnes Hosp., St. Louis, 1956-58; mem. plastic surgery staff Naval Hosp., St. Albans, 1958-60; chief plastic surgery Naval Hosp., Phila., 1960-63; chief plastice surgery Nat. Naval Med. Ctr., Bethesda, Md., 1963-67; asst. prof. surgery, plastic surgery U. N.C., Chapel Hill, 1967-69, prof. surgery, plastic surgery, 1976-85, prof. dental ecology Sch. Dentistry, 1976-85; assoc. prof., chief plastic surgery U. Ariz. Coll. Medicine, Tucson, 1969-76; prof. surgery U. Wash. Sch. Medicine, Seattle, 1985—; mem. com. on study evaluation procedures Am. Bd. Med. Specialties, 1981-85, research com. 1985—. Contbr. articles to profl. jours. Bd. dirs., pres. Pima County unit and Ariz. divs. Am. Cancer Soc., 1970-76, bd. dirs. N.C. div., pres. Orange County (Calif.) unit, 1976-82. Mem. AMA, ACS, Am. Assn. Plastic Surgeons (historian 1973-76, v.p. 1984-85, pres.-elect 1985-86, pres. 1986-87), Am. Soc. Plastic and Reconstructive Surgeons, Am. Soc. Aesthetic Plastic Surgery (at large bd. dirs. 1979-81, treas. 1984-87), Am. Burn Assn., Am. Cleft Palate Assn. (pres. 1980-81), Am. Cleft Palate Ednl. Found. (pres. 1984—), Gamma Delta Chi, Alpha Kappa Kappa. Episcopalian. Home: 7701 Lakemont Dr NE Seattle WA 98115 Office: U Wash Dept Surgery RF-25 Sch Medicine Seattle WA 98195

TRIFF, JOSEPH DAVID, electronic service executive, clergyman; b. Los Angeles, Oct. 15, 1931; s. John George and Elizabeth (Tamok) T.; student RCA Inst., 1963; m. Brenda Evelyne Rettig, June 20, 1965; children—Belisa Dawn, Joy Amber. Ordained to ministry Jehovah's Witnesses, 1941; pioneer minister, 1955-69; pres. Woodcrest Congregation of Jehovah's Witnesses, 1966-70, San Pedro Congregation, 1970-72; Watchtower condr. West Congregation, 1981-82; pres., owner Triffic Mobile Electronics, Long Beach, Calif., 1977—. Presiding overseer West Congregation, 1984—; city overseer, San Pedro, 1975-77; asst. assembly overseer Cir. 16C, 1984—. Recipient Am. Legion Citizenship award, 1946; Bank of Am. Vocational award, 1949; Sealbearer award, 1949. Club: Alignment.

TRIFFET, TERRY, college dean; b. Enid, Okla., June 10, 1922; B.A., U. Okla., 1945; B.S., U. Colo., 1948, M.S., 1950; Ph.D. in Structural Mechanics, Stanford U., 1957; married; 3 children. Instr. engring. U. Colo., 1947-50; gen. engr. rocket and guided missile research U.S. Naval Ordnance Test Sta., 1950-55; gen. engr. radiol. research, head radiol. effects br. U.S. Naval Radiol. Def. Lab., 1955-59; assoc. prof., then prof. mech. and materials sci., 1959-76; assoc. dean research Coll. Engring., U. Ariz., Tucson, 1976-84, acting dean, 1984—; mem. apex com. U.S. Naval Research Labs., 1959-65; cons. to govt. and industry. Grantee Australian Research Grants Com., 1966-67, 72-73. Mem. Am. Phys. Soc., Am. Math. Soc., Soc. Engring. Sci., Soc. Industry and Applied Math., IEEE, Assn. Computing Machinery. Address: Coll Engring Univ Ariz Tucson AZ 85721

TRIGG, CHARLES WILDERMAN, writer; b. Balt., Feb. 7, 1898; s. Samuel Holland and Mary E. (Wilderman) T.; grad. Balt. Poly. Inst., 1914; B.S. in Chem. Engring., U. Pitts., 1917; M.A., U. So. Calif., 1931, M.S., 1934, postgrad., 1950-55; postgrad. U. Calif. at Los Angeles, 1936-38; m. Ida Faye Conner, Dec. 17, 1932 (dec. Aug. 1973); m. 2d, Avetta Hoffman Danford, Jan. 11, 1975. Fellow Mellon Inst. Indsl. Research, Pitts., 1916-20; chemist, prodn. mgr. King Coffee Products Corp., Detroit, 1920-23; sales promotion mgr. John E. King Coffee Co., Detroit, 1923-24; with E.R. Bohan Paint Co., Los Angeles, 1924-27; tchr. Los Angeles Pvt. High Sch., 1927-30; asso. prof. chemistry Cumnock Coll., Los Angeles, 1930-36, dean men, 1936-38; tchr. Eagle Rock High Sch., Los Angeles, 1938; coordinator Air Corps Inst., 1941-43; instr. East Los Angeles Jr. Coll., 1945-46; instr. Los Angeles City Coll., 1938-43, 46-49, coordinator, 1949-50, asst. dean, 1950-55, dean instruction, 1955-63, dean emeritus, prof. emeritus, 1963—; lectr. U. So. Calif., 1946, 59-60. Served to lt. comdr. USNR, 1943-45. Named Eagle Scout Boy Scouts Am., 1914. Mem. Math. Assn. Am. (sect. chmn. 1952-53; mem. nat. bd. govs. 1953-56), Nat. Council Tchrs. Math., Sch. Sci. and Math. Assn., Assn. Los Angeles Jr. Coll. Adminstrs. (pres. 1957-58), Sigma Xi, Alpha Chi Sigma, Phi Lambda Upsilon, Phi Delta Kappa, Pi Mu Epsilon, Alpha Mu Gamma. Author: Mathematical Quickies, 1967. Mem. editorial bd. Los Angeles Math. Newsletter, 1954, Jour. Recreational Math., 1971—. Mem. editorial staff Math. Mag., 1949-63. Contbr. numerous articles to profl. jours. Book reviewer, 1961—. Patentee instant coffee. Address: 2404 Loring St San Diego CA 92109

TRIGIANO, LUCIEN LEWIS, physician; b. Easton, Pa., Feb. 9, 1926; s. Nicholas and Angeline (Lewis) T.; m. Christy; children: Lynn Anita, Glenn Larry, Robert Nicholas. Student Tex. Christian U., 1944-45, Ohio U., 1943-

44, 46-47, Milligan Coll., 1944, Northwestern U., 1945, Temple U., 1948-52. Intern, Meml. Hosp., Johnstown, Pa., 1952-53; resident Lee Hosp., Johnstown, 1953-54; gen. practice, Johnstown, 1953-59; med. dir. Pa. Rehab. Center, Johnstown, 1959-62, chief phys. medicine and rehab., 1964-70; fellow phys. medicine and rehab. N.Y. Inst. Phys. Medicine and Rehab., 1962-64; dir. rehab. medicine Lee Hosp., 1964-71, Ralph K. Davies Med. Center, San Francisco, 1973-75, St. Joseph's Hosp., San Francisco, 1975-78, St. Francis Meml. Hosp., San Francisco, 1978-83; asst. prof. phys. medicine and rehab. Temple U. Sch. Medicine; founder Disability Alert. Served with USNR, 1944-46. Diplomate Am. Bd. Phys. Medicine and Rehab. Mem. AMA, A.C.P., Pa., San Francisco County Med. socs., Am. Acad. Phys. Medicine and Rehab., Am. Congress Phys. Medicine, Calif. Acad. Phys. Medicine, Nat. Rehab. Assn., Babcock Surg. Soc. Author various med. articles. Home: 1050 Northpoint St San Francisco CA 94109 Office: 2000 Van Ness Suite 506 San Francisco CA 94109

TRIGLIA, DENNIS, research immunologist; b. Bronx, N.Y., Mar. 6, 1954; s. Aldo Joseph and Lorraine Marie (Ramocki) T. BS in Biology, Fordham U., 1975; MA in Biology, CUNY, 1979. Librarian N.Y. Pub. Library, Bronx, 1969-75; purchasing agt. Rockefeller U., N.Y.C., 1975-76; sr. research technician Sloan-Kettering Cancer Ctr., N.Y.C., 1976-79; research asst. The Salk Inst., San Diego, 1979-82, Scripps Clinic and Research Found., San Diego, 1982-83; research immunologist CYTOTECH Inc., San Diego, 1983—. Contbr. articles to profl. jours. Peer counselor San Diego A.I.D.S. Project, 1985—; vol. Cardinal Hayes Exceptional Childrens Program, Bronx, 1968-71. Mem. AAAS. Democrat. Avocations: camping in the desert, photography, gardening. Home: 1774 Klauber Ave San Diego CA 92114 Office: CYTOTECH Inc 11045 Roselle St Suite C San Diego CA 92121

TRIMINGHAM, WILLIAM EARL, manufacturing company executive; b. San Francisco, Feb. 27, 1928; s. George Earl and Edith C. (Christopherson) T.; m. Mary Trimingham, June 21, 1952; children: Terry Ann, Thomas, Patricia, Jill. BA, San Jose State U., 1951; postgrad., U. Santa Clara, 1955-57. Safety engr. Calif. Research Corp., Livermore, 1951-52; sales rep. Cutter Labs., Berkeley, Calif., 1952-62; sales mgr. hosp. div. Kendall Co., Los Angeles, 1962-70; exec. v.p., gen. mgr. Quinton Instruments, Seattle, 1970-82; v.p. mktg. MedPacific Corp., Seattle, 1982-83; pres. Myo-Tronics Research, Seattle, 1984—, also bd. dirs. Mem. Am. Heart Assn. Served with U.S. Army, 1946-47. Mem. Beta Beta Beta. Republican. Lodge: Elks. Avocations: skiing, writing. Office: Myo-Tronics Research Inc 720 Olive Way #800 Seattle WA 98101

TRIMM, MAUREEN PATRICIA, telecommunication specialist; b. Madison, Wis., Aug. 22, 1948; d. Meryl Daniel and Margery Lois (Pratt) Doyle; m. Sammy Gordon Trimm, May 21, 1977; 1 child, Margaret Louise. BA in Journalism, Humboldt State U., 1969; EdM, Utah State U., 1972; M in Pub. Adminstrn., U. So. Calif., 1977. Project dir. Mountain Valley Library System, Sacramento, Calif., 1975-78; systems coordinator South Bay Library System, Santa Clara, Calif., 1978-82; telecommunications ops. mgr. Stanford Univ., Stanford, Calif., 1983-84; communication services mgr. Stanford Univ., Stanford, 1984-86; asst. dir. Info. Tech. Services div. Stanford U., Stanford, 1986—. Mem. Telecommunications Assn., Assn. Coll. and Univ. Telecommunications Adminstrs. Office: Stanford Univ Communication Services Stanford CA 94305

TRIMMER, JOSEPH FRANCIS, transportation executive, consultant; b. McCook, Nebr., Dec. 5, 1928; s. Joe F. and Izella R. Trimmer; m. Barbara J. Robinson, June 20, 1954; children: Bret A., Linda A., Stacey Jo. BBA, U. Denver, 1953, MBA, 1954, J.D., 1962. Bar: Colo. 1962. Various positions, personnel clk. to sr. v.p. indsl. relations Ringsby Truck Lines, Inc., Denver, 1954-76; v.p., exec. v.p., pres., chief exec. officer Salt Creek Freightways, Casper, Wyo., 1976-86; mgmt. cons. Profl. Mgmt. Services, Aurora, Colo., 1986—; instr. motor carrier transp. U. Denver, 1954-59. Mem. Transp. Lawyers Assn., Colo. Motor Carriers Assn. (pres. 1973, dir. 1965—), Wyo. Trucking Assn. (dir. 1979—). Lodges: Rotary (Casper); Masons, Shriners (Denver). Office: 7100 E Evans #426 Denver CO 80224

TRIPOLI, GREGORY JOHN, meteorologist; b. Cleve., Oct. 13, 1950; s. Bart John and Therba Irene (Bucklad) T.; m. Bonnie Jean Hamaker, Aug. 25, 1973; children: Benjamin James, Theodore Russell. BS, Fla. State U., 1972, MS, 1974; PhD, Colo. State U., 1986. Meteorologist GFDL/NOAA/Dept. Commerce, Princeton, N.J., 1974-76; meteorologist, research assoc. Colo. State U., Fort Collins, Colo., 1976—; ptnr., cons. Aster, Ft. Collins, 1985—. Contbr. articles to profl. jours. Mem. Am. Meteorol. Soc., Sigma Xi, Chi Epsilon Pi. Democrat. Office: Colo State U Dept Atmospheric Sci Foothills Campus Fort Collins CO 80523

TRIPP, R(USSELL) MAURICE, geophysical engineer; b. Holten, Kans., July 12, 1916; s. Maurice Hall and Alma Belle (Cottrell) T.; m. Catherine Graham Burr, Aug. 12, 1937; children: Catherine Ann, Peggy Marie, Elizabeth Belle, R. Maurice II, David Graham, Timothy Lane, Mary Alice. Grad., Colo. Sch. Mines, 1939, M Geophys. Engring., 1943; ScD in Geology, MIT, 1948. Seismic observer Geotech. Corp., Dallas, 1936-37, 39-41; asst. to pres., dir. research Geotech. Corp., Cambridge, Mass., 1944-46; mem. faculty Colo. Sch. Mines, Golden, 1941-43; sr. scientist U.S. Bur. Ships, 1946; cons. in field Lincoln, Mass., 1946-48; v.p., dir. Research, Inc., Coffeyville, Kans., 1948-54; pres. Tripp Research Corp., Dallas, 1955—, Skia Corp., Santa Clara, Calif., 1972—, Aktina Corp., Santa Clara, 1984—. Contbr. articles to profl. jours.; patentee in field. Pres. El Camino Trust, San Jose, Calif., 1966-68; pres. Youth Park, Los Gatos, Calif., 1986; v.p. Santa Clara County Girl Scouts, Saratoga (Calif.) Hist. Found.; chmn. Calif. State Parks Adv. Com., 1967-81. Recipient Outstanding Contbn. to Preservation of Human Sight award Carbert Found., 1976, Service award San Jose Community YMCA, 1982. Mem. N.Y. Acad. Sci., Am. Inst. Mining Engrs. (com. chmn.), Am. Assn. Petroleum Geologists (com. chmn.), Soc. Exploration Geophysicists, Soc. Info. Display (v.p.), Soc. Photographic Scientists and Engrs. (treas.), Soc. Photographic Instrument Engrs., No. Calif. Crystal Growers, Calif. Acad. Sci., Golden C. of C. (v.p.). Republican.

TRISCHLER, THOMAS JOSEPH, architect, development consultant; b. Pitts., Sept. 27, 1952; s. Floyd David and Gloria Neldine (Fusting) T.; m. Jana Lee Abrams. Registered architect, Calif. B.S. in Architecture, U. So. Calif., 1974; MBA, degree in urban land economics, real estate fin., mktg. strategic analysis UCLA, 1986. Designer, Ben-Ami Shulman Registered Bldg. Designers, Los Angeles, 1972, George Barnes Architect, Northridge, Calif., 1973-74; assoc. urban planner, urban designer East Los Angeles Community Union Planning Dept., 1972-73; urban planner, urban designer Community Planning & Devel. Co., 1974-75, Irvine Co., 1975; project mgr. Danielian Moon, Ilg and Assocs., Newport Beach, Calif., 1975-77, Rolly Pulaski & Assocs., 1977-78; office mgr., project mgr. Brion Jeannette & Assocs., 1978; sr. design architect Albert C. Martin & Assocs., Los Angeles, 1978-80; project architect-dir., mgr. computer implementation WZMH Group, Inc., 1981—; prin. Trischler Assocs., Orange, 1981—, The TA/TAG Venture, Newport Beach, Calif., 1986—; active in reformation of archtl. licensing laws, 1977-80. Prin. works include Thousand Oaks Pub. Library, Calif. (design award), The Atrium Office Bldg., Irvine, Calif. (design award), Plaza Alicante Office Bldg., Garden Grove, Calif. (design award), Princess Hotel, Garden Grove (design award). Com. coordinator East Los Angeles Community Union, 1972-73; mem. Ad Hoc Com. to Incorp. East Los Angeles, 1972-74; speaker career day programs Boy Scouts Am., 1978—. Calif. State scholar, 1970-74; recipient cert. of appreciation East Los Angeles Area C. of C., 1974. Mem. AIA (assoc. pres.), U. So. Calif. Alumni Assn., Assn. U. Related Research Parks, Urban Land Inst., Am. Planning Assn.; pres. Orange County chpt. 1979-80, assoc. dir. Calif. council 1980, mem. coms. 1979-80, numerous certs. and awards 1977—). Roman Catholic. Clubs: Back Bay Rugby Football. Office: 1818 W Chapman Ave Suite B Orange CA 92668

TRISCIK, BETTE, speech pathologist; b. Ogden, Utah, Mar. 22, 1944; d. Charles Ernest and Chloe (Robison) T.; children: Gregory Ronald Carroll, Marcus Triscik Carroll. AA, San Jose City Coll., 1972; BA, San Jose State U., 1976, MA, 1983. Lic. speech pathologist Calif. Bd. Med. Quality Assurance. Tchr. San Jose (Calif.) Unified Schs., 1979-83, speech-lang. pathologist, 1983—; pvt. practice speech pathology San Jose, 1981—. Author: Language Therapy for Adolescents, 1984. Mem. NEA, Am. Speech-Lang. and Hearing Assn. (cert.), Santa Clara Speech-Lang. Assn. (treas. 1984-86, v.p. 1986-87), San Jose Unified Speech Council (pres. 1985-86), Calif. Speech-Lang. and Hearing Assn.

TRISKA, JAN FRANCIS, political science educator; b. Prague, Czechoslovakia, Jan. 26, 1922; came to U.S., 1948, naturalized, 1955; s. Jan and Bozena (Kubiznak) T.; m. Carmel Lena Burastero, Aug. 26, 1951; children: Mark Lawrence, John William. J.U.D., Charles U., Prague, 1948; LL.M., Yale U., 1952, J.S.D., 1950; Ph.D., Harvard U., 1957. Co-dir. Soviet treaties Hoover Instn., Stanford, Calif., 1956-58; lectr. dept. polit. sci. U. Calif.-Berkeley, 1957-58; asst. prof. Cornell U., Ithaca, N.Y., 1958-60; assoc. prof. Stanford U., Calif., 1960-65, prof. polit. sci., 1965—, assoc. chmn. dept., 1965-66, 68-69, 71-72, 74-75. Co-author: (with Slusser) The Theory, Law and Policy of Soviet Treaties, 1962, (with Finley) Soviet Foreign Policy, 1968, (with Cocks) Political Development and Political Change in Eastern Europe, 1977, (with Ike, North) The World of Superpowers, 1981, (with Gati) Blue Collar Workers in Eastern Europe, 1981, Dominant Powers and Subordinate States, 1986; bd. editors: East European Quar. Comparative Politics, Internat. Jour. Sociology, Jour. Comparative Politics, Studies in Comparative Communism, Soviet Statutes and Decisions, Documents in Communist Affairs. Recipient Research award Ford Found., 1963-68; fellow NSF, 1971-72; Fulbright-Hays faculty research fellow, 1973-74; fellow Woodrow Wilson Internat. Ctr. for Scholars, 1980-81. Mem. Am. Polit. Sci. Assn. (sec. pres. conf. on communist studies 1970-76), Assn. Advancement Slavic Studies (bd. dirs. 1975-83), Am. Soc. Internat. law (exec. council 1964-67), Czechoslovak Soc. Arts and Scis. (pres. 1978-80). Democrat. Club: Fly Fishers (Palo Alto, Calif.). Home: 720 Vine St Menlo Park CA 94025 Office: Stanford U Dept Political Sci Stanford CA 94305

TROAN, JANET LILLIAN, accountant; b. Mpls., Oct. 7, 1934; d. William Edward and Lillian (Bering) Cook; m. John Trygve Troan, Mar. 21, 1953; children: Gordon, Janine. BS in Acctg., Mpls. Sch. Bus., 1958; postgrad., Anoka-Ramsey Coll., Coon Rapids, Minn., 1963-66, Phoenix Coll., 1982-85. Controller Sanford, Inc., Mpls., 1955-67; account mgr. Troan Fin. Services, Phoenix, 1971-80; sec., bd. dirs. Five Star Corp., Phoenix, 1980—. Treas. Federated Women's Club, Coon Rapids, 1965-69; pres. Federated Women's Club, Phoenix, 1977-81; sec. Coon Rapids Dems., 1963-68; dep. registrar Phoenix Dems.; precint com. Ariz. Dems. Recipient Outstanding Achievement award Ariz. Dems., 1984. Lutheran. Lodge: Sons of Norway. Avocation: antiques. Home: 2403 W Cortez Ave Phoenix AZ 85029 Office: Five Star Enterprises Inc 10635 N 19th Ave Phoenix AZ 85029

TROCK, WARREN LEIGH, agricultural and natural resource economics educator; b. Pratt, Kans., June 30, 1926; s. Elmer and Lottie Marie (Lemons) T.; m. Bette Jene Sloan, Aug. 15, 1949; children: Daniel Leigh, Rebecca Ann, David Alan. BS in Agrl. Adminstrn., Kans. State U., 1950, MS in Agrl. Econs., 1957, PhD in Agrl. Econs., 1965. Extension economist Mont. State U., Bozeman, 1957-64; from asst. prof. to prof. agrl. econs. Tex. A&M U., College Station, 1964-73; extension economist Colo. State U., Ft. Collins, 1973—; dir. County Info. Service, Colo. State U. Contbr. articles to profl. jours. Served as cpl. U.S. Army, 1944-46, 50-51. Co-recipient award for Excellence Western Agrl. Econs. Assn., 1979. Mem. Sigma Xi, Gamma Sigma Delta (pres.-elect 1986—), Omicron Delta Epsilon. Democrat. Avocations: fishing, photography. Home: 1725 Essex Dr Fort Collins CO 80526 Office: Colo State U Dept Agrl and Natural Resource Econs Fort Collins CO 80523

TROLINGER, MILDRED SUE, social work program administrator; b. Clinton, Mo., Jan. 21, 1947; d. Robert Lee and Lillian Mildred (Cauthon) T.; children: Ray Eugene Parrish, Robin Sue Parrish. AA, Glendale Community Coll., 1977; B in Sociology, UCLA, 1979; MSW, San Diego State U., 1981. Lic. clin. social worker, Calif. Counselor Glendale (Calif.) Community Coll., 1975-77; research assoc. UCLA, 1977-79; psychiat. social worker VA Hosp., San Diego, 1980-81; psychiat. social worker VillaView Hosp., San Diego, 1982-85, clin. supr., 1985—. Scholar Am. Bus. Women's Assn., Los Angeles, 1976-80, Assistance League, Glendale, 1977; fellow Calif. State U. San Diego, 1979-81; grantee Ctr. for Study of Person, San Diego, 1981. Mem. Nat. Assn. Social Workers, Continuing Care Assn. San Diego. Office: VillaView Community Hosp 5550 University Ave San Diego CA 92105

TROUT, WILLIAM HOLLIS, architect; b. Cleve., June 29, 1935; s. William Henry and Margaret Marie (Pauer) T.; B.S., Kent State U., 1960; m. Beverly Heather Law, June 17, 1961; children—William Hollis, Peter Dunsmore, Timothy Pauer. With Hellman & Wilson, Falmouth, Mass., 1959-60, Visnapuu & Gaede, Cleve., 1962, John Terrance Kelly, Cleve., 1962, Houston Assos., Mentor, Ohio, 1964, William B. Morris Assos., Shaker Heights, Ohio, 1965; prin. The Trout Creek Architects, Inc., Vail, Colo., 1981—; lectr. in field. Formerly mem. Eagle County Planning Commn.; mem. Vail Planning and Environ. Commn.; mem. Design Rev. Bd. of Beaver Creek. Served with Ohio N.G., 1954. Recipient Cleve. Arts prize, 1978; 1st homor award Architects Soc. Ohio, 1969; design award AIA, 1970, for Schubert House, for DeBenedetto House, Ocepek House, Moore House, The Little House, 1971, Child Day Care Center T. Celeste, 1971, Office Interior of Trout Architects, 1972, Pirates' Cove, 1972, The Trout House, 1976, The Sciangula House, 1976; Craftsmanship award, Cleve. Builders Exchange, 1976, 77; Record House of the Yr., Archtl. Record Mag., 1978; nat. design award Nat. Assn. Home Builders and Better Home & Gardens mag., 1979, 78; Design for Better Living award Am. Wood Council, 1979. Mem. AIA, Architects Soc. Ohio, Am. Underground Space Assn., Eagle Valley Home Builders Assn. (dir., award for outstanding mem. 1983), Delta Tau Delta. Republican. Episcopalian. Clubs: Cleve. Yachting, Midget Ocean Racing Class Assn., Dillon Yacht. Author: Solar Houses, 1978; Modern Houses in America, 1978; contbr. articles to profl. jours. Address: PO Box 1956 Vail CO 81658 *

TROUTMAN, SAMUEL JACKSON, JR., engineering company executive, consultant; b. Washington, Pa., Mar. 4, 1936; s. Samuel Jackson and Emma Evlyn (Jackson) T.; m. Gisela Ingrid Roden, Nov. 7, 1961; children—Samuel David, Barbara Ann, Robert Andrew. B.S. in Electrical Engring., Ind. Inst. Tech., 1964; M.S., U. Dayton, 1974. Registered profl. engr., Ind. Radar specialist U.S. Army, 1958-60; prodn. engr. Curtis Wright Co., Albuquerque, 1960-61; research engr. Wabash Magnetics Co., Wabash, Ind., 1961-68; research assoc. Webb Assocs., Yellow Springs, Ohio, 1968-72, chief engr., 1972-80; v.p. Dynatech Frontier Corp., Albuquerque, 1980—; cons. Yellow Springs Athletic Boosters Club, Ohio, 1972-80, Center Stage Theater, Yellow Spring, 1974-78. Contbr. articles to profl. jours. Served with U.S. Army, 1958-60. Recipient New Tech. merit award NASA, 1969, 75. Mem. Nat. Soc. Profl. Engrs., Internat. Soc. Respiratory Protection, Assn. Contamination Contro. Mfrs., Iota Tau Kappa. Lutheran. Club: Yellow Springs Athletic Boosters (pres. 1978-79). Home: 7113 Marilyn Ave NE Albuquerque NM 87109 Office: Tri-Tech Enterprises 7113 Marilyn Ave NE Albuquerque NM 87109

TROVER, DENIS WILLIAM, microcomputer co. exec.; b. Columbus, Ohio, Feb. 1, 1945; s. Kenneth Harold and Virginia June (Denis) T.; B.S. in Physics, Mich. State U., 1967; M.B.A., Coll. William and Mary, 1972; M.S. in Physics, Vassar Coll., 1973; m. Florence Ellen Lloyd, June 12, 1971; 1 dau., Florence Emma. Optical physicist IBM, Fishkill, N.Y., 1967-71; staff assoc., systems programmer Rockwell Internat. Sci. Center, Thousand Oaks, Calif., 1974-78; pres., dir. Sonix Systems, Inc., Thousand Oaks, 1978-86; pvt. practice small bus. computer cons., Camarillo, Calif., 1986—. Mem. energy task force Conejo Future Found., 1975—, chmn., 1980-81. Club: Vassar So. Calif. (bd. dirs. 1982—). Home: 11355 Presilla Rd Camarillo CA 93010

TROVER, ELLEN LLOYD, lawyer; b. Richmond, Va., Nov. 23, 1947; d. Robert Van Buren and Hazel (Urban) Lloyd; m. Denis William Trover, June 12, 1971; 1 dau., Florence Emma. A.B., Vassar Coll., 1969; J.D., Coll. William and Mary, 1972. Asst. editor Bancroft-Whitney, San Francisco, 1973-74; owner Ellen Lloyd Trover Atty.-at-Law, Thousand Oaks, Calif., 1974-82; ptnr. Trover & Fisher, Thousand Oaks, 1982—; bd. dirs. Burco Mfg., Los Angeles. Editor: Handbooks of State Chronologies, 1972. Trustee, Conejo Future Found., Thousand Oaks, 1978—, vice chmn., 1982-84, chmn., 1984—; pres. Zonta Club Conejo Valley Area, 1978-79; trustee Hydro Help for the Handicapped, 1980-85. Mem. Conejo Simi Bar Assn. (pres. 1979-80, dir. 1983-85), Ventura County Bar Assn. (state del. 1984), State Bar Calif., Va. State Bar, Phi Alpha Delta. Democrat. Presbyterian. Home: 11355 Presilla Rd Camarillo CA 93010 Office: Trover and Fisher 1107E Thousand Oaks Blvd Thousand Oaks CA 91362

TROWBRIDGE, DALE BRIAN, educator; b. Glendale, Calif., May 17, 1940; s. Dale Beverly and Alison Amelia (Goldsborough) T.; m. Helen Elaine Turner, July 2, 1966; children: Katelin Elizabeth, David Brian. BA, Whittier Coll., 1961; MS, U. Calif., Berkeley, 1964, PhD, 1969. Chemist Aerojet Gen., Azusa, Calif., 1961-62; chemistry tchr. Berkeley (Calif.) High Sch., 1964-66; prof. chemistry Sonoma State U., Rohnert Park, Calif., 1969—; vis. prof. chemistry U. Calif., Berkeley, 1970-74. Contbr. articles to profl. jours. Mem. Am. Chem. Soc., Research Soc. N. Am. Home: 6039 Elsa Ave Rohnert Park CA 94928 Office: Sonoma State U 1801 E Cotati Ave Rohnert Park CA 94928

TROY, FREDERIC ARTHUR, II, medical biochemistry educator; b. Evanston, Ill., Feb. 16, 1937; s. Charles McGregor and Virginia Lane (Minto) T.; m. Linda Ann Price, Mar. 23, 1959; children: Karen M., Janet R. BS, Washington U., St. Louis, 1961; PhD, Purdue U., 1966; postdoctoral, Johns Hopkins U., 1968. Asst. prof. U. Calif. Sch. Medicine, Davis, 1968-74, assoc. prof., 1974-80, prof., 1980—; vis. prof. Karolinska Inst. Med. Sch., Stockholm, 1976-77; cons. NIH, Bethesda, Md., 1974—, NSF, Washington, 1975—, Damon Runyon Cancer Found., N.Y.C., 1980-81, VA, Washington, 1984—. Contbr. articles to profl. jours. Recipient Research Cancer Devel. award Nat. Cancer Inst., 1975-80; Eleanor Roosevelt Internat. Cancer fellow Am. Cancer Soc., 1976-77. Mem. Am. Soc. Biol. Chemistry, Am. Assn. Cancer Research, Am. Chem. Soc., Am. Soc. Enologists, Am. Soc. Microbiology, Biochemistry Soc., Biophysics Soc., Am. Fedn. for Clin. Research., N.Y. Acad. Sci., AAAS, Soc. Complex Carbohydrates, Sigma Xi. Office: U Calif Sch Medicine Dept Biol Chemistry Davis CA 95616

TROY, SHIRLEY LORETTA, speech pathologist; b. Hollywood, Calif., June 23, 1958; d. Robert Edward and Barbara (Russell) T. AA, Mt. San Antonio Coll., 1978; BA, Whittier Coll., 1980, MA in Communication Disorders, 1983. Lang. speech specialist Los Angeles Office of Edn., Downey, Calif., 1982—, leadership team mem., 1985—; master clinician Calif. State U., Los Angeles, 1985—. Mem. Am. Speech-Lang.-Hearing Assn. (cert.), Calif. Speech Hearing Assn., Phi Beta. Republican. Avocations: sailing, music. Home: 10635 Colima Rd Apt 24 Whittier CA 90604

TRUDELL, LAURENCE GREGORY, research geologist; b. St. Louis, Nov. 5, 1931; s. Roy Alfred and Myrtle Ruth (Mitchell) T. AB in Geology, U. Mo., 1956; student, U. Mich., 1957-58. Geophys. aide Fairchild Aerial Survey, Los Angeles, 1958-59; geologist U.S. Bur. Mines, Laramie, Wyo., 1961-75, U.S. Energy Research and Devel. Adminstrn., Laramie, 1976-77; supervisory geologist U.S. Dept. Energy, Laramie, 1978-83; sr. research geologist Western Research Inst., Laramie, 1983—. Contbr. articles to profl. jours. Served with U.S. Army, 1953-55, Korea. Mem. AAAS, Wyo. Geol. Assn., Rocky Mountain Assn. Geologists, VFW, Sigma Xi. Lodge: Elks. Avocations: skiing, boating. Office: Western Research Inst 365 N 9th St Laramie WY 82071

TRUE, DIEMER, state senator, trucking company executive; b. Cody, Wyo., Feb. 12, 1946; s. Henry Alfonso and Jean (Durland) T.; B.S., Northwestern U., 1968; m. Susie Lynn Niethammer, Aug. 28, 1967; children—Diemer Durland, Kyle Shawn, Tara Jeanine, Tracy Lynn. With Black Hills Trucking, Inc., Casper, Wyo., 1970—, v.p., 1974—; v.p. Toolpushers Supply Co., Casper, 1981—; dir. Hilltop Nat. Bank, Mountain Plaza Nat. Bank; mem. Wyo. Ho. of Reps., 1972-76; mem. Wyo. Senate, 1976—, chmn. minerals, bus. and econ. devel., mgmt. audit coms. 1979—, v.p. 1987—; adv. bd. U. Wyo. Enhanced Oil Recovery Inst., senate rules and procedures, judiciary coms.; mem. governing bd. Council State Govts., 1979—; mem. Council of State Govts. suggested state legislation com. and econ. devel. and internat. trade com., Am. Legis. Exchange Council, 1974-76. Pres. Natrona County United Way, 1976; mem. bus. adv. council Coll. Commerce and Industry, U. Wyo. Served with AUS, 1968. Mem. Wyo. Trucking Assn. (dir. 1972-80, pres. 1983-85), Ind. Petroleum Assn. Am. (bd. dirs.), Rocky Mountain Oil and Gas Assn. (chmn. transp. com.), Nat. Assn. Mfrs. (bd. dirs.), Western Hwy. Inst. (bd. dirs.). Republican. Methodist. Office: PO Box 2360 Casper WY 82602

TRUE, HENRY ALFONSO, III, oil company executive, financial executive, rancher; b. Hayden, Colo., Oct. 4, 1942; s. Henry Alfonso and Jean (Durland) T.; m. Karen S. Wright, Nov. 29, 1968; children—Thea Jean, Henry Alfonso, Barbara Bowles. B.A., U. Wyo., 1966, B.S., 1967. Landman Belle Fourche Pipeline Co., Casper, Wyo., 1969-72, sr. v.p., 1981—; crude oil products rep. Black Hills Oil Marketers, Inc., Casper, 1972-75; crude oil and products rep. Res. Oil Purchasing Co., Casper, 1975-77; v.p. True Oil Purchasing Co., Casper, 1977-80; ptnr. Eighty-Eight Oil Co., Casper, 1980—; ptnr. True Geothermal Energy Co., Casper, 1981—; pres. Midland Fin. Corp., Casper, 1980-84; dir. Hilltop Nat. Bank, Casper. Pres. United Way of Natrona County, Inc., Wyo., 1979; state chmn. Ducks Unltd., Inc., Casper, 1982-84. Mem. Ind. Petroleum Assn. Am. (v.p.), Mont./Wyo. Liquid Petroleum Gas Assn. (pres.), Petroleum Assn. Wyo. (pres.), Rocky Mountain Oil and Gas Assn., U.S. Bus. Industry Council (area v.p.), Cowboy Hall of Fame (Buckaroo life mem.), Sigma Nu. Republican. Episcopalian. Lodge: Elks. Office: Belle Fourche Pipeline Co 895 W Rivercross Rd Casper WY 82601

TRUE, HENRY ALFONSO, JR., oil and gas producer, drilling contractor, rancher, banker; b. Cheyenne, Wyo., June 12, 1915; s. Henry A. and Anna Barbara (Diemer) T.; m. Jean Durland, Mar. 20, 1938; children—Tamma Jean (Mrs. Donald Hatten), Henry Alfonso, III, Diemer D., David L. B.S. in Indsl. Engring., Mont. State Coll., 1937; Ph.D. (hon.) in Engring., Montana State U., 1983. Roustabout, pumper, foreman The Tex. Co., 1937-45, supt. drilling and prodn. for Wyo., 1945-48; mgr. Res. Drilling Co., 1948-51, pres., 1951-59; ptnr. True Drilling Co. and True Oil Co., Casper, Wyo., 1951—; v.p., sec. Toolpushers Supply Co., 1952-53, pres., 1954—; v.p., sec. True Service Co., 1953, pres., 1954-70; pres. True Bldg. Corp., 1956-67, Smokey Oil Co., 1975—, Belle Fourche Pipeline Co., 1957—, Black Hills Trucking, Inc., 1977—; owner True Ranches, Inc., 1957-76, pres., 1977-86; pres. True Oil Purchasing Co., 1977-81, True Geothermal Drilling Co., 1981—; ptnr. Eighty-Eight Oil Co., 1955—, Double Four Ranch Co., 1980—, True Geothermal Energy Co., 1981—, True Ranches, 1983—; chmn. Powder River Oil Shippers Service, Inc., 1963-67; pres. Camp Creek Gas Co., 1964-77; v.p. George Mancini Feed Lots, Brighton, Colo., 1964-72; v.p. Black Hills Marketers, Inc., 1966-72, pres., 1973-80; v.p. White Stallion Ranch, Inc., Tucson, 1965—; pres. Res. Oil Purchasing Co., 1972-73; bd. dirs. Midland Fin. Corp., Research Corp.; chmn. Hilltop Nat. Bank, 1977—, Mountain Plaza Nat. Bank, 1980—; mem. Wyo. adv. com., 1965-84; mem. exec. com. Wyo. Oil Industry Com., 1958-74, treas., 1958-59, pres. 1960-62; dir. Rocky Mountain Oil Show, 1955; mem. adv. bd. Internat. Oil and Gas Edn. Ctr., 1964—, vice chmn., 1969-73; mem. natural gas adv. council Fed. Power Commn., 1964-65, mem. exec. adv. com., 1971-74; mem. exec. co. com. Gas Supply Com., 1965-69, vice chmn., 1967-69; mem. adv. council Pub. Land Rev. Commn., 1965-70; dir. U.S. Bus. and Indsl. Council, 1971—, exec. com., 1974—; mem. Nat. Petroleum Council, 1962— , nat. oil policy com., 1965, vice chmn., 1970-71, chmn., 1972-73; mem. Rocky Mountain Petroleum Industry Adv. Com., Fed. Energy Office, 1973-77; hon. dir. Mountain Bell, bd. advisors, 1965-84. Chmn. advance gifts com. United Fund; nat. assoc. Boys Clubs Am., 1964-69, hon. chmn. local chpt. 1971; trustee Casper Air Terminal, 1960-71, pres. 1964-65, 67-68; mem. research fellows Southwestern Legal Found., 1968—; trustee U. Wyo., 1965-77, pres. bd., 1971-73, mem. adult edn. and community service council, 1961-64; bd. govs. Western Ind. Colls. Found., 1963-65; nat. trustee Voice of Youth, 1968; bd. dirs., trustee Nat. Cowboy Hall of Fame and Western Heritage Ctr., 1975—, pres. bd., 1978-80, chmn., 1980-82; trustee Buffalo Bill Meml. Assn., 1983—; Wyo. state fin. chmn. Reagan-Bush campaign '84. Named Oil Man of Yr., 1959, recipient Honored Citizen award, 1964, Casper C. of C.; Chief Roughneck of Yr. award, Lone Star Steel award 1965, ann. Indsl. award Wyo. Assn. Realtors, 1965, Pierre F. Goodrich Conservation award Polit. Econ. and Research Ctr., 1982; named Disting. Businessman for Small Bus. Mgmt., 1966-67, recipient Alumni Medallion U. Wyo., 1978; named to Wisdom Hall Fame; named Exec. of Year Teton chpt. Profl. Secs. Internat., 1985. Mem. Internat. Assn. Drilling Contractors (dir. 1950—), Am. Petroleum Inst. (dir. 1960—, exec. com. 1970—, Gold Medal for Disting.

Service award 1985), Rocky Mountain Oil and Gas Assn. (treas. 1954-55, v.p. Wyo. 1956-58, dir. 1950—, pres. 1962-63, exec. com. 1954—, hon. mem., 1978), Ind. Petroleum Assn. Am. (v.p. Wyo. 1960-61, exec. com. 1962—, pres. 1964-65; Russell B. Brown Meml. award 1975), Rocky Mountain Petroleum Pioneers, Wyo. Stockgrowers Assn., Casper Petroleum (dir. 1954), U.S. C. of C. (dir. 1975-81), Casper C. of C., All-Am Wildcatters, 25 Year Club Petroleum Industry, Ind. Petroleum Assn. Mountain States (Rocky Mountain Wildcatter of Yr. award 1982), Petroleum Assn. Wyo. (dir. 1974—), Am. Judicature Soc. (mem. com. just976), Sigma Chi (Significant Sig award, 1981), Beta Gamma Sigma (hon. mem., 1971 Alpha chpt. Wyo.). Republican. Episcopalian (vestry 1960-62). Lodge: Masons, Shriner, Elks. Office: Belle Fourche Pipeline Co 895 W Rivercross Rd PO Drawer 2360 Casper WY 82602

TRUEBLOOD, DONALD C., environmental scientist; b. Baton Rouge, Dec. 10, 1954; s. Malcolm Stanley and Audene Jane (Hoppe) T.; m. Linda L. Barrus, Dec. 28, 1974; children: Nena Ann, Eric Stanley. BS, U. Wyo., 1977, MS, 1980. Research asst. U. Wyo., 1978-80; project coordinator GPR Inc., Laramie, Wyo., 1980-82; reclamation supr. N. Antelope Coal Co., Gillette, Wyo., 1982-85; environ. supr. Powder River Coal Co., Gillette, 1985—. Mem. Soc. Range Mgmt., Sigma Xi, Alpha Zeta, Gamma Sigma Delta, Phi Kappa Phi. Republican. Home: 6506 Hendrich Ct Gillette WY 82716 Office: Powder River Coal Co Caller Box 3034 Gillette WY 82716

TRUEBLOOD, KENNETH NYITRAY, chemist, educator; b. Dobbs Ferry, N.Y., Apr. 24, 1920; s. Howard Moffit and Louise (Nyitray) T.; m. Jean Turner, Mar. 7, 1970. A.B., Harvard, 1941; Ph.D., Calif. Inst. Tech., 1947. Postdoctoral fellow chemistry dept. Calif. Inst. Tech., Pasadena, 1947-49; faculty UCLA, 1949—, prof. chemistry, 1960—, chmn. dept. chemistry, 1965-70, dean Coll. Letters and Sci., 1971-74, chmn. acad. senate, 1983-84; vis. prof. chemistry U. Ibadan, Nigeria, 1964-65; Mem. U.S. Nat. Com. on Crystallography, 1960-65, vice chmn., 1963-65; exchange visitor to USSR, 1965. Recipient Fulbright award Oxford (Eng.) U., 1956-57, UCLA Disting. Teaching award, 1961, award for excellence in teaching Mfg. Chemists Assn., 1978, Coll. prize Coll. Letters and Scis., UCLA, 1982; Guggenheim fellow Eidgenössiche Technische Hochschule Zurich, Switzerland, 1976-77. Mem. Am. Chem. Soc., Am. Crystallographic Assn., Phi Beta Kappa, Sigma Xi, Alpha Chi Sigma. Research and publs. on theory of chromatography, chem. crystallography including high speed computer applications; analysis of molecule motion in crystals. Home: 1089 Moraga Dr Los Angeles CA 90049

TRUEBLOOD, MARK H(ERVY), veterinarian; b. Phoenix, Dec. 14, 1947; s. Ralph Hervy and Crystal Joyce (Carlton) T.; m. Susan Lee Wallace, Jan. 24, 1970; children: Karen Joy, Jason Robert. BS, Ariz. State U., 1970; DVM, Wash. State U., 1974. Vet. East Maryland Animal Hosp., Phoenix, 1974-75, Moon Valley Animal Hosp., Phoenix, 1974-75; vet., owner Glenex Animal Clinic, Glendale, Ariz., 1975-80, Apollo Vet. Assn., Glendale, 1980—; med. cons. Ariz. Dept. Fish and Game, 1980—; speaker vet. confs. Mem. zoning and planning commn., Glendale, 1981-84. Mem. Ariz. Vet. Med. Assn. (pres. 1986-87), Cen. Ariz. Vet. Med. Assn. (pres. 1983-84), Ariz. Vet. Med. Assn. (pres., founder polit. action com. 1983-86), Am. Vet. Dental Soc., Ariz. Acad. Vet. Practice (bd. dirs. 1985-86), Companion Animal Assn. Ariz., Glendale C. of C., Ariz. State U. Alumni Assn. (bd. dirs. 1986—), Wash. State U. Alumni Assn. (Leadership award 1986), Alpha Psi, Alpha Zeta. Republican. Baptist. Avocations: alpine skiing, decoy collecting, trap shooting. Home: 5016 W Ruth Ave Glendale AZ 85302 Office: Apollo Vet Assn 5016 W Ruth Ave Glendale AZ 85302

TRUEX, GEORGE ROBERT, JR., banker; b. Red Bank, N.J., May 29, 1924; s. George Robert and Elsie D. (White) T.; m. Nancy Carroll Burt, May 10, 1947; children: Peter Barclay, Amy Dinsmore. A.B. in Econs., Rutgers U., 1949; LL.D. (hon.), Pacific Luth. U. Sr. v.p. Irving Trust Co., N.Y.C., 1949-66; exec. v.p. Bank of Am., San Francisco, 1966-73; vice chmn. Small Bus. Enterprises Co. (subsidiary), 1968-72; chmn., chief exec. officer Rainier Bancorp., Seattle, 1974—, Rainier Nat. Bank, from 1973; dir., mem. exec. com. Nat. Airlines, Inc., Miami, Fla., 1962-80, INA Life Ins. Co. N.Y., 1965-68; dir. Pan Am. World Airways, N.Y.C., Universal Furniture Ltd., Hong Kong, Seattle br. Fed. Res. Bank San Francisco. Bd. dirs. Calif. Bankers Assn., 1969-73, Wash. State China Relations Council, 1979-83; Fin. chmn. Calif. Gov.'s Task Force on Flood Relief, 1969-73; mem. fin. advisory com. CAB, 1970-71; mem. orthopaedic council Orthopaedic Hosp., Los Angeles, 1969-72; trustee Calif. Inst. Arts, 1968-72; dir., sec.-treas., mem. exec. com. Washington Roundtable, 1983—; bd. dirs. Walt Disney Assos. for Calif. Inst. Arts, 1972-81, San Francisco Planning and Urban Renewal Assn., 1973, East-West Ctr. Found., Hawaii; bd. dirs. Jr. Achievement So. Calif., 1967-72, pres., 1968-70, Western Regional bd. dirs., 1968-72; nat. bd. dirs. Jr. Achievement, Inc., 1968-75; bd. dirs. Jr. Achievement Greater Seattle, 1976-77; div. chmn. United Way, Inc., Los Angeles, 1970, 71; asso. gen. campaign chmn. United Way of King County, 1976, 78, gen. chmn., 1979, bd. dirs., 1979-83; bd. regents Seattle U., 1976-80; bd. dirs. Virgina Mason Hosp., 1976—, treas., 1982—; trustee Seattle U., 1980—, Bank of Am. Found., 1973; mem. adv. bd. Grad. Sch. Bus. Adminstrn., U. Wash., 1975—, chmn., 1978-80; co-chmn. fin. com. Wash. State Republican Com., 1983—. Served to capt., cav. AUS, World War II, ETO. Mem. Assn. Res. City Bankers, Seattle C. of C. (trustee 1975-78). Clubs: Bankers (San Francisco), Bohemian (San Francisco); Seattle Golf (Seattle), Wash. Athletic (Seattle), Rainier (Seattle), Broadmoor Golf (Seattle); Useless Bay Country (Langley, Wash.). Office: Rainier Nat Bank Box 3966 Seattle WA 98124 *

TRUEX, LEIGH PATRICIA, pickle company executive, real estate broker; b. N.Y.C., Jan. 18, 1926; d. Harry and Dorothy (Abrams) Mahl; m. Wendell R. Truex, Nov. 26, 1947 (dec. 1970); children—Wende Stewart, Timothy. B.A., U. Pacific, 1950. Owner, pres. Bubbies of San Francisco, 1981—, The Best Kosher Dill Pickle Co., San Francisco, 1981—. Judge, Marin County Fair. Named Pickle Queen, Pickle Packers Internat., 1963; recipient Blue Ribbon award Culinary Carnival, 1981. Mem. Nat. Acad. Sci., Junior Aid, Nat. Press Club, Nat. Assn. Specialty Food Trade, Inc. Democrat. Clubs: Golden Gateway Tennis (San Francisco); Profl. Women's. Patentee in field. Home: 405 Davis Ct Apt 1305 San Francisco CA 94111

TRUITT, HARRY ERWIN, diving equipment supply company executive; b. Weisbaden, W.Ger., Jan. 13, 1948; came to U.S., 1950, naturalized, 1952; s. Clarence James and Lidia (Basenko) T.; m. Laura Patricia Vazquez, June 30, 1978 (div. May 1981); m. Donna R. Franck, Oct. 17, 1986. B.S. in Indsl. Engring., Bradley U., 1970. Instr., Profl. Assn. Diving Instrn., Chgo., 1963—, master instr., Tacoma, Wash., 1971—; instr. Nat. Assn. Underwater Instrn., Seattle, 1971—; sec.-treas. Puget Sound Lighthouse, Renton, Wash, 1972-80; pres. Lighthouse Diving Ctr., Seattle, 1980—; founder, promoter Great Underwater Pumpkin Hunt, Seattle, 1975-81, producer, founder NW Dive Report, Seattle, 1984; founder First Nat. Scuba Week Chase's Calendar, 1983. Author: Guide to Our Underwater World, 1973. Contbr. articles to profl. jours.; underwater photographer for mags. Mem. Profl. Assn. Diving Instrn., Nat. Assn. Underwater Instrn. (Internat. Service award, 1980), Wash. Assn. Diving Retailers (pres. 1980—). Office: Lighthouse Diving Ctr Inc 5421-C 196th Ave SW Lynnwood WA 98036

TRUJILLO, LOUIS CELSO, insurance company executive; b. Albuquerque, Feb. 5, 1938; s. Pete and Jennie (Padilla) T.; m. Yvonne Ruth Chavez (div. 1960); 1 child, Michael Louis; m. Beatrice Silvia Tafoya, Apr. 27, 1962; children: Louie Gregory, Dolores Maria, Catherine Veronica. Student, U. N.Mex., Nat. Fire Acad., Albuquerque, Eastern N.Mex. U. Asst. chief Albuquerque Fire Dept., 1958-80; chief St. Petersburg (Fla.) Fire Dept., 1981-83; sr. field rep. Rockwood Ins., Albuquerque, 1983—. Chmn. Community Assn., Albuquerque, 1965-73; vice chmn. Ward 10, Albuquerque, 1984—; mem. City/County Unification Task Force, Albuquerque, 1983-85. Mem. Nat. Council on Compensation Ins., N.Mex. Workers Compensation Assn., N.Mex. Ins. Assn., Am. Assn. Safety Engrs., N.Mex. Ind. Ins. Agts. (assoc.), Ind. Order Fire Fighters (life). Democrat. Roman Catholic. Lodge: KC. Avocations: sports, hunting, fishing. Home: 2301 Malpaiz Rd SW Albuquerque NM 87105 Office: Rockwood Ins PO Box 35400 2201 San Pedro NE Albuquerque NM 87176-5400

TRUJILLO, RICHARD RAY, metallurgical research engineer; b. Albuquerque, Apr. 11, 1958; s. Ross and Mary (Gallegos) T. Student, USAF Acad., 1976-78; BSMetE, U. Wash., 1983. Chief metallurgist Litton Fastening Systems div. Litton Systems Inc., Los Angeles, 1983-84; sr. engr. Boeing Comml. Airplane Co., Seattle, 1984—. Active Seattle/King County Big Brothers Assn., 1982-83, Community Pheresis Donor Program, Seattle, 1984—. Mem. Am. Soc. Metals, Metall. Soc. of AIME. Democrat. Roman Catholic. Avocations: scuba diving, sailing, skiing. Home: 17127 56th Ave W Lynnwood WA 98037 Office: Boeing Comml Airplane Co PO Box 3707 MS 97-29 Seattle WA 98124

TRUJILLO-OVIEDO, PATRICIA ANN, environmental biologist, toxicologist; b. Los Alamos, N.Mex., Nov. 8, 1949; d. Jacobo Ortega and Isabelle (Garcia) Trujillo; m. Marco Antonio Oviedo, Aug. 18, 1980; 1 child, Jacobo Javier. BS in Agrl. Biology, N.Mex. State U., 1972, MS In Toxicology, 1984; MS in Biology, Utah State U., 1977. Research asst. N.Mex. State U., 1972, 1977-80, research specialist, 1980-85; chem. technician Los Alamos Nat. Lab., 1972; research technician Utah State U., 1973-76; environmentalist N.Mex. State Hwy. Dept., Santa Fe, 1985—; pub. involvement coordinator N.Mex. State Hwy. Dept., 1985—. Author pamphlet on local art, 1983 and contbr. chpt. to tech. book, 1975. Mem. AAAS (cert. merit Southwest chpt. 1983), Am. Inst. Biol. Sci., N.Mex. Acad of Sci., Sigma XI. Republican. Roman Catholic. Avocations: trail guide, burro trail rides. Home: Box 23A Centinela Ranch Chimayo NM 87522

TRULES, ALISON JUDY, social worker, psychotherapist; b. Mineola, N.Y., Apr. 7, 1952; d. Joseph and Rosalind (Rosenberg) T. BS cum laude, U. Vt., 1976; MSW, U. Calif., Berkeley, 1980. Intern in social work U. Calif. Med. Ctr., San Francisco, 1978-79; intern in psychiatry dept. Kaiser-Permanente, San Francisco, 1979-80; med. social worker dept. social services Kaiser-Permanente, Hayward, Calif., 1981; hospice social worker Home Health and Counseling, RIchmond, Calif., 1981; mental health specialist Youth Interagy. Assessment Consultation & Treatment Clinic, Concord, Calif., 1981—; field work instr., clin. supr. U. Calif., Berkeley, 1983—; pvt. practice psychotherapy, 1984—; group psychotherapist U. CAlif., San Francisco, 1986. Mem. Nat. Assn. Social Work (cert.), Berkeley Psychotherapy Inst., Walnut Creek Hosp. (affiliate), Contra Costa County Child Abuse Council, Contra Costa County Sexual Abuse Task Force, Bay Area Adolescent Offender Treatment Network. Democrat. Jewish.

TRULL, SAMUEL GEORGE, educator; b. Buffalo, Nov. 26, 1922; s. Samuel G. Trull; children: Robert, Deborah, Pamela. B.S.E.E., Union Coll., 1944; M.S.E.E., Renesselar Poly. Inst., 1947; Ph.D., Cornell U., 1956; lic. profl. engr., N.Y. 1950. Lighting and power engr., sales supr. Central Hudson Gas and Electric, Poughkeepsie, N.Y., 1947-55; instr. U. Calif.-Berkeley, 1957-62; prof. mgmt. San Francisco State U., 1964—; pres. Ednl. Mgmt., Inc., 1960—, Owner Builder Dir. Inc., 1980, Rancho Tres Mesas Inc., 1974. Served to lt. USN, 1943-46. Mem. Acad. Mgmt. Contbr. numerous articles to profl. jours. Office: Ednl Mgmt Inc 2831 7th St Berkeley CA 94710

TRULOVE, PAUL CHAPPELL, materials compatibility research scientist; b. Travis, Calif., Sept. 30, 1961; s. Donald George and Sarah Ann (Chappell) T.; m. Lona Lydia Mathes, Oct. 8, 1983; children: Katherine Ann, Margaret Chappel. BS in Chemistry, U. Kans., 1984; postgrad., Calif. State U., Northridge, 1985—. Research asst. U. Kans., Lawrence, 1982-83, teaching asst., 1983; chem. research officer Air Force Rocket Propulsion Lab., Edwards AFB, 1984—. Served to 1st lt. USAF, 1984—. Mem. Am. Chem. Soc. Republican. Club: Toastmaster (sec. 1986—). Avocations: fishing, golfing, gardening. Office: Air Force Rocket Propulsion Lab LKL Edwards AFB CA 93523

TRUMAN, ROLLAND A., judge; b. Loma Linda, Calif., Apr. 30, 1912; s. Archibald William and Daisy Ethel (Nary) T.; m. Iola LaVerne Gilbert, June 14, 1941 (div.); children—Rolland Gilbert, Norris Wesley; m. Laurel A. Weibel, Sept. 15, 1953; children—Tracy, Tammy, Trent, Tricia, Trina. B.A., U. So. Calif., 1940, J.D., 1943. Bar: Calif. 1942, U.S. Dist. Ct. (all dists.) Calif. 1942, U.S. Supreme Ct. 1957, U.S. Ct. Claims 1978, U.S. Tax Ct. 1978, U.S. Customs Ct. 1978, U.S. Ct. Customs and Patent Appeals 1978, U.S. Ct. Internat. Trade 1981. Atty., Pacific Electric Railway Co., Los Angeles, 1942-44; ptnr. Paap & Truman, Long Beach, Calif., 1944-48; sole practice, Long Beach, 1948-50; ptnr. Whitman & Truman, Southgate, Calif., 1950-58; sole practice, Southgate, 1958-63; superior ct. commnr. Los Angeles County, 1963-77, judge pro tem, 1980-81, 1982—; cons., referee, appeals hearing officer, arbitrator Los Angeles County, 1977—. Contbr. articles to profl. jours. Mem., Ch.-State Council, 1965—; trustee White Meml. Med. Ctr., Los Angeles, 1975-83; mem. Banjos-A-Plenty, El Monte, Calif., 1979—, Smithsonian Nat. Assocs., 1984—; performer Jerry Reilly and His Calif. Banjoleers, 1980—. Recipient numerous awards for community service and profl. excellence including Commendation, Congl. Record, 1983. Fellow Am. Acad. Matrimonial Lawyers; mem. ABA, Assn. Trial Lawyers Am., Calif. Bar Assn., Los Angeles County Bar Assn., Long Beach Bar Assn., Delta Theta Thi (Cert. of Honor). Democrat. Seventh-Day Adventist (elder). Clubs: Associated Radio Amateurs (Long Beach); Fretted Instrument Guild of Am.; Supreme Ct. Hist. Soc., Council on Religious Freedom (life, bd. dirs.). Home: 4522 Greenmeadow Rd Long Beach CA 90808

TRUMBULL, ROY HOWARD, electrical engineer; b. San Francisco, Nov. 28, 1939; s. Lyman Burr and Sue Helen (Higgins) T.; B.S.E.E., Heald Engring. Coll., 1959; A.A., Coll. of Marin, 1965; postgrad. San Francisco State U.; m. Patricia E. Pick, Aug. 28, 1965; children—Erica, David. Research engr. Autonetics, 1959-62; chief engr. Sundial Broadcasting, 1962-63, Apollo Broadcasting, 1963-66, Wright Broadcasting, 1966-68; supr. Metromedia, 1968-71, CBS, 1971-76; instr. Laney Coll., 1976-79; asst. chief engr. Chronicle Broadcasting Co., 1979; owner, operator Trumbull Co., El Cerrito, Calif., 1972—. Adult leader Boy Scouts Am. Mem. Calif. Council Electronic Instrs. (pres.; Allan Maxwell award), Soc. Broadcast Engrs. (cert.); Richard T. Parks award chpt. 40), Soc. Motion Picture and TV Engrs. Jewish. Author: Printed Circuit Techniques for the Hobbyist, 1974; contbr. articles to profl. jours. Office: 1001 Van Ness St San Francisco CA 94109

TRUSCINSKI, WAYNE FRANCIS, dentist; b. St. Paul, Aug. 9, 1948; s. Frank Joseph and Dorothy Marie (Herzog) T.; m. Anne Marie Honey, Aug. 18, 1971 (div. May 1982); m. Kelly Anne Hanley, Sept. 14, 1984. AA, Inver Hills Community Coll., 1972; BA cum laude, Augsburg Coll., 1974; DDS, U. Minn., 1979. Gen. dental officer Bremerhaven (Fed. Republic Germany) Dental Clinic, 1979-81; gen. dentist Siren (Wis.) Dental Clinic, 1983; facility dental officer Indian Health Service, Wolf Point, Mont., 1983-85; dental chief Ft. Peck Service Unit Indian Health Service, Poplar, Mont., 1985—. Served to capt. U.S. Army, 1967-70, Vietnam, also 1979-82. Decorated Bronze Star with V device, Purple Heart. Mem. Minn. Soc. Clin. and Exptl. Hypnosis. Democrat. Roman Catholic. Club: Ducks Unltd. Avocations: hunting, canoeing, weight tng., butterfly collecting. Home: 521 Johnson St Wolf Point MT 59201 Office: Verne E Gibbs Health Ctr PO Box 67 Poplar MT 54255

TRUSSEL, HAROLD JUNIOR, school principal; b. Montpelier, Idaho, July 4, 1936; s. William and Wanda Matilda (Jaussi) T.; m. Vilate Gardner, Jan. 21, 1961; children—Reed William, Bryan Gardner, Allison. B.S., U. Utah, 1963, M.S., 1968, Ednl. Specialist, 1972; postgrad. U. Fla., 1977. Tchr., South High Sch., Salt Lake City, 1970-73; acting prin. SE Jr. High Sch., Salt Lake City, 1972-73; prin. Lincoln Jr. High Sch., Salt Lake City, 1974-75, Jordan Intermediate Sch., Salt Lake City, 1975-78, Bryant Intermediate Sch., Salt Lake City, 1978-84, West High Sch., Salt Lake City, 1984—; chmn. Utah State Middle Sch. Com., 1981-83, Utah Jr. High Adv. Com., 1984—; dir. Nat. Tchr. Corps, Salt Lake, 1976-78. Organizer, officer Freedom Clubs for Am., Salt Lake City, 1979—; coach Little League Baseball, Salt Lake City, 1968-70; mem. Town Council Meeting, Salt Lake City, 1976; mem., speaker Utah Pub. Productivity Fair, 1983. Recipient Valley Forge Freedoms Found. medal, 1983; named Best High Sch. Prin. Utah, Utah Holiday Mag., 1985. Mem. Salt Lake Adminstrs. Exec. Council, Salt Lake Assn. Secondary Sch. Adminstrs. (chmn. adminstr. edn. com. 1981-82, chmn. profl. rights and responsibility com. 1979-80), Nat. Assn. Secondary Sch. Prins., Phi Delta Kappa. Republican. Address: West High Sch 241 N 300 W Salt Lake City UT 84103

TRUSSELL, FREDRICK GEORGE, reactor operator, consultant; b. Albuquerque, Mar. 5, 1950; s. Travis L. and Enid L. (Wells) T.; m. Kathryn D. Stringfellow, June 1, 1968 (div. Oct. 1968); m. Patricia Humphries, Oct. 23, 1974; children: Travis, Todd, Cody, Danny, Mike. B in Nuclear Engring., Columbia Pacific U., 1984. Reactor operator U.S. Navy, 1972-80; field technician Eberline Instrument Co., Albuquerque, 1980; reactor operator Sandia Nat. Labs., Albuquerque, 1981—. Author: ACRR Operators Manual, 1983, ACRR Experimenters Manual, 1984, Multiple Listing Software, 1984. Bernalillo County chmn. Am. Diabetes Assn. Bike Ride, 1984. Club: Optimists (charter, bd. dirs. 1981-83, 84-85, v.p. 1983-84). Office: 7256 Sandia Nat Labs Albuquerque NM 87185

TRUSSELL, R(OBERT) RHODES, environmental and sanitary engineer; b. National City, Calif; s. Robert L. and Margaret (Kessing) T.; m. Elizabeth Shane, Nov. 26, 1969; children—Robert Shane, Charles Bryan. BSCE, U. Calif.-Berkeley, 1966, MS, 1967, PhD, 1972. With J.M. Montgomery Cons. Engrs., Pasadena, Calif., 1972—, v.p., 1977, sr. v.p., 1986, mgr. water quality treatment, 1980—. Mem. com. on water treatment chems. Nat. Acad. Sci., 1980-82, mem. com. 3d part cert., 1982-83, com. on irrigation-induced water quality problems, 1985—, chmn. subcom. on treatment; mem. U.S./German research com. on corrosion of water systems, 1984-85; mem. U.S./Dutch research com. on organics in water, 1982-83; mem. U.S./USSR research com. on water treatment, 1985—. Mem. joint editorial bd. Standards Methods for Examination of Water and Wastewater, 1980—; mem. editorial adv. bd. Environ. and Sci. and Tech., 1977-83; contbr. articles to profl. publs. Mem. Am. Water Works Assn., Water Pollution Control Fedn., Internat. Water Pollution Research Assn., Am. Chem. Soc., Am. Inst. Chem. Engrs., Nat. Assn. Corrosion Engrs., Sigma Xi. Office: 250 N Madison PO Box 7009 Pasadena CA 91109-7009

TRYBUL, THEODORE N., government official; b. Chgo., Apr. 12, 1935; s. Theodore and Sophie T.; m. Barbara Reynolds, Aug. 22, 1959; children—Catherine, Barbara, Adrienne, Diane, Theodore. B.S. in Mech. Engring, U. Ill., 1957; M.S. in Mech. Engring, U. N.Mex., 1963; D.Sc. magna cum laude, George Washington U., 1976. Research staff Sandia (N.Mex.) Labs., 1957-64; engring. group supr. Gen. Dynamics Corp.; project mgr. Aerospace Corp., San Bernardino, Calif., 1965-67; program dir. Raytheon Co., Bedford, Mass., 1967-68; div. chief USA Advanced Materiel Concepts Agy., AMC, Washington, 1968-74; dir. TECOM, Md.; now project mgr. electronic warfare programs, advanced programs div. Hughes Aircraft Co., Los Angeles; prof. engring. George Washington U., 1976-83, Am. U., 1978-83, Calif. State Coll.; prof. mgmt. U. No. Colo.; prof. system scis. U. So. Calif.; mem. USN Bur. Weapons Adv. Council, joint study group on Mil. Resource Allocation Methodology, Army Sci. Bd. Author: Operations Research, 1968, Systems Analysis, 1971, Systems Engineering, 1974; contbr. numerous articles to profl. jours. Pres. Gunston Sch. PTA, Lorton, Va., Aquia Harbor Assn., Hollowing Point Potomac River Estates Assn., Assn. Sea Pines Plantation Oroperty Owners, Inc.; mem. council Our Lady of Angels Ch., Woodbride, Va. Served with U.S. Army, 1959-61. Recipient Marquette U. Scholarship award, U. Ill. Scholarship Key, U. N.Mex. Math. award, George Washington U. teaching fellowship, U.S. Govt. Long Term Tng. award. Mem. Internat. Soc. Tech. Assessment, Indsl. Research Inst., World Future Soc., Washington Acad. Sci., Armed Forces Mgmt. Assn., Military Ops. Research Soc. (chmn. research and devel.), Washington Ops. Research Council, AAAS (sci. reviewer, mem. govt. fluidics coordination group, standardization, reliability and fabrication com.), Am. Soc. Mil. Comptrollers, ASME, Am. Def. Preparedness Assn. (needs analysis and effictiveness analysis coms.), Assn. U.S. Army, Soc. Computer Simulation (chmn.), Sigma Xi, Kappa Mu Epsilon, Pi Tau Sigma, Tau Beta Pi. Roman Catholic. Clubs: Sea Pines, Millionaire's, KC. Patentee in field. Home: 950 Virginia St El Segundo CA 90245 Office: Hughes Aircraft Co Bldg R-10 MS12011 Los Angeles CA 90009

TRYNCHY, PETER, Canadian government official; b. Rochfort Bridge, Alta., Can., Aug. 22, 1931; s. Peter and Anna (Roszko) T.; m. Lorraine Mary Wilkinson, Oct. 29, 1952; children—Darlene Annette, Marlin Peter. Student pub. schs., Rochfort Bridge, Alta., Can. Past mem. Mayerthorpe (Can.) Town Council; mem. Alta. Legis. Assembly, Edmonton, 1971—, minister Recreation and Parks, 1979-86; chmn. Alta. Hail and Crop Ins. Bd. Conservative. Clubs: Masons, Royal Can. Legion, Mayerthorne Curling.

TRZYNA, THADDEUS CHARLES, academic institution administrator; b. Chgo., Oct. 26, 1939; s. Thaddeus Stephen and Irene Mary (Giese) T.; divorced; 1 child, Jennifer. BA in Internat. Relations, U. So. Calif., 1961; PhD in Govt., Claremont Grad. Sch., 1975. Vice consul U.S. Govt., Elisabethville and Katanga, Zaire, 1962-63; consul U.S. Govt., Leopoldville, Peoples Republic of Congo, 1963-64; sec. Nat. Mil. Info. Disclosure Policy Com. U.S. Govt., Washington, 1964-67; pres. Calif. Inst. Pub. Affairs, Claremont, 1969—; mem. commn. Environ. Planning Internat. Union for Conservation of Nature and Natural Resources, 1983—; chmn. Calif. Forum on Hazardous Materials, 1985—, Calif. Farmlands Project Task Force, 1981-84; cons. U.S. and Calif. State Agys. on environ. policy, cons. on devel. of natural resources Univ. for Peace, Costa Rica; lectr. internat. relations, Pomona Coll. Author: The California Handbook, rev. 5th edit. 1986. Mem. Am. Fgn. Service Assn., Sierra Club (v.p. 1975-77, chmn. internat. com. 1977-79). Democrat. Mem. Unitarian Ch. Office: Calif Inst Pub Affairs PO Box 10 Claremont CA 91711

TSAI, ROBERT CHINFU, engineer, consultant; b. Taipei, Taiwan, Republic of China, Aug. 15, 1941; came to U.S., 1966; s. Ching Liang and May Yee (Chen) T.; m. Rita Mei-Bao, June 1, 1968; children Albert Richard, Anthony R., Hubert R. BS, Chung Yuan Christian Coll. Sci. & Engring., Taipei, 1965; MS, Wichita State U., 1970; PhD, U. Va., 1973. Sect. head Engelhard Industries div. Engelhard Corp., Edison, N.J., 1974-75; sr. devel. engr. Intel Corp., Cupertino, Calif., 1975-77; group leader Hughes Aircraft Co., Carlsbad, Calif., 1977-79; dept. mgr. Singer Librascope, Glendale, Calif., 1979-86; sr. mgr. LASA Industries Inc., Santa Clara, Calif., 1986—. Patentee in field. Mem. Am. Phys. Soc., Am. Optical Soc., Soc. for Info. Display (program com. 1980—), Soc. Photooptical Engrs. (session chmn. 1982-83), Laser Inst. Am. (symposium chmn. 1984, Contribution of Service award 1984), United Chinese Am. League, Taiwanese Am. League, Sigma Xi, Sigma Pi Sigma. Home: 100 Hillview Ave Los Altos CA 94022 Office: LASA Industries Inc 3333C Octavius Dr Santa Clara CA 95054

TSAY, CHEN-HUI, process and device engineer; b. Chingshui, Republic of China, Oct. 23, 1952; came to U.S., 1979; s. Yi-Ian and Duey (Lee) T.; m. Mei-Chung P. Li, Sept. 6, 1981. BS, Tunghai U., Taichung, Republic of China, 1976; MSEE, U. So. Calif., 1981. Teaching asst. Tunghai U., 1978-79, U. Calif. San Diego, La Jolla, 1979-80, U. So. Calif., Los Angeles, 1981; process engr. Supertex, Inc., Sunnyvale, Calif., 1983—. Mem. IEEE. Home: 3241 Terra Cotta Dr San Jose CA 95135 Office: Supertex Inc 1225 Bordeaux Dr Sunnyvale CA 94088

TSCHOPP, JUERG FRIEDRICH, molecular biologist; b. Ziefen, Switzerland, July 10, 1950; came to U.S., 1979; s. Fritz and Verena Tschopp. BA, U. Basel, Switzerland, 1974, PhD, 1979. Cert. tchr. coll. Postdoctoral fellow U. Calif., Berkeley, 1979-83; staff research scientist Salk Inst. Biotech./Indsl. Assocs., Inc., La Jolla, Calif., 1983—. Contbr. articles to profl. jours. Served to lt. Swiss Nat. Army, 1976-79. Fellow Swiss Nat. Found., Bern, 1979-80, Janggen-Poehn Found., St. Gallen, Switzerland, 1981, U. Calif., Berkeley, 1982. Mem. Am. Soc. Microbiology, Am. Chem. Soc., Grad. Bus. Students Assn. Club: Swiss (San Diego). Avocations: skiing, running, cooking, classical guitar. Home: 12458 Carmel Cape San Diego CA 92130 Office: Salk Inst Biotech/Indsl Assocs 505 S Coast Blvd La Jolla CA 92037

TSENG, GAN-TAI, aerospace corporation official; b. Chungking, China, Sept. 9, 1938; came to U.S., 1962, naturalized, 1973; s. Shao-hsuen and Yunying (Shieh) T.; B.S., Nat. Taiwan U., 1960; M.S., U. Calif.-Berkeley, 1964; Engr. (univ. fellow), Stanford U., 1966; Ph.D. with distinction, UCLA, 1971; m. Joan J. Liu, Sept. 5, 1965; children—Carol, Michelle. Engring. specialist, cons. Garrett-AiResearch, Los Angeles, 1966-72; postgrad. research engr. UCLA, 1969-70; sr. engring. scientist RCA Astro-Electronics, Princeton, N.J., 1972-77; mgr., sr. engring. specialist Aerospace Corp., El Segundo, Calif., 1977—; cons. Garrett Corp.; instr. UCLA; mem. tech. com. Def. Advanced Research Projects Agy., NASA, Air Force Wright Aero. Labs., Air Force Weapons Lab. Strategic Def. Initiative Orgn. NASA; prin. investigator research and devel. projects Def. Advanced Research Projects Agy., Air Force Office Sci. Research Air Force Lab., RCA Corp., Aerospace Corp.

Recipient engring. recognition award RCA, 1973; NASA Big Dipper award, 1974; Aerospace Corp. Outstanding Accomplishment award, 1985. Fellow AIAA (assoc., tech. chmn., session chmn. confs.); mem. Am. Astronautical Soc., Sigma Xi. Editor: Advances in Astronautical Sciences; reviewer for NSF, 1977-78; reviewer profl. jours. and confs.; contbr. articles on dynamics and control to profl. publs. Office: 2350 E El Segundo Blvd Segundo CA 90245

TSINA, RICHARD VASIL, chemistry educator; b. Boston, Aug. 13, 1941; s. Vasil Anastas and Theodora (Kasuli) T.; m. Irene Wang, Nov. 28, 1970; children: Lesley, Katherine. BA, Boston U., 1963; MA, Duke U., 1965; PhD, Tufts U., 1968. Asst. prof. chemistry Rutgers U., New Brunswick, N.J., 1970-73; v.p. Sultra Corp., N.Y.C., 1973-76; dean continuing edn. Cogswell Coll., San Francisco, 1976-79; vice chmn. engring extension U. Calif., Berkeley, 1979—. Contbr. articles to profl. jours. Mem. IEEE (chmn. San Francisco sect. 1984-85, chmn. fin. council 1985-86, cert. appreciation 1984), Am. Soc. Engring. Edn. (chmn. continuing profl. devel. 1978-85), Am. Chem. Soc., Tau Beta Pi (eminent engr. com.). Avocations: music, reading, hiking. Home: 1424 Dana Ave Palo Alto CA 94301 Office: U Calif Continuing Edn Engring 2223 Fulton St Berkeley CA 94720

TSUE, JOHN MASAICHI, optometrist; b. Hilo, Hawaii, Sept. 6, 1949; s. Jackson Masami and Susan (Tatsue) T.; m. Shelley F. Tsue; 1 child, Matthew Teruo. B.A. in Zoology, U. Hawaii, 1971; O.D., Pacific U., 1978. Cert. optometrist, Hawaii. Intern, Forest Grove, Oreg., 1977-78; sole practice optometry, Kailua-Kona, Hawaii, 1979—; cons., lectr. Served with U.S. Army, 1971-73. Recipient Nat. Eye Research Found. award, 1978; Western Interstate Commn. Higher Edn. grantee, 1974-78. Mem. Hawaii Optometric Assn. (dir. 1983), Kona Coast C. of C., Better Vision Inst., Am. Optometric Found., Am. Optometric Assn. (charter mem. contact lens sect.), Nat. Eye Research Found., Kona Jaycees (v.p. 1983, pres. 1984-85), 100 Plus Club, Phi Theta Upsilon. Baptist. Club: Hualalai Exchange (past dir., sec.).

TSUJI, WAYNE HIROHARU, physician; b. Wailuku, Hawaii, Nov. 6, 1947; s. Yoshiharu and Tokie Ann (Maehara) T.; m. Judith Jeffers, Sept. 16, 1983. AB, U. Calif., Berkeley, 1970; MD, U. Calif., San Francisco, 1974. Cert. Am. Bd. Internat. Medicine, Am. Bd. Rheumatology. Intern San Francisco Gen. Hosp., 1974-75; resident U. Calif. Hosps., San Francisco, 1975-77, fellow rheumatology, 1978-80; ptnr. Summit Madison Med. Group, Seattle, 1980—; mem. internal rev. bd. Swedish Hosp., Seattle, 1984—; clin. instr. U. Wash. Med. Sch., Seattle, 1980-84, asst. clin. prof., 1985—; active staff Swedish Hosp., 1980—. Bd. dirs. United Nations Assn., Seattle, 1986—; fundraiser Community Home Health Care, 1983. NIH trainee, Berkeley, 1969, San Francisco, 1969-72. Mem. Am. Rheumatism Assn., Am. Soc. Internal Medicine, King County Med. Soc., N.W. Rheumatism Soc., Arthritis Found. (chmn. edn. com. Western Wash. chpt. 1985—, bd. dirs., exec. bd.), Japanese Am. Citizens League. Democrat. Congregationalist. Club: Washington Athletic (Seattle). Avocations: hiking, running, swimming, fishing, sailing. Home: 1721 Evergreen Pl Seattle WA 98122 Office: Summit Madison Med Group 1229 Madison St 15th Fl Seattle WA 98104

TSUTAKAWA, EDWARD MASAO, business consultant; b. Seattle, May 15, 1921; s. Jin and Michiko (Oka) T.; student U. Wash., 1941, Wash. State U., 1949; m. Hide Kunugi, Aug. 11, 1949; children—Nancy Joyce Tsutakawa Seigel, Margaret Ann Langston, Mark Edward. Free-lance comml. artist, Spokane, 1943-47; artist Maag & Porter Comml. Printers, Spokane, 1947-54; organizer Litho Art Printers, Inc., Spokane, 1954—, gen. mgr., pres., 1965-80; prin. E. M. Tsutakawa Co., bus. cons. and dir., 1980—. Pres. emeritus Spokane-Nishinomiya Sister City Soc.; pres. emeritus Sister Cities Assn. of Spokane, area adv. council SBA; bd. dirs. Fairmount Cemetery, Spokane Community Found. Recipient Disting. Service medal Boy Scouts of Japan, 1967, Cultural medal in Edn., Japan, 1985; Disting. Service award City of Nishinomiya, 1971; Disting. Service to Expo '74, State of Wash., 1974; Book of Golden Deeds award Exchange Club, 1978; Disting. Service award UN Assn., 1979; Order of Sacred Treasure medal Govt. of Japan, 1984. Mem. Eastern Wash. State Hist. Soc., Japanese Am. Citizens League. Methodist. Clubs: Kiwanis, Spokane. Home: S 4116 Madelia St Spokane WA 99203

TUCHMAN, RALPH GREGORY, clergyman, audio-visual consultant; b. N.Y.C., Sept. 21, 1919; s. Herman and Anna (Gregory) T.; m. Fran Harris, June 26, 1949. B.S., NYU, 1939; M.S., Northwestern U., 1941; D.D. (hon.), Ernest Holmes Coll. Ordained to ministry United Ch. of Religious Sci., 1976; reporter, West Coast editor Broadcasting Mag., 1942-49; head Harris-Tuchman Prodns., Inc., Burbank, Calif., 1950—; minister Burbank-Toluca Lake 1st Ch. of Religious Sci., 1973—. Founding incorporator Big Bros. Greater Los Angeles, 1953, past dir., now mem. adv. council. Served to capt. USAAF, 1943-46. Mem. Profl. Journalists Soc. Office: 260 N Pass Ave Burbank CA 91505

TUCK, MICHAEL RAY, technical services executive; b. Pocatello, Idaho, Aug. 9, 1941; s. Amos R. and Phyllis (Day) T.; m. Heather K. Fowler, Oct. 22, 1962; children: Lisa M., Jennifer A., M. Mark. BS in Math., Idaho State U., 1964; MS in Math., U. Idaho, 1971. Programmer analyst Argonne Nat. Labs., Idaho Falls, Idaho, 1964-69, computer scientist, 1969-76; engr., mgr. computer div. Montana Energy Inst., Butte, Mont., 1976-81; v.p. MultiTech Inc. div. MSE Inc., Butte, 1981-82, pres., 1982-83; vice pres. MSE Inc., Butte, 1983—; cons. TMA Assocs., Butte, 1982-83. Bd. dirs. Jr. Achievement of Butte. Mem. Am. Soc. Data Processing Profls., Butte C. of C. (bd. dirs.), Mont. Data Processing Soc. Methodist. Club: Exchange (Butte). Office: Multitech div of MSE Inc PO Box 4078 Butte MT 59701

TUCK, RUSSELL RUSSELL, JR., university president. m. Marjorie Gay Tuck; children: Russell R. III, Catherine Elizabeth. BS in Chemistry, Union U., 1956; MS in Biology, Vanderbilt U., 1957, PhD in Curriculum and Instrn., 1971; postgrad., Wash. U., 1960-61. Instr. biology, asst. coordinator Korean Tchr. Edn. Program George Peabody Coll. Vanderbilt U., Nashville, 1957-59; tchr. biology, chmn. sci. dept. University City (Mo.) Sr. High Sch., 1960-63, from asst. prin. to prin., 1963-70; prin. Parkway North Sr. High Sch., St. Louis County, Mo., 1971-78; asst. supt. Parkway Sch. Dist., St. Louis County, 1979-81, assoc. supt., 1981-84; pres. Calif. Bapt. Coll., Riverside, 1984—. Contbr. articles to profl. jours. Bd. dirs. Opera Assn., ARC; active Bapt. Ch., local Hosp. Assn. Bd., local Edn. Com. Mem. Calif. Bapt. Hist. Soc. (bd. dirs.), Calif. Bapt. Devel. Found. (bd. dirs.), Am. Assn. Sch. Adminstrs., Am. Assn. Pres.' of Ind. Colls. and Univs., Kappa Delta Pi, Phi Delta Kappa. Lodge: Rotary. Office: Calif Bapt Coll 8432 Magnolia Ave Riverside CA 92504

TUCKER, DAVID CHRISTIAN, chemistry educator, glassblower; b. Spokane, Wash., Oct. 24, 1944; s. William Dewey and Grace (Anderson) T.; m. Judith Marlene Scheele, May 25, 1945; children: Robert David, Tracy Lynn. BS, Washington State U., 1967, MA in Teaching Phys. Sci., 1969. Cert. secondary tchr., Wash. Tchr. sci. Morton (Wash.) High Sch., 1971; research asst. Wash. State U., Pullman, 1972; tchr. sci. Mt. Baker High Sch., Deming, Wash., 1973—. Contbr. articles to profl. jours. Named to Tchr. Honors Workshop AT&T Bell Labs., 1984; grantee NSF; recipient Presdl. award for excellence in sci. and math. teaching. 1986, Nat. Exemplary award, 1986. Mem. Nat. Sci. Tchrs. Assn. (Search for Excellence com. 1985—, Nat. Exemplary Chemistry Tchr. award 1984), Wash. Sci. Tchrs. Assn. (bd. dirs.), Am. Chem. Soc. (Tchr. of Yr. award Pacific N.W. chpt. 1985), Sigma Xi (Tchr. award 1985), Phi Kappa Phi. Home: 2618 Huron St Bellingham WA 98226 Office: Mt Baker High Sch PO Box 95 Deming WA 98244

TUCKER, GORDON CHARLES, archaeologist; b. Seattle, Dec. 20, 1950; s. Gordon C. and Maureen T. (Robbins) T.; m. Kathleen A. Rhudy, May 31, 1980; children: Jessica L., Christopher J., Jonathan E. BA in Sociology, Anthropology, Western Wash. State Coll., 1972; MA in Anthropology, Idaho State U., 1976; PhD, U. Colo., 1981. Teaching asst. Idaho State U., Pocatello, 1974-76, U. Colo., Boulder, 1977-80; sr. staff archaeologist Nickens & Assocs., Montrose, Colo., 1980—; tchr. Montrose Continuing Edn., 1984—. Contbr. articles to profl. jours. Mem. AAAS, N.Y. Acad. Scis., Soc. Am. Archaeology, Colo. Council Profl. Archaeologists, Colo. Archaeol. Soc. (v.p. Chipeta chpt. 1983-85), Sigma Xi. Democrat. Avocations: microcomputers, jogging, skiing, hiking. Office: Nickens & Assocs 834 N 1st Montrose CO 81401

TUCKER, LEONARD LEE, mechanical engineer, contractor; b. Los Angeles, June 27, 1947; s. Ralph Jr. and Evelyn Fay (Lane) T.; m. Elvira Garcia, Jan. 11, 1969; children: Leonard L. Jr., Richard A., Delfina. AA, El Camino Coll., 1974; BS summa cum laude, UCLA, 1976. Registered profl. engr., Calif. Gen. mgr. L&R Heating and Air Conditioning, Gardena, Calif., 1976-78; project engr. Ayres Assocs., Los Angeles, 1978-83; pres. Cool-Breeze, Simi Valley, Calif., 1983—. Served to sgt. USAF, 1966-73. Mem. Am. Soc. Plumbing Engrs., ASHRAE (assoc.), ASME (assoc.), Refrigeration Service Engrs. Soc., Tau Beta Pi. Lutheran. Lodge: Rotary. Office: Cool-Breeze 1910 Park St Simi Valley CA 93063

TUCKER, OWEN REUBEN, electronics company executive; b. Lake Charles, La., Jan. 25, 1956; s. Owen and Doris (Orosco) T.; m. Valerie Sharon Clarke, Sept. 25, 1976; children: Michelle, Lisel. BEE, U. Manchester, Eng., 1977; MBA, Pepperdine U., 1985. Registered profl. elec. engr., Calif. Research engr. Northrop Corp., Hawthorne, Calif., 1977-78; mem. tech. staff Teledyne Controls, West Los Angeles, 1978-79, sr. mem. tech. staff, 1979-81, engring. cons., 1981-84; systems engr. Excellon Industries, Torrance, Calif., 1981-82, mgr. test engring., 1982-85, dir. quality assurance, 1985-86; mgr. quality assurance and advanced mfg. Teradata Corp., Los Angeles, 1986—; Engring. cons. Acudata Systems Inc., Los Angeles, 1985—. Mem. IEEE, Am. Soc. Test Engrs., Am. Soc. Quality Control, Assn. MBA Execs., Am. Mgmt. Assn. Republican. Methodist. Avocations: tennis, photography, computers, travelling. Home: 11038 Ardath Ave Inglewood CA 90303 Office: Teradata Corp 12945 Jefferson Blvd Los Angeles CA 90066

TUCKER, SUZANNE MARIE, author, educator; b. Milw., Nov. 26, 1945; d. Jerome F. and Evelyn E. (Buero) Palmer; m. Michael Keith Tucker, Dec. 18, 1970; children: Michael Jr., Carole, Lawrence. BS, Colo. State U., 1967, M in Home Econs., 1969; EdD, U. No. Colo., 1981. Instr. Colo. State U., Ft. Collins, 1969-72, asst. prof., 1972-78, faculty affiliate, 1978—, author, instr. correspondence course, 1979—; editor Western Regional Educators Home Mgmt. Family Econs., 1971-74, 81-84. Co-author: Management in Family Living, 1975, Family Life Management, 1986; author ednl. materials, 1974—; contbr. articles to profl. jours. Proposal com. Ctr. for Enriched Communication, Grand Junction, 1985—; awards chmn. Cub Scout Pack 358, Grand Junction, 1985. Named Very Important Prof., Home Econs. Council. Colo. State U., 1975. Mem. Am. Home Econs. Assn. (nominating com. 1973-75), Colo. Home Econs. Assn. (regional coordinator 1985—), Sigma Xi, Omicron Nu (chpt. advisor 1972-76). Democrat. Methodist.

TUCKER, WALLACE HAMPTON, astrophysicist; b. McAlester, Okla., Nov. 4, 1939; s. Charles Brown and Josephing E. (Wilkinson) T.; m. Karen Allen Slagle, June 21, 1957; children: Kerry, Stuart. BS in Math., U. Okla., 1961, MS in Physics, 1962; PhD, U. Calif., San Diego, 1966. Research assoc. Cornell U., Ithaca, N.Y., 1966-67; asst. prof. astrophysics Rice U., Houston, 1967-69; sr. staff scientist Am. Sci. and Engring., Cambridge, Mass., 1969-72; astrophysicist Harvard-Smithsonian Obs., Cambridge, 1976—; vis. prof. U. Calif., Irvine, 1980—. Author: The Star Splitters, 1984; (with R. Giacconi) The X-ray Universe, 1985; (with K. Tucker) The Cosmic Inquirers, 1986; also articles to profl. jours. Mem. AAAS, Am. Astron. Soc., Internat. Astron. Union. Home: PO Box 266 Bonsall CA 92003

TUCKER, WANDA HALL, newspaper editor, columnist; b. Los Angeles, Feb. 6, 1921; d. Frank Walliston and Hazel Gladys (Smith) Hall; A.A., Citrus Coll., 1939; m. Frank R. Tucker, Apr. 16, 1943; children—Frank Robert, Nancy Irene. Society editor Azusa (Calif.) Herald, 1939-42, editor, 1942-43; city editor San Marino (Calif.) Tribune, 1943-45; editor Canyon City (Calif.) News, 1953; reporter Pasadena (Calif.) Star-News, 1953-73, city editor, 1973-75, day mng. editor, 1975, mng. editor, 1975-81, sr. mng. editor, 1981-84, dir. internship program, 1976-79, mem. editorial bd., 1982-84; editor, assoc. pub. Foothill Inter-City Newspapers, 1984-86; communications cons., Palm Desert, Calif., 1986—. Recipient writing award Calif. Newspaper Pubs. Assn., 1965; named Woman of Year, Pasadena Women's Civic League, 1974, Pasadena chpt. NAACP, 1977, Emer Bates Meml. award, 1981. Mem. Greater Los Angeles Press Club (writing awards 1971-72), Nat. Soc. Newspaper Columnists, Sigma Delta Chi.

TUELL, JACK MARVIN, clergyman; b. Tacoma, Nov. 14, 1923; s. Frank Harry and Anne Helen (Bertelson) T.; m. Marjorie Ida Beadles, June 17, 1946; children—Jacqueline, Cynthia, James. B.S., U. Wash., 1947, LL.B., 1948; S.T.B., Boston U., 1955; M.A., U. Puget Sound, 1961; D.D., Pacific Sch. Religion, 1966. Bar: Wash. bar 1948. Practice law with firm Holte & Tuell, Edmonds, Wash., 1948-50; ordained to ministry Methodist Ch., 1953; pastor Grace Meth. Ch., Everett, Wash., 1950-52, South Tewksbury Meth. Ch., Tewksbury, Mass., 1952-55, Lakewood Meth. Ch., Tacoma, 1955-61; dist. supt. Puget Sound dist. Meth. Ch., Everett, 1961-67; pastor 1st United Meth. Ch., Vancouver, Wash., 1967-72; bishop United Meth. Ch., Portland, Oreg., from 1972; now bishop Pacific and Southwest Conf., United Meth. Ch., Los Angeles.; Mem. gen. conf. United Meth. Ch., 1964, 66, 68, 70, 72. Author: The Organization of the United Methodist Church, 1970. Pres. Tacoma U.S.O., 1959-61, Vancouver YMCA, 1968; v.p. Ft. Vancouver Seamens Center, 1969-72; vice chmn. Vancouver Human Relations Commn., 1970-72; pres. Oreg. Council Alcohol Problems, 1972-76; Trustee U. Puget Sound, 1961-73, Vancouver Meml. Hosp., 1967-72, Alaska Meth. U., Anchorage, from 1972, Willamette U., Salem, Oreg., from 1972, Willamette View Manor, Portland, from 1972, Rogue Valley Manor, Medford, Oreg., 1972-76; pres. nat. div. bd. global ministries United Meth. Ch., 1972-76, pres. ecumenical and interreligious concerns div., 1976—. Jacob Sleeper fellow, 1955. Club: Rotarian. Office: 472 E Colorado Blvd PO Box 6006 Pasadena CA 91109 *

TUESDAY, DAVID SHEFFIELD, geochemist; b. Royal Oak, Mich., June 5, 1956; s. Charles Sheffield and Jean (Quallis) T.; m. Julie Anne Flammang, Sept. 11, 1982. BS in Geology, Mich. State U., 1978; MS in Geochemistry, Colo. Sch. Mines, 1983. Geochemist Anaconda Minerals Co., Denver, 1979-83; sr. geochemist Ecology and Environment, Inc., Denver, 1984-85, MultiTech., Inc., Butte, Montana, 1985—; cons. geologist Anaconda Mineral Co., Denver, 1984. Mem. Am. Chem. Soc., Nat. Assn. Environ. Profl. Avocations: woodworking, skiing, auto racing. Office: MultiTech Inc PO Box 4078 Butte MT 59702

TUFFILE, FRED MICHAEL, graphic arts executive; b. N.Y.C., May 12, 1941; s. Fred C. and Helen T. (Haubrich) T.; m. Constance Marie Langdeau, Aug. 3, 1963; children: Alexander, Charles, Anthony. BChemE, U. Detroit, 1963; MSChemE, Rensselaer Poly. Inst., 1965; PhD in Chemistry, Seton Hall U., 1971; postgrad., Dartmouth Coll., 1983. Sr. scientist Avon Products, Inc., Suffern, N.Y., 1965-71; various mgmt. positions Polaroid Corp. Inc., New Bedford, Mass., 1971-80, div. mgr., 1980-83; dir. films devel. Polaroid Corp. Inc., Cambridge, Mass., 1983-85; pres. and chief exec. officer Sage Technology, Inc. subs. Polaroid Corp., Inc., San Diego, 1985—; bd. dirs. Mass. Technology Park Corp., Westboro. Contbr. articles to profl. jours.; patentee in field. Com. chair Greater New Bedford C. of C., 1980-83; mem. bd. trustees St. Luke's Hosp., New Bedford, 1982—. Mem. Am. Inst. Chem. Engrs., Am. Chem. Soc., Soc. Photographic Scientists and Engrs., Am. Mgmt. Assn., Sigma Xi. Republican. Roman Catholic. Avocations: tennis, running, sailing, skiing, golf. Home: 12989 Abra Dr San Diego CA 92128 Office: Sage Technology Inc 10960 Via Frontera San Diego CA 92127

TUFT, DEAN BYARD, mechanical and safety engineer, consultant; b. Salt Lake City, Oct. 1, 1948; s. Byard Roy and Elda (Anderson) T.; m. Bonnie Jean Thomas, Jan. 23, 1970; children: Dean Chad, Brandie Marie. BSME, U. Utah, 1971, MSME, 1972; PhD, U. Calif., Davis, 1980. Registered prof. mech. engr., safety engr., Calif. Engr. LLNL, Livermore, Calif., 1972-83; prin., cons. Dean B. Tuft, Phd., Inc., Pleasant Hill, Calif., 1978—. Mem. ASME, Am. Soc. Safety Engrs., Soc. Automotive Engrs., Soc. Forensic Engrs. and Scientists. Office: 101 Gregory Ln #48 Pleasant Hill CA 94523

TUFTY, JAMES VAN WAGONER, advertising executive; b. Evanston, Ill., Mar. 11, 1929; s. Harold Guilford and Esther Ellen (Van Wagoner) T.; m. Mary Elizabeth White, June 3, 1967; children: Patti Alyn, James Jr., Valentina Ivern. BA in Journalism and Advt., Mich. State U., 1953; postgrad., Alliance Francaise, Paris, 1963. Field rep. Young and Rubicam, Inc., N.Y.C., 1956-58; asst. all-media buyer Young and Rubicam, Inc., Chgo., 1958-60; sr. all-media buyer Young and Rubicam, Inc., Los Angeles, 1960-62; journalist Tufty News Service, Paris, 1962-64; sec., treas. Tufty News Service, Washington, 1956-86; media dir. Am. Bakers Coop, Teaneck, N.J., 1964-65; supr., account rep. J. Walter Thompson Co., Washington, 1965-72; pres., chmn. bd. Ad Agy., Inc., Washington, 1971-81; pres., chmn. bd. dirs. Communications Sales, Inc., Washington, 1975-81; chmn. bd. Aloha Advt. Inc., Honolulu, 1981-86. Served with U.S. Army, 1953-56. Mem. Nat. Press Club. Presbyterian. Home: 6614 Kauna St Honolulu HI 96825

TUGEND, THOMAS JOSEPH, communications executive; b. Berlin, June 30, 1925; came to U.S., 1939; s. Gustav and Irene Frederika (Fontheim) Tugendreich; m. Rachel Spitzer, Oct. 7, 1956; children: Orlee, Alina, Ronit. BA, U. Calif., Berkeley, 1950; Bachelor's Cert., U. Madrid, 1954; MA, UCLA, 1957. Reporter San Francisco Chronicle, 1951-54; pub. info. officer UCLA, 1957-84, dir. communications Sch. Engring. and Architecture, 1984—; sr. assoc. editor Heritage Pubs., Los Angeles, 1958—; west coast corr. Jerusalem Post, 1974—; pub. relations cons. Weizmann Inst. Sci., Rehovot, Israel, 1963—, Sinai Temple, Los Angeles, 1965—. Bd. dirs. Internat. Alert, Los Angeles, So. Calif. Jewish Hist. Soc., Los Angeles. Served as sgt. U.S. Army, 1944-46, ETO, 1950-51; Israel Def. Forces, 1948-49. Recipient Journalism award for Excellence, Greater Los Angeles Press Club, 1984, 86. Mem. AAAS, Nat. Assn. Sci. Writers. Jewish. Avocations: tennis, swimming, gardening. Office: UCLA 7420 Boelter Hall Los Angeles CA 90024

TUKEY, HAROLD BRADFORD, JR., horticulture educator; b. Geneva, N.Y., May 29, 1934; s. Harold Bradford and Ruth (Schweigert) T.; m. Helen Dunbar Parker, June 25, 1955; children: Ruth Thurbon, Carol Tukey Schwartz, Harold Bradford. B.S., Mich. State U., 1955, M.S., 1956, Ph.D., 1958. Research asst. South Haven Expt. Sta., Mich., 1955; AEC grad. research asst. Mich. State U., 1955-58; NSF fellow Calif. Inst. Tech, 1958-59; asst. prof. dept. floriculture and ornamental horticulture Cornell U., Ithaca, N.Y., 1959-64, assoc. prof., 1964-70, prof., 1970-80; prof. urban horticulture U. Wash., Seattle, 1980—, dir Arboreta, 1980—, dir. Ctr. Urban Horticulture, 1980—; cons. Internat. Bonsai mag., Electric Power Research Inst., P.R. Nuclear Ctr., 1965-66; lectr. in field; mem. adv. com. Seattle-U. Wash. Arboretum and Bot. Garden, 1980—, vice chmn., 1982; vis. scholar U. Nebr., 1982; vis. prof. U. Calif.-Davis, 1973; mem. various coms. Nat. Acad. Scis.-NRC; bd. dirs. Arbor Fund Bloedel Res., 1980—, pres., 1983-84. Mem. editorial bd. Jour. Environ. Horticulture. Pres. Ithaca PTA; troop advisor Boy Scouts Am., Ithaca. Served to lt. U.S. Army, 1958. Fellow NSF, 1958-59; grantee NSF, 1962, 75, Bot. Soc. Am., 1964; hon. dr. Portuguese Soc. Hort., 1985. Fellow Am. Soc. Hort. Sci. (dir. 1970-71); mem. Internat. Soc. Hort. Sci. (U.S. del. to council 1971—, chmn. commn. for amateur horticulture 1974-83, exec. com. 1974—, v.p. 1978-82, pres. 1982-86), Internat. Plant Propagators Soc. (eastern region dir. 1969-71, v.p. 1972, pres. 1973, internat. pres. 1976), Am. Hort. Soc. (dir. 1972-81, exec. com. 1974-81, v.p. 1978-80, citation of merit 1981), Bot. Soc. Am., N.W. Horticulture Soc. (dir. 1980—), Arboretum Found. (dir. 1980—), Sigma Xi, Alpha Zeta, Phi Kappa Phi, Pi Alpha Xi, Xi Sigma Pi. Presbyterian. Lodge: Rotary. Home: 3300 E Saint Andrews Way Seattle WA 98112 Office: Ctr for Urban Horticulture U Wash GF-15 Seattle WA 98195

TULL, DONALD STANLEY, marketing educator; b. Mo., Oct. 28, 1924; s. Raymond Edgar and Ethel (Stanley) T.; m. Marjorie Ann Dobbie, May 15, 1948; children: Susan Margaret, David Dobbie, Brooks William. S.B., U. Chgo., 1948, M.B.A., 1949, Ph.D., 1956. Analyst U.S. Steel Corp., 1949-50; instr. U. Wash., 1950-52; mgr. adminstrn. N.Am. Aviation, 1954-61; prof. mktg. Calif. State U., Fullerton, 1961-67; dean Sch. Bus. Adminstrn. and Econs., 1966-67; prof. mktg. Coll. Mgmt. and Bus. U. Oreg., 1967—, chmn. dept. mktg., transp. and bus. environment, 1967-69, 73-81. Author: (with P.E. Green) Research for Marketing Decisions, 1978, (with G.S. Albaum) Survey Research, 1973, (with D.I. Hawkins) Marketing Research: Measurement and Method, 1987; contbr. articles to profl. jours. Served to lt. (j.g.) USNR, 1943-46. Mem. AAUP (pres. 1978-79), Am. Mktg. Assn., Beta Gamma Sigma. Home: 2580 Highland Oaks Eugene OR 97405 Office: U Oreg 171 Gilbert Hall Eugene OR 97405

TULLAR, (VICTOR) PHILIP, college administrator, counselor; b. Vom, Nigeria, Sept. 4, 1936 (parents Am. citizens); s. Leslie Erwin and Inga (Otteson) T.; m. Jo Ann Pearson, May 2, 1955; children—Vicki Ann, Philip Eugene. B.A., Howard Payne U., 1969; M.A., Wayne State U., 1972; M.Ed., U. Ariz., 1976, Ph.D., 1979. Lifetime teaching cert. for community coll. psychology and German, Ariz. Joined U.S. Army, 1955, advanced through grades to command sgt. maj., 1974; served in U.S., Europe, Vietnam, ret. 1975; counselor, faculty mem. Pima Community Coll., Tucson, 1976-79, asst. dean, 1979-80, dean for ednl. services, 1980-82; v.p., provost Cochise Coll., Sierra Vista, Ariz., 1982—. Decorated Bronze Star medal with 2 oak leaf clusters, Meritorious Service medal with oak leaf cluster, Army Commendation medal with 2 oak leaf clusters, Vietnamese Cross of Gallantry; recipient Meritorious Service recognition Pima Community Coll., 1982. Mem. Nat. Assn. Student Personnel Adminstrs., Ariz. Assn. Student Personnel Adminstrs., Phi Delta Kappa. Republican. Baptist.

TULLER, WENDY JUDGE, oil co. ofcl.; b. Cranston, R.I., Dec. 17, 1943; d. Alfred Carmen and Anna Louise (Waterman) Judge. A.B., Brown U., 1965; M.L.S., U. R.I., 1969. Librarian, Providence Public Schs., 1965-69; mgr. various locations Xerox Corp., 1969-75; mgr. Carter Hawley Hale Stores, Inc., Los Angeles, 1976; cons. Sibson & Co., Inc., Princeton, N.J., 1976-78; coordinator Atlantic Richfield Co., Los Angeles, 1978—. Mem. Am. Soc. Personnel Adminstrn., Am. Soc. Tng. and Devel., Internat. Assn. Personnel Women, AAUW (v.p. local chpt. 1979-80). Club: Los Angeles Athletic. Home: 222 S Figueroa St Los Angeles CA 90012 Office: Atlantic Richfield Co 515 S Flower St Los Angeles CA 90071

TULLIS, DAVID ALLEN, municipal official, safety consultant; b. Madison, S.D., Sept. 10, 1938; s. Ralph and Millie Grace (Hanneman) T.; m. Celia Kathleen Hagan (div. 1970); children: Christine Louise, David Bradford; m. Linda Pauline Sweat, Sept. 10, 1972; 1 child, Larry Allan. Student, U. Wash., 1963, Centralia (Wash.) Coll., 1969, South Sound Coll., 1975. Customer engr. IBM Corp., Seattle, 1963-69; bus. machine technician State of Wash., Olympia, 1969-77, safety compliance officer, 1977-80, sr. safety compliance officer, 1980-83; safety officer City of Tacoma, 1983—; mem. Employers Elec. Safety Commn., State of Wash., 1983—; chmn. utilities panel Gov.'s Conf. on Safety, State of Wash., 1985-86. Scoutmaster Boy Scouts Am., Olympia, 1977. Served with U.S. Army, 1959-62. Mem. Am. Pub. Works Assn. (chmn. northwest sect. 1985—), Am. Soc. Safety Engrs., Am. Pub. Power Assn. Lodge: Elks. Home: 2111 Tina Ct SE Olympia WA 98503 Office: City of Tacoma PO Box 11007 Tacoma WA 98411

TUNG, CHIANG-YING MEI, materials scientist; b. Chongqing, Republic of China, Dec. 10, 1945; came to U.S., 1968; d. Ju-long and Yu-ling (Wu) Mei; m. Paul P. Tung, Dec. 9, 1972; children: Yong-Jin, Elsa. BSc, Nat. Taiwan U., 1967; PhD, UCLA, 1973. Instr. Palomar Coll., San Marcoo, Calif., 1973-75, Pierce Coll., Woodland Hills, Calif., 1976-78; mem. tech. staff Rockwell Internat. Sci. Ctr., Thousand Oaks, Calif., 1978—. Patentee in field. Mem. Soc. Advancement Material and Processing Engring., Am. Chem. Soc., Polymer Chemistry div. Am. Chem. Soc. Democrat. Office: Rockwell Internat Sci Ctr PO Box 1085 Thousand Oaks CA 91360

TUNISON, ELIZABETH LAMB, education educator; b. Belfast, Northern Ireland, Jan. 7, 1922; came to U.S., 1923; d. Richard Ernest and Ruby (Hill) Lamb; m. Ralph W. Tunison, Jan. 24, 1947 (dec. Apr. 1984); children: Eric Arthur, Christine Wait, Dana Paul. BA, Whittier Coll., 1943, MEd, 1963. Tchr. Whittier (Calif.) Schs., 1943-59; tchr. TV pub. schs. Los Angeles, 1960-75; dir. curriculum Bassett (Calif.) Schs., 1962-65; elem. sch. prin. Rowland Unified Schs., Rowland Heights, Calif., 1965-68; assoc. prof. edn. Calif. State Poly. U., Pomona, 1968-71; prof. Whittier Coll., 1971—. Recipient Whittier Coll. Alumni Achievement award 1975; Helen Heferman scholar 1963. Mem. Assn. Calif. Sch. Adminstrs. (chmn. higher edn. com. 1983—, pres. region XV 1981-83, Wilson Grace award 1983), AAUP, Delta Kappa Gamma. Lodge: P.E.O. (chaplain 1975-77). Home: 5636 Ben Alder Whittier CA 90601 Office: Whittier Coll 13406 E Philadelphia Whittier CA 90601

TUOHEY, CONRAD GRAVIER, lawyer; b. N.Y.C., Dec. 27, 1933; s. James L. and Rose (Gravier) T.; B.A., George Washington U., 1957; J.D., U. Mich., 1960; m. Judith Octavia Jeeves, July 7, 1956; children—Octavia

Jeeves, Heather Gravier, Meighan Judith, Caragh Rose. Admitted to Calif. bar, 1962, N.Y. bar, 1980, D.C. bar, 1980; sr. mem. firm Tuohey & Prasse; dir. Fed. Home Loan Bank, San Francisco, 1980-83; legal cons., counsel Calif. State Senate, 1981—; counsel Senate Select Com. on the Pacific Rim, 1986—. Mem. citizens adv. bd. Orange County Transit Com., 1966-68; pres. Calif. Alliance Partners for Progress, 1969-72, Friends of Calif. State U. at Fullerton, 1969-71; mem. InterAm. bd. Partners Alliance for Progress, 1969-72, nat. bd. dirs., 1970-72. Served with AUS, 1951-54. Decorated Combat Infantryman's Badge, Korean Service medal with 3 battle stars; named Outstanding Young Man of Yr., Fullerton Jr. C. of C., 1967. Mem. State Bar Calif., ABA (internat., corp., banking and bus. law sects.), Los Angeles Bar Assn., Orange County Bar Assn. chmn. environ. law sect.), D.C. Bar Assn., N.Y. Bar Assn., Kent Inn of Phi Delta Phi, Phi Sigma Kappa. Home: 24762 Red Lodge Pl Laguna Hills CA 92653 Office: Suite 800 1200 N Main St Santa Ana CA 92701 *

TUPIN, JOE PAUL, hospital medical director, psychiatry educator; b. Comanche, Tex., Feb. 17, 1934; m. Betty Thompson, June 19, 1955; children: Paul, Rebecca, John. BS in Pharmacy, U. Tex., 1955, postgrad., 1955; MD, U. Tex., Galveston, 1959, Wash. Sch. Psychiatry, 1962, NIH Grad. Sch., 1962-64. Lic. psychiatrist, Tex., Calif. Intern U. Calif. Hosps., San Francisco, 1959-60; resident U. Tex. Med. br., Galveston, 1960-62, asst. prof. psychiatry, 1964-68, mem. staff John Sealy Hosp., 1964-69, dir. psychiatric consultation service, 1965-66, dir. psychiatric research, 1965-69, asst. dean medicine, 1967-68, assoc. prof., 1968-69, assoc. dean, 1968-69; resident NIMH div NIH, 1963-64; assoc. prof. psychiatry U. Calif., Davis, 1969-71, mem. staff Davis Med. Ctr., 1969—, vice-chmn. dept. psychiatry, 1970-76, prof., 1971—, acting chmn. dept. psychiatry, 1977, acting dir. admissions sch. medicine, 1977-78, chmn. dept. psychiatry, 1977-84; cons. staff St. Mary's Infirmary, Galveston, 1967-69, Moody House Retirement Home for the Aged, Galveston, 1967-69, VA Hosp., Martinez, 1977-82, Yolo Gen. Hosp., 1980—; dir. psychiatric consultation service U. Calif., Davis, 1969-74, co-director 1974-77; vis. prof. King's Coll. Med. Sch., London, 1974; acting dir. admissions sch. medicine, U. Calif., Davis, 1977-78; chief div. mental health U. Calif. Davis Med. Ctr., 1977-84, also mem. quality care com., 1979-85, chmn. com., 1981-85; med. dir. and assoc. dir. Hosp. and Clinics U. Calif., Davis, 1984—. Referee and book reviewer numerous pubs.; mem. sci. editorial bd. Am. Jour. Forensic Psychiatry, 1985—, Jour. Clin. Psychopharmacology, 1981—, Psychiatry, 1985, Tex. Reports on Biology and Medicine, 1965-67, 68-69; Western Jour. Medicine, 1979—; contbr. numerous articles to profl. jours. Mem. Academically Talented Child com. Galveston City Sch. Bd., 1966-67; chmn. bd. dirs. William Temple Found., Galveston, 1967-68; bd. dirs. Citizens for Advancement of Pub. Edn., Galveston, 1967-69, pres., 1968-69, Moody House Retirement Home for the Aged, 1968, Cal Aggie Athletic Assn., 1978-82; mem. Davis Master Plan com., 1971. Served to lt. commdr. USPHS, 1962-64, with Res. 1964-80. Recipient Career Teaching award NIMH, 1964-66; named to Friars Soc. U. Tex., 1954; Mosby scholar U. Tex., Ginsberg fellow Group for Advancement of Psychiatry, 1960-62, Nat. Found. Infantile Paralysis fellow, 1957; grantee U. Tex. Med. br., 1964-69, NIMH, 1965-68, 69-77, U. Calif. Davis and Sacramento Med. Ctr., 1973-77, U. Calif. Davis, 1969-77, 73—. Fellow Am. Psychiat. Assn., Am. Coll. Psychiatrists (mem. com., editorial com.); mem. AMA, Yolo County Med. Assn. (chmn. credentials com. 1974-75, nominating com. 1980-84), Calif. Med. Assn. (sec. psychiatry sect. 1977-78, 78-79, sci. adv. panel on psychiatry 1975—, psychiatry adv. sect. 1977—, sci. adv. bd. 1978-80), Titus Harris Soc., Cen. Calif. Psychiat. Soc. (chmn. mem. com. 1970-73, pres. 1976), AAAS, Soc. Health and Human Values (exec. council 1970-73), Am. Acad. Psychiatry and the Law, AAUP, West Coast Coll. Biol. Psychiatries Com., Sigma Xi, Rho Chi, Alpha Omega Alpha. Home: 1108 Kent Dr Davis CA 95616 Office: U Calif Davis Med Ctr 2315 Stockton Blvd Med Staff Office Sacramento CA 95817

TUPPER, JACK WILLIAM, hand surgeon; b. Ft. Worth, Jan. 19, 1925; s. Frank and Esther May (McArthur) T.; m. Joan Putnam, Oct. 28, 1961; 1 child, Shelby Putnam, B.S., U. Iowa, 1947, M.D., 1951. Diplomate Am. Bd. Orthopedic Surgery. Intern San Francisco County Hosp., 1951-52; resident U. Calif.-San Francisco, 1952-57; fellow in hand surgery, Los Angeles, 1957-58; clin. prof. hand surgery, U. Calif.-San Francisco, 1958—; dir. hand clinic Alameda County Hosp., Oakland, Calif., 1958-86, Children's Hosp. No. Calif., Oakland, 1958—. Contbr. chpts. to books, articles on arthritis and nerves to jours. U.S. and abroad. Served to ensign USNR, 1943-46, PTO. Fellow ACS, Internat. Soc. Reconstructive Microsurgery; mem. Sunderland Soc., Am. Soc. Reconstructive Microsurgery, Societe Internationale de Chirurgie, Orthopedique et de Traumatologie. Republican. Clubs: San Francisco Wine and Food (cellar master), Cercle de L'Union San Francisco. Office: 2938 Webster Oakland CA 94609

TURBAN, EFRAIM, inmation systems executive, educator; b. Tel Aviv, Oct. 5, 1930; came to U.S., 1961; s. Issac and Devora (Rosen) T.; children: Daphne, Sharon. BSc, Technion, Haifa, Israel, 1953; MBA, U. Calif., Berkeley, 1962, PhD, 1966. Dir. planning control Gen. Electric Co., Oakland, Calif., 1962-64; assoc. prof. Lehigh U., Bethlehem, Pa., 1966-70; prof. Fla. Internat. U., Miami, 1970-81; vis. prof. UCLA, 1982; prof. systems sci. U So. Calif., Los Angeles, 1983—; cons. Bank Am., San Francisco, 1984-85, Peat Marwick, Chgo., 1986—. Author: Applied Mathematical Programming, 1972, Hospital Cost Containment, 1981, Fundemental Management Science, 1985, Decision Support and Expert System, 1986. Mem. Am. Assn. Artificial Intelligence, Inst. Mgmt. Sci., Mgmt. Sci. Round Table Assn. (Artificial Intelligence and Mgmt. Nat. award 1985). Republican. Jewish. Home: 1020 Granville Ave #204 Los Angeles CA 90049 Office: Dept System Sci U So Calif Los Angeles CA 90089

TURBINI, LAURA JOSEPHINE, engineering manager; b. Coco Solo, Republic of Panama, July 19, 1941; dl Lauro Joseph and Margaret Frances (Vassalotti) T. AB in Chemistry cum laude, Regis Coll., 1965; MA in Inorganic Chemistry, Cornell U., 1972, PhD in Inorganic Chemistry, 1974. Tchr. chemistry Fontbonne Acad., Milton, Mass., 1965-69; teaching, research asst. dept. chemistry Cornell U., Ithaca, N.Y., 1969-74; postdoctoral research assoc. Boston U., 1974-75, MIT, Cambridge, 1975-76, U. Tex., Austin, 1976-77; mem. research staff Western Electric Research Ctr., Hopewell, N.J., 1977-79, research leader, 1979-82; tech. pubs. mgr. AT&T Techs., N.Y.C., 1982-85; product and processing engring. mgr. AT&T Info. Systems, Denver, 1985—; session chmn. soldering Nat. Electronic Packaging Conf./WEST, Anaheim, Calif., 1982, Nat. Electronic Packaging Conf./EAST, N.Y.C., 1982. Editor: The Western Electric Engineer, 1982-85; contbr. articles to profl. jours. Mem. budget com. United Way, Princeton, N.J., 1979-80, panel chmn., 1981-84; campaign chmn., co-chmn. AT&T United Way Campaign, Denver, 1985-86. Recipient Western Electric Excellence in Tech. Writing award, 1980; named to YWCA Acad. Women Achievers, YWCA, N.Y.C., 1982; Tribute to Women in Industry honoree YWCA, Princeton, 1984. Mem. Inst. Interconnecting and Packaging Electronic Circuity (chmn. soldering workshop 1981, vice chmn. cleaning and coating com. 1986, U.S. Tech. Advisor Group), Am. Chem. Soc., N.Y. Acad. Scis., Grad. Women in Sci., Future Pioneers (chmn., organizer Thayer chpt. 1981-82), Sigma Xi. Office: AT&T Info Systems 1200 W 120th Ave Westminster CO 80234-2795

TURBITT, SUSANA ALSINA, publishing executive; b. Buenos Aires, Jan. 9; came to U.S., 1967; d. F. Gustavo and Susana (Alvarez de Toledo) Alsina; m. Philip Mark Turbitt Jr., Mar. 26, 1976. BA in Langs. and Internat. Studies, U. Tex., 1970. Tech. editor and translator Gen. Dynamics Corp., Pomona, Calif., 1978-80, systems analyst, 1980-81; systems specialist Beckman Instruments, Fullerton, Calif., 1981-85, mgr. multilang. publs., 1985—. Mem. Assn. Systems Mgmt., Am. Translators Assn. Club: Racquetball World (Fullerton). Avocations: languages, traveling, interior decorating, sports. Office: Beckman Instruments Inc 2500 N Harbor Blvd Fullerton CA 92621

TURCHIK, STEVE PAUL, business educator; b. Ashtabula, Ohio, Feb. 23, 1927; s. Michael and Magda (Kerkes) T.; m. Wilma Turchik, Oct. 4, 1958; 1 child, Stephanie Ann. BSBA, BS in Edn., Kent State U., 1954; MS in Edn., U. So. Calif., 1956. Buyer trainee Carlisle-Allen Co., Ashtabula, 1955-56; tchr. bus. Twenty-nine Palms (Calif.) High Sch., 1956-57, Anaheim (Calif.) High Sch., 1957-60; instr. bus. Ventura (Calif.) Coll., 1960-65; tchr. bus. Santa Paula (Calif.) High Sch., 1963-82, treas., chmn. dept., 1966-71. Editor: TELL mag. Am. Helvetia Philatelic Soc., 1985—, KC News, 1972-76. Bd. dirs. Boys' Clubs Santa Paula, 1967-71; vice-chmn. Santa Paula Taxpayers Assn., 1976; trustee Santa Paula Sch. Dist., 1977-81. Recipient Edn. award Mexican-Am. Service Orgn., 1975; Best of Show, Venpex Philatelic Expn., 1973, 80, 82, State Editor of Yr. award KC, 1976. Mem. Ventura County Bus. Tchrs. Assn. (co-founder 1967), Internat. Platform Assn., Delta Pi Epsilon, Theta Chi. Lodges: Optimists (sec. 1987—, disting. sec. 1962-63, co-knight of yr. 1973-74, optimist of yr. 1976-77), Noble Grand IOOF. Home: 727 E Pleasant St Santa Paula CA 93060

TURK, HERMAN, sociologist, educator, researcher; b. N.Y.C., May 29, 1924; s. Leo F. and Lotta A.L. (Jaenke) T.; m. Elizabeth L. Branstrom, Aug. 5, 1978; children—Lawrence, Gregory, Norman; 1 stepchild, Mark. B.S. in Elec. Engring., U. Nebr., 1947; M.A. in Sociology, Columbia U., 1952; Ph.D. in Sociology, Am. U., Washington, 1959. Safety engr. Royal Liverpool Group, N.Y.C., 1947-51; research asst. Bur. Applied Social Research Columbia U., N.Y.C., 1951-52; research asst., research assoc., research scientist Human Resources Research Office, George Washington U., Washington, 1952-58; social sci. contractor U.S. Dept. State, Washington, 1957-58; social sci. analyst NIMH, Bethesda, Md., 1958-59; faculty research assoc., asst. prof. sociology and psychiatry Duke U., Durham, N.C., 1959-63; assoc. prof., dir. Bur. Sociol. Research U. Nebr., Lincoln, 1963-66; prof. sociology, dir. Lab. for Orgnl. Research U. So. Calif., Los Angeles, 1966—; vis. prof. U. Wis., Madison, 1969, Social Sci. Research Inst., U. Cologne, U. Kiel, Fed. Republic of Germany, 1972-73, U. Stockholm, 1973-74, 80, U. P.R., 1979-80, 83; rev. panelist NSF, Washington, 1972-79; mem. exec. com. Social Sci. Adv. Com. 1977-78; cons. NIH, 1964-74, Nat. Acad. Sci., 1973-75, White House Office of Budget, 1974, U. P.R. Med. Sch., 1979—. Author: (with Thelma Ingles) Clinic Nursing: Explorations in Role Innovation, 1963, (with others) Social Aspects of Aging, 1966, Interorganizational Acivation in Urban Communities: Deductions from the Concept of System, 1973 (Am. Sociol. Assn. Rose award 1973), , Organizations in Modern Life: Cities and Other Large Networks, 1977; author, editor: (with R.L. Simpson) Institutions and Social Exchange: The Sociologies of Talcott Parsons and George C. Humans, 1970; editor: Commentaries on the Social Research and Theorems of George C. Homans, 1964; assoc. editor Sociol. Inquiry, 1961-64, editor, 1964-67; assoc. editor Sociology and Social Research, 1966-85, book rev. editor, 1974-77; assoc. editor Sociol. Quar., 1970-72, 75-80, Sociol. Symposium, 1972—, Connections, 1978—, Social Welfare, Social Planning and Social Devel., 1980—, Social Forces, 1983-86 ; contbr. articles to profl. jours. and chpts. to books. NIH-Nat. Library Medicine health sci. scholar, 1968. Fellow Am. Sociol. Assn. (exec. councils sect. on theoretical sociology 1970-74, sect. on community 1975-78, chmn. com. on publs. 1981-83), Internat. Sociol. Assn. (research council 1976—), Pacific Sociol. Assn. (chmn. publs. 1968-73, 1st v.p. 1976-78), Internat. Network for Social Network Analysis (exec. com. 1977—), Fedn. Am. Scientists, AAUP, Alpha Kappa Delta (exec. council's 1964-74, 80, pres. 1968-70). Avocations: tennis; computers. Office: U So Calif Dept Sociology MC0032 Los Angeles CA 90089

TURK, RUDY HENRY, museum director; b. Sheboygan, Wis., June 24, 1927; s. Rudolph Anton and Mary Gertrude (Stanisha) T.; m. Wanda Lee Borders, Aug. 4, 1956; children: Tracy Lynn, Maria Teresa, Andrew Borders, Jennifer Wells. BS in Edn., U. Wis., 1949; MA in History, U. Tenn., 1951; postgrad., Ind. U., 1952-56. Instr. art history, gallery dir. U. Mont., Missoula, 1957-60; dir. Richmond (Calif.) Art Ctr., 1960-65; asst. dir. San Diego Mus. Art, 1965-67; dir. Ariz. State U. Art Mus., 1967—; from assoc. prof. to prof. art Ariz. State U., 1967-77; bd. dirs. Friends of Mexican Art, Tempe Arts Com.; mem. Ariz. Commn. Arts and Humanities, 1980-84. Painter, works exhibited in solo and group exhbns.; mus. cons., juror, art cons., art lectr; author: (with Cross and Lamm) The Search for Personal Freedom, 2 vols., 1972, 76, 80, 85, Merrill Mahaffey: Monumental Landscapes, 1979, Udinotti, 1973, (with others) Scholder, 1983, also commentaries. Bd. dirs. Chandler Arts Com., 1983-86. Served with USN, 1945-46. Recipient Merit award Calif. Coll. Arts and Crafts, 1965; named Hon. Ariz. Designer Craftsman, 1975; Fulbright scholar, U. Paris, 1956-57. Mem. Am. Assn. Mus., Western Assn. Art Mus. (Golden Crate award 1974), Phi Alpha Theta, Phi Kappa Phi. Democrat. Roman Catholic. Home: 2113 E Huntington Dr Tempe AZ 85282 Office: Ariz State U 200 Matthews Center Tempe AZ 85287

TURK, TASHA, artist, educator; b. Buffalo, Jan. 22, 1938; d. Avrom Maurice and Geraldine Lucille (Leff) Greenberg; m. Ronald Jay Turk, Dec., 1959 (div.); 1 child, Ethan David; m. Avery Sandberg, 1970. BA in Fine Arts, U. Calif.-Berkeley, 1966; MFA, SUNY-Buffalo, 1977. Cert. Community coll. art tchr., Ariz. Med. illustrator, designer Roswell Park Meml. Inst., Buffalo, 1962-64; tchr. Sequoia High Sch. Dist., Redwood City, Calif., 1966-67; art dir. Sanford Weiner Assocs., Menlo Park, Calif., 1967-68; med. illustrator, exhibit designer Laurel Schaubert Studio, San Francisco, 1968-70; photographer, iconographer Buffalo and Erie County Hist. Soc., 1978; arts coordinator Living Dance Co., Tucson, 1979; pub. relations/exhbn. coordinator Community Artists Project Administr., Tucson, 1979-80; instr. sci. illustration U. Ariz., Tucson, 1980; instr. drawing, composition, life drawing Glendale Community Coll., 1981-86; graphic artist edn. dept. W.O. Boswell Meml. Hosp., Sun City, Ariz., 1982-85; instr. drawing, painting Phoenix Inst. Tech., 1986—; freelance muralist, portraitist, comml. and fine artist; one woman shows: Hallwalls Gallery, Buffalo, 1977, Polish Community Ctr., Buffalo, 1978, Germanow Gallery, Rochester, N.Y., 1979, Mind, Matter & Metaphysics Symposium, Tucson, 1981, Glendale Community Coll. Women's Ctr., 1982, 83, 84; group shows include: Ariz. Women's Caucus for Art, Louise Kerr Ctr., 1982, Glendale Community Coll. Faculty Shows, Verde Valley Art Assn. 2d Ann. Women's Fine Arts Competition, Jerome, Ariz., 1982, Phoenix Artists Coalition State Capitol Show, 1983, 84, 86, Valley Nat. Bank Art Is My Life Show, 1986, Foothills Invitationsl Show, 1986, 3d Ann. Exotic Invitational Show, Phoenix, 1986, AVA/Alwun House, Phoenix, 1985, 87; muralist Pima County (Ariz.) Jail Women's Quarters, 1980; tchr., muralist Papago Reservation, Sells, Ariz., 1980. Recipient U. Calif.-Berkeley Gallery purchase award, 1965; Roswell Park Meml. Inst. muralist grantee, 1972; SUNY-Buffalo grantee, 1976. Mem. Ariz. Women's Caucus for Art, Ariz. Artists Guild, Assn. Sci. Communicators, Ariz. Visionary Alternative, Phoenix Artists Coalition. Subject of newspaper articles and revs.; contbr. to art catalogues, newsletters. Address: PO Box 17193 Phoenix AZ 85011

TURLEY, STANLEY F., state senator; b. Snowflake, Ariz., Feb. 27, 1921; s. Fred A. and Wilma (Fillerup) T.; m. Cleo Fern Olson, 1944; children: Tauna Lee, Margo Yvonne, Jana, Fredrick C., Miriam K., Lisa, Leslie. Student, Brigham Young U. Mem. Ariz. Ho. of Reps., 1964-72, speaker, 1967-72; mem. Ariz. Senate, 1973—, pres., 1983—; bd. dirs. Ariz. Cotton Growers. Served with USAF, 1944-46. Mem. Farm Bur., Ariz. Cattle Growers Assn. Mormon. Lodge: Rotary. Address: Pres of Senate State House Phoenix AZ 85007

TURLEY, WILLIAM DALE, research chemist; b. Escondido, Calif., Nov. 10, 1957; s. Earl Ray and Josephine Ellen (Watson) T. BS in Chemistry, U. Calif., Santa Barbara, 1979, MS in Chemistry, 1984. Lab. asst. Marine Sci. Inst., Santa Barbara, 1980-83; research and teaching asst. U. Calif., Santa Barbara, 1983-84; scientist Clorox Tech. Ctr., Pleasanton, Calif., 1985-86, EG&G Energy Measurements Inc., Goleta, Calif., 1986—. Contbr. articles to profl. jours. Mem. Am. Chem. Soc. Office: EG&G Energy Measurements Inc 130 Robin Hill Rd Goleta CA 93116

TURLEY-GRINE, ELIZABETH JANE, residential services specialist; b. Beresford, S.D., Apr. 5, 1933; d. Albert and Myrtle (Boster) Nelsen; m. Michael O. Turley, Sept. 20, 1967 (div. 1975); m. Alfonso G. Grine, Mar. 21, 1980; 1 child, Deborah. BA, St. San Antonio, 1965; postgrad., Chaffey Coll., 1965-67. Cert. residential specialist; cert. psychiat. technician. Supr. Pacific State Hosp., Pomona, Calif., 1953-65; owner, operator Turley-Grine, Pomona and La Mirada, Calif., 1965—; adv. cons. Merci, Alhambra, Calif., 1986, Inland Counties, San Bernardino, Calif., 1970-75. Served as pvt. U.S. Army, 1950-52. Named Outstanding Provider, Inland Counties Regional Ctr., San Bernardino, 1974, Outstanding Provider, Eastern Los Angeles Regional Ctr., Alahambra, 1985, State Council Devel. Disabilities, 1986. Republican. Avocations: china painting, traveling, sewing, arts and crafts. Home and Office: 14324 San Ardo Dr La Mirada CA 90638

TURMAN, GEORGE, lt. gov. Mont.; b. Missoula, Mont., June 25, 1928; s. George Fugett and Corinne (McDonald) T.; m. Kathleen Hager, Mar. 1951; children—Marcia, Linda, George Douglas, John, Laura. B.A., U. Mont., 1951. Various positions Fed. Res. Bank of San Francisco, 1954-64; mayor Missoula, 1970-72; mem. Mont. Ho. of Reps. from (Dist. 18), 1973-74; Mont. Pub. Service commr. (Dist. 5), 1975-80; lt. gov. Mont., 1981—. Served with U.S. Army, 1951-53. Decorated Combat Inf. badge. Address: 1300 Stuart St Helena MT 59601

TURNAGE, JEAN A., state supreme court chief justice; b. St. Ignatius, Mont., Mar. 10, 1926. LL.B., Mont. State U., 1951. Bar: Mont. 1951, U.S. Dist. Ct. Mont. 1963. Formerly ptnr. Turnage & McNeil, Polson, Mont.; formerly Mont. State senator from 13th Dist.; pres. Mont. State Senate, 1981-85; assoc. justice Supreme Ct. Mont., Helena, 1985-86; chief justice Supreme Ct. Mont., 1986—. Mem. Mont. State Bar Assn., ABA. Office: Mont Supreme Ct Justice Bldg Helena MT 59620

TURNBULL, MARY EDITH, painter, art educator; b. Surrey, B.C., Can., Oct. 24, 1927; came to U.S., 1943, naturalized, 1952; d. Henry Harvey and May Lavina (Winter) T.; m. Dudley Charles Ambrose, July 16, 1949 (div. Apr. 1977); children—Peter Charles, Janet Mary, Antoinette Carmen Theresa. B.S., U. Calif.-Berkeley, 1949; teaching credential Calif. Poly. State U., 1979; postgrad. UCLA, 1984, Calif. State U., Northridge, 1987. Contract art instr. San Luis Obispo Art Assn., Calif., 1978-82, Paso Robles Art Assn., Calif., 1977-85, Cuesta Coll., San Luis Obispo, 1976-82; art therapist Riverview Vol. Assn., New Westminster, B.C., summer 1985; art coordinator Culver City Unified Sch. Dist., Calif., 1985—; art specialist J. Paul Getty Inst. Culver City Unified Sch. Dist., 1985—. Painter in oils and watercolor; one-woman shows include: Western Orchid Congress, Anaheim, Calif., 1975, Calif. Poly. State U., San Luis Obispo, 1977, Santa Barbara Mus. Natural History, 1981, Descanso Gardens Hospitality House Gallery, 1986; exhibited group shows including: Fresno Arts Ctr., 1978, Art Ctr., San Luis Obispo, 1980, Mid-State Fair (1st prize for watercolor) 1980, San Bernardino County Mus., 1985. Leader 4-H Club, Atascadero, Calif., 1950-54, 70-75; condr. art tours San Luis Obispo Civic Assn., 1978; fund raiser Monday Club, San Luis Obispo, 1974-80, chmn. art com., 1973-82. Mem. Nat. Watercolor Soc., San Luis Obispo Art Assn. (chmn. bus. exhibits 1973-78), Women in Design, Artists Equity Assn. (chmn. programs, sec. 1983 86—), Exec. Female Art Educators of So. Calif. Democrat. Avocations: reading; writing; traveling. Home: 4309 Radford Ave Suite A Studio City CA 91604 Office: La Ballona Sch 10915 Washington Blvd Culver City CA 90230

TURNBULL, THOMAS KENT, Episcopalian priest; b. Lancaster, Ohio, Aug. 3, 1934; s. Donald Curtis and Lucy Gordon (Taylor) T.; m. Ingrid Johanne Moeller, Apr. 15, 1967; children: Michael David, John Christopher, Rachael Maria. BA in Theatre Arts, Denison U., 1959; BDiv., Episcopal Theol. Sch., 1965. Ordained to ministry Episcopal Ch. as deacon, 1965, as priest, 1966. Rector Christ Ch., Ironton, Ohio, 1967-71; vicar Ch. of the Holy Spirit, Cin., 1971-74; assoc. rector Christ Ch., Denver, 1974-75; vicar St. George's Ch., Leadville, Colo., 1975-78; rector Ch. of the Transfiguration, Vail, Colo., 1975-85; on sabbatical in England and Colo., 1985-86; interim rector Ch. of Holy Conforter, Broomfield, Colo., 1986-87; rector St. Andrew's Episc. Ch., Chelan, Washington; pres. standing com. Diocese of Colo., 1984-85, mem. examining chaplains, 1980-87; leader numerous workshops and retreats, 1967—; alt. gen. conv. The Episcopal Ch., 1985; del. Mutual Responsibility and Interdependance Conf. on Prayer From So. Diocese Ohio, 1972. Author numerous poems; photographer. Chaplain Vail Valley Med. Ctr., 1980-85, Vail Police Dept., 1982-85. Served as sgt. USMC, 1953-56. Mem. St. Gregory's Benedictine Abbey (assoc.), Evang. Sisters of Mary (Fed. Republic of Germany), The Anglican Soc. Lodge: Rotary. Avocation: photography. Office: St Andrew's Episcopal Ch 120 Woodin Ave Chelan WA 98816

TURNER, CHARLES INNES, optical engineer; b. Bklyn., Sept. 28, 1946; s. Norman Innes and Ellen Sue (Redinger) T.; m. Susan Elizabeth Oakley, Nov. 29, 1975 (div. June 1982). BArch, Princeton U., 1967; MME, U. Tex., 1970; BA in Mgmt., U. Redlands, 1982. Drafter S.W. Research Inst., San Antonio, 1963-69; jr. engr. J.J. Kassner & Co., N.Y.C., 1967-68; project leader S&W Design, Inc., Austin, Tex., 1972-74; drafting supr. U. Tex., Austin, 1974-78; design supr. Tracor, Inc., Austin, 1978-79; optics supr. Eaton Corp./ MSC Products, Costa Mesa, Calif., 1979—, lectr. tng. sessions, 1985—; lectr. training sessions Eaton Corp./MSC Products, 1985—. Served with USN, 1970-72, Vietnam. Avocations: race car driving, travel, music, art. Home: 25121 La Suen Rd Laguna Hills CA 92653 Office: Eaton Corp/MSC Products 1640 Monrovia Blvd Costa Mesa CA 92653

TURNER, DEAN EDSON, education educator, minister; b. Tyrone, Okla., May 24, 1927; s. Jesse Lee and Cora May (Luman) T.; m. Nancy Margaret Roche, Aug. 12, 1964; children: Taos Lee, Summer Marie. BA, Centro de Estudios Universitarios, Mexico City, 1953-55; MEd, Adams State Coll., 1959; PhD in Philosophy and History of Edn., U. Tex., 1966. Cert. tchr., Colo.; ordained to ministry Disciples of Christ Ch., 1967. English tchr. Instituto Taylor Comercial, Mexico City, 1953-55; Spanish tchr. Anchorage High Sch., 1956-58, Carmichael (Calif.) High Sch., 1958, Farmingdale (L.I.) High Sch., 1961, Rye (N.Y.) High Sch., 1963-64; prof. Spanish Sullins Women's Coll., Bristol, Va., 1962-63; prof. sociology, Spanish U. Md., 1959-61; prof. founds. of edn. U. No. Colo., Greeley, 1966—. Author: The Autonomous Man, 1970, Commitment to Care, 1978, The Einstein Myth, 1979 (Alt. Book of Myth award 1979); co-author: Classrooms in Crisis, 1986. Served to sgt. U.S. Army, 1950-52. Recipient Tchrs. Who Care award Channel 4, Denver, 1986, Lucille Harrison Outstanding Tchr. of Yr. award U. No. Colo., 1983. Mem. Soc. Christian Philosophers, Soc. Christian Ethics, Christian Educators Assn. Internat. Home: 1708 37th Ave Greeley CO 80634 Office: U No Colo Greeley CO 80639

TURNER, ED C., engineer; b. Santa Monica, Calif., Apr. 15, 1939; s. Herbert Chan and Helen Naomi (Hahn) T.; children—Michael Edwin, Lynn Elizabeth, Jennifer Sue. A.A., Santa Monica City Coll., 1963. Registered profl. engr., land surveyor, Idaho. With Mt. Whitney Pack Trains, Lone Pine, Calif., 1956-59; pub. works engr. City of Los Angeles, 1962-69; design engr., traffic engr., city engr. Idaho Falls, 1969—. Co-chmn., Conf. on Children, 1978; appeared before U.S. Senate Subcom. on Parental Kidnapping, Los Angeles. Mem. Am. Pub. Works Assn., Inst. Transp. Engrs. Office: PO Box 220 Idaho Falls ID 83402

TURNER, FRED, JR., soil scientist; b. Paris Crossing, Ind., Jan. 13, 1920; s. Fred and Laura Evangeline (Click) T.; m. Marilyn C. Cantelou, July 24, 1942 (dec. Jan. 1975); 1 child, Fred Lynwood; m. Lillian Irene Brewer, Dec. 31, 1976; children: Deanna Irene Butcher, Marjorie Carol Mathews. BS, U. Ariz., 1948; MS, Wash. State U., 1951; PhD, Mich. State U., 1958. Soil scientist Northern Great Plains Field Sta., Mandan, N.D., 1953-54; asst. prof. soil sci. U. Ariz., Tucson, 1957-61, supt. br. experiment sta., soil scientist, 1961-80, soil specialist, extension soil specialist, 1980-83, emeritus soil scientist, 1983—; head. agriculture dept. Regional Devel. Com., Oman, 1983-85; soil and water specialist USAID and U. Ariz., Yemen Arab Republic, 1979, World Bank, Yemen Arab Republic, 1981; advisor in soils USAID and U. Ariz., Fortaleza, Brazil, 1966-68. Contbr. articles to profl. jours. Pres. Copper Council Boy Scouts Am., Safford, Ariz., 1976-78; chmn. Mt. Graham chpt. ARC, Safford, 1968-80; mem. western nat. field office adv. council ARC, Burlingame, Calif., 1976-79. Served to col. USAFR, 1941-80, WWII and Korea. Recipient Appreciation award U. Ariz. Alumni Assn., 1966, Pub. Service award Nat. Weather Service, Washington, 1976, Silver Beaver award Boy Scouts Am., Phoenix, 1976. Mem. Internat. Soc. Soil Sci., Soil Sci. Soc. Am., Am. Soc. Agronomy, Am. Legion, Sigma Xi, Alpha Zeta (chronicler 1938-39, named Top Freshman 1938). Republican. Methodist. Lodge: Rotary (pres. Safford club 1978). Avocations: meteorology, photography, hunting, fishing. Home and Office: 46-283 Kahuhipa St #PH-6 Kaneohe HI 96744

TURNER, IRIS EVELYN NORTON, elementary educator, reading specialist; b. Truxton, Mo., Oct. 16, 1927; d. Walter Richard and Gwendolyn Evelyn (Anson) Norton; m. Frank David Turner, Sept. 7, 1952; 1 child, Thomas Richard. BS in Elem. Edn., U. Nev., 1964; MA in Elem. Edn., U. No. Ariz., 1983. Cert. elem. tchr., reading specialist. Tchr. history Wassuk Coll., Hawthorne, Nev., 1984; elem. tchr. Mineral City Dist., Hawthorne, 1964-81, tchr. math, reading, 1980—; speaker Internat. Reading Assn., Reno, 1986. Author: Preparing Your Child for School, 1983. Mem. Library

Bd. Mineral County, Hawthorne, 1985. Served to sgt. Women's Army Corps, 1950-52. Recipient Valley Forge Tchrs. medal Freedoms Found., 1973. Mem. Delta Kappa Gamma, Alpha Chi. Republican. Baptist. Home: 600 K St Box 363 Hawthorne NV 89415 Office: Mineral County Sch Dist Hawthorne NV 89415

TURNER, JAMES HARRIS, III, information systems executive; b. Richmond, Va., May 15, 1947; s. James Harris Jr. and Doris (Scroggs) T.; m. Kathy Nance, Aug. 12, 1978 (div. Apr. 1986); 1 child, James Harris IV. Student, Am. U., 1968, George Washington U., 1969. Police officer Washington Police Dept., 1968-70; supr. police Henrico Police Dept., Richmond, Va., 1970-78; gen. mgr. ATO Corp., Richmond, 1978-80; elected sheriff Henrico County, Richmond, 1980-85; cons. Turner and Assocs., Sacramento, 1985-86; dir. criminal justice info. systems Bus. Info. Systems, Ventura, Calif., 1986—; bd. dirs. Nat. Inst. Corrections, Washington. Sgt. at Arms Va. Rep. Conv., Richmond; del. Rep. Nat. Conv., Detroit, 1980. Served as sgt. U.S. Army, 1965-68, Vietnam. Named Outstanding Law Enforcement Officer, Jaycees, Richmond, 1979, one of Outstanding Young Men Am., Jaycees, Richmond, 1981. Mem. Nat. Sheriffs Assn., Am. Correctional Assn., Va. Sheriffs Assn., United Coml. Travelers, Am. Legion. Methodist. Avocations: golf, hunting, fishing, camping. Office: Business Info Systems 4880 Market St Ventura CA 93003

TURNER, JANET E., artist; b. Kansas City, Mo., 1914; d. James Ernest and Hortense (Taylor) T. A.B., Stanford U., 1936; diploma, postgrad., Kansas City Art Inst. (under Thomas H. Benton, John de Martelly), 5 years; student art, Claremont Grad. Sch. (Millard Sheets, Henry McFee), 2 years, M.F.A., 1947; student serigraphy, Edward Landon; Ed.D., Columbia, 1960. Faculty Girls Collegiate Sch., Claremont, Calif., 1942-47; asst. prof. art Stephen F. Austin State Coll., Nacogdoches, Tex., 1947-56; asst. prof. Chico State U., 1959-63, assoc. prof., 1963-68, prof., 1968-80, emeritus, 1980—. Works have been shown in painting, water colors and prints exhbns. throughout U.S.; exhibited over 200 one-man shows in U.S., Israel, Japan; exhibited in Internat. Biannual of Graphics, Krakow, Poland, Internat. Exchange Exhbn., Seoul, Korea, Artistes Contemporains Americains, Le Salon des Nations, Paris; represented in collections in U.S., fgn. countries. Illustrator: F. Smith. Recipient prizes including: (painting) 1st prize Tex. Fine Arts Assn., 1948; Dealey purchase prize and Comini popular prize 11th Tex. Gen. Exhbn.; R.D. Straus prize 13th Tex. Gen. Exhbn.; 3 prize oils 50th Anniversary Exhbn. Art Assn. New Orleans; S. Karasick prize 59th Ann. Nat. Assn. Women Artists; water colors purchase prize 2d Tex. Water Color Soc.; Sun Carnival prize 3d Ann. Southwestern Sun Carnival Fine Arts Exhbn., El Paso; purchase prize Smith Coll. Mus. Art, 37th Ann. Exhbn. Western Art, Denver; Marcia Tucker prize Nat. Assn. Women Artists; prints Nat. Assn. Women Artists, 1950; graphics 1st prize Painters and Sculptors Soc. N.J., 32d Ann. Springfield (Mass.) Art League, Pen and Brush Black and White Exhbn., N.Y.C.; purchase prize Soc. Am. Graphic Artists 36th Ann. A.N.A.; 2d prize, Springfield Art League, Mass., 1955; 1st prize, Pen and Brush, 1956; 8th ann. Boston Printmakers purchase prize; 6th Southwestern Dallas Mus. Fine Arts, 1st prize graphics, Painters Sculptors Soc. of N.J.; Tupperware Art Fund Fellowship award for painting; Los Angeles County Nat. purchase prize; purchase prize Calif. State Fair, 1960; Cannon prize N.A.D., 1961; Medal of Honor and Alice S. Buell Meml. prize Nat. Assn. Women Artists, 1963; Katheryn Colton prize, Medal of Honor and Mabel M. Garner award, 1967; A.P. Hankins Meml. prize Print Club Pa., 1972; Lessig Rosenwald prize Print Club, 1975; Medal of Honor, Nat. Assn. Women Artists, 1977; Guggenheim fellow, 1952; Tupperware fellow, 1956—; co-recipient Outstanding Prof. award Calif. State U. and Colls., 1975. Mem. League Am. Pen Women, Los Angeles Printmaking Soc. (Purchase prize 1971), Nat. Assn. Women Artists (Schafer prize 1983), Audubon Artists (award 1981), Am. Color Print Soc. (award 1981), Soc. Am. Graphic Artists (award 1982), N.A.D. (academician, Cook award 1985), AAUW, Calif. Soc. Printmakers, Los Angeles Printmaking Soc., Centro Studie Scambi Internazionale, Delta Kappa Gamma, Alpha Omicron Pi, Kappa Delta Pi, Pi Lambda Theta. Home: 567 E Lassen St Sp 701 Chico CA 95926

TURNER, JOHN FREELAND, state senator, rancher; b. Jackson, Wyo., Mar. 3, 1942; s. John Charles and Mary Louise (Mapes) T.; m. Mary Kay Brady, 1969; children—John Francis, Kathy Mapes, Mark Freeland. B.S. in Biology, U. Notre Dame, 1964; postgrad. U. Innsbruck, 1964-65, U. Utah, 1965-66; M.S. in Ecology, U. Mich., 1968. Rancher, outfitter Triangle X Ranch, Moose, Wyo.; chmn. bd. dirs. Bank of Jackson Hole; photo-journalist; state senator from Sublette, Teton County, pres. Wyo. Senate, chmn. legis. mgmt. audit com., rules com., vice chmn., Sec. of Interior's Nat. Parks adv. bd.; mem. state adv. bd. for Small Bus. Adminstrn., statewide coordinating Task Force U. Wyo., exec. commn. State Reps., adv. council Coll. Agriculture U. Wyo.; mem. Teton Sci. Sch. Bd.; mem. exec. com. Council of State Govt.; chmn. Pride in Jackson Hole Campaign, 1986; bd. dirs. Wyo. Waterfowl Trust. Mem. Western River Guides Assn., Jackson Hole Guides and Outfitters. Named Citizen of Yr. County of Teton, 1984; recipient Nat. Conservation Achievement award Nat. Wildlife Fedn., 1984. Author: The Magnificent Bald Eagle: Our National Bird, 1971. Republican. Roman Catholic. Address: Triangle X Ranch Moose WY 83012

TURNER, NELVIA FRANCES, hotel executive; b. Keiser, Ark., Sept. 28, 1934; d. James McKinley and Gladys Martha (Lyerly) T. Cert., Northwestern Bus. Coll., 1955. With front office, reservations, sales sec., dir. food and beverage, also catering Westin Hotels, Portland, Oreg., 1955—. Democrat. Methodist. Office: The Westin Benson Broadway and Oak Portland OR 97205

TURNER, RALPH B., biochemist professor; b. Lynchburg, Va., Mar. 1, 1931; s. Ralph Marshall and Helen Winifred (Burton) T.; m. Penelope Virginia Clark, Dec. 15, 1953; children: Burton, Ginger. BS, Va. Tech. Inst., 1952; PhD, U. Tex., Austin, 1963. Research biochemist USDA-Agrl. Research Services, Gainesville, Fla., 1963-68; research prof. N. Mex. State U., Las Cruces, 1968—. Editor: Analytical Biochemistry of Insects, 1978. Served with U.S. Army, 1951-56, Korea. Fellow AAAS, Am. Inst. Chemists; mem. Am. Soc. Biochemists, Am. Chem. Soc., Sigma Xi. Avocations: reading, exercise, fishing. Home: 300 Capri Arc Las Cruces NM 88005 Office: N Mex State Univ Box 3 BE Las Cruces NM 88003

TURNER, RALPH HERBERT, sociologist, educator; b. Effingham, Ill., Dec. 15, 1919; s. Herbert Turner and Hilda Pearl (Bohn) T.; m. Christine Elizabeth Hanks, Nov. 2, 1943; children: Lowell Ralph, Cheryl Christine. B.A., U So. Calif., 1941, M.A., 1942; postgrad., U. Wis., 1942-43; Ph.D., U. Chgo., 1948. Research assoc. Am. Council Race Relations, 1947-48; faculty UCLA, 1948—, prof. sociology and anthropology, 1959—, chmn. dept. sociology, 1963-68; chmn. Acad. Senate U. Calif. System, 1983-84; vis. summer prof. U. Wash., 1960, U. Hawaii, 1962; vis. scholar Australian Nat. U., 1972; vis. prof. U. Ga., 1975, Ben Gurion U., Israel, 1983; vis. fellow Nuffield Coll. Oxford U., 1980; disting. vis. prof. Am. U., Cairo, Egypt, 1983; adj. prof. China Acad. Social Scis., Beijing, People's Republic China, 1986; faculty research lectr. UCLA, 1986-87. Author: (with L. Killian) Collective Behavior, 1957, 2d edit., 1972, 3d edit., 1987, The Social Context of Ambition, 1964, Robert Park on Social Control and Collective Behavior, 1967, Family Interaction, 1970, Earthquake Prediction and Public Policy, 1975, (with J. Nigg, D. Paz, B. Young) Community Response to Earthquake Threat in Southern California., 1980, (with J. Nigg and D. Paz) Waiting for Disaster, 1986; editorial cons., 1959-62; editor: Sociometry, 1962-64; acting editor: Ann. Rev. of Sociology, 1977-78; assoc. editor, 1978-79, editor, 1980-86; adv. editor: Am. Jour. Sociology, 1954-56, Sociology and Social Research, 1961-74; editorial staff: Am. Sociol. Rev., 1955-56; assoc. editor: Social Problems, 1959-62, 67-69; cons. editor: Social Inquiry, 1968-73, Western Sociol. Rev., 1975-79; editorial bd. Mass Emergencies, 1975-79, Internat. Jour. Critical Sociology, 1974—, Symbolic Interactions, 1977—. Mem. behavioral scis. study sect. NIH, 1961-66, chmn., 1963-64; dir.-at-large Social Sci. Research Council, 1965-66; chmn. panel on pub. policy implications of earthquake prediction Nat. Acad. Scis., 1974-75, also mem. earthquqke study delegation to Peoples Republic of China, 1976; Mem. com. social edn. and action Los Angeles Presbytery, 1954-56. Served to lt. (j.g.) USNR, 1943-46. Recipient Faculty prize Coll. Letters and Scis. UCLA, 1985; Faculty Research fellow Social Sci. Research Council., 1953-56; Sr. Fulbright scholar U.K., 1956-57; Guggenheim fellow, U.K., 1964-65. Mem. Am. Sociol. Assn. (council 1959-64, chmn. social psychology sect. 1960-61, pres. 1968-69, chmn. sect. theoretical sociology 1973-74, chmn. collective behavior and social movements sect. 1983-84), Pacific Sociol. Assn. (pres. 1957), Internat. Sociol Assn. (council 1974-82, v.p. 1978-82), Soc. Study Social Problems (exec. com. 1962-63), Soc. for Study Symbolic Interaction (pres. 1982-83, Charles Horton Cooley award 1978), AAUP. Home: 1126 Chautauqua Blvd Pacific Palisades CA 90272 Office: UCLA 405 Hilgard Ave Los Angeles CA 90024

TURNER, ROBERT HAROLD, mechanical engineering educator; b. San Francisco, Sept. 20, 1941; s. Robert Harold and Teresa Mary (Meckel) T.; m. Nancy Ann Augden, Sept. 13, 1969; children: Alexa Gabriella, Eric Christian, Tobias Lee. BS, U. Calif., Berkeley, 1964, MS, 1965; PhD, UCLA, 1971. Registered profl. engr., Calif., Nev. Engr. AiResearch, Los Angeles, 1965-67; teaching and research asst. UCLA, 1968-71; head thermal sect. So. Research Inst., Birmingham, Ala., 1971-72; environ. analyst NUS Copr., Rockville, Md., 1972-74; solar systems researcher Jet Propulsion Lab., Pasadena, Calif., 1975-83; prof. mech. engring. U. Nev., Reno, 1983—; cons. Spectrolab, Sylmar, Calif., 1967-71, in field, Reno, 1983—. Author: High Temperature Thermal Energy Storage, 1978; also numerous articles to profl. jours. Mem. ASME, ASHRAE, Sigma Xi. Avocations: hiking, camping, backpacking, chess. Home: 12300 Westridge Dr Reno NV 89511 Office: U Nev Reno NV 89557

TURNER, RONALD MICHAEL, physician; b. Seattle, May 12, 1947; s. Raeburn Leslie and Barbara Rose (Hoffman) T.; 1 child, Sheryl Rose. BA, Eastern Wash. U., 1970; MD, Southwestern U., Cebu City, The Philippines, 1980. Residency Bapt. Hosp. Bowman Gray Med. Sch., Winston-Salem, N.C., 1981-82; pvt. practice medicine Walla Walla, Wash., 1982—. Served with U.S. Army, 1967-68.

TURNER, ROSS JAMES, corporate executive; b. Winnipeg, Man., Can., May 1, 1930; s. James Valentine and Gretta H. (Ross) T.; m. Helen Elizabeth Todd, June 9, 1950; children: Ralph, Rick, Tracy Lee. Student, U. Man. Extension, 1951, Banff Sch. Advanced Mgmt., 1956. Acct. Dominion Bridge Co., Winnipeg, 1951-53; controller Alta. div., Edmonton, 1958; mgr. acctg. service Alta. div., Montreal, 1959-61; sec.-treas. Standard Iron & Engring. Works, Ltd., Alta., 1954-57; div. v.p. BACM Industries, Ltd., Winnipeg, 1962-63, treas., dir., 1963-64, exec. v.p., 1965-68; pres., chief operating officer, dir. Neonex Internat., Ltd., 1969-71, Seaspan Internat., Ltd., North Vancouver, B.C., 1971-72; pres., dir. Genstar Western Ltd., Vancouver, 1973-76; pres., chief exec. officer Genstar Corp., San Francisco, 1976-86, chmn. bd. dirs., 1987—; vice chmn. Genstar Corp., 1986—; bd. dirs. Rio Algom Ltd., Gt. West Life Assurance Co., Fed. Industries Ltd. and Oxford Properties Can. Ltd. Bd. dirs. YMCA, San Francisco; mem. adv. council Faculty of Commerce and Bus. Adminstrn. U. B.C. Fellow Soc. Mgmt. Accts. Can.; mem. San Francisco C. of C. Clubs: Mount Royal (Montreal); Toronto (Toronto); Vancouver (Vancouver); Pacific Union (San Francisco), World Trade, Peninsula Golf and Country. Office: Genstar Corp 4 Embarcadero Center 3800 San Francisco CA 94111

TURNER, RUSSELL KENNETH, banking executive; b. Ogden, Utah, May 4, 1957; s. Wayne William Turner and Jackie (Bryant) Newman; m. Jill Buttars, Feb. 28, 1976; children: Racheal, R. Scott. BS in Data Processing, Weber State Coll., 1981; MBA, U. Alaska, 1986. Cert. data processor, 1982. Programmer, analyst Blue Cross/Blue Shield Co., Salt Lake City, 1979-80, mgr. claims systems, 1980-81; prin. Turner Software Cons., Anchorage, 1981-84; v.p. systems and devel. Alaska Mut. Bank, Anchorage, 1984-86, v.p. product devel. and planning, 1986—. Mem. Data Processing Mgmt. Assn., Assn. for Systems Mgmt. Lodge: Masons. Avocations: pilot, fishing, hunting, skiing. Office: Alaska Mut Bank 1500 W Benson Blvd Anchorage AK 99503

TURNER, TAMARA ADELE, medical librarian; b. Seattle, Mar. 27, 1940; d. Fredrick Patrick and Florence Elfreda (Puntenney) T. B.A., U. Wash., 1972, M.L.S., 1974. Staff librarian Rainier Sch., Wash. State Library, Buckley, 1974-77; dir. med. library Childrens's Hosp. and Med. Ctr., Seattle, 1977—. U.S. Dept. Edn. fellow, 1973-74. Mem. Wash. Med. Librarians Assn., Seattle Area Hosp. Library Consortium (pres. 1980), Med. Library Assn., Spl. Libraries Assn., Am. Soc. Info. Sci. Home: 1931 E Calhoun Seattle WA 98112 Office: Childrens Hosp and Med Ctr PO Box 5371 Seattle WA 98105

TURNER, WALTER FRANKLIN, electronics company executive; b. Chgo., Feb. 8, 1934; s. Walter Franklin and Mary (Campanale) T.; m. Jean Ann McDermott, Jan. 29, 1969; children: Paul E., Teresa E., Tracey L. BBA, Loyola U., Los Angeles, 1955. Mktg. rep. IBM, Los Angeles, 1959-69; regional mgr. Farrington Mfg. Co., Los Angeles, 1969-70; nat. acct. mgr. Telex Computer Products, Los Angeles, 1970-73; regional mgr. Value Computing, Los Angeles, 1973-82; pres. JCA Software, Inc., Irvine, Calif., 1982—. Served to lt. USN, 1955-59. Office: JCA Software Inc 18201 Von Karman Ave Irvine CA 92715

TURNER, WILLIAM BOB, management and financial consultant, educator, lecturer; b. Fresno, Calif., July 3, 1920; s. William Burton and Grace (Calhoun) T.; m. Phyllis Vivian Hain, Apr. 2, 1940; children—Jacqulyn Lee Turner Gruchala, Pamela Turner Kartiganer, Donna Turner Diaz. B.S., UCLA, 1948; M.S., Golden State U., 1952; B.A., Columbia Pacific U., 1980, Ph.D., 1984. Lic. nursing home adminstr., Calif. Mgr., contract adminstr. Sunstrand/Turbo, Pacoima, Calif., 1955-59; mgr. mgmt. control Marquardt Corp., Van Nuys, Calif., 1959-64; div. controller Purolator Products, Inc., Newbury Park, Calif., 1964-67; controller A. & W. Internat., Inc., Santa Monica, Calif., 1967-70; exec. v.p. Wyndon Corp., Century City, Calif., 1970-80, dir., 1972-80; pres. Del Rey Mgmt., Sherman Oaks, Calif., 1979—; v.p. Sandpebbles Corp., Canoga Park, Calif., 1976-82; prof. Golden State U., Los Angeles, 1985—; cons. in field, 1965—; asst. prof. Calif. State U.-Dominguez Hills, 1976-80, Golden State U., Los Angeles, 1952-56; quizmasters seminars, 1976—; exec. trustee Magnolia Investments, 1982; mem. Calif. Senate Select Som. on Small Bus., 1986—. Author: The Administrator, 1977; Study Manual for NHA Exam, 1980; A-I-T Study Manual for the California Exam, NHA, 1982. Republican precinct worker, 1952-68. Served with U.S. Army, 1944-45. Fellow Am. Coll. Health Care Adminstrs. (Educator of Yr. 1985); mem. Nat. Assn. Accts. Populist. Lodges: De Molay (past comdr., dean, chevalier, Cross of Honor, Legion of Honor, past master councilor), Masons. Home: 13902 Huston St Sherman Oaks CA 91423 Office: Golden State U 1210 W 4th St Los Angeles CA 90017

TURNER, WILLIAM COCHRANE, international management consultant; b. Red Oak, Iowa, May 27, 1929; s. James Lyman and Josephine (Cochrane) T.; m. Cynthia Dunbar, July 16, 1955; children: Scott Christopher, Craig Dunbar, Douglas Gordon. BS, Northwestern U., 1952. Pres., bd. dirs. Western Mgmt. Cons., Inc., Phoenix, 1960-74, Western Mgmt. Cons. Europe, S.A., Brussels, 1968-74; U.S. ambassador, permanent rep. OECD, Paris, 1974-77, vice chmn. exec. com., 1976-77, U.S. rep. Energy Policy Commn., 1976-77; mem. U.S. dels. internat. meetings, 1974-77; mem. western internat. trade group U.S. Dept. Commerce, 1972-74; chmn. Argyle Atlantic Corp., Phoenix, 1977—; chmn. European adv. council, 1981—, Asia Pacific adv. council AT&T Internat., 1981—; mem. European adv. com. IBM World Trade Europe, Africa, Middle East Corp., 1977-80; mem. Asia Pacific adv. council Am. Can Co., 1981-85; mem. Gen. Electric of Brazil adv. council Gen. Electric Co., Coral Gables, Fla., 1979-81 mem. Caterpillar of Brazil adv. council Caterpillar Tractor Co., Peoria, Ill., 1979-84; mem. Caterpillar Asia Pacific Adv. Council; mem. Adv. Com. for Trade Negotiations, 1982-84; bd. dirs. Goodyear Tire & Rubber Co., Akron, Ohio, Salomon Inc., N.Y.C., Atlantic Inst. Found., Inc., mem. internat. adv. council Avon Products, Inc., N.Y.C., 1985—; mem. Spencer Stuart adv. council Spencer Stuart and Assocs., N.Y.C., 1984—; chmn., mem. internat. adv. council Advanced Semiconductor Materials Internat. NV., Bilthoven, The Netherlands, 1985—; bd. dirs. The Atlantic Council of the U.S., Washington, 1977—; co-chmn. internat. adv. bd. Pacific & Asia Christian U., Kona, Hawaii, 1985—; bd. dirs. World Wildlife Fund/U.S., 1983—, The Conservation Found., 1985—; bd. govs. Joseph H. Lauder Inst. Mgmt. and Internat. Studies, U. Pa., 1983—; trustee Heard Mus., Phoenix, 1983—; chmn. bd. trustees Am. Grad. Sch. Internat. Mgmt., 1972—; bd. govs. Atlantic Inst. Internat. Affairs, Paris, 1977—; adv. bd. Ctr. Strategic and Internat. Studies, Georgetown U., 1977-81; mem. European Community-U.S. Businessmen's Council, 1978-79; bd. govs. Am. Hosp. of Paris, 1974-77; trustee Nat. Symphony Orch. Assn., Washington, 1973-83, Am. Sch., Paris, 1976-77, Orme Sch., Mayer, Ariz., 1970-74, Phoenix Country Day Sch., 1971-74; mem. nat. councils Salk Inst., 1978-82; mem. U.S. Adv. Com. Internat. Edn. and Cultural Affairs, 1969-74; nat. rev. bd. Ctr. Cultural and Tech. Interchange between East and West, 1970-74; mem. vestry Am. Cathedral, Paris, 1976-77; pres., bd. dirs. Phoenix Symphony Assn., 1969-70; chmn. Ariz. Joint Econ. Devel. Com., 1967-68; exec. com., bd. dirs. Ariz. Dept. Econ. Planning and Devel., 1968-70; chmn. bd. Ariz. Crippled Children's Services, 1964-65; treas. Ariz. Rep. Com., 1956-57; chmn. Ariz. Young Rep. League, 1955-56. Recipient East-West Ctr. Disting. Service award, 1977. Mem. U.S. Council Internat. Bus. (trustee, exec. com. 1977—), Council Fgn. Relations, Phoenix 40. Episcopalian. Clubs: Met., Links (N.Y.C.), Plaza (Phoenix), Paradise Valley (Ariz.) Country, Bucks (London). Office: 4350 E Camelback Rd Suite 240-B Phoenix AZ 85018

TURNER-MCFARLAND, ALICE ELIZABETH, librarian; b. Saskatoon, Sask., Can., Oct. 16, 1925; d. John Ross and Annie Louise (Jackson) Turner; m. R.B. McFarland, 1985. BA, U. Sask., 1946; BLS, McGill U., 1950. Librarian, U. Man. (Can.), Winnipeg, 1950-52; childrens librarian Saskatoon Pub. Library, 1952-53, head reference dept., 1953-61, asst. chief librarian, 1961-80, chief librarian, 1981—. Office: Saskatoon Public Library, 311 23d St E, Saskatoon, SK Canada S7K 0J6

TURNEY, JAMES EDWARD, II, computer scientist; b. Greenburg, Pa., May 14, 1933; s. James Edward and Mary Elizabeth (Koch) T.; m. Joan Lois Sweeney, Sept. 1, 1957 (dec. Jan. 1982); m. Audra Varnagy, Mar. 27, 1982; children: Audrey, Jennifer, Jill, Joy. BS in Indsl. Engring., Northeastern U., 1961; MS in Indsl. Mgmt., MIT, 1964; postgrad., Calif. Coast U. Sr. cons. Peat Marwick Mitchell Co., Los Angeles, 1965-68; gen. mgr. Technicolor, Inc., Hollywood, Calif., 1968-70; dir. Intercontinental Computing, Inc., Kansas City, Mo., 1970-72; v.p. Insight Systems, Ltd., Des Moines, 1972-76; pres. Pro Data Systems, Inc., Belmont, Calif., 1976—. Bd. dirs. Luth. Ch., Wayland, Mass., 1964-66, Palos Verdes, Calif., 1967-71, Overland Park, Kans., 1973-76. Served as sgt. U.S. Army, 1953-56. Mem. Am. Inst. Indsl. Engrs. (pres. 1966-67). Republican. Avocations: sailing, music, photography. Home and Office: Pro Data Systems Inc 2700 All View Way Belmont CA 94002

TURNLUND, JUDITH RAE, nutrition scientist; b. St. Paul, Sept. 28, 1936; d. Victor Emanuel and Vida Mae (Priddy) Hanson; m. Richard W. Turnlund, Nov. 9, 1957; children: Michael Wayne, Mark Richard, Todd Hanson. BS in Chemistry and Psychology, Gustavus Adolphus Coll., 1958; PhD in Nutrition, U. Calif., Berkeley, 1978. Postdoctoral fellow U. Calif., Berkeley, 1978-80, vis. lectr., 1981-82, 84—; research nutritionist Western Regional Research Ctr., USDA, Albany, Calif., 1980-84, Western Human Nutrition Research Ctr., USDA, Albany, 1984—; vis. asst. prof. Am. U., Beirut, 1979, 80. Editor: Stable Isotopes in Nutrition, 1984; contbr. articles to profl jours. Grantee USDA, Nat. Dairy Council. Mem. Am. Inst. Nutrition (chmn. adv. bd. Nutrition Notes, 1985-86), Am. Soc. Clin. Nutrition, Am. Chem Soc. (sec.-treas. nutrition sect. 1982-83), Am. Dietetics Assn. Home: 5061 Chelsea Dr Newark CA 94560 Office: USDA Western Human Nutrition Research Ctr 800 Buchanan St Albany CA 94710

TUROCZY, CHERYL LA RAE, institutional planning coordinator; b. Rupert, Idaho, Aug. 14, 1943; d. Arthur Ray and Dorothy LaBelle (Hart) Fike; 1 son, Richard. B.A., Whitman Coll., 1965; M.Ed. in Human Services, Boston U., 1979. Tchr., Sharpstein Elem. Sch., Walla Walla, Wash., 1965-68, Tyler Primary Sch., Naha AFB, Okinawa, Japan, 1968-69, Nurnburg (W.Ger.) Elem. Sch., 1969-70, Stuttgart (W.Ger.) Elem.-Jr. High Sch., 1977-81; program dir. Federally Funded Guardian Ad Litem Program, Twin Falls, Idaho, 1981-86, coordinator of institutional planning Coll. So. Idaho, Twin Falls, 1986—; cons., trainer child abuse prevention and treatment; state social services adv. bd; pres. Idaho Network for Children, chpt. of Nat. Com. for Prevention of Child Abuse, 1983-84, bd. dirs. 1983-86. Mem. Soc. Coll. and Univ. Planning, Am. Assn. Community and Jr. Colls., Nat. Council Research and Planning, World Future Soc., Am. Assn. Women in Community and Jr. Colls., Nat. Inst. Leadership Devel. Home: 1975 Sherry Ln Twin Falls ID 83301 Office: Coll So Idaho PO Box 1238 315 Falls Ave Twin Falls ID 83303-1238

TURPEN, FORREST LEE, education administrator; b. Peoria, Ill., Dec. 30, 1937; s. Emmett Belvie and Evelyn Emma Turpen; m. Judith Jean, July 1, 1963; children: Brian, David, Carol, Andrew. Student, Bradley U., 1957-58; BEd, No. Ill. U., 1963, postgrad., 1972-73; postgrad., Utah State U., 1965, U. Ga., 1966-68; MA, Stanford U., 1969. Cert. tchr., Ill.; cert. gen. adminstr., Ill. Machinist apprentice Caterillar Tractor Co., Peoria, Ill., 1956-59; co-mgr. Skate-A-Rama, 1976-78; prin. Christian Book and Gift Shop, 1979-83; agt. Franklin Life Ins. Co., Princeton, Ill., 1979-80; tchr. Hazel Crest (Ill.) Highlands Elem. Sch., 1963, Canterbury Jr. High Sch., Harvey, Ill., 1964-67, 69-70; prin., asst. supt. Wyanet Community Schs., 1970-74; prin. Lincoln Elem. Sch., Princeton, 1974-76, Washington Middle Sch., Princeton, 1976-83; exec. dir. Christian Educators Assn. Internat., Pasadena, Calif., 1983—. Pres. Sch. Dist. 144 Edn. Assn., Markham, Ill., 1967-68, sec., 1966-67; pres. Bur. Valley Elem. Conf., Princeton, 1971, 73, Bur. County Sci. Assn., Princeton, 1972-74; supt. Sunday sch. Princeton bible Ch., 1972-75; sponsor Ch. Youth Singing Group, Princeton, 1971-74; treas. Bur. County Youth Crusade, Princeton, 1971-76, pres., 1976-78; deacon Princeton Bible Cs., 1977-83; mem. Young Life Com., Princeton, 1980-83; active other orgns. Mem. Ill. Prin. Assn. (charter, treas. 1981-83, chmn. 1972-73, dir. 1974-75, chmn. state evaluation com. 1976-79), Bur. County Adminstrs. Assn., christian Educators Assn., Assn. Sch. Curriculum Dirs., Nat. Assn. Elem. Sch. Prins., Nat. Assn. Evangelicals. Republican. Home: 8541 E Sheffield Rd San Gabriel CA 91775

TURRENTINE, HOWARD BOYD, U.S. district judge; b. Escondido, Calif., Jan. 22, 1914; s. Howard and Veda Lillian (Maxfield) T.; m. Virginia Jacobsen, May 13, 1965; children: Howard Robert, Terry Beverly. A.B., San Diego State Coll., 1936; LL.B., U. So. Calif., 1939. Bar: Calif. 1939. Practice in San Diego, 1939-68; judge Superior Ct. County of San Diego, 1968-70; judge U.S. Dist. Ct. for So. Dist., Calif., San Diego, 1970—. Served with USNR, 1941-45. Mem. ABA, Fed. Bar Assn., Am. Judicature Soc. Office: US Courthouse #2 940 Front St San Diego CA 92189

TUTELMAN, ROBERT ALLEN, mechanical engineer; b. Bronx, N.Y., June 1, 1944; s. Herman Herbert and Marjory (Friedman) T. B MechE, CCNY, 1965; MS MechE, U. Mich., 1966. Engring. supr. Bell Telephone Labs., Holmdel, N.J., 1965-72; organisateur Club Mediterranee, Paris, 1972-76; sr. mech. engr. Sub-Sea Systems Inc., Escondido, Calif., 1977-84; engring. group leader Cipher Data Products, San Diego, 1984-86; mgr. mech. engring. Ametek Straza, El Cajon, Calif., 1986—. Author: How to Find, Clean and Collect Shells, 1975, (with others) Physical Design of Electronic Systems, 1970. Grad. fellow NSF, 1965. Mem. Mensa (far west regional vice chmn. 1985-87). Avocations: instrumental music, sailing, skiing.

TUTTLE, DANIEL WEBSTER, political science educator; b. Quincy, Ill., Feb. 25, 1925; s. Daniel Webster and Nellie Blanche (Hampton) T.; m. Elsie Eleanor Smith, June 28, 1947; children: Vera Kay, Daniel Webster, David B.H. AB, Ill. coll., 1945; MA, U. Minn., 1947, PhD, 1964. Instr. polit. sci. U. Wyo., Laramie, 1947-50; from asst. prof. to assoc. prof. U. Hawaii, Honolulu, 1950-66, spl. prof., 1971—; vis. faculty Stephens Coll., Columbia, Mo., 1956-57, UCLA, 1961; exec. dir. Hawaii Edn. Assn., Honolulu, 1966-71; polit. analyst Sta. KGMB-TV-Radio, Honolulu, 1958—. Author: State Elections Prior to Admittance to Union, 1951, Hawaii Voting Behavior, 1964-73, Papers on Hawaiian Politics, 1952-62, Religion and Politics, 1981; columnist Honolulu Star Bull. Advertiser, 1959-66, 81—. Chmn. bd. dirs., pres., dir. Pub. Affairs Adv. Service, Honolulu, 1973—; mem. Honolulu Charter Commn., 1971-72, Hawaii Ednl. Council, 1967-70; active PTA; bd. dirs. Big Bros. of Hawaii, 1964-79, advisor, 1979—, Aloha United Fund, 1967-71, Honolulu Youth Symphony Assn., 1965-71. Eagleton Found. grantee U. Hawaii, 1962. Mem. NEA, AAUP, Am. Polit. Sci. Assn., Western Polit. Sci. Assn., Am. Soc. Pub. Adminstrn., Phi Beta Kappa, Alpha Phi Omega, Tau Kappa Epsilon. Lodge: Kiwanis. Home: 14 Akilolo St Honolulu HI 96821

TUTTLE, JERRY, community education and devel. consultant; b. Long Beach, Calif., Sept. 5, 1926; s. Preston Lyons and Dorothy (Tuttle) Wilson;

m. M. Joan Lee, Oct. 26, 1955; children—Jerry Lee, Jon Wilson, Jana Lyn, Jeffrey David. B.A., U. Utah, 1950; M.A., Northwestern U., 1951; Ph.D., U. Nebr., 1958. Instr. in geography U. Colo., Boulder, 1955-56; water rights and resources engr. Water Resource Devel. and Regulation Agy., Utah Engrs. Office, 1957-61; tech. writer, missile research and devel. and prodn. Hercules Powder Co., Salt Lake City, 1961-62, Magna, Utah, tech. asst., 1962-63; with Bur. Indian Affairs, Regulatory and Devel. Agy., Dept. Interior, 1964-80, community devel. officer Albuquerque area, 1973-76, assigned chief, Washington, 1972-74, with detail to Zuni as fed.-officer-in-charge, 1975-76, indsl. devel. specialist, Albuquerque area, 1976-78, with detail to Western Fed. Regional Council at San Francisco, 1977, and as Albuquerque area coordinator Youth Conservation Corps-Young Adult Conservation Corps, 1978, program analyst So. Pueblos Agy., 1978-80; research assoc. Olivarez & Bowman Assocs., Albuquerque, 1980-83; br. mgr., program developer, project dir. Western Energy Planners, Ltd., cons., Albuquerque, 1980-82; dist. commr. Albuquerque Future Goals Commn., 1986—; cons. community edn. and community devel., Albuquerque, 1980-87; cons. on leadership devel. of Indians, Ford Found.; NSF rep. to 8th Quadrennial Internat. Geog. Congress, 1960; speaker, presenter in field. Treas., N. Mex. Swimming Assn.; treas. N. Mex. Pageant of Bands. Served with USNR, 1947-50, 52-53; PTO, Atlantic, Korea, Japan, Philippines. Recipient Spl. Achievement award U.S. Bur. Indian Affairs, 1971, Superior Performance award, 1965. Mem. Internat. Community Educators Assn. (founding), Sigma Xi. Democrat. Methodist. Club: Kirtland Officers. Contbr. articles to profl. publs. Home and Office: 12305 Eastridge Dr NE Albuquerque NM 87112

TUTTLE, STEPHANIE ELLEN, entertainment company executive; b. Pensacola, Fla., Feb. 1, 1954; d. William Edwin and Lillian Patricia (Kastuck) T. Student, Beaver Coll., 1972-76. Asst. account exec. McCaffrey & McCall, Inc., N.Y.C., 1978-79, account exec., 1980-82; dir. advt. services ABC Entertainment Ctr., Los Angeles, 1982-86, mgr. dramatic devel., 1986—. Mem. Los Angeles Arts Council. Mem. Acad. Arts and TV Soc. Republican. Episcopalian. Avocations: piano, water sports. Office: ABC Entertainment Ctr 2040 Avenue of Stars Los Angeles CA 90067

TWIGG-SMITH, THURSTON, newspaper publisher; b. Honolulu, Aug. 17, 1921; s. William and Margaret Carter (Thurston) Twigg-S.; m. Bessie Bell, June 9, 1942 (div. Feb. 1983); children: Elizabeth, Thurston, William, Margaret, Evelyn.; m. Laila Roster, Feb. 22, 1983. B.Engring., Yale U., 1942. With Honolulu Advertiser, 1946—, mng. editor, 1954-60, asst. bus. mgr., 1960-61, pub., 1961-86; pres., dir., chief exec. officer Honolulu Advertiser, Inc., 1962—; pres., dir., chief exec. officer Persis Corp.; chmn. Asa Properties Hawaii, Shiny Rock Mining Corp.; bd. dirs. First Fed. Am., Inc., Hawaiian Electric Industries, Inc., Hawaiian Electric Company, Tongg Pub. Co., Am. Fin. Services, Inc., Kamehameha Investment Corp. Trustee Punahou Sch., Old Sturbridge Inc., Honolulu Acad. Arts, Western States Art Found., Contemporary Arts Ctr., Hawaii. Served to maj. AUS, 1942-46. Mem. Honolulu C. of C. Clubs: Waialae (Honolulu), Pacific (Honolulu), Oahu (Honolulu). Office: PO Box 3110 Honolulu HI 96802

TWIST, ROBERT LANPHIER, farmer, rancher, cattle feeder; b. Memphis, Dec. 27, 1926; s. Clarence C. and Edith G. Twist; student Springfield (Ill.) Jr. Coll., 1943; B.S. in Agr., U. Ill., 1950; postgrad. U. Edinburgh (Scotland); 1 dau., Marilyn Edith. Owner, operator farm lands, Twist, Ark., 1949—, Bow Fiddle Ranch, Laramie, Wyo., 1961—, Lost Creek Ranch, Masters, Colo., 1963, Rolling T Ranch, Ft. Morgan, Colo., 1965—, R.L. Twist Ranches Cattle Feeding Enterprises, Greeley, Colo. and Ft. Morgan, 1974—; prin. R.L. Twist Land & Investments, Paradise Valley, Ariz., 1974—; Rocker M Ranch, Douglas, Ariz., 1981—; cons. agrl. mgmt. Justice of Peace, Twist, Ark., 1954. Served with USAAF, 1944-46. Mem. Colo. Farm Bur., Wyo. Farm Bur., Nat. Cattlemen's Assn. (charter). Republican. Presbyterian. Home: 4612 E Sparkling Ln Paradise Valley AZ 85253

TWOMEY, SEAN ANDREW, atmospheric scientist; b. Cork, Ireland, Nov. 30, 1928; came to U.S., 1959; s. Timothy C. and Elizabeth M. (Fogarty) T.; m. Marie McInerney; children: Adele, Patrick, Timothy, Kieran, Damian. MSc, Nat. U., Ireland, 1949, PhD, 1955. Physics cons. Naval Research Lab., Washington, 1963-68, 76-78; chief research scientist Commonwealth Sci. and INdsl. Research Orgn., Sydney, Australia, 1968-76; cons. Lawrence Livermore (Calif.) Nat. Labs., 1973-74. Author: Mathematics of Inversion in Remote Sensing, 1954, Atmospheric Aerosols, 1977; contbr. articles to profl. jours. Recipient C.G. Rossby medal Am. Meteorol. Soc., 1980. Office: U Ariz Inst Atmos Physics Tucson AZ 85721

TWOMLEY, BRUCE CLARKE, lawyer, state official, administrative law judge; b. Selma, Ala., Jan. 23, 1945; s. Robert Clarke and Eleanor Jane (Wood) Anderson T.; m. Sara Jane Minton, June 13, 1979. B.A. in Philosophy, Northwestern U., 1967; LL.M., Hastings Coll. Law, 1970; fair hearing cert. Nat. Jud. Coll., Reno, Nev., 1983. Bar: Calif. 1972, Alaska 1973, U.S. Dist. Ct. Alaska, 1973, U.S. Ct. Appeals (9th cir.) 1982. VISTA vol., Anchorage, 1972-73; lawyer Alaska Legal Services Corp., Anchorage, 1973-82; commr. Alaska Comml. Fisheries Entry Commn., Juneau, 1982-83, chmn., 1983—. Recipient Alaska Legal Services Disting. Service award, 1983. Mem. Kappa Sigma (pres. interfraternity council 1966-67), Gov.'s Fisheries Mini-Cabinet. Home: PO Box 020972 Juneau AK 99802-0972 Office: Alaska Comml Fisheries Entry Commn PO Box KB Juneau AK 99811

TYGIEL, JULES, history educator; b. Bklyn., Mar. 9, 1949; s. Gustave and Rose (Gross) T.; m. Luise Custer, Oct. 10, 1983; 1 child, Charles Custer. BA, Bklyn. Coll., 1969; MA, UCLA, 1973, PhD, 1977. Asst. prof. U. Tenn., Knoxville, 1976-77, U. Va., Charlottesville, 1977-78; asst. prof. Calif. State U., San Francisco, 1977-81, assoc. prof., 1981-85, prof. history, 1985—. Author: Baseball's Great Experiment, 1983; contbr. articles to profl. jours. Commr. Pacific Ghost League, San Francisco, 1980—; co-dir. Ghost League Baseball, San Francisco, 1985—. Named Ambassador of Honor, English Speaking Union, 1983. Mem. Orgn. Am. Historians, Am. Hist. Soc., N. Am. Soc. Sports History, Southwest Labor Studies Assn. Avocation: baseball. Office: Calif State U Dept History 1600 Holloway Ave San Francisco CA 94132

TYLER, CLIFFORD ERNEST, school superintendent; b. San Francisco, Feb. 12, 1944; s. Steve Allen and Helen Ernestine (Shores) T.; m. Anne Clare Davis, June 13, 1971. B.S., Oreg. State U., 1966; M.Ed., U. Oreg., 1968; postgrad. San Jose State U., 1970-71; Ed.D., U. Pacific, 1981. Tchr., Palo Alto Unified Sch. Dist., Calif., 1968-72; prin. Fern Ridge Sch. Dist., Elmira, Oreg., 1973-74, Modesto City Schs., Calif., 1974-78; supt., prin. Falls City Sch. Dist., Oreg., 1978-79, Aumsville Sch. Dist., Oreg., 1979-81; dist. supt. Cutler-Orosi Unified Sch. Dist., Calif., 1981-86, Amador County Unified Sch. Dist., Jackson, Calif., 1986—. Contbr. articles to profl. jours. Bd. dirs. Muir Trail council Girl Scouts U.S.A., Modesto, Calif., 1977. Oreg. State U. scholar, 1966. Mem. Assn. Calif. Sch. Adminstrs. (dir.), Confedn. Oreg. Sch. Adminstrs., Assn. Supervision and Curriculum Devel., Am. Assn. Sch. Adminstrs., C. of C., Phi Delta Kappa. Democrat. Methodist. Lodges: Lions, Kiwanis. Clubs: Sportsmen of Stanislaus, Visalia Racquet. Home: 12001 Colt Dr Sutter Creek CA 95685 Office: Amador County Unified Sch Dist 217 Rex Ave Jackson CA 95642

TYLER, DARLENE JASMER, dietitian; b. Watford City, N.D., Jan. 26, 1939; d. Edwin Arthur and Leola Irene (Walker) Jasmer; B.S., Oreg. State U., 1961; m. Richard G. Tyler, Aug. 26, 1977; children—Ronald, Eric, Scott. Clin. dietitian Salem (Oreg.) Hosp., 1965-73; sales supr. Sysco Northwest, Tigard, Oreg., 1975-77; clin. dietitian Physicians & Surgeons Hosp., Portland, Oreg., 1977-79; food service dir. Meridian Park Hosp., Tualatin, Oreg., 1979—. Registered dietitian. Mem. Am. Dietetic Assn., Oreg. Dietetic Assn., Portland Dietetic Assn., Am. Soc. Hosp. Food Service Adminstrs. Episcopalian. Home: 12800 SE Nixon Ave Milwaukie OR 97222 Office: 19300 SW 65th St Tualatin OR 97062

TYLER, DAVID LYNN, exploration geologist; b. Houston, Dec. 27, 1950; s. Carnie Collins and Alda Ray (Sisson) T.; m. Sandra Lee Ohlsson, June 9, 1973; 1 son: Grant. B.S. in Geology, U. So. Calif., 1973, B.S. in Petroleum Engring., 1973; M.A. in Geology, Rice U., 1976. Certified petroleum geologidt, Geologist Shell Oil Co., Houston, 1975-77; exploration geologist Terra Resources, Inc., Casper, Wyo., 1977-78; sr. geologist Chorney Oil Co., Denver, 1978-79, Tesoro Petroleum, Inc., Denver, 1979-81; dist. geologist Merland Oil & Gas, Inc., Denver, 1981-82, Farmer's Union Cen. Exchange Billings, Mont., 1982—. Recipient scholarship Standard Oil Co., 1968, 70, Union Oil Co., 1969, R.H. Baker Found., 1971, 72; research assistantship NSF, 1974. Mem. Am. Assn. Petroleum Geologists (cert.), Rocky Mountain Assn. Geologists, Soc. Econ. Paleontologists and Mineralogists, Mont. Geol. Soc., Wyo. Geol. Assn. Republican. Office: Farmer's Union Cen Exchange 1601 Lewis Ave Billings MT 59104

TYLER, DAVID RALPH, chemistry educator; b. Willimantic, Conn., Apr. 26, 1953; s. Varro Eugene and Virginia May (Demel) T.; m. Kim Elaine Baker, Aug. 18, 1973; children: Michael, Anna. BS, Purdue U., 1975; PhD, Calif. Inst. Tech., 1979. Asst. prof. chemistry Columbia U., N.Y.C., 1979-85; assoc. prof. U. Oreg., Eugene, 1985—. Contbr. numerous articles to profl. jours. Alfred P. Sloan fellow, 1986-88. Mem. Am. Chem. Soc. Home: 2055 W 28th Ave Eugene OR 97405 Office: U Oreg Dept Chem Eugene OR 97403

TYLER, FRANK HILL, medical educator; b. Villisca, Iowa, Jan. 5, 1916; s. Royal Frank and Fausta Alice (Hill) T.; m. Inez Betty Hannan, June 22, 1941 (dec.); children: Karen June, Royal Hannan, Frank Peter; m. Alida Woolley, Mar. 19, 1962. AB, Willamette U., 1938; MD, Johns Hopkins U., 1942. Diplomate Am. Bd. Internal Medicine. Mem. faculty U. Utah Coll. Medicine, Salt Lake City, 1947—, asst. prof., 1950-54, assoc. prof., 1954-59, prof. medicine, 1959—; mem. USPHS gen. med. study sect. NIH, 1957-63, mem. research career program com., 1967-71, gen. clin. research ctr. com., 1971-75; mem. nat. adv. com. Arthritis/Metabolic Disease Council, 1963-67. Author: Harrison's Principles of Internal Medicine, Strauss and Welt—Diseases of the Kidney; contbr. articles to profl. jours. Served to lt. (j.g.) MC, USNR, 1944-46, PTO. Recipient Disting. Research award, U. Utah, 1978. Mem. ACP (Master 1981), Assn. Am. Physicians, Western Assn. Physicians (pres. 1963-64), Am. Fedn. Clin. Research, Am. Soc. Clin. Investigation, Western Soc. Clin. Investigation (pres. 1957-58), Am. Clin. and Climatol. Assn. Home: 1130 Vine St Salt Lake City UT 84121 Office: U Utah Med Ctr 50 N Medical Dr Salt Lake City UT 84132

TYLER, GAIL MADELEINE, nurse; b. Dhahran, Saudi Arabia, Nov. 21, 1953 (parents Am. citizens); d. Louis Rogers and Nona Jean (Henderson) T. A.Sc., Front Range Community Coll., Westminster, Colo., 1979. R.N., Colo. Ward sec. Valley View Hosp., Thornton, Colo., 1975-79; nurse Scott and White Hosp., Temple, Tex., 1979-83, Meml. Hosp. Laramie County, Cheyenne, Wyo., 1983—. Mem. Critical Care Assn. Avocations: collecting international dolls; sewing; reading; traveling.

TYLER, JANE FORREST, speech pathologist, educational administrator; b. N.Y.C., Dec. 13, 1949; d. Irwin H. and Estelle Forrest; m. William Tyler, July 4, 1980; 1 child, Kaicy Alison. BS, Emerson Coll., 1971; MA, NYU, 1974; MS, U. N.Mex., 1977; postgrad., San Jose State U., 1986. Advt. and publicity coordinator Praeger Pubs., N.Y.C., 1972-74; speech pathologist Rio Grande Sch., Belen, N.Mex., 1976-77; dir. speech pathology services Behavioral Scis. Inst., Monterey, Calif., 1977-78; teaching prin., mentor tchr. Monterey County Office of Edn., Salinas, Calif., 1978—; leadership trainer The Essential Elements of Instrn., Salinas, 1984—. Columnist Demeter newspaper, 1978-81. Recipient Speakers award Head Start Program, 1983, Lions Club, Monterey, 1980, Kiwanis Club, Monterey, 1982, Mentor Tchr. award Calif. State Dept. Edn., 1986. Mem. Assn. Calif. Sch. Adminstrs., Assn. Supervision and Curriculum Devel., Am. Speech Lang. Hearing Assn., Calif. Speech Lang. Hearing Assn. (dist. officer 1982-84), Monterey County Speech and Hearing Assn. (pres. 1983-85), AAUW. Avocations: photography, travel, writing, tennis. Home: 25505 Hacienda Pl Carmel CA 93923 Office: Monterey County Office Edn PO Box 80851 901 Blanco Circle Salinas CA 93912

TYLYR, BRANDY JESSICA, engineering manager, consultant; b. Racine, Wis., Aug. 4, 1961. AA in Electronics Tech., Cleve. Inst. Electronics, 1984. Programmer Manu-Tronics, Kenosha, Wis., 1979-80; div. mgr. Solectron Corp., San Jose, Calif., 1980-84; test engring. mgr. Calif. Circuit Assembly, Mountain View, 1984; engring. mgr. Zyvex Corp., San Jose, 1984—; cons. in field; chief tech. dir. Custom Software Systems, Fremont, Calif., 1985—. Author: Love Is Forever, 1982; designer (software) Apple Custom Clock Peripheral, 1986; creator Software Application Quality Control Reporting, 1985. Mem. Am. Electronics Assn. Calif., Am. Electronics Assn., Apple Computer Devel. (cert.). Avocations: guitar, sports car racing, home crafts. Home: PO Box 8405 Fremont CA 94537-8405 Office: Custom Software Systems 3279 Langhorn Dr Fremont CA 94536

TYNES, REX A., consulting electrical engineer; b. Hereford, Tex., Apr. 7, 1915; s. Rex Arthur and Caroline (Avera) T.; m. Gladys Wright, Aug. 11, 1941; children: Rex, Virginia, Patricia, Kathleen. BSEE, Tex. Tech U., 1940. Registered profl. engr., Ariz., Colo., Nev.; registered land surveyor, Ariz. Ptnr. Tynes & Loftin, Albuquerque, 1948-58; exec. asst. Pub. Services Co. N.Mex., Albuquerque, 1958-63, Nev. Power Co., Las Vegas, 1963-74; pvt. practice cons. engr. Sun City, Ariz., 1974—; bd. dirs. Gila River Power Authority, Sacaton, Ariz.; chmn. N.Mex. Bd. Registration for Profl. Engrs., Santa Fe, 1959-63, vice chmn. Nev. Bd. Registration for Profl. Engrs., Las Vegas, 1966-74; sec. Colo. Bd. Registration for Profl. Engrs., Denver, 1978-81. Contbr. articles to profl. jours. V.p. Sun City Concert Band. Named Engr. of Yr., Nev. Soc. Profl. Engrs., 1972; recipient Disting. Service cert. Nat. Council Engr. Examiners, 1983. Fellow ASCE; mem. Sun City Engrs. Club. Democrat. Methodist. Avocations: amateur radio, music.

TYRE, TERIAN, editor; b. Malcomb, Ill., Aug. 19, 1956; s. Richard Thomas and Patricia Ann (McCarthy) T. BA, San Diego State U., 1978. Owner, operator Tyre Yacht Maintenance, Dana Point, Calif., 1978-82; sr. editor Profiles Mag., Solana Beach, Calif., 1982-85, co-editor, 1985—. Contbr. articles to mags. Mem. Internat. Assn. Bus. Communicators. Democrat. Lutheran. Avocations: scuba diving, disc golf. Office: Kaypro Corp/Profiles Mag 533 Stevens Ave Solana Beach CA 92075

TYSON, GRAHAM, computer company director; b. Pomona, Calif., Mar. 16, 1923; s. Graham and Ura E. (Henson) T.; m. Beth L. Burson, Aug. 5, 1947 (div. 1982); children: Terri P. Welker, John G.; m. ALicia Cuerbo, Jan. 16, 1982; 1 dau., Alyson C. BEE, U. So. Calif., 1949. Field engr. IBM, Santa Monica, Calif., 1949-53; group leader Northrop Corp., Hawthorne, Calif., 1953-57; application engr., gen. mgr. Amker-Telemeter Magnetics, Los Angeles, Calif., 1957-62; v.p., group v.p. Dataproducts Corp., Woodland Hills, Calif., 1961-82, pres., 1972-80, chmn. bd., 1980-86, dir.; dir. Measurex Corp., Cupertino, Calif. Methodist. Office: Dataproducts Corp 6200 Canoga Ave Woodland Hills CA 91365 *

TYTLER, LINDA JEAN, marketing executive, state legislator; b. Rochester, N.Y., Aug. 31, 1947; d. Frederick Easton and Marian Elizabeth (Allen) Tytler; m. George Stephen Dragnich, May 2, 1970 (div. July 1976). AS, So. Sem., Buena Vista, Va., 1967; student U. Va., 1973; student in pub. adminstrn. U. N. Mex., 1981-82. Spl. asst. to Congressman John Buchanan, Washington, 1971-75; legis. analyst U.S. Senator Robert Griffin, Washington, 1975-77; ops. supr. Pres. Ford Com., Washington, 1976; office mgr. U.S. Senator Pete Domenici Re-election, Albuquerque, 1977; pub. info. officer S.W. Community Health Service, Albuquerque, 1978-83; cons. pub. relations and mktg., Albuquerque, 1983-84; account exec. Rick Johnson & Co., Inc., Albuquerque, 1983-84; dir. mktg. and communications St. Joseph Healthcare Corp., 1984—; mem. N.Mex. Ho. of Reps., Santa Fe, 1983—, vice chmn. appropriations and fin. com., 1985-86, interim com. on children and youth, mem. voters and election com., chmn. Rep. caucus, 1985—; mem. hosp. cost containment task force Nat. Conf. State Legislatures. Bd. dirs. N. Mex. chpt. ARC, Albuquerque, 1984. Recipient award N.Mex. Advt. Fedn., Albuquerque, 1981, 82, 85, 86. Mem. Am. Soc. Hosp. Pub. Relations (cert.), Nat. Advt. Fedn., Soc. Hosp. Planning and Mktg., Am. Mktg. Assn. Republican. Baptist. Office: 400 Walter NE Albuquerque NM 87109

TYUS, HAROLD MAURICE, ichthyologist; b. Lake City, Fla., Mar. 8, 1942; s. Howard Kelly and Minnie (Louise) T.; m. Ruby J. Stone, Nov. 25, 1974 (div. 1979); 1 child, Christopher Scott; m. Lee Mary Hemhauser, Nov. 29, 1979. BS, Fla. So. Coll., 1964; MS, N.C. State U., 1969, PhD, 1971. Instr. Fla. So. Coll., 1965-66; field biologist State of Fla., Tampa, 1966; fishery biologist U.S. Army C.E., Wilmington, N.C., 1971-74; fishery biologist U.S. Fish and Wildlife Service, Miami, Fla., 1974, Raleigh, N.C., 1975-76, environ. specialist, Denver, 1976-79, field supr. Colorado River Fish Project, Vernal, Utah, 1979—; cons. Coastal Zone Resources Corp., Wilmington, 1973. Author sci. articles, govt. reports. Recipient Spl. Achievement award, U.S. Fish and Wildlife Service, Denver, 1982, appreciation award, U.S. Dept. Interior, 1978; NSF grad. trainee, 1965-69; Nat. Wildlife Fedn. grad. scholar, 1970-71. Mem. Am. Inst. Fishery Research Biologists, Am. Fisheries Soc. (cert. fisheries scientist), Am. Soc. Ichthyologists and Herpetologists, Desert Fishes Council, Sigma Xi, Lambda Chi Alpha. Democrat. Methodist. Home: 902 N 2100 W Vernal UT 84078 Office: US Fish and Wildlife Service 1680 W Hyw 40 #1210 Vernal UT 84078

TZAVELLA-EVJEN, HARA, classics educator; b. Pireus, Greece, June 27, 1936; came to U.S., 1966; d. Adam and Markella (Polymeri) Tzavellas; m. Harold D. Evjen, Jan. 30, 1967; 1 child, Harald. BA, U. Athens, Greece, 1959, PhD, 1970. Tchr. classics Pearce Coll., Athens, 1960-66; lectr. U. Colo., Denver, 1968-69; asst. prof. classics U. Colo., Boulder, 1966-67, 70-73, assoc. prof., 1973—; dir. excavation at Lithares Greek Archaeol. Service, Thebes, 1970-77. Author: The Winged Creatures in Aegaean Art, 1970, Lithares, 1984, Lithares An Early Helladic Settlement, 1985; contbr. articles to profl. jours. Mem. Archaeol. Inst. Am., Am. Philol. Assn., Archaeol. Soc. Athens, Classical Assn. Middle West and South, Assn. Greek Writers, Greek Archaeol. Soc. (dir. excavation at Chaeroneia 1983—). Home: 2123 4th Boulder CO 80302 Office: U Colo Dept of Classics Boulder CO 80309

UBER, CHET LEE, marketing professional; b. Miami, Fla., Aug. 17, 1962; s. Edwin Jay and Barbara Ann (Beiley) U. Student, Mont. State U., 1980. Asst. floor supr. World Wide Press, Great Falls, Mont., 1980-81; prin. Uber Advt., Great Falls, 1981-86; dir. new projects Girard Enterprises div. Venture Capital Co., Great Falls, 1986—; chief exec. officer Family Entertainment Co., Great Falls, 1984-86; cons. Hobbyworld Corp., Great Falls, 1981—, other corps. Vol. ARC, 1980—; co-chmn. Young Reps., Great Falls, 1983-84; bd. dirs. Mont. chpr. Multiple Sclerosis Assn., 1984—. Recipient 1st Place Ad awards (3), Rent-A-Wreck Internat., Los Angeles, 1983, Mont. Addy award Am. Advt. Fedn., 1983, 84, 85, Clara Barton award ARC, 1985. Mem. Great Falls Advt. Fedn., Downtown Bus. Council, Great Falls C. of C., Oppidans (bd. dirs. 1984-85). Jewish. Club: Ad II (chmn. 1984-85). Lodge: Optimists. Avocations: biochemistry, tennis, golf. Home: 2228 Juniper Great Falls MT 59404

UCHIDA, PRENTISS SUSUMU, computer electronics company executive; b. San Jose, Calif., Nov. 30, 1940; s. Fred Toshio and Elise Chioye (Kurasaki) U.; B.A., San Jose State U., 1963; postgrad. Santa Clara U. Bus. Sch., 1965; m. Patricia Ann White, Oct. 17, 1981; children—S. Akemi, Toshio C., Kamal K. P. Programmer, Lockheed Missiles & Space Co., Sunnyvale, Calif., 1963-66, Adage Inc., Los Angeles, 1966-69; founder, pres., chmn. Vector Gen. Inc., Woodland Hills, Calif., 1969-79; pres. InnerGame Corp., Los Angeles, 1979-83; chmn. bd., chief exec. officer Secom Gen. Corp., Calabasas, Calif., 1984-86; pres. Rice Systems Co., Calabasas, Calif., 1981—; chmn. bd. Instar Informatique, Paris, Potter Electronics, Inc., Yanceyville, N.C., Secom Communications Co., Southfield, Mich., 1984-86, Nickel Equipment Co., Grand Rapids, Mich., 1985-86; mgmt. cons., Agoura, Calif., 1986—. Mem. adv. com. Stanford U. Exec. Inst., 1975-76; bd. dirs. United Crusade/United Way, 1977-79. Mem. Assn. Computer Machinery, Am. Mgmt. Assn., Aircraft Owners and Pilots Assn. Democrat. Club: Te Ken Jutsu Kai. Office: 30423 Canwood St Agoura CA 91301

UDALL, MORRIS KING, congressman; b. St. Johns, Ariz., June 15, 1922; s. Levi S. and Louise (Lee) U.; m. Ella Royston, 1968; children by previous marriage: Mark, Judith, Randolph, Anne, Bradley, Katherine. LL.B. with distinction, U. Ariz., 1949. Bar: Ariz. bar 1949. Ptnr. firm Udall & Udall, Tucson, 1949-61; chief dep. county atty. Pima County, 1950-52, county atty., 1953-54; lectr. labor law U. Ariz., 1955-56; mem. 87th-100th Congresses, 2d Dist. Ariz., 1961—; chmn. House Com. on Interior and Insular Affairs; vice chmn. Com. on Post Office and Civil Service; vice chmn. Office Tech. Assessment.; mem. Com. on Fgn. Affairs; a founder Bank of Tucson, 1959, former dir.; former chmn. bd. Catalina Savs. and Loan Assn.; chmn. Ariz. Com. for Modern Cts., 1960. Author: Arizona Law of Evidence, 1960, Education of a Congressman, 1972; co-author: The Job of the Congressman, 1966. Del. Democratic Nat. Conv., 1956; chmn. Ariz. delegation, 1972, Ariz. Volunteers for Stevenson, 1956; candidate for Dem. nomination for Pres., 1976; keynote speaker Dem. Nat. Conv., 1980. Served to capt. USAAF, 1942-46, PTO. Mem. ABA, Ariz. Bar Assn. (bd. govs.), Pima County Bar Assn. (exec. com.), Am. Judicature Soc., Am. Legion, Phi Kappa Phi, Phi Delta Phi. Office: 235 Cannon House Office Bldg Washington DC 20515

UDEVITZ, NORMAN, journalist; b. Cheyenne, Wyo., Jan. 22, 1929; s. Jay and Edith (Stienberg) U.; m. Marsha Rae Dinner, Dec. 17, 1960; children: Jane, Kathryn, Andrew. Student, U. Colo., 1946-49. With Cheyenne Newspapers Inc. Cheyenne, 1949-54; editor-pub. Wyo. Buffalo, Cheyenne, 1954-63; account supr. Tilds & Cantz Advt. Agy., Los Angeles, 1963-66; exec. v.p. Fitzgerald, Maahs, Miller, Los Angeles, 1966-71; staff writer The Denver Post, 1971—. Served to sgt. USNG, 1950-53. Named Colo.'s Outstanding Journalist, U. Colo., 1977; recipient Pulitzer Prize Gold medal Columbia U., 1986. Mem. Investigative Reporters and Editors Inc., (bd. dirs. 1978-80, 81-83), The Newspaper Guild (McWilliams award 1976, 77). Jewish. Home: 4677 E Euclid Ave Littleton CO 80121 Office: care The Denver Post PO Box 1709 Denver CO 80201

UDICK, ROBERT E., newspaper executive; b. Colorado Springs, Colo., May 27, 1922; s. Albert Earl and Edna (Young) U. Student, Colo. Coll. Staff corr. Rocky Mountain News, Denver, 1947-49, United Press, Denver and Santa Fe, 1950-51; war corr. United Press, Korea, 1951-53; later became mgr. Hong Kong and Manila burs.; then mgr. for Southeast Asia, hdqrs., Singapore; editor, pub. Bangkok World, until 1967; pub. Pacific Daily News, Agana, Guam, until 1985; cons. Gannett Co., Inc., 1985—; Mem. civilian adv. bd. 8th Air Force; mem. Navy League, Guam Stock Exchange. Bd. regents U. Guam. Served with Coast Arty., Inf., Signal Corps, World War II. Mem. Fgn. Corr. Assn. Thailand (pres.), Phi Delta Theta. Club: Rotary. Office: Pacific Daily News PO Box DN Agana GU 96910

UDWADIA, FIRDAUS ERACH, engineering educator; b. Bombay, Aug. 28, 1947; came to U.S., 1968.; s. Erach Rustam and Perin P. (Lentin) U.; m. Farida Gagrat, Jan. 6, 1977; children: Shanaira, Zubin. BS, Indian Inst. Tech., Bombay, 1968; MS, Calif. Inst. Tech., 1969, PhD, 1972; MBA, U. So. Calif., 1985. Mem. faculty Calif. Inst. Tech., Pasadena, 1972-74; asst. prof. engring. U. So. Calif., Los Angeles, 1974-77, assoc. prof., 1977-83, prof., 1983—; also bd. dirs. Structural Identification Computing FacilityU. So. Calif.; cons. Jet Propulsion Lab., Pasadena, Calif., 1978—, Argonne Nat. Lab., Chgo., 1982-83, Air Force Rocket Lab., Edwards AFB, Calif., 1984—. Contbr. articles to profl. jours. Bd. dirs. Crisis Mgmt. Ctr., U. So. Calif. NSF grantee, 1976—. Mem. AIAA, ASCE, Am. Acad. Mechanics, Soc. Indsl. and Applied Math., Seismological Soc. Am., Sigma Xi (Earthquake Engring. Research Inst., 1971, 74, 84). Avocations: writing poetry, piano, chess. Home: 1708 N Roosevelt Altadena CA 91001 Office: U So Calif University Park 364 DRB Los Angeles CA 90089-1114

UECKER, MICHAEL EUGENE, military officer; b. Tulsa, Aug. 25, 1947; s. Louis Joseph and Ruth Elizabeth (Schnee) U.; m. Carolyn Ann Oliver, June 12, 1971. BS in History, USAF Acad., 1971; MS in Systems Mgmt., Air Force Inst. Tech., 1984. Commd. 2d lt. USAF, 1971, advanced through grades to maj., 1985; radar navigator USAF, Pease AFB, N.H., 1972-75, Grand Forks AFB, N.D., 1980-82; instr. navigator USAF, Plattsburgh AFB, N.Y., 1975-78; research and devel. program mgr. USAF, Wright-Patterson AFB, Ohio, 1982-86; dep. dir. comdr.'s action group Space div. USAF, Los Angeles, 1986-87, mgr. research and devel. program, 1987—; project engr. Ford Motor Co., Dearborn, Mich., 1978-80. Advisor 4-H Club, Fairborn, Ohio, 1982-86. Recipient Air Force Commendation medal, 1975, with oak leaf cluster, 1982, Air Force Meritorious Service medal, 1986; named one of Outstanding Young Men of Am., 1984. Mem. Air Force Assn., Soc. Automotive Engrs. (chmn. task force 1978-80), USAF Acad. Assn. Grads., Sigma Iota Epsilon. Roman Catholic. Avocations: horseback riding, choir. Home: 39 Silver Saddle Ln Rolling Hills Estates CA 90274 Office: SD/CLVH PO Box 92960 Los Angeles CA 90009-2960

UEHLING, BARBARA STANER, educational researcher; b. Wichita, Kans., June 12, 1932; d. Roy W. and Mary Elizabeth (Hilt) Staner; m. Stanley Johnson; children: Jeffrey Steven, David Edward. B.A., U. Wichita, 1954; M.A., Northwestern U., 1956, Ph.D., 1958; hon. degree, Drury Coll., 1978; LL.D. (hon.), Ohio State U., 1979. Mem. psychology faculty Oglethorpe U., Atlanta, 1959-64, Emory U., Atlanta, 1966-69; adj. prof. U. R.I., Kingston, 1970-72; dean Roger Williams Coll., Bristol, R.I., 1972-74; dean arts scis. Ill. State U., Normal, 1974-76; provost U. Okla., Norman, 1976-78; chancellor U. Mo.-Columbia, 1978-86, U. Calif., Santa Barbara, 1987—; sr. vis. fellow Am. Council Edn., 1987—; cons. higher edn. State of N.Y., 1973-74; cons. North Central Accreditation Assn., 1975—; mem. nat. educator adv. com. to Comptroller Gen. U.S., 1978; mem. commn. on mil.-higher edn. relations Am. Council on Edn., 1978; dir. Merc. Bancorp., Inc., Meredith Corp. Author: Women in Academe: Steps to Greater Equality, 1978; contbr. articles to profl. jours. Bd. dirs., chmn. Nat. Ctr. Higher Edn. Mgmt. Systems; bd. dirs. Am. Council on Edn., 1979-83, treas., 1982-83; trustee Carnegie Found. for Advancement of Teaching, 1980—; mem. adv. com. Nat. Ctr. for Food and Agrl. Policy; bd. dirs. Resources for the Future; mem. NCAA Select Com. on Athletics, 1983-84, NCAA Presdl. Commn.; mem. Nat. Council on Ednl. Research, 1980-82; mem. Bus.-Higher Edn. Forum, Am. Council on Edn. Social Sci. Research Council fellow, 1954-55; NSF fellow, 1956-57; NIMH postdoctoral research fellow, 1964-67; named one of 100 Young Leaders of Acad. Change Mag. and ACE, 1978; recipient Alumni Achievement award Wichita State U., 1978, Alumnae award Northwestern U., 1985. Mem. Am. Assn. Higher Edn. (dir. 1974-77, pres. 1977-78), Sigma Xi. Office: Office of Chancellor Univ Calif Cheadle Hall Santa Barbara CA 93106

UFERT, NANCY MARIE, advertising company executive; b. Denver, Dec. 21, 1947; d. Edwin Leo and Teresa Margaret (Elper) Doherty; m. Hans Herbert Ufert, June 8, 1968 (div. Nov. 1979); children: Stephan Hans, Kelly Marie. Student, Community Coll. Denver, Idaho State U. Nurse Kaiser Permanente Health Orgn., Denver, 1972-75; sales mgr. Sta. KSEI, Pocatello, Idaho, 1976-78; sales and mktg. dir. Holiday Inn, Pocatello, 1979-80; sales mgr., gen. sales mgr. Sta. KPVI-TV, Pocatello, 1980-83; prin. Intermedia, Pocatello, 1984—. Producer, dir. (TV comls.) Hydrotube Summer Just Went Indoors, 1984 (Idaho State Broadcasters Assn. award 1984). Named an Outstanding Young Woman of Am., 1982. Mem. Pocatello Advt. Fedn. (pres. 1981-82, bd. dirs. 1982-85, v.p. 1980-81), Idaho State U. Vocat. Home Econs. Adv. Com. Roman Catholic. Avocations: skiing, tennis, golf, reading. Home and Office: 227 S 7th St Pocatello ID 83201

UGLUM, JOHN RICHARD, optometrist; b. Wonewoc, Wis., Nov. 26, 1909; s. John R. and May (Dewey) U.; m. Frances T. Wikholm, Jan. 20, 1940 (dec. May 1984); children: Karen, Katherine. BS, Northwestern U., 1930; postgrad., Dakota Wesleyan U., 1946; OD, No. Ill. Coll. Optometry, 1932; DSc (hon.), Internat. Coll. Visual Sci., 1962, Philathea Coll., 1971, Ind. No. U., 1972. Diplomate Nat. Bd. Examiners in Optometry, Nat. Bd. Examiners in Podiatry. Pvt. practice optometry Reno, 1961, Brookings, S.D., 1964—; exec. sec. Nat. Bd. Examiners in Optometry, Reno, 1951-64; assoc. Watson Clinic, Brookings, 1964-72; tchr. devel. reading S.D State U.; bd. dirs. Daktronics Inc.; sec., fellow Disting. Service Found. Optometry, Reno, 1959; contract med. care officer USPHS; mem. Eye Research Found. Pres. Washoe Assn. for Mental Health; bd. dirs. Brookings Area Guidance Ctr., S.D. Bapt. Conv.; trustee Sioux Falls (S.D.) Bldg. Authority, 1972—; mem. S.D. Cen. Dem. Com., 1972—. Recipient medal Order of St. John of Jerusalem, knight of Honor, 1965; officer Order of Crown of Thorns, France, 1965; grand cross Fundacion Internationale Eloy Alfaro (Panama), 1966. Mem. Am. Optometric Assn., Am. Acad. Optometry, AAAS, Internat. Assn. Bds. Examiners Optometry, Nev. Optometric Assn., S.D. Optometric Assn. (hon.), Ariz. Optometric Assn. (hon.), Cen. Ariz. Optometric Assn. (hon.), Am. Geriatrics Assn., Contact Lens Soc. Am., Nev. Soc. for Crippled Children (pres.), Nat. Soc. Crippled Children and Adults (trustee), Illuminating Engrs. Soc., Safety Engring. Soc., Am. Orthopsychiat. Assn., Sons of Norway, Torske Klubben, Norske Stravangerlager, Soc. for Advancement Research in Ophthalmology, Soc. European Optometrics, Sigma Xi. Baptist (pres. ch. council, moderator). Masons, Shriners. Home: 9418 Manzanita Dr Sun City AZ 85373

UHL, PATRICIA SANDRA, software company executive; b. Bayonne, N.J., July 10, 1950; d. George Joseph and Veronia (Lukaszewich) U.; m. Michael De Rubertis, 1986. BS, U. Md., 1972. Account rep. Gen. Electric Co., San Francisco, 1975-77; tech. rep. Computer Scis. Corp., San Francisco, 1977-78; cons., pres. Uhl Assocs., Tiburon, Calif., 1978-81; cons. mgr. Ross Systems, Palo Alto, Calif., 1981-83; v.p. Distributed Planning Systems, Calabasas, Calif., 1983—. Troop leader San Francisco council Girl Scouts U.S., 1974; participant Women On Water, Marina Del Rey, Calif., 1983. Mem. Nat. Assn. Female Execs., Delta Delta Delta. Democrat. Club: San Fernando Valley Yacht (Marina Del Rey, Calif.). Office: Distributed Planning Systems 23632 Calabasas Rd Calabasas CA 91302

UHL, PHILIP EDWARD, marine artist; b. Toledo, Aug. 19, 1949; s. Philip Edward and Betty Jean (Mayes) U. Student, Dayton Art Inst., 1967-68, Art Students League, 1974. Creative dir. Ctr. for Civic Initiative, Milw., 1969-71; art dir. Artco Advt. Agy., Honolulu, 1972-73; artist, photographer Assn. Honolulu Artists, 1974-77; pres. Uhl Enterprises div. Makai Photography, Honolulu, 1977—, Videoscapes div. Channel Sea TV, Honolulu, 1977—; cons. Pan Am. Airways, N.Y.C. and Honolulu, 1979-84, ITTC Travel Ctr., Honolulu, 1982-83, Royal Hawaiian Ocean Racing Club, Honolulu, 1985-86, Sail Am.-Am.'s Cup Challenge, Honolulu, 1985-86. Co-producer video documentary White on Water, 1984 (Emmy 1984); pub., art dir. mags., promotional publs. Pan Am. Clipper Cup, 1980, 82, 84 and Kenwood Cup, 1986; photographer: (book) Nautical Quarterly, 1983 (Soc. Publ. Designers award 1984); contbr. numerous articles, photos to yachting publs. worldwide. Mem. Am. Soc. Mag. Photographers, U.S. Yacht Racing Union, Royal Hawaiian Ocean Racing Club (cons.), Royal Corinthian Yacht Club, Waikiki Yacht Club. Mem. Honolulu Creative Group. Office: UHL Enterprises Century Ctr Suite 3-757 1750 Kalakaua Honolulu HI 96826

UHLENHUTH, EBERHARD HENRY, psychiatrist, educator; b. Balt., Sept. 15, 1927; s. Eduard Carl Adolph and Elisabeth (Baier) U.; m. Helen Virginia Lyman, June 20, 1952; children: Kim Lyman, Karen Jane, Eric Rolf. B.S. in Chemistry, Yale U., 1947; M.D., Johns Hopkins U., 1951. Intern Harborview Hosp., Seattle, 1951-52; resident in psychiatry Johns Hopkins Hosp., Balt., 1952-56; asst. psychiatrist in charge outpatient dept. Johns Hopkins Hosp., 1956-61, psychiatrist in charge, 1961-62; chief adult psychiatry clinic U. Chgo. Hosps. Clinics, 1968-76; instr. psychiatry Johns Hopkins U., 1956-59, asst. prof., 1959-67, assoc. prof., 1967-68; assoc. prof. U. Chgo., 1968-73, prof., 1973-85, acting chmn., 1983-85; prof. psychiatry U. N.Mex., Albuquerque, 1985—; cons. in field; mem. clin. psychopharmacology research rev. com. NIMH, 1968-72, treatment devel. and assessment rev. com., 1987—; mem. psychopharmacology adv. com. FDA, 1974-78. Mem. editorial bd. Jour. Affective Disorders, 1978—; Psychiatry Research, 1979—, Jour. Human Stress, 1982—; contbr. articles profl. jours. Recipient Research Career Devel. award USPHS, 1962-68, Research Scientist award, 1976-81. Fellow Am. Coll. Neuropsychopharmacology (pres. 1986), Am. Psychiat. Assn., Am. Psychopathol. Assn.; mem. AAAS, Balt.-Washington Soc. for Psychoanalysis, Collegium Internationale Neuro-Psychopharmacologicum, Soc. Neurosci., Psychiat. Research Soc. Office: U NMex Dept Psychiatry 2400 Tucker NE Albuquerque NM 87131

UHLER, MICHAEL DAVID, molecular biologist; b. San Bernardino, Calif., Oct. 3, 1956; s. David Neville and Mary Louise (McConnville) U.; m. Kathryn Ann Nickson, Aug. 27, 1977; children: Sarah Ann, Alan Michael. BS in Chemistry and Clin. Chemistry, Seattle U., 1977; PhD in Biochemistry, U. Oregon, 1982. Postdoctoral fellow Stanford U., Palo Alto, Calif., 1982-84, grad. student advisor, 1983-84; postdoctoral fellow U. Wash., Seattle, 1984-86; asst. prof. Advanced Inst. Molecular Biology Oreg. Health Scis. U., 1986—. Contbr. articles to profl. jours. Recipient Orval Klose award 1976. Mem. AAAS. Democrat. Roman Catholic. Avocation: photography.

UHRICH, KENNETH DALE, human service educator; b. Seattle, Feb. 24, 1944; s. Oliver Norris Uhrich and Philamina Mary (Habets) Burdett. BS, U. Wash., 1968, MSW, 1970. Psychiat. technician Seattle Mental Health Inst., 1967-70; ednl. coordinator Wash. Dept. Social and Health Services, Tacoma, 1970-72; mem. faculty Seattle Community Coll., 1972—; assoc. Human Affairs Internat., Murray, Utah, 1984—; mental health cons. Saipan, Mariana Islands, 1978; mem. adv. com. Seattle Indian Health Bd., 1977-82; mem. cert. bd. Substance Abuse Profls., Seattle, 1980-84. Mem. Nat. Assn. Social Workers, Acad. Cert. Social Workers. Democrat. Roman Catholic. Home: 549 NE 92nd Seattle WA 98115 Office: Human Affairs Internat 1904 3rd Ave Seattle WA 98101

UHRICH, RICHARD BECKLEY, hospital executive, physician; b. Pitts., June 11, 1932; s. Leroy Earl and Mabel Hoffer (Beckley) U.; m. Susan Kay Manning, May 25, 1985; children by previous marriage—Mark, Karen, Kimberly. B.S., Allegheny Coll., 1954; M.D., U. Pa., 1958; M.P.H., U. Calif.-Berkeley, 1966. Diplomate: Am. Bd. Preventive Medicine. Intern Lancaster Gen. Hosp., (Pa.), 1958-59; commd. asst. surg. USPHS, 1959, advanced through grades to med. dir., 1967; resident U. Calif., 1965-66; various adminstrv. positions regional and service unit levels Indian Health Services, until 1971; dir. div. programs ops. Indian Health Service, Health Services Adminstrn. USPHS, Washington, 1971-73; assoc. dir. div. profl. resources Office Internat. Health, Office Asst. Sec. for Health, HEW, Washington, 1973-74; assoc. dir. for program devel. and coordination Office Internat. Health, 1974-78; dir. Phoenix Indian Med. Ctr. and Phoenix Services Unit, 1978-81, ret., 1982; sr. adminstr. Good Samaritan Med Ctr., Phoenix, 1981-82, chief exec. officer, 1982—; mem. Phoenix Regional Hosp. Council, 1981—, pres., 1982-83; bd. dirs. Med. Ctr. Redevel. Corp., Phoenix; v.p. Samaritan Redevel. Corp., 1983—. Bd. dirs. Phoenix Symphony Orch., 1984—, Ariz. Sr. Olympics Bd., 1985—. Recipient Meritorious Service medal USPHS, 1973; recipient citation USPHS, 1973, Commd. Officers award, 1981. Mem. Ariz. Hosp. Assn. (bd. dirs. 1980-86, chmn. council on planning 1980-81, council on human resources 1982-83, council on patient care 1983-84, fin. com. 1984—), Am. Coll. Health Care Adminstrs., Am. Pub. Health Assn. Clubs: Arizona, Kiva; Camelback Country (Phoenix). Office: Good Samaritan Med Ctr 1111 E McDowell Rd Phoenix AZ 85004

UHRICK, GENE ALLEN, sales engineer; b. Decatur, Ind., Oct. 19, 1931; s. Luzern Francis and Helen (Schmitz) U.; m. Patricia S. Lasch, June 25, 1955 (div.); children—Lisa and Lisbeth (twins), Steven, Anthony; m. 2d, Ann E. Belote, Nov. 10. 1981. B.S., Ind. U., 1960; M.S., U. Calif.-Berkeley, 1961. Sanitarian, Allen County Health Dept., Ft. Wayne, Ind., 1956-58; lab. technician Marion County (Ind.) Health Dept., 1958-60; field sanitarian San Diego Health Dept., 1961-62; water dist. sect. mgr. Leucadia County (Calif.), 1962-65; v.p. Western regional mgr. sales Walker Process div. Chgo. Bridge and Iron, Pasadena, Calif., 1965-81; pres. Uhrick Process, Glendale, Calif., 1981—. Served to staff sgt. USAF, 1951-55. Mem. Am. Water Works Assn. Office: Uhrick Process 65 West Del Mar Ave Pasadena CA 91105

UKROPINA, JAMES ROBERT, energy company executive, lawyer; b. Fresno, Calif., Sept. 10, 1937; s. Robert J. and Persida (Angelich) U.; m. Priscilla Lois Brandenburg, June 16, 1962; children—Michael Steven, David Robert, Mark Gregory. A.B., Stanford U., 1959, M.B.A., 1961; LL.B., U. So. Calif., 1965. Bar: Calif. 1966, D.C. 1980. Asso. firm O'Melveny & Myers, Los Angeles, 1965-72; partner O'Melveny & Myers, 1972-80; exec. v.p., gen. counsel Santa Fe Internat. Corp., Alhambra, Calif., 1980-84, dir., 1981-86; exec. v.p., gen. counsel Pacific Lighting Corp., Los Angeles, 1984-86, pres., dir., 1986—; bd. dirs. Security Pacific Corp.; lectr. in field. Editor-in-chief: So. Calif. Law Rev, 1964-65. Served with USAF, 1961-62. Mem. Am. Bar Assn., Calif. Bar Assn., Los Angeles County Bar Assn., Beta Theta Pi. Club: Calif. Office: Pacific Lighting Corp 810 S Flower St Los Angeles CA 90017

ULERY, DONALD EUGENE, rubber distributing company executive; b. Denver, Mar. 27, 1924; s. John W. and Lulena (Donaldson) U.; m. Bette J. Wakeland, Nov. 28, 1944; children: Donald Eugene, Jacqueline Sue Ulery Barshow. BA, Whitter Coll., 1949; MBA, Santa Clara U., 1962. Dist. sales mgr. West Am. Rubber Co., Orange, Calif., 1952-76; pres., gen. mgr. Western Rubber and Supply Co., San Francisco, 1976—; pres. Pacific Rubber Assocs. Inc., San Francisco, Haldon Leasing Corp., San Francisco. Served with USAF, World War II, Korea. Recipient award Sales Mktg. Execs Assn., Los Angeles, 1967. Mem. No. Calif. Rubber Mfg. Assn. (past pres.). Republican. Home: 1469 Holt Ave Los Altos CA 94022 Office: Western Rubber & Supply Co 1760 Yosemite Ave San Francisco CA 94124

ULLMAN, BUDDY, research biochemist; b. Bklyn., Aug. 10, 1949; s. Robert Julian and Nelly (Szabo) U. BA, Oberlin Coll., 1970; PhD, Harvard U., 1975. Postdoctoral researcher U. Calif., San Francisco, 1975-81; asst. prof. biochemistry, genetics U. Ky., Lexington, 1981-85, Oreg. Health Sci. U., Portland, 1985—. Office: Oreg Health Sci U Dept Biochemistry Dept L333 3181 SW Sam Jackson Park Rd Portland OR 97201

ULLMAN, CORNELIUS GUMBEL, conservation cons.; b. Cleve., Sept. 14, 1906; s. Lee J. and Daisy (Gumbel) U.; B.S. in Econs., U. Calif. at Berkeley, 1928; M.S. in Agr., U. Calif. at Davis, 1934; m. Robie Jenkins, Jan. 24, 1936; children—Cornell, Lorna, Maury. Area agronomist soil conservation service U.S. Dept. Agr., 1935-41, dist. conservationist, 1941-50; field rep. Calif. Soil Conservation Commn., Sacramento, 1950-57; program coordinator div. soil conservation Calif. Dept. Conservation, Ventura, 1957-68, resource conservationist, 1967-68; resource conservation cons., 1968—. Fellow Am. Geog. Soc.; mem. Am. Geophys. Union, AAAS, Western Soc. Soil Sci., Soil Conservation Soc. Am., Sigma Xi. Republican. Club: Commonwealth of Calif. Home and Office: 50 Debussy Ln Ventura CA 93003

ULLMAN, VIRGINIA MELODY, civic leader; b. St. Louis, Aug. 23; d. Paul and Ruth (Bill) Melody; m. George Walter Ullman, Feb. 12, 1952 (dec.). Student pub. schs., Ill., Mass. With Shriner's Hosp. Crippled Children, Chgo., Am. Vol. Fgn. Aid, N.Y.C., 1940-47, Elizabeth Arden, Inc., N.Y.C., Phoenix, 1947-50. Vol., Jr. League, Chgo., N.Y.C., 1933—, Lighthouse for Blind, 1952-70; v.p. Ariz. Zool. Soc., Phoenix, 1962-81; founder Canal Beautification; bd. dirs. Phoenix Art Mus., 1964-73, Taliesin Council, Costume Soc. Am., N.Y.C., 1974—, Am. Fedn. Arts, 1978—, Costume Inst. of Phoenix Art Mus., 1968—, Ariz. Sci. Mus., 1980—. Republican. Episcopalian.

ULLMER, FRED, manufacturing engineer, consultant; b. Michigan City, Ind., Sept. 25, 1926; s. Edmund Ullmer and Bessie (Wood) Heath; m. Elena Dei, July 16, 1948; children: John Richard, Marco Lee. BSME, Tri State U., 1948. Development engr. Aerojet Engring. Co., Azusa, Calif., 1951-60; engring. specialist NATO Licensees of Aerojet Engring. Co., Italy, Fed. Republic Germany, France, 1961-68; tech. asst. NATO Licensees of Aerojet Engring. Co., Rome, 1974-76; dir. internat. ops. Aerojet Solid Propulsion Co., Sacramento, 1968-72; mktg. cons. Rome, 1972-73; mgr. mfg. tech. Aerojet Strategic Propulsion Co., Sacramento, 1977—. Bd. dirs. UNICO Internat., Sacramento, 1981-85. Served as sgt. U.S. Army, 1944-46, ETO. Mem. Soc. Mfg. Engrs. (sr.). Democrat. Roman Catholic. Avocations: piano, organ, woodworking. Home: 1355 43d St Sacramento CA 95819 Office: Aerojet Strategic Propulsion Co PO Box 15699C Sacramento CA 95813

ULLSTROM, L. BERWYN, lawyer; b. Memphis, Nebr., Sept. 18, 1919; s. LeRoy and Myrtle Estella (Parrish) U.; m. Loine Evelyn Sloan, Sept. 11, 1942; children: Linda Louise Dixon, Jeanne Ann Cook, Bruce Richard. Student, Scottsbluff Coll., 1937-40; B.S., U. Mich., 1946; LL.B., U. Denver, 1948. Bar: Colo. 1948, U.S. Supreme Ct 1954; Licensed comml. pilot. Practice in Denver, 1948-51; instr. aviation law and legal subjects U. Denver, 1948-51; trial atty. CAA, 1951-54; asso. gen. counsel FCDA, 1954-56, dep. exec. asst. adminstr., 1956-58; observer Operation Redwing, Joint Task Force 7 Pacific Thermonuclear Bomb Drop Test, 1956; exec. asst. dir. Office Civil and Def. Mblzn., Exec. Office Pres., 1958-61; cons. Dept. Def., 1961; pvt. practice law Denver, 1961—. Served to comdr., aviation USNR, 1941-45; mem. Res. (ret.). Mem. ABA, Colo. Bar Assn., Denver Bar Assn., Lawyer-Pilots Bar Assn. (v.p. Rocky Mountain regional chpt. 1982-86), Am., Colo. Trial lawyers assns., Nat. Transp. Safety Bd. Bar Assn., Internat. Soc. Air Safety Investigators (pres. Rocky Mountain regional chpt. 1984-86), Aircraft Owners and Pilots Assn., Phi Delta Phi. Home: 13990 W 30th Ave Golden CO 80401 Office: Suite 400 601 Broadway Denver CO 80203

ULMER, HAROLD WILLIAM, electronic engineer, manufacturing company executive; b. Los Angeles, Oct. 1, 1912; s. Henry Charles and Elizabeth Anna (Baumetz) U.; m. Olga Katherine Koehlert, Jan. 2, 1943; children: Janice Irene, Ronalee Anne Ulmer Elsberry, James R. (dec.). Student Pasadena City Coll., 1930-31, student Oceanside-Carlsbad Coll., 1934-35, Palomar Coll., 1962. Registered profl. engr., Calif. Sr. vacuum tube engr. Fed. Telegraph Co., Newark, 1942; sect. head power tube div. Raytheon Mfg. Co., Waltham, Mass., 1942-45; research engr. Convair, San Diego, 1946-51; pres., chief engr. Vacuum Tube Products, Oceanside, Calif., 1951-58, dir., 1955-58; electron tube div. mgr. Hughes Aircraft Co., Los Angeles, 1959; pres., chief engr. H.W. Ulmer Co., Oceanside, 1960-64; chief engr. M U Inc., Oceanside, 1965—, pres., dir., 1965-83. Contbr. articles to profl. jours. Author engring. manuals. Mem. IEEE (sr., life), Calif. Soc. Profl. Engrs. (charter), NSPE, Am. Soc. Quality Control, Am. Vacuum Soc. Republican. Methodist. Club: Palomar Radio (North San Diego County). Home: 2550 Pahvant St Oceanside CA 92054

ULMER, HARRIET GLASS, health services adminstr.; b. St. Louis, June 7, 1940; d. Melvin Gabriel and Deenie Joy (Laskowitz) Shcolnik; m. Allen L. Glass, Sept. 4, 1956 (div.); children—Bonnie Glass Nielson, Bernard J., Laura L.; m. 2d, Raymond A. Ulmer, Feb. 26, 1980 (div.). A.B. in English, UCLA, 1976; M.P.A. in Health Services Adminstrn., U. So. Calif., 1980. Regional project coordinator Kaiser Found. Health Plan, Los Angeles, 1977-80; dir. planning and mktg. Hosp. of Good Samaritan, Los Angeles, 1981, v.p. mktg. and bus. devel., 1981-86; cons. healthcare Laventhol & Horwath, Los Angeles, 1986—; cons. Humana Corp., Los Angeles Health Planning and Devel. Agy. Mem. Coro Assocs.; mem. Los Angeles Area Planning Com. Mem. Am. Hosp. Assn., Am. Coll. Healthcare Execs., Women in Health Adminstrn., Healthcare Execs. of So. Calif., So. Calif. Soc. for Hosp. Planners, Am. Soc. Hosp. Planning, Am. Mktg. Assn. (pres. health care div. So. Calif. chpt. 1984-85), Am. Heart Assn. (chmn. pub. policy edn. com. Greater Los Angeles affiliate 1982-84), Acad. Health Services Mktg. (nominating com. 1985, award coordinator and presentation com. 1987), U. So. Calif. Health Services Adminstrn. Alumni Assn. (treas. 1983-84, v.p. 1984-85). Office: Laventhol & Horwath 3699 Wilshire Blvd Suite 700 Los Angeles CA 90010

ULRICH, PAUL GRAHAM, lawyer, author, editor; b. Spokane, Nov. 29, 1938; s. Donald Gunn and Kathryn (Vandercook) U.; m. Kathleen Nelson Smith, July 30, 1982; children—Kathleen Elizabeth, Marilee Rae, Michael Graham. B.A. with high honors, U. Mont., 1961; J.D., Stanford U., 1964. Bar: Calif. 1965, Ariz. 1966, U.S. Supreme Ct. 1969. Law clk. judge U.S. Ct. Appeals, 9th Circuit, San Francisco, 1964-65; assoc. firm Lewis and Roca, Phoenix, 1965-70; ptnr. Lewis and Roca, 1970-85; pres. Paul G. Ulrich PC, Phoenix, 1985—; owner Pathway Enterprises, 1985—; judge pro tem Ariz. Ct. Appeals Div. 1, Phoenix, 1986; instr. Thunderbird Grad. Sch. Internat. Mgmt., 1968-69, Ariz. State U., Coll. Law, 1970-73, 78, Scottsdale Community Coll., 1975-77, also continuing legal edn. seminars; owner Pathway Enterprises, 1985—. Author: Applying Management and Motivation Concepts to Law Offices, 1985; editor, contbr.: Working with Legal Assistants, 1980, 81; Future Directions for Law Office Management, 1982; People in the Law Office, 1985-86; contbr. numerous articles to profl. jours. Bd. visitors Stanford U. Law Sch., 1974-77. Served with U.S. Army, 1956. Recipient continuing legal edn. award State Bar Ariz., 1978, 86, Harrison Tweed Spl. Merit award Am. Law Inst./ABA, 1987. Mem. ABA (chmn. selection and utilization of staff personnel com., legal econs. sect. 1979-81, mem. standing com. legal assts. 1982-86, co-chmn. joint project on appellate handbooks 1983-85, co-chmn. fed. appellate handbook project 1985—, chmn. com. on liaison with non-lawyer orgns. Econs. of Law Practice sect. 1985-86), Ariz. Bar Assn. (chmn. econs. of law practice com. 1980-81, co-chmn. lower ct. improvement com. 1982-85, co-chmn. Ariz. Appellate handbook project 1976—), Maricopa County Bar Assn., Calif. Bar Assn., Am. Law Inst., Am. Judicature Soc. (Spl. Merit Citation 1987), Phi Kappa Phi, Phi Alpha Delta, Sigma Phi Epsilon. Republican. Presbyterian. Home: 107 E El Caminito Rd Phoenix AZ 85020 Office: 3030 N Central Ave Suite 501 Phoenix AZ 85012

ULRICH, VERA ELIZABETH, educator; b. Chippewa Falls, Wis., July 1, 1922; d. Albion Myles and Wilhelmina Josephine (Johnson) Britten; m. William Viorel Ulrich, Dec. 8, 1946; children:Susanna U. Barton, Cawley. BS, Wis. State U., 1953; MS Pepperdine U., 1976; postgrad. U. Minn., UCLA, U. So. Calif. Cert. tchr., Calif., Minn.; cert. Miller Unruh Reading Specialist. Tchr. pub. schs., Glidden and Beloit, Wis., 1943-44, 46, South St. Paul, Minn., 1946-53; tchr. Enterprise Sch., Compton, Calif., 1953-69, reading specialist, 1966-77; condr. pvt. reading clinic, Torrance, Calif., 1973-82. Leader, neighborhood chmn. Girl Scouts U.S.A., 1947-64; active VFW Aux., Centinella Hosp. Aux. Served with WAC, U.S. Army, 1944-45. Named hon. life mem. Enterprise PTA. Mem. NEA, Calif. Tachers Assn., Compton Faculty Assn. (pres. 1966-67), Reading Specialists Calif. (state exec. bd. 1972—, state pres. 1984-86), Nat. Reading Assn., Calif. Reading Assn., Torrance Reading Assn., Redondo Beach Tchrs. Assn., WAC Vets. Assn. Democrat. Lutheran. Club: Eastern Star. Author: Face Puppets, 1977; editor Reading Specialists Newsletter. Address: 3805 W 183d St Torrance CA 90504

ULVELING, ROGER ALAN, state government official; b. Detroit, Dec. 20, 1943; s. Ralph Adrian and Elizabeth (Baer) U.; m. Margaret Jane Eichelberger, Nov. 27, 1968; children: Jennifer Anne, Katherine Emily, Robert Adam. BA, U. Detroit, 1966; grad. advanced mgmt. program, Harbard U.Grad. Sch. Bus., 1981. Dir. mktg. Wailea Land Corp. (subsidiary of Alexander & Balwin, Inc.), Honolulu, 1970-73; project mgr. Pacific Resources, Inc., Portland, Oreg., 1973-75; asst. to exec. v.p. Pacific Resources, Inc., Honolulu, 1975-76, dir. adminstrn., 1976-77, dir. govt. affairs, 1977-80, v.p., 1980-86; dir. dept. planning and econ. devel. State of Hawaii, 1986—. Div. chmn. Aloha United Way, Honolulu, 1977-79; bd. dirs. Child and Family Service, Honolulu, 1982-83; trustee Le Jardin Acad., Kailua, Hawaii, 1978—, Palama Settlement, Honolulu, 1980-82. Served to lt. USNR, 1967-69. Named Hon. Consul of Belgium, Govt. of Belgium, 1980. Clubs: Pacific (Honolulu) (bd. dirs. and chmn. house com. 1981-85), Kaneohe (Hawaii) Yacht. Home: 1438 Mokolea Dr Kailua HI 96734 Office: Dept Planning and Econ Devel 250 S King St PO Box 2359 Honolulu HI 96804

ULVOG, CARL GERHARD, geologist, consultant; b. Elk Point, S.D., Apr. 11, 1918; s. Daniel Edward and Lydia Johanna (Ven) U.; m. Dorothy Jean Christon, Aug. 22, 1948; children—Peter, Paul, Randi-Marie, Eric. B.S., Sch. Mines, Rapid City, S.D., 1950. Geologist, U.S. Geol. Survey-Minerals, Custer, S.D., 1950; exploration geologist Pure Oil Co., Midland, Tex., 1951-56, Sunray DX Oil Co., Roswell, N.Mex., 1956-69; geol. cons. Huber Corp., Midland, Tex., 1969-70; dir. minerals dept. N.Mex. State Land Office, Santa Fe, 1970-73; chief geologist N.Mex. Oil Cons. Commn., Santa Fe, 1973-84; geol. cons., 1984—. Pres., Midland for Am., Tex., 1959; campaign mgr. Independent candidate for U.S. Congress, Midland, 1960; asst. scoutmaster Boy Scouts Am., 1962-66; pres. Band Boosters-High Sch., Roswell, N.Mex., 1966-68. Served with U.S. Army, 1940-46. Recipient 1st Good Citizen award Sunray DX Oil Co., Roswell, N.Mex., 1968. Republican. Lutheran. Mem. Am. Assn. Petroleum Geologists (dist. rep. 1960-63), N.Mex. Geol. Soc. (chmn. field conf. 1964-66), Soc. Econ. Paleontologists and Mineralogists (pres. 1958-60, chmn. field conf. 1960), S.D. Alumni Assn. (pres. 1951-55). Home: 218 Sereno Dr Santa Fe NM 87501

UMEMOTO, KAREN SHIGEMI, social worker; b. Berkeley, Calif., Jan. 23, 1958; d. Harry Hiroshi and Hatsumi (Sando) U. BA, U. Colo., 1979; MSW, U. Denver, 1984. Vol. coordinator Rocky Mountain Planned Parenthood, Boulder, Colo., 1979-80, edn. cons., 1979-80; youth treatment counselor Denver Children's Home, 1981-83; social work intern Denver Pub. Schs., 1982, The Children's Hosp., Denver, 1983-84; dir. social service DeHa Comml. Meml. Hosp., Delta, Colo., 1984-85; med. social worker Penrose Hosps., Colorado Springs, Colo., 1985-86, U. Colo. Health Services Ctr., Denver, 1986—. Bd. dirs. Am. Cancer Soc., Colorado Springs, 1985-86. Japanese-Am. Citizen's League scholar, 1979. Mem. Nat. Assn. Social Workers, Inc. Democrat. Avocations: sewing, knitting, cooking, reading camping. Home: 1329 Jasmine St Denver CO 80220 Office: U Colo Health Scis Ctr Med Social Services 4200 E Ninth Ave Denver CO 80262

UMEZAWA, HIROOMI, physics educator, researcher; b. Saitama-ken, Japan, Sept. 20, 1924; came to Can., 1975; s. Junichi and Takako (Sato) U.;

m. Tamae Yamagami, July 30, 1958; children: Rui, Ado. BSEE, U. Nagoya, Japan, 1947, DSc in Physics, 1952. Research asst. U. Nagoya, 1947-53, assoc. prof., 1953; assoc. prof. U. Tokyo, 1955, prof., 1960-64; prof. U. Napoli Inst. Theoretical Physics, Italy, 1964-66; prof. U. Wis., Milw., 1967-67, disting. prof., 1967-75; dir. Inst. Theoretical Physics, Helsinki, Finland, 1965; group leader on structure of matter Centre of Nat. Research Naples div., Italy, 1964-66; Killam Meml. prof. sci., prof. physics U. Alta., Edmonton, Can., 1975—; vis. prof. U. Wash., Seattle, 1956, U. Md., College Park, 1957, U. Iowa, Iowa City, 1957, U. Marseille, France, 1959. Mem. editorial bd. N.Am. Edition of Annals of Louis de Broglie Found.; contbr. numerous articles to profl. jours. ICI fellow U. Manchester, Eng., 1953-55. Fellow N.Y. Acad. Scis., Am. Phys. Soc. Office: U Alta, Dept of Physics, Edmonton, AB Canada T6G 2J1

UMILE, LAUREL FLANDERS, psychotherapist; b. Longmont, Colo., Aug. 15, 1942; d. Laurence Burdette and Eleanor (Carlson) F.; m. Anthony Umile, July 4, 1965; children: Mark Anthony, Barbara Lynette. BA, U. Colo., 1960; postgrad., U. Calif., Berkeley, 1965, MSW, 1969. Lic. social worker II, Colo. Caseworker Colo. Dept. Social Services, Boulder, 1969-70, 1975-79, supr. III, 1979-81, adminstr. IV, 1981-85; adoption caseworker Friends for All Children, Boulder, 1973-75; pvt. practice psychotherapy Longmont, Colo., 1985—; instr. intro. to social work Lees Jr. Coll., Jackson, Ky., 1970; trainer Family Resource Ctr., Boulder, 1974; field instr. Colo. State U., Ft. Collins, 1982, Denver U., 1983; presenter child abuse workshops, 1983-84. Cellist Longmont Symphony Orch., 1972-83; vol. Planned Parenthood, San Francisco, 1966, Telegraph Hill Neighborhood Ctr., San Francisco, 1965; chmn. Colo. Adoption Coalition, 1987—; vol. pilot project Futurist Century Sch., 1986; trustee Flanders Found., 1975—. Mem. Nat. Assn. Social Workers (diplomate), Boulder Psychiat. Inst. (affiliate), St. Vrain Women's Connection, Audubon Soc., Sierra Club, Phi Beta Kappa. Democrat. Mem. Soc. of Friends. Avocations: music, reading, camping, hiking, swimming. Office: 709 3d Ave Longmont CO 80501

UMINSKI, GEORGE JOSEPH, electronics engineer; b. Racine, Wis., Nov. 3, 1920; s. Leroy Joseph and Clara Adelle (Klein) U.; m. Eunice May Jensen, May 9, 1942; children: Joanne Carol, Marcia Lee, Scott Alan. Cert., Valparaiso Tech. Inst., 1943; AS, San Diego State Coll., 1970. Registered profl. engr. Calif. AM-FM-TV engr. Sta. WTMJ, Milw. Jour. Co., 1943-56; sr. electronics engr. Gen. Dynamics Convair, San Diego, 1956-70; sr. product engr. Gen. Dynamics Electronics, San Diego, 1976-84; sr. electronics engr. Rohr Aircraft Co., Chula Vista, Calif., 1970-72; sr. product engr. Solar Aircraft Co., San Diego, 1975-76; sr. engr. Access Research Corp., Encinitas, Calif., 1984—; engring. cons., San Diego, 1972-75. Editor (engring. manual) Factory Test Atlas Missile Factory Acceptance Test Plan, 1964. Served with U.S. Army, 1942-43. Mem. NSPE. Republican. Club: Palomar Amateur Radio (Vista, Calif.). Avocations: house building, photography, auto maintenance, amateur radio. Home: 13776 Mira Montana Dr Del Mar CA 92014 Office: Access Research Corp 9655 Towne Centre Dr San Diego CA 92121

UNANGST, GREGORY JOHN, aerospace executive; b. Detroit, July 8, 1946; s. Russell Samuel and Florence (Justewicz) U.; m. Catherine Howell, Dec. 28, 1968; children: Stephanie Ann, Geoffrey John. BS, U.S. Mil. Acad., West Point, N.Y., 1968; MBA, MS in Engring., U. Pa., 1974; M in Philosophy, NYU, 1985. Commd. 2d lt. U.S. Army, 1968, advanced through grades to capt., 1970; inf. officer U.S. Army, Alaska, Vietnam, U.S., 1968-74; ops. research system analyst U.S. Army, Ft. Monmouth, N.J., 1974-78; resigned U.S. Army, 1978; product planning analyst Ford Motor Co., Dearborn, Mich., 1978-80; mgr. system design Ford Aerospace, Palo Alto, Calif., 1980-83; tech. dir. Ford Aerospace, Colorado Springs, Colo., 1983-85, mgr. advanced systems, 1985-86, mgr. theater level programs, 1986—. Mem. IEEE, Armed Forces Communications Electronics Assn., Assn. of U.S. Army. Avocations: running, tennis, skiing, hiking, swimming. Home: 19335 Greenwood Dr Monument CO 80132 Office: Ford Aerospace and Communication Corp 10440 State Hwy 83 Colorado Springs CO 80908

UNDERHILL, ADNA HEATON, retired natural resource scientist, researcher; b. Jersey City, June 8, 1914; s. Elmer and Ethel (Buckingham) U.; m. Lucille Diamond, Feb. 13, 1942; children: Lynn, Pamela, Adna Heaton Jr., Leslie, John. AB in Forest Botany, Dartmouth Coll., 1936; PhD in Fisheries, Cornell U., 1948. Game research investigator N.Y. Conservation Dept., Albany, 1940-41, dist. game mgr., 1946-48; exec. sec. Fish and Game Assn. State of Mass., Boston, 1948-50; dir. div. Fish and Game State of N.J., Trenton, 1950-62; asst. dir. U.S. Bur. Outdoor Recreation, Washington, 1962-77; sr. research scientist Nat. Park Service, Tucson, 1977-86, ret., 1986; pres. N.E. Fish and Game Dirs., Trenton, 1955-56; chmn. Nat. Waterfowl Council, Washington, 1959-60; chmn. exec. com. Internat. Assn. Conservation Agys., Washington, 1961-62, interagy. com. nat. rivers and trails U.S. Dept. Interior, Washington, 1965-77. Contbr. numerous articles to profl. jours. Bd. dirs. Santa Catalina Home Owners Assn., Tucson, 1984-86. Served to maj. U.S. Army, 1941-46, ETO; col. Res. ret. 1975. Decorated 2 invasion spearheads, 6 battle stars, silver star, bronze star, purple heart. Mem. Internat. Assn. Fish and Wildlife Agys. (chmn. exec. com. 1961-62), Nat. Waterfowl Flyways Council (chmn. 1960-61), Nat. Wild and Scenic Rivers System (chmn. interagy. com. 1968-77), Am. Fisheries Soc. (pres. N.E. sect. 1956), Boone and Crockett Club, Nat. Parks and Recreation Assn. Home: 6540 N Calle Padre Felipe Tucson AZ 85718

UNDERWOOD, BERDETT PENIRD, electrical engineer; b. Auburn, N.Y., Jan. 13, 1932; s. Charles James and Leona Mae (Merithew) U.; m. Elaine Joyce Ripley, Jan. 14, 1969 (div. Jan. 1981); children: Bonnie Pamela, Berdett Penird Jr.; m. Shirley Dianne Boyd, Mar. 25, 1983. B.S.E.E., Syracuse U., 1958; Assoc., Capital Radio Engring. Inst., Washington, 1961; M.S.E.E., George Washington U., 1980. Sr. test engr. Litton Industries, New Rochelle, N.Y., 1963-66; site supr. Page Communications Engrs., S. Vietnam, Washington, 1967-68; mgr. Halifax Engring. Co., Alexandria, Va., 1969-71; sr. test engr. E Systems, Dallas, Iran, 1971-74; mgr. Computer Sci. Co., Falls Church, Va., 1974-82; sr. tech. specialist Northrop Corp., ASD, Pico Rivera, Calif., 1982-85; mgr. software qualtiy assurance Magnavox Advanced Products and Systems Co., 1985—; cons. Fairchild Space & Electronics, Germantown, Md., 1973, ITT Gilfillan, Van Nuys, Calif., 1978-79, Boeing Aerospace Corp., Seattle, 1980-82. Author: Software Reliability, 1983, Software Supportability, 1984. Scoutmaster Cayuga County Boy Scouts Am., 1969-71. Served to T/sgt. USMC, 1950-58, Korea. Decorated Achievement award, Appreciation award; recipient Appreciation award Electronics Internat. Adv. Panel, 1975. Mem. Assn. Computing Machinery, IEEE (sr.), Software Adatable Reliable Systems, Data Processing Mgmt. Assn., Nat. Mgmt. Assn., Am. Legion, VFW, DAV. Republican. Mem. Assembly of God. Clubs: Computer, Reliability (Washington). Lodge: Masons. Home: 2400 E Lincoln St #114 Anaheim CA 92806 Office: Magnavox Advanced Porducts and Systems Co 2829 Maricopa St Torrance CA 90503

UNDERWOOD, JAMES WALTON, coast guard officer; b. Loma Linda, Calif., June 11, 1950; s. Donald Charles and Jacqueline Louise (Thibault) U.; m. Katherine Ann Vaverchak, Apr. 27, 1973; 1 child, Katherine Louise. BS, U.S. Coast Guard Acad., 1972; grad. Def. Info. Sch., 1976, Maritime Law Enforcement Sch., 1979. Commd. ensign U.S. Coast Guard, 1972; advanced through grades to comdr., 1987; communications officer USCG Cutter Glacier, 1972-74; boating safety officer 11th Dist., Long Beach, Calif., 1974-76, pub. affairs officer, adm.'s aide, 1976-79; exec. officer USCG Cutter Citrus, Coos Bay, Oreg., 1979-81; comdg. officer USCG Tng. Team One, Alameda, Calif., 1981-84; comdg. officer USCG Cutter Sweetbrier, Cordova, Alaska, 1984—; instr. Maritime Law Enforcement; tng. dir. Pacific Area operational mobile tng. unit; instr. adult edn. english and history, 1973-74. Mem. policy adv. com. Prince William Sound Community Coll. Decorated Commendation medal, Achievement medal, Antarctic and Arctic service medals. Mem. Am. Polar Soc., Internat. Narcotic Enforcement Officers Assn., Internat. Non-Lethal Weapons Assn., U.S. Coast Guard Acad. Alumni Assn., Am. Legion. Republican. Roman Catholic. Lodge: Moose. Office: Comdg Officer USCGC Sweetbrier PO Box 300 Cordova AK 99574

UNDERWOOD, JANE HAINLINE HAMMONS, university official; b. Ft. Bliss, Tex., Oct. 30, 1931; d. Frank and Lydia (Williams) Hammons; m. Van K. Hainline, Oct. 20, 1947 (div. 1966); children: Michael K., Susan J.; m. John W. Underwood, July 4, 1968; 1 dau., Anne K. A.A., Imperial Valley Coll., 1957; B.A., U. Calif., Riverside, 1960; M.A., UCLA, 1962, Ph.D., 1964. Asst. prof. U. Calif., Riverside, 1963-68; research anthropology Yap Islands, 1964, 65-66; prof. anthropology U. Ariz., Tucson, 1968—; assoc. dean Grad. Coll. U. Ariz., 1979-80, asst. provost for grad. studies, 1980-82, acting dir. Sch. Health Related Professions, 1980-82, asst. v.p. research, assoc. dean Grad. Coll., 1982—. Contbr. articles to profl. jours. Woodrow Wilson fellow, 1960-61; UCR Jr. Faculty fellow, 1968. Fellow AAAS; mem. Am. Assn. Phys. Anthropologists (v.p. 1980-82), Assn. Study Human Biology, Internat. Assn. Human Biologists, Sigma Xi (pres. U. Ariz. chpt. 1981-82). Home: 2228 E 4th St Tucson AZ 85719 Office: U Ariz Grad Coll Adminstrn 101 Tucson AZ 85721

UNDERWOOD, RALPH EDWARD, computer scientist; b. Houston, Sept. 26, 1947; s. Harry Anson and Ethel Jackson (Burns) U.; m. Linda Sue Merkel, Apr. 10, 1976. BS in Biology, Baker U., 1969; JD, Washburn U., 1973; MS in Computer Sci., Kans. U., 1984. Bar: Kans, 1973. Freelance stock and options trader Prairie Village, Kans., 1974-79; mem. staff BDM Corp., Leavenworth, Kans., 1982-84; sr. research and devel. engr. Ford Aerospace and Communications Corp., Colorado Springs, Colo., 1984—. Patentee in field. Mem. ABA, IEEE, Armed Forces Communications and Electronics Assn., Kans. Bar Assn., Upsilon Pi Epsilon, Sigma Phi Epsilon (social chmn. 1968, asst. ho. mgr. 1968, sec./treas. sr. council 1969), Phi Alpha Delta. Avocations: hunting, fishing, tennis, competitive shooting, skiing. Office: Ford Aerospace and Communications Corp 10440 State Hwy 83 Colorado Springs CO 80908

UNMACK, JAMES LOUIS, industrial hygienist; b. South Gate, Calif., July 12, 1941; s. Louis L. and Eleanor F. (Hauser) U.; m. Carol Hiroko Tsuneta, Apr. 2, 1966; children: David E.T., Chanda M. Student, Long Beach City Coll., 1959-61; BS, U. Calif., Berkeley, 1964; MSEE, U. Santa Clara, 1966; postgrad., U. Calif., San Diego, 1970-71. Registered profl. engr., Calif.; cert. indsl. hygienist, cert. safety profl. Head environ. health and safety dept. Hughes Aircraft Co., Los Angeles, 1971-74; chief indsl. hygiene sect. Long Beach (Calif.) Naval Shipyard, 1974-75; mgr. environ. health and safety Northrop Electronics, Hawthorne, Calif., 1981-84; sr. applications engr. SKC West, Inc., Fullerton, Calif., 1985-86; sr. indsl. hygiene engr. State of Calif., Los Angeles, 1975-81; indsl. hygiene cons. State of Calif., Downey, 1986—; instr. U. So. Calif., Los Angeles, 1980, U. Calif., Irvine, 1980—; cons. in field, 1984-86; chmn. Pacific Occupational Safety and Health Conf., Anaheim, Calif., 1984, Torrance, Calif., 1986; indsl. hygiene cons., State of Calif. Regional commr. Am. Youth Soccer Orgn., Rancho Palos Verdes, Calif., 1980; chmn. Boy Scouts Am., Rancho Palos Verdes, 1983-85. Served to capt. USAF, 1967-70. Mem. IEEE, AIAA (vice chmn. 1969), Am. Conf. Govtl. Indsl. Hygienists (chmn. So. Calif. sect. 1981), Am. Indsl. Hygiene Assn. (pres. So. Calif. sect. 1983). Home: 31016 Hawksmoor Dr Rancho Palos Verdes CA 90274 Office: Cal OSHA Consultation Service 8535 E Florence Ave Downey CA 90240

UNRUH, JESSE MARVIN, state ofcl.; b. Newton, Kans., Sept. 30, 1922; s. Isaac P. and Nettie Laura (Kessler) U.; m. Virginia June Lemon, Nov. 2, 1943 (div.); children—Bruce, Bradley, Robert, Randall, Linda Lu; m. Chris Edwards , 1986. B.A., U. So. Calif., 1948, postgrad., 1949, LL.D., 1967. Dist. staff dir. Fed. Census, 1950; with Pacific Car Demurrage Bur., 1950-54; mem. Calif. Assembly, 1954-70, chmn. com. fin. and ins., 1957-59, chmn. ways and means com., 1959-61, speaker of assembly, 1961-68, Democratic leader, 1968-70, mem. adv. commn. on intergovtl. relations, 1967-70; vis. prof. polit. sci. San Fernando Valley State Coll., 1970; vis. prof. U. So. Calif. Sch. Law, 1971-72; now treas. State of Calif.; cons., prof. polit. sci. Eagleton Inst. Politics, Rutgers U., from 1965; co-chmn. Seminar Young Legislators, Carnegie Corp.; Chubb fellow Yale, 1962. Mem. Calif. Central Democratic Com., 1954—; So. Calif. mgr. John F. Kennedy presdl. campaign, 1960, So. Calif. co-chmn. gubernatorial campaign, 1962, statewide coordinator assembly, congl. campaigns, 1962; chmn. Robert F. Kennedy's Calif. presdl. campaign, 1968; chmn. Calif. del. Dem. Nat. Conv., 1968; pres. Nat. Conf. State Legis. Leaders, 1966; Dem. candidate for gov. Calif., 1970; bd. regents U. Calif., 1961-68; trustee Calif. State Colls., 1961-68, Inst. for Am. Univs., Citizens Conf. on State Legislatures, from 1968. Served with USNR, 1942-45. Office: PO Box 942809 Sacramento CA 94209-0001

UNTCH, KARL GEORGE, chemistry consultant; b. Cleve., Apr. 24, 1931; s. Michael and Maria (Kraus) U.; m. Constance Louise Ford, Dec. 26, 1953; children: Peter M., Katharine A. BA, Oberlin Coll., 1953; MS, U. N.D., 1955; MA, Columbia U., 1957, PhD, 1959. Postdoctoral fellow U. Wis., Madison, 1958-60; fellow fundamental research Mellon Inst., Pitts., 1960-66; assoc. prof. Belfer Grad. Sch. Sci., Yeshiva U., N.Y.C., 1966-68; dept. head. Syntex Research, Basic Chem., Palo Alto, Calif., 1968-80; prin. scientist Syntex Research, Palo Alto, 1980-81; instr. Evergreen Valley Coll., San Jose, Calif., 1982-84; cons. chemistry pvt. practice San Jose, Calif., 1981—; cons. Calsec., Inc. Contbr. articles to profl. jours.; patentee in field. Chmn. Santa Clara County Adv. Commn. Devel. Disabilities, San Jose, 1970-81; vol., pres., v.p., treas. for mental retardation and devel. disabilities orgns.; vol. spl. olympics. Fellow Alfred P. Sloan Found., 1967-69. Mem. Am. Chem. Soc., Inc., Sigma Xi, Phi Lamda Upsilon. Avocations: golfing, music. Home and Office: 7203 Via Carrizo San Jose CA 95135

UNTERMAN, RUTH, psychotherapist, consultant; b. N.Y.C., Mar. 9, 1924; s. Hyman and Clara (Battes) Dulitzky; m. Israel Unterman, Aug. 18, 1943; children: Lee David, Robert Todd. BA, Ind. U., 1946; MA, Columbia U., 1948; MSW, Adelphi U., 1963. Social worker Hillside Hosp., Great Neck, N.Y., 1963-65, League Sch., Boston, 1966-68, North Shore Hosp., Manhasset, N.Y., 1969-73; pvt. practice psychotherapy Managua, Nicaragua, 1974-76, La Jolla, Calif., 1976—, San Diego, 1978—; cons. Palomar Family Service, San Diego, 1977-78, in field, 1977—. Vol. Dem. Party, Long Island, N.Y., Long Island Arts Commn., LWV. Fellow Soc. Clin. Social Workers (chmn. San Diego chpt. 1979-80, cert.); mem. Nat. Assn. Social Workers (cert.), Referal Service Psychotherapy (bd. dirs.), Pvt. Practice Council (pres.).

UPADHYAYA, SHRINIVASA KUMBHASHI, agricultural engineering educator; b. Kumbhashi, India, Feb. 27, 1950; came to U.S., 1976; s. Krishna G. and Satyabhama G. (Bhat) U.; m. Jayashree S. Hebbar, Jan. 17, 1977; children: Arun, Amar. B Tech. with honors, Indian Inst. Tech., Kharagpur, 1972; MS, U. Man., Can., 1975; PhD, Cornell U., 1979. Research and devel. engr. Vicon Ltd., Bangalore, India, 1972-73; asst. prof. U. Agrl. Scis., Hebbal, Bangalore, 1973-74; research asst. agrl. engring. U. Man., 1974-75; teaching, research asst. agrl. engring. Cornell U., Ithaca, N.Y., 1976-79, research assoc. agrl. engring., 1979-81; asst. prof. agrl. engring. U. Del., Newark, 1981-83, U. Calif., Davis, 1983—. Contbr. numerous agrl. engring. papers to jours.; patentee in field. Energy Research grantee Univ. Wide Energy Research Group, 1985-86, Compactions Research grantee Kerney Found., 1986—, traction research grantee Good Yr. Rubber Co., 1986, Kelly Springfield Tire Co., 1986; U. Man. fellow, 1975. Mem. AAAS, Am. Soc. Agrl. Engrs. (Paper award 1982), Sigma Xi. Avocations: swimming, gardening. Office: U Calif Dept Agrl Enging Davis CA 95616

UPASANI, MOHAN BALWANT, soil engineer; b. Nandurbar, India, Mar. 8, 1956; came to U.S., 1981; s. Balwant S. and Shanta (Kulkarni) U.; m. Meera M. Aolaskar, Mar. 7, 1984. BE, U. Bombay, 1977; MS, U. Calif., Irvine, 1982. Found. engr. Found. Corp. India, Bombay, 1977-79; civil engr. Eastern Ltd., United Arab Emirates, 1979-81; sr. engr. Computech, Inc., Berkeley, Calif., 1983-84; soil engr. Nicoll & Assocs., Inc., Tustin, Calif., 1984—. Recipient Sir James Berkey Gold medal U. Bombay, 1977. Home: 1392 Walnut #201 Tustin CA 92680 Office: Nicoll & Assocs Inc 15621 Red Hill Ave Suite 210 Tustin CA 92680

UPATISRINGA, VISUTDHI, mathematics educator, investor; b. Phuket, Thailand, Sept. 2, 1936; came to U.S., 1955; s. Hun Kwan and Kim Lien (Chun) Goh; m. Sally Lea Bailey, Aug. 20, 1966. B.A. in Chemistry, Oreg. State Coll., 1959; M.A. in Math., Oreg. State U., 1967, Ph.D., 1975. Instr. Linn-Benton Community Coll., Albany, Oreg., 1967-68; asst. prof. math. Humboldt State U., Arcata, Calif., 1969-80, assoc. prof., 1980-86, prof., 1986—; bd. dirs. Univ. Ctr. Bd., 1976-79, chmn. personnel com. dept. math., 1983-84, chmn. placement examination rev. com., 1976-77, chmn. search com., 1982-83; vis. scholar UCLA, 1980-81. Chmn. Hun Kwan Goh Meml. Scholarship Fund, Humboldt Area Found. Mem. Am. Math. Assn., Math. Assn. Am., AAUP, Pi Mu Epsilon, Phi Eta Sigma. Contbr. in field. Home: 3315 H St Eureka CA 95501 Office: Dept Math Humboldt State Univ Arcata CA 95521

UPTON, JAMES SOUTHERLAND, musicologist, educator; b. Ft. Smith, Ark., Jan. 2, 1937; s. James Southerland and Virginia (Townsend) U.; m. Emma Jo Perry, Aug. 24, 1958; children: James, Miles, Ellen, Candace. BA, BM, Hendrix Coll., 1958; MusM, So. Meth. U., 1961; PhD, U. Tex., 1968. Band dir. Star City (Ark.) High Sch., 1958-59; music dir. Fordyce (Ark.) Pub. Schs., 1961-65; music instr. Alma (Mich.) Coll., 1965-68; prof. music U. No. Colo., Greeley, 1968—. Mem. Am. Musicology Soc. (chmn. local chpt. 1981-82), Am. Recorder Soc. Office: U No Colo Sch Music Greeley CO 80639

UPTON-KNITTLE, WILLIAM JOSEPH, media executive, psychologist; b. Santa Monica, Calif., June 11, 1945; s. William Joseph Knittle and Lahlee (Duggins) Morrell; m. Linda Catherine Black, Apr. 19, 1969 (div. Aug. 1977); 1 child, Kristen Elizabeth; m. Alexis Carrell Upton, Sept. 30, 1977; 1 child, Jonathan Kynan. BA in English, Loyola U., Los Angeles, 1966, MA in Communication Arts, 1970, MA in Counseling Psychology, 1973; PhD in Communication Theory and Social Psychology, Lawrence U., Santa Barbara, Calif., 1976; D of Dharma in Asian Religion and Philosophy, U. Oriental Studies, 1980; MBA, U. La Verne, 1983. Assoc. editor Black Belt mag., 1960-65; asst. news dir. Sta. KHJ-TV, Los Angeles, 1966-67; news editor Sta. KFWB Radio, Los Angeles, 1967-69; dir. news and pub. info. Loyola Marymount U., Los Angeles, 1969-75; gen. mgr. Media Five, Los Angeles, 1976-79, v.p., 1981-83; assoc. dir. div. of continuing edn. U. La Verne, Calif., 1979-81; pres. Western News Assocs., Los Angeles, 1983—; asst. to dean UCLA Sch. Medicine, 1985—. Author: Survival Strategies for the Classroom Teacher, 1982; columnist various newspapers, mags., 1970—; contbr. articles to profl. jours. Asst. abbot Internat. Buddhist Med. Ctr., Los Angeles, 1976-81; assoc. dir. Pasadena/San Gabriel Valley Counseling Ctr., 1973. Recipient Martial Arts Pioneer award Am. Tae Kwon Do-Kung Fu Assn., 1976, Nat. Headliners award Wash. Press Club, 1968, Internat. Journalism award Sigma Delta Chi, 1968. Mem. AAAS, Assn. for Transpersonal Psychology, Inst. for Holistic Edn., Soc. Interdisciplinary Study of Mind, Internat. Imagery Assn., Am. Soc. Tng. and Devel., Nat. Book Critics Circle, Investigative Reporters and Editors, Am. Fedn. Police (chaplian 1985—), Nat. Police Acad. Avocations: martial arts, memory, mentalism and pseudoscience, outdoor preservation. Office: Western News Assocs PO Box 9189 Van Nuys CA 91209

URBAN, ANDREW, III, manufacturing company executive; b. Chicago Heights, Ill., Nov. 8, 1938; s. Andrew Jr. and Violet Veryle (Allen) U.; m. Betty Gayle Bulifant, Aug. 10, 1960; 1 child, Andrew IV. AS, Thornton Jr. Coll., 1957; BS in Chemistry, U. Ill., 1959. Shift supr. Reynolds Metals, Avenel, N.Y., 1967-68, PLT supt., 1968-69, mgr. quality control, 1969-71; mgr. quality control Reynolds Metals, Torrance, Calif., 1971-74; mgr. quality control and tech. service Weyerhaeuser, Longview, Wash., 1974-79; dir. quality control Weyerhaeuser, Tacoma, 1979—. Served with U.S. Army, 1961-63. Mem. Am. Soc. Quality Control (sr.), Am. Chem. Soc., Master Brewers of the Ams. Republican. Lutheran. Avocations: reading, travelling, cooking. Home: 2909 204th Ave Ct E Sumner WA 98390 Office: Weyerhaeuser CCB-6D Tacoma WA 98477

URBANCZYK, ANDREW AUGUSTUS, explorer, author; b. Russia, Mar. 1, 1936; came to U.S., 1972, naturalized, 1982; s. Sigmund Michailowich and Monika Urbanczyk; M.S. in Chemistry and Physics, Tech. U. Gdansk (Poland), 1960; m. Saborowska Krystyna, Oct. 5, 1968. Instr., Tech. U. Gdansk, 1960-68; research cons. Am. Yachting Assn., 1965-70; licensed capt., skipper, organizer oceanic expdns., 1957—; solo circumnavigator 50,000 miles, 1983-84; mem. exam. bd. Amateur Yachting Assn., 1965—; author 15 books, 1957—, including Lonely Voyages, 1971; Raft Expeditions, 1973; Thank You Pacific, 1981; The Calms and the Storms, 1987; world champion transpacific record in singlehanding sailing, 1978. Named Meritorious Laborer of Seas, Baltic Soc., 1970; recipient various grants. Address: 428 Fallerone Ave PO Box 37-1090 Montara CA 94037

URI, GEORGE WOLFSOHN, accountant; b. San Francisco, Dec. 8, 1920; s. George Washington and Ruby (Wolfsohn) U.; m. Pamela Dorothy O'Keefe, May 15, 1961. A.B., Stanford U., 1941, I.A., 1943, M.B.A., 1946; postgrad., U. Leeds, Eng., 1945. C.P.A., Calif. Mem. acctg., econs. and stats. depts. Shell Oil Co., Inc., San Francisco, 1946-48; ptnr. Irelan, Uri, Mayer & Sheppie, San Francisco; pres. F. Uri & Co., Inc., Athos Corp., Irelan Accountancy Corp.; instr. acctg. and econs. Golden Gate Coll., 1949-50. Contbr. articles to profl. jours. Chmn. San Rafael Redevel. Adv. Com., 1977-78, mem., 1978—; bd. dirs. San Francisco Planning and Urban Renewal Assn., 1958-60. Served with AUS, 1942-46. Recipient Key Man award San Francisco Jr. C. of C.; Meritorious Service medal Sec. of Army, 1978. Mem. Inst. Mgmt. Scis. (treas. No. Calif. chpt. 1961-62), Am. Inst. C.P.A.s, Calif. Soc. C.P.A.s (sec.-treas. San Francisco chpt. 1956-57, dir. 1961-63, state dir. 1964-66, mem. Forbes medal com. 1968-69, chmn. 1969-71), Am. Econs. Assn., Nat. Assn. Accts., San Francisco Estate Planning Council (dir. 1965-68), Am. Statis. Assn., Assn. Mil. Comptrollers, Execs. Assn. San Francisco (pres. 1965-66), Inst. Mgmt. Acctg. (cert. mgmt. acctg.; Disting. Performance cert. 1978), Inst. Cert. Fin. Planners (chartered fin. cons., cert. fin. planner), Am. Soc. C.L.U.s. Clubs: Engrs. San Francisco, Commonwealth, Stanford, Farael Racquet; Army and Navy (Washington). Home: 11 McNear Dr San Rafael CA 94901 Office: Suite 2000 100 Pine St San Francisco CA 94111

URIARTE, JOHN PHILIP, social worker; b. San Francisco, Sept. 1, 1954; s. Luis Bolivar and Mary Natividad (Avila) U. BA, San Francisco State U., 1984; postgrad., U. Calif., Berkeley, 1987—. Cert. social services worker. Med. social worker VA Med. Ctr., Martinez, Calif., 1981-83, psychiat. social worker, 1983-84; child psychotherapist Marin Community Mental Health, Kentfield, Calif., 1985-86; clin. social worker Concord (Calif.) Vets Ctr., 1986—; cons. Calif. Autism Found., San Rafael, 1985-86. Author: The Military Experience, 1982. Mem. Nat. Assn. of Social Workers, San Francisco Psychoanalytic Inst. Roman Catholic. Avocations: sail boating, flying, scuba diving, hiking.

URNESS, PHILIP JOEL, range science educator; b. Wenatchee, Wash., Jan. 18, 1936; s. Emory Vance and Lana (Maupin) U.; m. Marylln Gerda Underwood, Oct. 27, 1956; children: Lisa Diane, Laura Anne. BS in Wildlife Sci., Wash. State U., 1958, MS in Wildlife Sci., 1960; PhD in Range Sci., Oreg. State U., 1965. Research biologist Wildlife Resources div. State of Utah, Logan, 1960-62; research asst. Oreg. Game Commn., Corvallis, 1962-65; research scientist Forest Service, USDA, Tempe, Ariz., 1965-73; assoc. prof. range sci. Utah State U., Logan, 1973—. Contbr. articles to profl. jours. Mem. The Wildlife Soc., Soc. Range Mgmt. (pres. Utah sect. 1986), Northwest Sci. Assoc., Sigma Xi. Home: 1454 N 1600 E Logan UT 84321 Office: Utah State U Range Sci Dept Logan UT 84322-5230

URSIN, BJARNE ELLING, manufacturing company executive; b. Bridgeport, Conn., Aug. 8, 1930; s. Bjarne and Esther (Schiott) U.; student Oberlin Coll., 1949-51; BS in Physics, MIT, 1957; m. Mary Elizabeth Locke, July 26, 1969; children: Stephanie, Lara, Matthew, Jonathan, Teri, Kristian. Project engr. Raytheon, Andover, Mass., 1957-60; prin. investigator Gen. Dynamics, San Diego, 1960-62; sr. scientist Philco-Ford, Newport Beach, Calif., 1962-67; with McDonnell Douglas Corp., Huntington Beach, Calif., 1967-76, sr. ops. project mgr., mgr. mfg., 1967-76; prodn. mgr. Eldec Corp., Lynnwood, Wash., 1976-78; v.p. mfg. TCS Inc., Redmond, Wash., 1978-80; dir. new bus. Data I/O Corp., Redmond, 1980-82; prodn. mgr. Atex Inc., A Kodak Co., 1982-83; quality assurance systems mgr. Boeing Electronics Co., Seattle, 1983—; assoc. Coldwell Banker Co., 1981-83, Wallace and Wheeler Realty, 1984—; owner Westechnology, Bellevue, Wash., 1980—; co-owner Lighthouse Interiors, 1982—; community chmn. City of Huntington Beach, 1975-76. Served with AUS, 1951-53, Korea. Recipient NASA Team award Saturn/Apollo, 1975, Nasa Design VIP award Skylab, 1976, Cert. Appreciation, McDonnell Douglas, 1976. Mem. Am. Assn. Physics Tchrs., AIAA, AAAS, U.S. Internat. Sailing Assn., Am. Mgmt. Assn. Republican. Roman Catholic. Clubs: Bahia Corinthian Yacht (dir. 1972-76, rear commodore 1974, vice commodore 1975, commodore 1976) (Corona Del Mar); Royal Norwegian Yacht (Oslo); Balboa Bay; Seattle Yacht, U.S. Power Squadron, MIT of Puget Sound (dir. 1979—). Home: 9520 SE 61st Pl Mercer Island

WA 98040 Office: PO Box 596 Mercer Island WA 98040 Office: PO Box 6968 Bellevue WA 98008

URTIEW, PAUL A., research engineer; b. Nish, Yugoslavia, Feb. 23, 1931; came to U.S. 1950, naturalized, 1957.; s. Andrei and Margaret (Grebner) U.; m. Svetlana Dombrovsky, July 16, 1961; children: Andrei, Natalia. BS, U. Calif., Berkeley, 1955, MS, 1959, PhD, 1964. Research asst. gasdynamic lab. U. Calif., Berkeley, 1957-64, project dir., 1964-67; research scientist physics dept. Lawrence Livermore (Calif.) Lab., 1967-73, research scientist chemistry dept., 1973—. Contbr. numerous articles to profl. publs. Served with U.S. Army, 1955-57. Mem. Combustion Inst., AIAA, St. George Pathfinders, Sigma Xi, Tau Beta Pi, Pi Tau Sigma. Home: 413 Bell Ave Livermore CA 94550 Office: Lawrence Livermore Nat Labs Livermore CA 94550

USHER, JULIA MARIE, mechanical engineer; b. New Haven, Nov. 30, 1962; d. Theron and Carol Ann (Denver) U. BSME summa cum laude, Yale U., 1984; MSME, U. Calif., Berkeley, 1987. Research asst. Yale U., New Haven, 1983-84; engr. nuclear energy bus. ops. Gen. Electric Co., San Jose, Calif., 1984-87; mgmt. cons. Bain and Co., San Francisco, 1987—. Mem. AAAS, ASME, Am. Vacuum Soc., Assn. Yale U. Alumni, Yale Sci. and Engring Assn., Phi Beta Kappa, Sigma Xi, Tau Beta Pi. Democrat. Clubs: Yale (Palo Alto, Calif.); Ivy (San Francisco). Avocations: gourmet cooking and fine dining, printmaking, aerobic dance and nautilus. Home: 2130 Shelter Creek Ln San Bruno CA 94066 Office: Bain and Co 1 Embarcadero Ctr San Francisco CA 94111-3723

USHIJIMA, JEAN MIYOKO, city official; b. San Francisco, Feb. 14, 1933; d. Toyoharu George and Frances Fujiko (Misumi) Miwa; m. Tad E. Ushijima, Dec. 30, 1951; 1 child, Carol M. B.S., U. San Francisco, 1981. City clk. City of Beverly Hills, Calif., 1973—. Bd. dirs. West Los Angels Japanese Am. Citizens League, 1979—, Leadership Edn. for Asian Pacifics, 1985—. Mem. Acad. Advanced Edn., City Clks. Assn. Calif. (pres. 1986), Calif. Women in Govt. (program chmn. 1978-79), Leadership Edn. for Asian Pacific (chmn. bd. 1987), League Calif. Cities (admisntrv. services com. 1982-86). Avocations: reading, Japanese dancing. Office: City Clerk 450 N Crescent Dr #102 Beverly Hills CA 90210

USSERY, HARRY MACRAE, lawyer; b. Rockingham, N.C., Jan. 27, 1920; s. Robert Roy and Maggie Estelle (MacRae) U.; m. Olive Dual Simmons, Mar. 19, 1949. A.A., Wake Forest U., 1947; J.D., George Washington U., 1950. Bar: D.C. 1950. Assoc. firm Geiger & Harmel, Washington, 1950-52; ptnr. firm McNeill & Ussery, Washington, 1952-53; gen. counsel, dir. Harry R. Byers, Inc., Washington and Denver, 1953-59; procurement counsel Martin Mariette Corp., Denver, 1959-62; authorized agt. RCA, Camden N.J., 1962-69; staff counsel, mgr. internat. subcontract ops. Burns and Roe Constrn. Corp., Paramus, N.J., 1969-74, legal counsel, 1975-78, asst. to pres., Oradell, N.J., 1978-81; investor, Santa Fe, 1981—; chief moderator, dir., Dist. Roundtable, Sta. WWDC, Washington, 1950-53. Served with USAAF, 1941-45. Recipient Community Chest campaign awards, 1951, 52. Mem. ABA, Am. Judicature Soc., Nat. Contract Mgmt. Assn., George Washington U. Law Assn., Wake Forest U. Alumni Assn., Geneal. Soc. Santa Fe (state commr.), Council Scottish Clans Assns., St. Andrew's Soc., Clan MacRae Soc., Delta Theta Phi. Republican. Presbyterian. Club: Vintage Car (pres. 1985—) (Santa Fe). Author: The Origin of the Surname of Ussery, 1983; contbr. articles to various publs. Address: 2953 Plaza Azul Santa Fe NM 87505

UTEVSKY, DAVID, lawyer; b. Dayton, Ohio, Aug. 29, 1951; s. Fred and Shirley (Fishman) U.; m. Reba Allyn Shangrow, Apr. 22, 1983. BA in Communications, U. Wash., 1972; JD, U. Calif., Berkeley, 1977. Bar: Wash. 1977, U.S. Dist. Ct. (we. dist.) Wash. 1978, U.S. Ct. Appeals (9th cir.) 1979, U.S. Dist. Ct. (ea. dist.) Wash. 1982, U.S. Tax Ct. 1984, U.S. Supreme Ct., 1985. Law clk. to dist. judge U.S. Dist. Ct., Conn., 1977-78; assoc. Foster Pepper & Riviera, Seattle, 1978-84, ptnr., 1984—. Mem. ABA, Assn. Trial Lawyers Am., Am. Bankruptcy Inst., ACLU of Wash.(cooperating attys. legal com. 1980—, bd. dirs. 1983—), Order of Coif. Office: Foster Pepper Riviera 1111 Third Ave 34th Floor Seattle WA 98101

UTHE, PAUL MICHAEL, instrument company executive; b. Watertown, S.D., May 12, 1930; s. Paul Michael and Kota Louise (Wishard) U.; m. Mavis Vihulda Himrich, June 8, 1952 (div. 1979); children—Hans, Michelle M., Karla K.; m. M. Louise Criter, Oct. 20, 1979. B.S., S.D. State U., 1952; M.S., Air U., 1957. Commd. 2d lt. USAF, 1952, advanced through grades to capt., 1960; physicist Lawrence Livermore Lab, Livermore, Calif., 1960-62; research engr. Stanford Research Inst., Menlo Park, Calif., 1962-64; prin. scientist Electronic Assocs., Palo Alto, Calif., 1964-66; founder, chmn. UTI Instruments, Sunnyvale, Calif., 1966—, also dir.; pres. Uthe Tech., Inc., Burlingame, Calif., 1966—; v.p. Crestek, Inc., Trenton, N.J.; dir., chmn. Database Applications, Redwood City, Calif., Patentee mass spectroscopy, ultrasonics. Mem. Planning Commn., Livermore, 1964-66; mem. Livermore City Council, 1966-70; chmn. Valley Planning Commn., Livermore Valley, 1968-70; dir., v.p. Alameda County Mental Health Assn., Calif., 1966-70. Mem. IEEE, Semiconductor Equipment Materials Inst., Internat. Soc. Hybrid Mfg., ASTM. Republican. Presbyterian. Home: 15 Admirality Pl Redwood City CA 94065

UTSUGI, MICHAEL YOSHI, mechanical engineer; b. Honolulu, Nov. 18, 1961; s. David Yoshiro and Geraldine Taeko (Misono) U. BSME, Seattle U., 1984. Engring. aide State of Hawaii, 1981-83; project mgr. Korry Electric Co., Seattle, 1984—. Mem. Soc. Automotive Engring., Am. Astronautical Soc., Nat. Space Inst., Honor Soc. Nat. of Mid-Pacific Inst., Polynesian Voyaging Soc. Avocations: flying, weightlifting, reading. Home: 7540 37th Ave NE Seattle WA 98115 Office: Korry Electronics 901 Dexter Ave N Seattle WA 98109

UTTERBACK, DAVID FRANCIS, occupational health educator; b. Kansas City, Mo., Jan. 11, 1952; s. Martin Albert and Areleta Laynelle (Burditt) U.; m. Mary Elizabeth McCutchen, June 12, 1982. BS, N.E. Mo. State U., 1977; MPH, U. N.C., 1982, PhD, 1983. Cert. indsl. hygienist Am. Bd. Indsl. Hygiene. Chemist EPA, Research Triangle Park, N.C., 1977-78; environ. chemist Research Triangle Inst., Research Triangle Park, N.C., 1978-80; asst. prof. health sci. Calif. State U., Fresno, 1983-85, assoc. prof., 1985-86; asst. prof. environ. health sci. sch. pub. health U. S.C., Columbia, 1986—; cons. indsl. hygiene, Fresno, 1983—. Served with USN, 1971-73. Research grantee Calif. State U., Fresno, 1984-86, NIOSH, Fresno, 1984-86. Mem. Am. Indsl. Hygiene Assn., Am. Conf. Govtl. Indsl. Hygienists, Am. Chem. Soc. Democrat. Avocations: computer programming, backpacking, reading. Home: 729 E University Ave Fresno CA 93704 Office: Calif State U Health Sci Dept Fresno CA 93740

UTTERSTROM, JOHN RAYMOND, missiles systems executive; b. Vancouver, B.C., Can., Oct. 8, 1922; s. John and Gertrude Wilhemina (Hanson) U.; m. Mary Agnes Deffries, Sept. 24, 1947; children—Vicki Ann, Thomas Raymond, Mary Susan, Kathy Jo. B.S.E.E., U. Wash., 1948. With Boeing Co., Seattle, 1948-83, successively analyst, successively group leader, dept. head, chief engr., dir. engring., program mgr., 1948-80, v.p. Missile Systems div., 1980-83; pres. Boeing Mgmt. Assn. Pres. bd. dirs. Wash. State Spl. Olympics. Served to lt., USAAF, 1942-45. Recipient Ann. Honors, Aviation Week, 1961. Fellow AIAA (assoc. dir. Outstanding Aerospace Engring. award 1980, Wright Meml. Lectureship 1985, Edward Wells award 1984); mem. Sigma Xi, Tau Beta Pi. Clubs: Overlake Golf and Country (Bellevue, Wash.); Seattle Yacht. Patentee AC modulation suppressor. Deceased Dec. 1986. Home: 9830 Shoreland Dr SE Bellevue WA 98004 Office: PO Box 3999 MS 84 30 Seattle WA 98124

UYEHARA-ISONO, JUNE MIEKO, audiologist, consultant; b. Honolulu, Nov. 28, 1953; s. Donald Masuo and Yoshika (Torigoe) Uyehara; m. Gary Akira Isono, June 23, 1979; children: Sean, Catherine. BS, U. Hawaii, 1974; MS Clin. Competence in Audiology, Purdue U., 1977. Audiologist Honolulu Med. Group, 1977-80; audiologist, pres. Audiol. Cons. and Services, Honolulu, 1980—. Fellow Am. Acad. Dispensing Audiologists; mem. Am. Speech-Lang.-Hearing Assn., Alexander Graham Bell Assn., St. Regulatory Bd. of Hearing Aid Dealers (chmn. 1979—). Office: Audiol Cons and Services 1380 Lusitana #209 Honolulu HI 96813

VACCARO, ROBIN COLLEEN, interior designer; b. Yuba City, Calif., Mar. 10, 1950; d. Howard Anthony and Starr Jacqueline (Barnett) Spalding; m. Al John Vaccaro, July 22, 1972; 1 child, Brandon Alexander. BFA, Calif. State U., Chico, 1973. Drapery salesman Lucia's Interiors, Yuba City, 1969; salesperson Brayton's Hallmark, Chico, 1973-75; retailer Colusa (Calif.) Country Club, 1976-83; freelance painter Colusa, 1976-83; interior designer House Parts, Danville, Calif., 1985—. Vol. Fremont Hosp., Yuba City, 1966-68, Driftwood Hosp., Yuba City, 1966-68. Mem. Lyon Furniture Mercantile Agy., Allied Bd. Trade Inc., AAUW, Omega Nu. Democrat. Roman Catholic. Avocations: painting, travelling, gardening, reading. Home and Office: 5154 Blackhawk Dr Danville CA 94526

VACHON, ROGATIEN ROSAIRE (ROGIE), professional ice hockey executive; b. Palmarolle, Que., Can., Sept. 8, 1945; m. Nicole Vachon; children: Nicholas, Jade, Mary Joy. Goaltender Montreal (Que) Canadiens, NHL, 1966-72, Los Angeles Kings, NHL, 1972-78, Detroit Red Wings, NHL, 1978-80, Boston Bruins, 1980-82; asst. coach Los Angeles Kings, 1982-84, gen. mgr., 1984—. Co-recipient Vezina Trophy, 1968. Office: care Los Angeles Kings PO Box 10 The Forum Inglewood CA 90306 *

VADLEJCH, JAN, nuclear engineer, consultant; b. Prague, Czechoslovakia, Apr. 27, 1944; came to U.S., 1979, naturalized, 1984; s. JUDr Jan and Marie (Strakova) V.; m. Natalia Borodin Ivancova, Dec. 29, 1969. M.S.M.E., Prague Tech. U., 1970. Sr. researcher Inst. of Thermomechanics, Prague, Czechoslovakia, 1969-75; dir. research Nuclear Research Inst., Prague, 1975-77; sr. sci. programmer World Computer Corp., Paris, 1977-79; mgr. mech. engring. Quadrex Corp., Campbell, Calif., 1979-82; mgr. engring. Quadrex Internat. Corp., Mannheim, Fed. Republic Germany, 1982-84, dir. SW Europe Ansaldo Divisone Nira, Quadrex Internat. Corp., Genova, Italy, 1984-86, v.p. European operation, Heidelberg, Fed. Republic Germany, 1986—. Contbr. articles to profl. jours. Mem. Am. Nuclear Soc. ASME, Republican Task Force. Home and Office: 1700 Dell Ave Campbell CA 95008-6986

VAGHEFI, MORTEZA MONIR, research chemist; b. Natanz, Iran, Oct. 12, 1948; came to U.S., 1977; s. Mohammad Monir Vaghefi and Robabeh MirToraby; m. Zahra Parandoosh, Nov. 21, 1977; 1 child, Kaveh. Doctorate in pharmacy, Tehran (Iran) U., 1972; MS, U. Utah, 1981; PhD, Brigham Young U., 1985. Quality control lab. asst. Abidi Pharms., Tehran, 1971-73; mgr. process control Tolidaru Pharms., Tehran, 1973-75, mgr. prodn. plant, 1973-77; research asst. U. Utah, Salt Lake City, 1978-80; head biomed. chemistry Nucleic Acid Research Inst., Costa Mesa, Calif., 1985—. Served to lt. Iranian Army, 1972-74. Mem. Am. Chem. Soc. Office: Nucleic Acid Research Inst 3300 Hyland Ave Costa Mesa CA 92626

VAGHEI, MOHAMAD, architect; b. Isfahan, Iran, July 26, 1960; came to U.S., 1975; s. Mostafa and Molouk (Etemadi) V. BSArch, Ohio State U., 1980; MArch, U. Ill., 1982, MSCE, 1983. Project engr. C.L. Peck Contractors, Los Angeles, 1983-84; sr. project designer S.G.P.A. Planning & Architecture, San Diego, 1984—; pres. Arcomp Internat., San Diego, 1983—. Named Best Designer Iranian Inst. Architects, 1983; recipient Merit award Nat. Endowment Arts 1985. Mem. AIA, Am. Inst. Advancement Scis. Moslem. Avocations: tennis, skiing, painting, music. Home: 4040-73 Porte Lapaz San Diego CA 92122 Office: SGPA Planning & Architecture 1565 Hotel Circle S San Diego CA 92103

VAGNEUR, KATHRYN OTTO, accountant, rancher; b. Aurora, Ill., Feb. 23, 1946; d. Harold William and Afton (Bryner) Otto; m. Gerald Ronald Terwilliger, Oct. 19, 1968 (div. 1974); 1 dau., Jocelyn Marie; m. 2d, Clyde O. Vagneur, Aug. 24, 1979. B.S. in Math., U. Utah, 1968; M.S. in Agribus. Mgmt., Ariz. State U., 1979. CPA, Colo. Computer systems designer U. Utah Libraries, Salt Lake City, 1966-68; research asst. in computer systems Carnegie-Mellon U., 1968-70; owner, mgr. Evening at Arthurs Restaurant, Aspen, Colo., 1973-76; self-employed tax cons. Phoenix, 1977-78; with Touche Ross & Co., Colorado Springs, Colo., 1978-82; ptnr., fin. mgr. V Bar Lazy V Ranch, Peyton, Colo., 1978—; ptnr. Vagneur & Co., Colorado Springs, 1982—; pres. The Marlwood Corp., Colorado Springs. Chmn. bd. dirs. Pikes Peak Ctr.; del. Rep. State Conv., 1982, White House Small Bus. Conf., 1986; mem. Gov.'s Econ. Devel. Action Council, 1987; 4-H leader. Mem. Am. Inst. CPAs, Nat. Soc. Accts. for Coops., Colo. Soc. CPAs, Nat. Assn. Accts., Jr. League, Am. Salers Assn., Nat. Cattlemen's Assn. (featured speaker 1986 Beef Profit Conf.), Nat. Fedn. Ind. Bus., Colorado Springs C. of C. (com. chmn.), Am. Quarter Horse Assn., Beta Alpha Psi, Alpha Zeta. Author: A Financial Analysis of Cooperative Livestock Marketing, 1978. Home: 14725 Jones Rd Peyton CO 80831 Office: 228 N Cascade Suite 202 Colorado Springs CO 80903

VAGO, MARTA, psychological consultant; b. Budapest, Hungary, May 5, 1944; came to U.S., 1956; d. Joseph and Sara (Groszman) V.; m. David Freundlich, Sept. 2, 1962 (div. May 1970). BS in Music, The Julliard Sch., 1966, MS in Music, 1968; MSW, Temple U., 1971; PhD in Psychology, Columbia Pacific U., 1983. Outpatient supr. Pa. Hosp., Phila., 1971-73; founder, dir. Laurel Inst. Inc., Phila., 1971-78; assoc. Phila. Profl. Assocs., 1978-79; pvt. practice psychotherapy Santa Monica, Calif., 1982—; lectr. The Broadway, Los Angeles, 1984-86; media spokesperson Tonka Toys, Minnetonka, Minn., 1985. Columnist Century City News, Los Angeles, 1986—; contbr. articles to profl. jours. Mem. Nat. Assn. Social Workers (cert.), Nat. Registry Health Care Providers in Clin. Social Work. Club: Inside Edge (Beverly Hills, Calif.). Avocations: arts, travelling, phys. fitness. Home: 1601 Veteran Ave #203 Los Angeles CA 90024 Office: 1421 Santa Monica Blvd Santa Monica CA 90404

VAIL, PATRICK VIRGIL, laboratory administrator, entomologist, researcher; b. Pasadena, Calif., Nov. 16, 1937; s. Virgil Parks and Mary Theresa McGuire V.; m. Susan Saroyan; children: Kimberly Ann, Patricia Lynn, Stacey Marie. BA, Calif. State U., Fresno, 1960, MA, 1962; PhD, U. Calif., Riverside, 1967. Cert. entomologist in insect ecology and biol. control. Research entomologist, Agrl. Research Service USDA, Riverside and Fresno, 1962-69, 1978-86; research leader, Agrl. Research Service USDA, Phoenix, 1969-75; lab. dir. Agrl. Research Service USDA, Fresno, 1982—; sect. head Insect and Pest Control sect. Internat. Atomic Energy Agy. UN, Vienna, Austria, 1975-78; cons. numerous state, fed., sci. and internat. orgns. Editor: Baculoviruses, 1975; contbr. over 80 articles to profl. jours. Mem. Soc. Invertebrate Pathology, Entomol. Soc. Am. (chair internat. affairs com. 1979-84), AAAS (steering com. consortium of affiliates for internat. programs), Internat. Plastic Modelers Assn. Roman Catholic. Club: Tempe Racquet (Ariz.) (bd. dirs. 1972-74). Avocations: tennis, squash, fishing, scale-model aircraft. Office: USDA Agrl Research Service Hort Crops Research Lab 2021 S Peach Ave Fresno CA 93727

VALADEZ, SUSAN GAYLE, vocational rehabilitation counselor; b. Yakima, Wash., Sept. 1, 1944; d. Homer Hudson Young and Hazel Ida (Kludas) Vasseur; m. Arthur J. Sweetland, June 21, 1969 (div. 1973); 1 child, jason; m. Larry David Valadez, May 5, 1979. BA in Psychology with honors, Eastern Wash. U., 1969, postgrad. counseling psychology, 1984; postgrad., Seattle U., 1973—. Neighborhood worker Spokane (Wash.) Mental Health, 1967-68; caseworker Pub. Assistance, Spokane, 1969-73; vocat. rehab. counselor State of Wash., Spokane, 1973—; sec., bd. dirs. liason EduCare Acad., Spokane, 1980—; liason Sacred Heart Kidney Ctr., Spokane, 1980—, Nancy Reagan Care Unit, 1986—, Mountain View Hosp., 1986—, Raleigh Hills Hosp., 1986—; handicapped employment Fairchild AFB Vets. Hosp., 1983—, mem. selective placement com., 1980-84. Mem. govs. com. on employment of the handicapped, Spokane, 1973—, Blue Ribbon Task Force in Mktg., Olympia, Wash., 1984-85; mem. Inland Empire Hispanic Assn. Mem. Nat. Rehab. Assn. (bd. dirs. 1973-76), Spokane Bus. Women's Assn. Democrat. Presbyterian. Office: Vocat Rehab S 9 Washington Room 510 Sopkane WA 99204

VALAREZO, TONI ANN, audiologist; b. Independence, Kans., July 27, 1957; d. Marlin A. and Norma Louise (Ross) T.; m. Walter O. Valarezo, May 26, 1985. BS, U. Wyo., 1977-80, MS, 1982. Audiologist Los Angeles Ear Med. Group, 1983-84, San Pedro (Calif.) Eye, Ear, Nose & Throat, 1984—; prin. Audio-Diagnostics, San Pedro, 1985—; cons. to med. practices, Los Angeles, 1982-83. Mem. Am. Speech Lang. Hearing Assn., Leads Club. Avocations: reading, sewing, needlecraft. Office: Audio-Diagnostics 571 W 7th St San Pedro CA 90731

VALDES, HALCEA MAXINE, social work administrator; b. Medford, Oreg., Dec. 13, 1928; d. Chester Arthur and Orpha Dell (Stevenson) Moore; m. Victor Mario Valdes, mar. 27, 1948 (div. Nov. 1966); children: Hayden McKie, Victor Mario Jr., Chester Moore. BS with honors, Tex. Women's U., 1962; MSW, U. Calif., Berkeley, 1967. Lic. clin. social worker, marriage-family and child counselor, Calif. Child welfare supr. Alameda County, Oakland, Calif., 1967-76; asst. dist. dir. Children's Home Soc., San Jose, Calif., 1976-80; program mgr. Children's Home Soc., Oakland, Calif., 1980-86; adoption supr. State of Calif. Social Services, Santa Rosa, 1986—; pvt. practice in psychotherapy 1969—; field work supr. U. Calif., Berkeley, 1969-84, San Francisco State U., 1980-85, Antioch Coll. West, Monterey, Calif., 1978-79. Mem. Nat. Assn. Social Workers (cert.), Bay Area Suprs. of Adoption. Democrat. Avocations: traveling, swimming, scuba diving, collecting antiques, backpacking. Home: 2001 Francisco St Berkeley CA 94709 Office: State Adoptions 50 D St Suite 301 Santa Rosa CA 95404

VALDEZ, VINCENT EMILIO, artist; b. Mora, N.Mex., Mar. 15, 1940; s. Jose Bartolo Valdez and Maria Natividad (Nolan) Henderson; m. Gloria Jean Skidgel; children: Trevor, Tiffney. Student in art, U. Wyo. Detective Laramie (Wyo.) Police Dept., 1964-84; free-lance artist Laramie, 1983—. Mem. Nat. Sculpture Ctr. Served with U.S. Army, 1964-68. Recipient Best of Show award Wildlife and Western Art Exhbn., Milw., 1985, 3d Place sculpture award George Phippen Meml. Art Show, Prescott, Ariz., 1986. Mem. Laramie Art Guild. Avocations: cross-country skiing, karate, fishing, photography. Office: Vince Valdez Studio PO Box 581 Laramie WY 82070

VALDOV, THOMAS, banker; b. Tallinn, Estonia, Feb. 24, 1942; came to U.S., 1949, naturalized, 1955; s. Richard Voldemar and Leida Marie (Kurema) V.; m. Vickie Lynn Christmas, Nov. 11, 1970; children—Mark, Brent, Gregory. B.S. in Bus., U. Nev., Las Vegas, 1969. Property mgr. Am. West Property Investments, Las Vegas, 1974—; trust officer 1st Interstate Bank, Las Vegas, 1969-81; v.p. Valley Bank, Las Vegas, 1981—; cons. property mgmt., 1974—. Served with USAF, 1962-66. Mem. Young Republicans, Am. Inst. Banking (gov. 1962-64). Presbyterian. Club: UNLV-Alumni, ATO-Alumni. Home: 3355 Southridge Ave Las Vegas NV 89121 Office: Valley Bank Nev PO Box 14527 Las Vegas NV 89114

VALENCIA, ED, savings institution executive. Pres. Citicorp Savs., Oakland, Calif., 1984—. Office: PO Box 2082 Citicorp Savs Office of Pres 180 Grand Ave Oakland CA 94111 *

VALENTINE, DAVID WADE, technology company executive; b. Los Angeles, June 16, 1942; s. Edward Lee and Murial Harline (Slocum) V.; m. Virginia Sue Stokes, Jan. 26, 1963; children: David Wade Jr., Merilee Jo. BS, U. Calif., Santa Barbara, 1965; MS, U. Calif., San Diego, 1970, DSci, 1972. Project scientist Dames & Moore, Westwood, Calif., 1973-74; sr. scientist Tetra Tech, Inc., Pasadena, Calif., 1974-81, dir. internat. ops., 1981—; pres. Nova Sci. Corp., La Jolla, Calif., 1981-83. Contbr. articles to profl. jours. Trainee NSF, 1966-68, NIH, 1969-72. Mem. AAAS. Avocations: fishing, swimming, skiing, scuba diving. Office: Tetra Tech Inc 11777 Sorrento Valley Rd San Diego CA 92037

VALENTINE, JAMES WILLIAM, geology educator, author; b. Los Angeles, Nov. 10, 1926; s. Adelbert Cuthbert and Isabel (Davis) V.; m. Grace Evelyn Whysner, Dec. 21, 1957 (div. 1972); children—Anita, Ian; m. Cathryn Alice Campbell, Sept. 10, 1978 (div. 1986); 1 child, Geoffrey; m. Diane Mondragon, Mar. 16, 1987. B.A., Phillips U., 1951; M.A., UCLA, 1954, Ph.D., 1958. From asst. prof. to assoc. prof. U. Mo., Columbia, 1958-64; from assoc. prof. to prof. U. Calif.-Davis, 1964-77; prof. geol. scis. U. Calif.-Santa Barbara, 1977—. Author: Evolutionary Paleoecology of the Marine Biosphere, 1973; editor: Phanerozoic Diversity, 1985; co-author: Evolution, 1977, Evolving, 1979; also numerous articles, 1954—. Served with USNR, 1944-46; PTO. Fulbright research scholar, Australia, 1962-63; Guggenheim fellow Yale U., Oxford U., Eng., 1968-69; Rockefeller Found. scholar in residence, Bellagio, Italy, summer 1974; grantee NSF, NASA. Fellow Am. Acad. Arts and Scis., AAAS, Geol. Soc. Am.; mem. Nat. Acad. Scis., Paleontol. Soc. (pres. 1974-75). Avocation: collecting works of Charles Darwin. Home: 475F Cannon Green Dr Goleta CA 93117 Office: U Calif Dept Geol Scis Santa Barbara CA 93106

VALENTINE, JOHN DALE, anesthesiologist; b. Wellington, Kans., June 21, 1951; s. Darrell Eugene and Lee Rose (DeBus) V.; m. Suzanne DuPont, Dec. 23, 1973; children: Seth Colter, Spencer Cade. BA in Biology, U. Kans., 1973, MD, 1976. Dir. emergency dept. Med. Ctr. of Independence, Mo., 1978-81; resident in anesthesiology U. Kans. Sch. Medicine, Kansas City, Kans., 1982-84; practice medicine specializing in anesthesiology Denver, 1984—; med. dir. Emergency Med. Services of Blue Springs, Mo., 1980-81, Gold Cross Ambulance Services, Independence, 1981. Fellow Am. Bd. Anesthesiologists; mem. Am. Soc. Anesthesiologists, Colo. Soc. Anethesiologists, Internat. Anesthesia Research Soc., Denver Med. Soc., Colo. Med. Soc., Phi Beta Kappa. Republican. Presbyterian. Club: Denver Athletic. Avocations: skiing, horses. Office: 3005 E 16th Ave #175 Denver CO 80206

VALENZUELA, FERNANDO, professional baseball player; b. Navajoa, Sonora, Mexico, Nov. 1, 1960; m. Linda, Dec. 29, 1981; 1 son, Fernando. Pitcher Mexican Leagues, 1978-79, minor league, 1979-80, Los Angeles Dodgers, Nat. League, 1980—; mem. Nat. League All-Star Team, 1981-86, World Series championsip team, 1981. Recipient Cy Young Meml. award Nat. League, 1981; named Rookie of the Yr. Nat. League, Rookie of Yr. Baseball Writers' Assn. Am., 1981. Office: Los Angeles Dodgers Dodger Stadium 1000 Elysian Park Ave Los Angeles CA 90012 *

VALENZUELA, WILFREDO RAMOS, computer specialist; b. Malolos, Bulacan, Philippines, July 9, 1949; came to U.S., 1971, naturalized, 1985; s. Mario Lopez and Felisa (Ramos) V. BS in Math., U. Philippines, Quezon City, 1968; MS in Computer Sci., UCLA, 1973. Instr. math. U. Philippines, Quezon City, 1968-71; research asst. UCLA, 1973; programmer, analyst McDonnell Douglas Corp., Carson, Calif., 1974-77, sect. mgr., 1977-82; mgr. McDonnell Douglas Corp., Cypress, Calif., 1982-84, dir. CAD/CAM, 1984—. Avocations: bridge, volleyball, swimming. Office: McDonnell Douglas Corp 5701 Katella Ave Cypress CA 90630

VALIERE, GARY MARK, business consultant; b. Valley City, N.D., Feb. 24, 1931; s. Eugene Anthony and Doris Lois (Keeler) V.; m. Delores Elaine Leick, Jan. 2, 1950; children—Steven Mark, Michael Gordon, Thomas Paul, Gary James. B.S., N.D. State Coll., Valley City, 1955; M.B.A., Calif. State U.-Fullerton, 1968; Ph.D., U.S. Internat. U., San Diego, 1980. Lab. foreman, research chemist Phillips Chem. Co., Borger, Tex., 1955-58; research design engr. Boeing Co., Seattle, 1958-61; sr. electronics engr., mgr. program mgmt. Raytheon Corp., Santa Barbara, Calif. 1961-62; project dir. Mgmt. Systems Corp., Boston and Newport Beach, Calif., 1962-65; dir. mgmt. analysis Douglas Aircraft, Santa Monica and Huntington Beach, Calif., 1965-68; asst. v.p., dir. program planning and control, mil. aircraft div. McDonnell Douglas Corp., Long Beach, Calif., 1968-69; mgr. cons. Peat, Marwick, Mitchell, Los Angeles, 1969-72; v.p., dir. Rex Land & Assocs., Los Angeles, 1972-77; pres., chmn. bd. Gary Valiere & Assocs., Irvine, Calif., 1977—, Office Word Processing, Irvine, 1982—, Astro Vista, Inc., Irvine, 1982—; dir. Cypress Internat., Dovaly, Inc., Garretson-Valiere & Assocs.; lectr. Am. Mgmt. Assn., Am. Inst. Indsl. Engrs., Nat. Contract Mgmt. Assn., UCLA, U. So. Calif. Active senatorial campaigns, 1960, 68. Served with U.S. Army, 1949-51. Mem. AIAA, Univ. Doctoral Soc., Am. Def. Preparedness Assn., ASSN. U.S. Army, U.S. Air Force Assn., Nat. Contract Mgmt. Assn., World Affairs Council, Nat. Security Council (adv. council), Am. Legion. Clubs: Congressional, Senatorial, Elks. Author books, manuals, papers on orgn. and mgmt. Office: 2151 Michelson Dr Suite 295 Irvine CA 92715

VANALLEN, WILLIAM GEORGE, educational administrator; b. New Brunswick, N.J., July 19, 1914; s. George and Emma May (Smith) VanA.; m. Victoria Dolores Caballero, Oct. 16, 1937. B.S. in Elec. Engring., Rutgers U., 1936; M.S. in Civil Engring., State U. Iowa, 1948; postgrad. Army War Coll., 1955. Registered profl. engr., Hawaii. Commd. 2d lt. C.E., U.S. Army, 1936, advanced through grades to col., 1952, ret., 1965; dir. land div. Kamehameha Schs./Bishop Estate, Honolulu, 1965-85. Decorated Legion of Merit with 2 oak leaf clusters, Bronze Star medal with 2 oak leaf clusters,

Army Commendation medal with oak leaf cluster; Croix de Guerre with palm. Mem. Hawaii Soc. Profl. Engrs. (pres. 1969-70), Soc. Am. Mil. Engrs. (pres. Honolulu chpt. 1963-64), Engrs. Assn. Hawaii, Hawaii Council Engring. Socs., Honolulu C. of C., Oahu Devel. Conf., Phi Beta Kappa, Tau Beta Pi. Club: Plaza. Home: 4340 Pahoa Ave Apt 14A Honolulu HI 96816 Office: 567 South St Honolulu HI 96813

VAN ARSDALE, DICK, sports broadcaster; b. Indianapolis, IN, Feb. 22, 1943; m. Barbara V.; children: Jill, Jason. AB in economics, Indiana U., 1965. Player New York Knicks (Nat. Basketball Assn.), N.Y.C., 1965-68; with Phoenix Suns, Phoenix, Ariz., 1968-77; color commentator, television broadcasts Phoenix Suns, 1977—, interim mgr., 1987. Named "Mr. Basketball" of Indiana during high school, NCAA All-American, Indiana U. Office: care Phoenix Suns 2910 N Central Phoenix AZ 85012 *

VAN ARSDALE, JAMES W., mayor; m. Eva Van Arsdale; three sons. B.S.B.A., U. Colo. Various sales mgmt. positions mktg. dept. Conoco, 1948-81; mayor City of Billings, Mont., 1984—; past chmn. Billings City Council. Bd. dirs. Mont. League Cities and Towns, Deaconess Hosp. Served with USN. Methodist. Office: City of Billings Office of Mayor PO Box 1178 Billings MT 59103 *

VAN ARSDOL, MAURICE DONALD, JR., sociologist, educator; b. Seattle, May 4, 1928; s. Maurice Donald and Madge (Belts) V.; m. Marian Clide Gatchell, Aug. 18, 1950; 1 child, Pece Durcinovski. B.A. in Sociology, U. Wash., 1949, M.A., 1952, Ph.D., 1957. Research asst. Office Population Research U. Wash., Seattle, 1950-54, doctoral assoc., 1953-57; asst. prof. dept. sociology U. So. Calif., Los Angeles, 1957-61, research coordinator youth studies ctr., 1959-60, assoc. prof. sociology, 1961-65, prof. sociology, 1965—, dir. population research lab., 1965—; vis. prof. dept. sociology U. Hawaii, Honolulu, 1966, Stockholm U., Sweden, 1978, 82; cons., lectr. in field. Co-author: Mortality Trends in the State of Washington, 1955, The Population of Bahrain, 1978, Changing Roles of Arab Women in Bahrain, 1985; contbr. chpts. to books, articles to profl. jours. Served with U.S. Army, 1952-53. Grantee in field from numerous profl. orgns. Fellow AAAS, Am. Sociol. Assn. (conf. com. 1963); mem. Internat. Union Sci. Study of Population, Population Assn. Am., Pacific Sociol. Assn. (adv. council 1965-68), Alpha Kappa Delta, Lambda Alpha. Office: Population Research Lab 3716 S Hope St Los Angeles CA 90007

VAN BROCKLIN, JUDITH BURNS, education educator; b. Los Angeles, Aug. 14, 1942; d. Ralph Harold and Esther (Posner) B.; children: Kyle, Gregory, David; m. Bruce James Van Brocklin, Sept. 1, 1979. BA in Edn., UCLA, 1964; MA in Spl. Edn., St. Mary's Coll., Moraga, Calif., 1980; EdD in Curriculum and Instruction, U. San Francisco, 1985. Tchr. Los Angeles and Beverly Hills (Calif.) elem. schs., 1964-67; cons., instr. and program developer San Jose, Calif., 1973-76; resource tchr. Murray Sch. Dist., Dublin, Calif., 1976; resource and reading specialist, cons. San Ramon Valley Schs., Danville, Calif., 1976-84; program rev. trainer Office Spl. Edn. Calif. Dept. Edn., Sacramento, 1982; asst. prof. edn. San Jose State U., 1984-86; program adminstr. II spl. edn. Contra Costa County, Calif., 1986—; spl. edn. and curriculum cons. to sch. dists. and pubs., Calif. Author: The Effects of Vigilance Stimuli, 1985; contbr. articles to profl. jours. Grantee Packard Found., 1984. Mem. Am. Ednl. Research Assn., Assn. Supervision and Curriculum Devel., Internat. Reading Assn., Calif. Reading Assn. (hon.), Council for Exceptional Children, UCLA Alumni Assn. (chmn. govtl. relations com. higher edn., mem. scholarship and advisory com.), Calif. Club (pres.), Save San Francisco Bay, Phi Delta Kappa. Club: Bay Area Bruins (San Francisco) (chmn. govtl. relations com. 1985—). Avocations: sailing, tennis, cooking, writing. Home: 5054 Blackhawk Dr Danville CA 94526 Office: Contra Costa County Office Edn 75 Santa Barbara Rd Pleasant Hill CA 94523

VAN CAMP, JULIE CHARLOTTE, academic administrator; b. Davenport, Iowa, June 5, 1947; s. Leon A. and Helen A. (Sander) Van C. AB cum laude, Mt. Holyoke Coll., 1969; JD cum laude, Georgetown U., 1980; PhD, Temple U., 1982. Bar: D.C. 1980, Calif. 1986. Tchr. philosophy various orgns., 1971-75; environ. protection specialist EPA, Washington, 1975-77; program office NEH, Washington, 1977-85; dir. sponsored research Calif. State U., Los Angeles, 1985—. Articles in field. Fellow Temple U., 1969-73. Mem. ABA (chmn. com. on pictorial, graphic, sculptural and choreographic works sect. trademark and copyrigth law 1986—), D.C. Bar Assn., Calif. Bar Assn., Vol. Lawyers for the Arts, Am. Soc. Aesthetics. Home: 4589 Via Marisol #162 Los Angeles CA 90042 Office: Calif State U 5151 State U Dr Los Angeles CA 90032

VANCE, CARRIE TEMPLE, nurse; b. Jackson, Miss., Nov. 20, 1944. A.A. in Nursing, San Joaquin Delta Coll., Stockton, Calif., 1974; BA in Health Service Adminstrn., St. Mary's Coll., Moraga, Calif., 1978; MS in Nursing Adminstrn. and Music, PhD in Music Performance, Columbia Pacific U., 1985. Lic. nurse, Calif. Staff nurse Dameron Hosp., Stockton, Calif., 1976-77, charge nurse, 1977-80, supr. nursery, 1980—. Mem. San Joaquin Gen. Hosp. Delta Coll. Nurse Alumni Assn., Soc. Nursing Service Adminstrs., Nat. Assn. Female Execs., Columbia Pacific U. Alumni Assn., Nat. Assn. Neonatal Nurses, St. Mary's Coll. Alumni Assn. Seventh-day Adventist. Office: Dameron Hosp Assn 525 W Acacia St Stockton CA 95203

VAN CITTERS, ROBERT LEE, medical educator, physician; b. Alton, Iowa, Jan. 20, 1926; s. Charles and Wilhemina (Heemstra) Van C.; m. Mary E. Barker, Apr. 9, 1949; children: Robert, Mary, David, Sara. A.B., U. Kans., 1949; M.D., U. Kans. Med. Ctr., Kansas City, 1953; Sc.D. hon., Northwestern Coll., Orange City, Iowa, 1977. Intern U. Kans. Med. Ctr., Kansas City, 1953-54, resident, 1955-57, fellow, 1957-58; research fellow Sch. Medicine, U. Wash., Seattle, 1958-61, asst. prof. physiology and biophysics, 1962-65, assoc. prof, 1965-70, prof., 1970—; prof. medicine Sch. Medicine, U. Wash., 1970—, assoc. dean Sch. Medicine, 1968-70, dean Sch. Medicine, 1970-81; mem. staff Scripps Clinic and Research Found., La Jolla, Calif., 1961-62; exchange scientist joint U.S.-U.S.S.R. Sci. Exchange, 1962; mem. Liason Commn. on Med. Edn., Washington, 1981-85; mem. nat. adv. research council NIH, Bethesda, Md., 1980-83; mem. Va. Spl. Med. Adv. Commn., 1974-78, chmn., 1976-78; mem. various com.s NIH, Bethesda, Md. Contbr. numerous articles to profl. jours. Bd. dirs. Pacific Sci. Ctr., Seattle; bd. dirs. Wash. State Heart Assn. Served to 1st lt. U.S. Army, 1943-46, PTO; to capt. M.C., USAF, 1953-55. Recipient research career devel. USPHS. Fellow AAAS; mem. Assn. Am. Med. Colls. (adminstrv. bd. and exec. council 1972-78, Disting. Service mem.), Am. Coll. Cardiology (Cummings medal 1970), Nat. Acad. Sci. Inst. Medicine, Am. Heart Assn., Wash. State Med. Assn. (hon. life). Club: Rainier (Seattle). Home: Edmonds WA 98020 Office: U Wash Seattle WA 98195

VAN CLEAVE, PHILIP FORD, naturalist; b. Urbana, Ill., Aug. 14, 1920; s. Harley Jones and Bernice (Ford) Van C; student U. Ill., 1938-40, U. Ariz., 1942; m. Winifred Louise Evans, May 21, 1950; children—Kent Bowen, Katherine Mary Van Cleave Parris, Lorna Louise. Acting custodian Wupatki Nat. Monument, Ariz., Nat. Park Service Dept. Interior, 1943-46, park ranger Lake Mead Recreation Area, Nev., 1946-47, archeologist Mesa Verde Nat. Park, Colo., 1947-56, chief park naturalist Petrified Forest Nat. Park, Ariz., 1956-64, chief park naturalist Carlsbad Caverns Nat. Park, N.Mex., 1964-68, chief interpretation and resource mgmt., 1968-71, chief tech. services, 1971-73, staff interpretive and environ. specialist, 1973-76, ret. Bd. advisers S.E. N.Mex. Regional Library. Recipient Meritorious Service award Dept. Interior, 1977. Mem. Southeastern N.Mex. Hist. Soc. (pres. 1971, 78-79, treas. 1980-82), Carlsbad Arts and Humanities Alliance (v.p. 1977-81), Early Am. Coppers Club, Am. Numismatic Assn., Cave Research Found. (hon.). Author: (with Lancaster, Pinkley and Watson) Archeological Excavations in Mesa Verde National Park, Colorado, 1950, 54; Contbg. author The Arms of Ethan Allen and Associates. Home: 1505 Westridge Rd Carlsbad NM 88220

VANDEGAER, SISTER PAULA, social worker; b. Kansas City, Mo., Feb. 14, 1936; d. Thomas James and Lillian Loretta (Lynn) V. BA, Immaculate Heart Coll., 1963; MSW, Cath. U. Am., 1965. Dir. br. Cath. Youth Orgn., Canoga Park, Calif., 1968-71; supr. casework Holy Family Services, Los Angeles, 1971-73; treas., first counselor Sisters of Social Services, Los Angeles, 1973-78; dir. br. Alternatives to Abortion, Internat., Los Angeles, 1978-85; exec. dir. Internat. Life Services, Inc., Los Angeles, 1985—. Editor Heartbeat mag., 1978-85, Living World mag., 1985—; contbr. articles to mags. and jours., 1978—. Presenter pregnancy/abortion-issue workshops worldwide, 1970—; founder 7 Right-to-Life/Pregnancy Ctrs., Los Angeles, Orange and Ventura, Calif., 1970-76; cons. Pro-Life counseling groups, 1978—; testifier Calif. Legislature, Sacramento, U.S. Senate, Washington. Mem. Nat. Orgn. Social Workers, Nat. Orgn. Christian Social Workers, Nat. Assn. Social Workers (cert.), Acad. Lic. Clin. Social Workers. Republican. Mem. Ch. Sisters Social Service. Avocations: music, art, reading, piano, guitar. Office: Internat Life Services Inc 260 1/2 W 8th St Los Angeles CA 90057

VAN DE KAMP, JOHN KALAR, state attorney general; b. Pasadena, Calif., Feb. 7, 1936; s. Harry and Georgie (Kalar) Van de K.; m. Andrea Fisher, Mar. 11, 1978; 1 dau., Diana. B.A., Dartmouth U., 1956; J.D., Stanford U., 1959. Bar: Calif. 1960. Asst. U.S. atty. Los Angeles, 1960-66, U.S. atty., 1966-67; spl. asst. Pres.'s Commn. on Campus Unrest, 1970; dep. dir. Exec. Office for U.S. Attys., Washington, 1967-68, dir., 1968-69; fed. pub. defender for Los Angeles 1971-75; dist. atty. Los Angeles County, 1975-83; atty. gen. State of Calif., 1983—; mem. Commn. on Jud. Appointments, Peace Officers Standards and Tng. Commn. Mem. Calif. Dist. Attys. Assn. (past pres.), Nat. Dist. Attys. Assn. (past v.p.), Peace Officers Assn. Los Angeles County (past pres.), Nat. Assn. Attys. Gen. (mem. exec. com.), Conf. Western Attys. Gen. (pres. 1986). Office: Office of Attorney General 3580 Wilshire Blvd Suite 800 Los Angeles CA 90010

VANDENBERG, EDWIN JAMES, chemistry educator, researcher; b. Hawthorne, N.J., Sept. 13, 1918; s. Albert J. and Alida C. (Westerhoff) V.; m. Mildred Elizabeth Wright, Sept. 9, 1950; children: David James, Jean Elizabeth. M.E. with distinction, Stevens Inst. Tech., 1939, Dr.Engring. (hon.), 1965. Research chemist Hercules Inc. Research Ctr., Wilmington, Del., 1939-44, asst. shift supr. Sunflower Ordnance Works, Kans., 1944-45, research chemist Research Ctr., Wilmington, 1945-57, sr. research chemist, 1958-64, research assoc., 1965-77, sr. research assoc., 1978-82; adj. prof. chemistry Ariz. State U., Tempe, 1983—. Author: Polyethers, 1975; Coordination Polymerization, 1983; Contemporary Topics in Polymer Science V, 1984. Patentee in field. Mem. adv. bd. Jour. Polymer Sci., 1967—, Macromolecules, 1979-81. Mem. Am. Chem. Soc. (councillor Del. sect. 1974-81, chmn. 1976, chmn. div. polychemistry 1979, coordinator indsl. sponsors 1982—, Del. sect. award 1965, Polymer Chemistry award 1981, Exceptional Service award 1983). Home: 16223 Inca Ave Fountain Hills AZ 85268 Office: Ariz State U Dept Chemistry Tempe AZ 85287

VANDENBERGHE, RONALD GUSTAVE, accountant, real estate developer; b. Oakland, Calif., July 1, 1937; s. Anselm Henri and Margaret B. (Bygum) V.; B.A. with honors, San Jose State Coll., 1959; postgrad. U. Calif. at Berkeley Extension, 1959-60, Golden Gate Coll., 1961-63; CPA, Calif.; m. Patricia W. Dufour, Aug. 18, 1957; children: Camille, Mark, Matthew. Real estate investor, pres. VandenBerghe Fin. Corp., Pleasanton, Calif., 1964—. Instr. accounting U. Cal., Berkeley, 1963-70; CPA, Pleasanton, 1963—. Served with USAF. Mem. Calif. Soc. CPAs. Republican. Presbyterian. Mason (Shriner). Home: PO Box 803 Danville CA 94526 Office: 20 Happy Valley Rd Pleasanton CA 94566

VANDENBURGH, WILLIAM GEORGE, physical education educator; b. Seattle, July 24, 1924; s. George Henry and Eva Mae (Wenger) V.; m. Rita C. Simon, Aug. 22, 1953; 1 child, Laura. BS, U. Wash., 1949, MS, 1950; EdD, Columbia U., 1953. Prof. Fresno (Calif.) State U., 1953-60; prof. Calif. State U., Hayward, 1960-65, exec. dean, 1965-84, prof., 1984—. Mem. Alameda County Juvenile Justice Com., Oakland, Calif, 1972; pres. Eden Housing Com., Hayward, 1984—; pres. 14th dist. Dem. Assembly, Hayward, 1982-85; bd. dirs. Bay Area United Way, 1984, Eden Youth Ctr., Hayward, 1978—. Mem. N. Am. Soc. for Sport History, Internat. Assn. for Health, Physical Edn., Recreation and Dance, Calif. Assn. for Health, Physical Edn., Recreation and Dance, Nat. Assn. of Physical Educators for Higher Edn., Phi Kappa Phi, Phi Delta Kappa. Democrat. Avocation: tennis. Home: 3972 Amyx Ct Hayward CA 94542 Office: Calif State U Hayward CA 94542

VAN-DEN-NOORT, STANLEY, physician, educator; b. Lynn, Mass., Sept. 8, 1930; s. Judokus and Hazel G. (Van Blarcom) van den N.; m. June Le Clere, Apr. 17, 1954; children—Susanne, Eric, Peter, Katherine, Elizabeth. A.B., Dartmouth, 1951; M.D., Harvard, 1954. Intern, then resident Boston City Hosp. Med. Center, 1954-56; resident neurology Boston City Hosp., 1958-60; research fellow neurochemistry Harvard, 1960-62; instr. medicine Case Western Res. U., Cleve., 1962-66; asst. prof. Case Western Res. U., 1966-69, assoc. prof., 1969-70; prof. neurology U. Calif., Irvine, 1970—; chief dept. neurology U. Calif., 1970-72, assoc. dean Coll. Medicine, 1972-73, dean, 1973-85; mem. cons. staff St. Joseph Hosp., U. Calif., Irvine Med. Center; mem. cons. staffs Long Beach (Calif.) Meml. Hosp., Long Beach VA Hosp., Children's Hosp. of Orange County. Mem. med. adv. bds. Orange County Epilepsy Soc., 1971—; mem. med. adv. bds. Nat. Multiple Sclerosis Soc./Myasthenia Gravis, 1971—, Orange County chpt. Nat. Multiple Sclerosis Soc., 1971—; mem. Orange County Health Planning Council, 1971-85. Served to lt. MC USNR, 1956-58. Fellow A.C.P.; mem. AAUP, Am. Acad. Neurology, Am. Neurol. Assn., Am. Assn. Neurol. Surgeons, Calif. Med. Assn., AMA Am. Cancer Soc., Am. Heart Assn., Nat. Com. for Research in Neurological and Communicative Diseases (chmn.). Home: 17592 Orange Tree Tustin CA 92680 Office: U Calif Coll of Medicine Irvine CA 92717

VANDERBEEK, MARK PATRICK, data processing administrator; b. Ft. Mead, Md., Sept. 27, 1960; s. Carlton Eugene Vanderbeek and Joan Anne (Fasani) Mills. Student, Cambridge (Eng.) U., 1978, U. Calif., Santa Barbara, 1979-80, Los Angeles Harbor Coll., 1981-82; AS in Computer Sci., Santa Barbara City Coll., 1983. Computer operator, programmer Dripcut Corp., Santa Barbara, Calif., 1983, mgr. data processing, 1983—; cons. Personal Software Design, Santa Barbara, 1984—. Mem. U.S. Soccer Fedn., So. Calif. Soccer Ofcls. Assn., Nat. Intercollegiate Soccer Ofcls. Assn., Referees Assn. United Kingdom, Santa Barbara Soccer Referees Assn. (sec., bd. dirs. 1985—, v.p. 1986—), Pacific Assn. Coll. and Univ. Residence Halls (editor newsletter 1979), U. Calif. at Santa Barbara Residence Halls Assn. (treas. 1979, editor newsletter 1978). Roman Catholic. Office: Dripcut Corp 400 Rutherford St Goleta/Santa Barbara CA 93117

VAN DER BIJL, WILLEM, meteorology educator; b. Alphen, The Netherlands, Aug. 15, 1920; came to U.S., 1956; s. Coenraad Johannes and Hillegonda Maria (Evenblij) Van Der B.; m. Godefrieda Judith Lemkes, Sept. 24, 1946; children: Joan Elizabeth, Baldwin John William. BS, Free U., Amsterdam, The Netherlands, 1941, MS, 1943; PhD, State U., Utrecht, The Netherlands, 1952. Research assoc. Royal Netherlands Meteorol. Inst., de Bilt, 1946-56; prof. meteorology Kans. State U., Manhattan, 1956-61, Naval Postgrad. Sch., Monterey, Calif., 1961—. Author: Long Range Weather Forecasts, 1951, Statistics in Climatology, 1952; contbg. author: Academic American Encyclopedia, 1980. Fellow U. Chgo., 1954-55. Mem. Am. Meterol. Soc., Am. Geophys. Union., Naval Postgrad. Sch. Soccer Club, Sigma Chi. Home: 791 Toyon Dr Monterey CA 93940-4226 Office: Naval Postgrad Sch Dept Meteorology Monterey CA 93943-5000

VANDERFORD, FRANK JOSIRE, engineer; b. Moose Lake, Minn., Oct. 19, 1921; s. William and Mary (Flaa) V.; m. Eleanor Marie Gibis, Feb. 8, 1945; children: Constance, Gail, Deborah. Cert. in Electronics, U. Minn., 1952. Engr. Remington Rand Univac, St. Paul, 1955-59, Collins Radio Co., Newport Beach, Calif., 1959-69, Control Data Corp., Santa Ana, Calif., 1969-71; staff engr. Hughes Aircraft Co., Fullerton, Calif., 1971—. Served with USN, 1940-46. Mem. Nat. Rep. Senatorial Com., U.S. Senatorial Club, Rep. Presdl. Task Force (charter), Nat. Rifle Assn. Mem. Assembly of God Ch. Avocations: mini horse rancher, sports car restoration, camping, music. Office: Hughes Aircraft Co 1901 W Malvern St Fullerton CA 92634

VANDERHOEF, LARRY NEIL, university administrator; b. Perham, Minn., Mar. 20, 1941; s. Wilmar James and Ida Lucille (Wothe) V.; m. Rosalie Suzanne Slifka, Aug. 31, 1963; children: Susan Marie, Jonathan Lee. B.S., U. Wis., Milw., 1964, M.S., 1965; Ph.D., Purdue U., 1969. Postdoctorate U. Wis., Madison, 1969-70; research assoc. U. Wis., summers 1970-72; asst. prof. biology U. Ill., Urbana, 1970-74; assoc. prof. U. Ill., 1974-77, prof., 1977—, head dept. plant biology, 1977-80; provost Agrl. and Life Scis., U. Md., College Park, 1980-84; exec. vice chancellor U. Calif.-Davis, 1984—; vis. investigator Carnegie Inst., 1976-77, Edinburgh (Scotland) U., 1978; cons. in field. NRC postdoctoral fellow, 1969-70; Dimond travel grantee, 1975; NSF grantee, 1972, 74, 76, 77, 78, 79; NATO grantee, 1980. Mem. AAAS, Am. Soc. Plant Physiology (bd. editors Plant Physiology 1977-82, trustee, mem. exec. com., treas. 1983—), Nat. Assn. State Univ. and Land Grant Colls. Home: 615 Francisco Pl Davis CA 95616 Office: U Calif-Davis Office of Exec Vice Chancellor Davis CA 95616

VANDER HOUWEN, BOYD ALBERT, bank communications officer; b. Yakima, Wash., Jan. 17, 1946; s. John W. and Elsie W. (Lanfear) V.; m. Loma Alene Madsen, June 27, 1970; children: Garth John, Dana Madsen. BA in Journalism, U. Mont., 1968; BA in Econs., U. Wash., 1971, MA in Communications/Bus., 1978. Editor, city hall reporter Idaho Falls (Idaho) Post-Register, 1971-72; farm bus. writer Tri-City Herald, Kennewick, Wash., 1973-74; bur. mgr., editor Yakima Valley Tri-City Herald, Sunnyside, Wash., 1974-76; editor Jour. Contemporary Bus., mgr. bus. publs. Grad. Sch. Bus. Adminstrn. U. Wash., Seattle, 1978-81; communications officer Rainier Nat. Bank, Seattle, 1981—. Mem. publs. redesign com. Hist. Seattle, 1982; mem. selection com. merit scholarship Rainier Nat. Bank, 1983; publicity chmn. United Way One to One Program, 1983, United Way Cabinet, 1982, mem. mktg. com. United Way of King County, 1984. Served with U.S. Army, 1969-71. NEH grantee, 1979; recipient Excellence in Publs. award Soc. Tech. Publs., 1979, 81. Mem. Pub. Relations Soc. Am., Internat. Assn. Bus. Communicators (Pacesetter awards com. 1981-83, internal communications award of excellence Pacific NW chpt. 1982, Silver 6 and Totem awards employee publs. Puget Sound chpt. 1983), Sigma Delta Chi (bus. writing editing awards 1971, 73, 74). Home: 8575 SE 76th Pl Mercer Island WA 98040 Office: Rainier Nat Bank PO Box 3966 Seattle WA 98124

VANDERHURST, STUART RANDALL, veterinarian, educator; b. San Francisco, Feb. 20, 1940; s. Stuart Randall and Athalea Jacquelyn (Long) V.; m. Charlotte Anne Lund, June 20, 1964; children—Dana Lynn, Stuart Randall. A.S., Coll. of San Mateo, 1960; B.S., U. Calif.-Davis, 1963, D.V.M., 1965; Diploma Vet. Clin. Sci. with distinction, Massey U., N.Z., 1983. Lic. veterinarian, Colo. Assoc. prof. vet. sci. SUNY-Delhi, 1968-73; assoc. prof. animal health Colo. Mountain Coll., Glenwood Springs, 1973-75, prof. 1975—; cons. in field. Contbr. chpts. to books. Served to capt. U.S. Army, 1966-68. Decorated Army Commendation medal; Rotary internat. scholar, 1983. Mem. AVMA, Assn. Vet. Technician Educators (sec.-treas, 1977-79), Colo. Vet. Med. Assn. Presbyterian. Home: 92 Marble Ct Carbondale CO 81623 Office: Colo Mountain Coll Vet Tech 3000 County Rd #114 Glenwood Springs CO 81601

VANDERKOLK, BARBARA ANNE, management consultant; b. Phila., Jan. 5, 1949; d. Walter William and Barbara (Jackson) Schwarz. BA, Calvin Coll., 1970; student U. Montpelier (France), 1967-68; postgrad. Cen. Wash. U. Tchr. high sch. English, Rochester, Wash., 1970-71; mem. faculty exec. mgmt. devel. program U. Wash. Grad. Sch. Pub. Affairs, 1984—; speaker commencement U. Wash. Sch. Pharmacy, 1987; speechwriter Speaker of House, Wash. Ho. of Reps., Olympia, 1972-73; lobbyist, polit. action dir. Wash. Edn. Assn., Olympia, 1974-78; pres., owner Barbara Vanderkolk & Assocs., Inc., Seattle, 1978—; gov.'s appointee State Bd. Pharmacy, 1984. Author: State Sex Equity in Education Act, 1975. Pres., Women's Polit. Caucus, 1978; dir. Seattle Voice mag., 1981-82; trustee Waldo Gen. Hosp.; vis. com. U. Wash. Sch. Psychology. Recipient B'nai B'rith award, 1966; Creative Leadership in Womens Rights award Wash. Edn. Assn., 1977; named to Seattle Times 81 Newsmakers of 1981. Mem. Nat. Assn. Female Execs., Women and Bus. (pres.-elect), Nat. Women's Polit. Caucus, World Affairs Council. Clubs: Seattle, City. Lodge: Rotary. Office: Peoples Bank Bldg 1415 Fifth Ave Suite 1000 Seattle WA 98171

VAN DER MEULEN, JOSEPH PIERRE, neurologist, medical school dean; b. Boston, Aug. 22, 1929; s. Edward Lawrence and Sarah Jane (Robertson) VanDer M.; m. Ann Irene Yadeno, June 18, 1960; children—Elisabeth, Suzanne, Janet. A.B., Boston Coll., 1950; M.D., Boston U., 1954. Diplomate: Am. Bd. Psychiatry and Neurology. Intern Cornell Med. div. Bellevue Hosp., N.Y.C., 1954-55; resident Cornell Med. div. Bellevue Hosp., 1955-56; resident Harvard U., Boston City Hosp., 1958-60, instr., fellow, 1962-66; assoc. Case Western Res. U., Cleve., 1966-67; asst. prof. Case Western Res. U., 1967-69, assoc. prof. neurology and bioned. engring., 1969-71; prof. neurology, chmn. dept. U. So. Calif., Los Angeles, 1971—; also dir. dept. neurology Los Angeles County/U. So. Calif. Med. Center; chmn. dept. U. So. Calif., 1971-78, v.p. for health affairs, 1977—, dean Sch. Medicine, 1985-86; vis. prof. Autonomous U. Guadalajara, Mex., 1974; pres. Norris Cancer Hosp. and Research Inst., 1983—. Contbr. articles to profl. jours. Mem. med. adv. bd. Calif. chpt. Myasthenia Gravis Found., 1971-75, chmn., 1974-75, 77-78; med. adv. bd. Amyotrophic Lateral Sclerosis Found., Calif., 1973-75, chmn., 1974-75; mem. Com. to Combat Huntington's Disease, 1973—; trustee Calif. Hosp. Med. Ctr., Good Hope Med. Found., Eisenhower Med. Ctr., Doheny Eye Hosp., House Ear Inst., Los Angeles Hosp. Good Samaritan, Children's Hosp. of Los Angeles. Served to lt. M.C. USNR, 1956-58. Nobel Inst. fellow Karolinska Inst., Stockholm, 1960-62; NIH grantee, 1968-71. Mem. Am. Neurol. Assn., Am. Acad. Neurology, Los Angeles Soc. Neurology and Psychiatry (pres. 1977-78), Mass., Ohio, Calif. med. socs., Los Angeles Acad. Medicine, Alpha Omega Alpha (councillor). Home: 39 Club View Ln Rolling Hills Estates CA 90274 Office: U So Calif 1985 Zonal Ave Los Angeles CA 90033

VAN DER PAS, PETER WILLIAM, scientist, historian; b. Helmond, Netherlands, Feb. 5, 1915; s. Petrus Wilhelmus and Gerarda Johanna (Kroese) V.; came to U.S., 1946; naturalized, 1958; M.S. in Physics, Inst. Tech., Delft, Netherlands; m. Mary Katherine Durr, Aug. 6, 1947 (dec. Oct. 1983); children—Margaret Mary, Elisabeth Katherine, Peter William; m. Priscilla L. Kepfer, Aug. 18, 1984. Asst. Inst. Tech., Delft, 1940-43; research and devel. engr. Royal Dutch Shell, The Hague and San Francisco, 1943-50; founder 1st Netherlands Bomb Disposal Co., 1944; process design engr. Ralph M. Parsons Co., Los Angeles, 1950-57; staff scientist Holmes and Narver, Inc., Los Angeles, 1957-67; dir. Pacific Library History of Sci. and Tech., 1976—. Served as lt. Netherlands Army, 1937-38, 39-40. Recipient Mendel medal, Japan, 1965. Mem. History of Sci. Soc., Soc. for the History of Tech., Netherlands Hist. Soc., Netherlands Soc. for History of Sci. San Diego, Nevada County hist. socs., Math. Assn. Am. Republican. Author: In Search of the Original Californian; Herman ten Kate's Expedition to Baja California, 1883-1884, 1977, articles to profl. jours. Home: 212 Hill St Grass Valley CA 95945 Office: Pacific Library History Sci/Tech Mt St Mary's Grass Valley CA 95945

VANDER SCHALIE, PAUL HENDRICK, viticulturist and vintager; b. Patterson, N.J., Oct. 13, 1949; s. Harry Hans and Marion (Hunter) V.S.; m. Peyton Carol McMahon, Feb. 15, 1975 (div. Apr. 1982); 1 child, Summer Peyton. Student, Coll. of Marin, 1971-72, Santa Rosa Jr. Coll., 1975-77; BS in Plant Sci., U. Calif., Davis, 1980. Winery worker Korbel Champaign Cellars, Guerneville, Calif., 1976-78; vineyard mgr. P. Sledge Vineyards, Guerneville; vineyard supr. Beringer Winery, St. Helena, Calif., 1980-83, Charles Krug Winery, St. Helena, 1983—; tchr. Santa Rosa (Calif.) Jr. Coll., 1981—; viticultural cons. Sugarloaf Farming Corp., Calistoga, Calif., 1982—. Mem. ligistics com. Napa Valley Wine Auction, St. Helena, 1985; exec. com., co-founder Sonoma County Vineyard Tech. Group, 1981—; mem. Napa Vineyard Tech. Group, 1980—. Mem. Am. Soc. Viticulture and Enology, Ducks Unltd. (St. Helena chpt. organizational com.). Avocations: tennis, jogging, skiing, jet skiing. Home: 3268 Ehlers Ln Saint Helena CA 94574 Office: Charles Krug Winery PO Box 191 Saint Helena CA 94574

VANDERSTAY, OTTO RANDOLPH, electronic engineer; b. Houston, Jan. 17, 1933; s. Otto Randolph, Sr. and Addie Byrd (Wallingford) V.; m. Jacqueline Paulette Douchet, Oct. 6, 1968; children—Natalie Michelle, Rachelle Monique. Student U. Tex., 1950-51, U. Houston, 1957. Engr. various cos., Ger. and Calif., 1956-68; owner, mfr.'s rep. Van Ness Assocs., Glendale, Calif., 1968-74; br. service mgr. Honeywell, Inc., Los Angeles, 1974-76; owner, mfr. Evaporation Apparatus Inc., Los Angeles, 1976-77; nat. service mgr. Vitek Systems, Pasadena, Calif., 1977-78; sr. engr. DuPont Instruments, Pasadena, 1978-79; dir. electronic engring. Children's Hosp. Los Angeles, 1980—; cons. analytical instrumentation Jet Propulsion Labs., DuPont Instruments, Pasadena. Mem. U.S. Congressional Adv. Bd., 1983; sustaining mem. Republican Nat. Com., 1982-83. Served with USAF, 1953-

61; to capt. Calif. State Mil. Res., 1981—. Mem. Res. Officers Assn. U.S., N.G. Assn. Calif., Assn. Advancement Med. Instrumentation, Assn. Field Service Mgrs., Alliance Francaise, French War Vets. Designed Air Force temp. hangar, Anchorage. Home: 1700 E Glenoaks Blvd Glendale CA 91206 Office: Children's Hospital Los Angeles 4650 Sunset Blvd Los Angeles CA 90027

VANDERVEST, JAN ANN, investment services counselor; b. Casco, Wis., July 25, 1934; d. Emil and Mabel (Gigot) V.; BS, U. Wis., Stevens Point, 1959; MSW, Cath. U. Am., 1968. With YWCA, 1961-83, recreation dir., Green Bay, Wis., 1961-66, br. dir., Hartford, Conn., 1968-75, assoc. dir., Rochester, N.Y., 1975-77, exec. dir., San Jose, Calif., 1977-83, dist. mgr., 1983—; NOW sit. mgr. Money Concepts Fin. Ctr., Campbell, Calif.; treas. United Way Execs., 1978-80, tech. com. for services, 1980; adv. bd. Women's Residence Ctr., San Jose, 1978-81, Career Outreach for Women, 1978-81; mem. task force on womens concerns sub com. on equal worth Santa Clara County. Mem. Internat. Assn. Fin. Planners, Nat. Assn. Social Workers, Am. Soc. Tng. and Devel., Bus. and Profl. Women's Club (sec. 1983, v.p. 1984, 87), Nat. Wilderness Soc., Quota Club of San Jose (v.p. 1981-82), AAUW, Sierra Club (Women in Bus. award 1979, Outstanding Service award 1981). Office: Money Concepts Fin Ctr 2155 S Bascom Ave #102 Campbell CA 95008

VANDER VORSTE, JAMES LEROY, architect; b. Bismark, N.D., Mar. 4, 1947; s. Martin and Marjorie (Jones) Vander V.; m. Joanne Marie Carlson, June 23, 1967; 1 dau., Gwyn. B.Arch. with honors, N.D. State U., 1970. Tech. asst. Elken, Geston & Hanson, Moorhead, Minn., 1968-70; designer Foss, Engelstad, Foss, Fargo, N.D., 1970; architect Hobart D. Wagener, Assocs., Boulder, Colo., 1970-78; ptnr. Wagener/Vander Vorste, Boulder, 1978—. Mem. AIA, Constrn. Specifications Inst., Kappa Tau Delta, Tau Beta Pi, Phi Kappa Phi. Methodist. Office: Wagener Vander Vorste Architects 737 29th St Boulder CO 80303

VANDER ZALM, WILLIAM NICK, government official; b. Noordwykerhout, Holland, May 29, 1934; came to Canada, 1947; s. Wilhelmus Nicholaas and Agatha C. (Warmerdam) van der Zalm; m. Lillian Vander Zalm, June 27, 1956; children: Jeffrey, Juanita, Wim, Lucia. Student pub. schs., Holland and Canada. Pres. Art Knapp Nurseries Ltd., 1956—; alderman Surrey Mcpl. Council, 1965-69, mayor, 1969-75; Minister of Human Resources Provincial Legis. for Social Credit Party, 1975-78; Minister Mcpl. Affairs and Minister of Urban Transit Authority B.C., 1978-82; Minister of Edn. and Minister responsible for B.C. Transit 1982-83; founder Fantasy Garden World, Richmond, Can., 1983; Premier of B.C. and leader of B.C. Social Credit Party Victoria, BC, Can., 1986—. Mem. B.C. C. of C. (pres. 1986). Roman Catholic. Avocations: gardening, fishing, soccer. Home: 19003-88 Ave, Surrey, BC Canada V3S 5X7 Office: Office of Premier, Legis Bldgs, Victoria, BC Canada V8V 4R3

VANDEVENTER, JANICE LEIGH, cartographer, flight instructor; b. Long Beach, Calif., Aug. 10, 1944; d. Owen Jerome and Laurence Elizabeth (Monninger) V.; B.A. in Geography, UCLA, 1966. Cartographer, Automobile Club So. Calif., Los Angeles, 1966-70, sr. cartographer, 1970-72, research coordinator, 1972-74, chief cartographer, supr. 1974—; flight instr. Falcon Air, Long Beach, 1975—. Recipient FAA Safety Pin, 1974. Mem. Am. Congress Surveying and Mapping, Nat. Computer Graphics Assn., Los Angeles Area C. of C., Aircraft Owners and Pilots Assn., Sweet Adelines, Goldenaires Quartet (lead singer, group named novice quartet champions 1982), UCLA Alumni Assn., Alpha Xi Delta. Home: 5141 E Burnett St Long Beach CA 90815 Office: Automobile Club So Calif 2601 S Figueroa St Los Angeles CA 90007

VAN DE WATER, SANDRA MANFIELD, audiologist; b. Cleve., Feb. 2, 1947; d. Jack Albert and Elsie Jane (Close) Mansfield; m. Gordon Budd Van De Water, Apr. 1, 1966; children: Julie Beth, Adam Michael. Student, St. Lawrence U., 1964-66, U. Mich., 1967; BA, SUNY, Potsdam, 1972; MS, Syracuse U., 1975. Clin. audiologist Otolaryngology Assn., Chestnut Hill, Pa., 1977-81; dir. audiology Colo. Ear Clinic, Denver, 1981-86, Denver Ear Assn., 1986—; cons. Colo. Otologic Research Ctr., Denver, 1982-86; co-dir. Denver Metro Area Audiology Group, 1984—. Contbr. articles to profl. jours. Mem. Am. Speech-Lang.-Hearing Assn., Colo. Speech-Lang.-Hearing Assn. Home: 8145 S Adams Way Littleton CO 80122 Office: Denver Ear Assn 2005 Franklin St Denver CO 80205

VAN DRESER, MERTON LAWRENCE, ceramic engineer; b. Des Moines, June 5, 1929; s. Joseph Jerome and Victoria (Love) Van D.; m. Evelyn Lenore Manny, July 12, 1952; children—Peter, Jennifer Sue. B.S. in Ceramic Engring., Iowa State U., 1951. Tech. supt. Owens-Corning Fiberglas Corp., Kansas City, Mo., 1954-57; research engr. Kaiser Aluminum & Chem. Corp., Milpitas, Calif., 1957-60; research sect. head Kaiser Aluminum & Chem. Corp., 1960-63, lab. mgr., 1963-65, assoc. dir. research, 1965-69; dir. refractories research Kaiser Aluminum & Chem. Corp., Pleasanton, Calif., 1969-72; dir. non-metallic materials research Kaiser Aluminum & Chem. Corp., 1972-83; v.p., dir. research Indsl. Chem. div. and Harshaw/Filtrol Partnership Kaiser Aluminum & Chem. Corp., Cleve., 1983-85; dir. bus. devel. Kaiser Aluminum & Chem. Corp., Pleasanton, 1985—; mem. adv. bd. dept. ceramic engring. U. Ill., 1974-78; chmn. tech. adv. com. Refractories Inst., 1980-84; mem. nat. materials adv. bd. Nat. Acad. Sci.; mem. Indsl. Research Inst. Contbr. articles to sci. jours. Sustaining membership chmn. local dist. Boy Scouts Am., 1980; pres. PTA, 1967-68. Served as aviator, C.E. U.S. Army, 1951-54. Recipient Profl. Achievement citation Iowa State U., 1978. Fellow Am. Ceramic Soc. (v.p. 1973-74); mem. ASTM (hon.; com.), Brit. Ceramic Soc., Nat. Inst. Ceramic Engrs., Keramos (pres. 1976-78, herald 1980-84, Greaves Walker Roll of Honor award), Metall. Soc., AIME. Lodges: Rotary (Paul Harris fellow), Masons. Patentee in field. Office: Kaiser Aluminum & Chem Corp 6177 Sunol Blvd Pleasanton CA 94566

VAN DYCK, MICHAEL, dentist; b. San Antonio, June 23, 1949; s. Louis Morris Van Dyck and Kathleen (Woodard) Thibodeaux; m. Janet Lynn Pastell, Aug. 20, 1977. B.S. (Duff scholar), Tex. A&M U., 1972; D.D.S. (Mosbey award), Baylor U., 1975. Gen. practice dentistry, Manhattan Beach, Calif., 1976—; advisor Centienella South-Bay Dental Assts. Soc., 1978-79; dental edn. advisor South Coast Regional Occupational Ctr., 1980—. Elder Neighborhood Ch., Palos Verdes, Calif., 1977-80; treas. South Bay Medal of Valor Com., 1978-80. Recipient service award Los Angeles County Bd. Suprs., 1982, archtl. design award City of Manhattan Beach, 1984. Mem. ADA, Calif. Dental Soc., Western Dental Soc. (bd. dirs. 1978-80, ethics com. 1978-81, lab. relations chmn., dental care chmn. 1978-79, table clinics chmn. 1979-80, peer rev. com. 1983—), Acad. Gen. Dentistry, Am. Acad. Periodontology, So. Calif. Quest Dental Study Group (founder, pres. 1981-82), Manhattan Beach C. of C. (bd. dirs. 1977-83, 84—, 2d v.p. 1979-80, 1st v.p. 1980-81, pres. 1981-82). Republican.

VANDYKE, JILL, geophysicist; b. Douglas, Mich., Apr. 11, 1954; d. Arthur John VanDyke and Suzanne (Leonard) Simmons. BA in Geophysics, Hope Coll., 1976; MS in Geophysics, U. Minn., 1979. Geophysicist Gulf Oil, Houston, 1979-81, exploration geophysicist, 1981, petroleum geophysicist, 1981-82, sr. geophysicist, 1982-84, project geophysicist, 1984-85; geophysicist Chevron U.S.A., San Ramon, Calif., 1985—. Recipient Bausch & Lombe Sci. award, 1972, Pres. scholarship, 1972-76; named one of Notable Women of Tex., 1984. Mem. Soc. Exploration Geophysicists, Am. Assn. Petroleum Geologists, Geophys. Soc. Houston, Geol. Soc. Houston, Bay Area Geophys. Soc., Geol. Soc. Am. Avocations: painting, organ, stained glass, photography, crafts. Office: Chevron Park San Ramon CA 94583

VANE, SYLVIA BRAKKE, anthropologist, cultural resource management company executive; b. Fillmore County, Minn., Feb. 28, 1918; d. John T. and Hulda Christina (Marburger) Brakke; m. Arthur Bayard Vane, May 17, 1942; children—Ronald Arthur, Linda, Laura Vane Spooner. A.A., Rochester Jr. Coll., 1937; B.S. with distinction, U. Minn., 1939; student Radcliffe Coll., 1944; M.A., Calif. State U.-Hayward, 1975. Med. technologist Dr. Frost and Hodapp, Willmar, Minn., 1939-41; head labs. Corvallis Gen. Hosp., Oreg., 1941-42; dir. lab. Cambridge Gen. Hosp., Mass., 1942-43, Peninsula Clinic, Redwood City, Calif., 1947-49; v.p. Cultural Systems Research, Inc., Menlo Park, Calif., 1978—; pres. Ballena Press, Menlo Park, 1981—; cons. cultural resource mgmt. So. Calif. Edison Co., Rosemead, 1978-81, San Diego Gas and Elec. Co., 1980-83, Pacific Gas and Elec. Co., San Francisco, 1982-83, Wender, Murase & White, Washington, 1983—, Yosemite Indians, Mariposa, Calif., 1982-84, San Luis Rey Band of Mission Indians, Escondido, Calif., 1986—, U.S. Ecology, Newport Beach, Calif., 1986. Author: (with L.J. Bean), California Indians, Primary Resources, 1977, The Cahuilla and the Santa Rosa Mountains, 1981. Contbr. chpts. to several books. Bd. dirs. Sequoia Area council Girl Scouts U.S., 1954-61; bd. dirs., v.p., pres. LWV, S. San Mateo County, Calif., 1960-65, cons. San Francisco council Girl Scouts U.S., 1962-69, Riverside County Flood Control and Water Conservation Dist., 1985—. Fellow Soc. Applied Anthropology; mem. Southwestern Anthrop. Assn. (program chmn. 1976-78, newsletter editor 1976-79), Am. Anthropology Assn., Soc. for Am. Archaeology. Mem. United Ch. of Christ. Office: Ballena Press 823 Valparaiso Ave Menlo Park CA 94025

VAN FLEET, BRIDGET BELLE, police department administrator; b. Gorham, Ill., Mar. 29, 1933; d. Henry Earl and Mathilda (Shields) Gale; m. Floyd J. Van Fleet Sr., Apr. 14, 1952; children: Monica, Floyd J. Jr., Rita, Ronald, Katherine. ATA in Secretarial Sci., Lower Columbia Coll., Longview, Wash., 1976; BSBA, City Coll., Seattle, 1981. Policewoman, clk. Longview Police Dept., 1969-75, policewoman, adminstrv. sec., 1975-83, records supr., 1983. Rec. sec. Cowlitz Cen. Rep. Com., Longview, 1980; active Am. Cancer Soc. Recipient Appreciation award Am. Cancer Soc., Longview, 1985, Teams Steering Com., Longview, 1985. Mem. Law Enforcement Info. and Records Assn. (bd. dirs., sec. Olympia chpt. 1985-86), Longview Police Benefit Assn. (treas. 1982-83). Roman Catholic. Club: Toastmasters (Longview)(treas. 1984-85). Avocations: interior decorating, landscaping, running. Home: 2824 Maryland Longview WA 98632 Office: Longview Police Dept PO Box 128 Longview WA 98632

VAN FLEET, WILLIAM MABRY, architect; b. Point Richmond, Calif., Jan. 22, 1915; s. Harvey Lorenz and Allie O'Dell (Taylor) Van F.; A.B., U. Calif., Berkeley, 1938; m. Colette Sims, Apr. 26, 1940; children—Christine, Ellen, Peter. Pvt. practice architecture, Eureka, Calif., 1951—; lectr. design Humboldt (Calif.) State U., 1965-66; ptnr. William & Colette Van Fleet, 1954—; prin. works include: Del Norte County Courthouse and Library, Crescent City, Calif., 1957, Freshwater (Calif.) Elementary Sch., 1954, Lee residence, Sunnybrae, Calif., 1962, Zane Jr. High Sch., Eureka, 1965, offices for Brooks-Scanlon Lumber Co., Bend, Oreg., 1967. Chmn., No. Humboldt Vocat. Council, 1964-65, Humboldt County Scenic Resources Com., 1965; pres. Humboldt-Del Norte Mental Health Soc., 1970-71; mem. Humboldt County Community Services Ctr. 1970, Humboldt Arts Council, 1970, Humboldt County Energy Adv. Com., 1979; chmn. Eureka Beautification Com., 1969, Humboldt Sr. Retirement Homes Com., 1979—; bd. dirs. Humboldt County Assn. Retarded Children, 1960-68, Humboldt Family Service Ctr., 1970, Redwoods United Workshop, 1973, Open Door Clinic, 1973, Coordinating Council Human Services Humboldt County, 1976, Calif.-Oreg. Community Devel. Soc., 1980—; mem. Humboldt Energy Adv. Com., 1980—, Eureka City Housing Adv. Bd., 1982. Recipient Merit award HHFA, 1964, 1st Honor award Pub. Housing Adminstrn., 1964, Gov. Calif. Design award, 1966, Outstanding Service award Far West Indian Hist. Soc., 1973, Man of Year award Redwood region Nat. Audubon Soc., 1976, resolutions of commendation Calif. State Senate and Assembly, 1982. Mem. AIA, Net Energy Assn. (dir.), Humboldt Native Plant Soc., Redwood Art Assn. (pres. 1970), Sierra Club (dir. 1972), Fifty-Plus Runners Assn. (1st place in age group Nat. Fifty-Plus Runners Meet 1981). Unitarian. Clubs: Kiwanis (pres. Eureka 1976-77; Disting. Service award 1968); Six Rivers Running (dirs., All Am. awards). Participant in various marathons and races, including Internat. Marathon, Sacramento, 1983 (1st in 65-69 age group), World Vet. Championships Marathon, Rome, Italy, 1984 (1st in U.S., 8th in World, 70-74 age group), Fifty-Plus 5 mile run, Stanford, Calif., 1985 (1st in 70-74 age group, 2d all-time nationally), others. Home: Route 1 Box 108 Eureka CA 95501 Office: 818 3d St Eureka CA 95501

VAN GYTENBEEK, RICHARD PETER, recreation organization executive; b. Paterson, N.J., Feb. 5, 1933; s. Rudolph Johann and Carrie (Rist) Van G.; m. Bette Fradd Tonge, June 18, 1955; children—Richard, Tony, Kate. B.A., Princeton, 1955. Salesman, sales mgr. Kendrick Bellary, Denver, 1958-61; br. mgr., div. mgr. Kistler/Kwill, Colorado Springs, 1961-67, Denver, 1967-69; exec. dir. Trout Unlimited, Denver, 1969-74; pres. Am. Sportsman's Club, Inc., Denver, 1975-77, Internat. Fedn. Fly Fisheries, 1983-85; v.p. Seal Furniture & Systems Inc.; pres. Chadwell Farms, Inc., 1966-69, The Office Place, Seattle; chmn. bd. United Sportsmen's Council of Colo. Author: The Way of a Trout, 1972, (with J. Michael Migrl) Streamside Conservation Guide, 1974. Pres. Colorado Springs Symphony, 1964-67; chmn. Colorado Springs Planning Commn., 1965-67; pres., founder Colorado Springs Racquet Club, 1965-67; Bd. dirs. Rocky Mountain Center on Environment, pres., 1979-82. Served to capt. AUS, 1956-58. Mem. South Park Sportsmen (chmn. bd.), Trout Unltd. (nat. dir.), Am. League Anglers (nat. dir.). Clubs: Alpine-Winter Park Ski (Denver) (v.p.); El Paso (Colorado Springs); Arapahoe Tennis (Cherry Hills, Colo.). Home: 6400 Plateau Drive Englewood CO 80110 Office: Federation of Fly Fishers PO Box 1088 West Yellowstone MT 59758

VAN HEMERT, WILLEM STEPHANUS, civil engineering consultant; b. Zaltbommel, The Netherlands, Oct. 12, 1950; s. Hendrik and Stephanie P. (Müeller) Van H.; m. Roswitha Julia Trendelenburg, Jan. 12, 1974; children: Caroline R., Ashley R., Hendrik P. BCE, U. Mich., 1972. Registered profl. engr., Alaska. Staff engr. Finkbiener, Pettis & Strout, Toledo, 1973-74; project engr. Arctic Engrs., Anchorage, 1974-75, chief engr., 1977-80; chief utility operator Atlantic Richfield Co., Anchorage and Prudhoe Bay, Alaska, 1976; prin. CRW Engring. Group, Anchorage, 1981—. Mem. Profl. Engrs. in Pvt. Practice, Alaska Water Mgmt. Assn. (com. chmn. 1984-85), Am. Pub. Works Assn. (exec. bd. 1985-86), Alaska Soc. Profl. Engrs., Fedn. Water Pollution Control. Avocations: hiking, mountain climbing, skiing, fishing, brewing beer. Office: CRW Engring Group 3900 Arctic Blvd Suite 203 Anchorage AK 99503

VAN HOLE, MILDRED MAE, manufacturer's representative; b. Littleton, Colo., Aug. 14, 1920; d. William and Ruth Belle (Pearman) DeKoevend; m. Joseph L. Van Hole, Dec. 13, 1941; children—Larry M., William R., Melanie An, Patricia L. Student Central Bus. Coll., 1938. Exec. sec. to pres. O.K. Rubber Co., 1939-45; exec. sec. The Thorson Co., Denver, 1960-80; pres. V-H Tech. Inc., Denver, 1981—. Bd. dirs. Englewood Sch., 1964-73, pres., 1971-73; mem. Southeast Met. Bd. Coop. Services, 1968-73; mem. Arapahoe County Sch. Planning commn., 1964-66; mem. Colo. State Bd. Community Colls. and Occupational Edn., 1983—. Named Bus. and Profl. Woman of Yr., Colo. Bus. and Profl. Women, 1973. Mem. Christian Ch. (Disciples of Christ). Office: V-H Tech Inc 2785 Speer Blvd Denver CO 80211

VAN HOUTEN, GENE STEVEN, industrial engineering executive; b. Chgo., June 18, 1946; s. Eugene Kazimier and Ann Geraldine (Durica) V.; m. Eileen Marie Meister, June 15, 1974; children—Steven, Heather, Kristopher. A.A., Riverside (Calif.) City Coll., 1973; student Calif. Poly. U., 1979-81; B.S., U. Redlands, 1982, M.A. in Bus. Adminstrn/Mgmt., 1983. Spl. equipment design and assembly engr. Deutsch Co., Banning, Calif., 1967-74; mgr. indsl. engring. Sunkist Growers Inc., Ontario, Calif., 1974—; gen. mgr. Digmor Engring., Redlands, Calif.; mem. Calif. Senatorial Productivity Rev. Bd. Cubmaster Boy Scouts Am., 1983. Recipient So. Calif. Edison Energy Mgmt. award, 1982; cert. of appreciation Productivity Council of S.W., 1982. Mem. Am. Concrete Inst., IEEE, Presdl. Energy Adv. Council, Am. Inst. Indsl. Engrs. (pres. Inland Empire chpt.), Nat. Council of Farmer Co-ops (rep.), Sunkist Growers Suprs. Club (pres.), Internat. Assn. Quality Circles, Assn. Standards and Research. Club: Kiwanis (Ontario and Riverside, Calif.). Democrat. Home: 5042 Red Bluff Rd Riverside CA 92503

VAN KREGTEN, ANTHONY GERARD LODEWYK WILLEM, JR., aerospace engineer, real estate broker; b. Middelburg, Netherlands, Dec. 7, 1906; s. Anthony Gerard Lodewyk Willem and Anna Hermanna (Rompelman) Van K.; came to U.S., 1953, naturalized, 1959; m. Lucille Plantenga, Sept. 26, 1935; children—Ronald, Fitzgerald. B.S., Holland Poly. U., Arnhem, 1930, M.S. in Aero. Engring., 1942. Mem. staff preliminary design Fokker Aircraft, Holland, 1931-45; asst. prof. aero. div. Delft (Holland) U., 1945-53; staff engr. Lockheed Aircraft Corp., Burbank, Calif., 1953-57, research specialist Lockheed Missile and Space Co., Sunnyvale, Calif., 1957-66; staff cons. engr., Lockheed Missile and Space Co. and Lockheed Ga. div., San Jose, Calif., 1966—; v.p. Pacific Tech. Inst., San Jose. Lic. aircraft pilot. Fellow AIAA (asso.); mem. ASTM, Am. Ordnance Assn., Aircraft Owners and Pilots Assn., Airmen's Assn. Santa Clara. Presbyn. Author: Directions Aircraft Design, 1953; Reliability Engineering Missile Systems, 1961; contbg. author Tech. Engring. Ency., 1948—; patentee antitank missile, 1965. Home: 258 Cronin Dr Santa Clara CA 95051 Office: Lockheed Missle & Space Co & Lockheed Ga div 100 N Winchester Blvd Suite 380 San Jose CA 95128

VAN KRIEDT, PHYLLIS PUBLOW, magazine publisher; b. Lansing, Mich., Dec. 12, 1921; d. Henry E. and Hazel (Powell) Publow; widowed; children; Nicolas, Mary. Student, Sweet Briar Coll., 1939-41, Katherine Gibbs Secretarial Sch., 1945-46; BA, Mich. State U., 1943; postgrad., Columbia U., 1944. Pub., editor Calif. Wineletter, Mill Valley, 1975—. Home: 76 Hillside Ave Mill Valley CA 94941 Office: Calif Wineletter PO Box 70 Mill Valley CA 94942

VAN LEEUWEN, MATTHEW JOHN, engineer; b. S'Gravenzande, The Netherlands, Jan. 30, 1942; came to U.S., 1946; s. Cornelius and Greta (Kruithof) Van L.; m. Toshiko Murata, Mar. 30, 1966; 1 child, Keith Tys. Student in mech. engring., Long Beach State Coll., 1962. Design engr., contractor various firms, 1964-71; project engr. Spectrolab Inc., Sylmar, Calif., 1971-77, Arco Solar Inc., Chatsworth, Calif., 1977-80; sr. engr. Applied Solar Energy Corp., Industry, Calif., 1980-81; sr. project engr. Hughes Aircraft Co., Long Beach, Calif., 1981—. Patentee in field. Served with USMCR, 1963-69. Recipient Excellence in Engring. Design award Design News mag., 1970. Mem. Seinan Judo Dojo. Avocations: aquatics, vehicle design and fabrication, judo. Office: Hughes Aircraft Co 2000 E Imperial Hwy El Segundo CA 90245

VAN LEEUWEN, WILLIAM HAROLD, insurance executive; b. Paducah, Ky., July 4, 1923; s. William Harold and Virginia Marie (Charles) VanL.; m. Lois Bolle, Aug. 18, 1948; children: Barbara Mullaney, Thomas M. AB, U. Ill., 1947, LLB, 1948. CPCU, CLU. Resident v.p. Sentry Ins., 1948-65; asst. v.p. Lumbermens Mut. Casualty Co. & Am. Motorists Ins. Co., Chgo., 1965-67, 2d v.p., 1967-71, v.p., 1971-73; chmn. bd. dirs., chief exec. officer Kemper Investors Life Ins., Los Angeles, 1972-76; pres., chief exec. officer Nat. Automobile and Casualty Ins. Co., Los Angeles and Pasadena, Calif., 1972—; pres. Pacific Ins. and Surety Conf. Chmn. bd. dirs. Ins. Council of Calif. for City of Hope, Los Angeles, 1986. Served to 1st lt. U.S. Army, 1943-46. Named Co. Person of Yr., Profl. Ins. Agts. Calif. and Nev., 1985. Mem. Am. Soc. Property and Casualty Underwriters Inc., Am. Coll. Life Underwriters, Assn. Calif. Ins. Co. (bd. dirs. 1986), Pacific Ins. and Surety Conf. (v.p. 1986). Clubs: Jonathan (Los Angeles); Annandale Golf (Pasadena). Office: Nat Automobile Casualty Ins Co 150 S Los Robles Ave Pasadena CA 91101

VAN LEIRSBURG, DEAN ALLEN, research chemist; b. Chicago Heights, Ill., May 24, 1940; s. Julius and Regina (Monahan) Van L. BA, St. Joseph's Coll., Rensselaer, Ind., 1962; MS, Iowa State U., 1969; PhD, Oreg. State U., 1973. Postdoctoral fellow Rice U., Houston, 1973-74; research assoc. Oreg. Grad. Ctr., Beaverton, 1974-79; research chemist Chevron Research Co., Richmond, Calif., 1979—, participating fellow Soviet Am. Exchange, 1974. contbr. articles to profl. jours.; patentee in field. Mem. Am. Chem. Soc., Sigma Xi. Democrat. Roman Catholic. Home: 1047 Helen Ct Petaluma CA 94952

VAN LEUVEN, ARTHUR EDWIN, JR., financial services executive; b. Redlands, Calif., Nov. 13, 1925; s. Arthur Edwin and Bessie Lee (Gotcher) Van L.; m. Charlotte Adele Miller, Apr. 21, 1946; children—Fred Arthur and Nancey Adele (twins). Student, Kans. State Coll. at Pittsburg, 1944-45, U. Kan., 1945-46; Exec. Degree in Credit and Financial Mgmt, Stanford, 1962-64. Field rep. Transam. Fin. Corp. (previously Pacific Fin. Corp.), Los Angeles, 1947-48; office mgr. Transam. Fin. Corp. (previously Pacific Fin. Corp.), 1948-52, credit supr., 1952-55, supr. operations, 1955-59, mgr. dist., 1959-62, various home office positions, 1962-66, v.p. region, 1967-69, v.p. adminstrn., 1969-72, exec. v.p., 1972-77, pres., chief exec. officer, 1977—, mem. exec. com., 1972—, also dir.; exec. v.p. Transam. Corp.; dir. Transam. Title Ins. Co., 1980—; dir. Transam. Investment Services Inc., Transam. Realty Services, Transam. Equipment Leasing Co., Transam. Interway, Transam. Occidental Life Ins. Co, Transam. Ins. Co., Transam. Corp. Served with USNR, 1943-46. Office: Transamerica Corp 1150 S Olive St Los Angeles CA 90015

VAN LINT, VICTOR ANTON JACOBUS, physicist; b. Samarinda, Indonesia, May 10, 1928; came to U.S., 1937; s. Victor J. and Margaret (DeJager) Van L.; m. M. June Woolhouse, June 10, 1950; children: Lawrence, Kenneth, Linda, Karen. BS, Calif. Inst. Tech., Pasadena, 1950, PhD, 1954. Instr. Princeton (N.J.) U., 1954-55; staff mem. Gen. Atomic, San Diego, 1957-74; physics cons. San Diego, 1974-75; staff mem. Mission Research Corp., San Diego, 1975-82, 83—; spl. asst. to dep. dir. sci. and tech. Def. Nuclear Agy., Washington, 1982-83. Author, editor: Radiation Effects in Electronic Materials, 1976; contbr. articles to profl. jours. Served with U.S. Army, 1955-57. Recipient Pub. Service award NASA, 1981. Fellow IEEE. Republican. Mem. United Ch. of Christ. Home: 1032 Skylark Dr La Jolla CA 92037

VAN LOAN, MARTA D., research physiologist; b. Springfield, Mass., May 29, 1951; d. Kenneth R. and Mary M. (Regan) Van L. BA, Doane Coll., 1973; MS, Eastern Ill. U., 1974; PhD, U. Ill., 1985. Instr. Northwestern Conn. Community Coll., Winstead, 1974-78; research physiologist USDA-Agrl. Research Service, San Francisco, 1982—. Contbr. articles to profl. jours. Mem. AAAS, Am. Coll. Sports Medicine, Human Biology Council. Office: USDA Agrl Research Service Western Human Nutrition Research PO Box 29997 Persidio of San Fran CA 94129

VAN MICHAELS, CHRISTOPHER, research engineer; b. Bulgaria, Feb. 14, 1924; came to U.S., 1967; s. Miho and Dragana (Ivanova-Dragneva) van M.; m. Anna Atanasova Vakarelyisky, Apr. 24, 1955; children: Diana Michaels, Julien Michaels. Grad. in theoretical and nuclear physics, U. Paris, 1962-66; diploma in physics, geophysics, chemistry, U. Sofia, Bulgaria, 1949; MSci of Research, Acad. Scis., Sofia, 1955. Research engr., physicist, indsl. chemist Sci. Research Inst. of Bulgaria Acad. Scis., Sofia, 1949-60; research engr. ESCOA Corp., Phoenix, 1967-73; pres. Montex Corp., Los Angeles, 1974—; cons. in physics, indsl. chemistry, math. Discovered the rotary ctrs. of the ellipse; patentee elliptic engines and compressors, bladeless turbines, gasiform engine pistons, internally cooling thermodynamic cycles, fuel alloys process for mfg. hydrocarbons, process for converting cellulose into edible flour, resonance quanto-ionic propulsion concept and contbrns. in Bulean Algebra; contbr. articles to profl. jours. Recipient Magnavox award, 1974. Mem. Internat. Physics Assn. Home: 1850 N Cherokee Ave Los Angeles CA 90028

VANN, BETH, medical social worker; b. Birmingham, Ala., Mar. 7, 1956; d. Robert Wood and Betty Jane (Barnett) V. BA in Psychology, U. Ill., 1978; MSW, U. Ga., 1982. Coordinator spouse abuse program U.S. Dept. Army, Ft. Richardson, Alaska, 1983, coordinator family advocacy program, 1983-84; med. social worker Home Health Care, Anchorage, 1984—; counselor family treatment Northpoint-Milam, Anchorage, 1985—; field instr. U. Alaska Sch. Social Work, Anchorage, 1983-84, 85—; vol. trainer Hospice of Anchorage, 1985—. Vol. Alaska Council Prevention of Drug and Alcohol Abuse, Anchorage, 1985—. Grantee U.S. Children's Bur., 1981-82. Mem. Nat. Assn. Social Workers (cert.), Nat. Assn. Home Care Forum for Social Workers, Humane Soc. U.S., Nat. Wildlife Fedn., Alaska Wildlife Fedn. Avocations: cross country skiing, backpacking, dogs, sewing, gardening. Office: Home Health Care 4107 Laurel St Anchorage AK 99508

VANNE, STEVEN LEE, energy company executive; b. San Jose, Calif., Oct. 24, 1956; s. Robert M. and Fairie L. (Havens) V.; m. Sonja A. Mosier, Nov. 28, 1980; children: Brionna A., John H. B in Bus., Western Ill. U., 1979. Market analyst Caterpillar Tractor Co., Peoria, Ill., 1979-80; regional sales rep. Caterpillar Ams. Co., Lima, Peru, 1981-83; regional product support mgr. Caterpillar Ams. Co., Santiago, Chile, 1984-86; pres. Advanced Energy

Concepts, Inc., Englewood, Colo., 1986. Mem. Blue Key, Sigma Pi (pres. 1978-79). Mem. Christian Ch. Avocations: skiing, climbing, reading. Office: Advanced Energy Concepts Inc 7304 S Alton Way Suite N Englewood CO 80112

VANNICE, KENNETH EARL, manufacturing engineering manager, consultant; b. Bozeman, Mont., Jan. 2, 1944; s. Daniel Bratschi and Catherine Naomi (Asimos) V. BSEE, Mont. State U., 1967, BS in Theatre Arts, 1967. Registered profl. engr., Calif. Tech. dir. Loft Theatre, Inc., Bozeman, 1964-66; tech. dir., lectr. Montana State U., Bozeman, 1965-67; engr. Kliegl Bros. Western, North Hollywood, Calif., 1967-74; mgr. Kliegl Bros. Western, North Hollywood, 1970-74; mgr., mfg. engr. Colortran, Inc., Burbank, Calif., 1975—; designer lighting control systems for entertainment; industry adv. council Underwriters Labs., 1985—. Treas. Sunset Junction Neighborhood Alliance, Los Angeles, 1984—. Mem. IEEE, Soc. of Motion Picture and TV Engrs., Illuminating Engring. Soc., U.S. Inst. for Theatre Tech. (sect. v.p. 1984-86, treas. 1986—). Republican. Club: Saga Ski (Los Angeles). Lodge: Masons. Avocations: photography, backpacking, camping. Home: 1707 Micheltorena St #418 Los Angeles CA 90026 Office: Colortran Inc 1015 Chestnut St Burbank CA 91506

VANNIX, C(ECIL) ROBERT, data processing professional; b. Glendale, Calif., June 14, 1953; s. Cecil H. Jr. and Gloria Jenny (Zappia) V.; married, 1980; 1 child, Robert Jeremy. AS in Plant Mgmt., BA in Indsl. Arts, Loma Linda U., 1977; AS in Info. Systems, Ventura City Coll., 1985. Instr. indsl. arts Duarte (Calif.) High Sch., 1977-79, Oxnard (Calif.) High Sch., 1979-81; computer cons. Litton Data Comand Systems, Agoura, Calif., 1976-81, sr. engr. instr., 1981-85; computer cons. McLaughlin Research Corp., Camarillo, Calif., 1976-77; sr. program analyst Mcglaughlin Research Corp., Camarillo, Calif., 1985—. Recipient Spl. Achievement award One Way Singers, Glendale, 1975. Republican. Adventist. Clubs: Apple PI Computer, Litton Computer (pres. 1975-76). Avocations: woodworking, automotives, photography, skiing. Home: 407 Appletree Ave Camarillo CA 93010 Office: McLaughlin Research Corp 275 E Pleasant Valley Rd Bldg 260 Camarillo CA 93010

VAN NORSDALL, BARBARA LOUISE, school administrator; b. Ft. Smith, Ark., Nov. 17, 1934; d. Ross Amos and Daphna (Louise) Van N. BA, Woodbury U., 1957; MBA, U. Nev., Las Vegas, 1973. Sec. Clark County Sch. Dist., Las Vegas, 1958-67, programmer, 1967-69, systems analyst, 1969-73, coordinator data processing, 1973-84, dir. mgmt. info. systems, data processing, 1984—. Democrat. Office: Clark County Sch Dist 2832 E Flamingo Rd Las Vegas NV 89121

VAN ORDEN, ROY CORTNEY, structural engineer; b. N.Y.C., Apr. 18, 1918; s. Harold M. and Lydia N. (Noack) Van O.; m. Betty M. Wagner, Nov. 14, 1942; children: Darole Ann Thorkildsen, Ronald C., Linda L. Mc Creight, Gretchen G. Berger, Heidi M. BS, Calif. Inst. Tech., 1942; MS, U. So. Calif., 1951, degree in Civil Engring., 1954. Cert. structural engr., civil engr., mech. engr., Calif. Leadman in structures engring. Douglas Aircraft Corp., Long Beach, Calif., 1942-46; assoc. structural engr. Los Angeles City Dept. Bldg., 1946-48; prin. assoc. engr. Bennett & Bennett, Pasadena, Calif., 1948-50; mgr. div. A.C. Martin & Assocs., Los Angeles, 1950-83; chief engr. Lindvall, Richter & Assocs., Los Angeles, 1983-86; cons. structural engr. R.C. Van Orden & Assocs., Newport Beach, Calif., 1986—; adj. instr. civil engring. Calif. Inst. Tech., Pasadena, 1943-44, U. So. Calif., Los Angeles, 1953-68. Chmn. interview bd. Los Angeles City Civil Services Commrs.; mem. Seismic Element Com. for City of San Marino. Mem. ASCE, Am. Concrete Inst., Soc. Am. Mil. Engrs., Cons. Engrs. Assn. Calif., Structural Engrs. Assn. So. Calif., Earthquake Engring. Research Inst., Chi Epsilon. Republican. Presbyterian. Club: U.S. Power Squadron (lt. 1964—). Office: RC Van Orden & Assocs 4012 Channel Pl Newport Beach CA 92663

VAN OSDEL, ROBERT LINN, medical device company executive, researcher; b. Bakersfield, Calif., May 27, 1946; s. Francis William and Gloria Mae (Hamilton) Van O.; m. Carol Brownlee Schwartz, June 16, 1968 (div.); children: Kristofer Jon, Eric Carter; m. Lucinda Marie Markey, Nov. 8, 1985. BS in Zoology, Calif. State U., Long Beach, 1970. Research assoc. Abbott Sci., Los Angeles, 1968-73; prodn. mgr. Internat. Med. Systems, Ltd., South El Monte, Calif., 1973-76; brewing supr. Miller Brewing Co., Azusa, Calif., 1976-79; regulatory mgr. Intermedics Intraocular, Inc., Pasadena, Calif., 1979-81; v.p. Ioptex, Inc., Azusa, 1981-87; ptnr. Biogeneral, San Diego, 1987—. Patentee in field. Served with USNR, 1964-68. Mem. AAAS, Am. Soc. Quality Control, Soc. Biomaterials. Republican. Presbyterian. Avocations: scuba diving, skiing, bicycling, photography, boating. Home: PO Box 583 Duarte CA 91010-0583 Office: Ioptex Inc 1301 Optical Dr Azusa CA 91702-1375

VAN PELT, W(ESLEY) AUSTIN, clergyman, educator; b. Rahway, N.J., Aug. 24, 1930; s. Charles Wesley and Grace Elizabeth (DeHart) Van P.; B.A., Maryville Coll., 1952; M.Div., Louisville Presbyn. Sem., 1955; M.A., U. Denver, 1964, Ph.D., 1970; m. Elenor Kramer, June 11, 1952; children—Mary, Anne, Peter, David. Ordained to ministry United Presbyn. Ch., mem. faculty Maryville (Tenn.) Coll., 1954-57, Sheldon Jackson Jr. Coll., Sitka, Alaska, 1957-59; gen. mgr. Sta. KSEW, 1959-61; pastor, New Castle, Pa., 1961-63; asst. prof. sociology Peru State Coll., 1964-68; dean Arapahoe Community Coll., Littleton, Colo., 1969-75, instr. sociology, 1976—; interim pastor chs., Colo., Alaska, Utah, Wyo., 1984—; adj. prof. U. Denver, 1976, McCormick Theol. Sem., Chgo., 1979-81. Mem. NEA, Colo. Edn. Assn., Presbytery of Denver. Office: 5900 S Santa Fe Dr Littleton CO 80120

VAN REMMEN, ROGER, advertising executive; b. Los Angeles, Sept. 30, 1950; s. Thomas J. and Elizabeth (Vincent) V.; m. Mary Anne Montague, Sept. 11, 1976. B.S. in Bus., U. So. Calif., 1972. Account mgr. BBDO, Los Angeles, 1972-78; account mgr. Dailey & Assocs. Advt., Los Angeles, 1978—, v.p., mgmt. supr., 1980-84, sr. v.p., 1985—; dir. Aux. Aids Inc., Richstone Family Ctr. Mem. adv. bd. El Segundo (Calif.) First Nat. Bank. Mem. Univ. So. Calif. Alumni Assn., Advt. Club of Los Angeles. Roman Catholic. Home: 441 2d St Manhattan Beach CA 90266 Office: Dailey & Assocs 3055 Wilshire Blvd 2d Fl Los Angeles CA 90010

VAN RIEL, EGBERT MATTHYS, chemical, industrial engineer; b. Amsterdam, The Netherlands, Aug. 15, 1926; came to U.S., 1958; s. Matthys Gerrit and Martha Johanna (Oostinga) Van R.; m. Theodora Willemina Lamers, Sept. 15, 1949; 1 child, Robert John. Diploma in sugar chemistry, Coll. for Sugar Industry, Amsterdam, 1947; BSChemE, Royal Inst. PBNA, Arnhem, The Netherlands, 1955; M in Engring. Adminstrn., U. Utah, 1966; cert. in Bus. Mgmt., UCLA. Registered profl. chem. engr., Calif. Project research engr. Am. Potash Co., Trona, Calif., 1958-63; proj. mgr. Stauffer Chem. Co., Salt Lake City, 1963-67; sr. chem. engr. C.F. Braun & Co. subs. Santa Fe Internat. Corp., Alhambra, Calif., 1967-79; prin. project engr. Fluor Corp., Irvine, Calif., 1980-83; indsl. engr. U.S. Dept. Def., Los Angeles, 1984—. Patentee shale oil extraction process. Vice-chmn. South African Health and Benefit Soc., New Castle, 1957. Served to 1st lt. Royal Dutch Air Force, 1948-50. Mem. AIME, Am. Inst. Chem. Engrs., Am. Chem. Soc., Minimax Investors Club. Club: Toastmasters (San Gabriel, Calif.)(pres. 1974). Avocations: travel, photography, gardening. Home: 2805 Flecha Ct Hacienda Heights CA 91745 Office: AFPRO-TRW One Space Park Redondo Beach CA 90278

VAN RIPER, CHARLES, III, wildlife science educator; b. Mahopac, N.Y., Sept. 24, 1943; s. Charles II and Dorothy (Wilson) van R.; m. Sandra Jean Guest, June 4, 1977; children: Kale, Jacqueline, Kimberly, Carena. BS in Zoology, Colo. State U., 1966, MEd in Sci., 1967; PhD in Zoology, U. Hawaii, 1978. Biol. technician Colo. Fish, Game and Parks Dept., 1963; instr. Mahopac (N.Y.) High Sch., 1967-68, Hawaii Preparatory Acad., Kamuela, Hawaii, 1968-72; teaching asst. zoology U. Hawaii, Honolulu, 1972-74, research asst., 1974-75, asst. researcher, 1977-79; wildlife biologist Dept. Interior-U.S. Fish and Wildlife Service, Hawaii, 1975-76; unit leader Coop. Nat. Park Resources Studies U. Calif., Davis, 1980—, assoc. adj. prof. wildlife and fisheries biology, 1985—; Mem. Western U.S. Peregrine Falcon recovery team U.S. Fish and Wildlife Service, 1982—, Hawaii endangered species recovery team, 1974—. Leader 4-H, Davis, 1984—. Grantee McInery Found., 1973, Internat. Council Bird Preservation, Frank M. Chapman Meml. Fund Am. Mus. Natural History, 1973, 79, NSF, 1974, Hawaii Nat. Park Service, 1974, World Wildlife Fund, 1974-75, Ctr. for Field Research, 1978-80, Inst. Ecology, 1980, others. Mem. Nat. Wildlife Soc. (Hawaii rep.), Am. Ornithologists Union (life, chmn. com. career opportunities in ornithology 1985-86), Aviculturists Soc., Calif. Field Ornithologists (life), Cooper Ornithol. Soc. (bd. dirs. 1986—), Ecol. Soc. Am., George Wright Soc., Hawaii Audubon Soc.(fellow 1972, grantee 1974, 78), Soc. Am. Naturalists, Western Bird-banding Assn. (life), Wilson Ornithol. Soc. (life), Wildlife Disease Assn. (asst. editor 1986—), Wildlife Soc., Sigma Xi (grantee 1979), Phi Si. Home: Rt 1 Box 776C Woodland CA 95695 Office: U Calif Dept Wildlife and Fisheries Biology and Coop Studies Unit 2148 Wickson Hall Davis CA 95616

VAN SANTEN, JOHN HENRY, III, electronics company manager; b. Washington, June 10, 1953; s. John Henry, Jr. and Lillian May (Whittenburg) van S.; m. Cheryl Denise Kincaid, Oct. 16, 1976 (div. Apr. 1983); 1 child, Nicholas John; m. Caroline Diann Terhune, July 20, 1985; 1 child, Kimberly Diann. BS, U. Calif., Davis, 1974, MS, 1976. Mem. tech. staff Hewlett-Packard Co., Cupertino, Calif., 1976-78, engring. services mgr., Corvallis, Oreg., 1978-80, engring. project mgr., Corvallis, 1980—. Mem. IEEE. Office: Hewlett-Packard Co 1000 NE Circle Blvd Corvallis OR 97330-4285

VAN SLYKE, SHERRIE MARIE, psychotherapist; b. Oceanside, Calif., Sept. 15, 1945; m. George Dudley Van Slyke, June 11, 1966; children: Sandra Marie, Kathryn Suzanne. AA, Palomar Jr. Coll., 1976; AA summa cum laude, Met. State Coll., 1977, BS summa cum laude, 1979; MSW, U. Denver, 1981. Probation officer Denver Juvenile Ct., 1978; psychotherapist Jefferson County Mental Health, Lakewood, Colo., 1978, 1979, 1981-82; social worker Kunsmiller Jr. High Sch., Denver, 1980-81; pvt. practice psychotherapy Littleton, Colo., 1982—; cons. Columbine United Ch., Littleton, 1982—, also lectr., 1982—, Christian Edn. dir., 1983-85, divorce group leader, 1985—. Bd. dirs. VOICES in Action. Mem. Nat. Assn. Social Workers, VOICES, Inc. Democrat. Avocations: painting, gardening, reading. Home and Office: 7973 S Lamar Ct Littleton CO 80123

VAN STEE, ROBERT CLAY, JR., engineering educator; b. Detroit, May 31, 1946; s. Robert Clay and Helene Rebecca (Grape) Van S.; m. Marilyn Kay Dammrose, June 22, 1969; children Vanessa Lynn, Dana Robert. BS in Engring., Walla Walla Coll., 1969; MS in Engring., UCLA, 1984. Registered profl. engr., Oreg., Wis. Mem. tech. staff Hughes Aircraft Co., Canoga Park, Calif., 1969-74; pvt. practice engring. Salem, Oreg., 1974-79, Arpin, Wis., 1979-84; asst. prof. engring. Walla Walla Coll., College Place, Wash., 1984—. Mem. ASME, Am. Soc. Engring. Edn., Am. Motorcyclist Assn. (life). Republican. Mem. Ch. Seventh Day Adventists. Avocations: photography, motorcycle touring. Office: Walla Walla Coll Sch Engring College Place WA 99324

VANTRESS, MARIAN CRAMPTON, commercial design company executive; b. July 17, 1934; d. Robert C. and Monica I. (Dempsey) Crampton; divorced; children: Robert M., Sarah L., Michael K., Mary E. Vantress Painter. BS, U. Calif., Berkeley, 1956. Pres. Vantress Design Assocs., Aptos, Calif., 1971—, Calif. Contract Furniture, 1986—. Mem. Inst. Bus. Designers (profl., cert.), Am. Soc. Interior Designers (profl., cert.), Children's Home Soc., Delta Gamma (treas.). Republican. Club: Jr. League (San Jose, Calif.). Avocations: skiing, tennis, art.

VAN TUYLE, ROBERT, health care facilities company executive; b. Manchester, Ill., 1912. Student, Univ of Cincinnati, MIT. Chmn., chief exec. officer Beverly Enterprises, Pasadena, Calif.; dir. Jacobs Engring. Group, Inc., Alpha Microsystems. Office: Beverly Enterprises 873 S Fair Oaks Pasadena CA 91105 *

VAN VALIN, ROBERT DETRICK, JR., linguistics educator; b. San Diego, Feb. 1, 1952; s. Robert Detrick and Rebecca Camp (Barge) Van V.; m. Jeri Juanita Jaeger, Dec. 29, 1978; children; Anna Rebecca, Alice Eileen, Robert Chester. AB in Linguistics, U. Calif., San Diego, 1973; MA in Linguistics, U. Calif., Berkeley, 1975, PhD in Linguistics, 1977. Vis. asst. prof. U. Ariz., Tucson, 1977-78; asst. prof. anthropology Temple U., Phila., 1978-80, 82-83; research fellow Australian Nat. U., Canberra, 1980-82; asst. prof. U. Calif., Davis, 1983-85, assoc. prof., program dir., 1985—; mem. adv. bd. Internat. Pragmatics Assn., 1986—. Co-author: Functional Syntax and Universal Grammar, 1984; editor (jour.) Davis Working Papers in Linguistics, 1986—; reviewer Univ. Presses and Fed. Granting Agys., 1978—; contbr. numerous articles to profl. jours. NSF fellow, 1973-76. Mem. Linguistic Soc. Am., Soc. Study Indigenous Langs. of Ams., Australian Linguistic Soc., Sigma Xi. Office: U Calif Linguistics Program Davis CA 95616

VAN VALKENBURG, FREDERICK ROBERT, II, lawyer; b. Denver, May 3, 1948; s. Fred R. and Aileen C. (Keough) VanV.; m. Carol Bulger, Sept. 4, 1971; children: Kevin Tobin, Kristin Anne. BBA, Gonzaga U., 1970; JD, U. Mont., 1973. Asst. atty. City of Missoula, Mont., 1973-75; ptnr. Smith, Connor & Van Valkenburg, Missoula, 1975-84; dep. county atty. Missoula County, 1985—; senator State of Mont., 1978—, majority leader, 1985—. Bd. dirs. Big Bros. and Sisters, Missoula, 1979—. Mem. State Bar Mont. Democrat. Roman Catholic. Home: 219 University Ave Missoula MT 59801 Office: Missoula County Courthouse Missoula County Attys Office Missoula MT 59802

VANVLEET, MARK RICHARD, manufacturing company transportation executive; b. Milw., Sept. 23, 1952. AA in Supervision, Ohlone Coll., 1978; AA in Transp., De Anza Coll., 1981; cert. in transp., Golden Gate U., 1982. Stockroom supr. Orroy Corp., Santa Clara, Calif., 1975-77; traffic supr. Ball Computer Products, Sunnyvale, Calif., 1977-79; traffic mgr. T.I.W. Systems, Sunnyvle, 1979-81; mgr. transp. Varian Assocs., Palo Alto, Calif., 1981—; mem. hazardous material task force Sci. Apparatus Makers Assn., 1982—; transp. adv. bd. Electronic Industry Assn., Washington, 1983—. Mem. Delta Nu Alpha. Avocation: surfing. Office: Varian Assocs 611 Hansen Way M/S S065 Palo Alto CA 94303

VAN VOLKENBURGH, ELIZABETH, plant physiologist; b. Ft. Sill, Okla., July 2, 1952; d. Robert Heber and Jean Fontaine (Brown) Van V.; m. William Henry Lippitt, July 27, 1974; children: Alice Brett, William Henry. BS, Duke U., 1973; PhD, U. Wash., 1980. Postdoctoral assoc. U. Ill., Urbana, 1980-81; NATO postdoctoral fellow U. Lancaster, Eng., 1981-82; postdoctoral assoc. U. Wash., Seattle, 1982-84, research assoc., 1984-85, research asst. prof. plant physiology, 1986—. Contbr. articles to profl. jours. Mem. AAAS, Am. Soc. Plant Physiologists, Sigma Xi. Avocations: sailing, hiking. Office: U Wash Botany Dept KB-15 Seattle WA 98195

VAN VOORHIS, THOMAS, lawyer; b. Great Falls, Mont., Feb. 24, 1930; s. George E. and Ruthe (Williams) V.; AA, U. Calif., 1955; LLB, JD, Hastings Coll. Law, 1959; m. Eleanor Cooper, Mar. 21, 1958; children: Kevin, Karen, Thomas. Admitted to Calif. bar, 1960; pres. Campbell & Van Voorhis, Walnut Creek, Calif., 1960-82; of counsel Van Voorhis & Skaggs, 1982-85; of counsel McCutchen, Brown, Doyle & Enersen, 1985—; judge pro tem Walnut Creek-Danville Municipal Ct., 1974-82; pres. Domino II Cattle Co., Walnut Creek, 1971-86; v.p. Blackhawk Devel. Co., Danville, Calif., 1972-75; corp. sec., dir. RWC Calif. Co., Danville, 1975-85, RWC Nev. Co., Reno; sec., dir. Woodhill Devel. Co., Danville, 1976-85; dir. First Security Savs. Bank. Pres. Rep. Assembly, Walnut Creek, 1964. Bd. dirs. Walnut Creek (Cal.) Action for Beauty Council, Pacific Vascular Found., 1986. Served with USAF, 1950-54. Mem. State Bar Calif., ABA (com. on devel. and mgmt. real estate 1975—), Contra Costa Bar Assn., Internat. Assn. Fin. Planning. Office: 1855 Olympic Blvd Walnut Creek CA 94596

VAN VRANKEN, NADINE, social worker; b. Pasadena, Calif., Nov. 19, 1958; d. Gilbert and Dora (Drumm) Van V. BA Sociology, Eng. Lit. with honors, U. Calif., Santa Cruz, 1980; MSW, U. Calif., Berkeley, 1985. Research asst. mental health and social welfare research group U. Calif., Berkeley, 1984-85; psychiat. social work intern U. Calif. Langley Porter Psychiat. Inst., San Francisco, 1984-85; research asst. Ctr. for Family in Transition, Corte Madera, Calif., 1985; social worker Mt. St. Joseph-St. Elizabeth Ctr., San Francisco, 1985—; adminstrv. intern congressman Dellums' 8th Dist. office, Oakland, Calif., 1983-84. Mem. Nat. Assn. Social Workers, U. Calif. Berkeley Alumni Assn. Democrat. Avocations: literature, theater. Home: 1729 Dolores St San Francisco CA 94110 Office: Mt St Joseph-St Elizabeth 100 Masonic Ave San Francisco CA 94118

VAN WAGENEN, STERLING GRAY, film producer, director; b. Provo, Utah, July 2, 1947; s. Clifton Gray and Donna Anna (Johnson) Van W.; m. Marilee Jeppson; children: Sarah, Kristina, Arthur, William, Hugh, Andrew. BA, Brigham Young U., 1972. Media coordinator Utah Arts Council, Salt Lake City, 1976-78; exec. dir. U.S. Film Festival, Park City, Utah, 1978-80; exec. dir. Sundance Inst., Salt Lake City, 1980-84, v.p., 1984—; asst. dir. Los Angeles Music Ctr., 1971, script reader Creative Mgmt. Assocs., 1971. Dir. plays include King Lear, 1974, Othello, 1984, Hamlet, 1972, The Flies, 1970; producer films include Faith of an Observer 1984, The Trip to Bountiful (Acad. Award Best Actress 1986). Office: Sundance Inst 19 Exchange Place 3d Floor Salt Lake City UT 84111

VAN WORMER, KATHERINE STUART, social worker; b. New Orleans, July 24, 1944; d. Rupert Alison Stuart and Elise (Talmage) Lieb; m. Robert Potter Van Wormer, Sept. 1, 1972; children: Flora Talmage, Rupert Talmage. BA, U. N.C., 1966; MEd., Queen's U., Belfast, Northern Ireland, 1967; MA, Western Ky. U., 1970; PhD, U. Ga., 1976; MS in Social Welfare, U. Tenn., 1984. Asst. prof. Bluefield (W. Va.) State Coll., 1975-76, Livingtone Coll., Salisbury, N.C., 1976-77, Kent (Ohio) State U., 1976-77; social worker Community Alcohol Ctr., Longview, Wash., 1984—. Author: Sex Role Behavior in a Woman's Prison, 1978; contbr. articles to profl. jours. Active U.S. Draft Bd., Kent, 1982-84, Fellowship of Reconciliation, Longview, Wash., 1984—. Mem. Nat. Assn. Social Workers, Quakers in Higher Edn. Avocation: tennis. Home: 209 SW 15th Ave Rochester MN 55902 Office: Community Alcohol Ctr 1260 Commerce St Longview WA 98632

VARGA, STEVEN CARL, reinsurance company official; b. Columbus, Ohio, Jan. 19, 1952; s. Stephen Thomas and Eva Jeney V.; B.A. in Psychology and Philosophy magna cum laude, Carthage Coll., 1977, MSA with honors Cen. Mich. U., 1986; m. Michelle L. Auld, Nov. 17, 1973; children—Zachary Steven, Joshua Lewis. Service mgr. Chem-Lawn Corp., Columbus, 1972-75; respiratory therapist St. Catherine's Hosp., Kenosha, Wis., 1975-77; policy analyst Nationwide Ins. Cos., Columbus, 1978-79, asst. mgr. Corp. Tng. Center, 1979-86; dir. ednl. tng. and devel. Sullivan Payne Co., Seattle, 1986—, mem. civic action program com., 1979—. Mem. Nat. Mental Health Assn., 1972—, v.p. Kenosha County chpt., 1975-77; mem. Franklin County (Ohio) Mental Health Assn., 1978—. Rhodes scholar, 1976-77. Mem. Am. Soc. Tng. and Devel., Soc. Broadcast Engrs., Internat. TV Assn., Am. Psychol. Assn., Am. Mgmt. Assn., Soc. of Ins. Trainers and Educators, Am. Film Inst., Carthage Coll. Alumni Assn., Phi Beta Kappa, Psi Chi. Home: 12111 SE 46th Ctd Bellevue WA 98006 Office: Sullivan Payne Co 1501 4th Ave Seattle WA 98101

VARGAS, MICHAEL PAUL, college administrator; b. San Jose, Calif., Apr. 10, 1947; s. Donald Joseph and Dollie Martha (Fuhrmann) V. BA in Art, San Jose State U., 1969; MA in History of Art, Ohio State U., 1972; MA in Museology, John F. Kennedy U., 1979. Cert. tchr. community colls., Calif. Instr. art history Coll. of Dayton (Ohio) Art Inst., 1973-75, Mission Coll., Santa Clara, Calif., 1977-84; instl. dean Mission Coll., Santa Clara, 1984—. Author (exhibition catalog): Life and Times of Elizabeth Boott Duveneck, 1980, A System for the Classification and Cataloging of Art Slides and Photographs, 1980. Advisor Triton Mus. Art, Santa Clara, 1983—; mem. Heritage Preservation Commn., Sunnyvale, Calif., 1983—. Office: Mission Coll 3000 Mission College Blvd Santa Clara CA 95054

VARNER, WILLARD CHARLES, sales executive; b. Columbus, Ohio, Nov. 4, 1940; s. Wilbur Willard and Helen Mae (Green) V.; m. Sandra Kay Winjum, July 3, 1969; children—Cathryn Ann, Lance Douglas, Jason Winjum; B.A. in Econs., Otterbein Coll., 1966; M.B.A., Pepperdine U., 1968; M.A. in Econs., Calif. State U.-Long Beach, 1973; M.S. in Fin., U. So. Calif., 1979. Market research analyst, Rockwell Internat., Los Angeles, 1967-69; sr. market research analyst, Douglas Aircraft Co., 1969-73; aviation systems cons., Daniel, Mann, Johnson & Mendenhall, Los Angeles, 1973-76; airline planning specialist Lockheed Aircraft Co., Burbank, 1977-79; sales mgr. Douglas Aircraft Co., 1979-84; sales mgr. Lockheed Aircraft Service Co., 1984—. Mem. ASCE (past chmn. air transport group Los Angeles sect.), Air Force Assn., Naval Inst., AIAA. Republican.

VARON, MICHAEL NATHAN, mechanical engineer; b. Bklyn., July 27, 1950; s. Jack and Ann (Cassuto) V.; m. Jane Renee Felland, June 21, 1981. BME, CCNY, 1973; MME, U. So. Calif., 1978. Sr. staff engr. Hughes Aircraft Co., El Segundo, Calif., 1973—. Mem. AIAA, ASME. Democrat. Avocations: cross country skiing, hiking. Office: Hughes Aircraft Co PO Box 92919 s/32/C327 Los Angeles CA 90009

VAS, IRWIN EMMANUEL, energy executive; b. Bombay, Apr. 16, 1931; came to U.S., 1948; s. Emmanuel Joseph Vas and Primrose Mary Johnson; m. Manya Mary Milun, Mar. 26, 1965; children: Catherine Mary, Joseph Irwin. BME, Cath. U. Am., 1952, B. in Aerospace Engring., 1953; MS in Engring., Princeton U., 1955; PhD, NYU, 1970. From research asst. to sr. research engr. Princeton (N.J.) U., 1955-77; program mgr. ERDA, N.Y.C., 1977-78; program mgr. wind energy Solar Energy Research Inst., Golden, Colo., 1978-80; dir. research and engring. Flo Wind Corp., Pleasanton, Calif., 1981-82; v.p. research and engring. Flo Wind Corp., Kent, Wash., 1982-85; v.p. internat. mktg. Flo Wind Corp., Kent, 1986—; cons. Gen. Electric Corp., Boeing Aerospace Corp., Bell Helicopters. Editor: (proceedings) Fifth Biennial Wind Energy Conf., 1981, Sixth Biennial Wind Energy Conf., 1983; author of numerous tech. reports. Fellow AIAA (assoc.); mem. ASME, Am. Solar Energy Soc. (chmn. wind div.), Sigma Xi. Home: 12533 SE 62d Pl Bellevue WA 98006

VASBINDER, JAMES DUANE, real estate company executive, civil engineer; b. Cadiz, Ohio, June 13, 1949; s. Jack D. and Wilma Irene (Delloma) V.; m. Diane Elaine (Little); children: Joshua, Joseph, Jordan. BSCE, Ohio U., 1971. Registered profl. engr., Ohio, Colo., Pa., W.Va. Project mgr. Metcalf & Eddy, Inc., Boston, 1971-76, Burgess & Niple Ltd., Columbus, Ohio, 1976-78; constrn. mgr. Don M. Casto Orgn., Columbus, 1978-80; dir. constrn. Linclay Corp., Columbus and Denver, Colo., 1980-84; v.p. RACO Devel. Corp., Denver, 1984—. Mem. Nat. Assn. Indsl. Office Parks. Methodist. Home: 7122 S Oliveway Englewood CO 80112 Office: RACO Devel Corp 8400 E Prentice Ave Englewood CO 80111

VASCONCELLOS, JOSE ANDRES, food technologist, nutrition and biochemistry educator; b. Guayaquil, Ecuador, May 31, 1938; came to U.S., 1969, naturalized, 1985; s. Jose Andres and Idalia (Rosado) V.; m. Marilyn Mathieu, Jan. 2, 1972; children—Miguel, Andres, Cristina, Eduardo. B.S. in Chem. Engring., U. Guayaquil, (Ecuador), 1969; M.S. in Food Sci., U. Calif.-Davis, 1972, M.S. in Nutrition, 1976; Ph.D. in Nutrition and Biochemistry, U. Ariz., 1979. Prodn. mgr. OLEICA, South Am., Guayaquil, 1966-69, 1972-73; research assoc. U. Ariz., Tucson, 1977-79; prof. U. Americas, Puebla, Mexico, 1979-81; project leader research and devel. Beatrice/Hunt-Wesson, Fullerton, Calif., 1981—; prof. food sci. and nutrition Chapman Coll., Orange, Calif., 1983—. Contbr. chpts. to New Sources of Fats and Oils, 1981. Contbr. articles to profl. jours. Orgn. Am. States scholar, 1973, 74. Mem. Inst. Food Technologists, Am. Inst. Nutrition, Latin Am. Soc. Nutrition, Am. Oil Chemists Soc., Smithsonian Instn. Clubs: So. Calif. Swimming (Orange). Home: 4620 E Golden Eagle Ave Orange CA 92669 Office: Beatrice/Hunt-Wesson Foods Inc 1645 W Valencia Dr Fullerton CA 92634

VASEEN, VESPER ALBERT, engineering company executive, environmental and sanitary engineer; b. Denver, Sept. 13, 1917; s. Albert and Ruby Cornelia (Weisz) V.; m. June L. Novak, Feb. 2, 1941; children: Gail C. Vaseen Moler, Dale A. MS, Colo. Sch. Mines, 1939; cert., Denver U., 1940; postgrad., U. Mich., 1941, Colo. State U., 1942-86; DSci, U. Del Norte, Coquimbo, Chile, 1981. Registered profl. engr., Colo., Kans., Utah, Pa., Alaska. Pres. Ripple & Howe Inc., Denver, 1946-79; project engr. Stearns Roger Corp., Denver, 1966-79; pres. AVASCO, Wheat Ridge, Colo., 1979—, Technometrics Inc., Wheat Ridge, 1982—; cons. Internat. Execs. Service Assn., N.Y.C., 1981. Contbr. articles to profl. jours; inventor, patentee in field. Served to maj. AUS, 1943-49. Recipient cert. of merit various C. of

C.'s nationwide, 1952—. Mem. Am. Water Works Assn. (life), Water Pollution Control Fedn. (life), U.S. Dept. Commerce (exec. res.). Republican. Lodges: Kiwanis, Masons, Order Rosicrucians (bd. chmn.). Home and Office: 9840 W 35th Ave Wheat Ridge CO 80033

VASQUEZ, EDMUNDO EUSEBIO, religious organization administrator; b. Chacon, N.Mex., May 14, 1932; s. Eusebio and Dora (Ortiz) V.; B.A., N.Mex. Highlands U., 1953; postgrad. U. Colo., 1958, Brigham Young U., 1959; M.A., Stanford U., 1961; postgrad. U. Costa Rica, 1966; m. Carol Vallendar, June 16, 1957 (div. Aug. 1978); children—Amarante, Daniel, Amalio; m. Jane Atkins, Nov. 1983. With Sta. KFUN, 1949-53; dean Wasatch Acad., Mt. Pleasant, Utah, 1955-65; dean Colegio Americano, Ibagué, Colombia, 1966-71; pres. Menaul Sch., (Albuquerque, 1971-78; agt. Nat. Life of Vt. and Northwestern Mut. Life, Albuquerque, 1978-81; dir. So. Calif. Found., 1981—; rep. United Presbyn. Found., 1981—; cons. in field; lectr., cons. Hispanic affairs; cons. multicultural edn. Bd. dirs. United Presbyn. Health, Edn. and Welfare Assn., 1975-78, March of Dimes, 1976-79, ARC, 1979-82; trustee San Francisco Theol. Sem., San Anselmo, Calif., 1982—; fundraiser charitable and polit. orgns. Served with USAF, 1953-55. Mem. Assn. Supervision and Curriculum Devel., Nat. Assn. Life Underwriters. Clubs: Rotary, Lions, Masons. Office: So Calif Found 1501 Wilshire Blvd Los Angeles CA 90017

VASSALLO, PAUL, academic administrator, library science educator; b. Marsa, Malta, Aug. 3, 1937; came to U.S., 1952, naturalized, 1954; s. Salvatore and Giuseppina (Gravino) V.; m. Benita Mae Weber, June 21, 1981. B.A. in Polit. Sci., Wayne State U., 1959, postgrad., 1959-61; M.A. in Library Sci., U. Mich., 1962. Spl. library recruit Library of Congress, Washington, 1962-63; asst. head Hispanic exchange sect. exchange and gift div. Library of Congress, 1963, subject cataloger, 1963-64, head newspaper and periodical sect. serial div., 1964-65, asst. head pub. reference sect. gen. reference and bibliography div., 1965-66, asst. chief serial record div., 1966-67, cons. serials data program, info. systems office, 1967-68, chief congl. reference div., 1968-72, dir. nat. serials data program, 1972-74; asst. to dean Sch. Library and Info. Services, U. Md., College Park, 1967-68; prof. librarianship U. N.Mex., Albuquerque, 1974—, dean library services, 1974-86, assoc. v.p. computer services and info. systems, 1985—; cons. Orgn. Am. States, Managua, 1976, U. Autonoma de Guadalajara, Mex., 1980-83, Inst. de Investigaciones Electricas, Cuernavaca, Mex., 1981, U. Autonoma de Chiapas, Mex., 1984, 85; initiator, chmn. Task Force on State-wide Interlibrary Cooperative System for N.Mex., 1977; mem. N.Mex. White House Conf. Planning Com., 1978, del., head N.Mex. delegation, 1979; founder Council Acad. Research Libraries in AMIGOS, 1979, chmn. 1981-84; del. OCLC Users Council, 1981-83; initiator, bd. dirs. Library of Congress Vol. Project at D.C. Correction Complex; con. Library of Congress Recruiting Program; mem. Fulbright Discipline Com. in Library Sci., 1984-86. Editor: The Magic of Words: Rudolfo A. Anaya and His Writings, 1982; contbr. articles to profl. jours. Trustee AMIGOS Bibliog. Council, 1979-82, sec., 1979, chmn., 1981; bd. dirs. N.Mex Symphony Orch., 1985—; pres. Mich. State Soc., Washington, 1974; v.p. Library of Congress Welfare and Recreation Assn., 1964, pres., 1965. Mem. ALA (exec. com. history sect. 1972-74, chmn. nominating com. serial sect. 1975-76, spl. com. on library edn. 1982-85), Am. Soc. Info. Sci., Spl. Libraries Assn., N.Mex. Library Assn. (chmn. fed. relations com. 1977-78), Greater Albuquerque Library Assn., Assn. Research Libraries (trustee 1982-85, ACRL legis. com. 1978-84, ALA nominating com. 1987—), Albuquerque C. of C. (cultural com. 1978—). Avocations: cooking; photography; sailing; hiking. Home: 2313 Artesanos Ct NW Albuquerque NM 87107 Office: U New Mexico Computer Services and Info Systems Albuquerque NM 87131

VAUGHAN, ALAN, parapsychologist; b. Akron, Ohio, Dec. 28, 1936; s. Robert L. and Millie M. (Denny) V.; m. Diane Dudley, June 20, 1975; children: Lauren, Thomas, Jonathan. AB in Greek and Latin, U. Akron, 1958; PhD in Parapsychology (hon.), El Inst. de Ciencias Parapsicologicas, Granada, Spain, 1977. Editor Psychic mag., San Francisco, 1970-77; parapsychology editor New Realities, San Francisco, 1977; editor Reincarnation Report, Malibu, Calif., 1982-83; intuitive cons. Los Angeles, 1981—. Author: Patterns of Prophecy, 1973, Incredible Coincidence, 1979, The Edge of Tomorrow, 1982; co-author: Dream Telepathy, 1973; contbr. Spirit Speaks, Los Angeles, 1985—. Research grantee Parapsychology Found., N.Y.C., 1967. Mem. Parapsychol. Assn. (assoc.), Assn. Past-Life Research and Therapy (assoc.). Home: 3223 Madera Ave Los Angeles CA 90039 Office: care Spirit Speaks PO Box 84304 Los Angeles CA 90073

VAUGHAN, JAMES ARTHUR, JR., physician, surgeon; b. Sherman, Tex., Aug. 16, 1914; s. James Arthur and Nola Beatrice (Lawrence) V.; B.S., East Tex. State Coll., 1947, M.S., 1950; D.O., Chgo. Coll. Osteopathy, 1951; M.D., Calif. Coll. Medicine, 1962; m. Betty Ruth Brecheen, June 19, 1942 (dec.); children: J.A., James A. III; m. 2d, Betty Jo Stewart, Nov. 14, 1958 (div.); 1 dau., Karen. Intern Dallas Osteo. Hosp., 1951-52; pvt. practice, Dallas, 1952-63; assoc. Antelope Valley Med. Clinic, 1963-77; practice medicine, 1977-86; vice chief staff Lancaster Community Hosp., 1968, chief of staff, 1980-86; staff mem. Antelope Valley Hosp.; bd. dirs. Dallas Osteo. Hosp. until 1963; mem. adv. com. LVN Sch. Nursing until 1963. Served from seaman 2d class to lt. comdr. USNR, 1941-46, now lt. comdr. ret. Decorated Air medal with 1 gold star; recipient Disting. Service award CAP. Mem. AMA, Los Angeles County Med. Assn., Ret. Officers Assn. (life), Nat. Aero. Assn., Flying Doctors Soc. Africa (life), D.A.V. (life), Am. Legion (life), VFW (life), Sigma Tau Gamma, Iota Tau Sigma, Sigma Sigma Phi. Mason (32 deg., Shriner); mem. Order Eastern Star, Amaranth. Democrat. Episcopalian. Club: Caterpillar. Office: Box 2988 Lancaster CA 93539-2988

VAUGHAN, JOHN H., physician, researcher; b. Richmond, Va., Nov. 7, 1921; s. Warren Taylor and Emma (Heath) V.; m. Marjorie E. Seybold, Mar. 19, 1983; children: John, Nancy, David, Margaret. AB cum laude, Harvard U., 1942, MD, 1945. Diplomate Am. Bd. Internal Medicine, Am. Bd. Allergy and Immunology. Intern in medicine Peter Bent Brigham Hosp., Boston, 1945-46, research fellow, 1948-50, sr. asst. resident in medicine, 1950-51; fellow in research NRC Columbia-Presbyn. Med. Ctr., N.Y.C., 1951-53; asst. prof. medicine Med. Coll. Va., Richmond, 1953-58; assoc. prof. medicine, asst. prof. bacteriology and immunology U. Rochester (N.Y.) Med. Sch., 1958-63, prof. med., head immunology and infectious diseases unit, 1963-70; adj. prof. medicine U. Calif., San Diego, 1970—; chmn. clin. divs. Scripps Clinic and Research Found., La Jolla, Calif., 1970-74, chmn. dept. clin. research, 1974-77, head div. clin. immunology, 1977—. Editor: Immunological Diseases, 1965, 3d rev. edit., 1978, Dermatology in General Medicine, 1971. Served with AUS, 1946-48. Mem. Am. Acad. Allergy (pres. 1966-67), Am. Assn. Immunologists, Am. Clin. Climatol. Assn., ACP, Am. Fedn. Clin. Research, Am. Rheumatism Assn. (pres. 1970-71), Am. Soc. Clin. Investigation, Assn. Am. Physicians, Infectious Diseases Soc., San Diego County Med. Soc., Western Assn. Physicians (councillor 1978-81), Western Soc. Clin. Research, NIH (gen. medicine study sect. 1956-60, allergy and immunology study sect. 1960-64, ad hoc coms. on arthritis ctrs. 1978-80, allergy and clin. immunology research com. 1981), Nat. Inst. Allergy and Infectious Diseases (bd. councillors for intramural program 1968-72), Yugoslavian Rheumatology Soc. (hon.), Brazilian Soc. Rheumatology (hon.), Alpha Omega Alpha. Home: 7936 Calle de la Plata La Jolla CA 92037 Office: Scripps Clinic & Research Found 10666 N Torrey Pines Rd La Jolla CA 92037

VAUGHAN, LYNDA DIANE JULIEN, educational administrator; b. Turlock, Calif., Apr. 8, 1941; d. Ronald Lyndon and Evelyn Gertrude (Eastman) Julien; m. Richard James Vaughan, Jan. 30, 1960; children: Lance Richard, Brent Alan, Brannan Paul, Julien Kristin. BA, Calif. State Coll.-Stanislaus, 1961; MA in Ednl. Adminstrn., St. Mary's Coll., 1983. Cert. tchr., adminstr. Calif. Tchr. Turlock (Calif.) High Sch., 1961-62; tchr., adminstr. Waterford (Calif.) Sch. Dist., 1966-82; project specialist, coordinator Stanislaus County Dept. Edn., Modesto, Calif., 1982-84, cons., 1982-86; adminstr. personnel services, ednl. services coordinator, 1987—. Mem. Family Service League, coordinator Stanislaus County Indsl. Edn. Council; past pres. Friends of Waterford Library, Waterford Tri-W; past bd. dirs. local heart assn., mem. city council City of Waterford (Calif.), vice mayor, 1984-85, mayor, 1985-86; mem. policy bd. Stanislaus Area Assn. Govts. Recipient Bank of Am. Achievement award, Math. Assn. Am. award, Bausch and Lomb Sci. award, 1958; Kettering Found. IDEA fellow, 1983-84. Mem. Assn. Calif. Sch. Adminstrs., Calif. Assn. for Gifted, Nat. Council Tchrs. Math., Calif. Scholarship Fedn. (life), P.E.O., Phi Delta Kappa. Office: 801 County Center 111 Ct Modesto CA 95355

VAUGHAN, THOMAS JAMES GREGORY, historian; b. Seattle, Oct. 13, 1924; s. Daniel George and Kathryn Genevieve (Browne) V.; m. Elizabeth Ann Perpetua Crownhart, June 16, 1951; children: Meagan, Margot, Stephen, Cameron. B.A., Yale U., 1948; M.A., U. Wis., 1950, doctoral residence, 1951-53; Litt.D., Pacific U., 1969; LL.D., Reed Coll., 1975. Exec. dir. Oreg. Hist. Soc., Portland, 1954—; editor-in-chief Oreg. Hist. Quar., 1954—; adj. prof. Portland State U., 1968—; chmn. bd. Salar Enterprises, Ltd.; dir. Am. Heritage Pub. Co., 1976—; film producer, 1958-76. Author: A Century of Portland Architecture, 1967, Captain Cook, R.N, The Resolute Mariner: An International Record of Oceanic Discovery, 1974, Portland, A Historical Sketch and Guide, 1976, 2d edit., 1983, Voyage of Enlightenment: Malaspina on the Northwest Coast, 1977; editor: Space, Style and Structure: Building in Northwest America, 2 vols., 1974, The Western Shore, 1975, Ascent of the Athabasca Pass, 1978, Wheels of Fortune, High and Mighty, 1981, Soft Gold, 1982; To Siberia and Russian America, Vols. I and II, also others.; mem. adv. bd.: Am. Heritage Mag., 1977—. First chmn. Oreg. State Com. for Humanities, NEH, 1969—; 1st chmn. Gov.'s Adv. Com. on Historic Preservation Oreg., 1970—; sec. Oreg. Geog. Names Bd., 1958—; adviser 1000 Friends of Oreg., 1972—; lay mem. Oreg. State Bar Disciplinary Rev. Bd., 1975—; vice chmn. adv. panel Nat. Endowment Arts, 1975—; mem. Nat. Hist. Publs. and Records Commn. Matrix, 1975-76. Served with USMC, 1942-45. Decorated comdr. Order Brit. Empire; recipient Aubrey Watzek award Lewis and Clark Coll., 1975; Edith Knight Hill award, 1977; recipient Disting. Service award U. Oreg., 1980, Portland State U., 1985; Tom McCall Broadcasting award, 1981; English Speaking Union grantee, 1961. Fellow Royal Geog. Soc.; mem. Am. Assn. State and Local History (dir. 1955-74, pres. 1976—), Am. Assn. Mus. (council, exec. com.), Nat. Trust Historic Preservation (adv. council). Clubs: City (Portland) (bd. govs.), Univ. (Portland) (bd. govs.). Home: 1634 SW Myrtle St Portland OR 97201 Office: Oreg Hist Quar 1230 SW Park Ave Portland OR 97205

VAUGHN, DONALD ALLEN, advertising executive; b. San Mateo Calif., Aug. 6, 1930; s. Edgar Allen and Flora May (Allen) V.; m. Cheryl Ann Lindsay, Jan. 31, 1970; children—Diana, Gregory, Jeffry, Jennifer, Meghan. Student Long Beach City Coll., 1952-54; B.F.A., Art. Ctr. Coll of Design, Pasadena, Calif., 1957. Sr. art dir. Young and Rubicam, N.Y.C., 1957-69; assoc. creative dir. McCann-Marshalk, N.Y.C., and Atlanta, 1969-70; creative dir. Adams and Assocs., Compton, Calif., 1970-73, Glenn Advt., Burlingame Calif., 1973-75; sr. art. dir. Doyle Dane, Bernbach, Honolulu, 1975-77; v.p. creative dir. Tom, Vaughn, Hayashi Advt., Honolulu, 1977-78; sr. art dir. J. Walter Thompson, San Francisco, 1978-87; prin. Schuller, Vaugan Communications, Calif., 1987—; instr. advt., art dir. U. Calif., Berkeley Extension. Served to sgt. USMCR, 1947-52, Korea. Recipient Clio Advt. awards, 1977; Best in West award Am. Advt. Fedn., 1978; Andy award, 1980. Mem. Art Ctr. Coll. of Design Alumni Assoc., Japanese-Am. Inst. Mgmt. Sci. Republican. Contbr. articles to profl. jours.

VAUGHN, STEPHANIE LEE, social work consultant; b. Albuquerque, Sept. 14, 1955; d. Harold Roy and Mary Jo (Tawzer) V. BA, Trinity U., 1977; MS, U. Tex., Arlington, 1980. Social worker Dept. Human Services, Albuquerque, 1980-85, social work cons., 1985—. Tchr. First Presbyn. Sch., Albuquerque, 1983—. Mem. Nat. Assn. Social Workers (bd. dirs. 1985—). Republican. Avocations: theatre, gardening. Home: 941 Calle Mejia Santa Fe NM 87501 Office: Dept Human Services PO Box 2348 Santa Fe NM 87504

VAUSHER, ABRAHAM LUKE, safety engineer; b. Mehalla-el-Koubra, Egypt, July 28, 1928; came to U.S., 1969—.; s. Naguib and Labieba Ibrahim; m. Afeefa Marie Vausher, July 24, 1954; children: Alexander, George, Phoebe. BS, U. Cairo, 1949; MA in Chemistry, Mankato State U., 1971; MPH, U. Minn., 1972. Assoc. chemist Midwest Research Inst., Hopkins, Minn., 1974-78; application engr. Gen. Resource Corp., Hopkins, 1978-81; staff chemist Goodyear Atomic Corp., Piketon, Ohio, 1981-85; engr. scientist McDonnell Douglas Astronautic Corp., Huntington Beach, Calif., 1986—. Contbr. articles to profl. jours.; inventor in field. Mem. Am. Inst. Chem. Engrs., Am. Chem. Soc. Coptic Orthodox.

VAVOULIS, ALEXANDER, chemistry educator; b. Pitts., Dec. 28, 1924; s. William and Katherine (Zervas) V.; m. Jean Carlisle, Mar. 12, 1955; children: Ted G., David W. AB, Bklyn. Coll., 1951, MA, 1953; EdD in Chemistry, U. Pacific, 1962. Prof. chemistry Davidson (N.C.) Coll., 1953-55; instr. Wright Jr. Coll., Chgo., 1958-59, U. Pacific, Stockton, Calif., 1959-62, Stockton Coll., 1961-63; mem. faculty Calif. State U., Fresno, 1963—. Author: (with A. Wayne Colver) Science and Society, 1966, Chemistry Calculations, 1966; contbr. articles to profl. jours. Pres. Fresno Free Coll. Found., 1973—; mgr. KFCF-FM, 1975—; bd. dirs. ACLU, Fresno, 1970-75. Served with USN, 1943-46. Dupont fellow, U. N.C., 1955-58, Zellerbach fellow, 1959-60. Home: 1203 E Santa Ana Ave Fresno CA 93704 Office: Calif State U Dept Chemistry Fresno CA 93740

VAWTER, DONALD GEORGE, personnel management consultant; b. Spokane, Wash., May 19, 1920; s. Edgar F. and Lina M. V.; student polit. sci. Wash. State U., 1946-49; m. Margaret Schroeder, May 5, 1950; children—Charlotte, Sara. Supr. employee services Wash. State Employment Service, Seattle, 1950-58; employment mgr. Sundstrand Data Control, Redmond, Wash., 1958-72; profl. recruiter DBA Bellevue Employment Agy., Bellevue, Wash., 1972-73; personnel mgr., workers compensation adminstr. Crown Zellerbach, Omak, Wash., 1973-82; bd. dirs. Pacific N.W. Personnel Mgmt. Assn., 1967-73. Bd. dirs. Area 7 Manpower Planning Bd., 1974-78; apptd. Gov's. Services Council, 1975-77; planning adv. council State of Wash., 1977—. Served with USCGR, 1942-46, 50-53, comdr. Res. ret., 1968. Mem. Am. Soc. Personnel Adminstrn. (accredited personnel mgr.). Clubs: Elks, Grey W (Wash. State U.). Home: PO Box 296 Tonasket WA 98855

VAYDA, STEPHEN HALL, engineer; b. Oxford, Eng., June 5, 1944; came to U.S., 1982; s. Raoul Imre and Joan Charlotte (Hall) V.; m. Cherrill Wendy Barron, Sept. 13, 1975; children: Daniel, Thomas, Sarah, Elizabeth. Diploma, Mical Coll., Liverpool, Eng., 1969; MS, Cranfield Inst. Tech., Eng., 1971. Registered profl. engr., Eng. Design engr. Hunting Engring. Ltd., Ampthill Bedford, Eng., 1973-74, Babcock and Wilcox, London, 1974-76; sr. design engr. Preece Cardew and Rider, Brighton, Eng., 1976-78; lead engr. Fluidized Combustion Contractors Ltd., Crawley, West Sussex, Eng., 1978-82; advanced engr. Simons Eastern Co., Atlanta, 1983; proposal engr. Pyropower Corp., San Diego, 1983, applications engr., 1985-86; cons. in fluidized bed combustion and energy cons. Poway, Calif., 1986—. Mem. Inst. Energy, Inst. Marine Engrs., ASME (advanced energy com. 1983—). Home: 14814 Derringer Rd Poway CA 92064 Office: 13715 Poway Road Poway CA 92064

VEAL, DONALD LYLE, former university president, aircraft instrumentation consultant and researcher, educator; b. Chance, S.D., Apr. 17, 1931; s. Boyd William and Esther Mabel (Iverson) V.; m. Bonita Dale Larson, May 8, 1953; children: Sherrill, Barbara. B.S.C.E., S.D. State U., 1953; M.S.C.E., U. Wyo., 1960, Ph.D. in Civil Engring., 1964. Lic. profl. engr. Wyo. Asst. prof. civil engring. U. Wyo., 1964-66, assoc. prof., 1966-71, prof., 1971—, head dept. atmospheric sci., 1971-76, 77-80, v.p. research, 1980-81, acting pres., 1981-82, pres., 1982-87; dir. nat. hail research expt. Nat. Center Atmospheric Research, Boulder, Colo., 1976-77; trustee Univ. Corp. for Atmospheric Research, Boulder, 1978—; chmn. Univ. Corp. for Atmospheric Research, 1980-82; commr. Western Interstate Commn. for Higher Edn., Salt Lake City, 1981—; mem. ROTC adv. com. U.S. Army Command and Gen. Staff Coll., Fort Leavenworth, Kans., 1982—; dir. Particle Measuring Systems, Inc., Boulder, 1982—, First Interstate Bank, Laramie, Wyo., 1974—; mem. Nat. Acad. Scis.-NRC panel on low-altitude wind variability. Mem. Brees Field Airport Authority, Laramie, 1962-76; pres. Bress Field Airport Authority, 1964-76; mem. Wyo. Congl. Award Council, 1983; pres. Western Athletic Conf. Found., 1983—. Served to 1st lt. USAF, 1953-57. Recipient Disting. Alumnus U. S.D., 1983. Fellow Am. Meteorol. Soc.; mem. Nat. Soc. Profl. Engrs., Am. Soc. Engring. Edn., ASCE, Weather Modification Assn., N.Y. Acad. Scis., Sigma Xi. Lodge: Rotary (Laramie). Office: U Wyo PO Box 3434 Univ Sta Laramie WY 82071

VEALE, J. B., JR., orthodontist; b. Dallas, Sept. 3, 1925; s. J. B. Veale and Lillian (Milliken) Cummings; m. Mary Katherine Bean, Feb. 22, 1947; children—Thomas S., Deborah Anne. Student U. Tex., Austin, U. Okla.-Norman; D.D.S., U. Tex.-Houston, 1950. Practice dentistry specializing in orthodontics, Pampa, Tex., 1950-82; pres. Red River Ski Area subs. Mt. Wheeler Corp., Red River, N.Mex., 1961-84, Mt. Wheeler Devel. Co., Red River, 1978-84; chmn. bd. TDA Ins. Co., Houston, 1979—. Editor Tex. Dental Jour., 1975-78. Founder, pres. United Fund, Pampa, 1954; pres. Community Concert Assn., Pampa, 1960; chmn. Santa Fe Dist. council Boy Scouts Am., Pampa, 1960. Served with USNR, 1943-46; PTO. Recipient Scouters Key award Boy Scouts Am., 1965. Mem. Tex. Dental Assn. (v.p. 1975-76, Pres.'s award 1979), Southwestern Soc. Orthodontists, ADA (del. 1950), Assn. Am. Dentists (pres. 1970). Republican. Methodist. Home: 9425 Oakmont NE Albuquerque NM 87111

VEALE, JOHN EDMOND (JACK), business executive; b. Winchester, Mass., July 12, 1954; s. Edmond John and Margaret Louise V.; BS in Bus. Adminstrn., Norwich U., 1976; m. Laurie Jean Howard, Apr. 29, 1978; children: Alex, Jason. With Southwest Hide Co., Boise, Idaho, 1976—, acct., 1977-78, office mgr., corp. office, 1978-79, corp. controller, 1979-81, chief fin. officer, 1981-87; div. pres. Northwest Mgmt. Assocs., Gt. West Data Systems, 1983—. Mem. Idaho Assn. Commerce and Industry, Boise Philharm. Assn., Idaho Golf Angels Assn., Bogus Basin Recreation Assn., Plantation C. of C., Alpha Kappa Psi. Republican. Clubs: Full Gospel Businessmen's Internat., Crane Creek Country, Nat. Ski Patrol. Home: 4062 Patton St Boise ID 83704 Office: Box 7946 Boise ID 83707

VEATCH, JOHN WILLIAM, speech pathologist; b. Mitchell, S.D., Dec. 9, 1923; s. William Homer and Helen Gwendolyn (Lowther) V.; m. Doris Lavelle Guthrie (dec. 1978); children: Dean, Joan; m. Winnifred Ann Sawin, Aug. 6, 1982; children: Shaun, Monicah. BA in Speech, Wash. State U., 1946, BEd, 1951; MA in Speech, U. Wash., 1950; DEd, U. Idaho, 1970. Pvt. practice speech pathology Spokane, Wash., 1950-79; pvt. practice speech pathology and ednl. cons. Tacoma, 1980—; pres., chief exec. officer and dir. research. Espial Inst., Tacoma, 1982—; cons. Kinetic Design, Inc., Ollalla, Wash., 1986—. Author (test profiles) Personal Stress Balance Profile, 1982, Info. Processing Style, 1984, The Deep Screening Profile of Tongue Thrusting Activity, 1985, The Tongue Thrust Screening Test, Learning Style Profile, 1986. Fellow Northwest Acad. Speech Pathology (pres. 1978-82, 86—); mem. Internat. Assn. Oral Myology, Am. Speech and Hearing Assn. Avocations: boating, fishing. Home: 4708 64th Ave W Tacoma WA 98466 Office: 4113 Bridge Port Way W Suite B Tacoma WA 98466

VEATCH, ROBERTA ANN, marketing executive, perfume company executive; b. Holdredge, Nebr., Oct. 8, 1955; d. Robert Wesley and Mildred Lillian (Pavelka) Hull; m. Thomas Dale Veatch, May 23, 1973; 1 child, Kyna Harmony. Student Ariz. State U., Scientia Coll. Make up artist, Houston, 1975-78; cosmetic trainer Dynige Internat., Phoenix, 1978-80; nat. tng. dir. Chem. Assocs., Phoenix, 1980-81; nat. cosmetic dir. d'Saison Cre Creative Color, Houston, 1981-82; exec. v.p., 1982-84; pres. Entourage Perfumery, Houston, 1984—. Author: Mirror Image, 1981; developed signature fragrance Amadeus, skin care and body products. Recipient top sales awards Home Care Internat., 1982, Dynique Internat., 1979. Mem. Fragrance Found., Nat. Female Execs., Delta Delta Delta. Avocations: hot air ballooning, painting, writing. Home: 1918 E Myrna Ln Tempe AZ 85284 Office: Entourage Internat Inc PO Box 19934 Houston TX 77024

VEBLEN, THOMAS THORSTEIN, ecology and geography educator; b. Seattle, Nov. 15, 1947; s. Robert Alfred and Lois Aileen (Oglesbee) V.; m. Arlene Shuey-Yuen Tseu, June 28, 1969; children: Kari Elizabeth, Conner Thorstein. BA, U. Calif., Berkeley, 1969, MA, 1970, PhD, 1975. Vis. prof. Universidad Austral, Valdivia, Chile, 1975-79; New Zealand Nat. Research Adv. Council fellow Forest Research Inst., Christchurch, 1979-81; asst. prof. geography U. Colo., Boulder, 1981-83, assoc. prof., 1983—; research assoc. Inst. Alpine and Arctic Research, Boulder, 1982-86. Mem editorial bd. Mountain Research and Devel., 1982—, Phys. Geography, 1985—; contbr. articles to profl. jours. Grantee Colo. Commn. Higher Edn., 1982-83, Nat. Geog. Soc., 1983-84; Guggenheim fellow, 1985-86, Nat. Sci. Found.. fellow, 1986-90. Mem. Conf. Latin Americanist Geographers (bd. dirs. 1982-85), Internat. Assn. Vegetation Sci., Brit. Ecol. Soc., Assn. Am. Geographers, Ecol. Soc. Am. Avocations: jogging, hiking. Home: 4170 Hunt Ct Boulder CO 80303 Office: U Colo Dept Geography Box 260 Boulder CO 80309-0260

VEEDER, GEORGE THOMAS, III, microbiologist; b. Franklin, La., Mar. 22, 1944; s. George Thomas Jr. and Mary Frances (Clyburn) V.; m. Peggy Auenson, June 13, 1966 (div. June 1975); children: George Thomas IV, Stephen; m. Jo Ann Chapman, June 21, 1975; children: Cheri, Tami, John. BS, U. Southwestern La., 1966; MS, La. State U., 1969. Sr. research microbiologist Kelco Co., San Diego, 1969-79; research fellow Kelco div. Merck & Co., Inc., San Diego, 1979-82, mgr., 1982—. Patentee in field, 1983. Mem. Am. Soc. Microbiology, Soc. Indsl. Microbiology, U.S. Fedn. Culture Collections. Republican. Avocations: golf, reading. Office: Kelco Div MercK & Co Inc 8225 Aero Dr San Diego CA 92123

VEGA, JOSE GUADALUPE, psychologist, clinical director; b. San Benito, Tex., June 4, 1953; s. Jose Guadalupe and Bertha (Saenz) V.; m. Beth Susan Brimmer, Aug. 20, 1979 (div. 1986); children: Lilian Anna, Jose Guadalupe III. BA, Pan. Am. U., Edinburg, Tex., 1975; MA, U. Denver, 1976, PhD, 1979. Lic. psychologist, Colo., 1983; lic. profl. counselor, Tex., 1983; diplomate Am. Bd. Med. Psychotherapists. With Oasis of Chandala, Denver, 1978-79, Maytag-Emrick Clinic, Aurora, Colo., 1979; psychologist Spanish Peaks Mental Health Ctr., Pueblo, Colo., 1980-85; pvt. practice Assocs. for Psychotherapy and Edn., Inc., 1985-86; co-owner Affiliates in Counseling, Psychol. Assessment and Consultation, Inc., Pueblo, 1986—. Active Colo. Inst. Chicano Mental Health Community Youth Orgn., Boys Club Pueblo. Mem. Am. Psychol. Assn., Nat. Acad. Neuropsychologists, Am. Assn. for Counseling and Devel. (health and human services com.), Colo. Psychol. Assn., Nat. Hispanic Psychol. Assn., Phi Delta Kappa, Kappa Delta Pi. Democrat. Roman Catholic. Office: 635 W Corona Suite 205 PO Box 2337 Pueblo CO 81005

VEGA, MICHAEL ROBLES, podiatrist; b. Loma Linda, Calif., June 18, 1955; s. Trinidad and Emelia (Robles) V.; m. Julie Louise Haak, Apr. 29, 1978; children: Bianca Pilar, Michael Louis. BA, U. San Diego, 1977; D in Podiatric Medicine, Ohio Coll. Podiatric Medicine, 1982. Podiatrist Community Health Found., Los Angeles, 1983-86; pvt. practice podiatry Montebello, Calif., 1985—; clin. asst. prof. podiatric medicine Calif. Coll. Podiatric Medicine, 1987—. Contbr. articles to profl. jours. Mem. Podiatry Soc. Los Angeles, Am. Podiatric Med. Assn., Am. Acad. Podiatric Sports Medicine, Am. Running and Fitness Assn., Am. Podiatric Med. Writers Assn., Pi Delta. Democrat. Roman Catholic. Avocations: golf, racquetball, tennis, painting. Home: 5509 Westmont Rd Whittier CA 90601 Office: West Beverly Podiatry Group 433 N 4th St Suite 202 Montebello CA 90640

VEGA, ROY DAVID, community official; b. San Jose, Calif., Dec. 6, 1946; s. Gabriel and Eloise (Osuna) V.; B.A. in Polit. Sci., U. Santa Clara, 1968; m. Kathy Marie Mestas, June 29, 1974; children: Angelene, David, Michael, Emily. Dir. Dept. Pub. Safety, Community of Pagosa Lakes (Colo.), 1974—. Contbr. articles to profl. jours. Served to capt., M.P. U.S. Army, 1969-74. Decorated Bronze Star, Joint Service Commendation medal Def. Nuclear Agy. Mem. Internat. Assn. Chiefs of Police. Republican. Nat. Sheriffs Assn., Upper San Juan Emergency Med. Technicians Assn., Upper San Juan Peace Officers Assn. Roman Catholic. Club: Rotary Internat. Office: 191 N Pagosa Blvd PO Drawer 4010 Pagosa Lakes CO 81157

VEITCH, ELWOOD N., minister of consumer and corporate affairs; b. Monk Township, Ont., Can., July 21, 1929; s. Wellington and Alice Alma (Brott) v.; m. Sheila Boyce; children: Barbara Anne McCallum, Brian Andrew, Gregory Neil. Diploma in Bus. Adminstrn., U. B.C., Vancouver, Can., 1969; MBA, Pacific Union Coll., 1979. Mem. Legis. Assembly, Victoria, B.C., 1975, 83; minister tourisms, small bus. devel. Govt. B.C., 1978, chief govt. whip, 1983, minister consumer corp. affairs, 1986—. Lodges: Rotary, Masons, Shriners (pres. Burnaby club 1976). Home: 4762 Carson Pl, Burnaby Can V5J 2Y5 Office: Parliament Bldg, Victoria Can V8V 1X4

VEJVODA, EDWARD, aerospace company executive; b. N.Y.C., Apr. 18, 1924; s. Emil and Mary (Stuzinsky) V.; m. Mary Ellen Smith, June 12, 1949; children: Mary Diane, Karl Spencer, Gail Denise. BA in Chemistry, U. No. Colo., 1949, MA in Chemistry, 1951; postgrad., U. Denver, 1956-69. Analytical chemist Dow Chem. Co., Golden, Colo., 1952-60, mgr. research and devel., 1961-64, 66-74; plutonium cons. ALKEM, Karlsruhe, Fed. Republic of Germany, 1964-65; dir. chem. ops. Rockwell Internat., Golden, 1975-85, exec. asst., 1986—; plutonium ops. cons., Rockwell Hanford Co., Richland, Wash., 1977—. Patentee in field; contbr. articles to profl. jours. Served as sgt. AC, U.S. Army, 1943-46, PTO. Mem. Am. Chem. Soc. (awards com.), Am. Electroplater's Soc., Inst. for Nuclear Materials Mgmt., Nat. Mgmt. Assn. (Excellence award 1986), Am. Legion, Sigma Xi. Republican. Methodist. Lodge: Elks. Avocations: hunting, fishing, boating. Office: Rockwell Internat PO Box 464 Golden CO 80401

VELA, CELIA TOMACITA, federal agent; b. Bremerton, Wash., Mar. 29, 1953; d. Jesse and Maria Juana (Lujan) Ramirez; m. Pedro Vela, Jr., Oct. 6, 1979 (dec. 1983). B.S. in Criminal Justice, San Diego, 1975, postgrad., 1976-78. Cert. explosive instr. Fed. agt. Alcohol, Tobacco & Firearms, Treasury Dept., Phoenix, 1978-82, San Diego, 1982—, vault custodian, 1982—, destruction officer, 1982—, recruiter, 1984—, explosive instr., 1986—, arson investigator, 1985—. Author recruitment manual: How to Fill Out 171, 1985. Local Bd. Selective Service System, Chula Vista, Calif., 1985—. Served with USAR, 1976-78. Recipient Outstanding Performance award Treasury Dept., 1981, Spl. Achievement award, 1986. Mem. Nat. Assn. Arson Investigators, Nat. Assn. Treasury Agts., Internat. Assn. Bomb Technicians and Investigators, Nat. Assn. Female Execs. Roman Catholic. Club: St. Mary's Women Choir (National City). Avocations: violin, running, swimming, bicycling. Office: Alcohol Tobacco and Firearms 880 Front St Room 6N16 San Diego CA 92188

VELDE, JOHN ERNEST, JR., business executive; b. Pekin, Ill., June 15, 1917; s. John Ernest and Alga (Anderson) V.; m. Shirley Margaret Walker, July 29, 1940 (dec. 1969); 1 dau., Drew; m. Gail Patrick, Sept. 28, 1974 (dec. July 1980); m. Gretchen Swanson Pullen, Nov. 7, 1981. A.B., U. Ill., 1938. Pres. Velde, Roelfs & Co., Pekin, 1955-60; dir. Herget Nat. Bank, 1948-75, Kroehler Mfg. Co., 1974-81; pres. Paisano Prodns., Inc., 1980—. Trustee Pekin Pub. Library, 1948-69, Pekin Meml. Hosp., 1950-69; chmn. Am. Library Trustee Assn. Found., 1976; trustee Am. Library Assn. Endowment, 1976-82, Everett McKinley Dirksen Research Center, 1965-74; chmn. trustees, bd. dirs. Center Ulcer Research and Edn. Found., 1977-82; mem. bd. councilors Brain Research Inst. UCLA, 1977-82; trustee Center for Am. Archeology, Evanston, 1978-83; mem. Nat. Commn. on Libraries and Info. Sci., 1970-79; mem. adv. bd. on White House Conf. on Libraries, 1976-80; trustee Joint Council on Econ. Edn., 1977-83; bd. dirs. U. Ill. Found., 1977-83, Omaha Pub. Library Found., 1985—; vice chmn. U. Ill. Pres.' Council, 1977-79, chmn., 1979-81, mem. fin. resources council steering com., 1976-78; mem. adv. council UCLA Grad. Sch. Library and Info. Sci., 1981-82; pres. Ill. Valley Library System, 1965-69; dir. Lakeview Center for Arts and Scis., Peoria, Ill., 1962-73; mem. Nat. Book Com., 1969-74. Served as lt. (j.g.) USNR, World War II. Mem. Am. Library Trustee Assn. (regional v.p. 1970-72, chmn. internat. relations com. 1973-76), Kappa Sigma. Clubs: Chgo. Yacht, Internat. (Chgo.); California (Los Angeles); Outrigger Canoe (Honolulu); Thunderbird Country (Rancho Mirage, Calif.); Chaine des Rotisseurs, Chevaliers du Tastevin; Circumnavigators (N.Y.C.); Omaha Country. Home: 8405 Indian Hills Dr Omaha NE 68114 : 40-231 Club View Dr Rancho Mirage CA 92270

VELEZ-IBANEZ, CARLOS GUILLERMO, anthropology educator, research lab. administrator; b. Nogales, Ariz., Oct. 27, 1936; s. Adalberto Garcia and Luz (Ibanez) Velez; children from previous marriage: Carlos, Lucy, Miguel, Carmelita; m. Maria Teresa Marquez, Jan. 28, 1974; 1 child, Mariel. BA, U. Ariz., 1961, MA, 1968; MA, U. Calif., San Diego, 1972, PhD, 1975. Assoc. prof. anthropology UCLA, 1982—; dir. Bur. Applied Research in Anthropology U. Ariz., Tucson, 1982—, prof., 1983—, assoc. dean Sch. Social and Behavioral Scis., 1984-86; vis. assoc. Smithsonian Inst., 1986—. Author: Bonds of Mutual Trust, 1983, Rituals of Marginality, 1983; assoc. editorHuman Organization, 1980—, Am. Ethnologist, 1984—; contbg. editor AZTLAN-Internat. Jour., 1981-85; contbr. articles to profl. jours., chpts. to books. Mem. Hispanic Profl. Action Com., Tucson, 1983—. Fellow Rockefeller Found., 1981-82, Ctr. Advanced Study Behavioral Scis., 1987—; named Disting. Phillips Visitor Haverford Coll., 1981. Fellow Soc. Applied Anthropology, Am. Anthrop. Assn. (mem.-at-large gen. anthrop. unit); mem. CIBOLA Anthrop. Assn. (pres. 1985—), Hispanic Alumni Assn. Avocations: running, martial arts, painting, creative writing. Office: U Ariz Bur Applied Anthrop Research Anthropology Bldg Room 317A Tucson AZ 85721

VELICK, PAUL (LIGHT BOB), artist, performer; b. Detroit, 1952. Student, Art Ctr. Coll., 1974; BFA, Antioch Coll., Los Angeles, 1975. lectr. Contemporary Art Ctr., New Orleans, CAGE Gallery, Cin., Calif. Inst. of Arts, and others, 1978—. Exhibitions with Francis G. Shishim (The Dark Bob) include Ruth S. Schaffner Gallery, Los Angeles, 1978, Swope Gallery/Art Garden, Venice, Calif., 1979, Los Angeles Inst. Contemporary Art, 1979, Vanguard Gallery, Los Angeles, 1980, Espace Gallery, Los Angeles, 1981, Upstairs Gallery, Tryon, N.C., 1981, WPA Gallery, Washington, 1981, Marianne Deson Gallery, Chgo., 1982; exhibited in group shows at Los Angeles Inst. Contemporary Art, 1976, 81, Craft and Folk Art Mus., Los Angeles, 1980, Long Beach (Calif.) Mus. Art, 1980, San Francisco Internat. Video Festival, 1980, Mus. Contemporary Art, Chgo., 1981, Downtown Gallery, Los Angeles, 1981, Tortue Gallery, Santa Monica, Calif., 1981, Am. Gallery, Los Angeles, 1982, UCLA, 1982, WPA Gallery, 1982, Calif. State U., Long Beach, 1983, traveling exhibitions, Los Angeles, Buffalo, 1983; appeared in numerous performances, recordings, radio interviews and videos, 1975—. Office: Bob & Bob PO Box 6461 Beverly Hills CA 90212

VELK, ROBERT JAMES, consulting psychologist; b. Chgo., Feb. 27, 1938; s. Jerry E. and Sylvia B. (Wladar) Vlk; m. Vera A. Kraml, Nov. 25, 1961; children—Robert Frank, Cheryl Anne. B.B.A., Northwestern U., 1963, M.B.A., 1968; M.A., Rutgers U., 1980, Ph.D., 1983. Asst. mgr. product decorations Meyercord Co., Carol Stream, Ill., 1959-65, nat. account mgr., 1965-68; assoc. Kepner Tregoe, Inc., Princeton, N.J., 1968-70, Western region mgr., 1970-72, dir. mktg. N.Am. ops., 1972-73; pres. Creative Leadership Inc., Princeton, 1973-83; pres. Cognitive Sci. Corp., Ft. Collins, Colo., 1983—. Author: Information and Imagination, 1978; Thinking About Thinking, 1978. Mem. Am. Psychol. Assn., Am. Soc. Tng. and Devel., Nat. Soc. Performance and Instrn. Clubs: Christian Businessmen's Com. of Central Jersey (chmn. 1974-75), Gideon's. Office: Cognitive Sci Corp PO Box 1487 Fort Collins CO 80522

VELONA, CHARLES SANTO, television executive; b. Jersey City, N.J., Feb. 1, 1941; s. Domenick N. and Rose V. (Impal) V.; m. Mary Kay Wathen, July 1, 1961; children—Gerard, Carrie, David, Christopher. Student, Tulane U., 1958-59, Local sales mgr. Sta.-KTLA-TV Los Angeles, 1959-71; salesman Sta-KHJ-TV, Los Angeles, 1972-74, sales mgr., 1974-80, v.p., gen. mgr., 1980—. Mem. Calif. Broadcasters, So. Calif. Broadcasters, Acad. TV Arts and Scis., Nat. Assn. TV Programming Execs., Assn. Ind. TV Stas. Office: Sta KHJ-TV 5515 Melrose Ave Los Angeles CA 90038 *

VELTRI, JOSEPH CHARLES, poison control center executive, pharmacy educator; b. San Francisco, Jan. 3, 1948; m. Elizabeth Cobain; children: Nicole, Charles A. BS in Pharmacy, U. Utah, 1971, PharmD, 1977. Dir. Intermountain Regional Poison Control Ctr., Salt Lake City, 1980—; assoc. prof. pharmacy U. Utah, Salt Lake City, 1980—; sr. staff fellow FDA, Rockville, Md., 1982-83, cons., 1982. Asst. editor Poisindex, 1978—; contbr. articles to profl. jours. Recipient commr.'s spl. citation FDA, Rockville, 1983. Fellow Am. Acad. Clin. Toxicology, mem. Am. Assn. Poison Control Ctrs. Office: Intermountain Poison Control Ctr 50 N Medical Dr Salt Lake City UT 84132

VENKATESH, ESWARAHALLI SUNDARARAJAN, engineering educator; b. Bangalore, India, Jan. 30, 1949; came to U.S., 1971; s. Eswarahalli R. Sundararajan and Lokamata (K.) Rangaiyengar; m. Vijaya H. Kasturi, Apr. 20, 1977; children: Sundararajan E.V., Vinita. BSc. in Phys. Math., Bangalore U., 1969; BE in Metallurgy, Indian Inst. Sci., Bangalore, 1971; MS in Materials, Brown U., 1973; PhD in Metallurgy, N.Mex. Tech.Inst., 1977; MS in Petroleum Engring., Okla. U., 1980. Instr. U. Okla., Norman, 1978-80; research engr., investigator INTEVEP div. Nat. Venezuelan Oil, Los Teques, Venezuela, 1980-81; research metallurgist Conoco Inc., Ponca City, Okla., 1981-83; asst. prof. mech. engring., petroleum engring. U. Alaska, Fairbanks, 1983—. Contbr. articles to profl. jours. Mem. Soc. Petroleum Engrs., AIME, Am. Soc. Metals, Nat. Assn. Corrosion Engrs., Metall. Soc. (founder of Bangalore chpt.), Sigma Xi, Alpha Sigma Mu, Tau Beta Pi, Pi Epsilon Tau. Hindu. Lodge: Rotary. Avocations: stamp collecting, coin collecting, music, travel. Home: 3020 Davis Rd D-06 Fairbanks AK 99709 Office: U Alaska Petroleum Engring Dept Fairbanks AK 99775

VERDIER, QUENTIN ROOSEVELT, personnel consultant; b. Mancelona, Mich., Mar. 19, 1921; s. John Walter and Louise (Hills) V.; m. Margaret Elizabeth Wells, Nov. 13, 1943; children: Margaret Louise, Quentin Wells, Nanette Marie Bloom. AB in Pub. Adminstrn., Kalamazoo Coll., 1943, MA in Pub. Adminstrn., 1947; postgrad., Am. U., 1948-51; PhD in Human Resource Devel., Columbia Pacific U., 1985. Cert. employment cons., personnel cons., forensic vocat. expert; lic. employment agt., Wis. Asst. personnel officer U.S. Savs. Bonds div. U.S. Govt., Washington, 1951-58; div. chief office of personnel Internat. Coop. Adminstrn./Agy. for Internat. Devel., Washington, 1959-63; dep. chief pub. adminstrn. div. U.S. Ops. Mission/Agy. for Internat. Devel., Saigon, South Vietnam, 1963-65; asst. dir. tng. Inst. Govt. Affairs U. Wis. Extension, Madison, 1966-67; v.p. adminstrn. Advance Mktg. Group, Madison, 1981-83; pres., chief ops. officer AvailABILITY of Madison, Inc., 1967—, also chmn. bd. dirs.; mem. adv. panel Nat. Forensic Ctr., Princeton, 1983—. Author City Employee Handbook-Better Pub. Service, 1947; editor hist. pamphlet series Understanding Backgrounds, 1964; contbr. articles to profl. jours. Bd. dirs. Capital Community Citizen's Assn., Madison, 1967; pres. Country Heights Homeowners Assn., Oregon, 1969. Served with U.S. Air Corps, 1943-46. Recipient Wm G. Howard prize, 1946; Upjohn fellow Kalamazoo Coll., 1946-47. Mem. Nat. Assn. Personnel Cons., Am. Soc. Personnel Adminstrn., Wis. Soc. Personnel Cons., Am. Arbitration Assn. (arbitrator, mem. panel Chgo. regional office), U.S.A. Tug-of-War Assn. (sec., parliamentarian 1978), Am. Assn. Ret. Persons. Club: Toastmasters (dist. 36 gov.). Lodge: Masons (32 degree), Rotary. Avocations: choral singing, genealogy.

VERHAEREN, PAUL VEN, computer consultant, artist; b. Detroit, Feb. 10, 1939; s. Victor and Rosemary Immaculata (Chauvin) V.; m. Karen Frankenfield, Oct. 7, 1970 (div. 1973). Student, U. San Diego, 1956-58; BA cum laude, Fordham U., 1982. Margin mgr., asst. to v.p. First Calif. Co., San Francisco, 1965-71; margin mgr. E.F. Hutton Co., San Francisco, 1971-73; performance analyst Mfrs. Hanover Trust Corp., N.Y.C., 1973-79; mgr., editor Swedenborg Found., N.Y.C., 1979-83; mgr., newsletter editor Calif. League Sr. Citizens, Los Angeles, 1983-85; ptnr. Verhaeren & Hay, Pacific Grove, Calif., 1985, Monarch Software, Newbury Park, Calif., 1986—; project dir. Calif. Sr. Discount Program, Los Angeles County, Calif., 1985. Editor Logos, N.Y.C., 1979-83, Senior Citizen Sentinel, 1984-85; one-man shows painting and drawing, Europe and U.S.; film works include Patterns, 1981, Liberty, 1982. Artist and sec. Affiliated Coms. on Aging, Los Angeles County, 1983-85; sec., bd. dirs., Calif. League and Affiliated Coms., Los Angeles, 1983-85. Mem. Pacific Grove C. of C., Swedenborg Found. (contbg., recording sec. 1979-83), Lotus Group (tiler, lectr. 1964-70), Geneal. Soc. Flemish-Ams. Democrat. Episcopalian. Avocations: writing, computer graphics, fabric arts. Home: 240 Walnut St Pacific Grove CA 93950 Office: Verhaeren & Hay PO Box 51999 Pacific Grove CA 93950

VERHEY, JOSEPH WILLIAM, psychiatrist; b. Oakland, Calif., Sept. 28, 1928; s. Joseph Bernard and Anne (Hanken) V.; B.S. summa cum laude, Seattle U., 1954; M.D., U. Wash., 1958; m. Darlene Helen Seiler, July 21, 1956. Intern, King County Hosp., Seattle, 1958-59; resident Payne Whitney Psychiatric Clinic, N.Y. Hosp., Cornell Med. Center, N.Y.C., 1959-62, U. Wash. Hosp., Seattle, 1962-63; practice medicine, specializing in psychiatry, Seattle, 1963—; mem. staff U. Hosp., Providence Hosp., Fairfax Hosp., VA Med. Center, Tacoma; clin. instr. psychiatry U. Wash. Med. Sch., 1963-68, clin. asst. prof. psychiatry, 1968-82, clin. assoc. prof., 1982—; cons. psychiatry U.S. Dept. Def., Wash. State Bur. Juvenile Rehab.; examiner Am. Bd. Psychiatry and Neurology. Diplomate Am. Bd. Psychiatry and Neurology. Fellow N. Pacific Soc. Psychiatry and Neurology, Am. Psychiat. Assn.; mem. AMA, Am. Fedn. Clin. Research, World Fedn. Mental Health, Soc. Mil. Surgeons of U.S. Clubs: Wash. Athletic, Swedish (life). Home: 1100 University St Seattle WA 98101 Office: VA Med Center Tacoma WA 98493

VERHEYDEN, JULIEN PIERRE, pharmaceutical company executive, organic chemist; b. Brussels, May 22, 1933; came to U.S., 1961; s. Jean Albert and Henriette (Crombez) V.; m. Danielle Lucia Isbecque, June 24, 1959; children: Evelyne, Anne. MS in Chemistry, U. Brussels, 1955, PhD, 1958. Researcher U. Brussels, 1958-61; postdoctoral fellow Syntex, Palo Alto, Calif., 1961-63; staff researcher Syntex, Palo Alto, 1963-71, dept. head, 1971-81, asst. dir. inst. bio-organic chemistry, 1981—. Patentee in field. Served to lt. Belgium Army, 1959-60. Mem. Am. Chem. Soc., Chem. Soc., Belgium Chem. Soc. Avocations: bee-keeping, photography, hiking, classical music, gardening. Office: Syntex R1-215 3401 Hillview Ave Palo Alto CA 94304

VERKAIK, GERARD, architect, consulting engineer; b. Zaandam, The Netherlands, Sept. 24, 1928; came to Can., 1953, came to U.S., 1957; s. Gerard and Sophia (Lengwin) V.; m. Willy Eeltink, July 19, 1953; children: James Peter, Tim Gerard, Lisa Sophia Jean. Ing. Architecture and Engring., U. Utrecht, The Netherlands, 1953; B of Applied Sci., Civil Engring., U. Toronto, 1955; MS in Structural Engring., U. Seattle, 1960. Registered profl. engr. Colo., La., Tex., Ariz. Cons. engr. Lane & Lane, Sudbury, Ont., Can., 1953-57; design engr. The Boeing Co., Renton, Wash., 1957-62; mgr. engring. The Boeing Co., New Orleans, 1962-72; prin. engr., architect Covington, La., 1972-80, Canon City, Colo., 1981—. Engring. mgr. design and mgmt. of the Lunar Roving Vehicle, 1970. Served as sgt. Royal Dutch Army, 1948-50. Mem. Am. Steel Inst., Am. Concrete Inst., Post Tensioning Inst., Internat. Conf. Bldg. Ofs., Canon City C. of C. Republican. Lodge: Rotary. Home: Park County Rd 104 Guffey CO 80820 Office: 831 Royal Gorge Blvd 418 Canon City CO 81212

VERNIERO, JOAN EVANS, educator; b. Wilkes-Barre, Pa., Nov. 30, 1937; d. Raymond Roth and Cary Hazel (Casano) Evans; m. Daniel Eugene Verniero Jr., Jan. 7, 1956; children: Daniel Eugene III, Raymond Evans. BA, Kean Coll., 1971; MS in Edn. Adminstrn., Monmouth Coll., West Long Branch, N.J., 1974; postgrad., Calif. Coast U., 1986—. Cert. elem. sch. tchr.; cert. spl. edn. tchr.; cert. sch. adminstr., N.J., N.Mex., Colo. Tchr. Children's Psychiat. Ctr., Eatontown, N.J., 1965-69; tchr. Arthur Brisbane Child Treatment Ctr., Farmingdale, N.J., 1969-71, prin., 1971-75; prin. S.A. Wilson Ctr., Colorado Springs, Colo., 1976-82; tchr. pub. schs. Aurora, Colo., 1982—; spl. edn. cons. Colo. Dept. Edn., Denver, 1976—; edn. rep. Aurora Public Schs. Citizen's adv. com. Mem. Econ. Devel. Commn., Middletown, N.J.; crew leader Black Forest (Colo.) Rescue Squad, 1979-85, treas., bd. dirs.fire protection dist., 1980-85. Mem. NEA, Colo. Edn. Assn., Aurora Edn. Assn. (faculty rep.), Phi Delta Kappa. Republican. Presbyterian. Avocations: nature photography, horseback riding. Home: 12244 E 2d Dr Aurora CO 80011 Office: Virginia Court Elem Sch 395 S Troy St Aurora CO 80012

VERNON, ROBERT GERARD, lawyer, oil company executive, consultant; b. N.Y.C., July 9, 1935; s. Weston, Jr., and Adelaide (Neilson) V.; m. Kathryn Barnes, Sept. 16, 1966; children: David Cannon, Linda, Richard Daniel. Student Columbia Coll., 1952-54; BA, U. Utah, 1956; postgrad. George Washington U. Law Sch., 1959; JD, Columbia U., 1963. Bar: Utah 1964, U.S. Dist. Ct. Utah 1964. Atty.-landman Skyline Oil Co., Salt Lake City, 1964-79, asst. sec., 1964-72, sec., 1972-77; sole practice, Salt Lake City, 1979-83; oil and gas lease investor and cons., Salt Lake City, 1979-83; v.p. Crossroads Oil Co., 1983—. Chmn. Rep. voting dist. 2644, Salt Lake City, 1970-71. Recipient E.B. Convers Prize, Columbia Law Sch., 1963. Mem. ABA, Utah State Bar (first chmn. oil and gas com. 1978-79), Utah Assn. Petroleum and Mining Landmen (pres. 1971), Am. Assn. Petroleum Landmen (cert. profl. landman). Mormon. Contbr. articles, papers to profl. publs. and confs. Home: 1782 S 2500 E Salt Lake City UT 84108 Office: 530 Kennecott Bldg 10 East S Temple Salt Lake City UT 84133

VERRAN, JOYCE ANN, nurse, researcher, educator; b. Detroit, Nov. 25, 1941; d. Melvin Roy and Dorothy Lucille (Rowe) V. Diploma, Sch. Nursing Los Angeles County-U. So. Calif. Med. Ctr., 1963; B.S., U. Ariz., 1969, M.S., 1970, Ph.D., 1982. Staff nurse Los Angeles County-U. So. Calif. Med. Ctr., Los Angeles, 1963-65, head nurse, 1965-69; asst. dir. med. nursing Ariz. Health Scis. Ctr. Univ. Hosp., Tucson, 1970-73, assoc. dir. clin. nursing, 1973-78, assoc. prof., div. coordinator med.-surg. nursing Coll. Nursing, 1978—. Trustee Kino Community Hosp., 1975-77. Recipient Nat. Research Service award Div. Nursing, HHS, 1979-82. Mem. Am. Nurses Assn., Nat. League for Nursing, Am. Assn. Neurosci. Nurses, Am. Statis. Assn., Sigma Xi, Sigma Theta Tau, Inc. Developed ambulatory care client classification instrument; contbr. articles to profl. jours. Office: Coll Nursing U Ariz Tucson AZ 85721

VERRUE, KAREN ANN, chemist; b. Riverside, Calif., Feb. 7, 1959; d. Henry and Mary (Hanna) V. AA in Math. and Phys. Scis., Am. River Coll., 1979; BS in Chemistry with honors, Calif. State U., Sacramento, 1983. Chemist Morse Labs., Sacramento, 1982-83, Canonie Engrs., Stockton, Calif., 1983—. Mem. AAAS, Am. Chem. Soc., Astrol. Soc. Avocations: macrame, karate, backpacking. Office: Canonie Engrs 212 Frank West Suite A Stockton CA 95206

VER STEEG, DONNA LORRAINE FRANK, nurse-sociologist, educator; b. Minot, N.D., Sept. 23, 1929; d. John Jonas and Pearl H. (Denlinger) Frank; B.S. in Nursing, Stanford, 1951; M.S. in Nursing, U. Calif. at San Francisco, 1967; M.A. in Sociology, UCLA, 1969, Ph.D. in Sociology, 1973; m. Richard W. Ver Steeg, Nov. 22, 1950; children—Juliana, Anne, Richard B. Clin. instr. U. N.D. Sch. Nursing, 1962-63; USPHS nurse research fellow U. Cal. Los Angeles, 1969-72; spl. cons., adv. com. on physicians' assts. and nurse practitioner programs Calif. State Bd. Med. Examiners, 1972-73; asst. prof. UCLA Sch. Nursing, 1973-79, assoc. prof., 1979—, asst. dean, 1981-83, chmn. primary ambulatory care, 1976— assoc. dean, 1983-86; co-prin. investigator PRIMEX Project, Family Nurse Practitioners, UCLA Extension, 1974-76; assoc. cons. Calif. Postsecondary Edn. Commn., 1975-76; spl. cons. Calif. Dept. Consumer Affairs, 1978; accredited visitor Western Assn. Schs. and Colls., 1985—; mem. Calif. State Legis. Health Policy Forum, 1980-81. Named Outstanding Faculty Mem., UCLA Sch. Nursing, 1982. Fellow Am. Acad. Nursing; mem. AAAS, Am. Pub. Health Assn., Am. Soc. Law and Medicine, Nat League Nursing, Calif. League Nursing, Soc. Study Social Problems, Assn. Health Services Research, Am., Calif. (pres. 1979-81) nurses assns., Am. Sociol. Assn., Stanford Nurses Club, Sigma Theta Tau. Contbr. articles to profl. jours., chpts. to books. Home: 708 Swarthmore Ave Pacific Palisades CA 90272 Office: UCLA Sch Nursing Los Angeles CA 90024

VERZINO, WILLIAM JOHN, JR., chemist; b. Easton, Pa., Oct. 28, 1940; s. William John and Regina Margaret (Noti) V.; m. Judith Ann Massey, June 27, 1964; children—William John, Robert Lee, Anthony James, Patricia Margaret. B.S., Muhlenberg Coll., 1962; M.S., John Carroll U., 1967; Ph.D. in Chemistry, Colo. State U., 1970. Sr. research chemist Am. Enka Corp. (N.C.), 1970-74, exchange research chemist Enka-Glanzstoff, A.G., Obernburg, W.Ger., 1972-73; mem. tech. staff Aerospace Corp., El Segundo, Calif., 1974-78; acting assoc. group leader Los Alamos Nat. Lab., 1978-82, staff mem., 1984—; assoc. prof. chemistry U.S. Naval Acad., 1982-84; served as ensign U.S. Naval Res., 1962-65, advanced to capt., 1985; fossil fuel/mil. cons. Los Alamos Cons., 1981—. Bd. dirs. Los Alamos YMCA, 1981-82. Fellow Am. Inst. Chemists (cert.); mem. Am. Chem. Soc., Royal Soc. Chemistry (chartered chemist) (London), N. Mex. Acad. Scis., Naval Res. Assn. (life), Res. Officers' Assn. (life), Sigma Xi, Phi Kappa Phi. Club: K.C. Author numerous govt. reports. Office: ESS-9 Mail Stop D-436 Los Alamos Nat Lab Los Alamos NM 87544

VESA, MANUEL GUILLERMO, design consultant; b. Camagüey, Cuba, July 29, 1946; came to U.S., 1960; s. Antonio Gregorio and Gliceria Maria (Alvarez) V. BFA, Art Ctr. Coll. Design, 1974. Dir. archtl. standards Med. Planning Assn., Malibu, Calif., 1974-76; dir. profl. services Herman Miller Inc., Venice, Calif., 1976-82; pvt. practice design cons. Woodland Hills, Calif., 1982—; bd. dirs. adv. bd. Art Ctr. Coll. Design, Pasadena, Calif; project dir. Psychiat. and Drug Rehab. Facilities Model Hosps. for Iran, 1976, Harrah's Hdqrs., Reno, Nev., 1980; design dir. Burroughs Corp. World Hdqrs., Detroit, 1985, Corp. Idenity New Am. Savs., Camarillo, Calif., 1984, Bank of H. Levy Hdqrs., Ventura, Calif., 1985; graphics cons. Tosco Corp., Santa Monica, Calif., 1983—, Hdqrs. EZ Sportswear, Chatsworth, Calif., 1986, showrooms Dallas, Los Angeles, N.Y.C., 1987; design cons. U.S. Naval Facilities Engring. Command, 1976-77, Harrah's Exec. Offices, Reno, Nev., 1978. Contbr. articles to profl. jours. Served as sgt. USAF, 1966-69. Mem. Indsl. Designers Soc. Am. Office: MGV Design Cons 4329 Saltillo Dr Woodland Hills CA 91364

VESELY, JARRY JOE, architect; b. Laramie, Wyo., May 28, 1951; s. Wayne H. and Alice Nadine (Oder) V.; m. Tricia Rose La Tendresse, July 20, 1985; children: Douglas Ballesteros, Manuel Ballesteros. BS in Architecture, Calif. State Poly. U., Pomona, 1975. Registered architect, Calif. Designer Tozier and Assocs., Claremont, Calif., 1973-79; project architect E.W. Bruce AIA, Riverside, Calif., 1979-83; archtl. mgr. LA Wainscott and Assocs., Grand Terrace, Calif., 1983—. Mem. AIA (dir. ICC chpt. 1987-90), Soc. Am. Mil. Engrs., Riverside Jaycees (pres. 1983-84, named Key Man 1982-83, Disting. Service award 1984). Republican. Club: 2% (Riverside). Lodge: Kiwanis. Avocations: bicycling, golfing, racquetball, woodworking. Home: 1420 Basel Pl Riverside CA 92506 Office: L A Wainscott and Assocs Inc 22400 Barton Rd #200 Grand Terrace CA 92324

VEST, GERALD WRIGHT, social work educator; b. Omaha, Mar. 20, 1935; s. Hubert Leslie and Mira M. (Patrick) V.; m. Louise Merck, Aug. 22, 1964; children: Patrick, Christiane. AA, Long Beach City Coll., 1959; BA, Calif. State U., Long Beach, 1961; MSW, U. Conn., 1966. Exec. dir. South Hills Area YMCA, Pitts., 1966-70, Chartiers Mental Health/Mental Rehab. Ctr., Pitts., 1970-74; pvt. practice in Gestalt Therapy Pitt., 1974-75; dir. social work program Rio Grande (Ohio) Coll., 1975-78; dir. Teaching-Learning Ctr. program and field coordinator N.Mex. State U. dept. social work, Las Cruces, 1978—; adminstr. Mental Retardation program, State of Pa., 1973; cons, trainer, instr. U.S. Army, Ft. Bliss, El Paso, Tex., 1986—; dir. health promotion team N.Mex. State U., Las Cruces, 1978—, adminstr. Social Health Services, 1980—; instr. stress mgmt. course, 1985. Author: Group Work with Youth, 1967; contbr. articles to profl. jours. Bd. dirs. Consortium of Human Services, Las Cruces, 1980—, Las Cruces Family YMCA, 1985—. NIMH grantee U. Conn., 1965. Mem. Nat. Assn. Social Workers (cert., chmn. Dona Ana program 1983-84), Wellness N.Mex. Assn. (presenter 1984-86), Council on Social Work Edn. (nat. conf. presenter 1981-83). Democrat. Episcopalian. Lodges: Kiwanis (program com. 1962-64), Rotary (youth advisor 1972-74). Avocations: martial arts, meditation, therapeutic massage, camping. Home: 472 Van Patten Las Cruces NM 88005 Office: N Mex State U Dept Social Work PO Box 3SW Las Cruces NM 88005

VESTAL, ROBERT, III, public relations and publishing executive; b. Elyria, Ohio, July 7, 1933; s. Robert and Frances A. (Whiteley) V.; children—Paul, Debra, Janice, William. B.A., U. Denver, 1957. Editor Shell Oil Co., Denver, 1957-62; pub. relations rep. AT&T, N.Y.C. and Denver, 1962-67; mgr. Botsford-Ketchum Co., Denver, 1971-76; mktg. dir. Potato Bd., Denver, 1976-81; v.p. advt. and pub. relations Fuller & Co., Denver, 1981-86. Mem. Denver Press Club, Denver Advt. Club.

VESTERFELT, COLIN EDWARD ANSON, investment executive, consultant; b. Belleville, Ont., Can., May 23, 1947; came to U.S., 1965; s. James Peter and Evelyn Elizabeth (Anson) V.; m. Rondee Allene Holmes, Jan. 31, 1969; children—Kirste, Ian, Carly, Devra, C. Christian, Candice, Jamie. B.S., Brigham Young U., 1969, M.A., 1974, M.B.A., 1981; postgrad. U. Utah, Salt Lake City, 1978-79. Cert. psychologist, Alta. Counselor, Glenwood State Hosp., Iowa, 1971-73; counselor Latter Day Saints Social Services, Calgary, Alta., Can., 1973-74; program adminstr., psychologist Alta. Mental Health, Medicine Hat, Alta., 1974-78; pres. Can Am Assocs., Orem, Utah, 1978—; sr. fin. advisor Music Tchrs. Supply, Omaha, 1978—; supr. new product devel. and fin. analysis Timp Industries, Pleasant Grove, Utah, 1982-83. Author; (with Karen Ireland) Five Year Projection for Handicapped, 1978. Contbr. articles to profl. jours. Mem. exec. bd., treas. Alta. Union of Provincial Employees, Edmonton, 1976-78; co-chmn. Joint Consultation Com., chmn. Profl. Affairs Com., Province of Alta., Edmonton, 1976-78; council chmn. Boy Scouts Am., Orem, 1984—. Skagg's scholar, 1980; Exxon scholar, 1981; Grad. Sch. Mgmt. scholar Brigham Young U., 1982. Mem. Am. Assn. Mental Deficiency, Psychologists Assn. Alta., Canadian Psychol. Assn., Am. Psychol. Assn., Brigham Young U. Mgmt. Soc. Mormon. Home: 227 W 2000 N Orem UT 84057

VETTERLEIN, RALPH ALAN, paper company executive; b. San Francisco, July 14, 1930; s. Raymond Herman and Juanita Dolores (Tricou) V.; m. Barbara Diane Carideo, June 26, 1955; 1 child, Ralph Andrew. AA, City Coll. San Francisco, 1951; MS, U. Calif., Berkeley, 1954. Salesman Internat. Paper Co., San Jose, Calif., 1955-59, sales mgr., 1959-65; gen. mgr. Internat. Paper Co., Los Altos, Calif., 1965-70; nat. acct. mgr. Internat. Paper Co., Los Altos Hills, Calif., 1970—; lectr. Am. Mgmt. Assn., 1973-78. Dir., campaign mgr. for Elected Mayor of Fremont, Calif., 1966-67; bd. dirs. Hills Little League, 1968-78, pres., 1973. Mem. Am. Arbitration Assn., Fibre Box Assn. No. Calif. (chmn. 1965), U. Calif. Bus. Sch. Alumni Assn. (bd. dirs. 1872), Alpha Kappa Lambda. Republican. Club: Calif. (Berkeley). Avocations: coaching baseball, collecting stamps, Civil War history. Home and Office: Internat Paper Co 26035 Todd Ln Los Altos Hills CA 94022

VEVANG, JAMES S., social worker; b. Bklyn., July 14, 1945; s. Selmer E. and Bernice S. (Sholl) V.; m. Jeanne E. Lussenhop, Dec. 19, 1964; children: Elizabeth, Jason. BA in Econs. and Sociology, Mankato (Minn.) State U., 1967; MSW, U. Wash., 1970. Probation officer King County Juvenile Ct., Seattle, 1967-73; social worker The Casey Family Program, Seattle, 1973. Mem. Nat. Assn. Social Workers, Acad. Cert. Social Workers (cert.), Nat. Assn. Foster Parents. Home: 414 156th SE Bellevue WA 98007

VIAN, WAYNE EDWIN, plant breeder, cytologist; b. Litchfield, Nebr., Oct. 26, 1942; s. Ray Edwin and Annie Ella (Easley) V.; m. Sharon Klare Clark, June 8, 1963; children: Carol Ann, James Edwin. BA in Edn., Kearney State Coll., 1966, MS in Edn., 1971; PhD, N.D. State U., 1975. Instr. Elm Creek (Nebr.) Pub. Sch., 1966-69; asst. prof. U. Ky., Lexington, 1975-80; breeder, sta. mgr. Coker's Pedigreed Seed Co., Richland, Ind., 1980-84; sr. breeder, sta. mgr. Rohm and Haas Seeds Inc., Berthoud, Colo., 1984—; affiliate faculty mem. Colo. State U., Ft. Collins, 1985—. Patentee in field. NDEA fellow, 1971-75; U. Ky. Research Found. grantee 1977-78, GAF Corp. grantee, 1977-81, Coker's Pedigreed Seed Co. grantee, 1979-84. Mem. Am. Soc. Agronomy, Crop Sci. Soc., Council Agrl. Sci. and Tech., Sigma Xi (life), Gamma Sigma Delta. Lodge: Masons (sec. 1985—), Order of Eastern Star. Avocations: woodworking, hunting, fishing.

VIANSON, PAOLO MARIO, engineer; b. Genoa, Italy, Sept. 20, 1959; s. Enrico Rinaldo Vianson and Elena Hardouin Di Gallese; m. Christie Lynn Hardwick, Aug. 31, 1985. M in Mech. Engring. magna cum laude, U. Milan Poly., 1983. Registered profl. engr., Italy. Researcher U. Milan Poly., 1980-83; sr. project engr. involved in switchgear design Square D Co., Yin Research Corp., Fremont, Calif., 1984—. Author: Research About the Periodical Irregularity of the Flow in Volumetric Pumps, 1983. Mem. Am. Soc. Metals, 1985—. Roman Catholic. Avocations: golf, rugby, sailing. Home: 48242 Purpleleaf St Fremont CA 94539 Office: Square D Co 4248 Solar Way Fremont CA 94538

VICARS, MARGARET ELAINE, municipal finance officer; b. Poplar Bluff, Mo., Dec. 3, 1947; d. Jeffrey Clifford and Velma Jean Louise (Davis) Dearing; B.A. in Econs., U. Mich., 1970; M.P.A., Golden Gate U., 1973; student extension cert. program in contract adminstrn. U.Calif.-Berkeley, 1981—. Bookkeeper/mgr. Feiner's Inc., Ann Arbor, Mich., 1971-72; acctg. asst. Lee Wilson, C.P.A., Oakland, Calif., 1974; grant programs coordinator Calif. Coll. Podiatric Medicine, San Francisco, 1974-78; controller Inst. for Research in Social Behavior, Oakland, 1978-83; fin. mgr. City of Pismo Beach (Calif.), 1983—. Mem. speakers bur. Planned Parenthood, Oakland, 1973-74; founder, coordinator Bed and Breakfast Program, San Francisco League Women Voters, 1977-80; bd. dirs. Vernon Villa Homeowners Assn., Oakland, 1979-81, pres., 1980-81; fin. dr. coordinator Oakland LWV, 1981-83; mem. Hearst Castle Citizens Com., 1982-84; treas. Friends of Hearst Castle, 1984—. Mem. Am. Soc. Public Adminstrn., Am. Bus. Women's Assn. (chmn. membership 1985—), San Luis Obispo LWV. Democrat. Office: City of Pismo Beach 1000 Bello St Pismo Beach CA 93449

VICERRA-MCGRATH, CRISTINO, social worker, psychotherapist; b. San Francisco, Mar. 21, 1935; s. Cristino Salvador and Evarista (Apolinar) V.; m. Delia McGrath, Oct. 12, 1969; children: Molly FitzRoy, Martina McGrath. Social worker Alameda County, Oakland, Calif., 1959-64; social worker San Francisco County, 1966-75, child welfare worker, 1975—; pvt. practice psychotherapy San Francisco, 1982—. Panel mediator Neighborhood Bds., San Mateo, Calif., 1986—. Mem. Nat. Assn. Social Workers, Sierra Club (life). Avocations: gardening, civic activities. Home: 239 Modoc Pl Pacifica CA 94044 Office: San Francisco County Dept Social Services 170 Otis St San Francisco CA 94103

VICIAN, THOMAS ALLEN, SR., educator; b. Mason City, Iowa, Jan. 31, 1935; s. Stephen Roy and Blanche (Lucas) V.; A.B., Luther Coll., 1957; B.D., Luther Theol. Sem., 1961; postgrad. San Jose State Coll., 1963-64; Ph.D., Claremont Grad. Sch., 1971; m. Elizabeth Ann Overgaard, Aug. 11, 1957; 1 son, Thomas Allen, Jr. Ordained minister Luth. Ch., 1961; asso. minister Gloria Dei Luth. Ch., Rochester, Minn., 1961-62, Grace Luth. Ch., Palo Alto, Calif., 1962-64; asst. prof. philosophy Calif. State Coll., Hayward, 1966-67, U. Nev., Reno, 1967-68; prof. philosophy De Anza Coll., Cupertino, Calif., 1968—, also chmn. dept.; philos.-religious cons., Palo Alto, Calif. Woodrow Wilson fellow, 1964-65, Nat. Endowment Humanities fellow, 1973. Mem. AAUP, Philosophy of Sci. Assn., Bay Area Ednl. TV Assn., World Future Soc., Sierra Club, Smithsonian Assos., Center Study Democratic Instns., Am. Philos. Assn. Home: 3718 Redwood Circle Palo Alto CA 94306 Office: De Anza Coll 21250 Stevens Creek Blvd Cupertino CA 95014

VICINI, HOWARD LOUIS, marketing executive; b. Warren, Pa., Jan. 6, 1949; s. Robert L. and Priscilla (Highfield) V. BSBA, Indiana (Pa.) U., 1973. Contract adminstr. ITT Arctic Services, Fairbanks, Alaska, 1973-75; mktg. research and advt. exec. Howard L. Vicini & Assocs., Anchorage, San Francisco, and Al Kabar, Saudi Arabia, 1977-81; agy. dir. Ampersand Design, San Francisco, 1985-86; v.p. mktg. and sales Bel Age Design, San Francisco, 1986—. Contbr. Anchorage Daily News, 1975-76, After Dark mag., 1980, S.F. Gentry mag., 1986. Democrat. Home: 645 14th St San Francisco CA 94114 Office: Bel Age Design Showplace Sq E 1775 Alameda St San Francisco CA 94103

VICK, AUSTIN LAFAYETTE, civil engineer; b. Cedervale, N.Mex., Jan. 28, 1929; s. Louis Lafayette and Mota Imon (Austin) V.; BSCE, N.Mex. State U., 1950, MSCE, 1961; m. Norine E. Melton, July 18, 1948; children: Larry A., Margaret J., David A. Commd. 2d lt. USAF, 1950, advanced through grades to capt., 1959, ret., 1970; ordnance engr. Ballistics Research Lab., White Sands Proving Ground, Las Cruces, N.Mex., 1950-51, civil engr., 1951-55, gen. engr. White Sands Missile Range, 1957-73, phys. scientist adminstr., 1955-57, 73—; owner A.V. Constrn., Las Cruces, 1979—; realtor Campbell Agy., Las Cruces, 1979-84; cons. instrumentation systems, ops. maintenance and mgmt., 1984—; pres., treas. Survey Tech., Inc., 1985—; cons. engr., pres. Survey Tech. Inc., Las Cruces, 1984—. Mem. outstanding alumni awards com. N.Mex. State U., 1980. Recipient Outstanding Performance award Dept. Army, White Sands Missile Range, 1972, Spl. Act awards, 1967, 71, 75. Mem. Mil. Ops. Research Soc. (chmn. logistics group 1968-69), Am. Def. Preparedness Assn. (pres. 1970-72), Assn. U.S. Army (v.p. 1970-71), Am. Soc. Photogrametry, Am. Astronautical Soc. (sr. mem.), N.Mex. State U. Acad. Civil Engring. Contbr. articles to profl. jours. Home and Office: 4568 Spanish Dagger Las Cruces NM 88001

VICK, WILLIAM HUGH, environmental scientist and engineer; b. Houston, July 15, 1952; s. Forest Burns and Frances (Hitch) V.; m. Linda Susan Tucker, Aug. 10, 1970 (div. Mar. 1973); m. Jenny Carol Vickers Feb. 7, 1975; children: Margaret Kimberly, Michele Rene. BS, U. Tex. Dallas, Richardson, 1977, MS, 1978, PhD, 1981. Research assoc. U. Tex. Dallas, 1978-81; lab. mgr. Tex. Instruments, Dallas, 1979-81; sr. program mgr., quality assurance/quality control dir. Sci. Applications Internat. Corp., La Jolla, Calif., 1981—; cons. Citizens Action Group Against Trash to Energy Programs, Encinitas, Calif., 1985, Citizens Action Group Against Ocean Discharge of Primarily Treated Sewage, Del Mar, Calif., 1984. Mem. AAAS, Am. Chem. Soc., Am. Water Works Assn., Am. Indsl. Hygiene Assn. Democrat. Avocations: golf, woodworking, camping. Office: SAIC PO Box 2351 476 Prospect St La Jolla CA 92038

VICKERS, GROVER WILLIAM, data processing administrator; b. Tyner, Ky., Jan. 16, 1927; s. Clifton Henry and Etta Mae (Cook) V.; m. Nancy Elizabeth Sanford, June 6, 1953; children—Elizabeth Ann Oliver, Donald William. B.S. in Commerce, U. Ky., 1951; grad. profl. mil. comptroller course, Air U., 1971. Commd. U.S. Air Force, 1951; advanced through grades to lt. col., 1968; mgr. data processing audit, 1954-59; mgmt. analyst, 1959-61; systems analyst USAF Hdqrs., Washington, 1967-70; mgr. systems analysis and programming, Colorado Springs, Colo., 1964-65; mgr. computer ctr. ops., various locations 1962, 63, 66, 71; dir. data automation, mgr. automated data processing, AFAFC, 1972-76; ret. 1976; dir. computer services Metropolitan State Coll., Denver, 1978—. Bd. dirs., treas. Chateau Claire, Inc., condominium complex. Decorated Legion of Merit, Commendation medal, Bronze Star, Vietnam Service medal, Republic of Vietnam medal. Mem. ACM, Data Processing Mgmt. Assn. (v.p. student chpts.), Colls. and Univs. Systems Exchange. Republican. Baptist. Office: 1006 11th St Box 15 Denver CO 80204

VICKERY, BYRDEAN EYVONNE HUGHES (MRS. CHARLES EVERETT VICKERY, JR.), library services administrator; b. Belleview, Mo., Apr. 18, 1928; d. Roy Franklin and Margaret Cordelia (Wood) Hughes; m. Charles Everett Vickery, Jr., Nov. 5, 1948; 1 dau., Camille. Student Flat River (Mo.) Jr. Coll., 1946-48; B.S. in Edn., S.E. Mo. State Coll., 1954; M.L.S., U. Wash., 1964; postgrad. Wash. State U., 1969-70. Tchr., Ironton (Mo.) Pub. Schs., 1948-56; elem. tchr. Pasco (Wash.) Sch. Dist. 1, 1956-61, jr. high sch. librarian, 1961-68, coordinator libraries, 1968-69; asst. librarian Columbia Basin Community Coll., Pasco, 1969-70, head librarian, dir. Instructional Resources Center, 1970-78, dir. library services, 1979—; chmn. S.E. Wash. Library Service Area, 1977-78. Bd. dirs. Pasco-Kennewick Community Concerts, 1977—, pres., 1980-81, 87-88; bd. dirs. Mid-Columbia Symphony Orch., 1983—; trustee Wash. Commn. Humanities, 1982-85. Author, editor: Library and Research Skills Curriculum Guides for the Pasco School District, 1967; author (with Jean Thompson), also editor Learning Resources Handbook for Teachers, 1969. Recipient Woman of Achievement award Pasco Bus. and Profl. Women's Club, 1976. Mem. AAUW (2d v.p. 1966-68, corr. sec. 1969), Wash. Dept. Audio-Visual Instrn., ALA, Wash. Library Assn., Am., Wash. assns. higher edn., Wash. State Assn. Sch. Librarians (state conf. chmn. 1971-72), Tri-Cities Librarians Assn., Wash. Library Media Assn. (community coll. levels chmn. 1986-87), Am. Assn. Research Libraries, Soroptimist Internat. Assn. (rec. sec. Pasco-Kennewick chpt. 1971-72, treas. 1973-74, pres. 1978-80), Columbia Basin Coll. Adminstrs. Assn. (sec.-treas. 1973-74), Pacific N.W. Assn. Ch. Libraries, Women in Communications, Pasco Bus. and Profl. Women's Club, P.E.O. Beta Sigma Phi, Delta Kappa Gamma, Phi Delta Kappa (sec. 1981-82, Outstanding Educator award 1983). Home: 4016 W Park St Pasco WA 99301 Office: Columbia Basin Community Coll 2600 N 20th Ave Pasco WA 99301

VIEGLAIS, NIKOLAJS, clergyman; b. Dundaga, Latvia, Mar. 31, 1907; s. Andrew P. and Eugenia (Jakobson) V.; grad. Theol. Sem., Latvia, 1928, Music Sch., 1932; baccalaureate Theol. Faculty, U. Latvia, 1940; m. Natalija Calders, Oct. 18, 1931; children: Natalija, Marina (Mrs. Alfredo Alva), Alexis, Olga (Mrs. J. Kuhlman), Tatjana (Mrs. C. Tressler); came to U.S., 1949, naturalized, 1955. Ch. choir dir., Cesis, Latvia, 1928-34; deacon cathedral, Riga, Latvia, 1934-37; ordained priest Eastern Orthodox Ch., Latvia, 1937; priest, Riga, 1937-44; priest refugee camps, Germany, 1944-49; apptd. priest Orthodox Ch. in Am., 1949; priest, Lykens, Pa., 1949-51, Berkeley, Calif., 1952—. Editor, pub. ch. books and music, Latvia, 1935-40, 41-44, Germany, 1946-49, U.S.A., 1950-79; dean No. Calif., Am.-Russian Orthodox Ch., 1955-74, 75-76; sec. Exarchate for Baltic States, 1942-44; sec. San Francisco Diocese, 1960-72, mem. council, 1952-76; spiritual adviser local chpt. Federated Russian Orthodox Clubs, 1964-70, Pacific-Alaska Dist., 1967-68. Home: 1908 Essex St Berkeley CA 94703 Office: 1900 Essex St Berkeley CA 94703

VIEIRA, DAVID JOHN, nuclear chemist; b. Oakland, Calif., May 5, 1950; s. Gerald John and Pauline (Dahlstrom) V.; m. Catherine Ann Evans, June 3, 1972; children: Mia Christine, Carrie Ann. BS in Chemistry with honors, Oreg. State U., 1972; PhD in Nuclear Chemistry, U. Calif., Berkeley, 1978. NSF research fellow Oreg. State U., summer 1971; research fellow Los Alamos (N.Mex.) Sci. Labs., summer 1972; research and teaching asst. Lawrence Berkeley (Calif.) Lab., 1972-77; dir.'s postdoctoral fellow Los Alamos (N.Mex.) Sci. Labs., 1978-79, staff scientist, 1979-85; leader nuclear chemistry sect. Los Alamos Meson Physics Facility, 1985—; adj. prof. Utah State U., Logan, 1984—. Contbr. articles to profl. jours. Mem. Am. Chem. Soc., Am. Phys. Soc. Avocations: golf, hiking. Office: Los Alamos Nat Lab Mail Stop H824 Isotope Nuclear Chemistry INC-11 Los Alamos NM 87545

VIESER, RICHARD WILLIAM, electrical manufacturing company executive; b. Newark, Nov. 14, 1927; s. William L. and Viola S. (Coltort) V.; m. Lois Barbara Johnson, Sept. 8, 1951; children: Richard, Cheryl, Cynthia, William, Jamie. A.B., Lafayette Coll., 1951. Mgmt. trainee Western Electric Co., N.Y.C., 1951-52; sales mgr. Chatham Electronics Corp., Livingston, N.J., 1954-56; from asst. div. mgr. to gen. mgr. Tung Sol Electric, Livingston, 1957-66; div. gen. mgr. Wagner Electric Corp., Livingston, 1966-70, v.p., 1970, group v.p., 1971-73, pres., 1973-74; chief exec. officer FL Industries, Inc., 1974-79; exec. v.p. McGraw-Edison, 1979-84, pres., chief operating officer, 1984-86; chmn., pres., chief exec. officer Midland Ross Corp., N.J., 1986—, Lear Siegler Holdings Corp., Santa Monica, Calif., 1987—; exec. v.p. Studebaker Worthington, 1979—. Bd. dirs. Hwy. Users Fedn. Served with U.S. Army, 1946-48, Korea. Mem. Automotive Presidents Council, Soc. Automotive Engrs., Motor Equipment Mfrs. Assn. (chmn.), Theta Delta Chi. Clubs: Baltusrol (Springfield, N.J.); Pine Valley (N.J.) Golf, Morris County Golf. Office: Lear Siegler Holdings Corp 2850 Ocean Park Blvd Santa Monica CA 90405 *

VIG, BALDEV KRISHAN, genetics educator, researcher; b. Lyalpur, Punjab, India, Oct. 1, 1935; came to U.S., 1964; s. Behari Lal and Sheela Wanti (Watta) V.; m. Gargi Dilawari, Dec. 13, 1964; children: Anjana, Pamela. BS, Khalsa Coll., Amritsar, India, 1957; MS, Punjab U., 1961; PhD, Ohio State U., 1967. Diplomate Am. Bd. Med. Genetics. Cytogeneticist Children's Hosp., Columbus, Ohio, 1967-68; asst. prof. U. Nev., Reno, 1968-72, assoc. prof., 1972-78, prof. genetics, 1978—, chmn. biology dept., 1985—; pvt. practice med. genetics Reno, 1982—; Dir. genetics program State of Nev., Reno, 1975-81; panel mem. environ. biology EPA, Washington, 1983—; chmn. Somatic Cell Genetics, 1982. Recipient Outstanding Researcher award Grad. Sch U. Nev., 1979; D.F. Jones fellow, 1974-75, Alexander vonHumboldt Found. fellow, 1975, Deutscher Akademischer Austauschdienst fellow, 1985, German Cancer Research Ctr. fellow, 1987. Mem. Genetics Soc. Am., Am. Soc. Human Genetics, Genetics Soc. Can., Sigma Xi, Phi Kappa Phi. Democrat. Hindu. Avocations: badmitton, swimming, cricket. Office: U Nev Dept Biology Reno NV 89557

VIGIL, CHARLES S., lawyer; b. Trinidad, Colo., June 9, 1912; s. J.U. and Andreita (Maes) V.; m. Kathleen A. Liebert, Jan. 2, 1943; children: David Charles Edward, Marcia Kathleen. LL.B., U. Colo., 1936. Bar: Colo. 1936. Dep. dist. atty. 3d Jud. Dist. Colo., 1937-42, asst. dist. atty., 1946-51; U.S. atty. Dist. Colo., 1951-53; pvt. practice law Denver.; Dir., sec. Las Animas Co. (Colo); ARC. Author: Saga of Casimiro Barela. Bd. dirs. Family and Children's Service Denver, Colo. Humane Soc. dir. Auraria Community Center; mem. Bishop's com. on housing. Served as ensign to lt. (s.g.) USCG, 1942-46. Recipient award of civil merit Spain, 1960, award of civil merit Colo. Centennial Expn. Bd., 1976; award Colo. Chicano Bar Assn., 1979. Mem. Internat. Law Assn., ABA, Fed. Bar Assn., Colo. Bar Assn. (bd. govs.), So. Colo. Bar Assn., Hispanic Bar Colo. (bd. dirs.), Am. Judicature Soc., Internat. Bar Assn., Inter-Am. Bar, V.F.W. (comdr.), Am. Legion (comdr.), Nat. Assn. Def. Lawyers, Am. Trial Lawyers Assn., Lambda Chi Alpha, Elk, Eagle, Cootie. Clubs: Lions, Denver Athletic, Columbine Country, City of Denver, Trinidad Country. Home: 1085 Sherman St Denver CO 80203 Office: 485 Capitol Life Center 225 E 16th Ave Denver CO 80203

VIGIL, MARIO OLIVER, social worker, family therapist; b. Taos, N.Mex., Nov. 20, 1956; s. Bences and Fabiola (Martinez) V. Student, U. N.Mex.; BA, N.Mex. Highlands U., 1979, MSW, 1980. Cert. sch. social worker. Clin. specialist Community Mental Health, Taos, 1980-82; program dir. Children In Need of Supervision Program, Taos, 1982-83; social worker Dept. Social Services, Albuquerque, 1983-84; sch. social worker Albuquerque Pub. Schs., 1984-85; coordinator Albuquerque Family Health Ctr., 1985—. Vol. Friends Ken Schutz for Mayor, Albuquerque, 1985-86. Recipient Service award Albuquerque Pub. Schs., 1985, engring. scholarship U. N.Mex., 1974. Mem. Nat. Assn. Social Workers. Democrat. Roman Catholic. Avocations: photography, archery, hiking, basketball, fishing. Home: 1014 Valencia SE Apt 19W Albuquerque NM 87108

VIGIL-GIRON, REBECCA D., Sec. of stateof New Mex., Santa Fe. Office: Office of the Sec of State 400 State Capitol Santa Fe NM 87503 *

VIHSTADT, ROBERT FRANCIS, real estate broker; b. Rochester, Minn., Oct. 6, 1941; s. Francis A. and Catherine P. (Condon) V.; m. Kathleen A. McGuire, Sept. 14, 1963 (div. Oct. 1976); children: Maureen T., Michael R., Mark T.; m. Leslie P. Teutsch, Mar. 16, 1979; children: Lynn P. Edmondson, April R. Edmondson. BA, Mankato State Coll., 1962. Employment counselor Minn. Dept. Employment Security, St. Paul, 1963-64; mktg. adminstr. IBM Corp., St. Paul, 1964-65; dir. mktg. adminstrn. Control Data Corp., Albuquerque, Los Angeles, and Bloomington, Minn., 1965-70; mgr. Ackerman-Grant, Inc., Realtors, Albuquerque, 1970-74; pres. Key Realty, Albuquerque, 1974—; dir. mktg. Stewart Title Co., Albuquerque, 1984-86. Active Ronald McDonald House, John Baker PTA, Mile-High Little League. Mem. Nat. Assn. Realtors, Realtors Assn. N. Mex., Albuquerque Bd. Realtors (bd. dirs., com. chmn.). Democratic. Roman Catholic. Lodge: Lions. Avocation: skiing. Office: Key Realty PO Box 11771 Albuquerque NM 87192

VILARDI, AGNES FRANCINE, real estate broker; b. Monson, Mass., Sept. 29, 1918; d. Paul and Adelina (Mastrioanni) Vetti; m. Frank S. Vilardi, Dec. 2, 1939; children—Valerie, Paul. Cert. of dental assisting Pasadena Jr. Coll., 1954. Lic. real estate broker. Real estate broker, owner Vilardi Realty, Yorba Linda, Calif., Placentia, Calif., Fullerton, Calif., 1968—; cons. in property mgmt. Mem. Am. Dental Asst. Assn., North Orange County Bd. Realtors (sec./treas. 1972). Clubs: Yorba Linda Country; Desert Princess (Palm Springs, Calif.). Home and Office: 18982 Vila Terr Yorba Linda CA 92686

VILKER, VINCENT LEE, chemical engineer educator; b. Beaver Dam, Wis., Jan. 17, 1943; s. Vincent Chester and Louise Marie (Frank) V.; m. Martha Rosmond Stone, Aug. 30, 1981. BSChemE, U. Wis., 1967; PhD, MIT, 1976. Research engr. Exxon Research and Engring. Co., Baton Rouge, 1967-70; asst. prof. UCLA, 1975-81, assoc. prof. chem. engring., 1981-86, prof. chem. engring., 1986—; mem. stringfellow sci. adv. panel Calif. State Senate, Sacramento, 1983—. Contbr. articles to profl. jours. and chpts. to books. Mem. Westside YMCA, Los Angeles. Recipient Fulbright Sr. Research award Netherlands Am. Commn., 1984-85; Sr. Research fellow The Agrl. U., 1984-85. Mem. AAAS, Am. Inst. Chem. Engrs., Am. Chem. Soc. Avocation: handball. Home: 247 N Bowling Green Way Los Angeles CA 90049 Office: UCLA 5531 Boelter Hall Los Angeles CA 90025

VILLABLANCA, JAIME ROLANDO, medical scientist, educator; b. Chillàn, Chile, Feb. 29, 1929; came to U.S., 1971; naturalized, 1985; s. Ernesto and Teresa (Hernàndez) V.; m. Guillermina Nieto, Dec. 3, 1955; children: Amparo C., Jaime G., Pablo J., Francis X., Claudio I. Bachelor in Biology, Nat. Inst. Chile, 1946; licentiate medicine, U. Chile, 1953, MD, 1954. Cert. neurophysiology. Postdoctoral fellow in physiology John Hopkins and Harvard Med. Schs., 1959-61; internat. research fellow in anatomy UCLA, 1966-68, assoc. research anatomist and psychiatrist, 1971-72, assoc. prof. psychiatry, 1972-76, prof. psychiatry, 1976—, prof. anatomy, 1977—; mem. faculty U. Chile Sch. Medicine, 1954-71, prof. exptl. medicine, 1970-71; vis. prof. neuro-biology Cath. U. Chile Sch. Medicine, 1974; cons. in field. Author of over 160 research papers, book chpts. Fellow Rockefeller Found., 1959-61, NIH, 1966-68; grantee USAF Office Sci. Research, 1962-65; found. Fund Research Psychiatry, 1969-72; USPHS-NICHD, 1972—; USPHS-NIDA, 1981-85. Mem. Mental Retardation Research Ctr., Brain Research Inst., Internat. Brain Research Orgn., Am. Physiol. Soc., Soc. Neurosci., European Neurosci. Assn., Sci. Council Internat. Inst. Research and Advice in Mental Deficiency, Sigma Xi. Home: 200 Surfview Dr Pacific Palisades CA 90272 Office: UCLA Dept Psychiatry Los Angeles CA 90024

VILLACRES, LINDA GRACE, controller; b. Royal Oak, Mich., July 5, 1935; d. Max E. Rubin and Esther Rosalie (Shoaff) Borroni; divorced; children: Gregory Robert, Cynthia Rae. BBA with distinction, U. Redlands, 1975. Cost acct. Douglas Aircraft Co., Long Beach, Calif., 1955-58; controller Wonder Bowl Inc., Downey, Calif., 1959-65; office mgr. El Fortin Bandido Inc., Anaheim, Calif., 1965-68; controller, asst. treas. Tishman W. Mgmt. Corp., Orange, Calif., 1968—. Mem. Brea (Calif.) Rep. Womens Group, 1986. Mem. Anaheim Jaycettes (treas. 1958-59). Avocations: golf, reading, traveling. Home: 892 N Grand Canyon Brea CA 92621 Office: Tishman West Mgmt Corp 1 City Blvd W Orange CA 92668

VILLAMOR, JOSEFINO REJUSO, pharmacist; b. San Jacinto, Philippines, Nov. 13, 1918; came to U.S., 1974; s. Nicomedes Almodal Villamor and Josefa (Esparrago) Rejuso; m. Maria Flores Sulatra, Feb. 24, 1941 (dec. Dec. 1983); children: Rogelio Sulatra, Ramon Sulatra; m. Maria Norma Reteracion, Dec. 14, 1985. BS in Pharmacy, U. Iloilo, Philippines. Owner, mgr. Farmacia Ester, Cabatuan, Philippines, 1945-54; chief pharmacist Merck Sharp and Dohme Labs., Manila, 1954-74; pharmacist, technician VA, West Los Angeles, Calif., 1978—; cons. So. Iloilo Sugar Planters Research, 1973-74. Contbr., literary editor Balita, 1969. Adv. Cabatuan Youth in Greater Manila, Philippines, 1955. Served as sgt. U.S. Army, 1942-45. Mem. Am. Pharm. Assn. Democrat. Roman Catholic. Clubs: Kawilihan (Long Beach, Calif.), Masbate (Los Angeles). Avocations: stamps, coins, cycling, contests. Home: 1026 Blaine St #207 Los Angeles CA 90015

VILLAVECES, JAMES WALTER, allergist, immunologist; b. San Luis Obispo, Calif., Nov. 4, 1933; s. Robert and Solita (Combariza) V. BA, UCLA, 1955; MD, U. Calif. Med. Sch., 1960. Cert. Am. Bd. Allergy and Immunology. Rotating intern Santelle VA Hosp., Los Angeles, 1960-61; practice medicine Ross Loos, Los Angeles, 1961-64; preceptor allergy U. So. Calif., Los Angeles, 1964-65; fellow allergy White Meml. CCM, Los Angeles, 1965-67; chief allergy div. Ventura (Calif.) Med. Ctr., 1969-87; practice medicine specializing in allergy-immunology Ventura, 1984-87; cons. Bio-Dynamics Co., Ventura, 1975-80, Norwich-Eaton and Pharmacia and Fisons, Ventura, 1980—; mem. bd. advisors Viral Response Systems, Inc., Greenwich, Conn. Contbr. articles to profl. jours. Bd. dirs. Am. Lung Assn., Ventura, 1969-85, pres., 1974, advisor air pollution control com., 1971-74; judge Ventura Sci. Fair, 1970-85. Recipient Commendation, County Bd. Suprs., Ventura, 1974. Fellow Am. Acad. Allergy, Am. Coll. Allergists, Am. Assn. Allergists immunologists; mem. AMA, Calif. Med. Assn., Audobon Soc., Native Plant Soc., Gold Coast Tri Co-Allergy Soc. (pres. 1987), CAL Club (hon.), Ventura County Sports Hall of Fame (founder), Mensa. Republican. Avocations: writing, photography, lecturing, bicycling. Home: 88 Eugenia Dr Ventura CA 93003 Office: Dudley Profl Ctr 4080 Loma Vista Rd Suite M Ventura CA 93003

VINATIERI, MICHAEL TODD, environmental scientist; b. Vallejo, Calif., Jan. 4, 1944; s. Felix William and Jean Ann (Smith) V.; m. Dolores Jeanette Huffman, June 18, 1966 (div. Feb. 1973); m. Glady Barbara Vinatieri, May 18, 1974; children: Michael Dante, Sarah Dawn, Monica Renee, Ryan Mathew. AA, Vallejo Jr. Coll., 1964; BA, San Jose (Calif.) State U., 1966, MPh, 1977. Environtl. health sanitarian Santa Clara County Pub. Health, Calif., 1974-77; supervising sanitarian Sonoma County Pub. Health Dept., Santa Rosa, Calif., 1977-79; dir. environtl. health Sonoma County Pub. Health Dept., 1979—; sec. Well adv. com. Sonoma County, 1984—, Sonoma County Hazardous Materials Mgmt. Council, 1986. Served to staff sgt.

USAF, 1968-72. Mem. Calif. Conf. Dirs. of Environ. Health (pres. 1986-87, various offices), Calif. Conf. Local Health Officers, Am. Pub. Health Assn., Nat. Environ. Health Assn., Calif. Environ. Assn., Empire Sports Car Assn., Calif. Assn. Environ. Health Adminstrs. Republican. Roman Catholic. Clubs: Valley CORSA (San Jose pres., founder 1975-77). Office: Sonoma County Pub Health Dept 3313 Chanate Rd Santa Rosa CA 95404

VINCENT, ALBERT VERNON, real estate executive; b. Rector, Ark., Sept. 4, 1921; s. Albert Wesley and Helen (Wilcher) V.; student pub. schs.; m. Kay Tokie Nagata, Sept. 4, 1960; children—Armond Vernon, Linda Carol, Sharon Lynn, Albert Vernon, Wendi Vernelle. Supr., Naval Supply Center, Pearl Harbor, 1942-48; div. mgr. Century Metalcraft Corp., 1948-54; gen. mgr. Saladmaster of Hawaii, 1954-56; realtor, 1957-60; pres. Tropic Shores Realty, Ltd., 1960—. Named Hawaii Realtor of Yr. Mem. Nat. (dir., v.p. 1970), Hawaii (pres. 1978) assns. realtors, Nat. Inst. Real Estate Brokers (gov.), Honolulu Bd. Realtors (pres.), Inst. Real Estate Mgmt., Nat. Inst. Farm and Land Brokers, Internat. Real Estate Fedn., Calif. Real Estate Assn., Realtors Nat. Mktg. Inst. (gov.), Real Estate Securities and Syndication Inst. (gov. 1973), Am. Soc. Real Estate Counselors (gov.), Internat. Platform Assn., Honolulu Press Club. Clubs: Pacific, Plaza, Honolulu. Home: 1920 Laukahi St Honolulu HI 96821 Office: 33 S King St Honolulu HI 96813 *

VINCENT, DAVID RIDGELY, information executive; b. Detroit, Aug. 9, 1941; s. Charles Ridgely and Charlotte Jane (McCarroll) V.; m. Margaret Helen Anderson, Aug. 25, 1962 (div. 1973); children—Sandra Lee, Cheryl Ann; m. Judith Ann Gomez, July 2, 1978; 1 child, Amber; stepsons—Michael Jr., Jesse Joseph Flores. B.S., B.A., Calif. State U.-Sacramento, 1964; M.B.A., Calif. State U.-Hayward, 1971. Sr. ops. analyst Aerojet Gen. Corp., Sacramento, 1960-66; controller Hexcel Corp., Dublin, Calif., 1966-70; mng. dir. Memorex, Austria, 1970-74; sales mgr. Ampex World Ops., Switzerland, 1974-76; dir. product mgmt. NCR, Sunnyvale, Calif., 1976-79; v.p. Boole & Babbage Inc., gen. mgr. Inst. Info. Mgmt., Sunnyvale, Calif., 1979-85; pres. The Info. Group, Inc., Santa Clara, Calif., 1985—. Trustee Republican Nat. Task Force; deacon Union Ch., Cupertino, Calif.; USSF/NCAA soccer referee. Author: Perspectives in Information Management, Information Economics, 1983, Handbook for Information Management and Data Administration, 1986; contbr. monographs and papers to profl. jours. Home: 2803 Kalliam Dr Santa Clara CA 95051 Office: PO Box Q Santa Clara CA 95055-3756

VINCENTI, SHELDON ARNOLD, legal educator, lawyer; b. Ogden, Utah, Sept. 4, 1938; s. Arnold Joseph and Mae (Burch) V.; m. Elaine Cathryn Wacker, June 18, 1964; children—Matthew Lewis, Amanda Jo. A.B., Harvard U., 1960, J.D., 1963. Bar: Utah 1963. Sole practice law, Ogden, 1966-67; ptnr. Lowe and Vincenti, Ogden, 1968-70; legis. asst. to U.S. Rep. Gunn McKay, Washington, 1971-72, adminstrv. asst., 1973; prof., assoc. dean U. of Idaho Coll. of Law, Moscow, Idaho, 1973-83, dean, prof. law, 1983—. Home: 2480 W Twin Rd Moscow ID 83843 Office: Coll Law U Idaho Moscow ID 83843

VINES, JEANETTE LORIS, retail executive; b. Birmingham, Ala., Oct. 25, 1949; d. James H. and Clifford (Cash) V.; m. C.L. Byrd; 1 child, Byron David. BSBA, U. So. Calif., 1971. Asst. buyer May Co. Calif., Los Angeles, 1971-72, mgr. dept., 1972-74, buyer, 1974-80; buyer J.W. Robinson's, Los Angeles, 1980-84, group buyer, 1984-86, gen. store mgr., 1987—. Mem. Ebonics Support Group (U. So. Calif. chpt.).

VINEYARD, C L, lawyer; b. Hale County, Tex., Nov. 9, 1927; s. Clarence Calvin and Louella Ruby (Ray) V.; m. Nora Lee Crawford, July 15, 1978; children from previous marriage: John, Paul, Anne. AA, Valley Coll., San Bernardino, Calif., 1953; BA in Admnstrn. and Acctg., Claremont Men's Coll., 1955; JD, U. Calif., Los Angeles, 1959. Bar: Calif. 1960. Ptnr. King & Mussell, San Bernardino, Calif., 1960-71; sole practice San Bernardino, Calif., 1971-74; ptnr. Eckhardt, Youmans & Vineyard, San Bernardino, Calif., 1974-75; assoc. Sprague, Milligan & Beswick, San Bernardino, Calif., 1975-76, sole practice, 1976—; judge pro tem San Bernardino County Mcpl. Ct., 1975-81; arbitrator personal injury panel San Bernardino Superior Ct., commr. 1975—; prin. referee Calif. State Bar, Los Angeles, 1979—. Served with USN, 1944-48. Mem. ABA, Am. Arbitration Assn. (arbitrator for claims, comml., constrn. and med. malpractice), San Bernardino County Bar Assn., Internat. Assn. for Ins. Counsel, Am. Bd. Trial Advocates, Calif. Trial Lawyers Assn., Calif. State Bar (prin. referee state bar ct.), Phi Delta Phi. Republican. Lodges: Lions, Elks, Masons, Shriners. Home: 808 E Avery San Bernardino CA 92404 Office: Pacific Savs Plaza 330 N D St Suite 430 San Bernardino CA 92401

VINEYARD, DAVID JESS, automobile club official; b. Hollywood, Calif., Feb. 12, 1926; s. Owen and Lucille (McKee) V.; student Oreg. State U., 1945-49. Asst. to divisional credit mgr. Comml. Credit Corp., Portland, Oreg., 1949-51; field investigator Fed. Res. Bank of San Francisco, Portland, 1951-52; zone mgr. Anglo-Calif. Nat. Bank, San Francisco, 1953-54; credit mgr. Calif. Electric Supply Co., San Francisco, 1954-57; sr. supr. collection sect. Calif. State Automobile Assn., San Francisco, 1957-64; field insp. Approved Accommodations, Restaurants, San Francisco, 1964-69, mgr. market research dept., 1969—; pres. Vigilantia, Inc., San Francisco, 1961-62, dir., 1959-62; pres. CSAA Employees Fed. Credit Union, San Francisco, 1973, treas., mgr., 1975-82, treas., 1975—; v.p., dir. Credit Union Assn. No. Calif., San Francisco, 1978—. Mem. adv. bd. Eugene S. Elkus Found., San Francisco, 1961-62. Served with USNR, 1944-46. Mem. Am. Mktg. Assn., Real Estate Research Council No. Calif. Club: Commonwealth. Office: 150 Van Ness Ave San Francisco CA 94102

VINGO, JAMES RAY, transportation executive; b. Oakland, Calif., Aug. 16, 1938; s. James Samuel and Pauline G. (Isbell) V.; m. Margaret Joanna Sheridan, Oct. 16, 1968; children: Andrea, Michael, Paul. BBA, U. Calif., Berkeley, 1960. Underwriter Calif. Compensation Fund, San Francisco, 1960-63, Fireman's Fund, San Jose, Calif., 1963-66; asst. treas. Western Temporary Services, San Francisco, 1966-68; casualty mgr. CNA Ins. Group, San Francisco, 1968-69; treas. Flying Tiger Line, Los Angeles, 1969-77, Shaklee Corp., San Francisco, 1977-83; v.p. fin. and chief fin. officer Alaska Airlines, Inc., Seattle, 1983—; v.p. fin. and chief fin. officer Alaska Air Group, Seattle, 1983—, also bd. dirs. Served with U.S. Army, 1960-61. Mem. Fin. Execs. Inst. Avocations: boating, sailing. Office: Alaska Air Lines Inc PO Box 68900 Seattle WA 98168

VINLOVE, DONALD JOHN, county official; b. Faribault, Minn., Dec. 18, 1942; s. Ray O. and Gladys M. (Dwyer) V.; m. Dianne Marie Nuese, Apr. 30, 1966; children: Dirk, Joshua. Student, St. John's U., 1961; BA, Mankato State U., 1965; postgrad., Ill. Benedictine Coll., 1981-82; student, No. Ill. U., 1982. Time study engr. McQuay Inc., Faribault, 1966-68; inventory analyst Honeywell, St. Louis Park, Minn., 1968-73; data processing coordinator Osseo (Minn.) Sch. Dist., 1973-78; asst. dir. N.E. Minn. Edn. Corp. Consortium, Duluth, 1976-78; data processing mgr. Valley View Sch. Dist., Romeoville, Ill., 1978-83; dir. mgmt. info services Jackson County, Medford, Oreg., 1983—. Served to 2d lt. USAR, 1966-72. Mem. Data Processing Mgmt. Assn. (exec. v.p. 1983-85, pres. 1986), Am. Motorcyclists Assn. Republican. Roman Catholic. Avocations: tennis, racquetball. Office: Jackson County 10 S Oakdale Medford OR 97501

VIOLA, JOHN THOMAS, aerospace company executive; b. Haverhill, Mass., Mar. 6, 1938; s. John and Antoinette (Pacitto) V.; m. Beverly Marie Gaunya, Sept. 3, 1960; children: Lisa, Julie. BS, U. N.H., 1960; MS, Pa. State U., 1961; PhD, MIT, 1967. Commd. 2d. lt. USAF, 1960-84, advanced through grades to col., 1980; program mgr. office of scientific research USAF, Washington, 1975-78; dir. bus. mgmt. electronic systems div. USAF, Hanscom AFB, Mass., 1978-82, dir. Joint Surveillance System electronic systems div., 1980-82; dep. for space trans. system space div. USAF, Los Angeles, 1982-83, dep. space test, space div., 1983-84; ret. USAF, 1984; program mgr. Rockwell Sci. Ctr, Thousand Oaks, Calif., 1984—; cons. Nat. Materials Adv. Bd., Washington, 1968-71, Dept Energy, Washington, 1976. Contbr. articles to profl. jours; inventor in field. Mem. AIAA, Air Force Assn., Sierra Club, Sigma Xi, Tau Beta Pi. Republican. Roman Catholic. Avocations: skiing, hiking, photography, art. Home: 1007 Brookview Ave Westlake Village CA 91361 Office: Rockwell Internat Sci Ctr 1049 Camino Dos Rios Thousand Oaks CA 91360

VIOLET, WOODROW WILSON, JR., retired chiropractor; b. Columbus, Ohio, Sept. 19, 1937; s. Woodrow Wilson and Alice Katherine (Woods) V.; student Ventura Coll., 1961-62; grad. Los Angeles Coll. Chiropractic, 1966; m. Judith Jane Thatcher, June 15, 1963; children—Woodina Lonize, Leslie Alice. Pvt. practice chiropractic medicine, Santa Barbara, Calif., 1966-73, London, 1973-74, Carpinteria, Calif., 1974-84; past mem. council roentgenology Am. Chiropractic Assn. Former mem. Parker Chiropractic Research Found., Ft. Worth. Served with USAF, 1955-63. Recipient award merit Calif. Chiropractic Colls., Inc., 1975, cert. of appreciation Nat. Chiropractic Antitrust Com., 1977. Mem. Nat. Geog. Soc., Los Angeles Coll. Chiropractic Alumni Assn., Delta Sigma. Patentee surg. instrument.

VIPPERMAN, CAROL FAYE, consultant; b. Renton, Wash., Feb. 24, 1948; d. James Riley and Lydia Bobbyette (Caldwell) V.; m. Jerry Lee Price, Mar. 10, 1979. BA, U. Wash., 1970. Service rep. Liberty Mut. Ins. Co., Seattle, 1970-72; group sales mgr. John A. Tetley Co., Seattle, 1972-76; regional sales mgr. Harrison Hotel, Seattle, 1976-78; pres. Carol Vipperman Inc., Seattle, 1978—; bd. advisers No. Sun, Inc., Lynnwood, Wash., 1983-84, W.I.S.E., Bellevue, Wash., 1984-85; mem. mktg. adv. bd. Seattle office Deloitte Haskins & Sells. Author: Solution to Sales Problems, 1983, Marketing Services, 1987; contbr. articles to profl. jours. Bd. dirs. Alki Found., Seattle, 1984, Seattle Enterprise Ctr.; advocate Seattle Children's Home, 1984; chmn. Wash. State Small Bus. Improvement Council, 1984-86; participant White House Conf. on Small Bus., 1986; mem. adv. bd. Sound Savs. & Loan. Mem. Travellarians (pres. 1974-75), Sales and Mktg. Execs. (pres. 1980-81), Internat. Transactional Analysis Assn. (spl. fields mem. 1982—), Women Bus. Owners (co-founder 1979-80), Greater Seattle C. of C. (vice chmn. 1984-86). Democrat. Clubs: Seattle; Rainier. Office: 1932 1st Ave Suite 609 Seattle WA 98101

VIRCA, GEORGE DUKE, research biochemist; b. Warren, Ohio, Mar. 11, 1952; s. George Francis and Mary (Stanceu) V.; m. Gabrielle Metz, Aug. 10, 1985. BA, Denison U., 1974; MS, U. Ga., 1977, PhD, 1982. Research assoc. Scripps Clinic and Research Found., La Jolla, Calif., 1984—. Contbr. articles to profl. jours. Postdoctoral research fellow CIBA-GEIGY, Ltd., Basel, Switzerland, 1982-84. Mem. AAAS. Avocations: traveling, reading, skiing, hiking, collecting and framing art. Office: Scripps Clinic Research Found 10666 N Torrey Pines Rd La Jolla CA 92037

VISCO, STEVEN JOSEPH, research chemist; b. Brookline, Mass., Mar. 23, 1955; s. Luciano S. and Muriel (Boudrot) V.; m. Donna Moran Mendes, Aug. 22, 1981. BS in Chemistry magna cum laude, U. Mass., 1977; PhD in Chemistry, Brown U., 1982. Postdoctoral researcher U. Calif., Santa Barbara, 1982-84; staff scientist Lawrence Berkeley (Calif.) Nat. Lab., 1984—; dir. research high tech. battery systems, Lawrence Berkeley Nat. Lab., 1984—. Contbr. articles to profl. jours.; patentee in field. Mem. Am. Chem. Soc., Sierra Club, Phi Eta Sigma. Democrat. Roman Catholic. Avocations: sports, guitar, photography. Home: 1330 Neilson St Berkeley CA 94702 Office: Lawrence Berkeley Lab 62-239 1 Cyclotron Rd Berkeley CA 94720

VISCONTI, RON MICHAEL, non-profit associan executive, career consultant, educator; b. Redwood City, Calif., Feb. 23, 1952; s. George Louis and Josephine (Abate) V.; m. Eve Young, Dec. 16, 1978. B.A. in Sociology, U. San Francisco, 1973; postgrad. San Francisco State U., 1978-80. Social services worker County San Mateo Social Services, Calif., 1974-80; adult tchr., San Mateo, 1978—, De Anza Coll., Foothill Coll., San Mateo Adult Schs., 1980-81, Mideast Am. Corp., Burlingame, Calif., 1981-82; salesman Haines & Co., San Mateo, Calif., 1982—; vocat. counselor Tng. Employment Ctr., 1983-84; dir. Community Career Edn. Ctr., 1984—; career cons. Mem. Am. Personnel and Guidance Assn., Am. Soc. for Tng. and Devel., Alpha Sigma Nu. Author: Is There Work after College? Career Planning from A to Z, 1983.

VISEL, DAVID P., advertising agency executive; b. Orange, Calif., May 25, 1938; s. Charles Wesley and Florence Adele (Rundstrom) V.; m. Karen L. Anderson, June 20, 1964; children: David Scott (dec.), Amy Louise. BA, U. So. Calif., 1961; postgrad., Boston U., 1965, Brookings Inst., Washington, 1972, 74; grad., Fgn. Service Inst., Washington, 1966. Prodn. asst. Disneyland, Anaheim, Calif., 1959-61; info. officer USAF, U.S. and Thailand, 1961-67; mgr. corp. news Aerospace Corp., El Segundo, Calif., 1967-75; sr. account exec. Burson-Marsteller, Los Angeles, 1975-76; pres. David Visel & Assocs., Los Angeles, 1977—; bd. dirs. Sales and Mktg. Execs. Los Angeles; cons. 35-40 orgs. U.S. Contbr. articles to profl. publs. Fund raiser YMCA, Boy Scouts Am., United Crusade, 1969-75; bd. dirs. Boys & Girls Club of Venice, Calif., 1972-76. Decorated D.S.C. with oak leaf cluster. Republican. Mem. Covenant Ch. Avocations: history, music, golf. Office: David Visel & Assocs 350 W 5th St San Pedro CA 90731

VISSCHER, ENGBERTUS HENDERIKUS, aerospace engineer; b. Smilde, Drente, The Netherlands, Jan. 29, 1922; came to U.S., 1956; s. Eise and Aaltien (de Vroome) V.; m. Lambertha Wiskerke, Dec. 30, 1949; children: Eise Jan, Françoise Janna, Irene Carol. BS, Tech. Evening Coll., Amsterdam, The Netherlands, 1943. Draftsman, designer Fokker Aircraft Co., Amsterdam, 1938-43, design engr., 1945-56; design engr. Messerschmitt Aircraft Co., Augsberg, Germany, 1943-45; design specialist Lockheed Missiles & Space Co., Sunnyvale, Calif., 1956-65, advanced systems staff engr., 1968-78, metric coordinator, 1978-84, metric cons., 1984—; chmn. metric adv. com. Lockheed Missiles & Space Co., 1978-84; staff cons. Lockheed Aircr Deutschland, Munich, 1966-67. Patentee in field. Mem. AIAA, U.S. Metric Assn. (chmn. cert. metrication specialist program bd.). Presbyterian. Home: 1922 Serge Ave San Jose CA 95130 Office: Lockheed Missles and Space Co 1111 Lockheed Way Box 504 Sunnyvale CA 94086

VISSCHER, WILLIAM MAURITS, physicist; b. Memphis, May 16, 1928; s. Maurice B. and Janet Gertrude (Pieters) V.; m. Jean Elizabeth Dininny, June 14, 1951; children: Wendy Ann, Judith Elaine, James William, Jonathan Maurits. BA, U. Minn., 1949; PhD, Cornell U., 1953. Research assoc. U. Md., College Park, 1953-56; mem. staff Los Alamos (N.Mex.) Nat. Lab., 1956—; vis. prof. U. Wash., Seattle, 1967. Contbr. numerous articles to profl. jours. Fellow Am. Phys. Soc.; mem. Sigma Xi, Phi Beta Kappa, Phi Kappa Phi. Democrat. Unitarian. Club: Toastmasters (various offices held 1965—). Avocations: sailing, backpacking, skiing. Home: 102 Loma del Escolar Los Alamos NM 87544 Office: Los Alamos Nat Lab MS B262 Los Alamos NM 87545

VISSER, LUCAS R., graphic designer, marketing consultant; b. Amsterdam, The Netherlands, Apr. 1, 1940; came to U.S., 1964; m. Sharon Eve White. Diploma, Graphic Arts Sch., Amsterdam, 1960; BS in Deaf Edn., U. Utah, 1963, BFA in Graphic Design cum laude, 1971. Quality control mgr. Deseret Press, Salt Lake City, 1966-72; art dir., mgr. U. Utah, Salt Lake City, 1972-75; art dir., pres. Design Communications, Salt Lake City, 1975-83; art dir., cons. Visser Design Group, Salt Lake City, 1983—; bd. dirs. Internat. Visitors, Salt Lake City; conf. chmn. Colls. Design Assn.; show chmn. Art Dirs., Salt Lake City, 1983. Bd. dirs. Sandy Arts Sch., Sandy, Utah, 1985—. Mem. Am. Inst. Graphic Artists. Republican. Mormon. Lodge: Rotary. Avocations: painting/illustration, skiing. Home: 488 E Floyd Dr Sandy UT 84070

VISWANATHAN, R(AMACHANDRAN), research physicist; b. Tenkasi, Madras, India, Dec. 17, 1938; came to U.S., 1965; d. S.V. And Lakshmi Ramachandran; m. Drowpadha Viswanathan, Feb. 21, 1965; children: Anand, Arvind. MA in Physics, U. Madras, India, 1959, MS in X-Rays, 1960; PhD in Physics, I.I. Sci., Bangalore, India, 1964. Research assoc. U. Ill., Champaign, 1965-66; research physicist Battelle, Columbus, Ohio, 1966-67; research assoc. U. Cin., 1967-69; asst. scientist U. Calif. San Diego, La Jolla, 1969-74; assoc. scientist Brookhaven Nat. Lab., Upton, N.Y., 1974-78; sr. staff mem. Hughes Aircraft Co., El Segundo, Calif., 1978—, prin. investigator, 1978-79, project mgr., 1981—; vis. prof. Inst. Solid State Physics, Julich, Fed. Republic of Germany, 1973. Contbr. articles to profl. jours. Mem. AIAA, AIME, AAAS, Am. Phys. Soc., Am. Vacuum Soc. Home: 30711 Casilina Dr Rancho Palos Verdes CA 90274 Office: Hughes Aircraft Co PO Box 92919 Bldg S33 MS C370 Los Angeles CA 90009

VITA, ANTHONY S., data processing consultant; b. Bklyn., Nov. 30, 1946; s. Salvatore and Carmela (Colacino) V.; m. Lisa Schooler, Jan. 14, 1973. BS in Math., Bklyn. Coll., 1969; MS in Ops. Research, NYU, 1970. Systems analyst Anchorage Borough, 1971-74; bus. systems analyst Alyeska Pipeline, Anchorage, 1974-77; data processing systems cons. Anchorage, 1979—. Served with U.S. Army, 1969-71. CUNY Regents scholar (N.Y.C), 1965. Mem. Data Processing Mgmt. Assn., Prime User Group, Theatre Guild, Synergy (bd. dirs. 1983—). Avocations: theatre. Office: 200 W 34th Ave #379 Anchorage AK 99503

VITALE, ELENA PERSIS, audio-visual production specialist, writer, producer; b. Santa Monica, Calif., Jan. 29, 1949; d. James and Ada (Tourtas) V. BA in Filmwriting, UCLA, 1970. Sect. supr. Becker & Hayes, 1971; clk./typist Comarco Engring Co., Ridgecrest, Calif., 1972-73; engring. technician Naval Weapons Ctr., China Lake, Calif., 1974-75, writer, editor, 1975-79, audio-visual prodn. specialist, 1979—, br. supr., 1984—. Mem. Community Light Opera and Theater Assn. (pres. 1981, 82, 85); charter mem., by-laws originating com. High Desert Council for Arts, Ridgecrest. Named Woman of Yr., Fed. Women's Program Naval Weapons Ctr., 1982; recipient Order Golden Sword, Am. Cancer Soc., 1981; Best actress award Community Light Opera and Theater Assn., 1974, 75, Best Supporting Actress award, 1977, 1980, Best Tech. Dir., 1980, Best Dir., 1978, 79, 85; Jane Bugay meml. award, 1984; Comdr.'s award Naval Weapons Ctr., 1983. Mem. Nat. Assn. Female Execs. Lutheran. Clubs: China Lake Players, Entertainers Network of Desert. Home: 1005 Riverside Dr Inyokern CA 93527 Office: PO Box 2168 Ridgecrest CA 93555

VITALIE, CARL LYNN, pharmacist, lawyer; b. Clinton, Ind., Aug. 31, 1937; s. Paul Gilman and Martha Irrydell (Heidrick) V. D. Pharm., U. So. Calif., 1961, JD, 1965; postgrad., UCLA, 1977. Lic. pharmacist, Calif., Nev., Tex.; diplomate Am. Bd. Diplomates in Pharmacy. Community pharmacy practice various pharmacies, So. Calif., 1961-65; staff atty. Am. Pharm. Assn., Washington, 1965-66; staff pharmacist Sav-On Drugs, Inc., Anaheim, Calif., 1966-69, asst. dir. indsl. and pub. relations, 1969-71, dir. pharmacies, 1971-74, v.p. pharmacy ops., 1974-85; v.p. pharmacy div. The Vons Cos., Inc., El Monte, Calif., 1985—; lectr. pharmacy law and ethics U. So. Calif., Los Angeles, 1968-70; mem. Calif. Bd. Pharmacy, 1968-76; bd. dirs. Bloomfield Leasing Corp., Chgo. Co-author: (with Nancy J. Wolff) Establishment and Maintenance of Membership Standards in Professional Societies of Pharmacists, 1967; mem. editorial adv. bd. Legal Aspects of Pharmacy Practice, 1978-80; also contbr. articles to profl. jours. Served with USAF, 1961-62, Calif. Air N.G., 1962-68. Mem. ABA, Va. State Bar Assn., State Bar Assn. Calif., Am. Mgmt. Assn., Soc. for Advancement of Mgmt., Am. Soc. Pharmacy Law, Am., Calif. Pharm. Assns., Nat. Assn. Bds. Pharmacy, Acad. Gen. Practice Pharmacy, Town Hall Calif., Delta Theta Phi, Phi Delta Chi. Lodge: Masons. Home: 3626 Bravata Dr Huntington Beach CA 92649 Office: Vons Cons Inc 10150 Lower Azusa Rd El Monte CA 91731

VITE, MARK STEVEN, educational administrator; b. Elkhart, Ind., Oct. 18, 1956; s. Frank Anthony and Barbara Ann (Decio) V. BS, Miami U., Oxford, Ohio, 1978. Educator Elkhart (Ind.) Commmunity Schs., 1979-81; asst. high sch. swim coach Elkhart Cen., 1980-81; educator Judson Sch., Scottsdale, Ariz., 1981-82; supr. Marriott's Mountain Shadows, Scottsdale, Ariz., 1982-83; educator Camelback Desert Sch., Scottsdale, Ariz., 1983-85; pres. Marc III Inc., Tempe, Ariz., 1985—. Water safety instr. ARC, Elkhart, 1973-81, Phoenix, 1981—. Named Employee of Month Marriott's Mountain Shadows, 1982-83. Republican. Roman Catholic. Avocations: deep sea fishing, camping, water skiing, reading. Home: 1616 E Fremont Dr Tempe AZ 85282 Office: Marc III Inc 1985 E 5th St Suite 12 Tempe AZ 85281

VITEK, JAMES ALLEN, nuclear engineer; b. Youngstown, Ohio, Mar. 30, 1958; s. John Paul and Eleanor Merrie (Sinclear) V. BE in Chem. Engring., Youngstown State U., 1983; MS in Nuclear Engring., Bettis Atomic Lab Nat. Research Found., 1984. Nuclear plant engr. Westinghouse, Idaho Falls, Idaho, 1983—, engring. officer of the watch, 1984, from engring. duty officer, to nuclear plant engr. of tng. to nulcear plant engr. of ops., 1985, quality control engr., 1986, nuclear plant engr. of tng., 1986—, sr. tng. asst., 1986—. Assoc. staff mem. Campus Life, Youngstown Ohio, 1976-82. Mem. NSPE, Am. Nuclear Soc., Am. Inst. Chem. Engrs., Idaho Soc. Profl. Engrs. (Engring. Deans Council pres. 1982-83), Omega Chi Epsilon (v.p. 1982-83). Republican. Mem. United Ch. Christ. Avocations: racquetball, climbing, working on cars. Home: 4970 Mohawk Pocatello ID 83204 Office: Westinghouse Electric NRF PO Box 2068 Idaho Falls ID 83401

VITOUSEK, PAIGE BOVEE, real estate educator, executive; b. Los Angeles, Dec. 30, 1936; d. Daniel Snyder and Doris (Hume) Bovee; m. Martin J. Vitousek, Mar. 12, 1965 (div.). BS, U. So. Calif., 1958; cert. real estate broker, Grad. Realtors Inst. Hawaii. Pres. Vitousek Real Estate Sch., Honolulu, 1970—; v.p. Vitousek & Dick, Inc., Honolulu, 1974. Co-author Principles and Practices of Hawaiian Real Estate, 1972, 10th rev. edit., Questions and Answers to Help You Pass the Real Estate Exam, 1980, 3d rev. edit. Mem. Mayor's Com. Status for Women, Honolulu, 1976. Mem. Hawaii Assn. Real Estate Schs. (pres. 1985—), Hawaii Assn. Realtors, Real Estate Educators Assn. (instr. 1985). Republican. Clubs: Outrigger Canoe, Honolulu. Avocations: golf, tennis, horseback riding, racquetball, flying. Office: Vitousek Real Estate Sch 657 Kapiolani Blvd #1 Honolulu HI 96813

VITTETOW, THOMAS LIGON, publisher; b. Sangly Point, Philippines, May 8, 1961; came to U.S., 1965; s. Francis Hoyt and Elizabeth (Prather) V. BA in Econs. and Bus., Rollins Coll., 1983. Computer programmer Zink Communications, Orlando, Fla., 1983; account exec. Zincom, Inc., Tampa, Fla., 1983-84; account exec., researcher Zink Pub., Inc., Maitland, Fla., 1984-85; assoc. pub. Zink Pub. West, Englewood, Colo., 1985—; directory organizer State of Colo., Denver, 1986—. Editor: Office Guide to Denver, 1985. Mem. Denver Advt. Fedn., Ad 2 of Denver (pres. 1986). Avocations: tennis, body building, reading, running, traveling. Office: Zink Communications Inc 7346A S Alton Way #118 Englewood CO 80112

VITTORI, RAMON DEL, city official; b. Oakland, Calif., Dec. 6, 1940; s. Peter and Cornelia Ardell (Nagle) V.; m. Jacky Ann Kohlberg, Nov. 9, 1963; children—Peter Dante, Christopher Lee. A.A., Merritt Coll., 1973, Diablo Valley Coll., 1975; B.A., St. Mary's Coll., Moraga, Calif., 1981. Cert. in fire sci.; cert. first aid instr.; cert. tchr., Calif. tool and die maker Fed. Stamping, St. Petersburg, Fla., 1962-63; machinist, Johnson Gear, Berkeley, Calif., 1964-65; from firefighter to fire chief, City of Emeryville, Calif., 1965—. Asst. scoutmaster Oakland Bay Area council Boy Scouts Am., Oakland, Calif., 1968-69. Served with USAF, 1959-62. Mem. Internat. Assn. Fire Chiefs, Nat. Fire Protection Assn., Western Fire Chiefs Assn., Calif. Fire Chiefs Assn., Bay Area Fire Forum, Internat. Assn. Firefighters, Alameda County Fire Chiefs Assn. (sec./treas. 1984, v.p. 1985—), Am. Fedn. Tchrs. Calif. Roman Catholic. Lodge: Lions. Office: City of Emeryville 2449 Powell St Emeryville CA 94608

VLAHOVICH, JOHN LOUIS, interior and graphic designer; b. Los Angeles; s. John and Katica (Kazulin) V.; m. Mary Victoria Himsl, Nov. 23, 1963; children: Max, Tyler, Sam. BA in Painting and Design, Seattle U., 1960. lectr. Wash. State U. Sch. Architecture Design, Pullman, 1974; invitational show presenter Pacific Luth. U. Sch. Art Design, Tacoma, 1978; instr. photography for gifted students, Tacoma, 1979; guest critic U. Wash. Grad. Sch. Architecture, Seattle, 1977; juror Am. Advt. Fedn. Competition, Colo., 1982. Prin. works include (sculpture) St. John's Hosp., 1963, U. Wash. Oceanography Bldg. Exterior, 1965; (painting) Gov.'s Invitational, 1969. Mem. Old City Hall Hist. Dist., Tacoma, 1981-85, Mcpl. League, Tacoma, 1983-85; commr. Landmarks Preservation Commn., Tacoma, 1984-85, Wash. State Arts Commn., Olympia, 1984—. Recipient Advt. Honor award Seattle Art Dirs. Show, 1976-77, Interior Design Honor award S.W. chpt. AIA, 1984, Spl. Citation S.W. chpt. AIA, 1982. Roman Catholic. Avocation: photography. Home: 517 N 6th St Tacoma WA 98403 Office: Vlahovich Design Assocs 821 Pacific Ave Tacoma WA 98402

VLAY, GEORGE JOHN, engineering executive; b. Buffalo, Dec. 1, 1927; s. John and Victoria (Mili) V.; B.S. in Elec. Engring., U. Buffalo, 1953, postgrad., 1954-56; m. Betty Jo Wayland, July 21, 1949; children—Vanessa Michelle, Susan Victoria, George John. Project engr. electronics R.B.

Warman, Buffalo, 1954-56, Aero Comdr. Corp., Norman, Okla., 1956-61, GTE/Sylvania, Williamsville, N.Y., 1961-66; mgr. advanced communications systems Philco-Ford, Palo Alto, Calif., 1966-78; dir. bus. devel. and planning Ford Aerospace Corp., Palo Alto, 1978-82; dir. tech. affairs Ford Aerospace and Communications Corp., Palo Alto, 1982—. Served with USAF, 1946-49. Registered profl. engr., Okla. Assoc. fellow AIAA; mem. Air Force Assn., Armed Forces Communications and Electronics Assn., IEEE (sr.), Pi Mu Epsilon. Republican. Methodist. Home: 32 Yerba Buena Ave Los Altos CA 94022 Office: Ford Aerospace & Communications Corp 3939 Fabian Way Palo Alto CA 94303

VOBEJDA, WILLIAM FRANK, aerospace engineer; b. Lodgepole, S.D., Dec. 5, 1918; s. Robert and Lydia (Stefek) V.; m. Virginia Parker, Oct. 24, 1942; children—William N., Margaret, Mary Joan, Barbara, Lori. B.C.E., S.D. Sch. Mines and Tech., 1942. Registered profl. engr., Colo. Stress analyst Curtiss Wright Corp., Columbus, Ohio, 1942-45; civil/hydraulic engr. Bur. Reclamation, Denver, 1945-54; mech. supr. Stearns Roger Corp., Denver, 1954-62; mgr. Martin Marietta Corp., Denver, 1962-86, mgr. engring. M-X Program, 1978-86; pres. BV Engring., Inc., Englewood, Colo., 1986—. Active Boy Scouts Am. Recipient Silver Beaver award. Mem. Englewood City Council 1984—. Mem. AIAA. Democrat. Roman Catholic. Clubs: St. Louis Men's, K.C., Martin Marietta Chess.

VOCATE, DONNA R., speech-language educator; b. Smith County, Kans., July 15, 1941; d. Ancel L. and Eva (Covey) Garrett; m. Gilbert E. Vocate, Feb. 28, 1964. BA, U. Colo., 1962; MA, U. Denver, 1977, PhD, 1980. Asst. prof. Eastern Mont. Coll., Billings, 1980-83, U. Colo., Boulder, Colo., 1983—; faculty research assoc. Inst. Cognitive Sci., Boulder, 1984—. Author: The Theory of A.R. Luria, 1986; contbr. articles to profl. jours. Grantee Pres. Com. Research and Creative Endeavor, 1982, EMC Found. and Dean's Office, 1983. Mem. Internat. Communication Assn., Western Speech Communication Assn., Am. Assn. Univ. Women, Nat. Speech Communication Assn. (chmn. Speech and Lang. Scis. div. 1985—). Office: U Colo Boulder Dept Communication Boulder CO 80309-0270

VOEGELI, PAUL THOMAS, JR., podiatric physician, surgeon; b. Boise, Idaho, Nov. 18, 1953; s. Paul Thomas and Nancy C. (Charuhas) V. BS in Biology cum laude, Regis Coll., 1976; BS, Calif. Coll. Podiatric Medicine, 1981, D in Podiatric Medicine, 1983. Diplomate Nat. Bd. Podiatry Examiners. Resident in surgery U.S. VA Med. Ctr., Albuquerque, 1983-84; practice medicine specializing in podiatry Foothills Podiatry Ctr., Lakewood, Colo., 1985—; tech. advisor, cons. Sanmarco Internat., Aspen, Colo., 1983—; cons. podiatry U.S. Nat. Disabled Ski Team, Winter Park, Colo., 1983—. Contbr. articles to profl. jours. Vol. med. staff Regional Health Fairs, Denver; lectr. sr. citizens groups, Denver. Mem. Am. Podiatric Med. Assn., Colo. Podiatric Med. Assn. Greek Orthodox. Avocations: Alpine and Nordic skiing, cycling, family. Office: Foothills Podiatry Ctr 405 Urban St Suite 201 Lakewood CO 80228 Address: PO Box 683 Tabernash CO 80482

VOEKS, VIRGINIA WILNA, educator; b. Champaign, Ill., May 9, 1921; d. B. Forrest and Dorothy (Wade) V.; B.S. summa cum laude, U. Wash., 1943, M.S., 1944; Ph.D., Yale U., 1947; m. William McBlair IV. Research asso. Yale U., New Haven, 1944-45; asst. prof. U. Wash., 1947-49; asst. prof. San Diego State U., 1949-55, asso. prof., 1955-58, prof., 1958-71, prof. emeritus, 1971—. Recipient Pres. medal U. Wash., 1943; Sterling award Yale, 1945. Fellow N.Y. Acad. Scis., Am. Psychol. Assn. (sec.-treas. div. I 1965-77, editor Newsletter); mem. Western Psychol. Assn., AAUP, AAAS, Nat. Geog. Soc., Psychonomic Soc. (charter), UN Assn. San Diego, U.S. Olympic Soc., San Diego Ballet Assn. (charter), Jacques Cousteau Soc. (charter), Am. Bible Soc., Nat. Wildlife Fedn., Asso. Council Arts, Phi Beta Kappa, Sigma Xi, Psi Chi (pres. U. Wash. chpt. 1942-44), Phi Kappa Phi, Sigma Epsilon Sigma, Alpha Lambda Delta. Episcopalian. Club: Heritage. Author: On Becoming an Educated Person, 1957, 64, 70, 79; contbr. article to Internat. Ency. Social Scis., 1971; contbr. articles to profl. jours. Editorial bd. Teaching Psychology. Home: PO Box 877 4319 Explorer Rd La Mesa CA 92044 Office: Dept Psychology San Diego State U San Diego CA 92182

VOELZ, GEORGE LEO, occupational physician; b. Wittenberg, Wis., Oct. 13, 1926; s. George Albert and Louise Amelia (Hacker) V.; m. Emily Jane Neunast, June 10, 1950 (widowed Mar. 1979); children: Valerie, David, Brian, Sharon; m. Mary Affleck Wesselman, Jan. 3, 1981; stepchildren: Eric Bartsch, Julie Bartsch. BS in Pre Medicine, U. Wis., 1948, MD, 1950. Diplomate Am. Bd. Preventative Medicine. Occupational physician Los Alamos (N.Mex.) Sci. Lab., 1952-57; med. dir. Idaho Ops. Office, AEC, Idaho Falls, 1957-70; health div. leader Los Alamos Nat. Lab., 1970-82, asst. div. leader, 1982—; cons., radiation specialist numerous cos. and legal firms; mem. Nat. Council on Radiation Protection and Measurements, Washington, 1973—, bd. dirs., 1975-79; com. mem. Internat. Commn. Radiol. Protection, London, 1984—. Contbr. over 50 articles to profl. jours., principally on ionizing radiation; also book chpts. Served with USN, 1945-46. Fellow Am. Acad. Occupational Medicine, Am. Coll. Preventative Medicine, Am. Occupational Medicine Assn.; mem. Internat. Commn. Occupational Health, Am. Indsl. Hygiene Assn. (J.M. Dallavalle award 1967), Health Physics Soc. Republican. Lutheran. Avocations: skiing, gardening, music. Home: 117 La Vista Dr Los Alamos NM 87544 Office: Los Alamos Nat Lab PO Box 1663 Mail Stop K491 Los Alamos NM 87545

VOGEL, DREW FRANKLIN, paint company executive; b. Orange City, Iowa, July 12, 1950; s. Franklin and Lois Betty (Boonstra) V.; m. Jean Ellen Tallman, June 25, 1977; children: Meika Marie, Trevor Andrew. B.S. in Indsl. Adminstrn., Iowa State U., 1973. With Diamond Vogel Paints, Des Moines, 1973-74, br. mgr., Omaha, 1975-77; v.p., gen. mgr. Diamond Vogel Paints, Mpls., 1977-82; exec. v.p. Komac Paint, Inc., Denver, 1982—. Bd. dirs. Bethesda Hosp. Found., 1987. Mem. Christian Reformed Ch. Office: Komac Paint Inc PO Box 546 Denver CO 80201

VOGELS, DAVID SELLERS, JR., lawyer; b. Phila., May 2, 1925; s. David Sellers and Irene Ambler (Wallace) V.; m. Mary Stetson Prescott, Sept. 1, 1951 (div. Oct. 1977); children: David Sellers III, Robert Prescott, Edward Page, Jonathan Bryant. AB, Dartmouth Coll., 1949; postgrad, Harvard U., 1949-50; MBA, Syracuse U., 1957; JD, St. Mary's U., San Antonio, 1959; MA, U. Calif., Riverside, 1967; PhD, Mich. State U., 1973. Bar: Colo. 1974. Enlisted USAF, 1943, advanced through grades to col., 1970, ret., 1975; legal adminstr. Weller, Friedrich, et al, Denver, 1977-80; dir. legal adminstrn. Mountain Bell, Denver, 1981—. Sr. warden St. James Episcopal Ch., Wheat Ridge, Colo., 1985—. Decorated DFC, Legion of Merit, 31 other decorations and awards; recipient George E. Williams award Federation of Geneal. Socs., 1985. Mem. Denver Bar Assn. (chmn. law office mgmt. com. 1980-83), Colo. Bar Assn. (chmn. law office mgmt. com. 1981-83), Assn. Legal Adminstrs. (v.p. 1984-86, pres.-elect 1986-87, pres. 1987—). Avocation: genealogy. Office: Mountain States Telephone & Telegraph Co 1801 California St Denver CO 80202

VOGT, EUGENIA F., speech pathologist, special education educator; b. Schenectady, N.Y., June 23, 1921; d. Clinton Forrest Sparta and Harriet (Lendrum) Felton; m. Charles Elonzo Mitchell, Oct. 16, 1947 (div. Aug. 1952); m. August H. Vogt, Feb. 12, 1953; children: August David, Lisa Marie. BA, Kenka Coll., 1945; MA, SUNY, Albany, 1947; PhD, U. So. Calif., 1973. Cert. clin. competence, Calif.; cert. tchr., Calif.; lic. speech pathologist, Calif. Instr. Emmetsburg (Iowa) Jr. Coll., 1947-48, U. Wash., Seattle, 1948-49; clinician Pub. Schs., Rapid City, S.D., 1950-51; pvt. practice speech pathologist Los Angeles, 1957—; clinician, coordinator Exceptional Children Found., Los Angeles, 1967-74; tchr., specialist Los Angeles County Office Edn., 1974—. Clinician Santa Monica (Calif.) Coordinating Council Deveopmentally Disabled, 1971-73; mem. coordinating council Parent and Profls. in Infant Devel., Los Angeles, 1973-74. Served with WAC, 1945. Mem. Am. Speech and Hearing. Assn., Calif. Speech and Hearing Assn. Lodge: Oddfellows. Avocations: dress designing, cooking. Office: Los Angeles County Office Edn 9300 E Imperial Hwy Downey CA 90242-2890

VOGT, ROCHUS EUGEN, physicist, educator; b. Neckarelz, Germany, Dec. 21, 1929; came to U.S., 1953; s. Heinrich and Paula (Schaefer) V.; m. Micheline Alice Yvonne Bauduin, Sept. 6, 1958; children: Michele, Nicole. Student, U. Karlsruhe, Germany, 1950-52, U. Heidelberg, Germany, 1952-53; S.M., U. Chgo., 1957, Ph.D., 1961. Mem. faculty dept. physics Calif. Inst. Tech., Pasadena, 1962—, assoc. prof., 1965-70, prof., 1970-82, R. Stanton Avery Disting. Service prof., 1982—, chmn. faculty, 1975-77, chmn. div. physics, math. and astronomy, 1978-83, v.p. and provost, 1983-87, chief scientist Jet Propulsion Lab., 1977-78; acting dir. Owens Valley Radio Obs., 1980-81. Fellow Am. Phys. Soc.; mem. Am. Assn. Physics Tchrs., AAAS. Research in astrophysics. Office: Calif Inst Tech 103-33 Pasadena CA 91125

VOIGHT, FRANK EDWARD, service organization executive; b. Redlands, Calif., Dec. 28, 1915; s. Julius Edward and Mary Lucille (Cordero) V.; B.A. in Polit. Sch., U. Redlands, 1949; M.S. in Public Adminstrn., U. So. Calif., 1950; m. Betty Lou Collins, June 15, 1947; children—Susan Lynn Voight Stoney, Steven E. (dec.), Cynthia L. With Allied Trades & Fire Prevention, 1935-43; with CSC, 1950-76, communications staff officer San Bernardino Air Materiel Area, Norton AFB, Calif., 1960-63, chief resources info. Space and Missile Systems Orgn., Los Angeles Air Force Sta., 1966-76; dir. community services Goodwill Industries of Inland Counties, Inc., San Bernardino, Calif., 1976-77. Chmn. heritage com. Bicentennial Commn., Rialto, Calif., 1975-76; chmn. adv. bd. ARC, San Bernardino County, 1982—; bd. dirs. Am. Lung Assn., San Bernardino County, 1982-84; interim exec. dir., 1982; pres. Cerebral Palsy Assn., City of Hope; mem. nat. adv. bd. Am. Security Council; elder Seventh-Day Adventist Ch., Fontana, Calif.; chmn. lay adv. com. S.E. Calif. Conf., Seventh-Day Adventist Ch., 1982-83; mem. Republican Nat. Com., Rep. Nat. Congl. Com., Rep. Presdl. Task Force, 1981-87. Served with M.C., U.S. Army, 1943-44. Recipient certificate of appreciation local lung assn., 1965-67, Cerebral Palsy Assn., 1963-64, City of Hope, 1964; named Citizen of Year, Rialto (Calif.) Inter-Service Club Council, 1961. Mem. Pub. Relations Soc. Am. (treas. Calif. Inland Empire chpt. 1978-79), Hist. Soc. Rialto, Am. Legion. Republican. Adventist. Club: Kiwanis (pres. local club 1976-77) (Rialto). Co-author: A History of Rialto, rev. edit., 1976.

VOIGT, MELVIN JOHN, editor, information scientist, librarian; b. Upland, Calif., Mar. 12, 1911; s. Adolf F. and Marie T. (Hirschler) V.; m. Susie M. Warkentin, Dec. 28, 1933; children: Marjorie Huskins, Dolores Scott, Paul W. Voigt. AB, Bluffton Coll., 1933; ABLS, U. Mich., 1936, AMLS, 1938. Librarian Bluffton (Ohio) High Sch. and Pub. Library, 1933-35, U. Mich., Ann Arbor, 1935-42; dir. library and pub. Gen. Mills, Inc., Mpls., 1942-46; librarian and prof. Carnegie Inst. Tech., Pitts., 1946-52; asst. univ. librarian U. Calif., Berkeley, 1952-59; univ. librarian U. Calif.-San Diego, La Jolla, 1960-76; editor communications Ablex Pub. Corp., La Jolla, 1976—; vis. prof. U. Mich., 1951, UCLA, 1977; vis. lectr. and scholar U. Ga.; cons. to numerous govt. agys., fed. and comml. orgns., 1960—. Editor: Advances in Librarianship (7 vols.), 1970-77, Communication and Information Science Series (55 vols.), 1976—, Progress in Communication Sciences (8 vols.), 1979—; author Scientists' Approaches to Information, Books for College Libraries; contbr. articles to profl. jours. Pres. Lung Assn. San Diego County, 1969-70. Fulbright sr. research scholar, U. Copengagen, 1958-59, Inst. für Dokumentation, Frankfurt, Fed. Republic Germany, 1974-75. Fellow AAAS; mem. Am. Library Assn. (pres. resources and tech. services div. 1960-61, library edn. div. 1962-63, com. chmn.), Spl. Libraries Assn. (v.p. 1947-48, pres. local chpt. 1943-46), Pa. Library Assn. (pres. 1951-52), Am. Soc. Info. Sci., Internat. Communication Assn., Speech Communication Assn. Democrat. Congregationalist. Office: U Calif-San Diego 624 Cen Univ Library La Jolla CA 92093

VOISENAT, FRANCIS (FRANK) WILLIAM, quality assurance engr.; b. Englewood, N.J., Aug. 21, 1935; s. Frank and Mary (Unalt) V.; B.S., Manhattan Coll., 1957; postgrad. U. Calif., Santa Barbara, 1969-71; m. Jan. 8, 1966 (div. Apr. 1972); children—Michelle Marie, Melissa Rene. Human engring. analyst Boeing A/C Co., Vandenberg AFB, Calif., 1965-66; sr. engr. scientist Manned Orbital Lab., McDonnel Douglas Co., Vandenberg AFB, 1966-70; sr. quality control engr. Lunar Rover, Gen. Motors Co., Goleta, Calif., 1970-71; project quality assurance engr. Infra red Components Santa Barbara Research Ctr., subs. Hughes Aircraft Co., Goleta, Calif., 1971—. Served with USAFR, 1957-77. Club: Elks. Office: 75 Coromar Goleta CA 93017

VOJTECKY, MICHAEL ALLEN, public health educator; b. Natrona Heights, Pa., July 30, 1953; s. Joseph Stephen and Margaret Mary (Hrnciar) V. BA, Pa. State U., 1974, MA, 1977; MPH, U. Pitts., 1980, PhD, 1981. Site dir. West Pa. Heart Assn. Exec. Program, Pitts., 1979; program coordinator indsl. health edn. Health Edn. Ctr. Pitts., 1980-81; asst. prof. pub. health UCLA, 1981—. Contbr. articles to profl. jours. Chmn. heart at work task force Am. Heart Assn., Los Angeles, 1985-86. Mem. AAAS, Am. Pub. Health Assn. (session chmn. 1985), Soc. Pub. Health Edn., Human Factors Soc. Republican. Roman Catholic. Office: UCLA Sch Pub Health 405 Hilgard Ave Los Angeles CA 90024

VOLLHARDT, KURT PETER CHRISTIAN, chemistry educator; b. Madrid, Mar. 7, 1946; came to U.S., 1972; Vordiplom, U. Munich, 1968; PhD, U. Coll., London, 1972. Postdoctoral fellow Calif. Inst. Tech., Pasadena, 1972-74; asst. prof. chemistry U. Calif., Berkeley, 1974-78, assoc. prof., 1978-82, prof., 1982—; prin. investigator Lawrence Berkeley Lab., 1975—; cons. Monsanto Corp., St. Louis, Exxon Corp., Annandale, N.J., Maruzen Corp., Tokyo. Co-author: Aromatizität; contbr. articles to profl. jours.; patentee in field. Sloan fellow, 1976-80; Camille and Henry Dreyfus scholar, 1978-83; recipient Adolf Windaus medal, 1983, Humboldt Sr. Scientist award, 1985; named One of Am.'s 100 Brightest Scientists Under 40 Sci. Digest, 1984. Mem. Am. Chem. Soc. (Organometallic Chemistry award 1987), German Chem. Soc., Chem. Soc. of London. Office: U Calif Dept Chemistry Berkeley CA 94720

VOLLMAR, ARNULF RICHARD, chemistry educator; b. Pluderhausen, Fed. Republic Germany, Apr. 15, 1928; came to U.S., 1958; s. Frederic and Johanna (Trauttmann) V.; m. Christa Lesle, Feb. 19, 1978. Student, Univ. Tubingen, Fed. Republic Germany, 1948-51, U. Heidelberg, Fed. Republic Germany, 1952-57; MS, U. Heidelberg, Fed. Republic Germany, 1956, PhD, 1957. Research assoc. U. Heidelberg, 1957-58; postdoctoral fellow UCLA, 1958-60; research chemist Chevron Research, Richmond, Calif., 1960-64; prof. chemistry Calif. State Poly. U., Pomona, 1965—; researcher Furan chemistry. Mem. Am. Chem. Soc., Sigma Xi. Office: Calif State Poly U Dept Chemistry Temple St Pomona CA 91768

VOLPE, JAMES ANTHONY, computer company executive, poet; b. Chgo., June 24, 1954; s. Vincent Francis and Bernice Stella (Piragis) V. BS in Mktg., No. Ill. U., 1975; postgrad. Santa Clara U., 1986—; Dale Carnegie Course grad, 1984. Br. adminstrv. specialist Four-Phase Motorola, Des Plaines, Ill., 1978-80, central regional adminstrv. mgr., 1980-84, mgr. customer order to billing, corp. offices, Cupertino, Calif., 1984-86; mgr. credit and collections, 1986-87. Author numerous poems. Recipient Golden Poet award World of Poetry Press, 1985, 86. Mem. Jammers Athletic Orgn., Phi Sigma Epsilon. Roman Catholic. Home: 7375 Rollingdell Dr Apt 76 Cupertino CA 95014 Office: Motorola Computer Systems 10700 N DeAnza Blvd Cupertino CA 95014

VOLPE, LEO, research physical chemist; b. Moscow, Jan. 19, 1955; came to U.S., 1976; s. Michael and Sofia (Kovnat) V. BS, Yale U., 1979; PhD, Stanford U., 1983. Staff engr./scientist IBM, San Jose, Calif., 1983—. Contbr. articles to profl. jours.; patentee in field. Mem. Am. Inst. Chem. Engrs., Am. Chem. Soc., Electrochem. Soc., Nat. Assn. Corrosion Engrs., Phi Beta Kappa, Tau Beta Pi. Avocation: tennis. Home: 2510 Emerson Palo Alto CA 94301 Office: IBM 5600 Cottle Rd San Jose CA 95193

VOLPERT, RICHARD SIDNEY, lawyer; b. Cambridge, Mass., Feb. 16, 1935; s. Samuel Abbot and Julia (Fogel) V.; m. Marcia Flaster, June 11, 1958; children: Barry, Sandy, Linda, Nancy. B.A., Amherst Coll., 1956; LL.B. (Stone scholar), Columbia U., 1959. Bar: Calif. bar 1960. Atty. firm O'Melveny & Myers, Los Angeles, 1959-86; ptnr. O'Melveny & Myers, 1967-86, Skadden, Arps, Slate, Meagher & Flom, Los Angeles, 1986—; pub. Jewish Jour. of Los Angeles, 1985—. Editor, chmn.: Los Angeles Bar Jour, 1965, 66, 67, Calif. State Bar Jour, 1972-73. Chmn. community relations com. Jewish Fedn.-Council Los Angeles, 1977-80; bd. dirs. Jewish Fedn.-Council Greater Los Angeles, 1976—, v.p., 1978-81; pres. Los Angeles County Natural History Mus. Found., 1978-84, trustee, 1974—; chmn. bd. councilors U. So. Calif. Law Center, 1979-85; vice chmn. Nat. Jewish Community Relations Adv. Council, 1981-84, mem. exec. com., 1978—; bd. dirs. U. Judaism, 1973—, bd. govs., 1973—; bd. dirs. Valley Beth Shalom, Encino, Calif., 1964—; mem. capital program major gifts com. Amherst Coll., 1978—; bd. dirs., mem. exec. com. Los Angeles Wholesale Produce Market Devel. Corp., 1978—, v.p., 1981—; mem. exec. bd. Los Angeles chpt. Am. Jewish Com., 1967—; vice-chmn. Los Angeles County Econ. Devel. Council, 1978-81; bd. dirs. Jewish Community Found., 1981—; mem. Pacific S.W. regional bd. Anti Defamation League B'nai B'rith, 1964—. Named Man of Year, 1978. Fellow Am. Bar Found.; mem. ABA, Am. Soc. Planning Ofcls., Urban Land Inst., Los Angeles County Bar Assn. (trustee 1968-70, chmn. real property sect. 1974-75), Los Angeles County Bar Found. (trustee 1977-80), Calif. Bar Assn. (com. on adminstrn. justice 1973-76), Am. Coll. Real Estate Lawyers. Jewish. Clubs: Amherst of So. Calif. (dir. 1968—, pres. 1972-73); University (Los Angeles). Home: 4001 Stansbury Ave Sherman Oaks CA 91423 Office: Skadden Arps Slate Meagher & Flom 300 S Grand Ave Los Angeles CA 90071

VOLPICELLI, FERRILL JOSEPH, real estate; b. Syracuse, N.Y., Dec. 30, 1955; s. Ferrill Joseph and Jessie A. (Semple) V.; m. Lori Ann Rowan, Apr. 20, 1981; children: Ashley, Chanel, Travis. B with honors in Biology, UCLA, 1974-78. Pvt. practice real estate, securities, ins. broker Reno, 1979-86. Office: Volpicelli Investment Mgmt Inc 316 California Ave Reno NV 89509

VOLZ, MICHAEL GEORGE, environmental biochemist; b. Long Beach, Calif., Nov. 30, 1945; s. Edgar Louis and Fannie Rae (Young) V.; m. Adrienne Jane Machado, Mar. 17, 1968; children: Carla Marie, Eric Michael, Raphael Francis. BS, U. Calif., Berkeley, 1967, PhD, 1972. Cert. profl. agronomist, soil scientist. Research biochemist U. Calif., Berkeley, 1972-75; plant physiologist Conn. Agrl. Experiment Sta., New Haven, 1975-77; assoc. sanitary microbiologist Calif. Dept. Health Services, Berkeley, 1977-82, pub. health chemist, 1982-85, environ. biochemist, group leader environ. measurements, 1985—. Contbr. articles to profl. jours. Mem. AAAS, Am. Soc. Agronomy, Soil Sci. Soc. Am., Soc. Environ. Geochem. and Health, Am. Water Works Assn., Water Pollution Control Fedn. Democrat. Roman Catholic. Avocations: running, gardening, travel. Office: Calif Dept Health Services Sanitation and Radiation Lab 2151 Berkeley Way Berkeley CA 94704

VON BARANDY, RICHARD DWIGHT, marketing company executive; b. South Bend, Ind., July 5, 1935; s. Oscar von Barandy and Thelma (Harris) W.; student William Jennings Bryan Coll., 1953-54, Ariz. State U., 1958-59; B.S.E.E., U. Ariz., 1960; m. Carol Jean Weber, Nov. 13, 1976; children—Richard Linn, Charla Diane, Michelle LeAnn, Michael Derek. Dir. reliability, product mktg. mgr., quality assurance mgr. Dickson Electronics Corp., Siemens, Ariz., 1960-67; mgr. reliability and quality assurance Transitron-Mexicana, 1967-68; v.p. mktg. Gen. Semiconductor Industries, Inc., Tempe, Ariz., 1968—. Recipient presdl. E award for export sales Ariz. Rep. Rhodes, 1980. Mem. Am. Soc. Quality Control (sr.), Am. Mgmt. Assn., Ariz. World Trade Assn. (dir.), Aircraft Owners and Pilots Assn., Internat. Aircraft Owners and Pilots Assn. Republican. Baptist. Patentee electromagnetic pulse suppressor; contbr. articles to profl. publs. and confs. Home: 2818 S Bala Tempe AZ 85281 Office: Gen Semiconductor Industries Inc 2001 W 10th Pl Tempe AZ 85281

VONBLUM, PAUL, educator, lawyer; b. Phila., Mar. 30, 1943; s. Peter W. and Selma E. VonB.; m. Ruth Chervin, Mar. 23, 1971; 1 child, Elizabeth Sarah. AB, San Diego State U., 1964; JD, U. Calif., 1967. Bar: Calif. 1969, U.S. Dist. Ct. Instr. Golden Gate Coll., San Francisco, 1967, Calif. Inst. of the Arts, Los Angeles, 1967-68, U. Calif., Berkeley, 1968-79, U. So. Calif., Los Angeles, 1979-80, UCLA, 1980—, U. Calif., San Diego, 1986; sole practice Calif., 1969—; evaluator and cons. Calif. State U. Chancellor's Office, Long Beach, 1983-87. Author: The Art of Social Conscience, 1976, Audrey Pressler, 1981, The Critical Vision, 1982, Stillborn Education, 1986; contbr. numerous articles and reviews to profl. jours. Program administr. NEH, Washington, 1979. Recipient Disting. Teaching award U. Calif., Berkeley, 1974, 1st prize Non.-Legal Pubs., Calif. State Bar Assn., 1977, Disting. Teaching award UCLA, 1986. Mem. Calif. Bar Assn., Assn. Integrative Studies (v.p. 1979). Home and Office: 2038 Louella Ave Venice CA 90291

VON DASSANOWSKY-HARRIS, ROBERT, writer, editor; b. N.Y.C., Jan. 28, 1956; s. Leslie Harris de Erendred and Elfriede Maria Baroness von Dassanowsky. Grad., Am. Acad. Dramatic Arts; BA with honors, UCLA, MA. Actor, dir. Los Angeles, N.Y.C., 1975—; freelance writer Los Angeles, 1979—; dir. Ind. Theatrical Prodns., Los Angeles, 1981—; bd. advisors Com. Art for Olympia, N.Y.C., 1984—, Arno Breker Soc., N.Y.C., 1983—. Author: Telegrams From the Metropole, 1987; (plays) The Birthday of Margot Beck, 1980, Briefly Noted, 1981, Vespers, 1982 (Beverly Hills Theater Guild award 1984), Tristan in Winter, 1986, Songs of a Wayfarer, 1986; editor Rohwedder Internat. Arts Mag., 1986—, New German Rev., 1987—; author numerous poems, contbr. articles and essays to profl. jours. Mem. German Am. Nat. Congress, Mt. Prospect, Ill., 1983, Peu-Aktion-Österreich, Vienna, Austria, 1983—, Paneuropa Union, Munich, 1982—. Recipient Residency award Karolyi Found., France, 1979, Man of Achievement award, U.K., 1986. Fellow World Lit. Acad.; mem. Dramatists Guild, Screen Actors Guild, Authors League, Heinrich-Von-Kleist-Gesellschaft, Goethe Soc. N.Am. Home: 4346 Matilija Ave 27 Sherman Oaks CA 91423

VONDERHEID, ARDA ELIZABETH, nursing administrator; b. Pitts., June 19, 1925; d. Louis Adolf and Hilda Barbara (Gerstacker) V.; diploma Allegheny Gen. Hosp. Sch. Nursing, 1946; B.S. in Nursing Edn., Coll. Holy Names, Oakland, Calif., 1956; M.S. in Nursing Adminstrn., UCLA, 1960. Head nurse Allegheny Gen. Hosp., Pitts., 1946-48; staff nurse Highland-Alameda County Hosp., Oakland, Calif., 1948-51, staff nurse poliomyelitis units, 1953-55; pvt. duty nurse Directory Registered Nurses Alameda County, Oakland, 1951-53; adminstrv. supervising nurse Poliomyelitis Respiratory and Rehab. Center, Fairmont, Alameda County Hosp., Oakland, 1955-58; night supr., relief asst. dir. nursing Peninsula Hosp., Burlingame, Calif., 1960, adminstrv. supr., 1961-62, inservice educator, 1963-69; staff nurse San Francisco Gen. Hosp., 1969, asst. dir. nurses, 1969-72; mem. faculty continuing edn. U. Calif., San Francisco, 1969-71; dir. nursing services Kaiser Permanente Med. Center, South San Francisco, 1973-1982, asst. adminstr. Med. Center Nursing Services, 1982-85; asst. adminstr. Kaiser Permanente Med. Ctr., 1985-87; ret. 1987. Chmn. edn. com. San Mateo County (Calif.) Cancer Soc., 1962-69; bd. dirs. San Mateo County Heart Assn., 1968-71; mem., foreman pro tem San Mateo County Civil Grand Jury, 1982-83; mem. San Mateo County Health Council, 1982-85, vice chmn., 1984. Cert. advanced nursing adminstrn. Mem. San Mateo County (dir. 1964-69, pres. elect 1967-68, pres. 1968-70), Golden Gate (1st v.p. 1974-78, dir. 1974-78), Calif., Am. nurses assns., Nat. League Nursing, Soc. for Nursing Service Adminstrs., State Practice and Edn. Council, AAUW, San Mateo County Grand Jury Assn., Calif. Grand Jury Assn., Sigma Theta Tau. Republican. Lutheran. Club: Kai-Perm. Contbr. articles in field to profl. jours. Home: 1047 Aragon Ct Pacifica CA 94044

VONHEEDER, GEORGEAN MARIE, vice mayor, city council member, accountant; b. Oakland, Calif., June 24, 1947; d. George M. and Minnie C. (Souza) Silva; m. Vincent H. Vonheeder, Mar. 19, 1966; children—Judy, Steve, Joe, David. Student, Chabot Jr. Coll., 1974-76, Calif. State U.-Hayward, 1965-66. With Denis Sherry, Acct., 1972-78, office mgr., 1973-84; owner, mgr. Bus. Assts./Valley Tax Service, Dublin, Calif., 1978-84. Active Girl Scouts U.S.A.; treas. Dublin Youth Softball, 1977; treas. Dublin/San Ramon Activities Council, 1979; mem. Com. Incorporate Dublin/San Ramon, 1980; mem. Dublin Mcpl. Adv. Com., 1981; campaigner for city and council candidates; mem. ad hoc com. for Parks and Recreation, Dublin, 1982; mem. Dublin Planning Com., 1982-84, vice chmn., 1982-84; mem. Dublin City Council, 1984—; mayor pro tempore City of Dublin, 1986—. Mem. Nat. Assn. Enrolled Agts., Calif. Soc. Enrolled Agts., Am. Bus. Women's Assn., Dublin C. of C. (bd. dirs. 1981-84, treas. 1983-84), Native Daus. of Golden West, Model A Ford Club Am. (regional treas. 1978-84, nat. treas. 1980).

VONKAENEL, JEFF P., newspaper executive; b. Columbus, Ohio, Mar. 10, 1951. Advt. mgr. Santa Barbara (Calif.) News and Rev., 1973-79; gen. mgr. Chico (Calif.) News and Rev., 1980—.

VON KALINOWSKI, JULIAN ONESIME, lawyer; b. St. Louis, May 19, 1916; s. Walter E. and Maybelle (Michaud) von K.; m. Penelope Jayne Dyer, June 29, 1981; children by previous marriage: Julian Onesime, Wendy Jean von Kalinowski Corzo. B.A., Miss. Coll., 1937; J.D. with honors, U. Va., 1940. Bar: Va. bar 1940, Calif. bar 1946. Asso. firm Gibson, Dunn and Crutcher, Los Angeles, 1946-52; partner Gibson, Dunn and Crutcher, 1953-62, mem. exec. com., 1962-82; dir. W. M. Keck Found.; mem. faculty Practising Law Inst. programs, 1971, 76, 78, 79, 80; instr. Columbia Law Sch., N.Y.C., summer 1981; mem. lawyer dels. com. to 9th Circuit Jud. Conf., 1953-73; UN expert Mission to People's Republic of China, 1982. Contbr. articles to legal jours.; author: Antitrust Laws and Trade Regulation, 1969, desk edit., 1981; gen. editor: World Law of Competition, 1978, Antitrust Counseling and Litigation Techniques, 1984. Mem. bd. regents So. Meth. U. Sch. Law. Served to lt. comdr. USN, 1941-46; capt. Res.; ret. Fellow Am. Bar Found., Am. Coll. Trial Lawyers; mem. ABA (ho. of dels. 1970), Am. Bar Assn. (chmn. antitrust law sect. 1972-73), State Bar of Calif., Los Angeles Bar Assn., U. Va. Law Sch. Alumni Assn., Phi Kappa Psi., Phi Alpha Delta. Republican. Episcopalian. Clubs: Calif, Los Angeles Country; Bohemian (san Francisco), Pacific-Union (san Francisco); Los Jolla Beach and Tennis; N.Y. Athletic (N.Y.C.), The Sky (N.Y.C.). Home: 12320 Ridge Circle Los Angeles CA 90049 Office: 333 S Grand Ave Los Angeles CA 90071

VON KOHORN, JEFFREY, clin. psychologist; b. N.Y.C., Mar. 31, 1949; s. Henry and Marcy Von K.; B.A., Northwestern U., 1971; M.A., Calif. Sch. Profl. Psychology, 1974, Ph.D., 1976; m. Nancy K. Lakeman, June 12, 1971; children—Daniel Adam, Jonathan Edward. Dir. client services Crisis House Work Devel. Center, El Cajon, Calif., 1976-78; cons. psychologist Mesa Vista Hosp., San Diego, 1980—; mem. faculty Edwards Inst. for Advanced Study, San Diego, 1980-81; dir. clin. psychology Tri-Community Service Systems, San Diego, 1978-82; sr. v.p., dir. Grid Research Corp., 1982-84 . Treas., bd. dirs. Crisis House, Inc., 1979-82. Mem. Am. Psychol. Assn., Assn. Advancement Psychology, Calif. State Psychol. Assn., Acad. San Diego Psychologists, San Diego Psychology and Law Soc. Office: 3655 Ruffin Rd Suite 320 San Diego CA 92123

VON KRENNER, WALTHER G., artist, writer, art consultant and appraiser; b. W. Ger., June 26, 1940; s. Frederick and Anna-Marie (von Wolfrath) von K.; m. Hana Renate Geue, 1960; children—Michael P., Karen P. Privately educated by Swiss and English tutors; student Asian studies, Japan, 1965-68; student of Southeast Asia studies, Buddhist U., Bankok, Thailand, Cambodia. Curator, v.p. Gallery Lahaina, Maui, Hawaii; pres. Internat. Valuation, Honolulu, 1974-84; researcher culture of Indians of No. Plains, Kalispell, Mont., 1980—; owner Al Hilal Arabians; instr. aikido, 1962—. Mem. Am. Soc. Appraisers (sr. mem.; pres., dir.). Author books on Oriental art.

VON POHLE, CHARLES LAWRENCE, physician; b. Balt., Aug. 28, 1899; s. William Richard and Ida May (Peregoy) von P.; m. Laura Maxine Ross, Mar. 21, 1906; 1 child, Carlos Ross. A.B. in Sci., Columbia Union Coll., 1924; M.D., Loma Linda U. Diplomate Nat. Bd. Med. Examiners. Practice, Chandler, Ariz., 1933-42, 46-56; chief-of-staff S.S. Dist. Hosp., Mesa, Ariz., 1947-48; bd. dirs. Ariz. Boys Ranch, Chandler, 1953-55; dir. U.S. Ops. Mission, Guatemale, 1956-63. Contbr. articles on health and sanitation, 1942-65. Mem. adv. bd. Chandler Golden Age Ctr., 1977—; trustee Chandler Sch. Bd., 1938-42. Served to col. AUSMC, 1942-46. Decorated Legion of Merit, Order of Quetzal, Condor de Los Andes, Cruz de Boyaca. Mem. Ariz. State Med. Soc., Maricopa County Med. Soc. Adventist. Republican. Clubs: White Mountain Country (Pinetop, Ariz.), San Marcos Resort (Chandler). Lodge: Rotary Internat. (past pres., Paul Harris fellow 1984).

VON REICHBAUER, PETER GRAVES, senator; b. Seattle, Dec. 30, 1944; s. Ludwig and Marian VonR.; m. Martha Ann Lindberg, June 26, 1983; children: Jeff, Jeremy, Katherine. BA, U. Ala., 1971. Senator State of Wash., Olympia, 1986—; Rep. whip Senate Rep. Caucus, Olympia, 1985—. Treas. St. Francis Community Hosp., Federal Way, Wash., 1986; vice chmn. U.S. Olympics Com., 1986; bd. dirs. Federal Way Boys and Girls Club, 1986. Served to capt. inf. U.S. Army. Roman Catholic. Lodge: Kiwanis (pres. Federal Way club 1986). Home: PO Box 3737 Federal Way WA 98063 Office: Senate Rep Caucus 113 Institutions Bldg Olympia WA 98504

VON STROH, GORDON E., business management educator, consultant; b. Lockwood, Mo., Jan. 21, 1943; s. Edward C. and Hulda A. (Mein) Von S.; m. S. Patrice Helland, Mar. 12, 1977; children: Christina, Johnathan, Justin. BA, Southwestern Coll., Winfield, Kans., 1963; MA, Kans. State U., 1964; PhD, U. Okla., 1967. Asst. prof. mgmt. U. Denver, 1967-71, assoc. prof. mgmt., 1972-78, dir. Sch. Pub. Mgmt.,, 1975-81, prof. mgmt., 1979—; economist, planner U.S. Dept. Transp., Washington, 1971-72. Bd. dirs. Cen. City Opera House Assn., Denver, 1981. Mem. Am. Mgmt. Assn., Am. Soc. Pub. Adminstrn., Am. Econs. Assn. Republican. Lutheran. Club: City (Denver). Home: 2881 S Sidney Ct Denver CO 80231 Office: U Denver Grad Sch Pub/Bus Mgmt 2020 S Race Denver CO 80208

VOORHEES, BRUCE DOUGLAS, lawyer; b. Boise, Idaho, Feb. 28, 1957; s. Donald A. and Thelma R. (Reynolds) V.; m. Debra Dibitonto, Feb. 2, 1985; 1 child, Brady Austin. BS, U. Nev.; JD, Southwestern U., Los Angeles. Bar: Nev. 1984, U.S. Dist. Ct. Nev. 1985, U.S. Ct. Appeals (9th cir.) 1985. Assoc. Paul J. Williams, Reno, 1984-85; sole practice Reno, 1985—. Mem. Washoe County Bar Assn., Nev. State Bar Assn., Nev. Trial Lawyers Assn. Republican. Presbyterian. Home: 561 W 10th St Reno NV 89503 Office: 328 California Ave Reno NV 89509

VOORHEES, DONALD SHIRLEY, judge; b. Leavenworth, Kans., July 30, 1916; s. Ephraim and Edna Mary (Oliphint) V.; m. Anne Elizabeth Spillers, June 21, 1946; children: Stephen Spillers, David Todd, John Lawrence, Diane Patricia, Richard Gordon. A.B., U. Kans., 1938; LL.B., Harvard U., 1946. Bar: Okla. 1947, Wash. State 1948. Practiced law Tulsa, 1946-47, Seattle, 1947-74; partner firm Riddell, Williams, Voorhees, Ivie, & Bullitt, Seattle, 1952-74; judge U.S. Dist. Ct., Western dist., Wash., 1974—; Bd. dirs. Fed. Jud. Center. Served with USN, 1942-46. Mem. Am., Washington State, Seattle-King County bar assns., Maritime Law Assn., Am. Judicature Soc., Phi Beta Kappa. Office: 502 US Courthouse Seattle WA 98104

VORIS, WILLIAM, educational administrator; b. Neoga, Ill., Mar. 20, 1924; s. Louis K. and Faye (Hancock) V.; m. Mavis Marie Myre, Mar. 20, 1949; children: Charles William II, Michael K. BS, U. So. Calif., 1947, MBA, 1948; PhD, Ohio State U., 1951; LLD, Sung Kyun Kwan U. (Korea), 1972, Eastern Ill. U., 1976. Teaching asst. Ohio State U., Columbus, 1948-50; prof. mgmt. Wash. State U., Pullman, 1950-52; prof., head dept. mgmt. Los Angeles State Coll., 1952-58, 60-63; dean Coll. Bus. and Pub. Adminstrn., U. Ariz., Tucson, 1963-71; pres. Am. Grad. Sch. Internat. Mgmt., Glendale, Ariz., 1971—. Ford Found. research grantee Los Angeles State Coll., 1956; prof. U. Tehran (Iran), 1958-59; Ford Found. fellow Carnegie Inst. Tech., Pitts., 1961; prof. Am. U., Beirut, Lebanon, 1961, 62; cons. Hughes Aircraft Co., Los Angeles, Rheem Mfg. Co., Los Angeles, Northrop Aircraft Co., Palmdale, Calif., Harwood Co., Alhambra, Calif., ICA, Govt. Iran. Served with USNR, 1942-45. Fellow Acad. Mgmt.; mem. Ariz. Acad., Beta Gamma Sigma, Alpha Kappa Psi, Phi Delta Theta. Author: Production Control, Text and Cases, 1956, 3d edit., 1966; Management of Production, 1960. Research in indsl. future of Iran, mgmt. devel. in Middle East. Home: Thunderbird Campus Glendale AZ 85306

VORZIMER, KENNETH DOUGLAS, interior designer and design company executive, consultant; b. N.Y.C., Nov. 6, 1941; s. Seymour Vorzimer and Roslyn (Lefkowitz) Rosenblum; m. Bonnie Sharon Marshall, Aug. 10, 1964 (div. 1973); children—Jay Scott, Adam Isaac, Jonas David; m. Janice Morein, Oct. 15, 1980 (div. 1982); 1 child, Rachel Anne. B.S. in Archtl. Engring., U. Miami, Coral Gables, Fla., 1964. Engr., U.S. Army C.E., Jacksonville, Fla. and Phila., 1964-66; facilities planner Gen. Electric Co., Phila., 1966-67; supr. facilities planning Philco Ford, Phila., 1967-68; project dir., supr. SLS Environetics, Los Angeles, 1968-72; sr. ptnr. Antonoff & Vorzimer, Century City, Calif., 1972-73; pres. Century Group Inc., Sherman Oaks, Calif., 1973—; instr. Los Angeles Community Coll., 1978-79. Artist various art and sculpture works, 1965—; designer interior design and lighting. Democrat. Jewish. Lodge: B'Nai B'rith (v.p. Century Hills Lodge 1975, Outstanding Service award 1972-73, Disting. Service award 1975). Home: 10200 Bianca Ave Northridge CA 91325 Office: Century Group Inc 14429 Ventura Blvd Sherman Oaks CA 91423

VOSS, DEBORAH LUPTON, hospital association executive, consultant; b. St. Louis, Jan. 13, 1952; d. Thomas Kidwell and Flavian Alyce (Kungle) Lupton; m. Duane K. Johnson, Dec. 5, 1969 (div. Aug. 1977); children: Ginger Lee, Robin Ann; m. Kurt R. Voss, May 8, 1982 (dec. Oct. 1986). Asst. supr. computer services Wyo. Legis. Service Office, Cheyenne, 1976-79; data processing cons. Colo. Legis. Drafting Office, Denver, 1979-80; communications cons. Wyo. Hosp. Assn., Cheyenne, 1980-81; account exec. Motorola C&E, Cheyenne, 1981; office mgr. Bagley, Hickey, Evans & Statkus, Attys. at Law, Cheyenne, 1981-83; v.p. Wyo. Hosp. Assn., Cheyenne, 1983—; communications cons. State of Wyo., Cheyenne, 1980-81, 83—; program dir., instr. Emergency Med. Dispatch, Wyo., 1983—; cons., instr. Emergency Mgmt. Planning, Wyo., 1983—. Contbr. articles on emergency med. dispatch. Bd. dirs. Cheyenne Little Theatre Players, 1984—; mem. Gov.'s Adv. Council on Emergency Med. Services, Cheyenne, 1984—, Cheyenne-Laramie County Ambulance Bd., 1984—; bd. dirs. Wyo. Commn. on Nursing and Nursing Edn., 1986—. Recipient Silver Poet award World of Poetry, 1985, 86. Mem. Associated Pub. Safety Communications Officers (pres. Wyo. chpt. 1985). Democrat. Presbyterian. Avocation: theatre, creative writing. Home: 416 E 27th St Cheyenne WY 82001 Office: Wyo Hosp Assn PO Box 5539 Cheyenne WY 82003

VOSS, KATHRYN ANN, religious administrator; b. Salida, Colo., Dec. 13, 1933; d. Edgar William and Helen Faye (Robertson) Lujan; m. Donald Paul Voss, June 15, 1957; children: Martin, Gregory, Annette, Rita, Theresa, Margaret, Cathy, Mary, Joanie, Jennifer. BA in Math., Immaculate Heart Coll., Los Angeles, 1955. Dance tchr. Louis DaPron Studio, Hollywood, Calif., 1945-52; prin. Westchester Sch. of Dance, Los Angeles, 1953-57; aero. engr. N.Am. Aviation, Los Angeles, 1955-59; dir. office of family life Roman Cath. Diocese, Phoenix, 1981—. Contbr. articles to profl jours.; performed with USO, 1950-57; free lance choreographer, Los Angeles, Phoenix, 1953-57; choreographer Washington Dist. Project Potential Choir, Phoenix, 1979-83; speaker on marriage and family topics, Phoenix, 1968—. Mem. resource com. State Task Force on Marriage and Family, Phoenix, 1977; mem. adv. bd. County Youth Service Bur., Maricopa County, Ariz., 1978-81; chmn. family affairs Phoenix Diocesan Council of Cath. Women, 1975-81. Mem. Nat. Assn. Cath. Diocesan Family Life Ministers (bd. dirs. 1983—, nat. treas. 1985—). Avocations: choreography, music, sports. Home: 347 W Pine Valley Dr Phoenix AZ 85023 Office: Cath Diocese of Phoenix 400 E Monroe Phoenix AZ 85004

VOY, ROBERT O., physician, sports medicine administrator; b. Denver, Aug. 8, 1933; m. Ann Voy; children: Kim, Bill, Dan. BS, S.D. State Sch.; MS, U. S.D.; MD, U. Oreg. Commd. 2d lt. U.S. Army, 1959; advanced through grades to capt. Madigan Med. Hosp., resigned, 1967; intern Madigan Med. Hosp., Takoma; resident San Bernardino (Calif.) Hosp.; pharmacist Village Drug Store, Lake Grove, Oreg., 1962-64; pvt. practice medicine Lake Arrowhead, Calif., 1967-71, Portland, 1971-73, Tualtin, Oreg., 1973-83; chief med. officer U.S. Olympic Tng. Ctr., Colorado Springs, Colo., 1984-85, chief med. officer, dir. sports medicine and sci., 1985—. Chmn. Rep. legis. for Oreg. State House, 1974; state co-chmn. Ford for Pres. campaign, 1976; state chmn. Oreg. Reps., 1979-83. Mem. Colo. Acad. Family Practice, El Paso County Med. Soc., Am. Acad. Family Physicians, Am. Coll. Sports Medicine, Oreg. Med. Assn. Republican. Office: US Olympic Tng Ctr 1750 E Boulder Colorado Springs CO 80901

VOYER, LARRIE DALE, infosystems specialist, real estate broker; b. Providence, Aug. 15, 1939; s. Oliver Joseph and Marie E. (Larrivee) V.; m. Karen Ruth, Aug., 22, 1964 (div. June 1984); children: Julie, Michele. BSBA, U. Redlands, 1983. Sr. mgmt. engr. Martin Marietta Corp., Vandenberg AFB, Calif., 1962-70; facility mgr. Union Am. Co., Los Angeles, 1970-72; data processing mgr. MGM Studios, Culver City, Calif., 1972-77; systems support mgr. Denny's, La Mirada, Calif., 1977-84; mgmt. info. systems dir. Data Products Corp., Woodland Hills, Calif., 1984—. Assessment appeals hearing officer Orange County, Santa Ana, Calif., 1979-80. Served with USAF, 1957-61. Recipient Outstanding Citizen award Orange County Bd. Suprs., 1980. Avocations: skiing, boating, off roading, hiking. Home: 4610 Park Granada #4 Calabasas CA 91302 Office: Dataproducts Corp 6200 Canoga Ave Woodland Hills CA 91365

VRAJICH, NICK, manufacturing engineer, educator, consultant, educator; b. Botos, Yugoslavia, Oct. 21, 1938; s. Ilija and Zagorka (Onjin) V.; came to U.S., 1967, naturalized, 1974; m. Carla Roberta Howarth, May 11, 1973; children—Sasha, Michael. B. Vocat. Edn., Calif. State U.-Los Angeles, 1976, M.A., 1978; Ph.D. in Indsl. Tech., Colo. State U., 1983. Instr. credential, Calif. Community Colls. Apprentice machinist LZTK, Kikinda, Yugoslavia, 1954-57; journey level machinist/tool maker, Yugoslavia, 1957-64, W.Ger., 1964-65, Toronto, and Windsor, Ont. Can., 1965-67, Los Angeles, 1967-73; instr. assoc. engring. and tech. div. Orange Coast Coll., Costa Mesa, Calif., 1973-75; instr. engring. tech. div. Cuesta Coll., San Luis Obispo, Calif., 1975—; lectr. engring. tech. dept. Calif. Poly. State U., San Luis Obispo; prof. indsl. and tech. edn. MSC, Ada, Yugoslavia, 1978-79; corp. rep. mktg. ops. LSB Industries, Bucharest, Rumania, 1979-80; pres. Am. R&D Engring. Co.; cons. mfg. engring. Served Yugoslav Armed Forces, 1957-59. Mem. Am. Vocat. Edn. Assn., Soc. Mfg. Engrs. (sr.), Smithsonian Inst., Iota Lambda Sigma. Democrat. Serbian-Orthodox. Home: 745 Evans Rd San Luis Obispo CA 93401 Office: Cuesta Coll PO Box J San Luis San Luis Obispo CA 93406

VRBA, FREDERICK JOHN, research astronomer; b. Cedar Rapids, Iowa, May 25, 1949; s. Fred and Emily Katherine (Dobry) V.; m. Sheryl Lynn Blunk, June 1, 1971; children: Marya Katherine, Sarah Elizabeth. BA, U. Iowa, 1971; PhD, U. Ariz., 1976. Astronomer U.S. Naval Obs., Flagstaff, Ariz., 1976—; Contbr. articles to profl. jours. Mem. Am. Astron. Soc., Internat. Astron. Union, Sigma Xi. Republican. Avocations: reading, hiking, rafting. Home: 6601 N Snowflake Dr Flagstaff AZ 86004 Office: US Naval Obs PO Box 1149 Flagstaff AZ 86002

VREELAND, PATRICIA PRIEST, biologist, researcher, environmental educator; b. Reno, Nev., Feb. 6, 1940; d. Ralph E. and Ann (Wiendl) Priest; m. Hamilton Vreeland, Feb. 14, 1974 (dec.). BS in Biology, U. Nev., 1974, MS in Biology, 1976, PhD in Biology, 1980. Asst. instr. biology U. Nev., Reno, 1971-76; prin. investigator Earthwatch, Belmont, Mass., 1976-80; researcher Western Analytical Biogeographers, Reno, 1976—; instr. Truckee Meadows Community Coll., Reno, 1978-83, Chapman Coll, Reno, 1978—; cons. NASA SIR-B project, Hawthorne, Nev., 1984—, also botanical researcher, cons. geothermal div. U.S. Dept. Energy, Nev., 1979, Bur. Land Mgmt., Nev. 1979. Co-author: Research Handbook on Deserts of North America, 1982; contbr. chpts. to books, articles to profl. jours. Grantee Earthwatch, 1976-80, U.S. Dept. Energy, 1979, Bur. Land Mgmt., 1979. Fellow Explorers Club; mem. May Arboretum Soc. (pres. 1984—), Westerners Internat. Nev. Corral (treas. 1985—), Sigma Xi, Phi Kappa Phi. Avocations: skiing, hiking, backpacking, photography, gardening. Home and Office: Western Analytical Biogeographers 1980 Carter Dr Reno NV 89509

VREELAND, ROBERT WILDER, electronics engineer; b. Glen Ridge, N.J., Mar. 4, 1923; s. Frederick King and Elizabeth Lenora (Wilder) V.; m. Jean Gay Fullerton, Jan. 21, 1967; 1 son, Robert Wilder. BS, U. Calif., Berkeley, 1947. Electronics engr. Litton Industries, San Carlos, Calif., 1948-55; sr. devel. electronics engr. U. Calif. Med. Ctr., San Francisco, 1955—; cons. electrical engring; speaker 8th Internat. Symposium Biotelemetry, Dubrovnik, Yugoslavia, 1984, RF Expo, Anaheim, Calif., 1985, 86, 87. Contbr. articles to profl. jours., also to internat. meetings and symposiums; patentee in field. Recipient Chancellor's award U. Calif., San Francisco, 1979; cert. appreciation for 25 years' service U. Calif., San Francisco, 1980. Mem. Nat. Bd. Examiners Clin. Engring. (cert. clin. engr.), IEEE, Assn. Advancement Med. Instrumentation (bd. examiner), Am. Radio Relay League (pub. service award 1962). Home: 45 Maywood Dr San Francisco CA 94127 Office: U Calif Med Ctr 4th and Parnassus Sts San Francisco CA 94143

VREMAN, HENDRIK JAN, biochemist, consultant; b. Soest, The Netherlands, Jan. 22, 1939; s. Gerrit Jan Engelbartus and Maria Sophia (de Back) V.; m. Pietje de Groot, May 16, 1964; children: Shirley, Gerrit John. Student, U. Pa., 1962-64; BA in Chemistry, U. N.C., 1968; PhD in Botany and Biochemistry, U. Wis., 1973. Analytical chemist Dutch Inst. of Health and U. Utrecht, The Netherlands, 1957-62, Duke U. Med. Ctr., Durham, N.C., 1964-68; postdoctoral research assoc. Western Regional Research Ctr. USDA-Sci. Edn. Administrn., Berkeley, Calif., 1973-75; lab. dir. Stanford (Calif.) U. Med. Ctr., 1975—; cons. in field, Los Altos, Calif., 1978—; prodn. mgr. Trace Analytical Inc., Menlo Park, Calif., 1983—. Contbr. articles to profl. jours. Coach Am. Youth Soccer Assn., Los Altos, 1976-80; leader Boy's Club, Palo Alto, Calif., 1979-82, Youth Group, Palo Alto, 1982-85. Nat. Research Council fellow. Mem. AAAS. Democrat. Avocations: orchid growing, hiking, skiing, camping. Home: 1283 Brentwood St Los Altos CA 94022 Office: Stanford U Med Ctr Dept Pediatrics Neonatology Div Stanford CA 94022

VRIELING, JOHN BERT, insurance consultant; b. Everett, Wash., Oct. 11, 1925; s. Gerrit and Jennie (DeHaas) V.; m. Bonnie Matter, June 17, 1949; children: Greg, Debbie, Mark, Scott. CLU; chartered fin. cons. Agt. Met. Life Ins. Co., Bellingham, Wash., 1948-52; ins. cons. Met. Life Ins. Co., Moses Lake, Wash., 1952-66; unit mgr. Met. Life Ins. Co., Tacoma, Wash., 1966-71; sr. sales rep. Met. Life Ins. Co., Moses Lake, 1971-82; gen. agt., cons. Vrieling & Assocs., Moses Lake, 1982—; pres. Columbia Basin Assn. Life Underwriters, Moses Lake, 1959-60. Pres. United Givers Moses Lake, 1963-64; mem. bd. Moses Lake Intermediate Sch. Dist., 1976-82. Served to sgt. USAF, 1945-47, PTO. Named Outstanding Veteran Met. Field Veteran Assn., Seattle, 1981. Mem. Million Dollar Round Table, Am. Soc. CLU's, Assn. Life Underwriters (past local pres., v.p.). Presbyterian (elder). Club: Moses Lake Golf and Country (charter mem.). Lodges: Elks, Rotary. Avocations: gardening, boating, golf, tennis. Home: 334 Crestview Dr Moses Lake WA 98837 Office: 1006 W Ivy Moses Lake WA 98837

VROOM, DAVID ARCHIE, chemical company executive; b. Vancouver, B.C., Can., Sept. 12, 1941; came to U.S., 1968; s. Nathaniel Ellenwood and Jean Ferriman (Salsbury) V.; m. Anna Elisabeth Stravers, Sept. 12, 1969; 1 child, Peter. BS in Chemistry with honors, U. B.C., 1963, PhD in Chem. Physics, 1967. Postdoctoral fellow FOM Lab., Amsterdam, The Netherlands, 1967-68; staff scientist Gen. Atomic Co., San Diego, 1968-71; mgr. IRT Corp., San Diego, 1971-81; sect. dir. Raychem Corp., Menlo Park, Calif., 1981-84, mfg. mgr., 1984-87, dir. radiation services, 1987—. Contbr. numerous articles to profl. jours. Served to lt. Royal Can. Navy, 1961-66. NRC Can. fellow, 1967-68. Mem. Am. Chem. Soc., Am. Phys. Soc. Lutheran. Avocation: woodworking. Home: 107 Walter Hays Dr Palo Alto CA 94303 Office: Raychem Corp 300 Constitution Dr Menlo Park CA 94303

VRYONIS, SPEROS, JR., historian, educator; b. Memphis, July 18, 1928; s. Speros Panayis, Sr., and Helen (Touliatou) V.; children—Speros Basil, Demetrios, Nikolas. B.A., Southwestern U., Memphis, 1950; M.A., Harvard U., 1952, Ph.D., 1956. Instr. history Harvard U., 1956-60; prof. history UCLA, 1960—, dir. G.E. von Grunebaum Ctr. of UCLA, 1972-75, 79-82; vis. prof. U. Chgo., 1966-67; fellow Dumbarton Oaks, Harvard U., 1979-84; chmn. medieval and modern history U. Athens, 1976-84. Recipient Kokkinos award Acad. Athens, 1974. Fellow Am. Mediaeval Acad. (Haskins medal); mem. Am. Philos. Soc., Am. Acad. Arts and Scis., Soc. Macedonian Studies. Author: Byzantium and Europe, 1967; Byzantium: Its Internal History and Relations with Muslim World, 1971; Decline of Medieval Hellenism in Asia Minor, Process of Islamization, 1971; Studies on Byzantium, Seljuks, Ottomans, 1981; Istoria ton valkanikon laon, 1979; Readings in Medieval Historiography, 1968; The Balkans: Continuity and Change, 1972; The Role of the "Past" in Medieval and Modern Greek Culture, 1978; editor: (with others Islam and Cultural Change in the Middle Ages, 1975; contbr. articles to profl. jours. Office: Dept History UCLA 405 Hilgard Ave Los Angeles CA 90024

VU, THANH HUU, molecular biologist, biochemist; b. Ninhbinh, Socialist Republic of Vietnam, Apr. 10, 1947; came to U.S., 1979; s. Thuan and Bien (Pham) V.; m. Shigeko Endo, July 7, 1979; children: Yuki T., Yurika B. BS, Saigon (Socialist Republic of Vietnam) U., 1969; MS, Tohoku U., Sendai, Japan, 1974, PhD with honors, 1977. Postdoctoral research assoc. Purdue U., West Lafayette, Ind., 1979-81, research biologist, 1981-84; research assoc. Stanford (Calif.) U., 1984—. Mem. AAAS. Home: 4263 Nerissa Circle Fremont CA 94536 Office: Stanford U Dept Biol Scis Keck Bldg Stanford CA 94305

VUCANOVICH, BARBARA FARRELL, congresswoman; b. Camp Dix, N.J., June 22, 1921; d. Thomas F. and Ynez (White) Farrell; m. Ken Dillon, Mar. 8, 1950 (div. 1964); children: Patty Dillon Cafferata, Mike, Ken, Tom, Susan Dillon Stoddard; m. George Vucanovich, June19, 1965. Student, Manhattanville Coll. of Sacred Heart, 1938-39. Owner, operator Welcome Aboard Travel, Reno, 1968-74; dist. rep. Nev. U.S. Senate, Reno, 1974-81; mem. 98th-100th Congresses from 2d Nev. Dist., 1983—, mem. coms. interior and insular affairs, house adminstrn. Pres. Nev. Fedn. Republican Women, Reno, 1955-56; former pres. St. Mary's Hosp. Guild, Lawyer's Wives. Roman Catholic. Club: Hidden Valley Country (Reno). Office: US Ho of Reps 312 Cannon House Office Bldg Washington DC 20515 •

VUNCANNON, DELCIE HOBSON, educator, librarian; b. Glendale, Calif., Apr. 26, 1925; d. Stephen Douglas and Erma Elsie (Hoffman) Hobson; m. James Mervin Parker, July 17, 1946 (div. 1960); children—Stephen, Jamie, Whitney, Michael, Timothy, Kelly. B.A., Pomona Coll., 1946; M.A. in Classics, U. Calif.-Berkeley, 1962, M.L.S., 1964. Reference librarian U. Calif.-Davis, 1964-68; reference librarian Calif. State U.-Sacramento, 1968-70, instr., San Bernardino, 1979-81; instr. Chapman Coll., Palms, Calif., 1974—, Coll. Desert, Palm Desert, Calif., 1973—; adminstrv. head No. Ariz. City Libraries, Flagstaff, 1970-72; cons. archaeologist. Contbr. articles to profl. jours. Mem. Am. Rock Art Research Assn. (bd. dirs. 1979), Rock Publs., Mus. of Man, Archaeol. Survey Assn. So. Calif. Republican. Home: PO Box 711 Yucca Valley CA 92286 Office: Coll Desert Rotary Rd Joshua Tree CA 92257

VYAS, GIRISH NARMADASHANKAR, immunologist; b. Aglod, India, June 11, 1933; came to U.S., 1965, naturalized, 1973; s. Narmadashankar P. and Rukshmani A. (Joshi) V.; m. Devi Ratilal Trivedi, Apr. 3, 1962; children—Jay, Shrikrishna. B.Sc., U. Bombay, 1954, M.Sc., 1956, Ph.D., 1964. Postdoctoral fellow Western Res. U., 1965-66; mem. faculty U. Calif., San Francisco, 1967—; prof. lab. medicine U. Calif., 1977—; WHO cons., S.E. Asia, 1980; cons. in field; mem. com. viral hepatitis NRC, 1974-76; mem. task force blood processing Nat. Heart and Lung Inst., 1972-73; sci. program com. Am. Assn. Blood Banks, 1971-76; com. immunoglobulin allotypes WHO, 1974—; mem. U.S. del. immunologists to, Romania and Hungary, 1980; mem. FDA com. on blood and blood products, 1985; cons. to VA on med. research, 1985; cons. UN Devel. Program in India, 1986; delivered Dr. R.G. Dhayagude Meml. oration, 1986. Author: Hepatitis and Blood Transfusion, 1972, Laboratory Diagnosis of Immunological Disorders, 1975, Membrane Structure and Function of Human Blood Cells, 1976, Viral Hepatitis, 1978, also research papers. Recipient Julliard prize Internat. Soc. Blood Transfusion, 1969; named Outstanding Immigrant in Bay Area Communities Mayor of Oakland, Calif., 1969; Fulbright scholar France, 1980. Mem. Am. Soc. Hematology, AAAS, Am. Assn. Immunologists, Am. Soc. Clin. Pathologists. Democrat. Hindu. Office: U California Lab Med M-523 San Francisco CA 94143

WACHTELL, THOMAS, petroleum company executive, lawyer; b. Crestwood, N.Y., Mar. 27, 1928; s. Theodore and Carolyn (Satz) W.; grad. Choate Sch., 1946; B.S., Syracuse U., 1950; LL.B., Cornell U., 1958; m. Esther Carole Pickard, Jan. 27, 1957; children—Roger Bruce, Wendy Ann, Peter James. Bar: N.Y. 1958. Assoc. Livingston, Wachtell & Co., C.P.A.s, N.Y.C., 1958-60; pres. Allied Homeowners Assn., Inc., White Plains, N.Y., 1960-63, pres. Gen. Factoring Co., White Plains, N.Y., 1960-63; exec. asst. to pres. Occidental Petroleum Corp., Los Angeles, 1963-65, v.p., exec. asst., chmn. bd., 1965-72, exec. v.p., 1972-73, officer, dir. numerous subs.; pres. Hydrocarbon Resources Corp., 1973-81; chmn. Oriental Petroleum Corp., 1982—; exec. v.p. Frontier Oil and Refining Co., Denver, 1985—, also bd. dirs.; chmn. bd. Frontier Oil Internat., 1985—; pres., chief exec. officer, dir.

NMR Ctrs., Inc., 1982-83; pres., dir. Cayman Petroleum Corp., 1974-75, Ridgecrest Energy Corp., 1979; dir. Tanglewood Consol. Resources, 1982-84. Panelist, lectr. Nat. Indsl. Conf. Bd.; bd. govs., performing arts council Los Angeles Music Center, 1973—; chmn., chief exec. officer, bd. dirs. Los Angeles Music Center Opera Assn., 1972—, chmn., chief exec. officer, 1981—; trustee Good Hope Med. Found., Los Angeles, 1974—. Served to lt. Office Naval Intelligence, USNR, 1952-56. Mem. Am. Mgmt. Assn., Los Angeles World Affairs Council, Choate Alumni Assn. So. Cal. (chmn. 1969—), Confrerie des Chevaliers du Tastevin, Beta Theta Pi, Phi Delta Phi.

WACK, PAUL EDWARD, physics educator; b. Council Bluffs, Iowa, Apr. 28, 1919; s. John Joseph and Mary Francis (Toller) W.; m. Mary Ellen Van Hoomissen, Dec. 30, 1952; children: Paul Joseph, Edwin John, Ellen Elizabeth, Mary Margaret. Student, St. Benedict's Coll., 1936-38; AB, Creighton U., 1941; MS, U. Notre Dame, 1942, PhD, 1947. Instr. U. Notre Dame, South Bend, Ind., 1943-45; chmn. dept. physics Creighton U., Omaha, 1947-49; asst. prof. physics U. Portland, Oreg., 1949-57, assoc. prof., 1957-66, prof., 1966—, chmn. dept. physics, 1966-73; vis. scientist Oreg. Acad. Sci., Portland, 1965-68; v.p. Wack Elec. Co., Council Bluffs, 1956-75; dir. NSF Summer Insts., Portland, 1965-73; radioactive surveyor Civil Def., Portland, 1950-55; air sampler Columbia-Willamette Air Pollution Authority, Portland, 1971. Author physics lab. manuals, 1982; contbr. articles to profl. jours. Recipient Culligan award U. Portland, 1961. Mem. Am. Assn. Physics Tchrs., Am. Phys. Soc., Sigma Xi. Democrat. Roman Catholic. Avocation: photography. Home: 6314 N Princeton St Portland OR 97203 Office: U Portland 5000 N Willamette Blvd Portland OR 97203

WADDELL, BETTY LOUISE, psychology educator; b. Billings, Mont., Dec. 17, 1941; d. Albert E. and Louise (Pospisil) Leuthold; m. Theodore J. Waddell, Mar. 6, 1965; children: Heather Clarisse Arin, Shanna Beth Louise. BA, U. Mont., 1963, MA, 1965, PhD, 1975. Psychologist Mont. State Hosp., Warm Springs, 1964-65; psychol. research assoc. Ammons' Lab., Missoula, Mont., 1965-74; mgr. Leuthold OK Ranch, Molt, Mont., 1976-87; assoc. prof. psychology Rocky Mountain Coll., Billings, 1980—; faculty chair Rocky Mountain Coll., Billings, Mont., 1985-86; instr. U. Mont., Missoula, 1972-73, Eastern Mont. Coll., Billings, 1978-79; v.p. Leuthold OK Ranch Corp.; bd. dirs. Leuthold Found. Mem. Mont. Psychol. Assn. (pres. 1986—), Am. Psychol. Assn. (assoc.), AAUP, Mental Health Assn. Yellowstone County (bd. dirs.), Sigma Xi. Republican. Mem. United Ch. Christ. Home: Molt MT 59057 Office: Rocky Mountain Coll 2812 Hoover Billings MT 59057

WADDELL, JOHN HENRY, sculptor; b. Des Moines, Feb. 14, 1921; s. William Wilder and Isabel Catherine (McGee) W.; m. Leslie Owen, 1942 (div. 1948); children—Sean Seamus, SeanChan; m. Ruth Holland, Mar. 24, 1949; children—Lindsey, William, Amy. BFA, Art Inst. Chgo., 1948; B in Art Edn., 1949, MFA, 1949, M in Art Edn., 1951; DFA (hon.), Nat. Coll. Edn., 1979. Instr. Nat. Coll. Edn., Evanston, Ill., 1949-55; asst. prof. Ill. Inst. Tech., Chgo., 1955-57; prof. Ariz. State U., Tempe, 1957-64; head Waddell Sculpture Fellowship, Cornville, Ariz., 1971—. Executed sculpture Dance, Phoenix Civic Ctr., 1974, The Family, Maricopa County, Phoenix, 1967, That Which Might, Unitarian Ch., Paradise Valley, Ariz., 1964, Backwalkover, Phoenix Sports Medicine Ctr., 1985; represented Scottsdale (Ariz.) Ctr. For the Arts, 1984, others. Served with AUS, 1943-45. Grantee Valley Beautiful Commn., Phoenix, 1965, Nat. Endowment Arts/Commn. Arts and Humanities, 1969-74, Nat. Endowment Arts, 1978. Unitarian. Home: HC 66 Box 2273 Cornville AZ 86325

WADDELL, WILLIAM HENRY, mental health therapist; b. Belo-Horizonte, Brazil, Oct. 30, 1939; s. Richard Lord and Margaret G. Waddell; m. Mary Ingalls, Dec. 27, 1969. BA, Whitworth Coll., 1962; MSW, Ariz. State U., 1975. Social worker San Diego County, 1966-68, State of Nev., Fallon, 1970-73; mental health therapist Grant County Mental Health Ctr., Moses Lake, Wash., 1975—. Del. Dem. County Conv., Grant County, 1986. Served with U.S. Army, 1962-65. NIMH fellow, 1974-75. Mem. Wash. Assn. County Designated Mental Health Profls., Nat. Assn. Social Workers (cert.). Presbyterian. Avocation: sailing. Home: 8920 A Travis Dr Moses Lake WA 98837 Office: PO Box 1057 Moses Lake WA 98837

WADDELL, WILLIAM RHOADS, general and thoracic surgeon, clinical oncologist, researcher; b. Ft. Smith, Ark., Oct. 12, 1918; s. William Turner and Bonnie (Roper) W.; m. Barbara Christie, July, 1944; children: Bonnie, Susan, Nancy, Sarah. BS, U. Ariz., 1940; MD, Harvard U., 1943. Diplomate Am. Bd. Surgery, Am. Bd. Thoracic Surgery. Intern Mass. Gen. Hosp., Boston, 1944, 1944, residency, 1945-51; practice medicine specializing in surgery Silver City, NM, 1983—; prof. surgery U. Colo., Denver, 1961-83, chmn. dept., 1961-72, prof. emeritus, 1983—. Editor clin. research in trauma pubs.; contbr. articles to profl. jours. Served to lt. (j.g.) USN, 1946. Grantee NIH, 1952-82; Cancer Research scholar Eleanor Roosevelt Cancer Research Inst., Denver, 1972-83. Mem. Am. Surgical Assn., Am. Assn. Thoracic and Cardiovascular Surgery, ACS, AAAS. Avocations: tennis, race walking. Home: 703 N Arizona Silver City NM 88061 Office: U Colo 1600 E 32d St Silver City NM 88061

WADE, CHARLES GORDON, technical manager; b. Griggsville, Ill.; s. Charles Delbert and Lucy (Kennedy) W.; m. Camille M. Gaudette, Nov. 24, 1964; children: Christopher, Jeffrey. BS, So. Ill. U., 1960; PhD, MIT, 1965. Prof. chemistry U. Tex., Austin, 1967-80; application scientist IBM, San Jose, Calif., 1980-83, tech. support mgr., 1983-84, mgr. customer support ctr., 1984—, mgr. magnetics ops. west div., 1986—. Author: Science, Energy and The Environment, 1976. Mem. Am. Chem. Soc., Am. Phys. Soc. Office: IBM Instruments Inc 40 Airport Pkwy San Jose CA 95110 Home: 40 W Brokaw Rd San Jose CA 95110

WADE, JON CHARLES, academic administrator; b. Flandreau, S.D., Oct. 3, 1938; s. Ross B. and Clara L. (Allen) W.; m. Marilyn Mae Wilkerson, May 29, 1960; children: Jean M., Lynn R. BS, No. State Coll., Vermillion, S.D., 1960; MA, U. S.D., 1965. Cert. tchr., secondary sch. adminstrn. Dir. Indian edn. State Dept. Pub. Instrn., Pierce, S.D., 1965-68; edn. specialist Aberdeen (S.D.) Area Office BIA, 1968-74; supt. Phoenix Indian Sch., 1974-75; div. chief Indian Edn. Resources Ctr., Albuquerque, 1975-79; pres. Inst. Am. Indian Arts, Santa Fe, 1979—; vice chmn. Flandreau Santer Sioux Tribe, 1964-66; mem. spl. subcom. Nat. Council on Indian Opportunity, Washington, 1971-72. Republican. Presbyterian. Avocations: history, psychology, hunting, fishing. Office: Inst Am Indian Arts Alexis Hall Coll Santa Fe St Michaels Dr Santa Fe NM 87501

WADE, LOUISE CARROLL, history educator; b. Toledo, Feb. 22, 1928; d. Benjamin H. and Louise H. (Lucas) C. BA, Wellesley Coll., 1948; PhD, U. Rochester, 1954. Lectr. (part-time) U. Chgo., 1963-67; assoc. prof. history U. Oreg., Eugene, 1975-83, prof. history, 1983—. Author: Graham Taylor: Pioneer for Social Justice, 1964, Chicago's Pride: Stockyards, Packingtown and Environs, 1986. Fulbright grantee, Australia, 1980. Mem. Am. Hist. Assn., Orgn. Am. Historians. Home: 1629 Braeman Village Eugene OR 97405 Office: U Oreg Dept History Eugene OR 97403

WADE, MICHAEL ROBERT ALEXANDER, Asian marketing specialist; b. N.Y.C., June 29, 1945; s. Burton Jean and Celia (Handleman) W.; student U. Rennes, France, 1964; AB, U. Chgo., 1967; postgrad. in pub. adminstrn., Am. U., 1967-71; MBA in Fin., N.Y. U., 1975; m. Carole Kay West, Aug. 25, 1974. Program analyst, mgmt. intern HUD, 1967-71; dep. dir. Mgmt. Communications and Briefing Center, U.S. Price Commn., 1972; asst. exec. sec. policy coordination U.S. Cost of Living Council, 1973-74; asso. dir. U.S. Indochina Refugee Program, 1975-76; pres. China Trade Devel. Corp. of Chgo., 1977—: participant with W.R. Grace & Co. in Okla. oil and gas prodn. Recipient Meritorious Service award Exec. Office of the Pres., 1972, Disting. Service award U.S. Cost of Living Council, 1974. Mem. Soc. Contemporary Art, Internat. Bus. Council MidAm. (bd. dirs.). Office: China Trade Devel Corp 2049 Century Park East Suite 416 Los Angeles CA 90067

WADE, NEIL HOWARD, geotechnical engineer; b. Fredericton, N.B., Can., Apr. 11, 1936; s. Paul Randal and Alma Elizabeth (McCracken) W.; B.Sc. in Civil Engring., U. N.B., 1959; Ph.D. in Soil Mechanics (Athlone fellow 1959-61, NRC scholar 1961-63), Imperial Coll., U. London, 1963; m. Louise Marie Nygren, May 15, 1981. Asst. prof. civil engring. U. Calif., Berkeley, 1963-64; asso. prof. Ga. Inst. Tech., 1964-68; sr. geotech. engr. Tippetts-Abbott-McCarthy-Stratton, N.Y.C., 1968-69, Tarbela, Pakistan, 1969-71; sr. geotech. engr. B.C. Hydro, Vancouver, 1971-74; exec. engr. Klohn Leonoff Cons., Vancouver, 1974-76; head geotech. engr. B.C. Hydro & Power Authority, Vancouver, 1976-80; head geotech. dept. Montreal Engring., Calgary, Alta., Can., 1980—; vis. lectr. U. Calif., Davis and U. B.C., Vancouver, 1976-80, U. Alta., Edmonton and U. Calgary, 1981-83; lectr. B.C. Inst. Tech., 1977-80; registered cons. Asian Devel. Bank, World Bank; cons. in field. NSF grantee, 1965-69; Ford Found. fellow, 1968-69. Mem. Assn. Profl. Engrs. B.C., Assn. Profl. Engrs. Alta., Assn. Profl. Engrs. Sask., Engring. Inst. Can., Canadian Geotech. Soc., ASCE, Internat. Assn. Engring. Geology, Internat. Soc. Soil Mechanics and Found. Engring. Home: 240 Valhalla Crescent, Calgary, AB Canada T3A 2A1 Office: Monenco Plaza 400, 801 6th Ave SW, Calgary, AB Canada T2P 3W3

WADE, RICHARD LINCOLN, scientist, technology company executive; b. Bath, Maine, Aug. 7, 1946; s. Walter Lorenzo and Viola (Bowie) W.; m. Reta Aldworth; 1 child, Kendra Sue. BS, U. N.H., 1968; MPH, U. Mich., 1970, PhD, 1972; postgrad., Harvard U., 1973. Scientist Am. Pub. Health Assn., Washington, 1972-73; cons. PAHO, Mexico City, 1973-74; dir. environ. program City of Seattle, 1974-76, State of Minn., Mpls., 1976-78; dep. chief Calif. Dept. OSHA, San Francisco, 1978-82; corp. dir. Internat. Tech. Corp., Martinez, Calif., 1982-86; pres. Risk Mgmt. Scis., Mill Valley, Calif., 1987—; asst. prof. toxicology and environ. engring. U. Wash., 1974-75, U. Minn., 1975-76; assoc. prof. U. Calif., 1979—. Author: Health Effects of Energy Generation, 1972, Health Issues in Semiconductor Industry, 1981; contbr. articles to profl. jours. Rockefeller fellow, U. Mich., 1969-71. Mem. Am. Pub. Health Assn. (policy bd. 1974-76), Nat. Environ. Health Assn. (action com. 1974-75), Am. Chem. Soc., Am. Indsl. Hygiene Assn., Alpha Zeta. Club: Sausalito (Calif.) Yacht. Avocation: sailing. Home: 232 Tiburon Blvd San Rafael CA 94901 Office: Risk Mgmt Scis 205 Camino Alto Suite 225 Mill Valley CA 94941

WADE, ROBERT ALAN, chemistry educator, researcher; b. Kalamazoo, Apr. 25, 1953; s. Richard Jr. Wade and Caroline Maitee (Lung) Bird; m. Wendy Jane Coysten, Jan. 7, 1979; children: Hilary Erin, Erica Megan. BA, Kalamazoo Coll., 1975; PhD, Oxford U., Eng., 1979. Research chemist Oxford U., 1975-78, Cornell U., Ithaca, N.Y., 1978-79; asst. prof. Walla Walla Coll., College Place, Wash., 1980-84, assoc. prof. chemistry, 1984—; research chemist U. Wash., Seattle, 1984—. Contbr. articles to sci. publs. Kalamazoo Coll. scholar, 1971-75; Kalamazoo Coll. fellow, 1975. Mem. Am. Chem. Soc. Adventist. Club: Walla Walla Proptwisters. Avocations: remote control aircraft, astronomy, backpacking. Home: 315 SE Valley Dr College Place WA 99324 Office: Walla Walla coll College Place WA 99324

WADE, ROBERT RICHARD, engineer; b. Nashville, Mar. 5, 1940; s. John and Emma Lake (Hutton) W.; m. Carol Louise Thompson, June 5, 1966 (div. June 1983); children: Angela C., Christopher R. AS in Engring., Allan Hancock Coll., 1970; BA in Math., LaVerne Coll., 1975; BS in Electronics Tech., Chapman Coll., 1980. Aerospace engr. Titan missle system Martin Marietta Corp., Vandenberg AFB, Calif., 1971-78, sr. flight safety system ops. engr., 1978-82, info. systems adminstr., 1982—; data adminstr. FOW Investors, Lompoc, Calif., 1980—. Author: Introduction to Digital Troubleshooting, 1977. Served to sgt. USAF, 1959-63. Recipient Gold Medallion award Martin Marietta Corp., 1976. Avocations: jazz record collecting, writing, fishing. Home: PO Box 611 Lompoc CA 93438 Office: Martin Marietta Corp PO Box 1681 Vandenberg AFB CA 93437

WADE, TERENCE CLIFFORD, psychologist, consultant; b. Greensboro, N.C., Jan. 1, 1947; m. Darlene Karen Peterson, Feb. 14, 1986. BA, Stanford U., 1972; MA, U. Utah, 1976, PhD, 1977. Lic. psychologist; cert. substance abuse counselor; cert. substance abuse program administrator. Psychologist Hawaii Dept. Health, 1977-78; pvt. practice psychology Honolulu, 1978—; pres. Anodyne Inc. and Cocaine Addiction Services of Hawaii, Honolulu, 1985—; cons. Hina Mauka, Kaneohe, Hawaii, 1978—; preceptor Counseling and Assistance Ctr. Pearl Harbor, 1986—, Barbers Point, Hawaii, 1986—; preceptor Alcohol Rehab. Ctr., Pearl Harbor, 1984—. Contbr. articles to profl. jours. Preceptor ARC, Pearl Harbor, Hawaii, 1984—. Grantee Nat. Inst. on Aging, C. of C., Kaiser Found; Graduate Research fellow U. Utah 1973-76. Mem. Am. Psychol. Assn., Hawaii Psychol. Assn. (pres. 1982). Lodge: Rotary. Avocations: sailing, skiing, swimming, running, bicycling. Office: 1188 Bishop St Suite 3204 Honolulu HI 96813

WADE, THEODORE EVERETT, JR., publisher, author; b. Pueblo, Colo., June 28, 1936; s. Theodore Everett and Zola Vivan (Talbott) W.; m. Karen Alene Peterson, July 8, 1956; children: Timothy, Dorothea, Melvin. BA, Union Coll., 1958; MA, U. Nebr., 1962, PhD, 1970. Missionary tchr. Seventh-day Adventist Ch., Rwanda, 1962-67; pres. Franco-Haitian Sem., Seventh-day Adventist, Port-au-Prince, Haiti, 1971-74; pub. Gazelle Publs., Auburn, Calif., 1976—; prof. Weimar (Calif.) Coll., 1980-84. Author: School at Home, 1980, Home School Manual, 1984, 2d rev. edit., 1986; editor With Joy: Poems for Children, 1976, 2d rev. edit., 1985; Bubbles, Poetry for Fun and Meaning, 1987. Avocations: computer programming, scripture study. Home and Office: Gazelle Publs 5580 Stanley Dr Auburn CA 95603

WADKINS, LANCING EATON, architect; b. Midland, Tex., Apr. 24, 1945; s. Lloyd Earl and Margie Estelle (McGuirk) W.; m. Debra Ann Pfeiffer, April 19, 1980; children: General Jeremiah Jessop, Zoe Pia Pfeiffer. BA in Architecture, U. Ark., 1970, BArch, 1976. Registered architect, Alaska, Ark., Ind., S.D., Wash. Project architect Rigg Nelson Architects, Seattle, 1977-79; prin. Rigg Wadkins Houlihan Architects, Seattle, 1979-82; architect Pool Engring. Inc., Ketchikan, Alaska, 1982-84; mgr. archtl. services Cooper Cons. Inc., Bellevue, Wash., 1984—. Author: The Listener, 1985, Wadkins Prod., 1984-86. Served to sgt. U.S. Army, 1971-74, Vietnam. Decorated Bronze Star. Mem. AIA, Architects, Engrs., and Planners Users Group. Avocations: music, art, sailing. Home: PO Box 2743 Kirkland WA 98033 Office: Cooper Cons Inc 1750 112th Ave NE Suite C225 Bellevue WA 98004

WADMAN, WILLIAM WOOD, III, health physicist, chemical company executive; b. Oakland, Calif., Nov. 13, 1936; s. William Wood, Jr., and Lula Fae (Raisner) W.; M.A., U. Calif., Irvine, 1978; children—Roxanne Alyce Wadman Hubbing, Raymond Alan (dec.), Theresa Hope Wadman Foster. Radiation safety specialist, accelerator health physicist U. Calif. Lawrence Berkeley Lab., 1957-68; campus radiation safety officer U. Calif., Irvine, 1968-79; dir. ops., radiation safety officer Radiation Sterilizers, Inc., Tustin, Calif., 1979-80; prin. Wm. Wadman & Assos., 1980—; pres. Intracoastal Marine Enterprises Ltd., Martinez, Calif.; mem. team No. 1, health physics appraisal program NRC, 1980-81; cons. health physicist to industry; lectr. dept. community and environ. medicine U. Calif., Irvine, 1979-80, Orange Coast Coll. Active Cub Scouts; chief umpire Mission Viejo Little League, 1973. Served with USNR, 1955-56. Recipient award for profl. achievement U. Calif. Alumni Assn., 1972, Outstanding Performance award U. Calif., Irvine, 1973. Mem. Health Physics Soc. (treas. 1979-81, editor proc. 11th symposium, pres. So. Calif. chpt. 1977, Professionalism award 1975), Internat. Radiation Protection Assn. (U.S. del. 4th Congress 1977), Am. Nuclear Soc., Am. Public Health Assn. (chmn. program 1978, chmn. radiol. health sect. 1979-80), Campus Radiation Safety Officers (chmn. 1975, editor proc. 5th conf. 1975), ASTM. Club: UCI Univ. (dir. 1976, sec. 1977, treas. 1978). Contbr. articles to tech. jours. Home: PO Box 562 Martinez CA 94553 Office: 1990 N California Blvd Suite 830 Walnut Creek CA 94596

WADSWORTH, ROLAND, JR., civil engineer; b. Salt Lake City, Mar. 27, 1924; s. Roland and Libbie Fern (Hudson) W.; m. Norma Lou Jones, June 19, 1953 (div. Mar. 1977); children—Janice Lee, Julie Ann, Jill Janine, Jeffrey Bryant; m. Lila Merle Kearns, July 1, 1977. C.E., U. Cin., 1951. Registered profl. engr., Ariz., Mont., Oreg. Stress analyst Douglas Aircraft Co., Long Beach, Calif., 1951; gen. mgr. Savage Mfg. Co., Phoenix, 1952-54; ptnr. Engring. Corp. Am., Phoenix, 1955—; pres. Wadsworth, Jensen & Assocs., Phoenix, 1975-84; assoc. Howard, Needles, Tammen & Bergendoff, Phoenix, 1982-84; with RW Group, Scottsdale, Ariz., 1985—. Served to 1st lt. F.A., U.S. Army, 1943-46, PTO. Decorated Bronze Star. Mem. ASCE, Nat. Soc. Profl. Engrs., Am. Concrete Inst., Ariz. Cons. Engrs. Assn., Stuctural Engrs. Assn. Ariz. Republican. Mem. Ch. of Jesus Christ of Latter-day Saints. Home: 8207 E Cholla St Scottsdale AZ 85260 Office: RW Group 8207 E Cholla St Scottsdale AZ 85260

WADT, WILLARD ROGERS, theoretical chemist; b. Bayonne, N.J., Jan. 6, 1949; s. Willard Frederick and Rena Rebecca (Mettam) W.; m. Ann Scholl McLaughlin, Nov. 23, 1984. BA in Chemistry summa cum laude, Williams Coll., 1970; PhD in Chemistry, Calif. Inst. Tech., 1975. Sr. research chemist Monsanto Research Mound Lab., Dayton, Ohio, 1974-76; mem. staff theoretical chemistry group Los Alamos (N.Mex.) Nat. Lab., 1976-81, dep. group leader theoretical chemistry group, 1981-85, tech. project mgr. SIS program, 1981-85, project mgr. optical damage program, 1984-85; v.p. Bi-oDesign Inc., Pasadena, Calif., 1986-87; assoc. div. leader chem. and laser scis. div. Los Alamos (N. Mex.) Nat. Lab., 1987—. Named one of 100 Outstanding Young Scientists in Am., Sci. Digest, 1984. Democrat. Office: Los Alamos Nat Lab CLS-DO MS-J563 Los Alamos NM 87545

WAER, EDWARD JACK, aerospace company executive; b. Long Branch, N.J., Feb. 4, 1936; s. Benjamin Lewis and Nora Ruth (Barker) W.; m. Becky Lynn Smithwick, May 1, 1977; children: Brian Jeffery, Deirdre Lynn. BSBA, U. Phoenix, 1982. Enlisted U.S. Army, 1953, advanced through grades to chief warrant officer 3, with intelligence, 1953-79, ret., 1979; area mgr. Goodyear Aerospace Corp., Litchfield Park, Ariz., 1980—; mem. adv. bd. Glendale (Ariz.) Coll., 1982—. Mem. Tech. Mktg. Soc. Am., A Touch of the Old West (founder, pres. 1983-84), VFW (life), DAV (life), Mensa. Avocation: Old West reenactments and shoot-outs. Office: Goodyear Aerospace Corp PO Box 85 Litchfield Park AZ 85340-0085

WAGATSUMA, BERT MAMORU, accountant; b. Hilo, Hawaii, Feb. 11, 1955; s. Shinichi and Kikue (Arai) W. BBA, U. Hawaii, 1977. CPA, Hawaii. Staff auditor U.S. Army Audit Agy., Ft. Lewis, Wash., 1978-79; mem. staff Thayer & Matsushita, Kahului, Maui, Hawaii, 1979-80; sr.-in-charge Lester Witte & Co., Honolulu, 1980-81; mgr. Thayer & Assocs., Kahului, 1981-83; controller Fuku Constrn., Wailuku, 1983, Build N Grow, Hilo, 1983; owner Bert M. Wagatsuma CPA, Hilo, 1983—. Mem. acctg. adv. com. Maui Community Coll., 1981-83; asst. treas. Dem. Party, 1984—. Mem. Am. Inst. CPA's, Hawaii Soc. CPA's, Hawaii State Bd. Pub. Accountancy, Lehua Jaycees (exec. v.p. 1986-87, treas. 1985-86, pres. 1987-88), Univ. Hawaii Alumni Assn. (treas. 1986—), Hilo High Sch. Alumni Assn. (auditor 1986—). Democrat. Office: 318 Kamehameha Ave Hilo HI 96720

WAGERS, PAMELA WEISBART, not-for-profit foundation administrator, writer; b. Brush, Colo., Jan. 15, 1950; d. Jack Weisbart and Verdie Jean (Reasoner) Carlson; m. Kenneth John Wagers, June 8, 1968. BA, U. Colo., 1971. Asst. mgr. Mountain Bell Telephone Co., Denver, 1972—; loaned exec. United Way, Boulder, Colo., 1985—. Author numerous poems. Vol. Polit. Action Coms., Boulder, 1982, 83; active campaign John Buechner Rep. for Colo. State Rep., 1983. Recipient Outstanding Vol. Service award Boulder County Assn. Agy. Execs., 1985. Mem. Profl. Women's Fellowship of Boulder, Women in Communications. Republican. Jewish. Club: Rep. Women's Forum. Avocations: classical piano, golf, skiing, reading, yoga. Home: 2510 Hawthorn Boulder CO 80302 Office: United Way Boulder County 2955 Baseline Rd Boulder CO 80303

WAGGAMAN, DOUGLAS SCOTT, lawyer; b. Greenwich, Conn., Nov. 25, 1956; s. Eugene Sauve and Nancy (Quinn) W.; m. Lorene Hiroko Abe, Jan. 9, 1982. BA in Polit. Sci., Boston Coll., 1980; JD, UCLA, 1983. Bar: Calif. 1983, U.S. Dist. Ct. (cen. dist.) Calif. 1984, U.S. Ct. Appeals (9th cir.) 1984. Assoc. Levy & Norminton, Los Angeles, 1983—. Atty. Los Angeles Pub. Counsel, 1984—. Mem. ABA, Los Angeles County Bar Assn., Am. Trial Lawyers Assn., Order of Coif. Republican. Roman Catholic. Avocations: automobile restoration, tennis. Home: 4534 Argentine Rd Woodland Hills CA 91364 Office: Levy & Norminton 815 Moraga Dr Los Angeles CA 90049

WAGNER, CHARLES NORMAN, banker, accountant; b. Fond du Lac, Wis., Aug. 19, 1947; s. Norman George and Louella Ann (Mehre) W.; m. A. Lorraine Hurteau, June 14, 1969; children—Laura Rene, Steven Charles. B.B.A., U. Wis.-Whitewater, 1973. C.P.A., Ariz. Acct., Ernst & Whinney, Tucson, 1973-77; controller Home Fed. Savs., Tucson, 1978-82; dep. auditor First Interstate of Ariz., Phoenix, 1982-83, comptroller, 1983—. Mem. adv. council Ariz. Sonora Desert Mus., Tucson, 1980-82; bd. dirs. Ariz. Boys Ranch, Phoenix, 1982—, Community Council, Phoenix, 1984—. Mem. Am. Inst. C.P.A.s, Ariz. Soc. C.P.A.s, Bank Adminstrn. Inst., Fin. Mgrs. Soc. (pres. Ariz. chpt. 1980-81, chmn. nat. com. 1979-82), Nat. Assn. Accts., Phi Kappa Phi. Republican. Lutheran. Lodge: Lions (treas. 1978-79, sec. 1979-80).

WAGNER, DEBORAH ANN, financial director; b. Syracuse, N.Y., Mar. 24, 1951; d. Bruce Earl and Barbara J. (Ward) W. BA in Polit. Sci and Sociology, SUNY, Buffalo, 1973; MPA, U. Denver, 1976. Adminstr. Colo. State Personnel Bd., Denver, 1977-79; sr. policy budget analyst State Office of Planning and Budgeting, Denver, 1979-80; budget dir. Colo. Dept. Personnel, Denver, 1980-84, Colo. Dept. Natural Resources, Denver, 1984—; bd. dirs. State Employees Group Ins. Bd., Denver, 1980—. Capt. Denver Dems., 1985—; bd. dirs. Mayor's Adv. Commn., Denver, 1986—, Denver Civil Service Commn., 1986—. Mem. Leadership Denver Assn. Avocations: skiing, swimming, diving, scuba diving. Office: Colo Dept Natural Resources 1313 Sherman St Room 718 Denver CO 80203

WAGNER, FRANCIS ROBERT, management educator, consultant; b. Santa Monica, Calif., Apr. 10, 1948; s. Francis Vincent and Virginia Mary (Heape) W.; m. Karen Yolanda Secchi, Sept. 13, 1969; children: James Francis, Jessica Monique. B in Commerce, Santa Clara U., 1969; MBA, UCLA, 1970, PhD, 1976, postdoctoral, 1976-78. Asst. prof. mgmt. Loyola Marymount U., Los Angeles, 1976-82; ptnr., dir. Keilty, Goldsmith & Boone, La Jolla, Calif., 1981-86; co-founder Prism Ltd., Santa Monica, 1986—; bd. advisors ACS, Concord, Calif., 1984—; cons. IBM, Coca-Cola, Dun & Bradstreet, IDS Fin. Services, Citibank, Warner Lambert, Can. Red Cross, Apple Computer, Inc. Contbr. articles to mgmt. and psychology jours. Co-leader CROP Hunger Walks, Pacific Palisades, Calif., 1980-81. Served to 1st lt. U.S. Army, 1971-72. Named one of Outstanding Young Men in Am., 1979. Roman Catholic. Avocations: surfing, skiing, running. Home: 832 Alma Real Dr Pacific Palisades CA 90272

WAGNER, JUDITH BUCK, investment advisory firm executive, banker; b. Altoona, Pa. Sept. 25, 1943; d. Harry Bud and Mary Elizabeth (Rhodes) B.; m. Mark S. Foster, June 17, 1967 (div. 1977); m. Joseph E. Wagner, Mar. 15, 1980; 1 child, Elizabeth. BA in History, U. Wash., 1965; grad. N.Y. Inst. Fin., 1968. Chartered fin. analyst; registered Am. Stock Exchange; registered N.Y. Stock Exchange; registered investment advisor. Security analyst Morgan, Olmstead, Kennedy & Gardner, Los Angeles, 1968-71; research cons., St. Louis, 1971-72; security analyst Boettcher & Co., Denver, 1972-75; pres. Wagner Investment Counsel, 1975-84; chmn. Wagner & Hamil, Inc., Denver, 1983—; chmn., bd. dirs. The Women's Bank, N.A., Denver, 1977—, organizational group pres., 1975-77; chmn. Equitable Bankshares Colo., Inc., Denver, 1980—; bd. dirs. Equitable Bank of Littleton, 1983—, pres., 1985; bd. dirs. Colo. Growth Capital, 1979-82; lectr. Denver U., Metro State, 1975-80. Author: Woman and Money series Colo. Woman Mag., 1976; moderator 'Catch 2' Sta. KWGN-TV, 1978-79. Pres. Big Sisters Colo., Denver, 1977-82, bd. dirs., 1973—; bd. fellows U. Denver, 1985—; bd. dirs. Red Cross, 1980, Assn. Children's Hosp., 1985, Colo. Health Facilities Authority, 1978-84, Jr. League Community Adv. Com., 1979—, Brother's Redevel., Inc., 1979-80; mem. Hist. Paramount Found., 1984, Denver Pub. Sch. Career Edn. Project, 1972; mem. investment com. YWCA, 1976—; mem. adv. com. Girl Scouts U.s.; mem. agy. relations com. Mile High United Way, 1978-81, chmn. United Way Venture Grant com., 1980-81; fin. chmn. Schoettler for State Treas., 1986. Recipient Making It award Cosmopolitan Mag., 1977, Women on the Go award, Savvy mag., 1983, Minouri Yasoni award, 1986, Salute Spl. Honoree award, Big Sisters, 1987; named one of the Outstanding Young Women in Am., Denver C. of C., 1979. Fellow Fin. Analysts Fedn.; mem. Women's Forum of Colo. (pres. 1979), Women's Found. Colo., Inc. (bd. dirs. 1986—), Denver Soc. Security Analysts (bd. dirs. 1976—, v.p. 1980-81, pres. 1981-82), Leadership Denver (Outstanding Alumna award 1986), Pi Beta Phi (pres. U. Wash. chpt. 1964-65). Office: Wagner & Hamil Inc 410 17th St #840 Denver CO 80202

WAGNER, KAREN JANE, data communications executive; b. Kansas City, Mo., July 27, 1954; s. Forrest E. Wagner and H. Jane (Kirby) McCamis; m. James H. Peterman, May 18, 1973 (div. Sept. 1981). Student, Maplewoods

Community Coll., 1971, 72, 75. Computer operator Mazda Motors Am. Cen. Inc., Rancho Dominguez, Calif., 1979-80, ops. supr., 1980-81, tech. services supr., 1981-83, ops. services supr., 1983-85, mgr. data communications, 1985—. Mem. Am. Mgmt. Assn., Nat. Assn. Female Execs. Avocations: golf, music, reading. Office: Mazda Motors of Am Cen Inc 3040 E Ana Rancho Dominguez CA 90221

WAGNER, KIT KERN, atmospheric scientist; b. Chickasha, Okla., Nov. 13, 1947. BS, U. Okla., 1970, MS, 1971, PhD, 1975. Meteorlogist Nat. Severe Storms Lab., Norman, Okla., 1975; asst. prof. meteorology U. Calif., Davis, 1975-81; air pollution research specialist State of Calif., Sacramento, 1981—. Contbr. articles to Jour. Applied Meteorology. Mem. Am. Meteorol. Soc. (cert.), Air Pollution Control Assn. Office: Air Resources Bd TSD PO Box 2815 Sacramento CA 95812

WAGNER, RAY JAY, editor; b. N.Y.C., June 30, 1931; s. Cornelius and Theresa (Hanghofer) W.; m. Carmela Matilda Sigari, Jan. 25, 1960; 1 child: Nicole. BA, CCNY, 1955. Editor Graybar, Burlingame, Calif., 1962—; cons. Ray Jay Studios, Foster City, Calif., 1980—. Author: 50 U.S. Treasure Wrecks, 1967; editor jour. Outlook, 1962-71, Counterpoints, 1971—. Mem. Authors League Am., Authors Guild. Republican. Roman Catholic. Lodge: Elks. Avocation: yachting. Home: 391 Port Royal Foster City CA 94404 Office: Graybar Electric Co Box 4454 Burlingame CA 94010

WAGNER, RAYMOND LEE, aerospace systems engineer, security engineer; b. Kansas City, Mo., Aug. 21, 1941; s. Albert Louis and Esther Pauline (Anderson) W.; m. Cheri C. Adams, Aug. 30, 1969; children: Richard, Frederek. AB in Physics, Rice U., 1968; PhD in Astrophysics, U. Tex., 1972. Asst. prof. astronomy U. Wash., Seattle, 1972-74; asst. prof. astronomy, physics La. State U., Baton Rouge, 1974-78; software engrng. specialist Ford Aerospace and Communications Corp., Colorado Springs, Colo., 1979-83, security engrng. supr., 1983-85, program mgmt. specialist, 1986—; lectr. physics U. Colo., Colorado Springs, 1984. Contbr. astrophysics articles to profl. jours. Cabot scholar Rice U., 1964-68; NSF summer fellow U. Tex., Austin, 1970, Univ. fellow U. Tex., 1970-72; NSF research grantee, La. State U., Baton Rouge, 1974-78. Mem. Am. Astron. Soc., Internat. Astron. Union, AIAA (nat. space sci. tech. com. 1984-87, space ops. tech. com. 1986—), Armed Forces Communications and Electronics Assn., Sigma Xi, Phi Kappa Phi. Republican. Avocations: hiking, fishing, antique glass collecting, philately. Home: 2610 Black Diamond Terr Colorado Springs CO 80918 Office: Ford Aerospace Communications Corp 10440 State Hwy 83 Colorado Springs CO 80908

WAGNER, ROGER FRANCES, choral director; b. LePuy, France, Jan. 16, 1914; came to U.S., 1921; s. Francis W. BA, Coll. of Montmorency, France; PhD cum laude, U. Montreal; hon. doctorates, Westminster Choir Coll., Princeton U., St. Norbert Coll., Wis. Organist, choir master St. Josephs Ch., Los Angeles, 1937-45; organizer Bur. of Music, 1945; head choral activities UCLA, 1949—, prof. emeritus, 1980—; formerly head music dept. Marymount Coll. Founder, Roger Wagner Chorale, 1946, nat. tours, 1956, Dept. State tours, Central Am., Mexico, S.Am., 1959, 64, Middle East, 1966, tours to Japan, 1965, 67, 78, 80, 82, 84; guest condr., Los Angeles Philharmonic Orch., Detroit Symphony, Royal Philharmonic, London, Orchestre des Conservatoires, Paris, Bolshoi Orch., Moscow, Concertgebouw Orch., Amsterdam, New Philharmonic, Paris, founder, Los Angeles Master Chorale and Sinfonia Orch., 1965, condr., Phila. Orch. and Los Angeles Master Chorale at Kennedy Center for presdl. inaugural concert, 1973, Symphony Orch. in, S.Am., Sao Paulo, 1973, toured Soviet Union with, Soviet Orch. and Los Angeles Master Chorale, 1974, condr. symphony concerts in, Montevido, Uruguay and Sodre Symphony, 1974; recs. with Allegro and Capitol Records, 1951—; condr., New Philharmonic and Radio France Chorale in, Royal Chapel of Versailles. Recipient Grammy award for album Virtuoso.; Decorated knight Pope Paul VI, Order St. Bridgette. Office: care Columbia Artists Mgmt Inc 165 W 57th St New York NY 10019 Office: Roger Wagner Chorale 5930 Penfield Ave Woodland Hills CA 91367 *

WAGNER, SAMUEL ALBIN MAR, records management executive, educator; b. Brighton, Colo., Feb. 23, 1942; s. Jacob Doer and Leota Garnet (Wilson) W.; m. Donna Dee Person, Mar. 20, 1987; 1 child, Andrea. BA in History, U. Colo., 1964, MA in History, 1965; STB (MTS) in History of World Religions, Harvard U., 1968. Cert. records mgr. Sr. asst. archivist Cornell U., Ithaca, N.Y., 1971-73; editor Brighton Blade Ft. Lupton Press, Brighton and Ft. Lupton, Colo., 1973-77; city archivist City of Providence, 1978-80; records analyst Wyo. State Archives, Cheyenne, 1979-83; records mgr. Ft. Collins (Colo.) Police Dept., 1984—; pres. Records Mgmt. Cons., Ft. Collins, 1985—; bd. dirs. Records, Inc., Cheyenne; instr. Chapman Coll., Cheyenne, 1981—. Author: Brighton Reflections: Bicentennial Years, 1976, Adams County: Crossroads of the West, 1977; editor: The Fort Lupton Story, 1976; contbr. numerous articles to profl. jours. county historian Adams County, Brighton, 1976-77; mem. Brighton Human Relations Commn., 1977-78; bd. dirs. Brighton Bicentennial Com., 1975-76, Brighton Centennial Com., 1986—. Recipient Hist. Preservations award Adams County Hist. Soc., 1978; Ethnic Heritage Project grantee Colo. Humanities Council, 1977; Ford Found. fellow, 1964. Mem. Microcomputer/PC Industry Action Com. (chmn. 1984—), Assn. Records Mgr. Adminstrs. (pres. No. Colo. chpt. 1984-85, chmn. various coms., Mem. of Yr. 1985), Inst. Cert. Records Mgrs. (regional coordinator, exam proctor 1982—), Soc. Am. Archivists, Am. Assn. State and Local History. Democrat. Unitarian. Avocations: local historian, art, photography, film, hiking. Home: 231 Hobbs Ave Cheyenne WY 82009 Office: City of Fort Collins 300 LaPorte Ave Fort Collins CO 80522

WAGNER, SUE ELLEN, state legislator; b. Portland, Maine, Jan. 6, 1940; d. Raymond A. and Kathryn (Hooper) Pooler; m. Peter B. Wagner, 1964: children—Kirk, Kristina. B.A. in Polit. Sci., U. Ariz., 1962; M.A. in History, Northwestern U., 1964. Asst. dean women Ohio State U., 1963-64; tchr. history and Am. govt. Catalina High Sch., Tucson, 1964-65; reporter Tucson Daily Citizen, 1965-68; mem. Nev. Assembly, 1975-83; now mem. Nev. Senate from 3d dist. Author: Diary of a Candidate, On People and Things, 1974. Mem. Reno Mayor's Adv. Com., 1973-84; chmn. Blue Ribbon Task Force on Housing, 1974-75; mem. Washoe County Republican Central Com., 1974-84, Nev. State Rep. Central Com., 1975-84; mem. Nev. Legis. Commn., 1976-77; del. social service com. Council State Govts.; v.p. Am. Field Service, 1973, family liaison, 1974, mem.-at-large, 1975. Kappa Alpha Theta Nat. Grad. scholar, also Phelps-Dodge postgrad. fellow, 1962; named Outstanding Legislator, Nev. Young Republicans, 1976, One of 10 Outstanding Young Women in Am. Mem. AAUW (legis. chmn. 1974), Bus. and Profl. Women, Kappa Alpha Theta. Episcopalian. Office: Nevada State Senate State Capitol Carson City NV 89710 Other Address: 845 Tamarack Dr Reno NV 89509 *

WAGNER, WAYNE HILBERT, investment officer; b. Milw., Sept. 5, 1938; s. Hilbert Jack and Gertrude (huss) W.; m. Mary Davey, June 30, 1963 (div. July 1974); 1 child, Jocelyn; m. Beth Corson, Jan. 25, 1975; children: Wendy, Eric. BBA, U. Wis., 1960; M in Stat, Stanford U., 1961. Registered prin., N.Y. Stock Exchange, Nat. Assn. Securities Dealers. Systems engr. IBM, San Francisco, 1961-64; asst. v.p. Wells Fargo Bank, San Francisco, 1964-73; chief investment officer Wilshire Assocs., Santa Monica, Calif., 1973-86; ptnr., chief investment officer Plexus Group, Santa Monica, 1986—. Author: (jour.) Reducing Cost of Trading, 1974, South African Divestment, 1984. Home: 14631 Bestor Blvd Pacific Palisades CA 90272 Office: Wilshire Assocs 1299 Ocean Ave Santa Monica CA 90401

WAGNER, WILLIAM GERARD, university dean, physicist, consultant, information scientist; b. St. Cloud, Minn., Aug. 22, 1936; s. Gerard C. and Mary V. (Cloone) W.; m. Janet Agatha Rowe, Jan. 30, 1968 (div. 1978); children: Mary, Robert, David, Anne; m. Christiane LeGuen, Feb. 21, 1985. B.S., Calif. Inst. Tech., 1958, Ph.D. (NSF fellow, Howard Hughes fellow), 1962. Cons. Rand Corp., Santa Monica, Calif., 1960-65; sr. staff physicist Hughes Research Lab., Malibu, Calif., 1960-69; asst. prof. physics U. Calif. at Irvine, 1965-66; assoc. prof. physics and elec. engring. U. So. Calif., Los Angeles, 1966-69; prof. depts. physics and elec. engring. U. So. Calif., 1969—, dean div. natural scis. and math. Coll. Letters, Arts and Scis., 1973-87, dean interdisciplinary studies and developmental activities, 1987—, spl. asst. automated record services, 1975-81; chmn. bd. Malibu Securities Corp., Los Angeles, 1971—; cons. to Janus Mgmt. Corp., Los Angeles, 1970-71, Croesus Capital Corp., Los Angeles, 1971-74; allied mem. Pacific Stock Exchange, 1974-82; fin. and computer cons. Hollywood Reporter, 1979-81. Contbr. articles on physics to sci. publs. Richard Chase Tolman postdoctoral fellow, 1962-65. Mem. Am. Phys. Soc., Nat. Assn. Security Dealers, Sigma Xi. Home: 2828 Patricia Ave Los Angeles CA 90064-4425 Office: Univ of So Calif 251 Allan Hancock Found Los Angeles CA 90089-0371

WAGONER, DAVID EVERETT, lawyer; b. Pottstown, Pa., May 16, 1928; s. Claude Brower and Mary Kathryn (Groff) W.; m. Landon Jensen; children—Paul R., Colin H., Elon D., Peter B. B.A., Yale U., 1950; LL.B., U. Pa., 1953. Bar: D.C. 1953, Pa. 1953, Wash. 1953. Law clk. U.S. Ct. Appeals (3d cir.), Pa., 1955-56; law clk. U.S. Supreme Ct., Washington, 1956-57; ptnr. Perkins & Coie, Seattle, 1957—. Mem. sch. com. Mcpl. League Seattle and King County, 1958—, chmn., 1962-65; mem. Seattle schs. citizens coms. on equal ednl. opportunity and adult vocat. edn., 1963-64; mem. Nat. Com. Support Pub. Schs.; mem. adv. com. on community colls., to 1965, legislature interim com. on edn., 1964-65; mem. community coll. adv. com. to state supt. pub. instrn., 1965; chmn. edn. com. Forward Thrust, 1968; mem. Univ. Congl. Ch. Council Seattle, 1968-70; bd. dirs. Met. YMCA Seattle, 1968; bd. dirs. Seattle Pub. Schs., 1965-73, v.p., 1966-67, 72-73, pres., 1968, 73; trustee Evergreen State Coll. Found., chmn. 1986; trustee Pacific NW Ballet, v.p. 1986. Served to 1st lt. M.C., AUS, 1953-55. Fellow Am. Coll. Trial Lawyers; mem. English Speaking Union (v.p. Seattle 1961-62), ABA (chmn. appellate advocacy com.), Wash. State Bar Assn., Seattle-King County Bar Assn., Nat. Sch. Bds. Assn. (bd. dirs., chmn. Council Big City Bds. Edn. 1971-72), Chi Phi. Home: 1150 22d Ave E Seattle WA 98112 Office: Perkins and Coie Washington Bldg Seattle WA 98101

WAGONER, MICHAEL DON, bank executive; b. Portland, Oreg., Dec. 4, 1952. BSBA, Portland State U., 1976. CPA, Oreg. Staff acct. Malcolm D. MacGregor, CPA, Gresham, Oreg., 1974-76; acctg. officer U.S. Bancorp, Portland, 1976-81, asst. controller, 1981-82, asst. v.p., 1982-85, v.p., corp. fin. officer, 1985—. Pres. Good News Foursquare Ch. Men's Ministry, Portland, 1982-85, council mem. Good News Ch., 1986; Rep. precinct person, Portland, 1985. Mem. Evangelical Ch. Avocations: running, reading. Office: US Bancorp 111 SW 5th Ave Portland OR 97204

WAHI, KRISHAN KISHORE, consulting engineer; b. Hardwar, India, Oct. 20, 1948; came to U.S., 1967, naturalized, 1980; s. Wazir Chand and Raj Karni (Malhotra) W.; B.S. (tuition scholarship 1968-69), U. Wash., Seattle, 1969, M.S. (grad. asst. 1970-74), 1971, Ph.D. in Mech. Engring., 1974; m. Natalie R. Todd, June 5, 1974; children—Rajeev K., Nikhil D., Arun K. Sr. physicist Physics Internat. Co., San Leandro, Calif., 1974-75; with Sci. Applications, Internat. Corp., 1975-85, sr. scientist, Fort Collins, Colo., 1979-80, Albuquerque, 1980-86, supr. waste mgmt. systems; pres. GRAM Inc., Albuquerque, 1986—. Mem. ASME, Sigma Xi. Author papers in field. Home: 1312 Michael Hughes St NE Albuquerque NM 87112 Office: GRAM Inc 1709 Moon St NE Albuquerque NM 87112

WAHL, IVER WILLIAM, aerospace company executive; b. Denver, Aug. 26, 1923; s. Iver William and Pearl Geneva (Warriner) W.; student U. Wichita, 1941-43; BSME, U. Colo., 1949; m. Clayta Winifred Davis, June 23, 1945; children: Michael Dan, Eileen Annette. Registered profl. engr., Calif.; cert. profl. property mgr. Stores supr. Cessna Aircraft Co., Wichita, Kans., 1941-43; tool design engr. Maytag Co., Newton, Iowa, 1949-51; insp. supr. Heckethorn Mfg. Co., Littleton, Colo., 1951-57; acting chief quality planning Martin-Marietta, Denver, 1957-64; mgr. quality assurance, material, property and prodn. Ball Aerospace Systems Div., Boulder, 1964—; cons. quality, property mgmt. Bd. dirs. Littleton YMCA, 1952-55; mem. adv. council Met. State Coll., 1972-77. Served with USAAF, 1943-45. Recipient Skylab achievement award NASA. Fellow Am. Soc. Quality Control (officer, regional reliability counselor, testimonial award); mem. Nat. Security Industries Assn. (com. chmn., Outstanding Achievement award), Electronics Industries Assn., Nat. Property Mgmt. Assn. (v.p. for communications, membership, chpt. property Person-of-Yr. award 1983, 86, regional personal property Person of Yr. award 1986), DAV. Presbyterian. Club: Knife and Fork (regional dir. and v.p.). Lodge: Elks. Home: 1205 Eastridge Boulder CO 80303 Office: PO Box 1062 Boulder CO 80306

WAHL, JOAN CONSTANCE, tech. writer, editor; b. Phila., Dec. 23, 1921; d. Frank L. and Sara E. (Timoney) O'Brien; B.A., Rosemont Coll., 1943; postgrad. U. Calif., Los Angeles, 1960-61; m. John Carl Wahl, Jr., Dec. 31, 1943 (div. 1959); children—John, Mark, David, Lawrence, Thomas, Jeanne, Madeleine Sophie, Eugene. Substitute tchr. Los Angeles City Bd. Edn., 1961; editor, proofreader Renner/Cal-Data Corp., Los Angeles, 1962-63; editor, tech. writer Volt Tech. Corp., 1964-66; sr. tech. editor, writer, project editor Aerospace Corp., El Segundo, Calif., 1966—. Sect. chmn. United Way, Los Angeles, 1963-64; mem. communications com. St. Paul the Apostle Roman Cath. Ch., Westwood, Calif., 1976-78. Recipient Outstanding Service award United Way, 1964. Mem. Soc. Tech. Communications (sr.), Aerospace Women's Com., Mental Health Assn. Los Angeles County, Kistler Honor Soc. Contbr. articles to profl. jours. Office: Aerospace Corp M3/377 2350 El Segundo Blvd El Segundo CA 90245

WAHLBERG, DAVID KARL LANE, retail industry executive; b. Great Falls, Mont., Nov. 18, 1930; s. John and Iola Mae (Lane) W. BS, U. Wis., 1955. Adminstrv. audit mgr. Montgomery Ward and Co., Chgo., 1964-65; field audit mgr. Montgomery Ward and Co., Balt., 1965-67; systems program mgr. Montgomery Ward and Co., Chgo., 1967-68; auditor Ohrbach's, Inc., Los Angeles, 1972-77; dir. of systems Daylin, Inc., Los Angeles, 1977-80; v.p. mgmt. info-systems The Federated Group, Commerce, Calif., 1980—; cons. Charles F. Kirn Co., Santa Rosa, Calif., 1985—. Served to 1st lt. U.S. Army, 1955-57, Korea. Office: The Federated Group Inc 5655 E Union Pacific Ave Commerce CA 90601

WAHLGREN, ERIK, emeritus foreign language educator; b. Chgo., Nov. 2, 1911; s. Oscar G. and Marion I. (Wilkins) W.; m. Dorothy Sly, Nov. 9, 1939 (div. 1951); children: Nils, Arvid; m. Beverly Pont, Dec. 18, 1952 (div. 1969); children: Siri Wahlgren Grochowski, Thor; m. Helen Gilchrist-Wottring, July 2, 1971; 2 stepchildren. Ph.B., U. Chgo., 1933, Ph.D., 1938; M.A., U. Neb., 1936. Mem. faculty UCLA, 1938—, prof. Scandinavian langs., 1955-70, prof. Scandinavian and Germanic langs., 1970-77, prof. emeritus, 1977—, vice chmn. dept. Germanic langs., 1963-69; dir. U. Calif. study centers at Univs. Lund (Sweden) and Bergen (Norway), 1972-74; lectr. Uppsala U., also vis. prof. Stockholm Sch. Econs., 1947-48; exchange instr. U. B.C., summer 1940; vis. prof. Augustana Coll., summer 1946, U. Calif. at Berkeley, 1968, U. Wash., 1970, Portland State U., 1979-80; U.S. mem. Commn. Ednl. Exchange U.S.-Sweden, 1973-74; sr. fellow, cons. Monterey Inst. Fgn. Studies, 1977-78; adv. NEH, 1978—; advisor Oreg. Gov.'s Commn. on Fgn. Langs. and Internat. Study, 1981-83; German lang. dir. Army Specialized Tng. Program, 1943-44. Author: The Kensington Stone: A Mystery Solved, 1958, The Vikings and America, 1986; also several other books, translations and numerous articles on Scandinavian philology.; appeared various documentary films. Mem. Mayor's Community Adv. Com., 1964-73. Am.-Scandinavian Found. fellow Sweden, 1946-47, recipient Gold medal, 1975; grantee to Scandinavia Am. Philos. Soc., 1954-55; Guggenheim Meml. Found. fellow Scandinavia, 1961-62; recipient pub. citation Icelandic Community Los Angeles, 1964; decorated knight Royal Swedish Order of Polar Star, knight Order Lion of Finland, knight Icelandic Order of Falcon. Fellow Internat. Inst. Arts and Letters (life); mem. Swedish Cultural Soc. Am. (dir. 1940-48, pres. Los Angeles 1941-46), MLA So. Calif. (exec. bd. 1950-53), MLA Assn. Am. (chmn. Scandinavian sect. 1955, 67), Am.-Scandinavian Found. (pres. Los Angeles chpt. 1958-60), Soc. Advancement Scandinavian Study (assoc. editor 1947-57, 70-73, assoc. mng. editor 1957-69), Am. Assn. Tchrs. German (nat. exec. council 1957-59, 60-63), Finlandia Found., Medieval Acad. Am., Am. Swedish Hist. Mus., Swedish-Am. Hist. Soc. Calif., Nordic Heritage Mus. (Viking ship com.), World Affairs Council Oreg., Wash., Seattle Swedish Club, Oreg. Internat. Council, Tau Kappa Epsilon, Delta Sigma Rho, Delta Phi Alpha. Home and Office: 4243 28th Pl W Seattle WA 98199

WAHLKE, JOHN CHARLES, educator; b. Cin., Oct. 29, 1917; s. Albert B.C. and Clara J. (Ernst) W.; m. Virginia Joan Higgins, Dec. 1, 1943; children: Janet Parmely, Dale. A.B., Harvard U., 1939, M.A., 1947, Ph.D., 1952. Instr., asst. prof. polit. sci. Amherst (Mass.) Coll., 1949-53; prof. polit. sci. Vanderbilt U., Nashville, Tenn., 1953-63, SUNY, Buffalo, 1963-66, U. Iowa, 1966-71, SUNY, Stony Brook, 1971-72, U. Iowa, Iowa City, 1972-79, U. Ariz., Tucson, 1979—. Author: (with others) The Legislative System, 1962, Government and Politics, 1966, The Politics of Representation, 1978; editor: Causes of the American Revolution, 1950, Loyalty in a Democratic State, 1952; co-editor: Legislative Behavior, 1959, The American Political System, 1967, Comparative Legislative Behavior, 1973. Served to capt., F.A. AUS, 1942-46. Decorated Air medal with 2 oak leaf clusters. Mem. AAAS, Am. Polit. Sci. Assn. (past pres.), Internat. Polit. Sci. Assn., So. Polit. Sci. Assn., Midwest Polit. Sci. Assn. (past pres.), Western Polit. Sci. Assn., Southwestern Polit. Sci. Assn. Home: 5462 N Entrada Catorce Tucson AZ 85718 Office: U Ariz Dept Polit Sci Tucson AZ 85721

WAHRHAFTIG, DAVID IRA, management consultant; b. Washington, Apr. 19, 1957; s. Leon and Betty Wahrhaftig. BA, Western Md. Coll., 1979; MBA, Wake Forest U., 1982. Cert. mgmt. acctg. Mgr. entrepreneurial services group Arthur Young, Washington, 1982-85; mgr. nat. high tech. group mergers and acquisitions West Region Group Arthur Young, San Francisco, 1985—. Mem. Babcock Grad. Sch. Mgmt. Admissions Council, Winston-Salem, N.C., 1983—; active Big Bros. Am., Winston-Salem, 1980-82, Washington, 1982-85. Recipient Outstanding Service award Big Bros. Am., 1983. Democrat. Home: 2100 Bay St San Francisco CA 94123 Office: Arthur Young 1 Sansome St San Francisco CA 94104

WAIDE, MARY MARIE, educator, artist; b. Portales, N.Mex., Nov. 8, 1946; d. Jack F. and Ruth M. (Wilson) W. BA, Eastern N.Mex. U., 1964, MEd, 1969, Degree in Edn. Specialists, 1973. Cert. tchr., N.Mex. Tchr. Roswell (N.Mex.) Pub. Schs.; cons. arts and crafts workshops; tchr. Roswell Mus. and Art Ctr., Roswell Adult Ctr., Eastern N.Mex. U. Vol. Easter Seals Work, Southeastern N.Mex. Mental Health Clinic. Recipient Artist for Humanities grantee Roswell Pub. Library, 1983; named one of Artists of Month, Eastern N.Mex. U., 1985, Roswell Pub. Library, 1983. Mem. Am. Bus. Women's Assn. (Woman of Yr.), AAUW, N.Mex. Reading Assn., Assn. Supervision and Curriculum Devel., Roswell Art Guild, Pecos Valley Potters Guild, Roswell Fine Arts League, United Council Artists, Roswell Alliance English Lang. Arts, Nat. Mus. Women in Arts, Mus. N.Mex. Found., Roswell Community Little Theater, Roswell Mus. and Art Ctr., Phi Kappa Phi. Democrat. Baptist. Home: 1117 S Lea Roswell NM 88201 Office: Roswell Pub Schs 1601 E Bland Roswell NM 88201

WAIHEE, JOHN DAVID, III, governor of Hawaii, lawyer; b. Honokaa, Hawaii, May 19, 1946; m. Lynne Kobashigawa; children: John David, Jennifer. B.A. in History and Bus., Andrews U., 1968; postgrad., Central Mich. U., 1973; J.D., U. Hawaii, 1976. Bar: Hawaii 1976. Community edn. coordinator Benton Harbor (Mich.) Area Schs., 1968-70, asst. dir. community edn., 1970-71; program evaluator, adminstrv. asst. to dirs., planner Honolulu Model Cities Program, 1971-73; sr. planner Office Human Resources City and County of Honolulu, 1973-74, program mgr. Office Human Resources, 1974-75; assoc. Shim, Sigal, Tam & Naito, Honolulu, 1975-79; ptnr. Waihee, Manuia, Yap, Pablo & Hoe, Honolulu, 1979-82; mem. Hawaiian Ho. of Reps., 1980-82; lt. gov. State of Hawaii, Honolulu, 1982-87, gov., 1987—. Del. 1978 Constnl. Conv.; del. Hawaii Dem. State Conv., 1972,74, 76, 78, 82; dir. and past pres. Kalihi-Palama Community Council; mem. steering com. Goals for Hawaii Orgn., past chmn. land use goals com., past co-chmn. outreach com.; past bd. dirs. Hawaii Sr. Citizens Travel Bd.; past mem. State Council on Housing and Constrn. Industry; mem. Kalihi-Palama Hawaiian Civic Club; past bd. dirs. Legal Aid Soc. of Hawaii, Alu Like. Mem. Hawaii Bar Assn. (chmn. unauthorized practice of law com. 1979, chmn. legis com. 1980), ABA, U. Hawaii Law Sch. Alumni, Filipino C. of C. Lodge: Kalakaua Lions. Office: Office of Gov 5th Fl State Capitol Honolulu HI 96813

WAINER, STANLEY ALLEN, electronics industry executive; b. Los Angeles, May 10, 1926; s. Calman and Katherine (Copeland) W.; m. Shirlene Joy Goldberg, Feb. 3, 1949; 1 child, William Edward. B.S. with honors, UCLA, 1950, grad. exec. program, 1958. Accountant Price Waterhouse & Co., Los Angeles, 1950-55; chief financial and adminstrv. officer Paramount Pictures Corp., and subsidiaries, 1955-60; v.p., sec.-treas. Royal Industries, Pasadena, Calif., 1960-61; with Wyle Labs., El Segundo, Calif., 1962—; pres. Wyle Labs., 1970-85, chief exec. officer, 1979—, chmn., 1984—, also dir., mem. exec. com.; dir. City Nat. Corp./City Nat. Bank; Pres., dir. UCLA Bus. Sch. Alumni Assn., 1968-69. Trustee, mem. exec. com. UCLA Found., 1972—; bd. visitors UCLA Grad. Sch. Mgmt., 1983—; bd. dirs. NCCJ, 1974-80, bd. govs., 1980—; bd. dirs. Los Angeles Urban League, 1978-80; regent U. Calif., 1980-82; trustee Orthopaedic Hosp., Los Angeles, 1974-81, adv. council, 1980—; bd. dirs. Coro Found., 1982—, El Segundo Ednl. Found., 1984—. Served with USNR, 1944-46. Named Man of Yr., City of Hope Aids, 1979, UCLA Alumnus of Yr., 1987; honoree NCCJ, 1981. Mem. Financial Execs. Inst., Technion Soc. (past dir.), Am. Inst. CPAs, C. of C. of U.S., Calif. C. of C. (dir.), Los Angeles C. of C. (dir. 1980—, chmn. fed. affairs com.), UCLA Alumni Assn. (dir. 1979—, pres. 1980-82), Soc. Order Blue Shield, Town Hall, Beta Gamma Sigma. Clubs: Regency, Riviera Tennis, Century West, Le Club de l'Ermitage. Home: 1151 Hilary Ln Beverly Hills CA 90210 Office: Wyle Labs 128 Maryland St El Segundo CA 90245 *

WAINESS, MARCIA WATSON, legal administrator; b. Bklyn., Dec. 17, 1949; d. Stanley and Seena (Klein) Watson; m. Steven Richard Wainess, Aug. 7, 1975. Student, UCLA, 1967-71, student interior design program, 1981. Office mgr., paralegal Lewis, Marenstein & Kadar, Los Angeles, 1977-81; office mgr. Rosenfeld, Meyer & Susman, Beverly Hills, Calif., 1981-83; adminstr. Rudin, Richman & Appel, Beverly Hills, 1983; dir. adminstrn. Kadison, Pfaelzer, Los Angeles, 1983—; faculty mem. UCLA Legal Mgmt. & Adminstrn. Program, 1983, Assn. Legal Adminstrs., Los Angeles, 1984, U. So. Calif. Paralegal Program, Los Angeles, 1985. Mem. ABA (chmn. Displaywrite Users Group 1986, legal tech. adv. council litigation support working group 1986—), State Bar Calif., Los Angeles County Bar Assn. (exec. com. law office mgmt. sect.), Assn. Profl. Law Firm Mgrs., Assn. Legal Adminstrs. (asst. regional v.p. Calif. 1987-88, pres. Beverly Hills chpt. 1985-86, membership chmn. 1984-85, chmn. new adminstrn. sect. 1982-84). Avocations: historic preservation, antiques, interior design. Office: Kadison Pfaelzer Woodard et al 707 Wilshire Blvd 40th Floor Los Angeles CA 90017

WAINIO, MARK ERNEST, loss control specialist; b. Virginia, Minn., Apr. 18, 1953. BA, Gustavus Adolphus Coll., 1975. Cert. safety profl., assoc. loss control mgmt., assoc. risk mgmt., CPCU. Carpenter ABI Contracting Inc., Virginia, 1975-77; co-owner Mesabi Builders, Albuquerque and Eveleth, Minn., 1977-79; sr. engring. rep. Aetna Life & Casualty, Albuquerque, 1979-86; loss control specialist CNA Ins. Cos., Albuquerque, 1986—. Mem. Am. Soc. Safety Engrs., CPCU. Avocations: golf, fishing, hunting, swimming, Karate. Home: 5525 Sonata Dr NE Albuquerque NM 87111 Office: CNA Ins Companies 8500 Menaul NE Albuquerque NM 87112

WAITE, SARITA CAMILLE, lawyer; b. San Jose, Calif., Apr. 27, 1941; d. Horace and Muriel (Scheffler) W. BA, U. Calif., Berkeley, 1963; JD, Golden Gate Coll., 1969. Bar: Calif. 1970. Ptnr. Waite & Reaves, Berkeley, 1981—. Mem. ABA, Calif. State Bar, Am. Acad. Matrimonial Lawyers. Democrat. Home: 1020 Miller Berkeley CA 94708

WAITE, WILLIAM DAVID, architect; b. Grangeville, Idaho, Apr. 12, 1950; s. Bob Judson and Vera Muriel (Lyda) W.; m. Janice Louise Wilbanks, Mar. 5, 1977; 1 child, Amber LaRee. BArch, U. Idaho, 1973. Registered architect, Idaho. Architect Peace Corps, Honduras, 1973-75, Trout-Gile & Assocs., Boise, Idaho, 1976, Ronald Thurber & Assocs., Boise, 1976-83, Gile-Armstrong Architects, Boise, 1983—. Community Spanish instr., Boise, 1977-79. Republican. Baptist. Avocations: skiing, photography, computers. Office: Gile-Armstrong Architects 4477 Emerald Suite A 100 Boise ID 83706

WAITMAN, B.A., investment banking company executive; b. Ft. Collins, Colo., May 17, 1946; d. Henry and Lydia (Frickel) Kerbel; 1 child, Craig A. Adminstrv. asst. Fleishcer & Co., Phoenix, 1970-78; legal adminstr. Shank, Irwin & Holmes, Denver, 1978-80; v.p. Franchise Fin. Corp. Am., Phoenix, 1980-86, sr. v.p., 1986—. Republican. Baptist. Avocations: golf, racquetball, bike riding, gardening. Office: Franchise Fin Corp Am 500 Financial Ctr 3443 N Central Ave Phoenix AZ 85012

WAITON, RUDOLPH O., physician; b. Monessen, Pa., June 11, 1922; s. Lawrence and Anna (Ostrander) W.; m. Marilyn Earle, Dec. 8, 1979; children: Richard, CorryAnn, Melanie, Thomas. BS, U. Pitts., 1949; MA, Stanford U., 1954, PhD, 1956; DO, Kirksville Coll., 1965; MD, U. Oreg., 1974. Diplomate Am. Bd. Osteo. Medicine. Intern Standring Meml. Hosp., Seattle, 1965-66; resident in rehab. medicine VA Hosp., Portland, Oreg., 1972-74; practice osteo. medicine and rehab. and phys. medicine Los Gatos, Calif., 1975—; mem. staff. Valley West Gen. Hosp.; pres., chmn. bd. dirs. Calif. Inst. Rehabilitative and Preventive Medicine; adj. prof. Coll. Osteo. Medicine of the Pacific. Served with USAAF, World War II, Korea. Decorated DFC with oak leaf cluster, Air medal with three oak leaf clusters, Purple Heart; recipient Nobel Peace Prize, 1985, diplomate Am. Osteo. Coll. Rehab. Medicine. Fellow Am. Acad. Med. Preventics, Internat. Coll. Gen. Practice (charter), Internat. Coll. Applied Nutrition; mem. AMA, Calif. Med. Assn., Am. Acad. Family Physicians, Am. Acad. Osteopathy, Santa Clara County Med. Assn., Osteo. Physicians and Surgeons Calif., Fed. Aviation Med. Assn., Am. Osteo. Assn., Am. Coll. Rehab. Medicine, Internat. Acad. Preventive Medicine, Orthomolecular Med. Soc., Union Concerned Scientists, Stanford chpt. Physicians for Social Responsibility Beyond War, Internat. Physicians for the Prevention of Nuclear War, Better World Soc., Plowshares, Inc., Sane. Lodges: Elks, Rotary, Masons. Home: 120 Carlton #54 Los Gatos CA 95030 Office: 221 Almendra Ave Los Gatos CA 95030

WAITS, ROBERT KING, technical film researcher; b. Chgo., Mar. 13, 1932; s. Harold F. and Edith (King) W.; m. Susie Arleane Tomlin, Dec. 12, 1964; children: Jennifer, Janine. BA cum laude, Tex. Christian U., 1955; MS, Stanford U., 1958. Research and devel. engr. Fairchild Camera & Instrument Corp., Palo Alto, Calif., 1962-73; project leader Hewlett-Packard Co., Cupertino, Calif., 1974-81; project leader Trilogy Systems, Cupertino, 1981-83, research and devel. mgr., 1983-86; sr. engring. mgr. Digital Equipment Corp., Cupertino, 1986—. Adv. editor Solid State Tech. mag., 1978—; contbr. articles to profl. jours.; patentee in field. Mem. Am. Vacuum Soc. (instr. 1973—), Sigma Xi. Avocation: collecting antiques. Office: Digital Equipment Corp 10500 Ridgeview Ct Cupertino CA 95014

WAKATSUKI, JAMES H., state supreme court associate justice; b. Honolulu, Aug. 17, 1929; m. Irene Natsuko Yoshimura; children—Janie, Stuart, Cora. Student, U. Hawaii, 1947, Bowling Green State U., 1949-51; LL.B., U. Wis., 1954. Mem. Hawaii Ho. of Reps., 1958-80, speaker, 1974-80; judge Circuit Ct., 1980-83; assoc. justice Hawaii Supreme Ct., Honolulu, 1983—. Served with U.S. Army, 1948-49; mem. Res. (ret.). Office: Hawaii Supreme Ct PO Box 2560 Honolulu HI 96804 *

WAKAYAMA, EDGAR JUNRO, clinical chemist, biochemist; b. Manzanar, Calif., Mar. 22, 1943; s. Kinzo Ernest and Toki June (Maruyama) W.; m. June D. Kang; children: Lisa Ann, Liane Kim. BA in Biology, Northeastern U., 1967; MS in Clinical Chemistry, U. Oreg., 1972; PhD in Biochemistry, U. Nev., 1985. Asst. prof. clin. lab. sci. U. Okla., Oklahoma City, 1978-79; asst. prof. clin. lab. sci. and biochemistry U. Nev., Reno, 1979-84, assoc. prof., 1985—. Served to capt. U.S. Army, 1968-70, lt. col. Res. Recipient Grand Diagnostic award Mass. Soc. Med. Technologists, 1967, Luis de Flores scholar Northeastern U., 1967; grantee NIH, 1971. Mem. Am. Assn. Clin. Chemists, Nat. Registry in Clin. Chemistry (clin. chemist), N.Y. Acad. Sci., Nat. Acad. Clin. Chemistry, Soc. Armed Forces Med. Lab. Scientists, Sigma Xi. Avocation: golf. Home: 4300 Camino Lindo Way Reno NV 89502 Office: U Nev 300 Mackay Sci Bldg Reno NV 89557

WAKE, DAVID BURTON, biology educator, researcher; b. Webster, S.D., June 8, 1936; s. Thomas B. and Ina H. (Solem) W.; m. Marvalee Hendricks, June 23, 1962; 1 child, Thomas Andrew. B.A., Pacific Luth. U., 1958; M.S., U. So. Calif., 1960, Ph.D., 1964. Instr. anatomy and biology U. Chgo., 1964-66, asst. prof. anatomy and biology, 1966-69; assoc. prof. zoology U. Calif., Berkeley, 1969-72, prof., 1972—; dir. Mus. Vertebrate Zoology U. Calif., Berkeley, 1971—. Author: Biology, 1979; co-editor: Functional Vertebrate Morphology, 1985. Recipient Quantrell Teaching award U. Chgo., 1967, Outstanding Alumnus award Pacific Luth. U., 1979; grantee NSF, 1965—; Guggenheim fellow, 1982. Fellow AAAS, Calif. Acad. Scis., NAS/NRC Bd. Basic Biology; mem. Soc. Study Evolution (pres. 1983, editor 1979-81), Soc. Systematic Zoology (council 1980-84), Herpetologist's League (Disting. Herpetologist 1984), Am. Soc. Ichthyologist and Herpetologists (bd. govs.). Home: 999 Middlefield Rd Berkeley CA 94708

WAKE, MARVALEE HENDRICKS, zoology educator; b. Orange, Calif., July 31, 1939; d. Marvin Carlton and Velvalee (Borter) H.; m. David B. Wake, June 23, 1962; 1 child, Thomas A. B.A., U. So. Calif., 1961, M.S., 1964, Ph.D., 1968. Teaching asst./instr. U. Ill., Chgo., 1964-68, asst. prof., 1968-69; lectr. U.Calif., Berkeley, 1969-73, asst. prof., 1973-76, assoc. prof., 1976-80, prof. zoology, 1980—, chmn. dept. zoology, 1985—, assoc. dean Coll. Letters and Sci., 1975-78. Editor, co-author: Hyman's Comparative Vertical Anatomy, 1979; co-author: Biology, 1978; contbr. articles to profl. jours. NSF grantee, 1978—. Fellow AAAS, Calif. Acad. Scis.; mem. Am. Soc. Ichthyology and Herpetology (pres. 1984, bd. govs. 1978—), Internat. Union Biol. Scis. (U.S. Nat. Com. 1986-92). Home: 999 Middlefield Rd Berkeley CA 94708 Office: Univ Calif Dept Zoology Berkeley CA 94720

WAKS, STEPHEN HARVEY, lawyer; b. Decatur, Ill., Apr. 9, 1947; s. Paul and Regina (Geisler) W. BA, U. Wis., 1969; JD, U. Calif., San Francisco, 1974. Bar: Calif. 1974, U.S. Ct. Appeals (9th cir.) 1977, U.S. Tax Ct. 1977. Assoc. Wohl, Cinnamon, Hagedorn, Dunbar & Johnson, Sacramento, 1978-79; mem. Stephen H. Waks, Inc., Sacramento, 1979—; instr. U. Calif.-Davis, 1982—, Golden Gate U., 1983—. bd. dirs. Am. River Bank, Sacramento. Mem. ABA, Calif. Bar Assn., Sacramento County Bar Assn., Real Estate Securities and Syndication Inst., Phi Delta Phi. Office: 555 Capitol Mall Suite 410 Sacramento CA 95814

WALBA, DAVID MARK, chemistry educator; b. Oakland, Calif., June 29, 1949; s. Harold and Beatrice (Alpert) W.; m. Cassandra Geneson, Oct. 30, 1981; 1 child, Paul Geneson. BS, U. Calif., Berkeley, 1971; PhD, Calif. Inst. Tech., 1975; postdoctoral, UCLA, 1977. Asst. prof. chemistry U. Colo., Boulder, 1977-83, assoc. prof., 1983—; cons. Displaytech Inc., Boulder, 1986—. Contbr. articles to profl. jours.; patentee in field. Sloan Found. fellow 1982-84; Dreyfus Tchr. scholar 1984-86. Mem. Am. Chem. Soc., Sigma Xi. Office: U of Colo Dept of Chemistry Box 215 Boulder CO 80309-0215

WALDEN, OLIVER JOHN, data processing specialist; b. Greenville, Tex., Mar. 23, 1946; s. Oliver John and Kate (Beene) W.; m. Janice Leona Payne, Mar. 4, 1966; children: John Andrew, Jennifer Lynn. AA, Fullerton Jr. Coll., 1967; BA, Calif. State U., Fullerton, 1979. Computer operator Anaheim (Calif.) Union High Sch. Dist., 1970-76, programmer, 1976-79, systems analyst, 1979-81, asst. dir. data processing, 1981, dir., 1981—; mem. adv. com. Calif. State Dept. Edn., Sacramento, 1985—. Deacon 1st So. Bapt. Ch., Anaheim, 1971-81, Crescent Bapt. Ch., Anaheim, 1981—. Served with U.S. Army, 1968. Mem. Assn. Computing Machinery, Calif. Assn. Sch. Bus. Ofcls., Calif. Ednl. Data Processing Assn. Democrat. Avocations: photography, flying. Home: 2775 E Verde Ave Anaheim CA 92806 Office: Anaheim Union High Sch Dist 501 Crescent Way Anaheim CA 92803-3520

WALDEN, RICHARD KEITH, agri-business executive; b. Santa Paula, Calif., July 4, 1913; s. Arthur Frisbie and Eva Juanita (Southwick) W.; m. Barbara Eldredge Culbertson, Sept. 25, 1938 (div.); 1 son, Richard Sheffield; m. 2d, Dorothy Dayton Beck, July 5, 1967. B.A., Pomona Coll., 1936; postgrad. UCLA, 1934, 39. With Limoneira Ranch Co., Santa Paula, 1936-40; mgr. Ford-Craig Ranch Co., San Fernando, Calif., 1940-46; founder, pres., chmn. bd. Farmers Investment Co., Calif., Ariz. and Fla., 1946—; dir. Ariz. Feeds Co., 1950-74, 1st Interstate Bank, 1962-84 , Cotton, Inc., 1961-73; cons. Ford Found., Pakistan, 1969; dir. agr. adv. com. Stanford Research Inst., 1960-66; chmn. Pima County Agr. and Stblzn. Com., 1956-61. Bd. trustees Pomona Coll., 1978-81, Continental Sch. Bd., 1950-67; bd. dirs. Tucson C. of C.; chmn. Ariz. Oil and Gas Commn., 1960-66, Green Valley Community Health Ctr., 1981—; mem. Gov.'s Emergency Resources Planning Com. Recipient Disting. Citizen award U. Ariz. Alumni Assn., 1973; named Citizen of Yr., Rotary Club, 1980. Mem. Nat. Pecan Council, Ariz. Cotton Growers, Nat. Cotton Council (dir. 1960), Western Pecan Growers Assn. (dir. 1972-82), Ariz. Cattle Growers Assn. (dir. 1954-60), Cotton Council Internat. (chmn., pres. 1961-66), Town Hall Ariz. Republican. Clubs: Balboa (Mazatlan, Sinaloa, Mex.), Old Pueblo (Tucson), Plaza (Phoenix), Green Valley (Ariz.) Country. Home: 635 W Twin Buttes Rd PO Box 504 Green Valley AZ 85614 Office: PO Box 7 Sahuarita AZ 85629

WALDER, ROBERT ALAN, biomedical engineer, consultant; b. Alhambra, Calif., June 13, 1952; s. Irvin and Alice (Myronick) W.; m. Kelli Suzanne Cason, Aug. 18, 1973; children—Suzanne, James, Jonathan. Student East Los Angeles Coll., 1970-71; A.A. in Elec. Engring., Los Angeles Tech. Coll., 1972; cert. in elec. engring. Foothill Coll., 1977; cert. in supervision and mgmt. Mission Coll., 1981; M.S. in Clin. Engring., U. So. Calif., 1972. Cert. clin. engr., Calif.; lic. physician's asst., Wyo., Colo.Chief biomed. engr. Amber Med., Culver City, Calif., 1971-73; field service mgr. Med. Life Systems, Mountain View, Calif., 1973-77; supr. clin. engring. Good Samaritan Hosp., San Jose, Calif., 1977—; owner Samaritan Med. Equipment Services, 1977—; cons. in field. Served with USNR, 1970-71. Mem. Assn. Advancement Med. Instrumentation, Calif. Med. Instrumentation Assn. Home: 6432 Ramblewood Dr San Jose CA 95124 Office: 2425 Samaritan Dr San Jose CA 95120

WALDMAN, BARBARA LEE, marketing executive; b. Akron, Ohio, Sept. 15, 1947; d. Jack L. and Betty (Klusner) W.; m. Dennis L. Winger, May 19, 1984. BA, U. Mich., 1969; PMD cert., Harvard U., 1978. Systems and procedures asst. Lommis Sayles & Co., Boston, 1969-71; sr. planning analyst Continental Can Co., Chgo., 1972-76; asst. to pres. Continental Can Co. (later Continental Can Internat.), Stamford, Conn., 1976-78, mgr. mktg. services, 1979-80; asst. v.p. mktg. Bank of America, San Francisco, 1981-82, v.p. mktg., 1982-86; prin. Decorator Previews, San Francisco, 1986—. Mem. Harvard Bus. Sch. Assn. No. Calif., San Francisco Advt. Club, Sales and Mktg. Execs. Assn. Avocations: art collecting, interior design. Home: 2425 Francisco St San Francisco CA 94123 Office: Decorator Previews 3025 Fillmore St San Francisco CA 94123

WALDORF, JEAN MOSELEY, publishing executive; b. Montgomery, Ala., Mar. 15, 1942; d. Max H. and Lillian (Campbell) Moseley; m. Ronald C. Waldorf, May 1983; children—Kathleen, Michael and Patrick Kotecki. Student U. Ala., 1959, U. Ill., 1960-63, Troy State U., 1972-74. Supr. dept. advt./layout Champaign-Urbana (Ill.) Courier, 1959-63; freelance advt. promotional work, 1963-68; freelance advt., Memphis, 1968-70; owner, operator Books-N-Things, Montgomery, 1970-73; advt. mgr. Daily Sentinel Star, Grenada, Miss., 1974-76; advt sales mgr. Sta. WRIL-FM, Grenada, 1977; owner, publisher, editor The Copper Era, Greenlee County, Ariz., 1977—; pres. New Horizons Pub. Co., Inc., Ariz. Corp., 1983—. County chmn. March of Dimes, Grenada; bd. dirs. Downtown Prescott Bus. Assn., Prescott, Ariz., 1982; job tng. partnership act Greenlee County Bd. Dirs., 1984. Recipient Jaycee's Disting. Young Woman award, Montgomery, 1972, State of Ala., 1972; Nat. Found. March of Dimes Vol. Appreciation award, 1973. Mem. Miss. Presswomens Assn., Nat. Press Women's Assn., Miss. Advt. Execs., Nat. Advt. Execs. Assn., Ariz. Newspapers Assn., Nat. Press Assn. Republican. Roman Catholic. Clubs: Ala. Fedn. Women's, Soroptimist Internat. Home: 704 Laine Blvd Clifton AZ 85533 Office: 55 N Coronado Blvd Clifton AZ 85533

WALDRIP, EDWINA (SALAZAR), social worker; b. Denver, Dec. 20, 1948; d. Rudolph Edward and Marie (Duran) Salazar; m. Cecil Mack Waldrip, Apr. 21, 1970; 1 child, Natalie. B of Social Work, Colo. State U., 1971; MSW, U. Denver, 1975. Clin. social worker S.E. Wyo. Mental Health Ctr., Cheyenne, 1972-81; pvt. practice social work Cheyenne, 1981-86; part-time instr. social work U. Wyo., Cheyenne, 1979-86, Laramie County Community Coll., Cheyenne, 1982-86; cons. S.E. Dialysis Unit, Cheyenne, 1983-86, Wyo. Home Health, Cheyenne, 1985-86, Luth. Health and Hosp., Wheatland, 1984-86. Bd dirs. YWCA-Rape Crisis Ctr., Cheyenne, 1977, Citizens for Mental Health Safe House, Cheyenne, 1979, Attention Home (Youth Crisis Ctr.), Cheyenne, 1985, Cath. Social Service, 1986. mem. Am. Assn. Marriage and Family Therapy (clin. pres. 1984-86), Nat. Assn. Social Workers (bd. dirs., pres. 1979, named Social Worker of Yr. 1980), Acad. Cert. Social Workers, Image De Cheyenne. Democrat. Avocations: cross country skiing, reading, walking. Home: 804 W Pershing Blvd Cheyenne WY 82001 Office: Bindschadler & Waldrip Assoc 502 E 19th St Cheyenne WY 82001

WALDROP, WILLIAM FRANKLIN, audiologist, speech pathologist, musician; b. Clayton, Ind., Aug. 2, 1905; s. Samuel DeForest and Maude Elenore (Wright) W.; m. Ruth Henry, Apr. 4, 1931 (dec.). BS, Millikin U., 1929; MA, U. Iowa, 1940. Tchr. music pub. high schs. Minn., Ill., Ind., 1929-39; instr. music Wesleyan Coll., Macon, Ga., 1940-42; with Ill. Regional Office VA, Chgo., 1946-50; dir. rehab. clinic Presbyn.-St. Luke's Hosp., Chgo., 1950-70; audiologist, speech pathologist Craw Meml. Hosp., Robinson, Ill., 1972-85; audiologist, speech pathologist Calif. Luth. Homes, Alhambra, 1985-86, retired, 1986, cons., 1986—. Co-author: Your New Voice, 1969 (Am. Cancer Soc. award 1970). Lodge: Masons. Avocations: music, electronics. Home: 2400 S Fremont Alhambra CA 91803

WALDSCHMIDT, PAUL EDWARD, clergyman; b. Evansville, Ind., Jan. 7, 1920; s. Edward Benjamin and Olga Marie (Moers) W. B.A., U. Notre Dame, 1942; student, Holy Cross Coll., Washington, 1942-45; S.T.L., Laval U., Que., Can., 1947; S.T.D., Angelicum U., Rome, Italy, 1948. Ordained priest Roman Catholic Ch., 1946; prof. apologetics and dogmatic theology Holy Cross Coll., 1949-55; v.p. U. Portland, 1955-62, dean faculties, 1956-60, pres., 1962-78; aux. bishop of Portland, 1978—; mem. NCCB Com. on Doctrine Bishops and Pres.'s; cons. Migration and Tourism; chmn. com. Sapientia Christiana. Mem. Cath. Theol. Soc. Am. (v.p. 1954-55), NEA, Delta Epsilon Sigma. Club: K.C. (4 deg.). Address: 5402 N Strong St Portland OR 97203

WALENDOWSKI, GEORGE JERRY, business management specialist, accounting educator; b. Han-Minden, W.Ger., Mar. 25, 1947; came to U.S., 1949; s. Stefan and Eugenia (Lewandowska) W. A.A., Los Angeles City Coll., 1968; BS, Calif. State U.-Los Angeles, 1970, MBA, 1972. Cert. community coll. instr. acctg. and mgmt., Calif. Acct., Union Oil Co. Calif., Los Angeles, 1972-76, data control supr., 1976-78, acctg. analyst, 1978-79; sr. fin. analyst Hughes Aircraft Co., El Segundo, Calif., 1979-83, fin. planning specialist, 1983-86; instr. bus. math. Los Angeles City Coll., 1976-80, instr. acctg., 1980—, mem. acctg. adv. com., 1984; bus. mgmt. specialist, 1986—. Contbr. articles to profl. jours. Softball co-organizer Precious Blood Ch., Los Angeles, 1979. Mem. Acad. Mgmt., Am. Acctg. Assn., Nat. Assn. Accts. (Robert Half Author's trophy Los Angeles chpt. 1980, cert. of appreciation 1980, 83, mem. Author's Circle 1980), Planning Forum (recognition award Los Angeles chpt. 1983), World Inst. Achievement, Beta Gamma Sigma. Republican. Roman Catholic. Home: 426 N Citrus Ave Los Angeles CA 90036 Office: Hughes Aircraft Co 2141 E Rosecrans El Segundo CA 90245

WALES, LARGO ANN, elementary education, special education and federal programs administrator; b. Seattle, July 22, 1948; d. Gilbert P. Wales and Mildred A. (Dooley) Shlosky. BA, Wash. State U., 1970; MA, U. Puget Sound, 1975; EdD, Seattle U., 1983. Cert. tchr., adminstr., supt., Wash. Nursery sch. dir. Clover Park Schs., Tacoma, 1969; tchr. Franklin Pierce Sch. Dist., Tacoma, 1970-79; prin. South Kitsap Sch. Dist., Port Orchard, Wash., 1979-82; dir. elem. and spl. edn. Auburn (Wash.) Sch. Dist., 1982—; adj. prof. Seattle Pacific U., 1980-84, Tacoma Community Coll., 1985—; chairperson spl. edn. adv. bd., Auburn, 1986. Author: Terry Tumbleweed, 1969. Chairperson United Way, Port Orchard, 1980, Sch. Levies, Tacoma and Port Orchard, 1977, 80. Named Outstanding Blue Bird Supporter, Camp Fire Girls, Washington, 1979, one of Outstanding Young Women in Am., 1983; Fulbright scholar U.S. Dept. Edn., 1987. Mem. Nat. Assn. for Supervision and Curriculum Devel., Wash. Assn. Sch. Adminstrs., Delta Kappa Gamma (Outstanding Woman Edn. Leader 1981). Home: 2910 28th St SE Auburn WA 98002 Office: Auburn Sch Dist 915 4th St NE Auburn WA 98002

WALKE, MARCIA GERRARD, advertising executive; b. Salt Lake City, Aug. 12, 1945; d. Theron (Jim) and Blanche (Robbins) Gerrard; m. William L. Walke, Nov. 6, 1966 (div. Apr. 1980); children: Kristia, Peter, Tiffany. Student, Knox Coll., 1963-65; BA, Westminster Coll., 1970; MFA, U. Utah, 1980. Advt. mgr. The Paris, Salt Lake City, 1970-72; freelance artist, writer Salt Lake City, 1972-74; writer, producer Collett Agy., Salt Lake City, 1979-80, art dir., 1980-81; exec. dir. Ten States Advt., Salt Lake City, 1981-86; dir. advt., mktg. Rick Warner Enterprises, Salt Lake City, 1986—; nat. mktg. dir. Taco Time Internat., Eugene, Oreg., 1984-85. Author (play) Ladies Night at the Orpheum, 1978 (Babcock Playwriting award U. Utah, 1978), The Nest, 1977. Bd. dirs. Salt Lake Acting Co., 1979-80; participant and local vol. State Dem. Conv., Salt Lake City, 1968; vol. Lalapalooza Children's Mus./Art Festival, Salt Lake City, 1978, 79, Sundance Playwright's Conf., Provo, Utah, 1984, Big Bros./Big Sisters, Salt Lake City, 1986; mem. Salt Lake Visitors and Conv. Bur. Mem. Utah Advt. Fedn., Salt Lake C. of C., U. Utah Alumni Group, Delta Delta Delta. Mormon. Avocations: scuba diving, skiing. Home: 7104 S Ponderosa Dr Salt Lake City UT 84121 Office: Rick Warner Ford 47 W 6th St Salt Lake City UT 84101

WALKER, ARNELL R., insurance executive; b. American Fork, Utah, Dec. 15, 1941; s. Thomas A. and Lucile (Allen) W.; m. Jaleen Jensen Walker, Nov. 20, 1962; children—J. Wallace. B.S., Utah State U., 1965. Tchr. Joint Sch. Dist. 150, Soda Springs, Idaho, 1966-72; safety mgr. B H & I Constrn. Co., Soda Springs, 1972-73; ins. agt., owner, mgr. Walker Ins., Soda Springs, 1973—. Mem. Soda Springs Bd. Edn., 1976-79, chmn., 1977-79; mem. Idaho Textbook Adoption Com., 1977-83, chmn., 1983. v.p. programs Tendoy area council Boy Scouts Am., 1982-84, council commr., 1984—, tng. com. Western region; comdr. Idaho Jeep Search and Rescue, 1973-74; mem. Caribou County Sheriff's Search and Rescue, 1968-77. Mormon. Lodge: Rotary (pres. Soda Springs chpt. 1985-86, dist. gov. rep. 1986-87, sec. 87—).

WALKER, BURTON LEITH, engineering writer, psychotherapist; b. Mt. Morris Twp., Mich., Oct. 23, 1927; s. Dalton Hugh and Muriel Joyce (Black) W.; m. Norva Jean Trochman, June 28, 1949; children—Paul, Cynthia Halverson, Mark; m. 2d, Carol Jean DeAndrea, July 31, 1982. Cert. psychology. tchr., lic. psychotherapist, hypnotherapist, Calif. A.A., Allan Hancock Coll., 1971; B.A., Chapman Coll., 1974, M.A., 1975. Contract estimator Ryan Aeronaut., San Diego, 1949-59; logistics rep. GD/A, San Diego, 1960-62; systems engr., cons. fgn. service Ralph M. Parsons, Los Angeles, 1962-68; lead engring. writer, sr. analyst Fed. Electric, Vandenberg AFB, Calif., 1969-86 ; psychotherapist St. Mary's Counseling Ctr., Lompoc, Calif., Employee Counseling Services, Vandenberg Village, Lamar Smith Counseling Ctr., Santa Maria, Calif., part time prof. Allan Hancock Coll., Santa Maria, Calif., small bus. owner 1974. Active Santa Ynez Valley Presbyn. Ch.; mem. Republican Nat. Com. Served with USN, 1946-48. Mem. Nat. Mgmt. Assn. (Outstanding Service award 1982), Am. Assn. Counseling and Devel., Calif. Assn. Marriage and Family Therapists, Solvang Bus. Assn., Assn. Advancement Ret. People. Republican. Home: 3149 Hwy 246 E Santa Ynez CA 93460

WALKER, DAVID RUDGER, horticulture educator; b. Ames, Iowa, Sept. 15, 1929; s. Rudger H. and Fawn L. (Davies) W.; m. Janee Smith; children: Brent, Steve, Ralph, Karen, Jan, Jill, Jennifer, Craig, Amy. BS, Utah State U., 1951, MS, 1952; PhD, Cornell U., 1955. Asst. prof. N.C. State U., Raleigh, 1955-58, assoc. prof., 1958-60; assoc. prof. Utah State U., Logan, 1960-65, prof. plant sci., 1965—; prin. horticulturist Coop. State Research Service, USDA, Washington, 1968-69. Contbr. numerous articles to profl. jours. Fellow AAAS (Pacific div. exec. bd. 1980-85, agr. com. 1979-86), Am. Soc. for Horticultural Sci. (bd. dirs. 1969-70). Mormon. Home: 429 Boulevard Logan UT 84321 Office: Utah State U Plant Sci Dept College Hill Logan UT 84322

WALKER, DEWARD EDGAR, JR., anthropologist, educator; b. Johnson City, Tenn., Aug. 3, 1935; s. Deward Edgar and Matilda Jane (Clark) W.; m. Candace A. Walker; children: Alice, Deward III, Mary Jane, Sarah, Daniel. Student, Eastern Oreg. Coll., 1953-54, 56-58, Mex. City Coll., 1958; BA in Anthropology with honors, U. Oreg., 1960-61, PhD in Anthropology, 1964; postgrad., Wash. State U., 1962. Asst. prof. anthropology George Washington U., Washington, 1964-65; asst. prof. anthropology Wash. State U., Pullman, 1965-67, research collaborator, 1967-69; assoc. prof., chmn. dept. sociology and anthropology, U. Idaho, Moscow, 1967-69; prof. U. Colo., Boulder, 1969—, research assoc. in population processes program of inst. behavioral sci., 1969-73, assoc. dean Grad. Sch., 1973-76; affiliate faculty U. Idaho, 1971—. Co-editor Northwest Anthropol. Research Notes, 1966—, editor, Plateau Vol: Handbook of North American Indians, 1971—; contbr. articles to profl. jours. Served with U.S. Army, 1954-62. Fellow NSF, 1961, NDEA, 1961-64. Fellow Am. Anthropol. Assn. (assoc. editor Am. Anthropologist 1973-74), Soc. Applied Anthropology (life, exec. com. 1970-79, treas. 1976-79, chmn. High Plains Regional sect. 1980-82, cons., expert witness tribes of N.W., editor Human Orgn. 1970-76); mem. AAAS, Am. Acad. Polit. Social Scis., Northwest Anthropol. Conf. Avocations: geology, mining. Home: PO Box 4147 Boulder CO 80306 Office: U Colo Dept Anthropology Box 233 Boulder CO 80309

WALKER, DONALD IRVING, chemist, association executive; b. Lombard, Ill., Jan. 13, 1922; s. George B. and Grace (Patrick) W.; B.S., U. Ill., 1948; Ph.D., U. Colo., 1956; m. Ruth Ellen Rouley, Feb. 15, 1944; children—Judith Elyn, Marc Stephen, David Lee. Research chemist Los Alamos Sci. Lab., 1950-53; teaching asst. U. Colo., 1953-56; dep. dir. health and safety div. AEC, Idaho Falls, Idaho, 1956-57, dir. licensee compliance div., 1957-62, dir. region IV div. compliance, Denver, 1957-62, dir. region IV div. compliance, 1962-70, dir. health services lab., Idaho Falls, 1970-76; exec. dir. Associated Western Univs., Inc., Salt Lake City, 1976—. Served with C.E., AUS, 1942-46. Mem. Am. Chem. Soc., Internat. Health Physics Soc., Am. Inst. Chemists. Home: 2609 E Sundance Dr Sandy UT 84092 Office: Assoc Western Univs Inc 142 E 200 South Salt Lake City UT 84111

WALKER, DUANE DENNIS, nursing adminstr., educator; b. Waterloo, Iowa, July 28, 1938; s. Robert T. and Margery E. (Hoppe) W.; children—Geoffrey, Robyn, Troy. B.S., Weber State Coll., 1969; M.S. in Psycho-Social Nursing, U. Utah, 1977. R.N., 1963. Instr., Weber State Coll., 1968-70, clin. instr. nursing, 1972-78; dir. clin. services Weber County Hosp., Roy, Utah, 1968-70; asst. adminstr., dir. nursing service Holy Cross Hosp., Salt Lake City, 1970-75; asst. adminstr., patient care service U. Utah Med. Ctr., 1975-78; clin. prof. dept. biol. dysfunctions U. Calif.-San Francisco, 1979—; assoc. adminstr. hosp., dir. nursing service Stanford U., 1978-85, lectr. dept. family, community and preventive medicine, 1979—; v.p. patient services Queen's Med. Ctr., Honolulu, 1985—; clin. prof. sch. nursing U. Hawaii, 1987—; mem. Hawaii State Council on Mental Health and Abuse, 1987—; bd. dirs. Hospice Hawaii. Bd. dirs. Lytton Gardens, 1981-82. Served with Nurse Corps, U.S. Army, 1966-68. Fellow Am. Acad. Nursing; mem. Nat. League Nursing, Am. Nurses Assn., Am. Hosp. Assn., Sigma Theta Tau (Media award). Republican. Roman Catholic. Contbr. articles to profl. jours. Home: 4358 Royal Pl Honolulu HI 96816 Office: The Queen's Med Ctr 1301 Punchbowl St Honolulu HI 96813

WALKER, DUNCAN EDWARD, air force officer; b. Washington, Aug. 2, 1942; s. Edward John and Katherine Edith (Duncan) W. BA in Indsl. Psychology, N.Mex. State U., 1965; MS in Systems Mgmt., U. So. Calif., 1978; MPA, Golden Gate U., 1980. Commd. 2d lt. USAF, 1965, advanced through grades to lt. col., 1981; grad. Squadron Officers Sch., 1973, Air Command and Staff Coll., 1974, Indsl. Coll. Armed Forces, 1977; chief devel. and deployment br. ICBM requirements SAC, Offutt AFB, Nebr., 1981-84; dep. for ICBM ops. and evaluation Air Force Operational Test and Evaluation Ctr., Vandenberg AFB, Calif., 1984—. Decorated Bronze Star, Meritorious Service medal with one oak leaf cluster, Air Force Commendation medal with three oak leaf clusters. Mem. Air Force Assn., Mental Health Assn., Mil. Order of World Wars, Am. Legion. Democrat. Methodist. Lodge: Elks. Home: 113 N Y St Lompoc CA 93436 Office: AFOTEC/OL-BC Vandenberg AFB CA 93437

WALKER, ELJANA M. DU VALL, civic worker; b. France, Jan. 18, 1924; came to U.S., 1948; naturalized, 1954; student Med. Inst., U. Paris, 1942-47; m. John S. Walker, Jr., Dec. 31, 1947; children—John, Peter, Barbara. Pres., Loyola Sch. PTA, 1958-59; bd. dirs. Santa Calus shop, 1959-73; treas. Archdiocese Denver Catholic Women, 1962-64; rep. Cath. Parent-Tchr League, 1962-65; pres. Aux. Denver Gen. Hosp., 1966-69; precinct committeewoman Arapahoe County Republican Women's Com., 1973-74; mem. reelection com. Arapahoe County Rep. Party, 1973-78, Reagan election com., 1980; block worker Arapahoe County March of Dimes, Heart Assn., Hemophilia Drive, Muscular Dystrophy and Multiple Sclerosis Drive, 1978-

81. Recipient Distinguished Service award Am.-by-choice, 1966; named to Honor Roll, ARC, 1971. Mem. Cherry Hills Symphony, Lyric Opera Guild, Alliance Franciase (life mem.), ARC, Civic Ballet Guild (life mem.), Needlework Guild Am. (v.p. 1980-82), Kidney Found. (life), Denver Art Mus., U. Denver Art and Conservation Assns. (chmn. 1980-82), U. Denver Women's Library Assn., Chancellors Soc. Roman Catholic. Clubs: Union (Chgo.); Denver Athletic, 26 (Denver); Welcome to Colo. Internat. Address: 6185 S Columbine Way Littleton CO 80121

WALKER, FRANCIS JOSEPH, lawyer; b. Tacoma, Aug. 5, 1922; s. John McSweeney and Sarah Veronica (Meechan) W.; m. Julia Corinne O'Brien, Jan. 27, 1951; children—Vincent Paul, Monica Irene Hylton, Jill Marie Nudell, John Michael, Michael Joseph, Thomas More. B.A., St. Martin's Coll., 1947; J.D., U. Wash., 1950. Bar: Wash. Asst. atty. gen. State of Wash., 1950-51; sole practice, Olympia, Wash., 1951—; gen. counsel Wash. Cath. Conf., 1967-76. Served to lt. (j.g.) USNR, 1943-46; PTO. Home: 2723 Hillside Dr Olympia WA 98501 Office: 203 E 4th Ave Suite 301 Olympia WA 98501

WALKER, HAROLD EMMETT, accountant; b. Columbus, Ga., Nov. 27, 1932; s. Emmett Boyd and Grace Truman (Wadsworth) W.; m. Janice Carter, June 9, 1956; children: Mark Jackson, Margaret Anne. BBA, U. Tenn., 1954. With audit staff Ernst & Whinney, Knoxville, Tenn., 1954-66; ptnr. Ernst & Whinney, Miami, Fla., 1966-71; mng. ptnr. Ernst & Whinney, Ft. Lauderdale, Fla., 1971-76, Miami, 1976-84, Honolulu, 1984—. Pres. Broward County United Way, Ft. Lauderdale, 1975; pres. Citizens Bd. U. Miami, 1979-80, trustee, 1980-81; mem. exec. com. Miami Citizens Against Crime, 1982-84; vice chmn. Econ. Devel. Corp. of Honolulu. Mem. Am. Inst. CPA's (nat. council 1977-82), Fla. Inst. CPA's (pres. 1977-78), Nat. Assn. Accts. (pres. Knoxville chpt. 1982), Greater Miami C. of C. (vice chmn. 1981-84). Republican. Congregationalist. Clubs: Oahu Country, Waialae Country, Pacific, Plaza, Miami (pres. 1981). Home: 1733 Kumakani Loop Honolulu HI 96821 Office: Ernst & Whinney 2400 Pauahi Tower Honolulu HI 96813

WALKER, HENRY ALEXANDER, JR., corporation executive; b. Honolulu, Mar. 5, 1922; s. H. Alexander and Una (Craig) W.; m. Nancy Johnston, Mar. 10, 1946; children: Henry Alexander III, Susan Walker Kowen. Student, Harvard U., 1940-42, Columbia U., 1946-47. With AMFAC, Inc., Honolulu, 1947—, v.p., ops., 1966, exec. v.p., 1966-67, pres., 1967-74, chief exec. officer, chmn. bd., 1974-78, chmn., chief exec. officer, pres., 1978-83, chmn., 1983—; bd. dirs. Hawaiian Telephone Co., Gulf Westerns, Inc. Bd. dirs. Hawaii Maritime Ctr., Straub Found., East-West Ctr. Found., Aloha United Way; mem. adv. bd. U. Hawaii Coll. Bus. Adminstrn.; mem. dean's adv. bd. Chaminade U. Sch. Bus. Served with USNR, 1944-46. Mem. Hawaiian Sugar Planters Assn. Clubs: Pacific Union (San Francisco); Phoenix S.K, Massachusetts, Harvard (N.Y.C.); Pacific, Waialae Country, Oahu Country (Honolulu). Office: Amfac Inc PO Box 3230 Honolulu HI 96801 also: Amfac Inc 44 Montgomery St San Francisco CA 94104 *

WALKER, HENRY GARY, real estate developer, management executive; b. Alta., Can., Oct. 1, 1921; s. Henry and Amalia (Nagel) W.; m. Alma Jane Eichinger, Oct. 1, 1951; children—Cynthia Louise, Henry Gary III, Catherine Ann. Ed. pub. schs. Photographer Silver Screen mag., 1939-41, San Francisco Examiner, 1941; White House photographer Life mag., 1949-59; fgn. corr. in Life mag., Berlin, U.K., Paris, Japan and Korea, 1948, 51, 60; with Curtis Pub. Co., 1962-65, mem. editorial bd., 1963-65, mng. dir. Photography, 1963-65; asst. mng. editor Sat. Eve. Post, 1962-65; pres. Walker Broadcasting Co., Ft. Pierce, Fla.; owner radio sta. WARN AM-FM, 1965-68; coordinator Manned Spaceflight Still Photo Pool, Cocoa Beach, Fla., 1965-68; sr. v.p. C.V.R. Industries, Inc.; pres. Scottie Craft Boat Corp. Am., 1968-72, Congress Industries; v.p., dir. Outdoor Supply Corp., Servinational Inc., 1972-79; owner I&W Properties Ltd., 1972-84, W & W Properties Ltd., 1984—. Served with USMCR, World War II. Home: 1424 W 28th St Sunset Island I Miami Beach FL 33140 Office: 20340 NE 15th Ct Miami FL 33179

WALKER, HENRY GILBERT, healthcare executive, consultant; b. Gowanda, N.Y., Feb. 16, 1947; s. Henry George and Grace Dayton (Moore) W.; m. Elaine Ruth Darbee, July 18, 1970 (div. Dec. 1979); 1 child, Matthew Case; m. Patricia Ann Andrade, May 14, 1983; children: Michael David, Christopher John. B.S. in Indsl. Engring., Cornell U., 1969; M.B.A., U. Chgo., 1975. Evening adminstr. Rush-Presbyn. St.-Luke's Med. Ctr., Chgo., 1973-75; mgmt. cons. Booz, Allen & Hamilton, Chgo., 1975-79; regional adminstr., v.p. S.W. Community Health Service, Albuquerque, 1979-83; adminstr., v.p. S.W. Community Health Service, 1983-86, v.p., 1986—; exec. v.p. Presbyn. Healthcare Services, Albuquerque, 1986—; dir. Centro Compesino de Salud, Española, N.Mex., Hosp. Home Health Care, Albuquerque. Campaign mgr. United Fund, Newport, R.I., 1971, 72; bd. dirs. Park Dist., Elmhurst, Ill., 1978, 79; mem. Dist. III Community Action Com., Albuquerque, 1985; area dir. United Way of Albuquerque., 1985. Recipient Hosp. Survey award U. Chgo., 1975, Bachmeyer award U. Chgo., 1975, Outstanding Midshipman award Cornell U., 1969; named one of Emerging Healthcare Leaders, Hosp. Forum Mag., 1985, 86. Mem. Am. Coll. Healthcare Execs.; Healthcare Fin. Mgmt. Assn., Am. Hosp. Assn., N.Mex. Hosp. Assn. (bd. dirs. 1983—). Democrat. Presbyterian. Avocations: reading; hiking; skiing; tennis.

WALKER, JAMES LEE, computer systems engineer; b. Washington, May 27, 1946; s. Lee Board and Helen Irene (Browning) W.; m. Sherri Lucille Owens, Mar. 18, 1967; children: Wendy Lee, Vaughn Christian, Joshua David. Student Ozark Bible Coll., 1964-65, U. Mo., Rolla, 1965-66, No. Va. Community Coll., 1970-72, U. Colo., Colorado Springs, 1976-79. Computer maintenance technician Philco-Ford Corp., Arlington, Va., 1970-72, tchr. computer theory, Colorado Springs, 1973-74, test writer, condr., supr., 1974-80; systems engr. Ford Aerospace and Communications Corp., Colorado Springs, 1980-83, mgr. test and integration, 1984-85, engring. supr. large space systems test and integration group, 1985—. Choir dir. Security Christian Ch., Colorado Springs, 1976-84, tchr., 1976-84. Served with USAF, 1966-70. Home: 1006 De La Vista Pl Widefield CO 80911 Office: Ford Aerospace & Communications Corp 10440 State Hwy 83 Colorado Springs CO 80908

WALKER, JAMES LYNWOOD, seminary group president. B.A., N.Carolina Central U., 1963; M.Div., Pacific Sch. Religion, 1967; Ph.D. Grad. Theol. Union/U. Calif.-Berkeley, 1970. Assoc. prof., asst. dean Grad. Theol. Union, 1970-73; exec. dir. Pastoral Inst. of Wash./Ida., 1973-78; pastor Magnolia Presbyn. Ch., Seattle, 1979-81; interim pastor Newport Presbyn. Ch., Bellevue, Wash., 1981-82; pres. Northwest Theol. Union, Seattle, 1984—; cons., therapist, 1982-84. Author: Body and Soul: Gestalt Therapy and Religious Experience, 1971; editor: Agendas for Black Churches, 1985. Office: Northwest Theol Union 914 E Jefferson St Seattle WA 98122 *

WALKER, JOHN DAVIES, agronomy educator, researcher, consultant; b. Logan, Utah, Apr. 26, 1941; s. Rudger Harper and Fawn Lucile (Davies) W.; m. Sharon Lee Powers, Sept. 12, 1961; children: Suzanne Rachel, Michael Powers. BS, Brigham Young U., 1963; PhD, U. Ill.-Urbana, 1973. Tchr. sci. pub. high schs., Salt Lake City, 1965-69; asst. prof. agronomy Ohio State U., 1973-76; prof. agronomy, chmn. dept. farm crops mgmt. Ricks Coll., 1976—; adj. prof. agronomy Brigham Young U., 1981—; seasonal researcher on range revegetation U.S. Forest Service, Utah, 1961-69; cons. in field; bd. dirs. Eastern Idaho Agrl. Hall of Fame, 1977—; producer, bd. dirs. ann. Idaho Field Days on Reduced Tillage Techniques; nat. and internat. speaker on reduced tillage; pres. Bd. Idaho Agrl. Hall of Fame, 1987. Author papers in field of agronomy. Served with U.S. Army N.G., 1963. Recipient Teaching award Ohio State U. Agrl. Tech. Inst., 1976, Teaching award Ricks Coll., 1979, Disting. Faculty award Ricks Coll., 1986, Disting. Service award Idaho Wheat Commn., 1986, 50th Yr. Anniversary award U.S. Soil Conservation Service; Farmer Merchant Speaker award Rexburg (Idaho) C. of C., 1977; agrl. chem. cos. grantee, 1974—; Idaho Wheat Commn. grantee, 1979—. Mem. Am. Soc. Agronomy, Soil Sci. Soc. Am., Crop Sci. Soc. Am., Weed Sci. Soc. Am. Republican. Mormon.inimum tillage wheat and barley prodn. Office: Ricks Coll Dept Farm Crops Rexburg ID 83440

WALKER, JOSEPH ROBERT, neurosurgeon; b. Atlantic City, N.J., Mar. 2, 1942; s. Joseph West and Helen (Mendte) W.; m. Mary Cynthia Long, Aug. 23, 1968; children: Joseph West II, Scott Robert, Heather Elizabeth. BS, St. Josephs Coll., 1964; MD, Creighton U., 1968. Diplomate Am. Bd. Neurol. Surgery. Intern Atlantic City (N.J.) Hosp., 1968-69; resident surgery Jefferson Med. Coll. Hosp., Phila, 1969-70; resident neurosurgery U. N.C., Chapel Hill, 1972-76, fellow, instr. neurosurgery, 1976-77; chief neurosurgery Washoe Med. Ctr., Reno, Nev., 1982, St. Mary's Hosp., Reno, 1982; asst. prof. U. Nev. Med. Sch., Reno, 1979—. Served as lt. comdr. USN, 1970-72. Office: 85 Kirman Reno NV 89502

WALKER, KEITH ALLEN, plant genetics company executive; b. Cleve., Oct. 17, 1948; s. Joseph Fordun and Audrey Marie (Brindley) W.; m. Marguerite Joyce Ming, Aug. 29, 1970; children—Kenneth Alec, Andrew Fordun. B.A., Coll. of Wooster, 1970; Ph.D., Yale U., 1974. Sr. research biologist Monsanto Chem. Co., St. Louis, 1974-76, research group leader, 1976-79, sr. research group leader, 1979-81; dir. product devel. Plant Genetics, Inc., Davis, Calif., 1981-82, v.p. research, dir. 1982—. Mem. Am. Soc. Plant Physiologists, Am. Soc. Agronomy, Soc. Devel. Biology, Am. Bot. Soc., Sigma Xi. Contbr. articles, chpts. to tech. jours., books. Office: Plant Genetics Inc 1930 5th St Davis CA 95616

WALKER, LELAND JASPER, civil engineer; b. Fallon, Nev., Apr. 18, 1923; s. Albert Willard and Grayce (Wilkinson) W.; m. Margaret Frances Noble, Jan. 21, 1946; children: Thomas, Margaret, Timothy. B.S. in Civil Engring, Iowa State U., 1944; D. Eng. (hon.), Mont. State U., 1983. Engr. with various govtl. depts. 1946-51, 53-55; v.p. Wenzel & Co. (cons. engrs.), Great Falls, Mont., 1955-58; pres., chmn. bd. No. Engring. and Testing, Inc., Great Falls, 1958—; v.p., dir. Service Corp. Mont.; pres. Ind. Labs. Assurance Co., 1977-79; v.p. Accrediting Bd. for Engring. and Tech., 1978-79, pres., 1980-83; dir. Great Falls Savs. & Loan Assn., Mont. Power Co., Sletten Constrn. Co., Entech Inc., TLC Co.,Danforth Instruments Co., also vice-chmn. Pres., trustee Endowment and Research Found., Mont. State U., 1969-82, Mont. Deaconess Hosp., Great Falls, 1959-67; trustee Mont. Sch. for Deaf and Blind Found., 1984—; trustee Rocky Mountain Coll., 1977-80, Dufresne Found., 1979—; chmn., dir. Mont. Tech. Services Adv. Council; mem. Engring. Coll. adv. council Mont. State U.; bd. visitors Engring. Coll. U. Calif., Davis; bd. dirs. Mont. State Fair, Engring. Socs. Commn. on Energy, 1977-79, Mont. Bd. Sci. and Tech., 1983—, Nat. Ctr. for Policy Analysis for Acid Rain, 1985—. Served with USNR, 1943-46, 51-53. Fellow ASCE (pres. 1976-77), Cons. Engrs. Council (pre. Mont. 1971), AAAS; mem. Nat. Acad. Engring., Am. Council Ind. Labs. (sec. 1973-76), Chi Epsilon (hon.), Tau Beta Pi (hon.). Republican. Methodist. Clubs: Montana, Meadowlark Country, Black Eagle Country. Lodge: Kiwanis (pres. Great Falls 1970). Home: 2819 8th Ave S Great Falls MT 59405 Office: 528 Smelter Ave PO Box 951 Great Falls MT 59403

WALKER, RAYMOND FRANCIS, business and financial consulting company executive; b. Medicine Lake, Mont., Nov. 9, 1914; s. Dennis Owen and Rose (Long) W.; m. Patricia K. Blakey, May 15, 1951; children: Richard A., Mark D., Maxie R. Forest, Victoria L. Le Huray, Suzanne J. Buhl, Tracy A. Grad. pub. schs.; student, Edison Vocat. Sch., 1935-39. Truck mgr. Pacific Food Products, Seattle, 1939-42; machinist Todd Shipyard, Seattle, 1943-45; owner Delbridge Auto Sales, Seattle, 1945-48; pres. Pacific Coast Acceptance Corp., 1949-60; v.p. West Coast Mortgage, Seattle, 1960-67, United Equities Corp., Seattle, 1965-69; pres. Income Mgmt. Corp., Seattle, 1970-87; v.p. Internat. Mint and Foundry, Redmond, Wash., 1983—; cons. Life Ins. Co. Am., Consumer Loan Service. Mem. Nat. Assn. Security Dealers. Methodist. Lodge: Elks. Home: 777 W Sequin Bay Rd Sequim WA 98382

WALKER, RICHARD FRANK, utility company executive; b. 1924; married. BEE, U. Colo., 1949. With Pub. Service Co. of Colo., Denver, 1949—, mgr. planning and analysis, 1964-66, asst. v.p. engring., 1966-68, v.p. engring. and planning elec. dept., 1968-76, pres., chief operating officer, 1976-78, pres., chief exec. officer, 1978-86, chmn., chief exec. officer, 1986—, also bd. dirs. Served with U.S. Army, 1943-46. Office: Pub Service Co of Colo 550 15th St PO Box 840 Denver CO 80202

WALKER, ROBERT EDWIN, protective services official; b. Calgary, Alta., Can., July 13, 1929; s. Edwin Maxwell and Winnifred Isabel Walker; m. Geraldine Sullivan, May 19, 1951; 1 child, Christine Hegi. Diploma in pub. adminstrn., Mt. Royal Coll. Adminstrn., U. Calgary., 1968. Firefighter Calgary Fire Dept., 1951-64, lt., 1964-68, capt., 1968-79, dep. chief, 1979-82; fire chief Dist. North Vancouver, B.C., Can., 1982-84, Edmonton Fire Dept., Alta., 1984—. Past mem. City of Calgary Exhbn. and Stampede Bd., Mount Royal Coll. Adminstrv. Studies Exec. Bd.; mem. med. tech. adv. bd. So. Alta. Inst. Tech. Served with RCAF, 1947-49. Mem. Internat. Assn. Fire Chiefs (urban com.), Can. Assn. Fire Chiefs (joint stats. com.), Alta. Provincial Assn. Fire Chiefs (bd. dirs.), Fire Marshal's Assn. N.Am., Edmonton C. of C., Inst. Pub. Adminstrn. Can., Nat. Fire Protection Assn. (past bd. dirs. fire service sect.), Calgary Firefighters' Credit Union (past pres.), Gyro Internat. (past dir. Calgary/Vancouver chpts.), So. Alta. Pioneers Assn., Lighthouse Keepers Soc. Edmonton, Tree Planters Soc. Edmonton, Edmonton Klondike Days Assn. (bd. dirs.). Conservative. Anglican. Lodges: Masons, KT, Shriners. Home: 2302 10011 123 St, Edmonton Can T5N 1M9 Office: City of Edmonton Fire Dept, 10351 96th St, Edmonton, AB Canada T5H 2H5

WALKER, ROBIN DEE, chemical technician; b. Iowa City, Nov. 23, 1948; d. Robert Cornelius and Dorothy (Ellen) Russell; m. Thomas Eugene Walker, Sept. 23, 1973. BA in Gen. Sci., U. Iowa, 1972. Biochem. technician U. Iowa, Iowa City, 1971-73; chem. technician Los Alamos (N.Mex.) Nat. Lab, 1976—. Co-author: Coal Science and Chemistry, 1986; also articles. Mem. Am. Chem. Soc. (sec. tech. affiliate group 1986—), N.Mex. Women in Sci. Republican. Methodist. Home: 65 Kachina Los Alamos NM 87544 Office: Los Alamos Nat Lab MS K484 Los Alamos NM 87545

WALKER, WALTER WYRICK, metallurgical engineer; b. Winslow, Ariz., Jan. 14, 1924; s. John Edward and Sadie Theresa (Moore) W.; B.S., U. Ariz., 1950, M.Sc. (NDEA fellow 1959-62), 1962, Ph.D. (NSF fellow 1966-67), 1968; Ph.D. (hon.), U. Phys. Sci., 1958; m. Frances Ellen Sprawls, Jan. 16, 1952. Metall. engr., chemist in automotive, nuclear energy and aerospace field, 35 yrs.; group leader metall. tech. Hughes Aircraft Co., Tucson, 1978-82, staff engr., 1982-84, sr. staff engr., 1984-86, sr. scientist, 1986—; mem. part-time and full-time faculty various univs. Mem. Pima County Pollution Control Hearing Bd., 1979—, Tucson Adv. Com. on Air Pollution, 1970-72. Served with USNR, World War II. Registered profl. engr., Ariz., Calif. Fellow Am. Inst. Chemists, AIME, Am. Soc. Metals, Nat. Soc. Profl. Engrs., AAAS, ASTM, Am. Geophys. Union, Am. Optical Soc., Nat. Assn. Corrosion Engrs., Ariz. Acad. Scis., N.Y. Acad. Scis., Brit. Inst. Metals, Mensa. German Shepherd Dog Club, So. Ariz. Rescue Assn., Sigma Xi. Democrat. Club: So. Ariz. Hiking. Author papers in field. Home: 5643 E 7th St Tucson AZ 85711 Office: Hughes Aircraft Co Bldg 802 M/SC-8 Tucson AZ 85734

WALL, BRIAN RAYMOND, research forest economist; b. Tacoma, Wash., Jan. 26, 1940; s. Raymond Perry and Mildred Beryl (Pickert) W.; m. Joan Marie Nero, Sept. 1, 1962; children—Torden Erik, Kirsten Noel. B.S., U. Wash., 1962; M.F., Yale U., 1964. Forestry asst. Weyerhaeuser Timber Co., Klamath Falls, Oreg., 1960; inventory forester West Tacoma Newsprint, 1961-62; timber sale compliance forester Dept. Nat. Resources, Kelso, Wash., 1963; research forest economist Pacific N.W. Forest and Range Experiment Station, U.S. Dept. Agr. Forest Service, Portland, Oreg., 1964—; co-founder, bd. dirs. Cordero Youth Care Ctr., 1970-81; cons. to govt. agys., Congress univs., industry; freelance photographer. Co-author: An Analysis of the Timber Situation in the United States, 1982; contbr. articles, reports to profl. publs., newspapers; staff photographer Soccer Am. mag. Interviewed and cited by nat. and regional news media. Recipient Cert. of Merit U.S. Dept. Agr. Forest Service, 1982. Mem. Soc. Am. Foresters (chmn. Portland chpt. 1973, Forester of Yr. 1975), Conf. of Western Forest Economists (treas. 1982—), Zeta Psi. Home: 7155 SW Alden St Portland OR 97223 Office: USDA Forest Service Pacific Northwest Research Sta PO Box 3890 Portland OR 97208

WALL, FRANCIS JOSEPH, statistical consultant; b. Moss Point, Miss., Mar. 22, 1927; s. Thomas J. and Nina B. (Brewer) W.; m. B. Jean, Apr. 15, 1950; children: David W., Karen S., Leslie J. BS, Sul Ross State U., 1947; MS, U. Colo., 1956; PhD, U. Minn., 1961. Statistician Dow Chem. Co., Boulder, Colo., 1952-57, Sperry Univac, St. Paul, 1957-61, Dikewood Corp., Albuquerque, 1961-69, Lovelace Found., Albuquerque, 1969-71; pvt. practice cons. Albuquerque, 1972—. Author: Statistical Data Analysis Handbook, 1986. Mem. Am. Statis. Assn., Biometric Soc., Sigma Xi. Republican. Mem. United Ch. of Christ. Home and Office: 290 Alamosa Rd NW Albuquerque NM 87107

WALL, LLOYD L., geological engineer; b. Jerome, Idaho, Feb. 2, 1936; s. Lloyd and Ola (Buck) W.; m. Myrna Bradshaw, Aug. 25, 1954; children: Jeffrey B., Julie, Neil S., Charlene, Gail, Matthew W., Suzzane, Michael L., Connie. AS, Coll. Eastern Utah, 1956; BS in Geology, Brigham Young U., 1958. Pres., owner Cons. Geologist, Salt Lake City and Brigham City, 1958—; plant mgr. Thiokol, Brigham City, Utah, 1958-66; mgr. ops. Sealcraft, Sal Lake City, 1966-68; mgr. programs Eaton-Kenway, Bountiful, Utah, 1968-76; pres., owner HydraPak, Inc., Salt Lake City, 1976—; pres. Kolt Mining Co., Salt Lake City, 1979—. Vol. tchr. Alta Acad., Salt Lake City, 1983—. Served as sgt. N.G., 1954-62. Mem. Geol. Soc. Am., Utah Geol. Assn. Republican. Mormon. Avocations: hunting, fishing, mountain climbing, photography. Home: 2180 East Clayborne Ave Salt Lake City CA 84109

WALL, MARK GEORGE, association administrator; b. Lawndale, Calif., Mar. 12, 1956; s. Samuel Garrett and Dorothy Lucille (Cerny) W. Grad., Calif. Scholastic Press Assn., Nat. Coop. Devel. Tng., USDA, Pierce Coll., 1976, El Camino Coll., 1978. Mgr. Gardena (Calif.) Cert. Farmers' Market, 1979-81; coordinator Southland Farmers' Market Assn., Los Angeles, 1981—; Founder Calif. Direct Mktg. Assn., 1981—; organizer Nat. Dir. Mktg. Conf., Des Moines, 1986. Author: Farmer's Guide, 1983; editor: Managing a Farmers' Market, 1981; contbr. articles to profl. jours. Antihunger grantee Kenny and Marianne Rogers, Los Angeles County Fair grantee, 1984; recipient mgr. award, Outstanding Exhibit, 1982. Mem. Calif. Assn. Family Farmers, Sustainable Agriculture Famers Adv. Bd. Univ. Calif. Coop. Extension. Avocations: beekeeping, toy bank collecting, backpacking, genealogy. Home: 14806 Osage Ave Lawndale CA 90260 Office: Southland Farmers Market Assn 1010 S Flower Suite 402 Los Angeles CA 90015

WALL, RICHARD VERN, corporate executive; b. Ogden, Utah, Nov. 22, 1932; s. Ernest Vern and Naomi (Allred) W.; m. Joyce Bartschi, June 13, 1962; children: Rebecca, Matthew, Timothy, Christopher, Judson, Heather, Jennifer, Rachel, Emily. AB in Architecture, Columbia U., 1954; BFA in Arch., U. Utah, 1961, MA in French Lang. and History, 1963; PhD in French lang. and lit., Mich. State U., 1971; postgrad., Johns Hopkins U., 1976, U.S. Naval War Coll., 1980. Missionary France, Belgium; br. and dist. pres., supervising elder Ch. Jesus Christ of Latter-day Saints, 1956-59; draftsman, asst. constrn. adminstr., constrn. adminstr. Ashton, Evans & Brazier Architects and Engrs., Salt Lake City, 1959-63; teaching asst. U. Utah, Salt Lake City, 1959-63; draftsman, job capt. Warren Holmes Co. Architects and Engrs., Lansing, Mich., 1964-65; instr. Mich. State U., East Lansing, 1965-67; lectr., chmn. French dept. Ind. Purdue U., Ft. Wayne, 1967-71, asst. prof., 1971, acting chmn. dept. modern fgn. langs., 1972-73; constrn. adminstr. Archonics Corp. Architects and Engrs., Ft. Wayne, 1972, Lee and Assocs. Architects and Engrs., Cleve., 1973-77; project dir., assoc. Louis Petro & Assocs., Ft. Wayne, 1981-82; cons., draftsman Irmscher & Sons Gen. Contractors, Ft. Wayne, 1982-83; dir. govt. programs Shipley Assocs., Bountiful, Utah, 1983—. Contbr. articles to profl. jours. Bishop Ft. Wayne First Ward Mormon Ch., 1977-82. Served to capt. USNR, 1954-56, ret., 1984. Recipient Mich. State Teaching award, 1967, Ind. U.-Purdue U. Outstanding Tchr. award, 1980; nominated Danforth Teaching Assn., 1981; Columbia Coll. nat. scholar, 1950-54; grantee Mich. State U., 1965-66; Ind. U., 1969, 76, NEH, 1976; fellow Ind. U., 1973, 78;. Mem. Am. Assn. Tchrs. Frech, Am. Council on Teaching Fgn. Langs., Deseret Lang. and Linguistic Soc., Soc. Mil. Engrs., Am. Soc. Tng. and Devel., Phi Sigma Iota. Republican. Home: 447 E 1700 S Bountiful UT 84010 Office: Shipley Assocs 390 N Main Bountiful UT 84010

WALL, ROBERT THOMAS, restaurant and hotel executive, chartered accountant; b. London, Oct. 21, 1932; came to Can., 1942; s. Cyril Edward and Mary Agnes (Christie) W.; m. Thelma Gertrude Lorne, Nov. 20, 1955; children—Kevin, Leslie Anne, Jennifer, John. Self-employed income tax cons., Vancouver, B.C., 1957-62; v.p. White Spot Restaurant, Vancouver, 1962-68; pres. Acadia Mgmt. Corp. Ltd., Vancouver, 1969-86; with Dorchester Hotels, Ltd., 1986—; dir. Circe Enterprises Ltd., Vancouver, 1977—, Village Carvery Rstaurant, Vancouver, 1982—. Author: (video tapes) Photography Techniques, 1982. Mem. Inst. Chartered Accts. Ont. and B.C. Conservative. Anglican. Club: Terminal City, Arbutus (Vancouver) (pres. 1984). Lodge: Masons. Home: 3122 O'Hara Ln, Crescent Beach, BC Canada V4A 3E7 Office: Dorchester Hotels Ltd, 320-1675 W 8th Ave, Vancouver, BC Canada V6J 1V2

WALL, RONALD WILLIAM, economist, consultant; b. Providence, May 5, 1944; s. Frederick Raymond and Rose Marion (Rooney) W.; m. Regina Christine Staud, June 7, 1969 (div. Sept. 1978); 1 child, Jamie Travis; m. Charlene Yap Simpson, July 7, 1985. Student, Cath. U., 1963-66; BA, U. Md., 1967, MA, 1974; PhD, Kans. State U., 1981. Tchr. McNamara High Sch., Forestville, Md., 1969-72; asst. prof. N.Mex. State U., Las Cruces, 1978-82; family econ. specialist Coop. Extension Service U. Hawaii, Honolulu, 1982—, chmn. dept. Human Resources, 1984-85. Author: (booklet) Calculating Your Finances, 1984; also articles. Tutor ESL Hawaii Literacy program, Honolulu, 1984-85. Mem. Hawaii Council on Family Relations (v.p. 1983-84, pres. 1985—), Hawaii Home Econ. Assn. (bd. dirs.), Am. Home Econ. Assn., Am. Council on Consumer Interests, Nat. Council on Family Relations, Omicron Nu, Gamma Sigma Delta. Avocations: golf, tennis, jogging, reading, travel. Office: U Hawaii Dept Human Resources Miller 10 Honolulu HI 96822

WALLACE, ARTHUR, agricultural educator; b. Bear River City, Utah, Jan. 4, 1919; s. James Newton and Clara Caroline (Mackay) W.; m. Elna Kemp, Apr. 16, 1943; children: Garn, Loretta, Marlin, Scott. BS, Utah State U., 1943; PhD, Rutgers U., 1949. Asst. prof. biomed. and environ. scis. UCLA, 1949-56, assoc. prof., 1956-62, prof., 1962—. Contbr. numerous articles to profl. jours. Served to sgt. U.S. Army, 1943-46. Fellow Am. Soc. Agronomy, Soil Sci. Soc. Am., Crop Sci. Soc. Am.; mem. Am. Soc. Hort. Sci., Am. Soc. Plant Physiologists, Internat. Soil Sci. Soc. Mormon. Home: 10215 Clematis Ct Los Angeles CA 90077 Office: UCLABiomed and Environ Scis Lab Biomet and Enviorn Scis 900 Veteran Ave Los Angeles CA 90024

WALLACE, BARBARA JEAN, educator, consultant; b. St. Marys, Pa., Dec. 30, 1947; d. Robert Russell and Marjorie Frances (Schreiber) Wilson; m. Michael H. Wallace, Oct. 20, 1976. B.S. cum laude, Old Dominion U., 1969; M.A., Calif. State U., 1977; Ed.D., U. So. Calif., 1981. Tchr. English, First Colonial High Sch., Virginia Beach, Va., 1969-70; tchr., team leader grades 4-6, Conejo Valley Unified Sch., Newbury Park, Calif., 1972-76, coordinator early childhood edn. project, 1976-79; supr. student tchrs. Calif. Poly. State U., San Luis Obispo, 1979-85, sr. v.p., dir. Westco Savings Bank, Culver City, Calif., 1985—; evaluator pre-delinquent intervention program Paso Robles (Calif.) Schs. Trustee Paso Robles Joint Union High Sch. Dist., 1981-85; pres. Paso Robles br. Calif. Fedn. Republican Women, 1983. Mem. Assn. Calif. Sch. Adminstrs., Assn. Supervision and Curriculum Devel., Calif. Sch. Bds. Assn., AAUW. Home: 4470 Golf Course Dr Westlake Village CA 91362 Office: PO Box 5367 Culver City CA 90231

WALLACE, CAROLE JEAN WICKSTROM, art educator; b. Munising, Mich., May 10. 1938; d. George Berger and Edith Ann (Webster) W.; m. Laird Edward Wallace, Oct. 12, 1957. BS in Sci. and Design, U. Mich., 1961; student, U. Ariz., Guadalajara, Mex., 1964; MEd, San Diego State U., 1969; cert. in adminstrn., Point Loma Coll., 1976. Tchr. art Castle Park Middle Sch., Chula Vista, Calif., 1961—, chmn. fine arts, 1964—; Cert. tchr. jr. high; cert. specialist art instrn. K-14; cert. in curriculum and instrn., SDS. Commr. Internat. Friendship Commn. (chmn. Chula Vista chpt. 1976-84). Recipient Plaque for Service, City of Chula Vista chpt. Internat. Friendship Commn., 1984. Mem. NEA, AAUW. Republican. Episcopalian. Club:

Chula Vista Women's. Avocations: gardening roses, bridge, swimming, travel, camping. Home: 315 Nolan Way Chula Vista CA 92011 Office: Castle Park Middle Sch 160 Quintard Chula Vista CA 92011

WALLACE, EDWARD ERNEST, leasing corporation executive; b. Kansas City, Mo., Sept. 3, 1948; s. Edward Cornell and Ruth Ultima (Fiss) W.; m. Patricia Ann Paris, Sept. 17, 1969; children: Edward Arthur, Christine Lynn, Nancy Jane. Student, U. Toledo; Exec. Program Bus. Adminstrn., Columbia U., 1983—, Exec. MBA program, U. Wash., 1986. Zone mgr. Hertz Corp., Pitts. and Atlanta, 1969-78; v.p., gen. mgr. Columbus Nat. Lease, Ohio, 1978-80; exec. v.p., gen. mgr. Paccar Leasing Corp., Bellevue, Wash., 1980—, also dir.; dir. PACCAR Fin. Corp., Railease Inc., Bellevue. Bd. dirs. Youth Eastside Services, Bellevue, 1983—, treas., 1984-85, v.p. 1986.

WALLACE, GARY DEAN, botanist, museum curator; b. Pasadena, Calif., Jan. 4, 1946; s. Milo Dean and Helen Grace (Dibbert) W.; m. Marianne Doumakes, Dec. 1, 1977; children: Zebulon James, Benjamin Kodiak. BA, Calif. State U., Los Angeles, 1967, MA, 1972; PhD, Claremont Grad. Sch., 1975. Taxonomist Los Angeles County Arboretum, Arcadia, Calif., 1975-81; assoc. curator botany Natural Hist. Mus., Los Angeles, 1982—; rotating chmn. regional planning com. Significant Ecol. Areas Tech. Adv. Com. NSF grantee, 1973. Mem. Internat. Assn. Wood Anatomists, Internat. Assn. Plant Taxonomy, Am. Soc. Plant Taxonomists, Bot. Soc. Am., Assn. for Tropical Biology. Avocations: woodworking, fishing. Office: Natural History Mus Botany Sect 900 Exposition Blvd Los Angeles CA 90007

WALLACE, GEORGE WASHINGTON, JR., infosystems specialist; b. Decatur, Ill., Nov. 24, 1930; s. George Washington Sr. and Sadie Alice (Strader) W.; m. Mary Katherine Glenn, Jan. 23, 1956; children: Elizabeth A. (dec.), Victoria L., Michael A., Kevin S. Student U. Wyo., 1958-60, U. Ariz., 1973-76. Enlisted USAF, 1947, advanced through grades to 1st sgt., 1966, retired, 1970; asst. dir. transp. and communications Tucson Med. Ctr., 1970-72; supr. U. Ariz., Tucson, 1975—; cons. Western Interpretive Services, Sheridan, Wyo., 1972-74. Pres. Montezuma Council PTA, Tucson, 1971-73; mem. com. Precinct 113, Tucson, 1971-75; insp. Pima County and City of Tucson Election Bd., 1972—; bd. dirs. Pima Assn. Govt. Planning Commn., Tucson. Recipient Award of Merit, Italian War Graves Commn., 1959, commendation medal, USAF, 1962, 69, 70. Mem. U.S. Naval Inst. (life), Assn. Record Mgrs. and Adminstrs. (v.p. 1982-83), Smithsonian Inst., Alpha Kappa PSI Frat. Democrat. Episcopalian. Avocations: Am. architecture, early Western cemetaries, mil. aircraft and ships. Office: U Ariz Room 311 Bldg 66 Tucson AZ 85721-0663

WALLACE, J. CLIFFORD, judge; b. San Diego, Dec. 11, 1928; s. John Franklin and Lillie Isabel (Overing) W.; m. Virginia Lee Schlosser, Apr. 8, 1957; children: Paige, Laurie, Teri, John. B.A., San Diego State U., 1952; LL.B., U. Calif., Berkeley, 1955. Bar: Calif. 1955. With firm Gray, Cary, Ames & Frye, San Diego, 1955-70; judge U.S. Dist. Ct. So. Dist. Calif., 1970-72, U.S. Ct. Appeals 9th Circuit, 1972—. Contrbr. articles to profl. jours. Served with USN, 1946-49. Mem. ABA, Am. Bd. Trial Advocates, Inst. Jud. Adminstrn. Mormon (stake pres. San Diego East 1962-67, regional rep. 1967-74, 77-79). Address: US Courthouse Room 4N25 940 Front St San Diego CA 92189

WALLACE, JAMES WENDELL, lawyer; b. Clinton, Tenn., July 13, 1930; s. John Nelson and Rose Ella (Carden) W.; m. Jeanne Mary Ellen Newlin; children—Karen Wallace Young, Michael James. Student Syracuse U., 1952-53; B.S., U. Tenn.-Knoxville, 1959, J.D., 1958. Bar: Calif. 1959, U.S. Dist. Ct. (cen. dist.) Calif. 1959, U.S. Ct. Appeals (9th cir.) 1977, U.S. Supreme Ct. 1964. Sec., legal counsel Guidance Tech., Inc., Santa Monica, Calif., 1958-65; sr. atty., asst. sec. Varian Assocs., Palo Alto, Calif., 1965-67; gen. counsel, asst. sec. Electronic Splty. Co., Pasadena, Calif., 1967-69; asst. gen. counsel, asst. sec. The Times Mirror Co., Los Angeles, 1969-75; assoc. gen. counsel, asst. sec. The Times Mirror Co., 1976-85, assoc. gen. counsel, sec., 1985—. Mem. editorial bd. Tenn. Law Rev., 1956-58. Served with USAF, 1951-55. Mem. ABA, Am. Soc. Corp. Secs. (dir. 1979-82), Los Angeles County Bar Assn., Phi Delta Phi, Phi Kappa Phi. Clubs: Oakmont Country (Glendale); Jonathan (Los Angeles). Office: Times Mirror Square Los Angeles CA 90053

WALLACE, JANE BRANDEBURY, sales manager; b. N.Y.C., Dec. 1, 1950; d. Kenneth Donald and Ida (Harvey) W. BA, Am. U., 1976. Account exec. Sta. WGMS-AM-FM, Washington, 1978-79, Sta. King-AM, Seattle, 1979-81; local sales mgr. Sta. King-FM, Seattle, 1981-82; gen. sales mgr. Sta. KLSY-AM-FM, Seattle, 1982—. Mem. Puget Sound Radio Broadcasters Assn. (treas. 1985-86). Home: 515 W Crockett Seattle WA 98119 Office: Sta KLSY 12011 NE 1st St Bellevue WA 98005

WALLACE, JOHN ROBERT, electronics executive, consultant; b. Columbus, Ohio, Aug. 22, 1948; s. Robert Edward and Nora Joan (Wright) W.; m. Shirley Gale Hengst, May 25, 1969 (div. Jan 1976); m. Christine Gale Connors, June 26, 1976; children: Melissa Erin, Chelsea Lin, Matthew Robert. BSEE, Rice U., 1969, MEE, 1970. Project engr. Garrett Comtronics, San Diego, 1971-73, Western Digital, Costa Mesa, Calif., 1973-75; pres. Precision Micro Design, Santa Cruz, Calif., 1975-78; dir. Western Devel. Ctr. (Perkin-Elmer), Santa Cruz, 1978-81; program mgr. INTEL, Chandler, Ariz., 1981-82; pres. Ford Microelectronics, Inc., Colorado Springs, Colo., 1982—; bd. dirs., cons. ABEK Corp., Colorado Springs; mem. adv. bd. U. Colo. at Colorado springs. Bd. dirs. Hospice, Colorado Springs, 1985—, United Way, Colorado Springs, 1985—. Mem. IEEE. Republican. Presbyterian. Office: Ford Microelectronics Inc 10340 State Hwy 83 Colorado Springs CO 80908

WALLACE, KENNETH ALAN, investor; b. Gallup, N.Mex., Feb. 23, 1938; s. Charles Garrett and Elizabeth Eleanor (Jones) W.; A.B. in Philosophy, Cornell U., 1960; postgrad. U. N.Mex., 1960-61; m. Rebecca Marie Odell, July 11, 1980; children—Andrew McMillan, Aaron Blue, Susanna Garrett. Comml. loan officer Bank of N.Mex., Albuquerque, 1961-64; asst. cashier Ariz. Bank, Phoenix, 1964-67; comml. loan officer Valley Nat. Bank, Phoenix, 1967-70; pres. WWW, Inc., Houston, 1970-72; v.p. fin. Hometels of Am., Phoenix, 1972-77, Precision Mech. Co., Inc., 1972-77; ptnr. Schroeder-Wallace, 1977—; mng. ptnr. Pala Partners, San Diego; pres. Blackhawk, Inc., Phoenix, 1977—; pres., dir. Kloron Corp., Johannesburg, South Africa, Blackhawk, Inc., Phoenix; exec. v.p. South African BMX; dir. Schroeder Constrn. Co., Inc., Phoenix; v.p., dir. C.G. Wallace Co., Albuquerque, Apache County Sand Corp., Sanders, Ariz.; ptnr. New Dynasty Mining Corp., Vancouver, FWS, Phoenix, Univ. Sq. Assocs., Flagstaff, Ariz., Banador, Mijas, Spain; bd. dirs. World Trading and Shipping, N.Y.C.; gen. ptnr. Diamond W Ranch, Ltd., Sanders, Ariz., Wallco Enterprises, Ltd., Mobile, Ala.; dir. Columbia Bank, Avondale, Ariz. Loaned exec. Phoenix United Way, 1966, Tucson United Way, 1967; mem. Valley Big Bros., 1970—; bd. dirs. Phoenix Big Sisters, 1985-87; mem. Alhambra Village Planning Com.; fin. dir. Ret. Sr. Vol. Program, 1973-76; mem. Phoenix Men's Arts Council, 1968—, dir., 1974-75; mem. Phoenix Symphony Council. Campaign committeeman Republican gubernatorial race, N.Mex., 1964; treas. Phoenix Young Reps., 1966; bd. dirs. Devel. Authority for Tucson, 1967. Mem. Soaring Soc. Am. (Silver badge), Am. Rifle Assn. (life), Nat. Mktg. Assn. (Mktg. Performance of Year award 1966), S.W. Profl. Geog. Assn., Nat. Assn. Skin Diving Schs., Pima County Jr. C. of C. (dir. 1967), Phoenix Little Theatre, Phoenix Musical Theatre, S.W. Ensemble Theatre (dir.), Alpha Tau Omega. Mason (Shriner). Clubs: Univ., Plaza (Phoenix); Kona Kai (San Diego). Home: 409 E Keim Dr Phoenix AZ 85012 Office: Schroeder-Wallace PO Box 7703 Phoenix AZ 85011

WALLACE, LEIGH ALLEN, JR., bishop; b. Norman, Okla., Feb. 5, 1927; s. Leigh Allen and Nellie Elizabeth (Whittemore) W.; m. Alvira Kinney, Sept. 2, 1949; children—Jenny Leigh, Richard Kinney, William Paul. B.A., U. Mont., 1950; M.Div., Va. Theol. Sem., 1962, D.Div., 1979. Ordained priest Episcopal Ch.; vicar chs., Sheridan, Virginia City, Jeffers, Mont., 1962-65; rector St. Luke's Ch., Billings, Mont., 1965-71, Holy Spirit Parish, Missoula, Mont., 1971-78; bishop of Spokane, 1979—. Served with USNR, 1945-46. Address: 245 E 13th Ave Spokane WA 99202

WALLACE, LEON, physician, psychoanalyst; b. Syracuse, N.Y., July 7, 1925; s. Rodney Louis and Bessie (Sacks) W.; 1 child, Rodney. AB, Syracuse U., 1944; MD, Case Western Reserve U., Cleveland, 1949. Diplomate Am. Bd. Psychiatry. Intern N.Y. Med. Coll., N.Y.C., 1949-50; resident in psychiatry Compton (Calif.) Sanitarium, 1950-52; resident in psychosomatics Los Angeles Gen Hosp., 1952-53; practice medicine specializing in psychiatry Torrance, Calif., 1955—. Author: Pleasure and Frustration, 1984; contbr. articles to profl. jours. Served to capt. M.C., U.S. Army, 1953-55. Mem. Los Angeles County Med. Assn. (chmn. impaired physician com. 1979). Jewish. Home: 27921 Palos Verdes Dr E Rancho Palos Verdes CA 90274 Office: 3400 Lomita Blvd Torrance CA 90505

WALLACE, LYNN PYPER, engineering educator; b. Salt Lake City, Feb. 5, 1934; s. William Henry and Lavelle (Pyper) W.; m. Kaye Mangum, Aug. 14, 1959; children: Bryan L., Kenneth M., Katherine K. Ashby, Robert M., Jennifer R., Allison P., Amy L., Sarah L. BSCE, U. Utah, 1963; MSCE, W.Va. U., 1968, PhD in Engring., 1970. Registered profl. engr. Utah, Ariz., Alaska, Ohio, Ky., W.Va. Project engr. Okland Constrn. Co., Salt Lake City, 1963-64; br. chief EPA, Cin., 1970-72; commd. USPHS, 1964, advanced through grades to capt., 1980, ret., 1984; assoc. prof. engring. Brigham Young U., Provo, Utah, 1983—; owner, prin. engr. Wallace Engring., Anchorage, 1972-78, Phoenix, 1978-81, Provo, 1983—. Contbr. articles to profl. jours. V.p. Anchorage council Boy Scouts Am., 1976-78, scoutmaster Salt Lake City, 1958, Phoenix, 1980, Covington, Ky., 1982, explorer advisor Salt Lake City, 1960, Phoenix, 1981, com. chmn. Provo, 1986. Recipient Silver Beaver award Boy Scouts Am., 1977. Mem. ASCE (br. pres. 1986—), Water Pollution Control Fedn. (v.p. 1986—), Am. Water Works Assn., Am. Congress Surveying and Mapping, Am. Acad. Environ. Engrs. (diplomate), Mensa, Sigma Xi. Republican. Mormon. Avocations: pvt. pilot, skiing, tennis, jogging, singing. Home: 3187 N Foothill Dr Provo UT 84604 Office: Brigham Young U Box 33 Clyde Bldg Provo UT 84602

WALLACE, MARY ANN, development company executive; b. Reno County, Kans., Feb. 19, 1939; d. Ivan Lewis and Vina Sue (Smith) Newell; m. Alexander Wallace III, Feb. 17, 1968 (div. June 1982); 1 child, Alexander IV. BS, Wichita State U., 1961. Property mgr. 650 S. Grand Bldg. Co., Los Angeles, 1961-68; v.p. Milner Devel., Santa Monica, Calif., 1981-83; chief fin. officer Milner Devel., Los Angeles, 1983—; cons. Kitty Prodns., Los Angeles, 1978—; cons., v.p. Am. Mut. Prodns., Redlands, Calif., 1975—. V.p. Sister Servants of Mary Guild, Los Angeles, 1970-77; treas. Hosp. of Good Samaritan Aux., Los Angeles, 1969-75; pres sec. Orphanage Guild Jrs., Los Angeles, 1974. Named Downtown Working Angel, Downtown Businessmen's Assn., Best Fund Raiser, Sister Servants of Mary Guild, 1974-76. Mem. Los Angeles World Affairs Council, Los Angeles Women in Bus., Nat. Art Assn. Republican. Roman Catholic. Club: Los Angeles Country (Beverly Hills, Calif.). Avocations: travel, collecting, reading for blind. Home: 458 S Rexford Dr Beverly Hills CA 90212

WALLACE, MATTHEW WALKER, real estate investment company executive, consultant; b. Salt Lake City, Jan. 7, 1924; s. John McChrystal and Glenn (Walker) W.; m. Constance Cone, June 22, 1954 (dec. May 1980); children—Matthew, Anne; m. Susan Struggles, July 11, 1981. B.A., Stanford U., 1947; M.C.P., MIT, 1950. Prin. planner Boston City Planning Bd., 1950-53; v.p. Nat. Planning and Research, Inc., Boston, 1953-55; pres. Wallace-McConaughy Corp., Salt Lake City, 1955-69; pres. Ariz. Ranch & Metals Co., Salt Lake City, 1969-84; chmn. Wallace Assocs., Inc., Salt Lake City, 1969—; dir. 1st Interstate Bank, Salt Lake City, 1956—; mem. adv. bd. Mountain Bell Telephone Co., Salt Lake City, 1975-85. Pres., Downtown Planning Assn., Salt Lake City, 1970; chmn. Utah State Arts Council, Salt Lake City, 1977; mem. Humanities and Scis. Council, Stanford U., also mem. athletic bd.; mem. nat. adv. bd. Coll. Bus., U. Utah; chmn. endowment com. Utah Symphony Orch. Served to lt. (j.g.) USN, 1944-46; PTO. Recipient Contbn. award Downtown Planning Assn., 1977. Mem. Am. Inst. Cert. Planners (charter). Clubs: Alta (dir.), Cottonwood (pres. 1959-63), Salt Lake Country (dir.). Lodge: Masons. Home: 2510 Walker Ln Salt Lake City UT 84117 Office: Wallace Assocs Inc 165 S Main St Salt Lake City UT 84111

WALLACE, ROBERT CAMPBELL, software executive; b. Washington, May 29, 1949; s. Robert Ash and Luna Agnes (Campbell) W.; m. Megan Mary Dana, July 4, 1986. Student, Brown U., 1967-69, U. Calif., Santa Cruz, 1969-71; BS, U. Wash., Seattle, 1974, MS, 1978. Programmer Brookings Inst., Washington, 1971-72; prdn. mgr. Microsoft, Bellevue, Wash., 1978-83; propr., pres. Quicksoft, Seattle, 1983—; bd. dirs. Wash. Software Bd., Bellevue, 1985—. Software designer and author, 1978-86. Unitarian. Avocation: cats. Home and Office: Quicksoft 219 First N #224 Seattle WA 98109

WALLACE, ROBERT EARL, geologist; b. N.Y.C., July 16, 1916; s. Clarence Earl and Harriet (Wheeler) W.; m. Gertrude Kivela, Mar. 19, 1945; 1 child: Alan R. BS, Northwestern U., 1938; MS, Calif. Inst. Tech., 1940, PhD, 1946. Registered geologist, Calif., engring. geologist, Calif. Geologist U.S. Geol. Survey, various locations, 1942—; regional geologist U.S. Geol. Survey, Menlo Park, Calif., 1970-74; chief scientist Office of Earthquakes, Volcanoes and Engring.; U.S. Geol. Survey, Menlo Park, 1974—; asst. and assoc. prof. Wash. State Coll., Pullman, 1946-51; mem. adv. panel Nat. Earthquake Prediction Evaluation, 1980—, Stanford U. Sch. Earth Sci., 1972-82. Contbr. articles to profl. jours. Recipient Meritorious Service award U.S. Dept. Interior, 1978, Disting. Service award U.S. Dept. Interior, 1978; Japanese Indsl. Tech. Assn. fellow, 1984. Fellow Geol. Soc. Am. (chair cordillidan sect. 1967-68), Earthquake Engring. Research Inst., mem. Seismol. Soc. Am. Avocations: bird watching, ham radio, water color painting. Office: US Geol Survey 345 Middlefield Rd Menlo Park CA 94025

WALLACE, RONALD WILLIAM, computer science educator; b. San Francisco, Oct. 17, 1953; s. Alan Lewis and Ruth Estelle (Williford) W.; m. Carolyn Joy Parker, July 12, 1975; children: Brandon Parker, Tyler Lewis. BA in Math., Azusa Pacific Coll., 1974; MS in Math., Calif. State Poly. U., 1978. Cert. community coll. and secondary tchr., Calif. Math tchr. Western Christian High Sch., Glendora, Calif., 1975-78; math instr., grad. asst. Calif. State Poly. U., Pomona, 1976-78, 82-83; asst. prof. math. Azusa (Calif.) Pacific U., 1978-83; instr. computer sci. Blue Mountain Community Coll., Pendleton, Oreg., 1983—; text book reviewer McGraw Hill Pub., N.Y.C., 1985—, CBS Coll. Pub., N.Y.C. Mem. Math. Assn. Am., Oreg. Council Tchrs. Math., Northwest Council Computer Edn., Alpha Chi. Republican. Baptist. Avocations: tennis, golfing, camping, music, racguetball. Home: 2218 SW Quinney Dr Pendleton OR 97801 Office: Blue Mountain Community Coll 2411 NW Carden Ave Pendleton OR 97801

WALLAR, ROBERT EDWARD, economic development consultant, author; b. St. Louis, Jan. 13, 1942; s. Robert E. and Anita E. (Krueger) W.; A.A., Santa Barbara City Coll., 1967; B.A., San Francisco State Coll., 1969; m. Kathleen A. Yett, Apr. 12, 1975; children by previous marriage—Jane Omunson, Lynn, Andrew. Assoc. planner City of Bellevue (Wash.), 1969-71, planning dir., 1971-73; v.p. Bert McNae, Inc., Bellevue, 1973-75; owner The Wallar Assocs., 1973-85, Bryant/Wallar Assocs., 1974-76; pres. Robert E. Wallar Real Estate, 1975-79, 83— ; gen. mgr., chief exec. officer Puyallup Tribal Enterprises, Tacoma, 1978-80; chief staff dept. planning and community devel. Puyallup Nation, Tacoma, 1980—; exec. dir. Puyallup Nation Port Authority, Tacoma, 1980-82; ptnr. Frolich-Wallar Assocs., 1984—; instr. urban planning Bellevue Community Coll., 1970-71. Co-author: (with Judith O. Frolich) A New Approach to Indian Sovereignty, 1986. Mem. King County Agrl. Preservation Task Force, 1977-78, King County Growth Mgmt. Forum, 1978-80; mem. Commencement Bay Environ. Impact Com., U.S.A.C.E., 1978-82. Served with AUS, 1962-65. Mem. Puyallup Tribal Bar, Washington State Hist. Soc., Mus. History and Industry, Puget Sound C. of C. (chmn. land use com. 1973-75), Kirkland C. of C., Seattle C. of C. (chmn. agrl. preservation com. 1977-78), Bellevue C. of C. (bd. dirs. 1973-76). Episcopalian. Home: 1356 Bellefield Ln Bellevue WA 98004 Office: 15 Brooks Bldg 611 Market St Kirkland WA 98083-2863

WALLEN-STONE, VERA, school system adminsitrator; b. Ft. Knox, Ky., Sept. 24, 1941; d. Glen Lockwood and Mary Elizabeth (DeMoulin) Foote; m. Gary Leon Stone, Apr. 13, 1968 (div. May 1975); m. Jack Allen Wallen, Oct. 24, 1982. BA in English and History, U. Calif., Berkeley, 1963, PhD in Edn. Leadership, 1979; MA in Ednl. Administration, San Francisco State U., 1974. Tchr. Oakland (Calif.) Sch. Dist., 1964-69, Weston (Mass.) Pub. Schs., 1969-72; asst. dir. spl. edn. Vallejo (Calif.) Sch. Dist., 1972-75; prin. Santa Clara County Schs., Gilroy, Calif., 1975-79; supt. Oak Valley Sch. Dist., Tulare, Calif., 1979-82, Richland Sch. Dist., Shafter, Calif., 1982-87, Rosemead Sch. Dist., Rosemead, Calif., 1987—; bilingual instrn. researcher Richland Schs.; curriculum developer Oak Valley, Springville, Richland Sch. Dists., 1981-83. Mem. Crime and Violence Prevention Team, Safter-Wasco, Calif., 1982—, Richland PTA, 1982—, Kern County Supts. Curriculum Adv. Com., 1983—, Kern County Master Plan Spl. Edn. Exec. Com., 1985—. Mem. AAUW (career workshop coordinator), Assn. Calif. Sch. Adminstrs., Assn. Suprvision and Curriculum Devel., Phi Delta Kappa. Clubs: Shafter Women's; Shafter-Wasco Investment Group. Avocations: travel, reading, ballet. Home: 3930 N Rosemead Blvd #S Rosemead CA 91770 Office: Richland Sch Dist 331 Shafter Ave Shafter CA 93263

WALLER, H. EDWARD, advertising executive; b. Lancaster, Pa., Nov. 12, 1928; s. H. Earl and Esther J. (Allen) W.; m. Barbara Jean Ritten, Dec. 13, 1934; children: John Allen, thomas Allworth. BS in Econs., U. Pa., 1954. Copywriter Cin. Milacron, 1954-61; account exec. David K. Burnap Advt., Inc., Dayton, Ohio, 1961-66; v.p. David K. Burnap Advt. Agy., Dayton, Ohio, 1966-83, exec. v.p., 1983—.

WALLER, ROBERT CARL, chiropractor, pharmacist; b. Chgo., Aug. 1, 1931; s. Morton Sam and Linea Matilda (Anderson) W.; children by previous marriage—Wendy, Jeff. B.S., U. Ill., 1957; D.Chiropractic, Los Angeles Coll. Chiropractic, 1979; postgrad. UCLA, 1968-74. Staff pharmacist Savon Drugs, Granada Hills, Calif., 1968-70; mgr. pharmacy Hy-Lo Drug Co., Sepulveda, Calif., 1970-79; practice chiropractic medicine, Santa Monica, Calif., 1980—. Served with USNR, 1949-50. Mem. Am. Pharm. Assn., Am. Chiropractic Assn., Calif. Chiropractic Assn., UCLA Alumni Assn., Mensa. Democrat. Home: 3611 Meier St Los Angeles CA 90066 Office: 1530 Lincoln Blvd Suite C Santa Monica CA 90066

WALLERICH, PETER KENNETH, banker; b. Tacoma, Mar. 4, 1931; s. Clarence W. and Ellen (Hansen) W.; m. Marylu Ann Oakland, July 9, 1954; children—Karen, Kristen, Karla, Kaari. B.A.A., U. Wash., 1953. Investment officer N.Pacific Bank, Tacoma, 1956-59, exec. v.p., 1959-71, chmn. bd., 1971-73, pres., 1973—; gen. mgr. Soutn Tacoma Motor Co., 1959-68, pres., 1968-71; dir. North Pacific Bank, Western Fin. Co., Mountain View Devel. Co. Pres. Design for Progress, 1970-71; bd. dirs. Goodwill Industries, Wash. Research Council; trustee, treas. U. Puget Sound.; chmn. bd. trustees Mary Bridge Children's Hosp; trustee Lakewood Gen. Hosp.; bd. visitors Sch. Law U. Puget Soun.; gen. chmn. Tacoma Pierce County United Way, 1981. Mem. Wash. Bankers Assn. (dir., treas.), Am. Bankers Assn. (nat. exec. planning com.), C. of C. (dir.), Mensa, Beta Gamma Sigma (chpt. award 1980). Home: 12111 Gravelly Lake Dr SW Tacoma WA 98499 Office: N Pacific Bank 5448 S Tacoma Way Tacoma WA 98409

WALLERSTEIN, RALPH OLIVER, physician; b. Dusseldorf, Germany, Mar. 7, 1922; came to U.S., 1938, naturalized, 1944; s. Otto R. and Ilse (Hollander) W.; m. Betty Ane Christensen, June 21, 1952; children—Ralph Oliver Jr., Richard, Ann. A.B., U. Calif., Berkeley, 1943; M.D., U. Calif., San Francisco, 1945. Diplomate: Am. Bd. Internal Medicine (bd. govs. 1975-83, chmn. 1982-83). Intern San Francisco Hosp., 1945-46, resident, 1948-49; resident U. Calif. Hosp., San Francisco, 1949-50; research fellow Thorndike Meml. Lab., Boston City Hosp., 1950-52; chief clin. hematology San Francisco Gen. Hosp., 1953—; faculty U. Calif., San Francisco, 1952—; clin. prof. medicine U. Calif., 1969—. Served to capt. M.C. AUS, 1946-48. Mem. Am. Soc. Hematology (pres. 1978), Am. Coll. Physicians (gov. 1977—, chmn. bd. govs. 1980-81, regent 1981-87, pres.-elect 1987—), San Francisco Med. Soc., AMA, Am. Clin. and Climatol. Assn., Am. Fedn. Clin. Research, Am. Soc. Internal Medicine, Am. Bd. Internal Medicine (bd. govs. 1975-83, chmn. 1982-83), Am. Assn. Blood Banks, Inst. Medicine, Calif. Acad. Medicine, Internat. Soc. Hematology, Western Soc. Clin. Research, Western Assn. Physicians. Republican. Home: 3447 Clay St San Francisco CA 94118 Office: 3838 California St Suite 707 San Francisco CA 94118

WALLERSTEIN, ROBERT SOLOMON, psychiatrist; b. Berlin, Germany, Jan. 28, 1921; s. Lazar and Sarah (Guensberg) W.; m. Judith Hannah Saretsky, Jan. 26, 1947; children—Michael Jonathan, Nina Beth, Amy Lisa. B.A., Columbia, 1941, M.D., 1944; postgrad., Topeka Inst. Psychoanalysis, 1951-58. Asso. dir., then dir. research Menninger Found., Topeka, 1954-66; chief psychiatry Mt. Zion Hosp., San Francisco, 1966-78; tng. and supervising analyst San Francisco Psychoanalytic Inst., 1966—; clin. prof. U. Calif. Sch. Medicine, Langley-Porter Neuropsychiat. Inst., 1967-75, prof., chmn. dept. psychiatry, also dir. inst., 1975-85, prof. dept. psychiatry, 1985—; vis. prof. psychiatry La. State U. Sch. Medicine, also New Orleans Psychoanalytic Inst., 1972-73, Pahlavi U., Shiraz, Iran, 1977, Fed. U. Rio Grande do Sul, Porto Alegre, Brasil, 1980; mem., chmn. research scientist career devel. com. NIMH, 1966-70; fellow Center Advanced Study Behavioral Scis., Stanford, Calif., 1964-65, 81-82. Author books and monographs; mem. editorial bd. 8 profl. jours.; contbr. articles to profl. jours. Served with AUS, 1946-48. Recipient Heinz Hartmann award N.Y. Psychoanalytic Inst., 1968, Distinguished Alumnus award Menninger Sch. Psychiatry, 1972, J. Elliott Royer award U. Calif. at San Francisco, 1973, Outstanding Achievement award No. Calif. Psychiat. Soc., 1987. Fellow Am. Psychiat. Assn., A.C.P., Am. Orthopsychiat. Assn.; mem. Am. Psychoanalytic Assn. (pres. 1971-72), Internat. Psychoanalytic Assn. (v.p. 1977-85, pres. 1985—), Group Advancement Psychiatry, Phi Beta Kappa, Alpha Omega Alpha. Home: 290 Beach Rd Belvedere CA 94920 Office: Langley-Porter Neuropsychiat Inst 401 Parnassus St San Francisco CA 94143

WALLET, STEPHEN SELIG, architect, educator; b. Fresno, Calif., Mar. 4, 1952; s. George Leo and Irene (Winocoor) W.; m. Lisa Marie Rini, July 10, 1982. Student, U. Calif., San Diego, 1969-72; BArch, Berkeley, 1974; MArch, U. Calif., Berkeley, 1976. Lic. architect, Calif. Project architect Gaede/Alcorn, La Jolla, Calif., 1978-81; assoc. Naegle Assocs., La Jolla, 1981—; asst. prof. New Sch. Architecture, Chula Vista, Calif., 1983—. Editor/pub. Off the Wall, 1984-86. Club: San Diego Architecture (v.p. 1984—). Home: 4324 Corinth St San Diego CA 92115

WALLING, CHEVES T., chemistry educator; b. Evanston, Ill., Feb. 28, 1916; s. Willoughby George and Frederika Christina (Haskell) W.; m. Jane Ann Wilson, Sept. 17, 1940; children—Hazel, Rosalind, Cheves, Janie, Barbara. A.B., Harvard, 1937; Ph.D., U. Chgo., 1939. Research chemist E. I. dePont de Nemours, 1939-43; research chemist U.S. Rubber Co., 1943-49; tech. aide Office Sci. Research, Washington, 1945; sr. research assoc. Lever Bros. Co., 1949-52; prof. chemistry Columbia U., N.Y.C., 1952-69; disting. prof. chemistry U. Utah, Salt Lake City, 1970—. Author: Free Radicals in Solution, 1957; also numerous articles. Fellow AAAS; mem. Nat. Acad. Scis., Am. Acad. Arts and Scis., Am. Chem. Soc. (editor jour. 1975-81, James Flack Norris award 1970, Lubrizol award 1984). Home: 2784 Blue Spruce Dr Holladay UT 84117 Office: U Utah Dept Chemistry Salt Lake City UT 84112

WALLIS, LYNN RUEL, electric manufacturing company consultant; b. Portland, Oreg., Mar. 14, 1934; s. Lynn R. and Monttie M. (Scott) W.; B.S. in Physics, U. Oreg.; postgrad. in Physics, Oreg. State U., 1960-65; m. Joan Smith, Aug. 30, 1954; children—Kathleen, Kim. With Gen. Electric Co., 1959—, mem. managerial engring. staff Vallecitos Nuclear Center, Pleasanton, Calif., 1967-71, mem. engring. and communication staff Nuclear Energy Bus. Group, San Jose, Calif., 1971—; instr. U. Calif., Berkeley, 1967, 68, 69; participant public service radio series on energy, atom, plutonium Am. Nuclear Soc., 1975, 77; contact for U.S. media on nuclear energy matters U.S. Atomic Indsl. Forum, Washington, 1977—; lectr. politics of nuclear power J.F. Kennedy Sch. Govt., Harvard U., 1977; instr. U. Mex., 1982, U. Brazil, 1982; bd. dirs. CAL RAD forum; mem. nat. steering com. public info. program Am. Nuclear Soc., chmn., 1983-84; U.S. del. Uranium Inst., London, 1982, chmn. pub. info. com., 1983-84; chmn. Atomic Indsl. Forum Radiation Com.; lectr. Named to Hon. Order of Ky. Cols. Mem. Calif. Legis. Adv. Com. Radioactive Waste. Registered profl. engr., Calif. Home: 2326 Fairfield Pleasanton CA 94566

WALLIS, RICHARD FISHER, physicist, educator; b. Washington, May 14, 1924; s. William F. and Alberta (Sigelen) W.; m. Mary Camilla Williams, Aug. 20, 1955; children: Maria Fisher, Sylvia Camilla. B.S., George Washington U., 1945, M.S., 1948; Ph.D., Cath. U. Am., 1952. Postdoctoral fellow

(U. Md.), College Park, 1951-53; chemist Applied Physics Lab., Johns Hopkins U., Silver Spring, Md., 1953-56; physicist Naval Research Lab., Washington, 1956-66, 67-69, head semiconductors br., 1965-66, 67-69; prof. physics U. Calif., Irvine, 1966-67, 69—, chmn. dept. physics, 1972-75, 80-83; cons. Gen. Motors, Naval Research Lab. Author: (with Maradudin and Dobrzynski) Handbook of Surfaces and Interfaces, 1980, (with Balkanski) Many-Body Aspects of Solid State Spectroscopy, 1986; editor: Lattice Dynamics, 1965, Localized Excitations in Solids, 1968; contbr. articles to profl. jours. Served with U.S. Army, 1945-46. Recipient Pure Sci. award Naval Research Lab., 1964. Fellow Am. Phys. Soc.; mem. AAAS, Philos. Soc. Washington, Phi Beta Kappa, Sigma Xi. Home: 2635 Alta Vista Dr Newport Beach CA 92660 Office: Dept Physics Univ Calif Irvine CA 92717

WALLMANN, JEFFREY MINER, author; b. Seattle, Dec. 5, 1941; s. George Rudolph and Elizabeth (Biggs) W.; B.S., Portland State U., 1962; m. Helga Reidun Eikefet, Dec. 1, 1974. Pvt. investigator Dale Systems, N.Y.C., 1962-63; asst. buyer, mgr. public money bidder Dohrmann Co., San Francisco, 1964-66; mfrs. rep. electronics industry, San Francisco, 1966-69; dir. public relations London Films, Cinelux-Universal and Trans-European Publs., 1970-75; editor-in-chief Riviera Life mag., 1975-77; realtor, mktg., pub. relations cons., 1978—; books include: The Spiral Web, 1969, Judas Cross, 1974, Clean Sweep, 1976, Jamaica, 1977, Deathtrek, 1980, Blood and Passion, 1980; Brand of the Damned, 1981; The Manipulator, 1982; Return to Conta Lupe, 1983; The Celluloid Kid, 1984; Business Basic for Bunglers, 1984, Guide to Applications Basic, 1984; (under pseudonym Leon DaSilva) Green Hell, 1976, Breakout in Angola, 1977; (pseudonym Nick Carter) Hour of the Wolf, 1973, Ice Trap Terror, 1974; (pseudonym Peter Jensen) The Virgin Couple, 1970, Ravished, 1971; (pseudonmy Jackson Robard) Gang Initiation, 1971, Present for Teacher, 1972, Teacher's Lounge, 1972; (pseudonym Grant Roberts) The Reluctant Couple, 1969, Wayward Wives, 1970; (pseudonym Gregory St. Germain) Resistance #1: Night and Fog, 1982, Resistance #2: Maygar Massacre, 1983; (pseudonym Wesley Ellis) Lonestar on the Treachery Trail, 1982, numerous others in the Lonestar series; (pseudonym Tabor Evans) Longarm and the Lonestar Showdown, 1986; (pseudonym Jon Sharpe) Trailsman 58: Slaughter Express, 1986, numerous others in Trailsman series; also many other pseudonyms and titles; contbr. articles and short stories to Argosy, Ellery Queen's Mystery Mag., Alfred Hitchcock's Mystery Mag., Mike Shayne's Mystery Mag., Zane Grey Western, Venture, Oui, TV Guide; also (under pseudonym William Jeffrey in collaboration with Bill Pronzini) Dual at Gold Buttes, 1980, Border Fever, 1982, Day of the Moon, 1983. Mem. Mystery Writers of Am., Sci. Fiction Writers Am., Western Writers Am., Crime Writers Assn., Eugene Bd. Realtors, Nat. Assn. Realtors.

WALLNER, RICHARD ALAN, physicist; b. Bklyn., Apr. 28, 1945; s. Mathias and Margaret Louise (Boss) W.; m. Barbara Ann Zurawel, July 27, 1969; children: Richard N., Mary Catherine T. BA, NYU, 1966, MS, 1968; postgrad., U. N.Mex., 1974-76. Commd. 2d lt. USAF, 1969, advanced through grades to capt., 1972; div. weapons controller, 20th air div. USAF, Petersburg, Va., 1969-73; chief wavefront analysis, weapons lab. USAF, Albuquerque, 1973-77; resigned USAF, 1981; asst. prof. physics USAF Acad., Colorado Springs, Colo., 1977-81; research scientist Kaman Scis. Corp., Colorado Springs, 1981—. Mem. Optical Soc. Am. Republican. Roman Catholic. Avocations: numismatics, genealogical research. Office: Kaman Scis Corp PO Box 7463 Colorado Springs CO 80933

WALLOP, MALCOLM, U.S. Senator; b. N.Y.C., Feb. 27, 1933; s. Oliver M. and Jean (Moore) W.; children: Malcolm, Amy, Paul, Matthew; m. French Wallop. B.A., Yale U., 1954. Owner, operator Canyon Ranch, Big Horn, Wyo.; mem. Wyo. Ho. of Reps., 1969-73, Wyo. Senate, 1973-77; mem. U.S. Senate from Wyo., 1976—, mem. coms. on energy and natural resources, fin., small bus.; ofcl. observer from Senate on arms control negotiations; mem. Commn. on Security and Cooperation in Europe. Served to lt. U.S. Army, 1955-57. Mem. Wyo. Stockgrowers Assn., Am. Nat. Cattleman's Assn., Am. Legion. Republican. Episcopalian. Office: 206 Russell Senate Bldg Washington DC 20510

WALLS, JOSEPH WARREN, insurance and healthcare executive; b. San Diego, Mar. 19, 1945; s. Warren Russell and Doris Pearl (Bellmyer) W.; m. Linda Marie Sandoval, Jan. 24, 1976; children: Kimberley, Erica, Nicholas. AS in Respiratory Therapy, Grossmont Coll., 1974; BS in Occupational Safety and Health, San Diego State U., 1977. Cert. respiratory therapist, healthcare safety profl., safety engr. Mgr. hosp. pulmonary medicine Sharp Meml. Hosp., San Diego, 1974-77; mgr. loss control Ins. Co. West, San Diego, 1977-82; exec. dir. state rehab. Prohealth Ctr. Diagnostics Rehab., San Diego, 1982-85; risk control cons. Indsl. Imdemnity Ins. Co., San Diego, 1985—; cons. coordinator Calif. Paramedic Law, San Diego, 1974-77; cons. Calif. Assn. Hosp. Risk Mgmt., Sacramento, 1979-81. Contbr. articles to profl. jours. Active YMCA Indian Guides. Served with U.S. Army, 1965-67, Vietnam. Named Hon. Faculty, Sun Coast Hosp., Key Largo, Fla., 1983, Author of Yr. Healthcare Edn., N.Y., 1982; recipient health educator award U. Calif., San Diego Med. Ctr., 1981. Mem. Profl. Healthcare Safety Assn. (bd. dirs. 1980-85, Safety award 1982), Calif. Assn. Hosp. Risk Mgmt. (bd. dirs. 1981-84, Safety award 1982), Am. Soc. Safety Engrs. (Safety award 1980), Am. Assn. Respiratory Therapists, Risk and Inst. Mgmt. Assn., ARC, Small Bus. Assn. Presbyterian. Club: Rotary. Avocations: designing landscaping, auto restoration, camping, family. Office: Risk Mgmt 1595-104 Grand Ave San Marcos CA 92069

WALLSTRÖM, WESLEY DONALD, bank exec.; b. Turlock, Calif., Oct. 4, 1929; s. Emil Reinhold and Edith Katherine (Lindberg) W.; student Modesto Jr. Coll., 1955-64; certificate Pacific Coast Banking Sch., U. Wash., 1974; m. Marilyn Irene Hallmark, May 12, 1951; children: Marc Gordon, Wendy Diane. Bookkeeper, teller First Nat. Bank, Turlock, 1947-50; v.p. Gordon Hallmark, Inc., Turlock, 1950-53; asst. cashier United Calif. Bank, Turlock, 1953-68, regional v.p., Fresno, 1968-72, v.p., mgr., Turlock, 1972-76; founding pres., dir. Golden Valley Bank, Turlock, 1976-84; pres. Wallström & Co., 1985—. Campaign chmn. United Crusade, Turlock, 1971; chmn., founding dir. Covenant Village, retirement home, Turlock, 1973—, treas. Covenant Retirement Communities West; founding pres. Turlock Regional Arts Council, 1974, dir., 1975-76. Served with U.S. N.G., 1948-56. Mem. Nat. Soc. Accts. for Coops., Ind. Bankers No. Calif., Am. Bankers Assn., U.S. Yacht Racing Union, No. Calif. Golf Assn., Turlock C. of C. (dir. 1973-75), Stanislaus Sailing Soc. (commodore 1980-81), Republican. Mem. Covenant Ch. Clubs: Turlock Golf and Country (pres. 1975-76, v.p., 1977, dir. 1977, 83), 1977), Masons, Rotary. Home: 1720 Hammond Dr Turlock CA 95380 Office: 2925 Niagara Turlock CA 95380

WALLWORK, GREGORY THOMAS, electronics company executive, leasing company executive; b. Portland, Oreg., Apr. 3, 1947; s. J. Bernard and Margaret Elizabeth (Thomas) W.; m. Judy Antoinette Bush, Nov. 13, 1971. B.S. in Engring., Portland State U., 1970. Vice pres.-gen. mgr. Electronic Controls Design, Mulino, Oreg., 1966—; ptnr.-acctg. BWT Leasing, Oregon City, Oreg., 1975—; mem. Clackamas Pvt. Industry Council. Mem. Molalla (Oreg.) Buckaroo Adv. Bd. Named Bus. Man of Yr. City of Molalla, 1986. Mem. Am. Prodn. and Inventory Control Soc. (chmn. mktg. com.), Electronics Mfg. Assn. (acting pres. 1979), Molalla C. of C. (v.p. 1986, treas. 1987). Republican. Presbyterian. Office: Electronic Controls Design Inc 13626 S Freeman Rd Mulino OR 97042

WALRATH, HARRY RIENZI, clergyman; b. Alameda, Calif., Mar. 7, 1926; s. Frank Rienzi and Cathren (Michlar) W.; A.A., City Coll. San Francisco, 1950; B.A., U. Calif. at Berkeley, 1952; M.Div., Ch. Div. Sch. of Pacific, 1959; m. Dorothy M. Baxter, June 24, 1961; 1 son, Gregory Rienzi. Dist. exec. San Mateo area council Boy Scouts Am., 1952-55; ordained deacon Episcopal Ch., 1959, priest, 1960; curate All Souls Parish, Berkeley, Calif., 1959-61; vicar St. Luke's, Atascadero, Calif., 1961-63, St. Andrew's, Garberville, Calif., 1963-64; asso. rector St. Luke's Ch., Los Gatos, 1964-65, Holy Spirit Parish, Missoula, Mont., 1965-67; vicar St. Peter's Ch., also headmaster St. Peter's Schs., Litchfield Park, Ariz., 1967-69; chaplain U. Mont., 1965-67; asst. rector Trinity Parish, Reno, 1969-72; coordinator counciling services Washoe County Council Alcoholism, Reno, 1972-74; adminstr. Cons. Assistance Services, Inc., Reno, 1974-76; pastoral counselor, contract chaplain Nev. Mental Health Inst., 1976-78; contract mental health chaplain VA Hosp., Reno, 1976-78; mental health chaplain VA Med. Ctr., 1978-83, staff chaplain, 1983-85, chief, chaplain service, 1985—, also triage coordinator for mental health; dir. youth Paso Robles Presbytery; chmn. Diocesan Commn. on Alcoholism; cons. teen-age problems Berkeley Presbytery; mem. clergy team Episcopal Marriage Encounter, 1979-85, also Episc. Engaged Encounter. Mem. at large Washoe dist. Nev. area council Boy Scouts Am., scoutmaster troop 73, 1976, troop 585, 1979-82, asst. scoutmaster troop 35, 1982—, also advisor Tannu Lodge 346; South Humboldt County chmn. Am. Cancer Soc. Trustee Community Youth Center, Reno. Served with USNR, 1944-46. Decorated Pacific Theater medal with star, Am. Theater medal, Victory medal, Fleet Unit Commendation medal; recipient dist. award of merit Boy Scouts Am., St. George award Episc. Ch.-Boy Scouts Am., Silver Beaver award Boy Scouts Am., 1986, Founders' award Order of the Arrow, Boy Scouts Am., 1985; performance awards VA-VA Med. Ctr., 1983, 84; named Arrowman of Yr., Order of Arrow, Boy Scouts Am. certified substance abuse counselor, Nev. Mem. Ch. Hist. Soc., U. Calif. Alumni Assn., Nat. Model R.R. Assn. (life), Sierra Club Calif., Missoula Council Chs. (pres.), Alpha Phi Omega. Democrat. Club: Rotary. Home: 580 Huffaker Ln E Reno NV 89511 Office: VA Med Ctr 1000 Locust St Reno NV 89520

WALSH, DANIEL FRANCIS, bishop; b. San Francisco, Oct. 2, 1937. Grad., St. Joseph Sem., St. Patrick Sem., Catholic U. Am. Ordained priest, Roman Catholic Ch., 1963. Ordained titular bishop of Tigia and aux. bishop of San Francisco 1981—. Office: 445 Church St San Francisco CA 94114 *

WALSH, DON, marine consultant, executive; b. Berkeley, Calif., Nov. 2, 1931; s. J. Don and Marguerite Grace (Van Auker) W.; m. Joan A. Betzmer, Aug. 18, 1962; children—Kelly Drennan, Elizabeth McDonough. B.S., U.S. Naval Acad., 1954; M.S., Tex. A&M U., 1967, Ph.D., 1968; M.A., San Diego State Coll., 1968. Commd. ensign USN, 1954, advanced through grades to capt., 1974; officer-in-charge Bathyscaph Trieste USN, Trieste, 1959-62; comdr. in USS Bashaw USN, 1968-69; dir. Inst. Marine and Coastal Studies, prof. ocean engring. U. So. Calif., Los Angeles, 1975-83; pres., chief exec. officer Internat. Maritime, Inc., Los Angeles, 1976—; dir. Ctr. for Marine Transp. Studies, U. So. Calif., 1980-83; mem. Nat. Adv. Com. on Oceans and Atmosphere, 1979-85; bd. govs. Calif. Maritime Acad., 1985—. Author: Law of the Sea: Issues in Ocean Resource Management, 1977, Energy and Resources Development of Continental Margins, 1980, Energy and Sea Power: Challenge for the Decade, 1981, Waste Disposal in the Oceans: Minimizing Impact, Maximizing Benefits, 1983; editor Jour. Marine Tech. Soc., 1975-80; mem. editorial bd. U.S. Naval Inst., 1974-75. Decorated Legion of Merit (2), Meritorious Service medal (2); Woodrow Wilson Internat. Ctr. for Scholars fellow, 1973-74. Fellow Marine Tech. Soc., Explorers Club; mem. Soc. Naval Architects and Marine Engrs., Am. Soc. Naval Engrs., Am. Geophys. Union, Navy League, Naval Inst., AAAS. Office: Internat Maritime Inc 839 S Beacon St Room 217 San Pedro CA 90731

WALSH, EDWARD JOSEPH, toiletries and food company executive; b. Mt. Vernon, N.Y., Mar. 18, 1932; s. Edward Aloysius and Charlotte Cecilia (Borup) W.; m. Patricia Ann Farrell, Sept. 16, 1961; children: Edward Joseph, Megan, John, Robert. B.B.A., Iona Coll., 1953; M.B.A., NYU, 1958. Sales rep. M & R Dietetic Labs., Columbus, Ohio, 1955-60; with Armour & Co., 1961—; v.p. toiletries div. Armour Dial Co., Phoenix, 1973-76; exec. v.p. Armour Dial Co., 1976-77; former pres., now dir. Armour Internat. Co., Phoenix, 1978—; pres. The Dial Corp. (formerly Armour-Dial Co.), Phoenix, 1984—, chief exec. officer, 1986—; pres., chief exec. officer Purex Corp., from 1985. Pres. Mt. Vernon Fire Dept. Mems. Assn., 1960-61. Served with U.S. Army, 1953-55, Germany. Mem. Am. Mgmt. Assn., Nat. Meat Canner Assn. (pres. 1971-72), Cosmetic, Toiletries and Fragrance Assn. (bd. dirs. 1985—), Nat. Food Processors Assn. (bd. dirs.). Republican. Roman Catholic. Office: The Dial Corp 111 W Clarendon Phoenix AZ 85077

WALSH, HOWARD BENJAMIN, business consultant; b. Hampton, Iowa, Sept. 25, 1919; s. Benjamin George and Caroline (Heeren) W.; student mil. sci. U. Md., 1951-55; grad. Air War Coll., 1959, U.S. Navy Postgrad. Sch., 1966, U. So. Calif. Mgmt. Policy Inst., 1977; m. Barbara Mary Eales, June 1, 1945; children—Michael Benjamin, Mary Elizabeth. Commd. 2d lt. U.S. Army Air Force, 1940, advanced through grades to col., 1954; combat pilot 8th Air Force, World War II; exec. officer Hdqrs. U.S. Army Air Force, 1945-47; air attache U.S. embassy, Stockholm, 1947-51; NATO adv. Office Sec. Def., Washington, 1951-55; wing comdr. SAC, Dyess AFB, Tex., 1955-59; in sr. mil. posts NATO, Washington, France, Belgium, 1959-70, ret., 1970; exec. dir. Nat. Alliance Bus., Santa Barbara, Calif., 1971-82; bus. cons., 1982—. Trustee, Santa Barbara Art Inst., 1971-73, Direct Relief Internat., 1978-83; city commr. City of Santa Barbara, 1974-75; mem. U. So. Calif. Adv. Council, 1975—; mem. CETA Manpower Planning Council, Santa Barbara County, 1975-79; mem. San Luis Obispo Trade Adv. Council Calif. Men's Colony, 1974-82; vice chmn. Pvt. Industry Council Santa Barbara County, 1979-82, chmn., 1982-84; bd. dirs. Interdenom, Ch. Camp, Camp Cachuma, Calif., 1975-80, ARC, 1976—; bd. dirs. United Way, Santa Barbara County, 1976-82, pres., 1979-80; vestry mem. All Saints by the Sea Episcopal Ch., Montecito, Calif., 1977-81. Decorated Legion of Merit, D.F.C.(2), Air medal (4), Purple Heart, Meritorious Service medal (U.S.); knight Royal Order of Sword (Sweden); Croix de Guerre avec Palme (France); recipient commendation Calif. Assembly, 1973, Sec. of Army, 1946, of Air Force, 1965, of Labor, 1973, County of Santa Barbara, 1980, 83, Pres. U.S., 1979; Disting. Citizens Community Service award Anti-Defamation League of B'nai B'rith, 1982. Mem. Council Fgn. Relations, Air Force Assn., Ret. Officers Assn., Am. Security Council. Republican. Clubs: Channel City, Santa Barbara Ret. Officers (pres. 1976), Rotary (pres. local club 1980-81). Home: 48 Alston Pl Santa Barbara CA 93108

WALSH, JAMES ANTHONY, psychology educator; b. Portland, Oreg., Apr. 13, 1938; s. James Anthony and Mary Norine (O'Shea) W.; m. Roberta Annette Blake, Sept. 17, 1957; children: Jennifer, Robert. BS, U. Wash., 1960, MS, 1961, PhD, 1963. Lic. psychologist, Mont. (mem. licensing bd. 1981-82, chmn. 1982-84). Asst. prof. psychology and stats. Iowa State U., Ames, 1965-66, assoc. prof., 1966-69, prof., 1969-72; prof. psychology Mont. State U., Missoula, 1972—, chmn. dept., 1972-76; cons. Mont . Gov., Helena, 1976-77, Mont. C. of C., Helena, 1978, Casey Family Program, Helena, 1980-84, McKenzie, Steele, Briggs, Crown Corp., Brandon, Man., Can., 1985; vis. lectr. Com. Pres. Statis. Socs., 1976—. Developer: Comprehensive Social Desirability Scale for Children, 1974; contbr. articles and revs. to profl. jours. Mem. Missoula Pub. Schs. Adv. Council, 1974-76; mem. program. com. Comprehensive Devel. Ctr., Missoula, 1980-83; bd. dirs. Crisis Ctr. of Missoula, 1984-85. Postdoctoral fellow NIMH, 1963-64, Soc. Sci. Research Council, 1970-71. Fellow Am. Psychol. Assn.; mem. Am. Statis. Assn., Psychometric Soc., Biometric Soc., Sigma Xi. Democrat. Avocations: fishing, hiking, botany, modern poetry. Office: U Mont Dept Psychology Missoula MT 59812

WALSH, JOHN, JR., museum director; b. Mason City, Wash., Dec. 9, 1937; s. John J. and Eleanor (Wilson) W.; m. Virginia Alys Galston, Feb. 17, 1961; children: Peter Wilson, Anne Galston, Frederick Matthiessen. B.A., Yale U., 1961; postgrad., U. Leyden, Netherlands, 1965-66; M.A., Columbia U., 1965, Ph.D., 1971. Lectr., research asst. Frick Collection, N.Y.C., 1966-68; asso. higher edn. Met. Mus. Art, N.Y.C., 1968-71; assoc. curator European paintings Met. Mus. Art, 1970-72, curator dept. European paintings, 1972-75, vice-chmn., 1974-75; adj. asso. prof. art history Columbia U., N.Y.C., 1969-72; adj. prof. Columbia U., 1972-75; prof. art history Barnard Coll., Columbia U., N.Y.C., 1975-77; Mrs. Russell W. Baker curator paintings Mus. Fine Arts, Boston, 1977-83; dir. J. Paul Getty Mus., Malibu, Calif., 1983—; vis. prof. fine arts Harvard U., 1979; mem. governing bd. Yale U. Art Gallery, 1975—. Contbr. articles to profl. jours. Mem. county com. Democratic party, N.Y.C., 1968-71; mem. vis. com. Fogg Mus., Harvard U. Served with USNR, 1957-59. Fulbright grad. fellow The Netherlands, 1965-66. Mem. Coll. Art Assn., Am. Assn. Mus., Archaeol. Inst. Am. Club: Century Assn. (N.Y.C.). Office: J Paul Getty Mus Box 2112 Santa Monica CA 90406

WALSH, MARY D., civic worker; b. Whitewright, Tex., Oct. 29, 1913; d. William Fleming and Anna Maud (Lewis) Fleming; B.A., So. Meth. U., 1934; LL.D. (hon.), Tex. Christian U., 1979; m. F. Howard Walsh, Mar. 13, 1937; children—Richard, Howard, D'Ann Walsh Bonnell, Maudi Walsh Roe, William Lloyd. Pres. Fleming Found.; v.p. Walsh Found.; partner Walsh Co.; mem. Lloyd Shaw Found., Colorado Springs, Big Bros. Tarrant County; guarantor Fort Worth Arts Council, Schola Cantorum, Fort Worth Opera, Fort Worth Ballet, Fort Worth Theatre, Tex. Boys Choir, Schola Cantorum; hon. mem. bd. dirs. Van Cliburn Internat. Piano Competition; cofounder Am. Field Service in Ft. Worth; mem. Tex. Commn. for Arts and Humanities, 1968-72, mem. adv. council, 1972-84; bd. dirs. Wm. Edrington Scott Theatre, 1977-83, Colorado Springs Day Nursery, Colorado Springs Symphony, Ft. Worth Symphony, 1974-81; hon. chmn. Opera Ball, 1975, Opera Guild Internat. Conf., 1976; co-presenter (with husband) through Walsh Found., Tex. Boy's Choir and Dorothy Shaw Bell Choir ann. presentation of The Littlest Wiseman to City of Ft. Worth; granter with husband land and bldgs. to Tex. Boy's Choir for permanent home, 1971, Walsh-Wurlitzer organ to Casa Manana, 1972. Sem. Recipient numerous awards, including Altrusa Civic award as 1st Lady of Ft. Worth, 1968; (with husband) Disting. Service award So. Bapt. Radio and Television Commn., 1972; Opera award Girl Scouts, 1977-79; award Streams and Valleys, 1976-80; named (with husband) Patron of Arts in Ft. Worth, 1970, Edna Gladney Internat. Grandparents of 1972, (with husband) Sr. Citizens of Yr, 1985; Mary D. and Howard Walsh Meml. Organ dedicated by Bapt. Radio and TV Commn., 1967, tng. ctr. named for the Walshes, 1976; Mary D. and Howard Walsh Med. Bldg., Southwestern Bapt. Theol. Sem.; library at Tarrant County Jr. Coll. N.W. Campus dedicated to her and husband, 1978; Brotherhood citation Tarrant County chpt. NCCJ, 1978; Spl. Recognition award Ft. Worth Ballet Assn.; Royal Purple award Tex. Christian U., 1979; Friends of Tex. Boys Choir award, 1981; appreciation award Southwestern Bapt. Theol. Sem., 1981, B. H. Carroll Founders award, 1982; numerous other award for civic activities. Mem. Ft. Worth Boys Club, Ft. Worth Children's Hosp., Jewel Charity Ball, Ft. Worth Pan Hellenic (pres. 1940), Opera Guild, Fine Arts Found. Guild of Tex. Christian U., Girl's Service League (hon. life, hon. chmn. Spring Ballet, 1985), AAUW, Goodwill Industries Aux., Child Study Center, Tarrant County Aux. of Edna Gladney Home, YWCA (life), Ft. Worth Art Assn., Ft. Worth Ballet Assn., Tex. Boys Choir Aux., Friends of Tex. Boys Choir, Round Table, Colorado Springs Fine Art Center, Am. Automobile Assn., Nat. Assn. Cowbelles, Ft. Worth Arts Council, Am. Guild Organists (hon., Ft. Worth chpt.), Am. Guild of Organists (hon. Ft. Worth chpt.), Rae Reimers Bible Study Class (pres. 1968), Tex. League Composers (hon. life), Chi Omega (pres. 1935-36, hon. chmn. 1986), others. Baptist. Clubs: The Woman's (Club Fidelite), Colorado Springs Country, Garden of Gods, Colonial Country, Ridglea Country, Shady Oaks Country, Chi Omega Mothers, TCU Woman's. Home: 2425 Stadium Dr Fort Worth TX 76109 Home: 1801 Culebra Ave Colorado Springs CO 80907

WALSH, PATI LUNDE, speech and language pathologist; b. Lake City, Minn., May 10, 1950; d. J.W. and Evelyn (Schmidt) Lunde; m. Timothy Daniel Walsh, Aug. 3, 1974; children: Maggie, Kay Leigh. BA in Social Sci., U. Calif., Irvine, 1972; MS in Communication Disorders, U. N.Mex., 1974. Cert. clin. competence. Speech pathologist Esperanza Para Nuestros Niños, Albuquerque, 1974-75, Newport Mesa Unified Sch., Newport Beach, Calif., 1975-77; speech/lang. pathologist Albuquerque Pub. Schs., 1984—, spl. edn. head tchr., 1985—. Author: American Anthology of Poetry, 1984-85. Pres. PTA, Griegos Sch., 1986-87. Office of Edn. fellow U. N.Mex., 1972-74. Avocations: investing, reading, cross country skiing. Home: 1334 Cherokee Ct NW Albuquerque NM 87107 Office: Albuquerque Pub Schs 4040 San Isidro Albuquerque NM 87107

WALSH, ROBERT MICHAEL, reprographics company executive; b. Wilmington, Del., Jan. 28, 1938; s. Michael Franklin and Mary Elizabeth (McAteer) W.; m. Mary Regan, June 24, 1961; children: Elizabeth, Maura, Michael, Christopher. BS, U. Del., 1960; PhD, U. Calif., Berkeley, 1965. With Hercules Inc., Wilmington, 1965-85; tech. dir. Esgraph Inc., Cerritos, Calif., 1985—. Patentee in field. Mem. Am. Chem. Soc., Soc. Photographic Scientists and Engrs., Sigma Xi. Home: 1800 Mount Salem Ln Wilmington DE 19806 Office: Esgraph Inc 16833 Edwards Rd Cerritos CA 90701 Address: 5600 Orangethorpe Apt 3307 La Palma CA 90623

WALSH, WILLIAM, professional football coach; b. Los Angeles, Nov. 30, 1931. Student, San Mateo Jr. Coll.; B.A., San Jose State U., 1954, M.A. in Edn, 1959. Asst. coach Monterey Peninsula Coll., 1955, San Jose State U., 1956; head coach Washington Union High Sch., Fremont, Calif., 1957-59; asst. coach U. Calif., Berkeley, 1960-62, Stanford U., 1963-65, Oakland Raiders, Am. Football League, 1966-67, Cin. Bengals, 1968-69, 70-75, San Diego Chargers, Nat. Football League, 1976; head coach Stanford U., 1977-78; head coach, gen. mgr. San Francisco 49ers, NFL, 1979—. Named NFL Coach of Yr. Sporting News, 1981. Coached Stanford U. winning team Sun Bowl, 1977, Bluebonnet Bowl, 1978. Coached NFL Championship team, 1981, 84. Office: San Francisco 49ers 711 Nevada St Redwood City CA 94061 *

WALSH, WILLIAM DESMOND, private investor; b. N.Y.C., Aug. 4, 1930; s. William J. and Catherine Grace (Desmond) W.; m. Mary Jane Gordon, Apr. 5, 1951; children: Deborah, Caroline, Michael, Suzanne, Tara Jane, Peter. B.A., Fordham U., 1951; LL.B., Harvard, 1955. Bar: N.Y. State bar 1955. Asst. U.S. atty. So. dist. N.Y., N.Y.C., 1955-58; counsel N.Y. Commn. Investigation, N.Y.C., 1958-61; mgmt. cons. McKinsey & Co., N.Y.C., 1961-67; sr. v.p. Arcata Corp., Menlo Park, Calif., 1967-82; gen. ptnr. Sequoia Assocs., 1982—; pres., chief exec. officer Atacra Liquidating Trust, 1982—; chmn. Sequoia Pacific Systems, Exeter, Calif., Timberjack Holding Inc., Woodstock, Ont., Can.; dir. Interstate Bakeries Corp., Kansas City, Mo., Advanced Systems Inc., Arlington Heights, Ill., Traditional Industries Inc., Westlake Village, Calif., Scandiline Furniture Corp., Compton, Calif. Chmn. Evergreen Assn., Menlo Park, Calif.; bd. dirs. Herbert Hoover Boys and Girls Club. Mem. Am., N.Y. State bar assns. Clubs: Harvard (N.Y.C. and San Francisco). Home: 279 Park Ln Atherton CA 94025 Office: 3000 Sand Hill Rd Bldg 2 Suite 140 Menlo Park CA 94025

WALSMITH, CHARLES RODGER, psychologist, educator; b. Denver, May 19, 1926; s. Joseph Francis and Florence Ophelia (Brown-Smith) W.; B.A. (Chancellor's Ednl. scholar), U. Denver, 1956, M.A., 1962; postgrad. U. Wash., 1968-76; Ph.D., Stanton U., 1976; children—Karen Frances, Cynthia Ann, Erik Konrad. Research psychologist Personnel Tng. and Research Center, Maintenance Lab., USAF Lowery AFB, Denver, 1956; research asst. U. Colo. Med. Center, Denver, 1956-57, research asso., 1957-64; asst. prof. psychology North Park Coll., Chgo., 1965-66; sr. human engring. analyst, psychoacoustics Boeing Co., Seattle, 1965-68; instr. emeritus psychology dept. behavioral scis. Bellevue (Wash.) Community Coll., 1968—, chmn. emeritus dept., 1968-87, Phi Theta Kappa adviser, 1981-87. Resident trainer Gestalt Inst. of Can., Lake Cowichan, B.C., summers 1969-71, assoc., 1969—; dir. Gestalt Inst. of Wash., Bellevue, 1970—. Democratic precinct chmn., Renton, Wash., 1966-68; patron BCC Found. Served with USNR, 1944-46. Mem. Wash. State, Psychol. Assn., NEA, Wash. Edn. Assn., Inst. for Advancement of Health, Phi Beta Kappa, Psi Chi. Home: Gestalt House 14909 SE 44th Pl Bellevue WA 98006

WALSTROM, THOMAS ARVID, agency administrator; b. Bellingham, Wash., June 3, 1933; s. Ernest Arvid and Winnifred Faye (Roberts) W.; m. Mary Lue Myrtle Henifin, Aug. 1, 1952; children: Kim F., Linda K., Richard A., Kevin T., Kristina J. Student, Olympic Jr. Coll., 1952-56. Supr. U.S. Dept. Energy Bonneville Power Adminstrn., Custer, Wash., 1966—; owner, operator Win's Drive-In, Bellingham, 1978—. Freeholder Whatcom County, Bellingham, 1978. Mem. Nat. Restaurant Assn., Wash. State Restaurant Assn. Lutheran. Club: Toastmasters (pres. 1976-77). Avocations: investments, politics, travel, salt water fishing, power boating. Office: Wins Drive-In 1315 12th St Bellingham WA 98225

WALTER, BRUCE ALEXANDER, physician, educator; b. Seattle, Apr. 15, 1922; s. Ernest R. and Marion (Alexander) W.; B.A., U. Wash., 1944, B.S., 1948, M.D., 1951; M.P.H., UCLA, 1962; m. Gloria Helen Parry, Feb. 4, 1956; children—Maia Marion, Wendy Diane, Shelley Kathleen, Allison Ann. Intern Los Angeles County Gen. Hosp., 1951-52; resident internal medicine Wadsworth Hosp., U. Calif., 1952-54; dir. grad. program hosp., health facilities adminstrn. UCLA, 1965-68; attending staff Salt Lake County Hosp., 1954-55; fellow medicine U. Utah, 1954-55; fellow medicine U. So. Calif., 1955-56, mem. faculty, 1956-65; attending staff Los Angeles County Hosp., 1956-65; physician internal medicine, Palm Springs, Calif., 1956-61;

chief staff Desert Hosp., 1960-61; dir. med. care studies Calif. Dept. Pub. Health, Berkeley, 1962-65; dir. Med. Care Services, State of Utah, 1969-71, dep. dir. health, 1971-79, acting dir. health, 1979; cons. Newport Med. Group and Advanced Health Systems, Inc., Newport Beach, Calif., 1979-84; practice medicine specializing in internal medicine, Costa Mesa, Calif., 1984—; asst. prof. community and family medicine U. Utah Sch. Medicine, Salt Lake City, 1969-79; mem. Utah State Bd. Aging; bd. dirs. Blue Shield of Utah, Utah Profl. Standards Rev. Orgn. Served to 1st lt. Signal Corps, AUS, 1943-46. Mem. AMA, Calif. Med. Assn., Nat. Assn. Health Facility Licensing and Certification Dirs. (pres. 1975-76), Orange County Med. Soc., Alpha Delta Phi, Alpha Kappa Kappa, Alpha Delta Sigma. Clubs: Balboa Bay. Home: 2821 Blue Water Dr Corona del Mar CA 92625 Office: 275 Victoria St Costa Mesa CA 92627

WALTER, GEORGE SIMON, physician, educator; b. Vom, Nigeria, Apr. 4, 1934; (parents Am. Citizens).; s. Victor Edson and Mabel Verona (Skogsberg) W.; m. Barbara W. Herlihy, June 11, 1955 (dec. Jan. 1977); children: Bryan K., Jeffrey M., Ann P., Katherine E.; m. Bonnie Rae Lockhart, Aug. 16, 1980. BS in Chemistry, U. Denver, 1957; MD, U. Colo., 1958; MPH, U. Calif., Berkeley, 1970. Cert. Am. Bd. Ob-Gyn; lic. med. practioner, Colo., Ariz., Calif. Intern Denver Gen. Hosp., 1958-59; resident ob-gyn. U. Colo. Med. Ctr., Denver, 1962-65; med. officer in charge USPHS, Pt. Barrow, Alaska, 1959-60, Owyee, Nev., 1960-62; chief ob-gyn USPHS Hosp., Ft. Defiance, Ariz., 1965-69; MCH cons. Navajo area USPHS Hosp., Window Rock, Ariz., 1970-71; field coordinator MCH Project U. Calif., Cotonou, Bénin, Africa, 1971-75; med. tng. coordinator internat. health program U. Calif., San Francisco, 1975—; project officer PL-480 Family Planning, Sarjevo, Yugoslavia, 1969-71; cons. aux. nurse mid-wives sch. USAID, Kabul, Afghanistan, 1976-79; cons., trainer USAID, 1978—, Family Circle Ministries, Enugu, Nigeria, 1985, 87, Inst. Maternal and Child Health, Metro Manila, Philippines, 1986. Bd. dirs. Planned Parenthood, Santa Cruz, Calif., 1978-85; pres. site counsel San Lorenzo Valley High Sch., Felton, Calif., 1979-82; family life educator various chs. and schs. in Santa Cruz County, 1978—. Fellow Am. Coll. Obstetricians and Gynecologists; mem. Am. Pub. Health Assn., Am. Assn. Planned Parenthood Profls., Am. Assn. Sex Educators, Counselors and Therapists, Commnd. Officers Assn. of U.S. Pub. Health Service. Democrat. Mem. Evang. Free Ch. Avocations: reading, music, hiking, gardening, travel. Home: 238 Union St Santa Cruz CA 95060 Office: U Calif Internat Health Programs 210 High St Santa Cruz CA 95060

WALTER, MARTIN EDWARD, mathematician, educator; b. Lone Pine, Calif., Jan. 26, 1945; s. Karl Emil and Clare Marie (Larsen) W.; m. Elaine I. Austin, June 24, 1967 (div. Nov. 85); 1 child, Liv Muir. BS, U. Redlands, 1966; MS, PhD, U. Calif., Irvine, 1971. Functional analysis yr. fellow UCLA, 1970-71; research assoc. Queen's U., Kingston, Ont., Can., 1971-73; asst. prof. math. U. Colo., Boulder, 1973-77, assoc. prof. math., 1977-84, prof. math., 1984—; cons. Rocky Mountain chpt. Sierra Club, 1973—. Contbr. articles to profl. jours. Fellow Alfred P. Sloan Found., 1976-78, Woodrow Wilson Found., 1966, NSF, 1966-70. Mem. Am. Math. Soc., AAAS, Sierra Club, Colo. Mountain Club (rock climbing instr.). Avocations: mountain and rock climbing, karate, guitar, scuba diving, farming.

WALTER, MICHAEL CHARLES, lawyer; b. Oklahoma City, Nov. 25, 1956; s. Donald Wayne and Viola Helen (Heffelfinger) W. BA in Polit. Sci., BJ, U. Wash., 1980; JD, Univ. Puget Sound, 1983. Bar: Wash. 1985, U.S. Dist. Ct. (9th cir. 1985). Assoc. Keating, Bucklin & McCormack, Seattle, 1985—; instr. Bellevue (Wash.) Community Coll., 1983—. Mem. Internat. Assn. Bus. Communicators, Reporters Com. for Freedom of Press, ACLU, ABA, Wash. State Bar Assn., Seattle-King County Bar Assn., Wash. Assn. Def. Counsel, Seattle Claims Adjustors Assn. Avocations: running, swimming, hiking, coin collecting, antiques. Home: 11552 3d Ave NW Seattle WA 98177 Office: Keating Bucklin & McCormack 4141 SeaFirst Fifth Ave Plaza Seattle WA 98104

WALTERMIRE, JIM, secetary of state Montana; b. Choteau, Mont., Feb. 15, 1949; s. Robert and Anne (Luinstra) W. B.S. in Bus. Adminstrn, U. Mont. Engaged in real estate, ranching, constrn. and banking 1972-75; partner Waltermire & Wicks (investments), Missoula, Mont., 1975-77; commr. Missoula County, 1977-80; sec. of state State of Mont., 1981—; Fellow Union Bank & Trust, Helena, 1970. Recipient Outstanding Young Alumnus award U. Mont., 1985—. Mem. Nat. Assn. Secs. State. Office: Room 225 State Capitol Bldg Helena MT 59620

WALTERS, ALTON JOSEPH, internist; b. Goldboro, N.C., Jan. 4, 1949; s. Alton Hodges and Ethel Lilian (Sharpe) W.; m. Sandra Lee, Nov. 1, 1982; children: Brett Alton, Casey Richard. BA, U. Calif., San Diego, 1969, MS, 1972; BS, U. N.D., 1977; MD, Chgo. Univ. Health Scis. Med. Sch., 1979. Intern U. N. Mex., Albuquerque, 1979, U. Nev., Reno, 1979-80; research asst. U. Calif., San Diego, 1969-72; facility cons. N.D. Dept. Health, Bismark, 1972-73; exec. dir. N.D. S.C. Health Planning Council, Bismark, 1973-75; resident in internal medicine U. Nev., Reno, 1979-82; practice medicine specializing in internal medicine Henderson, Nev., 1982—; chmn. ICU com. St. Rose de Lima Hosp., Henderson, 1983-84; v.p. Glassburn Constrn. Co., Henderson; pres. Atlantic City Apts., Henderson. Contbr. articles to profl. jours. Mem. AMA, ACP, Nev. State Med. Assn., Nev. Preferred Profls., Nev. Med. Legal Screening Panel, Clark County Med. Soc., Calif. Scholastic Fedn. (life). Office: 67 E Lake Mead Dr Henderson NV 89015

WALTERS, ANNA LEE, writer, administrator; b. Pawnee, Okla., Sept. 9, 1946; d. Luther and Juanita Mae (Taylor) McGlaslin; student U. N.Mex., 1977—; m. Harry Walters, June 1965; children—Anthony, Daniel. Dir. Navajo Community Coll. Press, Tsaile (Navajo Nation), Ariz., 1982—; contbg. author: The Man to Send Rainclouds, 1974, Warriors of the Rainbow, 1975, Shantih, 1976, The Third Woman, 1979, The Remembered Earth, 1979, American Indians Today, Thought, Literature, Art, 1981; co-author textbook: The Sacred Ways of Knowledge, Sources of Life, 1977; author: The Otoe-Missiouria Tribe, Centennial Memoirs, 1881-1981, 1981; Earth Power Coming, 1983; The Sum in not Merciful, 1985; contbr. articles to jours.; guest editor Frauen Offensive, 1978; also poet, feature writer. Recipient Am. Book award The Before Columbus Found., 1986, Virginia Scully McCormick Lit. award, 1986. Office: Navajo Community Coll Press Tsaile AZ 86556

WALTERS, DOROTHY MAE, publishing company executive; b. Los Angeles; s. Harold J. and Lillian C. (Soutter) Wells; m. Robert E. Walters; children: Robert Michael, Jeanine Diane, Lillet Ruthlyn. Grad. high sch., Alhambra, Calif. Cert. speaking prof. Chief exec. officer, founder R&D Walters Corp., Glendora, Calif., 1956—, Royal Pub., Glendora, 1976—. Author numerous articles in profl. jours. and books. Named Bus. Woman of Yr. San Gabriel Valley YWCA and San Gabriel Valley Trib., West Covina, Calif., 1985. Mem. Nat. Speakers Assn., Assn. of Assn. Execs. (mem. of yr. Los Angeles chpt. 1984), Internat. Group Agts. and Burs. (exec. dir., founder). Home: 18825 Hicrest Rd Glendora CA 91740 Office: PO Box 1120 Glendora CA 91740

WALTERS, EDWARD ALBERT, chemistry educator; b. Whitefish, Mont., Jan. 2, 1940; s. Eric Albert and Katie W. (Kuehn) W.; m. Susan Elaine Dally, June 24, 1964; children: Eric Nash, Gregory Edward, Elaine Mee Sun. BS, Pacific Luth. U., 1962; PhD, U. Minn., 1966. Research assoc. Cornell U., Ithaca, N.Y., 1966-68; asst. prof. U. N.Mex., Albuquerque, 1968-74, assoc. prof., 1974-85, prof. chemistry, 1985—; vis. staff mem. Los Alamos (N.Mex.) Nat. Lab., 1970—; research collaborator Brookhaven Nat. Lab., Upton, N.Y., 1980—. Author: Contemporary Chemistry, 1974. Mem. AAAS, Am. Chem. Soc. (councillor), Am. Vacuum Soc., Royal Soc. Chemistry. Lutheran. Avocations: backpacking, flyfishing, soccer. Home: 8109 Harwood Ave NE Albuquerque NM 87110 Office: U N Mex Dept Chemistry Albuquerque NM 87131

WALTERS, JESSE RAYMOND, JR., judge; b. Rexburg, Idaho, Dec. 26, 1938; s. Jesse Raymond and Thelma Rachael (Hodgson) W.; m. Harriet Payne, May 11, 1959; children—Craig T., Robyn, J. Scott. Student Ricks Coll., 1957-58; B.A. in Polit. Sci., U. Idaho, 1961, J.D., 1963; postgrad. U. Washington, 1962. Bar: Idaho 1963, U.S. Dist. Ct. Idaho 1964, U.S. Ct. Appeals (9th cir.) 1970. Law clk. to chief justice Idaho Supreme Ct., 1963-64; sole practice, Boise, Idaho, 1964-77; atty. Idaho senate, Boise, 1965; dist. judge 4th Jud. Dist., Idaho, Boise, 1977-82, adminstrv. dist. judge, 1981-82; chief judge Idaho Ct. Appeals, Boise, 1982—; chmn. magistrate's commn. 4th jud. dist.; chmn. Supreme Ct. mem. services; mem. Civil Pattern Jury Instrn. Com; Republican committeeman, Boise, 1975-77; mem. Ada County Rep. Central Com., 1975-77. Mem. Idaho Bar Assn. (bankruptcy com.), Idaho Adminstrv. Judges Assn., ABA, Am. Judicature Soc., Assn. Trial Lawyers Am. Idaho Trial Lawyers Assn., Council Chief Judges Ct. Appeals, Boise Estate Planning Council, Jaycees (nat. dir. 1969-70, pres. Boise chpt. 1966-67). Mormon. Lodges: Lions, Elks, Eagles. Office: State of Idaho Ct Appeals 537 W Bannock St Boise ID 83720

WALTERS, JOSEPH CURTIS, broadcasting educator; b. Buckeye, Ariz., June 22, 1939; s. George Curtis and Frances W. (Walker) W. BS, U. Ariz., 1965; MA, U. Tex., 1967; PhD, Fla. State U., 1977. Dir. radio-TV-film div. Baylor U., Waco, Tex., 1969-76; assoc. prof. broadcasting Northern Ariz. U., Flagstaff, 1977-81, assoc. dir. broadcasting, 1984—; prof. Middle Tenn. State U., Murfreesburo, 1981-82; assoc. prof. U. Tex., El Paso, 1982-83. Author mag. column Buck's Luck, 1971-72. Served with USMC, 1956-60. Mem. Speech Communication Assn., Soc. Profl. Journalists (pres. Grand Canyon Profl. chpt. 1984-86), Ariz. Communication Assn. (v.p.-elect 1985-86), Western Social Sci. Assn. Avocations: hunting, fishing, restoring old cars. Home: 27 Palomino Rd Flagstaff AZ 86004 Office: Northern Ariz U Box 6006 Flagstaff AZ 86011

WALTERS, LUCIA MARIE, lawyer; b. Kansas City, Mo.; d. Willard J. and Eileen Ruth (Biederman) W.; m. John L. Diamond, May 27, 1984. AB, UCLA, 1971; MLS, U. Calif., Berkeley, 1972; JD, U. Calif., San Francisco, 1982. Bar: Calif. 1982, U.S. Dist. Ct. (no. dist.) Calif. 1982, U.S. Dist. Ct. (cen. dist.) Calif. 1984, U.S. Ct. Appeals (9th cir.) 1984, U.S. Tax Ct. 1985. Librarian Nev. County Library, Nevada City, Calif., 1972-73, Stockton (Calif.)-San Joaquin County Pub. Library, 1973-79; law clk. to cir. judge U.S. Ct. Appeals (9th cir.), Los Angeles, 1983-84; assoc. Thelen, Marrin, Johnson & Bridges, San Francisco, 1984—. Stanford Law Sch. fellow, 1982-83. Mem. ABA, Beta Phi Mu, Phi Delta Phi. Club: Corinthian Yacht; Belvedere Tennis. Office: Thelen Marrin Johnson & Bridges Two Embarcadero Ctr San Francisco CA 94111

WALTERS, MARY COON, justice state supreme court; b. Baraga, Mich., Jan. 29, 1922; d. Marvin Leonard and Nancy C. (Conway) Coon; m. Asa Lane Walters, July 9, 1952 (dec. June 1974); 1 child, Mark Richard. J.D., U. N.Mex., 1962. Bar: N.Mex. 1962, U.S. Supreme Ct. Pvt. practice Albuquerque, 1962-71, 73-78; judge 2d Jud. Dist. N.Mex., Albuquerque, 1971-72; judge N.Mex. Ct. Appeals, Santa Fe, 1979-81, chief judge, 1981-83; justice N.Mex. Supreme Ct., Santa Fe, 1984—. Served with Women's Airforce Service Pilots, 1943-44, USAF, 1951-55. Mem. ABA, N.Mex. Bar Assn., Albuquerque Bar Assn., Santa Fe Bar Assn. Democrat. Roman Catholic. Office: N Mex Supreme Ct PO Box 848 Santa Fe NM 87501

WALTERS, RICHARD FRANCIS, computer science educator; b. Teleajen, Romania, Aug. 30, 1930; s. Ray Pearce and Gertrude (Gravett) W.; m. Shipley Newlin, Aug. 30, 1952; children: Leslie Walters Alexander, David Todd. BA magna cum laude, Williams Coll., 1952; MA, U. Wyo., 1953; Diplome superieur en scis. naturalles, U. Bordeaux, France, 1955; PhD, Stanford U., 1957. Geologist Humble Oil and Refining Co., Los Angeles, 1956-60; subsurface geologist Humble Oil and Refining Co., Chico, Calif., 1960-63; sr. subsurface geologist Humble Oil and Refining Co., New Orleans, 1963-66; sr. research geologist Esso Prodn. Research Co., Houston, Tex., 1966-67; lectr. computer sci. U. Calif., Davis, 1967-68, asst. prof. med. edn. and biomed. engirng., 1968-73, assoc. prof. med. edn. and biomed. engring., 1973-78, assoc. prof. community health, 1978-79, prof. community health, 1979-83, prof. elec. and computer engring., 1980-83, prof. computer sci. div., 1983-84, prof. family practice, 1984—. Editorial cons. Soc. for Computer Simulations, 1970-76; editorial rev. bd. mem. Jour. of Computer Basted Instrn., 1975—, Med. Informatics, 1977—, MUMPS Users' Group Quarterly, 1981—, Computers in Biology and Medicine, 1982; contbr. articles to profl. jours. Fellow: Am. Geol. Soc.; mem. Am. Arbitration Assn. Assn. Computing Machinery (mem. spl. interest group on programming langs. 1980—, mem. spl. interest group on computers in edn., 1974—, mem. spl. interest group on mgmt. data base, 1981), MUMPS Users' Group (vice chmn. 1974-75, chmn. 1975-77, 81-83, devel. com. chmn. 1977-79, 80-82, hon. life mem. Europe and Japan), Am. Assn. Med. Systems and Informatics, IEEE. Democrat. Episcopalian. Avocation: music. Home: 647 Elmwood Davis CA 95616 Office: U Calif Computer Sci Div Davis CA 95616

WALTHER, DALE JAY, lawyer; b. Elko, Nev., Oct. 15, 1948; s. Harold V. and Beryl H. (Brand) W.; m. Kazue Mori, Sept. 25, 1975; children—Kent, Brian, Nolan, Lisa, Curtis. B.A., Northwestern U., 1972; postgrad., Notre Dame U. summer law program, Japan, 1974; J.D., Calif. Western Sch. Law, 1975. Bar: Alaska 1975. Assoc. Law Offices Murphy Clark, Anchorage, 1975-80; ptnr. Clark, Walther & Flanigan, Anchorage, 1980—. Mem. Anchorage Bar Assn., Alaska Bar Assn., ABA, Order of Barristers, Am. Arbitration Assn., Phi Alpha Delta. Lodge: Elks. Home: PO Box 100428 Anchorage AK 99510 Office: Clark Walther & Flanigan 807 G St Suite 300 Anchorage AK 99501

WALTNER, JAMES DOUGLAS, pediatrician, educator; b. Yankton, S.D., Sept. 20, 1947; s. Glenn Hubert and Pauline Blanche (Hoffman) W. Student, U. S.D., 1965-68; MD, U. Tex., Dallas, 1972. Diplomate Am. Bd. Pediatrics. Pediatric intern Children's Med. Ctr., Dallas, 1972-73; resident in psychiatry Neuropsychiat. Inst., U. Mich., Ann Arbor, 1973-75; resident in pediatrics U. N.Mex. Sch. of Medicine/Bernalillo County Med. Ctr., Albuquerque, 1975-77, clin. asst. prof. pediatrics, 1978—; pvt. practice medicine specializing in pediatrics Espanola (N.Mex.) Pediatric Clinic, 1977-86; staff physician Los Lunas (N.Mex.) Hosp. and Tng. Sch., 1986-87; med. dir. Coordinated Community In-Home Care, Santa Fe, 1987—; chief of staff Espanola Hosp., 1980, trustee, 1980-85; med. dir. N.Mex. AIDS Services, Santa Fe, 1985—, mem. N.Mex. AIDS Task Force, 1983—. Contbr. articles to profl. jours. Fellow Am. Acad. Pediatrics; mem. AAAS, N.Mex. Med. Soc., N.Mex. Pediatric Soc., Am. Assn. Physicians for Human Rights, N.Mex. Assn. Physicians for Human Rights (pres. 1985-86). Recipient Upjohn Achievement award The Upjohn Co., Disting. Service award Espanola C. of C. 1980, Service and Edn. awards N.Mex. chpt. Am. Diabetes Assn., 1981. Fellow Am. Acad. Pediatrics; mem. AAAS, N.Mex. Med. Soc., N.Mex. Pediatric Soc., Am. Assn. Physicians for Human Rights, N.Mex. Assn. Physicians for Human Rights (pres. 1985-86). Avocations: music, hiking/camping, motorcycling, bicycling, physical fitness. Home: 3603 Calle del Sol NE Albuquerque NM 87110 Office: Coordinated Community In-Home Care PERA Bldg Room 516 PO Box 2348 Santa Fe NM 87504-2348

WALTON, JAMES STEPHEN, biomechanical engineer; b. Kingston-upon-Thames, Eng., Nov. 27, 1946; came to U.S., 1968, permanent resident, 1975; s. Ronald Walter and Jean Edna (Hudson) W.; m. Dorcas Ann Graham, July 20, 1974; children: Kirstyn Amy, Lars Timothy. Diploma in Phys. Edn., Leeds U., 1968; MA in Exercise Physiology, Mich. State U., 1970; MS in Applied Mechanics, Stanford U., 1976; PhD in Biomechanics, Pa. State U., 1981. Cert. tchr., Eng. Research asst. Stanford (Calif.) U., 1974-76; tchr. Gaynesford High Sch., Carshalton, Eng., 1969-70; dir. engring. Computerized Biomech. Analysis Inc., Amherst, Mass., 1979; sr. biomed. research scientist Gen. Motors Research Labs., Warren, Mich., 1979-85; applications engring. and product planning mgr. Motion Analysis Corp., Santa Rosa, Calif., 1985—; cons. Sci. mag., 1982, 83, Mich. State U., 1984-85; trampoline coach several gymnastics clubs and univ. teams, 1968—. Contbr. articles to profl jours. Mem. Nat. Boy's Club Gt. Britain, London, 1964—. Recipient Research award Nat. Collegiate Gymnastics Assn., 1968-69. Mem. Internat. Soc. Biomechanics (force platform group), Internat. Soc. Biomechanics in Sports, AAAS, Am. Acad. Forensic Scis. (provisional), Am. Coll. Sports Medicine, Am. Soc. Biomechanics, Am. Soc. Photogrammetry and Remote Sensing, Human Factors Soc., N.Y. Acad. Scis., Soc. Photo-Optical Instrumentation Engrs. (high-speed photography and photonics working group), Digital Equipment Computer User's Soc., Mensa, U.S. Gymnastics Fedn., Brit. Trampoline Fedn., Stanford Mechanics Alumni Club, Sigma Xi (several offices GM Research Labs. chpt. 1981-82, 84-86). Avocations: gymnastics, photography. Home: 3136 Pauline Dr Sebastabol CA 95472 Office: Motion Analysis Corp 93 Stony Circle Santa Rosa CA 95401

WALTON, ROGER ALAN, public relations executive, writer; b. Denver, June 25, 1941; s. Lyle R. and Velda V. (Nicholson) W. Attended, U. Colo., 1960-63. Govt. rep. Continental Airlines, Denver, 1964-72; dir. pub. affairs Regional Transp. Dist., Denver, 1972-77; pub. affairs cons. Denver, 1977—. Author: Colorado--A Practical Guide to its Government and Politics, 1973, 5th rev. edit., 1985; columnist The Denver Post newspaper, 1983—, The Rocky Mountain Jour., 1977-81. Mem. U.S. Presdl. Electoral Coll., Washington, 1968; commr. U.S. Bicentennial Revolution Commn., Colo., 1972-76, U.S. Commn. on the Bicentennial of the U.S. Constitution, Denver, 1985—, pres.; trustee Arapahoe County (Colo.) Library Bd., 1982-86. Republican. Avocations: reading, fishing. Home and Office: PO Box 10383 Denver CO 80210

WALTZ, MARYELLEN, chemical dependency hospital administrator, psychotherapist; b. San Rafael, Calif., Jan. 1, 1946; d. Charles Wayne and Betty (McCormack) W.; children: David D. Clark IV, Carrie Lee Marheuka. BA, U. Nev., 1977; MSW, U. Denver, 1985. Family therapist Phoenix Health, Alameda, Calif., 1980-82; therapist chemical dependency Care Unit div. Mercy Hosp., Denver, 1982-84, chem. dependency therapist and social worker, 1985-86; staff asst. Denver Dept. Social Services, 1984-85; pvt. practice psychotherapy Denver, 1982-86, Las Vegas, Nev., 1986—; program dir. Care Unit div. Hosp., Las Vegas, 1986—. Mem. Nat. Assn. Social Workers. Democrat. Lodge: Order Eastern Star. Avocations: swimming, piloting. Home: 6841 Caribbean Ct The Lakes NV 89117 Office: Care Unit Hosp Nev 5100 S Sahara Las Vegas NV 89102

WALZ, ALVIN EUGENE, chemistry educator; b. Hot Springs, S.D., Jan. 12, 1919; s. George Adam and Charlotte Ann (Guenthner) W. BS, No. State Coll., Aberdeen, S.D., 1943; MS, U. Iowa, 1945, PhD, 1950. Instr. sci. Univ. High Sch., Iowa City, 1943-48; from asst. prof. to prof. chemistry Mankato (Minn.) State U., 1950-63; prof. Calif. Luth. U., Thousand Oaks, 1963—. Mem. AAAS, Am. Chem. Soc., Sigma Xi. Republican. Lutheran. Home: 119 Sirius Circle Thousand Oaks CA 91360 Office: Calif Luth U 60 W Olson Rd Thousand Oaks CA 91360

WALZ, BETTY MARION, personnel service executive, dental management consultant; b. Big Timber, Mont., July 23, 1934; d. Milton Sureno and Donna Marion (Chapel) Willard; m. John William Walz, Aug. 30, 1963 (div. 1977); children—Mrs. Jemell Guiles, Mrs. Shawn Hooks. Registered dental asst., Calif. Dental asst. various offices, Seattle and San Diego, 1953-75; dental office mgr. various offices, San Diego, 1975-80; dental mgmt. cons., San Diego, 1980-81; founder, pres. Profl. Fill-Ins/PFI Personnel Services, San Diego, 1980—. Mem. adv. bd. San Diego Community Coll. Dist., 1982—; leader San Diego-Imperial council Girl Scouts U.S., 1959-69; youth chmn. Jr. Women's Club, Chula Vista, Calif., 1968; vol. Flying Samaritans, 1975, 76, 82, 83. Recipient State Service award Jr. Women's Club, 1968, Girl Scouts Service award Jr. Women's Club, 1968. Mem. San Diego County Dental Assts. Soc., So. Calif. Dental Assts. Assn. (del. 1985), Am. Dental Assts. Assn., Nat. Assn. Women Bus. Owners (2nd v.p. San Diego chpt. 1986-87), Beta Sigma Phi. Republican. Mem. Religious Sci. Ch. Avocations: oil paintng; fishing; walking; travel. Home: 4201 Bonita Rd #238 Bonita CA 92002 Office: PFI Personnel Services 1081 Camino del Rio S #221 San Diego CA 92108

WAMBA, JON MONTGOMERY, dentist; b. Seattle, Aug. 8, 1936; s. Freelyn Elwood and Clarice (Montgomery) W.; m. Sally Ann Black, July 2, 1961; children: Elizabeth, Jon Eric, Kristine. DDS, U. Wash., 1961. Gen. practice dentistry Dr. Jon Wamba & Assocs., Davenport, Wash., 1961—. Councilman City of Davenport, 1974-78. Served to lt. comdr., USN, 1961-68. Fellow Acad. Gen. Dentistry; mem. Dental Soc. N. Am., Am. Dental Assn., Wash. State Dental Assn., Spokane Dist. Dental Soc. Republican. Lutheran. Lodge: Lions (pres. local chpt. 1970-71). Avocations: golf, skiing, investments. Home: 810 Nichols Davenport WA 99122 Office: 707 Logan Davenport WA 99122

WAMBOLDT, RICHARD LEE, social worker; b. Dayton, Ohio, July 26, 1946; s. Henry and Frieda (Schmidt) W. Student, U. Ams., Cholula, Mex., 1972-73; BA, Wright State U., 1973; MSW, U. Louisville, 1981. Social service worker Greene County Pub. Welfare Dept., Xenia, Ohio, 1975-76; social service cons. Green County Community Action Council, Xenia, 1976; social work trainee VA Med. Ctr., Albuquerque, 1980; social worker Dayton (Ohio) Mental Health Devel. Ctr., 1976-82, VA Vet Ctr., Gallup, N.Mex., 1982—; part-time instr. U. N.Mex., Gallup, 1986. Served with U.S. Army, 1966-68. Recipient Performance award VA, Albuquerque, 1984. Fellow Inst. Rational Emotive Therapy (assoc., supr. 1985); mem. Nat. Assn. Social Workers, Acad. Cert. Social Workers (cert.), Registry Clin. Social Workers. Avocations: fishing, guitar, cross country skiing. Office: VA Vet Ctr 211 W Mesa Suite 6 Gallup NM 87301

WAMSER, CARL CHRISTIAN, chemistry educator; b. N.Y.C., Aug. 10, 1944; s. Christian A. and Madeline G. (Miller) W.; m. Laurie A. Schmidt, Aug. 12, 1984; children: Scott Christian, Kimberly Joy. ScB, Brown U., 1966; PhD, Calif. Inst. Tech., 1969. Postdoctoral research fellow Harvard U., Cambridge, Mass., 1969-70; prof. chemistry Calif. State U., Fullerton, 1970-83, Portland (Oreg.) State U., 1984—; vis. prof. U. So. Calif., Los Angeles, 1975-76, U. Hawaii, 1981; research felow U. Calif., Berkeley, 1980. Co-author Fundamentals of Organic Reaction Mechanisms, 1976, Organic Chemistry, 1985; contbr. articles to profl. jours. Named Outstanding Prof. Calif. State U., Fullerton, 1983, Disting. Faculty Alumni Assn. Calif. State U., Fullerton, 1983. Mem. Am. Chem. Soc., Inter-Am. Photochem. Soc. Home: 19440 Wilderness Dr West Linn OR 97068 Office: Portland State U Dept Chemistry Portland OR 97207

WAN, FREDERIC YUI-MING, applied mathematician; b. Shanghai, China, Jan. 7, 1936; s. Wai-Nam and Olga Pearl (Jung) W.; m. Julia Y.S. Chang, Sept. 10, 1960. S.B., M.I.T., 1959, S.M., 1963, Ph.D., 1965. Mem. staff M.I.T. Lincoln Lab., Lexington, 1959-65; instr. math. M.I.T., Cambridge, 1965-67, asst. prof., 1967-69, assoc. prof., 1969-74; prof. math., dir. Inst. Applied Math. and Stats., U. B.C., Vancouver, 1974-83; prof. applied math. and math. U. Wash., Seattle, 1983—, chmn. Dept. Applied Math., 1984—; program dir. Div. Math. Sci. NSF, 1986-87; cons. indsl. firms and govt. agys. Mem. M.I.T. Ednl. Council for B.C. Area of Can. Contbr. articles to profl. jours. Sloan Found. fellow, 1973; Killam sr. fellow, 1979. Fellow Am. Acad. Mechanics (sec. fellows 1985—); mem. Soc. Indsl. and Applied Math., Can. Applied Math. Soc. (council 1980-83, pres. 1983-84), Am. Math. Soc., AAUP, ASME, Sigma Xi. Home: 11680 Sunrise Dr NE Bainbridge Island WA 98110 Office: U Wash FS-20 Dept Applied Math Seattle WA 98195

WANDELL, MICHAEL GEORGE, genetic engineering company executive; b. Aberdeen, Wash., Mar. 4, 1947; s. Edward F. and Patricia G. (Knowles) W.; m. Linda A. McCorkle, Jan. 2, 1983; 1 child, Marcus Patrick. BS in Polit. Sci., Oreg. State U., 1969; BS in Pharmacy, U. Wash., 1975; PharmD, U. Mich., 1978. Fellow in clin. pharmacology NIH, Tucson, Ariz., 1978-80; mgr. clin. research Syva Co., Palo Alto, Calif., 1980-84; dir. med. affairs Genetic Systems, Seattle, 1984-86, dir. internat. bus., 1986—. Author/editor: Clinical Pharmaco Kinetics, 1983; contbr. articles to profl. jours. Fellow Am. Soc. Clin. Pharmacology; mem. AAAS, Am. Heart Assn., Am. Coll. Clin. Pharmacy, Drug Info. Soc. Democrat. Avocations: sailboarding, off road bicycling. Home: 1963 21st Ave E Seattle WA 98112 Office: Genetic Systems Corp 3005 First Ave Seattle WA 98121

WANG, ALAN PING-I, mathematics educator; b. Shanghai, Republic of China, Mar. 1, 1930; came to U.S., 1950; s. Jun Liang Wang and Jan Yan Pan; m. Cecilia Y. Wang, Aug. 30, 1957; children: Geoffrey, James, Eugene. BS, Wash. State U., 1954; MS, U. So. Calif., 1957; PhD, UCLA, 1962. Sr. research engr. Northrop Corp., Los Angeles, 1957-62; sr. staff mem. Hughes Aircraft, Los Angeles, 1962-69; sr. cons. Hughes /aircraft, IBM Corp., Los Angeles, 1969-74; prof. Ariz. State U., Tempe, 1970—. Contbr. articles to profl. jours. Mem. Am. Math Soc., Soc. Applied Math., Internat. Radiative Soc., Sigma Xi. Office: Ariz State U Tempe AZ 85281

WANG, CHARLES PING, scientist; b. Shanghai, Republic of China, Apr. 25, 1937; came to U.S., 1962; s. Kuan-Ying and Ping-Lu (Ming) W.; m. Lily L. Lee, June 29, 1963. BS, Taiwan U., Republic of China, 1959; MS,

Tsinghua U., Singchu, Republic of China, 1961; PhD, Calif. Inst. Tech., 1967. Mem. tech. staff Bellcomm, Washington, 1967-69; research engr. U. San Diego, 1969-74; sr. scientist Aerspace Corp., Los Angeles, 1976-86; pres. Optodyne, Inc., Compton, Calif., 1986—; adj. prof. U. Calif., San Diego, 1979—; pres. Chinese-Am. Engr. and Scientists Assn. So. Calif., Los Angeles, 1979-81; program chmn. Internation Conf. of Lasers, Shanghai, 1979-80; organizer and session chmn. Lasers Conf., Los Angeles, 1981-84, program chmn., Las Vegas, 1985. Editor in chief Series in Laser Tech., 1983—; contbr. articles to profl. jours.; inventor discharge excimer laser. Calif. Inst. Tech. scholar, 1965. Fellow Am. Optical Soc., AIAA (assoc., jour. editor 1981-83). Office: Optodyne Inc 1180 Mahalo Pl Compton CA 90220

WANG, CHEN CHI, electronics co. exec., real estate exec., fin. co. exec.; b. Taipei, Taiwan, China, Aug. 10, 1932; came to U.S., 1959, naturalized, 1970; s. Chin-Ting and Chen-Kim (Chen) W.; m. Victoria Rebisoff, Mar. 5, 1965; children: Katherine Kim, Gregory Chen, John Christopher, Michael Edward. B.A., Nat. Taiwan U., 1955; B.S.E.E., San Jose State U., 1965; M.B.A., U. Calif., Berkeley, 1961. With IBM Corp., San Jose, Calif., 1965-72; founder, chief exec. officer Electronics Internat. Co., Santa Clara, Calif., 1968-72, owner, gen. mgr., 1972-81, reorganized as EIC Group, 1982, now chmn. bd. and pres.; dir. Systek Electronics Corp., Santa Clara, 1970-73; founder, sr. partner Wang Enterprises, Santa Clara, 1974—; founder, sr. partner Hanson & Wang Devel. Co., Woodside, Calif., 1977-85; chmn. bd. Golden Alpha Enterprises, Foster City, Calif., 1979—; mng. ptnr. Woodside Acres-Las Pulgas Estate, Woodside, 1980-85; founder, sr. ptnr. DeVine & Wang, Oakland, Calif., 1977-83; Van Heal & Wang, West Village, Calif., 1981-82; founder, chmn. bd. EIC Fin. Corp., Redwood City, Calif., 1985—. Served to 2d lt., Nationalist Chinese Army, 1955-56. Mem. Internat. Platform Assn., Tau Beta Pi. Mem. Christian Ch. Author: Monetary and Banking System of Taiwan, 1955; The Small Car Market in the U.S., 1961. Home: 195 Brookwood Rd Woodside CA 94062 Office: EIC Fin Corp 2055 Woodside Rd Suite 100 Redwood City CA 94061

WANG, CHEN HWA, civil and safety engineer; b. Tsingtao, People's Rep. China, Nov. 6, 1930; came to U.S., 1957; s. Shie C. and Shou C. (Chen) W.; m. Betty C. Chao, Sept. 2, 1962; children: Jeffrey W., Patrick W. BS, Taiwan Coll. Engring., Tainan, 1954; MS, U. Notre Dame, 1959; PhD, U. Mo., 1965. Registered profl. engr., Md., Calif., Washington, Va. Assoc. prof. Cath. U. Am., Washington, 1964-69; staff engr. TRW System Group, McLean, Va., 1969-71; chief engr. Jolles Assocs., Silver Spring, Md., 1971-73; sr. safety engr. Occupational Safety and Health Adminstrn., Washington, 1973-79; pres. Cathay Devel. Corp., Monterey Park, Calif., 1979-83, Tritech Assocs., Inc., Monterey Park, 1983—; chmn. Tritech Dev., Inc. subs Tritech Assocs., Inc., Monterey Park, 1983—; cons. Montgomery Green Wrignt, Silver Spring, Md., 1965-66, Milton Gurweitz Assocs., Washington, 1967; expert witness The Travelers Ins. Co., Hartford, Conn., 1984. Contbr. articles to profl. jours. Recipient Accomplishment Award Taiwan Power Co., Taipei, 1953, Achievement Award, Occupational Safety and Health Adminstrn. Dept. Labor, Washington, 1979. Mem. ASCE, System Safety Soc., Am. Soc. Safety Engrs., Am. Concrete Inst., Sigma Xi. Lodge: Lions. Avocations: music, photography. Home: 1731 Camino Lindo South Pasadena CA 91030 Office: Tritech Assocs Inc 735 W Emerson Ave Monterey Park CA 91754

WANG, CHING CHUNG, biochemistry educator; b. Beijing, People's Republic China, Feb. 10, 1936; came to U.S., 1960; m. Alice Lee, Apr. 6, 1963; children: Charlotte I-Ting, Felix Yang-Yang. BSc in Chemistry, Nat. Taiwan U., Taipei, Republic China, 1958; PhD in Biochemistry, U. Calif., Berkeley, 1966. Research assoc. Columbia U., N.Y.C., 1966-67, Princeton (N.J.) U., 1967-69; sr. investigator Merck Inst., Rahway, N.J., 1969-81; prof. chemistry U. Calif., San Francisco, 1981—. Contbr. articles to profl. jours. Vice-chmn. Golden Gate Regional Ctr. for the Handicapped, San Francisco, 1982—. Grantee Burroughs Wellcome Found., 1983. Mem. Am. Chem. Soc., AAAS, Am. Soc. Biol. Chemists, Soc. Neurosci., Am. Soc. Parasitologists, Soc. Chinese Bioscientists in Am. (pres. 1986-87). Office: U Calif Sch Pharmacy San Francisco CA 94143

WANG, CHUN-I, pediatrician, educator; b. Peking, Peoples Republic of China, Jan. 10, 1921; came to U.S., 1950; d. Hung-Nien and Fu-Yun (Chang) W.; m. Ching-Hsien Chiang, May 12, 1948; children: Elizabeth Chiang Kuo, Frances Lucille Chiang. BS, Yenching U., Beijing, 1941; MD, West China Union U., Chengtu, 1945. Diplomate Am. Bd. Pediatrics. Asst. prof. medicine Nat. Def. Med. Coll., Shanghai and Taipeh, Republic of China, 1949-50; asst. prof. pediatrics Childrens Hosp. Los Angeles and U. So. Calif. Sch. Medicine, 1965-72, assoc. prof. pediatrics, 1972—; dir. cystic fibrosis ctr. Childrens Hosp. Los Angeles, 1965—. Contbr. articles to profl. jours. Bd. dirs. United Way, Los Angeles, 1975-79. Served to lt. col. Chinese Army, 1945-50. Mem. AMA (cert. merit 1952), Am. Thoracic Soc., Calif. Med. Assn., Los Angeles County Med. Assn., Los Angeles Pediatrics Soc., Chinese-Am. Faculty Assn. (liaison officer 1985—). Republican. Presbyterian. Office: Childrens Hosp of Los Angeles 4650 Sunset Blvd Los Angeles CA 90027

WANG, GEORGE SHIH CHANG, marketing executive; b. Anking, People's Republic China, May 4, 1933; came to U.S., 1951; s. Chien-Shun and Ai-Lan (Kwong) W.; m. Ann Chen, Dec. 21, 1957; children: Julia, Gregory, Tracy. BS, U. Mich., 1958, MSCE, MS in Nuclear Engring., 1960; PhD in Engring., UCLA, 1970. Research engr. Engring. Research Inst.-U. Mich., Ann Arbor, 1960-62; project engr. Bechtel Power Corp., Los Angeles, 1962-67, asst. chief nuclear engr., 1967-68, chief nuclear engr., 1968-72, engring. mgr., 1972-76, mgr. engring., 1977-80; v.p. Bechtel Nat., Inc., San Francisco, 1980-85, Bechtel N. Am. Power Corp., San Francisco, 1985-86, Bechtel Overseas Corp., San Francisco, 1985-86; gen. mgr. Helium Breeder Assocs., Newport Beach, Calif., 1976-77; v.p. strategic planning and market devel. Fluor Corp., Irvine, Calif., 1986—; dep. gen. mgr., gen. mgr. research and engring div. Bechtel Group, Inc., San Francisco, 1980-85, chief sci. officer, 1983-85, dirs. adv. group, 1974-75. Contbr. articles to profl. jours. Fellow NSF, 1960. Fellow ASCE; mem. Am. Nuclear Soc., Soc. Civil Engrs., Chi Epselon. Club: U. Mich. (Orange County) (pres. 1973-80). Office: Fluor Corp 3333 Michelson Dr Irvine CA 92730

WANG, I-TUNG, atmospheric scientist; b. Peking, China, Feb. 16, 1933; s. Shen and Wei-Yun (Wen) W.; m. Amy Hung Kong; children: Cynthia P., Clifford T. BS in Physics, Nat. Taiwan U., 1955; MA in Physics, U. Toronto, 1957; PhD in Physics, Columbia U., 1965. Research physicist Carnegie-Mellon U., Pitts., 1965-67, asst. prof., 1967-70; environ. systems engr. Argonne (Ill.) Nat. Lab., 1970-76; mem. tech. staff Environ. Monitoring and Services Ctr. Rockwell Internat., Creve Coeur, Mo., 1976-80, Newbury Park, Calif., 1980-84; sr. scientist, combustion engr. Environ. Monitoring and Services Inc., Newbury Park, 1984—; tech. advisor Bur. of Environ. Protection,Republic of China, 1985. Contbr. papers to profl. jours. First violin Conejo Symphony Orch., Thousand Oaks, Calif., 1981-83. Grantee Bureau of Environ. Protection, Taiwan, 1985. Mem. N.Y. Acad. of Scis., Air Pollution Control Assn., Sigma Xi. Avocations: violin and chamber music. Office: Environmental Monitoring & Services Inc 2421 W Hillcrest Dr Newbury Pk CA 91320

WANG, JAMES CHIA-FANG, political science educator; b. Nanling, China, Apr. 4, 1926; came to U.S., 1946, naturalized, 1962; s. Chien-Yu and Lilian W.; m. Sarah Cutter, May 7, 1960; children—Sarah, Eric. B.A. in Polit. Sci., Oberlin Coll., 1950; postgrad., N.Y. U., 1951; Ph.D. in Polit. Sci, U. Hawaii, 1971. Research asst., internat. study group Brookings Instn., 1951-53; adminstrv. and tng. officer UN Secretariat, N.Y.C., 1953-57; editor-in-charge UN Documents Edit., Readex Corp., N.Y.C., 1957-60; lectr. far eastern politics NYU, N.Y.C., 1957-60; instr. Asian history and econs. Punahou Sch., Honolulu, 1960-64; program officer Inst. Student Interchange, East-West Center, Honolulu, 1964-69; acting dir. participant services Inst. Student Interchange, East-West Center, 1970, adminstrv. officer admissions, 1969-71; dir. freshmen integrated program Hilo (Hawaii) Coll., 1971-72; asst. prof. polit. sci. and internat. studies U. Hawaii, Hilo, 1971-72; assoc. prof. U. Hawaii, 1973-76, prof., 1976—; mem. U. Hawaii (Contemporary China Study Group), 1971—, chmn. dept. polit. sci., 1973-75, 84—; profl. asso. East-West Communications Inst., Honolulu, 1978, East-West Communications Inst. (Resource System Inst.), 1980-81; adviser to AAUW, Hawaii, 1978—; cons. World Polit. Risk Forecast, Frost & Sullivan, Inc., N.Y.C., 1980-81. Author: The Cultural Revolution in China: An Annotated Bibliography, 1976, Contemporary Chinese Politics: Political Institutions and Process, 1980, 85, Hawaii State and Local Politics, 1982, Study Guide for Power in Hawaii; contbr. articles to scholarly jours. Mem. Hawaii County Bicentennial Commn., 1975-76; vice chmn. Democratic Party, County of Hawaii, 1972-76, chmn. 1982-84; mem. Dem. State Central Com., 1982-84; chmn. univ. adv. com. to Hawaii county council; mem. coordinating com. Hawaii Polit. Studies Assn., 1986—. U. Hawaii Research Found. grantee, 1972-78. Mem. Assn. Asian Studies, Assn. Chinese Lang. Tchrs., Am. Polit. Sci. Assn., Internat. Studies Assn. Home: PO Box 13 Hilo HI 86720 Office: U Hawaii at Hilo Political Science Dept 1400 Kapiolani St Hilo HI 96721

WANG, JAW-KAI, agricultural engineering educator; b. Nanjing, Jiangsu, People Republic China, Mar. 4, 1932; s. Shuling and Hsi-Ying (Lo) W.; m. Kwang Mei Chow, Sept. 7, 1957; children—Angela C.C., Dora C.C., Lawrence C.Y. B.S., Nat. Taiwan U., 1953; M.S. in Agrl. Engring., Mich. State U., 1956, Ph.D., 1958. Registered profl. engr., Hawaii. Faculty agrl. engring. dept. U. Hawaii, Honolulu, 1959—; assoc. prof., chmn. dept. U. Hawaii, 1964-68, prof., 1968—, chmn. dept. agrl. engring., 1968-75; pres. Wang & Assocs., 1979—; co-dir. internat. sci. and ednl. council U.S. Dept. Agr.; vis. assoc. dir. internat. programs and studies office Nat. Assn. State Univs. and Land-Grant Colls., 1979; vis. prof. Nat. Taiwan U., 1965, U. Calif., Davis, 1980; cons. U.S. Army Civilian Adminstrn., Ryukus, Okinawa, 1966, Internat. Rice Research Inst., Philippines, 1971, Pacific Concrete and Rock Co. Ltd., 1973, AID, 1973, Universe Tankships, Del., 1980-81, World Bank, 1981, 82, ABA Internat., 1981-85, Internat. Found. for Agrl. Devel./ World Bank, 1981, Rockefeller Found., 1980, Orizaba, Inc., 1983, Agrisystems/FAO, 1983, Info. Processing Assocs., 1984, County of Maui, 1984, Alexander and Baldwin, 1986; mem. expert panel on agrl. mechanization FAO/UN, 1984—; sr. fellow East-West Center Food Inst., 1973-74; dir. Info. Systems and Services Internat., Inc., 1986—; mem. Am. Soc. Agrl. Cons. Internat. Dept. of State, 1985. Author: Irrigated Rice Production Systems; editor: Taro—A Review of Colocasia esculenta and its Potential, 1983; mem. editorial bd. Internat. Jour. Aquacultural Engring. Fellow Am. Soc. Agrl. Engrs. (chmn. Hawaii sect. 1962-63, chmn. grad. instrn. com. 1971-73, chmn. aquacultural engring. com. 1977-79, chmn. Pacific region 1975-76, engr. of yr. 1976, Tech. Paper award 1978); mem. Chinese Soc. Agrl. Engrs., Emerging Tech. Task Force, Sigma Xi, Gamma Sigma Delta (pres. Hawaii chpt. 1974-75), Pi Mu Epsilon. Home: 1503 Uluhaku Pl Kailua HI 96734 Office: Dept Agrl Engring 3050 Maile Way U Hawaii Honolulu HI 96822

WANG, JIN-CHEN CAMILLA, medical geneticist; b. Lan-Chou, Republic of China, Oct. 28, 1945; m. J.C.T. Wang; children: David, James. MS, Purdue U., 1971; MD, Nat. Taiwan U., 1970. Diplomate Am. Bd. Pediatrics, Am. Bd. Med. Genetics. Intern Greater Balt. Med. Ctr., 1972; resident in pediatrics North Shore U. Hosp., Manhasett, N.Y., 1974-76; staff pediatrician Az. Children's Hosp., Tempe, Ariz., 1976-79; staff physician E.K. Shriver Ctr., Waltham, Mass., 1979-81; fellow in pediatrics Mass. Gen. Hosp., Boston, 1981-84; instr. pediatrics Harvard U., Cambridge, Mass., 1983-84; med. geneticist The Genetics Inst., Pasadena, Calif., 1985—. Author: numerous articles to profl. jours. Mem. Am. Soc. Human Genetics. Home: 30926 Oceangrove Dr Rancho Palos Verdes CA 90274 Office: The Genetics Inst 11 Del Mar Pasadena CA 91105

WANG, KUO-KAI GEORGE, technical marketing manager; b. Tainan, Taiwan, Sept. 19, 1951; came to U.S., 1975; s. Kai-Shung and Mei-Hwei W.; m. Menq-Yun Wu, Jan. 18, 1977; children: Charles, Albert. B.S., Nat. Taiwan U., 1973; M.S., SUNY-Stony Brook, 1976, Ph.D., 1979; M.B.A., U. Santa Clara, 1985; system design engr. dept. research and devel. Burroughs Corp., N.Y.C., 1979-81; staff engr. dept. strategic mktg., microprocessor div. Fairchild Corp., Santa Clara, Calif., 1981-84; tech. mktg. mgr. dept. microprocessor mktg. NEC Electronics, Inc., Mountain View, Calif., 1984—. Research in transient queueing theory and computer communication and digital electronics. Mem. IEEE Computer Soc., Communications Soc., Cybernetics Soc., N.Y. Acad. Scis., Sigma Xi. Home: 1425 Hawk Ct Sunnyvale CA 94087 Office: NEC Electronics Inc 401 Ellis St Mountain View CA 94043

WANG, MING-YU RACHEL, chemistry educator; b. Taipei, Taiwan, Republic of China, Nov. 29, 1951; came to U.S., 1973; d. Kwei-Jeo and Yet-Ken (Tu) W. BS, Nat. Taiwan U., Taipei, 1973; MS, U. Chgo., 1974; PhD, Northwestern U., 1979. Asst. prof. chemistry Whitworth Coll., Spokane, Wash., 1979-82, assoc. prof. chemistry, 1982-85; asst. prof. chemistry Eastern Wash. U., Cheney, 1986—; part time instr. Eastern Wash. U., Cheney, 1985-86, Spokane Community Coll., 1985-86; chief health sci. profl. advisor Whitworth Coll., Spokane, 1983-85. Contbr. articles to profl. jours. Recipient Dr. Sun Yat Sun's award Republic China, 1971. Mem. Am. Chem. Soc. (sect. officer 1982-85), Nat. Sci. Tchrs. Assn. Office: Eastern Wash U Cheney WA 99004

WANG, SHIH-HO, electrical engineer, educator; b. Kiangsu, China, June 29, 1944; came to U.S., 1968; s. C.C. Wang and Man Shih. BEE, Nat. Taiwan U., Taipei, 1967; MEE, U. Calif., Berkeley, 1970, PhD in Elec. Engring., 1971. Asst. prof. elec. engring. U. Colo., Colo. Springs, 1973-76, Boulder, 1976-77; asst. prof. electrical engring. U. Md., College Park, 1977-78, assoc. prof., 1978-84; prof. U. Calif., Davis, 1984—; cons. Lawrence Livermore (Calif.) Nat. Lab., 1986—; scientific officer Office Naval Research, Arlington, Va., 1983-84. Assoc. editor Internat. Jour. Robotics and Automation, 1986—. Served to 2d lt. China Air Force, Taiwan, 1967-68. Mem. IEEE (hon. mention award control systems soc. 1975). Office: Univ Calif Dept Elec and Computer Engring Davis CA 95616

WANG, TONY KAR-HUNG, automotive and defense company executive; b. Shanghai, People's Republic of China, Apr. 28, 1952; came to U.S., 1970; s. Kuo-Tung and Chien-Wen (Chu) W.; m. Vivian Wei-Pie, May 25, 1980; children: Stephen, Jason. BSEin Materials and Metall. Engring., U. Mich., 1973, MSE in Materials, 1975. Materials engr. Burroughs Corp., Detroit, 1976-78; sr. project mgr. Gen. Motors Corp., Warren, Mich., 1978-85; staff engr. Hughes Aircraft Co., El Segundo, Calif., 1985, Gen. Motors-Hughes Electronics Corp., El Segundo, 1986—. Contbr. articles to profl. jours. Goodrich scholar, U. Mich., Ann Arbor, 1974. Mem. Soc. Advanced Materials and Process Engring. Republican. Office: GM Hughes Electronics Corp 2000 E El Segundo Blvd El Segundo CA 90245

WANLASS, STANLEY GLEN, sculptor, painter; b. Am. Fork, Utah, Apr. 3, 1941; s. L. Glen and Alta (Butler) W.; m. Joy Erikson, Feb. 17, 1966; children—Lincoln Stanley, Amber Joy, Britton Stanley, Brandy Joy, Brandon Stanley. B.F.A., Brigham Young U., 1966, M.A., 1968. Instr. Brigham Young U., Provo, Utah, 1965-70; instr. European Art Acad., Paris, summer 1966; prof. Université de Grenoble (France), 1969-70; dir. art programs Study Guild Internat., Salt Lake City, 1970-71; prof. Medicine Hat Coll., Alta., summer 1970, 71; prof. Clatsop Coll., Astoria, Oreg., 1971—; owner, painter, sculptor Stanley Wanlass Studios, Astoria, 1971—; paintings and sculptures represented in collections including: Des Arts Graphiques, Palais Congres, Paris, Cour de Maison, Université de Grenoble, Ft. Clatsop Nat. Meml. Lewis and Clark, Los Angeles Mus. Natural History, Detroit Hist. Mus., Pebble Beach Concourse D'Elegance, Mus. Nat. Heritage, Lexington, Mass., City of Everett, Wash.; design cons. for corps. and architects. Served with U.S. Army, 1959-60. Recipient Merrill award Brigham Young U., 1965; Brock Bank award, 1966; Grand Sweepstakes award Oreg. Trail Nat. Show, 1981; 1st place Bronze award, 1981; Silver medal Springfield Mus. Art, 1981; Bluebribbon award Concourse d'Elegance Oakland U., Detroit, Mich., 1983, Grand Prize and First Place awards Auburn (Ind.) Cord Duesenberg Mus., 1985. Mormon. Author Dictionary of America's Early Automobiles and Their Radiator Emblems, 1974. Home: 907 5th St Astoria OR 97103 Office: 16th and Jerome St Astoria OR 97103

WANTIEZ, HAROLD NICHOLAS, aerospace engineer; b. Pitts., Oct. 15, 1938; s. Harold Blair and Ethel Edna (Ertman) W.; m. Yoshiko Yasuda, June 10, 1965. BS in Aerospace Engring., Northrop Inst., 1961. Registered profl. engr., Wash. Specialist engr. Boeing Co., Seattle, 1968-76; aerospace engr. FAA, Seattle, 1977-85, mgr. standardization br., 1986, project mgr. British Aerospace/Fokker cert. programs, 1987—; cons. Wash. State Bd. Engring. Examiners, Olympia, 1972-81. Co-author: Eaglets of Mitsubishi, 1981; contbg. editor: Live Steam mag., 1986—. Served to 1st lt. USAF, 1962-65. Fellow AIAA (assoc., sec. 1981-82, service award 1980, named disting. lectr. 1981). Republican. Roman Catholic. Avocations: theoretical physics, design and constn. of steam powered models. Office: FAA 17900 Pacific Hwy S Seattle WA 98168

WANTLAND, EARL, electronics company executive; b. 1931; married. Student, Portland State Coll. With Tektronix Inc., Beaverton, Ore., 1955—, exec. v.p., 1969-71, pres., 1971—, chief exec. officer, 1974—, also dir.; dir. Portland Gen. Electric Co., U.S. Bancorp., U.S. Nat. Bank Oreg., Floating Point Systems Inc. Bd. dirs. Portland State U. Found.; trustee Lewis and Clark Coll., Portland. Served with USNR, 1950-54. Office: Tektronix Inc Box 500 Beaverton OR 97077 *

WARD, ALBERT EUGENE, research center executive, archeologist, ethnohistorian; b. Carlinville, Ill., Aug. 20, 1940; s. Albert Alan and Eileen (Boston) W.; m. Gladys Anena Lea, Apr. 26, 1961 (div. Apr. 4, 1974); children—Scott Bradley, Brian Tod; m. Stefanie Helen Tschaikowsky, Apr. 24, 1982. A.A., Bethany Luth. Jr. Coll., Mankato, Minn., 1961; B.S., No. Ariz. U., 1968; M.A., U. Ariz., 1972. Lab. asst., asst. archeologist Mus. No. Ariz., Flagstaff, 1965-67; research archeologist Desert Research Inst., U. Nev., Las Vegas, 1968; research archeologist Archeol. Survey, Prescott Coll., Ariz., 1969-71, research assoc., 1971-73; research archeologist Ariz. Archeol. Ctr., Nat. Park Service, Tucson, 1972-73, research collaborator Chaco Ctr., Albuquerque, 1975; founder, dir. archeol. research program Mus. Albuquerque, 1975-76; founder, dir., pres. bd. dirs. Ctr. Anthrop. Studies, Albuquerque, 1976—; lectr. U. N.Mex. Community Coll., 1974-77, others; contract archeol. salvage and research projects in N.Mex. and Ariz. Editorial adv. bd. Hist. Archeology, 1978-80; editor publs. Ctr. Anthrop. Studies, 1978—. Contbr. articles to scholarly jours. Grantee Mus. No. Ariz., 1972, S.W. Monuments Assn., 1973, CETA, 1975-79, Nat. Park Service, 1978-79. Mem. Soc. Am. Archeology, Soc. Hist. Archeology, No. Ariz. Soc. Sci. and Art, Ariz. Archeol. and Hist. Soc., Archeol. Soc. N.Mex., Albuquerque Archeol. Soc., Am. Anthrop. Assn., S.W. Mission Research Ctr., Am. Soc. Conservation Archeology, Soc. Archeol. Scis., Southwestern Anthrop. Assn., N.Mex. Archeol. Council, Living Hist. Farms and Agrl. Mus. Assn. Republican. Lutheran. Office: Ctr Anthrop Studies PO Box 14576 Albuquerque NM 87191

WARD, ANTHONY JOHN, lawyer; b. Los Angeles, Sept. 25, 1931; s. John P. and Helen C. (Harris) W.; A.B., U. So. Calif., 1953; LL.B., U. Calif. at Berkeley, 1956; m. Marianne Edle von Graeve, Feb. 20, 1960 (div. 1977); 1 son, Mark Joachim; m. 2d, Julia Norby Credell, Nov. 4, 1978. Admitted to Calif. bar, 1957; asso. firm Ives, Kirwan & Dibble, Los Angeles, 1958-61; partner firm Marapese and Ward, Hawthorne, Calif., 1961-69; individual practice law, Torrance, Calif., 1969-76; partner firm Ward, Gaunt & Raskin, 1976—. Mem. Los Angeles World Affairs Council. Served to 1st lt. USAF, 1956-58. Mem. Am., Los Angeles County bar assns., Blue Key, Lambda Chi Alpha. Democrat. Home: 2136 Via Pacheco Palos Verdes Estates CA 90274 Office: Pavilion A 21525 Hawthorne Blvd Torrance CA 90503

WARD, CARL EDWARD, research chemist; b. Albuquerque, Oct. 16, 1948; s. Joe E. and Loris E. (Wenk) W.; m. Bertha R. Schloer, June 9, 1970. BS in Chemistry, N.Mex. Inst. Mining and Tech., 1970; MS in Chemistry, Oreg. Grad. Ctr., 1972; PhD in Chemistry, Stanford U., 1977. Research chemist Union Carbide Corp., Charleston, W.Va., 1977-79, Dynapol Corp., Palo Alto, Calif., 1979-80; research chemist Chevron Chem. Co., Richmond, Calif., 1980-85, sr. research chemist, 1986—. Referee Jour. Organic Chemistry, 1983—; patentee in field. Recipient NSF traineeship, Stanford U., 1972-73; Upjohn fellow, Stanford U., 1976-77. Mem. AAAS, Am. Chem. Soc., Plant Growth Regulatory Soc. Am., Stanford Alumni Assn. Democrat. Club: N.Mex. Inst. Mining and Tech. Pres.'s (Socorro). Avocations: gardening, camping, fishing. Home: 1355 Bagely Way San Jose CA 95122 Office: Chevron Chem Co Ortho Div PO Box 4010 C-322 Richmond CA 94804-0010

WARD, CHARLES RICHARD, research entomologist, educator; b. Tahoka, Tex., Mar. 25, 1940; s. James Henry and Bertrice Opha (Moore) W.; m. Norma Faye Martin, Aug. 25, 1960; children: Beverly Jan, Charles Edward. AA, South Plains Coll., 1960; BS, Tex. Tech U., 1962, MS, 1964; PhD, Cornell U., 1968. Entomology specialist N.Mex. State U., Santa Cruz, Bolivia, 1976-78; research assoc., assoc. prof. entomology N.Mex. State U., Las Cruces, 1978-80; pest mgmt. specialist N.Mex. State U., Artesia, 1980-82, 1985-86; chief party, entomologist N.Mex. State U., San Pedro Sula, Honduras, 1983-85; supt., prof. entomology N.Mex. State U., Alcalde, 1986—; supt. Agrl. Sci. Ctr., Alcalde, 1986—; entomologist Internat. Irrigation Ctr., Logan, Utah, 1985-86. Contbr. numerous articles to profl. jours. Mem. Am. Registry Profl. Entomologists (Outstanding Contbrn. award 1981), Entomol. Soc. Am., Southwestern Entomol. Soc., Extension Specialists Assn., N.Mex. Acad. Sci. Avocations: insect collecting, hunting, fishing. Home and Office: NMex State U Agrl Sci Ctr PO Box 159 Alcalde NM 87511

WARD, CONLEY RICHARD, technology services executive, environmental engineer; b. Indpls., Oct. 1, 1930; s. Leslie Isaac and Mabel Idas (Tucker) W.; m. Mary Lou Kennedy, Nov. 9, 1951; children: Marsha, Valerie, Cynthia, Kevin. BA in Chemistry, U. Louisville, 1952; BS in Meteorology, U.S. Naval Postgrad. Sch., 1960; MS in Oceanography, Old Dominion U., 1973. Commd. ensign USN, 1952, advanced through grades to capt., 1972; comdg. officer Fleet Numerical Weather Cen. USN, Monterey, Calif., 1974-76; comdr. Naval Weather Service USN, Washington, 1976-78; ret. USN, 1978; sr. tech. dir. Oceandata Systems, Monterey, 1979-81; v.p. Globalweather Dynamics, Inc., Monterey, 1981—; asst. oceanographer Navy for environ. prediction, Washington, 1976-78. Contbr. articles to profl. jours. NROTC scholar, Ind., 1949. Mem. Am. Meteorol. Soc. (councilor 1978-81), Sigma Xi. Republican. Home: 27570 Via Sereno Carmel CA 93923 Office: Globalweather Dynamics Inc 2400 Garden Rd Monterey CA 93940

WARD, DIANE KOROSY, lawyer; b. Cleve., Oct. 17, 1939; d. Theodore Louis and Edith (Bogar) Korosy; m. S. Mortimer Ward IV, July 2, 1960 (div. 1978); children: Christopher LaBruce, Samantha Martha; m. R. Michael Walters, June 30, 1979. AB, Heidelberg Coll., 1961; JD, U. San Diego, 1975. Bar: Calif. 1977, U.S. Dist. Ct. (so. dist.) Calif. 1977. Ptnr. Ward & Howell, San Diego, 1978-79, Walters, Howell & Ward, A.P.C., San Diego, 1979-81; mng. ptnr. Walters & Ward, A.P.C., San Diego, 1981— ; dir., v.p. Oak Broadcasting Systems, Inc., 1982-83; dir. Elisabeth Kubler-Ross Ctr., Inc., 1983-85; sheriff Ranchos del Norte Corral of Westerners, 1985—; trustee San Diego Community Defenders, Inc., 1986—. Pres. bd. dirs. Green Valley Civic Assn., 1979-80; trustee Palomar-Pomerado Hosp. Found., chmn., 1985—; trustee Episcopal Diocese of San Diego. Mem. ABA, Rancho Bernardo Bar Assn. (chmn. 1982-83), Lawyers Club San Diego, Profl. and Exec. Women of the Ranch (founder, pres. 1982—), San Diego Golden Eagle Club, Phi Delta Phi. Republican. Episcopalian. Club: Soroptimist Internat. (pres. chpt. 1979-80). Home: 16503 Avenida Florencia Poway CA 92064 Office: Walters & Ward 11665 Avena Pl Suite 203 San Diego CA 92128

WARD, GARETH RAY, electronic engineer; b. Hollomon AFB, N.Mex., May 24, 1957; s. Gareth Craig and Anita Marie (Lutman) W. BSEET, Oreg. Inst. Tech., 1979. With Litton Guidance and Control Systems, Grants Pass, Oreg., 1979-84, INTEL Corp., Hillsboro, Oreg., 1984-86; electronics engr. NEC Am., Inc., Hillsboro, Oreg., 1986—. Home: 1285 SE Jacquelin Hillsboro OR 97123 Office: NEC America Inc 3100 NE Shute Rd Hillsboro OR 97124

WARD, GORDON A(RTHUR), college president; b. Edgeley, N.D., May 22, 1926; s. Charles William and Eleanor Grace (Whitman) W.; B.S. in Edn., No. State Coll., 1950; M.A. in History, U. Wyo., 1958, Ph.D. in Higher Edn., 1969; postgrad. in econs. (Gen. Electric fellow) Stanford U., 1961; m. Betty Lou Butler, Aug. 27, 1958; children—Cheryl Denise (dec.), Kimberly Ann. Adminstr. pub. schs., Casper, Wyo., N.D. and S.D., 1950-67; adminstrv. asst. to pres. Casper Coll., 1967; dean instrn. Central Wyo. Coll., 1968; chmn. Wyo. Pres.'s Council, 1982-84; pres. Wyo. Community Coll. Athletic Conf., 1977. Mem. Wyo. Ho. of Reps., 1964-66; sec. No. Wyo. Community Found., 1973—; chmn. Legis.-Exec. Comm. on Reorgn. State Govt. Wyo., 1974-76, mem., 1974-78; mem. Wyo. Gov.'s Task Force on

Nondiscrimination on Basis of Handicap, 1976-77; v.p. Salvation Army Adv. Bd., Sheridan, 1977-78; mem. adv. bd. N.G., 1977-79; mem. adv. bd. Hugh O'Brian Found., 1981—; treas. Council Occupational Edn. Served with USN, 1944-45; PTO. Recipient Most Creative award Community Coll. Seminar, U. Wyo., 1967; Coe fellow, 1959. Mem. Am. Assn. Community and Jr. Colls., Mountain States Assn. Community Colls. (pres. 1982-83), Mountain Plains Adult Edn. Assn., Phi Delta Kappa, Delta Kappa Pi. Presbyterian (elder). Home: 510 S Jefferson Sheridan WY 82801 Office: PO Box 1500 Sheridan WY 82801

WARD, JOHN FREDERICK, landscape photographer; b. Washington, Mar. 23, 1943; s. Frederick Norville and Loraine (Lundeen) W.; m. Susan Charlotte Etter, June 9, 1966. BA, Harvard U., 1964; PhD, U. Colo., 1971. Asst. prof. physics Lawrence U., Appleton, Wis., 1971-72; freelance photographer Boulder, Colo., 1972—; artist-in-residence Nat. Park Service, Rocky Mountain Nat. Park, 1985. Photographer: (portfolio) Landscape, 1981; (also author) Colorado—Magnificent Wilderness, 1984. Lutheran. Avocations: classical music, physics. Office: PO Box 4576 Boulder CO 80306

WARD, JOHN J., bishop; b. Los Angeles, 1920. Student, St. John's Sem., Camarillo, Calif., Catholic U. Am. Ordained priest, Roman Catholic Ch., 1946. Ordained titular bishop of Bria, aux. bishop Diocese of Los Angeles Roman Cath. Ch., 1963; now vicar gen. Roman Cath. Ch., Los Angeles. Office: 10425 W PicoBlvd Los Angeles CA 90064 *

WARD, LANE DENNIS, university administrator, consultant; b. Salt Lake City, Apr. 22, 1948; s. Orville Milton and Mildred (Tyler) W.; m. Julie Glazier, Nov. 22, 1971; children: Glazier, Johnathan, Joseph, Christian, Julane. BA, Brigham Young U., 1972, M Edn. Adminstrn., 1976, EdD, 1979. Cert. educator, Utah. Cross-cultural trainer Lang. Tng. Ctr., Provo, Utah, 1969-72; educator Latter-Day Saints Edn. System, Salt Lake City, 1972-78; asst. dir. tng. Brigham Young U., Provo, 1978-80, assoc. dir. research devel., 1980-83, exec. asst. to pres., dir. planning and devel., 1983—; pres. L.Ward & Co., Orem, Utah, 1982—. Contbr. articles to profl. jours. Named to Nat. Nominating Com. Human Resource Devel. Orgn. Mag., 1985. Mem. Am. Mgmt. Assn., Am. Soc. Tng. and Devel., N.Y. Tng. Confr. Republican. Mormon. Home: 1304 N 800 W Orem UT 84057 Office: Brigham Young U 2005 N 900 E Provo UT 84604

WARD, LARRY DON, purchasing administrator; b. Odessa, Tex., July 27, 1951; s. John L. and Barbara (Howell) W.; m. Jamie Lynn Himes, June 3, 1978; children: Philip, Kristin, Amanda. BS, La. State U., 1975. Cert. purchasing mgr. Geophys. technician Decca Survey Systems, Houston, 1975; dir. purchasing Campus Crusade for Christ, San Bernardino, Calif., 1976-83; buyer Calif. Inst. Tech., Pasadena, 1983—. Mem. Nat. Contract Mgmt. Assn., Nat. Assn. Ednl. Buyers, Calif. Higher Edn. Assn. Purchasing (steering bd. 1986-87). Republican. Baptist. Avocations: tennis, outdoor team sports. Home: 1553 W Morgan Rd San Bernardino CA 92407 Office: Calif Inst Tech 1201 E California Blvd Pasadena CA 91125

WARD, LESTER LOWE, JR., lawyer; b. Pueblo, Colo., Dec. 21, 1930; s. Lester Lowe and Alysmai (Pfeffer) W.; m. Rosalind H. Felps, Apr. 18, 1964; children—Ann Marie, Alison, Lester Lowe. A.B. cum laude, Harvard U., 1952, LL.B., 1955. Bar: Colo. 1955. Sole practice Pueblo, 1957—; ptnr. Predovich, Ward & Banner, Pueblo, 1974—. Trustee, Thatcher Found., Frank I. Lamb Found., Helen G. Bonfils Found., Denver Ctr. for Performing Arts; pres. bd. trustees Pueblo Pub. Library, 1960-66; trustee St. Mary-Corwin Hosp., 1972—, pres., 1979-80. Served with U.S. Army, 1955-57. Named Outstanding Young Man of Yr., Pueblo Jaycees, 1964. Fellow Am. Coll. Probate Counsel; mem. ABA (house of dels. 1986—), Colo. Bar Assn. (bd. govs. 1977-79, 82—, pres. 1983-84), Pueblo County Bar Assn. (Outstanding Young Lawyer award 1965, 67, pres. 1976-77), Harvard Law Sch. Assn. Colo. (pres. 1972). Democrat. Roman Catholic. Lodge: Kiwanis (pres. 1969). Home: 118 Baylor St Pueblo CO 81005 Office: Predovich Ward & Banner 727 Thatcher Bldg Pueblo CO 81003

WARD, LOUIS EMMERSON, retired physician; b. Mt. Vernon, Ill., Jan. 19, 1918; s. Henry Ben Pope and Aline (Emmerson) W.; m. Nan Talbot, June 5, 1942; children—Nancy, Louis, Robert, Mark; m. Marian Mansfield, Jan. 27, 1979. A.B., U. Ill., 1939; M.D., Harvard, 1943; M.S. in Medicine, U. Minn., 1949. Intern Ill. Research and Ednl. Hosp., Chgo., 1943; fellow medicine Mayo Found., 1946-49; cons. medicine, rheumatology Mayo Clinic, 1950-83, chmn. bd. govs., 1964-75; dir. Northwestern Bell Telephone Co., Bankers Life, Des Moines. Contbr. articles to profl. jours. Vice chmn. bd. trustees Mayo Found., 1964-76; past bd. dirs. Fund for Republic; bd. dirs. Center for Study Democratic Instns.; past bd. dirs. Arthritis Found.; mem. Nat. Council Health Planning and Devel., 1976-83. Recipient U. Ill. Alumni Achievement award, 1968; recipient disting. alumnus award Mayo Found., 1983. Mem. Inst. Medicine (Nat. Acad. Scis.), AMA, Am. Rheumatism Assn. (pres. 1969-70), Nat. Soc. Clin. Rheumatologists (pres. 1967-69), Central Soc. Clin. Research, Minn., Zumbro Valley med. socs., So. Minn. Med. Assn., Phi Beta Kappa, Sigma Xi, Alpha Omega Alpha, Phi Delta Theta. Home: 30 Raeburn Ct Port Ludlow WA 98365

WARD, ORVILLE ELVIN, insurance company executive; b. Topeka, May 6, 1926; s. John Edward and Sylvia (Anderson) W.; m. Dorothy Kathryn Brainard, Jan. 8, 1949; children: Claudia Ward McGrath, Virginia Ward Klevjer, Dona Ward Tindall, Jay. Student U. Wash., 1944-45. Ind. ins. agt., Seattle, 1955-62; field rep. SAFECO Life Ins. Co., Seattle, 1962-64, ins. educator, 1964-65, div. life mgr., 1965-69, v.p., dir. pensions, 1969-86, also bd. dirs.; pres. Resource Planning Services Inc., 1986—; dir. Sound Bank, Federal Way, Wash.; chmn. bd. AeroFab, Inc.; lectr. in field. Bd. dirs. Seattle-King County ARC, St. Cabrini Hosp. Ethics Bd.; chairperson Ret. Sr. Vol. Program King County. Served with USAF, 1944-45. Named Seattle Citizen of Day, 1985. Mem. Internat. Assn. Fin. Planners. CLU. Contbr. articles to profl. mags. Home: 35790 27th Ave S Federal Way WA 98003 Office: Resource Planning Services 2615 4th Ave Seattle WA 98121

WARD, PAUL HUTCHINS, otolaryngologist; b. Lawrence, Ind., Apr. 24, 1928; s. Howard Hutchins and Lillian (Anderson) W.; m. Suzanne Fowler, Feb. 7, 1976; children: Walter, Judith. AB, Anderson Coll., 1953; MD, John Hopkins U., 1957. Diplomate Am. Bd. Otolaryngology; licensed physician, Ill., Calif., Tenn., Md. Intern Henry Ford Hosp., Detroit, 1957-58; resident U. Chgo., Detroit, 1958-61; spl. fellow U. Chgo., 1962-64; asst. prof. surgery, chief head and neck service U. Chgo. Sch. Medicine, 1962-64; assoc. prof., chmn. div. otolaryngology Vanderbilt U. Sch. Medicine, Nashville, 1964-68; prof. surgery, chief div. head and neck surgery UCLA Sch. Medicine, 1968—; Cons. Wadsworth VA Hosp., Los Angeles, 1968—, U.S. Naval Hosp., 1969—; staff UCLA Hosps. and Clinic, 1968—, Los Angeles County-Harbor Gen. Hosp., Torrance, Calif., 1968—, Cedars-Sinai Med. Ctr., Los Angeles, 1977—, Los Angeles County-Olive View Hosp., Van Nuys, Calif., 1978—; lectr. in field. Contbr. over 250 articles to profl. jours. Bd. dirs. Hope for Hearing Found., 1969—, UCAL Hosp. Chpalaincy Service, 1975-82, pres. 1977-81; trustee Blalock Found., 1979—. Served as staff sgt. Med. Service Corps, U.S. Army, 1946-49. Mem. ACS (sr. advisor com. on med. motion pictures, 1984—), Am. Acad. Ophthalmology and Otolaryngology, NIH, Calif. Med. Assn., Am. Acad. Facial Plastic and Reconstructive Surgery (com. on research 1973-80), Am. Council of Otolaryngology, Am. Laryngological Assn. Avocations: golfing, skiing, tennis, basketball. Office: UCLA Sch Medicine 10833 Le Conte St Los Angeles CA 90024

WARD, RAYMOND BUZZ, alcohol and drug therapist; b. Providence, Feb. 17, 1937; s. Raymond and Eleanor (Gleason) W.; m. Patricia Pina, Feb. 2, 1956 (div. Nov. 1966); children: Raymond, Lucielle, Marie, Troy; m. Ellen Warren, Aug. 8, 1986; children: John Warren, Fatima Kathleen, Elizabeth, Megan. Student, Harvard U., 1961-62, Stanford U., 1972-73, San Francisco State U., 1974-75, U. Calif., Berkeley, 1975-76. Cert. alcohol and drug counselor, Oreg. Therapist San Francisco Dept. Pub. Health, 1972-76, Jackson County Council on Alcoholism, Ashland, Oreg., 1976-78; clin. supr. Family Counseling Ctr., St. Helens, Oreg., 1978-86; bd. dirs. Benton/Linn County Council on Alcohol, Corvallis, Oreg., 1986—; designer, bd. dirs. "Getting Straight" Alcohol Drug Treatment Ctr., Scappose, Oreg., 1986—. Designer San Francisco Methadone Treatment Program, 1972, Project Cleen, Drug Treatment Program, San Francisco; mem. Scappose Alcohol Drug Com. Mem. AAAS, Oreg. Council Alcoholism, The New Profls., Ethno Pharmacology Soc. Democrat. Moslem. Lodge: Moose. Avocations: writing children's books, painting, golf. Home: PO Box 739 Scappoose OR 97056 Office: Family Counseling Ctr 636 NW 11th St Corvallis OR 97330

WARD, ROBERT EDWARD, political science educator, university administrator; b. San Francisco, Jan. 29, 1916; s. Edward Butler and Claire Catherine (Unger) W.; m. Constance Regina Barnett, Oct. 31, 1942; children: Erica Anne, Katherine Elizabeth. B.A., Stanford U., 1936; M.A., U. Calif.-Berkeley, 1938, Ph.D., 1948. Instr. in polit. sci. U. Mich., 1948-50, asst. prof. polit. sci., 1950-54, assoc. prof., 1954-58, prof., 1958-73; prof. Stanford U., 1973—, dir. Center for Research in Internat. Studies, 1973—; cons. in field; advisor Center for Strategic and Internat. Studies, Washington, 1968—. Author: Modern Political Systems: Asia, 1963, Political Modernization in Japan and Turkey, 1964. Mem. nat. council Nat. Endowment for Humanities, Washington, 1968-73; mem. Pres.'s Commn. on Fgn. Lang.-Internat. Studies, 1978-79; chmn. Japan-U.S. Friendship Commn., 1980-83; mem. Dept. Def. Univ. Forum, 1982—. Served to lt. (j.g.) USN, 1942-45. Recipient Japan Found. award Tokyo, 1976; recipient Order of Sacred Treasure 2d class (Japan), 1983. Fellow Am. Acad. Arts and Scis.; mem. Am. Polit. Sci. Assn. (pres. 1972-73), Assn. Asian Studies (pres. 1972-73), Social Sci. Research Council (chmn. 1969-71), Am. Philos. Soc. Home: 1385 Westridge Dr Portola Valley CA 94025 Office: Stanford U Center for Research in Internat Studies Stanford CA 94305

WARD, STEVEN MICHAEL, law enforcement administrator, management consultant; b. Oregon, Ill., May 12, 1945; s. Alfred Henry Ward and Jeanne Arlene (Stevens) Ward Eyrick; m. Pamela Jean McMillen, Aug. 15, 1965; children—Jason Brian, Joshua Ryan. B.S. cum laude in Criminology, Calif. State U.-Long Beach, 1967; M.P.A., U. So. Calif., 1970. Cert. delinquency control, Calif. Program officer U. So. Calif., Los Angeles, 1969-70, chief security, 1977—; staff assoc. Pub. Adminstrn. Service, Chgo., 1970-71; staff dir. Atty. Gen.'s Adv. Commn. on Community-Police Relations, Los Angeles, 1971-73; dir. Nat. Sheriffs' Inst., U. So. Calif., Los Angeles, 1973-80; cons. various pub. and pvt. orgns., 1970—. Editor: Police Programs for Preventing Crime and Delinquency, 1972. Contbr. articles to profl. jours. and books, 1975—. Served with USNR, 1968-69, Vietnam. Recipient distinctive honors Boys' Club, Los Angeles, 1976. Mem. Nat. Sheriffs Assn. (cons. 1973—), Internat. Assn. Chiefs of Police, Am. Soc. Pub. Adminstrn. Home: 2130 W Crescent St #2171 Anaheim CA 92081 Office: U So Calif 3667 S McClintock Ave Los Angeles CA 90089

WARD, WILLIAM OGDEN, finance co. exec.; b. Bismarck, N.D., Oct. 10, 1944; s. William O. and Kathryn C. Ward; B.A. in Econs., Wash. State U., 1966; M.B.A., U. Wash., 1969; postgrad. (fellow) U. Mich., 1970-71; M.B.A. in Taxation, Golden Gate U., 1973; m. Patricia E. Maffit, June 24, 1967. Nat. bank examiner U.S. Treasury Dept., Seattle, 1966-68; acct. Peat, Marwick, Mitchell & Co., San Francisco, 1971-74; div. v.p., dir. taxes Itel Corp., San Francisco, 1975-79; pres. Belvedere Equipment Fin. Co., San Francisco, 1979-82; ptnr. Ward Holmes & Co., Marin County, Calif., 1983—; chmn., pres. MICRO-RENT Corp., Marin County, 1983—; dir. Belvedere Holdings Ltd., Bermuda, Belvedere Corp., Del.; mem. faculty Golden Gate U., 1974-75. Bd. dirs., pres. Greenbrae Property Owners Assn., Named Outstanding Alumni, Golden Gate U. Sch. Taxation, 1979; C.P.A., Calif., Wash. Mem. Am. Inst. C.P.A.s, Calif. Soc. C.P.A.s, Beta Alpha Psi. Roman Catholic. Clubs: San Francisco Yacht. Office: 505 Tamal Plaza Corte Madera CA 94925

WARDEN, DAVID RUSSELL, literary agent; b. Sacramento, May 7, 1952; s. Russell and Dorothy Eleanor (Stiles) W. B.A., U. Calif.-Davis, 1973, M.A., 1976. Intern, Warner Bros. Inc., Burbank, Calif., 1974; literary agent William Morris Agy., Beverly Hills, Calif., 1976-80, Eisenbach-Greene Inc., Los Angeles, 1980-84, Agy. for the Performing Arts, Los Angeles, 1984—; lectr., adv. U. of Alberta, Edmonton, Alberta, Can., 1983—. Home: 633 S Bundy Dr Los Angeles CA 90049

WARDLAW, FRANCIS GLEN, audiologist, speech pathologist; b. Gravette, Ark., Sept. 2, 1930; s. Everette Dee and Eva Alter (Thrasher) W.; m. Mary Jane Moore, Aug. 30, 1955; children: Carol Jane, Steven Glen, Glenda Mae. BA, Northwest Nazarene Coll., 1956; MA, U. Denver, 1960, postgrad., 1961-64. Tchr. Kuna (Idaho) Sch. Dist., 1956-59, Hodgkins Jr. High Sch., Westminster, Colo., 1959-61; postdoctoral fellow U. Denver, 1961-64; audiologist Colo. Hearing Soc., Denver, 1964-66, Tri-county Dist. Health dept., Aurora, Colo., 1966-69, Nampa (Idaho) Sch. Dist., 1969—. Vol. Handicapped Camp, McCall, Idaho, 1973-77. Served with USN, 1950-54. Mem. NEA (life), Idaho Edn. Assn., Am. Speech and Hearing Assn. (cert.), Idaho Speech and Hearing Assn. Republican. Nazarene. Lodge: Civitan (pres. Nampa chpt. 1976-77). Avocations: hunting, fishing, cross-breeding cattle, sports, reading. Home: 716 Fern St Nampa ID 83651 Office: Nampa Sch Dist 131 619 S Canyon St Nampa ID 83651

WARDROP, JOHN DRISCOLL, manufacturing executive; b. Indpls., Jan. 23, 1937; s. John and Catherine (Driscoll) W.; m. Maribeth Gietzen, Dec. 18, 1966; children: Scott Christopher, Brett Matthew. BA, Dartmouth Coll., 1959. Tchr., coach Forest Hills High Sch., Grand Rapids, Mich., 1961-67; salesperson, mgr. Sparks Belting Co., Grand Rapids, 1967-78, v.p., 1978-81, pres., 1981—. Bd. dirs. S.E. YMCA, Grand Rapids, 1980—; account solicitor United Way, Grand Rapids, 1986. Mem. Nat. Indsl. Belting Assn. (v.p. 1985-86, pres. 1986—). Republican. Presbyterian. Office: Sparks Belting Co 3800 Stahl Dr SE Grand Rapids MI 49506

WARD-STEINMAN, DAVID, composer, music educator; b. Alexandria, La., Nov. 6, 1936; s. Irving Steinman and Daisy Leila (Ward) W.-S.; m. Susan Diana Lucas, Dec. 28, 1956; children: Jenna, Matthew. B.Mus. cum laude (Dohnanyi award 1965), Fla. State U., 1957; Mus.M., U. Ill., 1958, D.M.A., 1961; postgrad. study, Nadia Boulanger, Paris, 1958-59; postdoctoral vis. fellow, Princeton U., 1970. Grad. instr. U. Ill., 1957-58; mem. faculty San Diego State U., 1961—, prof. music, 1968—, dir. comprehensive musicianship program, 1972—, composer in residence, 1961—, univ. research lectr., 1986-87; mem. summer faculty Eastman Sch. Music Workshop, 1969; Ford Found. composer in residence Tampa Bay (Fla.) Area, 1970-72; acad. cons. U. North Sumatra (Indonesia), 1982; concert and lecture tour U.S. Internat. Communication Agy., Indonesia, 1982; mem. faculty Coll. Music Soc. Nat. Inst. for Music in Gen. Studies, U. Colo., 1983, 84; composer-in-residence Brevard Music Ctr., N.C., summer 1986; appointed research lectr. San Diego State U., 1986-87. Composer: Symphony, 1959, Prelude & Toccata for orch., 1962, Concerto No. 2 for chamber orch., 1962, ballet Western Orpheus, 1964, Cello Concerto, 1966, These Three ballet, 1966, The Tale of Issoumbochi chamber opera, 1968, Rituals for Dancers and Musicians, 1971, Antares, 1971, Arcturus, 1972, The Tracker, 1976, Brancusi's Brass Beds, 1977; oratorio Song of Moses, 1964; Jazz Tangents, 1967, Childs Play, 1968; 3-act opera Tamar, 1977; Golden Apples, 1981; choral suite Of Wind and Water, 1982; Christmas cantata And In These Times, 1982; Moiré for piano and chamber ensemble, 1983, And Waken Green, song cycle on poems by Douglas Worth, 1983, Olympics Overture for orchestra, 1984, Children's Corner Revisited, song cycle, 1984, Summer Suite for oboe and piano, 1984, Quintessence for double quintet and percussion, 1985, Chroma concerto for multiple keyboards, percussion and chamber orch., 1985, Winging It for chamber orchestra, 1986, Elegy for Astronauts, for orchestra, 1986; recs. include Fragments from Sappho, 1969; Duo for cello and piano, 1974, Childs Play for bassoon and piano, 1974, The Tracker, 1981, Brancusi's Brass Beds, 1984, concert suite from Western Orpheus, 1987, Moiré, 1987, 3 Songs for Clarinet and Piano, 1987; commd. by Chgo. Symphony, Joffrey Ballet, numerous others; author: (with Susan L. Ward-Steinman) Comparative Anthology of Musical Forms, 2 vols, 1976. Recipient Bearns prize Columbia U., 1961; SAI Am. Music award, 1962; annual BMI awards, 1970—; named Outstanding Prof. Calif. State Univs. and Colls., 1968; Outstanding alumnus of Year Fla. State U., 1976; Recipient Broadcast Music prize, 1954, 55, 60, 61, Exceptional Merit Service award San Diego State U., 1984. Mem. Broadcast Music, Inc., Am. Soc. Univ. Composers, Coll. Music Soc., Am. Music Center. Presbyterian. Club: Golden State Flying. Office: Music Dept San Diego State University San Diego CA 92182

WARE, GEORGE WHITAKER, JR., entomology educator; b. Pine Bluff, Ark., Aug. 27, 1927; s. George Whitaker and Dorothy Adelaid (Clark) W.; m. Doris Marie Adams, Oct. 7, 1952; children: Cynthia W., Samuel D., Julia L. BS, U. Ark., 1951, MS, 1952; PhD, Kans. State U., 1957. Diplomate Am. Acad. Toxicological Scis.; registered profl. entomologist. From asst. to assoc. prof. Ohio State U., Columbus, 1956-66; prof., head dept. entomology U. Ariz., Tucson, 1967-83, assoc. dir. agrl. experiment sta., 1983—; cons. Office of Pesticide Programs EPA, Washington, 1979—, various pesticide formulators and mfrs., 1972—. Author: Complete Guide to Pest Control, 1980, Pesticides: Theory and Application, 1983, Fundamentals of Pesticides, 1986; Editor: (book series) Reviews of Environmental Contamination Toxicology, 1985—. Scoutmaster Boy Scout Am., Tucson, 1969-71. Served to 1st lt. U.S. Army, 1952-54, Korea. Named Man of Yr. Ariz. Pest Control Operators, Tucson, 1976. Mem. Soc. Toxicology, Am. Chem. Soc., Entomol. Soc. Am., Council for Agrl. Sci. and Technology (chmn. task force 1980). Republican. Club: Exchange (Tucson pres. 1970-71). Avocations: running, stained glass, tennis, hunting, fishing. Home: 5794 Camino Celador Tucson AZ 85715 Office: U Ariz Coll Agr Tucson AZ 85721

WARE, PATRICIA LUCILLE, educator; b. Salt Lake City, Sept. 4, 1941; d. Daniel Beville Searcy (dec.) and Dorothy Melton Adkison; m. Willett Ware III (div. 1984); children—Kenton Daniel, Kimberly, Rebecca. Student Northwestern U., 1959-60; A.B., U. Calif.-Berkeley, 1963; M.A., Calif. State U.-Chico, 1978; postgrad. U. Calif.-Santa Barbara, 1966-67, U. Calif.-Santa Cruz, Calif. State U.-San Jose, La. State U. Cert. secondary and community coll. tchr., Calif. Tchr. Santa Barbara (Calif.) High Sch. Dist., 1967-69, Santa Cruz (Calif.) City Schs., 1969-73, Pajaro Valley (Calif.) Unified Schs., 1973-76; cons. Shasta County (Calif.) supt. schs., 1977-78; English tchr. Paradise (Calif.) Unified Sch. Dist., 1979—. pilot program summer seminars NEH, 1983; cons. Dept. Def. Dependents Schs., Giessen, Federal Republic of Germany, 1984-86; Active Chico (Calif.) Unified Dist. PTA. Recipient Genevieve Haight award, 1967; No. Calif. Writing Project fellow, 1977. Mem. Nat. Council Tchrs. English, Calif. Assn. Tchrs. English, Calif. Tchrs. Assn. (state mem. at large), AAUW, Calif. Reading Assn., Phi Delta Kappa, Delta Kappa Gamma. Democrat. Home: 165 Fairgate Ln Chico CA 95926 Office: 5911 Maxwell Dr Paradise CA 95969

WARE, RANDOLPH HOWARD, geophysicist; b. Santa Maria, Calif., June 13, 1944; s. Arnold Grassel and Freda (Cowperthwaite) W.; m. Maria Jesus Aragon, June 22, 1986; children: Davis Aragon, Marisa Aragon. BA in Chemistry, Math., Physics, U. Colo., 1966, MA in Physics, 1969, PhD in Nuclear Physics, 1974. Research assoc., joint instr. Lab. Astrophysics, Boulder, Colo., 1974-78; research assoc. Coop. Inst. for Research in Environ. Sci., Boulder, 1978-85, fellow, 1985—; adj. prof. Aerospace Engring. Scis. U. Colo., Boulder, 1985—; Congl. sci. fellow Office of Tech. Assessment, Washington, 1983-84; founder, bd. dirs., chmn. Boulder Brewing Co., 1979—; bd. dirs., chmn. U. Navstar Consortium, 1984—; chmn. Space Phoenix Task Force, 1985—; pres., bd. dirs. External Tanks Co., Boulder, 1986—. Contbr. articles to profl. jours. Mem. Am. Geophys. Union., Am. Astronautical Soc., U.S. Space Found., AAAS, Internat. Assn. Geodesy. Avocations: windsurfing, hiking, music. Office: CIRES/449 U Colo Boulder CO 80309

WARE, WILLIS HOWARD, computer scientist; b. Atlantic City, Aug. 31, 1920; s. Willis and Ethel (Rosswork) W.; m. Floy Hoffer, Oct. 10, 1943; children—Deborah Susanne Ware Pinson, David Willis, Alison Floy. B.S.E.E., U. Pa., 1941; M.S.E.E., MIT, 1942; Ph.D. in Elec. Engring, Princeton U., 1951. Research engr. Hazeltine Electronics Corp., Little Neck, N.Y., 1942-46; mem. research staff Inst. Advanced Study, Princeton, N.J., 1946-51, North Am. Aviation, Downey, Calif., 1951-52; mem. corp. research staff Rand Corp., Santa Monica, Calif., 1952—; adj. prof. UCLA Extension Service, 1955-68; first chmn. Am. Fedn. Info. Processing Socs., 1961, 62; chmn. HEW sec.'s Adv. Com. on Automated Personal Data Systems, 1971-73; mem. Privacy Protection Study Commn., 1975-77, vice chmn., 1975-77; mem. numerous other adv. groups, spl. coms. for fed. govt., 1959—. Author: Digital Computer Technology and Design, vols. I and II, 1963. Recipient Computer Scis. Man of Yr. award Data Processing Mgmt. Assn., 1975, Disting. Service award Am. Fedn. Info. Processing Socs. 1986, Exceptional Civilian Service medal USAF, 1979. Fellow IEEE (Centennial medal 1984); mem. Assn. Computing Machinery, AAAS, Nat. Acad. Engring., AIAA, Sigma Xi, Eta Kappa Nu, Pi Mu Epsilon, Tau Beta Pi. Office: The Rand Corp 1700 Main St Santa Monica CA 90406

WARFEL, GEORGE HUNTINGTON, JR., technology company executive; b. Chgo., Oct. 9, 1947; s. George Huntington Sr. and Joanne Stewart (Mitchell) W. BA, Claremont McKenna Coll., 1969, MBA, 1981; MA, Occidental Coll., 1971. Adminstr. U. Hawaii, Honolulu, 1975-79; dir. research Calif. Credit Union League, Pomona, Calif., 1979-81; mgr. retail cons. Fin. Industries Ctr. SRI Internat., Menlo Park, Calif., 1981-84; client exec. TFS, Berkeley, Calif., 1984; adj. faculty Antioch U., San Francisco, 1982—, Cen. Mich. U., 1972-82. Author: Credit Union Financial Management, 1980; contbr. articles to prfol. jours. Mem. Planning Commn., Hermosa Beach, Calif., 1980. Fellow Coro Found. Mem. Am. Assn. for Artificial Intelligence, Club of 1,000. Avocations: skiing, writing, drawing. Home: 6363 Christie Dr #2712 Emeryville CA 94608 Office: TFS 2001 Center St Berkeley CA 94707

WARGO, MICHAEL JOHN, JR., entomologist; b. Norwalk, Ohio, Apr. 1, 1940; s. Michael John and Gladys (Irene) W.; m. Diane Florence Morrow, Aug. 14, 1982; children: James, William, Gregory; 1 stepson: John. BS, U. Ariz., 1963; MS, U. Calif., Riverside, 1971. Foreman Libby Owens, City of Industry, Calif., 1972-76; photographer Riverside Photography, 1976-78; horticulturist Am. Nurseries, Riverside, 1978-79; mosquito operator N.W. Mosquito Abatement, Riverside, 1979-80; dist. mgr., entomologist Coachella Valley Mosquito Abatement, Thermal, Calif., 1980—. Contbr. articles to profl. jours. Pres. Riverside Lyons Little Leaque, 1977-78. Mem. Calif. Mosquito and Vector Control Assn. (regional rep. 1985-86), Soc. Vector Ecologists, Entomol. Soc. Am., Am. Mosquito Control Assn. Democrat. Rotary (local v.p., programs chmn. 1986, pres. Coachella Valley chpt. 1987—). Avocations: metal detecting, prospecting, gardening. Home: 83-731 Ave 55 Thermal CA 92274 Office: Coachella Valley Mosquito Abatement Dist 83-733 Ave 55 Thermal CA 92274

WARKENTIN, LARRY RAY, music educator, composer; b. Reedley, Calif., Aug. 14, 1940; s. Pete D. and Marie G. (Janzen) W.; m. Paula B. Berg, Aug. 17, 1962; children: Richard, Rhonda. AB, Tabor Coll., 1962; MA, Calif. State U., Fresno, 1964; DMA, U. So. Calif., 1967. Chmn. humanities div. Fresno Pacific Coll., 1966—. Composer: Invitation to Joy, 1981, This is a Holy Day, 1978, Koinonia, 1978 (comm. by Mennonite World Conf.). Recipient 1st prize for composition Calif. Music Tchrs. Assn., 1984. Mem. Music Tchrs. Assn. Calif. (chmn. composition competition, 1982-86), Fresno Nat. Soc. Arts and Letters (pres. 1984-86). Mem. Mennonite Brethren Ch. Avocations: travel, gardening. Office: Fresno Pacific Coll 1717 S Chestnut Ave Fresno CA 93702

WARLICK, MICHAEL DAVID, cosmetic company sales executive; b. Dallas, Dec. 5, 1949; s. Homer Elvy and Betty Jane (Ware) W.; A.A., North Tex. State U., 1974. Field rep. Redken Labs., San Francisco, 1975, asst. dist. mgr., So. Calif., 1975-76, dist. mgr., 1976-79, regional mgr., Western U.S., 1979-86; prin. Michael Warlick & Assocs., Santee, Calif., 1986—. Republican. Mem. Ch. of Christ.

WARME, JOHN EDWARD, geology educator; b. Los Angeles, Jan. 16, 1937; s. Clarence Herbert and Edna (Peterson) W.; m. Martha Fowler, 1959 (div. 1963); children: Susan Lynn, Jane Kathleen. BA, Augustana Coll., 1959; PhD, UCLA, 1966. Lectr. Calif. Luth. Coll., Thousand Oaks, 1961-62, instr., 1962-63; Fulbright fellow in geology U. Edinburgh, Scotland, 1966-67; prof. geology and oceanography Rice U., Houston, 1967-79; prof. geology Colo. Sch. Mines, 1979—, dir. exploration geosci. inst., 1986—. Co-editor: The Deep Sea Drilling Project: A Decade of Progress; contbr. sci. articles to geol. jours. Named Ewing Prof. Oceanography Rice U., 1976-79; NSF Research grantee, 1969—. Fellow AAAS, Geol. Soc. Am.; mem. Soc. Econ. Paleontologists and Mineralogists (pres. 1983-84), Palentol. Soc., Am. Assn. Petroleum Geologists, Internat. Assn. Sedimentologists, The Soc. Econ. Paleontologists and Mineralogists Found. (pres., co-founder 1983—, bd. dirs. 1984—). Home: 1420 Genesee Ridge Golden CO 80401 Office: Dept Geology Colo Sch Mines Golden CO 80401

WARNAS, JOSEPH JOHN, municipal official; b. Boston, Aug. 31, 1933; s. Augustas and Nellie (Pipiras) W.; m. Bernice Gearlene Sarver (dec. July 1983); children: Robert John, Kimberly Joanne; m. Ruth Ellen Haaker, Jan. 12, 1985. BS in Mgmt., Boston Coll., 1955; MBA in Mgmt., Ariz. State U., 1971. Adminstr. subcontract Gen. Motors, Oak Creek, Wis., 1958-65; mgr. purchasing Sperry Rand Corp., Phoenix, 1965-70; dir. material mgmt. dept. Maricopa County, Phoenix, 1970—; Mem. Joint Fed., State and local Govt. Adv. Bd GSA, Washington, 1974; mem. exptl. tech. adv. com. Nat. Inst. Govt. Purchasing & GSA, Washington, 1975; guest lectr. Ariz. State U., Tempe, Glendale Community Coll.; instr. seminars Nat. Inst. Govt. Purchasing, Washington. Assoc. editor Aljian's Purchasers Handbook, 4th rev. edit., 1982; contbr. articles to profl. jours. Mem. State Ariz. Purchasing Rev. Bd., Phoenix, 1980, Men's Zoo Aux., Phoenix, 1976—. Served as 1st lt. U.S. Army, 1956-58. Mem. Nat. Inst. Govtl. Purchasing (pres. 1971, bd. dirs. 1972—, sr. del. to Internat. Fedn. Purchasing and Mgmt. 1983), Ariz. State Capitol Chpt. Nat. Inst. Govtl. Purchasing Inc. (founder, pres. 1977), Purchasing Mgmt. Assn. Ariz. (pres. 1973), Sigma Iota Epsilon. Republican. Roman Catholic. Avocations: hunting, fishing, camping, hiking, literature. Home: 12511 N 76th Pl Scottsdale AZ 85260-4841 Office: Maricopa County Material Mgmt Ctr 320 W Lincoln St Phoenix AZ 85003

WARNATH, MAXINE AMMER, organizational psychologist, psychology educator, seminar leader; b. N.Y.C., Dec. 3, 1928; d. Philip and Jeanette Ammer; m. Charles Frederick Warnath, Aug. 20, 1952; children—Stephen Charles, Cindy Ruth. B.A., Bklyn. Coll., 1949; M.A., Columbia U., 1951, Ed.D., 1982. Lic. psychologist, Oreg. Various profl. positions Hunter Coll., U. Minn., U. Nebr., U. Oreg., 1951-62; asst. prof. psychology Oreg. Coll. Edn., Monmouth, 1962-77; assoc. prof. psychology, chmn. dept. psychology and spl. edn. Western Oreg. St. Coll., Monmouth, 1978-83, prof. 1986—, dir. organizational psychology program 1983—; pres. Profl. Perspectives, Salem, Oreg., 1987—; cons., dir. Orgn. Research and Devel., Salem, Oreg., 1982—, seminar leader Endeavors for Excellence program. Author: Power Dynamism, 1987. Mem. Oreg. Psychol. Assn. (pres. 1980-81, pres.-elect 1979-80, legis. liaison 1977-78), Am. Psychol. Assn. (com. pre-coll. psychology 1970-74), Western Psychol. Assn. Office: Orgn Research and Devel 708 Rural Ave S Salem OR 97302

WARNE, WILLIAM ELMO, irrigationist; b. nr. Seafield, Ind., Sept. 2, 1905; s. William Rufus and Nettie Jane (Williams) W.; m. Edith Margaret Peterson, July 9, 1929; children—Jane Ingrid (Mrs. David C. Beeder), William Robert, Margaret Edith (Mrs. John W. Monroe). A.B., U. Calif., 1927; D.Econs., Yonsei U., Seoul, 1959; LL.D., Seoul Nat. U., 1959. Reporter San Francisco Bull. and Oakland (Calif.) Post-Enquirer, 1925-27; news editor Brawley (Calif.) News, 1927, Calexico (Calif.) Chronicle, 1927-28; editor, night mgr. Los Angeles bur. A.P., 1928-31, corr. San Diego bur., 1931-33, Washington corr., 1933-35; editor, bur. reclamation Dept. Interior, 1935-37; on staff Third World Power Conf., 1936; assoc. to reviewing com. Nat. Resources Com. on preparation Drainage Basin Problems and Programs, 1936, mem. editorial com. for revision, 1937; chief of information Bur. Reclamation, 1937-42; co-dir. (with Harlan H. Barrows) Columbia Basin Joint Investigations, 1939-42; chief of staff, war prodn. drive WPB, 1942; asst. dir. div. power Dept. Interior, 1942-43, dept. dir. information, 1943; asst. commr. Bur. Reclamation, 1943-47; apptd. asst. sec. Dept. Interior, 1947, asst. sec. Water and Power Devel., 1950-51; U.S. minister charge tech. cooperation Iran, 1951-55, Brazil, 1955-56; U.S. minister and econ. coordinator for Korea, 1956-59; dir. Cal. Dept. Fish and Game, 1959-60, Dept. Agr., 1960-61, Dept. Water Resources, 1961-67; v.p. water resources Devel. and Resources Corp., 1967-69; resources cons. 1969—; pres. Warne & Blanton Pubs. Inc., 1985—; Disting. Practitioner in Residence Sch. Pub. Adminstrn., U. So. Calif. at Sacramento, 1976-78; adminstr. Resources Agy. of Calif., 1961-63; Chmn. Pres.'s Com. on San Diego Water Supply, 1944-46; chmn. Fed. Inter-Agy. River Basin Com., 1948, Fed. Com. on Alaskan Devel., 1948; pres. Group Health Assn., Inc., 1947-51; chmn. U.S. delegation 2d Inter-Am. Conf. Indian Life, Cuzco, Peru, 1949; U.S. del. 4th World Power Conf., London, Eng., 1950; mem. Calif. Water Pollution Control Bd., 1959-67; vice chmn. 1960-62; mem. water pollution control adv. bd. Dept. Health, Edn. and Welfare, 1962-65, cons., 1966-67; chmn. Calif. delegation Western States Water Council, 1965-67. Author: Mission for Peace—Point 4 in Iran, 1956, The Bureau of Reclamation, 1973, How the Colorado River Was Spent, 1975, The Need to Institutionalize Desalting, 1978; prin. author: The California Experience with Mass Transfers of Water over Long Distances, 1978. Served as 2d lt. O.R.C., 1927-37. Recipient Distinguished Service award Dept. Interior, 1951; Distinguished Pub. Service Honor award FOA, 1955; Order of Crown Shah of Iran, 1955; Outstanding Service citation UN Command, 1959. Mem. Nat. Acad. Pub. Adminstrn. (chmn. standing com. on environ. and resources mgmt. 1971-78), Nat. Water Supply Improvement Assn. (pres. 1978-80, Lifetime Achievement award 1984), Sigma Delta Chi, Lambda Chi Alpha. Clubs: Sutter (Sacramento); Nat. Press (Washington); Explorers (N.Y.C.). Home: 2090 8th Ave Sacramento CA 95818

WARNER, DAVID GILL, wholesale food distributing company executive; b. Salt Lake City, 1928. Grad., U. Utah, 1954. Dir. store devel. Fleming Foods Co., 1963-65; with Associated Food Stores, Inc., Salt Lake City, 1965—, asst. gen. mgr., mgr. Salt Lake div., exec. v.p., gen mgr., pres., 1972—; pres., bd. dirs. M & I Gen. Agy., Mcht., Inc.; bd. dirs. Rick-Warner Ford Co., Western Family Foods, Inc., Zions 1st Nat. Bank. Office: Associated Food Stores Inc 1812 S Empire Rd Salt Lake City UT 84130

WARNER, DEWEY WILLIAM, chemist, computer programmer; b. Bellingham, Wash., Jan. 26, 1948; s. Douglas E. and Grace C. (Ecklor) W.; m. Janet Seaman, Aug. 24, 1974; 1 child, James. BS, Western Wash. State Coll., 1970; MS, Wash. State U., 1978. Research technician II Wash. State U., Pullman, 1978—. Served as sgt. U.S. Army, 1971-74, Vietnam. Avocations: amateur radio, computer programming. Home: PO Box 192 Albion WA 99102 Office: Wash Animal Disease Diagnostic Lab PO Box 2037 CS Pullman WA 99165

WARNER, HAROLD CLAY, JR., banker, investment management executive; b. Knoxville, Tenn., Feb. 24, 1939; s. Harold Clay and Mary Frances (Waters) W.; m. Patricia Alice Rethorst, Sept. 1, 1961; children—Martha Lee, Carol Frances. B.S. in Econs, U. Tenn., 1961, Ph.D., 1965. Asst. to pres. First Fed. Savs., Savannah, Ga., 1965-67; v.p. and economist No. Trust Co., Chgo., 1967-73; sr. v.p. and chief economist Crocker Nat. Bank, San Francisco, 1974-79; sr. v.p. liability mgmt. Crocker Nat. Bank, 1979-82; exec. v.p., dir. fixed income mgmt. BA Investment Mgmt. Corp., 1982-84, dir., pres., chief operating officer, 1984-86; dir., pres. Montgomery St. Income Securities, Inc., 1984-86; sr. v.p. Bank of Am., San Francisco, 1982-86; chmn. BA Investment Mgmt. Internat., Ltd., 1985-86; pres. Arthur D. Gimbel, Inc., San Mateo, Calif., 1986—; lectr. dept. econs. U. Tenn., 1962-63, Grad. Sch. Bus., Loyola U., Chgo., 1969-73; lectr. Pacific Coast Banking Sch., U. Wash., 1978-79. Bd. dirs. Chgo. Commons Assn., 1973-74. NDEA fellow, 1961-64. Mem. Chgo. Commons Assn. (bd. dirs. 1973-74), Phi Gamma Delta, Phi Eta Sigma, Omicron Delta Kappa, Phi Kappa Phi. Clubs: Peninsula Golf and Country (San Mateo, Calif.); Bankers (San Francisco). Home: 167 Toyon Rd Atherton CA 94025 Office: 155 Bovet Rd #410 San Mateo CA 94402

WARNER, ILA JUANITA HARRIS, educational administrator; b. Malvern, Ark., May 2, 1929; d. Sylvester and Lola Aquila (Tyree) H.; m. Jarriet Wallace Warner, Apr. 26, 1953 (div. 1982); children: Karen Antoinette Warner Patterson, Sylvet Phern. AA, Ark. Bap. Coll., 1951; BA, Lincoln U., 1953; MA, San Francisco State U., 1972. Elem. sch. tchr. Bell City (Mo.) Sch. Dist., 1951-55, East St. Louis (Ill.) Sch. Dist., 1955-59; supr. Richmond (Calif.) Parks and Recreation, 1960-62; elem. sch. tchr. Richmond Unified Sch. Dist., 1962-70, elem. sch. v.p., 1973-76; supr. student tchr. San Francisco State U., 1970-72; elem. sch. prin. Pittsburg (Calif.) Unified Sch. Dist., 1976—; facilitator Sci. Inservice for Tea. Lawrence Livermore (Calif.) Nat. Lab., 1983—; cons. Harcourt, Brace, and Javonovich, Inc., San Francisco, Calif. Facilitator Fine Arts Black Cultural Polit. League, Pittsburg, 1981—; mem. planning com. Sch. Desegregation-Integration, Richmond, 1965-70; active Richmond-Shimada Friendship Commn., 1968—; active Internat. Inst. of the East Bay, Oakland, Calif., 1980—; v.p. Coalition 100 Black Women, San Francisco; star panalist Lou Rawls Parade of Stars, Nat. United Negro Coll. Fund., 1986. Named Outstanding Educator, 1976, Model Tchr. Far West Lab. Edn. Research, 1971. Mem. Pittsburg Assn. Sch. Adminstrs. (chmn. com. 1976, Letter of Recognition 1976), Calif. Assn. Compensatory Edn. (local com. mem., Letter of Recognition), Lincoln U. Alumni Assn. (chairperson souvenir book com. San Francisco Bay area chpt. nat. conv. 1987), Black C. of C., Phi Delta Kappa (bd. dirs. 1982—), Delta Kappa Gamma, Beta Pi Sigma Sorority, Inc. (named Nat. Soror of Yr., 1977). Clubs: Bulah Cluster (Richmond) (pres. 1965, 75), Bowling League. Avocations: traveling, bowling, playing bridge, reading, cooking. Home: 3019 Barkley Dr Richmond CA 94806 Office: Village Sch 350 School St Pittsburg CA 94565

WARNER, LAWRENCE ALLEN, retired professor, consultant; b. Monroe, Ohio, Apr. 20, 1914; s. Clarence F. and Mary B. (Wones) W.; m. R. Elizabeth Robinson, Oct. 17, 1942; children: Garett R., Susan E. BA, Miami U., Oxford, Ohio, 1937; PhD, Johns Hopkins U., 1942. Geologist U.S. Antarctic Service, Marie Byrd Land, 1939-41, U.S. Geol. Survey, Alaska, 1942-45; from asst. prof. to prof. geology U. Colo., Boulder, 1946-81; cons. Boston U., 1952-54, U.S. Geol. Survey, Rocky Mountain region, 1948-65, Denver Water Dept., 1956—. Contbr. numerous papers and profl. reports. Recipient Congl. medal, 1946, R.L. Stearns award, U. Colo., 1959. Fellow Geol. Soc. Am.; mem. Am. Geophys. Union, Colo. Sci. Soc., Sigma Xi. Congregationalist. Avocations: fishing, gardening, photography. Home: 2455 Kenwood Dr Boulder CO 80303 Office: U Colo CB250 Dept Geol Scis Boulder CO 80309

WARNER, PETER DERYK, psychotherapist, clinical director; b. Urmstom, Lancashire, Eng., Feb. 20, 1938; s. Hugh Francis and Belinda (Jones) W.; m. Susan Christine Halverson, Mar. 30, 1984; children—Andrew Peter, Sharon Ruth. Student Liverpool Sch. Architecture, 1954-56; D in Theology (hon.), Handsworth Coll., 1961; postgrad. Liverpool U. and U. West Indies, 1961-66. Diplomate Am. Inst. Counseling and Psychotherapy. Mgr., Norman Hurst Hotel, Rhyl, Wales, 1954; draftsman Jim Porter & Co., Colwyn Bay, Wales, 1954-56; pastor, supt. schs. Jamaica, W.I., 1961-68; pastor Harrisburg Methodist Ch., Harrisburg, 1968-71; sr. pastor Park Rose Meth. Ch., Portland, Oreg., 1971-78; psychotherapist N.W. Counseling Assocs., Portland, 1971-78; gen. mgr. La. Pacific Corp., Portland, 1978-81; pvt. practice psychotherapy, Portland, Oreg., 1981-82, Vancouver, Wash., 1982—; exec. dir. The Counseling Ctr.of Vancouver, Wash.; dir. East Portland Clinic, 1982-83; dir. N.W. Counseling Assn., 1975-83. Bd. dirs. Park Rose Sch. Dist., 1974-78, chmn. bd., 1977-78; Oreg. soccer commr., 1975-79; sec. Jamaica Council Chs., 1963-67; active Multnomah County Juvenile Services Commn., 1980-81. Served with Royal Air Force, 1956-58. Recipient NCCJ award, 1978. Fellow Am. Orthopsychiat. Assn.; mem. Am. Assn. Marriage and Family Therapy, Am. Mental Health Counselors Assn., Am. Bd. Med. Psychotherapists. Democrat. Office: 1112 Daniels St Vancouver WA 98660

WARNER, ROBERT COLLETT, biochemistry educator; b. Denver, Aug. 31, 1913; s. Hayward Dare and Grace Kendall (McKibben) W.; m. Myra Spector, Feb. 21, 1936 (div. June 1969); children: Peter David, Caroline Dare, Victoria Kaufman; m. Estelle Prussin, June 20, 1969. BS, Calif. Inst. Tech., 1935; MS, NYU, 1937, PhD, 1941. Chemist USDA, Phila., 1941-46; from asst. prof. to prof. biochemistry NYU Sch. Medicine, 1946-69; prof molecular biology and biochemistry U. Calif., Irvine, 1969—, chmn. dept., 1969-77; cons. NRC, 1955-62, NIH, 1962-73. Contbr. articles to profl. jours. Guggenheim fellow, Copenhagen, 1958. Mem. Am. Chem. Soc., Am. Soc. Biol. Chemists (assoc. editor 1968-72)), Biophys. Soc. Home: 1609 Temple Hills Dr Laguna Beach CA 92651 Office: U Calif Dept Molecular Biology/Biochemistry Irvine CA 92717

WARNER, THOMAS RICHARD, air force officer; b. Washington, Sept. 18, 1945; s. Richard Carelton and Mary Constance (Mayhew) W.; m. Martha Elizabeth Miller, Oct. 2, 1976; children: Rebecca, Jocelyn, Abigail. BA, Ind. U., 1968; MA, Cen. Mich. U., 1977. Commd. 2d lt. USAF, 1968, advanced through grades to lt. col., 1984; chief of base adminstrn. USAF, Rickenbacker AFB, Ohio, 1975-76, squadron comdr., 1976-77, exec. officer, 1977-78; chief, systems mgmt. div. Hdqrs. 8th Air Force, Barksdale AFB, La., 1978-80; dir. adminstrn. Hdqrs. Alaskan Air Command, Elmendorf AFB, Alaska, 1980-84, Hdqrs. 15th Air Force, March AFB, Calif., 1984; chief protocol Tactical Fighter Weapons Ctr., Nellis AFB, Nev., 1986—. Mem. Air Force Assn. (life), 15th Air Force Assn., March Field Mus. Found., Riverside Master Chorale, Riverside Opera Assn. Avocations: music, tennis, skiing.

WARNER, WILLIS LEE, consulting company executive; b. Endicott, N.Y., Jan. 28, 1930; s. Willis Eugene and Eva Mae (Zimmerman) W.; B.A., Syracuse U., 1950; M.D., SUNY, Syracuse, 1960. Intern, San Francisco Gen. Hosp., 1960-61; resident St. Mary's Hosp., San Francisco; asso. clin. researcher Baxter Labs., Morton Grove, Ill., 1963-66, asso. dir. clin. research, 1966-71; dir. clin. research, biologics Hoechst Pharm., Somerville, N.J., 1971-75; dir. med. ops. Cutter Labs., Berkeley, Calif., 1975-79; pres. Cons. for Health Care, San Rafael, Calif., 1979—, also dir. Served with U.S. Navy, 1950-55. Mem. Am. Soc. Hematology, Am. Soc. Clin. Pharmacology and Therapeutics, Am. Assn. Blood Banks, Am. Heart Assn. Editor: Plasma Forum, 1979-82; contbr. articles to profl. jours.; patentee in field. Home: 39 Bret Harte Rd San Rafael CA 94901

WARNER, WILSON KEITH, sociology educator; b. Heyburn, Idaho, Sept. 6, 1930; s. Wilson A. and Eva L. (Pratt) W.; m. Vila Jenks, Sept. 1, 1950; children—Karen, Janice, Randall, Neil. B.S., Utah State U., 1958, M.S., 1959; Ph.D., Cornell U., 1960. Asst. prof. rural sociology U. Wis.-Madison, 1960-66, assoc. prof., 1966-69, prof., 1969-71, vis. prof. dept. rural sociology, 1984; prof. sociology Brigham Young U., Provo, Utah, 1971—, assoc. dir. univ. honors program, 1978-79; Mem. steering com. for community progress program State of Utah, 1973. Served with U.S. Army, 1953-55. Named Outstanding Educator of Am., 1972, 1974-75. Mem. Am. Sociol. Assn., Rural Sociol. Soc. (pres. 1973-74, Disting. Rural Sociologist award 1985), Utah Acad. Scis., Arts and Letters, Sigma Xi. Contbr. articles to profl. jours.; editor Jour. Rural Sociology, 1968-69. Office: Brigham Young U Dept Sociology Provo UT 84602

WARNES, JILL RAND, nurse adminstrator; b. San Diego, Mar. 21, 1939; s. Frederick Edward and Barbara Rand (Wisdom) W. AA, Merritt Coll., 1966; BSN, U. Phoenix, Costa Mesa, Calif., 1985. RN, charge nurse coordinator Children's Hosp., Orange, Calif., 1966-80; RN, clinician Marilyn Myers, MD, Santa Ana, Calif., 1980-85; clin. coordinator Mason Clinic Cancer Ctr., Seattle, 1985—. Mem. edn. com. Am. Cancer Soc., Costa Mesa, 1975-85. Robbie Simpson fellow St. Jude Cancer Research Hosp., Memphis, 1975. Mem. Oncology Nurse Assn. (adminstrn. com.), Assn. Pediatric Oncology Nurses. Democrat. Roman Catholic. Avocations: sewing, knitting, embroidery, jogging, tennis. Home: 6001 219th St SW #202 Mountlake Terrace WA 98043 Office: Mason Clinic Cancer Ctr 1100 9th Ave Seattle WA 98101

WARNICK, CHARLES TERRY, research biochemist; b. Brigham City, Utah, Jan. 29, 1943; s. Charles W. and Blanche (Richards) W.; m. Sandra Hathaway, Sept. 2, 1970; children: Derek, Darren, Bryan, Amber, Ashlee. BS, Brigham Young U., 1965; PhD, U. Utah, 1971. Postdoctoral fellow U. Alta., Edmonton, Alta., Can., 1970-72; research assoc. U. Utah, Salt Lake City, 1972-74, research instr., 1974-79, asst. research prof., 1979-81; asst. prof. biochemistry Latter-day Saints Hosp. and U. Utah, Salt Lake City, 1981—, cons. clin. labs., 1985—, also dir. research lab. Contbr. articles to profl. jours. Fellow NASA, 1965, Nat. Cancer Inst. Can., 1970; grantee NIH, 1978, Utah Heart Assn., 1982. Mem. AAAS, Am. Chem. Soc., N.Y. Acad. Sci. Mormon. Avocations: marathon running, coin and stamp collecting. Office: Latter-day Saints Hosp Research Lab 325 8th Ave Salt Lake City UT 84143

WARNICK, G. RUSSELL, clinical chemist, biochemist; b. Great Falls, Mont., Mar. 25, 1944; s. George Webb and Donna (Blackburn) W.; m. Nancy Lynn Foster, Dec. 5, 1967; children: Karl Foster, Kristan, Maren, Kathryn, David Russell. BA cum laude, Utah State U., 1968, MS, 1970; MBA, City U., Seattle, 1982. Asst. chief chemistry 6th U.S. Army Med. Lab, Ft. Baker, Calif, 1971-73; supr. core lab. N.W. Lipid Research Ctr., U. Wash., Seattle, 1973-76, asst. lab. dir., 1976-82, lab. mgr., 1982-85, lab. dir., 1985—; chmn. lab. methods com. Lipid Research Clinics Program, Bethesda, Md., 1981—; adj. scientist NIH Study Cardiovascular Disease, Peoples Republic of China, 1983—; panelist lab. standardization Nat. Cholesterol Edn. Program, 1986—. Contbr. chpts. to profl. publications. Scout master, com. chmn. Boy Scouts Am., Issaquah, Wash., 1973—; mem. Issaquah Sch. Dist. Instructional Media Selection Com., 1980-83. Served to maj. Med. Service Corps, U.S. Army, 1971-73, with Res., 1973—. Mem. Am. Assn. Clin. Chemistry, Am. Chem. Soc., Soc. Armed Forces Med. Lab. Scientists, Clin. Lab. Mgmt. Assn. Republican. Mormon. Home: 10123 238 Way SE Issaquah WA 98027 Office: U Wash NW Lipid Research Ctr 326 9th Ave Seattle WA 98104

WARNKE, DETLEF ANDREAS, geologist, educator; b. Berlin, Fed. Republic of Germany, Jan. 29, 1928; came to U.S., 1955; s. Aloys and Martha (Konetzky) W.; m. Holly M. Menkel, Nov. 14, 1964; children: Erik, D. Christian. Diploma in Geology, U. Freiburg, Fed. Republic of Germany, 1953; PhD in Geology, U. So. Calif., 1956. Jr. exploitation engr. Shell Oil, Houston and Los Angeles, 1956-58; research asst. U. So. Calif., Los Angeles, 1959-61; instr. various colls., Los Angeles and Long Beach, Calif., 1959-63; research assoc., asst. prof. Fla. State U., Tallahassee, 1963-71; from asst. prof. to prof. geology Calif. State U., Hayward, 1971—; exchange prof. Free U. Berlin, 1980-81. Contbr. articles to profl. jours. NSF grantee. Mem. Geol. Soc. Am., Soc. Econs. Paleontologists and Mineralogists, Am. Geophys. Union, Am. Quaternary Assn., Geologische Vereinigung, Sigma Xi. Avocations: skiing, hiking. Office: Calif State U Dept Geol Scis Hayward CA 94542

WARNKEN, VIRGINIA MURIEL THOMPSON, social worker; b. Anadarko, Okla., Aug. 13, 1927; d. Sam Monroe and Ruth L. (McAllister) Thompson; A.B., Okla. U., 1946; M.S.W., Washington U., 1949; m. Douglas Richard Warnken, Sept. 16, 1957; 1 son, William Monroe. Med. social cons. Crippled Children's Services, Little Rock, 1950-54; supr. VA Hosp., Little Rock, 1954-55; asst. prof. U. Tenn. Sch. Social Work, Nashville, 1955-57; dir. social services N.Y. State Rehab. Hosp., Rockland County, 1957-58; asst. prof. U. Chgo. Sch. Social Service Adminstrn., 1958-59; free lance editor, 1960—; instr. evening div. Coll. of Notre Dame, Belmont, Calif., 1967-68; asso. Mills Hosp., San Mateo, Calif., 1978—; med. aux. Community Hosp., Pacific Grove, Calif., 1980—. Com. mem. C. of C. Miss Belmont Pageant, 1971-84, co-chmn., 1975-78. U.S. Children's Bur. scholar, 1947-49. Mem. Assn. Crippled Children and Adults (dir. 1952-55), Assn. Mentally Retarded (dir. 1953-55), Am. Assn. Med. Social Workers (practice chmn. 1954-55), Nat. Assn. Social Workers (dir. 1962-66), Acad. Cert. Social Workers, Am. Assn. Med. Social Workers, Nat. Rehab. Assn., Am. Psychol. Assn., Am. Orthopsychiat. Assn., Council Social Work Edn. Democrat. Presbyterian. Clubs: Carmel Valley Golf and Country, Peninsula Golf and Country, Monterey Golf and Country (Palm Desert, Calif.). Author: Annotated Bibliography of Medical Information and Terminology, 1956. Address: 1399 Bel Aire Rd San Mateo CA 94402

WARR, HOLLIS JEFFERSON, JR., communications educator; b. Amarillo, Tex., Oct. 16, 1949; s. Hollis Jefferson and Kathleen (Stevens) W.; m. Debra Hawk, July 3, 1982. BA, Abilene Christian U., 1972, MA, 1974; PhD, U. Tenn., 1982. Instr. Abilene (Tex.) Christian U., 1974-76, asst. prof., 1978-81; instr. U. Tenn., Knoxville, 1981-82; assoc. prof. Pepperdine U., Malibu, Calif., 1982—; cons. 1982—; v.p., co-owner Drake & Warr Communications, Abilene, 1972-74. Contbr. articles to profl. jours. Named Tchr. of Yr., Pepperdine U., 1985. Mem. Assn. for Edn. in Journalism and Mass Communication, Am. Acad. Advt., Phi Kappa Phi, Kappa Tau Alpha. Republican. Mem. Ch. of Christ. Home: 5560 N Buffwood Pl Agoura Hills CA 91301 Office: Pepperdine U Malibu CA 90265

WARR, ROBERT OSCAR, advertising agency executive; b. Montgomery, Ala., Oct. 15, 1937; s. Gilbert Henry and Grace (Hood) W.; m. Patricia Perlich, May 4, 1963; children—Kristin Ann, Darby Ann. B.S., U. Oreg., 1961. Copywriter, Allen de St. Maurice & Scroggin, San Francisco, 1964-66; creative dir. Pacific Nat. Advt., Portland, Oreg., 1966-68, Martel Scroggin Advt., San Francisco, 1968-70; account supr. Paul Pease Advt., Palo Alto, Calif., 1970-71; ptnr. Hommel Stanko Warr, Palo Alto, 1971; owner Warr Dept., Los Altos, 1972-74; pres., bd. chmn. Warr, Foote & Rose, Los Altos and Eugene, Oreg., 1974—; chmn. Pehaco Corp., Los Altos, 1975-80; pres. Warr Sports, Inc., Eugene, 1979—; promotion chmn. IEEE Computer Soc. Internat. Confs., 1971-75. Bd. dirs. Eugene Family YMCA; bd. trustees, treas. Kerns Art Ctr. Served with AUS, 1957-58. Mem. U. Oreg. Pres.'s Assos., Sigma Chi. Republican. Clubs: U. Oreg. No. Calif. Alumni (pres. 1977-78), Oregon. Lodge: Eugene Rotary. Writer numerous print advts., broadcast commls., mag. articles.

WARREN, BARBARA LEONARD, educator, author; b. Fall River, Mass., Nov. 3, 1943; d. John Morris and Jeanne Adrienne (Clement) Leonard; m. B. William Warren, Sept. 9, 1972. BA, Bridgewater State Coll., 1966; MA, Ariz. State U., 1976. Cert. secondary tchr., Mass, Ariz.; cert. community coll. tchr., Ariz. Tchr. B.M.C. Durfee High Sch., Fall River, 1966-69; women's editor Prescott (Ariz.) Courier, 1972; tchr. Casa Grande (Ariz.) High Sch., 1974—. Author: Capture Creativity: Photographs To Inspire Young Writers, 1982; contbr. articles to profl. jours. Mem. NEA, Ariz. Edn. Assn., Casa Grande Edn. Assn., Nat. Assn. Gifted Child, Ariz. Assn. Gifted and Talented, Nat. Council Tchrs. Eng., Ariz. Eng. Tchrs. Assn., Delta Kappa Gamma (chair communications com.). Home: PO Box 1282 Casa Grande AZ 85222 Office: Casa Grande High Sch 420 E Florence Blvd Casa Grande AZ 85222

WARREN, BRADLEY JOSEPH, sanitation executive; b. Lima, Ohio, July 23, 1953; s. Joseph E. and Doris June (Kiracofe) W.; m. Katie O. Gibson. Driver SCA Services Co., Lima, 1973-78, ops. mgr., 1978-80; dist. mgr. SCA Services Co., Pontiac, Mich., 1980-82, Oklahoma City, 1982-84; area mgr. GSX Corp., Phoenix, 1984—. Avocation: woodcarving, sports.

WARREN, DAVID HARDY, psychology educator; b. Chelsea, Mass., July 28, 1943; s. Roland Leslie and Margaret (Hodges) W.; 1 child, Michael Jonathan. A.B. in Psychology, Yale U., 1965; Ph.D. in Child Devel, U. Minn., 1969. Prof. psychology U. Calif., Riverside, 1969—, dean Coll. Humanities and Social Scis., 1977-85. Author: Blindness and Early Childhood Development, 1977, 84; contbr. articles profl. jours. Mem. Psychonomic Soc., AAAS. Office: U Calif Dept Psychology Riverside CA 92521

WARREN, EDWARD MCCOY, petroleum geologist; b. Barberton, Ohio, Oct. 10, 1925; s. Sherwood S. and Adelaide W. (McCoy) W.; m. Patricia Lou Parker, Nov. 23, 1949; children—Susan, David, Carol. Geol. E., Colo. Sch. Mines, 1950. Geologist, Texaco, Inc., San Antonio, 1950-51; mgr., geologist Petroleum Service & Research, San Antonio, 1951-53, various ind. cos., San Antonio, 1953-75; v.p., dir. Petrolero Corp., San Antonio and Evergreen, Colo., 1975-81; geol. cons., Evergreen, 1981—. Zoning commr. Town of Hollywood Park (Tex.), 1973; officer, com. chair Evergreen Meadows Homeowners Assn., 1978-80. Served with USN, 1943-46; PTO. Mem. Am. Inst. Profl. Geologists (sect. pres. 1981), Am. Assn. Petroleum Geologists, Rocky Mountain Assn. Geologists, Wyo. Geol. Assn., Four Corners Geol. Soc., N.Mex. Geol. Soc., S. Tex. Geol. Soc. (select adv. com.), Colo. Sch. Mines Found. (dir. 1985-87) Colo. Sch. Mines Alumni Assn. (sec.-treas., pres.-elect 1981-83, pres. 1984). Republican. Methodist. Clubs: Kiwanis (pres. 1982-83) (Evergreen); Optimists (pres. 1955) (San Antonio). Lodge: Elks. Home: 7945 S Native Dancer Trail Evergreen CO 80439

WARREN, EUGENE HOWARD, JR., economic consultant; b. Oak Park, Ill., Jan. 1, 1943; s. Eugene H. and Lorene Winifred (Long) W.; m. Linda Lou Glascock, Mar. 1, 1964; children: Kristen Lynn, Brooke Anne. AB, Ind. U., 1967; MS, Purdue U., 1969, PhD, 1975. Instr. econs. Western Mich. U., Kalamazoo, 1971-73; asst. prof. U. Tenn., Chattanooga, 1973-74; asst. prof. U. Calgary, Alta., Can., 1974-76, assoc. prof., 1976-78; sr. economist Jet Propulsion Lab., Pasadena, Calif., 1978-82; pvt. practice econ. cons. Claremont, Calif., 1982—. Co-author: The Solar Alternative, 1981; also articles to profl. jours. Treas. Mount Baldy Aquatics, Claremont, 1982-85; deacon Claremont Presby. Ch., 1982-85. Krannert Research fellow Purdue U., West Lafayette, Ind., 1971-72. Mem. AAAS, Am. Econ. Assn., Ops. Research So. Am. Republican. Home and Office: 691 Clarion Pl Claremont CA 91711

WARREN, GERALD LEE, newspaper editor; b. Hastings, Nebr., Aug. 17, 1930; s. Hie Elias and Linnie (Williamson) W.; m. Euphemia Florence Brownell, Nov. 20, 1965 (div.); children: Gerald Benjamin, Euphemia Brownell; m. Viviane M. Pratt, Apr. 27, 1986. A.B., U. Nebr., 1952. Reporter Lincoln Star, Nebr., 1951-52; reporter, asst. city editor San Diego Union, 1956-61; bus. rep. Copley News Service, 1961-63; city editor San Diego Union, 1963-68, asst. mng. editor, 1968-69, editor, 1975—; dep. press. sec. to Pres. Richard M. Nixon, 1969-74, Pres. Gerald Ford, 1974-75. Served to lt. (j.g.) USNR, 1952-56. Mem. Am. Soc. Newspaper Editors, Sigma Delta Chi, Sigma Nu. Republican. Episcopalian. Office: Copley Press 350 Camino de la Reina San Diego CA 92108

WARREN, JAMES RONALD, museum director, author, columnist; b. Goldendale, Wash., May 25, 1925; stepson H.S. W.; m. Gwen Davis, June 25, 1949; children: Gail, Jeffrey. B.A., Wash. State U., 1949; M.A., U. Wash., 1953, Ph.D., 1963. Adminstrv. v.p. Seattle Community Coll., 1965-69; pres. Edmonds Community Coll., Lynnwood, Wash., 1969-79; dir. Mus. of History and Industry, Seattle, 1979—. Author several history books; Columnist: Seattle Post Intelligencer, 1979—, Puget Sound Bus. Jour., 1980—. Served with U.S. Army, 1943-45. Mem. Am. Assn. Museum. Lodge: Rotary (Seattle). Home: 3235 99th NE St Bellevue WA 98004 Office: Mus of History and Industry 2700 24th Ave E Seattle WA 98112

WARREN, JEFFRY CLARY, clinical psychologist; b. Burbank, Calif., Nov. 1, 1949; s. Bernard W. and Florence S. W.; student Valley Coll., 1967-79; B.A., U. Calif.-Santa Barbara, 1971; Ph.D. in Clin. Psychology, Calif. Sch. of Profl. Psychology, 1976; 1 son, Adam Bernard. Registered psychologist Tech. Research, San Diego, 1976-78; developer, coordinator grad. tng. program Edwards Inst. for Advanced Studies, San Diego, 1980, dir. profl. and acad. tng., 1980; clin. psychologist TRI-Community Service Systems, San Diego, 1979-83; pvt. practice, La Jolla, Calif., 1983—; sr. v.p., dir. Grid Research Corp., 1982-83; cons. and educator in family therapy and child abuse. Developer task force on child abuse, San Diego, 1978-80. Mem. Am. Psychol. Assn., Nat. Register of Health Service Providers in Psychology, Calif. State Psychol. Assn., Acad. San Diego Psychologists, Western Psychol. Assn. Jewish. Contbr. papers to profl. assn. confs. Office: 7755 Fay St Suite I La Jolla CA 92037

WARREN, NICHOLAS WALTER, synergetics educator; b. Champaign, Ill., Apr. 12, 1941; s. William Joseph and Annette (Chemielewski) W.; m. Sally Lappen, Aug. 2, 1981; children: Adria, Caitrina, Kaitlin. BA in Physics, U. Calif., Berkeley, 1964; MA in Astronomy, Columbia U., 1966, PhD in Geophysics, 1971. Research geophysicist UCLA, 1971-80, assoc. research geophysicist, 1980-83; faculty Otis-Parsons Art Inst., Los Angeles, 1980—, Internat. Coll., Los Angeles, 1984-86; dean dept. natural sci. Sierra U., Santa Monica, Calif., 1986—; cons. in art and sci., Santa Monica, 1984—. Contbr. articles to profl. jours. Mem. AAAS, Internat. Soc. for the Arts Scis and Technology, Nat. Sci. Tchrs. Assn., N.Y. Acad. Sci., Union Concerned Scientists, Wilderness Soc., Amnesty Internat., Sigma Xi. Avocations: hiking, poetry. Home: 134 Hart Ave Santa Monica CA 90405 Office: Art/Sci Cons 134 Hart Ave Santa Monica CA 90405

WARREN, PETER, university dean; b. N.Y.C., Sept. 30, 1938. BA, U. Calif., Berkeley, 1950; MA with honors, U. Wis., 1965, PhD, 1970. Prof. math. and computer sci. U. Denver, 1970-78, dir. div. data processing, 1985-86, dean Univ. Coll., 1986—; dir. research Colo. Energy Research Inst., Denver, 1978-83; pvt. practice statistics cons., Denver, 1974-86. Contbr. over 40 articles to profl. jours. Pres., chmn. bd. Denver Internat. Film Festival, 1978-82; chmn. Urban Design Forum, Denver, 1983-85. Mem. Am. Assn. Computing Machinery, Am. Math. Soc. Democrat. Home: 936 Detroit St Denver CO 80206 Office: U. Denver Denver CO

WARREN, RAYMOND JOSEPH, lawyer; b. Syracuse, N.Y., Apr. 20, 1957; s. Raymond Arthur and Jean Marie (Clark) W.; m. Mary Ellen Simpson, Aug. 2, 1980; 1 child, Joseph. BSEE, U. Okla., 1980, JD, 1983. Bar: Okla. 1983, Ariz. 1984, U.S. Patent Office 1982. Patent atty. Motorola Inc., Phoenix, 1983—. Mem. ABA, Okla. Bar Assn., State Bar Ariz., Am. Intellectual Property Law Assn.

WARREN, RICHARD WAYNE, obstetrician and gynecologist; b. Puxico, Mo., Nov. 26, 1935; s. Martin R. and Sarah E. (Crump) W.; B.A., U. Calif., Berkeley, 1957; M.D., Stanford, 1961; m. Rosalie J. Franzola, Aug. 16, 1959; children—Lani Marie, Richard W., Paul D. Intern, Oakland (Calif.) Naval Hosp., 1961-62; resident in ob-gyn Stanford Med. Center (Calif.), 1964-67; practice medicine specializing in ob-gyn, Mountain View, Calif., 1967—; mem. staff Stanford and El Camino hosps.; pres. Richard W. Warren M.D., Inc.; assoc. clin. prof. ob-gyn Stanford Sch. Medicine. Served with USN, 1961-64. Diplomate Am. Bd. Ob-Gyn. Fellow Am. Coll. Ob-Gyn; mem. AMA, Calif. Med. Assn., San Francisco Gynecol. Soc., Peninsula Gynecol. Soc., Am. Assn. Gynecologic Laparoscopists, Assn. Profs. Gynecology and Obstetrics, Royal Soc. Medicine. Contbr. articles to profl. jours. Home: 102 Atherton Ave Atherton CA 94025 Office: 2500 Hospital Dr Mountain View CA 94040

WARTA, JOHN M., communications company executive. married; 4 children. Student, Met. State Coll., 1971-75, U. Pa., 1985. Systems mgr. Portland (Oreg.) Sch. Dist., 1975-77; supr. systems and programming Advanced Bus. Computers, 1977-78; gen. mgr. Data Mgmt. Systems, Inc., 1978-81; from systems and programming supr. to info. service ctr. mgr. Pacific Telecom, Inc., 1981-84; sr. v.p. Am. Network, Inc., 1984—; research and devel. cons. Columbine Systems. Served with USAF, Vietnam, 1966-69. Address: Rt 2 Box 461 BB La Center WA 98629

WARTEN, RALPH MARTIN, mathematics educator; b. Bielefeld, Fed. Republic Germany, Jan. 6, 1926; came to U.S., 1948; s. Bernhard and Ernestine (Isaac) Wartensleben; m. Winifred Grace Battelle, Oct. 14, 1950. BS, Bklyn Coll., 1957; MS, Purdue U., 1959, PhD, 1961. Researcher Math. Research Ctr. IBM Corp., Palo Alto, Calif., 1966-68, instr., adv. mathematician fed. systems div., 1961-65; research and teaching asst. Purdue U., Lafayette, Ind., 1957-60; prof. math. Calif. Poly. State U., San Luis Obispo, 1968—. Contbr. articles to profl. jours. Mem. AAAS, Am. Math. Soc., Math. Assn. Am., N.Y. Acad. Scis., Phi Beta Kappa, Sigma Xi, Kappa Mu Epsilon, Alpha Sigma Lambda, Pi Mu Epsilon. Home: 11 Mariposa Dr San Luis Obispo CA 93401

WARWICK, MAL, fund raising consultant, telemarketing executive. BA with distinction, U. Mich., 1963; postgrad. in Latin Am. Affairs, Columbia U., 1963-65. Freelance writer Calif., 1969-76; exec. editor, co-founder Alternative Features Service, Berkeley, Calif., 1971-73; campaign coordinator John George for Supr., Oakland, Calif., 1976; campaign mgr., coordinator Berkeley Citizens Action, 1976-80; pres., founder Mal Warwick & Assocs., Inc., Berkeley, 1979—; mktg. dir. Richard Parker & Assocs., San Francisco, 1981-82; chmn., co-founder The Progressive Group, Inc., Northampton, Mass., 1985—. Vol. Peace Corps, Ecuador, 1965-69; com. mem. Ronald V. Dellums, 1979—; mem. exec. bd. Calif. Dems., 1982—, co-founder Environ. Caucus, 1984, orgn. and devel. com., 1984-85, resolutions com., 1985—; bd. dirs. New Dem. Forum East Bay, (various offices held 1982-85); rec. sec. Nat. Women's Polit. Caucus, 1983-85; bd. dirs. Berkeley Support Services, 1980-83; chmn. Berkeley Citizens' Commn. Automatic Data Processing Ops., 1981-82. Mem. Direct Mktg. Assn., Nonprofit Mailers Fedn., Nat. Com. Responsive Philanthropy, Nat. Soc. Fund Raising Execs., Assn. Direct Response Fundraising. Office: Mal Warwick & Assocs Inc PO Box 1282 Berkeley CA 94701

WASDEN, WINIFRED SAWAYA, English educator, freelance writer; b. Kemmerer, Wyo., Apr. 15, 1938; d. George Sabeh and Letta Louise (Gerken) Sawaya; m. John Frederic Wasden, Dec. 20, 1960; children: Frederic Keith, Carol Elizabeth. BA with honors, U. Wyo., 1960, MA, 1961. Emergency instr. U. Wyo., Laramie, 1960-61; tchr. English Worland (Wyo.) High Sch., 1963; from instr. to assoc. prof. English Northwest Community Coll., Powell, Wyo., 1964—. Contbr. articles to pubs.; author numerous poems. Mem. Powell Bd. Adjustments, 1974—; chmn., bd. dirs. Civic Orch. and Chorus, Powell, 1981—; mem. Wyo. Council for the Humanities, 1978-79, coordinator Big Horn Basin Project, 1980-85. Mem. Wyo. Oral History and Folklore Assn. (v.p. 1984-85, bd. dirs. 1985-86), Wyo. Assn. Tchrs. English, N.W. Community Coll. Faculty Assn. (pres. 1977-78), AAAUW, Delta Kappa Gamma (pres. Powell chpt. 1978-80), Phi Rho Pi (hon.). Republican. Roman Catholic. Avocations: travel, reading. Office: Northwest Community Coll Powell WY 82435

WASHAM, GARY IVAN, marketing professional; b. Hickory, N.C., July 8, 1949; s. Troy L. and Martha C. (Gardner) W.; m. Connie L. Gell, Oct. 22, 1977. BS in Systems Engrng., U.S. Naval Acad., 1971; MS in Systems Mgmt., U. So. Calif., 1979. Commd. lt. commdr. USN, San Diego, 1971, res., 1980; dir. product mktg. Megatek Corp., San Diego, 1982-83, dir. mktg. support, 1983-84, dir. corp. devel., 1984-85, dir. mktg., 1985—. Mem. Soc. for Computer Simulation, Assn. Computing Machinery, Nat. Computer Graphics Assn. Republican. Avocations: hunting, camping, skiing. Office: Megatek Corp 9645 Scranton Rd San Diego CA 92121

WASHBURN, JAMES THOMAS, II, minister; b. Midland, Tex., Dec. 22, 1958; s. Almas Preston and Mary Wynola (Waters) W.; m. Julie Ellen Eakin, Dec. 27, 1983. BA in Bible, Lubbock Christian Coll., 1983. Ordained to ministry Ch. of Christ, 1979. Intern Broadway Ch. of Christ, Lubbock, Tex., 1979-82; youth minister Ft. Worth and Jax Ch. of Christ (now Fairmont Park Ch. of Christ), Midland, 1981-84, 3d and Kilgore Ch. of Christ, Portales, N.Mex., 1984—; adventure leader Adventures in Christian Living, 1985. Basketball official, 1984—, Football official, 1985—. Named one of Outstanding Young Men of Am., 1983. Mem. N.Mex. Activities Assn., N.Mex. Officials Assn. Republican. Avocations: backpacking, reading, golfing. Home: 1708 S Globe Portales NM 88130 Office: 3d and Kilgore Ch of Christ Box 450 Portales NM 88130

WASHBURN, JERRY MARTIN, accountant, company executive; b. Powell, Wyo., Dec. 31, 1943; s. Roland and Lavon (Martin) W.; B.S., Brigham Young U., 1969; m. Pamela Ruth Palmer, June 11, 1965; children—Garth, Gavin, Kristina. Staff acct. Arthur Andersen & Co., Seattle, 1969-71, sr. auditor, Boise, Idaho, 1971-73, audit mgr. Boise, Idaho, Portland, Oreg., 1976-79; controller Washburn Musicland, Inc., Phoenix, 1979-84; prin. Washburn Enterprises; Phoenix, 1979-82; pres. Total Info. Systems, Inc., Phoenix, 1982—; founding dir. Internat. and Commerce Bank, Phoenix, 1985—. C.P.A., Wash., Idaho, Oreg. Mem. Inst. Internal Auditors (past pres. Boise, dir. Boise and Portland), Am. Mgmt. Assn., Am. Inst. C.P.A.'s, Idaho, Wash. Socs. C.P.A.'s. Republican. Home: 5122 E Shea Scottsdale AZ 85254 Office: 4201 N 24th St Suite 150 Phoenix AZ 85016

WASHINGTON, FRANKIE MARIN, medical social worker; b. El Paso, Tex., July 4, 1953; d. Frank M. Viramontes and Ozella L. (Jones) Glaab; m. Thomas E. Renguul, July 27, 1974 (div. May 1982); children: Ozella, Anna; m. Stephen E. Washington, Aug. 8, 1984 (dec. Mar. 1986); 1 child, Bridget. BSW, Loma Linda Med. U., 1978; postgrad., Inst. Children's Lit., 1979; cert., SUNY Downstate Med. Ctr., Bklyn., 1982. Adminstrv. asst. tchr. Palau Acad. and Elem. Sch., Western Carolines Island, 1974-76; supr., counselor Option House Shelter, Rialto, Calif., 1978; social services asst. Dept. Social Services, Redlands, Calif., 1978; family planning counselor Women's Clin., San Bernardino, Calif., 1979; adminstrv. asst. counselor Cath. Charities, Bklyn., 1980-82; rehab. recreation dir. State of Ark., Hot Springs, 1982-83; rehab. vocational evaluator State of Ark., Little Rock, 1983-84; substitute tchr. Needles (Calif.) Sch. Dist., 1984-85; med. social worker Community Hosp., Needles, 1985—. Named Employee of Yr., West World Health Care Needles Hosp., 1985. Mem. Nat. Assn. Social Workers, Nat. Rehab. Assn. Lodge: Soroptomists (recipient Women Helping Women awards, Ont., Needles, 1986). Avocations: writing, public speaking, acting, dancing. Office: Needles Desert Communities Hosp Needles CA 92363

WASHINGTON, HAROLD J., elementary instructor, retired non-commissioned officer; b. New Iberia, La., Jan. 1, 1931; s. Paul and Venita (Jones) W.; m. Celia A. Marion; children: Jolene, Joseph, Sheona, Ginette, Roseann, Brianne, Eileen. BE, Seattle U., 1973, postgrad., 1975, MEd, 1983. Cert. prin., Wash. Enlisted U.S. Army, 1948, advanced through grades to sgt. 1st class, ret., 1969; advisor to Wash. N.G. Tacoma, 1963-69; tchr. Our Lady of the Lake Sch., Seattle, 1973—. Mem. Assn. Supervision and Curriculum Devel. Democrat. Mem. Christian Ch. Home: 19010 60th Ave W PO Box 551 Lynnwood WA 98036

WASHINGTON, NAPOLEON, JR., insurance agent, clergyman; b. Ft. Baker, Calif., Apr. 12, 1948; s. Napoleon and Annie D. (Carter) W.; A.A., Merced Coll., 1976; student Stanislaus State Coll., 1976-77; grad. Billy Graham Sch. Evangelism, 1983; m. Nadine Reed, Nov. 6, 1968; children—Gregory D., Kimberlee N., Geoffrey N. Lic. Baptist minister. Agt., Met. Life Ins. Co., Merced, Calif., 1970-72, sr. sales rep., 1972-83; broker Gen. Ins. Brokers, Merced, 1973—; owner Washington Assocs. Fin. Services; tchr. salesmanship Merced Coll., 1979—. Chmn. bd. trustees St. Matthew Baptist Ch., 1978—, ordained deacon, lic. minister, assoc. minister, 1982—; vice-chmn. Merced County Pvt. Industries Council, 1981-83; mem. ins. adv. council City of Merced Schs.; vocat. mgr. New Hope Found., Dos Palos, Calif., 1984-85. Served with U.S. Army, 1968-70. Recipient Nat. Quality award Nat. Assn. Life Underwriters, 1979, Nat. Sales Achievement award, 1979, Health Ins. Quality award, 1977; mem. Million Dollar Round Table, 1973, 74, 75, 76, 77, 78; teaching cert. Calif. community colls. Mem. Nat. Assn. Life Underwriters, Calif. Assn. Life Underwriters (dir. 1975-76), Merced County Assn. Life Underwriters (pres. 1976-77), Merced County Estate Planning Council (dir.), Merced County Pvt. Industries Council, NAACP, Phi Beta Lambda. Democrat. Club: Rotary (dir. 1974-76). Home: 1960 Cedar Crest Dr Merced CA 95340 Office: 935 W 18th St Merced CA 95340

WASHINGTON, REGINALD LOUIS, cardiologist, pediatrician, educator, administrator; b. Colorado Springs, Colo., Dec. 31, 1949; s. Lucius Louis and Brenette Y. (Wheeler) W.; m. Billye Faye Ned, Aug. 18, 1973; children: Danielle Larae, Reginald Quinn. BS in Zoology, Colo. State U., 1971; MD, U. Colo., 1975. Diplomate Nat. Bd. Med. Examiners, Am. Bd. Pediatrics, Pediatric Cardiology. Intern in pediatrics U. Colo. Med. Ctr., Denver, 1975-76, resident in pediatrics, 1976-78, fellow in pediatric cardiology, 1979-81, chief resident, instr., 1981-86, asst. prof. pediatrics, 1986—; staff cardiologist Children's Hosp., Denver, 1981—; asst. prof. pediatrics, mem. admissions com. U. Colo. Sch. Medicine, Denver, 1985-89; bd. dirs. Rocky Mountain Heart Found. for Children, Children's Health Care Assn. Adv. bd. dirs. Equitable Bank of Littleton, Colo., 1984—. Recipient Mosby award in Pediatrics, U. Colo. Med. Ctr., 1975. Fellow Am. Acad. Pediatrics (cardiology subsect.), Am. Coll. Cardiology, Am. Heart Assn., Soc. Critical Care Medicine; mem. Am. Acad. Pediatrics/Perinatology, N.Am. Soc. Pediatric Exercise Medicine (pres.), Colo. Heart Assn. (bd. dirs., exec. com. 1987—, grantee 1983-84). Democrat. Roman Catholic. Clubs: Denver Athletic, Oxford (Denver). Avocations: skiing, fishing. Home: 7423 Berkeley Circle Castle Rock CO 80104 Office: Dept Pediatric Cardiology 1056 E 19th Ave Denver CO 80218

WASIELEWSKI, RONALD DEAN, utilities company executive; b. Milw., Oct. 22, 1947; s. Henry John Wasielewski and Juanita (Sebastian) Baumhueter; m. Gilou Suissa, Nov. 15, 1969 (div. Dec. 1983); 1 child, Gregory Dean. AA in Bus., East Los Angeles Coll., 1975; BS in Mgmt., Calif. State U., Los Angeles, 1978. Various clerical positions So. Calif. Edison Co., Alhambra, 1971-75; material controller So. Calif. Edison Co., Barstow, 1975-76; mgmt. analyst So. Calif. Edison Co., Rosemead, 1976-77; methods and procedures analyst So. Calif. Edison Co., Long Beach, 1978-79; systems adminstr. So. Calif. Edison Co., Rosemead, 1979-83; mgmt. info. systems adminstr. So. Calif. Edison Co., Alhambra, 1983—; prof. East Los Angeles Coll., Monterey Park, Calif., 1976—. Served to sgt. USMC, 1965-69. Mem. Acad. Magical Arts. Democrat. Roman Catholic. Avocations: golf, water skiing, fishing, raquetball, making fine jewelry. Office: So Calif Edison Co 501 S Marengo Box 429 Alhambra CA 91802

WASLEY, RICHARD JUNIOR, engineer; b. Oakland, Calif., June 24, 1931; s. Richard John Wasley and Rosaline Sonora (Howell) Previati; m. Margery Louise Ziniker, Oct. 22, 1960; children: Richard, Anne, Pamela. BS, U. Calif., Berkeley, 1954; MS, Stanford U., 1958, PhD, 1961. Registered profl. engr., Calif. Div. leader Lawrence Livermore Nat. Lab., Livermore, Calif., 1972-85; research engr. Lawrence Livermore Nat. Lab., Livermore, 1985—. Author: Stress Wave Propagation, 1973; contbr. articles to profl. jours.; patentee in field. Served with AUS, 1953-55. Recipient A. Noble Prize Five Profl. Engrng. Orgns., 1961. Fellow ASCE; mem. ASME, Valley Trail Riders (pres. 1984-85). Republican. Lutheran. Avocations: camping, hiking, trail riding. Home: 4290 Colgate Way Livermore CA 94550 Office: Lawrence Livermore Nat Lab PO Box 808 L626 Livermore CA 94550

WASLIEN, GLENN SELMER, food store chain executive; b. Ithaca, N.Y., May 7, 1943; s. Palmer Jennings and Ann Helen (Larsen) W.; m. Sandra Lynne Hultman, July 14, 1968; children: Jennifer Victoria, Gary Steven. BA, Calif. Luth. Coll., 1965. Field rep. Southland Corp., La Mesa, Calif., 1965-69, dist. mgr., 1969-74, zone mgr., 1974-78, ops. mgr., 1978-79, div. mgr., 1979-87; gen. mgr. Video Ops., Dallas, 1987—. Served to 1st lt. U.S. Army, 1965-69. Republican. Lutheran. Avocation: golfing. Home: 5516 Club View Dr Yorba Linda CA 92686 Office: The Southland Corp 1240 S State Coll Blvd Anaheim CA 92806

WASSERMAN, ISAAC MILES, vocational evaluator; b. Richmond, Va., Sept. 25, 1932; s. Joseph Benjamin and Eva W.; A.B.A., Nichols Jr. Coll., 1956; student in bus. adminstrn. Lynchburg Coll., 1953-55; B.S. in Edn., Boston U., 1958, M.Ed., 1959; 1 dau., Erica Jacqueline. Tutorial and remedial tchr. White Plains (N.Y.) Public Schs., 1959-60; tchr. English and geography Newton (Mass.) Public Schs., 1960; instr. psychology and public speaking Cambridge Jr. Coll., 1961-62; vocat. counselor Jewish Vocat. Service, Boston, 1962-63; guidance counselor jr. high schs. Winthrop (Mass.) Public Schs., 1963-68; elem. counselor, sch. psychologist Andover (Mass.) Public Schs., 1968-76; sch. psychologist, core team chmn. Greater Lowell (Mass.) Regional Vocat. Tech. Sch., 1976-77; sch. psychologist Lawrence (Mass.) pub. schs., 1977; vocat. evaluator/rehab. counselor Goodwill Industries, San Jose, Calif., 1977-81, vocat. evaluator, 1982—; vocat. evaluator Westcom Industries, Richmond Calif., 1981; psychol. cons. Lawrence Public Schs. Recipient Dr. Quincy Merrill award Nichols Jr. Coll., 1959 Mem. Am. Personnel and Guidance Assn., Nat. Vocat. Guidance Assn., Am. Sch. Counselors Assn. Club: Masons (Richmond, Va.). Home: 5545 Tilden Pl Fremont CA 94536 Office: Goodwill Industries 1080 N 7th St San Jose CA 95112

WASSERMAN, LEW R., film, recording, publishing company executive; b. Cleve., Mar. 15, 1913; m. Edith T. Beckerman, July 5, 1936; 1 dau., Lynne Kay. D (hon.), Brandeis U., NYU. Nat. dir. advt. and publicity Music Corp. Am., 1936-38, v.p., 1938-39, became v.p. charge motion picture div., 1940; now chmn. bd., dir., chief exec. officer, mem. exec. com. MCA, Inc., also chmn. bd., chief exec. officer, dir. subsidiary corps.; dir. Am. Airlines; chmn. emeritus Assn. Motion Picture and TV Producers. Trustee John F. Kennedy Library, John F. Kennedy Center Performing Arts, Calif. Inst. Tech., Jules Stein Eye Inst., Carter Presdl. Ctr., Lyndon Baines Johnson Found.; pres. pres. Hollywood Canteen Found.; chmn. Research to Prevent Blindness Found.; hon. chmn. bd. Center Theatre Group Los Angeles Music Center; bd. dirs. Amateur Athletic Found. of Los Angeles (chmn. fin. com.), Los Angeles Music Ctr. Found.; bd. gov.'s Ronald Reagan Presdl. Found. Recipient Jean Hersholt Humanitarian award Acad. Motion Picture Arts and Scis., 1973. Democrat. Office: MCA Inc 100 Universal City Plaza Universal City CA 91608

WASSERMAN, MARK ROBERT, academic director; b. Boston, Nov. 2, 1956; s. Lawrence William and Della Mae (Keeran) W.; m. Judy Lynn Lake, Dec. 29, 1979. Student, Boston U., 1975-77; BBA, U. Okla., 1979; MBA, U. N.D., 1985. Commd. USAF, 1980, advanced through grades to capt.; missile competition instr. 321 Strategic Missile Wing, Grand Forks AFB, N.D., 1983-84, missile instr. comdr., 1984, missile competition comdr., 1984-85; instr. USAF Acad. CWIS, Colorado Springs, Colo., 1985-86, asst. course dir., 1986, course dir. freshman curriculum, 1986—; asst. prof. USAF Acad. CWIS, 1987—. Author: Special Operations, 1985-86, Surveillance and Reconnaissance, 1986-87; editor: Professional Foundations, 1987, U.S. Air Power and Force Application, 1987. Youth dir. Faith Evang. Free ch., Grand Forks, 1981-84, Wildwood community Ch., Norman, Okla., 1978-80; active Grand Forks Jaycees, 1982-84. Named one of Outstanding Young Men of Am., 1982-86. Mem. Air Force Assn., 321 Strategic Missile Wing Crew Mems. Assn. (treas. 1984-85). Republican. Avocations: sports, photography, biblical related activities. Home: 19050 Royal Archers Ln Monument CO 80132 Office: USAF Acad CWIS Colorado Springs CO 80840-5421

WASSERMAN, ROBERT, city official; b. Gary, Ind., Jan. 12, 1934; s. Morris K. and Alice W.; B.S., Calif. State U., 1963; M.P.A., U. So. Calif., 1975; m. Mary Linda Galantin, Sept. 13, 1958; children—Daniel Joseph, Jill Marie. Chief of police City of San Carlos (Calif.), 1969-72, City of Brea and Yorba Linda (Calif.), 1972-76, City of Fremont (Calif.), 1976—; chmn. adv. com. Calif. Commn. on Peace Officer Stds. and Tng., 1979-83; mem. Calif. Commn. on Peace Officer Standards and Tng.; mem. Pres.'s Adv. Com. Law Enforcement; cons. to police agys. Bd. mgrs. Fremont-Newark YMCA, 1978—. Served with U.S. Army, 1950-52. Mem. Calif. Peace Officers Assn. (pres. 1980), Internat. Assn. Chiefs of Police, Police Exec. Research Forum. Club: Rotary. Contbr. articles to profl. jours. Office: 39710 Civic Center Dr Fremont CA 94538

WASSERMAN, SAUL, child psychiatrist; b. N.Y.C., Apr. 22, 1942; s. David and Zelda (Luberoff) W.; m. Judy Ruskin, Dec. 25, 1963; 1 child, Rachel. BS in Engring. and Physics, Cornell U., 1963; MD, U. Chgo., 1967. Diplomate Am. Bd. Psychiatry and Neurology. Intern U. Chgo. Hosps., 1968; fellow in psychiatry Stanford U., 1971; psychiatrist Adult and Child Guidance Clinic, San Jose, Calif., 1971-73; asst. med. dir. Child and Adult Psychiat. Inst., San Jose Hosp., 1973-77, med. dir., 1977—; mental health chief San Jose Med. Group, 1985—; psychiatrist Santa Clara County Juvenile Probation Dept., 1973-75; assoc. clin. prof. child psychiatry Stanford U., 1983—; cons. Santa Clara County Dept. Social Services, 1983-84; child psychiatrist Multi-Discipline Child Abuse Team, Santa Clara County, 1984—; bd. dirs. Santa Clara County Maternal, Child and Adolescent Health Commn. Bd. dirs. E. Santa Clara St. Polit. Action Com., San Jose, 1984—. Mem. Am. Acad. Child Psychiatry, Am. Psychiat. Assn., No. Calif. Psychiat. Soc. (councilor 1986—), Santa Clara Med. Soc., Calif. Med. Assn. Democrat. Jewish. Avocations: collecting Japanese woodblock prints, marine aquaria. Home: 751 Southampton Dr Palo Alto CA 94303 Office: San Jose Hosp 675 E Santa Clara St San Jose CA 95112

WASSERMAN, STEPHEN IRA, physician, educator; b. Los Angeles, Dec. 17, 1942; m. Linda Morgan; children: Matthew, Zachary. BA, Stanford U., 1964; MD, UCLA, 1968. Intern, resident Peter B. Brigham Hosp., Boston, 1968-70; fellow in allergy, immunology Robert B. Brigham Hosp., Boston, 1972-75; asst. prof. medicine Harvard U., Boston, 1975-79, assoc. prof., 1979; assoc. prof. U. Calif.-San Diego, La Jolla, 1979-85, prof., 1985—, chief allergy tng. program Sch. Medicine, 1979-85, chief allergy div. Sch. Medicine, 1985—, acting chmn. dept. medicine, 1986—; co-dir. allergy sect. Robert B. and Peter B. Brigham Hosps., 1977-79. Contbr. articles to profl. jours. Served to lt. comdr. USPHS, 1970-72, San Francisco. Fellow Am. Acad. Allergy and Immunology; mem. AAAS, Am. Soc. Clin. Investigation, Am. Assn. Immunologists, Collegium Internationale Allergologicum, Phi Beta Kappa, Alpha Omega Alpha. Office: U Calif Med Ctr 225 W Dickinson St San Diego CA 92103

WASSERMAN, WILLIAM JACK, chemistry educator; b. N.Y.C., Apr. 27, 1925; s. Leon and Dora (Dyer) W.; m. Charlotte Freeman Kaufman, Apr. 15, 1950 (div. 1957); m. Harriet Jo Marsh, July 19, 1959; children: Wayland, Wyeth. BS in Chemistry, UCLA, 1947; MS in Organic Chemistry, U. So. Calif., 1950; PhD in Organic Chemistry, U. Wash., 1954. Asst. prof. Humboldt State U., Arcata, Calif., 1954-57; sr. research chemist Martin-Marietta Corp., Seattle, 1957-62, Truesdail Labs., Los Angeles, 1962-63; asst. prof. chemistry San Jose (Calif.) State U., 1963-67; instr. Seattle Cen. Community Coll., 1967—; cons. Counselors in Chemistry, Seattle, 1958—. Contbr. articles to profl. jours. Served with USN, 1944-46, PTO. Mem. Am. Chem. Soc. (chmn. Puget Sound sect. 1981, chmn. nat. meeting 1983), Sigma Xi, Phi Lambda Upsilon. Democrat. Avocations: collections, theater and concert events. Home: 1247 20th Ave E Seattle WA 98112 Office: Seattle Cen Community Coll 1701 Broadway Seattle WA 98122

WASSON, DAVID WESLEY, educational service agency director; b. Whitefish, Mont., Dec. 15, 1942; s. Lewis Henry and Betty F. (Bahm) Larter;

m. Sue Caroll Gentry, Aug. 25, 1964; children: Wesley, Tammy, Bonnie, Kimberly. AA, York (Nebr.) Coll., 1962; BSE, Abilene (Tex.) Christian U., 1965; MA, No. Ariz. U., 1971. Cert. tchr. Ariz., Tex. (life), Calif. (life). Tchr., dept. head Needles (Calif.) High Sch., 1965-73; curriculum specialist Mohave County Career Edn., Kingman, Ariz., 1973-76; exec. dir. Mohave Ednl. Services, Kingman, Ariz., 1976—; res. instr. San Bernadino Valley Coll., Needles, 1966-73, Mohave County Community Coll., Kingman, 1973—, No. Ariz. U., Kingman, 1976—; cons. office career edn. U.S. Office Edn., Washington, 1978-80; bd. dirs. Harper & Wasson Pubs., Inc., Kingman, 1984—. Author, dir. (TV spl.) Sky-12 Visits Ariz., 1984; producer: (videotape) How to Speak Indian Sign Language, 1984, Wovoka and the Ghost Dance, 1985; author: The Silent Language of the Plains, 1986. Bd. dirs. Mohave Mus. History and Arts, Kingman, 1979-82; mem. exec. bd. Kingman Centennial Commn., Kingman, 1979-83, vocat. edn. task force Ariz. Dept. Edn., 1980-86. TIPS fellow U. Colo., 1971, COE fellow Pepperdine U., 1972. Mem. Ariz. Assn. Career Edn. Republican. Club: Toastmasters. Avocations: philately, photography, freelance writing. Home: 2509 Valentine Ave Kingman AZ 86401 Office: Mohave Ednl Services 515 W Beale Kingman AZ 86401

WATANABE, CORINNE KAORU AMEMIYA, lawyer, state official; b. Wahiawa, Hawaii, Aug. 1, 1950; d. Keiji and Setsuko (Matsumiya) Amemiya; m. Edwin Tsugio Watanabe, Mar. 8, 1975; children: Traciann Keiko, Brad Natsuo, Lance Yoneo. BA, U. Hawaii, 1971; JD, Baylor U., 1974. Bar: Hawaii 1974. Dep. atty. gen. State of Hawaii, Honolulu, 1974-84, 1st dep. atty. gen., 1984-85, 87—, atty. gen., 1985-87. Mem. ABA, Hawaii Bar Assn. Democrat. Office: Atty Gen 415 S Beretania St 405 State Capitol Honolulu HI 96813 *

WATANABE, MARK DAVID, pharmacist; b. Santa Monica, Calif., Dec. 7, 1955; s. Jack Shigeru and Rose Nobuko (Iida) W. BA in Chemistry, U. Calif., Irvine, 1977, BS in Biol. Sci., 1978; PharmD, U. Calif., San Francisco, 1982, PhD in Pharm. Chemistry, 1987. Lic. pharmacist, Calif., Oreg., Hawaii. Pharmacy intern various locations, San Francisco, 1979-82; pharmacist Kaiser Permanente, San Francisco, 1981—; research asst. U. Calif., San Francisco, 1980—. Regents scholar U. Calif., San Francisco, 1979-82; recipient Excellence in Teaching award Long Found., San Francisco, 1984. Mem. Am. Pharm. Assn., Am. Chem. Soc., Am. Soc. Hosp. Pharmacists, Am. Assn. Colls. of Pharmacy, Calif. Pharmacists Soc. Unitarian Universalist. Avocations: individual and fitness sports, reading, travel, music. Home: 331 Carl St San Francisco CA 94117 Office: U Calif Dept Pharm Chemistry San Francisco CA 94143

WATERHOUSE, HOWARD NELSON, agricultural and food scientist; b. Bethel, Maine, Apr. 19, 1932; s. Cleveland Nelson and Alice Frances (Connor) W.; m. Doris Marie Carlberg, June 4, 1960; children: Nancy, Carol. BS, U. Maine, Orono, 1954; MS, U. Ill., 1958, PhD, 1960. Pet food group leader Gen. Mills, Inc., Indianola, Iowa, 1960-67; poultry group leader Allied Mills, Inc., Libertyville, Ill., 1967-70; dir. nutrition Robin Hood Multifoods, Inc., Montreal, Que., Can., 1970-74; sr. poultry nutritionist Cen. Soya, Inc., Decatur, Ind., 1974-78; dir. nutrition Bell Grain and Milling, Inc., Perris, Calif., 1978—, also bd. dirs. Served with U.S. Army, 1954-56. Mem. Poultry Sci. Assn., Calif. Animal Nutrition Council (chmn. 1982-83), Pacific Egg and Poultry Assn. (chmn. feed quality and nutrition subcom. 1985—). Club: Toastmaster (Iowa)(pres. 1955). Avocations: skiing, photography, woodworking, fishing. Home: 2837 Sandberg St Riverside CA 92506 Office: Bell Grain and Milling Inc PO Box 758 Perris CA 92370

WATERLOO, ROBERT FRANCIS, chemical company executive; b. Evanston, Ill., Apr. 16, 1942; s. Napoleon Nicholas and Emma Bridgett (Noslick) W.; m. Kathleen Marie Mechan, Oct. 26, 1963; children: Deborah Ann, Elizabeth Marie. Cert. in bus., Northwestern U., 1969; diploma in mgmt., Aurora Coll., 1979. Mgr. sales adminstrn. Internat. Minerals and Chem. Corp., Skokie, Ill., 1960-75; Sales mgr. Fed. Bentonite, Aurora, Ill., 1975-82; v.p. and gen. mgr. Eisenman Chem. Co., Greeley, Colo., 1982—. Office: Eisenman Chem Co 4687 18th St Greeley CO 80634

WATERMAN, MICHAEL SPENCER, mathematics educator, biology educator; b. Coquille, Oreg., June 28, 1942; s. Ray S. and Bessie E. (Payne) W.; m. Vicki Lynn Buss, Aug. 14, 1962 (div. Mar. 1977); 1 child, Tracey Lynn. B.S., Oreg. State U., 1964, M.S., 1966; M.A., Mich. State U., 1968, Ph.D., 1969. Assoc. prof. Idaho State U., Pocatello, 1969-75; mem. staff Los Alamos Nat. Lab., 1975-82, cons., 1982—; prof. math. and biology U. So. Calif., Los Angeles, 1982—; vis. prof. math. U. Hawaii, Honolulu, 1979-80; vis. prof. structural biology U. Calif.-San Francisco, 1982; cons. Simon Mktg., Los Angeles, 1984—, Schlumberger, Palo Alto, Calif., 1985—. Contbr. numerous research articles on math., stats., biology to profl. jours., 1970—. Grantee NSF, 1971, 72, 75, Los Alamos Nat. Lab., 1976, 81, System Devel. Found., 1982-87, NIH, 1986—. Mem. Inst. Math. Stats., AAAS, Am. Statis. Assn., Soc. Math. Biology, Soc. Indsl. and Applied Math. Office: U So Calif Dept Math Los Angeles CA 90089

WATERS, KENNETH R., retail computer stores executive. Pres., chief operating officer Computerland Corp., Oakland, Calif., 1986—. Office: Computerland Corp PO Box 5005 Hayward CA 94540-5005 *

WATERS, MAXINE, state legislator; b. St. Louis, Aug. 15, 1938; d. Remus and Velma (Moore) Carr; m. Sidney Williams, July 23, 1977; children by previous marriage—Edward, Karen. Grad. in sociology Calif. State U., Los Angeles. Former tchr. Head Start; mem. Calif. Assembly from dist. 48, 1976—, Democratic caucus chair, 1984. Mem. Dem. Nat. Com.; del. Dem. Nat. Conv., 1980; mem. Nat. Adv. Com. for Women, 1978—. Office: Calif State Assembly State Capitol Sacramento CA 95814 *

WATERS, RODNEY LEWIS, manufacturing executive; b. Long Beach, Calif., July 13, 1936; s. Harris Eades and Gladys Edna (Lippy) W.; B.A. in Physics, UCLA, 1963; M.B.A., Pepperdine U., 1979; m. Norma Hanson, Dec. 22, 1958 (div. 1978); children—Julie Anna Smith, Danae Lynn, John Davis; m. 2d, Diana Lee Johnson, Sept. 8, 1984. Research engr. N. Am. Rockwell, Downey, Calif., 1963-65; product mgr. Korad dept. Union Carbide Corp., 1965-73; mktg. mgr. Quantrad Corp., El Segundo, Calif., 1973-74; pres. Florod Corp., Hawthorne, Calif., 1974—; Pres. Gifted Childrens Assn., Hawthorne, 1971-72. Served with U.S. Army, 1958-60. Mem. Internat. Soc. Hybrid Microelectronics, Soc. Photog. Instrumentation Engrs. Republican. Contbr. articles to profl. jours. Office: 17360 Gramercy Pl Gardena CA 90247

WATERS, WILLIAM EUGENE, forestry scientist, entomology educator; b. Springfield, Mass., July 2, 1922; s. Francis Marland and Grace Elizabeth (Alden) W.; m. Harriet Fairbank Hume, June 11, 1943 (div. 1976); children: Ellen, William, Francis, Richard; m. Muriel Jane Dawson, Apr. 29, 1976. Student in Forestry, U. Maine, 1940-42; BS in Forestry, Syracuse U., 1948; M in Forest Entomology, Duke U., 1949; PhD in Ecology, Yale U., 1958. Research entomologist U.S. Forest Service, New Haven, 1949-66; chief of lab. U.S. Forest Service, Hamden, Conn., 1966-68; chief of forest insect research U.S. Forest Service, Washington, 1968-73; pioneering research scientist U.S. Forest Service, Berkeley, Calif., 1973-75; dean. coll. natural resources U. Calif., Berkeley, 1975-77, prof., 1977-86, prof. emeritus, 1986—; bd. dirs. Internat. Stat. Ecology Program, University Park, Pa., 1978—; cons. Boise Cascade Corp., Idaho, 1980-83, Sierra Club Legal Def. Fund, Denver, 1985—. Served to sgt. USAAF, 1942-46. Noyes-Clark fellow Yale U., 1955-57. Mem. Entomol. Soc. Am. (governing bd. 1974-76), Soc. Am. Foresters, Calif. Natural Resources Fedn. (pres. 1976-77), Sigma Xi. Republican. Avocations: hiking, fishing, tennis. Home: 3747 Painted Pony Rd El Sobrante CA 94803 Office: U Calif 201 Wellman Hall Berkeley CA 94720

WATKINS, DANE HANSEN, state senator, business executive; b. Idaho Falls, Idaho, Aug. 24, 1943; s. George W. and Hope C. (Hansen) W.; B.S., U. Utah, 1965; m. Sherry McNamara, Aug. 8, 1964; children—Tory, Tracey, Dane Hansen, Damond, Taryn, David, Tiffany. Ptnr. Watkins Enterprises, farming and investments, Idaho Falls, 1965—; mem. Idaho Senate, Idaho Falls, 1971—, chmn. local govt. and taxation com., 1980—, mem. agrl. affairs com., 1979-82, mem. fin. com., 1974-80, vice chmn. fin. com., 1982—. Pres. Idaho Employees Council, 1978-80; dir. Blue Cross Idaho, 1974-80; mem. Eastern Idaho Spl. Services Agy., 1981—, Bonneville County Home Health Agy., 1980-81; v.p. Teton Peaks Boy Scout Council, 1976-80; treas. Idaho Gasohol Commn., 1979—; mem. Nat. Gasohol Commn., 1978—; bd. dirs. Bonneville County United Way, 1968-74, YMCA, 1968-78, Eastern Idaho Regional Med. Ctr., 1983—; chmn. Bonneville County Republican Central Com., 1968-71; pres. Eastern Idaho Lincoln Day Assn., 1970-71. Bishop Ch. of Jesus Christ of Latter-day Saints. Office: PO Box 781 Idaho Falls ID 83402

WATKINS, JOHN JAMES, purchasing manager; b. Bellingham, Wash., Dec. 3, 1945; s. Robert Moore and Esther Mabel (Succetti) W.; m. Janet Elo, Sept. 12, 1971; 1 child, Elizabeth. BBA, Seattle U., 1973. Prodn. mgr. Modular Pacific Corp., Seattle, Wash., 1973-74; buyer purchasing div. State of Wash., Olympia, 1975; purchasing mgr. Green River Community Coll., Auburn, Wash., 1975—. Served to specialist 5th class USN, 1968-72. Mem. Wash. Community Colls. Purchasing Affairs Com. (v.p. 1980-82, pres. 1982-84, sec. 1984—). Avocations: snorkeling, hunting, water skiing. Office: Green River Community Coll 12401 SE 320th Auburn WA 98002

WATKINS, MICHAEL IRWIN, research chemist; b. Orange, Tex., Aug. 7, 1952; s. Francis Irwin and Patricia (Grilletti) W. BS in Chemistry, U. Calif., Berkeley, 1974; PhD in Chemistry, U. So. Calif., 1981. Postdoctoral fellow U. So. Calif., Los Angeles, 1981-82; research chemist Beckman Instruments, Brea, Calif., 1982—. Contbr. articles to profl. jours. Mem. AAAS, Am. Assn. Clin. Chemists, Am. Chem. Soc. Avocations: photography, hiking, camping, theatre, music. Office: Beckman Instruments 200 S Kraemer Blvd Brea CA 92621

WATKINS, ROBERT FRED, communications and electronics co. exec.; b. Pueblo, Colo., May 20, 1927; s. Robert F. and Ida C. (McDermott) W.; B.S., Calif. Coast U., 1976, M.B.A., 1977, Ph.D. in Bus. Adminstrn., 1979; LL.B., LaSalle Law U. and Calif. Coast U., 1977; m. Janice Tising, Nov. 7, 1948; children—James Leland, Jody Lynn, Julia Louise. Sr. tech. instr. Philco Corp., 1953-55; liaison engr. Boeing Aircraft Co., 1955-56; sr. engr. Bendix Corp., Balt., 1956-61; regional mgr. bus. devel. data systems div. Litton Industries, Boston and Rome, N.Y., 1961-63, Dayton, Ohio, 1963-66, Colorado Springs, 1966-68, Red Bank, N.J., 1967—, Van Nuys, Calif., 1968-71; mgr. advance systems and mktg. F&M Systems Co., Dallas, 1971-75; bus. devel. dir. Electrospace Systems, Inc., Richardson, Tex., 1975-83, strategic bus. planner, 1983—; cons. bus. planning and devel., 1979—; co-founder Integrated Mgmt. Tech., Inc., Colorado Springs, Colo., 1978; bd. dirs., chief fin. officer HOH Water Technology, Inc., 1986—, chief exec. officer and pres. 1987—. Served with USN, 1944-46, 48-49, USAF, 1951-53; PTO, Korea. Mem. Soc. Applied Learning (charter), Armed Forces Communications Electronics Assn., LaSalle U. Alumni Assn. Republican. Mem. Calvary Community Ch., Thousand Oaks, Calif. Author: Move Ahead in Selling, 1974; The Marketing Audit: A Positive and Dynamic Method for Directing the Company's Total Marketing Program, 1977; The Marketing Audit: A Major Step Toward Successful Marketing Control, 1979. Home: 57 La Palma Newbury Park CA 91320

WATKINS, SUSAN DIANE, office automation specialist; b. Olympia, Wash., Nov. 11, 1946; d. George S. and Sheilia I. (Gant) W. Student, U. Oreg., 1966-71, Lane Community Coll., 1974-75, Cuaunahuac Lang. Inst., Cuernavaca, Mexico, 1976, Portland Community Coll., 1979-80, Xiamen U., People's Republic of China, 1982. Sec. to dir. Learning Resource Ctr. Lane Community Coll., Eugene, Oreg., 1970-75, supr. word processing ctr., 1975-83; supr. word processing and copy ctr. Chemeketa Community Coll., Salem, Oreg., 1983-86, office automation specialist, 1986—; instr. word processing Lane Community Coll., 1977-78. Mem. Assn. Info. Systems Profls., Internat. Word Processing Assn. (pres. Willamette Valley chpt. 1982-83). Democrat. Methodist. Clubs: Nordic, Chemeketar Hiking and Climbing (Salem). Avocations: skiing, backpacking, langs., linguistics, traveling. Home: 2025 18th NE Salem OR 97303 Office: Chemeketa Community Coll 4000 Lancaster Dr NE Salem OR 97309

WATKINS, WILFRED EUGENE, physician, urologist; b. Hinsdale, Ill., May 2, 1934; s. John Pearl and Nancy Janette (Armstrong) W.; m. Barbara Jean Boinski, Oct. 31, 1959; children: Scott Alan, Gregory John, Lisa Janette, Amelia Elizabeth. BS, Ill. Wesleyan U., 1958; MD, U. Ill., 1962. Intern Presbyn.-St. Luke's Hosp., 1962-64; resident in urology Research and Ednl. Hosp., Chgo., 1964-67; gen. practice medicine Idaho Urology Clinic, Nampa, 1967—; v.p. Indsl. Corp., Nampa, 1984—. Contbr. articles to profl. jours. Rep. precinct coordinator, Nampa, 1984—. Served to lt. col. USAR, 1981—. Mem. Am. Urol. Assn., Am. Assn. Clin. Urology (pres. 1984-85), Idaho Med. Soc. (pres. 1982-83), S.W. Idaho Med. Soc. (pres. 1972-73). Club: Arid (Boise, Idaho). Lodge: Elks. Avocations: music, drama, hunting, fishing.

WATNE, DONALD ARTHUR, accountant, educator; b. Gt. Falls, Mont., Jan. 18, 1939; s. Arthur Leonard and Anne (Salo) W.; m. Patricia Elaine Schick, Aug. 12, 1961; children—Elizabeth Anne, Michael Arthur. B.A. with high honors, U. Mont., 1960, M.A., 1961; Ph.D., U. Calif.-Berkeley, 1977. C.P.A., Oreg. Acct., Piquet & Minihan, Eugene, Oreg., 1961-65; mgr. capital investment analysis Weyerhaeuser Co., Tacoma, 1965-68; mktg. rep. IBM Corp., Portland, Oreg., 1968-70; dir. EDP Ctr. in Concejo Mcpl., Barquisimeto, Venezuela, 1971-72; prof. acctg. Portland State U., 1976—; vis. prof. Xiamen (Fujian, People's Rep. China), 1985-86, U. Otago, Dunedin, New Zealand, 1985-86, U. Newcastle, Australia, 1985-86; cons. in field. Mem. Am. Inst. C.P.A.s, Am. Acctg. Assn., Oreg. Soc. C.P.A.s, Oreg. Soc. Individual Psychology (dir. 1977-83). Author: (with Peter B.B. Turney) Auditing EDP Systems, 1984; contbr. articles in field, chpts. in handbooks. Home: 2826 NE 26th Ave Portland OR 97212 Office: Sch Bus Adminstrn Portland State U PO Box 751 Portland OR 97207

WATRING, WATSON GLENN, gynecologic oncologist, educator; b. St. Albans, W.Va., June 2, 1936; s. Neva J. Louise Bullington; m. Roberta Watring. BS, Washington & Lee U., 1958; MD, W.Va. U., 1962. Diplomate Am. Bd. Ob-Gyn, Am. Bd. Gynecol. Oncology. Intern The Toledo Hosp., 1963; resident in ob-gyn Ind. U., Indpls., 1964-66, Tripler Gen. Hosp., Honolulu, 1968-70; resident in gen. and oncologic surgery City of Hope Nat. Med. Ctr., Duarte, Calif., 1970-71, assoc. dir. gynecol. oncology, sr. surgeon, 1973-77; fellow in gynecol. oncology City of Hope Nat. Med. Ctr. and UCLA Med. Ctr., 1972-74; asst. prof. ob-gyn UCLA Med. Ctr., 1972-77; assoc. prof., sr. gynecologist, sr. surgeon Tufts New Eng. Med. Ctr. Hosp., Boston, 1977-80, asst. prof. radiation therapy, 1978-80; practice medicine specializing in ob-gyn Boston, 1980-82; assoc. prof. ob-gyn U. Mass., Worcester, 1982; regional dir. gynecol. oncology So. Calif. Permanente Med. Group, Los Angeles, 1982—, asst. dir. residency tng., 1985—; dir. gynecol. oncology St. Margarets Hosp. for Women, Dorchester, Mass., 1977-80; clin. prof. ob-gyn U. Calif., Irvine, 1982—. Contbr. articles to profl. jours. Mem. ch. council Luth. Ch. of the Foothills, 1973-75. Served to lt. col. M.C., U.S. Army, 1965-71. Fellow Am. Coll. Ob-Gyn, Los Angeles Obstet. and Gynecol. Soc.; mem. AAAS, ACS (Calif. and Mass. chpts.), Boston Surg. Soc., AMA, Mass. Med. Soc., Mass. Suffolk Dist. Med. Soc., Internat. Soc. Gynecol. Pathologists, Western Soc. Gynecologists and Obstetricians, Am. Soc. Clin. Oncology, Soc. Gynecol. Oncologists, Western Assn. Gynecol. Oncologists (sec.-treas. 1976-81, program chmn. 1984, pres. 1985—), New Eng. Assn. Gynecol. Oncologists (chmn. charter com.), New Eng. Obstet. and Gynecol. Soc., Obstet. Soc. Boston, Am. Radium Soc., Soc. Study Breast Disease, New Eng. Cancer Soc., Internat. Gynecol. Cancer Soc., Daniel Morton Soc., Sigma Xi. Republican. Avocations: golf, skiing, horticulture. Office: So Calif Permanente Med Group 4950 Sunset Blvd Los Angeles CA 90027

WATSON, DAVID COLQUITT, elec. engr.; b. Linden, Tex., Feb. 9, 1936; s. Colvin Colquitt and Nelena Gertrude (Keasler) W.; m. Flora Janet Thayn, Nov. 10, 1959; children: Flora Janeen, Melanie Beth, Lorrie Gaylene, Cherlayn Gail, Nathan David, Amy Melissa, Brian Colvin. BSEE, U. Utah, 1964, PhD in Elec. Engring. (NASA fellow), 1968. Electronic technician Hercules Powder Co., Magna, Utah, 1961-62; research fellow U. Utah, 1964-65, research asst. microwave devices and phys. electronics lab., 1964-68; sr. mem. tech. staff ESL, Inc., Sunnyvale, Calif., 1968-78, head dept. Communications, 1969-70; sr. engring. specialist Probe Systems, Inc., Sunnyvale, 1978-79; sr. mem. tech. staff ARGO Systems, Inc., Sunnyvale, 1979—; mem. faculty U. Santa Clara, 1978—, San Jose State U., 1981—. Contbr. articles to IEEE Transactions, 1965-78; co-inventor cyclotron-wave rectifier; inventor gradient descrambler. Served with USAF, 1956-60. Mem. IEEE, Phi Kappa Phi, Tau Beta Pi, Eta Kappa Nu. Mormon. Office: Argo Systems Inc 884 Hermosa Ct Sunnyvale CA 94086

WATSON, DENISE ANN, state correctional department official, consultant; b. Baxter Springs, Kans., Aug. 6, 1952; d. James Oliver and Mamie Jewell (Reynolds) Watson; 1 son, Tige O'Dare. Student (scholar) San Francisco Sch. Ballet, 1969-70, (scholar) Harlem Ballet Theatre, N.Y.C., 1972; B.A. in Psychology, U. N.Mex., 1974; MA in Pub. Adminstrn., 1987. Profl. dancer Ashton-Kochmann Prodn., N.Y.C., 1972-73; research asst. Checkerboard Area Health System, Cuba, N. Mex., 1974-75; counselor Opportunities Industrialization Center, Albuquerque, 1975-76; diagnostic eval. specialist Penitentiary of N. Mex., Santa Fe, 1975-76; probation, parole officer N. Mex. Dept. Corrections, Albuquerque, 1976-78, trouble employee adviser, Santa Fe, 1978-80, tng. specialist, 1978-81, dir. staff devel. acad. edn. and tng. div., 1981—; cons. human resources devel. and tng. acad. devel. and orngl. devel. Coordinator Gov.'s Ann. Women's Career Conf., 1980; active Black Leadership Council, 1982; active Gt. SW council Boy Scouts Am. Served to capt. USAR, 1972—. Mem. N.Mex. Criminal Justice Profls. Assn., Western Correctional Assn., Am. Correctional Assn., Criminal Justice Trainers Assn., Am. Jail Assn., Nat. Council Crime and Delinquency, Res. Officers Assn., NAACP, Phi Kappa Phi, Alpha Kappa Alpha. Democrat. Baptist. Home: 7912 Southern SE Albuquerque NM 87108 Office: 113 Washington Ave Santa Fe NM 87501

WATSON, GEORGE A., pathologist; b. San Jose, Calif., March 4, 1905; s. John Gilchrist and Jessie Anna (Rood) W.; A.B., U. Calif.-Berkeley, 1932, M.D., 1940; m. Evelyn Boelter, June 1, 1931. Intern San Francisco City and County Hosp., 1939-40; resident pathologist Highland Alameda County Hosp., Oakland, Calif., 1940-42, Fairmount Hosp., 1940-42; sr. resident Henry Ford Hosp., Detroit, 1942-43; assoc. pathologist Santa Clara County Hosp., 1944-45; pathologist Vallejo (Calif.) Community Hosp., 1945-47, Hahnemann Hosp., San Francisco, 1945-66; sr. pathologist French Hosp., San Francisco, 1945-77; cons. pathologist Garden Hosp., San Francisco, 1959, Drs. Hosp., San Francisco, 1961, Polyclinic Hosp., 1965, Weimar (Calif.) Joint Sanitorium, 1948-62, Golden Gate Hosp., 1950, Laguna Honda Hosp., 1965. Diplomate Am. Bd. Pathology, 1946. Founding fellow Coll. Am. Pathologists; fellow Am. Geriatrics Soc., Am. Soc. Clin. Pathologists; mem. Soc. Nuclear Medicine, AMA, Calif. Soc. of Pathologists, San Francisco Path. Soc., San Francisco Med. Soc., Calif. Med. Assn., Royal Soc. Medicine. Home: Belvedere Av Belvedere CA 94920

WATSON, GERALD GLENN, lawyer, educator; b. Salem, Oreg., Aug. 17, 1945; s. Gerald D. and Lucille (Pavey) W.; m. Diane Lynn Peterson, June 24, 1967; children: Christina, Gregory, Matthew. BA, Willamette U., 1967; MA, U. Fla., 1969, PhD, 1971; JD, U. Colo., 1983. Bar: Colo. 1983, Oreg. 1984, U.S. Dist. Ct. Colo. 1984, U.S. Dist. Ct. Oreg. 1985. Asst. then assoc. prof. polit. sci. U. No. Colo., Greeley, 1973-85; assoc. prof. U. Portland, Oreg., 1986—; assoc. atty. Wyatt & Martell, Ft. Collins, Colo., 1983-84, Hershner & Hunter, Eugene, Oreg., 1985-86. Contbr. articles to profl. jours. Bd. dirs. Hospice of Weld Co., Inc., Greeley, 1984; mem. budget com. Chemeketa Community Coll., 1986—. Mem. ABA (YLD environ. law com. 1985-86), Oreg. Bar Assn., Marion County Bar Assn., Pacific NW Polit. Sci. Assn. Democrat. Mem. Christian Ch. Club: City (Salem). Avocations: gardening, reading, photography, jogging, tennis. Home: 1237 Manzanita Way NE Keizer OR 97303 Office: U Portland Dept Psychology and Social Scis 5000 N Willamette Blvd Portland OR 97203

WATSON, GREGORY ERNEST, clinical social worker; b. Oakland, Calif., July 31, 1955; s. Billy Joe and Ann Augusta (Picaso) W. AA, Moorpark (Calif.) Coll., 1976; BA, Calif. State U., Sacramento, 1978, MSW, 1982. Lic. clin. social worker, Calif. Intern El Dorado County Mental Health Ctr., Placerville, Calif., 1979-80, Cath. Social Services, Sacramento, 1980-81; state hosp. coordinator Orange County Mental Health, Children and Youth Services, Camarillo, Calif., 1982-84; clinician Plumas County Mental Health Ctr., Quincy, Calif., 1984—; mem. Plumas County Child Abuse Council, Quincy, 1984—; instr. Feather River Coll., Quincy, 1986; children and youth services coordinator Plumas County Mental Health Ctr., Quincy, 1984—. Bd. dirs. Plumas Rural Services, Inc., Quincy, 1985—; coach Plumas Cen. Little League, Quincy, 1985-86. Named one of Outstanding Young Men of Am., U.S. Jaycees, 1980. Mem. Nat. Assn. Social Workers (five-year mem. award, 1986), Calif. State U. Sacramento Alumni Assn., No. Calif. Children's Coordinators. Democrat. Lodge: Rotary. Avocations: fishing, cross-country skiing, traveling. Home: PO Box 3176 Quincy CA 95971 Office: Plumas County Mental Health Ctr PO Box 480 Quincy CA 95971

WATSON, GUY EDWARDS, mechanical engineer, consultant; b. Los Angeles, Nov. 1, 1923; s. Russell Allen and Sacca Mauree (Hardesty) W.; m. Margie Anne Ruffin, July 10, 1948; one child, Kimberly Anne. BS, U. Calif., Berkeley, 1950; MSME, Santa Clara (Calif.) U., 1967; degree engr. in mech. engring., Stanford U., 1972. Registered profl. engr., Calif., Kans. Rep., sr. service research and devel. staff Fed.-Mogul Corp., Detroit, 1950-54; design and research engr. Coleman Co. Inc., Wichita, Kans., 1954-60; pres. Midwest Plastics Corp., Wichita, 1960-63; technical cons. Lockheed Missiles & Space Co., Sunnyvale, Calif., 1963—; cons. Fahlin Propellers, Cupertino, Calif., 1980—. Patentee in field. Served to capt. USAAF, 1942-46, PTO. Mem. AIAA (sr.), Soc. Automotive Engrs., Quiet Birdmen. Home: 10682 Pebble Pl Cupertino CA 95014 Office: Lockheed Missiles & Space Co Systems Engring O/81-70 B/157 1111 Lockheed Way Sunnyvale CA 94088

WATSON, HAROLD GEORGE, ordnance company executive, mechanical engineer; b. Phoenix, Oct. 19, 1931; s. Clarence Elmer and Eunice A. (Record) W.; m. Ruth May Thomas, Aug. 30, 1951; children—Patricia Ruth, Linda Darlene, Harold George. B.S., U. Ariz., 1954. Engr., Shell Oil Co., Los Angeles, 1954; project engr. Talco Engring. Co., Hamden Conn., 1956, area mgr., Mesa, Ariz., 1956-57, chief engr. rocket power, 1958-61, dir. engring., 1961-64; dir. engring. Space Ordnance Systems, El Segundo, Calif., 1964-68; dir. engring. Universal Propulsion Co., Riverside, Calif., 1968-70, gen. mgr., v.p. engring., Tempe, Ariz., 1970-76, v.p., mgr., 1976-77, pres., gen. mgr., Phoenix, 1977—. Served to 1st lt. USAR, 1954-56. Mem. Am. Ordnance Assn., SAFE Assn. (pres.), AIAA, Air Force Assn., Internat. Pyronetics Soc., Am. Def. Preparedness Assn. Patentee aircraft escape systems. Office: Universal Propulsion Co Inc Box 1140 Black Canyon Stage Number 1 Phoenix AZ 85029

WATSON, HELEN RICHTER, educator, ceramic artist; b. Laredo, Tex., May 10, 1926; d. Horace Edward and Helen Mary (Richter) Watson. B.A., Scripps Coll., 1947; M.F.A., Claremont Grad. Sch. and U. Ctr., 1949; postgrad. Alfred U., 1966; Swedish Govt. fellow Konstfackskolan, Stockholm, 1952-53. Mem. faculty Chaffey Coll., Ontario, Calif., 1950-52; chmn. ceramics Mt. San Antonio Coll., Walnut, Calif., 1955-57; prof., chmn. ceramics dept. Otis Art Inst., Los Angeles, 1958-81; mem. faculty Otis-Parsons Sch. Design, 1983—; studio ceramic artist, Claremont, Calif. and Laredo, Tex., 1949—; design cons. Interpace, Glendale, Calif., 1963-64; artist-in-residence Claremont Men's Coll., 1977. Claremont Grad. Sch. fellow, 1948-49; Swedish Govt. grantee, 1952-53; recipient First Ann. Scripps Coll. Disting. Alumna award, Claremont, 1978. Mem. Artists Equity, Nat. Ceramic Soc., Am. Craftsmen's Council, Los Angeles County Mus. Art, Mus. Contemporary Art Los Angeles. Republican. Episcopalian. Address: 220 Brooks Ave Claremont CA 91711 Address: 1906 Houston St Laredo TX 78040

WATSON, JOANN LEATHERBY, lawyer; b. Los Angeles, May 13, 1955; d. Ralph William and Eleanor Augustine (Samson) Leatherby; m. Emroy Leonard Watson, Oct. 1, 1983. BA, Iowa Wesleyan Coll., 1977; JD, UCLA, 1980. Bar: Calif. 1980. Exec. dir. Women's Legal Clinic, Los Angeles, 1978-81, also bd. dirs.; v.p. administrn. UniCare Ins., Irvine, Calif., 1981-82; sole practice Newport Beach, Calif., 1982-84; gen. counsel Ricoh Electronics Inc., Santa Ana, Calif., 1984—; bd. dirs. UniCare Fin. Corp., Irvine. Mem. Irvine Valley Coll. Chamber Singers. Mem. State Bar Assn. Calif., Orange County Women Lawyers. Democrat. Home: 23 Rocky Knoll Irvine CA 92715 Office: Ricoh Electronics Inc 2320 Red Hill Ave Santa Ana CA 92705

WATSON, JOHN MILTON, nuclear engineer; b. Wilson, N.C., Aug. 8, 1945; s. Lewis Milton and Ruth Louise (Hawkes) W.; m. Gene Lee Airoldi,

June 7, 1972 (div. Jan. 1986); 1 child, Cynthia Ann. BS in Nuclear Engring., N.C. State U., 1975. Cert. engr.-in-tng. Nuclear engr. Mare Island Naval Shipyard, Vallejo, Calif., 1975—. Served with USN, 1967-72. Mem. Internat. Fedn. Profl. and Tech. Engrs. (pres. local chpt. 25 1982-85), NSPE, Am. Nuclear Soc., Am. Soc. Quality Control, Sierra Club. Democrat. Club: First Osborne Group (Daly City, Calif.). Avocations: computing, hiking, camping, gardening, carpentry. Home: 1727 Sacramento St Vallejo CA 94590 Office: Mare Island Naval Shipyard Code 2350 Stop T11 Vallejo CA 94592

WATSON, KENNETH MARSHALL, physicist, educator; b. Des Moines, Sept. 7, 1921; s. Louis Erwin and Irene Nellie (Marshall) W.; m. Elaine Carol Miller, Mar. 30, 1946; children: Ronald M., Mark Louis. B.S., Iowa State U., 1943; Ph.D., U. Iowa, 1948; Sc.D. (hon.), U. Ind., 1976. Research engr. Naval Research Lab., Washington, 1943-46; mem. staff Inst. Advanced Study Princeton (N.J.) U., 1948-49; research fellow Lawrence Berkeley (Calif.) Lab., 1949-52, mem. staff, 1957—; asst. prof. physics U. Ind., Bloomington, 1952-54; asso. prof. physics U. Wis., Madison, 1954-57; prof. physics U. Calif., Berkeley, 1957-81; prof. oceanography, dir. Marine Physics Lab., U. Calif., San Diego, 1981—; trustee LaJolla Inst.; cons. Mitre Corp., Sci. Application Corp.; mem. U.S. Pres's. Sci. Adv. Com. Panels, 1962-71; adviser Nat. Security Council, 1972-75; bd. dirs. Center for Studies of Dynamics, 1979—; mem. JASON Adv. Panel. Author: (with M.L. Goldberger) Collision Theory, 1964, (with J. Welch and J. Bond) Atomic Theory of Gas Dynamics, 1966, (with J. Nutall) Topics in Several Particle Dynamics, 1970, (with Flatté, Munk, Dashen) Sound Transmission Through a Fluctuating Ocean, 1979. Mem. Nat. Acad. Scis. Home: 2191 Caminito Circulo Norte La Jolla CA 92037 Office: Marine Phys Lab U Calif La Jolla CA 92093

WATSON, OLIVER LEE, III, aerospace engineering manager; b. Lubbock, Tex., Sept. 18, 1938; s. Oliver Lee Jr. and Sallie Gertrude (Hale) W.; m. Judith Valeria Horvath, June 13, 1964; 1 child, Clarke Stanford. BSEE, U. Tex., 1961; MSEE, Stanford U., 1963; MBA, Calif. State U., Fullerton, 1972; cert., U. So. Calif., 1980. Mgr. ballistic analysis Rockwell Internat. Autonetics Div., Anaheim, Calif., 1973-78, mgr. minuteman systems, 1978-83, mgr. preliminary engring., 1983-84, mgr. analysis group, 1984-85; mgr. aircraft systems Rockwell Internat. Autonetics Dept., Anaheim, Calif., 1985—; lectr. engring. Calif. State U., Fullerton, 1981—; ptnr. Hochman-Watson Pub., Orange, Calif., 1982—. Co-author Digital Computing Using Fortran IV, 1982; Fortran 77, A Complete Primer, 1986. Bd. dirs. Olive Little League, Orange, 1980, vol. Stanford U. Gen. Appeal Program, Orange County, Calif., 1983, regional chmn., 1984-86, So. Calif. chmn. 1986—. Named Div. Mgr. of Yr., Rockwell Strategic Systems, Anaheim, 1983; Inst. Advancement Engring. fellow, Los Angeles, 1976; North Am. Aviation Sci.-Engring. fellow, Los Angeles, 1962, 63. Mem. IEEE (sr.; sect. v.p. 1974-75, sect. chmn. 1975-76), Am. Assn. Artificial Intelligence, Inst. Navigation (corp.), Jaycees (v.p. Orange chpt. 1973-74), Beta Gamma Sigma. Republican. Club: Lido Sailing. Avocations: sailing, swimming, fiction writing, reading. Home: 3101 N Pinewood St Orange CA 92665 Office: Rockwell Internat 3370 E Miraloma Ave OB23 Anaheim CA 92803

WATSON, PEGGIE ALLEN, interior designer; b. Phoenix, Mar. 16, 1961; d. Jay H. and Nancy A. (Banker) Allen; m. Wayne E. Watson, Dec. 17, 1983. BA, Brigham Young U., 1983. Design technician Sverdrup & Parcel, Anchorage, 1984-85; prin. interior cons. PW Design, Tacoma, 1985—; comml. interior designer McGranahan, Messenger and Assocs., Tacoma, 1985—; lectr. in field, 1984-85. Counselor Ch. Womens Orgn., Tacoma, 1985—; tchr. Ch. Childrens Orgn., Los Angeles, 1979, Tacoma, 1985—. Recipient Best Design award Brigham Young U. Library Com., 1985. Mem. Am. Soc. Interior Design. Mormon.

WATSON, RONALD ROSS, immunology educator; b. Tyler, Tex., Dec. 9, 1942; s. Roscoe Derrick and Ellen (Kemp) W.; m. Anita Ann Hebert, May 27, 1966; children: Jon B.D., Britton K., Bethany L., Cali A. Student, U. Idaho, 1960-62, 64-65; BS, Brigham Young U., 1966; PhD, Mich. State U., 1971; postdoctoral, Harvard U., 1972-73. Research fellow Harvard U., Boston, 1971-73; asst. prof. immunology, microbiology U. Miss. Med. Ctr., Jackson, 1973-74; asst. prof. immunology Ind. U., Indpls., 1974-78; assoc. prof. Purdue U., West Lafayette, Ind., 1978-82; research assoc. prof. U. Ariz., Tucson, 1982-86, research prof., 1986-87; cons. Nutrition Inst., Cairo, 1980-87; co-investigator Internat. Ctr. Med. Research, Colombia, 1974-81. Editor: Nutrition, Disease Resistance and Immune Functions, 1984, Handbook of Nutrition in the Aged, 1985, Nutrition and Heart Disease in the Aging, 1987. Mem. Am. Inst. Nutrition (chmn. pub. affairs com. 1980-82), Am. Assn. Immunologists, Am. Soc. Clin. Nutrition, Can. Soc. Immunology, Mariposa Found. (bd. dirs. 1976—), Nutrition Found. (Future Leaders award 1976-78). Republican. Mormon. Office: U Ariz Dept Family and Community Medicine Tucson AZ 85724

WATSON, SHARON GITIN, psychologist, administrator; b. N.Y.C., Oct. 21, 1943; d. Louis Leonard and Miriam (Myers) Gitin; m. Eric Watson, Oct. 31, 1969; 1 child, Carrie Dunbar. B.A. cum laude, Cornell U., 1965; M.A., U. Ill., 1968, Ph.D., 1971. Psychologist City N.Y. Prison Mental Health, Riker's Island, 1973-74; psychologist Youth Services Ctr., Los Angeles County Dept. Pub. Social Services, Los Angeles, 1975-77, dir. clin. services, 1978, dir. Youth Services Ctr., 1978-80; exec. dir. Crittenton Ctr. for Young Women and Infants, Los Angeles, 1980—. Contbr. articles to profl. jours. Pres. Calif. Assn. Services for Children, chmn. program com. 1985-86, chmn. mgmt. info. services com., 1984-85, sec., treas., chmn. budget and fin. com., chmn. membership com., 1983-84; mem. community adv. com. Div. of Adolescent Medicine, Children's Hosp. of Los Angeles; mem. steering com. Los Angeles Children's Roundtable, Child Welfare League of Am. Western Region, Los Angeles Children's Planning Council (also co-chair); mem. Parents Council, Westridge Sch. for Girls; bd. dirs. Adolescent Pregnancy Child Watch. Mem. Am. Psychol. Assn. (pres.), Calif. Assn. Services for Children, Nat. Conf. Social Welfare, Am. Mgmt. Assn., Cornell Alumni Assn. of So. Calif., Assn. Children's Services Agys. of So. Calif. (pres. 1984-85, sec. 1981-83). Club: Pasadena (Calif.) Figure Skating (pres.). Home: 4056 Camino Real Los Angeles CA 90065 Office: Crittenton Ctr for Young Women and Infants 234 E Avenue 33 Los Angeles CA 90031

WATSON, TRACY JILL, speech-language pathologist; b. Milw., Mar. 18, 1958; d. Robert Louis and Shirley Ann (Adamson) Buhler; m. Jesse Watson, Aug. 4, 1979; children: Jared Jesse, Kelly Shea. BS, Cen. State U., Edmond, Okla., 1983; MS, U. N.Mex., 1984. Speech therapist Hinton (Okla.) Pub. Schs., 1983-84, Albuquerque Pub. Schs., 1984—. Mem. Am. Speech-Lang.-Hearing Assn. (cert.). Republican. Home: 1513 Gabablon NW Albuquerque NM 87104 Office: Atrisco Elem 1201 Atrisco SW Albuquerque NM 87105

WATSON, VIOLET PHELPS, librarian; b. Keokuk, Iowa, Nov. 4, 1903; d. Clinton Wayne and Emma (Jones) Phelps; m. Martin Vincent Fowler, July 23, 1926 (div. 1949); 1 child, Patricia Anne Fowler-Borzilleri; m. 2d Frederick Jenkins Watson, Dec. 14, 1950 (dec.). A.B., Simpson Coll., 1926; postgrad. U. So. Calif. Asst. city librarian City of Palm Springs, Calif., 1954-72; head librarian Palm Springs Desert Mus., 1972—. Republican. Presbyterian. Mem. DAR (regent). Club: Palm Springs Women's (pres. 1950-51, 1970-71). Home: 600 Grenfall Rd Palm Springs CA 92262 Office: Palm Springs Desert Mus Library PO Box 2288 101 Museum Dr Palm Springs CA 92262

WATSON, VIRGINIA DREW, anthropologist, researcher; b. Tomah, Wis., June 17, 1918; d. Francis Henry and Eunice (Williams) Drew; m. James Bennett Watson, Mar. 18, 1943; children: Anne Thaxter, James Bennett. PhB, U. Wis., 1940; AM, U. Chgo., 1943, PhD, 1965. Clk. Am. Consulate, Sao Paulo, Brazil, 1944-45; lectr. Washington U., St. Louis, 1948-53, Seattle U., Wash., 1957-63; affiliate curator Burke Mus. U. Wash., Seattle, 1969—. Author: Wulfing Plates, 1950, Prehistory of the Eastern Highlands of New Guinea, 1977; co-author 3 vols. Batainabura, 1972; contbr. numerous articles to profl. jours. Fellow Am. Anthropol. Assn., Royal Anthropol. Soc. of Great Britain; mem. AAAS, Soc. Am. Archaeology, Indo-Pacific Prehistory Assn. Office: U Wash Burke Mus Seattle WA 98195

WATSON-FRANKE, MARIA-BARBARA, womens studies anthropologist; b. Adorf, Germany, Sept. 14, 1938; came to U.S., 1967; d. Herwig Ortwin and Gudrun Maria (Haberkorn) Franke. MA, Goethe U., Frankfurt, Fed. Republic Germany, 1967; PhD, U. Vienna, 1970. Research assoc., Latin Am. Ctr. UCLA, 1971-78; prof. women's studies San Diego State U., 1974—, chair dept. women's studies, 1983-86; field worker with Guajiro Indians, Venezuela, 1967-68, 72, 75, 77, 78, 87; with women's carnival socs., Fed. Republic Germany, 1983. Co-author: Interpreting Life Histories, 1985; contbr. chpt. to book, articles to profl. jours. Research grantee Latin Am. Ctr., 1972, German Research Council, 1972-74, German Acad. Exchange Service, 1967-68. Fellow Am. Anthropol. Assn.; mem. Current Anthropology (assoc.), Nat. Women's Studies Assn., Soc. Applied Anthropology. Office: San Diego State U Dept Women's Studies San Diego CA 92182

WATT, DIANA LYNN, social worker; b. Leon, Iowa, Mar. 21, 1956; d. Charles Edward and Nora Eunice (Dickerson) W. BSW, Graceland Coll., 1980; postgrad., U. Kans., 1981-83. Social work intern St. Michael's (Ariz.) Sch., 1979, Mattie Rhodes Ctr., Kansas City, Mo., 1982-83; child care worker Gillis Home for Boys, Kansas City, 1980-84; community work experience program worker Social and Rehab. Services State of Kans., Kansas City, 1983-84; contractual assignee Reorganized Ch. of Jesus Christ of Latter-day Saints, San Jose, Calif., 1984-87. Counselor in tng. for camps and bible schs. Reorganized Ch. Jesus Christ Latter-day Saints, Iowa, 1969-73, counselor children's camp, San Jose, 1985, mem. ethnic community program com., East San Jose, 1984-87. Honored for Community Outreach in Ethnic Ministries, Reorganized Ch. Jesus Christ Latter-day Saints, 1986. Mem. Nat. Assn. Soc. Workers (cert.). Club: Intercultural (Lamoni, Iowa) (activity chmn. 1977-79). Avocations: horseback riding, sewing, crafts, reading, painting.

WATT, RICHARD STEVENSON, bank executive; b. Cleve., Jan. 15, 1935; m. Jean Mace; children: Kimberly, Richard. BS, U. Md., 1958, MA, 1959; postgrad., U. Calif., Berkeley, 1962, Harvard, 1971. Instr. Fla. So. U., Orlando, 1959-61; acct. mgr. sales IBM Corp., Washington, 1963-68; assoc. dir. dept. mgmt. FDIC, Washington, 1968-69; asst. dir. bd. govs. Fed. Res., Washington, 1969-74; pres., chmn., chief exec. officer United Banks Service Co., Englewood, Colo., 1974—; grad. instr. George Washington U., Washington, 1964-68; mem. planning com. ABA/NOAC, Dallas, 1985; cons. AT&T-IS Nat. Sales Sch. Chmn. community adv. bd. Shared Resource Computer Lab. George Washington High Sch., Denver, 1985—; mem. Metro Citizens' Light Rail Com., Denver, 1983. Served to capt. USAF, 1959-63. Mem. Denver C. of C. (metro bus. panel on light rail 1983, transp. steering council 1985—, chmn. light rail com. 1979-85). Avocation: tennis. Office: United Banks Service Co 5700 DTC Pkwy Englewood CO 80111

WATT, TOM, professional hockey team coach; b. Toronto, ON, Canada, June 17, 1935. Head coach Winnipeg Jets, NHL, Man., Can., 1981-83; head coach Vancouver Canucks, Brit. Col., 1985-87, asst. to gen. mgr., from 1985; coach Univ. of Toronto, 1965-79, 1984-85. Office: care Vancouver Canucks, 100 North Renfrew St, Vancouver, BC Canada V5K 3N7 *

WATTENBERG, MARTIN PAUL, educator; b. Washington, June 6, 1956; s. Leonard and Frances Anna (Marans) W. Teaching asst. U. Mich., Ann Arbor, 1978-82; vis. asst. prof. polit. sci. UCLA, 1982-83; asst. prof. U. Calif., Irvine, 1983-86, assoc. prof., assoc. dir. pub. policy research orgn., 1986—; cons. Ednl. Testing Service, Princeton, N.J., 1985. Author: The Decline of American Political Parties 1952-1984; editor: (assoc.) The Social Science Journal, 1984-87; contbr. articles to profl. jours. Mem. Am. Polit. Sci. Assn., Am. Assn. for Pub. Opinion Research, Inst. for Contemporary Studies (acad. assoc. 1984—). Democrat. Jewish. Avocation: tennis. Home: 240 Nice Ln 105 Newport Beach CA 92663 Office: U Calif Dept Social Scis Irvine CA 92717

WATTS, GEORGE BRYANT, air force officer; b. Boston, Sept. 3, 1946; s. Arthur Leighton Watts, Jr. and Eleanor (Darling) Crane; m. Mary Cunningham, Oct. 26, 1974; 1 child, George Bryant, Jr. B.A. in History, Denison U., 1968; M.S. in Systems Mgmt., U. So. Calif., 1980. Cert. command pilot, U.S. Air Force. Commd. 2d lt. U.S. Air Force, 1969, advanced through grades to lt. col., 1984. B-52 combat pilot, airborne command, S.E. Asia, 1971-73 (151 combat missions, 58 into North Vietnam); B-52 pilot instr., evaluator, 7th bomb wing Carswell AFB, Tex., 1970-74; FB-111A pilot instr., evaluator, 509th bomb wing Pease AFB, N.H., 1974-80; comdg. air officer U.S. Air Force Acad., Colorado Springs, Colo., 1981-83; space def. dir., chief spl. ops. NORAD Space Command, Colorado Springs, 1983—. Decorated D.F.C. with oak leaf cluster, Air medal with 8 oak leaf clusters. Named Outstanding FB-111A Crew in SAC, 1979. Recipient Fairchild Trophy, SAC, 1979, Honor Squadron Air Officer Comdg. award U.S. Air Force Acad., 1982. Mem. U.S. Jaycees (Outstanding Young Man Am. 1980), Air Force Assn., Air Force Acad. Athletic Assn., Sigma Alpha Epsilon. Republican. Episcopal. Home: 16810 Bar X Rd Colorado Springs CO 80908 Office: Space Defense Ops Ctr NORAD Space Command Peterson Colorado Springs AFB CO 80914

WATTS, LOU ELLEN, educator; b. Conway, S.C., Sept. 23, 1940; d. Bernie Louis and Dallie Ellen (Lemons) Overhultz; m. Ervin William Watts, Feb. 3, 1963; children: William Ashley. B in Music Edn., La. State U., 1962; postgrad. U. Ga., 1965, U. Ariz., 1972. Cert. elem. tchr., music tchr., Ind., Ga., La., Ariz. Music tchr. Westchester Twp. Sch., Chesterton, Ind., 1963-64; music cons. Clayton County Sch., Jonesboro, Ga., 1964-66; elem. and chorus tchr. Tucson Unified Sch. Dist., 1979—, intermediate head div. tchr., music cons., 1983-84, chorus dir., 1979-84; teacher, cons. archaeology, 1983—. Author (tchr./student manuals): Archaeology is More Than a Dig; contbr. articles to profl. jours. Pres., fine arts chmn., cons. Sahuaro Jr. Women's Club, Tucson, 1970-74; state consumer chmn., music award chmn. Ariz. Fedn. of Women's Club, 1970-72; mem. Tucson Panhellenic Council, 1971-72; project chmn. Southwest Children's Exploratory Ctr., Tucson. Tucson Enrichment Fund grantee, 1983—. Recipient Clubwoman of the Year Ariz. Fedn. Jr. Women's Club, 1972. Mem. NEA, Nat. Audubon Soc., Nat. Sci. Tchr. Assn., Music Educators Nat. Conf., Ariz. Edn. Assn., Ariz. Sci. Tchr.'s Assn. (Search for Excellence in Sci. award 1985), Tucson Edn. Assn., DAR, So. Ariz. Arabian Horse Assn., Delta Kappa Gamma, Sigma Alpha Iota. Home and Office: 8740 E Summer Terr Tucson AZ 85749

WATTS, OLIVER EDWARD, consulting engineer; b. Hayden, Colo., Sept. 22, 1939; s. Oliver Easton and Vera Irene (Hockett) W.; m. Charla Ann French, Aug. 12, 1962; children—Erik Sean, Oliver Eron, Sherilyn. B.S., Colo. State U., 1962. Registered profl. engr., Colo., Calif. Crew chief Colo. State U. Research Found., Ft. Collins, 1962; with Calif. Dept. Water Resources, Gustine and Castaic, 1964-70; land and water engr. CF&I Steel Corp., Pueblo, Colo., 1970-71; engring. dir. United Western Engrs., Colorado Springs., Colo., 1971-76; ptnr. United Planning and Engring Co., Colorado Springs., Colo., 1976-79; owner Oliver E. Watts, cons. engr., Colorado Springs., Colo., 1979—. Dir. edn. local Ch. of Christ, 1969-71, deacon, 1977-87, elder, 1987— . Served to 1st lt. C.E., AUS, 1962-64. Recipient Individual Achievement award Colo. State U. Coll. Engring., 1981. Fellow ASCE (v.p. Colorado Springs br. 1975, pres. 1978); mem. Nat. Soc. Profl. Engrs. (pres. Pikes Peak chpt. 1975, sec. Colo. sect. 1976, v.p. 1977, pres. 1978, 79, Young Engr. award 1976, Pres.'s award 1979), Cons. Engrs. Council Colo. (cert.; dir. 1981-83), Am. Cons. Engrs. Council, Profl. Land Surveyors Colo., Colorado Springs Homebuilders Assn., Colo. Engrs. Council (del. 1980—), Colo. State U. Alumni Assn. (v.p., dir. Pike's Peak chpt. 1972-76), Lancers, Lambda Chi Alpha. Home: 7195 Dark Horse Pl Colorado Springs CO 80919 Office: Oliver E Watts Cons Engr 614 Elkton Dr Colorado Springs CO 80907

WATTS, WILLIAM EDWARD, II, social worker; b. Honolulu, HI, Jan. 27, 1951; s. William E. and Dixie P. (Mears) W.; m. Susan Lynn Schmidt, July 13, 1986. MSW, U. Hawaii, 1981, MS, 1986. Research assoc. World Health Orgn., Honolulu, 1979-81; staff social worker Queen's Med. Ctr., Honolulu, 1981—. Pres. Diamond Head Hillside Assn., Honolulu, 1985—. Mem. Hawaii Pacific Gerontol. Soc. (chmn. membership com. 1983-86, editor jour. 1985—, bd. dirs. 1979—), Nat. Assn. Social Workers (cert.), Planetary Soc. Avocations: hot air ballooning, sky watching. Office: Queen's Med Ctr Dept Social Work 1301 Punchbowl St Honolulu HI 96813

WAUGH, SHIRLEY JEAN, educator; b. Elkland, Mo., May 25, 1934; d. Francis and Amy Evelyn (Price) Bath; m. Charles Alfred Waugh, May 16, 1951; children: Dennis Keith, Garry Lynn, Pamela Ann. AA, Fullerton Jr. Coll.; BA in History, U. Calif., Fullerton, 1968, MS in Reading, 1980. Tchr. Laurel Elem. Sch., Brea, Calif., 1970-75, 78-79, 85—, reading specialist, 1975-78, 79-85. Tchr.-rep. Brea PTA, 1980-81, mem. guidance com. 1975-78, 78-85; supt. Fullerton 1st So. Baptist Ch. Sunday Sch., 1981-84. Named Tchr. of Yr. Brea-Olinda Sch. Dist., 1980-81; recipient Hon. Service award Brea PTA, 1980-81. Mem. NEA, Calif. Tchrs. Assn., Internat. Reading Assn. (pres.'s club 1984-85), Calif. Reading Assn., Orange County Reading Assn. (chmn. publicity com. 1981-82, v.p. membership com. 1983-85), Brea-Olinda Tchrs. Assn. Democrat. Office: Laurel Elem Sch 200 S Flower Brea CA 92621

WAX, RAY VAN, state agency administrator; b. Sterling, Okla., June 7, 1944; s. Sam Van Wax and Betty Louise (Lucas) Landers; m. Linda Ann Willcutt, Dec. 31, 1972; children: Cody, Tiffany. Student, Pierce Coll., 1972-74, U. Wash., 1974, U. Ala., 1976. Safety inspector State Wash. Dept. Labor and Industry, Olympia, 1973-83; sr. safety inspector State Wash. Dept. Labor and Industry, Tacoma, 1983-84, mgr. safety regulations program, 1984—; cons. Wax Safety Services, Graham, Wash., 1980—. Editor numerous safety and health standards publs.; contbr. articles to profl. jours. Served with USN, 1962-68. Mem. Am. Soc. Safety Engrs., Am. Nat. Standards Insts. (coms.). Home: 24214 64th Ave E PO Box 353 Graham WA 98338 Office: Wash Dept Labor and Industries Div Indsl Safety and Health 805 Plum St SE Olympia WA 98504

WAXMAN, HENRY ARNOLD, congressman; b. Los Angeles, Sept. 12, 1939; s. Louis and Esther (Silverman) W.; m. Janet Kessler, Oct. 17, 1971; children: Carol Lynn, Michael David. B.A. in Polit. Sci, UCLA, 1961, J.D., 1964. Bar: Calif. 1965. Mem. Calif. State Assembly, 1969-74, 94th-100th Congresses from 24th Calif. Dist. Pres. Calif. Fedn. Young Democrats, 1965-67. Mem. Guardians Jewish Home for Aged, Am. Jewish Congress, Sierra Club. Club: B'nai B'rith. Office: 2418 Rayburn House Office Bldg Washington DC 20515 *

WAY, E(DWARD) LEONG, pharmacologist, toxicologist, educator; b. Watsonville, Calif., July 10, 1916; s. Leong Man and Lai Har (Shew) W.; m. Madeline Li, Aug. 11, 1944; children—Eric, Linette. B.S., U. Calif., Berkeley, 1938, M.S., 1940; Ph.D., U. Calif., San Francisco, 1942. Pharm. chemist Merck & Co., Rahway, N.J., 1942; instr. pharmacology George Washington U., 1943-46, asst. prof., 1946-48; asst. prof. pharmacology U. Calif., San Francisco, 1949-52; asso. prof. U. Calif., 1952-57, prof., 1957—, chmn. dept. pharmacology, 1973-78; USPHS spl. research fellow U. Berne, Switzerland, 1955-56; vis. prof. research fellow U. Hong Kong, 1962-63, China Med. Bd.; Sterling Sullivan disting. vis. prof. Martin Luther King U., 1982; hon. prof. pharmacology and neurosci. Guangzhon Med. Coll., 1987; mem. sci. adv. com. Pharm. Mfrs. Assn. Found., 1968—; mem. council Am. Bur. for Med. Advancement in China, 1982—; bd. dirs. Li Found., pres., 1985—; hon. prof. in pharmacology and neurosci. Guanghon Med. Coll., 1987. Contbr. numerous articles and revs. to profl. publs.; editor: New Concepts in Pain, 1967, (with others) Fundamentals of Drug Metabolism and Drug Disposition, 1971, Endogenous and Exogenous Opiate Agonists and Antagonists, 1979; editorial bd.: Clin. Pharmacology, Therapeutics, 1975—, Drug, Alcohol Dependence, 1976—, Progress in Neuro-psychopharmacology, 1977—, Research Communications in Chem. Pathology and Pharmacology, 1978—, Alcohol and Drug Dependence Research, 1986—. Recipient 1st Achievement award in Pharmacodynamics Am. Pharm. Assn. Found., 1962, Faculty Research Lectr. award U. Calif., San Francisco, 1974, San Francisco Chinese Hosp. award, 1976; Cultural citation and Gold medal Ministry of Edn. Republic of China, 1978; Nathan B. Eddy award Com. on Problems in Drug Dependence, 1979; Chancellor's award for pub. service U. Calif., 1986. Fellow Am. Coll. Neuropsychopharmacology, AAAS, Am. Coll. Clin. Pharmacology (hon.); mem. Am. Soc. Pharmacology, Exptl. Therapeutics (bd. editors 1957-65, pres. 1976-77), Fedn. Am. Socs. Exptl. Biology (exec. bd. 1975-79, pres. 1977-78), Am. Pharm. Assn. (life, co-recipient Ebert prize certificate 1962), AMA (affiliate), Soc. Aid and Rehab. Drug Addicts (Hong Kong) (life), Western Pharmacology Soc. (pres. 1963-64), Japanese Pharm. Soc. (hon.), Council Sci. Soc. Presidents (exec. com. 1979-84, treas. 1980-84), Com. on Problems of Drug Dependence (bd. dirs. 1978—, chmn. 1978-82), Chinese Pharmacology Soc. (hon.), Japanese Pharm. Soc. (hon.), Academia Sinica, Sigma Xi. Research on drug metabolism, analgetics, developmental pharmacology, drug tolerance and dependence. Office: Dept Pharmacology U Calif San Francisco CA 94143

WAY, JAMES DOUGLAS, chemical engineer; b. Dayton, Ohio, Feb. 17, 1956; s. James Harry and Rebekah (Upchurch) W.; m. Debra Jan Schlender, Nov. 22, 1986. B.S. in Chem. Engring., U. Colo., 1978, M.S. in Chem. Engring., 1980, PhD in Chem. Engring., 1986. Research engr. Nat. Bur. of Standards, Boulder, Colo., 1980-83, separation lab. team leader, 1983-86; chem. engr. SRI Internat., Menlo Park, Calif., 1987—. Editor spl. issue Jour. Membrane Sci., 1984; co-editor Am. Chem. Soc. syposium series Liquid Membranes Theory and Applications, 1987. Contbr. chpt. to symposium procs., 1982, 1984; contbr. articles to profl. jours. Pres. bd. dirs. Shanahan Trail Condominium Assn., Inc., Boulder, 1984-86, mem. bd. dirs. 1987. Recipient Outstanding Performance award Nat. Bur. of Standards, 1981, 82, 84, Special Service award, 1981, Sustained Superior Performance award, 1986; grantee Gas Research Inst., 1981, 82, Dept. Energy, 1984, 86, Nat. Bur. Standards, 1984. Mem. Am. Inst. Chem. Engrs., European Soc. Membrane Sci. and Tech., N.Am. Membrane Soc. Democrat. Methodist. Home: 6 Woodfern Portola Valley CA 94025 Office: SRI Internat Chem Engring Lab 333 Ravenswood Ave Menlo Park CA 94025

WAYBURN, EDGAR, physician; b. Macon, Ga., Sept. 17, 1906; s. Emanuel and Marian (Voorsanger) W.; m. Cornelia Elliott, Sept. 12, 1947; children: Cynthia, William, Diana, Laurie. AB, U. Ga., 1926; MD, Harvard U., 1930. Hosp. tng. Columbia-Presbyn. Hosp., N.Y.C., 1931-33; assoc. clin. prof. Stanford (Calif.) U., 1933-65, U. Calif., San Francisco, 1960-76; practice medicine specializing in internal medicine San Francisco, 1933-8588; mem. staff Pacific Presbyn. Med. Ctr., San Francisco, 1959-86, chief endocrine clinic, 1959-72, vice chief staff, 1961-63. Editor: Man Medicine and Ecology, 1970; contbr. articles to profl. and environ. jours. Mem. Sec. of Interior's Adv. Bd. on Nat. Park System, 1979-83, Citizen's Adv. Commn. Golden Gate Natural Recreation Area, San Francisco, 1974-86, I.U.C.N. Commn. on Nat. Parks and Protected Areas; leader nat. campaigns for Redwood Nat. Park, Golden Gate Recreation Area, Alaska Nat. Interest Lands Conservation Act; trustee Pacific Presbyn. Med. Ctr., 1978-86; bd. dirs. Garden Sullivan Hosp., 1965-78. Served to maj. USAF, 1942-46. Fellow ACP; mem. AMA, Am. Soc. Internal Medicine, Calif. Med. Assn. (del. 1958-83, Recognition award 1986, Leadership and Quality awards 1986), San Francisco Med. Soc. (pres. 1965, Resolution of Congratulations 1986), Sierra Club (pres. 1961-64, 67-69, John Muir award 1972), Fedn. Western Outdoor Clubs (pres. 1953-55). Avocations: exploration, hiking. Home: 314 30th Ave San Francisco CA 94121

WAYLAND, J(AMES) HAROLD, biomedical scientist, educator; b. Boise, Idaho, July 2, 1909; s. Charles William and Daisy (McConnell) W.; m. Virginia Jane Kartzke, June 24, 1933; children—Ann Marie Peters, Elizabeth Jane (Mrs. Paul T. Barber). B.S., U. Idaho, 1931, D.Sc. (hon.), 1977; M.S., Calif. Inst. Tech., 1935, Ph.D., 1937. Am. Scandinavian Found. fellow U. Copenhagen, 1937; asst. prof. physics U. Redlands, 1938-41; mil. research in mine warfare and torpedo devel. 1941-48; assoc. prof. applied mechanics Calif. Inst. Tech., Pasadena, 1949-57; prof. Calif. Inst. Tech., 1957-63, prof. engring. sci., 1963-79, prof. emeritus, 1979—; U.S. coordinator U.S.-Japan Coop. Seminars on Peripheral Circulation, 1967, 70; mem. cardiovascular and renal study sect. NIH, 1973-77; vis. prof. Shinshu U., Matsumoto, Japan, 1973, U. Limburg, Maastricht, The Netherlands, 1979, U. New South Wales, Australia, 1980; Disting. vis. prof. U. Del., 1985. Contbr. articles to profl. publs., also books and articles on history of playing cards. Recipient Ordnance Devel. award U.S. Navy, 1945; Certificate of Recognition NASA, 1975; Humboldt Sr. Scientist Research award U. Heidelberg, 1982; Guggenheim fellow, 1953-54; research grantee NIH; research grantee NSF; research grantee John A. Hartford Found.; research grantee Kroc Found. Fellow AAAS (chmn. med. scis. sect. 1976); mem. Microcirculatory Soc. (pres. 1971-72, Landis award 1981), Am. Phys. Soc., Am. Physiol. Soc.,

European Microcirculatory Soc. (hon.), German Microcirculatory Soc. (hon.), Internat. Soc. Biorheology, Am. Heart Assn., Am. Inst. Archeology, Am. Soc. Enologists, AAUP, Playing Card Soc., Sigma Xi, Phi Beta Kappa, Sigma Tau. Democrat. Unitarian. Club: Athenaeum. Patentee in field. Home: 361 S Greenwood Ave Pasadena CA 91107 Office: Calif Inst Tech Pasadena CA 91125

WAYLAND, JAMES ROBERT, JR., physicist, researcher; b. Plainview, Tex., May 3, 1937; s. James Robert and Edna (Earl) W.; m. Susan Martz, June 2, 1961; children: Sarah Catherine, Jennifer Sabrina. BS in Physics, U. of South, 1959; MS in Physics, U. Ariz., 1963, PhD in Physics, 1967. AEC Fellow U. Calif., Berkeley, 1959-60; teaching asst. and health physicist U. Ariz., Tucson, 1962-67; research assoc. U. Md., College Park, 1967-70; asst. prof. Tex. A&M U., College Station, 1970-74; mem. tech. staff Sandia Nat. Labs., Albuquerque, 1979—. Editor tech. books; contbr. tech. articles to profl. jours.; patentee in field. Pres. Mt. Doers, Albuquerque, 1979. Mem. Soc. Petroleum Engrs., Am. Phys. Soc., Am. Physicist Assn. (treas. 1968-75, Founders award 1975). Avocation: custom design furniture building. Office: Sandia Nat Labs PO Box 5800 Albuquerque NM 87185

WAYLAND, L. C. NEWTON, pub. health pediatrician; b. Plainview, Tex., May 4, 1909; s. Levi Clarence and Connie Onita (Newton) W.; student Wayland Coll., Plainview, 1925-26, West Tex. State Tchrs. Coll., 1926-30; A.B., Stanford U., 1932, M.D., 1936; postgrad. U. Calif. Med. Sch., Children's, Gen. hosps., Los Angeles; m. Helen Hart, June 18, 1938 (div. 1966); children—Newton, Elizabeth, Constance. Intern, San Francisco City and County Hosp., Stanford Service, 1936; house officer San Mateo County Hosp., 1937, Children's Hosp., Los Angeles, 1938; dir. child health Santa Barbara (Calif.) County Health Dept., 1938-44; dir. health Santa Barbara City Schs., 1944-74; dir. health Santa Barbara City Coll., 1946-74; pvt. practice medicine specializing in pediatrics, 1955-70; ret. mem. pediatric staffs Santa Barbara Gen., St. Francis, Cottage, Goleta Valley hosps.; ret. med. cons. Calif. State Dept. Rehab., 1974-78; emeritus mem. med. staff Calif. State Prison at Soledad. Past non-nurse dir. exec. com., sch. nursing sect. Nat. Orgn. Pub. Health Nurses; past mem. adv. com. Calif. Dept. Edn. on Pub. Sch. Health; mem. Pub. Citizen Inc. Past 1st bd. dirs. Get Oil Out!; mem. vol. staff. Santa Barbara Zool. Gardens. Recipient award Calif. Sch. Nurses Orgn., 1965, 71. Fellow Am. Sch. Health Assn. (past pres. Calif. div.), Am. Pub. Health Assn.; mem. NEA (ret.), Calif. Tchrs. Assn. (ret.), Calif. Med. Assn. (ret.), Santa Barbara County Med. Soc. (ret.), Am. Acad. Pediatrics, Los Angeles pediatric socs. (ret.), World Council Chs., Nat. Council Chs. (founding mem. laymen's commn.), No. Calif. Ecumenical Council, UN Assn. (past pres. Santa Barbara chpt.), Ams. for Democratic Action, NAACP, ACLU, So. Christian Leadership Conf., Calif. Congress Parents and Tchrs. (hon. life), Scholastic Socs. South, Assn. Am. Indian Affairs, Santa Barbara Democratic League (founding), Nat. Audubon Soc., Save the Redwoods League, Wilderness Soc., Isaac Walton League, Nat. Parks Assn., Sierra Club, So. Christian Leadership Conf., Cousteau Soc., Planned Parenthood Fedn. Am., Environ. Protective Assn., Trustees for Alaska, Fellowship Reconciliation, Inst. for Am. Democracy, Com. for Improvement Med. Care, SANE, Ams. for Indian Opportunity, Nat. Indian Youth Council, Am. Soc. Contemporary Medicine and Surgery, Nat. Wildlife Assn., Intern at Wildlife Assn., Riviera Assn. (past pres.), Common Cause, Episcopal Peace Fellowship, Fund for Peace, Nature Conservancy, Scenic Shoreline Preservation Conf., Nat. Trust for Historic Preservation, Santa Barbara Mus. Natural History, Friends of the Earth, Green Peace, Gray Panthers, Defenders of Wildlife, Internat. Physicians for Prevention of Nuclear War, Physicians for Social Responsibility, Nat. Urban League, Religious Coalition for Abortion Rights, Nat. Abortion Rights Action League, Freedom from Hunger Found., Alliance for Survival, Inst. Aerobic Research, Calif. Wilderness Coalition, Center War/Peace Studies, Am. Farmland Trust, Rural Advancement Fund, NOW, ERA, So. Poverty Law Center, United World Federalists, Zero Population Growth, Negative Population Growth, Amnesty Internat., Council for Livable World, Clergymen and Laymen Concerned, Community Environ. Council, Am. Horse Protection Assn., Am. Fedn. Scientists, Planning and Conservation League Calif., Am. Indian Fund, Humane Soc. U.S., Assn. for Vol. Sterilization, Council on Econ. Priorities, N. Am. Congress on Latin Am., Coalition for a New Fgn. and Mil. Policy, Met. Opera Assn., Nat. Council on Aging, The Africa Fund., Ams. United for Separation of Ch. and State, Am. Friends Service Com., Nat. Assn. fo R.R. Passengers, Calif. Tax Reform Assn., Nat. Com. for Peace in Cen. Am., LWV, Santa Barbara Citizens Planning Assn., Internat. Ctr. for Devel. Policy, Simon Wiesenthal Ctr., Am.-Israeli Civil Liberties Coalition, numerous others. Democrat. Episcopalian. Contbr. articles to ednl. and other profl. jours. Home: 1807 Paterna Rd Santa Barbara CA 93103

WAYMAN, COOPER HARRY, industrial hygiene specialist; b. Trenton, N.J., Jan. 29, 1927; s. Cooper Ott and Helen Viola (Unverzagt) W.; m. Ruth Treier, June 16, 1951; children: Carol Beth, Andrea Lee. BS, Rutgers U., 1951; MS, U. Pitts., 1954; PhD, Mich. State U., 1959; JD, U. Denver, 1967. Bar: Colo. 1969, Tex. 1972; registered profl. engr., Colo.; cert. real estate broker, Colo. Research chemist U.S. Geol. Survey, Lakewood, Colo., 1960-65; assoc. prof. chemistry Colo. Sch. Mines, Golden, 1965-70; asst. to regional adminstr. EPA, Denver, 1971-74, regional counsel, 1974-83; exec. asst. to mayor City of Denver, 1981-85; dir. environment compliance Cord Labs., Inc., Broomfield, Colo., 1986—; dir.energy office EPA, Denver, 1974-78; adj. prof. law U. Denver, 1981—; mem. State Colo. Air Pollution Commn., Denver, 1969-70. Author: Detergents and Environment, 1965, Permits Handbook, 1981; contbr. articles to profl. jours. V.p. WE Lockwood Civic Assn., Lakewood, 1985-86. Served with USNR, 1945-46. Grantee U.S. Fish and Wildlife Service, 1967; fellow MIT, 1956. Mem. Colo. Bar Assn. (tech. law com. 1985-86). Avocations: skiing, golf, photography, art. Home: 11022 W Oregon Pl Lakewood CO 80226 Office: Cord Labs Inc 2225 W Midway Blvd Broomfield CO 80020

WAYMAN, LANCE R., computer consulting company executive; b. Haywoods Heath, Eng., Dec. 15, 1938; came to U.S., 1968; s. Richard and Eileen Wayman; m. Nien-Ling Wayman, Dec. 17, 1966; children: Thomas, Peter. BS, U. Melbourne, Australia, 1964; MBA, U. So. Calif., 1971. Engr. United Concrete Pipe, Baldwin Park, Calif., 1968-70; cons. T. Barry & Assocs., Los Angeles, 1971-72, A.T. Kearney, Los Angeles, 1972-77; pres. Wayman & Assocs. Inc., Redondo Beach, Calif., 1977—. Mem. Inst. Engrs. Australia. Office: Wayman & Assocs Inc 217 S Pacific Coast Hwy Redondo Beach CA 90277

WAYNE, KYRA PETROVSKAYA, author; b. Crimea, USSR, Dec. 31, 1918; came to U.S., 1948, naturalized, 1951; d. Prince Vasily Sergeyevich and Baroness Zinaida Fedorovna (Von-Haffenberg) Obolensky; m. George J. Wayne, Apr. 21, 1961; 1 child, Ronald George. B.A., Leningrad Inst. Theatre Arts, 1939, M.A., 1940. Actress, concert singer, USSR, 1939-46; actress, U.S., 1948-51; enrichment lectr. Royal Viking Line cruises, Alaska-Can., Greek Islands-Black Sea, Russia/Europe, 1978-79, 81-82, 83-84. Author: Kyra, 1959; Kyra's Secrets of Russian Cooking, 1960; The Quest for the Golden Fleece, 1962; Shurik, 1971; The Awakening, 1972; The Witches of Barguzin, 1975; Max, The Dog That Refused to Die, 1979 (Best Fiction award Dog Writers Assn. Am. 1980); Rekindle the Dreams, 1979, Quest for Empire, 1986. Founder, pres. Clean Air Program, Los Angeles County, 1971-72; mem. women's council KCET-Ednl. TV. Served to lt. Russian Army, 1941-43. Decorated Red Star, numerous other decorations USSR; recipient award Crusade for Freedom, 1955-56; award Los Angeles County, 1972. Mem. Soc. Children's Book Writers, Authors Guild, P.E.N., UCLA Med. Faculty Wives (pres. 1970-71, dir. 1971-75) UCLA Affiliates (life), Los Angeles Lung Assn. (life). Home: 234 S Rimpau Blvd Los Angeles CA 90004

WEATHERFORD, GARY DEAN, lawyer, consultant; b. Riverside, Calif., Sept. 30, 1936; s. Clarence Austin and Bertha Mae (Bobbitt) W.; m. Jane Ann Gharst, Dec. 20, 1959 (div.); 1 child, Theodore Austin; m. Suzanne Marie Gassner, Oct. 29, 1985. BA magna cum laude, U. Redlands, 1958; BD, Yale U., 1961, LLB, 1964. Bar: Calif. Asst. prof. of law U. Oreg., Eugene, 1966-68; v.p. Ferris, Weatherford and Brennan, San Diego, 1968-76; dep. sec. Resources Agy. State of Calif., Sacramento, 1976-77; dir. John Muir Inst., Napa, Calif., 1977-81; vis. prof. law U. Santa Clara, Calif., 1982-84; pres. Watershed West, Berkeley, Calif., 1984-85; of counsel Ferris, Brennan & Britton, San Diego, 1986—; bd. dirs. Water Sci. and Tech. Bd. NRC, Washington, Western Network, Santa Fe, L'Enfant Trust, Washington;. Editor: Water and Agriculture in the Western U.S., 1982, Acquiring Water for Energy, 1982; co-editor: New Courses for the Colorado River, 1986; also articles. Mem. Calif. Bar Assn., AAAS, Am. Geophys. Union (policy scis. com. hydrology sect. 1984—), Am. Water Resources Assn., Internat. Water Resources Assn. Democrat.

WEATHERILL, ANNE SHARON, artist, writer; b. Ft. Lewis, Wash., Sept. 22, 1945; d. Kenneth M. and Mary H. (Smith) Roberts; m. James Vincent Weatherill, Dec. 20, 1966; children—Maryanne Marie, Christine Rose. B.A., U. Calif.-Riverside, 1969. Adminstrv. asst. Nez Perce County Hist. Soc., 1980-81, exec. dir., 1981-84; sec. chief examiner Asotin County Civil Service Commn., 1984—. Recipient Wakan Camp Fire award for exceptional and imaginative leadership and service to youth, 1980. Mem. Am. Assn. Museums, Hellsgate Graphics Assn. Home and Office: 2178 23d St Clarkston WA 99403

WEATHERUP, ROY GARFIELD, lawyer; b. Annapolis, Md., Apr. 20, 1947; s. Robert Alexander and Kathryn Crites (Hesser) W.; m. Wendy Gaines, Sept. 10, 1977; children: Jennifer, Christine. AB in Polit. Sci., Stanford U., 1968, JD, 1972. Bar: Calif. 1972, U.S. Dist. Ct. 1973, U.S. Ct. Appeals (9th cir.) 1975, U.S. Supreme Ct. 1980. Assoc. Haight, Dickson, Brown & Bonesteel, Los Angeles, Santa Monica and Santa Ana, Calif., 1972-78, ptnr., 1979—; Moot Ct. judge UCLA, Loyola U., Pepperdine U.; arbitrator Am. Arbitration Assn. Mem. Calif. Acad. Appellate Lawyers, ABA, Town Hall Calif., Los Angeles County Bar Assn. Republican. Methodist. Home: 17260 Rayen St Northridge CA 91325 Office: Haight Dickson Brown & Bonesteel 201 Santa Monica Blvd Santa Monica CA 90406

WEAVER, CHARLES RICHARD, household products company executive; b. Kingman, Ind., Sept. 16, 1928; s. Atha Lavern and Jennie Mildred (Best) W.; m. Phyllis Jane Plaster, Sept. 30, 1950 (div. 1982); children—Wendy, Cynthia, Daniel; m. Donna Lee Lambert, Nov. 21, 1982. B.S., Purdue U., 1950. Sales trainee Faultless Caster Co., Evansville, Ind., 1950-51; product mgr. Westinghouse Corp., Pitts., 1951-53; brand mgr. Procter & Gamble Co., Cin., 1953-69; advt. mgr. Clorox Co., Oakland, Calif., 1969-82; pres., chief operating officer Clorox Co., Oakland, 1982-85, pres., chief exec. officer, 1985-86; chmn., chief exec. officer Clorox Co., 1986—. Served with USMC, 1946-47. Office: Clorox Co 1221 Broadway Oakland CA 94612

WEAVER, DENNIS A(LOYSIUS), safety professional, consultant; b. South Waverly Sayre, Pa., Feb. 12, 1916; s. Dennis Percival and Margaret (Burke) W.; m. Eleanor Jackson Leatherman, Sept. 8, 1946; children: Jackson Dell, Cynthia Burke, Jann Cather, Gregory Stuart. BS, Pa. State U., 1939, MA, 1941. Cert. safety profl. Pub. safety officer Pa. State U., State College, 1948-52, Purdue U., West Lafayette, Ind., 1953-61; instr. traffic Northwestern U., Evanston, Ill., 1961-62; dir. policyholder edn. Wausau (Wis.) Ins. Co., 1962-78; safety mgr. Transp. Test Ctr. Dept. Transp., Pueblo, Colo., 1978-83; prin. D.A. Weaver & Assocs., Pueblo, 1983—; adj. instr. safety mgmt. U. Ariz., Tucson, 1977-78. Co-editor: Directions in Safety, 1976; contbr. articles to profl. jours. Served with Am. Field Service, 1942-45, ETO. Mem. Am. Soc. Safety Engrs. (1st prize 1983), Pueblo C. of C. (Pueblo Image award 1983). Lodge: Kiwanis. Avocations: bicycling, gardening, writing. Home and Office: 9 Brooks Pl Pueblo CO 81001

WEAVER, GERALD ELBERT, broadcasting educator; b. Los Angeles, May 25, 1938; s. Lauren A. and Margaret A. (Lind) W.; m. Bonnie Sasse, Sept. 1, 1963 (div. 1980); children: Robert, Chris. BA in Radio and TV, U. of the Pacific, 1960; MA in Radio and TV, U. Miss., 1977. Newsman, disc jockey Sta. KIST, Santa Barbara, Calif., 1960-61; newsman Sta. KCRA-TV, Sacramento, Calif., 1961-64; news bur. dir. U. of the Pacific, Stockton, Calif., 1964-69; pub. relations dir. Whitter (Calif.) Coll., 1969-71; asst. prof. Miss. U. for Women, Columbus, 1977-79, pub. info. dir., 1971-79; assoc. prof. journalism and broadcasting U. Alaska, Fairbanks, 1979-87; instr. Eastern Ill. State U., Charleston, 1987—; cons. Sta. KCIN, Victorville, Calif., 1980; newsman, prodn. asst. Sta. KIAK, Fairbanks, 1981-83; gen. mgr., co-owner Sta. KGHX, Fairbanks, 1983-85; pub. relations cons. Coll. of the Desert, Palm Desert, Calif., 1984. Exec. producer, narrator audio tape programs including Alaska, Trans-Alaska Pipeline; producer radio program Remembering, Stas. KAUC-FM, KGHX; co-producer TV programs On The Record, Newsmakers, Sta. KUAC-TV. Advance man The White House, Mobile, Ala., Jackson, Miss., 1976; mem. Nat. Adv. Council Women's Ednl. Programs, U.S. Dept. Edn., 1975-78. Recipient Coll. Radio Program of Yr. award Council Advancement and Support of Edn., 1976. Mem. Broadcast Edn. Assn., Radio/TV News Dirs. Assn., Sigma Delta Chi. Avocations: photography, travel. Home: PO Box 82131 Fairbanks AK 99708 Office: Dept Journalism-Broadcasting U Alaska Fairbanks AK 99775

WEAVER, HARRY EDWARD, JR., physicist; b. Phila., Feb. 1, 1923; s. Harry Edward Weaver; m. Ellen Cleminshaw, June 10, 1944; children: P. Lynne, Thomas S. BS, Case Western Res. U., 1943, MS, 1948; PhD, Stanford U., 1952. Instr. U. Zürich, Switzerland, 1952-54, 59-61; sr. scientist Varian Assocs., Palo Alto, Calif., 1954-59, 61-69, H.P. Labs., Palo Alto, 1969—; physicist Manhattan Project, Oakridge, Tenn., 1943-46. Chmn. Planning Commn., Portola Valley, Calif., 1981-85, Archtl. Com., Irish Beach, Calif., 1986—. Mem. Am. Phys. Soc., N.Y. Acad. Sci., Calif. Acad. Sci., Am. Inst. Physics (adv. com. corp. assocs. 1986—), Sigma Xi, Tau Beta Pi. Club: Commonwealth (San Francisco). Avocations: astronomy, sailing. Office: HP Labs 1651 Page Mill Rd Palo Alto CA 94304

WEAVER, HOWARD CECIL, newspaper editor; b. Anchorage, Oct. 15, 1950; s. Howard Gilbert and Lurlene Eloise (Gamble) W.; m. Alice Laprele Gauchay, July 16, 1970 (div. 1974); m. Barbara Lynn Hodgin, Sept. 16, 1978. B.A., Johns Hopkins U., 1972. Reporter, staff writer Anchorage Daily News, 1972-76, columnist, 1979-81, mng. editor, 1981—; editor, owner Alaska Advocate, Anchorage, 1976-79. Recipient Pulitzer prize, 1976; Pub. Service award AP Mng. Editor's Assn., 1976; Headliner award Press Club of Atlantic City, 1976. Mem. Am. Soc. Newspaper Editors, Investigative Reporters and Editors, Sigma Delta Chi. Episcopalian. Clubs: Alaska Press (bd. dirs. 1972-84), Upper Yukon River Press (pres. 1972). Address: 1001 Northway Dr Anchorage AK 99508

WEAVER, JOHN BARNEY, sculptor; b. Anaconda, Mont., Mar. 28, 1920; naturalized Can. citizen, 1972; s. John Bruce and Myrtle Lenore (Dragstedt) W.; m. Jane Clare Menke, June 30, 1949; children—Sara Marie, Henry Clement. Grad. Art Inst. Chgo., 1946; LL.D. (hon.), U. Alta., 1984. Tchr. Layton Sch. Art, Milw., 1946-51; state sculptor, curator Mont. Hist. Soc., Helena, 1954-61; sculptor Smithsonian Instn., Washington, 1961-66; provincial sculptor Provincial Mus. and Archives of Alta., 1966-71; sculptor, pres. John Weaver Fine Arts Ltd., Silver Creek-Hope, B.C., Can., 1978—. Author: Sculpture of John Weaver, 1980. Prin. works include sculpture Jubilee Auditorium, Edmonton, Alta., Can., capital bldg. rotunda, Helena, Centennial Library, Edmonton, Livingston Fish Hatchery, Calgary, Alta., Franklin Mint, Franklin Ctr., Pa., N.Y. State Mus., Albany, Libby Dam, Libby, Mont., Cypress Hills near Maple Creek, Sask., Pedestrian Mall, Last Chance Gulch, Helena, Madison County Courthouse, Virginia City, Mont., Ft. Edmonton Park, Edmonton, Keyano Coll. Fort McMurray, Alta., Alta. Gov. Telephones Telecommunications Mus., Calgary, Northland Park, Edmonton, City Hall grounds, Edmonton, Cochrane, Alta., Chilliwack B.C., Deerfoot Trail Mall, Calgary, Graceland Coll. Lamoni, Iowa; series include Carling O'Keefe Community Art Heritage Series, Carling Community Art Found., Roy Allen Oil Industry Series; Winter Olympic Series by Calgary Olympic Devel. Assn. Recipient Statue of Victory World Culture award, Acad. of Nations, 1984, Nation's Great prize Acad. Fine Art, Parma, Italy, 1983, Gold medal for Artistic Merit, Internat. Parliament for Peace and Security, 1983, Diploma of Merit, U. Art, Parma, 1981, Golden Flame award Internat. Parliament, 1986. Mem. La Salon des Nations, Paris (permanent), Centre Internatl. d'Art Contemporian, Paris, Acad. Fine Art, Parma (hon.), Mus. of Rockies, U. Mont., Mont. Hist. Soc., Nat. Sculptor Soc. Home: PO Box 1723, Hope, BC Canada V0X 1L0 Office: John Weaver Fine Arts Ltd, 19255 Silverhope Rd, Silver Creek-Hope, BC Canada V0X 1L0

WEAVER, JYOTI RAE, flight attendant; b. Bremen, India, Dec. 13, 1950; s. Maurice and Berthella Mae (Whitmyer) S.; m. Kevin Earl Weaver, Mar. 25, 1980; 1 child: Sierra Laakea Stevens. BA, U. Hawaii, 1981, MSW, 1983. Flight attendant Pan Am. World Airways, N.Y.C., 1972—; pvt. practice clin. social worker Honolulu, 1983-85, Phoenix, 1986—; dir. Divorce Services Hawaii, Honolulu, 1983-85. Contbr. chpt. in book and articles to profl. jours. Pres. Pan Am. Employees Recycling Fund, Honolulu, 1980-85, founder; vol. Neighborhood Justice Ctr., Honolulu, 1981-85, Handicapped Program Parks and Recreation, Glendale, 1986; bd. dirs. Spl. Olympics, 1985—. Mem. Nat. Assn. Social Workers. Home: 4511 W Vogel Ave Glendale AZ 85302

WEAVER, LOIS JEAN, physician, educator; b. Wheeling, W.Va., May 23, 1944; s. Lewis Everett and Ann (Novak) W.; m. James A. Burke, Apr. 14, 1985. BA, Oberlin Coll., 1966; MD, U. Chgo., 1970. Pulmonary fellow Northwestern U., Evanston, Ill., 1975-77; trauma fellow U. Wash. Harborview Hosp., Seattle, 1977-79, research assoc., instr. medicine, 1979-81, clin. asst. prof. medicine, 1983—; clin. research fellow Virginia Mason Med. Research Ctr., Seattle, 1981-82; mem. med. staff Swedish Hosp., Seattle, 1984—; pulmonary cons. Fred Hutchinson Cancer Research Inst., Seattle, 1984—, disability quality br. Social Security, Seattle, 1985—. Contbr. sci. articles to profl. jours. La Verne Noyes scholar U. Chgo., 1966; Parker B. Francis fellow Northwestern U., 1975. Mem. AMA, Am. Thoracic Soc., Wash. State Med. Assn., Wash. Lung Assn., Sigma Xi. Avocations: gardening, music. Home: 1221 Madison #918 Seattle WA 98104 Office: Seattle Pulmonary Assn 1221 Madison Suite 918 Seattle WA 98104

WEAVER, MAX KIMBALL, social worker, consultant; b. Price, Utah, Apr. 4, 1941; s. Max Dickson and Ruth (Kimball) W.; m. Janet Hofheins, Sept. 13, 1963; children: Kim, Cleve, Chris, Wendy, Michael, Amyanne, Heather. Student, So. Utah State Coll., 1959-60; BS, Brigham Young U., 1965; MSW, U. Utah, 1967. Lic. clin. social worker and marriage counselor, Utah. Cons. Utah State Tng. Sch., American Fork, 1966; dir. Dept. Pub. Welfare, Cedar City, Utah, 1967-70; social worker Latter Day St. Social Services, Cedar City, 1970-75; with Mental Retardation Devel. Disabled Adult Services Dept. Social Services, Cedar City, 1975—; cons. nursing homes, Utah, 1974—; tchr. So. Utah State Coll., Cedar City, 1972, 77. Contbr. articles to mags. Pres. Am. Little League Baseball, 1977-84, 86, Cedar High Booster Club, 1984—; chmn. Rep. Precinct #1, 1984; v.p. Big League Baseball, 1986—. Mem. Nat. Assn. Social Work (nominating com., licensing com.), Am. Pub. Welfare Assn., Utah Pub. Employees Assn. Mormon. Lodge: Rotary. Avocations: reading, sports, scouting, gardening. Home: 116 N 200 E Cedar City UT 84720 Office: Dept Social Services 1552 W 200 N Cedar City UT 84720

WEAVER, PAUL MARTIN, military officer; b. Trenton, Jan. 3, 1954; s. Ebon P. and Emerenciana Marie (Yeager) W.; m. Marja Ann Ross, June 30, 1984. BS, U.S. Air Force Acad., 1976; MS, Air Force Inst. Tech., 1982. Commd. 2d lt. USAF, 1976, advanced through ranks to capt., 1980; pilot USAF, McGuire AFB, N.J., 1978-80; instr. pilot USAF, Vance AFB, Okla., 1980-81; research and devel. flight test mgr. USAF, Wright-Patterson AFB, Ohio, 1983-86; pilot USAF, Travis AFB, Calif., 1986—. Vol. Dixon (Calif.) Community Ch., 1986, Emanuel Luth. Ch., Dayton, Ohio, 1986; dir., coordinator Christian Career Fellowship, Dayton, 1981-84. Named to Order of the Arrow, Boy Scouts Am., 1970. Mem. Tau Beta Pi. Avocations: woodworking, bicycling, outdoor sports, gardening. Office: 75 Mil Airlift Squadron Bldg 912 Travis AFB CA 94535

WEAVER, RACELLE FINKLEMAN, social worker; b. N.Y.C., Feb. 8, 1951; d. Richard and Roslyn (Bottner) Finkleman. AA in Elem. Edn., Ill. Cen. Coll., East Peoria, 1972; BA in Psychology, Calif. State U., Northridge, 1981; MSW, Calif. State U., Sacramento, 1983. Clin. counselor Midtown Manor, Sacramento, 1984-85; social service practitioner Child Protective Services, Stockton, Calif., 1985-87; treatment coordinator Child and Family Inst., Sacramento, 1987—. Mem. Nat. Assn. Social Workers. Democrat. Jewish. Club: Sacramento Tall. Avocations: needlepoint, reading, photography. Office: Chfld and Family Inst 5109 Florin-Perkins Rd Sacramento CA 95826

WEAVER, WILLIAM BRUCE, astronomer, research administrator; b. Catskill, N.Y., Sept. 1, 1946; s. William Ray and Bette (Martino) W.; m. Sandra Dale Wilford; children: Cristina Dawn, Robert Bruce Glen. BS, U. Ariz., 1968; MS, Case Western Res. U., 1971, PhD, 1972. Prin. staff mem. BDM, Monterey, Calif., 1973—; astronomer Montery Inst. for Research in Astronomy, 1972—, pres., 1986—, also bd. dirs. Contbr. articles to profl. jours. Recipient NSF traineeship, 1968-72. Fellow Royal Astron. Soc., Am. Astron. Soc.; mem. Calif. Acad. Sci., Astron. Soc. Pacific. Office: Monterey Inst Research Astronomy 900 Major Sherman Ln Monterey CA 93940

WEBB, ALBERT DINSMOOR, enology consultant, chemist, educator; b. Victorville, Calif., Oct. 10, 1917; s. Ralph Hough and Harriet Vida (Dinsmoor) W.; m. Nancy May Mathews, Sept. 5, 1943 (dec. Jan. 1984); children: Robert Dinsmoor, Bradford Clarke. Student, U. Calif., Davis, 1941-43; PhD, U. Calif., Berkeley, 1948; docteur honoris causa, U. Bordeaux, France, 1982. Chemist E&J Gallo Winery, Modesto, Calif., 1939, Petri Winery, Escalon, Calif., 1940; with U. Calif.-Davis and Manhattan Dist., Oak Ridge, Tenn., 1941-45; prof. U. Calif., Davis, 1945-82; dir. Wine Industry Tech. Symposiums, San Francisco, 1975—; pres. Willobank Club, Inc., Davis, 1985-86. Editor: Chemistry of Winemaking, 1974, Grape and Wine Centennial Symposium Process, 1982; Am. Jour. Enology and Viticulture, 1977-81: author (with others) Tech. of Winemaking, 4th rev. edit., 1980. Recipient Hon. Research award Med. Friends of Wine, San Francisco, 1968. Mem. Am. Soc. Enologists (pres. 1974-75), AAAS, Am. Chem. Soc. (emeritus), Sigma Xi. Avocations: gardening, stamp collecting. Office: U Calif Dept Viticulture and Enology Davis CA 95616

WEBB, DALE ALBERT, business administrator; b. Detroit, Feb. 25, 1941; s. Albert L. and Mary Louise (Burgess) W.; m. Judith Ann Kaster, June 16, 1962; children: Scott Allen, Susan Kaye Webb Schroeder, Todd Albert. BA, Kalamazoo Coll., 1962. Tchr. Roseville (Mich.) Pub. Schs., 1962-63; with labor relations dept. Ford Motor Co., Sterling Heights, Mich., 1963-66; mgr. personnel Control Data Corp., Rochester (Mich.) and Tucson, 1966-74; mgr. bus. Nat. Radio Astronomy Obs., Tucson, 1974—. Leader Tucson council Boy Scouts Am., 1970-76. Mem. Tucson Personnel Club (bd. dirs. 1972-73). Republican. Methodist. Avocation: antique vehicle restoration. Office: Nat Radio Astronomy Obs 949 N Cherry Ave Bldg 65 Tucson AZ 85721-0655

WEBB, DEAN LEROY, engineering executive, consultant, forensic, structural and investigative engineer; b. Murray, Utah, Feb. 18, 1949; s. Dean B. and Lawana (Williams) W.; m. Marla LaRue Wood, Aug. 6, 1971; children: Chanin Therin, Lacey LaRue. BCE, BEE, Utah State U., 1973. Registered profl. engr., Utah, Calif., Idaho, Wyo., Colo., Ariz., Mont. Structural engr. Coon, King & Knowlton, Salt Lake City, 1973-81, DMJM, Coon, King & Knowlton, Salt Lake City, 1981-84; pres. Dean L. Webb & Assocs., Salt Lake City, 1984—. Recipient 1983 Portland (Oreg.) Concrete Assn. Award of Excellence. Mem. NSPE (pres. Utah chpt. 1986-87), Salt Lake Area C. of C., Constrn. Specifications Inst. (pres. Salt Lake chpt. 1982-83), Utah Soc. Profl. Engrs. (pres. Salt Lake City chpt. 1983-84), Utah Engrs. Council (pres.-elect 1986-87, chmn. 1987-88), Am. Cons. Engring. Council, Structural Engrs. Assn. Utah (founding mem.), Am. Concrete Inst. (award of excellence, 1983), Nat. Forensic Ctr. Republican. Mormon. Avocation: golf. Office: 5330 S 900 E Salt Lake City UT 84117

WEBB, GEORGE WENDELL, physicist; b. Santa Monica, Calif., June 25, 1938; s. Donald A. and Ruth P. (Palmer) W.; m. Marielle van Thillo, Dec. 16, 1972; 1 child, Katherine. BA in Physics, U. Calif., Santa Barbara, 1961; PhD in Physics, U. Calif., San Diego, 1967. Research asst. U. Calif., San Diego, 1961-67, asst. research physicist, 1967-68, research physicist, 1974—; mem. tech. staff David Sarnoff Research Ctr.-RCA, Princeton, N.J., 1969-74; pres., bd. dirs. Energy Sci. Labs., San Diego; bd. dirs. Calif. Innovation Network; cons. Calif. Energy Commn., 1982-83. Contbr. articles to profl. jours.; patentee in field. Recipient Outstanding Achievement award RCA Labs., 1972; grantee NSF, 1977-80, NASA, 1975—, USAF, 1974—. Mem. Am. Phys. Soc. Avocations: jogging, canoeing. Office: Energy Sci Labs PO Box 85608 San Diego CA 92138

WEBB, JOHN DAY, III, chemist; b. Washington, Nov. 30, 1949; s. John Day II and Marjorie (Gash) W. BA in Chemistry, U. Colo., Denver, 1973; BSChemE, U. Colo., Boulder, 1977; MS in Chemistry, U. Denver, 1982.

Chemist Protex Industries Inc., Denver, 1973-75; process engr. Shell Chem. Co., Marietta, Ohio, 1977-78; sr. chemist Solar Energy Research Inst., Golden, Colo., 1978—. Contbr. articles to profl. jours.; patentee in field. Active Vols. for Outdoor Colo. Recipient Outstanding Performance award Solar Energy Research Inst., 1984. Mem. Am. Chem. Soc. Democrat. Avocations: skiing, backpacking, hunting, fishing. Home: 13251 W 20th Ave Golden CO 80401 Office: Solar Energy Research Inst 1617 Cole Blvd Golden CO 80401

WEBB, PATRICIA SHIRLEY, journalist, public relations counselor; b. Southampton, N.Y., Dec. 9, 1949; d. Frank A. and Leona C. (Deegan) Belson; m. James F. Webb, Jr., Mar. 22, 1969; children—Michelle M., James P. A.A., Honolulu Community Coll., 1980; B.A. in Journalism, U. Hawaii-Manoa, 1982. Asst. to sports info. dir., women's athletics dept. U. Hawaii-Manoa, 1981; journal intern Hawaii Statewide Vol. Services, 1982; account asst. in pub. relations Ogilvy & Mather, 1983-84; asst. editor Hawawaii Foodservice News, 1985—. Carol Burnett Fund for Responsible Journalism grantee, 1983. Mem. Pub. Relations Soc. Am., Sigma Delta Chi. Roman Catholic.

WEBB, WELLINGTON E., state official. Exec. dir. Colo. Regulatory Agys. Dept., Denver. Office: Colo Regulatory Agys Dept Room 110 1525 Sherman St Denver CO 80203 *

WEBB, WILLIAM CLEMENT, clergyman; b. Aransas Pass, Tex., Aug. 14, 1963; s. William Vernon and Maxine (Jordan) W.; B.A., Belmont Coll., 1968; M.Div., Midwestern Baptist Theol. Sem., 1971; M.A., U. No. Colo., 1976; m. Debra Ann Keenan, Dec. 15, 1972; children—Melinda Joy, Kristi Lin, William Robert. Dir. transp. Kemmerer (Wyo.) Sch. Dist. 1, 1973-74; ordained to ministry So. Bapt. Ch., 1964; pastor First Bapt. Ch., Kemmerer, 1973-74, First Bapt. Ch., Bamberg, W.Ger., 1974, Meml. Bapt. Ch., Wheatland, Wyo., 1975-76; social worker Platte County Dept. Social Services, Wheatland, 1975-76; counselor, chaplain Union Mission Settlement, Charleston, W.Va., 1976-77; dir. Nome (Alaska) Bapt. Ministries, 1977-83; clin. services dir. Alaska Bapt. Family Service Ctr., Anchorage, 1983-86; pastor, dir. Friendship Bapt. Mission, Fairbanks, Alaska, 1986—; mem. So. Bapt. conv. home mission bd.; publicity chmn. Wyo. Human Resouces Confedn., 1975-76; bd. dirs. Nome chpt. ARC, 1978; pres. Alaska Assn. Homes for Children. Mem. Am. Personnel and Guidance Assn., Am. Assn. Rehab. Counselors, Assn. Counselor Edn. and Supervision, Am. Assn. Specialists in Group Work, Am. Council on Alcohol Problems, Mental Health Counselor Assn., Assn. for Religious Issues and Values in Counseling. Democrat. Clubs: Rotary, Masons. Home: 1501 Lacey Fairbanks AK 99701

WEBB, WILMA J., state legislator. Mem. Colo. Ho. of Reps. from 8th Dist. Office: Colorado State Legislature Denver CO 80203 *

WEBBER, DONALD SALYER, consulting optical physicist; b. Los Angeles, Jan. 15, 1917; s. Frank Paul and Althea (Salyer) W.; m. Mary Elizabeth Boodakian, Aug. 26, 1951; children: Donald Aram, Zachary Michael Haik. BA in Physics, UCLA, 1938, MA in Physics, 1941, PhD in Physics, 1954; MS in Meteorology, Calif. Inst. Tech., 1942. Instr. physics UCLA, 1954-55; mem. sr. staff Ramo-Wooldridge, Hawthorne, Calif., 1955-61; mgr. astron. sci. lab. Lockheed Aerospace Corp., Burbank, Calif., 1961-65; sr. staff engr. TRW Systems, Redondo Beach, Calif., 1965-80; cons. optical physics Sherman Oaks, Calif., 1980—. Contbr. articles to profl. jours. Served to maj. USAAF, 1941-46, NATOUSA. Mem. Am. Phys. Soc., Optical Soc. Am., Sigma Xi. Democrat. Unitarian. Avocations: gardening, travel. Home and Office: 3551 Knobhill Dr Sherman Oaks CA 91423

WEBBER, PATRICK NEIL, Canadian provincial government official; b. Hanna, Alta., Can., Apr. 17, 1936; m. Dorothy Webber; children—Barbara, Carol, Dianne, Leonard, Lorne. B.Sc. in Math., U. Alta., 1957, Ph.D. in Curriculum and Instrn., 1973; B.Ed., U. Calgary, 1962; M.A., U. Mont., 1964. Formerly with research and devel. dept. Can. Industries Ltd.; meteorol. officer Can. Fed. Govt.; tchr. math. and physics various high schs., Calgary, Alta.; instr. math. Mt. Royal Coll., 1966-75, head math.-physics dept. several yrs.; mem. Alta. Legis. Assembly, 1975—, assoc. minister telephones, 1979-82, minister of social services and community health, 1982-86, minister edn., 1986, minister of energy, 1986—. Former mem. Coll. Bd. Govs., former mem. curriculum com. and fin. com. Office: Room 228, Legislature Bldg, Edmonton, AB Canada T5K 2B7

WEBER, CHARLENE LYDIA, social worker; b. Phila., Mar. 2, 1943; d. Walter Gotlieb and Dorothy (Peart) W.; m. Billy Mack Carroll, Oct. 3, 1959 (div. Sept. 1974); children: Dorothy Patricia, Robert Walter, Lydia Baker, Billy Bob, Elizabeth Louise; m. John Edward Thomaston, Sept. 26, 1974 (div. July 1986). BSW with honors, Coll. Santa Fe, 1983. Client service agt. I Social Services div. Dept. Human Services, Albuquerque, 1975-78, client service agt. IV, 1978-83; social worker II Social Services div. Dept. Human Services, Bernalillo, N.Mex., 1983, social worker III, 1983—. Mem. Nat. Assn. Social Workers, N.Mex. Council on Crime and Deliquency, Albuquerque Retarded Assn., Child Welfare League. Democrat. Home: 72 Umber Ct Rio Rancho NM 87124 Office: Dept Human Services div Social Services PO Box 820 Bernalillo NM 87004

WEBER, CHARLES WALTER, nutrition educator; b. Harold, S.D., Nov. 30, 1931; s. Walter Earl and Vera Jean (Scott) W.; m. Marylou Merkel Adam, Feb. 3, 1961; children: Matthew, Scott. BS, Colo. State U., 1956, MS, 1958; PhD, U. Ariz., 1966. Research asst. U. Ariz., Tucson, 1963-66, asst. prof., 1966-68, assoc. prof., 1969-72, prof. nutrition, 1973—; cons. Hermosillo, Mex., 1970-74, Inst. of Health, Cairo, 1981-82, U. Fortaleza, Rio de Janiero, 1986. Contbr. articles to sci. jours. Served as cpl. U.S. Army, 1952-54. Mem. Am. Inst. Nutrition, Inst. Food Technologists, N.Y. Acad. Scis., Am. Soc. Clin. Nutrition, Poultry Sci. Assn., Ariz. Referees Assn. Club: Randolph Soccer (Tucson) (pres. 1976-79). Avocation: stamp collection. Home: 4031 Calle de Jardin Tucson AZ 85721 Office: U Ariz Dept Nutrition and Food Sci 309 Shantz Bldg Tucson AZ 85721

WEBER, DARRELL JACK, plant biochemistry educator; b. Thornton, Idaho, Nov. 16, 1933; s. John and Norma (Severson) W.; m. Carolyn Foremaster, Aug. 24, 1962; children:Becky, Brian, Todd, Kelly, Jason, Trent. BS, U. Idaho, 1958, MS, 1959; PhD, U. Calif., Davis, 1963. Postdoctoral fellow U. Wis., Madison, 1963-65; assoc. prof. biology U. Houston, 1965-69; prof. botany Brigham Young U., Provo, Utah, 1969—; postdoctoral fellow Mich. State U., East Lansing, 1975-76. Author: (with others) Introductory Plant Biology Manual, 1973, Mechanisms of Pesticide Resistance in Non-Target Organisms, 1981; Principals and Application of Instrumentation in the Biological Sciences, 1976; contbr. numerous articles to profl. jours. Recipient Research Regulation award Karl G. Maeser, Provo, 1974; Utah Acad. Sci. fellow, Salt Lake City, 1972. Mem. Am. Mycol. Soc. (editor), Sigma Xi (sec. Brigham Young U. chpt. 1982-85). Republican. Mormon. Avocations: skiing, growing fruit. Office: Brigham Young U. 285 Widtsoe Provo UT 84602

WEBER, GEORGE RICHARD, accountant, author; b. The Dalles, Oreg., Feb. 7, 1929; s. Richard Merle and Maud (Winchell) W.; B.S., Oreg. State U., 1950; M.B.A., U. Oreg., 1962; m. Nadine Hanson, Oct. 12, 1957; children—Elizabeth Ann Weber Katooli, Karen Louise, Linda Marie. Sr. trainee U.S. Nat. Bank of Portland (Oreg.), 1950-51; jr. acct. Ben Musa, C.P.A., The Dalles, 1954; tax and audit asst. Price Waterhouse, Portland, 1955-59; sr. acct. Burton M. Smith, C.P.A., Portland, 1959-62; pvt. C.P.A. practice, Portland, 1962—; lectr. acctg. Portland State Coll.; expert witness fin. and tax matters. Sec.-treas. Mt. Hood Kiwanis Camp, Inc., 1965. Exec. counselor SBA; mem. fin. com., powerlifting team U.S. Powerlifting Fedn., 1984, ambassador People to People, China, 1987. Served with AUS, 1951-53. Decorated Bronze Star; C.P.A., Oreg. Mem. Am. Inst. C.P.A.s, Internat. Platform Assn., Council Fgn. Relations Portland com. 1985—). Oreg. City Traditional Jazz Soc., Order of the Holy Cross Jerusalem, Knightly Assn. St. George the Martyr., Beta Alpha Psi, Pi Kappa Alpha. Republican. Episcopalian. Clubs: Kiwanis, Portland Track, City (Portland); Multnomah Athletic; Sunrise Toastmasters. Author: Small Business Long-term Finance, 1962, A History of the Coroner and Medical Examiner Offices, 1963. Contbr. to profl. publs. and poetry jours. Home: 2603 NE 32d Ave Portland OR 97212 Office: 4380 SW Macadam Suite 400 Portland OR 97201

WEBER, HANS JURGEN, biologist, executive search consultant; b. Teplitz, Czechoslovakia, Feb. 12, 1942; came to U.S., 1973; s. Felix and Gerta (Stoeber) W. MS, Tech. U., Berlin, 1968; PhD, Free U. of Berlin, 1972. Postdoctoral researcher Calif. Inst. Tech., Pasadena, 1973-75; postdoctoral researcher U. Calif., Berkeley, 1975-77, research assoc., 1977-80; research biochemist U. Calif. Med. Ctr., San Francisco, 1980-83; v.p. Bio-Quest, Inc., San Francisco, 1985—; v.p. mktg. TUNGNAM, Los Gatos, Calif., 1985. Contbr. articles to profl. jours. Mem. AAAS, Bay Area OD Network. Avocations: backpacking, skiing, sailing. Office: BioQuest Inc 649 Mission St San Francisco CA 94105

WEBER, JOHN CHARLES, forest biologist; b. Yakima, Wash., Dec. 27, 1948; s. John Floyd and Meryl (Mehner) W.; m. Bonnie Elizabeth Avery, Aug. 4, 1975. BA, Gonzaga U., 1971; MS, U. Wash., 1980; postgrad., Oreg. State U., 1980—. Tchr. biology U.S. Peace Corps., Kenya, 1973-76; research asst. U. Wash., Seattle, 1977-80, Oreg. State U., Corvallis, 1980-86; statistician U.S. Forest Service, 1987—. Mem. Cen. Am. Task Force, Corvallis, 1980—. Mem. Am. Inst. Biological Scis., Western Forest Genetics Assn., Union Concerned Scientists, Sierra Club, Sigma Xi, Phi Kappa Phi, Alpha Sigma Nu. Democrat. Avocations: Hispanic and English lit., poetry, outdoor activities. Home: 203 NW 21st St Corvallis OR 97330 Office: Oreg State U Dept Forest Sci Corvallis OR 97330

WEBER, LARRY GLENN, sales and marketing company executive, real estate sales company executive; b. Los Angeles, July 5, 1951; s. Carl and Frances Helene (Tullius) W.; m. Nanette Walden, May 3, 1985. BA, U. So. Calif., 1973, MBA, 1976. Salesman, Mktg. West, Inc., North Hollywood, Calif., 1976-78, product mgr., 1978-79, sales mgr., 1979-80, sec.-treas., 1980-85, pres., owner, ptnr., 1985-86; sec.-treas., owner/ptnr. Ind. Rep. Sales, Inc., North Hollywood, 1980-86, Premium Sales & Distbg., Inc., North Hollywood, 1980-85; v.p. Weber & Assocs. Real Estate, Inc., Gardena, Calif., 1978—; founder, owner Weber Mktg. Assocs., 1986; founder, owner, ptnr., chief exec. officer Telesis Sales Group, Inc., 1987—. Mem. Los Solteros, 1981-85, v.p., 1983. Named Salesman of Year, Mktg. West, Inc., 1976, 77, Millionaire's Club, 1980, 81, Multi-Millionaire's Club, 1982, 83, 84, 85, 86, Mgr. of Year, 1982, 83, 85; Sales Performance award Sanyo Electric Inc., 1981. Mem. Calif. Assn. Realtors, Gardena Bd. Realtors, U. So. Calif. MBA Alumni Assn., U. So. Calif. Gen. Alumni Assn., Mensa, U.S. Recreational Ski Assn., BMW Automobile Club N.Am., Theta Xi, U.S. Ski Assn. Democrat. Roman Catholic. Office: Telesis Sales Group Inc 21000 Devonshire St #202 Chatsworth CA 91311

WEBER, PAUL R., computer graphics consultant; b. Colo., July 12, 1957; s. Ruben and Nettie Lea (Eaton) W. BS in Chemistry, Colo. Sch. Mines, 1979. Engr. Tosco, Golden, Colo., 1981-83; software engr. Interactive Systems Co., Littleton, Colo., 1983-84, Precision Visuals, Boulder, Colo., 1984-85; cons. NASA, Boulder, 1984—; cons. graphics Johnson Engring., Boulder, 1984—. Mem. Am. Chem. Soc., Arvada Ctr. Arts, Nat. Space Inst. Home: 6651 Everett St Arvada CO 80004-3006

WEBER, WILLIAM ALFRED, botany educator; b. N.Y.C., Nov. 16, 1918; s. Henry Paul and Emilie Agnes (Rilke) W.; m. Selma Ruth Herrmann, Aug. 5, 1940; children: Linna Louise, Heather Oma, Erica Marion. BS, Iowa State U., 1940; MS, Wash. State U., 1942, PhD, 1945. From instr. to assoc. prof. U. Colo., Boulder, 1946-62, prof. botany, 1962—; Herbarium curator U. Colo. Museum, Boulder, 1946—; cons. various orgns., 1946—. Author: Rocky Mountain Flora, 1976, T.D.A. Cockerell, 1976, Colorado Flora: Western Slope, 1987. Linnean Soc. fellow, 1985; recipient Robert L. Stearns award, 1986. Mem. Am. Inst. Bot. Scis., Am. Bryological and Lichenological Soc. (past sec. and pres.) Nordic Bot. Soc., Swedish Bot. Soc., Calif. Bot. Soc. Democrat. Congregationalist. Avocation: music. Office: U Colo Museum Campus Box 218 Boulder CO 80302

WEBER, WILLIAM JOHN, nuclear scientist; b. Watertown, Wis., July 19, 1949; s. Clarence Edward and Ramona Theresa (Jana) W.; m. Jan Carole Grunewald, Aug. 21, 1971 (div. May 1979); m. Reta Rennee Rodgers, Dec. 8, 1984;. BS in Physics, U. Wis., Oshkosh, 1971; MS in Nuclear Engring., U. Wis., 1972, PhD in Nuclear Engring., 1977. Research trainee Oak Ridge (Tenn.) Nat. Lab., 1970; student honors program Argonne (Ill.) Nat. Lab., 1971; research asst. U. Wis., Madison, 1971-77; sr. research scientist Battelle Northwest Labs., Richland, Wash., 1977ú; vis. scientist European Inst. Transuranium Elements, Karlsruhe, Fed. Republic of Germany, 1983. Contbr. numerous articles to profl. jours. Vol. instr. community fly-tying class, Richland, 1979-82. Mem. Materials Research Soc. (mem. com.), Am. Ceramic Soc. (Best Paper, 1982), Sigma Xi, Sigma Pi Sigma. Roman Catholic. Club: Columbia Basin Fly Casters (Richland) (pres. 1982-83). Avocations: hiking, backpacking, hunting, fishing, camping. Home: 5201 W 16th Ct Kennewick WA 99337 Office: Battelle Northwest Labs PO Box 999 Richland WA 99352

WEBER, WILLIS WILMER, chemical engineer; b. Waseca, Minn., Nov. 23, 1934; s. Rueben Martin and Gladys (Gibbs) W. B in Chem. Engring., U. Minn., 1957. Jr. research engr. Olin Matheson, Niagara Falls, N.Y., 1957-60, sr. research engr., 1960-62; sr. devel. engr. Union Carbide Corp., Tonawanda, N.Y., 1962-65, group leader, 1965-69, sr. devel. assoc., 1969-72, supr. mfg. process devel., 1972-76, sr. cons., 1976-83; sr. scientist ATEC, Inc., Riverton, Wyo., 1983—, also bd. dirs. Holder numerous patents in field. Mem. AAAS. Avocations: woodworking, lapidary. Home: Box 2120 E Riverview Rd Riverton WY 82501 Office: ATEC Inc 625 W Madison Ave Riverton WY 82501

WEBSTER, FRANCES MARGARET, health services director; b. Phoenix, Mar. 17, 1925; d. Arthur Richmond and Mary Ellen (White) W. Nursing diploma, St. Mary's Coll. Nursing, 1951; BS, Ariz. State U., 1969, MSW, 1971. RN; lic. clin. social worker; lifetime Calif. instr. credential; cert. med. hypnosis. Psychiat. social worker St. Joseph's Hosp., Phoenix, 1969-72; dir. social services Mercy Hosp., Bakersfield, Calif., 1972-75, project coordinator, 1983—; pain control therapist Mercy Hosp. Med. Ctr., San Diego, 1974-80; dir. health services Cath. Social Services, Bakersfield, 1980—; mem. health services adv. bd. Sisters of Mercy, Burlingame, Calif., 1973-75, planning com. Mercy Hosp., Bakersfield, 1983-85. Founder Bakersfield Cath. Charities Auxiliary, 1981. Mem. Nat. Assn. Social Workers (sec. Grand Canyon chpt. 1971-72). Democrat. Roman Catholic. Avocations: backpacking, gardening, crocheting. Home: 2615 21st St Bakersfield CA 93301 Office: Mercy Hosp 2215 Truxtun Ave Bakersfield CA 93302

WEBSTER, HARVEY CURTIS, journalist; b. Chgo., Nov. 6, 1906; s. Ira Gilbert and Beatrice Dunham (Curtis) W.; m. Lucille Audine Jones, Apr. 12, 1932 (dec. Mar. 1980); m. Joan Hildebrandt Miles, Jan. 4, 1982. AB, Oberlin Coll., 1927, AM, 1929; PhD, U. Mich., 1935. Teaching fellow U. Mich., Ann Arbor, 1929-35; instr. Colo. State Coll., Ft. Collins, 1935-36; from asst. prof. to prof. English U. Louisville, 1936-76, chmn. dept. English, 1967-68, prof. emeritus, 1976—. Author: On a Darkling Plain, 1947, After the Trauma, 1970; Selected Poems of Hortence Flexner, 1975; foreward Graham Breene: A Descriptive Catalog, 1979; lit. journalist New Leader, New Republic, Poetry, Contemporary Criticism, Austin, Tex., 1976—; also Louisville Courier-Jour. Chmn. West End Community Council, Louisville, 1966-67, Ky. Dems. for Adlai Stevenson, 1960. Recipient awards Yaddo Writers Colony, Saratoga Springs, N.Y., 1947, 54, 64, 65; Fulbright prof. U. Durham, Eng., 1950-51, U. Leeds, Eng., 1962-63. Mem. AAUP (pres. Louisville chpt. 1949-50), Am. Fedn. Tchrs. (pres. Louisville chpt. 1944-45, 49-50), NAACP, MLA, Modern Humanities Research Assn., Urban League. Mem. Soc. Friends. Home and Office: 245 W Lucero Las Cruces NM 88005

WEBSTER, ORRIN JOHN, agronomist; b. Arkansas City, Kans., June 26, 1913; s. Milo Edwin and Mary Gertrude (Witters) W.; m. LeVenia Hile, May 31, 1936; children: Dean G., Thomas J., Jean M. BS, U. Nebr., 1934, MS, 1940; PhD, U. Minn., 1950. With Soil Conservation Service, 1935-36, USDA, 1936-75; agronomist USDA, Africa, 1951, 63-71, P.R., 1971-75; adj. prof. U. Ariz., Tucson, 1975—. Contbr. articles to profl. jours. Mem. Am. Soc. Agronomy, Am. Genetics Soc., Sigma Xi, Gamma Sigma Delta, Alpha Zeta. Rebublican. Methodist. Home: 5649 E 7th St Tucson AZ 85711 Office: U Ariz Dept Plant Sci Tucson AZ 85721

WEBSTER, R. BRUCE, hypnotherapist, cons.; b. Glendale, Calif.; s. James Scott and Kathryn Glen (Loughman) W.; m. Toni Griffin, June 18, 1960 (div. 1972); 1 child, Robert Bruce Jr. BA, Calif. State U., Northridge, 1966; postgrad., Los Angeles U., 1974-77. Sales mgr. Culligan Deionized Water, Los Angeles, 1967-68; retail and pub. relations mgr. Talon Am. div. Textron Inc., Los Angeles, 1968-71; practice hypnotherapy, instr. Sydell, Webster & Assocs., Sherman Oaks, Calif., 1971—; motivational cons. profl. and Olympic athletes, univs., 1972—. Rep. vol., Los Angeles, 1976—;. Mem. Hypnotists Union (charter, exec. bd. 1972-75), Am. Hypnosis Assn., Sigma Chi. Episcopalian. Lodge: Lions (local bd. dirs. 1985-86, pres. 1986-87). Office: Sydell Webster & Assocs 13527-A Ventura Blvd Sherman Oaks CA 91423

WEDBERG, STANLEY EDWARD, microbiology educator; b. Bridgeport, Conn., Aug. 28, 1913; s. Frank Enock and Anna Mathilda (Osterlund) W.; m. Mary Elizabeth Stewart, June 28, 1941; children: Karen Elizabeth Wedberg Miller, Robin Carol Wedberg Brown. BS, U. Conn., 1937; PhD, Yale U., 1940. Instr. Yale U. Med. Sch., New Haven, Conn., 1941; instr. U. Conn., Storrs, 1941-43, asst. prof. microbiology, 1946-50, assoc. prof., 1950-59, prof., 1959-69, head dept., 1955-66; microbiologist Southwestern Coll., Chula Vista, Calif., 1969-80; free-lance lectr. and cons. San Diego, 1980—; pres. Conn. Pub. Health Assn., Hartford, 1960-61, Conn. Adv. Com. Food and Drugs, Hartford, 1952-53, 62-63, mem. 1952-69. Author: (texts) Microbes & You, 1954, Paramedical Microbiology, 1963, Introduction to Microbiology, 1966; also articles. V.p. Conn. Adv. Clean Air Task Force, Hartford, 1968-69; mem. Conn. Gov.'s Clean Water Task Force, Hartford, 1967-68. Served to capt. U.S. Army, 1943-46, ETO. Recipient Outstanding Tchr. award U. Conn., 1964. Fellow Am. Acad. Microbiology (charter); mem. AAAS, Zool. Soc. San Diego, Mil. Order World Wars, Phi Kappa Phi, Soc. Sigma Xi. Republican. Presbyterian. Club: Friends of Classics (San Diego) (dir. 1984—). Avocations: writing, lecturing. Home and Office: 3361 Ullman St San Diego CA 92106

WEDDINGTON, PATRICIA DIANE, journalist, educator; b. Mooresville, N.C., July 7, 1950; d. Luther Monroe and Annie Rowena (Cox) W. BA, Duke U., 1972, MDiv, 1976; MA, U. Mo., 1977; postgrad., U. Calif., Berkeley. Librarian Grad. Theol. U. Library, Berkeley, 1982; dir. admissions dept. psychology New Coll. Calif., San Francisco, 1983; mgr. Ctr. for Contextual Study, Berkeley, 1984, Calif. Planners, Berkeley, 1985; religion editor Contra Costa Times, Walnut Creek, Calif., 1986—. Author: (with others) Sexual Harassment, 1979, Media Ethics, 1983; contbr. articles to profl. jours. Ralph Stoody fellowship, 1976. Mem. Women in Communications, Am. Acad. Religion, Am. Soc. Poets, Sigma Delta Chi. Democrat. Episcopalian. Avocations: backpacking, gourmet cooking, cross-country skiing. Office: 2640 Shadelands Dr PO Box 5088 Walnut Creek CA 94596

WEDEL, MILLIE REDMOND, educator; b. Harrisburg, Pa., Aug. 18, 1939; d. Clair L. and Florence (Heiges) Aungst; B.A., Alaska Meth. U., 1966; M.Ed., U. Alaska, Anchorage, 1972; postgrad. in communications Stanford U., 1975-76; m. Frederick L. Wedel, Jr., Nov. 2, 1974; 1 son, Tom Redmond. Profl. model Charming Models & Models Guild of Phila., 1954-61; public relations staff Haverford (Pa.) Sch., 1959-61; asst. dir. devel. in charge public relations Alaska Meth. U., Anchorage, 1966, part-time lectr., 1966-73; communications tchr. Anchorage Sch. Dist., 1967—; owner Wedel Prodns., Anchorage, 1976-86; pub. relations staff Alaska Purchase Centennial Exhibit, U.S. Dept. Commerce, 1967; writer gubernatorial campaign, 1971; part-time instr. U. Alaska, Anchorage, 1976-79; cons. Cook Inlet Native Assn., 1978, No. Inst., 1979. Bd. dirs. Sta. KAKM, Alaska Public TV, membership chmn., 1978-80, elected nat. lay rep. to Pub. Broadcasting Service and Nat. Assn. Pub. TV Stas., 1979; bd. dirs. Ednl. Telecommunications Consortium for Alaska, 1979, Mid-Hillside Community Council, Municipality of Anchorage, 1979-80, 83-87, Hillside East Community Council, 1984—, pres. 1984-85; research writer, legal asst. Vinson & Elkins, Houston, 1981. Recipient awards for newspapers, lit. mags.; award Nat. Scholastic Press Assn., 1968, 74, 77, Am. Scholastic Press Assn., 1981, 82, 83, 84; Alaska Council Econs., 1982, Merits award Alaska Dept. Edn.; lic. third class broadcasting, FCC. Mem. Assn. Public Broadcasting (charter mem., nat. lay del. 1980), Indsl. TV Assn. (San Francisco), Alaska Press Club (chmn. high sch. journalism workshops, 1968, 69, 73, awards for sch. newspapers, 1972, 74, 77), Alaska Fedn. Press Women (dir. 1978-86, youth projects dir., award for brochures, 1978), NEA, Am. Educators in Communications Tech., World Affairs Council, Nat. Council Tchrs. English, Alaska Council Tchrs. of English, Houston Legal Assts. Assn., Delta Kappa Gamma. Presbyterian. Clubs: Stanford Alumni (pres. 1982-84) Capt. Cook Athletic (Anchorage). Office: PO Box 730 Girdwood AK 99587

WEDEMEYER, HENRY FREDERICK, health science facility administrator, consultant; b. St. Louis, June 27, 1942; s. Daniel Frederick and Eleanor (Masek) W.; m. Judith Diane Gragnani, Aug. 2, 1969; children: Christopher Robert, Kimberly Ann, Benjamin Michael. BS, U. Houston, 1974; MS, Ohio State U., 1976. Lic. pharmacist, Ohio, Colo., Tex. Asst. prof. U. Nebr. Med. Ctr., Omaha, 1976-79; dir. pharmacy and materials mgmt. St. Luke's Hosp., Denver, 1979—. Author: Administration of Medications-Handbook of Institutional Pharmacy Practice, 1984, Performing an Internal Audit of Pharmacy Services, 1980; co-author: Oral Syringe Use Survey, 1980, Medication Teaching Manual-A Guide for Patient Counseling, 1978. Served with U.S. Army, 1966-69. Recipient Upjohn Achievement award for Outstanding Pub. Service, 1974. Mem. AAAS, Am. Soc. Hosp. Pharmacists (alt. del. Colo. 1984, mem. council adminstrv. affairs, 1986—), Colo. Soc. Hosp. Pharmacists, Am. Pharm. Assn. (del. 1984, 85), Am. Pub. Health Assn., Am. Soc. of Law and Medicine, Colo. Pharmacal, Denver Area Pharmacists Assn., Acad. Pharmacy Practice, Internat. Chili Soc., Rho Chi. Republican. Roman Catholic. Avocations: fishing, exploring. Home: 642 Northridge Rd Highlands Ranch CO 80126 Office: St Luke's Hosp 601 E 19th Ave Denver CO 80203

WEDEMEYER, JOHN MILLS, JR., social worker, social service administrator, consultant, planner; b. Olympia, Wash., Aug. 4, 1945; s. John Mills, Sr. and Helen (Gullett) W.; m. Marianne Jensen Wedemeyer, June 28, 1969; 1 child, Anne Marie. BA in Polit. Sci., Univ. Calif.-Davis, 1967; MSW, San Diego State U., 1969. Social worker San Diego County Dept. Social Service, Calif., 1969-71; exec. dir. San Diego Youth and Community Service, 1970-76; exec. dir. Community Congress of San Diego, 1976-82; dir. Youth Services Santa Cruz Community Counseling Ctr., Calif., 1982-83, June Burnett Inst. for Children, Youth and Families, San Diego State U. Found., 1984—. Chmn. supervisory comn. Golden Hill Community Fed. Credit Union, San Diego, 1969-71; co-founder, exec. dir., chmn. planning com. The Bridge, 1970; treas. Community Congress of San Diego, 1972-73, vice chmn., 1974-75, chmn. San Diego county juvenile justice task force, 1974-76; sec. Nat. Network Runaway and Youth Services, Washington, 1975-76, nat. chmn., 1976-78, chmn. region IX, 1975-76; nominating com. chmn. Health Systems Agy. of San Diego and Imperial Counties, 1976-78; chmn. tng. com. Western States Youth Services Network, 1983-85. Named Alumnus of Yr., San Diego State U. Sch. Social Work, 1976. Mem. San Diego County Foster Parent Assn. (founding, parliamentarian, newsletter editor 1969-71), Nat. Assn. Social Workers, Am. Soc. Pub. Adminstrn., Calif. Child Youth and Family Coalition. Episcopalian. Home: 1438 Dale St San Diego CA 92102 Office: June Burnett Inst for Children Youth and Families 6310 Alvarado Ct San Diego CA 92120

WEDEMEYER, LOWELL REMY, lawyer; b. Adair, Iowa, June 27, 1941; s. Lawrence Theodore and Loretta Agnes (Donohue) W.; m. Linda Lee Downie, June 23, 1979; children: Michelle, Rebecca, Loretta. BSChemE, Iowa State U., 1963; JD, Harvard U., 1969. Bar: Calif. 1969, U.S. Dist. Ct. (no. dist.) Calif. 1976, U.S. Dist. Ct. (cen. dist.) Calif. 1969, U.S. Dist. Ct. (so. dist.) Calif., U.S. Patent Office 1986, U.S. Ct. Appeals (9th cir.) 1976, U.S. Supreme Ct. 1977. Research assoc. AEC Iowa State U., Ames, 1962-63; chem. engr. McDonnell Aircraft Co., St. Louis, 1963; vol. Peace Corps, Nigeria, 1964-65; assoc. Wyman, Bautzer, Rothman & Kuchel, Beverly Hills, Calif., 1969-70; dir., mng. officer Alexander, Inman, Tanzer & Wedemeyer, Beverly Hills, 1970-82; sole practice Davis, Calif., 1982—; plaintiff's lead trial counsel Securities Law Class Action, Los Angeles, 1971-75; plaintiff's lead appellate counsel State Employee's Class Action, 1983-85. Founder, pres. New Deal Dem. of Santa Monica, Calif., 1980-81; founder, speaker Santa Monica Citizen's Congress, 1980-81; lawyer enforcement of elections code, Los Angeles, 1980-83. Served to 2d lt. USAFR, 1968. Mem. ABA, Calif. State Bar Assn. (intellectual property sect. 1986), Tau Beta Pi, Phi Lambda Upsilon. Roman Catholic. Avocation: farming.

WEDGE, BARBARA LYNN, educational marketing professional; b. Livingston, Mont., Oct. 23, 1946; d. Ralph Henry and Mildred (Olund) George; children: Stephanie, Chelsey. BS in Speech Pathology, Mankato State Coll., 1969; MA in Speech Pathology, U. Kans., 1979. Speech pathologist Osseo (Minn.) Pub. Schs., 1969-72, Mankato (Minn.) and Shawnee Mission (Kans.) schs., 1972-80; Univ. rep. U. Phoenix, San Jose, Calif., 1980—; dir. mktg. U. Phoenix, San Jose and San Ramon, Calif., 1985—; dir. programs Lab. Sci. Interrogation, Falls Church, Va. and Pleasanton, Calif., 1985-86; rep. TelPlus Communications, Pleasanton, Calif., 1986—; cons. Corp. SpeakersTng. Bur., Pleasanton, 1985—. Contbr. articles to Jour. Speech and Hearing Disorders. Mem. Am. Soc. Indsl. Security, Am. Speech-Lang.-Hearing Assn. (cert. clin. competence). Club: Lakeview (Oakland, Calif.). Avocations: reading, research, archaeology, skiing.

WEDGWOOD, RALPH JOSIAH PATRICK, pediatrician, educator; b. London, Eng., May 25, 1924; came to U.S., 1940, naturalized, 1951; s. Josiah and Dorothy Mary (Winser) W.; m. Virginia Lloyd Hunt, Oct. 25, 1943; children—Josiah Francis, James Cecil (dec.), Jeffrey Galton, John Christopher Ralph. M.D., Harvard, 1947. Intern pediatrics Bellevue Hosp., N.Y.C., 1947-48; resident Bellevue Hosp., 1948-49; research fellow pediatrics Harvard Med. Sch., 1949-51; sr. instr. pediatrics and biochemistry Western Res. U. Med. Sch., 1953-57, asst. prof. pediatrics and preventive medicine, 1957-62; asso. prof. pediatrics U. Wash. Sch. Medicine, 1962-63, prof., 1963—, chmn. dept., 1963-72; Spl. cons., mem. gen. clin. research center com. NIH, 1962-66; mem. Nat. Adv. Research Resources Council, 1966-70; pres. Assn. Med. Sch. Pediatric Chairmen, 1966-68; chmn. Joint Council Nat. Pediatric Socs., 1967-69. Editorial bd.: Pediatrics, 1966-73; Contbr. numerous articles to profl. jours. Mem. several research adv. coms. Birth Defects Found., 1969—; mem. sci. adv. bd. St. Jude Hosp., Memphis, 1970-76. Served to capt. M.C. AUS, 1944-46, 51-53. Spl. USPHS research fellow Microbiol. Research Establishment, Porton, Eng., 1960-61; John and Mary Markle scholar med. scis., 1960-65; Rockefeller scholar Villa Serbelloni, 1985; vis. fellow St. John's Coll., Cambridge (Eng.) U., 1969-70; Distinguished service mem. Assn. Am. Med. Colls. Mem. numerous profl. socs. Home: 3717 41st Ave NE Seattle WA 98105

WEEKS, DONALD PAUL, molecular biologist; b. Terre Haute, Ind., Feb. 15, 1941; s. Paul Vaughn and Ruth Margaret (Gentry) W.; m. Rita Ann Stableton, June 6, 1964; children: Emily Jean, Jonathan Blaine, Derek Edward, Vaughn Andrew. BS, Purdue U., 1963; PhD, U. Ill., 1967. NIH postdoctoral fellow Inst. Cancer Research, Phila., 1968-73, asst. mem., 1973-78, assoc. mem., 1978-82; vis. prof. U. Geneva, 1982; sr. scientist, cons. Zoecon Research Inst., Palo Alto, Calif., 1982—; mem. study sections NIH, Bethesda, Md., USDA, Washington. Mem. AAAS, Am. Assn. Plant Physiologists, Am. Soc. Cell Biologists, Internat. Soc. Plant Moleculer Biologists. Home: 11238 Redondo Ct Cupertino CA 95014 Office: Zoecon Research Inst Sandoz Crop Protection Corp 975 California Ave Palo Alto CA 94304

WEEKS, GARY LYNN, bank executive; b. Smithfield, Utah, Sept. 14, 1936; s. Lawrence G. and Opal (Ahlstrom) W.; m. JoAnn Burzinski, Aug. 25, 1956; children: Randall L., Todd A., Julie Weeks Prawicki. BS in Math., Utah State U., 1959. Project engr. Sperry Utah Co., Salt Lake City, 1959-64; mgr. ops. research Kennecott Copper Corp., Salt Lake City, 1964-68; systems mgr. Calif. Blue Shield, San Francisco, 1968-69; sr. cons. Optimum Systems Inc., Palo Alto, Calif., 1969-70; v.p. Western States Bankcard Assn., San Francisco, 1970-77; sr. v.p. Fed. Home Loan Bank of San Francisco, 1977—. Mem. Am. Mgmt. Assn., Am. Bankers Assn. Republican. Mormon. Avocations: travel, classical music, arts. Home: 2337 Westbrook Ct Walnut Creek CA 94598 Office: Fed Home Loan Bank San Francisco 600 California St San Francisco CA 94108

WEEKS, HARVEY, therapist; b. Buffalo, June 26, 1925; s. Harvey and Elizabeth Maria (Kimbell) W.; m. Joan Remley, June 27, 1948; children: Florence Jane Spangler, Deborah Joan Tessmann. BA in Gen. Studies, U. Colo., 1949; MSW, UCLA, 1965. Lic. clin. social worker and marriage, family, and child counselor, Calif. Counselor Family Service Assn., San Diego, 1967-69; dir. social work services Northside Psychiat. Hosp., Fresno, Calif., 1970-73; psychiat. social worker Fresno County Health Dept., 1973-78; mental health specialist Pacific County, Long Beach, Wash., 1982-86; pvt. practice mental health cons. Long Beach, Wash., 1986—; instr. social work dept. Calif. State U., 1972-73, 76-77. Served as cpl. U.S. Army, 1943-46. Mem. Nat. Assn. Social Workers, Phi Beta Kappa. Home and Office: PO Box 1026 Long Beach WA 98631

WEEKS, JANET HEALY, judge; b. Quincy, Mass., Oct. 19, 1932; d. John Francis and Sheila Josephine (Jackson) Healy; A.B. in Chemistry, Emmanuel Coll., Boston, 1954; J.D., Boston Coll., 1958; LL.D. (hon.), U. Guam, 1984; m. George Weeks, Aug. 29, 1959; children—Susan, George. Admitted to Mass. bar, 1958, Guam bar, 1972; trial atty. Dept. Justice, Washington, 1958-60; trial atty. firm Trapp & Gayle, Agana, Guam, 1971-73; partner firm Trapp, Gayle, Teker, Weeks & Friedman, Agana, 1973-75; judge Superior Ct. Guam, Agana, 1975—; chmn. task force cts., prosecution and defense Terr. Crime Commn., 1973-76; mem. Terr. Crime Commn. Bd., 1975-76, Guam Law Revision Commn., 1981—; rep. Nat. Conf. State Trial Judges, 1982. Mem. Catholic Sch. Bd. Guam, 1973. Mem. Nat. Assn. Women Judges (charter), Am. Judges Assn., Am. Bar Assn., Fed. Bar Assn. (chpt. sec. 1974), Guam Bar Assn. Club: Internat. (Guam). Office: Superior Ct Guam 110 W O'Brien Dr Agana Guam GU 96910

WEEKS, WILFORD FRANK, glaciologist; b. Champaign, Ill., Jan. 8, 1929; married; 2 children. BS, U. Ill., 1951, MS, 1953; PhD in Geology, U. Chgo., 1956. Geologist mineral deposits br. U.S. Geol. Survey, 1952-55; glaciologist USAF Cambridge Research Ctr., 1955-57; asst. prof. Washington U., St. Louis, 1957-62; glaciologist Cold Regions Research & Engring. Lab., 1962—; prof. geophysics Alaskan Synthetic Radar Facility, Geophys. Inst. of U. Alaska, Fairbanks, 1985—; adj. assoc. prof. Dartmouth Coll., 1962-72, adj. prof., 1972-85; Japan Soc. Promotion Sci. vis. prof. Inst. Low Temperature Sci. Hokkaido U., Japan, 1973; chmn. div. River, Lake and Sea Ice, Internat. Commn. on Snow and Ice; mem. adv. panel Jet Propulsion Lab.; lectr. Advan Study Inst. Air Sea and Ice Interactions, NATO; chmn. arctic marine sci. Office Naval Research, USN Postgrad. Sch., 1978-79; mem. earth observation system team, Earth system sci. com. NASA; mem. Radarsat sci. group Can. Ctr. Remote Sensing; advisor U.S. Arctic Research Commn., NSF. Fellow Arctic Inst. N. Am., Geol. Soc. Am.; mem. NRC (chmn. panel on glaciology 1971-77, polar research bd.), Internat. Glaciological Soc. (v.p. 1969-72, pres. 1972-75), Nat. Acad. Engring. (chmn.), Am. Geophys. Union. Research on geophysics of sea, lake and river ice. Office: Geophys Inst Univ Alaska Fairbanks AK 99775-0800

WEEMS, FRANK TAYLOR, engineering and construction company executive, manufacturing company executive; b. Birmingham, Ala., Dec. 26, 1924; s. Ben Carpenter and Gladys (Taylor) W.; m. Kirsten Lee Borgen, Sept. 10, 1949 (dec. Feb. 23, 1985); children: Barbara Lee, William Taylor, Robert Chipley. BS ChemE, U. Ala., 1944; SM ChemE, M.I.T., 1950. Sales engr. Dorr Co., 1948-52; tech. dir. Eimco Corp., 1952-55, regional mgr., 1955-62, mgr. indsl. sales, 1962-66, mktg. dir., 1966-68, v.p. mktg., 1968-70, pres., 1970-72; exec. v.p., pres. Air Quality Control Group, Envirotech Corp., Menlo Park, Calif., 1972-82; exec. v.p., dir. Mountain States Mineral Enterprises, Tucson, 1982—; pres., dir. A.H. Ross & Assocs., Inc., Toronto, Ont., Can., 1982-86; v.p., dir. Mountain States Synfuels Corp., 1983-86; pres., chief fin. officer, chief exec. officer Cochlea Corp., 1984—, also bd. dirs.; bd. dirs. Granger Assocs., Santa Clara, Calif.; chmn. bd. Chem. Engring. Corp. of Tokyo, 1976-80, Bahnson Co. Inc., Winston Salem, N.C., 1976-81. Active Little League Baseball, Weston, Conn.; trustee Rowland Hall-St. Marks Sch., Salt Lake City. Served with USNR, 1943-46. NRC fellow. Mem. Am. Inst. Chem. Engrs., Am. Inst. Mining, Metall. and Petroleum Engrs., Tau Beta Pi, Theta Tau. Republican. Episcopalian. Clubs: Mining (N.Y.C.), Chemists (N.Y.C.); Alta (Salt Lake City); Los Altos Golf and Country; Old Pueblo (Tucson). Home: 610 Nandell Ln Los Altos CA 94022 also: 8166 E McLaren Dr Tucson AZ 85715 Office: 985 Timonthy Dr San Jose CA 95133

WEG, RUTH L.B., biologist, physiologist, educator; b. N.Y.C., Oct. 12, 1920; d. Morris and Ethel Cooper; m. Martin S. Weg, Sept. 23, 1962; children: Hanna, Robert Bass, Andrea Bass. BA, Hunter Coll., 1940; MS, U. So. Calif., 1954, PhD, 1958. Research assoc. U. So. Calif., Los Angeles, 1960-65; dir. summer inst. Andrus Gerontology Ctr., Los Angeles, 1969-71, assoc. dir. for tng., 1970-74, dean students, 1974-76, assoc. prof. biology and gerontology, Leonard Davis Sch., 1976-85, prof. gerontology (biology), 1985—, also cons.; Belle Boone Beard Meml. lectr. Lynchburg (Va.) Coll., 1987; lectr. and cons. Air Pollution Control Inst. Author: Nutrition in the Later Years, 1979; The Aged: Who, Where, How Well, 1981; editor, author 2 chpts. Sexuality in the Later Years: Roles and Behavior, 1983; mem. edit. bd. various jours. Recipient George C. Griffiths Mem. award, 1977; named Ida Beam Disting. Vis. Prof. U. Iowa, 1986; named to Hunter Coll. Hall of Fame, Hunter Coll. Alumni Assn., 1979. Mem. AAAS, Gerontol. Soc. Am., Am. Soc. on Aging, Assn. for Gerontology in Higher Edn. (pres. 1987—). Office: Andrus Gerontology Ctr U So Calif Univ Park MC0191 Los Angeles CA 90089-0191

WEGLOSKI, DANIEL JOSEPH, hydroelectric engineer; b. Chgo., July 11, 1949; s. Joseph Paul and Elenor (Shatkowski) W.; m. Madonna Marie Meller, Aug. 14, 1971. BSCE, Ill. Inst. Tech., 1971; MBA, Loyola U., Chgo., 1977. Registered profl. engr., Ill., N.Mex. Mem. engring. team Harza Engring., Chgo., 1971-81; project engr. Daverman & Assocs., Syracuse, N.Y., 1981-84; owners rep. Dept. Pub. Utilities, Los Alamos, N.Mex., 1984—. Mem. ASCE. Office: Dept Pub Utilities 901 Trinity Dr Los Alamos NM 87544

WEGMAN, DAVID HOWE, health science educator, consultant; b. Balt., Mar. 13, 1940; s. Myron Ezra and Isabel (Howe) W.; m. Cynthia Heynen, June 18, 1962 (div. Aug. 1968); m. Peggy Nelson, June 7, 1969; children: Jesse Howe, Maryа Nelson. BA, Swarthmore Coll., 1963; MD, Harvard U., 1966, MS in Pub. Health, 1972. Diplomate Am. Bd. Occupational Medicine, Am. Bd. Preventive Medicine. Intern Cleve. Met. Gen. Hosp., 1966-67; med. epidemiologist, N.Y.C Health Dept. Nat. Communicable Disease Ctr., USPHS, 1967-69; dir. indsl. hygiene project Urban Planning Aid, Inc., Cambridge, Mass., 1969-71; occupational hygiene physician Mass. Dept. Labor and Industry, Boston, 1972-78; asst. prof. pub. health Harvard U., Boston, 1972-77, assoc. prof. pub. health, 1977-83; prof., dir. environ. occupational health scis. UCLA, 1983—; vice-chmn. Occupational/Environ. Health Edn. Com., Am. Lung Assn., Los Angeles, 1985—; chmn. Occupational Health China Exchange Adv. Com., 1982—; chair Occupational Health and Safety Work group, HEW sec.'s Conf. on Preventing Disease/Promoting Health, Objectives for the Nation, 1979, Gen. Motors/United Auto Workers Occupation Health Adv. Bd., 1982—; mem. Sci. Com. Epidemiology, Internat. Commn. Occupational Health, 1982—, adv. bd. Mass. Coalition Occupational Safety and Health, 1981-85, TLV Com. Am. Conf. Govtl. Indsl. Hygienists, 1976-79, sub-com. Occupational Cancer, Nat. Cancer Inst., 1981-82, task force Occupational Lung Disease, Nat. Heart Lung Blood Inst., 1977, task force Occupational Respiratory Disease ALSOH, 1976, task group on Surveillance, Nat. Inst. Occupational Safety and Health, 1976-77, study sect. Nat. Inst. Occupational Safety and Health, 1980-83, bd. sci. advisors subcom. on Individual Worker Notification, Nat. Inst. Occupational Safety and Health, 1985, task force III Research Needs in Environ. Health, 1984, spl. commn. to evaluate extent of use of asbestos in pub. bldgs., Commonwealth Mass., 1977-83; monograph reviewer NRC, 1984-85; site visitor for ctr. grant proposal Nat. Inst. Environ. Health Scis., 1985; evaluator asbestos liability, U.S. Dept. Justice; com. mem. vinyl chloride standard, generic carcinogen standard, assess to med. records standard, U.S. Dept. Labor; cons. Boston Gas Co., Chem. Mfrs. Assn., Cin. Cen. Labor Council, W.R. Grace Co., McGill U. Sch. Occupational Health, Uncoal Med. Surveillance Program, B.C. Research Found.; chmn. occupational adv. bd. Gen. Motors/UAW, 1982—; adv. bd. Harvard U. Med. Sch. health letter, 1983—; adv. panel Health Effects of Air Pollution, Rand Corp., 1983—; prin. investigator Gen. Electric Co., U.S Borax Corp., 1985—. Author and editor Occupational Health, 1983; editor and manuscript reviewer var. health publications; contbr. 80 articles to profl. jours. Adv. Bd. mem. Working Women, 1981-85. Recipient Alfred L. Frechette award Mass. Pub. Health Assn., 1979. Fellow Am. Coll. Epidemiology, Am. Coll. Preventive Medicine; mem. Am. Conf. Govtl. Indsl. Hygienists, Am. Pub. Health Assn. (panel environ. studies 1976-78, exec. bd. 1982, chmn. occupational health and safety sect., 1976, governing council 1974-80, 1983-85), Am. Occupational Medicine Assn., Am. Soc. Epidemiology, Internat. Epidemiol. Assn., Internat. Commn. Occupational Health, Soc. Epidemiol. Research, Soc. Occupational and Environmental Health. Avocations: hiking, swimming, camping. Home: 10551 Rochester Ave Los Angeles CA 90024 Office: UCLA Sch Pub Health 650 Circle Dr S Los Angeles CA 90024

WEGNER, ELDON L., sociology educator; b. Detroit, Mar. 27, 1941; s. Herman Emil and Elsie (Locht) W. BA, U. Redlands, 1963; MA, U. Wis., 1965, PhD, 1967. Asst. prof. U. Hawaii, Honolulu, 1967-69, assoc. prof., 1975—; asst. prof. U. Calif., Riverside, Calif., 1970-75; vis. asst. prof. U. Pa., Phila., 1969-79. Contbr. articles to profl. jours. Grantee Nat. Cancer Inst., 1977-79; fellow German Acad. Exchange Service, 1982, Fulbright, 1982. Mem. Am. Sociol. Assn., Soc. for Study Social Problems, Pacific Sociol. Assn., Hawaii Pub. Health Assn. Democrat. Mem. United Ch. Christ. Lodge: Elks. Avocations: choir, swimming, jogging, bowling. Home: 1805 Poki St Apt 703 Honolulu HI 96822 Office: U Hawaii at Manda Porteus Hall Honolulu HI 96822

WEHAUSEN, JOHN VROOMAN, mathematician, educator; b. Duluth, Sept. 23, 1913; s. George W. and Elizabeth (Vroman) W.; m. Mary Katherine Wertime, Aug. 19, 1938; children—Sarah, Peter Vrooman, Julia, John David. B.S., U. Mich., 1934, M.S., 1935, Ph.D., 1938. Instr. math. Brown U., 1937-38, Columbia, 1938-40, U. Mo., 1940-44; mathematician David Taylor Model Basin, Carderock, Md., 1946-49; acting head mechanics br. Office Naval Research, 1949-50; exec. editor Math. Revs., 1950-56; asso. research mathematician Inst. Engring. Research, U. Calif. at Berkeley, 1956-57, research mathematician, 1957—, asso. prof. engring. sci., 1958-59, prof., 1959-84, prof. emeritus, 1984—; Fulbright lectr. U. Hamburg, 1960-61; Consultant Operations Research Group USN, 1944-46. vis. prof. Flinders U., Australia, 1967, U. de Nantes, 1973, U. Grenoble, 1979, Technion, Haifa, 1982, Chalmers Inst. Tech., Gothenburg, 1982, U. de Nantes, 1984. Mem. Am. Math. Soc., Math. Assn. Am., Soc. Naval Architects and Marine Engrs., Soc. Naval Architects of Japan, Nat. Acad. Engring. Home: 15 Hillside Ct Berkeley CA 94704

WEHDE, ALBERT EDWARD, lawyer; b. Milw., Feb. 14, 1935; s. Albert Christian and Mary Hubbel (Dewey) W.; m. Joan M. Forney, Nov. 4, 1978; children: John C., Edward T. BS, Marquette U., 1956, JD, 1960. Bar: Wis. 1960, Calif. 1968. Atty. AEC, Albuquerque, 1963-66; counsel Lockheed Aircraft Co., Sunnyvale and Redlands, Calif., 1966-73; assoc. Schultz & Manfield, Palo Alto, Calif., 1973-74; sr. counsel FMC Corp., Santa Clara, Calif., 1974—; bd. dirs. Tech. Fed. Credit Union, San Jose, Calif. Pres. Mountain View (Calif.) Babe Ruth League, 1976; trustee Mid-Peninsula Family Services Assn., Palo Alto, 1973-74. Served to capt. U.S. Army, 1960-63. Mem. ABA (region VII chmn. 1977-81, pub. contracts sect.), Santa Clara County Bar (co-chmn. corp. counsels sect. 1983-84, mem. exec. com.), Am. Corp. Counsels Assn. (chpt. sec., bd. dirs. 1983—). Democrat. Roman Catholic. Club: Decathalon (Santa Clara). Avocations: gourmet cooking, music, sports. Home: 1106 Lorne Way Sunnyvale CA 94087 Office: FMC Corp PO Box 58123 Santa Clara CA 95052

WEHNER, ALFRED PETER, inhalation toxicologist, biomedical scientist; b. Wiesbaden, Germany, Oct. 23, 1926; came to U.S., 1953, naturalized, 1958; s. Paul Heinrich and Irma (Schulze) Wl; m. Ingeborg Hella Miller, Aug. 30, 1955; children: Patricia Ingeborg, Alfred Peter, Jr., Jackie Diane, Peter Hermann. Cand. med., Johannes Gutenberg U., 1949, Zahnarzt DDS, 1951, D.M.D. cum laude, 1953. Individual practice dentistry Wiesbaden, 1951-53; fellow clin. pedodontia Guggenheim Dental Clinic, N.Y.C., 1953-54; dentist 7100th Hosp., USAF, 1954-56; research asst. Mobil Oil Co., Dallas, 1957-62; sr. research scientist Biometrics Instrument Corp., Plano, Tex., 1962-64; pres. Electro-Aerosol Inst., Plano, Tex.; dir. Electro-Aerosol Therapy Center, 1964-67; prof., chmn. dept. sci. U. Plano, Tex., 1966-67; sr. research scientist, biology dept. Battelle Pacific Northwest Labs., Richland, Wash., 1967-78; mgr. environ. and indsl. toxicology Battelle Pacific Northwest Labs., 1978-80, task leader indsl. toxicology, 1980—; Cons. VA Hosp., McKinney, Tex., 1963-65; chmn., guest speaker 16 internat. sci. congresses and symposia. Author: From Hitler Youth to U.S. Citizenship, 1972; more than 90 sci. publs., including chpts. to books.; reviewer various sci. jours.; patentee in field. Fellow Internat. Soc. Med. Hydrology, Tex. Acad. Sci.; mem. AAAS, Am. Inst. Med. Climatology (bd. dirs. 1972—, sec. 1972-83, pres. 1984—), Pacific NW Assn. Toxicologists, Internat. Soc. Biometeorology (U.S. rep. 1972-80), Soc. Exptl. Biology and Medicine, Internat. Soc. Aerosols in Medicine (mem. exec. bd. 1970-80), Dallas County Dental Soc. (hon.), Internat. Assn. Aerobiology, Sigma Xi. Office: Battelle Pacific Northwest Labs Biology and Chemistry Dept PO Box 999 Richland WA 99352

WEHR, C. TIMOTHY, chemist; b. San Francisco, Feb. 15, 1943; s. Carl Henry and Rosemary (Angelo) W.; m. Carol Meyer, Mar. 20, 1966; children: Michael Stephen, Kevin Christopher. BA, Whitman Coll., 1965; PhD, Oreg. State U., 1969. Postdoctoral fellow U. Calif., Davis, 1969-71; research assoc. U. Calif., Berkeley, 1971-74; research dir. AgriSci. Labs., Los Angeles, 1974-78; applications chemist Varian Assocs., Walnut Creek, Calif., 1978-80, mgr. liquid chromatography applications lab., 1980—; co. chmn. sci. com. Internat. Symposium on HPLC Proteins, Peptides and Polynucleotides, 1981—; exec. dir., 1984. Guest editor, mem. edit bd. various sci. jours. Bd. govs. Topanga (Calif.) Community House, 1977-78. Grantee Jane Coffin Child's Meml. Fund, 1969-71, Ford Found., 1964. Mem. AAAS, Am. Soc. Biol. Chemistry. Avocations: winemaking, automobile restoration. Home: 706 Gateview Dr Albany CA 94706 Office: Varian Instruments 2700 Mitchell Dr Walnut Creek CA 94598

WEHR, HERBERT MICHAEL, agricultural specialist; b. San Francisco, Feb. 15, 1943; s. Carl Henry and Rosemary (Angelo) W.; m. Nancy Briggs, Dec. 19, 1967; 1 dau., Anne Michelle. Student, U. Calif., Davis, 1961-63; BS, U. Calif., Berkeley, 1966; MS, Oreg. State U., 1968, PhD, 1972. Supr food sci. microbiology lab. services Oreg. Dept. Agr., Salem, 1971-74, asst. adminstr. lab. services, 1974-78, adminstr., dir. lab. services, 1978-84, chmn. Pesticide Analysis Response Ctr., 1984—; chmn. Oreg. Adv. Com. on Synthetic Chems. in the Environment, Oreg. Interagy. Pesticides Com., 1980—, Oreg. State Agy. Lab. Consortium, 1979—; chmn. sci. adv. commn. Dairy Research Found., 1986—. Mem. Assn. Ofcl. Analytical Chemists (planning com., internat. rep., chmn. ofcl. methods bd.), Inst. Food Technologists, Am. Pub. Health Assn. (com. standard methods for examination of dairy products), Nat. Conf. Interstate Milk Shipments (lab. com.), Am. Chem. Soc., Internat. Assn. Milk, Food and Environ. Sanitarians, Council Agrl. Sci. and Tech. Home: 460 Superior St S Salem OR 97302 Office: 635 Capitol NE Salem OR 97310

WEHRLY, JOSEPH MALACHI, mfg. co. exec.; b. County Armagh, Ireland, Oct. 2, 1915; s. Albert and Mary Josephine (Gribbon) W.; came to U.S., 1931, naturalized, 1938; student Los Angeles City Coll., evenings 1947-49; certificate indsl. relations U. Calif. at Berkeley Extension, 1957; m. Margaret Elizabeth Banks, July 3, 1946; children—Joseph Michael, Kathleen Margaret, Stephen Patrick. Mgr. interplant relations Goodyear Tire & Rubber Co., Los Angeles, 1935-42; dir. indsl. relations Whittaker Corp., Los Angeles, 1946-60, Meletron Corp., Los Angeles, 1960-61; asst. indsl. relations mgr. Pacific Airmotive Corp., Burbank, Calif., 1961-63; personnel mgr. Menasco Mfg. Co., Burbank, 1963-66; indsl. relations adminstr. Internat. Electronic Research, Burbank, 1966; dir. indsl. relations Adams Rite Industries, Inc., Glendale, Calif., 1966-75, cons., 1975-76; personnel mgr. TOTCO div. Baker Internat. Corp., Glendale, 1975-80; instr. indsl. relations and supervision Los Angeles Pierce Coll., 1949-76. Served with U.S. Army, 1942-46. Mem. Personnel and Indsl. Relations Assn., Mchts. and Mfrs. Assn. Republican. Roman Catholic. Home: 4925 Swinton Ave Encino CA 91436

WEI, JULIE LEE, science writer, editor; b. Shanghai, Republic of China; came to U.S., 1956.; d. Chih-fu and Lilian (Lay) Lee; m. Ta-hsien Wei (dec.). MA in Eng. Lit., Fordham U.; MA in Chinese Lit., U. Mich. Sr. sci. writer Univ. Mich., Ann Arbor, 1978-85; editor "Inside SRI" SRI Internat., Menlo Park, Calif., 1985—. Editor U. Mich. Research News, 1978-81. Mem. Nat. Assn. Sci. Writers. Home: 11 Agua Vista Ct Redwood City CA 94062 Office: SRI Internat 333 Ravenswood Menlo Park CA 94025

WEIDE, WILLIAM WOLFE, housing and recreational vehicles manufacturer; b. Toledo, Aug. 19, 1923; s. Samuel and Pearl Celia (Weide) W.; m. Beatrice Lieberman, June 4, 1950; children: Brian Samuel, Bruce Michael, Robert Benjamin. Student, U. Toledo, 1942, Marquette U., 1943-44; B.S., U. So. Calif., 1949. Asst. controller Eldon Mfg., 1950; mem. Calif. Franchise Tax Bd., 1951; controller Sutone Corp., 1951-53; treas. Descoware Corp., 1953-58; sr. v.p., dir. Fleetwood Enterprises, Inc., Riverside, Calif., 1958-73, pres., chief exec. officer, 1973-81, vice chmn., 1982—, dir.; treas. So. Eastern Manufactured Housing Inst., Atlanta. Mem. City of Riverside Housing Com.; mem. exec. com. of policy adv. bd. Joint Center for Urban Studies, Harvard-MIT, Cambridge; trustee City of Hope Hosp., Duarte, Calif.; Orange County chmn. United Jewish Welfare Fund, 1982-83; mem. Pres.'s Circle of U. So. Calif.; pres. Orange County Jewish Community Found., 1987—. Served with USNR, 1942-46, PTO. Recipient Jack E. Wells Meml. award for service to manufactured housing industry, 1976; named to Recreational Vehicle/Manufactured Housing Industry Hall of Fame Elkhart, Ind., 1981; named Man of Yr., City of Hope, 1986. Mem. Nat. Assn. Accts. (past v.p., dir. Los Angeles and Orange County chpt.), Manufactured Housing Inst. (chmn., founding com. Calif. chpt. 1986), Western Manufactured Housing Inst. (vice-chmn.), Trailer Coach Assn., NAM (public affairs com.), Riverside C. of C. Office: Fleetwood Enterprises Inc 3125 Myers St Riverside CA 92523

WEIDMANN, VICTOR HUGO, civil engineer; b. N.Y.C., Mar. 25, 1926; s. Victor Hugo and Dorothy Gilroe (Caldwell) W.; m. Judy Larue Henry, Oct. 2, 1982; children—Donna Lynn, Lisa Marlene, Suzanne V. B.S. in Civil Engring., Northeastern U., 1953. Registered profl. engr., Colo., Wyo., Ind., Nebr. registered land surveyor, Colo., Ind. cert. wastewater treatment plant operator, Class IV, Ind. diplomate Am. Acad. Environ. Engrs. Safety engr. Am. Associated Ins. Cos., N.Y.C., 1948-49; jr. detailer and cold test engr. Raytheon Mfg. Co., Waltham, Mass., 1949-50; survey party chief Harry Feldman, Boston, 1950-53; engr. U.S. Steel Corp., Pitts., 1953-54, Gary, Ind., 1954-56; assoc., br. mgr. Hurst-Rosche & Assos., Gary, 1956-63; owner, mgr. Weidmann Engring., Gary and Hobart, Ind., 1963-73; ptnr., v.p. James H. Stewart & Assocs., Inc., Ft. Collins, Colo., 1973-81; owner and prin. Weidmann Engring., Longmont, Colo., 1981—. Engring. works include Oak Knoll Terr. Housing Devel, Gary, 1966, Constrn. Engring. Twin Pipeline Arch Bridge over Ship Canal, Romeoville, Ill., 1971, Central Relief Sewer System, Terre Haute, Ind., 1962, Water and Sewer Systems, Black Butte Coal Mine, Point of Rocks, Wyo., 1977. Active Community Chest. Served with USCG, 1943-46, CBI, ETO, NATOUSA, MTO, PTO. Fellow ASCE (pres. N.W. br. Ind. sect. 1968-69), Am. Cons. Engrs. Council (nat. dir., Colo. chmn. govt. affairs advisory program); mem. Am. Water Works Assn., Am. Arbitration Assn. (nat. panel), Am., Rocky Mountain quarter horse assns., Nat. Rifle Assn. Lodges: Shriners, Masons. Home: 18 Ash Ct Apt 6 Longmont CO 80501

WEIGAND, WILLIAM KEITH, bishop; b. Bend, Oreg., May 23, 1937. Ed., Mt. Angel Sem., St. Benedict, Oreg., St. Edward's Sem. and St. Thomas Sem., Kenmore, Wash. Ordained priest Roman Catholic Ch., 1963; ordained bishop of Salt Lake City 1980. Office: Pastoral Ctr 27 C St Salt Lake City UT 84103

WEIGEND, GUIDO GUSTAV, geographer, educator; b. Zeltweg, Austria, Jan. 2, 1920; came to U.S., 1939, naturalized, 1943; s. Gustav F. and Paula (Sorgo) W.; m. Areta Kelble, June 26, 1947; children: Nina, Cynthia, Kenneth. B.S., U. Chgo., 1942, M.S., 1946, Ph.D., 1949. With OSS, 1943-45; with mil. intelligence U.S. War Dept., 1946; instr. geography U. Ill., Chgo., 1946-47; instr. then asst. prof. geography Beloit Coll., 1947-49; asst. prof. geography Rutgers U., 1949-51, assoc. prof., 1951-57, prof., 1957-76, acting dept. chmn., 1951-52, chmn. dept., 1953-67, assoc. dean, 1972-76; dean Coll. Liberal Arts, Prof. geography Ariz. State U., Tempe, 1976-83, prof. geography, 1976—; Fulbright lectr. U. Barcelona, 1960-61; vis. prof. geography Columbia U., 1963-67, NYU, 1967, U. Colo., summer 1968, U. Hawaii, summer 1969; liaison rep. Rutgers U. to UN, 1950-52; mem. U.S. nat. com. Internat. Geog. Union, 1951-58, 61-65; chmn. Conf. on Polit. and Social Geography, 1968-69. Author articles, monographs, bulls. for profl. jours.; contbr.: (4th edit.) A Geography of Europe, 1977; geog. editor-in-chief: Odyssey World Atlas, 1966. Bd. adjustment, Franklin Twp., N.J., 1959; mem. Bd. Edn., Highland Park, N.J., 1973-75, v.p., 1975; mem. Ariz. Humanities Council, 1976-80, Phoenix Com. on Fgn. Relations (vice-chmn. 1976-79, chmn., 1979-81), exec. com. Fedn. Pub. Programs in Humanities, 1977-82; mem. exec. bd. Fedn. Pub. Programs in Humanities, 1980-83; bd. dirs. Council Colls. Arts and Scis., 1980-83. Research fellow Office Naval Research, 1952-55, Rutgers Research Council, 1970-71; grantee Social Sci. Research Council, 1956, Ford Found., 1966, Am. Philos. Soc., 1970-71, German Acad. Exchange Service, 1984; Fulbright travel grantee Netherlands, 1970-71. Mem. Assn. Am. Geographers (chmn. N.Y. Met. div. 1955-56, editorial bd. 1955-59, mem. council 1965-66, chmn. N.Y.-N.J. div. 1965-66), Am. Geog. Soc., Assn. Pacific Coast Geographers, North Cen. Assn. Colls. and Schs. (comm. instns. higher edn. 1980-83, exec. com. fedn. pub. programs in humanities 1977-82, Ariz. counicl humanities and pub. policy 1976-80; commr. 1976-80), Am. Geog. Soc., German Studies Assn., Sigma Xi. Home: 2094 E Golf Ave Tempe AZ 85282 Office: Arizona State U Coll Liberal Arts & Scis Tempe AZ 85287 *

WEIGLE, WILLIAM OLIVER, immunologist, educator; b. Monaca, Pa., Apr. 28, 1927; s. Oliver James and Caroline Ellen (Alsing) W.; m. Kathryn May Lotz, Sept. 4, 1948 (div. 1980); children—William James, Cynthia Kay; m. Carole G. Romball. B.S., U. Pitts., 1950, M.S., 1951, Ph.D., 1956. Research assoc. pathology U. Pitts., 1955-58, asst. prof. immunochemistry, 1959-61; assoc. div. exptl. pathology Scripps Clinic and Research Found., LaJolla, Calif., 1961-62, assoc. mem. div., 1962-63, mem. dept. exptl. pathology, 1963-74, mem. dept. immunopathology, 1974-82, chmn. dept. immunopathology, 1980-82, mem., vice chmn. dept. immunology, 1982-85, chmn. dept. immunology, 1985—; adj. prof. biology U. Calif., San Diego; McLaughlin vis. prof. U. Tex., 1977; cons. in field. Author: Natural and Acquired Immunologic Unresponsiveness, 1967; assoc. editor: Clin. and Exptl. Immunology, 1972-79; Jour. Exptl. Medicine, 1974-84; Immunochemistry 1964-71; Procs. Soc. Exptl. Biology and Medicine, 1967-72; Jour. Immunology, 1967-71; Infection and Immunity, 1969—; sect. editor: Jour. Immunology, 1971-75; editorial bd.: Contempoaray Topics in Immunobiology, 1971—; Cellular Immunology, 1983—; contbr. articles to profl. jours. Served with USNR, 1945-46. Pub. Health Research fellow, Nat. Inst. Neurol. Diseases and Blindness, 1956-59; NIH sr. research fellow, 1959-61, Research Career award, 1962. Mem. Am. Assn. Immunologists, Am. Soc. Exptl. Pathology (Parke Davis award 1967), Am. Soc. Microbiology, N.Y. Acad. Scis., Am. Acad. Allergy, Western Assn. Clin. Research, Am. Assn. Pathologists, Soc. Exptl. Biology and Medicine. Home: 14018 Mango Dr Del Mar CA 92014 Office: Scripps Clinic Dept Immunology IMM9 10666 N Torrey Pines Rd La Jolla CA 92037

WEIHAUPT, JOHN GEORGE, scientist, university administrator; b. La Crosse, Wis., Mar. 5, 1930; s. John George and Gladys Mae (Ash) W.; m. Audrey Mae Reis, Jan. 28, 1961. Student, St. Norbert Coll., De Pere, Wis., 1948-49; B.S., U. Wis., 1952, M.S., 1953; M.S., U. Wis.-Milw., 1971; Ph.D., U. Wis., 1973. Exploration geologist Am. Smelting & Refining Co., Nfld., 1953, Anaconda Co., Chile, S.Am., 1956-57; seismologist United Geophys. Corp., 1958; geophysicist Arctic Inst. N. Am., Antarctica, 1958-60, Geophys. and Polar Research Center, U. Wis., Antarctica, 1960-63; dir. participating Coll. and Univ. program, chmn. dept. phys. and biol. sci. U.S. Armed Forces Inst., Dept. Def., 1963-73; assoc. dean for acad. affairs Sch. Sci., Ind. U.-Purdue U., Indpls., 1973-78; prof. geology Sch. Sci., Ind. U.-Purdue U., 1973-78; asst. dean (Grad. Sch., prof. geoscis. Purdue U.), 1975-78; prof. geology, assoc. acad. v.p., dean grad. studies and research, v.p. Univ. Research Found., San Jose (Calif.) State U., 1978-82; vice chancellor for acad. affairs U. Colo., Denver, 1982—; Sci. cons., mem. sci. adv. bd. Holt Reinhart and Winston, Inc., 1967—; sci. editor, cons. McGraw-Hill Co., 1966—; hon. lectr. U. Wis., 1963-73; geol. cons., 1968—; editorial cons. John Wiley & Sons, 1968; editorial adv. bd. Dushkin Pub. Group, 1971—. Author: Exploration of the Oceans: An Introduction to Oceanography; mem. editorial bd. Internat. Jour. Interdisciplinary Cycle Research, Leiden. Mem. Capital Community Citizens Assn.; mem. Madison Transp. Study Com., Found. for Internat. Energy Research and Tng.; U.S. com. for UN Univ.; mem. sci. council Internat. Center for Interdisciplinary Cycle Research; mem. Internat. Awareness and Leadership Council; mem. governing bd. Moss Landing Marine Labs.; bd. dirs. San Jose State U. Found. Served as 1st lt. AUS, 1953-55, Korea. Mt. Weihaupt in Antarctica named for him, 1966; recipient Madisonian medal for outstanding community service, 1973; Outstanding Cote Meml. award, 1974; Antarctic medal, 1968. Fellow Geol. Soc. Am., Explorers Club; mem. Antarctican Soc., Nat. Sci. Tchrs. Assn., Am. Geophys. Union, Internat. Council Corr. Edu., Soc. Am. Mil. Engrs., Wis. Alumni Assn., Soc. Study Biol. Rhythms, Internat. Soc. for Chronobiology, Marine Tech. Soc., AAAS, Univ. Indsl. Adv. Council, Am. Council on Edn., Expdn. Polaire France (hon.), Found. for Study Cycles, Assn. Am. Geographers, Nat. Council Univ. Research Adminstrs., Soc. Research Adminstrs., Man-Environ. Communication Center, Internat. Union Geol. Scis., Internat. Geog. Union, Internat. Soc. Study Time, Community Council Pub. TV, Internat. Platform Assn., Ind., Midwest assns. grad. schs., Western Assn. Grad. Schs., Council Grad. Schs. in U.S., Wis. Alumni Assn. of San Francisco. Clubs: Carmel Racquet (Rinconada Racquet); Kiwanis. Codiscoverer USARP Mountain Range (Arctic Inst. Mountain Range), in Victoria Land, Antartica, 1960; discoverer Wilkes Land Meteorite Crater, Antarctica. Home: 23906 Currant Dr Golden CO 80401 Office: Univ of Colorado at Denver 1100 14th St Denver CO 80202

WEIHRICH, HEINZ, management educator. came to U.S., 1959; s. Paul and Anna Weihrich; m. Ursula Weihrich, Aug. 3, 1963. BS, UCLA, 1966, MBA, 1967, PhD, 1973. Assoc. Grad. Sch. Mgmt. UCLA, 1968-73; from asst. to assoc. prof. Ariz. State U., Tempe, 1973-80; prof. mgmt. U. San Francisco, 1980—. Author: Management Excellence--Productivity Through MBO, 1985; co-author: Management, 8th rev. edit., 1984, Essentials of Management, 4th rev. edit., 1986, Management Basiswissen, 1986; contbr. numerous articles and papers to profl. publs. Grantee Am. Mgmt. Assn., 1970. Mem. Acad. Mgmt., Assn. Mgmt. Excellence (trustee 1985—), Assn. Bus. Simulation Exptl. Learning, Acad. Internat. Bus., Beta Gamma Sigma, Sigma Iota Epsilon. Roman Catholic. Office: U San Francisco Ignatian Heights San Francisco CA 94117-1080

WEIKEL, CHARLES PORTER, gerontologist; b. Troy, N.Y., Nov. 14, 1913; s. Charles Byers Weikel and Anita Inez Lugar; m. Miriam Louise Ogburn, Dec. 23, 1939; children: Susan Morrison, Wendy Madeline. AB, U. Calif., Berkeley, 1939; postgrad., U.S. Naval Acad., 1943, Am. U., 1950. From field rep. to asst. regional rep. Social Security Adminstrn., various locations, 1939-42, 47-64; regional dir. U.S. Adminstrn. Aging, San Francisco, 1964-70; v.p., dir. Retirement Housing Found., Long Beach, Calif., 1968-78; writer, cons. retirement planning Little River, Calif., 1978—; syndicated columnist, 1965-78; mem. adv. com. Coll. of The Redwoods. Contbr. articles to publs. Served with USMC, 1932-40, USN, 1942-46, PTO, lt. comdr. USNR ret. Mem. Marine's Meml. Assn., Navy League, Naval Res. Assn., Am. Radio Relay League, Calif. Alumni Assn., Social Security Alumni Assn., European Fedn. Welfare of Elderly (conf. del.), Park Hills Homes Assn. (pres. 1973-78, cert. appreciation 1960, 78), Delta Phi Epsilon, Epsilon Chi (pres. 1939, pres. NOCA alumni chpt. 1940-41). Home: PO Box E Little River CA 95456

WEIL, ANDREW THOMAS, physician; b. Phila., June 8, 1942; s. Daniel Pythias and Jenny (Silverstein) W. BA, Harvard U., 1964, MD, 1968. Intern Mt. Zion Hosp. Med. Ctr., San Francisco, 1968-69; assoc. Harvard Bot. Mus., Cambridge, Mass., 1971-84; fellow Inst. Current World Affairs, N.Y.C., 1971-75; lectr. U. Ariz., Tucson, 1983—; pres. Beneficial Plant Research Inst., Sausalito, Calif., 1979—; wellness counselor Canyon Ranch SPA, Tucson, 1985—. Author: Natural Mind, 1972, Marriage of the Sun and Moon, 1980, Chocolate to Morphine, 1983, Health and Healing, 1984. Served to lt. USPHS, 1969-70. Fellow Linnean Soc. London; mem. Sigma Xi. Democrat. Buddhist. Avocations: gardening, backpacking. Home: 1975 W Hunter Rd Tucson AZ 85737 Office: Ariz Health Scis Ctr Coll Medicine Rm 2102 1501 N Campbell Ave Tucson AZ 85724

WEIL, STUART JAMES, lawyer, accountant; b. Cleve., July 31, 1954; s. Bert S. and Marilyn Rose (Dworkin) W. Student, U. Mich., 1972-75; BS, Case Western Reserve, 1976, JD, 1981. Bar: Ohio, Calif. Acct. Berkman, CS&S, Cleve., 1977-78; lawyer Forest City Ent., Cleve., 1981-82; sole practice San Francisco, 1983—. Mem. Calif. State Bar Assn. (vols. in parole 1985—, vol. legal services program, 1985—). Avocations: swimming, numismatics, film, literature. Home: 601 24th Ave #301 San Francisco CA 94121 Office: 433 California St 11th Floor San Francisco CA 94104

WEILENMAN, JAMES AUSTIN, textile executive; b. Red Oak, Iowa, Sept. 5, 1933; s. Homer James and Lucille (Stover) W.; m. Bonnie Linda Bennett, Feb. 19, 1966. AB in Psychology, Stanford U., 1955; postgrad., U. So. Calif., 1958-60, Calif. State U., Los Angeles, 1960-66. With engring. dept. N.Am. Aviation, Inc., Los Angeles, 1955-60; unit supr., field rep. disability ins. div. Dept. Employment State of Calif., Los Angeles, 1960-66; office mgr., adminstr. State Mut. Am., Los Angeles, 1966-70; personnel mgr. Lewis Foods Nat. Can Corp., Long Beach, Calif., 1970-72, Kern Foods, Inc., City of Industry, Calif., 1972-81; plant personnel mgr. Star-Kist Foods, Inc., Terminal Island, Calif., 1981-83; apparel industry ofcl. Sirena, Inc., South El Monte, Calif., 1984—; v.p. Calif. State Employees Assn., 1960-66; trustee Fish Canners-United Cannery and Indsl. Workers Union Health and Pension trust funds, 1981-83. Mem. West San Gabriel Valley Mayor's Com. for Employment of Handicapped, 1978; advisor M&M Assn. Personnel Practices Com., 1975-77; advisor-employer adv. com., Employment Devel. Dept., State of Calif., 1974—; exec. com. officer council advisors on re-employment of ex-offenders State of Calif. Dept. Corrections, 1981—; employer advisor apparel arts dept. Los Angeles Trade Tech. Coll., 1984—; scoutmaster South Bay council Boy Scouts Am., 1951-52, scoutmaster Explorer Scouts, 1953. Served with U.S. Army, 1956-58. Recipient spl. citation El Monte Police Dept., 1976-78, Pub. Service award State Calif. Employment Devel. Dept., 1984. Mem. Personnel and Indsl. Relations Assn. (dist. chmn. 1971, dir. 1970-74, citation; chmn. ann. conf. 1973, 86, 87), Am. Soc. Personnel Adminstrn., Industry Personnel Council (chmn. 1977-81), Alpha Phi Omega. Republican. Mem. Christian Ch. Club: Brea Glenbrook. Avocations: art in oils, pen and ink, cartoonist, designer cards. Office: Sirena Inc 10333 Vacco St South El Monte CA 91733

WEILER, DOROTHY ESSER, librarian; b. Hartford, Wis., Feb. 21, 1914; d. Henry Hugo and Agatha Christina (Dopp) Esser; A.B. in Fgn. Langs., Wash. State U., 1935; B.A.L., Grad. Library Sch., U. Wash., 1936; postgrad. U. Ariz., 1956-57, Ariz. State U., 1957-58, Grad. Sch. Librarianship, U. Denver, 1971; m. Henry C. Weiler, Aug. 30, 1937; children—Robert William, Kurt Walter. Tchr.-librarian Roosevelt Elem. Schs., Dist. #66, Phoenix, 1956-59; extension librarian Ariz. Dept. Library and Archives, Phoenix, 1959-67; library dir. City of Tempe (Ariz.), 1967-79; asso. prof., dept. library sci. Ariz. State U., 1968; vis. faculty Mesa Community Coll., 1980—. Mem. public relations com. United Fund; treas. Desert Samaritan Hosp. and Health Center Aux., 1981, v.p. community relations Hosp., 1982. Named Ariz. Librarian of Yr., 1971; recipient Silver Book award Library Binding Inst., 1963. Mem. Tempe Hist. Soc., Ariz. Pioneers Hist. Soc., Am. Radio Relay League, Am. Bus. Women's Assn., ALA, Southwestern Library Assn., Ariz. State Library Assn. (pres. 1973-74). Roman Catholic. Clubs: Our Lady of Mt. Carmel Ladies' Sodality, Soroptimist Internat. Founder, editor Roadrunner, Tumbling Tumbleweed; author Ency. Americana article on Tempe. Home: PO Box 26018 Tempe AZ 85282

WEILER, KRISTI PAULETTE, lawyer; b. San Francisco, Apr. 1, 1958; d. Paul Harry and Thelma Jane (Schwabenland) W. BA, Calif. State U., Fresno, 1981; JD, Pepperdine U., 1984. Bar: Calif. 1984, U.S. Dist. Ct. (so. dist.) Calif. 1985. Clk. to justice Calif. Ct. Appeals, Los Angeles, 1984-85; assoc. Law Offices of Stanley B. Mann, Encino, Calif., 1984-86; ptnr. Law Offices of Herman J. Isman, Encino, 1986—. Mem. ABA, Calif. Bar Assn., Los Angeles County Bar Assn., Assn. Trial Lawyers Am., Calif. Trial Lawyers Assn. Democrat. Avocations: equestrian competition, skiing. Office: Law Offices Herman J Isman 5435 Balboa Blvd #105 Encino CA 91316

WEILL, SAMUEL, JR., automobile company executive; b. Rochester, N.Y., Dec. 22, 1916; s. Samuel and Bertha (Stein) W.; student U. Buffalo, 1934-35; m. Mercedes Weil, May 20, 1939 (div. Aug. 1943); children—Rita and Eric (twins); m. Cléanthe Kimball Carr, Aug. 12, 1960 (div. 1982); m. Jacqueline Natalie Bateman, Jan. 5, 1983. Co-owner, Brayton Air Coll., St. Louis, 1937-42; assoc. editor, advt. mgr., bus. mgr. Road and Track Mag., Los Angeles, 1951-53; pres. Volkswagen Pacific, Inc., Culver City, Calif., 1953-73, Porsche Audi Pacific, Culver City, 1953-73; chmn. bd. Minto Internat., Inc., London; v.p. fin. Chieftain Oil Co., Ventura, Calif. Recipient Tom May award Jewish Hosp. and Research Center, 1971. Served with USAAF, 1943-45. Home: 305 Palomar Rd Ojai CA 93023 Office: 1787 Mesa Verde Ave Suite 201 Ventura CA 93003

WEIMER, SHERRY J., occupational safety and health manager; b. Santa Monica, Calif., 1945; d. John B. and Rayola (Calaway) W. BS, U. Utah, 1969. Office mgr. Naval Air Reserve Sta., Oak Harbor, Wash., 1970-72, Naval Engring. Service Unit, Oak Harbor, 1972-74; asst. safety officer Naval Air Sta. Whidbey Island, Oak Harbor, 1974-78; occupational safety and health mgr. USCG 17th dist., Juneau, Alaska, 1978-87. Author: District Safety Manual, 1982 (spl. achievement award 1983). Pres. Big Dipper Sq. Dance Club, Auke Bay, Alaska, 1986-87; defensive driving instr. Alaska Peace Officers Assn., Juneau, 1985—. Mem. Am. Soc. Safety Engrs., Assn. Fed. Safety and Health Profls., Nat. Safety Mgmt. Soc., Nat. Assn. Female Execs. Club: Toastmasters (Juneau). Home: PO Box 020121 Juneau AK 99802-0121

WEIN, JERRY DOUGLAS, career military officer; b. Ingelwood, Calif., July 25, 1951; s. Jerry Clifford Wein and Glenna Jeana (Lopez) Fullerton; m. Alunya Wein, Nov. 15, 1974; children: Gregory, Sandra. B in Aerospace Engring., U. So. Calif. Enlisted USAF, 1970; sgt. in avionics maint. USAF, Bergestrom AFB, Tex., 1970-73; with avionics maint. squadron USAF, Udorn AFB, Thailand, 1973-75; with quality control div. USAF, Beale AFB, Calif., 1975-81; commd. 2d lt. USAF, 1984, advanced through grades to lt.; engr. missile div. USAF, Hill AFB, Utah, 1984—. Recipient John Laufer Meml. award U. So. Calif., Los Angeles, 1984, Logistice Mgmt. award Soc. Logistics Engrs., Ogden, Utah, 1985. Mem. Co. Grade Officers Council, Air Force Assn. (Auisition Logistics award 1986). Republican. Avocations: computer hardware and software design, water skiing, racquetball. Office: USAF Logistics Command OO-ALC/MMGXS Hill AFB UT 84056

WEIN, LIBBY (LILLIAN) RAPHAEL, social worker; b. Phila., Feb. 23, 1934; d. Samuel and Esther (Terry) Raphael; m. Joseph Alexander Wein, June 23, 1957; children: Michele Georgeanne, Paul Frederick. Cert., Franklin Sch. Sci. and Arts, 1955; AA, Santa Monica Coll., 1969; BA cum laude, UCLA, 1976; MSW, U. So. Calif., 1981. Lic. social work, Calif. Med. social worker Midway Hosp., Los Angeles, 1981-82; psychotherapist Airport Marina Counseling Service, Los Angeles, 1981-83; geriatric, psychiat. social worker Sr. Health and Peer Counseling Ctr., Santa Monica, Calif., 1983—; cons. Cedars-Sinai, Los Angeles, 1978, case mgr., 1979; ctr. fellow UCLA, U. So. Calif. Long Term Care Gerontology Ctr., 1985. Mem. Nat. Assn. Social Workers, Soc. Clin. Social Work. Avocation: dance study. Home: 324 S Clark Dr Beverly Hills CA 90211 Office: Sr Health & Peer Counseling Ctr 2125 Arizona Santa Monica CA 90404

WEINAND, GERALD ALLEN, architect; b. Warren, Mich., Sept. 12, 1948; s. Richard Gerald and Joan Rose (Geotz) W.; m. Gretchen Maricac, June 21, 1961 (dec. Mar. 1973); children: Michael Charles, Abra, Gregory Maricac. BArch, Lawrence Inst. Tech., 1960; MArch, Harvard U., 1964. Registered architect, Mich., N.Y., Calif., Eng. Architect apprentice SH&G, Detroit, 1958-61; assoc. designer Taft Architects, Boston, 1964-66; job capt. Roche & Dinkeloo, N.Y.C., 1967-74, SOM, Chgo., 1974-77; project architect Pflueger Architects, San Francisco, 1978-83; prin. in charge Weinand Architects, San Francisco, 1983—; design cons. Super-Graphique, San Francisco, 1981—. Author: Fun With Lego's, 1968; contbg. editor (jour.) San Francisco Archtl. Jour., 1984-86; writer, dir. (film) The Thing That Wouldn't Move, 1972. Planning commr. City of Oak Park, Ill., 1976-77. Recipient Jury award Chgo. chpt. AIA, 1975, Citation, Progressive Architecture, 1982. Mem. San Francisco Archtl. Soc. Democrat. Club: Pencil Pointers (Berkeley). Avocations: painting, sketching, ukulele, horseback riding, hang gliding.

WEINBERG, LAWRENCE, professional basketball team owner. Owner, formerly pres. Portland Trail Blazers, Nat. Basketball Assn., Oreg. Office: care Portland Tr Blazers 700 NE Multnomah St Suite 950 Lloyd Bldg Portland OR 97232 *

WEINBERG, OFRA, education director; b. Jerusalem, Sept. 28, 1949; came to U.S., 1971; d. Avraham and Margalit (Levy) Zadok; m. Norbert Weinberg, Oct. 24, 1971; children: Danit, Adi, Eran. Student, David Yellin Tchrs. Coll., Jerusalem; pub. relations cert., UCLA; postgrad., Pacific Oaks. Youth edn. dir. Temple Rodef Sholom, Newport News, Va., 1977-80; edn. dir. Temple Beth Sholom, Whittier, Calif., 1980-85; interim prin. Atid Hebrew Acad., Covina, Calif., 1985—. Mem. Conf. for Alternatives in Jewish Edn., Bur. Jewish Edn. (cert.). Avocation: art. Home: 13667 Dicky Whittier CA 90605 Office: Atid Hebrew Acad 1220 E Ruddock Covina CA 91724

WEINBERG, STEPHEN LEE, physics educator; b. Rochester, N.Y., Sept. 17, 1947; s. Sydney A. and Edith Weinberg. PhD, U. Calif., Berkeley, 1976. With physics and astronomy depts. U. Calif., Berkeley, 1969-75; with Physics and Astrophysics Inst., Munich, Republic of Germany, 1976; with chemistry, astronomy, math., physics dept. Berkeley Acad. Artsci., 1977—. Mem. Israel Math. Union, Polish Math. Soc., Am. Math. Soc., Am. Phys. Soc., Math. Assn. Am., MIT Faculty Club, U. Calif. Faculty Club. Clubs: U. Calif. Amateur Radio, Calif. Sailing Club (Berkeley). Office: Berkeley Acad Artsci 48 Shattuck Square Bin 76 Berkeley CA 94704 Address: U Rochester PO Box 29112 Rochester NY 14627

WEINBRANDT, RICHARD M., petroleum engineering consultant; b. July 20, 1944. B.S. in Mech. Engring., U. Calif.-Berkeley, 1967, M.S. in Mech. Engring., 1968; Ph.D. in Petroleum Engring., Stanford U., 1972. Pres. EORCO and Hoback Oil Co., Jackson, Wyo. Contbr. articles to profl. jours. Mem. Soc. Petroleum Engrs., Am. Petroleum Inst., Petroleum Soc. of Can. Inst. Mining and Metallurgy. Home: Skyline Ranch Box 20 Jackson WY 83001

WEINER, DORA B., medical humanities educator; b. Furth, Germany, 1924; d. Ernest and Emma (Metzger) Bierer; m. Herbert Weiner, 1953; children—Timothy, Richard, Antony. Baccalaureat, U. Paris, 1941; B.A. magna cum laude, Smith Coll., 1945; M.A., Columbia U., 1946, Ph.D., 1951. Lectr. gen. studies Columbia U., N.Y.C., 1949-50, instr., 1950-52, vis. lectr. Tchrs. Coll., 1962-63; instr. Barnard Coll., 1952-56; fellow in history of medicine Johns Hopkins U., Balt., 1956-57; mem. faculty dept. social sci. Sarah Lawrence Coll., 1958-62; asst. prof. history Manhattanville Coll., 1964-65, assoc. prof., 1966-78, prof., 1978-82; adj. prof. med. humanities UCLA Sch. Medicine, Los Angeles, 1982—; cons. and lectr. in field. Author: Raspail: Scientist and Reformer, 1968; The Clinical Training of Doctors: An Essay of 1793, 1980; co-editor: From Parnassus; Essays in Honor of Jacques Barzun, 1976; contbr. chpts. to books, articles to profl. jours. Grantee numerous profl. and ednl. instns. Mem. Am. Hist. Assn. (nominating com. 1979-82, Leo Gershoy award com. 1985—), AAUP, Am. Assn. History Medicine (past mem. numerous coms.), Soc. 18th Century Studies, Soc. for French Hist. Studies (exec. com. 1978-81), History of Sci. Soc. Office: UCLA 12-138 Ctr for Health Scis Los Angeles CA 90024

WEINER, ELLEN LUSTBADER, administrative assistant; b. Newark, June 2, 1947; d. Edwin Ira and Estelle (Farkash) Lustbader; m. Stewart George Weiner, Feb. 14, 1986. Student, Parsons Coll., 1965-67; grad., Katharine Gibbs Sch., 1968. Pvt. sec.to Jane Fonda, Hollywood, Calif., 1969-74, 75-76; pvt. sec. to Faye Dunaway, Hollywood, 1974-75, Lee Strasberg, N.Y. and Calif., 1976-77; asst. to v.p. The Lantz Office, Los Angeles, 1979—. Home: 8939 Keith Los Angeles CA 90069 Office: The Lantz Office 9255 Sunset Blvd Los Angeles CA 90069

WEINER, HERBERT, psychiatry educator; b. Vienna, Austria, Feb. 6, 1921; came to U.S., 1939; s. Ludwig and Hedwig Blanche (Monath) W.; m. Dora Bierer, Nov. 27, 1953; children: Timothy E., Richard A., Anthony P. AB magna cum laude, Harvard U., 1943; MD, Columbia U., 1946. Prof. psychiatry Albert Einstein Coll. Medicine, N.Y.C., 1966-82, chmn. dept. psychiatry Montefiore Hosp. Med. Ctr., 1969-82, prof. neurosci., 1974-82, Melitta Sperling lectr., 1982; chief behavioral medicine UCLA, 1982, dir. clin. research tng., dept. psychiatry, 1982, prof. psychiatry, 1982; cons. VA Wadsworth Med. Ctr., Los Angeles, 1982, VA Med. Ctr., Sepulveda, Calif., 1982, VA Brentwood (Calif.) Med. Ctr., 1984. Author: Psychobiology and Human Disease, 1977, Brain, Behavior & Bodily Disease, 1981. Research grantee NIMH, 1976-86, John D. and Catherine T. MacArthur Found., 1983—. Fellow Am. Psychiat. Assn., N.Y. Acad. Medicine; mem. Acad. Behavioral Med. Research (founder, pres. 1983-84), Internat. Coll. Psychosomatic Medicine (founder, pres. 1983), Los Angeles Psychoanalytic Soc. and Instn. Office: UCLA Adult Psychiatry 760 Westwood Plaza Los Angeles CA 90024

WEINER, ROBERTA HELENE, social worker; b. Pitts., Feb. 20, 1936; d. Daniel and Florence (Neil) W. BA, U. Miami, 1958; MSW, UCLA, 1977. Lic. clin. social worker. Children's services worker Dept. Pub. Social Services, Los Angeles, 1967-74, adminstrv. social worker, 1974-75; psychiat. social worker Dept. Mental Health, Los Angeles, 1977-81; program dir. Aviva Ctr., Los Angeles, 1981-87; clin. social worker Daniel Freeman Hosp., 1982-84; psychotherapist Children's Hosp., Los Angeles, 1985—; dir. treatment svcs. Fred Finch Youth Ctr., 1987—. Bd. dirs. Allen Ave. Square North Condominium Assn., Pasadena, Calif, 1985-86, pres; soloist Cambridge Singers, 1984-86. Mem. Nat. Assn. Social Workers.

WEINGARTEN, VICTOR I., engineering educator; b. N.Y.C., Jan. 18, 1931; s. Arnold and Sophia (Dickerman) W.; m. Myrna Marcia Rosenthal, July 31, 1954; children: Scott, Barbara. BME, CCNY, 1952; MSME, NYU, 1954; PhD in Engring., UCLA, 1964. Prof. computer structural mechanics U. So. Calif., Los Angeles, 1964—; br. head, cons. Northrop Aircraft, Hawthorne, Calif., 1964-66; cons. Hughes Aircraft, Canoga Park, Calif., 1964-86, Rockwell Internat., El Segundo, Calif., 1983—; pres. Structural Research and Analysis Corp., Santa Monica, Calif., 1983—. Contbr. articles to profl. jours. Mem. ASME, ASCE. Office: Structural Research & Analysis Corp 1661 Lincoln Blvd Suite 100 Santa Monica CA 90404

WEINHAUER, CARLIN EUGENE, clergyman, college administrator, consultant; b. Wellsville, N.Y., Oct. 31, 1939; s. Henry Frank and Thelma Ethel (Campbell) W.; m. Marcia Arlene Watne, Aug. 11, 1962; children—Cheri, Lynda, Becky. B.A. in Bibl. Edn., Columbia Bible Coll., S.C., 1964; M.A. in Practical Theology, Chgo. Grad. Sch. Theology, 1971; M.A. in Christian Edn., Trinity Evang. Div. Sch., Deerfield, Ill., 1974; Ph.D. in Ednl. Adminstrn., U. Alta., Can., 1979. Ordained to ministry, 1964. Sr. pastor Mt. Olivet Bapt. Ch., Camden, S.C., 1963, 66; missionary Am. Mission Fellowship, Gt. Falls, Mont., 1966-67; minister edn. and youth Bethel Community Ch., Chgo., 1967-68; faculty Briercrest Bible Coll., Caronport, Sask., Can., 1969-79, v.p. pub. ministries, 1979-84; assoc. pastor leadership devel. Willingdon Ch., Burnaby, B.C., 1984-85; sr. pastor, 1986—; tchr. devel. sem. cons. Scripture Press, Whitby, Ont., Can., 1975—; mem. pub. relations commn. Am. Assn. Bible Colls., 1981-84. Grantee U. Alta., 1978; recipient service award Briercrest Bible Coll., 1984. Mem. Delta Epsilon Chi. Mem. Mennonite Brethren Ch. Home: 6818 Acacia Ave, Burnaby, BC Canada V5E 3J7 Office: Willingdon Ch, 4812 Willingdon Ave, Burnaby, BC Canada V5G 3H6

WEININGER, JEAN, nutrition writer, editor, consultant; b. N.Y.C., Dec. 18, 1945; d. Benjamin Ide and Katharine (Spahr) W. AB, Vassar Coll., 1967; MS, Columbia U., 1970; PhD, U. Calif., Berkeley, 1977. Nutritionist Linus Pauling Inst. of Sci. and Medicine, Menlo Park, Calif., 1971-73; nutrition cons. Soc. for Nutrition Edn., Berkeley, 1973-74; lectr. U. Calif., San Francisco, 1977-81; lectr. U. Calif., Berkeley, 1978, research fellow, 1978—; contract faculty mem. Calif. Sch. Profl. Psychology, Berkeley, 1979-80; pvt. practice cons. Berkeley, 1973—. Co-editor books Nutrition Update, vols. 1 and 2, 1983, 85; contbr. articles to profl. jours. Mem. Community Health

Advisory Com., Berkeley, 1977-85. Mem. Soc. for Nutrition Edn., AAAS, Phi Beta Kappa, Phi Tau Sigma, Iota Sigma Pi.

WEINLAND, STUART LOUIS, ceramic engineering researcher; b. Dayton, Ohio, Sept. 25, 1940; s. Louis Albert and Mazel Clara (Schott) W. BS, Alfred U., 1962; MS, Miss. State U., 1965; postgrad., U. N.Mex., 1967. Assoc. ceramic engr. The Babcock and Wilcox Co., Alliance, Ohio, 1962-63; scientist Lockheed Missiles and Space Co., Sunnyvale, Calif., 1965-67; sr. engr. Martin Marietta Corp., Orlando, Fla., 1968-70; sr. sci. assoc. Lawrence Livermore (Calif.) Lab., 1976—. Contbr. articles to profl. jours.; patentee in field. Mem. Am. Ceramic Soc. Office: Lawrence Livermore Nat Lab 7000 E Ave L-369 Livermore CA 94550

WEINPEL, MARC JOHN, lawyer; b. Passaic, N.J., Apr. 14, 1949; s. Joseph A. and Eleanor G. (Vogel) W.; m. Mary E. Hones, June 4, 1971 (div. June 1986); children: Joseph B., Scott M., Jonathan. BA in Polit. Sci., Creighton U., 1971, JD, 1973. Bar: Nebr. 1974, N.J. 1974, Idaho. 1979, U.S. Fed. Dist. Cts. Nebr. N.J., Idaho. Assoc. atty. J. Peter Davidow, Millville, N.J., Peetz, Peetz & Weinpel, Sidney, Nebr., 1975-78, Cox, Ohman & Weinpel, Idaho Falls, Idaho, 1978-80; sole practice Idaho Falls, 1980—; sr. ptnr. Weinpel, Woolf, Just, Combo & Davis, Idaho Falls. Bd. dirs. Holy Rosary Sch. Found., Idaho Falls. Served to maj. USAR. Mem. Idaho Trial Lawyers Assn., Assn. Trial Lawyers of Am. Democrat. Roman Catholic. Club: Idaho Falls Country (pres. 1986—). Home: 1463 Vega Circle Apt 8 Idaho Falls ID 83402 Office: Weinpel Woolf Just Combo et al 545 Shoup Ave Suite 227 Box 936 Idaho Falls ID 83402

WEINRACH, ROY SYLVAN, oncology physician; b. Phila., Apr. 24, 1930; s. Lewis Samuel and Jeannette Edith (Weintraub) W.; m. Judith Marcie Borens, Jan. 1, 1967; children: Jonathan, David, Joshua. AB, Temple U., 1951, AM, 1954; PhD, U. Chgo., 1957; MD, Northwestern U., 1961. Diplomate Am. Bd. Internal Medicine, Am. Bd. Hematology, Am. Bd. Oncology. Intern Phila. Gen. Hosp., 1961-62; resident, fellow Mt. Sinai Hosp., N.Y.C., 1965-67; sr. surgeon USPHS, Bethesda, Md., 1963-65; asst. prof. Med. Coll., Phila., 1967-68; practice medicine specializing in oncology, hematology Phoenix, 1968—; mem. teaching staff St. Joseph's Hosp. and Good Samaritan Hosp., Phoenix, 1968—. Contbr. articles to profl. jours. Fellow ACP; mem. Ariz. Med. Soc., AMA, Maricopa County Med. Soc., Alpha Omega Alpha. Republican. Jewish. Club: Roosevelt Rough Riders (Phoenix). Avocations: deep sea fishing, horseback riding, wine collecting. Office: Affiliated Oncologists Ltd 333 E Virginia #113 Phoenix AZ 65004

WEINSHIENK, ZITA LEESON, federal judge; b. St. Paul, Apr. 3, 1933; d. Louis and Ada (Dubov) Leeson; m. Hubert Troy Weinshienk, July 8, 1956 (dec. 1983); children: Edith Blair, Kay Anne, Darcy Jill; m. James N. Schaffner, Nov. 15, 1986. Student, U. Colo., 1952-53; B.A. magna cum laude, U. Ariz., 1955; J.D. cum laude, Harvard U., 1958; Fulbright grantee U. Copenhagen, Denmark, 1959. Bar: Colo. 1959. Probation counselor, legal adviser, referee Denver Juvenile Ct., 1959-64; judge Denver County Ct., 1964-71; Denver dist. judge 1972-79, U.S. dist. judge for dist. Colo., 1979—. Precinct com.-woman Denver Democratic Com., 1963-64; bd. dirs. Crime Stoppers. Named One of 100 Women in Touch with Our Time Harper's Bazaar Mag., 1971. Mem. ABA, Colo. Bar Assn., Denver Bar Assn., Nat. Conf. Fed. Trial Judges, Colo. Women's Bar Assn., Women's Forum of Colo., Harvard Law Sch. Assn., Denver League Women Voters, Soroptimist Club Denver, Bus. and Profl. Women's Club Denver (Woman of Yr. 1969), Order of Coif (hon. Colo. chpt.). Office: US District Court 1929 Stout St Rm C-246 Denver CO 80294

WEINSTEIN, CHARLES DAVID, psychologist; b. Los Angeles, Oct. 1, 1953; s. Roy Cyril and Helen Bernice (Tellefsen) W.; m. Jane Duncan Bowman, Aug. 25, 1979. AB with honors, Brown U., 1975; MA in Psychology, U. So. Calif., 1981, PhD in Psychology, 1983. From asst. dir. to dir. Pomona (Calif.) Open Door Community Mental Health Clin., 1976-78; assessor Mid-Valley Diagnostic Ctr, Covina, Calif., 1979; psychology trainee Jerry L. Pettis VA Hosp., Loma Linda, Calif., 1979; program coordinator for human relations ctr. U. So. Calif., Los Angeles, 1979-80, teaching asst., 1980-81; project assoc. Univ. Family Studies Project, 1980-82; neuropsychol. assessor of children Children's Hosp. of Los Angeles, 1982-83; predoctoral intern U. So. Calif. Med. Ctr., Los Angeles, 1982-83, clin. asst. prof. psychiatry, 1984—, clin. assoc. dept. biology, 1985—; clin. onsite supr. Loyola Marmount U., Los Angeles, 1983-84; psychologist, postdoctoral fellow San Fernando Valley (Calif.) Child Guidance Clinic, 1983-84; psychologist Woodland Hills (Calif.) Med. Group, 1984—; clin. dir. Santa Clarita Valley Spl. Children's Ctr., Newhall, Calif., 1985—. Contbr. articles to profl. jours. Active Calif. Scholastic Fedn. NIMH fellow, 1979-80. Mem. Am. Psychol. Assn. (mem. com. clin. child psychology 1985), Calif. State Psychol. Assn., Los Angeles County Psychol. Assn., Sigma Xi (assoc.). Home: 1238 N Cordova Ave Glendale CA 91207 Office: 6150 Canoga Ave Suite 207 Woodland Hills CA 91367

WEINSTEIN, DONALD, history educator; b. Rochester, N.Y., Mar. 13, 1926; s. Harris and Rose (Shaywitz) W.; m. Anne Kingsley, Jan. 14, 1953 (div.); children: Jonathan, Elizabeth; m. Beverly J. Parker, June 1, 1979. BA, U. Chgo., 1947, MA, 1950; PhD, U. Iowa, 1957. Instr. U. Iowa, Iowa City, 1957-58; asst. prof. Roosevelt U., Chgo., 1958-59; from asst. prof. to prof. Rutgers U., New Brunswick, N.J., 1960-78; vis. assoc. prof. U. Calif., Berkeley, 1964-65; prof., chmn. dept. U. Ariz., Tucson, 1978—. Author: Ambassador from Venice, 1960, Savonarola and Florence, 1971, co-author Saints and Society, 1982; editor: Renaissance and Reformation, 1965. Served to cpl. U.S. Army, 1944-46. Am. Council Learned Socs. fellow U. Wis. Inst. for Research in Humanities, 1959-60. Mem. Inst. Advanced Study, Renaissance Soc. Am., Am. Hist. Assn. Home: 2237 E Blacklidge Dr Tucson AZ 85719 Office: U Ariz Dept History Social Science 215 Tucson AZ 85721

WEINSTEIN, JUDITH, art consultant; b. Chgo., Feb. 11, 1927; d. Julius and Charlotte (Brandau) Braun; m. Irwin Weinstein, Jan. 20, 1951; children: James, David. BS in Psychology, U. Wis., 1950. Tchr. N.Y. State Child Care Ctr., N.Y.C., 1950-52, U. Chgo., 1952-53; interior designer, color cons. Paul Bennett and Assocs., 1953-58; dir. Ethnic Arts Shop, Bookshop and George Page Mus. Shop, Los Angeles County Mus. Natural History; producer ethnic art shows and research asst. dept. anthropology Los Angeles County Mus. Natural History, 1971-77; dir., continuing edn. Artsreach program UCLA Extension, 1978-85; producer Judith Weinstein Prodns., 1985—; bd. dirs. T.S.B. Prodns., Humorx. Mem. polit. campaign coms. for U.S. Senate, mayor of Los Angeles, 1958-63; bd. dirs. Los Angeles Mcpl. Art Gallery Assocs., 1980—, Los Angeles Art Showcase, 1972-75, project developer Zev Braun Pictures; spl. advisor for art U.S. sen. Alan Cranston; mem. planning com. Dem. Nat. Telethon, 1960; bd. dirs. Calif. Chamber Symphony, 1960-71, Alternative Living for Aging, Los Angeles Street Scene Festival, 1978—, Israel Cancer Research Fund, 1986—; v.p. Pacific chpt. UN Assn., 1963-69, adv. bd., 1969-71; organizer, developer, dir. UN Ctr., Westwood, Calif., 1963-71; del. 1st women's conf. Dem. Nat. Com., 1971; adv. com. Los Angeles Children's Mus., 1978; mem. com. Corp. Disabilities and Telecommunication, 1981—.

WEINSTEIN, NANCY LOU, interior designer; b. Covington, Ky., Apr. 8, 1946; m. Mel Weinstein, Sept. 19, 1964; 1 child, Jennifer Nicole. Pvt. practice interior design Long Beach, Calif., 1966; dir. Easter Seals Internat. Design House, 1985. Contbr. articles to mags., newspapers. Named Hon. Order of Ky. Cols., 1959. Mem. Interior Design Soc., Design Internat., Orange County (Calif.) Charter 100, Women in Business, Nat. Assn. of Women Bus. Owners, Long Beach C. of C. Avocation: travel. Office: Nancy Weinstein Interior Design 4232 Heather Rd Long Beach CA 90808

WEINTRAUB, DEBORA SHARON, electrical engineer; b. N.Y.C., Nov. 12, 1953; d. David Weintraub and Norme Weintraub Fritz. B.S. in Microbiology, Ariz. State U., MS in indsl. engring., 1985. Assoc. programmer analyst Motorola GEG, Scottsdale, Ariz., 1979-81, programmer/analyst, 1981-82, sr. engr., electronics, 1982-84, staff engr. electronics, 1984—. Mem. Assn. Computing Machinery. Club: Team STRADA, U.S. Masters Swimmers.

WEINTRAUB, MICHAEL LAWRENCE, insurance company executive; b. Chgo., June 28, 1944; s. Max and Rosanne (Levatin) W.; m. Paula Green, Oct. 5, 1969; 1 child, Scott. CLU, Pa. Agt. Washington Nat. Ins. Co., Evanston, Ill., 1967—; pres. Contemporary Pensions, Inc., Walnut Creek, Calif., 1975—. mem. planning commn. City of Clayton, Calif., 1983—; pres. estate planning council, 1985—. Mem. Am. Soc. Pension Acturies, Million Dollar Roundtable (vice chmn. 1985—). Republican. Jewish. Avocations: tennis, photography, travel, biking, hiking. Home: 2 Nottingham Circle Clayton CA 94517 Office: Contemporary Pensions Inc 309 Lennon Ln Suite 101 Walnut Creek CA 94598

WEINY, GEORGE AZEM, physical education educator, consultant; b. Keokuk, Iowa, July 24, 1933; s. George Dunn and Emma Vivian (Kraushaar) W.; m. Jane Louise Eland, Sept. 29, 1956 (div. 1985); children: Tami L., Tomas A., Aaron A., Arden G.; m. Lori Arlene Rowe, Aug. 6, 1985; 1 child, Austin George. BA, Iowa Wesleyan Coll., 1957; MA, State U. Iowa, 1962; PhD, U. Beverly Hills, 1980. Phys. dir. YMCA, Keokuk, 1956-57; asst. dir. pub. relations Iowa Wesleyan Coll., Mt. Pleasant, Iowa, 1957-58; prin., tchr., coach Hillsboro (Iowa) High Sch., 1958-59; tchr., coach Burlington (Iowa) High Sch. and Jr. Coll., 1959-62, Pacific High Sch., San Bernardino, Calif., 1962-67; prof. phys. edn. Calif. State U., San Bernardino, 1967—; ednl. cons. Belau Modekngei Sch., West Caroline Islands, 1984-85; swim meet dir. Nat. Collegiate Athletic Assn., 1982-84, 86-87; tng. dir. for ofcls. So. Calif. Aquatics Fedn., 1967-78; scuba tour guide Dive Maui Resort, Hawaii, 1982-83; salvage diver U.S. Trust Territories, 1973; coach YMCA swim team, San Bernardino, 1962-77, 84-87. Editor: Swimming Rules and Case Studies, 1970-73; author: Snorkeling Fun for Everyone, 1982; contbr. articles to profl. jours. Mem. county water safety com. ARC, San Bernardino, 1968-80; bd. dirs. YMCA, San Bernardino, 1970-77; mem. Bicentennial Commn., San Bernardino, 1975-76. Served to sgt. U.S. Army, 1953-55. Recipient Outstanding Service award So. Calif. Aquatics Fedn., 1978. Mem. Profl. Assn. Diving Instrs. (cert.), Nat. Assn. Underwater Instrs. (cert.), Am. Assn. Health Phys. Edn. Recreation and Dance, Coll. Swim Coaches Assn., Am. Swim Coaches Assn. (cert.), Nat. Interscholastic Swim Coaches Assn. Club: Sea Sons Dive (Rialto, Calif.) (pres. 1982-83, sec. 1983-87). Avocation: scuba diving. Home: PO Box 30393 San Bernardino CA 92413 Office: Calif State U 5500 University Pkwy San Bernardino CA 92407

WEIR, ALEXANDER, JR., utility executive; b. Crossett, Ark., Dec. 19, 1922; s. Alexander and Mary Eloise (Feild) W.; BSChemE, U. Ark., 1943; MMSChemE, Poly. Inst. Bklyn., 1946; PhD, U. Mich., 1954; cert. U. So. Calif. Grad. Sch. Bus. Adminstrn., 1968; m. Florence Forschner, Dec. 28, 1946; children: Alexander III, Carol Jean, Bruce Richard. Analyst, chemist Am. Cyanamid and Chem. Corp. summers 1941, 42, chem. engr. Am. Cyanamid Co., Stamford Research Labs., 1943-47; with U. Mich., 1948-58, lectr., then asst. prof. chem. and metall. engring. dept. Engring. Research Inst., 1954-58; successively cons., mem. tech. staff, sect. head, asst. mgr.-in-charge Atlas Missile captive test program Ramo-Woolridge Corp. (now TRW, Inc.) Los Angeles, 1956-70; asst. to sr. v.p. tech., Corp. devel. planner, tech. adviser, corp. lab. dir. plans and programs, asst. corp. dir. tech. programs Northrop Corp. Corporate Office, Beverly Hills, Calif., 1960-70; prin. scientist for air quality, mgr. chem. systems research and devel. So. Calif. Edison Co., Los Angeles, 1970-86, chief research scientist, 1986—; rep. Am. Rocket Soc. to Detroit Nuclear Council, 1954-57; chmn. session on chem. reactions Nuclear Sci. and Engring. Congress, Cleve., 1955; U.S. del. AGARD (NATO) Combustion Colloquium, Liege, Belgium, 1955; Western U.S. rep. task force on environmental research and devel. goals Electric Research Council, 1971; indsl. adv. com. Calif. State U., Los Angeles, 1984—; electric utility advisor Electric Power Research Inst., 1974-78, 1984-87; mem. industry adv. com. Dept. Chemistry and Biochemistry, Calif. State U., Los Angeles, 1982—. Bd. govs., past pres. Civic Union Playa del Rey, chmn. sch., police and fire, nominating, civil def., army liaison coms.; mem. Senate, Westchester YMCA, chmn. Dads sponsoring com., active fund raising; chmn. nominating com. Paseco del Rey Sch. P.T.A., 1961; mem. Los Angeles Mayors Community Adv. Com.; asst. chmn. advancement com., merit badge dean Centinella dist. Los Angeles Area council Boy Scouts Am. Mem. Am. Geophys. Union, Electric Power Research Inst. (electric utility advisor, 1974-78, 84-87) Navy League U.S. (v.p. Palos Verdes Peninsula council 1961-62), N.Y. Acad. Scis., Sci. Research Soc. Am., Am. Chem. Soc., Am. Inst. Chem. Engrs., AAAS, Combustion Inst., Air Pollution Control Assn., U.S. Power Squadron, Sigma Xi, Phi Kappa Phi, Phi Lambda Upsilon, Alpha Chi Sigma, Lambda Chi Alpha. Club: Santa Monica Yacht. Author: Two and Three Dimensional Flow of Air through Square-Edged Sonic Orifices, 1954; (with R. B. Morrison and T. C. Anderson) Notes on Combustion 1955; also tech. papers. Inventor Weir power plant stack scrubber. Office: So Calif Edison Co PO Box 800 Rosemead CA 91770

WEIR, ROBERT CHARLES, electronics company executive; b. Cleve., July 13, 1953; s. Gordon Everett and Hope Marie (Smith) W. BS in Physics, Kent State U., 1976, BS in Math., 1976, MA in Physics, 1976, postgrad., 1976-77. Assoc. physicist in applied physics Johns Hopkins U., Laurel, Md., 1977-82; sr. engr. marine div. Westinghouse Electric Co., Sunnyvale, Calif., 1982-85, engring. supr. marine div., 1985—. Mem. Soc. Naval Architects and Marine Engrs.; BMW Motorcycles Owners of Am. Avocations: sailboat racing, scuba diving, backpacking, skiing, motorcycle touring. Home: 1041 Sherman Oaks Dr San Jose CA 95128 Office: Westinghouse Electric Corp 401 E Hendy Ave PO Box 3499 Sunnyvale CA 94088-3499

WEIR, THOMAS W(ILSON), dermatologist, dermal pathologist; b. St. Louis, Oct. 12, 1937; s. William Victor and Marion Susan (Wilson) W.; m. Kristina Lee Hagman, Sept. 2, 1961; children—Todd Hagman, Brian Wilson. A.B., Amherst Coll., 1959; M.D., U. Mo., 1963. Diplomate Am. Bd. Dermatology, Am. Bd. Dermal Pathology. Intern Letterman Gen. Hosp., San Francisco, 1963-64; resident in dermatology Temple U., Phila., 1966-69, fellow in dermatopathology, 1968-69; practice medicine specializing in dermatology and dermal pathology, Redmond, Wash., 1970—; clin. asst. prof. med. U. Wash., Seattle, 1970—; vis. lectr. dept. medicine U. Nairobi, Kenya, 1979-80. Served to capt. M.C., U.S. Army, 1963-66. Fellow Am. Acad. Dermatology, Am. Soc. Dermatopathology, Pacific Dermatol. Assn.; mem. Seattle Dermatol. Soc. (pres. 1974-75). Unitarian. Office: Group Health Cooperative of Puget Sound 2701 156th Ave NE Redmond WA 98052

WEISBERG, HOWARD LOUIS, physicist; b. Cleve., Nov. 12, 1939; s. Sidney M. and Margie (Peterman) W.; m. Suzanne Shatzberg, June 25, 1965; children: Seth, Jonathan. BS, Calif. Inst. Tech., 1960; PhD, Brandeis U., 1965. Research assoc. U. Calif., Berkeley, 1965-70; asst. prof. U. Pa., Phila., 1970-76; physicist Brookhaven Nat. Lab., Upton, N.Y., 1976-84, R&D Assocs., Marina del Rey, Calif., 1984—. NSF fellow, 1965-68. Mem. Am. Phys. Soc. Jewish. Home: 16001 Anoka Dr Pacific Palisades CA 90272

WEISIGER, RICHARD A., biomedical scientist, hepatologist; b. N.Y.C., Feb. 25, 1946; s. James Richard and Elisabeth Patricia (O'Brien) W.; m. Jane Eloise Martin, June 23, 1973; children: Alexander, Elizabeth, Christopher. AB, Princeton U., 1968; PhD, Duke U., 1973, MD, 1974. Diplomate Am. Bd. Internal Medicine. Housestaff intern Washington U., St. Louis, 1974-76; postdoctoral fellow NIH, Bethesda, Md., 1976-78; clin. fellow U. Calif., San Francisco, 1978-80, asst. prof. medicine, 1981—; cons. Am. Liver Found., Cedar Grove, N.J., 1984—. Assoc. editor: Gastroenterology, 1984-85; reviewer NIH and various med. jours.; contbr. numerous book chpts. and research papers. Elder Christ Presbyn. Ch., San Rafael, Calif., 1983-86; pres. Chancel Choir, Lakeside Ch., San Francisco, 1980-83. Served to lt. comdr. USPHS, 1976-78. NIH grantee Bethesda, Md., 1983—; Hartford Found. fellow, N.Y.C., 1981-83, Am. Liver Found. fellow, Cedar Grove, N.J., 1980-81. Mem. AAAS, Am. Assn. for Study of Liver Diseases, Western Soc. for Clin. Investigation, Western Soc. for Clin. Research. Avocations: woodworking, aviation. Home: 52 Millstone Terr San Rafael CA 94903 Office: U Calif Dept Med 1120 HSW San Francisco CA 94143

WEISMAN, MARTIN JEROME, manufacturing company executive; b. N.Y.C., Aug. 22, 1930; s. Lewis E. and Estelle (Scherer) W.; m. Sherrie Cohen, Jan. 27, 1952; children: Jane Dory, Andrea Sue, Amy Ellen. B in Chem. Engring., N.Y.U., 1951. Sr. chem. engr. Ideal Toy Corp., Hollis, N.Y., 1951-57; research chemist Chesebrough-Ponds, Stamford, Conn., 1957-62; mgr. nail products lab. Max Factor and Co., Hollywood, Calif., 1962-81; v.p., tech. dir. Sher-Mar Cosmetics div. Weisman Industries, Inc., Canoga Park, Calif., 1981—. Patentee in field. Mem. Soc. Cosmetic Chemists, Los Angeles Soc. Coatings Tech., Am. Chem. Soc. Office: Sher-Mar Cosmetics 8755 Remmet Ave Canoga Park CA 91304

WEISMAN, WALTER L., health care company executive. Pres. Am. Med. Internat., Inc., Beverly Hills, Calif., chief exec. officer, 1985—, former chief operating officer. Office: Am Med Internat Inc 414 N Camden Dr Beverly Hills CA 90210 *

WEISMEYER, RICHARD WAYNE, academic administrator; b. Loma Linda, Calif., Oct. 15, 1943; s. Norman Glenn and Nedra Aileen (McGinniss) W.; m. Carol Mae Siebenlist, Aug. 16, 1970; children: Michael Brett, Marci Diann. BA in English, Loma Linda U., Riverside, 1966. Editorial asst. Loma Linda (Calif.) U., 1966-70, editor, new publs., 1970-75, dir. pub. relations, 1975—; mem. panel Heart Transplantation and Pub. Relations sponsored by USA Today and Fellows ACS; bd. dirs. Sta. KSGN-FM, Riverside, Calif., Loma Linda U. Acad. Press. Editor Loma Linda Univ. Scope mag., 1978—. Mem. Pub. Relations Assn. So. Calif., Council for Advancement and Support of Edn., Am. Med. Colls. group on Pub. Relations. Adventist. Avocations: travel, astronomy, collecting stamps, rare books, memorabilia. Home: 143 Browning St Riverside CA 92507 Office: Loma Linda U Loma Linda CA 92350

WEISMULLER, THOMAS PAUL, chemist; b. Pomona, Calif., Feb. 26, 1949; s. Oliver Thomas and Jean Katherine (Nolan) W.; m. Penny Christine Klein, Oct. 17, 1975; children: Nathan Thomas, Sarah Elizabeth. AA, Fullerton Coll., 1969; BA, Calif. State U., Fullerton, 1971, MS, 1977. Cert. secondary tchr. Analytical chemist Rockwell Internat., Anaheim, Calif., 1974-77, sr. staff scientist, 1980—; tech. staff scientist Hughes Aircraft Co., Fullerton, 1978-79; sr. mfg. devel. engr. Gen. Dynamics Corp., Pomona, 1979-80. Contbr. articles to profl. jours.; patentee in field. Recipient Service award Rockwell Internat., 1984. Mem. Am. Chem. Soc., The Metall. Soc., U.S. Karate Assn. (cert. instr.). Democrat. Mormon. Office: Rockwell Internat PO Box 4192 MZ BD 14 Anaheim CA 92803-4192

WEISNER, STANLEY JAMES, social work educator; b. Oakland, Calif., Feb. 26, 1946; s. Gilbert Gerson and Beatrice Ruth (Ullman) W.; m. Constance Meyer, June 18, 1972; children: Aron Gilbert, Stephanie Marie, Julia Ruth. BA, U. Calif., Riverside, 1967; D in Social Work, U. Calif., Berkeley, 1975; MSW, U. Minn., 1969. Acting dir. internat. edn. U. Calif., Berkeley, 1978-81; assoc. dir. Coleman Advocates for Children and Youth, San Francisco, 1984—; lectr. in social welfare U. Calif., Berkeley, 1975—; vis. prof. U. San Francisco, 1983—. Author: Social Work in Kenya, 1971; co-author: Social Revenue Sharing, 1975, Impact of Proposition 13, 1978; also chpts. to books and articles. Mem. Mayor's Task Force on Child Abuse, San Francisco, 1986; contbr. Friends Com. on Legis., Sacramento, 1980—; mem. selection com. United Way, San Francisco Bay Area, 1983; contbr. Amnesty Internat. NIMH fellow 1971-73; Profl. Studies Program intern, New Delhi, India, 1973-74. Mem. Nat. Assn. Social Workers, Internat. Assn. Schs. Social Work, Com Health Rights Cen. Am., ACLU. Democrat. Unitarian. Avocations: sports, guitar. Home: 75 Weybridge Oakland CA 94611 Office: U Calif Sch Social Welfare Berkeley CA 94720

WEISS, CHARLES FREDERICK, holding company executive; b. Los Angeles, Nov. 9, 1939; s. Walter E. and Marie E. W.; m. Katherine Joyce Weiss, June 26, 1959; children: Bryan Scott, Michael Craig. B.S., Calif. State U., Los Angeles, 1963; M.B.A., U. So. Calif., 1965. Vice pres. Great Western Savs. & Loan Assn., Los Angeles, 1963-69; corp. dir. orgn. devel. Rep. Corp., Los Angeles, 1969-72; corp. v.p. Beverly Hills Bancorp, Calif., 1972-75, 20th Century Fox Film Corp., Los Angeles, 1975-82; acting chief exec. officer Sta. KCET-TV, Los Angeles, 1982-83; exec. Pacific Lighting Corp., Los Angeles, 1984—. Bd. dirs., exec. com. Calif. Found. on Employment and Disability. Clubs: Los Angeles Turf, Jonathan, Los Angeles. Home: 1542 Moreno Dr Glendale CA 91207 Office: Pacific Lighting Corp 810 S Flower St Los Angeles CA 90017

WEISS, HERBERT KLEMM, aeronautical engineer; b. Lawrence, Mass., June 22, 1917; s. Herbert Julius and Louise (Klemm) W.; m. Ethel Celesta Gitner, May 14, 1945; children—Janet Elaine, Jack Klemm (dec.). B.S., MIT, 1937, M.S., 1938. Engr. U.S. Army Arty. Bds., Ft. Monroe, Va, 1938-46; engr. U.S. Army Arty. Bds., Camp Davis, N.C., 1938-46, Ft. Bliss, Tex., 1938-46; chief WPN Systems Lab., Ballistic Research Labs., Aberdeen Proving Grounds, Md, 1946-53; chief WPN systems analysis dept. Northrop Aircraft Corp., 1953-58; mgr. advanced systems devel. mil. systems planning aeronutronic div. Ford Motor Co., Newport Beach, Calif., 1958-61; group dir., plans devel. and analysis Aerospace Corp., El Segundo, Calif., 1961-65; sr. scientist Litton Industries, Van Nuys, Calif., 1965-82; cons. mil. systems analysis 1982—; Mem. Sci. Adb. Bd. USAF, 1959-63, sci. adv. commn. Army Ball Research Labs., 1973-77; advisor Pres.'s Commn. Law Enforcement and Adminstrn. Justice, 1966; cons. Office Dir. Def., Research and Engring., 1954-64. Contbr. articles to profl. jours. Patentee in field. Recipient Commendation for meritorious civilian service USAF, 1964. Fellow AAAS, Am. Inst. Aeros. and Astronautics (assoc.); mem. Ops. Research Soc. Am., IEEE, Inst. Mgmt. Scis. Republican. Presbyterian. Club: Cosmos. Home: PO Box 2668 Palos Verdes Peninsula CA 90274

WEISS, JANET HARDCASTLE, auto dealerships business manager; b. San Jose, Calif., Sept. 8, 1935; d. C. Irvin and E. Berniece (Cottrell) Hardcastle; m. F. Douglas Weiss, Dec. 27, 1958 (div. 1968); children—Dana Christine, Kurt Douglas. B.A., San Jose State U., 1957. Tchr., Whisman Dist., Mountain View, Calif., 1957-58, Oakland Dist., Calif., 1960-61; cashier, sec. Himsl Volkswagen, San Jose, Calif., 1969-71; office mgr. Almaden Toyota, San Jose, 1971-74; bus. mgr., controller San Jose Datsun & Affiliate Cos., 1974—. Republican. Methodist. Avocations: reading, bridge. Home: 16470 Matilija Dr Los Gatos CA 95030 Office: San Jose Datsun & Affiliate Cos 4100 Stevens Creek Blvd San Jose CA 95129

WEISS, JOHN CHARLES, JR., design educator; b. Tulsa, Nov. 2, 1942; s. John C. Sr. and Mary M. (Welp) W.; m. Jean R. Stahlberg, Aug. 21, 1965; children: Neala, Michelle, David, Aaroon, Jenny, Mikel. BFA in Art, Okla. State U.; MFA in Design, Brigham Young U. Sales mgr. Internat. Funds, Hanau, Fed. Rep. Germany, 1969-71; dir. Spl. Services U.S.A., Heidelberg, Fed. Rep. Germany, 1971-72; program dir. Ch. of Jesus Christ of Latter-Day Saints, Klamath Falls, Oreg., 1972-74; instr. art Brigham Young U., Provo, Utah, 1974-80, asst. prof. design, 1980—, coordinator Design Found.,, 1980—. Rep. del. Utah State Conv., 1986, also county convs. Served to 1st lt. U.S. Army, 1967-69. Mem. Assn. Multi-Image Internat. (pres. Mountain chpt., advisor Brigham Young U. chpt., bd. dirs. Photo Safaris). Avocations: skiing, canoeing, tennis, cycling. Home: 1473 S 235 W Orem UT 84058 Office: Brigham Young Univ 210 BRMB Provo UT 84601

WEISS, JOHN WILLIAM, financial analyst; b. Chgo., June 21, 1947; s. Adolph Jack and Marget (Wrenn) W. BA in Econs., U. Calif., Santa Barbara, 1969; MBA, UCLA, 1971. Investment analyst The Ill. Co., Chgo., 1971-73, Schreck, Stein & Franc, St. Louis, 1973-76, The No. Trust Co., Chgo., 1976-79, Dean Witter Reynolds, N.Y.C., 1979-82, Montgomery Securities, San Francisco, 1982—. Avocations: golf, running. Office: Montgomery Securities 600 Montgomery St San Francisco CA 94111

WEISS, KARL WERNER, marketing research analyst; b. Lakewood, Ohio, Oct. 8, 1960; s. Michael Karl and Helene Kathyrn (Durst) W. BS in Mktg., Statistics, U. Oreg., 1983, MBA in Mktg., 1984. Data processing analyst Computer For Mktg. Corp., Denver, 1984-85; market research analyst Research Dimenions Inc., Arvada, Colo., 1985—; statistics advisor/tutor Learning Resource Ctr., Eugene, Oreg., 1983-84, Boulder, 1986. Mem. Am. Mktg. Assn. Democrat. Avocations: classical and jazz piano, skiing, bicycling touring, bodybuilding. Home: 20 S Boulder Circle #2206 Boulder CO 80303 Office: Research Dimensions Inc 5440 Ward Rd #101 Arvada CO 80002

WEISS, LAWRENCE ROBERT, investment banking executive; b. Pasadena, Mar. 8, 1937; s. Joseph B. and Elsie (Shaw) W.; B.S. in Applied Physics, UCLA, 1959; M.S. in Mgmt. Sci., U. So. Calif., 1974; m. Elaine Saxon, June 23, 1963; children—Jeffrey Arthur, Jason Ashley. Electronic systems engr., N.Am. Aviation, Inc., Los Angeles, 1960-62, Litton Systems, Inc., 1962-63; group head Hughes Aircraft Co., Culver City, Calif., 1963-67, group head, sales rep., br. sales mgr. 1967-70; with Sci. Data Systems, Systems Engring. Labs., Gen. Automation, Inc., Interdata Corp., Applied Digital Data Systems, Inc., 1973-80; co-founder, chmn., pres. Health-tronics Labs. Inc., Rochester, N.Y., 1970-72, Cal-trend Personality Systems, Inc., Los Angeles, 1973-85; co-founder, chmn. bd., v.p. Evolution Computer Systems Corp., (name changed to Evolution Techs., Inc. 1981), Irvine, Calif., 1980-82; co-founder, chmn., pres. Capital Tech. Group Inc., Irvine, 1981-83; co-founder, pres. Tek-Net Funding Corp., Irvine, 1984-85; fin. cons. Shearson Lehman Bros., Inc., Orange, Calif., 1985-86; v.p. investments Drexel Burnham Lambert Inc., Newport Beach, Calif., 1986—. Mem. Space Studies Inst., Planetary Soc., U.S. Naval Inst., Am. Def. Preparedness Assn., Mensa. Home: 22706 Islamare Ln El Toro CA 92630 Office: Drexel Burnham Lambert Inc 620 Newport Ctr Dr Newport Beach CA 92660

WEISS, LOUIS ISRAEL (LOU), marketing consultant; b. Bklyn., May 7, 1948; s. Lipman Leo and Frances (Markowitz) W.; m. Naomi Faith Gelman, July 19, 1970; children: Elan Stephen, Lavy Mikhael. BS, Bklyn. Coll., 1969; MBA, Baruch Coll., 1972. Supr. mktg. research Gen. Foods Corp., White Plains, N.Y., 1970-72; exec. v.p. Peter Honig Assocs., White Plains, 1972-78; sr. v.p. Yankelovich, Skelly & White, N.Y.C. and Newport Beach, Calif., 1978-80; pres. Am. Mktg. Services, Newport Beach, 1980—, also bd. dirs.; cheif operating officer, bd. dirs. Dursol of N.Am., Newport Beach; chief fin. officer, bd. dirs. AMS Holding Inc., Newport Beach; sr. assoc., bd. dirs. Innovative Coupon Systems, N.Y.C. Contbr. articles to profl. jours. Bd. dirs. Portafina Assn., Laguna Beach, Calif., 1980-85, Jewish Community Ctr., Laguna Beach, 1980-84; founder, bd. dirs. Chabad of Laguna, 1984—; v.p. Jewish Fedn. Orange County, Calif., 1985—. Honored at Banquet, Chabad of Irvine, Calif., 1985. Mem. Mktg. Research Assn. (pres. 1984-85). Democrat. Avocations: sailing, running, patenting, community service. Office: Am Mktg Services Inc 3822 Campus Dr Newport Beach CA 92660-2609

WEISS, MARTIN HARVEY, neurosurgeon, educator; b. Newark, Feb. 2, 1939; s. Max and Rae W.; m. R. Debora Rosenthal, Aug. 20, 1961; children: Brad, Jessica, Elizabeth. A.B. magna cum laude, Dartmouth Coll., 1960, B.M.S., 1961; M.D., Cornell U., 1963. Intern Univ. Hosps., Cleve., 1963-64; resident in neurosurgery Univ. Hosps., 1966-70; sr. instr. to asst. prof. neurosurgery Case Western Res. U., 1970-73; asso. prof. neurosurgery U. So. Calif., 1973-76, prof., 1976-78, prof., chmn. dept., 1978—; chmn. neurology B study sect. NIH.; bd. dirs. Am. Bd. Neurol. Surgery, 1983. Author: Pituitary Diseases, 1980; editorial bd.: Neurosurgery, 1979-84, Neurol. Research, 1980—; editor in chief: Clin. Neurosurgery, 1980-83; assoc. editor: Bull. Los Angeles Neurol. Socs, 1976-81, Jour. Clin. Neurosci., 1981—; mem. editorial bd. Jour. Neurosurgery, 1987—; contbr. articles sci. jours. Served to capt. USAR, 1964-66. Decorated; Army Commendation Medal; NIH spl. fellow in neurosurgery, 1969-70. Mem. Soc. Neurol. Surgeons, Am. Coll. Surgeons (adv. council neurosurgery 1985—), Neurosurg. Soc. Am., Am. Acad. Neurol. Surgery, Research Soc. Neurol. Surgeons, Am. Assn. Neurol. Surgeons, Congress Neurol. Surgeons (v.p. 1982-83), Western Neurosurg. Soc., Neurosurg. Forum, So. Calif. Neurosurg. Soc. (pres. 1983-84), Phi Beta Kappa, Alpha Omega Alpha. Home: 357 Georgian Rd Flintridge CA 91011 Office: 1200 N State St Box 1931 Los Angeles CA 90033

WEISS, MAX TIBOR, aerospace company executive; b. Hajduananas, Hungary, Dec. 29, 1922; came to U.S., 1929, naturalized, 1936; s. Samuel and Anna (Hornstein) W.; m. Melitta Newman, June 28, 1953; children: Samuel Harvey, Herschel William, David Nathaniel, Deborah Beth. B.E.E., CCNY, 1943; M.S., M.I.T., 1947, Ph.D., 1950. Research assoc. M.I.T., 1946-50; mem. tech. staff Bell Telephone Labs., Holmdel, N.J., 1950-59; assoc. head applied physics lab. Hughes Aircraft Co., Culver City, Calif., 1959-60; dir. electronics research lab. The Aerospace Corp., Los Angeles, 1961-63; gen. mgr. labs. div. The Aerospace Corp., 1963-67, gen. mgr. electronics and optics div., 1968-78, v.p., gen. mgr. lab. ops., 1978-81, v.p. engring. group, 1981-85; asst. mgr. engring. ops. TRW Systems, Redondo Beach, Calif., 1967-68. Contbr. articles to physics and electronics jours. Served with USNR, 1944-45. Fellow Am. Phys. Soc., IEEE; mem. Sigma Xi, Nat. Acad. Engrng. Patentee electronics and communications. Office: Aerospace Corp PO Box 92957 MS: M1-002 Los Angeles CA 90009

WEISS, RHODA ELAINE, hospital administrator, consultant; b. Detroit, Oct. 8, 1949; d. Harold Martin and Mildred (Million) W. BA in Communications, Mich. State U., 1971; MA in Psychology, Antioch U., 1980; postgrad., U. Calif., Berkeley, 1981. Reporter Gannett Newspapers, N.Y.C., 1971-72; editor Luth. Hosp. Soc., Los Angeles, 1973; pub. relations dir. St. John's Hosp., Santa Monica, Calif., 1974-75; pub. relations agt. The Rand Corp., Santa Monica, 1975-76; community relations dir. Torrance (Calif.) Meml. Hosp., 1976-78; asst. adminstr. Sisters of Providence, St. Joseph Med. Ctr., Burbank, Calif., 1978—; cons. Hosp. Home Health Care Agy., Torrance, 1977—, Beverly Enterprises, Pasadena, Calif., 1985—, cons. Interactive Health Systems, Santa Monica, 1986—, Am. Assn. Homes for Aged, Washington, 1986—, Univ. Hosps. Cleve., 1986—; adj. prof. Pepperdine U., Malibu, Calif., 1984—. Contbr. articles to profl. jours. Bd. dirs. Juvenile Justice Connection Project, Los Angeles, Watts-Willowbrook Boys and Girls Clubs, Watts, Calif.; mem. Hospice Adv. Bd., Torrance. Recipient 15 Lulu Awards Los Angeles Advt. Women, 1981-86, 4 Maggie Awards Western Pub. Assn., Los Angeles, 1983-84. Mem. Healthcare Pub. Relations and Mktg. Assn. (pres., 23 Golden Adv. awards 1982-86), Women in Communications (pres., Clarion award 1982, 83, 84, 85), Pub. Relations Soc. Am. (bd. dirs., 22 Prisms awards 1981-86), Calif. Hosp. Assn. (bd. dirs.), Hosp. Council of So. Calif. (bd. dirs.), Assn. of Western Hosps. (bd. dirs., 11 Best of West awards 1980-84), Nat. Hospice Orgns. (bd. dirs.), Internat. Assn. Bus. Communicators (12 Gold Quills, 25 Silver Quills, 48 Bronze Quills 1978-86), Am. Soc. Hosp. Mktg. (13 Touchstone awards 1983-86), Publicity Club (13 PRO awards 1981-86), Women in Health Adminstrn. (mem. chart bd. 1981—, pres. 1985), Am. Mktg. Assn., Alpha Delta Pi (alumna pres. 1978-80, local chpt. adv. 1977-81, Outstanding Alumni 1980). Jewish. Club: Health Care Execs. (Los Angeles). Avocations: traveling, internat. speaking and cons. Home: 307 Montana #203 Santa Monica CA 90403 Office: St Joseph Med Ctr Buena Vista and Alameda Burbank CA 91505

WEISS, RICHARD LAWRENCE, microbiology educator; b. N.Y.C., Dec. 28, 1940; s. Louis Lawrence and Annette (Bizzoco) W.; m. Marcia Mae Erisman, June 12, 1970 (div. 1980); children: Shaynon Andrew, Wendy Alicia. BA in Liberal Arts, U. Conn., 1962; MS in Microbiology, Calif. State U., Long Beach, 1970; PhD in Biophysics, Ind. U., 1972. EM lab. dir. Harvard U., Cambridge, Mass., 1974-75; assoc. med. microbiologist Med. Sch. U. Calif., Irvine, 1976-77; asst. prof. biology San Diego State U., 1977-81, assoc. prof. biology, 1981-85, prof. biology, 1985—; prin. investigator NIH Biomed. Research San Diego State U., 1985-87, NIH Gen. Med., San Diego State U., 1978-81, NSF, San Diego State U., 1986. Mem. Phycol. Soc. Am., Sigma Xi. Avocations: photography. Office: San Diego State U Dept Biology San Diego CA 92182-0057

WEISS, ROBERT STEPHEN, medical manufacturing company financial executive; b. Honesdale, Pa., Oct. 25, 1946; s. Stephen John and Anna Blanche (Lescinski) W.; B.S. in Acctg. cum laude, U. Scranton, 1968; m. Marilyn Annette Chesick, Oct. 29, 1970; children—Christopher Robert, Kim Marie, Douglas Paul. Supr., Peat, Marwick, Mitchell & Co., N.Y.C., 1971-76; asst. corp. controller Cooper Labs., Inc., Parsippany, N.J., 1977-78, v.p./corp. controller, Palo Alto, Calif., 1981-83; v.p., corp. controller CooperVision, Inc., Palo Alto, Calif., 1984— ; v.p. fin./controller CooperVision Pharms., Mountain View, Calif., 1979. Served with U.S. Army, 1969-70. Decorated Bronze Star with oak leaf cluster, Army Commendation medal; C.P.A., N.Y. State. Mem. N.Y. State Soc. C.P.A.s., Am. Inst. C.P.A.s. Republican. Roman Catholic. Home: 446 Arlington Ct Pleasanton CA 94566 Office: CooperVision Inc 3145 Porter Dr Palo Alto CA 94304

WEISS, SIEGFRIED ALMA, architect, planner; b. Salt Lake City, Mar. 28, 1926; s. Karl and Theresia (Baumgartner) W.; m. Kathleen King, July 29, 1944; children—Linda Kay Weiss Hovey, Marc Siegfried, Marie Michelle, Christina Weiss Karren. B.F.A., U. Utah, 1953, B.Arch., 1955. Registered architect, Utah, Idaho. Project leader Harold K. Beecher, Architect, Salt Lake City, 1958-62; project architect Ashton, Evans & Brazier, Architects, Salt Lake City, 1962-69, jr. ptnr. Snedaker, Budd & Watts, Architects, Salt Lake City, 1969-73; v.p. Budd, Weiss & Vincent, Architects, 1973-78, pres., 1978-82; owner, operator Weiss & Assocs., Architects/Planners, Salt Lake City, 1978—. Prin. work includes Friendship Manor Apts., 1969 (merit award, 1969), Adminstrn. Bldg. Dept. Natural Resources, State of Utah, 1981, First Fed. Plaza, 1981. Served with USN, 1943-47, PTO. Recipient Merit awards Utah State U., Concrete Inst., 1969, Constrn. Specifications Inst., 1969, Masonry award Design Excellence Utah Masonry Council, 1981. Mem. Nat. Council of Archtl. Registration Bds. (cert.), AIA (award of Merit Design Excellence and Use of Landscaping in Architecture, Utah chpt., 1981), Salt Lake Area C. of C. Lodges: Kiwanis (dir. Sandy chpt. 1978-79, dir. Salt Lake Bonneville chpt. 1983-85), Lions. Office: Weiss & Assocs Architects/Planners #8 E Broadway Salt Lake City UT 84111

WEISS, STEVEN ALAN, communications company executive; b. Glendale, Calif., Oct. 19, 1944; s. Adrian and Ethel (Long) W.; A.A., Los Angeles City Coll., 1964; B.S., U. So. Calif., 1966; M.S., Northwestern U., 1967; J.D., LaSalle Extension U., 1970; m. Laurie Charmak, Nov. 9, 1967; children—Ara Simon, Zachary Adam. Gen. mgr. Adrian Weiss Prodns., Beverly Hills, Calif., 1971-74; v.p., treas. Weiss Global Enterprises, Beverly Hills, 1974-76, sec.-treas., 1976—, dir., 1974—; sec.-treas. Film Investment Corp., Oxnard, Calif., 1975—. Charter mem. Republican Presdl. Task Force, U.S. Senatorial Club, Nat. Rep. Senatorial Com.; mem. Jewish Nat. Fund, Eddie Cantor Charitable Found., Simon Weisenthal Ctr., Scripps Inst.; sustaining mem. Rep. Nat. Com., Calif. Rep. Party. Served with USN, 1966-71. Mem. Nat. Cable TV Assn., Nat. Assn. TV Program Execs. Internat., Am. Film Inst., Assn. Program Distbrs. Jewish. Lodges: Masons, B'nai B'rith, Scottish Rite. Home: 4137 Sunset Ln Channel Islands CA 93035-8017 Office: 2055 S Saviers Rd Suite 12 Oxnard CA 93033-3693

WEISS, STEVEN NEIL, venture capitalist; b. Bklyn., May 4, 1946; s. Irving and Rose (Berger) W.; m. Sandra Jacob, June 14, 1969 (div. Dec. 1983); children: Ilene Stacy, Jason Yvan; m. Mary Alice Caldwell, May 28, 1984. BSEE, CCNY, 1968, MSEE, 1970; MBA, Fordham U., 1974; postgrad., NYU, 1970-72. Cert. med. technologist, N.Y. Engring. mgr. Cavitron Corp., Irvine, Calif., 1970-77; gen. mgr. Edwards Labs., Irvine, 1977-82; pres. Diasonics-Cardio-Imaging, Milpitas, Calif., 1982-83; pres., chief exec. officer Vitalog Corp., Palo Alto, Calif., 1983-84; gen. ptnr. Montgomery Med. Ventures, San Francisco, 1984—; bd. dirs. Pediatric Diagnostic Services, Boston, 1985—, Loredan, Inc., Davis, Calif., 1985—, Medinet, Inc., Purchase, N.Y., 1985—. Patentee in field. Mem. IEEE, Am. Inst. Ultrasound in Medicine, Assn. Advancement Med. Instrumentation, Eta Kappa Nu, Tau Beta Pi, Tau Epsilon Phi (treas. 1967). Avocations: raquetball, tennis, travel. Home: 112 Via Collado Los Gatos CA 95030 Office: Montgomery Med Ventures 600 Montgomery St San Francisco CA 94111

WEIST, ROBERT DUNCAN, corporation executive; b. Joliet, Ill., July 10, 1939; s. Gilbert H. and Kathryn (Turner) W.; m. Sally Carlson, Sept. 3, 1960; children: Sandra, Kari, Robert. BS in Chem. Engring., Purdue U., 1962; JD, NYU, 1966; MBA, U. Chgo., 1981. BAR: N.J. 1966, Ill. 1968. Primary patent atty. ESSO Research & Engring. Co., Elizabeth, N.J., 1962-67; dir. licensing CPC Internat., Chgo., 1967-70; ptnr. Merriam Marshall, Chgo., 1970-76; sr. strategic planner Abbott Labs., Chgo., 1976-82; sr. v.p., sec., gen. counsel Amgen Co., Thousand Oaks, Calif., 1982—. Mem. Chgo. Bar Assn., N.J. Bar Assn., Ill. Bar Assn., Licensing Execs. Soc. Office: Amgen 1900 Oak Terrace Ln Thousand Oaks CA 91320

WEITZ, ELLIOTT BARRY, consultant; b. Traverse City, Mich., Mar. 6, 1941; s. Harry L. and Ellamarie (Pearlman) W.; m. June Kantor, Dec. 31, 1966; children: Mark H., David J. BA in Sociology, Kalamazoo Coll., 1964; student U. Bonn, W.Ger., 1961-62. System programmer Codon Corp., Boston, 1970-71; system architect Index Systems, Inc., Boston, 1971-79, cons., Santa Monica, Calif., 1980-86, mgr. mgmt. info. systems, Irvine, Calif., 1986—. Served to capt. USAF, 1964-69. Mem. Data Processing Mgmt. Assn. (dir. 1977-79), Air Force Assn. Jewish. Lodge: Lions (service award 1977). Home: 15397 Feldspar Dr Chino CA 91709 Office: Nat Edn Corp 18400 Von Karman Irvine CA 92715

WEITZEL, DEE ANN, entrepreneur; b. San Jose, Calif., May 23, 1938; d. Cleo Francis Desbien and Bernice Georgina (Saindon) Trimmer; m. Fred R. Knowles, Feb. 15, 1960 (div. Nov. 1965) children: Scott, Kirk, Clay; m. D.K. Weitzel, Nov. 27, 1969; 1 child, Tim. Student, Mesa Coll., 1965-67. Bookkeeper Holmes Roberts & Owen, Denver, 1967-69; office adminstr. Ernst & Ernst, Denver, 1969-74; chief exec. officer Temporary Services, Inc., Grand Junction, Colo., 1974-85; planner Meetings, Etc., Tucson, 1985—; del. White House Conf. on Small Bus., Washington, 1986; organizer Mesa County Women's Network, 1984, Working Women's Conf., Grand Junction, 1985, Ariz. Awareness Forum on Small Bus., Tucson, 1986, Working Women's Conf., Tucson, 1986, So. Ariz. Working Women's Conf., 1986, Western Colo. Women's Conf., 1986; facilitator Nat. Issues Forum, Tucson, 1986; liaison for Network mag.; bd. dirs. Colo. Small Bus. Council, 1985, Small Bus. Council Denver, 1985. Contbr. articles to profl. jours. Vol. LWV, Tucson, 1986. Recipient Bus. Office Edn. Employer award Mesa County Sch. award, 1977-79, Summer Youth Employee award State Colo., 1980-82. Mem. Am. Soc. Personnel Adminstrs., Assn. Builders and Contractors, Meeting Planners Internat., Am. Soc. Trainers and Developers, Entrepreneurial Forum, Am. Bus. Womens Assn. (Boss of Yr. 1982), Tucson C. of C. (bus. and devel. com. 1986), Nat. Assn. Women Bus. Owners (chmn. polit. action com. So. Ariz. chpt.). Republican. Roman Catholic. Lodge: Monument Lioness (treas. Grand Junction 1980-81) Altrusa Internat. (sec. Grand Junction 1978). Avocations: downhill skiing, reading historical novels, swimmings, watching football. Home: 4020 S Lazy Palm Dr Tucson AZ 85730 Office: Meetings Etc 4020 S Lazy Palm Dr Tucson AZ 85730

WELARATNA, SRI RAMYA, engineering company executive; b. Colombo, Sri Lanka, July 6, 1945; came to U.S., 1979; s. Don Edmund and Lalitha (Rodrigo) W.; m. Usha Sripalee Bandaratilaka, June 19, 1971; children: Ruwan, Sumudu, Deepthi. BSc (with honors), U. Ceylon, Peradeniya, Sri Lanka, 1967; PhD, U. Bradford, Eng., 1975. Sr. applications engr. Hewlett Packard Co., Eng., 1976-79, Santa Clara, Calif., 1979-82; pres. Data Physics Corp., San Jose, Calif., 1984—; cons. signal processing, IBM, San Jose, 1982—. IEEE scholar, Bradford, Eng., 1973. Avocation: carpentry. Home: 767 Sunshine Dr Los Altos CA 94022 Office: Data Physics Corp 1210 S Bascom Ave #224 San Jose CA 95128

WELBORNE, JOHN HOWARD, lawyer; b. Los Angeles, July 24, 1947; s. William Elmo and Pauline Cornwell (Schoder) W. A.B., U. Calif.-Berkeley, 1969; M.P.A., UCLA, 1974; J.D., U. Calif.-Davis, 1977. Bar: Calif. 1977, D.C. 1980. Congl. intern Congressman John V. Tunney, Washington, 1969; assoc. firm Adams, Duque & Hazeltine, Los Angeles, 1979-84, of counsel, 1984—; mgmt. cons., 1971—; dir. Pueblo Viejo Devel. Corp., Union Hardware & Metal Co. Contbr. articles to profl. jours. Mem. cen. bus. dist. project adv. com., chmn. open space task force and South Park task force City of Los Angeles Community Redevel. Agy.; Mem. Los Angeles Philharmonic Men's Com.; pres. Los Angeles County Host Com. for Olympic Games, 1984; mem. exec. com. Citizens' Task Force for Cen. Library Devel., Los Angeles; bd. dirs. Los Angeles chpt. ARC, Children's Bur. Los Angeles, El Pueblo Park Assn., Los Angeles Library Assn., Windsor Sq. Assn., Los Angeles Beautiful, 1982-85, Pershing Sq. Restoration Campaign; bd. dirs. In the Wings div. Music Ctr. Los Angeles County, 1982-86, pres., 1984-85; bd. dirs., officer Los Angeles 200 Com.; bd. councilors U. So. Calif. Sch. Pub. Adminstrn.; mem. adv. bd. The Los Angeles Conservancy; trustee Windsor Sq.-Hancock Park Hist. Soc., 1983-86; fellow Amundsen Inst. U.S.-Mex. Studies. Served with Adj. Gen.'s Corps, U.S. Army, 1970-71, USAR, 1972-79. Decorated Army Commendation medal with oak leaf cluster; Cross of Merit 1st class (Fed. Republic Germany). Mem. ABA, D.C. Bar Assn., State Bar Calif., Los Angeles County Bar Assn. Democrat. Episcopalian. Office: Adams Duque & Hazeltine 523 W 6th St Room 1000 Los Angeles CA 90014

WELCH, BETTY LEONORA, accountant; b. Missoula, Mont., July 18, 1961; d. George Oliver and Betty June (Dolton) W. BBA, U. Mont., 1983. CPA, Mont. Staff acct. Ellis & Assocs., Boise, Idaho, 1984; acct. Glacier Electric Coop., Cut Bank, Mont., 1984-86, office mgr.m 1986—; income tax cons. Mem. Nat. Assn. Female Execs., Am. Inst. CPA's, Beta Gamma Sigma. Democrat. Roman Catholic. Avocations: skiing, sewing, reading, hunting. Office: Glacier Electric Coop Inc 4 410 E Main St Cut Bank MT 59427

WELCH, CARL MARTIN, consulting geologist; b. Manhattan, Kans., July 12, 1949; s. John Francis and Alberta Caroline (Doege) W.; m. Christine Marie Slifko, May 27, 1978; children: Colleen, Kathleen. BS in Geology, S.D. Sch. of Mines and Tech., 1971, MS in Geology, 1974. Registered profl. geologist, Calif. Project geologist Gulf Mineral Resources, Reno, 1974-77; geologist Bendix Corp., Reno, 1978; exploration geologist Continental Materials Corp., Reno, 1979-82; cons. geologist Reno, 1983—; pres. Renegade Resources Corp., Reno, 1984—. Served to 2d lt. U.S. Army, 1975. Mem. Geol. Soc. Am., Soc. Mining Engrs. of AIME, Soc. Econ. Geologists, Nev. Petroleum Soc., Geol. Soc. Nev.; assoc. Sigma Xi. Libertarian. Roman Catholic. Home and Office: Renegade Resources Corp 5335 Cedarwood Dr Reno NV 89511

WELCH, FERN STEWART, magazine editor; b. Redford, Mo., Aug. 13, 1934; d. Elza L. and Ruby I. (Bounds) DeMente; m. John M. Stewart Jr., May 24, 1954; children—Joni Stewart Olsen, Susan Stewart Caldwell, John D.; m. 2d, Kenneth A. Welch, Apr. 25, 1981. A.A., Phoenix Coll., 1953; student Ariz. State U., 1954, Phoenix Coll., 1965, Bellevue Community Coll., 1967, Lake Washington Community Coll., 1968. Writer-reporter, columnist Sammamish Valley News, Redmond Wash., 1967-71; staff writer, asst. to pub. relations dir. First Nat. Bank Oreg., Portland, 1971-72; asst. pub. relations dir. The Ariz. Bank, Phoenix, 1972-73, pub. relations dir., 1973-77; founder, prin. Fern Stewart and Assocs., Ltd., Phoenix, 1977—; editorial dir. Metro Phoenix Mag., 1984; lectr. pub. relations. Bd. dirs. Central Ariz. chpt. ARC, 1976—, Combined Met. Arts and Scis.; mem. Arizonans for Cultural Devel., Scottsdale (Ariz.) Art Ctr. Assn., Valley Shakespeare Co. Recipient awards of merit and excellence Internat. Assn. Bus. Communicators, 1975-77. Mem. Pub. Relations Soc. Am., Women in Communications. Republican. Clubs: Phoenix Country, Plaza (Phoenix). Contbr. numerous articles to local and regional mags. Office: Fern Stewart and Assocs Ltd 4707 N 12th St Suite C Phoenix AZ 85014

WELCH, KENNETH WAYNE, JR., marketing executive; b. Apr. 21, 1956; s. Kenneth W. Sr. and Anna Jean (Atkins) W. Grad. high sch., Antelope Valley. Freelance model Galveston, Tex., 1976-79; prin. Welch Landscaping, 1979; mgr. Pyramid Waterbeds, 1980-81, Water Wonderland, 1981; proprietor mail order sales corp. 1981-82; v.p. Whitmore and Assocs., 1982; sales mktg. cons. The Resort Ctr. Inc., Lancaster, Calif., 1982, pres., gen. ptnr., 1983—; chmn. bd., chief exec. officer Internat. Health Resorts, Inc., 1986; exec. producer Video Vacations, 1985. Mem. Antelope Polit. Action Com. Served with U.S. Army, 1974-76. Republican. Mormon. Avocations: building, designing. Office: The Resort Ctr 858 W Jackman Suite 202 Lancaster CA 93534

WELCH, LLOYD RICHARD, engineering educator, consultant; b. Detroit, Sept. 28, 1927; s. Richard C. and Helen (Felt) W.; m. Irene Althea Main, Sept. 12, 1953; children—Pamela Irene Welch Towery, Melinda Ann, Diana Lia Welch Worthington. B.S. in Math., U. Ill., 1951; Ph.D. in Math., Calif. Inst. Tech., 1958. Mathematician NASA-Jet Propulsion Lab., Pasadena, Calif., 1956-59; staff mathematician Inst. Def. Analyses, Princeton, N.J., 1959-65; prof. elec. engring. U. So. Calif., Los Angeles, 1965—; cons. in field. Contbr. articles to profl. jours. Served with USN, 1945-49, 51-52. Fellow IEEE; mem. Nat. Acad. Engring., Am. Math. Soc., Math. Assn. Am., Soc. for Indsl. and Applied Math., Phi Beta Kappa, Sigma Xi, Phi Kappa Phi, Pi Mu Epsilon, Eta Kappa Nu. Office: U So Calif University Park Dept Elec Engring Powell Hall Los Angeles CA 90089

WELCH, MARK RANDOLPH, mining company executive; b. Chuquicamata, Chile, Mar. 23, 1939; (parents Am. citizens); s. John R. and Aileen D. (Russell) W.; children: Kristina, Kenneth, Kimberly; m. Sharon S. Evans, Feb. 6, 1987. BS in Mining Engring., Wash. State U., 1962; MS in Mil. Sci., U.S. Army Command & Gen. Staff Coll., 1983. Project engr. Cleveland Cliffs Iron Co., Ishpeming, Mich., 1968-69; mine mgr. Interpace Corp., Ione, Calif., 1970-74; chief engr. Ranchers Exploration Corp., Albuquerque, 1974-84; pres. Western Resources Co., Albuquerque, 1984—; v.p. Western Resources Mont., Albuquerque, 1985—; ptnr. Amarillo Sand Co., Albuquerque, 1984—. Contbr. research papers to tech. jours. Served to 2d. lt. CE, U.S. Army, 1962-68, lt. col. Res. Mem. Soc. Mining Engrs., Can. Inst. Mining Engrs. Republican. Avocations: geology, hunting, photography. Office: Western Resources Co 10010 Indian School Rd NE Albuquerque NM 87112

WELCH, WILLIAM FRANCIS, mining engr.; b. Monarch, Wyo., Mar. 12, 1909; s. Frank and Mary Ellen (Scullen) W.; student Regis Coll., Denver, 1928-29; Engring. degree in metallurgy Colo. Sch. Mines, 1933; m. Lorene Elizabeth Wondra, Dec. 31, 1952. Mining engr. Sheridan-Wyo. Coal Co., Monarch, 1933-40; ranching and pvt. engring. practice, Acme, Wyo., 1940-48; supt. Welch Coal Co., Sheridan, 1948—, dir., 1948—; pres. Tongue River Ditch Co., 1951—; bd. dirs. Rocky Mountain Fed. Savs. and Loan, Steel Creek Producers, Ranchester State Bank, Capital Savs.; v.p. Wymo Oil Co. Treas. Sch. Dist. 24, 1955-58; pres., 1958-65; treas. Tongue River Soil Conservation Dist., 1949-60. Bd. dirs. Whitney Benefits Ednl. Found., 1964-69; pres. bd. Tongue River Fire Dist., 1954-78; mem. pres.'s council Regis Coll., Denver, Colo. Sch. Mines, Golden; bd. dirs. Billings (Mont.) Deaconess Hosp. Found. Life mem. Nat. Cowboy Hall of Fame; Paul Harris fellow; William F. Welch Mining Ctr. at Sheridan Coll. named for him; Welch Regional Heart Ctr., Billings Deaconess Hosp. named for him. Mem. Wyo. Mining Assn., Wyo. Stockgrowers, Wyo. Sch. Trustees Assn. AIME, Wyo. Water Resources Assn., Rocky Mountain Coal Mining Inst., Soc. Mining Engrs., Alpha Tau Omega, Theta Tau. Clubs: Elks, Rotary. Roman Catholic. Address: 155 Scott Dr Sheridan WY 82801

WELIKY, NORMAN, immunochemist, medical researcher; b. Bronx, N.Y., Nov. 1, 1919; s. Kopel and Mollie (Zimmerman) W.; m. Berta Gandelman, Aug. 4, 1955; children: Karen, Michael. BChemE, CCNY, 1939; postgrad., Columbia U., 1950-52; PhD, Polytech. Inst. Bklyn., 1957. Chemist Mineral Pigments Corp., Muirkirk, Md., 1946-47, Reichhold Chemicals, Inc., Bklyn., 1950-52; research fellow, dept. chemistry Harvard U., Cambridge, Mass., 1956-57; research fellow, dept. chemistry Calif. Inst. Tech., Pasadena, 1957-59, group supr., Jet Propulsion Lab., 1959-65; asst. mgr. bioscis. and electrochemistry dept. TRW Systems Group, Redondo Beach, Calif., 1966-75; research scientist allergy and immunology div. Dept. Pediatrics, UCLA Med. Ctr., Torrance, Calif., 1976-81; asst. research scientist cytology and cytogenics div. City of Hope Nat. Med. Ctr., Duarte, Calif., 1983-85; cons. Monterey Park, Calif., 1985—; cons. Nat. Cancer Inst., Bethesda, Md., 1968-71. Contbr. articles to profl. jours.; patentee in field. Served with USN, 1942-46. Recipient Technical Brief award NASA, 1973. Mem. Am. Chem. Soc. (councilor 1973-74, congl. sci. counselor 1978—, alternate legisltv. counselor 1974-78), So. Calif. sect. Am. Chem. Soc. (chmn., chemistry and pub. affairs 1969-72), Royal Soc. Chemistry, AAAS, Assn. Harvard Chemists, Sigma Xi. Home and Office: 1072 Ridge Crest St Monterey Park CA 91754

WELLER, EMY LU, teacher specialist, educator; b. Torrington, Wyo., Feb. 23, 1949; d. William Edward and Mary O. (Netherton) Warren; m. Steve Michael Weller, Aug. 6, 1969 (div. Mar. 1971); 1 child, Meri Kathryn. AA, Eastern Wyo. Coll., 1969; BA, U. Wyo., 1971, MA, 1975; PhD, UCLA, Calif. State U. Los Angeles (joint deg.), 1981. Cert. elem. edn. tchr., tchr. of severely handicapped, learning handicapped, Calif., Wyo. Asst. prof. Calif. State U., Los Angeles, 1976-85; chief cons. assessment and resource ctr. Pasadena (Calif.) Guidance Clins., 1981—; tchr. specialist, assoc. prof. Pasadena City Coll., 1979—; chief cons. learning disabilities assessment, Assessment and Resource Ctr., div. Pasadena Guidance Clins., 1981—. Mem. Calif. Assn. Neurologically Handicapped Children/Assn. Children and Adults with Learning Disabilities (exec. com., community coll. liason 1986-87, spl. award 1983), Orton Dyslexia Soc. Avocations: gardening, jogging, aerobics, camping. Home: 68 N Michigan #2 Pasadena CA 91106 Office: Pasadena City Coll Spl Services 1570 E Colorado Blvd Pasadena CA 91106

WELLER, GUNTER ERNST, geophysics educator; b. Haifa, June 14, 1934; came to U.S., 1968; s. Erich and Nella (Lange) W.; m. Sigrid Beilharz, Apr. 11, 1963; children: Yvette, Kara, Britta. BS, U. Melbourne, Australia, 1962,

MS, 1964, PhD, 1968. Meteorologist Bur. Meteorology, Melbourne, 1959-61; glaciologist Australian Antarctic Exps., 1964-67; from asst. prof. to assoc. prof. geophysics Geophys. Inst., U. Alaska, Fairbanks, 1968-72, prof., 1973—, dep. dir., 1984—; program mgr. NSF, Washington, 1972-74; pres. Internat. Commn. Polar Meteorology, 1980-83; chmn. polar research bd. Nat. Acad. Scis., 1985—. Contbr. numerous articles to profl. jours. Recipient Polar medal Govt. Australia, 1969; Mt. Weller named in his honor by Govt. Australia, Antarctica; Weller Bank named in his honor by U.S. Govt., Arctic. Fellow Arctic Inst. N.Am.; mem. Internat. Glaciological Soc., Am. Meteorol. Soc. (chmn. polar meteorology com. 1980-83), Am. Geophys. Union, AAAS. Home: Box 81024 Fairbanks AK 99708 Office: U Alaska Geophys Inst Fairbanks AK 99775-0800

WELLER, JAMES ROBERT, advertising executive, film director; b. Chgo., Jan. 10, 1940; s. Ross Russell and Mildred (Skerball) W.; m. Victoria Montgomery; 1 child, Barrett Elizabeth. BS, Northwestern U., 1961. Pres. Jim Weller & Ptnrs., Milw., 1969-74; sr. v.p. Clinton E. Frank Advt., Chgo., N.Y.C. and San Francisco, 1974-78; exec. v.p., ptnr. Van Levween & Ptnrs., N.Y.C., 1978-79, Della Femina, Travisano & Ptnrs., Los Angeles, N.Y.C. and Tokyo, 1979—; bd. dirs. Casablanca Industries, Los Angeles, 1985—. Creative dir. Tuesday Team-Reagan campaign, Washington, 1984, Ned Regan for State Comptroller, N.Y.C., 1978, 86. Recipient Gold Medal award Internat. Film Festival N.Y., Internat. Film Festival Chgo., N.Y. Art Dirs. Shows, Clio awards, Belding awards, Telly awards, Am. Advt. Show awards. Home: 1485 Stone Canyon Rd Old Bel-Air CA 90077 Office: Della Femina Travisano Ptnrs 5900 Wilshire Blvd Los Angeles CA 90036

WELLES, JOHN GALT, museum director; b. Orange, N.J., Aug. 24, 1925; s. Paul and Elizabeth Ash (Galt) W.; m. Barbara Lee Chrisman, Sept. 15, 1951; children: Virginia Chrisman, Deborah Galt, Barton Jeffery, Holly Page. BE, Yale U., 1946; MBA, U. Pa., 1949. Test engr. Gen. Electric Co., Lynn, Mass., 1947; labor relations staff New Departure div. Gen Motors Corp., Bristol, Conn., 1949-51; mem. staff Mountain States Employers Council, Denver, 1952-55; head indsl. econs. div. U. Denver Research Inst., Denver, 1956-74; v.p. planning and devel. Colo. Sch. Mines, Golden, 1974-83; regional adminstr. EPA, Denver, 1983-87; exec. dir. Denver Mus. Natural History, 1987—. Sr. cons. Secretariat, UN Conf. Human Environment, Geneva, 1971-72; cons. Bus. Internat., S.A., Geneva, 1972; dir. KCFR Pub. Broadcasting of Colo. Inc., Denver, 1985—; chmn. Colo. Front Range Project, Denver, 1979-80. Contbr. articles to profl. jours., newspapers. Recipient Disting. Service award Denver Regional Council Govts., 1980. Mem. Am. Econ. Assn., AAAS, World Future Soc., Tau Beta Pi, Blue Key. Republican. Episcopalian. Clubs: Arapahoe Tennis (pres. 1964-65); University (Denver). Office: Denver Mus Natural History City Park Denver CO 80252

WELLES, MELINDA FASSETT, educational psychologist, educator, consultant, artist; b. Palo Alto, Calif., Jan. 4, 1943; d. George Edward and Barbara Helena (Todd) W.; m. Robert Joseph Sbordone, June 30, 1972 (div. Aug. 1977). Student fine arts San Francisco Inst. Art, 1959-60, U. Oreg., 1960-62; BA in Fine Arts, UCLA, 1964, MA in Spl. Edn., 1971, PhD in Ednl. Psychology, 1976; student fine arts and illustration Art Ctr. Coll. Design, 1977-80. Cert. ednl. psychologist, Calif. Asst. prof. Calif. State U., Northridge, 1979-82, Pepperdine U., Los Angeles, 1979-82; assoc. prof. counseling and spl. edn. U. So. Calif., Los Angeles, 1980—; mem. acad. faculty Pasadena City Coll., 1973-79, Art Ctr. Coll. Design, 1978—, Otis Art Inst. of Parsons Sch. Design, Los Angeles, 1986—, UCLA Extension, 1980-84, Coll. Devel. Studies, Los Angeles, 1980—, El Camino Community Coll., Redondo Beach, Calif., 1982-86; cons. spl. edn.; pub. adminstrn. analyst UCLA Spl. Edn. Research Program, 1973-76; exec. dir. Atwater Park Ctr. Disabled Children, Los Angeles, 1976-78; coordinator Pacific Oaks Coll. in service programs for Los Angeles Unified Schs., Pasadena, 1978-81. Author, Calif. Dept. Edn. tech. reports, 1972-76; editor: Teaching Special Students in the Mainstream, 1981; group shows include: San Francisco Inst. Art, 1960, U. Hawaii, 1978, Barnsdall Gallery, Los Angeles, 1979, 80; represented in various pvt. collections. HEW fellow, 1971-72; grantee Calif. Dept. Edn., 1975-76, Calif. Dept. Health, 1978. Mem. Calif. Assn. Neurologically Handicapped Children, Am. Council Learning Disabilities, Clearing House for Info. on Learning Disabilities, Calif. Scholarship Fedn. (life), Alpha Chi Omega. Democrat. Office: U So Calif WPH 301 Univ Park Los Angeles CA 90089

WELLING, CONRAD GERHART, mining company executive; b. St. Louis, June 21, 1919; s. Conrad Author and Otillia (Brefeld) W.; m. Mary Katherine Henderson, Aug. 26, 1944; children: Bonnie Lynn Parks, Conrad G. II, Patricia Ann Leugers. MS, U.S. Naval Postgrad. Sch., 1948. Commd. ensign USN, 1936, advanced through grades to comdr., 1954, ret., 1959; program mgr. Lockheed Corp., Sunnyvale, Calif., 1959-77; v.p. Ocean Minerals Co., Mountain View, Calif., 1977-81; sr. v.p. Ocean Minerals Co., Santa Clara, Calif., 1981—; exec. com. Law-of-The-Sea Inst., 1980—. Inventor, patentee Ocean Mining System, 1980. Mem. AAAS, Off Shore Tech. Conf. (chmn. bd. dirs. 1983), Marine Tech. Soc., Am. Mining Congress. Republican. Home: 102 Catalpa Dr Atherton CA 94025 Office: Ocean Minerals Co 3385 Scott Blvd Santa Clara CA 95051

WELLING, DOUGLAS STEVEN, academic administrator; b. Kansas City, Mo., Feb. 6, 1952; s. Gordon Lilywhite and JoAnne (Purcell) W.; m. Kate Eleanor Dobos, Mar. 28, 1981. BS in Econs., Ariz. State U., 1976; MBA, U. Colo., 1983. Computer operator Phoenix Coll., 1973-76; operator power plant Salt River Project, Page, Ariz., 1976-78; instrumentation technician Colo.-Ute Elec. Assn., Hayden, 1978-80; cons. Utility Graphics Cons., Englewood, Colo., 1980-83; mgr. data processing Kellogg Corp., Littleton, Colo., 1983-85; dir. info. mgmt. Adams County (Colo.) Sch. Dist. 50, Westminster, 1985—; cons. Swedish Hosp., Englewood, 1983-84. Contbr. articles to profl. jours. Patron Denver Art Mus., 1986; vol. Denver VA, 1984—, Denver Spl. Olympics, 1983—. Served as cpl. USMC, 1971-72, Vietnam. Mem. Data Processing Mgmt. Assn., Assn. Computing Machinery (com. chmn. 1983-86), Assn. System Mgrs., Assn. Sch. Bus. Ofcls., AM/FM Internat. (mem. com. 1984-86), Sigma Alpha Epsilon (treas., bd. dirs. 1985-86). Republican. Mormon. Lodge: Elks. Avocations: skiing, rugby, photography. Home: 10615 Ash Ct Thornton CO 80233 Office: Ctr for Info Mgmt 7300 Lowell Blvd Westminster CO 80030

WELLINGTON, JOHN SESSIONS, medical school administrator, educator, physician; b. Glendale, Calif., Sept. 28, 1921; s. George Washington and Florence Eveline (Smith) W.; m. Mary Jane Evans, Feb. 26, 1944; children: Peter Evans, Ann Elizabeth. AB, U. Calif., Berkeley, 1942; MD, U. Calif., San Francisco, 1945. Diplomate Am. Bd. Surgery, Am. Bd. Pathology. Intern U.S. Naval Hosp., Oakland, Calif., 1945-46; resident VA Hosp., San Francisco, 1948-51; resident in pathology U. Calif. Hosp., San Francisco, 1951-52; resident San Francisco Gen. Hosp., 1952-53; from instr. to prof. pathology U. Calif., San Francisco, 1953-78, assoc. dean sch. med., 1968-78; prof. pathology U. Hawaii, Honolulu, 1978—, acting dean sch. med., 1978-79, acting provost, profl. schs., 1980-81, assoc. dean sch. med., 1982—; cons. UNESCO, Indonesia, 1970, AID, S.E. Asia Regional Ctr. Tropical Medicine, 1966-68. Contbr. articles on pathology, internat. med. edn. to profl. jours. Bd. dirs. Community Mental Health Services, Honolulu, 1985—. Served with USNR, 1942-48. Alan Gregg Travel fellow China Med. Bd., 1967-68. Fellow Am. Coll. Pathologists; mem. Internat. Acad. Pathologists, Am. Soc. Exptl. Pathology, Hawaii Soc. Pathologists (pres. 1986-87). Democrat. Home: 2064 Alihilani Pl Honolulu HI 96822 Office: U Hawaii 1960 East West Rd Honolulu HI 96822

WELLNER, JON AUGUST, statistician, educator; b. Portland, Oreg., Aug. 17, 1945; s. Charles August and Ethel Dorothy (Wolf) W.; m. Cathryn Joyce Holm, Oct. 18, 1969. BS in Math., U. Idaho, 1968; PhD in Stats., U. Wash., 1975. Asst. prof. stats. U. Rochester, N.Y., 1975-78, assoc. prof., 1978-83; prof. U. Wash., 1983—. Author: Empirical Processes with Applications to Statistics, 1986; contbr. articles to profl. jours. Served to lt. U.S. Army, 1969-71, Vietnam. Fellow Inst. Math. Stats. (assoc. editor Annals of Stats. 1983—). Avocations: mountain climbing, skiing, photography. Home: 1947 14th Ave E Seattle WA 98112 Office: U Wash Dept Stats GN-22 Seattle WA 98195

WELLS, ALAN HILARY, biomedical researcher; b. N.Y.C., Dec. 15, 1958. AB, Brown U., 1979; D Med. Sci., Karolonska Inst., Stockholm, 1982; postdoctoral studies, Brown U., 1981—. Assoc. prof. Okayama (Japan) U. Med. Sch., 1983-84; postdoctoral fellow U. Calif., San Francisco, 1984-86. Contbr. articles to profl. jours. Recipient ICRETT award Union Internat. Against Cancer, Geneva, 1980. Mem. AAAS, N.Y. Acad. Scis., Sigma Chi, Phi Beta Kappa, N.Y. Acad. Scis. Jewish. Avocations: hiking, skiing, reading, travelling. Home: 415 Warren 2 San Francisco CA 94131 Office: Hooper Found UCSF HSW 1501 San Francisco CA 94143

WELLS, ALBERT JOHN, JR., sales executive; b. Boston, Oct. 4, 1932; s. Albert John Sr. and Rena Louise (Duke) W.; m. Elizabeth-Ann Parr, Sept. 20, 1954 (div. 1978); children: Beth, Greg; m. Karen F. Rosen, Apr. 4, 1980. BSChemE, U. R.I., 1954. Systems engr. E.I. DuPont de Nemours, Newark, Del., 1959-65; sales engr. The Hays Corp., Michigan City, Ind., 1965-70; product mgr. The Foxboro (Mass.) Co., 1970-80; mgr. sales and mktg. BBN Instruments Corp., Cambridge, Mass., 1980-82; mgr. sales Automated Dynamics Co., San Jose, Calif., 1982-84; pres. Pantechnicon, Danville, Calif., 1984—; Mem. bd. trustees So. New Eng. Annual Conf., Boston, 1979-82. Served as lt. USNR, 1956-59. Mem. Instrument Soc. Am. (sr.), Am. Inst. Chem. Engrs. Methodist. Club: Toastmasters. Lodge: Masons. Avocation: sailing. Home and Office: Pantechicon 598 Sycamore Circle Danville CA 94526

WELLS, CECIL HAROLD, JR., consulting engineer; b. San Mateo, Calif., Apr. 21, 1927; s. Cecil H. and Bertha (Teeter) W.; m. Elizabeth Anne O'Leary (dec.); children—Cecilia E. A., Timothy; m. Christina Maria Poelzl; children—Kristy-Sue, Jeff-Dean. Student, Menlo Coll., 1948, San Jose State Coll., 1948, U. Calif., 1949, 52; BCE, U. Santa Clara, 1951. Registered profl. engr., Calif., Alaska, Ariz., Colo., Mont., Nev., Oreg., Tex., Utah, Wash. Engr. Hall & Pregnoff, San Francisco, 1951-56; engr. Graham Hayes, San Francisco, 1956-58; cons. engr. on bldgs. and structures Cecil H. Wells, Jr. & Assocs., San Mateo, 1953—; pres. 20th Ave. Catering Corp., 1971-72, 2031 Pioneer Ct. Corp., 1958-70; tchr. engring. Menlo Coll., 1948-62; lectr. lateral design of bldgs. Stanford U., 1956-61. Author: Structural Engineering Design for Architects and Design of Buildings for Earthquakes and Wind. Mem. San Mateo County Regional Planning Bd., pres., 1964-65; mem. San Francisco, San Mateo, Santa Clara Tri County Planning Bd., pres., 1959-60; chmn. Elks Charity, 1964-65; mem. Calif. Bay Conservation and Devel. Commn., 1965-67, Internat. Conf. World Planners, Mexico City, 1964; commr. San Mateo City Planning, 1956-67, chmn., 1958-59, 61-62, 64-67; mem. San Mateo City Govtl. Efficiency Commn., chmn. 1970-72; engr. San Mateo County Harbor Dist., 1969-83; active Boy Scouts Am., mem. exec. bd. county, 1969—, county v.p., exec. bd., 1972-75, chmn. Explorers, 1969-74; pres. Menlo Alumni Council, 1967-68; mem. men's adv. com. LWV, 1970-71, 73-74; trustee Drew Sch., 1972-73; bd. dirs. Purissima Mut. Water Dist., 1968-71, San Mateo County Devel. Assn., 1964—, San Mateo County Growth Policy Council, 1982—. Served with Submarine Service, USNR, World War II. Named Citizen of Day, Sta. KABL, 1970, 74; recipient 1st place award in apt. design City of Fremont Environ. Design Com., 1973, Silver Beaver award Boy Scouts Am., 1975; Paul Harris fellow Rotary Internat., 1980. Fellow ASCE; mem. ASTM, Structural Engring. Assn. Calif. (sec. 1954-58), Seismol. Soc. Am., Am. Concrete Inst., San Mateo C. of C. (bd. dirs. 1965—, pres. 1969-72), Nat. Soc. Profl. Engrs., Am. Soc. Mil. Engrs., Am. Inst. Timber Constrn., Prestressed Concrete Inst., Nat. Rifle Assn., San Mateo County Hist. Soc. Club: Peninsula Golf and Country. Lodges: Rotary (pres. 1972-73), Elks (exalted ruler 1966-67, trustee 1967-72, chmn. 1971-72). Office: 2031 Pioneer Ct Suite 12 San Mateo CA 94403

WELLS, DAVID CONRAD, lawyer; b. Los Angeles, June 22, 1938; s. Glenn W. and Maxine B. Wells; m. D. Charlene Moore, Apr. 6, 1963; children—Karen A., Michael V. B.A., U. Colo., 1960, LL.B., 1963. Bar: Colo. 1963. Assoc., Mack, Johnson & Doty, Boulder, Colo., 1963-66; ptnr. Zook & Wells, Boulder, 1966-68; sole practice, Boulder, 1969-75; ptnr. Wells, Love & Scoby, Boulder, 1975—; lectr. Constable, Boulder County, 1960-63; fire chief Boulder Heights Fire Protection Dist., 1972-78. Mem. ABA, Colo. Bar Assn., Boulder County Bar Assn., Am. Arbitration Assn. Author legal articles. Office: 225 Canyon Blvd Boulder CO 80302

WELLS, FRANK G., lawyer, film studio executive; b. Mar. 4, 1932. BA summa cum laude, Pomona Coll., 1953; MA in Law (Rhodes scholar), Oxford U., Eng., 1955; LLB, Stanford U., 1959. Former vice chmn. Warner Bros. Inc.; ptnr. Gang Tyre & Brown, 1962-69; pres., chief operating officer Walt Disney Prodns., Burbank, Calif., 1984—. Co-author: Seven Summits. Served to 1st lt. U.S. Army, 1955-57. Mem. Phi Beta Kappa, ABA, State Bar Calif. Club: Explorer's. Office: Walt Disney Productions 500 South Buena Vista St Burbank CA 91521 *

WELLS, GERTRUDE BEVERLY, speech language pathology educator; b. Harerhill, Mass., July 14, 1940; d. True Franklyn Wells and Priscilla Eleanor (Browne) Duerstling. BS, SUNY, Fredonia, 1962; MA, Coll. St. Rose, 1969; PhD, U. Mo., 1976. Tchr. speech pathology N.Y. Pub. Schs., Albany and Clifton Park, 1962-70; lectr. SUNY, Albany, 1970-73; asst. prof. Coll. St. Rose, Albany, 1975-77; assoc. prof. U. No. Iowa, Cedar Falls, 1977-78; prof. U. Southwestern La., Lafayette, 1978-85; prof., program dir. Calif. State U. Stanislaus, Turlock, 1985—; cons. in field. Author: Stuttering Treatment, 1987; contbr. articles to profl. jours. Mem. United Way of Stanislaus County, Modesto, Calif., 1985—, Stroke Services, Inc., Modesto, 1985—, Services to Older Adults Advisory Council, Modesto, 1985—. Mem. Am. Speech Lang. Hearing Assn., Calif. Speech Lang. Hearing Assn., AAUP, Nat. Assn. Women Deans Adminstrs. and Counselors, Kappa Delta Pi. Democrat. Mem. Unitarian Ch. Avocations: skiing, oil painting, writing. Home: 1413 Emigrant Way Modesto CA 95351 Office: Calif State U Stanislaus 801 W Monte Vista Ave Turlock CA 95380

WELLS, JOHN STEWART, physician, psychiatrist; b. San Francisco, June 15, 1934. BA, Stanford U., 1956; MD, U. Iowa, 1965. Diplomate Am. Bd. Psychiatry and Neurology. Practice medicine specializing in psychiatry Arcadia, Calif., 1969—; dist. dir. Los Angeles County Dept. Mental Health, Arcadia, 1970—; asst. clin. prof. psychiatry U. So. Calif., Los Angeles, 1978—. Officer Arcadia Reserve Police Dept., 1980; bd. dirs. Community Hotline, Arcadia, 1983. Served to lt. USN, 1957-61. Fellow Am. Psychiat. Assn. Democrat. Presbyterian. Avocation: skiing, backpacking, bridge, swimming, traveling. Office: PO Box 1309 735 W Duarte Rd Arcadia CA 91006

WELLS, MERLE WILLIAM, historian, state archivist; b. Lethbridge, Alta., Can., Dec. 1, 1918; s. Norman Danby and Minnie Muir (Huckett) W.; student Boise Jr. Coll., 1937-39; A.B., Coll. Idaho, 1941, L.H.D. (hon.), 1981; M.A., U. Calif., 1947, Ph.D., 1950. Instr. history Coll. Idaho, Caldwell, 1942-46; assoc. prof. history Alliance Coll., Cambridge Springs, Pa., 1950-56, 58, dean students, 1955-56; cons. historian Idaho Hist. Soc., Boise, 1956-58, historian and archivist, 1959—; hist. preservation officer, archivist State of Idaho, Boise, 1968-86. Treas., So. Idaho Migrant Ministry, 1960-64, chmn., 1964-67, 70—; nat. migrant adv. com. Nat. Council Chs., 1964-67, gen. bd. Idaho council, 1967-75; bd. dirs. Idaho State Employees Credit Union, 1964-67, treas., 1966-67; mem. Idaho Commn. Arts and Humanities, 1966-67; mem. Idaho Lewis and Clark Trail Commn., 1968-70, 84—; mem. Idaho Bicentennial Commn., 1971-76; bd. dirs. Sawtooth Interpretive Assn., 1972—, dept. history United Presbyn. Ch., 1978-84; v.p. Idaho Zool. Soc., 1982-84, bd. dirs., 1984—. State Hist. Preservation Officers (dir. 1976-81, chmn. Western states council on geog. names 1982-83), Am. Hist. Assn., Western History Assn. (council 1973-76), AAUP, Am. Assn. State and Local History (council 1973-77), Soc. Am. Archivists, others. Author: Anti-Mormonism in Idaho, 1978, Boise: An Illustrated History, 1982, Gold Camps and Silver Cities, 1984, Idaho: Gem of the Mountains, 1985. Office: Idaho Hist Soc 610 N Julia Davis Dr Boise ID 83702

WELLS, MICHAEL ARTHUR, biochemist, educator; b. Los Angeles, Nov. 8, 1938. BA, U. So. Calif., 1961; PhD, U. Ky., 1965. Asst. prof. U. Ariz., Tucson, 1967-72, assoc. prof., 1972-77, prof. biochemistry, 1977—; acting chmn. U. Ariz., Tucson, 1974-75, dept. head 1986—; vis. research scientist U. Calif., Santa Barbara, 1975-76. Macy Faculty scholar and vis. research scientist, U. Calif., 1975-76; predoctoral fellow U.S. Pub. Health Service, U. Ky., 1962-65, postdoctoral Am. Cancer Soc., U. Wash., 1965-67. Mem. Am. Chem. Soc., Am. Soc. Biol. Chemists, AAAS, Phi Beta Kappa, Phi Kappa Phi. Home: 3502 N Forgeus Pl Tucson AZ 85716 Office: U Ariz Dept Biochemistry Biological Sciences W Tucson AZ 85721

WELLS, PATRICIA BENNETT, business administration educator; b. Park River, N.D., Mar. 25, 1935; d. Benjamin Beekman Bennett and Alice Catherine (Peerboom) Bennett Breckinridge; A.A., Allan Hancock Coll., Santa Maria, Calif., 1964; B.S. magna cum laude, Coll. Great Falls, 1966; M.S., U. N.D., 1967, Ph.D., 1971; children—Bruce Bennett, Barbara Lea. Fiscal acct. USIA, Washington, 1954-56; public acct., Bremerton, Wash., 1956; statistician U.S. Navy, Bremerton, 1957-59; med. services accounts officer U.S. Air Force, Vandenberg AFB, Calif., 1962-64; instr. bus. adminstrn. Western New Eng. Coll., 1967-69; vis. prof. econs. Chapman Coll., 1971; vis. prof. U. So. Calif. systems Griffith AFB, N.Y., 1973-74; assoc. prof. bus. Va. State U., 1973-74; assoc. prof. bus. adminstrn. Oreg. State U., Corvallis, 1978-82, prof. mgmt., 1982—, coordinator, 1984-86, dir. adminstrv. mgmt. program, 1974-81, pres. Faculty Senate, 1981; cons. process tech. devel. Digital Equipment Corp., 1982. Pres., chmn. bd. dirs. Adminstrv. Orgnl. Services, Inc., Corvallis, 1976-83, Dynamic Achievement, Inc., 1983—. Cert. adminstrv. mgr. Fellow Am. Bus. Women's Assn. (named Top Businesswoman in Nation 1980, Bus. Assoc. Yr. 1986); mem. Am. Bus. Communication Assn. (mem. internat. bd. 1980-83, v.p. Northwest 1981, 2d v.p. 1982-83, 1st v.p. 1983-84, pres. 1984-85), Assn. Info. Systems Profls., Adminstrv. Mgmt. Soc., AAUP (chpt. sec. 1973, chpt. bd. dirs. 1982, 84-87, pres. Oreg. conf. 1983-85), Am. Vocat. Assn. (nominating com. 1976), Associated Oreg. Faculties, Nat. Bus. Edn. Assn., Nat. Assn. Tchr. Edn. for Bus. Office Edn. (pres. 1976-77, chmn. public relations com. 1978-81), Corvallis Area C. of C. (v.p. chamber devel. 1985-86, Pres.'s award 1986), Sigma Kappa. Roman Catholic. Contbr. numerous articles to profl. jours. Office: 208 Bexell Coll Bus Oreg State U Corvallis OR 97331

WELLS, RICHARD PAUL, chemist; b. Idaho Falls, Idaho, Mar. 12, 1959; s. Lyman G. and Barbara Ann (Lang) W. BS, U. Idaho, 1981; MS, U. Utah, 1983. Chemist Morton-Thiokol Inc., Brigham City, Utah, 1983-85, sr. chemist, 1985-86, sr. engr., 1986—. Mem. Am. Chem. Soc. (com. chmn. 1985—). Avocations: woodworking, skiing, softball, golf. Home: 1138 Connecticut Ave Ogden UT 84404 Office: Morton-Thiokol Inc PO Box 524 M S 732 Brigham City UT 84302

WELLS, THEODORA FRASER WESTMONT, communications cons.; b. Niagara Falls, N.Y., Apr. 18, 1926; d. Oscar B. and Marjorie Wells (Fraser) Westmont; B.S., U. Calif., Berkeley, 1947; M.B.A., U. So. Calif., 1965; divorced; children—David Kuettel, Steven Kuettel; 1 stepdau., Deanna Molina. Fin. dir. Los Angeles Council Girl Scouts U.S., 1954-58; asst. v.p., project coordinator, customer relations dir. Lytton Savs. & Loan Assn., Hollywood, Calif., 1961-68; tng. and customer relations mgr. First Charter Fin. Corp., Beverly Hills, Calif., 1968-69; partner Wells-Christie Assos., 1970-72; propr. Wells Assocs., Beverly Hills, 1970—; extension tchr. mgmt. devel. for women UCLA, 1968-79. Mem. Acad. Mgmt., Orgn. Devel. Network, Am. Soc. Tng. and Devel., World Future Soc., Assn. Humanistic Psychology, Delta Gamma, Beta Gamma Sigma. Author: Woman—Which Includes Man, of Course, 1970; (with Rosalind K. Loring) Breakthrough: Women into Management (Edn. award Delta Kappa Gamma 1973, Profl. Achievement award Phi Chi Theta 1974), 1972; Keeping Your Cool Under Fire: Communicating Non-Defensively, 1980; also articles to profl. jours. and chpts. in books on non-defensive communication, psychology of women. Home: 341 S Swall Beverly Hills CA 90211 Office: Box 3392 Beverly Hills CA 90212

WELLS-MORAN, JOLYN, social worker; b. Port Angeles, Wash., Jan. 27, 1953; d. Robert Earl and Lorna Jean (Cameron) W. B, Western Wash. U.; MSW, U. Wash. Therapist Lake Whatcom Ctr., Bellingham, Wash., 1980-82; case mgr. Seattle Psychiat. Clin., 1982-84; case mgr., dir. research Chinook Club of Valley Cities Mental Health Ctr., Auburn, Wash., 1986—. Mem. Nat. Assn. Social Workers, Wash. Community Mental Health Assn. Office: Chinook Club 602 W Main St Auburn WA 98001

WELSCH, JAMES LESTER, municipal judge; b. Catskill, N.Y., Oct. 2, 1917; s. Wolfgang Frederick and Hazel Juene (Lester) W.; m. Grace Warner, Oct. 23, 1963. B.S., Purdue U., 1942; M.A., Los Angeles State Coll., 1954; D. Naturopathy, Golden State U., 1956. Lic. ednl. adminstr., N. Mex., Ariz., Colo. real estate broker, N.Mex. Personnel mgr. Nat. Cash Register Co. electronics div., Hawthorne, Calif., 1952-55; dir. indsl. relations Mercast Mfg. Corp., LaVerne, Calif., 1955-57; asst. prof. mgmt. Eastern N.Mex. U., Portales, 1957-58; asst. prof. indsl. mgmt. Calif. Western U., San Diego, 1958-63; dir. Montelores Multicultural Ctr., Cortez, Colo., 1967-68; guidance counselor Dzilth-Na-o-dith-hle Sch., Bur. Indian Affairs, Bloomfield, N.Mex., 1974-76, supervisory guidance counselor, Huerfano, N.Mex., 1976-80, realty specialist, rights protection, Juneau, Alaska, 1980, supervisory realty specialist, Anchorage, 1981-83; mcpl. judge, Bloomfield, N.Mex., 1983—. Chmn. San Juan County (N.Mex.) planning and zoning commn., 1973; bd. dirs. San Juan County Mus. Assn., 1978-79, San Juan County chpt. ARC, 1980; del. N.Mex., State Republican Conv., 1974, 76; sustaining mem. Rep. Nat. Com. Served to lt. USN, 1942-46, 51-52. Mem. Am. Soc. Safety Engrs., Phi Delta Kappa (pres. Mesa Verde, Colo. chpt., 1979), Am. Legion, VFW. Clubs: Elks, Masons, Red Cross Constantine, Nat. Sojourners. Home: 226 Salmon Dr Bloomfield NM 87413 Office: 915 N First Bloomfield NM 87413

WELSH, ELIZABETH D'ANN, banker; b. Oklahoma City, Aug. 2, 1944; d. Gaynes A. and Juanita (Ivy) Garrett; m. Richard G. Welsh, Oct. 5, 1963; children: Wakonda Shawnee, Wyleah Shoshoni. Student N.Mex. State U.; grad. Nat. Sch. Retail Banking. File clk., teller, sec. First Nat. Bank Dona Ana County, Las Cruces, N.Mex., 1962-76, dealer loan officer, 1976-81, asst. v.p., 1982-86, br. mgr., 1986—. Bd. dirs., campaign chair, pres. United Way Las Cruces; co-leader Girl Scouts U.S.A., bd. dirs. Rio Grande council, 1986—. Mem. Am. Inst. Banking (instr. 1981—), Am. Heart Assn. (assoc. bd. dirs. Dona Ana Chpt.), VFW Ladies Auxiliary. Democrat. Home: PO Box 631 Mesilla Park NM 88047 Office: First Nat Bank 500 S Main St Las Cruces NM 88004

WELSH, LAWRENCE H., bishop; b. Winton, Wyo., Feb. 1, 1935. Ed., U. Wyo., St. John's Sem., Minn., Cath. U. Am. Ordained priest Roman Catholic Ch., 1962; bishop Diocese of Spokane, 1978—. Address: Spokane Diocese/Office of Bishop 1023 W Riverside Ave PO Box 1453 Spokane WA 99210 *

WELSH, MARY MCANAW, educator; b. Cameron, Mo., Dec. 7, 1920; d. Francis Louis and Mary Matilda (Moore) McA.; m. Alvin F. Welsh, Feb. 10, 1944; children: Mary Celia, Clinton F., M. Ann. AB, U. Kans., 1942; MA, Seton Hall U., 1960; EdD, Columbia U., 1971. Reporter, Hutchinson (Kans.) News Herald, 1942-43; house editor Worthington Pump & Machine Corp., Harrison, N.J., 1943-44; tchr., housemaster, coordinator Summit (N.J.) Pub. Schs., 1960-68; prof. family studies N.Mex. State U., Las Cruces, 1972-85; adj. faculty dept. family practice Tex. Tech. Regional Acad. Health Ctr., El Paso, 1978-82, Family Mediation Practice, Las Cruces, 1986—. Mem. AAUW (pres. N.Mex. 1981-83), AAUP, N.Mex. Council Women's Orgn. (founder, chmn. 1982-83), LWV, Nat. Council Family Relationships, Am. Home Econs. Assn., Western Gerontol. Soc., Theta Sigma Phi, Delta Kappa Gamma, Kappa Alpha Theta. Democrat. Roman Catholic. Author: A Good Family is Hard to Found, 1972; Parent, Child and Sex, 1970; contbr. articles to profl. jours.; writer, presenter home econs. and family study series KRWG-TV, 1974; moderator TV series The Changing Family in N.Mex./LWV, 1976. Home: PO Box 3483 University Park Las Cruces NM 88003

WELSH, TERRY COLLEEN, speech pathologist, educator; b. Pocatello, Idaho, Apr. 5, 1941; d. Kenneth F. and Merle J. (Williams) DeLate; m. Dennis R. Welsh, Aug. 24, 1963 (div. Dec. 1981); children: Greg, Scott, Julie. BA in Speech Pathology, Idaho State U., 1963; No. Ariz. U., MA in Counseling, 1983. Cert. speech and lang. therapist, elem. tchr., Ariz. Pvt. practice speech pathology Phoenix, 1970—; speech pathologist Washington Elem. Schs., Phoenix, 1972—. Mem. Am. Speech, Lang., Hearing Assn. (cert. clin. competence in speech, 1978), Delta Kappa Gamma.

WELSHANS, GARY KEITH, environmental engineer; b. Jersey Shore, Pa., June 3, 1945; s. Merrill Leroy and Janet Rae (Dieffenbach) W.; m. Carolyn Goudsmit. B.S., UCLA, 1968; M.S., Calif. State U.-Los Angeles, 1971; Ph.D., N.J. Inst. Tech., 1978. Registered profl. engr., Calif., N.J., N.Y. Civil and hydraulic engr. U.S. Army C.E., Los Angeles, 1968-73; project engr.

Ray Cons. Co., Highland Park, N.J., 1973-74; environ. engr. Stone & Webster Engring. Corp., N.Y.C., 1977-78, sr. environ. engr., N.Y.C., 1980-85; assoc. Fred C. Hart Assocs., Inc., N.Y.C., 1978-80; sr. environ. engr. Dames & Moore, San Francisco, Calif., 1985—; expert witness during fed. and state pub. hearings on stormwater mgmt., hazardous waste disposal, solid waste mgmt. facilities, N.Y., Ohio, Author: Paper Recycling: Recovery of Secondary Fibers by Selective Wettability, 1978. Contbr. articles to profl. jours. Mem. ASCE, Sigma Xi. Democrat. Avocations: handball; squash; racketball player; ballet and concert attendee. Office: Dames & Moore 500 Sansome St San Francisco CA 94111

WELTON, CHARLES EPHRAIM, lawyer; b. Cloquet, Minn., June 23, 1947; s. Eugene Frances and Evelyn Esther (Koski) W.; m. Nancy Jean Sanda, July 19, 1969; children—Spencer Sanda, Marshall Eugene. B.A., Macalester Coll., 1969; postgrad. U. Minn., 1969-70; J.D., U. Denver, 1974. Bar: Colo. 1974, U.S. Dist. Ct. Colo. 1974, U.S. Supreme Ct. 1979, U.S. Ct. Appeals (10th cir.) 1980. Assoc., Davidovich & Assocs., and predecessor firm, Denver, 1974-77; Charles Welton and Assocs., Denver, 1978-80, 1984—; ptnr. Davidovich & Welton, Denver, 1981-84; ptnr. OSM Properties, Denver, 1982—. Contbr. articles to profl. jours. Co pres. PTSA, Denver, 1983-84; coach Colo. Jr. Soccer League, 1980-85; co-coach Odessey of the Mind (formerly Olympics of the Mind), 1986—. Served alt. mil. duty Denver Gen. Hosp., 1970-72. Mem. Denver Bar Assn., Colo. Bar Assn. (legal fee arbitration com.), Assn. Trial Lawyers Am., Colo. Trial Lawyers Assn. (bd. dirs. 1985—, chmn. seminar com. 1986—), Americans Building a Lasting Earth (founder), Exec. Ventures Group of Am. Leadership Forum (adv. bd.). Democrat. Lutheran. Club: Midtown Athletic. Home: 5020 Montview Blvd Denver CO 80207 Office: Old Smith Mansion 1751 Gilpin St Denver CO 80218

WENDEL, DOUGLAS JOHN, petroleum engineer; b. Salt Lake City, May 26, 1951; s. Allen Martin and Rose Eileen (Chabot) W.; m. Sylvia Keding, Aug. 20, 1975; children: Chantelle Ann, Jared Richard, Jason Allen, Angela. BSChemE, U. Utah, 1975, MSChemE, 1977. Research technician Flammability Research, Salt Lake City, 1974-78; research engr. Conoco, Inc., Ponca City, Okla., 1978-84; research and devel. mgr. Petroleum Testing Service, Santa Fe Springs, Calif., 1984—. Contbr. articles to profl. jours. Asst. scoutmaster Boy Scouts Am., Ponca City, 1980-84, Whittier, Calif., 1984—. Internat. Isocyanate Inst. fellow, 1975-77; named Outstanding Young Man of Am., U.S. Jaycees, 1984. Fellow Am. Inst. Chemists; mem. Soc. Petroleum Engrs., Am. Inst. Chem. Engrs., Soc. Core Analysts. Mormon. Avocations: bicycling, camping, hiking. Office: Petroleum Testing Service 12051 Rivera Rd Santa Fe Springs CA 90670

WENDEL, ROBERT EDWIN, podiatrist; b. Seattle, July 5, 1935; s. Edwin A. and Lucille O. (Jansen) W.; m. Kayanne Ringo, June 8, 1963; children—Heidi Anne, Brent Robert. B.S., U. Wash., 1961; M.S., Wash. State U., 1963; D.P.M., Ohio Coll. Podiatry, 1975. Diplomate Am. Bd. Podiatric Orthopedists, Am. Bd. Podiatric Surgery. Tchr., Highline High Sch., Burien, Wash., 1961-64, Tyee High Sch., Burien, 1964-66; mem. faculty, div. chair Bellevue (Wash.) Community Coll., 1966-72; podiatric physician and surgeon, Seattle, 1976—; pres. Peak Performance Sports Medicine and Wellness Ctr., Seattle, 1983—; cons. Seattle Dept. Social and Health Services, 1977—. Contbr. articles to profl. jours. Pres., Pine Lake Community Club, Issaquah, Wash., 1970; bd. deacons Community Baptist Ch., Issaquah, 1983; bd. dirs. Issaquah Gliders Track Club, 1983-84. Served with USMC, 1954-57; Far East. Fellow Am. Coll. Foot Orthopedists; mem. Am. Podiatry Assn., Wash. State Podiatry Assn. (sec. 1982-83), Am. Coll. Sports Medicine, Phi Epsilon Kappa, Phi Kappa Phi. Clubs: Wash. Athletic, Northwest (Seattle). Home: 21817 SE 20th St Issaquah WA 98027 Office: Peak Performance Sports Medicine & Wellness Ctr 509 Olive Way Suite 321 Seattle WA 98101

WENK, JENNY, advertising executive; b. Pitts., Dec. 29, 1942; d. Samuel Augustine and Jean Lois (Barnes) W.; B.A., U. Calif., Berkeley, 1964; M.B.A., Golden Gate U., 1980; m. Paul R. Allman, Dec. 31, 1981. Advt. promotion and research asst. Richmond (Calif.) Independent, 1965-67; sales promotion writer Dow Jones & Co., Inc., N.Y.C., 1968-70; mem. advt. sales staff Nat. Observer, San Francisco, 1970-74, advt. mgr. Pacific coast, 1974-77; advt. sales rep. Wall Street Jour., San Francisco, 1977—. Mem. San Francisco Women in Advt. (hon. mem., past pres.), San Francisco Advt. Club (dir. 1979-80), Seattle Women in Advt. (hon.). Presbyterian. Office: Wall St Jour 220 Battery St San Francisco CA 94111

WENKERT, ERNEST, chemist, educator; b. Vienna, Austria, Oct. 16, 1925; came to U.S., 1941, naturalized, 1946; s. Moses and Elcie (Seidmann) W.; m. Ann Davis, June 22, 1948; children: Naomi, David, Daniel, Deborah. B.S., U. Wash., 1945, M.S., 1947; Ph.D., Harvard, 1951; Dr. honoris causa, U. Paris-Sud, 1978, U. Perugia, Italy, 1986. Faculty Lower Columbia Jr. Coll., Longview, Wash., 1947-48; faculty Ia. State U., Ames, 1951-61; prof. Ia. State U., 1959-61, Ind. U., Bloomington, 1961-69; Herman T Briscoe prof. chemistry Ind. U., 1969-73; E.D. Butcher prof. chemistry Rice U., Houston, 1973-80; chmn. dept. chemistry Rice U., 1976-80; prof. U. Calif., San Diego, 1980—; cons. chem. industry; Guggenheim fellow, 1965-66; vis. prof. U. Calif., Berkeley, 1961-62, U. Paris, 1968, 70, U. Calif., Santa Barbara, 1974, U. Colo., Boulder, 1975, U. Calif., San Diego, 1976, Irvine, 1978; Mellor vis. prof. U. Otago, Dunedin, N.Z., 1974; Fulbright lectr. Institut de Chimie des Substances Naturelles, Gif-sur-Yvette, France, 1963; prof., acting head dept. organic chemistry Weizmann Inst. Sci., Rehovoth, Israel, 1964-65. Contbr. articles to profl. jours. Mem. Am. Chem. Soc. (Ernest Guenther award 1971), Royal Soc. Chemistry, AAUP, Swiss Chem. Soc., Academia Brasileira de Ciencias (elected), Sigma Xi. Office: Dept of Chemistry D-006 U Calif-San Diego La Jolla CA 92093

WENNER, JACQUELINE MARIE, social worker; b. Doylestown, Pa., Nov. 11, 1936; d. Frank Andrew and Amelia Anna (DeMusz) W.; m. John Dixon Morrow, July 16, 1960 (div. Mar. 1972). BA, San Francisco State U., 1981; M in Social Welfare, U. Calif., Berkeley, 1985. Med. social worker St. Mary's Hosp., San Francisco, 1981-83, French Hosp., San Francisco, 1983; psychiat. social worker VA Med. Ctr., Menlo Park, Calif., 1985—, coordinator family psycho-ednl. project, 1986—. Mem. Nat. Assn. Social Workers, Soc. Clin. Social Workers, Bay Area Social Workers in Health Care, Phi Gamma Mu. Home: 160 21st Ave San Francisco CA 94121

WENNER, WALLIS, graphic designer; b. Yakima, Wash., Nov. 6, 1919; s. Charles Stanley and Florence Evelyn (Williams) W.; widowed; children: Wallis Elizabeth, Thorne Mary. Artist, designer Western Art Service, San Francisco, 1939-42; creative dir. Dealer Sales Builders, San Francisco, 1947-60, Brorsen & Wenner, San Francisco, 1960-66, Recorder Sunset Calif. Printing, San Francisco, 1966-80; graphics mgr. packaging Del Monte Corp., San Francisco, 1980—; art dir. Wayfarers Civic Rep., San Francisco, 1936-42, Hillbarn Theater, San Mateo, Calif., 1950-62. Served to 2nd lt., U.S. Army, 1942-46, PTO. Home: 783 Marin Dr Mill Valley CA 94941

WENTORF, ERIC TIM, pharmaceutical manufacturing company executive; b. Racine, Wis., Apr. 22, 1954; s. Fred G. and Gerry Mae (Ericson) W.; m. Susan M. McIntosh, July 1, 1978; children: Erin, Nicholas, Jessica. BS in Chemistry, U. Wis., Kenosha, 1977. Analytical chem. technician Abbott Labs., North Chicago, Ill., 1977-79, prodn. supr., 1979-81, prodn. foreman, 1981-83, incoming quality assurance group leader, 1983-84; dir. tech. services Ferguson Labs. div. Diet Ctr. Inc., Rexburg, Idaho, 1984—. Elder Community Presbyn. Ch., Rexburg, 1985—; scoutmaster Teton Peaks council Boy Scouts Am., Rexburg, 1985—. Mem. Am. Pharm. Assn. (assoc.), Inst. Food Technologists, Am. Soc. Quality Control, Assn. Ofcl. Analytical Chemists (assoc.), Am. Chem. Soc. Avocations: tech. rock climbing, camping, running, downhill skiing. Office: Ferguson Labs 350 S 5th W Rexburg ID 83440

WENTWORTH, THEODORE SUMNER, lawyer; b. Bklyn., July 18, 1938; s. Theodore Sumner and Alice Ruth (Wortmann) W.; A.A., Am. River Coll., 1958; J.D., U. Calif., Hastings Coll. Law, 1962; m. Sharon Linelle Arkush, Mar. 26, 1965; children—Christina Linn, Kathryn Allison. Admitted to Calif. bar, 1963; asso. Adams, Hunt & Martin, Santa Ana, Calif., 1963-66; partner Hunt, Liljestrom & Wentworth, Santa Ana, 1967-77; pres. Solabs Corp.; chmn. bd., exec. v.p. Plant Warehouse, Inc., Hawaii, 1974-82; prin. Law Offices of Theodore S. Wentworth, specializing in personal injury, product liability and profl. malpractice litigation, Irvine, Calif. Pres., bd. dirs. Santa Ana-Tustin Community Chest, 1972; v.p., trustee South Orange County United Way, 1973-75; pres. Orange County Fedn. Funds, 1972-73; bd. dirs. Orange County Mental Health Assn. Diplomate Nat. Bd. Trial Advocacy. Mem. State Bar Calif., ABA, Orange County Bar Assn. (dir. 1972-76), Am. Trial Lawyers Assn. (judge pro tem superior ct. attys. panel), Calif. Trial Lawyers Assn. (bd. govs. 1968-70), Orange County Trial Lawyers Assn. (pres. 1967-68), Lawyer-Pilots Bar Assn., Am. Bd. Trial Advs., Aircraft Owners and Pilots Assn. Clubs: Bahia Corinthian Yacht, Balboa Bay (Newport Beach, Calif.); Lincoln (Orange County); Corsair Yacht (Catalina, Calif.). Research in vedic prins., natural law, metaphysics. Office: 2112 Business Center Dr Suite 220 Irvine CA 92715

WENTZEL, MARK WILLIAM, physicist; b. Langenburg, Sask., Can., Sept. 29, 1963; s. Edwin Forest and Mary Magdalene (Derkson) Barnum. BS, Mont. State U., 1984. Physicist Naval Weapons Ctr., China Lake, Calif., 1984—. Active Immanuel Bapt. Ch., Ridgecrest, Calif., 1986—. Mem. N.Y. Acad. Scis., Internat. Soc. Hybrid Microelectronics, AAAS, Am. Inst. Physics. Republican. Mem. Evang. Ch. Avocations: basketball, skiing, hiking, bicycling. Home: 1036 Sherri St Ridgecrest CA 93555 Office: Naval Weapons Ctr Microelectronics Code 3318 China Lake CA 93555

WENZEL, CAROL MARION NAGLER, family therapist; b. Chgo., Nov. 17, 1936; d. Philip L. and Grace (Hindley) Nagler; m. Gene H. Wenzel, July 25, 1954; children: Scott, Jamie, Philip, Sue Ellen. BA in Communication and Social Scis., Marylhurst Coll., 1982; MSW, Portland State U., 1984. Registered clin. social worker. Family therapist Intensive Family Service, Inc., Portland, Oreg., 1984—; pvt. practice counseling Oreg., 1986—; trainer alcoholic family systems, various agys., Portland, 1982-86. Mem. Nat. Assn. Social Workers (cert.). Democrat. Lutheran. Avocations: reading, writing, bowling, swimming, going to beach. Home: 8325 SE Carnation Milwaukie OR 97267 Office: Intensive Family Services 815 NE Davis Portland OR 97232

WEPPNER, ROBERT STEPHENS, health care educator; b. Cheyenne, Wyo., Feb. 22, 1936; s. Albert Stanton and Hazel Irene (Stephens) W.; m. Gene Suzanne Riegel, Sept. 7, 1968; children: Kerrie, Sarah, Billy. PhD, U. Colo., 1968. Dir. addiction scis. div. Med. Sch. U. Fla., Miami, 1973-77; asst. dean U. Wis., Milw., 1977-81; prof. health care adminstrn. Idaho State U., Pocatello, 1981—; pres. Aspen Mgmt. Group Inc., Pocatello, 1985—. Author: The Untherapeutic Community, 1983; editor: Street Ethnography, 1977; contbr. articles to profl. jours. Trustees Sch. Dist. 25, Pocatello, 1986—. NIDA grantee for $847, 000, 1974. Fellow Am. Anthropol. Assn., Soc. Applied Anthropology. Democrat. Home: 457 S 19th Pocatello ID 83201 Office: Idaho State U Dept Health Care Adminstrn Pocatello ID 83209

WERNER, JOANNE ROTH, health care educator and researcher; b. Milw., Feb. 27, 1946; d. Jacob and Mildred (Satler) Roth; m. Jeffrey Allen Werner, June 17, 1973; children: Jeremy Matthew, Daniel Simon. BSN, Duke U., 1968; MS, U. Colo., 1972. From staff nurse to sr. staff nurse NYU Hosp., 1968-69; supr. psychiat. nursing U. B.C. Psychiat. Hosp., Vancouver, 1969-70; staff nurse Vis. Nurse Service of Denver, 1970-71; pub. health nurse Seattle King County Health Dept., 1972, with inservice, staff devel., 1977-80; instr. theory and practice community health nursing U. Wash. Sch. Nursing, Seattle, 1972-75, lectr., 1983-85, curriculum coordinator, 1985, project dir. Elderly Homecare Project Dept. Community Health, 1986-87; with inservice, staff devel. San Francisco Vis. Nurse Assn., 1975-77; research, devel. and tchg. cons. Seattle, 1980-83; cons. in field. Mem. Am. Nurses Assn., King County Nurses' Assn. (chmn. community health nurses's spl. interest group 1983), Nat. League for Nursing, Wash. State League for Nursing, Sigma Theta Tau (mem. nominating com. 1985, program com. 1983, research com., 1983).

WERNER, ROGER HARRY, archaeologist; b. N.Y.C., Nov. 11, 1950; s. Harry Emile and Rena (Roode) W.; m. Kathleen Diane Engdahl, Feb. 20, 1982; children: Meryl Lauren, Sarah Melise; 1 stepchild, Amber Fawn. BA, Belknap Coll., 1973; MA, Sonoma State U., Rohnert Park, Calif., 1982. Curatorial aide Anthro. Lab. Sonoma State Coll., 1975-76, curatorial asst., 1976-77, staff archaeologist, 1977-80; staff archaeologist Planning Dept., Lake County, Calif., 1977; cir. riding archaeologist western region Nat. Park Service, Tucson, Ariz., 1978; pres., investigator Archaeol. Services, Inc., Stockton, Calif., 1979—; cons. Calif. Indian Legal Services, Ukiah, 1977, Geothermal Research Impact Projection Study, Lakeport, Calif., 1977; instr. Ya-Ka-Ama Indian Ednl. Ctr., Santa Rosa, Calif., 1978-79; lead archaeologist No. Calif., WESTEC Services, Inc., San Diego, 1979-81. Sec. PTA, 1983-84, 2d v.p., 1985; cons., instr. Clovis Adult Sch., 1984-85; instr. U. Pacific Lifelong Learning Ctr., 1987—; bd. dirs. Valley Mountain Regional Ctr., 1987—; active, Spl. Olympics, Stockton, Calif., 1986, 87. Anthropology dept. research grantee, Sonoma State U., 1980. Mem. Great Basin Anthropol. Conf., Soc. for Am. Archaeology, Soc. for Calif. Archaeology, Soc. Profl. Archaeologists, Assn. for Retarded Citizens, Clearlake C. of C. Democrat. Lodge: Kiwanis. Avocations: reading, community activities, computers. Home: 117 Aberdeen Ave Stockton CA 95209 Office: Archaeol Services Inc PO Box 3127 Clearlake CA 95422

WERNER, RUTH MARGARET, retired social work educator, civic worker; b. Fond du Lac, Wis., May 15, 1913; s. Henry Charles and Elsa Elizabeth (Nast) W. BA, U. Wis., 1934; MA, U. Chgo., 1948, PhD, 1960. Social worker Wis. State Dept. Pub. Welfare, Madison, 1938-44, chief case work services, 1950-55; supr. Ill. Childrens Home Aid Soc., Chgo., 1945-50; from asst. prof. to prof. social work Case Western Res. U., Cleve., 1956-77, assoc. dean; cons. Fells Inst., Phila., 1961-62, other instns., workshops, 1949-63. contbr. articles to profl. jours. Mem. Santa Barbara (Calif.) Com. on Srs., 1985—; assembly woman Calif. Sr. Legis., Sacramento. Recipient Disting. Servce award So. Coast Coordinators Council, Santa Barbara, 1983. Mem. Nat. Assn. Social Workers (cert., Cleve. chpt. chmn. div. social policy 1957-58, 1st vice chmn. 1961-63, del. 1962), Child Welfare League (pub. vol. relations com. 1967-70), Nat. Council Social Welfare (vice chmn. program com. 1962). Democrat. Presbyterian. Home: 2665 Tallant Rd Santa Barbara CA 93105

WERNER, THEODORE ADOLPH, architect; b. Oakland, Calif., Sept. 5, 1934; s. Theodore Frederickson and Josephine (Flamick) W.; m. Mary Ellen Cheney, 1958 (div. 1971); children: Leslie Camille, Theodore, Denise; m. Constance Brooks Prescott, May 20, 1978; 1 child, Brooks. BSArchE, Calif. Poly. State Coll., San Luis Obispo, 1960. Registered architect, Calif., Oreg., Wash. Draftsman Dreyfuss & Blackford, Sacramento, 1960-63; project architect Caywood & Nopp, Architects, Sacramento, 1963-66, Lutes & Amundson, Architects, Springfield, Oreg., 1967-71, Lawrence Simons, Architects, Santa Rosa, Calif., 1971-73; assoc. James McGranahan Assoc., Tacoma, 1973-77; pvt. practice architecture Ted A. Werner, AIA, Architect, Tacoma, 1977—. V.p. Allied Arts of Tacoma, 1986, pres., 1987. Mem. AIA, (pres. Southwest Wash. Chpt. 1982). Lodge: Rotary. Avocations: gardening, hunting, fishing, snow skiing, hiking. Office: Ted A Werner AIA Architect 7 St Helens Suite 2 Tacoma WA 98402

WERSHING, SUSAN MEDLER, publishing executive; b. Bklyn., Aug. 9, 1938; d. Edwin Leo and E. Frances (Mantyniemi) Medler; m. Francis S. Wershing, Aug. 29, 1959 (div. 1978). Student, U. Vienna, Austria, 1959; BJ, Fairleigh Dickinson U., 1960, postgrad., 1963-64; cert. publishing course, Stanford U., 1981. Assoc. editor Med. Econs. mag., Oradell, N.J., 1974-78; sr. editor Audio-Digest Found., Glendale, Calif., 1978-79; founder, editor and publisher Dance Teacher Now mag., Davis, Calif., 1979—; corp. sec., also bd. dirs. The Videotape Catalog, Davis, 1985—; pres. Davis Comic Opera Co., also choreographer and lighting designer; performer and lighting designer Ridgewood (N.J.) Gilbert and Sullivan Co., 1968-78. Mem. Nat. Fedn. Ind. Bus., Davis Small Bus. Network, Rockette Alumnae Assn., AAHPERD, Nat. Assn. Regional Ballet. Republican. Avocations: choreography, theatrical lighting design. Home: 1333 Notre Dame Dr Davis CA 95616 Office: SMW Communications Inc 803 Russell Blvd Suite 2 Davis CA 95616

WERTHEIM, JOHN TAYLOR, banker; b. Flushing, N.Y., June 30, 1943; s. Edward Taylor and Elva Jean (Squires) W.; m. Mary Christine Pfouts, Sept. 3, 1966; children: John Jr., Peter. BBA, Kent State U., 1965; MBA, Ohio State U., 1966; Diploma in Banking, U. Wis. CPA, N.Y., Ohio. Sr. cons. Arthur Andersen & Co., N.Y.C., 1969-73; sr. v.p. AmeriTrust Co., Cleve., 1973-82; exec. v.p. Marine Bank of Appelton, Wis., 1982-84; pres., chief exec. officer First Bus. Bank Ariz., Phoenix, 1984—; mem. Robert Morris Assocs. Treas. Valley of Sun United Way, Phoenix, 1985—; mem. Ariz. Acad. Town Halls, Phoenix, 1985—. Served to 1st lt. U.S. Army, 1967-69. Mem. Am. Soc. CPA's, Ariz. Soc. CPA's. Lodge: Rotary. Office: 1st Bus Bank Ariz PO Box 33249 Phoenix AZ 85067

WERTHEIM, ROBERT HALLEY, aerospace company executive; b. Carlsbad, N.Mex., Nov. 9, 1922; s. Joseph and Emma (Vorenberg) W.; m. Barbara Louise Selig, Dec. 26, 1946; children: Joseph Howard, David Andrew. Student, N.Mex. Mil. Inst., 1940-42; B.S., U.S. Naval Acad., 1945; M.S. in Physics, M.I.T., 1954; grad., Advanced Mgmt. Program, Harvard U., 1969. Commd. ensign U.S. Navy, 1945, advanced through grades to rear adm., 1972; assigned Spl. Projects Office, Washington, 1956-61, Naval Ordnance Test Sta., China Lake, 1961-62, Office Sec. Def., Washington, 1962-65; head Missile br. Strategic Systems Project Office, Washington, 1965-67; dep. tech. dir. Missile br. Strategic Systems Project Office, 1967-68, tech. dir., 1968-77, dir., 1977-80; sr. v.p. Lockheed Corp., 1981—; dir. MCC Corp.; cons. Office Sec. Def.; mem. Charles Stark Draper Lab., Inc.; mem. sci. adv. groups Def. Nuclear Agy. and Joint Strategic Target Planning Staff, Nat. Security Adv. Group, Los Alamos Nat. Lab. Trustee Naval Undersea Warfare Mus. Found. Decorated Legion of Merit, D.S.M. with cluster, Navy Commendation medal, Joint Service Commendation medal; recipient Rear Adm. William S. Parsons award Navy League U.S., 1971. Fellow AIAA; mem. Am. Soc. Naval Engrs. (Gold Medal award 1972), Nat. Acad. Engring., U.S. Naval Inst., Sigma Xi, Tau Beta Pi. Clubs: Cosmos, Army-Navy Country, Woodland Hills Golf & Country, Bernardo Heights Country, Cosmos. Lodge: Masons. Home: 17032 Gledhill St Northridge CA 91325 Office: Lockheed Corp 4500 Park Granada Blvd Calabasas CA 91399

WERTHEIMER, RICHARD A., association executive; b. Moline, Ill., Nov. 11, 1958; s. Milton A. and Rhoda M. (Gellman) W. BS in Agrl. Bus. Mgmt., U. Wis., 1982. Performance testing specialist U. Wis., Madison, 1982; dir. mktg. info. Am. Sheep Producers Council, Denver, 1983—. Mem. Am. Mgmt. Assn., Colo. Livestock Leaders Council, Western Agri. Econs. Assn., Am. Soc. Assn. Execs. Jewish. Home: 1680 Pontiac Denver CO 80220 Office: Am Sheep Producers Council 200 Clayton Denver CO 80206

WERTHEIMER, THOMAS, business executive; b. N.Y.C., 1938. B.A., Princeton U., 1960; LL.B., Columbia U., 1963. Vice-pres. bus. affairs subs. ABC, 1964-72; with MCA, Inc., 1972—, v.p. Universal TV div., corp. v.p., 1974-83, exec. v.p., 1983—, dir. Office: MCA Inc 100 Universal City Plaza Universal City CA 91608

WESCHE, LILBURN EDGAR, director university graduate programs, educator; b. Taming, Hopel, Peoples Republic of China, Nov. 21, 1929; came to U.S., 1940; s. Kenneth P. and Pearl (Myers) W.; m. Esther Louise Rinker, Aug. 21, 1953; children: Kenneth, Cheryl, Barbara. AB, Northwest Nazarene Coll., 1951; MEd, Trinity U., San Antonio, 1955; EdD, U. No. Colo., 1961. Dir. tchr. edn. Northwest Nazarene Coll., Nampa, Idaho, 1961-81, dir. evening summer programs, 1981-84; dir. grad. studies Seattle Pacific U., 1984—. Author: (with others) AV Aids in the Church, 1968. Mem. Idaho Edn. Assn. (pres. 1964-65), NEA (bd. dirs. 1968-74), Am. Assn. Tchr. Edn. (liaison 1974-76), Assn. Sch. Adminstrn., Assn. Supervision and Curriculum Devel., C. of C. (edn. com. 1985—), Phi Delta Kappa (v.p. 1986—, pres. Seattle U. chpt.). Democrat. Mem. Nazarene Ch. Office: Seattle Pacific U Seattle WA 98119

WESLEY, PHILLIP, librarian; b. Los Angeles, June 3, 1930; s. George Gregor and Olive Vessie (Barnette) W.; A.A., Glendale, Coll., 1950; B.A., U. Calif. at Los Angeles, 1956; M.S., U. So. Calif., 1959. Sr. library asst. U. Calif. at Los Angeles Law Library, 1955-58; bindery clk., acquisitions librarian, cataloger Los Angeles County Law Library, 1958-59; ltd. loan and serials librarian Calif. State U. at Los Angeles Library, 1959-60; acquisitions librarian Los Angeles County Law Library, 1960-61, reference librarian, 1961-62, head catalog librarian, 1961-66; head catalog librarian Calif. State U., Northridge, 1966-67, chief tech. services, 1967-69, acting coll. librarian, 1969; dir. ednl. resources ctr. Calif. State U., Dominguez Hills, 1969-77, dean ednl. resources, 1977—. Mem. Am. Assn. Law Libraries, So. Calif. Assn. Law Libraries (pres. 1964-65), Spl. Libraries Assn. (chpt. treas. 1969-70), So. Calif. Tech. Processes Group (pres. 1972-74), Am., Calif. library assns. Home: 2287 Panorama Terr Los Angeles CA 90039 Office: 1000 E Victoria St Carson CA 90747

WESNICK, RICHARD JAMES, newspaper editor; b. Racine, Wis., Oct. 14, 1938; s. John and Julia (Kassa) W.; m. Elaine Apoline Smith, Sept. 30, 1967; children: Catherine Elaine, Julia Ann. BA, U. Houston, 1961. Reporter Jour. Times, Racine, 1965-76; mng. editor Ind. Record, Helena, Mont., 1976-80; editor Billings Gazette, Mont., 1980—. Editor: Death Sentences, 1984, Best of Bragg, 1985. Served with USMC, 1961-64. Mem. Mont. AP (chmn., bd. dirs. 1985—, freedom of info. com., legis. rev. com.), Soc. Newspaper Designers, Am. Soc. Newspaper Editors. Roman Catholic. Lodges: Kiwanis, Rotary. Avocations: hunting; fishing; gardening. Home: 2214 22d St W Billings MT 59102 Office: The Billings Gazette 401 N Broadway Billings MT 59101

WESSEL, JOHN EMMIT, chemical physicist; b. Los Angeles, Mar. 8, 1942; s. John B. and Lucy Wessel; m. Judith B. Herman, Dec. 20, 1978. BS, UCLA, 1965; PhD, U. Chgo., 1970. Postdoctoral fellow U. Pa., Phila., 1970-72, instr., 1972-74; mem. tech. staff The Aerospace Corp., El Segundo, Calif., 1974-78, research scientist, 1978-82, sr. scientist, 1982—. Contbr. articles to profl. jours.; inventor Molecular Detector Based on Multiplication Photoionization, 1978; patentee in field. Fellow Woodrow Wilson Found., 1975; grantee NSF, Dept. of Energy, Air Force Office of Sci. Research, the Aerospace Corp. 1976—; recipient Pres.' award Sci. Research, Aerospace Corp., 1982. Mem. AAAS, Am. Chem. Soc., Am. Phys. Soc., Sigma Xi. Avocations: cross country skiing, bicycle touring. Home: 919 Duncan Ave Manhattan Beach CA 90266 Office: The Aerospace Corp M2-253 PO Box 92957 Los Angeles CA 90009

WESSLER, MELVIN DEAN, farmer, rancher; b. Dodge City, Kan., Feb. 11, 1932; s. Oscar Lewis and Clara (Reiss) W.; grad. high sch.; m. Laura Ethel Arbuthnot, Aug. 23, 1951; children—Monty Dean, Charla Cay, Virgil Lewis. Farmer-rancher, Springfield, Colo., 1950—; dir., sec. bd. Springfield Co-op. Sales Co., 1964-80, pres. bd., 1980—. Pres., Arkansas Valley Co-op. Council, S.E. Colo. Area, 1965—, Colo. Co-op. Council, 1969-72; community com. chmn. Baca County, Agr. Stablzn. and Conservation Service, Springfield, 1961-73, 79—, vice chmn. Baca County Com., 1980—; mem. spl. com. on grain mktg. Far-Mar-Co.; mem. adv. bd. Denver Baptist Bible Coll., 1984—; chmn., bd. dirs. Springfield Cemetery Bd., 1985—. Mem. Colo. Cattlemen's Assn., Colo. Wheat Growers Assn., Southeast Farm Bus. Assn., Big Rock Grange (treas. 1964-76, master 1976-82). Baptist. Address: Route 2 Box 24 Springfield CO 81073

WESSON, DONALD RAY, health science facility administrator; b. Gadsden, Ala., Sept. 18, 1941. BS in Chemistry, U. Ala., 1963, postgrad., 1963; MD, Med. Coll. Ala., 1967. Diplomate Am. Bd. of Psychiatry and Neurology. Intern Gorgas Hosp., Balboa Heights, Calif., 1967-68; resident in psychiatry San Francisco Community Mental Health, 1968-71; chief psychiatrist Haight-Ashbury Free Med. Clin., San Francisco, 1970-73; dir. outpatient dept. Sunset Community Mental Health, San Francisco, 1971-72; pvt. practice specializing in psychiatry 1971-84; project dir. Nat. Clearinghouse for Drug Abuse Info., 1972-73; prin. investigator San Francisco Polydrug Project Nat. Inst. on Drug Abuse, 1973-76; contract instr. Calif. Sch. Profl. Psychology, Berkeley, 1974-84; assoc. dir. div. biol. research dept. psychol. and social medicine Pacific Med. Ctr., San Francisco, 1979-81; asst. dir. Amphetamine Research and Physician Tng. Project, San Francisco, 1981-83; research dir. Merritt Peralta Chem. Dependency Recovery Hosp., Oakland, Calif., 1981-84; assoc. dir. Benzodiazepine Research and Physician Tng. Project, San Francisco, 1982-84; research dir. Look-Alike Research and Physician Tng. Project, San Francisco, 1982-84; dir. substance abuse research VA Med. Ctr., San Francisco, 1986—; assoc. clin. prof. dept. psychiatry U. Calif. Med. Sch., San Francisco, 1986—; chmn. div. med. quality-liaison com. to BMQA's diversion program for impaired physicians, Calif. Soc. Treatment of Alcoholism and Other Drug Dependencies, 1984-86. Author book chptrs. and numerouse articles to profl. jours. Nat. Inst. on Drug Abuse grantee, 1985-88. Mem. Am. Med. Soc. on Alcoholism, Calif. Soc. Treatment of Alcoholism and Other Drug Dependencies (cert., newsletter editor, chmn. research com.), San Francisco Med. Soc., Calif. Med. Assn., Calif. State Research Adv. Panel, Nat. Inst. on Drug Abuse (services research subcom.). Office: San Francisco VA Med Ctr 116F 4150 Clement St San Francisco CA 94121

WEST, ANITA S., research director, researcher; b. N.Y.C., Oct. 21, 1930; d. Bert S. and Dorothy (Sandler) Wolfe; m. David Lee West, Feb. 18, 1955; children: David R., Laurie D. Student, Columbia U., 1952-55; BA, U. Denver, 1960, MS, 1962, PhD, 1969. Research systems analyst IBM, N.Y.C., 1962-63; research scientist Martin-Marietta, Denver, 1960-62; sr. research scientist Denver Research Inst., U. Denver, 1975-78, head research div., 1978—, dir., chief operating officer, 1986—; cons. U.S. Dept. Justice, 1978-87, USAF, Washington, 1972-86, Dept. Army, Washington, 1980, Nat. Inst. Edn., Washington, 1975-85, Nat. Inst. Corrections, Boulder, Colo., 1983-85, NSF, Washington, 1980—. Contbr. numerous articles and tech. papers to profl. jours. Mem. Gov.'s Adv. Commn. Sci. and Tech., Colo., 1978-85, Commn. on Conversion to Metric, Colo., 1981-83; chmn. Rocky Flats Monitoring Com. Evaluation, Colo., 1981-83, chmn. Mayor's Conf. on Women, Denver, 1974. Mem. AAAS, N.Y. Acad. Scis., Sigma Xi (former chpt. pres.). Jewish. Avocation: piano. Home: 3235 S St Paul Denver CO 80210 Office: U Denver Denver Research Inst Denver CO 80208

WEST, BARBARA JO, food company executive; b. Bishop, Calif., Apr. 10, 1945; d. James J. and Inez E. (Fackrell) Carberry; m. Robert M. West, Oct. 1, 1972 (div.); children—N. Dion, W. Todd. B.B.A., Boise State U. Mktg. asst. H.J. Heinz Co., Boise, Idaho, 1973-74, asst. product mgr., 1975-78, product mgr., 1978-80, sr. product mgr. new products Ore-Ida Brand div., 1980-81, sr. product mgr. product devel. dept. Weight Watchers div., 1981-83; sr. product mgr. Am. Home Products, 1983-84; pres. Barbstac Corp., 1984-86; mgr. promotions Commtek Publ., 1986—. Advisor Jr. Achievement, Boise, 1976-77; pub. relations dir. Idaho chpt. Cystic Fibrosis, 1979-80. Recipient Mktg. Achievement award Sales and Mktg. Execs., 1979; Jr. Achievement scholar, 1964. Mem. Am. Mktg. Assn., Idaho Advt. Fedn., Assn. Nat. Advertisers. Roman Catholic.

WEST, BILLY GENE, public relations and mktg. co. exec.; b. Richmond, Ind., Nov. 22, 1946; s. Billy D. and Jean C. (Cox) W.; A.A., Cerritos Coll., 1966; B.A., U. So. Calif., 1969; M.A., U. Minn., 1971. Salesman, Marina Art Products, Los Angeles, 1967-73; v.p. Am. Telecon Network, Dallas, 1974-77; gen. mgr. Phoenix Publs., Houston, 1977-78; pres. San Dark, Inc., San Francisco, 1978-82; gen. ptnr. Billy West & Assocs., 1982—; pres. V.G. Prodns., 1983—. Vice pres. Calif. Young Republican Coll. Fedn., 1966-67; exec. dir. Young Ams. for Freedom, Minn. and Wis., 1970-72; pres. S.F.P.A., San Francisco, 1982-83. Mem. Assn. M.B.A. Execs. Mem. Am. Ref. Ch.

WEST, CAROL ANNE, educator; b. Palo Alto, Calif., May 29, 1944; d. Robert George and Martha Geraldine (Michaelson) West; children—Robert Philip, Amy Trainor. A.B., U. Calif.-Davis, 1966, teaching cert., 1967. Tchr. A.M. Winn Elem. Sch., Sacramento, 1967—; rep. Calif. Tchrs. Assn., 1984—; artist. Docent, Capitol Vol. Mus. Assn., Sacramento, 1984—; bd. dirs. Homeowners Assn., Sacramento, 1984—. Robert A. Taft Inst. grantee, 1984. Mem. Calif. Alumni Assn., Art Mus. Assn., Opera Guild Assn., Sacramento Children's Home Guild. Republican. Presbyterian. Club: Sierra. Home: 2756 Catania Way Sacramento CA 95826

WEST, CLELL ALBERT, protective services official; b. Searcy, Ark., Aug. 23, 1934; s. Albert and Della Mae (Lawson) W.; m. Stella Ruth Webb, Sept. 4, 1953; children: Michael, Sherry, Rick. AA, Phoenix Coll., 1972; BA, U. Phoenix, 1981. Capt. Phoenix Fire Dept., 1968-72, bn. chief, 1973-76, dep. chief, 1978-82, asst. chief, 1983-84; fire chief Las Vegas (Nev.) Fire Dept., 1984—. Mem. Nat. Fire Protection Assn. (bd. dirs. 1985—), Internat. Assn. Fire Chiefs, Ariz. Fire Chief's Assn. (pres. 1984-85), Internat. Fire Service Tng. Assn. (com. chmn. 1981-85), Nev. Fire Chiefs Assn. Democrat. Lodge: Lions (sec. Las Vegas club 1985, Lion of Yr. 1985). Avocations: hunting, fishing, camping. Home: 6208 Peppermill Dr Las Vegas NV 89102 Office: City of Las Vegas Fire Dept 500 N Casino Center Blvd Las Vegas NV 89101

WEST, DARBY LINDSEY, manufacturing company executive; b. Melrose, N.Mex., Jan. 13, 1938; s. Wayne Burton and Mildred Minnie (Lindsey) W.; grad. high sch.; m. Angelina Loomis, Feb. 9, 1980; children—Rebecca, Darby, Jr., Johnny Wayne. Well attendant El Paso Natural Gas Co., Farmington, N.Mex., 1957-65, instrument technician, 1965-67, dehydrator man, 1967-77; v.p., partner Natural Gas Prodn. Equipment P & A, Inc., Farmington, 1977—. Republican. Baptist. Home: PO Box 2648 Bloomfield NM 87413 Office: Natural Gas Prodn Equipment P & A Inc 768 US Hwy 64 Farmington NM 87401

WEST, DONALD MARKHAM, chemistry educator, textbook co-author; b. Pasadena, Calif., Apr. 22, 1925; s. Donald and Hildreth Dana (Markham) W.; m. Marjorie Morris, Sept. 18, 1948. BS, Stanford U., 1949, PhD, 1958. Asst. prof. San Jose (Calif.) State U., 1956-61, assoc. prof., 1961-65, prof. chemistry, 1965—. Author: Fundamentals of Analytical Chemistry, 1963, 4th rev. edit., 1982, Analytical Chemistry: An Introduction, 1965, 4th rev. edit., 1986, Principles of Instrumental Analysis, 1971. Served to lt. USNR, 1942-65. Mem. Am. Chem. Soc., AAUP, AAAS, Sigma Xi, Phi Lambda Upsilon. Home: 1477 Firebird Way Sunnyvale CA 94087 Office: San Jose State U Dept Chemistry San Jose CA 95192

WEST, GEORGINA SUE (LANE), university public relations specialist; b. East St. Louis, Ill., Feb. 27, 1941; d. George Russell and Claire Belle (Stanley) Lane; m. James N. Heiligenstein, 1960 (div. May 1971); children: James Daniel, Cynthia Sue, Adam Noel; m. Lloyd S. West, Dec. 20, 1975. Student, Lindenwood Coll., St. Charles, Mo., 1959, U. Ill., 1960-62; BS, No. Ill. U., 1975. Reporter The Daily Times, Ottawa, Ill., 1970-76, Spokane (Wash.) Chronicle, 1976; communications officer Bancshares Mortgage, Spokane, 1976-78; dir. community relations Gonzaga U., Spokane, 1980—. Mem. Pub. Relations Soc. Am. (accredited, bd. dirs. Greater Spokane chpt., sec.-treas. 1985), Internat. Assn. Bus. Communicators, Soc. Profl. Journalists, SigmaDelta Chi. Presbyterian. Lodge: Job's Daughters (honored queen, 1957). Avocations: photography, needlepoint. Office: Gonzaga U E 502 Boone Spokane WA 99258

WEST, HUGH STERLING, aircraft leasing co. exec.; b. Kansas City, Kans., Apr. 5, 1930; s. Gilbert Eugene and Dorothy (Johnson) W.; B.S., U. Va., 1952; B.S. Aero., U. Md., 1959; grad. U.S. Naval Test Pilot Sch., 1959; m. Willa Alden Reed, Jan. 16, 1954; children—Karen, Phillip, Susan. Commd. 2d lt. U.S. Marine Corps., 1948, advanced through grades to maj., 1961; exptl. flight test pilot, U.S. Naval Air Test Center, Patuxent River, Md.; resigned, 1961; program mgr. Boeing Aircraft Co., Seattle and Phila., 1961-66, dir. airworthiness, comml. airplane div., 1969-71; dir. aircraft sales Am. Airlines, Tulsa, 1971-76; v.p. equipment mgmt. GATX Leasing Corp., San Francisco, 1976-80; v.p. tech., partner Polaris Aircraft Leasing Corp., San Francisco, 1980-85; v.p., co-founder U.S. Airlease, Inc., 1986—; aircraft cons. Mem. Soc. Exptl. Test Pilots. Republican. Episcopalian. Club: Army Navy Country. Home: 387 Darrell Rd Hillsborough CA 94010 Office: U S Airlease Inc 615 Battery St San Francisco CA 94111

WEST, JAMES HAROLD, accounting company executive; b. San Diego, Oct. 11, 1926; s. Robert Reed and Clara Leona (Moses) W.; m. Norma Jean, 1953 (div.); 1 son, Timothy James; m., Jerel Lynn Smith, Nov. 16, 1976; 1 son, James Nelson. B.S., U. So. Calif., Los Angeles, 1949. C.P.A., Calif. Ptnr., McCracken & Co., San Diego, 1950-61; mgr. Ernst & Ernst, San Diego, 1961-64; pres. West Johnston Turnquist & Schmitt, San Diego, 1964—. Bd. govs. ARC, Washington, 1981—; pres., bd. dirs. Combined Arts and Edn. Council, San Diego, 1980-83; bd. dirs. San Diego Hosp. Assn., 1981—; treas. Pioneer Hook & Ladder, San Diego, 1966—; trustee Calif. Western Sch. Law, 1985—; bd. advisors U. So. Calif. Sch. Acctg., 1985—. Served with AUS, 1945-46; PTO. Mem. Calif. Soc. C.P.A.s (bd. dirs. 1963-64), Am. Inst. C.P.A.s. Republican. Clubs: University (San Diego); Capital Hill (Washington). Lodge: Masons. Home: 3311 Lucinda St San Diego CA 92106 Office: West Johnston Turnquist & Schmitt 2550 5th Ave San Diego CA 92103

WEST, JERRY ALAN, professional basketball team executive; b. Chelyan, W.Va., May 28, 1938; s. Howard Stewart and Cecil Sue (Creasey) W.; m. Martha Jane Kane, May, 1960 (div. 1977); children: David, Michael, Mark; m. Karen Christine Bua, May 28, 1978; 1 son, Ryan. B.S., W.Va. Coll.; L.H.D. hon., W.Va. Wesleyan Coll. Mem. Los Angeles Lakers, Nat. Basketball Assn., 1960-74, coach, 1976-79, spl. cons., from 1979, gen. mgr., 1982—; mem. first team Nat. Basketball Assn. All-Star Team, 1962-67, 70-73, mem. second team, 1968, 69. Author: (with William Libby) Mr. Clutch: The Jerry West Story, 1969. Capt. U.S. Olympic Basketball Team, 1960; named Most Valuable Player NBA Playoff, 1969, Allstar Game Most Valuable Player, 1972; named to Naismith Meml. Basketball Hall of Fame, 1979, NBA Hall of Fame, 1980; mem. NBA 35th Anniversity All-Time Team, 1980. Office: Los Angeles Lakers 3900 W Manchester Blvd Inglewood CA 90306 *

WEST, JOHANNA DIXON, computer programmer; b. San Francisco, Apr. 8, 1947; d. Richard Ballantyne and Johanna (Dixon) W.; m. Albert Richard Hoersch, Jan. 25, 1972 (div. Feb. 1982); 1 child, Angela. Student and postgrad., Stanford U., summers 1965, 69; BA, Wheaton Coll., Norton, Mass., 1969; postgrad., U. Calif., Davis, 1969-70; BS, Coleman Coll., 1982. Cert. elem. tchr., Mass. (life). Clk. typist II Millersville (Pa.) State Coll., 1972-75; legal sec. Rogers, Eilers & Howell, St. Louis, 1975-77; computer programmer U.S. Dept. Defense, San Diego, 1983—. Republican. Episcopalian. Office: US Dept Defense Naval Facilities Command PO Box 205 San Diego CA 92136

WEST, JOHN BURNARD, physician, educator; b. Adelaide, Australia, Dec. 27, 1928; came to U.S., 1969; s. Esmond Frank and Meta Pauline (Spehr) W.; m. Penelope Hall Banks, Oct. 28, 1967; children: Robert Burnard, Joanna Ruth. M.B.B.S., Adelaide U., 1952, M.D., 1958, D.Sc., 1980; Ph.D., London U., 1960. Resident Royal Adelaide Hosp., 1952, Hammersmith Hosp., London, 1953-55; physiologist Sir Edmund Hillary's Himalayan Expdn., 1960-61; dir. respiratory research group Postgrad. Med. Sch., London, 1962-67; reader medicine Postgrad. Med. Sch., 1968; prof. medicine U. Calif. at San Diego, 1969—; leader Am. Med. Research Expdn. to Mt. Everest, 1981; mem. life scis. adv. com. NASA. Author: Ventilation/Blood Flow and Gas Exchange, 1965, Respiratory Physiology-The Essentials, 1974, Pulmonary Pathophysiology-The Essentials, 1977, High Altitude Physiology, 1981, Everest-The Testing Place, 1985, Best and Taylor's Physiological Basis of Medical Practice, 1986, also numerous articles. Recipient Ernest Jung Prize for Medicine, Hamburg, 1977. Fellow Royal Coll. Physicians (London), Royal Australasian Coll. Physicians, Royal Geographical Soc. (London); mem. AAAS, Nat. Acad. Scis. (com. space biology and medicine), Nat. Bd. Med. Examiners (physiology com. 1973-76), Am. Physiol. Soc., Am. Soc. Clin. Investigation, Brit. Physiol. Soc., Am., Brit. thoracic socs., Assn. Am. Physicians, Western Assn. Physicians, Explorers Club, Am. Alpine Club. Home: 9626 Blackgold Rd La Jolla CA 92037 Office: U Calif San Diego Sch Medicine M-023A Dept Medicine La Jolla CA 92037

WEST, JOHN LEROY, aerospace engineer; b. Los Angeles, Calif., June 18, 1947; s. John LeRoy and Margaret (Jones) W. B.S. in Aerospace Engring., U. So. Calif., 1970, M.S. in Mech. Engring., 1973. Engring. research asst. Air Force Rocket Propulsion Lab., Edwards AFB, Calif., summer 1968; systems engr. hdqrs. Air Force Satellite Control Facility, El Segundo, Calif., 1970-73; engring. research asst., Jet Propulsion Lab., Pasadena, Calif., summer 1969, systems engr., 1975-86, tech. group leader Inner Planets Spacecraft System Design Group, 1986—. Mem. AIAA. Mormon. Club: Corvair Soc. Am. Contbr. publs. in field of aerospace tech. Office: Inner Planets Spacecraft System Design Group 4800 Oak Grove Dr Pasadena CA 91103

WEST, JUDITH ANNE, librarian; b. Whittier, Calif., Mar. 14, 1940; d. Emile Roland and Florence Lucile (Binford) Crumly; m. Joseph West, Dec. 18, 1965; (div. 1974). BA, Whittier Coll., 1963; MLS, U. So. Calif., 1964. Librarian, Los Angeles County Library, 1965-69; city librarian Turlock Library, Calif., 1969-71; librarian Stanislaus County Free Library, Modesto, Calif., 1971-82, county librarian, 1982—. Mem. Ala, AAUW, Calif. Library Assn., Calif. County Librarians Assn. Democrat. Mem. Soc. of Friends. Lodge: Soroptimist. Office: Stanislaus County Library 1500 I St Modesto CA 95354

WEST, LOUIS JOLYON, psychiatrist; b. N.Y.C., Oct. 6, 1924; s. Albert Jerome and Anna (Rosenberg) W.; m. Kathryn Louise Hopkirk, Apr. 29, 1944; children—Anne Kathryn, Mary Elizabeth, John Stuart. B.S., U. Minn., 1946, M.B., 1948, M.D., 1949. Diplomate: Nat. Bd. Med. Examiners, Am. Bd. Psychiatry and Neurology. Mem. faculty Cornell U., 1950-52; chief psychiatry service USAF Hosp., Lackland AFB, San Antonio, 1952-56; prof. psychiatry, head dept. psychiatry, neurology and behavioral scis. U. Okla. Sch. Medicine, 1954-69; chief mental health sect. Okla. Med. Research Found., 1956-69; cons. psychiatry Oklahoma City VA Hosp., Tinker AFB Hosp., 1956-69; fellow Center for Advanced Study in Behavioral Scis., Stanford U., 1966-67; prof., chmn. dept. psychiatry and biobehavioral sci. UCLA, 1969—; dir. Neuropsychiat. Inst. at UCLA Center for Health Scis., 1969—; psychiatrist-in-chief UCLA Med. Ctr., 1969—; nat. cons. psychiatry Surgeon Gen. USAF, 1957-62; cons. psychiatry Brentwood and Sepulveda VA hosps., 1969—; mem. nat. adv. coms. NIMH, USAF Office Sci. Research, USPHS, VA, HEW, Nat. Acad. Scis., NRC, Nat. Inst. Medicine, U.S. Army Med. Research and Devel. Panel, A.M.A., White House Conf. Civil Rights; mem. internat. adv. bd. Israeli Center for Psychobiology, Jerusalem Mental Health Center. Author: Hallucinations, 1962; editor: Hallucinations: Behavior, Experience, and Theory, 1975, Treatment of Schizophrenia: Progress and Prospects, 1976, Research on Smoking Behavior, 1977, Critical Issues in Behavioral Medicine, 1982, Alcoholism and Related Problems: Issues for the American Public, 1984; mem. editorial bd. Directions in Psychiatry, Medical Update, Cultic Studies Jour., Violence Aggression, Terrorism; contbr. articles to profl. jours., chpts. in books. Bd. dirs. Brain Research Inst., UCLA Found., Alcoholism Council Calif. Fellow AAAS, Am. Coll. Neuropsychopharmacology (founding), Am. Coll. Psychiatrists, Am. Psychiat. Assn. (life), Soc. Behavioral Medicne; mem. AMA, Am. Acad. Psychiatry and Law, Soc. Biol. Psychiatry, Am. Orthopsychiat. Assn., Acad. Psychoanalysis, Assn. Psychophysiol. Study Sleep, Am. Psychosomatic Soc., Am. Psychopath. Assn., Am. Psychol. Assn., Assn. Research in Nervous and Mental Disease, Assn. Am. Med. Colls., Nat. Acad. Religion and Mental Health (founding), Nat. Council on Alcoholism, Pavlovian Soc. (pres. 1975), Soc. Biol. Psychiatry, Soc. Psychophysiol. Research, So. Profs. Psychiatry (pres. 1963), Soc. Clin. and Exptl. Hypnosis, Alpha Omega Alpha, Sigma Xi. Office: UCLA Neuropsychiatric Inst 760 Westwood Plaza Los Angeles CA 90024

WEST, RICHARD VINCENT, art museum official; b. Prague, Czechoslovakia, Nov. 26, 1934; came to U.S., 1938, naturalized, 1947; s. Jan Josef and Katherine Frieda (Mayer) Vyslouzil; m. Emily Ann Pagenhart, June 26, 1961; 1 child, Jessica Katherine. Student, UCLA, 1952-55; B.A. with highest honors, U. Calif., Santa Barbara, 1961; postgrad., Akademie der Bildenden Kuenste, Vienna, 1961-62; M.A., U. Calif., Berkeley, 1965. Curatorial intern Cleve. Art Mus., 1965-66; curatorial intern Albright-Knox Art Gallery, Buffalo, 1966-67; curator Bowdoin Coll. Mus. Art, 1967-69, dir., 1969-72; dir. Crocker Art Mus., Sacramento, Calif., 1973-83, Santa Barbara Mus. Art, Calif., 1983—; mem. Joint Yugoslav-Am. Excavations at Sirmium, 1971; bd. dirs. Sacramento Regional Art Council, 1973-77. Author: Language of the Print, 1968; The Walker Art Building Murals, 1972; exhbn. catalogues, also various monographs and articles. Served with USN, 1956-57. Ford Found. fellow, 1965-67; Smithsonian fellow, 1971. Mem. Assn. Art Mus. Dirs., Am. Assn. Mus., Coll. Art Assn., Internat. Council Mus., Western Assn. Art Mus. (pres. 1975-78), Calif. Assn. Mus. (bd. dirs. 1980-82). Club: Rotary Internat. Office: Santa Barbara Mus Art 1130 State St Santa Barbara CA 93101

WEST, ROBERT ALAN, planetary scientist; b. Valparaiso, Ind., June 14, 1951; s. Richard William and Anna Mae (Engwer) W.; m. Karen Jean Reinhard, June 23, 1979. BS, Calif. Inst. Tech., 1973; PhD, U. Ariz., 1977. Research assoc. Lab. Atmospheric and Space Physics, U. Colo., Boulder, 1978-84; mem. tech. staff Jet Propulsion Lab., Calif. Inst. Tech., Pasadena, 1984—. Recipient Group Pioneer award NASA, 1974, Group Voyager award NASA, 1982, 86, Group Solar Mesosphere Explorer award NASA, 1983. Mem. Internat. Astron. Union, Am. Astron. Soc., Am. Geophys. Union. Democrat. Club: Sierra (Los Angeles). Avocations: hiking, camping, mountaineering, climbing. Office: Jet Propulsion Lab MS 183-301 4800 Oak Grove Dr Pasadena CA 91109

WEST, RONALD EUGENE, medical equipment company executive; b. Hobbs, N.Mex., Sept. 19, 1943; s. Eugene Allen and Hazel Inez (Tarver) W.; married; children: Jon. M., Scott D., Daniel A. BEE, U. N.Mex., 1965; postgrad., U. Colo.; MBA, Denver U., 1978. Engr. Gen. Electirc, Phoenix, 1965-69; mem. technical staff Teledyne, Northridge, Calif., 1969; mgr. med. engring. Honeywell, Englewood, Colo., 1969-78; sr. v.p. Johnson & Johnson, Englewood, Colo., 1978-84; pres. Cochlear Corp., Englewood, Colo., 1984—. Patentee automatic brake sequencing for overhead arm assembly, 1982; contbr. articles to Honeywell Computer Jour. Mem. IEEE, Am. Inst. Ultrasound in Medicine, Nat. Electronics Mfrs. Assn. (chmn. imaging sect. 1984). Lodge: Rotary. Avocation: tennis, jogging. Home: 7048 S Louthan Circle Littleton CO 80120 Office: Cocklear Corp 61 Inverness Dr Englewood CO 80112

WESTALL, FREDERICK CHARLES, research institute administrator; b. Pasadena, Calif., Nov. 6, 1943; s. Edward Francis and Irene Mae (Berry) W.; m. Janet Lynn Robertson, Jan. 13, 1968; children: Andrew, Amy, Abby, Adrienne. BS, UCLA, 1964; MS, San Diego State Coll., 1966; PhD, U. Calif., San Diego, 1970. From asst. prof. to assoc. prof. Salk Inst., La Jolla, Calif., 1970-83; pres. Inst. Disease Research, Alta Loma, Calif., 1984—. Contbr. numerous articles to profl. jours. Nat. Multiple Sclerosis Soc. fellow, N.Y.C., 1970-72. Mem. Am. Chem. Soc., Am. Acad. Neurology, Soc. Neurosci. Episcopalian. Home: 6171 Kinlock Ave Alta Loma CA 91701 Office: Inst Disease Research PO Box 1293 Alta Loma CA 91701

WESTBERG, ROBERT NEIL, architect; b. Salina, Kans., Nov. 10, 1949; s. Harold Arnason and Margaret Elaine (McLean) W.; m. Janet Marie Kovanda, Apr. 1, 1978; children: Lindsey Ann, Megan Marie. Registered architect, Ariz., N.Mex., Kans. Architect, project mgr. Wilson & Co., Salina, 1970-85; dir. architecture Wilson & Co., Phoenix, 1985—. Presbyterian. Avocations: sailing, skiing, golf, tennis, gardening. Home: 3 W Caroline Ln Tempe AZ 85284

WESTBO, LEONARD ARCHIBALD, JR., electronics engr.; b. Tacoma, Wash., Dec. 4, 1931; s. Leonard Archibald and Agnes (Martinson) W.; B.A. in Gen. Studies, U. Wash., 1958. Electronics engr. FAA, Seattle Air Route Traffic Control Center, Auburn, Wash., 1961-72; asst. br. chief electronics engring. br. 13th Coast Guard Dist., Seattle, 1972-87. Served with USCG, 1951-54, 1958-61. Registered profl. engr., Wash. Mem. Aircraft Owners and Pilots Assn., I.E.E.E., Am. Radio Relay League. Home: 10528 SE 323d St Auburn WA 98002 Office: 10528 SE 323d St Auburn WA 98002

WESTER, F(RANK) MICHAEL, architect, planner, urban designer; b. San Diego, Dec. 30, 1947; s. Francis Bostick and Marcella Dee (Faulk) W.; B.Arch. (Nat. Found. Arts scholar), Tex. A&M U., 1971; M.Arch. and Urban Design, UCLA, 1977; m. Susan Murriel Hensley, Oct. 5, 1986; children—Travis Bostick, Austin Dwight. Designer Urban Design div. Dept. Urban Planning, Dallas, 1973-75, Urban Innovations Group, Inc., Los Angeles, 1975-76, Wallace, McHarg, Roberts, Todd, Los Angeles, 1976-77; chief planner Albert C. Martin & Assos., Los Angeles, 1977-81; prin. F. Michael Wester, AIA, Santa Monica, Calif., 1981-85; sr. project mgr. The Jerde Partnership, Inc., Los Angeles, 1985—; lectr. mem. archtl. juries Los Angeles area; works include EDS Center master plan, Dallas, Joaquin Ranch/Bear Creek Village specific plan, Riverside County, Calif., Union Terminal devel. study, Los Angeles, Loyola Law Sch. master plan, Los Angeles, IBM Tucson Facilities master plan. Bd. Dirs. UCLA Grad. Sch. Architecture Alimni Assn. Recipient merit award for community design Pacific Coast Builders Conf., 1980, HUD design award, 1974; Welton Becket fellow, 1976. Mem. AIA, Am. Planning Assn., Soc. Archtl. Historians. Nat. Trust Hist. Preservation. Democrat. Home: 3737 Fredonia Los Angeles CA 90068 Office: The Jerde Partnership 2798 Sunset Blvd Los Angeles CA 90026

WESTERDAHL, JOHN BRIAN, health educator, nutritionist; b. Tucson, Dec. 3, 1954; s. Jay E. and Margaret (Meyer) W. AA, Orange Coast Coll., 1977; BS, Pacific Union Coll., 1979; MPH, Loma Linda U., 1981. Registered dietitian. Nutritionist, health educator Castle Med. Ctr., Kailua, Hawaii, 1981-84, health promotion coordinator, 1984—; talk show host Nutrition and You, Sta. KGU-Radio, Honolulu, 1983—; nutrition com. mem. Hawaii Heart Assn., Honolulu, 1984—; mem. nutrition study group Govs. Conf. Health Promotion and Disease Prevention for Hawaii, 1985. Named Outstanding Young Men Am., 1984. Mem. AAAS, Am. Coll. Sports Medicine, Am. Dietetic Assn., Am. Pub. Health Assn., Hawaii Nutrition Council (v.p. 1983-86), Hawaii Dietetic Assn., Seventh-day Adventist Dietetic Assn., Soc. for Nutrition Edn., Soc. Pub. Health Edn., Assn. for Fitness in Bus., Nat. Wellness Assn., N.Y. Acad. Scis. Republican. Avocations: swimming, scuba diving, numismatics, photography, biblical studies. Office: Castle Med Ctr 640 Ulukahiki St Kailua HI 96734

WESTFALL, JEAN-RENE, fine arts appraiser; b. Chgo., July 10, 1928; s. John Galen and Juliet Renee (Duruet) W.; m. Martha Jean Hillings, June 24, 1950; children—Dennis, Philip, Brian, Randolph. B.A., Woodbury U., 1949; A.A., Citrus Coll., 1967 student in Chinese lang. Seton Hall U., 1980, U. Calif.-San Diego, 1983. Reliability engr. Calif. Inst. Tech., Pasadena, 1955-63; writer, enginring., art subjects, appraisal, Los Angeles and San Diego, 1963-70; dir. Fine Arts Studio, Lake San Marcos, 1970-75; pres. J. R. Westfall & Sons, Escondido, Calif., 1975-84; cons. museums and pvt. corps. Author: More than Words, 1970; Highlights, 1955, 65. Contbr. articles to jours. and mags. Mem. Pub. Arts Adv. Council, County of San Diego, 1983; founding mem. Felecita Found. for Arts, Escondido, 1982-83. Mem. Am. Soc. Appraisers (sr., bd. dirs. S.D. chpt. 1987), New Eng. Appraisers Soc., San Diego Mus. Art, Archaeol. Inst. Am., San Marcos Art League (pres. 1972), Escondido Hist. Soc. (life), San Marcos Hist. Soc., Republican. Roman Catholic. Office: J R Westfall & Sons PO Box 3377 Escondido CA 92025

WESTFALL, KIRK MATTHEW, chemical technologist, safety professional; b. Peoria, Ill., Mar. 27, 1953; s. Don Carlos Wesfall and Lois Emily Smith; m. Margaret Jane Westfall, Sept. 4, 1981 (div. 1987); 1 child, Kyle Addison. Student, U. N.Mex., 1971-73, U. Albuquerque, 1973-74; grad., BioCentrics Inst., 1984. Engring. asst. Monosil Inc., Cupertino, Calif., 1978-82; parametric test operator Monosil Inc., Santa Clara, Calif., 1981-82; spl. LCD operator Suncrux Inc., Sunnyvale, Calif., 1982; safety dir. S.P.I. Inc., San Jose, Calif., 1982-85; asst. tchr. Teledyne Semiconductor Inc., Mountain View, Calif., 1984-85, chem. technologist, safety specialist, 1985-86; chem. technologist, safety specialist BioCentrics Inst., Mountain View, 1986—; advt. cons. You Deserve Time Out, San Jose, Calif., 1985. Patentee in field. Mem. AAAS. Club: B.A.M.M.A. (Cupertino) (Buoy Tender 1980-85). Avocations: painting, cars, reading, inventing, builder radio controlled model scale ships and boats. Office: Teledyne Semiconductor Mountain View CA 94043

WESTFALL, RICHARD MERRILL, chemist, research administrator; b. Denver, Dec. 17, 1956; s. Robert Raymond and Madelyn Evastine (Cornwell) W. Student, U. Colo., 1976-80. Mem. lab. staff NOAA, Boulder, Colo., 1978-79, Solar Energy Research Inst., Golden, Colo., 1979-80; dir. research Galactic Products, Denver, 1981-82; pres., dir. research CEL Systems Corp., Arvada, Colo., 1982—; process chemist, engr. (temporary) Tex. Med. Instruments, Schertz, 1986—. Inventor electrolytic growth tin and other metals, and process, 1980-82; patentee in field. Mem. AIAA, Air Force Assn. Avocations: aerospace propulsion, electric thrust systems. Home: 4838 Stuart St Denver CO 80212

WESTMORE, JANET KAREN, telecommunications executive; b. Ross, Calif., July 7, 1947; d. John and Elizabeth Marshall (Chubb) Broman; m. William John Wright, Oct. 21, 1966; children—Karen Elizabeth, Jennifer Anne; m. Normand Earl Westmore, Jan. 20, 1980. B.A. in Math., Mills Coll., 1970. Asst. engr. Pacific Telesis, San Francisco, 1970, engr., 1971-75, adminstrv. mgr., 1975-78, switching mgr., 1978-81, dist. mgr., 1981—. Elder Presbyn. Ch., counselor Jr. High Youth Group, 1983-85; discussion leader Beyond War. Mem. Mills Coll. Alumnae Assn. (bd. govs. 1982-84), World Affairs Council, AAUW, Great Books Discussion Group. Democrat. Office: Pacific Telesis Co 633 Folsom St Room 680 San Francisco CA 94107

WESTON, DUANE RUSSELL, music educator; b. Fresno, Calif., June 21, 1929; s. John Charles and Marion Adella (Todd) W.; m. Ann Morrow Shelton, Sept. 16, 1950; children: Dwight, Deborah, Deniece. AA, Bakersfield Coll., 1949; BA, Fresno State U., 1951; Masters, Calif. Poly. State U., San Luis Obispo, 1970. Cert. secondary tchr., Calif.; cert. counselor, Calif. Tchr. music Kern County High Sch., Bakersfield, Calif., 1953-57, Fresno (Calif.) City Unified Sch., 1957-75, Coll. Sequoias, Visalia, Calif., 1975—; dir. student activities Roosevelt High Sch., Fresno, 1973-75, counselor, dir. work experience program, 1973-75. Composer Col. Moore March, 1955. Named Tchr. of Yr., Roosevelt High Sch., 1967, Tchr. of Yr., Coll. Sequoias, 1981; recipient Citizen's award Visalia City Council, 1981, Faculty Teaching award Coll. Sequoias, 1983. Mem. NEA, Music Assn. Calif. Community Colls. (bd. dirs.), Calif. Band Dirs. Assn. (pres. 1964), Calif. Music Edn. Assn. (band rep.). Republican. Club: Trade (Tulare, Calif.) (song leader). Avocations: golf, softball, umpiring, musician. Home: 3527 W Paradise Visalia CA 93277

WESTON, JOHN FREDERICK, educator; b. Ft. Wayne, Ind., Feb. 6, 1916; s. David Thomas and Bertha (Schwartz) W.; children: Kenneth F., Byron L., Ellen J.; m. Eva Dixon, Jan. 3, 1987. B.A., U. Chgo., 1937, M.B.A., 1943, Ph.D., 1948. Instr. Sch. Bus., U. Chgo., 1940-42, asst. prof., 1947-48; econ. cons. to pres. Am. Bankers Assn., 1945-46; prof. Grad. Sch. Mgmt., U. Calif., Los Angeles, 1949—; disting. lecture series U. Okla., 1967, U. Utah, 1972, Miss. State U., 1972, Miami State U., 1975. Author: Scope and Methodology of Finance, 1966, International Managerial Finance, 1972, Impact of Large Firms on U.S. Economy, 1973, Financial Theory and Corporate Policy, 1979, 2d edit., 1983, Managerial Finance, 8th edit, 1986; assoc. editor: Jour. of Finance, 1948-55; mem. editorial bd., 1957-59. Bd. dirs. Bunker Hill Fund. Served with Ordnance Dept. AUS, 1943-45. McKinsey Found. grantee, 1965-68; Gen. Electric Co. grantee, 1967; Ford Found. Faculty Research fellow, 1961-62. Mem. Am. Finance Assn. (pres. 1966, adv. bd. 1967-71), Am. Econ. Assn., Western Econ. Assn. (pres. 1962), Econometric Soc., Am. Statis. Assn., Royal Econ. Soc., Fin. Analysts Soc., Fin. Mgmt. Assn. (pres. 1979-80). Home: 500 Bonhill Rd Los Angeles CA 90049 Office: Grad Sch Mgmt U Calif Research Competition Bus Policy Los Angeles CA 90024

WESTON, WILLIAM FRANCIS, physicist; b. Oakland, Calif., May 31, 1946; s. Willard Francis and Ruth Mildred (Fields) W.; m. Gale Marsha Kozberg Tuneberg, Aug. 25, 1968 (div. Mar. 1977); m. Gay Elizabeth Sivers, Nov. 11, 1978; 1 child, Rachel Ann. BA, U. Calif., Berkeley, 1968; MS, U. Ill., 1970, PhD, 1973; MBA, U. Denver, 1981. Physicist Lawrence (Berkeley) Livermore Lab., 1968, 69; teaching asst. U. Ill., Champaign, 1968-69, 69-70, research asst., 1970-73; physicist Nat. Bur. Standards, Boulder, Colo., 1973-75; dir. Rockwell Internat., Golden, Colo., 1975—. Mem. Inst. Nuclear Materials Mgmt., Am. Phys. Soc., Sigma Xi. Avocations: running, weight lifting, swimming, softball. Office: Rockwell Internat PO Box 464 Golden CO 80402-0464

WESTOVER, TODD ROBERT, art director; b. Manitowoc, Wis., Apr. 14, 1962; s. Tom and Sally (Turney) W. Student, Saddleback Jr. Coll., 1980-82. Art dir. Hot Bike mag., Anaheim, Calif., 1982-85, Car Craft mag., Hollywood, Calif., 1986—. Art dir. Auto Accents catalogue, 1985. Avocations: drums, songwriting. Home: 1782 Brigden Rd Pasadena CA 91104 Office: Car Craft mag Petersen Pubs 8490 Sunset Blvd Los Angeles CA 90069

WESTOVER, VIRGINIA L. ((WEINER)), writer; b. Bay City, Mich., May 20, 1938; s. Edwin Frederick and Virginia Elizabeth (Snyder) Westover; m. Michael D. Ryan II, Apr. 23, 1960 (div. 1965); m. Joseph J. Weiner, Sept. 29, 1978. Student, Wheaton Coll., Norton, Mass., 1957-59; BA in English Lit., U. Mich., 1961. Pub. relations asst. Univ. Relations of U. Mich., Ann Arbor, 1961-62; reporter Ann Arbor News, 1962-66, Detroit News, 1966-67; reporter, writer San Franicsco Chronicle, 1967-71, soc. editor, 1971-73; asst. dir. devel. San Francisco Opera, 1974-76; publicity dir. San Francisco Symphony, 1976-78; project dir. The Presence of the Past, 1980-82; freelance writer San Francisco, 1984—. Active San Francisco Art Inst. Council, 1978—, Modern Art Council, San Francisco Mus. Modern Art., 1985—; trustee U. Art. Mus., U. Calif., Berkeley, 1985—. Democrat. Presbyterian. Club: Met. (San Francisco). Avocations: art collecting, hiking, swimming, bird watching, opera.

WETHERALL, ELOISE ANN, insurance executive; b. Mpls., Aug. 31, 1937; d. Emmet Nathan and Sylvia Marie (Kaufmann) W.; m. Francis F. Gomes, June 16, 1956 (div. Sept. 1967); 1 child, Kimberly Kanoelani. BA, U. Minn., 1959. CLU; cert. employee benefit specialist. Group mgr. N.Y. Life Ins. Co., Honolulu, 1959-69, Union Mut. Life Ins. Co., Honolulu, 1969-70; v.p. Johnson & Higgins of Hawaii Inc., Honolulu, 1970-86; pres. Gleason, Wetherall & Assocs., Honolulu, 1986—; chmn. Pub. Health Com., Honolulu, 1985—. Pres. United Cerebral Palsy Assn., Honolulu, 1984-86, regional dir., San Francisco, 1985-86; commr. Commn. on Handicapped, Honolulu, 1985—; bd. dirs. Oahu Pvt. Industry Council, Honolulu, 1985—. Mem. Sales and Mktg. Execs., Honolulu C. of C. (v.p. 1985—, treas. 1986-87). Democrat. Roman Catholic. Clubs: The Plaza (bd. govs. 1985-86), Honolulu. Home: 927 Prospect St #1503 Honolulu HI 96822 Office: Gleason Wetherall & Assocs 900 Fort St Mall Honolulu HI 96813

WETHERWAX, RITCHIE JEAN, hospital administrator; b. Belleville, Ill., July 28, 1928; d. Richard and Viola L. (Davis) Grossner; m. Richard R. Wills, Jan. 23, 1948; children—Valann M. Kampf, Sheila L. Ortiz; m. Lawrence G. Wetherwax, June 29, 1974. A.A., Crafton Hills Coll., 1976; B.A., Redlands U., 1977. Lic. nursing home adminstr., Calif. Patient service rep. Loma Linda U. Hosp., 1968-72; office mgr. Canyon Crest Convalescent Hosp., Colton, Calif., 1972-74, Highland House Healthcare (Calif.), 1974-76; adminstr. Beverly Manor Convalescent Hosp., Riverside, Calif., 1977-79, Terracina Convalescent Hosp., Redlands, Calif., 1979—. Fellow Am. Coll. Health Care Adminstrs.; mem. Am. Coll. Nursing Home Adminstrs. Nat. Assn. Female Execs., AAUW, Redlands C. of C. Republican. Adventist. Lodges: Order Eastern Star, Soroptimists.

WETMORE, RALPH FREDERICK, tool manufacturing company executive; b. Meriden, Conn., Nov. 17, 1934; s. James Russell Wetmore and Genevive Berniece (Modrejczwski) Meyers; m. Jennifer Louise Patterson, Nov. 22, 1969; children—James, Judith, Daniel, Suzanne. Student pub. schs., Downey, Calif. Registered profl. engr., Calif. With Wetmore Tool & Engring. Corp., Pico Rivera, Calif., 1956—, pres., 1976-83, chief exec. officer, 1983—. Cubmaster Boy Scouts Am., El Monte, Calif., 1964; pres. La Mirada Little League, Calif., 1981-83. Recipient resolution Calif. Assembly, 1982. Mem. Soc. Carbide Engrs. (chmn. Los Angeles chpt. 9, 1969), Am. Soc. Metals, Nat. Assn. Mfrs., Calif. Mfrs. Assn., Cutting Tool Mfrs. (bd. dirs. 1985-87), Nat. Fedn. Ind. Bus., Pico Rivera C. of C. Republican. Lodges: Elks, Masons, Shriners, Scottish Rite. Office: Wetmore Tool & Engring Co Inc 9129 Perkins St Pico Rivera CA 90660

WETTS, RICHARD WAYNE, biology researcher; b. Green Bay, Wis., May 28, 1956; s. Wayne Joseph and Hazel (Hansen) W.; m. Megan Valeria Wolff, Aug. 11, 1979; 1 child, Rachel Allison. BS in Psychobiology, U. So. Calif., 1978; PhD in Human Genetics, Yale U., 1982. Postdoctoral fellow U. Montreal, Can., 1982-83, Johns Hopkins U., Balt., 1983-85, U. Calif., Irvine, 1985—. Contbr. articles to profl. jours. Mem. Soc. Neurosci., Phi Beta Kappa, Phi Kappa Phi. Republican. Lutheran. Home: 1250 Adams Ave B103 Costa Mesa CA 92626 Office: U Calif Dept Physiology and Biophysics Irvine CA 92717

WETZEL, CHERIE LALAINE RIVERS, biologist; b. Lewiston, Idaho, June 20, 1930; d. Edwin Bagnal and Mary Elizabeth (Rose) Rivers; m. Herbert Don Wetzel, July 3, 1948; children: Margaret Elizabeth, Don Louis. AA, Chabot Coll., 1966; BA in Biology, Stanford U., 1968, MA, 1970; PhD in Botany, U. Calif., Berkeley, 1979. Asst. curator Dudley Herbarium Stanford (Calif.) U., 1968-70; instr. Calif. flora U. Calif., Berkeley, summer 1977, vis. assoc. prof. botany, biology, 1977-85; instr. gen. biology, ecology, microbiology Chabot Coll., Hayward, Calif., 1970-71, 74-77; instr. botany, field ecology, biology San Francisco City Coll., 1977—, chmn. dept. biol. scis., 1980-84; participant various profl. meetings; invited speaker XIV Internat. Bot. Conf., Berlin, 1987. Contbr. bot. and electron microscopy articles to profl. jours. Recipient Outstanding Scholarship Faculty award Chabot Coll., 1966, Gordon Ferris $1,000 award Stanford U., 1969; NIH grantee, 1976. Mem. AAAS, Am. Soc. Cell Biology, Bot. Soc. Am., Calif. Bot. Soc. (treas.), Calif. Native Plant Soc., Electron Microscope Soc., Am. Friends of U. Calif. Bot. Garden, No. Calif. Electron Microscope Soc., Sigma Xi. Home: 48 Starview Dr Oakland CA 94618 Office: San Francisco City Coll Dept Biol Scis 50 Phelan Ave San Francisco CA 94112

WETZEL, JOHN, professional basketball coach; b. Waynesboro, VA, Oct. 22, 1944; m. Diane W.; 2 children: Mark, Paul. Attended, Virginia Tech. Player Los Angeles Lakers, 1967-68, Atlanta Hawks, Phoenix Suns; asst. coach Phoenix Suns, 1979-87, head coach, 1987—. Office: care Phoenix Suns PO Box 1369 Phoenix AZ 85001 *

WEWER, DEE J., artist, educator, creative arts therapist; b. Mobile, Ala., Apr. 27, 1948; d. Gene B. and Juanita (Schmeckenbecher) Wewer; m. Doni Mitchell, Apr. 13, 1985. B.S., U. So. Miss., 1969; M.A., Am. U., 1974; postgrad. Georgetown U., 1981-82; Ph.D., Union Grad. Sch., 1986. With Dixie Press, Biloxi, Miss., 1968-70; tchr. St. Martin Public Sch., Biloxi, 1970; editor newspaper of Nat. War Coll., Ft. McNair, Washington, 1971-73; press and scheduling asso. and coordinator Nat. Fedn. State Chairmen, Office of Chmn., Republican Nat. Com., Washington, 1972-73; cons. Nat. Women's Edn. Fund, Nat. Women's Polit. Caucus, 1973-74; gen. mgr., treas. Printing Services Unltd., Washington, 1975; instr. Inst. Politics, Harvard U., Boston, 1976; media dir./prodn. mgr./creative group head Bailey, Deardourff & Assos., Washington, 1975-76; dir. mktg./account supr. Weitzman & Assocs., Washington, 1976-78; dir. mktg. Britches of Georgetown, Washington, 1978-79; instr. Coll. Bus. and Mgmt., U. Md., College Park, 1980-83; v.p. public affairs AMF Head Sports Wear, Columbia, Md., 1979-81; exec. v.p. Sport-Obermeyer, Aspen, Colo., 1982-85; creativity coach, painter, writer, cons., 1985—; instr. Colo. Mountain Coll., 1985—; paintings represented by Aspen Artists Gallery, R Collection, Los Angeles, Sheehan & Assocs., Balt.; owner The Mitchell Wewer Studios Design Group; dir. Monte/Edel Advt. Represented in permanent collection Aspen Art Mus. Charter mem. Aspen Initiative; active community affairs; vol. therapist Aspen Mental Health Clinic. Recipient Creative Design Distinction, Andy, Printing Industries Am., 1981; Distinctive Merit award Advt. Club of N.Y., 1980, Art Dirs. Club of Met. Washington, 1980; Clio awards, 1979; named Outstanding Working Woman, Glamour mag., 1978, Outstanding Tchr., Colo. Mountain Coll.; Nat. Newspaper Nat. Creativity award, 1974. Mem. Ski Industries of Am., Women in Advt. and Mktg., Am. Women in Radio and TV, Am. Mgmt. Assn., Advt. Club, Art Dirs. Club, NOW. Home: 790 W Hallam Aspen CO 81611 Studio: Mitchell & Wewer Studios 210-E Ventnor Ave Aspen CO 81611

WEYERHAEUSER, GEORGE HUNT, forest products company executive; b. Seattle, July 8, 1926; s. John Philip and Helen (Walker) W.; m. Wendy Wagner, July 10, 1948; children: Virginia Lee, George Hunt, Susan W., Phyllis A., David M., Merrill W. BS with honors in Indsl. Engring., Yale U., 1949. With Weyerhaeuser Co., Tacoma, 1949—, successively mill foreman, br. mgr., 1949-56, v.p., 1957-62, exec. v.p., 1962-66, pres., 1966—, also chief exec. officer, bd. dirs.; bd. dirs. Boeing Co., Fed. Res. Bank of San Francisco, SAFECO Corp., Chevron Copr.; mem. adv. bd. sch. of bus. adminstrn. U. Wash., the Bus. Council, Bus. Roundtable, Wash. State Bus. Roundtable. Office: Weyerhaeuser Co Tacoma WA 98477

WEYGAND, LAWRENCE RAY, insurance broker; b. South Haven, Mich., Jan. 5, 1940; s. Ray and Lorraine (Berkins) W.; B.A., Drake U., 1962, postgrad., 1962-63; m. Paula West, May 2, 1987; 1 son, Chad C. Comml. multi-peril ins. underwriter Aetna Casualty & Surety Co., Mpls., also Indpls., 1964-66, Safeco Ins. Co., Denver, 1966-69; pres., chmn. bd. Weygand & Co., ins. agts., brokers and consultants, Denver, 1969—; pres. Homeowners Ins. Agy., Inc., Scottsdale, Ariz., Homeowners Ins., Inc., Denver, Weygand & Co. of Ariz., Inc., Scottsdale, Transatlantic Underwriters, Inc.; owner U.S. Insurors, Inc., Ariz. Dealers Ins. Services, Inc., Colo. Dealers Ins. Services, Inc., Denver, Storage Pak Ins., Inc.; owner, pres. mng. gen. agy. serving Colo., Ariz., Nev., Utah and N.Mex.; asst. to Gov. State of Iowa, 1961-62. Mem. bus. community adv. council Regis Coll., 1976—. Mem. Ind. Ins. Agts. Colo. (chmn. fair and ethical practice com.), Ind. Ins. Agts. Am., Profl. Ins. Agts. Colo., Profl. Ins. Agts. Am., Alpha Tau Omega. Republican. Congregationalist. Clubs: Denver Athletic. Home: 10703 E Crestline Ave Englewood CO 80110 Home: 8415 E San Candido Dr Scottsdale AZ 85258 Office: 1582 S Parker Rd Denver CO 80231 Office: 3200 N Hayden St Scottsdale AZ 85258

WEYGAND, LEROY CHARLES, security cons.; b. Webster Park, Ill., May 17, 1926; s. Xaver William and Marie Caroline (Hoffert) W.; B.A. in Sociology cum laude, U. Md., 1964; m. Helen V. Bishop, Aug. 28, 1977; children—Linda M. Weygand Vance (dec.), Leroy Charles, Cynthia R., Janine P. Enlisted in U.S. Army, 1944, commd. 2d lt., 1950, advanced through grades to lt. col., 1966; service in Korea, 1950; chief phys. security U.S. Army, 1965-70; ret., 1970; pres. Weygand Security Cons. Services, Anaheim, Calif., 1970—, W & W Devel. Corp., 1979—; security dir. Jefferies Banknote Co., 1972-78; exec. dir Kern County Taxpayers Assn., 1986—; dir. Mind Psi-Biotics, Inc. Bd. dirs. Nat. Assn. Control Narcotics and Dangerous Drugs. Decorated Legion of Merit. Mem. Am. Soc. Indsl. Security. Contbr. articles profl. jours. Patentee office equipment locking device. Home and Office: PO Box 140 Tehachapi CA 93561

WHALEN, THOMAS JOHN, labor union representative; b. Pawtucket, R.I., June 2, 1937; s. Thomas J. Sr. and Ellen V. (Dempsey) W.; m. Patricia Ann Roberts, Oct. 3, 1959; children: Threasa, John, Sheryl, Michael. AA, Los Angeles Trade and Tech. Coll., 1959. Draftsman, loftsman/layout master N.Am. Aviation, Los Angeles, 1959-65; rep., editor UAW Local 887, Los Angeles, 1965-78; mgr. UAW Job Devel., Huntington Park, Calif., 1978-79; internat. rep. UAW Internat. Union, Bell, Calif., 1979—; pres. Rockwell Credit Union, Downey, Calif., 1968-82; trustee UAW Mgmt. Joint Bd., Los Angeles, 1980—. Editor: Propeller, 1966-79 (LUPA award 1976-79), Bettertimes, 1984— (AFL-CIO award 1985). Mem. Dem. County Com., Los Angeles, 1968-70, Dem. State Com., Calif., 1970-74; chmn. City of Inglewood Planning Com., Calif., 1971-74. Served with USCGR, 1955-59. Mem. United Aerospace Workers (local chmn. 1964-68), News Paper Guild Am. Roman Catholic. Avocations: fishing, reading, photography, traveling. Office: UAW Internat Union 17100 Pioneer Blvd Artesia CA 90701

WHAN, WEN JEA, geophysicist; b. Kaohsiung, Republic of China, May 8, 1951; came to U.S., 1977; s. Shie Yeng and Li-Kung W.; m. Kong Ming, May 1977; 1 child, E. Jin. MS, Nat. Taiwan U. Oceanography Inst., Republic of China, 1977; PhD, Colo. Sch. Mines, 1979. Geophysicist Edlon Group 7, Denver, 1978-79; researcher Colo. Sch. Mines, Golden, 1979-82; exec. pres. GeoPacific Resources, Inc., Golden, 1982—. Ministry Edn. grantee Republic of China, 1977. Mem. Soc. Exploration Geophysicists, Sigma Xi. Home: 263 Kimball Ave Golden CO 80401 Office: GeoPacific Resources Inc Bldg C 15985 S Golden Rd Golden CO 80401

WHARTON, THOMAS WILLIAM, health administration executive; b. St. Louis, Nov. 20, 1943; s. Thomas William and Elaine Margaret (Bassett) w.; divorced; children: Thomas William, Christopher John. BSc in Econs., U. Mo., 1967; M in Health Adminstrn., U. Ottawa, Ont., Can., 1978. Asst. to exec. dir. Ottawa Civic Hosp., 1978-80; exec. dir. Cariboo Meml. Hosp., Williams Lake, B.C., Can., 1980-83; dir. clinic and rehab. services Workers' Compensation Bd., Vancouver, B.C., 1983—. Mem. Vancouver Art Gallery, 1986, Physicians for Social Responsibility, Vancouver, 1986, Alliance Francaise, Vancouver, 1986. Recipient Founder award Cariboo Musical Soc., 1983. Mem. Can. Coll. Health Service Execs., Am. Coll. Health Execs., Am. Acad. Med. Adminstrs., Health Adminstrs. Assn. B.C., U. Ottawa Health Service Alumni Assn. (pres. 1983-84), Rolls Royce Owners Club. Club: Chevalier de Vin de France (Vancouver). Avocations: swimming, music, wine, art.

WHATMORE, GEORGE BERNARD, physician, clinical neurophysiologist; b. Seattle, Aug. 31, 1917; s. Harry Joseph and Delia (Frolich) W.; B.S., U. Wash., 1940, M.S., 1941; Ph.D. (Univ. fellow, Rawson fellow, Sheldon fellow), U. Chgo., 1946, M.D., 1948; m. Frances Maxwell Beatty, May 28, 1942; children—Pamela Frances, David Blake, Nancy Janice. Intern, King County Hosp., Seattle, 1948-49, resident, 1949-50; resident Lab. Clin. Physiology, Chgo., 1950-51; pvt. practice internal medicine, functional disorders, Seattle, 1951—; mem. staff Virginia Mason, Swedish, Med.-Dental Bldg. hosps. (all Seattle), 1951—, Eastern State Hosp., Medical Lake, Wash., 1955-58; prin. investigator Pacific N.W. Research Found., Seattle, 1966—. Recipient Ginsburg award U. Chgo., 1946. Mem. N.Y. Acad. Sci., AAAS, Am. Physicians Soc. for Physiologic Tension Control, Internat. Stress and Tension Control Assn., Behavior Therapy and Research Soc., Acad. Psychosomatic Medicine, AMA, Wash. Med. Assn., King County Med. Soc., Am., Wash. biofeedback socs., Western Acad. Beaux Arts, Sigma Xi. Author: (with Daniel R. Kohli) Dysponesis: A Neurophysiologic Factor in Functional Disorders, 1968, The Physiopathology and Treatment of Functional Disorders, 1974; contbr. articles to profl. jours. Home: 10524 SE 27th St Bellevue WA 98004 Office: 10524 SE 27th St Bellevue WA 98004

WHEABLE, BERT LOWELL, JR., corporate safety director, chiropractor; b. Salt Lake City, June 1, 1922; s. Bert Lowell and Eva Christina (Holm) W.; m. Iona Finch, Aug. 12, 1946; children—Michael, Melodee Wheable Kennedy, Barbara Wheable Sarrica, Kit Wheable Barlow. D. Chiropractic, Calif. Chiropractic Coll., 1951, philosopher chiropractic (hon.), 1954. Lic. chiropractor, Calif. Route mgr. Pepsi Cola Co., Oakland, Calif., 1967-72, area mgr., 1972-74, merchandising and tng. coordinator, 1974-77, corporate safety dir., 1977—. Active Boy Scouts Am., 1942—, including cubmaster, scoutmaster, council tng. chmn., dist. and council coms. Recipient Scouting Dist. award Merit, Oakland Area council, Mt. Diablo council; Nat. award Boy Scouts Am., Silver Beaver. Mem. Am. Soc. Safety Engrs., Internat. Chiropractic Assn., Calif. Chiropractic Assn. Mormon. Home: 201 Powell Ave Pleasant Hill CA 94523 Office: Pepsi Cola Co 940 81st Ave Oakland CA 94621

WHEADON, RICK DEAN, engineer, consultant; b. Murray, Utah, July 14, 1957; s. Dean A. and Sherrie (Fitzgerald) W.; m. Jana Fuhriman, Sept. 12, 1979; children: Jacob Dean, Whitney. BSCE, Brigham Young U., 1982, M Engring. Mgmt., 1983. Prin. Turf Irrigation Co., Provo, Utah, 1975-76; field technician Horrocks & Corrollo Engrs., American Fork, Utah, 1976; teaching asst. Brigham Young U., Provo, 1981-83; ptnr. Water and Wastewater Services, Springville, Utah, 1983-86; gen. mgr., ptnr. Community Cons., Springville, 1983-86; v.p., ptnr. Community Mgmt. Inc., Springville, 1983—. Author tech. articles to publs. Mem. ASCE, Am. Cons. Engrs. Council, Am. Water Works Assn. (grantee 1986), Am. Legion (boys state 1974). Mormon. Club: Sportsmen. Avocations: hunting, fishing, skiing, boating. Home: 1942 N Skyline Dr Orem UT 84057 Office: Community Mgmt Inc 1205 Springcreek Dr Springville UT 84663-0574

WHEATLEY, JEFF R., construction lawyer; b. Lawton, Okla., July 14, 1927; s. J. Carl and Dennis Belle (Roper) W.; m. Garline J. Johnson, Aug. 2, 1949; children—Michael Jeff, Kayci Garline, Kelly Donald. B.S.E.E., U. Okla., 1956; J.D. cum laude, Pepperdine U., 1970. Bar: Calif. 1971, U.S. Dist. Ct. (9th dist.) Calif. 1971. Sole practice, Long Beach, Calif., 1971-73, Placentia, Calif., 1973-77, Fullerton, Calif., 1977—; tchr. constrn. law 1981-82; mem. five atty. firm, Fullerton. Served with USN 1945-46. Recipient Charles R. Mower award Orange County Builders Assn., 1981. Mem. ABA (Constrn. Forum), Orange County Bar Assn., Am. Subcontractors Assn. (legal adv. com.), So. Calif. Builders Assn., USCG Aux. Producer audio tapes on constrn. law for Calif. contractors. Club: Dana Point Yacht. Office: 2600 E Nutwood Ave Suite 101 Fullerton CA 92631

WHEATMAN, VICTOR STEVEN, telecommunications consultant; b. N.Y.C., Nov. 14, 1945; s. Nathan E. and Helen (Silverstein) W.; m. Kathleen Murray, Aug. 21, 1971; 1 child, Laura. BA in Journalism, Fairleigh Dickinson U., 1968; MS in Broadcasting, Boston U., 1972; cert. in exec. mgmt., Harvard U., 1980; cert. in telecommunications, Golden Gate U., 1985. News, program dir. Sta. WBUR, Boston, 1972-77; radio mgr. Sta. KTEP-FM, El Paso, Tex., 1979-80, Sta. KCSM-FM, San Mateo, Calif., 1980-82; ind. cons. Wheatman Assocs., Hayward, Calif., 1982-84; mktg. dir. Creative Strategies, San Jose, Calif., 1984-85; cons. Input, Mountain View, Calif., 1985—; bd. dirs. Western Pub. Radio, San Francisco, 1980—; mem. exec. com. Calif. State Pub. Broadcasting Commn., Sacramento, 1980-82. Recipient Tom Phillips award UPI, 1974, Corp. Pub. Broadcasting award, Washington, 1975; NEH grantee, 1975, 80. Avocations: collector sound recordings and books about radio. Home: 41088 Bairo Ct Fremont CA 94539 Office: Input 1943 Landings Dr Mountain View CA 94043

WHEATON, JOHN SOUTHWORTH, distribution company executive; b. Balt., Dec. 26, 1928; s. Ezra Almon and Ruth Adelaide (Otis) W.; m. Joy Lorraine Thuressen, Dec. 16, 1950; children: Sandra, Jason, Christopher. B.A., Stanford U., 1951; M.B.A., Columbia U., 1953. Mgr. fin. TRW, Inc., Redondo Beach, Calif., 1956-60; v.p. ops. Bissett-Berman Corp., Santa Monica, Calif., 1960-71; v.p. ops. control Foremost-McKesson, Inc., San Francisco, 1971-74; v.p. planning and analysis McKesson Corp., San Francisco, 1974-86, exec. v.p. adminstrn., 1986—; bd. dirs. Armor All, Irvine, Calif., Pharm. Card Systems, Scottsdale, Ariz. Bd. dirs. Assn. Corp. Growth, San Francisco. Served to lt. USNR, 1953-56. Club: Olympic. Office: McKesson Corp 1 Post St San Francisco CA 94104

WHEELER, BONNIE G., author; b. Charleston, W.Va., July 12, 1943; d. Earnest A. and Virginia F. (Barker) Lindner; m. Dennis R. Wheeler, June 14, 1961; children—Julie Lynn, Timothy Dennis, Robert Grant; adopted children—Rebecca Anne, Benjamin Joel. Student pub. schs., Ft. Lauderdale, Fla. Free-lance writer, 1977—; tchr. and workshop leader Writers' Workshops and Confs.; co-founder No. Calif. Christian Writers Ann. Workshop; co-founder and pres. Sutter-Buttes Christian Writers Fellowship. Mem. Colusa County Children's Health Adv. Bd., 1980—; chmn. Colusa County Spl. Edn. Adv. Bd., 1981-83; mem. Williams Sch. Site Council, 1981-83, Colusa County Mother and Child Adv. Commn., 1983—; dir. Hurrier I Go...Time Workshops; mem. Nat. Right to Life Com.; cons. editor The Caring Congregation; task force del. Christian and Missionary Alliance. Recipient Inspiration award Mt. Hermon Christian Writers Conf., 1982. Mem. Christian Writers Guild. Republican. Author: Of Braces and Blessings, 1980; Challenged Parenting, 1983; Meet the Overcomers, 1984; The Hurrier I Go, 1985; contbr.: Chosen Children, 1978; Wondrous Power, Wondrous Love, 1984; contbr. articles to religious pubs. Home: 2409 Jasmine St Wasco CA 93280

WHEELER, CHARLES LYNN, music educator, pianist; b. Lebanon, Oreg., July 4, 1943; s. Charles Bland and Willa Roberta (Eberman) W.; m. Charlaine Patricia Amey, Aug. 14, 1966; 1 child, Charlynn Marie. MusB, Walla Walla Coll., 1966; MusM, Cath. U. Am., 1970; D in Music Arts, U. Oreg., 1976. Instr. music Campion Acad., Loveland, Colo., 1961-62, Portland (Oreg.) Union Acad., 1966-67, Columbia Union Coll, Takoma Park, Md., 1967-71; prof. music Pacific Union Coll., Angwin, Calif., 1971—, music dept. chmn., 1986—. Performer U.S. concert tour, 1978, U.S. and Caribbean concert tour, 1980. Mem. Music Tchrs. Assn. Calif. (Napa br. pres. 1974-75), Calif. Assn. Profl. Music Tchrs. (dist. pres. 1975-77), Music Tchrs. Nat. Assn., Am. Coll. Musicians, Piano Guild. Republican. Adventist. Home: 480 Bay St Angwin CA 94508-9797 Office: Pacific Union coll Dept Music Angwin CA 94508-9797

WHEELER, CHRIS LEE, state government administrator, water resources engineer; b. Milton-Freewater, Oreg., Dec. 30, 1927; s. Charles Oscar and Virgie Ann (Fugate) W.; m. Mildred Mae Pitzer, Dec. 23, 1949; children: Christi, Sharon, Michael, Jared. BS in Engring., Oreg. State U., 1950, postgrad., 1950; postgrad., U. Oreg., 1957. Registered profl. engr., Oreg. Project engr. Lamb Weston, Inc., Milton-Freewater, 1951; water rights engr. State Engr. Oreg., Salem, 1951-52, adminstr. water rights, 1952-58, asst. state engr. Hydro Com., 1958-62, state engr., 1962-75, dep. dir. water resources dept., 1975—; mem. Klamath R. Compact com., Klamath Falls, Oreg., 1962—; mem. nat. adv. com. water data for pub. use, U.S. Geol. Survey, Reston, Va., 1972—, State Sanitary Authority, Salem, 1962-67, Nuclear and Thermal Energy Council, Salem, 1971-75; bd. dirs. Oreg. Nuclear Emergency Orgn., Salem, 1967—; mem. Western States Water Council, Salt Lake City, 1965-79, vice chmn., 1975-77, chmn., 1977-78. Pres.

Active Salem Parent Tchr. groups, 1960-72, YMCA Indian Guide programs, Salem, 1960-68; coach Ch. League Basketball, Salem, 1967-74. Served with U.S. Army C.E., 1946-47, PTO. Mem. NSPE, Am. Soc. Agr. Engrs., Assn. Western State Engrs. (pres. 1965, 2d v.p. 1984), Sigma Tau, Alpha Zeta. Republican. Mem. Christian Ch. Clubs: Salem Pilots (pres. 1969-75), Great Western Investors (Salem). Home: 1970 John St South Salem OR 97302 Office: Oreg Water Resources Dept 555 13th St NE Salem OR 97310

WHEELER, ELTON SAMUEL, financial executive; b. Salinas, Calif., Oct. 25, 1943; s. Luther Elton and Naomi E. (Beatty) W.; B.S., Calif. State U., 1966; m. Patricia Lynne McCleary, Sept. 2, 1967; children—Pamela Kathleen, Leslie Elizabeth-Anne, Deborah Suzanne, Jonathan Samuel. Acct., Coopers & Lybrand, Oakland, Calif., 1967-70; controller Adams Properties, Inc., San Francisco, 1970-71, treas., 1972-75, v.p., chief fin. officer, 1976-77; v.p., chief fin. officer Adams Capital Mgmt. Co., San Francisco, 1977-79, pres., chief exec. officer, 1979—; pres., chief exec. officer, dir. Calif. Real Estate Investment Trust, 1980—; pres. Adams Mgmt. Co., 1977—; dir. Adams Properties, Inc., 1970—. Served with USMCR, 1966-72. C.P.A., Calif. Mem. Nat. Assn. Real Estate Investment Trusts, Inc. (treas., bd. govs.), Am. Inst. CPAs, Calif. Soc. CPAs. Club: Olympic. Address: Suite 800 601 Montgomery St San Francisco CA 94111

WHEELER, JUDITH PAYSON, aerospace company executive; b. Wilkes-Barre, Pa., Oct. 25, 1934; d. William Silver and Jane Park (Fowler) W. AB magna cum laude, Smith Coll., 1956. Researcher Aviation Week mag., N.Y.C., 1956-59, Fortune mag., N.Y.C., 1959-67, Carnegie Corp., N.Y.C., 1967-68; with pub. relations dept. Rand Corp., Santa Monica, Calif., 1968-70; mgr. sci. pub. relations ICN Pharms., Irvine, Calif., 1970-73; free lance writer, editor various clients, Los Angeles, 1973-76, 78-81; mgr. editorial services Northrop Corp., Los Angeles, 1976-78; dir. corp. publs. Lockheed Corp., Calabasas, Calif., 1981—. Republican. Episcopalian. Office: Lockheed Corp 4500 Park Granada Blvd Calabasas CA 91399

WHEELER, LARRY RICHARD, accountant; b. Greybull, Wyo., Nov. 30, 1940; s. Richard F. and Olive B. (Fredrickson) W.; m. Marjorie A. Frady, Dec. 20, 1961; m. Patricia C. Marturano, Dec. 3, 1977; children: Anthony, Richard, Teresa, Kara. BS, U. Wyo., 1965. CPA, Colo. Staff acct. H. Greger CPA, Ft. Collins, Colo., 1965-66, sr. acct. Lester Draney & Wickham, Colorado Springs, Colo., 1966-67; acct., controller/treas., J.D. Adams Co., Colorado Springs, 1967-74; ptnr. Wheeler Pierce & Hurd, Inc., Colorado Springs, 1974-80; gen. mgr., v.p. Schneebeck's, Inc., Colorado Springs, 1980-81; prin. L.R. Wheeler & Co., P.C., Colorado Springs, 1981—; dir. Schneebeck's Industries, Williams Printing, Inc. Bd. dirs. Domestic Violence Prevention Ctr. Paul Stock Found. grantee, 1962. Mem. Internat. Assn. Fin. Planners, Am. Inst. CPA's, Nat. Contract Mgmt. Assn., Colo. Soc. CPA's. Club: Colorado Springs Country. Office: 317 E San Rafael Colorado Springs CO 80903

WHEELER, MARILYN LEE, accountant, tax consultant; b. Inman, Nebr., May 15, 1936; d. Warren J. and Delia E. (Allyn) McClurg; children—Linda Wheeler Tarpeh-Doe, Steven, David. Student Nebr. Wesleyan U., 1953-55, U. Wyo., 1955-57; B.S., U. Colo., 1972; M.T., U. Denver, 1980. CPA, Colo. Acct. Hurdman & Cranstoun, now known as KMG Peat Marwick Main, Denver, 1973-82, ptnr., 1982-83; shareholder Wheeler Brunschwig Wasoff, P.C. Treas., Colo. affiliate Am. Diabetes Assn. Mem. Am. Inst. CPAs, Colo. Soc. CPAs, Am. Women's Soc. CPAs. (nat. dir.), Am. Soc. Women Accts. (past pres. Denver chpt., nat. treas. Ednl. Found.). Republican. Presbyterian. Clubs: Petroleum. Office: 303 E 17th Ave Suite 630 Denver CO 80203

WHEELER, RALPH ALLEN, surgeon, air force officer; b. Grand Forks, N.D., Nov. 17, 1942; s. George Carlos and Jeanette Elizabeth (Norris) W.; m. Margo Leslie Reierson, Dec. 19, 1964 (div. Aug. 1978); children: Lezlie Charlene, Scott Allen. Student, Rice U., 1960-62; BA, U. N.D., 1964, BS, 1965; MD, CM, McGill U., Montreal, Que., Can., 1967. Diplomate Am. Bd. Surgery, Nat. Bd. Med. Examiners. Intern Detroit Gen. Hosp., 1967-68; resident Wayne State U., Detroit, 1968-70, Walter Reed Army Med. Ctr., 1973-75; commd. capt. USAF, 1971, advanced through grades to col., 1982; chief trauma service Wilford Hall Med. Ctr., Lakeland AFB, Tex., 1978-84, asst. chmn. dept. gen. surgery, 1982-84; chief surg. services USAF Regional Hosp., Sheppard AFB, Tex., 1984-86; chmn. dept. surgery, asst. dir. hosp. services USAF Regional Med. Ctr., Clark AFB, Angeles City, 1986—; cons. Surgeon Gen., 1980—; asst. prof. surgery U. Tex., San Antonio, 1979—; assoc. prof. Uniformed Services U. Health Scis., 1983—; mem. trauma adv. group U.S. Army Research and Devel. Command, Letterman Army Med. Ctr., Calif., 1983-85. Decorated Bronze Star. Fellow ACS; mem. AAAS, AMA, So. Med. Assn., Soc. Air Force Clin. Surgeons.

WHEELER, ROBERT ROSS, physician; b. Milw., Sept. 12, 1949; s. Ross Wheeler; m. Anne C. Burke; children: Sarah, Cailin. AB, U. Calif., Berkeley, 1972; MD, U. Calif., San Francisco, 1976. Diplomate Am. Bd. Internal Medicine. Intern San Francisco Gen. Hosp., 1976-77; resident in internal medicine U. Calif., San Francisco, 1977-79; practice medicine specializing in internal medicine Cottage Grove, Oreg., 1981—; supervising physician Cottage Grove Emergency Med. Technicians, 1982—; chief of staff Cottage Grove Hosp., 1984, chmn. critical care com., 1986—. Mem. ACP, AAAS, Oreg. Med. Assn., Lane County Med. Assn., Am. Heart Assn., Oreg. Arthritis Assn., Phi Beta Kappa. Office: 1450 Birch Ave Cottage Grove OR 97424

WHEELER, THOMAS FRANCIS, data processing executive; b. Norristown, Pa., Jan. 27, 1937; s. Thomas Francis and Dorothy Marie (Kane) W.; m. Margaret Anne Raleigh, April 4, 1964; children: Thomas A., Michael T., Margaret T. BA, Villanova U., 1960; postgrad., Cath. U. Am., 1960-61. Physics, math. tchr. St. Pius X High Sch., Pottstown, Pa., 1962-63; computer programmer IBM Corp., Endicott, N.Y., 1963-68, mgr. programming, 1968-74; asst. to v.p. systems devel. IBM Corp., Poughkeepsie, N.Y., 1974-75; design mgr. communications and distributed systems IBM Corp., Kingston, N.Y., 1975-78; cons. for engring., programming, tech. IBM Corp., Armonk, N.Y., 1978-81; mgr. systems architecture IBM Corp., White Plains, N.Y., 1981-84; v.p. advanced systems Gen. Elec. Calma, San Diego, 1984—; mem. steering com. for engring. mgmt. edn. San Diego State U., 1985—; lectr. Mfg. Tech. Inst., 1981-84, devel. mgmt. tng. 1981-84; frequent speaker; mem. adv. com. U. Calif. San Diego Sch. Engring., 1986—. Author numerous research papers; contbr. articles to tech. jours. Various positions Boy Scouts Am., Binghamton, N.Y., Poughkeepsie, N.Y., White Plains N.Y., Dallas, 1969-84; mem. fin. com. campaign Sen. James Buckley, N.Y., 1976. Recipient Silver Beaver award Boy Scouts Am., Poughkeepsie, 1978. Mem. IEEE (computer soc., Disting. Lectr. award 1985), AAAS, N.Y. Acad. Sci., World Future Soc., Assn. of Computing Machinery, San Diego C. of C. Republican. Roman Catholic. Lodge: Kiwanis. Avocations: golf, camping, swimming, multilingual Scrabble. Office: Gen Electric Calma Advanced Systems 9805 Scranton Rd San Diego CA 92121

WHEELER, TREASURE ANN, optometrist; b. Phoenix, May 1, 1945; d. Charles Landis and Bette Jane (Oyler) Sullivan; m. Gary Hale Wheeler, May 13, 1968. B.S., Pacific U., 1968, O.D., 1969. Lic. optometrist Oreg. Assoc. Dr. Tole Greenstein, Oregon City, Oreg., 1968; civilian optometrist Bliss Army Hosp., Ft. Huachuca, Ariz., 1969-70; pvt. practice optometry, Medford, Oreg., 1970—; dir. Oreg. Optometric Extension Program, 1975-78, sponsor Northwest Optometric Assts. Program, 1975-80; mem. Oreg. Bd. Optometry, sec., 1984-88, pres., 1986-87, 87-88; lectr., advisor, cons. in field. Mem. Nat. Adv. Bd., Biosocial Med. Ctr.; charter mem., mem. at large Parents for Better Nutrition; vol. Community Bus. Edn. Resource; mem. Gov.'s Commn. for Women, Juvenile Services Commn., 1981-82; v.p. Jackson Josephine County 4C Council, 1983-85; mem. Oreg. Gov.'s Edn. Mission, 1985—. Fellow Coll. Optometrists in Vision Devel. (Oreg. dir. 1974-75); mem. Am. Optometric Assn. (edn. and manpower div. career guidance com.), Oreg. Optometric Assn. (chmn. Task Force Vision Screening, pres. 1979-80), So. Oreg. Optometric Soc. (Former v.p.), So. Oreg. Soc. Preventive Medicine, So. Oreg. Assn. Children with Learning Disabilities (v.p. 1984-85), Phi Theta Upsilon. Contbr. articles to profl. publs. Home: 303 Gennessee St Medford OR 97504 Office: 309 Genessee St Medford OR 97504

WHEELER, WALTER LEE, civil engineer; b. Annapolis, Md., Sept. 6, 1951; s. Ralph Philmore and Margaret C. (Meyer) W.; m. Leslie G. Richie, Mar. 23, 1974 (div. Apr. 1983). BSCE, Drexel U., 1974; MSCE in Transp., Georgia Inst. Tech., 1980. Registered profl. engr., N.J., Ga., Calif.; cert. profl. planner, N.J. Twp. engr., dir. pub. works Princeton (N.J.) Twp., 1980-82; project coordinator East Hanover (N.J.) sewers Van Note-Harvey Assocs., Princeton, 1983; supr. utilities, Metro Rail project Parsons Brinckerhoff, Los Angeles, 1983—. Contbr. articles to profl. jours. Active Inman Park Restoration, Inc., Atlanta, Atlanta Preservation Ctr., Atlanta Great Park Planning, Inc. 1981 Joel award for service to community. Mem. NSPE, ASCE (nat. pub. transp. com., urban transp. div., vice chmn. Los Angeles sect. history and heritage com.), Inst. Transp. Engrs. (nat. tech. council cons.), Am. Pub. Works Assn., Calif. Soc. Profl. Engrs., Pub. Works Hist. Soc., Princeton C. of C. Club: Couples (Los Angeles)(founder, co-chair 1985-87). Home: 7265 Franklin Ave Hollywood CA 90046 Office: Parsons Brinkerhoff/MRTC 548 S Spring St Los Angeles CA 90013

WHEELESS, KAREN JEAN, government official; b. Dallas, June 2, 1954; d. E.E. and Alleen (Witten) W. BA, Baylor U., 1976, MBA, 1979. Asst. mgr. direct mail clubs Word DMS Inc., Waco, Tex., 1976-77; account exec. Charles Wallis Inc., Waco, 1977-79; mktg. mgr. Smithsonian Sci. Info. Exchange, Washington, 1979-80; pub. affairs officer U.S. Forest Service, Gainesville, Ga., 1980-84; asst. dir. communications Dept. Energy, Richland, Wash., 1984—. Contbr. book revs. and feature articles to newspapers and mags. Publicity team leader Tri City council Girl Scouts U.S.; commr. Parks and Recreation Commn. City of Kennewick, Wash.; vol. Tri-City Voluntary Action Council. Mem. Pub. Relations Soc. Am. Baptist. Home: 8612 W Hood St Kennewick WA 99336

WHEELON, ALBERT DEWELL, physicist; b. Moline, Ill., Jan. 18, 1929; s. Orville Albert and Alice Geltz (Dewell) W.; m. Nancy Helen Hermanson, Feb. 28, 1953 (dec. May 1980); children—Elizabeth Anne, Cynthia Helen; m. Cicely J. Evans, Feb. 4, 1984. B.Sc., Stanford U., 1949; Ph.D., Mass. Inst. Tech., 1952. Teaching fellow, then research assoc. physics MIT, Boston, 1949-52; with Douglas Aircraft Co., 1952-53, Ramo-Wooldridge Corp., 1953-62; dep. dir. sci. and tech. CIA, Los Angeles, 1962-66; with Hughes Aircraft Co., Los Angeles, 1966—, chmn., chief exec. officer, 1970-87; mem. Def. Sci. Bd., 1967-77, adv. bd. Pres.'s Fgn. Intelligence, 1983, presdl. commn. on space shuttle Challenger accident, 1986; trustee Calif. inst. Tech. Author 30 papers on radiowaves propagation and guidance systems. Fellow IEEE, AIAA (Von Karman medal 1986); mem. Nat. Acad. Engring., Am. Phys. Soc., Sigma Chi. Republican. Episcopalian. Office: PO Box 92919 Los Angeles CA 90009

WHEELWRIGHT, RONALD VERN, credit manager; b. Ogden, Utah, June 12, 1957; s. Worth Pearse and Geniel Rae (Cullimore) W.; m. Rebecca Lynn Prout, June 20, 1980; children—Steven Ronald, Jonathan James. Student Brigham Young U., 1979-80; B.A. in Bus. Adminstrn. and Fin., Weber State Coll., 1982. Salesman, Wheelwright Lumber Co., Ogden, 1979-82; credit mgr. Albion Labs., Inc., Clearfield, Utah, 1982—. Mem. Phi Beta Lambda (v.p. 1981-82), Delta Sigma Pi (pres. Eta Lambda chpt. 1981-82). Republican. Mormon. Club: Jaycees (v.p. Ogden 1985-87). Home: 1314 Arlington Dr Ogden UT 84403 Office: Albion Labs Inc 101 N Main Clearfield UT 84015

WHELAN, FRANCIS C., federal judge; b. O'Neill, Nebr., Dec. 11, 1907; s. Edward H. and Susan (Quilty) W.; m. Marian Willette, Feb. 7, 1948 (dec.); stepchildren—Marianne Conway Laub, Francis W. Conway. Student, San Diego State Coll., 1925-28; LL.B., U. Calif., 1932. Bar: Calif. bar 1932. Pvt. practice San Diego, 1932-35, Los Angeles, 1948-61; asst. U.S. atty., 1935-39; spl. asst. Dept. Justice; also spl. asst. to U.S. atty. gen., 1939-48; U.S. atty. So. Dist. Calif., 1961-64; U.S. dist. judge Central Dist. Calif., 1964—; now sr. judge. Mem. ABA, Los Angeles County Bar Assn., Am. Judicature Soc. Roman Catholic. Club: K.C. Office: US Ct House 312 N Spring St Los Angeles CA 90012

WHELCHEL, SANDRA JANE, writer; b. Denver, May 31, 1944; d. Ralph Earl and Janette Isabelle (March) Everitt; m. Andrew Jackson Whelchel, June 27, 1965; children—Andrew Jackson, Anita Earlyn. B.A. in Elem. Edn., U. No. Colo., 1966; postgrad. Pepperdine Coll., 1971, UCLA, 1971. Elem. tchr. Douglas County Schs., Castle Rock, Colo., 1966-68, El Monte (Calif.) schs., 1968-72; br. librarian Douglas County Libraries, Parker, Colo., 1973-78; zone writer Denver Post, 1979-81; reporter The Express newspapers, Castle Rock, 1979-81; history columnist Parker Trail newspapers, 1985—; contbr. short stories and articles to various publs. including: Empire mag., Calif. Horse Rev., Host mag., Jack and Jill, Child Life, Children's Digest; author (non-fiction books): Your Air Force Academy, 1982, A Day at the Cave, 1985; (coloring book) A Day in Blue, 1984, Pro Rodeo Hall of Champions and Museum of the American Cowboy, 1985, Pikes Peak Country, 1986, Mile High Denver, 1987; lectr. on writing. Mem. Internat. Order of Foresters, Nat. Writers Club (treas. Denver Metro chpt. 1985-86, v.p. membership 1987), Parker Area Hist. Soc. (pres. 1987).

WHINNERY, JOHN ROY, electrical engineering educator; b. Read, Colo., July 26, 1916; s. Ralph V. and Edith Mable (Bent) W.; m. Patricia Barry, Sept. 17, 1944; children—Carol Joanne, Catherine, Barbara. B.S. in Elec. Engring, U. Calif. at Berkeley, 1937, Ph.D., 1948. Student engr. Gen. Electric Co., 1937-40, supr. high frequency course advanced engring. program, 1940-42, research engr., 1942-46; part-time lectr. Union Coll., Schenectady, 1945-46; asso. prof. elec. engring. U. Calif.-Berkeley, 1946-52, prof., vice chmn. div. elec. engring., 1952-56, chmn., 1956-59; dean Coll. Engring. U. Calif-Berkeley, 1959-63, prof. elec. engring., 1963-80, Univ. prof. Coll. Engring., 1980—; vis. mem. tech. staff. Bell Telephone Labs., 1963-64; research sci. electron tubes Hughes Aircraft Co., Culver City, 1951-52; bd. editors I.R.E., 1956. Author: (with Simon Ramo) Fields and Waves in Modern Radio, 1944, 2d edit. (with Ramo and Van Dozer), 1985, (with D. O. Pederson and J. J. Studer) Introduction to Electronic Systems, Circuits and Devices; also tech. articles. Chmn. Commn. Engring. Edn., 1966-68; mem. sci. and tech. com. Manned Space Flight, NASA, 1963-69; mem. Pres.'s Com. on Nat. Sci. Medal, 1970-73, 79-80; standing com. controlled thermonuclear research AEC, 1970-73. Recipient Edn. medal IEEE, 1967; Lamme medal Am. Soc. Engring. Edn., 1975; Microwave Career award IEEE Microwave Theory and Techniques Soc., 1977; Engring Alumni award U. Calif. at Berkeley, 1980; named to Hall of Fame Modesto High Sch. (Calif.), 1983; Guggenheim fellow, 1959. Fellow I.R.E. (dir. 1956-59), Optical Soc. Am., Am. Acad. Arts and Scis.; mem. Nat. Acad. Engring. (Founders award 1986), Nat. Acad. Scis., IEEE (life mem., dir. 1969-71, sec. 1971, Centennial medal 1984, Medal of Honor 1985), Phi Beta Kappa, Sigma Xi, Tau Beta Pi, Eta Kappa Nu. Conglist. Home: One Daphne Ct Orinda CA 94563 Office: U Calif Berkeley CA 94720

WHIPPLE, BRENT HANKS, retail controller; b. Salt Lake City, Oct. 29, 1954; s. Blaine Webb and E. Dianne (Hanks) W.; m. Mary Kay Wellington, Dec. 19, 1975; children: Kenneth, Jeffrey, Shannon. BS, U. Utah, 1978; MBA, U. Phoenix, 1986. Asst. to controller ZCMI, Salt Lake City, 1979-81, chief acct., 1981-84, asst. controller, 1984—; v.p. ZCMI Credit Union, Salt Lake City, 1986—. Mem. Utah Retail Fin. Execs. Assn. (pres. 1985-86), Nat. Retail Merchants Assn. Republican. Mormon. Avocations: stamp collecting, sports. Office: ZCMI 2200 S 9th W Salt Lake City UT 84137

WHIPPLE, CHRISTOPHER GEORGE, risk analyst; b. Columbus, Ohio, Feb. 17, 1949; s. George Henry and Joan (Pearlman) W.; m. Francine Ann Machfinger, June 7, 1970; children: Matthew, Allison. BS in Engring., Purdue U., 1970; MS in Engring., Calif. Inst. Tech., 1971, PhD in Engring., 1974. Mem. tech. staff Electric Power Research Inst., Palo Alto, Calif., 1974-77, mgr. spl. studies, 1977-78, tech. mgr., 1978—. Editor: Risk Analysis in the Private Sector, 1985, The Elements of Risk Assessment, 1983; contbr. articles to profl. jours. Mem. Soc. Risk Analysis (pres. 1982-83). Office: Electric Power Research Inst 3412 Hillview Ave Palo Alto CA 94303

WHIPPLE, ELEANOR BLANCHE, educational administrator, social worker; b. Bellingham, Wash., June 7, 1916; d. Charles William and Susan Blanche (Campbell) W.; B.A. in Sociology, U. Wash., 1938, M.S.W., 1949; Ph.D., U. Santa Barbara (formerly Laurence U.), 1982; m. Robert Auld Fowler, Oct. 1, 1938 (div. 1947); children—Lawrence William, Jeanice Marie Fowler Roosevelt. Lic. clin. social worker. Founder, dir. Camp Cloud's End, Deception Pass, Wash., 1939-42; therapist Family Counseling Service, Seattle, 1949-58; field instr. U. Wash., Seattle, 1954-57; pvt. practice counselling, Burbank, Calif., 1958-60; social service dir. Hollygrove Children's Residential Treatment Center, Hollywood, Calif., 1960-66, exec. dir., 1966-81; adj. faculty Biola U., La Mirada, Calif., 1972-80; dean Grad. Sch. Calif. Christian Inst., Orange, 1981-85, pres., 1985—. Bd. dirs. Christian Fellowship for the Blind, Inc. Mem. Nat. Assn. Social Workers (chartered), Acad. Cert. Social Workers, N.Am. Assn. Christians in Social Work (bd. dirs., disting. service award). Contbr. articles in field to profl. publs. Home: 1105 Mound Ave Apt 9 South Pasadena CA 91030 Office: Calif Christian Inst 1744 W Katella Ave Orange CA 92667

WHIPPLE, GEORGE STEPHENSON, architect, contractor; b. Evanston, Ill., Sept. 21, 1950; s. Taggart and Katharine (Brewster) W.; m. Lydia Buckley, May 30, 1981; children: Katherine Elizabeth, John Taggart. B.A., Harvard U., 1974; student Boston Architectural Ctr., 1975-76. Vice-pres., Call Us Inc., Edgartown, Mass., 1970-74; pres. Cattle Creek Assocs., Carbondale, Colo., 1976—, Earthworks Constrn., Carbondale, 1978—. Chmn., Redstone Hist. Preservation Commn., Colo. Mem. Rocky Mountain Harvard Club. Office: 3335 County Rd 113 Carbondale CO 81623

WHISLER, KIRK, publishing executive; b. Omaha, Calif., June 7, 1951; s. Donald Dee and Biddy Louise (Covert) W.; m. Magdalena Gonzalez, June 15, 1985. Student, U. Calif., Santa Barbara, 1969-72, Escuela de Artes Plasticas, Guadalajara, Mex., 1972; BA in History and Politics, U. Calif., Riverside, 1973. Pub. Somos Mag., San Bernardino, Calif., 1977-79, Caminos Mag., Los Angeles, 1979-86; dir. mktg. Embassy Pictures-Gregorio Cortez, Los Angeles, 1983-84; pres. Am. Internat. Hispanic Communications, Los Angeles, 1983—; pres. Nat. Assn. Hispanic Publs., Los Angeles, 1984—. Editor: National Hispanic Conventioneer, 3d rev. edit., 1985, National Hispanic Media Directory, 1986; author: National Hispanic Readership Study, 1985, Familia Latina Hispanic Market Fact Book, 1984; pub., editor Nevada Mag., 1986—. Del. Commn. of the Califs., Sacramento and Mex., 1977—; mem. Los Angeles Organizing Com., 1981-84, San Bernardino (Calif.) City Community Devel. Commn., 1979-83, San Bernardino City Econ. Devel. Council, 1981-83. Recipient Golden Eagle award Nosotros, 1979, Leadership award San Bernardino Unified Sch. Dist. Bilingual Dist. Adv. Com., 1981, Contributor award Children's Mus., Los Angeles, 1985. Mem. U.S. Hispanic C. of C., City of Los Angeles Hispanic Leadership Corps, Nat. Assn. Hispanic Journalists, Western Publs. Assn., San Bernardino County Mus. Assn. Democrat. Methodist. Avocations: collecting rare books, reading, photography, travel. Office: Am Internat Hispanic Communications Inc 1219 Palo Verde Carson City NV 89701

WHITAKER, CORINNE COOPER, financial executive; b. Stamford, Conn., Aug. 31, 1934; d. Samuel and Natalie Gordon; B.A. (Durant scholar), Wellesley Coll., 1956; postgrad. N.Y. Inst. Fin., 1972-73, U. Houston, 1974; children—Nanette Cooper McGuinness, Robin Cooper Feldman. Sr. account exec. Eppler, Guerin & Turner, Inc., Houston, 1972-76; fixed income liaison Loeb, Rhodes & Co., Los Angeles, 1976-77; cons. Edward T. Watkins & Co., Houston, 1977; account exec., asso. v.p. Bateman Eichler Hill Richards, Los Angeles, 1977-79; chmn. bd., chief adminstrv. officer Don C. Whitaker, Inc., Los Angeles, 1980-84; pres. Hillcreast Cons., Inc., 1984—; mem. Pacific Stock Exchange; organized seminars, courses in field; seminar coordinator Investment Dynamics series, Houston, 1975. Bd. dirs. women's div., nat. publicity chmn. Aerospace Med. Assn., 1964; lectr. African art, docent leader Rice U. Media Center Art to Schs. Program, 1974-75; mem. bus. and industry com. women's council Los Angeles Area C. of C., 1978. Recipient John Masefield award Wellesley Coll., 1956, Katherine Lee Bates award, 1956; Vol. Service award N.Y. Med. Coll., Flower and Fifth Ave. Hosps., 1958; Rookie of Yr. award Eppler Guerin & Turner, 1973, award of excellence, 1976, named to Millionaires Club 1973-75; commendation Houston Jr. C. of C., 1975; named to Century Club, Bateman Eichler Hill Richards Inc., 1978. Mem. Norton Simon Mus., Friends of Photography, Fellows of Contemporary Art, Soc. for Contemporary Photography, Nat. Mus. of Women in Arts (charter), Am. Crafts Council, Los Angeles Floor Brokers Assn. (founder), Phi Beta Kappa. Clubs: Wellesley Coll. Alumnae (chmn. spl. gifts div. Washington area 1964).

WHITAKER, MARY MANNING, journalist, photographer; b. Marlboro, Mass., Apr. 2, 1947; d. John Francis and Mary Virginia (Bordeleau) Manning; m. Frank D. Whitaker, July 15, 1975 (div. May 1980); 1 child, Michelle. BA in English, U. Nev., 1970. Copy girl Las Vegas Sun, Nev., 1965, reporter, 1966-71, Sunday editor, 1976-78, journalist, 1978—; info. officer Clark County Health Dist., Las Vegas, 1971-73; reporter AP Stanford, San Francisco, 1973-76. Mem. Pen Women of Am., Sigma Delta Chi (bd. dirs. 1986). Democrat. Unitarian. Avocations: reading, writing poetry. Office: Las Vegas Sun 121 S Highland Dr Las Vegas NV 89127

WHITCOMB, DONALD LEROY, chemist; b. Ilion, N.Y., Feb. 1, 1925; s. Arthur Leroy and Grace (Dubois) W.; m. Helen P. Johnson, Sept. 4, 1948; children: Diane, Patricia, Mary, Ronald. BS, U. Rochester, 1952, PhD, 1956. Research chemist Eastman Kodak Co., Rochester, N.Y., 1946-53; mem. tech. staff Bell Labs., Allentown, Pa., 1957-63, Hughes Aircraft Co., Los Angeles, 1963-66; sr. engr. Motorola Semiconductor Co., Phoenix, 1966-70; lab. mgr. State of Ariz., Phoenix, 1970-81; nuclear chemist Ariz. Pub. Service, Phoenix, 1981—. Contbr. articles to profl. jours. Served with USAF, 1943-46, PTO. Mem. Am. Chem. Soc., Phi Beta Kappa. Avocations: computers, ham radio, electronics, hiking, camping. Home: 7420 N 179th Ave Waddell AZ 85355

WHITE, ALLEN COLLIER, psychiatrist, educator; b. Los Angeles, Feb. 9, 1940. BA in Biology, Occidental Coll., 1961; MD, George Washington U., 1965; cert. neuropsychiatry Mental Health Retardation Program, UCLA, 1973. Lic. physician, surgeon, Calif., Wash.; cert. Nat. Bd. Med. Examiners; diplomate Am. Bd. Psychiatry and Child Psychiatry. Intern Santa Barbara County (Calif.) Cottage Hosp., 1965-66; resident in psyhiatry State of Calif. Dept. Mental Hygiene, 1966-69; postdoctoral fellow child psychiatry Stanford (Calif.) U. Med. Ctr., 1971-73, asst. prof., clin. faculty mem. dept. psychiatry and behavioral scis.; pvt. practice psychiatry Cupertino, Calif.; cons. in field. Served to maj. M.C., USAF, 1969-71. Fellow Am. Orthopsychiat. Assn.; mem. Am. Psychiat. Assn., No. Calif. Psychiat. Soc., Am. Acad. Psychiatry and Law, Clin. Faculty Assn. Avocations: backpacking, writing. Office: 20396 Town Center Ln Suite 9E Cupertino CA 95014

WHITE, ALVIN MURRAY, mathematics educator, consultant; b. N.Y.C., June 21, 1925; s. Max and Beatrice White; m. Myra Goldstein, Dec. 4, 1946; children: Louis, Michael. BA, Columbia U., 1949; MA, UCLA, 1951; PhD, Stanford U., 1961. Acting instr. Stanford (Calif.) U., 1950-54; asst. prof. U. Santa Clara, Calif., 1954-61; prof. Harvey Mudd Coll., Claremont, Calif., 1962—; mem. math. research ctr., U. Wis. Madison, 1961-62; vis. scholar MIT, 1975. Author: Interdisciplinary Teaching, 1981; contbr. articles to profl. jours. Served with USN, 1943-46, PTO. Grantee Fund for Improvement of Post-secondary Edn., Exxon Found. Mem. Am. Math. Soc., Math. Assn. Am., Profl. Organizational Developers Network, Fedn. Am. Scientists, AAUP, Sigma Xi. Office: Harvey Mudd Coll Dept Math Claremont CA 91711

WHITE, ANTHONY GENE, government official, educator; b. Eugene, Oreg., Nov. 8, 1946; s. Wallace Eugene and Vivian Arlene (Thomson) W.; m. Carole Ann Price, May 17, 1969. BS, Oreg. State U., 1967; MS, Portland State U., 1971, M in Pub. Adminstrn., 1977. Research asst. div. urban affairs U. Del., Newark, 1968-69; research assoc. City-County Commn., Portland, Oreg., 1972-74; property control officer Multnomah County, Portland, 1974-75; adminstrv. analyst, research Local Govt. Boundary Commn., Portland, 1975-76; evaluator, researcher Dist. Atty.'s Office, Portland, 1976-77; dir. pub. mgmt. programs Marylhurst (Oreg.) Coll., 1978-79; program coordinator Oreg. Pub. Utility Commn., Salem, 1979-86, local govt. mgmt. cons., 1986—; pres., editor N.W. Wine and Dine Inc., 1985—. Author: Returning Metropolitan Governments, Municipal Bonding and Taxation; also book chpts., monographs, papers, articles, reports. Bd. dirs. Oreg. Assn. for Children with Learning Disabilities, 1978-80; precinct committeeman Multnomah County Dem. cen. com., 1974-76; mem. Clackamas County Dem. cen. com., 1979-86; mem. West Linn (Oreg.) Comprehensive Plan Rev. Com., 1980; chmn. adminstrn. com., mem. ch. council West Linn Luth. Ch., 1980-83, v.p. ch. council, 1982-83. Served with AUS, 1969-72, lt. col. Oreg. N.G., 1978—. Mem. AAAS, Am. Math. Soc., Am. Acad. Polit. and Social Scis., Nat. Mcpl. League, Western Pacific N.W. Polit. Sci. Assns.,

World Future Soc., Columbia-Willamette Futures Forum, Western Govtl. Research Assn. Home and Office: 3270 Forest Ct West Linn OR 97068

WHITE, BOB ALLEN, architect; b. Denton, Tex., Jan. 6, 1938; s. Claude Allen and Margaret (Crosswhite) W.; m. Ruby Shuman, Mar. 12, 1960; children: Clint, Christie, Shawn. BArch, Tex. Tech U., 1964. Registered architect, Tex., Colo., Mont., Idaho, Wyo. Draftsman Atcheson, Atkinson & Cartwright, Architects, Lubbock, Tex., 1955-64; project architect Mills & King, Architects, Lubbock, Tex., 1964-69, James Sudler Assocs., Architects, Denver, 1969-71, Fisher, Reese & Johnson, Architects, Denver, 1971-73; pvt. practice architecture Denver, 1973—. Mem. Am. Inst. Architects, Water Pollution Control Fedn., Nat. Council Archtl. Registration Bds. Lodges: Paul Revere; Optimists (Lakewood, Colo.) (lt. gov. Colo./Wyo. dists. 1976), pres. 1975, 87). Office: Bob A White Arch Planning 5025 W 29th Ave Denver CO 80212

WHITE, BRITTAN ROMEO, manufacturing company executive; b. N.Y.C., Feb. 13, 1936; s. Brittan R. and Matilda H. (Baumann) W.; m. Esther D. Friederich, Aug. 25, 1958 (dec. May 1981); children: Cynthia E., Brittan R. VII. BSChemE, Drexel U., 1958; MBA, Lehigh U., 1967; JD, Loyola U., Los Angeles, 1974; MA, Pepperdine U., 1985. Bar: Calif., U.S. Dist. Ct. Calif.; registered profl. engr., Calif. Process engr. Air Reduction Co., Bound Brook, N.J., 1958-64; area supr. J.T. Baker Chem. Co., Phillipsburg, N.J., 1964-66; asst. plant mgr. Gamma Chem. Co., Great Meadows, N.J., 1966-69; plant mgr. Maquite Corp., Elizabeth, N.J., 1969-70; purchasing mgr. Atlantic Richfield Co., Los Angeles, 1970-79; dir. mfg. Imperial Oil, Los Angeles, 1979-82; mgr. infosystems and spl. projects Hughes Aircraft Co., Los Angeles, 1982—; bd. dirs. Diversified Resource Devel. Inc., Los Angeles, 1979—; seminar moderator and speaker Energy Conservation Seminars, 1979-83. Editor Rottweiler Rev., 1979-81; chief award judge Chem. Processing mag., 1976, 78, 80; contbr. articles to profl. jours. Vice chmn. Bd. Zoning and Adjustment, Flemington, N.J., 1970-72; pres. bd. dirs. Homeowners Assn., Palm Springs, Calif., 1983—. Served to capt. C.E., U.S. Army, 1958-60, Res., 1960-68. Mem. ABA, Am. Inst. Chem. Engrs., Am. Chem. Soc., Mensa, Psi Chi. Republican. Lodge: Elks. Avocations: antiques, show dogs, psychology. Home: 3664 Vigilance Dr Rancho Palos Verdes CA 90274 Office: Hughes Aircraft Co 7200 Hughes Terr Los Angeles CA 90045

WHITE, CANDACE COLLONS, public relations consultant, special projects coordinator; b. Los Angeles, Nov. 27, 1940; d. Burton and Evelyn K. (Bast) Collons; children from former marriage—Tracy White McDougal, Serena. Ed. U. Calif.-Santa Barbara, Antioch U.;market researcher Wright's Market Research, Santa Barbara, Calif., 1963-73; tchr. St. Michaels Sch., Goleta, Calif., 1971-77; Santa Barbara Community Coll., 1974-78; owner Santa Barbara Indls. Finishing, 1971-77; ind. artist rep., owner Blithe Spirits, Santa Barbara, 1976—; asst. to pres. Fin. Planning Services, Santa Barbara, 1978-79; pub. relations/spl. projects coordinator Aspen Club Internat., 1980-82. Bd. dirs. Aspen Women's Forum League Internat., Dallas, The Phoenix of Santa Barbara; creator dance communication program for young children Santa Barbara Recreation Dept. Address: 1170 Hill Rd Santa Barbara CA 93108-2815

WHITE, CAROL MAE, public relations executive; b. Davenport, Iowa, May 4, 1947; d. Hersel Francis and Eula Fern (Bultemeier) W. BA, Drake U., 1969; postgrad., Syracuse U., 1970. Staff writer Post-Standard, Syracuse, N.Y., 1969-70; staff writer, editorial asst. NOW The Mag. of North Tex., Dallas, 1970-71; editorial asst. The Dallas Morning News/S.W. Scene Mag., 1971-72; asst. dir. pub. relations Baylor U. Med. Ctr., Dallas, 1972-74; dir. pub. relations Ft. Worth Osteopathic Med. Ctr. Inc., 1974-80; dir. pub. relations Am. Med. Internat. Inc., Houston, 1980-83, asst. v.p., dir. mktg. plan devel., 1983, asst. v.p., dir. U.S. health care devel. pub. relations, 1984; asst. v.p., corp. dir. mktg. pub. relations Am. Med. Internat. Inc., Beverly Hills, Calif., 1985—. Loaned exec. United Way of Met. Tarrant County, Ft. Worth, 1976; bd. regents The Oakridge Sch., Ft. Worth, 1979-80. Mem. Pub. Relations Soc. Am. (assoc.), Fedn. Am. Hosps., Am. Hosp. Assn., Am. Soc. Hosp. Mktg. and Pub. Relations, Women in Communications Inc. (pres. Ft. Worth chpt. 1980). Republican. Avocations: golf, tennis, spectator sports, travel. Home: 26121 McBean Pkwy #23 Valencia CA 91355 Office: Am Med Internat Inc 414 N Camden Dr Beverly Hills CA 90210

WHITE, CECIL RAY, librarian, consultant; b. Hammond, Ind., Oct. 15, 1937; s. Cecil Valentine and Vesta Ivern (Bradley) W.; m. Frances Ann Gee, Dec. 23, 1960; children—Timothy Wayne, Stephen Patrick. B.S. in Edn., So. Ill. U., 1959; cert. in Czech., Syracuse, U., 1961; M. Div., Southwestern Bapt. Sem., 1969; M.L.S., N. Tex. State U., 1970, Ph.D., 1984. Librarian, Herrin High Sch. (Ill.), 1964-66; acting reference librarian Southwestern Sem., Ft. Worth, 1968-70, asst. librarian, 1970-80; head librarian Golden Gate Bapt. Sem., Mill Valley, Calif., 1980—; library cons. Hist. Commn., So. Bapt. Conv., Nashville, 1983-84, mem. Thesaurus Com., 1974-84. Bd. dirs. Hope and Help Ctr., 1986—, vice chmn. 1987—. Served with USAF, 1960-64. Lilly Found. grantee Am. Theol. Library Assn., 1969. Mem. Am. Theol. Library Assn. (coordinator consultation service 1973-78, program planning com. 1985—, chmn., 1986—), Nat. Assn. Profs. Hebrew (archivist 1985—), ALA, Calif. Library Assn., Phi Kappa Phi, Beta Phi Mu. Democrat. Baptist. Home: 161 Dolores St #5 San Francisco CA 94103 Office: Golden Gate Bapt Sem Strawberry Point Mill Valley CA 94941

WHITE, CHARLES RADCLIFFE, fish behavior researcher; b. Pitts., July 7, 1925; s. Charles Conley and Mary Louise (Radcliffe) W.; m. Anne Preston Anderson; children—Charles Leland, Kevin Radcliffe, David Radcliffe. B.S. in Civil Engring., Cornell U., 1946. Sales engr. Aluminum Co. of Am., Cleve., 1946-49; biologist, photographer Oreg. Fish Commn., 1950-52; exec. TV stas. KPTV, KLEW, CHEK, Portland, Oreg., Lewiston, Idaho, Victoria, B.C., Can., 1952-57; researcher Saltaire Products Ltd., Victoria, 1958-61; owner, operator Undersea Gardens Marine Exhibits, Can., U.S., 1962-69; writer, lectr. on marine life, 1970-73; fish behavior researcher for TV, films; lectr., 1974—; dir. B.C. TV Broadcasting Ltd.; lectr. Camosun Coll., Victoria, 1971—. Served with USN, 1944-46. Recipient Bartlett Cup, Bay of Island's Billfish Club, 1972. Author: How To Catch Salmon, 1971; contbr. numerous books on fish and marine life; patentee facility for viewing marine life, self extinguishing portable cooking unit, developer numerous fishing devices and remotely controlled underwater TV; camera system for studying fish behavior.

WHITE, DONALD HARVEY, physicist, educator, consultant; b. Berkeley, Calif., Apr. 30, 1931; s. Harvey Elliott and Adeline White; m. Beverly Evalina Jones, Aug. 8, 1953; children: Jeri M., Brett D., Holly G., Scott E., Erin N. AB, U. Calif., Berkeley, 1953; PhD, Cornell U., 1960. Lab. asst. Lawrence Berkeley Lab., summers 1949-57; teaching asst. Cornell U., Ithaca, N.Y., 1953-58, research asst., 1958-60; research physicist Lawrence Livermore (Calif.) Nat. Lab., 1960-71; prof. physics Western Oreg. State Coll., Monmouth, 1971—; cons. Lawrence Livermore Nat. Lab., 1971—. Author (with others): Physics, an Exact Science, 1968, Physics and Music, 1980; contbr. numerous articles to profl. jours. Pres. Monmouth-Independence Community Arts, 1983; pres.-elect E. Smith Fine Arts Program, Monmouth, 1987. DuPont Found. scholar, 1958; Minna-Heineman Found. fellow, Hannover, Fed. Republic Germany, 1977. Mem. Am. Phys. Soc., Am. Assn. Physics Tchrs. (pres. Oreg. sect. 1974-75), Oreg. Acad. Sci. (pres. 1979-80), Phi Kappa Phi. Presbyterian. Home: 411 Walnut Dr Monmouth OR 97361-1948 Office: Western Oreg State Coll Dept Physics Monmouth OR 97361

WHITE, DONALD HERBERT, aircraft company executive; b. Long Beach, Calif., Oct. 7, 1931; s. Orville Herbert and Mildred Florence (Spencer) W.; m. Janice Margaret Jacobs, Nov. 15, 1953; children: Marleigh Ellen, Spencer William. AB magna cum laude, Stanford U., 1953, MBA summa cum laude, 1958; SM, MIT, 1970. Sales trainee IBM, San Francisco, 1958-59; v.p., asst. gen. mgr. Northrop Archtl. Systems, City of Industry, Calif., 1959-67; v.p. fin. Northrop Corp. Aircraft Div., Hawthorne, Calif., 1967-74; sr. v.p., controller Hughes Aircraft Co., El Segundo, Calif., 1974-83, pres., chief operating officer, 1983—, also bd. dirs. Bd. govs. Music Ctr. Los Angeles County; bd. dirs. Nat. Action Council for Minorities in Engring., Inc. Served to lt. (j.g.) Signal Corps, USN, 1953-56, Japan. Mem. Nat. Contract Mgmt. Assn., Nat. Aero. Assn. (bd. dirs.), Am. Def. Preparedness Assn. (bd. dirs.), Calif. Bus. Roundtable. Republican. Clubs: Rolling Hills Country (Rolling Hills Estates, Calif.); Bel-Air Country (Los Angeles). Office: Hughes Aircraft Co 7200 Hughes Terr Los Angeles CA 90045 *

WHITE, EUGENE R., computer manufacturing company executive. With Gen. Electric Co., Fairfield, Conn., 1958-70, Fairchild Camera & Instrument Corp., 1970-74; chmn., chief exec. officer Amdahl Corp., Sunnyvale, Calif., 1974—, also bd. dirs. Office: Amdahl Corp 1250 E Arques Ave Sunnyvale CA 94086 *

WHITE, GEORGE HARVEY, supt. schs.; b. Durango, Colo., Feb. 5, 1939; s. Loyd Oscar and Sally Beatrice (Mullenix) W.; m. Janice Pope, Sept. 30, 1960. B.A. in History, U. Alaska, 1964; M.Ed. in Adminstrn., Eastern Wash. State Coll., 1969. Supt., div. regional schs. Beltz Regional High Sch., Nome, Alaska, 1968-69; regional supt. N.W. Region Div. State Operated Schs., Nome, 1970-71; assoc. supt. Alaska State Operated Sch. System, Anchorage, 1971-75; supt. Alaska Unorganized Borough Sch. Dist., Anchorage, 1975-76; dist. supt. N.W. Arctic Sch. Dist., 1976-82; supt. Kake (Alaska) City Sch. Dist., 1982—; vice chmn. Alaska Profl. Teaching Practices Commn., 1977-80; chmn. Alaska Public Offices Commn., 1980-84; mem. adv. bd. Alaska Airlines, 1980-81. Ex-officio mem. U. Alaska adv. council Kotzebue Community Coll., 1976-82; instl. rep. Boy Scouts Am., 1968-69; mem. Juvenile Adv. Com. to Superior Ct., Nome, 1968-69; mem. exec. com. N.W. Alaska Regional Strategy Planning Council, 1977-82; mem. Cross-Cultural Edn. Program Consortium, to 1980; bd. dirs. S.E. Regional Resource Center. Mem. State Operated Schs. Adminstrs. Assn., Am. Assn. Sch. Adminstrs., Rural Edn. Assn., Alaska Assn. Sch. Adminstrs. (pres.-elect, mem. exec. bd.; sec.-treas. 1979-80). Cert. prin., tchr., supt., Alaska. Home: Box 317 Kake AK 99830 Office: Box 450 Kake AK 99830

WHITE, GEORGE PHILIP, computer industry entrepreneur, computer designer; b. Hartford, Conn., July 8, 1948; s. Norman E. and Lucy (D'addario) W.; m. Madelyn M. Ball, June 4, 1970 (div. Nov. 1984); m. Diane L. Donaldson, Nov. 26, 1984. S.B. in Elec. Engring., MIT, 1971. Computer engr. Logicon Corp., Fairfax, Va., 1975-76, Computer Automation, Irvine, Calif., 1976-78, engring. mgr., 1978-80, dir. strategic planning, 1980; dir. engring. Western Digital, Irvine, 1980-83; mgr. Tex. Instruments, Irvine, 1983-85; founder Corollary, Inc., Irvine, 1985—. Contbr. articles to profl. jours. Mem. IEEE, Assn. for Computing Machinery. Office: Corollary Inc PO Box 18977 Irvine CA 92713

WHITE, H(AROLD) LORING, historian, former educator; b. New Britain, Conn., Nov. 17, 1928; s. Harold L. and Leone Virginia (Hathaway) W.; m. Louise Chandler, Aug. 24, 1951 (div. 1969); children—Harold Loring, Thomas Lloyd, William Arthur; m. Evelyn Gramse Smith, Sept. 17, 1978. B.A. magna cum laude, U. Conn., 1951, M.A., 1954; M.A., U. Colo., 1968; D.A., Ill. State U., 1983. Instr., U. Conn., Storrs, 1951-52; supt. schs. Stockville Schs., Nebr., 1952-53; chmn., English, Sidney Schs. Nebr., 1953-56; prof. English and history, Fla. State U., Balboa, C.Z., 1957-64; prof. history and English, Panama Canal Coll., Balboa, 1963-81, chmn. dept. English, 1976-81. Author: Schooling in the Canal Zone, 1904-1979, 1979; World History: Theories and Teaching Models, 1983. Pres., Theatre Guild, Ancon, C.Z., 1970-71, mem., 1957-81. Named Outstanding Prof., Panama Canal Co., Balboa Heights, C.Z., 1975; recipient cert. appreciation Dept. Def., 1981. Mem. Am. Hist. Assn., World History Assn., Internat. Soc. Comparative Study Civilization, Soc. for History Edn., Phi Delta Kappa, Phi Alpha Theta. Democrat. Lodge: Elks.

WHITE, HORACE FREDERICK, chemistry educator; b. Fresno, Calif., Apr. 25, 1925; s. Harry Edward and Meta Glades (Hansen) W.; m. Mary Ellen Wilde, June 7, 1952; children: H. Frederick, Suellen Martine, William H. AB, Calif. State U., Fresno, 1947; MS, Oreg. State U., 1950; PhD, Brown U., 1953. Postdoctoral fellow U. Minn., Mpls., 1952-54; chem. analytical supr. research dept. M.W. Kellogg Co., Jersey City, 1954-57; research analytical chemist Union Carbide Chem. Co., South Charleston, W.Va., 1957-65; prof. chemistry Portland (Oreg.) State U., 1965—, chmn. dept. chemistry, 1966-68. Contbr. articles to profl. jours. Grantee NSF, 1976. Mem. Am. Chem. Soc., Sigma Xi. Avocations: stamp and coin collecting, photography, model railroading. Home: 5918 SW Seville Lake Oswego OR 97034 Office: Portland State U Dept Chemistry PO Box 751 Portland OR 97035

WHITE, HOWARD ASHLEY, emeritus university president; b. Cloverdale, Ala., Sept. 28, 1913; s. John Parker and Mabel Clara (Hipp) W.; m. Maxcine Elliott Feltman, June 17, 1952; children—Ashley Feltman, Howard Elliott. Diploma, David Lipscomb Coll., 1932; B.A., Tulane U., 1946, M.A., 1950, Ph.D., 1956. Ordained to ministry Ch. of Christ, 1933; minister Carrollton Ave. Ch. of Christ, New Orleans, 1941-52; assoc. prof. history David Lipscomb Coll., Nashville, 1953-56; prof., chmn. dept. David Lipscomb Coll., 1956-58; chmn. social sci. dept. Pepperdine U., Malibu, Calif., 1958-65; dean grad. studies Pepperdine U., 1965-67, dean undergrad. studies, 1967-70, exec. v.p., 1970-78, pres., 1978-85, pres. emeritus, 1985—. Bd. dirs. Community Services Dist., Malibu, Calif., 1979—. Mem. Am. Hist. Assn., So. Hist. Assn., Orgn. Am. Historians, Phi Alpha Theta, Phi Delta Kappa. Clubs: Calif, Lincoln, Regency, Rotary. Home: 24440 Tiner Ct Malibu CA 90265 Office: Pepperdine U 24255 Pacific Coast Hwy Malibu CA 90265

WHITE, IAN MCKIBBIN, museum administrator; b. Honolulu, May 10, 1929; s. Osborne and Alice Aileen (Dowsett) W.; m. Florence Hildreth, June 27, 1959; children: Peter, Daniel, Susanna. A.B., Harvard U., 1951, postgrad., 1951-52; postgrad. in indsl. design, UCLA, 1957-58; D.F.A. (hon.), Bowdoin Coll., 1977. Adminstrv. asst. Bklyn. Botanic Garden, N.Y.C., 1959-60; supt. Bklyn. Mus., N.Y.C., 1961-63; asst. dir. Bklyn. Mus., 1964-67; dir. Calif. Palace of Legion of Honor, San Francisco, 1968—, M.H. de Young Meml. Mus., San Francisco, 1970—; adviser Archives of Am. Art; mem. mus. adv. panel Nat. Endowment for Arts, 1973-76. Designed: Frieda Shiff Warburg Sculpture Garden, Bklyn. Mus., 1966, Peary-MacMillan Arctic Mus. at Bowdoin Coll, Brunswick, Maine, 1967. Trustee Louise A. Boyd Natural Sci. Mus., Marin County, Calif., 1969-70, Corning (N.Y.) Mus. of Glass, 1977—. Served with USNR, 1953-56. Decorated Order of Republic of Egypt; recipient Chevalier de la Legion d'Honneur, 1984, Papal Knighthood of St. Gregory, 1984, Officer of Order of Arts and Letters French Minister of Culture, 1984. Mem. Am. Assn. Mus. (adv. council 1980-83), Am. Fedn. Arts (trustee 1971—), Internat. Council Mus. (U.S. nat. com. 1971-73, 83—), Internat. Com. for Mus. of Fine Art (v.p. 1983—), Am. Assn. Mus. Dirs. (pres. 1976-77), Mcpl. Art Soc. N.Y.C. (dir. 1966), Victorian Soc. Am. (adv. com. 1970). Clubs: Rembrandt (Bklyn.); Bohemian (San Francisco). Home: 2 Lagunitas Rd Ross CA 94957 Office: Calif Palace Legion Honor Dir Fine Arts Mus San Francisco Lincoln Park San Francisco CA 94115

WHITE, JACK RONALD, electronic engineer; b. Beeville, Tex., Sept. 23, 1943; s. Gene Wallace and Janet Marjorie (Copeland) W.; m. Junko Imaizumi, June 17, 1973; children—John Christopher, Jennifer Anne. B.S.E.E., U. Calif.-Santa Barbara, 1970. Electronics tech. Dynalectron Corp., Point Mugu, Calif., 1964-65, Electro Optical Inc., Santa Barbara, 1965-70; electronic engr. Pacific Missile Test Ctr., Point Mugu, 1970—. Patentee in field; author: The Invisible World of the Infrared, 1984; Satellites of Today and Tomorrow, 1985; How Computers Really Work, 1986. Served with USN, 1961-64. Recipient Design award EDN Mag, 1975, Spl. Achievement award Dept. Def., 1981, Outstanding Performance award Dept. Def., 1983. Mem. Soc. Children's Book Writers. Republican. Home and Office: 2641 Truman St Camarillo CA 93010

WHITE, JAMES EDWARD, geophysicist; b. Cherokee, Tex., May 10, 1918; s. William Cleburne and Willie (Carter) W.; m. Courtenay Brumby, Feb. 1, 1941; children: Rebecca White Vanderslice, Peter McDuffie, Margaret Marie White Curren, Courtenay White Rasmussen. B.A., U. Tex., 1941, M.A., 1946; Ph.D., MIT, 1949. Dir. Underwater Sound Lab., MIT, Cambridge, 1941-45; scientist Def. Research Lab., Austin, Tex., 1945-46; research assoc. MIT, 1946-49; group leader, field research lab. Mobil Oil Co., Dallas, 1949-55; mgr. physics dept. Denver Research Center, Marathon Oil Co., 1955-69; v.p. Globe Universal Scis., Midland, Tex., 1969-71; adj. prof. dept. geophysics Colo. Sch. Mines, Golden, 1972-73; C.H. Green prof. Colo. Sch. Mines, 1976—; L.A. Nelson prof. U. Tex., El Paso, 1973-76; Esso vis. prof. U. Sydney, Australia, 1975; vis. prof. MIT, 1982, U. Tex.-Austin, 1985; del. U.S.-USSR geophysics exchange Dept. State, 1965; mem. bd. Am. Geol. Inst., 1972; mem. space applications bd. Nat. Acad. Engring., 1972-77; exchange scientist Nat. Acad. Sci., 1973-74; del. conf. on oil exploration China Geophys. Soc.-Soc. Exploration Geophysicists, 1981. Author: Seismic Waves: Radiation, Transmission, Attenuation, 1965, Underground Sound: Application of Seismic Waves, 1983, (with R.L. Sengbush) Production Seismology, 1987; editor: Vertical Seismic Profiling (E.I. Galperin), 1974; contbr. articles to profl. jours. Fellow Acoustical Soc. Am.; mem. Soc. Exploration Geophysicists (hon., Maurice Ewing medal 1986, Halliburton award 1987), Sigma Xi. Unitarian. Club: Cosmos. Patentee in field. Office: Dept Geophysics Colo Sch Mines Golden CO 80401

WHITE, JAMES ROBERT, nuclear engineer consultant; b. Rotan, Tex., Oct. 10, 1946; s. James Calvin and May Bell (Smith) W.; m. Betty Jo McGaugh, Dec. 27, 1968; children: James David, Misty Dawn. BS, Tex. Tech U., 1970; MS, U. N.Mex., 1972. Engr. TVA, Chattanooga, 1972-75; supr. EG&G Idaho, Inc., Idaho Falls, 1975-80; sr. engr. ITI, Inc., Idaho Falls, 1980-85; pres. J.R. White Cons., Idaho Falls, 1985—; v.p. Snake River Software, Idaho Falls, 1984—. Mem. ASME, Am. Nuclear Soc., Tau Beta Pi, Sigma Pi Sigma. Baptist. Club: Eagle Rock Commodore (librarian 1985—). Home and Office: 2100 Belmont Ave Idaho Falls ID 83401

WHITE, JOAN MARIE, naturopathic physician; b. Seattle, Aug. 1, 1955; d. Edward James and Frances Marie (Ball) W. BS in Zoology, Howard U., 1976; BS in Human Biology, Kansas Newman Coll., 1979; D of Naturopathic Medicine, Nat. Coll. of Naturopathic Medicine, 1981. Research asst. U. Wash. Hosp., Seattle, 1976; research lab. technician NIH, Bethesda, Md., 1976-77; med. extern Portland (Oreg.) Clinic, 1979-81; mgr., sales assoc. Frederick & Nelson, Seattle, 1981-83; biologist The Seattle Aquarium, 1983-87, corp. mgmt. adv. com., 1983; program mgr. teen parents' transition to work program North Seattle Community Coll., Seattle, 1987—. Recipient Ebony Excellence award Portland Adv. Newspaper, 1981. Mem. Howard U. Alumni Assn. Home: 812 Lake Washington Blvd S Seattle WA 98144 Office: N Seattle Community Coll Teen Parents Transition Work Program 9600 College Way N Seattle WA 98103

WHITE, JOHN M(ARK), performance artist; b. San Francisco, May 10, 1937; s. John T. and Betty Jeanne (LaVelle) W.; m. Sylvia Haimoff, Mar. 24, 1975. M.F.A., Otis Art Inst., Los Angeles, 1969. One-man shows, Betty Gold Gallery, Los Angeles, 1974, Gallerie Doyle, Paris, 1975, Okum Thomas Gallery, St. Louis, 1977, Jan Baum Gallery, Los Angeles, 1978, 81, 83, Roy Boyd Gallery Chgo., 1981, Los Angeles Mcpl. Art Gallery, 1983, group shows include Contemporary Mus. Art, 1973, Los Angeles County Mus. Art, 1971, Newport Harbor Art Mus., 1975, Los Angeles Inst. Contemporary Art, 1975, St. Louis Mus. Art, 1977, U. B.C., 1977, Indspl. Mus. Art, 1979, Guggenheim Mus., N.Y.C., 1981; represented in permanent collections, Los Angeles County Mus. Art, St. Louis Mus. Contemporary Art, Smithsonian Archives of Am. Art, Indpls. Mus. Modern Art, Guggenheim Mus. Nat. Endowment for Arts fellow, 1975, 78, 83. Office: care Contemporary Artists Services 9520 Jefferson Blvd Culver City CA 90232

WHITE, JUDY A., journalist; b. Vallejo, Calif., Sept. 2, 1955; d. Andrew Beaton and Marion Lillieven (Hall) W. Student Heald Bus. Coll., 1973, Calif. Poly. State U.-San Luis Obispo, 1976-79. Free lance journalist Marysville, Calif., 1979-83; exec. sec. Fremont Med. Ctr., Yuba City, Calif., 1983-84; asst. editor Pacific Coast Jour., Sacramento, 1984; publicity dir. various events and fairs Calif. and Nev., 1979—; free lance journalist, Sacramento, 1984—. Contbr. articles to mags. Project leader 4-H, Marysville, 1985-87; mem. election bd. Yuba County, Marysville, 1985-86. Medal class champion Am. Horse Shows Assn., 1972-73, Internat. Stock Seat, 1972-73; year-end stock horse res. champion No. Calif. Horse Show Assn., 1973; champion stock horse Calif. State Horseman's Assn., Santa Rosa show, 1972, Nat. Am. Quarter Horse Cutting Champion. Mem. Sacramento Profl. Women's Network, Sacramento Zool. Soc. (author newsletter 1986—), Sigma Delta Chi and No. Calif. Chpt. Democrat. Roman Catholic. Clubs: Pacific Coast Cutting Horse Assn., Nat. Cutting Horse Assn., Calif. Writers Assn. Avocations: showing horses; scuba diving; reading. Home: 8725 Lodestone Circle Elk Grove CA 95624 Office: PO Box 1724 Marysville CA 95901

WHITE, LELIA CAYNE, librarian; b. Berkeley, Calif., Feb. 22, 1921; d. James Lloyd and Eulalia Fulton (Douglass) Cayne; children by previous marriage—Douglass Fulton, Cameron Jane. B.A., U. Calif., Berkeley, 1943, M.L.S., 1969. Bibliographer, lectr., asso. U. Calif. at Berkeley Sch. Library and Info. Studies, 1969-72; reference librarian Berkeley-Oakland (Calif.) Service Systems, 1970-76, supervising librarian, 1973-76; dir. Oakland Public Library, 1976—. Contbr. to: Public Library User Education, 1981. Mem. ALA, Calif. Library Assn., Public Library Assn., Calif. Inst. Libraries (pres.), Public Library Execs. Central Calif., LWV, Oakland Dalian (China) Friendship City Soc. (pres.). Office: Oakland Public Library 125 14th St Oakland CA 94612

WHITE, LORAINE PATRICIA, social work educator; b. St. Louis, July 18, 1930; d. John J. and Lucy L. (Brock) Williams; m. Waldo Rutledge White, Aug. 23, 1953; children: William L., Darryl C., Russlyn D., Bambia E. BS, Calif. State Poly U., Pomona, 1971; MSW, U. So. Calif., 1973. Psychiat. social worker Tri-City Mental Health Ctr., Pomona, 1972-74; med. social worker U. Med. Ctr., Tucson, 1974-76; lectr. psychiat. social work U. Ariz., Tucson, 1976—; assoc. faculty mem. Pima Community Coll., Tucson, 1975—, Ariz. State U., Tucson, 1977—; cons. Pima County Juvenile Ct., Tucson, 1984—. Mem. Nat. Assn. Social Workers (cert.), Nat. Assn. Black Social Workers (pres. 1985—), Am. Orthopsychiat. Assn., Clin. Social Work and Psychotherapy, Alpha Kappa Alpha. Democrat. Methodist.

WHITE, MARTIN ARTHUR, utilities company executive; b. Whitehall, Mont., Aug. 3, 1941; s. Stewart E. and Sylvia J. (Olson) W.; m. Kathy Francis Harrington, Aug. 1965 (div. Nov. 1969); m. Sheila Mary McMahon, Aug. 24, 1973; children: Matthew Thomas, Jonathan Lewis. BS in Math. and Econs., Mont. State U., 1966; AMP, Harvard U., 1980. Acctg. clk. Mont. Power Co., Butte, 1966-67; acct. Western Energy Co., Butte, Mont., 1967-72, asst. gen. mgr., 1972-74; project mgr. Colstrip, Mont., 1974-1979; v.p., gen. mgr. Butte, 1979-83; pres., chief exec. officer Entech, Inc. (formerly Western Energy Co.), Butte, 1983—; also bd. dirs.; chmn. bd. dirs. Northwestern Resources Co., MSE, Inc., Mont. State U. Endowment and Alumni Found.; bd. dirs. Mont. Bank, Butte, EnTech, Inc., Sunlight Devel., Inc., MERDI, Inc. Mem. exec. com. Mont. Internat. Trade Commn. Served with U.S. Army, 1966-70. Mem. Nat. Coal Council (exec. com. mem., adv. panel to dept. of energy), U.S. High Altitude Speed Skating Found, Inc. (pres.), Mont. Amateur Speed Skating Assn. (v.p.). Lutheran. Lodge: Elks.

WHITE, MORENO JONES, JR., engineer; b. Evergreen, Ala., Dec. 19, 1948; s. Moreno J. Sr. and Mamilu (Taylor) W.; m. Wendy Reeder, Aug. 11, 1978; children: Kristen, Kevin. BS in Aerospace Engring., U. Ala., 1972; MSME, Calif. State U., Long Beach, 1976. Engr. assoc. Sci. Applications, Santa Ana and Irvine, Calif., 1977-81; engr. Gen. Research, Santa Barbara, Calif., 1981-82; sr. engr. Sparta, Inc., Laguna Hills, Calif., 1982-85, prin. investigator thermostructural analysis/material sci., 1985—; bd. dirs. Little White House, Inc., El Toro, Calif., 1986—. Contbr. articles to sci. jours. Mem. Am. Assn. Artificial Intelligence, Phi Sigma Phi, Tau Beta Pi. Republican. Avocations: hiking, backpacking, skiing, racketball, traveling. Home: 22981 Hazelwood El Toro CA 92630 Office: Sparta Inc 23293 S Pointe Dr Laguna Hills CA 92653

WHITE, NANCY SANEN, librarian, administrator; b. Sharon, Pa., Oct. 1, 1953; d. William Roy and Lorraine Irene (Taylor) Aggers; 1 dau., Samantha Rae. B.A. in Latin, Oberlin Coll., 1975; M.L.S., U. Calif.-Berkeley, 1980. Library asst. Case Western Res. U., Cleve., 1976; clk. treas. Cleve. Area Met. Library System, 1976-78; med. library asst. Letterman Army Med. Ctr., San Francisco, 1978-79; research asst. Sta. KRON-TV, San Francisco, 1980; reference librarian Standard Oil Co. of Calif., San Francisco, 1980; library asst. Pacific Gas and Electric Co., San Francisco, 1980-81, info. specialist, 1981, dir. corp. library, 1981-83, administrv. asst. rate dept., 1983-84, cost acctg. supr., 1984-85, project mgr. fuel filings, 1985-86, forecasting supr., 1986—. Pres. alumni bd. dirs. Grad. Sch. of Library and Info. Sci., U. Calif.-Berkeley. Club: Commonwealth (San Francisco). Office: Pacific Gas and Electric Co 77 Beale St Suite 995 San Francisco CA 94106

WHITE, NATHANIEL MILLER, astronomer; b. Providence, Feb. 28, 1941; s. Russell Harkness and Anna Alila (Tuthill) W.; m. Jean Evelyn Moore, June 7, 1967; children: Grace, Andrew, Charles. AB, Earlham Coll., 1964; MSc, Ohio State U., 1967, PhD, 1971; BSEE, No. Ariz. U., 1985. Researcher Lowell Obs., Flagstaff, Ariz., 1969-71, staff astronomer, 1972-78, sr. staff astronomer, 1978—, dir. engring., 1979—; instr. Yarapai Community Coll., Prescott, Ariz., 1977-78. Contbr. articles to profl. jours. Active City Planning and Zoning, City Councils, Flagstaff, 1970—; dir. Local Foot Races, Flagstaff, 1975—; Cub Scout leader Boy Scouts Am., Flagstaff, 1979—. Mem. AAAS, Am. Astron. Soc., Internat. Astron. Union, IEEE, Sigma Xi. Mem. Soc. of Friends. Avocations: trombone playing, wood working, auto restoration, city politics, computers. Home and Office: Lowell Obs Mars Hill Rd 1400 W Flagstaff AZ 86001

WHITE, PAUL H., data processing professional; b. Hanford, Calif., Nov. 28, 1948; s. Frank J. and Frances (Pederson) W.; m. Jane W. Grant, July 23, 1983; 1 child, Lee Woodruff. BS in Math., Calif. Inst. Tech., 1970. Sci. programmer Calif. Inst. Tech., Pasadena, 1969-71; application programmer Lane County, Eugene, Oreg., 1973-76; system programmer Regional Info. System, Eugene, 1976-84, sr. system programmer, 1980-84, tech. support mgr., 1984—. Mem. Computer Measurement Group, Northwest System Programmers Group. Democrat. Avocations: outdoor sports. Office: Regional Info System 125 E 8th Ave Eugene OR 97401-2926

WHITE, ROBERT JOEL, lawyer; b. Chgo., Nov. 1, 1946; s. Melvin and Margaret (Hoffman) W.; m. Gail Janet Edenson, June 29, 1969 (div. Dec. 1982); m. Penelope K. Bloch, Dec. 22, 1985. BS in Accountancy, U. Ill., 1968; JD, U. Mich., 1972. Bar: Calif. 1972, N.Y. 1985, U.S. Dist. Ct. (cen., ea., so. dists.) Calif. 1972, U.S. Ct. Appeals (9th cir.) 1978, U.S. Ct. Appeals (5th cir.) 1983, U.S. Ct. Appeals (6th cir.) 1984, U.S. Supreme Ct. 1977. Staff auditor Haskin & Sells, Chgo., 1968-69; assoc. O'Melveny & Myers, Los Angeles, 1972-79, ptnr., 1980—; adjunct lectr. U. Mich. Law Sch., Ann Arbor, 1986. Contbr. articles to profl. jours. Active Constl. Rights Found., 1980—. Served with U.S. Army, 1968-74. Mem. Los Angeles County Bar Assn. (chmn. fed. cts. com. 1981-82, comml. law and bankruptcy sect., exec. com. 1982-84), Assn. Bus. Trial Lawyers (bd. govs. 1983-85), Fin. Lawyers Conf. (bd. govs. 1986—), ABA (comml. law, bankruptcy com., litigation sect. 1972—), Am. Bankruptcy Inst., Bankruptcy Study Group. Avocations: skiing, running, U.S. history. Office: O'Melveny & Myers 400 South Hope St Los Angeles CA 90071

WHITE, ROBERT LEE, electrical engineer, educator; b. Plainfield, N.J., Feb. 14, 1927; s. Claude and Ruby Hemsworth Emerson (Levick) W.; m. Phyllis Lillian Arlt, June 14, 1952; children: Lauren A., Kimberly A., Christopher L., Matthew P. B.A. in Physics, Columbia U., 1949, M.A., 1951, Ph.D., 1954. Assoc. head atomic physics dept. Hughes Research Labs., Malibu, Calif., 1954-61; head magnetics dept. Gen. Tel. and Electronics Research Lab., Palo Alto, Calif., 1961-63; William E Ayer prof. elec. engring. Stanford U., Palo Alto, 1963—, chmn. elec. engring. dept., 1981-86; William E. Ayer prof. elec. engring. Stanford U., 1985—; dir. Inst. for Electronics in Medicine, 1973—, The Exploratorium, San Francisco, 1987—; dir. Analog Design Tools Inc.; initial ltd. partner Mayfield Fund, Mayfield, II and Alpha II Fund, Rainbow Co-Investment Ptnrs.; cons. in field. Author: (with K.A. Wickersheim) Magnetism and Magnetic Materials, 1965, Basic Quantum Mechanics, 1967; Contbr. numerous articles to profl. jours. Served with USN, 1945-46. Fellow Guggenheim, Oxford U., 1969-70, Kantonsspital Zurich, 1977-78, Christensen fellow Oxford, 1986. Fellow Am. Phys. Soc., IEEE; mem. Sigma Xi, Phi Beta Kappa. Home: 450 El Escarpado Way Stanford CA 94305 Office: The Exploratorium 3601 Lyon St San Francisco CA 94123

WHITE, ROLAND JAMES, aeronautical engineer; b. Missoula, Mont., Dec. 13, 1910; s. Roland John and Mamie (Jacobsen) W.; m. Mary Cleeton, Feb. 10, 1948; children—Roland, Glenna. B.S., U. Calif., 1933; M.S. in Mech. Engring., Calif. Inst. Tech., 1934, M.S. in Aero Engring., 1935. Engr. Curtiss Wright, St. Louis, 1935-36, Lockheed Aircraft, Burbank, Calif., 1937-38; instr. U. Wash., Seattle, 1938-40; engr. Curtiss Wright Corp., St. Louis, 1940-45; unit chief transport div. Boeing, Seattle, 1945-71; engr. Aerophysics Research Corp., Bellevue, Wash., 1971, Bell Aerospace Co., New Orleans, 1972-76, Analytical Methods, Bellevue, 1976, Rohr Industries, San Diego, 1976, Gates Learjet, Wichita, Kans., 1977-81, Canadair Ltd., Mojave, Calif., 1982, Grumman Aero., N.Y., 1983, Cessna A/C, Kans., 1984, Gulfstream, Okla., 1985. Served as lt. (j.g.) USNR, 1937-57. Mem. AIAA. Patentee (12); contbr. articles to profl. jours. Home and Office: 4670 95th Ave NE Bellevue WA 98004

WHITE, RUSSELL LYNN, fashion designer; b. Omaha, May 8, 1950; s. Russell Alfred White and Jo Ann (Steepy) Blotti. AA, Modesto Jr. Coll., 1970; BA in Art, Calif. State U., San Francisco, 1971; student, Coll. of Alameda, 1971-72, Laney Coll., 1976-78, Pierce Coll., 1981-82, Otis Art Inst. of Parsons Sch. Design, 1984-85. Designer Levi Strauss & Co., San Francisco, 1976-79, Jantzen Inc., Los Angeles, 1979-80; head designer Keepers Industries, Woodland Hills, Calif., 1981-83; merchandiser, designer Domino/Victory Mens Wear, Los Angeles, 1983-85; merchandiser, designer Joel/Cal-Made, Ltd., Los Angeles, 1985-86, mdse. mgr., 1986; dir. design Balboa Sportswear Co., Los Angeles, 1986—; prin. BRW & Assocs., Los Angeles, 1986—. Music dir. Holy Trinity Community Ch., Los Angeles, 1981-85, v.p., sec., 1981-83, social dir., 1984-85, treas. 1987. Frank S. Ione Mancini scholar 1968. Mem. Am. Designer Guild (treas. Los Angeles steering com. 1987), Textile Assn. Los Angeles. Republican. Club: Mcpl. Election Com. of Los Angeles (election com. 1982, mem. adv. council) Lodge: Masons (De Molay of Yr. 1968, chevalier 1971). Home and Office: 20300 Valerio St Canoga Park CA 91306

WHITE, RUTH S., publisher; b. Pitts., Sept. 1, 1925; d. Leon H. and Rose (Stevenson) W. BA in Piano and Music Composition, Carnegie Mellon U., 1948, MFA, 1949; teaching cert., UCLA, 1951. Supr. UCLA Demonstration Sch., Los Angeles, 1951-59; pres. Rhythms Prodns., Los Angeles, 1955—, Cheviot Corp., Los Angeles, 1979—; guest lectr. various Los Angeles Colls., 1958—. Author numerous texts; composer classical, electronic music, over 60 children's albums; also music for dance, film scores and TV. Recipient first prize for composition, Nat. Soc. Arts and Letters, Los Angeles, 1950, first prize for film score Atlanta Film Festival, 1971, Parents Choice Award for Excellence in Childrens Rec., 1983, Notable Rec. award ALA, 1983; Huntington Hartford Found. fellow, Los Angeles, 1965. Mem. ASCAP, Nat. Assn. Rec. Arts and Scis. (trustee, bd. govs. 1970-76), Am. Fedn. Musicians, Nat. Assn. Am. Composers, Am. Women Composers, Inc., Internat. Congress Women Composers, Internat. Assn. Ednl. Dealers and Suppliers, Music Eductors Nat. Conf., Audio Engring. Soc., Nat. Sch. Suppliers and Equipment Assn., NOW, Direct Mktg. Assn., Sigma Alpha Iota. Office: Rhythms Prodns/Cheviot Corp Box 34485 Los Angeles CA 90034

WHITE, STANLEY ARCHIBALD, research electrical engineer; b. Providence, Sept. 25, 1931; s. Clarence Archibald White and Lou Ella (Givens) Arford; m. Edda María Castaño-Benítez, June 6, 1956; children: Dianne, Stanley Jr., Paul, John. BSEE, Purdue U., 1957, MSEE, 1959, PhD, 1965. Registered profl. engr., Ind., Calif. Engr. Rockwell Internat., Anaheim, Calif., 1959-68, mgr., 1968-84, sr. scientist, 1984—; adj. prof. elec. engring. U. Calif., 1984—; cons. and lectr. in field. Contbr. chpts. to books; articles to profl. jours.; patentee in field. Fellow N.Am. Aviation Sci. Engring, 1963-65; recipient Disting. Lectr. award Nat. Electronics Conf., Chgo., 1973, Engr. of Yr. award Orange County (Calif.) Engring. Council, 1984, Engr. of Yr. award Rockwell Internat., 1985, Leonardo Da Vinci Medallion, 1986. Fellow IEEE (chmn. various coms., Centennial medal 1984), AAAS, Inst. Advancement Engring., N.Y. Acad. Scis.; mem. Audio Engring. Soc. Avocation: choral music. Home: 433 E Ave Cordoba San Clemente CA 92672 Office: Rockwell Internat Corp 3370 Miraloma Ave Anaheim CA 92803-3170

WHITE, TIM DOUGLAS, anthropology educator; b. Los Angeles, Aug. 24, 1950; s. Robert Julian and Georgia Johnston (McDougall) W. B.S. in Biology, U. Calif., Riverside, 1972, B.S. in Anthropology, 1972; M.A., U. Mich., 1974, Ph.D., 1977. Paleontologist East Rudolf Research Project, N. Kenya, 1974-77, Laetolil Expdn., N. Tanzania, 1978, Middle Awash Valley, Ethiopia, 1981, Olduvai Gorge, 1985-86; prof. anthropology U. Calif., Berkeley, 1977—. Grantee NSF. Mem. Soc. Vertebrate Paleontology, AAAS. An excavator earliest human ancestor footprints, Tanzania, 1978; co-discoverer earliest human ancestor A. afarensis 1978-79. Office: Kroeber Hall Berkeley CA 94720

WHITE, VIRGINIA JOYCELYN, interior designer, consultant; b. Des Moines, April 25, 1924; d. William Wood White and Alwilda (Denning) W. Student, Art Inst. Chgo., 1942-43; B.F.A., Choinard Sch. Art, 1947; postgrad. Woodbury Coll. Design, 1947-48, UCLA, 1948-50, Southwestern U. Law, 1954-56. Designer Martin Young Furniture Mfg. Co., Los Angeles, 1947-52; owner, designer Virginia White Interiors Co., Los Angeles, 1952-57, Studio City, 1966-80, Palm Desert, 1980—; dir. design Gen. Fireproofing Co., Los Angeles 1957-63, Barker Bros. Co., Los Angeles, 1963-66; instr. design Woman's Workshop, Northridge, Calif., 1973-79; cons. to furniture mfrs. Bd. dirs. Spastic Children's Fund, Los Angeles, 1952-56. Recipient Nat. Instn. Mag. design award, 1958; McCall Mag. design award, 1963. Mem. Calif. Fedn. Bus. and Profl. Women (charter pres. Los Angeles chpt. 1957-58), Am. Soc. Interior Designers (cert. 1974) Sigma Tau Psi (chpt. pres. 1945-46, nat. pres. 1946-48). Republican. Mem. Ch. Religious Sci. Patentee in furniture field; contbr. articles to publs.

WHITEHEAD, ARDELLE COLEMAN, advertising and public relations executive; b. Carrollton, Ohio, May 13, 1917; d. James David and Gilsie Dale (Hendricks) Coleman; m. W. Wilson Whitehead, Mar. 9, 1974. B.S., Wittenberg U., 1938. Various advt. agy. and corp. exec. positions, N.Y.C., Los Angeles, until 1966; consumer affairs specialist Jennings/Thompson, Phoenix, 1966-73; pub. communications mgr. Valley Nat. Bank, Phoenix, 1974-76; pres. Whiteheads Inc., Phoenix, 1976—. Author, pub. various advt. booklets. Named Adperson of Yr., Phoenix, 1978. Mem. Women in Communications (chpt. dir. 1977—, named Woman of Achievement Phoenix chpt. and Far West region 1981), Pub. Relations Soc. Am. (chpt. dir. 1980-84, Percy award for excellence 1985). Clubs: Phoenix Advt. (dir. 1966-76, pres. 1974-75). Home: 337 E Pierson St Phoenix AZ 85012

WHITEHOUSE, CHARLES BARTON, avionics educator; b. Boston, Sept. 7, 1933; s. John Clifford and Pauline Barbara (Larkin) W.; m. Diana Bernier, June 9, 1962; 1 child, Clifford Bernard. B.S., Central Conn. State Coll., 1957; M.S., U. Northern Colo., 1974, D.Edn., 1977. Cert. profl. tchr., Colo.; cert. flight instr., aircraft & instrument, Colo. Electrician, Killywatt Elec. Co., Newington, Conn., 1951-56, Guerrard Elec. Co., New Britain, Conn., 1956-57; technician electric curriculum Opportunity Sch., Denver, 1958-60, elec. instr., 1960-68, avionics, communications instr., 1968—; founder, owner, seminar leader Intertech Aviation Services, Littleton, Colo., 1980—. Author of manual and study guide on avionics. Mem. Vcat. Tchrs. Fedn., Denver Radio League, Exptl. Aircraft Assn. Republican. Unitarian. Home: 3 Sunset Ln Greenwood Village Littleton CO 80121 Office: Opportunity Sch Room 455 1250 Welton St Denver CO 80204

WHITEKER, ROY ARCHIE, university administrator; b. Long Beach, Calif., Aug. 22, 1927; s. Ewing Harris and Mabel Mary (Williams) W.; m. Jean Fiske MacLean, June 3, 1960; 1 son, Scott MacLean. B.S., UCLA, 1950, M.S., 1952; Ph.D., Calif. Inst. Tech., 1956. Instr. chemistry M.I.T., 1955-57; asst. prof. Harvey Mudd Coll., Claremont, Calif., 1957-61; assoc. prof. Harvey Mudd Coll., 1961-67, prof. chemistry, 1967-73; assoc. dir. fellowships Nat. Acad. Scis., Washington, 1967-68; dep. exec. sec. Council Internat. Exchange Scholar, Washington, 1971-72; exec. sec. Council Internat. Exchange Scholar, 1972-75, dir., 1975-76; dean, prof. chemistry Coll. Pacific, Stockton, Calif., 1976—. Dir. Stockton Symphony Assn., 1978-80, Sta. KUOP Community Adv. Bd., 1981—. Served with USNR, 1945-46. Recipient Dow Chem. Co. fellowship, 1953-54; DuPont Teaching fellowship, 1954-55; NSF Sci. Faculty fellowship Royal Inst. Tech., Stockholm, Sweden, 1963-64. Mem. Am. Chem. Soc., Am. Council Acad. Deans, Alpha Chi Sigma, Phi Beta Kappa, Phi Kappa Phi, Sigma Xi. Home: 3734 Portsmouth Circle N Stockton CA 95209 Office: Coll Pacific 3601 Pacific Ave Stockton CA 95211

WHITEMAN, BETTY BLUE, retired teacher; b. Richey, Mont., June 2, 1914; d. William Millard and Blanche (Hott) Blue; m. George Dewey Whiteman, Feb. 23, 1935; children—Dewey Dean, Peggy L., Sharon E., Janice K. Diploma, Mont. State Normal Coll., 1937; B.A., Western Mont. Coll., 1976. Cert. elem. tchr., Mont. Tchr. Dawson & Richland Co., Richey, Mont., 1933-42, Richey Elem. Sch., 1950-78, ret. Compiler History of Richey and Community: Honyocker's Heritage, 1981. Sec., treas. Richey Hist. Soc., 1970—; treas. Richey Health Ctr., 1975-79; v.p. Richey Sr. Citizens, 1981-83; sec. United Meth. Ch., Richey, 1981—. Recipient Outstanding Citizen award Richey Jaycees, 1975. Mem. Am. Legion Aux. (v.p. 1978-84, historian, 1984—). Democrat. Office: Richey Hist Mus PO Box 218 Richey MT 59259

WHITESIDES, RANDY DALE, electronics executive; b. Long Beach, Calif., May 5, 1952; s. Lawrence Allen Whitesides and Elizabeth (Stockton) Gewin; m. Robin Erin Curley, Aug. 22, 1981; 1 child, Alexander Curley. BA, U. So. Calif., 1974; postgrad., U. Calif., Irvine, 1973—, UCLA, 1977. Exec. v.p. Y.Y., Inc., Tustin, Calif., 1976-77, Biraic, Newport Beach, Calif., 1976-82; v.p. mktg. The Mega Group, Irvine, 1983—, also bd. dirs.; chief exec. officer Spectra Scan, Newport Beach, 1986—; gen. ptnr. Micro Max, Ltd., Energy Storage Microtechs., Costa Mesa, 1982—; bd. dirs. Aridcor. Contbr. articles to profl. jours. Recipient Keystone award 1CP, Phoenix, 1984. Mem. Orange Coast Venture Group, U. So. Calif. Alumni Assn. (pres. Newport Harbor chpt., 1985). Republican. Avocations: sailing, scuba diving, tennis, gourmet cooking, wine collecting. Home: 1814-C Fullerton Ave Costa Mesa CA 92627 Office: Spectra Scan 500 Newport Ctr Dr Suite B Newport Beach CA 92660

WHITESON, LEON, journalist; b. Bulawayo, Zimbabwe, Oct. 19, 1930; came to U.S., 1984; s. Charles and Rececca (Goldman) W.; m. Janine Kahn, Mar. 18, 1950 (div. Sept. 77); children: Adam, Karen; m. Aviva Cantor, Sept. 7, 1978. Cambridge cert., Milton Sr., 1947; BArch, U. Cape Town, South Africa, 1953. Registered architect, U.K. Freelance architect London, 1954-65, freelance writer, 1965-80; architecture critic Toronto Star, 1980-83, Los Angeles Herald Examiner, 1984—. Author: Modern Canadian Architecture, 1982, The Livable City, 1982, White Snake, 1982, Fool, 1983. Founding mem. Watts Towers Community & Conservation Trust, Los Angeles, 1985; pres., bd. dirs. Urban Design Adv. Coalition, Los Angeles, 1985. Home: 9949 C Robbins Dr Beverly Hills CA 90212 Office: LA Herald Examiner 1111 S Broadway Los Angeles CA 90015

WHITFIELD, BELVA WIGGINS, speech pathologist; b. Lovington, N.Mex., Mar. 30, 1929; d. Ervin James and Maymie J. (Clayton) Wiggins; m. Willis James Whitfield, Sept. 3, 1949; children: Joe Ray, James Donald. BS, Hardin-Simmons U., 1951; MA, U. N.Mex., 1971. Speech pathologist Albuquerque Pub. Schs., 1971-76, adminstr., 1976—. Mem. Am. Speech Lang. and Hearing, Albuquerque Speech and Audiology Profls., Council Exceptional Children, N.Mex. Speech Lang. and Hearing Assn. Baptist. Home: 7004 Dellwood Rd NE Albuquerque NM 87110 Office: Albuquerque Pub Schs 120 Woodland NW Albuquerque NM 87107

WHITFIELD, BENJAMIN HATCH, JR., ins. agt.; b. Jackson, Miss., Jan. 10, 1947; s. Benjamin Hatch and Lucy (Sellers) W.; B.A., Ambassador Coll., Pasadena, Calif., 1969, M.A. in Edn., 1973; m. Mary-Pat Whitfield. June 1, 1969; children—Benjamin Michael, John Gregory. Tchr., Imperial Schs., Pasadena, 1969-74; minister Worldwide Ch. of God, 1975-77, now elder; marriage counselor Carbon County (Wyo.) Counseling Center, Rawlins, 1977-78; agt. State Farm Ins., Rawlins, 1979—. Bd. dirs. City of Rawlins Recreation Dept., Rawlins Fine Arts Council, Ryan Park Winter Sports Site Bd.; dist. chmn. Boy Scouts Am. Mem. Nat. Assn. Life Underwriters, Nat. Assn. Health Underwriters. Club: Rotary. Home: 1315 Date St Rawlins WY 82301 Office: PO Box 639 205 W Cedar Rawlins WY 82301

WHITHORN, DORIS SWENSON, civic worker, author; b. Davenport, Nebr., Dec. 18, 1916; d. Arthur Emmet and Minnie Lois (Rousch) Swenson; m. William Francis Whithorn, June 25, 1939; children—Bruce Allen, Carol Jean Whithorn Orr, Alta Joyce Whithorn Stands, Duane Arthur. Student Nebr. Wesleyan U., 1934, U. Nebr., 1937-39. Vol. caretaker Park County Museum, Livingston, Mont., 1976-86, pres. Mus. Assn., 1980-86. Author (with William Whithorn) books on local history, 1965, 76, also 13 paperback books on local history, 1965-83; compiler Bicentennial Tapestry of Yellowstone Conf., 1984. Contbr. articles to True West, Frontier Times and Hobbies. Mem. Park County Tax Appeal Bd., Livingston, 1972-76, Park County Design Rev. Bd., Livingston, 1983; chmn. bicentennial com. Yellowstone Conf., 1983-84, Park County History Book Com., 1984; mem. Commn. on Archives and History, Yellowstone Conf., United Meth. Ch. Mem. Park County Hist. Soc. (pres. 1972-74), Mont. Fedn. Women's Clubs (pres. dist. IV 1978-79). Republican. Clubs: Yellowstone (pres. 1972-73), United Meth. Women's (pres. 1983-84). Lodge: Royal Neighbors Oracle. Home: 510 S 8th Livingston MT 59047

WHITING, ALLEN SUESS, political science educator, writer, consultant; b. Perth Amboy, N.J., Oct. 27, 1926; s. Leo Robert and Viola Allen (Suess) W.; m. Alice Marie Conroy, May 29, 1950; children: Deborah Jean, David Neal, Jeffrey Michael, Jennifer Hollister. B.A., Cornell U., 1948; M.A., Columbia U., 1950, cert. Russian Inst., 1950, Ph.D., 1952. Instr. polit. sci. Northwestern U., 1951-53; asst. prof. Mich. State U., East Lansing, 1955-57; social scientist The Rand Corp., Santa Monica, Calif., 1957-61; dir. Office Research and Analysis Far East U.S. Dept. State, Washington, 1962-66; dep. consul gen. Am. Consulate Gen., Hong Kong, 1966-68; prof. polit. sci. U. Mich., Ann Arbor, 1968-82; prof. U. Ariz., Tucson, 1982—, dir. Ctr. for East Asian Studies, 1982—; cons. U.S. Dept. State, 1968—; dir. Nat. Com. on U.S.-China Relations, N.Y.C., 1977—; assoc. The China Council, 1978—; pres. Ariz. China Council, Tucson, 1983—. Author: Soviet Policies in China: 1917-1924, 1954, China Crosses the Yalu, 1968, Chinese Calculus of Deterrence, 1975, Siberian Development and East Asia, 1981, others; contbr. articles to profl. jours.; spl. commentator McNeil-Lehrer Program; CBS and NBC Spls. on China. Served with U.S. Army, 1945. Social Sci. Research Council fellow, 1950, 74-75; Ford Found. fellow, 1953-55; Rockefeller Found. fellow, 1978. Mem. Assn. Asian Studies, Council Fgn. Relations. Home: 125 Canyon View Dr Tucson AZ 85704 Office: Dept Polit Sci U Ariz Tucson AZ 85721

WHITLEY, WALKER, consultant; b. Evanston, Ill., June 7, 1927; s. William Richard and Margaret Lillian (Sullivan) W.; m. Nancy Ann Brickbauer, Nov. 16, 1957; children—William Walker, Virginia Lyn. B.A., Grinnell Coll., 1950; postgrad. Northwestern U., 1958-59. Appraiser, asst. br. mgr. Cadillac Motor Car div. Gen. Motors Corp., Evanston, Ill., 1950-53; investment banker, statistician Betts, Borland & Co., Chgo., 1953-58; auto fin. and wholesale credit mgr. Southeastern U.S. Gen. Fin. Corp., Evanston, 1958-59; instl. bond salesman, govt. bond trader N.Y. Hanseatic Corp., Chgo., 1959-63; recognition rep. O. C. Tanner Co., Chgo., 1963-65; regional rep. L. G. Balfour Co., Mpls., 1966-76; cons. Walker Whitley Co., Scottsdale, Ariz., 1976—. Mem. Edina Sch. Dist. Citizens Adv. Task Force, 1975-77. Served with USNR, PTO, 1945-46. Mem. Nat. Assn. Securities Dealers. Club: Rotary (chmn. community projects com.). Home and Office: 6059 N Granite Reef Rd Scottsdale AZ 85253

WHITLEY, WESLEY THOMAS, mechanical engineer; b. LaGrange, Ga., July 24, 1951; s. Robert Milligan and Hazal Theo (Partain) W.; m. Ruth Elaine Henry, Feb. 15, 1986; children: Nathan Thomas, Christina Rose, Susan Marie. BSME, U. N.Mex., 1979. Package design engr. Hewlett Packard, Boise, Idaho, 1980-82, mfg. devel. engr., 1982—. Served with USN, 1969-72. Avocations: gardening, woodworking. Office: Hewlett Packard 11413 Chinden Blvd Boise ID 83707

WHITLOW, GARRY DEE, physician; b. Taft, Calif., Nov. 21, 1940; s. Roy Rudolph and Elsie Catherine (Buck) W. BA summa cum laude, St. Mary's U., San Antonio, 1962; MD, UCLA, 1967. Intern St. Joseph's Hosp., Phoenix, 1967-68; chief resident in neurology Barrows Neurol. Inst., Phoenix, 1968-69, resident in neurology, 1968-70; dir. neurology clinic U.S. Naval Hosp., Port Hueneme, Calif., 1969-71; emergency physician South Bay Hosp., Redondo Beach, Calif., 1972—, dir. emergency dept., 1980—; med. cons. Emergency Med. mag., 1975—; paramedic liason physician, Redondo Beach, Manhattan Beach, Calif., Hermosa Beach, Calif., 1973—. Author: The Great Flagstad, 1984, The Basics of Baking, 1986. Med. dir. Operation Heart Start, Redondo Beach, 1975. Served to lt. comdr. USN, 1969-71. Charter mem. Am. Coll. Emergency Physicians, Am. Trauma Soc. Roman Catholic. Avocations: opera, classical music, baking, writing. Home: 7772 Torreyson Dr Hollywood CA 90046 Office: S Bay Hosp Emergency Dept 514 N Prospect Redondo Beach CA 90277

WHITMAN, DAVID LYNN, educator; b. Torrington, Wyo., Nov. 10, 1952; s. Donald Ray and Patricia Ann (Wilson) W.; m. Ellen Marie Griffith, Dec. 19, 1971; children—Andrea, Angela, Ashlee. B.S. in Elec. Engring., U. Wyo., 1975, Ph.D. in Mineral Engring., 1978. Registered profl. engr., Wyo. Vice pres. research and devel. World Energy, Inc., Laramie, Wyo., 1978—; assoc. prof. petroleum engring. U. Wyo., Laramie, 1981—. No. Natural Gas fellow, 1975. Mem. Nat. Soc. Petroleum Engrs., Sigma Xi, Phi Kappa Phi, Tau Beta Pi, Sigma Tau, Pi Epsilon Tau. Republican. Methodist. Contbr. articles to profl. jours. Home: 1666 N 23d St Laramie WY 82070 Office: PO Box 3295 University Station Laramie WY 82071

WHITMAN, KENNETH JAY, advertising executive; b. N.Y.C., May 4, 1947; s. Howard Jay and Suzanne Marcia (Desberg) W.; m. Linda Loy Meisnest, Nov. 25, 1968; 1 child, Tyler Ondine. Student, Berklee Sch. Mus., 1965-66, Hubbard Acad., 1968-70. Nat. dep. dir. Pub. Relations Bur., Los Angeles, 1970-75; pres. Creative Cons., Los Angeles, 1975-82; pres., creative dir. Whitman & Green Advt., Toluca Lake, Calif., 1982-86, Whitman-Olson, Toluca Lake, 1986—. Co-author: Strategic Advertising, 1986; editor Freedom news jour., 1971-79; contbr. newspaper column Shape of Things, 1971-79. Pres. Los Angeles Citizens Commn. Human Rights, 1971-75. Recipient Cert. of Design Excellence Print Regional Design Ann., 1985, Award of Excellence Consolidated Papers, 1985. Mem. Bus. and Profl. Advt. Assn. (award for Excellance 1987), Art Dirs. Club of Los Angeles, VSC (pres. 1964-65). Avocations: interior design, music. Office: Whitman-Olson 10200 Riverside Dr Toluca Lake CA 91602

WHITMER, JOHN CHARLES, chemistry educator; b. Kingfisher, Okla., Jan. 28, 1939; s. Charles Austin and Jeannette (Keys) W.; m. Kathryn M. Steenson, May 27, 1967; children: Charles, David. BS in Chemistry, U. Rochester, 1960, MS in Chemistry, 1962; PhD in Chemstry, U. Mich., 1965. Asst. prof. chemistry Western Wash. U., Bellingham, 1965-67, 1969-72, assoc. prof. chemistry, 1972-76, prof. chemistry, 1976—; lectr. in chemistry U. E. Africa, Kampala, Uganda, 1967-69. Contbr. articles to profl. jours. Mem. AAAS, Am. Chem. Soc., Sigma Xi. Home: 420 Morey Ave Bellingham WA 98225

WHITMORE, MICHAEL EUGENE, marketing professional; b. York, Pa., Nov. 11, 1946; s. Woodrow Wilson and Arlene Elizabeth (Bubb) W.; m. Elizabeth R. Yoder, Oct. 12, 1966 (div. Sept. 1985); 1 child, Andrew Michael. AA, York Jr. Coll., 1964-66. Bus. analyst Dunn & Bradstreet, Harrisburg, Pa., 1973-76; acct. exec. Susquehanna Broadcasting, York, 1976-79; owner Susquehanna Assocs., Ltd., York, 1979-81; dist. mgr. Larkey & Lamon, Inc., Richmond, Va., 1981-83; sec.-treas., sales mgr. Whitmore & Rodman Assocs., Ltd., Lancaster, Pa., 1983-85; mktg. mgr. Winston Network, Inc., Phoenix, 1985—. Rep. precinct committeeman Maricopa County, Scottsdale, Ariz., 1985—; active com. Phoenix Symphony Orch., 1986—. Recipient Medallion award Advt. Fed. Cen. Pa., Harrisburg, 1977. Mem. Phoenix Met. C. of C. (media com. 1986—), Phoenix Advt. Club., Advt. Fedn. Cen. Pa. (bd. dirs. 1975-78). Avocations: photography, skiing, racquetball. Home: 7521 E Cannon Dr Scottsdale AZ 85256 Office: Winston Network Inc 1835 E 6th St Suite 21 Tempe AZ 85281

WHITNEY, CONSTANCE CLEIN, psychologist, consultant; b. Seattle, Nov. 12, 1931; BA, Stanford U., 1952; M A, Washington U., St. Louis, 1977, PhD, 1984; children: Mark R. Wittcoff, Caroline C. Wittcoff. Writer, San Francisco Chronicle, 1953-55; dir. UN, St. Louis, 1956-60; lectr. St. Louis Art Mus., 1960-71; producer KETC-TV, 1973-75; instr. U. Mo., St. Louis, 1976-78; clin. research asst. psychiatry med. Sch., Washington U., 1977-80; motivation research dir. 1980-84, research asst. , 1983-84, lectr. organizational behavior, fellow in mgmt., research assoc., 1984-86; bd. dirs. Adult Edn. Council, 1977-82, Bd. dirs. St. Louis Symphony, 1959-63, Dance Concert Soc., 1965-70, Child Guidance Clinic, 1981-84,Am. Heart Assn., Women For: UN Com. to Eliminate Discrimination; exec. producer Forward-Looking Strategies for Women, 1986—; cons. Loyola Marymount U., Los Angeles; leadership cons. Girl Scouts Am., Greater Los Angeles,

1986—. Mem. Calif. Psychol. Assn., Am. Psychol. Assn., Calif. Psychol. Assn., Assn. for Advancement Behavioral Therapy, AAUP, Am. Ednl. Research Assn., Internat. Soc. for Polit. Psychology, Am. Soc. Tng., Devel., Orgn. Behavioral Teaching Soc., Acad. Mgmt. St. Louis Art Mus. (life), Stanford Alumni Assn. (life). Clubs: Bus. and Profl. Women, St. Louis. Author: Effective Learning Skills, 1977; What is Treatment?, 1977; (with Brim and Wetzel) Social Network Characteristics of Hospitalized Depressed Patients, 1982; writer, dir. film Women and Money: Myths and Realities, 1976. Home: 10601 Wilshire Blvd Los Angeles CA 90024

WHITNEY, DAVID CLAY, educator, consultant, writer; b. Astoria, Oreg., May 30, 1937; s. Rolla Vernon and Barbara (Clay) W.; m. Kathleen Donnelley, 1956 (div. 1963); children: David Jr., Gordon, Sara; m. Zelda Gifford, 1967 (div. 1973). BS in Chemistry, San Diego State U., 1959; PhD in Chemistry, U. Calif., Berkeley, 1963. Cert. data processor, cert. data educator. Acting asst. prof. U. Calif., Davis, 1962-63; chemist, mathematician Shell Devel. Corp., Emeryville, Calif., 1963-72; dir. computer services Systems Applications, Inc., San Rafael, Calif., 1973-77; prof. San Francisco State U. Sch. Bus., 1977—; info. systems cons. numerous cos., 1977—; textbook reviewer numerous pubs., 1979—. Author: Instructors' Guides to Understanding Fortran 77, 1983, 87, Understanding Fortran, 1984. Mem. Assn. Computing Machinery, Data Processing Mgmt. Assn., Soc. Data Educators, Mensa. Home: 624 Vendola Dr San Rafael CA 94903 Office: San Francisco State U Sch of Bus San Francisco CA 94132

WHITNEY, ELVIN DALE, research plant pathologist; b. Woods Cross, Utah, Mar. 23, 1928; s. Charles Leroy and Thelma Pearl (Reed) W.; m. Rochelle Agren, June 18, 1958; children: Christy, Charles Elmer, Annette. BS, Utah State U., 1946-50, cert. tchr., 1958; PhD, Cornell U., 1965. Research asst. Cornell U., Ithaca, N.Y., 1960-65; plant pathologist Agrl. Research Service USDA, Salinas, Calif., 1965—; bd. dirs. Whitney Ranches Inc., Cokeville, Wyo, pres., 1985—. Assoc. editor Am. Phytopathological Soc., St. Paul, 1984—; contbr. articles to profl. jours. Scoutmaster, chmn. com. Boy Scouts Am., Salinas, 1975-84; officer Ch. Jesus Christ Latter-day Saints, Ithaca and Salinas, 1960—. Served to 1st lt. USAF, 1952-54. USDA grantee, Colmar, France, 1984. Mem. Am. Pathol. Soc. (vice chmn. compendium com. 1983-84), Am. Soc. Sugar Beet Technologists, Sigma Xi. Republican. Avocations: skiing, backpacking, ranching, fishing, hunting. Home: 763 Carmelita Dr Salinas CA 93901 Office: Agrl Research Div USDA 1636 E Alisal St Salinas CA 93905

WHITNEY, LARRY KEITH, minister, business educator, lawyer; b. Marion County, Ill., Jan. 8, 1946; s. Charles Wayne and Doris R. (Mulvaney) W.; m. Karen Lynn Whitney, Feb. 6, 1971; children: Kirsten, Kari. MBA, Eastern Ill. U., 1972; JD, Tex. Tech. U., 1977. Bar: Ill. 1977. Tax acct. Arthur Andersen & Co., St. Louis, 1977-78; sole practice, Olney, Ill., 1978-81; atty. city of Olney, 1978-81; chmn. dept. bus. Freed-Hardeman Coll., Henderson, Tenn., 1981-83; assoc. prof. bus. law and fin. Pepperdine U., Malibu, Calif., 1983-86; sr. minister Northside Ch. of Christ, Santa Ana, Calif., 1986—. Author: Declaring the Dawn. Served with USAF, 1966-69. Decorated Air medal. Recipient Wall St. Jour. award. Mem. ABA, Ill. Bar Assn., Phi Delta Phi. Mem. Ch. of Christ.

WHITNEY, Q. LOUISE, cosmetology college executive; b. Artesia, N.Mex., Jan. 26, 1944; d. William Neil Jackson and Mary Lois (Pryor) Miller; children—Tammy, Lorrie, Billy, Orville, Jr., Christopher. Cert. cosmetology instr., N.Mex. Cosmetologist, Curl Cottage, Roswell, N.Mex., 1970-71, Dottie's Roswell, 1971-72, Maude's, Roswell, 1972-74, Lea's, Roswell, 1975-76; mgr. Louise's, Roswell, 1976-79; pres. Roswell Coll. Cosmetology, 1976—. Mem. Nat. Hairdressers and Cosmetologists Assn. (pres., v.p.), Tchr.'s Edn. Council, Nat. Assn. Cosmetology Schs., S.W. Assn. Fin. Aid Officers, Roswell C. of C. Democrat. Baptist. Office: Roswell Coll Cosmetology 112 N Virginia Roswell NM 88201

WHITNEY, ROBERT ELI, retail executive; b. Walla Walla, Wash., Mar. 27, 1947; s. Robert Bruce and Shirley Elizabeth (Gardner); 1 son, Peter Whitney. B.A., Whitman Coll., 1969. Owner Eli Whitney Office Supply, Kirkland, Wash., 1980-82; dist. mgr. J.K. Gill Co., Seattle, 1983—; ins. agt. A.L. Williams Co., 1984; v.p. Medford Merchants Assn., 1974; dir. Southcenter Inc., Seattle, 1976-78. Mem. Seattle Downtown Devel. Assn., 1977-79; council alt. mem. Jacksonville Oreg. City Council, 1973; pres. alumni bd. Whitman Coll. Mem. Nat. Office Products Assn., Phi Delta Theta. Club: Glen Acres Country. Home: 7500 39th NE Seattle WA 98715 Office: 10983 Via Frontera San Diego CA 92127

WHITNEY, STEPHEN L., librarian; b. Chgo., July 18, 1943. AB in Engring., Rockhurst Coll., 1965; MSLS, Case Western Res. U., 1966. Adult services librarian St. Louis Pub. Library, 1966-67; coordinator Mcpl. Library Coop. of St. Louis County, 1967-70; adminstrv. asst. to dir. St. Louis County Library, 1970-74; county librarian Broward County Library, 1974-77; city librarian San Bernardino (Calif.) Pub. Library, 1977—. Office: San Bernardino Pub Library 525 W Sixth St San Bernardino CA 92410 *

WHITSEL, RICHARD HARRY, biologist; b. Denver, Feb. 23, 1931; s. Richard Elstun and Edith Muriel (Harry) W.; B.A., U. Calif., Berkeley, 1954; M.A., San Jose State Coll., 1962; m. Joanne Elissa Cox, June 26, 1982; 1 son, Russell David; children by previous marriage: Robert Alan, Michael Dale, Steven Deane. Sr. research biologist San Mateo County Mosquito Abatement Dist., Burlingame, Calif., 1959-72; environ. program mgr., chief of planning Calif. Regional Water Quality Control Bd., Oakland, 1972—; mem. grad. faculty water resource mgmt. U. San Francisco, 1987—. Served with Med. Service Corps, U.S. Army, 1954-56. Mem. Entomol. Soc. Am., Entomol. Soc. Wash., Am. Mosquito Control Assn., Calif. Alumni Assn., Sierra Club. Democrat. Episcopalian. Contbr. articles to profl. jours. Home: 4331 Blenheim Way Concord CA 94521 Office: Calif Regional Water Quality Control Bd 1111 Jackson St Oakland CA 94607

WHITSELL, LEON JEFFERSON, psychiatrist, neurologist; b. Fernley, Nev., Sept. 6, 1914; s. Leon Otto and Betty Loren (McKaig) W.; m. Alice Jane Lawrence, Dec. 22, 1938; children—Leon Lawrence, George Edward, James Lawrence. A.B., Stanford U., 1935, M.D., 1939. Diplomate Am. Bd. Psychiatry and Neurology. Merril fellow in psychiatry Stanford Sch. Medicine, Calif., 1946-47; cons. psychiatrist U.S. Penitentiary, Alcatraz Island, Calif., 1947-63; practice medicine specializing in psychiatry and neurology, San Francisco, 1947—; asst. clin. prof. of medicine Stanford U., San Francisco, Palo Alto, 1947-62; attending physician, cons. in neurology VA Hosp., Martinez, Oakland, Calif., 1947-70; examiner for med. commn. Superior Court, San Francisco, 1952-54; asst. prof. to assoc. clin.l prof. U. Calif., San Francisco, 1962-84. Med. editor Internat. Trumpet Guild Publs., 1980—. Mem. sci. adv. bd. Orton Dyslexia Soc., 1976—. Served to lt. commdr. (j.g.) USNR, 1942-46, active duty med. corps. Fellow Am. Psychiat. Assn. (life), Am. Acad. Neurology; mem. San Francisco Neurol. Soc. (pres.), San Francisco Med. Soc., Calif. Med. Assn. (chmn. nervous and mental disease com. 1962). Republican. Clubs: Santa Cruz; San Francisco (pres.). Lodges: Masons, Deutscher Musik Verein. Office: Leon J Whitsell MD 909 Hyde St San Francisco CA 94109

WHITSON, DAVID ROBERT, financial planner; b. Tucson, Jan. 18, 1952; s. Robert W. Whitson and Margie Lou (Wright) Allen; m. Pamela Gail Thornsberry, Nov. 24, 1979; children—Amber Rose, Andrea Louise. Grad. high sch., Albuquerque. Cert. fin. planner. Sales mgr. Coast Plants, Vista, Calif., 1974-78; owner, mgr. David Whitson Co., Tempe, Ariz., 1979—; pres. Whitson Ins., Mesa, Ariz., 1980-84, Road Runner R.V. Rentals, Mesa, 1984—, Whitson Fin. Ins. Group, Tempe, 1984—, Whitson Fin., Tempe, 1984—. Chmn. Tri-City Civitan, Tempe, 1984. Served with USMC, 1970-74. Recipient Sales Master Round Table award Mut. Omaha, 1981, Pres. Club award Mut. Omaha, 1981, 82, 83. Republican. Home: PO Box 28275 Tempe AZ 85282 Office: PO Box 28275 Tempe AZ 85282

WHITSON, NANCY LEE MILLER, school administrator; b. Columbia City, Ind., Oct. 7, 1936; d. DeLoss Herbert and Mary Elizabeth (Willits) Miller; BS in Edn., Ind. U., 1958; MS in Edn., Seattle Pacific U., 1974; postgrad. Ind. U., U. Idaho, Central Wash. U., Seattle Pacific U., UCLA, 1959—; m. Leslie B. Whitson, Oct. 7, 1971; stepchildren: Rick, Gregory, Gary; children by previous marriage: Robert, Timothy. Elem. tchr., Calif., Ind., Idaho and Wash., 1958-66, 71-76; dist. reading coordinator, Snoqualmie, Wash., 1968-71; elem. sch. prin., Snohomish, Wash., 1976-78, adminstrv. asst. curriculum and instrn., 1978-81, elem. sch. prin., 1981—; coordinator elem. advanced placement program Snohomish Sch. Dist., 1985—; prin. Cen. Elem. Demonstration Sch., 1985—; nat. reading cons. Economy Co. Ednl. Pubs., 1963-70, 75-76; adj. prof. reading and instrnl. improvement colls. and univs., 1964—; adminstrv. asst. for curriculum and instrn. Snohomish Sch. Dist., 1978-81; cons. reading improvement and cons. programs for improvement of instructional skills of tchrs., supervisory skills of adminstrs., classroom mgmt. skills of tchrs. and learning styles, 1964—; mem. Puget Sound Ednl. consortium, facilitator prins'. leadership acad, mem. task force on equity and excellence in schs. 1986—. Mem. Wash. Assn. Sch. Adminstrs., Nat. Assn. Elem. Sch. Prins., Assn. Wash. Sch. Prins., Snohomish County Prins. Assn., Snohomish Prins. Assn., Assn. Supervision and Curriculum Devel., Wash. Assn. Supervision and Curriculum Devel. (Educator of Yr. 1979), Internat. Reading Assn., Wash. Orgn. Reading Devel., Nat. Staff Devel. Council, Nat. Council Tchrs. of English, Nat. Council Tchrs. of Math. Republican. Mormon. Home: 14202 92d St SE Snohomish WA 98290 Office: Snohomish Sch Dist 221 Union Ave Snohomish WA 98290

WHITT, KATHRYN LOUISE, educator; b. St. Louis, Nov. 17, 1936; d. Alvin Jobst and Mary Kathryn (Holzapple) Ritter; m. James Patrick Whitt, Dec. 3, 1955; children: Tammy Beth, Wesley Gordon II, Jacqueline Lois. AA, Boise Jr. Coll., 1955; LPN, St. Luke's Sch. Nursing, 1955. Pvt. practice acctg. Anchorage and Ft. Yukon, Alaska, 1978-84; teaching asst. Anchorage Sch. Dist., 1984—. Active campign Joe Josephson for Senate, Anchorage, 1982-83. Served to 2d lt. CAP, Alaska, 1978-83. Mem. Totem Assn. Avocations: backpacking, crocheting, raising collies. Office: Anchorage Sch Dist 4600 DeBarr Ave Anchorage AK 99519

WHITTEMORE, OSGOOD JAMES, ceramic engineering educator; b. Clear Lake, Iowa, Jan. 24, 1919; s. Osgood James and Bonnie Laurine (Beaumont) W.; m. Barbara Estelle Greenwood, Oct. 4, 1941; children: Donald, Bonnie, Julie. BS in Ceramic Engring., Iowa State U., 1940, profl. degree in ceramic engring., 1950; MS in Ceramic Engring., U. Wash., 1941. Registered profl. engr., Mass. Fellow Mellon Inst., Pitts., 1941-44; group leader MIT, Manhattan Project, Cambridge, 1944-46; research assoc. Norton Co., Worcester, Mass., 1946-64; prof. titular Universidade Federal de São Carlos, Brazil, 1976; prof. U. Wash., 1964—; cons. various cos., 1965—; dir. Wash. Mining and Mineral Resources Research Inst., 1982-87; mem. bd. editors Ceramics Internat., Faenza, Italy, 1982—. Patentee in field; contbr. articles to profl. jours. Mem. adv. bd. Town of Princeton, Mass., 1961-63; mem. Wachusett Regional Sch. Com., Holden, Mass., 1963-64. Recipient Admiral Earle medal Worcester Engring. Soc., Mass., 1949, Trinks Indsl. Heating award Indsl. Heating mag., Pitts., 1955. Fellow Am. Ceramic Soc. (v.p. 1975-76), Inst. of Ceramics; mem. AIME, Soc. Mining Engrs., Associacaõ Brasileira Ceramica (Azevedo Prize, 1979, 83), Internat. Inst. for Study of Sintering (full). Democrat. Club: Faculty (U. Wash.). Lodge: Elks. Avocations: kayaking, hiking, camping. Home: 10015 Lakeshore Blvd NE Seattle WA 98125 Office: U Wash Mail Stop FB10 Seattle WA 98195

WHITTEN, CHARLES ALEXANDER, JR., educator; b. Harrisburg, Pa., Jan. 20, 1940; s. Charles Alexander and Helen (Shoop) W.; m. Joan Emann, Nov. 20, 1965; 1 son, Charles Alexander. B.S. summa cum laude, Yale U., 1961; Ph.D. in Physics, Princeton U., 1966. Research asso. A.W. Wright Nuclear Structure Lab., Yale U., 1966-68; asst. prof. physics UCLA, 1968-74, assoc. prof., 1974-80, prof., 1980—, vice chmn. physics dept., 1982-86; vis. scientist Centre d'Etudes Nucléaires de Saclay-Moyenne Energie, 1980-81, 86-87. Contbr. articles to profl. jours. Mem. Am. Phys. Soc., Sigma Pi Sigma, Phi Beta Kappa. Home: 9844 Vicar St Los Angeles CA 90034 Office: Dept Physics U Calif 405 Hilgard Ave Los Angeles CA 90024

WHITTEN, ROBERT CRAIG, JR., research scientist; b. Bristol, Va., Dec. 6, 1926; s. Robert Craig and Adeline Anna (Gerke) W.; m. Sally Marie Kriz, Aug. 2, 1953; children: Robert Craig III, Lisa Marie Marchese. BS, U.S. Mcht. Marine Acad., 1947; BA, SUNY, Buffalo, 1955; PhD, Duke U., 1959; MS, San Jose State U., 1971. Research asst. Duke U., Durham, N.C., 1955-59; from physicist to sr. physicist SRI Internat., Menlo Park, Calif., 1959-67; research scientist NASA-Ames Research Ctr., Moffett Field, Calif., 1967—; instr. Stanford (Calif.) U., 1961-62, 64-66, Santa Clara (Calif.) U., 1964, 69, San Jose (Calif.) State U., 1972-73, 79, 84. Editor: Ozone in the Free Atmosphere, 1985, The Stratospheric Aerosol Layer, 1982; author: Fundamentals of Aeronomy, 1971; contbr. articles to profl. jours. Pres. Santa Clara Valley Council Navy League of U.S., 1986. Served to lt. USN, 1949-53. Recipient Group Achievement award NASA, 1980, 81. Mem. AIAA (tech. com. on atmospheric environment 1983-86, sr.), Am. Geophys. Union, U.S. Naval Inst., Air Force Assn. (governing council chpt. 361), St. Andrew's Soc. Republican. Lutheran. Avocations: naval and mil. history, free market econs., sailing, camping. Home: 1117 Yorkshire Dr Cupertino CA 95014 Office: NASA-Ames Research Ctr MS 245-3 Moffett Field CA 94035

WHITTINGTON, MARGARET ANN, business executive; b. Radford, Va., Aug. 3, 1948; d. David Kelsey and Margaret Ann (Kerns) W.; m. Edward Albert Wagner, Jr., Feb. 14, 1977. Student Blackburn Coll., 1967-68. Student employment coordinator Carneige Mellon U., Pitts., 1975-77; admissions asst. Calif. Inst. Arts, Valencia, 1977-80; adminstrv. mgr. G.W. Smith & Assocs., Inc., Valencia, 1980-82; v.p., sec. U.S. Fin. Cons., Inc., Burbank, 1983-85; asst. sec., treas. Chantal Pharm. Corp., Los Angeles, 1985—; dir. Metco Mining Corp., W.Va., 1983-85.

WHITTINGTON, OLIVER RAY, accounting educator; b. Mobile, Ala., June 20, 1948; s. Oliver Ray and Catharine Sage (Terrill) W.; m. Anne Laurel Jensen, Nov. 20, 1972 (div. June 1980). BBA, Sam Houston State U., 1971; MS, Tex. Tech. U., 1972; PhD, U. Houston, 1978. CPA, Tex., Calif. Sr. auditor Peat, Marwick & Mitchell, Houston, 1973-75; instr. U. Houston, 1975-78; prof. San Diego State U., 1978—. Author: Principles of Auditing, 1985, Income Tax Fundamentals, 1986; contbr. articles to profl. jours. Recipient Bronze medal Inst. Mgmt. Accts., 1980. Mem. Am. Inst. CPA's (acad. fellow 1980-81), Am. Acctg. Assn., Inst. Internal Auditors. Republican. Roman Catholic. Avocations: jogging, theatre, travel. Home: 4729 Natalie Dr San Diego CA 92115 Office: San Diego State U Sch Acctg San Diego CA 92182

WHITWORTH, KERNAN BRADLEY, III, corporate communications executive; b. Santa Monica, Calif., Dec. 4, 1953; s. Kernan Bradley Jr. and Carolyn Harkins (McGill) W.; m. Karen Elizabeth Nakano, July 10, 1982; one child, Kernan Bradley IV. BA, BJ, U. Mo., 1975. Advt. dir. OGR Service Corp., Springfield, Ill., 1976-78; mgr. employee communications Horace Mann Ins. Co., Springfield, Ill., 1978-80; mgr. internal communications Hewlett-Packard Inc., Palo Alto, Calif., 1980—. Mem. Internat Assn. Bus. Communicators (bd. dirs. 1984—, Gold Quill award 1985, 86). Home: 1463 Ormsby Dr Sunnyvale CA 94087 Office: Hewlett-Packard Co 3000 Hanover St Palo Alto CA 94304

WHYTE, HELENA MARY, chemistry educator, technical training specialist; b. Albuquerque, Dec. 19, 1948; d. Alexander Peter and Helen (Mriz) M.; m. Kent Neil Whyte, July 6, 1973; children: Stacey Helene, Kurt Neil. BS in Chemistry with honors, N.Mex. Inst. Mining Tech., 1970; MA in Sci. Teaching, U. N.Mex., 1971. Lab. asst. N.Mex. Bur. Mines, Socorro, 1966-70; research asst. Los Alamos (N.Mex.) Sci. Lab., 1970-71; chemistry tchr. Los Alamos High Sch., 1971-79; chemistry instr. U. N.Mex., Los Alamos, 1981-84; staff mem. Los Alamos Nat. Lab., 1979—; appointed to women's com. Los Alamos Nat. Lab., 1986—. Contbr. articles to profl. publs. Mem. Pajarito Art League, Los Alamos. Fellow Am. Inst. Chemists (cert.); mem. AAUW (ednl. founds. chair 1982—), Am. Chem. Soc., Nat. Sci. Tchrs. Assn., Women in Sci., Alpha Delta Kappa (local pres. 1979-80). Democrat. Roman Catholic. Avocations: ceramics, reading, travel. Office: Los Alamos Nat Lab M589 HRD3 Los Alamos NM 87545

WHYTLAW, ELIZABETH ELLEN, speech and language pathologist; b. Oklahoma City, Feb. 27, 1954; s. Edward Louis and Margaret Georgina (Egbert) W. BA in Psychology and Speech Sci., St. Olaf Coll., 1976; MS in Speech Pathology, Phillips U., 1978; postgrad., Idaho State U., 1982—. Speech/language pathologist, site supr. Adult/Child Devel. Ctr., Mountain Home, Idaho, 1978—. Coordinator, head coach Mountain Home Spl. Olympics, 1980-85. Mem. Am. Speech and Hearing Assn. (cert. clin. competence, continuing edn. award 1985), Idaho Speech and Hearing Assn. Republican. Methodist. Avocations: downhill skiing, handcrafts, softball, camping. Home: 512 W 2d N Mountain Home ID 83647 Office: Adult/Child Devel Ctr 809 N 6th E Mountain Home ID 83647

WIATROWSKI, CLAUDE ALLAN, computer executive; b. Chgo., Dec. 27, 1946; s. Alex F. and Emilie N. (Macias) W.; m. Margaret A. Ammeson, Nov. 23, 1967; children: Kevin Douglas, Karen Elaine. BS in Physics, Ill. Inst. Tech., 1968; MSEE, U. Ariz., 1970, PhDEE, 1973. Design engr. Burr Brown Research Corp., Tucson, 1973-75; asst. prof. engring. U. Colo., Colorado Springs, 1975-81; pres. Mountain Automation Corp., Woodland Park, Colo., 1976—; chief scientist Scott Sci. and Tech., Colorado Springs, 1981-84; v.p. Parkcon, Inc., Woodland Park, 1986—. Author: Logic Ckts and Microcomputer, 1980, Cog Wheel Route, 1982, From C To Modula-2 And Back, 1987, Teller County, 1987; VLSI editor Simulation mag., 1986—. Recipient Outstanding Teaching award U. Colo., 1978. Mem. IEEE, Soc. Computer Simulation, Nat. Ry. Hist. Soc. (bd. dirs. 1977-80). Avocations: RRs, music, photography. Home: PO Box 4590 Woodland Park CO 80866-4590 Office: Mountain Automation Corp PO Box 6020 Woodland Park CO 80866-6020

WIBERG, DONALD MARTIN, electrical engineering educator, consultant; b. Battle Creek, Mich., Sept. 20, 1936; s. Martin and Lina (Havstein) W.; m. Barbara Maynard Penney, Oct. 12, 1980; children: Erik M., Kristin A., Kenneth C., Laura J. Penney, John M. Penney. B.S., Calif. Inst. Tech., 1959, M.S., 1960, Ph.D., 1965. Registered profl. engr., Calif. Sr. design engr. Convair, San Diego, 1964-65; asst. prof. system sci. UCLA, 1965-71, assoc. prof., 1971-77, prof., 1977—, prof. anesthesiology, 1979—, vice chmn. dept. elec. engring., 1985—; cons. in field; vis. prof. German Research Orgn. for Air and Space Flight, Munich, 1969-70. Author: State Space and Linear Systems, 1971; co-editor: Regulation of Breathing, 1983. Mem. adv. bd. Parthenia Sch., Los Angeles, 1971-74. Sr. NATO research fellow KFZ Karlsruhe, W.Ger., 1973; sr. Fulbright fellow, Copenhagen, 1976-77, Trondheim, Norway, 1983-84. Mem. IEEE (applications assoc. editor Transactions on Automatic Control 1983), Sigma Xi. Office: UCLA Dept Electrical Engineering 7731 Boelter Hall Los Angeles CA 90024

WICHINSKY, GLENN ELLIS, lawyer; b. Monticello, N.Y., Dec. 22, 1952; s. Michael Wichinsky and Ann (Pesekow) Kaplan; m. Lillian Carol Rindom, June 6, 1976; 1 child, Laura Elyse. BA, U. Miami, Coral Gables, Fla., 1974; JD, U. Pacific, 1982. Bar: Nev., Fla. Exec. asst. Games of Nev., Las Vegas, 1974-78, legal cons., 1983—; legis. asst. Calif. State Legis., Sacramento, 1978-79; legal advisor Small Claims Advisors Clinic, Sacramento, 1980-82; atty. Rogers, Monsey, Woodbury, Philips, Perky & Berggreen, Las Vegas, 1983; sole practice Las Vegas and Reno, 1984—. Del. Dem. Conv., Miami, 1972. Mem. Fla. Bar Assn., State Bar. Nev., ABA (mem. Forum Com. on Air and Space Law 1983—), Interfraternity Council (rep. 1972-74), Tau Epsilon Phi (pres. 1973-74). Jewish. Home: 4180 Reno Ave Las Vegas NV 89120 Office: 2607 S Highland Dr Las Vegas NV 89109

WICHMAN, HERMAN LEE, III, lawyer, financial consultant; b. St. Louis, July 3, 1919; s. Herman Lee and Pearl (Wilson) W.; m. Betty Morse, Oct. 16, 1961 (div. 1982); children by previous marriage—Dwight Lloyd, Susan. B.S. in Bus. Adminstrn., Washington U., St. Louis, 1942, M.B.A., 1943, LL.B., 1942, J.D., 1945. Bar: Mo. 1941. Assoc. Buder & Buder, St. Louis, 1941-42; with McDonnell-Douglas Co., St. Louis, 1942-52, asst. sec., 1946-51, sec., 1951-52, v.p., gen. counsel, 1949-52; corp. fin. cons., Dallas, 1952-56; founder, pres. Wickfield, Inc., Dallas, 1956-59; founder, dir., chmn. bd. Union Fin. Corp. (name now Transohio Co.), Cleve., 1959-62; founder, exec. v.p., chmn. exec. com. Republic Nat. Corp., Cleve., 1962-65; pres. Wichman Assocs., Inc., corp. fin. cons. mergers and acquisitions, San Francisco, Los Angeles and Indian Wells, Calif., 1965—; dir. Platt-LePage Aircraft Corp., Phila., Rotary Research Corp., Phila.; chmn. legal com. Aerospace Industries, Washington. Vice chmn. campaign ARC, St. Louis, 1950, chmn., 1951; chmn. Greater Bay area Washington U. Alumni Council, San Francisco, 1967-68, chmn. fund campaign, 1968; chmn. bd. trustees Calvary Presbyn. Ch., San Francisco. Mem. ABA, Mo. Bar, St. Louis Bar Assn. (chmn. ethics com. 1940-50), Tex. Bar Assn., Dallas Bar Assn., Phi Delta Phi, Sigma Nu. Republican. Clubs: Olympic, Eldorado Country, Casa Dorada. Home: 75-707 Hwy 111 B-14 Indian Wells CA 92210 Office: Wichman Assocs Inc 2035 Westwood Blvd Los Angeles CA 90025

WICK, JAMES PHILIP, product manager; b. Pasadena, Calif., Mar. 20, 1953; s. Robert James and Marilyn Mae (Lubbring) W.; m. Cynthia June Brown, Dec. 19, 1976; children: Kimberly Anne, Trevor James. Bs, Calif. Poly. U., 1976. Chemist Harshaw/Filtrol, Los Angeles, 1977-78, sales coordinator, 1978-80, sales rep., 1980-82, group leader, 1982-83, tech. services mgr., 1983-86, product mgr., 1986—. Mem. Calif. Arboretum Found., Arcadia, 1979—. Mem. Am. Soc. for Testing Materials, Am. Chem. Soc., Soc. Applied Spectrascopy, Optical Soc., Fine Particle Soc. Democrat. Avocations: gardening, theatre, skiing. Home: 1398 Erin Ave Upland CA 91786 Office: Harshaw/Filtrol Ptnrship 5959 W Century Blvd Suite 1414 Los Angeles CA 90045

WICKE, DALLAS CLYDE, aerospace engineer; b. Atwood, Kans., Nov. 18, 1940; s. Ernest William and Edith (Wimer) W. B.S. in Aerospace Engring., U. Kans., 1962; M.S. in Aerospace Engring., U. So. Calif., 1968. Assoc. engr. McDonnell Douglas Corp., Huntington Beach, Calif., 1962-66, engr., 1966-67, engr. specialist, 1967-72, sr. engr., 1972-73, supr., 1973-75, sect. chief, 1975-85, staff mgr., 1985—. Mem. AIAA (adv. bd., sect. tech. com. for guidance, navigation, dynamics and control), U. Kans. Alumni Assn., U.S. Ski Assn. Republican. Contbr. articles to profl. jours. Home: 6877 Danvers Dr Garden Grove CA 92645 Office: McDonnell Douglas Corp 5301 Bolsa Ave Huntington Beach CA 92647

WICKERSHAM, ROBERT ELLIS, lawyer; b. Palo Alto, Calif., Sept. 8, 1917; s. Ellis Burton and Mary Ethel (Perkins) W.; m. Virginia Grace Voorheis, Feb. 14, 1943 (dec. Apr. 1983). B.A., Principia Coll., 1938; J.D., Stanford U., 1942. Bar: Calif., U.S. Dist. Ct. (no. and cen. dists.) Calif., U.S. Ct. Appeals (9th cir.), U.S. Supreme Ct. Assoc. A. Donham Owen, San Francisco, 1946-69; ptnr., v.p. Owen, Wickersham & Erickson, P.C., San Francisco, 1965—. Co-founder, exec. v.p. Albert Baker Meml. Scholarship Fund for Higher Edn., San Francisco, 1964—. Served with U.S. Army, 1942-46, ETO. Mem. ABA, Am. Patent Law Assn., Internat. Patent and Trademark Assn., Bar Assn. San Francisco, San Francisco Patent and Trademark Law Assn. (pres. 1966-67). Republican. Christian Scientist. Clubs: Sierra, Hort., Engrs. Home: 1 Glen Dr Mill Valley CA 94941 Office: Owen Wickersham & Erickson PC 433 California St 11th Fl San Francisco CA 94104

WICKES, DIANA CALISTA, social worker, trainer; b. Pitts., Jan. 2, 1930; d. Calista (Wedemier) Grabow; m. Thomas A. Wickes, Aug. 26, 1950; children: Aeron D., Brian G., Lisa D. BA in Psychology, U. Mont., 1956; MS in Social Adminstrn., Western Res. U., 1973; cert., Calif. State U., Northridge, 1983. Registered indsl. engr. Geographical planning specialist U.S. Census Bur., Los Angeles, 1980; student engr. Hughes Aircraft Co., El Segundo, Calif., 1981-83; quality circle adminstr. Rockwell Internat., El Segundo, 1983-84; dir. tng. Pioneer Magnetics, Santa Monica, Calif., 1984-85; field rep. Rand Corp., Santa Monica, 1986—; tchr. Santa Monica Coll., 1985—. Editor: Magnetic News, 1985. Mem. Nat. Assn. Social Workers (cert.), Am. Soc. Quality Control, Internat. Assn. Quality Circles (v.p. 1984-85), AAUW (local pres. 1985—, recipient Dorothy Mikesell award 1984, Named Gift award 1985), LWV (unit chmn. 1985-86). Democrat. Club: Toastmasters (El Segundo) (pres. 1983-84). Home: 640 Lorna Ln Los Angeles CA 90049

WICKMAN, PAUL EVERETT, public relations executive; b. Bisbee, Ariz., Aug. 21, 1912; s. Julius and Hilda Wilhelmina (Soderholm) W.; m. Evelyn Gorman, Nov. 22, 1969; children by previous marriage: Robert Bruce, Bette Jane, Marilyn Faye. Student, La Sierra Coll., Arlington, Calif., 1928-30, Pacific Union Coll., Angwin, Cal., 1931-32; spl. student, Am. U., 1946. Internat. traveler, lectr., writer 1937-44; assoc sec Internat. Religious Liberty Assn., 1944-46; travel lectr. Nat. Lecture Bur., 1944-55; exec. sec., dir. internat. radio and TV prodns. Voice of Prophecy Corp., Faith for Today Corp., 1946-53; v.p. Western Advt. Agy., Los Angeles, 1953-55; dir. devel.

Nat. Soc. Crippled Children and Adults, Inc., Chgo., 1955-56; exec. dir. Pub. Relations Soc. Am., Inc., N.Y.C., 1956-57; dir. corp. pub. relations Schering Corps., Bloomfield, N.J., 1957-58; pres. Wickman Pharm. Co., Inc., Calif. Mem. Newport Beach CSC; bd. dirs. U. Calif. at Irvine Found.; mem. Orange County Children's Hosp. Fund. Mem. Newcomen Soc., Pub. Relations Soc. Am. (accredited), Am. Soc. Assn. Execs., Am. Pharm. Assn., Calif. Pharm. Assn., Am. Hosp. Assn., Orange County C. of C. (bd. dirs.). Clubs: Swedish (Los Angeles) (past pres.); Newport Beach (Calif.) Country; Vikings, 552 Hoag Hospital. Lodges: Elks, Masons, Shriners, Royal Order Jesters, Kiwanis (Newport Beach past pres.). Home: 28 Point Loma Dr Corona Del Mar CA 92625

WICKS, PATRICK HEATH, chemical engring. consultant; b. Albany, Calif., Mar. 17, 1943; s. Alansen Heath and Lois Mariam (Thompson) W.; m. Patricia Anne Shafer, Apr. 8, 1967; 1 child, Tereia Shannon. BSChemE, U. Idaho, 1966. Registered profl. engr., Oreg. Engr. Shell Oil Co., Wilmington (Calif.), N.Y.C. and Houston, 1965-72; sect. supr. Dept. Environ. Quality, Portland, Oreg., 1972-76; mgr., pres. Chem-Security Systems, Bellevue, Wash., 1976-82; dir. Chem-Nuclear Systems, Bellevue, 1982-83; prin. Hazardous Waste Cons., Redmond, Wash., 1983-86; pres. ERM-Northwest, Redmond, 1986—. Author: Hazardous Waste Management Planning; contbr. articles to profl. jours. Mem. Hazardous Waste Task Force, Olympia, Wash., 1983—, Ad Hoc Com. Hazardous Wash., State of Wash., 1977-78; speaker numerous community and indsl. groups hazardous waste, 1973—. Mem. Am. Inst. Chem. Engring., Am. Chem. Soc., NSPE, Wash. Soc. Profl. Engrs., Redmond C. of C. (chmn. environ. com. 1984), Alpha Tau Omega, Sigma Tau, Phi Kappa Phi. Republican. Club: Bellevue Athletic. Avocations: fishing, jogging, golf. Home: 19708 182d Ave NE Woodinville WA 98072

WIDDER, BETTE WIENBERG, nursing adminstr.; b. Lafayette County, Mo., June 20, 1929; d. Elmer Arthur and Lorene Mathilda (Bodenstab) Wienberg; m. John Arthur Widder, July 7, 1953; children—John A., Anne Whiteley, Susan Jane, Scott Kevin. BA cum laude, Linfield Coll., 1976. R.N., Oreg., N.Y. Acting supr. U. Mo. Hosps., 1951-52; mem. staff Arlington (Va.) Community Hosp., 1960-61, W. Jefferson Gen. Hosp., Marrero, La., 1965, dispensary 8th Naval Dist., 1965; mem. rehab. staff A. Holly Patterson Home, Uniondale, N.Y., 1969-70; mem. staff St. Vincent Hosp. and Med. Ctr., Portland, Oreg., 1972-78, asst. dir. nursing services, 1978—. Founder, editor St. Vincent Nursing Newsletter. Contbr. articles to profl. jours. Mem. Oreg. Women's Polit. Caucus; leader Girl Scouts U.S.A., Virginia Beach, Va., 1963-64. Mem. AAUW, SEE Internat., Am. Hosp. Assn., Oreg. Hosp. Assn., Am. Soc. Nurse Adminstrs., Washington County Pub. Affairs Forum, Oreg. Soc. Nurse Adminstrs. (legis. com.). Home: 15095 NW Oakmont Loop Beaverton OR 97006 Office: St Vincent Hosp & Med Ctr 9205 SW Barnes Rd Portland OR 97225

WIDDER, JOHN ARTHUR, electrical engineer; b. Bethesda, Md., June 14, 1954; s. John Arthur and Bette June (Wienberg) W. A.A.S., Portland Community Coll., (Oreg.), 1974; B.S.E.E., U. Portland, 1977. Prodn. engr. Hewlett-Packard Co., Boise, 1978-79, design engr., Vancouver, Wash., 1979—. Mem. World Affairs Council of Oreg.; del., Wash. State Dem. Conv., Tacoma, 1984. Mem. IEEE, AAAS, Delta Epsilon Sigma. Club: City of Portland. Home: 15611 NE 189th Ave Brush Prairie WA 98606 Office: Hewlett Packard Co PO Box C 006 Vancouver WA 98668

WIDENER, DON, writer, film producer; b. Holdenville, Okla., Mar. 13, 1930; s. Carl James and Lucile Victoria (Cole) W.; A.A. in Journalism, Compton (Calif.) Coll., 1950; m. Veda Rose Pannell, June 13, 1953; children—Jeffrey, Christopher. Newspaper reporter, editor Herald Pub. Co., Los Angeles, 1954-58; aerospace writer various cos., 1958-64; press relations ofcl., producer, writer NBC-TV, 1964-70; ind. film producer, writer, Calif., 1970—; lectr. in field. Active environ. groups. Founding mem. adv. bd. Calif. Mus. Sci. and Industry. Served with USAF, 1950-53. Recipient Hugo award Chgo. Film Festival, 1967, A.I. duPont-Columbia U. Broadcast Journalism award, 1969, Silver award N.Y. Film Festival, 1969, Broadcast Media award San Francisco State Coll., 1970, Emmy awards Acad. TV Arts and Scis. (3). Methodist. Author: Timetable for Disaster, 1970; N.U.K.E.E., 1974; Lemmon (biography of Jack Lemmon), 1975; (screenplays) Night of the 'Possum, 1978, N.U.K.E.E., 1982, Perks, 1983, The Ballad of Bigfoot, 1984, The Search for Sunny Skies, 1985, Scuttle, 1985. Patentee nuclear warning system. Address: PO Box 247 Lake Arrowhead CA 92352

WIDENER, MICHAEL NEWTON, lawyer; b. Mt. Ranier, Md., June 10, 1950; s. Newton F. and Mary A. (Edwards) W.; m. Peggy Ann Tucker, May 20, 1978; children: Kathryn Emily, Alison Danielle, Victoria Paige. BA, U. Va., 1972; MS, U. Ill., 1974; JD, U. Ariz., 1982. Bar: Ariz. 1983, Tenn. 1983, U.S. Dist. Ct. Ariz., 1983, U.S. Ct. Appeals (9th cir.), 1983, U.S. Supreme Ct., 1986. Law clk. to justice Ariz. Supreme Ct., Phoenix, 1982-83; assoc. Beus, Gilbert, Wake & Morrill, Phoenix, 1983-86, Lowe & Berman, P.A., Phoenix, 1986—. Contbr. articles to Ariz. Law Review (Strouss Law Review prize, 1981). Mem. ABA, Tenn. Bar Assn., Maricopa County Bar Assn., State Bar Ariz., Ariz. Community Service Legal Asst. Found. (dir.). Republican. Presbyterian. Home: 6040 N 16th Dr Phoenix AZ 85015 Office: Lowe & Berman PA 3300 N Central Ave Phoenix AZ 85012

WIDMAN, LARRY ALLEN, physician, hospital administrator; b. Rosalia, Wash., Sept. 11, 1947; s. George Leonard and Erma Jean (O'Keefe) W.; m. Andrea Joyce Nelson, Sept. 14, 1968; children: Natalie, Laticia. BS in Zoology, Wash. State U., 1969; MD, U. Wash., 1973; MPH, U. Calif., Berkeley, 1977. Cert. Am. Bd. Preventive Medicine. Commd. ensign USN, 1972, advanced through grades to comdr., 1980; sr. med. officer USS Ranger USN, Western Pacific, 1977-80; chief aviation medicine Whidbey Naval Hosp. USN, Oak Harbor, Wash., 1980-83; sr. med. officer br. clinic Naval Air Sta. USN, Moffett Field, Calif., 1983-85; resigned USN, 1986; dir. Santa Clara (Calif.) Med. Ctr., 1986—. Contbr. articles to profl. jours. instr. advanced cardiac life support Am. Heart Assn. Fellow Am. Coll. Preventive Medicine; mem. AMA (rep. hosp. med. staff sect.), Aerospace Med. Assn., Am. Pub. Health Assn., Western Occupational Medicine Assn., Am. Occupational Medicine Assn. Methodist. Avocations: aerobic exercise, distance running, classical music. Office: Santa Clara Med Ctr 2794 El Camino Real Santa Clara CA 95051

WIEBE, LEONARD IRVING, radiopharmacist, educator; b. Swift Current, Sask., Can., Oct. 14, 1941; s. Cornelius C. and Margaret (Teichroeb) W.; m. Grace E. McIntyre, Sept. 5, 1964; children—Glenis, Kirsten, Megan. BSP, U. Sask., 1963, MS, 1966; PhD, U. Sydney, Australia, 1970. Pharmacist Swift Current Union Hosp., 1963-64; sessional lectr. U. Sask., Can., 1965-66; asst. prof. U. Alta., Can., 1970-73, assoc. prof., 1973-78, prof., 1978—, dir. Slowpoke Reactor Facility, 1975—, asst. dean research, 1984—; sessional lectr. U. Sydney, Australia, 1973; sec. Internat. Bionucleonics Cons. Lts., 1975—; research assoc. Cross Cancer Inst., Edmonton, Can., 1978—, Med. Research Council of Can.; vis. prof. Royal P.A. Hosp., Sydney, 1983-84, Toronto, 1987—; radiopharmacy cons. Autralian Atomic Energy Commn., Sydney, 1983-84. Editor: Liquid Scintillation: Science and Technology, 1976; Advances in Scintillation Counting, 1983. Guest editor Jour. of Radioanalytical Chemistry, 1981. Commonwealth Univs. Exchange grantee, 1966; Alexander von Humboldt fellow, 1976-79, 82. Mem. Pharm. Bd. of New South Wales, Sask. Pharm. Assn., Soc. Nuclear Medicine, Assn. Faculties of Pharmacy of Can., Can. Radiation Protection Assn., Can. Assn. Radiopharm. Scientists, Am. Pharm. Assn., Am. Assn. Pharm. Sci. Mem. Mennonite Ch. Club: University (Edmonton) (pres. 1985-86). Home: 11739 38A Ave, Edmonton, AB Canada T6J 0L8 Office: U Alberta, Edmonton, AB Canada T6G 2N8

WIEBE, MICHAEL EUGENE, microbiologist, cell biologist; b. Newton, Kans., Oct. 1, 1942; s. Austin Roy and Ruth Fern (Stucky) W.; m. Rebecca Ann Doak, June 12, 1965. BS, Sterling Coll., 1965; PhD, U. Kansas, 1971. Research assoc. Duke U. Med. Ctr., Durham, N.C., 1971-73; asst. prof. Cornell U. Med. Coll., N.Y.C., 1973-81, assoc. prof., 1981-85; assoc. dir. research and devel. N.Y. Blood Ctr., N.Y.C., 1980-83, dir. Leukocyte products, 1983-84; sr. scientist Genentech Inc., South San Francisco, Calif., 1984—. Contbr. articles to profl. jours. Postdoctoral fellow NIH, 1971-73. Mem. AAAS, Am. Soc. for Microbiology, Am. Soc. Virology, Am. Soc. Tropical Medicine and Hygiene, Soc. of Exptl. Biology and Medicine, Tissue Culture Assn., N.Y Acad. Sci. Presbyterian. Avocations: travel, photography, racquetball. Home: 44 Woodhill Dr Redwood City CA 94061 Office: Genentech Inc 460 Point San Bruno Blvd South San Francisco CA 94080

WIEDERHOLD, CHARLES WALLACE, education educator; b. Sacramento, Feb. 5, 1936; s. Wallace William and Emily Angelis (Eby) W.; divorced; children: Ann Kristin Carmack, Brian Dow. BA in Edn., Calif. State U., Sacramento, 1958, MA in Edn. Administrn., 1967, MA in Environ. Sic. Tchr. Rio Linda (Calif.) Sch. Dist., 1958-65, prin., 1965-66; dir. Area III Sci. Project, Auburn, Calif., 1967-71; cons. Placer County Office Edn., Auburn, 1971—; cons. Calif. State Dept. Edn., Sacramento; keynote speaker Calif. County Supts. Assn., Sci. Confs., Gibson Mgmt., N.Y. and Chgo. Author: (tv series) Time to Investigate, 1971, (text series) Man, Ecology and Change, 1973, (guidebook) Planning Science, Kindergarten-Eighth Grade, 1985. Pres. Rio Linda Edn. Assn., 1965, Placer County Edn. Assn., 1969; founder Ecology Info. Ctr., Sacramento, 1972. Recipient Commendation, State of Calif. Gov's. Office, 1981. Mem. AAAS, Assn. Calif. Sch. Adminstrs., Phi Delta Kappa. Democrat. Methodist. Lodge: Masons. Avocations: music, photography, artist. Home: 201 Chad Circle Applegate CA 95703 Office: Placer County Office Edn 360 Nevada St Auburn CA 95603

WIEDERHOLT, WIGBERT C., neurologist, educator; b. Germany, Apr. 22, 1931; came to U.S., 1956, naturalized, 1966; m. Carl and Anna-Maria (Hoffmann) W.; student (Med. Sch. scholar), U. Berlin, 1952-53; M.D., U. Freiburg, 1955; M.S., U. Minn., 1965; children—Sven, Karen, Kristin. Intern in Ob-Gyn, Schleswig (W. Ger.) City Hosp., 1955-56; rotating intern Sacred Heart Hosp., Spokane, Wash., 1956-57; resident in medicine Cleve. Clinic, 1957-58, 61-62, U.S. Army Hosp., Frankfurt, W. Ger., 1958-59; resident in neurology Mayo Clinic, Rochester, Minn., 1962-65; assoc. prof. medicine, dir. clin. neurophysiology Ohio State U. Med. Sch., Columbus, 1965-72; prof. neuroscis. U. Calif. Med. Sch., San Diego, 1972—, neurologist-in-chief, 1972-83, chmn. dept. and group in neuroscis. 1978-83; chief neurology VA Hosp., San Diego, 1972-79. Fulbright scholar, 1956-58. Diplomate Am. Bd. Psychiatry and Neurology. Fellow Am. Acad. Neurology (S. Weir Mitchell award 1965); mem. Internat. Brain Research Orgn., Am. Assn. EEG and Electrodiagnosis (sec.-treas. 1971-76, pres. 1977-78), AAAS, Soc. for Neurosci., Am. Neurol. Assn., Am. EGG Soc., Western EEG Soc., Calif. Neurol. Soc., San Diego Neurol. Soc., N.Y. Acad. Scis., AMA, Calif. Med. Assn., San Diego County Med. Soc. Club: La Jolla Tennis. Contbr. numerous articles to med. jours. Home: 6683 La Jolla Scenic Dr La Jolla CA 92037 Office: Dept Neuroscis M-024 Univ Calif at San Diego La Jolla CA 92093

WIEDERSPAHN, ALVIN LEE, senator, lawyer; b. Cheyenne, Wyo., Jan. 18, 1949; s. John Arling and Edvina (Fahrenbruch) W.; m. Cynthia Marie Lummis, May 30, 1983; 1 child, Annaliese. BS, U. Wyo., 1971; JD, U. Denver, 1976. Bar: Wyo. 1978, U.S. Dist. Ct. Wyo. 1978, U.S. Ct. Appeals (10th cir.) 1985. Assoc. Guy, Williams & White, Cheyenne, 1977-79, Kline & Swainson, Cheyenne, 1979-81, Holland & Hart, Cheyenne, 1981-85; sole practice Cheyenne, 1985—; senator State of Wyo., Cheyenne, 1985—. Rep. Wyo. Legis., Cheyenne, 1978-84; chmn. Devel. Disabilities Protection and Advocacy System, Cheyenne, 1978-83, Downtown Devel. Authority, Cheyenne, 1984—, Southeast Wyo. Mental Health Ctrs., Cheyenne, 1982-85, Gov.'s Task Force on Chronically Mentally Ill., Cheyenne, 1984—, Wyo. Energy Conservation Office, Cheyenne, 1980-83; pres. Assn. for Retarded Citizens, Cheyenne, 1979-81; bd. dirs. Symphoney and Choral Soc., Cheyenne, 1984-86, Rocky Mountain Fed. Savs. and Loan Assn., Wyoming Taxpayers Assn. Named Outstanding Vol., Youth Alternatives, 1982, one of Outstanding Young Men of Am., 1980, 81, 83; recipient Disting. Service award Rocky Mountain Conf. Community Mental Health Ctrs., Outstanding Service award Assn. for Retarded Citizens, 1986. Mem. ABA (pub. utility sect.), Wyo. State Bar. Democrat. Congregationalist. Club: Cheyenne Athletic. Avocations: Western art, tennis, skiing, lapidary. Home: 3905 Bent Ave Cheyenne WY 82001 Office: 2020 Carey Ave Cheyenne WY 82001

WIEDEWITSCH, LEWIS GRANT, safety administrator; b. Hillsboro, Oreg., Oct. 8, 1947; s. Lloyd Lewis and Viola Evelyn (Schlee) W.; m. Lonamae Tamee Baker, Jan. 23, 1982. BA in Chemistry, Linfield Coll., 1971. Chief chemist and safety dir. N.L. Industries, Portland, Oreg., 1971-72; lab. tech. Pennwalt Corp., Portland, 1972-75, plant chemist, 1975-81, safety supr., 1981—. Served with USAR, 1967—. Mem. Am. Chem. Soc., Am. Soc. Safety Engrs. Republican. Club: Grange. Lodges: Oddfellows, Shriners. Home: 19220 NE Williamson Rd Newberg OR 97132 Office: PO Box 4102 Portland OR 97208

WIEDMANN, TIEN-WEN TAO, medical scientist; b. Shanghai, China, Jan. 12, 1938; came to U.S., 1955; d. Pai-chuan and Su-chuin (Chang) T.; m. Walter Wiedmann, June 20, 1966; children: Christian, Ulrich. Student, Nat. Taiwan U., Republic of China, 1953-55; BS, U. Okla., 1957; MS, Harvard U., 1958, PhD, 1963. Research assoc. Harvard U., Boston, 1965-69; scientist Basel (Switzerland) Inst. for Immunology, 1970-74, Bioctr., Basel, 1975-80; sr. research assoc. Stanford (Calif.) U., 1980-84, assoc. prof. biology, 1984—; vis. assoc. prof. Nat. Taiwan U., 1969. Contbr. articles to profl. jours. Home: 50 Peter Cts Stanford CA 94305 Office: Stanford U Med Ctr Dept Nuclear Medicine Stanford CA 94305

WIEDOW, CARL PAUL, electromech. and geophys. instruments company executive; b. Pasadena, Calif., Dec. 3, 1907; s. Carl and Clara Minna (Matthes) W.; m. Mary Maletia Foulks, 1935 (div. Jan. 1946); m. Mary Louise Montesano, Nov. 27, 1947. A.B. in Math., Occidental Coll., 1933; M.S. in Physics, Calif. Inst. Tech., 1945, M.S. in Elec. Engring., 1946; Ph.D. in Elec. Engring., Oreg. State U., 1956. Registered profl. engr., Calif. Assoc. prof. electronics U.S. Naval Postgrad. Sch., Monterey, Calif., 1956-59; design specialist Gen. Dynamics Astronautics, San Diego, 1955-61, Ryan Aerospace div., San Diego, 1961-62; prof., head dept. physics Calif. Western U., San Diego, 1962-66; staff engr. Marine Advisors, La Jolla, Calif., 1966-67; chief of research Humphrey Inc., San Diego, 1967—; cons. engr. Elgin Nat. Watch Co., West Coast Micronics div., 1959-60, Gen. Dynamics Astronautics, San Diego, 1963-64, Havens Industries, San Diego, 1962-64, Solar, San Diego, 1964-66, Anka Industries, Chula Vista, Calif., 1979—. Counselor, judge Sci. Fair, San Diego, 1962—; acad. asst. NSF, 1966-68. Mem. Optical Soc. San Diego, AAUP, Sigma Xi, Sigma Tau, Sigma Pi Sigma, Pi Mu Epsilon. Clubs: Soc. Wireless Pioneers, Quarter Century Wireless Assn., Old Time Communicators.

WIEGAND, JAMES HERMAN, mechanical engineering educator; b. Traverse City, Mich., Sept. 11, 1915; s. Herman Leopold and Minnie Marie (Dunn) W.; m. Florence Amelia Wransky, Aug. 12, 1944; 1 child, Elissa Marie. BS, U. Mich., 1937, MS, 1939, PhD, 1941. Chem. engr. E.I. du Pont de NeMours Co., Wilmington, Del., 1941-42; mgr. propellant devel. Naval Ordnance Test Sta., China Lake, Calif., 1946-53; chmn. chemistry and chem. engring. dept. S.W. Research Inst., San Antonio, 1953-56; dept. head propellant evaluation Aerojet-Gen. Corp., Sacramento, 1956-70; dept. head solid propellants research and devel. Naval Ordnance Sta., Indianhead, Md., 1970-77; adj. prof. mech. engring. San Diego State U., 1978—; mem. joint U.S. Army/USN/NASA/USAF com. structures and mech. behavior solid propellants, 1960—. Contbr. articles to profl. jours. Served to capt. U.S. Army, 1942-46. E.I. du Pont de Nemours Co. fellow, 1940. Mem. Sigma Xi. Republican. Unitarian. Avocations: photography, woodworking, gardening, music. Home and Office: 5181 College Gardens Ct San Diego CA 92115

WIEGAND, SIEDFRIED, food service, culinary educator; b. Dortmund, Fed. Republic Germany, July 2, 1932; came to U.S., 1954; s. August Ferdinand and Maria (Kölling) W.; m. Elke Schmidt, Aug. 6, 1966; children: Andreas Michael, Siegfried Georg. M in Food Service, Dortmund State Culinary Inst., 1955; BE, U. Hawaii, 1972, MEd, 1974. Chief instr. food service and hospitality edn. Kapiolani Community Coll., Honolulu, 1963—; TIM instr., 1975; instr. Sear's Famous Chef Cooking Courses, 1970-72; chef de partie Ambassador Hotel, coconut Grove, Calif.; chef Hillcrest Country Club, Calif., Valley Club, Montecedo, Calif.; host internat. restaurants Honolulu Exec. chef, 1962-63; vis. prof. Culinary Leader Seminar, Palau, Caroline Islands, 1978; food cons. L.J. Minor Corp., Cleve., 1979-85; mem. adv. com. Nat. Vocat. Ednl. Leadership program, U. Hawaii, 1976-79; mem. exec. faculty com. Kapiolani Community Coll., 1980-83, faculty com., 1983—. Narrator Continental Cuisine program Sta. KNDI, 1964-68, TV program Past Time, 1968-78. Recipient Bronze Medal Culinary Excellence award German Chancellor, 1955, Gold Medal Culinary Competition of Pacific, 1982; E.P.D.A. fellow U. Hawaii, 1972. Mem. Am. Culinary Fedn., Chefs de Cuisine Assn. of Hawaii (pres. 1980—, treas. 1968-79, 81—, Chef of Yr. 1979). Home: 944 Kaluanui Rd Honolulu HI 96825 Office: U Hawaii Kapiolani Community Coll Dept Food Service 620 Pensacola St Honolulu HI 96814

WIEGAND, VIRGINIA ANN KEISTER, computer company executive; b. Buffalo, July 21, 1928; d. Forest Glen and Bess Katherine (Baughman) Keister; m. William Charles Wiegand Jr., Feb. 20, 1947; children: William, Cort, Ronn, James, Carley, Scott, Wenden. BA, U. Calif., Berkeley, 1962, MA, 1966, PhD, 1969. Assoc. dir. Jack and Jill Nursery Sch., Walnut Creek, Calif., 1960-62; tchr. Lafayette (Calif.) Sch. Dist., 1963-64; research asst. Lafayette (Calif.) Sch. Dist., Berkeley, 1964-69; teaching asst. U. Calif., Berkeley, 1965-69; asst. prof. ednl. psychology Calif. State U., Hayward, 1969-71; research psychologist Stanford Research Inst., Menlo Park, Calif., 1971-75; pvt. practice cons. psychology Walnut Creek, 1977—; pres. Wiegand System Design, Walnut Creek, 1977; instr. computer sci. Diablo Valley Coll., Pleasant Hill, Calif., 1980. Author: Social Inquiry: An Overview, 1979; contbr. articles to profl. jours. Mem. Am. Psychol. Assn., Western Psychol. Assn., Am. Ednl. Research Assn., AAAS, Assn. Computing Machinery. Democrat. Club: Commonwealth. Home: 31 Ellery Ct Walnut Creek CA 94595

WIEMAN, LESLIE ANN, CAD software executive; b. Santa Ana, Calif., June 30, 1945; d. Robert Eisley and Lois Helen Bowyer; m. Howard Henry Wieman, June 19, 1965; children: Benjamin, Seth. BA, U. Wash., 1968, MA, 1970, PhD, 1974. V.p. Digital Microsystems, Oakland, Calif., 1977-82; pres., chief exec. officer Dasoft Design Systems, Berkeley, Calif., 1982—. Mem. Phi Beta Kappa, Phi Kappa Phi. Avocations: volleyball, bowling, silversmithing. Home: 862 Hillside Albany CA 94706 Office: Dasoft Design Systems Inc 1827B 5th St Berkeley CA 94710

WIEMAN, TERRY LYNN, lawyer; b. Montrose, Colo., Oct. 9, 1951; s. Simon William and Martha Elizabeth W.; BS cum laude, Wichita State U., 1974; JD, Washburn U., 1981. Bar: Colo. 1982, U.S. Dist. Ct. Colo. 1982. Propr., Smith & Co. Realty, Inc., Wichita, Kans., 1974-75; job supr. Thousand Oaks Enterprises, Inc., Ltd., Wichita, 1975-79; jr. ptnr. Colo. Law Ctrs. of Falcone and Alexander, Colorado Springs, 1981—; ptnr. Alexander & Wieman; real estate investor. Mem. ABA, Colo. Bar Assn., El Paso County Bar Assn., Delta Theta Phi, Phi Delta Theta. Republican. Methodist.

WIEMER, ROBERT DALE, agricultural research executive; b. Creston, Nebr., Aug. 31, 1931; s. August and Almuth Fredericka (Bruhn) W.; m. Barbara Lou Schicks, Sept. 16, 1961; children: Debra Carol, Scott Dale, Bruce Alan. BS, U. Nebr., 1958; MS, U. Hawaii, 1963. Agrl. trainee Experiment Station, Hawaiian Sugar Planters Assn., Honolulu, 1958-60, asst. weed scientist, 1960-62, asst. mgr. substation, 1962-64, mgr. substation, 1964—, asst. to pres., 1986—; pres. Hawaiian Sugar Technologists, 1983; cons. Hawaiian Sugar Planters Assn., Saipan and Bangladesh, 1982, 84, 85. Bd. dirs. St. Louis Heights Community Assn., Honolulu, 1967-76, pres., 1977-78, 80, treas., 1981-86. Served to cpl. U.S. Army, 1952-54. Mem. Hawaii Acad. Sci., Soil Conservation Soc. Am., Hawaii Assn Conservation Dist. (v.p. 1969-72, pres. 1972-76), Sigma Xi. Republican. Congregationalist. Avocations: gardening, photography. Home: 1504 Kalaepohaku Pl Honolulu HI 96816 Office: Hawaiian Sugar Planters Assn 99-193 Aiea Heights Dr Aiea HI 96701

WIENER, JON, history educator; b. St. Paul, May 16, 1944; s. Daniel N. and Gladys (Aronsohn) Spratt. B.A., Princeton U., 1966; Ph.D., Harvard U., 1971. Vis. prof. U. Calif.-Santa Cruz, 1973; acting asst. prof. UCLA, 1973-74; asst. prof. history U. Calif.-Irvine, 1974-83, prof., 1984—; plaintiff Freedom of Info. Lawsuit against FBI for John Lennon Files, 1983-86. Author: Social Origins of the New South, 1979; Come Together: John Lennon in his Time, 1984. Contbr. articles to profl. jours. including The Nation, The New republic and new York Times Book Review. Rockefeller Found. fellow, 1979; Am. Council Learned Socs.-Ford Found. fellow, 1985. Mem. Am. Hist. Assn., Nat. Book Critics Circle, Orgn. Am. Historians, Nat. Writers' Union, The Authors' Guild, So. Hist. Assn. Office: Dept History U Calif Irvine CA 92717

WIENER, STUART ALAN, medical school business executive, accountant; b. N.Y.C., Oct. 18, 1948; s. Joseph Wiener and Pearl (Schachter) Altner; m. Wendi Kraslow, June 20, 1971; 1 dau., Jennifer Lyn. B.A., Queens Coll., 1970. Cert. N.Y. Inst. Fin. Sr. acct., office mgr. New Court Securities Corp., N.Y.C., 1970-74; chief acct. Am. Orgn. for Rehab. through Tng. Fedn., N.Y.C., 1974-78; asst. controller City of Hope, Los Angeles, 1978-82; asst. treas. Claremont Colls. (Calif.), 1981-82; v.p. Coll. Osteopathic Medicine of the Pacific, Pomona, Calif., 1982-86, v.p. fin. and bus., 1986—. Bd. dirs. Vis. Nurse Service. Served with Army N.G., 1964-70. Recipient Torch of Hope award, City of Hope, 1981. Mem. Nat. Assn. Accts., Am. Mgmt. Assn., Am. Assn. Higher Edn., Med. Group Mgmt. Assn., Am. Assn. Coll. Fiscal Officers (sec.), Vis. Nurse Assn. (bd. dirs.). Republican. Jewish. Lodge: Kiwanis. Home: 5110 Webb Pl Yorba Linda CA 92686 Office: Coll Osteopathic Medicine Pacific College Plaza Pomona CA 91766

WIENER, SYDNEY PAUL, mortgage broker; b. N.Y.C., Aug. 18, 1918; s. Nathan and Lillian (Fortunoff) W.; m. Charlotte Rosen, Jan. 28, 1945; children: Laura Jane Mills, Barbara Hanawalt. DMD, U. Louisville, 1943. Gen. practice dentistry Flushing, N.Y., 1947-68; pvt. investor El Cajon, Calif., 1968—; mortgage sales rep. El Cajon, 1972—; dentist Booth Meml. Hosp., Flushing, 1963-68; researcher Anti-Coronary Club N.Y.C. Dept. Health, 1962-67. Contbr. articles on coronary disease, remedial edn. to profl. jours. Bd. dirs. Calif. Community and Jr. Colls., Calif. Community Coll. Trustees, Sacramento, 1975—; trustee Grossmont-Cuyamaca Community Coll. Dist., El Cajon, 1973—; dep. sheriff San Diego Sheriff Aerosquadron, 1971-82; pres. El Cajon San Diego County civic Ctr. Authority, 1973-77. Served to capt. U.S. Army, 1941-47. Recipient Commendation, Sheriff Maricopa County, Phoenix, 1981, Commendation, Sheriff San Diego County, 1981; award, City El Cajon, 1973-74, award Associated Students Grossmont Coll., El Cajon, 1975, Grossmont Coll. Learning Skills award, 1983, Calif. Community Coll. Trustees award, 1987. Democrat. Jewish. Avocations: pvt. pilot, collecting Edison phonographs.

WIERER, OTTO, lawyer, lecturer, translator, university librarian; b. Prague, Czechoslovakia, Jan. 8, 1912; came to U.S., 1956; s. Alois and Emilie (Prokop) W.; m. Maria-Magdalena Rohrer, May 17, 1958. JD, Charles U. Faculty Law, Prague, 1938; diploma in polit. sci., Free Sch. Polit. Sci., Prague, 1938; postgrad., Maximilian U., Munich, 1945-46; MLS, Columbia U., 1958, postgrad., 1958-60. Sec. Cen. European Press, Prague, 1933-37; asst. Czech Charles U. Faculty Law, 1937-39; editor, head translating dept. Melantrich Publ. House, Prague, 1937-41; legal advisor, prosecutor U.S. High Commn. Cts. for Germany, Munich, 1946-51; external researcher RFE, Munich, 1951-54; export-import RMT, Rio de Janeiro, 1955; legal collaborator, translator Munich br. Internat. Commn. Jurists, 1956; cataloguer EIS N.Y. Pub. Library, 1956-60; asst. head lang. div. Queens Borough Pub. Library, 1960-65; cataloguer Gibb Coll., Harvard U., 1965-66; head Internat. Info. Ctr. SUNY, Oyster Bay, 1966-68; univ. librarian, lectr. U.S. Internat. U., San Diego, 1968-76; lectr., librarian San Diego Community Coll., 1976-77; vis. prof. LATF, 1977-79; mem. faculty La Jolla (Calif.) U., 1978-79; instr. U. Humanistic Studies, San Diego, 1982-83; long-term care ombudsman Calif. Dept. Aging, 1982—. Mem. Spl. Libraries Assn., Am. Oriental Soc., Am. Soc. Info. Sci., Assn. Holistic Health (founding). Home: 1815 Magdalene Way San Diego CA 92110

WIERZBA, HEIDEMARIE B., infosystems specialist; b. Heinrichswalde, Fed. Republic of Germany, Sept. 26, 1944; came to U.S., 1967; s. Heinz Hugo and Kaethe Liselotte (Trutnau) Krink; m. Leonard Bernard Wierzba, May 14, 1969 (div. 1980). Buchhandel, Dt. Buchh. Schule, Kiel, Republic of Germany, 1965; profl. cert., Coll. of Further Edn., Oxford, Eng., 1966; BA, Calif. State U., Fullerton, 1979. Library asst. Allergan, Inc., Irvine, Calif., 1975-76; info. analyst Allergan Pharms., Irvine, Calif., 1976-79, library supr., 1979-81, mgr. corp. info. ctr., 1982—; cons. in field, Tustin, Calif., 1975-77; translator Unitran, Mission Viejo, Calif., 1980—. Editor sci. articles. Bd.

dirs. Nat. Woman's Polit. Caucus, Irvine, 1984-85. Mem. Indsl. Tech. Info. Mgmt. Group (steering com. mem. 1984—, acting pres. 1986) Cooperative Library Agy. for Systems and Services (com. mem.), Am. Soc. Info. Sci., Spl. Library Assn., Med. Libraries of O.C. (pres. 1978), Pharm. Mfg. Assn. (com. mem. 1985—). Democrat. Avocations: dramatic arts, horseback riding, tennis. Home: 23306 Copante Mission Viejo CA 92692 Office: Allergan Inc 2525 Dupont Dr Irvine CA 92715

WIESE, WILLIAM HASTINGS, medicine educator; b. Boston, Nov. 5, 1938; s. Robert George and Esther (Wurst) W.; m. Janislee Arvanites, Jan. 18, 1964; children: Michael, Andrew, Brian. BA, Yale U., 1960; MD, Harvard U., 1964, M in Pub. Health, 1971. Diplomate Am. Bd. Internal Medicine. Resident in medicine Boston City Hosp., 1964-66, 68-69; research assoc. NIH, Bethesda, Md., 1966-68; mem. faculty U. N.Mex., Albuquerque, 1971—; mem. test com. Nat. Bd. Med. Examiners, Phila., 1984—; pres. HealthNet N.Mex., 1985—. Mem. U.S. Preventive Services Task Force, Washington, 1984—. Served with USPHS, 1966-68. Mem. Am. Pub. Health Assn., Assn. Tchrs. Preventive Medicine (bd. dirs. 1978-81, steering com. 1985—), Soc. Tchrs. of Family Medicine, N.Mex. Med. Soc., Greater Albuquerque Med. Assn., Alpha Omega Alpha. Office: U NMex Sch Medicine 2400 Tucker Ave Albuquerque NM 87131

WIESELMANN, PAUL ALBERT, aircraft company executive; b. Denver, May 27, 1939; s. Egon W.G. and Florence E. (Riede) W. BSME, Colo. State U., 1961; MSME, Rensselaer Poly. Inst., 1963; PhDME, MIT, 1969. Program mgr. Kaman Scis. Corp., Colorado Springs, 1970-84; chief engr. Lockheed Calif. Co, Burbank, 1984—; advisor Am. Security Council, Boston, Va., 1982—. Contbr. articles on air combat and air superiority to publs. Mem. Mus. Neon Art, Los Angeles, 1984—. Mem. Nat. Mgmt. Assn., Am. Def. Preparedness Assn., Am. Craft Council, Sigma Xi. Club: U.S. Senatorial Com. (Washington).

WIESENDANGER, HANS U.D., university administrator; b. Zurich, Switzerland, Jan. 13, 1928; came to U.S., 1955; s. Karl Ulrich and Sella Wiesendanger; m. Elfriede Michel, May 26, 1954; children: Thomas H.U., Brigitte E., Markus D., Felix P. DSc, Swiss Fed. Inst. Tech., Zurich, 1954; diploma in Chemistry, Swiss Fed. Inst. Tech., 1951. Sr. research chemist Stanford Research Inst., Menlo Park, Calif., 1959-66; mktg. mgr. Electronic Assocs., Palo Alto, Calif., 1966-70, Uthe Tech., Sunnyvale, Calif., 1970-72; internat. dir. Barnes-Hind Pharm., Sunnyvale, 1972-74; mktg. dir. Plessey Environ., San Diego, 1975-77; internat. dir. Chemetrics Inc., Burlingame, Calif., 1977-82, Sequoia-Turner Corp., Mountain View, Calif., 1982; licensing assoc. Stanford U., Palo Alto, 1984—; cons., Los Altos, Calif., 1974-75, 82-84; pres. Orbiotech Internat., Los Altos, 1981—. Contbr. articles to profl. jours. Mem. Am. Chem. Soc., Licensing Execs. Soc., Soc. Univ. Patent Adminstrs. Home: 1151 Buckingham Dr Los Altos CA 94022 Office: Tech Licensing Office Stanford U 350 Cambridge Ave Palo Alto CA 94022

WIESENFELD, IRVING HAROLD, otolaryngologist; b. San Francisco, June 14, 1912; s. Louis and Ann (Berke) W.; A.B., U. Calif., 1934, M.D., 1938, C.P.H. (Calif. State fellow), 1939, M.S., 1941, Dr.P.H., 1947; m. Betsey Ramsay Straub, May 11, 1939; children—Stephen Lee, Ramsay. Intern, U. Calif. Hosp., San Francisco, 1937-38; chief bur. maternal and child health Calif. Dept. Health, San Francisco, 1939-41; resident in otolaryngology Los Angeles County Hosp. on U. So. Calif. Service, 1941-42; chief otolaryngology service Kaiser Found. Hosp., Oakland, Calif., 1942-46; practice medicine specializing in otolaryngology, Oakland, 1946—; mem. staffs Herrick Meml. Hosp., Berkeley, Calif., Providence Hosp., Oakland, Children's Hosp., Oakland, Cowell Hosp., Berkeley; med. dir. Oakland Unified Sch. Dist., 1949—. Diplomate Am. Bd. Otolaryngology, Internat. Bd. Surgery. Fellow ACS, Internat. Coll. Surgeons; mem. AMA, Calif., Alameda-Contra Costa med. assns., Am. Med. Tennis Assn., Phi Beta Kappa, Sigma Xi, Alpha Omega Alpha. Republican. Jewish. Club: Oakland Athletic. Home: 120 Monte Ave Piedmont CA 94611 Office: 400 30th St Suite 206 Oakland CA 94609

WIESER, SIEGFRIED, planetarium director; b. Linz, Austria, Oct. 30, 1933; came to Can., 1955; s. Florian Wieser and Michaela Josepha (Kaufmann) Wieser-Burgstaller; m. Joan Xaven Quick, Sept. 8, 1962; children: Leonard Franz, Bernard Sidney. BS in Physics, U. Calgary, Alta., Can., 1966. Lead chorus singer, dancer Landes Theatre, Linz, 1949-53; project engr. EBG, Linz, 1952-54; with Griffith Farms Ltd., Eng., 1954-55; seismic computer operator Shell Can., Calgary, 1956-61; GTA systems analyst U. Calgary, 1961-66; planetarium dir. Centennial Planetarium, Calgary, 1966—; cons. Electro Controls, Salt Lake City, 1978-79. Contbr. articles to profl. publs. Recipient Violet Taylor award U. Calgary, 1964; Queen Elizabeth scholar Province Alta., 1961. Mem. Royal Astron. Soc. Can., Internat. Planetarium Soc., Can. Planetarium Soc., Can. Mus. Assn., AAAS. Anglican. Club: Magic Circle (Calgary). Avocations: swimming, hiking, astronomy, lecturing. Office: Centennial Planetarium, PO Box 2100, 701 11 St SW, Calgary, AB Canada T2P 2M5

WIESNER, ERHARD, management consultant; b. Giersdorf, Germany, Sept. 22, 1943; came to U.S., 1969; s. Herbert A. and Margarete C. (Hartelt) W.; m. Marian Jean Koopman, May 6, 1978; children: Erik Michael, Martin Andreas. BS, Tech. U., Hannover, Fed. Republic Germany, 1964; diplom-Kaufmann degree, Georgia Augusta U., Goettingen, Fed. Republic Germany, 1969; MBA, Columbia U., 1970. Asst. prof. mktg. Georgia Augusta U., 1969; sr. cons. Quickborner Team, Inc., Hamburg, Fed. Republic Germany, 1970-72, ptnr., 1972—; v.p. Quickborner Team, Inc., Millburn, N.J., 1972-78; pres. Plan-Consult, Inc., Evergreen-Hiwan, Colo., 1978—; lectr., various orgns.; cons. in field. Contbr. articles to profl. jours. Fellow, Columbia U. German Acad. Exchange program (DAAD), Bonn, Fed. Republic Germany, 1969, 70; grantee German Acad. Exchange program, 1960-70. Mem. Am. Mgmt. Assn., Adminstrv. Mgmt. Soc. Avocations: skiing, hiking, photography.

WIETECHA, EDWARD ALBERT, chemical engineer; b. Chgo., Oct. 10, 1950; s. Edward John and Katherine Agnes (Czekalski) W. BS in Chemistry, Ill. Inst. Tech., 1974, BS in Chem. Engring., 1979. Chemist Daubert Chem. Co., Chgo., 1975, project engr., 1976-78; project engr. Brand Indsl. Service Co., Park Ridge, Ill., 1978; plant engr. Borden Chemical Co., Sheboygan, Wis., 1979-83; project engr. Borden Chemical Co., Bellevue, Wash., 1984—. Mem. Sheboygan City Council, 1982-83. Mem. Am. Chem. Soc., Instrument Soc. Am. Avocations: investment analysis, woodworking, fishing.

WIGAL, IRIS SELIGMAN, educator; b. Madison, Wis., Aug. 7, 1947; d. Daniel Samuel and Birdie (Ginsburg) Seligman; m. Dennis Dean Wigal, Aug. 13, 1974; 1 dau., Amanda Michele. B.A. in Elem. Edn. summa cum laude, Ariz. State U., 1969, M.A. in Spl. Edn., 1971. Cert. tchr., Ariz. Tchr., Cartwright Sch. Dist., Phoenix, 1969—. Mem. Valley Leadership; treas., bd. dirs. Valley Leadership Alumni Assn., 1982-84; rec. sec. Women's Orgn. for Rehab. Tng., 1979-80, v.p., 1980-81; mem. Maricopa County Child Services Task Force, 1981; bd. dirs. Childsplay, 1984-85, Phoenix Town Hall. Mem. NEA, Ariz. Edn. Assn., Cartwright Edn. Assn. (bldg. rep. 1970-74), AAUW (program v.p. 1986-87, community area rep. 1986), Ariz. State U. Alumni Assn. (homecoming steering com., editorial adv. bd.), Phoenix Panhellenic, Alpha Lambda Housing Corp. (sec. 1983—), Alpha Epsilon Phi (nat. rush chmn. 1979-81, co-nat. conv. chmn. 1979-81, nat. province supr. 1981-83, nat. alumnae sec. 1983-85, nat. v.p. alumnae 1985-87, Phoenix Alumni pres. 1975-77), Order of Omega. Democrat. Jewish. Club: Phoenix City. Home: 1735 W Seldon Ln Phoenix AZ 85021 Office: 2252 N 55th Ave Phoenix AZ 85035

WIGET, ANDREW O., educator; b. Richmond, Calif., Nov. 28, 1945; s. Orville Lewis Wiget and Marie (Baptista) Clement; m. Linda Green, Sept. 1968 (div. 1970); m. Catherine Herbison, Dec. 19, 1971; children: Sarah Catherine, Paul Andrew. BA, John Carroll U., 1967, MA, 1973; PhD, U. Utah, 1977. Teaching fellow U. Utah, Salt Lake City, 1973-77; instr. of English U. New Orleans, 1978-79; asst. prof. English Native Am. Studies Dartmouth Coll., Hanover, N.H., 1979-83; asst prof. English N.Mex. State U., Las Cruces, 1983-87, assoc. prof., 1987—; dir. N.Mex. Heritage Ctr., Las Cruces, 1986. Author: Native American Literature, 1985; editor: Critical Essays on Native American Literature, 1985, ASAIL Notes, 1983; contbr. articles to profl. jours. Mem. MLA, Rocky Mt. MLA, Assn. Study of Am. Indian Lits. (pres. elect. 1984, pres. 1985, first v.p. 1985), N.Mex. Folklore Soc., Am. Folklore Soc. Democrat. Roman Catholic. Avocations: hiking, painting. Home: 4732 Doña Ana Rd Las Cruces NM 88005 Office: NMex State U Dept English/3E Las Cruces NM 88003

WIGGETT, HOWARD JOHN DASH, mining company executive; b. London, Eng., Oct. 28, 1939; came to U.S., 1974; s. Kenneth Heath and Jacqueline Suzanne (Crocker) W.; B.Sc., Sir George Williams U., 1962; M.S.C. Applied, McGill U., 1966; D.B.A., U. Toronto, 1972; m. Sheridan Diane Coates, Aug. 19, 1972. Exploration geologist ASARCO, Inc., London, Eng., 1967-70; mgr. field exploration Watts, Griffis, McQuat Ltd., Toronto, Ont., Can., 1970-71; mining analyst Wood Gundy Ltd., Toronto, 1971-74; mgmt. cons. Theodore Barry & Assocs., Los Angeles, 1974-78; mgr. fin. services NERCO, Inc., Portland, Oreg., 1978-79, controller, 1979-81, mgr. tech. services, 1981-82, mgr. tech. rev., 1982-83; v.p. minerals UNC Teton Exploration Drilling, Inc., Gallup, N.Mex., 1983-85; v.p. fin. John E. Brown & Assocs., Inc., Marina Del Rey, Calif., 1985—. Profl. engr., Ont.; profl. geologist Geol. Assn. Can. Mem. Can. Inst. Mining and Metallurgy, N.W. Mining Assn., Am. Mgmt. Assn., Soc. Mining Engrs. of AIME, Planning Execs. Inst. (past officer), B.C. and Yukon Chamber of Mines. Clubs: West Hills Racquet, City (Portland); Gallup Country. Home: 3025 Thatcher Ave Marina del Rey CA 90292 Office: John E Brown & Assocs 4676 Admiralty Way Suite 522 Marina del Rey CA 90292

WIGGINS, ALVIN DENNIE, statistics educator, researcher; b. Harrisburg, Ill., May 5, 1922; s. Archie and Jessie (Kaid) Slavish; m. Margaret Louise Deal, July 1, 1950; children: Michael, Karl, Phillip, Frederick, Elizabeth, Andrew. AB, U. Calif., Berkeley, 1951, MA, 1953, PhD, 1957. Sr. statistician Gen. Electric Co., Richland, Wash., 1957-63; assoc. research biostatistician U. Calif., Berkeley, 1963-69; from asst. prof. to prof. U. Calif., Davis, 1969—, dir. statis., 1979-82; cons. Cutter Labs., Berkeley, 1963, State Water Resources Control Bd., Sacramento, 1977. Contbr. articles to profl. jours. Served to sgt. U.S. Army, 1944-46. Fellow Am. Heart Inst., Royal Statis. Soc. of London; mem. Inst. Math. Stats., Am. Statis. Assn. (pres. elect San Francisco chpt. 1986—), Biometric Soc. Avocations: long distance running, fine woodworking, carpentry and bldg. Home: 1709 Willow Ln Davis CA 95616 Office: U Calif Davis CA 95616

WIGGINS, WALTON WRAY, publisher; b. Roswell, N.Mex., May 13, 1924; s. Miles Burgess and Mona Cecil (Brown) W.; grad. Motion Picture Cameraman Sch., Astoria, N.Y., 1945; m. Roynel Fitzgerald, Apr. 30, 1963; children—Walton Wray, Kimberly Douglas, Lisa Renee. Free-lance photojournalist for nat. mags., 1948-60; dir. public relations Ruidoso Racing Assn., Ruidoso Downs, N.Mex., 1960-69, v.p., 1967-68; founder, pub. Speedhorse Publs., Roswell, N.Mex. and Norman, Okla., 1969-78; owner/operator Wiggins Galleries Fine Art, 1978—; pres. Quarter Racing World, 1970-78, Am. Horse Publs., Washington, 1978; del. leader People to People, Internat. Served with U.S. Army, 1943-46. Recipient Detroit Art Dirs. award, 1955, Greatest Contbr. award Quarter Racing Owners Am., 1974. Mem. Overseas Press Club, Am. Soc. Mag. Photographers, Am. Horse Publs. Republican. Author: The Great American Speedhorse, 1978; Cockleburs and Cowchips, 1975; Alfred Morang-A Neglected Master, 1979; Ernest Berke-Paintings and Sculptures of the Old West, 1980; Juan Dell-The First Lady of Western Bronze, 1981; Go Man Go-The Legendary Speedhorse, 1982. Office: 1085 Mechem Dr Ruidoso NM 88345

WIKER, STEVEN FORRESTER, industrial research engineer; b. Alhambra, Calif., Sept. 29, 1952; s. Bruce Forrester and Joan (Centers) W.; m. Jody Louise Wiker, Jan. 24, 1976; children: Douglas Forrester, James McCallum. BS in Physiology, U. Calif., Davis, 1975; MS in Biol. Scis., Washington U., 1981; MS in Indsl. Engring., U. Mich., 1982, PhD in Indsl. Engring., 1986. Research project officer USCG, Washington, 1976-79; research asst. U. Mich., Ann Arbor, 1979-86; research engr. Naval Ocean Systems Ctr. Lab., Kailua, Hawaii, 1986-87, Naval Ocean Systems Ctr., San Diego, 1987—; sr. research engr. James Miller Engring., Inc., Ann Arbor, 1981—. Contbr. articles to profl. jours. Fellow Ford Motor Co., Detroit, 1983-86; grantee Nat. Inst. Occupational Safety and Health, Washington, 1979-84. Mem. Am. Soc. Safety Engrs., Inst. Indsl. Engrs., Internat. Soc. Biomechs., Aerospace Med. Soc., Human Factors Soc., Res. Officers Assn., Sigma Xi, Alpha Pi Mu. Avocations: pvt. pilot, amateur photography. Home: 2116 Lemon Ave Escondido CA 92025 Office: Naval Ocean Systems Ctr Code 5301 San Diego CA 92152-5000

WILBANKS, ROBERT LEROY, finance company executive; b. St. James, Mo., Aug. 30, 1937; s. Kenneth Leroy and Hallie Ellen (Shepherd) W.; m. Mary Roques Peyrefitte, May 7, 1959; children: Ann Marie, Kenneth Perry. BS in Bus., Ariz. State U., 1972. Commd. USAF, 1957, advanced through grades to maj., res., 1969; dist. dir. Verex Assur Corp., Tex., 1973-80; v.p. Valley Nat. Bank, Ariz., 1980-84; sr. v.p. Otero-Savs. Co., Colorado Springs, Colo., 1984—. Active Colorado Springs Symphony Council, 1985—. Decorated D.F.C. and Air medal with 10 oak leaf clusters. Mem. Mortgage Bankers Am. Republican. Methodist. Club: Colo. Country. Avocations: hunting, fishing, skiing, tennis.

WILBER, CHARLES GRADY, forensic science educator, consultant; b. Waukesha, Wis., June 18, 1916; s. Charles Bernard and Charlotte Agnes (Grady) W.; m. Ruth Mary Bodden, July 12, 1944 (dec. 1950); children: Maureen, Charles Bodden, Michael; m. Clare Marie O'Keefe, June 14, 1952; children: Thomas Grady (dec.), Kathleen, Aileen, John Joseph. B.Sc., Marquette U., 1938; M.A., Johns Hopkins U., 1941; Ph.D., Johns Hopkins, 1942. Asst. prof. physiology Fordham U., 1945-49; assoc. prof. physiology, dir. biol. labs. St. Louis U., 1949-52; leader Arctic expdns. 1943-44, 48, 50, 51; physiologist Chem. Corps, U.S. Army, 1952-61; assoc. physiology and pharmacology U. Pa., 1953-61, chief comparative physiology, 1956-61; profl. lectr. biol. scis. Loyola Coll., Balt., 1957-61; dir. Loyola Coll. (In-Service Inst. Sci. Tchrs.), 1958-61; prof. biol. scis., univ. research coordinator, dean Grad. Sch., Kent State U., 1961-64; dir. marine laboratories U. Del., 1964-67; chmn. prof. dept. zoology Colo. State U., 1967-73, prof., 1973—, also dir. forensic sci. lab.; dep. coroner, Larimer County, Colo., 1968-78; mem. Center for Human Identification; expert witness fed. and state cts. on poisons, firearms, others. mem. Marine Biol. Lab., Woods Hole, Mass., 1947—; mem. U.S. Army Panel Environ. Physiology, 1952-61; mem. study group Nat. Acad. Scis.-USAF, 1958-61; Wellcome vis. prof. basic med. scis. Ohio U. Med. Sch., 1983-84. Author: Biological Aspects of Water Pollution, 2d edit, 1971, Japanese edit., 1970, Forensic Biology for the Law Enforcement Officer, 1975, Contemporary Violence, 1975, Ballistic Science for the Law Enforcement Officer, 1977, Medicolegal Investigation of The President John F. Kennedy Murder, 1978, Chemical Trauma from Pesticides, 1979, Forensic Toxicology, 1980, Beryllium, 1980, Agent Orange, 1980; Author: Turbidity, 1983, Selenium, 1983; contbr. articles to profl. jours.; exec. editor: Adaption to the Environment, vol. in series, 1962; editor: Am. Lecture Series in Environ. Studies; mem. editorial bd.: Am. Jour. Forensic Medicine and Pathology; contbr.: Harper Ency. Nat; vis. lectr.: Am. Inst. Biol. Scis, 1957—. Served to capt. USAAF, 1942-46; col., ret. USAF. Fellow N.Y. Acad. Scis., Am. Acad. Forensic Sci.; mem. Am. Physiol. Soc., Phi Beta Kappa, Sigma Xi, Phi Sigma, Gamma Alpha. Republican. Catholic. Club: Cosmos (Washington). Home: 900 Edwards St Fort Collins CO 80524 Office: Dept Zoology Colo State U Fort Collins CO 80523

WILBER, DONALD BLAINE, medical psychotherapist, clergyman; b. Albuquerque, Oct. 5, 1952; s. M. Blaine and S. June (Warren) W.; m. Janet Marie Scott, Sept. 14, 1973; children—Eric, Casey, Ty, Daniel. B.A. in Religion, N.W. Nazarene Coll., 1976; M.A. in Gen. Counseling, Coll. Idaho, 1980; Ph.D. in Counseling Psychology, Columbia Pacific U., 1982. Ordained to ministry Ch. of the Nazarene, 1978; cert. Nat. Bd. Med. Psychotherapists. Pastor marriage and family counselor Ch. of the Nazarene, Harper, Oreg., 1976-79; intern, behavior health counselor, Mountain State Tumor Inst., Boise, 1980; dir., therapist Treasure Valley Counseling, Ontario, Oreg., 1980-82; pastor Ch. of the Nazarene, Prosser, Wash., 1983—. bd. dirs. Lower Valley Pregnancy Ctr.; adv. bd. Prosser Schs.; cons. Valley Family Medicine and Valley Family Dental Clinics; zone chmn., advisor to Chrisitian Action Standing Com., Ch. Nazarene; dir. Concerned Pastors for Traditional Values. Mem. Prosser Ministerial Assn. (pres.). Contbr. articles to profl. jours. Home: 1006 Burgundy Pl Prosser WA 99350 Office: Ch of the Nazarene 1937 Highland Dr Prosser WA 99350

WILBURN, RONALD PAUL, controller; b. East St. Louis, Ill., Aug. 10, 1937; s. Frank Cecil and Virginia Catherine (Shephard) W. m. Frances Rose Sever, Nov. 6, 1965 (div. Nov. 1985); children: Rhonda Lynn, Landon Aron, Amanda Lynette. BA in Acctg., So. Ill. U., 1960; student, U. Paris-Sorbonne, 1963; BA in Acctg., Pacific Western Coll., 1968, MBA in Fin., 1970. Pres., fin. cons. Fin. Systems, Inc., Bellevue, Wash., 1970-80; pres., fin. cons. Questron Fin. Services, Inc., Bellevue, 1981, founder, chief exec. officer, 1981—; controller Mon Arc Electric Corp., Redmond, Wash., 1979, Synetix Industries, Inc., Redmond, Wash., 1980—; tchr. acctg. City Coll. Seattle; chief fin. officer Precision Engine Specialists, Inc., Seattle, 1986—, Craftech Pressworks, Inc., Bellevue, Washington, 1987—. Rep. precinct committeeman, 1976—; active budget bldg. com. Issaquah (Wash.) Sch. Dist.; founder, past pres. Issaquah Commn. Edn. Served with USMC, 1960-66. Decorated Purple Heart. Mem. Internat. Assn. Fin. Planners, Nat. Assn. Accts. Mormon. Lodges: Masons, Shriners, Order of Eastern Star. Home: 6624 161st Pl SE Edmonds WA 98020 Office: 999 Third Ave #1050 Seattle WA 98104

WILBURN, STEVE, energy executive, consultant; b. Chgo., Dec. 19, 1948; s. Melvin Wren and Joan June (Evans) W.; m. Cherri Lynn Renner; children: Stephanie, Nathan. BCE, Washington U., St. Louis, 1972. Research asst. Monsanto Corp., St. Louis, 1973-77; dir. tech. mktg. Gundlach Machine Co., St. Louis, 1977-79; pres. Steve Wilburn & Assocs., Tucson, 1980—. Served as cpl. USMC, 1967-69, Vietnam. Decorated Purple Heart. Mem. Internat. Cogeneration Soc. (chmn. midwest region 1983), Assn. Energy Engrs. Republican. Roman Catholic. Club: Engineers (St. Louis). Lodge: Optimists (v.p. 1981-82). Avocations: tennis, golf, swimming. Home and Office: 3681 N Tres Lomas Tucson AZ 85749

WILCOX, COLLEEN BRIDGET, special education administrator; b. Rock Island, Ill., July 24, 1949; d. Wayne Eugene and Virginia Mae (Dewrose) W. B.S., U. Iowa, 1971; M.S., U. Ariz., 1974; PhD U. So. Calif., 1986; ednl. adminstrn. credential U. So. Calif. Asst. dir. parks and recreation City of Moline (Ill.), 1969-74; dir. speech pathology Instituto Guatemalteca Sequiridad, Peace Corps., Guatemala City, 1971-72; speech and lang. specialist Tucson Sch. Dist., 1974-75; aphasia tchr. specialist, itinerant specialist Los Angeles County Schs., 1975-77; program specialist in severe lang. disorder/aphasia Los Angeles County Supt. Schs., 1977-79, program adminstr./communication disorders, Baldwin Park, 1979-83, mem. budget standards com. 1979-82; mem. credential adv. bd., communications dept. Calif. State U., Los Angeles, 1978, asst. prof., 1977-83, chmn. sabbatical rev. com.; dir. spl. edn. Tucson Unified Sch. Dist.; art dir. the Great Stampede, 1981-83; Bd. dirs. dept. developmental disabilities Assn. Retarded Citizens; bd. dirs. Pima Council on Developmental Disabilities; chmn. spl. edn. adv. council Pima Coll. Spl. Edn.; co-chair Mayor's Com. Constitution Celebration, 1986. Recipient Harriett Rutherford Johnstown award Pi Beta Phi, 1971; Barnes Drill award U. Iowa, 1971; lic. speech pathologist, cert. tchr. speech and hearing therapy, severely handicapped credential, learning handicapped credential, Calif.; cert. speech and lang. therapist, Ariz. Mem. Calif. Speech and Hearing Assn. (exec. council 1986—), Am. Speech and Hearing Assn. (cert. clin. competence in speech pathology, conv. com. 1979, com. on manpower 1982-83, Ariz. legis. councilor 1986—), Jr. League of Tucson (state polit. action delegate 1986), Council Exceptional Children (legis. com.), Assn. Calif. Sch. Adminstrs., UN Assn., Pi Beta Phi Alumnae, Phi Delta Kappa. Co-author, illustrator: Let's Share, 1983, Super Soup, 1986, Understanding and Preventing AIDS, 1987. Home: 820 Placita del Mirador Tucson AZ 85718

WILCOX, DANIEL EDWARD, III, state employee; b. Bryn Mawr, Pa., Dec. 27, 1946; s. Daniel Edward and Laura Elsie (Church) W.; m. Anita Leah Warwick, July 7, 1949; children: Crystal, Heather, Daniel. BS in Occupational Edn., So. Ill. U., 1982. Enlisted USAF, 1966; adminstrv. technician, McChord AFB, Tacoma, Wash., 1966-71; edn./tng. supt. Fairchild AFB, Spokane, Wash., 1971-82; personnel supt. Travis AFB, Calif., 1982-86, ret., 1986; trades name specialist dept. licensing Wash. State Bus. License Service, Olympia, 1986—. Decorated Meritorious Service medal, Air Force Commendation medal with two oak leaf clusters. Mem. Am. Vocat. Assn., Noncommd. Officer Acad. Grad. Assn., Air Force Assn., Nat. Thespian Soc. Democrat. Methodist.

WILCOX, DAVID ALBERTSON, urban planner, economics consultant; b. Grand Rapids, Mich., Aug. 11, 1938; s. David Albertson and Florence Sanfield (McDonell) W.; m. Carol Francis Brian, Aug. 26, 1967; children—Wendy, Michele, Wilcox. B.A., U. Mich., 1961, M.A., 1961; M.R.P., Harvard U. Grad. Sch. Design, 1967. Vol., U.S. Peace Corps, 1962-64; planning asst. City of Lynn (Mass.), 1965-66; mgmt. analyst, urban planner U.S. Bur. Budget, Washington, 1966-68; planning dir., dep. administr. Community Redevel. Agy., City of Los Angeles, 1968-76; ptnr., v.p. Econ. Research Assocs., Los Angeles, 1977—; instr. community redevel. Sch. Urban and Regional Planning, U. So. Calif., 1977—. Bd. dir. Los Angeles Beautiful, 1978—. Mem. Am. Inst. Cert. Planners (Lasker fellow 1964-66), Nat. Assn. Housing Redevel. Ofcls. Democrat. Roman Catholic. Office: 10960 Wilshire Blvd Suite 2400 Los Angeles CA 90024

WILCOX, EVLYN, city mayor. children: Wayne, Moire, Marlene. Owner, pres. Manpower, Inc., San Bernardino, Riverside, Upland, San Gabriel Valley, Calif.; mayor City of San Bernardino. Pres. Arrowhead United Way, 1983, campaign chmn., 1981; pres. Community Arts Prodns.; treas., bd. dirs. Nat. Orange Show; bd. dirs. YMCA; bd. councillors Calif. State U., San Bernardino. Named Citizen of Yr. Inland Empire mag., 1979. Mem. Exec. Women Internat. (pres Inland Empire chpt. 1975), Uptown Bus. and Profl. Women, Bus. and Profl. Women USA (pres. San Orco dist.), San Bernardino Area C. of C. (pres. Athena award 1986). Lodge: Zonta Internat. Avocations: gardening, collecting porcelain, oriental art and antiques, traveling. Office: Office of the Mayor 300 North D St San Bernardino CA 92418

WILCOX, JOHN STEWART, manufacturing company executive; b. Pierce, Ariz., Dec. 31, 1908; s. Ellis Neriah and Helen Margret (Stewart) W. Student, Phoenix Jr. Coll., 1926-28; corr. student, Wash. State U., 1930-35. Shop supt. TOTCO, Los Angeles, 1940-42, TILAB, Inglewood, Calif., 1942-49; owner Wilcox Lab., Reseda, Calif., 1952—. Patentee in field of hydraulics. Mem. Inventors Workshop Internat. Edn. Found. (v.p. 1972—). Mem. United Lodge of Theosophists. Avocations: hiking, camping, sailing. Office: Wilcox Lab 7024A Darby Ave Reseda CA 91335

WILCOX, LYNN ESSLINGER, psychology educator; b. Huntsville, Ala., Sept. 4, 1935; d. William Francis and Anna Mae (Linthicum) Esslinger; 1 child, Gregory C. Haun. BS cum laude, Southwest Mo. State U., 1959; MEd, U. Mo., 1961, PhD, 1968. Cert. sch. counselor and sch. psychologist, Calif.; lic. marriage, family and child counselor, Calif. Tchr. high sch. Springfield, Mo., 1958-60; grad., research asst. U. Mo., Columbia, 1960-64; counselor elem. sch. Smyrna, Ga., 1965-67; asst. prof. Ga. State U., Atlanta, 1968-69; prof. edn., dept. chmn., coordinator Calif. State U., Sacramento, 1969—. Pres. Wayfinders Inc., Sacramento, 1986—; chmn. Am. Personnel & Guidance Assn. Com. for Women, 1972-74; bd. dirs. Community Interaction Program, Sacramento, 1982; prof. adv. com. Suicide Prevention Service, Sacramento, 1970-72; rep. Sacramento Community Commn. for Women, 1971-73. Fellow Gregory 1962, Danforth 1975; recipient Profl. Promise award Calif. State U., Sacramento, 1986. Mem. Am. Psychol. Assn., Am. Assn. for Counseling and Devel., Faculty Women's Assn. (v.p. 1971-73, pres. 1973-74), Western Psychol. Assn., Assn. for Counselor Edn. and Supervision, Middle Eastern Studies Assn., Western Assn. for Counselor Edn. and Supervision. Republican. Home: 619 Commons Dr Sacramento CA 95825 Office: Calif State U 6000 J St Sacramento CA 95819 Office: Wayfinders Inc 1555 River Park Dr #206 Sacramento CA 95815

WILCOX, W(EBSTER) WAYNE, forest products pathologist, educator; b. Berkeley, Calif., Oct. 28, 1938; s. Webster Williamson and Edith Jeanette (La Belle) W.; Margaret Ruth Starkweather, Aug. 7, 1960; children: Melissa Margaret, Wynn William. BS in Forestry, U. Calif., Berkeley, 1960; MS in Plant Pathology, U. Wis., 1962, PhD in Plant Pathology, 1965. Plant pathologist U.S. Forest Products Lab., Madison, Wis., 1960-64; assoc. forest products pathologist, lectr. U. Calif. Forest Products Lab., Richmond, Calif., 1964-77, forest products pathologist, prof., 1977—; mem. Structural Pest Control Bd., Sacramento, Calif., 1979-81; cons. in field. Contbr. more than 65 articles to profl. jours. Fulbright-Hays sr. postdoctoral fellow, 1973-74.

Fellow Internat. Acad. Wood Sci.; mem. Forest Products Research Soc. (Wood award 1965), Soc. Wood Sci. and Tech., Internat. Assn. Wood Anatomists, Am. Inst. Biol. Scis., Sigma Xi, Xi Sigma Pi. Avocations: sailing, vocal music, backpacking. Office: U Calif Forest Products Lab 1301 S 46th St Richmond CA 94804

WILCZAK, JOHN JOSEPH, JR., marketing and financial management executive; b. Queens, N.Y., Jan. 2, 1952; s. John Joseph and Vivian (Laura) W. AB in Anthropology, Brown U., 1974; MBA in Fin. and Internat. Bus., Columbia U., 1978. Mktg. rep. Gen. Motors Corp., N.Y.C., 1975-76; internat. fin. cons. Am. Can Co., Greenwich, Conn., 1979; corp. mktg. cons. Gen. Electric Co., Bridgeport, Conn., 1979-82; sr. gen. mgmt. cons. Touche Ross & Co., N.Y.C., 1982-83; corp. dir. mktg. IPCO Corp., White Plains, N.Y., 1984-85; v.p. mktg. services Bermudez and Assocs., Los Angeles, 1986—. Author: (with others) Integrated Direct Marketing, 1986. Cons. Multiple Sclerosis Soc., Westchester, N.Y., 1985. Fellow Gen. Electric Alumni; mem. Am. Mgmt. Assn., Assn. Corp. Growth, Direct Mktg. Assn. (cons., disting. leader award 1985). Republican. Club: Brown (N.Y.C.). Avocations: restoring classic fgn. sports cars, tennis, sailing, skiing, surfing. Office: Bermudez and Assocs 12400 Wilshire Blvd Suite 1100 Los Angeles CA 90025

WILD, CLAUDE CHARLES, III, federal agency counselor; b. Austin, Tex., Sept. 18, 1949; s. Claude Charles Jr. and Nadine (King) W.; m. Mary Ann Voress, June 30, 1984. AB, Duke U., 1972; JD, Georgetown U., 1975. Bar: Colo. 1976, DC 1979. Intern U.S. Dept. Justice, Washington, 1973; ptnr. Makaroff & Wild, PC, Denver, 1976-78; assoc. Wiggins & Smith PC, Denver, 1978-83; regional dir. FTC, Denver, 1983—. Pres. Cinnimon Down the Street Homeowners Assn., Denver, 1978-82. Mem. ABA (antitrust sect.), Colo. Bar Assn., Denver Bar Assn., Siberian Husky Club Am. Republican. Baptist. Club: Lone Tree Country (bd. govs. 1986). Avocations: breeding and exhibiting dogs, sled dog racing. Office: FTC 1405 Curtis St #2900 Denver CO 80202

WILD, ROBERT LEE, physics educator; b. Sedalia, Mo., Oct. 9, 1921; s. Alwin Bernard and Nellie Marie (Nowlin) W.; m. Frances Elleta Wheeler, Oct. 7, 1943; children: James Robert, Janet Gayle, Margaret Nell. B.S., Central Mo. State U., 1943; M.A., U. Mo., 1948, Ph.D., 1950. Asst. prof. physics U. N.D., Grand Forks, 1950-52; prof. physics U. Calif., Riverside, 1953—; Fulbright lectr. U. Philippines, 1981-82. Contbr. articles profl. jours. Served with AUS, 1943-45. NSF fellow, 1959-60; recipient Disting. Teaching award U. Calif., Riverside, 1973. Mem. Am. Phys. Soc., Am. Assn. Physics Tchrs. (v.p. sect. 1983-84, pres. So. Calif. sect. 1985-86, pres., 1986-87, award 1966), Sigma Xi. Baptist. Home: 5709 Durango Rd Riverside CA 92506 Office: U Calif Dept Physics Riverside CA 92521

WILDE, CHARLES BROADWATER, investment banker, oil company executive; b. Oakland, Calif., July 22, 1940; s. Willard Henry and Elizabeth M. (Broadwater) W.; A.B., U. Calif. at Berkeley, 1962; m. Molly Burnett, June 23, 1962 (div. July 1986); children—Charles Broadwater, Stephen Burnett; m. Dori Sternberg, Aug. 3, 1986. Salesman Procter & Gamble, San Francisco, 1963-64, dist. head salesman, 1964-65, unit mgr., 1965-67; account exec. Dean Witter, Reynolds, Inc., Hayward, Calif., 1967-70, asst. v.p., divisional syndicate mgr., 1972-74, v.p., nat. dir. tax advantaged investments, 1974-79; v.p. Winthrop Fin. Co., Inc., San Francisco, 1979-82; sr. v.p. Winthrop Securities Co., Inc., 1979-82; exec. v.p. Peregrine Oil & Gas Co., Burlingame, Calif., 1982-83, Western Dominion Capital Corp., Denver; exec. v.p., ptnr., dir. Splty. Shelter Inc., Walnut Creek, Calif., 1983-85; pres. GRZ & Assocs., 1983; sr. v.p. sales and mktg. Traweek Investment Co., Marina del Rey, Calif., 1983—; dir. Allen & Dorward Advt., Jimmie Huega Ctr., Vail, Colo.; cons. indsl. solar energy conversions Dept. Energy; co-founder, dir., exec. v.p. Interflight Corp., Long Beach, Calif., 1970-72. Vice pres. Tahoe Pines Assn., 1968-71. Fin. chmn. No. Calif. com. for Brian Van Camp, candidate Calif. sec. state, 1974. Bd. dirs. Golden Bear Athletic Found.; pres. No. Calif. chpt. Nat. Multiple Sclerosis Soc., 1980. Mem. Big C Soc. (dir. 1972-77, fin. chmn. 1973-77), U. Calif. Young Alumni Assn. (dir. 1968-70). Clubs: Bohemian (San Francisco); Claremont Country (Oakland). Home: 310 Tahiti Way #211 Marina del Rey CA 90292 Office: Traweek Investment Co 4720 Lincoln Blvd Marina del Rey CA 90292

WILDE, CHRISTINE BUCEY, physical sciences educator; b. Chula Vista, Calif., Nov. 9, 1949; d. Charles Clair Bucey and Clare Patricia Palardy; m. Daniel L. Wilde, June 12, 1983. Student, Russell Coll., 1967-71; BS, Stanford U., 1973. cert. tchr., Calif. Chemistry and earth sci. tchr. Mercy High Sch., San Francisco, 1973-75; tchr. Yosemite Inst., Yosemite Nat. Park, Calif., 1975-76; physics, chemistry, earth sci. tchr., dept. head, gifted edn. coordinator Cen. Cath. High Sch., Modesto, Calif., 1976—; cons., Modesto, 1983—; lectr. Calif. Assn. for Gifted state conv., Oakland, Calif., 1986, seminars on improving sci. teaching, Calif. Author: (with others) Chemistry Demonstrations, 1984; book reviewer Charles Merrill Publ. Co., 1985. Host family Youth for Understanding, Turlock, Calif., 1985-86. Mem. Nat. Sci. Tchrs. Assn. (speaker conv. 1986), Calif. Sci. Tchrs. Assn. (contbr. articles to jour.), Am. Assn. Physics Tchrs., Calif. Assn. Chemistry Tchrs., Calif. Sect. Am. Chem. Soc., AAUW, Sierra Club, Sigma Xi. Roman Catholic. Avocations: sports, needlecrafts, gardening, reading, writing. Office: Cen Cath High Sch PO Box 4878 Modesto CA 95352

WILDE, NED, electrical engineer, rancher; b. Milw., Aug. 23, 1924; s. Edwin and Erna Betty (Speiker) W.; m. Wanita C. Weber, June 28, 1947 (dec. Dec. 1980); children—Keith, Glenn, Lynn; m. D. Marie Jensen, July 11, 1981. B.S. in Elec. Engring., Milw. Sch. Engring., 1949; M.S. in Elec. Engring., U. Wis.-Madison, 1951. Registered profl. engr., Idaho. Mem. staff Sandia Nat. Lab., Albuquerque, 1951-56; assoc. prof. U. Ariz., Tucson, 1957-61; pres. Wilde Engring., Idaho Falls, Idaho, 1961—; engr., cons. Idaho Nat. Engring. Lab., Idaho Falls, 1961—; affiliate prof. U. Idaho, Idaho Falls, 1961—; owner, mgr. Wilde Angus Ranch, Arco, Idaho, 1962—. Served to pfc. U.S. Army, 1943-46; ETO. Mem. IEEE (sr.), Instrument Soc. Am. (sr.), Idaho Angus Assn. (pres. 1971-73), Theta Tau. Home: 1587 Garfield St Idaho Falls ID 83401

WILDER, JAMES D., geology and mining administrator; b. Wheelersburg, Ohio, June 25, 1935; s. Theodore Roosevelt and Gladys (Crabtree) W.; children: Jaymie Deanna, Julie Lynne. Graduated high sch., Wheelersburg. Lic. real estate agt. Portsmouth, Ohio; mgr. comml. pilots, fixed base operator Scioto County Airport, Ohio; mgr. and part owner sporting goods store, Portsmouth; cons. geologist Paradise, Calif., 1973-81; pres. Mining Consultants, Inc., Paradise, 1981-84; dir. Geology and Devel. Para-Butte Mining, Inc., Paradise, 1984—. Served with U.S. Army, 1956-57. Avocations: hunting, fishing, camping. Home and Office: Para-Butte Mining Inc 1737 Drayer Dr Paradise CA 95969

WILDER, MARTA MARIE KICK, state official; b. Everett, Wash., Dec. 11, 1954; d. Clayton Jack and Mary Viola (Ogle) Kick. B.A., Evergreen State Coll., 1977, M.P.A., 1984. Writer Wash. Ho. of Reps., Olympia, 1977-79; pub. affairs ofcl. Wash. Dept. Ecology, Olympia, 1979-83; pub. info. and planning ofcl., coordinator, writer, Wash. Gov.'s Office and Dept. Emergency Services, Olympia, 1983; pub. info. dir., spokesperson Nuclear Waste Bd. Writer speeches, brochures, and newsletters; editor Newsletter '85, 1984-85, Newsletter '86; prin. Wilder Enterprises, 1986—. Mem. Gov.'s Pub. Info. Com., 1982-83; v.p. Wash. State Info. Council, 1982-83, pres., 1983-84; counselor 6th grade camp, Olympia, 1972; singer Evergreen State Coll. Chambers Singers, Olympia, 1974-75. Mem. Am. Soc. Pub. Adminstrn., Evergreen State Coll. Alumni Assn. Clubs: Capitol City Press (sec. 1982-83), Toastmasters. Office: Dept Ecology High-Level Nuclear Waste Mgmt PV 11 Olympia WA 98504

WILDER, RAYMOND LEIGH, statistician, management consultant; b. Tacoma, Aug. 19, 1927; s. Raymond Dabney and Edna Mabel (Leigh) W.; m. Marion Shirley Champagne, Jan. 22, 1972; children—Michael Jon, Leslie Ann. B.S. in Math., Oreg. State U., 1952; postgrad. U. Wash., 1952-53, 55, U. Oreg., 1956-57, U. Del., 1958-59; M.S. in Quantitative Bus. Analysis, U. So. Calif., 1965. Applied statistician U. Wash. Pub. Opinion Lab., Seattle, 1953; computing analyst Douglas Aircraft Co., Long Beach, Calif., 1953-55; computing engr. N.W. Natural Gas Co., Portland, Oreg., 1956, 57; cons. statistician E.I. du Pont de Nemours & Co., Wilmington, Del., 1957-59, Niagara Falls, N.Y., 1959-60; group engr. McDonnell Douglas Corp., Culver City, Calif., 1960-63, Huntington Beach, Calif., 1972-74, asst. to dir., Santa Monica, Calif., 1963-72; sr. assoc. Wilder Assocs., Sunset Beach, Calif. and Seal Rock, Oreg., 1974—; cons., tchr. in field. Mem. adv. com. Waldport (Oreg.) Sch., 1978-79; treas., bd. dirs. Seal Rock Rural Fire Protection, 1979-87; mem. Beaver Creek Citizens Adv. Com., Oreg. Land Conservation Devel. Commn., 1980-81; mem. endowment com. YMCA, Newport, Oreg., 1983—. Served with USN, 1945-48. Mem. Am. Statis. Assn. Phi Kappa Phi, Pi Mu Epsilon, Chi Phi. Democrat. Episcopalian. Home and office: 6408 NW Pacific Coast Hwy Seal Rock OR 97376

WILDHAGEN, DWAYNE LLOYD, audiologist; b. Denver, Mar. 31, 1952; s. Lloyd Merle and Eileen Hilda (McIntosh) W.; m. Linda Susan Zimmerman, Aug. 29, 1975; children: Jill Linda, Matthew Dwayne. BS, Colo. State. U., 1974; MA, U. No. Colo., 1975. Audiologist Hastings (Nebr.) Ednl. Service Unit, 1975-77, Easter Seal Soc. of Fla., Orlando, 1977-79, Steven Borsanyi, MD, Melbourne, Fla., 1979-84, Armando Jimenez, MD, Winter Haven, Fla., 1981-85; audiologist, dir. Audiol. Services of Winter Haven, 1981-85, Rocky Mountain Ear Inst., Denver, 1985—. Mem. Am. Speech and Hearing Assn., Am. Auditory Soc., Colo. Speech and Hearing Assn. Republican. Roman Catholic. Lodge: Sertoma (Merit award, Pres. award 1983). Avocations: chess, woodworking, raquetball, golf. Home: 533 W Beech Pl Louisville CO 80027 Office: Rocky Mountain Ear Inst 4701 E 9th Ave Denver CO 80220

WILDIN, MAURICE WILBERT, mechanical engineering educator; b. Hutchinson, Kans., June 24, 1935; s. John Frederick and Mildred Minerva (Dawson) W.; m. Mary Ann Brovan Christiansen, Aug. 9, 1958; children: Molly, Mildred. AA, Hutchinson Jr. Coll., 1955; BSME, U. Kans., 1958; MSME, Purdue U., 1959, PhD, 1963. Grad. asst. and instr. mech. engring. Purdue U., West Lafayette, Ind., 1958-61; asst. prof. U. N.Mex., Albuquerque, 1961—, prof. mech. engring., 1973; mem. tech. staff Sandia Nat. Labs., Albuquerque, 1984-85, cons., 1985—; cons. Bridgers & Paxton, Albuquerque, 1985—, T.Y. Lin, 1986—, Honeywell, 1986—. Contbr. articles to profl. jours. Mem. ASME, Am. Soc. Heating Ventilating and Air-Conditioning Engrs., Am. Solar Energy Soc. Office: U NMex Dept Mech Engring Albuquerque NM 87131

WILDSCHUETZ, HARVEY FREDERICK, electric utility executive; b. Independence, Mo., Sept. 3, 1943; s. George Frederick and Dorothy Mae (Knapheide) W.; m. Sharon Kay Eigenmann; children: Holly Dawn, Michael Dean. BSEE, U. Mo., Rolla, 1966. Registered profl. engr., Ill., Mo., N.Mex.; real estate broker, N.Mex. Elec. engr. power div. Burns & McDonnell Engring. Co., Kansas City, Mo., 1966-69; supt. elec. engring. City Water Light & Power, Springfield, Ill., 1969-76; dir. of generation Plains Electric G&T Corp., Albuquerque, 1976—. Coach Little League. Mem. IEEE, NSPE, N.Mex. Soc. Profl. Engrs. Club: Exchange. Avocations: camping, fishing, hunting, golf, pool. Home: 6600 Renee NE Alubuquerque NM 87109 Office: Plains Electric G&T Corp 2401 Aztec NE Albuquerque NM 87110

WILES, LAURENTIA RAMOS, businesswoman; b. Ewa, Honolulu, Feb. 28, 1924; d. Eugenio Lesperilles and Pelajia (Addion) R.; m. Henry Wiles, May 18, 1956. Cert., Honolulu Bus. Coll., 1942; diploma Dolores Premier Cosmetology Sch., San Francisco, 1944. Clk. typist, U.S. Army Civil Service, San Francisco, 1944-59; owner, mgr. Hobbitt Beauty Salon, San Francisco, 1956—. Community organizer Filipino Adult and Youth Cath. Orgn., San Francisco, 1959—; sr. commr. Commn. Status of Women of City and County San Francisco, 1975—; pres. Filipino Adult and Youth Cath. Orgn., 1970—, Filipino Community San Francisco, 1964-76, 84—; pres. Filipino Am. Coordinating Conf., 1976-82; bd. dirs. YWCA, San Francisco, 1970-81; appointed by mayor of San Francisco to the San Francisco-Manila Sister City; mem. women's adv. com. legis. issues. Recipient Spl. Recognition resolution Calif. Senate, 1974, 76, 79; Key to City of Sacramento, 1970; Cert. of Honor, City and County of San Francisco, 1974, 79; Outstanding Woman Leadership plaque Philippine Consulate Gen., 1970. Democrat. Roman Catholic. Avocation: dancing. Home: 214 Rutland St San Francisco CA 94134 Office: Hobbitt Beauty Salon 323 Geary St Suite 820 San Francisco CA 94102

WILETS, LAWRENCE, physics educator; b. Oconomowoc, Wis., Jan. 4, 1927; s. Edward and Sophia (Finger) W.; m. Dulcy Elaine Margoles, Dec. 21, 1947; children—Ileen Sue, Edward E., James D.; m. Vivian C. Wolf, Feb. 8, 1976. B.S., U. Wis., 1948; M.A., Princeton, 1950, Ph.D., 1952. Research asso. Project Matterhorn, Princeton, N.J., 1951-53, U. Calif. Radiation Lab., Livermore, 1953; NSF postdoctoral fellow Inst. Theoretical Physics, Copenhagen, Denmark, 1953-55; staff mem. Los Alamos Sci. Lab., 1955-58; mem. Inst. Advanced Study, Princeton, 1957-58; mem. faculty U. Wash., Seattle, 1958—; prof. physics U. Wash., 1962—; cons. to pvt. and govt. labs.; vis. prof. Princeton, 1969, Calif. Inst. Tech., 1971. Author: Theories of Nuclear Fission, 1964, also over 130 articles. Del. Dem. Nat. Conv., 1968. NSF Sr. fellow Weizmann Inst., Rehovot, Israel, 1961-62; Nordita prof. and Guggenheim fellow Lund (Sweden) U., also Weizmann Inst., 1976—; Alexander von Humboldt sr. U.S. scientist award, 1983. Fellow Am. Phys. Soc., AAAS; mem. Fedn. Am. Scientists, AAUP (pres. chpt. 1969-70, 73-75, pres. state conf. 1975-76), Phi Beta Kappa, Sigma Xi. Club: Explorers. Research on theory of nuclear structure and reactions, nuclear fission, atomic isotope shifts, atomic collisions, many body problems, elementary particles.

WILEY, BILL BEAUFORD, microbiology educator; b. St. Joseph, Mo., Nov. 12, 1923; s. Beauford John and Esther Adelyn (Dennis) W.; m. Avis Mary Dew; children: Karen Sue, Sharon Mary. BA, U. Kans., 1949, MA, 1950; PhD, U. Rochester, 1956. Asst. prof. microbiology U. Satchewan, Can., 1956-62; asst. prof. microbiology U. Utah, Salt Lake, 1952-70, assoc. prof., 1970-81, prof., 1981—. Contbr. articles to profl. jours. Served with U.S. Army, 1943-45. Research grantee Nat. Research Council Can., 1956-62, NIH, 1963-74. Mem. AAAS, Am. Soc. Microbiology, Can. Soc. Microbiology, AAUP, N.Y. Acad. Sci. Home: 4041 Lisa Dr Salt Lake City UT 84124 Office: U Utah Med Ctr Dept Cellular Viral and Molecular Biology Salt Lake City UT 84132

WILEY, DAVID OWEN, public relations executive; b. Philipsburg, Pa., Jan. 26, 1935; s. Franklin Williams and Mary (Owens) W.; divorced; children: Bethalee Dawn Jones, Jeffrey Brian. Student, Mich. State U., 1959-62. Editor Ford Motor Co., Dearborn, Mich., 1966-70; pubs. specialist Goodyr. Tire and Rubber Co., Akron, Ohio, 1970-74; mgr. communication services Wean United Inc., Warren, Ohio, 1974-78; dir. pub. relations The Patton Agy., Phoenix, 1978-79; pres. Petroglyph Communications, Inc., Phoenix, 1979-86; prin. Cook, Riggs & Wiley, Inc., Phoenix, 1986—. Mem. speakers bur. New Detroit Inc., 1969; bd. dirs. West Side Neighborhood Inc., Akron, 1971-72; chmn. state pub. info. Ariz. Chpt. Nat. Cancer Soc., Phoenix, 1980. Served as sgt. USMC, 1955-59. Mem. Pub. Relations Soc. Am. (bd. dirs. Phoenix chpt. 1979—, pres.-elect 1987—), Internat. Assn. Bus. Communicators (pres. Phoenix chpt. 1979-80, dist. v.p., bd. dirs. 1975-77, Gold Quill award 1973). Democrat. Episcopalian. Club: Phoenix City. Avocations: hiking, photography, reading, writing. Office: Cook Riggs & Wiley Inc 2600 N Central Ave #800 Phoenix AZ 85004

WILEY, DONOVON LINN, banker; b. Oregon City, Oreg., Oct. 20, 1938; s. Donovan Jean and Thelma Maxine (Linn) W.; m. Nancy Leigh White, Aug. 22, 1964; children: Jeffrey Richard, Kristen Linn. B.A. in Econs, U. Calif.-Davis, 1964; M.B.A., Calif. State U.-Long Beach, 1971; grad., Grad. Sch. Credit and Financial Mgmt., Harvard U., 1972, Grad. Sch. Sales Mgmt. and Mktg., Syracuse U., 1978. With First Western Bank & Trust Co., 1964-72; mgr. Santa Ana corp. office, 1969-72; sr. v.p., dir. Kans. State Bank & Trust Co., Wichita, 1972-73; pres. Ahmanson Bank & Trust Co., Beverly Hills, Calif., 1973-74; v.p. corp. banking div. Lloyds Bank Calif., 1974-75, sr. v.p., dir. mktg., dir. planning, 1975-77; regional v.p. Lloyds Bank Calif., No. Calif., 1977-81; exec. v.p. Banking div. Lloyds Bank Calif., Los Angeles, 1981-83; pres., chief exec. officer Am. Nat. Bank, Bakersfield, Calif., 1983—. Chmn. 3d Ann. Wichitennial; bd. dirs. Orange County Heart Assn., Orange County Lung Assn., 1970-72, Calif. Pediatric Center, 1974-78, Los Angeles Central City Assn., 1976-77; mem. com. for new dimensions Calif. Luth. Coll., 1975—; bd. dirs. Bridgemont Found., 1981, Golden Gate Energy Center., Calif. Hosp., 1983, Am. Cancer Soc. Kern County, 1983—. Served with USMC, 1956-60. Named Boss of Year Orange County chpt. Am. Inst. Bankers, 1969-70; Mgr. of Year First Western Bank and Trust Co., 1971. Mem. Robert Morris Assos. Republican. Roman Catholic. Clubs: Rotary, The Family. Office: 5016 California Ave Bakersfield CA 93309 *

WILEY, MICHAEL EDWARD, social services administrator; b. Longview, Tex., Nov. 16, 1954; s. Charles E. and Jolene (McCormick) W.; m. Carrie Lynn Mori, Aug. 12, 1978. BSW, Colo. State U., 1978; MSW, U. Denver, 1985. Caseworker Morgan County Dept. Social Services, Ft. Morgan, Colo., 1979-84; coord. youth services City of Lakewood, Colo., 1985—. Mem. Nat. Assn. Social Workers, Family Therapy Network. Democrat. Lodge: Kiwanis (treas. Ft. Morgan chpt. 1982-84). Avocations: skiing, bicycling, bird watching. Home: 1150 Galapago #310 Denver CO 80204 Office: Lakewood Youth Services Program 12100 W Alameda Pkwy Lakewood CO 80228

WILEY, RICHARD HAVEN, chemist, educator; b. Mattoon, Ill., May 10, 1913; s. John Frederick and Mary Frances (Moss) W.; m. Marybeth Signaigo, Dec. 28, 1940; children: Richard Haven, Frank Edmund. A.B., U. Ill., 1934, M.S., 1935; Ph.D., U. Wis., 1937; LL.B., Temple U., 1943. Fellow Wis. Alumni Research Found., 1935-37; research chemist E.I. duPont de Nemours & Co., Wilmington, Del., 1937-45; asso. prof. chemistry U. N.C., 1945-49; prof. chemistry, chmn. dept. U. Louisville, 1949-65; NSF sr. postdoctoral fellow Imperial Coll., London, 1957-58; vis. prof. grad. div. CUNY, 1963-64, exec. officer chemistry, 1965-68; prof. chemistry Hunter Coll., 1965-79, prof. emeritus, 1979—; vis. scholar Stanford U., 1978-80; vol. employee San Jose State U., 1980-85. Author: (with P.F. Wiley) Pyrazolones, Pyrazolidones and Derivatives, 1963; Editor: (with P.F. Wiley) Five and Six Membered Compounds with Nitrogen and Oxygen, 1963, Pyrazoles, Pyrazolines, Pyrazolidine and Condensed Ring Systems, 1967; asso. editor: Jour. Chem. and Engring. Data, 1966-71; past mem. editorial bd.: Jour. Polymer Sci, Jour. Macromolecular Chemistry; Contbr. to textbook articles on organic and polymer chemistry sci. jours. Fellow AAAS, Am. Inst. Chemists, N.Y. Acad. Scis.; mem. Am. Chem. Soc. (Midwest award St. Louis sect. 1965), N.Y. Acad. Scis., Phi Beta Kappa, Sigma Xi, Phi Eta Sigma, Phi Lambda Upsilon, Phi Kappa Psi. Patentee in field. Home: 8 Roosevelt Circle Palo Alto CA 94306

WILEY, WILLIAM RODNEY, microbiologist, administrator; b. Oxford, Miss., Sept. 5, 1931; s. William Russell and Edna Alberta (Threlkeld) W.; m. Myrtle Louise Smith, Nov. 10, 1952; 1 child: Johari. B.S., Tougaloo Coll., Miss., 1954; M.S., U. Ill., Urbana, 1960; Ph.D., Wash. State U., Pullman, 1965. Instr. electronics and radar repair Keesler AFB-U.S. Air Force, 1956-58; Rockefeller Found. fellow U. Ill., 1958-59; research assoc. Wash. State U., Pullman, 1960-65; research scientist dept. biology Battelle-Pacific N.W. Labs., 1965-69, mgr. cellular and molecular biology sect. dept. biology, 1969-72, inst. coordinator, life scis. program, assoc. mgr. dept. biology, 1972-74, mgr. dept. biology, 1974-79, dir. research, 1979-84; dir. Pacific N.W. div. Battelle Meml. Inst., Richland, Wash., 1984—; adj. assoc. prof. microbiology Wash. State U., Pullman, 1968—; cons. and lectr. in field. Contbr. chpts. to books, articles to profl. jours. Co-author book in microbiology. Mem. Wash. Tech. Ctr., 1984, sci. adv. panel Wash. Tech. Ctr., 1984—; mem. adv. com. U. Wash. Sch. Medicine, 1976-79; trustee Gonzaga U., 1981—; bd. dirs. MESA program U. Wash., Seattle, 1984—, United Way of Benton & Franklin Counties, Wash., 1984—, Tri-City Indsl. Devel. Council, 1984—; mem. Wash. Council Tech. Advancement, 1984-85 ; bd. dirs. Econ. Devel. Partnership for Wash., 1984—, N.W. Coll. and Univ. Assn. for Sci., 1985—; mem. Tri-City Univ. Ctr. Citizens Adv. Council, 1985—; mem. Wash. State Higher Edn. Coordinating Bd., 1986—, Wash. State Found., 1986— . Served with U.S. Army, 1954-56. Mem. Am. Soc. Biol. Chemists, Am. Soc. Microbiology, AAAS, Soc. Exptl. Biology and Medicine, Sigma Xi. Office: Battelle Meml Inst Pacific NW Div Battelle Blvd Richland WA 99352

WILFLEY, GEORGE MERRITT, mfg. co. exec.; b. Denver, May 23, 1924; s. Elmer R. and Margaret W., B.A. U. Colo., 1950, postgrad., 1977; m. Eleanore Breitenstein; children—George Michael, John Frederick. With A.R. Wilfley & Sons, Inc., Denver, 1950—, pres., 1958—, also dir.; pres., dir. Western Foundries, Inc.; chmn. bd., dir. Conveying Industries, Inc.; dir. First Interstate Bank of Denver, Olson Industries. Vice pres. bd. trustees U. Denver, chmn. bd. Boys Club of Denver, Inc. Served with F.A., AUS, 1943-46. Mem. AIME, Nat. Assn. Corrosion Engrs., Colo. Mining Assn., NAM (dir.). Home: 34 Polo Club Circle Denver CO 80209 Office: PO Box 2330 Denver CO 80201

WILHELM, JAMES RAYMOND, aviation educator; b. Paulding, Ohio, Apr. 6, 1940; s. Louis Albert and Rae Deane (Klingler) W.; m. Linda Rose Trausch, Sept. 17, 1970; children: Jay, Heidi, Erica, Cheryl, Dean. B in Gen. Studies, U. Nebr., 1975; MBA, M in Aviation, Embry-Riddle Aero. U., 1979, M in Aero. Sci., 1980. Commd. officer USAF, 1959, advanced through ranks to maj., 1971, retired, 1979; dept. chmn. Embry-Riddle Aero. U., Prescott, Ariz., 1981-84, 86—, assoc. prof., 1984—; Bd. dirs. CDC Investments Corp., Cedar City, Utah. Councilman City of Prescott, 1983-87. Decorated DFC; recipient Air medal with six oak leaf clusters. Mem. U. Aviation Assn., Am. Assn. Airport Execs., Ariz. Airports Assn., VFW (coordinator nat. polit. action com.), Am. Assn. Airport Execs. Republican. Roman Catholic. Avocations: flying, boating, gardening. Home: 12 Bar Heart Dr Prescott AZ 86301 Office: Embry-Riddle Aero U Bldg 37 3-200 Willow Creek Rd Prescott AZ 86301

WILHELM, ROBERT OSCAR, lawyer, civil engineer; b. Balt., July 7, 1918; s. Clarence Oscar and Agnes Virginia (Grimm) W.; m. Grace L. Sanborn Luckie, Apr. 4, 1919. B.S. in Civil Engring., Ga. Tech. Inst., 1947, M.S.I.M., 1948; J.D., Stanford U., 1951. Bar: Calif. 1952, U.S. Sup. Ct. Mem. Wilhelm, Thompson, Wentholt and Gibbs, Redwood City, Calif., 1952—; gen. counsel Bay Counties Gen. Contractors; pvt. practice civil engring., Redwood City, 1952—; pres. Bay Counties Builders Escrow, Inc., 1972—. Served with C.E., AUS, 1942-46. Mem. Bay Counties Civil Engrs. (pres. 1957), Peninsula Builders Exchange (pres. 1958-71, dir.), Calif. State Builders Exchange (tres. 1971). Clubs: Mason, Odd Fellows, Eagle, Elks. Author: The Manual of Procedures for the Construction Industry, 1971; columnist Law and You in Daily Pacific Builder, 1955—; author: Construction Law for Contractors, Architects and Engineers. Home: 463 Raymondo Dr Woodside CA 94062 Office: 600 Allerton Redwood City CA 94063

WILHELM, STEPHEN PAUL, business executive; b. Berkeley, Calif., Oct. 28, 1948; s. Stephen and Elizabeth Ruth (Wilson) W.; m. Lila Marie Osborn, Aug. 21, 1971. B.A. in Physiology and Psychology, U. Calif.-Berkeley, 1971. Sr. claim rep., med. cost containment analyst Aetna Life Ins. Co., Oakland, Calif., 1971-81; v.p. Nematode Farm, Inc., Palo Alto, Calif.; founder, pres. NEMATEC-Biol. Control Agts., San Leandro, Calif. Chmn. community adv. council Mt. Diablo Hosp. Med. Ctr., Concord, Calif., 1978-82. Home: 65 Thousand Oaks Oakland CA 94605 Office: NEMATEC PO Box 758 San Leandro CA 94577-0958

WILHELM, WILLIAM GREGORY, electronics executive; b. La Jolla, Calif., May 9, 1952; s. John Irving and Rose Marie (Macatee) W. BA, U. San Diego, 1974; JD, Calif. Western U., 1978. Bar: Calif. 1978, U.S. Dist. Ct. (so. dist.) Calif. 1979. Assoc. Schofield & McGowan, La Jolla, 1978-80; sole practice La Jolla, 1980-85; pres. Sector Research and Devel., Inc., La Jolla, 1981-82, Cordic, Inc., San Diego, 1982—; bd. dirs. Trigomatic, Inc., San Diego, 1986—. Inventor electronics equipment. Republican. Home: 711 Fern Glen La Jolla CA 92037 Office: Cordic Inc 7162 Convoy Ct San Diego CA 92111

WILK, STEPHEN RICHARD, research assistant; b. New Brunswick, N.J., Dec. 1, 1955; s. Joseph Stephen and Maria (Szlachtowicz) W. BS in Physics, MIT, 1977; MS in Optics, Rochester U., 1983. Research asst. U. Utah, 1983—. Contbr. articles to profl. jours. Mem. Am. Inst. Physics, Optical Soc. Am., Sigma Xi. Avocations: writing, cycling, racquetball, karate, skiing. Home: 120 Colfax St South River NJ 08882 Office: Physics Dept U Utah Salt Lake City UT 84112

WILKENFELD, JEROME, environmental, health and safety consultant; b. Bklyn., Oct. 25, 1920; s. Elias and Pauline (Nadel) W.; m. Rhoda B. Barandes, Dec. 21, 1969; children—Richard S., Robert M. B.Chem. Engring., CCNY, 1943. Successively operating and tech. assignments, dir. process engring. group, quality control and product specification, mgr. research and control Hooker Chems. & Plastics Corp., 1943-65, dir. corp. program environ. health, 1966-78, dir. environ. health, 1970-78; dir. health, environ. and safety, Occidental Petroleum Corp., Los Angeles, 1978-86; cons. environ., health and safety programs, Los Angeles, 1986—; mem. N.Y. State Air Pollution Control Bd., 1958-70, N.Y. State Environ. Bd., 1970-80, N.Y. State Health Planning Adv. Council, 1972-76; adv. com. Calif. Occupational Health Ctrs., 1982—; solvents adv. com. EPA, 1970-72. Bd. dirs. Am. Lung Assn., 1971-78. Mem. Mfg. Chemists Assn. (chmn. environ. coms.), Am. Petroleum Inst., Chlorine Inst., Air Pollution Control Assn. (chmn. Niagara Frontier sect., Outstanding Contbn. award for air pollution control 1964), Environ. Health Commn. (chmn.), N.Y. State Chem. Industries Council, Am. Inst. Chem. Engrs., Am. Chem. Soc., Water Pollution Control Fedn. Contbg. author: Waste Management and Control, 1966; Industrial Pollution Control Handbook, 1971; Occupational Safety and Health Handbook. Office: Wilkenfeld Assocs 5757 Owensworth Ave Suite 10 Woodland Hills CA 91367

WILKENING, JANE SHEPARD, secondary school teacher; b. Jacksonville, N.C., Jan. 24, 1943; s. Percil Henry and Margaret Susan (King) S.; m. Peter Kohler Wilkening, Feb. 12, 1970; children: Brent Colin, Derek Stefan. BA, Atlantic Christian Coll., 1965. Cert. English, mental retarded educator, learning handicapped educator, resource specialist. English tchr. Perry High Sch., Pitts., 1965-67, Northwoods Park Jr. High, Jacksonville, N.C., 1967-68; tchr. of the educable retarded Sun Valley Jr. High, Los Angeles Unified Sch. Dist., 1968-73, reading coordinator, 1973-80; tchr. of educable retarded Sun Valley Jr. High, Los Angeles, 1980—; lectr. ednl. colloquium LAUSD, Calif., 1984, spl. edn. fall conf., LAUSD, Calif., 1985; leader staff devel. programs: needs assessment for spl. edn., Sun Valley, Calif., 1983-85. Contbr. articles to profl. jours. Sec. Laurel Hall Day Sch. Com., North Hollywood, Calif., 1984-87; mem. ch. council Emmanuel Lutheran Ch., 1984-87. Mem. Spl. Educator's Resource Network, Downs Syndrome Parent's Group, Council for Exceptional Children, Computer Using Educators, NEA, United Tchrs. Los Angeles. Avocations: needlework, photography, computers, reading. Home: 14032 Hartsook St Sherman Oaks CA 91423 Office: Sun Valley Jr High Sch 7330 Bakman Ave Sun Valley CA 91352

WILKENING, LAUREL LYNN, university official and dean, planetary scientist; b. Richland, Wash., Nov. 23, 1944; d. Marvin Hubert and Ruby Alma (Barks) W.; m. Godfrey Theodore Sill, May 18, 1974. B.A., Reed Coll., 1966; Ph.D., U. Calif.-San Diego, 1970. Asst. prof., assoc. prof. U. Ariz., Tucson, 1973-80, dir. Lunar and Planetary Lab., head planetary scis., 1981-83, vice provost, prof. planetary scis., 1983-85, v.p. research, dean Grad. Coll., 1985—; div. scientist NASA Hdqrs., Washington, 1980; vice chmn. Nat. Commn. on Space, Washington, 1984-86; co-chmn. primitive bodies mission study team NASA/European Space Agy., 1984-85; chmn. com. rendezvous sci. working group NASA, 1983-85; mem. panel on internat. cooperation and competition in space Congl. Office Tech. Assessment, 1982-83. Author: (monograph) Particle Track Studies and the Origin of Gas-Rich Meteorites, 1971; editor: Comets, 1982. Mem. Ariz. Gov.'s Adv. Com., 1984-86. U. Calif. Regents fellow, 1966-67; NASA trainee, 1967-70. Fellow Meteoritical Soc. (councilor 1976-80), AAUW; mem. Am. Astron. Soc. (chmn. div. planetary scis. 1984-85), Am. Geophys. Union, AAAS, Internat. Astron. Union (orgn. com. 1979-82), Phi Beta Kappa. Democrat. Avocations: gardening; camping; swimming. Office: U Ariz Adminstrn 601 Tucson AZ 85721

WILKER, LEN, marketing executive; b. Boston, Jan. 8, 1931; s. Harry and Bessie (Deckelbaum) W.; m. Louise Margot Kaplan, June 25, 1985; children: Gregory, Leah, Aaron, Rivka. BS, Northeastern U., 1954; M, West Coast U., 1964. Western regional sales mgr. Computer Automation, Irvine, Calif., 1970-75; nat. sales mgr. Qume, San Jose, Calif, 1975-80; pres. Wilken, Inc., Dublin, Calif., 1980-83; v.p. mktg. CXI, Palo Alto, Calif., 1983-85, mktg. cons., 1983; dir. mktg. Matrix Impact Tech., Fremont, Calif., 1985-86; v.p. sales Solana Electronics, San Diego, 1986—. Pres. SOS Community Service, Sierra Madre, Calif., 1972-75; scoutmaster Boy Scouts Am., Hayward, Calif., 1979-85; bd. dirs. Webloe Scouts, Sierra Madre, 1973-75. Served as cpl. U.S. Army, 1954-56. Recipient Community Service awart St. Rita's Ch., Sierra Madre, 1973; named Outstanding Scoutmaster Boy Scouts Am., Hayward, 1981. Mem. IEEE, Instrumentation Soc. Am. Democrat. Jewish. Lodge: B'nai Brith. Home: 905-A Menlo Ave Menlo Park CA 94025-4625 Office: Matrix Impact Tech 7887 Dunbrook Rd Suite A San Diego CA 92126

WILKERSON, KENNETH DWAYNE, speech-language pathologist; b. Roswell, N.Mex., Mar. 27, 1954; m. Tammie D. Hall, Mar. 9, 1979; children: Heather, Dane. BS summa cum laude, Eastern N.Mex. U., 1981, MS, 1983. Speech-lang. pathologist in charge of ancillary services Portales (N.Mex.) Mcpl. Sch. Dist., 1983—. Mem. Am. Speech Lang. Hearing Assn. (cert. clin. competency), Phi Kappa Phi, Blue Key. Republican. Mem. Assembly of God. Avocation: calligraphy. Home: 725 W 17th Ln Portales NM 88130 Office: Portales Mcpl Schs PO Box 779 Portales NM 88130

WILKES, LINDA MARIE, chemistry educator; b. Los Angeles, Nov. 23, 1947; d. Warner Thomas Wilkes and Rena (D'Arcy) Jones. BA, Calif. State U., Sacramento, 1970; PhD, U. Nev., 1981. Instr. chemistry Sierra Nev. Coll., Incline Village, 1975-78; research assoc. chemistry U. Nev., Reno, 1981-82; head analytical lab. Nev. Bur. Mines, Reno, 1982-83; assoc. prof. chemistry U. So. Colo., Pueblo, 1983—. Contbr. articles to profl. jours. Mem. Am. Chem. Soc., Sigma Xi, Sigma Sigma Kappa. Avocations: reading, music, skiing, biking, weight-lifting. Office: U So Colo Dept Chemistry Pueblo CO 81001

WILKIE, DONALD WALTER, biologist, aquarium museum director; b. Vancouver, B.C., Can., June 20, 1931; s. Otway James and Jessie Margaret (McLeod) W.; m. Patricia Ann Archer, May 18, 1980; children: Linda, Douglas, Susanne. B.A., U. B.C., 1960, M.Sc., 1966. Curator Vancouver Pub. Aquarium, 1961-63, Phila. Aquarama, 1963-65; dir. aquarium-mus. Scripps Instn. Oceanography, La Jolla, Calif., 1965—; aquatic cons. Contbr. numerous articles to profl. jours. Bd. dirs. Univ. State Employees Credit Union. Fellow San Diego Mus. Natural History.; mem. Am. Assn. Zoo Parks and Aquariums, Internat. Assn. Aquatic Animal Medicine, Nat. Marine Edn. Assn., Am. Assn. Mus., Am. Soc. Ichthyologists and Herpetologists. Home: 4548 Cather Ave San Diego CA 92122 Office: Scripps Instn Oceanography 8602 La Jolla Shores Dr La Jolla CA 92093

WILKIN, EDITH ESTHER, editor; b. Boise, Idaho, Feb. 2, 1922; d. Rolfe Jay and Edith Adair (Young) Denniston; m. Harry Thomas Wilkin, Apr. 6, 1963 (dec. 1968). A.A., Antelope Valley Jr. Coll. Stenographer, U.S. Air Force, Norton AFB, Calif., 1942-52, sec., Rabat, Morocco, 1952-54, editorial sec., March AFB, Calif., 1955-73; editor/author newsletter Jurupa Cultural Ctr., Riverside, Calif., 1979—; co-editor Riverside County Republican Mo. Newsletter, 1978-80. Author: St. John's Bread, 1975. Editor: The Great Gymnosperms, 1979, Putting the Sun to Work, 1980. Pres. bd. dirs. Jurupa Mountains Cultural Ctr., Riverside, Calif., 1975, dir., 1972-84; bd. dirs. Parents of Jurupa, Riverside, 1974-84. Recipient Spl. Achievement award, 15th Air Force, 1969. Mem. SCRIBE. Republican. Office: Jurupa Mountains Cultural Ctr 6721 Granite Hill Dr Riverside CA 92509

WILKINS, BRYAN JAMES, religious organization administrator; b. Fairbury, Nebr., Apr. 22, 1961; s. James Duane and Verna Mae (Kisser) W. BA in Bus. Adminstrn., Evangel Coll., 1983. House framer Horner Constrn., Grand Island, Nebr., 1976-78; with Chief Industries, Grand Island, 1979; salesman Davey's Locker Sportfishing, Newport Beach, Calif., 1980-82; valet mgr. Antonello Ristorante, Santa Ana, Calif., 1983-84; bus. mgr., treas. Colonial Bible Ch., Tustin, Calif., 1984—, athletic dir., 1985—; salesman Omega C.G. Ltd., Chgo., 1986. Recipient Gold Key Art award Nebr. Scholastic Art Soc., 1976; Basic Ednl. Opportunity Grants, 1979-81. Mem. Christian Ministries Mgmt. Assn. Clubs: Chess, Lettermen's (Grand Island) (sec. 1978-79). Avocations: bicycling, running, racquetball, music, drawing. Home: 258 Flower Apt C Costa Mesa CA 92627 Office: Colonial Bible Ch 13601 Browning Ave Tustin CA 92680

WILKINS, FLOYD, JR., lawyer; b. Fowler, Calif., Sept. 8, 1925; s. Floyd and Kathryn (Springborg) W.; m. Holly Blee, June 18, 1949 (div. Jan. 1964); children: Douglas B., Janet H., Steven B., Kevin D.; m. Sybil Ann Perrault, Feb. 22, 1964. BS, U. Calif., Berkeley, 1946; LLB, Harvard U., 1952. Bar: N.Y. 1953, Calif. 1959. Assoc. Dwight, Royall, Harris, Koegel & Caskey, N.Y.C., 1952-58; v.p., trust officer San Diego Trust & Savs. Bank, 1958-63; assoc., then ptnr., prin. Seltzer Caplan Wilkins & McMahon, P.C. and predecessors, San Diego, 1963—; lectr. U. So. Calif. Tax Inst., Los Angeles, 1975, Title Ins. and Trust Co., Los Angeles and Santa Ana, Calif., 1973, 78, 83, Trust Services of Am. Tax Forum, San Diego, U. Calif. Continuing Edn. of Bar, San Diego, 1977—. Bd. dirs., pres. San Diego County Citizens Scholarship Found. Served with USNR, 1944-46. Mem. ABA, State Bar Calif., San Diego County Bar Assn. Republican. Avocations: travel, photography, wine, gardening. Home: 2005 Soledad Ave La Jolla CA 92037 Office: Seltzer Caplan Wilkins & McMahon PC 3003-3044 4th Ave PO Box X33999 San Diego CA 92103

WILKINS, ROBERT MASON, physician, rancher; b. Durham, N.C., Apr. 18, 1937; s. Robert Bruce and Lillian Marguerite (Mason) W.; m. Gloria Charlotte Heil, Feb. 13, 1968; children—Marguerite Davis, Robert Bruce. A.B. in English, U. N.C., 1959; M.D., Wake Forest U., 1963. Diplomate Am. Bd. Internal Medicine. Intern, U. Colo. Med. Ctr., Denver, 1963-64; fellow in gastroenterology Duke U. Med. Ctr., Durham, 1964-65, resident in internal medicine, 1967-68, fellow in gastroenterology, 1968-69; practice medicine specializing in gastroenterology Croasdaile Clinic, Durham, 1969-72; practice medicine specializing in gastroenterology, Nampa, Idaho, 1972—; assoc. med. staff Watts Hosp., Durham, cons. gastroenterology VA Hosp., Fayetteville; clin. assoc. community health scis. Duke U. Med. Ctr.; mem. staff Mercy Med. Ctr., Nampa, 1972—; clin. asst. prof. medicine U. Wash., 1977—. Served with USN, 1965-67. Fellow ACP (gov. Idaho), Am. Coll. Gastroenterology; mem. Am. Soc. Gastrointestinal Endoscopy, Am. Gastroent. Assn., AMA, Am. Soc. Internal Medicine, Idaho Med. Assn., Idaho Soc. Internal Medicine, Idaho Angus Assn. (pres. 1980-82), Western States Angus Assn. (pres. 1981-83). Episcopalian. Contbr. articles to med. jours. Home: Route 4 Dry Lake Rd Nampa ID 83651 Office: Med Ctr Physicians 215 E Hawaii St Nampa ID 83651

WILKINSON, C. GERALD, clinical social work; b. Pocatello, Idaho, Jan. 29, 1930; s. J.R. and Gladys H. (England) W.; m. Barbara G. Elliott; children: Nancy Anne, Robert Elliott. BA, Idaho State U., 1953; MSW, Wash. U., 1957. Social worker Mendota St. Hosp., Madison, Wis., 1957-59; chief social worker Milw. Psychiat. Found., 1959-62, Child Psychiatry Clinic, Milw., 1962-64; coordinator profl. services Wolworth County Counseling, Elkhorn, Wis., 1964-69; social work specialist Region I Mental Health Ctr., Coeur d'Alene, Idaho, 1969—; pvt. practice clin. social work, Coeur d'Alene, 1983—. Mem. Acad. Cert. Social Workers (cert.), Register of Clin. Social Workers, Nat. Assn. Social Workers (Social Worker of Yr. award 1986), Idaho Bd. Social Work Examiners (bd. dirs. 1985—). Home: 830 N 17th St Coeur d'Alene ID 83814 Office: Region I Mental Health 2195 Ironwood Ct Coeur d'Alene ID 83819

WILKINSON, CHARLES THOMAS, safety administrator; b. Mansfield, Ohio, Nov. 22, 1932; s. Ralph Armstrong and Susan Anne (Franko) W.; B.A., U. Md., 1965; student Indsl. Coll. Armed Forces, 1973; M.A., Ball State U., 1976; postgrad. Ariz. State U., 1976; m. Shirley Jean Steward, Aug. 21, 1954; children: Scott Alan, Sandra Sue, Gail Ann. Cert. safety exec. World Safety Orgn. Joined USAF, 1953, commd. aviation cadet USAF, 1953, advanced through grades to lt. col., 1970; dir. safety Hahn Air Base, Germany, 1974-77; dir. Battle Staff Support Center, 25th Norad Region, McChord AFB, Wash., 1977-79; ret., 1979; chief safety and security services Western State Hosp., Ft. Steilacoom, Wash., 1979-80; Western Wash. field safety officer Dept. Social and Health Services, Tacoma, 1980-81, safety program mgr., 1981-85, loss control mgr., 1986—. Decorated Air medal with 2 oak leaf clusters. Recipient Community Service award United Way, 1974. Mem. Am. Soc. Safety Engrs., Nat. Safety Mgmt. Soc., Air Force Assn., VFW, Order Daedalians. Lodges: Elks, Kiwanis (bd. dirs. Clover Park 1978-80, v.p. 1980-81, pres. 1982-83). Home: 7920 98th Ave SW Tacoma WA 98498 Office: Western Wash Dept Social & Health Services 8815 S Tacoma Way Suite 220 Tacoma WA 98499

WILKINSON, DAVID LAWRENCE, state government official; b. Washington, Dec. 6, 1936; s. Ernest LeRoy and Alice Valera (Ludlow) W.; m. Patricia Anne Thomas, Dec. 30, 1976; children: David Andrew, Samuel Thomas, Margaret Alice. B.A. cum laude in History, Brigham Young U., 1961; B.A. in Jurisprudence, Oxford U., Eng., 1964, M.A., 1969; J.D., U. Calif.-Berkeley, 1966. Bar: Calif. 1966, Utah 1972. Assoc. Lawler, Felix & Hall, Los Angeles, 1966-71; ptnr. Cook & Wilkinson, Los Angeles, 1971-72; asst. atty. gen. State of Utah, Salt Lake City, 1972-76, 77-79; chief dep. to Salt Lake County Atty., 1979-80; atty. gen. State of Utah, Salt Lake City, 1981—; spl. instr. Brigham Young U. Sch. Law, 1976-77, bd. visitors Sch. of Law, 1983-85; panelist Robert A. Taft Inst. Of Govt., Salt Lake City, 1974-76, 83-84; founder, mgr. Utah Bar. Rev. Course, 1973-76. Mem. Utah Council Criminal Justice Adminstrn., 1974-76, 77, Council Criminal and Juvenile Justice, 1984—. Served with U.S. Army, 1961-62. Rhodes scholar, 1961-64. Mem. Utah Bar Assn. (chmn. eminent domain sect. 1979-80); mem.. Nat. Assn. Attys. Gen. (exec. com. 1984-85); mem. Statewide Assn. Prosecutors (chmn. bd. 1983-84). Republican. Mormon. Office: Utah State Attorney General 236 State Capitol Salt Lake City UT 84114

WILKINSON, DAVID ORMOND, political scientist. s. Theodore Leonard and Helen Stephanie (Brink) W. AB, Harvard U., 1960; MA, Columbia U., 1962, PhD, 1965. Instr. govt. Columbia U., N.Y.C., 1963-64; asst. prof. polit. sci. UCLA, 1964-69, assoc. prof., 1969-73, prof., 1973—. Author: Malraux, 1967, Comparative Foreign Relations, 1969, Revolutionary Civil War, 1975, Deadly Quarrels, 1980, Gen. War, 1986. Office: UCLA Dept Polit Sci Los Angeles CA 90024

WILKINSON, GREGG STUART, epidemiologist; b. Alexandria, Va., July 25, 1942; s. Stanley Stuart and Erna G. (Adleff) W.; m. Jacqueline Neil Roemer, Nov. 12, 1966; children: Julie Caroline, Garret Stuart, Glen Jeffrey, Scott Graham. BA, SUNY, Buffalo, 1969, MA, 1971, PhD, 1973. Assoc. cancer research scientist Rosewell Park Meml. Inst., Buffalo, 1974-78; sr. epidemiologist EPA, Research Triangle Park, N.C., 1978-80; epidemiology group leader Los Alamos (N.Mex.) Nat. Lab., 1980—; cons. U. Tex. Sch. Health Scis., Houston, 1980-82, NSF, Washington, 1985—. Author: An Evaluation of a Cancer Information Telephone Facility: Candial, Praeger Scientific, 1985; contbr. articles to profl. jours. Del. Buffalo Council of Chs., 1977, 78. Grantee Nat. Cancer Inst., 1974-78, U.S. Dept. Energy, 1980—, Nat. Inst. Occupational Health and Safety, 1985—. Mem. Soc. Epidemiologic Research, Am. Sociol. Assn. (assoc.), Am. Pub. Health Assn., AAAS, Phi Kappa Psi (chpt. chaplain 1961-62). Mem. United Ch. Christ. Avocations: gardening, fishing, hunting, horseback riding, camping. Home: 1360 Barranca Rd Los Alamos NM 87544

WILKINSON, JOAN KRISTINE, nurse; b. Rochester, Minn., June 15, 1953; d. A. Ray and Ruth Audrey (Wegwart) Kubly; m. Robert Morris Wilkinson, June 14, 1975; children: Michael Robert, Kathryn Ann. BS in Nursing, U. Wis., 1975; MS, U. Colo., 1986. RN. Team leader Mendota Mental Health Inst., Madison, Wis., 1975-76; care leader Boulder (Colo.) Psychiat. Inst., 1976-78; pub. health nurse, head nurse Rocky Mountain Poison Ctr., Denver, 1978-84; research teaching asst. U. Colo. Health Scis. Ctr., Denver, 1986—. Participant community service United Way, Denver, 1981-84; disaster nurse ARC, Boulder, 1976—, vol. swim instr., 1976-83; vol. nurse Channel 9 Health Fair, Boulder, 1983. Recipient Gold award United Way, Denver, 1981, Cert. of Recognition, ARC, Madison, 1978; U. Colo. Health Scis. Ctr. fellow, 1986. Mem. Colo. Nurses Assn. (dist. 12 scholar 1983-86), Am. Nurses Assn., World Health Assn., Sigma Tau Theta. Lutheran. Home: 1195 Hancock Dr Boulder CO 80303 Office: U Colo Health Scis Ctr Sch Nursing 9th and Colorado Denver CO 80206

WILKINSON, LAWRENCE HAMLETT, film and television producer; b. Greensboro, N.C., Jan. 2, 1950; s. William Cook and Joy (Morgan) W.; m. Joy Draper Williams, June 5, 1972 (div. June 1978). BA summa cum laude, Davidson Coll., 1972; BPhil, Oxford U., 1974; MBA with distinction, Harvard U., 1976. Dir. planning and mktg. Sta. WNET, N.Y.C., 1976-79; dir. prodn. and mktg. Sta. KQEO Inc., San Francisco, 1979-81; mng. ptnr. Wilkinson & Assocs., San Francisco, 1981-84; gen. mgr. Colossal Pictures, Inc., San Francisco, 1984—, also bd. dirs.; cons. EEN (Pub. Broadcasting System Network), Boston, 1981—, SRI Internat., Menlo Park, Calif., 1981-83, Varitel Communications, San Francisco, 1982-84; pres., co-founder Friends of KQEO, San Francisco, 1982—. Author: Public Broadcasting in the U.S., 1976; co-editor: Paradise Lost, (John Milton); producer, writer, reporter numerous T.V. news programs, 1976—. Fellow: Love, 1974-76, Sloan, 1968-72; Marshall scholar, 1972-74, Nat. Merit scholar, 1968-72; recipient Pub. Broadcasting System Devel. award, 1979-80, Emmy award, 1978, 79. Mem. Nat. Acad. T.V. Arts and Scis., Advt. Assn. San Francisco, Film Arts Found. Clubs: Commonwealth (San Francisco); Harvard (N.Y.C. and San Francisco). Avocations: traveling, reading. Home: 2012 Broadway San Francisco CA 94115 Office: Colossal Pictures Inc 2800 Third St San Francisco CA 94107

WILKINSON, PHILIP CHARLES, television advertising executive; b. Chgo., Apr. 14, 1956; s. Francis Xavier and Mary Elizabeth (Sprissler) W.; m. Wendy Marthe Kruidenier, Aug. 11, 1985. BBA, San Diego State U., 1979. Account exec. Info-Radio Broadcasting, San Diego, 1980-81; advt. dir. U.S.D. Sports Publs., San Diego, 1981-82; sales mgr. Univision TV Network, Beverly Hills, Calif., 1982—. Coordinator La Gloria Sch. Toys for Tots Drive, Tijuana, Mex., 1984—. Mem. Hollywood Radio and TV Soc., Adclub of Los Angeles, San Diego State U. Alumni and Assocs. Republican. Roman Catholic. Clubs: Fairbanks Ranch Country (Rancho Santa Fe, Calif.). Avocations: scuba diving. Home: 719 Chapala Dr Pacific Palisades CA 90272 Office: Univ TV Network 9200 Sunset Blvd #1100 Los Angeles CA 90069

WILL, OTTO ALLEN, JR., psychiatrist; b. Caldwell, Kans., Apr. 26, 1910; s. Otto August and Florence Sarah (Keeling) W.; A.B. with gt. distinction in Econs. and Sociology, Stanford U., 1933, M.D., 1940; grad. Washington Sch. Psychiatry, 1950, Washington Psychoanalytic Inst., 1953; m. Beulah Parker, Oct. 23, 1980; children by previous marriage—Patrick Terence, Deirdre Gwen. Intern, Stanford Lane Hosps., San Francisco, 1939-40, asst. resident in pediatrics, 1940-41, asst. resident in internal medicine, 1941-42; practice medicine specializing in psychiatry, Washington, 1943-67, Rockville, Md., 1947-67, Stockbridge, Mass., 1967-78, San Francisco and Richmond, Calif., 1978—; staff psychiatrist Chestnut Lodge, Rockville, 1947-54, dir. psychotherapy, 1954-67; mem. faculty Washington Sch. Psychiatry, 1950-67, trustee, 1953—; mem. faculty Washington Psychoanalytic Inst., 1953-67, tng. analyst, 1958-67; asso. clin. prof. dept. psychiatry, U. Md. Sch. Medicine, Balt., 1956-64, clin. prof., 1964-67; part-time lectr. dept. psychiatry Johns Hopkins U., Balt., 1962-67; vis. prof. dept. psychiatry U. Chgo. Sch. Medicine, 1963-64; clin. prof. dept. psychiatry Cornell U., N.Y.C., 1967-75; med. dir. Austen Riggs Center, Inc., Stockbridge, 1967-78; vis. prof. dept. psychiatry U. Cin., 1972; mem. faculty U. Mass. Sch. Medicine, Amherst, 1976-78; clin. dir. adolescent and young adult sect. dept. psychiatry Mt. Zion Hosp., San Francisco, 1978-79; pvt. practice, 1979—. Trustee, Austen Riggs Center, 1967—. Served to lt. comdr., M.C., USN, 1942-47. Life fellow Am. Psychiat. Assn., Am. Acad. Psychoanalysis; life mem. Washington Psychoanalytic Soc., Western Mass. Psychiat. Soc., Am. Psychoanalytic Assn., Internat. Psychoanalytic Assn.; mem. No. Calif. Psychiat. Soc., William Alanson White Psychoanalytic Soc. (hon. mem.), Am. Psychosomatic Soc., AAAS, Med. Soc. of St. Elizabeth's Hosp., Phi Beta Kappa, Alpha Omega Alpha. Contbr. articles on psychotherapy and psychiat. illness to prof. jours. Address: 307 Western Dr Richmond CA 94801

WILLARD, H(ARRISON) ROBERT, elec. engr.; b. Seattle, May 31, 1933; s. Harrison Eugene and Florence Linea (Chelquist) W.; B.S.E.E., U. Wash., 1955, M.S.E.E., 1957, Ph.D., 1971. Staff asso. Boeing Sci. Research Labs., Seattle, 1959-64; research asso. U. Wash., 1968-72, sr. engr. and research prof. applied physics lab., 1972-81; sr. engr. Boeing Aerospace Co., Seattle, 1981-84; dir. instrumentation and engring. Tech. Dynamics Inc., 1984—. Served with AUS, 1957-59. Lic. profl. engr., Wash. Mem. IEEE, Am. Geophys. Union, Phi Beta Kappa, Sigma Xi, Tau Beta Pi. Contbr. articles to tech. jours. Patentee in field. Office: 18800 142 Ave NE Suite 4 Woodinville WA 98072

WILLARD, JAMES DOUGLAS, health care administrator; b. St. Edward, Nebr., Aug. 13, 1945; s. Merrell and Eloise Vanell (Andreasen) W.; m. Sylvia Lawrence, Jan. 2, 1970; children: James Christopher, Elizabeth. B.S., Colo. State U., 1967; M.H.A., U. Minn., 1972. Asst. adminstr. People to People Health Found (HOPE), Washington, 1968-70; assoc. dir. Comprehensive Health Plan Agy., Worcester, Mass., 1973-74; v.p., adminstr. Luth. Med. Ctr., Wheat Ridge, Colo., 1974-80, exec. v.p., 1980-82, pres., 1982—, chief exec. officer, 1984—, also dir.; dir. Hosp. Shared Services, Denver, 1981-85, COPAC, Denver, 1982-85, Northeast Central Health Systems, Denver, Interhealth, 1985; dir., treas. InterHealth, 1985—. Mem. Jefferson County Pvt. Industry Council; mem. Met. Denver Hosp. Council, past pres. Mem. Am. Hosp. Assn., Colo. Hosp. Assn. (chmn. council data mgmt., bd. dirs. 1986—, med. indigent com.), Denver C. of C. (leadership roundtable). Mem. United Ch. of Christ. Club: Rotary of Denver. Home: 10888 W 30th Pl Lakewood CO 80215 Office: Luth Med Ctr 8300 W 38th Ave Wheat Ridge CO 80033

WILLARDSON, LYMAN SESSIONS, agricultural engineering educator; b. Ephraim, Utah, May 10, 1927; s. Lyman Young and Alice (Sessions) W.; m. Vivian Berrey, Oct. 8, 1948; children: L. William, Kathleen, Timothy M., Mark B., Paul B., Laura. BCE, Utah State U., 1950, MCE, 1955; PhD in Agrl. Engring., Ohio State U., 1967. Instr. tng. course Peace Corps, San Luis Obispo, Calif., 1963; instr. irrigation sci. Utah State U., Logan, 1964, instr. Utah Agr. Exptl. Sta., prof., 1974—; cons. WMS II, Africa, 1985, Keller-Bliesner Engrs., Mescalero, Calif., 1985; expert witness Lewis, D'Amato, Brisbois & Bisgaard, San Diego, 1985; researcher Agrl. Research Service USDA, Calif., 1957-74. Contbr. articles to profl. jours. Mem. Mcpl. Golf Course Planning Com., Logan, 1986. Served with USN, 1945-46. Mem. ASCE (tech. com. mem.), Am. Soc. Agrl. Engrs. (vice chmn., mem. tech. com.), Internat. Commn. Irrigation and Drainage (chmn. of research and spl. studies, bd. dirs.), NSPE, ASTM (chmn.), Sigma Tau, Gamma Sigma Delta. Avocations: woodwork, photography. Home: 146 North 500 West Logan UT 84321 Office: Utah State U Dept Agr Irrigation UMC 4105 Logan UT 84322

WILLARDSON, ROBERT KENT, physicist, manufacturing technology executive; b. Gunnison, Utah, July 11, 1923; s. Anthony Robert and Alice Eva (Pierce) W.; m. Beth Marie Bennett, Sept. 12, 1947; children—Amanda Marie Ballou, Elizabeth Ann Engar, Jennie Lynette. B.S in Physics, Brigham Young U., 1949; M.S in Solid State Physics, Iowa State U., 1951. Asst. chief phys. chemistry div. Battelle Meml. Inst., Columbus, Ohio, 1951-60; gen. mgr. electronic materials div. Bell & Howell Co., Pasadena, Calif., 1960-72; pres. Electronic Materials Corp., Pasadena, 1973; sales mgr. Cominco Am. Inc., Spokane, Wash., 1973-82; pres. Willardson Cons., Spokane, 1982-84; pres., dir. Cryscon Techs. Inc., Phoenix, 1984-87. Editor: Compound Semiconductors, 1962; Semiconductors and Semimetals, 29 vols., 1966—. Served as sgt. USAF, 1942-46. Mem. Components, Hybrids and Mfg. Tech. (chmn. TC-5), Am. Phys. Soc., IEEE (sr., chmn. San Gabriel chpt. 1967-68), Am. Chem. Soc., Electrochem. Soc., Internat. Soc. Hybrid Microelectronics. Democrat. Mormon. Home: E 12722 23d Ave Spokane WA 99216

WILLBANKS, ROGER PAUL, publishing and book distributing company executive; b. Denver, Nov. 25, 1934; s. Edward James and Ada Gladys (Davis) W.; m. Beverly Rae Masters, June 16, 1957; children—Wendy Lee, Roger Craig. B.S., U. Denver, 1957, M.B.A., 1965. Economist, bus. writer, bus. forecaster Mountain States Telephone Co., Denver, 1959-66; dir. pub. relations Denver Bd. Water Commrs., 1967-70; pres. Royal Publs. Inc., Denver, 1971—, Nutri-Books Corp., Denver, 1971—. Editor Denver Water News, 1967-70, Mountain States Bus., 1962-66. Mem. Gov. of Colo.'s Revenue Forecasting Com., 1963-66. Served with U.S. Army, 1957-58. Recipient pub. relations award Am. Water Works Assn., 1970. Mem. Am. Booksellers Assn., Nat. Nutritional Foods Assn., Pub. Relations Soc. Am. (charter mem. health sect.), Denver C. of C., SAR. Republican. Lutheran. Clubs: Columbine Country, Denver Press, Auburn Cord Duesenberg, Rolls Royce Owners, Classic Car of Am., Denver U. Century (Denver). Address: Royal Publs Inc PO Box 5793 Denver CO 80217

WILLBANKS, SUE SUTTON, investment executive, writer, artist; b. Luling, Tex., Sept. 24, 1935; d. William Herbert and Melba Ophelia (Ward) Sutton; m. Charles Walter Willbanks, Nov. 21, 1953 (dec. Feb. 1979); children—Jill Ann, Brenda Kay. B.S., Tex. Tech. U., 1955; M.A., U. Tex. Permian Basin, 1980. Cert. secondary, vocat. and elem. tchr., Tex. Tchr., Big

Spring Ind. Sch. Dist., Tex., 1964-68, 1972-79, dept. chmn., 1980-82; owner, pres. Sutwill Co., Aiea, Hawaii, 1981—; pvt. practice psychotherapy, Tex., Hawaii, 1979—. Author short stories and poems. Contbr. articles to profl. jours. Organizer Silver Heels Vol. Fire Dept., Howard County, Tex., 1970-71; bd. dirs. Permian Basin Planned Parenthood Assn., Odessa, Tex., 1980-82; organist Immaculate Heart of Mary Ch., Big Spring, Tex., 1975-78;Mem. Nat. Assn. Female Execs., Psi Inst. Hawaii, Common Boundary,Planetary Citizens. Methodist. Avocations: interior decorating; acting. Home: 98-1457 B Kaahumanu St Aiea HI 96701

WILLEY, DARRELL S., education educator; b. Farmington, Utah, May 9, 1925; s. R.C. Willey and Helen (Swaner) Barber; m. Velma Roush, June 7, 1947 (dec. May 1971); children: Randie Carol Boldra, Trica L. Hazelton, Jacqui I. Clements; m. Irene Knox, May 30, 1972; 1 foster child, Roger E. Mayfield III. AB, Denver U., 1948; MS, Utah State U., 1949; EdD, U. Utah, 1953; postdoctoral, U. So. Calif. Cert. sch. mgmt., Utah, Colo., N.Mex. Prin. Wendover (Utah) Sch., 1949-50, West Sch., Littleton, Colo., 1952-53; from asst. prof. to assoc. prof. edn. mgmt. and devel. N.Mex. State U., Las Cruces, 1953-82, prof., 1982—, dir. edn. research ctr., 1969-82, head dept. edn. mgmt. and devel., 1962-70, dir. ERIC-CRESS program, 1966-68, dir. edn. research tng. program, 1966-72; cons. NIH, NSF, U.S. Dept. Edn., U.S. Civil Rights Commn., 1963—. Author N.Mex. Survey Vocat. Tech. Ednl. Needs, 1963-64. Senator's del. White House Conf. on Children, 1970. Served as sgt. USAAF, 1943-45, CBI. Mem. AAAS, Am. Assn. Sch. Administrs., Am. Edn. Research Assn., Hump Pilots Assn., Phi Delta Kappa. Democrat. Mormon. Lodge: Elks. Avocations: travel, color photography, coins. Home: PO Box 486 Mesilla NM 88046

WILLHITE, CALVIN CAMPBELL, toxicologist; b. Salt Lake City, Apr. 27, 1952; s. Jed Butler and Carol (Campbell) W.; m. Tandra Pauline Jorgensen, Aug. 14, 1982. BS, Utah State U., 1974, MS, 1977; PhD, Dartmouth Coll., 1980. Toxicologist Western Region Lab. USDA, Berkeley, Calif., 1980-85; toxicologist dept. health services State of Calif., Berkeley, 1985—. Contbr. articles to profl. jours. Nat. Inst. Child Health and Human Devel. grantee, 1986; recipient Research award Calif. Assn. Profl. Scientists, 1986. Mem. Soc. Toxicology (Frank R. Blood award 1986), Teratology Soc., Sigma Xi, Alpha Zeta. Republican. Mem. United Ch. of Christ. Home: 33029 Korbel St Union City CA 94587 Office: Community Toxicology Unit 2151 Berkeley Way Berkeley CA 94704

WILLI, EDWARD FREDERICK, fire protection equipment company executive; b. Sacramento, July 20, 1920; s. Edward Frederick and Elsie Eleanor (Orr) W.; B.S., U. Calif.-Berkeley, 1942; M.B.A., Harvard U., 1949; m. Helena Wendy Carey, May 20, 1950; children—Wendy, Leslie. Adminstrv. asst. to pres. Avoset Co., Oakland, Calif., 1949-60; pres. Wilkirk Inc., Hayward, Calif., 1961—, also chmn. bd.; founding stockholder Bay Area Bank, Redwood City, 1979; dir. Bell Plaza Travel Inc., 1981. Mem. adv. bd. Assistance League Santa Clara County. Served to lt. USN, 1942-47. Kiwanis Clubs scholar, 1937. Mem. Nat. Fire Protection Assn., Harvard U. Bus. Sch. Assn., U. Calif.-Berkeley Alumni Assn., Phi Delta Theta (pres. 1941). Republican. Episcopalian. Clubs: Kiwanis, Masons, Elks. Office: Wilkirk Inc 25634 Nickel Pl Hayward CA 94545

WILLIAM, RAYMOND D., horticulture educator, agricultural consultant; b. Denver, Oct. 1, 1946; s. Ray D. and Elizabeth Jane (Anderson) W.; m. Nancy Lee Garber, June 21, 1969; children: Brian Keith, Kamala Lynn. BS, Wash. State U., 1968; MS, Purdue U., 1971, PhD, 1974. Fgn. area fellow U. de Vicosa, Brazil, 1972-74; tng. officer and crop mgmt. specialist Asian Vegetable Research and Devel. Ctr., Tainan, Taiwan, 1974-77; extension vegetable specialist U. Fla., Gainesville, 1977-80; extension weed specialist Oreg. State U., Corvallis, 1980—; cropping systems specialist U. Fla, El Salvador, Bolivia, 1977-80; crop-based erosion control specialist Devel. Alternatives, Inc., Jamaica, 1983; farming systems research and extension U. Wis. and U. Fla., The Gambia, 1985; weed mgmt. shortcourse instr. Wash. State U., Jordan, 1986; advisor horticulture and farming systems Ministry of Agricultuer, Malawi, 1986—. Author and translator: Weed Control, 1974; editor: Horticultural Rev.; contbr. articles to profl. jours. Coach Am. Youth Soccer Orgn., Corvallis, 1983-86; mem. Internat. 4-H Youth Exchange; bd. dirs. FarmHouse Fraternity Assn., Corvallis, 1984-86. Extension and Research grantee vaious agrl. orgns., Oreg. State U., 1980—. Mem. Am. Soc. Horticultural Sci. (chmn. workgroups and symposiums 1980—), Weed Sci. Soc. Am., Western Soc. Weed Sci., Internat. Weed Sci. Soc., Oreg. Weed Sci. Soc. Republican. United Ch. Christ. Clubs: Corvallis Gourmand, IFYE Alumni. Avocations: hiking, clamdigging, fishing, camping, jogging. Office: Oreg State U Dept Horticulture Corvallis OR 97331

WILLIAMS, ALBERT PAINE, economist; b. Elgin, Tex., Mar. 5, 1935; s. Albert Paine and Mary Dempes (Hudler) W.; m. Elizabeth Ann Whitaker, June 22, 1957; children: Albert, Robert, John. B.S., U.S. Naval Acad., 1957; M.A., Fletcher Sch., Tufts U., 1963; M.A.L.D., Tufts U., 1964, Ph.D., 1967. Budget examiner, internat. economist Bur. Budget, Washington, 1965-67; adv. on fgn. assistance strategy and econ. policy White House Staff, Washington, 1967-68; economist Rand Corp., Santa Monica, Calif., 1968-72; sr. economist Rand Corp., 1972—, dir. health scis. program, 1976—; dir. Rand/UCLA Ctr. for Health Policy Study, 1982—; prof. Rand Grad. Inst., 1971—, mem. adv. bd., 1975—. Scoutmaster Great Western council Boy Scouts Am., 1971-78, 82—. Served with USN, 1957-62. Recipient Profl. Achievement award Exec. Office of Pres., 1967. Mem. AAAS, Am. Econ. Assn., Assn. Pub. Policy Analysis and Mgmt., Sierra Club. Unitarian. Home: 508 12th St Santa Monica CA 90402 Office: 1700 Main St Santa Monica CA 90406

WILLIAMS, ANGELA ANDERSON, health care administrator; b. Columbus, Ga., Aug. 12, 1956; d. Homer C. and Bernice Willene (Davis) Anderson; m. Charles Arthur Williams, June 3, 1978; children—Kimberly Faith, Angela Renee. A.A. in Nursing, Columbus Coll., Ga., 1977, B.S. in Health Sci., 1978; M.S. in Health Sci. Adminstrn., Jersey City State Coll., 1986; postgrad. SUNY-Albany, 1986—. Registered nurse Ga., Wash., N.J. Nursing supr. Stewart Webster Hosp., Richland, Ga., 1978; therapist St. Peters' Hosp., Olympia, Wash., 1979-80; anesthesia asst. St. Peter's Hosp., Olympia, 1980-82; head nurse Nutri-System Weight Loss Clinic, Columbus, Ga., 1983; staff nurse Vet.'s Med. Ctr., East Orange, N.J., 1984-85; asst. adminstr. North Jersey Community Union Health Ctr., Newark, 1985—. Tchr. Sunday Sch., Army Chapel, Bayonne, 1985-86. Mem. Am. Pub. Health Assn., Nat. Assn. Female Execs., Officer's Wives Club, ARC, N.J. Pub. Health Assn. Clubs: Internat Order Rainbow (Columbus), Order Eastern Star. Avocations: sewing; painting; restoring antiques. Home: 4024 Apollo Dr Anchorage AK 99504

WILLIAMS, ANTHONY JOSEPH, state senator, lawyer; b. Las Cruces, N.Mex., Dec. 17, 1949; s. James S. and Anne T. (Tondre) W. B.S., U. Mex., 1975, J.D., 1979. Bar: N.Mex. 1979, U.S. Dist. Ct. N.Mex. 1979. Ptnr. Skyline Constrn., 1977-78; shareholder, v.p. Wilco Builders, Inc., 1979-81; sole practice law, 1979-85; ptnr. Williams, Conroy and Sims, Belen, N.Mex., 1985—; mem. N.Mex. Senate from 29th Dist., 1985—.

WILLIAMS, BETTY, corporate professional; b. Los Angeles, Nov. 27, 1920; d. John D. Rasmussen and Muriel Grace (Kay) Winters; children—Derek Allen, Diane Lee Gilmore. Student Los Angeles City Coll., 1938-40, Occidental Coll., 1940, Los Angeles Jr. Coll. Bus., 1954-55, Loretta Young Way Sch. Modeling, 1959-61; Fellow of Religious Sci., Ernest Holmes Coll. Sch. Ministry, 1985. Lic. practitioner of religious sci. Exec. sec., asst. mgr. research dept. Los Angeles C. of C., 1957-63; exec. sec. McCann Erickson-Advt., Los Angeles, 1963-66, U. So. Calif., 1966-71, League of Calif. Cities, Los Angeles, 1972-77, Getty Oil Co. Texaco Inc., Los Angeles, 1980-86; exec. sec., writer Soc. West Mag./Patte Barham Edn., Los Angeles, 1977-79, 86-87; recording sec. So. Calif. Assn. C. of C. Mgrs., 1957-63, San Gabriel Valley Assn. C. of C., 1957-63; asst. mgr. Los Angeles C. of C. Alaska Good Will Tour, 1960. Author poetry, letters to high officials. Charter mem. Republican Presdl. Task Force, Washington, 1982; worker Rep. party, Los Angeles, 1978; mem. church choir Founder's Religious Sci. Ch., 1972-84, sec., practitioner, 1974-84. Mem. Am. Stats. Assn., Am. Mktg. Assn., Internat. Soc. Gen. Semantics, Classroom Tchrs. Gen. Semantics, League of Religious Sci. Practitioners. Avocations: singing; piano; dancing; swimming. Home: 820 Gramercy Pl Apt 11 Los Angeles CA 90005 Office: care Patte Barham 100 Fremont Pl Los Angeles CA 90005

WILLIAMS, BRIAN ROBERT, dentist; b. Mpls., Aug. 5, 1939; s. Donald Edwin Williams and Constance Barbara (Davis) Nyman. B.S. in Aero. Engring., U. Minn., 1962; M.S. in Aerospace Engring., U. So. Calif., 1968; D.D.S., UCLA, 1977. Staff engr. McDonnell Douglas Co., Huntington Beach, Calif., 1963-71; practice dentistry, Fountain Valley, Calif., 1978—; mem. med. adv. com. Orange County Head Start Program, Santa Ana, Calif., 1979—. Contbr. articles to profl. jours. Hon. President's Undergrad. fellow UCLA, 1976. Mem. Delta Sigma Delta. Republican. Home: 367 N Richard St Orange CA 92669 Office: Gonzales Underwood Williams 18444 Brookhurst St Fountain Valley CA 92708

WILLIAMS, C. BASIL, cardiologist; b. Salt Lake City, Mar. 29, 1931; s. Carroll B. and Gurtha (Petersen) W.; m. Stephanie Rich, Aug. 24, 1954; children—Deborah, Barton, Megan, Raquel, Rebecca, Melissa. B.S., U. Utah, 1953, M.D., 1956. Fellow in cardiology, resident in medicine U. Utah, 1956-58, 59-61, Boston City Hosp., 1958-59; cardiologist Ogden Clinic, Utah, 1961—. Fellow ACP, Am. Coll. Cardiology; mem. Utah Heart Assn. (pres. 1968), Utah Soc. Internal Medicine (pres. 1969), Phi Beta Kappa, Alpha Omega Alpha. Mormon. Office: Ogden Clinic 4650 Harrison Ogden UT 84403

WILLIAMS, COLQUITT LAMAR, mechanical engineer; b. Valdosta, Ga., June 20, 1944; s. Walter Henzle Jr. and Martha Ada (Johnson) W.; m. Carrolyn Jo Lovering, Jan. 27, 1973; children: Curtis Lamar, Caryn Leigh. BSME, Ga. Inst. Tech., 1967, MSME, 1968, PhD, 1973. Sr. engr. Bettis Atomic Power Lab., West Mifflin, Pa., 1973-79; project mgr. Electric Power Research Inst., Palo Alto, Calif., 1979—; co-owner Williams Software and Services, San Jose, Calif., 1983-86, PEP Outreach, San Jose, Calif., 1986—. Author computer program; contbr. articles to profl. jours. Fellow Nat. Def. Edn. Act, Ga. Inst. Tech., 1967. Mem. ASME, Sigma Xi, Phi Kappa Phi, Tau Beta Pi, Pi Tau Sigma. Republican. Methodist. Avocations: math. puzzles, digital graphics. Office: Electric Power Research Inst 3412 Hillview Ave Palo Alto CA 94303

WILLIAMS, DAVID CARY, nuclear power safety analyst; b. Santa Monica, Calif., June 22, 1935; s. Donald Cary and Katherina Pressly (Adams) W. AB in Chemistry, Harvard Coll., 1957; PhD in Nuclear Chemistry, MIT, 1962. Postdoctoral research fellow in nuclear chemistry Princeton (N.J.) U., 1962-64, Los Alamos (N.Mex.) Sci. Lab., 1964-66; mem. tech. staff Sandia Nat. Labs., Albuquerque, 1966-87, safety analyst nuclear power reactors, 1975—, disting. mem. tech. staff, 1987—. Chmn. nuclear div. Ams. for Rational Energy Alternatives, 1978-85, bd. dirs. 1980-85. Mem. Am. Nuclear Soc., Am. Phys. Soc., Am. Chem. Soc., AAAS, Sigma Xi. Republican. Club: N.Mex. Mountain. Home: 1300 Espanola St NE Albuquerque NM 87110 Office: Sandia Nat Labs Div 6419 Albuquerque NM 87185

WILLIAMS, DAVID S., vision research scientist; b. Kaikoura, New Zealand, Dec. 30, 1954; came to U.S., 1982; s. John S. and Frances Ruth (Lindsay) W. BS with honors, U. Canterbury, Christchurch, New Zealand, 1978; PhD, Australian Nat. U., Canberra, 1982. Postdoctoral fellow U. Calif., Santa Barbara, 1982-84; asst. research prof. UCLA, 1984—. Contbr. articles to profl. jours. Grantee NSF, NIH, Retinitis Pigmentosa Internat. Soc., Nat. Soc. to Prevent Blindness. Mem. AAAS, Assn. for Research in Vision and Ophthamology. Home: 564 Midvale Ave Los Angeles CA 90024 Office: Jules Stein Eye Inst UCLA Sch Medicine Los Angeles CA 90024

WILLIAMS, DAVID WELFORD, U.S. district judge; b. Atlanta, Mar. 20, 1910; s. William W. and Maude (Lee) W.; m. Ouida Maie White, June 11, 1939; children: David Welford, Vaughn Charles. A.A., Los Angeles Jr. Coll., 1932; A.B., UCLA, 1934; LL.B., U. So. Calif., 1937. Bar: Calif. 1937. Practiced in Los Angeles, 1937-55; judge Mcpl. Ct., Los Angeles, 1956-62, Superior Ct., Los Angeles, 1962-69, U.S. Dist. Ct., Central Dist. Calif., Los Angeles, 1969—; now sr. judge U.S. Dist. Ct., Central Dist. Calif.; judge Los Angeles County Grand Jury, 1965. Recipient Russwurm award Nat. Assn. Newspapers, 1958; Profl. Achievement award UCLA Alumni Assn., 1966. Mem. ABA, Los Angeles Bar Assn., Am. Judicature Soc. Office: US District Court 312 N Spring St Los Angeles CA 90012

WILLIAMS, DENNIS BUCHER, actor, nutritionist, food products executive; b. Tulsa; s. Paul Dennis and Catherine Susan (Krischan) B. BFA, Kans. U., 1967; diploma, Royal Acad. Dramatic Arts, London, 1971; assoc. deg., Pasadena (Calif.) Playhouse, 1973; cert. nutritionist, Donsbach Sch., 1982. Actor Universal Studios, Inc., Universal City, Calif., 1974-85; actor, contract player 20th Cent. Fox Studios, Century City, Calif., 1973-74; pres., owner Nutritional Needs Co., Hollywood, Calif., 1982—; dir. and instr. Pasadena Playhouse, 1983-85; instr. Hollywood, Calif., 1983—; bd. dirs. USO, Hollywood. Author: Basic Health and Nutrition, 1986; screenwriter Sunset Heaven, 1978, The Illuminati, 1984. Founding member Hollywood Preservation Orgn., 1985; mem. Hollywood Heritage, Inc., 1985; mem. com. Save Medicare and Social Security, 1986—. Recipient Resolution award City of Los Angeles, 1985, Disting. Service award Hollywood Heritage, Inc., 1985, Bronze Halo award So. Calif. Motion Picture Council, Star Sapphire award So. Calif. Motion Picture Council, 1985, Jennie award So. Calif. Motion Picture Council, 1986; named Celebrity of Yr. Calif. Spl. Olympics, 1984. Mem. Screen Actors Guild, Am. Fedn. TV and Radio Artists, Actors Equity Assn., WHO, Royal Acad. Dramatic Arts, Acad. TV Arts and Scis. (Emmy award nominee 1985). Avocations: horseback riding, oil painting and watercolor art.

WILLIAMS, DENNIS LEE, church administrator; b. Merced, Calif., June 19, 1958; s. James Kent and Ruby Mae (Zweimiller) W.; m. Vonda Jaine Nieves, April 16, 1983. AA, Centralia (Wash.) Coll., 1978; BA, Western Wash. U., 1981; postgrad., Berean Sch., 1983—. Supr. Payless Northwest, Lacey, Wash., 1981-83; minister Evergreen Christian Ctr., Olympia, Wash., 1983-84; bus. administr. Christian Life Assembly, Federal Way, Wash., 1985—. Mem. Am. Mgmt. Assn., Assembly of God Musicians Fellowship. Republican. Avocations: music, theater, sports, camping. Home: 2731 SW 332d Ct Federal Way WA 98023 Office: Christian Life Assembly PO Box 3799 Federal Way WA 98063

WILLIAMS, DONALD KEITH, power company official; b. Wilder, Idaho, Apr. 13, 1921; s. Floyd W. and Bernice M. (Hatfield) W.; m. Alyce L. Craven, Sept. 8, 1946; children—Ronald E., Conrad L., Douglas K. B.A., George Fox Coll., Newberg, Oreg., 1948. Notary pub. Farmer, Caldwell, Idaho, 1948-49; exec. sec. Canyon County Farm Bur., Caldwell, 1949-55; orgn. dir. Mont. Farm Bur., Bozeman, 1955-56, exec. sec., 1956-63; exec. sec. Mont. Taxpayers Assn., Helena, 1963-65; agr. rep. Mont. Power Co., Butte, 1965-86, also real estate agt. until 1986. Mem. exec. com. Mont. Rural Area Devel. Assn., 1970-83; chmn. council Faith Evang. Ch., Billings, 1983-84; beef supt. Yellowstone Exhbn., Billings, 1978-84. Mem. Mont. Farm Bur. Fedn. (exec. sec. 1956-63), Mont. Pork Producers Assn. (dir. 1976-80; Friend of the Industry 1978), Mont. Stockgrowers Assn., Nat. Water Resources Assn. (life, bd. dirs. 1980-85, chmn. underground water com. 1984), Mont. Woolgrowers Assn., Mont. Wheatgrowers Assn., Mont. Water Devel. Assn. (dir., sec. 1969-84), Mont. Rural Area Devel. Com. (life), Billings C. of C. (chmn. agrl. com. 1972, chmn. tax com. 1974, chmn. water com. 1966-67). Republican. Mem. Evangelical Ch. N.Am. Home and Office: 2445 Custer Ave Billings MT 59102

WILLIAMS, DONALD SPENCER, scientist; b. Pasadena, Calif., May 28, 1939; s. Charles Gardner and Delia Ruth (Spencer) W.; B.S., Harvey Mudd Coll., 1961; M.S., Carnegie Inst. Tech., 1962; Ph.D., Carnegie-Mellon U., 1969. Asst. project dir. Learning Research and Devel. Ctr., Pitts., 1965-67; cons. system design, Pitts., 1967-69; mem. tech. staff RCA Corp., Palo Alto, Calif., 1969-72; prin. investigator robot vision Jet Propulsion Lab., Calif. Inst. Tech., Pasadena, 1972-80; mgr. tech. accessment TRW Inc., Redondo Beach, 1980—; producer indsl. shows and films, 1970-84; cons system design, 1984—. Mem. Am. Assn. Artificial Intelligence, AAAS, Assn. Computing Machinery, Audio Engring. Soc., Nat. Fire Protection Assn., IEEE, Soc. Motion Picture and TV Engrs., Soc. Preservation Variety Arts, Town Hall of Calif. Contbr. articles to profl. jours. Home: 1210 N Allen Ave Pasadena CA 91104 Office: One Space Park Redondo Beach CA 90278

WILLIAMS, DOUGLAS, management consultant; b. Newburgh, N.Y., Oct. 13, 1912; s. Everett Frank and Marjorie Tuthill W.; m. Esther Grant, Sept. 23, 1939; children—Penelope Williams Winters, Grant. A.B., Cornell U., 1934; M.B.A., Harvard U., 1936. With Air Reduction Co., 1936-37, Am. Inst. Pub. Opinion, 1938, Elmo Roper Co., 1939-40; assoc. dir. Nat. Opinion Research Ctr., U. Denver, 1940-42; pres. Douglas Williams Assos., Carefree, Ariz. and N.Y.C., 1948—. Pres. Community Chest, Larchmont, N.Y., 1959; bd. mgrs. West Side YMCA, N.Y.C., 1957-60; bd. dirs. Ariz. State U. Coll. Bus.; mem. nat. adv. bd. Heard Mus.; mem. Ariz. State U. Council of 100, Ariz. State U. Council of Emeritus Advisers. Served to lt. col. U.S. Army, 1942-45. Republican. Episcopalian. Clubs: Larchmont Yacht, Univ. (pres.) (Larchmont), Harvard, Union League, Cornell, Winged Foot Golf, Desert Forest Golf. Home: 7612 E Horizon Dr PO Box 941 Carefree AZ 85377 Office: Executive Center PO Box 941 Carefree AZ 85377

WILLIAMS, DWIGHT DAVID, electronics superintendent; b. San Diego, Nov. 18, 1936; s. Stafford Miller and Mildred (Standridge) W.; children: Michelle Lyn and Kristin Kay (twins). A.A., Los Angeles City Coll., 1966; B.S., U. San Francisco, 1980; postgrad. Golden Gate U., 1987. Field engr. Gen. Electric Co., Los Angeles, 1966-72; electronics supt. Turlock Irrigation Dist., Calif., 1972—. Mem. adv. bd. Modesto Jr. Coll., Calif., 1974-76, 79—, tchr. electronics, 1976-79. Served with U.S. Army, 1957-62. Recipient Letter of Appreciation for development of message distbn. system U.S. Army, 1961; Royal Order of Lobster award Gen. Electric Co., 1970, Safety award, 1972. Mem. Nat. Assn. Radio and Telecommunications Engrs., Instrument Soc. Am., Utilities Telecommunications Council. Republican. Lodge: Masons. Home: 1115 N Quincy Rd Turlock CA 95380 Office: Turlock Irrigation Dist 333 E Canal Dr Turlock CA 95380

WILLIAMS, EARL FREDERICK, social worker; b. Glendale, Calif., Jan. 23, 1937; s. Rawson Oliver and Harriet Mony (Eidmann) W.; m. Fidelina Maria Moscote, Apr. 20, 1968; 1 child, Diana. BA, St. John's U., Camarillo, Calif., 1963; MSW, Calif. State U., Fresno, 1971; MPA, Calif. State U., Fullerton, 1978. Tchr. Claretian Jr. Sem., Compton, Calif., 1965-67; contract counselor Family Services, Tustin, Calif., 1977-78; social worker Dept. Children's Services, Long Beach, Calif., 1977-84; contract counselor Psychiat. Clinic for Youth, Long Beach, Calif., 1978-79; social worker supr. Dept. Children's Services, Long Beach, 1984—. Sponsor Parents Anonymous, Santa Ana, Calif., 1973-78; vol. supr. Concern Counseling Services, Anaheim, Calif., 1983—. Recipient stipend State Dept. Social Services, 1969, grad. study item Dept. Social Services, Los Angeles, 1970. Mem. Nat. Assn. Social Workers (cert.), Am. Pub. Welfare Assn. Democrat. Roman Catholic. Avocations: music, vocal and instrumental. Home: 3205 S Lowell St Santa Ana CA 92707

WILLIAMS, EVELYN METOYER, educator; b. Evergreen, La., May 27, 1937; d. Steven and Alnetter T. Metoyer; B.S., Tex. So. U., 1959; M.Ed., So. U., 1965; Reading Specialist degree, U. So. Calif., 1979; m. Lindbergh Williams, Feb. 2, 1975. Master tchr. E. Baton Rouge Parish Sch. Dist., 1966-71; supr. aids and tchrs. Southeastern La. U. Lab. Sch., Hammond, 1971-73; asso. prof. So. Univ., New Orleans, 1973-74; Children's Center tchr., Los Angeles Unified Sch. Dist., 1977—, cons., tchr. in field. Com. mem. Calif. Tchrs. State Council; life mem. NAACP. Mem. NEA (women's caucus), Calif. Tchrs. Assn. (women's caucus), Black Women's Forum, Assn. for Supervision and Curriculum Devel., United Tchrs. Los Angeles; Internat. Reading Assn., Calif. Reading Assn., United Tchrs. Los Angeles, Calif. Ednl. Assn. for Young Children, Phi Beta Kappa, Phi Delta Kappa. Roman Catholic. Lodges: Order Eastern Star, Dau. of Isis.

WILLIAMS, FRANCIS LEON, retired engineering executive, consultant; b. McGill, Nev., Sept. 19, 1918; s. Leon Alfred and Mazie Arabella (Blanchard) W.; m. Ailsa Bailey, Oct. 1944 (div.); children: Rhonda, Graham, Alison; m. Marita I. Fury, Feb. 23, 1974. Student, Calif. Inst. Tech., 1940-41, UCLA, 1946-47, Am. TV Labs., 1948; BME, Sydney U., Australia, 1952; postgrad., San Jose State Coll., 1958-60, Foothill Coll., 1961, Regional Vocat. Ctr., San Jose, Calif., 1962, Alexander Hamilton Inst., 1971-72, Lane Community Coll., 1978-85. Project engr., prodn. supr. Crompton, Parkinson, Australia Pty., Ltd., Sydney, 1949-50; field and sales engr. Perkins Australia Pty., Ltd., Sydney, 1951-54; chief mech. engr. Vicon Corp., San Carlos, Calif., 1955-60; design engr., group leader Lockheed Missiles and Space Co., Sunnyvale, Calif., 1960-70; prin. Astro-Tech Cons. Co., Los Altos, Calif., 1971-72; mech. designer Morvue and Morden Machines, Portland, Oreg., 1973-74; sr. mech. design engr. Chip-N-Saw div. Can-Car of Can., Eugene, Oreg., 1974-75; sales mgr. Indsl. Constrn. Co., Eugene, 1975-76, gen. mgr., 1977-78; ops. mgr. Steel Structures, Eugene, 1976-77; mech. design and project engr. Carothers Co., Eugene, 1978-80; chief engr. Bio Solar and Woodex Corps., Eugene and Brownsville, Oreg., 1980-83; cons. and design engr. Am. Fabricators, Woodburn, Oreg., 1983-84; design engr., draftsman Peterson Pacific Corp., Pleasant Hill, Oreg., 1984-85, Jensen Drilling Co., Glenwood, Oreg., 1985; design engr. Judco & Ball Flight Dryers, Inc., Harbor City, Calif., 1985-86; sr. v.p. The Richelsen Co., also cons.; advisor solid waste recovery County Bd. Commr.'s Office, Eugene, 1984-85. Contbr. articles to profl. jours.; patentee in field. Chmn. bldg. and grounds Westminster Presbyn. Ch., Eugene, 1984-86. Served with USAF, 1941-45. Democrat. Lodge: Elks. Avocation: writing. Home: 2324 Lillian St Eugene OR 97401

WILLIAMS, FREDERICK WALLACE, civil engineer; b. Spokane, Wash., June 11, 1923; s. Frederick Wallace and Rowetta (Toulouse) W.; m. Azalea Lora Perry, Feb. 9, 1946; children: James Terrance, Paul Frederick, David Lee. BSCE, U. Wash., 1949, MSCE, 1950. Registered profl. engr., Wash. Sales engr. H.D. Fowler Co., Seattle, 1950-51; designer Western Engrs., Seattle, 1951-52; jr. engr. Seattle Engring., 1952-53, assoc. engr., 1953-63, mgr. X, 1963—. Instnl. rep. cub pack 144 Boy Scout Am., Seattle, 1959-67, chmn. food com., 1967. Served with U.S. Army, 1943-46. Mem. ASCE, Sigma Xi. Club: Evergreen Rock (Seattle) (pres. 1984-85, treas.). Lodge: Elks. Avocations: geology, lapidary, fishing, hunting. Home: 5050-36th Ave NE Seattle WA 98105

WILLIAMS, GEORGE JOSEPH, III, author, publisher; b. Springfield, Mass., Mar. 3, 1949; s. George Joseph Jr. and Millie (Dalton) W.; m. Edie Karen Godfrey, Sept. 18, 1976; children—Sarah, Michael. Student Riverside (Calif.) City Coll., 1967-69; B.A. in Music Composition, Calif State U.-Fullerton, 1971; B.A. in English, U. Calif.-Riverside, 1974. Owner, operator recording studio, Riverside, Calif., 1976-84; owner, pub. Tree by the River Pub. Co., Riverside, 1980—. Author: Rosa May: The Search for a Mining Camp Legend, 1980; The Guide to Bodie, 1981; The Murders at Convict Lake, 1984; The Songwriter's Demo Manual and Success Guide, 1984; The Redlight Ladies of Virginia City, Nevada, 1984; Mark Twain: His Adventures at Aurora and Mono Lake, 1986; Mark Twain: His Life in Virginia City, Nevada, 1986. Recipient John Stone award Riverside City Coll., 1969; nominated for Nobel Prize in Lit., 1984, Pulitzer prize, 1986. Mem. Publishers Assn. So. Calif. Office: Tree by the River Pub Co PO Box 881 Virginia City NV 89440

WILLIAMS, GORDON LEE, molecular genetics research scientist; b. Mechanicsburg, Pa., Sept. 9, 1947; s. Frank Billmeyer and Eva May (Bowman) W.; m. Phyllis Jaye Reynolds, June 14, 1969 (div. Feb. 1985); children: Eric Alan, Paul Andrew, Jennifer Lynn; m. Jill Jewell, Nov. 1, 1986. BA in Biology and Psychology, Lehigh U., 1969; PhD in Genetics and Biochemistry, U. N.H., 1972. Asst. prof. biology Wilmington (Ohio) Coll., 1972-76, chmn. coll. council, 1974-76, chmn. search com. for acad. dean, 1975-76; assoc. prof. biology SUNY, Fredonia, 1976-79, dir. biomed. sci. programs, 1976-80, chmn. biology dept., 1979-80; sr. research scientist Battelle Northwest, Richland, Wash., 1980-83, mgr. biotech. devel., 1983-85; v.p., chief sci. officer Biolife Techs. Inc., Pomona, Calif., 1985—; bd. dirs., exec. v.p. Zelenka Ltd., Hong Kong; bd. dirs., pres. Biolife Inst., Pomona; bd. dirs. Microlife Ltd., Jersey, U.K., 1985—; cons. M.J. Pharms. Ltd., Bombay, 1985—; vis. clin. prof. Jiangxe Tumor Hosp., Nanchang, Peoples Republic of China, 1985—; cons. Mitsubishi Internat., Tokyo, 1983-85; adj. prof. genetics Wash. State U., Pullman, 1982-85; research fellow U. Calif., Davis, 1980; cons. scientist Jamestown (N.Y.) Gen. Hosp., 1977-80. Patentee in field; contbr. articles to profl. jours. Grantee N.Y. Pub. Health Service, NSF, NIH; recipient Acad. Program award Am. Soc. Allied Health Professions, 1969. Mem. AAAS, Am. Soc. Microbiology, N.Y. Acad. Scis., Sigma Xi (local chpt. v.p. 1978-80, lectr. 1980). Avocations: gardening, hiking, camping, carpentry, astrology. Home: 450 W Foothill Blvd Apt 138

Pomona CA 91767 Office: Biolife Techs Inc 337 E Foothill Blvd Pomona CA 91767

WILLIAMS, HARRIETTE FLOWERS, educational administrator; b. Los Angeles, July 18; d. Orlando and Virginia (Carter) Flowers; BS, UCLA, 1952, EdD, (HEW fellow), 1973; MA, Calif. State U., Los Angeles, 1956; m. Irvin F. Williams, Apr. 9, 1960; children: Lorin Finley, Lori Virginia. Tchr., Los Angeles Unified Sch. Dist., 1952-59, counselor, 1954-59; psychometrist, 1958-62, faculty chmn., 1956-57, student activities coordinator, 1955-59, leader insts. and workshops, 1952-67, dir. counseling, 1960-65, supr. Title I programs Elem. Secondary Edn. Act, 1965-68, asst. prin., 1968-76, prin., 1976-82, dir. instrn. sr. high sch. div., 1982-85, adminstr. ops., 1985—; asst. dir. HEW project for high sch. adminstrn. UCLA, 1971-72; adj. prof. in Masters in Sch. Adminstrn. program Pepperdine U., Los Angeles, 1974-78. Recipient Sojourner Truth award Nat. Assn. Negro Bus. and Profl. Women's Clubs, Los Angeles, 1968; Life Membership Service award Los Angeles PTA, 1975; Los Angeles Mayor's Golden Apple award for ednl. excellence. Mem. Los Angeles Assn. Secondary Sch. Adminstrs., Assn. Calif. Sch. Adminstrs. (state chmn. urban affairs com. 1985—), Nat. Assn. Secondary Sch. Prins., Sr. High Sch. Asst. Prins. Assn. of Los Angeles (dir. 1974-76), Sr. High Sch. Prins. Orgn., Nat. Council of Negro Women (life mem.), Lullaby Guild of Children's Home Soc. Los Angeles, UCLA Gold Shield, Los Angeles PTA, NAACP, Urban League, Inglewood-Pacific cpt. Links Inc., Jack and Jill of Am., Inc., UCLA Alumni Assn. (dir.), Delta Sigma Theta (pres. Los Angeles chpt. 1964-66, regional dir. 1968-72, nat. committeewoman 1966—), Pi Lambda Theta, Kappa Delta Pi, Delta Kappa Gamma. Baptist. Office: 644 W 17th St Los Angeles CA 90015

WILLIAMS, HOWARD WALTER, aerospace executive; b. Evansville, Ind., Oct. 18, 1937; s. Walter Charles and Marie Louise (Bollinger) W.; m. Phyllis Ann Scofield, May 4, 1956 (div. Sept. 1970); m. Marilee Sharon Mulvane, Oct. 30, 1970; children: Deborah, Steven, Kevin, Glenn, Lori, Michele. AA, Pasadena City Coll., 1956; BSME, Calif. State U., Los Angeles, 1967; BSBA, U. San Francisco, 1978. Turbojet, rocket engr. Aerojet-Gen. Corp., Azusa, Calif., 1956-59, infrared sensor engr., 1959-60, rocket, torpedo engr., 1960-66; power, propulsion mgr. Aerojet-Gen. Corp., Sacramento, 1967-73, high speed ship systems mgr., 1974-78, combustion, power mgr., rocket engine mktg. mgr., 1979—. Author: (with others) Heat Exchangers, 1980, Industrial Heat Exchangers, 1985; co-inventor Closed Cycle Power System, 1969. Recipient Energy Innovations award U.S. Dept. Energy, 1985. Mem. AIAA (sr.; Best Paper 1966), Am. Soc. Metals (organizing dir. indsl. heat exchange confs. 1985—). Avocations: bicycling, computers, scuba, skiing. Office: Aerojet TechSystems Co Aerojet Rd & Folsom Blvd Rancho Cordova CA 95670

WILLIAMS, JAMES MARVIN, science facility administrator; b. Denver, Apr. 27, 1934; s. Marvin Julius and Royalene Grace (Bogue) W.; m. Dottie L. Powers, May 6, 1961; children: Brentley James, Marcy Lynne. B-SChemE, U. N.Mex., 1957, MS, 1964. Br. chief. AEC, Washington, 1969-72; group leader Los Alamos (N.Mex.) Sci. Lab., 1972-74, div. leader, 1978-79, asst. dir., 1979-86, deputy office leader indsl. applications, 1987—; asst. dir. Dept. Energy, Washington, 1974-78; pres. TRADE, Los Alamos, 1985—, Los Alamos Econs. Devel. Corp., 1983-85; chmn. Los Alamos Med. Ctr., 1983-86; bd. dirs. Fusion Power Assn., Washington, 1979-81. Vestry Trinity on the Hill Episc. Ch., Los Alamos, 1979-83; fin. chmn. People for Pete, Los Alamos, 1984; vice chmn. N.Mex. Energy Research Inst., Santa Fe, 1985-86. Served to lt. commdr. USN., 1957-60. Fellow Am. Inst. Chemists. Republican. Episcopalian. Avocations: running, swimming, sailing, gardening.

WILLIAMS, JOEL MANN, polymer material scientist; b. Suffolk, Va., Apr. 6, 1940; s. Joel Mann and Mildred (Barlow) W.; m. Mary Carol Gregory, Sept. 1, 1962; children: Catherine Reine, Michael Gregory. BS, Coll. William and Mary, 1962; PhD, Northwestern U., 1966. Asst. prof. chemistry U. Minn., Mpls., 1967-68; research chemist E.I. DuPont de Nemours, Waynesboro, Va., 1968-72; mem. staff Los Alamos (N.Mex.) Nat. Lab., 1972—; cons. G.V. Med., Mpls., 1986—. Co-author: Advances in Physical Organic Chemistry, 1968, Analytical Chemistry of Liquid Fuel Sources, 1978, Coal Science and Chemistry, 1986. Fellow NIH, 1963-66, NSF, 1966-67. Mem. Sigma Xi. Republican. Roman Catholic. Clubs: Tennis (Los Alamos) (tres. 1984-86), Mountain Mixers Square Dance (treas. 1977-79), Barranca Mesa Pool Assn. (treas. 1975-76). Avocations: skiing, camping. Home: 51 Zuni Los Alamos NM 87544 Office: Los Alamos Nat Lab MST-7 E549 Los Alamos NM 87545

WILLIAMS, JOHN ANDREW, physiologist, consultant; b. Des Moines, Aug. 3, 1941; s. Harold Southall and Marjorie (Larsen) W.; m. Christa A. Smith, Dec. 26, 1965; children: Rachel Jo, Matthew Dallas. BA, Cen. Wash. State Coll., 1963; MD, U. Wash., Seattle, 1968, PhD, 1968. Staff fellow NIH, Bethesda, Md., 1969-71; research fellow U. Cambridge, Eng., 1971-72; from asst. to prof. physiology U. Calif., San Francisco, 1973—; cons. U. Mich. Gastrointestinal Peptide Ctr., Ann Arbor, Mich., 1985—; me. gen. medicine study sect. NIH, Bethesda, 1985. Contbr. numerous articles to profl. jours. NIH grantee, 1973. Mem. Am. Physiol. Soc. (Hoffman LaRoche prize 1985), Am. Soc. of Cell Biology, Am. Soc. for Clin. Investigation, Am. Gastroenterology Assn., Am. Pancreatic Assn. (pres. 1985-86). Democrat. Home: 148 Dorchester Way San Francisco CA 94127 Office: U Calif Dept of Physiology S762 San Francisco CA 94143

WILLIAMS, JOHN JAMES, JR., architect, golf clubhouse design consultant; b. Denver, July 13, 1949; s. John James and Virginia Lee (Thompson) W.; m. Mary Serene Morck, July 29, 1972. BArch, U. Colo., 1974. Registered architect, Colo. Project architect Gensler Assoc. Architects, Denver, 1976, Heinzman Assoc. Architects, Boulder, Colo., 1977, EZTH Architects, Boulder, 1978-79; prin. Knudson/Williams PC, Boulder, 1980-82, Faber, Williams & Brown, Boulder, 1982-86, John Williams & Assocs., Boulder, 1986—; panel chmn. U. Colo. World Affairs Conf.; vis. faculty U. Colo. Coll. Design and Planning, Coll. Environtl. Design. Author (with others) State of Colorado architect licensing law, 1986. Commr. Downtown Boulder Mall Commn., 1985-86; bd. dirs. U. Colo. Fairway Club, 1986-87. Recipient Teaching Honorarium, U. Colo. Coll. Design and Planning, 1977, 78, 79, 80, Excellence in Design and Planning award City of Boulder, 1981, 82, Citation for Excellence, WOOD Inc., 1982. Mem. Nat. Council Architect Registration Bd., AIA, (bd. dirs. Colo. North chpt. 1985-86, sec. 1987), Architects and Planners of Boulder (v.p. 1982), Nat. Golf Found. (sponsor), Am. Philatelic Soc., Kappa Sigma (chpt. pres. 1970). Avocations: golf, polit. history, African cichlids, fitness and health. Home: 3345 16th ST Boulder CO 80302 Office: John Williams & Assocs 1137 Pearl St Suite 203 Boulder CO 80302

WILLIAMS, KEN MICHAEL, logistics engineer; b. Charleston, W. Va., Mar. 7, 1944; s. R. Don and Ruth Norma (Berg) W.; m. Khanh Thi Tran, July 26, 1973; children: Xali Khanh, Donn Christopher. BA, Ohio State U., 1968; MA, Mich. State U., 1977. Cert. bus. and indsl. mgmt. tchr., Calif. Commd. U.S. Army, 1968, resigned, 1984; logistics specialist McDonnell Douglas, Long Beach, Calif., 1985; asst. material mgmt. officer State Agy., Long Beach, 1986—; bd. dirs. TFW Scis., Long Beach; pres. Wms. Scis., Westminster, Calif., 1984-86; cons. Success Strategy Tng., Orange, Calif., 1985-86; logistics instr. Cerritos Coll., Norwalk, Calif., 1985. Bd. dirs. Site Council Clegg Sch., Westminster, 1985—; recorder Westminster Jr. All-Am. Football League and Little League Baseball, 1985—. Recipient Community Service award Camp Zama, 1978; numerous awards U.S. Army, 1968-84. Mem. Soc. Logistics Engrs. (vice-chmn. ops. 1986-87, newsletter editor 1985-86, Award of Excellence 1986), Am. Prodn. Inventory Control Soc., Retired Officers Assn., VFW. Republican. Methodist. Lodges: Masons, Shriners. Avocations: little league activities, coaching, cons. Home: 14082 Rondeau #1 Westminster CA 92683 Office: Div Material Mgmt Office 3700 Spring St Long Beach CA 90822

WILLIAMS, KENNETH JAMES, retired county official; b. Eureka, Calif., Apr. 28, 1924; s. E. J. and Thelma (Hall) W.; student Humboldt State Coll., 1942-43; B.S., U. Oreg., 1949, M.Ed., 1952; m. Mary Patricia Warring, Sept. 3, 1949; children—James Clayton, Susan May, Christopher Kenneth. Engaged as mountain triangulation observer with U.S. Coast and Geodetic Survey, 1942; instr. bus. and geography Boise (Idaho) Jr. Coll., 1949-51; tchr. Prospect High Sch., 1952-54; prin. Oakland (Oreg.) High Sch., 1954-58; supt. prin. Coburg Public Schs., 1958-64; supt. Yoncalla (Oreg.) Public Schs., 1964-66, Amity (Oreg.) Public Schs., 1966-72; adminstr. Yamhill County, McMinnville, Oreg., 1974-85; cons., 1985—; county liaison officer Land and Water Conservation Fund, 1977-85. Dist. lay leader Oreg.-Idaho ann. conf. United Methodist Ch., 1968-80, bd. dirs. western dist. Ch. Extension Soc., 1976; mem. Mid-Willamette Manpower Council, 1974-85; bd. dirs. Lafayette Noble Homes, 1970-72; mem. adv. com. local budget law sect. State of Oreg. Served with AUS, 1943-46. Recipient Purple Heart, Good Conduct medal, battle stars. Mem. NEA, Oreg. Edn. Assn., Oreg. Assn. Secondary Prins., Nat. Assn. Secondary Prins., AAUP, Oreg., Am. assns. sch. adminstrs., Assn. Supervision and Curriculum Devel., Nat. Sch. Pub. Relations Assn., Phi Delta Kappa. Mason (Shriner), Lion. Home: 21801 SE Webfoot Rd Dayton OR 97114

WILLIAMS, KENNETH OWEN, pediatric hematologist, oncologist; b. Wales, May 23, 1925; came to U.S., 1930; s. Thomas and Margaret Lydia (Evans) W.; m. Sally Barber, Apr. 26, 1956; children: Eric Matthew, James Christopher. BA, U. Vt., 1950, MD, 1954. Cert. Am. Bd. Pediatrics, Am. Bd. Pediatric Hematology-Oncology. Assoc. prof. pediatrics U. So. Calif., Los Angeles, 1960—; assoc. hematologist, oncologist Children's Hosp. Los Angeles, 1960—. Vol. med. dir. St. John's Well Child Ctr., Los Angeles, 1964—; active Los Angeles City-County AIDS task force, 1984—. Served with USN, 1943-46. Fellow Am. Acad. Pediatrics; mem. Los Angeles County Med. Assn. (chmn. AIDS com. 1985—), Los Angeles Figure Skating Assn. Episcopalian. Avocations: bicycling, skiing, photography, supporter ice skating. Home: 1916 Micheltorena St Los Angeles CA 90039 Office: Children's Hosp Los Angeles 4650 Sunset Blvd Los Angeles CA 90027

WILLIAMS, KNOX, water conditioning company executive; b. Grandfield, Okla., Aug. 9, 1928; s. Knox B. and Clara Mae (Butler) W.; m. Juanita June Wood, Sept. 9, 1951; children—Jodi Ann and Jeri Ruth (twins), Drue Knox. B.A., UCLA, 1951. With Wilson-McMahan Furniture Stores, Santa Barbara, Calif., 1951-61; prin., pres. Rayne of North San Diego County, Vista, Calif., 1961—, Aqua Fresh Drinking Water Systems, Inc., San Diego, 1980—. Mem. bd. counsellors UCLA. Served with USNR, 1947-48. Mem. Carlsbad C. of C., Pacific Water Quality Assn. (pres. 1975-76), Water Quality Assn. (bd. dirs. 1980-83). Republican. Presbyterian. Clubs: El Camino Rotary (Oceanside, Calif.), Masons (Santa Barbara). Office: Rayne of North San Diego County 2011 W Vista Way Vista CA 92083 Office: Aqua Fresh Drinking Water Systems 7370 Opportunity Rd Suite I San Diego CA 92111

WILLIAMS, L. JAY, public relations executive, communications consultant; b. Cedar City, Utah, Feb. 20, 1943; s. Max and Edna (Walker) W.; m. Carol Dean Seay, June 2, 1967; children: Reuben, Daniele, John, George. BA, Brigham Young U., 1967, MA, 1970. Ordained bishop Mormon Ch., 1979. Advt. mgr. Orem (Utah)-Geneva Times, 1965; prodn. photographer WIS-TV, Columbia, S.C., 1968; dir. pub. relations Brazosport Coll., Lake Jackson, Tex., 1970, Converse Coll., Spartanburg, S.C., 1973; dir. advt. Arnold Machinery Co., Salt Lake City, 1980; dir. pub. relations Utah Tech. Coll., Salt Lake City, 1982—; cons. Progressive Music, Salt Lake City, 1985—. Active Boy Scouts Am., 1956—; Bishop Mormon Ch., Salt Lake City, 1982—. Named Master M-Man Mormon Ch., Houston, 1971, recipient Palmetto award Boy Scouts Am., Spartanburg, 1978. Mem. Pub. Relations Soc. Am., Advt. Fedn., Council Advancement and Support Edn., Kappa Tau Alpha. Republican. Lodge: Order of the Arrow. Avocations: camping, cycling, short wave radio, gardening. Home: 4172 S 1540 W Salt Lake City UT 84123 Office: Utah Tech Coll Salt Lake 4600 S Redwood Rd Salt Lake City UT 84107

WILLIAMS, LAWRENCE ERNEST, physicist; b. Youngstown, Ohio, Nov. 29, 1937; s. William Karapanza and Dorothy (Randulovich) W.; m. Sonia Bell Bredmeyer, Nov. 12, 1966; children: Erica, Beverley. BS in Physics, Carnegie-Mellon U., 1959; MS, U. Minn., 1962, PhD, 1965. Asst. prof. physics Western Ill. U., Macomb, 1968-70; asst. prof. radiology U. Minn., Mpls., 1973-78, NIH fellow, 1971-73, assoc. prof., 1978-80; imaging physicist City of Hope, Duarte, Calif., 1980—; adj. assoc. prof. UCLA, 1982—; prof. Eurotech. Research U., Palo Alto, Calif., 1983—; cons. Jet Propulsion Lab, Pasadena, Calif., 1981-84; bd. dirs. Epidaurus Corp., Mission Viejo, Calif., 1985—. Co-author: Biophysical Science, rev. 2d edit., 1979; contbr. articles to med. jours.; patentee in field. Treas. United Meth. Ch., West Covina, Calif., 1982-83. Westinghouse Sci. Talent Search scholar, 1955, R.J. Wean scholar, 1957; NSF fellow U. Minn., 1961-62. Mem. AAAS, Soc. Nuclear Medicine (Gold medal 1983), Am. Coll. Radiology, Am. Assn. Physicists in Medicine, N.Y. Acad. Scis., Sigma Xi. Democrat. Methodist. Avocations: furniture refinishing, music, sketching. Office: City of Hosp Med Ctr 1500 E Duarte Rd Duarte CA 91010

WILLIAMS, LESLIE WEGENER, veterinarian, consultant; b. Raytown, Md., Aug. 14, 1930; s. Leslie Nathan and Velma Slee (Phillips) W.; m. Lois Jeanette Hasse, Dec. 21, 1952 (div. June 1976); children: Gregory S., Cheryl D., Valerie J., René J. BS in Agriculture, DVM, U. Mo., 1954; MS in Veterinary Sci., U. Fla., 1980; student, U. Wis., 1954-56. Diplomate Am. Coll. Veterinary Ophthalmology. Veterinary officer U.S. Army Chem. Corp, Washington, 1954-57; meat inspector and food hygienist USDA, Washington, 1958-60; mgr., chief exec. officer 5-W Farms, Inc., Kansas City, Mo., 1960-75; veterinarian Kansas City, 1960-75; post doctoral research fellow U. Fla., Gainesville, 1975-80; cons. Vet. Ophthalmology Cons. and Animal Eye Clinic, Las Vegas, Nev., 1980—; city veterinarian City of Las Vegas, 1980-86. Contbr. articles to profl. jours. Active First Baptist Ch., Gainesville; pres. K.C. C. of C.; bd. dirs Mo. C. of C.; mem. Mo. Bond ADv. Com., Citizen's Adv. Council, Democratic Forum, Inc. Served to capt. U.S. Army, 1954-56. Recipient Outstanding Citizen award, State of Mo., Norden Outstanding Student award, Community Council Leadership award, Richard Rebauer AFB; named Man of Yr., Mo. C. of C. Mem. AVMA, Am. Soc. Vet. Ophthalmologists, Mo. Vet. Med. Assn. (continueing edn. chmn., legis. chmn.), Nev. Vet. Med. Assn., Am. Assn. Mgr. Am. Royal Livestock and Horse show (official veterinarian), Mo. Dept. Agriculture (animal disease adv. com.), Am. Hereford Assn. Republican. Lodge: Lions (pres.). Avocations: golfing, gold prospecting, traveling. Home: 3165 E Rochelle Las Vegas NV 89121-5114 Office: Vet Ophthalmology Cons & Animal Eye Clinic 1914 E Sahara Ave Las Vegas NV 89104

WILLIAMS, LUKE G., financial consultant; b. Spokane, Wash., 1923. Former chmn. Nat. Assn. Mfrs., now corp. dir. *

WILLIAMS, LYNNE HUIE, psychiatrist; b. Evanston, Ill., Aug. 23, 1943; d. Virgil Clifford and Vivian (Brown) W.; B.A., U. Mich., 1965; M.D., Wayne State U., 1969; children—Tavis Randall, Shepherd Subhan. Intern, Bronx Mcpl. Hosp., 1969-70, resident in pediatrics, 1970-72; resident in psychiatry U. Miami (Fla.), 1973-74, fellow developmental pediatrics, 1972-73; practice medicine, specializing in developmental pediatrics, gestalt therapy, Asheville, N.C., 1974-79; med. dir. Devel. Evaluation Center, Asheville, 1976-79; fellow in child and adolescent psychiatry U. Miami, 1979-81; practice medicine specializing in infant, child, adolescent and adult psychiatry, Spokane, Wash., 1981—. Diplomate Am. Bd. Pediatrics. Author: The Too Precious Child, 1987. Mem. Human Potential Inst. Gt. Smokies (dir. 1975—), Am. Soc. Adolescent Psychiatry, Gestalt Therapy Inst. Fla. (asso.), Am. Psychiat. Assn., Am. Orthopsychiat. Assn., N.C. Group Behavior Soc. Research on developmental effects of early parent-infant interactions. Home: E4518 Silver Pine Rd Colbert WA 99005 Office: E 12 5th Spokane WA 99207

WILLIAMS, MARSHALL MACKENZIE, utility company executive; b. Londonderry, N.S., Can., Dec. 11, 1923; s. Millard Filmore Williams and Gladys Christine Williams MacKenzie; m. Joan Atlee Ross, Sept. 6, 1952; children—Peter, Alex, Stephen, Margot. Student, Acadia U.; B.Engring., Tech. U. N.S., Halifax, Can., 1947, M.Engring., 1949, D.Engring. (hon.), 1978. Exec. v.p. TransAlta Utilities Corp., Calgary, Alta., Can., 1968-73, pres., 1973-80, pres., chief exec. officer, 1980-84, chmn. bd., pres., 1984-85, chmn. bd., chief exec. officer, 1985—; dir. Royal Trustco Ltd., Toronto, Ont., Can., PanCan. Petroleum Ltd., Calgary, Alta., Nfld. Light & Power Co. Ltd., St. John's, Can., Sun Life Assurance Co., Toronto. Mem. Assn. Profl. Engrs., Geologists and Geophysicists Alta., Can. Elec. Assn. (past pres.), N.W. Electric Light and Power Assn. (past pres.). Club: Ranchmen's (Calgary, Alta., Can.). Avocations: skiing; fishing; hiking.

WILLIAMS, MARVIN LEON, structural engineer, consultant; b. Payson, Utah, July 24, 1944; s. Charles R. and Elda (Sorensen) W.; m. Barbara Lynn Clark, Sept. 17, 1964; children: Kellie, Justin Kale, Burke Leon, Jeremy Clay, Brooke Lynn. BES, Brigham Young U., 1968, MS, 1969. Registered profl. engr., Utah, Alta., Can. Engr. Hugh A. McKellar Co., Provo, Utah, 1967-69; plant engr. Kennecott Copper Co., Salt Lake City, 1969-70; structural engr. R.L. Wadsworth Co., Salt Lake City, 1970-71; chief engr. Pullman/Torkelson Co., Salt Lake City, 1971-73; mgr. engring. Ch. of Jesus Christ of Latter-day Saints, Salt Lake City, 1973—. Rep., Earthquake Awareness Com., Alpine, Utah, 1979; mem. Alpine City Planning Com., 1983. Mem. Structural Engrs. Assn. Utah (founding mem., tech. com. 1980-81, tech. chmn. 1981-83, membership chmn. 1984-85, bd. dirs. 1986-87), Am. Concrete Inst. Republican. Mem. Ch. of Jesus Christ of Latter-day Saints. Home: 838 S Alpine Hwy Alpine UT 84003 Office: M Leon Williams Engr 838 S Alpine Hwy Alpine UT 84003

WILLIAMS, MICHAEL ALLEN, religious educator; b. Paducah, Ky., Aug. 30, 1946; s. Gerald Leon and Mary Sue (Walker) W.; m. Mary Louise Rodriguez, May 21, 1968; children: Melissa Ann, Mary Elizabeth. BA, Abilene Christian U., 1968; MA, Miami U., Oxford, Ohio, 1970; PhD, Harvard U., 1977. Asst. prof. religion U. Wash., Seattle, 1976-83, assoc. prof., 1983—, chmn. comparative religion program, 1985—; com. mem. Christian Century Lectureship N.W., Seattle, 1983-87; adj. faculty mem. N.W. Theol. Union, Seattle, 1985—. Author: The Immovable Race, 1985; editor: Charisma and Sacred Biography, 1982; translator: Martin Dibelius' Commentary on the Epistle of James, 1976; contbr. numerous articles to profl. jours. and essay collections. Research grantee U. Wash., Seattle, 1979. Mem. Am. Acad. Religion, Soc. Bibl. Lit., Internat. Assn. Coptic Studies, Am. Research Ctr. Egypt. Office: U Wash Comparative Religion Program DR-05 Seattle WA 98195

WILLIAMS, MICHAEL CHARLES, architect; b. Long Beach, Calif., Jan. 17, 1952; s. Owen Charles and Patricia Eileen (Judge) W.; m. Vicki Lynette Ware (div. Apr. 1980); 1 child, Michele Kathleen. BArch, Calif. Poly. State U., San Luis Obispo, 1978. Draftsman Collins & Wright, AIA, Irvine, Calif., 1978-82; designer, project mgr. South Shore Builders, Costa Mesa, Calif., 1980-83; job capt. Lewis Homes Calif., Upland, 1983-85; constrn. adminstr. WWAT&G Architects Ltd., Newport Beach, Calif., 1985—. Mem. AIA, Am. Inst. Archeologists, Archeol. Inst. Am., Bibl. Archaeology Soc., Constrn. Specifications Inst. Republican. Mem. Christian Ch. Avocations: photography, art. Home: 9100 Meadow Creek Dr #334 Orlando FL 32821 Office: WWAT&G 140 Newport Ctr Dr #200 Newport Beach CA 92660

WILLIAMS, NANCY ELLEN-WEBB, social services administrator; b. Quincy, Ill., Aug. 1; d. Charles and Garnet Naomi (Davis) Webb; m. Jesse B. Williams, Apr. 11, 1959; children: Cynthia L. Williams Clay, Troy Andrea Williams Redic, Bernard Peter. BA, Quincy Coll., 1957; postgrad., Tenn. A&I U., 1961; M Pub. Adminstrn., U. Nev., Las Vegas, 1977; LHD (hon.), U. Humanistic Studies, 1986. Cert. peace officer, Nev. (chmn. Standards and Tng. Com., 1978-81). Tchr. Shelby County Tng. Sch., Memphis, 1957-61; dep. probation officer Clark County Juvenile Ct., Las Vegas, 1961-66, supervising probation officer, 1966-74, dir. probation services, 1974-80, dir. intake admissions, 1980-81, dir. Child Haven, 1981—; mem. Nev. Crime Commn., 1970-81. Author: When We Were Colored, 1986; contbr. poetry to various mags. Mem. exec. com. Clark County Econ. Opportunity Bd., Las Vegas, 1963-71; chmn. So. Nev. Task Force on Corrections, 1974-81; mem. Gov.'s Com. on Justice Standards and Goals, 1979-81; bd. dirs. U. Humanistic Studies, Las Vegas, 1984—. Recipient Friend of the Golden Gloves award Golden Gloves Regional Bd., 1981, Tribute to Black Women award U. Nev., Las Vegas, 1984. Fellow Am. Acad. Neurol. and Orthopedic Surgeons (assoc.); mem. AAUW, Nat. Council Juvenile Ct. Judges, Nat. Writers Assn. Democrat. Avocations: writing, comparative religions, camping, hiking, racquetball. Office: Child Haven 3401 E Bonanza Rd Las Vegas NV 89101

WILLIAMS, NOEL ALTON, psychiatrist, pharmacologist; b. Shawnee, Okla., Dec. 25, 1933; s. Alton Phillips and Alpha Mae (McAdams) W.; m. Ardelia Ruth Max, June 15, 1957; children: Sean, Stewart, Anne. Student, U. Okla., 1951-54; BS, Northwestern U., 1954, MS in Pharmacology, MD, 1958. Diplomate Am. Bd. of Psychiatry. Resident in psychiatry Menninger Found., Topeka, 1959-62; chief psychiatrist USPHS, Chillicothe, Ohio, 1960-64; pvt. practice psychiatry Walnut Creek, Calif., 1967—; cons. psychiatrist Dept. Energy, San Francisco, 1967—, U.S. Dept. Justice, Chillicothe, 1964-66. Founder, chmn. Scioto-Paint Valley Guidance Ctr., Chillicothe, 1962. Served to surgeon USPHS, 1960-64. Mem. Am. Psychiat. Assn., East Bay Psychiat. Assn. (treas. 1984-85), No. Calif. Psychiat. Soc., Contra Costa Assn. of Psychiatrists (founder 1970), Pe-Et Soc., Sigma Xi, Phi Eta Sigma. Republican. Methodist. Avocations: travel, photography, coin collecting, antique guns, archaeology. Office: 130 La Casa Via Bldg 3 Walnut Creek CA 94598

WILLIAMS, PAT, congressman; b. Helena, Mont., Oct. 30, 1937; m. Carol Griffith, 1965; children: Griff, Erin, Whitney. Student, U. Mont., 1956-57, William Jewell U.; B.A., U. Denver, 1961; postgrad., Western Mont. Coll. Mem. Mont. Ho. of Reps., 1967, 69; exec. dir. Hubert Humphrey Presdl. campaign, Mont., 1968; exec. asst. to U.S. Rep. John Melcher, 1969-71; mem. Gov.'s Employment and Tng. Council, 1972-78, Mont. Legis. Reapportionment Commn., 1973; co-chmn. Jimmy Carter Presdl. campaign, Mont., 1976; mem. 96th-100th Congresses from 1st Mont. dist. Coordinator Mont. Family Edn. Program, 1971-78. Served with U.S. Army, 1960-61; Served with Army N.G., 1962-69. Mem. Mont. Fedn. Tchrs. Democrat. Lodge: Elks. Office: 2457 Rayburn House Office Bldg Washington DC 20515

WILLIAMS, PHARIS EDWARD, physicist; b. Seligman, Mo., July 13, 1941; s. Opal Glenn and Hazel Virginia (Lawson) W.; B.S. in Elec. Engring., U. Colo., 1968; M.S., Naval Postgrad. Sch., 1976; m. Geraldine Williams, May 29, 1961; children—Cynthia Lynn, Deborah Ann, Timothy Pharis, David Matthew, Daniel Ross. Commd. ensign U.S. Navy, 1968. advanced through grades to lt. comdr., 1977; ret., 1983; pres. Williams Research Corp., Socorro, N.Mex., 1984—; instr. U.S. Naval Acad., Annapolis, Md., 1976-78; naval research assoc. Los Alamos Sci. Lab., 1978-83, asst. dir. Ctr. for Explosives Tech. Research, N.Mex. Tech., 1985—. Grantee Naval Acad. Research Council, 1976-77, Office Naval Research, 1976-77. Mem. Sigma Xi. Office: Williams Research Corp PO Box 795 Socorro NM 87801

WILLIAMS, RICHARD HIRSCHFELD, professional baseball manager; b. St. Louis, May 7, 1929; s. Harvey Grote and Kathryn Louise (Rohde) W.; m. Norma Marie Mussato, Oct. 23, 1954; children: Kathi, Richard Anthony, Marc Edmund. Student, Pasadena City Coll., 1946-47. Profl. baseball player 1947-64; mem. Bklyn. Dodgers, 1951-56, Balt. Orioles, 1956-58, 61-62, Cleve. Indians, 1957, Kansas City Athletics, 1959-60, Boston Red Sox, 1963-64; baseball mgr. Toronto Maple Leafs, 1965-66, Boston Red Sox, 1967-69, Oakland A's, 1971-73, Calif. Angels, 1974-76, Montreal Expos, 1977-81, San Diego Padres, 1982-86; mgr. Seattle Mariners, 1986—. Served with U.S. Army, 1951. Named All Star Mgr., 1968, 73-74, 85; Am. Mgr. of Yr., 1967; Nat. League Mgr. of Yr. AP, 1979. Mem. Baseball Players Assn. Am. Roman Catholic. Played in World Series, 1952-53, managed teams in World Series, 1967, 72-73, 84. Office: care Seattle Mariners PO Box 4100 100 S King St Seattle WA 98104

WILLIAMS, RICHARD STANLEY, chemistry educator; b. Kodiak, Alaska, Oct. 27, 1951; s. Bobby Lebe and Shirley Ann (Tweten) W. BA, Rice U., 1974; MS, U. Calif., Berkeley, 1976, PhD, 1978. Mem. tech. staff AT&T Bell Labs., Murray Hill, N.J., 1978-80; asst. prof. chemistry UCLA, 1980-84, assoc. prof., 1984—, assoc. dir. lab. for synchrotron radiation research, 1982—. Mem. editorial bd. Chem. Physics Letters Sci. Jour., 1986—; contbr. articles to profl. jours. Fellow NSF, 1974-77, Alfred P. Sloan Found., 1984-86; scholar Camille and Henry Dreyfus Found. scholar, 1983—. Mem. Am. Chem. Soc., Am. Phys. Soc., Am. Vacuum Soc., Materials Research Soc., Alpha Chi Sigma. Office: UCLA Dept Chemistry 405 Hilgard Ave Los Angeles CA 90024

WILLIAMS, ROBERT C., paper company executive; b. 1930. B.S. in Mech. Engring., U. Cin.; M.B.A., Xavier U.; postgrad., Inst. Paper

Chemistry, Rochester Inst. Tech. Various tech. and supervisory positions Gardner div. Diamond Internat. Corp., 1947-59; with research and devel. dept. Albermarle Paper Co., 1963-68; co-founder James River Corp. of Va., Richmond, 1969—; now pres., chief operating officer James River Corp. of Va.; pres. Crown Zellerbach Corp. San Francisco. Office: James River Corp Va Box 2218 Richmond VA 23217 Office: Crown Zellerbach Corp One Bush St San Francisco CA 94104

WILLIAMS, ROBERT STONE, city official; b. Mathews, Va., Jan. 22, 1952; s. Charles H. and Anne (Stone) W. A.A.S., Rowan Tech. Inst., 1972; B.S. in Fire Protection and Safety Engring., Okla. State U., 1975, M.B.A., 1976. Adminstrv. specialist Oklahoma City Fire Dept., 1977-79; dep. fire chief Clovis Fire Dept., N.Mex., 1979-82; fire chief Billings Fire Dept., Mont., 1982—. Bd. dirs. Salvation Army, Billings, 1984-85, Am. Heart Assn., Clovis, N.Mex., 1980-82. Mem. Western Fire Chiefs Assn. (1st v.p. 1984-85, pres. 1985-86), Internat. Assn. Fire Chiefs, Nat. Fire Protection Assn., Curry County Jaycees (v.p. 1981-82, Jaycee of Yr. 1982), Billings Jaycees (bd. dirs. 1983—, v.p. community devel. 1985, Outstanding Jaycee 1983, Disting. Service award 1985), Mont. Jaycees (treas. 1986-87, speak-up program mgr. 1986-87, Yount Montanan award 1985-86). Methodist. Office: City of Billings Fire Dept 2305 8th Ave N Billings MT 59101

WILLIAMS, RONALD OSCAR, systems engineer; b. Denver, May 10, 1940; s. Oscar H. and Evelyn (Johnson) W. B.S. in Applied Math., U. Colo. Coll. Engring., 1964, postgrad. U. Colo., U. Denver, George Washington U. Computer programmer Apollo Systems dept., missile and space div. Gen. Electric Co., Kennedy Space Center, Fla., 1965-67, Manned Spacecraft Center, Houston, 1967-68; computer programmer U. Colo., Boulder, 1968-73; computer programmer analyst def. systems div. System Devel. Corp. for NORAD, Colorado Springs, 1974-75; engr. def. systems and command-and-info. systems Martin Marietta Aerospace, Denver, 1976-80; systems engr. space and communications group, def. info. systems div. Hughes Aircraft Co., Englewood, Colo., 1980—. Vol. fireman Clear Lake City (Tex.) Fire Dept., 1968; officer Boulder Emergency Squad, 1969-76, rescue squadman, 1969-76, liaison to cadets, 1971, personnel officer, 1971-76, exec. bd., 1971-76, award of merit, 1971, 72, emergency med. technician 1973—; spl. police officer Boulder Police Dept., 1970-75; spl. dep. sheriff Boulder County Sheriff's Dept., 1970-71; nat. adv. bd. Am. Security Council, 1979—, Coalition of Peace through Strength, 1979—; mem. Republican Nat. Com., Nat. Rep. Senatorial Com. Served with USMCR, 1958-66. Decorated Organized Res. medal; recipient Cost Improvement Program award Hughes Aircraft Co., 1982, Systems Improvement award, 1982, Top Cost Improvement Program award, 1983. Mem. AAAS, Math. Assn. Am., Am. Math. Soc., Soc. Indsl. and Applied Math., AIAA, Armed Forces Communications and Electronics Assn., Assn. Old Crows, Am. Def. Preparedness Assn., Marine Corps Assn., Air Force Assn., Nat. Geog. Soc., Smithsonian Instn. (assoc.), Met. Opera Guild, Colo. Hist. Soc., Hist. Denver, Inc., Historic Boulder, Inc., Denver Art Mus., Denver Botanic Gardens, Denver Mus. Natural History, Denver Zool. Found., Inc., Am. Mensa Ltd., Denver Mile Hi Mensa. Republican. Lutheran. Club: Hour of Power Eagles (Garden Grove, Calif.). Home: 7504 W Quarto Ave Littleton CO 80123-4332 Office: Def Info Systems div Hughes Aircraft Co 8000 E Maplewood Ave Englewood CO 80111-4999

WILLIAMS, RUSSELL BROWNELL, biology educator; b. Los Angeles, Aug. 28, 1936; s. Howard Brownell and Florence Arlene (Swanson) W.; m. Rebecca Clara Stuart, May 16, 1964; children: Jonathan, Michael, Stephen. AB, U. Calif., Santa Barbara, 1959; MA, UCLA, 1960; PhD, Laurence U., 1974. Cert. jr. coll. tchr., secondary tchr.; lic. real estate broker. Research assoc. U. Calif., Santa Barbara, 1960-61; NDEA research fellow U. Hawaii, Honolulu, 1961-63; instr. biology Pioneer High Sch., Whittier, Calif., 1964-65; instr. Pasadena (Calif.) City Coll., 1967-68; prof. S.W. Coll., Los Angeles, 1968—, chmn. div., 1975-78, cons. real estate, 1975—. Vol. YMCA, Calif., 1956—; contbr. Halley Watch, So. Calif., 1985—. Mem. AAAS, Ventura Astron. Soc., Western Soc. Naturalists, Am. Fedn. Tchrs., Nat. Assn. Realtors. Republican. Baptist. Avocations: astronomy, camping, nature study. Home: 10630 Flaxton St Culver City CA 90230 Office: SW Coll 1500 W Imperial Hwy Los Angeles CA 90047

WILLIAMS, RUTH LEE, clinical social worker; b. Dallas, June 24, 1944; d. Carl Woodley and Nancy Ruth (Gardner) W. BA, So. Meth. U., 1966; M Sci.in Social Work, U. Tex., Austin, 1969. Milieu coordinator Starr Commonwealth, Albion, Mich., 1969-73; clin. social worker Katherine Hamilton Mental Health Care, Terre Haute, Ind., 1973-74; clin. social worker, supr. Pikes Peak Mental Health Ctr., Colorado Springs, Colo., 1974-78; pvt. practice social work Colorado Springs, 1978—; pres. Hearthstone Inn, Inc., Colorado Springs, 1978—; practitioner Jin Shin Jyutsu, Colorado Springs, 1978—; pres., bd. dirs. Colorado Springs Mental Health Care Providers, Inc., 1986—. Author, editor: From the Kitchen of The Hearthstone Inn, 1981, 2d rev. edit., 1986. Mem. Nat. Registry Health Care Providers in Clin. Social Work (charter mem.), Colo. Soc. Clin. Social Work (editor 1976), Nat. Assn. Soc. Workers (cert.), Nat. Assn. Ind. Innkeepers, So. Meth. U. Alumni Assn. (life). Avocations: gardening, hiking, sailing. Home: 11555 Howell Rd Colorado Springs CO 80908 Office: 536 E Uintah Colorado Springs CO 80903

WILLIAMS, STANLEY CLARK, medical entomologist, educator; b. Long Beach, Calif., Aug. 24, 1939; s. Thomas and Sadie Elenore (Anderson) W.; m. Charlene E. Fernald; children: Lisa M., Thomas S.; m. Roxanna Berlin, Aug. 30, 1981; 1 child, Erin B. AB, San Diego State Coll., 1961, MA, 1963; postgrad., U. Kans., 1963-64; PhD, Ariz. State U., 1968. Cert. secondary tchr., Calif. Instr. San Diego Mus. Nat. History, 1957-59, asst. curator herpetology, 1957-61; park naturalist U.S. Nat. Park Service, San Diego, 1960-62; instr. Grossmont (Calif.) High Sch. Dist., 1962-63, Ariz. State U., Tempe, 1964-66; prof. biology San Francisco State U., 1967—; bd. dirs. West Point Acad. Sci., Calif.; mem. adv. bd. San Francisco Insect Zoo. Contbr. over 60 articles to profl. jours. Grantee NSF, 1968-72; recipient Travel grant T.P. Hearne Co. Fellow Calif. Acad. Sci.; mem. Am. Arachnological Soc. (editorial bd.), Ecol. Soc. Am., San Francisco Beekeepers Assn. (pres. 1984-85), Pacific Coast Entomol. Soc. (pres. elect 1986, pres. 1987—), Assn. Biologists for Computing (pres. 1986—), Soc. Vector Ecologists (edit. bd. 1986—), Western Apicultural Soc., Sigma Xi.. Avocations: photography, apiculture, horticulture, backpacking, bicycling. Office: San Francisco State U Dept Biology San Francisco CA 94132

WILLIAMS, TALMAGE THEODORE, JR., physicist; b. Atlanta, Jan. 20, 1933; s. Talmage Theodore and Maye (Lamb) W.; m. Judy Ann Bain, Dec. 15, 1964; children—Angelyn Patricia, Patrick Dewey. B.S. in Physics, Ga. Inst. Tech., 1955; postgrad. Fla. Inst. Tech., 1965-71, U. So. Calif., 1976-77. Physicist, E.I. DuPont Co., Aiken, S.C., 1958-62; leader RCA Apollo Ships Evaluation, Patrick AFB, Fla., 1962-68, staff physicist, chief scientist's office RCA Missile Test Project, 1968-72, mgr. land and air systems analysis, 1972; mgr. sci. analysis dept. ITT Fed. Electric Corp., 1972-75, dep. dir. for plans and analysis, 1975-79, dir. advanced systems, 1979-83, dir. ops. and evaluation, 1983-86, dir. range ops. and systems support, 1986—. Served to lt. (j.g.) USN, 1955-58. Fellow AIAA (assoc., nat. flight test com.); mem. AAAS, Am. Phys. Soc., Am. Inst. Physics, Internat. Test and Evaluation Assn., Inst. Nav., Sigma Pi Sigma. Contbr. articles to profl. jours. Home: 725 Doverlee Dr Santa Maria CA 93454 Office: ITT Fed Electric Corp Vandenberg AFB CA 93437

WILLIAMS, TERRY WAYNE, biomedical research scientist, consultant; b. Los Angeles, Dec. 24, 1945; s. Ben Harris and Esther Sibyle (Karr) W. Student San Diego State U.; B.A., U. Calif.-San Diego; Ph.D., U. Calif.-Irvine. Research assoc. U. Calif.-San Diego, 1972-78; research cons., San Diego, 1979-81; sr. staff assoc. Georgetown U., Washington, 1982-84; research specialist Monsanto Co., St. Louis, 1984-85; sr. scientist Cancer Biologics Inc., Santa Ana, 1985-86; sr. research assoc. Brunswick Technetics, San Diego, 1986; sr. fellow U. Wash., Seattle, 1970-71. Recipient Research award NSF, Irvine, Calif., 1968, predoctoral fellow, 1968, postdoctoral fellow, Seattle, 1970; recipient Nat. Research Service award, Washington, 1982. Mem. Am. Assn. Immunologists, Am. Soc. Cell Biology, Soc. Sci. Exploration, Tissue Culture Assn. Home: 1546 Flair Encinitas Encinitas CA 92024 Office: Brunswick Technetics 4116 Sorrento Valley Blvd San Diego CA 92121

WILLIAMS, TESS MERN, education administrator; b. Declo, Idaho, Mar. 23, 1924; s. Elmer and Laurine (Olsen) W.; m. Maxine Hoggan, Dec. 23, 1949; children: Dorice, Alan Mern. BS in Agrl. Engring., Oreg. State U., 1950; MS in Tech. Journalism, Iowa State U., 1954; PhD in Speech and Drama, Mich. State U., 1971. Dir. film graphics Sta. KOIN-TV, Portland, Oreg., 1953-57; ETV cons. Oreg. System Higher Edn., Eugene, 1957-60; dir. broadcast services Brigham Young U., Provo, Utah, 1960-66; prof. communications Brigham Young U., 1967-70; dir. learning systems Mich. State U., East Lansing, 1966-67; dir. telecommunications and info. technologies Utah Bd. Regents, Salt Lake City, 1970—; TV cons. various orgs., 1953-60; vis. prof. several univs., 1953—. Author: Handbook of Films for TV, 1954; numerous TV/movie scripts. Chmn. sub-com. Gov.'s Adv. Com. on Community Affairs, Utah, 1970-78; del. Utah State Pol. Conv. Mem. Utah Telecommunications Assn. (pres. 1972-78), Soc. Motion Pictures/TV Engrs., Assn. Edn. Communications and Tech. (chmn. 1958—). Club: Toastmasters. Avocations: music, gardening, hiking, freelance writing. Home: 1025 E Center St Bountiful UT 84101

WILLIAMS, VALENA MINOR, radio station official; b. New Orleans, Apr. 6, 1923; d. Norman Selby and Grace Claudia (Jones) Minor; m. John B. Williams, June 6, 1948 (dec. Oct. 1976); children—Valena Marie, Allison Grace, Jennifer Minor, Kimberley Susan. B.S., Bennett Coll., Greensboro, N.C., 1943; M.Jour., U. Calif.-Berkeley, 1981. Broadcaster Stas. WABQ, WHK, WTAM, Cleve., 1955-64; producer, coordinator univ. relations President's Office, U. Calif.-Berkeley, 1967-83; sta. mgr. Sta. KQED-FM, San Francisco, 1983—; pub. mem. Pub. Broadcasting Service, 1977-83; profl. mem. bd. dirs. Nat. Pub. Radio, 1985-87. Producer radio series U.C. Drum (African series), 1970-71, U.C. News Service, 1975-77. Recipient Golden Mike award McCall/Am. Women in Radio and TV, 1961. Home: 2207 Braemar Rd Oakland CA 94602

WILLIAMS, VERLE ALVIN, consulting engineer; b. New Virginia, Iowa, Apr. 8, 1933; s. Donald Oliver and Josephine Emily (Read) W.; A.A., Pueblo Jr. Coll., 1957; B.S. in M.E., B.S. in Bus., Colo. U., 1960; m. Mary Sue Earley, June 2, 1957; children—Steven Lee, Randall Joe, LeAnne Sue. Sales engr. Johnson Controls, Inc., Portland, Oreg., 1960-67, Los Angeles, 1967-68, San Diego, 1968-69, br. mgr., 1970-79; assoc. in charge of energy conservation systems dept. Dunn-Lee-Smith-Klein & Assos., National City, Calif., 1979-81; owner Verle A. Williams & Assos., Inc., profl. energy and control cons., San Diego, 1981—; lectr. in field. Founding mem. Rancho Bernardo Bapt. Ch., chmn., treas., 1970—. Served with U.S. Army, 1953-55. Registered profl. engr., Calif.; cert. energy auditor, Calif. Mem. Am. Mgmt. Assn., ASHRAE (chmn. energy mgmt. com. 1979-81, past pres., v.p., bd. govs.), Soc. Level Tech. Com. on Automatic Control Systems, Assn. Energy Engrs. (cert. energy mgr.; founding pres. San Diego chpt. 1981; Engr. of Yr. 1982, Regional Engr. of Yr. 1983, Internat. Energy Engr. of Yr. 1984, v.p. Region V 1984—), Soc. Energy Mgmt. (vice chmn. energy mgmt. 1985—), Energy Monitoring and Control Soc. Clubs: Rancho Bernardo Bowleros (pres. 1969-71). Home: 12394 Fairway Pointe Row San Diego CA 92128 Office: Williams Engring Ctr 7047 Carroll Rd San Diego CA 92121

WILLIAMS, WALTER, public affairs educator; b. Houston, Dec. 13, 1932; s. Walter and Rosalie (Lazarus) W.; m. Jacqueline Block, Jan. 30, 1958; children: Stuart, David. BBA, U. Tex., 1955, MBA, 1956; PhD, Ind. U., 1960. Asst. prof. Ind. U., Bloomington, 1960-64; assoc. prof. U. Ky., Lexington, 1964-65; chief research and plans div. OEO, Washington, 1967-69; dir. Inst. Pub. Policy and Mgmt., Seattle, 1980-84; prof. pub. affairs U. Wash., Seattle, 1970—; vis. scholar London Sch. Econs., 1983. Author: Social Policy Research and Analysis, 1971, Implementation Perspective, 1980, Government By Agency, 1980, Disaster Policy Implementation, 1986. Served to 1st lt. U.S. Army, 1955-57. Postdoctoral fellow Ford Found., 1962-63; grantee NSF, 1974-84, German Marshall Fund, 1980-82. Mem. Assn. Pub. Policy Analysis and Mgmt. (policy council). Democrat. Jewish. Home: 1235 22d Ave E Seattle WA 98112 office: U Wash Grad Sch Pub Affairs DP-30 Seattle WA 98195

WILLIAMS, WILHO EDWARD, consulting engineering executive; b. Spokane, Wash., Mar. 7, 1922; s. Emil Wilho and Lulu May (Johnson) W.; m. Virginia May Knudsen, June 26, 1954; children: Craig Wilho, Kim Ann, Kevin Jon. BSCE, Wash. State U., 1944; MSCE, U. Ill., 1947. Registered profl. engr., Wash., Idaho, Oreg., N.Mex.; registered profl. land surveyor, Idaho. Ptnr. Culler, Gale, Martell, Ericson and Norrie, Spokane, 1958-73; assoc. Bovay Engrs., Inc., Spokane, 1973-85; v.p. Bovay Northwest, Inc., Spokane, 1985—; mem. State of Wash. Bd. Registration for Profl. Engrs. and Land Surveyors, 1978-83, 85—. Mem. City of Spokane Bldg. Commn., 1980-83. Served to capt. USNR, 1942-75, Korea. Fellow ASCE (Engr. of Merit 1986); mem. Wash. Soc. Profl. Engrs. (pres. 1979-80), Structural Engrs. Assn. of Wash. (pres. 1975, Engr. of Yr. 1976), Am. Concrete Inst. Republican. Lutheran. Home: E 2332 34th Ave Spokane WA 99223 Office: Bovay Northwest Inc E 808 Sprague Ave Spokane WA 99202

WILLIAMS, WILLIAM IVOR, journalist; b. Easton, Pa., Aug. 31, 1923; s. William A. Williams and Annie Jones; m. Dulcie Williamson, Sept. 1, 1943; children—Wyn Garry, Judith Brenda. Reporter, editor London Free Press, Ont., Can., 1945-73; editor in chief Regina Leader Post, Sask., Can., 1973—. Served with RCAF, 1941-53, ETO. Mem. Can. Daily Newspaper Pub. Assn. (chmn. editorial div. 1974-76), Can. Mng. Editors Conf. (pres. 1970-73), Am. Soc. Newspaper Editors. Presbyterian. Avocations: golfing; flying; traveling; hunting. Home: 4011 Gordon Rd, Regina, SK Canada S4S 6G6 Office: Regina Leader Post, 1964 Park St, Regina, SK Canada S4P 3G4

WILLIAMS, WILLIS RAY, paint manufacturing company executive; b. Iaeger, W. Va., Mar. 8, 1937; s. Hobart Virgil and Thelma Belle (Blankenship) W.; m. Gale Jacqueline Scott, Aug. 27, 1957; children: Ray, Scott, Michael, Mark. B.S. in Chemistry, Marshall U., 1963. Chemist, Columbia Paint Co., Huntington, W.Va., 1957-63, tech. dir., 1963-66, v.p., 1966-71, pres., 1971-79; pres., owner Wiltech Corp., Wash., 1979—. Mem. Nat. Paint and Coatings Assn., Portland Paint and Coatings Assn. (pres. 1984-85). Methodist. Lodge: Huntington Kiwanis (pres. 1978). Home: 4400 Sunset Way Longview WA 98632 Office: Wiltech Corp 1203 California Way Longview WA 98632

WILLIAMS, YVONNE ELAINE, home economist, teacher; b. Colorado Springs, Colo., Oct. 13, 1944; d. William Dean and Martha LaVerna (Golding) Sams; m. Lawrence Richard Williams, Dec. 22, 1967; 1 son, Jeremy Za. B.S., Bob Jones U., 1966; M.A., U. No. Colo., 1968; postgrad. U. Colo., 1980, 83, 86. Cert. tchr. Colo. Tchr. home econs., phys. edn. Kit Carson (Colo.) Sch. Dist., 1966-68; tchr. home econs. Elkhart (Kans.) High Sch., 1968-73, Russell Jr. High Sch., Colorado Springs, Colo., 1974-75; home econs. tchr. Doherty High Sch., Colorado Springs, 1975—, chmn. home econs. dept., cheerleader sponsor, 1975-76; mem. curriculum writing com. Colorado Springs Sch. Dist. 11; tchr. adult edn. classes in sewing and tailoring; judge Colo. Beef Cook-off, local and dist. clothing exhibits El Paso County Fair. Mem. Gifted and Talented Parent Group Lincoln Elem. Sch., 1980-83; asst. cub scout den mother local Boy Scouts Am., 1981-83; Bible sch. tchr. Calvary Bible Ch., 1982-83, 86. Recipient Bob Jones U. Outstanding Achievement in Home Econs. award, 1966; named Young Career Woman of Elkhart, Kans., 1969; Colo. Home Econs. Tchr. of Yr., 1984. Mem. Colo. Home Econs. Assn. (nominating com. 1987), Am. Home Econs. Assn., Bob Jones U. Alumni Assn. (2d v.p.), Delta Kappa Gamma. Republican. Home: 1720 Applewood Ridge Ct Colorado Springs CO 80907 Office: Doherty High Sch 4515 Barnes Rd Colorado Springs CO 80917

WILLIAMSON, DORIS, business education educator; b. Salt Lake City, July 1, 1937; d. Frank Farrow and Ruby Dean (Andersen) W. A.S., Coll. So. Utah, Cedar City, 1957; B.S. in Bus. Edn., Brigham Young U., 1959; M.S. in Bus. Edn., Utah State U., 1974. Cert. secondary tchr., Utah. Tchr., Salt Lake City Schs., 1959-64; tchr. typewriting Granite Sch. Dist., Salt Lake City, 1964-70; asst. prof. bus. edn. Idaho State U., 1973-76; assoc. prof. So. Utah State Coll., Cedar City, 1976—, pres. Faculty Senate, 1983-84; lectr. workshops in teaching methodology and secretarial sci. Trustee Utah Summer Games, 1985—. EDPA fellow, 1971-73; recipient Leadership award Delta Pi Epsilon, 1976; Outstanding Tchr.-Bus. Edn. award Utah Bus. Edn. and Utah Vocat. Assns. 1979; Disting. Educator award So. Utah State Coll., 1983. Mem. Utah Bus. Edn. Assn., Utah Vocat. Edn. Assn., Nat. Bus. Edn. Assn., Am. Vocat. Assn., Bus. and Profl. Women Internat. (Woman of Achievement award Cedar City 1983), Utah Shakespeare Guild (pres. 1983—), Cedar City C. of C. (bd. dirs. 1981-83, pres. 1982-83), Western Bus. Edn. Assn., Classroom Edn. of Bus. Assn., Delta Pi Epsilon, Delta Kappa Gamma, Phi Kappa Phi. Mormon. Home: 17 W Robbers Roost Ln Cedar City UT 84720 Office: Bus So Utah State Coll Cedar City UT 84720

WILLIAMSON, HARWOOD DANFORD, utility company executive; b. Waimea, Kauai, Hawaii, 1932. Grad., Stanford U., 1956. Pres., chief operating officer Hawaiian Electric Co., Inc., also bd. dirs.; v.p., bd. dirs. Hawaiian Electric Industries, Inc.; chmn. Hawaii Electric Light Co., Inc., Maui Electric Co., Ltd. Office: Hawaiian Electric Co Inc 900 Richards St Honolulu HI 96813 *

WILLIAMSON, (JOHN STEWART) JACK, writer; b. Bisbee, Ariz., Apr. 29, 1908; s. Asa Lee and Lucy Betty (Hunt) W.; m. Blanche Slaten Harp, Aug. 15, 1947 (dec. Jan. 1985); stepchildren: Keign Harp (dec.), Adele Harp Lovorn. BA, MA, Eastern N.Mex. U., 1957, LHD (hon.), 1981; PhD, U. Colo., 1964. Prof. English Eastern N.Mex. U., Portales, 1960-77. Author numerous sci. fiction books including The Legion of Space, 1947, Darker Than You Think, 1948, The Humanoids, 1949, The Green Girl, 1950, The Cometeers, 1950, One Against the Legion, 1950, Seetee Shock, 1950, Seetee Ship, 1950, Dragon's Island, 1951, The Legion of Time, 1952, Dome Around America, 1955, The Trial of Terra, 1962, Golden Blood, 1964, The Reign of Wizardry, 1965, Bright New Universe, 1967, Trapped in Space, 1968, The Pandora Effect, 1969, People Machines, 1971, The Moon Children, 1972, H.G. Wells: Critic of Progress, 1973, Teaching SF, 1975, The Early Williamson, 1975, The Power of Blackness, 1976, The Best of Jack Williamson, 1978 Brother to Demons, Brother to Gods, 1979, Teaching Science Fiction: Education for Tomorrow, 1980, The Alien Intelligence, 1980, The Humanoid Touch, 1980, Manseed, 1982, The Queen of a Legion, 1983, Wonder's Child: My Life in Science Fiction, 1984 (Hugo award 1985), Lifeburst, 1984, Firechild, 1986; (with Frederik Pohl) Undersea Quest, 1954, Undersea Fleet, 1955, Undersea City, 1956, The Reefs of Space, 1964, Starchild, 1965, Rogue Star, 1969, The Farthest Star, 1975, Wall Around a Star, 1983; (with James Gunn) Star Bridge, 1955; (with Miles J. Breuer) The Birth of an New Republic, 1981. Served as staff sgt. USAAF, 1942-45. Mem. Sci. Fiction Writers Am. (pres. 1978-80, Grand Master Nebula award 1976), Sci. Fiction Research Assn. (Pilgrim award 1968), World Sci. Fiction, Planetary Soc. Avocations: travel, astronomy, photography. Home: PO Box 761 Portales NM 88130 Office: Eastern N Mex U Golden Library Portales NM 88130

WILLIAMSON, KENNETH DONALD, JR., chemical engineer; b. Williamsport, Pa., July 30, 1935; s. Kenneth Donald and Martha (Cockburn) W.; m. Ruth Sollitt, Dec. 27, 1958; children: Kenneth III, Kimberly, Karen. BS, Pa. State U., 1957, MS, 1960, PhD, 1961. Mem. staff Los Alamos (N.Mex.) Nat. Lab., 1961-73, assoc. group leader, 1973-79, group leader, 1979—. Editor: Hydrogen Its Technology, 1977, Liquid Cryogens, 1983, Recent Development H2 Technolgoy, 1985. Treas. N.Mex. Citizens for Clean Air and Water, Los Alamos, 1978—. Mem. Internat. Assn. Hydroged Energy. Republican. Lutheran. Lodges: Kiwanis (pres. 1976, lt. gov. 1978), Masons. Avocations: stamp and coin collecting, fishing, hiking. Home: 436 Estante Way Los Alamos NM 87544 Office: Los Alamos Nat Lab PO Box 1663 MS F611 Los Alamos NM 87545

WILLIAMSON, NEIL SEYMOUR, III, aircraft company executive, retired Army officer; b. Dumont, N.J., Jan. 5, 1935; s. Neil Seymour and Mary Louise (Bittenbender) W.; m. Sue Carrole Cooper, Dec. 15, 1985; children: Deborah D., Leisa L., Neil S. IV, Dirk A., Wendy L. BS, U.S. Mil. Acad., 1958; MSME, U. Mich., 1963. Commd. 2d lt. U.S. Army, 1958, advanced through grades to col.; assoc. prof. dept. earth, space and graphic scis. U.S. Mil. Acad., West Point, N.Y., 1965-68; chief edn. sect. U.S. Army, Ft. McNair, D.C., 1970-71; analyst armor infantry systems group Pentagon U.S. Army, Washington, 1972-73, systems analyst requirements office Pentagon, 1974-75, program analyst, 1975-76; chief advanced systems concept office U.S. Army, Redstone Arsenal, Ala., 1976-77; comdr., dir. fire control & small caliber weapon systems lab. U.S. Army, Dover, N.J., 1977-78; project mgr. TOW U.S. Army, Redstone Arsenal, 1978-81; ret. U.S. Army, 1981; program mgr. Hughes Aircraft Co., El Segundo, Calif., 1981—. Decorated Bronze Star with one oak leaf cluster, Legion of Merit with one oak leaf cluster, Air medal with seven oak leaf clusters, Purple Heart. Mem. Soc. Automotive Engrs., Am. Def. Prepardness Assn., Army Aviation Assn. (pres. Tenn. Valley chpt. 1980), Am. Helicopter Soc., U.S. Armor Assn., Disabled Am. Vets. Office: Hughes Aircraft Co PO Box 902 El Segundo CA 90245

WILLIAMSON, RICHARD SCOTT, water resources engineer; b. Oxnard, Calif., Apr. 26, 1954; s. John Arthur and Mari Louise (Richards) W. m. Jill Robin Arend, Sept. 23, 1983; children—Jenna Lynn, Alex Jesse. B.S. in Water Resources Engring., UCLA, 1975; postgrad. in mgmt. Golden Gate U., 1978. Registered profl. engr., Calif., Ariz. San. engr. region IX, EPA, San Francisco, 1975-79; mgr. safe drinking water program Ariz. Dept. Health Services, Phoenix, 1979-81; prin. Williamson & Assocs., Environ. Engring., Phoenix, 1981—; gen. mgr. No. Gila County (Ariz) San. Dist., 1982—; pres. Utility Mgmt. & Ops. Services Inc., 1985—; prin. Williamson Engrs., 1985—; mem. Ariz. Water and Sewer Commn. Mem. Am. Water Works Assn., Water Pollution Control Fedn., Ariz. Water and Pollution Control Assn., Assn. Ariz. San. Dists. (pres.), Sigma Chi. Presbyterian. Lodge: Rotary (Payson). Home: PO Box 1586 Payson AZ 85547 Office: Northern Gila County Sanitary Dist PO Box 591 Payson AZ 85547

WILLIAMSON, STEPHEN VICTOR, state official; b. Tulare, Calif., May 20, 1950; s. Grady Edgar and June Bernice (Gragg) W. B.A., U. Calif.-Davis, 1971. Sr. coordinator U. Calif. Statewide Student Body Presidents Council-Student Lobby, 1971-73; cons. budget div. Calif. Dept. Fin., 1973-74, Systems Research Inc., Los Angeles, 1974-76, Calif. Research, Sacramento, Calif., 1976-78; dir. Calif. State Clearinghouse, Gov.'s. Office Planning and Research, Sacramento, 1978-82; exec. com. State EDP Policy, 1983-84; mgr. info. systems Calif. Housing Fin. Agy., Sacramento, 1983-84; sr. mgr., mgmt. cons. Price Waterhouse, 1984—. Mem. Assn. Environ. Profls. (Achievement of Yr. award 1982), Assn. for Computing Machinery, Data Processing Mgmt. Assn., Assn. Systems Mgmt., Am. Soc. Pub. Adminstrs., Chi Phi. Office: Price Waterhouse 455 Capitol Mall Sacramento CA 95814

WILLIAMSON-SPARKS, CONSTANCE MAY, chemistry educator; b. Ft. Defiance, Ariz., Apr. 11, 1944; d. Ray Clyde and Ann (May) Clark; m. Lance Williamson, Dec. 23, 1963 (div. Oct. 24, 1977); children: Narayin Singh Khalsa, Laurence; m. Don Sparks, Dec. 23, 1985. BS, U. Ariz., 1968; MA, Calif. State U., Los Angeles, 1979. Cert. tchr. Tchr., prin. Rambam High Sch., Beverly Hills, Calif., 1968-75; tchr. Newbridge High Sch., Beverly Hills, 1975-77; tchr. chemistry Los Angeles City Schs., 1977—; cons., Los Angeles, 1980—; workshop leader UCLA, 1983—; tchr. summer sch. Westlake Sch. for Girls, Los Angeles, 1984-86. Bd. dirs. Greater Los Angeles Sci. Tchrs. Assn., 1983—, pres. 1987-88; mem. Ho. Reps. United Tchrs. Los Angeles, 1982—, legis. contact for Tom Hayden, 1983-84. Recipient Math./Sci. fellowship Los Angeles Edn. Ptnrship, 1985; STUP grantee State of Calif., Sacramento, 1984; Videodisc grantee, 1983—. Mem. Nat. Sci. Tchrs. Assn., Calif. Assn. Chemistry Tchrs. (sec. 1986—), NEA, Am. Chem. Soc. (Videodisc grantee 1985-86), NOW (chmn. edn. task force 1983-85), Sierra Club. Democrat. Unitarian. Avocations: folk dancing, acting at Renaissance Faires. Office: Kennedy High Sch 11254 Gothic Ave Granada Hills CA 91344

WILLIE, ELVIN, JR., Indian tribal executive; b. Schurz, Nev., Sept. 15, 1953; s. Elvin and Rosalie Irene (McKay) W.; m. Georgina A. Willie; children: James X. II, Everett Z. B.A., U. Calif.-Berkeley, 1976. Media coordinator native Am. studies U. Calif.-Berkeley, 1973-76; curriculum devel. coordinator tribal edn. program Walker River Paiute Tribe, Schurz, Nev., 1976-77, tribal chmn., 1979—; smokeshop mgr. Walker River Tribal Enterprise, 1977-79. Election bd. chmn. precinct 11, Mineral County, Nev., 1980-83. Mem. Western Nev. Dirt Track Racing Assn.

WILLING, JAMES RICHARD, computer technician; b. Portland, Oreg., Apr. 1, 1958; s. James Albert and Venita Faye (Fishburn) W.; m. Carole Marguerite Babbitt, Feb. 10, 1979; 1 child, Robert James. Grad. Beaverton High Sch., Oreg. Shop technician Byte N.W. Inc., Beaverton, 1976-79; field service technician N.W. Computer Support, Beaverton, 1979-81; systems programmer Johnson-Laird Inc., Portland, 1982; project dir. CB CBBS/NW, Beaverton, 1979—; lead technician Computerland, Tigard, Oreg., 1982-86; field engr., tech. Compu-Shop, 1986—; mem. steering com. Portland Computer Arts Resource Ctr., 1986—. Mem. computer edn. task force Oreg. Mus. Sci. and Industry, Portland, 1984. Mem. Control Program for Microcomputers User's Group NW (founder 1979), pres. 1979-82). Republican. Methodist. Home: 14120 SW 20th Beaverton OR 97005-4971 Office: Compu-Shop 851 SW 6th Portland OR 97204

WILLING, THOMAS SHIPPEN, purchasing administrator; b. Phila., Aug. 8, 1950; s. E. Shippen Willing and Martha (Kent) Denniston; m. Mary Burgess, June 14, 1975; children: Nathaniel, Charles. BA, U. Oreg., 1974; MA, Ohio State U., 1977. Purchasing mgr. Mantra Marine, Seattle, 1978-80; sr. buyer Fed. Res. Bank, Portland, Oreg., 1981-84; purchasing mgr. Smith Bros. Office Outfitters, Portland, 1984—. Coordinator Galer St. Community, Seattle, 1977-80. Mem. Purchasing Mgmt. Assn. Oreg (trustee 1986—, v.p. 1987), Nat. Assn. Purchasing Mgmt. (named Profl. Devel. Person of Yr., 1986). Avocations: fly fishing, furniture building, Riparian biology. Office: Smith Bros Office Outfitters 135 NW Park Portland OR 97209

WILLIS, HAROLD WENDT, SR., real estate developer; b. Marion, Ala., Oct. 7, 1927; s. Robert James and Della (Wendt) W.; student Loma Linda U., 1960, various courses San Bernardino Valley Coll.; m. Patsy Gay Bacon, Aug. 2, 1947 (div. Jan. 1975); children: Harold Wendt II, Timothy Gay, April Ann, Brian Tad, Suzanne Gail; m. Vernette Jacobson Osborne, Mar. 30, 1980 (div. 1984); m. Ofelia Alvarez, Sept. 23, 1984; 1 child, Ryran Robert, Samantha Ofelia. Ptnr., Victoria Guernsey, San Bernardino, Calif., 1950-63, co-pres., 1963-74, pres., 1974—; owner Quik-Save, 1966—, K-Mart Shopping Ctr., San Bernardino, 1969—; pres. Energy Delivery Systems, Food and Fuel, Inc. San Bernardino City water commr., 1965—. Bd. councillors Loma Linda (Calif.) U., 1968-85, pres., 1971-74. Served as officer U.S. Mcht. Marine, 1945-46. Recipient Silver medal in 3000 meter steeplechase Sr. Olympics, U. So. Calif., 1979, 81, 82, 83; lic. pvt. pilot. Mem. Calif. Dairy Industries Assn. (pres. 1963, 64), Liga Internat. (2d v.p. 1978, pres. 1982, 83). Seventh-day Adventist (deacon 1950-67). Home: 207 W Sunset Redlands CA 92373 Office: PO Box 5607 San Bernardino CA 92412

WILLIS, RODNEY LEE, photographer; b. Kirksville, Mo., Oct. 16, 1953; s. Robert Lee and Glaza Beth (Haynes) W. B.A., No. Mo. State U., 1979; postgrad., San Jose State U., 1982-84. Audio-visual technician, No. Mo. State U., Kirksville, 1977-79; photographer Coppinger Inc., Cleveland, Tenn., 1979-80; audio-visual specialist Focus Communication Group, San Jose, Calif., 1980-85; free-lance photographer, 1985—; cons., photographer Prestige Portraits, Emeryville, Calif., 1981-82. Designer, Cameraman slide shows; photographer video tape, mag. Cameraman, Catholic Youth Orgn., San Jose, 1982; audio-visual contbr. San Jose Film Festival, 1984. Recipient BPAA award for Excellence, Gold award N.Y. Film Festival. Mem. Assn. for Multi-Image (Gold award), Phi Sigma Epsilon. Democrat. Club: Flying Twenty (San Jose). Home: 124 Rancho Dr #2 San Jose CA 95111

WILLIS, WAYNE OWEN, agricultural scientist, researcher; b. Paonia, Colo., Jan. 21, 1928; m. Sally R., Mar. 18, 1951; children: David, Donald, Diane, Daniel. BS, Colo. State U., 1952; MS, Iowa State U., 1953, PhD, 1956. Soil scientist Agrl. Research Service, USDA, Prosser, Wash., 1956-57, Riverside, Calif., 1957-58, Mandan, N.D., 1958-71, Beltsville, Md., 1971, Mandan, N.D., 1971-76, Ft. Collins, Colo., 1976—. Co-editor: Dryland Agriculture, 1983, Plant Product Management Under Drought, 1983; contbr. numerous chpts. to books. Served with USN, 1946-48. Fellow Am. Soc. Agronomy, Soil Sci. Soc. Am. (bd. dirs. 1973-75), Soil Conservation Soc. Am. (water resource div. 1980-82); mem. Internat. Soil Sci. Soc., Can. Soc. Soil Sci. Lodge: Elks. Avocations: outdoor fishing, photography. Home: 721 Cherokee Dr Fort Collins CO 80525 Office: USDA-ARS Agronomy Dept Colo State U Fort Collins CO 80523

WILLMAN, WARREN WALTON, mathematician; b. Chgo., May 24, 1943; s. Warren Page and Marguerite Susan (Dietrich) W. BA, BS in Engring., U. Mich., 1965; MA, Harvard U., 1966, PhD, 1969. Mathematician Shell Devel. Co., Houston, 1969-70; ops. research analyst Naval Research Lab., Washington, 1971-82; mathematician Naval Weapons Ctr., China Lake, Calif., 1982—; mem. thesis examination bd. Indian Inst. Tech., Delhi, 1977. Contbr. articles to profl. jours. Recipient Disting. Scholar award U. Mich., 1964, Research Publ. award U.S. Naval Research Lab., 1973, 74. Mem. AIAA, Sigma Xi. Home: 1400 N Richmond Rd Apt A Ridgecrest CA 93555 Office: Naval Weapons Ctr Code 3807 China Lake CA 93555-6001

WILLMS, JAMES A., company executive; b. Gooding, Idaho, Feb. 23, 1947; s. Alton William and Harriett (Lamb) W.; m. Paula Jean Cruikshank, Aug. 17, 1974; children: David James, Ashley Ann. Cert., Colo. Sch. Mines, 1964, W. Va. U., 1965; BSME, U. Idaho, 1970; MBA, Harvard U., 1972. Asst. brand mgr. Procter & Gamble, Cin., 1973-75, brand mgr., 1975-80; v.p. mktg. Unicover Corp., Cheyenne, Wyo., 1980-82, exec. v.p., 1982—; lectr. U. Wyo. Coll. Commerce and Industry, 1981-85. Chmn. bus. adv. council to U. Wyo., Laramie, 1986, pub. info. Water Bond Commn., Cheyenne, 1982; pres.-elect Cheyenne Symphony Orch., 1986. Boise Cascade scholar Harvard U., 1970; recipient Arthur L. Williston award ASME, 1971. Mem. Rocky Mountain Direct Mktg. Club, U. Idaho Alumni Assn. (bd. dirs. 1970, fund-raising chmn. Ohio 1972-79, Wyo. 1980-84). Republican. Roman Catholic. Club: Harvard U. (Denver). Lodge: Rotary. Avocations: hunting, fishing, gardening, pub. speaking. Home: 114 Ponderosa Trail Cheyenne WY 82009 Office: Unicover Corp One Unicover Ctr Cheyenne WY 82008

WILLNER, JAY R., consulting company executive; b. Aurora, Ill., Sept. 22, 1924; s. Charles R. and Ida (Winer) W.; m. Suzanne Wehmann, July 17, 1958; 1 child, Adam Wehmann. Student U. Calif., Los Angeles, 1946-48; BS, MIT, 1950; MBA, Rutgers U., 1959. Researcher Andrew Brown Co., Los Angeles, 1950-52; tech. salesman Glidden Co., Los Angeles, 1952-54; market researcher Roger Williams Inc., N.Y.C., 1954-59; sr. market analyst Calif. Chem. Co., San Francisco, 1959-63; mgr. planning chem. coatings div. Mobil Chem. Co., N.Y.C., 1963-68; pres. WEH Corp., San Francisco, 1968—; lectr. U. Calif., Berkeley, 1962—; adj. faculty U. San Francisco, 1977—; U.S. corr. German mag. Farbe & Lack. Contbg. editor Jour. Protective Coatings & Linings. Served to 2d lt. A.C., AUS, 1943-46. Mem. Am. Chem. Soc., Chem. Market Research Assn., Golden Gate Paint and Coatings Assn., Chem. Coaters Assn. Clubs: Chemists (N.Y.C.), M.I.T. No. Calif. Home: 2011 Vallejo St San Francisco CA 94123 Office: WEH Corp PO Box 40066 San Francisco CA 94140

WILLOUGHBY, KENNETH WAYNE, physicist, telecommuter consultant; b. Chgo., May 4, 1935; s. Lester Keith and Louise Christine (Vogrig) W.; m. Cosette Theda Jarboe, July 13, 1961. Student Nebr. U., 1953-54; B.A., Nebr. Wesleyan U., 1958; postgrad N.Mex. State U., 1958-61. Physicist, White Sands Missile Range, N.Mex., 1958-61; flight test analysis engr. Lockheed Missiles and Space Co., Sunnyvale, Calif., 1961-67, sr. research engr., 1967-70; sr. data processor, 1970-72; mgr., sr. research engr. Willoughby Research Co., Fairacres, N.Mex., 1972—, mgr., owner, Potter, Nebr., 1973-74, Fairacres, 1977—. Author: Secrets of EGO Power and Control, 1973. Republican. Methodist. Office: Willoughby Research Co Box 317 Fairacres NM 88033

WILLS, ARNOLD JAMES, mechanical engineer; b. Denver, July 24, 1941; s. William Welcome and Ella (Phillips) W.; m. Ruth Marie Eppler, Sept. 5, 1964; children: Victoria Lynn, Raymond John, Dorothy Jean. BSME, U. Colo., 1964. Project mgr. Gates Rubber Co., Denver, 1964—. Bd. dirs. Parker (Colo.) United Meth. Ch., 1970-72; mem. com. Boy Scouts Am., Parker, 1984—. Recipient Exceptional Contbn. award Gates Rubber Co., 1984. Avocations: automotive design and constn., water skiing. Home: 16717 E Davies Ave Aurora CO 80016 Office: Gates Rubber Co PO Box 5887 Denver CO 80217

WILLS, PATRICK LYNN, military officer; b. Longview, Wash., Apr. 23, 1950; s. John Leslie and Pearl Ellen (Forslin) W.; m. Terri Adele McLucas, Apr. 28, 1972 (div. Dec. 1974); 1 child, Teri; m. Michalene Sue Walker, May 18, 1978; children: Leilani, Peter, Kasja. BA, Columbia Coll., 1984; postgrad., Tulane U., 1984-85, U. Calif., Sonoma, 1986. Tchr. Storekeeper Sch., Petaluma, Calif., 1976-78, Leadership Sch., Yorktown, Va., 1980-81; chief pay sect. 12th dist. USCG, San Francisco, 1978-80; chief br. 8th dist. USCG, New Orleans, 1981-84; officer Nonappropriated Funds Activity, USCG Training Ctr., Petaluma, 1985—. Author: 13th USCG District HAIL, 1974; various training manuals, 1978-84. Chmn. cub pack com. Boy Scouts Am., Seattle, 1974, chmn. troop com., Slidell, La., 1983-84, cubmaster cub pack, Petaluma, 1977-78. Mem. Chief Warrant Officer Assn., Chief Petty Officer Assn. Republican. Mormon. Avocations: scuba diving, genealogy, ranching. Home: 7315 Elphick Rd Sebastopol CA 95472 Office: USCG Training Ctr Petaluma CA 94952

WILMETH, ERNEST WILLIAM, II, painter, potter; b. Perryton, Tex., Dec. 21, 1952; s. Ernest William and Doris Jean W. Student, W. Tex. State U., 1971-72; B.F.A., No. Ariz. U., 1976. One-man shows: Statesman's Club, Albuquerque, 1982; exhibited in group shows Tri-State Fair, Amarillo, Tex., 1979, Arts and Crafts Show, U. N.Mex. Christmas Show, 1982, 83, 84; Contemporary Crafts Exhibit, 1984, 85, N.Mex. Arts and Crafts Fair, 1985, 87, N.Mex. Potters Assn. Exhibit, 1986, Spring Expo, Albuquerque, 1986, 87; represented in permanent collection Hansford County Library, Spearman, Tex., Angel Fire (N.Mex.) Art Gallery, Canyon (Tex.) Art Gallery, Gallery G. Fine Arts, Albuquerque, The Variant Gallery, Santa Fe, N.Mex., Taos, N.Mex. Recipient 1st place award in oil painting Tri-State Fair, Amarillo, Tex., 1979, hon. mention in watercolors, 1979. Mem. Royal Soc. Arts Gt. Britain (life), N. Mex. Potters Assn. (Exhibit 1985-86), N. Mex. Watercolor Soc. Methodist. Home: 1521 Bryn Mawr Dr NE Albuquerque NM 87106

WILSON, ANN, singer, recording artist; b. 1950; d. John and Lou Wilson. Ed., Cornish Allied Inst. Fine Arts, Seattle. Lead singer rock group Heart, 1975—. Albums include: Dreamboat Annie, 1975, Magazine, 1975, Little Queen, 1977, Dog and Butterfly, 1978, Bebe le Strange, 1980, Heart Live-Gr, Private Audition, 1982, Passionworks, 1983, Heart, 1985; single recs. include: Magic Man, 1976, Barracuda, 1977, Crazy on You, 1976, Straight On, 1978, Even It Up, 1980, Sweet Darlin', 1980, Tell It Like It Is, 1981, Unchained Melody, 1981, This Man is Mine, 1982, City's Burning, 1982, Bright Light Girl, 1982, How Can I Refuse, 1983, Sleep Alone, 1983, Almost Paradise, 1984, The Heat, 1984, What About Love, 1985, Never, 1985, These Dreams, 1986, Nothin' at All, 1986. Office: Suite 333 219 1st Ave N Seattle WA 98109

WILSON, BARRY WILLIAM, biology educator; b. Bklyn., Aug. 20, 1931; s. Albert Abraham Wilson and Ethel (Lubart) Bedsow; m. Joyce Ann Sisson, June 7, 1957; 1 child, Sean. BA, U. Chgo., 1950; BS, MS, Ill. Inst. Tech., 1957; PhD, UCLA, 1962. Asst. prof. biology U. Calif., Davis, 1962-1972, prof., 1972—; mem. drug task force Muscular Dystrophy Assn., N.Y.C., 1980—; councilor NeuroToxicology subsect. Soc. Toxicology, Washington, 1985-86; pres. Calif. br. Tissue Culture Assn., Washington, 1978; mem. editorial bd. NeuroToxicology, Little Rock, 1986—; ad hoc mem. NIH Toxicology Study Sect., Washington, 1985. Editor: Birds: Readings From Science American, 1980; contbr. numerous articles to profl. jours. Mem. Am. Physiol. Soc., Soc. Neurosci., Soc. Toxicology, Soc. Devel. Biology, Am. Soc. Cell Biology. Avocations: bird watching, photography, music. Office: U Calif Dept Avian Scis Davis CA 95616

WILSON, BRANDON LAINE, advertising and public relations executive, writer, photographer; b. Sewickley, Pa., Oct. 2, 1953; s. Edgar C. and Mary Beth (Tuttle) W.; m. Kathryn Langton Ward, Oct. 3, 1974 (div. 1977). B.A., U. N.C., 1973; Cert. Am. Acad. Dramatic Arts, 1974; lic. in broadcasting 3d class, FCC. Asst. acct. exec. Hill & Knowltin Pub. Relations, Pitts., 1973; dir. video Seattle Repertory Co., 1975-76; floor mgr. ENG prodn. UNC-TV Network, Chapel Hill, 1976-77; dir. advt. N.Am. Films, Eugene, Oreg., 1977-79; gen. mgr. Boulder Community Coops., 1980-81; pub. info. officer, asst. to mayor City of Barrow, Alaska, 1981-82; dir. promotion Anchorage Conv. and Visitors Bur., Anchorage, 1983-85; mgr. mktg. communications Hawaiian Tel, Honolulu, 1986-87; prin., pres. Wilson and Assoc., 1987—. Prin. works (TV) include: The General Assembly Today, 1976-77, (films) Sasquatch, Mystery of the Sacred Shroud, Buffalo Rider; contbr. articles to nat. mags. and newspapers. Recipient Eagle Scout award Boy Scouts Am.; named one of Exceptionally Able Youth, 1970, one of Outstanding Young Men in Am., 1986. Mem. Honolulu Advt. Fedn., Pub. Relations Soc. Am. (accredited), Cousteau Soc., Mensa. Mem. Soc. Friends.

WILSON, BRIAN LEONARD, entrepreneur; b. Long Beach, Calif., Nov. 25, 1948; s. Robert Hayse and Bettie Elaine (Radcliffe) W.; m. Candyce Lee Stewart, Dec. 16, 1971. AA, Diablo Valley Coll., 1969. Mgr. Saga Foods, Aspen, Colo., Portland, Oreg., Larkspur and Fresno, Calif., 1971-78; owner, mgr. Sam's Anchor Cafe, Tiburon, Calif., 1978—; prin. Sam's Beachside Grill, Maui, Hawaii, 1987—; ptnr., cons. Restcon, San Rafael, Calif., 1980-85. Democrat. Avocations: travel, fishing, golf. Home: 37 Marguerite Mill Valley CA 94941 Office: Anchor Restaurant Corp 27 Main St Tiburon CA 94920

WILSON, CARL ANTHONY JR., business managment consultant; b. Boston, Nov. 25, 1934; s. Carl Anthony Wilson and Anne (Piniak) Norton; m. Barbara Ann Glass, Sept. 15, 1956 (div. Aug. 1965); children: Marc, Terri, Scott; m. Antoinette Loui Lewis, Dec. 6, 1965. BS, U. Omaha, 1966. Enlisted U.S. Army, 1953, advanced through grades to lt. col., 1968, ret., 1973; sec., treas. Shatzer & Gaillard, Inc., Honolulu, 1973-77; ops. mgr. Lewers & Cooke, Inc., Honolulu, 1977-79; mgmt. cons. Hawaii Econ. Devel. Corp, Honolulu, 1979—; cons. pvt. practice, 1982—. Mem. Assn. U.S. Army, The Retired Officers Assn., Assn. of U.S. Army, Nat. Contract Mgmt. Assn. Republican. Episcopalian. Club: Mariner Meml. (San Francisco). Avocations: physical fitness, gardening. Home: 95-204 Alaalaa LP Mililani Town HI 96789 Office: Hawaii Economic Devel Corp 1405 N King St Suite 302 Honoulu HI 96817

WILSON, CARL ARTHUR, real estate broker; b. Manhasset, N.Y., Sept. 29, 1947; s. Archie and Florence (Hefner) W.; m. Mary Elizabeth Coppes; children: Melissa Starr, Clay Alan. Student UCLA, 1966-68, 70-71. Tournament bridge dir. North Hollywood (Calif.) Bridge Club, 1967-68, 70-71; computer operator IBM, Los Angeles, 1967-68, 70-71; bus. devel. mgr. Walker & Lee Real Estate, Anaheim, Calif., 1972-76; v.p. sales and mktg. The Estes Co., Phoenix, 1976-82, Continental Homes Inc., 1982-84; pres. Roadrunner Homes Corp., Phoenix, 1984-86, Lexington Homes, Inc., 1986, Barrington Homes, 1986—; adv. dir. Liberty Bank. Mem. Glendale (Ariz.) Citizens Bond Council, 1986-87, pres.'s council Am. Grad. Sch. Internat. Mgmt., 1985—; vice-chmn. Glendale Planning and Zoning Comm., 1986—, chmn., 1987—; mem. bd. trustees Valley of Sun United Way, 1987—. Mem. Nat. Assn. Homebuilders (bd. dirs. 1985—), Cen. Ariz. Homebuilders Assn. (adv. com. 1979-82, treas. 1986, sec. 1987, v.p. 1987—, bd. dirs. 1985—); mem. bd. adjustments City of Glendale, 1976-81, chmn., 1980-81, mem. bond council, 1981—; planning and zoning commr. City of Glendale, 1981—; mem. real estate edn. adv. council State Bd. Community Coll., 1981—; precinct committeeman, dep. registrar, 1980-81. Served with U.S. Army, 1968-70. Mem. Glendale C. of C. (dir. 1980-83), Sales and Mktg. Council (chmn. edn. com. 1980, chmn. council 1981—, Mame grand award 1981). Home: PO Box 10141 Phoenix AZ 85064

WILSON, CAROL SCROGGINS, library literacy program administrator; b. Fayetteville, Ark., May 1, 1950; d. Jack Sam and Lelah Francine (Stewart) Scroggins; m. Jimmy Lee Jones, Dec. 25, 1969 (div. Feb. 1975); m. Joseph Walter Wilson, Mar. 19, 1980 (div. Mar. 1987); 1 stepchild—Joseph Jeffrey. B.S. in Social Work, U. Ark., 1979, M.Ed., 1980; postgrad. U. San Francisco, 1984—. Research asst. Antaeus Research Inst., Fayetteville, 1980-81; mem. faculty Clovis Adult and Vocat. Edn., Calif., 1983—; mem. faculty women's studies Calif. State U.-Fresno, 1983-85; coordinator Library Literacy Program, Fresno, 1985—; advisor bd. dirs. McCarthy Inst. Learning and Edn., Madera, Calif., 1983—; founding mem. Literacy Coalition of Fresno, 1985—. Works of poetry include: Rain Goddess, 1984 (Golden Poet award 1985), Wishing Star, 1985. Mem. Central Calif. Forum Refugees, Fresno, 1986, Women's Caucus, Fresno, 1985; advisor Disabled Students Assn., Fresno, 1984; alt. Central Calif. Democratic Com., Fresno, 1983. Recipient certs. of recognition Coalition on Parenting Edn., 1979, Northwest Ark. Hospice, 1981; named One of Outstanding Young Women Am., 1981; recipient Com. Service award Internat. Readers Assn., 1987; honarary mention Innovation in Library Service, ALA, 1987. Mem. Nat. Assn. Female Execs., Am. Soc. Tng. and Devel., Nat. Assn. for Ethnic Studies, Council for Advancement Experiential Learning. Democrat. Lodge: Order Rosae Crucis (chpt. dep. master 1985-86, master 1986—). Avocations: writing; poetry; sewing. Home: 4888 E Clinton #107 Fresno CA 93703 Office: Library Literacy Program 2420 Mariposa Fresno CA 93721

WILSON, CHARLES OREN, JR., chemist, consultant; b. Salt Lake City, May 9, 1926; s. Charles Oren Sr. and Phyllis Lucille (Sparks) W. BS, Stanford U., 1949. Prodn. chemist Transandino Co., South Palo Alto, Calif., 1949-51; research chemist Olin-Mathieson & Chem., Niagara Falls, N.Y., and Pasadena, Calif., 1951-59, Nat. Engring. Sci., Pasadena, 1959-61, Am. Potash Co., Whittier, Calif., 1961-67; chemist Xerox MDO, Pasadena, 1967-69; chemist C-14 synthesis ICN, Irving, Calif., 1969-70; research chemist Abbott Diagnostics, South Pasadena, Calif., 1970—; cons. South Pasadena; teaching Pasadena-Glendale area, 1972—. Contbr. articles to profl. jours. Served with U.S. Army, 1944-46. Mem. Am. Chem. Soc. Republican. Clubs: Brookside (Pasadena), Whittier (Pasadena), Narrows Golf (San Gabriel, Calif., pres. 1970-72), De Belle Golf (Burbank, Calif.). Avocation: golf. Home: 2055 Eleanore #1 Glendale CA 91206 Office: Abbott Diagnostics 820 Mission St South Pasadena CA 91030

WILSON, CHARLES R., research chemist; b. San Francisco, Oct. 11, 1946; s. Charles G. Wilson Jr. and Eleanore R. (Muzzin) Samarzes. BS, St. Mary's Coll. of Calif., 1968; PhD in Inorganic Chemistry, Stanford U., 1973. Research chemist Corning (N.Y.) Glass Works, 1973-74, ARCO Chem. Co., Glenolden, Pa., 1974-77; sr. research chemist Air Products and Chem., Inc., Marcus Hook, Pa., 1977-81; sr. research assoc. Chevron Research Co., Richmond, Calif., 1981—. Patentee in field. Mem. AAAS, Am. Chem. Assn., Phila. Catalysis Soc., Calif. Catalysis Soc. Home: 1101 Diamond St San Francisco CA 94114 Office: Chevron Research Co 576 Standard Ave Richmond CA 94802

WILSON, CHARLES ZACHARY, JR., newspaper publisher; b. Greenwood, Miss., Apr. 21, 1929; s. Charles Zachary and Ora Lee (Means) W.; m. Doris J. Wilson, Aug. 18, 1951 (dec. Nov. 1974); children: Charles III, Joyce Lynne, Joanne Catherine, Gary Thomas, Jonathan Keith; m. Kelly Freeman, Apr. 21, 1986. BS in Econs., U. Ill., 1952, PhD in Econs. and Stats., 1956. Asst. to v.p. Commonwealth Edison Co., Chgo., 1956-59; asst. prof. econs. De Paul U., Chgo., 1959-61; assoc. prof. bus. SUNY, Binghamton, 1961-67, prof. econs. and bus., 1967-68; prof. mgmt. and edn. UCLA, 1968-84, vice chancellor acad. programs, 1969-84; pub./pres. Cen. News-Wave Publs., Los Angeles, 1985—; mem. adv. council Fed. Res. Bank, San Francisco, 1986—, 2001 com. Office of Mayor of Los Angeles, 1986—. Author: Organizational Decision-Making, 1967; contbr. articles on bus. to jours. Bd. dirs. Los Angeles County Mus. Art, 1972-84; com. on Los Angeles City Revenue, 1975-76, United Nations Assn. panel for advancement of U. and Japan Relations, N.Y.C. 1972-74; chmn. Mayor's task force on Africa, 1979-82. Fellow John Hay Whitney, U. Ill., 1955-56, Ford Found., 1960-61, 81-82, 84, Am. Council of Edn., UCLA, 1967-68, Aspen Inst. for Human Studies; named one of Young Men of Yr., Jaycees, 1965. Mem. AAAS, Am. Econ. Assn., Nat. Newspaper Pub. Assn., Am. Mgmt. Assn., Alpha Phi Alpha (pres., pledgemaster 1952-54), Phi Kappa Phi, Order of Artus (pres.). Avocations: tennis, jogging, collecting old bus. texts. Home: 1053 Tellem Dr Pacific Palisades CA 90272 Office: Cen Newspaper Publs 2621 W 54th St Los Angeles CA 90043

WILSON, CONRAD RITCHIE, English instructor, writer; b. Alexandria, Ind., Mar. 23, 1935; s. Everett Lee and Addie Mildred (Ritchie) W.; divorced; children: Lolita Louise, Marta Raquel Claudia, Anthony Alexander Carlos. Student, Mexico City Coll., 1953-54; BA in English, Ball State U., 1960; postgrad., Calif. State U., Long Beach, 1985. Cert. tchr., Ind. Chmn. Eng. dept. Nkubmi Internat. Coll., Kobwe, Zambia, 1965-67; instr. lang. U. Petroleum and Minerals, Dhahran, Saudi Arabia, 1968-73; instr. lang. Northrop Corp., Dhahran, 1973-77, Khamis Mushayt, Saudi Arabia, 1979-85; freelance writer fiction. non-fiction and travel articles Hermosa Beach and Long Beach, Calif., 1978—.

WILSON, DENNIS ARNOLD, brokerage executive; b. Payson, Utah, Sept. 5, 1953; s. Arnold and Joyce (Hutchings) W.; m. Pamela Roylance, Aug. 1, 1975; children: Emily, Stacy Ann, Jeremy, Amy Lynn, Jeffrey. BA in Physics, Brigham Young U., 1976, MBA in Fin., 1978. Realtor assoc. Century 21-All Western, Springville, Utah, 1976-78; v.p. sales Smith Barney Inc., Salt Lake City, 1978—; instr. econs. and fin. U. Phoenix, 1985—. Scoutmaster Utah Nat. Parks council Boy Scouts Am., Provo, 1975-77, dist. cubmaster, Springville, Utah, 1977-78, asst. scoutmaster, Salt Lake City, 1984—; Rep. voting dist. chmn., Salt Lake City, 1982-83. Mormon. Home: 1533 Tallowood Circle Sandy UT 84092 Office: Smith Barney Inc 36 S State St Suite 1000 Salt Lake City UT 84111

WILSON, DENTON ALVIN (AL), marketing professional, sales executive; b. Wichita Falls, Tex., May 4, 1941; s. James Woodrow and Laura Virginia (Wigington) W.; m. Barbara Diane Needham, Nov. 14, 1959 (div. 1980); children: Starlette Ann Wilson Gerik, Denton Alvin Jr.; m. Patricia Sue Holbrook, Nov. 8, 1980; children: Mark David, Jon Russell. AA in Mktg., Jackson State Coll., 1975. Field service engr. Ling Temco Vaught, Dallas, 1966-70; systems test engr. ITT Telecommunications, Milan, Tenn., 1970-76; systems engr. Am. Bus. Electronics, Dallas, 1976-78; nat. field service mgr. Tidel Systems, Dallas, 1978-80; nat. sales mgr. Dynair Electronics, San Diego, 1981—. Chmn. Wheelchair Regatta, 1983-84, liason, 1985-86. Served with USN, 1959-66, Vietnam. Mem. Armed Forces Communications and Electronics Assn., Sports Car Club of Am., Nat. Field Archery Assn. Republican. Club: Silver Gate Yacht (Fleet Capt. 1986), Order of the Iron Test Pattern (officer 1980—). Avocation: sailboat cruising. Home: 7096-57 Park Mesa Way San Diego CA 92111 Office: Dynair Electronics Inc 5275 Market St San Diego CA 92114

WILSON, DIERDRE, theatre and dance educator, choreographer, author, performer, researcher, therapist; b. La Mesa, Calif., Feb. 21, 1945; d. Joseph Herbert Wilson and Audrie Ilene (Branin) W.; m. Douglas John Hammel, Aug. 18, 1978; children: Devon, Galen. A.A., Grossmont Coll., 1977; B.A. in Clin. Psychology, Antioch U., 1979; M.Ed. in Counseling Psychology, Wash. State U., 1983, M.A. in Theatre, 1983, now intern Counseling Services; dance and theatre tng. Agnes Moorehead Actor's Workshop, Los Angeles, 1967, Lee Strasberg Inst., Los Angeles, 1969, Odyssey Improvisation Theatre, Los Angeles, 1969, Theatre East Actor's Workshop, Los Angeles, 1969, Am. Conservatory Theatre, San Francisco, 1970-71; City Coll. San Francisco, 1975; dance tng. San Francisco Ballet, San Francisco Dance Spectrum, San Francisco Dance Theatre, Marguerite Ellicot Sch. Ballet, Pacific Ballet Acad., Gene Maranaccio Sch. Ballet, Roland Dupree Dance Acad., Wash. State U. Registered drama therapist. Ballet instr. Ed Mock Studios, San Francisco, 1974-75, San Francisco Dance Theatre, 1974-75; tchr. creative dramatics Ballet Folk, Moscow, Idaho, 1980; instr., curriculum designer creative arts for handicapped Wash. State U., Pullman, 1980, instr. ballet, 1980, instr. acting, 1982-83, mem. senate, 1981; dir., owner, adminstr. Acad. Performing Arts, Pullman; founding dir. Acad. Performing Arts, Pullman, 1986—; dir. Wash. Jr. Concert Ballet; dance cons., choreographer; mem. San Francisco Ballet; soloist San Francisco Opera Co.; appeared in numerous musicals, with various ballet cos., in several films; cons. Wash. Commn. for Humanities, 1984. Chmn. disabled services adv. council San Diego Parks and Recreation Dept., 1978. San Diego Theatre for Disabled grantee, 1978; Wash. State U. grantee, 1982; Wash. Commn. for Humanities grantee, 1983, 84. Mem. Actor's Equity Assn., Am. Guild Musical Artists, Nat. Assn. Drama Therapists, Am. Personnel and Guidance Assn., Phi Delta Kappa. Author: Introduction to Theatre for the Aged Disabled, 1977. Office: Acad Performing Arts NW 115 State St Pullman WA 99163

WILSON, DONALD ALAN, neurobiologist; b. York, Nebr., Sept. 30, 1957; s. James B. and Kay (Becker) W.; m. Regina Sullivan, Dec. 3, 1985. BS summa cum laude, U. Nebr., 1979; PhD, McMaster U., 1983. Research assoc. U. Calif., Irvine, 1983—. Contbr. articles to sci. jours. Clifton W. Sherman scholar, 1979-83, Yates 1981-82, Kayser 1978-79; NSF grantee, 1986. Mem. AAAS, Soc. Neurosci., Phi Kappa Phi, Delta Phi Alpha.

Avocations: woodworking, bicycling, hiking. Office: U Calif Dept Psychobiology Irvine CA 92717

WILSON, DONTE, corporate executive, software developer; b. Los Angeles, May 18, 1949; s. LeRoy Delano and Leola Wilson. Grad. in computer design, Cleve. Inst., 1974. Title officer Title Ins. and Trust Co., Los Angeles, 1969-70; v.p. Farrington-Hart, Encino, Calif., 1970-74; pres. OP II Corp., San Francisco, 1974-77, Arion II, Gardena, Calif., 1977—; cons. Andromeda, Inglewood, Calif., 1977—. author: (software) Account Pac, Sched. I. Mem. The Computer User's Group. Democrat. Roman Catholic. Home Office: Arion II 41369 154th St Lancaster CA 93535 Office (regional): Arion II Arifaxx Systems div 22232 S Vermont Ave Bldg #104 Torrance CA 90502

WILSON, DOUGLAS EDWIN, lawyer; b. Sacramento, Apr. 23, 1917; s. Richard Matthew and Ruth (O'Brien) W.; A.B., U. of Pacific, 1940; J.D., U. Calif. at San Francisco, 1948; m. Helen Marie Lewis, Apr. 5, 1942; children—Sandra Jane (Mrs. Kenneth Arthur Olds), Kent Lewis, Jay Douglas. Admitted to Calif. bar, 1949; partner Forslund & Wilson, Stockton, 1949-83, Wilson & Wison, 1983—; U.S. magistrate Stockton, Eastern Dist. of Calif., 1962-76. Mem. San Joaquin County Retirement Bd., 1952-72. Served to capt. AUS, 1941-46. Recipient Silver Beaver award Boy Scouts, 1955, Distinguished Eagle Scout award, 1971. Mem. San Joaquin County, Calif. State bars, Am. Legion. Republican. Methodist. Mason (Shriner, K.T.), Elk, Rotarian. Club: Commonwealth (San Francisco). Home: 2134 Gardena Ave Stockton CA 95204 Office: 11 S San Joaquin Stockton CA 95202

WILSON, ELIZABETH ALLEN, consulting geologist; b. Bridgeport, Conn., Jan. 6, 1950; d. Ethan and Margaret Elizabeth (Boyle) Allen; m. John Thomas Wilson, May 26, 1979; one child, Edward Allen. AB, Mt. Holyoke Coll., 1972; MS, U. Del., 1974, PhD, 1978. Exploration geologist Shell Oil Co., New Orleans and Houston, 1977-80; cons. Evergreen, Colo., 1980—. Contbr. articles to profl. jours. Devel. vol. Mt. Holyoke Coll., South Hadley, Mass., 1982-83, 85, mem. sesquicentennial com., 1986. Mem. Am. Assn. Petroleum Geologists (cert., mem. research com. 1982—), Rocky Mountain Assn. Geologists, Internat. Assn. Sedimentologists, Soc. Econ. Paleontologists and Mineralogists, Am. Geol. Inst. (mem. women geoscientists com. 1975-79, edn. com. 1978-80). Democrat. Episcopalian. Club: Mt. Holyoke (Colo.)(v.p. 1980—). Avocations: skiing, sailing, traveling. Home and Office: 375 Aspen Dr Evergreen CO 80439

WILSON, EMILY MARIE, manufacturing company sales executive; b. Aberdeen, Wash., Mar. 24, 1951; d. Charles Robert and Alice Adele (Robinson) W.; m. Michael A. Rich, July 1, 1976. Student, U. Puget Sound, 1969-71, Austro-Am. Inst., Vienna, 1971; BA in Polit. Sci., U. Wash., 1973. Tour counselor, documents and receipts, air reservationist Princess Cruises and Tours, Seattle, 1973-75; with Clairol, Inc., Seattle, 1975—, sales rep. N.W. Wash., drug-mass mdse. div., 1975-77, sales rep. Met. Seattle, 1977-78, dist. mgr. sales Western Wash., 1978-81; trainer territorial sales reps., mgr. dist. dollar sales, and dist. sales mgr. of Wash., Oreg., Idaho and Mont., Clorox, Inc., Seattle, 1981-82, assoc. regional mgr. Western div. spl. markets, 1982-83; regional mgr. Olympic Stain Co., Bellevue, Wash., 1983-86; nat. sales mgr. specialty plants The Weyerhauser Co., Tacoma, 1987—. Mem. Transcendental Meditation Soc., Oreg. Hist. Soc., Sons and Daus. of Oreg. Pioneers, Pioneer Assn. Wash., Seattle Hist. Soc., Sidha of the Age of Enlightenment World Govt. Assn., Grad. Sci. of Creative Intelligence, Women's Profl. Managerial Network (bd. dirs. Seattle chpt.). Club: Zonta (Seattle). Office: 4417 54th Ave NE Seattle WA 98105

WILSON, EVIE CHRISTINA, county data processing manager; b. Ft. Hood, Tex., Jan. 5, 1953; d. John and Wanda (Filinsky) Barnett; m. Scott Lange Wilson, Nov. 4, 1978. Student City Coll. San Francisco, 1971-73, U. Calif.-Berkeley, 1973. Ops. mgr. C.I.C.S.-Pacific, San Francisco, 1977-79; data processing ops. mgr. Victoria Sta., Greenbrae, Calif., 1975-77; data processing ops. mgr., div. chief County of Marin, San Rafael, Calif., 1979—. Recipient Resolution of Commendation County of Marin, Commn. on Status of Women, 1981. Mem. Nat. Assn. Female Execs. Office: Civic Center Room 215 San Rafael CA 94903

WILSON, FREDERIC ROWLAND, educator; b. Council Bluffs, Iowa, Dec. 14, 1947; s. Frederic Clarke and Hazel (Burke) W.; m. Sallie Anjeanette Hall, May 17, 1969; children: Fred, Gregory, Anjeanette, Thomas. BS in Bible/Missions, Phila. Coll. of Bible, 1970; ThM, Dallas Theol. Sem., 1975; PhD in Adult Edn., Kans. State U., 1983. Licensed to ministry, Bapt. Ch. Dir. youth St. Paul's Evang. Ch., Camden, N.J., 1969-70; mem. campus staff InterVarsity Christian Fellowship, Madison, Wis., 1972-75, cons., 1975—; asst. prof. Christian Edn. Can. Bible Coll./Can. Theol. Sem., Regina, Sask., Can., 1975-80; asst. prof. youth leadership Sterling (Kans.) Coll., 1980-83; assoc. prof. Christian Edn. Biola U., La Mirada, Calif., 1983—, dir. D of Edn. program, 1985—; dir. Christian Edn. Whittier (Calif.) Hills Bapt. Ch., 1984—; interim pastorate Reformed Presbyn. Ch., Sterling, 1980-82; cons. Can. Sunday Sch. Mission, Sask., 1976-80. Contbr. articles, revs. to jours. Mem. Nat. Assn. Profs. Christian Edn., Conf. on Faith and History, Religious Edn. Assn., Assn. Profs. and Researchers in Religious Edn. Avocations: baseball, basketball, bicycle trips. Office: Biola U 13800 Biola Ave La Mirada CA 90639

WILSON, GAIL GARDEN, chemistry educator; b. Montour Falls, N.Y., May 9, 1939; d. Frank Eugene and Harriet (Saunders) G.; m. Walter Davis Wilson, Oct. 9, 1959; children: Kenneth M., Douglas F., Catherine J. BS with honors, U. Calif., Berkeley, 1961, MS, 1964. Cert. chemistry tchr., Calif. Lit. chemist Shell Devel. Corp., Emeryville, Calif., 1961-62; part time chemistry lectr. Calif. Poly. State U., San Luis Obispo, 1976—. Mem. Concerned Calif. Poly. Faculty, 1981, Environ. Ctr. San Luis Obispo. Mem. Am. Chem. Soc. Democratic. Avocations: swimming, bowling, photography. Office: Calif Poly State U Chemistry Dept San Luis Obispo CA 93407

WILSON, GRANVILLE GENE, dentist; b. Sacramento, June 10, 1930; s. Samuel Forest and Thelma Irene (Purdy) W.; m. Blanche Evelyne Nicola, Aug. 18, 1957; children—Della Louise, Diane Janene, Rodney Clyde, Barry Douglas, Danny. B.A., Pacific Union Coll., 1957; D.D.S., Coll. Med. Evangelists, 1961; M.S., Loma Linda U., 1984. Practice dentistry specializing in orthodontics, Fort Bragg, Calif., 1962-70; clinic dir. Loma Linda U. Sch. Dentistry Extension, Monument Valley, Utah, 1970-82, student orthodontics, Loma Linda, Calif., 1982-84, dir. orthodontic, Monument Valley, 1984—. Served with U.S. Army M.C., 1951-53; Germany. Mem. ADA, Utah Dental Assn., Utah Tri-County Dental Soc. Seventh-Day Adventist. Home: PO Box 12 Monument Valley UT 84536 Office: Loma Linda Univ Sch of Dentistry Extension PO Box 9 Monument Valley UT 84536

WILSON, GREGORY BRUCE, anaesthesiologist; b. St. Paul, Nov. 20, 1949; s. Bruce Evans and Jane (Schroeder) W.; m. Yvonne H. Nakamoto, Sept. 26, 1980; children: Nicholas Kenji, Erik Akihito. BS, U. Wash., 1972, MD, 1976. Cert. Am. Bd. Anesthesiologists. Intern U. Hawaii, Honolulu, 1977; resident Virginia Mason Hosp., Seattle, 1980; staff anaesthesiologist The Queen's Med. Ctr., Honolulu, 1980—, St. Francis Hosp., Honolulu, 1980—; med. dirs. Surgicare, Honolulu, 1984—. Mem. AMA, Am. Soc. Anesthesiologists. Unitarian. Avocations: astronomy, hiking, basketball. Office: 1520 Liliha Suite 608 Honolulu HI 96817

WILSON, J. ROBERT, utility company executive; b. Meade, Kans., Dec. 3, 1927; s. Robert J. and Bess O. (Osborne) W.; m. Marguerite Jean Reiter, Nov. 27, 1960; 1 son, John Ramsey. B.A., Kans. U., 1950, LL.B., 1953. Bar: Kans. 1953, Nebr. 1961, Colo. 1981. Practiced in Meade, 1954-57; county atty. Meade County, Kans., 1954, 56; city atty. Meade, 1954-57; asst. gen. counsel Kans. Corp. Commn., 1957-59, gen. counsel, 1959-61, mem., 1961; atty. KN Energy, Inc., 1961-75, personnel dir., 1964-67, v.p., treas., 1968-75, exec. v.p., 1975-78, pres., chief operating officer, 1978-82, chief exec. officer, 1982-85, chmn., pres., chief exec. officer, 1985—. With USNR, 1945-46. Mem. Phi Kappa Sigma. Democrat. Home: 1725 Foothills Dr S Golden CO 80401 Office: KN Energy Inc 12055 W 2d Pl Lakewood CO 80228

WILSON, JOHN ABRAHAM ROSS, academic administrator; b. Trout Lake, B.C., Can., Aug. 25, 1911; s. Henry and Grace Ellen (Ross) W.; m. Nora Margaret (Mains) June 28, 1940; children: John Richard Meredith, Douglas Gordon. BA, U. B.C., 1932, MA, 1939; EdD, Oreg. State U., 1951. Tchr., counselor various schs., B.C., 1934-51; prof. U. Calif., Santa Barbara, 1951-79; prof., adminstr. Laurence U., Santa Barbara, 1979—; chmn. bd. Acoustic Mktg. of Can. Ltd., Vancouver, Can., 1979—. Author: (with others) Psychological Foundation of Learning and Teaching, 1969, Kind Evaluation of Learning Potential, 2d edit. 1967, Psychology of Reading, 1974; editor; Diagnosis of Learning Difficulties, 1971. Mem. Calif. Ednl. Research Assn. (pres. 1968-69), Nat. Edn. Assn., Nat. Assn. for Study Edn., Phi Delta Kappa. Club: Cosmopolitan (Santa Barbara). Home: 2519 Chapala St Santa Barbara CA 93105 Office: Laurence U 30 W Mission St Santa Barbara CA 93101

WILSON, JOHN PASLEY, law school dean; b. Newark, Apr. 7, 1933; s. Richard Henry and Susan Agnes (Pasley) W.; m. Elizabeth Ann Reed, Sept 10, 1955; children—David Cables, John, Jr., Cicely Reed. A.B., Princeton U., 1955; LL.B., Harvard U., 1962. Bar: N.J. 1963, U.S. Dist. Ct. N.J. 1963, Mass. 1963, U.S. Dist. Ct. Mass. 1963. Budget examiner Exec. Office of Pres., Bur. of Budget, Washington, 1955-56; assoc. Riker, Danzig, Scherer & Brown, Newark, 1962-63; asst. dean Harvard U. Law Sch., Cambridge, Mass., 1963-67; assoc. dean Boston U. Law Sch., 1968-82; dean Golden Gate U. Law Sch., San Francisco, 1982—; cons. Nat. Commn. for the Protection of Human Subjects of Biomed. and Behavioral Research; mem. Mass. Gov's. Commn. on Civil and Legal Rights of Developmentally Disabled. Author: The Rights of Adolescents in the Mental Health System. Contbr. chpts. to books, articles to profl. jours. Bd. dirs. Greater Boston Legal Services, Chewonki Found., Concord Home Owning Corp.; mem. Health Facilities Appeals Bd., Commonwealth of Mass.; mem. Concord Moderate Income Housing Com.; assoc. mem. Democratic Town Com., Concord; chmn. Bd. Assessors, Concord; bd. overseers Boston Hosp. for Women, past chmn. med. affairs com. Served to lt. (j.g.) USN, 1956-59. NIMH grantee, 1973. Mem. Am. Arbitration Assn., Am. Law Inst. (ex officio), Alameda/Contra Costa Med. Assn. (bioethics com.). Office: Golden Gate U Sch Law 536 Mission St San Francisco CA 94105

WILSON, JUDY ELAINE, banker; b. Lander, Wyo., June 16, 1950; s. Karl Martin and Mary Margaret (Barrett) Johnson; m. Ray Wilson, Sept. 3, 1971; children—Sara Rae, Janie Marie. Student Central Wyo. Coll., 1968-69; cert. Nat. Personnel Sch., Boulder, Colo., 1981. Proof operator First Interstate Bank, Riverton, Wyo., 1968-74, teller, 1974-75, teller supr., 1976-78, gen. ledger, 1977-79, ops. officer, 1979-80, v.p., personnel officer, 1979—. Speaker job search Wyo. Job Service, Riverton, 1983. Mem. Nat. Assn. Bank Women (chmn. Mountain Valley chpt. 1984-85), Big Horn Basin Bankers, Riverton Council of Cath. Women. Roman Catholic. Home: Box 2745B Dubois Rt Riverton WY 82501 Office: First Interstate Bank of Riverton 323 E Main St Riverton WY 82501

WILSON, KAY, medical research coordinator; b. Cleve., Dec. 22, 1944; d. Alvin Eugene and Therese (Eroskey) W.; m. George Edward Popyack, Jan. 30, 1970; 1 child, Lara Natasha. BA in Social Welfare, U. Calif., Berkeley, 1970. Researcher in psychiatry Stanford (Calif.) U., 1972-78; bioanalyst Syntex Pharm., Palo Alto, Calif., 1978; researcher Boystown Ctr., Stanford, 1978-80; researcher heart disease prevention program Stanford U., 1980—; computer cons., 1972—; tng. cons., 1978—. Contbr. articles to profl. jours. Bd. dirs. Palo Alto Community Child Care Bd., 1972-75; mem., mediator Rental Housing Mediation Task Force, Palo Alto, 1975-76; mem., advisor Calif. Child Care Adv., Sacramento, 1976-77; mem., speaker Child Care Advocacy Council, Palo Alto, 1978—. Mem. Soc. Behavioral Medicine, SCAN. Avocations: skiing, physical fitness. Office: Stanford Ctr Research in Disease 730 Welch Rd Room #234 Palo Alto CA 94304

WILSON, KEVIN MARK, oil services company executive, geological consultant; b. Lansing, Mich., Sept. 3, 1952; s. George Dillard and Florine Alice (Skiffington) W.; m. Robin Raley, Aug. 2, 1975; children: Katherine G.L., Morgan O.R. BS in Geology, Western Mich. U., 1977; postgrad. Ind. U., 1977; MS in Earth Scis., U. N.H., 1979; postgrad. U. Colo., 1985—. Geologist, cons. Phillips Petroleum Co., Bartlesville, Okla., 1979-80; instr. U. N.H., Durham, 1980-81; sr. geologist Weeks Energy Minerals Corp., Denver, 1981-84; v.p., dir. Cougar Exploration Services, Golden, Colo., 1984; pres., dir. Wildhorse Exploration, Inc., Boulder, 1984—; cons. Phillips Petroleum Co., 1980; self-employed cons., Denver, 1984—. Grantee U. N.H., 1978, Geol. Soc. Am., 1978, 86, grantee-in-aid, Sigma Xi Soc., 1978. Mem. Geol Soc. Am., Am. Assn. Petroleum Geologists, Soc. Econ. Paleontologists and Mineralogists, AAAS, Am. Geophys. Union.. Office: Wildhorse Exploration Inc 3880 Britting Ave Boulder CO 80303

WILSON, LEE, hydrologist, consultant; b. Wichita Falls, Tex., Apr. 15, 1942; s. William Haynie and Sidney Jean (Main) W.; m. Gladys Danielle Freudmann, June 26, 1969; 1 child, Dana. BA, Yale U., 1964; PhD, Columbia U., 1971. Cert. profl. hydrogeologist. Tchr. geology Briarcliff Coll., Briarcliff Manor, N.Y., 1968-69, Brock U., St. Catherine, Ont., Can., 1969-70; cons. Le Nickel, N.Y.C., 1971-72; sr. scientist Environment Cons., Dallas, 1972-73; pres. Lee Wilson and Assocs., Santa Fe, 1973—; expert witness for Fed. and State Cts. Contbr. articles to profl. jours. Columbia U. Faculty fellow 1971. Fellow Geol. Soc. Am. Democrat. Home and Office: PO Box 931 Santa Fe NM 87501

WILSON, LIONEL J., mayor Oakland (Calif.); b. New Orleans, 1915; m. Dorothy P.; children: Robin and Lionel (twins), Steven. A.B., U. Calif., 1939, J.D., 1949. Judge Superior Ct. Calif., to 1977; mayor of Oakland, 1977—; mem. State CETA Bd., Com. on Selection of Fed. Jud. Officers, U.S. Ct. of Patents and Appeals. Recipient numerous awards including West Coast Merit award NAACP; Outstanding Profl. Service award Calif. Med., Dental, and Pharm. Assn.; Judge for all Seasons award Oak Center Inc.; Man of Yr. award Oakland Lodge, B'nai B'rith, 1978; Leadership award Chinese Am. Citizens Alliance, 1979; award Marcus Foster Inst.; Outstanding Alumnus award Oakland Public Schs., 1979. Mem. League Calif. Cities (past dir.), U.S. Conf. Mayors (various coms.), Nat. League Cities (various coms.). Democrat. Office: Room 302 City Hall One City Hall Plaza Oakland CA 94612

WILSON, MARK WAYNE, optical physicist, physics instructor; b. Chgo., Sept. 14, 1955; s. William O. and Mary E. (Carroll) W.; m. Michele Maria Marcheschi, Aug. 1977; children: Jennifer A., Matthew C., Rebecca A. BS in Physics, Math., Psychology, Ill. Benedictine Coll., 1977; MS in Physics, U. Ill., Chgo., 1979, PhD, 1982. Research asst. U. Ill., Chgo., 1979-82; research physicist SRI Internat., Menlo Park, Calif., 1982-86; program mgr. Sci. Applications Internat. Corp., Los Altos, Calif., 1986—; instr. Triton Coll., River Grove, Ill., 1981-82, Calif. State U., Hayward, 1986. Contbr. articles to sci. jours. Mem. IEEE, Optical Soc. Am., Sigma Pi Sigma. Office: Sci Applications Internat Corp 5150 El Camino Real Suite A-30 Los Altos CA 94022

WILSON, MICHAEL MANOR, correctional specialist; b. Phoenix, July 3, 1950; s. Alvin and Ruth (Jackson) W. B.Social Work, Ariz. State U., 1973. Dep. adult probation officer Maricopa County, Phoenix, 1974-79, coordinator of vol. employment services, 1979-81, counselor Ariz. Dept. Corrections, Maricopa County, Phoenix, 1982-83, correctional programs officer, 1983-84, programs and projects specialist, 1984-85, correctional program supr., 1985—. Bd. dirs. Okemah Day Care Center, 1978-80, Phoenix South Mental Health Center, 1980, Ariz. State Foster Care Rev. Bd., 1980-81, Community Orgn. for Drug Abuse Mental Health and Alcoholism Services, Inc., 1984—; team building trainer Am. Cancer Soc. Recipient 25th Anniversary award Vols. in Criminal Justice, 1983. Fellow Am. Soc. Tng. and Devel., Am. Correctional Assn. Roman Catholic. Club: Toasmasters (v.p. 1978-79). Office: Ariz State Dept Corrections 1210 S 7th Ave Phoenix AZ 85007

WILSON, PAULA FRANCELLE, marketing professional; b. Long Beach, Calif., July 18, 1945; d. ElRoy Lewis and Lucelle Evelen (Barnette) Childs; m. Don LeRoy, Aug. 29, 1964; children: Jason Allen Wilson, Krisha Kim Wilson. Diploma, Lee Cosmetology Coll., 1965, Merle Norman Cosmetics, 1966. Cert. cosmetologist, Wash. Cosmetics cons. Merle Norman Cosmetics, Seattle, 1965-67; owner, mgr. Merle Norman Cosmetics, Tukwilla, Auburn, Wash., 1968-78; image cons. Color 1 Assocs., Bellevue, Wash., 1979—; regional dir. Transart, Bellevue, Wash., 1981-82; pres. Shopping Trips to Exotic Places, Bellevue, Hong Kong and Republic of Korea, 1985—. Home: 4700 155th Pl SE Bellevue WA 98006

WILSON, PETE, senator; b. Lake Forest, Ill., Aug. 23, 1933; s. James Boone and Margaret (Callaghan) W.; m. Betty Robertson (div.); m. Gayle Edlund, May 29, 1983. B.A. in English Lit., Yale U., 1955; J.D., U. Calif.-Berkeley, 1962; LL.D., Grove City Coll., 1983, U. Calif.-San Diego, 1983, U. San Diego, 1984. Bar: Calif. 1962. Mem. Calif. Legislature, Sacramento, 1966-71; mayor City of San Diego, 1971-83; U.S. Senator from Calif. 1983—. Trustee Conservation Found.; mem. exec. bd. San Diego County council Boy Scouts Am.; hon. trustee So. Calif. Council Soviet Jews; adv. mem. Urban Land Inst., 1985-86; founding dir. Retinitis Pigmentosa Internat.; hon. dir. Alzheimer's Family Ctr., Inc., 1985; hon. bd. dirs. Shakespeare-San Francisco, 1985. Recipient Golden Bulldog award, 1984, 85, 86, Guardian of Small Bus. award, 1984; ROTC scholar Yale U., 1951-55; named Legislator of Yr., League Calif. Cities, 1985; Man of Yr. award Nat. Guard Assn. Calif., 1986, Man of Yr. citation U. Calif. Boalt Hall, 1986. Mem. Nat. Mil. Family Assn. (adv. bd.), Phi Delta Phi, Zeta Psi. Republican. Episcopalian. Office: US Senate 720 Hart Senate Bldg Washington DC 20510

WILSON, RAYMOND LAURENCE, art historian, writer; b. Dayton, Ohio, Apr. 17, 1946; s. Frank Caswell and Florence Berry (Ballinger) W.; m. Susan Emily Holmer. PhD, Ohio U., 1980. Teaching fellow Ohio U., Athens, 1975-78; vis. lectr. Calif. State U. Stanislaus, Turlock, 1980-81, Fresno (Calif.) State U., 1981-82, U. Calif., Davis, 1985; lectr. San Francisco State U., 1983—. Mem. Assn. Historians Am. Art. Republican. Presbyterian.

WILSON, RAYMOND RUPERT, marine biologist, researcher; b. Newport, Ark., Dec. 10, 1952; s. Raymond Rupert and Betty Bonner (McKenzie) W.; m. Bette Ellan Chetwood, Feb. 4, 1984. BA in Biology, U. Calif., San Diego, 1978; PhD in Marine Biology, U. Calif., La Jolla, 1984. Research biologist Scripps Inst. Oceanography, U. Calif., La Jolla, Calif., 1984-86; NFS fellow Oreg. State U., Corvallis, 1986—. Contbr. articles to profl. jours. Mem. Am. Soc. Ichthyologists and Herpetologists, Western Soc. Naturalists. Democrat. Club: Balboa Chess (San Diego) (pres. 1976-78). Avocations: biking, music. Home: 14227 Recuerdo Dr Del Mar CA 92014 Office: Scripps Inst Oceanography A-002 La Jolla CA 92093

WILSON, ROBERT MONTAGUE, computer company executive; b. Portsmouth, Va., Jan. 19, 1942; s. Robert Elmore and Martha Jane (Flanagan) W.; m. Janet Carol Disinger; children: John Eric, Michael Patrick. BJ, U. Mo., 1963. Commd. ensign USNR, 1963, advanced through grades to comdr., 1980, ret., 1984; pilot Continental Airlines, Los Angeles, 1969-70, 77—; chief exec. officer Hi-Country Data Systems, Colorado Springs, Colo., 1981—. Decorated Air medal, DFC. Mem. Air Line Pilots Assn. (sec., treas. 1984), Assn. Computing Machinery, Kappa Alpha Mu (pres. 1962-63). Democrat. Methodist. Home: PO Box 4095 Woodland Park CO 80863 Office: Hi-Country Data Systems 819 E Lovell Rd Woodland Park CO 80863

WILSON, (ROBERT) ROBIN H. H., transportation executive; b. Dublin, Ireland, June 18, 1936; came to U.S., 1962; s. L. Cecil and Eileen M. Wilson; m. Glenda Christiana Ploger, Oct. 26, 1968; children: Siobhan, Christopher. BA, Cambridge U., Eng., 1958; MBA, Harvard U., 1964; LLD, Adelphi U., 1983. With Trans World Airlines, N.Y.C. and San Francisco, 1964-76; v.p. tech. services Trans World Airlines, Kansas City, Mo., 1976-78; sr. v.p. ops. Trans World Airlines, N.Y.C., 1978-81; pres., gen. mgr. L.I. R.R., Jamaica, N.Y., 1981-85; pres., chief ops. officer Western Airlines, Los Angeles, from 1985. Trustee Intermountain Health Care, Salt Lake City, 1985—. Mem. SKAL Los Angeles, Wings Club, Newcomen Soc., Aero Club of So. Calif. Office: Western Air Lines Inc Box 92005 World Way Postal Ctr 6060 Avion Dr Los Angeles CA 90045

WILSON, ROBIN SCOTT, university president, writer; b. Columbus, Ohio, Sept. 19, 1928; s. John Harold and Helen Louise (Walker) W.; m. Patricia Ann Van Kirk, Jan. 20, 1951; children: Kelpie, Leslie, Kari, Andrew. B.A., Ohio State U., 1950; M.A., U. Ill., 1951, Ph.D., 1959. Fgn. intelligence officer CIA, Washington, 1959-67; prof. English Clarion State Coll., (Pa.), 1967-70; assoc. dir. Com. Instnl. Cooperation, Evanston, Ill., 1970-77; assoc. provost instrn. Ohio State U., Columbus, 1977-80; pres. Calif. State U., Chico, 1980—. Author: Those Who Can, 1973; short stories, criticism, articles on edn. Mem. Calif. Council Humanities, 1983—; mem. lay bd. Clarion Mission Episcopal Ch., 1967-70. Served to lt. USN, 1953-57. Mem. MLA, AAAS, Phi Kappa Phi. Democrat. Office: California State University 105 Kendall Hall Chico CA 95929

WILSON, ROGER LAVERN, federal agency administrator, agronomist; b. Siloam Springs, Ark., Oct. 22, 1936; s. Frank L. and Naomi A. (Babb) W.; m. Orma A. Griffith, Sept. 14, 1956; children: Randall A., Lorna J., Loren D. BS in Agronomy Sci., Utah State U., 1958; MS in Agronomy, Mont. State U., 1963, PhD in Agronomy and Soils, 1970. Soil scientist Soil Conservation Service, Philipsburg, Mont., 1958-63; county agt. Coop. Extension Service, Bozeman, Mont., 1963-70, soil scientist, 1970-79; area dir. Tenn. Valley Authority, Pullman, Wash., 1979—. Author: Handbook on Soil Fertility, 1973; contbr. articles to profl. jours. Deacon, elder, chmn. bd. dirs. Christian Ch., Bozeman, 1970-79; mem. leadership com. Assembly of God, Pullman, 1981—. Mem. Northwest Plant Food Assn. (5 state regional soil improvement com., Wash. soil improvement com.), Far West Fertilizer Assn., Am. Soc. Agronomy, Soil Sci. Soc. Am., Western Soc. Soil Sci., Soil Conservation Soc. Am., Soc. for Range Mgmt., Council for Agrl. Sci. and Tech., Sigma Xi. Lodges: Kiwanis, Rotary. Avocations: carpentry, hunting, fishing. Home: SE 305 Bellevue Pullman WA 99163 Office: Tenn Valley Authority Area Dir 169B Johnson Wall Pullman WA 99164-6420

WILSON, ROSEMARY DIANE NEWHOUSER LITTRELL, communications counselor; b. Fremont, Nebr., June 14, 1939; d. Lawrence Emerson and Rosemary Ann (Check) Littrell; m. Marc Anthony Wilson, Apr. 7, 1961; children: Charles Christopher, Alexandria Michelle, Roger Huntington. Student Colo. Womans Coll., 1958-59, Mills Coll., 1959-60, U. Hawaii, 1960-65. In radio and television prodn. and sales, Honolulu, 1961-66; radio salesperson stas. KZEL, KASH, KEED, KORE, Eugene, Oreg., 1967-74; media buyer Cochrane Chase & Co., Newport Beach, Calif., 1974-76; pub. relations cons. Cook Communications Services, Inc., Newport Beach, 1976-81; account exec. Five Star Mktg., Santa Ana, Calif., 1981-82; communications counselor Wilson/Creative Assocs., Irvine, Calif., 1982—; pub. relations cons. U. Calif., Irvine; instr. Golden West Coll., Huntington Beach, Calif. Past pub. relations dir. Orange County Philharm. Soc., active women's coms.; dir. Hands Across Am. Orange County; active women's coms. promotion and publicity dir. Tri-County chpt. Leukemia Soc. Am. Super Swim Classic. Mem. Pub. Relations Soc. Am. (Orange County chpt.). Republican. Office: 5232 Michelson Dr Ste 20D Irvine CA 92715

WILSON, ROY WOODROW, computer scientist; b. Milw., Oct. 2, 1950; s. LeRoy Woodrow and Rosemary Agnes (Lee) W.; m. Diane Lieb, Apr. 2, 1976. M.A. in Math., Denver U., 1978; M.S. in Computer Sci., 1983. Instr. computer sci. Denver U., 1978; research assoc. Denver Research Inst., 1978-80; assoc. programming engr. Burroughs Corp., Northglenn, Colo., 1980-81; prin. Computerized Employee Benefit Systems, Denver, 1982-83; instr. computer sci. Met. State Coll., Denver, 1984-85; mem. tech. staff Hughes Aircraft, Denver, 1984-85; staff engr. Martin Marietta Corp., Denver, 1985—. Mem. Assn. Computing Machinery, Sigmetrics, Home: PO Box 2216 Littleton CO 80161

WILSON, SODONIA MAE, psychologist; b. Galveston, Tex., Feb. 25; d. Jasper and Willie Mae (Reed) Moore; m. James Wilson, Jr., Mar. 24, 1957; 1 son, Demetrius D. R.N., French Hosp. Sch. Nursing; AS, City Coll. San Francisco; BA, MA, San Francisco State U.; PhD, Calif. Sch. Profl. Psychology. Staff nurse French Hosp., San Francisco, 1956-57, Ft. Miley VA Hosp., San Francisco, 1957-60; counselor San Francisco Youth Guidance Ctr., 1966, probation officer, 1967; head start analyst Office Econ. Opportunity, San Francisco, 1968; social service rep. San Francisco Redevel. Agy., 1969; coll. counseling coordinator Sequoia Union High Sch. Dist., Redwood

City, Calif., 1969-72; counselor Contra Costa Coll., San Pablo, Calif., 1972-73, dir. spl. programs and services, 1973-85, 86—, mgr. instrn. and tech. support services 1985-86; mem. San Francisco Bd. Edn., 1982—, pres. 1987. Mem. Student Aid Commn., State of Calif., 1982-85; commr. San Francisco Bd. Edn., 1982—. Mem. Calif. Sch. Bd. Assn., Am. Psychol. Assn., Assn. Calif. Community Coll. Adminstrs., Calif. Community Coll. Extended Opportunity Programs and Services Assn. (pres. 1977-78), Women in Higher Edn. Assn., NAACP, Nat. Black Caucus, Bay Area Black Women United, Nat. Women's Polit. Club, Black Women Organized for Action, Bus. and Profl. Women's Club, Nat. Assn. Negro Bus. and Profl. Women's Club. Democrat. Baptist. Home: 540 Darien Way San Francisco CA 94127 Office: Contra Costa Coll 2600 Mission Bell Dr San Pablo CA 94806

WILSON, STANLEY CHARLES, visual arts educator; b. Los Angeles, Feb. 2, 1947; s. Ernest Charles and Eleanor (Reid) W.; m. Jacquelyne Bellard, June 3, 1978; 1 child, Jendayi Asabi. BFA, Otis Art Inst., 1969, MFA, 1971. Asst. prof. Southwestern Coll., Chula Vista, Calif., 1972-73; prof. art. Calif. Poly U., Pomona, 1973—; instr. Otis Parsons Watts Towers, Los Angeles, 1981—; Bd. artists Brockman Gallery Prodns., Los Angeles, 1980-85; bd.dirs. Watts Towers Art Ctr., Los Angeles. One-man shows include Sol Del Rio Gallery, San Antonio, 1980, Daniel Maher Gallery, 1983, Southwest Coll., 1984; exhibited in group shows at Oranges/Sardines Gallery, 1984, Sparc Gallery, 1985, Mus. Of African Am. Art, 1985, Los Angeles Art Gallery, 1986; represented in permanent collections Calif. Mus. Afro-Am. History and Culture, Prairie View Coll., 1977, Tex. A&M U., 1977, Atlanta Life Ins. Co., 1984, Golden State Life Ins., 1985; contbr. articles to profl. jours. Fellow NEA, 1986. Democrat. Avocations: sports, landscape, gardening, camping. Office: Calif Poly U Dept Art 3801 W Temple Pomona CA 91768

WILSON, STEPHEN EDWARD, military officer; b. Ellensburg, Wash., May 12, 1945; s. Edward and Marjorie Louise (Tucker) W.; m. Mary Lynne Halwas, Aug. 28, 1966; children: Troy, Aubree-Anna. BA in English, Cen. Wash. State Coll., 1967; MA in Guidance Counseling, Wayne State U., 1973. Commd. USAF, 1967, advanced through grades to lt. col., 1983; chief intelligence career mgmt. USAF Mil. Personnel Ctr. USAF, Randolph AFB, Tex., 1976-80; br. chief Intelligence Ctr. Pacific, USAF, Camp Smith, Hawaii, 1980-81; Commdr. in Chief Pacific Staff USAF, Camp Smith, 1981-83; dir. Alert Ctr. Hdqrs. Electronic Security Command USAF, Kelly AFB, Tex., 1983-84, dir. tng., 1984-85; commdr. 6981 Electronic Security Squadron USAF, Elmendorf AFB, Alaska, 1985—; mem. USAF Intelligence Career Field Study Group, Washington, 1978-84, Dept. Def. Intelligence Career Devel. Panel, Washington, 1976-80; chmn. Computer Intelligence Officer Study Group, Washington, 1979-80, Pacific Target Actions Group, Honolulu, 1981-83. Author: North Vietnamese Use of Inland Waterways, 1970, Petroleum Pipelines in the Laotian Panhandle, 1971. Founding mem. San Antonio Council of Adoptable Children, 1976-80; charter mem. Hosanna! Luth. Ch., San Antonio, 1983-85; mem. Friends of Luth. Social Services Tex., San Antonio, 1976-80. Decorated Bronze Star. Mem. Air Force Assn., Assn. Old Crows. Home: 6-200-B H St Elmendorf AFB AK 99506 Office: 6981 Electronic Security Squadron Elmendorf AFB AK 99506

WILSON, STEPHEN MARK, social worker; b. Dayton, Ohio, May 21, 1948; s. Sigmund and Sylvia Renee (Lewis) W.; m. Christine Claire Dom, Sept. 15, 1973; children: Graham Mead, Daniel Sigmund Henry. BS in Edn., Ohio State U., 1972; MS in Social Work, U. Wis., 1982. Social worker Div. Family and Youth Services, Ft. Yukon, Alaska, 1976-80, Family Service Agy., Madison, Wis., 1980-82, Div. Family and Youth Services, Fairbanks, Alaska, 1982—; cons. trainer Women In Crisis, Fairbanks, 1982-85. Named Outstanding Alaskan Family Violence Counselor, Inst. on Family Violence, 1985. Mem. Nat. Assn. Social Workers, Community Sexual Abuse Treatment Team, Domestic Violence Task Force, Academy of Cert. Social Workers (cert.). Democrat. Jewish. Avocations: Alpine mountain skiing, whitewater canoeing, hiking. Home: 293 Paystreak Dr Fairbanks AK 99701 Office: Interest Counseling Consultation PO Box 10401 Fairbanks AK 99712

WILSON, STEPHEN ROLAND, financial consultant; b. Toronto, Ont., Can., Jan. 14, 1941; came to U.S., 1981; s. Roland Frederick and Bernice Sill (Langrill) W. B.A., U. Western Ont., London, 1963; LL.B., Osgoode Hall Law Sch., Toronto, 1966; M.B.A., Stanford U., 1969. Chartered acct. Inst. Chartered Accts. of Ont., 1972. Auditor, Price Waterhouse, Toronto, 1966-67, 69-71; exec. asst. Toronto Dominion Bank, 1971-77; sr. mng. project fin. Bank of Montreal, Toronto, 1977-79; v.p. spl. financing Bank of Montreal Trust Co., N.Y.C., 1979-81; v.p. Bechtel Financing Services Inc., San Francisco, 1981—; lectr. Grad. Sch. Internat. Affairs Columbia U. Mem. Inst. Chartered Accts. of Ont., Toronto Soc. Fin. Analysts. Clubs: Met. (N.Y.C.); Univ. (Toronto). Home: 55F Red Hill Circle Tiburon CA 94920 Office: Bechtel Financing Services Inc 50 Beale St San Francisco CA 94105

WILSON, THOMAS RAYBURN, III, urban planner, consultant; b. Midland, Tex., Sept. 5, 1946; s. Thomas Rayburn Jr. and Bennie Lee (Harlow) W.; m. Melody Harp, Oct. 28, 1967. BA in Geography, Tex. Tech U., 1972. Asst. planner City of Lubbock, Tex., 1973-74, assoc. planner, 1974-78; prin. planner City of Odessa, Tex., 1978-85; pvt. practice planning cons. Santa Fe, 1985—; dir. Office Land Use, Santa Fe County, 1986—. Co-author: Land Use Report, 1974, Community Facilities Report, 1974, Urban Image Analysis, 1974, Rural Land Use Study, 1976. Served with U.S. Army, 1969-72, Vietnam. Mem. Am. Inst. Cert. Planners, Am. Soc. Photogrammetry and Remote Sensing, Am. Planning Assn. (N.Mex. chpt.). Republican. Presbyterian. Avocations: skiing, hiking, running, photography, reading. Home and Office: 144 Verano Loop Santa Fe NM 87505

WILSON, THORNTON ARNOLD, aerospace company executive; b. Sikeston, Mo., Feb. 8, 1921; s. Thornton Arnold and Daffodil (Allen) W.; m. Grace Miller, Aug. 5, 1944; children: Thornton Arnold III, Daniel Allen, Sarah Louise Wilson Anderson. Student, Jefferson City (Mo.) Jr. Coll., 1938-40; B.S., Iowa State Coll., 1943; M.S., Calif. Inst. Tech., 1948; M.S. Sloan fellow, MIT, 1952-53. With Boeing Co., Seattle, 1943—, asst. chief tech. staff, project engring. mgr., 1957-58, v.p., mgr. Minuteman br. aerospace div., 1962-64, v.p. ops. and planning, 1964-66, exec. v.p., dir., 1966-68, pres., 1968—, chief exec. officer, 1969-86, chmn. bd., 1972—; dir. PACCAR, Inc., Weyerhaeuser Co., USX Corp., Hewlett Packard, Inc. Bd. govs. Iowa State U. Found.; trustee Seattle U.; mem. Bus. Council; mem. corp. MIT, Nat. Acad. Engring. Fellow Am. Inst. Aeronautics and Astronautics; mem. Aerospace Industries Assn. Office: The Boeing Co PO Box 3707 Seattle WA 98124

WILSON, WARREN BINGHAM, artist, art educator; b. Farmington, Utah, Nov. 4, 1920; s. Alma L. and Pearl E. (Bingham) W.; B.S. in Edn., Utah State U., 1943; M.F.A., Iowa State U., 1949; m. Donna Myrle VanWagenen, Dec. 22, 1948; children—Vaughn Warren, Michael Alma, Annette, Pauline, Douglas George, Craig Aaron, Robert Kevin. Asst. prof. art Utah State U., Logan, 1949-54; vis. instr. Salt Lake Art Center, Utah, 1952-53; prof. art and edn. Brigham Young U., Provo, Utah, 1954-83; ret., 1983 vis. lectr. ceramics U. Calif., Davis, 1968; fellow in residence Huntington Hartford Found., Pacific Palisades, Calif., 1960-61; vis. instr. Pioneer Crafthouse, Salt Lake City, 1969-70; one-man shows of paintings and/or sculpture include: Salt Lake Art Center, 1951, Yakima Valley Coll., 1962, UCLA, 1962, Mont. State U., Bozeman, 1963, Stanford U., 1963, Wash. State U., Pullman, 1964, Central Wash. State Coll., Ellensburg, 1964, Nev. So. U., Las Vegas, 1967, Ricks Coll., Rexburg, Idaho, 1976, 80, Brigham Young U., Provo, Utah, 1970, 75, 79, 82, retrospective retirement exhbn. of sculpture, ceramics and paintings, 1983; group shows include: Denver Art Mus., 1951, Colorado Springs (Colo.) Fine Arts Center, 1951, Santa Fe Art Mus., 1953, Madison Sq. Gardens, N.Y.C., 1958, Wichita Art Center, 1960, Ceramic Conjunction Invitational, Glendale, Calif., 1973; represented in permanent collections: Utah State Inst. Fine Arts Salt Lake City, Utah State U., Logan, Utah State Fair Assn., Utah Dixie Coll., St. George, Coll. So. Utah, Cedar City, Brigham Young U., also numerous pvt. collections. Asst. dist. commr. Boy Scouts Am., 1975-80; counselor in Ward Bishopric, Ch. of Jesus Christ of Latter-day Saints, 1981-83. Served with USAAF, 1943-46. Recipient Am. Craftsman Council merit award, 1964; Silver Beaver award Boy Scouts Am. Mem. Nat. Council for Edn. in Ceramic Arts. Republican. Home: 1000 Briar Ave Provo UT 84604

WILSON, WAYNE ROBERT, communications executive; b. Clawson, Mich., Aug. 3, 1940; s. Robert Grant and Marguerite Isabella (Kohen) W.; divorced; children: Christopher Wayne, Roberta Marie, Cheryl Marguerite, Rebecca Lyn. Student, Elmhurst Coll., 1983-85, U. Phoenix, 1986. Engr. GTE, Northlake, Ill., 1966-77, mgr. customer support, 1977-84; mgr. tech. assistance ctr. GTE, Northlake and Phoenix, 1984-85; mgr. research and devel. GTE, Phoenix, 1985-86, dir. research and devel., 1986-87; dir. tech. service Siemens Transmission Systems, Inc., 1987—. Adult leader Boy Scouts Am., Ill., Wis., 1966-77; mem. exec. com. Community Chest, Glendale Heights, Ill., 1966-70. Served with U.S. Army, 1961-64. Mem. Salem (Wis.) Jaycees (sec. 1972-74). Home: Box 4228 New River Stg II Phoenix AZ 85028 Office: Siemens Transmission Systems Inc 2411 W 14th St T-4 5th Fl Tempe AZ 85281

WILSON, WILLETTA, research scientist; b. Chgo., May 31, 1931; d. Stanley and Mabel Wilson. BA, Roosevelt U., 1959; MEd, Chgo. Tchrs. Coll., 1962; PhD, U. Oreg., 1980. Cert. spl. edn. tchr., Chgo. Spl. edn. tchr. Chgo. Pub. Sch. System, 1959-65; research asst. U. Oreg., Eugene, 1973-74, asst. dean, 1975-77; cons. Oreg. State U., Corvallis, 1980-81, asst. prof., 1982-83; research scientist Oreg. Research Inst., Eugene, 1981—, also bd. dirs. Mem. Lane County Social Services Adv. Council, Eugene, 1976. U. Chgo. scholar, 1961. Mem. Am. Assn. Diabetes Educators, Am. Diabetes Assn. (bd. dirs. Lane County chpt. 1981-82), Am. Psychol. Assn., Am. Pub. Health Assn., Western Gerontol. Assn., Pi Lambda Theta. Democrat. Office: Oreg Research Inst 1899 Willamette Eugene OR 97401

WILSON, WILLIAM GEORGE, natural gas and chemical company executive; b. Toronto, Ont., Can., May 19, 1935; m. Marilyn Jean Eagleson; children: Kevin David, Catherine Leslie. With Clarkson, Gordon & Co., 1954, partner, 1965; dir. fin. Cominco Ltd., Vancouver, B.C., Can., 1973, v.p. fin., 1974-79, exec. v.p., 1979, former pres.; exec. v.p. Nova Corp., Calgary, Alta., Can., 1986—; dir. Cominco Am. Inc.; dir. Western Can. Steel Ltd., West Kootenay Power and Light Co. Ltd., Pine Point Mines Ltd., Arvik Mines Ltd., Cominco Australia Pty. Ltd., Aberfoyle Ltd., Pacific Coast Terminals Co. Ltd. Club: Vancouver. Office: Nova Corp, PO Box 2535, Sta M, Calgary, AB Canada T2P TN6

WILSON, YVONNE CHANTILOUPE, marriage, family, child counselor; b. Mandeville, Jamaica, Mar. 26, 1944; d. Raphael Wilburn and Leila May (Mahoney) Chantiloupe; m. Robert Lee Wilson, Jr., Dec. 23, 1967 (div. 1978); children: Robert Lee III, Kurt Olaf; m. Godfrey Alexander Phillip, Aug, 29, 1985. AA, Laguardia Community Coll., 1977; BA, Calif. State U., San Bernardino, 1981; MA, Azusa Pacific U., 1983. Lic. marriage, family and child counselor. Social service counselor Casa De San Bernardino, 1978-80; mental health asst. County Mental Health, San Bernardino, 1980-84; instr. Adelphi Bus. Coll., San Bernardino, 1984-85; adminstrv. dir., owner Home Tutoring Service, Rialto, 1984-86; marriage, family counselor Psychology Ctr., San Bernardino, 1983—; social service practitioner Dept. Psych. Social. Services, Riverside, Calif., 1985—; bd. dirs. Sch.. Attendance Review Bd., Rialto Sch. Dist., 1978-85, Casa de Ayuda, San Bernardino, 1984-85; mem. adv. bd. Chaffey Coll., Alta Loma, Calif, 1983-84; cons. Daughters United Dept. Pub. Soc. Service, Riverside, 1986—. Mem. Calif. Assn. Marriage, Family Therapist, Calif. State Alumni Assn. (sec., treas. 1984-86). Avocations: traveling, writing, reading, dancing, exercising. Home: 150 E Morgan St Rialto CA 92376

WILTON, HENRY, journalist, editor; b. Kolozsvar, Hungary; came to U.S., 1929; m. Irene Gertrude (dec. Feb., 1985). Student, City Coll. N.Y., 1938-39. Editor Grass Roots Forum, San Gabriel, Calif., 1967—; founder Henry Wilton Cancer Research Lab. Semmelweiss Med. U., Budapest, Hungary. Mem. Unitarian Universalist Assn. (founder Henry Wilton Peace award). Home: 1507 Sierra Vista Alhambra CA 91801 Office: PO Box 472 San Gabriel CA 91776

WILTSE, CHLORYCE JERENE, home economics and computer science educator, computer software development company exectuive; b. Arnolds Park, Iowa, Nov. 25, 1933; d. Carl J. and Leila L. (Gibbs) Ode; m. Gary L. Wiltse, June 9, 1957; children—Mark, Lynn Wiltse Braswell. B.S., U. Nebr., 1955; postgrad. Iowa State, 1982, Mont. State U., 1968-81, U. Mont., 1967-72, Eastern Mont. Coll., 1965. Tchr. home econs. Osceola (Nebr.) High Sch., 1955-57; rural tchr. Billup Sch., Powder River County, Mont., 1957-58; tchr. home econs., computer sci. Powder River High Sch., Broadus, Mont., 1964-83; lectr. computers in home econs. edn., rural family fin. mgmt. Named Mont. Home Econs. Tchr. of Yr., Mont. Home Econs. Assn. and Family Circle mag., 1976. Mem. Am. Home Econs. Assn., Mont. Home Econs. Assn., Assn. for Devel. Co. Instrnl. Systems, Internat. Council for Computers in Edn., NW Council for Computer Edn., Mont. Council Computers in Edn., Mortar Bd., Delta Kappa Gamma, Phi Upsilon Omicron, Omicron Nu, Gamma Alpha Chi, Alpha Lambda Delta, Phi Sigma Chi, Kappa Delta, Women in Farm Econs. Republican. Lutheran. Order of Eastern Star. Author publs. in field. Home: Box 72 Volborg MT 59351

WILTSE, RICHARD CHARLES, osteopath, anesthesiologist; b. Detroit, Feb. 16, 1933; s. Cecil Clark and Mary Goe (Brashear) W.; m. Beatrice Grace Coveyou, June 20, 1959. BS in Pharmacy summa cum laude, U. Mich., 1955; DO, Kirksville (Mo.) Coll. Osteo. Medicine, 1964. Diplomate Am. Osteo. Bd. Anesthesiology. Pharmacist Plymouth, Mich., 1955-60; gen. practice osteo. medicine Houston, 1965-67; practice osteo. medicine specializing in anesthesiology Cuyahoga Falls, Ohio, 1969-73, Houston, 1974-80, Tucson, 1982—. Served with U.S. Army, 1956-58. Fellow Am. Osteo. Coll. Anesthesiologists (program chmn. 1984, annual meeting coordinator 1986); mem. Am. Osteo. Assn., Midwest Osteo. Soc. Anesthesiologists (program chmn. annual seminar 1984, pres. 1985), Ariz. Osteo. Med. Soc., Undersea Med. Soc., Beta Theta Pi (sec. 1952-53, exec. com. 1986). Presbyterian. Lodge: Elks. Avocations: skiing, golf, hiking, backpacking, scuba diving. Home: 5530 Arroya Grande Dr Tucson AZ 85718 Office: Aiz Profl Anesthetic Corp 2455 E Speedway #201 Tucson AZ 85719

WIMBERLY, RUSSELL JOSEPH, operations research analyst; b. Mobile, Ala., Feb. 6, 1950; s. John Joseph Wimberly and Florence Ethyl (Spikes) Jones; m. Carlita Idell Antoine, May 29, 1971; children: Kimberly, Shannon, William, Christian. BS in Math., U. So. Ala., 1972; MS in Ops. Research, Ga. Inst. Tech., 1981. Commd. 2d lt. U.S. Army, 1972, advanced through grades to maj., 1983; analyst, faculty mem. U.S. Army Logistics Mgmt. Ctr., Ft. Lee, Va., 1981-85; ops. research analyst U.S. Army Tng. and Doctrine Command Analysis Ctr., Monterey, Calif., 1985—; statis. cons. Ft. Lee Community Hosp., 1983. Contbr. articles to profl. jours. Mem. Ops. Research Soc. Am., Soc. Computer Simulation, Les Amis du Vin. Roman Catholic. Avocation: oenology.

WIMMER, GAYLE, artist, educator; b. Pitts., Oct. 2, 1943; d. Emanuel H. and Frances (Bernstein) W. BFA, Pratt Inst., 1967; MFA, Tyler Sch. of Art, 1970. Lectr. art Hunter Coll., N.Y.C., 1972-77; instr. The New Sch. for Social Research, N.Y.C., 1973-77; assoc. prof. U. Ariz., Tucson, 1977—; artistic designer Wimmer, Wimmer and Dancers, Phila., 1979-83. One-man shows include Galerie Faust, Geneva, 1986, Galeria Rzezby, Warsaw, 1986, Mandell Theatre, Phila., 1983, Annenberg Ctr., U. Pa., 1982, The Armory for the Arts, Santa Fe, 1979, Mus. of Fine Arts, Salt Lake City, 1979, Hadler Gallery, Houston, 1978, 101 Gallery, Tucson, 1977, Slocumb Gallery, Johnson City, Tenn., 1976, Paley Library, Temple U., Phila., 1973; represented in permanent collections U.S. Nat. Park Service, Nat. Steel Corp., Kino Hosp., U. Ariz., Pitts. Glove Mfg. Co., Stedman Gallery, The Textile Mus., Lodz, Poland, Roda Macchine, Ticino, Switzerland; contbr. articles to profl. jours. Grantee Pa. Council for Arts, 1981, U.S. Nat. Park Service, 1976, NEA, 1973; Internat. Research and Exchanges Bd. fellow to Acad. of Fine Art, Warsaw, Poland, 1971; Internat. Research and Exchanges Bd. research fellow to Poland, 1982-83. Home: 3468 N Richland Circle Tucson AZ 85719 Office: U Ariz Art Dept Tucson AZ 85721

WIMMER, JOHN CHARLES, building company executive; b. Albany, Calif., May 25, 1944; s. Herbert Fredrick and Cornelia Marie (Rothove) W. BSBA with distinction, San Jose State U., 1974; MBA, Stanford U., 1977. Real estate salesman Security Pacific Real Estate Co., Walnut Creek, Calif., 1971-73; adminstrv. asst. to pres. Anthony Sch. of Santa Clara Valley. Inc., 1973-75, v.p., dir., 1977-81; pres. Lifestyle Homes Inc., Santa Clara, Calif., 1977-81; v.p. constrn. The Meads Group, Santa Clara, 1981-82, Heflin Corp., Palo Alto, Calif., 1982-84; project mgr. First S.W. Constrn. Co., Temple, Tex., 1984-85, Lincoln Properties, Foster City, Calif., 1985-86; sr. project mgr. Oxford Constrn. Services, Inc., Encino, Calif., 1986—. Home: 9930-2 Sepulveda Blvd Mission Hills CA 91345 Office: Oxford Constrn Services Inc 16133 Ventura Blvd Suite 1270 Encino CA 91436

WINARSKI, DANIEL JAMES, mechanical engineer; b. Toledo, Dec. 16, 1948; s. Daniel Edward and Marguerite (Pietersien) W.; B.S. in Engring., U. Mich., 1970, Ph.D. (NSF fellow), 1976; M.S., U. Colo., 1973; m. Donna Ilene Robinson, Oct. 10, 1970; 1 son, Tyson York. Mech. engr. Libbey Owens Ford Co., Toledo, summers 1968, 69, 72; petroleum engr. Exxon Production Research, Houston, 1976-77; staff engr. mech. engring. sect. IBM, Tucson, 1977-84, adv. engr., 1984-86, systems engr., performance evaluator, 1986—; assoc. prof. dept. mechanics U.S. Mil. Acad., 1980—; instr. minority computer edn. No. Ariz. U., 1983-85. Served to 1st lt. U.S. Army, 1970-72; maj. Res., 1984. Recipient IBM Invention Achievement award, 1981, 82, 83, IBM Mfg. award, 1986; registered profl. engr., Ariz., Colo. Mem. ASME (pub. chmn. U. Mich. 1974), Am. Inst. Aeros., Sharlot Hall Mus., Mus. No. Ariz., Phi Eta Sigma, Pi Tau Sigma, Tau Beta Pi. Republican. Methodist. Club: So. Ariz. Rd. Runners. Designer adjustable artificial leg; patentee tape reel hub, tape loose-wrap check, tape reel sizing, tape reel-cartridge. Home: 647 S Woodstock Tucson AZ 85710 Office: IBM Corp 67E/060-1 Tucson AZ 85744

WINBURN, DUANE CLINTON, metallurgical engineer; b. Hecla, S.D., July 11, 1921; m. Yvonne Lois Marr, June 11, 1944; children: Vicki, Barry, Randy. BS in Metall. Engring., S.D. Sch. Mines and Tech., 1943. Metall. engr. Wright Aeronautical Corp., Paterson, N.J., 1943-46; staff mem. Los Alamos (N.Mex.) Nat. Lab., 1947-82, lectr., 1982—; cons. Los Alamos, 1982—; cons. Fred Reed Optical Co., Albuquerque, 1973—; laser adv. com. Univ. N.Mex., Los Alamos, 1973-80, Tech. Vocat. Inst., Albuquerque, 1975-80. Author: Practical Laser Safety, 1985, What Every Engineer Should Know About Lasers, 1987; contbr. articles to profl. jours. County commr. Los Alamos County, 1955-56; pres. Los Alamos Family YMCA, 1963-64, Los Alamos Recycle Ctr., 1973—; trustee Los Alamos United Ch.; active Democratic Cen. Com., Los Alamos, 1955-65. Served with U.S. Army, 1946-47. Recipient Outstanding Physical Fitness, Jaycees, 1964, Appreciation award United Fund, 1969, Gov.'s Vol. Service award, Gov. Anaya's Com., 1986. Mem. Laser Safety Inst. (founder, pres. 1985—), Am. Soc. Safety Engrs., Optical Soc. Am., Laser Inst. Am. (sec. 1975-80, Outstanding Service award, 1980). Club: Los Alamos Golf (bd. dirs. 1950-51). Lodge: Kiwanis (lt. gov. Los Alamos club 1966-67, Kiwanian of Yr. 1971, 82, 83, 86). Avocations: golf, basketball, traveling. Home and Office: 348 Andanada Los Alamos NM 87544

WINCHELL, ROBERT ALLEN, government agency administrator, accountant; b. Ft. Monmouth, N.J., Oct. 28, 1945; s. Robert Winslow Winchell; B.A., U. Calif., Santa Barbara, 1967; M.B.A., U. Pa., 1969. Auditor, Air Force Audit Agy., El Segundo, Calif., 1972-73; accountant Scholefield, Bellanca & Co., W. Los Angeles, 1974-75, So. Calif. Gas Co., Los Angeles, 1975-76; auditor Def. Contract Audit Agy., Dept. Def., Los Angeles, 1976—. Served with AUS, 1969-71; Vietnam. Decorated Bronze Star. Mem. Assn. Govt. Accountants, Am. Inst. C.P.A.'s, Alpha Kappa Psi. Republican. Presbyterian. Club: Los Angeles Country. Home: 2008 California Ave Santa Monica CA 90403

WINCHELL, VERNE H., retired restaurant chain executive; b. 1915; married. Propr. Winchell Music, 1938-45, Winchell Motors, 1945-48; propr. Winchell Donut House (acquired by Dennys Restaurant, Inc. 1968), 1948-54, pres., chief exec. officer, 1955-68; formerly chmn., pres., chief exec. officer Denny's Inc., La. Mirada, Calif., from 1968, now dir. Office: Dennys Inc 16700 Valley View Ave La Mirada CA 90638

WINCHESTER, PAUL DELBERT, neonatologist; b. Fargo, N.D., Sept. 7, 1948; s. Burl and Carolyn (Gay) W.; m. Sylvia Marie Telfer, Aug. 14, 1974; children: Sage Elizabeth, Cody Ray. BA, Stanford U., 1970; MA, U. Mich., 1972; MD, U. Colo., Denver, 1976. Diplomate Am. Bd. Pediatrics. Resident pediatrician U. Colo. Med. Ctrs., Denver, 1976-79, fellowship neonatology, 1979-81; dir. neonatology Meml. Hosp., Colorado Springs, Colo., 1981—; clin. prof. pediatrics U. Colo., Colo. Springs, 1985-86. Fellow Am. Acad. Pediatrics. Avocation: archaeology. Home: 820 Northfield Rd Colorado Springs CO 80919

WINCKEL, AUGUST, physician; b. Veendam, Netherlands, May 17, 1916; came to U.S., 1953, naturalized, 1959; s. August and Josephine Aleida (Van Heest) W.; M.D., U. Amsterdam, 1946; m. Joanne Kozlowski, July 29, 1975; children—August Henry, Paul, Joy, Michele. Resident in internal medicine and rheumatology U. Utrecht (Netherlands), 1949-53; rotating intern Seaside Meml. Hosp., Long Beach, Calif., 1954, Santa Monica (Calif.) Hosp., 1954-55; resident in emergency medicine Daniel Freeman Hosp., Inglewood, Calif., 1955-56; pvt. practice medicine, specializing in family practice, Santa Monica, 1956-85; mem. staff Santa Monica Hosp., 1956-66, sr. staff, 1966-85, mem. tumor bd., 1976-85; ret., 1986. Diplomate Am. Bd. Family Practice. Fellow Am. Acad. Family Physicians; mem. Loa Angeles County Med. Assn., AMA, Calif. Med. Assn. Republican. Presbyterian. Office: 4225 Longridge Ave #210 Studio City CA 91604

WINCOR, MICHAEL Z., psychopharmacology educator, researcher; b. Chgo., Feb. 9, 1946; s. Emanuel and Rose (Kershner) W.; m. Emily E.M. Smythe, Sept. 14, 1980; children: Meghan Heather, Katherine Rose. SB in Zoology, U. Chgo., 1966; PharmD, U. So. Calif., 1978. Research project specialist U. Chgo. Sleep Lab., 1968-75; psychiat. pharmacist Brotman Med. Ctr., Culver City, Calif., 1979-83; asst. prof. U. So. Calif., Los Angeles, 1983—; cons. Fed. Bur. Prisons Drug Abuse Program, Terminal Island, Calif., 1978-81, Nat. Inst. Drug Abuse, Bethesda, Md., 1981, The Upjohn Co., Kalamazoo, Mich., 1982-85, Area XXIV Profl. Standards Rev. Orgn., Los Angeles, 1983. Contbr. articles to jours. and chpts. to books. Recipient Cert. Appreciation, Mayor of Los Angeles, 1981; Faculty scholar U. So. Calif. Sch. Pharmacy, 1978. Mem. Am. Coll. Clin. Pharmacy, Am. Soc. Hosp. Pharmacists, Am. Pharm. Assn., Sleep Research Soc., Clin. Sleep Soc., Rho Chi. Avocation: photography. Office: U So Calif 1985 Zonal Ave Los Angeles CA 90033

WINDER, SCOTT ROBERTS, television producer, director; b. Craig, Colo., Aug. 4, 1958; s. John Robert Winder and Barbara Joan (Roberts) Rees. Student, Oreg. State U., 1976-77, So. Oreg. State Coll., 1978; AS in TV Broadcasting, Lane Community Coll., 1982. Producer, dir. Sta. KEZI-TV, Eugene, Oreg., 1980—; freelance producer, dir. Eugene, Oreg., 1986—; bd. dirs. Caldwell-Ryder Advt., Eugene, 1986—. Producer, dir. TV program The Amazing Feats of Wilt Chamberlain, 1986, Youth Sports Edn. Series. Recipient Addy award of Merit NW Addy Award, 1985. Mem. Mid Oreg. Ad Club (Merit award 1984). Republican. Avocations: golf, travel, softball. Home and Office: 2915 Norkenzie Rd Eugene OR 97401

WINDER, WILLIAM BURCH, investment company executive; b. Hayden, Colo., Sept. 13, 1928; s. George Norman and Mary (Burch) W.; m. Jeanne Wells, June 26, 1954; children—Cameron Brooks, Paige Normandy. S.B., MIT, 1950. Engr., Am. Tel.&Tel. Co., Denver, 1953-56; mgr. power sources div. Whittaker Corp., Denver, 1956-66; pres. Mate Sales Co., Denver, 1966-74; regional mgr. The PACE Orgn., Denver, 1968-74; pres. Blue Mountain Corp., Denver, 1972-80; pres. Two Bar Ranch Co., Denver, 1977-79, dir., 1950-79; mgmt. cons., 1974-83; pres. The Winder Corp., Denver, 1983—. Chmn. men's task force Denver Art Mus., 1969-71. Served to 1st lt. U.S. Army, 1951-53. Mem. Am. Soc. Profl. Cons., Sales and Mktg. Execs., Phi Gamma Delta. Republican. Clubs: Athletic, City, Toastmasters (Denver). Editor: Mineral Resources in Wilderness, 1982. Home: 2672 S Jackson St Denver CO 80210

WINDERMAN, JAY BENJAMIN, engineer, writer; b. Bklyn., Dec. 9, 1940; s. Milton and Elsie (Cohen) W.; m. Rochelle Rudoff, Mar. 21, 1971; children: Susan, Robin. BEE, Rensselaer Poly. Inst., Troy, N.Y., 1962; MEE, NYU, 1963. Asst. instr. in elec. engring. NYU, Bronx, 1962-63; engring. specialist Gen. Dynamics, Pomona, Calif., 1963—. Author short stories; contbr. articles to profl. jours.; patentee in field. Named Engr. of Yr. Gen. Dynamics, Pomona, 1981. Mem. IEEE (sr.). Club: Calif. Turtle and

Tortoise (Pasadena chpt.). Avocations: bridge, turtles, gardening. Office: Gen Dynamics PO Box 2507 Pomona CA 91769

WINDHAM, EDWARD JAMES, bank executive, leasing company executive; b. Salt Lake City, Dec. 13, 1950; s. James Rudolph and Margaret Ann (Griffith) W.; m. Marilyn Ann Kenyon, Mar. 27, 1973; children: Ian James, Kendra Ann. Student, U. Calif., San Diego, 1969-70, 72-74, U. Calif., Santa Barbara, 1970-72. Cert. mortgage credit examiner HUD. Emergency med. technician Hartson's Mobile Intensive Care Unit, San Diego, 1973-76; salesman Bonanza Properties, Tustin, Calif., 1976; loan officer Medallion Mortgage, Santa Cruz, Calif., 1976-80; sr. loan officer Cen. Pacific Mortgage, Santa Cruz, 1980-83, v.p., 1983-86; ptnr. Winn Leasing Co., Santa Cruz, 1983—; v.p. Community West Mortgage, 1986—; cons. Contour Inc., San Jose, Calif., 1983-85. Pres. Evergreen Estates Homeowners Assn., Soquel, Calif., 1983-85. Recipient Best Havana Brown award S.W. region Cat Fanciers Assn., 1976,77. Mem. Nat. Assn. Rev. Appraisers and Rev. Underwriters (sr., cert.), Mortgage Bankers Assn., Calif. Mortgage Bankers Assn., Mensa, Intertel. Republican. Lodge: Masons (master Santa Cruz 1986—, sr. warden 1985-86). Avocations: computer science, gifted children, skiing. Home: 3907 Adar Ln Soquel CA 95073 Office: Community West Mortgage PO Box 939 Capitola CA 95010-0939

WINDOFFER, BRUCE CRAIG, sales executive; b. Whittier, Calif., July 11, 1955; s. Don Duane and Dorothy Virginia (Brothers) W.; m. Karen Elizabeth Becker, Dec. 9, 1978; children: Lindsay Ann, Nathan Andrew. BS in Chemistry, Point Loma Nazarene Coll., 1978. From sr. a.p. chemist to sr. test engr. Truesdail Labs., Inc., Tustin, Calif., 1978-82; tech. sales rep. Fisher Sci. Co., Tustin, 1982-86, Beckman Instruments, Inc., Fullerton, Calif., 1985—. Vol. chief fin. officer P.F. Breese Found., Los Angeles, 1986—. Mem. Am. Chem. Soc., Research Assocs. of Point Loma Coll. Republican. Avocations: competitive volleyball, computing, alpine skiing, instrumental and vocal music. Home: 1321 Oak Hill Pl South Pasadena CA 91030 Office: Beckman Instruments 2500 Harbor Blvd E-20-E Fullerton CA 92634-0031

WINDREM, ORVILLE CECIL, oil company executive; b. Briercrest, Sask., Can., Aug. 31, 1925; s. Cecil Joseph and Mildred (Munn) W.; m. Trudy Johnson, June 21, 1947. B in Commerce, U. Sask., 1949. Clk. Texaco Exploration co., Calgary, Alta., Can., 1952-54, tax agt., 1954-58, tax adminstr., 1959-60; tax adminstr. Tex. Petroleum Co., Caracas, Venezuela, 1960-62, Tex. Can., Ltd., Montreal, Que., Can., 1962-70; asst. to v.p. Texaco, Inc., N.Y.C., 1970-72, asst. to gen. tax counsel, 1972-75; asst. to v.p. Texaco Exploration Can., Ltd., Calgary, 1975-78; corp. tax officer Texaco Can., Inc., Don Mills, Ont., 1978-80; v.p. Texaco Can. Resources, Ltd., Calgary, 1980-86, also bd. dirs.; v.p. Texaco Can. Resources, Calgary, 1985—. Served with Can. Army, 1944-46. Recipient Overseas Service award Can. Army, 1946. Mem. Can. Petroleum Assn. (bd. govs. 1979-81, bd. dirs. Sask. div. 1976-83, chmn. bd. dirs. B.C. div. 1978-79, bd. dirs. B.C. div. 1976—). Club: Calgary Petroleum. Office: Texaco Can Resources, PO Box 3333 Sta M, Calgary Can T2P 2P8

WINDUS, WALTER BRISTOL, quality assurance executive; b. Albany, N.Y., Nov. 10, 1938; s. Charles Edward and Lowene Elizabeth (Bristol) W.; m. Susan Paige Clow, Aug. 26, 1961; 1 child, Karen Gayle. BSEE, Wash. State U., 1961, MSEE, 1962; MBA, U. Santa Clara, 1964. Supr. Signetics Corp., Sunnyvale, Calif., 1966-74; mgr. Fairchild Semiconductor, Palo Alto, Calif., 1974-78, Kasper Instruments, Sunnyvale, 1979, DMC Systems, Inc., Santa Clara, 1979-83; dir. Televideo Systems, San Jose, Calif., 1983-85; v.p. Molecular Computer, San Jose, 1985—. Contbr. articles on aviation to jours. Mem. San Jose Mcpl. Airport Adv. Com., 1976; sr. pilot USCG Aux., San Jose, 1976—; bd. dirs. Frazier Lake Airpark, Hollister, Calif., 1983—. Recipient Engring. Excellence award Tau Beta Pi, 1960, Outstanding Leadership award Omicron Delta Kappa, 1961. Mem. IEEE, NSPE, Calif. State Aviation Adv. Com., Seaplane Pilots Assn. (west coast dir. 1976—, v.p. 1983—, Outstanding Service award 1984), Santa Clara County Airmen's Assn. (pres. 1974). Republican. Presbyterian. Clubs: Santa Clara County Kennel (treas.); Intermountain Kennel (Salt Lake City) (pres. 1969); Skyview Flying (San Jose) (pres., chief exec. officer 1966—). Avocation: aviation. Home: 12681 Saratoga Creek Dr Saratoga CA 95070 Office: Molecular Computer Inc 1983 Concourse Dr San Jose CA 95131

WINETROUT, C.A., III, real estate investor; b. Medford, Oreg., May 18, 1946; s. C.A. and Bettie (Hobbs) W.; m. Linda Jo Frederick, June 8, 1968 (div. Aug. 1977); children: Rence, Wendy; m. Pamie L. Polivka, Apr. 13, 1979. BS, U. Oreg., 1968, postgrad. in real estate, 1968-69. Builder, developer Winetrout Investments, Eugene, Oreg., 1970-84, Solana Beach, Calif., 1984—; pres. Fine Homes, Inc., Solana Beach, 1986—. Mem. Nat. Assn. Gen. Contractors, Nat. Bldg. Industry Assn. Republican. Avocations: golf, volleyball, sailing, traveling. Home and Office: 707 S Sierra Ave #12 Solana Beach CA 92075

WINFIELD, ARMAND GORDON, international plastics consultant; b. Chgo., Dec. 28, 1919; student Newark Acad. 1937; B.S., Franklin and Marshall Coll., 1941; postgrad. U. N.Mex., 1941, State U. Iowa, 1944, Washington U., St. Louis, 1948-50; m. Lillian Tsukea Kubota, June 8, 1951 (dec. Dec. 1965); m. 2d, Barbara Jane La Barge, July 23, 1966. Owner, Winfield Fine Art in Jewelry, N.Y.C., 1945-48; research dir. Hanley Plastics Co. div. Wallace Pencil Co., St. Louis, 1955-57; plastic cons. engr. DeBell & Richardson, Inc., Hazardville, Conn., 1957-64; exec. v.p. Crystopal Ltd., Hazardville, Conn., 1963—; pres. Armand G. Winfield Inc., Santa Fe, 1964—; also lectr., writer; mem. faculty Harris Tchrs. Coll., 1950, Washington U., 1956; lectr. Yale U., 1960-61; adviser USIA on plastics show to tour USSR, 1960-61; vis. critic in plastics Sch. Architecture, CCNY, 1968-69; plastics cons. indsl. design dept., faculty Pratt Inst., Bklyn., 1964-70, instr. prodn. methods, 1968-70; lectr. U. Hartford, U. Kans., 1970, U. Ariz., 1978; adj. prof. plastics engring. U. Lowell (Mass.), 1978-81, Calif. Poly. State U., 1980. Bd. dirs. Santa Fe Crime Stoppers, chmn. 1986, 87, carnival chmn. 1983, 84. U.S. State Dept. grantee to USSR, 1961; UN grantee for study plastics in low cost housing for developing countries, 1968-69; UN grantee, Vienna, Austria, 1971; UNIDO expert in newer fibers and composites, India, 1977, cons. glass fibers and composites, Colombia, 1979. Fellow Plastics and Rubber Inst. (Eng.); mem. Soc. for Advancement Materials and Process Engring. (charter, chpt. chmn. 1986, 87), Soc. Plastics Engrs. (pres. Western New Eng. sect. 1963-64, v.p. N.Y. sect. 1968-69, chmn. regional tech. conf. 1967, historian ann. tech. conf. 1968), Soc. Plastic Industry, Plastics Pioneers Assn., Plastics Inst. Australia, Internat. Assn. Housing Sci. (charter), Santa Fe C. of C. Author: The Alexian Brothers, 1951; The Merchants Exchange of St. Louis, 1953; Plastics For Architects, Artists and Interior Designers, 1961; 100 Years Young, 1968; also chpts. in books, monthly column in Display World Mag., 1965-68, Designer Mag., 1971-72, Museum Scope, 1976-77; numerous articles on plastics. Patentee in field. Office: 3 Siler Ln PO Box 1296 Santa Fe NM 87504

WING, DAVID ALLAN, biochemistry educator, research chemist; b. Chgo., Sept. 19, 1948; s. Richard Wallace and Darlene (Cross) W.; m. Ruth Ellyn Anderson, June 6, 1970; children: Emily, Rebecca, Daniel. BS in Chemistry, Wheaton (Ill.) Coll., 1970; PhD in Chemistry, Northwestern U., 1977. Postdoctoral fellow St. Louis U. Med. Sch., 1978, Washington U. Med. Sch., St. Louis, 1979-80; asst. prof. Grand Canyon Coll., Phoenix, 1980-82, assoc. prof., 1983-85, prof. biochemistry and chemistry, 1985—; mem. Project Seraphim, NSF. Contbr. articles to profl. jours. Served to capt. U.S. Army, 1975-77. Fellow Mo. Heart Assn., 1979-80. Mem. Am. Chem. Soc. Baptist. Avocation: music. Office: Grand Canyon Coll PO Box 11097 Phoenix AZ 85061

WING, HAROLD RAY, businessman; b. Springville, Utah, Mar. 5, 1940; s. Arthur and Mary Margurite (Falkner) W.; student Springville public schs.; m. Brigitte Mayer, Dec. 23, 1960; children—Dennis, Harold, Michael, Michelle, Douglas, Christina, Heidi. Asst. mgr. Carson's Market, Provo, Utah, 1961-63; mem. quality control staff Munz Castings, Heilbronn, W. Ger., 1963-65; mem. prodn. control staff Hercules, Inc., 1965-70; agt. Beneficial Life Ins. Co., 1970-74; owner, pres., dir. Little Giant Industries, Provo, Utah, 1974-86; owner, pres. Wing Enterprises, Springville, Utah, 1981—; vol. cons. small bus. Dist. pres., high councilman Ch. of Jesus Christ of Latter-day Saints; mem. U.S. Congl. Adv. Com., Utah State Gov.'s Council on Small Bus.; del. White House Conf. On Small Bus., 1986. Patentee (7), inventor in field. Served with U.S. Army, 1958-61. Home: 1185 E 225 N Springville UT 84663 Office: 2241 S Larsen Pkwy Provo UT 84601 also: Wing Enterprises 1325 West Indsl Circle Springville UT 84663

WING, IRA JOHN, II, construction company executive; b. San Diego, Oct. 18, 1945; s. Robert Curran and Helen Irene (Burgess) W.; m. Sheila Mae, June 26, 1971; children: Terri Lynn, Robert Lawrence, Ira John III, Adrianne Helen Elizabeth. Cert., San Diego City Coll., 1968; L.S. teaching cert., Mesa Jr. Coll., 1972. Lic. gen. bldg. contractor, Calif. Journeyman carpenter Constrn. Industry, San Diego, 1963-72; pvt. practice contractor Calif., 1972—; pres. Sheila Corp., San Marcos, Calif., 1976—; constrn. inspector, Calif., 1984—; instr. Palomar Coll., San Diego, 1973—. Served with U.S. Army, 1968-70, Vietnam. Decorated Purple Heart, Bronze Star V device. Mem. Nat. Assn. Women in Constrn. (hon., Instr. of Yr. 1979, 80, 84). Democrat. Presbyterian. Avocations: vegetable gardening, woodworking, soccer. Home: 1345 Tower Dr Vista CA 92083 Office: Sheila Corp 256 E Myrtle Ave San Marcos CA 92069

WING, JANET ELEANOR SWECDYK BENDT, nuclear scientist; b. Detroit, Oct. 12, 1925; s. Jack and Florence C. (Springman) Sweedyk; m. Philip J. Bendt, Sept. 4, 1948 (div. Jan. 1972); children: Karen Ann Bendt Sox, Paul Philip, Barbara Jean Bendt Medlin, Linda Sue; m. G. Milton Wing, Aug. 26, 1972 (div. Jan. 1987). BSEE with distinction, Wayne State U., 1947; MA in Physics, Columbia U., 1950; postgrad., U. Oreg., 1966-67, U. N.Mex., 1968-71. Research engr. Gen. Motors Corp., Detroit, 1944-48; physicist, mathematician Manhattan Project Columbia U., N.Y.C., 1950-51; mem. research staff Los Alamos (N.Mex.) Nat. Lab, 1951-57, 68—, project leader, 1976-81, asst. group leader, 1980-84, assoc. group leader, 1985—. Bd, dirs., treas. Esperanza Shelter, Santa Fe, N. Mex., 1984—. Mem. Am. Nuclear Soc., AAAS, Women in Sci. and Engring., Los Alamos Women in Sci., Sigma Xi, Tau Beta Pi. Avocations: karate, skiing, swimming. Office: Los Alamos Nat Lab Los Alamos NM 87545

WING, RICHARD CHOW, restauranteur; b. Hanford, Calif., June 20, 1921; s. Chow Gong and Shee Chan W.; B.A., U. So. Calif., 1953; m. Mary Lo, Jan. 25, 1965. Import-export rep. Fook Wah Co., Hong Kong, 1956-57; owner, operator, chef Imperial Dynasty 2, Hanford, 1957—; cons. in field. Recipient Man of Yr. award Chinese-Am. Citizen Alliance, 1960, Calif. Wine Patrons award, 1978. Mem. Chefs de Cuisine Assn. Calif., Am. Culinary Fedn., Am. Acad. Chefs, Les Amis d'Escoffier, Internat. Wine and Food Soc. (Cordon Bleu award 1960, 64), Chinese Hist. Soc., Confrerie Des Chevaliers du Tastevin, Soc. Bacchus, Calif. Wine Patrons. Democrat. Home: 854 Laurence Ln Hanford CA 93230 Office: Imperial Dynasty 2 China Alley Hanford CA 93230

WING, ROGER, management consultant; b. N.Y.C., May 26, 1945; s. John A. and Norma M. (LeBlanc) W.; m. Judith A., June 7, 1963 (div. 1980); m. Peggy J. McFall, Aug. 27, 1983; children: Roger, Karin. BBA, Cleve. State U., 1972, MBA, 1975. Supr. Am. Greetings Co., Brooklyn, Ohio, 1969-74; dir. Revco D.S. Inc., Twinsburg, Ohio, 1974-78; mgr. Hughes Aircraft Co., Los Angeles, 1978-79; sr. dir. Continental Airlines, Los Angeles, 1979-81; dir. Coopers & LyBrand, Los Angeles, 1981-83; pres. Huntington Cons. Group, Huntington Beach, Calif., 1983—; prof. Cleve. State U., 1977-78. Named Systems Man of Yr., Assn. Systems Mgmt., 1978. Avocations: tennis, skiing, photography, traveling. Office: The Huntington Cons Group 8531 Topside Circle Huntington Beach CA 92646

WING, WILLIAM HINSHAW, research physics educator; b. Ann Arbor, Mich., Jan. 11, 1939; s. Leonard William and Anne Marie (Hinshaw) W.; m. Jennifer Patai, June 10, 1967 (div. Aug. 18, 1979); children: Benjamin Patai, Jessica Grace. BA, Yale U., 1960; MS, Rutgers U., 1962; PhD, U. Mich., 1968. Research assoc., research staff physicist Yale U., New Haven, 1968-72, asst. prof. physics, 1972-74; assoc. prof. U. Ariz., Tucson, 1974-78, prof., 1978—; vis. prof. U. Colo., Boulder, 1979-80; prof. associé École Normale Supérieure, Paris, 1981; chmn. atomic and molecular div. Ariz. Research Labs. of U. Ariz., Tucson, 1983-86; chmn. com. on fundamental constants Nat. Acad. Scis./Nat. Research Council, 1983-87; founder, pres. Odyssey in Tech., Inc., Tucson, 1986—. Named U.S. Sr. Scientist Alexander Von Humboldt Stiftung, Fed. Republic of Germany, 1981; fellow John Simon Guggenheim Meml. found., 1980-81; vis. fellow Joint Inst. Lab. Astrophysics, Boulder, 1979-80. Fellow Am. Phys. Soc. (exec. com. div. atomic, molecular and optical physics, 1984-87), Optical Soc. Am.; mem. IEEE, N.Y. Acad. Scis., Am. Chem. Soc., Sigma Xi. Office: U Ariz Dept Physics Tucson AZ 85721

WINGATE, WILLIAM PETER, theatre executive; b. N.Y.C., Mar. 2, 1944; s. Henry Smith and Ardis (Swenson) W.; m. Anne Homstad, July 1, 1965; 1 child, William John. BA, Carleton Coll., 1965; MBA, Harvard U., 1968. Adminstrv. intern Ford Found., N.Y.C., 1968. Intern Ctr. Theatre Group of Los Angeles/Mark Taper Forum, Los Angeles, 1968-69, subscription mgr., 1970-72, mgr. New Theatre for Now, 1972-75, mng. dir., 1975-85, exec. mng. dir. Ctr. Theatre Group, 1985—, v.p. Taper Media Enterprises, 1983—; bus. mgr. Tyrone Guthrie Theatre, Mpls., 1969-70; dir. Am. Arts Alliance, Washington, 1984-87, Theatre Communications Group, 1985—; cons. NEH, Alaska State Arts Council, Anchorage, Denver Ctr. for Performing Arts; mem. theatre panel Nat. Endowment for Arts, 1984-86, chmn. 1986. Coproducer: (feature film) Zoot Suit, 1980; assoc. producer (broadway play) Children of a Lesser God, 1981 (Tony award 1981). Recipient Alumni Disting. Achievement award Carleton Coll., 1985. Mem. League of Resident Theatres (v.p. 1979-83), Music Ctr. Operating Com. (chmn. 1982—), Calif. Confedn. Arts (chmn. prominent orgns. com. 1982-83, Calif. Theatre Council (v.p. 1975-77). Democrat. Club: Harvard (N.Y.C.).

WINGER, LAURA, marketing director; b. Torrance, Calif., Aug. 16, 1961; s. Ronald Conway and Virginia Lee (Parker) W. BA, Ariz. State U., 1983. Retail exec. tng. program Robinson's, Los Angeles, 1984; asst. mktg. dir. The Hahn Co., Thousand Oaks, Calif., 1984-85; mktg. dir. The Hahn Co., Santa Barbara, Calif., 1985, Thousand Oaks, 1985-86, Pasadena, Calif., 1986—. Mem. City and County Affairs Com., Pasadena, 1986. Mem. So. Calif. Mktg. Dirs. Assn., Internat. Council Shopping Ctrs., Pasadena C. of C. Republican. Avocations: snow skiing, golf, dance. Home: 465 S Los Robles #15 Pasadena CA 91101 Office: The Hahn Co 202 Plaza Pasadena Pasadena CA 91101

WINGER, WAYNE D., electrical engineer, computer designer; b. Marion, Ind., Oct. 21, 1923; s. Lewis D. and Gladys S. (Small) W.; m. Marie Frances, Jan. 26, 1946; children: Wendell D., Janis E., Melissa L. BEE, Purdue U., 1949, MEE, 1950. Tech. engr. product devel. lab. IBM, Poughkeepsie, N.Y., 1950-51, various engring. positions, 1951-57, mgr. tech. planning, 1957-58, devel. mgr., 1958-59, machine tech. mgr., 1959-60; mgr. component plans IBM, Poughkeepsie and East Fishkill, N.Y., 1960-65; mgr. new tape device devel. IBM, Poughkeepsie and Boulder (Colo.), 1965-68; product mgr. library storage products IBM, Boulder, 1968-72, mgr. storage systems devel., 1972-73, lab. mgr., 1974-76, lab. ops. mgr., 1976-79; lab. ops. mgr. IBM, Tucson, 1979-84; cons. to IBM v.p. of tech. personnel devel., 1984-85. Inventor Taple Lookup Multiplying Computer, 1959 (Outstanding Invention, 1963), Data Transmission System, 1957 (Outstanting Invention, 1962). Served to 1st lt. U.S. Army, 1942-46. Recipient Pres.'s award for excellence as a Way of Life, IBM Gen. Product Div. Pres., Tucson, 1984. Mem. IEEE, Sigma Xi. Republican. Presbyterian. Avocations: photography, fishing, backpacking. Home: 6137 E Paseo Cimarron Tucson AZ 85715

WINGERD, BRUCE DELBERT, biology educator; b. Pasadena, Calif., Sept. 18, 1954; s. Delbert Jesse and Joanne Marie (Mergenthaler) W.; m. Mala Samia Wingerd, July 15, 1979; children: Joshua Seth, Ryan Joseph. AA in Biology, Orange Coast Coll., 1974; BS in Biology, San Diego State U., 1977, MS in Biology, 1980. Instr. biology San Diego City Coll., 1980-85; instr. biology San Diego State U., 1985—, adminstr., 1983—. Author: Human anatomy and Rabbit Dissection, 1984, Rabbit Dissection Manual, 1985. Office: San Diego State U Dept Biology 5300 Campanile Dr San Diego CA 92182

WINGET, CHARLOTTE LOUISE, association executive; b. Northwood, N.D., Mar. 19, 1939; d. Franklin Woodrow and Margaret Christina (Egland) Hagert; m. William Peter Winget, Sept. 17, 1960; children—William Brian, Marcelle Denise, David Matthew. B.A., U. Minn., 1962; B.A., Baldwin-Wallace Coll., Berea, Ohio, 1977; M.A., Mills Coll., 1973. Dir. movement therapy Ellen K. Raskob Learning Inst., Oakland, Calif., 1974; dir. student tax clinic Baldwin-Wallace Coll., Berea, 1977; jr. acct. Aloha Hawaii Travel, Ltd., Honolulu, 1978; membership/exhibits coordinator Pan-Pacific Surg. Assn., Honolulu, 1978-79; controller, 1979-80, controller-office mgr. 1980-82, exec. dir., 1982—. Mem. Hawaii Visitors Bur., 1980-85; hon. bd. dirs. Hawaii chpt. Just Say No. Mem. Nat. Assn. Accts., Profl. Conv. Mgmt. Assn., Nat. Assn. Female Execs., Hawaii Assn. Exposition Mgrs., Delta Zeta. Republican.

WINKELHAKE, JEFFREY LEE, pharmacologist, educator; b. Champaign, Ill., Oct. 5, 1945; s. Claude Arhtur and Marjorie Elsie (Seigwart) W. BS, U. Ill., 1967, MS, 1969, PhD, 1974. From asst. to assoc. prof. Med. Coll. Wis., Milw., 1976-84, prof., 1985; dir. pharmacology Cetus Corp., Emeryville, Calif., 1985—; cons. Blood Ctr. SE Wis., Milw., 1977-85; adj. prof. U. Calif. Berkeley, 1985—. Contbr. over 50 articles to profl. jours. Served with U.S. Army, 1970-72. Recipient 5 NIH grants, 2 NSF grants, 2 Am. Cancer Soc. grants, Arthritis Found. grant. Mem. Am. Assn. Immunology, Am. Soc. Biol. Chemists, Am. Assn. Cancer Research, Am. Chem. Soc., Biochem Soc., Am. Soc. Pharmacological Exptl. Therapists. Club: Encinal Yacht. Avocations: sailing, skiing, tennis. Office: Cetus Corp 1400 53d St Emeryville CA 94608

WINKELMAN, GORDEN KEITH, training analyst, consultant; b. Lawton, Okla., Sept. 18, 1952; s. Gorden Keith and Doris Joanne (Henderson) W.; m. Ann Elizabeth Myers, May 13, 1972 (div. May 1985); children: Erin Gaile, Heather Lyn; m. Cynthia Anne McCabe, June 21, 1986; stepchildren: Shannon Annette, Timothy Neal, Irene Lynn. Student U. Okla., Norman, 1970-71, De Anza Coll., 1979-81, BSBA U. Phoenix, 1987. Tech. trainer Measurex, Inc., Cupertino, Calif., 1979-80; tng. design specialist Rolm Corp., Santa Clara, Calif., 1980-82, tng. analyst, sr. course developer, 1982-85; instr., designer Pro-Log Corp., Monterey, Calif., 1985—; cons. Gt. Wall Industries, Beijing, People's Republic of China. Served to sgt. USAF, 1973-79. Mem. Am. Soc. Tng. and Devel. Methodist. Club: Santa Cruz Gem Soc. (Calif.).

WINKELMAN, LA MONT RAY, small business owner; b. Sparta, Wis., June 8, 1949; s. Frederick Arthur and Jean Marie (Tatu) W.; m. Janice Kay Stratton, Dec. 26, 1969; children: Shanon Ray, Chad La Mont. Student pub. schs., Tomah, Wis., grad. high sch. Foreman Band Box Cleaners, Tomah, 1965-67; operator 3M Co., St. Paul, 1967-75; quality control inspector Toro Co., Tomah, 1975-78; asst. gen. mgr. VCA Duplicating, Huntington Beach, Calif., 1978-85; v.p., gen. mgr. Crest Nat. Video, Hollywood, Calif., 1985—. Served as cpl. U.S. Army, 1969-71, Vietnam. Republican. Baptist. Avocations: basketball, football. Home: 5111 Sparrow Dr Huntington Beach CA 92649 Office: Crest Nat Video 1000 Highland Ave Hollywood CA 90019

WINKLER, IRWIN, motion picture producer; b. N.Y.C., May 28, 1931; s. Sol and Anna W. B.A., N.Y. U., 1955. Mailroom messenger William Morris Agy., N.Y.C., 1955-62. Producer: Rocky, 1976 (10 Acad. award nominations, winner 3 including best picture, Los Angeles Film Critics award for best picture), They Shoot Horses Don't They, 1969 (9 Acad. award nominations), Nickelodeon, 1976, The Gambler, 1974, Up the Sandbox, 1972, The New Centurions, 1972, Point Blank, 1967, Double Trouble, 1967, Leo the Last (Best Dir. award Cannes Film Festival 1970, Belgrade Film Festival 1970), The Strawberry Statement, (Jury prize Cannes Film Festival 1970), The Split, 1968, Breakout, 1975, Believe in Me, 1971, The Gang That Couldn't Shoot Straight, 1971, The Mechanic, 1972, Busting, 1974, SPYS, 1974, Peeper, 1975, New York, New York, 1977, Valentino, 1977, Uncle Joe Shannon, 1978, Comes A Horseman, 1978, Rocky II, 1979, Raging Bull, 1980 (8 Acad. award nominations, winner 2 Los Angeles Film Critics award for best picture), Rocky III, 1981, True Confessions, 1981, Author, Author, 1982, The Right Stuff, 1983 (8 Acad. award nominations), Rocky IV, 1984, Revolution, 1985, 'Round Midnight, 1986 (2 Acad. award nomiations, Acad. award Best Original Score). Served with U.S. Army, 1951-53. Named Commander d'Artes et de Letres, French Govt. Minister of Culture, 1985. Office: Chartoff-Winkler Prodns 10125 W Washington Blvd Culver City CA 90230

WINKLER, VICTOR WENDELL, chemical company executive; b. Columbus, Ohio, Aug. 19, 1940; s. John J. and Emma J. (Zesiger) W.; m. Theresa M. Kovach, Sept. 1, 1962; children: John J., Peter M. BA, Ohio State U., 1963, MS, 1964; PhD, Purdue U., 1969; MBA, Roosevelt U., Chgo., 1974. Jr. chemist State Chem. Lab., Lafayette, Ind., 1964-68; sr. scientist Abbott Labs., North Chicago, Ill., 1969-74, research fellow, 1975-78; group leader Sandoz Inc., East Hanover, N.J., 1979-82; mgr. Zoecon Corp., Wasco, Calif., 1983—; adj. prof. chemistry Calif. State U., Bakersfield, 1984—. Contbr. articles to profl. jours.; patentee in field. Advisor Explorer Scouts, North Chicago, 1970-71; coach Chester (N.J.) Little League, 1980-81; referee Am. Youth Soccer, Bakersfield, 1983. Fulbright fellow, 1968. Mem. Am. Chem. Soc. (lectr. 1981). Avocations: golf, tennis, skiing. Home: 1404 Corte Canalete Bakersfield CA 93309 Office: Zoecon Corp 5th and G Sts PO Box 220 Wasco CA 93280

WINKLER, WILLIAM HARRY, psychologist, sex therapist; b. Balt., June 20, 1949; s. Irving and Sally Myra (Wechsler) W.; 1 child, Eli. B.A., U. Vt., 1971, Ph.D., 1976. Lic. psychologist, Oreg.; lic. psychologist, Oreg. Dir. psychology Hallgarth Inst., Bourne, Mass., 1976-79; clin. asst. prof. Boston U., 1979-80; dir. crisis intervention Kaiser Permanente, Portland, 1980-83; pres., dir. Assocs. Psychol. Health, Portland; adj. clin. prof. Mass. Sch. Profl. Psychology, Boston, 1977-79; team psychologist Portland Trailblazers, 1985-86; cons. in field. Pub. Sexuality and Trauma In Rehabilitation in Trauma, 1987. N.J. State scholar, 1967-71, Rotary Internat. scholar, 1967. Mem. Am. Psychol. Assn., Oreg. Psychol. Assn., Am. Assn. Sex Counselors and Therapists (cert. sex therapist), Nat. Register of Health Service Providers in Psychology, Oreg. Acad. Profl. Psychologists, Tau Epsilon Phi. Home: 610 SE Linn St Portland OR 97202

WINN, FLORA BELLE, educator; b. Burnet, Tex., Feb. 25, 1940; d. Russell and Grace Marian (Ferguson) Schraeder; m. Luther Allen Winn, June 14, 1958; children: Cindy Ann, Gregory Hunter. AA (hon.), Yavapai Coll., 1978; BS summa cum laude, No. Ariz. U., 1981; MA No. Ariz. U., 1985. Cert. secondary sch. tchr., Ariz. Para-profl. Page (Ariz.) High Sch., 1967-78, reading tchr., 1979—; dist. coordinator Reading is a Family Affair; reading cons. Mem. NEA, Ariz. Edn. Assn., Page Edn. Assn., Ariz. Council Reading, Assn. Supervision and Curriculum Devel., Phi Kappa Phi. Democrat. Mem. Ch. of Christ. Clubs: Para Recreational, Tennis Racquet, Seasonal (Page). Home: 324 Elm St PO Box 374 Page AZ 86040 Office: Page High Sch PO Box 1927 Page AZ 86040

WINN, GEORGE, electrical equipment company executive. Pres. John Fluke Mfg. Co., Everett, Wash. Office: Office of Pres John Fluke Mfg Co 6920 Seaway Blvd Everett WA 98206 *

WINN, WILLIAM VINCENT, retail executive; b. St. Louis, Jan. 18, 1932; s. James and Mildred (Crume) W.; m. Rubia La Pearl, May 1965 (dec. May 1983); m. Katharine Menardi Stieglitz, June 15, 1984. Cert. data processing, NYU, IBM, UNIVAC, Gen. Electric, and Burroughs. V.p. data processing DiamonData, Chgo., 1969-75; data processing mgr. Trinair Industries, Lomita, Calif., 1975-79, Chase-Revel Co., Los Angeles, 1980-82; system coordinator Mattel Electronics Corp., Hawthorne, Calif., 1982-83; dir. data processing Judy's Merchandise Inc., Van Nuys, Calif., 1983—; v.p., treas. Data Processing Mgmt. Assn., Chgo., 1970, 73, 74; active Common, Hawthorne, Calif., 1983. Contbr. articles on computers to mags. Home: 11469 Stranwood Ave Granada Hills CA 91344 Office: Judy's Merchandise 7710 Haskell Ave Van Nuys CA 91406

WINNINGSTAD, C. NORMAN, computer company executive; b. Berkeley, Calif., Nov. 5, 1925; s. Chester Hafdan and Phyllis Amy (Whichello) W.; m. Dolores Constance Campbell, Mar. 24, 1948; children: Richard Norman, Dennis Steven, Joanne. B.S., U. Calif.-Berkeley, 1948; M.B.A., Portland State U., 1973; LL.D., Pacific U., 1982. Engr., TV Calif., San Francisco, 1948-50, Lawrence Berkeley Labs., 1950-58; mgr. Tektronix, Beaverton,

Oreg., 1958-70; chmn. Floating Point Systems Inc., Beaverton, 1970-76, vice chmn. 1976—; chmn. Lattice Internat., Inc., Portland, Oreg., 1984—; pres. Aircraft at your Call, Hillsboro, Oreg., 1982—; dir. Optical Data, Inc. Patentee in field. Trustee Oreg. Mus. Sci. and Industry 1983-86. Served with USNR, 1942-44. Named Free Enterprise Man of Yr., Nat. Mgmt. Assn., 1981; Oreg. Bus. Leader of Yr., Assn. Oreg. Industries, 1984. Mem. IEEE. Clubs: Arlington, University, Columbia Aviation Country.

WINOGROND, MARK HOWARD, city planner; b. Celina, Ohio, Jan. 18, 1947; s. Henry Roe and Esther (Thurmon) W.; m. Melanie Brown, Dec. 20, 1969 (div. 1980); 1 child, Gabriel; m. Jean Geisberg, Oct. 1, 1983. B.A., U. Wis.-Madison, 1969; M. City Planning, U. R.I., 1973. Riot photographer, U.S. New and World Report Mag., Washington, 1968-70; research analyst Children's Treatment Ctr., Madison, 1970; restoration carpenter Roger Wells, Inc., South Deerfield, Mass., 1971; teaching asst. U. R.I., Kingstown, 1972-73; sr. planner planning dept. City of San Francisco, 1973-80; dir. dept community devel. City of Lawndale, Calif., 1980-85; dirs. dept. community devel. City of West Hollywood, Calif., 1985—; dir. So. Calif. Planning Congress, Los Angeles; pres. Southwest Area Planning Council, Los Angeles, 1981-82; seismic element com. Gov.'s Seismic Safety Commn., Sacramento, 1983—. Co-author booklet, 1983. Bd. dirs. Tuum Est Inc., Substance Abuse Rehab. Ctr., Venice, Calif., 1980—; mem. criminal justice adv. com. NCCJ, 1984-85. Recipient Urban Design award Progressive Architecture Mag., 1978. Mem. Jaycees (named an Outstanding Young Man of Am., 1977), Am. Planners Assn. (award of Merit 1975, Nat. Merit Program award 1978), Am. Inst. Cert. Planners (cert.), Nat. Assn. Housing and Redevel. Officials, Nat. Trust Hist. Preservation, Inst. Urban Design., Urban Land Inst. Jewish. Home: 4305 Chase Ave Mar Vista CA 90066 Office: Dept Community Devel 8611 Santa Monica Blvd West Hollywood CA 90069

WINSEN, LOIS, entrepreneur; b. Detroit, Jan. 23, 1926; s. Maurice Jack and Cecelia (Bernstein) Kritchman; children: David, Janet, Julie. BBA, U. Mich., 1947; MA, Wayne State U., 1972. Creative dir. Simons Michelson Co., Detroit, 1965-70; pres. Imagination Communications, Inc., Southfield, Mich., 1970-78, Wolk Winsen, Inc., Southfield, 1979-81, Gemvest, Inc., San Diego, 1981-84, Market W. Prodns., Inc., San Diego, 1984—; gen. ptnr. Mood Ptnrs., Ltd., San Diego, 1984—. Producer/author (videocassette programs) Less Stress in 5 Easy Steps, 1984 (John Muir Med. Film Festival award 1986); author (videocassettes) The Lamaze Method, 1984, Exercises for Mothers to Be, 1983; contbr. articles to profl. jours. Mem. San Diego Venture Group, Mensa (treas. 1971-72). Home and Office: 3309 Caminito Gandara La Jolla CA 92037

WINSHIP, MYRON JAY, physician, microbiologist; b. Casper, Wyo., July 21, 1941; s. Myron Glean and Betty Jo (Harrington) W.; m. Marilynn Diane Louquet, Sept. 9, 1961; children: Rebecca Lynn, Amy Kathleen. Student, U. Mont., 1959-61, Mont. State U., 1961-62; BS, Northwestern U., 1964, MD, 1966. Diplomate Am. Bd. Internal Medicine, Am. Bd. Infectious Diseases, Am. Bd. Med. Microbiology; cert. in infection control. Intern Riverside (Calif.) Gen. Hosp., 1961-67, resident, 1969-71; fellow in infectious disease U. Calif. Davis, Sacramento, 1971-72; practice medicine Missoula, Mont., 1972—; bd. dirs. Missoula Community Microbiology Lab., 1981—; cons. Mont. Dept. Health, Helena, 1981—; cons. infectious disease Vets. Hosp., Ft. Harrison, Mont., 1976—; clin. asst. prof. U. Wash., Seattle, 1974-86; faculty affiliate in microbiology and pharmacy U. Mont., Missoula, 1976—. Contbr. articles to profl. jours. Mem. adv. com. Missoula C. of C., 1985; trustee Missoula Community Hosp., 1985-86; mem. Mont. Adv. Com. Biotech., Helena. Served to capt. USAF, 1967-69. Fellow ACP, Am. Acad. Microbiology; mem. Am. Soc. Internal Medicine, Am. Soc. Microbiology, Infectious Disease Soc. Avocations: reading, jazz, aviation. Office: 2825 Fort Missoula Rd Missoula MT 59801

WINSLOW, NICHOLAS SCOTT, economics consultant; b. Los Angeles, Feb. 24, 1943; s. Benjamen J. and Mary (Scott) W.; 1 child, Benjamen Scott. BA, Pomona Coll., 1964; MBA, Stanford U., 1966. V.p. Econs. Research Assocs., Los Angeles, 1967-74, Paramount Pictures subs. Gulf & Western Industries Inc., Hollywood, Calif., 1974-79; exec. v.p. United Video Industries, Hollywood, 1979-80; pres. Harrison Price Co., Los Angeles, 1980—. Exec. v.p., bd. dirs. Los Angeles Master Chorale; bd. dirs. Live Aid Found., Los Angeles, 1985, Liason Citizens Inc., Los Angeles, 1982-85. Mem. Pomona Coll. Alumni Assn. (pres. 1981-82), Econ. Round Table. Republican. Avocations: music, reading, skiing. Office: Harrison Price Co 876 S Bronson Ave Los Angeles CA 90005

WINSOR, TRAVIS WALTER, physician; b. San Francisco, Dec. 1, 1914; s. Samuel Wiley and Mabel Edna (Mc Carthy) W.; B.A., Stanford U., 1937, M.D., 1941; m. Elizabeth Adams, Sept. 1, 1939; children—David Wiley, Susan Elizabeth. Intern, Alameda County Hosp., Oakland, Calif., 1940-41; asso. fellow and instr. in medicine and cardiology Tulane U. Sch. Medicine, New Orleans, 1941-45; practice medicine specializing in cardiovascular disease; mem. staff Los Angeles County Hosp., Hosp. of Good Samaritan (hon.), St. Vincent's Med. Center, Los Angeles; clin. instr. in medicine U. So. Calif., Los Angeles, 1945-47, asst. clin. prof. medicine, 1947-61, asso. clin. prof. medicine, 1961-75, clin. prof. medicine, 1975—; dir. Meml. Heart Research Found., Inc., Los Angeles, 1957—. Diplomate Am. Bd. Internal Medicine. Fellow ACP, Am. Coll. Cardiology, Am. Coll. Chest Physicians, Internat. Coll. Angiology, Am. Coll. Angiology (pres. 1982-83), AMA, Am. Heart Assn.; mem. Am. Therapeutic Soc., Calif. Med. Assn., Los Angeles County Med. Assn., Calif. Soc. Internal Medicine, Los Angeles Soc. Internal Medicine, Am. Thermographic Soc. (pres. 1968-69), Royal Soc. Medicine London, Calif. Heart Assn., Internat. Cardiovascular Soc., Sigma Xi. Club: Los Angeles. Author: (with George E. Burch) A Primer of Electrocardiography, 1944; (with C. Hyman) A Primer of Peripheral Vascular Diseases, 1965; A Primer of Vectorcardiography, 1972; (with A. Kappert) Diagnosis of Peripheral Vascular Diseases, 1972; contbr. articles on cardiology to profl. jours. Home: 541 S Lorraine Blvd Los Angeles CA 90020 Office: 4041 Wilshire Blvd Los Angeles CA 90010

WINSTON, BRUCE EDWARD, printing co. exec.; b. Fairbanks, Alaska, July 19, 1950; s. William Barrett and Hulda Louise (Goodfellow) W.; student Wayne State Coll., 1968-69; B.S. in Psychology, U. Alaska, 1973; B.S. with highest honors in Printing Mgmt. and Tech. Rochester Inst. Tech., 1975; m. Kristie Sybil Collyer, Aug. 29, 1970; children—Kenneth Wray, Adam Collyer, Alexander Edward. With Ken Wray's Printing Inc., Anchorage, 1971—, now pres., also pres. Printmore Corp., 1983—. Mem. Wash.-Alaska Printing Industries Assn. (dir. 1976-77, 83-85), Printing Industries Am. (prodn. mgmt. com.), Nat. Assn. Printers and Lithographers, Graphic Arts Tech. Found., Am. Mgmt. Assn., Phi Kappa Phi. Lodge: Rotary (dir. 1978-81, pres. 1984-85). Home: 3421 Purdue St Anchorage AK 99508 Office: Ken Wrays Printing Inc 323 E Fireweed Ln Anchorage AK 99503

WINTER, IRWIN FLOYD, radiologist; b. Parkston, S.D., June 12, 1914; s. John G. and Aline Louise (Jaton) W.; m. Leona LaVon Luchsinger, June 23, 1939; children: Kathleen Dee, Brian Irwin, Kent Louis. BA, Huron (S.D.) Coll., 1935; BS, U. S.D., 1937; MD, Rush Med. Sch., Chgo., 1939; MS in Radiology, U. Minn., 1945. Intern Washington Blvd. Hosp., Chgo., 1939-40; resident St. Mary's and Pima County Hosps., Tucson, 1940-41; fellow in radiology Mayo Clinic, Rochester, Minn., 1941-44, jr. staff dept. radiology, 1944-46; practice medicine specializing in radiology Seattle, 1946-48; radiologist Swedish Hosp., Seattle, 1946-48, Salt Lake Clinic, Salt Lake City, 1948-51; instr. radiology U. Utah, 1948-50; practice medicine specializing in radiology Salt Lake City, 1948—. Mem. Utah Med. Soc., Salt Lake County Med. Soc., Am. Coll. Radiology, Utah Radiol. Soc. Club: Safari Internat. Lodge: Masons. Home: 900 Donner Way Apt #508 Salt Lake City UT 84108 Office: 508 E S Temple St Salt Lake City UT 84102

WINTER, JAMES, radiologist; b. N.Y.C., July 30, 1947; s. Alexander and Ruth (Cohen) W.; m. Donna Laure Cooper, Dec. 19, 1972; one child, Rebecca Cooper Winter. BS summa cum laude, Pa. State U., 1967; MD, Jefferson Med. Coll., 1969; MS, UCLA, 1972, PhD, 1978. Diplomate Nat. Bd. Med. Examiners, Am. Bd. Radiology. Intern U. Chgo., 1969-70; resident in radiology UCLA, 1970-74, fellow in neuroradiology, 1973-75, instr. diagnostic radiology, 1973-74, asst. prof., 1974-83, assoc. prof. diagnostic radiology and biomed. physics, 1983—; founder, chief scientist Info. Appliance Inc., Menlo Park, Calif., 1982—. Mem. editorial bd. Med. Imaging, 1976-79, Acta Thermografica, 1976-84; contbr. articles and revs. to profl. jours. Recipient James T. Case Meml. prize 1972; Picker found. fellow, 1974-77. Mem. AAAS, IEEE., Computer Soc. of IEEE, Am. Inst. Ultrasound in Medicine, Am. Coll. Radiology (com. computers), Am. Soc. Neuroradiology (sr.), Assn. Univ. Radiologists, Radiologic Soc. N.Am., Soc. Magnetic Resonance Imaging, Soc. Nuclear Medicine, Western Neuroradiol. Soc., Am. Assn. Physicists in Medicine, Am. Inst. Physics, Am. Soc. Photogrammetry and Remote Sensing, Assn. Computing Machinery, Optical Soc. Am., Pattern Recognition Soc., Soc. Photo-Optical Instrumentation Engrs., Sigma Xi, Phi Eta Sigma, Alpha Omega Alpha, Phi Delta Epsilon. Office: UCLA Med Ctr Dept Radiology Los Angeles CA 90024

WINTER, PHILLIP RAYMOND, insurance company executive; b. Meadville, Pa., Sept. 6, 1941; s. Philip Aloysius and Marion (Hovis) W.; m. Rhonda Lenore Jones, Apr. 13, 1966 (div. May 1970); 1 child, Phillip Raymond II. BA, San Diego State U., 1964. Asst. br. mgr. 1st Nat. Bank San Diego, 1967-69; polit. cons. San Diego, 1969-70; dir. exploring Boy Scouts Am., San Diego, 1970-72; underwriter properties Indsl. Indemnity, San Diego, 1972-75; acct. exec. John Burnham, San Diego, 1975-78; exec. v.p., chief ops. officer E.H. Crump of Calif., San Diego, 1985—; bd. dirs. San Diego Rescue Mission. Key mem. United Way San Diego, 1975-76; mgr. campaign Hubbard for County Supr., San Diego, 1978. Served as 1st. lt. U.S. Army, 1964-67. Mem. Nat. Assn. Profl. Surplus Lines Brokers. Republican. Lodge: Kiwanis. Avocations: stamp collecting, racquetball. Home: 1703 Primrose Dr El Cajon CA 92020 Office: E H Crump of Calif 9089 Clairemont Mesa Blvd San Diego CA 92123

WINTER, SHARON LEE, science educator; b. Tacoma, Aug. 12, 1951; d. Stanley Leon and Dorothy Elizabeth (Clawson) W. BS in Chemistry, U. Wash., 1974, MEd in Ednl. Adminstrn., 1984. Cert. tchr.; principal's credential. Urinalysis lab. asst. Children's Orthopedic Hosp., Seattle, 1975-78; sci. tchr. Rose Hill Jr. High Sch., Redmond, Wash., 1978-86, sci. dept. chmn., 1984-86; sci. tchr. Lake Washington High Sch., Kirkland, Wash., 1986—; lead secondary sci. tchr. Lake Washington Sch. Dist., 1987—; cons. Project STAR Harvard U., Cambridge, Mass., 1986—. Sorority advisor U. Wash. Mem. Nat. Sci. Tchrs. Assn. (conv. presenter 1986, honors tchr. award. 1985), Wash. Sci. Tchrs. Assn. (conf. presenter 1985). Avocations: music, dance. Home: 8009 NE 142d Pl Bothell WA 98001 Office: Lake Washington High Sch 12033 NE 80th St Kirkland WA 98033

WINTERS, MICHAEL ORIN, architect; b. Chgo., May 10, 1954; s. Jack Arthur and Cynthia Lee (Hanna) W.; m. Linda Torres, Sept. 1, 1978; 1 child, Stevan Michael Torres. BArch, U. Wis., Milw., 1977; MArch, U. Colo., 1980. Registered architect, Colo. Comml. designer Am. Timber Homes, Escanaba, Mich., 1975-78; designer Skidmore, Owings & Merrill, Denver, 1978-81; sr. assoc. C.W. Fentress & Assoc. P.C., Denver, 1981—. Prin. works include 1999 Broadway, Tucson City Ctr., Welton St. Garage. Recipient 2d place nat. design competition Precast Concrete Inst., 1980. Avocation: tournament racquetball. Office: CW Fentress and Assoc 1800 Grant #600 Denver CO 80203

WINTHROP, JOHN, real estate executive, lawyer; b. Salt Lake City, Apr. 20, 1947; m. Marilyn MacDonald, May 17, 1975; children: Grant Gordon, Clayton Hanford. AB cum laude, Yale U., 1969; JD magna cum laude, U. Tex., 1972. Bar: Calif. 1972. Law clk. U.S. Ct. of Appeals, Los Angeles, 1972-73; conseil juridique Coudert Freres, Paris, 1973-75; v.p. gen. counsel MacDonald Group, Ltd., Los Angeles, 1976-82, pres., chief exec. officer, 1982—, also bd. dirs. Mem. Calif. Bus. Properties Assn. (bd. advisors), Internat. Council Shopping Ctrs., Urban Land Inst., Nat. Realty Bd. Republican. Episcopalian. Clubs: California, The Beach. Office: The MacDonald Group Ltd 10100 Santa Monica Blvd Los Angeles CA 90067

WINTHROP, ROBERT HOMAN, cultural anthropologist, consultant; b. San Francisco, Apr. 29, 1950; s. Arnold Michael and Jane Gertrude (Jacobi) W.; m. Kathryn Eleanor Rice, Mar. 26, 1972; children: Rebecca, Anna. AB, U. Calif., Berkeley, 1972; MA, U. Minn., 1977, PhD, 1981. Vis. asst. prof. So. Oreg. State Coll., Ashland, 1982-86; prin. Winthrop Assocs. Cultural Research, Ashland, 1986—; cons. U.S. Dept. Energy, Albuquerque, 1985, U.S. Forest Service, Yreka, Calif., 1983-85. Mem. planning commn. City of Ashland, 1985—. Kraft scholar U. Calif., Berkeley, 1969; Nat. Fgn. Lang. Grad. fellow U.S. Office Edn., 1974-77. Fellow Am. Anthropol. Assn., Soc. Applied Anthropology, AAAS. Home and Office: 347 Guthrie St Ashland OR 97520

WINTON, DAVID LOUIS, aerospace company specialist; b. Bronx, N.Y., Nov. 12, 1950; s. Arthur and Florence Betty (Edelson) W. BA, U. Fla., 1972, MEd, 1973; JD, Western State U., 1975. Tchr. Fullerton (Calif.) Union High Sch. Dist., 1974-78; account rep. Civic Data Corp., Newport Beach, Calif., 1978-79; mgmt. tng. specialist Batten Seminars, Irvine, Calif., 1979-83; adminstr. profl. devel. McDonnell Douglas Corp., Long Beach, Calif., 1984-87; sr. specialist proposals devel. Douglas Aircraft Co., Long Beach, Calif., 1986—. Editor: (assoc.) Western State U. Law Rev., 1974-75. Vice-chmn. Women's Transitional Living Ctr., Orange County, Calif., 1980-81. Mem. Alpha Epsilon Pi (pres. 1970-71), Omicron Delta Kappa, Fla. Blue Key. Democrat. Jewish. Avocations: golf, reading. Home: 34122 Selva Rd #277 Laguna Niguel CA 92677

WINTON, JOHN DELBERT, civil engineer; b. June 10, 1944; s. Glenn Delbert and Victoria Ann (Ahlson) W.; m. Lynn Jonell Yaryan, Jan. 25, 1969; children—Jonell Marie, James David, Jerald Paul. B.S., N.Mex. State U., 1969. Registered profl. engr., N.Mex. Student trainee N.Mex. State Hwy. Dept., Santa Fe, 1962-68, asst. engr., 1969-71, geometric design engr., 1972-74, urban hwy. engr., 1975-78, engr. tech. services, 1979-82, dir. engring., 1983—. Bd. dirs. Christian Life Fellowship, Santa Fe, 1977-86, v.p., 1986—; active Gideons Internat., Santa Fe, 1982—. Mem. Am. Pub. Works Assn. Republican. Office: N Mex State Hwy Dept PO Box 1149 Santa Fe NM 87501

WIRT, MICHAEL JAMES, library director; b. Sault Ste. Marie, Mich., May 21, 1947; s. Arthur James and Blanche Marian (Carruth) W.; m. Barbara Ann Hallesy, Aug. 12, 1972; 1 child, Brendan. B.A., Mich. State U., 1969; M.L.S., U. Mich., 1971. Cert. librarian, Wash. Acting librarian Univ. Mich., Ctr. for Research on Econ. Devel., Ann Arbor, 1971-72; instnl. services librarian Spokane County Library Dist., Wash., 1972-76, asst. dir., 1976-79, acting dir., 1979, dir., 1980—. Mem. Adv. com. Partnership for Rural Improvement, Spokane, 1982-85, Wash. State Library Planning and Devel. Com., 1984—. Mem. Wash. Library Assn. (2d v.p. 1984-86, Merit award 1984, v.p., treas. State Users Group, 1986—), Wash. Library Network (rep. Computer Service Council 1983-86), Spokane Valley C. of C.

WIRTH, TIMOTHY ENDICOTT, senator from Colo.; b. Santa Fe, Sept. 22, 1939; s. Cecil and Virginia Maude (Davis) W.; m. Wren Winslow, Nov. 26, 1965; children: Christopher, Kelsey. B.A., Harvard U., 1961, M.Ed., 1964; Ph.D., Stanford U., 1973. White House fellow, spl. asst. to sec. HEW, Washington, 1967; asst. to chmn. Nat. Urban Coalition, Washington, 1968; dep. asst. sec. for edn. HEW, Washington, 1969; v.p. Great Western United Corp., Denver, 1970; mgr. Rocky Mountain office Arthur D. Little, Inc. (cons. firm), Denver, 1971-73; mem. 94th-99th congresses from 2d Colo. Dist., 1975-87, mem. energy and commerce com., sci. and tech. com., budget com.; chmn. subcom. telecommunications, fin. and consumer protection 94th-99th congresses from 2d Dist. Colo.; U.S. senator from Colo. 1987—, mem. arms services com., energy and natural resources com., budget com. Mem. Gov.'s Task Force on Returned Vietnam Vets., 1970-73; mem. bd. visitors U.S. Air Force Acad., 1978—; advisor Pres.'s Commn. on the 80's, 1979-80; trustee Planned Parenthood, Denver Head Start. Recipient Disting. Service award HEW, 1969; Ford Found. fellow, 1964-66. Mem. White House Fellows Assn. (pres. 1968-69), Denver Council Fgn. Relations (exec. com. 1974-75). Office: US Senate Office Senate Members Washington DC 20510 *

WIRTHLIN, DAVID BITNER, hospital administrator; b. Salt Lake City, Sept. 19, 1935; s. Joseph L. and Madeline (Bitner) W.; m. Anne Goalen, Apr. 25, 1961; children: Kimberly, Jennifer, David, Deborah, John, Marianne. B.S. in Bus. Adminstrn. cum laude, U. Utah, 1960; M.H.A., U. Minn., 1963. Asst. adminstr. Idaho Falls (Idaho) Latter Day Saints Hosp., 1963-66; asst. to adminstr. Latter Day Saints Hosp., Salt Lake City, 1966-67; 1st asst. adminstr. Latter Day Saints Hosp., 1967-70, asso. adminstr., 1970-73, adminstr., 1973-85; regional v.p. IHC Hosps., Inc., 1985—, Primary Children's Med. Center, 1973-75; v.p. cen. region Intermountain Health Care, Salt Lake City, 1984—; trustee Utah State Hosps.; mem. rev. com. Great Salt Lake Health Planning Agy., 1974; mem. Comprehensive Health Planning Rev. Com., 1975; chmn. Met. Hosp. Council, 1975; mem. bd. Utah Profl. Rev., 1975-77; adv. com. Robert Wood Johnson Found.'s Hosp.-based Rural Health Care Program. Fellow Am. Coll. Hosp. Adminstrs. (regent); mem. Am. Hosp. Assn., Utah Hosp. Assn. (past pres.), Western Assn. Hosps. (del. from Utah Hosp. Assn.), Council Teaching Hosps. Republican. Mormon. Clubs: Timpanogos, Bonneville Knife and Fork. Lodge: Kiwanis. Home: 2757 Saint Marys Way Salt Lake City UT 84108 Office: Intermountain Health Care 36 S State St Suite 2100 Salt Lake City UT 84111

WIRTZ, SHARON COLLEEN, retired guidance counselor; b. Great Falls, Mont., Aug. 18, 1934; d. Thomas Day and Ann Marie (Jorgensen) Pearson; m. Richard Andrew Tomcheck, June 7, 1958; 1 dau., Tracie Jo; m. Ronald LeRoy Wirtz, July 27, 1979. B.S., Mont. State U., 1956, M.Ed. in Guidance and Counseling, 1969; postgrad. U. Mont., Caroll Coll. Tchr., Great Falls High Sch., 1956-58; tchr., counselor Helena (Mont.) Sr. High Sch., 1959-69, counselor, 1969-74; dir. guidance Capital High Sch., Helena, 1974-86; workshop presenter; sec., dir. Helena Industries, Helena Family Teaching Ctr./Achievement Home. Publicity chmn. St. Peter's Hosp. Charity Ball; mem. adv. bd. Mont., Am. Coll. Testing; bd. dirs. Helena Symphony Soc.; sci. scholarship judge Mont. high schs. Helena Scottish Rite Educators scholar, 1968; Newspaper Fund Journalism fellow, 1965. Mem. Mont. Personnel and Guidance Assn., NEA, Mont. Edn. Assn., Helena Edn. Assn., Helena Mental Health Assn., Am. Personnel and Guidance Assn., Am. Sch. Counselors Assn., Alpha Omicron Pi, Delta Kappa Gamma (participant leadership/mgmt. seminar). Clubs: Helena Soroptimist (past pres.), Green Meadow Country. Home and Office: 5121 W Aster Dr Glendale AZ 85304

WIRZ, EDWIN FREDERICK, architect, interior designer; b. Denver, Oct. 4, 1955; s. Edwin and Rita (Hofer) W.; m. Roberta Lynn Scharringhausen, Sept. 6, 1980; 1 child, Tania Marie. BArch, U. Ill., 1977. Lic. architect, Colo., N.Y., Mich., Ga., Tex., Md., Va., Washington. Draftsman W.G. Karson & Assocs., Northbrook, Ill., 1978-80; architect Victor Huff & Assocs., Denver, 1980-84, Arthur Swords, Architects, Denver, 1984-85, R.N.M. Assocs., Conifer, Colo., 1985-86; prin. Design Services Inc., Englewood, Colo., 1986; corp. architect LePeeps Restaurants Inc., Denver, 1986—. Vol. St. Joseph's Blood Bank, Denver, 1980—. Mem. AIA, Nat. Council Archtl. Registration Bds. (cert.), Motoguzzi Nat. Owner's Club. Presbyterian. Avocations: skiing, motorcycles, mountain climbing, hiking, stamp collecting. Home: 16001-A E Radcliff Pl Aurora CO 80015 Office: LePeep Restaurants Inc 1777 S Harrison St Suite 802 Denver CO 80210

WISE, DALE ALAN, psychology educator; b. Borger, Tex., Nov. 22, 1936; s. Arjorie Lent and Mildred Elizabeth (Bowden) W.; m. Frances Ann McShane, June 20, 1961; (div. Nov. 1971); children: Bowden, Steven; m. Toni Lee Pryor, June 10, 1972; children: Christopher, Graham, Joshua. Student, U. N.Mex., 1954; BA, U. Ark., 1958, MA, 1960; PhD, U. Calif., Berkeley, 1971. Asst. prof. psychology Mt. Holyoke Coll., South Hadley, Mass., 1969-75; lectr., assoc. prof. San Jose (Calif.) State U., 1975—. Contbr. articles to profl. jours. Served to lt. USNR, 1960-64. Rigall scholar U. Ark., 1960. Mem. Am. Psychol. Assn., Animal Behavior Soc., Internat. Soc. Research on Aggression, Sigma Xi. Democrat. Office: San Jose State U Dept Psychology San Jose CA 95172

WISE, JANET ANN, university program administrator; b. Detroit, Aug. 8, 1953; d. Donald Price and Phyllis (Licht) W.; m. Peter Anthony Eisenklam, Oct. 16, 1976 (div. Aug. 1982); m. Edward Henry Moreno, Mar. 31, 1984; 1 child, Talia. Student, U. N.Mex., 1971-73. Editorial asst., writer The New Mexican, Santa Fe, 1975-77; press asst., press sec. Office of Gov. N.Mex., Santa Fe, 1979-82; dir. pub. relations City of Santa Fe, 1983-84, Coll. Santa Fe, 1984—. Bd. dirs. Santa Fe Better Bus. Bur., 1984—, Santa Fe Girl's Club, 1986—. Recipient Exemplary Performance award Office Gov. of N.Mex., Santa Fe, 1981, Outstanding Service award United Way of Santa Fe, 1982. Mem. Pub. Relations Soc. Am., N.Mex. Press Women. Democrat. Unitarian. Avocation: piano. Home: 104 Lugar de Oro Santa Fe NM 87501 Office: Coll Santa Fe La Salle Hall St Michael's Dr Santa Fe NM 87501

WISE, MICHAEL EDWIN, electrical engineer; b. Granite City, Ill., Jan. 20, 1954; s. Maynard Leo, and Arlene Rose (Overy) W.; m. Joan Marie Schulte, Apr. 24, 1982. Student, St. Louis U., 1971-72, U. Mo., St. Louis, 1972-74, U. Mo., Columbia, 1974-77; BSEE, U. Mo., 1977. Registered profl. engr., Calif., N.Y., Mo. Elec. engr. HOK Inc., St. Louis, 1978-80; mgr., elec. engr. EDM Inc., Kansas City, Mo., 1980-83; dir. elec. engring. HNTB, Kansas City, 1983-85; industry appications specialist IBM Corp., Los Angeles, 1985—. Asst. coach Northwest High Sch. Hockey Team, Kansas City, 1982-84. Named one of Outstanding Young Men of Am., Internat. Jaycees, 1983. Mem. IEEE, Computer Soc. of IEEE, NSPE. Republican. Roman Catholic. Avocations: racquetball, ice hockey, reading, films. Home: 1434 19th St 103 Santa Monica CA 90404 Office: IBM 11601 Wilshire Los Angeles CA 90025-1738

WISEMAN, JAY DONALD, photographer, heating contractor; b. Salt Lake City, Dec. 23, 1952; s. Donald Thomas and Reva (Stewart) W.; m. Barbara Helen Taylor, June 25, 1977; children: Jill Reva, Steve Jay. Ed. Utah State U., Logan, U. Utah. Cert. profl. photographer. Pvt. practice photography; v.p. A&T Heating. Recipient Grand prize Utah State Fair, 1986, Kodak Crystal for Photographic Excellence, 1986. Mem. Profl. Photographers Assn. Am., Rocky Mountain Profl. Photographers (Best of Show 1987), Toronto Camera Club, Inter-Mountain Profl. Photographers Assn. (Master's Trophy 1982, 86, Photographer of Yr. award 1986), Photographers Soc. Am (Best of Show award Utah chpt. 1986). Mormon. One man shows include Busath's 701 Gallery, Salt Lake City; represented in Salt Lake City Internat. Airport permanent photo exhibit; photographs published profl. jours. Office: 540 W 600 S Bountiful UT 84010

WISEMAN, JOHN RANDLE, mechanical engineer; b. Paterson, N.J., Dec. 27, 1923; s. John and Elizabeth (Heatley) W.; m. Edna M. Davis, July 12, 1946 (June 1985); children: Steven, Susan, Lynn, Randy; m. Florence Elizabeth Schillmoeller, Nov. 11, 1985. BSME, Stevens Inst. Tech., 1949. Project engr. Bendix, Teterboro, N.J., 1949-55; dir. engring. Thiokol, Denville, N.J., 1955-69, Fairchild Control Systems, Manhatten Beach, Calif., 1969—. Sr. warden St. Alban's Episcopal Ch., Oakland, N.J., 1962-68. Served with USNR, 1943-45. Mem. Am. Def. Preparedness Assn., Soc. Automotive Engrs., Assn. Old Crows, Navy League of U.S. Republican. Avocations: cycling, cabinet making. Home: 17671 Wrightwood Ln Huntington Beach CA 92649 Office: Fairchild Control Systems Co 1800 Rosecrans Ave Manhatten Beach CA 90266-3797

WISEMAN, T. JAN, association executive, educator, consultant; b. Prairie du Chien, Wis., Mar. 26, 1941; s. C. Edward and Gertrude Jeanette (Roth) W. J.B.S., U. Wis., 1964; M.S.Ed., No. Ill. U., 1968, C.A.S., 1979; m. Evelyn J. Knell. Journalism tchr. Glenbrook North High Sch., Northbrook, Ill., 1966-68; dean community edn. Kishwaukee Coll., Malta, Ill., 1968-79; staff v.p., dir. edn., mktg. Farm and Land Inst., Nat. Assn. Realtors, Chgo., 1979-81; exec. v.p. Am. Soc. Farm Mgrs. and Rural Appraisers, Denver, 1982-85; exec. v.p. Profl. Ins. Agts. of Colo., Inc., 1984—; dir. Profl. Devel. Inst., Denver, 1982-85; exec. v.p. Profl. Ins. Agts. Colo., 1985—; human devel. cons. Bd. dirs. DeKalb-Kane County (Ill.) CETA, 1976-77, Nat. Scholastic Press Assn., 1974-79; co-founder Community Enrichment Assn., 1975. Mem. Am. Soc. Assn. Execs., Am. Soc. Tng. and Devel., Nat. Assn. Realtors, Journalism Edn. Assn. (nat. pres. 1973-75 Carl Towley award 1977). Author: Creative Communications: Teaching Mass Media, 1971, 74. Home: 13569 Antares Littleton CO 80124 Office: 8100 E Arapahoe Rd Suite 305 Englewood CO 80112

WISKOCIL, ROBERT LAFE, physician; b. San Francisco, Aug. 5, 1949; s. John Clement Wiskocil and Elizabeth (Monson) Worthington; m. Sharon Olsen, June 30, 1976. BS, Stanford U., 1971; MD, U. Calif.-San Diego, La Jolla, 1976. Diplomate Am. Bd. Internal Medicine, Rheumatology. Resident in internal medicine UCLA Med. Ctr., Los Angeles, 1976-78; research assoc. biochemistry lab. NIH, Bethesda, Md., 1978-80; rheumatology fellow

U. Calif.-San Francisco Med. Ctr., 1980-82, asst. prof. medicine, 1982-83; rheumatologist Kaiser Med. Group, Fremont, Calif., 1984—. Contbr. numerous articles to profl. jours. U. Calif. Regent's scholar, 1971-76. Mem. AMA, AAAS, Phi Beta Kappa. Republican. Avocations: photography, music. Home: 29 Horseshoe Ct Walnut Creek CA 94596

WISKOFF, MARTIN FRED, research psychologist; b. N.Y.C., Mar. 12, 1935; s. Sam and Sonia (Sulzberg) W.; children: Mindy, Julie, Sharon. BA, CCNY, 1956; MA, U. Md., 1959, PhD, 1963. Research psychologist NIMH, Bethesda, Md., 1958-59, Army Research Inst., Washington, 1959-63; mgr. selection research program Bur. Naval Personnel, Washington, 1963-67, head psychol. research br., 1967-72; research mgr. Navy Personnel Research and Devel. Ctr., San Diego, 1972-83, lab. dir., 1983-87; sr. scientist Def. Personnel Security Research and Edn. Ctr., Monterey, Calif., 1987—; vis. prof. Naval Postgrad. Sch., Monterey, 1970-71. Editor Mil. Psychology jour.; contbr. articles to profl. jours. Pres. Kingswood Civic Assn., 1966-67. Served with AUS, 1958-59. Fellow Am. Psychol. Assn., Inter-Univ. Seminar; mem. Tech. Coop. Program, Mil. Testing Assn., Psi Chi. Office: Def Personnel Security Research and Edn Ctr 99 Pacific St Monterey CA 93940

WISOTSKY, JERRY JOSEPH, graphic arts company executive; b. N.Y.C., Oct. 22, 1928; s. Abraham I. and Anna P. (Slipoy) W.; student CCNY, 1946-48; m. Helen E. Lerner, Nov. 12, 1949; children—Pearle Eve Wisotsky Marr, Ronald Ian. Apprentice, Triplex Lithographic Corp., N.Y.C., 1949-51; pres. Kwik Offset Plate Inc., N.Y.C., 1952-59; chmn. bd. Imperial Litho/Graphics Inc., Phoenix, 1959—; ptnr. M.J. Enterprises, Phoenix, 1959—. Mem. bd. appeals, Phoenix, 1974-76; pres. Ariz. Found. for Handicapped, 1976—; campaign chmn. corp. div. United Way, 1975, gen. campaign chmn., 1977; trustee St. Luke's Hosp. Med. Center; pres. Phoenix Jewish Community Center, 1970-71; v.p. bd. dirs. United Way; pres. United Way Phoenix-Scottsdale, 1981; chmn. Valley of Sun United Way, 1981; chmn. Ariz. bd. dirs. Anti-Defamation League, also nat. commr.; bd. dirs. NCCJ; charter pres. Metro-Phoenix Citizens Council, 1986-87; bd. dirs. Boys' Clubs Met. Phoenix, 1986-87, v.p., 1987—; bd. dirs. Ariz.-Weizmann Inst., 1984, Phoenix Community Alliance, 1984, Ariz. Mus. Sci. and Tech., 1984, Golden Gate Settlement Devel. Council; treas. Dean's Council of 100 Coll. Bus. Ariz. State U.; chmn. Combined Health Resources, 1984; bd. adv. Mountain Bell-Ariz., 1984; bd. dirs. Phoenix Community Alliance; mem. 1986 Nat. UN Day Program; hon. bd. dirs. Valley of the Sun United Way; past chmn. bd. dirs. St. Luke's Hosp., Phoenix; bd. dirs. Combined Health Resources, 1982-83. Recipient Disting. Service award Rotary Internat., Phoenix, 1985, Humanitarian award Nat. Asthma Ctr. Nat. Jewish Hosp., Torch of Liberty award Anti-Defamation League, 1977; 12 Who Care Hon Kachina award, 1980; Tom Chauncey award, 1984; Volunteerism award Valley of the Sun United Way; named Phoenix Man of Yr., 1985. Mem. Am. Greyhound Found. (bd. dirs.), Nat. Jewish Ctr. Immunology & Respiratory Medicine, Met. C. of C. (intercity com.), Ariz. Jewish Hist. Soc. (bd. dirs. 1984), Valley Forward Assn., Econ. Club Phoenix (founding bd. dirs. 1984). Home: 7520 N 1st St Phoenix AZ 85020 Office: M J Enterprises 210 S 4th Ave Phoenix AZ 85003

WISSLER, GEORGE DENNIS, sales and marketing executive; b. Olney, Ill., June 23, 1939; s. Orpha Dill and Marjory Helen (Stettler) W.; m. Beverly J. Trueblood, June 23, 1962 (div. 1979); m. Janice B. Pascoe, Mar. 23, 1980; chidlren—Kelley Gayle, Wendy Carol. Student Ind. Central U., 1960-62. Sales dir. Howard W. Sams & Co., ITT, Indpls., 1965-77; pres. Green-Wissler Sales Co., Indpls., 1977-83; gen. sales mgr. Formaster Corp., San Jose, Calif., 1983-84; v.p. sales and mktg. Mag-Media, Santa Rosa, Calif., 1984-86, gen. mgr. media products Mountain Computer, Scotts Valley, Calif., 1986— . Served with USN, 1958-60. Mem. Electronic Industry Assn. (Chmn., co-chmn. 1974-77), Electronic Rep. Assn. (coms., Man of Yr. 1976). Republican. Methodist. Home: 305 W Main St Los Gatos CA 95030 Office: Mountain Computer 360 El Pueblo Rd Scotts Valley CA 95066

WISSLER, STANLEY GEBHART, cons. geologist; b. N.Y.C., Mar. 31, 1900; s. Clark and Viola (Gebhart) W.; B.S., Earlham Coll., 1922; M.A., Columbia U., 1923; m. Agnes Elizabeth Meerhoff, Oct. 26, 1926; children—Ann Elizabeth Wissler Malcolm, Clark William, John Benjamin. Grad. asst. in geology and paleontology Columbia U., 1923-25; various positions oil and gas exploration and research and adminstrn., Alaska, contiguous U.S., Can., Mex., Costa Rica, Philippines, Indonesia, Malaysia, Thailand, Burma, Pakistan, Ecuador, Union Oil Co. Calif., 1925-65; oil and gas cons., 1965-68; cons. Internat. Resources Co., S.E. Asia, 1969-70; partner Hazzard, Morris & Assos., Los Angeles, 1970-73; cons. geologist, Long Beach, Calif., 1973—. Registered geologist, Calif. Fellow Geol. Soc. Am., AAAS; mem. Am. Assn. Petroleum Geologists (cert. petroleum geologist, hon. life mem. Pacific sect.), Soc. Econ. Paleontologists and Mineralgists (hon. life mem. pres. 1937, pres. Pacific sect., 1928), Am. Inst. Profl. Geologists (cert.), Geol. Soc. Malaysia, Am. Security Council, Sigma Xi. Republican. Congregationalist. Clubs: Petroleum of Los Angeles, Retired Oil Man's. Contbr. sci. papers to profl. publs. in field. Home: 4245 Chestnut Ave Long Beach CA 90807

WITCHER, JOHN EDGAR, manufacturing company executive; b. Indpls., May 11, 1938; s. Edgar and Grace L. (Shrum) W.; m. Marilyn Jean Minor, Mar. 26, 1942; children—John M., Mark A. B.S., Ind. U.-Bloomington, 1961; LL.B. Blackstone Sch. Law, 1969. Quality engr. Cummins Engine Co., Inc., Columbus, Ind. and divs., 1961-70, materials dir., 1969-70; ops. mgr., v.p. ops. Remcom Systems, Inc., Garland, Tex., 1970-72; v.p., pres. Transtronics Corp., Garland, 1972-74; dir. purchasing, dir. materials Mitsubishi Aircraft Internat., Inc., San Angelo, Tex., 1975-80; dir. material Weber Aircraft div. Kidde, Inc., Burbank, Calif., 1980-82; dir. ops. control, 1982—. Mem. Am. Statis. Assn., Soc. Mfg. Engrs. Club: Masons. Office: Weber Aircraft Div 2820 Ontario St Burbank CA 91510

WITEK, GARY HERBERT, marketing professional; b. Denver, Mar. 26, 1948; s. Rudy Herbert Witek and Lilah (Hayes) Neal; m. Gloria Lee Gevara, Jan. 29, 1971 (div.); m. Loretta Baretta, June 6, 1984; children: Christina, Todd, Gina. Student, U. Denver, 1966-69. Sales assoc. May D & F, Denver, 1964-68; sales rep. Witek Assocs., Inc., Denver, 1968-70, v.p., 1970-73, pres., 1973—. Recipient Million Dollar Sales award Metal Masters Co., Smyrna, Del., 1976, 77, 80, Million Dollar Sales award Cambro, Inc., Huntington Beach, Calif., 1979, 82, 83, 84; named Salesman of Yr., Toastmaster Comml., Algonquin, Ill., 1977, 78, 79, 80. Mem. Mktg. Agts. for Food Service Industry (Denver regional chmn. 1976—). Home: 3555 E Euclid Ave Littleton CO 80121 Office: Witek Assocs 2496 W 2nd Ave Unit 1 Denver CO 80223

WITHAM, BARRY BATES, drama educator; b. Newcastle, Maine, Dec. 11, 1939; s. Cecil Leroy Witham and Afton Eloise Bates; m. Sheila Ann McNamara, Dec. 28, 1964 (div. June 1972); children: Michael Bates, Drake Sean; m. Margaret Ann Thomas, Aug. 13, 1976. BA in English magna cum laude, Tufts U., 1961; MA in Drama, U. Iowa, 1964; PhD in Theatre, Ohio State U., 1968. Asst. prof. drama Miami U., Oxford, Ohio, 1968-72, assoc. prof., 1972-78, prof., 1978-80; prof. U. Wash., Seattle, 1980—; dramaturge Seattle Repertory Theatre, 1983—. Co-author: Uncle Sam Presents, 1982; contbr. numerous articles to profl. and scholarly jours. Vol. Big Bros., Inc., Seattle, 1984—. Grantee NEA, 1982; named Outstanding Tchr. Miami U., 1978. Mem. Am. Soc. Theatre Research (exec. com. 1982-84), Am. Theater Assn. (chmn. commn. theater research 1982). Democrat. Avocations: golf, running. Home: 11909 80th Pl NE Kirkland WA 98034 Office: U Wash Dept Drama Seattle WA 98195

WITHERSPOON, JAMES DONALD, biology educator; b. Springfield, Mo., Dec. 19, 1933; s. Harry H. and Lucy Catherine (Applegate) W.; m. Rebecca Jane Hutto, Jan. 24, 1958; children: Sarah Jane, John Edward. BS, Purdue U., 1955, MS, 1960, PhD, 1963. From instr. to asst. prof. biology Western Md. Coll., Westminster, 1960-68; assoc. prof. Southwestern at Memphis Coll., 1968-76; free-lance writer Phoenix, 1976-82; adj. prof. Grand Canyon Coll., Phoenix, 1982-84, prof., 1984—, chmn. dept. scis., 1985—; cons. Doubleday & Co., Garden City, N.Y., 1960-62, Narco Bio-Systems, Houston, 1972-76. Author: The Functions of Life, 1970, Human Physiology, 1984; co-author: The Living Laboratory, 1960; co-author numerous tapes and programs, 1973—. Grantee Grass Found., 1962-72, Ariz. Commn. for Postsecondary Edn., 1985-87. Mem. AAAS, Am. Inst. Biol. Scis., Ariz. Alliance for Sci. (bd. dirs. 1986—, exec. bd. dirs.), Sigma Xi. Republican. Presbyterian. Avocations: hiking, camping. Home: 17122 Grande Blvd Fountain Hills AZ 85268 Office: Grand Canyon Coll 3300 W Camelback Phoenix AZ 85061

WITHNER, CARL LESLIE, retired botany educator, orchid consultant, writer, researcher; b. Indpls., Mar. 3, 1918; s. Carl Leslie and Martha (Myers) W.; m. Patricia d'Almeida Maxwell, June 4, 1941; children: Dennis, Rika, Holly. AB, U. Ill., 1941; MA, Yale U., 1943, PhD, 1948, postgrad. med., 1946-47. Tchr. CUNY, Bklyn., 1948-79; curator orchids Bklyn. Botanic Garden, 1948-75, N.Y. Botanical Garden, 1975-79; accredited judge Am. Orchid Soc., West Palm Beach, Fla., 1961—. Author: A Book of Orchids, 1985; editor: The Orchids: A Scientific Survey, 1959, The Orchids: Scientific Studies, 1972, Encyclopedia of Rose Culture, 1957; contbr. articles on horticulture to profl. jours. Served as pvt. U.S. Army, 1943-46. Fellow Guggenheim Found., U.S., South Am., England, 1962. Mem. Botanical Soc. Am., Am. Soc. Plant Physiologists, Am. Orchid Soc. (hon. life), Torrey Botanical Club. Avocations: growing orchids, collecting Paisley shawls, pressed glass, glass canes. Home and Office: 2015 Alabama St Bellingham WA 98226

WITKAY, CATHY SUNDERLAND, telephone company executive; b. Orange, N.J., May 16, 1955; d. Charles Benjamin and Gladys Ann (Ludwig) Sunderland; m. Paul Richard Witkay, Jan. 2, 1977. BA in Spanish, U. Ill., 1977; MBA, St. Mary's Coll., Moraga, Calif., 1986. Cert. tchr., Ill., Mich. Product mgr. Sunset Designs, San Ramon, Calif., 1978-81, mktg. communications mgr., 1981-83; staff mgr. advt. Pacific Bell, San Francisco, 1983-85, mgr. corp. advt., corp. indentity, 1985-86; mgr. corp. advt., corp. identity Pacific Telesis Group, 1986—. Recipient Best Informational Brochure award Pub. Relations Soc. Am., 1986. Mem. Am. Mktg. Assn., San Francisco Advt. Club (silver award 1986), Alpha Gamma Delta. Avocations: aerobics, skiing, calligraphy. Home: 24 Benthill Ct Lafayette CA 94549 Office: Pacific Telesis 140 New Montgomery Room 904 San Francisco CA 94105

WITKAY, PAUL R., chemical company executive; b. Evanston, Ill., Oct. 9, 1954; m. Cathy Jean Sunderland, Jan. 2, 1977. BSChemE, U. Ill., 1976; MBA, St. Mary's Coll., Moraga, Calif., 1986. Process engr. Dow Chem. Co., Midland, Mich., 1976-77; tech. specialist Betz Labs., Concord, Calif., 1977-79; prin., exec. dir. Witkay Assocs., Concord, 1979-83; dir. resource mgmt. Cardox Corp. div. Liquid Air, Walnut Creek, Calif., 1983—. Mem. Pvt. Industry Council of Contra Costa County, Concord, 1980—, vice chmn. 1982-83, chmn. 1983-85. Mem. Calif. Assn. Personnel Cons. (bd. dirs. 1981-83), Concord C. of C. (bd. dirs. 1981-83), Am. Inst. Chem. Engrs. Home: 24 Benthill Ct Lafayette CA 94549

WITMER, FRANK JOSEPH, chemist, consultant; b. Lewiston, Idaho, June 10, 1924; s. Frank Joseph and Ocie Belle (Croy) W.; m. Marilyn O'Malley, June 3, 1955; children: Moira F., Frank J. III. SCD (hon.), Nat. Med. Coll. China, Shanghai, 1947; BS in Chemistry, Denver U., 1950, MS in Chemistry, 1951; postgrad., U. Calif., Berkeley, 1953, MIT, 1959. Chief chemist USAF/SAC, Vandenberg AFB, 1961-62; project engr. Lockheed Missile/Space Ctr., Sunnyvale, Calif., 1962-65; prin. engr. The Boeing co., Seattle, 1965—; cons. USAF, 1970—, U. Colo. Med. Sch., Denver, 1970—, various nat. and internat. airlines. Contbr. articles (with others) to profl. jours. Served to 1st lt. USAF, 1942-46. Mem. AAAS, Am. Chem. Soc., Coblenz Soc. Republican. Roman Catholic. Club: AERO (Portland). Avocations: exploring white water rivers, Indian lore. Home: 16538 27th Ave NE Seattle WA 98155 Office: The Boeing Co 7700 E Marginal Way S Seattle WA 98124

WITT, NEIL ORAND, educator, management consultant; b. Milw., Oct. 30, 1941; s. Orand A. and Ruth E. W.; A.S., Clark County Community Coll., 1974; B.S., U. Nev., 1976; M.B.A., Golden Gate U., 1980; student Nev. So. U., 1965. Radiol. tech. So. Nev. Meml. Hosp., Las Vegas, 1965-79; instr. in mgmt. Clark County Community Coll., North Las Vegas, 1976—, instr. CETA program, 1979-80, coordinator intermurals, student activities Clark County Community Coll., 1986—; instr. psychology and human behavior Nat. U., 1985—; tech. cons. Lincoln County Hosp., Caliente, Nev., 1974; mgmt. cons. MCS Assos., 1979—; coordinator bus. lab. Clark County Community Coll.; instr. bus. mgmt. Nev. State Prison, 1980-82; instr. psychology & human behavior, Nat. U., N. Las Vegas, Nev.; promotions and fundraising, Radio Sta. KFM-Radio, Las Vegas, 1979—, pub. relations 1980-82; owner Neil O. Witt & Assocs., Mgmt. and Tng. Cons. Mem. Nat. Bus. Edn. Assn., AAUP, Am. Registry Radiologic Techs., Am. Soc. Radiologic Techs. (speakers bur.), Am. Mgmt. Assn. Home: 5809 Granada Ave Las Vegas NV 89107

WITT, SUSAN VIRGINIABETH, social worker; b. San Antonio, Apr. 27, 1945; d. Patrick W. and Ardeth F. (Yeargan) Armstrong; m. Robert G. Witt, Apr. 1, 1966. BA, U. Okla., 1966; MSW, U. Denver, 1974. Caseworker Adams County Social Services, Commerce City, Colo., 1967-76; social worker Sch. Dist. 50, Westminster, Colo., 1976—. Facilitator adventures in faith program Ch. Religious Sci., Lakewood, Colo., 1985—. Mem. Nat. Assn. Social Workers (cert.), Just As You Are. Democrat. Mem. Ch. Religious Sci. Club: Toastmasters (Lakewood, Colo.) (pres., 1986, sec. 1986—). Home: 5400 Estes Ct Arvada CO 80002 Office: Sch Dist 50 4476 W 68th Ave Westminster CO 80030

WITTBERGER, RUSSELL GLENN, advertising executive; b. Milw., July 7, 1933; s. Anton George and Libbie Elizabeth (Kresnicka) W.; m. Patricia Elizabeth Bradley, June 26, 1971; children: Steven, Robert, Elizabeth, Gary, Scott, Jennifer. BS in Journalism, Marquette U., 1955. Pres. Rand Broadcasting Corp., Miami, Fla., 1970-73; v.p., gen. mgr. KCBQ Inc., San Diego, 1973-78; pres. Charter Broadcasting Co., San Diego, 1978-83; exec. v.p. Cantor Advt. Corp., San Diego, 1983-85; v.p., gen. mgr. Boyd and Farmer Advt., San Diego, 1985-86; v.p., gen. mgr., prin. KLZZ-FM, San Luis Obispo, Calif., 1987—. Mem. Bldg. Industry Assn., San Diego Broadcasters (pres. 1973-75). Republican. Avocations: swimming, travel, sports. Home: 451 Camino Elevado Bonita CA 92002 Office: KLZZ-FM 321 Madonna Rd Suite 23 San Luis Obispo CA 93401

WITTE, CAROL ROSE, editor; b. Norfolk, Nebr., Dec. 9, 1938; d. Herman F.C. and Gertrude (Richter) Pohlman; m. Arvel B. Witte, June 28, 1959; children: Gretchen, John. BA, Calif. State U., Los Angeles, 1960. Cert. tchr. (life), Calif. Resource tchr. for gifted students Pasadena (Calif.) Unified Sch. Dist., 1965-68, Torrance (Calif.) Unified Sch. Dist., 1968; resource tchr. for gifted students and fifth grade tchr. Palos Verdes Peninsula Unified Sch. Dist., Rolling HIlls, Calif., 1968-83; pub., author Tchrs. Publ., Manhattan Beach, Calif., 1973-83; editor-in-chief Frank Schaffer Publs., Torrance, 1983—. Author: Fun with Metric Measurement, 1973, Early Childhood Metric Fun, 1974, Learing About the Computer, 1983, Simple Computer Programs, Daily Writing Activities; editor numerous books, editor Schooldays mag., 1983—, Classmate mag., 1985—. Chmn. Christian Edn. Bd. Rolling HIlls Covenant Ch., 1983-84. Mem. Nat. Council Tchrs. of Math., Nat. Council Tchrs. of English. Republican. Avocations: traveling, reading. Office: Frank Schaffer Publs 19771 Magellan Dr Torrance CA 90502

WITTE, MATTHEW LLOYD, real estate developer; b. Greenwich, Conn., July 19, 1957; s. Martin W. and Carol (Siff) W.; m. Elizabeth Anne Leyburn, June 23, 1985. BSArch, Cornell U., 1979. Registered architect, Calif. Architect Wudtke Watson Davis, San Francisco, 1979-80; real estate developer Grosvenor Internat., San Francisco, 1980-84, Bay West Devel., San Francisco, 1984—. Mem. Nat. Assn. Office and Indsl. Parks, Urban Land Inst., Cornell Real Estate Council. Club: Belden (San Francisco). Office: Bay West Devel 450 Sansome St San Francisco CA 94111

WITTELES, ELEONORA MEIRA, physicist; b. Jerusalem, July 14, 1938; d. Salomon and Rivka (Komornik) Witteles. B.S., Fordham U., 1962, M.S., 1963; M.S., N.Y.U., 1965; Ph.D. (research fellow), Yeshiva U., 1969. Postdoctoral fellow Bar-Ilan U., Israel, 1969-70, asst. prof., 1970-72; ind. cons., 1972-80; sr. research scientist Atlantic Richfield Co., Los Angeles, 1980-84; sr. scientist Hughes Aircraft Co., El Segundo, Calif., 1984—. Mem. Am. Phys. Soc., N.Y. Acad. Scis., IEEE, IEEE Engring. in Medicine and Biology Soc., IEEE Magnetics Soc., Com. on Status of Women in Physics. Research on solid state physics, superconductivity, applied material scis., inventor med. instrumentation and cryogenic instrumentation. Home: 4714 Browndeer Ln Palos Verdes CA 90274 Office: Electro-Optical and Data Systems Group Hughes Aircraft Co 2000 El Segundo Blvd El Segundo CA 90245

WITTEMYER, JOHN, lawyer; b. Boulder, Colo., Dec. 19, 1939; s. Leonard and Beatrice Augusta (Dickhut) W.; m. Nancy Jean Vincent, June 6, 1964; children—Jon Vincent, Christopher Glen, Luke Leonard. B.S.C.E., U. Colo., 1962, B.S. in Bus., 1962, LL.B., 1965. Bar: Colo. 1965, Alaska 1965. Law clk. U.S. Supreme Ct. Alaska, 1965; dist. atty. 1st Jud. Dist. Alaska, Juneau, 1966-67; sole practice, Boulder, 1967-73; ptnr. Moses, Wittemyer, Harrison & Woodruff, P.C., Boulder, 1973—; gen. counsel Platte River Power Authority, 1975—; chmn. bd., chief exec. officer Crowley land and Devel. Co., subs. Aetna Casualty and Surety Co., Ordway, Colo., 1970-75. Mem. ABA, Colo. Bar Assn., Boulder Bar Assn., Colo. Cattlemen's Assn. Republican. Methodist. Club: Country. Home: Sunshine Canyon Boulder CO 80302 Office: PO Box 1440 Boulder CO 80306

WITTENBERG, GEORGE KARL, chemistry educator; b. Chgo., Apr. 25, 1948; s. George Martin and Myrtle E. (Olsen) W. BA in Chemistry magna cum laude, Elmhurst Coll., 1970; PhD in Chemistry, Ariz. State U., 1979. Instr. Phoenix Coll., 1978-84; vis. asst. prof. chemistry Ariz. State U., Tempe, 1981—; instr. PSAP, Tempe, 1981-83, John Hopkins U., Tempe, 1984; cons. Eagle Resources, Phoenix, 1986. Mem. Am. Chem. Soc., Soc. Applied Spectroscopy, ARiz. ARms Assn. (bd. dirs. 1981-86), Phi Lambda Upsilon. Club: Ariz. Arms Assn. (dir. 1981-86). Avocations: poetry writing, arms collecting, leather work, hunting. Home: 1022 S Butte Ave Tempe AZ 85281 Office: Ariz State U Chemistry Dept Tempe AZ 85287

WITTENBERG, LAWRENCE JAMES, labor relations consultant; b. San Mateo, Calif., May 6, 1944; s. Weston W. and Mildred Ruth (Selfridge) W.; m. Patricia Nelle (Thorne), June 18, 1968; children—Andrew, Laura. A.A. in Polit. Sci., Foothill Coll., 1964; B.A. in Polit. Sci., U. Wash., 1966; M.Pub. Adminstrn., San Diego State U., 1971. Adminstrv. analyst City of San Diego, 1970-73; dep. city mgr. City of Chula Vista, Calif., 1973-79; asst. city mgr. City of Yakima, Wash., 1979-84; cons. Cabot Dow Assocs., Bellevue, Wash., 1984—; lectr. San Diego State U., 1974-77; instr. Labor Relations Inst., Assn. Wash. Cities, 1981-83; instr. City U., 1984-86, Yakima Valley Community Coll., 1987—. Author: (with Litzenberger) City Council Agenda Manual, 1981. Served to lt. (j.g.) USN, 1967-69, Vietnam. Mem. Internat. City Mgmt. Assn., Am. Soc. For Personnel Adminstrn., Nat. Pub. Employee Labor Relations Assn., Wash. Council Pub. Personnel Adminstrs., Wash. City Mgmt. Assn. Office: Cabot Dow Assocs Chinook Tower Suite 360 Box 4033 Yakima WA 98901

WITTENBURG, MICHAEL CRAIG, marketing executive; b. Waterloo, Iowa, Apr. 21, 1948; s. Donald D. and Esther Madeline (Henn) W.; m. Gretchen Hall-Gerrans, July 15, 1967 (div. May 1975); 1 child, Christopher Michael, m. Cheryl Bogue, Apr. 19, 1978. BA, Wartburg Coll., 1970; postgrad., U. No. Iowa, 1972. Dist. mgr. Koehring Co., Milw., 1972-76; mgr. distbr. devel. Clark Equipment Co., Benton Harbor, Mich., 1976-77; mgr. internat. dealer devel. Euclid div. Daimler Benz A.G., Cleve., 1978-79; dir. nat. accounts Plains Machinery Co., Houston, 1979-82; mgr. nat. accounts Physio Control div. Eli Lilly, Redmond, Wash., 1982—; bd. dirs. Axiom Corp., Houston, Wittenburg Inc., Waterloo; cons. Plains Overseas Group, Houston, 1981-82. Com. chmn. Young Reps., St. Joseph, Mich., 1977. Named Exec. of Month, County Jaycees, Cleve., 1976. Mem. Corp. Philanthropic Soc. (adv. bd. Blackhawk County chpt. 1973), Sugar Creek C. of C. (mng. sec. 1981-82). Lutheran. Home: 3335 Country Blvd Sugarland TX 77477 Office: Physio Control Corp 23275 S Pointe Dr Laguna Hills CA 92653

WITTER, ROBERT EDWARD, consulting engineering executive; b. Houston, Jan. 16, 1948; s. Robert Bruce and Mildred Ann (Jensen) W.; m. Joyce Ann Wilson, June 28, 1969; children: Larissa, Robin, Kara. BSEE, N.Mex. State U., 1971, MSEE, 1972. Registered profl. engr., N.Mex., Ariz., Tex., Colo., Calif. Operation and constrn. engr. Plains Electric Generation and Transmission Coop. Inc., Albuquerque, 1972-73; mgr. engring. services Continental Divide Electric Grants, N.Mex., 1973-75; cons. engr. A.D. Loftin and Assocs., Albuquerque, 1975-79; pres. Robert Witter and Assocs., Albuquerque, 1979—; mem. adv. com. Electric Utility Mgmt. Program N.Mex. State U., Las Cruces, 1983—; disting. engr. N.Mex. State U., 1980—. Elder, clk. Chelwood Christian Reformed Ch., Albuquerque, 1983-84; ham radio operator N.Mex. Lions Eye Bank, Albuquerque, 1978—. Grad. fellow N.Mex. State U., 1971. Mem. IEEE (sr.), NSPE (pres. chpt. 1982-83, PEPP bd. govs. 1983-86), Nat. Acad. Forensic Engrs. (charter, contbr. article to jour.), Am. Acad. Forensic Scis (provisional, contbr. article to meeting), N.Mex. Soc. Profl. Engrs. (Profl. Devel. award 1984, Outstanding Service award 1981). Republican. Avocations: amateur radio, golf, fishing. Home: 1805 Kriss Pl NE Albuquerque NM 87112 Office: Robert Witter and Assocs Inc 9301 Indian Sch Rd NE Albuquerque NM 87112

WITTMEYER, WILLIAM BRUCE, venture capitalist, electrical engineer; b. Calgary, Alta., Can., Mar. 26, 1950; came to U.S., 1956; s. William Woolsey and Elizabeth Johanna (Sheedy) W.; m. Maggie Tham, Jan. 24, 1980; 1 child, Alicia Ping-Quon. BS in Engring., USCG Acad., 1972; MBA in Fin., Columbia U., 1979. Commd. USCG, 1972, advanced through ranks to lt., 1977, resigned, 1977; fin. analyst Exxon Enterprises, N.Y.C., 1979-83; v.p. Grace Ventures, Cupertino, Calif., 1984—; cons. Witham Internat., N.Y.C., 1983-84; bd. dirs. Trans Image Corp., Menlo Park, Calif., Protolite Corp., San Jose, Calif. Mem. N.Y. Acad. Scis. Republican. Jewish. Avocations: diving, skiing. Home: 35 9th Ave #2 San Mateo CA 94401 Office: Grace Ventures Corp 20300 Steven Creek Blvd Cupertino CA 95014

WITTROCK, MERLIN CARL, educational psychologist, educator; b. Twin Falls, Idaho, Jan. 3, 1931; s. Herman C. and Mary Ellen (Baumann) W.; m. Nancy McNulty, Apr. 3, 1953; children: Steven, Catherine, Rebecca. B.S. in Biology, U. Mo., Columbia, 1953, M.S. in Ednl. Psychology, 1956; Ph.D. in Ednl. Psychology, U. Ill., Urbana, 1960. Prof. grad. sch. edn. UCLA, 1960—, founder Ctr. Study Evaluation, 1966, chmn. div. ednl. psychology; fellow Center for Advanced Study in Behavioral Scis., 1967-68; vis. prof. U. Wis., U. Ill., Ind. U., Monash U., Australia. Author or editor: The Evaluation of Instruction, 1970, Changing Education, 1973, Learning and Instruction, 1977, The Human Brain, 1977, Danish transl., 1980, Spanish transl., 1982, The Brain and Psychology, 1980, Instructional Psychology: Education and Cognitive Processes of the Brain; Neuropsychological and Cognitive Processes of Reading, 1981, Handbook of Research on Teaching, 3d edit., 1986; editor-in-chief: Readings in Educational Research, 7 vols, 1977; assoc. editor: Ednl. Psychologist; contbr. articles to profl. jours. Served to capt. USAF. Ford Found. grantee. Fellow Am. Psychol. Assn. (pres. div. ednl. psychology 1984-85), AAAS; mem. Am. Ednl. Research Assn. (chmn. ann. conv., chmn. publs. 1980-83, bd. dirs.), Phi Delta Kappa. Office: UCLA 321 Moore Hall Los Angeles CA 90024

WITTY, THOMAS ROBERT, director research and development; b. Fond du Lac, Wis., Aug. 1, 1947; s. Robert Isaac and Minette Novy (Smith) W.; m. Jane Louise Abrahamson; children: Heather, Tara. BA in Chemistry with hons., Macalester, 1969; PhD in Med. Chemistry, Purdue U., 1974. Postdoctoral fellow U. Ill., Urbana, 1974-76; synthesis dept. head Micromedic Diagnostics, Ft. Collins, Colo., 1976-77; research group leader Becton Dickinson, Salt Lake City, 1977-80, assoc. dir. biochemistry research and devel., 1980-84, dir. research and devel., 1984—; affiliate prof. Colo. State U., Ft. Collins, 1976-77. Contbr. articles to profl. jours.; patentee in field. Served to 1st lt. U.S. Army, 1974. NDEA fellow, 1970-76, Disting. Medicinal Chemistry fellow Purdue U., 1975. Mem. Am. Chem. Soc., Am. Assn. Clin. Chemistry. Avocation: skiing. Office: Becton Dickinson 810 N 2200 W Salt Lake City UT 84115

WITZELING, KENNETH FRANKLIN, pharmacist; b. Hartford, Wis., Feb. 27, 1927; s. Frank and Bertha Hulda (Serrow) W.; m. Elizabeth Ann Minch, June 23, 1951; children—David Kent, Todd Michael. B.S. in Pharmacy, U. Wyo., 1951. Registered pharmacist, Wyo. Owner, operator, pharmacist Skyline Drug, Powell, Wyo., 1968—; dir. Am. Nat. Bank, Powell, Clarks Fork Nat. Bank, Fromberg, Mont.; pres. Wyo. Bd. Pharmacy, 1984-85; mem. Nat. Assn. Bds. Pharmacy. Served to sgt. USAAF, 1945-46. Recipient Disting. Service award Worland Jaycees, Wyo.,

1962, Boss of Yr. award Powell Jaycees, 1974; named Man of Yr., C. of C., 1985. Mem. Nat. Assn. Retail Druggists, Wyo. Pharm. Assn. (pres. 1971, A. H. Robins award 1972), Aircraft Owners and Pilots Assn., U. Wyo. Alumni Assn. (life). Republican, Lutheran. Lodge: Kiwanis (pres. Worland club 1954, lt. gov. Rocky Mountain dist. 1961, life mem. Powell club 1976). Office: Skyline Drug 235 N Bent St Powell WY 82435

WODTLI, GERALD LEWIS, optometrist; b. Sweet Home, Oreg., Feb. 11, 1947; s. John E. and Verna M. (Pittsley) W.; m. Shirley Rae Lamphear, June 21, 1969; children—Jeremy Jonathan, Jill Jennifer. B.A. in Biology, U. Oreg., 1969; O.D., Pacific U., 1973. Prin., Pasco (Wash.) Vision Clinic, 1975—. Served to 1st lt. USAF, 1973-75. Fellow Coll. Vision Devel., Wash. state dir.; mem. Am. Optometric Assn., Wash. Optometric Assn. (Young O.D. of Year, 1980-81), Optometric Extension Program Found. (asst. state dir.), Tri-Cities Optometric Soc. Lutheran. Club: Rotary (Pasco-Kennewick). Office: Pasco Vision Clinic 1906 N 20th St Pasco WA 99302

WOELBER, CAROL J., marketing executive. d. Alfred Karl and Louise (Howell) W. BA, Colo. State U., 1974; postgrad. in edn., U. So. Colo., 1975-76; postgrad., U. San Diego, 1984. Mktg. dir. E.W. Hahn, Inc., San Diego, Calif., 1977-81, dir. media services, 1981-84; regional dir. mktg. E.W. Hahn, Inc., Denver, 1984—. Vol. Denver Pub. Library, 1986. Named one of Outstanding Young Women Am., 1985; recipient Creative Arts scholarship Colo. State U., 1971. Mem. Internat. Council Shopping Ctrs. (cert. mktg. dir.), Denver Advt. Fedn., Am. Mktg. Assn., Women in Communications. Office: E W Hahn Inc 901 Larimer B50 Denver CO 80204

WOELFEL, ROBERT WILLIAM, radio stations manager, mayor; b. Los Angeles, Nov. 5, 1944; s. William Herman and Mary Jane (Hiatt) W. A.A., Mt. San Antonio Coll., 1965; B.S. in Bus., Calif. State U.-Los Angeles, 1969; M.B.A., U. So. Calif., 1972. Salesman, Burroughs Corp., El Monte, Calif., 1969-71; sales mgr., announcer Sta. KMFB/KPMO, Mendocino, Calif., 1973-81; gen. mgr. Sta. KOZT, Ft. Bragg, 1981-85, Sta. KBLC, Lakeport, Calif., 1984-85; v.p., sales mgr., Sta. KZOZ/KKAL, San Luis Obispo, Calif., 1985-86, corp. gen. mgr. Visionary Radio Euphonics, Santa Rosa, Calif., 1986—; instr. advt. community coll.; advt. cons. Vice mayor City of Ft. Bragg, 1982-84, mayor, 1984-85; mem. City Council, 1977-85; v.p. bd. dirs. Mendocino Coast Ednl. TV Assn., 1983-85. Served with USN, 1966-68. Presbyterian. Contbr. articles to photog. jour. also: PO Box 1712 Santa Rosa CA 95402

WOELPER, ALEXANDER ELLIOTT, environmental engineer; b. El Paso, Nov. 8, 1957; s. Walter E. and Elvira O. (Lopez) W. B.S. in Civil Engring., Va. Mil. Inst., 1980; M.A. in Edn., Mich. State U., 1984. Supt./engrs. asst. Borsberry Constrn. Co., El Paso, 1977-78; engr. Mobil Oil Corp. 1985—. Named Outstanding Young Man, U.S. Jaycees, 1982. Served with U.S. Army, 1980-85. Mem. ASCE, Soc. Am. Mil. Engrs., Am. Water Works Assn. Republican. Methodist. Club: Tokyo Pegasus Running.

WOHLENHAUS, WILLIAM JEROME, banker; b. Browns Valley, Minn., Dec. 27, 1935; s. Robert Johnson and Fern Avis (Walker) W.; m. Helen Ann Swearingen, July 13, 1963; children: Kimberly Ann, William Eric. Student Moorhead State U., 1954-56, San Fernando Coll., 1963-64, student U. Minn., 1964-65; grad. U. Okla., 1976. Asst. v.p. Nat. City Bank, Mpls., 1964-70; v.p. Savage State Bank, Minn., 1970-72, First Nat. Bank, Phoenix, 1972-76; sr. v.p. United Bank of Ariz., Phoenix, 1976—; mem. adv. council U. Ariz. Sch. Engring., Tucson, 1980—. Served to sgt. U.S. Army, 1957-58. Mem. Ariz. Bankers Assn. (chmn. 1979-80), Robert Morris Assocs. (pres. 1981-82, nat. dir.), Tucson Clearing House Assn. (pres. 1981-84), Tucson Met. C. of C., Leadership Tucson Alumni. Methodist. Clubs: Old Pueblo (Tucson); Plaza (Phoenix). Office: United Bank of Ariz 3300 N Central Ave Phoenix AZ 85062

WOITASZEWSKI, DONNA MARIE, county extension agent; b. Kimball, Nebr., Apr. 30, 1952; d. Donald George and Elizabeth Ann Shandera; m. Ronald Paul Woitaszewski, May 29, 1982; 1 son, Andrew Paul. B.S. in Home Econs., Chadron State Coll., 1974; postgrad Mid-Plains Community Coll., 1978-79, U. Wyo., 1981, 82. Extension home economist Central Sandhills Area U. Nebr., Thedford, 1974-79, Natrona County, Casper, Wyo., 1979—. Mem. Nat. Assn. Extension 4-H Agts. (Disting. Service award 1983), Wyo. Assn. Extension 4-H Agts. (Disting. Service award 1982). Office: U Nebr 2011 Fairgrounds Rd Casper WY 82604

WOLBERD, PATRICK MCDANIEL, mental health administrator; b. Santa Monica, Calif., Sept. 25, 1942; s. Elmer John and Barbara Ruth (McDaniel) W.; m. Anita Marie Page, June 26, 1977; children: Aaron, Lysandra. BA in Social Work, Calif. State U., Sacramento, 1968; MSW, U. So. Calif., 1970. Lic. social worker, Mont., lic. clin. social worker, Calif. Program coordinator U. So. Calif. Sch. Medicine, Los Angeles, 1971-73; group home adminstr. Hillsides Home for Children, Pasadena, Calif., 1973-76; exec. dir. Unfinished Symphony Ranch, Agoura, Calif., 1976-79; licensing rep. State of Calif., Southern Calif., 1979-81; dir. Erikson Ctr., Tarzana, Calif., 1981-85; supt. Mont. Youth Treatment Ctr., Billings, 1985—; mem. Calif. State Gov.'s task force for Emergency Preparedness; examiner Calif. Social Work Licensing Bd. Mem. Mont. State com. for Emotionally Disturbed Youth. Served with USAF, 1961-65. Mem. Nat. Assn. Social Workers (cert.), Mental Health Assn. Mont., U. So. Calif. Alumni Support Group (past pres.). Lodge: Rotary (bd. dirs.).

WOLCHOK, ROBERT LLOYD, civil engineer; b. N.Y.C., Oct. 18, 1954; s. Sidney S. and Silkaly M. (Moskowitz) W. B.S. in Civil Engring. magna cum laude, Tufts U., 1977; M.S. in Civil/Water Resources Engring., Stanford U., 1978. Registered profl. engr., Calif., 1980, N.Y., 1986. Assoc. civil engr. Boyle Engring. Corp., Newport Beach, Calif., 1978-82; civil/water resources engr. Kennedy/Jenks Engrs., Irvine, Calif., 1982-83; project engr. water resources Robert Bein, William Frost & Assocs., Newport Beach, Calif., 1983-85; cons. civil engr. Vol. operating room U. Calif.-Irvine Med. Center, 1982. Mem. ASCE (William P. Morse scholar Boston sect. 1977), Am. Water Works Assn., Orange County Water Assn., Calif. Water Pollution Control Assn., Tau Beta Pi. Club: Toastmasters. Home: 20 Mamaroneck Road Scarsdale NY 10583 Office: 1401 Quail St Newport Beach CA 92663

WOLD, JOHN SCHILLER, geologist, former congressman; b. East Orange, N.J., Aug. 31, 1916; s. Peter Irving and Mary (Helff) W.; m. Jane Adele Pearson, Sept. 28, 1946; children: Peter Irving, Priscilla Adele, John Pearson. A.B., St. Andrews U., Scotland and Union Coll., Schenectady, 1938; M.S., Cornell U., 1939. Dir. Fedn. Rocky Mountain States, 1966-68; v.p. Rocky Mountain Oil and Gas Assn., 1967, 68; mem. Wyo. Ho. of Reps., 1957-59; Republican candidate for U.S. Senate, 1964, 70; mem. 91st Congress at large from, Wyo.; pres. BTU, Inc., J & P Corp., Wold Nuclear Co., Wold Mineral Exploration Co., Casper, Wyo.; founding pres. Wyo. Heritage Found., Central Wyo. Ski Corp.; bd. dirs. 1st Interstate Bank, Casper, Plains Petroleum Co., Coca Mines, Inc. Contbr. articles to profl. jours. Chmn. Wyo. Rep. Com., 1960-64, Western State Rep. Chmns. Assn., 1963-64; mem. exec. com. Rep. Nat. Com., 1962-64; chmn. Wyo. Rep. State Fin. Com.; Active Little League Baseball, Boy Scouts Am., United Fund, YMCA, Boys Clubs Am.; pres. Wyo. Heritage Soc.; former pres. bd. trustees Casper Coll.; trustee Union Coll. Served to lt. USNR, World War II. Named Wyo. Man of Yr. AP-UPI, 1968; Wyo. Mineral Man of Yr., 1979. Mem. Wyo. Geol. Assn. (hon. life, pres. 1956), Am. Assn. Petroleum Geologists, Ind. Petroleum Assn. Am., AAAS, Wyo. Mining Assn., Sigma Xi, Alpha Delta Phi. Espicopalian (past vestryman, warden). Home: 1231 W 30th Casper WY 82601 Office: Suite 200 Mineral Resource Centre Casper WY 82604

WOLD, JOHN THEODORE, political science educator, researcher; b. Fort Worth, Tex., Nov. 4, 1943; s. Erling Henry and Margaret Eugenie (Barth) W.; m. Diane Louise Peter, Nov. 4, 1967; children—Natalie Louise, Jonathan Sebastian. B.A., Calif. Luth. U., 1965; M.A., Johns Hopkins U., 1968, Ph.D., 1972. Asst. prof. polit. sci. Calif. State U.-Stanislaus-Turlock, 1970-74, assoc. prof., 1974-79, prof., 1979—, pre-law advisor, 1972—, coordinator social scis. program, 1982—, dir. legal and pub. service intern program, 1982—. Contbr. articles to profl. jours. Vestryman St. Francis Episcopal Ch., Turlock, 1978-81; lay reader Diocese of San Joaquin, Calif., 1978—; chalice bearer, 1985—. Recipient Bobbs-Merrill award for Excellence in Polit. Sci., 1968; Dept. Justice grantee, 1978-79. Mem. Am. Polit. Sci. Assn., Western Polit. Sci. Assn. Democrat. Episcopalian. Home: 2895 Colorado Ave Turlock CA 95380 Office: Dept Politics and Pub Adminstrn Calif State U Stanislaus 801 W Monte Vista Ave Turlock CA 95380

WOLD, NANA BEHA, social services administrator; b. N.Y.C., Nov. 4, 1943; d. William John and Margaret (Robinson) Beha. BA, Tex. Women's U., 1965; M in Social Welfare, U. Calif., Berkeley, 1967. Psychiat. social worker Mendocino State Hosp., Talmage, Calif., 1967-70, Calif. State Dept. Mental Health, San Diego, 1972-74; supervising psychiat. social worker Calif. State Dept. Health, San Diego, 1974-81; asst. chief, case mgmt. services San Diego Regional Ctr. Devel. Disabled, 1981—; instr. social work Chapman Coll., San Diego, 1972; mem. adv. com. Community Living Project, San Diego, 1973-76, Sr. Citizens Day Care Ctr., San Diego, 1976-77; mem. Sen. Ellis' Task Force for Devel. Disabled, San Diego, 1984—; co-chair Com. Community Care for Devel. Disabled, San Diego, 1978—. Co-author: Sex Education for the Mentally Retarded, 1975, (pamphlet) Happiness is a Good Home, 1977. Vol. Army Community Services, Ft. Wolters, Tex., 1968-69. Mem. Nat. Assn. Social Workers, Am. Assn. Mental Deficiency. Republican. Roman Catholic. Avocations: music, physical fitness. Office: San Diego Regional Ctr Devel Disabled 4355 Ruffin Rd #306 San Diego CA 92123

WOLD, ROBERT NORMAN, satellite communications executive; b. Mpls., Sept. 11, 1925; s. Albert Nelson and Margaret (Pederson) W.; m. Mary Angell, Dec. 1, 1956 (div. 1982); children—Peter, Margaret, Molly. B.A., U. Minn., 1949. Promotion mgr. Knox Reeves Advt., Mpls., 1950-51, WCCO TV, Mpls, 1951-52; sales rep. CBS, Chgo., 1952-54; account dir. Campbell Mithun Inc., Mpls., 1954-61; v.p. NW Ayer Inc., San Francisco and Los Angeles, 1962-71; chmn., chief exec. officer Robert Wold Co., Inc., Los Angeles, 1971—; dir. Advanced Bus. Communications, San Diego, Pacific Telecommunications Co., San Diego. Trustee U. Minn. Found. Served as ensign USN, 1943-46. Mem. Soc. Satellite Profls. (internat. pres.), Acad. TV Arts and Scis., Internat. Radio and TV Soc., Broadcast Pioneers, Hollywood Radio and TV Soc., Soc. Profl. Journalists. Club: Bel Air Country. Office: Robert Wold Co 10880 Wilshire Blvd Los Angeles CA 90024

WOLF, ARON S., psychiatrist; b. Newark, Aug. 25, 1937; B.A., Dartmouth Coll., 1959; M.D., U. Md., 1963; married; children—Jon, Lisa, Laurie. Intern, U. Md. Hosp., Balt., 1963-64; resident in psychiatry Psychiat. Inst., U. Md. Hosp., Balt., 1964-67, chief resident, 1966-67; practice medicine specializing in psychiatry, Anchorage, 1967—; dir. Springfield Hosp. Alcoholic Clinic, Balt., 1966-67; psychiat. cons. Levindale Hebrew Home and Infirmary, Balt., 1966-67, McLaughlin Yough Center, Anchorage, 1969-72; mem. staff Providence Hosp., chief psychiatry sect., 1977-81; mem. staff Humana Hosp., Alaska, Kodiak Island Hosp., Palmer Valley Hosp., Valdez Community Hosp., Bethel Community Hosp., Cordova Alaska Hosp.; mem. staff Charter North Hosp., exec. com., 1984—; staff psychiatrist Langdon Psychiat. Clinic, 1970-71; partner Langdon Clinic, Anchorage, 1971—, clinic pres., 1981; med. dir. Cordova Community Mental Health Center, 1976-80, 84—; cons. Alaska Native Med. Center, 1975-77, Woman's Resource Center, Anchorage, 1977-81; instr. dept. psychology U. Alaska, Anchorage, 1968-75; assoc. clin. prof. psychiatry U. Alaska, Fairbanks, 1974-85, clin. prof., 1985—; assoc. clin. prof. U. Wash., 1974-85, clin. prof., 1985—; participant weekly mental health TV talk show, Anchorage, 1970—; guest lectr. to various profl. and civic groups, 1967—. Vice pres. Greater Anchorage Area Borough Sch. Bd., 1971-72, pres., 1973-74; pres. Chugach Optional Sch. Parent Adv. Bd., 1976-77; mem. med. adv. com. Alaska Kidney Found., 1977-82; mem. Alaska Gov.'s Mental Health Adv. Bd., 1976-84, chmn., 1983; mem. Gov.'s Task Force on Criminally Committed Patients, 1980—; bd. dirs. Greater Anchorage Drug Mgmt. Group, 1972-73. Served with M.C., USAF, 1967-70. Recipient Wendell-Muncie award Md. Med. Soc., 1967; diplomate Am. Bd. Psychiatry and Neurology, Am. Bd. Forensic Psychiatry. Fellow Am. Psychiat. Assn. (pres. Alaska VII dist. br. 1975, sec. Alaska br. 1984-85, del. assembly 1975-81, area III chmn. assembly procedures com. 1982—, nat. planning com. 1981, nat. membership com. 1981—, chmn. confidentiality com., 1986—, recorder of assembly 1984-85, Alaska del., 1986—); mem. Am. Acad. Psychiatry and Law (mem. ethics com., 1987) , Am. Soc. Law and Medicine, Soc. Air Force Psychiatrists, ACLU, AMA (chmn. mental health com. 1971-75, medicine and law com. 1980-81), Alaska Med. Assn., N.Y. Acad. Scis. Contbr. articles on psychiatry to profl. jours. Home: 8133 Sundi Dr Anchorage AK 99502 Office: 4001 Dale St Anchorage AK 99504

WOLF, CHARLES, JR., economist, educator; b. N.Y.C., Aug. 1, 1924; s. Charles and Rosalie W.; m. Theresa van de Wint, Mar. 1, 1947; children: Charles Theodore, Timothy van de Wint. B.S., Harvard U., 1943, M.P.A., 1948, Ph.D. in Econs., 1949. Economist, fgn. service officer U.S. Dept. State, 1945-47, 49-53; mem. faculty Cornell U., 1953-54, U. Calif., Berkeley, 1954-55; sr. economist The Rand Corp., Santa Monica, Calif., 1955-67; head econs. dept. The Rand Corp., 1967-81; dean The Rand Grad. Sch., 1970—, dir. internat. econ. policy program, 1981—; dir. Fundamental Investors Fund, 1985—, Found. for 21st Century, 1986—; co-chmn., mem. exec. com. Calif. Seminar on Internat. Security and Fgn. Policy; mem. exec. com. Rand-UCLA Health Policy Ctr.; bd. visitors Duke U. Inst. Policy Scis.; mem. adv. com. UCLA Clin. Scholars Program; lectr. econs. UCLA, 1960-72; mem. exec. com. Rand-UCLA for Study of Soviet Internat. Behavior. Author: Foreign Aid: Theory and Practice in Southern Asia, 1960, United States Policy and the Third World: Problems and Analysis, 1967, Rebellion and Authority: An Analytic Essay on Insurgent Conflicts, 1970, The Costs and Benefits of the Soviet Empire, 1986, Markets or Governments; Choosing Between Imperfect Alternatives, 1986; contbr. articles to profl. jours. Mem. Assn. for Public Policy Analysis and Mgmt. (pres. 1980-81, policy council), Am. Econs. Assn., Econometric Soc., Council Fgn. Relations, Internat. Inst. Strategic Studies London. Clubs: Cosmos (Washington); Riviera Tennis (Los Angeles). Office: The Rand Grad Sch 1700 Main St Santa Monica CA 90406

WOLF, EDWARD CHARLES, biochemist, educator; b. Los Angeles, Jan. 8, 1954; s. August C. and Muriel M. (McCarry) W.; m. Janet L. Kearns, Aug. 9, 1980. BA in Chemistry, Calif. State U., 1976; PhD in Biochemistry, UCLA, 1981. Tchg. and research assoc. UCLA, 1976-81; lectr. Calif. State U., Fresno, 1982-83; asst. prof. U. Nev., Las Vegas, 1983—. Contbr. articles to profl. jours. Mem. Am. Chem. Soc., AAAS, Sigma Xi. Avocations: scuba diving, mountaineering. Office: Univ Nev Dept Chemistry 4505 Maryland Pkwy Las Vegas NV 89154

WOLF, FRANK L(EWELLYN), accountant; b. N.Y.C., Mar. 15, 1928; s. Morris and Pearl (Falk) W.; m. Judy Efron, Aug. 23, 1953; children—Arthur, Madeline, Phyllis. B.B.A., U. Mich., 1949, M.B.A., 1950. C.P.A., N.Y., Calif. Ptnr. Ernst & Whinney, N.Y.C., 1950-74; ptnr. Ernst & Whinney, Los Angeles, 1975—; vis. lectr. UCLA Grad. Sch. Mgmt. Bd. dirs. Block & Hexter Vacation Ctr. for Aged, N.Y.C., 1970-75; mem. adv. bd. Concern Found., Los Angeles, 1982—. Served to sgt. U.S. Army, 1950-52. Mem. Am. Inst. C.P.A.s, Calif. Soc. C.P.A.s. Office: Ernst & Whinney 1875 Century Park E Suite 2200 Los Angeles CA 90067

WOLF, FREDERICK GEORGE, hydrogeologist; b. Paterson, N.J., Aug. 30, 1952; s. Frederick George and Doris (Miller) W. BS, U. S.C., 1974; postgrad. Clemson U., 1976-77; MS, East Tenn. State U., 1978. Cert. profl. geologist, Alaska. Phys. scientist U.S. Army Environ. Hygiene Agy., Edgewood, Md., 1974-75; environ. engr. S.C. Dept. Health and Environ. Control, Columbia, 1977-78; hydrogeologist EPA, Atlanta, 1978-79, hydrologist, Boston, 1979-81, regional hydrogeologist, Seattle, 1981-86; mgr. hazardous waste sect. Parametrix Inc., Bellevue, Wash., 1986—. Author: Lakewood Groundwater Investigation, 1982. Served to lt. USN, 1974-75, now Res. Recipient spl. service award EPA, 1982, bronze medal 1983. Mem. Am. Inst. Profl. Geologists (cert. profl. geol. scientist), Assn. Engring. Geologists, U.S. Naval Inst., Soaring Soc. Am., Sigma Xi, Epsilon Nu Eta. Democrat. Unitarian. Home: 10029 NE 143 Ct Bothell WA 98011 Office: Parametrix 13020 Northrup Way Bellevue WA 98005

WOLF, MARVIN JULES, journalist, author; b. Chgo., July 23, 1941; s. Frank and Ceceille (Singer) W.; m. Kyong Cha Choi, Mar. 29, 1969 (div. 1976); 1 child, Laura Choi. AA, U. Md., 1974; BA, Calif. State U., Fullerton, 1977. Enlisted U.S. Army, 1959, advanced through grades to capt., 1969; served in Vietnam, Korea, Fed. Republic Germany and U.S; resigned U.S. Army, 1974; editor Avco Corp., Newport Beach, Calif., 1974-76, TransAmerica Corp., Los Angeles, 1976-77; freelance photojournalist Huntington Beach, Calif., 1978-85; freelance writer Los Angeles, 1986—. Author: The Japanese Conspiracy, 1983, Fallen Angels, 1986, Platinum Crime, 1987. Decorated Bronze Star; recipient Disting. Service award USMC Combat Corrs. Assn., 1982, Gold Quill, Internat. Assn. Bus. Communicators, 1977. Mem. Am. Soc. Journalists and Authors, Am. Soc. Mag. Photographers (v.p. 1981-85), Ind. Writers of So. Calif. (pres. 1985-86). Avocations: travel, photography. Home: 13237 Warren Ave Los Angeles CA 90066

WOLF, MONICA THERESIA, procedures analyst; b. Germany, Apr. 26, 1943; came to U.S., 1953, naturalized, 1959; d. Otto and Hildegard Maria (Heim) Bellemann; children—Clinton, Danielle. BBA, U. Albuquerque, 1985. Developer Word Processing Ctr., Pub. Service of N.Mex., Albuquerque, 1971-74, word processing supr., 1974-78, budget coordinator, 1978-80, lead procedures analyst, 1980—; mem. adv. bd., student trainer APS Career Enrichment Ctr. Instr. firearm safety and pistol marksmanship. Mem. Internat. Word Processing Assn. (founder N.Mex. chpt.), Nat. Assn. Female Execs., Nat. Rifle Assn., N.Mex. Shooting Sports Assn. Democrat. Club: Sandia Gun (adv. bd., coach). Home: 305 Alamosa Rd NW Albuquerque NM 87107 Office: 414 Silver Ave SW Albuquerque NM 87103

WOLF, PETER STEVEN, wine industry executive, consultant; b. N.Y.C., Sept. 28, 1943; s. Felix and Betty (Kaufman(W.; m. Carolyn Saula Deich, Mar. 18, 1973; children: Jenna, Shari, Adam. BBA, U. Miami, 1965; MBA, U. Ga., 1970. Div. mgr. Schenley Distilling Co., Miami, Fla., 1972; product mgr. Schenley Distilling Co., N.Y.C., 1973; v.p., regional mgr. Fleischmann Distilling Co., San Francisco and Houston, 1974-79; sr. v.p. mktg. Weibel Vineyards, Fremont, Calif., 1979-85; pres. The Wine Steward Co., Fremont, 1985—, Nova Mktg. Assn., Fremont, 1985—; tchr. Ohlone Coll., Fremont, 1984—, mem. mktg. adv. bd. 1983-86. Contbr. articles on mktg. to profl. jours. Bd. dirs. Chadbourne Sch., Fremont, 1983-85, Temple Beth Torah, Fremont, 1982-83. Served to capt. USAF, 1966-69. Mem. Les Amis Du Vin, Chaine des Rotisseur (chevelier), Wino, Fremont C. of C. (bd. dirs.). Republican. Avocation: sailing, biking, skiing. Home: 2750 Latham Dr Sacramento CA 95825 Office: Wine Steward Co Inc Zinfandel Sq 11099 Olson Dr Suite 4 Rancho Cordova CA 95670

WOLF, WALTER, chemist, pharmacist, educator; b. Frankfurt, Germany, May 25, 1931; came to U.S., 1958, naturalized, 1965; B.S. in Natural Scis, U. of Republic, Montevideo, Uruguay, 1949; M.S., Licenciado en Ciencias-Quimica, U. of Republic, 1952; Ph.D., U. Paris, 1956. Stagiaire Centre National de la Recherche Scientifique, Paris, 1955-56; attache de recherches 1956; assoc. prof. organic and biol. chemistry U. Concepcion, Chile, 1956-58; research assoc. Amherst Coll., Mass., 1958-59; research assoc. U. So. Calif., Los Angeles, 1959-62, lectr. organic pharm. chemistry, 1959-60, vis. asst. prof., 1961-62, asst. prof., 1962-65, dir. NSF undergrad. research participation program, 1963-72, assoc. prof. biomedicinal chemistry, 1965-70, prof., 1970—, acting chmn. grad. div. pharm., 1966-68; dir. radiopharmacy program U. So. Calif., 1968—, chmn. dept. biomedicinal chemistry, 1969-73; dir. radiopharmacy service Los Angeles County/U. So. Calif. Med. Center, 1970—; cons. VA, 1968—, Oak Ridge Assoc. Univs., 1967—, IAEA, 1969—. Co-editor: Radiopharmacy, 1976; contbr. numerous articles to profl. jours. McGill U. fellow, 1958; Hoffman LaRoche fellow, 1954-55; Ministere des Affaires Estrangeres (France) fellow, 1953; Intra-Sci. Research Found. fellow, 1971. Fellow Acad. Pharm. Scis.; mem. Radiation Research Soc., Am. Chem. Soc. (nat. councilor 1968-74, alt. councilor 1976-80, chmn. ad hoc com. pharm. chemistry 1966-80), Swiss Chem. Soc., Societe de Chimie Biologique, Academie de Pharmacie (Paris) (fgn. corr.), Soc. Nuclear Medicine (chpt. exec. com. 1973-78, nat. trustee 1974-78, sci. affairs com. 1973—, radiopharm. sci. com. 1974-76, sci. policy com. 1977-78, world fedn. com. 1977-78, editor Highlights of Nuclear Medicine 1975-78, pres. edn. and research found. 1982-86), AAUP, Sigma Xi, Rho Chi. Home: 12221 Sarazen Pl Knollwood Estates Granada Hills CA 91344 Office: Sch Pharmacy U So Calif 1985 Zonal Ave Los Angeles CA 90033

WOLFE, CLIFFORD EUGENE, architect, author; b. Harrington, Wash., Mar. 26, 1906; s. Delwin Lindsley and Luella Grace (Cox) W.; m. Frances Lillian Parkes, Sept. 12, 1936 (dec.); children—Gretchen Yvonne Wolfe Mason, Eric Von; m. Mary Theye Worthen. A.B. in Architecture, U. Calif.-Berkeley, 1933. Registered architect, Calif. Assoc. architect John Knox Ballantine, Architect, San Francisco, 1933-42; supervising architect, prodn. engr. G.W. Williams Co. Contractors, Burlingame, Calif., 1942-44; state-wide coordinator med. schs. and health ctrs. U. Calif.-Berkeley, San Francisco and Los Angeles, 1944-52; sec. council on hosp. planning Am. Hosp. Assn., Chgo., 1952-59; dir. planning dept. Office of York & Sawyer, Architects, N.Y.C., 1959-74; prin. Clifford E. Wolfe, AIA-E, Oakland, Calif., 1974—; assoc. designer State of Calif. Commn. for Golden Gate Internat. Exposition, San Francisco, 1938-39; cons. Fed. Hosp. Council, Washington, 1954-60; mem. Pres.'s Conf. on Occupational Safety, Washington, 1955; research architect Hosp Research and Ednl. Trust, Chgo., 1957-59; instr. hosp. planning Columbia U., N.Y.C., 1961-73. Author, editor manuals on hosp. planning, engring. and safety, 1954-58. Author: Ballad of Humphrey The Humpback Whale, 1985; contbr. poetry to Tecolote Anthology, 1983, The Ina Coolbrith Circle, 1985 (Grand prize Ina Coolbrith award 1986), Islandia, 1986. Hosp. planning research grantee USPHS, 1956. Mem. AIA (chmn. honor awards com. Chgo. chpt. 1958-59, chmn. activities com. N.Y. chpt. 1972-74, mem. emeritus East Bay chpt. 1974—). Address: 3900 Harrison St Apt 306 Oakland CA 94611

WOLFE, JAMES WALLACE, research neurophysiologist; b. Ludlowville, N.Y., Apr. 11, 1932; s. William Aaron Mattis and Hazel Marie (Riey) W.; m. Beverly Jane Langetieg, Sept. 11, 1954; children: Mark William, Jamie Lynn. AA, Riverside City Coll., 1960; BA, U. Calif., Riverside, 1963; PhD, U. Rochester, 1966. Field service rep. Link Aviation, Binghamton, N.Y., 1954-59; flight trainer analyst U.S. Govt., San Bernardino, Calif., 1959-63; research psychologist U.S. Army., Ft. Knox, Ky., 1966-68; chief vestibular lab. USAF, San Antonio, 1968-74, chief neurosci., 1974-86, chief tech. advisor Sch. Aero Medicine, 1986—; assoc. dir. ONR/AFOSR/FE USAF, Tokyo, 1985-86; mem. San Antonio Area Found. Eye Research Com., U. Space Research Assn.'s Sci. Council for Space Biomedicine, ad hoc com. availability on nonhuman primates Soc. Neurosci., ad hoc com. space motion sickness Am. Inst. Biol. Scis. Contbr. articles to profl. jours.; mem. editorial bd. Jour. Aviation Space and Environ. Medicine; editorial referee Annals of Otology, Rhinology and Laryngology. Served as staff sgt. USAF, 1950-54. Recipient Otis Benson Sci. award USAF Sch. Aerospace Medicine, 1982, Am. Acad. Otolaryngology Honor award, 1982, Outstanding Profl. award USAF Sch. Aerospace Medicine, 1983-84, Comdr.'s award USAF Sch. Aerospace Medicine, 1984. Fellow Aerospace Med. Assn. (assoc.); mem. Barany Soc., Internat. Brain Research Orgn., Sigma Xi, Alpha Gamma Sigma. Lodges: Masons (master mason 1977-78), Shriners. Avocations: flying, orchid growing, stained glass.

WOLFE, MARGARET ROUSE, social services director, consultant; b. Bemidji, Minn., July 17, 1935; d. Willard Hammond and Frances Dorothy (Lloyd) Rouse; m. John G.R. Wolfe, Aug. 8, 1969; children: John G.R., David F.G. BS, U. Minn., 1957; MSW, Nat. Cath. Sch. Social Services, 1965. Day care licensing, cons. States of Alaska and Minn., 1965-69; head start tng. officer Mpls., 1967; dir. family services unit Greater Anchorage Area Borough; mental health program mgr. Municipality of Anchorage, 1969-65; dir. Fedn. of Community Councils, Anchorage, 1979-83; dir., owner Midtown Day Care Ctr., Anchorage, 1983—. Mem. Acad. Cert. Social Workers, Anchorage Assn. Edn. Young Children. (legis. com. chairperson, conf. coordinator, pres.), Anchorage Child Protection Assn. (legis. com. chairperson, conf. coordinator). Avocations: music, reading. Home: PO Box 1572 Anchorage AK 99510 Office: Midtown Day Care Ctr Inc 1677 Juneau Dr Anchorage AK 99501

WOLFE, PHILIP MAURICE, manufacturing systems administrator; b. Minden, Nebr., July 17, 1941; s. Earl M. and Helen G. (Peterson) W.; m. Laura Lee Donalson, Jan. 26, 1964; children: Scot, Jaree, Jennifer. BSBA, BS in Indsl. Engring., U. Mo., 1964; MS in Indsl. Engring., Ariz. State U., 1966, PhD in Indsl. Engring., 1968. Sr. ops. research analyst Motorola Corp., Phoenix, 1967-71, systems mgr., 1971-76; prof. indsl. engring. Okla.

State U., Stillwater, 1976-84; mgr. ops. planning Garrett Turbine Engring. Co., Phoenix, 1984-85, mgr. mfg. systems engring., 1985—. Author: BASIC Engineering and Scientific Programs for the IMB PC, 1984. Fellow Inst. Indsl. Engrs. Home: 2318 W Galveston Chandler AZ 85224

WOLFF, MARTIN JOEL, space systems engineer; b. N.Y.C., May 13, 1959; s. Peter Ludwig and Paula Nan (Klopfer) W. BS in Engring. cum laude, Princeton U., 1981, MS in Engring., 1984. Project engr. Space and Communications Group Hughes Aircraft Co., El Segundo, Calif., 1984—. Contbr. articles to profl. jours. Mem. AIAA, Sigma Xi. Jewish. Club: Princeton Quadrangle (social chmn. 1980-81). Avocations: skiing, softball, travel. Home: 344 Penn St Apt A El Segundo CA 90245 Office: Hughes Aircraft Co 909 Sepulveda Blvd El Segundo CA 90245

WOLFF, SIDNEY CARNE, astronomer, observatory administrator; b. Sioux City, Iowa, June 6, 1941; d. George Albert and Ethel (Smith) Carne; m. Richard J. Wolff, Aug. 29, 1962. BA, Carleton Coll., 1962, DSc (hon.), 1985; PhD, U. Calif., Berkeley, 1966. Postgrad. research fellow Lick Obs. Santa Cruz, Calif., 1969; asst. astronomer U. Hawaii, Honolulu, 1967-71, assoc. astronomer, 1971-76; astronomer, assoc. dir. Inst. Astronomy, Honolulu, 1976-83, acting dir., 1983-84; dir. Kitt Peak Nat. Obs., Tucson, 1984—; acting dir. Nat. Optical Atronomy Observatories, 1987—; acting. dir. nat. Optical Astronomy Observatories, 1987—. Author: The A-Type Stars—Problems and Perspectives, 1983; (with others) Exploration of the Universe, 1987; contbr. articles to profl. jours. Research fellow Lick Obs. Santa Cruz, Calif., 1967. Mem. Astron. Soc. Pacific (pres. 1984-86, bd. dirs. 1979-85), Am. Astron. Soc. (council 1983-86), Internat. Astron. Union. Office: Kitt Peak Nat Obs PO Box 26732 Tucson AZ 85726

WOLFF, WARREN A., electrical engineer; b. San Angelo, Tex., Aug. 19, 1935; s. Albert William and Alberta Belle (Carlin) W.; m. Joanne Catherine Terrien, Jan. 24, 1958; children: Wendy Sue, Randy Lee, Stephanie Jo. BSEE, N.Mex. A&M, 1958; MSEE, N.Mex. State U., 1971. Field engr. Signal Corps, USAF, 1954-58, commd., 1958, advanced through grades to maj., ret., 1978; sr. program mgr. Lockheed Aircraft Service, Ontario, Calif., 1978—; sec. Advanced Ballistic Missile Systems working group, 1967-69; rep. Anti-Ballistic Missile working group, 1967-74; mem. working group on configuration mgmt. Software/Firmware, 1976-78. Coach San Bernardino (Calif.) Little League, 1963-72, San Bernardino Girls Softball League, 1968-71, Calif. Youth Tennis Found., San Bernardino, 1979-86; Mars dir. USAF Hawaiian Civil Def., 1960-62. Mem. Lockheed Computer Users Group (sec. 1985-86), N.Mex. State Amateur Radio Club (trustee 1958—), Nat. Mgmt. Assn., U.S. Racket Stringers. Republican. Avocations: tennis, amateur radio, philately, astronomy, bonsai. Home: 1742 E Foothill Dr San Bernardino CA 92404 Office: Lockheed Aircraft Service co Box 33 Bldg R-22 Ontario CA 91762-8033

WOLFLE, DAEL LEE, educator; b. Puyallup, Wash., Mar. 5, 1906; s. David H. and Elizabeth (Pauly) W.; m. Helen Morrill, Dec. 28, 1929; children—Janet Helen (Mrs. Wilhelm G. Christophersen), Lee Morrill, John Morrill. B.S., U. Wash., 1927, M.S., 1928; postgrad., U. Chgo., summers 1929, 30; Ph.D., Ohio State U., 1931, D.Sc., 1957; D.Sc., Drexel U., 1956, Western Mich. U., 1960. Instr. psychology Ohio State U., 1929-32; prof. psychology U. Miss., 1932-36; examiner in biol. scis. U. Chgo., 1936-39, asst. prof. psychology, 1938-43, assoc. prof., 1943-45; on leave for war work with Signal Corps, 1941-43; with OSRD, 1944-45; exec. sec. Am. Psychol. Assn., 1946-50; dir. commn. on human resources and advanced tng. Assoc. Research Councils, 1950-54; exec. officer AAAS, 1954-70; editor Sci., 1955, pub., 1955-70; prof. pub. affairs U. Wash., Seattle, 1970-76; prof. emeritus U. Wash., 1976—; mem. sci. adv. bd. USAF, 1953-57; mem. def. sci. bd. Dept. Def., 1957-61; mem. adv. council on mental health NIMH, 1960-64; mem. nat. adv. health council USPHS, 1965-66; mem. commn. on human resources NRC, 1974-78; mem. adv. bd. Geophys. Inst., Fairbanks, Alaska., 1970—, chmn. adv. bd., 1972-81. Author: Factor Analysis to 1940, 1941, Science and Public Policy 1959, The Uses of Talent, 1971, The Home of Science, 1972; editor: America's Resources of Specialized Talent, 1954, Symposium on Basic Research, 1959. Trustee Russell Sage Found., 1961-78, Pacific Sci. Cent. Found., 1962-80, Biol. Scis. Curriculum Study, 1980-85; chmn. bd. J. McK. Cattell Fund, 1962-82. Named Alumnus Summa Laude Dignatus, U. Wash., 1979. Mem. Am. Acad. Arts and Scis. (exec. com. western sect. 1985—), Am. Psychol. Assn., AAAS, AAUP, Sigma Xi. Home: 4545 Sand Point Way NE Seattle WA 98105 Office: Grad Sch Public Affairs U Wash Seattle WA 98195

WOLFORD, RICHARD HOWARD, lawyer; b. Chgo., Aug. 12, 1922; s. Darwin H. and Lila (Ferguson) W.; AB, Harvard U., 1944, JD, 1948; m. Helen Moore, Feb. 13, 1943; children—Richard George, Felicia Jane, Peter Arlington. Admitted to Calif. bar, 1949; law clk. U.S. Ct. of Appeals for 9th Circuit, San Francisco, 1948-49; pres. Los Angeles Jr. Bar Assn., 1957-58; mem. Calif. Law Revision Commn., Los Angeles, 1968-70; sr. partner Gibson, Dunn & Crutcher, Los Angeles, 1963-80, of counsel, 1981—; adj. prof. law (antitrust) U. Hawaii Law Sch., 1983. Mem. Los Angeles County Bar Assn. (trustee 1957-58), Am. Bar Assn., Internat. Bar Assn., Hawaii State Bar Assn., Am. Judicature Soc. Clubs: Los Angeles Country, California. Home: 751 E Pulehuiki Rd Kula Maui HI 96790

WOLFRAM, JAMES HIGGINS, research biotechnologist; b. Sandusky, Ohio, Aug. 14, 1943; m. Jean C. Dziamba, Aug. 31, 1968; children: Jeffrey, Jennifer. BS in Biochemistry, Ohio State U., 1965; postgrad., U. N.H., 1970-74, PhD in Biochemistry, 1974. Postdoctoral scientist USDA, Phila., 1976-78; research supr. USAID/USDA, Kenya, 1978; research scientist Joseph E. Seagram, Louisville, 1978-80; biotech. mgr. EG & G Idaho, Inc., Idaho Falls., 1980—; adjunct prof. Idaho State U., Pocatello, 1984—; cons. ethanol prodn., Idaho Falls., 1980—. Contbr. articles to profl. jours. Served as capt. USAF, 1965-70, Vietnam. Decorated Silver Star. Mem. Am. Soc. Microbiology, Am. Chem. Soc., Sigma Xi. Lodge: Elks. Home: 1263 Londonberry Idaho Falls ID 83401 Office: Inel/Idaho Nat Engring Po Box 1625 Idaho Falls ID 83415

WOLFSBERG, MAX, chemist, educator; b. Hamburg, Germany, May 28, 1928; came to U.S., 1939, naturalized, 1945; s. Gustav and Ida (Engelmann) W.; m. Marilyn Lorraine Fleischer, June 23, 1957; 1 dau., Tyra Gwendolen. A.B., Washington U., St. Louis, 1948, Ph.D., 1951. Asso. chemist Brookhaven Nat. Lab., Upton, N.Y., 1951-54; chemist Brookhaven Nat. Lab., 1954-63, sr. chemist, 1963-69; prof. chemistry SUNY, Stony Brook, 1966-69; vis. prof. chemistry Ind. U., Bloomington, 1965, Cornell U., Ithaca, N.Y., 1963; prof. chemistry U. Calif., Irvine, 1969—, chmn. dept., 1974-80; Deutsche Forschungs Gemeinschaft guest prof. U. Ulm, Fed. Republic Germany, 1986. Assoc. editor: Jour. Chem. Physics, 1968-70; editor: Comments on Chemical Physics, 1986—; contbr. articles to profl. jours. AEC fellow, 1950-51; NSF sr. postdoctoral fellow, 1958-59; Alexander von Humboldt awardee, 1977. Mem. Am. Chem. Soc., Phi Beta Kappa, Sigma Xi. Jewish. Home: 4533 Gorham Dr Corona del Mar CA 92625 Office: U Calif Dept Chemistry Irvine CA 92717

WOLFSON, FRANKLIN ALLEN, vitamin distributing company executive; b. Queens, N.Y., Jan. 20, 1943; s. Leon Bernard and Ruth (Levine) W. BBA, CCNY, 1966; MBA, NYU, 1969. Pres. Kostar, North Hollywood, Calif., 1976-80, Buckeroo Internat., Woodland Hills, Calif., 1980-81, Taxshelter Securities Corp., Los Angeles, 1981; v.p. mktg. Jones & Newman, Van Nuys, Calif., 1982-83; pres. 21st Century Nutritionals, Beverly Hills, Calif., 1985—. Editor (newsletter) Successful Real Estate Investor, 1985. Served with USAR. Jewish. Avocations: running, tennis, racquetball, collecting art and antiques. Home: 358 S Roxbury Dr Beverly Hills CA 90212 Office: Jones & Newman 6454 Van Nuys Blvd Van Nuys CA 91401

WOLFSON, ROBERT PRED, research engineer; b. Miami, Fla., May 29, 1926; s. O. Philip and Nora Jacqueline (Pred) W.; m. Helene Clare Abrahm, Nov. 12, 1949; children: Philip Michael, Robert P. BE, Tulane U., 1948; postgrad., Pa. State U., 1962-64, Poly. Inst. Bklyn., 1965. Air conditioning engr. Equitable Equipment Co., New Orleans, 1948-49, Wood-Leppard Air Conditioning Co., Houston, 1949, Conditioned Air Corp., Miami, 1949-50, Lewco Co., Miami, 1950-54, Hill-York Corp., Miami, 1954-55; thermoelectric energy research engr. The Franklin Inst Labs. Research and Devel., Phila., 1955-59; thermoelectric research and devel. mgr. Tenn. Products & Chem. Corp., Nashville, 1959-61; energy engr., systems engr. Gen. Electric Co., Phila., 1961-71; sci. contamination specialist Bionetics Corp., Hampton, Va., 1972; planetary quarantine project mgr., Mars/Earth back contamination research mgr., dir. energy programs Exotech. Inc., Gaithersburg, Md., 1972-80; project engr. The Aerospace Corp., El Segundo, Calif., 1980—. Contbr. articles to profl. jours. Served with USNR, 1944-46. Mem. IEEE, Wash. Acad. Scis. Home: 19 Laguna Ct Manhattan Beach CA 90266

WOLKOVITS, PAUL DENNIS, banker, educator; b. N.J., Dec. 22, 1948; s. Paul A. Wolkovitsch and Virginia V. Lauro. B.A., Columbia U., 1975; M. Div., Harvard U., 1978. Vice pres. employment and tng. mgmt. Mitsui Mfrs. Bank, Los Angeles, 1980—. Mem. Am. Soc. Tng. and Devel., Am. Inst. Banking (bd. dirs. Calif. chpt.).

WOLLENBERG, RICHARD PETER, paper manufacturer; b. Juneau, Alaska, Aug. 1, 1915; s. Harry L. and Gertrude (Arnstein) W.; m. Leone Bonney, Dec. 22, 1940; children: Kenneth Roger, David Arthur, Keith Kermit, Richard Harry, Carol Lynne. BS in Mech. Engring, U. Calif.-Berkeley, 1936; MBA, Harvard U., 1938; grad., Army Indsl. Coll., 1941; D in Pub. Affairs (hon.), U. Puget Sound, 1977. Prodn. control Bethlehem Ship, Quincy, Mass., 1938-39; with Longview (Wash.) Fibre Co., 1939—, safety engr., asst. chief engr., chief engr., mgr. container operations, 1951-57, v.p., 1953-57, v.p. ops., 1957-60, exec. v.p., 1960-69, pres., 1969-78, pres., chief exec. officer, 1978-85, also chmn. bd., bd. dirs.; mem. Wash. State Council for Postsecondary Edn., 1969-79, chmn., 1970-73; mem. western adv. bd. Allendale Ins. Bassoonist SW Washington Symphony. Chmn. bd. trustees Reed Coll., Portland. Served to lt. col. USAAF, 1941-45. Mem. NAM (bd. dirs. 1981-86), Pacific Assn. Pulp and Paper Mfrs. (pres. 1982—), Inst. Paper Chemistry (trustee), Wash. State Roundtable. Home: 1632 Kessler Blvd Longview WA 98632 Office: Longview Fibre Co PO Box 606 Longview WA 98632

WOLLENBERGER, LAURIE J., social worker; b. N.Y.C., July 25, 1959; d. Kurt Leo and Margot (Lahnstein) W. BA in Sociology, SUNY, Binghamton, 1981; MSW, NYU, 1984. Geriatric social work intern Kingsbridge Heights Nursing Home, N.Y.C., 1983-84; clin. social worker Multipurpose Sr. Service Program, San Francisco, spring 1985; med. social worker St. Mary's Hosp. and Med. Ctr., San Francisco, 1985; social worker VA Med. Ctr., Palo Alto, Calif., 1985—. Asst. editor newsletter The Respite Rev., 1986—. Active Big Bros./Big Sisters, Inc., San Francisco. Mem. Nat. Assn. Social Workers. Democrat. Jewish. Avocations: camping, hiking, rock music. Office: VA Med Ctr 3801 Miranda Ave Suite 331B Palo Alto CA 94304

WOLLMAN, NATHANIEL, emeritus educator, economist; b. Phila., May 15, 1915; s. Leon and Rose (Schimmel) W.; m. Lenora Levin, Dec. 25, 1939; children: Stephen, Eric. A.B., Pa. State U., 1936; Ph.D., Princeton U., 1940; LL.D., Colo. Coll., 1972. Instr., asst. prof. Colo. Coll., 1939-48; asso. prof., prof. econs. U. N.Mex., 1948-81, prof. emeritus, 1981—, chmn. dept. econs., 1960-81; dean Coll. Arts and Scis., 1969-81; Economist Resources for the Future, 1959-60, 64-65; Chmn. Internat. Environ. Programs Com., 1976-79. Author: (with others) Alternative Uses of Water, 1960, Water Supply and Demand, 1960, Water Resources of Chile, 1968, (with Gilbert Bonem) The Outlook for Water: Quality, Quantity and National Growth, 1971, (with others) Man, Materials and Environment, 1973. Served with USNR, World War II. Mem. Am. Econs. Assn. Home: 7010 Phoenix Ave NE #714 Albuquerque NM 87110

WOMACK, SHARON G., librarian. Dir. archives and pub. records dept. Ariz. Library, Phoenix. Office: Library Archives and Pub Records Dept Old State Capitol 1700 W Washington Phoenix AZ 85007

WOMELDORF, MARDIE GAIL, film director; b. Morristown, N.J., Apr. 11, 1950; s. William Benjamin and Marguerite (Heipertz) Womeldorf. B.A., Stetson U., 1972; M.A., U. Maine, 1974. Film and videotape editor Sta. KMPH-TV, Visalia, Calif., 1976-80; service rep. Pacific Telephone Co., Tulare, Calif., 1980-82; curator Tulare County Mus., Visalia, 1982; local origination dir. Sequoia Cablevision, Tulare, 1983; film dir. Sta. KDVR-TV, Denver, 1983—. Active Visalia Community Players; mem. East Hampden Players; mem. adv. council R.S.V.P.; vol. Denver Mus. Natural History. Office: Sta KDVR-TV 100 Speer Blvd Denver CO 80203

WON, KWANG WOONG, chemical engineer; b. Seoul, Korea, Dec. 24, 1940; came to U.S., 1965; s. Dong Shick and Dal Mak (Yoon) W.; m. Christina C. Kim, May 31, 1969; children: Alvina J., Erik J. BS, Seoul Nat. U., 1964; MS, Wayne State U., 1967; PhD, U. Calif., Berkeley, 1974. Registered profl. engr., Calif.; lic. chem. engr. Research and teaching asst. U. Calif., Berkeley, 1970-74; prin. process engr. Fluor Corp., Irvine, Calif., 1974-83; sr. tech. specialist Fluor Tech., Inc., Irvine, Calif., 1983—; lectr., adj. prof. U. So. Calif., 1977—. Author: Chemical Engineering of Supercritical Fluids, 1985; contbr. articles to profl. jours.; patentee infinite dilution volatilities of polar organic solutes in hydrocarbons, a gel layer effect on ultrafiltration mass flux. Referee Am. Youth Soccer Orgns. Orange County, Calif., 1983—. Served to cpl., Army, Republic of Korea, 1964-65. Mem. AAAS, Am. Inst. of Chem. Engrs. (prof. devel. cert.1985, referee Jour. 1979—), Am. Chem. Soc. Republican. Roman Catholic. Club: Toastmasters, Irvine. Avocations: tennis, skiing, marine water study. Home: 24141 Snipe Ln Laguna Nighel CA 92677 Office: Fluor TechInc 3333 Michelson Dr Irvine CA 92730

WON, KYUNG-SOO, symphony conductor, director; b. Korea, Dec. 4, 1928; m. Hae-Ja (Won). Nov. 18, 1965; children—Alisa, Justin. Mus.M., Cin. Conservatory, 1957; diploma Mozarteum, Salzburg, Austria, protege of Pierre Monteux; postgrad. Ind. U. Cert. tchr., Calif. Formerly prof. Seoul (Korea) Nat. U., music dir. Modesto (Calif.) Symphony, Seoul Philharmonic Orch.; currently music dir., condr. Stockton (Calif.) Symphony; guest condr. orchs., London, Berlin, Paris, Vienna, Austria, Ireland, Mexico City, S. Am. cities, Orient. Served with Korean Navy. Recipient Bartok award, Emeel Hermann award. Mem. Am. Symphony League. Home: 8034 Heather Dr Stockton CA 95209 Office: Stockton Symphony PO Box 4273 Stockton CA 95204

WON, VANN YUEN, physical chemist; b. Canton, China, Feb. 27, 1925; came to U.S., 1951; s. Yuen Cheng Won; m. Lily Fong; children: Joe, Synthia, Erwin, Julie. BS, Nat. Chekiang U., China, 1946. Research engr. paper and sugarcane byproduct Taiwan, China, 1946-51; chemistry engr. USAF Dept. Def., Sacramento, Calif., 1951-87, phys. scientist. Patentee in field. Home: 6697 Gloria Dr Sacramento CA 95831

WON, WILLIAM W.T., neurosurgeon; b. Honolulu, Sept. 7, 1931; s. K.F. and S.Y. (Young) W.; m. Margaret Lai, Nov. 12, 1961; 1 child, Eric C. BA, Columbia Coll., 1953; MD, SUNY, Bklyn., 1957. Diplomate Am. Bd. Neurol. Surgery. Intern surg. King's County Hosp., Bklyn., 1957-58; resident in neurosurgery Neurol. Inst. Columbia Prsbyn. Hosp., N.Y.C., 1961-64; staff neurosurgeon St. Francis Hosp., Honolulu, 1965—; cons. Queens Hosp., Honolulu, 1965—, Children's Hosp., Honolulu, 1965—, Kuakini Hosp., Honolulu, 1965—. Contbr. med. reports to Hawaii Med. Jour., 1985. Elder Presbyn. Ch., Honolulu, 1980—. Served to capt. M.C., USAF, 1958-60. Fellow ACS; mem. Am. Assn. Neurol. Surgeons, Congress Neurol. Surgeons, Pan Pacific Surg. Assn. Republican. Office: St Francis Med Office Bldg 2228 Liliha St #400 Honolulu HI 96817

WONDERS, WILLIAM CLARE, educator; b. Toronto, Ont., Can., Apr. 22, 1924; s. George Clarence and Ann Mary (Bell) W.; m. Lillian Paradise Johnson, June 2, 1951; children—Karen Elizabeth, Jennifer Anne, Glen William. B.A. with honors, Victoria Coll., U. Toronto, 1946; M.A., Syracuse U., 1948; Ph.D., U. Toronto, 1951; Fil. Dr. h.c., Uppsala U., 1981. Teaching asst. dept. geography Syracuse U., 1946-48; lectr. dept. geography U. Toronto, 1948-53; asst. prof. geography dept. polit. economy U. Alta., 1953-55, assoc. prof. geography, 1955-57, prof., head dept. geography, 1957-67, prof. dept. geography, 1967-83, Univ. prof., 1983—; vis. prof. geography U. B.C., 1954; U. Okla., 1965-66, St. Mary's U., 1977; guest prof. Inst. Geography, Uppsala (Sweden) U., 1962-63; research fellow in geography U. Aberdeen, Scotland, 1970-71, 78. Author: Looking at Maps, 1960; co-author: (with T. Drinkwater et al.) Atlas of Alberta, 1969, (with J. C. Muller et al.) Junior Atlas of Alberta, 1979; Contbr., editor: Canada's Changing North, 1971, The North, 1972, The Arctic Circle, 1976; Contbr. articles to jours., encys., chpts. to books. Mem. Nat. Adv. Com. on Geog. Research, 1965-69; mem. Canadian Permanent Com. on Geog. Names, 1981—, Alta. Historic Sites Bd., 1978-83; mem. policy bd. Canadian Plains Research Centre, U. Regina (Sask.), 1975-86; mem. adv. bd. Tyrrell Mus. Paleontology, 1984—; bd. dirs. The Muttart Found., 1986—. NSF sr. fgn. scientist fellow, 1965-66; Canada Council leave fellow, 1969-70, 77-78; Nuffield Found. fellow, 1970-71; Alta. vis. fellow U. Edinburgh, 1987. Fellow Arctic Inst. N. Am., Royal Soc. Can.; mem. Canadian Assn. Geographers (past pres.), Assn. Am. Geographers, Royal Scottish Geog. Soc., Canadian Assn. Scottish Studies (councillor 1974-77), Am.-Scandinavian Found., Canadian Scandinavian Found., Royal Canadian Geog. Soc., Champlain Soc. (councillor 1981—), Sigma Xi, Gamma Theta Upsilon. Office: Dept Geography U Alta, Edmonton, AB Canada T6G 2H4

WONDRA, JANET CLARE, poet, educator; b. Van Nuys, Calif., Sept. 20, 1952; d. Gerald Lloyd and Elizabeth Ellen (Rau) W. Student, Occidental Coll., 1970-72, U. Calif., Santa Cruz, 1977; BA in Philosophy, UCLA, 1977; MA in English, Creative Writing, San Francisco State U., 1983. Cert. community coll. tchr., Calif. Poet, tchr. Calif. Poets in the Schs., 1983—; lectr. Golden Gate U., San Francisco, 1983-86, U. San Francisco, 1983—, San Francisco State U., 1983—; poet, cons. San Francisco Mus. Modern Art, Fine Arts Mus. of San Francisco, 1985—. Co-Author: Emerging Island Cultures: A Collection of Stories and Poems, 1984; also numerous poems and non-fiction; co-pub./editor Emerging Island Cultures Press, San Francisco, 1984—. Mem. MLA, Acad. Am. Poets (recipient 1st prize 1982, hon. mention 1981), Phi Beta Kappa. Home and Office: 1212 Versailles Ave Alameda CA 94501

WONG, ALFRED MUN KONG, lawyer; b. Honolulu, Sept. 12, 1930; s. Inn and Mew Kung (Choy) W.; m. Laureen Hong, Nov. 20, 1965; children—Peter Marn On, Julie Li Sharn. Student U. Hawaii, 1948-50; B.S., Marquette U., 1953; J.D., U. Calif., 1964. Bar: Hawaii 1964. With Thomas Lee, C.P.A., 1961-62, firm Scott and Balacco, San Francisco, 1962-64; contract atty. Honolulu Redevel. Agy., 1968-71; mng. dir. Okumura, Takushi, Funaki & Wee, Attys. at Law, A Law Corp., Honolulu, 1964—; adj. prof. U. Hawaii Law Sch., 1980-82; mem. bd. bar examiners State of Hawaii, 1968-79; mem. Hawaii Jud. Selection Commn., 1979-85, chmn., 1983-85. Bd. dirs. Pacific council Girl Scouts U.S.A., 1973-78 (Outstanding Service award 1978); pres. Niu Valley Community Assn., 1975, bd. dirs., 1974, 76, 77. Served to capt. C.E., U.S. Army, 1953-61. Recipient Chicago Tribune medal, 1952, 83. Mem. ABA Hawaii Bar Assn. (dir., chmn. unauthorized practice of law com., nominating com.), Hastings Coll. Law Alumni Assn. (bd. govs., Disting. Service award 1987), Am. Judicature Soc., Friends of U. Hawaii Law Sch. (bd. dirs.), Am. Soc. Engrs. Clubs: Waialae Country (Honolulu), Honolulu (founding dir.), Beverly Hills Country. Office: Okumura Takushi Funaki Wee 733 Bishop St Honolulu HI 96813

WONG, ASTRIA WOR, cosmetic business consultant; b. Hong Kong, Oct. 23, 1949; came to U.S., 1970; B in Vocat. Edn., Calif. State U., Long Beach, 1976. Cert. coll. tchr. (life), Calif. West coast sales trainer Revlon Inc., N.Y.C, 1975-82; nat. tng. dir. diReniel Internat., Palm Springs, Calif., 1982; dir. Beauty Cons. Service Agy., Long Beach, Calif., 1983—. Author: The Art of Femininity, 1971; editor (newsletter) So. Calif. Cosmetic, 1983-86. Named Salesperson of Yr., Revlon, Inc., N.Y.C., 1978. Mem. So. Calif. Cosmetic Assn. (correspondence sec. 1982—), Women's Council, Cosmetologist Tchr. Assn., Bus. and Profl. Women. Republican. Office: Beauty Cons Service Agy 1731 Appleton St Long Beach CA 90802

WONG, BENEDICT NORBERT, direct marketing design consultant; b. Fresno, Calif., Jan. 1, 1943; s. Hon Way and Nellie Sue (Lee) W.; B.A., UCLA, 1964; postgrad. Calif. State U.-Los Angeles, 1967-68; m. Virginia Joyce Joke, Mar. 16, 1968; children—Cara Lisa, Matthew Jason. Graphics designer Autonetics, Anaheim, Calif., 1967-68; art dir. Bostelman Advt. Inc., Newport Beach, Calif., 1968-69; sr. art dir. Reach, McClinton & Co., Inc., Los Angeles, 1969-70; creative supr. Barnes-Champ Advt., Los Angeles, 1970-71; creative dir. Wenger-Michael Inc., San Francisco, 1971-75; owner, creative dir. Benedict Norbert Wong Mktg. Design, San Francisco, 1975—; guest speaker direct mktg. confs., Los Angeles and San Francisco. Vol. cons. Big Bros., Girl Scouts, Coll. Notre Dame, Crystal Springs Uplands Schs. Served with USN, 1964-66; Vietnam. Recipient awards N.Y. Art Dirs. Club, Communication Arts Soc. of Los Angeles, others. Mem. San Francisco Soc. Communicating Arts, Direct Mktg. Creative Guild (pres., bd. dirs.) Democrat. Roman Catholic. Clubs: San Francisco Tennis, Les Amis du Vin. Designer catalogs, Asian Art Mus. San Francisco, 1976-77; designs in Graphis, Communications Arts, Print, Art Dir. mags.; designer books: Guatemala: Faces of the Earth, 1976, Inflation Tax Planning, 1980; We Need a Cook, 1980, Equitec Annual Reports, 1982-86, The Pioneer Awards Annual, 1985. Home: 50 Bates Rd Hillsborough CA 94010 Office: 55 Osgood Pl San Francisco CA 94133

WONG, BENJAMIN YAU-CHEUNG, med. care delivery exec.; b. Hong Kong, July 15, 1943; s. Hung and Ku (Yip) W.; came to U.S., 1964, naturalized, 1979; B.C.E., Hong Kong Bapt. Coll., 1964; postgrad in Math., Baylor U., 1965; Ph.D. in C.E., Vanderbilt U., 1968; m. Beatrice Loh, Nov. 15, 1969; children—Carolyn, Jeffrey. Sr. structural engr. Smith, Hinchman & Grylls Assos., Inc., 1968-72; research fellow computer based tech. transfer Carnegie Mellon U., 1972-74; mgr. bldg. systems and computer applications devel. Architecture/Engring. Services, Kaiser Permanente Med. Care Program, Kaiser Found. Hosps., Inc., Oakland, Calif., 1974—. Recipient Scholastic award Hong Kong Bapt. Coll., 1964. Mem. Nat., Calif. (v.p. East Bay chpt., Achievement award) socs. profl. engrs., AAUP, ASCE, Am. Soc. Engring. Edn., Earthquake Engring. Research Inst., Structural Engring Assn. No. Calif., Med. Entities Mgmt. Assn., Tau Beta Pi. Contbr. articles on engring., bldg. systems, computer application, tech. transfer and health care delivery systems to profl. jours. Office: Kaiser Permanente Med Care Program Box 12916 Oakland CA 94604

WONG, CHARLES C., mathematics educator; b. Hong Kong, Hong Kong, June 10, 1944; came to U.S., 1958; s. Sik to and Kai Lui (Ho) W.; m. Celia Lam, Aug. 10, 1970 (div. Sept. 1972). BS in Math., U. Notre Dame, 1962; MS in Math. and Computer Sci., Stanford U., 1964; PhD in Math., Ohio State U., 1968. Lectr. Ohio State U., Columbus, 1966-70; dir. studies, chmn. dept. math. Columbus Sch. for Girls, 1970-83; prof. math. Albuquerque Acad., 1983—. Republican. Anglican. Avocations: fishing, poker, horse racing, Chinese gourmet cooking, soccer. Home: 2937 Madison NE Albuquerque NM 87110

WONG, CHRISTIAN CHARLES, aerospace company executive; b. Honolulu, July 16, 1946; s. Charles Wing Chin and Carole Yit Ho (Lum) W.; m. Colleen Jung, June 8, 1968 (div. Mar. 1973); m. Darcy Anne Decker, May 17, 1975; children—Karena, Kevin, Karianne. B.S. in Marine Engring., U.S. Mcht. Marine Acad., 1968; M.S. in Ops. Mgmt., Northrup Inst. Tech., 1972. Registered profl. engr., Calif. Design engr. Litton Industries, Los Angeles, 1970—, section mgr., 1972, design group mgr., 1977; cons., Canoga Park, Calif., 1976—. Patentee in field. Deacon, Calvary Assembly of God Ch., Hawaii, 1970; treas. Retinitus Pigmentosa Found., Woodland Hills, Calif., 1976—. Served to lt. (j.g.) USNR, 1968-69. Mem. IEEE, Soc. Naval Architects & Marine Engrs., So. Calif. Computer Soc. Republican. Clubs: Litton Computer (Woodland Hills) (v.p. 1975—), Chambers Landing. Office: Litton Industries 5500 Canoga Ave Woodland Hills CA 91364

WONG, CORINNE GAIL, biochemical pharmacologist, educator; b. Sacramento, Oct. 20, 1953; d. Joey Shaw and Lily (Tso) W. BA, U. Calif., Davis, 1975, BS, 1975; PhD, U. Calif., San Francisco, 1981. Postdoctoral fellow pharmacology Harvard U. Med. Sch., 1981-83; postdoctoral fellow Bascom Palmer Eye Inst., U. Miami, Fla., 1983-84; asst. prof. U. So. Calif., Los Angeles, 1984—. Contbr. articles to profl. jours. Recipient Long Found. prize for Excellence in Teaching Organic Chemistry, U. Calif., San Francisco, 1980, Patent Fund award U. Calif., San Francisco, 1980-81; U. So. Calif. Faculty Research and Innovation Fund grantee, 1985. Mem. Neuroscis., AAAS, Assn. Research in Vision and Ophthalmology. Office: U So Calif Dept Opthalmology 1355 San Pablo St Los Angeles CA 90033

WONG, DEANNA TOBY, university administrator; b. San Francisco, Mar. 14, 1939; d. Thomas Francis Leong and Rosaline S. Wong; children—Thomas M., Terri D., Darren J. Bookkeeper, Boston Ins. Co., San Francisco, 1958-61; office mgr. Sener Assocs., San Francisco, 1961-62; adminstrv. sec. City and County of San Francisco, 1962-64; sr. sec. San Francisco Unified Sch. Dist., 1964-74, tng. officer, 1974-76; adminstrv. asst. San Francisco State U., 1976-79, asst. dir. admissions and records, 1979-82, instr, 1981—dir. admissions and records, 1982—; exec. dir. B&D Cons., 1981—. Recipient Spl. Achievement award Calif. Dept. Edn., 1978; cert. of appreciation U.S. Navy Recruiting Dist., 1981, U.S. Army, 1982, U.S. Air Force, 1983. Mem. Nat. Assn. Female Execs., Am. Record Mgrs. Assn., Pacific Assn. Collegiate Registrars and Admissions Officers, Am. Assn. Collegiate Registrars and Admission Officers, Assn. Supervision and Curriculum Devel., Univ. Adminstrs. Assn., Phi Delta Kappa, Fedn. Chinese Golf Clubs. Mem. St. Mary's Chinese Catholic Mission. Club: Marin County Chinese Golf. Office: 1600 Holloway Ave San Francisco CA 94132

WONG, DONA LEE, biochemist/neurochemist educator; b. San Francisco, Dec. 12, 1946; d. Donald Sam and Mary (Lee) W.; m. Kym Francis Faull, July 21, 1979; 1 child, David Christopher. BS, Stanford U., 1968, PhD, 1983; MA, U. Calif., Berkeley, 1971. Research asst. dept. neuropathology Harvard U. Sch. Medicine-Children's Hosp. Med. Ctr., Boston, 1971-74; sr. research asst. Dept. Psychiatry and Behavioral Scis. Stanford (Calif.) U. Med. Ctr., 1974-83, research assoc., 1983-85, asst. prof. psychiatry, behavioral scis., 1985—. Contbr. articles to profl. jours. Scholar Calif. State Scholarship Fedn. Mem. AAAS, Am. Chem. Soc. (cert.), N.Y. Acad. Sci., Soc. Neurosci., Internat. Brain Research Orgn., World Fedn. Neuroscientists, Am. Soc. Neurochem., Iota Sigma Pi. Avocations: skiing, running, sewing, knitting. Home: 4170 Wallis Ct Palo Alto CA 94301 Office: Stanford U Sch Medicine Dept Psychiatry/Behavioral Scis Stanford CA 94305

WONG, ELLEN JEAN, securities trader, executive; b. Los Angeles, Jan. 5, 1939; d. Calvin Ngan and June Ruth (Wright) Locke; m. Victor D. Wong, July 22, 1958 (div. 1960); 1 child, Tracy Victor. Trader Black & Co., Inc., Portland, 1964-65, Hinton-Jones & Co., Seattle, 1965-66, Shaw Hooker & Co., San Francisco, 1966-68; corp. sec. McDonald, Shobar & Co., Inc., San Francisco, 1968-70; head trader Legg Mason & Co., Inc., San Francisco, 1970-72; asst. v.p. U.S. Nat. Bank of Oreg., Portland, 1972-84; prin., head trader Qualivest Capital Mgmt., Portland, 1984-86; assoc. Coldwell-Banker, 1985-86, Barbara Sue Seal Properties Inc., 1986. Bd. dirs. Sta. KBOO Community Radio, Portland, 1982-83, Jazz Soc. of Oreg., Portland, 1982-84, vice chmn., commr. met. Arts Commn., Portland, 1983—; bd. dirs. Greater Portland Vol. Bur., 1981-82; sec. Young Republicans Multnomah County, 1964-65; mem. City of Portland-Multnomah County Services Evaluation Task Force, 1984-86. Republican. Club: Multnomah Athletic. Office: Barbara Sue Seal Properites Inc 2275 W Burnside Portland OR 97210

WONG, EUGENE, engineering educator; b. Nanking, Peoples Republic of China, Dec. 24, 1934; came to U.S., 1949; s. Jennings and May (Yang) W.; m. Joan Chang, Sept. 8, 1956; children: Linda, David, Michael. BS, Princeton U., 1955, AM, 1958, PhD, 1959. Staff researcher IBM Corp., Yorktown, N.Y., 1960-62; asst. prof. elec. engring. U. Calif., Berkeley, 1962-65, assoc. prof., 1965-69, prof., 1969-83, Miller prof., 1983—, chmn. dept. elec. engring and computer sci., 1985—; cons. Ampex Corp, Redwood City, Calif., 1963-79, Computer Corp. Am., Cambridge, Mass., 1976-80; founder, cons. Relational Tech. Inc., Alameda, Calif., 1980—. Author: Stochastic Processes, 1971, Introduction to Random Processes, 1983; also articles. Guggenheim fellow, 1968, Sci. Research Council sr. fellow, 1973, Vinton Hayes fellow, 1976. Fellow IEEE; mem. Assn. Computing Machinery, Nat. Acad. Engring. Home: 97 Stonewall Rd Berkeley CA 94705 Office: Dept EECS U Calif Berkeley CA 94720

WONG, GLEN, industrial engineer; b. Vancouver, B.C., Can., May 7, 1961; came to U.S., 1966; s. Gim Sing and Wah Chun (Cheung) W. BS in Indsl. Engring., U. So. Calif., 1982, MS in Indsl. Engring., 1985. Jr. indsl. engr. R&G Sloane, Sun Valley, Calif., 1982-85, sr. indsl. engr., 1985, sr. project engr., 1985—. Mem. Inst. Indsl. Engring. (sr.), Soc. Mfg. Engrs., MENSA. Office: R&G Sloane 7660 N Clybourn Sun Valley CA 91352

WONG, HENRY LI-NAN, banker, economist; b. Rangoon, Burma, Nov. 3, 1940; s. Chew King and Jenny (Yu) W.; came to U.S., 1946. m. Laurie Yap, Apr. 11, 1968; children: Rachael S.Y., Remle S.M. BS, Waynesburg Coll., 1965; MS, U. Hawaii, 1968, PhD, 1969. Economist, Econ. Research Service U.S. Dept. Agr., Washington, 1969-70; economist Hawaii Dept. Budget and Fin., Honolulu, 1970-73; dir. Hawaii film office Hawaii Dept. Planning and Econ. Devel., Honolulu, 1973-84; exec. adminstr., v.p. to office of chmn. City Bank, Honolulu, 1984—. V.p. bd. dirs. Friends of East West Ctr., Honolulu, 1983-84. NDEA fellow, 1965-69. Mem. Assn. Film Commrs. (pres. 1980), Am. Econ. Assn., Am. Agrl. Econs. Assn., Hawaii Internat. Film Festival, Chinese C. of C., Hawaii Soc. Corp. Planners, Lanakila Crafts (trustee), Alpha Kappa Psi, Theta Chi. Democrat. Presbyterian. Lodges: Elks, Masons (trustee), Shriners. Office: City Bank 810 Richards St Honolulu HI 96813

WONG, JAMES BOK, economist, engineer, technologist; b. Canton, People's Republic of China, Dec. 9, 1922; came to U.S., 1938, naturalized, 1962; s. Gen Ham and Chen (Yee) W.; m. Wai Ping Lim, Aug. 3, 1946; children: John, Jane Doris, Julia Ann. BS in Agr., U. Md., 1949, BS in Chem. Engring., 1950; MS, U. Ill., 1951, PhD, 1954. Research asst. U. Ill., Champaign-Urbana, 1950-53; chem. engr. Standard Oil of Ind., Whiting, 1953-55; process design engr., research engr. Shell Devel. Co., Emeryville, Calif., 1955-61; sr. planning engr., prin. planning engr. Chem. Plastics Group, Dart Industries, Inc. (formerly Rexall Drug & Chem. Co.), Los Angeles, 1961-66, supr. planning and econs., 1966-67, mgr. long range planning and econs., 1967, chief economist, 1967-72, dir. econs. and ops. analysis, 1972-78, dir. internat. techs., 1978-81; pres. James B. Wong Assocs., Los Angeles, 1981—; chmn. exec. com., dir. United Pacific Bank, 1982-84; tech. cons. various corps. Contbr. articles to profl. jours. Bd. dirs., pres. Chinese Am. Citizens Alliance Found. Served with USAAF, 1943-46. Named to Exec. Order Ohio Commodores Commr. Asian Am. Edn. Commn., 1971-81; recipient Los Angeles Outstanding Vol. Service award, 1977. Mem. Am. Inst. Chem. Engrs., Am. Chem. Soc. VFW (vice comdr. 1959), Sigma Xi, Tau Beta Pi, Phi Kappa Phi, Pi Mu Epsilon, Phi Lambda Upsilon, Phi Eta Sigma. Home: 2460 Venus Dr Los Angeles CA 90046

WONG, JOEL KAM-HONG, industrial hygienist; b. Hong Kong, Sept. 22, 1940; came to U.S., 1963; s. Daniel Polam and Rita Sheung-Tsoh (Fung) W.; m. Shue Lin Ho, Feb. 22, 1966; children: Daniel A., Monica F. BA, Internat. Christian U., Tokyo, 1963; MS, U. Houston, 1966. Plant mgr. Gulf Oil Research and Devel. Co., Pitts. Pa, and Wasco, Calif., 1966-72; claims mgr. San Joaquin Found. Med. Care, Stockton, Calif., 1972-74; assoc. indsl. hygienist Div. Occupational Safety and Health, San Francisco, 1974-78; sr. indsl. hygienist Calif. OSHA Cons. Service, San Francisco, 1978-85; indsl. hygienist Lawrence Livermore (Calif.) Nat. Lab., 1985—; cons. Safety Specialist Inc., Santa Clara, Calif., 1985—; lectr. U. Calif., Davis, 1983—; adj. prof. Calif. State u., Hayward, 1978-83. Patentee in field. Mem. Am. Conf. Govtl. Indsl. Hygienists (profl. devel. com. 1984—). Office: Lawrence Livermore Nat Lab U Calif Chemistry Materials Sci PO Box 808 Livermore CA 94550

WONG, KWEE CHANG, research chemist; b. Rangoon, Burma, Dec. 13, 1939; came to U.S., 1971; s. Liu Hain and Kyin Chee (Hoo) W.; m. Yi Liang, May 12, 1981; 1 child, Jane. BS, Rangoon U., 1965; postgrad., Western Ill. U., 1978. Chemist Chamberlain Mfg. Co., Clinton, Iowa, 1971-74; chief chemist Bonewitz Chems., Burlington, Iowa, 1974-79; prin. chemist Electrochems., Youngstown, Ohio, 1979-84; research chemist Inland Specialty Chems., Costa Mesa, Calif., 1984—. Patentee in field. Mem. Am. Chem. Soc., Am. Phys. Soc., Electrochem. Soc., AAAS, N.Y. Acad. Scis. Office: Inland Specialty Chem Corp 3189 C Airway Ave Costa Mesa CA 92626

WONG, MARGIE JEAN, social worker; b. Hanford, Calif., Sept. 13, 1935; d. Wilfred Hertzel and Byllee (Brenes) Goodman; m. Trevor O. Wong, Feb. 14, 1965 (div. 1984); children: Michael, Jeffrey, Susan Hyman. BA, UCLA, 1977, MSW, 1980. Intake worker child psychiatry dept. Cedars Sinai Med. Ctr., Los Angeles, 1974-76; social work intern, probation officer Camp David Gonzales, Calabasas, Calif., 1978-79; social work intern UCLA Neuropsychiat. INst., 1979-80; pvt. practice social work Kailua-Kona, Hawaii, 1980—; mem. adv. bd. Med. Personnel Pool, Kailua-Kona, 1985—; personnel cons., Kailua-Kona, 1986—; presenter workshops and seminars on mental health issues; founder World Youth Video Exchange, Kailua-Kona, 1986—. Columnist, newspaper, 1981—; author poems. Active Big Bros. and Big Sisters Corp., Kailua-Kona, mem. selection com. 1983—; guardian ad litum 3d Cir. Ct., Hawaii County, 1985—; cons. Compassionate Friends, Kailua-Kona, 1985—; mem. adv. bd. Child and Family Services, Kailua-Kona, 1983—. Recipient Work toward World Peace Recognition award Baha'i Ch., 1985. Mem. Nat. Assn. Social Workers, Hawaii County Mental Health Assn. (adv. bd. 1982-83), Nalu Maluhia (founder, bd. dirs.). Club: Kona Outdoor Circle. Avocations: swimming, bicycling, yoga, aerobics, travel. Home: 77-6452 Alii Dr #213 Kailua-Kona HI 96740 Office: Kona Inn Shopping Village Kailua-Kona HI 96740

WONG, MARY KAMM, rental company executive; b. Honolulu, Feb. 11, 1904; d. Charles Seu and Kim Kyau (Goo) Kamm; B.S., U. Hawaii, 1927; M.A. (scholar), Boston U., 1930; m. Duke Bung Yai Wong, July 12, 1945. With Pineapple Research Lab., U. Hawaii, 1927; lab. technician Children's Hosp., 1930; tchr. pub. schs. Hawaii Dept. Pub. Instrn., 1931-65; v.p., treas. Ala Moana Broadcasting Co., Inc., 1957-59; pres., treas. Polynesian Broadcasting Co. Inc., 1960-66, Rural Broadcasting Co. Inc., 1969-72, Leilani Enterprises, 1968— (all Honolulu); dir. Kam Travel Agy., Inc., Big 88. Mem. NEA, Kam Soc., Outdoor Circle, AAUW, Boston U. Alumni Assn., Am. Legion Aux., Theta Upsilon. Episcopalian.

WONG, MITCHELL GARY, investment banker; b. Fresno, Calif., Sept. 16, 1951; s. Wyman C.H. and Wanda Cecilia (Yee) W.; m. Emily Tsao Wen, Mar. 22, 1986. AB, U. Calif., Berkeley, 1972, MBA, 1975. Assoc. Shuman, Agnew & Co., San Francisco, 1974; credit officer Wells Fargo Bank, San Francisco, 1972-74; asst. treas. Mfrs. Hanover, N.Y.C., 1975-76; v.p., sect. head Bank of Am., San Francisco, 1976-82; pres. Wedbush Leasing Inc., Los Angeles, 1982-87. Author: (jour.) Leasing on the West Coast, 1985, Tax Oriented Financing under the Tax Reform Act of, 1986, 87. Chmn. Asian/Pacific Rim Council, United Way, 1987. Mem. Asian Bus. League (pres. San Francisco chpt. 1981-82, pres. Los Angeles chpt. 1984, chmn. So. Calif. div. 1986), Assn. for Corp. Growth, Am. Assn. Equipment Lessors. Clubs: Stock Exchange, Los Angeles. Avocations: tennis, skiing, travel. Home: 2122 Veteran Ave Los Angeles CA 90025 Office: Wedbush Leasing Inc 615 S Flower St Los Angeles CA 90017

WONG, OTTO, epidemiologist, biostatistician; b. Canton, China, Nov. 14, 1947; came to U.S., 1967, naturalized, 1976; s. Kui and Foon (Chow) W.; m. Betty Yeung, Feb. 14, 1970; children—Elaine, Jonathan. B.S., U. Ariz., 1970; M.S., Carnegie Mellon U., 1972; M.S., U. Pitts., 1973, Sc.D., 1975. Cert. epidemiologist, Am. Coll. Epidemiology, 1982. USPHS fellow U. Pitts., 1972-75; asst. prof. epidemiology Georgetown U. Med. Sch., 1975-78; mgr. epidemiology Equitable Environ. Health Inc., Rockville, Md., 1977-78; dir. epidemiology Tabershaw Occupational Med. Assocs., Rockville, 1978-80; dir. occupational research Biometric Research Inst., Washington, 1980-81; pres. scientific affairs, sr. epidemiologist Environ. Health Assocs., Inc., Oakland, Calif., 1981—; cons. Nat. Cancer Inst., Nat. Inst. Occupational Safety and Health, Occupational Safety and Health Adminstrn., Nat. Heart, Lung and Blood Inst., Ford Motors Co., Gen. Electric, Mobil, Chevron, Union Carbide, Fairfax Hosp., Va. U. Ariz. scholar, 1967-68. Fellow Am. Coll. Epidemiology, Human Biology Council; mem. Am. Pub. Health Assn., Biometric Soc., Soc. Epidemiologic Research, Phi Beta Kappa, Pi Mu Epsilon. Democrat. Contbr. articles to profl. jours. Office: Environ Health Assocs Inc 520 3d St Suite 208 Oakland CA 94607

WONG, RONALD JAMES, pediatric dental surgeon; b. Fresno, Calif., Dec. 21, 1931; s. Raymond Arthur and Ruth (Moe) W.; B.S., U. So. Calif., 1954, D.D.S., 1956; m. Edith Mok, June 21, 1962 (div. 1986); children: Gary Hunter, Julie, Christy, Carina, Lara, Sabrina. Intern, P.T.A. Clinic, Los Angeles Sch. Dist., 1956-57; resident Greenpark Sch. dental clinic, Chofu, Japan, 1958-59; practice dentistry specializing in pediatric dental surgery, Hollywood, Calif., 1959—; mem. staff Hollywood Presbyn. Hosp.; asst. clin. prof. pedodontics U. So. Calif., Los Angeles, 1959-68; cons. Children's Hosp. Los Angeles, 1960-73, head dental div., 1973-78. Coordinator Lang. Services Archery Venue XXIII Olympics, Los Angeles. Served to capt. USAF, 1957-59. Nat. Flight Archery Champion U.S.A., 1984; First place winner 25 KG class U.S. Nat. Archery Flight Championship, 1982, Silver Wescott medal No. 2 amateur flight archer in U.S., 1983. Mem. Hollywood, Los Angeles dental socs., Hollywood Acad. Medicine, Am. Stomatological Soc. Japan, Am. Analgesia Soc., Am. Acad. Pedodontics, Am., So. Calif. (pres. 1968-69) socs. dentistry for children, So. Calif., Am. dental assns., Calif. Pedodontic Research Group, Western Pedodontic and Odontic Soc., Am. Endodontic Soc., Am. Hypnodontic Soc., Acad. of Dentistry for the Handicapped, Chinese Am. Citizen's Alliance, Delta Sigma Delta, Alpha Tau Omega. Rotarian. Author: Pedodontic Dental Preparations, 1961. Home: 3372 Rowena Ave #1 Los Feliz CA 90027 Office: 1616 Hillhurst Ave Hollywood CA 90027

WONG, STELLA MEE QUE, social work educator; b. Honolulu, May 29, 1950; d. Yuen Kong and Margaret (Lum) W. BS, U. Hawaii, 1972, MSW, 1976. Lectr., acad. advisor U. Hawaii, Honolulu, 1972-86; med. social worker, community rep. Med. Personnel Pool, Honolulu, 1982—, dir. mktg., 1986—; inservice coordinator Convalescent Ctr., Honolulu, 1981-82; bd. dirs. adv. bd. M.P.P., Honolulu. Bd. dirs., Hawaii Council Camp Fire Girls, Honolulu, 1972-80, v.p. 1977, pres. 1978-80; mem. nominating com. YWCA, Honolulu, 1978. Recipient Shawnequas award Hawaii Council Camp Fire Girls, 1974. Mem. Nat. Council Family Relations (treas. Hawaii Council chpt. 1977-80), Nat. Assn. Social Workers, Hosp. Assn. Social Work Dirs. Avocations: woodwork, tennis, camping. Office: Med Personnel Pool 1441 Kapiolani Blvd #1320 Honolulu HI 96822

WONG, STEPHANIE LAM, columnist, educator; b. San Francisco, July 16, 1949; d. Franklin Mager and Suey Quon (Wong) Lam; m. Darryl Eugene Wong, July 29, 1978; children: Jessica Marie, Marshall. AA in Gen. Edn., Coll. of Marin Jr. Coll., 1969; B in Spanish, U. Calif., Santa Barbara, 1972; M in Spl. Edn., U. Santa Clara, 1983. Cert. spl. edn. credential, community coll. instr. credential. Tchr. East Side Union, San Jose, Calif., 1976—; program dir. San Jose Community Coll., 1982-83, spl. projects coordinator, 1983—; syndicated columnist Tribune Media, Orlando, Fla., 1983-85; columnist Chronicle, San Francisco, 1986—; spl. projects coordinator and adv. com. mem. Am. Med. Tech. Program, San Jose, 1983—. Photographer: La Cumbre, 1972 (spl. judges award for black and white photography, intercollegiate press award 1972). Avocations: photography, contests. Office: care San Jose City Coll 2100 Moorpark Ave San Jose CA 95128

WONG, STEVEN WYMANN, social service and economic development consultant, accounting, business and computer science educator; b. Honolulu, Oct. 24, 1946; s. Gerald Y.K. and Amy (Gwendolyn (Chun) W.; B.A., Claremont McKenna Coll., 1968; M.A., San Diego State U., 1969; M.B.A., So. Ill. U., Edwardsville, 1976. Exec. asst. to exec. dept. Pacific Fruit Express div. So. Pacific Industries, San Francisco, 1970; actuarial analyst Judson Branch Research Ctr. div. Allstate Ins. Co. subs. Sears & Roebuck, Inc., Menlo Park, Calif., 1971; econ. devel./manpower coordinator Oakland (Calif.) Model Cities Program, 1972-73; econ. cons. Marshall Kaplan, Gans & Kahn, San Francisco, 1973; econ. devel. dir. Econ. and Social Opportunities, Inc., San Jose, Calif., 1974-76; cons. to bus. and social services on fin. and mgmt., 1976—; prof. accountancy Merritt Coll., Oakland, Calif.; mem. faculty U. San Francisco, 1976—, Vista Coll., Berkeley, Calif., 1979—, Chapman Coll., Orange, Calif., 1980—, Columbia Coll., 1983—. Home: 5817 Mendoza Dr Oakland CA 94611 Office: 12500 Campus Dr Oakland CA 94619

WONG, YEN LU, choreographer, educator; b. Kunming, Yunnan, China, Mar. 27, 1942; d. Tsinforn Charles and Chun May (Wei) W.; came to U.S., 1958; m. Herbert Shore; children—Pia Ilyen, Maya Iming Wong. B.S., Tufts U., 1962; M.A., U. Kans., 1972; cert. Laban/Bartenieff Inst. Movement Studies, N.Y.C., 1975; student Martha Graham Sch., 1961-63. Founder (with Herbet Shore) TNR/The New Repertory, Los Angeles, 1972—, also dir.; vis. prof. div. drama Sch. of Cinema-TV, U. So. Calif., Los Angeles, 1980; Editorial cons. Jour. Congress Research in Dance, 1977—. Choreographic works include: Documents from Hell, Cicada Images, Moulting, Between Silence and Light, I and II, Call of Ancient Voices, Golden Mountain, Moebius Moments, Shi-Mé with visual artist, Françoise Gilot. Mem. dance panel Nat. Endowment Arts, 1980-83; panelist cons. Nat. Endowment Humanities, 1977-79. Nat. Endowment Arts fellow, 1980, 81, 84, Rockefeller Found. fellow, 1979; U. Calif. Regents Creative Arts fellow, 1976, Nat. Endowment Humanities fellow, 1974-75; Martha Graham Sch. Contemporary Dance/deRothschild fellow 1962-64; grantee: Australian Council, China Acad., Ministry Edn. Taiwan, Mobil Corp. Mem. Conseil Internat. de la Danse (founding; exec. bd. Am. br. 1979), Calif. Dance Educators Assn. (pres. 1978-79). Office: 4091 W 8th St Los Angeles CA 90005

WONG-DIAZ, FRANCISCO RAIMUNDO, lawyer; b. Havana, Cuba, Oct. 29, 1944; came to U.S., Nov. 1961; s. Juan and Teresa (Diaz de Villegas) Wong; m. Maria Victoria Campos, 1986; 1 child, Richard Alan. B.A. with honors, No. Mich. U., 1963; M.A. with highest honors, U. Detroit, 1967; Ph.D., M.A., U. Mich., 1973; J.D., U. Calif.-Berkeley, 1976. Bar: Calif. 1980, U.S. Dist. Ct. (no. dist.) Calif. 1985, Fla. 1987. Asst. prof. San Francisco State U., 1977; vis. scholar U. Calif. Berkeley Sch. Bus., Berkeley, 1983-84; prof. City Coll. San Francisco, 1975—, dept. chmn., 1978—; sole practice, Kentfield, Calif., 1980—; assoc. dean Miami-Dade Coll., 1986; dir. Cutcliffe Consulting, Inc., Hawthorne, LaFamila Ctr., Inc., San Rafael, Calif., Small Bus. Inst., Kentfield. Bd. editors Indsl. Relations Law Jour., 1975-76. Diplomat-scholar U.S. Dept. State, Washington, 1976; Horace C. Rackham fellow U. Mich., 1970; NEH fellow, summer 1981. Mem. ABA, Am. Polit. Sci. Assn., Cuban Am. Nat. Council, World Affairs Council (seminar leader San Francisco 1980). Pan-Am. Soc. Roman Catholic. Club: Commonwealth.

WOO, CHIA-WEI, university president, physicist, educator; b. Shanghai, China, Nov. 13, 1937; came to U.S., 1955, naturalized, 1972; s. Chih-Ming and Janet (Hsia) W.; m. Yvonne Lo, Jan. 23, 1960; children: De-Kai J., De-Yi Y., De-Hwei M, Detian A. B.S., Georgetown Coll., Ky., 1956; M.A., Washington U., 1961, Ph.D., 1966. Applied mathematician Monsanto Co., St. Louis, 1959-62; research asso. Washington U., St. Louis, 1966; asst. research physicist U. Calif. at San Diego, La Jolla, 1966-68; provost Revelle Coll., prof., 1979-83; pres., prof. San Francisco State U., 1983—; asst. prof. physics Northwestern U., Evanston, Ill., 1968-70, assoc. prof., 1971-73, prof., 1973-79, chmn. dept. physics and astronomy, 1974-79; vis. asso. prof. U. Ill., Urbana, 1970-71; hon. prof. Inst. Physics, Chinese Acad. Scis., Beijing, 1978—, Fudan U., Shanghai, 1978—, Shenzhen U., 1986—; cons. Argonne Nat. Lab., 1967—, NSF, 1977-81, Exxon Research and Engring. Co., 1982—. Alfred P. Sloan Research fellow, 1971-73. Fellow Am. Phys. Soc. Office: San Francisco State Univ Office of the President 1600 Holloway Ave San Francisco CA 94132

WOO, DEXTER JU-WEI, chemist; b. Mar. 28, 1952; s. Wei Yen and Lucie (Feng) W.; m. Helen Mar, Aug. 26, 1984. AB, U. Calif., Berkeley, 1976. Jr. chemist Colgate-Palmolive Co., Berkeley, 1976-79; research chemist Stanford U., Palo Alto, Calif., 1979-81; applications chemist Chromatics, Sunnyvale, Calif., 1981-82, Interaction Chems., Mountain View, Calif., 1982—. Contbr. articles to profl. jours. Mem. AAAS, Inst. Food Technologists (profl.), Am. Chem. Soc., Assn. Ofcl. Analytical Chemists. Avocations: running, swimming, painting, Schutzhund tng. Home: 313 Klamath Rd Milpitas CA 95035 Office: Interaction Chemicals Inc 1615 Plymouth St Mountain View CA 94043

WOO, SAVIO LAU-YUEN, bioengineering educator; b. Shanghai, Peoples Republic of China, June 3, 1942; s. Kwok CHong and Fung Sing (Yu) W.; m. Patricia Tak-kit Cheong, Sept. 6, 1969; children: Kirstin Wei-Chi, Jonathan I-Huei. BSME, Chico State U., 1965; MS, U. Wash., 1966, PhD, 1971. Research assoc. U. Wash., Seattle, 1968-70; asst. research prof. U. Calif.-San Diego, La Jolla, 1970-74, assoc. research prof., 1974-75, assoc. prof., 1975-80, prof. surgery and bioengring., 1980—; prin. investigator VA Med. Ctr., San Diego, 1972—; cons. bioengr. Childrens Hosp., San Diego, 1973-80; cons. med. implant cos., 1978-85; vis. prof. biomechanics Kobe, Japan U., 1981-82; dir., chief exec. officer M&D Coutts Inst. for Joint Reconstrn. and Research, 1984—. Assoc. editor: Jour. Biochem. Engring., 1979—, Jour. Biomechanics, 1978—, Jour. Orthopedic Research, 1983—; contbr. articles to profl. jours. Recipient Elizabeth Winston Lanier Kappa Delta Award, 1983, 85, award for excellence in basic sci. research Am. Orthopaedic Soc. Sports Medicine, 1983, 86; Japan Soc. of Promotion of Sci. fellow, 1981; Research Career Devel. award NIH, 1977-82. Mem. ASME (sec., chmn. biomechanics com., chmn. honors com. bioengring. div., mem. exec. com., 1983—, sec. 1985-86, chmn. 1986-87), Western Orthopaedic Assn., Biomed. Engring. Soc. (bd. dirs. 1984-86), Am. Acad. Orthopedic Surgeons, Orthopaedic Research Soc. (exec. com. 1983—, sec., treas. 1977-80, pres. 1985-86), Am. Soc. Biochemics. Home: 4455 Heritage Glen Ln San Diego CA 92310 Office: U Calif San Diego Div Orthopaedic Surgery M-030 La Jolla CA 92093

WOOD, BRIAN WALLACE, optometrist, consultant; b. Des Moines, May 1, 1951; s. Wallace Glen and Evelyn Irene W. B.S., U. Iowa, 1973; postgrad. Drake U., 1973; O.D., Ill. Coll. Optometry, 1977. Lab./teaching asst. Ill. Coll. Optometry, 1974-77; practice optometry, Denver, 1977—; mem. Eye Clinic staff Denver Gen. Hosp., 1977-81; cons., investigator mapping div. U.S. Geol. Survey; investigator explt. soft contact lenses FDA. Bd. dirs. Denver County (Colo.) Young Republicans, 1978-80; chmn. Leadership Lakewood, 1987—. Merit scholar U. Iowa, 1969-70. Mem. Am. Optometric Assn., Lakewood C. of C., Colo. Optometric Assn., Jefferson County Optometric Soc., Phi Gamma Delta (bd. chpt. advs. 1982—), Beta Sigma Kappa. Republican. Club: Mt. Vernon Country (Golden, Colo.). Designer various optical aids for map makers Denver Fed. Center, U.S. Geol. Survey. Office: 8600 W 14th Ave Lakewood CO 80215

WOOD, DAVID JAMES, academic administrator, educator; b. Lima, Ohio, Mar. 21, 1948; s. Floyd Arley and Erma Vondale (Briggs) W.; m. Linda Louise Tropf, Aug. 18, 1973; children: Joann, Sara. BA, Ohio State U., 1970; MEd, St. Francis Coll., 1975; PhD, U. Toledo, 1978; postgrad., Bowling Green U., Ind. U., Ohio No. U., Wright State U. Tchr. Lima City Schs., 1970-75; supr. student tchrs., adminstrv. asst. to dean U. Toledo Coll. Edn., 1975-77; asst. dir. N.W. Ind. Spl. Edn. Coop., Crown Point, 1977-85; exec. dir. spl. edn. Aurora (Colo.) Pub. Schs., 1985—; asst. prof. edn. Bluffton (Ohio) Coll., 1975-77; adj. asst. prof. Purdue U., Hammond, Ind., 1977-80, Ind. U., Gary, 1979-85; ednl. cons. The Cedars, 1979-82; activity therapy dir. N.W. Community Mental Health Clinic and St. Rita's Hosp. Psychiat. Wards, Lima, 1972-74. Coordinator coop. programs Lucas County Schs. and Med. Coll. Ohio, Toledo, 1976-77; mem. Ind. U. Field Experiences Adv. Com., 1978-83; mem. Ind. Task Force on Emotional Disturbance, 1980—; mem. Ind. Dept. Edn. and Dept. Mental Health Com. task force on Interagy. Planning and Programming, 1983—; coordinator Lake County Tchr. Inst. on Tchr. Burnout, Merrillville, Ind., 1980; bd. dirs. Southlake Ctr. for Mental Health, 1978-82, Aurora Community Mental Health Ctr., 1986—. Mem. Am. Assn. Sch. Adminstrs., Assn. Supervision and Curriculum Devel., Nat. Orgn. Legal Problems in Edn., Ind. Assn. Sch. Bus. Ofcls., Council for Exceptional Children, Council for Adminstrn. of Spl. Edn., Council for Adminstrn. of Spl. Edn. in Colo. (pres.-elect 1986), Phi Delta Kappa (editor 1985-86). Avocations: water and snow skiing, internat. travel, writing, pub. speaking. Home: 13906 E Hamilton Dr Aurora CO 80014 Office: Aurora Pub Schs 11023 E 5th Ave Aurora CO 80010

WOOD, DENNIS PATRICK, clinical psychologist, educator; b. Oakland, Calif., Aug. 5, 1949; s. Donald James and Helen Winfred (Reimann) W.; m. Joan Anne Treinen, Feb. 14, 1971; children—Ross, Trevor, Megan. B.A. (Coll.-scholar 1967-71), St. Mary's Coll., Moraga, Calif., 1971; M.A. (Univ. scholar 1972-73), U. Nebr., 1973; Ph.D., Calif. Sch. Profl. Psychology, 1976. Lic. psychologist, Nev., Calif. Psychology intern In-Between Youth Ctr., San Diego, 1973-74, Golden State Community Mental Health Ctr. (now Hope Community Mental Health Ctr.), Lakeview Terrace, Calif., 1974-75, Alcohol Rehab. Ctr., Naval Sta., San Diego; postdoctoral intern dept. psychiatry Balboa Navy Hosp., San Diego, 1976-77; staff psychologist dept. psychiatry, 1976-80; co-dir. La Jolla (Calif.) Profl. Workshops, 1977-84; pvt. practice clin. and health psychology, San Diego and Las Vegas, Nev., 1980—; clin. instr. Sch. Medicine, U. Calif.-San Diego, 1979—; cons. to bus. and med. facilities. Vice pres. Donald James Wood Found., Oakland, Calif., 1971-77, trustee, 1977—. Served to lt. comdr. USNR, 1976-80. Recipient Outstanding Service cert. Commandant of 11th Naval Dist., 1975. Mem. Am. Psychol. Assn., Med. Psychology Network (program coordinator Western U.S.), Calif. Psychology Assn., Navy League, Res. Officers Assn., Naval Res. Assn., Am. Soc. Clin. Hypnosis. Democrat. Roman Catholic. Co-author: Clinical Hypnosis Primer, 1984. Contbr. articles on psychology, hypnosis and alcoholism to profl. jours. Office: 4230 S Burnham Ave Suite 244 Las Vegas NV 89109 Also: 550 Washington St #215 San Diego CA 92103

WOOD, DONALD JAMES, newspaper publishing executive; b. Modesto, Calif., Apr. 7, 1922; s. Ezra Benjamin and Maude Emma (Gardenhire) W.; m. Helen Winifred Reimann, Oct. 26, 1946; children: James, Dennis, Kathleen, Matthew. BS in Econs., St. Mary's Coll. of Calif., Moraga, 1946; MBA, Armstrong U., 1954; MJ, U. Calif., Berkeley, 1956; MA in Theology, Grad. Theol. Union, 1983; PhD in Edn., Walden U., 1972. Circulation supr. The Oakland (Calif.) Tribune, 1941-52; asst. to publ. San Francisco Call-Bulletin, San Francisco, 1952-59; mgr. circulation and promotion Berkeley Gazette, 1959-65; gen. mgr. Voice, Oakland, 1965—; pres. Am Cal Printing and Mailing Co., 1972—; prof. Oakland City Coll., 1956-62, Armstrong U., Berkeley, 1956-77; adj. prof. Dominican Sch. Philosophy and Theology, 1984; prin. cons. Wood Found., 1972-86. Author: Newspaper Circulation Management; William Randolph Hearst-His First Years in Journalism; A Media Doctor Needed; co-author (with Helen Winifred Wood) Men: Ideas, Issues (4 vols.); contbr. articles to newspapers and mags. Served with USN, 1943-44. Recipient Circulation Promotion award Editor and Publ., 1956, Newspaper Publicity award Calif. Circulation Mgrs. Assn., 1964, Sales Promotion award Internat. Circulation Mgrs. Assn., 1965, Advt. award Cath. Press Assn., 1972. Democrat. Roman Catholic. Avocation: swimming.

WOOD, ERNEST WILLIAM, university official; b. West Point, Ill., Feb. 1, 1934; s. William E. and Martha E. (Hess) W.; B.S., Central Coll., 1957; M.A., San Jose State U., 1979; Ed.D., U. of Pacific, 1983; 1 child, Tamara Dawn. Ordained to ministry Am. Evang. Christian Chs., 1960; cert. fund raising exec. Assoc. pastor 1st Assembly of God Ch., Memphis, 1959-65; missionary, Philippines, 1965-72; exec. v.p., dir. devel. Bethany Bible Coll., Santa Cruz, Calif., 1972-79; asst. v.p. devel. U. of Pacific, Stockton, 1979—; cons. and lectr. in field. Republican. Mem. Nat. Soc. Fund Raising Execs. (pres. No. Calif. chpt., nat. dir., nat. vice chair, v.p. found.), Council for Advancement and Support of Edn., Phi Delta Kappa. Club: Rotary. Home: 3632 Wood Duck Circle Stockton CA 95207 Office: Univ of Pacific Stockton CA 95211

WOOD, FERGUS JAMES, geophysicist, consultant; b. London, Ont., Can., May 13, 1917; came to U.S., 1924, naturalized, 1932; s. Louis Aubrey and Dora Isabel (Elson) W.; student U. Oreg., 1934-36; A.B., U. Calif.-Berkeley, 1938, postgrad., 1938-39; postgrad. U. Chgo., 1939-40, U. Mich., 1940-42, Calif. Inst. Tech., 1946; m. Doris M. Hack, Sept. 14, 1946; children—Kathryn Celeste Wood Madden, Bonnie Patricia Wood Ward. Teaching asst. U. Mich., 1940-42; instr. in physics and astronomy Pasadena City Coll., 1946-48, John Muir Coll., 1948-49; asst. prof. physics U. Md., 1949-50; assoc. physicist Johns Hopkins U. Applied Physics Lab., 1950-55; sci. editor Ency. Americana, N.Y.C., 1955-60; aero. and space research scientist, sci. asst. to dir. Office Space Flight Programs, Hdqrs., NASA, Washington, 1960-61; program dir. fgn. sci. info. NSF, Washington, 1961-62; phys. scientist, chief sci. and tech. info. staff U.S. Coast and Geodetic Survey (now Nat. Ocean Service), Rockville, Md., 1962-66, phys. scientist Office of Dir., 1967-73, research asso. Office of Dir., 1973-77; cons. tidal dynamics, Bonita, Calif., 1978—. Served to capt. USAAF, 1942-46. Recipient Spl. Achievement award Dept. Commerce, NOAA, 1970, 74, 76, 77. Mem. Sigma Pi Sigma, Pi Mu Epsilon, Delta Phi Alpha. Democrat. Presbyterian. Author: The Strategic Role of Perigean Spring Tides in Nautical History and North American Coastal Flooding, 1635-1976, 1978; Tidal Dynamics; Coastal Flooding and Cycles of Gravitational Force, 1986; contbr. numerous articles to encys., reference sources, profl. jours.; writer, tech. dir. documentary film: Pathfinders from the Stars, 1967; editor-in-chief: The Prince William Sound, Alaska, Earthquake of 1964 and Aftershocks, vols. 1-2A and sci. coordinator vols. 2B, 2C and 3, 1966-69. Home: 3103 Casa Bonita Dr Bonita CA 92002

WOOD, GEORGE, workers' compensation adjusting firm executive; b. Bisbee, N.D., Nov. 29, 1926; s. George Portarlington and Gladys Iola (Jennings) W.; m. Sally Ann Pearson, June 19, 1949 (dec. Aug. 1974); children—Susan HagEstad, Harry P., Nancy V. Davis, Barbara J. Student N.D. State U., 1946-48; B.A.E. with honors, U. Mont., 1950. Registered lobbyist. High sch. tchr., Helena, Mont., 1950-51; field adjuster Liberty Nat. Ins. Co., Helena, 1951-54; claims mgr., 1954-57; hearings officer Mont. State Indsl. Accident Bd., Helena, 1957-60; founder, owner, mgr. Compensation Adjusters, Missoula, Mont., 1960—. Pres. Ponderosa council Camp Fire Girls, 1970-73; mem. Gov.'s Adv. Council, 1970—. Recipient Appreciation award Mont. Bar Assn., 1979, Mont. Student Bar Assn., 1979; Sebago award Camp Fire Girls, 1971, Luther Halsey Gulick award, 1975; cert. of Outstanding Achievement, Mont. Div. Labor and Industry, 1973. Mem. Nat. Council Self-Insurers (bd. mgrs. 1974—, exec. com. 1980—). Served with inf. U.S. Army, 1944-45, PTO. Episcopalian. Club: Missoula Country. Lodge: Elks. Home: 409 Agnes Ave Missoula MT 59803 Office: Compensation Adjusters 321 SW Higgins Ave Missoula MT 59803

WOOD, GERALD LEE, consulting engineer; b. San Saba, Tex., Feb. 24, 1943; s. C.B. Jr. and Nellie V. (Brown) W.; m. Elizabeth Ann Lofgren, Aug. 10, 1973; children—Peter, John, Kristine, Daniel, Vincent, Jennifer. B.S. in Agrl. Engring., Tex. A&M, 1965. Registered profl. engr., Ariz., Mo.; registered land surveyor. Research asst. Tex. Agrl. Exptl. Sta., College Station, 1965-66; engr. Allis Chalmers, Independence, Mo., 1966-72; test engr. Massey-Ferguson, Detroit, 1972-78; mech. engr. Nat. Pump, Glendale, Ariz., 1979-82; cons. engr. W&W Engring., Scottsdale, Ariz., 1982—. Mem. Am. Soc. Agrl. Engrs. (state officer 1979-82), ASME, Soc. Automotive Engrs., Systems Safety Soc. Home: 6602 E Mountain View Rd Scottsdale AZ 85253 Office: W&W Engring PO Box 6393 Scottsdale AZ 85261

WOOD, HARRY GEORGE, packaging engineering and electrostatic discharge control consultant; b. Orchard Park, N.Y., Jan. 22, 1915; s. William A. and Marie E. (Schmidt) W.; m. Ruth Farber, Oct. 20, 1939; children—Keith F., Eugene F. B.S. in Edn., SUNY-Buffalo, 1936. Planning supr. Morrison Steel Products, Buffalo, 1944-51; sr. methods engr., materials handling supr. Schlage Lock Co., San Francisco, 1953-57; prodn. mgr. M. Greenberg's Sons Foundry & Machine Shop, San Francisco, 1957-58; packaging mgr. Hewlett-Packard Co., Santa Clara, Calif., 1959-83, established electrostatic discharge control program, 1981-83; cons. on packaging engring. and electrostatic discharge. H.G. Wood & Assocs., Palo Alto, 1983—; instr. factory planning and plant layout Foothill Jr. Coll., Los Altos, 1959-60; mem. nat. packaging industry adv. council U. Calif.-Davis, 1971-73; chmn. Internat. Air Cargo Forum, 1968-71; designed and built Ruth Wood Nursery Sch., 1962, ptnr. and bus. mgr., 1962—. Contbr. articles to profl. jours. Patentee in field. Recipient Grayson Lynn award for package design Lockheed Missile & Space Div., 1964, ann. achievement award Nat. Inst. Packaging Handling and Logistics Engrs., 1974. Fellow Soc. Packaging and Handling Engrs. (hon. life mem.; cert. profl. in packaging; 5 nat. design awards; (exec. v.p., program chmn. Golden Gate chpt. 1955, 63, pres. chpt. of yr. 1964-65, chmn. bd. dirs. 1966); Internat. Materials Mgmt. Soc. (nat. bd. dirs. 1956-57, pres. No. Calif. chpt. 1956-57). Home and Office: 849 Mesa Ave Palo Alto CA 94306

WOOD, JOHN DENISON, utility company executive; b. Calgary, Alta., Can., Sept. 28, 1931; s. Ernest William and Ellen Gartshore (Pender) W.; m. Christena Isabel; 1 dau., Donna M. BS in Civil Engring., U. B.C., 1953; MSCE of in Structures, Stanford U., 1954, PhD in Civil Engring. and Engring. Mechs., 1956. Research asst. in civil engring. and engring. mechs. Stanford U., Palo Alto, Calif., 1953-56; assoc. mgr. dynamics dept. Engring. Mechs. Lab. Space Tech. Labs., Inc., Redondo Beach, Calif., 1956-63; pres., dir. Mechs. Research, Inc., El Segundo, Calif., 1963-66; sr. v.p. engring. and research ATCO Ind., Ltd., 1966-68, sr. v.p. eastern region, 1968-75, sr. v.p. planning, 1975-77; pres., chief exec. officer ATCO Industries N.A., Ltd., 1977-82, AtCOR Resources Ltd., 1982-84; pres., chief operating officer Can. Utilities, Ltd., 1984—, also bd. dirs.; bd. dirs. Nat. Trust Co. Ltd., ATCO Ltd., ATCOR Resources Ltd., Can. Western Natural Gas Co. Ltd., Alta. Power Ltd., BioTechnica Internat., Inc., Vencap Equities Alta. Ltd. Co-author: Ballistic Missile and Space Vehicle Systems, 1961. Mem. pres.'s club adv. com. U. Alta. Athlone fellow. Mem. Engring. Inst. of Can., Sci. Research Soc. Am., Assn. Profl. Engrs. Alta., Sigma Xi, Tau Beta Pi. Baptist. Clubs: Glencoe, Earl Grey, Calgary Petroleum, Mayfair Golf and Country. Avocations: golf, badminton. Office: Canadian Utilities Ltd, 10035 105th St, Edmonton, AB Canada T5J 2V6 *

WOOD, LARRY (MARY LAIRD WOOD), journalist, author, environmental consultant, university educator; b. Sandpoint, Idaho; d. Edward Hayes and Alice (McNeel) Small; married; children: Mary, Marcia, Barry. BA magna cum laude, U. Wash., Seattle, 1938, MA with highest honors, 1940; postgrad., Stanford U., 1941-42, U. Calif., Berkeley, 1943-44; cert. in photography, U. Calif., Berkeley, 1971; postgrad. journalism, U. Wis., 1971-72, U. Minn., 1971-72, U. Ga., 1972-73; postgrad. in art, architecture and marine biology, U. Calif., Santa Cruz, 1974-76, Stanford Hopkins Marine Sta., Santa Cruz, 1977-80. By-line columnist (home and gardens, archtl. editor and real estate/fin. feature writer) Oakland (Calif.) Tribune, 1946—, San Francisco Chronicle, 1946—, Parade mag., Chevron U.S.A., Motorland, Westways, Accent; feature writer Western region Christian Sci. Monitor, CSM Radio Syndicate and Internat. News, 1973—, Register and Tribune Syndicate, Des Moines, 1975—, Calif. Today Mag., 1976—; No. Calif. contbg. editor Fashion Showcase, Dallas, Los Angeles, Chgo., N.Y.C., Linguapress, Besancon, France, 1981—, Parents mag., 1950-68; regional corr. Spokane mag.; by-lined feature writer and archtl. writer Calif. Living and Travel mag., San Jose Mercury News, 1978—, Parade mag., 1980—; archtl. writer Calif. Today mag., 1978—; by-lined feature writer and archtl. writer Oakland Calif. C. of C., 1983—; photographer/feature writer nat. geographic World Scholastic Publs., Nat. Geographic's World; photographer/feature writer Xerox Edn. Publs.and Scholastic Publs., 1974—; Calif. corr. Seattle Times Sunday mag.; feature writer East/West Network, 1980—, airline in-flight mags., 1980—, Travel and Leisure mag., 1984—, Chevron U.S.A., Times Mirror Syndicate and Knight Ridder Syndicate; writer In Paradise, 1987—; freelance writer mags. including Parents', Time, Sports Illus., Family Circle, Popular Mechanics, Family Handyman, House and Garden, Mechanix Illus., Indsl. Progress, Fawcett Boating Books, Hearst Publs., Oceans (award), Sea Frontiers (award), House Beautiful, Am. Home, Off-Duty, other nat. mags., 1946—; feature writer Meridian Publs., Ogden, Utah, Donnelley Bus. Publs. Country Roads, Indsl. Progress, Oak Brook, Ill.; programming cons. KRON-TV, 1985—; pub. relations cons. Bay Area Hosp. Assn., 1946-62; cons. Soc. Profl. Journalists Nat. Bd. for Hist. Sites, 1986—, Bay Area Hosp. Assn. and hosps. in 9 bay area cities, 1946-75; cons., reviewer for sci. textbooks, author sci. features on frontiers and scientists profiles Focus on Science Series, Charles E. Merrill div. Bell & Howell Co., 1983—; co-author Seeing The Golden State, 1986—; dir. pub. relations No. Calif. Assn. Phi Beta Kappa, 1969—; works used worldwide by USIA; cons., feature writer Met. Transp. Commn. No. Calif., 1970—; vis. prof. San Diego State U., 1974; asst. pprof. journalism San Diego State U., 1975—; disting. vis. prof. journalism San Jose State U., spring 1976; assoc. prof. journalism Calif. State U., Hayward, Calif. 19-univ. State U. system, 1976—; prof. environ./sci. journalism U. Calif. Berkeley Journalism Extension, 1979—; prof. journalism U. of Pacific, spring 1979; Western regional v.p., nat. bd. officer Women In Communication, 1975-77; key speaker Calif. Writers Club, 1987; cons. Soc. Profl. Journalists Nat. Bd. for Hist. Sites, 1986—; mem. and cons. Nat. Forensic Ctr., Lawrenceville, N.J.; keynote speaker Calif. State U. Women in Communications Conf., 1979, Nat. Assn. Edn. Journalism/Soc. Profl. Journalism Conf., 1979, Soc. Am. Travel Writers Conv., 1979, Harvard U., panel chmn., 1980; main speaker med. pub. relations Am. coll. Surgeons Nat. Conf., 1970; panelist sta. KRON-TV Doctor's News Conf., 1946-70; chmn. nat. travel writing contest for U.S. univ. journalism students Assn. for Edn. in Journalism/Soc. Am. Travel Writers, 1979-83; dir. pub. relations/cons. in field of sci., environ. affairs and recreation to numerous, firms, instns.; press del. Internat. Conf. Am. Geophys. Union./Newspapers Assn. for Edn. in Journalism, 1973-80; del. Nat. Press Photographers Flying Short Course, 1979, Asilomar Conf., FACS, Calif., 1982, Calif. Inst. Tech., 1984, 35th Nat. Conf. Pub. Relations Soc. Am., 1982, Nat. Trust for Hist. Preservation nat. conf., 1982, EXPO 86 Nat. Press Preview and Opening by Prince Charles and Princess Diana, 1986; Internat. Press Trip at Festival de los Vaqueros and Southwest Rodeo, Tucson, 1986, State of Hawaii/United Airlines Media Tour, 1985; press del. to Fla., Alaska, Mexico, Hawaii, Tex., Ga., Tenn., La. Media Tours, 1980-84, Washington State Nat. Press Trip, 1985, IEEE, 1985-86, conf. Lassen Nat. Park Sec. Interior and Dir. Nat. Park Service, 1986—; lead feature writer for CSM Internat.; press participant in U.S. Fish and Wildlife Service, Calif. Fish and Games Wild Elk Roundup for relocation, 1985. Syndicate's spl. edition Democratic Conv. in San Francisco, 1984 (awards); mem. nat. tasks AAAS, Assn. Med. Writers, Nat. Trust Hist. Preservation and exec. bd. mem.; cons. programming Sta. KRON-TV, 1985—. Author/reviewer Focus on Science series, Bell & Howell; author: Journalism Quarterly, 1978—; (with Charles Merrill) Principles of Science, 1982, 84, 87, (with Barry Wood) Fodor's California and San Francisco, 1982—; Railroads of the West; Pacific Coast Ports; Showcase Cities of the West; America's Estuaries, California's Underwater Parks; Megamouth, A New Species of Shark; Restorations in the West; Columbia-Glacier in Retreat, Youth Gangs in Los Angeles, Endangered Species series; Brown Pelican, Calif. Sea Otter, Blue Whales on Whales on Pacific Coast, Calif. Condor, Calif. Mountain Lion, Elephant Seals; Receding Columbia Glacier, Alaska; Fodor Travel Guide, Pacific N.W. works in archives of U. Wash. Library, Calif. writings in archives of Oakland Pub. Library; author features on Calif. Sea Otter, Wild Burro, Wild Mustang, Yellowstone Grizzlies and Wild Rivers Controversies; other writings include: Railroads Look again at Land Holdings, Seattle's Fire-Safe Federal Office Building, Homesteading in Cities, Turn of the Century San Francisco, Santa Cruz-Fusion of Architectural Gems, Pruneyard: A New Concept in Shopping, also lead feature on ports and San Francisco Cultural Scene for CSM Syndicate, July, 1984, Megamouth--New Species of Shark, 1986, Columbia--Alaska's Receding Glacier, 1986, L.A. Youth Gangs, 1985, Relocation of Wild Elk in West, 1985, Wild Burro/Wild Mustang Adoption Program, BLM, 1986; lead coverage Vallejo (Calif.)/USN Mare Island Nat. Wooden Boat Competition and Internat. Air Show featuring Canada's Snow Birds, Salinas, Calif., 1986; panelist Doctors' News Conference weekly show KRON-TV, 1946-70. Pub. relations dir. YWCA, YM-YW USO, Seattle, 1942-48, YWCA, Oakland Calif., 1946-56, Children's Home Soc. Calif., 1946-56, Children's Med. Ctr. No. Calif., 1946-70, Eastbay Regional Park Dist., 1946-58, Calif. Spring Garden Shows, 1948-58, Girl Scouts U.S.A., Oakland, 1948-56, others; speaker for ednl. insts., profl. groups, A.C.S., World Wildlife Fund, 1946—; sec. Jr. Ctr. of Arts, Oakland, 1952—; vol. pub. relations Am. Cancer Soc., YMCA, Oakland, 1946-52; pub. relations writer ARC, 1946-56; pres. Larry Wood Pub. Relations, 1947—; judge Nat. Book Awards, 1980—, Nat. Assn. Real Estate Editors ann. real estate contest, 1982—; Oakland Park Dept., YMCA, Seattle, Oakland; guest, press del. Govt. of Mexico, Mass., Dept. Econ. Devel. and City of Boston, Costa Rica, Wash., Oreg., Calif., Alaska, 1980-82, Fla., San Antonio, Atlanta, Chattanooga, Baton Rouge, Houston, Galveston, 1983; bd. dirs. Camp Fire Girls, Oakland, Joaquin Miller PTA, Oakland; trustee Calif. State Parks Found., 1976—; mem. Pres.'s Commn. on Families, 1984—; disting. mem. press pool Calif. Acad. Scis., Fine Arts Mus. of San Francisco, San Francisco Mus. Modern Art, 1960—; sponsor Nat. Mortar Bd. Alumni Music Scholarship, 1985 - . Recipient citations U. S. Forest Service, 1975, Bur. Land Mgmt., 1977, citation for coverage 1st nat. hist. preserve Ebey's Landing, San Juan Island, Wash., Nat. Park Service, 1976, citation and award for writings Oakland Mus. Assn., 1978-79, Hall of Fame award Broadway High Sch. U. Wash., Seattle, 1984; named Calif. Woman of Achievement, 1979; USN award for writings on hydrofoil missleships, 1983; co-recipient citation Oakland Mus., Nat. Headliners award San Hose Mercury News, Nat. Headliner award for Best Sunday Mag.; honoree for features Oakland C. of C. and Standard Oil USA, 1983, San Francisco C. of C. Mem. Pub. Relations Soc. Am., Nat. Sch. Pub. Relations Assn., Environ. Cons. N. Am., Internat. Environ. Cons., Oceanic Soc., Internat. Oceanographic Soc., Am. Assn. Edn. in Journalism (exec.bd. nat. mag. div. 1978 -, newspaper div. 1974-77, nat. exec. bd. mag./newspapers 1976-79), U. Wash. Ocean Scis. Alumni Assn. (charter), U. Calif.-Berkeley Alumni Assn., Investigative Reporters and Editors, Soc. Travel Writers Am., Women in Communications (nat. bd., western regional v. p. 1979, nat. constn. com. 1984-, panel chmn. assn. edn. journalism nat. conf. 1980, journalism ethics 1980), Calif. Acad. Environ. News Writers, Nat. Assn. Sci. Writers, No. Calif. Assn Sci. Writers, Am. Mgmt. Assn., AAAS, Nat. Press Photographers Assn., San Francisco Press Assn., Am. Med. Writers Assn. (nat. conf. del. 1985), Nat. Acad. TV Arts and Scis., Council Advancement of Sci. Writing, Eastbay Women's Press Club, Calif. Writers Club, Mortar Bd. Alumni Assn., Bay Area Ad Club (AdMark), Sigma Delta Chi, Theta Sigma Phi. Home: 6161 Castle Dr Oakland CA 94611 Office: San Diego CA

WOOD, LINDA MAY, librarian; b. Fort Dodge, Iowa, Nov. 6, 1942; d. John Albert and Beth Ida (Riggs) Wiley; m. C. James Wood, Sept. 15, 1964 (div. 1984). B.A., Portland State U., 1964; M.Librarianship, U. Wash., 1965. Reference librarian Library Assn. Portland (Oreg.), 1965-67, br. librarian, 1967-72, adminstrv. asst. to the librarian, 1972-73, asst. librarian, 1973-77; asst. city librarian Los Angeles Pub. Library, 1977-80; library dir. Riverside (Calif.) City and County Pub. Library, 1980—. Chmn. bd. dirs. Inland Library System, 1983-84; League of Calif. Cities Community Services Com., 1985—. Mem. AAUW, ALA, Pub. Library Assn., Library Adminstrn. and Mgmt. Assn., Calif. Library Assn. (pres. 1985), Calif. County Librarians Assn., LWV, OCLC Users Council . Democrat. Office: Riverside City and County Pub Library PO Box 468 Riverside CA 92502

WOOD, PAUL FOSTER, owner wholesale company, legislative aide; b. Adrian, Mo., May 8, 1911; s. Robert Lee and Edna (Foster) W.; m. Mable Irene Dye, Nov. 1, 1965. Student Huntsville Tchrs. Coll.; grad. Washington U., St. Louis; hon. degree in Psychology, 1934. Cert. med. lab. tech., criminal justice and criminology. Security rep. T.J. Pendergast and Truman, Kansas City, Mo., 1936-40; undercover agt. Bur. Narcotics, overseas, 1948-57; mgr. Buick Motor Div., Calif., Tex., Colo., 1958-63; investigator HUD, 5 western states, 1967-76; now owner Diversified Products Wholesale Co., Elko, Nev.; active Sr. Citizens Club, Elko County, 1978-81. Developer cleaning fluid, 1971; author: How to Sell Real Estate, 1970. Active fundraising Democratic campaigns, Tom Eagleton, Mo., 1974, Lloyd Benson, Tex., others. Served to lt. comdr. USN, 1940-46; PTO. Decorated Silver Star, Bronze Star, D.F.C., Purple Heart. Mem. VFW. Club: Lions (bd. dirs. Elko 1977-83, Spring Creek Nev. 1983—). Home: PO Box 1808 Elko NV 89801

WOOD, SHEILA KAY, chemist; b. Phoenix, June 29, 1959; d. Ralph E. And Anna E. (Leuning) Danielson; m. Daniel Steven Wood, Nov. 12, 1983. BS, Ariz. State U., 1981. Chemist City of Phoenix, 1981—. Recipient Productivity Improvement award City of Phoenix, 1985. Mem. Nat. Assn. Female Execs., Nat. Assn. Environ Profls., Inst. Indsl. Engrs. Republican. Avocations: home renovation, interior decoration. Home: 311 W Stella Ln Phoenix AZ 85013 Office: City of Phoenix 5615 S 91st Ave Phoenix AZ 85353

WOOD, WAYNE BARRY, photojournalist; b. Oakland, Calif., June 23, 1958; s. Wilbur and Larry Marylaird (Small) W. B.S. in Bus. and Transp. Mgmt. with highest honors, Calif. State U.-Hayward and San Francisco, 1980; M.B.A., with highest honors, Calif. State U.,Hayward, 1982; cert. of photography U. of Calif.-Berkeley, 1974-77. Freelance photojournalist numerous mags. and newspapers including Spectrum, San Jose Mercury News, Seattle Times, CSM News Syndicate, Off Duty, Model Railroader, Passenger Train Journ. Fashion Showcase, Sea Frontiers, Linguapress, Freeway, and others; mem. press corps for U.S. visit of Queen Elizabeth and Prince Philip, EXPO '86 visit of Prince Charles and Lady Diana to Vancouver, B.C.; guest Dept. of Tourism of Fla., Ariz., Alaska, Cape Cod, Houston, Chattanooga, Amtrak, Grand Tetons, Yellowstone, Wash., Hawaii. Co-author: Fodor's San Francisco, 1982, 84, 85, 86, 87; Fodor's California, 1984, 85, 86, 87; Official State Tour Guide of California, 1985. Photographer: Focus on Science, 1983, 87. Orland A. Close scholar Calif. State U.-Hayward, 1979. Mem. Nat. Press Photographers Assn, Soc. Profl. Journalists, U. Calif. Alumni Assn., Calif. Chpt. Sci. Writers, Nat. Assn. Sci. Writers. Home: 6161 Castle Dr Oakland CA 94611

WOOD, WILLIAM BARRY, aerospace engineer; b. Phila., Nov. 23, 1946; s. John Robert and Dorothy Eleanor (Wagner) W.; m. Kathryn Rose Porter, June 7, 1968; children: William Jr., Robert, Aimee, Dennis. BS in Math., USAF Acad., 1968; MA in Bus., U. Nebr., 1974; MS in Applied Math., U. Denver, 1977; cert. program mgmt., Def. Systems Mgmt. Coll., 1985. Commd. 2d lt. USAF, 1968, advanced through grades to capt., 1971, resigned, 1972; mem. tech. staff Hughes Aircraft Co., Denver, 1972-76, staff engr., 1976-78, sect. head, sr. project engr., 1978-83, project mgr., 1983—. Coach, referee Littleton (Colo.) Soccer Assn., 1977—; group leader St. Thomas More Parish Godparent Program, Englewood, Calif., 1984—. Mem. IEEE, Assn. Grads. USAF Acad. (v.p. Colo. chpt. 1979-80). Republican. Roman Catholic. Avocations: skiing, tennis, swimming. Home: 7889 S Garfield Way Littleton CO 80122 Office: Hughes Aircraft Co 8000 E Maplewood Ave Suite 226 Englewood CO 80111

WOOD, WILLIAM IRWIN, molecular biologist; b. Bloomington, Ind., Nov. 8, 1947; s. Willis Avery and Alice Jane (Spencer) W.; m. Bethe Lee Moulton, July 14, 1973. BA, Cornell U., 1970; MA, Harvard U., 1971, PhD, 1977. Staff fellow NIH, Bethesda, Md., 1978-81; scientist Genentech Inc., San Francisco, 1982-84, sr. scientist, 1985—. Mem. AAAS, Am. Soc. Biol. Chemists (assoc.). Avocation: computer sci. Home: 1400 Tarrytown St San Mateo CA 94402 Office: Genentech Inc 460 Point San Bruno Blvd South San Francisco CA 94080

WOOD, WILLIS BOWNE, JR., utility company executive; b. Kansas City, Mo., Sept. 15, 1934; s. Willis Bowne Sr. and Mina (Henderson) W.; m. Dixie Gravel, Aug. 31, 1955; children: Bradley, William, Josh. BS in Petroleum Engring., U. Tulsa, 1957; grad. advanced mgmt. program, Harvard U., 1983. Various positions So. Calif. Gas Co., Los Angeles, 1960-74, v.p. then sr. v.p., 1975-80, exec. v.p., 1983-84; pres., chief exec officer Pacific Lighting Gas Supply Co., Los Angeles, 1981-83; exec. v.p. Pacific Lighting Corp., Los Angeles, 1984—. Trustee Harvey Mudd Coll., Claremont, Calif, Calif. Med. Ctr., Los Angeles. Mem. Soc. Petroleum Engrs., Am. Gas Assn., Pacific Coast Gas Assn., Pacific Energy Assn. Republican. Presbyterian. Clubs: Calif., Los Angeles (Los Angeles); Center (Orange County); International (Washington). Office: Pacific Lighting Corp 810 S Flower St Los Angeles CA 90017

WOOD, YVONNE ANN, hospital administrator; b. Albuquerque, Oct. 22, 1949; d. John Eugene and Connie Molchan. BS cum laude, Calif. Poly. State U., Pomona, 1982. Cert. tchr., Calif. Program dir. Casa de Vida, San Luis Obispo, Calif., 1973-80, adminstr., 1980-82; adminstr. Paso Robles (Calif.), 1980-82, San Jose (Calif.) Care and Guidance, 1982—; cons. Am. Health, Newport Beach, Calif., 1976-80, San Luis Obispo Spl Edn., 1973-74, Am. Health Ctrs. Friendship Sch., San Luis Obispo, 1974-80; bd. dirs. Econ. Opportunity Commn., San Luis Obispo. Recipient Outstanding Achievement award Beverly Enterprises, Austin, Tex., 1984. Mem. Calif. Assn. Health Facilities (bd. dirs 1983—, treas. 1984—). Republican. Presbyterian. Avocations: reading, boating. Home: 4763 Golden Rd Pleasanton CA 94566 Office: San Jose Care and Guidance 401 Ridge Vista Dr San Jose CA 95127

WOODARD, DOROTHY MARIE, insurance broker; b. Houston, Feb. 7, 1932; d. Gerald Edgar and Bessie Katherine (Crain) Floeck; student N.Mex. State U., 1950; m. Jack W. Woodard; June 19, 1950 (dec.); m. Norman W. Libby, July 19, 1982. Partner, Western Oil Co., Tucumcari, N.Mex., 1950—; owner, mgr. Woodard & Co., Las Cruces, N.Mex., 1959-67; agt., dist. mgr. United Nations Ins. Co., Denver, 1968-74; agt. Western Nat. Life Ins. Co., Amarillo, Tex., 1976—. Exec. dir. Tucumcari Indsl. Commn., 1979—; dir. Bravo Dome Study Com., 1979—; owner Libby Cattle Co., Libby Ranch Co.; regional bd. dirs. N.Mex., Eastern Plains Council Govts., 1979—. Mem. Tucumcari C. of C. Club: Mesa Country. Home: PO Box 823 Tucumcari NM 88401 Home: 415 E Washington St Bueyeros Ranch NM 88412 Office: PO Box 1003 Tucumcari NM 88401

WOODARD, DUANE, attorney general of Colorado; b. Kansas City, Mo., Jan. 12, 1938; s. Duane and Maxine (Reed) W.; m. Thelma Hanser, Apr. 11, 1964; children—Elizabeth, Mary. B.A., U. Wyo., 1963; J.D., U. Okla., 1967. Bar: Okla. 1967, Colo. 1968, U.S. Dist. Ct. Colo. 1968, U.S. Supreme Ct. 1972, U.S. Ct. Appeals (10th cir.) 1986. Practice law Fort Collins, Colo., 1967—, dep. dist. atty., 1970-72; mem. Colo. State Senate Denver, 1977-80; pub. utility commr. State of Colo., 1980-82, atty. gen., 1982—. Mem. Fort Collins Planning and Zoning Commn., 1974-76. Lodge: Rotary. Home: 1749 Grape St Denver CO 80220 Office: Office of Colo Atty Gen 1525 Sherman St Denver CO 80203 *

WOODBURY, GEORGE WALLIS, JR., chemistry educator; b. Moscow, Idaho, Oct. 13, 1937; s. George Wallis and Kathryn (Schanley) W.; m. Carolyn Anderson, June 11, 1960; children: Joan Ruth, David Lynn. BS, U. Idaho, 1959; PhD, U. Minn., 1964. Research assoc. chemistry Cornell U., Ithaca, N.Y., 1965-66; mem. faculty U. Mont., Missoula, 1966-70, assoc. prof. chemistry, 1970-74, prof., 1974—. Contbr. articles to profl. jours. Mem. Am. Chem. Soc., Phi Beta Kappa, Sigma Xi. Home: 215 Eddy Missoula MT 59801 Office: U Mont Dept Chemistry Missoula MT 59812

WOODHOUSE, CLIVE SMITH, immunologist; b. Ashton Under Lyne, Eng., Jan. 29, 1955; came to U.S., 1982; s. Arnold and Jane (Smith) W.; m. Elaine Dawn Hardcastle, Apr. 3, 1976. BS, U. Hull, Eng., 1978; PhD, U. Birmingham, Eng., 1982. Biochemist U. Birmingham, 1979-82, research fellow, 1982; research fellow NCI, Frederick, Md., 1982-85; sect. head Neorx Corp., Seattle, 1985—. Contbr. articles to jours. Fogarty Internat. Vis. fellow NIH, 1982-85. Mem. AAAS, N.Y. Acad. Sci., Inst. Biology. Office: Neorx Corp 410 W Harrison St Seattle WA 98119

WOODHOUSE, GAY VANDERPOEL, lawyer; b. Torrington, Wyo., Jan. 8, 1950; d. Wayne Gaylord and Sally (Rouse) Vanderpoel; m. Randy Leon Woodhouse, Nov. 26, 1983. B.A. with honors, U. Wyo., 1972. J.D., 1977. Bar: Wyo. 1978, U.S. Dist. Ct. Wyo., U.S. Supreme Ct. Dir. student Legal Services, Laramie, Wyo., 1976-77; assoc. Jones Law Offices, Torrington, Wyo., 1977-78; asst. atty. gen. State of Wyo., Cheyenne, 1978—; chmn. Wyo. Telephone Consumer Panel, Casper, 1982—. Bd. dirs. Pathfinder, Cheyenne, Wyo., 1983—. Republican. Unitarian. Home: 13432 Stewart Rd Cheyenne WY 82009 Office: Atty Gen's Office 123 Capitol Bldg Cheyenne WY 82002

WOODLAND, WESLEY KEITH, information systems manager, computer programmer; b. Salt Lake City, Nov. 8, 1943; s. Keith Henry and Norma Louis (Harris) W.; m. Mary Ellen Farrer, Mar. 17, 1967; children: David, Wendy, Donna, Jenny, Ellen. BSEE, U. Utah, 1969, postgrad., 1985—; MS in Engring., Ariz. State U., 1971; MBA, U. Utah, 1987. Info. systems mgr. Educators Mut. Ins. Assn., Murray, Utah, 1969—; system programmer U. Utah Med. Biophysics., Salt Lake City, 1970-77; system analyst Corp. of the Pres., Salt Lake City, 1977-79. Bd. dirs. Murray Youth Football Conf., 1982-84. Mem. Utah Pick Users Group (pres. 1984-86, bd. dirs. 1986—, organizing com. 1984). Mormon. Home: 5958 Roanoke Murray UT 84123

WOODLE, ALAN STUART, podiatrist, surgeon; b. Vancouver, Wash., July 31, 1953; s. Malcolm Stuart and Lorraine Marie (Evans) W.; m. Roslyn Louise Knodel. BS (2), U. Wash., 1975, 76; D in Podiatric Medicine, Calif. Coll. Podiatric Medicine, 1979. Resident in surgery Valley West Gen. Hosp., Los Gatos, Calif., 1981; practice medicine specializing in foot and ankle surgery, also sports medicine Seattle, 1980—; clin. asst. prof. foot and ankle surgery VA Med. Ctr. Seattle, 1984—; lectr. U. Wash. Med Sch.; exec. com. Waldo Gen. Hosp., Seattle, 1985—, Northwest Hosp., 1986—; trustee Wash. State Podiatric Med. Assn., 1986—. Contbr. chpts. to textbooks, articles to profl. jours. Bd. dirs. Wash. State div. U.S. Olympic Com., Seattle, 1984, Home Health Care, Okanogan County, Wash., 1984, Multiple Sclerosis Assn., King County, Wash., 1986, Arthritis Found., 1986—. Fellow Am. Acad. Podiatric Sports Medicine; mem. Am. Coll. Sports Medicine, Am. Coll. Foot Surgeons (assoc.). Presbyterian. Avocations: skiing, running, tennis. Office: 9730 3rd NE Suite 208 Seattle WA 98115

WOODMANSEE, RAYMOND KURTH, aircraft service company executive; b. Chgo., Dec. 18, 1928; s. Elmer O. and Corrine (Kurth) W.; children—Karen, Paul, Kennith, Diana. Student Mt. San Antonio Coll., 1956-60. Mgr. Grants Air Service, Grants, N.Mex., 1960-63; owner, operator Ray's Aircraft Service, Porterville, Calif., 1964—. Author of maintenance and parts guide for Cessna airplanes. Pres. Tulare County Sheriff Aero Squadron, 1983-84. Mem. Cessna 195 Club, Porterville Area Pilots Assn. (pres. 1966), Fresno Early Ford V-8 Club. Democrat. Home: 22251 Ave 168 Porterville CA 93257 Office: Ray's Aircraft Service 1893 S Newcomb St Porterville CA 93257

WOODRIFF, ROGER LEE, mathematics educator, consultant; b. Bozeman, Mont., Apr. 30, 1942; s. Ray Alan and Margaret O. Woodriff. BS in Math., Mont. State U., 1964; MS in Math., U. Wis., Milw., 1965; postgrad., Columbia Pacific U., 1985—. Asst. prof. math. Hacetteppe Med. Sch., Ankara, Turkey, 1965-67, Middle East Tech., Ankara, 1965-67, Humboldt State U., Arcata, Calif., 1967-70; prof. math. Menlo Coll., Atherton, Calif., 1970—; cons. Menlo Research Assocs., Menlo Park, Calif., 1981—; v.p. engring. Pacific Investment Systems Inc., Palo Alto, Calif., 1978-82. Contbr. articles to profl. jours. Mem. Assn. Computing Machinery, Math. Assn. Am., AAUP. Avocations: sailing, skiing.

WOODRUFF, SHIRLEY JO, elementary school educator; b. Richmond, Calif., May 30, 1951; d. Vern LeRoy and Betty Jo (Salyer) Cole; m. Carl Perry Woodruff, June 21, 1973; children: Daniel, David, Ben, Mark, Joseph. AA, Solano Community Coll.; BA in Social Sci., Calif. State U., Sacramento; postgrad., Idaho State U., 1984—. Cert. elem. tchr., Idaho, Calif. Tchr. aide Richmond (Calif.) Unified Sch. Dist., 1971-72; student tchr. Calif. State U., Sacramento, 1973; art and music tchr. Dist. 91, Idaho Falls, Idaho, 1973-74; chpt. 1 reading tchr. Dist. 93, Idaho Falls, 1979-81, kindergarten tchr., 1981-85, mem. screening com. for testing entrance into kindergarten, 1983, 3rd grade tchr., 1985—. Editor: Hi-Hopes, newsletter, 1984-85. Facilitator MS-Read-a-thon, 1981. Mem. East Idaho Reading Council (v.p. 1982-83, pres. 1983-84, chmn. 1984-85, publicity chair, newsletter editor 1984-86.), NEA. Mormon. Avocations: sightseeing, coaching baseball, reading. Home: 580 Foster Dr Idaho Falls ID 83401 Office: Fairview Sch Rt 2 Box 389 Idaho Falls ID 83401

WOODRUM, DONALD, advertising company executive; b. N.Y.C., Aug. 6, 1917; s. Donald and Gertrude (Conn) W.; m. Mary Harvey, Mar. 18, 1944 (div. 1956); 1 child, Mary Lynn; m. Dorothea Enzor, Nov. 27, 1957. AB, U. Calif., Berkeley, 1937. Pres. Woodrum & Staff Ltd., Honolulu, 1946—. Author: This is Hawaii, 1974. Served with USNR, 1941-45, 50-53; now comdr. ret. Mem. Honolulu Advt. Fedn. (founding pres., awards of distinction 1977, 84, Ad Man of Yr. award 1986), Honolulu C. of C., Advt. Assn. West (lt. gov. 1965-67), Advt. Agy. Assn. Hawaii (past pres.), Bishop Mus. Assn., Alpha Sigma Phi. Republican. Club: Outrigger Canoe (Honolulu). Home: 207 Kawaikui Pl Honolulu HI 96821 Office: Woodrum & Staff Ltd 720 Kapiolani Blvd Honolulu HI 96813

WOODS, ALISON HALL, graphic designer; b. San Francisco, Oct. 29, 1954; d. Wendell Lawson and Janet Counsil (Schrock) J.; m. Paul Osiecki Woods, May 13, 1979; 1 child, Alexander Osiecki. BFA, Calif. Coll. Arts and Crafts, 1977. Dir. art Concept, Sacramento, 1977-78; graphic designer Michael Abramson & Assocs., N.Y.C., 1978-80, Lister Butler, N.Y.C., 1980-81, Robert Ross Design Assocs., San Francisco, 1981-82; prin. Woods Woods Graphic Communications, San Francisco, 1982—. Pub. works include Graphis, 1979, Print Regional, 1985. Recipient Silver award N.Y. Art Dirs. Club, N.Y.C., 1979, Spl. Show award N.Y. Art Dirs. Club, N.Y.C., 1985; Award Merit 4th Ann. Murphy Awards, San Francisco, 1983. Home: 4501 Elinora Ave Oakland CA 94619 Office: Woods Woods Graphic Communications 1810 Harrison St San Francisco CA 94103

WOODS, BOBBY JOE (BOB), transportation executive; b. Frederick, Okla., June 20, 1935; s. Vivin Richard and Mattie Marie (Malone) W.; m. O. Dell Smith, July 21, 1957; children: Donald B., Kathryn M., David R., Lynda J. Student, U. Calif., Berkeley, 1955-56; AA, Phoenix Coll., 1955; student, Glendale (Ariz.) Coll., 1968, 75. Credit mgr. Sam Boren Tire Co., Albuquerque, 1966-67; office mgr. Menke Transp., Albuquerque, 1967-68; dist. exec. Boy Scouts Am., Phoenix, 1968-76; pres. Southwest Prorate Inc., Phoenix, 1976—; owner Southwest Vehicle Title Service, Phoenix, 1985—. Commr. Boy Scouts Am., Ariz., N.Mex. Mem. Profl. Trucking Services Assn. (2d vice pres.). Republican. Mem. Evangelical Free Ch. Lodge: Lions (zone chmn. South Phoenix 1983-84, dep. dist. gov. 1984-85). Avocations: hiking, camping, stamp collecting, computers. Home: 918 W Cochise Phoenix AZ 85021 Office: Southwest Prorate Inc 8902 N Central Phoenix AZ 85020

WOODS, J. JAMEELAH, personnel agency executive; b. Oklahoma City, June 1, 1945; d. Julius Joseph Border and Elnora (Williams) Doolittle; m. Wayne Evan Woods (dec. Nov. 1978); children: Steven L., Nadiyah. Student, Cen. Bus. Coll., Oklahoma City, 1964-65, El Centro Jr. Coll., 1973-74, Sacramento City Coll., 1977-79. Adminstrv. sec. Dallas Ind. Sch. Dist., 1965-72; sec., unit supr. Dallas Welfare Dept., 1972-73; dir., owner Asian House Pre-Sch./Day Care and Restaurant, 1973-75; sec. Los Rios Coll. Dist., 1976-83; pres., dir. Ynobe Internat., Sacramento, 1983—. Producer various fashion shows and seminars in Calif. area, 1983-84. Active Sacramento Foster Parent Program, 1979, Friends of State Fair, Sacramento, 1985, Girl Scouts Am., Sacramento, 1985—; mem. exec. bd. Sacramento PTA, 1985. Democrat. Moslem. Avocations: swimming, walking, drawing, chess. Office: Ynobe Internat 9723-A Folsom Blvd Sacramento CA 95826

WOODS, JAMES DUDLEY, manufacturing company executive; b. Falmouth, Ky., July 24, 1931; s. Alva L. and Mabel L. (Miller) W.; m. Darlene Mae Petersen, Nov. 8, 1962; children: Linda, Debbie, Jeffrey, Jamie. A.A., Long Beach City Coll., 1958; B.A., Calif. State U.-Fullerton, 1967, postgrad., 1968-70. Mgr. planning and control Baker Internat. Corp., Los Angeles, 1965-68, v.p. fin. and adminstrn. Baker div., 1968-73, corp. v.p., group fin. officer, 1973-76, corp. v.p., 1977, past exec. v.p.; now pres., chief operating officer Baker Internat. Corp., Houston; also dir. Baker Internat. Corp.; pres. Baker Packers, Houston, 1976-77, Baker Oil Tools, Orange, Calif., 1977—. Served with USAF, 1951-55. Republican. Lutheran. *

WOODS, JAMES STERRETT, toxicologist; b. Lewistown, Pa., Feb. 26, 1940; s. James Sterrett and Jane Smith (Parker) W.; m. Nancy Fugate, Dec. 20, 1969; 1 dau., Erin Elizabeth. AB, Princeton U., 1962; MS, U. Wash., 1968, PhD, 1970; MPH, U. N.C., 1978. Diplomate Am. Bd. Toxicology. Research assoc. dept. Pharmacology Yale U. Sch. Medicine, New Haven, 1970-72; staff fellow environ. toxicology. Nat. Inst. Environ. Health Scis. br. NIH, Research Triangle Park, N.C., 1972-75, head biochem. toxicology sect., 1975-77; program leader epidemiology and environ. health research program Battelle Research Ctr., Seattle, 1978—; research prof. U. Wash., Seattle, 1979—. Contbr. articles to profl. jours. Served with USN, 1962-66. Scholar USPHS, 1966-70, Am. Cancer Soc., 1970-72. Mem. AAAS, Am. Cancer Research, Am. Pub. Health Assn., Am. Soc. Pharmacology and Exptl. Therapeutics, N.Y. Acad. Sci., Pacific NW Assn. Toxicologists (founding pres.), Soc. Epidemiology Research, Soc. Exptl. Biology and Medicine, Soc. Occupational and Environ. Health, Soc. Toxicology, Western Pharmacology Soc., Pacific Sci. Ctr., Am. Coll. of Epidemiology. Home: 4820 Stanford Ave NE Seattle WA 98105 Office: Battelle Research Ctr 4000 NE 41st St Seattle WA 98105

WOODS, LESLIE VICTOR, optometrist; b. Los Angeles, Dec. 26, 1925; s. Kenneth Campbell and Ada Lucille (Meyers) W.; student U. B.C., 1944-46; B.S., Pacific U., 1948, O.D., 1949; m. Noreen Ellen Barry, Nov. 23, 1950; children—Deirdre Ann, Megan Louise. Individual practice optometry, Sedro Wooley, Wash., 1949, Spokane, 1950, 65—, Chelan, Wash., 1951-65; optometrist dept. ophthalmology Pacific Med. Ctr.; mem. faculty Columbia-Pacific U.; mem. optometric faculty Spokane Community Coll., 1975-78. Chmn. optometric affairs State and County CD, 1958-65; dir. Chelan CD, 1951; mem. Wash. Welfare Med. Care Com., 1958-66; councilman, Chelan, 1952; trustee Fort Wright Coll. of the Holy Names, Spokane; vice-chmn. bd. trustees Ft. Wright Coll., 1978-79. Mem. Wash. Optometric Assn. (pres. Inland soc. 1975-77), North Central Wash. Optometric Soc. (pres. 1954-56, 63-64, state trustee 1954-56, 63-64), Calif. Optometric Assn., Am. Optometric Assn., Omega Delta, Delta Upsilon. Democrat. Roman Catholic. Club: Lions (dir. N. Spokane 1975-76, v.p. 1976, pres. 1977-78). Home: 1979 Clay St San Francisco CA 94109 Office: 2340 Clay St Room 635 San Francisco CA 94115

WOODS, MELFORD ALLAN, retired sugar company executive; b. San Bernardino, Calif., Sept. 4, 1913; s. Melford Allan and May Herand (Rogers) W.; m. Thelma M. Reed, Apr. 18, 1936; children: Susan May (dec.), Roberta Ann. AB, U. Redlands, 1936; MS, Oreg. State U., 1938. Registered profl. engr., Calif. Plant engr. Union Sugar Co., Santa Maria, Calif., 1940-49; supt., plant engr. Union Sugar Co. div. Consol. Foods, Santa Maria, 1949-69; v.p. ops. Sara Lee, Santa Maria, 1969-82; cons. in field; pres. Beet Sugar Devel. Found., 1972-74. Contbr. articles to profl. jour. Former mem. Oycult Sch. Bd., Santa Maria Sch. Bd., 1952-61, Santa Maria Joint Union High Sch. Bd., 1962-69. Mem. Am. Inst. Chem. Engrs., Am. Chem. Soc., Am. Soc. Beet Sugar Technologists (pres. 1970-71, 80). Republican. Lodges: Rotary (pres. Santa Maria 1967-68), Shriners. Avocation: golfing. Home: 125 E Camino Colegio Santa Maria CA 93454

WOODS, NORMAN JAMES, academic administrator; b. Springfield, Mo., Mar. 5, 1934; s. Norman O. and Doris Ena (Noblitt) W.; m. Phyllis Darlene Foster, Aug. 16, 1959; children: Michael J., Julie L. BA, Union Coll., Lincoln, Nebr., 1960; MEd, Central Wash. U., 1966; PhD, U. Oreg., 1969. Tchr., asst. dean men Auburn Acad., Wash., 1960-61; asst., then assoc. and later dean of men Walla Walla Coll., College Place, Wash., 1961-66; dean students Loma Linda U., Calif., 1966-67, asst. then assoc. dean admissions and student affairs, 1969-74, v.p. for acad. adminstrn., 1974-84, pres., 1984—. Served with U.S. Army, 1956-58. Mem. Am. Assn. Pres. Ind. Colls. and Univs. Seventh-day Adventist. Avocations: golf, tennis. Office: Loma Linda U Loma Linda CA 92350

WOODS, ROBERT LAWRENCE, life ins. exec., agy. mgmt. cons.; b. Los Angeles, May 17, 1911; s. Walter A. and Alice (Strang) W.; A.B., U. Calif. at Los Angeles, 1933; C.L.U., Am. Coll. Life Underwriters, 1937; m. Dorothy Welbourn, Oct. 10, 1942; children—Robert Lawrence, Susan Welbourn Woods. With Los Angeles agy. of Mass. Mut. Life Ins. Co., 1934-—, asst. gen. agt., 1938-46, assoc. gen. agt., 1946-49, gen. agt. in partnership, 1949-57, sole gen. agt., 1957-73. Fund raising chmn. Los Angeles chpt. ARC, 1961, dir., 1960-63. Trustee Am. Coll., 1958-61, 71-79. Served to lt. col., inf., AUS, 1941-46. Recipient John Newton Russell award Nat. Assn. Life Underwriters, 1971, Will G. Farrell award Los Angeles Life Ins. Assns., 1974; named to Mgmt. Hall of Fame, Nat. Gen. Agts. and Mgrs. Conf., 1974. Mem. Am. Soc. C.L.U.'s (pres. Los Angeles 1953-54, nat. pres. 1959-60), Mass. Mut. Gen. Agts. Assn. (pres. 1959-60), Gen. Agts. and Mgrs. Assn. (pres. Los Angeles 1957-58, nat. pres. 1967-68), Phi Gamma Delta. Home: 720 N Oakhurst Dr Beverly Hills CA 90210 Office: Mass Mut Life Ins Co 4401 Wilshire Blvd Los Angeles CA 90010

WOODS, ROBERT OCTAVIUS, aerospace engineer; b. Evanston, Ill., Feb. 17, 1933; s. Robert and Anna Margaret (Welch) W.; m. Judith Charlene Neese, Dec. 27, 1965; children: Lisa Ann, Robert David. BS in Engring., Princeton U., 1962, MS in Engring., 1964, MA, 1965, PhD, 1967. Registered profl. engr., Pa., N.Mex. From draftsman to profl. engr. Allstates Engring. Co., Trenton, N.J., 1950-60; mem. tech. staff Sandia Nat. Labs., Albuquerque, 1967—. Contbr. articles to profl. jours.; patentee in field. Fellow Ford Found., 1963, NSF, 1965. Fellow Brit. Interplanetary Soc.; mem. ASME, Am. Phys. Soc., Am. Geophys. Union, Albuquerque Soaring Club (v.p. 1972-74), Sigma Xi, Tau Beta Pi (Eminent Engr. award 1978). Republican. Presbyterian. Club: Princeton (N.Mex.)(pres. 1976—). Avocations: soaring, sailing, bicycle touring. Home: 7513 Harwood Ave NE Albuquerque NM 87110 Office: Sandia Nat Labs 9323 Albuquerque NM 87185

WOODS, WENDY, reporter, editor; b. Newark, Nov. 16, 1952; d. Julian Jonathan and Eileen Margaret (Woods) A.; m. Nicholas Cobalt Gorski, May 29, 1983. Student Wilkes Coll., Wilkes-Barre, Pa., 1970-72; B.A. in Film, Syracuse U., 1976. News reporter Sta. WILK, Wilkes-Barre, 1971-72; reporter, anchor Sta. WIXT-TV, Syracuse, N.Y., 1975-81; corr. Cable News Network, San Francisco, 1981-82; news reporter Sta. KGO-TV (ABC), San Francisco, 1982-84; reporter Computer Chronicles (PBS TV show), 1984—; lectr. in field. Editor newsletter Newsbytes, 1983—(Best Online Publ. award Computer Press Assn. 1985). . Recipient best environ. reporting award Central N.Y. Environ. Assn., 1979; best reporting under deadline pressure award Syracuse Press Club, 1980, best investigative reporting award, 1981. Mem. Nat. Assn. Broadcast Employees and Technicians, Computer Press Assn. (pres.), Democrat. Roman Catholic. Club: Sierra.

WOODSIDE, JEFFREY ROBERT, urologist; b. Pasadena, Calif., Nov. 24, 1942; s. Albion Belmont and Marianne (Starbuck) W.; m. Marilyn Elizabeth Duke, Aug. 29, 1964; children: Pamela Michelle, Shauna Janelle. BS, Oreg. State U., 1964; MD, U. Oreg., 1968. Diplomate Nat. Bd. Med. Examiners, Am. Bd. Urology. Intern Oreg. Health Scis. U., Portland, 1968-69; resident in urology U. N.Mex., Albuquerque, 1973-77; prof. urology U. N.Mex. Sch. Medicine, Albuquerque, 1977—. Contbr. chpts. to books; articles to profl. jours. Bd. dirs. Resolve of N.Mex., Albuquerque, 1978—; mem. med. adv. bd. Kidney Foun. N.Mex., Albuquerque, 1984—. Served to lt. comdr. USN, 1969-73. Mem. Am. Urological Assn., Internat. Continence Soc., Urodynamics Soc. (membership chmn. 1984—), Am. Fertility Soc., Alpha Omega Alpha. Republican. Baptist. Avocations: fishing, squash, fly tying. Home: 7501 Arroyo del Oso NE Albuquerque NM 87109 Office: U N Mex Sch Medicine Div Urology 2211 Lomas NE Albuquerque NM 87131

WOODSON, WELDON DWIGHT, nature writer; b. Ft. Worth, Feb. 17, 1907; s. Neal William and Mary Margaret (Hooser) W.; B.S., Wheaton (Ill.) Coll., 1931; M.A., Columbia U., 1938; m. Eva Freada Husted, Sept. 15, 1943. Asso. editor Welcome News, Los Angeles, 1933-43; writer Make It With Leather (formerly The Craftsman), Ft. Worth, 1965-85; stringer Modern People, Franklin Park, Ill., 1974-76; reviewer On Target With Books, AIM, Chgo., 1978-79; co-author: Black Widow, America's Most Poisonous Spider, 1945; The Basics of Saddlemaking, 1984; author articles condensed in publs. including Magazine Digest, Science Digest, Everybody's Digest, World Digest, Restaurant Digest; writings included sci. and reference publs. including Ency. Britannica, Jour. AMA, Zoological Record, Bibliography of Animal Venoms, Herpetologica, Our Scientific World; free lance contbr. to publs. including Christian Sci. Monitor, Desert Mag., Westways, Natural History, American Forests, Travel, Scientific American, Audubon Mag., Pacific Discovery, Frontiers, A Magazine of Natural History; author: Natural History Roundup, 1934; Nature Writing—From Pliny to Peattie, 1935; Nutria — From Pen to Fur Salon, 1955; contbg. author Illustrated Library of the Natural Sciences, 1958. Pvt. tutor in writing; nature counselor youth groups; author film scripts in field; lectr. writers week Redlands (Calif.) U., 1954, 55, 56. Mem. AAAS, Herpetologists League. Democrat. Baptist. Condr. research on poisonous reptiles, spiders, insects. Home and Office: 340 N Stoneman Ave Alhambra CA 91801

WOODWARD, JOHN RUSSELL, motion picture production executive; b. San Diego, July 10, 1951; s. Melvin C. and Dora M. (Rorabaugh) W. BA in Visual Arts, U. Calif., San Diego, 1973; MA in Cinema Prodn., U. So. Calif., 1978. V.p. prodn. World Wide Motion Pictures Corp., 1982—. Prodn. asst. various commls., 1977; asst. producer The Manitou, 1977; 1st asst. dir. Mortuary, 1981, They're Playing With Fire, 1983, Prime Risk, 1984, Winners Take All, 1986, Kidnapped, 1986, Slam Dance, 1986, Honor Betrayed, 1986, Hidden, 1987; location mgr. Star Chamber, 1982, To Be or Not To Be, 1983, Flashdance, 1983, Two of a Kind, 1983, Touch and Go, 1984, Explorers, 1984, Sweet Dreams, 1985, The Long Shot, 1985, The Running Man, 1985, A Different Affair, 1985, Bobo, 1986, others. Avocations: fishing, camping.

WOODWARD, OSCAR JAMES, III, lawyer, real estate developer; b. Oakland, Calif., Oct. 14, 1935; s. Oscar James II and Beatrice (Denke) W.; A.B., U. Calif.-Berkeley, 1958, J.D., 1964; M.B.A., Stanford U., 1961; children—Baron James, Skye Lynne. Teaching asst. U. Calif., Berkeley, 1962-64; admitted to Calif. bar, 1965; asst. gen. counsel Regents of U. Calif., 1966-67; partner firm Gallagher, Baker, Manock & Woodward, Fresno, Calif., 1967-72; regional mgr., counsel Kaiser Aetna, Newport Beach, Calif., 1972-77; v.p., counsel 1st Savs. & Loan Assn., Fresno, also exec. v.p. Uniservice Corp., 1977-83; v.p. Central Savs. & Loan Assn., 1983-85; sr. v.p. Guarantee Savs. & Loan Assn., 1985—; lectr. Calif. State U., Fresno. Pres., Fresno Arts Center, 1968-69, Storyland of Fresno, 1970, Fresno County Taxpayers Assn., 1981-82; treas. United Crusade, 1972; bd. dirs. Urban Coalition, 1969-71, Community Theatre, 1969-72 Pub. Radio, 1979-80, Hist. Soc., 1983-85, Fresno Met. Mus., 1986—, Madden Library Assocs., 1983-86, Fresno State U., 1984-86; chmn. bd. trustees Fresno Regional Found., 1980—; trustee Fresno County Bd. Rev., 1980-82, St. Agnes Hosp. Found. Council, 1983-85. Served to capt. U.S. Army, 1958-66. Cert. tchr. community coll., Calif. Mem. ABA, Urban Land Inst., Fresno C. of C., Fresno County Bar Assn., Estate Planning Council, Phi Delta Phi, Phi Delta Theta. Republican. Clubs: Sierra Sport and Racquet, Fig Garden Swim and Racquet, Stanford, Golden Bear, Commonwealth. Home: 2573 W Calimyrna Ave Fresno CA 93711 Office: Guarantee Savs & Loan Assn 2680 W Shaw Ln Fresno CA 93711

WOODWARD, STEPHEN RICHARD, newspaper editor; b. Fukuoka City, Japan, July 27, 1953; came to U.S., 1954; s. Leonard Edwin and Etsuko (Okumura) W.; m. Sandra Elizabeth Richardson, Dec. 31, 1979; children: Daniel Joseph, Elizabeth Etsuko. BA in English, Wright State U., 1975; MA in Journalism, U. Mo., 1979. Advt. coordinator Wright State U., Dayton, Ohio, 1976-77; reporter Kansas City (Mo.) Star, 1979-82; assoc. editor then editor Kansas City Bus. Jour., 1982-83; editor then gen. mgr. Portland (Oreg.) Bus. Jour., 1984-86; exec. bus. editor The Hartford (Conn.) Courant, 1986—. Recipient 1st Place Investigative Reporting award Assn. Area Bus. Publs., 1983, 1st Place Column Writing award Assn. Area Bus. Publs., 1985. Mem. Investigative Reporters and Editors Inc. Avocations: astronomy, chess, creative writing.

WOODWORTH, HARRY EADES, III, brokerage house executive; b. Honolulu, Sept. 26, 1941; s. Harry Eades Woodworth Jr. and Catherine Rose (Maier) Williams. AA, Hartnell Coll., 1966; BSBA, Armstrong Coll., 1968. Stockbroker Dean Witter, Anchorage, 1973-76; sr. v.p. Dean Witter Reynolds (formerly Dean Witter), Anchorage, 1981—; stockbroker Merrill Lynch, Anchorage, 1976-81; Prin. Eagle Land Assocs, Anchorage, 1983—, prin. Eagle Investments, Anchorage, 1983; bd. dirs. L. Nebel and Assocs. Landscape Architects, Anchorage, 1983—, bd. dirs. Eagle Broadcasting, Inc., Anchorage, 1983-85, bd. dirs. Pacific Rim Broadcasting, Inc., Anchorage, 1985—. Recipient Pacesetters award Dean Witter Reynolds, Inc., 1983-85. Mem. N.Y. Stock Exchange (registered rep.), Nat. Assn. Security Dealers (registered rep.), N.Y. Commodities Exchange (registered rep.), Chgo. Commodities Exchange (registered rep.), Chgo Bd. Options Exchange (registered rep.), Ducks Unltd.,Nat. Rifle Assn., Ferrari Owners Club, Mercedes Owners Club. Republican. Roman Catholic. Club: U.S. Boat, Ducks Unltd. Lodge: Elks. Avocations: travel, skiing, fishing, skeet, boating. Home: 13900 Jarvi Dr Anchorage AK 99515 Office: Dean Witter Reynolds Inc 3601 C St Anchorage AK 99503

WOODWORTH, SEARCY J., radio station executive; b. Oklahoma City, Sept. 12, 1921; s. Lemuel Allen and LaVerne Ellen (Landes) W.; m. Dorothy Mae Litchfield, 1951; children—Searcy F., Gary S., Ronald K., Gregory M. Grad. high sch., Oklahoma City. Ground radio operator Am. Airlines, Ft. Worth, 1942-44; flight radio operator Consolidated-Vultee Airlines, San Diego, 1944-45, Pan Am. Airways, San Francisco, 1945-48; chief engr. sta. KVNC, Winslow, Ariz., 1954-56; owner, mgr. sta. KVWM-AM-FM, Show Low, Ariz., 1957—. Served with USNR, 1945-48. Republican. Home: PO Box 970 Show Low AZ 85901 Office: Radio Station KVWM AM/FM 3150 S White Mountain Rd Show Low AZ 85901

WOOLHEATER, ROBERT LEROY, electronics company executive; b. Sioux Falls, S.D., May 17, 1930; s. Bernard L. and Adeline (Lass) W.; m. Lorna Colquhoun, Feb. 11, 1956; children—Richard Stellabotte, Carol, Dale, Robert D. B.S., UCLA, 1952. Office mgr. Bekins Van & Storage, Torrance, Calif., 1952-60; controller Vernitron Corp., Torrance, 1960-64; mgr. fin. FMA Inc., Los Angeles, 1964-68; treas. Anthony Industries, Los Angeles, 1968-69; v.p., treas., controller Craig Corp., Compton, Calif., 1969—. Mem. curriculum adv. com. Los Angeles Harbor Coll., 1980—. Served with U.S. Army, 1952-54. Named Citizen of Yr., City of Lomita (Calif.), 1965. Mem. Nat. Assn. Accts. (internat. v.p. 1974-75; Disting. Mem. 1975), Fin. Execs. Inst., Fgn. Trade Assn. So. Calif. (v.p. 1984, pres. 1986—), Assn. Electronic Importers (pres. 1982—). Republican. Roman Catholic. Home: 115 N Wetherly Dr #104 Los Angeles CA 90048 Office: 116 N Robertson Blvd Suite #609 Los Angeles CA 90048

WOOLSEY, JAMES ELMORE, clinical psychologist, consultant, educator; b. Evansville, Ind., July 29, 1940; s. Joseph Orval and Mary Lois (Bone) W.; m. Sandra Carolyn Fisher, Sept. 16, 1962; children—Sandra Darlene, James II, Kathleen, Sharlene. B.A. in Psychology, Fresno Pacific Coll., 1971; M.A. in Counseling, Calif. State U.-Fresno 1975; postgrad., Laurence U., 1981—. Cert. counselor-psychologist, N.Mex.; lic. tchr., Calif. Pastor Ch. of God, Fresno, Eureka, Napa, Calif., 1965-73; adminstr., coordinator Alcohol First Offender Programs, Silver City (N.Mex.) Area Human Resources, 1976-81; occupational program cons. State of N.Mex., Santa Fe, 1978-79; clin. psychologist, tng. dir. Ft. Bayard (N.Mex.) Med. Ctr., 1979-84; clin. psychologist Las Vegas (N.Mex.) Med. Ctr., 1984—; also pvt. cons.; cons. N.Mex. Nurses Assn. Continuing Edn. Mem. SW Services to Handicapped; Civil Rights Com.; Gov.'s Council Criminal Justice. Served with USN, 1958. Named Disting. Citizen, N.Mex. Sec. State; First Offender Program grantee; Alcohol and Family Services grantee. Mem. Am. Soc. Tng. and Devel., N.Mex. Hosp. Adminstrs. Assn., Assn. Labor-Mgmt. Adminstrs and Cons. on Alcoholism. Democrat. Methodist. Clubs: Kiwanis, Masons. Home: PO Box 2972 Las Vegas NM 87701 Office: Las Vegas Med Ctr Las Vegas NM 87701

WOOLSEY, ROY BLAKENEY, electronics company executive; b. Norfolk, Va., June 12, 1945; s. Roy B. and Louise Stookey (Jones) W. Student, Calif. Inst. Tech., 1962-64; BS with distinction, Stanford U., 1966, MS, 1967, PhD, 1970. Sr. physicist Tech. for Communications Internat., Mountain View, Calif., 1970-75; mgr. radio direction finding systems Tech. for Communications Internat., Mountain View, 1975-80, program mgr., 1980-83, dir. strategic systems, 1983—. Contbr. articles to profl. jours. Active YMCA, Palo Alto, Calif. Fellow NSF, 1966-70. Mem. Sierra Club, Sigma Xi, Phi Beta Kappa. Republican. Presbyterian. Avocations: sailing, tennis, racquetball, skiing, contract bridge. Home: 26649 Snell Ln Los Altos Hills CA 94022 Office: Tech for Communications Internat 34175 Ardenwood Blvd Fremont CA 94536

WOOLSON, STEVEN THURBER, orthopaedic surgeon; b. Detroit, Sept. 28, 1943; s. George Thurber and Helen Elizabeth (Lund) W.; divorced; children: Christopher, Melissa, Grace. BA, Hamilton Coll., 1965; student, U. Del., 1965-66; MD, U. Mich., 1970. Diplomate Am. Bd. Orthopaedic Surgery. Intern Univ. Hosp., U. Mich., Ann Arbor, Mich., 1970-71; resident in orthopaedics Univ. Hosp., U. Mich., Ann Arbor, 1971-75; practice medicine specializing in orthopaedic surgery Albuquerque, 1975-81; fellow in hip surgery Mass. Gen. Hosp., Boston, 1981-82; mem. facutly Stanford (Calif.) U. Med. Sch., 1982-84; practice medicine specializing in orthopaedic surgery Palo Alto (Calif.) Med. Clinic, 1984—. Contbr. articles on orthopaedic surgery to profl. jours. Mem. AMA, Western Orthopaedic Assn., Am. Acad. Ortho Surgeons, Orthopaedic Research Soc., Alpha Omega Alpha. Presbyterian. Home: 100 Higgins Ave Los Altos CA 94022 Office: Palo Alto Med Clinic 300 Homer Ave Palo Alto CA 94301

WOOLSTON, MICHAEL JON, lawyer; b. Salt Lake City, Nov. 30, 1955; s. Paul Strasburg and Margery (Peay) W. AA with highest honors, Chabot Coll., 1979; BA with highest honors, Calif. State U., Hayward, 1981; JD with honors, Brigham Young U., 1984. Bar: Calif. 1984, U.S. Dist. Ct. (no. dist.) Calif. 1984. Assoc. Abel & Abel Law Offices, Hayward, 1984-87, Bancroft-Whitney Co., San Francisco, 1987—. Served with U.S. Army, 1974-77. Mem. ABA, Calif. State Bar (Pro Bono Service award 1985). Democrat. Mormon. Home: 1182 E St #411 Hayward CA 94541 Office: Bancroft-Whitney Co 301 Brannan St San Francisco CA 94107

WOOSTER, WARREN S(CRIVER), marine educator; b. Westfield, Mass., Feb. 20, 1921; s. Harold Abbott and Violet (Scriver) W.; m. Clarissa Pickles, Sept. 13, 1948; children: Susan Wooster Allen, Daniel, Dana Wooster Pawka. Sc.B., Brown U., 1943; M.S., Calif. Inst. Tech., 1947; Ph.D., UCLA, 1953. From research asst. to prof. Scripps Instn. Oceanography, U. Calif., 1948-73; dir. UNESCO Office Oceanography, 1961-63; dean Rosenstiel Sch. Marine Atmospheric Sci., U. Miami, 1973-76; prof. marine studies and fisheries U. Wash., Seattle, 1976—; dir. Inst. Marine Studies U. Wash., 1979-82. Contbr. to books, profl. jours. Served with USNR, 1943-46. Fellow Am. Geophys. Union, Am. Meterol Soc.; mem. Sci. Com. Oceanic Research, Sigma Xi. Office: U Wash Inst for Marine Studies Seattle WA 98195

WORDEN, EARL FREEMONT, physical chemist; b. Portsmouth, N.H., Nov. 30, 1931; s. Earl F. and Nona B. (Odiorne) W.; m. Marlys K. Winter, Aug. 23, 1960; 1 child, Seth Langdon. BS, U. N.H., 1953, MS, 1955; PhD, U. Calif., Berkeley, 1959. Research chemist Lawrence Livermore (Calif.) Nat. Lab., 1958—. Contbr. articles to profl. jours. Fellow Optical Soc. Am; mem. Am. Chem. Soc., No. Calif. Soc. for Spectroscopy (chmn. 1983, Strait award, 1985). Home: Box 631 Diablo CA 94550 Office: Lawrence Livermore Reseach Lab Box 808 Livermore CA 94550

WORDEN, PAUL WELLMAN, physicist; b. San Angelo, Tex., Mar. 1, 1945; s. Paul Wellman Worden and Olga Meda Beck. BA, Rice U., 1967; MS, Stanford U., 1969, PhD, 1976. Postdoctoral scholar Stanford (Calif.) U., 1976-78, research assoc. Hansen Labs., 1978-80, sr. research assoc. Hansen Labs., 1980—; research affiliate Johns Hopkins Applied Physics Lab., Balt., 1973-74; cons. Jet Propulsion Lab., Pasadena, Calif., 1983-84. Editor: Gravity and Inertia: Selected Reprints, 1983; contbr. articles to profl. jours. Recipient C.W. Heaps prize Rice U., Houston, 1967. Mem. AAAS, Am. Phys. Soc., Sierra Club, Stanford Aviation Assn., Sigma Xi. Avocations: aviation, outdoors, travel, culture. Home: 2284 Williams St Palo Alto CA 94306 Office: Stanford U WW Hansen Labs of Physics Palo Alto CA 94305

WORDEN, ROBERT PASCAL, marketing executive, consultant; b. Houston, Sept. 23, 1960; s. Euclid Paul Worden and Nancy Elaine (Pinches) Ferguson. BS, Calif. State U., Sacramento. Real estate appraisor Nancy Ferguson, Inc., Oroville, Calif., 1978-80; coll. mktg. rep. Markstein Beverage Co., Sacramento, 1980-82, mktg. coordinator, 1982-86, account exec., 1987—; cons. Calif. State U. mktg. dept., Sacramento, 1984—, Snap-Crackle Popcorn Co., 1985—. V.P. No. Calif. chpt. Muscular Dystrophy Assn., 1985-86; bd. dirs. Sacramento Water Festival Assn., 1984-86, River Park Little League, Sacramento, 1985. Named hon. brewmaster Anheuser-Busch Sch., Fairfield, Calif., 1984. Mem. Sacramento Women in Adv., Sacramento Adv. Club, Big Brothers of Am., Sigma Alpha Epsilon (Brother of Yr. local chpt. 1984, 86). Republican. Club: 20/30 (Sacramento). Avocations: running, skiing, tennis, coaching, softball. Office: Sta KZAP 298 Commerce Circle Sacramento CA 95815

WORKMAN, CLAIR BLAINE, religious organization administrator; b. Salt Lake City, Apr. 11, 1951; s. Clair McKee and Donna (Thompson) W.; m. Marian Schlange, Aug. 7, 1980; children: Lily Ann, Kathryn Marie, Ellen Jane. BS, Brigham Young U., 1975; MBA, U. Utah, 1984. Auditor Peat, Marwick and Mitchell, Los Angeles, 1975-77; controller Deseret Industries, Los Angeles, 1977-80, Salt Lake Deseret Industries, Salt Lake City, 1980-81; fin. analyst Latter-day Saints Welfare Services, Salt Lake City, 1981-85; area fin. mgr. Latter-day Saints Welfare Services, Seattle, 1985—. Missionary Jesus Christ Latter-day Saints, French Polynesia, 1970-72; treas. So. Calif. Mormon Choir, Los Angeles, 1978-80; mem. Salt Lake Symphonic Choir, 1981-85. John Einer Anderson scholar Brigham Young U., Provo, Utah, 1974, Dean's scholar Brigham Young U., 1969-70, Acad. scholar Brigham Young U., 1972-73. Mem. Phi Kappa Phi. Republican. Avocations: music, skiing, swimming. Office: Latter-day Saints Welfare Services 220 S 3d Pl Renton WA 98055

WORKMAN, LAURAL ANN, retail association executive; b. Monrovia, Calif., Feb. 13, 1960; d. Albert Robert and Laura Louise (Benton) W. B.Mus., U. Oreg., 1983. Acctg. clk. Renfield Importers, N.Y.C., 1981-82; adminstrv. asst. Internat. Council Shopping Ctrs., N.Y.C., 1983-84, meetings mgr., 1984-85, western meetings dir., San Francisco, 1986—. Co-author: Guide to ICSC Idea Exchanges, 1985. Mem. NOW, Nat. Assn. Female Execs., Phi Beta (pres. 1981-82). Democrat. Avocations: classical musician; tennis; traveling; swimming. Home: 500 Stanyan St Apt 602 San Francisco CA 94117 Office: Internat Council Shopping Ctrs 353 Sacramento St Suite 400 San Francisco CA 94111

WORONOFF, DAVID SMULYAN, lawyer; b. Balt., June 20, 1937; s. Samuel Murray and Ella Sarah (Smulyan) W.; m. Karen Gail Scholz, Apr. 18, 1978; children—Jamie, Keith, Robin; children by previous marriage—Stefan, Bonnie. B.S. in Elec. Engring., M.I.T., 1959; J.D. (scholar), Boston Coll., 1962; postgrad. Utica Coll., 1965-66, Rutgers U., 1968-69. Bar: Conn. 1962 U.S. Dist. Ct. Conn. 1963, U.S. Patent Office 1965, N.J. 1972, U.S. Dist. Ct. N.J. 1972, R.I. 1979, U.S. Dist Ct. R.I. 1979. U.S. Ct. Customs and Patent Appeals 1980, U.S. Ct. Appeals (Fed. cir.) 1981. Mem. patent dept. Western Electric Co., Washington, 1961-62; law clk. Conn. Supreme Ct., 1962-63; sole practice, Bridgeport, Conn., 1972-75; patent atty. Bendix Corp., 1964-66; patent counsel Vitramon, Inc., 1966-68; line, staff mgmt. positions Singer Co., 1968-70, Xerox Corp., 1970-72; exec. v.p. Servco Leasing Corp., N.Y.C., 1972-74; sole practice, Bridgewater, N.J., 1972-77, Ormond Beach, Fla., Windsor, Colo., 1977—; of counsel Wood, Herzog, Osborn & Bloom, Ft. Collins, Colo., 1986—; ptnr. Colo. land devel.; cons. to industry on tech. devel.; lectr., tchr. profl. seminars various schs., univs., and govt. agys. Vol., United Jewish Appeal, 1974-76 M.I.T. Alumni Assn., 1975-78, Am. Cancer Soc., 1978-82; dir. N. Colo. Med. Ctr. Found., Inc.; mem. accountability com. RE-4 Sch. Dist.. Mem. ABA (litigation, patent sects., ethics com. patent sect.) N.J. Bar Assn., R.I. Bar Assn. Editor: Boston Coll. Bus. and Comml. Law Rev., 1961-62. Lodge: Rotary (local officer and dir.).

WORRALL, JOSEPH H., III, architect; b. Honolulu, Aug. 22, 1956; s. Joseph H. Worrall Jr. and Marian Christine (Hill) Artzt; m. Allyn B. Engman, June 9, 1984. BFA, R.I. Sch. Design, 1979, BArch, 1980; M in Environ. Planning, Ariz. State U., 1982. Registered architect. Draftsman Robinson, Green & Beretta, Providence, 1978-80; expediter Marshall Contractor, Rumford, R.I., 1980; draftsman, project mgr. Weymiller & Assocs., Tempe, Ariz., 1980-83; project. mgr., CADD system mgr. Cornoyer Hedrick Architects, Phoenix, 1983—, CADD system mgr., 1985—. Mem. Decus, McDonnell-Douglas GDS User's Group (host nat. conv. 1986), S.W. Region GDS User's Group. Republican. Congregationalist. Avocations: tennis, hiking, camping, sailing, motor sports. Home: 2504 E Devonshire Phoenix AZ 85016 Office: Cornoyer Hedrick Architects 1515 E Missouri Phoenix AZ 85014

WORRELL, GARY LEE, health science facility administrator; b. Detroit, Oct. 4, 1943; s. Hubert Lee Worrell and Margie Marie (Grablick) Dunstan; m. Sandra Joyce Brodine, June 19, 1965; children: Brandon Lee, Lisa Marie. BBA, Menlo Sch. Bus. Adminstrn., 1965; MA in Health Care Adminstrn., George Washington U., 1971. Adminstr. River Park Hosp., McMinnville, Oreg., 1973-75, Kishwaukee Community Hosp., DeKalb, Ill., 1975-76, McMinnville Community Hosp., 1976-83, Black Hills Community Hosp., Olympia, Wash., 1983—. Bd. dirs. Thurston County Econ. Devel. Council, Olympia, 1985-86, Evergreen State Coll. Found., Olympia, 1985-86. Served to capt. U.S. Army, 1966-69. Mem. Wash. State Hosp. Assn., Am. Coll. Health Care Execs. Republican. Lutheran. Lodge: Rotary (McMinnville) (pres. 1981-82). Avocations: white water rafting, skiing, travel. Home: 3407 Country Club Rd NW Olympia WA 98502 Office: Black Hills Community Hosp 3900 Capital Mall Dr SW Olympia WA 98502

WORRELL, PAUL MARTIN, physician; b. Seattle, Dec. 15, 1942; s. Jack Martin and Lucille Fern (Little) W.; m. Mary Lea Congdon, June 11, 1966; children: Lisa, Sharyl, April, Trevor. BA, U. Wash., 1965, MD, 1969. Resident in internal medicine U. Hawaii, Honolulu, 1980-81; pvt. practice medicine, Anchorage, 1971-78; orthopedic resident U. Colo., Denver, 1979; practice medicine, specializing in internal medicine, Anchorage, 1982—; founder, pres. Third World Missions, Anchorage, 1983—. Mem. ACP, Anchorage Med. Soc., Alaska Med. Soc., AMA, Alaska Acad. Family Physicians (pres. 1978). Office: 3650 Lake Otis Pkwy Anchorage AK 99504

WORREST, ROBERT CHARLES, radiation biologist; b. Hartford, Conn., July 6, 1935; s. Ralph N. and Ruth E. (Shafer) W.; m. Virginia Louise Peplaw, Aug. 24, 1957; 1 child, Colleen Emilie. BA, Williams Coll., 1957; MA, Wesleyan U., Middletown, Conn., 1964; PhD in Radiation Biology, Physiology and Zoology, Oreg. State U., 1975. Tchr. biology, chemistry, math. Canterbury Sch., New Milford, Conn., 1957-59; tchr. biology and math. Belmont (Mass.) Hill Sch., 1959-70; teaching asst. biology Oreg. State U., Corvallis, 1970, instr., 1971-72, research assoc. dept. gen. sci., 1975-77, asst. prof., 1977-81, assoc. prof., 1981-87, prof., 1987—; project leader photobiology program EPA, Corvallis, 1980-82, mem. sci. liaison photobiology program, 1983-86, project leader atmospheric effects program on global climate change and stratospheric modification, 1986—. Editor: Stratospheric Ozone Reduction, Solar Ultraviolet Radiation and Plant Life, 1986; contbr. articles to profl. jours. Mem. AAAS, Am. Soc. Limnology and Oceanography, Ecol. Soc. Am., Am. Soc. Photobiology, Soc. Risk Analysis, N.Y. Acad. Scis. Office: Environ Research Lab EPA 200 SW 35th St Corvallis OR 97333

WORTHINGTON, DAVID ALLEN, safety and occupational protection administrator; b. Kansas, Mo., July 23, 1952; s. Litton Lee and Alice Marie (Eder) W.; m. Joyce Irene Lasley, May 25, 1973; children: Alicia S., Andrew D. BS in Indsl. Psychology, Pittsburg (Kans.) State U., 1975, BSBA, 1976; MS in Indsl. Safety, Cen. Mo. State U., 1979. Cert. safety profl., cert. hazard control mgr. Safety mgr. Daniel Internat., Fulton, Mo., 1976-79; safety advisor Exxon Co. USA, Houston, 1979-81; sr. safety engr. Arco Project, Prudhoe Bay, Alaska, 1981-83, Arco Exploration and Tech., Prudhoe Bay, 1985; safety supr. Arco Alaska, Inc., Prudhoe Bay, 1983-85; dir. safety and occupational protection Arco Petroleum Products Co., Anaheim, Calif., 1985—. Mem. System Safety Soc., Am. Soc. Safety Engrs., Am. Indsl. Hygiene Assn., Veterans of Safety Soc. (assoc.). Avocations: fishing, hunting, camping. Home: 467 Westridge Circle Anaheim CA 92807 Office: PO Box 64001 Anaheim CA 92803-6401

WORTHINGTON, JOSEPH EDWARD, geologist; b. East Orange, N.J., June 18, 1931; Joseph Edward and Eleonore G. (Heyden) W.; m. Helen Weissenborn, June 13, 1959; children: Edward William, Sarah Ann, Joseph Edward IV. AB in Geology cum laude, Williams Coll., 1953; MA in Econ. Geology, Columbia U., 1954. Registered profl. geologist, Idaho. Geol. field work Bear Creek Mining Co., Mont., Idaho, Wash., summers 1953-54; exploration geologist Bear Creek Mining Co., Ariz., Mont., Idaho, 1960-67; geol. office work, drafting Behre, Dolbear & Co., 1954; geol. field work Am. Smelting and Refining Co., Idaho, 1955; mil. terrain analyst beach erosion bd. Office of Chief of Engrs. U.S. Army, 1956-57; pvt. practice exploration cons. U.S., Can., Mex., 1958-59, 78-82; regional mgr. exploration Cyprus Mines Corp., northwestern U.S., 1967-72; U.S. mgr. exploration Cyprus Mines Corp., nationwide, 1971-78; regional mgr. Tenneco Minerals Co., eastern U.S., Rocky Mountains, 1982-85; cons. for numerous corps., 1985—. Contbr. numerous articles to profl. jours. Mem. AAAS, Soc. Econ. Geologists, Soc. Mining Engrs. of AIME (editor Rock in the Box1965-68), Can. Inst. Mining and Metall. Engrs., Internat. Assn. Genesis Ore Deposits, Assn. Exploration Geochemists, Mining Club of Southwest, Northwest Mining Assn. (trustee 1970-72, v.p. 1973-75), Ariz. Geol. Soc., Outdoors Unltd., Denver Region Exploration Geologists Soc. Address: 29294 Roan Dr Evergreen CO 80439

WORTHINGTON, RALPH EUGENE, geologist; b. Flagler, Colo., Jan. 20, 1953; s. Robert Riley Worthington and Shirley Margaret (Cronkhite) Morris; m. Tina Marie Wray, June 23, 1973; children—Geoffrey Allan, Karen Ann, Bradley David. A.A.S., Morgan County Community Coll., Ft. Morgan, Colo., 1973; A.S., Pikes Peak Community Coll., 1978; B.S., U. So. Colo., 1980; M.S., U. Iowa, 1982. Geologist ARCO Exploration Co., Denver, 1982-84, ARCO Oil and Gas Co., Midland, Tex., 1984—. Served with USN, 1973-77. Recipient Geosci. honors U. So. Colo., 1981. Mem. Am. Assn. Petroleum Geologists, Soc. Econ. Paleontologists and Mineralogists, West Tex. Geol. Soc., N.Mex. Geol. Soc. Republican. Baptist.

WORTMAN, ROBERT HILTON, engineering educator; b. Dexter, N.Mex., Apr. 8, 1934; s. Frank and Anna B. (Wattenbarger) W.; m. Jean Henderson Metcalf, Aug. 15, 1959; children: Sallie Anne, Robert Alan, Richard Hilton. BSCE, U. N.Mex., 1957; cert., Yale U. Bur. Hwy. Traffic, 1962; MS, U. Ill., 1963, PhD, 1970. From instr. to asst. prof. engring. U. Ill., Urbana, 1965-73; assoc. prof. U. Conn., Storrs, 1973-76, U. Ariz., Tucson, 1976—. Co-author: Design and Planning of Engineering Systems, 1973, 2d rev. edit. 1985; contbr. articles to profl. jours. Served to 1st lt. USAF, 1958-60. Mem. ASCE (sec. Ariz. sect. 1979-80), Inst. Transp. Engrs., So. Ariz. Interscholastic Soccer Referees' Assn. (pres. 1985-87), Transp. Research Bd. (assoc.), Sigma Xi, Chi Epsilon, Tau Beta Pi. Office: U Ariz Dept Civil Engring Tucson AZ 85721

WOSKOW, ROBERT MARSHALL, management consultant; b. N.Y.C., Aug. 1, 1951; s. Martin and Marion (Kloder) W.; m. Gail Berrin, Apr. 1, 1979; children: Belle Ilysa, Benjamin Hale. BSEE, UCLA, 1973; MSEE, Calif. State U., Northridge, 1976; MBA, Pepperdine U., 1982. Elec. engr. various orgns., Los Angeles, 1973-84; engring. dir. Arts and Sci. Tech., Los Angeles, 1984-85; programs mgr. Pacesetter Systems, Sylmar, Calif., 1985—; chief exec. officer Robert Marshall and Assocs., Encino, Calif., 1982—. Patentee in field. Home and Office: Robert Marshall and Assocs 16801 Severo Pl Encino CA 91436

WOTHE, CAROLE ANN, speech pathologist; b. DeKalb, Ill., Aug. 30, 1944; d. Clifford W. and Lois M. (Nelson) Andersen; m. Jerry D. Wothe, Sept. 3, 1966; children: Clark J., Barbara J. BA, U. Denver, 1966, MA, 1967; postgrad., San Diego State U., 1983-85. Speech pathologist Children's Hosp., San Diego, 1967-71, Grossmont Hosp., La Mesa, Calif., 1978-85, Edgemoor Hosp., Santee, Calif., 1984—; cons. in field San Carlos Presch., San Diego, 1978—. Troop leader Girl Scouts U.S., San Diego, 1978—, troop organizer, 1978-85, cookie coordinator, 1986. Recipient Hon. Service award PTA, San Diego, 1985. Mem. Am. Speech-Lang.-Hearing Assn., DAR (local scholarship chmn. 1985). Mem. Unity Ch. Avocations: music, genealogy. Office: Speech Pathology Dept Edgemore Hosp 9065 Edgemore Dr Santee CA 92071

WOYAMES, GEORGE MOREIRA, social worker, gerontologist; b. Rio De Janeiro, May 26, 1944; came to U.S., 1969, naturalized, 1975; s. Hercules and Almerinda (Moreira) W. BA in Journalism, U. Brazil, Rio De Janeiro, 1965; BS in Edn., Boston State Coll., 1971; MA in Ibero Am. Studies, N.Y.U., 1973; MSW, U. Tex., 1981. Lic. clin. social worker, Calif. Program asst., interpreter Am. Embassy, Rio De Janeiro, 1967-69; tchr. English as second lang., social studies Cambridge (Mass.) High and Latin Sch., 1970-72; social worker Dallas County Child Welfare, 1974-79; instr. English as second lang. El Centro Coll., Dallas, 1974-78; clin. social worker Children's Med. Ctr., Dallas, 1981-83; med. social worker San Francisco Home Health and Hospice, 1983-85, Laguna Honda Hosp., San Francisco, 1985-86, San Francisco Gen. Hosp., 1986—; presenter Cultural Aspects in Health Care, Vis. Nurses Assn. of San Francisco, 1984-85; cons. in field; workshop leader on Stress Reduction for the Elderly, Dallas, San Francisco; bd. dirs. Hope and Help Project. Contbr. articles to profl. jours. Election campaign vol. San Francisco Nuclear Freeze, 1984; mem. YMCA. Mem. Nat. Assn. Social Workers (cert., pub. relations chmn. of Golden Gate Redwood Empire Ctr. 1986), Am. Soc. on Aging, Bay Area Bicultural Assn. Spanish Speaking Therapists, Calif. Specialists on Aging. Democrat. Roman Catholic. Avocations: hiking, camping, fine arts. Home: 77 Herman Apt #47 San Francisco CA 94102 Office: San Francisoc Gen Hosp 10001 Potrero Ln San Francisco CA 94102

WRAY, KARL, former newspaper owner and publisher; b. Bishop, Tex., June 8, 1913; s. Ernest Paul and Gertrude (Garvin) W.; m. Flora-Lee Koepp, Aug. 11, 1951; children: Diana, Mark, Kenneth, Norman, Thomas. A.B., Columbia U., 1935. Auditor U.S. Dept. Agr., Washington, also Little Rock, 1935-37; salesman O'Mara & Ormsbee, Inc., N.Y.C., 1937-42; advt. mgr. Lompoc (Calif.) Record, 1947-54; owner, pub. San Clemente (Calif.) Daily Sun-Post, 1954-67, Coastline Dispatch, San Juan Capistrano, Calif., 1956-67, Dana Point (Calif.) Lamplighter, 1966-67; cons. Lear Siegler, Inc., Washington, 1967-68; pub. Daily Star-Progress, La Habra, Calif., 1969-74, Anaheim (Calif.) Bulletin, 1974-86. Mem. Calif. State Park Commn., 1960-64, vice chmn., 1961-62; mem. exec. bd. Orange County council Boy Scouts Am., 1961-64, 76-87; mem. citizens adv. com. Orange Coast Coll., 1963-66; bd. dirs. Calif. Newspaper Youth Found., 1978-84; pres. Freedom Bowl, Inc., Anaheim, Calif., 1981-84, chmn. bd., 1984-86, bd. dirs., 1986— . Served to capt. USMC, 1942-46. Mem. Calif. Newspaper Advt. Execs. Assn. (pres. 1952-53), Calif. Newspaper Pubs. Assn. (dir. 1960-64), Am. Theatre Critics Assn., Baseball Writers Assn. Am., Football Writers Assn. Am., Calif. Press Assn., San Juan Capistrano C. of C. (pres. 1966), San Clemente C. of C. (pres. 1956-57), La Habra C. of C. (dir. 1970-74), Anaheim C. of C. (dir. 1974-86). Presbyterian (elder). Office: Anaheim Bulletin 2420 S Ola Vista San Clemente CA 92672-4360

WRAY, WINONA KAY, marketing professional; b. Boise, Idaho, Sept. 8, 1941; d. Marshall R. Smith and Leola (Jackson) Helvin; m. Richard D. Alter, Aug. 16, 1985; children: Van John Wray, Summer Celine Wray. BA in English, Calif. State Stanislaus, 1981, MA in Mktg., 1986. Adminstrv. asst. U. Wash., Seattle, 1968-72; asst. Turlock (Calif.) Mosquito Abatement Dist., 1972-76; alumni advisor Calif. State U. Stanislaus, Turlock, 1976-81; community relations dir. Doctors Med. Ctr., Modesto, Calif., 1981-86; mktg. dir. Psychiat. Inst., Modesto, Calif., 1986—; bd. dirs. Doctors Med. Ctr. Found., Modesto. Author: Poetry Anthology, 1975; (syndicated column) Funny Farm, 1972-76; also articles. Bd. dirs. Women's Resource Ctr., Modesto, 1984-85, Modesto Community Hospice, 1986—. Recipient Rotary scholarship, 1980. Mem. Modesto C. of C. (bd. dirs. 1986—), Women in Communications, Am. Mktg. Assn., Am. Hosp. Pub. Relation and Mktg. Assn., Hosp. Pub. Relations Assn. No. Calif., Cen. Calif. Devel. Council (sec.). Avocations: writing, photography, stained glass. Home: 920 Foxcraft Ln Modesto CA 95355 Office: Modesto Psychiat Ctr 1501 Claus Rd Modesto CA 95355

WREDE, KENNETH LAWRENCE, mining engineer; b. Rapid City, S.D., June 24, 1954; s. Burton Lyle and Helen Brennan (Hill) W. BS in Mining Engring., S.D. Sch. Mines, 1977. Mining engr. Gulf Mineral Resources, Grants, N.Mex., 1977-78; from mining engr. to foreman to quality control engr. to engring. supr. Wyodak Resources, Gillette, Wyo., 1978—. Named to All-S.D. Intercollegiate Conf. Basketball team, 1976, to All-Nat. Assn. Intercollegiate Athletics Conf. Dist. 12 Basketball team, 1976; named one of Outstanding Young Men in Am., 1986. Mem. AIME, Nat. Rifle Assn., Soc. Mining Engrs. Republican. Baptist. Club: Lions (Gillette). Avocations: water and snow skiing, hang gliding, fly fishing, photography. Home: #9 Gerrans Ave Gillette WY 82716 Office: Wyodak Resources Devel Corp RR 81 Box G90 Gillette WY 82716

WREN, ANTHONY GORDON, chemistry educator; b. Pasadena, Calif., Oct. 27, 1949; s. William Franklin and Emily Virginia (Zeger) W.; m. Marja Johanna Van Koppen, Aug. 28, 1976; children: David Andrew, Scott William (twins). Student, Monterey Peninsula Coll., 1967-69, Monterey Inst. Internat. Studies, 1969; BS in Chemistry, U. Calif. Santa Barbara, Goleta, 1972, MA in Chemistry, 1976. Research assoc. U. Calif., Santa Barbara, 1974-75, univ. assoc., 1975-76; research assoc. Aerospace Corp., El Segundo, Calif., 1976-78; instr. chemistry Butte Coll., Oroville, Calif., 1978—. Contbr. articles to profl. jours. Pres. Paradise (Calif.) Westside Homeowners Assn., 1983-85. Mem. Am. Chem. Soc., Calif. Assn. Chemistry Tchrs., Conf. on 2-Yr. Colls., Faculty Assn. Calif. Community Colls., Nat. Wildlife Fedn., Sierra Club, No. Calif. Community Coll. Computer Consortium (v.p. 1985-86, pres. 1986—), Paradise Runner's Club. Republican. Congregationalist. Avocations: woodworking, computers, hist. research, fishing, running. Home: 5883 Oakmore Dr Paradise CA 95969 Office: Butte Coll 3536 Butte Campus Dr Oroville CA 95965

WRIEDEN, JAMES ERIK, real estate broker; b. Bklyn., June 7, 1943; s. William and Isabel (Ryan) W.; B.S., San Diego State U., 1968; children—Wendy, Jamie. Owner, Mariposa Mgmt., Citrus Heights, Calif., 1979—, Century 21 Antelope Properties (formerly Antelope Properties), 1979—, James E. Wrieden & Assocs., Inc., 1969—. Served to lt. USN, 1968-71. Mem. Better Bus. Bur., Sacramento Real Estate Bd., Nat. Assn. Real Estate Brokers, Sacramento Apt. Assn., Calif. Assn. Realtors. Offices: Century 21 Antelope Properties 5727 Sunrise Blvd Citrus Heights CA 95610

WRIGHT, ARTHUR EDWIN, photography educator; b. Albany, Oreg., July 4, 1940; s. Lloyd Evert and Florence Lavon (McClain) W.; m. Beverly Ellis, Feb. 28, 1960 (div. 1968); children: Becky, Brian; m. Janet Kathleen Spurlock, Aug. 12, 1972; children: Cassie, Maggie. BS, U. Oreg., 1968, MS, 1971. Instr. Upward Bound, Eugene, Oreg., 1971, Linn-Benton Community Coll., Albany, 1972-74; cinematographer KOIN TV, Portland, Oreg., 1973—; assoc. prof. Idaho State U., Pocatello, 1974—, mem. Idaho State U. faculty senate., 1985. Producer, dir. Brett Weston: Photographer, 1974; photography exhibit Latin Am. Photography, 1985—. Chmn. Pocatello Area Cable Commn., 1983—. Grantee NEH, 1972, Idaho State U., 1975, 77, 86. Mem. Soc. Photographic Edn. (chmn. 1984—), Kappa Tau Alpha. Democrat. Avocations: cross-country skiing, long distance land travel. Home: 0123 SW Curry Portland OR 97201 Office: Idaho State U Liberal Arts Bldg Pocatello ID 83209

WRIGHT, ARTHUR LARRY, mathematics educator; b. Pasadena, Calif., Oct. 8, 1941; s. Arthur R. and Jessie Lucille (Wineman) W.; m. Photini Daskalaki, July 7, 1968; children: Lauren, Lia. BA, UCLA, 1964; MA, U. Calif., Irvine, 1972, PhD, 1974. Statistician IBM Corp., Los Angeles and Westlake, Calif., 1966-75; faculty U. Ariz., Tucson, 1976—, prof. math. Mem. Inst. Math. Stats. Avocation: running. Office: U Ariz Tucson AZ 85721

WRIGHT, ARTHUR VERN, insurance company executive; b. Colorado Springs, Colo., Sept. 25, 1946; s. Wilbur Vern and Maybelle (Denton) W.; m. Gail Marie Carter, Sept. 7, 1968; 1 child, Tammara Kay. BSBA, Colo. State U., 1968. CPCU. Underwriter Aetna Life and Casualty Ins. Co., Denver,

1974-78; mgr. casualty underwriting Reliance Ins. Co., Denver, 1978-82, regional mgr. spl. accounts, 1982-83; br. mgr. United Pacific Ins. Co., Albuquerque, 1983-85, Phoenix, 1985—. Served with USAF, 1969-71. Mem. Soc. CPCU's, Property and Casualty Mgrs. Ariz., Ariz. Ins. Mgrs. Republican. Presbyterian. Avocations: photography, woodworking, jogging, bicycling, jazz and classical music. Home: 9248 N 28th St Phoenix AZ 85028 Office: United Pacific Ins Co 2390 E Camelback Rd Suite 230 Phoenix AZ 85016

WRIGHT, BERNARD, artist; b. Pitts., Feb. 23, 1938; s. Garfield and Emma (Wesley) W.; m. Corrine Westley, Mar. 7, 1964; 1 son, Jeffrey. Student Otis Art Inst., Los Angeles, 1969-70, Los Angeles Trade Tech. Coll., 1971-73. Exhibited traveling art show Moscow, Baku, Leningrad, Alma Alta, USSR, European capitals, 1966, Los Angeles City Hall Rotunda Gallery, 1967, Calif. Lutheran Coll., Thousand Oaks, 1967, Alley Gallery, Beverly Hills, 1968, Florenz Art Gallery, Los Angeles, 1969, San Diego Mus., 1969, Phillip E. Freed Gallery of Fine Arts, Chgo., 1969, Art West Gallery, Los Angeles, 1973, N.J. State Mus., Trenton, Detroit Inst. Arts, Mich., 1974, U. So. Calif., Calif. Mus. Sci. and Industry, 1974, City Art Mus., St. Louis, 1976, N.Y.C. Pub. Library, 1977, Pitts. City Hall Rotunda, 1982, The Mus. of African Am. Art, Los Angeles, 1982, Main Bridge Art Gallery, Los Angeles City Hall, 1983; represented in pvt. and pub. collections including Howard U., Library of Congress. collections past pres. co-founder Wright's & Westley Prodns., furniture and garment designers. Cited by U.S. Rep. Cardiss Collins, Ill., 1978, state senator Bill Greene, Calif, 1981, Mayor Richard S. Callguiri, Pitts., 1981, Mayor Coleman A. Young, Detroit, 1981, Mayor Tom Bradley, Los Angeles. bd. supr. Kenneth Hahn, Los Angeles, 1981; active community involvement Sta. KHJ-TV, 1982. Mem. Art West Assn. (bd. dirs.). Contbr. articles to profl. jours. Home: PO Box 8990 Los Angeles CA 90008

WRIGHT, CAROLE YVONNE, chiropractor, consultant; b. Long Beach, Calif., July 12, 1932; d. Paul Burt and Mary Leoan (Staley) Fickes; 1 dau., Morgan Michelle. D. Chiropractic, Palmer Coll., Davenport, Iowa, 1975. Instr. Palmer Coll., 1975-76; dir., owner Wright Chiropractic Clinic, Rocklin, Calif., 1978—, Woodland, Calif., 1980-81; dir., co-owner Ft. Sutter Chiropractic Clinic, Sacramento, 1985—; cons. in field; lectr., speaker on radio programs, at seminars. Contbr. articles to profl. jours. Co-chmn. Harold Michaels for Congress campaign, Alameda, Calif., 1972; dist. dir. 14th Congl. Dist., 1983—. Mem. Internat. Chiropractic Assn. Calif. (bd. dirs. 1978-81, pres. 1983-85), Palmer Coll. Alumni Assn. (Calif. state pres. 1981-83), Rocklin C. of C. (bd. dirs. 1979-81), Chiropractic Info. Bur. Downtown Sacramento (pres. 1986—), Rocklin-Loomis Bus. and Profl. Women. Republican. Avocations: reading; travel. Home: 4270 Cavitt Stallman Rd Roseville CA 95678 Office: Wright Chiropractic Clinic 3175 Sunset Blvd Suite 105 Rocklin CA 95677

WRIGHT, CHARLES LEE, information systems consultant; b. Dalton, Ga., Dec. 18, 1949; s. Charlie William and Catherine Christine (Quarles) W.; m. Lora Langford, May 11, 1968; children: Charles Lee, Christina. AA in Bus., Dalton Jr. Coll., 1971; BS in Bus., U. Tenn., Chattanooga, 1977; also numerous IBM classes on various machines and systems;. Trainee Ludlow Carpets, Dalton, 1971, EDP supr., 1971-73, EDP mgr., 1973-77; ops. mgr. Walter Carpet Mills, Industry, Calif., 1977-80; ptnr., cons. TCT Systems, San Dimas, Calif., 1978-81; ptnr., chief exec. officer Williams, Wright and Assocs., Upland, Calif., 1981—. Served as sgt. U.S. Army, 1969-71; Vietnam, Cambodia. Decorated Bronze Star, Army Commendation medal with oak leaf and oak leaf cluster, Air medal. Mem. Data Processing Mgmt. Assn., Am. Mgmt. Assn., Small Systems User Group, COMMON. Home: 2410 Sandpiper Pl Ontario CA 91761 Office: 400 N Mountain Ave Upland CA 91786 Also: 3311 Clearwater #175 Kennewick WA 99336

WRIGHT, CHERYL SAWYER, nursing coordinator; b. Norfolk, Va., June 18, 1947; s. David Warren and Lucy Elizabeth (Hunter) Sawyer; m. Daniel Ray Wright, July 27, 1968; children: Jason Bryant. RN, Norfolk Gen. Hosp., 1968; BA in Health Services Adminstrn., St. Mary's Coll., Moraga, 1980. Vascular head nurse Med. Ctr. Hosp., Norfolk, 1976-79; adminstrn. coordinator O'Connor Hosp., San Jose, Calif., 1979-81; staff nurse, operating room Kaiser Hosp., Santa Clara, Calif., 1981-84, Kalispell (Mont.) Regional Hosp., 1984; supr. operating room North Valley Hosp., Whitefish, Mont., 1984-85; nurisng coodinator Northwest Neurosurg. Ctr., Kalispell, 1986—. Mem. Assn. Operating Room Nurses, Calif. Nurses Assn., Concerned Nurses Mont. Republican. Avocations: fishing, music, reading, knitting, hunting. Home: PO Box 653 Whitefish MT 59937 Office: Northwest Neurosurg Ctr 1280 Burns Way Kalispell MT 59901

WRIGHT, COLIN RICHARD, psychotherapist; b. San Francisco, Jan. 24, 1937; s. John Richard and Elizabeth (Larke) W.; m. Elizabeth Brown Churchwell, Aug. 16, 1962; children: Kevin John, Brian William. BA, San Jose State U., 1960; MSW, U. Calif., Berkeley, 1968; PhD, Union Grad. Sch., 1979. Lic. clin. social worker, marriage family and child counselor, Calif. Social services research coordinator Santa Clara County, San Jose, Calif., 1970-72; psychiat. social worker Kaiser Med. Ctr., Santa Clara, 1972-75; mgr. med. intervention program Kaiser Med. Ctr., San Jose, 1975-80; chief spl. services Northland Mental Health Ctr., Grand Rapids, Minn., 1980-83; pvt. practice psychotherapy San Jose, 1983—. Bd. dirs. Council for Community Action Planning, San Jose, 1968-73. Served with U.S. Army, 1960-62. Mem. AAAS, Nat. Assn. Social Workers (bd. dirs. 1968-73, bd. dirs. psychotherapy referral service 1983-84, Social Worker of Yr. 1974), Am. Psychol. Assn., Soc. Behavioral Medicine, Biofeedback Soc. Am. (cert.), Profl. Standards Rev. Orgn. (bd. dirs. 1976-80). Avocations: do-it-yourself projects. Home: 7183 Chantilley Ct San Jose CA 95139 Office: 2211 Moorpark Ave Suite 150 San Jose CA 95128

WRIGHT, CURTIS LYNN, advt. agy. exec.; b. Beloit, Wis., Sept. 16, 1944; s. Kenneth Archie and Lorraine Millicent (Hanamann) W.; student Purdue U., 1963-66; m. JoAnn Margaret Korn, Apr. 16, 1966; children: Christopher Michael, Bryan Edward. Advt. prodn. mgr. L.S. Ayres & Co., Indpls., 1962-66; advt. mgr. John Bean div. FMC Corp., Tipton, Ind., 1966-67, mktg. asst. Riverside (Calif.) div., 1967-68, asst. advt. mgr. ordnance div., San Jose, Calif., 1968-69; pres. Battenberg, Fillhardt & Wright, Inc., San Jose, 1969—. Bd. dirs. San Jose Symphony, 1971-72, Santa Clara (Calif.) County Performing Arts League, 1972, San Jose Community Theater, 1972, Santa Clara County Jr. Achievement, 1973—, Better Bus. Bur., 1977-78, Live Oaks Found., 1982—; elected councilman City of Morgan Hill, Calif., 1986—. Recipient Ad Man of Yr. award Am. Advt. Fedn., 1973, Andy award Advt. Club N.Y.C., 1973, 74, 75, 77, 79, 80, 81, 82, 84, 1st pl. awards (21) San Francisco Soc. Communicating Arts, 1973, 75, 76, 77, 78, 79, 80, 81, 82, 83, 84, Western Art Dirs. competition award, 1973, 75, 76, 77, 78, 79, 80, 81, 82, Communication Arts competition award, 1974, 77, 79, 81, others. Mem. Am. Assn. Advt. Agys. (gov. No. Calif. council 1974-75), San Jose C. of C. (chmn. communications com. 1974-76), No. Calif. Assn. Indsl. Advertisers (dir. 1973-74), Santa Clara Valley Assn. Advt. Agys. (bd. dirs. 1982—), San Jose Advt. Club (pres. 1974-76). Home: 18540 Castle Hill Dr Morgan Hill CA 95037 Office: 70 N Second St San Jose CA 95113

WRIGHT, DONALD FRANKLIN, newspaper executive; b. St. Paul, July 10, 1934; s. Floyd Franklin and Helen Marie (Hansen) W.; m. Sharon Kathleen Fisher, Dec. 30, 1960; children: John, Dana, Kara, Patrick. B.M.E., U. Minn., 1957, M.B.A., 1958. With Mpls. Star & Tribune Co., 1958-77, research planning dir., then ops. dir., 1971-75, exec. editor, 1975-77; exec. v.p., gen. mgr. Newsday, Inc., L.I., N.Y., 1977-78, pres., chief operating officer, 1978-81; pres., chief operating officer Los Angeles Times, 1981—; vice chmn. Internat. Press Telecommunications Council; mem. adv. bd. World Press Inst.; mgmt. task force Inst. Journalism Edn. City councilman, Mahtomedi, Minn., 1967-69, 71; chmn. Citizens Com. Sch. Dist. 832, Mahtomedi, 1970; bd. dirs. United Way L.I., Calif. Tech. Assocs.; bd. fellows Claremont U. Ctr., Claremont Grad. Sch.; co-chmn. Neighborhood Housing Services; bd. dirs., 1st vice chmn. Boy Scouts Am. Los Angeles area council. Mem. Am. Newspaper Pubs. Assn. (chmn. prodn. mgmt. com. 1975-77, chmn. telecommunications com.), L.I. Assn. Commerce and Industry (dir.), Nat. Soc. Profl. Engrs., ASME, Am. Mktg. Assn. (exec. mem.), Merchants and Mfrs. Assn. (bd. dirs.). Presbyterian. Club: U. Minn. Alumni. Office: Los Angeles Times Times Mirror Sq Los Angeles CA 90053

WRIGHT, DONNA MARIE, real estate company owner; b. Wenatchee, Wash., Feb. 17, 1940; d. Donald O. and Marie A. (Ritter) Doud; m. Gary Donald Wright, June 26, 1962; children: Donald, Pamela, Penny, Gregory, Theodore. Student, Shoreline Community Coll., Everett Community Coll., 1976-78. With traffic dept. Cedargreen Frozen Foods, Wenatchee, 1959-62; owner Gary Wright Realty, Inc., Marysville, Wash., 1974—. Active community theater performances, 1985—; Dem. precinct committeeman, Marysville, 1980-84, del., com. chmn. county and state conventions, Wash., 1974, 76, 78, 80, 82; region dir. Fedn. Dem. Women, 1977-79, edn. chmn., 1973-76; pres. Cascade Dem. Women, Snohomish County, Wash., 1976-80. Mem. Wash. Assn. Realtors (com. chmn. 1984—, bd. dirs.), Nat. Assn. Realtors (sub-com. 1982-83), Snohomish County Bd. Realtors (sec., treas. 1979—, bd. dirs., Outstanding Service award 1983, Community Service award 1985). Mem. Ch. Assemblies of God. Club: Bus. and Profl. Women (Marysville) (pres. 1981-82). Lodge: Soroptimists (local pres. 1985-86). Avocations: community involvement, traveling. Home: 5533 Parkside Dr Marysville WA 98270 Office: Gallery of Homes 9323 Hwy 99 Marysville WA 98270

WRIGHT, ERNEST MARSHALL, physiologist, consultant; b. Belfast, Ireland, June 8, 1940; came to U.S., 1965; m. Brenda Winifred Keys, Sept. 30, 1961; children: John, Neill. BSc, U. London, 1961, DSc, 1978; PhD, U. Sheffield, Eng., 1964. Research fellow Harvard U., Boston, 1965-66; from asst. prof. to full prof. physiology UCLA Med. Sch., 1967—; cons. NIH, Bethesda, Md., 1982—, Senator Jacob K. Javits neurosci. investigator, 1985. Office: UCLA Med Sch Dept Physiology Los Angeles CA 90024

WRIGHT, EUGENE ALLEN, federal judge; b. Seattle, Feb. 23, 1913; s. Elias Allen and Mary (Bailey) W.; m. Esther Ruth Ladley, Mar. 19, 1938; children: Gerald Allen, Meredith Ann Wright Morton. AB, U. Wash., 1935, JD, 1937; LLD, U. Puget Sound, 1984. Bar: Wash. 1937. Assoc. Wright & Wright, Seattle, 1937-54; judge Superior Ct. King County, Wash., 1954-66; v.p., sr. trust officer Pacific Nat. Bank Seattle, 1966-69; judge U.S. Ct. of Appeals 9th Circuit, Seattle, 1969—; acting municipal judge, Seattle, 1948-52; mem. faculty Nat. Jud. Coll., 1964-72; lectr. Sch. Communications, U. Wash., 1965-66, U. Wash. Law Sch., 1952-74; lectr. appellate judges' seminars, 1973-76, Nat. Law Clks. Inst., La. State U., 1973; chmn. Wash. State Com. on Law and Justice, 1968-69; mem. com. on appellate rules Jud. Conf., 1978-85, mem. com. on courtroom photography, 1983-85, com. jud. ethics, 1984—, com. Bicentennial of Constrn., 1985—. Author: (with others) The State Trial Judges Book, 1966; also articles; editor: Trial Judges Jour., 1963-66; contbr. articles to profl. jours. Chmn. bd. visitors U. Puget Sound Sch. Law, 1979-84; bd. dirs. Met. YMCA, Seattle, 1955-72; lay reader Episc. ch. Served to lt. col. AUS, 1941-46; col. Res.; ret. Decorated Bronze Star, Combat Inf. badge; recipient Army Commendation medal, Disting. Service award U.S. Jr. C. of C., 1948, Disting. Service medal Am. Legion. Fellow Am. Bar Found.; mem. ABA (council div. jud. adminstrn. 1971-76), Fed. Bar Assn. (Disting. Jud. Service award 1984), Wash. Bar Assn. (award of merit 1983), Seattle-King County Bar Assn. (Spl. Disting. Service award 1984), Appellate Judges Conf., Ret. Officers Assn., Order of Coif, Delta Upsilon, Phi Delta Phi. Clubs: Nat. Lawyers, Wash. Athletic. Lodges: Masons (33 degree), Shriners, Rainier. Office: 902 US Courthouse Seattle WA 98104

WRIGHT, FRANCES JANE, educational psychologist; b. Los Angeles, Dec. 22, 1943; d. step-father John David and Evelyn Jane (Dale) Brinegar. B.A., Long Beach State U., 1965, secondary tchr. cert., 1966; M.A., Brigham Young U., 1968, Ed.D., 1980; postgrad. U. Nev., 1970, U. Utah, 1972-73; postdoctoral Utah State U., 1985-86. Cert. tchr., adminstr. Utah. Asst. dir. Teenpost Project, San Pedro, Calif., 1966; caseworker Los Angeles County, 1966-67; self-care inservice dir. Utah State Tng. Sch., American Fork, Utah, 1968, vocat. project designer, 1968; tchr. mentally handicapped Santa Ana Unified Schs., Calif., 1968-69; state specialist intellectually handicapped State Office Edn., Salt Lake City, 1969-70; vocat. counselor Manpower, Salt Lake City, 1970-71; tchr. severely handicapped Davis County Schs., Farmington, Utah, 1971-73, diagnostician, 1973-74, resource elem. tchr., 1974-78; instr. Brigham Young U., Salt Lake City, 1976—; resource tchr. jr. high Davis County Schs., Farmington, 1978—; ednl. cons., Murray, Utah, 1973—; cons. and lectr. in field. Author curriculums in spl. edn.; contbr. articles to profl. jours. Named Profl. of Yr., Utah Assn. for Children with Learning Disabilities, 1985. Mem. Assn. Children/Adults with Learning Disabilities (del. 1979-85, 87, nat. nominating com. 1985-86), NEA, Nat. Assn. Female Execs., Utah Assn. Children/Adults with Learning Disabilities (exec. bd. 1978-84, profl. adv. bd. 1985—), Council Exceptional Children (div. learning disabilities, ednl. diagnostics, behavioral disorders), Utah Ednl. Assn., Davis County Edn. Assn., Council Learning Disabilities, Windstar Found., Smithsonian Found., Nat. Hist. Preservation Found., Nat. Assn. Sch. Adminstrs. Democrat. Mormon. Lodge: Job's Daughters. Avocations: geneology research, horseback riding, sketching, crafts, reading. Home: 5212 Gravenstein Park Murray UT 84123 Office: Kaysville Jr High Sch Kaysville UT 84037

WRIGHT, GLORIA DAWN OLSEN, social worker; b. Salt Lake City, Sept. 2, 1932; d. Clair and Ina Elizabeth (Lund) Olsen; m. James Owen Wright, Dec. 15, 1952; children: Rodney, Debra, Mark, Laurie, Scott, Kari. BS magna cum laude, Weber State Coll., 1981; MSW, U. Utah, 1983. Project dir. Parent Edn. Ctr., Farmington, Utah, 1984; alternatives counselor Council on Aging, Farmington, 1984-85; youth in custody worker Davis County Pub. Schs., Farmington, 1985—. Dist. sec. Davis County PTA, 1978; dist. vice-chmn. Rep. com., Kaysville, Utah, 1985—. Mem. Nat. Assn. Social Workers (cert.), Phi Kappa Phi, Alpha Delta Mu. Mormon. Avocations: public speaking, writing poetry, piano, sewing, genealogy. Home: 1084 Cambridge Rd Kaysville UT 84037 Office: Davis County Schs 45 E State Farmington UT 84025

WRIGHT, GORDON BROOKS, musician, conductor, educator; b. Bklyn., Dec. 31, 1934; s. Harry Wesley and Helen (Brooks) W.; m. Inga-Lisa Myrin Wright, June 13, 1958 (div. 1979); children—Karin-Ellen, Charles-Eric, Daniel Brooks. B.Mus., Coll. Wooster, 1957; M.A., U. Wis., 1961; postgrad., Salzburg Mozarteum, 1972, Loma Linda U., 1979. Prof. music U. Alaska, College, 1969—. Founder, condr. Wis. Chamber Orch., 1961-69; condr. Fairbanks Symphony Orch., Arctic Chamber Orch.; guest condr. Philarmonia Hungarica, Philomusica London, Siegerland Orch. Westfalia, Anchorage Symphony Orch.; composer: Suite of Netherlands Dances, 1965, Six Alaskan Tone Poems, 1974, Symphony in Ursa Major, 1979, 1984 Overture; columnist Alaska Advocate, Fairbanks Daily News-Miner; writer. Served with AUS, 1957-59. Mem. Am. Musicol. Soc., Internat. Musicol. Soc., Am. Symphony Orch. League, Galpin Soc., Dolmetsch Found., Arturo Toscanini Soc., Alaska Assn. Arts, Am. Fedn. Musicians, Royal Mus. Assn., Sierra Club (chmn. Fairbanks Group 1969-71), Friends of Earth, Wilderness Soc., Audubon Soc., Alaska Conservation Soc. (editor Rev. 1971-78), China Poot Bay Soc. Home: Box 80051 Fairbanks AK 99708 Office: Fairbanks Symphony Orch PO Box 82104 Fairbanks AK 99708

WRIGHT, HARRY ALLEN, chemistry educator; b. Oregon City, Oreg., Aug. 13, 1931; s. Merle Ewart and Beulah Belle (Wilson) W. BS in Chemistry, Pacific U., 1953; postgrad., Portland State U., 1954, 80, 84, So. Oreg. State Coll., 1958, U. Calif., Berkeley, 1960; MAT in Chemistry, Stanford U., 1962; postgrad., Hope Coll., 1966, U. Wash., 1970, Denver U., 1972. Tchr. math. and sci. Ontario (Oreg.) High Sch., 1953-56; tchr. chemistry Ashland (Oreg.) Sr. High Sch., 1956—, chmn. dept. sci., 1968-74, 80-85; advisor student govt. Ashland High Sch., 1958-84, Nat. Honor Soc., 1957—, also dir. sports info., 1958—; mem. state adv. bd. Oreg. Assn. Student Councils, 1982-84; bd. dirs. Rogue Fed. Credit Union, Jackson County, Oreg., 1967—, chmn. bd. 1970-85. Bd. dirs. Ashland Community YMCA, 1958-66, also sec. bd., 1959-63, v.p. bd. 1964-66; pres. bd. dirs. Meals on Wheels, Ashland; pres. Jr. C. of C., Ashland, 1960, also state chmn. religious activities, 1964. Recipient Disting. Service award Jr. C. of C., Ashland chpt., 1960, 64, People to People Exchange to Italy award John F. Kennedy Living Meml., Jackson County, 1964. Mem. NEA (life), Ashland Edn. Assn. (treas., v.p., pres.), Oreg. Edn. Assn., Nat. Sci. Tchrs. Assn (life), Oreg. Sci. Tchrs. Assn. (regional v.p. 1978-80), Am. Chem. Soc. Republican. Clubs: Siskiyou Knife and Fork (Ashland) (bd. dirs. 1974-79, 83—), Grange (Molalla, Oreg.). Lodges: Kiwanis (pres. Ashland club 1958), Ind. Order Odd Fellows. Avocations: sports statistician, community service, reading, gardening, stamp and coin collecting. Home: 1069 Henry St Ashland OR 97520 Office: Ashland High Sch 201 S Mountain Ave Ashland OR 97520

WRIGHT, HELENE SEGAL, editor; b. Los Angeles, Jan. 31, 1955; d. Alan and Lila E. (Hambro) Segal; m. David Scott Wright, May 6, 1979. Student, Calif. State U., Fullerton, 1973-75; BA in English, U. Calif., Santa Barbara, 1978. Library asst. Sta. ABC-CLIO, Santa Barbara, 1979-80, editorial asst., 1980-81, asst. editor, 1981-83, mng. editor, 1983—. Avocations: reading, collecting, swimming. Home: 142 La Vista Grande Santa Barbara CA 93103 Office: Sta ABC-CLIO 2040 Alameda Padre Serra Santa Barbara CA 93103

WRIGHT, JAMES REUBEN, air force officer, chemistry educator; b. Gooding, Idaho, Sept. 22, 1938; s. Reuben Albert and Vera (Toone) W.; m. Sue Ann Allen, Sept. 10, 1960 (div. May 1967); children: Lisa Annette, Trisha Carrie; m. Janice Ann Cheney, June 14, 1968; 1 child, James Gregory. Student, Brigham Young U., 1956-57; BS, U. Idaho, 1960, MS, 1962, PhD, 1964; postgrad., Air Command and Staff Coll., 1976-77. Acting asst. prof. dept. agrl. biochemistry U. Idaho, Moscow, 1964-65; commd. 2d lt. USAF, 1960, advanced through grades to col., 1986; biochemist Air Force Weapons Lab., Kirtland AFB, N.Mex., 1965-68; assoc. prof. chemistry USAF Acad. DFC, Colorado Springs, Colo., 1968-72, tenure prof. chemistry, 1977-86; nuclear research officer McClellan (AFB, Calif.) Cen. Lab., 1972-76, dir., 1986—. Explorer advisor Boy Scouts Am., Colorado Springs, 1977-80. Mem. Am. Chem. Soc. (bd. dirs. internat. chemistry olympiad study camp 1984-86),Sigma Xi, Phi Beta Kappa, Phi Kappa Phi. Republican. Mormon. Avocation: sports. Home: 4985 Primrose Dr Fair Oaks CA 95628 Office: McClellan Cen Lab Tech Ops Div/DL McClellan AFB CA 95652-6437

WRIGHT, JANET SCRITSMIER, investment consultant; b. Pomona, Calif., May 21, 1960; d. Jerome Lorenzo and Mildred Joan (Lloyd) Scritsmier; m. James Calvin Wright, Mar. 26, 1983; children—Justin Michael, Corey Gray. Student Calif. State Poly. U., 1978-79. Vice pres. sales E.L.A. Co., Industry, Calif., 1979-84; investment cons. Cameron Properties Inc., Covina, Calif., 1980—. Asst. instr. Dale Carnegie Sales Course, 1981-82, Human Relations, 1983. Republican. Mormon. Avocation: snow skiing. Home: 2454 N Cameron Ave Covina CA 91724

WRIGHT, JOAN, psychiatric nurse, consultant; b. Lewistown, Mont., July 18, 1934; d. Emmett Patrick and Francisca (Laux) O'Sullivan; m. Corley Hutching Wright, Mar. 21, 1953; children: Elizabeth Ann, Clare Maria, Wilma Harriet, William Harrison, Barbara Jo. AAS in Nursing, Ulster County Community Coll., Stone Ridge, N.Y., 1970; BS cum laude in Psychology, N.Y. Inst. Tech., 1978; MS in Edn., L.I. U., 1980. Staff nurse to adminstr. hosps. in N.Y. and Conn., 1970-75; asst. supervising nurse Dutchess County chpt. ARC, Poughkeepsie, N.Y., 1975-76; cons., dir. residential care Ann Storcks Nursery, Norfolk, Conn., 1977, 78; substitute tchr. Amenia, N.Y., 1977-79; psychiat. nurse Harlem Valley Psychiat. Ctr., Wingdale, N.Y., 1979-81, adminstr. crisis residence, 1980-81; psychiat. staff nurse Hilo Hosp., Hawaii, 1981-83; cons. in field, 1983—; disaster nurse ARC, 1975-81, home nurse instr., 1975-81; community mental health nurse, 1980-81; instr. CPR Am. Heart Assn. Recipient Clara Barton medal ARC, 1975. Mem. Am. Assn. Mental Deficiency, Am. Personnel and Guidance Assn., Am. Mental Health Counselors Assn., N.Y. State Personnel and Guidance Assn., N.Y. State Assn. Mental Deficiency, N.Y. State Mental Health Counselors Assn., Hawaii Personnel and Guidance Assn., Hawaii Mental Health Counselors Assn. (chmn. 1984, treas. 1987—), Dutchess County Nurses Assn. (treas. 1976). Roman Catholic.

WRIGHT, JOHN A., engineering, construction, and mining company executive; b. 1942; married. BS, C.W. Post Coll. of Long Island Univ., 1966; MS, Adelphi U., 1973. With Internat. Paper Co., 1964-71; pres. St. Joe Lead Co., 1977, Pea Ridge Iron Ore Co., 1978, St. Joe Resources Co., 1978; dir. corp. devel. St. Joe Minerals Corp., Clayton, Mo., 1971-75; v.p. sales St. Joe Minerals Corp., 1975-80, exec. v.p., 1980-82, pres., from 1982, then chmn., chief exec. officer; chmn. natural resources group, then exec. v.p. Fluor Corp. (parent co.), Irvine, Calif., 1983-86, pres., chief operating officer, 1986—; also bd. dirs. Fluor Corp. (parent co.). Served with U.S. Army, 1966-68. Office: Fluor Corp 3333 Michelson Dr Irvine CA 92730

WRIGHT, JOHN GEORGE, JR., manufacturing company executive; b. Cleve., June 5, 1947; s. John George and Margaret Josephine (Laumer) W.; m. Isabelle H. Pasquier, Dec. 21, 1976; children—Daniel William, Marie-Christine, Nicholas Fernand. B.S., Wharton Sch., U. Pa., 1969; M.S. summa cum laude, U. Minn., 1970; M.B.A., M.A.M., Claremont Grad. Sch., 1982, Ph.D., 1984. Mktg. rep. Columbia-Great Lakes Corp., Northridge, Calif., 1970-73, corp. gen. mgr., 1973-80, v.p., 1980-87, pres., 1987—, also bd. dirs.; pres. Columbia France, .S.A., 1987—. Mem. Data Processing Mgrs. Assn., U. Pa. Alumni Assn. (v.p., exec. com.), Beta Gamma Sigma, Delta Upsilon (life), Delta Sigma Pi (life). Office: Columbia-Great Lakes Corp 21823 Plummer St Chatsworth CA 91311

WRIGHT, KENNETH JAMES, chemistry and environmental science educator; b. Pitts., Aug. 26, 1939; s. William Orville and Laura Louise (Husted) W.; m. Virginia Louise Brodin, Jan. 1, 1966; children: Kody James, Clark William. Student, Harvey Mudd Coll., 1957-59; BS in Chemistry, Portland State U., 1962; postgrad., Oreg. State U., 1962-63; PhD in Chemistry, U. Idaho, 1971. Analytical and research chemist Harvey Aluminum Corp., The Dalles, Oreg., 1963-66; prof. chemistry and environ. sci. N. Idaho Coll., Coeur d'Alene, 1971—, chmn. div. sci., 1972-77, chmn. faculty, 1982-83; research trainee NSF, U. Idaho, 1967; ednl. cons. The Bunker-Hill Co., Kellogg, Idaho, 1977. Contbr. articles to profl. jours. Founder Hanford Edn. Action League, Spokane, Wash, 1985; appointee Hazardous Waste Cm., Coeur d'Alene, 1986, chmn., 1987. Fellow NDEA, U. Idaho, 1968-70. Mem. Am. Chem. Soc. (sect./treas. Inland Empire sect. 1979, vice-chmn. 1980, chmn. 1981), Idaho Conservation League, Sierra Club (chmn. Idaho-Mont. chpt. 1976, NW regional conservation com. 1977-79), Sigma Xi. Avocations: photography, backpacking, hunting, tennis, skiing. Office: N Idaho Coll 1000 W Garden Ave Coeur d'Alene ID 83814

WRIGHT, KENNETH LYLE, psychologist; b. American Falls, Idaho, Sept. 11, 1911; s. Jesse Joshua and Martha Sophia (Dickenson) W. children—Anne Collins, Corrella Carmelette Brown, Sandra Lynne Sutherland. B.A., U. Wash., 1941; M.A., U. So. Calif., 1957; Ph.D., San Gabriel Coll., 1958. Coach State Tng. Sch. for Boys, Chehalis, Wash., 1941; dep. probation officer, Los Angeles County, Calif., 1954-56; vis. lectr. Whittier Coll. (Calif.), 1955-56; dist. sch. psychologist Anaheim Union High Sch. Dist. (Calif.); guidance counselor, vice prin. Orleans Am. High Sch., Dept. Army (France), also psychol. services and spl. edn. coordinator Dependent Edn. Group Hdqrs., Karlsruhe, W.Ger., 1959-62; edn. specialist U.S. Navy, San Diego, 1962-63; pvt. practice psychology, San Diego, 1963-64, 69—; psychol. cons. Clin. Bd. Speech Therapy, Children's Hosp., San Diego, 1963-64; vis. prof. U. Western Ont., lectr., sch. psychologist London Bd. Edn. (Ont., Can.), 1964-66; dir. psychol. services Niagara Falls Dist. Bd. Edn. (N.Y.), 1966-69; lectr. Syracuse U., 1968. Pres. Whittier Coordinating Council; a founder Can. Sch. Vol. Program; founder Niagara Inst. Human Devel., European Assns. Am. Personnel and Guidance and Speech and Hearing in Dependent Schs. Served with USNR, 1941-46. Recipient outstanding award San Diego County Assn. Retarded Children. Fellow San Diego Biomed. Research Inst. (past pres.); mem. Assn. Children with Learning Disabilities, Council Exceptional Children (past pres. Niagara Falls chpt.), Royal Soc. Medicine, Am. Psychol. Assn., Calif. Psychol. Assn., San Diego County Psychol. Assn., Am. Soc. Clin. Hypnosis, Calif. Soc. Clin. Hypnosis (sec.), San Diego County Soc. Clin Hypnosis (pres. 1975-76), San Diego Assn. Clin. Psychologists (past pres.), Mensa. Club: Koha Kai. Lodge: Masons. Author: My Name Is Kim; The American Symbol; The Fantastic Journey with Visualization and Imagery; The Psychological Effects of Allergy; Allergy and Learning Disabilities in Children. Home: 751 Amiford Dr San Diego CA 92107 Office: 4070 Goldfinch San Diego CA 92103

WRIGHT, LIN M., theater educator; b. Mpls., Jan. 19, 1933; d. Nathanial F. and Mary F. (Hargarten) Sommers; m. James L. Wright, Aug. 5, 1963; 1 child, Miriam Sommers. BS, U. Minn., 1954, MA, 1960, PhD, 1973. Cert. secondary tchr., Minn. Tchr. Gilbert (Minn.) High Sch., 1954-55, Mounds View High Sch., New Brighton, Minn., 1955-63; asst. prof. theatre U. Minn., Mpls., 1965-73; prof. theatre Ariz. State U., Tempe, 1973-84, chmn. theatre dept., 1984—. Recipient Outstanding Contbns. award So. Calif. Edn. Theatre Assn., 1984. Mem. Am. Assn. Theatre for Youth (chair, founding bd. dirs., research citation 1986), Children's Theatre Assn. Am. (pres. 1981-83, v.p. research 1977-79, Human Awareness award 1976). Office: Ariz State U Dept Theater Tempe AZ 85287

WRIGHT, MAYNARD LATTIMER, research scientist; b. Chattanooga, Dec. 25, 1935; s. Maynard Lattimer and Clara W.; m. Phyllis Carol. BSEE, MIT, 1957; MS in Electrophysics, Poly. Inst. Bklyn., 1962. Research engr. AIL, Mineola, N.Y., 1957-65; staff scientist Watkins-Johnson, Palo Alto, Calif., 1965-66; research scientist H-P Labs., Palo Alto, 1966-67, Stanford U., Calif., 1967-69; staff scientist SRI Internat., Menlo Park, Calif., 1969—; cons. in field, Menlo Park, 1968—; instr. Foothill Coll., Los Altos Hills, Calif., 1976-77, De Anza Coll., Cupertino, Calif., 1977-78. Contbr. articles to profl. jours.; patentee in field. Served to capt. U.S. Army, 1958-66. Mem. Am. Assn. Artificial Intelligence, IEEE, Sigma Xi. Avocations: mountaineering, scuba diving, photography, sculpture. Home: 2071 Oakley Ave Menlo Park CA 94025 Office: SRI Internat 333 Ravenswood Ave Menlo Park CA 94025

WRIGHT, RALPH ROLAND, JR., holding company executive; b. Louisville, Jan. 15, 1948; s. Ralph Roland and Violet Clare (Bollinger) W.; m. Lynda Jane Hebson, July 20, 1968; children: Elizabeth, Janissa, Kathleen, Mary, Charles. BS, U. Ala., 1969, MBA, 1970. Assoc. corp. banking officer 1st Nat. Bank, Louisville, 1972-75, sr. regional banking officer, 1978-79; corp. banking officer 1st State Bank Oreg., Portland, 1975-78; pres. Internat. Enterprises/Rol-Away, Portland, 1979-80; exec. v.p. The Cutler Corp., Portland, 1980—. Chmn. Oregonians for Cost Effective Govt., Portland, 1985—; v.p., bd. dirs. Oreg. Taxpayers Assn., Salem, 1983-85. Served as 1st lt. USAF, 1970-72. Named to Hon. Order Ky. Col., Gov. Louis Nunn, 1969; recipient Ambassador of Goodwill award Mayor Kenneth Schmeid, Louisville, 1969. Mem. Portland C. of C. (bd. dirs. 1983—). Roman Catholic. Club: Multnomah Athletic (Portland). Avocations: sports, reading, family. Office: The Cutler Corp 4512 SW Kelly Ave Suite 300 Portland OR 97201

WRIGHT, RICHARD FORREST, cardiologist; b. Chgo., Nov. 2, 1952; m. Christina Weisner; children: Richard, Katherine. BA, U. Calif., Santa Barbara, 1973; MD, Harvard U., 1977. Diplomate Am. Bd. Internal Medicine, Am. Bd. Cardiology. Intern U. So. Calif., Los Angeles County Hosp., 1977-78; resident in internal medicine Peter Bent Brigham Hosp., Boston, 1981-84; cardiology and research fellow Harvard Med. Sch. and Brigham and Women's Hosp., Boston, 1981-84; dir. research Pacific Heart Inst., Santa Monica, Calif., 1986—. Fellow Am. Coll. Cardiology; mem. AMA, Am. Fedn. Clin. Research, ACP, Los Angeles Soc. Echocardiography (officer). Office: Pacific Heart Inst 2001 Santa Monica Blvd Santa Monica CA 90404

WRIGHT, ROBERT WILLIAM, building construction technology educator; b. Ogden, Utah, Aug. 28, 1945; s. Roland C. and Ruth (Barnett) W.; m. Janice Alder, Aug. 27, 1968; children: Melanie, Michelle, Bryan, Melinda, Brad. B, Weber State Coll., 1969; MS in Indsl. Edn., Brigham Young U., 1975. Cabinetmaker Davis Mill & Cabinet, Bountiful, Utah, 1975-76, Granite Mill, Salt Lake City, 1976-79; from instr. to prof. Snow Coll., Ephraim, Utah, 1979—. City inspector, Ephraim, 1983—. Grantee U.S. Office Edn., 1981-83, 85-86. Mem. Am. Vocat. Assn., Am. Solar Energy Soc., Utah Professiona Teaching Assn., Vocat. Indsl. Clubs of Am. (advisor 1983-84). Mormon. Avocations: woodworking, outdoor sports, stereos, computers, scouting. Home: 375 E 300 S Ephraim UT 84627 Office: Snow Coll 150 College Ave Ephraim UT 84627

WRIGHT, ROSALIE MULLER, newspaper and magazine editor; b. Newark, June 20, 1942; d. Charles and Angela (Fortunata) Muller; m. Lynn Wright, Jan. 13, 1962; children: James Anthony Meador, Geoffrey Shepard. B.A. in English, Temple U., 1965. Mng. editor Suburban Life mag., Orange, N.J., 1960-62; assoc. editor Phila. mag., 1962-64, mng. editor, 1969-73; founding editor Womensports mag., San Mateo, Calif., 1973-75; editor scene sect. San Francisco Examiner, 1975-77; exec. editor New West mag., San Francisco and Beverly Hills, Calif., 1977-81; features and Sunday editor San Francisco Chronicle, 1981—; tchr. mag. writing U. Calif.-Berkeley, 1975-76; participant pub. procedure's course Stanford U., 1977-79; chmn. mag. judges Council Advancement and Support Edn. Conf., 1980, judge, 1984. Contbr. numerous mag. articles, critiques, revs., Compton's Ency. Mem. Am. Assn. Sunday and Feature Editors (treas. 1984, sec. 1985, 1st v.p. 1986, pres. 1987). Office: Chronicle Pub Co 901 Mission St San Francisco CA 94119

WRIGHT, TIM EUGENE, packaging development executive; b. Weed, N.Mex., Oct. 13, 1943; s. Clyde Everett and Juanita Delores (Barrett) W.; m. Nancy Ann Ausenbaugh, Oct. 2, 1965 (div. 1975); 1 child, Ramsey Jordan. Diploma, Dayton Art Inst., 1967, M.F.A., U. Idaho, 1969. Designer, Lawson Mfg. Co., Troy, Idaho, 1968-70, Boise Cascade, Burley, Idaho, 1970-72; project coordinator Boise Cascade, Golden, Colo., 1972-76, product devel. mgr., Wallula, Wash., 1976-84; mng. ptnr. Matrix Applications Co., Pasco, Wash., 1984—. Patentee folding carton. Recipient Silver award for packaging, 1978. Mem. Soc. Packaging and Handling Engrs., Western Packaging Assn., TAPPI. Office: Matrix Applications Co PO Box 1407 Pasco WA 99301

WRIGHT, VALETA METCALF, school administrator; b. Albion, Ill., Feb. 3, 1930; d. Thomas Edward and Mary Laura (Bunting) Metcalf; m. Robert Cade Wright, June 12, 1956; children: Leta K., M. Kristine. BS, Eastern Ill. U., 1951; BA in Ministry, Lincoln Christian Coll., 1953; MA in Ministry, Pacific Christian Coll., 1979. Cert. community coll. tchr., Ariz. Adminstr. Lincoln Heights Sch. Young Children, Phoenix, 1971-79, Hillcrest Christian Sch., Granada Hills, Calif., 1979-81, Cen. Christian Sch., Mesa, Ariz., 1982-85, Eastside Christian Sch., Mesa, 1985—; instr. Maricopa County Community Coll., Phoenix, 1974-79; cons. Ft. McDowell Indian Reservation, Scottsdale, Ariz., 1974-78; presch. cons., Ariz. and Calif., 1970-75. Contbr. articles to profl. jours. Pres. Hollywood Women's Rep. Club, Inglewood, Calif., 1966; mem. Calif. Rep. Cen. Com. 1964-68, editor S.W. Rep. Newsletter, 1967. Recipient commendation Los Angeles County Bd. Suprs., 1971. Mem. Assn. Christian Sch. Internat. (cert.), Kappa Pi, Kappa Omicron Phi. Home: 2011 E Gary Cir Mesa AZ 85302

WRIGLEY, ELIZABETH SPRINGER (MRS. OLIVER K. WRIGLEY), found. exec.; b. Pitts., Oct. 4, 1915; d. Charles Woodward and Sarah Maria (Roberts) Springer; B.A. U. Pitts., 1935; B.S., Carnegie Inst. Tech., 1936; m. Oliver Kenneth Wrigley, June 16, 1936 (dec. July 1978). Procedure analyst U.S. Steel Corp., Pitts., 1941-43; research asst. The Francis Bacon Found., Inc., Los Angeles, 1944, exec., 1945-50, trustee, 1950—, dir. research, 1951-53, pres., 1954—, dir. Francis Bacon Library; mem. adv. council Royal Skakespeare Revels in the Ojai; mem. regional Fine Arts adv. council Calif. State Poly. U., Pomona. Mem. ALA, Calif. Library Assn., Renaissance Soc. Am., Modern Humanities Research Assn., Cryptogram Assn., Alpha Delta Pi. Presbyn. Mem. Order Eastern Star, Damascus Shrine. Editor: The Skeleton Text of the Shakespeare Folio L.A. (by W.C. Arensberg), 1952. Compiler: Short Title Catalogue Numbers in the Library of the Francis Bacon Foundation, 1958; Wing Numbers in the Library of the Francis Bacon Foundation, 1959; Supplement To Francis Bacon Library Holdings in the STC of English Books, 1967; (with David W. Davies) A Concordance to the Essays of Francis Bacon, 1973. Home: 4805 N Pal Mal Ave Temple City CA 91780 Office: Francis Bacon Library 655 N Dartmouth Ave Claremont CA 91711

WROBLESKI, JOHN JOSEPH, naval officer; b. Cleve., Dec. 31, 1948; s. John Joseph and Kathleen Jane (Connor) W.; m. Karen Agnes Johnson, Oct. 7, 1972; children: Michael, John III, Catherine. B in Aerospace Engring., U. Minn., 1975; MS in Aerospace Engring. and Aero. Engring., Naval Postgrad. Sch., 1981. Commd. USN, 1975, advanced through grades to lt. comdr., 1984; now Advanced Medium Range Air-to-Air Missile program officer Pacific Missile Test Ctr., USN. Mem. Am. Inst. for Aeros. and Astronautics, Sigma XI. Roman Catholic. Avocations: amateur radio, model aircraft. Home: 9346 Halifax St Ventura CA 93004 Office: Pacific Missile Test Ctr Code 1097 Naval Air Station Point Mugu CA 93042

WROBLICKY, THEODORE PETER, management consultant; b. Harvey, Ill., Sept. 9, 1937; s. Nestor Peter and Helen Marie (Hajek) W.; m. Barbara Kathryn Bukowski, Aug. 12, 1961; children: Gregory, Peter, Nicholas, Alexander. BS, No. Ill. U., 1963; MBA, Golden Gate U., 1970. Programmer Sears Roebuck & Co., 1963; application engr. Gen. Electric Co., 1964-67; asst. dir. mgmt. services Western Pacific R.R., 1967-71; cons. Ill. Central Gulf R.R., 1971-73; mgr. Haskins & Sells, Chgo., 1973-77; prin. Arthur Young & Co., Sacramento, 1978-82, dir. EDP cons., dir. mgmt. cons. Touche, Ross & Co., Sacramento, 1982—; mem. faculty Calif. State U., Sacramento, 1980; data processing adv. Reagan-Bush Com., Arlington, Va., 1980, mem. transition team, Washington, 1980-81; mem. Calif. Govt. Efficiency Team, 1983. Served with U.S. Army, 1956-59. Mem. Assn. Computing Machinery, Data Processing Mgmt. Assn., EDP Auditors Assn. Republican. Byzantine Catholic. Clubs: Sutter, Polish Am., Ukrainian Heritage No. Calif. Lodge: KC. Office: Touche Ross & Co 100 Howe Ave Suite 100 S Sacramento CA 95825

WU, FANG-SHENG, research biologist; b. Republic of China, May 4, 1941; came to U.S., 1973; s. Shu-Sheng and Yeh-Chi (Cheng) W.; m. Melanie Chang; children: Minming, Helen, Constance, Eaming. BS, Nat. Taiwan N. U., Taipei, 1967, M.Sc., 1972; PhD, Mich. State U., 1977. Asst. research fellow Academia Sinica, Taipei, 1972-73; research asst. Mich. State U., East Lansing, 1973-77; postdoctoral fellow U. Conn., Storrs, 1977-79; research asst. prof. SUNY, Syracuse, 1979-81; sr. research biologist Zoecon Corp., Palo Alto, Calif., 1981—. Contbr. articles to profl. jours. Recipient Bessey award Mich. State U., 1979. Mem. AAAS, Am. Soc. Plant Physiologists, Tissue Culture Assn., N.Y. Acad. Sci., Am. Soc. Horticulture Sci. Home: 3304 Plateau Dr Belmont CA 94002 Office: Zoecon Research Inst 975 Calif Ave Palo Alto CA 94304

WU, PO-SHUN, biochemical researcher; b. Taipei, Republic of China, July 26, 1947; came to U.S., 1969; s. Ann-Pan and Zuei-Mei (Lee) W.; m. Susan H.W. Chen, Apr. 1, 1981; 1 child, Martin Jason. BS, Nat. Taiwan U., Taipei, 1969; MS, U. Akron, 1972; PhD, Georgetown U., 1977. Research fellow Albert Einstein Coll. Medicine, Bronx, N.Y., 1977-79, Calif. Inst. Tech., Pasadena, 1980-82; asst. prof. Calif. State U., Los Angeles, 1982; research scientist Pacific Med. Ctr., San Francisco, 1982-84; mgr. quality control Xoma Corp., Berkeley, Calif., 1984-85; mgr. tech. ops. Gene Labs Inc., San Carlos, Calif., 1985—. Contbr. articles to profl. jours. and chpts. to books. Mem. AAAS, Am. Chem. Soc., N.Y. Acad. Scis. Home: 267 25th Ave San Francisco CA 94121 Office: Gene Labs Inc 505 Penobscot Dr Redwood City CA 94063

WU, TE-KAO, electrical engineer; b. Feng-Shan, Taiwan, Republic of China, Oct. 12, 1948; came to U.S., 1971; s. Pao-Ding and Yen Mei (Yao) W.; m. Tsan-Sheng Chang, Aug. 14, 1976; children: Angela, David. BSEE, Nat. Taiwan U., Taipei, Republic of China, 1970; MSEE, U. Miss., 1973, PhD, 1976. Scientist assoc. Lockheed Corp., Sunnyvale, Calif., 1978-79; mem. tech. staff TRW Corp., Redondo Beach, Calif., 1979-80; sr. staff engr. Sperry Corp., Clearwater, Fla., 1980-81; mem. tech. staff ECI div. E-Systems, St. Petersburg, Fla., 1981-83; sr. staff engr. Hughes Aircraft Co., El Segundo, Calif., 1983—; adj. prof. U. South Fla., Tampa, 1980-81. Inventor in field. Recipient Outstanding Acad. award Nat. Taiwan U., 1967. Mem. IEEE (sr., contbr. to Jour.), Eta Kappa Nu, Sigma Xi, Phi Kappa Phi. Avocations: table tennis, gardening, bridge. Office: Hughes Aircraft Co PO Box 92919 Los Angeles CA 90009

WUBBEN, HUBERT HOLLENSTEINER, history educator; b. Houston, Feb. 4, 1928; s. John Hubert and Neola Augusta (Hollensteiner) W.; m. Shirley Lois Griffith, Nov. 23, 1950; children: Nancy, Thomas. AA, Mesa Coll., 1948; BA, Cornell Coll., 1950, MA, 1958; PhD, Iowa U., 1963. Tchr. Oskaloosa (Iowa) High Sch., 1950-51, Davenport (Iowa) High Sch., 1951-52, 54-57, Univ. High Sch., Iowa City, Iowa, 1957-63; prof. Oreg State U., Corvallis, 1963—. Author: Civil War Iowa and the Copperhead Movement, 1980; contbr. articles to profl. jours. Mem. NAACP, ACLU. Served to sgt. U.S. Army, 1952-54, Korea. Decorated Bronze Star with "V". Mem. Orgn. Am. Historians, Iowa Hist. Soc. Democrat. Avocations: jazz piano, jogging. Home: 2400 NW 13th Corvallis OR 97330 Office: Oreg State U History Dept Corvallis OR 97331

WULZ, SUSAN VANOST, vocational rehabilitation counselor; b. Los Angeles, Mar. 3, 1954; d. Sanford Lansing and Loretta (Bailey) Van Ost; 1 child, Kevin Daniel Vanost Wulz. BA, U. Calif., Santa Barbara, 1975; MA, U. Kans., 1978, PhD, 1982. Research asst. U. Calif., Santa Barbara, 1972-75, Bur. Child Research, Lawrence, Kans., 1976-78; psychologist I Kans. Neurol. Inst., Topeka, 1978-82; dir. rehab. Goodwill, Santa Ana, Calif., 1982-86; pvt. cons. Irvine, Calif., 1986—; instr. spl. edn. Calif. State U., Fullerton, 1985—; bd. dirs. So. Calif. Rehab. Exchange, 1983—. Author: Directory of Workers' Compensation Professionals, 1984-85, (with others) Rehabilitation: The California System 1978-Present, 1985; contbr. articles to profl. jours. Mem. Calif. Assn. Rehab. Profls. (cert. bd. dirs. 1985), Nat. Assn. Autistic Children, Assn. Severely Handicapped, Nat. Rehab. Assn. Avocations: fictional writing, being with children. Office: 200 N Tustin Santa Ana CA 92705

WUNDER, BRUCE ARNOLD, zoologist, educator; b. Monterey Park, Calif., Feb. 10, 1942; s. Edwin Claude and Phyllis Viviene (Lehman) W.; m. Gayle Virginia Anderson, June 16, 1963; children—Michael Brent, Kristin Kathleen. B.A., Whittier Coll., 1963; Ph.D., UCLA, 1968. Teaching asst. in zoology UCLA, 1963-65, assoc. in zoology, 1965-66, USPHS trainee in cardiovascular zoophysiology, 1966-68; postdoctoral fellow NIH, 1968-69; asst. prof. zoology Colo. State U., Ft. Collins, 1969-76, assoc. prof. zoology and entomology, 1976-84, prof., 1984—, asst. chmn. zoology and entomology, 1978-79, 83-84, interim chmn. zoology, 1984-85, chmn., 1985—; small mammal and physiol. ecologist Ecology Cons., Inc., Biol. Research Assocs., Inc., Fort Collins, Thorne Ecol. Inst., Boulder, U.S. Army C.E., U.S. Fish and Wildlife Service; vis. investigator at biotron U. Wis., Madison, 1971; summer faculty Nat. Wildlife Fedn. Conservation Summit, Estes Park, Colo., 1972-77; summer faculty U. Mich. Biol. Sta., Douglas Lake, 1976, 78; Alexander von Humboldt Research fellow J.W. Goethe U., Frankfort, W.Ger., 1979-80; vis. prof. zoology U. Mont. Biol. Sta., Flathead Lake, 1981, 83, 85. Mem. AAAS, Am. Soc. Zoologists, Am. Soc. Mammalogists, Ecol. Soc. Am., Sigma Xi, Omicron Delta Kappa. Contbr. numerous articles to profl. jours. Home: 505 Canadian Pkwy Fort Collins CO 80524 Office: Dept Zoology Colo State Univ Fort Collins CO 80523

WUNSCH, JAMES PATRICK, JR., investment advisor; b. Wausau, Wis., July 15, 1948; s. James Patrick Sr. and Gertrude (Zona) W.; m. Kelly Wunsch, July 11, 1986; children: Jennifer, Jeffery. BBA, U. Wis., 1971; JD, U. Pacific, 1977. Agt. Bankers Life of Iowa, Sacramento, Calif., 1976-78; mgr. Calif. Western States Life, Chico, 1978-85; pres. Wunsch Ins. and Fin. Services Inc., Chico, 1984—. Named to Pres.'s Top 10, Calif. Western States Life, 1982-83; named Rookie of Yr., Sacramento Life Underwriters, 1976; named to Pres.'s Top Club, Am. Gen., 1986. Mem. Internat. Assn. Fin. Planning, Nat. Assn. Life Underwriters (pres. local chpt. 1982, bd. dirs., 1982), Chico C. of C., Million Dollar Round Table. Republican. Roman Catholic. Avocations: skiing, sailboat racing, photography. Home: 4707 Songbird Chico CA 95926 Office: Wunsch Ins and Fin Services 383 Connors Ct Suite E Chico CA 95926

WÜRSIG, BERND GERHARD, marine biology educator; b. Barsinghausen, Hanover, Federal Republic of Germany, Nov. 9, 1948; s. Gerhard Paul and Charlotte Annemarie (Yorkowski) W.; m. Melany Ann Carballeira, Nov. 19, 1969; children: Kim, Paul. BS, Ohio State U., 1971; PhD, SUNY, Stony Brook, 1978. Postdoctoral researcher U. Calif., Santa Cruz, 1978-81; prof. Moss Landing (Calif.) Marine Labs., 1981—; govt. cons. Minerals Mgmt. Service, Washington, 1980—. Contbr. articles to profl. jours. Recipient Dean's award for Excellence in Teaching, 1986. Mem. Marine Mammal Soc., N.Y. Acad. Scis., Soc. Cryptozoology, Am. Behavior Soc., LAm. Mus. Natural History, Soc. Archimedes. Club: Explorers (N.Y.C.) (fellow of research). Avocations: photography, diving, airplane piloting, skiing, hiking. Home: 2479 Tuckahoe Terr Watsonville CA 95076 Office: Moss Landing Marine Labs Moss Landing CA 95039

WURSTER, CARL FREEMAN, surgeon; b. Twin Falls, Idaho, July 30, 1953; s. Clarence Freeman and Geraldine Meta (Scott) W.; m. Lorie Josephine Nies, May 31, 1981. BS, U. Idaho, 1975; MD, Northwestern U., 1978. Diplomate Am. Bd. Otolaryngology. Intern Northwestern Univ. Med. Ctrs., Chgo., 1978-83; head and neck surgery fellow Northwestern U., Evanston, Ill., 1983-84; asst. prof. Med. U. S.C., Charleston, 1984-85; attending surgeon St. Luke's Regional Med. Ctr., Boise, Idaho, 1985—, St. Alphonsus Regional Med. Ctr., Boise, 1985—; cons. Mountain States Tumor Inst., Boise, 1985—. Contbr. articles to profl. jours. Bd. dirs. Idaho Epilepsy League, Boise, 1985—, Am. Cancer Soc., Ada County, 1985—. Recipient Lederer-Pierce award Chgo. Laryngol. Soc., 1983, 84. Mem. AMA, Am. Acad. Otolaryngology Head and Neck Surgery. Office: St Alphonsus Regional Med Ctr 100 Warm Springs Ave Boise ID 83702

WYAND, MARTIN JUDD, economics educator, retired military officer; b. Greenwich, Conn., May 28, 1931; s. Charles Samuel and Marian (Winter) W.; m. Margaret Alison Knox, May 26, 1974. BA in Social Sci., Pa. State U., 1953, MA in Econs., 1954; JD in Law, U. Denver, 1969; PhD, U. Ill., 1964. Graduate teaching asst. Pa. State U., Univ. Park., 1953-54; grad. teaching asst. U. Ill., Urbana, 1960-64; from asst. prof. to prof. U. Denver, 1964-82; adj. prof. econs. Metro State Coll., Denver, 1982—; instr. Armed Forces Intelligence Tng. Ctr., 1974. Contbr. articles to profl. jours. Adminstrv. bd. dirs. Washington Park Meth. Ch., Denver, 1977-85. Served to col. USAFR, 1953-83. Grantee Shell Oil Co., 1966, U. Denver, 1976. Mem. Am. Econ. Assn., Am. Collegiate Schs. Bus., Rocky Mountain Social Sci. Assn., Reserve Officers Assn. (pres. Geddes chpt. 1978-82), Air Force Assn., Alpha Kappa Psi, Pi Gamma Mu. Avocations: reading, chess, classical music, swimming. Home: 15740 E Greenwood Dr Aurora CO 80013 Office: Metro State Coll Dept Econs Denver CO 80204

WYATT, JOSEPH LUCIAN, JR., lawyer, author, educator; b. Chgo., Feb. 21, 1924; s. Joseph Lucian and Cecile Gertrude (Zadico) W.; m. Marjorie Kathryn Simmons, Apr. 9, 1954; children: Daniel, Linn, Jonathan. AB in English Lit. with honors, Northwestern U., 1947; LLB, Harvard U., 1949. Bar: Calif. 1950, U.S. Dist. Ct. (cen. dist.) Calif. 1950, U.S. Ct. Appeals (9th cir.) 1950, U.S. Tax Ct., U.S. Supreme Ct. 1965. Assoc. firm Brady, Nossaman & Walker, Los Angeles, 1950-58, ptnr., 1958-61; sole practice Los Angeles, 1961-71; sr. mem. firm Cooper, Wyatt, Tepper & Plant, P.C., Los Angeles, 1971-79; of counsel firm Beardsley, Hufstedler & Kemble, Los Angeles, 1979-81; ptnr. firm Hufstedler, Miller, Carlson & Beardsley, Los Angeles, 1981—; mem. faculty Pacific Coast Banking Sch., Seattle, 1963—. Author: Trust Administration and Taxation, 4 vols., 1964—; editor: Trusts and Estates, 1962-74. Lectr., trustee Pacific Oaks Coll. and Children's Sch., 1969—; counsel, parliamentarian Calif. Democratic party and presdl. conv. dels., 1971—; mem. Calif. State Personnel Bd., 1961-71, v.p., 1963-65, pres., 1965-67; bd dirs. Calif. Pub. Employees Retirement System, 1963-71. Served as 1st sgt. USAAF, 1943-45. Fellow Am. Coll. Probate Counsel; mem. ABA, Am. Law Inst., Los Angeles Bar Assn. (trustee 1956), Internat. Acad. Estate and Trust Law, Calif. State Bar Assn. (del. state bar conf. 1956, 62-67). Democrat. Christian Scientist. Avocations: poetry, fishing, skiing. Home: 1119 Armada Dr Pasadena CA 91103 Office: Hufstedler Miller Carlson & Beardsley 700 S Flower St Suite 1600 Los Angeles CA 90017-4286

WYCKOFF, ALEXANDER, stage designer, educator; b. Leonia, N.J., Aug. 17, 1898; s. James Talmage and Wilhelmina (Ludwig) W.; 1 child, Peter Talmage. Student, Columbia Coll., 1916-17, 19, Carnegie Inst. Tech., 1920. Designer, H. Robert Law Studios, N.Y.C., 1920-21, 24-25; instr., designer drama dept. Carnegie Inst. Tech., Pitts., 1921-24; dir. Memphis Little Theatre, 1927-30; art dir. U. Mich., Ann Arbor, 1932-41, 50; supr. design Phila. Mus. Sch., 1933-43; writer, illustrator, stage designer, Leonia, N.J., 1950-69 Tustin, Calif., 1971—; art dir. pageant Rensselaer Poly. Inst., 1924, U.S. Govt., Yorktown, Va., 1931, Joint City/Producers Corp., Alexandria, Va., 1949; art dir. Cin. Art Theatre, 1925-26. Author: (with Edward Warwick and Henry Pitz) Early American Dress, 1964; editor: Arts of Design-Dunlap, 1965; author/illustrator: 19th Century Dress, 1966-81, 1600 World Dress, 1982-83. Pres., bd. dirs. Leonia players Guild, N.J., 1920-53, Leonia Pub. Library, 1962-69, Wyckoff House Found. (hon.); vol. advisor Performing Arts, Tustin High Sch., Calif., 1975—. Served with U.S. Army, 1917-18. Mem. Nat. Theatre Conf. (founding, bd. dirs.). Address: 12937 B Newport Ave Tustin CA 92680

WYCKOFF, SUSAN, astronomy researcher; b. Santa Cruz, Calif., Mar. 18, 1941; d. Stephen and Jean (Taft) W.; m. Peter Augustus Wehinger, July 29, 1967. BA in Astronomy, Mount Holyoke, 1962; student, Swarthmore Coll., 1962-63; PhD in Astronomy, Case Inst. Technology, 1976. Postdoctoral fellow U. Mich., Ann Arbor, 1967-68; asst. prof. Albion (Mich.) Coll., 1968-70; research assoc. U. Kans., Lawrence, 1970-72; sr. lectr. Tel-Aviv U., Israel, 1972-75; prin. research scientist Royal Greenwich Observatory, Sussex, Eng., 1975-78; vis. prof. Ohio State U., Columbus, 1978-79; assoc. prof. Ariz. State U., Tempe, 1979-82, prof., 1982—; adj. prof. Sussex U., 1975-77, U. Heidelberg Theoretical Astrophysics Inst., 1980, U. Ariz., Tucson, 1984—; vis. com. Aura, Inc., Tucson, 1985—. Contbr. articles profl. jours. Mem. Gov.'s Disease Control Commn., Phoenix, 1985—. Fellow Royal Astronomical Soc. (Eng.); mem. NSF (adv. com. 1983—), Nat. Acad. Sci. (space sci. bd. 1984—), Ariz. State U. Faculty Women's Assn. (pres. 1983-84, exec. bd. 1983—), Am. Astron. Soc. (A.J. Cannon award comm. 1982—), Internat. Astron. Union, Sigma Xi. Avocations: jogging, swimming. Home: 2135 E Loma Vista Dr Tempe AZ 85282 Office: Ariz State U Physics/Astronomy Dept Tempe AZ 85287

WYCKOFF, THEODORE, political science educator; b. N.Y.C., Feb. 24, 1922; s. Wallace Hook and Helena (Schmid) W.; m. Ludmilla Dmitrieff, Apr. 22, 1945; children—Ann Wyckoff-Lancero, Barbara Wyckoff-Siris, Cathryn. B.A., UCLA, 1942, M.A., M.P.A., Princeton U., 1957; Ph.D., Bonn, Germany, 1967. Commd. 2d lt. U.S. Army, 1942, advanced through grades to lt. col., 1960; ret., 1968; assoc. prof. polit. sci. No. Ariz. U., Flagstaff, 1968-83, assoc. prof. emeritus, 1983—; lectr. U. Md., 1958-60; prof. mil. sci. Ariz. State U., 1961-64; vis. scholar U. Mich., 1978-79. Active Mus. No. Ariz., Bd. Cert. Holders, Flagstaff Hosp.; mem. Diocesan Council Episcopal Diocese Ariz. Mem. Internat. Polit. Sci. Assn., Am. Polit. Sci. Assn., Internat. Studies Assn., Phi Beta Kappa, Pi Sigma Alpha. Democrat. Episcopalian. Clubs: Wyckoff Assn. Am. (v.p.), Rotary (past pres. Flagstaff). Contbr. articles to publs. in U.S., Ger.; patentee Wyckoff's automatic transmission. Home: 515 E David Dr Flagstaff AZ 86001

WYCOFF, CHARLES COLEMAN, retired physician, anesthesiologist; b. Glazier, Tex., Sept. 2, 1918; s. James Garfield and Ada Sharpe (Braden) W.; m. Gene Marie Henry, May 16, 1942; children: Michelle, Geoffrey, Brian, Roger, Daniel, Norman, Irene, Teresa. AB, U. Calif., Berkeley, 1941; MD, U. Calif., San Francisco, 1943. Diplomate Am. Bd. Anesthesiology. Founder The Wycoff Group of Anesthesiology, San Francisco, 1947-53; chief of anesthesia St. Joseph's Hosp., San Francisco, 1947-52, San Francisco County Hosp., 1953-54; asst. prof. anesthesiology Columbia U., N.Y.C., 1955-63; creator residency tng. program in anesthesiology St. Joseph's Hosp., San Francisco, 1950, San Francisco County Hosp., 1954; practice anesthesiology, tchr. Presbyn. Med. Ctr., N.Y.C., 1955-63; clin. practice anesthesiology St. Francis Meml. Hosp., 1963-84; councilor at large Alumni Faculty Assn. Sch. Medicine U. Calif., San Francisco, 1979-80. Producer, dir. films on regional anesthesia; contbr. articles to sci. jours. Scoutmaster Boy Scouts Am., San Francisco, 1953-55. Served to capt. M.C., U.S. Army, 1945-47. Republican. Avocations: research in religion, hiking, gardening, constrn. of houses. Home: 870 Joost Ave San Francisco CA 94127

WYDEN, RONALD LEE, Congressman; b. Wichita, Kans., May 3, 1949; s. Peter and Edith W.; m. Laurie Oseran, Sept. 5, 1978; 1 child, Adam David. Student, U. Santa Barbara, 1967-69; A.B. with distinction, Stanford U., 1971; J.D., U. Oreg., 1974. Campaign aide Senator Wayne Morse, 1972, 74; co-founder, co-dir. Oreg. Gray Panthers, 1974-80; dir. Oreg. Legal Services for Elderly, 1977-79; instr. gerontology U. Oreg., 1976, U. Portland, 1980, Portland State U., 1979; mem. 97th-100th congresses from 3d Oreg. Dist. Recipient Service to Oreg. Consumers award Oreg. Consumers League, 1978, Citizen of Yr. award Oreg. Assn. Social Workers, 1979, Significant Service award Multnomah County Area Agy. on Aging, 1980; named Young Man of Yr. Oreg. Jr. C. of C., 1980. Mem. Am. Bar Assn., Iowa Bar Assn. Democrat. Jewish. Office: 1406 Longworth House Office Bldg Washington DC 20515 *

WYETH, HENRIETTE, artist; b. Wilmington, Del., Oct. 22, 1907; d. Newell Convers and Caroline (Bockius) W.; m. Peter Hurd, June 28, 1929; children—Peter Wyeth, Ann Carol, Michael. Student Pa. Acad. Fine Arts, 1922-25; pvt. study with N.C. Wyeth. One-man shows: Phila., 1932, Washington, 1934, Wilmington, Del., 1938, N.Y.C., 1942, Brandywine Mus., Chadds Ford, Pa., 1980, Santa Fe, 1982; exhibited in numerous group shows; represented in pvt. and pub. collections; commd. work includes portrait Mrs. Richard Nixon, White House, 1979, Andrew Wyeth, 1986. Address: Sentinel Ranch San Patricio NM 88348

WYLAND, DAVID CARL, electrical engineer; b. Monterey Park, Calif., Feb. 4, 1942; s. John Donald and Marie Ann (Norden) W.; m. Kathleen Ann Baltutat, Aug. 8, 1964; children: Christopher Paul, Chantell Jean, Charmaine Rae. BSEE, UCLA, 1964. Engr. Sci. Data Systems, 1964-65; sr. assoc. engr. IBM Systems Devel., 1965-71; devel. engr. L-S Computing, 1971-72; mem. tech. staff SCM Corp., 1972-73; mgr. Microprocessor Design, Monolithic Memories, 1973-76, Raytheon Semiconductor, 1976-78; pres. Aldebaran Corp., 1978-81; tech. dir. Astrel Ltd., 1981-83; sr. research engr. SRI Internat., 1983-86; mgr. Integrated Devic Tech., 1986—. Contbr. articles to profl. jours.; patentee in field. Home: 4804 Tonino Dr San Jose CA 95136 Office: IDT 3236 Scott Blvd Santa Clara CA 95052-8015

WYLE, EWART HERBERT, clergyman; b. London, Eng., Sept. 12, 1904; s. Edwin and Alice Louise (Durman) W.; B.A., U. Louisville, 1930; B.D., Lexington Theol. Sem., 1933; postgrad. Louisville Presbyn. Theol. Sem., Temple U., 1933-35; D.D., Tex. Christian U., 1953; m. Prudence Harper, June 12, 1959; 1 son, Ewart Herbert. Ordained to ministry Christian Ch., 1935; pastor First Ch., Palestine, Tex., 1935-37, First Ch., Birmingham, Ala., 1937-41, First Ch., Tyler, Tex., 1944-54, Country Club Ch., Kansas City, Mo., 1954-59; minister Torrey Pines Ch., La Jolla, Calif., 1959-79, minister emeritus, 1979—. Bd. dirs. Scripps Meml. Hosp., pres., 1980-81. Served as chaplain, maj., AUS, 1941-44. Mem. Mil. Order World Wars, Am. Legion, Tau Kappa Epsilon, Pi Kappa Delta. Clubs: Masons (32 deg.), Shriners, Rotary, LaJolla Beach and Tennis. Home: 8850 LaJolla Scenic Dr N La Jolla CA 92037

WYLLIE, F(RANCES) ROSEMARY (ROMY), interior designer, educator; b. Hull, England, Nov. 6, 1932; came to U.S., 1961; d. Robert Bertram and Frances Mary (Woodhouse) Blair; m. Peter John Wyllie, June 9, 1956; children; Andrew James, Elizabeth Jean (dec.), Lisa Margaret, John David. MA, U. St. Andrews, Scotland, 1955; diploma in design, Harrington Inst. Interior Design, Chgo., 1974. Sec. Pa. State U., State College, 1956-59; mng. editor Jour. Geology U. Chgo. Press, 1967-72; designer Space Design Group, Chgo., 1974-77; pres. Intekton, Inc., Pasadena, Calif., 1977—; substitute instr. Harrington Inst. Interior Design, Chgo., 1974-77, instr., 1977-83. Mem. Caltech. Archtl. Tour Service (founding dir., bd. dirs. 1985—). Club: Caltech Women's (pres. 1985-86). Avocations: tennis, hiking, art, photography, travel. Home: 2150 Kinclair Dr Pasadena CA 91107 Office: Intekton Inc 2150 Kinclair Dr Pasadena CA 91107

WYMAN, CHARLES ELY, biotechnologist, research director, chemical engineer; b. Greenfield, Mass., Oct. 23, 1944; s. Ely Warren and Ruth Harriott (Aschenbach) W.; m. Carol Joy Wroblewski, Feb. 17, 1968; children: Marc Ely, Kristin Lee. BS Chem. Engring. summa cum laude, U. Mass., 1967; MA Chem. Engring., Princeton U., 1969, PhD in Chem. Engring., 1971. Sr. chem. engr. Monsanto Co., Springfield, Mass., 1971-74; asst. prof. U. N.H., Durham, 1974-78; sr. engr., group mgr. Solar Energy Research Inst., Golden, Colo., 1978-81, dep. div. mgr., 1981, biotech. br. mgr., 1984—; mgr. process devel. Badger Co., Inc., Cambridge, Mass., 1981-84; adj. prof. Colo. Sch. Mines, Golden, 1986—; thesis com. U. Mass., Amherst, 1973-74; spl. mem. grad. faculty U. Colo., Boulder, 1987, mem. adv. bd. dept. biology U. Colo., Denver, 1987; vis. fellow Colo. State U., Ft. Collins, 1986-87; mobilization analyst U.S. Army, Charlottesville, Va., 1974-78. Coach Cohasset (Mass.) Boys Soccer team, 1982-83, Lakewood (Colo.) Advanced Soccer team, 1986—. Served to capt. U.S. Army, 1970-78. Mem. Am. Inst. Chem. Engrs., Am. Sect. Internat. Solar Energy Soc., ACS div. Microbial and Biochem. Tech., Sigma Xi, Phi Kappa Phi, Tau Beta Pi. Congregationalist. Avocations: sports, stained glass, carpentry. Office: Solar Energy Research Inst 1617 Cole Blvd Golden CO 80401

WYMAN, RICHARD VAUGHN, engineering educator, exploration company executive; b. Painesville, Ohio, Feb. 22, 1927; s. Vaughn Ely and Melinda (Ward) W.; m. Anne Fenton, Dec. 27, 1947; 1 son, William Fenton. B.S., Case Western Res. U., 1948; M.S., U. Mich., 1949; Ph.D., U. Ariz., 1974. Diplomate: registered profl. engr., Nev.; lic. water right surveyor, Nev.; registered geologist, Ariz., Calif. Geologist N.J. Zinc Co., 1949, 52-53, Cerro de Pasco Corp., 1950-52; chief geologist Western Gold & Uranium, Inc., St. George, Utah, 1953-55, gen. supt., 1955-57, v.p., 1957-59; pres. Intermountain Exploration Co., Boulder City, Nev., 1959—; tunnel supt. Reynolds Electric & Engring. Co., 1961-63, mining engr., 1965-67; asst. mgr. ops. Reynolds Electric and & Engring. Co., 1967-69; constrn. supt. engr. Sunshine Mining Co., 1963-65; lectr. U. Nev.-Las Vegas, 1969-73, assoc. prof., 1973-76, dept. chmn., 1976-80, prof., 1980—, chmn. dept. civil and mech. engring., 1984—; mineral rep. Ariz. Strip Adv. Bd., 1976-80; chmn. Pacific S.W. Minerals Conf., 1972; peer rev. com. Nuclear Waste Site, Dept. of Energy, Las Vegas, 1978-82; pres. Ariz. Juno Resources, Boulder City, 1980-83; cons. Corp. Andina de Fomento, Caracas, Venezuela, 1977-78; v.p. Comstock Gold, Inc., 1984—. Contbr. articles to profl. jours. Sec. Washington County Republican Party, Utah, 1958-60; del. Utah Rep. Conv., 1958-60; scoutmaster Boy Scouts Am., 1959-69. Served with USN, 1944-46. Mem. AIME (chmn. So. Nev. sect. 1971-72, dir. 1968—, sec.-treas. 1974—, gen. chmn. nat. conv. 1980), Assn. Engring. Geologists, Soc. Econ. Geologists (life), ASCE, Nev. Mining Assn. (assoc.), Ariz. Small Mine Operators Assn., Arctic Inst. N.Am. (life), Internat. Glaciol. Soc., Geol. Soc. Am., Sigma Xi (pres. Las Vegas sect. 1986—), Phi Kappa Phi (pres. UNLV chpt. 100, 1982-83), Sigma Gamma Epsilon. Congregationalist. Home: 610 Bryant Ct Boulder City NV 89005 Office: Dept Civil and Mech Engring U Nevada 4505 Maryland Pkwy Las Vegas NV 89154

WYMORE, A(LBERT) WAYNE, systems engineering educator; b. New Sharon, Iowa, Feb. 1, 1927; s. Darcy Bryan and Vera (Leatherman) W.; m. Muriel Lorraine Farrell, Mar. 19, 1949; children: Farrell Wade, Darcy Lorraine, Melanie Louise, Leslie Maureen. B.S., Iowa State U., 1949, M.S., 1950; Ph.D., U. Wis., 1955. Math. cons. Pure Oil Co., Chgo., 1955-57; dir. computer center U. Ariz., Tucson, 1957-67; head dept. systems and indsl. engring. U. Ariz., 1959-74, prof. systems and indsl. engring., 1959—; cons. 32 firms, 1954—. Author: A Mathematical Theory of Systems Engineering: The Elements, 1967, Systems Engineering Methodology for Interdisciplinary Teams, 1975; founding editor: Jour. Systems Engring., 1969. Served with USAAF, 1944-47. Mem. Am. Math. Soc., Am. Inst. Indsl. Engring., Sigma Xi, Phi Kappa Phi, Pi Mu Epsilon, Tau Beta Pi. Home: 4301 N Camino Kino Tucson AZ 85718

WYNHOLDS, PAUL FERDINAND, entomologist; b. Hackensack, N.J.; s. Wynhold Heiko and Nannie Sybilla (Zaalberg van Zelst) W.; m. Stephenie Jeanne Gaustad, June 21, 1969 (div. Oct. 1983); children: Jan Christopher, Laura Anne. BS with honors, U. Calif., Irvine, 1971; MS, U. Calif., Davis, 1974. Staff research assoc. II dept. entomology U. Calif., Davis, 1974—. Contbr. articles to profl. jours. Mem. AAAS, San Joaquin Entomology Assn. (sec.-treas. 1977-84), Entomol. Soc. Am., Western Apicultural Soc., Sigma Xi. Home: 211 Oleander Ave Bakersfield CA 93304 Office: U Calif 17053 N Shafter Ave Shafter CA 93263

WYNN, STEPHEN A., hotel, entertainment facility executive; b. 1941; married. Pres., chief exec. officer Best Brands, Inc., 1969-72; pres., chmn. bd. dirs. Golden Nugget, Inc., 1973—, now also chief exec. officer, bd. dirs. Office: Golden Nugget Inc 129 E Fremont St Las Vegas NV 89101 *

WYROBEK, ANDREW JULIUS, biomedical scientist; b. Hannover, Fed. Republic Germany, Sept. 13, 1948; came to U.S., 1957; BS, U. Notre Dame, 1970; PhD in Med. Biophysics, U. Toronto, Can., 1975. Biomed. scientist and sr. staff biophysicist Lawrence Livermore (Calif.) Nat. Lab., 1975—. Contbr. articles to profl. jours. Grantee EPA, 1975-83, U.S. Dept. Energy, 1983—, NIH, 1984, Nat. Inst. Environ. Health Scis., 1982—. Mem. Environ. Mutagen Soc., Human Genetics. Office: Lawrence Livermore Nat Labs Biomed Scis Div PO Box 5507 Livermore CA 94550

WYSZYNSKI, VALENTINE ANTHONY, sound design engineer, producer, consultant; b. Chgo., Dec. 24, 1941; s. Anthony Marion and Genevieve Ann (Stabosz) W.; m. Joy Anne Halverson, Oct. 5, 1966 (div. July 1976); children: April Suzanne, Brian Matthew, Charlotte Lillian. Student U.S. Air Force Inst., 1965-68, Nat. Tech Schs., 1968-70; BSEE, N.Mex. State U., 1980, BS in Music Engring. and Drama Tech., 1981. With U.S. Post Office, Lyons, Ill., 1959-64, Circle News, Joliet, Ill., 1971-73; mgr. So. N.Mex. region Combined Ins. Co. of Am., Chgo., 1973-76; sound design engr. drama dept. N.Mex. State U., University Park, 1977-81; ptnr., gen. mgr. Desert Distbg., Las Cruces, N.Mex., 1978-84; editor, photographer Coomes Advt./Entertainment Guide, Las Cruces, 1981-84; gen. mgr. Heartline Prodns., Wood Dale, Ill., 1984—; sound design engr. Candlelight Dinner Playhouse, Summit, Ill., 1985; sales engring. cons. Kayak Mfg. Corp., Westmont, Ill., 1985-86; mgr., lead guitarist The Majextics, 1959-64, The 1st Nat. Bank, 1968-73. Composer original music for original prodn. Equus, 1977, Children of a Lesser God, 1979 (Tony award 1980). Served to staff sgt.USAF, 1964-70. Mem. Soc. Broadcast Engrs., Soc. Electronic Musicians, U.S. Inst. Theatre Tech., Satellite Antenna Specialists Am., Jaycees (life Romeoville, Ill. chpt., editor Monitor mag. 1969-71, Spoke of Yr. award 1970, Editor of Yr. award 1971). Democrat. Roman Catholic. Avocations: music, photography, creative writing, crafts design.

X, LAURA, professional association adminstrator, consultant; b. St. Louis, Nov. 2, 1940; d. William Robert and Laura Hale (Rand) Orthwein. Student, Vassar Coll., 1958-61; BA, U. Calif., Berkeley, 1971. Day care tchr. City System, N.Y.C., 1960-62; pres., dir. Women's History Research Ctr. and Nat. Clearinghouse on Marital and Date Rape, Berkeley, 1968—. Editor: Women's Songbook, 1971, Film by and/or About Women, 1972, Female Artists, Past & Present, 1974, supplement, 1975; It Ain't Me Babe newspaper, 1970, Spazm newsletter, 1969; International Women's Directory, 1969; numerous microfilms, bibliographies. Active Berkeley Citizens' Action Com. Recipient Women of Achievement award Mademoiselle, 1974, Innovative Programs and Services award 1st World Congress on Victimology, Honorarium Soroptimists, 1974; Diana award nominee, 1974. Mem. ACLU, Nat. Action Against Rape, Coalition for Med. Rights for Women, Am. Library Assn., Am. Hist. Assn., Coordinating Com. on Women in Hist. Profession, Am. Anthrop. Assn., Assn. For Women in Psychology, Sociologists for Women in Soc., Assn. Feminist Cons. Presbyterian. Address: Womens History Research Ctr Nat Clearinghouse Marital Rape 2325 Oak St Berkeley CA 94708

XAVIER, NORINE BETTE, dance theatre director; b. Oakland, Calif., July 23, 1953; d. Thomas Mathew Xavier and Tillie Dolores (Souza) Grappo. BA, U. Calif., Berkeley, 1973. Artistic dir. West Coast Dance Theatre & Gymnastics Sch., Alameda, Calif., 1973—; also working as profl. actress and dancer; chmn. bd. West Coast Performers and Gymnastic Team Corp., Alameda, 1982—; dir. and sponsor childrens' dance, gymnastics programs in Calif. schs. with emphasis on low-income students. Mem. Delta Gamma. Democrat. Roman Catholic. Avocations: snow skiing, water skiing, tennis, softball, football. Home: 23530 Summit Dr Calabasas CA 91302

XIDIAS, ANGELOS GEORGE, aeronautical engineer; b. Chios, Greece, Oct. 3, 1952; came to U.S., 1975, naturalized, 1985; s. George A. and Stamatia K. (Chaviaros) X.; m. Mary A. Psillos, Dec. 5, 1962; children—Tina, George. B.S. in Math. and Physics, U. Patras, Greece, 1975; M.S. in Aero. Engring., U. Wash., 1979. Teaching asst. U. Wash., 1977-78; sr. aero. engr. Boeing Comml. Airplane Co., Seattle, 1980—. Contbr. articles to profl. jours. Recipient Pride of Excellence award Boeing Co., 1983. Mem. Am. Inst. Aero. and Astronautics (chmn. honors and awards com. Northwest sect.). Home: 11414 81st St NE Kirkland WA 98034 Office: Boeing Co MS 6W-29 PO Box 3707 Seattle WA 98124

YABLON, HARVEY STEVEN, real estate developer; b. Bklyn., July 24, 1947; s. Irving and Sadie (Shinofsky) Y.; m. Roberta Seifert (div. 1971); m. Jana Yablon, 1974; children: Benjamin, Liberty. BA in history, U. Wis., 1969. Pres. Santa Fe Mgmt. Co., 1971-80, Yablon and Schriber, Inc., Santa Fe, 1980-83, Yablon Real Estate Corp., Santa Fe, 1983—. V.p. bd. trustees Rio Grande Sch., Santa Fe, 1982-83. Mem. Santa Fe Bd. Realtors. Avocations: skiing, sailing. Home: PO Box 1794 Santa Fe NM 87501

YABUTANI, KOICHI MOLE, aerospace exec.; b. Brawley, Calif., Jan. 21, 1931; s. Shunzo K. and Toyoko (Kondo) Y.; B.S., U. Utah, 1958; M.Engring., U. Calif. at Los Angeles, 1975; m. Pauline T. Tanabe, Oct. 8, 1960. Equipment engr. RCA, Riverton, N.J., 1959-62; engr. Northrop Corp., Hawthorne, Calif., 1962-63; mem. tech. staff Hughes Aircraft Co., Culver City, 1958-59, group head, 1965-67, staff engr., 1967-68, sr. system engr., 1968-70, section head, 1970-72, asst. dept. mgr., 1972-79, asso. lab. mgr., 1979-82, lab. mgr., 1982—. Served with USAF, 1950-54. Mem. IEEE, Eta Kappa Nu, Tau Beta Pi, Phi Kappa Phi. Home: 4665 Guava St Seal Beach CA 90740 Office: MX 1088 Bldg R7 Hughes Aircraft Co PO Box 92426 Los Angeles CA 90009

YACENDA, JAMES EDMUND, banker; b. Los Angeles, Aug. 6, 1949; s. Dominick Anthony and Flavia Julia (Maechler) Y.; m. Rebecca Louise Cooper, Aug. 14, 1976; children—Carla Marie, Julia Lauren. B.A., St. John Coll., 1971. Street worker Gary Ctr., LaHabra, Calif., 1972-73, asst. dir., 1973-76, exec. dir., 1976-77; exec. dir. Neighborhood Housing Services, 1977-79; adminstr. community investment Fed. Home Loan Bank of San Francisco, 1979-81, community investment officer, 1981—. Contbr. articles to profl. jours. Bd. dirs. Glendale Fed. Community Found., Calif., 1982—, Bay Area Council on Housing Task Force, San Francisco, 1982—, Chinese Community Housing Corp., 1984—, Pacific Inst. for Community Orgns., Oakland, Calif., 1979—, Low-Income Housing Fund, San Francisco, 1984—; mem. The Traveling Squad, Los Angeles, 1971—. Democrat. Roman Catholic. Office: Fed Home Loan Bank of San Francisco 600 California St San Francisco CA 94120

YACOUBI, M. ABDUH, agronomist; b. Oujda, Morocco, Feb. 26, 1945; s. Adelkader and Aicha (Yacoubi) Y.; m. Annette Gibson, Nov. 11, 1982. B.S. in Soil and Irrigation Engring., Am. U. Beirut, 1970; M.S. in Agronomy, U. Ariz., 1973, Ph.D., 1974. Asst. wheat project mgr. Govt. Morocco, 1970-75; assoc. prof. Agronomic Inst., Rabat, Morocco, 1975-82; agronomist research advisor U. Ariz., 1981-82; tng. officer Icarda, Aleppo, Syria, 1982-83; pres. Sedima Cons. Co. Internat., Tucson, 1983—; agronomist African DEvel. Bank, Ivory Coast, 1987—. U.S. AID grantee, 1965-70, 72-73. Mem. Am. Soc. Agronomy, Soil Sci. Soc. Am., Internat. Soil Sci. Soc., Moroccan Soc. Soil Sci. (founding; pres.), Sigma Kappa Gamma, Assn. Moroccan Alumni, Orgn. African Students. Moslem. Club: Internat. (Tucson). Contbr. articles to profl. publs. Office: Box 3397 Tucson AZ 85722

YADON, VERNAL LEE, museum director, artist; b. Exeter, Calif., Feb. 18, 1930; s. Jacob Nelson and Hazel Winifred (Miller) Y. B.S., Oreg. State U., 1952, M.S., 1954. Dir. Pacific Grove (Calif.) Mus. Natural History, 1957—. Active Calif. Native Plant Soc., Audubon Soc.; former chmn. Ventura Chpt. Sierra Club. Served with U.S. Army, 1954-56. Mem. Am. Assn. Mus. (sr. counselor accreditation commn.; former pres. Western Regional Conf.), AAAS.

YAGER, EDWIN GEORGE HARLAND, mgmt. edn. cons.; b. Detroit, July 13, 1938; s. William Edwin and Myrtle Veronica (Harland) Y.; student U. Detroit, 1956-57, Brigham Young U., 1958-60; M.B.A., Mich. State U., 1966; m. Judith Mae Hartmann, June 14, 1960; children—Juline Lambert, Lori, Jon, Suzanne, Carol, Karen. With J. L. Hudson Co., Detroit, 1960-68; corp. staff Ford Motor Co., Dearborn, Mich., 1968-73, dir. mgmt. devel., 1971-73; pres. Consulting Assocs., Inc., Novi, Mich., 1973-81; pres. Yager Assocs., 1981—; lectr. Brigham Young U., U. Pitts., U. Colo., U. Mich., Eastern Mich. U., Wayne State U. Cons. to urban groups through Profl. Skills Alliance, Detroit, 1967-73; active numerous civic coms., election campaigns, others. Mem. Am. Soc. Tng. Devel., Coll. Placement Council, Internat. Assn. Quality Circles, Orgn. Devel. Network. Mormon (former bishop). Club: Mich. Mormon Concert Choir (condr. 1975-80). Author: Making The Training Process Work, 1979; Organization Development for Managers, 1981; Is There Life After Assessment; contbr. articles on human resource devel. to profl. publs. Office: 6560 Landmark #250 Park City UT 84060

YAGIELA, JOHN ALLEN, dental educator; b. Washington, July 23, 1947; s. Stanley and Kathryn Marie (Gilkeson) Y.; m. Dolores Jean Mitchell, Mar. 21, 1970; children: Gregory, Leanne. Student, U. Calif., Riverside, 1965-67; DDS, UCLA, 1971, postgrad., 1982-83; PhD in Pharmacology, U. Utah, 1975. Asst. prof. dentistry Emory U., Atlanta, 1975-78, assoc. prof., 1978-82; assoc. prof. UCLA, 1982-83, prof., 1983—, assoc. dean acad. affairs, 1984—; cons. Astra Pharm. Products, Inc., Worcester, Mass., 1982—, VA Wadsworth div. Los Angeles, 1983—. Co-author: Regional Anesthesia of the Oral Cavity, 1981; co-editor Pharmacology and Therapeutics for Dentistry, 2d edit., 1985; contbr. articles on dental therapeutics to profl. jours. Recipient Award of Achievement Am. Coll. Dentists, 1971; Regents scholar UCLA, 1968-71; Alpha Omega award, 1971. Fellow Am. Dental Soc. Anesthesiology; mem. Internat. Assn. Dental Research (sec.-treas. PTTG group 1984—), Am. Assn. Dental Schs. (chmn. pharmacology therapeutics sect. 1983), Am. Dental Assn., AAAS, Omicron Kappa Upsilon. Methodist. Avocations: photography, hiking. Home: 7956 Glade Ave Canoga Park CA 91304 Office: UCLA Sch Dentistry Ctr for Health Scis Los Angeles CA 90024

YALOF, STANLEY ARTHUR, chemical company executive; b. Bklyn., Aug. 6, 1930; s. Henry Isadore Yalof and Hilda Berniece (Katz) Cobert; m. Gloria Anna Boeck, July 1, 1956. BS, Bklyn. Coll., 1952; MS, U. Iowa, 1955. Mgr. physics dept. Narmco, San Diego, 1963-68; design specialist Micronetics, San Diego, 1968-69; pres. Tetrahedron Assocs., San Diego, 1969-85, K-4 Kaleidoscope, Inc., Carlsbad, Calif., 1986—. Contbr. articles to profl. jours.; patentee in field. Served as sgt. USAF, 1946-49. Mem. Am. Chem. Soc., Soc. Advancement of Materials and Process Engring. Avocations: nature, photography, playwriting. Home: Rte 1 Box 720 Escondido CA 92025 Office: K-4 Kaleidoscope Inc 2080 Las Palmas Dr Carlsbad CA 92008

YAMADA, RICHARD HARUICHI, engineer; b. Honolulu, Mar. 1, 1941; s. Robert Haruo and Ruby Chieko (Kadoi) Y.; m. Renu Wongduongsai, Jan. 4, 1972; children: Cheryll Ann, Robert Harold. Student, Pierce Coll., 1984-87. From technician to sr. technician Contel Page, Vienna, Va., 1963-69, field service and test engr., 1969-76, quality assurance engr., 1976-81, mgr. quality assurance and logistics, 1981-84; engring. specialist Litton Data Command Systems, Agoura Hills, Calif., 1984—. Served with U.S. Army, 1959-62. Mem. IEEE, Nat. Assn. Radio & Telecommunications Engrs., Armed Forces Communication and Elec. Assn., Am. Mgmt. Assn., U.S. Golf Assn. Avocations: personal computers, stamp collecting, golf, fishing, bowling. Home: 1620 Casarin Ave Simi Valley CA 93065 Office: Litton Data Command System 29851 Agoura Rd Agoura Hills CA 91301

YAMADA, TETSUJI, meteorologist; b. Osaka, Japan, May 9, 1942; s. Kozo and Kamiko (Juen) Y.; m. Sueko Fukumoto, Nov. 1, 1967; children: Sayuri, Tetsuhiro. BE, Osaka U., 1965, ME, 1967; PhD, Colo. State U., 1971. Mem. research staff Princeton (N.J.) U., 1972-76; meteorologist Argonne (Ill.) Nat. Lab., 1976-81; mem. staff Los Alamos (N.Mex.) Nat. Lab., 1981—. Contbr. numerous articles on atmospheric turbulence, transport and diffusion of air pollutants in complex terrain. Mem. Am. Meteorol. Soc., Royal Meteorol. Soc., Japanese Meteorol. Soc. (award 1984), Sigma Xi. Home: 147 Monte Rey Dr S Los Alamos NM 87544 Office: Los Alamos Nat Lab PO Box 1663 MS F665 Los Alamos NM 87545

YAMAGUCHI, KAZUO, sociology educator; b. Tokyo, Aug. 6, 1946; came to U.S., 1978; s. Kazuo Kozaki and Machie Yamaguchi; m. Tokue Tamura, Sept. 19, 1978; children: Yuki, Kohki. BS in Math., U. Tokyo, 1971; MA in Sociology, U. Chgo., 1979, PhD in Sociology, 1981. From research officer to sr. research officer Bur. Stats. Japanese Govt., Tokyo, 1971-74, 76-78; research assoc. dept. psychiatry Columbia U., N.Y.C., 1982-83, asst. prof. sch. pub. health, 1983-85; asst. prof. dept. sociology UCLA, 1985—; cons. in field, 1985—. Cons. editor Am. Jour. Sociology, Chgo., 1986—; contbr. articles to profl. jours. Recipient Susan Colver Rosenberger prize U. Chgo., 1984; Spencer Found. grantee, 1985. Mem. Am. Sociol. Assn., Internat. Sociol. Assn., Population Assn. Am., Japan Sociol. Soc. Office: UCLA Dept Sociology Los Angeles CA 90024

YAMAGUCHI, YUKIO, chemical research scientist; b. Hiroshima, Japan, Feb. 22, 1941; came to U.S., 1970; s. Tameo and Miyuki (Kodama) Y. BE, Kyushu U., Fukuoka, Japan, 1964, ME, 1966; PhD, U. Tex., Austin, 1978. Research assoc. Kyushu U., Fukuoka, 1966-70; postdoctoral fellow U. Tex., Austin, 1979-80; postdoctoral fellow U. Calif. and Lawrence Berkeley Lab., Berkeley, 1980-82, chemistry research scientist, 1982—. contbr. articles to profl. jours. Mem. Am. Chem. Soc., Chem. Soc. of Japan. Avocations: reading. Office: U Calif Chemistry Dept Berkeley CA 94720

YAMAKAWA, DAVID KIYOSHI, JR., lawyer; b. San Francisco, Jan. 25, 1936; s. David Kiyoshi and Shizu (Negishi) Y. B.S., U. Calif.-Berkeley, 1958, J.D., 1963. Bar: Calif. 1964, U.S. Supreme Ct. 1970. Prin. Law Offices of David K. Yamakawa Jr., San Francisco, 1964—. Dep. dir. Community Action Agy., San Francisco, 1968-69; dir. City Demonstration Agy., San Francisco, 1969-70; mem. adv. council Calif. Senate Subcom. on the Disabled, 1982-83; chmn. community residential treatment system adv. com. Calif. Dept. Mental Health, 1980-85; bd. dirs. Family Survival Project, 1981—; mem. San Francisco Human Rights Commn., 1975—; sr. v.p. Japanese Cultural and Community Ctr. of No. Calif., 1981-86; pres. Legal Assistance to the Elderly, 1981-83, Council of Internat. Programs, San Francisco, 1987—; 2d v.p. Nat. Conf. Social Welfare, 1983—; sec. Rescue Now, 1979—; v.p. Region IX, Nat. Mental Health Assn., 1981-83; bd. dirs. Mt. Zion Hosp. and Med. Ctr., 1983—; bd. dirs. United Neighborhood Ctrs. of Am., 1977-83; chmn. bd. trustees United Way Bay area, 1983-85; bd. dirs. Children's Home Soc. Calif., 1985—; v.p. Friends of Legal Assistance to the Elderly, 1984—; vice chmn. Friends of the San Francisco Human Rights Commn., 1985—; bd. dirs. Ind. Sector, 1986—, Keep Libraries Alive, 1986—, La Madre de los Pobres, 1982—, Nat. Concilio of Am., 1987—; pres. Council Internat. Programs, San Francisco, 1987—. Recipient John S. Williams Outstanding Planning and Agy. Relations vol. award United Way of the Bay Area, 1980, Mortimer Fleishhacker Jr. Outstanding Vol. award, United Way, 1985; Spl. Recognition award Legal Assistance to the Elderly, 1983, commendation Bd. Suprs. City and County of San Francisco, 1983, cert. Honor, Bd. Suprs. City and County San Fracnsico, 1985; San Francisco Found. award, 1985; October 10, 1985 proclaimed as David Yamakawa Day in San Francisco, 1985. Mem. ABA (Liberty Bell award 1986). Office: 582 Market St Suite 410 San Francisco CA 94104

YAMAMOTO, GAYLE YOOKO, speech pathologist; b. Honokaa, Hawaii, Sept. 30, 1956; s. Takashi and Chizuko (Fujimoto) Honma; m. Benny Wataru Yamamoto, June 8, 1985. BS, U. Hawaii at Manoa, 1978, MS, 1980. Speech pathologist Dept. Edn., Leeward Oahu Dist., Waipahu, Hawaii, 1981-85, Dept. Edn., Maui Dist., Wailuku, Hawaii, 1985—. Mem. Am. Speech-Lang.-Hearing Assn., Hawaii Speech-Lang.-Hearing Assn. Democrat. Buddhist.

YAMAMOTO, JOHN HIROSHI, engineering executive; b. Tokyo, June 10, 1940; came to U.S., 1954; s. Thomas Hiraaki and Jeanne-Marie (Kitazawa) Y.; children—Jeanne-Marie, Tamiko, Julianne, Kimiko. B.C.E., Manhattan Coll., 1963. Registered profl. engr., Mass.; diplomate Am. Acad. Environ. Engrs. Project mgr. TAMS, N.Y.C., 1963-66; chief engr. E.P. Snow Co., Boston, 1966-69; asst. v.p. CE Maguire, Inc., Providence, 1969-74; v.p., dir. Orogonics, Inc., Slatersville, R.I., 1975-80; v.p. CE Maguire, Inc., Honolulu, 1981-85; pres. PEMCO; Ltd., Honolulu, 1985—, also dir.; dir. YMA Internat., Inc. Editor Environ. Mgmt. Jour., Springer-Verlag, 1977-79. Contbr. articles to profl. jours. Recipient Cert. of Appreciation, Naval Facilities Engring. Command, Honolulu, 1982, Rotary, 1970, Lions, 1972. Mem. Nat. Soc. Profl. Engrs. (treas. 1981-82), ASME, Soc. Am. Mil. Engrs., Water Pollution Control Fedn., others. Democrat. Roman Catholic. Home: 877 Hahaione St Honolulu HI 96825 Office: PEMCO Ltd 1600 Kapiolani Blvd Suite 622 Honolulu HI 96814

YAMANE, STANLEY JOEL, optometrist, contact lens consultant; b. Lihue, Kauai, Hawaii, Mar. 13, 1943; s. Tooru and Yukiko (Miura) Y.; m. Joyce Mitsuko Tamura; children—Stanley Tooru Aiichi, Karen Margaret. B.S. in Optometry, Pacific U., 1966, O.D., 1966. Diplomate Am. Acad. Optometry. Practice optometry Waipahu, Hawaii, 1967-73; ptnr. with Dr. Dennis M. Kuwabara 1973-81; ptnr. Drs. Kuwabara & Yamane,

Optometrists, Inc., Waipahu, 1981—; lectr., cons. in field; sec.-treas. Hawaii Bd. Examiners in Optometry, 1975-76, v.p., 1976-78, pres., 1978-80; mem. adj. faculty Coll. Optometry, Pacific U., 1977—, Pa. Coll. Optometry, 1981—, So. Coll. Optometry, 1982—. Contbr. articles to profl. jours. Bd. mgrs. Leeward Oahu Br. YMCA, 1967-70, Hi-Y advisor, 1967—, mem. Century Club, 1967—, bd. mgrs. West Oahu Br., 1971-78, gen. chmn. sustaining membership, 1976; 2d v.p. August Ahrens Elem. Sch. PTA, 1969; mem. Leeward Mental Health Adv. Council, 1975-76, Friends of Waipahu Cultural Garden Park Found., 1976—, Aloha council Boy Scouts Am., 1976—; mem. bus. adv. council Waipahu High Sch., 1976-81, Parent-Tchr.-Community Adv. Council, 1978-80; bd. dirs. Central/Leeward unit Am. Cancer Soc., 1977-80, pub. edn. dir., 1978-79, v.p., 1979-80, founder, chmn. Celebrity Auction, 1980, dir. Oahu Baseline Survey, 1978; bd. dirs. Barbers Point council Navy League Am., 1981—. Recipient Merit award Nat. Eye Research Found., 1974, Disting. Service award, 1976. Fellow Am. Acad. Optometry (cornea and contact lens cert., corp. support for Jour. com. 1981—), AAAS, Am. Optometric Assn. (ann. congress del. 1978, pub. health com. 1978, optometric paraoptometric personnel com. 1978-79, contact lens project team 1979-80, task force on research and devel. 1984—), Leeward Oahu Jaycees (Disting. Service award 1969, Top Outstanding Young Man award 1975), Hawaii State Jaycees, Am. Optometric Found. (bd. dirs. 1981—, chmn. task force clin. research 1981—, nominations com. 1982, treas. 1985-86), Am. Pub. Health Assn., Better Vision Inst., Coll. Optometrists in Vision Devel., Hawaii Optometric Assn. (corr. sec. 1968-70, state newsletter editor 1968-70, rec. sec. 1971, 2d v.p. 1972, pres. 1974-75; Man of Yr. 1975, Optometrist of Yr. 1979), Hawaii Vision Assn. Professions, Nat. Eye Research Found. (fellow Internat. Orthokeratology sect.; editorial bd. Contacto Jour. 1979, contact lens cert. com. 1981—), Nat. Fedn. Ind. Bus., Optometric Cons. in Contact Lens Optometric Extension Program Found. (chmn. study group 1969-70, state dir. 1971-73), Optometric Hist. Soc., Optometric Polit. Action Coms., Soc. Contact Lens Specialists, Hawaii Assn. Children with Learning Disabilities, Hawaii Assn. Intellectually Gifted Children (pub. relations chmn. 1st Ann. State Conf. 1975, legis. lobbyist 1975-76), Waipahu Bus. Assn. (bd. dirs. 1974-78, chmn. pub. relations 1974-75, legis. lobbyist 1974-75, pres. 1974-75), Nat. Acad. Practice in Optometry (mem.-at-large on exec. com., disting. practitioner in optometry). Democrat. Baptist. Home: 98-336 Kaonohi St Apt 3 Aiea HI 96701 Office: 94-748 Hikimoe St Suite C Waipahu HI 96797

YAMAOKA, GARY KIYOSHI, government accounting executive; b. Honolulu, Mar. 23, 1947; s. Fred Yoshito and Edna Fumiko (Yamamoto) Y.; m. Aimee Nobuko Yamashita, July 16, 1972; 1 child, Neil Takio. B.B.A., U. Hawaii, 1969. C.P.A., Hawaii. Auditor, Harris, Kerr, Forster, Honolulu, 1969-71; systems acct. State of Hawaii, Honolulu, 1972-78, fiscal officer, 1978-79, acctg. supr., 1979-81, acctg. system mgr., 1981-86, bus. mgmt. officer, 1986—; owner, cons. Gary K. Yamaoka, C.P.A., Honolulu, 1973—, Gary K. Yamaoka, Real Estate Sales, Honolulu, 1980—; bd. dirs. Hawaii State Employees Fed. Credit Union, 1984—, vice chmn., 1985—. Mem. Assn. Govtl. Accts., Am. Inst. C.P.A.s, Beta Gamma Sigma. Home: 3320 Niolopua Dr Honolulu HI 96817 Office: Hawaii Acctg and Gen Services Dept PO Box 119 Honolulu HI 96810

YAMAOKA, SEIGEN H., church official. Bishop Buddhist Ch. Am., San Francisco. Office: Hdqrs Buddhist Ch Am 1710 Octavia St San Francisco CA 94109 *

YAMASAKI, MAMORU, state senator; b. Paia, Hawaii, Sept. 6, 1916. Marine terminal clk. Kahului R.R. Co.; asst. clk. Senate Ways and Mean Com., Territorial Legislature, 1959; mem. Hawaii Ho. of Reps., 1959-67, Hawaii Senate, 1968—. Past mem. adv. bd. Maui County council Boy Scouts Am., Salvation Army; formerly active Maui United Fund, Big Bros., J. Walter Cameron Center; mem. Hawaii Democratic Central Com., 1956-64, del. Dem. Nat. Conv., 1960. Office: Room 211 State Capitol Bldg Honolulu HI 96813

YAN, JOHNSON FAA, research chemist; b. Amoy, Fujian, Peoples Republic of China, May 21, 1934; came to U.S., 1963; s. Gian and K.C. (Loo) Y.; m. Suzie Chiu, Dec. 26, 1970; children: Alexander K., Benjamin C. BS, Nat. Taiwan U., Taipei, 1959; MS, Kent State U., 1965, PhD, 1967. Postdoctoral assoc. Cornell U., Ithaca, N.Y., 1967-69; devel. assoc. Bowater Carolina, Catawba, S.C., 1969-77; sci. specialist Weyerhauser, Tacoma, 1977-84; prin. research assoc. U. Wash., Seattle, 1984—; chief scientist Yan Research, Federal Way, Wash., 1984—. Contbr. articles to profl. jours. Mem. AAAS, Am. Chem. Soc. Home and Office: 3801 SW 326th St Federal Way WA 98023

YANCEY, PAUL HERBERT, biology educator, researcher; b. Whittier, Calif., July 4, 1951; s. Herbert W. and S. Barbara (Druilard) Y.; m. C. Susan Weiler, Sept. 24, 1978; 1 child, Ross. BS in Biology, Calif. Inst. Tech., 1973; PhD in Marine Biology, Scripps Inst. Oceanography, 1978. Postdoctoral fellow U. St. Andrew's, Scotland, 1978-81; asst. prof. biology Whitman Coll., Walla Walla, Wash., 1981-86, assoc. prof., 1986—. Contbr. articles to profl. jours. NSF grantee, 1985. Mem. AAAS, Am. Inst. Biol. Scis., Soc. Devel. Biology, Am. Soc. Zoologists, Sigma Xi (grantee 1984). Avocations: woodworking, camping, cross country skiing, photography. Office: Whitman Coll Biology Dept Walla Walla WA 99362

YANG, FEI PHIL, marketing professional; b. Taiwan, Republic of China, Sept. 2, 1958; came to U.S., 1971; s. Y.H. and W.H. (Sun) Y. BArch, U. Calif., Berkeley, 1980, MBA, 1982. Asst. product mgr. Gen. Mills, Inc., Mpls., 1982-84; product mgr. Nabisco Brands, Inc., San Francisco, 1984—. Vol. Guthrie Theatre Supporting Cast, Mpls., 1983-84, Univ. Art Mus., Berkeley, 1985-86; advisor Youth Advs., Mpls., 1983-84. Fellow Order of Golden Bear; mem. Commonwealth Club Calif., Calif. Alumnus Assn., Calif. Bus. Alumni, Delta Chi Alumni (advisor 1981-82, trustee 1984—, name Alumnus of Yr., 1982, 85). Avocations: snow skiing, tennis, volleyball. Office: Nabisco Brands/Del Monte One Market Plaza 533 Steuart San Francisco CA 94105

YANG, LINDA TSAO, financial consultant; b. Shanghai, China, Sept. 5, 1926; came to U.S., 1946; d. Ying Yung and Yu-shun (Ng) Tsao; m. An Tzu Yang, June 20, 1953; children—Yeulin T., Eton Y. B.A., St. John's U., Shanghai, 1945; M.S., Grad. Sch. Bus., Columbia U., 1948, M.Phil. in Econs., 1975. Instr. econs. and fin. Rutgers U., Newark, 1952-54; econ. analyst Am. Overseas Fin. Corp., N.Y.C., 1955-58; founder, dir. Mother Lode Savs., Sacramento, 1977-80; savs. and loan commr. State of Calif., San Francisco and Los Angeles, 1980-82; prin. Linda Tsao Yang & Assocs., Davis, Calif., 1983—; vice chmn. investment com., v.p. bd. adminstrn. Pub. Employees Retirement System, State of Calif., 1977-80; invited expert on restructuring fin. instrn. Senate Banking Com., Senate Fin. Com., Washington, 1981-82. Author article in field. Mem. policy adv. com. Coll. Agrl. and Environ. Scis., U. Calif.-Davis, 1979-85; mem. policy adv. com. Ctr. for Real Estate and Urban Econs., Grad. Sch. Bus., U. Calif.-Berkeley, 1980-82; mem. fairness commn. Dem. Nat. Com., 1984-85, compliance assistance commn., 1986—; commr. Calif. Commn. on Teaching Profession, 1984—. Recipient award Am. Savs. and Loan League, 1982, Achievement award Los Angeles YWCA, 1982, Outstanding Service award United Chinese-Am. League, 1982. Mem. Nat. Assn. Bus. Economists, Am. Econ. Assn., Acad. Polit. Sci., Orgn. Chinese-Ams., Trusteeship for Betterment of Women, Los Angeles, Asian-Pacific Women's Network Calif., Nat. Assn. State Savs. and Loan Suprs. (bd. dirs., nat. legis. com. 1980-82). Clubs: Nat. Economists (Washington); Downtown Economists Luncheon Group (N.Y.C.). Office: 1619 Holly Ln Davis CA 95616

YANG, TRACY CHUI-HSU, research biophysicist; b. Changsha, Hunan, China, Nov. 19, 1938; came to U.S., 1961; s. Yeh-Kung and Chin (Huang) Y.; m. Esther M.S. Lee; children: Tony T., Judith C. BS, Tunghai U., Taichung, Taiwan, Republic of China, 1959; MS, North Tex. State U., 1963; PhD, U. Ill., 1967. Postdoctoral trainee Argonne (Ill.) Nat. Lab., 1967-69; biophysicist Lawrence Berkeley (Calif.) Lab., 1969—. Recipient Group Achievement award NASA, 1975. Mem. Radiation Research Soc., Biophysics Soc., Internat. Council Sci. Unions (exec. sub-commn. radiation biology 1984-88). Home: 5145 Heavenly Ridge Ln Richmond CA 94803 Office: Lawrence Berkeley Lab 1 Cyclotron Rd Berkeley CA 94720

YANG, WILLIAM JIH-SHENG YANG, mechanical engineer, consultant; b. Shanxi, Peoples Republic of China, Sept. 12, 1932; s. A.Y. and S.H. (Shu) Y.; m. Diana H. Feng, Jan. 22, 1955; children: Esther Shaw, Ivy Leeson. BS, Calif. State U., Los Angeles, 1958. Registered profl. engr., Ala., Ariz., Calif., Colo., Fla., Hawaii, Ill., La., Mass., Mo., Nev., Ohio, Oreg., Tex., Wash. Prin., founder William J. Yang & Assocs., Burbank, Calif., 1966—; spl. tech. cons. The Royal Com. of Jubail & Yanbu Kingdom of Saudi Arabia, 1978-79. Contbr. articles to profl. jours. Recipient Spl. Outstanding Profl. award bldg. dept. Ch. of Jesus Christ Latter-day Saints, 1980; named Engr. of Yr., Asian-Am. Architects/Engrs., 1985. Mem. ASHRAE, Mech. Engrs. Assn. Calif. (pres. 1978-80), Cons. Engrs. Assn. Calif., Am. Cons. Engrs. Council, The Soc. Am. Mil. Engrs., Gen. Alumni Assn. U. So. Claif. (life). Democrat. Office: William J Yang & Assocs 847 N Hollywood Way Burbank CA 91505-2826

YANG, YUH-LIN ALLEN, chemist, researcher; b. Chiayi, Taiwan, Republic of China, Jan. 10, 1950; came to U.S., 1974; s. Arh-Jan and Orh (Chen) Y.; m. Leena Huang, Apr. 28, 1980; children: Ted H., Patrick H. BS in Chemistry summa cum laude, Tamkang U., Taipei, Republic of China, 1972; MS in Chemistry, Nat. Taiwan U., Taipei, 1974; PhD in Chemistry, U. Tex., Austin, 1980. Research assoc. U. Wis., Madison, 1980-81, Southwestern Med. Sch., Dallas, 1981-84; research chemist Chevron Chem. Co., Richmond, Calif., 1984—. Contbr. articles to profl. jours.; inventor new fungicides. Am. Heart Assn. research fellowship, 1982-84. Mem. Am. Chem. Soc. Home: 1988 Redwood Rd Hercules CA 94547 Office: Chevron Chem Co 15049 San Pablo Ave Richmond CA 94804

YANNI, JOHN OLIVER, advertising executive; b. Salt Lake City, July 26, 1951; s. Francis Joseph and Mary Catherine (Oliver) Y.; m. Gladys Elizabeth Limb, Feb. 24, 1979; children: Timothy John, Heather Elizabeth. BS, U. Utah, 1975. Advt. copywriter George Assoc., Salt Lake City, 1977-84; advt. mgr. Sun-Progress Inc., Price, Utah, 1984—. Mem. Utah Press Assn., Carbon County C. of C., Young Alumni Assn. Avocations: reading, fishing, photography, camping, sports. Home: 891 N Ninth E Price UT 84501 Office: Sun-Progress Inc 76 W Main Price UT 84501

YANOSKO, BARBARA JUR, mathematics, educator; b. Chgo., May 28, 1945; d. Frank and Ann Marie (Cap) Jur; m. Kenneth Yanosko, June 4, 1966 (div. Aug. 1984); children: John, Janet. BA in Sociology, U. Chgo., 1966; MS in Math., Ohio State U., 1971; EdD, U.S. Internat. U., San Diego, 1985. Cert. community coll. tchr. Asst. to notes editor MAA Monthly mag., Tallahassee, 1972-73; lectr. math. Fla. A&M U., Tallahassee, 1973-75, curriculum coordinator, Upward Bound/Special Services, 1975-77; instr., cons. Upward Bound/Spl. Services Humboldt State U., Arcata, Calif., 1978-79, extension coordinator, continuing edn., 1979-81, adj. assoc. prof. bus., 1982—; presenter summer MAA meeting, Laramie, Wyo., 1985; cons. remedial math., San Antonio, Tex., 1980. Bd. dirs. Expanding Your Horizons, Arcata, 1982-86, treas., textbook evaluator Legal Compliance Com., Arcata, 1983-84. Mem. AAAS, United Profs. Calif. (bd. dirs. 1985—), Am. Bus. Women's Assn. Woman of Yr. 1982), Math. Assn. Am., Assn. for Women in Math., Am. Contract Bridge League (bd. dirs. 1983-85), Mensa, Sigma Delta Epsilon (Omega com. 1981—). Democrat. Roman Catholic. Avocations: piano, needlework, indoor gardener, sci. fiction reading, writing. Home: 3170 Brian Ct Arcata CA 95521 Office: Humboldt State U Bus Adminstrn Arcata CA 95521

YARANOFF, CHRISTO DIMITER, advertising agency executive, graphic designer, photographer; b. Berlin, Germany, June 2, 1943; came to U.S., 1967; s. Dimiter A. and Vera C. (Vavov) Y.; m. Karen E. Jacobson, Feb. 18, 1968 (div. May 1976); children—Christo D. Jr., Victoria E. Diploma artist, Art Inst., Sofia, Bulgaria, 1964; M.A., Beaux Arts, Paris, 1967; M.A. (hon.), Profl. Graphic Inst., Chgo., 1969. Art dir. Swingline Corp., Chgo., 1968-71; design dir. Alphatype Corp., Chgo., 1971-72; mem. faculty Ariz. State U., Tempe, 1972-75; pres. Slesinger, Yaranoff & Assocs. Advt. Inc., Phoenix, 1975—. Served with Bulgarian Army, 1960-63. Recipient numerous awards including: Merit award Art Dirs. Club N.Y., Clio award, Phoenix Art Dirs. Club awards. Mem. Am. Assn. Advt. Agys., Am. Mktg. Assn., Phoenix Art Dirs. Club, Phoenix C. of C., Pub. Relations Soc. Am. Republican. Eastern Orthodox. Club: University (Phoenix). Home: 2323 N Central Ave Phoenix AZ 85004 Office: Slesinger Yaranoff & Assocs Advt Inc 2214 N Central Ave Phoenix AZ 85004

YARKONI, BARRY NEIL, marketing executive; b. N.Y.C., July 15, 1952; s. Fred and Elinor (Klarman) Y.; m. Nancy Jolles Friedman, Aug. 7, 1977; 1 child, Elizabeth Diane. BEE, U. Rochester, 1974. Engr. Leeds and Northrup, North Wales, Pa., 1974-75; mktg. mgr. Intel Corp., Santa Clara, Calif., 1975-79, Apple Computer, Cupertino, Calif., 1979-83; v.p. mktg. Bus. and Profl. Software, Cambridge, Mass., 1983-84; mktg. mgr. Rolm Corp., Santa Clara, 1984—. Pres. Cong. AM Echad, San Jose, Calif. 1983—. Jewish. Avocation: music. Home: 419 S McCadden Pl Los Angeles CA 90020 Office: Rolm Corp 23801 Calabasas Rd Calabasas CA 91302

YARRA, ROBERT WARREN, lawyer; b. N.Y.C., Oct. 20, 1952; s. Murray and Golda (Leifer) Y.; m. Elinor Naiburg, Apr. 16, 1977; children: Gabriel, Alexandria. BA magna cum laude, CCNY, 1975; JD, Southwestern U., 1980. Sole practice San Francisco, 1980—; mem. faculty Nat. Hispanic U., Oakland, Calif., 1984. Counselor SOS Racisme, Berkeley, Calif., 1985. Tom Bradley scholar, Southwestern Univ., 1980. Mem. Am. Immigration Lawyers Assn., San Francisco Bar Assn., Fresno County Bar Assn. Avocations: lit., travel, sports. Office: 500 Sansome St Suite 506 San Francisco CA 94111

YARYMOVYCH, MICHAEL IHOR, manufacturing company executive; b. Bialystok, Poland, Oct. 13, 1933; came to U.S., 1951, naturalized, 1956; s. Nicholas Joseph and Olga (Kruczowy) Y.; m. Roxolana Abramiuk, Nov. 21, 1951; children—Tatiana, Nicholas. B.Aero. Engring., NYU, 1955; M.S. in Engring. Mechanics, Columbia U., 1956, D. Engring. Sci., 1969. Dep. asst. sec. research and devel. U.S. Air Force, Washington, 1967-70; dir. AGARD, NATO, Paris, 1970-73; chief scientist U.S. Air Force, 1973-75; asst. adminstr. field ops. ERDA, 1975-77; v.p. engring. N.Am. aerospace ops. Rockwell Internat. Corp., El Segundo, Calif., 1977-81, v.p. advanced systems devel., 1981-86, v.p., assoc. dir. Strategic Defense Ctr., 1986—; cons. in field. Author papers in field. Translator Russian books and periodicals. Recipient Exceptional Civilian Service award Dept. Air Force, 1968, 73, 75, Disting. Service award ERDA, 1977; Guggenheim fellow, 1956-58. Fellow AIAA (dir., pres., gen. chmn. ann. meeting 1978), Air Force Assn., Nat. Mgmt. Assn., Nat. Security Industries Assn., AAAS, Am. Astronautical Soc., Internat. Acad. Astros. (v.p. sci. programs), Aerospace Industry Assn., Internat. Acad. Astronautics (v.p. sci. programs). Office: Rockwell Internat Corp 2230 E Imperial Hwy El Segundo CA 90245

YASHAR, FRANK DAVID, optical engineer; b. Tehran, Iran, Apr. 10, 1958; came to U.S., 1964; s. Samuel and Sheba Yashar. BS, UCLA, 1979. Registered profl. engr., Calif. Analysis engr. Litton Systems, Woodland Hills, Calif., 1980-81; mem. tech. staff KLA Instruments, Santa Clara, Calif., 1982—. Inventor in field. Democrat. Office: KLA Instruments 2051 Mission Coll Blvd Santa Clara CA 95054

YASNYI, ALLAN DAVID, TV production company executive; b. New Orleans, June 22, 1942; s. Ben Z. and Bertha R. (Michalove) Y.; B.B.A., Tulane U., 1964; m. Lesley E. Behrman, Dec. 8, 1968; children—Benjamin Charles, Evelyn Judith. Free-lance exec. producer, producer, writer, actor and designer for TV, motion picture and theatre, 1961-73; dir. fin. and adminstrn. Quinn Martin Prodns., Hollywood, Calif., 1973-76, v.p. fin., 1976-77, exec. v.p. fin. and corp. planning, 1977; vice chmn., chief exec. officer QM Prodns., Beverly Hills, Calif., 1977-78, chmn. bd., chief exec. officer, 1978-80; pres., chief exec. officer The Synapse Group, Inc. (formerly Vitrus Prodns., 1981—; dir. Found. for Global Broadcasting. Mem. adv. bd. Filmex; trustee Hollywood Arts Council; exec. v.p., trustee Hollywood Hist. Trust; bd. dirs. Am. Asthma and Allergy Found.Served with U.S. Army, 1964-66. Mem. Acad. TV Arts and Scis., Am. Advt. Fedn., Am. Mgmt. Assn., Hollywood Radio and TV Soc., Hollywood C. of C. (dir., vice-chmn.), Screen Actors Guild. Home: 3343 Laurel Canyon Blvd Studio City CA 91604

YASUDA, NAOKI, physician, educator; b. Tokyo, Mar. 12, 1945; came to U.S., 1972; s. Tatsuo and Ai (Hikone) Y.; m. Yuko Hoshino, May 1, 1971; children—Hajime, Makiko, Tsutomu. M.D., Tokyo Med. and Dental U., 1969. Intern, Mercy Hosp., Chgo., 1972-73; resident Toranomon Hosp., Tokyo, 1970-72; fellow in endocrinology Oreg. Health Scis. U., Portland, 1973-76, asst. prof. medicine, 1976-82, assoc. prof. medicine, 1982—. Tartar Research fellow Med. Research Found. Oreg., 1980; NIH grantee, 1982. Mem. Am. Endocrine Soc., AAAS, Am. Fedn. Clin. Research, Internat. Soc. Neuroendocrinology, Western Soc. for Clin. Research, N.Y. Acad. Scis. Office: Oreg Health Scis U 3181 SW Sam Jackson Park Rd Portland OR 97201

YATES, ALDEN PERRY, engineering and construction company executive; b. Los Angeles, July 12, 1928; s. John Perry and Sybill Norma (Kerr) Y.; m. Dawn Blacker, Dec. 16, 1950; children: Stephen, Michael, Karen, Jeffrey, Russell, Patricia. B.S.C.E., Stanford U., 1951. Field engr. Bechtel Corp., San Francisco, 1953-70; v.p. Bechtel Power Corp., San Francisco, 1970-75; v.p., dep. div. mgr. Internat. Bechtel, Inc., Kuwait City, Kuwait, 1975-78, Bechtel Overseas Corp., London, 1978-80; pres. Bechtel Petroleum, Inc., Houston, 1980-83, Bechtel Group, Inc., San Francisco, 1983—; dir. 1st City Bancorp. of Tex., Inc. Served to lt. j.g. USCG, 1951-53. Republican. Clubs: Pacific Union (San Francisco); San Francisco Golf. Office: Bechtel Group Inc 50 Beale St San Francisco CA 94105

YATES, GEORGE THOMAS, mechanical engineer, researcher; b. Youngstown, Ohio, Jan. 28, 1949; s. Horace Thomas and Verna (Hughes) Y. BS, Purdue U., 1971; MS, Calif. Inst. Tech., 1972, PhD, 1976. Research fellow Calif. Inst. Tech., Pasadena, 1976-78, lectr., 1980-82, sr. research fellow, 1978-85, sr. scientist, 1985—; cons. mech. engring., Pasadena, 1982—. Contbr. articles to profl. jours. Mem. ASME, So. Calif. Collegiate Hockey Assn. (treas. 1984—, sec. 1986—), Sigma Xi. Club: Calif. Inst. Tech. Hockey (pres. 1977—). Avocations: skiing, hockey, racquetball. Home: 3831 Blanche St Pasadena CA 91107 Office: Calif Inst Tech Dept Engring Sci 104-44 1201 E California Blvd Pasadena CA 91125

YATES, JAMES KAMMERER, government official; b. Peiping, China, Dec. 22, 1923 (parents Am. citizens); s. Theodore Markland and Jean Robinson (Kammerer) Y.; m. Dorothy Louise Gregory, May 20, 1950; children—James Gregory, Theodore Kammerer. B.S., U. S.C., 1949. Commd. 2d lt. USAF, 1944, advanced through grades to capt., 1954, resigned, 1963; engaged in adjudication VA, San Francisco, 1963—, mem. rating bd., 1978—. Presbyterian. Home: 30 San Felipe Way San Francisco CA 94127 Office: US VA RO 211 Main St San Francisco CA 94105

YATES, ROBERT EDMUNDS, physical chemist; b. Bisbee, Ariz., Aug. 15, 1926; s. Charles Francis and Gladys (Sisk) Y.; m. Lesley Louise Ward, Apr. 6, 1947; children: Kathleen, Richard, Susan, Carole. BS, U. Ariz., 1948, MS, 1949; PhD, Mich State Coll., 1952. Research chemist Dow Chem. Co., Freeport, Tex., 1952-58, Aerojet Gen. Corp., Azusa, Calif., 1958-61, Rocket Power, Inc., Pasadena, Calif., 1961-65, Aerojet Gen. Corp., Sacramento, 1966-71; phys. scientist USAF, Sacramento, 1971—. Contbr. sci. articles to profl. jours. Served to lt. (j.g.) USN, 1944-46. Mem. Am. Chem. Soc. Episcopalian. Avocations: golf, skiing, hiking. Office: Phys Sci Br SM-ALC/MAQCA McClellan AFB CA 95652

YAW, CHARLES EDWARD, quality control manager; b. Battle Creek, Mich., Nov. 12, 1938; s. Victor Lenard and Brittie (Parker) Y.; m. Phyllis Thayer, June 20, 1962 (div. Oct. 1965); children: Shelly, Cyntha; m. Audrey M. Howell, May 12, 1967; 1 child, Chalres E. II. BS in Quality Control Engring., Kellogg Community Coll., 1960. Quality control leader Tex. Aluminum, Mojave, Calif., 1967-72; shift supr. Cadillac Plastics, Kalamazoo, 1972-73; shift foreman Swanson Pipe Co., Phoenix, 1973-76; electrician's asst. Thermoliac Systems, Phoenix, 1976-77; mgr. quality control Ariz. Aluminum Co., Phoenix, 1977—; bd. dirs. 47 Place, Phoenix, Almex, Phoenix. Mem. ASTM, Am. Soc. Quality Control (cert.). Democrat. Roman Catholic. Avocations: golf, flying. Home: 5137 W Vogel Glendale AZ 85302 Office: Ariz Aluminum 249 S 51 Ave PO Box 6736 Phoenix AZ 85005

YEAGER, JACQUES S., construction company executive; b. Riverside, Calif., Oct. 26, 1921; s. Ernest Louis and Emma (Leah) Y.; m. Mary Barbara Gibbs, July 1, 1948; 5 children. BSCE, U. Calif., Berkeley, 1947. With E.L. Yeager Constrn. Co. Inc., Riverside, 1947-56, pres., 1956—; bd. dirs. Security Pacific Nat. Bank, Inland, Security Pacific Nat. Bank, Los Angeles, First Am. Title Ins. Co., Ri. Bd. dirs. Riverside Community Hosp., 1960-70, chmn. bd. dirs. 1959-60, mem. exec. com. 1979—, nominating com., 1979—, spl. contributions com., 1979-80, Founder's Club, (charter), 1974—, Monday Morning Group, 1960—, pres. Monday Morning Group, 1974-75; bd. dirs. Riverside Community Hosp. found. Ventures Corp., 1985—; bd. dirs. United Fund Riverside, 1966-74, chmn. 1975-76, mem. 1965—; active U. Calif. Riverside, 1969—; mem. Riverside County Energy Task Force, 1974-75, Riverside and San Bernardino Counties Transp. Support Group, 1974—, chmn. Riverside Civic Ctr. Art Fund Raising Com., 1974-76; bd. dirs. Riverside Internat. Raceway, 1975-78; com. mem. Inland Empire Cultural Found., 1980—; mem. Loma Linda (Calif.) U. Community Adv. Com., 1981-84; dir. at large Calif. Water Resources Assn., 1983—; hon. com. mem. ARC, 1984—; mem. needs assessment steering com. Riverside County Local Streets and Hwys., 1984—; chmn. Riverside Transp. Com., 1984—; bd. dirs. Regional Inst. So. Calif., 1985—. Served with USN, WWII. Mem. Greater Riverside C. of C. (2% Club, 1982—, co-chmn. Keep Riverside Ahead, 1983—, named Citizen of Yr. 1984), U. Calif. Berkeley Alumni Assn. (steering com. Coll. Engring., 1979—, Inland Colls. chpt. Alumni Associates, 1979—), Calif. C. of C. (statewide indsl.safety and health com. 1984—). Club: Exchange (Riverside) (recipient The Book Golden Deeds 1984) Lodge: Kiwanis. Office: EL Yeager Constrn Co Inc PO Box 87 Riverside CA 92502

YEAGER, KURT ERIC, research inst. ofcl.; b. Cleve., Sept. 11, 1939; s. Joseph Ellsworth and Karolyn Kristine (Pedersen) Y.; m. Rosalie Ann McMillan, Feb. 5, 1960; children—Geoffrey, Phillip; m. 2d, Regina Ursula Querfurt, May 12, 1970; 1 dau., Victoria. B.A. in Chemistry, Kenyon Coll., 1961; postgrad. Ohio State U., 1961-62; M.S. in Physics, U. Calif.-Davis, 1964. Teaching asst. Ohio State U., 1961-62; officer, program mgr. Air Force Tech. Applications Ctr., Alexandria, Va., 1962-68; assoc. dept. dir. Mitre Corp., McLean, Va., 1968-72; dir. energy research and devel. planning EPA, Washington, 1972-74; dir. fossil power plants dept. Electric Power Research Inst., Palo Alto, Calif., 1974-79, dir. coal combustion systems, 1979-83, v.p. coal combustion systems, 1983—; commerce tech. adv. bd., Oak Ridge fossil energy adv. bd. Nat. Acad. Engring., Nat. Coal Council. Pres. No. Va. Youth Football Assn., 1973-74; mem. Palo Alto C. of C. Served to capt. USAF, 1962-68. Decorated Air Force Commendation medals (2); recipient Outstanding Service award EPA, 1974. Mem. ASME (Research Policy Bd.), AAAS, Am. Chem. Soc. Republican. Episcopalian. Contbr. articles profl. jours.

YEAGLEY, MARYCATHERINE, manufacturing company executive; b. Seattle, July 23, 1947; d. Darrell Hutchison and Edith (Irene) Allsopp; m. Lawrence R. Yeagley, Sept. 27, 1975. Student, Seattle U., 1965-67, U. Wash., 1968-69; BA in Polit. Sci., U. Utah, 1969; cert. exec. devel., Northwestern U., 1985. Mgr. library U. Wash., Seattle, 1970-76; systems analyst PACCAR, Renton, Wash., 1977-78, asst. to gen. mgr., 1978-80; mgr. mng. devel. PACCAR, Bellevue, Wash., 1981-83, dir. human resource mgmt., 1984—; v.p. bd. dirs. Custom Industries, Bellevue, 1983—. Bd. dirs. Jr. Achievement, Seattle, 1985—. Mem. Human Resource Planning Soc. Democrat. Avocations: working small farm, traveling. Office: PACCAR PO Box 1518 Bellevue WA 98009

YEAMAN, JACK MICHAEL, social service administrator; b. Afton, Wyo., May 8, 1920; s. Michael Daniel and Mary Edith (Meacham) Y.; m. Ruth Reynolds, June 2, 1950. BS, U. Utah., 1948, postgrad., 1949, MSW, 1961. Cert. secondary tchr., Utah. Home tchr. for blind Wyo. State Dept. Edn., Cheyenne, 1949-50, dir. deaf and blind div., 1950-55; dir. tng. and adjustment services Utah State Div. Services for Visually Handicapped, Salt Lake City, 1955—; pres. Western Conf. Tchrs. of Adult Blind, 1952-57; cons. artificial eye project U. Utah Dept. Med. Research, Salt Lake City, 1974-80. Mem. Am. Assn. Edn. Rehab. for Blind, Nat. Assn. Social Workers (cert.). Mormon. Avocations: amateur radio, computer programming, gardening.

Home: 409 S 1300 E Salt Lake City UT 84102 Office: State Div Services for Visually Handicapped 309 E 1st S Salt Lake City UT 84111

YEAP, ARTHUR K., electronics co. exec.; b. Hong Kong, Feb. 15, 1956; s. Choong Yow and Alice Miu-Lan (Ko) Y.; came to U.S., 1963, naturalized, 1972; student U. Calif., Berkeley, 1973-74, Foothill Coll., 1975. Spl. programs engr. Hewlett Packard Central Research Labs., Palo Alto, Calif., 1974-75, cons. Hewlett Packard Studios, 1973; co founder, bd. chmn., pres. ADI-Audio Developments Internat., Palo Alto, 1975-83; chief exec. officer, bd. dirs. Innova Group, Inc., San Francisco, 1984—; mng. dir. Alembic, Inc., Santa Rosa, Calif., 1979-80; v.p., dir. Shama Sound Corp., San Francisco, 1981—; cons. to TV and recording studios and recording groups; advisor spl. scis. Foothill Coll., 1975. Recipient contbns. to sci. awards NASA, USAF, USN, also 2d place Sci. Clubs Am., 1970. Bd. dirs. judges San Francisco/Bay Area Science Fair, 1975—; mem. com. French-Am. Sch., 1986; mem. Learning Edn. Through Arts Project, 1986—. Mem. Audio Engring. Soc. (chmn. San Francisco sect., 1976-78, chmn. Internat. Conv. on Sound Reinforcement in New York, 1977). Evangelical. Asst. concertmaster San Francisco All City Orch., 1971-72. Contbr. articles to profl. jours., newspapers. Patentee in field. Home: 1722 38th Ave San Francisco CA 94122

YEARSLEY, DEWAINE, computer engineer; b. Safford, Ariz., Sept. 24, 1943; s. Karl Gibbs and Netta (Hancock) Y.; m. Carol Sue Delhagen, Apr. 5, 1969; children: Dawn Sharlet, Beth Alison, Kent Edward. BA in Physics, Brigham Young U., 1972, postgrad., 1972-74; postgrad., Pacific Luth. U., 1975-76, Wash. State U., 1978-79. Software engr. Boeing Aerospace, Kent, Wash., 1974-76; software devel. mgr. Azurdata, Richland, Wash., 1976-78; sr. engr. Westinghouse Hanford Co., Richland, Wash., 1978-80; supr. cen. area ARAMCO, Dhahran, Saudi Arabia, 1980-82; chief ILMF Martin Marietta of Denver, Vandenberg AFB, Calif., 1982-83; specialist lead engr. Northrop-Ventura, Newbury Park, Calif., 1984-86; software lead Delco Systems Orgn., Goleta, Calif., 1986—; tchr. Carden Conejo Sch., Westlake Village, Calif., 1985—; cons. in field. Co-editor lab. manual Physics of Photography, 1967; inventor food dehydrator kit, 1976. Troop leader Boy Scouts Am., Alaska and Wash., 1970-80; Rep. precinct rep., Richland, 1980. Served with U.S. Army, 1967-70. Mem. Am. Orchid Soc. Mormon. Avocations: reading, gardening, teaching children's computer sci. Home: PO Box 2766 Orcutt CA 93455 Office: Delco Systems Orgn 6767 Hollister Goleta CA 93117

YEATS, ROBERT SHEPPARD, geologist, educator; b. Miami, Fla., Mar. 30, 1931; s. Robert Sheppard and Carolyn Elizabeth (Rountree) Y.; m. Lillian Eugenia Bowie, Dec. 30, 1952; children: Robert Bowie, David Claude, Stephen Paul, Kenneth James, Sara Elizabeth. B.A., U. Fla., 1952; M.S., U. Wash., 1956, Ph.D., 1958. Registered geologist, Oreg., Calif. Geologist, petroleum exploration and prodn. Shell Oil Co., Ventura and Los Angeles, Calif., 1958-67; Shell Devel. Co., Houston, 1967; assoc. prof. geology Ohio U., Athens, 1967-70; prof. Ohio U., 1970-77; prof. geology Oreg. State U., Corvallis, 1977—; chmn. dept. Oreg. State U., 1977-85; geologist U.S. Geol. Survey, 1968, 69, 75; Glomar Challenger scientist 1971, co-chief scientist, 1973-74, 78; mem. Oreg. Bd. Geologist Examiners, 1981-83; vis. scientist N.Z. Geol. Survey, 1983-84. Mem. Ojai (Calif.) City Planning Commn., 1961-62, Ojai City Council, 1962-65. Served to 1st lt. U.S. Army, 1952-54. Ohio U. research fellow, 1973-74; grantee NSF; grantee U.S. Geol. Survey. Fellow Geol. Soc. Am.; mem. Am. Assn. Petroleum Geologists, Am. Geophys. Union, Seismol. Soc. Am., AAAS, Oreg. Acad. Sci. Research on Cenozoic tectonics of So. Calif., N.Z. and Pakistan, active faults of Calif. Transverse Ranges, deep-sea drilling in Eastern Pacific, structural geology North Cascade Range. Home: 1654 NW Crest Pl Corvallis OR 97330 Office: Dept Geology Oreg State U Corvallis OR 97331

YEATTS, REBECCA DIANE, speech-language pathologist; b. Coshocton, Ohio, Jan. 18, 1953; s. Roy Charles and Audrey Eileen (Barnes) Welker; m. James Edward Yeatts, Dec. 29, 1977; 1 child, Vanessa Erin. Student, Bowling Green U., 1971-75; BS in Speech-Lang. Pathology, U. Utah, 1978, MS in Speech-Lang. Pathology, 1981. Speech pathologist Primary Children's Hosp., Salt Lake City, 1980-82, U. Hosp., Tucson, 1982-83, Tucson Unified Sch. Dist., 1983-85; pvt. practice speech pathology Tucson, 1985—. Author: (article, workshop) Downs' Syndrome, 1982. Vol. Jr. League Tucson, 1981— (v.p. chmn. com. 1986-87); sec. Southwestern Inst. of Human Devel., Tucson, 1986—; active Pima Council on Developmental Disabilities, Tucson, 1986—; mem. steering com. and community awareness Let's Talk Program for Responsible Parenthood, Tucson, 1986—; program originator, co-chmn. Intergenerational Day Care, Tucson, 1984—. Recipient grants Talking Tapes, 1984 ($500), Intergenerational Day Care ($12,803 Am. Express). Mem. Am. Speech-Lang.-Hearing Assn. (cert.). Avocations: golf, racquetball, reading. Home and Office: 1791 E Hampton Tucson AZ 85719

YEAW, JAMES RAYMOND DONALD, marketing executive; b. Pictou, N.S., Can., Oct. 14, 1943; s. Ernest Donald McKay and Marguerite Elizabeth Joan (Hayward) Y.; came to U.S., 1945, naturalized, 1949; B.A., Rio Hondo Coll., 1974; postgrad. Calif. State U., Los Angeles, 1974-77; m. Beverly Jean Grigsby, Apr. 27, 1962; children—Susanne Noma Joan, Timothy Earl McKay, m. Gretjen Vanderveer Anderson, Oct. 21, 1983; children—Daniel William Anderson Yeaw and Katrina Elizabeth Anderson Yeaw (twins). Ins. agt. Automobile Club So. Calif., Los Angeles, 1966-74, supr. sales, 1974-76, mgr. mem. service tng., 1976—; pres. Educative Services, Inc., 1980-84; dir. mktg. The Dentists Co. div. Calif. Dental Assn., 1984-86; mktg. cons., Rocklin, Calif., 1986—. Named Outstanding Producer, Automobile Assn. Am., 1968. Mem. Am. Soc. Tng. and Devel., Nat. Soc. Performance Instrn., Western Heritage Assn. (pres.), Calif. Hist. Soc., Sierra Club, Am. Philatelic Soc., Am. Soc. Tng. and Devel., Assn. Advancement Adult Edn. Author: Strategies for Success in Auto Club Selling, 1976, Dental Computing, 1987; contbr. articles to travel and history jours. Home: 5325 Comstock Ct PO Box 1077 Rocklin CA 95677

YEE, EDWARD SHERWOOD, cardiothoracic surgeon; b. Canton, People's Republic of China, Dec. 17, 1949; s. Hoy Fow and Yet Wing (Chung) Y.; m. Victoria Jean Neel, Sept. 16, 1972; children: Andrea, Brandon. BS, U. Calif., Berkeley, 1971; MD, U. Calif., San Francisco, 1974; MPH, U. Calif., Berkeley, 1975. Intern in gen. surgery U. Calif., San Francisco, 1976-80, resident in thoracic surgery, 1981-83; staff physician VA Med. Ctr., San Francisco, 1983—, Peninsula Med. Ctr., Burlingame, Calif., 1983—, Moffitt Hosp., San Francisco, 1983—; mem. courtesy staff San Francisco Gen. Hosp., 1984—; asst. prof. surgery U. Calif., San Francisco, 1983—; bd. gov's. Am. Heart Assn., 1983—, CPR com., 1971—, program council, 1983—, exec. com. 1983—, Calif. del. 1985. Bd. dirs. San Francisco Med. Service, 1984; sec. Yee Shew Benevolent Assn., 1985. Mem. AAAS, San Francisco Surg. Soc., Internat. Soc. Heart Transplantation, Am. Fedn. Clin. Research, Am. Coll. Chest Physicians, Am. Coll. Cardiology. Home: 95 Saint Germain Ave San Francisco CA 94114 Office: U Calif San Francisco 896 Moffitt Hosp San Francisco CA 94143

YEE, JANICE KWAI LIN CHING, publisher, poetess, author, dress designer; b. Honolulu, Nov. 15, 1929; d. Kim Ak and Katherine Choy See (Lum) Ching; m. Alfred A. Yee, Jan. 29, 1953 (div. Mar. 1973); children: Alethea Lailan (Mrs. Robert Fell), Mark K.K., Eric K.S., Malcolm K.O., Ian K.P. B.S. in Bus. Adminstrn., Northwestern U., 1951. Account clk. Universal Motor Co., Honolulu, 1951; cost acct. Alfred Shaheen Co., Honolulu, 1952; chief acct. Honolulu Credit & Fin. Co., 1952-53; silent ptnr. Alfred A. Yee, Honolulu, 1952-53; pres., treas. Pi Press, Inc., Honolulu, 1973—, chairwoman, 1976—; pres., Fresh Ideas, Hawaii, 1978; pres., treas. Dress Investment Hawaii, 1983—. Author: (poetry) This Gift I Present, 1974, 76, 80, This Gift of Poetry for Children, 1975, This Gift of Poetry for Law, 1976, This Gift of Poetry for Competition, 1984; The Fast Gourmet from Hawaii, 1977, 1986; others. Trustee, bd. dirs. Chinese Youth of Hawaii, 1982-84. Mem. Hawaii Pubs. Assn., Assoc. Chinese Univ. Women, Nat. Assn. Female Execs., Hawaii United Gifts and Garments Salespersons, Nat. Fedn. Press Women, Honolulu Press Club, Am. Assn. Retired Persons, League of Republican Women. Episcopalian. Clubs: Punti Ching Clan Soc., See Dai Doo Soc. (Honolulu). Home: 3169 Alika Ave Honolulu HI 96817

YEE, PHILLIP KOON HIN, engineer; b. Honolulu, Feb. 19, 1916; s. Sheong and Shee (Leong) Y.; m. Maybelle W.Y. Lee, May 6, 1939; children—Curtis Q.H., Gary Q.L., Stephen Q.S. B.S. in Civil Engring., U. Hawaii, 1938. Registered profl. engr., Hawaii. Sports cartoonist Honolulu Star-Bull., 1934-45; planning draftsman Territorial Planning Bd., Honolulu, 1938-39; civil engr. U.S. Engrs. Office, Honolulu, 1940-41, head water supply sect., 1941-45; asst. supt. Suburban Water System, City and County Honolulu, 1945-60; engr. P. Yee & Assocs. Inc., Honolulu, 1960—; pres. Ala Moana Investment Corp., Honolulu, 1960-65, Intercontinental Corp., Honolulu, 1965-70; dir. Phillip K.H. Yee & Assocs., Honolulu. Mem. Cons. Engrs. Council Trade Mission IV, S.E. Asia, 1968; mem., citizen ambassador People to People waste water mgmt. delegation People's Republic of China, 1983. Recipient Cert. of Appreciation, U.S. Dept. Commerce, Washington, 1968. Mem. Cons. Engrs. Council, Am. Security Council, U.S. Congl. Adv. Bd. (state advisor). Astarian, Ashtar Command. Club: Engring. Assocs. (Honolulu). Home: 1885 Paula Dr Honolulu HI 96816 Office: Phillip KH Yee & Assocs Inc 243 Liluokalani AVe Honolulu HI 96815

YEE, ROY JENSON, electrical sales and service company executive; b. Honolulu, Sept. 29, 1943; s. Ken and Nancy (Wong) Yee; m. Andre Yvonne McIntosh, Dec. 18, 1975; children: Traci, Allison, Todd. BSEE, Oreg. State U., 1967. Registered profl. engr., Hawaii. Field engr. Gen. Electric, San Francisco, Honolulu, N.Y.C., Boston, 1967-69; v.p. KEMS Inc., Honolulu, 1969—, Honolulu Shipyard Inc., 1986—. Chmn. Homeport Hawaii Task Force, Honolulu, 1983-85, project mgr., 1984; mem. Kaneohe Neighborhood Bd., 1983-84; vice chmn. Mil. Affairs Council, Honolulu, 1985—. Mem. IEEE (sr., chmn. regional mem. devel. com.), NSPE, Soc. Naval Architects and Marine Engrs., Hawaii C. of C. (bd. dirs. 1986—). Avocations: amateur radio, computers, raquetball. Home: 46 Lilipuna Rd Kaneohe HI 96744 Office: KEMS Inc 2234 Hoonee Pl Honolulu HI 96819

YEGGE, ROBERT BERNARD, lawyer, educator; b. Denver, June 17, 1934; s. Ronald Van Kirk and Fairy (Hill) Y. A.B. magna cum laude, Princeton U., 1956; M.A. in Sociology, U. Denver, 1958, J.D., 1959. Bar: Colo. 1959, D.C. 1978. Partner firm Yegge, Hall and Evans, Denver, 1959-78; with Nelson & Harding, 1979—; prof. U. Denver Coll. Law, 1965—, dean, 1965-77, dean emeritus, 1977—; asst. to pres. Denver Post, 1971-75. Author: Colorado Negotiable Instruments Law, 1960, Some Goals; Some Tasks, 1965, The American Lawyer: 1976, 1966, New Careers in Law, 1969, The Law Graduate, 1972, Tomorrow's Lawyer: A Shortage and Challenge, 1974, Declaration of Independence for Legal Education, 1976. Mng. trustee Denver Center for Performing Arts, 1972-75; chmn. Colo. Council Arts and Humanities, 1968-80, chmn. emeritus, 1980—; mem. scholar selection com. Henry Luce Found., 1975—; Active nat. and local A.R.C., chmn. Denver region, 1985—; Trustee Denver Symphony Soc., Inst. of Ct. Mgmt.; trustee, vice chmn. Nat. Assembly State Arts Agys.; vice chmn. Mexican-Am. Legal Edn. and Def. Fund, 1970-76. Recipient Disting. Service award Denver Jr. C. of C., 1965; Harrison Tweed award Am. Assn. Continuing Edn. Adminstrs., 1985. Mem. Law and Soc. Assn. (life, pres. 1965-70), ABA (chmn. lawyers conf. 1987—, chmn. accreditation commn. for legal assistant programs 1987—), Colo. Bar Assn. (bd. govs. 1965-77), Denver Bar Assn., D.C. Bar Assn., Am. Law Inst., Am. Judicature Soc. (bd. dirs. 1968-72, 75—, Herbert Harley award 1985), Am. Acad. Polit. and Social Sci., Am. Sociol. Soc., Assn. Am. Law Schs., Order St. Ives, Phi Beta Kappa, Beta Theta Pi, Phi Delta Phi, Alpha Kappa Delta, Omicron Delta Kappa. Home: 4209 W 38th Ave Denver CO 80212

YEH, HSU-CHI, research aerosol scientist; b. Taipei, Taiwan, Republic of China, Sept. 30, 1940; came to U.S., 1964, naturalized, 1974; s. Ping-Hui and Ah-Zu Yeh; m. Terry S.H. Lin, Dec. 31, 1966; children: Eric, Stephen. BS, Nat. Taiwan U., 1963; MS, U. Minn., 1967, PhD, 1972. Teaching asst. U. Minn., Mpls., 1964-65, research asst., 1965-72; aerosol scientist Lovelace Inhalation Toxicol. Research Inst., Albuquerque, 1972—, group supr., 1982—. Mem. editorial bd. Aerosol Sci. and Tech. Jour., 1985—. Mem. AAAS, Am. Assn. Aerosol Research, Am. Indsl. Hygiene Assn., Health Physics Soc., Air Pollution Control Assn. Office: Lovelace Inhalation Toxicol Research PO Box 5890 Albuquerque NM 87185

YEH, YEA-CHUAN MILTON, electrical engineer; b. Yuan-chuan, Republic of China, Apr. 16, 1943; came to U.S., 1967; s. Sing-min and Dahchwen (Wang) Y.; m. Grace Ching-hsia Shen, June 7, 1969; children: Caroline, Christopher. BS, Nat. Taiwan U., Taipei, 1965; MS, UCLA, 1969, PhD, 1973. Head Radio Multiplex Relay Sta., Peng-Ho, Taiwan, Republic of China, 1965-66; asst. instr. Nat. Taiwan U., 1966-67; mem. tech. staff Jet Propulsion Lab., Pasadena, Calif., 1972-82; dir. advanced research Applied Solar Energy Corp., City of Industry, Calif., 1982—; pres. MYK Tech., Inc., City of Industry, 1983—. Contbr. articles to profl. jours.; patentee in field. Disting. fellow UCLA, 1969-70; cert. Recognition NASA, Washington, 1976, 77, 81, 82. Mem. IEEE, Internat. Solar Energy Soc., Sigma Xi. Office: MYK Tech Inc 1140-P Centre Dr City of Industry CA 91789

YELLIN, HERB, publisher; b. Malden, Mass., Jan. 24, 1935; s. Edward and Frances (Pally) Y.; m. Patricia Ann Casker, Sept. 12, 1960; children—Mark, William. Student Los Angeles City Coll., 1956-58. Dist. mgr. Zodys, Los Angeles, 1966-71; stockbroker Stern, Frank, Los Angeles, 1971-73; mktg. dir. Sega, Los Angeles, 1974-77; pub. Lord John Press, Northridge, Calif., 1977—; cons. Calif. Suppression Systems, Long Beach, 1981—. Trustee, Calif. State U., Northridge, 1980—. Served with USN, 1952-56. Mem. Bibliog. Soc. (pres. 1979). Republican. Jewish. Home: 19073 Los Alimos St Northridge CA 91326 Office: Lord John Press 19073 Los Alimos St Northridge CA 91326

YEN, JAMES CHING NING, architect, planner, analyst; b. Nanking, Republic of China, Feb. 5, 1946; came to U.S., 1971; s. Mon Hwa and Peilan (Kou) Y.; s. Essie Chin Yen, Apr. 18, 1975; children: Peter J., Kristine D. BArch, Chung Yuan Coll., 1970; MArch, Pratt Inst., 1974. Sr. design architect Grazen & Ptnrs., N.Y.C., 1974-75, P. Friedberg & Ptnrs., N.Y.C., 1975-76; architect Harry Weese & Assocs., Washington, 1976-80, supr. architect, 1982-85; project architect Cathy Devel. Corp., Los Angeles, 1980-82; prin. planning and analysis So. Calif. Rail Cons., Los Angeles, 1985—; project architect Architecture Cons., Los Angeles, 1983—. Served to lt. Chinese Marine Corps, 1970-71. Mem. AIA. Avocations: swimming, sightseeing, music, movies. Home: 16717 Green Coach Rd Hacienda Heights CA 91745 Home: 17514 Orlon Dr Rowland Heights CA 91748 Office: So Calif Rail Cons 403 W 8th St Los Angeles CA 90014

YEN, SAMUEL SHOW-CHIH, obstetrics and gynecology educator; b. Beijing, Feb. 22, 1927; s. K.Y. and E.K. Yen; m. Kathryn Bachman, July 26, 1958; children: Carol Amanda, Dolores Amelia, Margaret Rae. BS, Cheeloo U., China, 1949; MD, U. Hong Kong, 1954, DSc (hon.), 1980. Diplomate Am. Bd. Ob-Gyn (bd. examiners 1973-78), Am. Bd. Reproductive Endocrinology (bd. examiners 1976-82). Intern Queen Mary Hosp., Hong Kong, 1954-55; resident Johns Hopkins U., Balt., 1956-60; assoc. prof. reproductive biology Case Western Res. U., Cleve., 1967-70; prof. ob-gyn U. Calif., San Diego, 1970-72, chmn. dept. reproductive medicine, 1972-83, prof. reproductive medicine, 1983—; dir. reproductive endocrinology U. Calif. Med. Ctr., San Diego, 1983—; assoc. dir. obstetrics Univ. Hosp., Cleve., 1968-70; cons. FDA, Calif. 1979—; Howard and Georgianna Jones lectr. Johns Hopkins Med. Ctr., Balt., 1984. Editor: Reproductive Endocrinology—Physiology, Pathophysiology and Clinical Management, 1978, 2d rev. edit., 1986; editorial cons. Current Ob-Gyn Techniques, 1975—; mem. editorial bd. Endocrine Revs., 1984—. Oglebay fellow 1968-69; recipient Axel Munthe award Govt. Italy, 1982. Mem. Am. Gynecol. Soc. (fellowship com. 1978-81), Inst. Medicine-the Nat. Acad. Sci. Office: U Calif-San Diego Reproductive Medicine T-002 La Jolla CA 92093

YEN, TEH FU, civil engineering and environmental educator; b. Kun-Ming, China, Jan. 9, 1927; s. Kwang Pu and Ren (Liu) Y.; m. Shiao-Ping Siao, May 30, 1959. B.S., Cen. China U., 1947; M.S., W.Va. U., 1953; Ph.D., Va. Poly. Inst. and State U., 1956; hon. doctoral degree, Pepperdine U., 1982. Sr. research chemist Good Yr. Tire & Rubber Co., Akron, 1955-59; fellow Mellon Inst., Pitts., 1959-65; sr. fellow Carnegie-Mellon U., Pitts., 1965-68; assoc. prof. Calif. State U., Los Angeles, 1968-69; assoc. prof. U. So. Calif., 1969-80, prof. civil engring. and environ. engring., 1980—; cons. Universal Oil Products, 1968-76, Chevron Oil Field Research Co., 1968-75, Finnigan Corp., 1976-77, Gen. Electric Co., 1977-80, United Techs., 1978-79, TRW Inc., 1982-83, Exxon, 1981-82, DuPont, 1985—, Ministry of Petroleum, Bejing, Peoples Republic China. Author over ten tech. books; contbr. articles to profl. jours. Recipient Disting. Service award Tau Beta Pi, 1974; Imperial Crown Gold medal, Iran, 1976; Achievement award, Chinese Engring. and Sci. Assocs. of So. Calif., 1977; award Phi Kappa Phi, 1982; outstanding contbn. honor Pi Epsilon Tau, 1984. Fellow Royal Chem. Soc., Inst. Petroleum, Am. Inst. Chemists; mem. Am Chem. Soc. (chmn. geochemistry div. 1979-81). Home: 2378 N Morslay Rd Altadena CA 91001 Office: Univ So Calif University Park BHE 213A Los Angeles CA 90089

YEN, YEN-CHEN, chemical engineer, consultant; b. Shanghai, Peoples Republic of China, June 21, 1912; came to U.S., 1964; s. Chin-Chuen Yen and Pei Y.; m. Er-Ying, Sept. 9, 1939; children: Martha Meng, Madeline Chu, Rosa Chin, Margaret Chu, Benedict Tien-Sze. Diploma Engring., Tech. Hochschule, Berlin, 1937. Prof. various U.'s, Peoples Republic of China; v.p. Taiwan (Republic of China) Fertilizer Co., 1950-53; commr. Indsl. Devel. Committee, Taiwan, 1953-59; cons. Singapore and Taiwan, Republic of China, 1960-64; sr. chem. engr. SRI Internat., Menlo Park, Calif., 1965-81; cons. SRI Internat., Menlo Park, 1981—. Contbr. articles to profl. jours. Mem. Am. Chem. Soc., Am. Electrochem. Soc., Am. Inst. Chem. Engring. Home: 3373 St Michael Dr Palo Alto CA 94306 Office: SRI Internat 333 Ravenswood Ave Menlo Park CA 94025

YEO, RONALD FREDERICK, librarian; b. Woodstock, Ont., Can., Nov. 13, 1923; s. Frederick Thomas and Jugertha Aleda (Vansickle) Y.; m. Margaret Elizabeth Horsley, Oct. 12, 1953; children: Joanne, Peter. B.A., U. Toronto, 1948, B.L.S., 1966. Mgr. book dept. Am. News Co., Toronto, 1948-53; sales mgr., dir. Brit. Book Service, Toronto, 1953-63; mgr. trade div. Collier-Macmillan Can., Ltd., Toronto, 1963-65; pub. services coordinator North York (Ont.) Pub. Library, 1971; chief librarian Regina (Sask.) Pub. Library, 1971—; mem. Nat. Library Adv. Bd., 1982-87, chmn., 1986-87. Served with RCAF, 1942-45. Recipient Silver Jubilee medal, 1977. Mem. Can. Library Assn. (pres. 1978-79), Can. Assn. Pub. Libraries (chmn. 1975-76), Sask. Library Assn., Adminstrs. of Large Pub. Libraries (chmn. 1973-74). Club: Regina Kiwanis. Office: Regina Pub Library, 2311 12th Ave, Regina, SK Canada S4P 0N3

YERXA, CHARLES TUTTLE, agriculturist; b. Colusa, Calif., Nov. 29, 1918; s. Max N. and Charlotte (Tuttle) Y.; m. Virginia Wilson, Mar. 8, 1947; children—Woodford, Alison, Dorothy, Charles Tuttle. B.S., U. Calif., Berkeley, 1941. Pres. Charles T. Yerxa Farms Inc., Colusa, 1960—, Colusa-Glenn Prodn. Credit Assn., 1965-79; chmn. bd. Sunsweet Inc., Stockton, Calif., 1975—, Calif. Tomato Processing Bd., 1970-78; dir. Fed. Land Bank, 1962-75; bd. dirs. Prune Adminstrn. Com. Vice pres. Woodland Meml. Hosp., 1960-70; trustee Colusa Mosquito Abatement Com., 1965—. Served to lt. comdr. USNR, 1941-46. Republican. Episcopalian. Home: Box 269 Colusa CA 95932 Office: Sun-Diamind Growers of Calif 1050 S Diamond St Stockton CA 95201

YESINOWSKI, JAMES PAUL, chemist; b. LaSalle, Ill., Mar. 22, 1950; s. Andrew John and Agnes Agatha (Naujalis) Y. BS, U. Ill., 1971; PhD, Cambridge (Eng.) U., 1974. Research assoc. MIT, Cambridge, 1974-76; research chemist Miami Valley Labs. Procter & Gamble Co., Cin., 1976-84; mgr. So. Calif. Regional Nuclear Magnetic Resonance Facility, Pasadena, Calif., 1984—; profl. staff div. chemistry and chem. engring. Calif. Inst. Tech., 1987—. Contbr. articles to profl. jours. Mem. Am. Chem. Soc., Am. Geophys. Union. Avocations: piano playing. Home: 980 Alta Vista Dr Altadena CA 91001 Office: Calif Inst Tech 164-30 Pasadena CA 91125

YETTER, CAROL JOAN JOHNSON, audiologist; b. Portland, Oreg., May 6, 1943; d. Edwin Lawrence and Eloise Vera (Hale) Johnson; m. Richard Clarke, Aug. 21, 1965; children: Brook Barrett, Katheryn Lynn. BS, U. Oreg., 1965. Cert. tchr., Oreg. Speech pathologist Salem (Oreg.) Pub. Schs., 1965-68; speech-hearing clinician Salem Pub. Schs., 1985—; ednl. audiologist Cen. Oreg. Regional Program for Hearing/Vision Impaired, Bend, 1985—; audiology cons. St. Charles Med. Ctr., Bend, 1986. Chairperson AAUW, Salem, 1967-68; edn. chairperson St. Barnabas Episcopal Church Vestry, Portland, 1977-79; pres. Stephenson Sch. PTA, Portland, 1979-80; exec. bd. Tryon Creek State Park, Portland, 1980-82. Named Outstanding Vol. Bend-Lapine Sch. Dist., 1985. Mem. Am. Speech Lang. Hearing Assn., Oreg. Speech and Hearing Assn., Computer Users in Speech and Hearing. Democrat. Clubs: Quota Internat. (cons. 1984—, adminstr. 1985-86), P.E.O. (Bend) (edn. com. 1986-87). Home: 1426 NW Trenton Bend OR 97701 Office: Pilot Butte Med Ctr 2275 NE Doctors Dr Suite 7 Bend OR 97701

YETWIN, RICHARD MARK, lawyer; b. Elizabeth, N.J., Feb. 15, 1946; s. I. Jacques and Ruth (Horowitz) Y.; m. Deborah Joan Clark, Aug. 8, 1971; children—Jennifer, Brian. B.S., Tufts Coll., 1967; J.D., Boston U., 1971. Bar: Ariz. 1972, Mass. 1972, U.S. Supreme Ct. 1975. Atty. DeConcini, McDonald, Brammer, Yetwin, Lacy and Zimmerman, P.C., Tucson, Ariz., 1972—, mng. shareholder, 1981—; lectr. U. Ariz. Coll. Law, Tucson, 1977-82. Bd. dirs., pres. Beacon Found. for Mentally Retarded, Tucson, 1980—; bd. dirs. Jewish Family Service, 1984; head profl. div. United Way, Tucson, 1979; mem. Ariz. cancer adv. bd. U. Ariz., Tucson, 1983—. Served to capt. USAR, 1971-79. Mem. ABA, Mass. Bar Assn., Ariz. Bar Assn. Democrat. Jewish. Club: Old Pueblo (Tucson), La Paloma. Office: DeConcini McDonald Brammer Yetwin & Lacy Phelps Dodge Bldg 16th Fl 2600 N Central Phoenix AZ 85012 Office: 640 Gt Western Bank Bldg 4041 N Central St Phoenix AZ 85012

YEUNG, PETER FAI, development engineer; b. Chungking, Republic of China, Dec. 26, 1949; s. S.W. and Wai-C. (Sum) Yang. BS in Engring., U. Mich., 1972; MS, Stanford U., 1973. Staff engr. Aerotherm, Mountain View, Calif., 1973-74; mfg. engr. Hubbard & Co., Emeryville, Calif., 1974-76; sr. devel. engr. Solar Turbines Inc., San Diego, 1977—.

YGUADO, ALEX ROCCO, economics educator; b. Lackawanna, N.Y., Jan. 17, 1939; s. Manuel and Rose (Barrillio) Y.; m. Patricia Ann Rieker; children: Gary Alexander, Melissa Rose, Charissa Ann. BA, San Fernando State Coll., Northridge, 1968; MA, Calif. State U., Northridge, 1970; MS, U. So. Calif., 1972. Contractor Los Angeles, 1962-69; instr. Calif. Poly. State U., San Luis Obispo, 1969-70, U. So. Calif., Los Angeles, 1970-74; prof. econs. Mission Coll., San Fernando, Calif., 1975—; cons. Community Service Orgn., Los Angeles, 1969-71. Contbr. chpts. to books. Served with U.S. Army, 1957-58. Recipient: Blue Ribbon landscape design City of Albuquerque, 1962, Cert. Appreciation Los Angeles Mission Coll., 1978; Fulbright scholar, 1986-87. Democrat. Roman Catholic. Clubs: Newman (Los Angeles), Sierra Retreat (Malibu) (sponsor). Avocations: gardening, skiing, photography. Home: 31373 N Old Rd #F Castaic CA 91310 Office: Los Angeles Mission Coll 1212 San Fernando Rd San Fernando CA 91340

YIH, MAE DUNN, state legislator; b. Shanghai, China, May 24, 1928; d. Chung Woo and Fung Wen (Feng) Dunn; m. Stephen W.H. Yih, 1953; children—Donald, Daniel. B.A., Barnard Coll., 1951; postgrad. Columbia U., 1951-52. Asst. to bursar Barnard Coll., N.Y.C., 1952-53; mem. Oreg. Ho. of Reps. from 36th dist., 1977-83, Oreg. Senate from 19th dist., 1983—. State Democratic precinct woman; mem. Clover Ridge Elem. Sch. Bd., Albany, Oreg., from 1969, Albany Union High Sch. Bd., from 1975; mem. adv. com. Environ. Health Dept., Linn County, Oreg., from 1977. Mem. AAUW, LWV, Linn County Citizens for Retarded, Linn County Mental Health Assn., Oreg. Sch. Bd. Assn. Episcopalian. Office: Oreg Senate State Capitol Salem OR 97310 Other Address: 34465 Yih Ln NE Albany OR 97321 *

YING, KUANG LIN, cytogeneticist; b. Kiangsu, China, June 12, 1927; s. Shao Chen and Suan (Sun) Y.; m. Sun Chyi, Mar. 5, 1954; children—May Ying Wong, Bonni, Edward. B.S., Nat. Taiwan U., 1952; Ph.D., U. Sask., 1961. Sr. specialist plant industry div. Sino-Am. Joint Commn. on Rural Reconstrn., Taipei, Taiwan, 1961-64; research assoc. dept. pediatrics U. Sask., 1964-67, asst. prof. div. med. genetics, 1967-73, assoc. prof., 1973-78; dir. cytogenetics and prenatal detection lab. Valley Childrens Hosp., Fresno, Calif., 1978-81; dir. sect. cytogenetics Med. Genetics div. dept. pediatrics Childrens Hosp. Los Angeles, 1981—; assoc. prof. dept. botany Nat. Taiwan U., 1962-63; asst. prof., dir. cytogenetics lab. Meharry Med. Coll., 1970-71; vis. research scientist div. med. genetics UCLA, 1977-78; assoc. research cytogeneticist U. Calif.-San Francisco, 1978-81; assoc. clin. prof. pediatrics U. So. Calif., 1981—. NRC Can. assistantship 1957-61. Mem. Genetics Soc.

Can., Am. Soc. Human Genetics, Tissue Culture Assn. Contbr. articles to profl. jours. Office: Childrens Hosp 4650 Sunset Blvd PO Box 54700 Los Angeles CA 90054

YINGLING, ROY DONALD (DON), JR., technical engineer, researcher; b. Dallas, Apr. 26, 1943; s. Roy Donald Sr. and Lucienne (McNiel) Y. AS, El Centro Coll., 1970; student, Tex. Tech U., 1961-64. Sr. engring. tech. Tex. Instruments, Dallas, 1964-76; mem. tech. staff Rockwell Internat., Anaheim, Calif., 1976-79; mem. research staff Xerox Palo Alto (Calif.) Research Ctr., 1979—. Contbr. chpt. to book, articles to profl. jours. Recipient Spl. Service award Tex. Instruments, 1973, Spl. Recognition award Xerox Corp., 1984. Mem. Am. Vacuum Soc. Democrat. Unitarian. Avocations: photography, home remodeling. Home: 46 Clipper St San Francisco CA 94114 Office: Xerox Palo Alto Research Ctr 3333 Coyote Hill Rd Palo Alto CA 94304

YOCAM, DELBERT WAYNE, computer company executive; b. Long Beach, Calif., Dec. 24, 1943; s. Royal Delbert and Mary Rose (Gross) Y.; m. Janet McVeigh, June 13, 1965; children—Eric Wayne, Christian Jeremy, Elizabeth Janelle. B.A. in Bus. Adminstrn., Calif. State U.-Fullerton, 1966; M.B.A., Calif. State U., Long Beach, 1971. Mktg.-supply changeover coordinator Automotive Assembly div. Ford Motor Co., Dearborn, Mich., 1966-72; prodn. control mgr. Control Data Corp., Hawthorne, Calif., 1972-74; prodn. and material control mgr. Bourns Inc., Riverside, Calif., 1974-76; corp. material mgr. Computer Automation Inc., Irvine, Calif., 1976-78; prodn. planning mgr. central staff Cannon Electric div. ITT, World hdqrs., Santa Ana, Calif., 1978-79; exec. v.p., chief operating officer Apple Computer Inc., Cupertino, Calif., 1979—; mem. faculty Cypress Coll., Calif., 1972-79. Active Los Angeles County Heart Assn., 1966. Mem. Control Data Corp. Mgmt. Assn. (co-founder 1974). Republican. Methodist. Office: Apple Computer Inc 20525 Mariani Ave Cupertino CA 95014

YOCHELSON, SAUL B., electrical engineer; b. Cleve., Dec. 1, 1925; s. Julius and Etta (Lesser) Y.; m. Barbara Baturin, Dec. 7, 1952; children: Alan Scott, Karen Ann. BEE, Ohio State U., 1948; MSEE, U. Ill., 1950. Registered profl. engr., Ohio. Aero. research scientist NACA, Cleve., 1948-51; sr. engring. specialist Goodyear Aircraft, Akron, Ohio, 1951-61; staff engr. Librascope, Glendale, Calif., 1961-62, Lockheed Missile and Space Co., Van Nuys, Calif., 1962-64; chief scientist Hughes Aircraft Co., El Segundo, Calif., 1964—. Patentee in field; contbr. articles to profl. jours. Served with Merchant Marine, 1944-46. Mem. IEEE. Avocation: amateur radio. Home: 10010 Lasaine Ave Northridge CA 91325 Office: Hughes Aircraft Co PO Box 92426 MS R11/11044 Los Angeles CA 90009

YOCUM, HAROLD AMOS, physician; b. Chambersburg, Pa., June 1, 1942; s. John Francis and Evelyn Mary (Frye) Y.; m. Paula Rae Ross, Aug. 30, 1969 (div. June 1978); m. Maryjo Gilbert, July 15, 1978; children: (stepson) Michael Moritz, Heather Maryjo, Holly Roselyn. BS, Juniata Coll.; MD, Jefferson Med. Coll. Intern, then resident Sacred Heart Hosp., Spokane, Wash., 1968-70; commd. 2d lt. U.S. Army, 1970, advanced through grades to lt. col., resigned, 1981; orthopedic surgeon Kaiser Perm. of Colo., Denver, 1981-84; practice medicine specializing in hand surgery Lakewood, Colo., 1984—; cons. orthopedic surgery U.S. Army, Europe, 1978-81; chief med. officer Boy Scout Jamboree, Va., 1985; assc. clin. prof. orthopedics U. Colo. Sch. Medicine, Denver, 1985-86. Mem. health and safety com. Boy Scouts Am. Nat. Council, Irvine, Tex., 1983—. Served to col. USAR, 1986. Recipient Silver Beaver award Boy Scouts Am., Tex., 1975, Religion and Youth award Unitarian/Universalist, Boston, 1985. Fellow ACS, Am. Acad. Orthopedic Surgeons; mem. Western Orthopedic Assn., Soc. Mil. Orthopedic Surgeons, Nat. Eagle Scout Assn. (nat. com. 1982—, Disting. Service award, 1984). Lodges: Masons, Shriners. Avocations: skiing, camping, art, birdwatching, scout leader. Home: 3140 Alkire St Golden CO 80401 Office: 2020 Wadsworth Lakewood CO 80215

YODER, GENE FRANCIS, geologist; b. Washington, Iowa, May 17, 1934; s. Glenn Clayton and Elizabeth Margaret (Bauer) Y.; student U. Iowa, 1952-56; B.S. in Geology, Western State Coll. of Colo., 1959; m. Marilyn L. Scott, June 19, 1954; children—Christy Moore, Jene, Beth, David. Jr. geologist Pinnacle Exploration, Inc., Gunnison, Colo., 1956-60; asst. store mgr. oil field supply Franklin Supply Co., Moab, Utah, 1960-63; sr. geologist, mine supt. Homestake Mining Co., Kenedy, Tex., Casper, Wyo., Gunnison, Colo., and La Sal, Utah, 1963-74; land mgr. metals div. Union Carbide Corp., Grand Junction, Colo., 1974—; uranium cons., 1974. Mem. Grand Junction dist. adv. council Bur. Land Mgmt. Served with U.S. Army, 1954-56. Mem. Am. Mining Congress (public lands com. 1976—), Am. Assn. Petroleum Landmen (chmn. mining and geothermal com. 1979), Rocky Mountain Assn. Mineral Landmen, N.Mex. Mining Assn., Colo. Mining Assn., AIME, Soc. Mining Engrs. Republican. Lutheran. Home: 2813 Mesa Ave Grand Junction CO 81501 Office: PO Box 1029 Grand Junction CO 81502

YODER, JAMES EDWARD, ranch executive; b. Wooster, Ohio, Aug. 19, 1934; s. Harold James and Zella Mae (Yoder) Y.; m. Nancy Rose Bibler, Aug. 23, 1953; children: Vicki Lynn, Kinzie Mae, James Albert, Edward Allen. BS, Andrews U., 1956; postgrad., UCLA, 1963-64, IBM Corp., 1959-75, Control Data Inst., 1975. Acct. Loma Linda (Calif.) Found., 1956-59; dir. data processing Loma Linda U., 1959-75; mgr. Double "D" Land and Cattle Co., Lakeview, Oreg., 1975-78; instr. vocat. edn. Klamath-Lake County Youth Ranch, Bonanza, Oreg., 1978-80, exec. dir., 1980—; instr. computers San Bernardino (Calif.) Valley Coll., 1966-69, health-related professions Loma Linda U., 1969-75; treas. and mgr. La Loma Employees Fed. Credit Union, Loma Linda, 1958-74. Coordinator Youth Activities Dept., Southeast Calif. Conf. Seventh-Day Adventists, Riverside, 1973-75; treas. local Seventh-day Adventist Chs., Calif. and Oreg., 1958-75, elder, 1958-86. Recipient Charles Palmer Davis award Am. Ednl. Press, 1951-52. Mem. Oreg. Assn. Residential Youth Care Ctrs. (steering com. 1984-86), Loma Linda Flying Club (treas. 1970-75). Republican. Club: Pathfinders (bd. dirs. 1965-73). Avocations: hiking, backpacking, reading, bird watching, flying. Home and Office: Rt 1 Box 751 Bonanza OR 97623

YOKELL, MICHAEL DAVID, economist; b. Plattsburgh, N.Y., Nov. 21, 1946; s. Stanley Yokell and Edith Helen Gersen. Asst. prof. Wash. State U., 1975-76, U. Calif., Berkeley, 1976-77; sr. economist Solar Energy Research Inst., Berkeley, 1977-79; pres. Energy & Resource Cons., Boulder, Colo., 1979—; mng. ptnr. RRR Leasing Co.; course dir. Ctr. Profl. Advancement, New Brunswick, N.J. Author: (with June Taylor) Yellowcake: The International Uranium Cartel, 1979, The Environmental Benefits and Costs of Solar Energy, 1980. Chmn. Fellowship com. Am. Alpine Club, 1977-80. Named Colo./Okla. Bus. Man of Year. Mem. Nat. Assn. Bus. Economists, Internat. Assn. Energy Economists, AAAS, Am. Arbitrator Assn. Avocations: mountaineering, langs., travel. Office: Energy & Resource Cons Inc PO Drawer 0 Boulder CO 80306

YOKOM, DIANE ELAINE, retail design consultant; b. Detroit, Aug. 11, 1949; d. Robert William and Dorothy Mae (Leddick) Y.; m. John Richard Houghtaling, June 29, 1985. BS in Interior Design, Mich. State U., 1971. Designer Morse Shoe, Canton, Mass.; then designer Creative Atmospheres, Boston, Yokom Design, Boston, The Architects Collaborative, Cambridge, Mass.; then retail design cons. The Rouse Co., Columbia, Md., Durango, Colo.; lectr. The Rouse Co., 1983—, Melvin Simon and Assocs.; photographer workshops, seminars, shops and developers, 1985—; mfr. Sugarplum Stockings, Durango, 1986. Author: Retail Design Idea Book, 1985; (instrnl. videotape) Visual Merchandising-10 Steps to Success; designer The Chocolate Rule, 1980— (Silver medal 1980). Recipient Merit award Communication Arts, 1980, Merit award Art Dirs. Club Boston, 1978, 80. Mem. Nat. Trust for Hist. Preservation, Save the Children Found. Avocations: skiing, graphic design, sewing. Office: Yokom Design Cons PO Box 1091 Durango CO 81302

YOKOTA, GLEN ISAO, wholesale co. exec.; b. Kyoto, Japan, Apr. 25, 1938; s. Aguru and Shizue Yokota; B.S. in Aero. Engring., Osaka Furitsu U., 1962; m. Yoko Hamano, Oct. 12, 1966; children—Osamu, Yumi, Jake. Supr., C. Itoh & Co., Tokyo, 1962-68, asst. mgr., N.Y.C., 1968-70, mgr., 1970-73; exec. v.p. C. Itoh Aviation, Inc., Los Angeles, 1973-74; pres. Nat. Dynamics Corp., Lomita, Calif., 1975—; pres. CTK Industries, Inc., Lomita, 1980—. Home: 26392 Via Conchita Mission Viejo CA 92691 Office: 3001 Redhill Ave Suite 5-104 Costa Mesa CA 92626

YONISH, BRIAN GEORGE, lawyer; b. Rantoul, Ill., Mar. 24, 1958; s. George and Irene Rose (Charinko) Y.; m. Kersten Ann Luebbers, Sept. 17, 1983. BA, Creighton U., 1980, JD, 1983; postgrad., Naval Justice Sch., 1983. Bar: Nebr. 1983, U.S. Dist. Ct. Nebr. 1983, U.S. Ct. Appeals (8th cir.) 1983, U.S. Ct. Mil. Appeals, 1986. Def. and trial counsel USN, Seattle, 1984-85; staff judge advocate USN, San Diego, 1985—. Served to lt. USNR, 1981—. Mem. ABA, Nebr. State Bar, Assn. Trial Lawyers Am., U.S. Naval Inst., Pi Sigma Alpha. Democrat. Roman Catholic. Avocations: private pilot, running, skiing, tennis, racquetball. Home: 4547 Rueda Dr San Diego CA 92124 Office: USS McKee FPO San Francisco CA 96621-2620

YOO, JAY KUN, lawyer; b. Seoul, Republic of Korea, Sept. 19, 1937; came to U.S., 1969; s. Byung Yol and Sang Lim (Kim) Y.; m. Sungsoo Yoo, Mar. 7, 1968; children: Sarah, Peter, Andrew. BA, Yonsei U., Seoul, 1960, MA, 1965; MS, Brigham Young U., 1971; JD, U. Calif., Davis, 1977. Bar: Hawaii 1982, D.C. 1986, U.S. Supreme Ct. 1986. Sole practice Los Angeles, 1983—. Author: Guidebook for Naturalization, 1986, Immigration Law Theory and Practice, 1978. Mem. Human Right Commn., Sacramento, 1982-83. Recipient Civil Right Service award Koreatimes, 1979. Mem. Am. Immigration Lawyers Assn., Korea Am. Coalition (bd. dirs. 1983—). Office: 3424 Wilshire Blvd Suite 1000 Los Angeles CA 90010

YOON, DO YEUNG, polymer physicist, physical chemist; b. Inchon, Republic of Korea, Jan. 22, 1947; came to U.S., 1969; s. Pyung-Tae and Ok-Soon (Lee) Y.; m. Ki-Seup Hyun, June 5, 1971; children: Eunice, Jean, Hayne. BS, Seoul Nat. U., Republic of Korea, 1969; MS, U. Mass., 1971, PhD, 1973. Postdoctoral research assoc. Stanford U., Palo Alto, Calif., 1973-75; research staff mem. IBM, San Jose, Calif., 1975—, mgr. polymer physics, 1978—. Co-author: Selected Works of Paul J. Flory, 1985; contbr. articles to profl. jours. Mem. AAAS, Am. Phys. Soc., Am. Chem. Soc. Home: 17521 Pine Cone Ct Monte Sereno CA 95030 Office: IBM Almaden Research Ctr Dept K91-801 650 Harry Rd San Jose CA 95120-6099

YORDON, JEAN WALZER, social worker; b. Mt. Vernon, N.Y., Jan. 3, 1933; d. Ralph S. and Pearl (Silver) Gelardo; m. Herman Walzer, Oct. 2, 1954 (dec. Aug. 1974); children: Christopher John, Nancy Jean Walzer; m. Wesley James Yordon Jr., Oct. 23, 1982. BA, CCNY, 1954; MSW, U. Denver, 1970. Lic. social worker II, Colo. Caseworker Dept. Welfare, Denver, 1956-60, 63-64; adult program dir. YWCA, Boulder, Colo., 1966; psychiat. social worker Adams County Mental Health Ctr., Adams City, Colo., 1971-72; master social worker St. Vrain Valley Pub. Schs., Longmont, Colo., 1972-73; psychiat. social worker Mental Health Ctr. Boulder County, 1973-80; pvt. practice psychotherapy Boulder, 1981—; dep. probation officer Boulder Junvenile Dept., 1967. Chmn., sec., co-founder CORE, Denver, 1962-63; chmn. program com. Older Women's League, 1986—. Mem. Nat. Assn. Social Workers. Democrat. Congregationalist. Avocations: acting, playing piano. Home and Office: 1655 Dogwood Ln Boulder CO 80302

YORK, CARL MONROE, director philanthropic foundation; b. Macon, Ga., July 2, 1925; s. Carl Monroe and Eugenia (Anderson) Y.; m. Nancy Joan Sutton, Mar. 21, 1952 (div. June 1968); children: Christopher, Paul, Leila; m. Mary Nell Lewis, June 21, 1969. BA, U. Calif., Berkeley, 1946, MA, 1950, PhD, 1951. Asst. prof. physics U. Chgo., 1954-60; prof., asst. chancellor UCLA, 1960-69; tech. asst. U.S. Exec. Office of Pres., Washington, 1969-72; vice chancellor U. Denver, 1972-75; pres. York & Assocs., Oakland, Calif., 1975-84; dir. System Devel. Found., Palo Alto, Calif., 1984—. Fellow Guggenheim, 1959-60, Fulbright, 1951-52, Atomic Energy Commn., 1950-51. Mem. AAAS, Am. Phys. Soc. Home: 62 Starview Dr Oakland CA 94618 Office: System Devel Found One Maritime Plaza Suite 1770 San Francisco CA 94111

YORK, HARRY LAWRENCE, chamber of commerce executive; b. Grants Pass, Oreg., Aug. 8, 1944; s. Evans H. and Clara A. (Zumstein) Y.; m. Patricia M. Wolfe, Feb. 21, 1964 (div. Oct. 1977); children: John F., David A.; m. Sharon Kay Grisham, Dec. 26, 1977; 1 child, Christina Ruth. Student, Diablo Valley Coll.; grad., Inst. Organizational Mgmt. Mgr. Silver Dollar Garden Ctr., Concord, Calif., 1960-72; adminstrv. asst. Calif. Legis., Concord, 1972-80; exec. v.p. Concord C. of C., 1980—; pres. York & Assocs., Concord, 1978-81. Mem. park and recreation commn., Concord, 1970-73, planning commn., Concord, 1970-79, chmn. 1973, 76; mem. Mt. Diablo Sch. Dist. Bd., Concord, 1979-83, pres. 1982. Mem. Am. Assn. Chamber Execs., Calif. Assn. Chamber Execs. (bd. dirs. 1982-84). Democrat. Roman Catholic. Lodge: Rotary. Avocations: photography, hiking. Home: 36 Kirkwood Ct Concord CA 94521 Office: Concord C of C 2151 Salvio St Suite A Concord CA 94520

YORK, HERBERT FRANK, educator, government official; b. Rochester, N.Y., Nov. 24, 1921; s. Herbert Frank and Nellie Elizabeth (Lang) Y.; m. Sybil Dunford, Sept. 28, 1947; children: David Winters, Rachel, Cynthia. A.B., U. Rochester, 1942, M.S., 1943; Ph.D., U. Calif.-Berkeley, 1949; D.Sc. (hon.), Case Inst. Tech., 1960; LL.D., U. San Diego, 1964, Claremont Grad. Sch., 1974. Physicst Radiation Lab., U. Calif., Berkeley, 1943-58; asso. dir. Radiation Lab., U. Calif., 1954-58; asst. prof. physics dept. U. Calif., 1951-54, assoc. prof., 1954-59, prof., 1959—; dir. Lawrence Radiation Lab., Livermore, 1952-58; chief scientist Advanced Research Project Agy., Dept. Def., 1958; dir. advanced research projects div. Inst. for Def. Analyses, 1958; dir. def. research and engring. Office of Sec. Def. 1958-61; chancellor U. Calif.-San Diego, 1961-64, 70-72, prof. physics, 1964—, chmn. dept. physics, 1968-69, dean grad. studies, 1969-70, dir. program on sci., tech. and pub. affairs, 1972—; dir. Inst. Global Conflict and Cooperation, 1983—; ambassador Comprehensive Test Ban Negotiations, 1979-81; trustee Aerospace Corp., Inglewood, Calif., 1961—; mem. President's Sci. Adv. Com., 1957-58, 64-68, vice chmn., 1965-67; trustee Inst. Def. Analysis, 1963—; gen. adv. com. ACDA, 1962-69; mem. Def. Sci. Bd., 1977-81; spl. rep. of sec. def. at space arms control talks, 1978-79; cons. Stockholm Internat. Peace Research Inst.; mem. assessment adv. com. Office Sci. and Tech. Author: Race to Oblivion, 1970, Arms Control, 1973, The Advisors, 1976, Making Weapons, Talking Peace, 1987, Does Strategic Defense Breed Offense?, 1987; also numerous articles on arms or disarmament.; bd. dirs. Bull Atomic Scientists. Trustee Bishop's Sch., La Jolla, Calif., 1963-65. Recipient E.O. Lawrence award AEC, 1962; Guggenheim fellow, 1972. Fellow Am. Phys. Soc. (Forum on Physics and Society award 1976), Am. Acad. Arts and Scis.; mem. Inst. Aero. Scis., Internat. Acad. Astronautics, Fedn. Am. Scientists (chmn. 1970-71, mem. exec. com. 1969-76), Phi Beta Kappa, Sigma Xi. Research in application atomic energy to nat. def., problems of arms control and disarmament, elementary particles. Home: 6110 Camino de la Costa La Jolla CA 92037 Office: Mail Code Q-060 U Calif-San Diego La Jolla CA 92093

YORK, ROBERT EARL, elementary education administrator, fruits and vegetables grader; b. Goodland, Kans., Aug. 8, 1931; s. George Earl and Perna (Ransier) Y.; m. Mary Ann Albers, Dec. 23, 1961; children—Robert Earl, Sherri Ann. B.A., San Francisco State Coll., 1959; M.A., U. Pacific, 1968. Tchr., Ceres Unified Sch. Dist. (Calif.), 1953-62; grader U.S. Dept. Agr., Stockton, Calif., summers 1957—; supt., prin. Paradise Sch. Dist., Modesto, Calif., 1962—. Mem. Calif. Tchrs. Assn. Democrat. Mem. Assembly of God Ch. Home: 1800 Bannister Pl Modesto CA 95355 Office: Paradise Sch Dist 3361 California Ave Modesto CA 95351

YORK, RUTH B., educator; b. Boston, June 20, 1924; d. V. Everett and Beatrice C. (McGuire) Y. A.A., Graceland Coll., 1943; B.A., U. Iowa, 1945, M.A., 1947; Ph.D., Columbia U., 1963. Instr. Graceland Coll., Lamoni, Iowa, 1947-56; asst. prof. Ill. Coll., Jacksonville, 1956-59; lectr., then asst. prof. Columbia U., N.Y.C., 1959-65; asst. prof. U. Calif.-Davis, 1965-71, lectr., 1971-82, sr. lectr., chmn., 1981—, com. French XX Bibliography, 1961—. Contbr. articles and revs. to profl. jours. Fulbright fellow, 1954; Columbia U. Pres.'s fellow, 1959, 60; Samuel Fels Found. fellow, 1962. Mem. MLA, Am. Assn. Tchrs. French, Philological Assn. Pacific Coast, Assn. Internat. des Amis de Valery Larbaud. Home: 818 Barcelona Davis CA 95616 Office: Dept French and Italian U Calif Davis CA 95616

YORK, SUSAN DEBORAH, marketing professional; b. Newark, N.J.. Student, Rutgers U.; BA, U. S. Fla., 1978. Retail services dir. Bonne Bell, Tampa, Fla., 1976-78; with admissions Barbizon Schs., Tampa, 1978; advt. sales Clouds Jeans, N.Y.C., 1978-79; advt., mktg. dir. Ditto of Calif., Los Angeles, 1979-81; mktg. editor, dir. Miss Teenage Am. program and Gt. Model search Teen mag., Los Angeles, 1979-86; pres. Inserts, Los Angeles, 1986—; dir. Miss Teenage Am. Program, 1981—, Teen Mag's Great Model Search, 1981—. Office: Teen Mag 8490 Sunset Blvd Los Angeles CA 90292

YORK, TINA, artist; b. Bautzen, Fed. Republic Germany, Feb. 9, 1951; came to U.S., 1962; d. Albert Max and Erika (Bernd) Huhle. Student, N.Y. Med. Coll., 1980-83; BA cum laude, Brandeis U., 1978. Exhibited at Palais des Congress, Paris, 1975; one-man shows include Copley Soc., Boston, 1972-73, Cambridge (Mass.) Art Assn., 1975; prin. works include The Creation, 1975; complete 45 painting series involving medicine, physics, astronomy, philosophy and chemistry 1986. Mem. art commn. Columbia U., N.Y.C., 1985, Harkness Eye Inst. Hon. mention Lowell (Mass.) Internat. Festival of Art, 1973, Beverly Hills (Calif.) Spring Festival of Arts, 1984; recipient 1st prize Scitvate (Mass.) Internat. Festival of Art, 1975. Office: PO Box 10842 Beverly Hills CA 92130

YOSHIMOTO, HIROKO, art educator; b. Kobe, Japan, Apr. 23, 1943; came to U.S., 1958; d. Akira and Teiko (Takahashi) Y.; m. Allen Walton Jue, June 19, 1977 (separated). BA with highest honors, UCLA, 1965, MA with highest honors, 1967. Cert. tchr., Calif. Freelance designer Los Angeles, 1967-68; graphic designer Zamparelli Graphics, Los Angeles, 1968; with IBM Japan, Tokyo, 1968-70; instr. studio art Ventura (Calif.) Coll., 1970—; instr. Santa Ana (Calif.) Coll., 1970; artistic dir. Studio 83, Ventura, 1983-85. One-woman shows include Ventura Hist. Mus., 1978, Gallery 932, Ventura, 1982, Ventura County Govt. Ctr. Atrium Gallery, 1983; exhibited in group shows at Grandview Gallery, Los Angeles, Los Angeles Artcore Gallery, 1984, 86, Los Angeles County Mus. Art Rental Gallery, 1987. Mem. Am. Fedn. Tchrs., Ventura Art Assn. Democrat. Avocation: tennis. Home: 352 Lupine Way Ventura CA 93001 Office: Ventura Coll 4667 Telegraph Rd Ventura CA 93001

YOSHIOKA, VERNON TADAO, aerospace engineer; b. Hayward, Calif., Feb. 21, 1938; s. Giichi and June Noriko (Nishi) Y.; m. Shinobu Kobayashi, Sept. 18, 1965; children: Charles O. Bender, Carol A. Sainz, Linda L. Bender, Christine M. BS in Aero. and Astronautical Engring., MIT, 1960. Aero. engr. Ryan Aero. Co., San Diego, 1960-62; dynamics Gen. Dynamics Astronautics, San Diego, 1962-64; dynamics engr. Teledyne Ryan Aero. San Diego, 1964-68, tech. specialist, 1968—. Mem. San Diego Japanese Am. Citizens League, 1960—, bd. dirs., 1970-80, 82—, v.p. membership and services, 1980-83, pres. San Diego chpt., 1986—; founding chmn. Union of Pan Asian Communities, San Diego, 1973-76, bd. dirs., 1973-86; mem. citizens adv. com. San Diego City Coll., 1974—; bd. dirs. Kiku Gardens Inc., San Diego, 1979-86; chmn. San Diego Noise Abatement and Control Bd., 1980-84. Mem. AIAA, Assn. of Unmanned Vehicle Systems. Republican. Mem. United Church of Christ. Home: 6968 Glenflora Ave San Diego CA 92119 Office: Teledyne Ryan Aero 2701 Harbor Dr San Diego CA 92138

YOSHIZUMI, DONALD TETSURO, dentist; b. Honolulu, Feb. 18, 1930; s. Richard Kiyoshi and Hatsue (Tanouye) Y.; B.S., U. Hawaii, 1952; D.D.S., U. Mo., 1960, M.S., 1963; m. Barbara Fujiko Iwashita, June 25, 1955; children—Beth Ann E., Cara Leigh S, Erin Yuri. Clin. instr. U. Mo. Sch. Dentistry, Kansas City, 1960-63; gen. practice dentistry Santa Clara, Calif., 1963-70, San Jose, Calif., 1970—. Served with USAF, 1952-56. Mem. Am., Calif. dental assns., Santa Clara County Dental Soc., Omicron Kappa Upsilon, Delta Sigma Delta. Contbr. articles to profl. jours. Home: 5054 Parkfield Ave San Jose CA 95129 Office: 2011 Forest Ave San Jose CA 95128

YOST, GEORGE PALMER, physics researcher; b. Pitts., Mar. 7, 1942; s. George and Frances (Palmer) Y.; m. Frances Elizabeth Farrington, June 10, 1966; children: Eve Christina, Chelsea Sarah. AB, Princeton U., 1963; PhD, U. Md., 1969. Research assoc. Fla. State U., Tallahassee, 1968-71; asst. research physicist U. Calif., Berkeley, 1971-74, 1976-81, full specialist, 1981—; physicist P5 Lawrence Berkeley Lab., 1974-76, dir. particle data group, 1982-83. Contbr. articles to profl. jours. Mem. Am. Inst. Physics. Avocations: squash, weightlifting, chess. Home: 615 36th St Richmond CA 94805 Office: Lawrence Berkeley Lab 1 Cyclotron Rd MS 50/308 Berkeley CA 94720

YOUMANS, ANNE STEWART, research microbiologist; b. Springfield, Mo., Sept. 26, 1916; d. Roscoe and Clara Louise (Bell) Stewart; m. Guy Parry Youmans, Mar. 17, 1945. AB, Stanford U., 1938; MS, PhD, Northwestern U. Med. Sch., 1946. Diplomate Am. Bd. Microbiology. Asst. in bacteriology Northwestern U. Med. Sch., Chgo., 1946-49, instr. microbiology, 1949-61, asst. prof., 1961-64, assoc. prof., 1964-71, prof., 1971-76, prof. emeritus, 1976—; vis. prof. U. Ariz., Tucson, 1976—. Contbr. articles and monographs to profl. jours. Recipient Pasteur award Ill. Soc. Microbiology, 1970. Fellow AAAS, Am. Acad. Microbiology; mem. Am. Assn. Immunologists, Am. Soc. Microbiology, Reticuo-endotheral Soc., Sigma Xi. Republican. Presbyterian. Home: 2134 E Adams Tucson AZ 85719

YOUMANS, PAUL EDWIN, investment banker; b. Fort Smith, Ark., June 1, 1902; s. Frank Abijah and Delia (Enroughty) Y.; B.S. in Bus. and Public Adminstrn., U. Mo., 1923; m. Katherine St. John Carter, June 7, 1928 (dec.); 1 dau., Anne Carter Youmans Mason. Entered investment banking through Nat. Bank of Commerce, St. Louis, 1923; joined Internat. Trust Co., Denver, 1927; with Nat. City Co., 1928-29; joined Sullivan & Co., 1930, partner 1941-46; dir. Bosworth, Sullivan & Co., Inc., Denver, mem. N.Y. Stock Exchange, 1952-74; exec. v.p. Dain, Bosworth, Inc., 1979-80; dir. emeritus Inter-Regional Fin. Group, Inc.; bd. govs. Midwest Stock Exchange, 1969-71. Trustee, Blue Shield Plan, Denver, 1962-70. Mem. Investment Bankers Assn. Am. (gov. 1952-55), Nat. Assn. Securities Dealers (gov. 1960-63), Assn. Stock Exchange Firms (gov. 1965-70), Phi Delta Theta. Episcopalian. Clubs: Univ., Rotary (Denver), Mile High. Home: 480 S Marion St Pkwy Denver CO 80209 Office: 1225 17th St Denver CO 80202

YOUNG, C. CLIFTON, state supreme court justice; b. Nov. 7, 1922. B.A., U. Nev., 1943; LL.B., Harvard U., 1949; justice Nev. Supreme Ct., Carson City, 1985—. Office: Nev Supreme Ct Supreme Ct Bldg Carson City NV 89710

YOUNG, CHARLES EDWARD, university chancellor; b. San Bernardino, Calif., Dec. 30, 1931; s. Clayton Charles and Eula May (Walters) Y. A.A., San Bernardino Coll., 1954; A.B., U. Calif.-Riverside, 1955; M.A., U. Calif.-Riverside, Los Angeles, 1957, Ph.D., 1960; D.H.L. (hon.), U. Judaism, Los Angeles, 1969. Congl. fellow Washington, 1958-59; adminstrv. analyst Office of the Pres., U. Calif., Berkeley, 1959-60; asst. prof. polit. sci. U. Calif., Davis, 1960; asst. prof. polit. sci. UCLA, 1960-66, assoc. prof., 1966-69, prof., 1969—, asst. to chancellor, 1960-62, asst. chancellor, 1962-63, vice chancellor, adminstrn., 1963-68, now chancellor.; dir. UMF Systems, Inc., Intel Corp., Am. Savs. and Loan Assn., Fin. Corp. Am.; Cons. Peace Corps., 1961-62, to Ford Found. on Latin Am. Activities, 1964-66. Mem. Nat. Com. on U.S.-China Relations; mem. chancellor's assos. UCLA; past chair. Assn. Am. Univs.; mem. adminstrv. bd. Internat. Assn. Univs.; bd. govs. Found. Internat. Exchange Sci. and Cultural Info. by Telecommunications, The Theatre Group Inc.; mem. founding com., chair Mansfield Center for Pacific Affairs; v.p. Young Musicians Found.; bd. dirs. Los Angeles Internat. Visitors Council, Greater Los Angeles Energy Coalition; Trustee UCLA Found. Served with USAF, 1951-52. Named Young Man of Year Westwood Jr. C. of C., 1962. Office: UCLA Chancellor's Office 405 Hilgard Ave Los Angeles CA 90024

YOUNG, DAVE JESSE, mining company executive; b. Sheridan, Wyo., July 24, 1949; s. James Marshall Young and Phyllis Irene (Davis) Young Doyle; m. Julieanne Elaine Kastens, Mar. 20, 1977 (div. Mar. 1982); one child, Nathan; m. Karen Elizabeth Rogers, Aug. 12, 1983; stepchildren: Jade Harney, Michele Harney. Grad. high sch., Buffalo, Wyo. 2d class FCC lic. Warehouse mgr. Contractors Supply, Gillette, Wyo., 1973-75; inside sales mgr. Dakota Steel, Gillette, 1975-77; sr. warehouse technician Amax Coal Co., Gillette, 1977—. Del. Wyo. Rep. State Conv., 1985; state v.p. Young Ams. for Freedom, 1969. Mem. Nat. Metallic Handgun Shooters Assn., Nat. Rifle Assn., Wyo. State Shooters Assn., No. Rodeo Assn. Club: Gillette Gun. Avocations: handgun shooting, rodeo, auto restoration, bowling. Home: 3005 Foothills Rd Gillette WY 82716

YOUNG, DAVID ALLYN, clinical psychologist; b. Sacramento, Calif., Jan. 3, 1956; s. Bing Hin and Evelyn (Yuen) Y. BA, U. Calif., Santa Barbara, 1978; MA, Calif. Sch. Profl. Psychology, Los Angeles, 1980; PhD, Calif. Sch. Profl. Psychology, 1982; M in Pub. Health, Harvard U., 1984. Lic. psychologist, Calif. Intern Orange County Dept. Mental Health, Fullerton, Calif., 1980-81, U. So. Calif., Los Angeles, 1981-82; spl. scientific assoc. Boston City Hosp., 1984; orgnl. cons. ABA Groups, Inc., Hermosa Beach, Calif., 1984-85; pediatric psychologist Childrens Hosp. Orange County, Orange, Calif., 1985-86; pvt. practice psychology Health Psychology Assocs., Inc., 1986—; coordinator psychol. services for hematology and oncology Childrens Hosp. Orange County, 1985—, coordinator clin. tng. program, 1985—; behavioral cons. Behavioral Edn. and Learning Inst., Los Angeles, 1980-81; instr. Calif. State Univ., Fullerton, 1985—. Interviewed for feature series on cancer treatment, childhood illnesses to Los Angeles Times, Orange County Register, 1985-86, interviewed for video presentation, Teenage Suicide: Preventive Advice, 1986; contbr. research papers to psychol. and med. jours. Active Pediatric Cancer Research Found., Orange, 1986—, spl. populations task force Am. Cancer Soc. Postdoctoral teaching fellow Boston U. Sch. Medicine, 1982-83; named one of Outstanding Young Men Am. U.S. Jaycees, 1984. Mem. Am. Psychol. Assn. (chmn. ethnic minority affairs com. 1984-86), Calif. State Psychol. Assn., Soc. Pediatric Psychologists, Asian-Am. Psychol. Assn., Assn. for Advancement Psychology, Inst. for Advancement Health. Democrat. Avocations: surfing, skiing, tennis, people watching. Office: Health Psychology Assocs Inc 705 W LaVeta Suite 208 Orange CA 92668

YOUNG, DAVID EUGENE, physician; b. Chgo., June 28, 1953; s. Wilbur E. and Jane H. (Lundgren) Y.; m. Renée Roxanne Young, Feb. 11, 1978. BA, Hope Coll., 1975; MD, U. Ill., Rockford, 1979. Diplomate Am. Bd. Internal Medicine. Intern then resident San Joaquin Gen. Hosp., Stockton, Calif., 1979-83; staff physician Colo. Permanente Med. Group, Denver, 1983-86; fellow in oncology Harbor-UCLA Med. Ctr., Torrance, 1986—. Mem. AMA, ACP, Phi Beta Kappa. Avocations: composing concert music, traveling. Home: 16712 Saybrook Ln #218 Huntington Beach CA 92649

YOUNG, DAVID THAD, astrophyscist; b. Port of Spain, Trinidad and Tobago, Apr. 18, 1943; s. Mayo Thad and Alma Marie (David) Y.; m. Jane Stephanie Dunlap, Sept. 6, 1966; children: Matthew, Amy, Jacob, Jessica. BS, U. Southwestern La., 1964; MS, Rice U., 1967, PhD, 1970; Venia Docendi, U. Berne, Switzerland, 1980. Vis. scientist Royal Inst. Tech., Stockholm, 1971; sr. research assoc. U. Berne, 1971-80, privat docent, 1980—; mem. staff Los Alamos (N.Mex.) Nat. Lab., 1981—; cons. European Space Agy., Paris, 1976-77, 80-85, Southwest Research Inst., San Antonio, Tex., 1982—, NASA, Washington, 83, 84, 85. Contbr. articles to profl. jours.; inventor spacecraft instruments. Woodrow Wilson fellow 1964. Mem. Am. Geophys. Union, European Geophys. Soc., Internat. Assn. Geomagnetism Aeronomy (reporter 1981—), Hill City Pacers (founder, pres. 1983-85). Avocations: running, skiing. Home: 2159-B 43d St Los Alamos NM 87544 Office: Los Alamos Nat Lab PO Box 1663 MS D438 Los Alamos NM 87545

YOUNG, DON ANDREW, urologist; b. Detroit, Oct. 26, 1937; s. Don A. and Stella M. (Orlow) Y.; m. Elaine Ann Hurney, Dec. 3, 1967; children: Kelly Elizabeth, Holly Cambridge, Meghan Andrea. BA, U. Colo., 1959; MD, Wayne State U., 1963, degree in urology, 1971. Diplomate Am. Bd. Urology. Intern in surgery Emanuel Hosp., Portland, Oreg., 1963-65; resident in urology Detroit Gen. Hosp., 1967-71; practice medicine specializing in urology Portland, 1971—. Served to capt. USAF, 1965-67, Vietnam. Mem. AMA, Oreg. Med. Assn. (trustee 1985—), Multnomah County Med. Assn. (pres. 1986), Northwest Urologica, Oreg. Urol. Soc., Portland Rose Soc. (Shrunk award 1981). Republican. Episcopalian. Avocations: fishing, hunting, rose growing. Office: 510 NE 49th Portland OR 97213

YOUNG, DONALD CHARLES, research chemist; b. Fremont, Ohio, June 29, 1944; s. Charles William and Mildred Murlyleen (Miller) Y.; m. Janet Weaver, June 29, 1968 (div. May 1979); children: Steven Donald, Michael Justin; m. Mary Katherine Garland, Nov. 1, 1980; 1 child, Justin Thomas. AB, Harvard U., 1966; PhD, U. N.C., 1971. Postdoctoral research assoc. Purdue U., West Lafayette, Ind., 1971-72; asst. prof. chemistry Oakland U., Rochester, Mich., 1972-78; project chemist Gulf Oil Corp., Harvarville, Pa., 1978-84; sr. research chemist Chevron Oil Corp., Richmond, Calif., 1984—. Contbr. articles to profl. jours. Mem. Am. Chem. Soc., Soc. Applied Spectroscopy, Sigma Xi. Republican. Presbyterian. Office: Chevron Research Corp PO Box 1627 Richmond CA 94802-0627

YOUNG, DONALD E., congressman; b. Meridian, Calif., June 9, 1933; m. Lula Fredson; children—Joni, Dawn. Grad., Chico (Calif.) State Coll. Former educator, river boat capt.; mem. Fort Yukon City Council, 6 years, mayor, 4 years; mem. Alaska Ho. of Reps., 1966-70, Alaska Senate, 1970-73, 93d-100th congresses from Alaska. Republican. Office: 2331 Rayburn House Office Bldg Washington DC 20515

YOUNG, DONALD E., computer manufacturing company executive; b. Pitts., July 23, 1920; s. William P. and Helen (Bollenberg) Y.; m. Pauline Schloesser; children: Leigh, Anna Dey, Lance. B.A., George Washington U., 1948; M.B.A., Harvard U., 1951. Spl. agt. FBI, 1948-49; with FBI (Office Spl. Investigations), 1951-53; asst. to pres. G.H. Packwood Co., 1953-56; asst. to v.p. and treas., bank sales rep., regional bank mgr. Todd Co., 1956-60; with Burroughs Corp., Detroit, 1960—; v.p. corp. communications Burroughs Corp., 1966-76, sr. v.p., 1976-79, exec. v.p., 1980—; chmn. bd. Systems Devel. Corp., A Burroughs Co., Camarillo, Calif.; dir. Mich. Bank Bank, Detroit, Blue Cross/Blue Shield Mich. Bd. dirs. Detroit Conv. Bur., Boys Club Met. Detroit, Police Athletic League Detroit; bd. govs. Nat. Invest-in-Am., Greater Mich. Found.; mem. bd. mems. Mich. Coll. Found.; trustee Met. Fund Detroit, Founders Soc. of Detroit Inst. Arts, William Beaumont Hosp., Detroit, Detroit Renaissance. Served to capt. USAAF, 1941-46, ETO. Decorated D.F.C. with oak leaf cluster, Air medal with 5 oak leaf clusters. Mem. Soc. Former Agts. FBI, Mich. C. of C. (charter), Computer and Bus. Equipment Mfrs. Assn. (dir.), Econ. Club Detroit (v.p. 1975—). Clubs: Adcraft (Detroit), Detroit (Detroit), Detroit Athletic (Detroit), Harvard Bus. Sch. (Detroit); Harvard (N.Y.C.); Bloomfield Hills Country (pres. dir. 1979). Office: Burroughs Corp Burroughs Pl Detroit MI 48232 Office: System Devel Corp 5151 Camino Ruiz Camarillo CA 93010 *

YOUNG, ELVAN SHIU, microelectronics engineer; b. Helena, Ark., Aug. 25, 1948; s. Gene and Kim Ying (Wong) Fong; m. Nancy Marie Lucarotti, Mar. 23, 1980; 1 child, Tracy Allison. BS in Electron Physics cum laude, La. State U., 1970; MSEE, U. Ill., 1972. Engr. Rockwell Internat., Anaheim, Calif., 1972-74; sr. design engr. Intel Corp., Santa Clara, Calif., 1974-80; mgr. advanced memory devel. Synertek, Inc., Santa Clara, 1978-80; dept. mgr. design engring. Advanced Micro Devices, Sunnyvale, Calif., 1980-84; project mgr. research and devel. Cypress Semiconductor, Inc., San Jose, Calif., 1984—. Patentee in field. Mem. Phi Beta Kappa, Sigma Pi Sigma. Republican. Baptist. Avocations: photography, music, computers, science fiction, basketball. Home: 1342 Casa Ct Santa Clara CA 95051 Office: Cypress Semiconductor Inc 3901 N 1st St San Jose CA 95134

YOUNG, ETHEL RUTH, schoolteacher; b. Havelock, N.S., Can., Aug. 15, 1934; d. Handley Chipman and Ethel Ring (Sabine) Mullen; m. Harold Edwin Young, June 7, 1955; children: Jennifer Lorraine, Patricia Elaine. AB in Lit., Eastern Nazarene Coll., Quincy, Mass., 1955; MA, Pasadena (Calif.) Coll. (now Point Loma Nazarene Coll.), 1971; teaching credentials, Calif. State U., Fullerton, 1964; postgrad., UCLA, 1965-67, Claremont (Calif.) Grad. Sch., 1980—. Cert. lifetime elem. tchr., Calif.; cert. elem. sch. adminstr., cert. jr. coll. instr., cert. Miller-Unruh reading specialist, Calif. Tchr. pub. schs. Kans., Ohio, and Calif., 1955—; chmn. english dept. Green Twp. High Sch., Franklin Furnace, Ohio, 1961-62; spl. edn. tchr. Centralia Sch. Dist., Buena Park, Calif., 1965-67, 79-81, reading specialist, 1967-79, elem. tchr., 1981—; instr. children's lit. Santa Ana (Calif.) Coll., 1973-75; adj. prof. edn. Point Loma Nazarene Coll., 1975—; speaker nat. conv. Nat. Elem. Edn. Assn., 1981, 82. Author curricula for ch. sch. pubs., 1976-83. Mem. NEA, Calif. Tchrs. Assn., Centralia Edn. Assn. (sec. 1970-72), Pi Lambda Theta, Phi Delta Lambda. Home: 2437 Deerpark Dr Fullerton CA 92635 Office: Buena Terra Sch 8299 Holder St Buena Park CA 90620

YOUNG, FRANCIS ALLAN, psychologist; b. Utica, N.Y., Dec. 29, 1918; s. Frank Allan and Julia Mae (McOwen) Y.; m. Judith Wadsworth Wright, Dec. 21, 1945; children—Francis Allan, Thomas Robert. B.S., U. Tampa, 1941; M.A., Western Res. U., 1945; Ph.D., Ohio State U., 1949. Instr. Wash. State U., Pullman, 1948-50; asst. prof. Wash. State U., 1950-56, assoc. prof., 1956-61, prof. psychology, 1961—, dir. primate research center, 1957—; vis. prof. ophthalmology U. Oreg., Portland, 1964; vis. prof. pharmacology U. Uppsala (Sweden) Med. Sch., 1971; vis. prof. optometry U. Houston, 1979-80. Editor: (with Donald B. Lindsley) Early Experience and Visual Information Processing in Perceptual and Reading Disorders, 1970. Named Disting. Psychologist State of Wash., Wash. Psychol. Assn., 1973; recipient Paul Yarwood Meml. award Calif. Optometric Assn., 1978; Apollo award Am. Optometric Assn., 1980; Nat. Acad. Sci.-NRC sr. postdoctoral fellow in physiol. psychology U. Wash., 1956-57; research grantee NSF, 1950-53; research grantee USAF, 1965-72; research grantee NIH, 1960-78. Fellow Am. Acad. Optometry, Am. Pychol. Assn. ((pres. Div. 31) 1974-75); mem. Common Cause, Ams. Dem. Action, Assn. Research in Vision and Ophthalmology, Internat. Soc. Myopia Research (sec.-treas. 1978—), AAAS, Psychonomic Soc., Wash. State Psychol. Assn. (exec. sec. 1965-77), Western Psychol. Assn.; Mem. N.Y. Acad. Scis.; mem. Sigma Xi, Psi Chi (nat. pres. 1968-70). Home: NW 344 Webb St Pullman WA 99163 Office: Wash State U Pullman WA 99164

YOUNG, FRANK NOLAN, JR., commercial building contracting company executive; b. Tacoma, Wash., Feb. 26, 1941; s. Frank N. and Antoinette (Mahncke) Y.; m. Susan E. Bayley, Aug. 13, 1965; children—Sandra Susanne, Frank Nolan. B.A. in Bus. and Fin., U. Wash., 1963. Vice pres. Strand Inc., Bellevue, Wash., 1966-73; pres., treas., chief exec. officer, dir. Gall Landau Young Constrn. Co. Inc., Bellevue, 1973—; v.p., sec., dir. Cascade Structures, Kirkland, Wash., 1972—. Mem. Assoc. Gen. Contractors (pres. Seattle 1985, trustee 1968—, nat. dir.). Republican. Episcopalian. Clubs: Rainier, TAS Ski Found. (pres. 1983-84), Overlake Golf and Country; Seattle Yacht. Lodges: Elks, Masons, Shriners, Royal Order Jesters (impresario 1983—). Home: 5005 E Mercer Way Mercer Island WA 98040 Office: Gall Landau Young PO Box 6728 Bellevue WA 98008

YOUNG, GEORGE WALTER, lawyer; b. Los Angeles, May 15, 1950; s. George Albert and Edna Margaret (Hill) Y.; m. Marian Eileen Bement, May 29, 1982; children: George Eric, Ryan Walter. B.A., UCLA, 1972; J.D., Southwestern U., 1976. Bar: Calif. 1976, U.S. Supreme Ct. 1981. Mem. Young & Young, Los Angeles, 1976-82, Pepper, Hamilton & Scheetz, Los Angeles, 1982-84, ptnr. 1984—. Mem. John Marshall High Sch. Alumni Assn. (pres.), UCLA Alumni Assn., UCLA Bruin Bench. Republican. Presbyterian. Clubs: Los Angeles Athletic. Lodges: Lions, Masons. Office: Pepper Hamilton & Scheetz 606 S Olive St 20th Floor Los Angeles CA 90014

YOUNG, GERALD LEONARD, SR., farm equipment manufacturing executive; b. Billings, Mont., June 18, 1937; s. Leonard V. and Gladys (Laughery) Y.; m. Georgia M. Hartman, Mar. 5, 1982; children: Gerald L. Jr., Robert C. Student, Eastern Mont. Coll.; BA, Mont. State U., 1962. Territory mgr. Cert. Labs., Dallas, 1968-72, Midland Implement, Billings, 1972-75; ops. mgr. Renn U.S. div. Anthes Industries, Billings, 1975-80; gen. mgr. Renn U.S. div. Anthes Industries, Ft. Benton, Mont., 1980-84; dir. mktg. Renn div. Anthes Industries, Edmonton, Alta., Can., 1984-85, gen. mgr., 1985—; corp. officer Anthes Industries Mississaqua, Ont., Can., 1985—. Served with USN, 1954-58, Korea. Republican. Lodge: Elks. Avocations: hunting, fishing, golf, carpentry. Home: 1344 Pine Tree Dr Billings MT 59105 Office: Anthes Industries, Renn div, 12555 127th Ave, Edmonton Can T5L 3E5

YOUNG, HERBERT J., financial executive; b. 1931. Attended, Los Angeles City Coll. Chmn., chief exec. officer Gibraltar Savs. Co., Beverly Hills, Calif.; also chmn., pres. Gibralter Fin. Corp., Beverly Hills. Office: Gibralter Fin Corp 9111 Wilshire Blvd Beverly Hills CA 90213 *

YOUNG, HO LEE, environmental scientist; b. Canton, China, July 15, 1920; s. Hee B. and Check-K. (Tsang) Lee; married; 1 child, Linda. BS in Biology, Lingnan U., China, 1943; postgrad. Zoology, Mills Coll., 1949; PhD in Cellular Physiology, U. Calif., Berkeley, 1954. Research physiologist U. Calif., Berkeley, 1952-56, research chemist, 1962-63; research assoc. dept. radiation Stanford U., San Francisco, 1956-57; research chemist U. Calif., San Francisco, 1957-62; research biochemist, physiologist NASA Ames Research Ctr., Moffitt Field, Calif., 1963-72; supervisory chemist, environ. scientist EPA, San Francisco, 1973-85; pvt. cons. Bur. of Reclamation, Dept. Interior, Sacramento, 1985-87; cons. scientist United Nat., Manila, 1985. Co-author: Membrane Transport and Metabolism, 1960; contbr. articles to profl. jours. Abraham Rosenberg research fellow U. Calif., Berkeley, 1950-52, sr. research fellow San Francisco Heart Assn., 1960-62. Mem. Am. Chem. Soc., Chinese-Am. Chem. Soc., Am. Physiol. Soc., Sigma Xi. Home: 5978 Greenridge Rd Castro Valley CA 94552

YOUNG, HOPE THREADGILL, psychotherapist; b. Wadesboro, N.C., July 5, 1953; d. Henry Frank and Audrey Ann (Carter) Threadgill; m. David Pingwah Young, Nov. 6, 1973; children: Daniel Frank Shungchi, Steven Shunming. Student Winthrop Coll., 1971-72; BS in Psychology, U. S.C., 1974; MA in Counseling and Student Personnel Psychology, U. Minn., 1982; postgrad. in counseling psychology U. No. Colo., 1986—. Residential dir., clin. counselor Whitten Village Mental Retardation Inst., Clinton, S.C., 1974-76; coordinator patient services Muscular Dystrophy Assn., St. Paul, 1976-77; counselor, teaching asst. counseling and student personnel psychology U. Minn., Mpls., 1978-79; counselor, program dir. Women's Info. Ctr., U. Colo., Colorado Springs, 1980-85; edn. cons. Penrose Hosp., Colorado Springs, 1985-86; psychotherapist, cons., 1986—. Bd. dirs. Women's Resource Agy., Colorado Springs. Mem. Am. Psychol. Assn., Am. Assn. for Counseling and Devel., Am. Soc. Tng. and Devel., Nat. Assn. Women Adminstrs. and Counselors, Colo.-Wyo. Assn. Women Adminstrs. and Counselors, Colo. Psychol. Assn., Colo. Assn. Counseling Devel. Methodist. Office: 6009 W 28th St Greeley CO 80634

YOUNG, JAMES ALLAN, physicist; b. Hamilton, Ont., Can., Mar. 9, 1934; came to U.S., 1957, naturalized, 1967; s. Jack and May (Jones) Y.; m. Tanis Ruth Dalrymple, June 26, 1982; children: Carol Darlene, Kathryn Joan. B.S., McMaster U., 1957; Ph.D., U. Calif.-Berkeley, 1961. Physicist Gen. Electric Co., Pleasanton, Calif., 1960-63; asst. chmn. accelerator physics dept. Gen. Atomic, San Diego, 1963-68; sci. asst. to dep. dir. sci. and tech. Def. Nuclear Agy., Washington, 1968-70; mgr. theoretical div. Sci. Applications, Inc., La Jolla, Calif., 1970-75; pres., chmn. bd. Jaycor, San Diego, 1975—. Author: Aswan High, 1983. Mem. Chancellor's Assn., U. Calif.-San Diego, 1983—. Episcopalian. Office: PO Box 85154 San Diego CA 92138

YOUNG, JAMES BREWSTER, computer systems company executive; b. Ogdensburg, N.Y., Dec. 10, 1945; s. Robert Jay and Doris Blanch (LaRock) Y.; m. Glenna Sue Burns, July 19, 1980, children—Aaron Jay, Adam Lee, Steven William, Nannette Suzanne. B.A., Lycoming Coll., 1968; M.S., Pa. State U., 1971; M.B.A., Calif. Western U., 1976, Ph.D., 1978. Systems engr. Quaker Oats (Chgo., 1968-73, Pet, Inc., St. Louis, 1973-76; with process control dept. Standard Brands, N.Y.C., 1976-81; pres., chief exec. officer Universal Intergraphix Corp., Ontario, Calif., 1981-85; pres., chief exec. officer Designer's Internat., Chino Hills, Califj., 1985—. Author: Business Acquisitions, Mergers, 1978. Chief adminstr. Eastman Fire Dept., Ga., 1975; Olympics adminstr. Brea-Olinda council Girl Scouts U.S., 1980—. Republican. Lodge: Masons.

YOUNG, JOAN CRAWFORD, advertising executive; b. Hobbs, N.Mex., July 30, 1931; d. William Bill and Ora Maydelle (Boone) Crawford; m. Herchelle B. Young, Nov. 23, 1971 (div.). B.A., Hardin Simmons U., 1952; postgrad. Tex. Tech. U., 1953-54. Reporter, Lubbock (Tex.) Avalanche-Jour., 1952-54; promotion dir. KCBD-TV, Lubbock, 1954-62; account exec. Ward Hicks Advt., Albuquerque, 1962-70; v.p. Mellekas & Assocs., Advt., Albuquerque, 1970-78; pres. J. Young Advt., Albuquerque, 1978—. Bd. dirs. N.Mex. Symphony Orch., 1970-73, United Way of Greater Albuquerque, 1985—. Recipient Silver medal N.Mex. Advt. Fedn., 1977. Mem. N.Mex. Advt. Fedn. (dir. 1975-76), Am. Advt. Fedn., Greater Albuquerque C. of C. (dir. 1984). Republican. Author: (with Louise Allen and Audre Lipscomb) Radio and TV Continuity Writing, 1962. Home: 3425 Avenida Charada NW Albuquerque NM 87107 Also: 303 Roma NW Albuquerque NM 87102

YOUNG, JOHN ALAN, electronics company executive; b. Nampa, Idaho, Apr. 24, 1932; s. Lloyd Arthur and Karen Eliza (Miller) Y.; m. Rosemary Murray, Aug. 1, 1954; children: Gregory, Peter, Diana. B.S. in Elec. Engring, Oreg. State U., 1953; M.B.A., Stanford U., 1958. Various mktg. and finance positions Hewlett Packard Co. Inc., Palo Alto, Calif., 1958-63, gen. mgr. microwave div., 1963-68, v.p. electronic products group, 1968-74, exec. v.p., dir., 1974-77, pres., 1977—, chief exec. officer, 1978—; dir. Wells Fargo Bank, SRI Internat. Chmn. ann. fund Stanford, 1969-73, nat. chmn. corp. gifts, 1973-77; Bd. dirs. Mid-Peninsula Urban Coalition, 1972-80, co-chmn., 1976-80; mem. adv. council Grad. Sch. Bus., Stanford U., 1968-73, 75-80, univ. trustee, 1977—, chmn. Pres. Reagan's Commn. Indsl. Competitiveness, 1983; chmn. Nat. Jr. Achievement, 1983-85. Served with USAF, 1954-56. Mem. Am. Electronics Assn. Home: 26 Arastradero Rd Portola Valley CA 94025 Office: Hewlett-Packard Co 3000 Hanover St Palo Alto CA 94304 *

YOUNG, JOHN ANTHONY, food processing executive; b. Nelson, B.C., Can., May 12, 1931; came to U.S., 1969; s. John Albert and Margaret Alma (Sarvis) Y.; m. Nina Ruth Corry, Aug. 9, 1952; (div. Feb. 1970); m. Shirley Ann Kempster, Aug. 14, 1970; children: Michael, Lisa. Diploma, Lincoln Extension Inst. Mfg. mgr. Nalley's Fine Foods, Tacoma, 1968-75; ops. mgr. Basic Vegetable Produce Inc., King City, Calif., 1975-80; productivity devel. mgr. McCormick & Co., Gilroy, Calif., 1980; ops. dir. Gilroy Foods, 1980-85, also bd. dirs.; ops. dir. Gilroy Farms, 1985—. Elder Gilroy Presbyn. Ch., 1983—. Mem. Gilroy C. of C. (bd. dirs. 1985—). Republican. Lodge: Rotary (bd. dirs.). Avocations: camping, hiking, tennis. Office: Gilroy Farms 8333 Swanston Ln Gilroy CA 95020

YOUNG, JON NATHAN, archeologist; b. Hibbing, Minn., May 30, 1938; s. Robert Nathan Young and Mary Elizabeth (Barrows) Roy; m. Karen Sue Johnson, June 5, 1961 (div. May 1980); children: Shawn Nathan, Kevin Leigh. BA magna cum laude, U. Ariz., 1960, PhD, 1967; MA, U. Ky., 1962. Archeologist Nat. Park Service Southwest Archeol. Ctr., Globe and Tucson Ariz., Ariz., 1967-76; exec., camp dir. YMCA of Metro. Tucson, 1976-78; asst. dir. Kit Carson Meml. Found., Taos, N.Mex., 1978-79; co-dir. Las Palomas de Taos, 1979-80; archeologist Nat. Forest Service, Carson Nat. Forest, Taos, 1980—; exec. order cons. U.S. Sec. Interior, 1973-76. Author: The Salado Culture in Southwestern Prehistory, 1967; co-author: Excavation of Mound 7, 1981. Grantee NEH, 1977; Ariz. Wilson Found, NSF, Ky. Research Found fellow, 1960-66; Baird Found., Bausch and Lomb, Elks, Nat. Honor Soc. scholar, 1959-60. Fellow: AAAS, Am. Anthrop. Assn., Explorers Club, Royal Anthrop. Inst.; mem. Current Anthropology (assoc.), Ariz. Archaeol. and Hist. Soc., Ariz. Hist. Soc., Colonial N.Mex. Hist. Found., Council on Am's. Mil. Past., Four Corners Archaeol. Forum, Soc. Am. Archaeology, Harwood Found., Millicent Rogers Mus., Wheelwright Mus. Am. Ind., Sigma Xi, Phi Beta Kappa, Alpha Kappa Delta, Phi Kappa Phi, Delta Chi. Home: Box 2007 Taos NM 87571 Office: Nat Forest Service Suprs Office Box 558 112 Cruz Alta Rd Taos NM 87571

YOUNG, LEONARD GEE LING, marine biologist; b. Honolulu, July 1, 1948; s. Mun Jip and Shuit Ching (Lee) Y. BA in Zoology, U. Hawaii, 1970; MA in Biology, U. S.C., 1972; PhD in Zoology, Tex. A&M U., 1977. Asst. prof. biology Am. U., Beirut, 1980-85; aquatic biologist Queen Lili'uokalani Childrens Ctr., Kailua-Kona, Hawaii, 1985-86; aquaculture specialistaquaculture devel. program Dept. Land and Natural Resources State of Hawaii, Honolulu, 1987—. Mem. AAAS, Am. Soc. Zoologists. Avocations: cooking, reading, jazz music. Home: PO Box 1675 Honolulu HI 96806 Office: Aquaculture Devel Program Dept Land and Natural Resources State of Hawaii 335 Merchant St Room 359 Honolulu HI 96813

YOUNG, LOUISA FRANCES, interior designer; b. Dayton, Ohio, Mar. 12, 1907; d. William Frederick and Bertha Elizabeth (Kurtz) Kennell; m. Dallas M. Speer, Mar. 14, 1970 (dec.). Student Ohio Tchr.'s Coll., Dayton, 1926-27, Heatherley's Art Sch., London, 1931-32, Sch. of Art Inst. Chgo., 1932-33. Illustrator, Aero-Med. Lab., Wright Field, Dayton, 1941-45; interior designer Rike's, Dayton, 1958-71. Sec. Women's Civic Group, Dayton, 1935-40. Recipient: Disting. Service award Am. Soc. Interior Designers, 1980. Mem. Am. Soc. Interior Designers, Dayton Painter and Sculptor Soc. (founder). Republican. Episcopalian. Clubs: Ohio Fedn. Women's Clubs. One woman show: U. Dayton, 1969; portrait: Martha, 1969. Address: 205 S Belardo Rd Palm Springs CA 92262

YOUNG, MICHAEL BALDWIN, utility company executive; b. Santa Monica, Calif., May 4, 1941; s. Jesse and Eleanora (Baldwin) Y.; m. Cheryl Grace Hoiseth, Feb. 14, 1965; children: Michael Alan, Kellie Ann. AA, Glendale Coll., 1969; BA, U. LaVerne, 1979. Mgr. system ops. Met. Water Dist. So. Calif., Los Angeles, 1961—; instr. Coll. of Canyons, Valencia, Calif., 1974-77, West Coast U., Los Angeles, 1984—; tng. cons. U.S. corps., 1982—; bd. dirs. Inter Talk, Los Angeles. Cons. editor: Water Treatment, 1983, Water Distribution, 1984; contbr. articles to profl. jours. Recipient Honors for Outstanding Youth Leadership, Mayor Bradley, Los Angeles, 1982. Mem. Am. Water Works Assn. (chmn. 1987—, bd. dirs. Calif.-Nev. sect. 1983-85) (bd. dirs. Calif. Nev. sect. 1983-85), Am. Soc. Tng. and Devel., Glendale C. of C., Internat. Platform Assn., Marvin Gaye Found. (bd. dirs. 1984—). Club: Toastmasters (Los Angeles club extension chmn. 1982-84, chmn. speaker bur. 1986. Avocation: pub. speaking. Home: 2301 Janet Lee Dr La Crescenta CA 91214 Office: Met Water Dept So Calif 1111 Sunset Blvd Los Angeles CA 90054

YOUNG, PATRICIA JANEAN, speech pathologist; b. San Diego, Nov. 30, 1953; d. Bernarr Elbert and Janean Elizabeth (Romig) Y. AA, Palomar Community coll., 1974; BA, Calif. State U., Chico, 1976; MA, Calif. State U., Long Beach, 1981. Mgmt. trainee J.W. Robinson's Dept. Store, Los Angeles, 1977-78; screening coordinator Riverview Hearing, Speech and Lang. Ctr., Long Beach, 1978-81, speech pathologist, 1981-84; speech pathologist, dir. Speech Pathology Services, Carlsbad, Calif., 1984—; mem. pub. info. subcom. Senator Ellis' Adv. Com. for Developmentally Disabled, San Diego, 1985; coordinator for Pub. Service Announcement for Disabilities Awareness Week, ABC TV, 1986. Producer (cable TV show), Communicative Disorders, 1983. Mem. social com. Condominium Assn., Carlsbad, 1985—. Recipient Outstanding Young Women award, 1983. Mem. Am. Speech Lang. and Hearing Assn. (cert.), Calif. Speech Lang. and Hearing Assn. (div. rep. 1985—, Outstanding Achievement award 1986), Calif. Speech Pathologist Audiologists in Pvt. Practice, Nat. Assn. for Hearing and Speech Action (chmn. Disney benefit 1983-84), Assn. for Retarded Citizens, Calif. Scholastic Fedn., Zeta Tau Alpha, Phi Delta Gamma (sec. 1982-83, v.p. 1983-84). Republican. Home: 2880 Andover Ave Carlsbad CA 92008 Office: Speech Pathology Services PO Box 4355 Carlsbad CA 92008

YOUNG, PAUL RUEL, computer scientist; b. St. Marys, Ohio, Mar. 16, 1936; s. William Raymond and Emma Marie (Steva) Y.; children: Lisa Robin, Neal Eric. BS, Antioch Coll., 1959; PhD, MIT, 1963. Tchr. math. Harley Sch., Rochester, N.Y., 1957; asst. prof. Reed Coll., 1963-66; NSF postdoctoral fellow in math. Stanford U., 1965-66; asst. prof. computer sci. and math. Purdue U., Lafayette, Ind., 1966-67, assoc. prof., 1967-72, prof., 1972-83; chmn., prof. computer sci. U. Wash., 1983—; chmn., prof. computing and info. scis., prof. math. U. N.Mex., 1978-79; vis. prof. elec. engring. and computer sci. U. Calif.-Berkeley, 1972-73, 82-83; mem. adv. com. math. and computer scis., NSF, 1977-80, chmn., 1979-80. Author: (with Michael Machtey) An Introduction to the General Theory of Algorithms, 1978. NSF and Woodrow Wilson fellow, MIT, 1963. Mem. IEEE (chmn. tech. com. on math. founds. of computing 1981-83), Assn. Computing Machiney. Office: U Wash Dept Computer Sci FR-35 Seattle WA 98195

YOUNG, ROBERT EDWARD, institutional investment officer; b. Los Angeles, Nov. 28, 1943; s. David and Sue (Wise) Y.; m. Sharon Johnson, Dec. 8, 1967. Student, E. Los Angeles Coll., 1973, Santa Monica Coll., 1975; BA, UCLA, 1978. Cert. securities analyst N.Y. Inst. Fin., 1972. Computer operator Rocketdyne Corp., Canoga Park, Calif., 1963-65; computer ops. supr. Hughes Aircraft Corp., El Segundo, Calif., 1965-67; with investment securities dept. Smith, Tilton & Co., Inc., Santa Ana, Calif., 1967-70, Morton Seidel & Co., Inc., Los Angeles, 1970-78; sales mgr. of comml. interior constrn. NICO Constrn. Co., Inc., Los Angeles, 1978-80; sales mgr. Strauss Constrn. Co., Inc., Los Angeles, 1981-82; v.p., instl.

investment officer FCA Asset Mgmt./Am. Savs., Los Angeles, 1982—; bd. dirs. RESA Prodns. 1973-80, Edu Care, Los Angeles, 1981—, ASC Edn. Services Inc., Los Angeles, chmn. fin. com.; mktg. cons. Shehata Enterprises, Los Angeles, 1978-79; sales tng. cons. Versailles Gallery, Los Angeles, Schwartz Constrn., Los Angeles, 1982. Photographer: prin. works include Man at Work or Play UN, Geneva, 1976, Cat of Yr. photo, 1977, Photomontage U. So. Calif. Early Childhood Edn. Ctr., 1977; producer weekly pub. affairs program for family fin. planning sta. KPOL Radio, 1974, Stocks and bonds show KWHY-TV, 1975-78. Served with USCGR, 1964-70. Mem. AIA, Cosmopolitan Internat. (pres. 1967-68), Soc. Archtl. Historians, Los Angeles Conservancy, West Los Angeles Constitution Observance Day (chmn. 1970), Archtl. Hist. Soc. (life mem. So. Calif. chpt.), Valley MacIntosh User Group. Clubs: Downtown High Twelve (past. pres.). Lodges: Masons, Toastmasters (Outstanding Toastmaster 1973, 74, 76). Avocations: skiing, photography, computers. Home: 945 Hauser Blvd Los Angeles CA 90036 Office: FCA Asset Mgmt/Am Savs 10701 W Pico Blvd Los Angeles CA 90064

YOUNG, ROBERT SCOTT, insurance company executive; b. Denver, Nov. 25, 1951; s. Keith Eugene and Patricia (Eubank) Y.; m. Karen Young, May 14, 1976; children: Scott, Elizabeth, Jill, Kristin, Jeff. BS, Brigham Young U., 1977; MBA, Utah State U., 1982. CPCU, 1986. Spl. agt. Continental Ins., Salt Lake City, 1977-78, service ctr. mgr., 1978-80; mktg. rpe. TransAm. Ins., Salt Lake City, 1980-84, per-lines mgr., 1984-86, br. mgr., 1986—. Author: Go Ye Into All the World, 1980, Industry Savings Agency, 1982. Group leader Utah Reps., Salt Lake City, 1978. James S. Kemper scholar, Kemper Found., 1975. Blue Goose of Utah. Democrat. Mormon. Lodge: Toastmasters (sgt. at arms Salt Lake City chpt. 1978-81). Home: 5142 S Ryan Hill Circle Salt Lake City UT 84118

YOUNG, ROGER CARL, computer company executive; b. Clayton, Mo., Mar. 21, 1932; s. Gerald Lee Young and Bertha Augusta (Schlottach) McCulloh; m. Nadine Fay Basch, Apr. 27, 1952; children: Julia Allyn, David Ford. Student, Washington U., St. Louis, 1956-57, U. Calif., Berkeley, 1957-60, Contra Costa Coll., 1970. V.p. and div. mgr. Crocker Nat. Bank, San Francisco, 1967-75; nat. accts. mgr. Wang Labs., San Francisco, 1975-78; industry cons. Fortune 500, 1978-81; pres. ComTrak, Richmond, Calif., 1981-83; dir. mktg. Delphi Systems, Inc., Westlake Village, Calif., 1983—. Served with USAF, 1951-55. Mem. Data Processing Mgmt. Assn. (cert., dir., sec. San Francisco chpt. 1965-67), Am. Contract Bridge League (life master 1959). Republican. Club: Concord (Calif.) Mens Golf. Avocations: golf, tennis, computer product design, tournament bridge. Home: 1064 Sunwood Ln Agoura CA 91301

YOUNG, RUSSEL RAY, safety professional, public transportation executive; b. Portland, Oreg., Dec. 14, 1934; s. Walton Meyers and Charlotte Francis (Bottemiller) Y.; m. Barbara Jean Koonce, Mar. 24, 1956; children—Russel Ray, Cheryl Lynne. B.S. in Mgmt., Golden Gate U., 1974; M.S. in Safety, U. So. Calif., 1984. Cert. safety profl. Bd. Cert. Safety Profls. Commd. officer U.S. Air Force, 1954, advanced through grades to maj., 1966; transport pilot U.S. and Orient, 1955-61; acad. instr. aircraft maintenance, 1961-63; aircraft instrument pilot instr., 1963-65; aircraft comdr., Vietnam, 1965-66; chief command post European Hdqrs. Command and Control Ctr., 1966-70; chief flight safety br. Mather AFB, Calif., 1970-74, ret., 1974; loss control rep. Continental Ins. Co., Sacramento, Calif., 1974-76, loss control mgr., 1976-79; loss control mgr. Mission Ins. Co., Sacramento, 1979—; mgr. systems safety, Sacramento Regional Transit dist., 1986— . Decorated Bronze Star, D.F.C., Air medal with 8 clusters, Air Force Commendation medal with cluster, Meritorious Service medal, Air Force Expeditionary medal, Republic of Vietnam Service medal. Mem. Am. Soc. Safety Engrs. (chpt. v.p.), Exptl. Aircraft Assn. Home: Roseville CA 95678 Office: 1400 29th St Sacramento CA 95816

YOUNG, SALLY SATTERTHWAITE, retail buyer; b. Detroit, Feb. 14, 1940; d. Philip Conde and Pauline (Glidewell) Satterthwaite; m. Bob Grant Dunn, Dec. 22, 1962 (div. Aug. 1978); children: Lori Sue, Kevin Grant; m. Edsel Ford Young, Sept. 7, 1978. BBA, Nat. U., 1980, MBA, 1981. Pub. relations, social dir. Guam Reef Hotel, Tumon Bay, Guam, 1974; mktg. mgr. Global Mktg., Inc., Honolulu, 1974-76; buyer Navy Exchange, Mare Island, Calif., 1977-78; assoc. registrar Nat. U., Vista, Calif., 1979-82; buyer Marine Corps Exchange, Santa Ana, Calif., 1982-85, Camp Pendleton, Calif., 1985—. Fund raising chmn. St. John's Episcopal Ch., Tamuning, Guam, 1971, 72, 74. Named to Ancient Order Chamorri Govt. Guam, 1977. Mem. Nat. Assn. Female Execs., Women's Internat. Ctr., Vista C. of C. (fund raising chmn. 1980, Appreciation award 1980), Fallbrook C. of C., P.E.O. Sisterhood. Republican. Club: Guam Press. Lodge: Elks. Avocation: piano. Home: 852 Willow Tree Ln Fallbrook CA 92028 Office: Marine Corps Exchange 0141 Marine Corps Base Camp Pendleton CA 92055

YOUNG, SAMUEL DOAK, JR., banker; b. El Paso, Mar. 15, 1930; s. Samuel Doak and Elizabeth (Goodman) Y.; m. Marilyn Mays, July 16, 1969; children—Elizabeth Beard Roesler, Emily Beard Williams, M. Allison Beard McGuire, Whitney Blair, Samuel Doak III. B.A. in Econs. cum laude, Stanford U., 1951; cert. with distinction Southwestern Grad. Sch. of Banking, 1960. With 1st State Bank, El Paso, 1953-54; asst. nat. bank examiner Office of Comptroller of Currency, 11th Fed. Res. Dist., 1955-57; v.p. El Paso Nat. Bank, 1957-62, dir., 1957—, exec. v.p., 1962-64, pres., 1964-82, chief exec. officer, 1975-85, chmn. bd., 1982-85; pres., chief exec. officer El Paso Nat. Corp. (formerly Trans Tex. Bancorp.), 1971-85, chmn. bd., chief exec. officer, 1982-85; pres., chief exec. officer La Jolla Village Savs. Bank, 1985—; dir. Tex. Commerce Bancshares, Inc., 1982—, 1st State Bank, El Paso, 1958—; v.p. Trans Tex. Bancorp., Inc., 1967-85; mem. adv. com. Fed. Res. Bank, 1981-84; dir. Hilton Hotels Corp. Trustee El Paso YWCA, also chmn., 1959—; mem. Tex. Research League, 1971-85; bd. dirs. Providence Meml. Hosp., El Paso, 1973—, hon. bd. dirs. Spirit of Love Crisis Nursery, El Paso, 1981—; dirs. Nat. Alliance of Businessmen El Paso, 1969, El Paso Internat. City Assn., 1962-72, El Paso YMCA, 1962-63, El Paso Mcpl. Parking Authority, 1961-64, Tex. United Fund, 1959-66, Better Bus. Bur. El Paso, 1958-61, Blue Cross-Blue Shield, 1977-81, El Paso chpt. Jr. Achievement Program, 1966-79; mem. bus. adminstrn. adv. council U. Tex.-El Paso, 1965—, adv. council found., 1970—; charter mem. Tex. Council on Econ. Edn. 1969—; coordinating bd. Tex. Coll. and Univ. System, 1969-81, mem. Gov.'s Adv. Com. on Edn., 1979-81; vice chmn. Tex. Tchrs. Retirement System, 1961-73. Served with USAF, 1951-53. Mem. Tex. Bankers Assn. (pres. 1980-81, chmn. long range planning com. 1981-82, budget com. 1979-81, mem. exec. com. 1979-81, legis. com. 1981-82, dir. 1977-79, v.p. 1979-80), El Paso Assn. Banks (pres. 1978-79), Southwest Automated Clearing House Assn. (dir. 1980-81), Am. Bankers Assn., Assn. Res. City Bankers (com. on pub. affairs 1981-83), El Paso C. of C., Tex. Mfrs. Assn. (state affairs com. 1969-79), Beta Theta Pi. Episcopalian. Clubs: El Paso Country, La Jolla Beach and Tennis, La Jolla Country, Fairbanks Ranch Country. Lodges: Masons, Shriners. Office: La Jolla Village Savs Bank PO Box 8169 La Jolla CA 92038

YOUNGBLOOD, DEBORAH SUE, speech-language pathologist; b. Fairview, Okla., July 29, 1954; d. G. Dean and Beatrice J. (Heibert) W. BS with honors, Okla. State U., 1976, MA, 1979. Speech-lang. pathologist Mesa Sch. Dist. 51, Grand Junction, Colo., 1979-82, Fed. Migrant Presch., Grand Junction, 1980-81; dir. clin. services Idaho Easter Seal Soc., Boise, 1982-84; chief audiology and speech pathology Boise VA Med. Ctr., 1984-86; pvt. practice speech pathology Boise, 1986—; grad. asst. Okla. State U., Stillwater, 1976-78; speech-lang. cons. Boise Cleft Lip-Palate Team, 1982-84, Idaho Migrant Council, Boise, 1982-86, St. Alphonsus Med. Ctr., Boise, 1984-86. Recipient Superior Performance award VA, 1985. Mem. Am. Speech-Lang.-Hearing Assn. (cert.), Idaho Speech Hearing Assn., Colo. Speech-Hearing Assn. (mem. exec. council 1981), Internat. High IQ Soc., Mensa, Phi Kappa Phi. Avocations: skiing, backpacking, travel.

YOUNGQUIST, TED NOWAK, mining engineer; b. Stockton, Calif., Sept. 5, 1947; s. Herbert John and May A. (Nowak) Y; student public schs., Stockton; m. Lillie Ellen Younquist, Jan. 16, 1967; children—Philip, Thad, Leif. Lic. state safety instr. Operator own mines, Calif., 1970—; miner El Dorado Limestone, Shingle Springs, Calif., 1970; foreman Alhambra Atlanta Gold Mines, El Dorado County, Calif., 1971, Am. Hill Mine, Placer County, Calif., 1974; cons. engr. French Corral Mine, Nevada County, Calif., 1974; core drilling engr. Mine Rite Corp., El Dorado, Calif., 1974; cons. engr., assayer Manzinita Mine, El Dorado County, 1974; cons. engr. Trail Claim Mine, El Dorado, 1974—; engr. Sergeant Jacobs Placer Mines, Nevada County, 1975; cons. engr. Pease Mining Co., 1976, Horseshoe Bar Mining Co., 1976-77, Glacier King Uranium Mine, Carson City, Nev., 1978, Rolfe Ranches, Coulterville, Calif., 1979, Troy Gold Industries, 1979, Superior Extension Mine, Placerville, Calif., 1980, Relief Silver mine, Asarco County, Nev., 1980; cons. Teritary, Inc., 1977—, Benchmark Mining, Bishop, Calif., 1978—; owner, operator Tungo Mine, El Dorado County, 1977—; cons. Houston Mining & Resources, 1979—, Bentley Internat., Liberia, 1980; owner Youngquist Assaying, Georgetown, Calif., 1980—; operator Wind River Mining Project, 1983—; Calif. safety instr., 1978—. Mem. Dem. Central Com., 1972-73. Mem. AIME, ASME, Constrn. Specifications Inst. Liberian Fellowship of Mining Engrs. Lodge: Masons. Address: 4052 S Royal Links Circle Antioch CA 94509

YOUNGQUIST, WALTER LEWELLYN, geologist; b. Mpls., May 5, 1921; s. Walter Raymond and Selma Regina (Knock) Y.; m. Elizabeth Salome Pearson, Dec. 11, 1943; children: John, Karen, Louise, Robert. BA in Zoology, Gustavus Adolphus Coll., 1942; MS in Geology, U. Iowa, 1943, PhD in Geology, 1948. Registered profl. geologist, Oreg. Jr. geologist U.S. Geol. Survey, Baton Rouge, 1943-44; asst. prof. geology U. Idaho Sch. Mines, Moscow, 1948-51; sr. geologist Internat. Petrol. Corp., Talara, Peru, 1951-54; prof. geology U. Kans., Lawrence, 1954-57, U. Oreg., Eugene, 1957-66; cons. Exxon Corp., 1957-67, Amoco, 1968-70, Sun Oil Co., 1971, Eugene (Oreg.) Water and Electric Bd., 1973—. Author: Over the Hill and Down the Creek, 1966, Investing in Natural Resources, 1980, (with others) Ordovician Cephalopod Fauna of Baffin Island, 1954. Chmn. Gov.'s Geothermal Task Force, Oreg., 1978-79. Served with USNR, 1944-45. Recipient Lowden Prize in Geology U. Iowa, 1943. Fellow: AAAS, Geol. Soc. Am.; mem. Am. Assn. Petroleum Geologists, Geothermal Resources Council, Sigma Xi. Republican. Avocations: photography, fly-tying. Office: PO Box 5501 Eugene OR 97405

YOUNGS, JACK MARVIN, cost engineer; b. Bklyn., May 2, 1941; s. Jack William and Virginia May (Clark) Y.; B.Engring., CCNY, 1964; M.B.A., San Diego State U., 1973; m. Alexandra Marie Robertson, Oct. 31, 1964; 1 child, Christine Marie. Mass properties engr. Gen. Dynamics Corp., San Diego, 1964-68, research engr., 1968-69, sr. research engr., 1969-80, sr. cost devel. engr., 1980-81, cost devel. engring. specialist, 1981—. Dist. dir. Scripps Ranch Civic Assn., 1976-79; pres. Scripps Ranch Swim Team, 1980-82; dir., 1986; judge Greater San Diego Sci. and Engring. Fair, 1981-86. Mem. AIAA, Inst. Cost Analysis (cert., charter mem., treas. Greater San Diego chpt. 1986), Internat. Soc. Parametric Analysts, Nat. Mgmt. Assn. (award of honor 1975), Assn. MBA Execs., San Diego State U. Bus. Alumni Assn. (charter mem. 1986), Beta Gamma Sigma, Chi Epsilon, Sigma Iota Epsilon. Club: Scripps Ranch Swim and Racquet (dir. 1977-80, treas. 1978-79, pres. 1979-80). Research in life cycle costing and econ. analysis. Home: 11461 Tribuna Ave San Diego CA 92131 Office: PO Box 85900 San Diego CA 92138

YOUNGSTRUM, DAVID MANSFIELD, financial executive; b. Racine, Wis., Sept. 2, 1942; s. George Gustav and Marion E. (Lundberg) Y.; m. Dorothy M. Oldham Smedly, May 25, 1985. B.S. in Stats., Colo. State U., 1964; M.S. in Bus. Adminstrn., U. No. Colo., 1980. Cert. fin. examiner. Asst. actuary United Am. Life Ins. Co., Denver, 1964-73; asst. treas. United Am. Securities, Denver, 1973; chief actuary Colo. Div. Ins., Denver, 1973-86; chief fin. officer Metlife HealthCare Network of Colo., Golden, 1986—. Recipient award Am. Math. Assn., 1964. Fellow Life Mgmt. Inst.; mem. Internat. Actuarial Assn., Am. Statis. Assn., Denver Soc. Security Analysts, Am. Pub. Health Assn., Soc. Fin. Examiners, Mensa, Nat. Eagle Scout Assn. Republican. Presbyterian. Clubs: Denver Execs., Denver Actuarial, Denver Bot. Gardens, Collie of Colo. Office: MetLife HealthCare Network of Colo 534 Commons Dr Golden CO 80401

YOUNT, DAVID EUGENE, physicist, university official; b. Prescott, Ariz., June 5, 1935; s. Robert Ephram and Jeannette Francis (Judson) Y.; m. Christel Marlene Notz, Feb. 22, 1975; children—Laura Christine, Gregory Gordon, Steffen Jurgen Robert, Sonja Kate Jeannette. B.S. in Physics, Calif. Inst. Tech., 1957; M.S. in Physics, Stanford U., 1959, Ph.D. in Physics, 1963. Instr. Princeton U., 1962-63, asst. prof. physics, 1963-64, Minn. Mining and Mfg. fellow, 1963; NSF postdoctoral fellow U. Paris, Orsay, France, 1964-65; research asso. Stanford Linear Accelerator Center, Stanford U., 1965-69; assoc. prof. U. Hawaii, 1969-73, prof., 1973—, chmn. dept. physics and astronomy, 1979-85, acting asst. v.p. for acad. affairs, 1985-86, v.p. research and grad. edn., 1986—. Mem. Am. Phys. Soc., Undersea Med. Soc., Am. Chem. Soc., U.S. Tennis Assn., Sigma Xi. Republican. Lutheran. Research, numerous articles in elem. particle physics, undersea medicine and acoustics, 1962. Home: 5468 Opihi St Honolulu HI 96821 Office: U Hawaii 2505 Correa Rd Honolulu HI 96822

YOUNT, GEORGE STUART, paper company executive; b. Los Angeles, Mar. 4, 1949; s. Stanley George and Agnes (Pratt) Y.; m. Geraldine Marie Silvio, July 18, 1970; children: Trisha Marie, Christopher George. Grad. student, Harvard U., 1983-86. Mgmt. trainee Fortifiber Corp., Los Angeles, 1969-71, asst. to v.p. ops., 1971-75, adminstrv. v.p., treas., sec., 1975-85, exec. v.p., treas., sec., 1985—; treas., bd. dirs. Stanwall Corp., Los Angeles; past pres. Hollister Ranch Cattle Coop., Gaviota, Calif. Bd. dirs. Big Bros. of Greater Los Angeles, 1985-86. Mem. Am. Paper Inst. Clubs: Jonathan (Los Angeles); San Marino City (Calif.). Lodge: Rotary. Avocations: scuba diving, electronics, cattle ranching. Home: 684 Winston Ave San Marino CA 91108 Office: Fortifiber Corp 4489 Bandini Los Angeles CA 90023-4777

YOUNT, STANLEY GEORGE, paper co. exec.; b. Ketchum, Idaho, Feb. 15, 1903; s. George and Cansada (Smith) Y.; student U. Nev., 1924; m. Agnes Pratt, Feb. 17, 1944; children—Ann E., George S. Div. sales mgr. Crown Zellerbach Corp., 1926-40; pres. Southland Paper Converting Co., 1940-56; pres. Fortifiber Corp. and affiliates, Los Angeles, 1956-77, chmn., 1977—, also dir.; dir. Stanwall Corp. Served with U.S. Army, World War I; AEF in France. Mem. Nat. Flexible Packaging Assn. (pres. Indsl. Bag and Cover div. 1954-56), Barrier Paper Mfrs. Assn. Mason (Shriner). Clubs: Jonathan (Los Angeles), Rotary. Home: 2260 Robles Ave San Marino CA 91108 Office: Fortifiber Corp 4489 Bandini Blvd Los Angeles CA 90023-4777

YOUSEF, FATHI SALAAMA, communication studies educator, management consultant; b. Cairo, Jan. 2, 1934; came to U.S., 1968, naturalized, 1973; s. Salaama and Rose (Tadros) Y.; m. Caroline Droge, Nov. 27, 1969. B.A., Ain Shams U., Cairo, 1955; M.A., U. Minn., 1970, Ph.D., 1972. Service ctr. supt. Shell Oil Co., Cairo, 1955-61; indsl., mgmt. tng. instr. ARAMCO, Dhahran, Saudi Arabia, 1961-68; teaching assoc. U.-Minn., Mpls., 1968-72; speech communication prof. Calif. State U.-Long Beach, 1972—; with ARAMCO, 1978-80. Grantee NSF, 1981, 82, 83. Mem. Am. Mgmt. Assn., Internat. Communication Assn., AAUP, Am. Soc. Tng. and Devel., Soc. Cross-Cultural Research, Speech Communication Assn., Internat. Soc. Intercultural Edn., Tng. and Research, World Communication Assn., Wstern Speech Communication Assn., Assn. Egyptian Am. Scholars. Democrat. Co-author: An Introduction to Intercultural Communication, 1975, 1986; contbr. articles to profl. jours. Office: Calif State U Dept Speech Communication Long Beach CA 90840

YOUSOUFIAN, EUGENIA LITWORNIA, computer software company executive; b. Newark, Sept. 8, 1947; d. Eugene Ignatz and Helen Catherine (Adamczyk) Litwornia; m. Armen Zareh Yousoufian, Aug. 21, 1971; 1 child, Maria Anna. BA, Rutgers U., 1969; MBA, Seattle U., 1975. Cert. data processor. Programmer trainee Mobil Oil Co., N.Y.C., 1968; systems engr. IBM, Springfield, N.J., 1969-71; programmer analyst County of King, Seattle, 1971-74; programmer analyst/systems analyst Safeco Ins. Co., Seattle, 1974-76; instr. data processing Bellevue (Wash.) Community Coll., 1976-80; pres. Yousoufian Software, Inc., Vashon, Wash., 1981—. Roman Catholic. Avocations: cooking, travelling. Home: Route 3 Box 293 Vashon WA 98070-9803 Office: Yousoufian Software Inc 17230-99th Ave SW PO Box 950 Vashon WA 98070

YOUSSEFI, KOUROSH (KEN), mechanical engineering educator; b. Tehran, Iran, Oct. 21, 1948; came to U.S., 1968; s. Ali and Heshmat (Shafii) Y.; m. Karel A. Allen, June 17, 1972. BS, Sacramento State U., 1973; MS, U. Calif., Berkeley, 1974; PhD, U. Calif., 1978. Lectr. U. Calif., Berkeley, 1978, lectr., researcher, 1983—; cons. Ahvaz (Iran) Steel Mills, 1978-79; assoc. prof. U. Sci. and Tech., Tehran, 1979-82; researcher Lawrence Berkeley (Calif.) Lab., 1983; sr. mech. engr. Failure Analysis Assocs., Palo Alto, Calif., 1983-85, cons., 1985; lectr. San Jose (Calif.) State U., 1985—. Mem. ASME (assoc.). Avocations: bridge, skiing, tennis. Office: U Calif Berkeley Etcheverry Bldg Rm 5106 Berkeley CA 94720

YRIBIA, VIRGINIA WILSON, behavioral science educator; b. Syracuse, N.Y., Nov. 28, 1939; d. James Robert and Anna May (Caldwell) Wilson; m. William A. Yribia, May. 30, 1969; children: Laura E., Peter A. BA, U. N.Mex., 1961; MSW, U. Chgo., 1964; MA, U. Colo., 1986. Psychiat. social worker Bur. Mental Health, Prince Georges County, Md., 1969-70; adminstr., program dir. Barney Neighbor House, Washington, 1970-72; social worker Rosemount Day Care Ctr., Washington, 1972-74; pvt. practice, cons. social work Denver, 1975-85; mem. faculty U. Colo., Denver, 1983—; mem. Med. Adv. Bd. Comcare, Denver, 1984—, Bodimetric Health Services, 1982-85. Mem. Nat. Assn. Social Workers (cert.), Soc. Tchrs. Family Medicine, Colo. Gerontol. Soc., Am. Sociol. Soc., World Future Soc., Rocky Mountain Future Assn. (bd. dirs. 1983—). Home: 2375 Locust St Denver CO 80207 Office: U Colo Health Sci Ctr Dept Family Medicine 1180 Claremont St Denver CO 80220

YTURRALDE, DAVID JAVIER, construction management professional; b. El Paso, Tex., Sept. 21, 1944; s. David and Concepcion (Portugal) Y. B.Arch., U. Tex., 1973; M.S. in Engring., U. Wash., 1982. Registered architect, Wash. Architect Pellati & Herrera, El Paso, 1973-75; constrn. engr. OICC Trident, Bangor, Wash., 1975-80; project mgr. Criton Fentron Co., Seattle, 1980-81; cost/scheduling engr. Bechtel Power Inc., San Francisco, 1982-83; constrn. project mgr. CH2M Hill, Inc., Emeryville, Calif., 1983-86; project ops. mgr. Profl. Mgmt. Assocs., San Francisco, 1986— ; cons. Citicorp Real Estate, San Francisco, 1983-86. Served with U.S. Army, 1968-70, Vietnam. Mem. AIA (bldg. codes com. San Francisco chpt.), Project Mgmt. Inst., Constrn. Mgmt. Assn. Am., Soc. Mktg. Profl. Services, Am. Arbitration Assn., Assn. Preservation Tech. Club: Sierra. Home: 8029 Kittyhawk Ave Westchester CA 90045 Office: Profl Mgmt Assocs 455 Beach St San Francisco CA 94133

YU, DONALD ROBERT, consumer electronics products executive; b. Shanghai, China, Sept. 12, 1937; came to U.S., 1955, naturalized, 1958; s. Robert and Lillian (King) Y.; m. Jean King, Nov. 25, 1963; children—David Richard, Jennifer Katherine. A.A., Menlo Coll., Menlo Park, Calif., 1959, B.S., 1961; postgrad. Hastings Coll. Law, 1961. With consumer products div. Sharp Electronics Corp., 1968-72; pres., chief exec. officer Sheen Industries Ltd., San Rafael, Calif., 1973-75; mem. Hutchison Internat. Ltd., Hong Kong, 1973-75; pres., chmn., chief exec. officer Elint Semiconductors, Inc., Santa Clara, Calif., 1976—; pres., founder U.S. Games Corp., Santa Clara, 1980-82; chmn., chief exec. officer Toryo Tech. Corp., Santa Clara, 1982—; dir. Westin Internat. Corp. Office: 1245 Pear St Mount View CA 94043

YU, DOROTHY DO-SUN, gas company professional; b. Chuang King, Peoples Republic of China, Feb. 6, 1937; came to U.S., 1962; d. Yuan-Suan and Tao-Tien (Chu) Yu; m. Jason Chia Yu, May 26, 1965; children: William, Danny, Angela. BBA, Chuan Hsing U., Taipei, Republic of China, 1960; MSLS, George Peabody U., 1963. Asst. head. librarian Drexel U., Phila., 1968; head of sci. sect. Va. Poly. Inst. and State U., Blacksburg, 1968-74; sr. cataloger Utah State Library Commn., Salt Lake City, 1975-76; dir. of library Academia Sinica, Nankang, Republic of China, 1976-77; library specialist Earth Sci. Lab., Salt Lake City, 1977-79; records coordinator Northwest Pipeline Corp., Salt Lake City, 1979—; founder, pres. Library Faculty Assn., Blacksburg, 1972-73; vice prin. Salt Lake Chinese Sch., 1974-76. Bd. dirs. Great Salt Lake Chinese Sch., Salt Lake City, 1985—. Mem. Desk and Derrick Club, Assn. Records Mgrs., and Adminstrs. (advisor 1981-83), Office Automation Soc. Internat., Chinese Engrs. and Scientists Soc. of Utah. Roman Catholic. Avocation: educating community in the appreciation of various ethnics' culture. Home: 4845 Bron Breck St Salt Lake City UT 84117 Office: Northwest Pipeline Corp 295 Chipeta Way PO Box 8900 Salt Lake City UT 84108-0900

YU, ELMER, surgeon; b. Balt., Sept. 27, 1946; s. Shao-Chi and Shao-Chen Yu. BA, U. N.H., 1968; MD, George Washington U., 1973. Resident in gen. surgery U. N.Mex., Albuquerque, 1973-76, resident in plastic surgery, 1977-79, fellow in hand surgery, 1979. Office: 1010 Las Lomas NE Suite #2 Albuquerque NM 87102

YU, LOH-CHUNG, cell biologist; b. Taichung, Taiwan, Republic of China, Dec. 2, 1946; came to U.S., 1968; d. Ming-tung and Jeih-Jen (Kuang) Yu; m. Kenneth Lang Lum, Dec. 24, 1976; children; Christina, Kimberly. BS, Nat. Taiwan U., 1968; MS, U. Pitts., 1969; PhD, U. Calif., San Francisco, 1975. Postdoctoral fellow, assoc. researcher Sloan-Kettering Inst. for Cancer Research, N.Y.C., 1975-77, research assoc., 1978; sr. biomed. scientist Lawrence Livermore (Calif.) Nat. Lab., 1979—. Author: Human Cytogenetics, 1977, Research Perspectives in Cytogenetics, 1984, Muntjak Repetitive DNA, 1986. Fellow Earle C. Anthony, U. Calif., Berkeley, 1969-70, Genevieve McEnerney, U. Calif., Berkeley, 1970-71, NIH, Washington, 1976-78. Mem. AAAS, Tissue Culture Assn. Club: Toastmasters. Avocations: gardening, astronomy. Office: Lawrence Livermore Nat Lab East Ave Livermore CA 94550

YU, RAYMOND K., engineer; b. Shanghai, People's Republic of China, July 3, 1953; came to U.S., 1972; s. Jaw-Jang and Wei-Lien (Yang) Y.; m. Sabrina Pang, May 30, 1981; children: Claudia, Jessica. BS, U. Calif., Berkeley, 1976; MS, MIT, 1978. Research asst. MIT, Cambridge, Mass., 1977-78; chem. engr. GCA Tech. Corp., Bedford, Mass., 1978-79; process devel. engr. Hydrocarbon Research Inc., Lawrenceville, N.J., 1979-84; sr. process engr. Intel, Santa Clara, Calif., 1984-86, Monolithic Memories, Santa Clara, 1986—. Mem. Am. Chem. Soc., Am. Inst. Chem. Engrs., Combustion Inst., Sigma Xi. Avocations: photography, tennis, skiing, hiking.

YUEN, WING, food scientist, consultant; b. China, Sept. 29, 1914; came to U.S., 1957; s. Chung Kuen and Lan (Chan) Y.; m. Josie Fung, Dec. 1941; children: David Y.H., Judy K.C., Janni B.C., Joyse P.C. PhD, Free Protestant U., London, 1968; D. Sc., Sussex (England) Coll. Tech., 1969. Lectr. Lingnan U., Republic of China, 1940-41; sr. technologist China Food Industries Corp., Chung King, Republic of China, 1942-45; tech. splist. Agri-Machinery Ops. and Mgmt. Office, UN, Republic of China, 1947-49; chemist Sunkist Growers Inc., Ontario, Calif., 1957-58; research supr. Ventura (Calif.) Costal Corp., 1958-80; cons. Yuen & Assocs., Ventura, 1980—; cons. Inst. Food Technologists and Vols. for Internat. Tech. Assistance, 1964—; 1st choice rep. UN Indsl. Devel. Orgn. to advise Israel's citrus industry, 1968; vis. prof., advisor Ministry Agr., Agr. Univs. and the Food Industries, Republic of China, 1984—. Contbr. articles to profl. jours. Recipient citation Proposal to Developing Countries, U.S. Pres. Lyndon Johnson, 1966, citation Food for Peace Programs, Inst. Food Technologists, 1965. Fellow Royal Soc. Health (England), AAAS; mem. Am. Chem. Soc. (emeritus), Inst. Food Technologists (emeritus). Home: 3173 Preble Ave Ventura CA 93003

YULE, DOROTHY ANN, art director, graphic designer; b. Mineola, N.Y., Jan. 1, 1950; d. William Alan and Dorothy Elizabeth (Hunt) Y. BA, Barnard Coll., 1972; cert. in printmaking, St. Martin's Sch. Art., 1975. Adminstrv. asst. Kidder, Peabody and Co., Inc., N.Y.C., 1979-82; asst. to art dir. Inside Sports Mag., N.Y.C., 1982; assoc. art dir. Savvy Mag., N.Y.C., 1982-84; freelance graphic designer N.Y.C. and San Francisco, 1984-85; art dir. Women's Sports and Fitness Mag., Palo Alto, Calif., 1985-86. Mem. Am. Inst. Graphic Design. Home: 2666 Shasta Rd Berkeley CA 94708

YURIST, SVETLAN JOSEPH, mechanical engineer; b. Kharkov, USSR, Nov. 20, 1931; came to U.S., 1979, naturalized, 1985; s. Joseph A. and Rosalia S. (Zoilman) Y.; m. Imma Lea Erlikh, Oct. 11, 1960; 1 child, Eugene. M.S. in Mech. Engring. with honors, Poly. Inst., Odessa, USSR, 1954. Engr. designer Welding Equipment Plant, Novaya Utka, USSR, 1954-56; sr. tech. engr. Heavy Duty Automotive Crane Plant, Odessa, 1956-60, asst. chief matallugist, 1971-78; supr. research lab. Inst. Spl. Methods in

Foundry Industry, Odessa, 1960-66, project engr. sci. research, 1966-71; engr. designer Teledyne Cast Product, Pomona, Calif., 1979-81; sr. mech. engr. Walt Elliot Disney Enterprises, Glendale, Calif., 1981-83; foundry liaison engr. Pacific Pumps div. Dresser Industries, Inc., Huntington Park, Calif., 1984-86; casting engr. Superior Industries Internat., Inc., Van Nuys, Calif., 1986—. Recipient award for design of automatic lines for casting electric motor parts USSR Ministry Machine Bldg. and Handtools Mfr., 1966, for equipment for permanent mold casting All Union Exhbn. of Nat. Econ. Achievements, 1966-70. Mem. Am. Foundrymen's Soc. Contbr. reports, articles to collections All Union Confs. Spl. Methods in Foundry, USSR; USSR patentee permanent mold casting. Home: 5050 Lyman Ave Covina CA 91724 Office: Superior Industries Internat Inc 7800 Woodley Ave Van Nuys CA 91406-1788

ZABALA, THOMAS MICHAEL, architect; b. Boise, Idaho, Feb. 7, 1946; s. Thomas Floyd and Conchita Juanita (Arostegui) Z.; m. Jayne Abbe McMillen, Sept. 15, 1972; 1 son, Jeffrey Mark. BArch., U. Oreg., 1969. Registered architect Idaho, Mont., Colo., Oreg., Nev., Wash. Draftsman, N.W. Illustrations, 1967-68; architect intern Hamill/Shaw Assocs., 1968-69, Cline/Smull/Hamill/Shaw Assocs., 1969-72; architect Cline/Smull/Hamill Assocs., 1972-73; prin./ptnr. Zabala-Giltzow-Albanese, Boise, 1973—. Chmn., Boise City Design Rev. Com., 1976-80; mem. Boise City Planning and Zoning Commn., 1984—; mem. Citizens Adv. Com. on Downtown Renewal, 1979-80; mem. Idaho Hist. Preservation Council, Capitol Blvd. Design Plan Steering and Adv. com., Idaho Tech. Adv. Council; bd. dirs. Basque Cultural Ctr. Idaho. Served with U.S. Army, 1969-76. Recipient Honor award, 1984, 85. Mem. AIA (merit award 1978, citation award 1982, chmn. design awards com. 1976, 78, 82, mem. legis. law com. 1973—), Am. Arbitration Assn. (panel of arbitrators), Nat. Council Archtl. Registration Bds., Idaho State Bd. Archtl. Examiners. Democrat. Roman Catholic. Mem. editorial adv. bd. Symposia Mag., 1981-83, N.W. Architecture Mag., 1982—. Home: 3974 Oak Park Pl Boise ID 83703 Office: 815 Park Blvd Suite 350 Boise ID 83712

ZACCONE, TERRY SANTO, physicist; b. Madison, Wis., Nov. 18, 1936; s. Santo Lilo and Charlotte Elizabeth (Terrell) Z.; m. Judith A. Stark, Jan. 28, 1962; children: Julie Ann, Vincent Lilo. AA, Sacramento City Coll., 1958; BA, U. Calif., Berkeley, 1961; MS, San Jose State U., 1966; PhD, Stanford U., 1982. Cert. tchr., Calif. Statistician Aerojet-Gen., Sacramento, 1956-58, Lawrence Radiation Lab., Berkeley, 1959-61; sr. research specialist Space Systems div. Lockheed Corp., Sunnyvale, Calif., 1961-64, 72-80; sr. staff scientist Research and Devel. div. Lockheed Corp., Palo Alto, Calif., 1980—; research engr. Advanced Tech. div. Am. Standard, Mountain View, Calif., 1965-67, Philco-Ford, Calif., 1967-72. Served with USAFR, 1954-62. Fellow Brit. Interplanetary Soc.; mem. Optical Soc. Am., Acoustical Soc. Am., Am. Assn. Physics Tchrs., Porsche Club Am. (pres. 1985). Democrat. Avocations: race car driving, fencing, racquetball, classical music, writing. Home: 13046 Anza Dr Saratoga CA 95070 Office: Lockheed Research and Devel 3251 Hanover St Palo Alto CA 94304

ZACHARY, RAYMOND AUGUST, software company manager; b. Tyler, Tex., June 15, 1934; s. Raymond A. Zachary and Amy Elizabeth Frakes; m. Mary Katherine Barnet, May 30, 1951 (div. Apr. 1964); m. Nacia Anderson, Apr. 1964 (div. Sept. 1980); children: April, Brian, Austin; m. Karin Nicholette Steiner, July 4, 1981. BA, U. Tex., 1956, MA in Math., 1958. Programmer, analyst Boeing Airplane Co., Renton, Wash., 1958-59; ops. research analyst Tex. Instruments, Dallas, 1959-63, systems supr., 1967-75; systems analyst Hayes Internat. Corp., Birmingham, Ala., 1963-65; mgr. math. scis. Western Co. N.Am., Richardson, Tex., 1965-67; mgr. software engring. GTE Sylvania, Mountain View, Calif., 1976-77; mgr. software engr. Ford Aerospace and Communications Corp., Palo Alto, Calif., 1977—. Avocations: photography, skiing, hunting, reading, tennis. Office: Ford Aerospace & Communications Corp 3939 Fabian Way Palo Alto CA 94303

ZACHRISSON, CARL UDDO, political scientist, educator; b. San Francisco, Dec. 4, 1940; s. Carl Uddo and Erma Christiana (Luce) Z.; m. Adele Lee Hall, Dec. 30, 1971; children: Carl Frederick, Christopher Dawes. B.A., Stanford U., 1962; Lic. es Sci. Politiques, Grad. Inst. Internat. Studies, U. Geneva (Switzerland); D.Phil., Oxford U. (Eng.), 1972. Instr. to asst. prof. polit. studies Pitzer Coll., Claremont, Calif., 1967-74; assoc. prof. internat. relations Pomona Coll., Claremont, 1974-81; from asst. prof. to prof. govt. and internat. relations Claremont Grad. Sch., 1972—; dir. West Coast Region, Inst. Internat. Edn., San Francisco, 1983—; pres. Internat. Studies Assocs. Inc., 1981-83; lectr. USIS, West Africa, 1972; dir. Edn. Abroad, Pomona and Scripps Colls., 1973-81; v.p. So. Calif. div. UN Assn., 1976-79; bd. dirs. Council Internat. Ednl. Exchange, 1978-81, So. Calif. Global Edn. task force, 1978-81. Treas. Calif. Council UN U., 1979-81; bd. dirs. Internat. Visitors Ctr., San Francisco, 1986—, San Francisco-Abidjan Sister City Com., 1986—; mem. Am. Com. East-West Accord; mem. San Francisco Com. on Fgn. Relations, 1984—; pres. bd. trustees Internat. Exchange Network of No. Calif., 1985—; chmn. bd. trustees Town Sch. Boys, 1986—; sr. warden St. Mary the Virgin Episcopal Ch., San Francisco, 1986-88. Mem. African Studies Assn., Am. Polit. Sci Assn., Am. Soc. Internat. Law, Nat. Assn. Fgn. Student Affairs, Soc. Internat. Edn., Tng. and Research, Soc. Internat. Devel. Clubs: Bohemian, Oxford Union Soc.; Norfolk Country (Conn.). Author: (with R. Tebbets) Educating for International Competence, 1984. Office: Inst Internat Edn 312 Sutter St Suite 610 San Francisco CA 94108

ZADOROZNY, EDWARD ALEXANDER, design products supervisor; b. Pitts., Dec. 24, 1956; s. Edward and Helen Catherine (Kurtaneck) Z. B.S. in Mech. Engring., U. Pitts., 1978. Design engr., space div. Rockwell Internat., Downey, Calif., 1978—, program mgr. Dept. Def. materials research and devel. program, 1985—, now supr. involved in research and devel. of Space Shuttles Columbia, Challenger, Discovery, and Atlantis, also teaching asst. for computer aided design 1980-82; research in materials, computer tools and space problems, 1982—. Mem. AIAA (chpt. pres. 1977-78), Planetary Soc., Nat. Space Inst., Am. Space Found. Tau Beta Pi, Phi Eta Sigma, Pi Tau Sigma. Democrat. Orthodox Catholic. Researcher on design for artificial heart, 1975, on ground effects aircraft design, 1978. Office: MC AD36 12214 Lakewood Blvd Downey CA 90241

ZADOW, ROBERTA PAULINE, teacher; b. Los Angeles, Oct. 9, 1939; d. Abraham David and Sarah (Davidson) Z.; 1 child, Kira Zadow-Colley. BS, San Francisco State U., 1963, MA, 1980. Cert. gen. social scis. and reading specialist tchr. Tchr. San Francisco Unified Sch. Dist., 1965—; owner Roberta Zadow Artists Mgmt., San Francisco, 1970-75; cons. in field, San Francisco, 1975—; bd. dirs. Corp. Action Com., San Francisco. Editor: Northern California Counseling, 1979-86, Directions Work Now, 1981-86. Sec. Haight Ashbury Neighborhood Council, San Francisco, 1971-72; vol. Dem. Nat. Conv., San Francisco, 1984. Mem. Am. Fedn. Tchrs. (union leadership council 1979—), San Francisco Zool. Soc., Southern Calif. Acad. Scis., San Francisco Art Mus. Avocations: writing prose and poetry, wine making, renovating Victorian houses. Office: St Wilson High Sch 400 Mansell St San Francisco CA 94117

ZAERR, JOE BENJAMIN, forest tree physiologist; b. Los Angeles, Sept. 9, 1932; s. John L. and Mary Eleanor (Jones) Z.; m. Louis Marie Bingham, Jan. 26, 1954; children: Linda Marie, Laura Susan, Jon Benjamin. BS, U. Calif., Berkeley, 1954, PhD, 1964. Research assoc. Agrl. Research Service, USDA, Beltsville, Md., 1964-65; from asst. prof. to prof. forest tree physiology Oreg. State U., Corvallis, 1965-81, prof. forestry, 1981—, asst. dean grad. sch., 1977-80. Served to lt. comdr. USNR, 1954—. Named sr. researcher Fulbright Commn., Fed. Republic Germany, 1981-82. Mem. Soc. Am. Foresters, Am. Soc. Plant Physiologists, Northwest Sci. Assn. Republican. Club: Toastmasters (pres. local club 1978). Home: 5945 NW Rosewood Dr Corvallis OR 97330 Office: Oreg State U Coll of Forestry Corvallis OR 97331

ZAFFARONI, ALEJANDRO C., medical research company executive; b. Montevideo, Uruguay, Feb. 27, 1923; came to U.S., 1944; s. Carlos and Luisa (Alfaro) Z.; m. Lyda Russomanno, July 5, 1946; children—Alejandro A., Elisa. B., U. Montevideo, 1943; Ph.D. in Biochemistry, U. Rochester, 1949; Doctorate (hon.), U. Republic, Montevideo, 1983. Dir. biochem. research Syntex S.A., Mexico City, 1951-54, v.p., dir. research, 1954-56; exec. v.p., dir. Syntex Corp., Palo Alto, Calif., 1956-68; pres. Syntex Labs. Inc., Palo Alto, Calif., 1962-68, Syntex Research, Palo Alto, Calif., 1962-68; founder, chmn. bd., chief exec. officer ALZA Corp., Palo Alto, Calif., 1968—; founder, mem. policy bd. and exec. com. DNAX Research Inst. of Molecular and Cellular Biology, Inc., Palo Alto, Calif., 1980—; chmn. Internat. Psoriasis Research Found., Palo Alto; incorporator Neuroscis. Research Found. MIT, Brookline, Mass.; bd. govs. Weizmann Inst. Sci., Rehovot, Israel; mem. pharm. panel of com. on tech. and internat. econs. and trade issues Nat. Acad. Engring. Office of Fgn. Sec. and Assembly of Engring., Washington; hon. prof. biochemistry Nat. U. Mex., 1957, U. Montevideo, 1959. Contbr. numerous articles to profl. jours.; patentee in field. Recipient Barren medal Barren Found., Chgo., 1974; Pres.'s award Weizmann Inst. Sci., 1978; Chem. Pioneer award Am. Inst. Chemists, Inc., 1979. Fellow Am. Acad. Arts and Scis., Am. Pharm. Assn.; mem. AAAS, Am. Chem. Soc., Am. Found. Pharm. Edn., Am. Inst. Chemists, Inc., Am. Soc. Biol. Chemists, Inc., Am. Soc. Microbiology, Am. Soc. Pharmacology and Exptl. Therapeutics, Biomed. Engring. Soc., Calif. Pharmacists Assn., Internat. Pharm. Fedn., Internat. Soc. Chronobiology, Internat. Soc. Study of Biol. Rhythms, Soc. Exptl. Biology and Medicine, Sociedad Mexicana de Nutricion y Endocrinologia, Biochem. Soc. Eng., Endocrine Soc., Internat. Soc. Research in Biology of Reproduction, N.Y. Acad. Scis.

ZAFFOS, GERALD, federal agency executive; b. N.Y.C., July 26, 1950; s. Abraham and Lillian (Goldberg) Z.; m. Nydia Picayo, May 10, 1980; 1 child, Aaron Manuel. BA, CCNY, 1972; MA, Queens Coll., 1976. Clk. typist Presidio of San Francisco, 1975-77, engring. technician, 1977-80; procurement agt. GSA, San Francisco, 1980-83, supervisory procurement agt., 1983-85, chief commodity ops. br., 1985-86, chief procurement br., 1986—. Office: Gen Services Administrn 525 Market St San Francisco CA 94105

ZAHARY, ROBERT GENE, accounting educator; b. West Frankfort, Ill., Sept. 30, 1942; s. Joe and Iona Madge (Culley) Z. BS, Oreg. State U., 1965; MBA, U. So. Calif., 1972, PhD, 1982; BA, Calif. State U., Los Angeles, 1975. CPA, Calif. Mng. ptnr. Pasadena (Calif.) Vinyl Products, 1967-69; acct. Lee Sheridan & Co., Los Angeles, 1969-70; assoc. prof. biology Calif. State U., Los Angeles, 1982-84, asst. prof. acctg., 1984—; coordinator Orgn. Tropical Studies, San Jose, Costa Rica, 1983. Editor: Tropical Biology: An Ecological Approach, 1985; contbr. articles to profl. jours. Grantee Lerner Grey Fund for Marine Research, Theodore Roosevelt Meml. Fund for Wildlife Research, Janss Found., ARC. Mem. Am. Inst. CPA's, So. Calif. Acad. Scis. (treas. 1983-84, v.p. 1985-87—, pres. 1987—, bd. dirs. 1980—), Calif. State Soc. CPA's, Sigma Xi (grantee). Home: 1480 N Mentor Pasadena CA 91104 Office: Calif State U 5151 State Univ Dr Los Angeles CA 90032

ZAIDI, SHUJA HAIDER, oil company executive; b. Faisalbad, Punjab, Pakistan, Sept. 10, 1952; came to U.S., 1973; s. Syed Zahir Hussain and Syeda Raisa (Rizvi Khatoon) Z. BS, Govt. Coll., Punjab, 1972; MS, Birmingham U., 1976. Mgr. Caleb Brett/Aramco London, Dhahran, Saudi Arabia, 1977-81; cons., area mgr., v.p. Robinson Internat., Los Angeles, 1981-83; mgr. Chemoil Corp., Long Beach, Calif., 1983-85; v.p. Gustafson Oil Co., Los Angeles, 1985-86, Poly-Fuels Inc., Laguna Hills, Calif., 1986—; v.p. Gustafson Oil, Los Angeles, 1985—. Fellow Inst. Petroleum; mem. ASTM, Soc. Petroleum Engrs. Republican. Moslem. Home: 1846 Via Quinto Oceanside CA 92056 Office: Poly Fuels Inc 23276 S Pointe Dr Laguna Hills CA 92653

ZAISER, SALLY SOLEMMA VANN (MRS. FOSTER E. ZAISER), retail book company executive; b. Birmingham, Ala., Jan. 18, 1917; d. Carl Waldo and Einnan (Herndon) Vann; student Birmingham-So. Coll., 1933-36, Akron Coll. Bus., 1937; m. Foster E. Zaiser, Nov. 11, 1939. Acct., A. Simionato, San Francisco, 1958-65; head acctg. dept. Richard T. Clarke Co., San Francisco, 1966; acct. John Howell-Books, San Francisco, 1967-72, sec., treas., 1972-83, 84-85, dir., 1982-85; sec. Great Eastern Mines, Inc., Albuquerque, 1969-81, dir., 1980-85. Braille transcriber for ARC, Kansas City, Mo. 1941-45; vol. worker ARC Hosp. Program, São Paulo, Brazil, 1952. Mem. Book Club Calif., Calif. Hist. Soc., Soc. Lit. and Arts, Gleeson Library Assocs. (dir. 1984—, editor GLA newsletter 1984—), Nat. Notary Assn., Theta Upsilon. Republican. Episcopalian. Club: Capitol Hill. Home: 355 Serrano Dr Apt 4-C San Francisco CA 94132 Office: 434 Post St San Francisco CA 94102

ZAJAC, JOHN, semiconductor equipment company executive; b. N.Y.C., July 21, 1946; s. John Andrew and Catherine (Canepa) Z.; m. Vera Barbagallo, Jan. 13, 1973; children: Jennifer, Michelle. AAS, NYU, 1966; BEE, U. Ky., 1968. Project engr. B.C.D. Computing, N.Y.C., 1968-70; v.p. Beacon Systems, Commack, N.Y., 1970-73, E.T. Systems, Santa Clara, Calif., 1973-77; v.p. research and devel. Eaton Corp., Sunnyvale, Calif., 1977-81; pres. Semitech/Gen. Signal, Los Gatos, Calif., 1981-83; mgr. advanced product div. Tegal/Motorola Inc., Novato, Calif., 1983-86; v.p. research and devel. U.S.A. Inc., San Jose, Calif., 1986—. Author: Delecate Balance, 1987; patentee in field. Home: 1137 Angmar Ct San Jose CA 95121

ZAJDEL, WILLIAM JOHN, chemist, educator; b. Gary, Ind., July 5, 1954; s. Thaddeus Leo and Shirley Ann (Friel) Z. Student, U. London, 1974-75; BA in Chemistry summa cum laude, Wabash Coll., Crawfordsville, Ind., 1976; PhD in Chemistry, U. Ill., 1982. Teaching asst. Wabash Coll., Crawfordsville, 1973-76; researcher Monsanto, St. Louis, 1976; teaching asst. U. Ill., Urbana, 1976-80, research asst., 1980-82; asst. prof. chemistry Calif. Poly. Inst., San Luis Obispo, 1982-84, U. Redlands, Calif., 1984—. Coauthor: (chpt.) Amide Directed Lithiations, 1985; contbr. articles to profl. jours. Mem. Internat. Union of Pure and Applied Chemists (affiliate), Am. Chem. Soc., ACLU, Phi Beta Kappa, Phi Kappa Phi, Sigma Xi, Phi Lambda Upsilon, Alpha Chi Sigma, Phi Kappa Psi. Democrat. Home: 933 College St Redlands CA 92374 Office: Univ Redlands Redlands CA 92374

ZALETEL, JOHN, commercial laboratory executive, environmental and petroleum consultant; b. Pueblo, Colo., Feb. 20, 1943; s. John J. and Anna M. (Zobec) A.; m. Jacqueline A. Biondolillo, June 19, 1965; children—John, Paul, Regina, Nicole. B.S. in Chemistry, Regis Coll., Denver, 1965; M.S. in Chemistry, U. Iowa, 1968, Ph.D. in Chemistry, 1972. Teaching and research asst. U. Iowa, Iowa City, 1965-70; research chemist Lorillard Corp., Greensboro, N.C., 1970-76; chief chemist Agrl. Tech. Service, Bakersfield, Calif., 1976-79; instr. chemistry Calif. State Coll.-Bakersfield, 1979-80; pres. Zalco Labs. Inc., Bakersfield, 1979—; presenter profl. confs. Contbr. articles to profl. jours. Pres. Our Lady of Grace Parish Bd. Edn., Greensboro, 1976; bd. dirs. Vaughn Water Co., Bakersfield, 1981, 83, pres., 1982. Denver Metro Research Found. research grantee, 1964. Mem. Am. Chem. Soc. (sec. 1977-78, chmn.-elect 1978-79, chmn. 1979-80), Am. Petroleum Inst., Am. Water Works Assn. Republican. Roman Catholic.

ZALTA, EDWARD, otorhinolaryngologist; b. Houston, Mar. 2, 1930; s. Nouri Louis and Marie Zahde (Lizmi) Z.; m. Carolyn Mary Gordon, Oct. 8, 1971; 1 child, Ryan David; children by previous marriage: Nouri Allan, Lori Ann, Barry Thomas, Marci Louise. B.S., Tulane U., 1952, M.D., 1956. Diplomate Am. Bd. Quality Assurance and Utilization Rev. Physicians. Intern Brooke Army Hosp., San Antonio, 1956-57; resident in otolaryngology U.S. Army Hosp., Ft. Campbell, Ky., 1957-60; practice medicine specializing in otolaryngology Glendora, West Covina and San Dimas, Calif., 1960-82; ENT cons. City of Hope Med. Center, 1961-76; mem. staff Foothill Presbyn.; past pres. Los Angeles Found. Community Service, Los Angeles Poison Info. Center, So. Calif. Physicians Council, Inc.; founder pres., chmn. bd. CAPP CARE, Inc.; chmn. bd. MDM; founder Inter-Hosp. Council Continuing Med. Edn. Contbr. articles to profl. jours. Pres. bd. govs. Glendora Unified Sch. Dist., 1965-71; mem. Calif. Cancer Adv. Council, 1967-71, Commn. of Californias, Los Angeles County Commn. on Economy and Efficiency. Served to capt. M.C. AUS, 1957-60. Recipient Award of Merit Order St. Lazarus, 1981. Mem. AMA, Calif. Med. Assn., Los Angeles County Med. Assn. (past pres.), Am. Acad. Otolaryngology, Am. Council Otolaryngology, Kappa Nu, Phi Delta Epsilon. Republican. Jewish. Clubs: Glendora Country, Centurion, Sea Bluff Beach and Racquet. Home: 207 Whispering Oaks Glendora CA 91740 Office: 17390 Brookhurst Ave Fountain Valley CA 92708

ZALUTSKY, MORTON HERMAN, lawyer; b. Schenectady, Mar. 8, 1935; s. Albert and Gertrude (Daffner) Z.; m. Audrey Englebardt, June 16, 1957; children—Jane, Diane, Samuel. B.A., Yale U., 1957; J.D., U. Chgo., 1960. Bar: Oreg. 1961. Law clk. Oreg. Supreme Ct., 1960-61; assoc. Hart, Davidson, Veazie & Hanlon, 1961-63, Veatch & Lovett, 1963-64, Morrison, Bailey, Dunn, Cohen & Miller, 1964-69; prin. Morton H. Zalutsky, P.C., 1970-76; ptnr. Dahl, Zalutsky, Nichols & Hinson, 1977-79, Zalutsky & Klarquist, P.C., Portland, Oreg., 1980-85, Zalutsky, Klarquist & Johnson, P.C., Portland, 1985—; instr. Portland State U., 1961-64, Northwestern Sch. Law, 1969-70; assoc. prof. U. Miami Law Sch.; lectr. Practicing Law Inst., 1971—, Oreg. State Bar Continuing Legal Edn. Program, 1970, Am. Law Inst.-ABA Continuing Legal Edn. Program, 1973—, 34th, 37th NYU ann. insts. fed. taxation, So. Fed. Tax Inst., U. Miami Inst. Estate Planning, Southwestern Legal Found., Internat. Found. Employee Benefit Plans, numerous other profl. orgns. Author: (with others) The Professional Corporation in Oregon, 1970, 82; contbg. author: The Dentist and the Law, 3d edit.; contbr. to numerous publs. in field. Mem. ABA (vice chairperson profl. services 1987—, mem. council tax sect. 1985—, spl. coordinator 1980-85, vice chair profl. services 1987—), Multnomah County Bar Assn., Oreg. State Bar Assn., Oreg. Estate Planning Council. Jewish. Home: 3118 SW Fairmount Blvd Portland OR 97201 Office: 215 SW Washington St 3d Floor Portland OR 97204

ZAMBRANA, BERNARD, engineering and graphics design company executive, consultant; b. Cochabamba, Bolivia, Nov. 22, 1947; s. Rene Delgado and Elsa Alicia (Barragan) Z.; m. Paula England, Oct. 26, 1982 (div. Nov. 1983); 1 child, Zach. Registered profl. engr., Colo.; licensed pilot. Office mgr., project engr. Engring. Service Co., Aurora, Colo., 1971-75; project mgr. Ortloff Corp., Golden, Colo., 1976-82; owner, prin. cons. Zambrana and Assocs., Lakewood, Colo., 1983—; owner, designer Eagle 1 Graphics, Arvada, Colo., 1986—; ptnr. Lakewood Mag., 1986—. Mem. Instrument Soc. Am. (pres. 1978-79, sec., v.p. 1976-78, Leadership award 1979), Lakewood C. of C. (mem. task force 1985-86, exec. dialog 1985), Denver C. of C. (chief exec. officer connection group). Democrat. Roman Catholic. Avocations: triathelons, swimming, skiing, flying, hang gliding. Home: 5114 Bristol St Arvada CO 80002 Office: Zambrana and Assocs 10576 W Alameda Ave Lakewood CO 80226

ZAMONSKI, STANLEY WALTER, museum curator; b. Shenandoah, Pa., Aug. 7, 1919; s. Stanley Walter and Cecilia (Walishewski) Z.; student New Eng. Aircraft-Wentworth Inst., 1940-42, Mass. Inst. Tech., 1940-42, Georgetown U., 1943. Engring. draftsman Colo. Dept. Hwys., 1947-54; freelance photographer-writer, Denver, 1954-70; prof. photo-journalism Instituto Allende, San Miguel Allende, Mexico, 1970-72; engring. draftsman Denver Planning Dept., 1973-78; curator Buffalo Bill Meml. Mus., Golden, Colo., 1978—. Dep. sheriff Denver Posse Westerners. Served to 2d lt. USAAF, 1939-45. Decorated Air medal with two oak leaf clusters; recipient Braum award Denver Art Dirs. and Advt. Assn., 1959; named Colo. Press Photographer of Year, 1965, 66, 67. Mem. Polish Am. Hist. Assn., Nat. Historic Assn., Am. Assn. State and Local History, Nat. Writers Club, Am. Assn. Tchrs. Slavic and East European Langs., Polish Inst. Arts and Scis. Am., Colo. Authors League, Colo. Hist. Assn., Colo.-Wyo. Assn. Mus., Western History Assn., Colo. Authors League, Denver Press Club, Denver Art Club, Industries Jefferson County, Lakewood C. of C. Clubs: Polish (Denver); Am. Council Polish Cultural. Author: The 59'ers, Roaring Denver, 1961, The Westernaires on the Gallop, 1967, Grunwald, 1981, Gentleman Rogue, 1982, The Legacy of Buffalo Bill, 1986; (with O.J. Seiden) Buffalo Bill: His Life and Legend, 1983. Home: 800 S Vallejo St Denver CO 80223 Office: Box 950 Route 5 Golden CO 80401

ZAMZOW, DALE R., consultant; b. Beaver Dam, Wis., May 9, 1935; s. Alfred Eric and Viola I. (Dinkel) Z.; student U. Wis., 1953-54, Heidelberg U., 1959-60, Am. U. Beirut, 1960-61; m. Claudia Gooch, Dec. 15, 1962. Mgr. O/R Theatre Group, Milw., 1954-59; adminstrv. asst. Am. embassy, Lebanon, 1959-61; pres. IPC-Licensing, Santa Clara, Calif., 1962-81; exec. dir. U.S. Bear Force, Sunnyvale, Calif., 1982—, Trust Mgmt, Group, 1986—; dir. The Pinewood Sch., 1985—; cons. systems analyst, 1969-80. Founder, pres. Sunnyvale Art League, 1964; sec. Burbank Sanitary Dist., 1966-69; pub. relations dir. Lace Mus., 1979-81. Served with USAF, 1957-61. Decorated Award of Merit, Lebanese Air Force; recipient Presdl. Fitness awards, 1978, 79, U.S. Olympic Assn. award, 1980. Mem. Pub. Relations Roundtable, Vols. in Tech. Assistance, Nirvana Assn., Am. Soc. Systems Analysts (cert.). Clubs: Brit. Am., German Service, Good Bears of the World. Patentee packaging; designer 12 trademarks; author book and articles; Appropriate Tech. editor Vita News; pub. relations cons. Le Cav, Beirut, Lebanon; editor, publisher The Bear Force Times; cons. editor: Matchmaking News. Office: PO Box 4610 Santa Clara CA 95054

ZANDER, AXEL ROLF, physician, hospital administrator; b. Bielefeld, Fed. Republic Germany, Oct. 22, 1943; came to U.S., 1970;. Candidate in medicine, U. Munich, 1965; MD, Medizinische Akademie, Lübeck, Fed. Republic Germany, 1969. Fellow in hematology, oncology U. Ill., Chgo., 1973-76; asst. prof. U. Tex., Houston, 1977-81; assoc. prof. MD Anderson Tumor Instn., Houston, 1981-85, clin. dir. bone marrow transplantation, 1980-85; chief div. bone marrow transplantation Pacific Presbyn. U. Med. Ctr., San Francisco, 1985—. Contbr. articles to profl. jours. Home: 255 Glenn Dr Sausalito CA 94965

ZANDERS, CLAUDIA BOND, social worker; b. Beaumont, Tex., Oct. 11, 1939; d. Charles Senters and Ula Rae (Reinarz) Bond; m. John Zanders, Mar. 4, 1964 (div. 1965); 1 child, Anthony. BA, Trinity U., 1960; MSW, Our Lady of Lake Coll., 1964. Jr. psychiat. social worker Community Guidance Ctr., Austin, Tex., 1964, Child Guidance Clinic, San Antonio, 1966; med. social worker Foster Grandparent project, San Antonio, 1966-68; psychiat. social worker Desert Counseling Clin., China Lake, Calif., 1968-70; sr. social worker Santa Cruz (Calif.) Mental Health Ctr., 1970-73, adoption social worker, 1974—. Mem. Nat. Assn. Social Workers, Acad. Cert. Social Workers (cert.). Democrat. Home: PO Box 531 Ben Lomond CA 95005 Office: PO Box 1320 Santa Cruz CA 95061

ZANE, ALVIN YUN SHIN, structural engineer; b. Honolulu, Feb. 15, 1934; s. Kim Sang and Eunice C. K. (Ching) Z.; m. Mayette Lum, June 24, 1956; children—Kimeece, Darryl, Kareece. B.S.C.E., U. Hawaii, 1956. Lic. profl. structural and civil engr., Hawaii. Stress analyst N.Am. Aviation, Los Angeles, 1956-57; civil engr. Harland Bartholomew & Assocs., Honolulu, 1959-64; structural engr. Wilson Okamoto & Assocs., Honolulu, 1964-73; pres. Alvin Zane & Assocs., Honolulu, 1974—. Served to capt. U.S. Army, 1957-59. Mem. ASCE, Prestressed Concrete Inst., Structural Engring. Assn. Hawaii (v.p. 1980, pres. 1981), Soc. Am. Mil. Engrs., Am. Concrete Inst., Am. Welding Soc., Cons. Engrs. Council Hawaii, Mcpl. Toastmasters Honolulu (sec., treas., v.p., pres., 1976-80), Am. Inst. Steel Constrn., Post Tensioning Inst. Clubs: Hawaii Kai Game Fishing (Honolulu); The Presidents. Office: Alvin Zane & Assocs Inc 1314 S King St Suite 964 Honolulu HI 96814

ZANES, MARY BETH, social work consultant; b. Ft. Worth, Mar. 6, 1938; d. Jack R. Ball and Hazel Caroline Coward; m. Charles A. Zanes, Jan. 14, 1967; children: Charles, Douglas. AA, Christian Coll., 1958; EdB, Tex. Tech U., 1960; MSW, Fla. State U., 1962. Caseworker Ga. Dept. Pub. Health, Atlanta, 1962-64; cons. migrant health Maricopa County Health Dept., Phoenix, 1964-66, dir. social services, 1966-68; field instr. Ariz. State U., Tempe, 1966-68; social service coordinator Cath. Social Services, Douglas, Ariz., 1968; cons. health care programs Douglas, 1970—; mem. adv. bd. Cochise County Behavioral Health Service, Bisbee, Ariz., 1977-79. Bd. dirs. Ariz. State Liquor Control, 1986—, YWCA, Douglas, 1970-74, ARC, Douglas, 1974-77, Jr. Achievement, Douglas, 1983-84, Douglas Clean and Beautiful Com., 1985—; session mem. First Presbyn. Ch., Douglas, 1983—. Named one of Outstanding Young Women of Am., 1971. Mem. Nat. Assn. Social Workers (cert.), AAUW. Club: PEO.

ZANINOVICH, KAREN IRENE, business consultant, former telecommunications company executive; b. Bakersfield, Calif., Jan. 15, 1956; d. Jack Marion and Beatrice Carolyn (Perry) Z.; m. Joseph Philip Cavalli, Nov. 3, 1984; children: Jeremy, Stephanie. BS in Fin., San Jose State U., 1980; MBA in Mktg., U. Santa Clara, 1984. Acct., Memorex Corp., Santa Clara, Calif., 1978-81, fin. analyst, 1981-82; fin. systems analyst ROLM Corp., Santa Clara, 1982-83, fin. analyst, 1984-86; bus. counselor Success Alliance, Inc., 1986-87; prin. Zaninovich Cons., 1987—; v.p. sales, Applied Scholastics,

Inc., 1987—; bus. cons., 1987—. Mem. Assn. MBA Execs., Nature Conservancy, Nat. Wildlife Fedn. Avocations: tennis, outdoor activities. Home: 35050-I Lido Blvd Newark CA 94560

ZANOLINI, STEPHEN JEFFERY, banking executive; b. Clinton, Tenn., Sept. 25, 1947; s. Albert Silvio and Helen Mary (Burress) Z.; m. Claudia Cameron Debow, Mar. 14, 1981; children: Elizabeth Annette, Rebecca Helen. AA, Santa Rosa Jr. Coll., 1972; BA in English, Calif. State U., Sonoma, 1972-74; MBA, John F. Kennedy U., 1983. Gen. mgr. Herbie Green ENT, Redwood City, Calif., 1974-76; branch mgr. TransAm. Title Ins. Co., Concord, Calif., 1976-79, Founders Title Ins. Co., Fremont and Oakland, Calif., 1979-82; v.p., dir. adminstrn. IMI, San Francisco, 1982-84; v.p., mgr. adminstrv. services Farmers Savs., Davis, Calif., 1984—. Served to 1st lt. USMC, 1966-72. Mem. Internat. Facilities Mgmt. Assn. (sec. 1986—). Rebublican. Baptist. Avocations: running, chess, bridge. Home: 1712 Cork Pl Davis CA 95616 Office: Farmers Savs PO Box 4500 Davis CA 95616

ZARCONE, VINCENT PETER, JR., psychiatry educator; b. Decatur, Ill., July 10, 1937; s. Vincent P. and Alice E. (Irving) Z.; m. Joyce Ann Cale, July 13, 1958; children: Julia, Laura. Degree, U. Ill., 1958; MD, U. Ill., Chgo., 1962. Physician chief grade Palo Alto (Calif.) VA Med. Ctr., 1971—; clin. assoc. prof. psychiatry, sr. attending physician Stanford (Calif.) U. Sch. Medicine, 1973—, assoc. prof. clin. psychiatry, 1977-79; prof. clin. psychiatry Stanford U. Sch. Medicine, 1979—; staff psychiatrist Stanford U. Sleep Disorders Ctr., 1973—. Author: Drug Addicts In A Therapeutic Community: The Satori Approach, 1975; contbr. articles to profl. jours. Recipient Cert. Merit AMA (sect. on psychiatry), 1972. Mem. AAAS, Sleep Research Soc., Soc. Biol. Psychiatry, Am. Psychiat. Assn. (Rush Silver Medal award, 1972), Assn. Profl. Sleep Socs., West Coast Coll. Biol. Psychiatry (founding mem.). Republican. Roman Catholic. Avocations: skiing, mountain climbing, marathon running.

ZARE, RICHARD NEIL, chemistry educator; b. Cleve., Nov. 19, 1939; s. Milton and Dorothy (Amdur) Z.; m. Susan Leigh Shively, Apr. 20, 1963; children—Bethany Jean, Bonnie Sue, Rachel Amdur. B.A., Harvard, 1961; postgrad., U. Calif. at Berkeley, 1961-63; Ph.D. (NSF predoctoral fellow), Harvard, 1964. Postdoctoral fellow Harvard, 1964; postdoctoral research asso. Joint Inst. for Lab. Astrophysics, 1964-65; asst. prof. chemistry Mass. Inst. Tech., 1965-66; asst. prof. dept. physics and astrophysics U. Colo., 1966-68, assoc. prof. physics and astrophysics, asso. prof. chemistry, 1968-69; prof. chemistry Columbia, 1969-77, Higgins prof. natural sci., 1975-77; prof. Stanford U., 1977—, Shell Disting. prof. chemistry, 1980-85; cons. Aeronomy Lab., NOAA, 1966-77, radio standards physics div. Nat. Bur. Standards, 1968-77, Lawrence Livermore Lab., U. Calif., 1974—, Stanford Research Inst., 1974—, Los Alamos Sci. Lab., U. Calif., 1975—; fellow adjoint, Joint Inst. Lab. Astrophysics, U. Colo.; mem. IBM Sci. Advisory Com., 1977—. adv. bd. Chem. and Engring. News; editor Chem. Physics Letters, 1982-85. Recipient Fresenius award Phi Lambda Upsilon, 1974; Michael Polanyi medal, 1979; Nat. Medal Sci., 1985 award Spectroscopy Soc. Pitts., 1983, Michelson-Morley award, Case Inst. Tech./Case Western Res. U., 1986; nonresident fellow Joint Inst. for Lab. Astrophysics, 1970—; Alfred P. Sloan fellow, 1967-69; Christensen fellow St. Catherine's Coll., Oxford U., 1982; Stanford U. fellow, 1984—. Fellow AAAS; mem. Nat. Acad. Sci., Am. Acad. Arts and Scis., Am. Phys. Soc. (Earle K. Plyler prize 1981, Irving Langmuir prize 1985), Am. Chem. Soc. (Harrison Howe award Rochester sect. 1985, Remsen award Md. sect. 1985, Kirkwood award, Yale U., New Haven sect. 1986), Chem. Soc. London, Phi Beta Kappa. Research and publs. on laser chemistry and chem. physics. Office: Stanford U Dept Chemistry Stanford CA 94305

ZARIAN, LARRY, mayor. Mayor City of Glendale, Calif. Office: Office of Mayor 613 E Broadway Room 200 Glendale CA 91206 *

ZARUTSKIE, PAUL WALTER, reproductive endocrinoloigst, obstetrician/gynecologist.; b. Darby, Pa., May 4, 1951; s. Michael Andrew and Nita (Tatusko) Z. BS, Duke U., 1972; MD, Hahnemann Med. Coll., 1976. Cert. Am. Bd. Obstetrics and Gynecology. Resident Duke U. Med. Ctr., Durham, N.C., 1976-79, chief resident, 1979-80; clin. fellow reproductive endocrinology Brigham and Women's Hosp., Boston, 1980-82; instr. ob-gyn Harvard U., Boston, 1980; asst. prof. U. Pitts., 1982-84; asst. prof. U. Wash., Seattle, 1984—, clin. dir. in vitro fertilization program, 1984—. Contbr. articles to profl. jours. Fellow Am. Coll. Ob-gyn; mem. Am. Fertility Soc., Am. Andrology Soc., Bayard Carter Soc., Alpha Omega Alpha, Sigma Xi. Office: U Wash Dept Ob-Gyn RH-20 1959 NE Pacific St Seattle WA 98195

ZATULOVE, MICKIE ISAAC, social worker; b. New Orleans, Dec. 13, 1932; d. Solomon Charles and Leona (Minville) Isaac; m. Paul Myron Zatulove, Aug. 18, 1957; children: Brett Isaac, Tracy Marjorie. BS, La. State U., 1954; MSW, Ariz. State U., 1984. Elem sch. tchr. Lusher, New Orleans, 1954-57; adminstr. Nursey Sch. Temple Beth Am, Buffalo, 1966-79; parent aide Crisis Ctr., Phoenix, 1979-81; social worker Muscular Dystrophy Assn., Phoenix, 1984-85; therapist Jewish Family Service, Phoenix, 1985—. Bd. dirs. Planned Parenthood, Kivel; pres. Am. Jewish Com., 1985—; mem. planning commn. Hands Across Am., 1986, Consortium for the Homeless, 1986-87. Mem. Nat. Assn. Social Workers, Jewish Women's Profl., Opera Dames, Ladies Symphony (bd. dirs.), Brandeis Union Women (life). Democrat. Jewish. Avocations: tennis, gourmet cooking. Home: 2133 E Pasadena Phoenix AZ 85016 Office: Jewish Family Service 2033 N 7th St Phoenix AZ 85006

ZATZKIS, MARK ASHER, cardiologist; b. Newark, Jan. 9, 1954; s. Henry and Natalie (Serlin) Z.; m. Melissa Harris, Aug. 25, 1984. AB, Harvard U., 1975; MD, Columbia U., 1979. Dimplomate Am. Bd. Internal Medicine, 1982, Am. Bd. Cardiology, 1985. Fellow in cardiology U. Calif., San Francisco, 1983-85; sr. fellow in angioplasty San Francisco Heart Inst., 1985-86; clin. faculty memb. cardiology UCLA Hosp., 1986—; cons. in coronary angioplasty, Calif. Fellow Am. Coll. Cardiology; mem. Am. Heart Assn., Alpha Omega Alpha. Avocations: bicycling, music. Office: UCLA Hosp 11980 San Vicente Blvd Suite 901 Los Angeles CA 90049

ZAVALA, ALBERT, research psychologist; b. Chgo., Mar. 10, 1930; s. Edward and Maria Soledad (Herrejon) Z.; div.; children—Camille, Sally, Elena, Jenifer, Alexis. B.A., Willamette U., Salem, Oreg., 1959; M.A. Mich. State U., 1961; Ph.D., Kans. State U., 1966. Prof., head life scis. Calspan, Buffalo, 1967-73; prof. SUNY Coll. at Buffalo, 1968-78; exec. dir. Corp. IV, Cheektowaga, N.Y., 1973-77; dir. projects Inpsych, Cupertino, Calif., 1978-80; sr. research psychologist SRI Internat., Menlo Park, Calif., 1980-85; staff human factors engr., Lockheed Missiles and Space Co., Sunnyvale, Calif., 1985—. Mem. Erie County (N.Y.) sheriff's sci. staff, 1972-78. Served with U.S. Army, 1955-57. Dunlap fellow, 1964; Greater Kans. City Mental Health Found. fellow, 1962-63. Mem. Am. Psychol. Assn., Human Factors Soc., Sigma Xi, Psi Chi, Phi Kappa Phi. Author: (with J.J. Paley) Personal Appearance Identification, 1972. Contbr. numerous articles to profl. jours. Office: 1111 Lockheed Way Sunnyvale CA 94089-3504

ZAVARIN, EUGENE, forestry science educator; b. Sombor, Yugoslavia, Feb. 21, 1924; came to U.S., 1950; s. Alexey K. and Iya A. (Shepkin) Z.; m. Valentina S. Kusubov, July 15, 1956; children: Ksenya, Sergey, Michael, Nina, Mavrick. BS, U. Goettingen, Fed. Republic Germany, 1949; PhD, U. Calif., Berkeley, 1954. Sr. lab. technician U. Calif., Berkeley, 1952-54; asst. specialist Forest Products Lab., Richmond, Calif., 1954-57, asst. forest product chemist, 1957-62, assoc. forest product chemist, 1962-68, forest product chemist, 1968—; lec'. wood chemistry U. Calif., Berkeley, 1962-75, prof. forestry, 1975—; Reviewer grant proposals NSF. Mem. editorial adv. bd. Jour. Wood Chemistry and Tech.; contbr. articles to profl. jours. Fellow NIH, Institut de Chimie des Substances Naturelle, Gif-sur-Yvette, France, 1963; NSF grantee, 1965-67. Fellow Internat. Acad. Wood Sci.; mem. AAAS, Am. Chem. Soc., Sigma Xi. Republican. Avocations: travel, gardening, photography. Home: 280 Edgehill Way San Francisco CA 94127 Office: U Calif Forest Products Lab 1301 S 46th St Richmond CA 94804

ZAWACKI, GAIL MARIE, educator, school principal; b. Bridgeport, Conn., Apr. 25, 1947; d. Raymond Walter and Marie Fausta (Homza) Z. B.A. in Psychology, Sacred Heart U., 1969. Tchr., Westport, Conn., 1969-74, San Marino, Calif., 1974-81; prin., San Marino, Calif., 1981-82, Montrose, Calif., 1982—. Mem. Nat. Cath. Ednl. Assn., Assn. Supervision and Curriculum Devel. Office: 2361 Del Mar Rd Montrose CA 91020

ZBOZINEK, JASENKA VUCETA, environmental engineer; b. Karlovac, Yugoslavia, Oct. 19, 1945; came to U.S., 1968; d. Ivan Nickolas and Marija (Burany) Vuceta; m. Ladislav Bozidar Zbozinek, July 2, 1983; children: Berislav Dragan, Ivana Katarina . BS, U. Zagreb, Yugoslavia, 1968; MS, Calif. Inst. Tech., 1971, PhD, 1976. Postdoctorate researcher Calif. Inst. Tech., Pasadena, 1973; environ. engr. J.J. Momper Engring., Inc., Pasadena, 1977-78; engr. Bechtel Power Corp., Norwalk, Calif., 1978-79; project dir. SCS Engrs., Long Beach, Calif., 1979—. Contbr. articles to profl. jours. Mem. Water Pollution Control Fedn., Am. Chem. Soc. Republican. Roman Catholic. Office: SCS Engrs 4014 Long Beach Blvd Long Beach CA 91789

ZDERIC, JOHN ANTHONY, pharmaceutical company executive; b. San Jose, Calif., Jan. 25, 1924; s. Stephen Anthony and Florence Mathilda (Bush) Z.; m. Marie Alice Lobrovich, Sept. 24, 1949; 1 son, Stephen Anthony. AB, San Jose State Coll., 1950; MS, Stanford U., 1952, PhD, 1955. Research chemist Syntex Corp., Mexico, 1956-59, asst. dir. chem. research, 1959-61; dir. labs. Syntex Inst. Molecular Biology, Palo Alto, Calif., 1961-62; v.p. comml. devel. Syntex Internat., Mexico City, 1965-70, Syntex Labs., Palo Alto, 1970-72; v.p. research adminstrn. and tech. affairs Syntex U.S.A., Inc., Palo Alto, 1973—. Contbr. articles to profl. jours.; patentee in field. Served with USN, 1942-46. Fellow Eidig. Tech. hoch., Zurich, Switzerland, 1963-64; mem. Am. Chem. Soc., Sigma Xi. Home: 2369 Sharon Oaks Dr Menlo Park CA 94025 Office: Syntex USA Inc 3401 Hillview Ave Palo Alto CA 94304

ZEATON, ROBERT PAUL, transportation engineering executive; b. Winnipeg, Man., Can., Sept. 7, 1948; s. Paul and Stella (Sokulsky) Z.; m. Dorothy Sandra Milan, Sept. 25, 1971; children: Christine, Laurie, Karin, Gregory. BSME, U. Man., 1971. Asst. prodn. engr. Temro Ltd. div. J.B. Carter Ltd., Winnipeg, 1971-72; prodn. engr., asst. plant mgr. Temro Ltd. div. J.B. Carter Ltd., Toronto, Ont., Can., 1972-75; design, prodn. engr. Fort Garry Industries Ltd., Winnipeg, 1975-77; dir. engring. Motor Coach Industries Ltd., Winnipeg, 1977-80, Transp. Mfg. Corp., Roswell, N.Mex., 1980—. Mem. Am. Soc. Automotive Engrs., Am. Soc. Metals. Lodge: Rotary. Avocations: golf, camping, stamp collecting. Home: 2606 A Sherrill Ln Roswell NM 88201 Office: Transp Mfg Corp PO Box 5670 Roswell NM 88201

ZEBROSKI, EDWIN L., consultant, risk management, nuclear scientist; b. Chgo., Apr. 1, 1921; s. Peter Paul and Sophie (Rydz) Z.; m. Gisela Karin Rudolph, Sept. 6, 1969; children: Lars, Zoe, Susan, Peggy. BS, U. Chgo., 1941; PhD, U. Calif., Berkeley, 1947. Registered prof. engr., Calif. Project engr. Gen. Electric Co., Schenectady, N.Y., 1947-53; mgr. devel. engring. Gen. Electric Co., San Jose, Calif., 1958-73; mgr. engring. SRI Internat., Menlo Park, Calif., 1954-58; chief nuclear scientist EPRI, Palo Alto, Calif., 1974-80; v.p. engring. INPO, Atlanta, 1981-83, sr. tech. advisor, 1983—; vis. prof. Purdue U., West Lafayette, Ind., 1977-78; cons. OTA, Washington, 1980, 82-83, Dept. Energy, Washington, 1985—; mem. commn. engring. edn. Nat. Research Council, Washington, 1970-73. Contbr. chpts. to books, numerous articles to profl. jours.; patentee in field. Pres. bd. Unitarian Ch., Palo Alto, 1965-68. Recipient Charles A. Coffin award Gen. Electric Co., Schenectady, 1954. Fellow AAAS, Am. Nuclear Soc. (bd. exec. com. 1970), Am. Inst. Chemists; mem. Am. Phys. Soc., Nat. Acad. Engring. (chmn. peer com. 1984-86, chmn. mem. com. 1986-87). Avocations: tennis, music, hiking, photography, writing. Office: Electric Power Research Inst 3412 Hillview Ave Palo Alto CA 94303

ZECCHIN, MARCO PETER, photographer; b. San Diego, Apr. 1, 1955; s. Luciano Georgio and Enes (Della Santina) Z.; m. Mary Kay Jones, Oct. 22, 1983. B.S., U. Calif.-Davis, 1979. Photog. asst. U. Calif.-Davis, 1974-75; instr. Evelyn Wood Reading Dynamics, Walnut Creek, Calif., 1975-77; career counselor Work Learn Ctr., U. Calif.-Davis, 1978-79; pharm. rep. Ross Labs., Reno, Nev., 1979-84; guest lectr. U. Calif.-Davis, 1979-83; dietetic cons. St. Mary's Hosp. Neonatal Intensive Care Unit, Reno, Nev., 1983-84; instr. photography Hartnell Coll., Salinas, Calif., 1985—; owner, mgr. Image Ctr., Los Gatos, Calif., 1984—; photog. cons. Community Coop. Services, Reno, 1984—. Named Outstanding Sales Person of the Year for Dist. 9500, Ross Labs., 1982. Mem. Reno Dietetic Assn., Golden Empire Dietetic Assn., Calumet Photog. Soc., Am. Modelers Assn., Fedn. Aeronautique Internationale, Salinas Jaycees. Democrat. Roman Catholic. Club: Toastmasters. Lodge. Sons of Italy. Home: 704 Sherman Circle Salinas CA 93907 Office: Image Center PO Box 2087 Los Gatos CA 95031

ZEE, YUAN-CHUNG, veterinary medicine educator; b. Shanghai, Peoples Republic of China, Aug. 29, 1935; came to U.S., 1951; s. Y.C. and King-Ngu (Wong) Z.; m. Ming-Wei Lena, Aug. 20, 1966; children: Yvette, Colette. AB, U. Calif., Berkeley, 1957, MA, 1959, PhD, 1966; DVM, U. Calif., Davis, 1963. Lic. vet., Calif. Postgrad. research virologist U. Calif., Berkeley, 1963-66; asst. prof. vet. sci. U. Calif., Davis, 1966-68, assoc. prof., 1968-74, prof., chmn. dept. vet. microbiology, 1974—. CSIRO fellow, Australian Govt., 1973. Mem. AAAS, American Soc. for Microbiology (virology sect.), Sigma Xi. Home: 1015 Kent Dr Davis CA 95616 Office: U Calif Dept Vet Medicine Davis CA 95616

ZEHR, NORMAN ROBERT, alumni association administrator; b. Niagara Falls, N.Y., May 19, 1930; s. George Andrew and Ina Kate (Morrell) Z.; Engr. of Mines, Colo. Sch. Mines, 1952, M.S., 1956; m. Janet Hutchinson, Apr. 24, 1976; children—Jeannette Ann, Leslie. Sales trainee Ingersoll-Rand Co., N.Y.C., 1955-56, sales engr., Lima, Peru, 1956-64, regional mgr. mining and constrn. sales, Lima, Peru and N.Y.C., 1964-68, gen. sales mgr. Latin Am., N.Y.C., 1968-69, gen. mgr. Latin Am. ops., N.Y.C., 1969-71, v.p. Ingersoll Rand Internat., Woodcliff Lake, N.J., 1971-72, pres., 1972-83, , v.p. Ingersoll-Rand Co., 1975-83; exec. dir. Colo. Sch. Mines Alumni Assn., 1984—. Served with AUS, 1952-54. Recipient Colo. Sch. Mines Disting. Achievement medal, 1977. Mem. AIME, Scabbard and Blade, Nat. Soc. Pershing Rifles, Mining and Metall. Soc. Am., Sigma Nu. Club: Mining. Office: Chauvenet Hall Colo Sch Mines Golden CO 80401

ZEIDLER, ANDY GEORG, marketing professional; b. Selb, Fed. Republic of Germany, June 6, 1950. Diploma in applied physics, Fachhochschule Heilbronn, Fed. Republic Germany, 1975. Cert. engr. in applied physics. Regional sales mgr. Linseis GMBH, Frankfurt, Fed. Republic of Germany, 1975-78, Linseis, Inc. subs. Linseis GMBH, Princeton, N.J., 1978-79, Soltec Corp., Sun Valley, Calif., 1979-80; gen. mgr. BBC-Metrawatt/Goerz, Edison, N.J., 1980-84; mktg. mgr. BBC-Brown Boveri subs. BBC-Metrawatt/Goerz, Broomfield, Colo., 1984—. Mem. Instrument Soc. Am. Avocation: skiing, hiking. Home: 2185 Goddard Pl Boulder CO 80303

ZEIGEL, HENRY ALAN, architect; b. Vernal, Utah, Aug. 17, 1933; s. Emmett Ray and Willa Meddie (Hahn) Z.; m. Laura Belle Miller, Dec. 21, 1953; children: Shonda G. Zeigel Cortez, Désha K. Zeigel Davis, Brad A. BArch, U. Colo., 1957, postgrad., 1981-83. Lic. architect. Assoc. J.H. Johnson, FAIA, Denver, 1961-64; prin. Everett-Zeigel, Boulder, Colo., 1965—. Prin. works include Chautauqua Auditorium. Chmn. City Landmarks Bd., Boulder, 1975-79, Com. on Ch. Architecture and Arts, 1970-80; active Nat. Trust for HIst. Preservation, Washington, 1970—. Served to 1st lt. U.S. Army, 1957-60. Mem. AIA, Boulder C. of C. Episcopalian. Avocations: bicycle racing, tennis. Home: 603 Spruce Boulder CO 80302 Office: Worthington/Everett Zeigel Tumpes 1215 Spruce Boulder CO 80302

ZEIGLER, JOHN MARTIN, research chemist; b. Greensburg, Ind., Dec. 5, 1951; s. Ralph Martin and Peggy Jane Zeigler. BA, Wabash Coll., 1974; PhD, U. Ill., 1979. Research chemist Am. Cyanamid Co., Stamford, Conn., 1979-81; mem. tech. staff Sandia Nat. Labs., Albuquerque, 1981-85, supr. phys. chemistry and mech. properties of polymers div., 1985—; organizer Internat. Conf. in Silicon Polymer Chemistry. Contbr. articles to profl. jours.; patentee in field. Recipient Howell Prize in Chemistry, Wabash Coll., Crawfordsville, Ind., 1973, 74, Britton award in Chemistry, Wabash Coll., 1974, IR-100 award Research and Devel. mag., 1986. Mem. AAAS, Am. Chem. Soc., Soc. Photo-optical Inst. Engrs., Phi Beta Kappa, Phi Lambda Upsilon, Alpha Chi Sigma, Phi Kappa Psi. Avocations: wine collecting, gourmet cooking, classical music, hiking, golf. Home: 2208 Lester Dr NE #421 Albuquerque NM 87112 Office: Sandia Nat Labs Div 1812 PO Box 800 Albuquerque NM 87185

ZEIHEN, LESTER GREGORY, geology educator; b. Stevensville, Mont., Feb. 8, 1913; s. Gregory Sylvester and Francis M. (Haigh) Z.; m. Jeannette A. McMahon, July 10, 1941; children—Marilyn, Nancy, Donna, Gregory. B.S. in Geol. Engring., Mont. Sch. Mines, 1935, M.S., 1937, profl. degree, 1961. Jr. engr. Anaconda Copper Mining Co., Butte, 1937-38; mine geologist Chile Exploration Co., Chuquicamata, 1938-52; research geologist The Anaconda Co., Butte, 1952-73, cons. mineralogist, 1973-79; adj. assoc. prof. geology, adj. curator mineral mus. Mont. Coll. Mining Sci. and Tech., Butte, 1979—. Author in field. Pres., Silver Bow Humane Soc., Butte, 1984-86; bd. dirs. Butte Sheltered Workshop, 1984-86, Butte Silver Bow Arts Found., 1984-86, World Mus. Mining, Butte, 1984. Recipient Service Above Self award Butte Rotary, 1976. Mem. Am. Mineral. Assn. (life), AIME (chmn. sect. 1964, Legion of Honor), Soc. Econ. Geologists, Geochem. Soc., Sci. Research Soc., Mineral. Assn. Can., Mont. Tech. Alumni Assn. (sec.-treas. 1984), Sigma Xi. Republican. Roman Catholic. Lodge: Rotary (pres. 1980-81) (Butte). Home: 834 W Silver St Butte MT 59701 Office: Mont Coll Mineral Sci and Tech W Park St Butte MT 59701

ZEILIG, NANCY MEEKS, magazine editor; b. Nashville, Apr. 28, 1943; d. Edward Harvey and Nancy Evelyn (Self) Meeks; m. Lanny Kenneth Fielder, Aug. 20, 1964 (div. Dec. 1970); m. Charles Elliot Zeilig, Jan. 6, 1974: 1 child, Sasha Rebecca. BA, Birmingham-So. Coll., 1964; postgrad., Vanderbilt U., 1971-73. Editorial asst. Reuben H. Donnelley, N.Y.C., 1969-70; asst. editor Vanderbilt U., Nashville, 1970-74; editor U. Minn., St. Paul, 1975; asst. editor McGraw Hill Inc., Mpls., 1975-76; mng. editor Denver mag., 1976-80; editor Jour. Am. Water Works Assn., Denver, 1981—. Editor, co-pub.: WomanSource, 1982, rev. edit. 1984; editor: 100 Years, 1975; contbr. articles to profl. jours. Avocations: travel, reading British and Am. fiction, cooking. Subject of NBC News documentary Women Like Us, 1980. Office: Jour Am Water Works Assn 6666 W Quincy Denver CO 80235

ZEILIK, MICHAEL, astronomy educator; b. Bridgeport, Conn., Sept. 26, 1946; s. Michael and Margaret (Sabo) Z.; m. Kimberly Lesser, Aug. 31, 1985. BA in Physics, Princeton U., 1968; MA in Astronomy, Harvard U., 1969, PhD in Astronomy, 1975. Asst. prof. astronomy U. N.Mex., Albuquerque, 1975-80, assoc. prof., 1980-85, prof., 1985—, assoc. dir. Inst. Astrophysics, 1986—. Author: (with others) Astronomy—The Cosmic Perspective, 1983, Introductory Astronomy and Astrophysics, 1986; author: Astronomy—The Evolving Universe, 1985; mem. editorial bd. Jour. Coll. Sci. Teaching, 1983—. Woodrow Wilson fellow, 1968-69, NSF fellow, 1968-69; named Presdl. lectr. U. N.Mex., 1984-86. Mem. Internat. Astron. Union (commn. 46), Am. Astron. Soc. (edn. bd.), Am. Assn. Physics Tchrs. (astronomy com.), Astron. Soc. Pacific. Democrat. Roman Catholic. Avocations: hiking, camping, skiing, river rafting. Office: U NMex Dept Physics and Astronomy Albuquerque NM 87131

ZEILINGER, ELNA RAE, educator; b. Tempe, Ariz., Mar. 24, 1937; d. Clayborn Eddie and Ruby Elna (Laird) Simpson; B.A. in Edn., Ariz. State U., 1958, M.A. in Edn., 1966, Ed.S., 1980; m. Philip Thomas Zeilinger, June 13, 1970; children—Shari, Chris. Bookkeeper, First Nat. Bank of Tempe, 1955-56; with registrar's office Ariz. State U., 1956-58; piano tchr., recreation dir. City of Tempe, tchr. Thew Sch., Tempe, 1958-61, elem. tchr. Mitchell Sch., 1962-74, intern prin., 1976, personnel intern, 1977; specialist in gifted edn. Tempe Elem. Schs., 1977—; grad. asst. ednl. adminstrn., Iota Workshop coordinator Ariz. State U., 1978; presenter Ariz. Gifted Conf., 1978-81; condr. survey of gifted programs, 1980; reporter public relations Tempe Sch. Dist., 1978-80, Access com. for gifted programs, 1981-83. Freedom Train com. Ariz. Bicentennial Commn., 1975-76. Named Outstanding Leader in Elem. and Secondary Schs., 1976' Ariz. Cattle Growers scholar, 1954-55; Elks scholar, 1954-55; recipient Judges award Tempe Art League, 1970, Best of Show, Scottsdale Art League, 1976. Mem. Council Exceptional Children, Ariz. Assn. Gifted and Talented, Ariz. Sch. Adminstrs., Tempe Hist. Assn. (liaison 1975), Scottsdale Artists League, Tempe Art League, Am. Bus. Women's Assn. (Woman of Yr. 1983), Phi Kappa Phi, Pi Lambda Theta, Kappa Delta Pi, Phi Delta Kappa, Kappa Delta. Democrat. Congregationalist. Club: Eastern Star. Author: Leadership Role of the Principal in Gifted Programs: A Handbook, 1980; Classified Personnel Handbook, 1977, also reports and monographs. Home: 610 E Colgate St Tempe AZ 85283 Office: Tempe Elem Schs 1975 E Cornell St Tempe AZ 85283

ZEIND, SAMIR MAURICE, medical librarian; b. Egypt, Oct. 1, 1939; s. Maurice R. and Georgette F. (Hag) Z.; m. Jeanne F., June 28, 1969; 1 dau., Rita Marie-Noelle. B.S. in Chemistry, Am. U., Cairo, 1967; M.L.S., U. So. Calif., 1976. Library asst. U. So. Calif. Sch. Dentistry, 1970-76; asst. mgr. library Huntington Meml. Hosp., Pasadena, Calif., 1976-80, mgr., 1980—. Mem. ALA, Med. Library Assn., Med. Library Group So. Calif. and Ariz. Home: 14610 Runnymede St Van Nuys CA 91405 Office: Huntington Meml Hosp 100 Congress St Pasadena CA 91105

ZEITLER, BILL LORENZ, aviation engineer; b. Columbus, Ohio, July 14, 1920; s. Walter Andrew and Naomi Lee (Limes) Z.; B.S.C.E., Calif. State U.-Long Beach, 1965; m. Betty Eileen Thomas, Nov. 8, 1942; children—Eddie, Naomi Parker. Loftsman, Curtiss Wright Corp., Columbus, 1941-43, 44-46; linesman Lockheed Corp., Burbank, Calif., 1943-44; linesman N.Am. Rockwell (and predecessor firms), Inglewood, Calif., 1946-50, airframe designer, 1950-62, supr., 1962-65, project engr. life scis., health care delivery systems, 1965-68, project dir., Princeton, W.Va., 1968-69, mem. tech. staff, Downey, Calif., 1956—, project engr. space shuttle design, 1971-75, shuttle alignment and mating, 1975-77, space shuttle design support extra vehicular stowage and testing, 1978—; mem. Space Shuttle Speakers Bur. Cert. vocat. tchr., Calif. Mem. AIAA, Nat. Space Inst., Nat. Geog. Soc., Smith Instn. Assocs. Republican. Clubs: Rockwell Mgmt., Toastmasters.ers. Office: 12241 Lakewood Blvd AE47 Downey CA 92041

ZEITLER, EDDIE LORENZ, information systems executive; b. Hollywood, Calif., Aug. 24, 1943; s. Bill Lorenz and Betty Eileen (Thomas) Z.; m. Victoria Lee Duncan, Sept. 21, 1968 (div. Apr. 1984); children: Viena Lee, Erin Lynne. BS in Math., U. Ariz., 1968, MS in Systems Engring., 1970; postgrad., U. Alta., Can., 1971-73. Radar systems analyst ITT Gilfillan, Van Nuys, Calif., 1970-71; computer performance analyst Rockwell Internat., Downey, Calif., 1973-75; mgr. computer capacity mgmt. Transam. Info. Systems, Los Angeles, 1975-76; dir. tech. services Federated Dept. Stores, Cin., 1976-78, dir. computer ops., 1978-79; v.p. info. systems security Security Pacific Nat. Bank, Glendale, Calif., 1979—; mem. U.S. Dept. Treas. FMS security adv. panel, Washington, 1985. Author: Information Retrieval Systems, 1970. Mem. Los Angeles County Computer Crime task force, 1984-86; vol. guide Los Angeles Zoo Assn. Served with USAF, 1963-67. Mem. IEEE, Assn. Computing Machinery, Am. Nat. Standards Inst. (subcom. secure sign-0n standard fin. community), Security Pacific Nat. Bank Securiteam, Am. Bankers Assn. (data jewelry com.), Theta Tau, Alpha Sigma Phi. Baptist. Club: Beachcraft Flying (Van Nuys). Avocations: piloting, off shore sailboat racing. Home: 520 S 6th St Apt R Burbank CA 91501 Office: Security Pacific Nat Bank 611 N Brand Blvd G12-01 Glendale CA 91203

ZEITLIN, GERALD MARK, electrical engineer; b. Phila., May 7, 1937; s. David Edward and Charlotte (Freedman) Z.; m. Frances Loretta Scherr, May 17, 1983. BEE, Cornell U., 1960; MSEE, U. Colo., 1969. Electronic engr. Nat. Security Agy., Ft. Meade, Md., 1962-64, Westinghouse Georesearch Lab., Boulder, Colo., 1966-69; owner Sunrise Books, Estes Park, Colo., 1969-71; asst. research computer sci. U. Calif., San Francisco, 1972-78; assoc. devel. engr. U. Calif., Berkeley, 1978-82; sr. systems engr. EEG Systems Lab., San Francisco, 1982-86; computer cons., expert systems design Pacific Bell, San Francisco, 1986—. Contbr. articles to profl. jours. Served to 1st lt. U.S. Army, 1960-62. Summer Faculty fellow NASA-Am. Soc. Engring. Edn., Ames Research Ctr., 1981. Mem. AAAS, IEEE, Computer Soc. IEEE, Assn. Computing Machinery, Profl. Tech. Cons. Assn. Democrat. Jewish. Avocation: pvt. airplane pilot. Home: 2910 Hillegass Ave Berkeley CA 94705 Office: Pacific Bell 120 Montgomery St Room 330 San Francisco CA 94104

ZEITLIN, JACOB ISRAEL, rare book dealer; b. Racine, Wis., Nov. 4, 1902; s. Yehuda Louis and Bessie Fanny (Hurwitz) Z.; m. Edith Matheral, 1925 (div. 1929); 1 child, Judith Louah; m. Jean Weyl, 1931 (div. 1938); 1 child, David John; m. Josephine Adriana Ver Brugge, Oct. 29, 1939; children—Joel, Adriana. D.H.L. (hon.), LittD (Hon.) Occidental U., 1981. Owner, mgr. Jake Zeitlin Books, Los Angeles, 1927-36; pres. Jake Zeitlin Inc., Los Angeles, 1936-42, Zeitlin & Ver Brugge, Los Angeles, 1943—. Contbr. articles and poetry to mags. Mem. Am. Antiquarian Soc., Am. Antiquarian Booksellers Assn. (pres. 1955-59), Assn. Internal du Bibliophile (hon.). Clubs: Grolier, Zamorano, Century. Home: 907 N Alfred St Los Angeles CA 90069 Office: Zeitlin & Ver Brugge 815 N La Ciengega Blvd Los Angeles CA 90069

ZEITLIN, MAURICE, sociology educator, author; b. Detroit, Feb. 24, 1935; s. Albert J. and Rose (Goldberg) Z.; m. Marilyn Geller, Mar. 1, 1959; children: Michelle, Carla, Erica. BA cum laude, Wayne State U., 1957; MA, U. Calif.-Berkeley, 1960, PhD, 1964. Instr. anthropology and sociology Princeton (N.J.) U., 1961-64, research assoc. Ctr. Internat. Studies, 1962-64; asst. prof. sociology U. Wis.-Madison, 1964-67, assoc. prof., 1967-70, prof., 1970-77, dir. Ctr. Social Orgn., 1974-76; prof. sociology UCLA, 1977—, also research assoc. Inst. Indsl. Relations; vis. prof. polit. sci. and sociology Hebrew U., Jerusalem, 1971-72. Author: (with R. Scheer) Cuba: An American Tragedy, 1964, Revolutionary Politics and the Cuban Working Class, 1967, 1970, The Civil Wars in Chile, 1984, Landlords and Capitalists, 1987; Latin Am. editor Ramparts mag., 1967-73; editor-in-chief: Political Power and Social Theory, 1980—; editor: (with J. Petras) Latin America: Reform or Revolution, 1968, American Society, Inc., 1970, 77, Father Camilo Torres: Revolutionary Writings, 1972, Classes, Class Conflict, and the State, 1980, How Mighty a Force?, 1983, Insurgent Workers: The Origins of Industrial Unionism, 1987. Chmn. Madison Citizens for a Vote on Vietnam, 1967-68; chmn. Am. Com. for Chile, 1973-75; mem. exec. bd. U.S. Com. for Justice to Latin Am. Polit. Prisoners, 1977-84; mem. exec. com. Calif. Campaign for Econ. Democracy, 1983-86. Ford Found. fellow, 1965-67, 70-71; Guggenheim fellow, 1981-82; NSF grantee, 1981, 82; recipient Project Censored award Top Censored Story, 1981; named to Ten Best Censored list, 1978. Mem. Am. Sociol. Assn. (governing council 1977-80), Internat. Sociol. Assn. (editorial bd. 1977-81), Latin Am. Studies Assn., Orgn. Am. Historians. Democrat. Jewish. Office: UCLA Haines 237 405 Hilgard Ave Los Angeles CA 90024

ZEITLIN, MICHAEL DONALD, accountant; b. Denver, Apr. 20, 1951; s. Eugene Louis and Sylvia Myra (Weiss) Z.; m. Cheryl Ann Scott, Aug. 3, 1975. B.S., U. Colo., 1976, M. Taxation, U. Denver, 1978. C.P.A. Colo., 1978. Staff acct. Arthur Andersen & Co., San Diego, 1978-79; sr. tax acct. Zaveral, Boosalis & Raisch, Denver, 1980; tax mgr. Louis L. Fox & Co., Denver, 1980-82; owner Michael D. Zeitlin, CPA, Denver, 1982-85; pres. Zeitlin & Assocs., P.C., Englewood, Colo., 1986—; pub. speaker contbr. artilces on taxation to profl. jours. Mem. Denver Estate Planning Council. Mem. Am. Inst. C.P.A.s, Nat. Assn. Accountants, Colo. Soc. C.P.A.s. Lodge: B'nai B'rith. Office: Zeitlin & Assocs PC 2303 E Dartmouth Ave Englewood CO 80110

ZEKMAN, TERRI MARGARET, graphic designer; b. Chgo., Sept. 13, 1950; d. Theodore Nathan and Lois (Bernstein) Z.; m. Alan Daniels, Apr. 12, 1980. BFA, Washington U., St. Louis, 1971; postgrad, Art Inst. Chgo., 1974-75. Graphic designer (on retainer) greeting cards and related products Recycled Paper Products Co., Chgo., 1970—; apprenticed graphic designer Helmuth, Obata & Kassabaum, St. Louis, 1970-71; graphic designer Container Corp., Chgo., 1971; graphic designer, art dir., photographer Cuerden Advt. Design, Denver, 1971-74; art dir. D'Arcy, McManus & Masius Advt., Chgo., 1975-76; freelance graphic designer Chgo., 1976-77; art dir. Garfield Linn Advt., Chgo., 1977-78; graphic designer Keiser Design Group, Van Noy & Co., Los Angeles, 1978-79; owner and operator graphic design studio Los Angeles, 1979—. Recipient cert. of merit St. Louis Outdoor Poster Contest, 1970, Denver Art Dirs. Club, 1973.

ZELEZNY, WILLIAM FRANCIS, retired physical chemist; b. Rollins, Mont., Sept. 5, 1918; s. Joseph Matthew and Birdie Estelle (Loder) Z.; m. Virginia Lee Scarcliff, Sept. 14, 1949. BS in Chemistry, Mont. State Coll., 1940; MS in Metallurgy, Mont. Sch. Mines, 1941; PhD in Phys. Chemistry, State U. Iowa, 1951. Scientist NACA, Cleve., 1951-54; metallurgist div. indsl. research Wash. State Coll., Pullman, 1954-57; scientist atomic energy div. Phillips Petroleum Co., Idaho Falls, Id., 1957-66, Idaho Nuclear Corp., Idaho Falls, 1966-70; mem. staff Los Alamos (N.Mex.) Sci. Lab., 1970-80; instr. metallurgy State U. Iowa, Iowa City, 1948-49; asst. prof. metallurgy Wash. State Coll., 1956-57; instr. U. Idaho, Idaho Falls, 1960-68. Contbr. articles to profl. jours.; patentee in field. Bd. dirs. Biol. Sta. Univ. Mont., Polson, Mont., 1984—. Served with AUS, 1944-46. Mem. Am. Chem. Soc. (sec. N.Mex. sect. 1978-79), Microbeam Analysis Soc., Am. Soc. Metals, Am. Inst. Mining Metall. and Petroleum Engrs., N.Mex. Solar Energy Assn., Sigma Xi, Alpha Chi Sigma. Democrat. Methodist. Avocation: gardening. Home: PO Box 37 Rollins MT 59931

ZELLER, SUZANNE JEANNINE, applications chemist; b. Lansing, Mich., May 30, 1959; d. Arthur Carl Sr. and Ellen Grace (Reiher) Z. BA, Lindenwood Coll., 1981. Assoc. chemist TOSCO Corp., Golden, Colo., 1981-84; applications chemist Coulometrics, Inc., Golden, 1984—. Mem. Am. Chem. Soc., ASTM. Office: Coulometrics Inc 4630 Indiana Unit 3 Golden CO 80403

ZELLMER, WILLIAM EDWARD, architect; b. Monrovia, Calif., Nov. 16, 1961; s. Richard Gregory Zellmer and Joanne Zuerlien; m. Susan Anne Moore, Aug. 16, 1986. BArch, Calif. Poly. State U., San Luis Obispo, 1984. Registered architect, Calif. Architect Edward T. Murray and Assocs., Placerville, Calif., 1979-84, Takata & Sugioka, Sacramento, 1984—. Mem. AIA (assoc. dir. 1985-86). Republican. Roman Catholic. Avocations: bicycling, politics. Office: Takata & Sugioka 5660 Freeport Blvd #201 Sacramento CA 95682

ZELNA, DIANE, accountant; b. Los Angeles, Jan. 13, 1941; d. John S. and Katherine Zelna. Diploma, Life Bible Coll., 1965; A.A. in Bus. Mgmt., Fullerton Coll., 1978; postgrad. U. Calif.-Fullerton, 1979-83. Mgr., Am. Telecom, Inc., Anaheim, Calif., 1978-79; assoc. Edward Tuck & Co., Inc., W. Covina, Calif., 1979-81; pres., owner Assoc. Bus. Services Co., Placentia, Calif., 1981—, owner Gold Medal Sales, Orange, 1984—; corp. sec. Briarcrest, Inc., Covina, 1981; corp. sec., dir. Creative Frameworks, Inc., Santa Ana, Calif., 1982-83; v.p., corp. sec. bd. dirs. Creative Fundraising, Inc., Orange, 1985—. Mem. Am. Soc. Tng. and Devel., Alpha Gamma Sigma. Republican. Christian Ch. Office: Gold Medal Sales 1525 W Orangewood Ave Orange CA 92667

ZELUFF, GARY RICHARD, orthopedic surgeon; b. San Antonio, July 5, 1949; s. R.J.M. and Laura Ruth (Weakley) Z.; m. Bonnie Michelle Dunn, July 23, 1970 (div. Mar. 1983); 1 child, Jon Richard; m. Jamie Gay Fuller, Sept. 13, 1983. BSEE, U. Ariz., 1972, MD, 1975. Diplomate Am. Bd. Orthopedic Surgery. Intern Orange Meml. Hosp., Orlando, Fla., 1975-76; resident in ortho-surgery U. Utah, Salt Lake City, 1976-81; practice medicine specializing in ortho-surgery Salt Lake City, 1981—; assoc. prof. orthosurgery U. Utah, Salt Lake City, 1981—; assoc. v.p., chief of staff Holy Cross West Jordan Hosp., Salt Lake City, 1986—; cons. engr. Sorensen Research, Salt Lake City, 1976-78; team physician United State Ski Team, 1983; bd. dir. Energy Tech. Constructors, Salt Lake City; pres. Zohoz Funding, Salt Lake City, 1985—. Patentee in field. Bd. dirs. N.Am. Freestyle Com., 1985—. Mem. Salt Lake County Med. Soc., Utah State Med. Assn., Western Orthopedic Assn. Avocations: skiing, electronics, competitive marksmanship. Office: 1002 E S Temple #302 Salt Lake City UT 84102

ZEMACH, CHARLES, research physicist; b. Los Angeles, Sept. 15, 1930; s. Nahum David and Miriam (Goldina) Z.; m. Mary Merrill St. John, Feb. 7, 1958; children: Arthur Merril, dorothy Ellen, Kenneth David. BA, Harvard U., 1951, PhD, 1955. Prof. physics U. Calif., Berkeley, 1958-70; mem. staff, dep. spl. asst. to dir. U.S. SALT Del., Washington, 1970-74; mem. policy planning staff U.S. Dept. State, Washington, 1974-76; mem. staff Los Alamos (N.Mex.) Nat. Lab., 1976-81, dep. div. leader, 1981—. Contbr. articles to profl. jours. Fellow Alfred P. Sloan Found., 1959-63, John Simon Guggenheim Found., 1966-67. Mem. AAAS, Am. Phys. Soc. Club: Adobe Whitewater of N.Mex., Inc. (pres. 1984-86). Home: 740 Canyon Rd Los Alamos NM 87544 Office: Los Alamos Nat Lab Theoretical div Los Alamos NM 87545

ZENKA, DANIEL RICHARD, public relations agency executive; b. Hollis, N.Y., Aug. 2, 1958; s. Daniel Albert and Nellie (Civinskas) Z.; m. Mary Ellen Lennox, June 8, 1985. Student, Cambridge (Eng.) U.; BA in Journalism/Pub. Relations and Communications Arts, U. So. Calif., 1980. Pub. relations asst. account exec. Georgeson & Co., Los Angeles, 1980-81; pub. relations account exec. Spencer & Rubinow, Ltd., N.Y.C., 1981-82; sr. account exec. David Parry & Assocs., Los Angeles, 1983-85, sr. v.p., 1985—. Pub. relations dir. Gold Coast Theatre Co., Los Angeles, 1981, Arpeggio Ballet Co., Los Angeles, 1984. Mem. Pub. Relations Soc. Am. (bd. dirs. Los Angeles chpt. 1986—, Prisms award 1985, accredited). Club: Greater Los Angeles Press. Home: 6100 Pacific Coast Hwy #17 Redondo Beach CA 90277 Office: David Parry & Assocs 5900 Wilshire Blvd Suite 1435 Los Angeles CA 90036

ZENONE, RONALD JOSEPH, engineer, consultant; b. Latrobe, Pa., Dec. 9, 1941; s. Joseph and Teresa (Demangone) Z.; m. Patricia Mary Ann Orselli, Aug. 10, 1963; children: Annette, Michael, Steven. BSEE, Northrop Inst. Tech., 1962; MSEE, West Coast U., 1967. Sr. engr. Electronic Specialty, Los Angeles, 1962-66; project engr. Ralph M. Parsons Co., Pasadena, Calif., 1966-67; group supr. Jet Propulsion Lab., Pasadena, 1967-82; program mgr. Aerojet Electrosystems, Azusa, Calif., 1982—. Recipient Mgmt. Team Group Achievement award, NASA, 1974. Republican. Roman Catholic. Avocations: amateur radio, tennis, photography. Home: 1026 Entrada Way Glendora CA 91740 Office: Aerojet Electrosystems Co 1100 W Hollyvale St Azusa CA 91702

ZENZ, BARBARA ELIZABETH, advertising executive; b. Stockton, Calif., Jan. 24, 1956; d. Robert Lee and Patricia Frances (Lowdon) Zenz; m. Kim K. Yamaguchi Sept. 29, 1979. A.A., Sacramento City Coll., 1976; B.A., San Jose State U., 1979; postgrad. U. Santa Clara, 1979-80. Ops. mgr. Hotel Ste. Clair, San Jose, Calif., 1976-78; pub. relations specialist Santa Clara County Housing Authority, 1978-80; pres. The Stephenz Group, Inc., Campbell, Calif., 1980—; advt./mktg. communications cons. Mem. Project Area Com. for Redevel. of Downtown Campbell, 1983—. Republican. Roman Catholic. Club: Campbell Culture, Western Art Dirs. Address: 300 Orchard City Dr Ste 133 Campbell CA 95008

ZERELLA, JOSEPH T., pediatric surgeon; b. Youngstown, Ohio, Mar. 7, 1941; s. Atilio and Ann (Capuzello) Z.; m. Diana Isabelle Talbot, Aug. 5, 1967; children—Ann, Michael, Mark. B.S., Northwestern U., 1962, M.D., 1966. Diplomate Am. Bd. Surgery, Am. Bd. Pediatric Surgery. Intern Med. Coll. Wis., Milw., 1966-67, resident in surgery, 1967-68, 70-73; tng. fellow in pediatric surgery Children's Hosp. Med. Ctr., Cin., 1973-75; staff pediatric surgeon Phoenix Children's Hosp., 1975—, chmn. dept. surgery 1987—; staff Ariz. Children's Hosp., Phoenix, 1975—; pvt. practice medicine specializing in pediatric surgery, Phoenix, 1975—; mem. staff Good Samaritan Hosp., Phoenix, 1975—, sect. chief pediatric surgery, 1979—; mem. staff St. Joseph's Hosp., Phoenix, 1975—, sect. chief pediatric surgery, 1980—; Contbr. articles to profl. jours. Served as capt. U.S. Army, 1968-70. Fellow ACS, Am. Acad. Pediatrics, Am. Pediatric Surg. Assn., Pacific Assn. Pediatric Surgeons; mem. AMA. Roman Catholic. Home: 841 W Glenn Dr Phoenix AZ 85021 Office: Associated Pediatric Surgeons 1010 E McDowell Rd LL4 Phoenix AZ 85006

ZERLAUT, GENE ARLIS, chemist; b. Bailey, Mich., June 23, 1930; s. George David and Glenna Mae (Palm) Z.; student Western Mich. U., 1948-49; B.S., U. Mich., 1956; m. Cecelia Gail McGukin, Mar. 4, 1961; children—Scott Michael, Christopher Robert. Chemist, U.S. Army Ballistic Missle Agy., Huntsville, Ala., 1958-60; aerospace technologist, chemist NASA, Huntsville, 1960-62; sr. chemist, mgr. polymer chemistry research Ill. Inst. Tech. Research Inst., Chgo., 1962-73; pres., tech. dir. DSET Labs., Inc., Phoenix, 1973—. Coach, Little League Baseball, 1974-76; bd. dirs., vice chmn. bd. Solar Energy Research and Edn. Found., 1978-79; commr. Ariz. Solar Commn., 1979-83. Served with U.S. Army, 1956-58. Recipient Invention awards NASA, 1968, Innovation award, 1973. Mem. Solar Energy Industries Assn. (bd. govs. 1976, v.p. 1978-79, exec. com. 1979-81, bd. dirs. 1981-86), Am. Inst. Chemists (dir. 1975), ASTM (nat. chmn. solar energy conversion com. 1978-83, award of merit 1987), Am. Council Ind. Labs., Am. Inst. Aeros. and Astronautics, Am. Nat. Standards Inst. (mem. solar energy standards coordinating com. 1979-83, tech. adv. group on plastics, 1974—,), Internat. Solar Energy Soc., Internat. Standards Orgn. (chmn. U.S. tech. adv. com. on solar energy), Soc. Plastics Engrs., Fedn. Paint Socs. Patentee in field. Contbr. articles to profl. jours. Research in spectral solar radiometry and accelerated environ. testing. Home: 346 W Pine Valley Dr Phoenix AZ 85023 Office: Box 1850 Black Canyon Stage I Phoenix AZ 85029

ZERZAN, CHARLES JOSEPH, JR., physician; b. Portland, Oreg., Dec. 1, 1921; s. Charles Joseph and Margaret Cecelia (Mahony) Z.; B.A., Wilamette U., 1948; M.D., Marquette U., 1951; m. Joan Margaret Kathan, Feb. 7, 1948; children—Charles Joseph, Michael, Kathryn, Paul, Joan, Margaret, Terrance, Phillip, Thomas, Rose, Kevin, Gregory. Commd. 2d. lt., U.S. Army, 1940, advanced through grades to capt., 1945, ret., 1946, re-enlisted, 1951, advanced through grades to lt. col., M.C., 1965; intern Madigan Gen. Hosp., Ft. Lewis, Wash., 1951-52; resident in internal medicine Letterman Gen. Hosp., San Francisco, 1953-56, Walter Reed Gen. Hosp., Washington, 1960-61; chief of medicine Rodriquez Army Hosp., 1957-60, U.S. Army Hosp., Fort Gordon, Calif., 1962-65; chief gastroenterology Fitzsimmons Gen. Hosp., Denver, 1965-66; chief profl. services U.S. Army Hosp., Ft. Carson, Colo., 1967-68; dir. continuing med. edn. U. Oreg., Portland, 1968-73; partner Permanente Clinic, Portland, 1973—; assoc. clin. prof. medicine U. Oreg., 1973—; individual practice medicine, specializing in gastroenterology, Portland, 1968—; staff Northwest Permanente, P.C.; dir., 1980-83. Mem. Portland Com. Fgn. Relations, 1986—. Decorated Legion of Merit, Army Commendation medal with oak leaf cluster. Diplomate Am. Bd. Internal Medicine. Fellow A.C.P.; mem. Am. Gastroenterol. Assn., Oreg. Med. Assn. (del. Clackamas County, membership task force), Ret. Officers Assn. Republican. Roman Catholic. Home: 6364 SE McNary Rd Milwaukie OR 97222 Office: 10200 SE Sunnyside Rd Clackamas OR 97015

ZGUT, JO ELEN KATHERINE, academic administrator; b. Walsenburg, Colo., Apr. 5, 1939; d. Joseph Thomas and Helen Z. B.S. in Vocat. Home Econs. Edn., Colo. Stat U., 1961, M.Ed. in Vocat. Adminstrn. and Supervision, 1967. Vocat. credential, Colo. Tchr. home econs. Aurora (Colo.) Pub. Schs., 1961-67; grad. research asst. Colo. State U., Ft. Collins, 1967-69; dir. community and personal service occupations Community Coll. Denver, 1969-75, dir. resource devel., 1975-82; dir. human resources and services div. Red Rocks Community Coll., Golden, Colo., 1982-85, dir. bus. and human services, 1985-86; assoc. dir. Colo. Law Enforcement Tng. Acad., Golden, 1986—. Mem. Am. Vocat. Assn. (life; regional v.p., dir.), Colo. Vocat. Assn. (life; pres., mem. exec. bd.; Outstanding Service award), Nat. Council Local Adminstrs. (sec.), Colo. Council Local Adminstrs. (dir.), Colo. Assn. Vocation Adminstrs., Colo. Assn. Community/Jr. Colls., NEA, Colo. Edn. Assn., Aurora Edn. Assn. (sec.), Nat. Assn. Pub. Sch. Adult Edn., Colo. Assn. Continuing Adult Edn. (v.p.), Adult Edn. Assn. U.S.A., Mountain Plains Adult Edn. Assn., Nat. Assn., Vocat. Home Econs. Tchrs., Colo. Assn. Vocat. Home Econs. Tchrs., Nat. Environ. Educators Assn., Air Pollution Control Assn., Nat. Council Research Devel. (sec. region VIII), Delta Kappa Gamma. Roman Catholic. Club: Altrusa (dir.) (Denver). Office: Colo Law Enforcement Tng Acad 12600 W 6th Ave Golden CO 80401

ZHLAVODKA, ZEKE ALOYSIUS, computer operations director; b. Hays, Kans., Oct. 10, 1945; Ezekial K. and Isabella Marie (Tuzicka) Z.; m. Janine Frances Rowell, Jan. 29, 1969; children: Sasha Nicol, Erin Roscoe. BSBA, Colo. U., 1968; MS in Computer Sci., UCLA, 1970; PhD in Pub. Adminstrn., Notre Dame U., 1972. Cert. systems analyst. Asst. personnel mgr. Prudential Life, Chgo., 1972-74, dir. pub. relations, 1974-76, sr. systems analyst, 1976-80; cons. Dept. Def., Washington, 1980-83; dir. computer ops. State of Colo., Denver, 1983—; cons. Dept. Def., 1980—. Mem. City Council, Canon City, Colo., 1983-84. Mem. Nat. Assn. Computer Sci. (Outstanding Computer Analyst 1984). Lodge: Elks. Avocations: photography, caligraphy, ham radio, running, cycling. Home: 1346 Park Ave Canon City CO 81212 Office: State of Colo 1575 Sherman St Denver CO 80203

ZICHERMAN, JOSEPH B., fire safety consultant, building products researcher; b. N.Y.C., Feb. 8, 1946; s. Nelson R. and Mariam (Sumpf) Z.; children: Nona, Ben. BS in Forestry, SUNY, Syracuse, 1967; MS, N.C. State U., 1970; PhD, U. Calif., Berkeley, 1978. Chemist Glidden div. SCM, Stroysville, Ohio, 1970-72; sect. head Glidden div. SCM, Stroysville, 1972-73; asst. specialist U. Calif., Berkeley, 1973-78, asst. research engr., 1978-82, assoc. research wood tech., 1982—; prin. cons. IFT Inc., Berkeley, 1978—; assoc. research wood tech., U. Calif., Berkeley, 1982—. Contbr. articles to profl. jours. Served with USMCR, 1968-71. Mem. Am. Chem. Soc., Soc. Testing and Materials, Soc. Fire Protection Engrs., Forest Products Research Soc. (trustee N. Calif. sect., 1980—), Internat. Conf. Bldg. Officials, Nat. Inst. Bldg. Sci. (council mem., cons. 1978—). Office: IFT Inc 2550 9th St Berkeley CA 94710

ZIEMANN, DAVID ALAN, biological oceanographer, researcher, consultant; b. Madison, Wis., July 23, 1944; s. Clarence L. and Harriet E. (Everson) Z.; m. Karen R. Jennings, Dec. 31, 1971 (div. Jan. 1985). BS, Pa. State U., 1966; MS, U. Hawaii, 1970, PhD, 1975. Oceanographer AECOS Inc., Kailua, Hawaii, 1977-81, v.p., 1981-83; research scientist Oceanic Inst., Waimanalo, Hawaii, 1983—; mem. water quality standards tech. adv. com. State of Hawaii, Honolulu, 1983—. Mem. Am. Soc. Limnology and Oceanography. Democrat. Avocations: swimming, orchid culture. Home: 45-206 Puali Koa Pl Kaneohe HI 96744 Office: Oceanic Inst Makapuu Point Waimanalo HI 96744

ZIER, CHRISTIAN JOHN, archaeologist; b. White Plains, N.Y., Jan. 28, 1950; s. Carl Christian and Joan (Carey) Z.; m. Anne G. Hummer, June 12, 1976 (div. May 1982); m. Denise Patricia Fallon, Feb. 2, 1983; children: Caroline Grace, Abigail Fallon. BA, U. Colo., 1972, MA in Anthropology, 1976, PhD in Anthropology, 1981. Coordinator field projects Powers Elevation Co., Denver, 1979-80; prin., co-dir. Metcalf-Zier Archaeologists Inc., Eagle, Colo., 1980-84; prin., dir. Centennial Archaeology Inc., Ft. Collins, Colo., 1984—; asst. dir. U. Colo. Protoclassic Project, El Salvador, 1978-79. Author (monograph) Excavations Near Zuni, N.Mex., 1976; contbr. chpts. to books; articles to profl. jours. Fellow Mus. No. Ariz., Flagstaff, 1973-74; U. Colo. Fellowship Competition scholar, Boulder, 1978. Mem. Colo. Council Profl. Archaeologists (exec. com.), Colo. Archaeol. Soc., Soc. Am. Archaeology, Sigma Xi, Sigma Nu. Methodist. Avocations: whitewater boating, skiing, outdoor photography, hiking, fishing. Home and Office: Centennial Archaeology Inc 2400 Hawthorne Ct Fort Collins CO 80524

ZIERENBERG, ROBERT A., geologist; b. Merced, Calif., Apr. 12, 1952; s. Henry L. and Norma J. Zierenberg. BA, U. Calif., Berkeley, 1974; PhD, U. Wis., 1983. Geologist U.S. Geol. Survey, Menlo Park, Calif., 1984—. Mem. Am. Geophys. Union, Penninsula Geol. Soc., Mineralogic Assn. Can., Geochem. Soc., Soc. Econ. Geologist (assoc.). Office: US Geol Survey 345 Middlefield Rd MS901 Menlo Park CA 94025

ZIGMAN, PAUL EDMOND, environmental consultant executive; b. Los Angeles, Mar. 10, 1924; s. Fernand and Rose (Orligan) Z.; children: Andrea, Eric. BS in Chemistry, UCLA, 1948. Supr., applied research U.S. Naval Radiol. Def. Lab., San Francisco, 1949-59, head tech. mgmt. office, 1961-69; supr., analytical chemistry Atomics Internat., Canoga Park, Calif., 1960-61; pres. Environ. Sci. Assocs., San Francisco, 1969—. Contbr. articles to profl. jours. Served as pvt. U.S. Army, 1943. Recipient USN Meritorious Civilian Service award, 1968. Mem. Am. Chem. Soc., Nat. Assn. Environ. Profls. (v.p. 1977), Assn. Environ. Profls. (pres. 1974-76) (Outstanding Service award 1977, Cert. Appreciation 1984). Office: Environ Sci Assocs 760 Harrison San Francisco CA 94107

ZIKMUND, BARBARA BROWN, minister, educator; b. Ann Arbor, Mich., Oct. 16, 1939; d. Henry Daniels and Helen (Langworthy) Brown; m. Joseph Zikmund II, Aug. 26, 1961; 1 child, Brian Joseph. BA, Beloit Coll., 1961; BDiv, Duke U., 1964, PhD, 1969; D in Div (hon.), Doane Coll., 1984, Chgo. Theol. Sem., 1985. Ordained to ministry United Ch. of Christ, 1964. Instr. Albright Coll., Reading, Pa., 1966-67, Temple U., Phila., 1967-68, Ursinus Coll., Collegeville, Pa., 1968-69; asst. prof. religion studies Albion Coll., Mich., 1970-75; asst. prof. ch. history, dir. studies Chgo. Theol. Sem., 1975-80; dean and assoc. prof. ch. history Pacific Sch. Religion, Berkeley, Calif., 1981-85, dean and prof. ch. history, 1985—; chmn. United Ch. of Christ Hist. Council, 1983-85, mem. council for ecumenism, 1983—; mem. Nat. Council Chs. Commn. on Faith and Order, 1979—, World Council of Chs. Programme Theol. Edn., 1984—. Author: Discovering the Church, 1983. Editor: Hidden Histories in the UCC, 1984; (with Manschreck) American Religious Experience, 1976. Contbr. articles to profl. jours. Mem. City Council, Albion, Mich., 1972-75. Woodrow Wilson fellow, 1964-66; NEH grantee, 1974-75. Mem. Assn. Theol. Schs. (v.p. 1984-86, pres. 1986—, issues implementation grantee 1983-84), Am. Soc. Ch. History (council 1983-85), Internat. Assn. Women Ministers (v.p. 1977-79), AAUW (v.p. 1973-75). Democrat. Home: 1281 Peachwood Ct San Bruno CA 94066 Office: Pacific Sch Religion 1798 Scenic Ave Berkeley CA 94709

ZIL, JOHN STEPHEN, psychiatrist, physiologist; b. Chgo., Oct. 8, 1947; s. Stephen Vincent and Marilyn Charlotte (Jackson) Zilius. BS magna cum laude, U. Redlands, 1969; MD, U. Calif.-San Diego, 1973; MPH, Yale U., 1977; JD, Jefferson Coll., 1985. Intern, resident in psychiatry and neurology U. Ariz., 1973-75; fellow in psychiatry, advanced fellow in social and community psychiatry, Yale community cons. to State Dept. Corrections, Yale U., 1975-77, instr. psychiatry and physiology 1976-77; instr. U. Mass., 1976-77; acting unit chief Inpatient and Day Hosp. Conn. Mental Health Ctr., Yale-New Haven Hosp. Inc., 1975-76, unit chief, 1976-77; asst. prof. psychiatry U. Calif., San Francisco, 1977-82, assoc. prof. psychiatry and medicine, 1982-86, vice-chmn. dept. psychiatry, 1983-86; chief psychiatry and neurology VA Med. Ctr., Fresno, Calif., 1977-86, prin. investigator Sleep Research & Physiology Lab., 1980-86; dir. dept. psychiatry and neurology U. Calif.-Fresno-Central San Joaquin Valley Med. Edn. Program and Affiliated Hosps. and Clinics, 1983-86; chief psychiatrist State of Calif. Dept. Corrections cen. office, 1986—; mental health rep. med. adv. com. State Personnel Bd., 1986—; invited faculty contbr. and editor Am. Coll. Psychiatrist's Resident in Tng. Exam., 1981—. Assoc. editor: Corrective and Social Psychiatry Jour., 1978—, referee, 1980—, reviewer, 1981—. Contbr. articles in field to profl. jours. Nat. Merit scholar, 1965; recipient Nat. Recognition award Bank of Am., 1965; Julian Lee Roberts award U. Redlands, 1969; Kendall award Internat. Symposium in Biochemistry Research, 1970. Fellow Royal Soc. Health, Am. Assn. Social Psychiatry; mem. Am. Assn. Mental Health Profls. in Corrections (nat. pres. 1978—), Calif. Scholarship Fedn. (past pres.), AAUP, Am. Psychiat. Assn., Nat. Council on Crime and Delinquency, Am. Pub. Health Assn., Delta Alpha, Alpha Epsilon Delta.

ZILAITIS, FRANK DAVID, electrical engineer; b. Pottsville, Pa., Apr. 11, 1960; s. Frank William and Irene Hlatky Z.; m. Laura Lee Zilaitis, Aug. 30, 1985. BSEE, Drexel U., 1983; MSEE, U. So. Calif., 1985. Coop. assoc. Pa. Power and Light Co., Allentown, 1979-80; jr. engr. Harris Corp., Palm Bay, Fla., 1981-82; mem. tech. staff Hughes Aircraft Co., Los Angeles, 1983-86; elec. design engr. Norden Systems, Norwalk, Conn., 1986—. Mem. IEEE, Aircraft Owners and Pilots Assn., Drexel U. Alumni Assn. (chmn. Los Angeles Ambassadors com. 1986). Avocation: flying. Home: 93D Penny Meadow Ln Stratford CT 06497 Office: Norden Systems PO Box 5300 Norden Pl Norwalk CT 06856

ZILBERBERG, NAHUM NORBERT, video film and software prodn. exec., publisher; b. Manheim, Germany, Feb. 13, 1925; s. Mendel Max and Pasia Paula (Morgenstern) Z.; came to U.S., 1957, naturalized, 1961; grad. Sem. for Art Tchrs., Tel Aviv, 1952; BFA, Yale U., 1960, MFA, 1961; m. Rita Orechovsky, 1946 (div.); children: Oded, Doron; m. Barbara Cahn, 1968 (div.); children: Jedediah, Noah. Print shop apprentice, 1936; master of trade, lectr. on printing, 1940; prof. Sem. for Art Tchrs., Tel Aviv, also tchr. arts and crafts in elementary and high sch., 1952-57; teaching fellow Yale U., New Haven, 1958-61; designer Macmillan Pub. Co., Inc., 1963; asst. designer, Harcourt Brace & World (name changed to Harcourt Brace Jovanovich, Inc.), 1964-72, v.p. Center for Study of Instrn. div., San Francisco,

1972-73, pres. Harcourt Brace Jovanovich Films div., San Francisco, 1973-80; founder, pres. NZ Videodisc Prodns., Mill Valley, Calif., 1980—; founder, pres., chmn. bd. Silver Mountain Pubs., Mill Valley, 1986—; founder You're Publishing, Inc., Mill Valley, 1987—; adj. prof. edn. tech. San Francisco State U. Served with Israel Def. Forces, 1948-5. Recipient film and audio-visual awards including: Grand award Internat. Film and TV Festival N.Y., 1976, 80, Gold awards 1977, 78, 79, 80; Cindy award Info. Film Producers Am., 1976, Gold Camera award U.S. Indsl. Film Festival, 1977, Gold Camera award for videodisc U.S. Indsl. Film Festival, 1979, Gold Hugo award Chgo. Internat. Film Festival, 1980, Gold awards, 1977, 78; Gold award 10th Ann. Festival of Ams., 1977; Disting. Tech. Service awards Soc. Tech. Communication, 1979; Gold award Houston Internat. Film Festival, 1979; grand award Film Council Greater Columbus, 1981. Mem. Bookbuilders West, Am. Inst. Graphic Arts, Calif. Humanities Assn., Assn. Ednl. Communications and Tech. (study com. on videodisc).

ZIMMERMAN, CURTIS ROY, Episcopal priest; b. Santa Monica, Calif., Dec. 22, 1942; s. Thomas Henry and Verna Ruth (Naylor) Z. BMus, U. Redlands, 1966; MDiv, Ch. Div. Sch. of the Pacific, 1974. Ordained Episc. priest, 1974. Asst. to rector St. Francis Ch., San Jose, Calif., 1971-74; canon St. Andrew's Cathedral, Honolulu, 1974-79; rector Christ Ch., Puyallup, Wash., 1979—; lectr., advisor Anglican Liturgical Renewal, 1967—. Contbr. articles to ch. jours. Served as staff sgt. USAF, 1966-70. Recipient Oscar Greene Meml. Preaching Prize, Ch. Div. Sch. of Pacific, 1974. Mem. Acad. Parish Clergy, Clergy Assn. Puyallup (co-founder 1982-85), Order of the Holy Cross (assoc.), Aircraft Owners and Pilots Assn. Avocations: flying, computer programing, traveling, photography. Home: 301 21st St NW Puyallup WA 98371 Office: Christ Episcopal Ch 210 Fifth St SW Puyallup WA 98371

ZIMMERMAN, DANIEL FRANKLIN, publishing executive; b. Springfield, Mo., Feb. 18, 1947; s. Jac W. and Rheba I. (Wade) Z.; m. Dianne L. Maly, Jan. 31, 1970; 1 child, Adam Wade. BJ, U. Mo., 1969. Editor Herald-Free Press, Bolivar, Mo., 1969-72; pub. Valley Herald, Milton-Freewater, Oreg., 1972-82; gen. mgr. Whidbey Press, Oak Harbor, Wash., 1983—. Columnist local newspapers. Pres. Milton-Freewater C. of C., 1975; chmn. United Way, Milton-Freewater, 1974; mem. adv. bd. St. Mary Community Hosp., Walla Walla, Wash., 1978-82. Recipient Key to City award Milton-Freewater Govt., 1983; Ruhl fellow U. Oreg., 1980. Mem. Wash. Newspaper Pubs. Assn., Oak Harbor C. of C. (bd. dirs. 1985-87). Republican. Episcopalian. Lodge: Rotary (pres. Milton-Freewater club 1976-77). Avocations: skiing, golf, tennis, photography, astronomy. Home: 1365 N West Beach Rd Oak Harbor WA 98277 Office: Whidbey Island Pub Co PO Box 10 Oak Harbor WA 98277

ZIMMERMAN, DANIEL RAY, religious educator; b. Chgo., Nov. 22, 1948; s. Raymond Zimmerman and Kathleen (Benton) Dickie. AA, Triton Coll., 1968; BS in Edn., No. Ill. U., 1970; PhD, Universal Life U., 1982, DD (hon.), 1978; postgrad., Inst. Advanced Study of Human Sexuality, 1984—. Cert. tchr., Ill., Iowa. Tchr., spl. edn. tchr. Cedar Rapids (Iowa) Schs., 1970-86; minister Universal Life Ch., Cedar Rapids, 1976-86; administr. Universal Life Ch., Modesto, Calif., 1980—, supr., 1982—, at. law witness, 1982—; assoc. prof. religion Universal Life U., Modesto, 1983—, counselor sexual minorities, 1984—; presenter seminars in field; govtl. rep. Kingsom of Aqualandia, 1986—. Author: Universal Life Church Principles and Practices, 1983. Foster parent Linn County Human Services, Cedar Rapids, 1976-83; active Civil Rights Advocates, Washington, 1985. Recipient Tchr. Incentive award Dept. Edn. State of Iowa, 1974. Mem. Am. Humanist Assn., Am. Fedn. Tchrs., NEA. Democrat. Avocations: group presentations, networking and network information. Office: Universal Life Ch 601 3d St Modesto CA 95351

ZIMMERMAN, HAROLD SAMUEL, newspaper executive, state senator; b. Valley City, N.D., June 1, 1923; s. Samuel Alwin and Lulu (Wylie) Z.; m. Julianne Williams, Sept. 12, 1946; children—Karen, Steven, Judi Jean (dec.). B.A., U. Wash., 1947. News editor Sedro-Woolley (Wash.) Courier Times, 1947-50; editor, pub. Advocate, Castle Rock, Wash., 1950-57; pub. Post-Record, Camas, Wash., 1957-80; assoc. pub., columnist, 1980; assoc. pub., columnist, dir. Eagle Publs., Camas, 1980—. Mem. Wash. Ho. of Reps., 1967-80; mem. Wash. Senate, 1981—. Served with USAAF, 1943-46. Mem. Grange, Sigma Delta Chi, Sigma Chi. Republican. Methodist. Clubs: Lions, Kiwanis.

ZIMMERMAN, HOWARD CLINTON, education educator, consultant; b. Quilcene, Wash., Jan. 16, 1926; s. William Truesdale and Malvina Elizabeth (Langworthy) Z.; m. Lydia Koch, July 14, 1956 (div.); children—Sylvia, Angela, Joan, Garth. B.A., N.W. Nazarene Coll., Nampa, Idaho, 1948; M.A., U. Oreg., 1954, D.Ed., 1967; postdoctoral NDEA Insts., Kellogg Found. Inst., Kellogg-West retreat. Tchr. English and drama Nampa Sr. High Sch., 1948, Collinsview Grade Sch., Portland, Oreg., 1948-49; tchr., chmn. dept. English, Willamette High Sch., Eugene, Oreg., 1950-65; teaching asst., doctoral fellow U. Oreg., 1949-50, 53-54, 61-62, 64-65; prof. edn. U. Toledo, 1965-70, Calif. State U.-Bakersfield, 1970—; assoc. vis. prof. English, Bowling Green State U., 1968; cons. Am. Book Co.; cons. tech. edn. Advisor, Calif. Democratic party; mem. Kern Philharm. Soc. Served with USNR, 1943-44. Mem. NEA, Calif. Tchrs. Assn. (Who award 1976), Oreg. Edn. Assn. (pres. Lane County), Bethel Edn. Assn. (pres.), Calif. Higher Edn. Assn. (pres.), Nat. Council Tchrs. of English, Assn. Supervision and Curriculum Devel., Calif. Poetry Soc., Calif. Assn. Tchrs. of English, Calif. Reading Assn., Congress Faculty Assns. (local pres., state dir.), Calif. Profs. Reading, Council Exceptional Children, Kern County Assn. Neurol. Handicapped Children (pres.), Calif. Coll. and Univ. Faculty Assn. (pres.), Phi Delta Kappa (Outstanding Man in Edn. 1965). Author: Dico Ergo sum: An Introduction to the Nature of Language, 1961; Ideal Designs for English Programs, 1968; contbr. poetry to Orpheus, 1971-83; contbr. articles profl. jours.

ZIMMERMAN, MICHAEL DAVID, judge; b. Chgo., Oct. 21, 1943. B.S., U. Utah, 1967, J.D., 1969. Bar: Calif. 1971, Utah 1978. Law clk. to Chief Justice Warren E. Burger U.S. Supreme Ct., Washington, 1969-70; assoc. O'Melveny & Myers, Los Angeles, 1970-76; assoc. prof. law U. Utah, 1976-78, adj. prof. law, 1978-84; of counsel Kruse, Landa, Zimmerman & Maycock, Salt Lake City, 1978-80; staff Gov. of Utah, Salt Lake City, 1978-80, spl. counsel, 1980-84; ptnr. Watkiss & Campbell, Salt Lake City, 1980-84; justice Supreme Ct. of Utah, Salt Lake City, 1984—. Editor: Utah Law Rev., 1968-69. Mem. ABA, Jud. Conf. of U.S. (adv. com. civil rules 1985—), Utah Jud. Council, Salt Lake County Bar Assn., Order of Coif, Phi Kappa Phi. Office: Capitol Bldg Salt Lake City UT 84114

ZIMMERMAN, MURIEL, university administrator; b. Boston, Nov. 22, 1938; d. Nathan and Edna (Droz) Laden; m. Everett Zimmerman, Apr. 28, 1963; children: Andrew, Daniel. BS, Temple U., 1959, PhD, 1967. Lectr. tech. communications MIT, Cambridge, 1983-85; dir. interdisciplinary writing program U. Calif., Santa Barbara, 1985—. Editor Energy Rev., 1974-82; contbr. articles to profl. jours. Mem. Phila. Dem. City Com., 1964-68. NDEA fellow, 1960-63. Mem. Soc. Tech. Communication, Calif. Assn. Tchrs. Tech. and Profl. Writing, Assn. Tchrs. Tech. Writing, Profl. Communication Soc. of IEEE. Home: 1822 Prospect Ave Santa Barbara CA 93103 Office: U Calif Office Interdisciplinary Writing Santa Barbara CA 93106

ZIMMERMAN, RICHARD K., exploration geologist; b. Rochester, Minn., Apr. 8, 1954; s. Warren Wirth and Helen Marie (Garlock) Z.; m. Annette Louise Campbell, Aug. 20, 1977; children: Matthew Scott, Christina Marie, Daniel Robert. BA, Carleton Coll., 1976; MS, U. Mich., 1980. Mine geologist Rosario Resources, Honduras, 1980-81; exploration geologist Phelps Dodge Corp., Tucson, 1981—. Mem. Soc. Mining Engrs. of AIME, Sigma Xi. Home: 4989 W Spoonbill Dr Tucson AZ 85741 Office: Phelps Dodge Corp 1810 W Grant Rd Suite 103 Tucson AZ 85703-1427

ZIMMERMAN, SHIRLEY JEAN, business executive; b. Ohio, Jan. 1, 1942; d. Clifford Leo Buop and Laverne Mary (Woodmansee) Buop Mills; m. Michael Andrew Zimmerman, Aug. 27, 1965 (div.); 1 child, Shona Leah. BA, Earlham Coll., 1963; MA, U. Chgo., 1966. Cert. jr. coll. tchr., Calif. Asst. dir. Valley Med. Ctr., San Jose, 1976-77; human resources mgr. Raychem Corp., Menlo Park, Calif., 1978-80, mfg. planning mgr., 1980-81; pres. Orchard Farms Inc., Grass Valley, Calif., 1981—. Mem. com. Mcpl. Incorps. Ananda Village, Nev. City, Calif. Indsl. Areas Found. scholar, 1970. Mem. NOW, Am. Logistics Assn., Nat. Food Brokers Assn., Exec. Women's Roundtable, Nat. Fedn. Ind. Bus. Democrat. Jewish. Lodge: Soroptimists. Home: 287 Ball Rd Grass Valley CA 95945 Office: 13321 Grass Valley Dr Suite 10 Grass Valley CA 95945

ZIMMERMAN, THEODORE SAMUEL, physician, researcher, educator; b. St. Louis, May 3, 1937; s. Julius Aaron and Rose Bernice (Hammerman) Z.; m. Frances O'Neill, July 29, 1961; children: Grace Ann, Clare Elizabeth. AB magna cum laude, Harvard U., 1959, MD, 1963. Diplomate Am. Bd. Internal Medicine, Am. Bd. Hematology. Intern then resident U. Minn. Hosp., Mpls., 1963-65; with medicine br. NIH, Nat. Cancer Inst., Bethesda, Md., 1965-67; resident in medicine Barnes Hosp., St. Louis, 1967-68; fellow in hematology Case Western Res. U., Cleve., 1968-70; assoc. Scripps Clinic and Research Found., La Jolla, Calif., 1972-74, chief coagulation lab., 1972—, assoc. prof. immunology, 1974-82, prof., 1982—, mem. hematology staff, 1976—, dir. biomed. research lab., 1974—; asst. clin. prof. U. Calif. San Diego, La Jolla, 1972—; mem. rev. and adv. coms. NIH, 1974-77, Am. Heart Assn., 1975-77, and others. Mem. editorial bd. BLOOD, 1981-85; contbr. numerous chpts. to books and articles to profl. jours. Served to lt. comdr. USPHS, 1968-72. Recipient Research Career Devel. award NIH, 1972-77, Merit award Nat. Heart Lung and Blood Inst., 1985. Fellow ACP; mem. Assn. Am. Physicians, Am. Assn. Immunologists, Am. Fedn. Clin. Research., Am. Soc. Clin. Investigation, Am. Soc. Exptl. Pathology, Am. Soc. Hematology (councillor, mem. rev. and adv. coms.), Interat. Soc. Thrombosis and Haemostasis, World Fedn. Hemophilia, Nat. Hemophilia Found. (chmn. med. sci. adv. council). Home: 544 Bon Air St La Jolla CA 92037 Office: Scripps Clinic Research Found 10666 N Torrey Pines Rd La Jolla CA 92037

ZIMMERMAN, WAYNE, electronic company executive; b. Chgo., Sept. 13, 1936; s. Irving and Ann Honey (Diamond) Z.; m. Kimberly Kell, Sept. 10, 1981; children: Cathy, Scott, Paul, April. LLB, Glendale Coll. Law. Mktg. mgr. Amphenol, Broadview, Ill., 1969-77, Cramer Electronics, Newton, Mass., 1977-79; div. mgr. Wyle EMG, El Segundo, Calif., 1979-81, Time Electronics, Tempe, Ariz., 1981-85; gen. mgr. Dalis Electronics, Phoenix, Ariz., 1985—. Mem. Electronic Connector Study Group. Home: 16217 E Park Ave Gilbert AZ 85234 Office: Dalis Electronics 2829 E McDowell Phoenix AZ 85008

ZIMMERMANN, STEPHAN FRITZ-PETER, investment management company executive; b. Leipzig, Sachsen, Germany, Nov. 28, 1945; came to U.S., 1956; s. Andreas and Senta Agnes Klara (Bergmann) Z.; m. Pamela Clare Dawson, Mar. 29, 1980 (div. Aug. 1984); 1 child, Helen Jennifer. BA, U. Calif., Berkeley, 1971; cert. in econs., Cambridge U., 1975; MA, Monterey Inst. Internat. Studies, 1976. Underwriter Home Ins. Co., San Francisco, 1968-70; stockbroker Dean Witter Reynolds, Berkeley, Calif., 1971-73; analyst Bartle Wells Assocs., San Francisco, 1973-74; pres. Zimmermann, Wilson & Co. Inc., Carmel, Calif., 1976—. Producer record albums Pat DuVal-Old Monterey, 1985, Heartsounds, 1986; columnist Zimmermann Notes, 1971—. Bd. dirs. Monterey County Rep. Cen. Com., Salinas, Calif., 1976. Served with USAF, 1966-67. Recipient Dow Jones award in Econs., 1976. Avocations: novelist, poet, recording producer. Office: Zimmermann Wilson & Co Inc 533 Carmel Rancho Carmel CA 93923

ZINK, WAYNE PHILLIP, public relations executive; b. Phoenix, Feb. 20, 1961; s. Phillip Walter and Peggy Yvonne (Moehl) Z.; m. Francine Olman, Apr. 27, 1986. BS, Grand Canyon Coll., 1983. Sales rep. Broadway S.W., Phoenix, 1982-83; adolescent counselor Camelback Hosp., Phoenix, 1983-84; v.p. Francine Hardaway Connections, Phoenix, 1984—; bd. dirs. Palmer Drug Abuse Program, Phoenix, 1985—. Mem. Ariz. State U. Enterprise Network, Tempe, 1984-86, Phoenix Community Alliance, 1984-86, Phoenix Film Commn., 1984-86, Valley Forward, Phoenix., 1986. Mem. Pub. Relations Soc. Am. Republican. Club: Phoenix City. Lodge: Rotary. Avocations: snow and water skiing, aerobics, running. Home: 9031 N 15th St Phoenix AZ 85020 Office: Camelback Hosp 3550 N Central Phoenix AZ 85020

ZINKLE, THOMAS EDWARD, clinical psychologist; b. Prairie du Chien, Wis., Feb. 22, 1944; s. Thomas Francis and Anne (Honzel) Z.; B.A., St. Louis U., 1968; M.A., U.S. Internat. U., San Diego, 1970, Ph.D., 1974. Lic. clin. psychologist, Calif. Intern, Community Mental Health Ctr., San Bernardino, Calif., 1974, Community Mental Health Ctr., Pensacola, Fla., 1974-78; pvt. practice psychology, Riverside, Calif., 1978-79; clin. psychologist Kaiser Permanente, Fontana, Calif., 1979—. Mem. Am. Psychol. Assn., Calif. Psychol. Assn., Inland Counties Psychol. Assn., Nat. Registry Psychologists, Am. Contract Bridge League. Democrat. Home: 1227 Mira Monte Dr Redlands CA 92373 Office: 325 W Hospitality Ln Suite 312 San Bernardino CA 92408

ZINS, GEORGE BRIAN, association executive; b. Great Falls, Mont., Sept. 26, 1942; s. Leo George and Marion Frances (O'Leary) Z.; m. Diana Mae Dirkson, June 7, 1969; children—Erica Ann, Kendra Lee, Ryan Leo, Scott Raymond. B.S., Coll. Great Falls, 1969. Account mgr. Mont. Deaconess Hosp., Great Falls, 1966-69; dir. bus. Central Mont. Hosp., Lewistown, 1969-70; exec. dir. Mont. Med. Assn., Helena, 1970—. Served with AUS, 1964-66. Decorated Army Commendation medal. Mem. Am. Soc. Assn. Execs., Am. Assn. Med. Soc. Execs. Club: Lions. Home: 1055 Flathead Rd Helena MT 59601 Office: 2021 11th Ave Suite 12 Helena MT 59601

ZION, LETTIE BACKUS, civic worker; b. Yuma County, Colo., May 11, 1910; d. Elmer Abram and Valeria Anna (Hampton) Backus; m. Theodore Charles Zion, Aug. 17, 1947 (dec. 1976). B.A., U. Colo.-Boulder, 1932; M.A., U. Fla., 1943. Tchr., Yuma County High Sch., Colo., 1932-34, rural schs., Wray-Vernon, Colo., 1934-36, DeSoto County High Sch., Arcadia, Fla., 1936-42, Leesburg pub. schs., Fla., 1942-43, Vernon High Sch., Colo., 1943-44, St. Petersburg pub. schs., Fla., 1944-45, Lamoni pub. schs., Iowa, 1945-46, Laird pub. schs., Colo., 1946-47. Editor: East Yuma County History, 1978, Wray Centennial History, 1986; contbr. articles to profl. jours. Tchr. Vacation Bible Sch., Wray, Colo., 1932-87; precinct committeewoman Democrat Party, Yuma County, 1980-84; vol. ARC, first aid instr., 1941-87. Named Woman of the Year, Bus. and Profl. Women, Wray, Colo., 1970; mem. NEA, Colo. Edn. Assn., Ret. Tchrs. Assn. (v.p. 1983-85), Farmers Union. Mem. Reorganized Ch. of Jesus Christ of Latter Day Saints. Clubs: Extension Homemakers, Woman's Christian Temperance Union (Colo.) (v.p., pres. 1986-87). Home: 1132 W 7th St Wray CO 80758 Office: Wray Mus 140 W 4th Wray CO 80758

ZISHKA, RONALD LOUIS, sociologist, psychologist, educator, marriage and family therapist; b. Sheldon, Iowa, Mar. 27, 1935; s. Louis Frank and Wilma Marie (Plautz) Z.; B.A., Capital U., 1958; M.Div., Trinity Theol. Sem., 1962; M.A., Case Western Res. U., 1965; Ph.D., Ohio State U., 1973; postdoctoral psychotherapy tng. Pastoral Counseling Services, Columbus, Ohio, 1973-75; children from previous marriage—Mary, John, Cathy. Asst. prof. sociology Ohio U., Athens, 1966-79; assoc. prof. sociology Christ Coll. of Irvine, Calif., 1979-86, dir. social work program, 1981-86; pvt. practice marriage, family and child counseling and psychotherapy, Anaheim, Calif., 1979—; ordained to ministry Luth. Ch., 1962. Lic. marriage, family and child counselor, Clin. Mem. Am. Assn. Marriage, Family and Child Psychotherapists, Calif. Assn. Marriage, Family and Child Psychotherapists, Am. Sociol. Assn., Pacific Sociol. Assn., Soc. Sci. Study Social Problems. Home and Office: Family Enrichment Ctr 314 S Brookhurst Suite 103 Anaheim CA 92804

ZISMAN, FRANK, optometrist, psychophysicist; b. Los Angeles, July 18, 1948; s. Max and Celia (Kinsbursky) Z.; m. Katerina R. Rohan, Nov. 19, 1977; children: Emily Rebecca, Sarah Michelle, Celia Nicole. BS, U. Calif., Berkeley, 1972, OD, 1974; PhD, U. Manchester, Eng., 1977. Lic. optometrist, Calif., Eng. Ocular photographer Lawrence Donner, Berkeley, Calif., 1972-74; practice medicine specializing in optometry Calif. and Eng., 1975—; clin. instr., asst. research specialist U. Calif., Berkeley, 1978-80, asst. clin. prof., assoc. research specialist, 1980—; cons. U.S. Forestry Service, Berkeley, 1980-82, Alameda County Health Dept., Oakland, Calif., 1980—, San Jose Health Dept., 1984—, San Diego Health Dept., 1985—. Contbr. articles to profl. jours. Nikon scholar Nikon Ophthalmics, U. Calif., Berkeley, 1972; recipient Borisch award Am. Optometric Found., St. Louis, 1974. Fellow Am. Acad. Optometry; mem. Internat. Research Group on Color Vision Deficiencies, Am. Optometric Assn., Assn. Research in Vision and Ophthalmology, Alameda County Optometric Assn., Contra Costa County Optometric Assn., AAAS. Avocations: stamp collecting, hiking, camping, photography, sports. Office: U Calif Sch Optometry Berkeley CA 94720 Office: 1500 Sycamore Ave Suite B1 Hercules CA 94547

ZITZOW, RICHARD EDWARD, hospital administrator; b. Newark, Aug. 26, 1937; s. August and Genevieve (Katloski) Z.; m. Caroline Bernadette Zitzow, June 10, 1962; children: Patricia, Richard E. Jr., Vera. AA, Fairleigh Dickinson U., 1960, BS, 1962; MPH in Health Care Adminstrn., U. Minn., 1976. Cert. health care adminstr. Dir. clin. lab. USPHS, Mount Edgecumbe, Alaska, 1962-66, Gallup, N.Mex., 1966-71; dir. hosp. USPHS, Kayenta, Ariz., 1971-73, Barrow, Alaska, 1973-76; dir. program devel. Alaska Native Health Service, Anchorage, 1976-80, exec. officer, 1980—; v.p. Fed. Credit Union, Mount Edgecumbe, 1964-66; v.p. council of service unit dirs. USPHS, 1974-76. Mem. mayor's adv. com. health and social services, Anchorage, 1979, mayor's planning com. community planning Gov.'s Adv. Group, Anchorage, 1983-86. Recipient Profl. award State Hosp. Assn., 1975, Outstanding Performance award USPHS, 1975, Adminstrs. award for Excellence USPHS, 1980. Mem. Am. Coll. Health Care Execs., Fed. Health Care Execs. Assn., Health Care Execs. Alaska. Democrat. Roman Catholic. Lodge: Elks. Avocations: boating, flyfishing, astronomy. Home: 3871 Amber Bay Loop Anchorage AK 99515 Office: Alaska Native Med Ctr PO Box 7-741 Anchorage AK 99510

ZIVIC, WILLIAM THOMAS, artist, sculptor, gallery owner; b. Ironwood, Mich., Aug. 31, 1930; s. Stephan and Anna Louise (Herbenar) Z.; m. Carol Jean Engebretsen, July 11, 1959; children—William, John. Student pub. schs., Ironwood, Mich. Mcht. seaman, Atlantic and Pacific oceans, 1948; surveyor, Canada-U.S. oil pipeline, 1949; mcht. seaman, Gt. Lakes; iron miner, Ironwood, 1958-61; detective, Tucson Police Dept., 1961-67; now owner, Trail Dust Gallery; art lectr. Work represented in Pro Rodeo Cowboy Hall of Fame. Bd. dirs. YMCA. Served in U.S. Army, 1950-52, 1954-58. Decorated Bronze Star. Awards include: 1st place in watercolor Huachuca Art Show, Ariz., 1973-75; best of show Internat. Fine Arts Exhbn., Palm Springs, Calif., 1977; 1st place in oil painting Wis. Art Festival, 1978; 1st place in bronze sculpture Internat. Fine Arts Exhibition, Tucson, 1980. Roman Catholic. Author: Southwest Memories, 1975; painted official bicentennial painting for Ariz., 1976. Mem. Ariz. Cowboy Artists, Huachuca Art Assn., Southwest Profl. Artists, Old Pueblo Artisans, League of Southwest Artists.

ZIVIN, JUSTIN ALLEN, neurologist, neuroscientist, educator; b. Chgo., Aug. 17, 1946; s. Simon and Mabel Edith (Libert) Z.; m. Reni-Zoe Mandell, June 23, 1968; children: Kara, Leslie. BS, Northwestern U., 1967, MS, 1970, PhD, 1971, MD, 1972. Diplomate Am. Bd. Psychiatry and Neurology. Asst. prof. neurology U. Mass., Worcester, 1978-80, assoc. prof. neurology and pharmacology, 1980-85; assoc. prof. neurosci. U. Calif., San Diego, 1985—. Contbr. articles to profl. jours. Served as surgeon USPHS, 1973-75. Research grantee Nat. Inst. Neurol. and Communicative Disorders and Stroke, 1979—. Fellow Am. Heart Assn. (stroke council); mem. Am. Acad. Neurology, Soc. Neurosci., Soc. Neurochemistry. Office: U Calif Sch Medicine Dept Neurosci M-024 La Jolla CA 92093

ZMAK, WILLIAM THOMAS, insurance company executive, consultant; b. Reno, Aug. 18, 1940; s. William Valentine and Faye (Bedell) Z.; m. Claire Stephenson, Aug. 19, 1962; children: Stephen Michael, Gregory William. BS, U. Oreg., 1962. CPCU. Underwriting mgr. Allstate Ins. Co., various locations, 1965-77; casualty mgr. Mission Ins. Co., Tustin, Calif., 1977-80; underwriting mgr. Ins. Co. N. Am., Los Angeles, 1980-81; v.p. Dealer Cover Inc., Torrance, Calif., 1981-85; pres. Thomas Sinclaire & Assocs., Huntington Beach, Calif., 1985—. Chmn. Bd. W. County Family YMCA, Huntington Beach, 1985-86; co-chmn. Parents Council Warren Coll., U. Calif., San Diego, 1986-87; treas. Bldg. Fund Trustees St. Wilfrid's Episcopal Ch., Huntington Beach, 1982-87. Mem. Soc. CPCU's, U. Oreg. Alumni Assn. (v.p. So. Calif. chpt.1985-86). Republican. Avocations: photography, vintage wines. Home and Office: 17172 Englewood Circle Huntington Beach CA 92647

ZOBEL, DONALD BRUCE, botany educator; b. Salinas, Calif., July 17, 1942; s. Bruce John and Barbara June (Lemon) Z.; m. Priscilla Fay Matthews, July 9, 1966; children: Cheryl, Gregory. BS, N.C. State U., 1964; MS, Duke U., 1966, PhD, 1968. Asst. prof. Oreg. State U., Corvallis, 1968-74, assoc. prof., 1974-82, prof., 1982—; vis. researcher, Taiwan Forestry Research Inst., Taipei, 1976-77; Fulbright lectr. Tribhuvan U., Kathmandu, Nepal, 1984-85. Author: Ecology, Pathology and Management of Port-Orford-cedar (Chamaecyparis lawsoniana), 1985; contbr. articles to profl. jours. Grantee NSF, 1974-77, 1980-85. Mem. AAAS, Ecol. Soc. Am., NW Sci. Assn. (bd. trustees 1980-83), Brit. Ecol. Soc. Republican. Mem. Christian Ch. Home: 2310 NE Seavy Circle Corvallis OR 97330 Office: Oreg State U Botany and Plant Pathology Corvallis OR 97331-2902

ZOBELL, KARL, lawyer; b. La Jolla, Calif., Jan. 9, 1932; s. Claude E. and Margaret (Harding) ZoB.; m. Barbara Arth, Nov. 22, 1968; children: Bonnie, Elizabeth, Karen, Claude, Mary. Student, Utah State U., 1949-51, Columbia U., 1951-52; AB, Columbia U., 1953, student of law, 1952-54; JD, Stanford U., 1958. Bar: Calif., 1959. Assoc., lawyer Gray, Cary, Ames and Frye, San Diego, 1959-64, ptnr., lawyer, 1964—; bd. dirs. La Jolla (Calif.) Bank and Trust Co. Trustee La Jolla Town Council, 1962—, chmn. bd. dirs., 1967-68, pres. 1976-77, 80-81, v.p., 1986—; trustee La Jollans Inc., 1974-77, founder, 1964, 78-80, pres. 1965-68, 73-76, 78-89; mem. charter rev. com. City San Diego, 1968-73; trustee La Jolla Mus. Art, 1964-72, pres. 1967-70, bd. dirs Scripps Meml. Hosp. Found., 1980-84, bd. overseers, Stanford Law Sch., 1977-80, U. Calif., San Diego, 1974-76. Served to lt. USCG, 1954-57. Fellow Am. Coll. Probate Counsel; mem. ABA, Calif. Bar. Republican. Clubs: La Jolla Beach and Volleyball (pres. 1982—), La Jolla Beach and Tennis. Home: 1555 Coast Walk PO Box 1 La Jolla CA 92037 Office: Gray Cary Ames & Frye 1200 Prospect St La Jolla CA 92037

ZODL, JOSEPH ARTHUR, international trade executive, consultant; b. Hackensack, N.J., Aug. 13, 1948; s. Joseph Frank and Edna Josephine (Hokanson) Z. BA in Polit. Sci., Fordham Coll., 1970. Lic. customhouse broker U.S. Treasury Dept. Export mgr. Savage Universal Corp., Tempe, Ariz., 1984—. Contbr. articles to profl. jours. Vice chmn. Legis. Dist. 20 Dems., 1978-80, chmn., 1980-82; mem. Ariz. State Dem. Com., 1978—; candidate Ariz. Ho. Reps., 1986. Named Eagle Scout, Boy Scouts Am., 1966. Mem. Am. Polit. Sci. Assn., Ariz. World Trade Assn., Phoenix Traffic Club, Delta Nu Alpha (pres. 1980-81, Ariz. Transp. Man of Yr. 1980), Alpha Phi Omega. Roman Catholic. Address: Box 20232 Phoenix AZ 85036-0232

ZOELLNER, ROBERT WILLIAM, chemistry educator; b. Marshfield, Wis., May 30, 1956; s. Willard Rudolph and Marie Martha (Prihoda) Z.; m. Barbara Moore, Feb. 5, 1983; 1 child, Joan Moore. BS, St. Norbert Coll., De Pere, Wis., 1978; PhD, Kans. State U., 1983. Postdoctoral assoc. Cornell U., Ithaca, N.Y., 1983-84; vis. scientist Université d'Aix-Marseille (France) III, 1984-85; asst. prof. No. Ariz. U., Flagstaff, 1986—. Mem. AAAS, Am. Chem. Soc., N.Y. Acad. Sci., N.D. Acad. Sci., Wis. Acad. Sci., Arts and Letters, Sigma Xi, Alpha Chi Sigma, Phi Lambda Upsilon. Office: No Ariz U Dept Chemistry Box 5698 Flagstaff AZ 86011-0003

ZOLBER, KATHLEEN KEEN, nutrition educator, mgmt. cons.; b. Walla Walla, Wash., Dec. 9, 1916; d. Wildie H. and Alice (Johnson) Keen; m. Melvin L. Zolber, Sept. 19, 1937. BS in Foods and Nutrition, Walla Walla Coll., 1941; MA, Wash. State U., 1961; PhD, U. Wis., 1968. Registered dietitian. Dir. food service Walla Walla Coll., 1941-50, mgr. coll. store, 1951-59, asst. prof. food and nutrition, 1959-62, assoc. prof., 1962-64; assoc. prof. nutrition Loma Linda (Calif.) U., 1964-72, prof. nutrition, 1973—, dir. dietetic edn., 1967-84, dir. dietetics Med. Ctr., 1972-84, dir. nutrition program, 1984—. Mead Johnson grantee, 1965-67; recipient Alumna of Yr. award Walla Walla Coll., 1977; Delores Nyhus award Calif. Dietetic Assn., 1978. Mem. Am. Dietetic Assn. (pres. 1982—), Am. Pub. Health Assn., Am. Home Econs. Assn., Am. Mgmt. Assn., AAUP, Soc. Food Service

Research, Soc. Personnel Adminstrn., Omicron Nu, Delta Omega. Home: PO Box 981 Loma Linda CA 93354 Office: Loma Linda U Sch Health Dept Nutrition Loma Linda CA 93354

ZOLEZZI, SAMUEL MAURICE, airline pilot; b. San Diego, Oct. 5, 1949; s. Albert and Jo Noveline (Williams) Z.; m. Victoria Brooke Strickler, Mar. 22, 1980. AB in Theater and TV, San Diego State U., 1971. Lic. airline transport pilot; lic. instrument flight instr. Commd. 2d lt. USAF, 1971, advance through grades to capt., 1978; pilot active duty USAF, Southeast Asia, 1971-74; reserve pilot USAF, San Bernardino, Calif., 1974-80; resigned USAF, 1980; first officer New World Airways, Chula Vista, Calif., 1974-75; asst. chief pilot 21st Century Aviation, Chula Vista, 1975-76; first officer World Airways, Oakland, Calif., 1978-86, Pacific S.W. Airlines (bought by US Air), San Diego, 1986—. Home: 6057 Estelle St San Diego CA 92115

ZOLLARS, RICHARD LEE, chemical engineering educator; b. Mpls., Nov. 9, 1946; s. John Wesley and Jean Isabel (Wesner) Z.; m. Diane Michele Dillner, Dec. 20, 1968; children: Melanie Lindsey, Andrew David. BChemE, U. Minn., 1968; MS, U. Colo., 1972, PhD, 1974. Registered profl. engr., Wash. Lab. technician 3M Co., St. Paul, 1966-68; sr. engr. Union Carbide Corp., South Charleston, W.Va., 1974-77; asst. prof. chem. engring. U. Colo., Boulder, 1977-78; dir. program NSF, Washington, 1983-84; from asst. prof. to assoc. prof. Wash. State U., Pullman, 1978—. Contbr. articles to profl. jours. Served as sgt. U.S. Army, 1969-70, Vietnam. Named Outstanding Prof. Chem. Engring. Wash. State U. Coll. Engring., 1981, 82, 86. Mem. AAAS, Am. Inst. Chem. Engrs., Am. Chem. Soc., Am. Soc. Engring. Edn., Tau Beta Pi. Avocations: skiing, stained glass. Home: SE 745 Green Hill Ct Pullman WA 99163 Office: Wash State U Dept Chem Engring Pullman WA 99164-2710

ZOLTAN, LES LASZLO, computer company executive, engineer; b. Can., Dec. 11, 1947; s. Alex and Elizabeth (Gold) Z. B.S.E.E., U. Waterloo, Ont., Can., 1973; M.B.A., McGill U., Montreal, Que., Can., 1977. Mktg. mgr. Intel Corp., Santa Clara, Calif., 1977-79; sales mgr. Advanced Micro Devices, Sunnyvale, Calif., 1979-81; pres. Computer Modules, Inc., Sunnyvale, 1981—. Mem. IEEE. Office: Computer Modules Inc 1190 Miraloma Way #Y Sunnyvale CA 94086

ZOMMERS, G. JURIS, interior designer, consultant; b. Riga, Latvia, Dec. 13, 1938; s. Hermanis Rudolfs Zommers and Milda (Makars) Z.; m. Dzintra Aina Zamelis, June 15, 1963 (div.); children—Andrejs Markus, Karlis Eduards, Pauls Hermanis; m. 2d, Stephanie Lee Harris, Dec. 23, 1982. B.S. in Interior Design, U. Wash., 1962. Designer, Aaron's Interiors Co., Bellevue, Wash., 1962-65, Western Internat. Hotels, Seattle, 1965-68; mgr. interior design dept. Allied Stores (The Bon Marche), Seattle, 1968-73; dir. design Mayer Baron Assos., Seattle, 1973; ptnr., operator Daina Design-Interior Design Studio, 1973-83; ptnr. Harris/Zommers Interiors, 1984—; advisor career seminars. Active Boy Scouts Am., Nat. Right to Work Found. Served with USAR 1962-68. Patentee in field. Recipient Edward E. Carlson creativity award, 1972. Mem. Am. Soc. Interior Designers (cert. 1980). Republican. Lutheran. Club: American-Latvian, Seattle. Office: 126 Madrone Ln PO Box 10255 Bainbridge Island WA 98110

ZONER, CAROL FITZPATRICK, health systems administrator; b. Pitts., Dec. 5, 1958; s. Robert Bernard and June Lorraine (Purvis) F.; m. Steven Eric Zoner, Apr. 9, 1983. BA in Spanish, BA in Econs., Thiel Coll., 1981; MBA, Ariz. State U., 1986. Fin. tech. Samaritan Health Services, Phoenix, 1981-82, compensation tech., 1982, compensation analyst, 1982-83, compensation specialist, 1983-84; compensation adminstr. Blood Systems, Inc., Scottsdale, Ariz., 1984-86; compensation mgr. Pacific Med. Ctr., San Francisco, 1986—; mem. adv. bd. Am. Assn. Med. Transcription, Phoenix, 1984—. Exchange student Am. Field Service, South Africa, 1977. Mem. Am. Compensation Assn. (cert. compensation profl.), Am. Soc. Personnel Mgmt., Sigma Delta Pi, Chi Eta Sigma. Democrat. Lutheran. Avocations: backpacking, rock climbing, traveling, photography. Home: 744 20th Ave San Francisco CA 41575-1382 Office: Pacific Med Ctr 2340 Clay St San Francisco CA 94115

ZONGOLOWICZ, HELEN MICHAELINE, school principal; b. Kenosha, Wis., July 22, 1936; d. Edmund S. and Helen (Ostrowski) Z.; Ed.B., Dominican Coll., 1966; M.A., Cardinal Stritch Coll., 1973; Ed.D., U. No. Colo., 1977. Tchr. elem. schs. Kenosha, 1956-58, Center Line, Mich., 1958-59, Taft, Calif., 1960-61, Lake Wales, Fla., 1962-63, Albuquerque, 1963-65; tchr., asst. prin. St. Mary's Sch., Taft, 1965-69; asst. sch. supt. Diocese of Fresno, Calif., 1969-70; tchr. primary grades Greasewood Boarding Sch., Ganado, Ariz., 1970-72, coordinator spl. projects, 1972-75, liaison to parent adv. council, 1972-75, tchr. supr., 1972-76; ednl. specialist Ft. Defiance Agy., Navajo Area, Ariz., 1974-75, ednl. diagnostician, 1979-80; vis. asst. prof. U. Colo., 1976; asst. prof. Auburn (Ala.) U., 1977-79, U. N.Mex.-Gallup, 1981—; prin. Chuska Tohatchi (N.Mex.) Consol. Sch., 1980—. Recipient Spl. Achievement award U.S. Dept. Interior, 1971, 73, Superior Performance award, 1982. Mem. Am. Assn. Mental Deficiency, Assn. for Supervision and Curriculum Devel., Council for Exceptional Children, Council for Basic Edn., Am. Ednl. Research Assn., Nat. Assn. Female Execs., Navajo Nation North Cen. Assn. (chmn.), Kappa Delta Pi, Phi Delta Kappa. Address: Chuska Tohatchi Consol Sch Box 321 Tohatchi NM 87325

ZOOK, A(LMA) C(LAIRE), physics educator; b. Los Angeles, June 27, 1950; d. Morris Alva and Caroline Clara (Erskine) Z. BA, Pomona Coll.; PhD, U. Calif., Berkeley. Asst. prof. physics Hamilton Coll., Clinton, N.Y., 1978-82, Pomona Coll., Claremont, Calif., 1982—. Contbr. articles to profl. jours. Mem. Am. Astron. Soc., Astron. Soc. of Pacific, Optical Soc., Am. Assn. Women in Sci., Sigma Xi (sec.). Home: 1670 Lowell Ave Claremont CA 91711 Office: Pomona Coll Dept Physics 610 Coll Ave Claremont CA 91711

ZOOK, JOHN EDWIN, physician, surgeon, missionary; b. Tabor, Iowa, Oct. 3, 1924; s. Abram Eyster Zook and Eunice (Francis) Brenneman; m. Jeanne Pierson, Sept. 7, 1952; children—Rebecca Clair, Daniel John, Paul Michael. B.A., Lewis and Clark Coll., 1950; M.D., U. Oreg., 1954; cert. tropical medicine Antwerp Sch. Tropical Medicine, Belgium, 1956. Diplomate Am. Bd. Surgery. Intern Emanuel Hosp., Portland, Oreg., 1954-55; resident in surgery Good Samaritan Hosp., Portland, 1965-69; ednl. missionary Unevangelized Tribes Mission, Congo, 1943-46; med. missionary Congo Inland Mission, 1955-65; dir. med. activities Africa Intermennonite Mission, Zaire, 1961-65, surgeon, 1969-77; practice medicine specializing in gen. surgery, Portland, 1977—; chief staff Mt. Hood Med. Ctr., 1982; exchange physician China Ednl. Exchange Program, Chungquin Med. Coll., 1984—. V.p. Mennonite Men of Gen. Conf., Mennonite Ch., 1982-87. Fellow ACS, Internat. Coll. Surgeons (Oreg. regent 1980-84, v.p. 1985), Portland Surg. Soc. Republican. Office: East Portland Surg Clinic 169 NE 102d St Portland OR 97220

ZOPF, GEORGE WALTER, computer educator; b. Dayton, Ohio, Mar. 21, 1925; s. George W. and Lois (Bedford) Z.; m. Dorothy F. Richards, May 5, 1949; children: Richard, Amy, Sarah, Emily. BS, Union Coll., Schenectady, N.Y., 1949. Electronics engr. U. Ill. Dept Elec. Engring., Urbana, 1959-63; research assoc. Inst. Fisica Teorica, Naples, Italy, 1963-64; adminstrv. sec. Stazione Zoologica, Naples, Italy, 1964-65; sr. research chemist Vernay Labs. Inc., Yellow Springs, Ohio, 1965-73; tchr. Yellow Springs Schs., 1973-80; propr., owner PAIDEIA, Arroyo Seco, N.Mex., 1981—. Co-author: (with Dorothy F. Richards) Patchworks, 1985; editor (book) Principles of Self-Organization, 1962; contbr. articles to profl. jours.; patentee in field. Served with U.S.N., 1943-45. Mem. AAAS. Home and Office: Box 239 Arroyo Seco NM 87514

ZORICH, ROBERT SAM, process engineer; b. Montgomery, Ala., Oct. 14, 1957; s. Sam and Mary Jeanne (Hestand) Z.; m. Cathleen Mary Coles, Oct. 19, 1985; 1 child, Michelle. BS in Physics, U. Idaho, 1979. Process engr. Nat. Semiconductor, Salt Lake City, 1980-83; product engr., engring. data processing mgr. Intel Corp., Santa Clara, Calif., 1983-85; sr. process engr. LSI Logic Corp., Santa Clara, 1985—; chief exec. officer, programmer ACRO Tech., Sunnyvale, Calif., 1983—. Author (software) Scicalc Math Utilities, 1985. Mem. AAAS, Am. Phys. Soc., The Planetary Soc., Nature Conservancy, Union Concerned Scientists. Democrat. Avocations: backpacking, stamp and coin collecting. Home: 954 Aster Ct Sunnyvale CA 94086 Office: ACRO Tech 1111 W El Camino Real #331 Sunnyvale CA 94086

ZORITCH, GEORGE, dance educator, choreographer; b. Moscow, June 6, 1917; came to U.S., 1936; s. Serge and Helen (Grunke) Z. Diploma Lady Detterling's Russian Sch., Paris, 1933. Mem. Ida Rubinstein Ballet Co., Paris, 1933-34, Pavlova's Co., West Indies, Australia, India, Egypt and Eng., 1934-35, Col. de Basil's Ballet Russe de Monte-Carlo, U.S.A., S. Am., Europe, 1936-37; soloist Denham Ballet Russe de Monte-Carlo, U.S.A., Can., S. Am., Europe, 1938-42; actor, dancer plays, musicals, concert tours, Broadway and throughout U.S., S. Am., Europe, 1943-51: actor 17 movies in Hollywood, Calif. and Rome; premier danseur noble Grand Ballet du Marquis de Cuevas, Europe, Africa, S.Am., 1951-57, Denham Ballet Russe de Monte Carlo, U.S.A., 1957-62; founder George Zoritch Sch. Classical Ballet, West Hollywood, Calif., 1963-73; prof., lectr., mem. dance com., U. Ariz., Tucson, 1973—. Editor records: George Zoritch for Classical Ballet, 1962-65. Mem. Ariz. Dance Arts Alliance (hon. life mem.), Phoenix Ballet Guild (hon. mem.). Office: U Ariz Com on Dance Faculty Fine Arts Tucson AZ 85721

ZORN, GLENN ALLEN, biological research director; b. Rockville Center, N.Y., Apr. 6, 1950; s. Leroy Paul and Bernice Christine (Horkey) Z.; m. Marie Elizabeth Ciano, Sept. 7, 1969; children: Amy Marie, Julie Anne, Douglas Michael. Wyatt Matthew. BS, SUNY, Stony Brook, 1972, PhD in Biology, 1977. Postdoctoral fellow Brookhaven (N.Y.) Nat. Lab., 1978-80; asst. research cell biologist Children's Hosp., Oakland, Calif., 1980-82; in vitro lab. dir. John Muir Meml. Hosp., Walnut Creek, Calif., 1983—; cons. human in vitro fertilization Hanna Media, Inc., Berkeley, Calif., 1984; pres. Ygnacio Andrology Services, Walnut Creek, 1986—. Contbr. articles to profl. jours. N.Y. State Regents scholar., 1968-72, N.Y. State Predoctoral grantee, 1975-77, NIH postdoctoral fellow. Mem. Soc. Exptl. Biology and Medicine, Am. Fertility Soc., Am. Soc. Cell Biology, Tissue Culture Assn., AAAS. Republican. Supervised 2d frozen embryo pregnancy in U.S. Home: 1202 Chesterton Ct Walnut Creek CA 94596 Office: John Muir Meml Hosp 1601 Ygnacio Valley Rd Walnut Creek CA 94598

ZUBERI, SHAKIR HUSAIN, management consultant; b. Aligarh, India, July 1, 1940; came to U.S., 1970; s. Sabir Husain and Niaz Bano Zuberi; m. Shaila K., Mar. 12, 1972; children: Sana, Sahar. BS in Geology with honors, U. Sind, Hyderabad, Pakistan, 1962; MS in Internat. Bus., MBA, St. Marey's Coll., Moraga, Calif., 1978. Registered geologist, Calif. Jr. geologist Water and Power Devel. Authority, Lahore, Pakistan, 1962-65; geologist Khanpur (Pakistan) Dam Project, 1966-69; sr. project geologist Woodward-Clyde Cons., San Francisco, 1970-77, program mgr., 1978—. State advisor U.S. Congl. Adv. Bd., Washington, 1985; constrn. panel mem. Am. Arbitration Assn., N.Y.C., 1986. Mem. Project Mgmt. Inst. (chmn. contract and procurement com. 1985—), Am. Security Council, Internat. Strategic Studies Assn. Moslem. Avocations: photography, reading, travel. Home: 903 Alcosta Dr Milpitas CA 95035 Office: Woodward-Clyde Cons 1390 Market St Suite 250 San Francisco CA 94102

ZUCAL, STEVEN JOSEPH, priest; b. Denver, Sept. 3, 1959. BA in Communications, Regis Coll. Ordained priest Western Orthodox Ch. in Am., 1983. Pastor St. Ignatius of Antioch Parish, Englewood, Colo., 1983—; resident dir. Adsum House, Englewood, 1984-86; dir. mktg. Diakonia Credit Union, Denver, 1981—; regional dir. Servants of the Good Shepherd, 1982—; vol. chaplain Dept. Institutions Div. Youth Services, 1980—; mem. Commn. on Western Orthodox Liturgy, 1983—; co-dir. Info. Services Team, Englewood, 1983—. Co-author (calendar) Ecclesiastical Calendar, 1984, 85; editor: The Ch. Manual, 1984-85. Mem. Ad hoc Com. Juvenile Advocacy, Denver, 1985; advisor Colo. Teen. Inst., Denver, 1984, steering com., 1985; bd. dirs. Youth in Prison, Denver, 1984. Named Outstanding Vol., Colo. Teen Inst., 1984; recipient Appreciation award St. Luke's Hops. Addictions Recovery Unit, 1983. Mem. Nat. Chaplains Assn. Youth Rehab., Mile High Council on Alcoholism and Drug Abuse, Colo. Juvenile Council, Met. Child Protection Council. Home: 2842 S Broadway Englewood CO 80110 Office: St Ignatius of Antioch Parish 2842 S Broadway Englewood CO 80110

ZUCCA, RICARDO, physicist; b. Trieste, Italy, Feb. 7, 1936; came to U.S., 1966; s. Ricardo and Gemma (Illini) Z.; m. Olga Fongi, Oct. 16, 1958; children: Gerry, Silvana, Rudy, Fernando. MCE, U. Rosario, Argentina, 1960; PhD in Physics, U. Calif., Berkeley, 1971. Prof. physics U. Rosario, 1969-72; mem. tech. staff Rockwell Internat. Sci. Ctr., Thousand Oaks, Calif., 1972—. Contbr. numerous articles to profl. jours.; patentee semiconductor tech. Pan Am. Union fellow, 1967-69. Mem. IEEE (sr.). Home: 1404 Ellsworth Circle Thousand Oaks CA 91360 Office: Rockwell Internat PO Box 1085 Thousand Oaks CA 91360

ZUCKER, ALFRED JOHN, educator, sch. adminstr.; b. Hartford, Sept. 25, 1940; s. Samuel and Rose (Zucker) Z.; A.A., Los Angeles Valley Coll., 1960; B.A., U. Calif. at Los Angeles, 1962, M.A., 1963, Ph.D., 1966; m. Sallie Lea Friedheim, Dec. 25, 1966; children—Mary Anne, John James, James Patrick, Patrick Jonathan, Anne-Marie Kathleen, Kathleen Mary. Lectr. English, Los Angeles City Coll., 1963-68; prof. English, philosophy, chmn. div. humanities Los Angeles Southwest Coll., 1968-72, chmn. English dept., 1972-74, asst. dean instruction, 1974—; prof. English El Camino Coll., 1985—. Mem. Los Angeles Jr. Coll. Dist. Senate, 1969—. Mem. Los Angeles Coll. Tchrs. Assn. (dir.), Calif. Jr. Coll. Assn., Calif. Tchrs. Assn., AAUP, Phi Beta Kappa, Phi Delta Kappa (pres. U. Calif. at Los Angeles chpt. 1966-67, v.p. 1967-68). Lodge: KC. Contbr. articles to profl. jours. Office: 1600 W Imperial Hwy Los Angeles CA 90047

ZUCKER, HANK, computer software company executive; b. N.Y.C., June 10, 1950; s. Leon William and Arline (Davidson) Z.; m. Lisa Bacon, Oct. 10, 1982. A.B., Cornell U., 1972; M.A., SUNY-Buffalo, 1975; Ph.D., U. Calif.-Irvine, 1978. Survey analyst CBS News, N.Y.C., 1978, dir. news research, 1978-80; research dir. ERA Research, San Francisco, 1980-82; pres. Creative Research Systems, Petalumna, Calif., 1982—. Author computer program: The Survey System, 1983. Vol. Oceanic Soc., San Francisco, 1981—. Named Student of Yr., Internat. Communications Assn., 1978; SUNY-Buffalo fellow, 1974; Disting. scholar, U. Calif.-Irvine, 1975. Mem. Am. Assn. for Pub. Opinion Research, Am. Mktg. Assn., Internat. Communications Assn. Democrat. Jewish.

ZUCKER, ROBERT STEPHEN, neurophysiologist, physiology educator; b. Phila., Apr. 18, 1945; s. Irving Aaron and Dorothy Ruth (Pittenturf) Z.; m. Glenda Anita Teal, Sept. 1, 1968 (div. Apr. 1982); 1 child, David Aaron; m. Susan Henrietta Schwartz, Jan. 3, 1983; children: Mark Daniel Isaac, Ariel Dana. SB in Physics, MIT, 1966; PhD in Neurol. Sci., Stanford U., 1971. Asst. prof. physiology U. Calif., Berkeley, 1974-80, assoc. prof., 1980-85, prof., 1985—; vis. investigator Univ. Coll. London, 1971-73, Ctr. Nat. de la Recherche Sci., Gif-sur-Yvette, France, 1973-74; corp. mem. Marine Biology Lab., Woods Hole, Mass., 1981—; mem. bd. sci. counselors Nat. Inst. Neurol. And Communicative Disorders and Stroke, Washington, 1982; mem. study sects. NIH, 1983-84. Mem. editorial bd. Jour. Neurobiology, 1982-86; contbr. articles to profl. jours. Fellow Helen Hay Whitney Found., NIH, NSF, NATO, Alfred P. Sloan Found.; grantee NIH, NSF, 1976—; recipient Jacob Javitts award, 1987—. Mem. AAAS, AAUP, Soc. Neurosci., Biophys. Sci., Fedn. Am. Scientists, Union Concerned Scientists, Common Cause, ACLU, Sierra Club, Sigma Xi. Democrat. Jewish. Home: 1236 Oxford St Berkeley CA 94709 Office: U Calif Dept Physiology-Anatomy Berkeley CA 94720

ZUCKERKANDL, EMILE F., molecular evolutionary biologist, scientific institute executive; b. Vienna, Austria, July 4, 1922; came to U.S., 1975; s. Frederic and Gertrude (Stekel) Z.; m. Jane Gammon Metz, June 2, 1950. M.S., U. Ill., 1947; Ph.D., Sorbonne, Paris, 1959. Postdoctoral research fellow Calif. Inst. Tech., Pasadena, 1959-64; research dir. CNRS, Montpellier, France, 1967-80, dir. Ctr. Macromolecular Biochemistry, 1965-75; pres. Linus Pauling Inst., Palo Alto, Calif., 1980—; cons. in genetics Stanford U., 1963, vis. prof., 1964; vis. prof. U. Del., 1976. Contbg. author: Evolving Genes and Proteins, 1965; co-author: Genetique des Populations, 1976; editor Jour. Molecular Evolution, 1971—. Decorated Order of Merit (France). Mem. AAAS, Societe de Chimie Biologique, N.Y. Acad. Scis., Internat. Soc. Study Origin of Life. Home: 565 Arastradero Rd Palo Alto CA 94306 Office: Linus Pauling Inst Sci and Med 440 Page Mill Rd Palo Alto CA 94306

ZUCKERMAN, LAURENCE DAVID, fish ecology researcher; b. Flushing, N.Y., Dec. 2, 1955; s. Max and Jeanette (Cutler) Z. BS in Marine Ecology, SUNY, Stony Brook, 1976; MS in Environ. and Forest Zoology, SUNY, Syracuse, 1979; PhD in Fishery Biology, Colo. State U., Ft. Collins, 1986. Research assoc. Colo. State U., Ft. Collins, 1979—; fishery biologist Colo. Div. of Wildlife, Montrose, 1979-81; species expert-fish Colo. Div. of Wildlife, Denver, 1981-83; research assoc. Colo. Northwestern Wildlife Consortium, Boulder, 1982-83; limnologist Colo. Corp Fishery Research Unit, Ft. Collins, 1982-84; research contractor U.S. Army and U.S. Fish and Wildlife Service, Pinjon Canyon, Colo., 1983-84; fisheries cons. Binckley Ranch, Chama, N.Mex., 1985—; species expert Colo. Nongame Com., Denver, 1985—; cons. San Luis Valley Colo. Nature Conservancy, Denver, 1985—. Contbr. profl. papers to profl. confs. Organizer N.Y. Pub. Interest Research Group, Stony Brook, 1976, recruiter. Grantee in field; recipient Time Current Events award, Times/Mirror Publ. Co., 1962; Boettcher Found. fellow, Shell Oil Environ. fellow, Nat. Wildlife Fedn. Environ. fellow, Hill Meml. fellow, James Bennett Gordon Meml. scholar. Mem. AAAS, Trout Unlimited, Nature Conservancy, Am. Fisheries Soc. Exotic Fish Sect., Internat. Wildlife Soc., Internat. Apple Corps. Am. Soc. Ichthyologists and Herpetologists, Desert Fishes Council, Am. Mus. Natural History, Am. Rivers Conservation Council, Soc. Am. Naturalists, Soc. for Study Evolution, Sigma Xi. Democrat. Jewish. Club: Rocky Mountain Anglers. Avocations: rare book collecting, fishing, stamp collecting, windsurfing, canoeing. Home: 408 E Douglas Rd Fort Collins CO 80524 Office: Colo State U Dept Fishery and Wildlife Biology Fort Collins CO 80523

ZUENDEL, CARL SHERMAN, architect; b. Starr, Pa., June 13, 1927; s. Floyd Clifford Z. and Ruth Marie (Dickrager) Korb. Student Columbia Tech. Inst., Washington, 1946-51, George Washington U., 1951-55, U. So. Calif., 1955-58. Registered architect, Calif., Alaska. Job capt. Daniel, Mann, Johnson & Mendenhall, Los Angeles, 1955-62, project architect, Washington office, 1962-65; architect Alaska Archtl. and Engring Co., Fairbanks, 1965-71, Gray, Rogers, Myers, & Morgan, Fairbanks, 1971-73, Ellerbe-Alaska Co., Fairbanks, 1973-78, GDM & Assocs., Fairbanks, 1978—; mem. Code Rev. Commn., City of Fairbanks, 1980—; mem. Alaska Bd. Registration for Architects, Engrs. and Land Surveyors, 1968-75. Served with USN, 1945-46. Mem. AIA (corp. mem. Alaska chpt., chmn. Fairbanks sect. 1972, 82), Tanana Valley Sportsmen's Assn. (trustee 1968-70), Fairbanks Rifle and Pistol Club, (sec. 1966-76) Nat. Rifle Assn. (endowment mem.), Nat. Wilflife Fedn., Found. N.Am. Wild Sheep, Fedn. of Fly Fishers, Ruffed Grouse Soc., Nat. Sporting Fraternity Ltd. Lodge: Two Rivers Grange. Home: PO Box 16201 Two Rivers AK 99716 Office: PO Box 73768 Fairbanks AK 99707

ZUFELT, JACK M., equity capital consultant; b. Montrose, Colo.; s. Robert Floyd and Lillian Rosalie Zufelt; m. Marcia Ruby Baker, Sept. 8, 1985; children: Crystal, Heidi, Darren, Arianne, Rebecca. Dept. mgr. Elias Morris & Sons Co., 1971-74; mgr. State Stone Co., 1974-77; pres. Quest Co. Mktg. & Devel. Corp., 1977-81, Quest Pub. Corp., Salt Lake City, 1981—; v.p. real estate syndication Denver, 1981-83; pres. Am. Equity Resource, Inc., Littleton, Colo., 1983—; pub. speaker on investments and motivation; producer, host TV series Balanced Living, 1986. Contbr. articles to profl. jours. Mem. Internat. Assn. Fin. Planners, Nat. Assn. Securities Dealers (lic.), Internat. Assn. Financiers, Nat. Speakers Assn. Mormon. Home: 3228 E Phillips Dr Littleton CO 80122 Office: 2 W Dry Creek Circle Suite 190 Littleton CO 80120

ZUGSMITH, MICHAEL ALBERT, real estate executive; b. Los Angeles, Mar. 10, 1951; s. Albert and Ruth (Feldman) Z.; m. Rachel Susan Howitt; 1 child: Michele Ruth. AA, Los Angeles Valley Coll., 1973; BA, UCLA, 1976. Prin. Zugsmith & Assoc. Inc., Studio City, Calif., 1979—; bd. dirs. First Pacific Bank. Bd. dirs. So. Calif. Comml. Property Owners Assn., Glendale, Calif., 1984—. Mem. Royce 270, Beta Phi Gamma. Avocations: snow skiing, reading. Home: 3929 Mary Ellen Ave Studio City CA 91604 Office: Zugsmith & Assoc Inc 12711 Ventura Blvd Suite 230 Studio City CA 91604

ZULEEG, RAINER, physicist; b. Erlangen, Bavaria, Fed. Republic Germany, Sept. 23, 1927; came to U.S., 1953; s. Hans Jacob and Meta (Roedl) Z.; m. Maria Anne Ott, Dec. 12, 1958; children: Regina Uta, Christopher Rainer. BS, Hochschule, Bamburg, Fed. Republic Germany, 1948; MS, U. Munich, 1951; PhD, Tohoku U., Sendai, Japan, 1972. Engr. Radio Free Europe, Munich, 1952-53, Wash. Inst. Tech., College Park, Md., 1953-54; sect. head Sprague Electric, North Adams, Mass., 1954-58; sr. staff physicist Hughes Research Ctr. subs. Hughes Aircraft Co., Newport Beach, Calif., 1958-67; staff dir. McDonnell Douglas Corp., Huntington Beach, Calif., 1967—; lectr. U. Calif., Irvine, 1972—; vis. prof. Royal Melbourne (Australia) Inst. Tech., 1978, 82, U. Duisberg, Fed. Republic Germany, 1984. Co-author: Semiconductor Devices, 1963, 3d rev. edit., 1985; contbr. articles to profl. jours.; patentee semiconductors. Served with German Air Force, 1944-45. Fellow AIAA (assoc.); mem. IEEE, Am. Phys. Soc., Electrochem. Soc., Soaring Soc. Am. Lodge: Masons (32 degree). Avocation: soaring. Home: 33571 Avenida Calita San Juan Capistrano CA 92675 Office: McDonnell Douglas 5301 Bolsa Ave Huntington Beach CA 92647

ZUMBERGE, JAMES HERBERT, university president, geologist; b. Mpls., Dec. 27, 1923; s. Herbert Samuel and Helen (Reich) Z.; m. Marilyn Edwards, June 21, 1947; children: John Edward, JoEllen, James Frederick, Mark Andrew. Student, Duke, 1943-44; B.A., U. Minn., 1946, Ph.D., 1950; LL.D., Grand Valley State Coll., 1970, Kwansei Gakuin U., Japan, 1979; L.H.D., Nebr. Wesleyan U., 1972. Instr. Duke U., 1946-47; mem. faculty U. Mich., 1950-62, prof. geology, 1960-62; pres. Grand Valley State Coll., Allendale, Mich., 1962-68; prof. geology, dean U. Ariz. Coll. Earth Sci., Tucson, 1968-72; chancellor U. Nebr. at Lincoln, 1972-75; pres. So. Meth. U., Dallas, 1975-80, U. So. Calif., Los Angeles, 1980—; Cons. geologist ground water and non-metallic minerals, 1950-62; chief glaciologist Ross Ice Shelf Project, IGY, 1957-58; dir. Litton Industries, Pacific Lighting Corp., Security Pacific Nat. Bank; U.S. del., 1970-76; pres. Sci. Com. on Antarctic Research, 1982-86; chmn. Ross Ice Shelf Project NSF, 1970-73, also mem. steering group Greenland Ice Sheet Program, 1971-82; del. numerous internat. confs. on polar research, Moscow, 1958, Chamonix, 1958, Helsinki, 1960, Obergurgl, Austria, 1962, Poland, 1967, Oslo, 1970, Sydney, Australia, 1972, Mendoza, Argentina, 1976, Warsaw, 1978, New Zealand, 1980; mem. Nat. Sci. Bd., 1974-80. Author: The Lakes of Minnesota, 1952, Laboratory Manual for Physical Geology, 1967, 6th edit., 1983, Elements of Geology, 1963, 72, Elements of Physical Geology, 1976; numerous jour. articles and papers. Bd. overseers Hoover Instn. on War, Revolution and Peace, 1978-84; chmn. U.S. Arctic Research Commn., 1984—. Recipient Antarctic Service medal, 1966; Distinguished Alumni award U. Minn., 1972; James H. Zumberge Library, Grand Valley State Coll., named, 1968; Cape Zumberge, Antarctica named, 1960. Mem. Geol. Soc. Am., Am. Geophys. Union, Soc. Econ. Geologists, Internat. Glaciological Soc., AAAS, Mich. Acad. Scis. (pres. 1967); Conf. Bd.; Mem. Sigma Xi (nat. lectr. 1978-80). Clubs: Cosmos (Washington); Calif; University (N.Y.C.), Explorers (N.Y.C.); Bohemian (Los Angeles), One Hundred (Los Angeles). Address: U So Calif Office of Pres Los Angeles CA 90089-0012

ZUMBERGE, MARK ANDREW, research geophysicist; b. Ann Arbor, Mich., Nov. 23, 1954; s. James Herbert and Marilyn (Edwards) Z.; m. Catherine Jean Laskey, Jan. 1, 1977; children: Andrew, Allison. BS, U. Mich., 1976; MS, U. Colo., 1978, PhD in Physics, 1981. Research assoc. Nat. Bur. Standards, Boulder, Colo., 1982-83; asst. research geophysicist U. Calif. Inst. Geophysics and Planetary Physics, Scripps Instn. Oceanography, San Diego, 1984—. Contbr. articles to profl. jours. C.H.&I. Green Scholar, U. Calif., San Diego, 1983-84. Mem. Am. Phys. Soc., Am. Geophys. Union, Optical Soc. Am. Avocations: carpentry, running.

ZUMBRUNNEN, CRAIG, geography educator and researcher; b. Monticello, Minn., Apr. 3, 1944; s. Marcus and Helen Florence (Chesney) ZumB.; m. Carol Jean Brevik, Dec. 25, 1968; 1 child, Annika. BA cum laude, U. Minn., 1966; MS, Calif. Inst. Tech., 1968; PhD, U. Calif., Berkeley, 1973. Teaching asst. U. Calif., Berkeley, 1969, vis. asst. prof., 1974; asst. prof. Ohio State U., Columbus, 1972-77; research assoc. U. Wash., Seattle,

1975-76, asst. prof., 1977-79, assoc. prof. geography, 1979—; cons. IBM, Boca Raton, Fla., 1985-87, U.S. EPA, Washington, 1975. Co-author: A Geography of Europe, 1983, Soviet Resources in the World Economy, 1983, The Soviet Iron and Steel Industry, 1986; editor (book revs.) Soviet Geograhy, 1980—; contbr. articles to profl. jours. Democratic county and dist. del. King County, Wash., 1982, county del., 1984. NEA fellow, 1966-68. Mem. AAAS, Am. Assn. Advancement Slavic Studies, Assn. Am. Geographers (vice-chmn. 1984—, chmn. Soviet spl. interest group, 1985—), Computer Simulation Soc., Canadian Assn. Geographers, Sigma Xi. Avocations: furniture making, gardening, skiing, bicycling, hiking. Home: 18921 NE 20th Ct Redmond WA 98052 Office: U Wash Dept Geography Seattle WA 98052

ZUNKER, GEORGE ALLEN, lawyer; b. Spruce Center, Minn., July 29, 1940; s. George William and Elda Louise (Wilke) Z.; m. Jo. Patricia Rheingnas, June 6, 1964; children: L. Karl, Kurt. BS, St. Cloud State U., 1962; MA, U. N.C., 1968; JD, U. Wyo., 1975. Bar: Wyo. 1975, U.S. Ct. Appeals (10th cir.) 1979, U.S. Supreme Ct. 1983. Tchr. Ind. Sch. Dist. 858, St. Charles, Minn., 1962-65, Laramie County Sch. Dist. 1, Cheyenne, Wyo., 1965-72; law clk. to presiding justice U.S. Dist. Ct. Wyo., Cheyenne, 1975-77; ptnr. Whitehead, Zunker, Gage, Davidson and Shotwell P.C., Cheyenne, 1977—. Ticket chmn. Cheyenne Frontier Days, 1985-87, mem. gen. com.; Dem. chmn. Laramie County, Cheyenne, 1985-87; mem. bd. trustees Laramie County Sch. Dist. 1, Cheyene, 1973-79, chmn., 1977-79. Served with USAR, 1957-61. Mem. ABA, Laramie County Bar Assn., Wyo. Bar Assn., Wyo. Trial Lawyers Assn., Ciminal Def. Lawyers, Cheyenne C. of C. Democrat. Episcopalian. Avocations: fishing, photography, hiking, camping, riding. Home: 6116 Shaun Ave Cheyenne WY 82009 Office: Whitehead Zunker Gage Davidson & Shotwell PC 1920 Thomes Ave Cheyenne WY 82001

ZUSSY, NANCY LOUISE, librarian; b. Tampa, Fla., Mar. 4, 1947; d. John David and Patsy Ruth (Stone) Roche; m. R. Mark Allen, Dec. 20, 1986. B.A. in Edn., U. Fla., 1969; MLS, U. So. Fla., 1977, M.S. in Pub. Mgmt., 1980. Cert. librarian, Wash. Ednl. evaluator State of Ga., Atlanta, 1969-70; media specialist DeKalb County Schs., Decatur, Ga., 1970-71;

researcher Ga. State Library, Atlanta, 1971; asst. to dir. reference Clearwater (Fla.) Pub. Library, 1972-78, dir. libraries, 1978-81; dep. state librarian Wash. State Library, Olympia, 1981-86, state librarian, 1986—; chmn. Consortium Automated Libraries, Olympia, 1982—; cons. various pub. libraries, Wash., 1981—; exec. officer Wash. Library Network, 1986—. Contbr. articles to profl. jours. Treas. Thurston-Mason Community Mental Health Bd., Olympia, 1983-85, dir., 1982-85; mem. credentials com. Seafair Hydroplane Race, Seattle, 1986. Mem. ALA (Assn. Specialized and Coop. Library Agys. legis. com. 1983—, chmn. legis. com. 1985-87, vice chmn. state library agys. sect. 1985-86, chmn. state ibrary agys. sect. 1986-87, chmn. govt. affairs com. Library Adminstrn. and Mgmt. Assn. 1986-87), Wash. Library Assn. (co-founder legis. planning com. 1982—, fed. relations coordinator 1984—), Fla. Library Assn. (legis. and planning com. 1978-81), Pacific Northwest Library Assn., Phi Kappa Phi, Phi Beta Mu. Avocations: hiking, music, hydroplane racing, cross country skiing. Home: 904 East Bay Dr #B-404 Olympia WA 98506 Office: Wash State Library AJ-11 Olympia WA 98504-0111

ZWEIG, BRUCE MARTIN, computer scientist; b. Washington, Apr. 20, 1949; s. Oscar and Norma Marie (Garfinkle) Z. BS, MIT, 1971; MBA, Stanford U., 1978. Programmer AUI, Washington, 1972-76; pres. Lightning Software, Palo Alto, Calif., 1980-83, Bruce Zweig and Assocs., Palo Alto, 1983—; cons. Scarborough Systems, Tarrytown, N.Y., 1983—. Author computer program Master Type, 1981. Mem. Sigma Xi (assoc.). Democrat. Jewish. Avocations: saxophone, piano. Office: Bruce Zweig & Assocs 2160 Yale Palo Alto CA 94306

ZWEIG, STEPHEN ELIOT, biochemist, diagnostics company executive; b. Rochester, N.Y., Dec. 7, 1952; s. Hans J. Zweig and Marilyn Grace (Broadribb) Holly; m. Gail Ann Boyd, Nov. 17, 1984. BA in Physics and Biology, U. Calif., Santa Barbara, 1974; PhD in Biophysics, U. Calif., San Diego, 1980. Asst. prof. Baylor Sch. Medicine, Houston, 1982-84; sr. research scientist Miles Labs., Elkhart, Ind., 1984-85; dir. Lifescan Inc., Mountain View, Calif., 1985—. Contbr. articles to profl. jours. Fellow NIH, 1980-82, Arthritis Found., 1980. Mem. AAAS, Am. Chem. Soc., Am.

Assn. Clin. Chemists, Mensa. Avocations: computers, photography, sailing, reading. Office: Lifescan Inc 2443 Wyandotte Mountain View CA 94043

ZWIEBEL, IMRE, chemical, biological and materials engineering educator; b. Budapest, Hungary, June 13, 1932; came to U.S., 1948, naturalized, 1954; s. Herman and Bella (Schonberg) Z.; m. Barbara E. Copeland, Dec. 23, 1962; children: Karen, Jeffrey, Kenneth, Hannah. B.S., U. Mich., 1954; M.S., Yale U., 1959, Ph.D., 1961. Registered profl. engr., Mass. Devel. engr. E. I. DuPont Co., Wilmington, Del., 1954-57; research engr. Exxon (Esso) Research Co., Linden, N.J., 1960-64; prof. Worcester Poly. Inst., (Mass.), 1964-79; prof. and chmn. Ariz. State U., Tempe, 1979—. Served with U.S. Army, 1956-57. Mem. Am. Inst. Chem. Engrs., Am. Chem. Soc., Am. Soc. for Engring. Edn., AAAS, Sigma Xi, Phi Lambda Upsilon. Jewish. Home: 642 W Linger Ln Phoenix AZ 85021 Office: Ariz State U COB-B210 Tempe AZ 85287

ZWOYER, EUGENE MILTON, consulting engineer; b. Plainfield, N.J., Sept. 8, 1926; s. Paul Ellsworth and Marie Susan (Britt) Z.; m. Dorothy Lucille Seward, Feb. 23, 1946; children: Gregory, Jeffrey, Douglas. Student, U. Notre Dame, 1944, Mo. Valley Coll., 1944-45; B.S., U. N. Mex., 1947; M.S., Ill. Inst. Tech., 1949; Ph.D., U. Ill., 1953. Mem. faculty U. N.Mex., Albuquerque, 1948-71, prof. civil engring., dir. Eric Wang Civil Engring. Research Facility, 1961-70; research assoc. U. Ill., Urbana, 1951-53; owner Eugene Zwoyer & Assocs., cons engrs., Albuquerque, 1954-72; exec. dir., sec. ASCE, N.Y.C., 1972-82; pres. Am. Assn. Engring. Socs., N.Y.C., 1982-84; exec. v.p. T.Y. Lin Internat., San Francisco, 1984-86, pres., 1986—. Trustee Small Bus. Research Corp., 1976-80; trustee Engring. Info., Inc., 1981-84; internat. trustee People-to-People Internat. 1974-86; v.p. World Fedn. Engring. Orgns., 1982-85. Served to lt. (j.g.) USN, 1944-46. Named Outstanding Engr. of Yr. N.Mex Soc. Profl. Engrs., 1969. Mem. ASCE (dist. dir. 1968-71), Nat. Soc. Profl. Engrs., Am. Concrete Inst., Am. Soc. Engring Edn., AAAS, Nat. Acad. Code Adminstrn. (trustee, mem. exec. com. 1973-79), Engrs. Joint Council (dir. 1978-79), Engring. Soc. Commn. on Energy (dir. 1977-82), Sigma Xi, Sigma Tau, Chi Epsilon. Home: 6363 Christie Ave Apt 1326 Emeryville CA 94608 Office: T Y Lin International 315 Bay Street San Francisco CA 94133